TEXAS CRIMINAL AND TRAFFIC LAW MANUAL

2021–2022 EDITION

As updated through the 87th Legislature
First Special Session, 2021

Blue360°
Media

PREFACE

We are pleased to offer to the law enforcement community the 2021–2022 edition of **Texas Criminal and Traffic Law Manual.** This compilation of selected laws is fully up to date through the 2021 First Special Session of the 87th Legislature. We have included a Table of Sections Affected by 2021 Legislation. This volume is intended to be used throughout 2021, 2022, and 2023 until publication of the 2023–2024 edition in September 2023.

This volume includes a valuable presentation of Texas Police Procedure: Arrest, Search and Seizure, and Confession Law. Also available in the eBook is Government Code, Chapter 418 (Emergency Management).

We are indebted to the Texas Department of Public Safety, which provided us with direction and guidance in developing the contents of this volume.

We are committed to providing law enforcement professionals with the most comprehensive, current, and useful publications possible. If you have comments and suggestions please call the Blue360° Media Publisher, 1-844-599-2887; email us at *support@blue360media.com*; or visit our website at *www.blue360media.com.* Your valuable comments help keep this publication handy and more useful every year.

Visit the Blue360° Media home page at *www.blue360media.com* for an online bookstore, technical support, customer service, and other company information.

September 2021

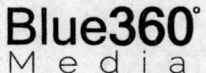

Blue360°
Media

IMPORTANT RESOURCES FOR TEXAS LAW ENFORCEMENT OFFICERS

Pub. #	Featured Law Enforcement Titles
29589	Texas Penal Code: Peace Officers' Field Manual and Study Guide
31081	Texas Criminal and Traffic Law Field Guide
31105	Texas Criminal and Traffic Procedural Manual *Larry E. Holtz and Warren J. Spencer*
31121	Texas Traffic Laws
33525	Texas Criminal and Traffic Law Manual
36185	Civil Process for Texas *Chief Deputy John Steinsiek (Retired)*
80042	Texas Controlled Substances Sourcebook: Peace Officer's Field Manual and Study Guide *M. Vasquez, Chief of Police (Ret.)*
80062	Texas Search & Seizure Survival Guide: A Field Guide to Law Enforcement *Anthony Bandiero, JD, ALM*

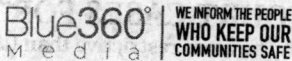

Blue360° Media | WE INFORM THE PEOPLE WHO KEEP OUR COMMUNITIES SAFE

Active Shooter Response Checklist for Patrol Officers

Since the Columbine High School (Colorado) shooting in 1999, response tactics by police to an active shooter incident have evolved. There is an ever-increasing number of active shooter events which calls for quick, effective response by police. (Complete this form and email completed version to yourself for your log or to facilitate reporting.)

Email address: ____________________ Case Number: ____________________

1. Development of an Action Plan

check all that apply

- ☐ Be aware of potential targets in your jurisdiction.
- ☐ Create a repository and access to floor plans for schools and other structures such as malls, etc.
- ☐ Conduct frequent tabletop exercises that include SWAT and all first responders such as the fire department, EMS etc.

Blue360° Media
2020 EDITION
Preparing for an Active Shooter Threat
The Law Enforcement Response Guide
Ken Wallentine
Chris Walden
Buy Now From Blue360Media.com

2. Immediate Deployment

- ☐ Respond in emergency mode with lights and siren.
- ☐ All available officers in the area will be dispatched to the scene and should be en-route immediately advising dispatch.
- ☐ First responders will expect the school or other facility to be in a "lockdown" when they arrive.
- ☐ If any students or other bystanders are outside, move them to a safe area quickly.
- ☐ GO IMMEDIATELY AND DIRECTLY toward the sound of the gunshots or threat; DO NOT WAIT for back-up or SWAT to arrive before you enter; follow your training and agency's policies and procedures.
- ☐ Ideally, at least two officers should enter at the same time, but current training emphasizes going directly to the threat even if you are alone—follow your agency's training and protocol!
- ☐ Dispatch will follow protocol by requesting other first responders and notifying surrounding schools or other public sites of the incident to accomplish lockdown of the sites, restricting exterior access.
- ☐ Perimeters and traffic control should be set up as soon as possible.

3. Locate and Engage the Active Shooter

- ☐ Move quickly and directly toward the sound of gunshots.
- ☐ Do not stop to help injured students or others.
- ☐ If you must enter a closed room, enter quickly announcing yourself.
- ☐ Always use cover and concealment as you move through the building, move as quickly as possible—it may take only a few minutes for casualties to happen.
- ☐ Keep in mind that there may be more than one shooter in one or more different locations.
- ☐ Maintain radio contact with dispatch as much as possible but try to keep your radio at a lower volume than normal.
- ☐ When you locate the suspect, use the necessary level of force to stop the shooter, which may include deadly force to protect your life or the life of others.
- ☐ After the encounter is made with the shooter, advise of your actions and the need for the type of assistance based on your actions and on the observations you made as you came through the building.

4. Command Posts

- ☐ An initial secure, safe area should be set up as soon as possible after the responding officers are inside to stop the shooting or threat.
- ☐ Immediate and special consideration for parents who respond to the scene must be in place.
- ☐ Parents and other non-tactical personnel should be moved away from the command post to a safe venue, such as a neighboring church, school, etc. with adequate manpower to secure the area.
- ☐ Remember to have enough officers at the scene to direct traffic and maintain a perimeter.
- ☐ The process of responding to the shooter, providing emergency medical assistance, rendering the scene safe and collecting evidence may take hours. Lockdown will remain in effect during this time.
- ☐ All of these elements are normally contained in an Incident Command System (ICS) where all first responders have been trained to follow specific protocol and training. Again, rely on your training and agency protocol.

Add any other comments, information, or details for this incident.

____

____

____

____

____

Mistakes for Active Shooter Incident

Lack of Action Plan and Floor Plans to Potential Targets

-No awareness and information on targets in your jurisdiction.
-No floor plans for schools, other structures, malls etc. to refer to.
-Lack of joint training with first responders from within your agency, such as specialty units, and others such as the fire department, EMS.

Deployment

-Lack of *or* miscommunication of exact direction, location, and emergency response.
-Not dispatching all available manpower and resources to the scene.
-If you are the first officer at the scene, ***NOT ENTERING IMMEDIATELY*** and going directly to the active shooter or other threat.
-Not setting up a perimeter, when possible, after entry to locate the threat or active shooter.

Locating and Engaging the Active Shooter

-Waiting for back-up officers.
-Not entering immediately.
-Stopping to help injured students or others.
-Not using "cover and concealment" as you move through the building.
-Lack of "situational awareness;" there may be more than one shooter.
-Not keeping dispatch and supervisory staff updated of the incident.

Command Post

- Not expediting a secure, safe area to set up a command post (ICS-Incident Command Center) with sufficient supervisors or command staff in place to coordinate emergency resources such as EMS, fire department, etc.
- Not keeping non-essential personnel away from the scene, especially concerned parents or others.

KEY U.S. SUPREME COURT CASES FOR LAW ENFORCEMENT

Jurisdictions may be more restrictive than US Supreme Court

US Constitution *Preamble*	*"We the people of the United States, in order to form a more perfect union, establish justice, insure domestic tranquility, provide for the common defense, promote the general welfare and secure the blessings of liberty to ourselves and our posterity, do ordain and establish this Constitution for the United States of America."*	
Bill of Rights Selected Amendments	1st Amendment	**Religion, Speech, Press, Public Assembly**
	2nd Amendment	**To Keep and Bear Arms**
	4th Amendment	**Search & Seizure**
	5th Amendment	**Due Process, Eminent Domain, Self-Incrimination, Grand Jury, Double Jeopardy**
	6th Amendment	**Speedy Trial, Informed of Accusations, Confront Accuser, Obtain Witnesses**
	8th Amendment	**No Excessive Bail, or Cruel & Unusual Punishment**
	14th Amendment	**Citizenship, Civil Rights, Due Process**

1st Amendment	Religion, Speech, Press, Public Assembly
Freedom of Speech	**Political Speech - NAACP v. Claiborne Hardware Co.**, 458 U.S. 886 (1982): Nonviolent political speech is entitled to the protection of the 1st Amendment.
	Public Figures - Hustler Magazine v. Falwell, 485 U.S. 46 (1988): Parodies of public figures, including those intended to cause emotional distress, are protected by the 1st Amendment.
	Fighting Words - Chaplinsky v. New Hampshire, 315 U.S. 568 (1942): Words to inflict injury, or incite a breach of the peace, are not protected by the 1st Amendment. **Snyder v. Phelps**, 562 U.S. 443 (2011): Updates this stance, and while **Chaplinsky** is cited often, its rule has not been enforced by a government action since its decision. **Snyder** holds that "speech cannot be restricted simply because it is upsetting or arouses contempt."
	Flag Burning - Texas v. Johnson, 491 U.S. 397 (1989): Flag burning as political protest symbolic speech is protected by the 1st Amendment.
	Symbolic Speech - Tinker v. Des Moines Independent Community School District, 393 U.S. 503 (1969): Public school students may wear armbands in protest at school as a form of protected symbolic speech.
	School Speech - Bethel School District v. Fraser, 478 U.S. 675 (1986): Students do not have a 1st Amendment right to make obscene speeches in school.
	Obscenity - Miller v. California, 413 U.S. 15 (1973): Obscene material is not protected by the 1st Amendment. Obscene works fail the Miller test, which determines if it has any "serious literary, artistic, political, or scientific value."
	Child Pornography - New York v. Ferber, 458 U.S. 747 (1982): Laws that prohibit child pornography are constitutional even if the content is not "obscene."
	Restraint Must Be Narrowly Tailored - Reno v. American Civil Liberties Union, 521 U.S. 844 (1997): Overbroad regulation of certain content on the internet is an unconstitutional restraint on the 1st Amendment.
Freedom of Peaceful Assembly, Expression	**Peaceful Protests - Edwards v. South Carolina**, 372 U.S. 229 (1963): 1st Amendment Free Protest Clause extends to the states.
	Prohibition of Inciting Others - Brandenburg v. Ohio, 395 U.S. 444 (1969): The mere advocacy of the use of force or of violation of the law is protected by the 1st Amendment. Only inciting others to take direct and immediate unlawful action is without constitutional protection. Overruled **Schenck v. United States**, 249 U.S. 47 (1919), which previously allowed speech limits during wartime when there was "clear and present danger."
	Public Demonstration May Exclude Groups - Hurley v. Irish-American Gay, Lesbian, and Bisexual Group of Boston, 515 U.S. 557 (1995): Private citizens organizing a public demonstration have the right to exclude groups whose message they disagree with from participating.
Freedom of Religion	**Establishment Clause - Town of Greece v. Galloway**, 572 U.S. 565 (2014): A town council's practice of opening its sessions with a sectarian prayer does not violate the Establishment Clause. **Free Exercise + Establishment Clause = Freedom of Religion**
	Religious Belief is no Defense - Reynolds v. United States, 98 U.S. 145 (1879): Religious belief or duty cannot be used as a defense against a criminal indictment.

2nd Amendment	To Keep and Bear Arms
18 U.S.C. § 921 et seq. 18 U.S.C. § 845	**The Gun Control Act (1968)** US federal law that regulates the firearms industry and firearms owners. It primarily focuses on regulating interstate commerce in firearms by generally prohibiting interstate firearms transfers except among licensed manufacturers, dealers and importers. **The Firearm Owners Protection Act of 1986 (FOPA)** is a United States federal law that revised many provisions of the Gun Control Act of 1968
Gun Ownership Lawful Purposes	**District of Columbia v. Heller**, 554 U.S. 570: The 2nd Amendment protects an individual's right to keep and bear arms for lawful purposes, such as self-defense within the home, and that the DC's handgun ban and requirement that lawfully owned rifles and shotguns be kept "unloaded and disassembled or bound by a trigger lock" violated this guarantee. The right to bear arms is not unlimited and it will continue to be regulated. Check your jurisdiction for relevant restrictions. **McDonald v. City of Chicago**, 561 U.S. 742 (2010): Protections of the 2nd Amendment are incorporated by the Due Process Clause of the 14th Amendment to states. **Nunn v. Georgia**, 1 Ga. (1 Kel.) 243 (1846): This was the first gun control measure to be overturned on 2nd Amendment grounds; a GA law ban on handguns was ruled a violation of the 2nd Amendment. **Presser v. Illinois**, 116 U.S. 252 (1886): No 2nd Amendment violation for law prohibiting citizens from forming personal military organizations and activities as it does not limit the personal right to keep and bear arms. **United States v. Miller**, 307 U.S. 174 (1939): The federal government and the states can limit access to all weapons that do not have "some reasonable relationship to the preservation or efficiency of a well regulated militia." Here, sawed-off shotgun did not have any reasonable relationship.
Stun Gun	**Caetano v. Massachusetts**, 577 U.S. 411 (2016): 2nd Amendment extends to all types of bearable arms, including stun guns; however, the 2nd Amendment does not protect weapons not typically possessed by law-abiding citizens for lawful purposes. (Remember that state and local laws can be more restrictive).
"Castle Doctrine"	The castle doctrine and **"stand-your-ground"** laws provide legal defenses to persons who have been charged with various use of force crimes when they reasonably believe it to be necessary to defend against deadly force, great bodily harm, kidnapping, rape, or (in some jurisdictions) robbery or some other serious crime in their home or places they legally occupy (such as a vehicle). This doctrine has many variations and has been controversial. Check your jurisdiction.
4th Amendment	Searches are Presumed Unreasonable Unless There is a Warrant or Recognized Exception
Search	**Secure in Persons, Houses, Papers & Effects - Search** happens when government makes 1) a physical trespass into a constitutionally protected area (i.e., persons, houses, papers, and effects); and 2) with the purpose of obtaining information. **Expectation of Privacy - Katz v. United States**, 389 U.S. 347, 353 (1967): A reasonable expectation of privacy will be violated if: 1) the person exhibited an actual (subjective) expectation of privacy; and 2) his expectation is one that society is prepared to recognize as reasonable (objective). Under the 4th Amendment a warrant issued by a "neutral and detached magistrate" must be obtained before police officers may lawfully search personal property, absent an exception. Superseded by statute in CA and NY; check your jurisdiction.
No Arbitrary Arrests or Unreasonable Searches	**4th Amendment Protections - Payton v. New York**, 445 U.S. 573 (1980): Protect against arbitrary arrests as well as against unreasonable searches **Reasonableness** **U.S. v. Jacobsen**, 503 U.S. 540 (1992): "An otherwise lawful seizure can violate the 4th Amendment if it is executed in an unreasonable manner. **U.S. v. Rohrig**, 98 F.3d 1506 (6th Cir. 1996): The 4th Amendment "does not mandate that police officers act flawlessly, but only that they act reasonably." **U.S. v. Goddard**, 312 F.3d 1360 (11th Cir. 2002): The "reasonable person" test asks, "not … what the defendant himself … thought, but what a reasonable man, innocent of any crime, would have thought had he been in the defendant's shoes." **Government Searches** - The 4th Amendment controls government officials, not private actors. If search directed by government and undertaken with intent to help police discover evidence, a private search may be turned into a government search so long as scope is not exceeded making it unreasonable. **Coolidge v. New Hampshire**, 403 U.S. 443 (1971): No government search evidence simply handed over. **Warrantless Arrest in Public -** **United States v. Watson**, 423 U.S. 411 (1976): Warrantless arrests in public are allowed. **United States v. Santana**, 427 U.S. 38 (1976): Warrantless arrest in suspect's home when she was initially approached in her doorway and then retreated into house was reasonable. **Atwater v. Lago Vista**, 532 U.S. 318 (2001): In most states, the misdemeanor must occur "in the officer's presence" to arrest without a warrant (needed for probable cause).

Hunches	**Request to Exit Vehicle** **- Driver - Pennsylvania v. Mimms**, 434 U.S. 106 (1977): A police officer may order the driver of a lawfully stopped car to exit his vehicle. **- Passenger - Maryland v. Wilson**, 519 U.S. 408 (1997): Extends Pennsylvania v. Mimms, 434 U.S. 106 (1977) to allow officers to request passengers of a lawfully stopped car may also be asked to exit the vehicle. The officer may more than a hunch but less than reasonable suspicion -- check your jurisdiction as application varies. **Demeanor - I.N.S. v. Delgado**, 466 U.S. 210, 216 (1984): Being uncooperative is a hunch, not reasonable suspicion
4th Amendment	**Reasonable Suspicion**
Terry Stop & Frisk	**Terry v. Ohio**, 392 U.S. 1 (1968): A "stop and frisk" is a "search and seizure" and does not violate the 4th Amendment when police have reasonable suspicion that 1) suspects may be (or have, or are about to) commiting a crime, and 2) may be armed and dangerous. Note: states differ, with about half of the states believing that suspects who are armed are dangerous. Seized items may be used as evidence.
Stop & Frisk - Vehicle Passenger	**Arizona v. Johnson**, 555 U.S. 323 (2009): Police may conduct a pat down search of a passenger in an automobile that has been lawfully stopped for a minor traffic violation, if the police reasonably suspect the passenger is armed and dangerous.
Stop & Identify	**Hiibel v. Sixth Judicial District Court of Nevada**, 542 U.S. 177 (2004): Laws requiring suspects to provide their names during a valid Terry stop by law enforcement officers do not violate the 4th Amendment, nor necessarily the 5th Amendment. Officers in Nevada must have a reasonable and articulable suspicion of criminal involvement to request that the person detained "identify himself", but the law there does not compel the person to answer any other questions. About half of the states have a stop & identify law for motorists, and several versions of stop & identify laws have been challenged. Generally to compel ID you need reasonable suspicion of a crime (plain view, plain smell, or commission of an offense), even though a suspect's refusal to identify coupled with surrounding events may give rise to probable cause in certain instances and jurisdictions. Be aware that some detainees ditch their ID if they anticipate police questioning so that they may confuse matters by providing someone else's name.
Reasonable Inference	**Kansas v. Glover**, 589 U.S. ___ (2019): When an officer runs a license plate and learns that the owner has a violation—absent knowledge of any contradictory facts—it is reasonable for the officer to infer that the driver is also the owner of the vehicle, and the traffic stop is justified.
Confidential Informant	**Adams v. Williams**, 407 U.S. 143 (1972): Confidential informant may be used to build reasonable suspicion.
Warrantless Vehicle Stop	**United States v. Cortez**, 499 U.S. 411 (1981): Reasonable suspicion means a suspicion particularized for a given person or persons. The 1) objective facts and 2) circumstantial evidence together justified the investigative stop of the vehicle.
4th Amendment	**Probable Cause**
Traffic Offense	**Whren v. United States**, 517 U.S. 806 (1996): Any traffic offense committed by a driver is a legitimate legal basis for a traffic stop. A concern with this holding is that police may controversially racially profile through traffic stops.
Totality of the Circumstances	**Draper v. U.S.**, 358 U.S. 307 (1959): Probable cause to arrest exists "where 'the facts and circumstances' known to be reasonably trustworthy information warrant the belief that an offense has been or is being committed."
Search Warrant Requirements	**Groh v. Ramirez**, 540 U.S. 551 (2004): A search warrant is a court order that a magistrate or judge issues to authorize law enforcement officers to conduct a search of a person, location, or vehicle for evidence of a crime and to confiscate evidence they find. An incorrectly written search warrant could result in any evidence obtained being excluded from trial. Here, the particularity of items sought repeated the address description in error, rather than drugs. The result was a narrowing of the mistake justification for qualified immunity.
Knock-and-Announce	**Wilson v. Arkansas**, 514 U.S. 927 (1995): "Reasonable entry" considers whether knock-and-announce (wait) was adhered to as a factor. Should law enforcement fail to knock and announce, then the search may violate the 4th Amendment. **Hudson v. Michigan**, 547 U.S. 586 (2006): When the police violate the knock-and-announce rule, the appropriate remedy is not generally suppression of the evidence.
No-Knock Warrant	**United States v. Ramirez**, 523 U.S. 65 (1998): A no-knock warrant is issued by a judge and allows law enforcement to enter a property without immediate prior notification of the residents, such as by knocking or ringing a doorbell. A no-knock entry is justified if police have a reasonable suspicion that knocking and announcing their presence before entering would be dangerous or futile, or inhibit the effective investigation of the crime. There have been some high profile media about no-knock warrants, so make sure you know your jurisdiction and you are compliant.
Search Warrants to Third Parties	**Zurcher v. Stanford Daily**, 436 U.S. 547 (1978): the 4th Amendment does not prevent issuing a warrant against a third party not suspected of committing a crime. Preconditions for the issuance of a search warrant must be applied with "particular exactitude" if the materials being searched are protected by the 1st Amendment. Be aware some legislation such as the Privacy Protection Act of 1980 has tried to codify sections from this decision to supersede it; however, this case is still cited for reasonable cause and specificity for a warrant.
Vehicle Search	**Carroll v. U.S.**, 267 U.S. 132 (1925): Police may conduct a warrantless search of a vehicle stopped in traffic if there is probable cause to believe that the vehicle contains contraband or evidence.

Confidential Informant	**Aguilar–Spinelli test:** former test for the validity of a search warrant or a warrantless arrest based on a confidential informant or an anonymous tip which was abandoned in favor of the **"totality of the circumstances"** evaluation per **Illinois v. Gates**, 462 U.S. 213 (1983); however, a few states (AK, HI, MA, NY, VT, OR, WA) retain the Aguilar-Spinelli test under their state constitutions. This former two-prong test based on **Aguilar v. Tex.**, 378 U.S. 108 (1964) (overruled) and **Spinelli v. United States**, 393 U.S. 410 (1969) required the issuing magistrate to be informed 1) why the informant is reliable and credible, and 2) underlying circumstances relied on by the CI.

4th Amendment	Exceptions to Search Warrant
C Consent	**Schneckloth vs. Bustamonte**, 412 U.S. 218 (1973): The consent given police to search the car of a driver stopped for a traffic violation is valid even if the driver was unaware he had the right to refuse. Usually the police have no duty to warn a person that he has a right to refuse consent to a warrantless search. **Illinois v. Rodriguez**, 497 U.S. 177 (1990): If consent is given by a person reasonably believed by an officer to have authority to give such consent, no warrant is required for a search or seizure.
A Arrest	**Chimel v. California**, 395 U.S. 752 (1969): A search incident to lawful arrest does not require issuance of a warrant. If someone is lawfully arrested, the police may search her person and any area surrounding the person that is within reach (within his or her "wingspan") as a protective measure for police and to secure evidence that might be destroyed. However, the arrest of a person in his home does not allow the warrantless search of the whole house incident to arrest. **United States v. Robinson**, 414 U.S. 218 (1973): In the case of a lawful custodial arrest, a full search of the person is reasonable. **United States v. Leon**, 468 U.S. 897 (1984): Evidence will be admitted when it was seized in reasonable, good-faith reliance on a search warrant, even if the warrant was subsequently found to be defective. **Arizona v. Gant**, 556 U.S. 332 (2009): During a lawful investigative traffic stop, with reasonable suspicion and clear facts that permit officer to conclude that the person is, has been, or will be engaged in criminal activity, police may conduct search. Police may search a vehicle of the arrestee only if the arrestee is within reaching distance (e.g., weapon) or if it is reasonable to believe that crime-related evidence will be found/disposed of in the vehicle.
P Plain View	**- PLAIN VIEW - Arizona v. Hicks**, 480 U.S. 321 (1987): Requires the police to have probable cause to seize items in plain view; **Horton v. California**, 496 U.S. 128 (1990): Warrantless seizure of evidence which is in plain view does not violate 4th Amendment; **Coolidge v. New Hampshire**, 403 U.S. 443 (1971): Police may not rely on the plain view doctrine when conducting a warrantless search of an automobile if the police expected in advance to find evidence and failed to secure a warrant. **- PLAIN FEEL / SMELL - Minnesota v. Dickerson**, 508 U.S. 366 (1993): The 4th Amendment permits the seizure of contraband detected through a police officer's sense of touch during a protective pat down search. **Texas v. Brown**, 460 U.S. 730 (1983): Probable cause that balloons contained drugs based on officer's experience. **- HEAR/SOUND - United States v. Hairston**, 402 F. App'x 84, 88 (6th Cir. 2010): Extends Terry Stop of individual near sound of recent gunshots fired; **Katz v. United States**, 389 U.S. 347, 353 **(1967)**: Warrantless use of listening and recording device placed on outside of phone booth violates 4th Amendment. Superseded by statute in CA and NY, check your jurisdiction. **- FLASHLIGHT/ILLUMINATE - United States v. Dunn**, 480 U.S. 294 (1987): Officer may use flashlight to illuminate barn interior; **Texas v. Brown**, 460 U.S. 730 (1983): Officer allowed to shine flashlight in interior of car; **United States v. Lee**, 274 U.S. 559 (1927): A search light may be used by police; **Kyllo v. United States**, 533 U.S. 27 (2001): Thermal imaging device to detect activity within a building by measuring heat outside the home is unreasonable absent a warrant or exception.
E Exigent	**Carroll v. U.S.**, 267 U.S. 132 (1925): Police may conduct a warrantless search of a vehicle stopped in traffic if there is probable cause to believe that the vehicle contains contraband or evidence. **Chambers v. Maroney**, 90 S. Ct. 1975 (1970): Applied the Carroll doctrine the warrantless search of the suspects' car, although at the police station (rather than during exigent traffic stop), after Chambers and the other occupants were arrested for robbery did not violate the 4th Amendment. **Cady v. Dombrowski**, 413 U.S. 433 (1973): Police have a community caretaking imperative to ensure that impounded automobiles do not contain revolvers or other dangerous items. **Kentucky v. King**, 563 U.S. 452 (2011): Warrantless searches conducted in exigent circumstances do not violate the 4th Amendment so long as the police did not create the exigency by violating or threatening to violate the 4th amendment. **Warden v. Hayden**, 387 U.S. 294 (1967): "Mere evidence" may be seized and held as evidence in a trial. **Schmerber v. California**, 384 U.S. 757 (1966): The 4th Amendment's protection against warrantless searches that intrude into the human body means that police may not conduct warrantless blood testing on suspects absent an emergency that justifies acting without a warrant. A state may draw blood for the purpose of determining intoxication in a drunken driving case without a warrant. The withdrawal of blood does not equate to giving a statement and therefore is not a 5th Amendment violation nor does it invoke the 6th Amendment right to counsel.
R Roadside	**United States v. Martinez-Fuerte**, 428 U.S. 543 (1976): Allows a brief, warrantless seizure at fixed roadside checkpoints aimed at intercepting illegal aliens to protect the nation's border (narrowly tailored reason). **Mich. Dep't of State Police v. Sitz**, 496 U.S. 444 (1990): sobriety checkpoint program to ensure roadway safety does not violate 4th Amendment. **Indianapolis v. Edmond**, 531 U.S. 32 (2000): When detecting ordinary criminal activity is the primary purpose of a checkpoint, it violates the 4th Amendment.

4th Amendment	Seizure
Of a Person	**Brower v. County of Inyo**, 489 U.S. 593 (1989): A seizure of a person occurs under the 4th Amendment when force is used with the intent to seize. **California v. Hodari**, 499 U.S. 621 (1991): Person seized when there is a sufficient show of authority that would lead a reasonable person to believe he was not free to leave.
Of Property	A **seizure** of property occurs under the **4th Amendment** when there is meaningful interference with someone's possessory interest in his property.
Consent	**United States v. Mendenhall**, 446 U.S. 544 (1980); Fla. v. Bostick, 501 U.S. 429 (1991): No seizure if there is consent. The test for a consensual encounter is not only the ability to leave, but also the ability to terminate the encounter.
Exclusionary Rule	**Mapp v. Ohio**, 367 U.S. 643 (1961): Evidence seized unlawfully, without a search warrant, and derivative evidence cannot be used. "Fruit of the Poisonous Tree."
Break in Chain	**Wong Sun v. United States**, 371 U.S. 471 (1963): verbal evidence and recovered narcotics where they were both fruits of an illegal entry are inadmissible in court except where there is a break in chain of evidence.
Unlawful Seizure	**Soldal v. Cook County**, 506 U.S. 56 (1992): Officers that "kept the peace" liable for unlawful seizure of property.
PC Hearing After Arrest	**Gerstein v. Pugh**, 420 U.S. 103 (1975): to keep arrestee in custody following a warrantless arrest, a "prompt" "administratively convenient" hearing to determine probable cause is needed. **County of Riverside v. McLaughlin**, 500 U.S. 44, 56 (1991): detention for up to 48 hours without a probable-cause hearing shifts the burden to the government to demonstrate extraordinary circumstances justifying further detention.

4th Amendment	Use of Force
Breaking Doors & Windows	**8 U.S.C. § 3109** governs breaking doors and windows if law enforcement is refused entrance.
Use of Force	**Graham v. Connor**, 490 U.S. 386 (1989): An objective reasonableness standard should apply to a free citizen's claim that law enforcement officials used excessive force in the course of making an arrest, investigatory stop, or other "seizure."
Fleeing Felon	**Tennessee v. Garner**, 471 U.S. 1 (1985): Deadly force OK if necessary to stop a fleeing felon from escaping, and the suspect poses a significant threat of death or serious physical injury to the officer or others.
Lesser Force	**Plakas v. Drinski**, 19 F.3d 1143 (7th Cir. 1994): When deadly force is authorized, there is no constitutional duty to use a lesser force.
Failure to Train	**City of Canton, Ohio v. Harris**, 489 US 378 (1989): Inadequacy of police training and § 1983 liability where failure to train was "deliberate indifference" to the rights of persons with whom the police came into contact.

5th Amendment	Due Process, Eminent Domain, Self-Incrimination, Grand Jury, Double Jeopardy
Due Process Equal Liberty	**United States v. Windsor**, 570 U.S. 744 (2013): The federal government cannot define the terms "marriage" and "spouse" in a way that excludes married same-sex couples from the benefits and protections that married opposite-sex couples receive.
Felonies are Infamous Crimes	**United States v. Moreland**, 258 U.S. 433 (1922): incarceration in a prison or penitentiary, as opposed to a correction or reformation house, attaches infamy to a crime. **Green v. United States**, 356 U.S. 165 (1957): "imprisonment in a penitentiary can be imposed only if a crime is subject to imprisonment exceeding one year."
Coercion/Duress	**Chambers v. Florida**, 309 U.S. 227 (1940): Confessions compelled by police through duress are inadmissible at trial.
Double Jeopardy	**Blockburger v United States**, 284 U.S. 299 (1932): Double jeopardy is not absolute. Using the "Same elements test," defendant could be convicted of two crimes arising from one fact situation so long as there is a unique element to each crime making them separate charges rather than lesser included offenses.

5th / 6th Amendments

Miranda Rights

1. You have the right to remain silent
2. Anything you say can be used against you
3. You have the right to an attorney
4. If you cannot afford an attorney, one will be appointed for you
5. This means you can choose not to answer an officer's questions and may request an attorney.

Understand? Proceed?

Miranda Warning	**Miranda v. Arizona**, 384 U.S. 436 (1966): Presumption that a statement is involuntary if made during a custodial interrogation without the "Miranda Warnings" given. Not only must the statement not be coerced, the suspect must know their rights when being interrogated and in custody (arrest, or when freedom is significantly deprived). "Interrogation" is the use of words or actions to elicit an incriminating response from an average person. Some exceptions to the Miranda Warnings have been carved out either by statute or case law (i.e., when necessary for public safety questioning is permitted, see **New York v. Quarles**, 467 U.S. 649 (1984); statute and case law regarding criteria for "voluntariness" of confession is varied).

Right to Counsel	**Edwards v. Arizona**, 451 U.S. 477 (1981): Once a defendant invokes his 6th Amendment right to counsel, police must cease interrogation until defendant's counsel has been made available to him, or he himself initiates further communication, exchanges, or conversations with the police. Statements obtained in violation of this rule are a violation of a defendant's 5th Amendment rights.
Re-Questioning	**Maryland v. Shatzer**, 559 U.S. 98 (2010): Police may re-open questioning of a suspect who has asked for counsel after there has been at least a 14-day break since Miranda custody.
Inmates	**Illinois v. Perkins**, 496 US 292 (1990): The Miranda Warnings are not required when an incarcerated person speaks freely to another inmate who is actually an undercover officer.
Juvenile	**Kaupp v. Texas**, 538 U. S. 1 (2003): Removing an adolescent from his home in handcuffs and improperly clothed for interrogation about a murder without probable cause resulted in the exclusion of the confession because the officers violated his 4th Amendment rights. Reading of the Miranda warnings did not overcome the officers' illegal actions.
"Garrity Warning"	**Garrity v. New Jersey**, 385 U.S. 493 (1967): Law enforcement and other public employees have the right to be free from compulsory self-incrimination. The "Garrity Warning," is administered to suspects in internal and administrative investigations in a similar manner as the Miranda warning is administered to suspects in criminal investigation.
6th Amendment	**Speedy Trial, Informed of Accusations, Confront Accuser, Obtain Witnesses**
Unanimous Verdict	**Ramos v. Louisiana**, 590 U.S. ___ (2020): The 6th Amendment right to a jury trial requires a unanimous verdict to convict a defendant of a serious offense.
Right to Counsel	**Texas v. Cobb**, 532 U.S. 162 (2001): The right to counsel attaches only to charged offenses, and there is no exception for crimes that are uncharged, yet "factually related" to a charged offense. Cobb burglarized a home, then he murdered to conceal the burglary. Cobb was charged with the burglary and obtained counsel. He was later Miranda-ized and questioned about the murders for which he had not been charged. These related crimes are separate crimes. The confession to the murders was properly obtained.
	Powell v. Alabama, 287 U.S. 45 (1932: that indigent or illiterate defendants charged with a capital crime must be given competent counsel at the expense of the public.
	United States v. Ash, 413 U.S. 300 (1973): The accused does not have a right to have counsel present when the Government conducts a post-indictment photographic display, containing a picture of the accused, for the purpose of allowing a witness to attempt an identification of the offender.
8th Amendment	**No Excessive Bail, or Cruel & Unusual Punishment**
Punishment Must be Proportional	**Kennedy v. Louisiana, 554 U.S. 407 (2008)**: The 8th Amendment bars the execution of a child rapist where the crime did not result, and was not intended to result, in the victim's death. The punishment must be proportional to the seriousness of the crime. There are many cases with various fact patterns regarding the principle of proportionality introduced in **Weems v. United States**, 217 U.S. 349 (1910). Note: less than half of the states authorize capital punishment for any offense as states may be more restrictive than federal laws.
Juvenile Sentence	**Roper v. Simmons**, 543 U.S. 551 (2005): A death sentence may not be imposed on juvenile offenders. **Graham v. Florida**, 560 U.S. 48 (2012): Juvenile offenders cannot be sentenced to life imprisonment without parole.
Intellectually Disabled Cannot Be Executed	**Madison v Alabama**, 586 U.S. ___ (2019): Executing a person currently suffering from dementia would be cruel and unusual punishment; however, the 8th Amendment may permit executing a prisoner with psychotic delusions or no memory of committing the crime. **Atkins v. Virginia**, 536 U.S. 304 (2002): death sentence may not be imposed on intellectually disabled defendants, but the states define "intellectual disability."
Addiction is a Condition	**Robinson v. California**, 370 U.S. 660 (1962): 1) The cruel and unusual punishment clause applies to the states, and 2) punishing a person for a medical condition is a violation of the 8th Amendment ban on cruel and unusual punishment. Addiction to narcotics is a "condition."
No Excessive Bail	**United States v. Salerno**, 481 U.S. 739 (1987): The Bail Reform Act's authorization of pretrial preventive detention on the ground of future dangerousness was not facially unconstitutional, and violated neither the due process clause of the 5th Amendment nor the excessive bail language of the 8th Amendment.
14th Amendment	**Citizenship, Civil Rights, Due Process**
Due Process	**Gitlow v. New York**, 268 U.S. 652 (1925): 1st Amendment freedoms apply to states via 14th Amendment due process.
Civil Rights	**Color of Law** - Criminal Civil Rights Violations (**18 U.S.C. § 242)**: It a crime for government officials to deprive any person of protected rights or to impose different punishments based on a person's race. The DOJ must prove the defendant: (1) acted "under color of" law; (2) acted "willfully"; and (3) deprived the victim of rights or was subjected to different punishments on account of the victim's race, color, or alien status. **Hernandez v. Texas**, 347 U.S. 475 (1954): The **equal protection** of the laws guaranteed by the 14th Amendment applies against discrimination.
	No Sexual Harassment - Meritor Savings Bank v. Vinson, 477 U.S. 57 (1986): sexual harassment is unlawful discrimination too; **Oncale v. Sundowner Offshore Services, Inc.**, 523 U.S. 75 (1998): no same-sex harassment.
	Gender Identity or Sexual Orientation - Bostock v. Clayton County, 590 U.S. ___ (2020): Title VII protects employees against discrimination due to their sexual orientation or gender identity.
	Right to Liberty - O'Connor v. Donaldson, 422 U.S. 563 (1975): The states cannot involuntarily commit individuals unless they are a danger to themselves or others.

TABLE OF CONTENTS

TABLE OF SECTIONS AFFECTED BY 2021 LEGISLATION

SECTION	EFFECT	BILL NUMBER
	Penal	
1.10	Added	HB2622
3.03	Amended	HB1403
9.54	Added	HB1758
12.50	Amended	HB3607
12.501	Added	HB624
15.031	Amended	HB1540
20.01	Amended	SB576
20.05	Amended	SB576
20A.01	Amended	HB1540
20A.01	Amended	HB3521
20A.01	Amended	SB1831
20A.02	Amended	SB1831
20A.02	Amended	HB375
20A.02	Amended	HB1540
20A.02	Amended	HB3521
21.01	Amended	HB246
21.02	Amended	HB375
21.12	Amended	HB246
22.01	Amended	HB1306
22.011	Amended	SB1164
22.011	Amended	HB3607
22.02	Amended	HB1306
22.04	Amended	SB1354
22.041	Amended	SB768
25.07	Amended	HB39
25.07	Amended	HB3607
25.08	Amended	HB1540
25.081	Amended	HB1540
28.03	Amended	SB516
28.03	Amended	SB705
30.05	Amended	SB550
30.05	Amended	HB1927
30.05	Amended	SB20
30.05	Amended	HB1540
30.05	Amended	HB2112
30.06	Amended	HB1069
30.06	Amended	SB20
30.06	Amended	HB1927
30.07	Amended	HB1069
30.07	Amended	HB1927
30.07	Amended	SB20
30.07	Amended	HB2112
32.46	Amended	SB109
32.55	Added	HB1156
33.021	Amended	HB1540
33.021	Amended	SB1831
37.09	Amended	HB3607
37.10	Amended	HB4555
39.04	Amended	HB3157
39.04	Amended	SB312
42.03	Amended	SB1495
42.03	Amended	HB9
42.0601	Added	SB1056
42.07	Amended	SB530
42.13	Amended	HB2366

SECTION	EFFECT	BILL NUMBER
43.01	Amended	HB1540
43.01	Amended	SB1831
43.02	Amended	HB1540
43.02	Amended	SB1831
43.021	Added	HB1540
43.021	Amended	HB1540
43.031	Amended	HB1540
43.041	Amended	HB1540
43.251	Amended	SB315
43.251	Amended	SB766
46.01	Amended	HB1069
46.01	Amended	HB957
46.02	Amended	HB1927
46.02	Amended	HB2112
46.02	Amended	SB550
46.03	Amended	HB1927
46.03	Amended	HB1920
46.035	Repealed	HB1927
46.035	Amended	HB1407
46.035	Amended	HB2112
46.035	Amended	SB550
46.04	Amended	HB1927
46.05	Amended	HB957
46.06	Amended	SB162
46.15	Amended	HB1069
46.15	Amended	HB1927
46.15	Amended	HB2112
46.15	Amended	SB550
46.15	Amended	HB3607
48.05	Added	HB1925
50.01	Added	HB2366
50.02	Added	HB2366
71.02	Amended	HB375

SECTION	EFFECT	BILL NUMBER
71.023	Amended	SB768
71.028	Amended	HB1540

Code of Criminal Procedure

SECTION	EFFECT	BILL NUMBER
2.12	Amended	SB1550
2.122	Amended	HB3452
2.1387	Added	SB69
2.1397	Added	SB111
2.26	Amended	HB3607
2.305	Amended	SB800
2.32	Amended	HB375
2.33	Added	SB69
4.01	Amended	HB3774
4.14	Amended	HB3774
7A.01	Repealed	HB3607
7A.02	Repealed	HB3607
7A.03	Repealed	HB3607
7A.035	Repealed	HB3607
7A.07	Repealed	HB3607
7B.001	Amended	HB39
7B.001	Amended	HB3607
7B.001	Amended	SB623
7B.002	Amended	HB3607
7B.002	Amended	SB623
7B.003	Amended	HB39
7B.003	Amended	HB3607
7B.004	Amended	HB3607
7B.007	Amended	HB39
7B.007	Amended	HB3607
11.07	Amended	HB3774
11.072	Amended	HB3774
12.01	Amended	HB375
12.01	Amended	SB109

TABLE OF SECTIONS AFFECTED BY 2021 LEGISLATION

SECTION	EFFECT	BILL NUMBER	SECTION	EFFECT	BILL NUMBER
13.40	Added	SB1056	38.01	Amended	HB3774
14.03	Amended	HB1927	38.071	Amended	HB375
15.051	Amended	HB1172	38.37	Amended	HB375
16.22	Amended	SB49	38.435	Added	HB2706
16.22	Amended	HB3607	38.50	Amended	SB335
17.03	Amended	HB375	42.01	Amended	HB3607
17.032	Amended	HB375	42.014	Amended	SB1056
17.04	Amended	SB49	42.01991	Added	HB465
17.081	Added	HB1005	42.037	Amended	SB1056
17.41	Amended	HB1005	42.15	Amended	SB1373
17.45	Amended	HB1540	42.152	Amended	SB1923
17.465	Added	HB1005	42.25	Added	HB3774
17.50	Added	HB766	42A.052	Amended	HB385
18.01	Amended	HB3363	42A.054	Amended	SB768
18.01	Amended	SB112	42A.056	Amended	SB768
18.021	Amended	HB375	42A.102	Amended	HB3607
18.06	Amended	HB3363	42A.102	Amended	SB768
18.06	Amended	SB112	42A.111	Amended	HB757
18.067	Added	SB1047	42A.301	Amended	HB385
18.07	Amended	HB3363	42A.303	Amended	SB1923
18.07	Amended	SB112	42A.303	Amended	HB385
18.10	Amended	SB1047	42A.403	Amended	SB1480
18B.001	Amended	HB3363	42A.403	Amended	HB385
18B.001	Amended	SB112	42A.404	Amended	SB1480
18B.151	Amended	HB3363	42A.404	Amended	HB385
18B.151	Amended	SB112	42A.4045	Amended	HB385
18B.202	Amended	SB112	42A.405	Repealed	SB1480
18B.321	Added	HB3363	42A.406	Amended	HB385
18B.322	Added	HB3363	42A.406	Amended	SB1480
18B.323	Added	HB3363	42A.407	Amended	SB1480
18B.324	Added	HB3363	42A.408	Amended	HB3607
18B.325	Added	HB3363	42A.453	Amended	HB1540
18B.326	Added	HB3363	42A.511	Amended	SB48

TABLE OF SECTIONS AFFECTED BY 2021 LEGISLATION

SECTION	EFFECT	BILL NUMBER
42A.514	Amended	SB1480
42A.515	Renumbered to Crim. Pro. art. 42A.516	HB3607
42A.516	Renumbered from Crim Pro. art. 42A.515	HB3607
42A.517	Added	HB9
42A.562	Amended	HB2352
42A.655	Amended	HB385
42A.701	Amended	HB385
42A.702	Amended	HB385
42A.751	Amended	HB1540
43.015	Amended	SB1373
44.2811	Amended	HB2669
45.004	Amended	SB1373
45.014	Amended	HB569
45.0217	Amended	HB2669
45.0241	Added	HB3774
45.041	Amended	HB80
45.041	Amended	HB569
45.0445	Amended	HB3774
45.048	Amended	HB569
45.051	Amended	SB1480
45.051	Amended	HB1560
45.0511	Amended	HB1560
46B.0735	Added	SB49
46B.080	Amended	SB49
46B.090	Amended	SB49
46B.091	Amended	SB49
46B.1055	Added	SB49
46C.102	Amended	SB49
49.04	Amended	HB1419
49.25	Amended	HB1419
49.25	Amended	HB2357
55.01	Amended	HB1927
55.02	Amended	HB1927
56.021	Repealed	HB3607
56.065	Repealed	HB3607
56.54	Repealed	HB3607
56.81	Repealed	HB3607
56A.001	Amended	HB3607
56A.052	Amended	HB3607
56A.052	Amended	HB2462
56A.052	Amended	HB39
56A.2505	Added	HB2462
56A.2506	Added	HB2462
56A.251	Amended	HB2462
56A.251	Amended	HB3607
56A.251	Amended	HB1172
56A.252	Amended	HB2462
56A.252	Amended	HB2706
56A.252	Amended	HB3607
56A.254	Amended	HB2706
56A.256	Added	HB3607
56A.301	Amended	HB3607
56A.302	Amended	HB2462
56A.302	Amended	HB2706
56A.303	Amended	HB2462
56A.303	Amended	HB2706
56A.303	Amended	HB3607
56A.304	Amended	HB2462
56A.304	Amended	HB2706
56A.304	Amended	HB3607
56A.305	Amended	HB2706
56A.306	Amended	HB3607
56A.307	Amended	HB2462
56A.3515	Added	HB1172

SECTION	EFFECT	BILL NUMBER
56A.352	Amended	HB1172
56B.003	Amended	HB3607
56B.106	Amended	HB3607
56B.107	Amended	SB957
56B.453	Amended	HB2462
56B.453	Amended	HB3607
58.051	Amended	HB3607
59.01	Amended	HB2315
59.06	Amended	HB402
62.001	Amended	HB375
62.001	Amended	HB1540
62.055	Amended	SB906
63.009	Amended	HB1419
66.102	Amended	HB375
66.252	Amended	HB3774
101.004	Added	SB1923
102.011	Amended	SB1923
102.014	Amended	SB1923
102.017	Amended	SB41
102.0173	Amended	HB3607
102.0179	Added	SB181
102.018	Amended	SB1923
102.020	Amended	HB3607
102.022	Amended	HB3607
102.030	Amended	HB3607
103.003	Amended	HB3774
103.0081	Amended	HB3774
103.0081	Amended	SB1373
Transportation Code		
391.256	Added	SB941
501.023	Amended	SB876
501.0234	Amended	SB876
501.030	Amended	SB876
501.0301	Amended	HB3607
501.051	Amended	SB1817
501.052	Amended	SB1817
501.053	Amended	SB1817
501.138	Amended	HB4472
502.0023	Amended	SB876
502.0025	Added	SB1064
502.040	Amended	SB876
502.041	Amended	SB876
502.0435	Added	HB2152
502.402	Amended	HB1698
502.407	Amended	SB1923
502.407	Amended	SB876
502.410	Amended	SB792
502.416	Added	HB2633
502.453	Amended	SB1064
502.473	Amended	SB1923
502.475	Amended	SB1923
503.009	Amended	HB3514
503.033	Amended	HB3533
503.0626	Amended	HB3927
503.063	Amended	HB3927
503.0631	Amended	HB3927
503.0632	Added	HB3927
503.067	Amended	HB3927
504.202	Amended	SB792
504.202	Amended	HB1081
504.202	Amended	HB1936
504.202	Amended	HB3401
504.315	Amended	HB912
504.3161	Amended	HB3607
504.327	Added	HB1081
504.327	Added	HB1936
504.327	Added	HB3401

SECTION	EFFECT	BILL NUMBER
504.327	Added	SB791
504.6012	Amended	HB2896
504.671	Renumbered to Transp. Code § 504.674	HB3607
504.671	Renumebred to Transp. Code § 504.672	HB3607
504.671	Renumbered to Transp. Code § 504.673	HB3607
504.672	Renumbered from Transp. Code § 504.671	HB3607
504.673	Renumbered from Transp. Code § 504.671	HB3607
504.674	Renumbered from Transp. Code § 504.671	HB3607
504.675	Added	HB1863
504.675	Added	HB2633
504.675	Added	HB4080
504.675	Added	SB1123
504.943	Amended	SB1923
504.945	Amended	SB1923
520.006	Amended	SB876
520.063	Amended	HB3514
521.013	Added	HB2497
521.013	Added	HB2633
521.026	Amended	SB1923
521.054	Amended	SB1134
521.054	Amended	SB1923
521.1016	Added	SB798
521.102	Amended	HB911
521.121	Amended	SB1134
521.1211	Amended	HB368
521.1235	Amended	HB911
521.142	Amended	SB1134
521.144	Amended	SB876
521.165	Amended	HB1560
521.1655	Amended	HB1560
521.168	Added	SB2054
521.1811	Amended	SB798
521.206	Amended	HB1560
521.221	Amended	SB1923
521.222	Amended	HB1560
521.372	Amended	SB181
521.374	Amended	SB181
521.374	Amended	SB1480
521.375	Amended	SB181
521.375	Amended	SB1480
521.376	Amended	SB181
521.376	Amended	SB1480
521.421	Amended	HB4544
521.4265	Amended	SB2054
521.4265	Amended	SB798
521.460	Amended	HB3374
522.023	Amended	HB3395
522.0296	Added	HB2633
541.201	Amended	HB3665
541.304	Amended	HB1560
542.304	Amended	HB3607
544.007	Amended	SB1055
545.001	Amended	HB1759
545.157	Amended	HB2048
545.251	Amended	HB1759
545.253	Amended	HB1759

SECTION	EFFECT	BILL NUMBER
545.2535	Amended	HB1759
545.254	Amended	HB1759
545.255	Amended	HB1759
545.3051	Amended	HB1257
545.3075	Added	HB3286
545.3531	Added	HB3282
545.412	Amended	HB1560
545.413	Amended	HB1560
545.4205	Added	SB1495
545.428	Added	SB1055
545.452	Amended	HB3026
547.004	Amended	SB1923
547.618	Added	HB3026
547.701	Amended	SB445
548.601	Amended	SB15
548.605	Amended	SB1923
551.107	Amended	HB3607
551.403	Amended	HB1281
551.4031	Amended	HB1281
551.404	Amended	HB1281
551A.001	Amended	HB3607
552.002	Amended	SB1055
552.003	Amended	SB1055
552.006	Amended	SB1055
601.455	Added	HB1693
622.151	Added	SB1815
622.152	Added	SB1815
622.153	Added	SB1815
622.902	Amended	SB1815
622.952	Amended	SB1815
622.955	Amended	SB1815
623.0112	Amended	SB1814
623.012	Amended	SB1814
623.013	Amended	SB1814

SECTION	EFFECT	BILL NUMBER
623.015	Amended	SB1814
623.016	Amended	SB1814
623.071	Amended	SB1815
623.0711	Amended	SB1814
623.075	Amended	SB1814
623.093	Amended	SB1814
623.0975	Added	SB1814
623.323	Amended	SB1814
643.002	Amended	HB3607
644.101	Amended	HB2748
644.101	Amended	HB3607
644.101	Amended	SB901
681.004	Amended	SB792
681.008	Amended	SB792
681.009	Amended	SB792
681.011	Amended	SB792
681.013	Amended	SB1923
721.003	Amended	SB795
724.012	Amended	HB558
724.013	Amended	HB558
724.015	Amended	SB335
730.003	Amended	SB15
730.006	Amended	SB15
730.007	Amended	SB15
730.0121	Added	SB15
720.0122	Added	SB15
730.0123	Added	SB15
730.013	Amended	SB15
730.014	Amended	SB15
730.016	Amended	SB15
731.001	Amended	HB3607

Alcoholic Beverage

SECTION	EFFECT	BILL NUMBER
1.04	Amended	SB911

TABLE OF SECTIONS AFFECTED BY 2021 LEGISLATION

SECTION	EFFECT	BILL NUMBER
101.673	Added	HB1957
103.06	Amended	HB763
105.01	Amended	HB1518
105.04	Amended	HB1518
105.05	Amended	HB1518
105.06	Amended	HB1518
105.091	Added	HB1518
106.115	Amended	SB1480
106.115	Amended	HB1560
106.17	Added	SB766
Agriculture		
122.201	Amended	SB703
Business and Commerce		
102.101	Amended	HB3721
Civil Practice & Remedies Code		
125.0015	Amended	HB375
125.0015	Amended	HB1540
125.0015	Amended	SB315
125.0015	Amended	SB766
125.0017	Repealed	HB1540
125.070	Amended	HB1540
Education Code		
33.0531	Added	SB2158
33.057	Amended	SB2158
37.0813	Amended	SB741
37.0815	Amended	HB1927
Family Code		
45.102	Amended	HB2301
45.103	Amended	HB2301

SECTION	EFFECT	BILL NUMBER
51.02	Amended	HB3774
51.03	Amended	HB1540
51.03	Amended	SB1056
51.04	Amended	HB3774
51.0414	Amended	HB3774
51.11	Amended	SB2049
53.03	Amended	SB1480
54.01	Amended	SB2049
54.02	Amended	SB2049
54.032	Amended	SB41
54.0325	Amended	SB41
54.04	Amended	SB2049
54.04012	Amended	HB2633
54.0405	Amended	HB1560
54.041	Amended	SB41
54.0411	Repealed	SB41
54.0461	Repealed	SB41
54.0462	Repealed	SB41
54.047	Amended	SB1480
54.047	Amended	SB41
54.05	Amended	SB2049
54.06	Amended	SB41
54.11	Amended	SB2049
58.106	Amended	HB4158
58.256	Amended	HB1401
58.258	Amended	HB1401
61.002	Amended	SB41
65.003	Amended	HB3165
85.005	Amended	HB39
85.006	Amended	HB39
85.0225	Added	HB1372
85.026	Amended	HB39
86.0011	Amended	HB39
261.001	Amended	HB375

SECTION	EFFECT	BILL NUMBER	SECTION	EFFECT	BILL NUMBER
261.001	Amended	HB1540	262.411	Added	HB3041
261.001	Amended	HB567	262.412	Added	HB3041
261.101	Amended	HB3379	262.413	Added	HB3041
261.3017	Amended	SB1578	262.414	Added	HB3041
261.30171	Added	SB1578	262.415	Added	HB3041
261.30175	Added	SB1578	262.416	Added	HB3041
261.3027	Added	HB135	262.417	Added	HB3041
261.3091	Added	HB135			
261.504	Amended	SB1578	**Government Code**		
262.102	Amended	SB1578	102.021	Repealed	HB3607
262.104	Amended	SB1578	102.021	Repealed	SB41
262.1095	Amended	HB3041	102.0211	Repealed	SB41
262.1095	Amended	HB2926	102.0212	Repealed	HB3607
262.113	Repealed	HB567	102.0212	Repealed	SB41
262.1131	Repealed	HB567	102.0213	Repealed	HB3607
262.114	Amended	HB2926	102.0213	Repealed	SB41
262.116	Amended	HB567	102.102	Repealed	HB3607
262.116	Amended	HB2536	102.102	Repealed	SB41
262.201	Amended	HB567	411.0074	Amended	HB1560
262.201	Amended	SB1578	411.0132	Amended	HB2343
262.2015	Amended	HB375	411.02096	Added	HB1927
262.2015	Amended	HB2924	411.02097	Added	HB1927
262.351	Amended	SB642	411.033	Added	SB2222
262.353	Added	SB642	411.042	Amended	HB1540
262.401	Added	HB3041	411.0745	Amended	SB41
262.402	Added	HB3041	411.077	Amended	SB41
262.403	Added	HB3041	411.1471	Amended	HB1540
262.404	Added	HB3041	411.172	Amended	HB918
262.405	Added	HB3041	411.1735	Added	HB918
262.406	Added	HB3041	411.177	Amended	HB2675
262.407	Added	HB3041	411.179	Amended	SB1134
262.408	Added	HB3041	411.179	Amended	HB918
262.409	Added	HB3041	411.179	Amended	HB2675
262.410	Added	HB3041	411.184	Added	HB2675

SECTION	EFFECT	BILL NUMBER
411.186	Amended	HB1927
411.198	Amended	HB1927
411.203	Amended	HB1927
411.2031	Amended	HB1927
411.204	Amended	HB1927
411.205	Amended	HB918
411.206	Amended	HB1927
411.209	Amended	HB1927
411.301	Added	SB3
411.302	Added	SB3
411.303	Added	SB3
411.304	Added	SB3
411.305	Added	SB3
411.306	Added	SB3
411.307	Added	SB3
411.308	Added	SB3
411.371	Added	HB103
411.372	Added	HB103
411.373	Added	HB103
411.374	Added	HB103
411.375	Added	HB103
411.376	Added	HB103
411.377	Added	HB103
411.378	Added	HB103
411.379	Added	HB103
411.380	Added	HB103
423.0045	Amended	SB149
	Health & Safety Code	
142.0062	Amended	HB797
161.081	Amended	SB248
161.083	Amended	SB248
161.0901	Added	SB248
161.0903	Added	SB248
169.001	Amended	HB1540
169.002	Amended	HB1540
169.003	Amended	HB1540
169.004	Amended	HB1540
169.005	Amended	HB1540
169.006	Amended	HB1540
170A.001	Added	HB1280
170A.002	Added	HB1280
170A.003	Added	HB1280
170A.004	Added	HB1280
170A.005	Added	HB1280
170A.006	Added	HB1280
170A.007	Added	HB1280
481.002	Amended	SB768
481.102	Amended	SB768
481.1022	Added	SB768
481.106	Amended	SB768
481.1123	Added	SB768
481.115	Amended	HB1694
481.115	Amended	SB768
481.1151	Amended	HB1694
481.116	Amended	HB1694
481.1161	Amended	HB1694
481.117	Amended	HB1694
481.118	Amended	HB1694
481.119	Amended	HB1694
481.121	Amended	HB1694
481.122	Amended	SB768
481.124	Amended	SB768
481.125	Amended	HB1694
481.134	Amended	HB1540
481.134	Amended	SB768
481.140	Amended	SB768
481.141	Amended	SB768

SECTION	EFFECT	BILL NUMBER
481.151	Amended	SB1125
481.152	Amended	SB1125
481.153	Amended	SB1125
481.159	Amended	SB1125
481.160	Amended	SB1125
481.161	Added	SB1125
483.041	Amended	HB1694
485.031	Amended	HB1694
552.002	Amended	HB1927
822.042	Amended	HB3340
841.041	Amended	SB906
841.061	Amended	SB906
841.062	Amended	SB906
841.063	Amended	SB906
841.064	Amended	SB906
841.0834	Amended	SB906
841.0837	Amended	SB906
841.084	Amended	SB906
841.146	Amended	SB906
841.151	Amended	SB906

Labor Code

SECTION	EFFECT	BILL NUMBER
52.062	Amended	HB1927

Occupations Code

SECTION	EFFECT	BILL NUMBER
169.001	Amended	HB1535
169.002	Amended	HB1535
169.003	Amended	HB1535
551.003	Amended	SB768
1701.3071	Amended	HB786
1701.351	Amended	HB3712
1701.352	Amended	HB786
1701.357	Amended	SB198
1701.451	Amended	SB24
1701.456	Amended	SB24
1701.601	Amended	SB1191
1701.621	Added	SB64
1701.622	Added	SB64
1701.623	Added	SB64
1701.624	Added	SB64
1701.625	Added	SB64
1701.626	Added	SB64
1701.6521	Added	HB1938
1701.655	Amended	HB929
1701.657	Amended	HB929
1701.658	Amended	HB1938
1956.001	Amended	HB4110
1956.0321	Added	HB4110
1956.033	Amended	HB4110
1956.034	Amended	HB4110
1956.035	Amended	HB4110
1956.036	Amended	HB4110
1956.037	Amended	HB4110
1956.040	Amended	HB4110
1956.051	Amended	SB1132
1956.052	Repealed	SB1132
1956.053	Repealed	SB1132
1956.054	Repealed	SB1132
1956.0612	Amended	SB1132
1956.0613	Amended	SB1132
1956.06131	Added	SB1132
1956.0616	Added	SB1132
2002.003	Amended	HB2757
2002.052	Amended	HB2757
2002.056	Amended	HB2757
2302.009	Renumbered to Occ. Code § 2302.010	HB3607

SECTION	EFFECT	BILL NUMBER
2302.010	Renumbered from Occ. Code § 2302.009	HB3607
2303.056	Amended	HB1560
2303.154	Amended	SB1817
2303.201	Added	SB1181
2303.202	Added	SB1181
2303.203	Added	SB1181
2303.204	Added	SB1181
2305.0051	Added	HB4110
2308.002	Amended	SB860
2308.055	Repealed	HB1560
2308.157	Amended	HB1560
2308.159	Amended	HB1560
2308.354	Amended	HB914
2308.457	Repealed	SB41
2309.056	Amended	HB1560
2309.106	Amended	HB1560
	Parks & Wildlife Code	
90.0035	Added	HB4436
	Property Code	
24A.002	Amended	HB1012
24A.0021	Amended	HB1012
24A.003	Amended	HB1012

SUMMARY OF SECTIONS AFFECTED BY 2021 LEGISLATION

ACTIVE SHOOTER

Requires that the Department of Public Safety develop and implement an alert system to be activated when there is a report of an active shooter; provides that the system must notify persons within a 50-mile radius of an active shooter's location at the request of a local law enforcement agency that determines it is necessary. [HB 103 adds Government Code §§ 411.371 to 411.380]

ASSAULT

Makes the assault of a process server a third-degree felony. [HB 1306 amends Penal Code §§ 22.01, 22.02]

BLOOD SPECIMENS

Requires that a blood specimen be taken on arrest if (1) the person is arrested for an offense under Chapter 49 (Intoxication and Alcoholic Beverage Offenses), (2) the person refuses to submit to the taking of the specimen voluntarily, (3) the person was operator of the motor vehicle or watercraft involved in an accident that the officer reasonable believes occurred as a result of the offense, and (4) at the time of the arrest, the officer "reasonably believes that as a direct result of the accident any individual has died, will die, or has suffered serious bodily injury." [HB 558 amends Transportation Code §§ 724.012, 724.013]

Allows the blood draw for an intoxication offense to be done in an adjacent county and by a law enforcement officer authorized to make an arrest in the county of execution. [SB 1047 adds Criminal Procedure art. 18.067; amends Criminal Procedure art. 18.10]

CONTROLLED SUBSTANCES

Creates a criminal offense specifically for fentanyl; creates a new group for fentanyl (1-B); increases the criminal penalties for possessing, manufacturing, and distributing fentanyl. [SB 768 adds Health and Safety §§ 481.1022, 481.1123]

Provides limited legal liability to overdose victims and those who seek help for them in order to encourage people to call for help in an overdose emergency. [HB 1694 amends Health & Safety Code §§ 481.115, 481.1151, 481.116, 481.1161, 481.117, 481.118, 481.119, 481.121, 481.125, 483.041, 485.031]

CPR TRAINING

Requires that the continuing education provided to telecommunicators include CPR training. [HB 786 amends Occupations Code §§ 1701.3071, 1701.352]

CRIMINAL MISCHIEF

Increases the criminal penalty for the offense of criminal mischief involving impairment or interruption of access to an automated teller machine to a third-degree felony. [SB 516 amends Penal Code § 28.03]

DOMESTIC VIOLENCE

Protects survivors of family violence by authorizing the separation of the wireless telephone numbers of a petitioner and any applicable children from the account of a primary account holder via court order. [HB 1372 adds Family Code § 85.0225]

DRIVER'S LICENSES

Reforms mandatory 180-day driver's license suspensions for anyone convicted of any drug offense by reducing suspensions to a minimum of 90 days and allowing a judge to waive suspensions for defendants with misdemeanor drug convictions who do not have prior drug convictions within the past 36 months. [SB 181 adds Criminal Procedure art. 102.0179; amends Transportation Code §§ 521.372, 521.374, 521.375, 521.376]

Establishes an alternative, no-cost process for obtaining a state-issued ID for victims of dating violence, victims of family violence, or a child of a victim dating or family violence. [SB 798 adds Transportation Code adds § 521.1016]

DRONES

Requires that each state or local law enforcement agency that plans to use drones in the field submit to the Texas Commission on Law Enforcement a written drone policy that sets forth the agency's rules of engagement and details when the use of force by drone is allowed;

prohibits the use of deadly force by means of a fully autonomous drone. [HB 1758 adds Penal Code § 9.54]

Adds military installations to the definition of "critical infrastructure facility" in connection with the restrictions on the operation of drones near those facilities. [SB 149 amends Government Code § 423.0045]

ELDERLY INDIVIDUALS

Creates the new offense of financial abuse of an elderly individual. [HB 1156 adds Penal Code § 32.55]

EMERGENCY VEHICLES

Makes it a state jail felony to intentionally, knowingly, or recklessly block an emergency vehicle operating its emergency lights or siren or near a hospital entrance. [HB 9 adds Criminal Procedure § 42A.517; amends Penal Code § 42.03]

EXCESSIVE FORCE

Provides that a peace officer has a duty to intervene to stop or prevent another peace officer from using force against a person who is committing an offense in certain circumstances; requires that a peace officer who witnesses the use of excessive force by another officer promptly make a detailed report. [SB 69 adds Criminal Procedure art. 2.1387]

FALSE REPORTS

Creates the offense of false report to induce emergency response; makes it a criminal offense to knowingly make a false report that is reasonably likely to cause an emergency response from a law enforcement agency or other emergency responder and causes the report to be made with reckless disregard about whether the response may result in bodily harm to any individual. [SB 1056 adds Penal Code § 42.0601, Criminal Procedure art. 13.40; amends Criminal Procedure art. 42.014, 42.037, Family Code § 51.03]

FIREARMS

Makes it legal for individuals who are 21 years of age or older and who can legally possess a firearm to carry a handgun without first obtaining a license. [HB 1927 adds Government Code §§ 411.02096, 411.02097; repeals Penal Code § 46.035; amends Penal Code §§ 30.05,

30.06, 30.07, 46.02, 46.03, 46.04, 46.15; Criminal Procedure arts. 14.03, 55.01, 55.02; Education Code § 37.0815; Government Code §§ 411.186, 411.198, 411.203, 411.2031, 411.204, 411.209; Health and Safety Code § 552.002; Labor Code § 52.062]

Prohibits the enforcement of certain federal regulations on firearms, firearm accessories, or ammunition that are not in state law. [HB 2622 adds Penal Code § 1.10]

Protects hotel guests from being prosecuted for possessing a handgun or ammunition in their vehicle or room on the hotel premises. [SB 20 amends Penal Code §§ 30.05, 30.06, 30.07; SB 550 amends Penal Code §§ 30.05, 30.07, 46.02, 46.035, 46.15]

Allows for the use of any type of holster for properly carrying a gun. [HB 2112 amends Penal Code §§ 30.05, 30.07, 46.02, 46.035, 46.15]

Establishes the right of certain first responders who are handgun license holders to carry a handgun while carrying out their duties, contingent on the first responder obtaining liability insurance and completing training. [HB 1069 amends Penal Code §§ 30.06, 30.07, 46.01, 46.15,

Removes firearm suppressors from the list of prohibited weapons; makes a firearm suppressor that is manufactured and remains in Texas not subject to federal law or federal regulation. [HB 957 amends Penal Code §§ 46.01, 46.05

Allows license holders to have a handgun visible in their vehicle, regardless of whether it is on their person, as long as it is in a holster. [HB 1407 amends Penal Code § 46.035]

Makes it a criminal offense to knowingly make a materially false or misleading statement when providing information for the purposes of complying with the National Instant Criminal Background Check system. [SB 162 amends Penal Code § 46.06]

Allows a school marshal to carry or possess a handgun on the physical premises of a school, but only in the manner provided by the governing body's regulations; requires (1) that the regulations provide that the school marshal may carry a concealed handgun unless the marshal's primary duty involves regular, direct contact with students and (2) that, if the marshal's duties require regular, direct contact, the handgun must be kept in a locked and secured safe on the physical premises of the school and that the marshal is authorized to access the handgun only under circumstances that would justify the use of deadly force. [SB 741 amends Education Code § 37.0813]

Makes a person who is at least 18 years of age but not yet 21 years of age eligible for a handgun license if the person meets all other license requirements except the minimum age under federal law to purchase a handgun and is protected under an active protective order or magistrate's order for emergency protection issued with respect to an offense involving family violence or with respect to stalking, compelling prostitution, or certain sexual or trafficking offenses. [HB 918 adds Government Code § 411.1735; amends Government Code §§ 411.172, 411.179, 411.205]

Creates an at-risk designation for a handgun license and provides for the expedited processing of an application for a license with that designation. [HB 2675 adds Government Code § 411.184; amends §§ 411.177, 411.179]

GOLF CARTS

Removes the license plate requirement for golf carts only operating in master planned communities. [HB 1281 amends Transportation Code §§ 551.403, 551.4031, 551.404]

HARASSMENT

Creates a criminal offense for harassment published on an Internet website that causes distress, abuse, or torment to another person; rules out communications made in connection with a matter of public concern to make sure that there would no chilling effect on political speech. [SB 530 amends Penal Code § 42.07]

LOCATION INFORMATION

Gives law enforcement the ability to obtain location information from electronic devices used by those suspected of committing serious offenses, who are considered felony fugitives, and their attempts to avoid apprehension; requires that law enforcement and prosecutors apply for a search warrant based on probable cause to obtain location information from devices used by suspects from electronic communications companies; permits a law enforcement agency to obtain location information without a warrant in life-threatening situations but requires that the warrant be obtained within 48 hours. [HB 3363 adds Criminal Procedure arts. 18B.321 to 18B.326; amends Criminal Procedure arts. 18.01, 18.06, 18.07, 18B.001, 18B.151

Applies the probable cause standard to require a peace officer's affidavit to state facts and circumstances related to the case that would leave the officer to believe that criminal activity has been or will be committed to request the installation of a mobile tracking device. [SB 112 amends Criminal Procedure arts. 18.01, 18.06, 18.07, 18B.001, 18B.151, 18B.202]

MOVE OVER LAW

Adds vehicles operated in connection with toll project entities to the list of vehicles that drivers are instructed to move over and slow down for while driving. [HB 2048 amends Transportation Code § 545.157]

NECK RESTRAINTS

Prohibits the use of neck restraints during a search or arrest. [SB 69 adds Criminal Procedure art. 2.33]

PEDESTRIANS

Expands the duties of a driver under the Transportation Code by providing for penalties for drivers who inflict bodily injury or series bodily injury on a pedestrian or individual who is lawfully using a crosswalk in a roadway. [SB 1055 adds Transportation Code § 545.428; amends Transportation Code § 544.007, 552.002, 552.003, 552.006]

POLICE OFFICERS

Increases the penalty for using a laser against a law enforcement officer by making it (1) a third-degree felony if it causes bodily injury to the officer and (2) a first-degree felony if it causes serious bodily injury to the officer. [HB 2366 amends Penal Code § 42.13]

Creates the offense of unlawful use of fireworks, which occurs when a person ignites or explodes a firework with the intent (1) to interfere with lawful performance of an official duty of a peace officer, (2) to flee from a person the actor knows is a peace officer, or (3) to cause bodily injury to a person the actor knows is a peace officer lawfully discharging their official duty. [HB 2366 adds Penal Code §§ 50.01, 50.02]

Requires that a law enforcement agency filing a case with the state's attorney submit a written statement from an officer attesting that all exculpatory, impeaching, or mitigating evidence in possession of the investigating agency has been released to the state's attorney at the time the case is filed; also requires that any exculpatory, impeaching, or mitigating evidence collected after the agency files a case is also promptly turned over to the state's attorney. [SB 111 adds Crim Pro art. 2.1397]

Directs that bullet-resistant windshields be provided for all Department of Public Safety patrol vehicles. [SB 2222 adds Government Code § 411.033]

Adds to the basic peace officer training course training on the prohibition and use of chokeholds, carotid artery holds, and neck restraints during certain encounters with members of the public; also requires training (1) on an officer's duty to intervene if the officer observes another officer using force he or she believes to be more than is required under the circumstances and (2) on the officer's duty to render aid to a person who he or she observes to have sustained serious injury during a use of force and the conditions under which aid should be rendered. [HB 3712 adds Occupations Code §§ 1701.2551, 1701.269, 1701.270; amends Occupations Code § 1701.351]

Creates a voluntary peer-to-peer support network focused on training law enforcement officers to provide support to each other. [SB 64 adds Occupation Code §§ 1701.621 to 1701.626]

Identifies video and audio recorded by a body worn camera as evidence; requires that the camera work by an officer who is actively involved in an investigation remain activated for the entirety of the investigation consistent with the law enforcement agency's policy. [HB 929 amends Occupations Code §§ 1701.655, 1701.657]

PROHIBITED CAMPING

Makes it a Class C misdemeanor for intentionally or knowingly camping in a public place without the consent of the legal authority that manages the public places; bars local entities from adopting or enforcing a policy that prohibits or discouraging enforcement of a public camping ban. [HB 1925 adds Penal Code § 48.05]

PUBLIC SERVANTS

Increases the criminal penalty for certain offenses committed in retaliation for or on account of a person's service or status as a public servant. [HB 624 adds Penal Code § 12.501]

SEXUAL OFFENSES

Establishes the same criminal penalties for continuous sexual abuse of a child (first-degree felony punishable by imprisonment for life or for a minimum of 25 years or maximum of 99 years) for continuous sexual abuse of a person with a disability. [HB 375 amends Penal Code § 20A.02, 21.02, 71.02, 71.023; Criminal Procedure §§ 2.32, 12.01, 17.03, 17.032, 18.021, 38.071, 38.37, 62.001, 66.102; Civil Practice and Remedies Code § 125.0015; Family Code §§ 261.001, 262.2015]

Increases the severity of the criminal offense of improper sexual activity with a person in custody from a state jail felony to a second-degree felony. [SB 312 amends Penal Code § 39.04]

SEXUALLY ORIENTED BUSINESSES

Raises the age of employment in sexually oriented businesses from 18 to 21; prohibits a sexually oriented business from allowing minors on the premises. [SB 315 amends Penal Code § 43.251

SMUGGLING OF PERSONS

Revises the conduct constituting a smuggling of persons offense and enhances the penalty for the offense under certain circumstances; includes an agent of the U.S. Department of Homeland Security as a special investigator; removes the condition of intent to obtain a pecuniary benefit in committing the offense and instead enhances the penalty for the offense from a third-degree felony to a second-degree felony if the offense was committed with that intent; provides a penalty for assisting, guiding, or directing two or more individuals onto agricultural land without consent. [SB 576 amends Penal Code §§ 20.01, 20.05]

SPEED LIMITS

Allows a district engineer of the Texas Department of Transportation of temporarily lower the speed limit at a highway maintenance activity site under certain circumstances. [HB 3282 adds Transportation Code § 545.3531]

STREET RACING

Makes it a Class C misdemeanor to knowingly attend or assist in the preparation for a "reckless driving exhibition" or street racing event; enhances the misdemeanor penalties for anyone who participates in the reckless driving at these events. [SB 1495 adds Transportation Code § 545.4205; amends Penal Code § 42.03]

TRUANCY

Establishes an affirmative defense to an allegation of truant conduct in cases where one or more of the absences where due to the child's voluntary absence from his or her home because of abuse as shown by a preponderance of the evidence. [HB 3165 amends Family Code § 65.003]

TEXAS POLICE PROCEDURE

Arrest, Search and Seizure, and Confession Law

Note: *This is a general overview of the classical and current United States and Texas court decisions related to the Laws of Arrest, Search and Seizure, and Confession Law. As an overview, it should be used for a basic analysis of the general principles but not as a comprehensive presentation of the entire body of law. It is not to be used as a substitute for the opinion or advice of the appropriate legal counsel from the reader's department. To the extent possible, the information is current. However, very recent statutory and case law developments may not be covered.*

1. CONSTITUTIONAL CRIMINAL PROCEDURE

1.1. Constitutional Analysis

The Bill of Rights in the federal Constitution, and corresponding provisions in each state's constitution, provide citizens with certain fundamental safeguards from intrusive governmental conduct. Particularly relevant to situations involving law enforcement officials are the Fourth, Fifth, Sixth and, to a lesser extent, the First and Fourteenth Amendments.

The Fourth Amendment to the federal Constitution safeguards the "right of the people to be secure in their persons, houses, papers, and effects, against unreasonable searches and seizures[.]" Additionally, the Amendment commands that "no Warrants shall issue, but upon probable cause, supported by Oath or affirmation, and particularly describing the place to be searched, and the persons or things to be seized." The "ultimate touchstone of the Fourth Amendment is 'reasonableness.'"[1]

Similarly, Article 1, § 9 of the Texas Constitution provides: "The people shall be secure in their persons, houses, papers and possessions, from all unreasonable seizures or searches, and no warrant to search any place, or to seize any person or thing, shall issue without describing them as near as may be, nor without probable cause, supported by oath or affirmation."

1.1.1. New Federalism

When confronted with an unreasonable search and seizure, a state court is free, and indeed encouraged, to rely on its own constitution to provide greater protection to the privacy interests of its citizens than that afforded under parallel provisions of the federal Constitution. As a well-established principle of our federalist system, state constitutions may be the source of "individual liberties more expansive than those conferred by the federal Constitution."[2] This means that a state court is free as a matter of its own law to impose greater restrictions on police activity than those the United States Supreme Court holds to be necessary under federal constitutional standards. The federal Constitution represents the baseline or "floor" of protection and, of course, a state may not drop below the federal floor;[3] it may, however, rely on its own state constitution to heighten that floor of protection. State law enforcement officers are cautioned, therefore, that their state may establish, as a matter of its own law, a ceiling of protection for its citizens which may have the effect of placing additional restrictions upon, or requiring the exercise of additional precautions by, its officers.[4]

1.1.2. Interpreting the Texas Constitution

In interpreting the Texas Constitution, courts are not bound by the United States Supreme Court's interpretation of the United States Constitution, even where the language is identical.[5] Texas law enforcement officers are cautioned, therefore, that Texas may, from time to time, establish, as a matter of Texas constitutional law, a ceiling of protection for Texas citizens which may have the effect of placing additional restrictions upon, or requiring the exercise of additional precautions by, local, county and Sate officers. Indeed, this

---

[1] *Brigham City v. Stuart*, 547 U.S. 398, 403, 126 S. Ct. 1943 (2006).

[2] *Pruneyard Shopping Center v. Robins*, 447 U.S. 74, 81, 100 S. Ct. 2035, 2040 (1980).

[3] Note also that in *Timbs v. Indiana*, 586 U.S. ___, 139 S.Ct. 682, 686-87 (2019), the United States Supreme Court held that the states cannot impose excessive fees, fines and forfeitures as criminal penalties. The Court's decision underscores that the Eighth Amendment's prohibition against "excessive fines" applies to states and localities as well as the federal government. Said the Court: "The Excessive Fines Clause is therefore incorporated by the Due Process Clause of the Fourteenth Amendment." *Id.*, 139 S.Ct. at 687.

[4] *See generally* Linde, *E. Pluribus – Constitutional Theory and State Courts,* 18 Ga. L. Rev. 165 (1984); Brennen, *State Constitutions and the Protection of Individual Rights,* 90 Harv. L. Rev. 489 (1977); Note, *The New Federalism, Toward a Principled Interpretation of the State Constitution,* 29 Stan. L. Rev. 297 (1977); Feldman & Abney, *The Double Security of Federalism: Protecting Individual Liberty Under the Arizona Constitution,* 20 Ariz. St. L.J. 115 (1988).

[5] *Heitman v. State*, 815 S.W.2d 681 (Tex. Crim. App. 1991).

is exactly what the Texas Court of Criminal Appeals did in *Heitman v. State*[6] wherein it declared, "Today we reserve for ourselves the power to interpret our own constitution."[7]

Nonetheless, even though Texas courts "are not bound by Supreme Court case law when it comes to interpreting [the Texas] Constitution, [they] are not precluded from following it either. This reasoning is particularly appropriate when the state constitutional provision ... and its federal constitutional counterpart are almost identically worded."[8] Thus, for purposes of arrests, searches and seizures effected by Texas law enforcement officers, the Fourth Amendment still remains the foundational source for the applicable rules, procedures and analyses.

1.1.3. Rights of Crime Victims

Pursuant to Tex. Code Crim. Proc. Art. 56.02(a): A victim, guardian of a victim, or close relative of a deceased victim is entitled to the following rights within the criminal justice system:

(1) the right to receive from law enforcement agencies adequate protection from harm and threats of harm arising from cooperation with prosecution efforts;
(2) the right to have the magistrate take the safety of the victim or his family into consideration as an element in fixing the amount of bail for the accused;
(3) the right, if requested, to be informed:
(A) by the attorney representing the state of relevant court proceedings, including appellate proceedings, and to be informed if those proceedings have been canceled or rescheduled prior to the event; and
(B) by an appellate court of decisions of the court, after the decisions are entered but before the decisions are made public;
(4) the right to be informed, when requested, by a peace officer concerning the defendant's right to bail and the procedures in criminal investigations and by the district attorney's office concerning the general procedures in the criminal justice system, including general procedures in guilty plea negotiations and arrangements, restitution, and the appeals and parole process;
(5) the right to provide pertinent information to a probation department conducting a presentencing investigation concerning the impact of the offense on the victim and his family by testimony, written statement, or any other manner prior to any sentencing of the offender;
(6) the right to receive information regarding compensation to victims of crime as provided by Subchapter B, including information related to the costs that may be compensated under that subchapter and the amount of compensation, eligibility for compensation, and procedures for application for compensation under that subchapter, the payment for a medical examination under Article 56.06 for a victim of a sexual assault, and when requested, to referral to available social service agencies that may offer additional assistance;
(7) the right to be informed, upon request, of parole procedures, to participate in the parole process, to be notified, if requested, of parole proceedings concerning a defendant in the victim's case, to provide to the Board of Pardons and Paroles for inclusion in the defendant's file information to be considered by the board prior to the parole of any defendant convicted of any crime subject to this subchapter, and to be notified, if requested, of the defendant's release;
(8) the right to be provided with a waiting area, separate or secure from other witnesses, including the offender and relatives of the offender, before testifying in any proceeding concerning the offender; if a separate waiting area is not available, other safeguards should be taken to minimize the victim's contact with the offender and the offender's relatives and witnesses, before and during court proceedings;

[6] *Heitman v. State*, 815 S.W.2d 681 (Tex. Crim. App. 1991).
[7] *Heitman v. State*, 815 S.W.2d 681, 682 (Tex. Crim. App. 1991).
[8] *Hankston v. State*, 517 S.W.3d 112, 120 (Tex. Crim. App. 2017). In *Hankston v. Texas*, ___ U.S. ___, 138 S. Ct. 2706 (2018), the United States Supreme Court vacated the judgment and remanded it to the Court of Criminal Appeals of Texas for further consideration in light of *Carpenter v. United States*, 585 U.S. ___, 138 S. Ct. 2206 (2018). The Texas Court of Criminal Appeals has ordered briefing pursuant to that remand to further consider the issue.

(9) the right to prompt return of any property of the victim that is held by a law enforcement agency or the attorney for the state as evidence when the property is no longer required for that purpose;
(10) the right to have the attorney for the state notify the employer of the victim, if requested, of the necessity of the victim's cooperation and testimony in a proceeding that may necessitate the absence of the victim from work for good cause;
(11) the right to request victim-offender mediation coordinated by the victim services division of the Texas Department of Criminal Justice;
(12) the right to be informed of the uses of a victim impact statement and the statement's purpose in the criminal justice system, to complete the victim impact statement, and to have the victim impact statement considered:
(A) by the attorney representing the state and the judge before sentencing or before a plea bargain agreement is accepted; and
(B) by the Board of Pardons and Paroles before an inmate is released on parole;
(13) for a victim of an assault or sexual assault who is younger than 17 years of age or whose case involves family violence, as defined by Section 71.004, Family Code, the right to have the court consider the impact on the victim of a continuance requested by the defendant; if requested by the attorney representing the state or by counsel for the defendant, the court shall state on the record the reason for granting or denying the continuance; and
(14) if the offense is a capital felony, the right to:
(A) receive by mail from the court a written explanation of defense-initiated victim outreach if the court has authorized expenditures for a defense-initiated victim outreach specialist;
(B) not be contacted by the victim outreach specialist unless the victim, guardian, or relative has consented to the contact by providing a written notice to the court; and
(C) designate a victim service provider to receive all communications from a victim outreach specialist acting on behalf of any person.

In addition, "[a] victim, guardian of a victim, or close relative of a deceased victim is entitled to the right to be present at all public court proceedings related to the offense, subject to the approval of the judge in the case. The office of the attorney representing the state, and the sheriff, police, and other law enforcement agencies shall ensure to the extent practicable that a victim, guardian of a victim, or close relative of a deceased victim is afforded the rights granted by this article and Article 56.021 and, on request, an explanation of those rights."[9]

Article 1, § 30 of the Texas Constitution provides similar rights to crime victims, including:

(1) the right to be treated with fairness and with respect for the victim's dignity and privacy throughout the criminal justice process; and
(2) the right to be reasonably protected from the accused throughout the criminal justice process. In addition, on the request of a crime victim, the crime victim has the following rights:
(1) the right to notification of court proceedings;
(2) the right to be present at all public court proceedings related to the offense, unless the victim is to testify and the court determines that the victim's testimony would be materially affected if the victim hears other testimony at the trial;
(3) the right to confer with a representative of the prosecutor's office;
(4) the right to restitution; and
(5) the right to information about the conviction, sentence, imprisonment, and release of the accused.

1.2. The Fifth Amendment

The Fifth Amendment provides, in part, that no person shall be compelled to be a witness against oneself in a criminal case. The Supreme Court has also found that an integral part of an accused's right to be free

[9] Tex. Code Crim. Proc. art. 56.02(b) and (c).

from compelled incrimination is a judicially created right to have counsel present and a right to refuse to answer questions during a custodial interrogation, even though the Constitution does not specifically provide such a safeguard.

Similarly, Article 1, § 10 of the Texas Constitution provides, in part: "In all criminal prosecutions the accused shall have a speedy public trial by an impartial jury. He shall have the right to demand the nature and cause of the accusation against him, and to have a copy thereof. He shall not be compelled to give evidence against himself, and shall have the right of being heard by himself or counsel, or both, shall be confronted by the witnesses against him and shall have compulsory process for obtaining witnesses in his favor." Article 1, § 19 of the Texas Constitution provides: "No citizen of this State shall be deprived of life, liberty, property, privileges or immunities, or in any manner disfranchised, except by the due course of the law of the land."

The Fifth and Fourteenth Amendments of the federal Constitution, and Article I, § 19 of the Texas Constitution each contain a "Due Process" clause. Due process means that no person shall be deprived of life, liberty or property without the due process of law. In the context of the rights of a criminal suspect, this provision has been construed as offering protection against certain fundamentally unfair governmental conduct, particularly the use of suggestive, prejudicial or discriminatory identification procedures.[10]

1.3. The Sixth Amendment

The Sixth Amendment provides that a defendant in a criminal case — and a suspect in a criminal investigation when the investigation has reached a critical stage — shall enjoy the right to counsel to aid in his defense. Article 1, § 10, of the Texas Constitution provides a similar right.

The Sixth Amendment is applicable to all state court proceedings by virtue of the Due Process Clause of the Fourteenth Amendment.[11] The right to counsel provided by the Sixth Amendment attaches when adversarial judicial proceedings are commenced against a defendant and remains throughout all critical stages of the proceedings.[12] The right attaches to initial proceedings, including formal charges, preliminary hearings, indictments, bills of information and arraignments.[13]

1.4. The Exclusionary Rule

1.4.1. General aspects

Although the Fourth Amendment does not specifically prohibit the use of evidence seized in violation of its terms, the Supreme Court has created a tool designed ultimately to safeguard Fourth Amendment rights. The tool is called the exclusionary rule and, since 1961, it has been disallowing the use of evidence obtained in violation of the Fourth Amendment in state as well as federal prosecutions.[14] Rather than a personal constitutional right belonging to the victim of an illegal search or seizure, the exclusionary rule operates as a judicially created remedy which protects Fourth Amendment rights generally by deterring wrongful police conduct.[15] "Deterrence," then, is the linchpin of the exclusionary rule.[16]

---

[10] *See Simmons v. United States,* 390 U.S. 377, 384, 88 S. Ct. 967, 971 (1968).

[11] This was made clear in *Gideon v. Wainwright*, 372 U.S. 335, 344, 83 S. Ct. 792, 796 (1963).

[12] *See Kirby v. Illinois*, 406 U.S. 682, 689, 92 S. Ct. 1877 (1972).

[13] *See Kirby v. Illinois*, 406 U.S. 682, 689, 92 S. Ct. 1877 (1972).

[14] *See Mapp v. Ohio*, 367 U.S. 643, 81 S. Ct. 1684 (1961) ("all evidence obtained by searches and seizures in violation of the Constitution is, by that same authority, inadmissible in a state court").

[15] *United States v. Leon*, 468 U.S. 897, 104 S. Ct. 3405 (1984).

[16] *See United States v. Janis*, 428 U.S. 433, 96 S. Ct. 3021 (1976) (The "prime purpose" of the exclusionary rule, if not the sole one, is "to deter future unlawful police conduct."). As further explained in *United States v. Calandra,* 414 U.S. 338, 347-48, 94 S. Ct. 613, 619-20 (1974), "[t]he purpose of the exclusionary rule is not to redress the injury to the privacy of the search victim.... Instead, the rule's prime purpose is to deter future unlawful police conduct and thereby effectuate the guarantee of the Fourth Amendment against unreasonable searches and seizures." The rule "is calculated to prevent, not to repair. Its purpose is to deter — to compel respect for the constitutional guaranty in the only effectively available way — by removing the incentive to disregard it." *Elkins v. United States,* 364 U.S. 206, 217, 80 S. Ct. 1437, 1444 (1960).

Simply stated, the exclusionary rule is a judicially created device which is employed by the courts to prohibit the use of evidence at a criminal trial when that evidence has been seized by law enforcement officials in violation of the Constitution.

The Texas legislature has codified the exclusionary rule at Tex. Code Crim. Proc. art. 38.23 which states, in part: "No evidence obtained by an officer or other person in violation of any provisions of the Constitution or laws of the State of Texas, or of the Constitution or laws of the United States of America, shall be admitted in evidence against the accused on the trial of any criminal case."

The federal exclusionary rule does not generally apply to actions taken under a statute that is subsequently ruled to be invalid.[17] The rule also does not apply to private searches.[18]

Other than deterrence, the exclusionary rule advances the imperative of judicial integrity and removes the profit motive from unconstitutional actions. As Justice Clark, writing for the Supreme Court in *Mapp v. Ohio*,[19] declared:

> There are those who say, as did Justice (then Judge) Cardozo, that under our constitutional exclusionary doctrine "the criminal is to go free because the constable has blundered."... In some cases this will undoubtedly be the result. But, ... "there is another consideration — the imperative of judicial integrity." ... The criminal goes free, if he must, but it is the law that sets him free. Nothing can destroy a government more quickly than its failure to observe its own laws, or worse, its disregard of the charter of its own existence.[20]

The remedy of exclusion applies generally to criminal prosecutions, prohibiting the use of evidence obtained in violation of federal or state constitutional rights.[21] The exclusionary rule has never been interpreted, however, to prohibit the use of illegally seized evidence in all proceedings or against all persons. As with any remedial device, the application of the rule has been restricted to those areas where its remedial objectives are thought to be best served.[22] If application of the exclusionary rule in a particular situation "does not result in appreciable deterrence," its use may be "unwarranted."[23]

1.4.2. "Fruit of the Poisonous Tree" Doctrine

The Fourth Amendment's exclusionary rule encompasses both the "primary evidence obtained as a direct result of an illegal search or seizure," and evidence later discovered and found to be derivative of an illegality.[24] This derivative, or secondary evidence, including an officer's testimony based on knowledge garnered as a result of the illegal conduct, is often referred to as the *"fruit of the poisonous tree."*[25] The

---

17 *See, e.g., Illinois v. Krull*, 480 U.S. 340, 107 S. Ct. 1160 (1987) (suppression is not required "when an officer's reliance on the constitutionality of a statute is objectively reasonable, but the statute is subsequently declared unconstitutional."). *See also Michigan v. DeFillippo*, 443 U.S. 31, 99 S. Ct. 2627 (1979) (An arrest "made in good-faith reliance on an ordinance, which at the time had not been declared unconstitutional, is valid regardless of a subsequent judicial determination of its unconstitutionality").

18 *See United States v. Calandra*, 414 U.S. 338, 94 S. Ct. 613 (1974) (Exclusionary rule is "wholly inapplicable 'to a search or seizure, even an unreasonable one, effected by a private individual not acting as an agent of the Government or with the participation or knowledge of any governmental official.'") (citation omitted). *See also Burdeau v. McDowell,* 256 U.S. 465, 41 S. Ct. 574 (1921).

19 *Mapp v. Ohio*, 367 U.S. 643, 81 S. Ct. 1684 (1961).

20 *Mapp v. Ohio*, 367 U.S. 643, 659, 81 S. Ct. 1684, 1693-1694 (1961) (quoting *People v. Defore*, 242 N.Y. 13, 150 N.E. 585, 587 (1926)).

21 *James v. Illinois*, 493 U.S. 307, 311, 110 S. Ct. 648, 651 (1990).

22 *See United States v. Calandra,* 414 U.S. 338, 348, 94 S. Ct. 613, 620 (1974).

23 *Compare United States v. Janis*, 428 U.S. 433, 459-60, 96 S. Ct. 3021, 3034 (1976) (illegally seized evidence may be used in a federal civil tax proceeding); *United States v. Calandra,* 414 U.S. 338, 348, 94 S. Ct. 613, 621-22 (1974) (illegally seized evidence may be used in grand jury proceedings); *United States v. Havens*, 446 U.S. 620, 627, 100 S. Ct. 1912, 1916-17 (1980) (illegally seized evidence may be used to impeach a defendant who takes the stand and testifies), *with I.N.S. v. Lopez-Mendoza,* 468 U.S. 1032, 104 S. Ct. 3479 (1984) (exclusionary rule not applicable to a civil deportation proceeding).

24 *See Segura v. United States*, 468 U.S. 796, 804, 104 S. Ct. 3380 (1984).

25 *Wong Sun v. United States,* 371 U.S. 471, 83 S. Ct. 407 (1963) (emphasis added).

fruit-of-the-poisonous-tree doctrine is an outgrowth of the exclusionary rule providing that the Fourth Amendment violation is deemed the "poisonous tree," and any evidence obtained by exploiting that violation is subject to suppression as the "fruit" of that poisonous tree.

To invoke the protection of the "poisonous tree" principle, the defendant must first demonstrate there was a primary illegality (i.e., an unconstitutional search or arrest, or a coerced confession), and secondly, a nexus, or connection, between the illegality and the derivative evidence. The nexus between the illegal act and the subject evidence must be so strong that police can be said to have obtained the evidence only by an exploitation of their illegal actions. If another event or outside factor weakens the connection between the illegality and the evidence, a principle referred to as attenuation, so that the evidence can no longer be said to be a by-product of the unlawful conduct, then suppression would not be appropriate. The attenuating factor removes the stigma of the illegal law enforcement action, so that denying the admission of the seized evidence does not serve the deterrent purposes of the exclusionary rule.

Thus, the exclusionary rule is not monolithic. Even when there is a Fourth Amendment violation, the rule of exclusion will not apply when the costs of exclusion outweigh its deterrent benefits. As indicated above, when the link between the unconstitutional conduct and the discovery of the evidence is too attenuated to justify suppression the rule will not be applied.[26] In this regard, the United States Supreme Court has held that, pursuant to the "attenuation doctrine," evidence will be "admissible when the connection between unconstitutional police conduct and the evidence is remote or has been interrupted by some intervening circumstance, so that 'the interest protected by the constitutional guarantee that has been violated would not be served by suppression of the evidence obtained.'"[27]

There are three factors for a court to consider when determining whether unlawful conduct has been adequately attenuated. Those factors are "(1) the elapsed time between the misconduct and the acquisition of the evidence, (2) the occurrence of intervening circumstances, and (3) the flagrancy and purpose of the improper law enforcement action."[28]

1.4.2.1. An unlawful stop and the subsequent discovery of an arrest warrant

In *Utah v. Strieff*,[29] during an unlawful investigative detention of defendant Edward Strieff, the investigating officer learned that Strieff had an outstanding arrest warrant for a traffic violation. The officer arrested Strieff pursuant to that warrant and a search incident to arrest uncovered a baggie of methamphetamine and drug paraphernalia. At court, the prosecution conceded that the officer lacked reasonable suspicion for the stop but argued that the evidence should not be suppressed because the existence of a valid arrest warrant attenuated the connection between the unlawful stop and the discovery of the contraband. *The United States Supreme Court agreed*, holding that the attenuation doctrine applies when an officer makes an unconstitutional investigatory stop; learns during that stop that the suspect is subject to a valid arrest warrant; and proceeds to arrest the suspect and seize incriminating evidence during a search incident to that arrest.[30] In this regard, the "valid arrest warrant was a sufficient intervening event to break the causal chain between the unlawful stop and the discovery of drug-related evidence on Strieff's person."[31]

---

[26] *See Utah v. Strieff*, 579 U.S. ___, 136 S. Ct. 2056, 2059 (2016).

[27] *See Utah v. Strieff*, 579 U.S. ___, 136 S. Ct. 2056, 2059 (2016) (quoting *Hudson v. Michigan*, 547 U.S. 586, 593, 126 S. Ct. 2159, 2164 (2016)).

[28] *See Brown v. Illinois*, 422 U.S. 590, 603-04, 95 S. Ct. 2254, 2261-62 (1975); *see also Utah v. Strieff*, 579 U.S. ___, 136 S. Ct. 2056, 2061-62 (2016). *Accord Martinez v. State*, 620 S.W.3d 734, 742 (Tex. Crim. App. 2021) ("The purpose and flagrancy of the official misconduct is one of the most important factors"); (citing *Self v. State*, 709 S.W.2d 662, 668 (Tex. Crim. App. 1986).

For example, in *Green v. State*, police misconduct was flagrant because they arrested 18-year-old Green at gunpoint at his home in the middle of the night without probable cause and then drove him around for an hour to investigate the offense before taking him to the station. 615 S.W.2d 700, 707 (Tex. Crim. App. 1980) (*en banc*). Similarly, police misconduct was flagrantly abusive in *Duncan v. State* where they arrested Duncan at home at 3:00 a.m. without a warrant for the express purpose of interrogating her and subjected her to nearly continuous interrogation for over three hours until she signed a written confession. 639 S.W.2d 314, 318 (Tex. Crim. App. 1982).

[29] *Utah v. Strieff*, 579 U.S. ___, 136 S. Ct. 2056 (2016).

[30] *Utah v. Strieff*, 579 U.S. ___, 136 S. Ct. 2056, 2059 (2016).

[31] *Utah v. Strieff*, 579 U.S. ___, 136 S. Ct. 2056, 2061 (2016).

Another exception involving the causal relationship between the unconstitutional act and the discovery of evidence is the "independent source" doctrine. This "allows trial courts to admit evidence obtained in an unlawful search if officers independently acquired it from a separate, independent source."[32] Similarly, the "inevitable discovery" rule "allows for the admission of evidence that would have been discovered even without the unconstitutional source."[33] And then there's the exclusionary rule's "good faith" exception.

1.4.3. The good-faith exception

In *United States v. Leon*,[34] the U.S. Supreme Court held that evidence should not be excluded from the prosecution's case if it was obtained by officers acting in reasonable reliance upon a search warrant, even if the warrant was ultimately found to be invalid. According to the Court, the primary benefit of the exclusionary rule is that it deters official misconduct by removing incentives to engage in unreasonable searches and seizures. The Court noted, however, that "the marginal or nonexistent benefits produced by suppressing evidence obtained in objectively reasonable reliance on a subsequently invalidated search warrant cannot justify the substantial costs of exclusion."[35] No deterrence of police misconduct occurs when the police reasonably rely on a warrant later found to be deficient.

The United States Supreme Court has also held that suppression is inappropriate where an officer conducts a search or arrest in reasonable, good-faith reliance on a warrant issued by a neutral and detached magistrate, and that warrant is later found to be invalid due to a defect in form or because of a "technical error on the part of the issuing judge."[36] Similarly, the exclusionary rule will not apply to evidence seized pursuant to a warrant executed in good faith, where the warrant is subsequently deemed defective because of clerical errors.[37]

In *Arizona v. Evans*, a motorist was pulled over for a routine traffic stop. The officer's in-dash computer indicated the motorist had an outstanding warrant for his arrest. He was placed under arrest, and a search of his car revealed a bag of marijuana. The officer did not know that the warrant under which he arrested the motorist had been quashed, and a clerk forgot to make the appropriate entry. The motorist sought to have the evidence suppressed as the fruit of an unlawful arrest. The Supreme Court denied suppression, holding that the exclusionary rule does not require suppression of evidence seized in violation of the Fourth Amendment by an officer who acted in reasonable reliance upon a police record indicating the existence of an outstanding arrest warrant – a record that is later determined to be erroneous due to a clerical error of a court employee."[38] Similarly, the Court has held that when a police mistake is the result of isolated negligence, rather than systemic error or reckless disregard of constitutional requirements, suppression of evidence is not required.[39]

In *Davis v. United States*,[40] the federal Supreme Court expanded the good-faith exception to the exclusionary rule to include good-faith reliance upon binding appellate precedent that specifically authorized a particular practice but was subsequently overruled.

The United States Supreme Court also recognizes a good-faith exception to the exclusionary rule for actions taken under a statute that is subsequently ruled to be invalid.[41]

---

[32] *See Utah v. Strieff*, 579 U.S. ___, 136 S. Ct. 2056, 2059 (2016).
[33] *See Utah v. Strieff*, 579 U.S. ___, 136 S. Ct. 2056, 2059 (2016).
[34] *United States v. Leon*, 468 U.S. 897, 104 S. Ct. 3405 (1984).
[35] *United States v. Leon*, 468 U.S. 897, 922, 104 S. Ct. 3405 (1984).
[36] *Massachusetts v. Sheppard*, 468 U.S. 981, 104 S. Ct. 3424, 3426 (1984).
[37] *Arizona v. Evans*, 514 U.S. 1, 115 S. Ct. 1185 (1995).
[38] *Arizona v. Evans*, 514 U.S. 1, 3, 14, 115 S. Ct. 1185, 1187, 1193 (1995).
[39] *Herring v. United States*, 555 U.S. 135, 129 S. Ct. 695 (2009). The mistake here was an arrest on a warrant that had been recalled five months earlier. The failure to update the computer database was deemed to be a "negligent omission."
[40] *Davis v. United States*, 564 U.S. 229, 240, 131 S. Ct. 2419, 2429 (2011).
[41] *See, e.g., Illinois v. Krull*, 480 U.S. 340, 107 S. Ct. 1160 (1987) (suppression is not required "when an officer's reliance on the constitutionality of a statute is objectively reasonable, but the statute is subsequently declared unconstitutional."); *Michigan v. DeFillippo*, 443 U.S. 31, 99 S. Ct. 2627 (1979) (An arrest "made in good-faith reliance on an ordinance, which at the time had not been declared unconstitutional, is valid regardless of a subsequent judicial determination of its unconstitutionality").

The Supreme Court has additionally recognized a reasonable mistake of law as a "good faith" exception to the exclusionary rule. In *Heien v. North Carolina*,[42] the Court held that, under the Fourth Amendment, an officer's reasonable suspicion for a motor vehicle stop can rest on a reasonable mistake of law. According to the Court, the Fourth Amendment is not violated when a police officer pulls over a vehicle based on an "objectively reasonable, although mistaken, belief" that the traffic laws prohibited the conduct which was the basis for the stop. The defendant in *Heien* was a passenger in a car that was stopped by the police because the car had only one working brake light. Cocaine was recovered from the defendant during the stop. Upon appeal, defendant contended that driving with only one brake light was not a violation and thus there was no basis for the traffic stop. Since the statute was an "ambiguous one," the Court determined that the officer's mistake was reasonable.[43]

The Texas Legislature has codified a version of the good-faith exception at Tex. Code Crim. Proc. art. 38.23(b), which states: "It is an exception to the [exclusionary rule] that the evidence was obtained by a law enforcement officer acting in objective good faith reliance upon a warrant issued by a neutral magistrate based on probable cause." This statutory exception is more restrictive than the federal exception. It will only save evidence seized by an officer acting in good faith reliance on a warrant based upon probable cause. Thus, if the warrant relied upon was not supported by probable cause, the evidence seized will be suppressed even if the officer relied upon it in good faith. In *McClintock v State*,[44] the Texas Court of Criminal Appeals explained, "It is plain enough from the language of Article 38.23(b) that, before its good-faith exception to Subsection (a)'s exclusionary rule may apply, there must be (1) objective good-faith reliance upon (2) a warrant (3) issued by a neutral magistrate that is (4) based upon probable cause. With respect to the fourth requirement, we long ago declared that '[t]he plain wording of Art[icle] 38.23(b) requires an initial determination of probable cause.'"[45]

In *Wheeler v. State*,[46] in applying for a blood-alcohol search warrant, a police officer submitted an unsworn probable-cause affidavit. Finding that the affidavit articulated probable cause but not realizing that it was unsworn, the magistrate signed and returned the search warrant. The same police officer then executed that search warrant. Here, there was no question that the officer's failure to take the oath and swear to his probable-cause affidavit was improper. The critical question was whether the good-faith exception to the Texas exclusionary rule applied such that the blood-alcohol evidence is admissible. According to the Court, under the facts of this case, the good-faith exception is inapplicable and the evidence is subject to suppression. "[T]he officer in this case was objectively unreasonable in executing a search warrant he knew was unsupported by a sworn probable-cause affidavit, such that he cannot be said to have acted in objective good-faith reliance upon the warrant."[47]

1.4.4. The "Independent Source" Doctrine

"The Fourth Amendment does not require the suppression of evidence initially discovered during a police officer's illegal entry of private premises, if that evidence is also discovered during a later search pursuant to a valid warrant that is wholly independent of the initial illegal entry."[48] In this regard, the "independent source" doctrine "permits the introduction of evidence initially discovered during, or as a consequence of, an unlawful search, but later obtained independently from lawful activities untainted by the initial illegality."[49] The circumstances that justify the second lawful search must have no connection to the initial, unlawful

[42] *Heien v. North Carolina*, 574 U.S. 54, 135 S. Ct. 530 (2014).

[43] *Heien v. North Carolina*, 574 U.S. 54, 135 S. Ct. 530, 539 (2014).

[44] *McClintock v. State*, 541 S.W.3d 63 (Tex. Crim. App. 2017).

[45] *McClintock v. State*, 541 S.W.3d 63, 67 (Tex. Crim. App. 2017) (quoting *Curry v. State*, 808 S.W.2d 481, 482 (Tex. Crim. App. 1991)). *see also* George E. Dix & John M. Schmolesky, 40 Texas Practice: Criminal Practice and Procedure § 7.67, at 395 (3d ed. 2011) ("If probable cause is found to be lacking, Article 38.23 – although not federal constitutional considerations – requires that the evidence be excluded regardless of whether the officer relying on the warrant believed that it had been issued on facts sufficient for probable cause.").

[46] *Wheeler v. State*, 616 S.W.3d 858 (Tex. Crim. App. 2021).

[47] *Wheeler v. State*, 616 S.W.3d 858, 860 (Tex. Crim. App. 2021).

[48] *Murray v. United States*, 487 U.S. 533, 108 S. Ct. 2529, 2536 (1987).

[49] *Murray v. United States*, 487 U.S. 533, 108 S. Ct. 2529, 2536 (1987).

conduct. In other words, the facts supporting the second search must arise wholly apart from those that purportedly justified the initial search (*e.g.*, a judicial finding of probable cause, and a warrant issued based on that finding, where the facts in the supporting affidavit derive completely from a source independent of facts garnered during an initial, illegal search).

In *Murray v. United States,*[50] officers conducting a narcotics investigation had probable cause to believe a large quantity of drugs was being stored in a warehouse. Before securing a warrant, they illegally entered the warehouse and confirmed their beliefs, finding several bales of marijuana. The officers subsequently applied for and obtained a search warrant but made no mention of their entry to the issuing judge, basing their application only on facts they had accumulated prior to the unlawful entry. The Supreme Court held that if the earlier information in the affidavit in fact supported the probable cause determination, so that the later seizure of the marijuana was not a result of the illegal entry, but rather the result of a warrant executed pursuant to the independent probable cause finding, the evidence should not be suppressed.

Texas courts recognize the "independent source" doctrine but have drawn a distinction between it and the "inevitable discovery" doctrine.[51] For example, in *Howard v. State,*[52] Agents Peck and Papanos of the Texas Department of Public Safety approached and knocked on defendant's door for a "knock-and-talk" investigation of suspected drug activity. "Both officers were in plain clothes, wearing bulletproof vests, with their badges hanging from chains around their necks. Peck knocked on the door and stood to the side of the door awaiting a response." Defendant answered the door wearing gym shorts, no shirt, and no shoes. As the officers spoke to defendant outside his apartment, they could smell the odor of marijuana through the opened door. Peck asked if anyone else was at home and when defendant said yes, Peck asked him to go back into the apartment to retrieve his house guest, a Mr. Pierce. While defendant was in the apartment, Peck leaned his head and part of his body through the door.

Once defendant and Pierce exited the apartment, Peck advised defendant that the officers had received a tip about the smell of marijuana coming from the apartment. Defendant admitted that there may be a small amount of marijuana in the kitchen; he also acknowledged that there were weapons in the apartment. When defendant refused to consent to a search, the officers decided to obtain a search warrant. Prior to that, the officers performed a "protective sweep" of defendant's apartment. During the sweep, they noticed marijuana on the kitchen counter, and in an open safe, the officers also saw pills that appeared to be ecstasy.

After the protective sweep, Agent Papanos left to get the search warrant. The affidavit in support relied on the odor of marijuana, as well as defendant's admission that there was marijuana in his kitchen. "The affidavit did not rely on any information obtained during the protective sweep, such as the marijuana seen in the kitchen or the ecstasy pills seen in the open safe."

The search conducted under the authority of the warrant uncovered 3.7 pounds of marijuana, 335 grams of hashish oil, 1,865 grams of ecstasy, 319 grams of methamphetamine, 343 grams of psilocybin, 29.1 grams of cocaine, 17.2 grams of Xanax, 20.9 grams of LSD, as well as 3 rifles, 6 pistols, and 3 shotguns.

Upon appeal, the court held that the "knock and talk" procedure was lawful, but the protective sweep was not. Nonetheless, the court determined that that the evidence was admissible under the "independent source" rule. Here, the police officers' initial illegal entry did not require suppression of evidence because they subsequently obtained a search warrant to search the same premises based on information acquired independently of the illegal initial entry." Significantly, the officers did not seize any evidence as a result of their illegal entry, nor did they use any information obtained from their illegal entry to establish probable case for the search warrant; and they had probable cause prior to their illegal entry and search of the defendant's apartment under the guise of a protective sweep. Said the court:

> Indeed, Officer Papanos testified that the officers decided to get a warrant as soon as they had evidence of (1) the odor of marijuana emanating from the apartment, and (2) [defendant's] admission that

---

[50] *Murray v. United States,* 487 U.S. 533, 108, S. Ct. 2529 (1988).

[51] *Wehrenberg v. State*, 416 S.W.3d 458 (Tex. Crim. App. 2013). For a more comprehensive discussion of the Texas exclusionary statute *see* Larry E. Holtz & Warren J Spencer, *Texas Criminal and Traffic Procedural Manual – An In-Depth Guide on How to Apply the Laws of Arrest, Search and Seizure, Confessions, & Eyewitness Identification* (Blue360° Media).

[52] *Howard v. State,* ___ S.W.3d ___ (2021 Tex. App. LEXIS 2185).

he had marijuana in the kitchen. Because both of these pieces of information were available to the officers before they conducted the illegal sweep, and none of the evidence observed in the unconstitutional sweep was used to obtain the warrant, the trial court did not abuse its discretion in concluding that the "independent source" doctrine applied, under circumstances similar to those presented in *Segura*.[53]

1.4.5. The "Inevitable Discovery" Doctrine

The "inevitable discovery" doctrine is similar to the independent source doctrine; it enables courts to look to the facts and circumstances surrounding the discovery of the tainted evidence and asks whether the police would have discovered the evidence despite the illegality. "If the prosecution can establish by a preponderance of the evidence that the information ultimately or inevitably would have been discovered by lawful means, then the deterrence rationale has so little basis that the evidence should be received."[54] Generally, courts will find evidence would have been inevitably discovered if the evidence would have been discovered, in the same condition, through an independent line of investigation, and where the independent investigation was already in progress at the time of the illegal search. Thus, "[t]he inevitable discovery doctrine, with its distinct requirements, is in reality an extrapolation from the independent source doctrine: Since the tainted evidence would be admissible if in fact discovered through an independent source, it should be admissible if it inevitably would have been discovered."[55]

In *Nix*,[56] two officers illegally obtained from a suspect the location of the body of a child he had murdered. The defendant argued that testimony concerning the location and condition of the body should be suppressed as a result of this illegality. The Supreme Court disagreed, holding that if the prosecution could demonstrate that the child's body would have been discovered without the benefit of the defendant's statements, suppression was not appropriate. In this case, there was an extremely good chance that the state could demonstrate the body's location would have been inevitably discovered, as there was a 200-member search party combing the area, which in fact was scheduled to search the area where the body was found.

Texas courts recognize the "independent source" doctrine but not the "inevitable discovery" doctrine.[57] In *Wehrenberg v. State*,[58] the court explained the difference between the two. "The independent source doctrine [] removes from the scope of the exclusionary rule evidence actually obtained pursuant to an independent source, so long as the source (such as a valid search warrant) is truly independent and untainted by the prior police conduct. The doctrine is distinct from other exceptions to the exclusionary rule because it requires that there be a complete break in the causal chain between the illegality and the acquisition of evidence; it asks a court to decide whether the evidence was actually discovered lawfully through an independent source. If so, exclusion is not required." By contrast, "the inevitable discovery doctrine applies to situations involving an actual unlawful seizure or discovery of evidence and serves to permit use of that evidence when the evidence would have eventually been discovered in a lawful manner had it not first been seized unlawfully."[59] Accordingly, in Texas, because of the statutory restrictions of Tex. Code Crim. Proc. art. 38.23(a), the "inevitable discovery" doctrine is not recognized.[60]

---

53 *Howard v. State*, __ S.W.3d __, __ (2021 Tex. App. LEXIS 2185).

54 *Nix v. Williams*, 467 *U.S.* 431, 104 S. Ct. 2501, 2511 (1984).

55 *Murray v. United States*, 487 U.S. 533, 539, 108 S. Ct. 2529, 2534 (1988).

56 *Nix v. Williams*, 467 *U.S.* 431, 104 S. Ct. 2501, 2511 (1984).

57 *Wehrenberg v. State*, 416 S.W.3d 458 (Tex. Crim. App. 2013); *State v. Daugherty*, 931 S.W.2d 269 (Tex. Crim. App. 1996); *Garcia v. State*, 829 S.W.2d 796 (Tex. Crim. App. 1992).

58 *Wehrenberg v. State*, 416 S.W.3d 458 (Tex. Crim. App. 2013).

59 *Wehrenberg v. State*, 416 S.W.3d 458, 472 (Tex. Crim. App. 2013) (citing *United States v. Stabile*, 633 F.3d 219, 243 (3d Cir. 2011); *United States v. Scott*, 270 F.3d 30, 44-45 (1st Cir. 2001); *Nix v. Williams*, 467 U.S. 431, 104 S. Ct. 2501 (1984); *United States v. Lazar*, 604 F.3d 230, 239 (6th Cir. 2010)).

60 *State v. Daugherty*, 931 S.W.2d 269 (Tex. Crim. App. 1996). *Garcia v. State*, 829 S.W.2d 796 (Tex. Crim. App. 1992). For a more comprehensive discussion of the Texas exclusionary statute *see* Larry E. Holtz & Warren J Spencer, *Texas Criminal and Traffic Procedural Manual – An In-Depth Guide on How to Apply the Laws of Arrest, Search and Seizure, Confessions, & Eyewitness Identification* (Blue360° Media).

2. INVESTIGATIVE DETENTIONS

2.1. Levels of encounters

When reviewing the legality of police interactions with citizens, courts initially assess the nature and extent of the contact. To aid in this analysis, interactions, or encounters, are divided into three conceptual categories.[61] First, there are encounters of a consensual nature. These are sometimes called "mere inquiries" or "mere field inquiries," which include a common law right to inquire – a right to ask a question enjoyed by all citizens, whether they work in law enforcement or not.

Occupying the next tier of encounters are interactions of a more intrusive character. These encounters are commonly called detentions, investigatory stops or *Terry* stops. An investigative detention ("*Terry* stop") is a "seizure" for purposes of the Fourth Amendment.[62] Such a "*Terry* stop" is reasonable when a law enforcement officer possesses specific and articulable facts which generate a "reasonable suspicion of criminal activity."[63] A "reasonable articulable suspicion" entails something more than an inchoate or unparticularized suspicion or "hunch," but less than the level of suspicion required for probable cause.[64] Since it is a less stringent standard than the probable cause standard, it certainly requires a quantum of proof that is less than preponderance of the evidence. In *State v. Woodard*,[65] the Texas Court of Criminal Appeals explained that there is no "bright-line" rule that determines when a consensual encounter becomes a seizure. "Generally, however, when an officer through force or a showing of authority restrains a citizen's liberty, the encounter is no longer consensual. This is the point at which an encounter becomes a detention or arrest, both of which are seizures under the Fourth Amendment."[66]

The final level of encounter is a formal arrest. To justify this action, law enforcement officials must possess a higher degree of suspicion, *i.e.*, "probable cause" to believe that a crime is being, or has been, perpetrated and that a specific person committed that crime.

This initial categorization of encounters is essential to a determination of the rights of the individual. If the encounter is consensual, the federal Constitution is not implicated because no seizure of a person, within the meaning of the Fourth Amendment, has taken place. However, if the encounter rises to the level of a detention or a full-scale arrest, then that person has been seized, and law enforcement conduct will be judged according to the standards of the Fourth Amendment. The person seized can then avail himself of Fourth Amendment protections.

2.2. Consensual encounters; the "mere inquiry"

There are some police-citizen encounters that do not require any level of constitutional justification because the interaction does not involve a "significant interference" with an individual's life, liberty or property. Law enforcement "officers do not violate the Fourth Amendment by merely approaching an individual on the street or in another public place, by asking him if he is willing to answer some questions, by putting questions to him if the person is willing to listen, or by offering in evidence in a criminal prosecution his voluntary answers to such questions."[67] Thus, when an officer approaches an individual in a public place and seeks voluntary cooperation though noncoercive questioning, there is no restraint on that person's liberty, and the person is not seized.

---

[61] *State v. Woodard*, 341 S.W.3d 404, 410-11 (Tex. Crim. App. 2011) (recognizing "three distinct types of interactions: (1) consensual encounters; (2) investigatory detentions; and (3) arrests"). *See also Johnson v. State*, 414 S.W.3d 184 (Tex. Crim. App. 2013).

[62] *See Terry v. Ohio,* 392 U.S. 1, 20-21, 88 S. Ct. 1868 (1968).

[63] *Terry v. Ohio,* 392 U.S. 1, 20-21, 88 S. Ct. 1868 (1968).

[64] *See United States v Sokolow*, 490 U.S. 1, 109 S. Ct. 1581 (1989).

[65] *State v. Woodard*, 341 S.W.3d 404 (Tex. Crim. App. 2011).

[66] *State v. Woodard*, 341 S.W.3d 404, 411 (Tex. Crim. App. 2011).

[67] *Florida v. Royer,* 460 U.S. 491, 497, 103 S. Ct. 1319, 1324 (1983); *see also Utah v. Strieff*, 579 U.S. ___, 136 S. Ct. 2056, 2063 (2016) ("[A] 'seizure does not occur simply because a police officer approaches an individual and asks a few questions.'") (quoting *Florida v. Bostick*, 501 U.S. 429, 434, 111 S. Ct. 2382 (1991)).

"Nor would the fact that the officer identifies himself as a police officer, without more, convert the encounter into a seizure requiring some level of objective justification."[68] "Even when law enforcement officers have no basis for suspecting a particular individual, they may pose questions, ask for identification, and request consent to search luggage provided they do not induce cooperation by coercive means[.] If a reasonable person would feel free to terminate the encounter, then he or she has not been seized."[69] These consensual encounters, called *"mere inquiries"* or *"field inquiries,"* require no constitutional justification because the interaction does not register on the constitutional scale; the encounter is not a "seizure" within the meaning of the Fourth Amendment.

Naturally, the person approached "need not answer any question put to him; indeed, he may decline to listen to the questions at all and may go on his way[.] He may not be detained even momentarily without reasonable, objective grounds for doing so; and his refusal to listen or answer does not, without more, furnish those grounds. [Thus,] if there is no detention – no seizure within the meaning of the Fourth Amendment – then no constitutional rights have been infringed."[70]

In *Terry v. Ohio*, the United States Supreme Court held that a seizure occurs "when the officer, by means of physical force or show of authority, has in some way restrained the liberty" of the individual.[71] Thereafter, in *INS v. Delgado*,[72] the Court refined this standard to mean that a seizure has occurred only "if, in view of all the circumstances surrounding the incident, a reasonable person would have believed that he was not free to leave." The Court further refined this standard in *Michigan v. Chesternut*,[73] by focusing not on whether a reasonable person would feel free to leave but on whether the officer's conduct would "have communicated to a reasonable person that he was not at liberty to ignore the police presence and go about his business." In *Chesternut*, the Court held that the defendant was not seized when an officer accelerated his patrol car and began to drive alongside him. The officer did not activate his siren or flashers, did not command defendant to halt, did not display a weapon, and did not drive aggressively so as to block defendant's path.

In 1991, the United States Supreme Court once again redefined the concept of "seizure" in *California v. Hodari D.*[74] The Court held that, even when an officer has manifested a "show of authority," a seizure within the meaning of the Fourth Amendment further "requires either physical force [or], where that is absent, submission to the assertion of authority."[75] Thus, under federal law, a seizure does not occur until either the suspect complies with an officer's "show of authority" or there is an application of physical force (however slight) to the suspect by the officer.

An Unsuccessful Attempt to Stop a Suspect is a "Seizure." In *Torres v. Madrid*,[76] the United States Supreme Court addressed the question whether a seizure occurs when an officer shoots someone who temporarily eludes capture after the shooting. The answer, according to the Court, "is *yes: The application of physical force to the body of a person with intent to restrain is a seizure, even if the force does not succeed in subduing the person*."[77]

The facts of the case unfolded at dawn in the middle of July, when four New Mexico state police officers went to an apartment complex in Albuquerque to execute an arrest warrant for a woman accused of white collar crimes, but also suspected of having been involved in drug trafficking, murder, and other violent crimes.

Upon arrival, the officers saw the plaintiff, Roxanne Torres, standing with another person near a Toyota FJ Cruiser in the parking lot of the complex. The officers did not believe either that Torres or her companion was the target of the warrant. As the officers approached the vehicle, the companion ran into the apartment, "while Torres—who at the time was experiencing methamphetamine withdrawal—got into the driver's seat

[68] *Florida v. Royer*, 460 U.S. 491, 497, 103 S. Ct. 1319, 1324 (1983).
[69] *United States v. Drayton*, 536 U.S. 194, 122 S. Ct. 2105, 2110 (2002).
[70] *Florida v. Royer*, 460 U.S. 491, 498, 103 S. Ct. 1319, 1324 (1983). *See also Illinois v. Wardlow*, 528 U.S. 119, 125, 120 S. Ct. 673, 676 (2000) (Since a "mere field inquiry" may be conducted without reasonable suspicion, the individual approached "has a right to ignore the police and go about his business.").
[71] *Terry v. Ohio*, 392 U.S. 1, 19, n.16, 88 S. Ct. 1868 (1968).
[72] *INS v. Delgado*, 466 U.S. 210, 215 104 S. Ct. 1758 (1984).
[73] *Michigan v. Chesternut*, 486 U.S. 567, 569 108 S. Ct. 1975 (1988).
[74] *California v. Hodari D.*, 499 U.S. 621, 111 S. Ct. 1547 (1991).
[75] *California v. Hodari D.*, 499 U.S. 621, 626, 111 S. Ct. 1547 (1991).
[76] *Torres v. Madrid*, 592 U.S. ___, 141 S. Ct. 989 (2021).
[77] *Torres v. Madrid*, 592 U.S. ___, 141 S. Ct. 989, 994 (2021).

and started the engine. The officers attempted to speak with her, but she did not notice their presence until one of them tried to open the door of her car."[78]

"Although the officers wore tactical vests marked with police identification, Torres saw only that they had guns. She thought the officers were carjackers trying to steal her car, and she hit the gas to escape them. Neither Officer Madrid nor Officer Williamson, according to Torres, stood in the path of the vehicle, but both fired their service pistols to stop her. All told, the two officers fired 13 shots at Torres, striking her twice in the back and temporarily paralyzing her left arm."[79]

In the court below, Officer Madrid testified that the Cruiser "drove at [her]" and she fired "at the driver through the windshield" in order "to stop the driver from running her over." Officer Williamson said that he shot at the driver because he feared being "crush[ed]" between the Cruiser and the neighboring car, as well as to stop the vehicle from going towards Officer Madrid.

Torres accelerated away from the officers' use of force, drove a short distance, and stopped in a parking lot. After asking a bystander to report an attempted carjacking, Torres stole a car that happened to be idling nearby and drove 75 miles to Grants, New Mexico. Ultimately, she was airlifted to a hospital in Albuquerque, properly identified, and arrested by police.

Torres sued the officers in federal court, under 42 U.S.C. §1983, asserting that the officers used excessive, unreasonable force. In the appeal to the Tenth Circuit, the court held that the officers were entitled to qualified immunity, for the officers had not "seized" Torres at the time of the shooting. The United States Supreme Court disagreed.

"This case concerns the 'seizure' of a 'person,' which can take the form of 'physical force' or a 'show of authority' that 'in some way restrain[s] the liberty' of the person." The main question here is "whether the application of physical force is a seizure if the force, despite hitting its target, fails to stop the person."[80] In short, the Court held:

> [T]he application of physical force to the body of a person with intent to restrain is a seizure even if the person does not submit and is not subdued. Of course, a seizure is just the first step in the analysis. The Fourth Amendment does not forbid all or even most seizures—only unreasonable ones. All we decide today is that the officers seized Torres by shooting her with intent to restrain her movement. We leave open on remand any questions regarding the reasonableness of the seizure, the damages caused by the seizure, and the officers' entitlement to qualified immunity.[81]

According to the Court, this rule is narrow. "In addition to the requirement of intent to restrain, a seizure by force—absent submission—lasts only as long as the application of force. That is to say that the Fourth Amendment does not recognize any "*continuing* arrest during the period of fugitivity."[82]

Applying these principles, the Court held that "the officers' shooting applied physical force" to Torres' body "and objectively manifested an intent to restrain her from driving away." Therefore, "the officers seized Torres for the instant that the bullets struck her."

During the course of its opinion, the Court stressed that the application of this rule "does not transform every physical contact between a government employee and a member of the public into a Fourth Amendment seizure. A seizure requires the use of force with intent to restrain. Accidental force will not qualify...." In this opinion, the Court considered "only force used to apprehend." Thus, the "appropriate inquiry is whether the challenged conduct objectively manifests an intent to restrain[.]"

"While a mere touch can be enough for a seizure, the amount of force remains pertinent in assessing the objective intent to restrain. A tap on the shoulder to get one's attention will rarely exhibit such an intent.... Nor does the seizure depend on the subjective perceptions of the seized person. Here, for example, Torres claims to have perceived the officers' actions as an attempted carjacking. But the conduct of the

---

[78] *Torres v. Madrid*, 592 U.S. ___, 141 S. Ct. 989, 994 (2021).
[79] *Torres v. Madrid*, 592 U.S. ___, 141 S. Ct. 989, 994 (2021).
[80] *Torres v. Madrid*, 592 U.S. ___, 141 S. Ct. 989, 995 (2021).
[81] *Torres v. Madrid*, 592 U.S. ___, 141 S. Ct. 989, 1003 (2021).
[82] *Torres v. Madrid*, 592 U.S. ___, 141 S. Ct. 989, 999 (2021) (Court's emphasis).

officers – ordering Torres to stop and then shooting to restrain her movement – satisfies the objective test for a seizure, regardless whether Torres comprehended the governmental character of their actions."[83]

The determination of whether a police-citizen encounter has elevated to one requiring a constitutional justification is measured from a "reasonable person's" perspective. A police officer's belief that the citizen was "free to leave" is not probative. Rather, the correct inquiry is whether the citizen, under all of the attendant circumstances, *reasonably believed* he could walk away without answering any of the officer's questions. Therefore, officers who wish to maintain a police-citizen encounter as a mere inquiry should: (1) pose their questions in a conversational manner; (2) avoid making demands or issuing orders; and (3) ensure that the questions they ask are not overbearing or harassing in nature.

"On the other hand, an encounter becomes a seizure if the officer engages in conduct a reasonable person would view as threatening or offensive[.] This would include such tactics as pursuing a person who has attempted to terminate the contact by departing, continuing to interrogate a person who has clearly expressed a desire not to cooperate, renewing an encounter with a person who earlier responded fully to police inquiries, calling to such a person to halt, holding a person's identification papers or other property, conducting a consensual search of the person in an 'authoritative manner,' bringing a drug-sniffing dog toward the person or his property, intercepting a phone call for the suspect, blocking the path of the suspect, physically grabbing and moving the suspect, drawing a weapon, calling for backup, and encircling the suspect by many officers[.]"[84]

Texas courts have acknowledged that there are many factors that will affect the analysis as to which level an encounter should be designated. In *State v. Garcia-Cantu*,[85] the court examined the distinction between a citizen-police "encounter" and a "detention." The facts unfolded at approximately 4 a.m., when Conroe Police Officer Okland saw a truck parked at the end of a dead-end street. The dome light was on inside the truck and he saw two people sitting in the truck. Officer Okland characterized this location as a "high crime" area for drugs and prostitution, but at trial he admitted there had been only two drug arrests in the prior six months and none for prostitution. Okland parked his patrol car behind and to the left of the truck and illuminated its interior with his spotlight. The officer got out of his patrol car and walked towards the driver's side of the truck with his flashlight illuminated and pointed at the truck. The driver got out of the truck and met the officer in the street. Officer Okland asked, "What are you doing here?" The defendant challenged the admission of the evidence, arguing that this encounter was not consensual and was not supported by reasonable suspicion.

The trial court noted that the defendant's vehicle was essentially blocked in by the patrol car and that it would be difficult, if not impossible, for the defendant to leave without Officer Okland first moving his police vehicle. The trial court also considered the use of the spotlight and did not believe Officer Okland's assertions that a person would feel free to drive away once illuminated by a police car's spotlight. Lastly, the trial court considered the effect of the officer's statement, "What are you doing here?" In addressing this statement, the Texas Court of Criminal Appeals explained:

> Although these words are not, by themselves, sufficient to convert an otherwise consensual encounter into a detention, much depends on the tone and level of voice, as well as the questioner's demeanor. The trial judge could have concluded that, based upon Officer Okland's tone and demeanor on the witness stand, as well as his tone and demeanor as seen and heard on the video recording, that the officer's questioning was more in the nature of an official command than a friendly or neutral inquiry.[86]

Once it is determined that a police-citizen encounter has constitutional implication – that is, it has advanced beyond the point of a "mere inquiry" and now registers on the constitutional scale as a

---

[83] *Torres v. Madrid*, 592 U.S. ___, 141 S. Ct. 989, 998-99 (2021).

[84] *See* 4 Wayne R. LaFave, *Search and Seizure, A Treatise on the Fourth Amendment* § 9.4(a), at 601-06 (6th ed. 2020) (citing cases); *see also United States v. Lowe*, 791 F.3d 424 (3d Cir. 2015) (a seizure occurred when "three marked police cars nearly simultaneously arrived on the scene and [f]our uniformed police officers" approached defendant and his companion, "commanding them to show their hands").

[85] *State v. Garcia-Cantu*, 253 S.W.3d 236 (Tex. Crim. App. 2008).

[86] *State v. Garcia-Cantu*, 253 S.W.3d 236, 248 (Tex. Crim. App. 2008).

seizure – courts will examine the totality of the circumstances to determine whether this seizure was justified by the required level of constitutional justification. In this case, the court ruled that "a reasonable person in [defendant's] position would not have felt free to leave or terminate this encounter with Officer Okland."[87]

2.2.1. Working the buses

Often an officer will approach a person in a public place (*i.e.,* airport, bus station, train, plane or bus, *etc.*). The officer needs no reasonable suspicion to ask questions, or ask for a person's identification, as long as a reasonable person would understand that he could refuse to cooperate. Thus, in *Florida v. Bostick,*[88] the United States Supreme Court held that a Fourth Amendment "seizure" does *not* occur when the police board a public bus during a scheduled stopover, approach a passenger at random, ask a few questions, ask to see the passenger's identification, and then request consent to search his bags – "so long as the officers do not convey a message that compliance with their request is required."[89] "[I]n order to determine whether a particular encounter constitutes a seizure, a court [will] consider all the circumstances surrounding the encounter to determine whether the police conduct would have communicated to a reasonable person that the person was not free to decline the officers' requests or otherwise terminate the encounter. That rule applies to encounters that take place on a city street, [on a train,] or in an airport lobby, and it applies equally to encounters on a bus."[90]

Similarly, in *United States v. Drayton,*[91] the Court held that defendant was not seized when officers boarded a Greyhound bus during a scheduled stop in Tallahassee and began questioning the passengers, even when an officer asked consent to search defendant's bag. Although the officers displayed their badges, they did not brandish weapons or make intimidating moves. They gave the passengers no reason to believe that they were required to answer the officers' questions and they left the aisle free so that passengers could exit the bus. Only one officer did the questioning and he spoke in a polite, quiet (not authoritative) voice: "Nothing he said would suggest to a reasonable person that he or she was barred from leaving the bus or otherwise terminating the encounter."

However, consider *Bond v. United States,*[92] wherein the Supreme Court held that, even if lawfully on a public bus during a scheduled stopover, an officer's physical manipulation of a bus passenger's carry-on luggage constitutes an unreasonable search and seizure under the Fourth Amendment.[93]

2.3. Investigative detentions; "stop and frisk"

Once it is determined that a police-citizen encounter has constitutional implications, that is, it has advanced beyond the point of a "mere inquiry," courts will examine, by reference to the totality of the circumstances, whether the official action was constitutionally justified. The circumstances will be viewed from the vantage point of a prudent and reasonable law enforcement officer on the scene at the time of the encounter, who possesses a reasonable degree of training, experience and skill.

The next conceptual category in the hierarchy of encounters involves interactions that courts refer to as investigatory stops, temporary detentions, or *Terry* stops. In *Terry v. Ohio,*[94] the United States Supreme Court instructed:

> Where a police officer observes unusual conduct which leads him reasonably to conclude in light of his experience that criminal activity may be afoot and that the persons with whom he is dealing may be armed and presently dangerous, where in the course of investigating this behavior he identifies himself as a police [officer] and makes reasonable inquiries, and where nothing in the initial stages of

---

[87] *State v. Garcia-Cantu*, 253 S.W.3d 236, 249 (Tex. Crim. App. 2008).
[88] *Florida v. Bostick*, 501 U.S. 429, 111 S. Ct. 2382 (1991).
[89] *Florida v. Bostick*, 501 U.S. 429, 111 S. Ct. 2388 (1991).
[90] *Florida v. Bostick*, 501 U.S. 429, 111 S. Ct. 2388, 2389 (1991).
[91] *United States v. Drayton*, 536 U.S. 194, 122 S. Ct. 2105 (2002).
[92] *Bond v. United States*, 529 U.S. 334, 120 S. Ct. 1462 (2000).
[93] *Bond v. United States*, 529 U.S. 334, 120 S. Ct. 1462, 1465 (2000).
[94] *Terry v. Ohio*, 392 U.S. 1, 26, 88 S. Ct. 1868, 1882 (1968).

the encounter serves to dispel his reasonable fear for his own or others' safety, he is entitled for the protection of himself and others in the area to conduct a carefully limited search of the outer clothing of such persons in an attempt to discover weapons which might be used to assault him.[95]

2.3.1. Reasonable articulable suspicion for a stop

The police-citizen encounter authorized by *Terry v. Ohio* has several distinct components. The first component concerns the level of "reasonable suspicion" that must exist before an "investigatory stop" may be conducted. This standard involves a level of belief which is something less than the probable cause standard needed to support an arrest. To justify such an intrusion, a law enforcement officer "must be able to point to specific and articulable facts which, taken together with rational inferences from those facts," collectively provide "'a particularized and objective basis' for suspecting the person stopped of criminal activity."[96] "Reasonable suspicion" as a "common sense, nontechnical conception[,]" deals with "'the factual and practical considerations of everyday life on which reasonable and prudent [persons], not legal technicians, act.'"[97]

The question whether an officer had a reasonable suspicion to support a particular investigative detention will be addressed by the courts by reference to an "objective" standard: Would the facts available to the officer at the moment of the stop or frisk warrant an officer "of reasonable caution in the belief that the action taken was appropriate."[98] To determine if the standard has been met in a particular case, a court will give due weight, not to an officer's "unparticularized" suspicions or hunches, but to the "specific reasonable inferences" which the officer is entitled to draw from the facts in light of his or her experience.[99] Thus, more is required than mere generalizations and subjective impressions. The officer must be able to articulate specific facts gleaned from the "totality of the circumstances" – the whole picture – from which he or she reasonably inferred that the person confronted was involved in criminal activity.[100] Reasonable suspicion will be evaluated in the context of the totality of the circumstances as viewed through the eyes of a reasonable, trained officer in the same or similar circumstances, combining objective facts with such an officer's subjective interpretation of those facts.

In *United States v. Arvizu*,[101] the U.S. Supreme Court further explained that the "totality of the circumstances" approach for determining whether a detaining officer has a "particularized and objective basis" for suspecting legal wrongdoing "allows officers to draw on their own experience and specialized training to make inferences from and deductions about the cumulative information available to them that 'might well elude an untrained person.'"[102] In this analysis, the officer is not required to rule out "the possibility of innocent conduct."[103] Many times, facts and circumstances susceptible to innocent explanation when considered in isolation will, when viewed together, as a whole, suffice to form a reasonable and articulable suspicion of criminal activity. Moreover, a police officer's deductions are particularly entitled to deference because, in analyzing the totality of the circumstances, law enforcement officers are permitted, if not required, to consider "the modes or patterns of operation of certain kinds of lawbreakers. From these data, a trained officer draws inferences and makes deductions – inferences and deductions that might well elude an untrained person."[104]

---

[95] *Terry v. Ohio*, 392 U.S. 1, 30-31, 88 S. Ct. 1868, 1884-85 (1968).

[96] *Terry v. Ohio*, 392 U.S. 1, 21, 88 S. Ct. 1868, 1880 (1968); *Ornelas v. United States*, 517 U.S. 690, 116 S. Ct. 1657, 1661 (1996) (quoting *United States v. Cortez*, 449 U.S. 411, 417-18, 101 S. Ct. 690, 694-95 (1981)); *see also United States v. Arvizu*, 534 U.S. 266, 122 S. Ct. 744 (2002) ("the Fourth Amendment is satisfied if the officer's action is supported by reasonable suspicion to believe that criminal activity 'may be afoot'"); *Derichsweiler v. State*, 348 S.W.3d 906 (Tex. Crim. App. 2011).

[97] *Ornelas v. United States*, 517 U.S. 690, 695, 115 S. Ct. 1657, 1661 (1996) (quoting *Illinois v. Gates*, 462 U.S. 213, 231, 103 S. Ct. 2317 (1983)).

[98] *Terry v. Ohio*, 392 U.S. 1, 22, 88 S. Ct. 1868, 1880 (1968).

[99] *Terry v. Ohio*, 392 U.S. 1, 27, 88 S. Ct. 1868, 1883 (1968); *see also Ornelas v. United States*, 517 U.S. 690, 116 S. Ct. 1657, 1663 (1996) (due deference should be given to the inferences drawn by an officer who necessarily "views the facts through the lens of his police experience and expertise").

[100] *Haas v. State*, 172 S.W.3d 42 (Tex. App. 2005).

[101] *United States v. Arvizu*, 534 U.S. 266, 122 S. Ct. 744 (2002).

[102] *United States v. Arvizu*, 534 U.S. 266, 122 S. Ct. 744, 750-51 (2002) (citation omitted).

[103] *United States v. Arvizu*, 534 U.S. 266, 122 S. Ct. 744, 753 (2002).

[104] *United States v. Cortez*, 449 U.S. 411, 418, 101 S Ct. 690, 695 (1981).

In *Arguellez v. State*,[105] the court reiterated that "actions in a series may each seem innocent enough in isolation. If, however, when examined in the context of the totality of the circumstances, they reasonably suggest recent or imminent criminal conduct, an investigative detention is justified."[106] There, officers stopped defendant after receiving information that an "unnamed man in a described motor vehicle was seen taking photographs of people at a public swimming pool. When the first officer arrived at the pool, he observed the described vehicle being driven away from the scene by a lone man."[107] The totality of the circumstances was not sufficient to justify the stop. The court reasoned, "Photographs are routinely taken of people in public places, including at public beaches, where bathing suits are also commonly worn, and at concerts, festivals, and sporting events. Taking photographs of people at such public venues is not unusual, suspicious, or criminal. The generally matching description of the vehicle simply connects appellant to the 'suspicious' photography, but does not in any way suggest that, by taking pictures in a public place, appellant was, had been, or soon would be, engaged in criminal activity."[108]

In *Worley v. State*,[109] police saw a car parked outside a known drug house. The driver, still in the vehicle, gave the officers "a good hard stare." Soon after, defendant walked out of the house with his attention focused on something in his cupped left hand. As defendant drew nearer, the officers could see that the something was a handful of capsules. Defendant was concentrating on them so hard he did not see the officers until he was almost at the curb. When he finally did look up and notice the officers, he "froze and stared at them." One of the officers later testified defendant "was looking real nervous, looking scared." One of the officers approached on foot, and when he was within arm's reach, defendant clinched his left hand to conceal the capsules and began to turn away.[110] The officer then had reasonable suspicion to seize defendant by grabbing his arm.

In *Johnson v. State*,[111] shortly after midnight, patrol Sergeant Cox noticed a vehicle parked in the park-and-ride parking lot where, at that time of night, "a variety of criminal activity" took place, including burglaries of motor vehicles, public lewdness, and illicit drugs. The vehicle was parked by itself away from where other vehicles were parked. This solitary vehicle's headlights and other outside lights were off, and there were no lights on inside the vehicle. When he shined his spotlight on the vehicle, Sergeant Cox could tell that there were two occupants and that there was movement inside the vehicle. In Sergeant Cox's experience, it was out of the ordinary for someone to be inside a vehicle at the park-and-ride after midnight "[w]ith no other vehicle there to pick them up and give them a ride."[112] The sergeant pulled to a stop 10 to 15 yards behind the vehicle and activated his overhead emergency lights. He activated those lights to start the recording equipment and also to let the occupants of the vehicle know he was a police officer. He approached the vehicle, made contact on the driver's side, and identified himself. At some point, the driver's side window was rolled down, and once that occurred, Sergeant Cox smelled marijuana.

Assuming without deciding that the use of the patrol vehicle's emergency lights constituted a "seizure," the Court held that the sergeant had a reasonable suspicion to conduct an investigative detention:

> The unusual and secretive behavior of the occupants of [defendant's] vehicle at least gave rise to an objectively reasonable suspicion that some sort of crime was being committed or contemplated. Drug crimes had occurred with at least some frequency at the park-and-ride, and a dark, isolated vehicle would easily facilitate such crimes. Or such a vehicle could be a waiting spot for the commission of some other crime, such as burglarizing someone else's vehicle or burglarizing a business, such as the nearby bar. Or there might be some other unknown crime that the occupant of such a vehicle intends to commit. As we have explained, an officer does not have to pinpoint an exact penal offense. Here,

---

105 *Arguellez v. State*, 409 S.W.3d 657 (Tex. Crim. App. 2013).
106 *Arguellez v. State*, 409 S.W.3d 657, 663 (Tex. Crim. App. 2013).
107 *Arguellez v. State*, 409 S.W.3d 657, 664 (Tex. Crim. App. 2013).
108 *Arguellez v. State*, 409 S.W.3d 657, 664 (Tex. Crim. App. 2013).
109 *Worley v. State*, 912 S.W.2d 869 (Tex. App.-Fort Worth 1995).
110 *Worley v. State*, 912 S.W.2d 869, 871 (Tex. App. 1995).
111 *Johnson v. State*, 2021 Tex. Crim. App. LEXIS 434.
112 *Johnson v. State*, 2021 Tex. Crim. App. LEXIS 434, at *2-*3.

the unusual and secretive nature of [defendant's] behavior was sufficient to give rise to a reasonable suspicion "that *something* of an apparently criminal nature is brewing."[113]

2.3.1.1. The scope of an investigative detention

A determination that an officer possessed reasonable suspicion, justifying a detention, is only the first step in determining the legality of a stop. A reviewing court will ask initially if the officer's action was justified at its inception, and secondly whether it was reasonably related in scope to the circumstances which justified the interference in the first place. An examination of the scope of the stop addresses the following: (i) the length of the detention, and (ii) the methods employed during the stop. The duration and methods employed during the stop must be tailored to serve the purpose of confirming or dispelling the officer's suspicions. If those concerns are confirmed, and an officer's observations during the detention create probable cause, an arrest may be made. If the suspicions are dispelled, then the suspect should be let go. The detention must be sufficiently limited in temporal duration to satisfy the conditions of an investigative seizure. The nature of the questioning and level of force employed during the detention must be similarly limited. Even though an initial stop may be justified, if the detention exceeds the scope authorized by its justification, *i.e.*, "reasonable suspicion of criminal activity," it will be deemed an illegal stop, and any incriminating evidence found thereafter will not be admissible in court.

In *United States v. Sharpe*,[114] the Supreme Court would not hold that an investigative detention, based on reasonable suspicion, which lasts 20 minutes or longer, is a violation of the Fourth Amendment's prohibition on unlawful seizures. "Obviously, if an investigative stop continues indefinitely, at some point it can no longer be justified as an investigative stop." However, the Court refused to place a rigid time limitation on *Terry*-type investigatory stops. "While it is clear that the brevity of the invasion of the individual's Fourth Amendment interests is an important factor in determining whether the seizure is so minimally intrusive as to be justifiable on reasonable suspicion," courts will also consider the law enforcement purposes to be served by the stop as well as the time reasonably needed to effectuate those purposes.[115]

Therefore, when a court determines whether a detention is too long in duration to be justified as an investigative stop, it will examine whether the police "diligently pursued a means of investigation that was likely to confirm or dispel their suspicions quickly, during which time it was necessary to detain the defendant." The court will make this assessment by considering whether the police acted swiftly in developing the situation. The question will not be whether some other alternative was available, but "whether the police acted unreasonably in failing to recognize or to pursue it."[116] As the court stated in *United States v. McCarthy*[117]: "There is no talismanic time beyond which any stop justified on the basis of *Terry* becomes an unreasonable seizure under the Fourth Amendment." Rather, in determining whether an investigative stop is too long, "common sense and ordinary human experience must govern over rigid criteria."

2.3.1.2. Stop and identify

Texas's "stop and identify" law, Tex. Penal Code § 38.02, provides, in part:

(a) A person commits an offense if he intentionally refuses to give his name, residence address, or date of birth to a peace officer who has lawfully arrested the person and requested the information.
(b) A person commits an offense if he intentionally gives a false or fictitious name, residence address, or date of birth to a peace officer who has:
(1) lawfully arrested the person;
(2) lawfully detained the person; or

[113] *Johnson v. State*, 2021 Tex. Crim. App. LEXIS 434, at *18-*19.
[114] *United States v. Sharpe*, 470 U.S. 675, 105 S. Ct. 1568 (1985).
[115] *Haas v. State*, 172 S.W.3d 42 (Tex. App. 2005).
[116] *United States v. Sharpe*, 470 U.S. 675, 105 S. Ct. 1568, 1576 (1985).
[117] *United States v. McCarthy*, 77 F.3d 522, 530 (1st Cir. 1996).

(3) requested the information from a person that the peace officer has good cause to believe is a witness to a criminal offense.

The United States Supreme Court has addressed the issue of whether the police can insist on identification. In *Hiibel v. Sixth Judicial Dist. Court of Nevada, Humboldt Co.*,[118] the United States Supreme Court, in upholding Nevada's "stop and identify" law, declared that the *Terry* line of cases "permit a State to require a suspect to disclose his name in the course of a Terry stop." The officer may not, however, "stop a citizen and demand identification without any specific basis for believing he is involved in criminal activity."[119] The officer must have a reasonable suspicion to support the investigative stop.

In *Hiibel*, the defendant was arrested for obstruction because he refused to provide his identity to the police during a valid *Terry* stop. Hiibel argued that Nevada's "stop and identify" statute, which requires a person detained by the police to disclose his identity, violated the Fourth Amendment. The Court disagreed, noting that "[o]btaining a suspect's name in the course of a *Terry* stop serves important government interests" because "[k]nowledge of identity may inform an officer that a suspect is wanted for another offense, or has a record of violence or mental disorder."[120]

2.3.1.3. The "least intrusive means" test

In *Florida v. Royer*,[121] the U.S. Supreme Court instructed that a reasonable investigative detention is one that is "temporary," lasting "no longer than is necessary to effectuate the purpose of the stop." The Court then went on to state that "the investigative methods employed should be the least intrusive means reasonably available to verify or dispel the officer's suspicion in a short period of time."[122] The "least intrusive means" language is "directed at the length of the investigative stop, not at whether the police had a less intrusive means to verify their suspicions before stopping *Royer.* The reasonableness of the officer's decision to stop a suspect does not turn on the availability of less intrusive investigatory techniques. Such a rule," noted the Court, "would unduly hamper the police's ability to make swift, on-the-spot decisions."[123]

Naturally, if the detention lasts too long, or if the officers' conduct is too intrusive, the stop may transform into an arrest. As explained by the court in *United States v. Ruiz*:[124]

> A *Terry* stop based on reasonable suspicion can ripen into a *de facto* arrest that must be based on probable cause if it continues too long or becomes unreasonably intrusive.... The investigation following a *Terry* stop must be reasonably related in scope and duration to the circumstances that justified the stop in the first instance so that it is a minimal intrusion on the individual's Fourth Amendment interests.

With respect to the duration of the stop, there is no rigid time limit placed on *Terry* stops; and a defendant's actions can contribute to a permissible extension of the stop. For example, in *United States v. Vega*,[125] the court held that a 62-minute delay was reasonable given that the defendant initially consented to a search of his garage, but then changed his mind. Assuming reasonable suspicion exists (as it did in *Ruiz*), "a reasonable delay attributable to arranging for a canine unit to conduct a sniff may permissibly extend the duration of a stop."[126] The officers in *Ruiz* detained defendant "for less than 20 minutes prior to obtaining his consent to search the car, which," the court held, was "a reasonable duration, given that there is nothing in the record to suggest that the officers acted less than diligently."[127]

---

[118] *Hiibel v. Sixth Judicial Dist. Court of Nev.*, 542 U.S. 177, 185, 124 S. Ct. 2451 (2004).
[119] *United States v. Henderson*, 463 F.3d 27, 45 (1st Cir. 2006).
[120] *Hiibel v. Sixth Judicial Dist. Court of Nev.*, 542 U.S. 177, 186, 124 S. Ct. 2451 (2004).
[121] *Florida v. Royer*, 460 U.S. 491, 500, 103 S. Ct. 1319, 1325 (1983).
[122] *Florida v. Royer*, 460 U.S. 491, 500, 103 S. Ct. 1319, 1325 (1983).
[123] *United States v. Sokolow*, 490 U.S. 1, 11, 109 S. Ct. 1581, 1587 (1989).
[124] *United States v. Ruiz*, 785 F.3d 1134, 1143 (7th Cir. 2015) (citations and internal quotes omitted).
[125] *United States v. Vega*, 72 F.3d 507, 515 (7th Cir. 1995).
[126] *United States v. Ruiz*, 785 F.3d 1134, 1144 (7th Cir. 2015).
[127] *United States v. Ruiz*, 785 F.3d 1134, 1144 (7th Cir. 2015).

2.3.1.4. Transporting suspects

In *Dunaway v. New York*,[128] the Supreme Court held that officers are not permitted to transport a suspect to police headquarters for questioning without his consent and without probable cause for an arrest. According to the Court, whenever a law enforcement officer removes a suspect from where he is found and transports that suspect to police headquarters for questioning without his consent and without probable cause (for his arrest), the detention is, in all important respects, indistinguishable from a traditional arrest and is unlawful. Merely because a suspect is not told he is under arrest, is not "booked," and would not have an arrest record if the interrogation proves fruitless, does not make such a detention analogous to the type authorized by *Terry v. Ohio*. Rather, such a "detention for custodial interrogation — regardless of its label — intrudes so severely on interests protected by the Fourth Amendment" that the familiar requirement of probable cause is thereby triggered.

In *Kaupp v. Texas*,[129] the Supreme Court reaffirmed that, in the absence of probable cause for an arrest, it is unlawful for law enforcement officials to transport a suspect, against his will, to the station for questioning.

This principle was underscored in *Lincoln v. Barnes*,[130] where members of the police SWAT team fatally shot John Lincoln at his mother's residence. The shooting took place in front of John's eighteen-year-old daughter, Erin. After the shooting, Erin was removed from the home, placed in handcuffs, and put in the backseat of a police vehicle. Although she did not fight, struggle, or resist, she did ask the officer why she was being taken into custody. According to the officers, they were holding Erin because they needed to get a statement from her. After being held in the back of the patrol car for about two hours, Erin was transported to the police station where she was interrogated for five hours, and was "forced to write out a statement. After the officers obtained her statement, Erin was permitted to leave."[131]

In this appeal, Erin asserted that the police violated her Fourth Amendment right to be free from unreasonable seizure by taking her into custody without a warrant, probable cause, or justifiable reason and interrogating her against her will for five hours, during which she was forced to write out a statement. She argue[d] that her detention constituted a *de facto* arrest. *The Fifth Circuit Court of Appeals agreed.*

Here, there was no dispute that the officers involved in the incident did not have a reasonable suspicion that Erin was involved with any criminal wrongdoing or that there was probable cause to believe she had committed or was committing a crime. The rationale for her detention rested solely on her status as a witness to her father's shooting.

As emphasized in *Dunaway v. New York*, "detention for custodial interrogation — regardless of its label — intrudes so severely on interests protected by the Fourth Amendment as necessarily to trigger the traditional safeguards against illegal arrest."[132] This principle had been made clear in *Davis v. Mississippi* — namely, "that an investigatory detention that, for all intents and purposes, is indistinguishable from custodial interrogation, requires no less probable cause than a traditional arrest."[133]

"Accordingly, police violate the Fourth Amendment when, absent probable cause or the individual's consent, they seize and transport a person to the police station and subject her to prolonged interrogation."[134]

In *Hayes v. Florida*,[135] however, the Supreme Court indicated that, with prior judicial authorization (such as an investigative detention order), the police may be authorized to transport a suspect to the police station for fingerprinting, even in the absence of probable cause or consent. Here, the Court noted that there have been a number of cases that have suggested that "the Fourth Amendment would permit seizures for the purpose of fingerprinting, if there is reasonable suspicion that the suspect has committed a criminal act, if there

---

[128] *Dunaway v. New York*, 442 U.S. 200, 99 S. Ct. 2248 (1979).
[129] *Kaupp v. Texas*, 538 U.S. 626, 123 S. Ct. 1843 (2003).
[130] *Lincoln v. Barnes*, 855 F.3d 297 (5th Cir. 2017).
[131] *Lincoln v. Barnes*, 855 F.3d 297, 300 (5th Cir. 2017).
[132] *Lincoln v. Barnes*, 855 F.3d 297, 302 (5th Cir. 2017) (citation and internal quotes omitted).
[133] *Davis v. Mississippi*, 394 U.S. 721, 726-27, 89 S. Ct. 1394 (1969). *See also Hayes v. Florida*, 470 U.S. 811, 815, 105 S. Ct. 1643 (1985) ("None of our later cases have undercut the holding in Davis that transportation to and investigative detention at the station house without probable cause or judicial authorization together violate the Fourth Amendment.").
[134] *Lincoln v. Barnes*, 855 F.3d 297, 302 (5th Cir. 2017).
[135] *Hayes v. Florida*, 470 U.S. 811, 105 S. Ct. 1643 (1985).

is a reasonable basis for believing that fingerprinting will establish or negate the suspect's connection with that crime, and if the procedure is carried out with dispatch."

2.3.1.5. Handcuffing suspects

While the use of handcuffs to restrain the person being detained is an indication that the detention is an arrest rather than a *Terry* stop, courts have held that a law enforcement officer's act of handcuffing a suspect during the course of a *Terry* stop will not *automatically* transform the investigative detention into an arrest. As observed by the court in *United States v. Glenna*,[136] "'neither handcuffing nor other restraints will *automatically* convert a *Terry* stop into a *de facto* arrest requiring probable cause.'"[137] If, in a rare case, common sense and ordinary human experience reasonably convince an officer that an investigative stop could be effectuated safely only in this manner, a court should uphold the officer's chosen method to investigate. Naturally, the "use of handcuffs substantially heightens the intrusiveness of a temporary detention."[138]

When the prosecution "seeks to prove that an investigatory detention involving the use of handcuffs did not exceed the limits of a *Terry* stop, it must be able to point to some specific fact or circumstance that could have supported a reasonable belief that the use of such restraints was necessary to carry out the legitimate purposes of the stop without exposing law enforcement officers, the public, or the suspect himself to an undue risk of harm."[139]

A number of other courts have held that the placing of a person in handcuffs may fall within the permissible scope of a temporary investigative detention under *Terry v. Ohio*. For example, in *United States v. Kapperman*,[140] the Eleventh Circuit noted that "neither handcuffing nor other restraints will *automatically* convert a *Terry* stop into a *de facto* arrest requiring probable cause. Just as probable cause to arrest will not justify using excessive force to detain a suspect[,] the use of a particular method to restrain a person's freedom of movement does not necessarily make police action tantamount to an arrest. The inquiry in either context is reasonableness."[141]

2.3.2. Reasonable suspicion for a protective "frisk"

Another component of the *Terry* rule involves an inquiry separate from whether the initial stop and detention was permissible. This component questions whether there was sufficient cause for an officer to conduct a protective pat-down search or "frisk" of the person being detained. It permits an officer to protect himself and others by conducting a limited search of the person's outer clothing for weapons "where he has reason to believe that he is dealing with an armed and dangerous individual, regardless of whether he has probable cause to arrest the individual for a crime. The officer need not be absolutely certain that the individual

---

136 *United States v. Glenna*, 878 F.2d 967 (7th Cir. 1989).

137 *United States v. Glenna*, 878 F.2d 967, 972 (7th Cir. 1989) (quoting *United States v. Kapperman*, 764, F.2d 786, 790 n.4 (11th Cir. 1985)).

138 *United States v. Glenna*, 878 F.2d 967, 972 (7th Cir. 1989).

139 *United States v. Acosta-Colon*, 157 F.3d 9, 18-19 (1st Cir. 1998).

140 *United States v. Kapperman*, 764 F.2d 786 (11th Cir. 1985).

141 *United States v. Kapperman*, 764 F.2d 786, 790 n.4 (11th Cir. 1985); *see also United States v. Tilmon*, 19 F.3d 1221, 1228 (7th Cir. 1994) ("handcuffing — once highly problematic — is becoming quite acceptable in the context of a *Terry* stop"); *United States v. Miller*, 974 F.2d 953, 957 (8th Cir. 1992) (handcuffing of *Terry* detainee permitted where the police were badly outnumbered); *Halvorsen v. Baird*, 146 F.3d 680, 683, 685 (9th Cir. 1998) (holding that handcuffing a person and moving him three blocks for questioning did not automatically turn a detention into an arrest when such actions were justified by reasons of officer safety and security); *United States v. Perdue*, 8 F.3d 1455, 1463 (10th Cir. 1993) (noting "recent trend allowing police to use handcuffs or place suspects on the ground during a *Terry* stop," and that "nine courts of appeal, including the Tenth Circuit, have determined that such intrusive precautionary measures do not necessarily turn a lawful *Terry* stop into an arrest"); *United States v. Purry*, 545 F.2d 217, 220 (U.S. App. D.C. 1976) (handcuffing of defendant was reasonable, as a corollary of the lawful *Terry* stop, in order to maintain status quo while the officer sought more information); *United States v. Crittendon*, 883 F.2d 326, 329 (4th Cir. 1989) (upholding the use of handcuffs in the context of a *Terry* stop where it was reasonably necessary to protect the officer's safety); *United States v. Taylor*, 716 F.2d 701, 709 (9th Cir. 1983) ("use of handcuffs, if reasonably necessary, while substantially aggravating the intrusiveness of an investigatory stop, [does] not necessarily convert a *Terry* stop into an arrest necessitating probable cause").

is armed. The issue is whether a reasonably prudent [officer] in the circumstances would be warranted in the belief that his safety or that of others was in danger."[142] The scope of a pat-down search is limited to that which is reasonably designed to discover guns, knives, clubs, or other hidden instruments that could be used to assault an officer.[143] In this regard, courts will determine whether a reasonably prudent officer in the circumstances would be warranted in the belief that [the officer's] safety or that of others was in danger. The officer must be able to articulate specific facts, which together with rational inferences from those facts, reasonably warrant the intrusion. The determination whether a pat-down search is justified is made by examining the totality of the circumstances with which the police officer is confronted. Factors to weigh in deciding whether a pat-down search ("frisk") is justified include: any furtive gestures or movements made in response to the officers' presence; the location of the encounter; the time of day; whether the suspect ignored requests to stop; and whether the suspect's clothing could conceal a weapon.

In *Arizona v. Johnson*,[144] the U.S. Supreme Court addressed the authority of a police officer to conduct a frisk of a passenger in a motor vehicle which was temporarily seized for a traffic infraction. According to the Court, "in a traffic-stop setting, the first *Terry* condition – a lawful investigatory stop – is met whenever it is lawful for police to detain an automobile and its occupants pending inquiry into a vehicular violation. The police need not have, in addition, cause to believe any occupant of the vehicle is involved in criminal activity. To justify a pat-down of the driver or a passenger during a traffic stop, however, just as in the case of a pedestrian reasonably suspected of criminal activity, the police must harbor reasonable suspicion that the person subjected to the frisk is armed and dangerous."[145]

In *Carmouche v. State*,[146] the Texas Court of Criminal Appeals explained that "[l]aw enforcement personnel may conduct a limited search for weapons of a suspect's outer clothing, even in the absence of probable cause, where an officer reasonably believes that the suspect is armed and dangerous. However, 'the purpose of a limited search after [an] investigatory stop is not to discover evidence of a crime, but to allow the peace officer to pursue investigation without fear of violence.'"[147] Thus, in *Furr v. State*,[148] when defendant failed to respond after Officer Ayala asked him if he was carrying any weapons, the police had received an anonymous tip that defendant was using drugs in a "high drug, high crime" area and defendant appeared "anxious, nervous, sweating, and evasive," the protective frisk was justified. However, in *Wade v. State*,[149] a warden did not have reasonable suspicion to detain and frisk defendant based only on defendant's nervousness and his withdrawal of his consent to the encounter by demanding to know why he was being targeted. Therefore, defendant's statement about the pipe in his truck was fruit of the poisonous tree and could not provide probable cause for searching his truck.

In *State v. Castleberry*,[150] "Officer Barrett [found] Castleberry behind a closed business in a high crime area. And when asked for his identification, Castleberry reached for his waistband, an act that could be reasonably construed as reaching for a weapon. At that point, Officer Barrett did not know if Castleberry was carrying a weapon." The court concluded that "a reasonably prudent person in the same circumstances as Officer Barrett would be warranted in believing that his or her safety may be in danger. Officer Barrett's brief detention and weapons frisk of Castleberry was justified under these circumstances."[151]

Significantly, there are no "routine" or "automatic" frisks; the reasonable suspicion must be that the person may be "armed and dangerous," not "drunk or impaired." In *O'Hara v. State*,[152] the State argued that a routine frisk after ordering a suspect out of the car is permissible, the Texas Court of Criminal Appeals disagreed

---

[142] *Terry v. Ohio*, 392 U.S. 1, 27, 88 S. Ct. 1868, 1883 (1968).
[143] *Adams v. Williams*, 407 U.S. 143, 146, 92 S. Ct. 1921 (1972).
[144] *Arizona v. Johnson*, 555 U.S. 323, 129 S. Ct. 781 (2009).
[145] *Arizona v. Johnson*, 555 U.S. 323, 129 S. Ct. 781, 784 (2009).
[146] *Carmouche v. State*, 10 S.W.3d 323 (Tex. Crim. App. 2000).
[147] *Carmouche v. State*, 10 S.W.3d 323, 329 (Tex. Crim. App. 2000) (citing *Terry v. Ohio*, 392 U.S. 1, 27, 88 S. Ct. 1868, 1883; *Davis v. State*, 829 S.W.2d 218, 220 (Tex. Crim. App. 1992); quoting *Wood v. State*, 515 S.W.2d 300, 306 (Tex. Crim. App. 1974)). *See also Lerma v. State*, 543 S.W.3d 184 (Tex. Crim. App. 2018).
[148] *Furr v. State*, 499 S.W.3d 872 (Tex. Crim. App. 2016).
[149] *Wade v. State*, 422 S.W.3d 661 (Tex. Crim. App. 2013).
[150] *State v. Castleberry*, 332 S.W.3d 460 (Tex. Crim. App. 2011).
[151] *State v. Castleberry*, 332 S.W.3d 460, 496 (Tex. Crim. App. 2011).
[152] *O'Hara v. State*, 27 S.W.3d 548 (Tex. Crim. App. 2000).

and reasoned, "Under the State's theory, once an officer has ordered a person out of his car, the officer could always, as a matter of routine, order the person to sit in the patrol car, and then always, as a matter of routine, frisk for weapons before allowing the suspect into the car. So every single traffic stop could be transformed, as a matter of routine, into a *Terry* stop. This would violate the "narrow scope" of *Terry* and dispense with any need for an officer to have specific and articulable facts to justify his actions.... We reject the State's argument that routine alone is sufficient to justify a pat-down."[153]

In *Glazner v. State*,[154] a deputy stopped defendant after noticing that the registration on defendant's vehicle had expired. While explaining why he stopped him and asking for his license, the deputy noticed a clip on defendant's pocket which he suspected was connected to a knife. The deputy then had reasonable suspicion for a pat-down.

Clearly, *Terry v. Ohio* does not permit police officers to engage in a practice of routinely frisking individuals, without concern for whether a particular person poses a danger. Accordingly, the *Furr* court refused to "adopt a rule that it is per se reasonable for the police to pat down a suspect for weapons if they are accused of possessing drugs."[155] Nonetheless, that knowledge coupled with a few other facts would support the pat-down.

2.3.2.1. Anonymous tip—"Man with a gun" call

In *Florida v. J.L.*,[156] the U.S. Supreme Court cautioned that an anonymous tip that a person is carrying a gun, *without more*, will not be sufficient to justify a police officer's stop and frisk of that person.

In *J.L.*, an anonymous tipster called the Miami-Dade Police and reported that "a young [B]lack male standing at a particular bus stop and wearing a plaid shirt was carrying a gun." Two officers responded to the tip and arrived at the bus stop about six minutes after receiving the dispatch. At the bus stop, the officers noticed three Black males "just hanging out." One of the three, defendant J.L., was wearing a plaid shirt. "Apart from the tip, the officers had no reason to suspect any of the three of illegal conduct." One officer "approached J.L., told him to put his hands up on the bus stop, frisked him, and seized a gun from J.L.'s pocket." A second officer frisked the other two individuals but found nothing.

The pivotal issue was whether the Court should adopt a "gun exception" to the general rule, originated in *Terry v. Ohio*, which prohibits stops and frisks on the basis of "bare-boned anonymous tips." Refusing to do so, the Court instructed that to justify a stop based solely on an anonymous tip, police must take steps to establish the reliability of the tip. If the anonymous tip is found to be so lacking in reliability that the constitutional standard of a "reasonable articulable suspicion" of criminal activity has not been satisfied, the stop and frisk will not be justified, even if it alleges "the illegal possession of a firearm." Said the Court: "An accurate description of a subject's readily observable location and appearance is of course reliable in this limited sense: It will help the police correctly identify the person whom the tipster means to accuse. Such a tip, however, does not show that the tipster has knowledge of concealed criminal activity. *The reasonable suspicion here at issue requires that a tip be reliable in its assertion of illegality, not just in its tendency to identify a determinate person.*"[157]

With regard to the issue whether an anonymous tip supports a reasonable suspicion to stop a suspect, Texas case law tracks federal precedent.[158]

2.3.3. The scope of the protective frisk

Yet another component of the *Terry* process concerns the permissible scope of the protective pat-down search or "frisk." Once a sufficient basis has been established for the investigatory detention and the limited pat-down search, the final inquiry is whether the search was narrowly restricted to the purpose such an intrusion is supposed to serve. Because the "sole justification" of the limited pat-down "is the protection of

153 *O'Hara v. State*, 27 S.W.3d 548, 553 (Tex. Crim. App. 2000).
154 *Glazner v. State*, 175 S.W.3d 262 (Tex. Crim. App. 2005).
155 *Furr v. State*, 499 S.W.3d 872, 880-81 (Tex. Crim. App. 2016).
156 *Florida v. J.L.*, 529 U.S. 266, 120 S. Ct. 1375 (2000).
157 *Florida v. J.L.*, 529 U.S. 266, 272, 120 S. Ct. 1375, 1379 (2000) (emphasis added).
158 *See Glenn v. State*, 967 S.W.2d 467 (Tex. App. 1998); *Zone v. State*, 84 S.W.3d 733 (Tex. App. 2002).

the police officer and others nearby," it must be "confined in scope to an intrusion reasonably designed to discover guns, knives, clubs, or other hidden instruments for the assault of the police officer."[159] As the U.S. Supreme Court explained in *Adams v. Williams*[160]: "The purpose of this limited search is not to discover evidence of crime, but to allow the officer to pursue his investigation without fear of violence." In *Adams*, the Court upheld a protective frisk based on an informant's tip that a described suspect seated in a specific area at 2:15 a.m. was carrying narcotics and had a gun at his waist.

Accordingly, investigative stops or detentions may only be conducted when an officer has an objective reasonable suspicion that criminal activity may be afoot. The protective frisk of a suspect's outer clothing may be conducted only when the officer is in possession of additional specific and articulable facts from which he can reasonably infer that the individual he is confronting is armed and presently dangerous. Moreover, the frisk must be strictly limited in scope; designed solely to uncover hidden weapons. The facts must be objectively realistic and not be grounded in speculation, subjective feelings or intuition. To allow anything less "would invite intrusions upon constitutionally guaranteed rights based on nothing more substantial than inarticulate hunches," a result which courts will not allow.[161] In *Baldwin v. State*,[162] an officer went beyond the bounds of a lawful pat-down search when he removed defendant's wallet to check his identification. "Though an officer may ask a defendant to identify himself during a valid investigative detention, that does not automatically mean that the officer can search a defendant's person to obtain or confirm his identity."[163]

In *State v. Williams*,[164] defendant was a rear seat passenger in a car stopped for a defective taillight. The driver was arrested when, after a pat-down, numerous prescription pills were found on his person. The driver then said that defendant had a steak knife, and she had been threatening to stab the other passengers. As the officer was a male and defendant a female, he did not want to pat her down. Instead, he asked her to "kind of reach underneath [her bra] and just pull it out a little bit and kind of shake it a little bit . . . and maneuver it." (Because defendant was relatively well-endowed – "more than average" – the officer was concerned she may have concealed the steak knife in her bra.) Defendant initially refused and cried, but after a second request complied. When she did, numerous pills fell out. The court ruled this search unconstitutional. The court found that the officer's reluctance to pat-down a female did not justify broadening the scope of this search beyond a simple frisk, noting that a pat-down would not have been dangerous or ineffective and that no legal authority prohibits the pat-down of a female suspect by a male officer. The pills were suppressed.

2.3.4. Plain touch

During the course of a pat-down, if a weapon is found, the officer may seize the item, and retain it, if its possession is unlawful. If the officer determines that the suspect is not armed, the purpose of the frisk is satisfied and the probing can proceed no further. However, if in the frisking process an object is detected, in a pocket or under clothing, that is clearly not a weapon, but rather, and just as obviously, contraband, the item may be seized under the "plain touch" or "plain feel" doctrine.[165] The rule here is that officers conducting a *Terry* frisk are entitled to seize any item whose contour, shape or mass make its identity immediately apparent as contraband. The officer must be able to immediately identity the item as contraband, without resort to further manipulation of the item.

Minnesota v. Dickerson set out the three requirements for "plain touch."[166] First, the officer must be lawfully *in the touching area*; that is, the officer must not violate the Fourth Amendment by arriving at the place from which the evidence could be tactilely perceived. Second, the officer must have some independent constitutional justification for placing his or her hands on the property or person in question. This

---

159 *Terry v. Ohio*, 392 U.S. 1, 29, 88 S. Ct. 1868, 1884 (1968).
160 *Adams v. Williams*, 407 *U.S.* 143, 146, 92 S. Ct. 1921, 1923 (1972).
161 *Terry v. Ohio*, 392 U.S. 1, 22, 88 S. Ct. 1868, 1880 (1968).
162 *Baldwin v. State*, 278 S.W.3d 367 (Tex. Crim. App. 2009).
163 *Baldwin v. State*, 278 S.W.3d 367, 372 (Tex. Crim. App. 2009).
164 *State v. Williams*, 312 S.W.3d 276 (Tex. App. 2010).
165 *See Minnesota v. Dickerson*, 508 U.S. 366, 113 S. Ct. 2130 (1993). For a comprehensive discussion of the "plain touch" corollary, *see* Holtz, *The "Plain Touch" Corollary: A Natural and Foreseeable Consequence of the Plain View Doctrine*, 95 Dickinson L. Rev. 521 (1991). *See also* Larry E. Holtz, *Criminal Procedure for Law and Justice Professionals* (Blue360° Media).
166 *Minnesota v. Dickerson*, 508 U.S. 366, 113 S. Ct. 2130 (1993).

requirement — though not unrelated to the mandate that the officer be lawfully in the perceiving area — should receive separate scrutiny which probes the independent and distinct constitutional justification for the touching of the person or evidentiary item. In this regard, the second prong of the plain touch formulation requires the officer's hands to be lawfully *on the touching area.* Finally, upon touching the area in question, the officer must, through the process of tactile recognition, garner probable cause to believe the object which she is touching constitutes evidence of crime, contraband, or is otherwise subject to official seizure. Additionally, the development of probable cause should be reasonably contemporaneous with the initial touching to avoid the danger of an inoffensive touching graduating into a governmental massage which, "by virtue of its intolerable intensity and scope," may violate the Fourth Amendment. In this respect, the recognition of the item as contraband must be *immediately apparent.*[167]

In *Griffin v. State,*[168] a reliable confidential informant told an investigator that defendant was dealing crack cocaine. The investigator knew that just two days earlier, defendant had been arrested for possession of a small amount of cocaine residue found in a "long plastic tube." About five minutes after receiving the tip, the investigator intercepted defendant, then stopped and frisked him. The investigator felt two long cylindrical tubes in defendant's left front pocket. He immediately recognized these as contraband without the need to "squeeze, slide, [or] otherwise manipulate" them. He also knew that defendant had used these types of containers to carry narcotics just two days earlier. The investigator's seizure of the tubes was therefore lawful.

However, in *Campbell v. State,*[169] the court held that the officer exceeded the scope of the *Terry* frisk when he seized a film canister from Campbell's pocket. The court reasoned that the incriminating character of the film canister was not immediately apparent based on the officer's testimony that the canister did not feel like a weapon. Similarly, in *Graham v. State,*[170] the officer exceeded the scope of the *Terry* frisk when he seized cocaine from defendant's watch pocket. There, "the officer testified that during his initial search he felt something 'puffy' and heard a 'crackling sound' but that it did not sound like anything. The officer acknowledged that the pocket contained no weapons and continued the search. Only after returning to feel the pocket for a second time did he determine that there were drugs in the pocket. The officer had to rub and pinch the pocket to feel the two capsules on the inside of the pocket."[171] The court concluded that "the 'incriminating character' of the capsules in the watch pocket was not 'immediately apparent' to justify their seizure."[172]

"The 'immediately apparent' requirement does not require actual knowledge of the contraband." But it does require that the officer have "probable cause to believe an item in plain view [or feel] is contraband before seizing it."[173] In *Young v. State,*[174] the court reviewed a case in which the officer, while conducting a lawful frisk, discovered a pill bottle. The officer reached into the pocket and removed the pill bottle, opened it and found 10 grams of an illegal narcotic. The court noted: "Central to the plain feel doctrine's application is that, through touch, the officer 'plainly know[s]' (i.e. has probable cause that) the object is contraband."[175] The court, noting there were no additional facts or circumstances present to support a finding of probable cause, held that the removal of the pill bottle from the defendant's pocket, and its subsequent opening, were not supported by the plain feel doctrine.

2.3.5. Various factors to consider

As the previous discussion indicates, the police may briefly detain and question a person upon a reasonable suspicion, short of probable cause for arrest, that the person is involved in criminal activity. What is, or is not, reasonable suspicion depends on balancing, weighing and examining a variety of factors, taking into

---

167 *Minnesota v. Dickerson*, 508 U.S. 366, 375, 113 S. Ct. 2130, 2137 (1993).
168 *Griffin v. State*, 215 S.W.3d 403 (Tex. Crim. App. 2007).
169 *Campbell v. State*, 864 S.W.2d 223 (Tex. App. 1993).
170 *Graham v. State*, 893 S.W.2d 4 (Tex. App. 1994).
171 *Graham v. State*, 893 S.W.2d 4, 8 (Tex. App. 1994).
172 *Graham v. State*, 893 S.W.2d 4, 8 (Tex. App. 1994).
173 *Young v. State*, 563 S.W.3d 325, 329 (Tex. App. 2018) (citing *Williams v. State*, 668 S.W.2d 692, 700 n.12 (Tex. Crim. App. 1983)).
174 *Young v. State*, 563 S.W.3d 325 (Tex. App. 2018).
175 *Young v. State*, 563 S.W.3d 325, 331 (Tex. App. 2018).

account the particular factual setting with which an officer is confronted. Some factors commonly cited by courts when determining the existence or absence of reasonable suspicion are set forth below.

2.3.5.1. A suspect's prior criminal record

A law enforcement officer's knowledge of a suspect's criminal history, especially where that history involves weapons offenses, is a relevant factor in judging the reasonableness of a *Terry* frisk. Although an officer's knowledge of a suspect's criminal record *alone* is not sufficient to justify the initial stop of a suspect or to justify a frisk of a suspect once stopped, an officer's knowledge of a suspect's prior criminal activity in combination with other factors may lead to a reasonable suspicion that the suspect is presently armed and dangerous. Indeed, *Terry* itself acknowledges that police officers must be permitted to use their knowledge and experience in deciding whether to frisk a suspect. In many instances, a reasonable inference may be drawn that a suspect is armed and dangerous from the fact that he or she is known to have been armed and dangerous on previous occasions.[176]

Accordingly, given the volatile times in which we live, courts certainly cannot require police officers to ignore the fact that a suspect whom they are confronting has a history of criminal behavior, particularly weapons offenses. While a suspect's criminal history alone will not justify a *Terry* frisk, that history, coupled with other facts, may be sufficient.

2.3.5.2. An officer's training and experience

Officers are entitled to rely on their own knowledge, training and experience in forming reasonable suspicion, and even probable cause. State and federal courts have "long recognized the police officer's investigatory insight in evaluating probable cause."[177] The courts are consistently deferential to police officer training and experience. Otherwise, there would be little merit in securing able, trained officers to guard citizens and the public peace if their actions were to be measured by what might be probable cause to an untrained civilian.

In *United States v. Foster*,[178] an officer was patrolling an apartment complex where he had made 85 PCP-related arrests. He saw defendant emerge from a still-running vehicle and walk toward a dumpster; the officer knew that PCP traffickers often hid their drugs in this dumpster area. The officer approached defendant in the hope of initiating a consensual encounter; as soon as he stood face-to-face with him, he could smell PCP coming from defendant's person. The officer asked defendant his name and what he was doing in the area. Defendant was nervous during this brief conversation and attempted to return to his vehicle after about one minute. Based on his observations, the officer had reasonable suspicion to detain defendant by handcuffing him and further questioning him. Because PCP users have a tendency to become violent, the officer had reasonable suspicion to frisk defendant as well.

In *United States v. Orrego-Fernandez*,[179] a state trooper was driving along the highway when he noticed defendant's pick-up truck, which appeared to have been altered. The truck frame was noticeably lower in the back than the front, so low that the leaf springs on the rear axle were only 5 inches above the pavement. The wheel well was solid black, with no metal slats visible, indicating that the bed was sitting directly on the frame. In addition, the trooper noticed that the gas tank was hanging 2 to 3 inches below the frame. The trooper had trained on a similar truck with a lowered gas tank; that truck had been equipped with a hidden compartment. Defendant's truck had a fresh, glossy coat of paint, which would have concealed any dents removed after altering the truck. Because this truck had several alterations consistent, in the trooper's experience, with a hidden compartment, he had reasonable suspicion for a stop.

In *Ramirez-Tamayo v. State*,[180] the deputy had "about seven years of experience as a licensed Texas peace officer conducting drug interdiction on highways. During this time, he came to know that 'very commonly'

---

176 *See, e.g., Ybarra v. Illinois*, 444 U.S. 85, 93, 100 S. Ct. 338, 343 (1979) (implying that knowledge of a person's criminal history would be a factor supporting a legitimate frisk).

177 Anna Lvovsky, *The Judicial Presumption of Police Expertise*, 130 Harv. L. Rev. 1995, 2026-27 (2017) (citing cases).

178 *United States v. Foster*, 376 F.3d 577 (6th Cir. 2004).

179 *United States v. Orrego-Fernandez*, 78 F.3d 1497 (10th Cir. 1996).

180 *Ramirez-Tamayo v. State*, 537 S.W.3d 29 (Tex. Crim. App. 2017).

illegal narcotics can be hidden inside car doors resulting in the windows becoming inoperable, and he had personally observed such instances on I-40 'a few times.'" Moroever, "a peace officer who spends his days patrolling on the highways could reasonably infer that a new-model car, serviced by a rental company, without visible signs of damage to the door or window, should have operable power windows that can easily be activated from the driver's seat," and "a peace officer with several years of experience would be aware that strong odors are often used to mask the smell of drugs, and he would be able to recognize an abnormal degree of nervousness compared to a more usual level of nervousness attending police-citizen encounters[.] Deputy Simpson knew that drug couriers commonly use rental cars rather than personally owned vehicles."[181] Thus, the deputy had reasonable suspicion to detain defendant.

In *Curtis v. State*,[182] at around 1 a.m., two officers saw defendant's car weave twice across "the inside fog line" (the left-most white line along the shoulder) and once across "the broken lane divider line" in the span of "several hundred yards."[183] The officers had extensive experience and training in detecting drunk drivers, and knew such weaving to be a sign of intoxication. The officers had reasonable suspicion for a stop.

In *Tanner v. State*,[184] at around 3 a.m., an officer on routine patrol saw defendant and a young woman pushing bicycles out from a dark area behind a bar. The officer knew the bar had been closed for at least an hour. Because the officer "made an on-the-spot observation of conduct that, by any standard, is unusual and highly consistent with criminal behavior,"[185] he had reasonable suspicion to stop and question the pair.

However, in *Parks v. State*,[186] officers did not have reasonable suspicion to stop four young men solely because they had blue rags hanging from their pockets, which the officers associated with gang membership. There was no individualized suspicion linking the men to any criminal activity.

Tribal police. In *United States v. Cooley*, [187] the United States Supreme Court held: "On a public right-of-way that traverses an Indian reservation and is primarily patrolled by tribal police, a tribal police officer has the authority to (a) stop a non-Indian motorist if the officer has reasonable suspicion that the motorist may violate or has violated federal or state law, (b) conduct a search to the extent necessary to protect himself or others, and (c) if the tribal officer has probable cause, detain the motorist for the period of time reasonably necessary for a non-tribal officer to arrive on the scene."[188]

2.3.5.3. Knowledge of a recent crime in the area

An officer's awareness that a crime was recently committed in the vicinity is a pertinent consideration. In *Balentine v. State*,[189] Amarillo officers responded to a shots-fired call at 2:26 a.m. in a residential, low-traffic area. While searching the area, they saw defendant, two houses down from the complainant's home and walking away at a brisk pace with his hands in his pockets. He appeared nervous and was constantly looking over his shoulder. The officers had reasonable suspicion to detain him for questioning. Similarly, in *Hammond v. State*,[190] at around 11 p.m., an officer heard a report of a burglary on Vine Street but was not assigned the call. Shortly thereafter, he was called to a disturbance at another address on Vine. While turning onto that street, he saw defendant "kind of run" in front of his patrol car, carrying a television. Reasonable suspicion was established for a stop.[191]

---

181 *Ramirez-Tamayo v. State*, 537 S.W.3d 29, 37-38 (Tex. Crim. App. 2017).
182 *Curtis v. State*, 238 S.W.3d 376 (Tex. Crim. App. 2007).
183 *Curtis v. State*, 238 S.W.3d 376, 377 n.2 (Tex. Crim. App. 2007).
184 *Tanner v. State*, 228 S.W.3d 852 (Tex. App. 2007).
185 *Tanner v. State*, 228 S.W.3d 852, 858 (Tex. App. 2007).
186 *Parks v. State*, 330 S.W.3d 675 (Tex. App. 2010).
187 *United States v. Cooley*, 593 U.S. ___, 141 S. Ct. 1638 (2021).
188 *United States v. Cooley*, 593 U.S. ___, 141 S. Ct. 1638, 1646 (2021) (Alito, J., concurring).
189 *Balentine v. State*, 71 S.W.3d 763 (Tex. Crim. App. 2002).
190 *Hammond v. State*, 664 S.W.2d 838 (Tex. App. 1984).
191 *See also Thomas v. State*, 297 S.W.3d 458 (Tex. App. 2009); *Malone v. State*, 734 S.W.2d 50 (Tex. App. 1987); *Sheffield v. State*, 647 S.W.2d 413 (Tex. App. 1983); *State v. Lopez*, 148 S.W.3d 586 (Tex. App. 2004); *Livingston v. State*, 739 S.W.2d 311 (Tex. Crim. App. 1987).

2.3.5.4. High-crime/high drug-trafficking areas

A suspect's presence in a high-crime area, or an area known for drug trafficking, standing alone, is not a basis for reasonable suspicion. But a suspect's presence in such an area is an articulable fact. Coupled with other more solid observations, such presence can create reasonable suspicion that the suspect is engaged in the unlawful activity for which the neighborhood is known.[192]

2.3.5.5. Time period

The time of day or night in which the individual is observed is relevant, and a late hour may be a factor contributing to a reasonable suspicion. For example, in *Adams v. Williams*,[193] while properly investigating the activity of a person who was reported to be carrying narcotics and a concealed weapon and who was sitting alone in a car in a high-crime area at 2:15 in the morning, the officer was held to have had ample reason to fear for his safety. However, merely being out in public at a late hour, without more, will not justify a stop.

2.3.5.6. Wanted flyers

In *United States v. Hensley*,[194] the United States Supreme Court held that "where police have been unable to locate a person suspected of involvement in a past crime, the ability to briefly stop that person, ask questions, or check identification in the absence of probable cause promotes the strong government interest in solving crimes and bringing offenders to justice." Thus, the law enforcement interests promoted by allowing one department to conduct investigative detentions based upon another department's bulletins or "Wanted Flyers" are considerable, while the intrusions on a person's Fourth and Fourteenth Amendment rights are minimal.

This was the first time the federal Supreme Court specifically addressed the issue of whether the police may stop and detain a person on information from a wanted flyer from another jurisdiction when the investigation is of a past or completed crime. Hensley was wanted for questioning in reference to an armed robbery. The Court held that the justification for the stop did not evaporate merely because the armed robbery had been completed. Therefore, when police have a reasonable suspicion, grounded in specific and articulable facts, that a person they encounter was involved, or wanted, in connection with a completed crime, then a *Terry*-type stop may be made to investigate that suspicion.

As explained in *Whiteley v. Warden*,[195] where the arresting officer relied on a radio bulletin advising officers that a warrant had been issued for the defendant's arrest:

> Certainly, police officers called upon to aid other officers in executing arrest warrants are entitled to assume that the officers requesting aid offered the magistrate the information requisite to support an independent judicial assessment of probable cause. Where, however, the contrary turns out to be true, an otherwise illegal arrest cannot be insulated from challenge by the decision of the instigating officer to rely on fellow officers to make the arrest.[196]

---

[192] *See e.g., See Illinois v. Wardlow*, 528 U.S. 119, 123-24, 120 S. Ct. 673 (2000). ("flight combined with the fact that it occurred in a high crime area supported a finding of reasonable suspicion"); *Furr v. State*, 499 S.W.3d 872 (Tex. Crim. App. 2016) (concluding pat-down justified when circumstances included anonymous tip, personal observations of police and a "high drug, high crime" area); *Brodnex v. State*, 485 S.W.3d 432 (Tex. Crim. App. 2016) (concluding observation of defendant walking through an area known for narcotics activity at 2 a.m. did not justify stop when not coupled with suspicious behavior).

[193] *Adams v. Williams*, 407 U.S. 143, 147-48, 92 S. Ct. 1921, 1924 (1972).

[194] *United States v. Hensley*, 469 U.S. 221, 105 S. Ct. 675 (1985).

[195] *Whiteley v. Warden*, 401 *U.S.* 560, 91 S. Ct. 1031 (1971).

[196] *Whiteley v. Warden*, 401 *U.S.* 560, 568, 91 S. Ct. 1031 (1971). *See also United States v. Hensley*, 469 U.S. 221, 231, 105 S. Ct. 675 (1985). ("*Whiteley* supports the proposition that when evidence is uncovered during a search incident to an arrest in reliance merely on a flyer or bulletin, its admissibility turns on whether the officers who *issued* the flyer possessed probable cause to make the arrest.") (emphasis in original).

2.3.5.7. Evasive conduct, furtive gestures, etc.

Evasive conduct and furtive gestures, along with concealing or attempting to conceal one's identity, are criteria an officer may weigh in assessing if his suspicion is reasonable. However, each individual observation, without more, will not create a reasonable suspicion of criminal activity. As to the furtive gesture, the law is clear that a furtive gesture alone is not a sufficient basis for probable cause. A furtive gesture in conjunction with other facts certainly could generate a reasonable suspicion, as well as probable cause.

2.3.5.8. Flight

A suspect's flight, when confronted with police presence, may give the officer reasonable suspicion to pursue and detain the suspect. Note, however, that not all conduct that merely avoids contact with a law enforcement officer is considered flight from the officer.

In *Illinois v. Wardlow*,[197] the U.S. Supreme Court held that the sudden, unprovoked flight of a person in a high drug-trafficking area, upon sighting a police vehicle, creates a reasonable suspicion of criminal activity to support a temporary investigative detention (*Terry* stop) of the person. In this case, two uniformed officers were in the last car of a four-car police caravan that converged on an area of Chicago known for heavy narcotics trafficking, in order to investigate drug transactions. The officers observed defendant, who was standing next to a building holding an opaque bag, look at the police caravan, then run in the opposite direction. Given the character of the area and defendant's headlong flight ("the consummate act of evasion"), the officers had reasonable suspicion to stop him.[198] The Court in *Wardlow* would not, however, adopt a bright-line rule authorizing the temporary detention of *anyone* who flees at the mere sight of a police officer. Rather, reasonable suspicion to support such a detention must be determined by looking to the totality of the circumstances – the whole picture.

In *Livingston v. State*,[199] at around 9 p.m., an unidentified man told two Houston officers of a shooting in a nearby Weingarten store parking lot. Moments later, the officers saw defendant emerge from the dimly lit, isolated area behind the store. He was not carrying any grocery bags. As soon as he saw the officers' patrol car, he turned and walked in the opposite direction. The officers could see that his pants were ripped from knee to crotch and he was sweating profusely. Based on all these observations, they had reasonable suspicion to stop and question him.

In *Salazar v. State*,[200] at around 5:30 a.m. officers were called to the scene of a burglary in progress at unit 13D in Dry Dock Apartments. When the first officer arrived, he saw a small car parked outside the apartment. Defendant was inside the car, but he ducked down upon seeing the officer. He then repeatedly looked over the seat, only to duck down again upon still seeing the officer. The officer radioed his colleagues about this suspicious behavior, and his col-

leagues then had reasonable suspicion for an investigatory stop.

In *Arguellez v. State*,[201] it was not flight when defendant drove away from a pool area as the officers were arriving. There, officers were responding to a call of "suspicious photography" at a public pool. However, because there was no suggestion that, "by taking pictures in a public place, appellant was, had been, or soon would be, engaged in criminal activity[,] ... leaving the scene of such photography does not constitute flight or evasion."[202]

2.3.5.9. Tips provided by informants

Information provided by someone outside the circles of law enforcement may provide sufficient justification for a stop if it carries with it sufficient indicia of reliability. Factors that bolster the reliability of information may include: the reliability and reputation of the person providing the tip; corroboration of the

197 *Illinois v. Wardlow*, 528 U.S. 119, 120 S. Ct. 673 (2000).
198 *Illinois v. Wardlow*, 528 U.S. 119, 124, 120 S. Ct. 673, 676 (2000).
199 *Livingston v. State*, 739 S.W.2d 311 (Tex. Crim. App. 1987).
200 *Salazar v. State*, 805 S.W.2d 538 (Tex. App. Fort Worth 1991).
201 *Arguellez v. State*, 409 S.W.3d 657 (Tex. Crim. App. 2013).
202 *Arguellez v. State*, 409 S.W.3d 657, 664 (Tex. Crim. App. 2013).

details contained in the tip by independent police work; and the extent to which any information provided by the informant has proved to be accurate or useful in the past. Anonymous tips, however, must be corroborated by other observations and supported by indicia of reliability, in order to generate a reasonable suspicion.

For example, in *Alabama v. White*,[203] Montgomery police received an anonymous tip stating that defendant, carrying a brown briefcase filled with cocaine, would leave a specific unit of an apartment building and travel in her brown Plymouth station wagon, which had a broken taillight, to a specific motel. Police watched the apartment complex and saw a brown Plymouth wagon with a broken taillight. They then watched defendant, empty-handed, exit the specified apartment, get into the car and drive directly toward the motel. Even though not every detail in the tip turned out to be totally correct, the partial corroboration by police alone provided reasonable suspicion for a stop. Here, the United States Supreme Court found it

> important that "the anonymous [tip] contained a range of details relating not just to easily obtained facts and conditions existing at the time of the tip, but to future actions of third parties ordinarily not easily predicted." The fact that the officers found a car precisely matching the caller's description in front of the 235 building is an example of the former. *Anyone could have "predicted" that fact because it was a condition presumably existing at the time of the call. What was important was the caller's ability to predict [White's] future behavior, because it demonstrated inside information – a special familiarity with [White's] affairs....* Because only a small number of people are generally privy to an individual's itinerary, it is reasonable for police to believe that a person with access to such information is likely to also have access to reliable information about that individual's illegal activities.[204]

In *Carmouche v. State*,[205] a confidential informant phoned a narcotics investigator with the Texas Department of Public Safety. The investigator recognized her because she had provided accurate information about at least eight of her co-defendants in a pending federal drug conspiracy case. The CI said that she and defendant (whom she only described as a Black male with "sleepy" eyes) would drive from Houston to Nacogdoches that evening, and that defendant would be carrying approximately 10 ounces of cocaine. She also stated that defendant would be renting a car, but she could not provide a description. The investigator asked her to stop at a specific gas station in Corrigan so he could identify her. At 8:45 that evening, the CI and a Black male (later identified as defendant) pulled into the specified gas station. Because of the CI's previous history of reliability, police had reasonable suspicion to stop the car and investigate further.[206]

Citizen informants. Courts have found citizen informants credible because historically a citizen informant would have been a victim or a witness to criminal activity. Greater credibility has traditionally been accorded such persons who have been witnesses to criminal activity and who act with the intent to aid the police in law enforcement efforts rather than for any personal gain or payment for the information. "It has been widely recognized that the reliability of a citizen-informant is generally shown by the very nature of the circumstances under which the incriminating information became known to him or her."[207] For example, in *Turley v. State*,[208] an officer received a call from a gas station clerk named Angela at around 3 a.m. (The officer knew Angela immediately because he often stopped at her station.) Angela told the officer that defendant had almost hit a gas pump while driving into the gas station parking lot and that when he entered the store, she immediately smelled alcohol on him and suspected he was intoxicated. Angela described defendant's car, including the license plate number. The officer arrived at the station two to three minutes later, and quickly located defendant's vehicle. Even though he observed no traffic violations, he stopped it. The court ruled that

---

[203] *Alabama v. White*, 496 U.S. 325, 110 S. Ct. 2412 (1990).

[204] *Alabama v. White*, 496 U.S. 325, 332, 110 S. Ct. 2412, 2417 (1990) (quoting *Illinois v. Gates*, 462 U.S. 213, 245, 103 S.Ct. 2317, 2335 (1983)) (emphasis added).

[205] *Carmouche v. State*, 10 S.W.3d 323 (Tex. Crim. App. 2000).

[206] See also *Williams v. State*, 924 S.W.2d 189 (Tex. App. 1996); *Turley v. State*, 242 S.W.3d 178 (Tex. App. 2007); *Bilyeu v. State*, 136 S.W.3d 691 (Tex. App. 2004).

[207] *Brother v. State*, 166 S.W.3d 255, 258 (Tex. Crim. App. 2005), *cert. denied sub nom. Brother v. Texas*, 546 U.S. 1150, 126 S. Ct. 1172 (2006).

[208] *Turley v. State*, 242 S.W.3d 178 (Tex. App. 2007).

the officer had reasonable suspicion, based on Angela's tip. The officer "knew" Angela – at least her first name and place of work – so she could be held accountable if she gave false information. Moreover, she relayed events she had observed first-hand, and continued to observe as she called. This added to her reliability. There was no indication that Angela was a paid informant, which might decrease her reliability. Finally, her description of the car was sufficiently detailed.[209]

2.3.5.10. Drug courier profiles

A drug courier profile is a collection of objective factors which may be innocent in and of themselves, but in conjunction with each other or other facts, lead officers to believe that the suspect is engaging in drug trafficking. In general, most courts consider those factors actually exhibited by a suspect to determine if they collectively demonstrate reasonable suspicion, without accepting any set or combination of factors as demonstrating reasonable suspicion *per se*. Although it has not addressed the specific question whether drug courier profiles alone can provide a basis for reasonable suspicion, the United States Supreme Court has approved the use of profile characteristics as permissible factors to be considered in the totality of circumstances analysis of reasonable suspicion.[210]

Thus, the "drug courier profile" is merely a shorthand way of referring to a group of characteristics that may indicate that a person is a drug courier. One word of caution: While conformity with just a few aspects of the profile may not sufficiently support a reasonable and articulable suspicion that criminal activity may be afoot in order to warrant a *Terry* stop of a suspect,[211] as explained by Justice Rehnquist, a police officer is nonetheless entitled to assess the totality of the circumstances surrounding the subject of his or her attention in light of that officer's experience and training, which, of course, may include "instruction on a 'drug courier profile.'"[212]

Often, undercover officers will survey airport or bus terminals for individuals matching a certain profile. Factors utilized in compiling this profile may include: a journey that originated in a source city for narcotics, or a short round trip, with a brief stay in such a city; the suspect carrying a hard-sided suitcase; the suspect appearing nervous when questioned; tickets that were paid for in cash; the suspect providing inconsistent or wavering answers to inquiries; furtive movements (*e.g.*, glancing over one's shoulder, not making eye contact, etc.).[213]

However, as the Court instructed in *Royer*, the "drug courier profile," while not an end in itself, is an effective means or investigative tool utilized by trained law enforcement officers as a systematic method of recognizing characteristics repeatedly found among those who traffic in illicit drugs. In his dissenting opinion, Justice Rehnquist described the profile as "the collective or distilled experience of narcotics officers concerning characteristics repeatedly seen in drug smugglers."[214]

Thus, in *Reid v. Georgia*,[215] the Court held that a DEA agent had no reasonable suspicion to detain defendant where (1) defendant had arrived from a source city for cocaine; (2) he arrived in the early morning; (3) he and his companion appeared to be trying to conceal that they were traveling together; and (4) they had no luggage other than their shoulder bags. The Court determined that defendant's early morning arrival from a source city for drugs, carrying only a shoulder bag, "describe[s] a very large category of presumably innocent travelers, who would be subject to virtually random seizures were the Court to conclude that as little foundation as there was in this case could justify a seizure."[216]

---

[209] *See also Brother v. State*, 166 S.W.3d 255, 258-59 (Tex. Crim. App. 2005), *cert. denied sub nom. Brother v. Texas*, 546 U.S. 1150, 126 S. Ct. 1172 (2006).

[210] *See Florida v. Royer*, 460 U.S. 491, 494 n.2, 103 S. Ct. 1319, 1322 n.2 (1983) ("The 'drug courier profile' is an abstract of characteristics found to be typical of persons transporting illegal drugs."); *United States v. Sokolow*, 490 U.S. 1, 10, 109 S. Ct. 1581, 1587 (1989).

[211] *See Reid v. Georgia*, 448 U.S. 438, 100 S. Ct. 2752 (1980).

[212] *Florida v. Royer*, 460 U.S. 491, 525 n.6, 103 S. Ct. 1319, 1339 n.6 (1983) (Rehnquist J., dissenting).

[213] *See e.g., United States v. Sokolow*, 490 U.S. 1, 109 S. Ct. 1581 (1989).

[214] *Florida v. Royer*, 460 U.S. 491, 525 n.6, 103 S. Ct. 1319, 1339 n.6 (1983) (Rehnquist, J., dissenting).

[215] *Reid v. Georgia*, 448 U.S. 438, 100 S. Ct. 2752 (1980).

[216] *Reid v. Georgia*, 448 U.S. 438, 441, 100 S. Ct. 2752, 2754 (1980).

In *Royer*, "the detectives' attention was attracted by the following facts which were considered to be within the profile: Royer was carrying American Tourister luggage, which appeared to be heavy; he was young, apparently between 25-35; he was casually dressed; he appeared pale and nervous, looking around at other people; he paid for his ticket in cash with a large number of bills; and rather than completing the airline identification tag to be attached to checked baggage, which had space for a name, address, and telephone number, he wrote only a name and the destination."[217] Upholding Royer's initial investigatory detention, the Court reasoned that when the officers learned that Royer was traveling under an assumed name, that fact, coupled with the facts already known by the officers which constituted a "drug courier profile" – "paying cash for a one-way ticket, the mode of checking the two bags, and Royer's appearance and conduct in general – were adequate grounds for suspecting Royer of carrying drugs and for temporarily detaining him and his luggage while they attempted to verify or dispel their suspicions."[218]

In a typical scenario, a suspect matching the profile is approached by officers and asked a few questions. Often, a threshold issue in such cases is the nature of the questioning. If the encounter is consensual, then no Fourth Amendment concerns arise. If, however, the officers' suspicions are aroused and a more aggressive investigatory posture is assumed, the encounter may escalate into a *Terry*-type detention, and the scope of the encounter must conform to constitutional guidelines. The method employed by investigating officers should be of the least intrusive means reasonably necessary to verify or dispel the officer's suspicion in a short period of time. Although the initial stop may be justified, it may become so protracted, exceeding a time limit that the officer would reasonably need to confirm or dispel his or her suspicions about possible trafficking activity, that it becomes unreasonable. To pass constitutional muster, a detention not only must be justified at its inception, but also must be reasonably related in scope to the circumstances that justified it in the first instance.

If, and when, such an encounter progresses into a full-blown detention, another frequently adjudicated question involves the seizure of a suspect's luggage, purse, handbag or other personal item. The general rule is that officers may temporarily detain the property if they have reasonable suspicion that the item contains contraband. The seizure must be brief and related in duration to dispelling any suspicion about what the luggage contains.[219] Frequently, the luggage is subjected to a sniff-test (by a dog trained to recognize, by smell, the presence of narcotics or other drugs), or officers try to obtain consent to search the luggage. In such cases, a distinction must be drawn between detaining and actually opening and searching a container. Although police may temporarily detain a container based upon reasonable suspicion, they generally may not open it without a warrant, or some recognized exception to the warrant requirement.

2.3.6. Mere inquiries, investigative stops and *Miranda*

In consensual encounters and in investigatory stops, the police are not required to administer the *Miranda* warning.[220] Inherent in the concept of a *Terry* stop is the right of the police to temporarily detain an individual to confirm or dispel their suspicions. Therefore, it is erroneous to focus solely on whether defendant was free to leave. Rather, the proper inquiry is whether the individual was "in custody." Indeed, *Miranda* itself instructed that "[g]eneral on-the-scene questioning as to facts surrounding a crime or other general questioning of citizens in the fact-finding process is not affected by our holding."[221] Rather, the safeguards outlined in *Miranda* become applicable as soon as the suspect's freedom of action is curtailed to a degree associated with a formal arrest.

---

[217] *Florida v. Royer,* 460 U.S. 491, 494 n.2, 103 S. Ct. 1319, 1322 n.2 (1983).

[218] *Florida v. Royer,* 460 U.S. 491, 502, 103 S. Ct. 1319, 1326 (1983).

[219] *United States v. Place,* 462 U.S. 696, 103 S. Ct. 2637 (1983).

[220] *Berkemer v. McCarty,* 468 U.S. 420, 437-442, 104 S. Ct. 3138, 3149-50 (1984).

[221] *Miranda v. Arizona,* 384 U.S. 436, 477, 86 S. Ct. 1602, 1629 (1966); *see also Miranda,* 384 U.S. at 477-78, 86 S. Ct. at 1629-30, where the Court pointed out that it "is an act of responsible citizenship for individuals to give whatever information they may have to aid in law enforcement. In such situations the compelling atmosphere inherent in the process of in-custody interrogation is not necessarily present.").

Once an arrest is made, however, or there is a detention equivalent to arrest, the person must be advised of his or her *Miranda* rights if the officer plans on questioning the person while he or she is in custody.[222]

2.3.7. Investigative detentions of vehicles; the "motor vehicle or traffic stop"

2.3.7.1. General aspects

In *Terry v. Ohio*,[223] the U.S. Supreme Court authorized a temporary investigative detention of a person when a law enforcement officer possesses a reasonable suspicion, based on "specific and articulable facts which, taken together with rational inferences from those facts, reasonably warrant" the belief that criminal activity may be afoot. Thereafter, in *Delaware v. Prouse*,[224] the Court extended the rationale of *Terry* to circumstances involving the temporary detention of motor vehicles. The officer in *Prouse* stopped defendant's vehicle merely to check his driver's license and registration. The officer had observed neither traffic, equipment violations nor any other suspicious activity associated with the vehicle. In applying the exclusionary rule to the seizure of marijuana observed in plain view on the vehicle's floor, the Court held:

> [E]xcept in those situations in which there is at least articulable suspicion that a motorist is unlicensed or that an automobile is not registered, or that either the vehicle or an occupant is otherwise subject to seizure for violation of the law, stopping an automobile and detaining the driver in order to check his driver's license and the registration of the automobile are unreasonable under the Fourth Amendment.[225]

Thus, in Fourth Amendment terms, "a traffic stop entails a seizure of the driver 'even though the purpose of the stop is limited and the resulting detention quite brief.'"[226] The stop also entails a seizure of every passenger in the vehicle, along with the driver.[227] In *Brendlin v. California*, the United States Supreme Court observed that during a routine traffic stop, all passengers are subject to some scrutiny.[228]

Accordingly, the "[t]emporary detention of individuals during the stop of an automobile by the police, even if only for a brief period and for a limited purpose, constitutes a 'seizure' of 'persons' within the meaning of the [Fourth Amendment]."[229]

The propriety of conducting motor vehicle stops on the basis of a reasonable and articulable suspicion that an occupant is or has been engaged in criminal activity, including a motor vehicle violation, has been consistently upheld.[230] In upholding the lawfulness of investigative detentions of vehicles on the basis of a

---

222 This topic is further explored in Section 8.3.2.

223 *Terry v. Ohio*, 392 U.S. 1, 88 S. Ct. 1868, 1880 (1968).

224 *Delaware v. Prouse*, 440 U.S. 648, 99 S. Ct. 1391 (1979).

225 *Delaware v. Prouse*, 440 U.S. 648, 663, 99 S. Ct. 1391, 1401 (1979); *see also United States v. Shabazz*, 993 F.2d 431, 434 (5th Cir. 1993) ("It is clear that, as in the case of pedestrians, searches and seizures of motorists who are merely *suspected* of criminal activity are to be analyzed under the framework established in *Terry v. Ohio*[.]") (emphasis in original).

226 *Brendlin v. California*, 551 U.S. 249, 127 S. Ct. 2400, 2406 (2007) (internal citations omitted).

227 *Brendlin v. California*, 551 U.S. 249, 127 S. Ct. 2400, 2406 (2007).

228 *Brendlin v. California*, 551 U.S. 249, 257, 127 S. Ct. 2400 (2007).

229 *Whren v. United States*, 517 U.S. 806, 809-10, 116 S. Ct. 1769 (1996).

230 *See e.g., Ornelas v. United States*, 517 U.S. 690, 116 S. Ct. 1657, 1660 (1996) ("An investigatory stop is permissible under the Fourth Amendment if supported by reasonable suspicion[.]"); *Alabama v. White*, 496 U.S. 325, 110 S. Ct. 2412 (1990) (motor vehicle stop on the basis of reasonable suspicion that the driver was in possession of cocaine upheld); *United States v. Cortez*, 449 U.S. 411, 101 S. Ct. 690 (1981) (totality of the circumstances "must yield a particularized suspicion" that the vehicle or its occupant was engaged in wrongdoing); *United States v. Brignoni-Ponce*, 422 U.S. 873, 95 S. Ct. 2574 (1975) (motor vehicle stop upheld where officers were "aware of specific and articulable facts, together with rational inferences from those facts, that reasonably warrant suspicion" that the vehicle contains illegal aliens); *New York v. Class*, 475 U.S. 106, 106 S. Ct. 960 (1986) (upholding stop of defendant for driving above speed limit in a car with a cracked windshield in violation of traffic laws); *Pennsylvania v. Mimms*, 434 U.S. 106, 98 S. Ct. 330 (1977) (upholding motor vehicle stop where police officers observed expired license plate). *See also United States v. Hensley*, 469 U.S. 221, 226, 105 S. Ct. 675, 679 (1985)

reasonable suspicion, courts have recognized that the physical characteristics of a motor vehicle and its use result in a lessened expectation of privacy therein:

> One has a lesser expectation of privacy in a motor vehicle because its function is transportation and it seldom serves as one's residence or as the repository of personal effects. A car has little capacity for escaping public scrutiny. It travels public thoroughfares where both its occupants and its contents are in plain view.[231]

Moreover, motor vehicles are "justifiably the subject of pervasive regulation by the State. Every operator of a motor vehicle must expect that the State, in enforcing its regulations, will intrude to some extent upon that operator's privacy[.]"[232] In this respect, the Supreme Court has observed:

> Automobiles, unlike homes, are subject to pervasive and continuing governmental regulation and controls, including periodic inspection and licensing requirements. As an everyday occurrence, police stop and examine vehicles when license plates or inspection stickers have expired, or if other violations, such as exhaust fumes or excessive noise, are noted, or if headlights or other safety equipment are not in proper working order.[233]

It is clear, therefore, that "[a]lthough stopping a car and detaining its occupants constitute a seizure within the meaning of the Fourth Amendment, the governmental interest in investigating an officer's reasonable suspicion, based on specific and articulable facts, may outweigh the Fourth Amendment interest of the driver and passengers in remaining secure from the intrusion."[234]

Nonetheless, "[a]n individual operating or traveling in an automobile does not lose all reasonable expectation of privacy simply because the automobile and its use are subject to government regulation."[235]

> Automobile travel is a basic, pervasive, and often necessary mode of transportation to and from one's home, workplace, and leisure activities. Many people spend more hours each day traveling in cars than walking on the streets. Undoubtedly, many find a greater sense of security and privacy in traveling in an automobile than they do in exposing themselves by pedestrian or other modes of travel. Were the individual subject to unfettered governmental intrusion every time he entered an automobile, the security guaranteed by the Fourth Amendment would be seriously circumscribed. As *Terry v. Ohio*,[236] recognized, people are not [stripped] of all Fourth Amendment protection when they step from their homes onto the public sidewalks. Nor are they [stripped] of those interests when they step from the sidewalks into their automobiles.[237]

2.3.7.2. A tip of dangerous or erratic driving

In *Navarette v. California*,[238] in Mendocino County, California, a driver called 911 to report that a silver Ford F-150 pickup truck with a specified license plate had just run her off the road, at mile marker 88 on southbound Highway 1. Roughly 18 minutes after the call, a California Highway Patrol officer spotted the same truck at mile marker 69, 19 miles south of the reported incident. The U.S. Supreme Court ruled that, assuming the 911 call was anonymous, the officer nevertheless had reasonable suspicion to stop the truck.

("law enforcement agents may briefly stop a moving automobile to investigate a reasonable suspicion that its occupants are involved in criminal activity").

231 *Cardwell v. Lewis*, 417 U.S. 583, 590, 94 S. Ct. 2464, 2469 (1974).

232 *New York v. Class*, 475 U.S. 106, 113, 106 S. Ct. 960, 965 (1986).

233 *South Dakota v. Opperman*, 428 U.S. 364, 368, 96 S. Ct. 3092, 3096 (1976); *see also Cady v. Dombrowski*, 413 U.S. 433, 441-42, 93 S. Ct. 2523, 2528 (1973); *California v. Carney*, 471 U.S. 386, 392, 105 S. Ct. 2066, 2069-70 (1985).

234 *United States v. Hensley*, 469 U.S. 221, 226, 105 S. Ct. 675, 679 (1985).

235 *Delaware v. Prouse*, 440 U.S. 648, 662, 99 S. Ct. 1391, 1400 (1979).

236 *Terry v. Ohio*, 392 U.S. 1, 88 S. Ct. 1868, 1880 (1968).

237 *Delaware v. Prouse*, 440 U.S. 648, 662-63, 99 S. Ct. 1391, 1400-01 (1979).

238 *Navarette v. California*, 572 U.S. 393, 134 S. Ct. 1683 (2014).

By reporting that she had been run off the road by a specific vehicle, the caller necessarily claimed eyewitness knowledge of the alleged dangerous driving — a driver's claim that another vehicle ran her off the road implies that the informant knows the other car was driven dangerously. That basis of knowledge lent significant support to the tip's reliability. In addition, the officer saw the truck in a location suggesting that the caller must have reported the incident soon after she was run off the road. The Court noted: "That sort of contemporaneous report has long been treated as especially reliable." In addition, 911 calls are recorded, which provides victims with an opportunity to identify the false tipster's voice and subject him to prosecution; a 911 caller's cell phone number can also be easily identified, further discouraging its use in giving false tips. Thus, the caller's use of the 911 system was another factor suggesting reliability. Finally, the Court noted that running another vehicle off the road "suggests lane positioning problems, decreased vigilance, impaired judgment, or some combination of those recognized drunk driving cues." Thus, there was reason to believe the driver of the truck might be intoxicated and therefore committing a crime. Under the totality of these circumstances, an investigatory stop was justified.

Accordingly, "The factual basis for stopping a vehicle need not arise from the officer's personal observation, but may be supplied by information acquired from another person."[239] For example, in *Brother v. State*,[240] defendant's erratic driving was reported by a citizen who called "911" on her cell phone after she witnessed defendant speeding, tailgating, and weaving across several lanes of traffic. The court reasoned, "Here, the citizen gave a detailed description of [defendant's] car and location, as well as his erratic driving. As requested by the '911' dispatcher, the citizen followed behind the suspect with her emergency lights on, which assisted the officer in identifying the proper vehicle. Throughout the incident, the citizen kept in contact with the '911' dispatcher, and she remained at the scene after [defendant's] car was stopped by police.... Relying on the information supplied by the citizen, the officer...was able to locate and identify [defendant's] vehicle. And,...the facts relayed to [the officer] through the '911' dispatcher caused him to believe that [defendant] was driving while intoxicated."[241]

2.3.7.3. Observed violations

Driving in an erratic manner in and of itself justifies a stop. Officers do not violate the Fourth Amendment by stopping and questioning someone who just committed a traffic violation in the officer's presence. Moreover, routine traffic infractions, even minor ones, can provide the requisite reasonable suspicion to stop a vehicle.[242]

For example, stops have been upheld for:

- turning without signaling[243]
- failing to maintain a single lane[244]
- traveling in the left lane when not passing[245]
- traveling below the prima facie limit of 65 miles per hour and impeding traffic[246]
- license plate partially obscured by a license plate frame[247]
- defective license plate light[248]
- swerving within lane[249]

---

239 *Brother v. State*, 166 S.W.3d 255, 257 (Tex. Crim. App. 2005), *cert. denied sub nom. Brother v. Texas*, 546 U.S. 1150, 126 S. Ct. 1172 (2006).

240 *Brother v. State*, 166 S.W.3d 255 (Tex. Crim. App. 2005), *cert. denied sub nom. Brother v. Texas*, 546 U.S. 1150, 126 S. Ct. 1172 (2006).

241 *Brother v. State*, 166 S.W.3d 255, 258 (Tex. Crim. App. 2005), *cert. denied sub nom. Brother v. Texas*, 546 U.S. 1150, 126 S. Ct. 1172 (2006).

242 *United States v. Palomino*, 100 F.3d 446 (6th Cir. 1996); *Haas v. State*, 172 S.W.3d 42 (Tex. App. 2005).

243 *Wehring v. State*, 276 S.W.3d 666 (Tex. App. 2008).

244 *Leming v. State*, 493 S.W.3d 552 (Tex. Crim. App. 2016).

245 *Jaganathan v. State*, 479 S.W.3d 244 (Tex. Crim. App. 2015).

246 *Delafuente v. State*, 414 S.W.3d 173 (Tex. Crim. App. 2013).

247 *State v. Johnson*, 219 S.W.3d 386 (Tex. Crim. App. 2007).

248 *Palacios v. State*, 319 S.W.3d 68 (Tex. App. 2010).

249 *State v. Alderete*, 314 S.W.3d 469 (Tex. App. 2010); *Mitchell v. State*, 187 S.W.3d 113 (Tex. App. 2006).

- traveling without control and unsafely[250]
- changing lanes without signaling[251]
- following too closely[252]
- operating a vehicle without wearing a seatbelt[253]
- failing to stop behind the line at a stop light and failing to use a turn signal at least 100 feet prior to the intersection[254]

2.3.7.3.1 The "owner is the driver" assumption

May a law enforcement officer, consistent with the Fourth Amendment, initiate an investigative traffic stop after running a vehicle's license plate and learning that the registered owner has a revoked driver's license? According to the Court in *Kansas v. Glover,*[255] the answer is ***yes.***

In *Glover,* while on patrol in Douglas County, Kansas, Sheriff's Deputy Mark Mehrer ran a registration check on a Chevy pickup truck. This revealed that the truck was registered to Charles Glover, Jr., and that his license was revoked. The deputy did not observe any traffic violations but initiated a traffic stop based on his assumption that the driver was the registered owner. The driver (Glover) turned out to be the registered owner and the officer issued him a citation.

Finding the stop lawful, the Court held that, so long as there are no facts negating the "inference that the owner is the driver of the vehicle, the stop is reasonable."[256] In this case, before initiating the traffic stop, Deputy Mehrer observed an individual operating a pickup truck with a specific Kansas license plate. He also knew that the registered owner of the truck had a revoked license and that the model of the truck matched the observed vehicle. "From these three facts, Deputy Mehrer drew the commonsense inference that Glover was likely the driver of the vehicle, which provided more than reasonable suspicion to initiate the stop."[257]

"The fact that the registered owner of a vehicle is not always the driver of the vehicle does not negate the reasonableness of Deputy Mehrer's inference." Such is the case with all reasonable inferences, for "[t]o be reasonable is not to be perfect." Glover's revoked license does not render the inference unreasonable either. "Empirical studies demonstrate what common experience readily reveals: Drivers with revoked licenses frequently continue to drive and therefore to pose safety risks to other motorists and pedestrians."[258]

The Court cautioned, however, that the presence of additional facts might dispel reasonable suspicion. "For example, if an officer knows that the registered owner of the vehicle is in his mid-sixties but observes that the driver is in her mid-twenties, then the totality of the circumstances would not raise a suspicion that the particular individual being stopped is engaged in wrongdoing."[259]

2.3.7.4. Permissible activities at, and length of, a traffic stop

During a traffic stop, an officer may take certain actions and make various inquiries that are deemed to be within the scope of investigation related to the stop.[260] This assists the officer in addressing the violation and making a determination whether to issue a citation or warning or make an arrest. In this regard, the officer –

---

[250] *Fernandez v. State*, 306 S.W.3d 354 (Tex. App. 2010).
[251] *Coleman v. State*, 188 S.W.3d 708 (Tex. App. 2005).
[252] *Stoker v. State*, 170 S.W.3d 807 (Tex. App. 2005).
[253] *Morrison v. State*, 71 S.W.3d 821 (Tex. App. 2002).
[254] *Lerma v. State*, 543 S.W.3d 184 (Tex. Crim. App. 2018).
[255] *Kansas v. Glover,* 589 U.S.___, 140 S. Ct. 1183 (2020).
[256] *Kansas v. Glover,* 589 U.S.___, 140 S. Ct. 1183, 1186 (2020).
[257] *Kansas v. Glover,* 589 U.S.___, 140 S. Ct. 1183, 1188 (2020).
[258] *Kansas v. Glover,* 589 U.S.___, 140 S. Ct. 1183, 1188 (2020).
[259] *Kansas v. Glover,* 589 U.S.___, 140 S. Ct. 1183, 1191 (2020).
[260] *See, e.g., Pennsylvania v. Mimms*, 434 U.S. 106, 111, 98 S. Ct. 330 (1977) (an officer may, as a matter of course, order the driver to either step out of or remain inside the vehicle); *Maryland v. Wilson*, 519 U.S. 408, 414-15, 117 S. Ct. 882, 886 (1997) (the *Mimms* rule extends to passengers).

- may request the motorist's driver's license, registration and proof of insurance.[261]
- may run a computer check.[262]
- may ask the driver out of the vehicle.[263]
- may ask a passenger out of the vehicle.[264]
- may advise the motorist of the reason for the stop.
- may ask questions reasonably related to the reason for the stop.[265]
- may ask questions about the purpose and itinerary of the motorist's trip, such as his or her point of origin, destination and travel plans.
- may ask reasonable questions in order to obtain additional information about the violation.[266]
- may ask questions regarding the circumstances leading to the violation of the law.
- may ask unrelated questions so long as the questions do not measurably prolong the stop.[267]
- need not give *Miranda* warnings *unless* the driver is placed "in custody."

As the United States Supreme Court instructed in *Arizona v. Johnson,*[268] "[a]n officer's inquiries into matters unrelated to the justification for the traffic stop ... do not convert the encounter into something other than a lawful seizure, so long as those inquiries do not measurably extend the duration of the stop."

In *Rodriguez v. United States,*[269] the Court further instructed that "[b]eyond determining whether to issue a traffic ticket, an officer's mission includes ordinary inquiries incident to [the traffic] stop" Typically, "such inquiries involve checking the driver's license, determining whether there are outstanding warrants against the driver, and inspecting the automobile's registration and proof of insurance[.] These checks serve the same objective as enforcement of the traffic code: ensuring that vehicles on the road are operated safely and responsibly."[270]

Once the traffic stop is completed, however, officers may not continue to detain a car for the purpose of asking unrelated questions without a reasonable suspicion of criminal behavior. Generally, the permissible duration of a traffic stop depends on the reason the police officer pulls the car over. The duration and execution of a traffic stop is necessarily limited by the initial purpose of the stop. This rule grows out of the United States Supreme Court's explanation of a broader Fourth Amendment principle: "An investigatory detention must be temporary and last no longer than is necessary to effectuate the purpose of the stop."[271] In this regard, any investigation of the vehicle or its occupants beyond that required to complete the purpose of the traffic stop constitutes a separate seizure that must be supported by independent facts sufficient to justify the additional intrusion.

As stated in *Rodriguez v. United States,*[272] "a police stop exceeding the time needed to handle the matter for which the stop was made violates the Constitution's shield against unreasonable seizures. A seizure justified only by a police-observed traffic violation, therefore, 'become[s] unlawful if it is prolonged beyond the time reasonably required to complete th[e] mission' of issuing a ticket for the violation."[273] In *Rodriguez,*[274] the U.S.

---

261 *Lerma v. State*, 543 S.W.3d 184 (Tex. Crim. App. 2018).
262 *Lerma v. State*, 543 S.W.3d 184 (Tex. Crim. App. 2018).
263 *Lerma v. State*, 543 S.W.3d 184 (Tex. Crim. App. 2018).
264 *Lerma v. State*, 543 S.W.3d 184 (Tex. Crim. App. 2018).
265 *Lerma v. State*, 543 S.W.3d 184 (Tex. Crim. App. 2018).
266 *Lerma v. State*, 543 S.W.3d 184 (Tex. Crim. App. 2018).
267 *Lerma v. State*, 543 S.W.3d 184 (Tex. Crim. App. 2018).
268 *Arizona v. Johnson*, 555 U.S. 323, 333, 129 S. Ct. 781, 788 (2009).
269 *Rodriguez v. United States,* 575 U.S. 348, 135 S. Ct. 1609, 1615 (2015).
270 *See also Arizona v. Johnson*, 555 U.S. 323, 333, 129 S. Ct. 781, 788 (2009) ("An officer's inquiries into matters unrelated to the justification for the traffic stop ... do not convert the encounter into something other than a lawful seizure, so long as those inquiries do not measurably extend the duration of the stop.").
271 *Florida v. Royer,* 460 U.S. 491, 500, 103 S. Ct. 1319, 1325 (1983).
272 *Rodriguez v. United States,* 575 U.S. 348, 135 S. Ct. 1609 (2015).
273 *Rodriguez v. United States,* 575 U.S. 348, 350, 135 S. Ct. 1609, 1612 (2015) (quoting *Illinois v. Caballes,* 543 U.S. 405, 407, 125 S. Ct. 834, 837 (2005)).
274 *Rodriguez v. United States,* 575 U.S. 348, 135 S. Ct. 1609 (2015).

Supreme Court held that the Fourth Amendment does not permit a dog sniff conducted after completion of a traffic stop.[275]

In *Illinois v. Caballes,*[276] the investigative activity at issue did not impact the duration of the stop *at all*, as the police dog sniff was conducted by the K-9 officer *at the same time* the traffic officer was writing out a warning for the violation. The U.S. Supreme Court cautioned, however, that a "motor vehicle stop that is justified solely by the interest in issuing a warning or a ticket to the driver can become an unlawful seizure if it is prolonged beyond the time reasonably required to complete that mission."[277] Thus, the use of a drug-detection dog during an "unreasonably prolonged traffic stop" may "lead to the suppression of evidence if the dog sniff is conducted while the motorist is being unlawfully detained."[278]

Once an officer has determined that the driver has a valid license and the citation or ticket has been issued, the driver must be allowed to proceed on his or her way, without being subjected to further delay by police for additional questioning, unless the driver consents to such questioning or the officer discovers evidence establishing a reasonable suspicion of criminal activity unrelated to the initial traffic violation.

In *St. George v. State*,[279] two deputies stopped a vehicle for having an inoperative license plate light. After receiving the driver's license, one of the deputies asked the passenger for his identification. The passenger identified himself as John Michael St. George and told the deputy he did not have his driver's license with him. Both deputies returned to the patrol unit to run the information they received. The license and warrant checks for the driver came back clear, but there was no record matching the name the passenger provided. The officers issued the driver a warning citation approximately nine minutes into the stop and indicated to the driver that the traffic stop was complete, by giving the driver a warning. Thereafter, the other officer began to question the passenger. During that questioning, the deputy learned that the passenger's real name was Jeffrey Michael St. George. After a further ten minutes of questioning upon completion of the traffic stop, the deputies arrested St. George on warrants they identified when they ran his proper name. The officers found marijuana on St. George during a search incident to arrest.

The Texas Court of Criminal Appeals found that the deputies unlawfully prolonged the detention because they lacked reasonable suspicion to continue questioning St. George once the initial reason for the traffic stop ended. Said the court, "At the time the driver was issued the warning citation, the deputies did not have specific articulable facts to believe that Appellant was involved in criminal activity, thus, the questioning of [defendant] regarding his identity and checks for warrants, without separate reasonable suspicion, went beyond the scope of the stop and unreasonably prolonged its duration."[280] The court further explained, "We do not intend to create a bright line rule that would automatically make an investigative detention unreasonable the moment that the initial reason for the traffic stop ends. Because the officers failed to show reasonable suspicion in this case, it was unreasonable for them to continue detaining [defendant] long after the warning citation was issued."[281]

The court came to the opposite conclusion in *Lerma v. State*.[282] There, Officer Salinas stopped a vehicle for failing to stop behind the line at a stop light and failing to use a turn signal at least 100 feet prior to the intersection. Lerma was a passenger in the car. After asking the driver for identification and insurance, Salinas asked Lerma for identification. Lerma indicated that he did not have any identification on him. Salinas observed Lerma fidgeting in his seat and determined that Lerma appeared nervous. Salinas asked Lerma to exit the vehicle and again inquired as to his name. Lerma said his name was "Bobby Diaz." According to the court, "Salinas then went back to his patrol unit and ran the personal information [Lerma] had given him. At 11 p.m., five minutes after the initial stop, Salinas determined that [Lerma] did not match the physical

---

[275] As stated in *Rodriguez*, the question is not "whether the dog sniff occurs before or after the officer issues a ticket," but "whether conducting the sniff prolongs – *i.e.*, adds time to – the stop[.]"

[276] *Illinois v. Caballes*, 543 U.S. 405, 125 S. Ct. 834 (2005).

[277] *Illinois v. Caballes*, 543 U.S. 405, 125 S. Ct. 834, 837 (2005).

[278] *Illinois v. Caballes*, 543 U.S. 405, 125 S. Ct. 834, 837 (2005); *see also Arizona v. Johnson*, 555 U.S. 323, 330, 129 S. Ct. 781 (2009) (The seizure remains lawful only so long as [unrelated] inquiries do not measurably extend the duration of the stop.").

[279] *St. George v. State*, 237 S.W.3d 720 (Tex. Crim. App. 2007).

[280] *St. George v. State*, 237 S.W.3d 720, 726 (Tex. Crim. App. 2007).

[281] *St. George v. State*, 237 S.W.3d 720, 727 (Tex. Crim. App. 2007).

[282] *Lerma v. State*, 543 S.W.3d 184 (Tex. Crim. App. 2018).

description of the 'Bobby Diaz,' with a birth date of September 22, 1984, that he had obtained from his computer. Salinas then returned to [Lerma] and asked where he was from and when he had last 'smoked weed.' [Lerma] replied that it was 'a while ago.' Salinas told [Lerma] that he could smell marijuana on him. [Lerma] then admitted that he had smoked synthetic marijuana that day and that he had some on him. At 11:04 p.m., Salinas searched [Lerma's] pockets and found synthetic marijuana, at which point [Lerma] took off running. The officers chased [Lerma] and caught him about 15 seconds later."[283] Lerma was arrested and a search incident to arrest uncovered a bag of synthetic marijuana and 17 crack cocaine rocks.

The Texas Court of Criminal Appeals distinguished the *Rodriquez* facts and reasoned, "Unlike the officer in *Rodriguez*, Salinas was still actively involved in the traffic stop when he questioned [Lerma] and he had not yet completed all aspects of the traffic stop at the point that [Lerma] fled. Most obviously, Salinas had not yet conducted a computer warrant check on the driver of the vehicle."[284] The court also distinguished the *St. George* facts:

> One clear difference between *St. George* and the case at hand is the presence of a second officer in *St. George*. In *St. George*, both deputies were involved in issuing the traffic citation and it wasn't until after the citation was given that they turned their attention to St. George. In this case, Salinas was the sole officer at the scene. He was required to conduct all aspects of the traffic stop by himself until his backup arrived. Given that he was alone, it was reasonable for Salinas to briefly question and attempt to identify the occupants of the car before running the driver's information through his computer system in his patrol car. As we have noted, an officer does not have to follow a particular order of events when conducting a stop. Almost immediately after another officer arrived, Salinas did in fact return to his patrol car to run the information through his system.
>
> Another key difference between *St. George* and the case at bar is the timing in which the events occurred. In *St. George*, the deputy did not begin questioning St. George until after he had completed a computer check on the driver and issued a citation, nine minutes into the traffic stop. Further, the deputies questioned St. George for an additional ten minutes before they obtained enough information to arrest him. Here, Salinas was still actively engaged in the purposes of the traffic stop when he asked [Lerma] to exit the vehicle and briefly questioned him.[285]

Accordingly, the court found that the detention did not unduly prolong the traffic stop.[286]

In *Haas v. State*,[287] Officer Frye had reasonable suspicion to prolong Haas's detention so that Frye could conduct a canine sniff on Haas's car. There, "Frye articulated three basic grounds for his decision to detain Haas so that his dog could sniff the car: (1) Haas volunteered a lot of information; (2) Frye thought the story was implausible and inconsistent and became more implausible and inconsistent as Frye questioned Haas; and (3) Haas was increasingly nervous and avoided eye contact."[288] Noting that "[i]ncreasing or extreme nervousness and conflicting or implausible information can, along with other factors, raise a reasonable suspicion,"[289] the court upheld the detention.

When the reason for the stop evaporates upon approach of the motorist. In *United States v. McSwain*,[290] a police officer saw a vehicle with no front or rear license plate, but a temporary registration sticker in the rear window. The officer was unable to read the sticker, so he stopped the vehicle to verify the validity of the sticker. As he approached the vehicle, the officer observed that the sticker was valid, but he spoke to the driver and requested identification from the driver and a passenger. The driver did not have a license, but he provided other identification. The officer conducted a computer search and learned that the driver had a suspended license and a prior record of drug and gun violations. The officer returned to the vehicle, questioned the driver about his travel plans, and asked for consent to search. The subsequent search of the vehicle's

---

283 *Lerma v. State*, 543 S.W.3d 184, 188 (Tex. Crim. App. 2018).
284 *Lerma v. State*, 543 S.W.3d 184, 194 (Tex. Crim. App. 2018).
285 *Lerma v. State*, 543 S.W.3d 184, 196-97 (Tex. Crim. App. 2018).
286 *See also Kothe v. State*, 152 S.W.3d 54 (Tex. Crim. App. 2004).
287 *Haas v. State*, 172 S.W.3d 42 (Tex. App. 2005).
288 *Haas v. State*, 172 S.W.3d 42, 54 (Tex. App. 2005).
289 *Haas v. State*, 172 S.W.3d 42, 54 (Tex. App. 2005).
290 *United States v. McSwain*, 29 F.3d 558 (10th Cir. 1994).

trunk revealed drugs and a gun. On appeal from defendant's unsuccessful motion to suppress, the court of appeals reversed, holding that the initially valid stop evolved into an unreasonable detention because once the officer saw that the sticker was valid, the purpose of the stop was satisfied and further detention to question the driver about his itinerary and to request his license and registration "exceeded the scope of the stop's underlying justification."[291] Because the officer's reasonable suspicion regarding the validity of the sticker was "completely dispelled *prior* to the time" he questioned the driver and requested his license, he lacked reasonable suspicion to prolong the detention.[292]

The reasoning of *McSwain* was initially adopted by the Illinois Supreme Court in *People v. Cummings*,[293] In *Cummings*, an officer checked a vehicle's registration and saw that its owner, a woman, had an outstanding warrant for her arrest. When he pulled the van over, he saw that the driver was a man. He still asked for license and insurance as "standard operating procedure" after pulling over a car, which led to a citation of the driver for driving with a suspended driver's license. In the first round of proceedings, the state Supreme Court determined that while the officer initially had a reasonable suspicion that the driver was subject to seizure, that suspicion disappeared when he saw that the driver was a man. The court stated that requesting the defendant's license impermissibly prolonged the stop because it was not related to the reason for the stop, and it violated the fourth amendment.[294]

On further appeal, the United States Supreme Court vacated the *Cummings* decision, remanding the case to the Illinois Supreme Court to reconsider its opinion in light of *Rodriguez v. United States*.[295]

Upon remand, the Court, in *People v. Cummings*,[296] determined that the "sole question" was whether, in light of *Rodriguez*, the officer's request for a driver's license after concluding defendant was not the woman wanted on the warrant, "impermissibly prolonged the stop, violating the fourth amendment."[297] The Court ruled:

> A traffic stop is analogous to a *Terry* stop, and its permissible duration is determined by the seizure's mission. The seizure's mission consists of the purpose of the stop – in *Rodriguez*, traffic enforcement – and "related safety concerns." Those related safety concerns include "ordinary inquiries incident to [the traffic] stop," and typically "involve checking the driver's license, determining whether there are outstanding warrants against the driver, and inspecting the automobile's registration and proof of insurance." Those checks serve also to enforce the traffic code.
>
> Ordinary inquiries incident to the stop do not prolong the stop beyond its original mission, because those inquiries are a part of that mission.... Nothing in *Rodriguez* suggests that license requests might be withdrawn from the list of ordinary inquiries for a nontraffic enforcement stop....
>
> Thus, where a traffic stop is lawfully initiated, the interest in officer safety entitles the officer to know the identity of a driver with whom he is interacting. If the permissible inquiries include warrant and criminal history checks, as the *Rodriguez* Court found, they necessarily include less invasive driver's license requests.[298]

Accordingly, the Court held that "Officer Bland's stop of defendant was lawfully initiated. Though his reasonable suspicion the driver was subject to arrest vanished upon seeing defendant, Bland could still make the ordinary inquiries incident to a stop. The interest in officer safety permits a driver's license request of a driver lawfully stopped. Such ordinary inquiries are part of the stop's mission and do not prolong the stop, for fourth amendment purposes."[299] This ruling, determined the Court, is consistent with the decision in

291 *United States v. McSwain*, 29 F.3d 558, 561 (10th Cir. 1994).
292 *United States v. McSwain*, 29 F.3d 558, 561-62 (10th Cir. 1994) (emphasis in original).
293 *People v. Cummings*, 2014 IL 115769, 6 N.E.3d 725 (2014).
294 *People v. Cummings*, 2014 IL 115769, 6 N.E.3d 725, 731, 734 (2014).
295 *Rodriguez v. United States*, 575 U.S. 348, 135 S. Ct. 1609 (2015); *see also Illinois v. Cummings*, 135 S. Ct. 1892 (2015).
296 *People v. Cummings*, 2016 IL 115769, 46 N.E.3d 248 (2016).
297 *People v. Cummings*, 2016 IL 115769, 46 N.E.3d 248, 250 (2016).
298 *People v. Cummings*, 2016 IL 115769, 46 N.E.3d 248, 251-252 (2016).
299 *People v. Cummings*, 2016 IL 115769, 46 N.E.3d 248, 252-253 (2016).

Rodriguez v. United States, which "makes clear that a driver's license request of a lawfully stopped driver is permissible irrespective of whether that request directly relates to the purpose for the stop."[300]

2.3.7.4.1. The VIN of a motor vehicle

The vehicle identification number (VIN), located inside the passenger compartment of a vehicle but visible from outside, does not receive Fourth Amendment protection; police may run a computer search on the number without probable cause or even reasonable suspicion.[301] In *New York v. Class,* two New York City police officers observed defendant, Class, driving above the speed limit in an automobile with a cracked windshield. When the officers stopped his vehicle, defendant exited and approached one of the officers. The other officer approached defendant's vehicle to inspect the Vehicle Identification Number (VIN). The officer first checked the left door jamb in which pre-1969 automobiles had the VIN located. When the VIN was not found there, the officer reached into the interior of the vehicle to move some papers obscuring the area of the dashboard where the VIN is located in all post-1969 automobiles. "In doing so, [the officer] saw the handle of a gun protruding about one inch from underneath the driver's seat."[302] The officer immediately seized the gun and arrested defendant.

Finding the officer's actions proper, the U.S. Supreme Court held that, in light of the "pervasive governmental regulation of the automobile and the efforts by the Federal Government to ensure that the VIN is placed in plain view," there is "no reasonable expectation of privacy in the VIN," and the viewing of the formerly obscured VIN was "not a violation of the Fourth Amendment."[303] According to the Court, "it is unreasonable to have an expectation of privacy in an object required by law to be located in a place ordinarily in plain view from the exterior of the automobile."[304] Analogous to the exterior of the automobile, the VIN "is thrust into the public eye, and thus to examine it [from the outside of the auto] does not constitute a search [within the meaning of the Fourth Amendment]."[305]

Here, it made no difference that the papers in the defendant's automobile obscured the VIN from the sight of the officer. Persons may not create a reasonable expectation of privacy where none would otherwise exist.

Similarly, reasonable suspicion is not required to run a computer check on a randomly selected license plate.

2.3.7.5. Roadblocks and checkpoints

In *Brower v. County of Inyo,*[306] the United States Supreme Court held that a Fourth Amendment "seizure" occurs when, during a motor vehicle pursuit of a fleeing suspect, police officials (1) place an unilluminated 18-wheel tractor-trailer across both lanes of a two-lane highway, (2) "effectively conceal" the truck behind a curve in the road in order to (3) block the path of the fleeing suspect, while at the same time, (4) positioning a police car with its headlights on, between the suspect's oncoming vehicle and the truck, so that the suspect would be "blinded" on his approach, and (5) this official conduct results in the suspect's death when he crashes into the police roadblock. According to the Court, a "seizure" occurs "when there is a governmental termination" of an individual's "freedom of movement *through means intentionally applied.*"[307] "[A] roadblock is not just a significant show of authority to induce a voluntary stop, but is designed to produce a stop by physical impact if voluntary compliance does not occur."[308]

---

300 *People v. Cummings,* 2016 *IL* 115769, 46 N.E.3d 248, 253 (2016). *See also United States v. Holt,* 264 F.3d 1215, 1221-22 (10th Cir. 2001), *abrogated on other grounds by United States v. Stewart,* 473 F.3d 1265, 1269 (10th Cir. 2007), cited with approval in *Rodriguez* and *Cummings,* which approved criminal record and warrant checks, "even though the purpose of the stop had nothing to do with such prior criminal history."

301 *See New York v. Class,* 475 U.S. 106, 106 S. Ct. 960, 966 (1986).

302 *New York v. Class,* 475 U.S. 106, 106 S. Ct. 960, 963 (1986).

303 *New York v. Class,* 475 U.S. 106, 106 S. Ct. 960, 966 (1986).

304 *New York v. Class,* 475 U.S. 106, 106 S. Ct. 960, 966 (1986).

305 *New York v. Class,* 475 U.S. 106, 106 S. Ct. 960, 966 (1986).

306 *Brower v. County of Inyo,* 489 U.S. 593, 109 S. Ct. 1378 (1989).

307 *Brower v. County of Inyo,* 489 U.S. 593, 109 S. Ct. 1378, 1381 (1989) (emphasis in original).

308 *Brower v. County of Inyo,* 489 U.S. 593, 109 S. Ct. 1378, 1382-83 (1989).

In *Michigan Dept. of State Police v. Sitz,*[309] the Supreme Court held that, when properly conducted, a state's use of highway sobriety checkpoints does not violate the Constitution. According to the Court, "the balance of the State's interest in preventing drunken driving, the extent to which [this state's] system can reasonably be said to advance that interest, and the degree of intrusion upon individual motorists who are briefly stopped, weighs in favor of [this state's] highway sobriety checkpoint] program."[310]

In *Sitz,* Michigan implemented a program where checkpoints would be set up at predetermined sites along state roads. All drivers passing through would be stopped and checked for obvious signs of intoxication. If such indications were detected, the motorist would be taken out of the flow of traffic and an officer would check his or her license and registration. If warranted, the officer would conduct field sobriety tests. All other motorists would continue unimpeded after the initial screening. The check lasted 75 minutes, during which 126 vehicles passed through. The average delay was 25 seconds. Three motorists were detained on suspicion of intoxication, and two were arrested. Finding that the checkpoint passed constitutional muster, the Court noted:

(i) The State had a substantial interest in eliminating drunken driving, noting that "no one can seriously dispute the magnitude of the drunken driving problem [or the] State's interest in eradicating it."

(ii) This checkpoint advanced the State's interest in curbing the drunk driving problem, noting that the use of a permissible checkpoint is but one of many reasonable alternatives to remedying the problem, and "the choice among such reasonable alternatives remains with the governmental officials who have a unique understanding" of the problem and the resources available to combat it.

(iii) The intrusion, both objective and subjective, was slight, pointing out the brevity (25 seconds) of the average encounter. The Court also noted that any subjective intrusion, such as making a motorist fearful or annoyed, was diminished by the fact that motorists could plainly see all vehicles were being stopped.

In upholding the lawfulness of sobriety checkpoints, courts around the nation have identified several critical features that Driving While Intoxicated (DWI) Sobriety Checkpoints should have. These include:

GUIDELINES GOVERNING ROADSIDE CHECKPOINTS

DWI Roadblocks; Safety Checkpoints; Etc.

1. There must be a *legitimate State interest* – for the checkpoint, for example drunk driving, safety checkpoints, etc.

2. When establishing the checkpoint, there must be participation of command or high-ranking supervisory authority in the formulation of an administrative plan for the checkpoint consisting of a uniform set of written, standardized guidelines setting forth proper procedures to reduce officer discretion, and for checkpoint officers to follow when approaching vehicles, observing motorists, requesting drivers' licenses, checking for other violations, and sidetracking those drivers found to have violations. (Ideally, roadblock decisions should be made by the chief of police or other high-ranking supervisor officials).

a. The Guidelines should set forth explicit, neutral and predetermined limitations on the conduct of officers participating in the checkpoint. Discretion should be minimized by directing checkpoint officers to stop cars at predetermined intervals, *e.g.*, every vehicle, or every 3rd, 4th, or 10th, and vehicles having observable violations.

b. *Site selection.* The Guidelines must include the selection of the time, place and duration of the checkpoint, which should be based on identifiable statistical data showing the need for the

---

309 *Michigan Dept. of State Police v. Sitz*, 496 U.S. 444, 110 S. Ct. 2481 (1990).

310 Not all states permit DUI checkpoints. The following 12 states have held that DUI checkpoints are unlawful: Alaska, Idaho, Iowa, Michigan, Minnesota, Montana, Oregon, Rhode Island, Texas, Washington, Wisconsin and Wyoming. Although Missouri law allows checkpoints, the state prohibits the public funding of checkpoint programs.

checkpoint at the respective time and place. Consideration should be given to (1) areas known for high incidents of accidents, drunk driving or other traffic violations, (2) traffic volume, and (3) motorist and pedestrian safety. For example, a checkpoint established during the late evening hours on a weekend may be reasonable to detect drunk drivers, while continuing the roadblock through Monday morning during rush hour might not be reasonable.

c. The Guidelines must set forth the required number of checkpoint officers that will be needed to ensure that delays are held to a minimum. If an executive-level officer did not participate in the plan's formulation, it should not be implemented until that officer has reviewed and approved it.

3. The safety of the motoring public and the field officer must be given proper attention. To avoid frightening the travelling public, adequate on-the-scene warnings must be given (*for example, a large, obvious sign indicating that the motorist is about to be stopped, the nature of the checkpoint, and that all motorists must pass through; flashing lights; marked police vehicles; flares; and other reflectorized equipment*). In addition, advance general publicity of the checkpoint may be provided to deter drunk drivers from getting in cars in the first place.

4. The checkpoints must be sufficiently staffed by uniformed officers to ensure safety and prevent undue inconvenience to motorists and unreasonable interference with normal traffic flow. A predetermined, safe and convenient "pull over" or parking area should be established and used for vehicles or motorists having violations.

5. Officers participating in the checkpoint should be provided with specified, neutral and courteous procedures to follow when stopping motorists; and the officers chosen for the process should have sufficient experience to quickly identify intoxicated motorists (motorists should be detained only briefly); and carefully planned and predetermined procedures must be in place for operations that will involve the moving of a checkpoint from one location to another.

6. Upon completion of the checkpoint operation, the participating officers should submit, through the appropriate chain of command, full reports in writing of the conduct and results of the checkpoint to the administrative officer(s) who initiated or planned the operation.

7. Advance publicity of the intention of the police to establish DUI roadblocks, without designating specific locations at which they will be conducted, also serves to minimize any apprehension motorists may otherwise experience upon encountering one (although the lack of advance publicity is not sufficient to invalidate a roadblock).

Roadside checkpoints may not be performed where the program's primary purpose is to "detect evidence of ordinary criminal wrongdoing."[311] In order to conduct a motor vehicle stop for the purpose of discovering or interdicting illegal drugs, police officers must first possess a reasonable articulable suspicion that the motorist or other vehicle occupant is engaged in unlawful activity.

Also, under the Fourth Amendment, brief "information-seeking" highway checkpoints are not unconstitutional *per se*. In *Illinois v. Lidster*,[312] the police checkpoint involved a brief stop of motorists to ask for information about a recent hit-and-run accident that resulted in a death. The stop's objective was to ask for public assistance in finding the perpetrator of this "specific and known crime." The checkpoint was "appropriately tailored" to this goal; its interference with the liberty of motorists was minimal; and all vehicles were stopped in a systematic and non-discriminatory manner. As such, it was constitutional.

An attempt to avoid a checkpoint. Evading a marked DWI checkpoint is a specific and articulable fact that is sufficient to predicate reasonable suspicion for an investigatory stop. However, an officer's conclusion that a driver is attempting to avoid a checkpoint may be unreasonable in light of the circumstances of the stop — the time of day, the proximity of the turn to the checkpoint, or whether the driver's actions were typical considering the layout of the area and the normal flow of traffic.

In Texas, because no governing body has ever authorized a statewide procedure for DWI roadblocks, they are not permitted.[313] In *Holt v. State*,[314] the court also suggested that such roadblocks may be barred under the

---

[311] *City of Indianapolis v. Edmond,* 531 U.S. 32, 121 S. Ct. 447, 454 (2000).

[312] *Illinois v. Lidster*, 540 U.S. 419, 124 S. Ct. 885 (2004).

[313] *Holt v. State*, 887 S.W.2d 16 (Tex. Crim. App.1994).

[314] *Holt v. State*, 887 S.W.2d 16 (Tex. Crim. App.1994).

Texas Constitution, but did not rule specifically on that issue. However, in *Schenekl v. State*,[315] the court upheld a statute which permits routine water safety checks of boaters. Noting that a checkpoint of boaters is impractical as there are no established avenues of transport on the water, and that "[b]oating is not basic, pervasive, or generally necessary, as is motor vehicle transportation," the court found that "the State has a high interest in promoting recreational water safety. That interest can be realistically promoted only through the means the Legislature has provided here – random water safety checks."[316]

2.3.7.6. Removing drivers or passengers from the motor vehicle

During a lawful traffic stop, the police may, as a matter of course, order the driver out of the vehicle pending completion of the stop. This was made clear in *Pennsylvania v. Mimms*,[317] where the United States Supreme Court observed: "Rather than conversing while standing exposed to moving traffic, the officer may prefer to ask the driver of the vehicle to step out of the car and off onto the shoulder of the road where the inquiry may be pursued with greater safety to both."[318]

In *Maryland v. Wilson*,[319] the Court further held that rule of *Pennsylvania v. Mimms* – that a police officer may, as a matter of course, order the driver of a lawfully stopped car to exit his vehicle – extends to passengers.

2.3.7.7. A "Terry frisk" of the vehicle's passenger compartment

The United States Supreme Court has noted that "roadside encounters between police and suspects are especially hazardous, and danger may arise from the possible presence of weapons in the area surrounding a suspect."[320] Thus, "the search of the passenger compartment of an automobile, limited to those areas in which a weapon may be placed or hidden, is permissible if the police officer possesses a reasonable belief based on 'specific and articulable facts which, taken together with the rational inferences from those facts, reasonably warrant' the officer in believing that the suspect is dangerous and the suspect may gain immediate control of weapons."[321] The search must be limited in scope to the area that the suspect can reach easily, sometimes called the "zone within the wingspan" or "grabbable area." Officers must also limit the scope of the search solely to weapons, not evidence. A search can be valid even if the suspect has already been removed from the vehicle.

The Texas Court of Criminal Appeals has recognized the safety issue addressed in *Long*, and has approved the *Long* "frisk," or protective inspection of a car's passenger compartment for weapons. Adopting the rationale of *Long*, the court, in *Goodwin v State*,[322] reiterated:

> Our past cases indicate [] that protection of police and others can justify protective searches when police have a reasonable belief that the suspect poses a danger, that roadside encounters between police and suspects are especially hazardous, and that danger may arise from the possible presence of weapons in the area surrounding a suspect. These principles compel our conclusion that the search of the passenger compartment of an automobile, limited to those areas in which a weapon may be placed or hidden, is permissible if the police officer possesses a reasonable belief based on "specific and articulable facts which, taken together with the rational inferences from those facts, reasonably

---

315 *Schenekl v. State*, 30 S.W.3d 412 (Tex. Crim. App. 2000).
316 *Schenekl v. State*, 30 S.W.3d 412, 416 (Tex. Crim. App. 2000).
317 *Pennsylvania v. Mimms*, 434 U.S. 106, 111, 98 S. Ct. 330 (1977) (an officer may, as a matter of course, order the driver to either step out of or remain inside the vehicle).
318 *Pennsylvania v. Mimms*, 434 U.S. 106, 111, 98 S. Ct. 330, 333 (1977).
319 *Maryland v. Wilson*, 519 U.S. 408, 414-415, 117 S. Ct. 882, 886 (1997).
320 *Michigan v. Long*, 463 U.S. 1032, 1049, 103 S. Ct. 3469, 3481 (1983).
321 *Michigan v. Long*, 463 U.S. 1032, 1049, 103 S. Ct. 3469, 3481 (1983).
322 *Goodwin v. State*, 799 S.W.2d 719 (Tex. Crim. App. 1990).

warrant" the officer in believing that the suspect is dangerous and the suspect may gain immediate control of weapons.[323]

Naturally, an officer may pat-down a driver or passenger during a traffic stop if there is a reasonable suspicion that they may be armed and dangerous.[324]

2.3.7.8. Pretextual stops

A "pretextual stop" may be defined as a traffic stop that occurs when an officer has probable cause or reasonable suspicion to believe that a motorist has violated a traffic law, but which the officer would not have made absent a desire, not supported by probable cause or reasonable suspicion, to investigate some other more serious offense.[325] For example, such a stop can arise when an officer observes a vehicle driving 26 miles per hour in a 25-m.p.h. zone, has some subjective reason to suspect that the vehicle is involved in the drug trade, and uses this minor violation of the traffic laws to investigate his hunch further.

Under the Fourth Amendment and federal case law, a stop is justified following any traffic violation, no matter how minor, even if the officer's true purpose is to investigate criminal activity completely unrelated to driving. Thus, in *Whren v. United States*,[326] the United States Supreme Court determined that when a motor vehicle stop is supported by probable cause or reasonable suspicion that the motorist committed a traffic violation, the stop is not invalid simply because the officer's underlying motivation was to investigate criminal activity unrelated to the traffic violation. Said the Court: "Ulterior motives do not invalidate police conduct that is justified on the basis of probable cause to believe a violation of the law has occurred."[327] The Court in *Whren* did pause to note that a motor vehicle stop motivated by an intent to single out members of a suspect class, such as race, would be obviously impermissible.

Thus, if there is an objectively valid reason for the stop, even one involving a minor traffic infraction, subjective intentions are irrelevant.[328]

Note also that an arrest is valid even if the criminal offense for which probable cause actually exists is not "closely related to the offense stated by the arresting officer at the time of arrest."[329] In other words, the officer's "subjective reason for making the arrest need not be the criminal offense as to which the known facts provide probable cause."[330] As the Supreme Court has consistently held:

> The fact that the officer does not have the state of mind which is hypothecated by the reasons which provide the legal justification for the officer's action does not invalidate the action taken as long as the circumstances, viewed objectively, justify that action.[331]

---

323 *Goodwin v. State*, 799 S.W.2d 719, 727-28 (Tex. Crim. App. 1990) (quoting *Terry v. Ohio*, 392 U.S. 1, 21, 88 S. Ct. 1868, 1880 (1968)).

324 *Arizona v. Johnson*, 555 U.S. 323, 129 S. Ct. 781, 784 (2009).

325 *See, e.g., Whren v. United States*, 517 U.S. 806, 116 S. Ct. 1769 (1996); *Scott v. United States*, 436 U.S. 128, 138, 98 S. Ct. 1717 (1978).

326 *Whren v. United States*, 517 U.S. 806, 116 S. Ct. 1769 (1996).

327 *See also Arkansas v. Sullivan*, 532 U.S. 769, 121 S. Ct. 1876 (2001) (rejecting defendant's argument that his arrest was merely a "pretext and sham to search" him and, therefore, violated the Fourth Amendment.)

328 *See, e.g., United States v. Hill*, 195 F.3d 258 (6th Cir. 1999) (the stop of defendant's rented U-Haul truck valid after the officer paced defendant's speed at 62 m.p.h. in a 55 m.p.h. zone, even though he initially began following defendant because, in his experience, rental trucks are often used to carry contraband); *Garcia v. State*, 827 S.W.2d 937, 943 (Tex. Crim. App. 1992) (adopting solely "objective" approach); *Crittenden v. State*, 899 S.W.2d 668, 673 (Tex. Crim. App. 1995) (adopting purely "objective" approach).

329 *Devenpeck v. Alford*, 543 U.S. 146, 153, 125 S. Ct. 588, 594 (2004).

330 *Devenpeck v. Alford*, 543 U.S. 146, 153, 125 S. Ct. 588, 594 (2004).

331 *Whren v. United States*, 517 U.S. 806, 813, 116 S. Ct. 1769 (quoting *Scott v. United States*, 436 U.S. 128, 138, 98 S. Ct. 1717 (1978)). In this regard, "evenhanded law enforcement is best achieved by the application of objective standards of conduct, rather than standards that depend upon the subjective state of mind of the officer." *Horton v. California*, 496 U.S. 128, 138, 110 S. Ct. 2301 (1990).

2.3.8. Investigative detentions of property

Persons and vehicles are not the only potential subjects of a temporary investigative detention. Officers may temporarily seize and detain items of personal property when they possess a reasonable suspicion that the property is connected with criminal activity. The detention must last no longer than reasonably necessary for the purpose of determining if the item is in fact linked to a criminal endeavor. If a brief investigation reveals that it is not, then the property should be returned to the owner. The Fourth Amendment protects property as well as privacy.[332] Therefore, similar to the seizure of an individual, "seizures of property are subject to Fourth Amendment scrutiny."[333] This is true even when no search within the meaning of the Amendment has taken place.

For example, in *Soldal*, deputy sheriffs assisted the owners of a mobile home park in evicting the Soldal family. As the deputies stood and watched, the park owners wrenched the sewer and water connections off the side of the Soldal trailer, disconnected the telephone, tore the trailer's canopy and skirting, pulled it free from its moorings and towed it away. Finding the Fourth Amendment clearly applicable, the United States Supreme Court held:

> As a result of the state action in this case, the Soldals' domicile was not only seized, it literally was carried away, giving a new meaning to the term "mobile home." We fail to see how being unceremoniously dispossessed of one's home in the manner alleged to have occurred here can be viewed as anything but a seizure invoking the protection of the Fourth Amendment.... The Amendment protects the people from unreasonable searches and seizures of "their persons, houses, papers, and effects."... [A]nd our cases unmistakably hold that the Amendment protects property as well as privacy.... We thus are unconvinced that... the Fourth Amendment protects against unreasonable seizures of property only where privacy or liberty is also implicated.[334]

Property is detained most often when the police wish to detain luggage or a package to search it for drugs. In *United States v. Place*,[335] the U.S. Supreme Court held that the Fourth Amendment permits law enforcement officials to temporarily detain an individual's luggage for exposure to a trained narcotics detection dog on the basis of a reasonable suspicion that the luggage contains narcotics. Thus, "the limitations applicable to investigative detentions of the person should define the permissible scope of an investigative detention of the person's luggage on less than probable cause."[336]

The Court in *Place* went on to hold, however, that the 90-minute detention of defendant's personal luggage for the purpose of arranging its exposure to a narcotics detection dog violated the Fourth Amendment because the investigating officers, although having ample time to do so, failed to diligently pursue a means of investigation which would have greatly minimized the length of the detention. Although the Court would not "adopt any outside limitation for a permissible *Terry* stop," it has never approved a seizure of the person for the prolonged 90-minute period involved in this case.

2.3.8.1. A trained "sniff" by a "canine cannabis connoisseur"[337]

During the course of its opinion in *Place*,[338] the Supreme Court had occasion to address the constitutionality of employing a narcotics-detection dog for the purpose of determining whether a particular item of property contains a controlled substance. Writing for the Court, Justice O'Connor instructed:

> We have affirmed that a person possesses a privacy interest in the contents of personal luggage that is protected by the Fourth Amendment[.] A "canine sniff" by a well-trained narcotics detection dog, however, does not require opening the luggage. It does not expose non-contraband items that otherwise

[332] *Soldal v. Cook Co.*, 506 U.S. 56, 113 S. Ct. 538 (1992).
[333] *Soldal v. Cook Co.*, 506 U.S. 56, 113 S. Ct. 538 (1992).
[334] *Soldal v. Cook Co.*, 506 U.S. 56, 113 S. Ct. 538, 543-45 (1992).
[335] *United States v. Place*, 462 U.S. 696, 103 S. Ct. 2637 (1983).
[336] *United States v. Place*, 462 U.S. 696, 103 S. Ct. 2637, 2645 (1983).
[337] *United States v. Bronstein*, 521 F.2d 459, 460 (2d Cir. 1975).
[338] *United States v. Place*, 462 U.S. 696, 103 S. Ct. 2637 (1983).

would remain hidden from public view, as does, for example, an officer's rummaging through the contents of the luggage. Thus, the manner in which information is obtained through this investigative technique is much less intrusive than a typical search. Moreover, the sniff discloses only the presence or absence of narcotics, a contraband item. Thus, despite the fact that the sniff tells the authorities something about the contents of the luggage, the information obtained is limited. This limited disclosure also ensures that the owner of the property is not subject to the embarrassment and inconvenience entailed in less discriminate and more intrusive investigative methods.

In these respects, the canine sniff is *sui generis* [*i.e.*, unique, in its own class]. We are aware of no other investigative procedure that is so limited both in the manner in which the information is obtained and in the content of the information revealed by the procedure. *Therefore, we conclude that the particular course of investigation that the agents intended to pursue here – exposure of [defendant's] luggage, which was located in a public place, to a trained canine – did not constitute a "search" within the meaning of the Fourth Amendment.*[339]

In *United States v. Jacobsen*,[340] the Court gave *Place* a broad interpretation and concluded that a police investigatory tool is not a "search" if it merely discloses the presence or absence of contraband. According to the *Jacobsen* Court, similar to the *Place* canine sniff, the likelihood that chemical tests (which merely disclose whether or not a certain substance is an illicit drug), "will actually compromise any legitimate interest in privacy seems much too remote to characterize the testing as a search subject to the Fourth Amendment."[341]

Finally, in *Smith v. Ohio*,[342] the Supreme Court emphasized that reasonable suspicion permits a brief detention of property, but not a search of it. "Although the Fourth Amendment may permit the detention for a brief period of property on the basis of only 'reasonable, articulable suspicion' that it contains contraband or evidence of criminal activity," it prohibits – "except in certain well-defined circumstances – the search of that property unless accomplished pursuant to a judicial warrant issued upon probable cause.... That guarantee protects alike the 'traveler who carries a toothbrush and a few articles of clothing in a paper bag' and 'the sophisticated executive with the locked attaché case.'"[343]

3. THE LAW OF ARREST

3.1. General aspects

An "arrest" may be defined as a substantial physical interference with the liberty of a person, resulting in his apprehension and detention. It is generally effected for the purpose of preventing a person from committing a criminal offense, or calling upon a person to answer or account for an alleged completed crime.

An arrest may be effected "actually" or "constructively." An *actual* arrest occurs when a duly empowered law enforcement officer intentionally employs physical force (*e.g.*, a physical touching of the person), and delivers a formal communication of a present intention to arrest (*e.g.*, "You are under arrest!"). A *constructive* arrest occurs without an intentional use of physical force and without a formal statement indicating an intention to take the person into custody. Moreover, in constructive arrest situations, the power or authority of the arresting officer, along with his or her intention to effect the arrest, is implied by all the circumstances surrounding the encounter. In either case, to determine whether an arrest has occurred, a court will examine whether physical force has been applied – which may be accomplished by a mere touching of the suspect – *or*, where that is absent, whether there has been a "*submission* to the assertion of authority."[344]

An arrest signifies the initial step toward a prospective prosecution and, as a governmental intrusion upon the "person," must be effectuated according to the dictates of the Fourth Amendment. Although the

---

339 *United States v. Place*, 462 U.S. 696, 103 S. Ct. 2637, 2644-45 (1983) (emphasis added).

340 *United States v. Jacobsen*, 466 U.S. 109, 104 S. Ct. 1652 (1984).

341 *United States v. Jacobsen*, 466 U.S. 109, 122-24, 104 S. Ct. 1652, 1661-62 (1984).

342 *Smith v. Ohio*, 494 U.S. 541, 110 S. Ct. 1288 (1990).

343 *Smith v. Ohio*, 494 U.S. 541, 110 S. Ct. 1288, 1289 (1990) (quoting *United States v. Ross*, 456 U.S. 798, 822, 102 S. Ct. 2157, 2171 (1982)).

344 *California v. Hodari D.*, 499 U.S. 621, 626, 111 S. Ct. 1547, 1551 (1991) (emphasis in original).

word "arrest" does not appear in the language of the Amendment, courts have consistently equated "arrest" with "seizure." In this respect, the United States Supreme Court has declared that "it is the command of the Fourth Amendment that no warrants either for searches or arrests shall issue *except upon probable cause*[.]"[345]

Accordingly, "the Fourth Amendment speaks equally to both searches and seizures, and ... an arrest, the taking hold of one's person, is quintessentially a seizure."[346]

3.2. The objective standard

To determine whether an arrest has taken place, a court will apply an objective standard, focusing on the reasonable impression conveyed to the person subjected to the apprehension and detention. In this respect, the relative inquiry is whether, in view of all the circumstances surrounding the police-citizen encounter, "a reasonable person would have believed that he was not free to leave" at the conclusion of the officer's inquiry.[347] Thus, a law enforcement officer's subjective view that a suspect was not free to leave – so long as that view has not been conveyed to the person confronted – will not transform an objectively casual, voluntary encounter, or even a temporary investigative detention, into a full-blown arrest. Significantly, the United States Supreme Court, almost without exception, has evaluated alleged violations of the law of arrest (as well as the law of search and seizure) by undertaking "an objective assessment of an officer's actions in light of the facts and circumstances then known to him."[348] So long as the facts and circumstances, viewed objectively, justify an officer's course of action, such action will not be invalidated merely because the officer does not have the state of mind which technically parallels the constitutional rules which provide the legal justification for that course of action.[349]

The objective standard uniformly applied by the courts utilizes a "reasonable person" test to determine whether a particular police-citizen encounter requires a certain level of constitutional justification. The determination proceeds by reference to the "totality of the circumstances," *i.e.*, the whole picture.[350] Although the federal Supreme Court in *Michigan v. Chesternut* recognized that the reasonable person test may be "imprecise," for "what constitutes a restraint on liberty prompting a person to conclude that he is not free to 'leave' will vary, not only with the particular police conduct at issue, but also with the setting in which the conduct occurs[,]" it nonetheless concluded:

> The test's objective standard – looking to the reasonable man's interpretation of the conduct in question – allows police to determine in advance whether the conduct contemplated will implicate the Fourth Amendment.... This "reasonable person" standard also ensures that the scope of the Fourth Amendment protection does not vary with the state of mind of the particular individual being approached.[351]

3.3. Factors to consider

To determine whether a police-citizen encounter has elevated into a Fourth Amendment arrest, courts will consider such factors as –

- whether the encounter was consensual;
- the basis for the encounter (whether the officers had reasonable grounds to believe a criminal offense had occurred and the grounds for that belief);

---

[345] *Henry v. United States*, 361 U.S. 98, 100, 80 S. Ct. 168, 170 (1959) (emphasis added.)

[346] *United States v. Watson*, 423 U.S. 411, 428, 96 S. Ct. 820, 830 (1976); *see also District of Columbia v. Wesby*, 583 U.S. ___, 138 S. Ct. 577, 585 (2018) ("Because arrests are 'seizures' of 'persons,' they must be reasonable."). Excerpts from the comprehensive discussion of the laws of arrest, search and seizure in Larry E. Holtz, *Criminal Procedure for Law and Justice Professionals* (Blue360° Media).

[347] *United States v. Mendenhall*, 446 U.S. 544, 554, 100 S. Ct. 1870, 1877 (1980).

[348] *Scott v. United States*, 436 U.S. 128, 137, 98 S. Ct. 1717, 1723 (1978).

[349] *Scott v. United States*, 436 U.S. 128, 138, 98 S. Ct. 1717, 1723 (1978); *see also Devenpeck v. Alford*, 543 U.S. 146, 125 S. Ct. 588, 593 (2004); *United States v. Robinson*, 414 U.S. 218, 236, 94 S. Ct. 467, 477 (1973).

[350] *Michigan v. Chesternut*, 486 U.S. 567, 108 S. Ct. 1975, 1979 (1989); *INS v. Delgado*, 466 U.S. 210, 215, 104 S. Ct. 1758, 1762 (1984).

[351] *Michigan v. Chesternut*, 486 U.S. 567, 108 S. Ct. 1975, 1979-80 (1989).

- the duration of the encounter;
- the investigative methods used to confirm or dispel suspicions;
- an officer's statement that the individual is the subject of an investigation;
- an officer's statement that the individual is or is not free to leave;
- whether the officer(s) blocked the individual's path or impeded his progress;
- whether weapons were displayed, enforcement canines employed, or the use of force in any other way threatened;
- the number of law enforcement officers present and their demeanor;
- the location of the encounter (public or private);
- the extent to which the officer(s) restrained the individual;
- whether the individual was transported to another location against his will (how far and why);
- whether the individual was free to choose between terminating or continuing the encounter with the officer(s);
- whether the individual was transported to the police station in a patrol car or arranged his own transportation; and
- whether the individual was placed in a closed-off interview room or in an open, common area.[352]

3.4. The probable cause requirement

While the law, both on the state and federal levels, certainly prefers that an arrest be effected pursuant to a warrant, it is well settled that a law enforcement officer may effect a warrantless arrest when he or she has probable cause to believe that a crime has been or is being committed and that the person to be arrested has committed or is committing it.[353] Moreover, when an officer must decide whether a warrantless arrest in a given set of circumstances is justified, he is not limited to consideration only of evidence admissible in a courtroom. Rather, the officer may consider all the facts and circumstances surrounding the prospective arrest, even that information coming from (preferably reliable) hearsay sources, when making the probable cause determination. Thus, "[t]he validity of the arrest does not depend on whether the suspect actually committed a crime[, and] the mere fact that the suspect is later acquitted of the offense for which he is arrested is irrelevant to the validity of the arrest."[354]

The constitutional justification for an arrest, whether on the federal or state level, and whether effected with or without a warrant, is "probable cause."[355] An arrest based on probable cause serves several important interests that serve to justify the seizure. An arrest —

- ensures that the suspect appears in court to answer charges;
- prevents the suspect from continuing his offense;
- safeguards evidence; and
- enables officers to conduct a more thorough in-custody investigation.[356]

"An arrest without probable cause that is investigatory or was designed to cause fright, surprise, and confusion is flagrant police misconduct."[357]

---

[352] *See United States v. Mendenhall*, 446 U.S. 544, 554-55, 100 S. Ct. 1870, 1877-78 (1980); *Florida v. Royer*, 460 U.S. 491, 499-503, 103 S. Ct. 1319, 1324-27 (1983); *United States v. Novak*, 870 F.2d 1345, 1351-52 (7th Cir. 1989); *United States v. Hammock*, 860 F.2d 390, 393 (11th Cir. 1988). Excerpts from the comprehensive discussion of the laws of arrest, search and seizure in Larry E. Holtz & Warren J Spencer, *Texas Criminal and Traffic Procedural Manual – An In-Depth Guide on How to Apply the Laws of Arrest, Search and Seizure, Confessions, & Eyewitness Identification* (Blue360° Media).

[353] Larry E. Holtz & Warren J Spencer, *Texas Criminal and Traffic Procedural Manual – An In-Depth Guide on How to Apply the Laws of Arrest, Search and Seizure, Confessions, & Eyewitness Identification* (Blue360° Media).

[354] *Michigan v. DeFillippo*, 443 U.S. 31, 36, 99 S. Ct. 2627, 2631 (1979).

[355] *See e.g., Michigan v. Summers*, 452 U.S. 692, 700, 101 S. Ct. 2587, 2593 (1981) (It is a "general rule that every arrest, and every seizure having the essential attributes of a formal arrest, is unreasonable unless it is supported by probable cause.").

[356] *See Virginia v. Moore*, 553 U.S. 164, 128 S. Ct. 1598, 1605 (2008) ("[T]he police do not violate the fourth amendment when they make an arrest that is supported by probable cause but is prohibited by state law.").

[357] *Martinez v. State*, 620 S.W.3d 734, 742 (Tex. Crim. App. 2021).

Probable cause is an elusive term which seems to carry varied meanings depending upon who is making the analysis. Virtually all courts and commentators tend to agree that it is generally more than "reasonable suspicion" but less than actual proof. In this respect, the United States Supreme Court has made it "clear that the kinds and degree of proof and the procedural requirements necessary for a conviction are not prerequisites to a valid arrest."[358] The question, of course, then becomes *how much* more than suspicion and *how much* less than proof?

Probable cause does not mean that the arrestee actually committed the suspected crime, or that the officer possesses enough proof to convict the suspect at a trial, or even that the arrestee will go to trial for the alleged offense. It does mean that at the time of the arrest, a prudent, objective person in the position of the officer, taking into account his or her experience, knowledge and observations, would reasonably believe that a crime has been or is being committed. It is interesting to note at this juncture that the police are not required to effect an arrest the moment they believe probable cause has materialized. In this regard, the United States Supreme Court has observed:

> There is no constitutional right to be arrested. The police are not required to guess at their peril the precise moment at which they have probable cause to arrest a suspect, risking a violation of the Fourth Amendment if they act too soon, and a violation of the Sixth Amendment if they wait too long. Law enforcement officers are under no constitutional duty to call a halt to a criminal investigation the moment they have the minimum evidence to establish probable cause, a quantum of evidence which may fall far short of the amount necessary to support a criminal conviction.[359]

Analysis of legal proof standards suggests that probable cause must find its place somewhere above reasonable suspicion but below a preponderant level of proof.[360] It is established by building upon reasonable suspicion those additional facts necessary to indicate an objectively reasonable probability that an offense has been committed and the person in question is, in fact, a criminal participant. The officer builds his probable cause by a *step-by-step ascent* from his reasonable suspicion. Depending upon the nature of the activity and the particular investigation, this ascent may take days, weeks, or months; then again, it might literally occur in seconds.[361]

Naturally, before reaching the threshold, or *landing*, of "reasonable suspicion," there must be some sort of *stimulus* which evokes the attention of the officer. In this respect, an assortment of stimuli may be acquired through the officer's contact with persons, places, vehicles or property, including any information received in such regard. The stimuli then mix with the officer's experience, training and education, and law enforcement intuition to build a reasonable basis for the activity which will follow. The officer now begins his ascent toward the "reasonable suspicion" threshold, or *landing*.

As the officer follows up or investigates each aspect of the "seasoned" stimuli, he either begins to corroborate and strengthen it, or he dispels it from his agenda. If the investigation proves fruitful, the officer now begins to enter the realm of "reasonable suspicion." He then must be able to collect all the steps of the ascent and articulate them in specific and objectively reasonable language. Once this is accomplished, the officer is safely on the *landing* of "reasonable suspicion."

The officer builds his "probable cause" by a *step-by-step ascent* from his reasonable suspicion. Its threshold is reached when the "specific and articulable facts," aided by the rational inferences drawn therefrom, not only support a reasonable basis for suspicion,[362] but magnify that suspicion to such an extent that a reasonable person, objectively viewing all the facts, would be convinced that an offense did, in fact, occur, and the person in question is, in fact, a criminal participant.

---

358 *Michigan v. DeFillippo*, 443 U.S. 31, 36, 99 S. Ct. 2627, 2631 (1979).
359 *Hoffa v. United States*, 385 U.S. 293, 310, 87 S. Ct. 408, 417 (1966).
360 *See e.g., Gerstein v. Pugh*, 420 U.S. 103, 121, 95 S. Ct. 854, 867 (1975) (probable cause "does not require the fine resolution of conflicting evidence that a reasonable-doubt or even a preponderance standard demands").
361 *See also Florida v. Harris*, 568 U.S. 237, 133 S. Ct. 1050, 1055 (2013) (probable cause is the kind of "fair probability" on which "reasonable and prudent" people act).
362 *Terry v. Ohio*, 392 U.S. 1, 88 S. Ct. 1868 (1968).

Significantly, the degree or quantum of belief required before a court may conclude that probable cause exists is virtually the same for purposes of an arrest or a search. A court should not apply two standards when assessing the sufficiency of probable cause, that is, there should not be a dual determination of probable cause – one related to the probability level necessary for a search and seizure, and one related to a different probability level necessary for an arrest. Rather, the focus of the court's attention should always be on the quantum or sufficiency of those objective facts and circumstances surrounding the particular police procedure at the relevant time in order to determine whether the police possessed the requisite *degree* of belief prior to engaging in the challenged procedure.[363]

The application of the same degree or quantum of belief – the probable cause standard – will take on a different analysis when the probabilities must be assessed against the facts and circumstances justifying an arrest as opposed to the facts and circumstances justifying a search and seizure. In this respect, *probable cause to arrest* may be found to exist when the facts and circumstances within the officer's knowledge are sufficient to permit a prudent person, or one of reasonable caution, to conclude that there is a fair probability that a criminal offense is being or has been committed, and the suspect is or has been a criminal participant. *Probable cause to search* may be found to exist when the facts and circumstances within the officer's knowledge are sufficient to permit a prudent person, or one of reasonable caution, to conclude that there is a fair probability that particularly described property which is subject to official seizure may be presently found in a particular place.

Finally, it is important for the officer to realize that his or her probable cause determinations, many times made in the haste and hustle of dangerous investigations, will not be judged by after-the-fact, desk-side analyses made by legal scholars using strict standards and exacting calculations. Rather, probable cause will be assessed by everyday commonsensical probabilities upon which ordinary, reasonable people act.[364]

Retaliatory arrest claims. In *Nieves v. Bartlett*,[365] the United States Supreme Court made it clear that the existence of probable cause to arrest will defeat a claim that the police retaliated against a person for his or her protected First Amendment speech.

Russell Bartlett was arrested by police officers Luis Nieves and Bryce Weight for disorderly conduct and resisting arrest on the last night of "Arctic Man," a week-long raucous winter sports festival held in a remote part of Alaska. According to Sergeant Nieves, at about 1:30 a.m., he was speaking with a group of partygoers when a seemingly intoxicated Bartlett started shouting at them not to talk to the police. When Nieves approached him, Bartlett began yelling at the officer to leave. Rather than escalate the situation, Nieves left. Minutes later, Bartlett saw Trooper Weight asking a minor whether he and his underage friends had been drinking. According to Weight, Bartlett approached in an aggressive manner, stood between Weight and the teenager, and yelled with slurred speech that Weight should not speak with the minor. Weight indicated that Bartlett then stepped very close to him in a combative way, so Weight pushed him back. Sergeant Nieves saw the confrontation and rushed over, arriving right after Weight pushed Bartlett. Nieves immediately initiated an arrest, and when Bartlett was slow to comply with his orders, the officers forced him to the ground. After he was handcuffed, Bartlett claims that Nieves said "bet you wish you would have talked to me now."

Bartlett sued under 42 U. S. C. §1983, claiming that the officers violated his First Amendment rights by arresting him in retaliation for his speech – *i.e.*, his initial refusal to speak with Nieves and his intervention in Weight's discussion with the minor.[366] The Supreme Court held that the existence of probable cause to arrest

---

[363] *See e.g., California v. Acevedo*, 500 U.S. 565, 111 S. Ct. 1982, 1989 (1991) ("the same probable cause to believe that a container holds drugs will allow the police to arrest the person transporting the container [in the passenger compartment of an automobile] and search it"); *Ybarra v. Illinois*, 444 U.S. 85, 105, 100 S. Ct. 338, 350 (1979) (Rehnquist, J., dissenting) ("Given probable cause to believe that a person possesses illegal drugs, the police need no warrant to conduct a full body search. They need only arrest that person and conduct the search incident to that arrest.").

[364] Excerpts from the comprehensive discussion of the laws of arrest, search and seizure in Larry E. Holtz & Warren J Spencer, *Texas Criminal and Traffic Procedural Manual – An In-Depth Guide on How to Apply the Laws of Arrest, Search and Seizure, Confessions, & Eyewitness Identification* (Blue360° Media).

[365] *Nieves v. Bartlett*, 587 U.S. ___, 139 S. Ct. 1715 (2019).

[366] "[A]s a general matter the First Amendment prohibits government officials from subjecting an individual to retaliatory actions" for engaging in protected speech. *Hartman v. Moore*, 547 U.S. 250, 256, 126 S. Ct. 1695 (2006). If an official takes

Bartlett precluded his First Amendment retaliatory arrest claim as a matter of law.[367] In rejecting Bartlett's contention that the issue is simply whether the officer "intended to punish the plaintiff for the plaintiff's protected speech," the Court said:

> Police officers conduct approximately 29,000 arrests every day – a dangerous task that requires making quick decisions in "circumstances that are tense, uncertain, and rapidly evolving." ... To ensure that officers may go about their work without undue apprehension of being sued, we generally review their conduct under objective standards of reasonableness.... Thus, when reviewing an arrest, we ask "whether the circumstances, viewed objectively, justify [the challenged] action," and if so, conclude "that action was reasonable whatever the subjective intent motivating the relevant officials." ... A particular officer's state of mind is simply "irrelevant," and it provides "no basis for invalidating an arrest."[368]

3.5. Involuntary transportation to the police station

In *Dunaway v. New York*,[369] the Supreme Court held that officers are not permitted to transport a suspect to police headquarters for questioning without his consent and without probable cause for an arrest. According to the Court, whenever a law enforcement officer removes a suspect from where he is found and transports that suspect to police headquarters for questioning without his consent and without probable cause (for his arrest), the detention is, in all important respects, indistinguishable from a traditional arrest and is unlawful. Merely because a suspect is not told he is under arrest, is not "booked," and would not have an arrest record if the interrogation proves fruitless, does not make such a detention analogous to the type authorized by *Terry v. Ohio*. Rather, such a "detention for custodial interrogation – regardless of its label – intrudes so severely on interests protected by the Fourth Amendment" that the familiar requirement of probable cause is thereby triggered. This principle had been made clear in *Davis v. Mississippi*—namely, "that an investigatory detention that, for all intents and purposes, is indistinguishable from custodial interrogation, requires no less probable cause than a traditional arrest."[370]

The Court, in *Kaupp v. Texas*,[371] reaffirmed that, in the absence of probable cause for an arrest, it is unlawful for law enforcement officials to transport a suspect, against his will, to the station for questioning. According to the Court, the "involuntary transport to a police station for questioning is sufficiently like arrest to invoke the traditional rule that arrests may constitutionally be made only on probable cause."

In *Hayes v. Florida*,[372] however, the Supreme Court indicated that, with prior judicial authorization (such as an investigative detention order), the police may be authorized to transport a suspect to the police station for fingerprinting, even in the absence of probable cause or consent. Here, the Court noted that there have

---

adverse action against someone based on that forbidden motive, and "non-retaliatory grounds are in fact insufficient to provoke the adverse consequences," the injured person may generally seek relief by bringing a First Amendment claim. *See also Crawford-El v. Britton*, 523 U. S. 574, 593, 118 S. Ct. 1584 (1998); *Mt. Healthy City Bd. of Ed. v. Doyle*, 429 U. S. 274, 283-284, 97 S. Ct. 568 (1977).

[367] While the existence of probable cause will generally defeat a retaliatory arrest claim, officers may not exercise their discretion not to arrest for the purpose of "exploit[ing] the arrest power as a means of suppressing speech." *Nieves v. Bartlett*, 587 U.S. ___, 139 S. Ct. 1715, 1727 (2019). "For example, at many intersections, jaywalking is endemic but rarely results in arrest. If an individual who has been vocally complaining about police conduct is arrested for jaywalking at such an intersection, it would seem insufficiently protective of First Amendment rights to dismiss the individual's retaliatory arrest claim on the ground that there was undoubted probable cause for the arrest." *Id.*

[368] *Nieves v. Bartlett*, 587 U.S.___, 139 S. Ct. 1715 (2019) (quoting *Graham v. Connor*, 490 U.S. 386, 397, 109 S. Ct. 1865 (1989); *Atwater v. Lago Vista*, 532 U.S. 318, 351 & n.22, 121 S. Ct. 1536 (2001); *Harlow v. Fitzgerald*, 457 U.S. 800, 814-819, 102 S. Ct. 2727 (1982); *Devenpeck v. Alford*, 543 U.S. 146, 153, 155, 125 S. Ct. 588 (2004)).

[369] *Dunaway v. New York*, 442 U.S. 200, 99 S. Ct. 2248 (1979).

[370] *Davis v. Mississippi*, 394 U.S. 721, 726-27, 89 S. Ct. 1394 (1969). *See also Hayes v. Florida*, 470 U.S. 811, 815, 105 S. Ct. 1643 (1985) ("None of our later cases have undercut the holding in Davis that transportation to and investigative detention at the station house without probable cause or judicial authorization together violate the Fourth Amendment."). For an extended discussion of this topic, *see* §2.3.1.4.

[371] *Kaupp v. Texas*, 538 U.S. 626, 123 S. Ct. 1843 (2003).

[372] *Hayes v. Florida*, 470 U.S. 811, 105 S. Ct. 1643 (1985).

been a number of cases that have suggested that "the Fourth Amendment would permit seizures for the purpose of fingerprinting, if there is reasonable suspicion that the suspect has committed a criminal act, if there is a reasonable basis for believing that fingerprinting will establish or negate the suspect's connection with that crime, and if the procedure is carried out with dispatch.

In *Livingston v. State*,[373] the Texas Court of Criminal Appeals explained, "where a person voluntarily accompanies investigating police officers to a certain location, and he knows or should know that the police officers suspect that he may have committed or may be implicated in committing a crime, that person is not 'restrained' or 'in custody'...so that his Fourth Amendment or Art. I, § 9 rights are implicated."[374] Accordingly, the cornerstone of the issue will be the voluntariness of the transport.

3.6. An officer's training, experience and expertise

An officer' specialized training, experience and expertise provide the officer with a unique ability to make judgments and assessments as to whether the law is or is not being violated. Unlike a layman, most law enforcement officials receive initial and continuing training for the job. Through years of experience, they also develop a specialized expertise in recognizing criminality in all its forms. In addition, "a good patrol officer considers it his business to develop so complete familiarity with his 'beat' that he is alerted by anything suspicious or unusual."[375]

As a general matter, courts will take into account an officer's training, experience and expertise in determining whether probable cause exists. In this regard, what constitutes probable cause for an arrest or a search and seizure must be determined from the standpoint of the officer, with his skills and knowledge, rather than from the standpoint of an average citizen under similar circumstances. Thus, probable cause is to be viewed from the vantage point of a prudent, reasonable, cautious police officer guided by his experience and training.[376]

3.7. The "fellow officer"/ "collective knowledge" rule

Police are also entitled to rely on facts garnered by those with whom they work. When more than one officer is working on a particular case, a reviewing court will take into account all of the information known to all of the officers on the case (not just the information known to the one who made the arrest) to determine if there was probable cause to arrest. Thus, in *Karr v. Smith*,[377] the court held that, under the "fellow officer" rule, "probable cause is to be determined by the courts on the basis of the collective information of the police involved in the arrest, rather than exclusively on the extent of the knowledge of the particular officer who may actually make the arrest." Rather than focusing exclusively on the extent of the knowledge of the particular officer who may actually have made the arrest, courts will determine the existence of probable cause "on the basis of the collective information" known to the police — all the officers involved in the arrest. This is known as the *fellow officer rule*. Under this rule, "the collective information" of all the law enforcement officers "involved in an arrest can form the

373 *Livingston v. State*, 739 S.W.2d 311 (Tex. Crim. App. 1987).
374 *Livingston v. State*, 739 S.W.2d 311, 327 (Tex. Crim. App. 1987).
375 *Model Code of Pre-Arraignment Procedure* 297 (1975).
376 *See United States v. Ortiz*, 422 U.S. 891, 95 S. Ct. 2585 (1975) ("officers are entitled to draw reasonable inferences from these facts in light of their knowledge of the area and their prior experience"); *Johnson v. United States*, 333 U.S. 10, 68 S. Ct. 367 (1948) (probable cause may be based on a distinctive odor where the officer is "qualified to know the odor"); *United States v. Smith*, 789 F.3d 923 (8th Cir. 2015) (probable cause established from officer's smell of marijuana in car, where officer "testified that he had been trained in the detection of controlled substances, including the odor of both raw and burned marijuana"); *United States v. Clarke*, 564 F.3d 949 (8th Cir. 2009) (probable cause established where officer "smelled an odor which, based on his training and extensive experience, he recognized as consistent with methamphetamine manufacturing"); *see also United States v. Peters*, 743 F.3d 1113 (7th Cir. 2014) (probable cause established where officer with 15 years of "significant training and experience in traffic enforcement" judged the distance between the vehicles "to be too short for cars moving so quickly").
377 *Karr v. Smith*, 774 F.2d 1029, 1031 (10th Cir. 1985).

basis for probable cause, even though that information is not within the knowledge of the arresting officer."[378]

The Texas Court of Criminal Appeals has stated, "when there has been some cooperation between law enforcement agencies or between members of the same agency, the sum of the information known to the cooperating agencies or officers at the time of an arrest or search by any of the officers involved is to be considered in determining whether there was sufficient probable cause therefor."[379] Accordingly, "under this 'collective knowledge' doctrine, when several officers are cooperating, their cumulative information may be considered in assessing reasonable suspicion or probable cause."[380] In *State v. Martinez*,[381] the court further held that "evidence of communication between officers is not always a necessary requirement to apply the collective knowledge doctrine."[382] Rather, in certain circumstances, the cumulative information of the cooperating officers should be considered in assessing probable cause. In *Martinez*, because "all of the officers were responding to the same call, all were present at the scene, all had some degree of communication with [defendant], and all were present at the time of the arrest,"[383] it was apparent that the officers were working as a team responding to the call.

3.8. Other factors to consider

3.8.1. High crime areas

In addition to an officer's training and experience, the known reputation of an area for crime is also a relevant factor in determining whether probable cause or reasonable suspicion exists.[384]

3.8.2. Identification of suspect

An officer must be sure that the description of a suspect is sufficiently detailed before she can effectuate an arrest. If the description is too vague or general, the officer should refrain from making the mistake of arresting the suspect prematurely. Instead she should ask the suspect certain questions or keep the suspect under surveillance. Obviously, if those procedures are not practical, the officer should use common sense and take reasonable steps to keep the suspect under observation.

The victim is the best source of identification of a suspect. The courts will assume that the victim is reliable and obviously knows what he or she is talking about. Unless a police officer has reason not to believe a victim (*i.e.*, if he or she exhibits emotional or mental problems), the officer can rely on the victim for sufficient identification and probable cause to make an arrest, without having to verify the information.[385]

In *Ahlers v. Schebil*,[386] plaintiff had been arrested for solicitation and was being kept in the Washtenaw County Jail. Her allegation that defendant, a corrections officer, had sexually assaulted her the night before, standing alone, established probable cause for defendant's arrest, especially when bolstered by Sheriff's Department records that confirmed that there was a window of time when the assault could have occurred.

378 *See also Whiteley v. Warden*, 401 U.S. 560, 568, 91 S. Ct. 1031, 1037 (1971) ("Certainly, police officers called upon to aid other officers in executing arrest warrants are entitled to assume that the officers requesting aid offered the magistrate the information requisite to support an independent judicial assessment of probable cause."); *United States v. Rocha*, 916 F.2d 219, 238 (5th Cir. 1990) (the arresting officer "need not have personal knowledge of all the facts constituting probable cause but can rely upon the collective knowledge of the police when there is a communication among them").

379 *Woodward v. State*, 668 S.W.2d 337, 344 (Tex. Crim. App. 1984).

380 *State v. Martinez*, 569 S.W.3d 621, 626 (Tex. Crim. App. 2019) (citing *State v. Duran*, 396 S.W.3d 563, 569 n.12 (Tex. Crim. App. 2013)).

381 *State v. Martinez*, 569 S.W.3d 621, 626 (Tex. Crim. App. 2019).

382 *State v. Martinez*, 569 S.W.3d 621, 627 (Tex. Crim. App. 2019).

383 *State v. Martinez*, 569 S.W.3d 621, 627 (Tex. Crim. App. 2019).

384 *See Illinois v. Wardlow*, 528 U.S. 119, 125, 120 S. Ct. 673, 676 (2000) ("[T]he fact that the stop occurred in a 'high crime area' [is] among the relevant contextual considerations in a *Terry* analysis.").

385 *See Ahlers v. Schebil*, 188 F.3d 365, 370 (6th Cir. 1999) ("[S]ince eyewitness' statements are based on firsthand observations, they are generally entitled to a presumption of reliability and veracity."); *Casarez v. State*, 504 S.W.2d 847 (Tex. Crim. App. 1974).

386 *Ahlers v. Schebil*, 188 F.3d 365 (6th Cir. 1999).

Occasionally a victim will tell a police officer that he or she is not absolutely certain of an identification or that a person only looks like the perpetrator of the crime. This information is usually insufficient to provide an officer with probable cause. However, probable cause will exist if the victim picks out a suspect's photograph.[387]

In *Romero v. State*,[388] an officer responded to a family disturbance call. He found the defendant's ex-wife with a cut lip, blood in her hair, scratches on her arm, and a swollen right eye; she said that defendant had come over and hit her. She then showed the officer a recent picture of defendant and described his vehicle. Less than an hour later, the officer found defendant near the described vehicle, a block away from the victim's home. He had probable cause to arrest.

A police officer can also rely on a citizen who is not the victim of a crime to provide information which will constitute probable cause to make an arrest. While the courts have also found this type of citizen to be trustworthy, an officer must still verify that the citizen knows what he or she is talking about. This is known as the citizen's "basis of knowledge."

3.8.3. Informants

When a police officer relies upon a confidential informant for information, there are certain points that the officer must keep in mind. Before the courts will find probable cause based on the informant's information, the officer must be sure that the tip is reliable.[389] Two important considerations in making this determination are the informant's "veracity" and "basis of knowledge."

In order to establish an informant's "veracity," an officer should determine the following: (i) whether the informant came forward in the past with accurate information (including the number of times, the nature of the prior cases, how often the information was true and correct, and how often the information has led to a successful arrest, prosecution or conviction); (ii) whether the informant made any criminal admissions (called declarations against his or her penal interest); (iii) whether the informant has a proper motive; (iv) whether the informant has a close relationship to key criminal targets; (iv) whether the officer can confirm details of the informant's story; and (v) whether the informant is an ordinary citizen who provides information solely to help solve a crime or prevent a future crime.[390]

In order to establish an informant's "basis of knowledge," the officer should consider the following: (i) whether the informant provided detailed information and a factual account *i.e.*, no rumors or innuendo; (ii) whether the informant spoke from personal knowledge; (iii) whether the information is provided with a relevant time frame; (iv) whether the informant was able to provide predictive information; and (v) whether the officer observed conduct directly corroborating the informant's report.[391]

If, under the totality of the circumstances — including the informant's "veracity" and "basis of knowledge" — the reliability of the tip can be established by the officer, probable cause for an arrest will exist. If an officer cannot fully establish an informant's "veracity," "reliability" or "basis of knowledge," a deficiency in either may be made up by independent police corroboration and an application of the totality of the circumstances. This approach was adopted by the United States Supreme Court in *Illinois v. Gates*.[392] Stating that probable cause is a fluid concept that is not readily or usefully reduced to a neat set of legal rules, the Court said:

> We agree ... that an informant's "veracity," "reliability," and "basis of knowledge" are all highly relevant in determining the value of [the informant's] report. We do not agree, however, that these elements should be understood as entirely separate and independent requirements to be rigidly exacted in every case.... Rather, ... they should be understood simply as closely intertwined issues that may usefully

---

387 *Ahlers v. Schebil*, 188 F.3d 365, 370 (6th Cir. 1999).
388 *Romero v. State*, 709 S.W.2d 53 (Tex. App. 1986).
389 *Amores v. State*, 816 S.W.2d 407 (Tex. Crim. App. 1991).
390 *See* Larry E. Holtz & Warren J Spencer, *Texas Criminal and Traffic Procedural Manual – An In-Depth Guide on How to Apply the Laws of Arrest, Search and Seizure, Confessions, & Eyewitness Identification* (Blue360° Media).
391 *See* Larry E. Holtz & Warren J Spencer, *Texas Criminal and Traffic Procedural Manual – An In-Depth Guide on How to Apply the Laws of Arrest, Search and Seizure, Confessions, & Eyewitness Identification* (Blue360° Media).
392 *Illinois v. Gates*, 462 U.S. 213, 232, 238, 103 S. Ct. 2317 (1983).

illuminate the common-sense, practical question whether there is "probable cause" to believe that contraband or evidence is located in a particular place.[393]

Under the "totality of the circumstances" approach, the facts are to be viewed collectively, not in isolation. Many times, when the facts are viewed separately and in isolation, they may be prone to innocent explanation. But "this kind of divide-and-conquer approach is improper."[394] Instead, we must look at "the whole picture."

For example, in *Guzman v. State*,[395] police officers received a tip that defendant was hiding heroin in his mouth. The tip was then corroborated by the suspect's failure to comply with an order to stop swallowing. Moreover, the suspect was found in an area well-known for drug trafficking and he "walked hurriedly away from the police"[396] when they asked him what he had in his mouth. "Under the totality of the circumstances, the officers had probable cause to justify a warrantless arrest of [defendant]."[397]

3.8.4. Flight, nervousness or evasive maneuvers

Flight, nervousness or evasive maneuvers when confronted with police presence, although not sufficient to create probable cause when standing alone, may create probable cause for arrest if coupled with a suspicion centering on the suspect.

For example, in *Illinois v. Wardlow*,[398] the defendant fled upon seeing police officers patrolling an area known for heavy narcotics trafficking. Two officers caught the defendant on the street, stopped him, and conducted a pat-down search for weapons. Upon discovering a .38 caliber handgun, the defendant was arrested. Finding the stop proper, the Court noted that an officer may, consistent with the Fourth Amendment, conduct a brief, investigatory stop when the officer has a reasonable, articulable suspicion that criminal activity is afoot.[399] Here, the fact that the stop occurred in a "high crime area" is among the relevant contextual considerations in a *Terry* analysis. However, in *Wardlow*, it was not merely defendant's presence "in an area of heavy narcotics trafficking that aroused the officers' suspicion but his unprovoked flight upon noticing the police."[400] And in developing a reasonable articulable suspicion, "nervous, evasive behavior" may be considered as a "pertinent factor." Said the Court:

> Headlong flight — wherever it occurs — is the consummate act of evasion: it is not necessarily indicative of wrongdoing, but it is certainly suggestive of such. In reviewing the propriety of an officer's conduct, courts do not have available empirical studies dealing with inferences drawn from suspicious behavior, and we cannot reasonably demand scientific certainty from judges or law enforcement officers where none exists.[401]

As discussed above, the *Guzman* court considered defendant's evasive behavior as part of the totality of the circumstances justifying his warrantless arrest. The court asserted its previous holding that "avoiding officers is a factor to consider when determining probable cause."[402] You will additionally remember that in *Lerma v. State*,[403] the defendant ran from Officer Salinas after Salinas found marijuana in defendant's pocket. There, defendant's flight was one justification for his arrest.

---

[393] *Illinois v. Gates*, 462 U.S. 213, 232, 230, 103 S. Ct. 2317 (1983). The law related to informants is further explored at Section 4.1.7.

[394] *District of Columbia v. Wesby*, 583 U.S. ___, 138 S. Ct. 577, 589 (2018).

[395] *Guzman v. State*, 955 S.W.2d 85 (Tex. Crim. App. 1997).

[396] *Guzman v. State*, 955 S.W.2d 85, 90 (Tex. Crim. App. 1997).

[397] *Guzman v. State*, 955 S.W.2d 85, 91 (Tex. Crim. App. 1997).

[398] *Illinois v. Wardlow*, 528 U.S. 119, 120 S. Ct. 673 (2000).

[399] *Illinois v. Wardlow*, 528 U.S. 119, 120 S. Ct. 673, 675 (2000).

[400] *Illinois v. Wardlow*, 528 U.S. 119, 120 S. Ct. 673, 675 (2000).

[401] *Illinois v. Wardlow*, 528 U.S. 119, 120 S. Ct. 673, 676 (2000).

[402] *Guzman v. State*, 955 S.W.2d 85, 90 (Tex. Crim. App. 1997).

[403] *Lerma v. State*, 543 S.W.3d 184 (Tex. Crim. App. 2018).

3.9. Arrest with a warrant

An arrest warrant has the purpose of interposing a probable cause determination by a neutral and detached magistrate or judge between the law enforcement officer and the person to be arrested. Placing this "check-point between the Government and the citizen implicitly acknowledges that an 'officer engaged in the often competitive enterprise of ferreting out crime' may lack sufficient objectivity to weigh correctly the strength of the evidence supporting the contemplated action against the individual's interests in protecting his own liberty and ... privacy[.]"[404]

Under Texas law an officer may arrest a person when the officer has a warrant.[405] When an arrest warrant issues, it demonstrates that a detached and neutral magistrate or judge has determined that probable cause exists to believe that the subject of the warrant has committed an offense. As such, the warrant necessarily serves to protect individuals from unreasonable searches and seizures.

Once armed with an arrest warrant, a police officer has the right to execute the warrant by the arrest of the accused not only in a public place but also at his or her home.[406]

3.9.1. Contents of the arrest warrant

An arrest warrant must be in the name of the State of Texas, specify the name of the person to be arrested (or, if unknown, some reasonably definite description of the person), name the offense the person is accused of committing, and be signed by the magistrate with his or her office named in the body of the warrant or in connection with his or her signature.[407]

An arrest warrant issued by any county or district clerk or by any magistrate may be executed in any county in the State.[408]An arrest warrant may be served at any time of the day or night.[409] The officer need not have physical possession of the warrant before making the arrest, but must show the warrant to the arrestee as soon as possible, if the arrestee so requests. If the officer does not possess the warrant at the time of arrest, the arrestee must be informed of the offense charged and the fact that a warrant has been issued.[410]

3.9.1.1. Media ride-alongs

In executing an arrest warrant, the United States Supreme Court has held that a "media ride-along," where a reporter and photographer accompanied police while an arrest warrant was served in a suspect's home, violated the Constitution.[411]

In *Wilson v. Layne*, as officers executed an arrest warrant in a private home, invited members of the media accompanied them. The officers were looking for a fugitive, Dominic Wilson, who had violated his probation on previous charges of robbery, theft, and assault. The computer report contained certain "caution indicators" that Wilson was "likely to be armed, to resist arrest, and to assaul[t] police."[412] Three arrest warrants issued for Wilson, one for each of the probation violations. Each warrant was addressed to "any duly authorized peace officer," and commanded the officer to arrest the subject and bring him "immediately" before the court. The warrants contained no reference to the presence or assistance of the media.

Holding that such a "media ride-along" violated the Fourth Amendment, the Court's analysis began with the famous *Semayne's Case* of 1603, where the English Court observed that "the house of every one is to

404 *Steagald v. United States*, 451 U.S. 204, 212, 101 S. Ct. 1642, 1648 (1981) (quoting *Johnson v. United States*, 333 U.S. 10, 14, 68 S. Ct. 367, 369 (1948)).
405 *Tex. Code Crim. Proc.* Art. 15.01.
406 *Payton v. New York*, 455 U.S. 573, 100 S. Ct. 1371 (1980).
407 Tex. Code Crim. Proc. art. 15.02.
408 Tex. Code Crim. Proc. art. 15.06.
409 Tex. Code Crim. Proc. art. 15.23.
410 Tex. Code Crim. Proc. art. 15.26.
411 *See Wilson v. Layne*, 526 U.S. 603, 119 S. Ct. 1692 (1999).
412 *Wilson v. Layne*, 526 U.S. 603, 119 S. Ct. 1692, 1695 (1999).

him as his castle and fortress, as well for his defence against injury and violence, as for his repose."[413] This "centuries-old principle of the respect for the privacy of the home," is embodied in the Fourth Amendment.[414]

Although the officers in this case were entitled to enter the Wilson home in order to execute the arrest warrant for Dominic Wilson, they were not entitled to bring a newspaper reporter and a photographer with them. Clearly, the presence of reporters inside the home "was not related to the objectives of the authorized intrusion.... [T]he reporters did not engage in the execution of the warrant, and did not assist the police in their task."[415] Rather, the "Washington Post reporters in the Wilsons' home were working on a story for their own purposes. They were not present for the purpose of protecting the officers, much less the Wilsons."[416] Accordingly, the "media ride-along," employed in this case violated the Fourth Amendment.

3.9.2. Delay in making an arrest

A criminal suspect has no constitutional right to be arrested. There is no requirement that once law enforcement possesses probable cause to arrest, they do so immediately. Although the Sixth Amendment guarantees a defendant the right to a speedy trial, it does not guarantee the right to a speedy arrest.[417] However, a gap between the commission of the offense (or the time law enforcement becomes aware of it), and the arrest may be so protracted that it violates the Due Process Clause of the Fourteenth Amendment.

To prevail on such a claim, a defendant must show that (i) the delay caused actual and substantial prejudice to the defendant; and (ii) the delay was the product of deliberate action or inaction by law enforcement in order to gain a tactical advantage. To demonstrate prejudice, the defendant must show that real and tangible harm was done to his or her defense. The mere passage of time, and its effects, is not sufficient. The fact that "memories will dim, witnesses become inaccessible, and evidence will be lost" during the gap is inadequate to demonstrate that the defendant cannot receive a fair trial and insufficient to show a due process violation.[418]

3.9.3. Protective sweeps

In *Maryland v. Buie*,[419] the Supreme Court held that, during the course of an in-home arrest, law enforcement officers may conduct a "protective sweep" of the premises so long as the officers possess specific and articulable facts which, taken together with the rational inferences from those facts, give rise to a reasonable suspicion "that the area to be swept harbors an individual posing a danger to those on the arrest scene." In addition, "as an incident to the arrest, the officers [may], as a precautionary matter and *without probable cause or reasonable suspicion*, look in closets and other spaces immediately adjoining the place of arrest from which an attack could be launched."[420] Such a protective sweep, however, is aimed only at protecting the arresting officers; it is *not* a full search of the premises, but only a brief "cursory inspection of those spaces where a person may be found."[421]

In *Ramirez v. State*,[422] an officer went to defendant's residence to investigate a report that he was selling marijuana. Defendant's young son answered the door and said his father was in the garage. The officer went around to the garage door and knocked. When defendant opened the door, the officer could see a set of scales with marijuana seeds and residue and a large green pipe on a table, as well as rolling papers and baggies on the floor; he could also smell the odor of fresh marijuana. Defendant stepped outside to speak with the officer, closing the door behind him. While they were speaking, another man, Pedro Reynosa, came out of

---

[413] *Semayne's Case*, 77 Eng.Rep. 194, 195 (K.B. 1603).

[414] *Wilson v. Layne*, 526 U.S. 603, 119 S. Ct. 1692, 1697 (1999).

[415] *Wilson v. Layne*, 526 U.S. 603, 119 S. Ct. 1692, 1698 (1999).

[416] *Wilson v. Layne*, 526 U.S. 603, 119 S. Ct. 1692, 1698 (1999).

[417] *See Hoffa v. United States*, 385 U.S. 293, 310, 87 S. Ct. 408, 417 (1966).

[418] *United States v. Marion*, 404 U.S. 307, 92 S. Ct. 455 (1971) (without an arrest, the period of three years that lapsed between the end of defendants' crime and their indictment did not implicate the Sixth Amendment speedy trial provision).

[419] *Maryland v. Buie*, 494 U.S. 325, 110 S. Ct. 1093, 1098-99 (1990).

[420] *Maryland v. Buie*, 494 U.S. 325, 110 S. Ct. 1093, 1098-99 (1990) (emphasis added).

[421] *Maryland v. Buie*, 494 U.S. 325, 110 S. Ct. 1093, 1099 (1990) (emphasis added).

[422] *Ramirez v. State*, 105 S.W.3d 730 (Tex. App. 2003).

the garage, leaving the door partially open behind him. The officer recognized Reynosa as someone who "had been handled for weapons before," and was a suspect in an assault that took place a week earlier. The officer frisked both men, and found a knife on Reynosa. The garage was lighted poorly, and the partially open door blocked the officer's view. Moreover, he did not know if there were any more adults inside, but did know that one of the adults who had been inside was armed. He therefore made a valid *Buie* sweep of the garage after arresting both men, to ensure the safety of himself and the other officers on the scene. However, the officer exceeded the scope of a valid *Buie* sweep when he looked inside a portable cooler, as this container was far too small to conceal a person.

In *Beaver v. State*,[423] police served an arrest warrant and a search warrant for drugs at defendant's radiator shop. Defendant was not present when they arrived. However, officers saw an unknown individual going in and out of the mobile home where defendant resided, approximately 200 feet from the shop. The officers went to the mobile home, knocked on the door, and were invited in by defendant. They entered to find defendant sitting at a table, drinking beer with another individual. Because the officers did not know exactly how many people were in the trailer, they were justified in conducting a sweep of the adjoining rooms, to ensure that no one was waiting to ambush them. The court noted with favor that the officers did not look in drawers or other closed areas, and that the search lasted less than a minute.

In *Reasor v. State*,[424] the Texas Court of Criminal Appeals was unable to uphold a protective sweep under the *Buie* test. There, the officer did not express a belief that any third person was inside defendant's home. Nor did he articulate a belief that a third person inside the home was attempting to jeopardize either his or the public's safety.

In *State v. Sheppard*,[425] Deputy Smith placed the defendant in handcuffs before performing a sweep of the residence. There, the deputy had been informed that three people had been present when the witness was threatened with a knife. Thus, his brief sweep of the home was justified to see if somebody else was present either as a victim or as a danger to the officer as he continued with his investigation of the complaint.

3.10. Arrest without a warrant

While the law certainly prefers that an arrest be made pursuant to a warrant, a law enforcement officer is nonetheless permitted to effect a *warrantless* arrest when she has probable cause to believe that a crime has been or is being committed and that the person to be arrested is a criminal participant. In this context, the term "crime" many times referred to as "felony," encompasses those offenses which carry a penalty of imprisonment for a year or more.

In Texas, "[a] police officer may arrest an individual without a warrant only if (1) there is probable cause with respect to that individual and (2) the arrest falls within one of the statutory exceptions."[426]

An officer may make a warrantless arrest for any offense committed within his presence or view.[427] An officer may also arrest for a felony or breach of the peace committed within the presence or view of a magistrate, if the magistrate so directs.[428] An offense is committed within an officer's "presence" when "any one of his senses afford him an awareness of its occurrence."[429] However, the information afforded to the officer must give him reason to believe a particular suspect committed the offense before an arrest can be made.

An officer may also make a warrantless arrest when a person is found in a "suspicious place" and the circumstances reasonably show that the person has committed a felony, disorderly conduct, breach of the peace

[423] *Beaver v. State*, 942 S.W.2d 626 (Tex. App. 1996).
[424] *Reasor v. State*, 12 S.W.3d 813 (Tex. Crim. App. 2000).
[425] *State v. Sheppard*, 271 S.W.3d 281 (Tex. Crim. App. 2008).
[426] *State v. Steelman*, 93 S.W.3d 102, 107 (Tex. Crim. App. 2002) (citing *Beverly v. State*, 792 S.W.2d 103, 104-105 (Tex. Crim. App. 1990)); *Lunde v. State*, 736 S.W.2d 665, 666 (Tex. Crim. App. 1987). For a more comprehensive discussion of the Texas law of arrest, *see* Larry E. Holtz & Warren J Spencer, *Texas Criminal and Traffic Procedural Manual – An In-Depth Guide on How to Apply the Laws of Arrest, Search and Seizure, Confessions, & Eyewitness Identification* (Blue360° Media).
[427] Tex. Code Crim Proc. art. 14.01(b).
[428] Tex. Code Crim Proc. art. 14.02.
[429] *State v. Steelman*, 93 S.W.3d 102, 107 (Tex. Crim. App. 2002) (holding no probable cause to arrest when defendant stepped out of his house and officers could smell marijuana in the air, but not on defendant himself).

or public intoxication, or is about to commit some offense against the laws.[430] Few, if any, places are suspicious in and of themselves. There must be additional facts to arouse justifiable suspicion.[431] The determination that a place is "suspicious" is highly fact-specific.[432] The time between the commission of the crime and the apprehension of the suspect is an "important factor" in determining if a place is suspicious.[433]

A place can be suspicious because (i) an eyewitness or officer connected the place to the crime; (ii) a crime occurred there or police reasonably believe a crime occurred there; (iii) there is specific evidence directly connecting the defendant or the place with the crime; or (iv) the defendant's behavior indicates that the place is suspicious.[434]

An officer may also make a warrantless arrest at any public place (i) a suspect who has assaulted another causing bodily injury, if there is probable cause to believe there is danger of further bodily injury; (ii) for violation of a protective order; (iii) for an assault resulting in bodily injury to a family or household member; (iv) for prevention or interference with an individual's ability to place a call in an emergency; or (v) of a person who has made a statement that establishes probable cause to believe the person has committed a felony.[435]

An arrest for a felony committed outside the officer's presence may also be made if: (i) a credible person alleges that the crime was committed, and (ii) the suspect is about to escape.[436] The State must prove by a clear showing that the suspect was about to escape, so that there was no time to procure an arrest warrant.[437]

Any person, including an officer, may arrest a suspect if there is probable cause to believe the suspect is in possession of stolen property.[438]

The Fourth Amendment does not prohibit a custodial arrest for a minor, fine-only offense.[439]However, in lieu of making an arrest for a Class C misdemeanor (other than public intoxication), an officer may issue a citation to the person that contains written notice of the time and place the person must appear before a magistrate, the name and address of the person charged, and the offense charged.[440] In lieu of making an arrest for public intoxication, an officer may release the suspect if (i) the officer believes detention in a penal facility is unnecessary for the protection of the suspect or others and (ii) the individual is released to the care of an adult who agrees to assume responsibility or the suspect verbally agrees to enter a treatment program.[441]

---

[430] Tex. Code Crim Proc. art. 14.03(a)(1).

[431] *Johnson v. State*, 722 S.W.2d 417 (Tex. Crim. App. 1986).

[432] *Holland v. State*, 788 S.W.2d 112 (Tex. App. 1990).

[433] *Dyar v. State*, 125 S.W.3d 460 (Tex. Crim. App. 2003).

[434] *Dror Haim Goldberg v. State*, 95 S.W.3d 345 (Tex. App. 2002). *See, e.g., Dyar v. State*, 125 S.W.3d 460 (Tex. Crim. App. 2003) (hospital a suspicious place when defendant was taken there following a single- car accident on New Year's Eve and showed signs of intoxication); *Adams v. State*, 552 S.W.2d 812 (Tex. Crim. App. 1977) (defendant's car a suspicious place when he drove it at 12:15 a.m. near the motel room of a known fence with the trunk open and a television in plain view inside); *Mitchell v. State*, 756 S.W.2d 71 (Tex. App. 1988) ("The presence of a stolen vehicle in [defendant's] yard [could] reasonably be considered to qualify the yard and house as a suspicious place"); *Wilson v. State*, 722 S.W.2d 3 (Tex. App. 1986) (defendant's apartment a suspicious place when a car registered to him was used in a bank robbery and his apartment manager identified him from a composite drawing of the robber); *Thomas v. State*, 681 S.W.2d 672 (Tex. App. 1984) (street in a neighborhood where a least one home had been recently burglarized suspicious when three men were walking down it carrying a television); *Douglas v. State*, 679 S.W.2d 790 (Tex. App. 1984)(defendant's house was a suspicious place when a dead body was found lying in the front yard and defendant had been seen near the body, had put something in a car parked outside the house, and had then run back inside after being seen by a witness); *Battles v. State*, 626 S.W.2d 149 (Tex. App. 1981) (defendant was in a suspicious place when he was found in the complainant's home with a gun in his hand after a call for discharge of a firearm).

[435] Tex. Code Crim Proc. art. 14.03(a)(2)-(6).

[436] Tex. Code Crim Proc. art. 14.04.

[437] *Fry v. State*, 639 S.W.2d 463 (Tex. Crim. App. 1982).

[438] Tex. Code Crim Proc. art. 18.16.

[439] *Atwater v. City of Lago Vista*, 532 U.S. 318, 121 S. Ct. 1536 (2001) (upholding arrest of motorist for failure to wear a seatbelt).

[440] Tex. Code Crim Proc. art. 14.06.

[441] Tex. Code Crim Proc. art. 14.031.

If a person who commits one of the following resides in the county where the offense occurred, and the offense is a Class A or B misdemeanor, an officer may issue a citation rather than taking the person before a magistrate:

- Possession of four ounces or less of marihuana (Health & Safety Code § 481.121(b)(1)-(2));
- Possession of four ounces or less of substance listed in Penalty Group 2-A (Health & Safety Code § 481.1161(b)(1)-(2));
- Criminal mischief involving pecuniary loss less than $500 (Penal Code § 28.03(b)(2));
- Graffiti involving pecuniary loss less than $500 (Penal Code § 28.08(b)(2) or (3));
- Theft of property with a value less than $500 (Penal Code § 31.03(e)(2)(A));
- Theft of services with a value less than $500 (Penal Code § 31.04(e)(2));
- Contraband in a correctional facility (Penal Code § 38.114);
- Driving while license invalid (Transportation Code § 521.457).[442]

When an officer must decide whether a warrantless arrest in a given set of circumstances is justified, he or she is not confined to consideration only of evidence admissible in a courtroom. Rather, the officer may consider all the facts and circumstances surrounding the prospective arrest, even that information coming from (preferably reliable) hearsay sources, when making the probable cause determination.

Once probable cause exists for the arrest of an individual, the arrest may take place without a warrant when it is effected in a public place. The Fourth Amendment permits such warrantless (felony) arrests even though the law enforcement officer had sufficient time to obtain a warrant.[443]

In *United States v. Watson*,[444] the Supreme Court refused to place a requirement of more than probable cause in a warrantless arrest situation. According to the Court, to require more than probable cause – *e.g.*, probable cause and exigent circumstances – would "encumber criminal prosecutions with endless litigation with respect to the existence of exigent circumstances, whether it was practicable to get a warrant, whether the suspect was about to flee, and the like."[445] Accordingly, the two critical components for warrantless criminal arrests remain: (1) probable cause, and (2) an offense punishable by imprisonment for a year or more.[446]

Respecting lower level offenses, *i.e.*, offenses punishable by imprisonment for less than one year, most jurisdictions require that the offense occur *in the presence* of the law enforcement officer. *"Presence,"* in this respect, means that the arresting officer has gained knowledge of the offense directly, and this may be accomplished by the use of any of his or her senses.[447]

Most commonly, the "in presence" requirement is satisfied by an officer directly viewing or seeing the offense occur, even if the officer uses a telescope or binoculars. The "in presence" requirement may also be satisfied if the officer witnesses the offense through his or her sense of hearing, smell or touch. In this regard, it is not enough that an officer uses his or her senses *to learn that an offense has been committed.* The offense must be committed at the time the officer is on the scene. For example, an officer would not be authorized to make an in-presence arrest for a minor assault merely because he has been told by the victim that the perpetrator, who is still present at the scene, struck her prior to the arrival of the officer. This is so even if the victim's story is largely corroborated by the officer's observation of signs of injury on the victim's body. It has also been held

---

442 Tex. Code Crim Proc. art. 14.06(d).

443 *United States v. Watson*, 423 U.S. 411, 96 S. Ct. 820 (1976) (upholding a warrantless arrest, based upon probable cause, effected by a postal inspector at a public restaurant).

444 *United States v. Watson*, 423 U.S. 411, 96 S. Ct. 820 (1976).

445 *United States v. Watson*, 423 U.S. 411, 423-24, 96 S. Ct. 820, 828 (1976).

446 For a more comprehensive discussion of the administration of *Miranda* warnings in Texas, *see* Larry E. Holtz & Warren J Spencer, *Texas Criminal and Traffic Procedural Manual – An In-Depth Guide on How to Apply the Laws of Arrest, Search and Seizure, Confessions, & Eyewitness Identification* (Blue360° Media).

447 *See Atwater v. City of Lago Vista*, 532 U.S. 318, 354, 121 S. Ct. 1536, 1557 (2001) ("If an officer has probable cause to believe that an individual has committed even a very minor criminal offense in his presence, he may, without violating the Fourth Amendment, arrest the offender.").

that a minor theft offense did not occur in the officer's presence in a case where the officer viewed a grocery store's videotape of the offender engaging in the alleged shoplifting offense.[448]

In *Maryland v. Pringle*,[449] a car with three male occupants was stopped for speeding in the early morning hours. When the driver retrieved his license from the glove compartment, an officer noticed a large amount of cash. Because he found this suspicious, the officer asked for and received consent to search the car. Police found $763 in the glove compartment and five glassine bags of cocaine between the back-seat armrest and the back-seat. All three men denied ownership of the drug. Because the cocaine was accessible to all the men, it was reasonable to infer all three had knowledge of it and exercised domain and control over it. Police therefore had probable cause to arrest all three occupants, including defendant, the front-seat passenger.

Note: *Private persons.* A private person may make a citizen's arrest when the offense is committed in his presence or within his view, if the offense is one classed as a felony or as an offense against the public peace.[450]

3.11. Entry of a dwelling to effect an arrest

In a landmark decision, the United States Supreme Court, in *Payton v. New York*,[451] held that, absent exigent circumstances, a law enforcement officer may not make a warrantless, nonconsensual entry into a suspect's home to arrest him, even though probable cause exists to believe the suspect is, in fact, the perpetrator of a felony. "[T]he Fourth Amendment has drawn a firm line at the entrance to the house. Absent exigent circumstances, that threshold may not reasonably be crossed without a warrant."[452]

According to the court, "physical entry of the home is the chief evil against which the wording of the Fourth Amendment is directed."[453] In the context of warrantless home entries, it should be emphasized that the doctrine of "exigent circumstances" will permit such an intrusion only where there is also probable cause to enter the home.

The federal Supreme Court has also accorded Fourth Amendment protection to hotel rooms. Similar to the home,[454] absent exigent circumstances or consent, police officers need to meet the requirements of the Fourth Amendment before searching or seizing things or persons from hotel or motel rooms.[455]

"As such, hotel staff may not consent to a law enforcement search of an occupied room in which a guest retains an expectation of privacy.... Hotel guests, however, lose that expectation of privacy in their room at the time their occupancy is scheduled to end or upon their eviction from the room by the hotel.[456] Moreover, if hotel management needs assistance with carrying out an eviction of a hotel guest (for example, based

---

[448] *See Forgie-Buccioni v. Hannaford Bros., Inc.*, 413 F.3d 175, 180 (1st Cir. 2005) (a videotape alone does not provide a sufficient basis to satisfy the "in presence" requirement for warrantless arrests).

[449] *Maryland v. Pringle*, 540 U.S. 366, 124 S. Ct. 795 (2003).

[450] Tex. Code Crim Proc. art. 14.01(a).

[451] *Payton v. New York*, 445 U.S. 573, 100 S. Ct. 1371, 1374-75 (1980).

[452] *Payton v. New York*, 445 U.S. 573, 100 S. Ct. 1371, 1374-75 (1980).

[453] *United States v. United States Dist. Court*, 407 U.S. 297, 313, 92 S. Ct. 2125, 2134 (1972).

[454] "A person always maintains a reasonable expectation of privacy in his or her home." *Tilghman v. State*, 2021 Tex. Crim. App. LEXIS 607 (citing *Kyllo v. United States*, 533 U.S. 27, 34-40, 121 S. Ct. 2038 (2001)).

[455] *See, e.g., Stoner v. California*, 376 U.S. 483, 490, 84 S. Ct. 889 (1964) ("No less than a tenant of a house ... a guest in a hotel room is entitled to constitutional protection against unreasonable searches and seizures."); *Moberg v. State*, 810 S.W.2d 190, 194 (Tex. Crim. App. 1991). *See also United States v. Jeffers*, 342 U.S. 48 51-52, 72 S. Ct. 93 (1951) (search of a hotel room not exclusively used by a defendant invalid absent exigent circumstances or consent); *McDonald v. United States*, 335 U.S. 451, 454, 69 S. Ct. 191 (1948) (no compelling reason to justify the search of a hotel room); *Johnson v. United States*, 333 U.S. 10, 14-15, 68 S. Ct. 367 (1948) (search of a hotel room without a warrant constitutionally invalid).

[456] *Tilghman v. State*, 2021 Tex. Crim. App. LEXIS 607, at *11-*12 (citing *Comm. v. Molina*, 459 Mass. 819, 948 N.E.2d 402, 408 (Mass. 2011) ("When a guest's hotel rental period has been lawfully terminated, the guest no longer has a legitimate expectation of privacy in the hotel room."); *State v. Williams*, 2016 N.D. 132, 881 N.W.2d 618, 624 (N.D. 2016) ("Once Williams was evicted, the hotel room reverted to the control of the hotel management, Williams no longer had a privacy interest in the hotel room, and the hotel manager could consent to the officers entering the room to remove Williams' belongings."); *United States v. Bautista*, 362 F.3d 584, 586 (9th Cir. 2004) (concluding that, because defendant "was not evicted from his motel room by the manager, he retained a legitimate expectation of privacy at the time of the warrantless entry by the police.")).

on expiration of the occupancy period or for a violation of hotel policies), police are allowed to assist with facilitating the eviction, and that is not considered a violation of the person's Fourth Amendment rights.[457]

Thus, in *Tilghman v. State*,[458] after hotel management smelled marijuana smoke coming from a guest room, a hotel employee knocked on the door in an attempt to evict the guests. After this attempt was unsuccessful, a manager later requested police assistance with evicting the guests. In assisting with the eviction, police entered the hotel room and witnessed drugs in plain view. Police then arrested the occupants of the room, conducted a search of the room incident to arrest, and seized the drugs. Upon appeal, the Court held that there was no Fourth Amendment violation. Once the hotel took affirmative steps to evict the occupants of the room, those occupants no longer had a reasonable expectation of privacy in the room. As a result, the evidence seized was admissible.

3.11.1. The requirement of exigent circumstances in addition to probable cause

In *Kirk v. Louisiana*,[459] police officers conducted a surveillance of defendant's home, based on an anonymous tip that drug sales were occurring there. After witnessing what appeared to be several drug purchases and allowing the buyers to leave the area, the officers stopped one of the buyers on the street outside defendant's apartment. Immediately thereafter, the officers knocked on the door of the apartment, entered, and placed defendant under arrest. A search incident to the arrest uncovered a vial of cocaine found in defendant's underwear. In addition, while in the apartment, the officers observed other contraband in "plain view." Finding the entry, arrest and search invalid under the rule set forth in *Payton*, the United States Supreme Court said:

> Here, the police had neither an arrest warrant for [defendant], nor a search warrant for [his] apartment, when they entered his home, arrested him, and searched him. The officers testified at the suppression hearing that the reason for their actions was a fear that evidence would be destroyed, but the Louisiana Court of Appeal did not determine that such exigent circumstances were present.... As *Payton* makes plain, police officers need either a warrant or probable cause plus exigent circumstances in order to make a lawful entry into a home.[460]

3.11.2. Exigent circumstances further explored

Generally, exigent circumstances are explained as those surrounding a fast moving, often tense, series of events which call for quick and decisive law enforcement action. These are factors that allow law enforcement agents to conduct a warrantless arrest, based on probable cause, when there exists an urgent need for official action and time to secure a warrant is not available. Factors considered in determining if exigent circumstances are present include: (i) whether the crime under investigation was recently committed; (ii) whether the offense was violent in nature; (iii) whether there was a reasonable belief the suspect was armed; (iv) the level of certainty that the suspect committed the offense; (v) the level of certainty that the suspect is in the building; (vi) whether the circumstances indicate that the suspect is a flight risk; (vii) the time of day; and (viii) the level of force officers need to obtain entry to the premises.[461]

The police generally must be unable to obtain a warrant in the time necessary to meet and defuse the situation, or at the very least, contacting a magistrate must be extremely impractical (*e.g.*, late hour, remote location). In such situations, the requirement of a warrant may be excused. The presence of these extreme circumstances mandates the compelling need for quick activity and makes warrantless in-home arrests reasonable within the meaning of the Fourth Amendment. If such circumstances were not present, a warrant

---

457 *See Voelkel v. State*, 717 S.W.2d 314, 315-16 (Tex. Crim. App. 1986) (concluding that a motel guest who had stayed past checkout time and had been asked to leave by manager had "a substantially diminished expectation of privacy" in her room, such that officers who arrived and entered her room to "facilitate her eviction" did not "infringe upon [her] Fourth Amendment expectation of privacy").

458 *Tilghman v. State*, 2021 Tex. Crim. App. LEXIS 607.

459 *Kirk v. Louisiana*, 536 U.S. 635, 122 S. Ct. 2458 (2002).

460 *Kirk v. Louisiana*, 536 U.S. 635, 122 S. Ct. 2458, 2459 (2002).

461 *See, e.g., Dorman v. United States*, 435 F.2d 385 (D.C. Cir. 1970).

would be required. Often cited examples of the risks created when officers hesitate in making a warrantless in-home arrest and instead seek to obtain a warrant before acting include the following: (i) the risk of injury or death to officers or bystanders; (ii) the potential destruction or concealment of valuable evidence; or (iii) the possibility that the suspect may flee and elude capture.

3.11.2.1. Community caretaking and emergency aid

Police officers may also enter a premise without a warrant to protect individuals in distress, to assist victims of crimes that have just occurred, or to investigate suspicious signs of impending danger. For an extended discussion of the "community caretaking" function of the police and the "emergency aid" exception to the warrant requirement, refer to Sections 4.2.2.4 and 4.2.2.5.

Entering a home to stop a fight. In *Brigham City v. Stuart,*[462] four officers responded to a loud party at a residence at around 3 a.m. When they arrived, they heard sounds of an altercation occurring inside – "thumping and crashing" as well as people yelling "stop, stop" and "get off me." The officers looked in the front window but saw nothing; because the sounds seemed to be coming from the back of the house, they proceeded down the driveway to investigate further. From the end of the driveway, they could see two juveniles drinking beer in the back yard. When they entered the back yard, they saw an altercation taking place in the kitchen through a screen door and windows. "[F]our adults were attempting, with some difficulty, to restrain a juvenile." The juvenile, fists clenched, eventually "broke free, swung a fist and struck one of the adults in the face."[463] That adult then spit blood into the sink. The other three adults continued to restrain the juvenile, pressing him against a refrigerator with such force that it slid across the floor. The officers called out but were ignored. They then entered the residence and broke up the fight. The adults were arrested for contributing to the delinquency of a minor (because of the juveniles outside with beer), disorderly conduct and intoxication. The U.S. Supreme Court upheld this warrantless entry under the Fourth Amendment. According to the Court, the officers were confronted with ongoing violence. They had an objectively reasonable belief that "both the injured adult might need help and that the violence in the kitchen was just beginning." The Court noted that police are not required to wait until someone is unconscious (or semi-conscious) before entering: "The role of a peace officer includes preventing violence and restoring order, not simply rendering first aid to casualties; an officer is not like a boxing (or hockey) referee, poised to stop a bout only if it becomes too one-sided."[464]

It should be noted that law enforcement's "community caretaking" function is not a "freestanding" Fourth Amendment category which would permit warrantless searches or seizures in the home.[465] For an extended discussion of the "community caretaking" function of the police and the "emergency aid" exception to the warrant requirement, refer to Sections 4.2.2.4 and 4.2.2.5.

3.11.2.2. Hot pursuit

Hot pursuit can be thought of as a specific application of the general "exigent circumstances" exception. In *Warden v. Hayden,*[466] the U.S. Supreme Court held that if police were in hot pursuit of a fleeing suspect, they were entitled to make a warrantless entry to effectuate the arrest if they had probable cause to believe the suspect committed a felony, and they believed he entered a specific dwelling. For example, if a drug dealer runs into a house when police approach her after a controlled buy and after they identify themselves, the officers may follow her into the house to make their arrest.[467] In *Welsh v. Wisconsin,*[468] however, the United States Supreme Court held this exception was not always applicable in situations where the suspect

---

462 *Brigham City v. Stuart,* 547 U.S. 398, 126 S. Ct. 1943 (2006).
463 *Brigham City v. Stuart,* 547 U.S. 398, 126 S. Ct. 1943, 1946 (2006).
464 *Brigham City v. Stuart,* 547 U.S. 398, 126 S. Ct. 1943, 1949 (2006).
465 *Caniglia v. Strom,* 593 U.S.___, 141 S. Ct. 1596, ___ (2021).
466 *Warden v. Hayden,* 387 U.S. 294, 87 S. Ct. 1642 (1967).
467 *See Smith v. Stoneburner,* 716 F.3d 926 (6th Cir. 2013).
468 *Welsh v. Wisconsin,* 466 U.S. 740, 104 S. Ct. 2091 (1984).

commits a misdemeanor, traffic offense, or other non-jailable or minor infraction.[469] In *Stanton v. Sims,* the U.S. Supreme Court pointed out that *Welsh* did not hold that a warrantless entry to arrest a misdemeanant is never justified, "but only that such entry should be rare."[470]

In *Lange v. California,*[471] the Supreme Court emphasized that the pursuit of a fleeing misdemeanor suspect does not *always*, or more legally put, does not *"categorically"* qualify as an exigent circumstance. The circumstances in *Lange* unfolded at about 10:20 p.m., when a California highway patrol officer noticed defendant's car playing music "very loudly" near Route 12 in Sonoma County. The driver – later identified as Arthur Lange – honked the car's horn four or five times, which the officer thought strange because there were no vehicles in front of Lange. The officer began following Lange intending to conduct a traffic stop, and turned on his overhead lights to signal Lange to pull over. By that time, Lange was only about a hundred feet from his home. Lange did not stop but continued to his driveway and entered his attached garage. The officer followed him in and began questioning him. This resulted in Lange's arrest for drunk driving, and a later blood test showed a blood-alcohol content of more than three times the legal limit.

Subsequently, Lange was charged with the misdemeanor of driving under the influence of alcohol, plus a (lower-level) noise infraction. At his motion to suppress, the prosecutor argued that Lange committed a "jailable" misdemeanor when he failed to stop after the officer activated his overhead lights. According to the state, "the pursuit of a suspected misdemeanant *always* qualifies as an exigent circumstance authorizing a warrantless home entry."[472] *The United States Supreme Court disagreed.*

Said the Court:

> The flight of a suspected misdemeanant does not *always* justify a warrantless entry into a home. An officer must consider all the circumstances in a pursuit case to determine whether there is a law enforcement emergency. On many occasions, the officer will have good reason to enter – to prevent imminent harms of violence, destruction of evidence, or escape from the home. But when the officer has time to get a warrant, he must do so – even though the misdemeanant fled."[473]

Stated another way, "an officer may make a warrantless entry into a home when pursuing a fleeing misdemeanant if an exigent circumstance is also present – for example, when there is a risk of escape, destruction of evidence, or harm to others."[474]

To justify a warrantless in-home arrest based on this exception, the prosecution must generally demonstrate that: (i) the pursuit was undertaken immediately after the crime (*i.e.*, it was "hot"); and (ii) there was a continuity of pursuit from the crime to the place of arrest. Note also that a suspect may not, however, defeat an arrest which has been set in motion in a public place (*e.g.,* outside the doorway of the suspect's home), by retreating into the home.[475]

In *Winter v. State,*[476] at 11:33 p.m., Deputy Constable Travitz was on patrol in Kingwood, traveling behind a gold Corvette. His attention was first drawn to the car when he noticed it bump the right-hand curb. Travitz then noticed the vehicle "cross over the center line seven or more times." He also noticed that the speed of the car was very erratic, varying "between 32 and 50 miles per hour."[477]

The constable activated his emergency lights and air horn and attempted to stop the driver. The driver, subsequently identified as defendant John Winter, looked in his rearview mirror, but continued driving, making two turns without signaling. Ultimately, defendant turned into the driveway of his own home and pulled into the open garage. Travitz followed behind him, pulling his patrol unit into defendant's driveway, then entering the garage. As soon as defendant opened his car door, Travitz detected the odor of alcohol. "Travitz

---

469 *But see Stanton v. Sims*, 571 U.S. 3, 134 S. Ct. 3 (2013) (recognizing that courts are divided on the legality of warrantless hot-pursuit home entries for minor offenses).

470 *Stanton v. Sims*, 571 U.S. 3, 134 S. Ct. 3, 6 (2013).

471 *Lange v. California*, 594 US. ___, ___ S. Ct. ___ (2021).

472 *Lange v. California*, 594 US. ___, ___ S. Ct. ___, ___ (2021) (emphasis added).

473 *Lange v. California*, 594 US. ___, ___ S. Ct. ___, ___ (2021) (emphasis added).

474 *Lange v. California*, 594 US. ___, ___ S. Ct. ___, ___ (2021) (Kavanaugh, J., concurring).

475 *United States v. Santana*, 427 U.S. 38, 96 S. Ct. 2406 (1976).

476 *Winter v. State*, 902 S.W.2d 571 (Tex. App. 1995).

477 *Winter v. State*, 902 S.W.2d 571, 573 (Tex. App. 1995).

asked [him] to step out of the car, and appellant 'practically fell out of the vehicle.'"[478] When defendant refused to take a field sobriety test, Travitz placed him under arrest.

The court held that the warrantless "hot pursuit" entry into defendant's garage was lawful. "Travitz followed [defendant] from the time he first saw [him] bump the curb until [he] parked his car in his own garage. Travitz's pursuit of [defendant] was both immediate and continuous ... [and he] was entitled to follow [defendant] into the garage to complete the arrest."[479]

3.11.3. Consent

Naturally, an entry to a home for an arrest will be lawful when based on a valid consent. Valid consent to enter may be given by the owner, or one entitled to possession of the premises, or one with common control or joint access to the premises for most purposes. Valid consent is that which is given voluntarily (*i.e.*, in the absence of overbearing conduct on the part of the law enforcement officials seeking permission), knowingly and intelligently. Consent may be either actually given or implied from conduct or acts. The validity, or voluntariness, of consent is determined by examining all of the facts and circumstances surrounding the encounter.

Under the "consent once removed" doctrine, if: (i) an undercover officer or informant enters a residence at the express invitation of someone with authority to consent; (ii) probable cause to arrest is established; and (iii) the officer or informant immediately summons help, then other officers may enter the residence to make an arrest.[480]

3.11.4. *Payton* violations and the limits of the exclusionary rule

Exactly how far will the exclusionary rule reach when a court determines that officers have violated the rule in *Payton* by effecting a warrantless nonconsensual entry into a suspect's home in order to make a routine felony arrest? In *New York v. Harris*,[481] the Supreme Court held that only that evidence which is obtained inside the home is the proper subject of suppression. So long as police have the requisite probable cause for the suspect's arrest (for a crime), any physical evidence or statements validly obtained after the arrest and outside the home will not be suppressed when neither is "the fruit of the fact that the arrest was made in the house rather than someplace else."[482] In this respect, the Court reasoned: "Even though we decline to suppress statements made *outside* the home following a *Payton* violation, the principal incentive to obey *Payton* still obtains: the police know that a warrantless entry will lead to the suppression of any evidence found or statements taken *inside* the home." Further, the Court observed:

> Nothing in the reasoning of [the *Payton*] case suggests that an arrest in a home without a warrant but with probable cause somehow renders unlawful continued custody of the suspect once he is removed from the house. There could be no valid claim here that Harris is immune from prosecution because his person was the fruit of an illegal arrest.... Nor is there any claim that the warrantless arrest required the police to release Harris or that Harris could not be immediately rearrested if momentarily released. Because the officers had probable cause to arrest Harris for a crime, Harris was not unlawfully in custody when he was removed to the station house, given *Miranda* warnings and allowed to talk.[483]

3.11.4.1. Minor offenses

In *Welsh v. Wisconsin*,[484] the Supreme Court held that the Fourth Amendment prohibits the warrantless entry into a suspect's home to effect his arrest when the underlying offense is a "nonjailable traffic offense,"

---

478 *Winter v. State*, 902 S.W.2d 571, 573 (Tex. App. 1995).
479 *Winter v. State*, 902 S.W.2d 571, 574-75 (Tex. App. 1995).
480 *See United States v. Pollard*, 215 F.3d 643 (6th Cir. 2000).
481 *New York v. Harris*, 495 U.S. 14, 110 S. Ct. 1640 (1990).
482 *New York v. Harris*, 495 U.S. 14, 110 S. Ct. 1640, 1644 (1990).
483 *New York v. Harris*, 495 U.S. 14, 110 S. Ct. 1640, 1643 (1990).
484 *Welsh v. Wisconsin*, 466 U.S. 740, 104 S. Ct. 2091, 2093 (1984).

and the circumstances do not amount to an exigency. Hot-pursuit entries may receive different treatment by the courts.[485]

For further analysis of this issue, refer to Section 3.11.2.2 and the extended discussion of *Lange v. California*.[486]

3.12. Entry of the home of a third party

Absent consent or exigent circumstances, law enforcement officers may not lawfully "search for the subject of an arrest warrant in the home of a third party without first obtaining a search warrant." This was made clear by the United States Supreme Court in *Steagald v. United States*.[487]

In *Hudson v. State*,[488] two Department of Public Safety (DPS) investigators, obtained a warrant for the arrest of Harvey Nichols. Thereafter, the investigators set up a surveillance near the home of defendant, Kenneth Hudson, a residence where Nichols had been seen. "After some time, the agents saw Nichols enter the house. Although there was no evidence indicating Nichols was armed, dangerous, or about to escape, the agents called in two more DPS officers. After the reinforcements arrived, they rang the doorbell of [Hudson's] house, and, when no one answered, an agent kicked in the door."[489] As the officers entered, they immediately saw Nichols, "who took a 'dive' for the couch, but did not try to resist or escape. The agents then went through the residence to 'secure' it. During this process, they saw [Hudson] coming out of a bedroom, and he was taken, without resistance, to the living room and told to sit down. Because the officers had seen a bong pipe containing marihuana on the coffee table when they first entered the house, they placed all occupants of the house under arrest."[490] A further search of the premises uncovered a small quantity of methamphetamine.

The Texas Court of Criminal Appeals observed that:

> The conduct of the DPS agents clearly violates *Steagald*'s dictates. In truth, their conduct exemplifies the fear expressed in *Steagald* that, when armed with an arrest warrant, officials are free to search any house where they are "reasonably certain" the subject may be. The objectionable feature of this use of the arrest warrant is that it provides no judicial check on the police officer's assessment that the evidence available justifies an intrusion into a home of a third party.[491]

The court held that "the intrusion and subsequent search of [Hudson's] house were invalid and the methamphetamine should have been suppressed"[492] because "officers must be armed with a search warrant if they are seeking to arrest a suspect in the home of a third person, absent consent or exigent circumstances."[493]

3.13. The "knock and announce" rule

When executing an arrest warrant, law enforcement officers should knock on the door of a residence or business, announce their purpose and authority, and give the occupants a reasonable opportunity to answer before forcing their way inside.[494]

Under the rule, in order to enter a private home to make an arrest or to carry out a search, a police officer must expressly announce the purpose of his coming.[495] Along with a statement of the purpose of his coming,

---

485 *See, e.g.*, *Stanton v. Sims*, 571 U.S. 3, 134 S. Ct. 3 (2013).
486 *Lange v. California*, 594 US. ___, ___ S. Ct. ___ (2021).
487 *Steagald v. United States*, 451 U.S. 204, 101 S. Ct. 1642 (1981).
488 *Hudson v. State*, 662 S.W.2d 957 (Tex. Crim. App. 1984).
489 *Hudson v. State*, 662 S.W.2d 957, 958 (Tex. Crim. App. 1984).
490 *Hudson v. State*, 662 S.W.2d 957, 958 (Tex. Crim. App. 1984).
491 *Hudson v. State*, 662 S.W.2d 957, 959 (Tex. Crim. App. 1984).
492 *Hudson v. State*, 662 S.W.2d 957, 960 (Tex. Crim. App. 1984).
493 *Hudson v. State*, 662 S.W.2d 957, 960 (Tex. Crim. App. 1984).
494 Tex. Code Crim. Proc. art. 15.25. *See also Ker v. California*, 374 U.S. 23, 83 S. Ct. 1623 (1963).
495 *Miller v. United States*, 357 U.S. 301, 78 S. Ct. 1190 (1958).

the officer must make a request for admittance before entering the house. These requirements have the two-fold purpose of protecting the privacy of residents by preventing police entry of the home without reasonable warning; and it reduces the possibility of danger to officer and citizen alike which might result from misunderstanding and misinterpretation of the purpose of the entry.

Strict compliance with the rule may be excused in cases where exigent circumstances are present, or if events indicated that compliance with the "knock and announce" statute would be a useless gesture. Exigent circumstances exist where there is a good faith belief by the officer that evidence will be destroyed, an arrest will be frustrated or that lives will be endangered by delay. This rule applies even if a door is found open.[496] As held in *Richards v. Wisconsin*,[497] "[a] no-knock entry is justified when the police have a reasonable suspicion that knocking and announcing their presence, under the particular circumstances, would be dangerous or futile, or that it would inhibit the effective investigation of the crime, for example, allowing the destruction of evidence." This standard, held the Court, "as opposed to a probable cause requirement, strikes the appropriate balance between the legitimate law enforcement concerns at issue in the execution of search warrants and the individual privacy interests affected by no-knock entries[.] This showing is not high, but the police should be required to make it whenever the reasonableness of a no-knock entry is challenged."[498]

Pursuant to a federal Supreme Court ruling, a knock-and-announce violation does not trigger the exclusionary rule, particularly when the discovery of the evidence was independent of the officers' failure to comply with the statutory knock-and-announce requirement.[499]

3.14. Use of force to effect an arrest

Pursuant to Tex. Code Crim. Proc. art. 15.24, "In making an arrest, all reasonable means are permitted to be used to effect it. No greater force, however, shall be resorted to than is necessary to secure the arrest and detention of the accused." The general rule is that reasonable force may be used to place a suspect under arrest. The permissible quantum of force employed varies from situation to situation. The analysis applied by courts to determine the reasonableness of an officer's actions, focuses on the police conduct, viewed objectively, in light of the circumstances confronting the officers at the time, without regard to their subjective intent or motivation.

All claims that "law enforcement officers have used excessive force – deadly or not – in the course of an arrest, investigatory stop, or other 'seizure' of a free citizen should be analyzed under the Fourth Amendment and its 'reasonableness' standard, rather than under a 'substantive due process' approach."[500] In this context, a "seizure" "triggering the Fourth Amendment's protections occurs only when government actors have, by means of physical force or show of authority," in some way "restrained the liberty of a citizen."

The proper application of force in the context of an arrest or investigatory stop requires "careful attention to the facts and circumstances of each particular case, including *the severity of the crime at issue, whether the suspect poses an immediate threat to the safety of the officers or others, and whether he is actively resisting arrest or attempting to evade arrest by flight*."[501]

The ultimate inquiry is whether a reasonable officer, confronted with the same circumstances, would have reacted in the same way. Once a use of force is deemed reasonable under *Graham v. Connor,* it may not be found unreasonable by reference to some separate, earlier constitutional violation.[502]

Officers cannot use force – including pepper spray – on a detainee who has been subdued, has not been told he is under arrest, or has not been resisting arrest. Even when a suspect verbally and physically resists arrest, the use of pepper spray may constitute excessive force – for example if the crime was minor and the

---

[496] *Richards v. Wisconsin*, 520 U.S. 385, 117 S. Ct. 1416, 1421-2 (1997).

[497] *Richards v. Wisconsin*, 520 U.S. 385, 117 S. Ct. 1416 (1997).

[498] *Richards v. Wisconsin*, 520 U.S. 385, 117 S. Ct. 1416, 1421-22 (1997).

[499] *See Hudson v. Michigan*, 547 U.S. 586, 599, 126 S. Ct. 2159 (2006) ("[T]he social costs of applying the exclusionary rule to knock-and-announce violations are considerable; the incentive to such violations is minimal to begin with, and ... the massive remedy of suppressing evidence of guilt is unjustified.").

[500] *Graham v. Connor*, 490 U.S. 386, 109 S. Ct. 1865, 1871 (1989).

[501] *Graham v. Connor*, 490 U.S. 386, 109 S. Ct. 1865, 1871-72 (1989) (emphasis added).

[502] *See County of Los Angeles v. Mendez*, 581 U.S. ___, 137 S. Ct. 1539 (2017).

arrestee does not pose an immediate threat to officers. Finally, even when the use of pepper spray is justified, using a large amount (for example, enough to make a suspect pass out) or using the spray at a very close distance may constitute excessive force.[503]

In some situations, the use of deadly force is reasonable within the meaning of the Fourth Amendment. Deadly force does not mean force that necessarily results in the death of the suspect, but rather a level of force that is reasonably likely to cause death or serious bodily injury resulting in death. In *Tennessee v. Garner*,[504] the United States Supreme Court described the circumstances under which the use of deadly force may be reasonable for purposes of the Fourth Amendment. The Court said: "Where the officer has probable cause to believe that the suspect poses a threat of serious physical harm, either to the officer or to others, it is not constitutionally unreasonable to prevent escape by using deadly force." Thus, if the suspect threatens the officer with a weapon or there is probable cause to believe that he has committed a crime involving the "infliction or threatened infliction of serious physical harm," the use of deadly force is permissible. If the officer does not have probable cause to believe the above, reasonable, non-deadly force must be used to effect the arrest.

3.15. Procedures after arrest

When an individual is the subject of a warrantless arrest, he or she is entitled to a prompt judicial determination of probable cause. Note that if the person had been arrested pursuant to a warrant, a judge has already made a probable cause determination as a prerequisite to issuing the warrant.

A prompt judicial determination of probable cause has been held to mean that a judicial hearing must be held as soon as is reasonably feasible, and that should be *within 48 hours of the arrest.*[505]

A hearing provided within 48 hours may violate the promptness requirement if the arrested individual can prove that the probable cause determination was delayed in an unreasonable manner. Examples of unreasonable delays are ones for the purpose of gathering additional evidence against the defendant, or ones motivated by ill will toward the defendant. The judicial probable cause determination may be combined with other proceedings, like an arraignment. If the state fails to provide a determination within this 48-hour window, the burden of proof shifts to the government to demonstrate the existence of an emergency or other extraordinary circumstance justifying the delay. In evaluating whether a delay in a particular case is unreasonable, courts will allow a substantial degree of flexibility.

The government cannot justify the failure to provide a determination within 48 hours on the basis of an intervening weekend (*e.g.*, a person arrested on Thursday not given a hearing until Monday).

An individual arrested pursuant to a warrant must also be brought before a magistrate within 48 hours, to be informed of the accusation against him or her and of his or her rights. Be aware that this may be done via videoconference.[506]

When a student (or person believed to be a student) at a public primary or secondary school is arrested for a felony, unlawful restraint, indecent exposure, deadly conduct, terroristic threat, street gang activity, sale or possession of drugs or paraphernalia, or unlawful possession of a weapon, the arresting law enforcement agency must orally notify the superintendent in the arrestee's school district within 24 hours of the arrest or before the next school day, whichever is earlier. Within 7 days after the date the oral notice is given, the agency must mail written notification, marked "PERSONAL and CONFIDENTIAL" on the mailing envelope, to the superintendent. The written notification must include the facts contained in the oral notification, the name of the person who was orally notified, and the date and time of the oral notification. When a student at a private primary or secondary school, the agency must make the oral and written notifications to the principal of that school.[507]

No right to delay an arrest for prayer. In *Sause v. Bauer*,[508] the Supreme Court held that once an officer places a suspect under arrest and orders the suspect to enter a police vehicle for transportation to jail, the suspect has no right to delay that trip by insisting on first engaging in prayer – "conduct that, at another

---

[503] *Grawey v. Drury*, 567 F.3d 302 (6th Cir. 2009).
[504] *Tennessee v. Garner*, 471 U.S. 1, 105 S. Ct. 1694 (1985).
[505] *County of Riverside v. McLaughlin*, 500 U.S. 44, 111 S. Ct. 1661 (1991). *See also* Tex. Code Crim. Proc. art. 14.06(a).
[506] Tex. Code Crim. Proc. art. 15.17.
[507] Tex. Code Crim. Proc. art. 15.27.
[508] *Sause v. Bauer*, ___ U.S. ___, 138 S. Ct. 2561 (2018).

time, would be protected by the First Amendment." According to the Court, there is "no doubt that the First Amendment protects the right to pray. Prayer unquestionably constitutes the 'exercise' of religion. At the same time, there are clearly circumstances in which a police officer may lawfully prevent a person from praying at a particular time and place. For example, if an officer places a suspect under arrest and orders the suspect to enter a police vehicle for transportation to jail, the suspect does not have a right to delay that trip by insisting on first engaging in conduct that, at another time, would be protected by the First Amendment."[509] However, "[w]hen an officer's order to stop praying is alleged to have occurred during the course of investigative conduct that implicates Fourth Amendment rights, the First and Fourth Amendment issues may be inextricable."[510]

3.15.1. Authority to obtain fingerprints and photographs

Once a person is lawfully arrested and brought to police headquarters to be detained in custody, the person must be accurately identified. In this regard, "criminal identification is said to have two main purposes: (1) The identification of the accused as the person who committed the crime for which he is being held; and (2) the identification of the accused as the same person who has been previously charged with, or convicted of, other offenses against criminal law."[511] Thus, courts have determined that the process of fingerprinting and photographing arrestees is "a natural part of 'the administrative steps incident to arrest.'"[512] In fact, by the "middle of the 20th century, it was considered 'elementary that a person in lawful custody may be required to submit to photographing and fingerprinting as part of routine identification process.'"[513]

When the arrest is for a serious offense, taking and analyzing a cheek swab of the arrestee's DNA is, like fingerprinting and photographing, a legitimate police booking procedure that is reasonable under the Fourth Amendment.[514]

4. SEARCH & SEIZURE

4.1. The Warrant Requirement

4.1.1. Preliminary

The Fourth Amendment to the Constitution safeguards the "right of the people to be secure in their persons, houses, papers, and effects, against unreasonable searches and seizures[.]" Additionally, the Amendment commands that "no Warrants shall issue, but upon probable cause, supported by Oath or affirmation, and particularly describing the place to be searched, and the persons or things to be seized."

Generally, the United States Supreme Court has viewed a search and seizure as "*per se* unreasonable within the meaning of the Fourth Amendment unless it is accomplished pursuant to a judicial warrant issued upon probable cause and particularly describing the [places to be searched and] the items to be seized."[515] As a fundamental principle of constitutional criminal procedure, search warrants are strongly favored under both the federal Constitution and all state constitutions. The judicial preference which underscores the written warrant requirement is predicated upon the proposition that the necessity, validity and reasonableness of a prospective search or seizure can best be determined by a "neutral and detached magistrate" instead of a law enforcement officer. As the Supreme Court has stated, the warrant procedure serves primarily "to advise the citizen that the intrusion is authorized by law and [is] limited in its permissible scope[,] and to interpose

[509] *Sause v. Bauer*, ___ U.S. ___, 138 S. Ct. 2561 (2018).

[510] The Freedom of Religion clause set forth in the First Amendment clearly applies to the States through the Due Process Clause of the Fourteenth Amendment. *See Cantwell v. Connecticut*, 310 U.S. 296, 303-04, 60 S. Ct. 900, 903 (1940) (As is true with Congress, state legislatures shall make no law respecting an establishment of religion or prohibiting the free exercise thereof.).

[511] *Maryland v. King*, 569 U.S. 435, 133 S. Ct. 1958, 1975 (2013) (internal quotes and citation omitted).

[512] *County of Riverside v. McLaughlin,* 500 U.S. 44, 58, 111 S. Ct. 1661 (1991); *Maryland v. King*, 569 U.S. 435, 133 S. Ct. 1958, 1976 (2013).

[513] *Maryland v. King*, 569 U.S. 435, 459, 133 S. Ct. 1958, 1976 (2013) (quoting *Smith v. United States*, 324 F.2d 879, 882 (D.C. Cir. 1963)).

[514] *Maryland v. King*, 569 U.S. 435, 133 S. Ct. 1958, 1980 (2013).

[515] *United States v. Place*, 462 U.S. 696, 701, 103 S. Ct. 2637, 2641 (1983).

a neutral magistrate between the citizen and the law enforcement officer 'engaged in the often competitive enterprise of ferreting out crime.'"[516]

The warrant procedure is not a mere formality. As the Court put it in *McDonald v. United States*:[517]

> The presence of a search warrant serves a high function. Absent some grave emergency, the Fourth Amendment has interposed a magistrate between the citizen and the police. This was done not to shield criminals nor to make the home a safe haven for illegal activities. It was done so that an objective mind might weigh the need to invade that privacy in order to enforce the law. The right of privacy was deemed too precious to entrust to the discretion of those whose job is the detection of crime and the arrest of criminals.... And so the Constitution requires a magistrate to pass on the desires of the police before they violate the privacy of the home. We cannot be true to that constitutional requirement and excuse the absence of a search warrant without a showing by those who seek exemption from the constitutional mandate that the exigencies of the situation made that course imperative.

The driving force behind the Fourth Amendment, along with the history of its application, demonstrates that the Amendment's purpose and design is the protection of the "people" against arbitrary action by their own government. "People," for purposes of the Fourth Amendment means "people of the United States,"[518] referring to "a class of persons who are part of a national community or who have otherwise developed sufficient connections with this country to be considered part of that community."[519] Thus, it has been held that the Fourth Amendment has no application to an unlawful search and seizure conducted by federal agents outside the United States of premises owned by an alien, even though that alien (a Mexican citizen) is physically (and involuntarily) present in the United States for purposes of criminal prosecution.[520] Significantly, aliens receive constitutional protection only "when they have come within the territory of the United States and developed substantial connections with this country."[521] Consequently, "'once an alien lawfully enters and resides in this country he becomes invested with the rights guaranteed by the Constitution to all people within our borders.'"[522]

Similarly, Article 1, § 9 of the Texas Constitution provides: "The people shall be secure in their persons, houses, papers and possessions, from all unreasonable seizures or searches, and no warrant to search any place, or to seize any person or thing, shall issue without describing them as near as may be, nor without probable cause, supported by oath or affirmation." As with the Fourth Amendment, a search will be unreasonable unless it is made pursuant to a valid search warrant or justified by a recognized exception.

When an officer has obtained a warrant, upon review, an appellate court will accord "great deference" to the magistrate's finding of probable cause.[523] The federal Supreme Court's preference for a written warrant requires the reviewing court to ask only whether a reasonably cautious person could have concluded that there was a "substantial basis" for the finding of probable cause. If so, the warrant was properly issued.[524] Thus, search warrants and the underlying affidavits will be "read in a common-sense and realistic manner."

4.1.2. The search warrant affidavit

Generally, it is the law enforcement officer's responsibility to present the facts and circumstances comprising his or her probable cause to the appropriate issuing authority (judge, justice of the peace or magistrate) by

---

516 *National Treasury Employees Union v. Von Raab*, 489 U.S. 656, 109 S. Ct. 1384, 1391 (1989) (quoting *Johnson v. United States*, 333 U.S. 10, 14, 68 S. Ct. 367, 369 (1948)).

517 *McDonald v. United States*, 335 U.S. 451, 455-56, 69 Ct. 191 (1978).

518 *United States v. Verdugo-Urquidez*, 494 U.S. 259, 110 S. Ct. 1056, 1061 (1990).

519 *United States v. Verdugo-Urquidez*, 494 U.S. 259, 110 S. Ct. 1056, 1061 (1990).

520 *United States v. Verdugo-Urquidez*, 494 U.S. 259, 110 S. Ct. 1056, 1064 (1990).

521 *United States v. Verdugo-Urquidez*, 494 U.S. 259, 110 S. Ct. 1056, 1064 (1990).

522 *United States v. Verdugo-Urquidez*, 494 U.S. 259, 110 S. Ct. 1056, 1064 (1990) (citations omitted).

523 *Illinois v. Gates*, 462 U.S. 213, 103 S. Ct. 2317 (1983); *see also United States v. Leon*, 468 U.S. 897, 914, 104 S. Ct. 3405, 3416 (1984).

524 *See Illinois v. Gates*, 462 U.S. 213, 103 S. Ct. 2317 (1983); *see also United States v. Ventresca*, 380 U.S. 102, 85 S. Ct. 741 (1965); *Brinegar v. United States*, 338 U.S. 160, 69 S. Ct. 1302 (1949).

way of application. This document is the search warrant "affidavit" and the officer who swears to the facts and circumstances contained in the affidavit is referred to as the "affiant." The warrant and the affidavit or testimony on which it is based must be legally sufficient, *i.e.*, they must contain sufficient facts demonstrating probable cause to believe that evidence will be found at the house, building, or other location or place where the person, property, or thing to be searched for and seized is situated.

Pursuant to Tex. Code Crim. Proc. art. 18.01(b), "[n]o search warrant shall issue for any purpose in this state unless sufficient facts are first presented to satisfy the issuing magistrate that probable cause does in fact exist for its issuance. A sworn affidavit setting forth substantial facts establishing probable cause shall be filed in every instance in which a search warrant is requested."

4.1.3. Issuance of the warrant

Search warrants may be issued by a magistrate. A warrant may be issued to search for and seize any property or other thing that is one or more of the following:

(a) Property acquired by theft or in any other manner which makes its acquisition a penal offense;
(b) Property specially designed, made, or adapted for or commonly used in the commission of an offense;
(c) Arms and munitions kept or prepared for the purposes of insurrection or riot;
(d) Weapons prohibited by the Penal Code;
(e) Gambling devices or equipment, altered gambling equipment, or gambling paraphernalia;
(f) Obscene materials kept or prepared for commercial distribution or exhibition, subject to the additional rules set forth by law;
(g) A drug, controlled substance, immediate precursor, chemical precursor, or other controlled substance property, including an apparatus or paraphernalia kept, prepared, or manufactured in violation of the laws of this state;
(h) Any property the possession of which is prohibited by law;
(i) Implements or instruments used in the commission of a crime;
(j) Property or items, except the personal writings by the accused, constituting evidence of an offense or constituting evidence tending to show that a particular person committed an offense;
(k) Persons;
(l) Contraband subject to forfeiture under Chapter 59 of this code;
(m) Electronic customer data held in electronic storage, including the contents of and records and other information related to a wire communication or electronic communication held in electronic storage; or
(n) A cellular telephone or other wireless communications device, subject to Article 18.0215.[525]

Be aware that Justices of the Peace may not issue an evidentiary warrant pursuant to Tex. Code Crim. Proc. art. 18.02(10), although they may issue all other types of warrant included in that article, to be served within the geographical limits of the J.P.'s county.[526] In addition, a statutory county court judge lacks the authority to issue a search warrant to be executed outside of the judge's county (in contrast to an arrest warrant, which may be executed anywhere in the State).[527]

4.1.4. The particularity requirement

Under both the United States and Texas Constitutions, a warrant must "particularly describe" the place to be searched and the person and things to be seized. As stated in Article 1, § 9 of the Texas Constitution: "no

[525] Tex. Code Crim. Proc. art. 18.02(a).
[526] Tex. Code Crim. Proc. art. 18.01(c). *See also State v. Acosta*, 99 S.W.3d 301 (Tex. App. 2003); *Bitner v. State*, 135 S.W.3d 906 (Tex. App. 2004).
[527] *Sanchez v. State*, 365 S.W.3d 681 (Tex. Crim. App. 2012).

warrant to search any place, or to seize any person or thing, shall issue without describing them as near as may be, nor without probable cause, supported by oath or affirmation."

The "particularity" requirement was designed to prevent "the issue of warrants on loose, vague or doubtful bases of fact."[528] "The manifest purpose" of the requirement "was to prevent *general searches*."[529] Even before our Government came into existence, such general searches had been "deemed obnoxious to fundamental principles of liberty[, and are presently] denounced in the constitutions or statutes of every State in the Union."[530] As the Supreme Court explained in *Coolidge v. New Hampshire*,[531] the problem posed by the general warrant "is not that of intrusion *per se*, but of a general exploratory rummaging in a person's belongings." The problem is addressed by the Fourth Amendment's "particularity" requirement.[532] "By limiting the authorization to search to the specific areas and things for which there is probable cause to search, the requirement ensures that the search will be carefully tailored to its justifications and will not take on the character of the wide-ranging exploratory searches the Framers [of our Constitution] intended to prohibit."[533]

Accordingly, the specific "requirement that warrants shall particularly describe the *things to be seized* makes general searches under them impossible and prevents the seizure of one thing under a warrant describing another. As to what is to be taken, nothing is left to the discretion of the officer executing the warrant."[534] The companion requirement, that warrants shall particularly describe the *place to be searched*, is satisfied where "the description is such that the officer with a search warrant can with reasonable effort ascertain and identify the place intended."[535]

A valid warrant authorizes the executing officer to look for a particular item in any place it could logically be found. For example, illegal narcotics may be reasonably expected to be found in a dresser drawer; a stolen Harley Davidson motorcycle, on the other hand, would not.

There are two prongs of the particularity requirement: (i) a particularly described place, and (ii) particularly described items.

4.1.4.1. The places to be searched

The test for whether a sufficient description of the premises to be searched is given in a search warrant has been stated as follows: "It is enough if the description is such that the officer with a search warrant can, with reasonable effort, ascertain and identify the place intended."[536] The Texas Court of Criminal Appeals has explained, "The constitutional objectives of requiring a "particular" description of the place to be searched include: (1) ensuring that the officer searches the right place; (2) confirming that probable cause is, in fact, established for the place described in the warrant; (3) limiting the officer's discretion and narrowing the scope of his search; (4) minimizing the danger of mistakenly searching the person or property of an innocent bystander or property owner; and (5) informing the owner of the officer's authority to search that specific location."[537]

Generally, a description containing the address as it would appear on a mailing envelope, along with the name of the resident, and a cursory listing of the physical appearance of the building itself, is sufficient for single unit dwellings. Thus, in *Bonds v. State*,[538] "[d]espite listing an incorrect address and roof color, the balance of the description was sufficient to enable an officer to distinguish which property was intended to be searched.... [The officer's] familiarity with the location to be searched and that he was both the affiant

528 *Go-Bart Importing Co. v. United States*, 282 U.S. 344, 357, 51 S. Ct. 153, 158 (1931).
529 *Maryland v. Garrison*, 480 U.S. 79, 107 S. Ct. 1013, 1017 (1987) (emphasis added).
530 *Go-Bart Importing Co. v. United States*, 282 U.S. 344, 357, 51 S. Ct. 153, 158 (1931).
531 *Coolidge v. New Hampshire*, 403 U.S. 443, 467, 91 S. Ct. 2022, 2038 (1971).
532 *Coolidge v. New Hampshire*, 403 U.S. 443, 467, 91 S. Ct. 2022, 2038 (1971).
533 *Maryland v. Garrison*, 480 U.S. 79, 107 S. Ct. 1013, 1017 (1987).
534 *Marron v. United States*, 275 U.S. 192, 196, 48 S. Ct. 74, 76 (1927) (emphasis added).
535 *Steele v. United States*, 267 U.S. 498, 503, 45 S. Ct. 414, 416 (1925).
536 *Steele v. United States*, 267 U.S. 498, 503, 45 S. Ct. 414, 416 (1925) (upholding the search of 609 West 46th Street under a warrant describing the premises as 611 West 46th Street, where the building was a large warehouse having both numbers and being only partly partitioned).
537 *Bonds v. State*, 403 S.W.3d 867, 874-75 (Tex. Crim. App. 2013).
538 *Bonds v. State*, 403 S.W.3d 867 (Tex. Crim. App. 2013).

and participated in the warrant's execution were circumstances that resolved any ambiguity created by the description's errors and rendered the warrant sufficiently particular."[539]

A problem arises, however, when the place to be searched is in a multi-unit structure, like an apartment in a complex or an office in a professional building. The general rule is that the description must describe the specific sub-unit to be searched, not the whole building, unless the multi-unit character of the building is not apparent and the searching officers had no knowledge of it. If the description merely lists the address of a building which itself contains many residences or offices, and the law enforcement agents executing the warrant have no means to determine which of the individual units is to be searched, the warrant may be invalid.

Property that is within the curtilage of any dwelling house must also be described with specificity in a search warrant in order to justify a search of such property pursuant to that search warrant.

4.1.4.2. The things to be seized

The search warrant must also describe the items authorized to be seized, so that officers can reasonably identify the things intended, thus preventing a general exploratory rummaging in a person's belongings. The degree of particularity with which the items must be described will fluctuate, depending on the circumstances and individual attributes of the subject items.

Note, however, that when executing a warrant, officers may seize contraband or other evidence not listed in the warrant, in plain view, if the requirements of that doctrine are met.[540]

4.1.4.2.1. Contraband goods

Generally, a lesser standard or degree of particularity is required in a search warrant for contraband goods such as illicit drugs, automatic weapons, explosives and the like.[541]

However, in *Groh v. Ramirez*,[542] the United States Supreme Court found a search warrant was plainly invalid when it provided no description of the type of evidence sought. The fact that the *application* for the warrant adequately described the "things to be seized" did not save it, because there were no words in the warrant incorporating other documents by reference and the application did not accompany the warrant (it had been sealed). Even though the search was conducted with restraint and only items listed in the application were seized, the search was deemed to be unlawful.

4.1.5. Judicial requirements

From the foregoing discussion, it is clear that the rules require issuance of a warrant by a magistrate or judge who must, after receiving an "oath or affirmation" from the warrant applicant, make an independent, "neutral and detached" determination whether probable cause exists to believe that (1) particularly described property, (2) which is subject to official seizure, (3) may be presently found, (4) at a particular place.

4.1.5.1. The neutral and detached magistrate

A search warrant must be issued by a neutral and detached magistrate.[543] "Neutral and detached" means that the warrant must be issued by a removed, impartial judge. Neutrality and detachment require "severance

---

539 *Bonds v. State*, 403 S.W.3d 867, 876-77 (Tex. Crim. App. 2013). *See also Long v. State*, 132 S.W.3d 443 (Tex. Crim. App. 2004) (holding search of red caboose was illegal where search warrant described a silver train car but not the red caboose).

540 For a further discussion of this area of law, refer to the Plain View Doctrine, Section 5.3.

541 *United States v. Rome*, 809 F.2d 665, 670 (10th Cir. 1987); *see also United States v. Caves*, 890 F.2d 87, 93 (8th Cir. 1989) (the degree of specificity required in a search warrant varies; less specificity is required when the object of the search constitutes controlled substances); *United States v. Grimaldi*, 606 F.2d 332 (1st Cir. 1979) (finding the phrase, "other paraphernalia used in the manufacture of counterfeit federal reserve notes" to be a sufficient description of items of contraband in a search warrant).

542 *Groh v. Ramirez*, 540 U.S. 551, 124 S. Ct. 1284 (2004).

543 *State v. Duarte*, 389 S.W.3d 349, 354 (Tex. Crim. App. 2012); *State v. McLain*, 337 S.W.3d 268, 271 (Tex. Crim. App. 2011) ("As long as the magistrate had a substantial basis for concluding that probable cause existed, we will uphold the magistrate's probable cause determination.").

and disengagement" from the activities of law enforcement.[544] This requirement is premised on the notion "that a warrant authorized by a neutral and detached judicial officer is a more reliable safeguard against improper searches than the hurried judgment of a law enforcement officer[.]"[545] As stated by Justice Jackson in *Johnson v. United States*:[546] "The point of the Fourth Amendment, which often is not grasped by zealous officers, is not that it denies law enforcement the support of the usual inferences which reasonable men draw from evidence. Its protection consists in requiring that those inferences be drawn by a neutral and detached magistrate instead of being judged by the officer engaged in the often-competitive enterprise of ferreting out crime."

In *Lo-Ji Sales Inc. v. New York*, the warrant was invalid when the magistrate who issued it went along on the raid he had authorized, and determined only when he saw certain materials what was obscene, and therefore what was to be seized. Similarly, in *Coolidge v. New Hampshire*,[547] where a warrant was issued by the state attorney general, who was also actively involved in the investigation, and later prosecuted the case at trial, the initial probable cause determination was patently improper, for it was not made by an impartial and remote observer. To ensure the requisite neutrality, the issuing judge must not play a role in the investigation or the search itself.

4.1.5.2. Oath or affirmation

The Texas and United States Constitutions require that search warrants must be supported by "Oath or affirmation." As stated by the Court in *Wheeler v. State*,[548]

> [O]ne of the most fundamental tenets of search and seizure law is that a search warrant must be supported by a probable-cause affidavit that is sworn "by oath or affirmation."[549] This oath or affirmation requirement is so critical that our Legislature codified it numerous times in the Texas Code of Criminal Procedure.[550] Thus, it is well established under Texas law that a search warrant cannot properly issue without a probable-cause affidavit made under oath. "An oath is any form of attestation by which a person signifies that he is bound in conscience to perform an act faithfully and truthfully."[551] "The difference between an affidavit and an oath is that an affidavit consists of a statement of fact, which is sworn to as the truth, while an oath is a pledge."[552] Texas law has always required that the oath must be made "before" or in the presence of another to convey the solemnity and critical nature of being truthful.[553]
>
> The oath requirement is for good reason. After all, in a probable-cause affidavit, the police officer is asking that the government be allowed to invade someone's constitutional right to privacy. It is not too much to ask that the officer swear before another that he or she is telling the truth about the necessity of such a violative intrusion.... Thus, while we have recognized that certain types of procedural

---

544 *Shadwick v. City of Tampa*, 407 U.S. 345, 350, 92 S. Ct. 2119 (1972).
545 *Lo-Ji Sales Inc. v. New York*, 442 U.S. 319 (1979).
546 *Johnson v. United States*, 333 U.S. 10, 13-14, 68 S. Ct. 367, 369 (1948).
547 *Coolidge v. New Hampshire*, 403 U.S. 443, 91 S. Ct. 2022, 2029 (1971).
548 *Wheeler v. State*, 616 S.W.3d 858 (Tex. Crim. App. 2021).
549 *Tex. Const.* art. I, § 9.
550 *See Tex. Code Crim. Proc.* art. 1.06 ("No warrant to search any place or to seize any person or thing shall issue without... probable cause supported by oath or affirmation."); art. 18.01(b) ("A sworn affidavit setting forth substantial facts establishing probable cause shall be filed in every instance in which a search warrant is requested."); art. 18.01(b-1)(1) ("The magistrate may examine an applicant for a search warrant... [but that] person must be placed under oath before the examination"); art. 18.01(c) (stating that a search warrant may not be issued under Article 18.02(a)(10) unless the "sworn affidavit required by Subsection (b) sets forth sufficient facts to establish probable cause"); art. 18.01(f) (same, with respect to warrants issued under Article 18.021); art. 18.01(g) (same, with respect to warrants issued under Article 18.02(a)(12)).
551 *Vaughn v. State*, 146 Tex. Crim. 586, 589, 177 S.W.2d 59, 60 (1943).
552 *Vaughn v. State*, 146 Tex. Crim. 586, 589, 177 S.W.2d 59, 60 (1943).
553 *See Clay v. State*, 391 S.W.3d 94, 98-99 (Tex. Crim. App. 2013) ("[T]his Court has held for the better part of a hundred years that, before a written statement in support of a search warrant will constitute a 'sworn affidavit,' the necessary oath must be administered 'before' a magistrate or other qualified officer.").

irregularities may not affect the validity of a search warrant, we have been unwavering in emphasizing that the oath requirement is essential.[554]

4.1.6. The probable cause requirement

After the application and affidavit for a search warrant is submitted to the magistrate, a review is conducted to determine whether probable cause exists sufficient to warrant a reasonable person to believe that seizable property would be found in a particular place or on a particular person. The probable cause standard for issuance of a search warrant is essentially the same as that for arrest, the difference being that police must have probable cause to believe that a crime has been committed, and that there is a substantial basis for inferring a fair probability that they will find certain evidence or contraband in a particular place. Probable cause "exists when reasonably trustworthy facts and circumstances within the knowledge of the officer on the scene would lead a man of reasonable prudence to believe that the instrumentality of a crime or evidence pertaining to a crime will be found."[555] When making a probable cause determination, the issuing magistrate is entitled to consider all the circumstances surrounding an alleged crime, *i.e.*, "the totality of the circumstances."

The Texas Court of Criminal Appeals has explained:

> Neither federal nor Texas law defines precisely what degree of probability suffices to establish probable cause, but that probability cannot be based on mere conclusory statements of an affiant's belief. An affiant must present an affidavit that allows the magistrate to independently determine probable cause and the magistrate's "'action[s] cannot be a mere ratification of the bare conclusions of others.'"[556]

In addition, "although the magistrate's determination of probable cause must be based on the facts contained within the four corners of the affidavit, the magistrate may use logic and common sense to make inferences based on those facts."[557] In *Rodriguez v. State*,[558] an experienced narcotics officer received information that defendant's uncle, Cantu, was selling and transporting large amounts of cocaine in Fort Worth. Officers thereafter observed Cantu exit defendant's garage with a package which he threw into the backseat of his vehicle. After having been stopped for a traffic violation and consenting to a search of his car, the package was discovered to contain cocaine. It was fair for the magistrate to draw inferences from these facts and issue a search warrant for defendant's garage.

In *Davis v. State*,[559] a magistrate issued a search warrant based on the affiant's statement that a patrol officer drove past the defendant's residence and "could smell a strong chemical odor he has associated with the manufacture of methamphetamine emitting from the residence."[560] The Texas Court of Criminal Appeals reasoned that it was a logical inference that a police officer who smells something that he "'associat[es]' with the manufacture of methamphetamine" has had prior experience with methamphetamine.[561] Otherwise he would not recognize the smell of methamphetamine. The court concluded that when the officer's statement and its supporting inferences were combined with the other facts in the affidavit (including an informant's tip), the totality of the information provided enough support for the magistrate's decision to issue a warrant.

---

[554] *Wheeler v. State*, 616 S.W.3d 858, 863-64 (Tex. Crim. App. 2021). *See also Smith v. State*, 207 S.W.3d 787 (Tex. Crim. App. 2006) (explaining that Tex. Code Crim. Proc. art. 18.01(b) and the Fourth Amendment specifically require an oath but not a signature). *But see Hunter v. State*, 92 S.W.3d 596 (Tex. App. 2002) (concluding that although the search warrant was fatally defective, the evidence obtained when the officers executed it was admissible under the good-faith exception).

[555] *Washington v. State*, 660 S.W.2d 533, 535 (Tex. Crim. App. 1983).

[556] *Rodriguez v. State*, 232 S.W.3d 55 (Tex. Crim. App. 2007) (quoting *Illinois v. Gates*, 462 U.S. 213, 238-39, 103 S. Ct. 2317 (1983)).

[557] *State v. Elrod*, 538 S.W.3d 551, 554 (Tex. Crim. App. 2017).

[558] *Rodriguez v. State*, 232 S.W.3d 55 (Tex. Crim. App. 2007).

[559] *Davis v. State*, 202 S.W.3d 149 (Tex. Crim. App. 2006).

[560] *Davis v. State*, 202 S.W.3d 149, 150-52 (Tex. Crim. App. 2006).

[561] *Davis v. State*, 202 S.W.3d 149, 157 (Tex. Crim. App. 2006).

A criminal defendant may challenge the validity of a warrant, or the sufficiency of an affidavit, on constitutional grounds, or may allege the warrant does not fulfill the requirements of the warrant statute. A constitutional challenge would, for example, involve assertions that the facts as alleged do not establish "probable cause," or that the warrant did not "particularly" describe the place to be searched or things to be seized, as required by the Fourth Amendment. A statutory challenge would involve allegations that the procedures required by the statute were not followed by the authorities.

If the defendant shows that a search warrant contains false statements or material omissions made by the affiant either knowingly or with reckless disregard for the truth, then the remaining information in the affidavit must independently establish probable cause, or else the warrant will be invalid.[562] In this respect, the United States Supreme Court in *Franks v. Delaware*[563] set forth the procedure as follows:

> [W]here the defendant makes a substantial preliminary showing that a false statement knowingly and intentionally, or with reckless disregard for the truth, was included by the affiant in the warrant affidavit, and if the allegedly false statement is necessary to the finding of probable cause, the Fourth Amendment requires that a hearing be held at the defendant's request. In the event that at that hearing the allegation of perjury or reckless disregard is established by the defendant by a preponderance of the evidence, and, with the affidavit's false material set to one side, the affidavit's remaining content is insufficient to establish probable cause, the search warrant must be voided and the fruits of the search excluded to the same extent as if probable cause was lacking on the face of the affidavit.[564]

There is, however, "a presumption of validity with respect to the affidavit supporting the search warrant. To mandate an evidentiary hearing, the challenger's attack must be more than conclusory and must be supported by more than a mere desire to cross-examine. There must be allegations of deliberate falsehood or of reckless disregard for the truth, and those allegations must be accompanied by an offer of proof. They should point out specifically the portion of the warrant affidavit that is claimed to be false; and they should be accompanied by a statement of supporting reasons. Affidavits or sworn or otherwise reliable statements of witnesses should be furnished, or their absence satisfactorily explained. Allegations of negligence or innocent mistake are insufficient. *The deliberate falsity or reckless disregard whose impeachment is permitted today is only that of the affiant, not of any nongovernmental informant.*"[565]

4.1.6.1. The "totality of the circumstances" test

In order to determine whether probable cause exists, the magistrate or judge will utilize the "totality of the circumstances" test, which was first announced by the United States Supreme Court in *Illinois v. Gates*.[566] In *Gates*, the Court redefined over 15 years of law governing the issuance of search warrants based upon information received from police informants. The Court abandoned the rigid "two-pronged test" originally established in *Aguilar v. Texas* and *Spinelli v. United States*, and determined that in its place, the "totality of the circumstances" analysis should be used to test the sufficiency of probable cause.[567]

In so doing, the Court said: "We are convinced that this flexible, easily applied standard will better achieve the accommodation of public and private interests that the Fourth Amendment requires." According to the Court in *Gates*, the "task of the issuing magistrate is simply to make a practical, common-sense decision

---

[562] *Hyland v. State*, 574 S.W.3d 904 (Tex. Crim. App. 2019).
[563] *Franks v. Delaware*, 438 U.S. 154, 98 S. Ct. 2674 (1978).
[564] *Franks v. Delaware*, 438 U.S. 154, 155-56, 98 S. Ct. 2674, 2676 (1978).
[565] *Franks v. Delaware*, 438 U.S. 154, 171, 98 S. Ct. 2674, 2684 (1978) (emphasis added).
[566] *Illinois v. Gates*, 462 U.S. 213, 103 S. Ct. 2317 (1983).
[567] *Illinois v. Gates*, 462 U.S. 213, 232, 103 S. Ct. 2317 (1983) (citing *Aguilar v. Texas*, 378 U.S. 108, 84 S. Ct. 1509 (1964); *Spinelli v. United States*, 393 U.S. 410, 89 S. Ct. 584 (1969)).

whether, given *all the circumstances* set forth in the affidavit before him, there is a fair probability that contraband or evidence of a crime will be found in a particular place."[568]

The *Gates* Court went on to say that it considered the "totality of the circumstances" approach to be a more "practical, non-technical" concept. Thus, the "assessment of probabilities" that flows from the evidence presented in support of the warrant must be seen and weighed not in terms of library analysis by scholars, but as understood by those versed in the field of law enforcement. Under the "totality of the circumstances" approach, the facts are to be viewed collectively, not in isolation. Many times, when the facts are viewed separately and in isolation, they may be prone to innocent explanation. But "this kind of divide-and-conquer approach is improper."[569] Instead, we must look at "the whole picture."

In *Hyland v. State*,[570] the totality of circumstances gave rise to probable cause that evidence of driving while intoxicated would be found in defendant's blood. There, defendant was "known to be the driver of a motorcycle that had recently been involved in a serious, single-vehicle accident that resulted in a fatality and serious injuries to himself. Also, [the officer] detected the strong odor of alcohol emanating from [defendant's] person. Taken together, these were 'reasonably trustworthy facts and circumstances within the knowledge of' [the officer] that 'would lead a man of reasonable prudence to believe that … evidence pertaining to a crime [would] be found' in a search of Appellant's blood."[571]

Likewise, in *State v. Cuong Phu Le*,[572] the totality of the circumstances gave rise to probable cause to search. There the totality of the circumstances included: (1) a tip from a concerned citizen that was verified by police over a three-week investigation; (2) the mini blinds were drawn tightly on every window; (3) the air conditioner was running continuously on a relatively cool day; (4) no lights were visible at night; and (5) the smell of raw marijuana at the door, on defendant's person and in his car. Accordingly, "the independent and lawfully acquired information in the search-warrant affidavit — when viewed as a whole and in a common-sense manner — clearly established probable cause."[573]

Three specific aspects of the subject, regarding the nature and quality of the information itself, or the specific source from which it came, pose special problems for courts when ascertaining the existence of probable cause: (i) the facts relied upon may be too old or no longer accurate (staleness); (ii) the use of third party informants, rather than direct observation or personal knowledge; and (iii) the facts relied upon establish that a crime may take place, and evidence of that crime may be found in a certain place in the future, but not at present (anticipatory warrants).

4.1.6.2. Staleness of probable cause

The age of the information supporting a warrant application is a factor in determining probable cause. If too old, the information is stale, and probable cause may no longer exist. It is critical that probable cause to search exists *at the time a warrant is issued.* Probable cause to search is concerned with whether certain identifiable objects are probably to be found *at the present time* in a certain identifiable place. It cannot be assumed that evidence of a crime will remain indefinitely in a given place. Thus, staleness is a factor to weigh in determining if there is probable cause to search.[574]

Age alone, however, does not determine staleness. Determining whether probable cause exists is not merely an exercise in counting the days or even months between the facts relied on and the issuance of the warrant. Rather, courts will also examine the nature of the crime and the type of evidence. The circumstances will vary depending upon such factors as whether the crime is a single instance or an ongoing pattern of

568 *Illinois v. Gates*, 462 U.S. 213, 103 S. Ct. 2317 (1983) (emphasis added); *see also Massachusetts v. Upton*, 466 U.S. 727, 104 S. Ct. 2805, 2088 (1984) (The "totality of the circumstances" analysis, *i.e.*, examining the "whole picture," is "more in keeping with the practical, common-sense decision demanded of the magistrate.").

569 *District of Columbia v. Wesby*, 583 U.S. ___, 138 S. Ct. 577, 589 (2018).

570 *Hyland v. State*, 574 S.W.3d 904 (Tex. Crim. App. 2019).

571 *Hyland v. State*, 574 S.W.3d 904, 913 (Tex. Crim. App. 2019) (quoting *Washington v. State*, 660 S.W.2d 533, 535 (Tex. Crim. App. 1983)).

572 *State v. Cuong Phu Le*, 463 S.W.3d 872 (Tex. Crim. App. 2015).

573 *State v. Cuong Phu Le*, 463 S.W.3d 872, 879-80 (Tex. Crim. App. 2015).

574 *See Sgro v. United States*, 287 U.S. 206, 210-12, 53 S. Ct. 138, 140-41 (1932) ("it is manifest that the proof must be of facts so closely related to the time of the issue of the warrant as to justify a finding of probable cause at that time").

protracted violations, whether the inherent nature of a scheme suggests that it is probably continuing, and the nature of the property sought, that is, whether it is likely to be promptly disposed of or retained by the person committing the offense.[575]

There are, therefore, a number of factors that a court may consider when determining whether the information supporting the issuance of a warrant has grown stale. These factors include: (1) the nature and quality of the seized evidence (whether perishable and easily transferable or of enduring utility to its holder); (2) the ease with which the evidence may be disposed of; (3) the character of the place to be searched (whether one of incidental use for mere convenience or a secure base of operations); (4) the lapse of time between the information and the warrant; (5) the character of the criminal (whether isolated and fleeting or entrenched); and (6) the character of the crime (whether chance encounter or an entrenched, continuing illegal scheme).

Texas courts have rejected staleness claims when an affidavit recites observations that are consistent with ongoing drug activity at a defendant's residence. In *Jones v. State*, the court observed, "'evidence of ongoing criminal activity will generally defeat a claim of staleness.'"[576] Noting that, in appropriate circumstances, "years could pass without information becoming stale," the court explained that the passage of time is less significant in cases of criminal activity of a "protracted or continuous nature."[577]

4.1.6.3. The "four corners" test

In analyzing whether probable cause exists to issue a search warrant, a reviewing court will use the "four corners test." This test requires that sufficient facts must appear on the face of the affidavit so that the reviewing court may judge whether the factual basis in the document alone provides probable cause. Thus, "[t]he core of the Fourth Amendment's warrant clause and its Texas equivalent is that a magistrate may not issue a search warrant without first finding 'probable cause' that a particular item will be found in a particular location. The test is whether a reasonable reading by the magistrate would lead to the conclusion that the four corners of the affidavit provide a "substantial basis" for issuing the warrant."[578]

The "four corners" test appears frequently in case law to support the principle that reviewing courts should consider only that information contained in the underlying affidavit in their probable cause review. In this regard, sufficient facts must appear on the face of the affidavit so that a magistrate's personal knowledge notwithstanding, a reviewing court can verify the existence of probable cause.[579]

In *State v. Duarte*,[580] the court did not allow an affidavit that was "based almost entirely on hearsay information supplied by a first-time confidential informant."[581] The court observed that the affiant's basis for finding the informant reliable were not demonstrated within the four corners of the affidavit. Moreover, the court took issue with the "boilerplate" nature of the affidavit noting that "it contained insufficient particularized facts about appellee's alleged possession to allow the magistrate to determine probable cause to issue a search warrant."[582] The motion to suppress was properly granted.

---

[575] *See, e.g., United States v. Foster*, 711 F.2d 871, 878 (9th Cir. 1983) ("The passage of time is not necessarily a controlling factor in determining the existence of probable cause. The court should also evaluate the nature of the criminal activity and the kind of property for which authorization to search is sought."); *Andresen v. State*, 24 Md. App. 128, 331 A.2d 78 (1975), *aff'd sub nom. Andresen v. Maryland*, 427 U.S. 463, 96 S. Ct. 2737 (1976) (considering the character of the crime, the criminal, the thing to be seized, and the place to be searched). The staleness inquiry is another component of the overall inquiry, which requires that the factual information provided in the affidavit establishes a fair probability that the evidence sought will be found at the location sought to be searched. *See United States v. Spikes*, 158 F.3d 913, 923-24 (6th Cir. 1998).

[576] *Jones v. State*, 364 S.W.3d 854, 861 (Tex. Crim. App. 2012) (quoting *United States v. Greene*, 250 F.3d 471, 481 (6th Cir. 2001)).

[577] *Jones v. State*, 364 S.W.3d 854, 861 (Tex. Crim. App. 2012).

[578] *State v. Duarte*, 389 S.W.3d 349, 354 (Tex. Crim. App. 2012) (citations omitted).

[579] *See Illinois v. Gates*, 462, U.S. 213, 238, 103 S. Ct. 2317, 2332 (1983) ("The task of the issuing magistrate is simply to make a practical, common-sense decision whether, given all the circumstances set forth in the affidavit before him, including the 'veracity' and 'basis of knowledge' of persons supplying hearsay information, there is a fair probability that contraband or evidence of a crime will be found in a particular place.").

[580] *State v. Duarte*, 389 S.W.3d 349 (Tex. Crim. App. 2012).

[581] *State v. Duarte*, 389 S.W.3d 349, 355 (Tex. Crim. App. 2012).

[582] *State v. Duarte*, 389 S.W.3d 349, 357 (Tex. Crim. App. 2012).

4.1.7. Sources of information/informants

Law enforcement officers do not often rely on their own direct observations to provide the underlying facts supporting a warrant. In so many cases, a third-party will provide documentation of a crime's commission, and detail where evidence or contraband can be found. In this regard, one of the most valuable assets in the law-enforcement battle against crime is the police informant. In fact, over the course of time, the proper utilization of information imparted by informants has led the courts to "consistently accept the use of informants in the discovery of evidence of a crime as a legitimate investigatory procedure consistent with the Constitution."[583]

Generally, informants are classified into three distinct types: criminal informants, citizen informants, and anonymous tips. The "type" of informant becomes important when a determination must be made as to whether the information imparted provides a sufficient constitutional justification for a particular police action. Moreover, knowledge of the type of informant the police are dealing with becomes critical when a determination must be made as to how much independent police investigation must be employed to verify or corroborate the information reported. Thus, courts will consider the following factors in determining whether the hearsay information provided by an informant generates probable cause: (1) the reliability of the informant; (2) the details contained in the informant's tip; and (3) the degree to which the tip is corroborated by independent police surveillance and information. One factor alone should not control the judge's decision. For example, if an informant's tip is sufficiently corroborated by independent police work, then the tip may form the basis for probable cause even if little is known about the informant's reliability.

4.1.7.1. Criminal informants

In the totality-of-the-circumstances analysis, the reliability of a criminal informant's hearsay information, along with the informant's credibility, remains a relevant inquiry. In fact, the hallmark of the competent criminal investigator is the ability to clearly and thoroughly document in an affidavit not only the credibility of his or her confidential informant but the reliability of the information relayed and the informant's basis of knowledge. These items are "closely intertwined issues" which make up the "commonsense, practical question whether there is 'probable cause' to believe that contraband or evidence is located in a particular place."[584]

Perhaps the most common way reliability is established is by documenting the past use of the particular informant and the number of times the information imparted by that informant proved not only to be true and correct but also led to the arrest and successful prosecution of the subject of the information. A mere bare bones statement in an affidavit that an informant is reliable and has proved to be reliable in the past is not enough. Officers should strive to include: (1) how often the informant has been used; (2) the nature or character of the investigations in which the informant has previously supplied information (*e.g.*, narcotics, burglary, stolen property, arson, etc.); (3) how many times the information proved to be true and correct; (4) whether the information led to the arrest of the subject of the information; and (5) whether the subsequent prosecution led to conviction. Naturally, if any of the aforementioned indicators of reliability is absent or unknown, the affidavit would merely be silent in that regard.[585]

In *State v. Duarte*,[586] a first-time CI told a San Antonio officer that he had seen cocaine "in the possession of defendant" within the previous 24 hours; the CI gave the tip in the hope of having pending charges reduced or dismissed. Never having given information before, this CI obviously was untested. Nor did the CI make a statement against penal interest – there was no indication the CI was the one who supplied this cocaine or shared possession of it with defendant. Moreover, the court noted that this CI was from the criminal milieu – a "snitch" whose motive was entirely self-serving – not a citizen-informant who could be presumed to be

[583] *Arizona v. Fulminante*, 499 U.S. 279, 111 S. Ct. 1246, 1262-63 (1991) (Rehnquist, C.J., dissenting in part).

[584] *Illinois v. Gates*, 462 U.S. 213, 103 S. Ct. 2317, 2328 (1983).

[585] Excerpts from the comprehensive discussion of the laws of arrest, search and seizure in Larry E. Holtz, *Criminal Procedure for Law and Justice Professionals* (Blue360° Media); *see also United States v. Winarske*, 715 F.3d 1063 (8th Cir. 2013) (informant deemed reliable because of his "track record of providing accurate information on local criminal activity" where "his tips were accurate enough to lead police to solve about a dozen open burglary cases").

[586] *State v. Duarte*, 389 S.W.3d 349 (Tex. Crim. App. 2012).

honest. While the CI gave first-hand information, the tip contained no particular level of detail describing defendant's premises or his criminal activity. The court noted that the CI did not indicate how much cocaine defendant had – "A couple of lines worth, laid out at a party and fully consumed? A kilo?'' – or where defendant kept the drug – "In the pocket of his jeans? Hidden in the attic? Was it piled on the kitchen table being weighed and packaged for sale?" There was no evidence defendant was engaged in drug-dealing, so it was possible he already had used whatever cocaine the CI had seen him possess. Nor was there a prediction of future behavior, or corroboration by other informants. In addition, police only confirmed that defendant lived at the address given by the CI; there was no surveillance of defendant's house, or research into his criminal record. In sum, the affidavit for the warrant contained insufficient particularized facts about defendant's alleged possession to allow the magistrate to determine probable cause to issue a search warrant. Evidence found pursuant to the warrant was suppressed.

In *Blake v. State*,[587] a Texas City officer received information from a confidential informant that persons living at 1024 Pin Oak in Dickinson were in possession of methamphetamine, cocaine, and crack cocaine. The officer had successfully executed several search warrants in the past based on this CI's information. The CI had also provided information to an agent with the Galveston County Narcotics Task Force which "resulted in the arrest of numerous defendants and the seizure of crack cocaine, marijuana, and currency." Therefore, the CI was credible and reliable. In addition, the CI claimed to have been in the suspect residence within the past two days, and described the glassware, tubes, and microwaves used to manufacture the methamphetamine, as well as the strong smell of chemicals that permeated the residence. Thus, the informant's basis of knowledge was clearly first-hand, personal observation. The CI's tips established probable cause to search the Pin Oak residence.

Reliability may also be adequately established if, during the course of supplying information, the informant supplies his own name to the police and includes a "statement against his penal interest."[588] For example, consider the case where the informant admits to buying narcotics on several occasions from a named individual. In such a case – where the informant admits to criminal conduct during the course of supplying information to the police – "[c]ommon sense in the important daily affairs of life would induce a prudent and disinterested observer to credit these statements. People do not lightly admit a crime and place critical evidence in the hands of the police in the form of their own admissions."[589] As the D.C. Circuit Court pointed out in *United States v. Clark*,[590] "officers could reasonably believe that precisely because [the informant] was actively engaged in drug trafficking, he would know – and thus be able to identify – the source of his trading goods; furthermore, because he was seeking leniency at the hands of the law, [the informant] would have little reason to prove himself an unreliable informant."

State v. Elrod[591] is a good example. There, the named informant, Stovall, was an eyewitness to the criminal activity because she was involved in it. Her statement gave investigators detailed information. The court commented favorably, "Investigator Smith's affidavit is sufficiently detailed to suggest direct knowledge on Stovall's part. Stovall was able to give details about the alleged criminal activity because she was participating in it, and she had first-hand knowledge of the alleged counterfeit and mail and identity theft operation she was describing. The magistrate did not have to rely upon a presumption of reliability, but rather was able to assess Stovall's reliability based upon the details she provided."[592]

Reliability may be further enhanced if the informant provides the police with such information with the hope of changing his or her criminal ways. Indeed, we are in a time when cocaine addiction is on the verge of epidemic proportion, and the public is extensively aware of the devastation created by it. Consequently, when a cocaine user voluntarily turns in his supplier to the police in the hope of shaking his reliance on the drug, and in doing so admits to his own criminal conduct, *such evidence sharply increases the degree of reliability* needed for the issuance of a search warrant.

---

587 *Blake v. State*, 125 S.W.3d 717 (Tex. App. 2003).
588 *United States v. Harris* 403 U.S. 573, 583, 91 S. Ct. 2075, 2081-82 (1971).
589 *United States v. Harris* 403 U.S. 573, 583, 91 S. Ct. 2075, 2082 (1971).
590 *United States v. Clark*, 24 F.3d 299, 303 (D.C. Cir. 1994).
591 *State v. Elrod*, 538 S.W.3d 551 (Tex. Crim. App. 2017).
592 *State v. Elrod*, 538 S.W.3d 551, 559 (Tex. Crim. App. 2017).

The informant's basis of knowledge may be established by documenting, in as much detail as possible, the informant's personal observations. This establishes how (and when) the informant came by his or her information, and demonstrates what precisely the informant personally saw, heard, smelled, tasted or touched. Persuasive in this regard would be details of the physical appearance of the target residence, exactly where in the residence the subject keeps or conceals the evidence or contraband, what the evidence or contraband looked like, how it was packaged, the name and detailed physical description of the subject and others who may also live at or occasion the target premises, and so on.[593] This type and degree of detail not only fortifies the reliability of the information supplied but constitutes a material consideration in the totality-of-the-circumstances analysis. Indeed, even if the informant's statements and the events the informant describes "diverge in minor ways, the magistrate may reasonably choose to credit the statements and disregard petty inconsistencies."[594]

The final ingredient in the totality-of-the-circumstances approach calls for the independent corroboration of as many of the facts relayed by the informant as possible. If time permits, all the information relayed should be confirmed by independent investigation. In this respect, a deficiency in any of the foregoing elements may be counterbalanced by the officer's independent investigation – the touchstone of the totality-of-the-circumstances approach.[595]

4.1.7.2. Citizen informants

In marked contrast to the criminal informant, an ordinary citizen presumably has no ties or connections with the criminal world. In this respect, courts will impart an assumption grounded in common experience that such a person, regarded as a law-abiding and cooperative member of the general public, is motivated by factors that are consistent with law enforcement goals. Consequently, an individual of this kind may be regarded as trustworthy and the information imparted by him or her to a law enforcement officer concerning a criminal episode would not especially entail further exploration or verification of the citizen's personal credibility or reliability before suitable action may be taken.

Clearly, a different rationale exists for establishing the reliability of named "citizen-informers" as opposed to the traditional idea of unnamed police contacts or informers who usually themselves are criminals. Information supplied to officers by the traditional police informer is not given in the spirit of a concerned citizen, but often is given in exchange for some concession, payment, or simply out of revenge against the subject. The nature of these persons and the information which they supply convey a certain impression of unreliability, and it is proper to demand that some evidence of their credibility and reliability be shown. As previously noted, one practical way of making such a showing is to point to accurate information which they have supplied in the past.

However, an ordinary citizen who reports a crime which has been committed in his presence, or that a crime is being or will be committed, stands on much different ground than a police informer. He is a witness to criminal activity who acts with an intent to aid the police in law enforcement because of his concern for society or for his own safety. He does not expect any gain or concession in exchange for his information. An informer of this type usually would not have more than one opportunity to supply information to the police.

Credibility and reliability in this respect may be further enhanced if the particular citizen is "more than the ordinary citizen," for example, fire fighters, first aid or ambulance squad members, security personnel and the like. These individuals, while not sworn law enforcement officers, are more involved and presumably more public spirited than the average citizen, and in and of themselves may be considered credible sources of information.

---

[593] *See, e.g., United States v. Hill*, 91 F.3d 1064, 1069 (8th Cir. 1996) (confidential informant's report was based on *direct observations* of the subject, entitling "'his tip to greater weight than might otherwise be the case'") (quoting *Illinois v. Gates*, 462 U.S. 213, 234, 103 S. Ct. 2317, 2330 (1983)).

[594] *See United States v. Schaefer*, 87 F.2d 562, 567 (1st Cir. 1996); *United States v. Zayas-Diaz*, 95 F.3d 105, 112 (1st Cir. 1996).

[595] Excerpts from the comprehensive discussion of the laws of arrest, search and seizure in Larry E. Holtz & Warren J Spencer, *Texas Criminal and Traffic Procedural Manual – An In-Depth Guide on How to Apply the Laws of Arrest, Search and Seizure, Confessions, & Eyewitness Identification* (Blue360° Media).

Finally, the information imparted by a citizen-informer who is himself or herself a victim or complainant, should be taken at face value.[596] Particularly when an informant is named, his or her reliability may be presumed, and the affidavit need only establish that his observations arise from personal knowledge.

In *Flores v. State*,[597] a Hayes County officer received a call from a concerned citizen reporting drug activity at a residence on Ramona Circle in San Marcos. The caller wished to remain anonymous for personal safety. Although the caller could not give an exact address, he stated that a black F-150 truck and gold Firebird were usually parked outside and that defendant Felix Flores resided there with his girlfriend, a white female he knew only as "Tiffany." The caller claimed to have observed a quantity of cocaine inside the residence in the past. The officer drove to Ramona Circle and found a residence with a black F-150 and gold Firebird parked outside. A license plate check revealed the truck was registered to Felix Flores. A utility subscriber check of the residence revealed the residence's account was in the name of "Tiffany Wardell"; a check of Ms Wardell's license indicated she lived at the residence. Police then performed two trash pulls, warrantless searches of trash left outside the curtilage for collection. The first pull discovered two empty packs of rolling papers and a plastic bag with a small amount of marijuana residue; the second pull, four days later, located several marijuana stems, seeds and marijuana residue. The officer's investigation sufficiently confirmed the anonymous caller's tip, giving police probable cause to obtain a warrant.

In *State v. Cuong Phu Le*,[598] the informant was a concerned neighbor. The citizen "observed young Asian males arriving at the residence though no one had moved any furniture into the home. The young Asian males would arrive at the residence in the early evening hours, remain for a short period of time, and then depart. They did not engage in any normal household activities such as yard work or washing cars. The concerned citizen did not see any lights inside the residence even when the young males visited the home during the evening hours."[599] The court noted with favor that the tip came from a citizen in good standing in the community. Said the court, "A citizen-informer is presumed to speak honestly and accurately; the criminal snitch who is making a quid pro quo trade enjoys no such presumption. The citizen informant in this case had no criminal history or driver's license suspensions and had been a home owner in Harris County for numerous years. The citizen informant remained accountable to [the police] despite requesting anonymity due to safety considerations. And ... the citizen informant ... provided sufficient information to evaluate the basis of the informant's knowledge or veracity."[600] Based on the totality of circumstances, including the tip, the information contained in the search warrant established probable cause to search.

4.1.7.3. Fellow officers

During the course of various types of investigations, police must rely on facts and information imparted by fellow officers. As a general rule, courts will consider information stemming from the observations and discoveries of fellow officers inherently trustworthy, and consequently, further exploration or verification of a fellow officer's personal credibility or reliability is not required. In this respect, the Supreme Court has determined that "[o]bservations of fellow officers of the Government engaged in a common investigation are plainly a reliable basis for a warrant applied for by one of their number."[601]

---

[596] *See, e.g., Easton v. City of Boulder*, 776 F.2d 1441, 1449 (10th Cir. 1985) ("[T]he skepticism and careful scrutiny usually found in cases involving informants, sometimes anonymous, from the criminal milieu, is appropriately relaxed if the informant is an identified victim."); *see also Sharrar v. Felsing*, 128 F.3d 810, 818 (3d Cir. 1997) ("When a police officer has received a reliable identification by a victim of his or her attacker, the police have probable cause to arrest.").

[597] *Flores v. State*, 319 S.W.3d 697 (Tex. Crim. App. 2010).

[598] *State v. Cuong Phu Le*, 463 S.W.3d 872 (Tex. Crim. App. 2015).

[599] *State v. Cuong Phu Le*, 463 S.W.3d 872, 874 (Tex. Crim. App. 2015).

[600] *State v. Cuong Phu Le*, 463 S.W.3d 872, 878 (Tex. Crim. App. 2015) (citing *State v. Duarte*, 389 S.W.3d 349, 356 (Tex. Crim. App. 2012)).

[601] *United States v. Ventresca*, 380 U.S. 102, 111, 85 S. Ct. 741, 747 (1965); *see also United States v. Griffin*, 827 F.2d 1108, 1112 (7th Cir. 1987) (the "'affiant's fellow agents'" may "'plainly [] be regarded as a reliable source by the magistrate'") (quoting *United States v. Pritchard*, 745 F.2d 1112, 1120 (7th Cir. 1984)). *Accord United States v. Cooper*, 949 F.2d 737, 745 (5th Cir. 1991) (if the combined knowledge of police from two different jurisdictions was such that they collectively had probable cause to believe criminal evidence was located in a robbery suspect's car, officers from either jurisdiction could lawfully have conducted a warrantless search).

4.1.7.4. Anonymous tips

Of all the types of information acted upon by law enforcement, the anonymous tip requires the most independent verification. By its very nature, the anonymous tip carries with it none of the traditional indicators of reliability which may attach to information imparted by citizen informants or even criminal informants. Thus, to develop the reliability of information imparted by the anonymous tip, officers must engage in two critical procedures: (1) comprehensive detail development; and (2) independent verification.[602]

First, the individual who takes the call or receives the information must elicit as much detail as possible from the informer. Comprehensive detail development is crucial; it demonstrates the anonymous informant's "basis of knowledge," and provides substance and meaning to the second procedure in the development of reliability. Naturally, the call-taker should not initially attempt to ascertain the caller's identity. It is all too often that the question, "What is your name?", is followed by the sound of a dial tone. Rather, the call-taker should try to ascertain as much detail as possible as to what exactly the caller has observed (or is presently observing), the physical description of the subject of the caller's observations, how far away the subject was (or is presently) from the caller, whether the caller is presently watching the subject and if not, how long ago the observations were made, the exact location of the subject, whether there were or presently are any other people or vehicles in the area, and whether the caller would stay on the line while officers are dispatched. Once the call-taker has elicited as much detail as possible from the caller, the call-taker may then consider asking more "dangerous" questions, such as, "Are you a resident of the neighborhood?" "Do you live next to where these things are taking place?" "Where do you live?" "What is your name?"

The second step requires independent investigation directed at confirming or verifying each of the facts related in the anonymous tip. It is this independent corroboration which provides a foundation for a reviewing court to conclude that a substantial basis exists for crediting the hearsay information imparted by the anonymous tip. Significantly, as the officer proceeds to corroborate each of the details of the tip, it becomes increasingly evident that "'[b]ecause [the] informant is right about some things, he is more probably right about other facts[.]'"[603] Once an officer has personally verified every possible facet of the information contained in the tip, reasonable grounds may then exist to believe that the remaining unverified bit of information – that a criminal offense is occurring, or has occurred – is likewise true.[604] As the United States Supreme Court has stated, "such tips, particularly when supplemented by independent police investigation, frequently contribute to the solution of otherwise 'perfect crimes.'"[605]

4.1.8. Warrant execution; serving the warrant

4.1.8.1. Service

In general, a search warrant must be executed within three whole days, exclusive of its day of issuance and day of execution.[606] This means three calendar days – a warrant may be executed up until midnight of the last day, even if more than 72 hours have passed since its issuance.[607]However, officers have up to 15 whole days to execute a warrant solely to search for and seize a blood or saliva sample from a specific person for DNA analysis and comparison.[608]

A warrant issued for electronic customer data held in electronic storage, including the contents of and records and other information related to a wire or electronic communication held in electronic storage, by

---

[602] Larry E. Holtz & Warren J Spencer, *Texas Criminal and Traffic Procedural Manual – An In-Depth Guide on How to Apply the Laws of Arrest, Search and Seizure, Confessions, & Eyewitness Identification* (Blue360° Media).

[603] *Illinois v. Gates*, 462 U.S. 213, 234, 103 S. Ct. 2317, 2335 (1983) (quoting *Spinelli v. United States*, 393 U.S. 410, 427, 89 S. Ct. 584, 594 (1969) (White, J., concurring)).

[604] *Draper v. United States*, 358 U.S. 307, 79 S. Ct. 329 (1959).

[605] *Illinois v. Gates*, 462 U.S. 213, 234, 103 S. Ct. 2317, 2332 (1983). Excerpts from the comprehensive discussion of the laws of arrest, search and seizure in Larry E. Holtz, *Criminal Procedure for Law Enforcement and Criminal Justice Professionals* (Blue360° Media).

[606] Tex. Code Crim. Proc. art. 18.07(a)(3).

[607] *Gonzalez v. State*, 768 S.W.2d 436 (Tex. App. 1989).

[608] Tex. Code Crim. Proc. art. 18.07(a)(1).

a provider of an electronic communications service or a provider of a remote computing service must be executed within 10 whole days.[609]

If a warrant is issued to search for and seize data or information contained in or on a computer, disk drive, flash drive, cell phone, or other electronic, communication, or data storage device, the warrant is considered to have been executed within three days if the device was seized before the expiration of the time allowed. Any data or information contained in or on a device seized may be recovered and analyzed after the expiration of the three-day limitation on the warrant.[610]

A search warrant may be served at any time of the day or night. The timing of the search is generally within the discretion of police officers — for example, they may delay a search until an individual arrives or leaves the location involved.[611]

Not later than three whole days after executing a search warrant, the officer shall return the search warrant. Upon returning the search warrant, the officer shall state on the back of the same, or on some paper attached to it, the manner in which the warrant has been executed.[612]

4.1.8.2. Entry and the "knock and announce" rule

Prior to entering a dwelling to execute a search warrant, police must knock and announce their presence, authority and purpose, and demand entry. This common law "knock and announce" principle "forms a part of the reasonableness inquiry under the Fourth Amendment."[613] The rule requires "notice in the form of an express announcement by the officers of their [authority and] purpose for demanding admission."[614] Compliance with the rule "is also a safeguard for the police themselves who might be mistaken for prowlers and be shot down by a fearful householder."[615] The roots of the "knock and announce" rule can be traced back through the English common law at least as far as the 1603 opinion in *Semayne's* case.[616]

Accordingly, the "knock and announce" rule has three underlying purposes: (1) to reduce the risk of violence that inheres in an unannounced, forced entry; (2) to protect privacy by reducing the risk of entering the wrong premises; and (3) to prevent unnecessary physical damage to the property.

Officers are required to adhere to the "knock and announce" rule even if the entry could be made without the use of force, *i.e.*, by merely opening a closed but unlocked door,[617] or by the use of a passkey.[618] As the Supreme Court stated in *Sabbath*: "An unannounced intrusion into a dwelling ... is no less an unannounced intrusion whether officers break down a door, force open a chain lock on a partially open door, open a locked door by use of a passkey, or, as here, open a closed but unlocked door."[619]

There is no constitutional mandate that an officer must knock and announce before entering a dwelling in every instance. Over the course of time, courts have recognized several exceptions to the "knock and announce" rule. Exceptions recognized to date include a reasonable suspicion that knocking and announcing would:

(1) present a threat of physical violence, *e.g.*, where the officers' peril would be increased if knocking preceded entry;
(2) be futile or a "useless gesture" (for example, where a prisoner escapes from the police and retreats to his dwelling, knocking and announcing would be considered a "useless gesture" or a "senseless ceremony" prior to entering the premises to regain custody of the escaping offender; *or* when no one is home at the target premises, knocking and announcing would be futile or a "useless gesture" when there is no one present to hear the police knocking);

609 Tex. Code Crim. Proc. art. 18.07(a)(2).
610 Tex. Code Crim. Proc. art. 18.07(c).
611 *Allen v. State*, 249 S.W.3d 680 (Tex. App. 2008).
612 Tex. Code Crim. Proc. art. 18.10.
613 *Wilson v. Arkansas*, 514 U.S. 927, 115 S. Ct. 1914 (1995).
614 *Miller v. United States*, 357 U.S. 301, 309, 78 S. Ct. 1190, 1196 (1958).
615 *Miller v. United States*, 357 U.S. 301, 313 n.12, 78 S. Ct. 1190, 1198 n.12 (1958).
616 *Semayne's* case, 5 Coke 91, 77 Eng.Rep. 194 (K.B. 1603).
617 *Sabbath v. United States*, 391 U.S. 585, 88 S. Ct. 1755 (1968).
618 *Munoz v. United States*, 325 F.2d 23 (9th Cir. 1963).
619 *Sabbath v. United States*, 391 U.S. 585, 590, 88 S. Ct. 1755, 1798 (1968).

(3) cause the arrest to be frustrated, when entry of a premises is necessary to execute an "arrest" warrant or effect a warrantless arrest with exigent circumstances; or

(4) result in the loss or destruction of evidence, and immediate action is required to preserve the evidence.[620]

Thus, in *Jeffrey v. State*,[621] the court found sufficient evidence of exigent circumstances to allow a mere five-second delay between the knock and the entry. There, after knocking three times on the front door, the deputy heard the sound of running. The court held, "The approximately five second wait, combined with the sound, coming from inside the house, of someone running in reaction to the knocking, provided the deputies with specific articulable facts creating reasonable suspicion that further delay would result in the suspects fleeing the scene or destroying evidence."[622]

In *Richards v. Wisconsin*,[623] however, the United States Supreme Court refused to adopt a blanket exception for felony drug investigations, rejecting the Wisconsin rule that

> police officers are never required to knock and announce their presence when executing a search warrant in a felony drug investigation." Rather, in order "to justify a no-knock entry, *the police must have a reasonable suspicion that knocking and announcing their presence, under the particular circumstances, would be dangerous or futile, or that it would inhibit the effective investigation of the crime by, for example, allowing the destruction of evidence.* This standard – as opposed to a probable cause requirement – strikes the appropriate balance between the legitimate law enforcement concerns at issue in the execution of search warrants and the individual privacy interests affected by no-knock entries.... This showing is not high, but the police should be required to make it whenever the reasonableness of a no-knock entry is challenged.[624]

Naturally, if at the time of search warrant procurement, the affiant possesses a reasonable suspicion that one or more of the foregoing factors are present, a judge would be "acting within the Constitution to authorize a 'no knock' entry."[625]

4.1.8.2.1. The time between the announcement and the entry

Officers may not knock and announce their presence, authority, and purpose and *immediately* enter the target premises. Although there is no set time for every case, to pass constitutional muster, the time lapse between the police announcement and any forced entry must be reasonable under the circumstances, but not necessarily extensive in length.

In *United States v. Banks*,[626] the U.S. Supreme Court held that, under the "totality of the circumstances" presented, a 15- to 20-second wait between an officer's knock and announcement of authority and the forcible entry satisfied the Fourth Amendment. In *Banks*, based on information that Banks was selling cocaine at his home, police officers and FBI agents obtained a warrant to search his two-bedroom apartment. "As soon as they arrived there, about 2 o'clock on a Wednesday afternoon, officers posted in front called out 'police search warrant' and rapped hard enough on the door to be heard by officers at the back door. There was no indication whether anyone was home, and after waiting for 15 to 20 seconds with no answer, the officers broke open the front door with a battering ram."[627] Banks was in the shower at the time. The search uncovered weapons, crack cocaine, and other evidence of drug dealing.

---

[620] *See Wilson v. Arkansas*, 514 U.S. 927, 115 S. Ct. 1914, 1919 (1995); *United States v. Banks*, 540 U.S. 31, 124 S. Ct. 521, 525 (2003).

[621] *Jeffery v. State*, 169 S.W.3d 439 (Tex. App. 2005).

[622] *Jeffery v. State*, 169 S.W.3d 439, 445 (Tex. App. 2005).

[623] *Richards v. Wisconsin*, 520 U.S. 385, 117 S. Ct. 1416 (1997).

[624] *Richards v. Wisconsin*, 520 U.S. 385, 117 S. Ct. 1416, 1421-22 (1997) (emphasis added).

[625] *United States v. Banks*, 540 U.S. 31, 124 S. Ct. 521, 525 (2003).

[626] *United States v. Banks*, 540 U.S. 31, 124 S. Ct. 521 (2003).

[627] *United States v. Banks*, 540 U.S. 31, 124 S. Ct. 521, 523 (2003).

As a general rule, held the Court, the police must wait "a reasonable time under all the circumstances." Here, the 15- to 20-second wait was reasonable.

Although officers should make every effort to comply with the "knock and announce" requirement, under the Fourth Amendment, a violation of the rule will not necessarily lead to the suppression of evidence. In this regard, the federal Supreme Court, in *Hudson v. Michigan*,[628] determined that "the social costs of applying the exclusionary rule to knock-and-announce violations are considerable; the incentive to such violations is minimal to begin with, and the extant deterrences against them are substantial[.] Resort to the massive remedy of suppressing evidence of guilt is unjustified."[629] The Court did note, however, that officers who violate the rule still face the threat of possible civil remedies (such as a lawsuit under 42 U.S.C. § 1983) or internal discipline by their employer.

4.1.9. Inventory and return

The inventory and return of seized items are governed by Tex. Rule Crim. Proc. art. 18.06(b), which provides in part: "Before the officer takes property from the place, he shall prepare a written inventory of the property to be taken. He shall legibly endorse his name on the inventory and present a copy of the inventory to the owner or other person in possession of the property. If neither the owner nor a person in possession of the property is present when the officer executes the warrant, the officer shall leave a copy of the warrant and the inventory at the place." Pursuant to *Tex. Rule Crim. Proc.* art. 18.10, "The officer shall also deliver to the magistrate a copy of the inventory of the property taken into his possession under the warrant. The failure of an officer to make a timely return of an executed search warrant or to submit an inventory of the property taken into the officer's possession under the warrant does not bar the admission of evidence under Article 38.23. The officer who seized the property shall retain custody of it until the magistrate issues an order directing the manner of safekeeping the property. The property may not be removed from the county in which it was seized without an order approving the removal, issued by a magistrate in the county in which the warrant was issued; provided, however, nothing herein shall prevent the officer, or his department, from forwarding any item or items seized to a laboratory for scientific analysis."

4.1.9.1. Police Need Not Inform Owner of the Procedures for Property Return

When law enforcement officers seize property under the authority of a search warrant, "due process requires them to take reasonable steps to give notice that the property has been taken so that the owner can pursue available remedies for its return."[630] Moreover, when the owner of the property is not present at the time of the search, such individualized notice that law enforcement officials have taken property is necessary "because the property owner would have no other reasonable means of ascertaining who was responsible for his loss."[631] There is no requirement, however, that officers inform the property owner of the procedures for seeking return of the seized property. As emphasized by the U.S. Supreme Court in *Perkins*, the Due Process Clause does not require law enforcement officials "to give detailed and specific instructions or advice to owners who seek return of property lawfully seized but no longer needed for police investigation or criminal prosecution."[632] Once the property owner is informed that his property has been seized, he or she can turn to published statutes, court rules, or case law to learn about the remedial procedures available for property return.[633]

4.1.10. Anticipatory warrants

An "anticipatory" search warrant is a warrant that is signed and issued by a judge based on an affidavit demonstrating probable cause to believe that, within a reasonable time in the future (but not at the time

---

628 *Hudson v. Michigan*, 547 U.S. 586, 126 S. Ct. 2159 (2006).
629 *Hudson v. Michigan*, 547 U.S. 586, 126 S. Ct. 2159, 2168, 2170 (2006).
630 *City of West Covina v. Perkins*, 525 U.S. 234, 119 S. Ct. 678, 681 (1999).
631 *City of West Covina v. Perkins*, 525 U.S. 234, 119 S. Ct. 678, 681 (1999).
632 *City of West Covina v. Perkins*, 525 U.S. 234, 119 S. Ct. 678, 679 (1999).
633 *City of West Covina v. Perkins*, 525 U.S. 234, 119 S. Ct. 678, 681-82 (1999).

the affidavit is presented), contraband or criminal evidence will arrive at a particular place. When applying for an anticipatory warrant, the affiant-officer is, in essence, asserting that probable cause does not exist presently, but will exist following the occurrence of some "triggering event." The affidavit must demonstrate a fair probability that evidence of a crime or contraband will be found at the place to be searched if the triggering condition occurs, and probable cause to believe that the triggering condition will occur. When properly drafted and used, anticipatory warrants have been held to be constitutional and a valuable law enforcement tool.[634]

Such warrants are typically used when law enforcement officials have arranged or will be monitoring a controlled delivery of contraband. The anticipatory search warrant and the affidavit in support thereof must demonstrate several things not normally found in the traditional search warrant. First, the affidavit must set forth facts demonstrating a *strong probability* that the sought-after evidence will be at the target premises when the warrant is executed. A judge must be able to conclude from the affidavit that there is a strong probability that the continuation of the process already initiated by the shipment of contraband will in the natural course of events result in the consummation of the crime at the time and place anticipated.

In *United States v. Grubbs*,[635] defendant purchased a videotape of child pornography from a website operated by an undercover postal inspector. Authorities arranged a controlled delivery of the videotape, then obtained a search warrant for defendant's home; the affidavit in support of the warrant specifically provided that the warrant was not to be executed "unless and until the parcel has been delivered by a person(s) and has been physically taken into the residence." After defendant's wife signed for the videotape, the warrant was lawfully executed. The affidavit in this case clearly established that contraband would be present in defendant's home once the videotape was delivered — child pornography is obviously illegal. In addition, there was probable cause to believe this condition would be satisfied; although it was possible defendant might have refused delivery, he was unlikely to do so after having ordered the videotape. Therefore, this was a valid anticipatory warrant.

In *State v. Toone*,[636] the Texas Court of Criminal Appeals upheld a federal anticipatory search warrant but cautioned, "We emphasize that our holding in this case does not reflect upon the validity of an anticipatory search warrant under the Texas Constitution, nor does it reflect upon the validity of an anticipatory search warrant which is otherwise governed by article 18.01."[637]

4.1.11. Scope of the search

As a general rule, the "scope" of a lawful search is "defined by the object of the search and the places in which there is probable cause to believe that it may be found."[638] Whenever a search is made pursuant to the authority of a valid search warrant, it may naturally extend to the entire area covered by the warrant's description. Therefore, if the residence to be searched is identified by street number, the search is not limited to the dwelling house, but may also extend to the garage and other structures deemed to be within the curtilage and the yard within the curtilage.

When a law enforcement officer executes a warrant authorizing the search of only a portion of a particular structure, only that portion may be searched. Thus, if the warrant specifically authorized a search of the third floor of a building, the officer may not lawfully search any other floor. And when the probable cause delineated in the warrant describes stolen property believed to be in the garage, that information would not support a search for that item in an upstairs bedroom.[639]

Individual rooms, places or objects within the described premises do not require any additional showing of probable cause when their access requires an additional act of entry. As the United States Supreme Court explained in *Ross*:

---

634 *United States v. Grubbs*, 547 U.S. 90, 126 S. Ct. 1494, 1499 (2006).
635 *United States v. Grubbs*, 547 U.S. 90, 126 S. Ct. 1494 (2006).
636 *State v. Toone*, 872 S.W.2d 750 (Tex. Crim. App. 1994).
637 *State v. Toone*, 872 S.W.2d 750, 752 (Tex. Crim. App. 1994).
638 *United States v. Ross*, 456 U.S. 798, 824, 102 S. Ct. 2157, 2172 (1982).
639 *United States v. Ross*, 456 U.S. 798, 824, 102 S. Ct. 2157, 2172 (1982).

A lawful search of fixed premises generally extends to the entire area in which the object of the search may be found and is not limited by the possibility that separate acts of entry or opening may be required to complete the search. Thus, a warrant that authorizes an officer to search a home for illegal weapons also provides authority to open closets, chests, drawers, and containers in which the weapon might be found. A warrant to open a footlocker to search for marijuana would also authorize the opening of packages found inside. A warrant to search a vehicle would support a search of every part of the vehicle that might contain the object of the search.[640]

Accordingly, when law enforcement officers are engaged in a legitimate search pursuant to a warrant whose "purpose and limits have been precisely defined, nice distinctions between glove compartments, upholstered seats, trunks, and wrapped packages, in the case of a vehicle, must give way to the interest in the prompt and efficient completion of the task at hand."[641]

A critical distinction, however, must be drawn between the premises to be searched and vehicles at the premises. In this respect, a warrant to search a building does not include authority to search vehicles at the premises, and, the authority to search a vehicle does not include authority to enter private premises to effect a search of a vehicle within those premises.

4.1.11.1. The authority to detain occupants

The United States Supreme Court has also held that, "for Fourth Amendment purposes," a "warrant to search for contraband founded on probable cause implicitly carries with it the limited authority to detain the occupants of the premises while a proper search is conducted."[642] Officers may detain anyone found in the residence, regardless of whether or not the occupant is a suspect named in the warrant, and may use reasonable force in detaining the occupants.[643]

In *Michigan v. Summers*, the U.S. Supreme Court observed that there are three important law enforcement interests that, taken together, justify the detention of an occupant who is on the premises during the execution of a search warrant: (1) officer safety; (2) facilitating the orderly completion of the search; and (3) preventing flight.[644]

A person may not, however, be detained incident to the execution of a search warrant unless the person is within the *immediate vicinity* of the premises to be searched — in other words, that area in which an occupant poses a real threat to the safe and efficient execution of the warrant. Courts can consider a number of factors to determine whether an occupant was detained within the immediate vicinity of the premises to be searched, including the lawful limits of the premises, whether the occupant was within the line of sight of his dwelling, and the ease of reentry from the occupant's location.[645] In *Bailey*, defendant's detention was unlawful when he left the house to be searched and had driven about a mile from the home before the officers stopped and searched him.

The authority to detain those present but not named in the warrant does not include the authority to search those persons, absent an independent justification for the search. Thus, in *Ybarra v. Illinois*,[646] the Court held that a valid warrant to search for narcotics at a particular tavern did not also provide the officers with the authority to automatically search or frisk any person who happens to be on the premises during the execution of that warrant. According to the Court, a person's mere presence at the target premises, standing

[640] *United States v. Ross*, 456 U.S. 798, 821, 102 S. Ct. 2157, 2170-71 (1982).

[641] *United States v. Ross*, 456 U.S. 798, 820-821, 102 S. Ct. 2157, 2171 (1982).

[642] *Michigan v. Summers*, 452 U.S. 692, 705, 101 S. Ct. 2587, 2595 (1981).

[643] *Muehler v. Mena*, 544 U.S. 93, 125 S. Ct. 1465 (2005) (police justified in handcuffing woman for two to three hours while executing search warrant for weapons at the residence of a suspected gang member); *cf. Illinois v. McArthur*, 531 U.S. 326, 121 S. Ct. 946 (2001) (Police could detain defendant on the front porch outside his home for two hours while they obtained a search warrant when they had probable cause to believe that marijuana was hidden inside the home, and that defendant would destroy this contraband if allowed to enter unescorted; noting with favor that detention lasted only long enough for police, acting with diligence, to obtain a warrant.).

[644] *Michigan v. Summers*, 452 U.S. 692, 101 S. Ct. 2587 (1981).

[645] *Bailey v. United States*, 568 U.S. 186, 133 S. Ct. 1031 (2013).

[646] *Ybarra v. Illinois,* 444 U.S. 85, 100 S. Ct. 338 (1979).

in close proximity "to others independently suspected of criminal activity does not, without more, give rise to probable cause to search that person.... This requirement cannot be undercut or avoided by simply pointing to the fact that coincidentally there exists probable cause to search or seize another or to search the premises where the person may happen to be."[647] Additionally, the "'narrow scope' of the *Terry* [rule] does not permit a frisk for weapons on less than reasonable belief or suspicion directed at the person to be frisked, even though that person happens to be on the premises where an authorized narcotics search is taking place."[648]

Likewise, in *Lippert v. State*,[649] the Texas Court of Criminal Appeals did not allow a search of a non-occupant during the otherwise lawful execution of a search warrant. In doing so the court explained the following:

> (1) that the combination arrest and search warrant did not specifically authorize appellant's arrest; (2) that appellant's mere presence on the premises at the time of the execution of the search warrant, without more, did not authorize his detention and subsequent frisk or search; (3) that while an occupant may be detained during the execution of a residential search warrant, this limited exception to the probable cause requirement does not extend to those merely on the premises; (4) that the discovery of evidence of criminal activity during the execution of the search warrant does not, without more, establish probable cause to arrest all persons present; (5) that since the officer had no reasonable belief that appellant was armed and presently dangerous, the pat-down frisk violated his personal rights of privacy; and (6) that even if the initial pat-down frisk was justified under the circumstances when no weapon was found, further intrusions were constitutionally impermissible absent probable cause to arrest, thus subsequent detention and frisk or search were invalid under the Fourth and Fourteenth Amendments, United States Constitution, and Article I, § 9, Texas Constitution.[650]

4.1.11.2. Media ride-alongs

In *Wilson v. Layne*,[651] and *Hanlon v. Berger*,[652] the United States Supreme Court held that "it is a violation of the Fourth Amendment for police to bring members of the media or other third parties into a home during the execution of a warrant when the presence of the third parties in the home was not in aid of the execution of the warrant."

4.2. Exceptions to the warrant requirement (warrantless searches)

As an established principle of contemporary criminal procedure, searches and seizures conducted without a written warrant are "*per se* unreasonable within the meaning of the Fourth Amendment,"[653] unless they fall within one of the recognized exceptions to the Fourth Amendment's written warrant requirement.[654] There is a strong judicial preference for the acquisition of a search warrant by a law enforcement officer prior to intruding into an individual's realm of privacy, and this requirement is not to be dispensed with lightly. The rule demonstrates the desirability of placing a judge's probable cause determination, and assessment of whether the circumstances are exigent (where applicable), between the law enforcement officer and the victim of the search or seizure, to provide the necessary security against unreasonable intrusions into an individual's right to privacy.[655]

As observed in *United States v. Ventresca*,[656] "an evaluation of the constitutionality of a search warrant should begin with the rule that the informed and deliberate determinations of magistrates empowered to

647 *Ybarra v. Illinois*, 444 U.S. 85, 100 S. Ct. 338, 342 (1979).
648 *Ybarra v. Illinois*, 444 U.S. 85, 100 S. Ct. 338, 342 (1979).
649 *Lippert v. State*, 664 S.W.2d 712 (Tex. Crim. App. 1984).
650 *Lippert v. State*, 664 S.W.2d 712, 721-22 (Tex. Crim. App. 1984).
651 *Wilson v. Layne*, 526 U.S. 603, 119 S. Ct. 1692, 1699 (1999).
652 *Hanlon v. Berger*, 526 U.S. 808, 119 S. Ct. 1706 (1999).
653 *United States v. Place*, 462 U.S. 696, 701, 103 S. Ct. 2637, 2641 (1983).
654 *See, e.g., Thompson v. Louisiana*, 469 U.S. 17, 105 S. Ct. 409, 411 (1984); *Mincey v. Arizona*, 437 U.S. 385, 98 S. Ct. 2408, 2412 (1978); *United States v. Edwards*, 415 U.S. 800, 802, 94 S. Ct. 1234, 1236 (1974).
655 *See Hyland v. State*, 574 S.W.3d 904 (Tex. Crim. App. 2019); *Bonds v. State*, 403 S.W.3d 867, 872-73 (Tex. Crim. App. 2013).
656 *United States v. Ventresca*, 380 U.S. 102, 105-06, 85 S. Ct. 741 (1965) (citations and internal quotes omitted).

issue warrants ... are to be preferred over the hurried action of officers who may happen to make arrests. This preference for a written warrant indicates that in a doubtful or marginal case, a search may be sustainable where without one it would fall."

Once a search or seizure is conducted without a warrant, the burden is upon the Government, as the party seeking to validate the warrantless search, to bring it clearly within one of the recognized exceptions created by the United States Supreme Court.[657] Thus, the Constitution does not, however, prohibit all warrantless searches or seizures; the Constitution only forbids "unreasonable searches and seizures."[658]

Over the course of time, the United States Supreme Court has carved out of the Fourth Amendment several carefully tailored exceptions to its warrant requirement. Those formally recognized include:

(1) Search incident to a lawful arrest
(2) Exigent circumstances
(3) Consent
(4) Automobile exception
(5) Impound/inventory
(6) Open fields
(7) Plain view
(8) Abandonment
(9) Administrative and Regulatory searches
(10) Non-governmental (private) searches

The following materials discuss each of the judicially recognized exceptions to the written warrant requirement and explore the impact each has on law enforcement.

4.2.1. Search incident to a lawful arrest

Generally, the courts address this exception in two broad areas: a search of a person incident to arrest and a search of a vehicle incident to arrest.

4.2.1.1. The person of the arrestee and the area within his immediate control

When a law enforcement officer effects a lawful custodial arrest based on probable cause, he or she is permitted to conduct a contemporaneous search of the person of the arrestee. Such a search safeguards the arresting officer and others nearby from harm while ensuring that the arrestee will not discard or destroy evidence.

Before a search incident to an arrest may be deemed valid, however, the arrest itself must be lawful. An officer may not justify an arrest by the search and at the same time justify the search by the arrest.[659] In this respect, if an officer makes an unlawful arrest, any evidence seized during the search incident to that arrest will be inadmissible in court. Thus, the propriety of the incident search depends upon the validity of the arrest.[660]

An incident search of an individual's person may not, therefore, be undertaken for the purpose of gathering evidential justification for that individual's arrest. Even if the desired evidence is found on the individual's person, an arrest thereafter will not be valid in the absence of probable cause for the arrest based on information separate and distinct from that which the search of the person disclosed. As the Supreme Court

---

657 *See, e.g., Riley v. California*, 573 U.S. 373, 134 S. Ct. 2473, 2482 (2014) ("In the absence of a warrant, a search is reasonable only if it falls within a specific exception to the warrant requirement."); *see also Kentucky v. King*, 563 U.S. 452, 131 S. Ct. 1849, 1856-57 (2011); *Wilson v. State*, 621 S.W.2d 799 (Tex. Crim. App. 1981).

658 *Terry v. Ohio*, 392 U.S. 1, 9, 88 S. Ct. 1868, 1873 (1968); *Elkins v. United States*, 364 U.S. 206, 222, 80 S. Ct. 1437, 1446 (1960).

659 *Johnson v. United States*, 333 U.S. 10, 16-17, 68 S. Ct. 367, 370 (1948).

660 *Baldwin v. State*, 278 S.W.3d 367 (Tex. Crim. App. 2009).

stated in *Sibron v. New York*: "It is axiomatic that an incident search may not precede an arrest and serve as part of its justification."[661]

It has been held, however, that so long as probable cause for an arrest exists prior to the undertaking of any search of the prospective arrestee's person, it does not matter whether the search immediately precedes or follows the formal arrest.[662] As the United States Supreme Court explained in *Rawlings v. Kentucky*,[663] "where the formal arrest followed quickly on the heels of the challenged search of [an individual's] person, we do not believe it particularly important that the search preceded the arrest rather than vice versa," so long as what the search disclosed was "not necessary to support probable cause to arrest." In these circumstances, if the arrest is lawful – apart from the search or what the search disclosed – and if the arrest and the search occurred as continuous steps in a single, integrated transaction, then the evidence disclosed by the search should not be lost merely because, in the precise sequence of events, the search preceded the arrest. It has been held, however, that a search will be unconstitutional, even if the officer had probable cause to arrest at the time, if an actual arrest is not made subsequent to the search.[664]

There is no requirement that the probable cause justifying the lawful custodial arrest, and therefore a search incident to that arrest, be "for the charge eventually prosecuted."[665] "Probable cause need only exist as to any offense that *could be charged* under the circumstances."[666] This means that an officer with probable cause to believe a person has committed *any offense justifying a full custodial arrest* has the authority to conduct a search incident to that arrest.

Once an individual has been lawfully arrested, not only may the police conduct a full search of the individual's person but they may also conduct a search of the area within that person's immediate control. This rule was pronounced by the United States Supreme Court in the landmark case of *Chimel v. California*,[667] where it was held that a valid custodial arrest creates the circumstance which justifies the contemporaneous warrantless search of the person arrested and of the immediately surrounding area. According to the Court, such contemporaneous searches incident to arrest have long been considered valid because of the law enforcement need "to remove any weapons that [the arrestee] might seek to use in order to resist arrest or effect his escape" and the need to prevent the destruction or concealment of evidence.[668] The Court said: "A gun on a table or in a drawer in front of one who is arrested can be as dangerous to the arresting officer as one concealed in the clothing of the person arrested."[669]

The reasons underlying such search need not, however, be litigated in every case.[670]

4.2.1.1.1. Strip searches

Naturally, a "full search of the person" does not include a strip search. A "strip search" requires a person to remove his or her clothing to expose underclothing, breasts, buttocks, or genitalia. It is no doubt a severe intrusion into one's privacy. Nonetheless, strip searches are not per se illegal or unconstitutional.

A strip search shall be performed by a person of the same sex as the person being searched and shall be performed in a place that prevents the search from being observed by a person not conducting or necessary to assist with the search.

---

[661] *Sibron v. New York*, 392 U.S. 40, 63, 88 S. Ct. 1889, 1902 (1968); *see also Smith v. Ohio*, 494 U.S. 541, 110 S. Ct. 1288, 1290 (1990) (The exception for searches incident to arrest "does not permit the police to search any citizen without a warrant or probable cause so long as an arrest immediately follows.").

[662] *See Williams v. State*, 726 S.W.2d 99 (Tex. Crim. App. 1986); *State v. Sanchez*, 538 S.W.3d 545 (Tex. Crim. App. 2017).

[663] *Rawlings v. Kentucky*, 448 U.S. 98, 111, 100 S. Ct. 2556, 2564-65 (1980).

[664] *See Bennett v. City of Eastpointe*, 410 F.3d 810 (6th Cir. 2005).

[665] *United States v. Bizier*, 111 F.3d 214, 218 (1st Cir. 1997).

[666] *Barna v. City of Perth Amboy*, 42 F.3d 809, 819 (3d Cir. 1994) (emphasis added).

[667] *Chimel v. California*, 395 U.S. 752, 89 S. Ct. 2034 (1969).

[668] *Chimel v. California*, 395 U.S. 752, 763, 89 S. Ct. 2034, 2040 (1969).

[669] *Chimel v. California*, 395 U.S. 752, 763, 89 S. Ct. 2034, 2040 (1969). *See also Lerma v. State*, 543 S.W.3d 184 (Tex. Crim. App. 2018).

[670] *See New York v. Belton*, 453 U.S. 454, 460-61, 101 S. Ct. 2860, 2864 (1981); *United States v. Robinson*, 414 U.S. 218, 235, 94 S. Ct. 467, 476 (1973); *see also Agnello v. United States*, 269 U.S. 20, 30, 46 S. Ct. 4, 5 (1925).

4.2.1.1.2. Fingerprints, photographs and DNA

As part of the authority to conduct a search incident to arrest, once a person is brought to police headquarters to be detained in custody, the person must be accurately identified. In this regard, "criminal identification is said to have two main purposes: '(1) The identification of the accused as the person who committed the crime for which he is being held; and (2) the identification of the accused as the same person who has been previously charged with, or convicted of, other offenses against criminal law.'"[671] Thus, courts have determined that the process of fingerprinting and photographing arrestees is "a natural part of the administrative steps incident to arrest."[672] In fact, by the "middle of the 20th century, it was considered 'elementary that a person in lawful custody may be required to submit to photographing and fingerprinting as part of routine identification processes.'"[673]

The United States Supreme Court has also held that the DNA identification of an arrestee "is a reasonable search that can be considered part of a routine booking procedure. When officers make an arrest supported by probable cause to hold for a serious offense and they bring the suspect to the station to be detained in custody, taking and analyzing a cheek swab of the arrestee's DNA is, like fingerprinting and photographing, a legitimate police booking procedure that is reasonable under the Fourth Amendment."[674]

4.2.1.1.3. The search must be substantially contemporaneous with the arrest

In *Vale v. Louisiana*,[675] the federal Supreme Court re-emphasized that "[a] search may be incident to an arrest 'only if it is substantially contemporaneous with the arrest and is confined to the *immediate* vicinity of the arrest.'"[676] Donald Vale was arrested on the steps leading to his home. Incident to the arrest, a search was conducted inside Vale's home, and a quantity of narcotics was found in the rear bedroom. Finding the search unlawful, the Court stated: "If a search of a house is to be upheld as incident to an arrest, that arrest must take place *inside the house*, * * * not somewhere outside — whether two blocks away, * * * twenty feet away, * * * or on the sidewalk near the front steps."[677] Naturally, even if the arrest does take place inside the house, the search incident to the arrest must be confined to the area within the arrestee's "immediate control." [678]

While a proper search incident to an arrest should be conducted contemporaneously with the arrest, *i.e.*, immediately preceding or succeeding the actual physical act of arrest, it has been held that a search of articles in the possession of the defendant at the time of arrest may not only be conducted at the time of the arrest, but may instead be conducted later, and at a different location, if a reasonable explanation for the delay is put forth.[679] Thus, searches and seizures that could be made on the spot at the time of arrest may legally be conducted later when the accused arrives at the place of detention.

4.2.1.1.3.1. Items carried by the arrestee

In addition to the person of the arrestee and the area into which the arrestee might reach, courts have addressed the question of searching receptacles in the possession of the arrestee. In *Price v. State*,[680] the Court of Criminal Appeals reviewed a case involving the search of luggage that was in the possession of the arrested person.

---

671 *Maryland v. King*, 569 U.S. 435, 458, 133 S. Ct. 1958, 1975 (2013) (internal citation omitted).

672 *County of Riverside v. McLaughlin*, 500 U.S. 44, 58, 111 S. Ct. 1661 (1991); *Maryland v. King*, 569 U.S. 435, 133 S. Ct. 1958, 1976 (2013).

673 *Maryland v. King*, 569 U.S. 435, 459, 133 S. Ct. 1958, 1976 (2013) (quoting *Smith v. United States*, 324 F.2d 879, 882 (CADC 1963)).

674 *Maryland v. King*, 569 U.S. 435, 133 S. Ct. 1958, 1980 (2013).

675 *Vale v. Louisiana*, 399 U.S. 30, 90 S. Ct. 1969 (1970).

676 *Vale v. Louisiana*, 399 U.S. 30, 90 S. Ct. 1969, 1971 (1970) (citations omitted; emphasis added).

677 *Vale v. Louisiana*, 399 U.S. 30, 90 S. Ct. 1969, 1971 (1970) (citations omitted; emphasis added).

678 *Chimel v. California*, 395 U.S. 752, 89 S. Ct. 2034 (1969).

679 *See United States v. Edwards*, 415 U.S. 800 (1974) (delay of ten hours between arrest and station house search permissible).

680 *Price v. State*, 2020 Tex. Crim. App. LEXIS 709, ___ S.W.3d ___ (Tex. Crim. App. 2020).

The Court acknowledged that there are two lines of cases addressing parcels. "Searches of the person, or of property within the *immediate* control of the person – property 'immediately associated with the person of the arrestee,'[681] ... are always justified under the search incident to arrest exception to the warrant requirement, upon no more justification than the arrest itself.[682] The second category involves those parcels that had been in the possession of the arrestee but are now in the control of the police. The federal Supreme Court explained in *Chadwick*: "Once law enforcement officers have reduced luggage or other personal property not immediately associated with the person of the arrestee to their exclusive control, and there is no longer any danger that the arrestee might gain access to the property to seize a weapon or destroy evidence, a search of the property is no longer an incident of the arrest."[683]

In *Price*, Detective Carl Bishop of the San Antonio Police Department received information from an Austin police officer that Price would be flying into the San Antonio airport with a quantity of marijuana purchased from out of state. Upon the flight's arrival, a drug dog alerted to the presence of contraband in suitcases bearing Price's name. Price retrieved the bags and rolled them out to the curb. The detectives then detained Price, handcuffed him, and seized the suitcases. Price was taken to a secure office in the airport and read his *Miranda* warnings. At this point Detective Bishop acknowledged that Price was under arrest. The detectives then opened the suitcases and discovered a large quantity of marijuana in vacuum-sealed bags.

In this appeal, Price argued that the search of the suitcases was unlawful. He claimed the suitcases were under the control of the police and he could not access them, so the bags fell under the rule in *Chadwick*, and could not qualify as a search incident to arrest under *Robinson*. The Court of Criminal Appeals based its opinion, in part, on the fact that the suitcases would "inevitably accompany him into custody" and as such fell under the search incident to arrest option in *Robinson*. The Court stated:

> We hold that, at least where – as in the instant case – an arrestee is in actual possession of a receptacle at the time of, or reasonably contemporaneously to, his custodial arrest, and that receptacle must inevitably accompany him into custody, a warrantless search of that receptacle at or near the time of the arrest is reasonable under the Fourth Amendment as a search incident to the arrestee's person. Such a search requires no greater justification than the fact of the lawful arrest itself. Application of this principle does not turn on the specific nature or character of the receptacle, as the court of appeals believed, but merely on whether it was in the arrestee's possession at the time of arrest, and whether it would inevitably accompany him into custody.[684]

In *United States v. Fleming*,[685] the Seventh Circuit upheld the seizure and search of two closed paper bags which were in the possession of the individuals arrested. The search of defendant Fleming's bag occurred immediately upon his arrest. The search of defendant Rolenc's bag occurred approximately five minutes after his arrest, when additional backup officers arrived on the scene. Fleming's bag contained $10,000 in cash and Rolenc's bag contained a quantity of cocaine. In the appeal which followed their conviction, the defendants argued that the searches of the bags, after the bags had been recovered from them and were securely in police custody, were illegal in the absence of a warrant, consent, or exigent circumstances. The court, however, refused "to impose on police a requirement that the search be absolutely contemporaneous with the arrest, no matter what the peril to themselves or to bystanders."[686] In this respect, the court stated: "It is surely possible for a *Chimel* search to be undertaken too long after the arrest and too far from the arrestee's person. That is the lesson of *Chadwick*. But we do not consider that the presence of more officers than suspects invalidated the immediate search of Fleming's bag. Nor do we think that a five-minute delay between seizing Rolenc's bag and opening it, occasioned by [the officer's] handcuffing Rolenc and moving with him to

---

[681] *United States v. Chadwick*, 433 U.S. 1, 15, 97 S. Ct. 2476, 2485 (1977) (emphasis in original).

[682] *Price v. State*, 2020 Tex. Crim. App. LEXIS 709, ___ S.W.3d ___ (Tex. Crim. App. 2020) (citing *United States v. Robinson*, 414 U.S. 218, 235, 94 S. Ct. 467, 477 (1973)).

[683] *Price v. State*, 2020 Tex. Crim. App. LEXIS 709, ___ S.W.3d ___ (Tex. Crim. App. 2020) (citing *United States v. Chadwick*, 433 U.S. 1, 15, 97 S. Ct. 2476, 2485 (1977)).

[684] *Price v. State*, 2020 Tex. Crim. App. LEXIS 709, at *20-*21, ___ S.W.3d ___ (Tex. Crim. App. 2020)

[685] *United States v. Fleming*, 677 F.2d 602 (7th Cir. 1982).

[686] *United States v. Fleming*, 677 F.2d 602, 607 (7th Cir. 1982).

the street, defeated [the officer's] right to search under *Chimel* principles."[687] Significantly, at the point when the police first seized the bags, "the bags were within Fleming's and Rolenc's grabbing area."[688]

4.2.1.1.4. Minor offenses

When a law enforcement officer has effected a full custodial arrest of a motorist for driving with a revoked license, that officer may thereafter conduct a full search of the person of that motorist as a contemporaneous incident of that lawful arrest. In *United States v. Robinson*,[689] the Court held that the general authority to search incident to a lawful custodial arrest should not be qualified or limited on "an assumption that persons arrested for the offense of driving while their licenses have been revoked are less likely to possess dangerous weapons than are those arrested for other crimes." The Court wrote, "*A custodial arrest of a suspect based on probable cause is a reasonable intrusion under the Fourth Amendment; that intrusion being lawful, a search incident to the arrest requires no additional justification. It is the fact of the lawful arrest which establishes the authority to search*[.]"[690] Accordingly, "in the case of a lawful custodial arrest a full search of the person is not only an exception to the warrant requirement of the Fourth Amendment, but is also a 'reasonable' search under that Amendment."[691]

4.2.1.1.5. Search incident to citation rejected

In *Knowles v. Iowa*,[692] the Supreme Court rejected the contention that the "search incident to arrest" exception to the written warrant requirement includes searches "incident to citation." According to the Court, "[o]nce Knowles was stopped for speeding and issued a citation, all the evidence necessary to prosecute that offense had been obtained. No further evidence of excessive speed was going to be found either on the person of the offender or in the passenger compartment of the car."[693] On this basis, the Court also expressly rejected the Iowa Supreme Court's reasoning that, "so long as the arresting officer had probable cause to make a custodial arrest, there need not in fact have been a custodial arrest."[694]

4.2.1.1.6. Blood and breath alcohol

In *Birchfield v. North Dakota*,[695] the United States Supreme Court addressed the issue whether motorists lawfully arrested for drunk driving may be convicted of a crime or otherwise penalized for refusing to submit to blood-alcohol testing. According to the Court, the answer was yes for breath, but no for blood. In this regard, incident to a lawful drunk-driving arrest, "the Fourth Amendment allows warrantless breath tests, but as a general rule does not allow warrantless blood draws[.]"[696]

4.2.1.1.7. Cell phones

In *Riley v. California*,[697] the U.S. Supreme Court addressed searches of data contained in modern-day cell phones. Finding that a warrant is generally required for such searches, the Court held that the digital data on a suspect's cell phone – including texts, e-mails, photos and call logs – may not be searched incident to arrest.[698] In this respect the Texas Court of Criminal Appeals has explained that "a person has a legitimate

---

[687] *United States v. Fleming*, 677 F.2d 602, 607-08 (7th Cir. 1982).
[688] *United States v. Fleming*, 677 F.2d 602, 607 (7th Cir. 1982).
[689] *United States v. Robinson*, 414 U.S. 218, 94 S. Ct. 47 (1973).
[690] *United States v. Robinson*, 414 U.S. 218, 94 S. Ct. 47 (1973) (emphasis added).
[691] *United States v. Robinson*, 414 U.S. 218, 235, 94 S. Ct. 467, 477 (1973).
[692] *Knowles v. Iowa*, 525 U.S. 113, 119 S. Ct. 484 (1998).
[693] *Knowles v. Iowa*, 525 U.S. 113, 119 S. Ct. 484, 487 (1998).
[694] *Knowles v. Iowa*, 525 U.S. 113, 119 S. Ct. 484, 487 (1998).
[695] *Birchfield v. North Dakota*, 579 U.S. ___, 136 S. Ct. 2160 (2016).
[696] *Birchfield v. North Dakota*, 579 U.S. ___, 136 S. Ct. 2160, 2185 n.8 (2016).
[697] *Riley v. California*, 573 U.S. 373, 134 S. Ct. 2473 (2014).
[698] *See also State v. Granville*, 423 S.W.3d 399 (Tex. Crim. App. 2014).

expectation of privacy in the contents of his cell phone because of its 'ability to store large amounts of private data' both in the cell phone itself and by accessing remote services. This data may involve the most intimate details of a person's individual life, including text messages, emails, banking, medical, or credit card information, pictures, and videos. A cell phone is unlike other containers as it can receive, store, and transmit an almost unlimited amount of private information. The potential for invasion of privacy, identity theft, or, at a minimum, public embarrassment is enormous."[699] However, officers may examine the physical aspects of a phone to ensure that it will not be used as a weapon – for example, to determine whether there is a razor blade hidden between the phone and its case.

4.2.1.1.7.1. Cell phone location data

In *Carpenter v. United States*,[700] the Court held that a Fourth Amendment search occurs when law enforcement officials access historical cell phone records that provide a comprehensive chronicle of the user's past movements. The case involved the Government's acquisition of wireless carrier cell-site records revealing the location of Carpenter's cell phone whenever it made or received calls. In all, the Government was able to obtain cell-site location information (CSLI) documenting 12,898 location points that cataloged Carpenter's movements over 127 days – an average of 101 data points per day.

The question before the Court was how to apply the Fourth Amendment to the personal location information maintained by a third party (Carpenter's wireless carriers Sprint and MetroPCS) and law enforcement's "ability to chronicle a person's past movements through the record of his cell phone signals." Much like GPS tracking of a vehicle addressed in *United States v. Jones*,[701] CSLI is detailed, encyclopedic, and effortlessly compiled. In fact, "when the Government tracks the location of a cell phone it achieves near perfect surveillance, as if it had attached an ankle monitor to the phone's user." Accordingly, the Court concluded:

> Given the unique nature of cellphone location records, the fact that the information is held by a third party does not by itself overcome the user's claim to Fourth Amendment protection. Whether the Government employs its own surveillance technology as in *Jones* or leverages the technology of a wireless carrier, we hold that an individual maintains a legitimate expectation of privacy in the record of his physical movements as captured through CSLI. The location information obtained from Carpenter's wireless carriers was the product of a search [, and]...the Government must generally obtain a warrant supported by probable cause before acquiring such records.[702]

The Government, in *Carpenter*, acquired the cell-site records pursuant to a court order issued under the Stored Communications Act, which required the Government to show "reasonable grounds" for believing that the records were "relevant and material to an ongoing investigation."[703] That showing, according to the Court, falls well short of the probable cause required for a warrant. "Under the standard in the Stored Communications Act[,] law enforcement need only show that the cell-site evidence might be pertinent to an ongoing investigation – a 'gigantic' departure from the probable cause rule...Consequently, an order issued under Section 2703(d) of the Act is not a permissible mechanism for accessing historical cell-site records. Before compelling a wireless carrier to turn over a subscriber's CSLI, the Government's obligation is a familiar one – get a warrant."[704]

Emergency circumstances. Even though the Government will generally need a warrant to access cell-site location information, "case-specific exceptions may support a warrantless search of an individual's cell-site records under certain circumstances. 'One well-recognized exception applies when the exigencies of the situation make the needs of law enforcement so compelling that [a] warrantless search is objectively

---

[699] *State v. Granville*, 423 S.W.3d 399, 408-09 (Tex. Crim. App. 2014) (citations and internal quotes omitted).
[700] *Carpenter v. United States*, 585 U.S.___, 138 S. Ct. 2206 (2018).
[701] *United States v. Jones*, 565 U.S. 400, 132 S. Ct. 945 (2012).
[702] *Carpenter v. United States*, 585 U.S.___, 138 S. Ct. 2206, 2217 (2018). In deciding this case, the Court rejected the contention that Carpenter lacked a reasonable expectation of privacy in the location information collected by the FBI because he had shared that information with his wireless carriers.
[703] 18 U.S.C. § 2703(d).
[704] *Carpenter v. United States*, 585 U.S.___, 138 S. Ct. 2206, 2221 (2018).

reasonable under the Fourth Amendment.'... Such exigencies include the need to pursue a fleeing suspect, protect individuals who are threatened with imminent harm, or prevent the imminent destruction of evidence."[705]

"As a result, if law enforcement is confronted with an urgent situation, such fact-specific threats will likely justify the warrantless collection of CSLI. Lower courts, for instance, have approved warrantless searches related to bomb threats, active shootings, and child abductions[, and the Carpenter case] does not call into doubt warrantless access to CSLI in such circumstances."[706]

In *Sims v. State*,[707] the Texas Court of Criminal Appeals addressed the issue of real-time location records as opposed to the historical records in *Carpenter*. There, police accessed the real-time CSLI records of defendant for a short amount of time. The court explained, "Whether a particular government action constitutes a 'search' or 'seizure' does not turn on the content of the CSLI records; it turns on whether the government searched or seized 'enough' information that it violated a legitimate expectation of privacy. There is no bright-line rule for determining how long police must track a person's cell phone in real time before it violates a person's legitimate expectation of privacy in those records. Whether a person has a recognized expectation of privacy in real-time CSLI records must be decided on a case-by-case basis."[708] Because the intrusion in *Sims* was minimal, the court concluded that defendant "did not have a legitimate expectation of privacy in his physical movements or his location as reflected in the less than three hours of real-time CSLI records accessed by police by pinging his phone less than five times."[709]

4.2.1.2. Motor vehicle searches incident to arrest

In *Chimel v. California*,[710] the U.S. Supreme Court held that, as a permissible incident of a lawful custodial arrest, the police may not only conduct a warrantless search of the person of the arrestee, but also of the area within the arrestee's immediate control, meaning the area within his reach.

> [I]t is entirely reasonable for the arresting officer to search for and seize any evidence on the arrestee's person in order to prevent its concealment or destruction. *And the area into which an arrestee might reach in order to grab a weapon or evidentiary items must, of course, be governed by a like rule.* A gun on a table or in a drawer in front of one who is arrested can be as dangerous to the arresting officer as one concealed in the clothing of the person arrested. There is ample justification, therefore, for a search of the arrestee's person *and the area "within his immediate control" – construing that phrase to mean the area from within which he might gain possession of a weapon or destructible evidence.*[711]

Although the *Chimel* principle may be stated simply enough – that a search incident to arrest may not go beyond the area within the immediate control of the arrestee – many courts have struggled with determining the precise area that would be within the immediate control of the arrestee, particularly when that area arguably includes the interior of an automobile and the arrestee is its recent occupant.

In *New York v. Belton*,[712] the U.S. Supreme Court established a bright-line rule for "the proper scope of a search of the interior of an automobile incident to a lawful custodial arrest of its occupants" after the arrestees are no longer in it. The *Belton* "bright line" rule provided: When an officer has made "a lawful custodial arrest of the occupant of an automobile," the officer "may, as a contemporaneous incident of that arrest, search the passenger compartment of that automobile" including "any containers found within the passenger compartment."[713]

---

705 *Carpenter v. United States*, 585 U.S. ___, 138 S. Ct. 2206, 2222-23 (2018) (citations and internal quotes omitted).
706 *Carpenter v. United States*, 585 U.S. ___, 138 S. Ct. 2206, 2223 (2018).
707 *Sims v. State*, 569 S.W.3d 634 (Tex. Crim. App. 2019).
708 *Sims v. State*, 569 S.W.3d 634, 645-46 (Tex. Crim. App. 2019).
709 *Sims v. State*, 569 S.W.3d 634, 646 (Tex. Crim. App. 2019).
710 *Chimel v. California*, 395 U.S. 752, 89 S. Ct. 2034 (1969).
711 *Chimel v. California*, 395 U.S. 752, 763, 89 S. Ct. 2034, 2040 (1969) (emphasis added).
712 *New York v. Belton*, 453 U.S. 454, 101 S. Ct. 2860, 863 (1981).
713 *New York v. Belton*, 453 U.S. 454, 101 S. Ct. 2860, 863 (1981).

In *Thornton v. United States*,[714] the U.S. Supreme Court determined that the rule of *Belton* was not limited to situations where the officer made contact with the occupant while the occupant was inside the vehicle. According to the Court, "*Belton* governs even when an officer does not make contact until the person arrested has left the vehicle."[715] Similar to Belton, Thornton was arrested for the possession of marijuana and cocaine.

Justice Scalia's concurrence in *Thornton* emphasized that –

> conducting a *Chimel* search is not the Government's right; it is an exception – justified by necessity – to a rule that would otherwise render the search unlawful. If "sensible police procedures" require that suspects be handcuffed and put in squad cars, then police should handcuff suspects, put them in squad cars, and not conduct the search. Indeed, if an officer leaves a suspect unrestrained nearby just to manufacture authority to search, one could argue that the search is unreasonable precisely because the dangerous conditions justifying it existed only by virtue of the officer's failure to follow sensible procedures....
>
> If *Belton* searches are justifiable, it is not because the arrestee might grab a weapon or evidentiary item from his car, but simply because the car might contain evidence relevant to the crime for which he was arrested....
>
> I would therefore limit *Belton* searches to cases where it is reasonable to believe evidence relevant to the crime of arrest might be found in the vehicle. In this case, as in *Belton*, [defendant] was lawfully arrested for a drug offense. It was reasonable for Officer Nichols to believe that further contraband or similar evidence relevant to the crime for which he had been arrested might be found in the vehicle from which he had just alighted and which was still within his vicinity at the time of arrest. I would affirm the decision below on that ground.[716]

Thereafter, in *Arizona v. Gant*,[717] the United States Supreme Court abandoned the *Belton* rule and held that the police "may search a vehicle incident to a recent occupant's arrest only if the arrestee is within reaching distance of the passenger compartment at the time of the search or it is reasonable to believe the vehicle contains evidence of the offense of arrest. When these justifications are absent, a search of an arrestee's vehicle will be unreasonable unless police obtain a warrant or show that another exception to the warrant requirement applies."[718]

In *State v. Sanchez*,[719] the search of the vehicle was justified by the discovery of a different offense after the initial arrest. There, defendant was arrested for outstanding warrants. During that arrest, the officer searched defendant's person and discovered illegal drugs. The officer then searched defendant's Jeep and discovered more illegal drugs. The Texas Court of Criminal Appeals held that "discovery of drugs on a suspect's person, after an arrest on traffic warrants but before the search of the suspect's vehicle, can supply a new basis for arrest that would justify search of the vehicle as a search incident to arrest."[720] Note that defendant was not formally arrested for the drug charge until after the search of his vehicle. With regard to that issue the court stated, "If an officer has probable cause to arrest, a search incident to arrest is valid if it is conducted before a formal arrest – at least if it is immediately before the arrest."[721] Thus, the search of the car was a valid search incident to arrest.

The two components of *Arizona v. Gant* are outlined below.

1) *The "possibility of access" component.* The police may search a vehicle incident to a recent occupant's arrest "when the arrestee is unsecured and within reaching distance of the passenger

---

714 *Thornton v. United States*, 541 U.S. 615, 124 S. Ct. 2127 (2004).
715 *Thornton v. United States*, 541 U.S. 615, 124 S. Ct. 2127 (2004).
716 *Thornton v. United States*, 541 U.S. 615, 124 S. Ct. 2127, 2133-38 (2004).
717 *Arizona v. Gant*, 556 U.S. 332, 129 S. Ct. 1710 (2009).
718 *Arizona v. Gant*, 556 U.S. 332, 129 S. Ct. 1710, 1723 (2009).
719 *State v. Sanchez*, 538 S.W.3d 545 (Tex. Crim. App. 2017).
720 *State v. Sanchez*, 538 S.W.3d 545, 546 (Tex. Crim. App. 2017).
721 *State v. Sanchez*, 538 S.W.3d 545, 550 (Tex. Crim. App. 2017).

compartment at the time of the search."[722] A critical aspect of this "possibility of access" component is that it is to be applied "at the time of the search," not at some earlier time. This is significant because, as pointed out by the dissent, "in the great majority of cases, an officer making an arrest is able to handcuff the arrestee and remove him to a secure place before conducting a search incident to the arrest."[723] "Because officers have many means of ensuring the safe arrest of vehicle occupants, it will be the rare case in which an officer is unable to fully effectuate an arrest so that a real possibility of access to the arrestee's vehicle remains."[724] Nonetheless, so long as the arrestee is "unsecured" *and* "within reaching distance of the passenger compartment" "a search incident to arrest is reasonable under the Fourth Amendment."[725]

2) *The "likelihood of discovering offense-related evidence" component.* Recall that *Chimel v. California* limited searches incident to arrest to "the arrestee's person and the area 'within his immediate control' – construing that phrase to mean the area from within which he might gain possession of a weapon or destructible evidence." Although it does not follow from *Chimel*, the *Gant* Court also held that "circumstances unique to the vehicle context" justify a search incident to a lawful arrest when it is "reasonable to believe the vehicle contains evidence of the offense of arrest."[726] This component appears to contain a new and additional power for officers conducting searches of vehicles incident to arrest – a power having nothing to do with the *Chimel* rationale. Nonetheless, officers are cautioned that "[i]n many cases, as when a recent occupant is arrested for a traffic violation, there will be no reasonable basis to believe the vehicle contains relevant evidence."[727] What remains to be seen is whether this component of *Gant* requires a simple purpose or nature-of-the-offense analysis, or whether there needs to be an inquiry into the "likelihood," "probability" or "possibility" that the vehicle contains relevant evidence.

In *United States v. McCraney*,[728] defendant was stopped for failure to dim his high beams upon the approach of an oncoming car, then arrested for driving while suspended. An officer then searched defendant's car, finding a gun under the driver's seat. At the time of the search, defendant and his passenger were standing two to three feet behind the car's rear bumper. Although neither had been handcuffed yet, they were surrounded by three officers. Thus, they were no longer within "reaching distance" of the passenger compartment. Because police could not reasonably expect to find evidence of defendant's suspension in the car, neither component of *Gant* was applicable, and the court determined that the search was unconstitutional, and that the gun should be suppressed.

4.2.2. Exigent circumstances

The situations that often fall under the exigent circumstances exception to the warrant requirement can be grouped into three general categories. Texas courts have "identified three categories of exigent circumstances that justify a warrantless intrusion by police officers: 1) providing aid or assistance to persons whom law enforcement reasonably believes are in need of assistance; 2) protecting police officers from persons whom they reasonably believe to be present, armed, and dangerous; and 3) preventing the destruction of evidence or contraband."[729] The rationale advanced for permitting warrantless searches under such circumstances is that extreme situations dictate that police act quickly, where there is no time to secure a warrant.

---

[722] *Arizona v. Gant*, 556 U.S. 332, 129 S. Ct. 1710, 1719 (2009).
[723] *Arizona v. Gant*, 556 U.S. 332, 129 S. Ct. 1710, 1730 (2009) (Alito, J., dissenting).
[724] *Arizona v. Gant*, 556 U.S. 332, 129 S. Ct. 1710, 1719 n.4 (2009).
[725] *Arizona v. Gant*, 556 U.S. 332, 129 S. Ct. 1710, 1719 n.4 (2009).
[726] *Arizona v. Gant*, 556 U.S. 332, 129 S. Ct. 1710, 1719 (2009) (citing *Thornton v. United States*, 541 U.S. 615, 124 S. Ct. 2127, 2137 (2004) (Scalia, J., concurring)).
[727] *Arizona v. Gant*, 556 U.S. 332, 343, 129 S. Ct. 1710, 1719 (2009) (citing *Atwater v. Lago Vista*, 532 U.S. 318, 324, 121 S. Ct. 1536, 1541 (2001)).
[728] *United States v. McCraney*, 674 F.3d 614 (6th Cir. 2012).
[729] *Gutierrez v. State*, 221 S.W.3d 680, 685 (Tex. Crim. App. 2007) (citing *McNairy v. State*, 835 S.W.2d 101, 107 (Tex. Crim. App. 1991)).

The warrant requirement may be dispensed with when officers take actions that are necessary responses to an emergency situation. Courts permit warrantless searches where officers have probable cause and a qualifying emergent set of circumstances. The Texas Court of Criminal Appeals has explained that "if police have probable cause coupled with an exigent circumstance, or they have obtained voluntary consent, or they conduct a search incident to a lawful arrest, the Fourth Amendment will tolerate a warrantless search. Yet, the warrant requirement is not lightly set aside, and the State shoulders the burden to prove that an exception to the warrant requirement applies."[730]

In *Pache v. State*,[731] Beaumont police received a tip that drugs were being sold from a specified trailer home. Three officers drove through an open gate up a dirt driveway to the trailer and performed a "knock-and-talk." As they walked up to the trailer, they smelled a very strong odor of marijuana emanating from inside it. After the officers knocked, defendant answered the door, and the lead officer identified himself. Defendant responded by trying to slam the door, but the officer prevented him from doing so for safety reasons. Defendant then turned and ran back into the trailer. The officers made a valid warrantless entry to pursue defendant. The tip combined with the odor of marijuana established probable cause to believe a crime was being committed. Given the context, the officers could reasonable conclude defendant was trying to reach the illegal drug in order to destroy it, so exigent circumstances were present. Had the officers delayed their entrance to obtain a search warrant, evidence would likely have been destroyed.[732]

Thus, in determining whether exigent circumstances exist to justify a warrantless seizure, courts will examine a number of factors to determine whether the police actions were reasonable. First and foremost, the police must have probable cause to believe that the premises contain contraband or evidence of a crime. In addition to probable cause, the police must demonstrate the existence of an actual emergency and articulate specific and objective facts which reveal a necessity for immediate action. In determining whether an exigency exists, court will examine such factors as: (1) the degree of urgency involved and amount of time necessary to obtain a warrant; (2) the reasonable belief that contraband is about to be removed or destroyed; (3) the possibility of danger to the police officers guarding the site of the contraband; (4) information indicating the possessors of contraband are aware that the police are on their trail; and (5) the ready destructibility of the contraband and the police knowledge that traffickers of the suspected contraband characteristically attempt to dispose of the destructible contraband and escape.[733]

In *Dorman v. United States*,[734] the court set forth several additional factors (often cited by numerous courts around the nation) as helpful in assessing whether exigent circumstances are present in cases involving serious crimes and a reasonable probability of imminent danger to life, serious damage to property, destruction of evidence, or the likelihood of flight. These factors include whether: (1) the crime under investigation was recently committed; (2) there was any deliberate or unjustified delay by the police during which time a warrant could have been obtained; (3) a grave offense was involved, particularly a crime of violence; (4) there was reasonable belief that the suspect was armed; (5) the police officers were acting on a clear showing of probable cause; (6) there was a likelihood that the suspect would escape if he or she was not swiftly apprehended; (7) there was strong reason to believe that the suspect was on the premises; and (8) the police entry was made peaceably, albeit nonconsensually.[735]

4.2.2.1. Destruction or removal of evidence

4.2.2.1.1. Crime scenes

Preliminarily, it is important to note that there is no "crime scene" exception to the written warrant requirement. This was made clear in *Mincey v. Arizona*,[736] where the United States Supreme Court held that

[730] *Gutierrez v. State*, 221 S.W.3d 680, 685 (Tex. Crim. App. 2007) (citing *McGee v. State*, 105 S.W.3d 609, 615 (Tex. Crim. App. 2003); *United States v. Robinson*, 414 U.S. 218, 243, 94 S. Ct. 467, 38 L. Ed. 2d 427 (1973)).
[731] *Pache v. State*, 413 S.W.3d 509 (Tex. App. 2013).
[732] *See also Wisenbaker v. State*, 311 S.W.3d 57 (Tex. App. 2010); *Effler v. State*, 115 S.W.3d 696 (Tex. App. 2003).
[733] *United States v. Rubin*, 474 F.2d 262, 268 (3d Cir. 1973).
[734] *Dorman v. United States*, 435 F.2d 385 (D.C. App. 1970).
[735] *Dorman v. United States*, 435 F.2d 385, 392-93 (D.C. App. 1970).
[736] *Mincey v. Arizona*, 437 U.S. 385, 98 S. Ct. 2408 (1978).

the exigent circumstances surrounding the investigation of a serious crime does not permit the creation of a "crime scene exception" to the written warrant requirement. According to the Court, the seriousness of the offense under investigation does not itself create "exigent circumstances of the kind that under the Fourth Amendment justify a warrantless search." Therefore, "the warrantless search of Mincey's apartment was not constitutionally permissible simply because a homicide had recently occurred there."[737]

Similarly, the United States Supreme Court in *Thompson v. Louisiana*,[738] held that the Fourth Amendment will not tolerate a "murder scene exception" to the written warrant requirement.[739]

4.2.2.1.1.1. Protective, victim/suspect fan-out searches

In one portion of the United States Supreme Court's opinion in *Mincey v. Arizona*, the Court recognized "the right of the police to respond to emergency situations [and to make] warrantless entries and searches when they reasonably believe that a *person* within is in need of immediate aid."[740] Additionally, "when the police come upon a scene of a homicide they may make a prompt warrantless search of the area to see if other victims or if a killer is still on the premises."[741] In this respect, "*[t]he need to protect or preserve life or avoid serious injury is justification* for what would be otherwise illegal absent an exigency or emergency."[742] Naturally, during the course of this protective, victim/suspect fan-out search, "police may seize any evidence that is in plain view[.]"[743]

4.2.2.1.1.2. Evidence about to be destroyed

Where police have an objectively reasonable belief that evidence is being or about to be destroyed, a warrantless entry may be permitted under this exception. In order to invoke this exception, the state must demonstrate that the seized evidence is of an "evanescent" nature (*i.e.*, an easily destructible item, like narcotics, which can be easily burned, secreted or flushed).

However, the Texas Court of Criminal Appeals has been clear that "the odor of marijuana alone is not enough to allow officers to conduct a warrantless search. This is because it is clear under both United States constitutional law and Texas constitutional law that a warrantless search of a residence is illegal unless probable cause exists in combination with exigent circumstances."[744] In *Estrada v. State*,[745] Officer Baladez responded to a call complaining of loud music and vehicles traveling at high speeds up and down a road next to Defendant's house. Upon approaching the house, Baladez observed people running from a car into the residence and cups containing alcoholic beverages on the hood of the car. There was no answer when Baladez knocked on the door and identified himself as a police officer. After responding to another call in the area, Baladez returned to the home and observed two vehicles exiting the driveway at a high rate of speed. He stopped the vehicles and discovered that the occupants were minors. He smelled marijuana on the occupants' clothes and breath. Ultimately, Baladez entered and searched the house.

Noting that in order to support a warrantless search, Baladez needed probable cause plus an exigent circumstance, the court held that the smell of marijuana provided probable cause. With regard to the exigent circumstances, "the warrantless search was justified by the need to prevent destruction of evidence or contraband in the time it would have taken for him to procure a warrant."[746]

---

737 *Mincey v. Arizona*, 437 U.S. 385, 98 S. Ct. 2408, 2415 (1978).
738 *Thompson v. Louisiana*, 469 U.S. 17, 105 S. Ct. 409 (1984).
739 *See also Flippo v. West Virginia*, 528 U.S. 11, 120 S. Ct. 7 (1999).
740 *Mincey v. Arizona*, 437 U.S. 385, 392, 98 S. Ct. 2408, 2413 (1978) (emphasis added). *See also Brimage v. State*, 918 S.W.2d 466 (Tex. Crim. App. 1996).
741 *Mincey v. Arizona*, 437 U.S. 385, 392, 98 S. Ct. 2408, 2413 (1978).
742 *Mincey v. Arizona*, 437 U.S. 385, 392, 98 S. Ct. 2408, 2413 (1978) (emphasis added).
743 *Mincey v. Arizona*, 437 U.S. 385, 392, 98 S. Ct. 2408, 2413 (1978).
744 *Estrada v. State*, 154 S.W.3d 604, 608 (Tex. Crim. App. 2005).
745 *Estrada v. State*, 154 S.W.3d 604, 608 (Tex. Crim. App. 2005).
746 *Estrada v. State*, 154 S.W.3d 604, 610 (Tex. Crim. App. 2005). *See also Wisenbaker v. State*, 311 S.W.3d 57 (Tex. App. 2010); *Effler v. State*, 115 S.W.3d 696 (Tex. App. 2003); *Pache v. State*, 413 S.W.3d 509 (Tex. App. 2013).

4.2.2.1.3. Narcotics and other dangerous drugs

The fact that the grounds for arrest involve narcotics, standing alone, does not create an exigent circumstance. In this regard, the U.S. Supreme Court in *Vale v. Louisiana,*[747] held that a narcotics arrest, which takes place on the steps outside the arrestee's home, does not provide its own "exigent circumstance" so as to justify a warrantless entry or search of the home.

4.2.2.1.4. Pending the arrival of a search warrant

It has been held, however, that when the police have probable cause to believe a person has hidden contraband or criminal evidence within his home, the officers may prevent that person from entering his home while officers obtain a search warrant. Thus, in *Illinois v. McArthur,*[748] the U.S. Supreme Court observed: "[T]he police officers in this case had probable cause to believe that a home contained contraband, which was evidence of a crime. They reasonably believed that the home's resident, if left free of any restraint, would destroy that evidence." It was reasonable, therefore, for the officers to restrict the resident from entering the home pending the acquisition of a search warrant. The period of restraint — two hours — was "no longer than reasonably necessary for the police, acting with diligence, to obtain the warrant." In *McArthur,* the Court also held that, pending the arrival of a search warrant, if a person detained outside of his home asks to enter the home, officers may enter with him to ensure that evidence is not destroyed. The need to "preserve evidence" of this "jailable" drug offense "was sufficiently urgent or pressing to justify" the restriction that entry would be permitted only in the company of an officer. "In this case, the police had good reason to fear that, unless restrained, McArthur would destroy the drugs before they could return with a warrant. The reasonable restraint imposed by the police merely prevented McArthur from entering his home 'unaccompanied.'"[749] In this respect, the Court said, "the reasonableness of the greater restriction (preventing reentry) implies the reasonableness of the lesser (permitting reentry conditioned on observation)."[750]

4.2.2.1.4.1. When the knock and announce prompts the sound of evidence destruction

In *Kentucky v. King,*[751] the Supreme Court determined that a warrantless home entry will be justified by "exigent circumstances" in a situation where the police, by knocking on the door of a residence and announcing their presence, cause the occupants to attempt to destroy evidence. Here, even though this exigency may have been "police created," the officers' actions prior to their entry into the apartment were "entirely lawful."[752] "[T]he exigent circumstances rule applies when the police do not gain entry to premises by means of an actual or threatened violation of the Fourth Amendment."[753]

The United States Supreme Court remanded the case to the Kentucky Supreme Court for a determination as to whether an exigency was in fact present. The state court concluded that "the Commonwealth failed to meet its burden of demonstrating exigent circumstances justifying a warrantless entry." During the suppression hearing, the officer repeatedly referred to the "possible" destruction of evidence. He stated that he heard people moving inside the apartment. He never articulated the specific sounds he heard which led him to believe that evidence was about to be destroyed. "In fact, the sounds as described at the suppression hearing were indistinguishable from ordinary household sounds, and were consistent with the natural and reasonable result of a knock on the door. Nothing in the record suggests that the sounds officers heard were anything more than the occupants preparing to answer the door."[754] Consequently, the court, concluded that exigent circumstances did not exist when police made a warrantless entry of the apartment.

---

747 *Vale v. Louisiana,* 399 U.S. 30, 90 S. Ct. 1969, 1972 (1970).
748 *Illinois v. McArthur,* 531 U.S. 326, 121 S. Ct. 946 (2001).
749 *Illinois v. McArthur,* 531 U.S. 326, 332, 121 S. Ct. 946, 950 (2001).
750 *Illinois v. McArthur,* 531 U.S. 326, 335, 121 S. Ct. 946, 952 (2001).
751 *Kentucky v. King,* 563 U.S. 452, 131 S. Ct. 1849 (2011).
752 *Kentucky v. King,* 563 U.S. 452, 131 S. Ct. 1849, 1854 (2011).
753 *Kentucky v. King,* 563 U.S. 452, 131 S. Ct. 1849, 1862 (2011).
754 *King v. Commonwealth,* 386 S.W.3d 119, 122 (Ky. 2012).

4.2.2.1.5. Blood alcohol

The natural dissipation of alcohol in the blood does not automatically justify a warrantless blood test of a drunk-driving suspect.[755] In those drunk-driving investigations where police officers can reasonably obtain a warrant before a blood sample can be drawn without significantly undermining the efficacy of the search, the Fourth Amendment mandates that they do so.

The Texas Court of Criminal Appeals has emphasized that there is an expectation of privacy in a person's own blood. Thus, absent an exigency, a warrant is required to test the blood for evidence of driving while impaired. In *State v. Martinez*,[756] defendant was involved in a traffic accident. He was taken to a hospital where his blood was drawn for medical purposes. The State later acquired and tested the blood, both without a warrant. In concluding that the test results should be suppressed, the court reasoned, "There are private facts contained in a sample of a person's blood beyond simple confirmation of a suspicion that a person is intoxicated. These private facts are those that a person does not voluntarily share with the world by the mere drawing of blood and may be subject to Fourth Amendment protection. We hold that there is an expectation of privacy in blood that is drawn for medical purposes."[757] Exceptions to this requirement must be decided on a case to case basis, based on facts showing that securing a warrant would have been impractical.[758]

For example, in *Mitchell v. Wisconsin*,[759] the U.S. Supreme Court held that a warrant is not required for a blood test when an officer has probable cause to believe a motorist has been driving while under the influence of alcohol, but the motorist is unconscious and cannot be given a breath test. In such cases, held the Court, "the exigent circumstances rule almost always permits a blood test without a warrant. When a breath test is impossible, enforcement of the drunk-driving laws depends upon the administration of a blood test. And when a police officer encounters an unconscious driver, it is very likely that the driver would be taken to an emergency room and that his blood would be drawn for diagnostic purposes even if the police were not seeking BAC information. In addition, police officers most frequently come upon unconscious drivers when they report to the scene of an accident, and under those circumstances, the officers' many responsibilities – such as attending to other injured drivers or passengers and preventing further accidents – may be incompatible with the procedures that would be required to obtain a warrant. Thus, *when a driver is unconscious, the general rule is that a warrant is not needed*."[760]

The Court, in *State v. Ruiz*,[761] held that it is unreasonable under the Fourth Amendment for an officer to rely on an unconscious driver's implied consent for a blood draw when the unconsciousness prevents the officer from seeking actual consent. According to the Court, "irrevocable implied consent is not free and voluntary and does not satisfy the consent exception to the warrant requirement of the Fourth Amendment." *Id.* at 785. Nonetheless, the Court remanded the matter for reconsideration in light of *Mitchell v. Wisconsin* for a determination of whether exigent circumstances justified the blood draw. On remand the appellate court determined there were sufficient exigent circumstances to justify the warrantless blood draw.[762]

In *Cole v. State*,[763] at 10:30 p.m. defendant Steven Cole drove his truck 110 miles per hour down a city street in Longview. He ran the red light at a busy intersection and struck Jim Hightower's truck. The impact from the crash caused Hightower's truck to explode in flames, killing Hightower instantly.

Officer Castillo arrived on the scene and approached the burning truck, but he could not tell if Hightower was dead or alive at the time. At the other end of the accident scene, was Cole's truck resting against a building with flames approaching it. Cole was in the truck yelling for help, but Castillo could not open the doors. At this point, other officers arrived and helped to put out the flames. With their assistance, Castillo was able

---

755 *See Missouri v. McNeely*, 569 U.S. 141, 165, 133 S. Ct. 1552, 1568 (2013); *State v. Villarreal*, 475 S.W.3d 784 (Tex. Crim. App. 2014).
756 *State v. Martinez*, 570 S.W.3d 278 (Tex. Crim. App. 2019).
757 *State v. Martinez*, 570 S.W.3d 278, 291 (Tex. Crim. App. 2019).
758 *Missouri v. McNeely*, 569 U.S. 141, 151, 133 S. Ct. 1552, 1560 (2013).
759 *Mitchell v. Wisconsin*, 588 U.S. ___, 139 S. Ct. 2525 (2019).
760 *Mitchell v. Wisconsin*, 588 U.S. ___, 139 S. Ct. 2525, 2531 (2019) (emphasis added).
761 *State v. Ruiz*, 581 S.W.3d 782 (Tex. Crim. App. 2019).
762 *See State v. Ruiz*, 2021 Tex. App. LEXIS 1837, at *12 (Tex. App.—Corpus Christi 2021).
763 *Cole v. State*, 490 S.W.3d 918 (Tex. Crim. App. 2016).

to remove Cole from the driver's seat. Castillo then began securing the accident scene, making sure nobody entered the area, as there was still considerable traffic in the area.

From a law enforcement perspective, Castillo needed to get as many officers to the area as possible because the fire and continued explosions caused a serious threat to public safety. Moreover, several major intersections had to be blocked off in order to keep the public at a safe distance. The accident occurred around a shift change, further complicating the manpower needed to secure the scene, conduct the investigation, and maintain public safety.

Meanwhile, defendant was sitting on a curb mumbling to himself. He told EMS that he had taken "some meth."[764] He was transported to the hospital. Thereafter, it took the lead investigator, Officer Higginbotham, over three hours to investigate the accident scene, which encompassed a debris field approximately one block long. The scene was not cleared until 6 a.m. the following morning.

At the hospital, Officer Wright arrested defendant at 11:38 p.m. When defendant refused to provide a voluntary blood sample, Wright directed hospital staff to draw his blood. The warrantless blood-draw was performed at 12:20 a.m. Defendant argued that the warrantless blood-draw violated *McNeeley*. The Texas Court of Criminal Appeals disagreed.

According to the court, a combination of factors served to create an exigency to justify the warrantless blood draw: (1) the length of time to process the accident scene and determine there was probable cause to believe the defendant had caused Hightower's death; (2) the large debris field; (3) Higginbotham could not leave the scene because he was the only qualified accident investigator; (4) Officer Wright could not leave the hospital to process a warrant because she was guarding the defendant who was in custody; (5) other officers could not be spared from the accident scene due to public safety concerns; (6) the number of officers required to work the scene made up nearly half of the officers required to cover the city of Longview; (7) the hour-and-a-half deal it would take to obtain the warrant; (8) the concern over the metabolization of the methamphetamine in the defendant's body; and (9) the negative impact any medications given to the defendant would have on the blood tests for methamphetamine.[765]

In *State v. Garcia*,[766] Officers Rodriquez and Torres responded to the scene of a horrific car accident in which three people would ultimately die as a result of the crash. They quickly learned that Garcia was one of the drivers and that he was being transported to a nearby hospital. The officers suspected that Garcia was under the influence of alcohol so, when he refused to provide a sample of breath or blood, Rodriquez returned to the station to prepare a search warrant. In the meantime, Torres accompanied Garcia to the hospital. At the hospital, Torres became concerned that Garcia would receive an IV prior to the warrant being approved. However, Garcia initially refused an IV and the nurse did not administer one. In spite of that fact, Torres requested the phlebotomist to draw Garcia's blood prior to obtaining the warrant. An analysis of Garcia's blood showed that he had a blood-alcohol concentration of 0.268 at the time of the draw. The analysis also detected the presence of "Benzoylecgonine," a cocaine metabolite, in Garcia's blood.

The court recognized that the dilemma faced by an officer attempting to obtain blood from a patient in need of medical treatment is more like a "now or never" situation than it is like a "natural dissipation" situation. "In the emergency-room setting, the officer faces an impossible choice between (1) delaying a potentially life-saving treatment to obtain the best possible evidence or (2) allowing that evidence to be spoiled so that a suspect's life might be saved. With these concerns in mind, we do not believe the Fourth Amendment requires police officers to wait until an I.V. needle is inches away from the suspect's arm before they may legally intervene – at which time, paradoxically, they might be duty-bound not to intervene. [Accordingly], if an officer is actually aware of facts from which an objectively reasonable officer could conclude that an evidence-destroying medical treatment is imminent, the Fourth Amendment allows the officer to take any reasonable steps to preserve the integrity of the imperiled evidence."[767] However, the court concluded that, in this case, Officers Torres and Rodriquez were not actually in this difficult situation. Rather, "at the time the

---

[764] *Cole v. State*, 490 S.W.3d 918, 920 (Tex. Crim. App. 2016).

[765] *Cole v. State*, 490 S.W.3d 918, 926 (Tex. Crim. App. 2016). *See also Weems v. State*, 493 S.W.3d 574 (Tex. Crim. App. 2016) (finding no exigency where no practical problems in obtaining warrant).

[766] *State v. Garcia*, 569 S.W.3d 142 (Tex. Crim. App. 2018).

[767] *State v. Garcia*, 569 S.W.3d 142, 154-55 (Tex. Crim. App. 2018).

officers ordered the phlebotomist to take a sample of Garcia's blood, all medical treatment of Garcia had stopped."[768] Thus the evidence found in the blood was suppressed.

What are the options in Texas for seeking blood evidence from an unconscious DWI suspect? Following the U.S. Supreme Court decisions invalidating implied consent for blood draws, the Texas courts have consistently required exigent circumstances to support a warrantless blood draw from a DWI suspect. As a result, there has been considerable focus on blood search warrants. Texas has two separate statutory provisions authorizing blood draw warrants: articles 18.01(j) and 18.02(10) of the Code of Criminal Procedure. In this regard, Article 18.01(j) provides:

Art. 18.01. Search Warrant.

* * * *

(j) Any magistrate who is an attorney licensed by this state may issue a search warrant under Article 18.02(a)(10) to collect a blood specimen from a person who:

(1) is arrested for an offense under Section 49.04, 49.045, 49.05, 49.06, 49.065, 49.07, or 49.08, Penal Code; and

(2) refuses to submit to a breath or blood alcohol test.

If a suspect does not refuse a request for a breath or blood sample, then article 18.01(j) could not authorize a warrant. Additionally, if there are insufficient exigent circumstances, then a warrantless blood draw would not be authorized. However, 18.01(j) is not the only search warrant option for blood discussed in article 18.01. The Amarillo appeals court rendered an opinion regarding the interplay between a warrant issued under 18.01(j) and one issued pursuant to 18.01(c), generally referred to as an evidentiary search warrant. Section 18.01(c) states:

(c) A search warrant may not be issued under Article 18.02(a)(10) unless the sworn affidavit required by Subsection (b) sets forth sufficient facts to establish probable cause: (1) that a specific offense has been committed, (2) that the specifically described property or items that are to be searched for or seized constitute evidence of that offense or evidence that a particular person committed that offense, and (3) that the property or items constituting evidence to be searched for or seized are located at or on the particular person, place, or thing to be searched. Except as provided by Subsections (d), (i), and (j), only a judge of a municipal court of record or a county court who is an attorney licensed by the State of Texas, a statutory county court judge, a district court judge, a judge of the Court of Criminal Appeals, including the presiding judge, a justice of the Supreme Court of Texas, including the chief justice, or a magistrate with jurisdiction over criminal cases serving a district court may issue warrants under Article 18.02(a)(10).

In *Henslee v. State*,[769] the court held:

[W]here there is no showing that the accused citizen has refused to give a specimen of breath or blood, as required for a warrant under subsection (j), law enforcement is not barred from seeking a general evidentiary warrant under subsection (c), on the grounds set forth in article 18.02(a)(10). The grounds for an evidentiary warrant issued under article 18.02(a)(10) do not include a suspect's refusal to voluntarily provide a breath or blood sample. Tex. Code Crim. Proc. Ann. arts. 18.01(c), 18.02(a)(10) (West Supp. 2018).

---

768 *State v. Garcia*, 569 S.W.3d 142, 155 (Tex. Crim. App. 2018).

769 *Henslee v. State*, No. 07-17-00285-CR, 2019 Tex. App. LEXIS 33, at *8 (Tex. App.–Amarillo, Jan. 3, 2019, pet. ref'd) (mem. op., not designated for publication).

In *Barrios v. State*,[770] an earlier case addressing a similar issue, the Amarillo court considered the purpose of article 18.01(j). The court determined that the purpose was to expand the number of magistrates available to issue search warrants for blood. According to the court, article 18.01(j) was not intended to limit the application of the other provisions of article 18.01:

> Simply put, subsection (c) of article 18.01 limits the magistrates who may sign search warrants. It is also clear that the passage of subsection (i) of article 18.01 was intended to expand the number of magistrates who could sign warrants in rural areas where there were none of the magistrates listed in subsection (c) to be found.[771] ... By passing the exception in subsection (j), it is this Court's view that the legislature was intending to expand, not contract, the number of magistrates available to sign search warrants for blood. Very consciously, the legislature used the term "any" in crafting this statute. Thus, it is apparent that the legislature wanted more magistrates available to review search warrants for blood, not less. This interpretation of the two provisions effectuates and harmonizes the statute so that all portions of the statute may be given effect.[772]

Indeed, one Texas court has held that 18.01(j) does not preclude the issuance of a search warrant for blood even if the suspect consented to a breath test:

> [Defendant's] consent to a breath test did not deprive the magistrate of authority to issue a warrant for [defendant's] blood draw under article 18.01(j). Even though the breath test indicated appellant's blood-alcohol content was 0.00, the warrant for the blood draw was supported by probable cause because, under the totality of the circumstances presented to the magistrate, there was a fair probability or substantial chance that evidence of a crime – that appellant had been driving while intoxicated – would be found in appellant's blood.[773]

4.2.2.2. Safety of the officer or others

If the officer believes that the suspect is armed or that the suspect presents a real and immediate danger to the officers or other people, a warrantless entry may be permitted.

For example, in *Brigham City, Utah v. Stuart*,[774] the U.S. Supreme Court held that the police "may enter a home without a warrant to render emergency assistance to an injured occupant or to protect an occupant from imminent danger." The facts of the case unfolded in late July, at about 3 a.m., when "four police officers responded to a call regarding a loud party at a residence. Upon arriving at the house, they heard shouting from inside, and proceeded down the driveway to investigate. There, they observed two juveniles drinking beer in the backyard. They entered the backyard and saw – through a screen door and windows – an altercation taking place in the kitchen of the home."[775] At the time, "four adults were attempting, with some difficulty, to restrain a juvenile. The juvenile eventually broke free, swung a fist and struck one of the adults in the face." The victim of the blow was then observed spitting blood into a nearby sink. "The other adults continued to try to restrain the juvenile, pressing him up against a refrigerator with such force that the refrigerator began moving across the floor. At this point, an officer opened the screen door and announced the officers' presence. Amid the tumult, nobody noticed. The officer entered the kitchen and again cried out, and as the occupants slowly became aware that the police were on the scene, the altercation ceased."[776] The officers subsequently arrested the adults, charging them with various offenses.

---

[770] *Barrios v. State*, 452 S.W.3d 835 (Tex. App.– Amarillo [7th Dis.] 2014).

[771] *See Muniz v. State*, 264 S.W.3d 392, 398 (Tex. App.– Houston [1st Dist.] 2008).

[772] *Barrios v. State*, 452 S.W.3d 835, 846 (Tex. App.– Amarillo [7th Dis.] 2014) (citing *Tex. Gov't Code* § 311.021; *Clinton v. State*, 354 S.W.3d 795, 800 (Tex. Crim. App. 2011) (holding that to determine the collective intent of the legislature in passing legislation, we look first to the literal text).

[773] *Thom v. State*, 437 S.W.3d 556, 564 (Tex. App.– Houston [14th Dist.] 2014).

[774] *Brigham City, Utah v. Stuart*, 547 U.S. 398, 126 S. Ct. 1943 (2006).

[775] *Brigham City, Utah v. Stuart*, 547 U.S. 398, 126 S. Ct. 1943, 1946 (2006).

[776] *Brigham City, Utah v. Stuart*, 547 U.S. 398, 126 S. Ct. 1943, 1946 (2006).

Finding the officers' actions proper, the Court said: "Here, the officers were confronted with *ongoing* violence occurring *within* the home.... We think the officers' entry here was plainly reasonable under the circumstances." It was clear to the Court that "the officers had an objectively reasonable basis for believing both that the injured adult might need help and that the violence in the kitchen was just beginning. Nothing in the Fourth Amendment required them to wait until another blow rendered someone 'unconscious' or 'semi-conscious' or worse before entering. The role of a peace officer includes preventing violence and restoring order, not simply rendering first aid to casualties; an officer is not like a boxing (or hockey) referee, poised to stop a bout only if it becomes too one-sided."[777]

In Michigan v. Fisher,[778] several officers responded to a complaint of a disturbance – a man was reportedly "going crazy" at a residence. Upon arrival, the officers found a household in considerable chaos: a pickup truck in the driveway with its front smashed, damaged fenceposts along the side of the property, and three broken house windows, the glass still on the ground outside. The officers also noticed blood on the hood of the pickup and on clothes inside of it, as well as on one of the doors to the house. Through a window, the officers could see defendant inside, screaming and throwing things. The back door was locked, and a couch had been placed to block the front door. The officers knocked, but defendant would not answer. They saw defendant had a cut on his hand and asked if he needed medical help, but defendant ignored these questions and demanded, with accompanying profanity, that they get a search warrant. One of the officers then pushed his way inside. The Court ruled that this warrantless entry was justified under the "Emergency Aid" doctrine because of defendant's violent behavior. Although the officers had not seen defendant hit anyone, they did see him throwing things, and it was objectively reasonable to believe that these projectiles might have a human target (perhaps a spouse or a child), or that defendant would hurt himself in the course of his rage.

4.2.2.2.1. When there is an imminent threat of violence

In *Ryburn v. Huff*,[779] two Burbank, California, officers responded to a call at a high school. The principal informed them that a student, Vincent Huff, was rumored to have written a letter threatening to "shoot up" the school and asked them to investigate. In interviewing Vincent's classmates, the officers learned he was a frequent target of bullying who had been absent from school for two days. The officers found this to be a cause for concern, as they had received training on targeted school violence and were aware that these characteristics are common among perpetrators of school shootings. The officers decided to continue their investigation by interviewing Vincent. At his house, the officers knocked on the door and announced several times they were with the Burbank Police Department. No one answered the door or otherwise responded to the knocks. One of the officers then called the home telephone. The officers could hear the phone ringing inside the house, but no one picked up. They next tried calling the cell phone of Vincent's mother, Mrs. Huff. When Mrs. Huff answered the phone, she indicated that both she and Vincent were inside the house; however, when the officers indicated they were outside and asked to speak with her, she hung up. One or two minutes later, Mrs. Huff and Vincent walked out of the house and stood on the front steps. The officers advised Vincent that they were there to discuss the threats. Vincent, apparently aware of the rumor that was circulating at his school, responded, "I can't believe you're here for that." An officer asked Mrs. Huff if they could continue the discussion inside the house, but she refused; in the officer's experience, it was "extremely unusual" for a parent to decline an officer's request to interview a juvenile inside. He also found it odd that Mrs. Huff never asked the officers the reason for their visit. The officer then asked if there were any guns in the house. Mrs. Huff responded by immediately turning around and running into the house. The officers followed her in. There, after a brief argument with Vincent's father, the interview continued for 5 to 10 minutes. The officers concluded the rumor about Vincent was false and left. The Huffs brought an action claiming the police violated their rights by entering their home without a warrant. The Supreme Court disagreed, finding that Mrs. Huff's odd behavior, combined with the information the officers gathered at the school, could have led reasonable officers to believe "that there could be weapons inside the house, and that family members or the officers themselves were in danger."

---

777 *Brigham City, Utah v. Stuart*, 547 U.S. 398, 126 S. Ct. 1943, 1949 (2006).
778 *Michigan v. Fisher*, 558 U.S. 45, 130 S. Ct. 546 (2009).
779 *Ryburn v. Huff*, 565 U.S. 469, 132 S. Ct. 987 (2012).

4.2.2.2.1.1. Burglary in progress

When a law enforcement officer has probable cause to believe that a burglary or other crime is in progress, or has just occurred, and that someone within the premises might be in need of assistance, sufficient exigent circumstances arise to justify an immediate warrantless entry of the premises.[780]

4.2.2.3. Hot/fresh pursuit

This doctrine may be analyzed as a specific application of the exigent circumstance doctrine discussed above. A warrantless entry of a private dwelling will be allowed when police are in hot pursuit of a suspect who they have probable cause to believe committed a felony. The pursuing officers must also have probable cause to believe the suspect entered a specific dwelling. After following the suspect into a dwelling, the police may seize contraband, weapons, instrumentalities or fruits of crime that are in plain view.[781]

In *United States v. Johnson*,[782] the police watched as defendant sat on his great-grandmother's front porch while other people on the porch made their way out into the street to engage in apparent drug transactions with passing cars; defendant seemed to be in charge of the operation. Eventually, a Geo Tracker drove up in front of the house, and defendant walked down to meet it; when the Tracker drove off, defendant had a white baggie and a scale in his hands. Two officers, wearing tactical vests with patches reading "POLICE" moved in to attempt to stop the Tracker, but could not. Upon seeing the officers, defendant ran up the stairs and into the house. According to the Sixth Circuit, the officers made a valid hot pursuit entry when they followed him inside, even though they did not have a warrant.

4.2.2.4. Emergency aid

There are many situations in which the police are required to enter premises without a warrant and without probable cause to believe a crime has occurred. Police officers perform various tasks in addition to conducting criminal investigations and identifying and apprehending criminal suspects. Beyond the "crime fighting" function, the police are also expected to: (1) "reduce the opportunities for the commission of some crimes through preventative patrol and other measures"; (2) "aid individuals who are in danger of physical harm"; (3) "assist those who cannot care for themselves"; (4) "resolve conflict"; (5) "create and maintain a feeling of security in the community"; and (6) "provide other services on an emergency basis."[783]

As observed by the former Chief Justice (then Judge) Burger in *Wayne v. United States*,[784] in such situations there must be a "balancing of interests and needs." In this regard, "[w]hen policemen, firemen or other public officers are confronted with evidence which would lead a prudent and reasonable official to see a need to act to protect life or property, they are authorized to act on that information, even if ultimately found erroneous."[785]

Thus, when an emergency arises – for example, a medical emergency – the police should not be required to hold a belief that the imminent death of a person is probable, or that there is a near certainty as to the presence of a person at risk in a premises. Rather, the test should be whether the police have "a prudent and reasonably based belief" that, at the premises, there is a potential medical or other emergency of unknown dimension. As stated in *Wayne*:

---

[780] *See Murdock v. Stout*, 54 F.3d 1437, 1442 (9th Cir. 1995); *see also United States v. Brown*, 449 F.3d 741, 748 (6th Cir. 2006) ("This and other circuits have held that an officer may lawfully enter a residence without a warrant under the exigent circumstances exception when the officer reasonably believes a burglary is in progress."); *see also Reardon v. Wroan*, 811 F.2d 1025, 1029-30 (7th Cir. 1987).

[781] *See, e.g., Warden v. Hayden*, 387 U.S. 294, 299 (1967) (while police are engaged in hot pursuit of a suspect and weapons, any other evidence of criminal behavior may be seized and admitted if it was discovered in a place where the suspect or weapons might be located).

[782] *United States v. Johnson*, 488 F.3d 690 (6th Cir. 2007).

[783] *ABA Standards for Criminal Justice* § 1-1.1 (2d ed. 1980).

[784] *Wayne v. United States*, 318 F.2d 205, 212 (D.C. Cir. 1963).

[785] *Wayne v. United States*, 318 F.2d 205, 212 (D.C. Cir. 1963).

> [A] warrant is not required to break down a door to enter a burning home to rescue occupants or extinguish a fire, to prevent a shooting or to bring emergency aid to an injured person. The need to protect or preserve life or avoid serious injury is justification for what would be otherwise illegal absent an exigency or emergency. Fires or dead bodies are reported to the police by cranks where no fires or bodies are to be found.... But the business of policemen and firemen is *to act*, not to speculate or meditate on whether the report is correct. People could well die in emergencies if police tried to act with the calm deliberation associated with the judicial process. Even the apparently dead often are saved by swift police response.[786]

What gives rise to the genuine exigency is the police need to protect or preserve life or prevent serious injury.

The "emergency aid" doctrine has been treated by most courts as a recognized exception to the written warrant requirement.[787] A close examination of it, however, reveals that it is nothing more than a "species of exigent circumstances."[788] The "emergency aid" doctrine stems from a common sense understanding that *exigent circumstances* may require public safety officials, such as the police, firefighters, or paramedics, to enter a dwelling without a warrant for the purpose of protecting or preserving life, or preventing serious injury. The primary rationale for the doctrine is that the Fourth Amendment does not require that public safety officials stand by in the face of an imminent danger and delay potential lifesaving measures while critical and precious time is expended obtaining a warrant.

In *In re J.D.*,[789] officers responded at around 8 a.m. to a report of two juveniles carrying a rifle in the vicinity of an elementary school. While searching the alley where they had last been seen, a witness approached and said that he saw the juveniles enter a yard on the other side of the alley and thought they may have gone into the adjoining house. As the officers approached the house, they heard loud noises from within that "sounded like running and an object hitting the wall." The front door had been tampered with; the screen was torn, the window was broken, and the door was slightly ajar. Police had probable cause to believe a burglary was in progress, and made a valid warrantless entry to investigate.

In *Brimage v. State*,[790] "when the officers decided to search [defendant's] home without a warrant the following facts were known to them:

> (1) Complainant had been missing for over two days;
> (2) [Defendant] was acquainted with complainant and her car had been found, unlocked and with her purse in plain view, parked near his residence in an area where she never parked according to her boyfriend;
> (3) Complainant was observed on the morning of her disappearance driving near [Defendant's] residence;
> (4) Six weeks earlier, another young lady reported to the police that [defendant] lured her to his house and attempted to assault her;
> (5) Complainant was wearing a red blouse when last seen;
> (6) A suitcase abandoned by [defendant] contained what appeared to be a piece cut from a red blouse which appeared to have a bloodstain on it as well as other cut-up women's clothing, a pair of scissors and a piece cut from a pair of blue pajama pants.

---

786 *Wayne v. United States*, 318 F.2d 205, 212 (D.C. Cir. 1963) (emphasis in original).

787 *See* 3 Wayne R. LaFave, *Search and Seizure, A Treatise on the Fourth Amendment* § 6.6(a) (6th ed. 2020), at 633-48 (and the cases listed therein); *see also id.* 2017-2018 Pocket Part, §6.6(a), at 87.

788 *But see Sutterfield v. City of Milwaukee*, 751 F.3d 542 (7th Cir. 2014), where the court identified a distinction between the emergency aid doctrine and exigent circumstances. "Exigency," observed the court, "is defined by a time-urgent need to act that makes resort to the warrant process impractical." *Id.*at 559. But here, where the police were responding to a psychiatrist's 911 call about a suicidal patient, "it is not at all clear to us, nor would it have been to the police, that the mere passage of time without apparent incident was sufficient to alleviate any concern that Sutterfield might yet harm herself." *Id.* at 562. Moreover, "in emergency aid cases, where the police are acting to protect someone from imminent harm, there frequently is no suspicion of wrongdoing at the moment that the police take action." *Id.* at 564.

789 *In re J.D.*, 68 S.W.3d 775 (Tex. App. 2001).

790 *Brimage v. State*, 918 S.W.2d 466 (Tex. Crim. App. 1996).

(7) A report from Judge Bennett who, on his own, entered [defendant's] residence (Judge Bennett is [defendant's] uncle) and who reported finding part of a pair of blue pajamas, other cut-up women's clothing and evidence of a "violent struggle" in the master bedroom."[791]

The police were justified in concluding that an emergency was taking place and entering the home without a warrant. The evidence they found in plain view was allowed.

Texas uses an objective standard of reasonableness in determining whether a warrantless search is justified under the Emergency Doctrine. This objective standard takes into account the facts and circumstances known to the police at the time of the search.[792]

In Texas, "to justify the search of a residence under the emergency doctrine, the State must show 1) that the officers had probable cause to search the residence, and 2) that obtaining a search warrant was impracticable because the officers reasonably believed there was an immediate need to act in order to protect or preserve life or to prevent serious bodily injury."[793]

Once the police respond and enter a premises pursuant to this exigency, they have the right to restore or maintain the status quo during the emergency to control the dangerous or dynamic situation. This right enables the officer to take a number of intrusive actions ranging from a command to halt to a seizure of an individual. During the investigation of an emergency situation, the police may search for weapons to protect themselves and others and may look for injured or missing persons.

In upholding warrantless entries based on the "emergency aid" doctrine, many courts have observed that the officers would have been derelict in their duty had they not acted. In the final analysis, the prosecution is not required to prove that an actual emergency existed at the time of the officers' warrantless entry. Rather, the government need only show that the facts and circumstances surrounding the entry and search were such that the officers reasonably believed there existed an emergency that made obtaining a search warrant impracticable.

Thus, the key factor in such cases is the officer's objectively reasonable belief that, given the totality of the circumstances, a person is in need of assistance. For example, warrantless entries have been upheld where immediate police action was necessary to:

- rescue people from a burning building;
- seek an occupant reliably reported to be missing;
- seek a person known to be suffering from a gunshot or knife wound;
- seek a person who was so badly beaten that he or she is probably dead;
- seek a person who had been repeatedly struck with a pipe until he stopped moving;
- check on an odor of rotting flesh;
- check on the well-being of unattended children;
- ensure that a weapon within the premises does not remain accessible to children there;
- assist a person reported to be ill or injured;
- seek possible victims of violence in premises recently burglarized;
- seek possible victims in premises where shots have been fired;
- investigate where disarray and blood stains indicate a recent affray has occurred;
- discover the location of explosives;
- retrieve an object which had obstructed the breathing passage of a child, where the child's doctor needed to examine the object to provide proper medical treatment;
- locate a high school student who, a short time earlier, swallowed an undetermined amount of cocaine and ran home;
- attempt to discover what substance might have been eaten by several children who were critically ill;

791 *Brimage v. State*, 918 S.W.2d 466, 501-02 (Tex. Crim. App. 1996).
792 *Brimage v. State*, 918 S.W.2d 466 (Tex. Crim. App. 1996).
793 *In re J.D.*, 68 S.W.3d 775, 779 (Tex. App. 2001).

- respond to a credible threat of suicide;[794]
- ensure the prompt involuntary commitment of a person who is apparently mentally ill and dangerous;
- respond to a fight within a premises;
- check out an occupant's hysterical telephone call to the police;
- determine the well-being of the occupants of a residence where screams were recently heard by neighbors who were unable to get anyone to answer the phone at the residence;
- seek persons possibly affected by detected noxious fumes in the home; and
- enter a hotel room based on a hotel guest's report of an armed robbery and the reasonable belief that a victim or gunman was still in the room.[795]

Once inside the premises, an officer's conduct "must be carefully limited to achieving the objective which justified the entry – the officer may do no more than is reasonably necessary to ascertain whether someone is in need of assistance and to provide that assistance."[796] If the officer determines that his or her assistance is, in fact, not needed, the officer must immediately depart the premises, rather than exploring further. If, however, the officer's "emergency aid" entry results in the "plain view" discovery of evidence of a crime or contraband, that evidence may be admissible under "plain view" principles.

In *Laney v. State*,[797] shortly after midnight, deputies responded to a dispute between neighbors at defendant's mobile home park. While the deputies were speaking with his neighbors, defendant came out of his trailer, approached the officers, and explained that he had turned off the electricity to a neighbor's trailer in retaliation for the neighbor doing the same to him. Defendant was placed in the back of a patrol car pending possible charges for criminal mischief. While the deputies continued their investigation, two young boys came out of defendant's darkened trailer onto the front porch. When asked if these were his sons, defendant said they were not. One of the boys, who appeared to be about 10 years old, made eye contact with a deputy and then went back inside. The deputies then asked defendant if he had ever been arrested, and he admitted that he had, for indecency with a child. Because defendant was possibly going to jail, the deputies had a responsibility to get the children out of the trailer and find out who their parents were. As they approached the trailer, one of the boys came out. He said the other boy, his brother, was in a back bedroom. The deputies called out to the other boy, but received no response. One deputy then entered to find the boy. While searching with a flashlight, he saw sexually explicit pictures of young boys on a shelf; he did not touch the pictures, but instead led the boy out of the trailer. His observations later served as the basis for a search warrant. The court upheld the deputy's entry under the emergency doctrine; his actions were directed solely toward securing the well-being of the child, not toward continuing the investigation of defendant.

When a homeowner makes a 911 call and requests immediate assistance because of an emergency, he is indicating his consent to (i) the arrival and entry of the responding officers to resolve that emergency and, (ii) absent any evidence of the revocation of that consent, an objectively reasonable limited investigation by the responding officers into the emergency that the homeowner reported.[798] Therefore, in *Johnson v State*,[799]

---

[794] *See, e.g., Sutterfield v. City of Milwaukee*, 751 F.3d 542 (7th Cir. 2014); *Rice v. ReliaStar Life Ins. Co.*, 770 F.3d 1122 (5th Cir. 2014) (no Fourth Amendment violation where officers entered house in attempt to prevent suicide); *United States v. Timmann*, 741 F.3d 1170, 1180 (11th Cir. 2013) (discussing *Roberts v. Spielman*, 643 F.3d 899, 902 (11th Cir. 2011) (warrantless entry justified on sister-in-law's report of possible suicide based on prior attempts, bipolar disorder, presence of vehicle, televisions on, and no answer at door)); *United States v. Uscanga-Ramirez*, 475 F.3d 1024 (8th Cir. 2007) (warrantless entry into locked bedroom justified by potential for suicide where wife told officers husband was not suicidal but was armed with gun and distraught over end of marriage); *Seibert v. State*, 923 So.2d 460, 467-68 (Fla. 2006) (officers' forced entry justified by roommate report of suicidal threat with large kitchen knife nearby).

[795] *See* 3 Wayne R. LaFave, *Search and Seizure, A Treatise on the Fourth Amendment* § 6.6(a) (6th ed. 2020), at 633-48, and the cases listed therein. *See also Brigham City, Utah v. Stuart*, 547 U.S. 398, 126 S. Ct. 1943 (2006); *Michigan v. Fisher*, 558 U.S. 45, 130 S. Ct. 546 (2009).

[796] 3 Wayne R. LaFave, *Search and Seizure, A Treatise on the Fourth Amendment* § 6.6(a) (6th ed. 2020), at 649-52.

[797] *Laney v. State*, 117 S.W.3d 854 (Tex. Crim. App. 2003).

[798] *Johnson v. State*, 226 S.W.3d 439 (Tex. Crim. App. 2007).

[799] *Johnson v. State*, 226 S.W.3d 439 (Tex. Crim. App. 2007).

warrantless entry into defendant's home was lawful after she called 911 and told the dispatcher that she had just shot her husband in self-defense.

4.2.2.4.1. Firefighters

Clearly, firefighters may make a warrantless entry into a burning building and seize any evidence of arson in plain view. As Justice Stewart explained:

> A burning building clearly presents an exigency of sufficient proportions to render a warrantless entry "reasonable." Indeed, it would defy reason to suppose that fire[fighters] must secure a warrant or consent before entering a burning structure to put out the blaze.[800]

They may also remain for a reasonable time after the blaze is extinguished to investigate its cause.[801] However, additional entries to investigate further must be made pursuant to the search warrant requirement.[802]

There are two types of warrants available to the investigating fire official, and the "object of the search determines the type of warrant required."[803] If the fire official's prime objective is to determine the cause and origin of a recent fire, an "administrative warrant" must be obtained. "Probable cause to issue an administrative warrant exists if reasonable legislative, administrative, or judicially prescribed standards for conducting an inspection are satisfied with respect to a particular dwelling."[804] This procedural requirement is accomplished by the official personally appearing before a judge, who will examine the official's affidavit and/or take his or her sworn testimony. At this meeting, the official must show that (1) a "fire of undetermined origin has occurred on the premises," (2) the "scope of the proposed search is reasonable[,]" (3) the "search will not intrude unnecessarily on the fire victim's privacy," and (4) the "search will be executed at a reasonable and convenient time."[805]

If, however, the fire official's prime objective is to gather evidence of criminal activity, *e.g.*, arson, a "criminal search warrant" must be secured. This is accomplished only upon a showing (before a judge) of probable cause to believe that relevant evidence will be found in the place to be searched.

Naturally, if, during the course of a valid administrative search, evidence of arson is discovered, the official may lawfully seize that evidence under the "plain view" doctrine. "This evidence may then be used to establish probable cause to obtain a criminal search warrant."[806]

4.2.2.5. Community caretaking

Care should be taken to distinguish the "emergency aid" doctrine from the "community caretaking" function of the police, which is very often used in the motor vehicle stop context. In this regard, it is now well recognized that, in addition to investigating crimes, the police also engage in "community caretaking" functions, which are "totally divorced from the detection, investigation, or acquisition of evidence relating to the violation of a criminal statute."[807] The Texas Court of Criminal Appeals explained the difference between "emergency aid" and "community caretaking" in *Laney v. State*.[808] "[W]hile both doctrines are based on an officer's reasonable belief in the need to act pursuant to his or her 'community caretaking functions,' the emergency

---

[800] *Michigan v. Tyler*, 436 U.S. 499, 509, 98 S. Ct. 1942, 1950 (1978).

[801] *Hummel v. State*, 2013 Tex. Crim. App. Unpub. LEXIS 1239 (Tex. Crim. App. Nov. 20, 2013).

[802] *See Michigan v. Tyler*, 436 U.S. 499, 509, 98 S. Ct. 1942, 1950 (1978); *see also Steigler v. Anderson*, 496 F.2d 793, 795-96 (3d Cir. 1974).

[803] *Michigan v. Clifford*, 464 U.S. 287, 294, 104 S. Ct. 641, 647 (1984).

[804] *Michigan v. Clifford*, 464 U.S. 287, 294 n.5, 104 S. Ct. 641, 647 n.5 (1984); *see also Camara v. Municipal Court*, 387 U.S. 523, 538, 87 S. Ct. 1727, 1735-36 (1967).

[805] *Michigan v. Clifford*, 464 U.S. 287, 294, 104 S. Ct. 641, 647 (1984).

[806] *Michigan v. Clifford*, 464 U.S. 287, 294, 104 S. Ct. 641, 647 (1984); *see also Martin v. State*, 620 S.W.3d 749, 767 (Tex. Crim. App. 2021).

[807] *Cady v. Dombrowski*, 413 U.S. 433, 441, 93 S. Ct. 2523, 2528 (1973).

[808] *Laney v. State*, 117 S.W.3d 854 (Tex. Crim. App. 2003).

doctrine is limited to the functions of protecting or preserving life or avoiding serious injury. Additionally, the [community caretaking] doctrine deals primarily with warrantless searches and seizures of automobiles (and will be limited to those circumstances except in unusual circumstances), while the emergency doctrine deals with warrantless entries of, but is not limited to, private residences."[809]

Cady v. Dombrowski was the first United States Supreme Court case to recognize a community-caretaking exception. It involved the search of an automobile operated by Chester Dombrowski, a Chicago police officer, who had been involved in an accident while visiting Wisconsin. During the accident investigation, local police became concerned that Dombrowski's service revolver was in the vehicle. At the time, Dombrowski appeared intoxicated to the officers, and offered conflicting versions of the accident. When no gun was found on Dombrowski's person, an officer checked the front seat and the glove compartment of the wrecked car, but to no avail. The officers' effort to find the weapon was motivated by the obligation of the police "to protect the public from the possibility that a revolver would fall into untrained or perhaps malicious hands."[810] Although no weapon was found in the vehicle, the Wisconsin officers did discover, in the trunk, various items that linked Dombrowski to a murder.

The Court held that the police search for the gun was lawful under the officers' "community caretaking" function.

> Because of the extensive regulation of motor vehicles and traffic, and also because of the frequency with which a vehicle can become disabled or involved in an accident on public highways, the extent of police-citizen contact involving automobiles will be substantially greater than police-citizen contact in a home or office.... Local police officers ... frequently investigate vehicle accidents in which there is no claim of criminal liability and engage in what, for want of a better term, may be described as *community caretaking functions, totally divorced from the detection, investigation, or acquisition of evidence relating to the violation of a criminal statute.*[811]

In *Cady*, the Court clearly distinguished automobile searches from searches of a home, pointing out that a search of a vehicle may be reasonable "although the result might be the opposite in a search of a home."[812] That distinction led to the Third Circuit declaring that the "community caretaking" doctrine simply "cannot be used to justify warrantless searches of a home."[813]

So, according to the United States Supreme Court, the defining characteristic of community-caretaking functions is that they are totally unrelated to the criminal investigation duties of the police.

In *Caniglia v. Strom*,[814] the Supreme Court clarified that law enforcement's "community caretaking" function is not a "freestanding" Fourth Amendment category which would permit warrantless searches or seizures in the home.[815] In *Caniglia*, during an argument with his wife, Edward Caniglia placed a handgun on the dining room table and asked his wife to "shoot [him] and get it over with." She did not; she left and spent the night at a hotel. The next morning, she was unable to reach Edward by phone, so she called the police to request a welfare check. The officers accompanied Caniglia's wife to the home, where they found Edward on the porch. The officers called an ambulance believing that Edward posed a risk to himself or others. Edward agreed to go to the hospital for a psychiatric evaluation on the condition that the officers not confiscate his firearms. But once he left, the officers entered his home and located and seized his weapons.

In discussing *Cady*, the *Caniglia* Court noted that while *Cady* did involve a warrantless search for a firearm, the location of that search was an impounded vehicle – not a home – and that is an important "constitutional difference." *Cady*'s unmistakable distinction between vehicles and homes also places into proper

---

809 *Laney v. State*, 117 S.W.3d 854, 861 (Tex. Crim. App. 2003).

810 *Cady v. Dombrowski*, 413 U.S. 433, 443, 93 S. Ct. 2523, 2528 (1973).

811 *Cady v. Dombrowski*, 413 U.S. 433, 442, 93 S. Ct. 2523 (1973) (emphasis added).

812 *Cady v. Dombrowski*, 413 U.S. 433, 440, 93 S. Ct. 2523 (1973) (emphasis added).

813 *See Ray v. Township of Warren*, 626 F.3d 170, 177 (3d Cir. 2010). *Compare State v. Bogan*, 200 NJ. 61, 975 A.2d 377 (2009) (upholding the warrantless entry of an apartment under the community caretaking function of the police). *See* Larry E. Holtz, *Criminal Procedure for Law Enforcement and Criminal Justice Professionals* (Blue360° Media), for a further discussion of this issue.

814 *Caniglia v. Strom*, 593 U.S. ___, 141 S. Ct. 1596 (2021).

815 *Caniglia v. Strom*, 593 U.S. ___, 141 S. Ct. 1596, ___ (2021).

context its reference to "community caretaking," where the Court discussed the frequency with which vehicles can become disabled or involved in accidents on public highways – often requiring the police to perform noncriminal "community caretaking functions," such as providing aid to motorists. Thus, "[w]hat is reasonable for vehicles is different from what is reasonable for homes. *Cady* acknowledged as much, and this Court has repeatedly 'declined to expand the scope of... exceptions to the warrant requirement to permit warrantless entry into the home.'"[816] Thus, there is "no special Fourth Amendment rule for a broad category of cases involving 'community caretaking.'"[817]

The Texas Court of Criminal Appeals first recognized the existence of the community-caretaking function in *Wright v. State*.[818] There, the court announced, "As part of his duty to 'serve and protect,' a police officer may stop and assist an individual whom a reasonable person – given the totality of the circumstances – would believe is in need of help. In determining whether a police officer acted reasonably in stopping an individual to determine if he needs assistance, the following factors are relevant to said determination:

(1) the nature and level of the distress exhibited by the individual;
(2) the location of the individual;
(3) whether or not the individual was alone and/or had access to assistance independent of that offered by the officer; and
(4) to what extent the individual – if not assisted – presented a danger to himself or others."[819]

The court additionally cautioned that the community-caretaking function is a narrow one. "Only in the most unusual circumstances will warrantless searches of private, fixed property, or stops of persons located thereon, be justified under the community caretaking function, given the greater expectation of privacy inherent with respect to residences and other private real property."[820]

In *Gonzales v. State*,[821] an Abilene officer stopped at a red light around 1 a.m. saw defendant's vehicle pull off the road and come to a stop on the shoulder just a short distance ahead of him. This area was "way out of town" with only a few businesses, no nearby houses, and minimal traffic. Believing defendant might need assistance, the officer activated his red and blue lights (to identify himself as a police officer and "not some bad guy") and pulled behind defendant's car. Defendant began to drive away, but quickly stopped. He later testified his sole reason for pulling in behind the car was "to check on them, see if they had a flat tire, if everything was okay, if maybe they were lost" and "to see if he was... having trouble, if he needed assistance...." The officer initiated contact with defendant and asked if everything was okay; he immediately noticed an odor of alcohol, as well as defendant's bloodshot eyes and slurred speech, which led to a DWI arrest. The court held the officer reasonably exercised his community-caretaking function in seizing defendant because, under the totality of the circumstances, it was reasonable to believe defendant was in need of help.

In *Byram v. State*,[822] a Fort Worth officer was monitoring the downtown bar district on Fourth of July. While stopped at a red light around 4:30 p.m., an SUV pulled beside him. The officer's window was down and an odor of alcohol wafted into his patrol car from the SUV. A woman was "hunched over" motionless in the passenger seat of the SUV. Concerned, the officer yelled to the driver (defendant), asking if his passenger was ok. Defendant did not respond, driving off when the light turned green. Despite observing no traffic violations, the officer pulled the SUV over. He discovered the female passenger was "barely conscious," and also observed an open container. After he called for an ambulance, he arrested defendant for DUI. The court ruled this was a valid caretaker stop. The officer was reasonably concerned that defendant's passenger was suffering from alcohol poisoning, and her motionless state suggested that she was in need of assistance. The precariousness of her situation was exacerbated by the fact that defendant appeared unconcerned, suggesting that, though the passenger was not alone in the car, she was not likely to receive assistance without the office's intervention. It was also possible that the passenger was incapacitated and had no control over

---

816 *Caniglia v. Strom*, 593 U.S. ___, 141 S. Ct. 1596, ___ (2021).
817 *Caniglia v. Strom*, 593 U.S. ___, 141 S. Ct. 1596, ___ (2021) (Alito, J., concurring).
818 *Wright v. State*, 7 S.W.3d 148 (Tex. Crim. App. 1999).
819 *Wright v. State*, 7 S.W.3d 148, 151-52 (Tex. Crim. App. 1999).
820 *Wright v. State*, 7 S.W.3d 148, 152 (Tex. Crim. App. 1999).
821 *Gonzales v. State*, 369 S.W.3d 851 (Tex. Crim. App. 2012).
822 *Byram v. State*, 510 S.W.3d 918 (Tex. Crim. App. 2017).

where defendant was taking her. Considering the totality of the circumstances, a reasonable person would believe she was in need of help. The officer's sole motivation was to assist her, not to enforce criminal laws.[823]

In *Corbin v. State*,[824] in late January, at approximately 1 a.m., Officer Benson noticed a vehicle approaching his patrol car. The vehicle crossed over the fog line and traveled on the shoulder of the road for about twenty feet before returning to its lane of travel. Using his radar gun, the officer clocked the vehicle traveling at fifty-two miles per hour; the speed limit was sixty-five. Because of the time of night, the relatively low speed of travel, and the motorist's crossing onto the shoulder of the road, Benson was concerned that the driver might be drunk or sleepy and thus in need of assistance. As a result, Benson pulled out and followed the car for a little over a mile. As he followed, Benson saw no traffic violations or indications that the driver was either drunk or fatigued. Benson then turned on his overhead lights, and the motorist pulled over without incident.

Officer Benson approached the car and asked the driver, identified as Bruce Corbin, to step out. The officer then conducted an immediate pat-down of Corbin for weapons and felt something on Corbin's back. Corbin explained that he was wearing a back brace for a back injury. As Officer Benson prepared a written warning, the dispatcher informed him that Benson had an extensive criminal history involving illegal narcotics. Benson then returned to Corbin and discovered that the back-brace was really a package of cocaine taped to Corbin's back. At this point, Corbin was placed under arrest.

The Texas Court of Criminal Appeals observed that Benson's stop of Corbin was a "seizure" within the meaning of the Fourth Amendment. The court then applied the *Wright* factors to the seizure to determine if Benson's belief that Corbin needed help was reasonable. The court determined that it was not.

> Although it certainly would be reasonable for a police officer to stop an individual who appears to be falling asleep while driving, the level of distress exhibited here does not reflect such an individual. [Corbin] crossed over the side stripe for only twenty feet and then continued to drive normally. If [he] was sleepy or falling asleep while driving, a reasonable person would expect to see more indications of fatigue. Here, we have one isolated incident of crossing the side stripe for less than one second. After the incident, [Corbin] drove in a normal fashion and did not present a risk to himself or other drivers. Although it is true that [Corbin] was traveling under the speed limit, we do not think that his speed was so low that a reasonable person would believe that [he] was in distress.... The level of distress exhibited by [Corbin] was simply too minor for Benson to reasonably believe that [Corbin] was falling asleep and in need of assistance.[825]

Accordingly, the court concluded that the community-caretaking function of the police could not be used to justify the stop and subsequent police action in this case.

4.2.2.5.1. Protective custody

Should an officer observe an individual conducting himself or herself in a manner that causes the officer to reasonably believe that the individual is a person requiring treatment for mental illness, the officer may take the individual into protective custody and transport the individual to a medical center or other community mental health crises intervention center for services.

Pursuant to Tex. Health & Safety Code § 573.001(a):

> A peace officer, without a warrant, may take a person into custody, regardless of the age of the person, if the officer:
>
> (1) has reason to believe and does believe that:
>
> (A) the person is a person with mental illness; and
>
> (B) because of that mental illness there is a substantial risk of serious harm to the person or to others unless the person is immediately restrained; and

[823] *See also Gonzalez v. State*, 563 S.W.3d 316 (Tex. App. 2018).
[824] *Corbin v. State*, 85 S.W.3d 272 (Tex. Crim. App. 2002).
[825] *Corbin v. State*, 85 S.W.3d 272, 278 (Tex. Crim. App. 2002).

(2) believes that there is not sufficient time to obtain a warrant before taking the person into custody.

A substantial risk of serious harm to the person or others may be demonstrated by:

(1) the person's behavior; or
(2) evidence of severe emotional distress and deterioration in the person's mental condition to the extent that the person cannot remain at liberty.[826]

The peace officer may form the belief that the person meets the criteria for apprehension:

(1) from a representation of a credible person; or
(2) on the basis of the conduct of the apprehended person or the circumstances under which the apprehended person is found.[827]

A peace officer who takes a person into protective custody shall immediately —

(1) transport the apprehended person to:
(A) the nearest appropriate inpatient mental health facility; or
(B) a mental health facility deemed suitable by the local mental health authority, if an appropriate inpatient mental health facility is not available; or
(2) transfer the apprehended person to emergency medical services personnel of an emergency medical services provider in accordance with a memorandum of understanding executed under Tex. Health & Safety Code § 573.005 for transport to a facility.[828]

A peace officer who takes a person into protective custody shall immediately inform the person orally in simple, nontechnical terms:

(1) of the reason for the detention; and
(2) that a staff member of the facility will inform the person of the person's rights within 24 hours after the time the person is admitted to a facility.[829]

A peace officer who takes a person into protective custody may immediately seize any firearm found in possession of the person.[830]

4.2.3. Consent searches

4.2.3.1. General aspects

As a recognized exception to the written warrant requirement, consensual searches continue to provide the law enforcement community with access to those areas in which an officer, desirous of searching, has less than the requisite probable cause to conduct a constitutional search or to secure a warrant. When a search is conducted pursuant to a valid consent, it may be conducted without a warrant and without probable cause.[831]

---

826 Tex. Health & Safety Code § 573.001(b).
827 Tex. Health & Safety Code § 573.001(c).
828 Tex. Health & Safety Code § 573.001(d).
829 Tex. Health & Safety Code § 573.001(g).
830 Tex. Health & Safety Code § 573.001(h).
831 *United States v. Matlock*, 415 U.S. 164, 165, 94 S. Ct. 988, 990 (1974); *Schneckloth v. Bustamonte*, 412 U.S. 218, 222, 93 S. Ct. 2041, 2045 (1973); *see also Balentine v. State*, 71 S.W.3d 763 (Tex. Crim. App. 2002).

As observed by the United States Supreme Court:

> "Consent searches are part of the standard investigatory techniques of law enforcement agencies" and are "a constitutionally permissible and wholly legitimate aspect of effective police activity." It would be unreasonable — indeed, absurd — to require police officers to obtain a warrant when the sole owner or occupant of a house or apartment voluntarily consents to a search. The owner of a home has a right to allow others to enter and examine the premises, and there is no reason why the owner should not be permitted to extend this same privilege to police officers if that is the owner's choice. Where the owner believes that he or she is under suspicion, the owner may want the police to search the premises so that their suspicions are dispelled. This may be particularly important where the owner has a strong interest in the apprehension of the perpetrator of a crime and believes that the suspicions of the police are deflecting the course of their investigation. An owner may want the police to search even where they lack probable cause, and if a warrant were always required, this could not be done. And even where the police could establish probable cause, requiring a warrant despite the owner's consent would needlessly inconvenience everyone involved — not only the officers and the magistrate but also the occupant of the premises, who would generally either be compelled or would feel a need to stay until the search was completed.[832]

When a person consents to a search of his property, he relinquishes his or her constitutional right to be free from unreasonable searches and seizures. Therefore, in order to be valid, the consent must be "voluntarily" given.[833] To be voluntary, the consent must be unequivocal and specific. In this respect, mere acquiescence cannot substitute for free consent. The consent must also be freely and intelligently given, uncontaminated by any duress or coercion, actual or implied. In all cases, "the question whether a consent to a search was in fact 'voluntary' or was the product of duress or coercion, express or implied, is a question of fact to be determined from the totality of the circumstances."[834] "The federal constitution requires the State to prove voluntary consent by a preponderance of the evidence. Under Article I, Section 9 of the Texas Constitution, however, the State must prove by clear and convincing evidence that consent was given voluntarily."[835]

4.2.3.2. The right to refuse

There is no requirement that officers tell an individual he or she has a right to refuse permission to search. "The law today is that knowledge of the right to refuse is but one factor in the totality of the circumstances to be examined in construing the reasonability of a search."[836] This aspect of the law of consent was underscored in *United States v. Drayton*, where the Court "rejected in specific terms the suggestion that police officers must always inform citizens of their right to refuse when seeking permission to conduct a warrantless consent search."[837] While knowledge of the right to refuse consent is one factor to be taken into account, there is no *per se* rule calling for a presumption of invalidity if a citizen consented without explicit notification that he or she was free to refuse to cooperate.[838]

---

[832] *Fernandez v. California*, 571 U.S. 292, 134 S. Ct. 1126, 1132 (2014) (quoting *Schneckloth v. Bustamonte*, 412 U.S. 218, 228, 231-32, 93 S. Ct. 2041, 2045 (1973)).

[833] *Bumper v. North Carolina*, 391 U.S. 543, 548, 88 S. Ct. 1788 (1968).

[834] *Schneckloth v. Bustamonte*, 412 U.S. 218, 227, 93 S. Ct. 2041, 2047-48 (1973).

[835] *Montanez v. State*, 195 S.W.3d 101, 105 (Tex. Crim. App. 2006); *see also State v. Ibarra*, 953 S.W.2d 242 (Tex. Crim. App. 1997).

[836] *Schneckloth v. Bustamonte*, 412 U.S. 218, 227, 93 S. Ct. 2041, 2047-48 (1973); *see also State v. Kelly*, 204 S.W.3d 808 (Tex. Crim. App. 2006); *United States v. Drayton*, 536 U.S. 194, 206, 122 S. Ct. 2105, 2113 (2002) (Officers do not have a constitutional duty to inform a suspect of his "right to refuse when seeking permission to conduct a warrantless consent search.")

[837] *United States v. Drayton*, 536 U.S. 194, 206, 122 S. Ct. 2105, 2113 (2002); *see also Ohio v. Robinette*, 519 U.S. 33, 39-40, 117 S. Ct. 417 (1996).

[838] *United States v. Drayton*, 536 U.S. 194, 207, 122 S. Ct. 2105, 2113 (2002).

4.2.3.3. Determining whether the consent was voluntary or coerced

There are several factors that a court will examine to determine whether a consent was voluntarily given or coerced. Factors which may suggest that consent was coerced include: (1) the presence of abusive, overbearing, or dictatorial police procedures; (2) police use of psychological ploys, or subtle psychological pressure or language, or a tone of voice which indicates that compliance with the request might be compelled; (3) statements or acts on the part of the police which convey to the consenting party that he is not free to refuse the search or to walk away from the officer; (4) that consent was obtained despite the consenting party's denial of guilt; (5) that consent was obtained only after the consenting party had refused initial requests for consent to search; (6) that consent was given after the police blocked or otherwise impaired the consenting party's progress, or in some other way physically restrained the individual, for example, by the use of handcuffs, by surrounding the individual with uniformed officers, by physically maneuvering the individual in a particular direction, by coercing the individual to move from a public area to a private area or office, or by the intimidating use of enforcement canines; (7) that consent was obtained only after the investigating officer retained possession of the consenting party's identification or plane, train or bus ticket; (8) that consent was obtained only after an officer informed the consenting party that if he were innocent, he would cooperate with the police; and (9) that the consent was given by a person already in custody or placed under arrest, and (i) the arrest occurred late at night, (ii) the arrest was made with a display of weaponry, (iii) the arrest was made by a forcible entry or by use of force against the person, (iv) the arrestee was placed in handcuffs or otherwise kept under close restraint after his arrest, (v) the police used the custody to make repeated requests for consent, and (vi) that the custody was used as leverage, in the sense that the arrestee was told he would be released if he gave consent.

Among the factors suggesting that the consent was voluntarily given are: (1) that the consenting party was not under arrest or in custody at the time the consent was given; (2) that (if in custody) the consenting party's custodial status was voluntary; (3) that consent was given where the consenting party had reason to believe that the police would find no contraband; (4) that the consenting party was aware of his constitutional right to refuse consent; (5) that the consenting party was informed by the police prior to the request for consent of what exactly they were looking for; (6) that the consenting party signed a "consent-to-search" form prior to the search; (7) that the consenting party admitted his guilt before giving consent; (8) that the consenting party affirmatively assisted the police in conducting the search; (9) that the consenting party used his own key to provide the police with access to the area to be searched; (10) that the consenting party demonstrated a cooperative posture throughout the encounter; (11) that the consenting party was not in any way restrained by the police; (12) that the consenting party knew the officers conducting the search; (13) that the consenting party was educated or intelligent; and (14) that the consenting party was no stranger to the criminal justice system.[839]

Note that if, in an attempt to gain consent to search a residence, officers mislead a person by saying or implying they have a warrant and will search anyway, when in reality they do not, any permission given is invalid.[840] However, the threat to obtain a warrant, while bearing on the voluntariness of consent, is not treated the same. Stating that a warrant can and will be obtained, if police in fact have the requisite grounds, will not automatically vitiate an ensuing consent.[841]

In *Meekins v. State*,[842] Officer Williams asked defendant six times whether he would consent to a search of his car. Defendant repeatedly stalled and evaded the question. After William's asked one final time, defendant either answered "yes" or "I guess." The record was unclear as to defendant's specific answer. The Texas Court of Criminal Appeals explained, "Not all compliance is mere acquiescence to official authority, however. 'Mere acquiescence' may constitute a finding of consent. Furthermore, repeatedly asking for consent does not result

---

839 *United States v. Mendenhall*, 446 U.S. 544, 555-57, 100 S. Ct. 1870, 1877-78 (1980); *United States v. Watson*, 423 U.S. 411, 424, 96 S. Ct. 820, 828 (1976); *United States v. Carter*, 854 F.2d 1102, 1106 (8th Cir. 1988); *United States v. Galberth*, 846 F.2d 983 (5th Cir. 1988); *United States v. Morrow*, 731 F.2d 233, 236 (4th Cir. 1984); *United States v. Ruigomez*, 702 F.2d 61, 65 (5th Cir. 1983); *United States v. Robinson*, 690 F.2d 869, 875 (11th Cir. 1982); *United States v. Setzer*, 654 F.2d 354, 357-58 (5th Cir. Unit B 1981), *cert. denied*, 459 U.S. 1041, 103 S. Ct. 457 (1982).

840 *Bumper v. North Carolina*, 391 U.S. 543, 549, 88 S.Ct. 1788, 1792 (1968).

841 *United States v. Salvo*, 133 F.3d 943 (6th Cir. 1998); *Fienen v. State*, 390 S.W.3d 328 (Tex. Crim. App. 2012).

842 *Meekins v. State*, 340 S.W.3d 454 (Tex. Crim. App. 2011).

in coercion, particularly when the person refuses to answer or is otherwise evasive in his response."[843] In *State v. Kelly*,[844] the court relied on the dictionary to define acquiescence as consent:

> [A]n express or implied finding of "mere acquiescence" to [a] blood draw also constitutes a finding of consent to the blood draw. Webster's II New Collegiate Dictionary defines "consent" as, among other things, "[v]oluntary allowance of what is planned or done by another." We further note that this same dictionary defines "acquiesce" as, among other things, "[t]o consent or comply without protest." Also, according to the Roget's Desk Thesaurus, "consent" and "acquiesce" are synonymous terms.[845]

In *Reasor v. State*,[846] defendant voluntarily consented to a search of his home after an illegal protective sweep. Although defendant was handcuffed and arrested at gunpoint, the guns were no longer drawn when he gave his consent. Also, the defendant had been given his *Miranda* warnings prior to his consent and was therefore warned that he had the right to remain silent. The court concluded, "[W]e hold that the State proved by clear and convincing evidence that appellant consented to the police search of his home. In fact, not only did he consent, but he cooperated with the police officers and showed them the illegal narcotics hidden in his home."[847] Note that consent to search is not rendered involuntary merely because the suspect has been placed under arrest at the time consent is given.[848]

4.2.3.4. Express or implied consent

A consent sufficient to avoid the necessity of a warrant may be express or implied from the circumstances surrounding the police-citizen encounter. In fact, an *implied* consent has been held to be as effective as any express consent to search. A consent may be "implied" when it is found to exist merely because of the person's particular responses to police inquiry or the person's conduct in engaging in a certain activity.[849] Thus, an implied voluntary consent may be found where the defendant has initiated police contact and has adopted a cooperative posture in the mistaken belief that he could thereby divert or prevent police suspicion of him.

4.2.3.5. Common authority

A valid consent may also be obtained from one other than the accused, *i.e.*, from a third party, so long as the consenting third party has the authority to bind the accused. In these circumstances, the inquiry whether a third-party consent is constitutionally valid focuses on whether the consenting third party possesses *common authority* over or other sufficient relationship to the premises or effects sought to be inspected.[850] The concept of third-party consent rests not upon the law of property, however, but upon the "mutual use of the property by persons generally having joint access or control for most purposes, so that it is reasonable to recognize that any of the cohabitants has the right to permit the inspection in his own right and that others have assumed the risk that one of their number might permit the common area to be searched."[851] Naturally, the prosecution must also demonstrate that the third-party consent was given freely and voluntarily.

---

[843] *Meekins v. State*, 340 S.W.3d 454, 463-64 (Tex. Crim. App. 2011) (citing *State v. Kelly*, 204 S.W.3d 808, 820-21 (Tex. Crim. App. 2006); *United States v. Pulvano*, 629 F.2d 1151, 1157 (5th Cir. 1980)).

[844] *State v. Kelly*, 204 S.W.3d 808 (Tex. Crim. App. 2006).

[845] *State v. Kelly*, 204 S.W.3d 808, 821 (Tex. Crim. App. 2006) (citations and internal quotes omitted).

[846] *Reasor v. State*, 12 S.W.3d 813 (Tex. Crim. App. 2000).

[847] *Reasor v. State*, 12 S.W.3d 813, 819 (Tex. Crim. App. 2000).

[848] *Harrison v. State*, 205 S.W.3d 549 (Tex. Crim. App. 2006).

[849] *See, e.g., United States v. Price*, 599 F.2d 494 (2d Cir. 1979) (valid search where defendant told police he did not care if they searched bag because it was not his and he had picked it up by mistake); *cf. North Carolina v. Butler*, 441 U.S. 369, 375-76, 99 S. Ct. 1755, 1758-59 (1979) (an express waiver is not invariably necessary to support a finding that the defendant waived his rights).

[850] *Matlock v. United States*, 415 U.S. 164, 169-172, 94 S. Ct. 988, 993 (1974).

[851] *Matlock v. United States*, 415 U.S. 164, 169-172, 94 S. Ct. 988, 993 (1974); *see also Limon v. State*, 340 S.W.3d 753 (Tex. Crim. App. 2011).

In *Balentine v. State*,[852] the owner of a "rear" house that defendant resided in had the power to consent to a search of the house; the utilities were in the owner's name and he paid them, and the owner allowed the defendant to occupy the rear house in exchange for cleaning up around the property. In *Patrick v. State*,[853] the defendant's girlfriend had power to consent to a search of the residence she had shared with the defendant. Although the girlfriend had left the premises the night before, she had signed the lease, she was responsible for one-half the utility bills, she told defendant she would return, and she returned several times to pick up personal effects. In *Garcia v. State*,[854] the landlord of a garage apartment rented to the defendant had the power to consent to a search of it. The owner kept some of his personal belongings in the garage and had an agreement with the defendant that he could enter whenever he wished.

Moreover, even where the party granting permission does not in fact have legally sufficient control over the premises, the consent may nonetheless be valid under the Fourth Amendment if the officer reasonably believes that the party had common control.[855] This is the rule for "apparent authority."

4.2.3.5.1. Parental consent

In *Sorensen v. State*,[856] defendant's mother consented to a search of his bedroom. Said the court:

> [W]e do not find that the "area" in which the marihuana was found was reserved to the use of appellant to the exclusion of all others. It is clear that appellant's mother, who had equal, if not superior right to be on the premises, was not restricted in any way from being in this "area." On the contrary, appellant's mother was in both his room and the closet in question with some regularity as a matter of course. Appellant had no "reasonable expectation of privacy" in this particular "area." His mother had a right to be where the marihuana was found, she could consent to a search of that area, and her consent would vitiate the need for any search warrant and would be binding upon anyone having rights in that "area."[857]

Similarly, in *Hubert v. State*,[858] defendant's grandfather allowed the police to search defendant's bedroom, located in the house that defendant and his grandfather shared. The court explained, "under the 'common authority' test, where the defendant lives 'with a parent or other close relative,' and the relative consents to a search of defendant's bedroom, most courts presume that the relative has sufficient common authority over the bedroom to authorize the consent to search."[859] Accordingly, the court concluded that –

> the appellant, lacking any proprietary interest in the house, or even any possessory right other than by the grace of his grandfather, assumed the risk that his grandfather might permit the search of any area of the house that he might reasonably suspect the appellant was using for criminal purposes, even including the appellant's bedroom – at least in the absence of any agreement between the two that would expressly prohibit the grandfather from making such an intrusion, or some other obvious indicium of exclusion, such as a lock on the door.[860]

4.2.3.6. Co-occupants

When one co-occupant of a residence consents to a search, but another co-occupant is also physically present and expressly objects to the search, then any subsequent search and seizure is unreasonable and invalid as to the objecting party.[861] In *Randolph*, defendant's wife called police regarding a domestic

---

[852] *Balentine v. State*, 71 S.W.3d 763 (Tex. Crim. App. 2002).
[853] *Patrick v. State*, 906 S.W.2d 481 (Tex. Crim. App. 1995).
[854] *Garcia v. State*, 887 S.W.2d 846 (Tex. Crim. App. 1994).
[855] *Illinois v. Rodriguez*, 497 U.S. 177, 110 S. Ct. 2793 (1990).
[856] *Sorensen v. State*, 478 S.W.2d 532 (Tex. Crim. App. 1972).
[857] *Sorensen v. State*, 478 S.W.2d 532, 534 (Tex. Crim. App. 1972).
[858] *Hubert v. State*, 312 S.W.3d 554 (Tex. Crim. App. 2010).
[859] *Hubert v. State*, 312 S.W.3d 554, 563 (Tex. Crim. App. 2010).
[860] *Hubert v. State*, 312 S.W.3d 554, 564 (Tex. Crim. App. 2010).
[861] *Georgia v. Randolph*, 547 U.S. 103, 120, 126 S. Ct. 1515, 1527 (2006).

disturbance. When officers arrived, defendant was not home, but his wife alleged that he had a cocaine habit, and that he had drug paraphernalia in the house. While officers were speaking with defendant's wife, defendant returned home. He denied he had a drug habit, but also refused to consent to a search of the residence. Undeterred, the officer who asked defendant for consent then turned to defendant's wife and asked her; she readily agreed to let him search, leading the officer to a bedroom, where the officer saw a section of a drinking straw covered with a powdery residue. Because defendant had been present at the start of the search and objected to it, the contraband the officer observed could not be used against him.

The rule in *Randolph* does not apply, however, if the objecting occupant is not physically present at the residence – this is true even if police are the reason for the occupant's absence (*i.e.*, if the occupant was lawfully detained or arrested prior to the request for consent to search being made).[862] Although a police officer may not remove someone from the premises for the purpose of preventing an objection, the officer is not required to locate an absent person to obtain the person's consent.[863] Two Texas cases illustrate this rule.

Just after the Supreme Court decided *Randolph*, *Odom v. State*[864] was decided in Texas. There, a search of a residence where defendant had been living for three months was unlawful when Sims, defendant's brother-in-law, who claimed to own the building, consented to a search. Defendant, who was present during the search, expressly objected and demanded that the officers obtain a warrant. Said the court, "Pursuant to *Randolph*, we conclude that the consent exception to the Fourth amendment's warrant requirement is inapplicable to the evidence seized and introduced against [defendant] at trial. After securing the residence and detaining [defendant], the officers should have abided by [defendant's] request that they obtain a search warrant because Sims's third-party consent was invalid in light of appellant's objection."[865]

In *Beall v. State*,[866] however, the defendant had no opportunity to object to the search because he was in the shower when the police arrived. Ronnie, another occupant of the motel room, provided consent. The court, citing *Randolph*, observed, "[Defendant] stands on the wrong side of the 'fine line' drawn by the Supreme Court in *Randolph*; as a potential objector, nearby but not invited to take part in the colloquy between Ronnie and the police, he loses out."[867]

4.2.3.7. Consent provided by a minor

In *Limon v. State*,[868] in response to a knock on the door by police at 2 a.m., a 13- or 14-year-old boy answered the door to his parents' home by himself. The Texas Court of Criminal Appeals cited *Randolph* and stated, "the Fourth Amendment does not prohibit a minor child from consenting to entry when the record shows the officer's belief in the child's authority to consent is reasonable under the facts known to the officer."[869] As to the officer's belief, the court concluded, "Under the facts available to Officer Perez at the moment, a mature teenager, possibly an adult, opened the front door to him at 2:00 a.m. and, after hearing that he was investigating a shooting, gave him consent to enter through the front door. We find that a person of reasonable caution could reasonably believe that [the child] had the authority to consent to mere entry under those circumstances."[870]

4.2.3.8. Traffic stops

Following a valid traffic stop, there is no requirement that an officer tell an individual that he or she is free to leave before asking for permission to search his or her vehicle.[871] It has been held, however, that a

---

[862] *See Fernandez v. California*, 571 U.S. 292, 134 S. Ct. 1126 (2014).
[863] *Georgia v. Randolph*, 547 U.S. 103, 121-122, 126 S. Ct. 1515, 1527 (2006).
[864] *Odom v. State*, 200 S.W.3d 333 (Tex. App. 2006).
[865] *Odom v. State*, 200 S.W.3d 333, 337 (Tex. App. 2006).
[866] *Beall v. State*, 237 S.W.3d 841 (Tex. App. 2007).
[867] *Beall v. State*, 237 S.W.3d 841, 847 (Tex. App. 2007).
[868] *Limon v. State*, 340 S.W.3d 753 (Tex. Crim. App. 2011).
[869] *Limon v. State*, 340 S.W.3d 753, 758 (Tex. Crim. App. 2011).
[870] *Limon v. State*, 340 S.W.3d 753, 758-59 (Tex. Crim. App. 2011).
[871] *Ohio v. Robinette*, 519 U.S. 33, 117 S. Ct. 417 (1996).

driver's right to refuse consent falls within constitutional protections against unreasonable searches. The exercise of that right cannot be penalized by making the refusal part of the foundation for a search.

4.2.3.9. Scope of the consent

The search must be limited to those areas to which the defendant actually or implicitly gives permission to search. The scope of the search is generally determined with reference to that which the officer is seeking, *i.e.*, to areas or containers where the stated subject of the search could be located. For example, in *Florida v. Jimeno*,[872] the U.S. Supreme Court approved the search of a paper bag, found on the floor of a car, for narcotics, after the defendant had given consent to a general search of his car. The Court concluded that, based on these facts, it was reasonable for the searching officer to believe the scope of the consent given permitted him to open the bag. The defendant knew the purpose of the search was to look for drugs, and it was objectively reasonable to assume drugs could be found there.

Consent to search may be limited in scope, and consent may be revoked. Any evidence obtained up to the time wherein the suspect revoked his consent is admissible. Once the suspect revokes his consent to search, however, the police must stop the search, unless some other basis justifies a continuation. If the police, for example, find illegal drugs during a consent search, they may arrest the suspect. They may then conduct a search incident to arrest, even if the suspect withdraws his consent to search after the discovery of illegal drugs. Because the illegal drugs were discovered before the withdrawal of the consent, they would be admissible. The continued search after the withdrawal of consent would be permitted because it would be based on a search incident to arrest rather than consent.

In *Lemons v. State*,[873] a father contacted police to complain that defendant had taken inappropriate pictures of his 14-year-old daughter. Officers went to question defendant at his place of employment. One of the officers asked defendant if he could see his cell phone. Defendant responded by handing the phone over. The officer examined the calling information on the phone, then hit the "camera" button. As a result, he observed several pictures stored on the phone, including one of the 14-year-old girl lying naked on a bed. The court found it reasonable to conclude that defendant's surrender of his phone in response to the officer's "open-ended request" implied a "grant of equally unbridled consent for the [officer] to examine the phone and the information contained therein."[874] The court also noted defendant did not object to the search as it was taking place. The scope of the search was within defendant's consent.

In *State v. Garrett*,[875] during a traffic stop for speeding and mud flap violations, a state trooper asked defendant if he could search defendant's truck for any "illegal contraband." Defendant said, "Yes," and did not limit his consent to any particular area of the truck. Because defendant's consent was so open-ended, the court concluded that the trooper did not exceed its scope by removing the driver's side door panel and looking inside (where he found nine balls of cocaine, three ecstasy pills, two sacks of clomiphene citrate pills, one bottle of liquid steroids and two baggies of powder cocaine).

In *Stokvis v. State*,[876] the male driver of a pick-up truck consented to a search of the vehicle. This consent did not extend to defendant's purse, which she had left on the passenger seat, because defendant was the only woman in the truck and the officer never asked for her consent or told her he planned to search the purse.

In *State v. Bagby*,[877] a deputy responded to a disturbance call. Defendant's neighbor said he had heard a sound like a .22 gunshot, saw his car window was shot out, then saw defendant "hunker down." Defendant denied shooting out the window, saying he had been in his shed the entire time. When asked, he did admit that he owned weapons, which were in his shed. He agreed to let the deputy inspect the weapons to see if they had been fired recently, but added that he did not want his property searched. When the deputy entered the shed, he immediately saw a small amount of marijuana in plain view. Then, after inspecting the weapons,

---

872 *Florida v. Jimeno*, 500 U.S. 248, 111 S. Ct. 1801 (1991).
873 *Lemons v. State*, 298 S.W.3d 658 (Tex. App. 2009).
874 *Lemons v. State*, 298 S.W.3d 658, 662 (Tex. App. 2009).
875 *State v. Garrett*, 177 S.W.3d 652 (Tex. App. 2005).
876 *Stokvis v. State*, 147 S.W.3d 669 (Tex. App. 2004).
877 *State v. Bagby*, 119 S.W.3d 446 (Tex. App. 2003).

he continued to search the shed, finding more drugs. The court held that while the marijuana was lawfully seized, all the contraband found after the deputy had completed his inspection of the firearms had to be suppressed, because the officer exceeded the scope of defendant's consent by remaining in the shed after the stated purpose of the search had been accomplished.

4.2.4. Automobile exception

4.2.4.1. General aspects

One of the "specifically established and well-delineated exceptions" to the warrant requirement is the "automobile exception," created by the United States Supreme Court in *Carroll v. United States*.[878] In that case, the United States Supreme Court established the exception as a result of an automobile's mobility, which makes it impractical to obtain a warrant.[879]

Under the Fourth Amendment, and the so-called "automobile exception," if police have probable cause to believe a readily mobile automobile contains contraband or evidence of a crime, they may lawfully conduct a warrantless search of the entire automobile, and any containers therein that may reasonably be expected to conceal the object of their search.[880] This rule applies equally to all compartments, containers and packages found within the vehicle "in which the object of the search may be found."[881]

Under the Fourth Amendment, separate exigent circumstances are not required.[882] Even if the officers have time to obtain a warrant before searching, they are not required to do so. In *Keehn v. State*,[883] an officer looked inside a minivan parked in a residential driveway as he was walking to the front door to question the suspects in an unrelated matter. He saw a 5-gallon propane tank in the back of the minivan; the "cutting of the tank" had a bluish-greenish discoloration. Based on his experience, the officer concluded that the tank held anhydrous ammonia, which he knew is used in the manufacture of methamphetamine. He lawfully seized the tank under the automobile exception. The court explained, "The automobile exception gave Officer Spragins the right to enter the van and seize the propane tank. The van was readily mobile, as demonstrated by Keehn's use of it days before the search, and it was subject to regulation. And based on his training and investigative experience concerning the production of methamphetamine, Officer Spragins had probable cause to believe that the tank contained anhydrous ammonia."[884]

State v. Crawford,[885] an officer approached defendant at a gas pump in response to a reckless driver call. The officer immediately saw that defendant's eyes were "bloodshot and glassy" and noticed "a light odor of burned marijuana coming from [defendant]." The car's window was open, and as the officer passed it, he could detect "the strong odor of burned marijuana coming from inside the vehicle."[886] The officer had probable cause to believe he would find drugs in the vehicle, so he was justified in conducting a warrantless search of it.

---

878 *Carroll v. United States*, 267 U.S. 132, 153-54, 45 S. Ct. 280, 285 (1925).

879 *Carroll v. United States*, 267 U.S. 132, 153, 45 S. Ct. 280, 285 (1925) (acknowledging the difference in practicality of obtaining a warrant for stationary objects like a store or dwelling and obtaining a warrant for objects like a ship or automobile, given the fact that "[a] vehicle can be quickly moved out of the locality or jurisdiction in which the warrant must be sought").

880 *See United States v. Ross*, 456 U.S. 798, 820-21, 102 S. Ct. 2157, 2172-73 (1982) (The scope of a warrantless search of a lawfully stopped vehicle based on probable cause "is no narrower – and no broader – than the scope of a search" that could be authorized by a search warrant.).

881 *United States v. Ross*, 456 U.S. 798, 820-21, 102 S. Ct. 2157, 2160, 2172-73 (1982); *see also California v. Carney*, 471 U.S. 386, 105 S. Ct. 2066 (1985) (automobile exception justified based on lower expectation of privacy in a vehicle); *Carroll v. United States*, 267 U.S. 132, 153-54, 45 S. Ct. 280 (1925) (warrantless automobile search supported by probable cause of a crime is lawful due to the mobility inherent in an automobile).

882 *See Pennsylvania v. Labron*, 518 U.S. 938, 116 S. Ct. 2485 (1996). *See also Maryland v. Dyson*, 527 U.S. 465 (1999).

883 *Keehn v. State*, 279 S.W.3d 330 (Tex. Crim. App. 2009).

884 *Keehn v. State*, 279 S.W.3d 330, 336 (Tex. Crim. App. 2009).

885 *State v. Crawford*, 120 S.W.3d 508 (Tex. App. 2003).

886 *State v. Crawford*, 120 S.W.3d 508, 509 (Tex. App. 2003).

In *Blaylock v. State*,[887] a named informant told a Kilgore detective that she could arrange a drug deal with defendant, from whom she had purchased cocaine on several prior occasions. Forty minutes later, she called the detective back to say that she had arranged the purchase of 2 ounces of cocaine, and that defendant would deliver it within 20 minutes to a specified convenience store, adding that he would have the drug hidden under the hood of the car. When defendant arrived at the store as predicted, police could search his car without first obtaining a warrant.

4.2.4.2. Closed packages in an automobile

In *California v. Acevedo*,[888] the U.S. Supreme Court held that the police are not required to obtain a warrant to open a closed package located in a motor vehicle when their probable cause relates to the package and not the entire vehicle. The Court wrote, "The line between probable cause to search a vehicle and probable cause to search a package in that vehicle is not always clear." The better rule is that "the police may search an automobile and the containers within it where they have probable cause to believe contraband or evidence is contained."

In *Micael v. State*,[889] a search of a sealed container seized from defendant's vehicle was allowed where the officers had reasonably trustworthy information that led them to believe there was probable cause that the vehicle contained evidence of the crime defendant was committing or about to commit. In *Robino v. State*,[890] "officers . . . responding to a report of an attempt to pass a counterfeit bill located a vehicle matching the description of the suspect's vehicle travelling on the same street which the victim reported it to be travelling, and only a short distance from the location of the offense. Almost immediately, Robino offered a story to the officers about being given counterfeit currency the night before, indicating his and the other occupant's probable involvement in the attempt to pass the counterfeit bill. Then, as the officers were interviewing the occupants, [the passenger] exited the vehicle, exposing a crumpled counterfeit bill on the front passenger's seat. These facts would warrant an objectively reasonable police officer to believe that items connected with the crime of forgery would be found in the vehicle or its contents. Since probable cause existed for the search, the officers were authorized to search the entire vehicle and all of its contents that may conceal evidence of forgery."[891]

4.2.4.3. Passengers belongings

When police have probable cause to believe an automobile contains contraband or evidence of a crime, they may search the entire car, including the contents of a *passenger's* personal belongings that may be capable of holding the object of the search.[892] According to the Supreme Court in *Wyoming v. Houghton*, effective law enforcement "would be appreciably impaired without the ability to search a passenger's personal belongings when there is reason to believe contraband or evidence of criminal wrongdoing is hidden in the car. As in all car-search cases, the 'ready mobility' of an automobile creates the risk that the evidence or contraband will be permanently lost while a warrant is obtained."[893] Thus, "police officers with probable cause to search a car may inspect passengers' belongings found in the car that are capable of concealing the object of the search." Moreover, such property may be searched, "whether or not its owner is present as a passenger or otherwise, because it may contain the contraband that the officer has reason to believe is in the car."[894]

---

[887] *Blaylock v. State*, 125 S.W.3d 702 (Tex. App. 2003).
[888] *California v. Acevedo*, 500 U.S. 565, 111 S. Ct. 1982 (1991).
[889] *Micael v. State*, 2018 Tex. App. LEXIS 6925 (Tex. App. Aug. 29, 2018).
[890] *Robino v. State*, 548 S.W.3d 108 (Tex. App. 2018).
[891] *Robino v. State*, 548 S.W.3d 108, 114 (Tex. App. 2018).
[892] *Wyoming v. Houghton*, 526 U.S. 295, 119 S. Ct. 1297 (1999).
[893] *Wyoming v. Houghton*, 526 U.S. 295, 119 S. Ct. 1297, 1302 (1999).
[894] *Wyoming v. Houghton*, 526 U.S. 295, 119 S. Ct. 1297, 1304 (1999).

4.2.4.4. Delayed searches

In *United States v. Johns*,[895] the U.S. Supreme Court held that a law enforcement officer may conduct a warrantless search of packages several days after those packages were removed from a lawfully stopped vehicle when the officer had probable cause to believe the packages contained contraband. When police have probable cause to believe a lawfully stopped vehicle contains contraband, they are entitled to conduct a warrantless "search of every part of the vehicle and its contents that may conceal the object of the search." The warrantless search of packages taken from that vehicle will not be deemed unreasonable merely because it occurs several days after the packages were unloaded from the vehicle. According to the Court, where officers are entitled to seize a package "and continue to have probable cause to believe that it contains contraband, ... delay in the execution of the warrantless search is [not] necessarily unreasonable."[896]

4.2.4.5. K-9 searches

The Fourth Amendment does not require that police have a reasonable, articulable suspicion of criminal activity before allowing a well-trained narcotics detection dog to sniff the exterior of a vehicle during a lawful traffic stop, as long as this does not prolong the duration of the stop.[897] Officers may not, however, extend an otherwise completed traffic stop in order to conduct a dog sniff, absent reasonable suspicion that there is contraband in the vehicle.[898]

A reliable drug dog's alert on the exterior of a vehicle may be sufficient, in and of itself, to establish probable cause for a warrantless search of the interior. Note also that a positive alert followed by a negative alert does not necessarily eliminate an officer's probable cause.

In this regard, a narcotics detection dog's failed alert is not *per se* dispositive of probable cause, but merely one factor to be considered, and, more specifically, that the subsequent failed alert did not necessarily negate an earlier positive alert.

4.2.4.6. Odor of contraband

When a qualified person smells an odor sufficiently distinctive to identity contraband, the odor alone may provide probable cause to believe that contraband is present.[899]

Thus, when an officer detects an odor of a controlled substance coming from a vehicle, an officer has probable cause to conduct a search of the vehicle if testimony has been elicited that the officer has training and experience in the detection of the controlled substance.[900]

4.2.4.7. Motor homes

Does a fully mobile motor home, which is located in a public parking lot, fall within the "automobile exception" to the Fourth Amendment warrant requirement? In *California v. Carney*,[901] the United States

---

895 *United States v. Johns*, 469 U.S. 478, 105 S. Ct. 881 (1985).

896 *United States v. Johns*, 469 U.S. 478, 105 S. Ct. 881, 886-87 (1985); *see also Florida v. White*, 526 U.S. 559 (1999) (noting that if there is probable cause to believe that a vehicle itself is contraband, it may be seized from a public place without a warrant); *Texas v. White*, 423 U.S. 67, 68, 96 S. Ct. 304, 305 (1975) (As long as probable cause exists for a warrantless search of a vehicle on the scene, the search may also be conducted later after the vehicle has been moved to the station house.); *see also Chambers v. Maroney*, 399 U.S. 42, 52, 90 S. Ct. 1975, 1981 (1970) ("The probable-cause factor" that developed on the scene "still obtained at the station house[.]").

897 *Illinois v. Caballes*, 543 U.S. 405, 125 S. Ct. 834 (2005).

898 *Rodriguez v. United States*, 575 U.S. 348, 135 S. Ct. 1609 (2015).

899 *Taylor v. United States*, 286 U.S. 1, 52 S. Ct. 466 (1932); *Johnson v. United States*, 333 U.S. 10, 15, 68 S. Ct. 367 (1948).

900 *Levine v. State*, 794 S.W.2d 451, 453 (Tex. App. 1990) ("probable cause to search a validly stopped vehicle without a warrant exists when the searching officer, experienced in detecting the odor of marihuana, smells burnt marihuana emanating either from the vehicle itself"); *Razo v. State*, 577 S.W.2d 709 (Tex. Crim. App. 1979); *Moulden v. State*, 576 S.W.2d 817 (Tex. Crim. App. 1978); *Luera v. State*, 561 S.W.2d 497 (Tex. Crim. App. 1978).

901 *California v. Carney*, 471 U.S. 386, 105 S. Ct. 2066 (1985).

Supreme Court said *yes*. The warrantless search of a fully mobile motor home, based upon probable cause, is proper under the "automobile exception" to the Fourth Amendment warrant requirement.[902]

The automobile exception will not apply, however, if the motor home is situated in such "a way or place that objectively indicates that it is being used as a residence."[903] Each of the following factors should be considered in determining whether the vehicle is being used as a residence and, therefore, whether a warrant must be obtained before its search: (1) the vehicle's location; (2) whether the vehicle is readily mobile or, instead, elevated on blocks or connected to utilities; (3) whether the vehicle is licensed; and (4) whether the vehicle has convenient access to a public road.[904]

4.2.4.8. GPS tracking

In *United States v. Jones*,[905] FBI agents installed a GPS tracking device on the undercarriage of defendant's Jeep while it was parked in a public parking lot. Over the next 28 days, the agents used the device to track the vehicle's movements (and once had to replace the device's battery when the Jeep was parked in a different public lot). By means of signals from multiple satellites, the device established the vehicle's location within 50 to 100 feet and communicated that location by cellular phone to an FBI computer. It relayed more than 2,000 pages of data over the four-week period. The U.S. Supreme Court found that installation of a GPS device, and the subsequent use of that device to monitor the vehicle's movements, constitutes a "search" within the meaning of the Fourth Amendment. The agents did more than conduct a visual inspection of the Jeep; by attaching the device to it, they encroached on a protected area. Because they did not first obtain a warrant, the Court held that the search was unlawful.

4.2.4.9. Driveway searches

In *Collins v. Virginia*,[906] the United States Supreme Court held that the automobile exception does not permit a law enforcement officer, uninvited and without a warrant, to enter the curtilage of a home in order to search a vehicle parked at the top of the home's driveway. According to the Court, "[t]he automobile exception does not afford the necessary lawful right of access to search a vehicle parked within a home or its curtilage because it does not justify an intrusion on a person's separate and substantial Fourth Amendment interest in his home and curtilage."[907]

4.2.5. Impound and inventory searches

4.2.5.1. General aspects

It is well recognized that police may conduct an inventory of the contents of lawfully impounded vehicles as a routine, administrative community-caretaking function, in order to protect the vehicle and the property in it, to safeguard the police and others from potential danger, and to insure against claims of lost, stolen, or vandalized property.[908]

---

902 *California v. Carney*, 471 U.S. 386, 105 S. Ct. 2066, 2070 (1985).

903 *California v. Carney*, 471 U.S. 386, 105 S. Ct. 2066, 2071 n.3 (1985).

904 *California v. Carney*, 471 U.S. 386, 105 S. Ct. 2066, 2071 n.3 (1985).

905 *United States v. Jones*, 565 U.S. 400, 132 S. Ct. 945 (2012).

906 *Collins v. Virginia*, 584 U.S. ___, 138 S. Ct. 1663 (2018).

907 The United States Supreme Court remanded the case for a state court determination of whether the officer's warrantless intrusion may have been reasonable on a different basis. Upon remand, the Virginia Supreme Court held that the evidence discovered during the warrantless search was admissible under the good-faith exception to the exclusionary rule. Said the Court: "The exclusionary rule does not apply under the facts of this case because, at the time of the search, a reasonably well-trained police officer would not have known that the automobile exception did not permit him to search a motorcycle located a few feet across the curtilage boundary of a private driveway." *Collins v. Commonwealth*, 297 Va. 207, 227, 824 S.E.2d 485, 496 (2019).

908 *South Dakota v. Opperman*, 428 U.S. 364, 369, 96 S. Ct. 3092, 3097 (1976).

In *South Dakota v. Opperman*,[909] the defendant's illegally parked car was towed to the city impound lot where an officer of the Vermillion Police Department observed several articles of personal property within the vehicle. As the officer proceeded to inventory the contents of the car, he discovered a plastic bag containing marijuana in the unlocked glove compartment.

Finding the initial impoundment lawful, the United States Supreme Court determined that the automobile impoundment was sanctioned by the "community caretaking functions" incumbent upon law enforcement officials in situations wherein the public safety and efficient movement of vehicular traffic are in jeopardy.[910] Respecting the inventory, the Court ruled that such intrusions into automobiles legally "impounded or otherwise in lawful police custody" have been widely sustained as reasonable under the Fourth Amendment "where the process is aimed at securing or protecting the car and its contents."[911]

As a result, the Court declared that the officer in *Opperman* was

> indisputably engaged in a caretaking search of a lawfully impounded automobile.... The inventory was conducted only after the car had been impounded for multiple parking violations. The owner, having left his car illegally parked for an extended period, and thus subject to impoundment, was not present to make other arrangements for the safekeeping of his belongings. The inventory itself was prompted by the presence in plain view of a number of valuables inside the car.... [T]here is no suggestion whatever that this standard procedure, essentially like that followed throughout the country, was a pretext concealing an investigatory police motive. [Accordingly,] in following standard police procedures, prevailing throughout the country and approved by the overwhelming majority of courts, the conduct of [this officer] was not "unreasonable" under the Fourth Amendment.[912]

4.2.5.2. Pre-existing standardized procedures

In *Colorado v. Bertine*,[913] the Court held that law enforcement officers may, consistent with the Fourth Amendment, open closed containers while conducting a routine inventory search of an impounded vehicle. So long as the police department has "reasonable police regulations relating to inventory procedures" in place, such impound and inventory procedures, administered in good faith, "satisfy the Fourth Amendment."[914]

In *Florida v. Wells*,[915] the Court re-emphasized the importance of "standardized criteria" in the area of impounded motor vehicle inventory searches, and delivered a strong message to law enforcement agencies that a pre-existing *department policy* or written *general order* covering the subject of impounded motor vehicle inventories is required before the procedure will receive judicial approval.[916] In the absence of a standardized policy covering the subject of impounded vehicle inventory searches, and the opening of closed containers encountered during such procedures, a vehicle search will not be "sufficiently regulated to satisfy the Fourth Amendment."[917]

Accordingly, in *Marcopoulos v. State*,[918] the inventory search was not allowed where the State failed to carry its burden of establishing the search qualified as an inventory pursuant to an impoundment of a vehicle. The officer who testified was not the officer who performed the purported inventory and there was not testimony confirming the the inventory was completed. In addition, there was no testimony with regard to the police procedure for searching a vehicle or whether that procedure was followed. Finally, there was no testimony or other evidence of anything recovered from the vehicle other than evidence later used against the defendant.

---

909 *South Dakota v. Opperman*, 428 U.S. 364, 96 S. Ct. 3092 (1976).

910 *South Dakota v. Opperman*, 428 U.S. 364, 368, 96 S. Ct. 3092, 3096 (1976); *see also Cady v. Dombrowski*, 413 U.S. 433, 441, 93 S. Ct. 2523, 2528 (1973).

911 *South Dakota v. Opperman*, 428 U.S. 364, 373, 96 S. Ct. 3092, 3099 (1976).

912 *South Dakota v. Opperman*, 428 U.S. 364, 375-76, 96 S. Ct. 3092, 3100 (1976).

913 *Colorado v. Bertine*, 479 U.S. 367, 107 S. Ct. 738 (1987).

914 *Colorado v. Bertine*, 479 U.S. 367, 107 S. Ct. 738, 742 (1987).

915 *Florida v. Wells*, 495 U.S. 1, 110 S. Ct. 1632 (1990).

916 *Florida v. Wells*, 495 U.S. 1, 110 S. Ct. 1632, 1635 (1990).

917 *Florida v. Wells*, 495 U.S. 1, 110 S. Ct. 1632, 1635 (1990).

918 *Marcopoulos v. State*, 548 S.W.3d 697 (Tex. App. 2018).

By contrast, in *Moskey v. State*,[919] the deputies needed to impound defendant's vehicle and conduct an inventory search because there was no one to whom they could release the vehicle after they arrested defendant. Both deputies "testified that Harris County Sheriff's Department policy requires deputies to impound a vehicle whose occupants have been arrested and to conduct an inventory search when there is no one to whom the officers can release the vehicle. In this situation, the officer conducting the search must complete an inventory form documenting the personal property found within the vehicle in an effort to protect the owner's valuables. Pursuant to the departmental policy, officers search closed and locked containers, as well as unlocked glove compartments. If, however, the glove compartment is locked, the searching officer must contact a supervisor and obtain a search warrant or get the owner's consent to search."[920] The glove compartment was unlocked and a deputy discovered marijuana inside. The court held that the deputies conducted the inventory search in accordance with standardized police procedures.

4.2.5.3. Booking procedures

In *Illinois v. Lafayette*,[921] the U.S. Supreme Court held that, in accordance with the routine booking process, it is reasonable under the Fourth Amendment "for police to search the personal effects of a person under lawful arrest as part of the administrative procedure at a police station house incident to booking and jailing the suspect."[922] According to the Court, "[a]t the station house, it is entirely proper for police to remove and list or inventory property found on the person or in the possession of an arrested person who is to be jailed."[923] Such a standardized procedure not only deters false claims, but also guards against theft or careless handling of property taken from the arrestee. Moreover, the Court observed that: "Arrested persons have also been known to injure themselves – or others – with belts, knives, drugs, or other items on their person while being detained. Dangerous instrumentalities – such as razor blades, bombs, or weapons – can be concealed in innocent-looking articles taken from the arrestee's possession."[924] Additionally, this procedure assists "the police in ascertaining or verifying the arrestee's identity."[925] These considerations therefore suggest that "a stationhouse search of every item carried on or by a person who has lawfully been taken into custody by the police will amply serve the important and legitimate governmental interests involved."[926]

In *Lafayette*, police arrested defendant and transported him to precinct headquarters. At the time he was carrying a shoulder bag. The bag was opened, emptied, and found to contain contraband. Defendant argued that the search exceeded the scope of a permissible booking search. The Court disagreed, reasoning that the search served the important government interests of protecting the property of the arrestee, as well as protecting the police department from false claims. A routine booking and search is a reasonable way to promote these interests and thus is valid under the Fourth Amendment.

5. PRIVACY EXPECTATIONS

5.1. Preliminary

At the federal level, in order to determine whether a particular area or object warrants Fourth Amendment protection, courts will engage in a two-part inquiry. The first part of the inquiry questions whether an individual has exhibited "an actual (or subjective) expectation of privacy" in the area or item in question.[927] Next, it

---

919 *Moskey v. State*, 333 S.W.3d 696 (Tex. App. 2010).
920 *Moskey v. State*, 333 S.W.3d 696, 701 (Tex. App. 2010).
921 *Illinois v. Lafayette*, 462 U.S. 640, 103 S. Ct. 2605 (1983).
922 *Illinois v. Lafayette*, 462 U.S. 640, 103 S. Ct. 2605, 2608, 2611 (1983).
923 *Illinois v. Lafayette*, 462 U.S. 640, 103 S. Ct. 2605, 2609 (1983).
924 *Illinois v. Lafayette*, 462 U.S. 640, 103 S. Ct. 2605, 2609 (1983).
925 *Illinois v. Lafayette*, 462 U.S. 640, 103 S. Ct. 2605, 2610 (1983).
926 *Illinois v. Lafayette*, 462 U.S. 640, 103 S. Ct. 2605, 2610 (1983).
927 *Katz v. United States*, 389 U.S. 347, 361, 88 S. Ct. 507, 516 (1967) (Harlan, J., concurring).

must be determined whether the expectation is "one that society is prepared to recognize as 'reasonable.'"[928] Taken as a whole, the *Katz v. United States* "twofold requirement" stands for the proposition that "wherever an individual may harbor a reasonable 'expectation of privacy,' ... he is entitled to be free from unreasonable governmental intrusion."[929] On the other hand, one cannot have a reasonable expectation of privacy in what is knowingly exposed to public view.[930]

The Texas Court of Criminal Appeals has explained that "[t]he factors that courts use in deciding whether a person has a reasonable expectation of privacy in the place or object searched include the following:

> (1) whether the defendant had a proprietary or possessory interest in the place or object searched;
> (2) whether the defendant's presence in or on the place searched was legitimate;
> (3) whether the defendant had a right to exclude others from the place or object;
> (4) whether the defendant took normal precautions, prior to the search, which are customarily taken to protect privacy in the place or object;
> (5) whether the place or object searched was put to a private use;
> (6) whether the defendant's claim of privacy is consistent with historical notion of privacy."[931]

"The touchstone of Fourth Amendment analysis is whether a person has a 'constitutionally protected reasonable expectation of privacy.'"[932] In this respect, police conduct will implicate the Fourth Amendment only if it intrudes into an area (or significantly interferes with the possession of an item) in which an individual has "manifested a subjective expectation of privacy ... that society accepts as objectively reasonable."[933]

In *Davidson v. State*,[934] the defendant pleaded guilty to killing her husband, who was an airman in the Air Force and disposing of his body in a pond. The investigation led to a field near defendant's veterinary clinic. The property was owned by Terrell Sheen, a local businessman, who reported that defendant had access to the property and kept a horse there. The victim's body was eventually found in one of the ponds on the property. Although the land was "in an area not visible from the public road, to which the public did not have access," the court found "nothing in the record ... to show that appellant had a property or possessory interest, unrestricted access, complete dominion and control, the right to exclude others, or any other expectations of privacy in the property that were of the types that society views as objectively reasonable. Nor was there any evidence that appellant intended to or had stayed overnight. At best, appellant's evidence addresses one of the six relevant factors to be considered – that she had legitimate presence in the place searched."[935] The court held that defendant did not have a reasonable expectation of privacy in the field.

In certain cases, however, the constitutional protection may extend directly to a person's property, even though privacy or liberty interests may not be immediately implicated. For example, in *Soldal v. Cook County, Ill.*,[936] deputy sheriffs assisted the owners of a mobile home park in evicting the Soldal family. As the deputies stood and watched, the park owners wrenched the sewer and water connections off the side of the Soldal trailer, disconnected the telephone, tore the trailer's canopy and skirting, pulled it free from its moorings and towed it away. Finding the Fourth Amendment clearly applicable, the U.S. Supreme Court held:

> As a result of the state action in this case, the Soldals' domicile was not only seized, it literally was carried away, giving a new meaning to the term "mobile home." We fail to see how being unceremoniously dispossessed of one's home in the manner alleged to have occurred here can be viewed as anything but a seizure invoking the protection of the Fourth Amendment.... The Amendment protects the

---

928 *Katz v. United States*, 389 U.S. 347, 361, 88 S. Ct. 507, 516 (1967) (Harlan, J., concurring).
929 *Terry v. Ohio*, 392 U.S. 1, 9, 88 S. Ct. 1868, 1873 (1968).
930 *See Katz v. United States*, 389 U.S. 347, 88 S. Ct. 507 (1967).
931 *State v. Granville*, 423 S.W.3d 399, 407 (Tex. Crim. App. 2014) (citing *Granados v. State*, 85 S.W.3d 217, 223 (Tex. Crim. App. 2002)).
932 *California v. Ciraolo*, 476 U.S. 207, 211, 106 S. Ct. 1809, 1811 (1986) (quoting *Katz v. United States*, 389 U.S. 347, 361, 88 S. Ct. 507, 516 (1967) (Harlan, J., concurring)).
933 *California v. Greenwood*, 486 U.S. 35, 39, 108 S. Ct. 1625, 1628 (1988).
934 *Davidson v. State*, 249 S.W.3d 709 (Tex. App. 2008).
935 *Davidson v. State*, 249 S.W.3d 709, 725-26 (Tex. App. 2008).
936 *Soldal v. Cook County, Ill.*, 506 U.S. 56, 113 S. Ct. 538 (1992).

people from unreasonable searches and seizures of "their persons, houses, papers, and effects."... [A]nd our cases unmistakably hold that the Amendment protects property as well as privacy.... We thus are unconvinced that ... the Fourth Amendment protects against unreasonable seizures of property only where privacy or liberty is also implicated.[937]

In *State v. Granville*,[938] the constitutional protection extended to the defendant's cell phone. The court explained that "courts commonly find that a person has a legitimate expectation of privacy in the contents of his cell phone because of its 'ability to store large amounts of private data' both in the cell phone itself and by accessing remote services. This data may involve the most intimate details of a person's individual life, including text messages, emails, banking, medical, or credit card information, pictures, and videos. A cell phone is unlike other containers as it can receive, store, and transmit an almost unlimited amount of private information. The potential for invasion of privacy, identity theft, or, at a minimum, public embarrassment is enormous."[939]

5.1.1. Listening devices

In *Katz v. United States*,[940] the Court determined that the police will violate the Fourth Amendment by electronically listening to and recording a person's words spoken into a telephone receiver in a public telephone booth without prior judicial authorization. In this regard, the Court determined that "the Fourth Amendment governs not only the seizure of tangible items, but extends as well to the recording of oral statements overheard without any 'technical [physical intrusion].'"[941] Thus, the FBI agents' conduct "in electronically listening to and recording the [defendant's] words violated the privacy upon which he justifiably relied while using the telephone booth and thus constituted a 'search and seizure' within the meaning of the Fourth Amendment. The fact that the electronic device employed to achieve that end did not happen to penetrate the wall of the booth can have no constitutional significance."[942]

5.1.2. Presence of the media during warrant execution

In *Wilson v. Layne*,[943] the Supreme Court held that "it is a violation of the Fourth Amendment for police to bring members of the media or other third parties into a home during the execution of [an arrest] warrant when the presence of the third parties in the home was not in aid of the execution of the warrant."[944]

5.1.3. Thermal imaging devices

In *Kyllo v. United States*,[945] the U.S. Supreme Court held that using a thermal imaging device to detect relative amounts of heat within the home, constitutes a Fourth Amendment "search." According to the Court where law enforcement officers use "a device that is not in general public use, to explore details of the home that would previously have been unknowable without physical intrusion, the surveillance is a 'search' and is presumptively unreasonable without a warrant."[946]

---

[937] *Soldal v. Cook County, Ill.*, 506 U.S. 56, 113 S. Ct. 538, 543-45 (1992).
[938] *State v. Granville*, 423 S.W.3d 399 (Tex. Crim. App. 2014).
[939] *State v. Granville*, 423 S.W.3d 399, 408-09 (Tex. Crim. App. 2014).
[940] *Katz v. United States*, 389 U.S. 347, 88 S. Ct. 507 (1967).
[941] *Katz v. United States*, 389 U.S. 347, 88 S. Ct. 507, 512 (1967).
[942] *Katz v. United States*, 389 U.S. 347, 88 S. Ct. 507, 512 (1967).
[943] *Wilson v. Layne*, 526 U.S. 603, 119 S. Ct. 1692 (1999).
[944] *Wilson v. Layne*, 526 U.S. 603, 119 S. Ct. 1692, 1699 (1999); *see also Hanlon v. Berger*, 526 U.S. 808, 119 S. Ct. 1706 (1999) (reaching the same result in a situation involving the execution of a search warrant and the invited presence of a crew of photographers and reporters from the Cable News Network, Inc.).
[945] *Kyllo v. United States*, 533 U.S. 27, 121 S. Ct. 2038 (2001).
[946] *Kyllo v. United States*, 533 U.S. 27, 121 S. Ct. 2038, 2046 (2001).

5.1.4. Use of a flashlight

A person's subjective expectation of privacy as to that which is located in an area of common access or view will be deemed unreasonable, and consequently, unworthy of Fourth Amendment protection. Therefore, visual observation of evidence located in such an unprotected area does not constitute a search within the meaning of the Fourth Amendment. Moreover, it has been held that no "search" takes place when police use artificial means, such as a flashlight, to illuminate a darkened area.[947] As explained in *Marshall v. United States*,[948]

> When the circumstances of a particular case are such that the police officer's observations would not have constituted a search had it occurred in daylight, then the fact that the officer used a flashlight to pierce the nighttime darkness does not transform his observation into a search. Regardless of the time of day or night, the plain view rule must be upheld where the viewer is rightfully positioned.... The plain view rule does not go into hibernation at sunset.[949]

5.1.5. Drug field test not a search

In *United States v. Jacobsen*,[950] the U.S. Supreme Court held that a chemical field test "that merely discloses whether or not a particular substance is cocaine does not compromise any legitimate interest in privacy."[951] Here the Court explained that a field test discloses "only one fact previously unknown to [an officer] – whether or not a suspicious [substance is an illegal drug]."[952] "It is probably safe," stated the Court, "to assume that virtually all of the tests conducted under the circumstances [of this case] would result in a positive finding; in such cases, no legitimate interest has been compromised. But even if the results are negative – merely disclosing that the substance is something other than [a particular illegal drug] – such a result reveals nothing of special interest."[953] As in the case of the "sniff test" conducted by a trained narcotics detection dog, the likelihood that a chemical field test of suspected narcotics will actually compromise any legitimate interest in privacy "seems too remote to characterize the testing as a search subject to the Fourth Amendment."[954]

5.1.6. Use of a drug-sniffing dog on a homeowner's porch

In *Florida v. Jardines*,[955] the Court held that an officer's "use of a trained drug-sniffing dog to investigate the home and its immediate surroundings is a 'search' within the meaning of the Fourth Amendment."[956] Since the canine search in this case was performed without a warrant or probable cause, it was an illegal search. It therefore rendered invalid the warrant that issued based upon the information gathered in that search, and inadmissible the evidence so obtained.

---

[947] *See, e.g.*, *United States v. Dunn*, 480 U.S. 294, 107 S. Ct. 1134, 1141 (1987) ("officers' use of the beam of a flashlight, directed through the essentially open front of [defendant's] barn, did not transform their observations into an unreasonable search within the meaning of the Fourth Amendment"); *Texas v. Brown*, 460 U.S. 730, 739-40, 103 S. Ct. 1535, 1542 (1983) (officer's "action in shining his flashlight to illuminate the interior of [defendant's] car trenched upon no right secured to the latter by the Fourth Amendment"); *United States v. Lee*, 274 U.S. 559, 563, 47 S. Ct. 746, 748 (1927) ("[The] use of a search light is comparable to the use of a marine glass or a field glass. It is not prohibited by the Constitution."); *United States v. Rickus*, 737 F.2d 360, 366 n.3 (3d Cir. 1984) (The "use of a flashlight to aid the officer's vision did not transform the observations justified under the 'plain view doctrine' into an illegal search.").

[948] *Marshall v. United States*, 422 F.2d 185 (5th Cir. 1970).

[949] *Marshall v. United States*, 422 F.2d 185, 189 (5th Cir. 1970).

[950] *United States v. Jacobsen*, 466 U.S. 109, 104 S. Ct. 1652 (1984).

[951] *United States v. Jacobsen*, 466 U.S. 109, 104 S. Ct. 1652, 1662 (1984).

[952] *United States v. Jacobsen*, 466 U.S. 109, 104 S. Ct. 1652, 1661 (1984).

[953] *United States v. Jacobsen*, 466 U.S. 109, 104 S. Ct. 1652, 1662 (1984).

[954] *United States v. Jacobsen*, 466 U.S. 109, 104 S. Ct. 1652, 1662 (1984).

[955] *Florida v. Jardines*, 569 U.S. 1, 133 S. Ct. 1409 (2013).

[956] *Florida v. Jardines*, 569 U.S. 1, 11-12, 133 S. Ct. 1409, 1417-18 (2013).

Rather than using a pure "expectation of privacy" analysis under *Katz v. United States*, the Court reasoned: "[W]e need not decide whether the officers' investigation of Jardines' home violated his expectation of privacy under *Katz*. One virtue of the Fourth Amendment's property-rights baseline is that it keeps easy cases easy. That the officers learned what they learned only by physically intruding on Jardines' property to gather evidence is enough to establish that a search occurred."[957] Here, the *Jardines* Court required not only a trespass, but also some attempted information-gathering, to find that a search had occurred. The *Jardines* information-gathering was the use of a drug-sniffing dog — conduct that the Supreme Court has held is not a search when the police have not trespassed.

In a trio of Texas cases, police conducted a dog sniff in the curtilage of a home without a warrant. Subsequently, the Supreme Court decided *Jardines*. Accordingly, the Texas Court of Criminal Appeals found the dog sniff unconstitutional in each case.[958]

5.1.7. The VIN of an automobile

In *New York v. Class*,[959] the federal Supreme Court held that there is "no reasonable expectation of privacy in the VIN" of an automobile. As a result, the police may run a computer search on the number without probable cause or even reasonable suspicion. Similarly, reasonable suspicion is not required to run a computer check on a randomly selected license plate.

5.1.8. Reasonable expectations of privacy and a person's physical appearance

5.1.8.1. Facial characteristics

In *United States v. Dionisio*,[960] the U.S. Supreme Court announced that no person has a reasonable expectation of privacy in his or her "facial characteristics" for one cannot reasonably expect that his face will be a mystery to the world.

5.1.8.2. Fingerprints

Similarly, no person can have a reasonable expectation of privacy in his or her fingerprints.[961]

5.1.8.3. The physical characteristics of a person's voice

In *United States v. Dionisio*,[962] the U.S. Supreme Court held that "[t]he physical characteristics of a person's voice, its tone and manner, as opposed to the content of a specific conversation, are constantly exposed to the public," so that "[n]o person can have a reasonable expectation of privacy that others will not know the sound of his voice[.]"[963] "Like a man's facial characteristics, or handwriting, his voice is repeatedly produced for others to hear."[964]

957 *Florida v. Jardines*, 569 U.S. 1, 11-12, 133 S. Ct. 1409, 1417-18 (2013); *see also Kyllo v. United States*, 533 U.S. 27, 121 S. Ct. 2038 (2001) (surveillance is a search when the government uses a physical intrusion to explore details of the home, including its curtilage; "the antiquity of the tools that they bring along is irrelevant").

958 *McClintock v. State*, 541 S.W.3d 63 (Tex. Crim. App. 2017); *State v. Cuong Phu Le*, 463 S.W.3d 872 (Tex. Crim. App. 2015); *State v. Rendon*, 477 S.W.3d 805 (Tex. Crim. App. 2015).

959 *New York v. Class*, 475 U.S. 106, 106 S. Ct. 960 (1986).

960 *United States v. Dionisio*, 410 U.S. 1, 14, 93 S. Ct. 764, 771 (1973).

961 *See Cupp v. Murphy*, 412 U.S. 291, 295, 93 S. Ct. 2000, 2003 (1973) (no reasonable expectation of privacy attaches to one's fingerprints, which are mere "physical characteristics" that are "constantly exposed to the public").

962 *United States v. Dionisio*, 410 U.S. 1, 93 S. Ct. 764 (1973).

963 *United States v. Dionisio*, 410 U.S. 1, 14, 93 S. Ct. 764, 771 (1973).

964 *United States v. Dionisio*, 410 U.S. 1, 14, 93 S. Ct. 764, 771 (1973).

5.1.8.4. Handwriting

In *United States v. Mara*, a companion case to *United States v. Dionisio*, the United States Supreme Court reached the same result as to a person's handwriting.[965]

5.1.8.5. Soles of a person's shoes

The visual inspection of the soles of a detainee's shoes has been held not to constitute a "search" within the meaning of the Fourth Amendment.

5.1.8.6. Dental implants

There is no constitutional impediment preventing the taking of dental impressions. In *Patterson v. State*,[966] the Texas Court of Criminal Appeals likened dental casts to fingerprints for constitutional purposes. The court later stated, "We hold this type of relatively unintrusive identification evidence to be seizable without constitutional implication."[967]

5.1.9. Arrest records

In *Paul P. v. Verniero*,[968] in upholding sex offender registration and community notification laws, the Third Circuit determined "that arrest records and related information are not protected by a right to privacy."

5.1.10. The passenger area of a commercial bus

In *United States v. Ramos*,[969] defendant hid a clear plastic bag containing drug paraphernalia between the seats of a commercial bus when, during a scheduled stop, the bus was boarded by police officers. One of the officers recovered the bag, placed defendant under arrest and discovered another plastic bag on defendant's person, this one containing cocaine base.

In the appeal following the denial of his motion to suppress, defendant argued that when he hid "the bag containing empty vials in the crevice between the seats, he clearly possessed a reasonable expectation of privacy in that bag[,]" just as he would were he instead traveling with "a valise or a suitcase."[970] Additionally, defendant argued that the crevice between the seats should be treated as "the constitutional equivalent of an opaque container," with the seats constituting "an area in which an occupant may reasonably expect fourth amendment protection."[971] The court disagreed.

Preliminarily, the court noted that the plastic bag defendant hid between the seats was transparent. Therefore, "he could have no expectation of privacy in the bag itself," for the Fourth Amendment "provides protection to the owner of only a 'container that conceals its contents from plain view.'"[972]

In addition, the court determined that the area in which defendant secreted the plastic bag is not one in which he could reasonably expect any degree of privacy. According to the court, "[a] passenger on a commercial bus certainly has no property interest in the crevice between the seats or for that matter in the rack

---

965 *See United States v. Mara*, 410 U.S. 19, 93 S. Ct. 774 (1973) ("Handwriting, like speech, is repeatedly shown to the public, and there is no more expectation of privacy in the physical characteristics of a person's script than there is in the tone of his voice."); *see also United States v. Euge*, 444 U.S. 707, 100 S. Ct. 874 (1980) ("compulsion of handwriting exemplars is neither a search nor a seizure subject to Fourth Amendment protections").

966 *Patterson v. State*, 509 S.W.2d 857 (Tex. Crim. App. 1974).

967 *Marquez v. State*, 725 S.W.2d 217, 234 (Tex. Crim. App. 1987).

968 *Paul P. v. Verniero*, 170 F.3d 396 (3d Cir. 1999).

969 *United States v. Ramos*, 960 F.2d 1065 (D.C. Cir. 1992).

970 *United States v. Ramos*, 960 F.2d 1065, 1067 (D.C. Cir. 1992).

971 *United States v. Ramos*, 960 F.2d 1065, 1067 (D.C. Cir. 1992).

972 *United States v. Ramos*, 960 F.2d 1065, 1067 (D.C. Cir. 1992) (citations omitted).

above the seats, the area beneath the seats, or anywhere else that personal effects may be stowed. Nor are we aware of any socially recognized expectation of privacy in the interior of a bus."[973]

5.1.11. Rental cars

In *Byrd v. United States*,[974] the United States Supreme Court held that a driver of a rental car has a reasonable expectation of privacy in the car, even when he or she is the sole occupant of the vehicle and is not listed as an authorized driver on the rental agreement. According to the Court, permitting an unauthorized driver to take the wheel of a rental car may be a violation of the rental agreement, but that has nothing to do with the driver's reasonable expectation of privacy in the rental car.

The facts of the case unfolded in mid-September, when the state police pulled over a car driven by defendant Terrence Byrd, the only person in the car. During the stop, "the troopers learned that the car was rented and that Byrd was not listed on the Budget rental-car agreement as an authorized driver. For this reason, the troopers told Byrd they did not need his consent to search the car, including its trunk where he had stored personal effects. A search of the trunk uncovered body armor and 49 bricks of heroin."[975] Byrd moved to suppress the evidence as the fruit of an unlawful search. The trial court denied the motion, reasoning that, because Byrd was not listed on the rental agreement, he lacked a reasonable expectation of privacy in the car. *The United States Supreme Court disagreed*, holding that, "as a general rule, someone in otherwise lawful possession and control of a rental car has a reasonable expectation of privacy in it even if the rental agreement does not list him or her as an authorized driver."[976]

Naturally, the person must be in lawful possession of the vehicle.

> A burglar plying his trade in a summer cabin during the off season, for example, may have a thoroughly justified subjective expectation of privacy, but it is not one which the law recognizes as "legitimate." Likewise, a person present in a stolen automobile at the time of the search may not object to the lawfulness of the search of the automobile. No matter the degree of possession and control, the car thief would not have a reasonable expectation of privacy in a stolen car.[977]

5.1.12. Parking lots

There is no legitimate expectation of privacy in an open parking lot, visible to the public.[978]

5.1.13. Bank records

The United States Supreme Court recognizes a distinction under the Fourth Amendment between information "a person keeps to himself and what he shares with others."[979] Under what has come to be known as the third-party doctrine, when a person voluntarily shares information with a third party, a person generally

[973] *United States v. Ramos*, 960 F.2d 1065, 1067-68 (D.C. Cir. 1992).
[974] *Byrd v. United States*, 548 U.S.___, 138 S. Ct. 1518 (2018).
[975] *Byrd v. United States*, 548 U.S.___, 138 S. Ct. 1518, 1523 (2018).
[976] *Byrd v. United States*, 548 U.S.___, 138 S. Ct. 1518, 1524 (2018).
[977] *Byrd v. United States*, 548 U.S.___, 138 S. Ct. 1518, 1529 (2018).
[978] *See United States v. Ludwig*, 10 F.3d 1523 (10th Cir. 1993) (defendant could claim no reasonable expectation of privacy in a motel parking lot that was open, unfenced, and visible from the public roads bordering it); *United States v. Dunkel*, 900 F.2d 105, 107 (7th Cir. 1990) (defendant had no legitimate expectation of privacy in the parking lot of a private office; lot was open to invitees of eight tenants and was not fenced), *vacated on other grounds*, 498 U.S. 1043, 111 S. Ct. 747 (1991); *United States v. Reed*, 733 F.2d 492, 501 (8th Cir. 1984) (officer's initial entry into business lot was not a search where lot was bound on three sides by public streets and visible from streets on two sides, and its fenced gate was completely open to a public street); *United States v. Edmonds*, 611 F.2d 1386, 1388 (5th Cir. 1980) (no legitimate expectation of privacy found in a business loading dock and parking lot).
[979] *Carpenter v. United States*, ___ U.S.___, 138 S. Ct. 2206, 2216 (2018).

has no legitimate expectation of privacy in that information. "As a result, the Government is typically free to obtain such information from the recipient without triggering Fourth Amendment protections."[980]

The United States Supreme Court has held that a person has no legitimate expectation of privacy under the Fourth Amendment in bank records which consist of information voluntarily shared with third parties. In *United States v. Miller*,[981] the Government acquired several months of Miller's checks, deposit slips, and monthly statements from his banks. The US Supreme Court held that Miller had no protected Fourth Amendment interest in those records. In this regard, the Court reasoned that Miller could not assert "ownership" or "possession" of the documents, which were "business records of the banks."[982] Second, the "nature of those records confirmed Miller's limited expectation of privacy[.]"[983] The checks were "not confidential communications but negotiable instruments to be used in commercial transactions," and the statements and deposit slips contained information "exposed to [bank] employees in the ordinary course of business."[984] Accordingly, the Court concluded that Miller had taken the risk, in revealing his affairs to another, that the information would be conveyed by that person to the Government, and held that "there was no intrusion into any area in which [Miller] had a protected Fourth Amendment interest."[985]

The following doctrines concern areas, and objects within those areas, or classes of property, with respect to which courts have consistently held individuals do not have a reasonable expectation of privacy. Because there is no privacy expectation, no search within the meaning of the Constitution may be deemed to have taken place. Technically, the Fourth Amendment is not implicated.

5.2. Open fields

The "open fields" doctrine, originally set forth in *Hester v. United States*,[986] authorizes law enforcement officers to enter and search an "open" field without a warrant. In *Hester*, Justice Holmes explained that the special and unique safeguards provided by the Fourth Amendment to the people in their "persons, houses, papers, and effects," is not extended to open fields. Open fields are not "houses" nor may they be considered "effects."

In *Oliver v. United States*, the United States Supreme Court held that the defendant's act of fencing in a secluded field and placing locked gates and "No Trespassing" signs on the property did not create a constitutionally protected area where one never existed. As a result, the police did not need a search warrant or probable cause to search the "open field."[987]

It is important to recognize that the phrase "open field" is a term of art that applies to any unoccupied or undeveloped area outside of the curtilage. Areas may fall within this legal definition that are neither "open" nor a "field" as those terms are used in common speech.[988] As explained in *Oliver*, "open fields do not provide the setting for those intimate activities that the [Fourth] Amendment is intended to shelter from government interference or surveillance."[989] Not only is there no societal interest in protecting the privacy of crop cultivation or field irrigation, "as a practical matter, these lands usually are accessible to the public and the police in ways that a home, an office, or commercial structure would not be."[990] A typical example would be the common viewing of such fields by airplane or helicopter. The final analysis always boils down to the question of

---

980 *Carpenter v. United States*, ___ U.S. ___, 138 S. Ct. 2206, 2216 (2018).
981 *United States v. Miller*, 425 U.S. 435, 438, 96 S. Ct. 1619, 1621 (1976).
982 *United States v. Miller*, 425 U.S. 435, 440, 96 S. Ct. 1619, 1622 (1976).
983 *Carpenter v. United States*, ___ U.S. ___, 138 S. Ct. 2206, 2216 (2018).
984 *United States v. Miller*, 425 U.S. 435, 442, 96 S. Ct. 1619 (1976).
985 *United States v. Miller*, 425 U.S. 435, 440, 96 S. Ct. 1619, 1622 (1976).
986 *Hester v. United States*, 265 U.S. 57, 44 S. Ct. 445 (1924).
987 *Oliver v. United States*, 466 U.S. 170, 104 S. Ct. 1735 (1984); *see also Goehring v. State*, 627 S.W.2d 159 (Tex. Crim. App. 1982).
988 *See, e.g., United States v. Hatfield*, 333 F.3d 1189 (10th Cir. 2003).
989 *Oliver v. United States*, 466 U.S. 170, 179, 104 S. Ct. 1735, 1741 (1984).
990 *Oliver v. United States*, 466 U.S. 170, 179, 104 S. Ct. 1735, 1741 (1984).

whether a person has a "constitutionally protected reasonable expectation of privacy" in the particular area in question.[991]

5.2.1. The "curtilage."

The home, of course, since the inception of this Nation, has been one of these areas which commands the sanctity and privacy recognized by our society. Privacy has also been extended to the "curtilage" – the "land immediately surrounding and associated with the home."[992] This land, termed the "curtilage," of the home, is treated as a part of the home; it is not only separate, but distinguished from neighboring open fields.

Generally, the "curtilage" is the enclosed space of the grounds and buildings immediately surrounding a dwelling house. It is an area to which extends the intimate activity associated with the sanctity of a person's home and the privacies of life, and therefore has been considered part of the home itself for Fourth Amendment purposes.

In *United States v. Dunn*,[993] the Supreme Court held that the area near defendant's barn, located approximately 50 yards from a fence surrounding a ranch house, was not within the curtilage of the house for Fourth Amendment purposes. Citing *Oliver v. United States*, the Court in *Dunn* reiterated that "the Fourth Amendment protects the curtilage of a house and that the extent of the curtilage is determined by factors that bear upon whether an individual reasonably may expect that the area in question should be treated as the home itself."[994] The "central component" of the curtilage inquiry is "whether the area harbors the 'intimate activity associated with the sanctity of a man's home and the privacies of life.'"[995] Thus, "curtilage questions should be resolved with particular reference to four factors:

(1) the proximity of the area claimed to be curtilage to the home;
(2) whether the area is included within an enclosure surrounding the home;
(3) the nature of the uses to which the area is put; and
(4) the steps taken by the resident to protect the area from observation by people passing by."[996]

While not a finely tuned mechanical formula, these factors nonetheless are "useful analytical tools" which may be used to determine "whether the area in question is so intimately tied to the home itself that it should be placed under the home's 'umbrella' of Fourth Amendment protection."[997]

Be aware that police do not violate the curtilage merely by walking up to the front door and knocking, just as any other member of the public might do. In *Florida v. Jardines*,[998] however, the Court held that an officer's "use of a trained drug-sniffing dog to investigate the home and its immediate surroundings is a 'search' within the meaning of the Fourth Amendment."[999] Since the canine search in this case was performed without a warrant or probable cause, it was an illegal search. It therefore rendered invalid the warrant that issued based upon the information gathered in that search, and inadmissible the evidence so obtained.

Rather than using a pure "expectation of privacy" analysis under *Katz v. United States*,[1000] the Court reasoned: "[W]e need not decide whether the officers' investigation of Jardines' home violated his expectation of privacy under *Katz*. One virtue of the Fourth Amendment's property-rights baseline is that it keeps easy cases

---

[991] *See Katz v. United States*, 389 U.S. 347, 88 S. Ct. 507 (1967) (The Fourth Amendment will only protect those expectations that society is prepared to recognize as "reasonable.").
[992] *See Oliver v. United States*, 466 U.S. 170, 180, 104 S. Ct. 1735, 1742 (1984).
[993] *United States v. Dunn*, 480 U.S. 294, 107 S. Ct. 1134 (1987).
[994] *United States v. Dunn*, 480 U.S. 294, 107 S. Ct. 1134, 1139 (1987).
[995] *United States v. Dunn*, 480 U.S. 294, 107 S. Ct. 1134, 1139 (1987) (citations omitted).
[996] *United States v. Dunn*, 480 U.S. 294, 107 S. Ct. 1134, 1139 (1987).
[997] *United States v. Dunn*, 480 U.S. 294, 107 S. Ct. 1134, 1139 (1987).
[998] *Florida v. Jardines*, 569 U.S. 1, 133 S. Ct. 1409 (2013).
[999] *Florida v. Jardines*, 569 U.S. 1, 133 S. Ct. 1409, 1417-18 (2013).
[1000] *Katz v. United States*, 389 U.S. 347, 361, 88 S. Ct. 507, 516 (1967).

easy. That the officers learned what they learned only by physically intruding on Jardines' property to gather evidence is enough to establish that a search occurred."[1001]

5.2.1.1. A home's driveway

In *Collins v. Virginia*,[1002] the United States Supreme Court held that the automobile exception does not permit a law enforcement officer, uninvited and without a warrant, to enter the curtilage of a home in order to search a vehicle parked at the top of the home's driveway.

During the investigation of two traffic incidents involving violations committed by an operator of an orange and black motorcycle with an extended frame, Officer David Rhodes learned that the motorcycle likely was stolen and in the possession of defendant Ryan Collins. While investigating, Officer Rhodes discovered photographs on Collins' Facebook page of an orange and black motorcycle parked at the top of a driveway of a house. The officer tracked down the address of the house, drove there, and parked on the street. "It was later established that Collins' girlfriend lived in the house and that Collins stayed there a few nights per week."

"From his parked position on the street, Officer Rhodes saw what appeared to be a motorcycle with an extended frame covered with a white tarp, parked at the same angle and in the same location on the driveway as in the Facebook photograph." The officer took a photograph of the covered motorcycle from the sidewalk, and then walked onto the residential property and up to the top of the driveway to where the motorcycle was parked. "Officer Rhodes pulled off the tarp, revealing a motorcycle that looked like the one from the speeding incident. He then ran a search of the license plate and vehicle identification numbers, which confirmed that the motorcycle was stolen. After gathering this information, Officer Rhodes took a photograph of the uncovered motorcycle, put the tarp back on, left the property, and returned to his car to wait for Collins." When Collins returned home and admitted that the motorcycle was his, the officer arrested him.

In this case, the Court initially decided that the part of the driveway where Collins' motorcycle was parked and subsequently searched was "curtilage." Just like "the front porch, side garden, or area outside the front window, the driveway enclosure where Officer Rhodes searched the motorcycle constitutes an area adjacent to the home and to which the activity of home life extends, and so is properly considered curtilage."

"In physically intruding on the curtilage of Collins' home to search the motorcycle, Officer Rhodes not only invaded Collins' Fourth Amendment interest in the item searched, i.e., the motorcycle, but also invaded Collins' Fourth Amendment interest in the curtilage of his home." And the automobile exception, held the Court, cannot be used to justify the invasion of the curtilage.

"Just as an officer must have a lawful right of access to any contraband he discovers in plain view in order to seize it without a warrant, and just as an officer must have a lawful right of access in order to arrest a person in his home, so too, an officer must have a lawful right of access to a vehicle in order to search it pursuant to the automobile exception. The automobile exception does not afford the necessary lawful right of access to search a vehicle parked within a home or its curtilage because it does not justify an intrusion on a person's separate and substantial Fourth Amendment interest in his home and curtilage."[1003]

1001 *Katz v. United States,* 389 U.S. 347, 361, 88 S. Ct. 507, 516 (1967); *see also Kyllo v. United States*, 533 U.S. 27, 121 S. Ct. 2038 (2001) (surveillance is a search when the government uses a physical intrusion to explore details of the home, including its curtilage; "the antiquity of the tools that they bring along is irrelevant").

1002 *Collins v. Virginia*, 584 U.S. ___, 138 S. Ct. 1663 (2018).

1003 The United States Supreme Court remanded the case for a state court determination of whether the officer's warrantless intrusion may have been reasonable on a different basis. Upon remand, the Virginia Supreme Court held that the evidence discovered during the warrantless search was admissible under the good-faith exception to the exclusionary rule. Said the Court: "The exclusionary rule does not apply under the facts of this case because, at the time of the search, a reasonably well-trained police officer would not have known that the automobile exception did not permit him to search a motorcycle located a few feet across the curtilage boundary of a private driveway." *Collins v. Commonwealth*, 297 Va. 207, 227, 824 S.E.2d 485, 496 (2019).

5.2.2. The "knock and talk"

In general, the "knock and talk" procedure is a law enforcement tactic in which the police, who possess some information that they believe warrants further investigation, but that is insufficient to constitute probable cause for a search warrant, approach the person suspected of engaging in illegal activity at the person's residence (even knock on the front door), identify themselves as police officers, and request consent to search for the suspected illegality or illicit items.

Thus, absent signs or other indications to the contrary, police may enter the curtilage of a home to the extent that they can just walk up to the front door, the same way any other visitor might, with the intent to gain the occupant's consent to a search or to otherwise acquire information from the occupant. Clearly, a "knock and talk" procedure, when performed within its scope, is not a search at all. The proper scope of a knock and talk is determined by the "implied license" that is granted to solicitors, hawkers, and peddlers of all kinds. In this regard, an officer not armed with a warrant may approach a home and knock, precisely because that is "no more than any private citizen might do."[1004] As explained in *Kentucky v. King*,[1005]

> When law enforcement officers who are not armed with a warrant knock on a door, they do no more than any private citizen might do. And whether the person who knocks on the door and requests the opportunity to speak is a police officer or a private citizen, the occupant has no obligation to open the door or to speak.... When the police knock on a door but the occupants choose not to respond or to speak, "the investigation will have reached a conspicuously low point," and the occupants "will have the kind of warning that even the most elaborate security system cannot provide."...And even if an occupant chooses to open the door and speak with the officers, the occupant need not allow the officers to enter the premises and may refuse to answer any questions at any time.[1006]

In *Howard v. State*,[1007] in upholding the lawfulness of a "knock and talk" procedure, the court instructed:

> As long as a person in possession of property has not made express orders prohibiting trespass, a police officer may enter upon residential property, follow the usual path to the home's front door, and knock on it for the purpose of asking the occupant questions.[1008]
>
> Federal and state laws provide that a police officer may approach a citizen in a public place or knock on a door to ask questions or seek consent to search.... Courts have defined a knock-and-talk as a noncustodial procedure in which the officer identifies himself and asks to talk to the home occupant, and then eventually requests permission to search the residence.... The knock-and-talk strategy is a reasonable investigative tool.[1009] ...The purpose of a knock-and-talk is not to create a show of force, make demands on occupants, or to raid a residence.... Instead, the purpose of a knock-and-talk

---

[1004] *Florida v. Jardines*, 569 U.S. 1, 6, 8, 133 S. Ct. 1409, 1415 (2013); *see also Carroll v. Carman*, 574 U.S. 13, 135 S. Ct. 348, 351 (2014) (open to the suggestion that an unsuccessful attempt at a "knock and talk" visit at the front door does not automatically prohibit officers from trying the back door or other parts of the property that are open to visitors); *United States v. Titemore*, 335 F. Supp. 2d 502, 505-06 (D. Vt. 2004) ("[T]he law does not require an officer to determine which door most closely approximates the Platonic form of 'main entrance' and then, after successfully completing this metaphysical inquiry, approach only that door. An officer making a 'knock and talk' visit may approach any part of the building where uninvited visitors could be expected."), *aff'd*, 437 F.3d 251 (2d Cir. 2006).

[1005] *Kentucky v. King*, 563 U.S. 452, 131 S. Ct. 1849 (2011).

[1006] *Kentucky v. King*, 563 U.S. 452, 469-70, 131 S. Ct. 1849, 1862 (2011); *see also Florida v. Jardines*, 569 U.S. 1, 21, 133 S. Ct. 1409, 1423 (2013) ("Even when the objective of a 'knock and talk' is to obtain evidence that will lead to the homeowner's arrest and prosecution, the license to approach still applies. In other words, gathering evidence – even damning evidence – is a lawful activity that falls within the scope of the license to approach. And when officers walk up to the front door of a house, they are permitted to see, hear, and smell whatever can be detected from a lawful vantage point.") (Alito, J., dissenting, joined by Roberts, C.J., Kennedy, J, and Breyer, J). *See also Fuentes-Sanchez v. State*, No. 03-12-00281-CR, 2014 Tex. App. LEXIS 4222 (Tex. App. Apr. 17, 2014).

[1007] *Howard v. State*, ___ S.W.3d ___, ___ (2021 Tex. App. LEXIS 2185).

[1008] *See Cornealius v. State*, 900 S.W.2d 731, 733-34 (Tex. Crim. App. 1995); *Nored v. State*, 875 S.W.2d 392, 396-97 (Tex. App.—Dallas 1994).

[1009] *See United States v. Lewis*, 476 F.3d 369, 381 (5th Cir. 2007).

approach is to make investigatory inquiry or, if officers reasonably suspect criminal activity, to gain the occupant's consent to search....

A police officer need not have reasonable suspicion or a basis for suspecting a particular person to simply ask questions of that individual or request consent to search, so long as the officer does not indicate that compliance with his request is required.... Such an encounter is a consensual interaction, which the citizen is free to terminate at any time.... The encounter is not considered a seizure, triggering Fourth Amendment scrutiny or constitutional analysis, unless it loses its consensual nature.[1010] ...

Naturally, the implied license to approach a house and knock "has certain spatial and temporal limits. A visitor must stick to the path that is typically used to approach a front door, such as a paved walkway. A visitor cannot traipse through the garden, meander into the backyard, or take other circuitous detours that veer from the pathway that a visitor would customarily use.... Nor, as a general matter, may a visitor come to the front door in the middle of the night without an express invitation."[1011]

5.3. Plain view

5.3.1. General aspects

The "plain view" doctrine, as originally set forth in *Coolidge v. New Hampshire*,[1012] and later modified by *Texas v. Brown*,[1013] authorizes law enforcement officers to seize evidence of a crime, contraband, or other items subject to official seizure without first obtaining a search warrant. So long as an officer has a prior constitutional justification for an intrusion into an individual's realm of privacy, and in the course thereof discovers a piece of incriminating evidence, a warrantless seizure of that evidence is authorized.

Although the "plain view" doctrine is often characterized as one of the exceptions to the written warrant requirement, the Supreme Court has indicated that "[i]f an article is already in plain view, neither its observation nor its seizure would involve any invasion of privacy."[1014] Thus, it may be said that the plain view doctrine simply "provides the grounds for seizure of an item when an officer's access to an object has some prior justification under the Fourth Amendment."[1015] In this respect, rather than being viewed as an independent exception to the warrant requirement, the doctrine merely "'serves to supplement the prior justification — whether it be a warrant for another object, hot pursuit, search incident to lawful arrest, or some other legitimate reason for being present'" in the viewing area.[1016] The constitutional requirements that follow, therefore, must attach, not to the government's *observation* of an item lawfully discovered in plain view, but to its *seizure* of that item. In these circumstances, it is the seizure by the government of a citizen's property which clearly invades the owner's possessory interest, and as a result, the dispossession must be constitutionally justified.[1017]

Historically, the Supreme Court required three conditions to be satisfied before the "plain view" doctrine could be invoked. First, the law enforcement officer must have been lawfully in the viewing area. This required the initial intrusion to be constitutionally reasonable, *i.e.*, officers may not violate the Constitution in arriving at the place from which the evidence could be plainly viewed. Second, an officer's discovery of the incriminating evidence must have been inadvertent. The officer could not have known in advance where the items were

---

1010 *Howard v. State*, ___ S.W.3d ___, ___ (2021 Tex. App. LEXIS 2185).

1011 *Florida v. Jardines*, 569 U.S. 1, 19-20, 133 S. Ct. 1409, 1422 (2013) (Alito, J., dissenting, joined by Roberts, C.J., Kennedy, J, and Breyer, J).

1012 *Coolidge v. New Hampshire*, 403 U.S. 443, 91 S. Ct. 2022 (1971).

1013 *Texas v. Brown*, 460 U.S. 730, 103 S. Ct. 1535 (1983).

1014 *Horton v. California*, 496 U.S. 128, 110 S. Ct. 2301, 2306 (1990).

1015 *Texas v. Brown*, 460 U.S. 730, 738 103 S. Ct. 1535, 1541 (1983).

1016 *Horton v. California*, 496 U.S. 128, 110 S. Ct. 2301, 2307 (1990) (quoting *Coolidge v. New Hampshire*, 403 U.S. 443, 466, 91 S. Ct. 2022, 2038 (1971)).

1017 *Horton v. California*, 496 U.S. 128, 110 S. Ct. 2301, 2306 (1990); *see also United States v. Jacobsen*, 466 U.S. 109, 113, 104 S. Ct. 1652, 1656 (1984); *United States v. Jackson*, 131 F.3d 1105, 1108 (4th Cir. 1997) ("The 'plain view' doctrine provides an exception to the warrant requirement for the *seizure* of property, but it does not provide an exception for a search.") (emphasis in original).

located nor intend to seize them beforehand. This requirement traditionally guarded against the transformation of an initially valid (and therefore limited) search into a "general" one. Finally, the incriminating character of the evidence must have been "immediately apparent," and since 1987, this has meant that the officer must have "probable cause" to associate the item with criminal activity.[1018] Naturally, even with all the requirements met, the officer must still "'have a lawful right of access to the object itself.'"[1019]

In *Horton v. California*,[1020] the Supreme Court eliminated the "inadvertence" requirement, reasoning that "evenhanded law enforcement is best achieved by the application of objective standards of conduct, rather than standards that depend upon the subjective state of mind of the officer."[1021] Thus, even though an officer may be interested in an item of evidence and fully expects to find it in the course of a search, that subjective fact "should not invalidate its seizure if the search is confined in area and duration by the terms of a warrant or a valid exception to the warrant requirement."[1022]

Accordingly, under the "plain view" doctrine, a warrantless seizure of an object is lawful if the following requirements are met:

(1) The officer must be lawfully in the viewing area; that is, an officer may not violate the Constitution in arriving at the place from which the evidence could be plainly viewed;
(2) The item's incriminating character is immediately apparent (here, the officer must have probable cause to believe the evidence is somehow associated with criminal activity); and
(3) The officer must have a lawful right of access to the evidence.

If these requirements are satisfied, the evidence may then be immediately seized without a search warrant. This seizure is constitutional, for it "involves no invasion of privacy and is presumptively reasonable[.]"[1023] In *State v. Dobbs*,[1024] officers were executing a search warrant for marijuana and cocaine in defendant's home. They found two sets of golf clubs in the middle of the floor in a bedroom – the clubs looked brand new. On a shelf in the bedroom closet, they found t-shirts with the logo of the Los Rios Country Club embroidered on them. At the time of discovery, the officers lacked probable cause to connect the clubs or shirts to any crime, but they were suspicious. They contacted dispatch to inquire if there had been any recent burglaries, particularly of country clubs. They learned the Los Rios Country Club had indeed reported a theft of golf merchandise. Because the officers were justified in searching the bedroom and closet pursuant to the search warrant, and still lawfully on the premises searching for drugs when they learned of the stolen merchandise, this was a valid plain view seizure.

In *Walter v. State*,[1025] a police officer observed defendant committing a traffic violation and pulled him over. While he was running a records check on defendant's license and registration, the officer called a canine unit. The canine unit arrived during the warrant check. Thereafter, the canine unit officer, who was standing next to defendant's truck, observed a clear plastic bag of marijuana on the floorboard. Because the officer "had every right to be standing where he was at the time he observed the drugs,"[1026] the seizure was permitted under the plain view doctrine.

[1018] *Arizona v. Hicks*, 480 U.S. 321, 327, 107 S. Ct. 1149, 1153 (1987).

[1019] *Collins v. Virginia*, 584 U.S. ___, 138 S. Ct. 1663, 1672 (2018) (quoting *Horton*); *see also Commonwealth v. McCree*, 592 Pa. 238, 255, 924 A.2d 621, 631 (2007) ("the plain view exception to the warrant requirement requires a determination of whether the police have a lawful right of access to the object seen in plain view").

[1020] *Horton v. California*, 496 U.S. 128, 110 S. Ct. 2301 (1990).

[1021] *Horton v. California*, 496 U.S. 128, 110 S. Ct. 2301, 2309 (1990).

[1022] *Horton v. California*, 496 U.S. 128, 110 S. Ct. 2301, 2309 (1990).

[1023] *Horton v. California*, 496 U.S. 128, 110 S. Ct. 2301, 2310 (1990); *Texas v. Brown*, 460 U.S. 730, 741-42, 103 S. Ct. 1535, 1543 (1983); *see also Payton v. New York*, 445 U.S. 573, 587, 100 S. Ct. 1371, 1380 (1980); *Collins v. Virginia*, 584 U.S. ___, 138 S. Ct. 1663, 1672 (2018).

[1024] *State v. Dobbs*, 323 S.W.3d 184 (Tex. Crim. App. 2010).

[1025] *Walter v. State*, 28 S.W.3d 538 (Tex. Crim. App. 2000).

[1026] *Walter v. State*, 28 S.W.3d 538, 544 (Tex. Crim. App. 2000). *See also Holman v. State*, 474 S.W.2d 247 (Tex. Crim. App. 1971); *Casarez v. State*, 504 S.W.2d 847 (Tex. Crim. App. 1974).

5.3.2. Use of a flashlight

No "search" takes place when police use artificial means, such as a flashlight, to illuminate a darkened area.[1027] Accordingly, the use of a flashlight to view an object does not make a plain-view observation unlawful.[1028]

5.3.3. Aerial observations

Courts have found that it is unreasonable to have a privacy expectation in the aerial view of one's property. This is due to the fact that any private citizen may obtain such a view. Since there is no protected privacy interest in the view, police may conduct aerial searches without a warrant.[1029] In *California v. Ciraolo*,[1030] the U.S. Supreme Court held that the Fourth Amendment was not violated by the warrantless, naked-eye aerial observation, at an altitude of 1,000 feet, of marijuana plants growing in a person's fenced-in backyard, within the curtilage of his home. The Court wrote: "In an age where private and commercial flight in the public airways is routine, it is unreasonable for [a person] to expect that his marijuana plants [growing in his fenced-in backyard curtilage] were constitutionally protected from being observed with the naked eye from an altitude of 1,000 feet."[1031]

In *Florida v. Riley*,[1032] the U.S. Supreme Court similarly determined that the surveillance of the interior of a partially covered greenhouse in a residential backyard from the vantage point of a helicopter located 400 feet above the greenhouse did not constitute a "search" for which a warrant is required under the Fourth Amendment.

5.4. Abandonment

5.4.1. General aspects

The relevance of abandoned property in the realm of constitutional criminal procedure lies in the notion that the safeguards of the Fourth Amendment simply do not extend to it. When a person abandons property, he is said to bring his right of privacy therein to an end and may not later complain about its subsequent seizure and use in evidence against him.

The keynote to the concept of abandonment is the actor's intention to relinquish all claim to the property — either personal or real — with the concomitant intention of not reclaiming or resuming ownership, possession, or control over it. The Texas Court of Criminal Appeals has explained, "Abandonment is primarily a question of intent to be inferred from words spoken, acts done, and other objective facts and relevant circumstances. Abandonment consists of two components: (1) a defendant must intend to abandon property, and (2) a defendant must freely decide to abandon the property."[1033] Once this situation exists, it may then be said that the actor's relinquishment took place under circumstances which demonstrate that he retained no reasonable expectation of privacy in the property so discarded. For example, in *Abel v. United States*,[1034] an FBI agent undertook a warrantless search of defendant's hotel room immediately after defendant had paid his bill and vacated the room. During the search, the entire contents of the room's wastepaper basket were seized and found to contain evidence which was subsequently used against defendant in his espionage prosecution. Finding the search and seizure entirely lawful, the Supreme Court explained:

1027 *See, e.g.*, *United States v. Dunn*, 480 U.S. 294, 107 S. Ct. 1134, 1141 (1987) (The officers' flashlight beam, directed through the essentially open front of defendant's barn, "did not transform their observations into an unreasonable search within the meaning of the Fourth Amendment.").

1028 *United States v. Reed*, 114 F.3d 644 (6th Cir. 1998). *See also Walter v. State*, 28 S.W.3d 538 (Tex. Crim. App. 2000).

1029 *Dow Chemical Co. v. United States*, 476 U.S. 227, 234-35, 106 S. Ct. 1819, 1824 (1986).

1030 *California v. Ciraolo*, 476 U.S. 207, 106 S. Ct. 1809 (1986).

1031 *California v. Ciraolo*, 476 U.S. 207, 106 S. Ct. 1809, 1813 (1986).

1032 *Florida v. Riley*, 488 U.S. 445, 109 S. Ct. 693 (1989).

1033 *State v. Martinez*, 570 S.W.3d 278, 286 (Tex. Crim. App. 2019) (citing *McDuff v. State*, 939 S.W.2d 607 (Tex. Crim. App. 1997); *Comer v. State*, 754 S.W.2d 656 (Tex. Crim. App. 1988); *Matthews v. State*, 431 S.W.3d 596 (Tex. Crim. App. 2014)).

1034 *Abel v. United States*, 362 U.S. 217, 80 S. Ct. 683 (1960).

> [A]t the time of the search, [defendant] had vacated the room. The hotel then had the exclusive right to its possession, and the hotel management freely gave its consent that the search be made. Nor was it unlawful to seize the entire contents of the wastepaper basket, even though some of its contents had no connection with crime.... *[Defendant] had abandoned these articles.* He had thrown them away. [So there] can be nothing unlawful in the Government's appropriation of such abandoned property.[1035]

As a result, for criminal procedure purposes, the relevant inquiry is whether the actor, by dispossessing himself of his property, has so relinquished his reasonable expectation of privacy in that property that a subsequent government inspection and appropriation of that property cannot be said to constitute a "search and seizure" within the meaning of the Fourth Amendment. As the federal Supreme Court noted, there can be "no seizure in the sense of the law" when law enforcement officers examine "the contents of [personal property] after it ha[s] been abandoned."[1036]

When an individual abandons an item of personal property, such as by dropping evidence while fleeing from police, he relinquishes a reasonable expectation of privacy in the discarded item.[1037] A showing of actual intent to abandon is not necessary. It is only necessary to show that the individual asserting a privacy interest in the property in question had relinquished sufficient control over the property so that he no longer had any reasonable expectation of privacy in the object or item.

For example, in *Matthews v. State*,[1038] Officer Zimpelman responded to a tip that Matthews was selling crack cocaine out of a white van parked in front of a store. Zimpelman located the van and, for reasons of officer safety, told Matthews to exit the van. At that point, Matthews refused to consent to a search of the van. Thereafter, when Matthews heard Zimpelman request a K-9 unit, defendant took flight. Zimpelman pursued Matthews for several blocks, caught him and returned to the squad car. The court held that Matthews had a reasonable expectation of privacy in the van *before* he fled. "[Defendant] exercised a subjective expectation of privacy when he refused to consent to the search of the vehicle.... Furthermore, [his] expectation of privacy was reasonable. [He] had permission to use the vehicle.... [He] was in the driver's seat, the doors were closed, and the keys were in the ignition."[1039] However, *after* he fled, Matthews abandoned his reasonable expectation of privacy in the van. The court explained that defendant "'took off running,' leaving the keys in the ignition of the vehicle. [Defendant] ran for two blocks and entered a vacant field. He stopped only when Officer Zimpelman activated his taser and pointed it at [him]. These circumstances show that [defendant] intended to abandon any expectation of privacy in the van he left behind."[1040]

In *McDuff v. State*,[1041] defendant was also found to have abandoned his vehicle. There, he pushed his car into a motel parking lot and left it there for six days. The court noted that there was no evidence of police involvement in his doing so. In addition, defendant used another car to push the vehicle into the parking lot, thus an indication that he had possession of another operable vehicle. Moreover, defendant did not return to his school classes and was found to be living under an alias in Kansas City, Missouri. The court found that there was sufficient evidence of abandonment and the evidence discovered in the car was admissible.

5.4.1.1. Throwing or discarding property

In *Smith v. Ohio*,[1042] the Supreme Court disallowed a search of property that had been placed on the hood of defendant's car. There, plainclothes police officers observed defendant carrying a grocery bag in what one of them described as a "gingerly" manner. When the officers identified themselves as police officers and approached defendant, he threw the bag onto the hood of his car. The officer asked the defendant what the bag contained but defendant did not answer, whereupon the officer opened the bag and found drug

---

[1035] *Abel v. United States*, 362 U.S. 217, 241, 80 S. Ct. 683 (1960) (emphasis added).
[1036] *Hester v. United States*, 265 U.S. 57, 58, 44 S. Ct. 445 (1924).
[1037] *Morrison v. State*, 71 S.W.3d 821 (Tex. App. 2002).
[1038] *Matthews v. State*, 431 S.W.3d 596 (Tex. Crim. App. 2014).
[1039] *Matthews v. State*, 431 S.W.3d 596, 609 (Tex. Crim. App. 2014).
[1040] *Matthews v. State*, 431 S.W.3d 596, 609 (Tex. Crim. App. 2014).
[1041] *McDuff v. State*, 939 S.W.2d 607 (Tex. Crim. App. 1997).
[1042] *Smith v. Ohio*, 494 U.S. 541, 110 S. Ct. 1288, 1290 (1990).

paraphernalia inside. In holding that the search was not justified, the court accepted the Ohio Supreme courts conclusion that "a citizen who attempts to protect his private property from inspection, after throwing it on a car to respond to a police officer's inquiry, clearly has not abandoned that property."[1043]

Note also that where officers do not have a justification for their initial actions (*e.g.*, detaining without reasonable suspicion), and the item is discarded in response to this unlawful activity, the evidence may be suppressed as the fruit of illegal law enforcement activity. In this instance, courts say that the unlawful police action forced the abandonment. Thus, in *Comer v. State*,[1044] although defendant dropped a syringe and attempted to kick it under his truck as he exited the vehicle, legally there was no "abandonment" of the syringe. The court found that the arresting officer was illegally pursuing the vehicle in which defendant was a passenger. Accordingly, defendant's attempt to relinquish the syringe was not voluntary but a direct result of the illegal police conduct.

5.4.2. Abandoned structures

Police do not need a search warrant before entering structures that, by all objective manifestations, appear abandoned. A court will weigh the totality of the circumstances in determining whether police could reasonably believe a structure has been abandoned, including (i) its outward appearance; (ii) its overall condition; (iii) the state of the vegetation on the premises; (iv) whether barriers have been erected and securely fastened in all openings; (v) indications that the home is not being serviced with gas or electricity; (vi) a lack of appliances or furniture typically found in a dwelling home; (vii) the length of time it takes for temporary barriers to be replaced with functional doors and windows; (viii) the history surrounding the premises and its prior use; and (ix) any complaints of illicit activity occurring in the structure.

5.4.3. Curbside garbage

The Supreme Court, in *California v. Greenwood*,[1045] held that the Fourth Amendment does not prohibit the warrantless seizure and search of garbage left for collection outside the curtilage of a home. According to the U.S. Supreme Court, when garbage is left for collection outside the curtilage of one's home, it is sufficiently exposed to the public so that any search or seizure thereof falls outside the parameters of the Fourth Amendment.[1046] Thus, a person will have no reasonable expectation of privacy in items deposited in a public area, conveyed to a third-party for collection, and "readily accessible to animals, children, scavengers, snoops, and other members of the public."[1047]

5.4.4. Denying ownership

If a defendant disclaims ownership of property or any possessory interest, police may use such a denial as sufficient proof of either an intent to abandon the property or a lack of ownership of the property. In *State v. Velasquez*,[1048] an officer saw defendant board a Greyhound bus carrying a black duffel bag. Before the bus was ready to leave, the officer and his partner (both in plain clothes) also boarded the bus and began to hold consensual interviews with the passengers. Without blocking defendant in, the officer squatted down next to defendant and asked – in addition to a few insignificant questions – to see his ticket and identification. He then asked if defendant had any luggage, to which defendant replied that he did not, even though the black bag he had carried on was in the seat next to him. The officer asked if it was his, and defendant replied, "No, that's not my bag." When the officer went to grab the bag, defendant placed his hands across it and asked, "What are you doing?" The officer said, "I'm getting this bag. Is this your bag?" Defendant replied, "Uh, no, it's

---

1043 *Smith v. Ohio*, 494 U.S. 541, 543-544,110 S. Ct. 1288, 1290 (1990). *See also Hudson v. State*, 205 S.W.3d 600 (Tex. App. 2006).

1044 *Comer v. State*, 754 S.W.2d 656 (Tex. Crim. App. 1988).

1045 *California v. Greenwood*, 486 U.S. 35, 108 S. Ct. 1625 (1988).

1046 *California v. Greenwood*, 486 U.S. 35, 108 S. Ct. 1625, 1628 (1988).

1047 *California v. Greenwood*, 486 U.S. 35, 108 S. Ct. 1625, 1629 (1988). *See also Flores v. State*, 319 S.W.3d 697 (Tex. Crim. App. 2010).

1048 *State v. Velasquez*, 994 S.W.2d 676 (Tex. Crim. App. 1999).

not." Because defendant disclaimed any ownership interest in the bag, it was effectively abandoned, and he could no longer legally object to the officer's search. Therefore, the marihuana the officer found in the bag was admissible.

A number of circuits have similarly held that an abandonment occurs where, in response to police questioning, a suspect denies ownership of the property in question.[1049] Accordingly, discarding something while fleeing, tossing something in the trash, or denying ownership are all ways that a person may be found to have abandoned property so as to relinquish a reasonable expectation of privacy in it.

5.4.4.1. Silence in response to a police inquiry about ownership

An abandonment of property would not be found solely from a person's silence or failure to respond to a police officer's questions regarding ownership of an item. As one commentator reasoned, "To equate a passive failure to claim potentially incriminating evidence with an affirmative abandonment of property would be to twist both logic and experience in a most uncomfortable knot."[1050]

6. ADMINISTRATIVE AND REGULATORY SEARCHES

6.1. Administrative searches

Searches and seizures may be undertaken by a state and its agents wholly apart from those pursued by law enforcement agencies. Whether the search or seizure is reasonable under the Fourth Amendment depends on an analysis of the totality of the circumstances and the nature of the search or seizure itself. In most typical cases involving law enforcement practice and procedure, there is a constitutional preference for a judicial determination of probable cause and the issuance of a written warrant. Yet, there are recognized exceptions to the warrant requirement, and in the area of regulatory and administrative searches, the courts will apply two types of analyses: "balancing of interests" and "special needs."

6.1.1. The "balancing of interests" analysis

In some circumstances, courts will apply a general Fourth Amendment "balancing test," examining the totality of the circumstances to assess, on the one side, the degree to which a search or seizure intrudes upon a person's reasonable expectation of privacy, and, on the other side, the degree to which it is needed for the promotion of legitimate governmental interests.[1051]

For example, in *Michigan Dept. of State Police v. Sitz*,[1052] the Supreme Court utilized a "balancing of interests" analysis in upholding the constitutionality of highway sobriety checkpoints. According to the Court, this test involved balancing the state's substantial interest in preventing harm caused by drunk drivers, the degree to which sobriety checkpoints advance that public interest, and the minimal level of intrusion upon individual motorists who are briefly stopped.[1053]

1049 *See United States v. Carrasquillo*, 877 F.2d 73 (D.C. Cir. 1989) (abandonment found where train passenger denied ownership of garment bag under his feet and no other person claimed it); *United States v. McBean*, 861 F.2d 1570 (11th Cir. 1988) (defendant abandoned any reasonable expectation of privacy in the contents of luggage in the trunk of his car when he told police that it was not his luggage and that he knew nothing of its contents); *United States v. Roman*, 849 F.2d 920 (5th Cir. 1988) (abandonment found where defendant checked his suitcases at an airport and then told agents that he had not checked any luggage and had no baggage other than his carry-on bag). *See also United States v. Clark*, 891 F.2d 501 (4th Cir. 1989); *United States v. Moskowitz*, 883 F.2d 1142 (2d Cir. 1989); *United States v. Nordling*, 804 F.2d 1466 (9th Cir. 1986); *United States v. Lucci*, 758 F.2d 153 (6th Cir.), *cert. denied*, 474 U.S. 843, 106 S. Ct. 129 (1985).

1050 *State v. Joyner*, 66 Haw. 543, 669 P.2d 152 (1983). *But see United States v. Adams*, 583 F.2d 457 (6th Cir. 2009) (police, in a hotel room by consent, asked to whom jacket on the floor belonged, and no one, including defendant, claimed ownership; defendant had thus abandoned any privacy interest in the jacket).

1051 *Brown v. Texas*, 443 U.S. 47, 99 S. Ct. 2637 (1979); *Samson v. California*, 547 U.S. 843, 126 S. Ct. 2193, 2197 (2006).

1052 *Michigan Dept. of State Police v. Sitz*, 496 U.S. 444, 110 S. Ct. 2481 (1990).

1053 *See also United States v. Martinez-Fuerte*, 428 U.S. 543, 96 S. Ct. 3074 (1976) (applying the "balancing of interests" approach to approve highway checkpoints for detecting illegal aliens).

Similarly, the Supreme Court, in *Illinois v. Lidster,*[1054] upheld the brief stop of motorists at a roadside checkpoint, where police sought information about a recent hit-and-run fatal accident. Utilizing the *Brown v. Texas* "balancing of interests" approach, the Court looked to the gravity of the public concerns served by such a seizure, the degree to which the seizure advanced the public interest, and the severity of the interference with individual liberty.

6.1.2. The "special needs" analysis

There are some areas of law enforcement and criminal procedure, where "special needs," beyond the normal need for law enforcement, authorize government action without the standard constitutional justifications which typically apply. In this regard, the Supreme Court has utilized a "special needs" analysis to carve out an exception to the familiar probable cause and judicial warrant requirements normally associated with the Fourth Amendment.

The first use of the "special needs" analysis may be found in Justice Blackmun's concurrence in *New Jersey v. T.L.O.,*[1055] where it was determined that a school official's search of a student's belongings based on individualized suspicion was reasonable. In this regard, Justice Blackmun explained that probable cause and a warrant were not required where "special needs, beyond the normal need for law enforcement, make the warrant and probable-cause requirements impracticable."[1056]

While the "balancing of interests" approach is an easier test for the prosecution to satisfy, the "special needs" approach involves a more stringent analysis. In this regard, if a "special need" does exist, courts may then make an exception to the probable cause and warrant requirements only after balancing the nature and quality of the intrusion on the individual's constitutional rights against "the importance of the governmental interests alleged to justify the intrusion."[1057]

6.1.2.1. School searches

In *New Jersey v. T.L.O.,* the Supreme Court held that the Fourth Amendment's prohibition on unreasonable searches and seizures applies to searches conducted by public school officials. "In carrying out searches and other disciplinary functions pursuant to [publicly mandated educational and disciplinary] policies, [public] school officials act as representatives of the State, not merely as surrogates for the parents, and they cannot claim the parents' immunity from the strictures of the Fourth Amendment."[1058] The Court balanced the student's legitimate expectation of privacy and personal security against such public school needs as maintaining discipline and order in the classrooms and on school grounds, and preservation of the educational environment.

In striking that balance, the Court ruled: First, public school officials are not subject to the warrant requirement.[1059] Requiring a warrant would "unduly interfere with the maintenance of the swift and informal disciplinary procedures needed in schools."[1060] Second, the level of suspicion applicable to public school officials has been reduced from probable cause to a standard which turns "simply on the reasonableness, under all of the circumstances, of the search."[1061] Reasonableness will be assessed by a two-fold inquiry: "first, one must consider whether the action was justified at its inception[;] second, one must determine whether the search as actually conducted was reasonably related in scope to the circumstances which justified the interference in the first place."[1062]

1054 *Illinois v. Lidster,* 540 U.S. 419, 427-28, 124 S. Ct. 885, 890-91 (2004).

1055 *New Jersey v. T.L.O.*, 469 U.S. 325, 351, 105 S. Ct. 733, 747-48 (1985) (Blackmun, J., concurring).

1056 *New Jersey v. T.L.O.*, 469 U.S. 325, 351, 105 S. Ct. 733, 748 (1985) (Blackmun, J., concurring).

1057 *See United States v. Place*, 462 U.S. 696, 703, 103 S. Ct. 2637, 2642 (1983).

1058 *New Jersey v. T.L.O.*, 469 U.S. 325, 105 S. Ct. 733, 741 (1985).

1059 *New Jersey v. T.L.O.*, 469 U.S. 325, 105 S. Ct. 733, 743 (1985).

1060 *New Jersey v. T.L.O.*, 469 U.S. 325, 105 S. Ct. 733, 743 (1985).

1061 *New Jersey v. T.L.O.*, 469 U.S. 325, 105 S. Ct. 733, 744-45 (1985).

1062 *New Jersey v. T.L.O.*, 469 U.S. 325, 105 S. Ct. 733, 744 (1985) (citations omitted); *see also Board of Educ. of Indep. Sch. Dist. No. 92 v. Earls*, 536 U.S. 822, 829-30, 122 S. Ct. 2559, 2564 (2002) (applying "special needs" principles to validate school's drug testing of all students participating in competitive extracurricular activities); *Vernonia Sch. Dist. 47J v. Acton*, 515 U.S.

6.1.2.1.1. An unreasonable strip search

In *Safford Unified School District #1 v. Redding*,[1063] the U.S. Supreme Court applied the rationale of *New Jersey v. T.L.O.* to hold that school officials violated a 13-year-old student's Fourth Amendment rights when the school nurse and an administrative assistant searched the student's bra and underpants acting on reasonable suspicion that she had brought forbidden prescription and over-the-counter drugs to school. According to the Court, because there were no reasons to suspect the drugs presented a danger or were concealed in her underwear, "the search did violate the Constitution[.]"[1064]

6.1.2.2. Government employers

In *O'Connor v. Ortega*,[1065] the Supreme Court held that the "special needs" of government workplaces permit government employers and supervisors to conduct warrantless, work-related searches of employees' desks, file cabinets and offices without a warrant or probable cause. Moreover, the same principles applicable to a government employer's search of an employee's office, desk, or file cabinet applies when the employer examines text messages sent and received on a device the employer owned and issued to employees.[1066]

6.1.2.3. Probation and parole

Similarly, in *Griffin v. Wisconsin*,[1067] the Court held that "a State's operation of a probation system, like its operation of a school, government office or prison, or its supervision of a regulated industry, likewise presents 'special needs' beyond normal law enforcement that may justify departures from the usual warrant and probable-cause requirements." According to the Court, "supervision" in the probation system is the "special need" of the state "permitting a degree of impingement upon privacy that would not be constitutional if applied to the public at large."[1068]

Accordingly, "probationers and parolees do not enjoy the same level of Fourth Amendment protection accorded defendants only suspected of a crime."[1069] "Rather, persons subject to community supervision enjoy 'only conditional liberty properly dependent on observance of special supervisory restrictions.'"[1070] Thus, in *Cochran v. State*,[1071] although Cochran did not consent to the search of his motel room, it was nonetheless allowed because he had in essence agreed to it as a condition of receiving his bargained-for community supervision. The court explained that "[a] condition of community supervision is invalid if it has all three of the following characteristics:

(1) it has no relationship to the crime;
(2) it relates to conduct that is not in itself criminal; and
(3) it forbids or requires conduct that is not reasonably related to the future criminality of the defendant or does not serve the statutory ends of probation."[1072]

646, 653, 115 S. Ct. 2386, 2391 (1995) (applying a "special needs" analysis to sustain drug-testing programs for student athletes).

1063 *Safford Unified Sch. Dist. #1 v. Redding*, 557 U.S. 364, 129 S. Ct. 2633 (2009).

1064 *Safford Unified Sch. Dist. #1 v. Redding*, 557 U.S. 364, 129 S. Ct. 2633, 2637 (2009).

1065 *O'Connor v. Ortega*, 480 U.S. 709, 107 S. Ct. 1492 (1987).

1066 *See City of Ontario v. Quon*, 560 U.S. 746, 130 S. Ct. 2619 (2010).

1067 *Griffin v. Wisconsin*, 483 U.S. 868, 873-74, 107 S. Ct. 3164, 3168 (1987).

1068 *Griffin v. Wisconsin*, 483 U.S. 868, 875, 107 S. Ct. 3164, 3169 (1987); *see also United States v. Knights*, 534 U.S. 112, 122 S. Ct. 587 (2001) (The warrantless search of a probationer's home, supported by a reasonable suspicion and authorized by his probation, was reasonable under the Fourth Amendment.); *Pennsylvania Bd. of Probation v. Scott*, 524 U.S. 357, 118 S. Ct. 2014 (1988) (The exclusionary rule, which generally prohibits the use at criminal trials of evidence obtained in violation of the Fourth Amendment, does not apply in parole revocation hearings.).

1069 *Garrett v. State*, 791 S.W.2d 137, 140 (Tex. Crim. App. 1990).

1070 *Cochran v. State*, 563 S.W.3d 374, 379 (Tex. App. 2018) (quoting *McArthur v. State*, 1 S.W.3d 323, 332 (Tex. App. 1999)).

1071 *Cochran v. State*, 563 S.W.3d 374 (Tex. App. 2018).

1072 *Cochran v. State*, 563 S.W.3d 374, 381 (Tex. App. 2018).

Because the condition requiring Cochran to submit to law enforcement searches was limited in scope to searches for illegal drugs or contraband, bore a direct relationship to the underlying crime and related to criminal acts, it did not infringe on Cochran's constitutional rights to privacy.

By contrast, the condition in *Tamez v. State*[1073] was not so limited. There, the Texas Court of Criminal Appeals found invalid a condition of community supervision requiring a defendant to "[s]ubmit his person, place of residence and vehicle to search and seizure at any time of the day or night, with or without a search warrant, whenever requested to do so by the Probation Officer or any law enforcement officer."[1074] Noting that a probationer's "expectations may be diminished only to the extent necessary for his reformation and rehabilitation,"[1075] the court concluded that "the probationary condition in the instant case is too broad, too sweeping and infringes upon the probationer's rights under the Fourth and Fourteenth Amendments to the United States Constitution and Article I, Sec. 9, of the Texas Constitution."[1076]

6.1.2.4. Drug testing

In upholding mandatory, suspicionless drug testing of U.S. Customs Service employees seeking promotion to drug-interdiction positions, the U.S. Supreme Court in *National Treasury Employees Union v. Von Raab*[1077] instructed:

> [W]here a Fourth Amendment intrusion serves special governmental needs, beyond the normal need for law enforcement, it is necessary to balance the individual's privacy expectations against the Government's interests to determine whether it is impractical to require a warrant or some level of individualized suspicion in the particular context.[1078]

In *Chandler v. Miller*,[1079] however, the Supreme Court struck down a Georgia statutory provision requiring that candidates for specified state political offices pass a urinalysis drug test within 30 days prior to qualifying for election. The Court reasoned that Georgia had failed to show a special need important enough to override the individual privacy interests of the candidates. The Court found that the "certification requirement is not well designed to identify candidates who violate anti-drug laws" and that the statute failed to show any concrete danger posed by a state official possibly using drugs.[1080]

6.1.2.4.1. Hotel/motel registries

In *City of Los Angeles v. Patel*,[1081] the Supreme Court struck down a City of Los Angeles law that required hotel/motel operators to make their registries available to the police on demand. The purpose of the record-keeping requirement was "to deter criminal conduct, on the theory that criminals will be unwilling to carry on illicit activities in motel rooms if they must provide identifying information at check-in. Because this deterrent effect will only be accomplished if motels actually do require guests to provide the required information, the ordinance also authorize[d] police to conduct random spot checks of motels' guest registers

1073 *Tamez v. State*, 534 S.W.2d 686 (Tex. Crim. App. 1976).
1074 *Tamez v. State*, 534 S.W.2d 686, 690 (Tex. Crim. App. 1976).
1075 *Tamez v. State*, 534 S.W.2d 686, 692 (Tex. Crim. App. 1976).
1076 *Tamez v. State*, 534 S.W.2d 686, 692 (Tex. Crim. App. 1976).
1077 *National Treasury Employees Union v. Von Raab*, 489 U.S. 656, 109 S. Ct. 1384 (1989).
1078 *National Treasury Employees Union v. Von Raab*, 489 U.S. 656, 665, 109 S. Ct. 1384, 1390 (1989).
1079 *Chandler v. Miller*, 520 U.S. 305, 117 S. Ct. 1295 (1997).
1080 *See also Ferguson v. City of Charleston*, 532 U.S. 67 (2001) (Court struck down a policy which required state hospital employees to perform drug tests on urine samples taken from pregnant women, without the informed consent of the women, then to report positive results to police, who arrested the women if they refused to enter a drug treatment program. The Court found that the "central and indispensable" purpose of this policy was to generate evidence for law enforcement purposes, not to provide medical treatment, and noted that police were actively involved in the development of this policy as well as its day-to-day administration.).
1081 *City of Los Angeles v. Patel*, 576 U.S. 409, 135 S. Ct. 2443 (2015).

to ensure that they are properly maintained."[1082] According to the Court, the provision of the "Los Angeles Municipal Code that requires hotel operators to make their registries available to the police on demand" – is "facially unconstitutional because it penalizes them for declining to turn over their records without affording them any opportunity for precompliance review."[1083]

6.2. Regulatory searches

As a general principle, the Fourth Amendment's prohibition against unreasonable searches and seizures is applicable to commercial businesses as well as private dwellings.[1084] While an owner or operator of a commercial establishment may have a lesser expectation of privacy in the establishment's premises than that enjoyed by a homeowner in his dwelling place, the owner or operator nonetheless maintains a legitimate expectation of privacy in the commercial establishment.[1085] This expectation of privacy exists with respect to administrative inspections designed to enforce regulatory schemes as well as to traditional searches conducted by police for the gathering of evidence of a crime.[1086]

Normally, prior to conducting a regulatory search, officers are required to obtain an administrative search warrant. In "closely regulated industries," however, "an exception to the warrant requirement has been carved out for searches of premises pursuant to an administrative inspection scheme."[1087] As the Third Circuit stated in *Lovgren v. Byrne*,[1088]

> [O]ne who is engaged in an industry, that is pervasively regulated by the government or that has been historically subject to such close supervision, is ordinarily held to be on notice that periodic inspections will occur and, accordingly, has [a significantly reduced] expectation of privacy in the areas where he knows those inspections will occur.[1089]

Thus, it has been held that in certain circumstances, government investigators conducting searches or inspections of "closely regulated" businesses need not adhere to the usual warrant or probable-cause requirements as long as their searches meet reasonable legislative or administrative standards.[1090]

In order to be constitutionally valid, a warrantless, administrative inspection of a closely regulated commercial establishment must satisfy three requirements:

1) There must be a substantial government interest in the regulatory scheme under which the warrantless, administrative inspection is conducted;

2) The warrantless, administrative inspection must be necessary to further the regulatory scheme; and

3) The warrantless inspection, by reason of the certainty of its terms and regularity of its application, must provide a constitutionally sufficient substitute for a search warrant. In this respect, similar to a search warrant, the regulatory scheme under which the inspection is conducted must

---

1082 *City of Los Angeles v. Patel*, 576 U.S. 409, 428, 135 S. Ct. 2443, 2457 (2015) (Scalia, J., dissenting).

1083 *City of Los Angeles v. Patel*, 576 U.S. 409, 412, 135 S. Ct. 2443, 2447 (2015).

1084 *New York v. Burger*, 482 U.S. 691, 107 S. Ct. 2636 (1987); *see v. City of Seattle*, 387 U.S. 541, 543, 546, 87 S. Ct. 1737, 1739, 1741 (1967).

1085 *Donovan v. Dewey*, 452 U.S. 594, 101 S. Ct. 2534 (1981).

1086 *See New York v. Burger*, 482 U.S. 691, 699, 107 S. Ct. 2636, 2642 (1987); *see also Marshall v. Barlow's Inc.*, 436 U.S. 307, 312-13, 98 S. Ct. 1816, 1820 (1978).

1087 *Shoemaker v. Handel*, 795 F.2d 1136, 1142 (3d Cir. 1986).

1088 *Lovgren v. Byrne*, 787 F.2d 857 (3d Cir. 1986).

1089 *Lovgren v. Byrne*, 787 F.2d 857, 865 (3d Cir. 1986).

1090 *See, e.g., New York v. Burger*, 482 U.S. 691, 702-03, 107 S. Ct. 2636, 2643 (1987) (warrantless inspections of automobile junkyard businesses come within exception for closely regulated industries); *Donovan v. Dewey*, 452 U.S. 594, 605, 101 S. Ct. 2534, 2541 (1981) (warrantless inspections under the Federal Mine Safety and Health Act); *United States v. Biswell*, 406 U.S. 311, 316-17, 92 S. Ct. 1593, 1596-97 (1972) (warrantless inspection of pawnshops licensed to sell guns); *Colonnade Catering Corp. v. United States*, 397 U.S. 72, 76-77, 90 S. Ct. 774, 777 (1970) (liquor industry); *Shoemaker v. Handel*, 795 F.2d 1136, 1142(3d Cir. 1986) (horse racing).

advise the property owner that: (a) the administrative inspection is being conducted under legal authority; (b) by reason of that authority, the scope of the inspection is clearly defined; and (c) the discretion of the inspecting officer is appropriately limited.[1091]

When each of the three requirements is satisfied, the warrantless, administrative inspection is constitutionally reasonable and the discovery of evidence of crimes in the course of an otherwise proper administrative inspection should not render the search illegal or the administrative scheme suspect.[1092]

6.3. Fire Scenes

6.3.1. Preliminary considerations

An individual's reasonable expectation of privacy and his Fourth Amendment protections are not diminished simply because the official conducting the search at the fire scene "wears the uniform of a firefighter rather than a policeman, or because his purpose is to ascertain the cause of a fire rather than to look for evidence of a crime, or because the fire might have been started deliberately."[1093] Firefighters, like police officers, are public officials, and as such, are subject to the constraints of the federal and state constitutions.[1094]

A hot fire scene, *i.e., a burning building,* "clearly presents an exigency of sufficient proportions to render a warrantless entry 'reasonable.' Indeed, it would defy reason to suppose that firemen must secure a warrant or consent before entering a burning structure to put out the blaze."[1095] If a firefighter — once inside the building and during the course of fighting the blaze — discovers evidence of arson that is in "plain view," he may lawfully seize that evidence. Accordingly, "an entry to fight a fire requires no warrant," and, once inside the building, if evidence of arson is discovered, it is seizable and "admissible at trial[.]"[1096] If, however, investigating fire officials during this time period "find probable cause to believe that arson has occurred and require further access to gather evidence for a possible prosecution, they [must] obtain a warrant ... upon a traditional showing of probable cause applicable to searches for evidence of crime."[1097] Fire officials do not, however, need a "warrant to remain in a building *for a reasonable amount of time* to investigate the cause of a blaze after it has been extinguished."[1098]

When a firefighter, in the line of duty, asks law enforcement for a safety check after seeing drug paraphernalia, guns, and flammable liquids in an apartment, is the officer's entry into the apartment reasonable under the Fourth Amendment, and can that officer's discovery of drug paraphernalia in plain view provide probable cause for a search warrant? In *Martin v. State,*[1099] the Court held that it was. In this regard, "where fire or police officials enter a structure during or in the immediate aftermath of a fire to conduct legitimate duties connected to the original exigency of the fire, no search warrant is required." In this case, the Court held that the officer's "conduct was justified in response to the firefighters' legitimate safety concerns pursuant to the exigency of the fire and its immediate aftermath."[1100]

In reaching this conclusion, the Court was guided by the federal Supreme Court's opinion in *Michigan v. Tyler,*[1101] which held:

> [W]here fire or police officials enter a structure during or in the immediate aftermath of a fire to conduct legitimate duties connected to the original exigency of the fire, no search warrant is required....

1091 *New York v. Burger,* 482 U.S. 691, 702, 713, 107 S. Ct. 2636, 2644, 2649 (1987).

1092 *See New York v. Burger,* 482 U.S. 691, 716, 107 S. Ct. 2636, 2651 (1987); *Santikos v. State,* 836 S.W.2d 631 (Tex. Crim. App. 1992); *Nesloney v. State,* 711 S.W.2d 636 (Tex. Crim. App. 1986).

1093 *Michigan v. Tyler,* 436 U.S. 499, 506, 98 S. Ct. 1942, 1948 (1978).

1094 *Michigan v. Tyler,* 436 U.S. 499, 506, 98 S. Ct. 1942, 1948 (1978).

1095 *Michigan v. Tyler,* 436 U.S. 499, 509, 98 S. Ct. 1942, 1950 (1978).

1096 *Michigan v. Tyler,* 436 U.S. 499, 512, 98 S. Ct. 1942, 1951 (1978).

1097 *Michigan v. Tyler,* 436 U.S. 499, 511, 98 S. Ct. 1942, 1951 (1978).

1098 *Michigan v. Tyler,* 436 U.S. 499, 511, 98 S. Ct. 1942, 1951 (1978) (emphasis added); *see also Hummel v. State,* 2013 Tex. Crim. App. Unpub. LEXIS 1239 (Tex. Crim. App. Nov. 20, 2013).

1099 *Martin v. State,* 620 S.W.3d 749 (Tex. Crim. App. 2021).

1100 *Martin v. State,* 620 S.W.3d 749, 767 (Tex. Crim. App. 2021).

1101 *Michigan v. Tyler,* 436 U.S. 499, 98 S. Ct. 1942 (1978).

> Applying that principle here, Officer Hart's warrantless entry into [defendant's] apartment was lawfully permitted.... [The facts show]: (1) Officer Hart was dispatched to assist the fire department with a structure fire; (2) the fire battalion chief informed Hart of the various safety concerns that had arisen while firefighters were still working on the scene and asked Hart to conduct a safety check; and (3) based on the facts known to him at the time, Hart reasonably believed that the safety check was necessary to allow the firefighters to complete their ventilation efforts. Given these facts, it was objectively reasonable for Hart to enter the apartment to conduct the requested safety check without first securing a search warrant.... [Since we] hold that Officer Hart's conduct was justified in response to the firefighters' legitimate safety concerns pursuant to the exigency of the fire and its immediate aftermath, we need not address the court of appeals' broader bright-line rule that would always permit an officer to "step into the shoes" of a firefighter and seize plain-view contraband.[1102]

6.3.2. The warrant requirement and fire scene entries

Whenever a fire official wishes to re-enter a "cold" fire scene in the absence of consent, exigent (emergency) circumstances, or complete devastation or destruction, a warrant is required. A "cold" fire scene may be defined as an area containing property which has been freshly fire-damaged, existing at a time when the fire has been completely extinguished and all fire and police officials have departed. Any entries during this "cold" period will be considered by the courts as being *beyond* the "reasonable time to investigate the cause of a blaze after it has been extinguished," in the absence of consent, exigent circumstances, or total devastation.[1103] Cold-scene entries and searches require a warrant.

There are two types of warrants available to the investigating fire official, and the "object of the search determines the type of warrant required."[1104]

6.3.2.1. To determine cause and origin

If the fire official's prime objective is to determine the *cause* and *origin* of a recent fire, an "administrative warrant" must be obtained. "Probable cause to issue an administrative warrant exists if reasonable legislative, administrative, or judicially prescribed standards for conducting an inspection are satisfied with respect to a particular dwelling."[1105] This procedural requirement is accomplished by the official personally appearing before a judge, who will examine the official's affidavit and/or take his or her sworn testimony. At this meeting, the official must show that: (1) a "fire of undetermined origin has occurred on the premises"; (2) the "scope of the proposed search is reasonable"; (3) the "search will not intrude unnecessarily on the fire victim's privacy"; and (4) the "search will be executed at a reasonable and convenient time."[1106]

Before a judge will authorize the issuance of an administrative warrant to conduct an investigation into the cause of a fire, he or she will want to know: (1) the "number of prior entries"; (2) the "scope of the search"; (3) the "time of day when it is proposed to be made"; (4) the "lapse of time since the fire"; (5) the "continued use of the building"; and (6) the "owner's efforts to secure it against intruders[.]"[1107]

6.3.2.2. To search for evidence of arson

If, however, the fire official's prime objective is to gather evidence of criminal activity, *e.g.*, arson, a "criminal search warrant" must be secured. This is accomplished only upon a showing (before a judge) of "probable cause to believe that relevant evidence will be found in the place to be searched."[1108] Probable cause

---

[1102] *Martin v. State*, 620 S.W.3d 749, 767 (Tex. Crim. App. 2021).

[1103] *Michigan v. Tyler*, 436 U.S. 499, 510, 98 S. Ct. 1942, 1950 (1978).

[1104] *Michigan v. Clifford*, 464 U.S. 287, 294, 104 S. Ct. 641, 647 (1984).

[1105] *Michigan v. Clifford*, 464 U.S. 287, 294 n.5, 104 S. Ct. 641, 647 n.5 (1984); *see also Camara v. Municipal Court*, 387 U.S. 523, 538, 87 S. Ct. 1727, 1735-36 (1967).

[1106] *Michigan v. Clifford*, 464 U.S. 287, 294,104 S. Ct. 641, 647 (1984). Note that "convenience" here refers to that time convenient to the fire victim, not the fire official.

[1107] *Michigan v. Tyler*, 436 U.S. 499, 98 S. Ct. 1942, 1949 (1978).

[1108] *Michigan v. Tyler*, 436 U.S. 499, 98 S. Ct. 1942, 1949 (1978).

will be found to exist "where the facts and circumstances within a person's knowledge and of which he has reasonably trustworthy information are sufficient in themselves to warrant a man of reasonable caution and prudence in the belief that an offense has been or is being committed."[1109]

Naturally, if, during the course of a valid administrative search, evidence of arson is discovered, the official may lawfully seize that evidence under the "plain view" doctrine. "This evidence may then be used to establish probable cause to obtain a criminal search warrant."[1110] The *Clifford* Court warns, however, that "[f]ire officials may not ... rely on this evidence to increase the scope of their administrative search without first making a successful showing of probable cause to an independent judicial officer."[1111] Additionally, the keynote to an administrative warrant is the "specific limitation" in the scope of the official inspection. Therefore, "[a]n administrative search into the cause of a recent fire does not give fire officials license to roam freely through the fire victim's private residence."[1112]

Because there is no bright line separating the firefighter's investigation into the cause of a fire from an investigatory search for evidence of arson, questions naturally arise as to when the administrative search becomes "excessive in scope," and whether the scope of such a search should necessarily expand or constrict in relation to the nature of the particular structure involved.

6.4. Border Searches

From before the adoption of the Fourth Amendment, to today, border searches "have been considered to be 'reasonable' by the single fact that the person or item in question had entered into our country from outside. There has never been any additional requirement that the reasonableness of a border search depended on the existence of probable cause. This longstanding recognition that searches at our borders without probable cause and without a warrant are nonetheless 'reasonable' has a history as old as the Fourth Amendment itself."[1113]

In *United States v. Oriakhi*,[1114] the Fourth Circuit held that the border search exception "extends to all routine searches at the nation's borders, irrespective of whether persons or effects are entering or exiting from the country."[1115] Regarding such exit searches, every other federal circuit addressing this issue has held that the exception applies regardless of whether the person or items are entering or leaving the United States.[1116]

The statutory authority of customs officers to conduct searches at the borders is derived from several sources. For example, federal law provides that "all persons coming into the United States from foreign countries shall be liable to detention and search by authorized officers and agents of the Government under [Treasury Department] regulations."[1117] One such regulation provides that "all persons, baggage, and merchandise arriving in the Customs territory of the United States from places outside thereof are liable to inspection and search by a customs officer."[1118] In addition, federal law provides that such officers "may stop, search and examine, any vehicle, beast or person, on which or whom he or they shall suspect there is merchandise which is subject to duty, or shall have been introduced into the United States in any manner contrary to law[.]"[1119]

1109 *Draper v. United States*, 358 U.S. 307, 313, 79 S. Ct. 329, 333 (1959).
1110 *Michigan v. Clifford*, 464 U.S. 287, 294, 104 S. Ct. 641, 647 (1984).
1111 *Michigan v. Clifford*, 464 U.S. 287, 294, 104 S. Ct. 641, 647 (1984).
1112 *Michigan v. Clifford*, 464 U.S. 287, 298, 104 S. Ct. 641, 649 (1984).
1113 *United States v. Ramsey*, 431 U.S. 606, 619, 97 S. Ct. 1972, 1980 (1977).
1114 *United States v. Oriakhi*, 57 F.3d 1290 (4th Cir. 1995).
1115 *United States v. Oriakhi*, 57 F.3d 1290, 1297 (4th Cir. 1995).
1116 *See, e.g., United States v. Ezeiruaku*, 936 F.2d 136, 143 (3d Cir. 1991); *United States v. Hernandez-Salazar*, 813 F.2d 1126, 1137 (11th Cir. 1987); *United States v. Des Jardins*, 747 F.2d 499, 504 (9th Cir. 1984); *United States v. Udofot*, 711 F.2d 831, 839-40 (8th Cir. 1983); *United States v. Ajlouny*, 629 F.2d 830, 834 (2d Cir. 1980); *see also Julian v. United States*, 463 U.S. 1308, 103 S. Ct. 3522 (1983) (Rehnquist, C.J.) (a chambers opinion applying the border search exception articulated in *Ramsey* to a person and his effects as he attempted to *depart* the country on a flight destined for Peru).
1117 19 U.S.C. § 1582.
1118 19 C.F.R. § 162.6.
1119 19 U.S.C. § 982.

Case law interpretation of these enactments provides that "routine searches" of the persons and effects of entrants are "not subject to any requirement of reasonable suspicion, probable cause or warrant."[1120] With respect to such "routine searches," there need not be any suspicion of illegality directed to the particular person or thing to be searched.

Not all border searches are exempt from the Fourth Amendment requirement of reasonableness. Rather, the exemption relates to only those border searches that are considered "*routine*." The main question is what constitutes a routine border search as opposed to one that is not routine.

The cases point to the following parameters constituting a "routine" border search requiring no particularized suspicion:

a) An initial stop and detention of an individual for questioning is permissible;
b) Searches of a traveler's luggage and personal effects, including the contents of a purse, wallet or pockets are deemed routine;
c) A request to remove outer garments, such as a coat, jacket, shoes or boots for the purpose of a search is likewise considered routine; and
d) A pat-down, commonly referred to as a frisk, is within the permissible limits of a routine border search.

Naturally, if a search is deemed to be non-routine, reasonable suspicion is required. In the context of a border search, customs officers may consider such factors as excessive nervousness, unusual conduct, loose fitting or bulky clothing, an itinerary showing brief stops in known drug source countries, lack of employment, inadequate or unusual luggage, and evasive or contradictory answers. While these factors are not exhaustive, they provide useful guideposts in analyzing the numerous factual variations customs officials may encounter.

In *United States v. Flores-Montano*,[1121] the United States Supreme Court addressed the question whether the removal or dismantling of a motorist's fuel tank was a "routine" border search for which no suspicion whatsoever is required. In this case, at the international border in southern California, customs officials seized 37 kilograms — a little more than 81 pounds — of marijuana from defendant Manuel Flores-Montano's gas tank. Chief Justice Rehnquist, speaking for a unanimous Court, held that the routine border search in question did not require reasonable suspicion. According to the Court,

> The Government's interest in preventing the entry of unwanted persons and effects is at its zenith at the international border. Time and again, we have stated that "searches made at the border, pursuant to the longstanding right of the sovereign to protect itself by stopping and examining persons and property crossing into this country, are reasonable simply by virtue of the fact that they occur at the border." ... That interest in protecting the borders is illustrated in this case by the evidence that smugglers frequently attempt to penetrate our borders with contraband secreted in their automobiles' fuel tank. Over the past 5½ fiscal years, there have been 18,788 vehicle drug seizures at the southern California ports of entry. Of those 18,788, gas tank drug seizures have accounted for 4,619 of the vehicle drug seizures, or approximately 25%.[1122]

The Court rejected defendant's contention that he had "a privacy interest in his fuel tank, and that the suspicionless disassembly of his tank [was] an invasion of his privacy."[1123] According to the Court, "the expectation of privacy is less at the border than it is in the interior.... We have long recognized that automobiles seeking entry into this country may be searched.... It is difficult to imagine how the search of a gas tank, which should be solely a repository for fuel, could be more of an invasion of privacy than the search of the automobile's passenger compartment."[1124]

[1120] *United States v. Montoya de Hernandez*, 473 U.S. 531, 537, 105 S. Ct. 3304, 3309 (1985).
[1121] *United States v. Flores-Montano*, 541 U.S. 149, 124 S. Ct. 1582 (2004).
[1122] *United States v. Flores-Montano*, 541 U.S. 149, 124 S. Ct. 1582, 1585-86 (2004) (citations omitted).
[1123] *United States v. Flores-Montano*, 541 U.S. 149, 124 S. Ct. 1582, 1586 (2004).
[1124] *United States v. Flores-Montano*, 541 U.S. 149, 124 S. Ct. 1582, 1586 (2004).

Accordingly, the Court held that "the Government's authority to conduct suspicionless inspections at the border includes the authority to remove, disassemble, and reassemble a vehicle's fuel tank. While it may be true that some searches of property are so destructive as to require a different result, this was not one of them."[1125]

7. PRIVATE SEARCHES

7.1. General aspects

The Fourth Amendment to the federal Constitution begins by commanding that the "right of the people to be secure in their persons, houses, papers, and effects, against unreasonable searches and seizures, shall not be violated...." A *search* compromises an individual's interest in privacy and takes place "when an expectation of privacy that society is prepared to recognize as reasonable is infringed."[1126] A *seizure* "deprives the individual of dominion over his or her ... property,"[1127] and constitutes a "meaningful interference" with the owner's possessory interests in that property.[1128]

These principles do not, however, apply to private action. In fact, over the course of time, they have been consistently interpreted as prohibiting only unreasonable *government* action; they are "wholly inapplicable 'to a search or seizure, even an unreasonable one, effected by a private individual not acting as an agent of the Government or with the participation or knowledge of any governmental official.'"[1129] Therefore, evidence obtained by private citizens in pursuit of personal goals will not implicate the commands of the Fourth Amendment, and may thereafter be turned over to the government, so long as no government official played a part in the search or in the acquisition of the evidence. In this respect, the United States Supreme Court has explained:

> Although the Fourth Amendment does not apply to a search or seizure, even an arbitrary one, effected by a private party on his own initiative, the Amendment protects against such intrusions if the private party acted as an instrument or agent of the government.[1130]
>
> "Whether a private party should be deemed an agent or instrument of the Government for [constitutional] purposes necessarily turns on the degree of the Government's participation in the private party's activities[,] a question that can only be resolved 'in light of all the circumstances.'"[1131]

7.2. The target of the exclusionary rule

Accordingly, the target of the exclusionary rule is "official," not "private," misconduct.[1132] For purposes of the discussion which follows, the pivotal factor will be whether the private individual, in light of all the circumstances, must be regarded as having acted as an "instrument" or "agent" of the police.

1125 *United States v. Flores-Montano*, 541 U.S. 149, 124 S. Ct. 1582, 1587 (2004).
1126 *United States v. Jacobsen*, 466 U.S. 109, 113, 104 S. Ct. 1652, 1656 (1984); *see also Horton v. California*, 496 U.S. 128, 110 S. Ct. 2301, 2306 (1990).
1127 *Horton v. California*, 496 U.S. 128, 110 S. Ct. 2301, 2306 (1990).
1128 *Maryland v. Macon*, 472 U.S. 463, 469, 105 S. Ct. 2778, 2782 (1985); *United States v. Jacobsen*, 466 U.S. 109, 113, 104 S. Ct. 1652, 1656 (1984).
1129 *United States v. Jacobsen*, 466 U.S. 109, 113-14, 104 S. Ct. 1652, 1656 (1984) (quoting *Walter v. United States*, 447 U.S. 649, 662, 100 S. Ct. 2395, 2404 (1980)); *see also Burdeau v. McDowell*, 256 U.S. 465, 41 S. Ct. 574 (1921).
1130 *Skinner v. Railway Labor Executives Ass'n.*, 489 U.S. 602, 614, 109 S. Ct. 1402, 1411 (1989).
1131 *Skinner v. Railway Labor Executives Ass'n.*, 489 U.S. 602, 614, 109 S. Ct. 1402, 1411 (1989) (quoting *Coolidge v. New Hampshire*, 403 U.S. 443, 91 S. Ct. 2022, 2026 (1971)); *see also Hoagburg v. Harrah's Marina Hotel Casino*, 585 F. Supp. 1167, 1171, 1174 (D.N.J. 1984).
1132 *United State v. King*, 55 F.3d 1193 (6th Cir. 1995).

A person will act as a "police agent" if:

(a) The police instigate, encourage, or foster the search;
(b) There is joint participation between private citizens and police officers;
(c) The police have significantly involved themselves in the search; or
(d) The police have pre-knowledge of the private individual's expressed intent to conduct a search or seizure and acquiesce in its effectuation.

If an unlawful private search or seizure is performed with any of the aforementioned relationships existing between the police and the private person(s) effecting the search or seizure, the Fourth Amendment's exclusionary rule will bar the admissibility of any evidence obtained. On the other hand, if it is found that the police had no significant connection with the private search or seizure, or any knowledge of it until after the fact, the evidence delivered to them may be admitted.[1133]

In *United States v. Jacobsen*,[1134] the Supreme Court ruled that the following set of circumstances *did not* give rise to a "governmental" search within the meaning of the Fourth Amendment to the Constitution:

> Federal Express employees opened a damaged cardboard box and, pursuant to written company policy regarding insurance claims, examined the contents. Within the box they found five to six pieces of crumbled newspaper covering a tube about 10 inches long. The tube was made of silver duct tape. The employees then cut into the tube and found a series of four ziplock plastic bags, the outermost enclosing the other three, and the innermost containing about six ounces of a suspicious-looking white powder.
>
> The employees then notified the DEA. Before the DEA agent arrived, the Federal Express employees put everything back into the cardboard box. When the DEA agent arrived, he opened the box, opened the duct tape tube, opened the plastic baggies, and conducted a field test of the white powder. The powder tested positive for cocaine. The DEA agent seized the cocaine.

According to the Court, the owner of the package "could have no privacy interest in the contents of the package, since it remained unsealed and since the Federal Express employees had just examined the package and had, on their own accord, invited the federal agent to their offices for the express purpose of viewing its contents."[1135] As a result, the DEA agent's inspection "of what a private party had freely made available for his inspection did not violate the Fourth Amendment."[1136]

This case is a prime example of the typical "third-party intervention" case. Because the initial violation of Jacobsen's privacy was the result of private action, the Court determined that the Fourth Amendment was not violated when the DEA agents re-examined the package.

Where the police expand the scope of the initial private search, however, the third-party intervention exception may no longer apply to the fruits of the expanded search. Thus, in *Walter v. United States*,[1137] where a shipping company erroneously delivered 12 cartons to "L'Eggs Products, Inc." instead of to "Leggs, Inc." When the L'Eggs Products employees opened the cartons, they discovered film canisters inside, with labels that indicated that they contained scenes of sexual activity. The employees did not screen the films or otherwise view their content. They did, however, call the FBI, whose agents picked up the cartons and viewed the films utilizing a projector.

The Supreme Court held that the FBI agents' viewing of the films was a warrantless search which violated the Fourth Amendment. According to the Court, the FBI's viewing of the films was a separate search that had expanded the scope of the private search. "The projection of the films was a significant expansion of the search that had been conducted previously by a private party and therefore must be characterized as a

---

[1133] *See Coolidge v. New Hampshire*, 403 U.S. 443, 487-88, 91 S. Ct. 2022, 2048-49 (1971). *But see Flagg Bros. v. Brooks*, 436 U.S. 149, 98 S. Ct. 1729 (1978) (where the Court intimated that where state involvement in private action constitutes *no more* than mere acquiescence or tacit approval, the private action is not automatically transformed into state action).
[1134] *United States v. Jacobsen*, 466 U.S. 109, 104 S. Ct. 1652 (1984).
[1135] *United States v. Jacobsen*, 466 U.S. 109, 104 S. Ct. 1652, 1659-60 (1984).
[1136] *United States v. Jacobsen*, 466 U.S. 109, 104 S. Ct. 1652, 1660 (1984).
[1137] *Walter v. United States*, 447 U.S. 649, 100 S. Ct. 2395 (1980).

separate search. That separate search was not supported by any exigency, or by a warrant even though one could have been obtained.... Since the additional search conducted by the FBI – the screening of the films – was not supported by any justification, it violated that Amendment."[1138]

In *State v. Rodriquez*,[1139] the Texas Court of Criminal Appeals refused "to extend the private-party-search doctrine to a residence, in this case, a college dorm room."[1140] Therefore, the defendant "retained her expectation of privacy in her room even though school officials had already entered the room pursuant to the housing agreement."[1141]

In *State v. Martinez*,[1142] defendant was involved in a serious traffic accident. He was taken to a hospital where his blood was drawn for medical purposes. The State later acquired and tested the blood, both without a warrant. Thereafter, defendant filed a motion to suppress, arguing that the blood was obtained unlawfully. Finding the search unlawful, the court said:

> There are private facts contained in a sample of a person's blood beyond simple confirmation of a suspicion that a person is intoxicated. These private facts are those that a person does not voluntarily share with the world by the mere drawing of blood and may be subject to Fourth Amendment protection. We hold that there is an expectation of privacy in blood that is drawn for medical purposes. The expectation is not as great as an individual has in the sanctity of his own body against the initial draw of blood.... But it is greater than an individual has in the results of tests that have already been performed on the blood.[1143]
>
> In this case, medical staff at the hospital performed a private search by beginning trauma procedures and drawing [defendant's] blood for medical purposes. The government's actions consisted of subjecting [defendant's] blood to testing at the DPS laboratory. [This] testing itself constitutes a search, and this search was not done by the hospital. [Defendant's] privacy interest vis-a-vis the contents of the blood – the blood's "informational dimension" – had not been frustrated by the actions of the hospital. The State, and only the State, tested and therefore searched the blood, and, ipso facto, the government search went beyond the scope of the private search.[1144]

Accordingly, the *Martinez* Court held that "there is a Fourth Amendment privacy interest in blood that has already been drawn for medical purposes. In this case, [defendant] had a subjective expectation of such a privacy interest in his blood, and the State's subsequent testing of the blood was a Fourth Amendment search separate and apart from the seizure of the blood by the State. Because no exception to the warrant requirement applied, the State was required to obtain a warrant before testing [the] blood."[1145]

8. CONFESSION LAW

8.1. Introduction

8.1.1. The Fifth Amendment

The Fifth Amendment to the Federal Constitution commands that *no person "shall be compelled in any criminal case to be a witness against himself."*[1146]This provision represents the constitutional right which has come to be recognized as the "privilege against self-incrimination." It has been made applicable to the states through the Fourteenth Amendment by the United States Supreme Court's decision in *Malloy v.*

1138 *Walter v. United States*, 447 U.S. 649, 657-59, 100 S. Ct. 2395, 2402-03 (1980).
1139 *State v. Rodriguez*, 521 S.W.3d 1 (Tex. Crim. App. 2017).
1140 *State v. Rodriguez*, 521 S.W.3d 1, 15 (Tex. Crim. App. 2017).
1141 *State v. Rodriguez*, 521 S.W.3d 1, 15 (Tex. Crim. App. 2017).
1142 *State v. Martinez*, 570 S.W.3d 278 (Tex. Crim. App. 2019).
1143 *State v. Martinez*, 570 S.W.3d 278, 291 (Tex. Crim. App. 2019).
1144 *State v. Martinez*, 570 S.W.3d 278, 292 (Tex. Crim. App. 2019) (citing *United States v. Jacobsen*, 466 U.S. 109, 115, 104 S. Ct. 1652 (1984); *Walter v. United States*, 447 U.S. 649, 657, 100 S. Ct. 2395, 2402-03 (1980)).
1145 *State v. Martinez*, 570 S.W.3d 278, 292 (Tex. Crim. App. 2019).
1146 U.S. Const. amend. V (emphasis added).

Hogan.[1147] In *Malloy*, the Supreme Court ruled that the privilege against self-incrimination is a "fundamental right," and, as such, is binding upon the states in the same manner the Fifth Amendment safeguards persons from the federal government. The Court employed the Fourteenth Amendment's Due Process Clause as the vehicle through which the privilege was made binding upon the states. In pertinent part, the Due Process Clause provides that no state shall "deprive any person of life, liberty, or property, without *due process of law*...."[1148] On the state level, Article 1, § 10 of the Texas Constitution provides in pertinent part:

> In all criminal prosecutions the accused shall ... not be compelled to give evidence against himself. He shall have the right of being heard by himself, or counsel, or both....

In comparing the state and federal provisions, the Texas Court of Criminal Appeals has held that Article 1, §10 does not provide "broader protection than the Fifth amendment *because of differences in language*."[1149] Yet, while Article 1, § 10 may in many respects be deemed "comparable in scope to the Fifth Amendment," the court has made clear that it shall continue its case-by-case approach to Fifth Amendment/Article 1, § 10 issues, examining the underlying "history, policy, and precedent" for its decisions in future cases.[1150]

The privilege to be free from self-incrimination has been described as the "essential mainstay of our adversary system," and "the constitutional foundation underlying the privilege is the respect a government – state or federal – must accord to the dignity and integrity of its citizens."[1151]

The Supreme Court in *Miranda* perceived an intimate connection between the constitutional privilege against self-incrimination and "police custodial questioning" which takes place in a "police dominated atmosphere."[1152]

8.1.2. The *Miranda* Requirements

Miranda dealt with "the admissibility of statements obtained from an individual who is subjected to custodial police interrogation and the necessity for procedures which assure that the individual is accorded his privilege under the Fifth Amendment to the Constitution not to be compelled to incriminate himself."[1153]

Chief Justice Warren, speaking for the U.S. Supreme Court, concluded that "the privilege is fulfilled only when the person is guaranteed the right 'to remain silent unless he chooses to speak in the unfettered exercise of his own free will.'"[1154]

"Coercive" custodial interrogation is the "evil" which the Court addressed in *Miranda*. "Custodial interrogation" is defined as "questioning initiated by law enforcement officers after a person has been taken into custody or otherwise deprived of his freedom of action in any significant way."[1155] This concept of custodial interrogation is what the Court had in mind when it previously "spoke of an investigation which had focused on an accused."[1156]

The necessary procedural safeguards emanating from *Miranda* are as follows:

> Prior to any questioning, the person must be warned that he has the right to remain silent, that any statement he does make [can and will] be used [against him in a court of law], and that he has a right

---

1147 *Malloy v. Hogan*, 378 U.S. 1, 84 S. Ct. 1489 (1964).
1148 U.S. Const. amend. XIV § 1 (emphasis added).
1149 *Thomas v. State*, 723 S.W.2d 696, 703 (Tex. Crim. App. 1986) (emphasis in original).
1150 *Thomas v. State*, 723 S.W.2d 696, 702 (Tex. Crim. App. 1986).
1151 *Miranda v. Arizona*, 384 U.S. 436, 460, 86 S. Ct. 1602, 1620 (1966).
1152 *Miranda v. Arizona*, 384 U.S. 436, 458, 86 S. Ct. 1602, 1619 (1966).
1153 *Miranda v. Arizona*, 384 U.S. 436, 439, 86 S. Ct. 1602, 1609 (1966).
1154 *Miranda v. Arizona*, 384 U.S. 436, 460, 86 S. Ct. 1602, 1620 (1966) (quoting *Malloy v. Hogan*, 378 U.S. 1, 8, 84 S. Ct. 1489, 1493 (1964)).
1155 *Miranda v. Arizona*, 384 U.S. 436, 444, 86 S. Ct. 1602, 1612 (1966).
1156 *Miranda v. Arizona*, 384 U.S. 436, 444 n.4, 86 S. Ct. 1602, 1612 n.4 (1966) (referring to *Escobedo v. Illinois*, 378 U.S. 478, 84 S. Ct. 1758 (1964)).

> to the presence of an attorney, . . . and that if he cannot afford an attorney one will be appointed for him prior to any questioning if he so desires.[1157]

Good practice dictates that the individual also be clearly informed that he or she may ask for counsel at any time during custodial questioning, and, in addition, that the questioning will cease at any time the person desires counsel. In addition, the warning given must convey that the suspect has the right to have an attorney present not only at the outset of interrogation, but at all times. In this regard, the Supreme Court, in *Florida v. Powell*,[1158] emphasized that, as a matter of law, an individual held for questioning "must be clearly informed that he has the right to consult with a lawyer *and to have the lawyer with him during interrogation*." These rights apply regardless of the nature or severity of the offense.[1159]

Accordingly, prior to custodial interrogation, the person must be informed of the following:

- You have the right to remain silent.
- Anything you say can and will be used against you in a court of law.
- You have the right to consult with an attorney and have an attorney present during questioning.
- If you cannot afford an attorney, one can be provided to you before questioning at no cost.
- You may ask for an attorney at any time during questioning, and questioning will stop if at any time you ask for an attorney.

Thereafter, if the individual —

> *indicates in any manner* and at any stage of the process that he wishes to consult with an attorney before speaking there can be no questioning. Likewise, if the individual is alone and *indicates in any manner* that he does not wish to be interrogated, the police may not question him. The mere fact that he might have answered some questions on his own does not deprive him of the right to refrain from answering any further inquiries until he has consulted with an attorney and thereafter consents to be questioned.[1160]

Thus, as a general matter, the prosecution must demonstrate that the *Miranda* warnings were administered to the accused prior to any custodial interrogation. At the time of questioning, the accused may, of course, waive his or her *Miranda* rights, provided the waiver is made *voluntarily, knowingly, and intelligently*.[1161] Failure to establish adherence to *Miranda*'s procedural safeguards — the administration of the warnings and receipt of an appropriate waiver — renders any and all statements obtained from an accused in any ensuing custodial interrogation inadmissible at trial, at least in the prosecution's case-in-chief.[1162]

"The *Miranda* Court did of course caution that the Constitution requires no 'particular solution for the inherent compulsions of the interrogation process,' and left it open to a State to meet its burden by adopting 'other procedures . . . at least as effective in apprising accused persons' of their rights[.] The Court indeed acknowledged that, in barring introduction of a statement obtained without the required warnings, *Miranda* might exclude a confession that [] would not [be] condemn[ed] as 'involuntary in traditional terms,' . . . and for this reason [the Court has] sometimes called the *Miranda* safeguards 'prophylactic' in nature."[1163]

1157 *Miranda v. Arizona*, 384 U.S. 436, 444, 479, 86 S. Ct. 1602, 1612, 1630 (1966).

1158 *Florida v. Powell*, 559 U.S. 50, 130 S. Ct. 1195, 1203 (2010).

1159 *See Berkemer v. McCarty*, 468 U.S. 420 (1984).

1160 *Miranda v. Arizona*, 384 U.S. 436, 444-45, 86 S. Ct. 1602, 1612 (1966) (emphasis added).

1161 *Miranda v. Arizona*, 384 U.S. 436, 444-45, 86 S. Ct. 1602, 1612 (1966).

1162 *See Michigan v. Tucker*, 417 U.S. 433, 444, 94 S. Ct. 2357, 2364 (1974) (recognizing that *Miranda*'s "procedural safeguards were not themselves rights protected by the Constitution but were instead measures to insure that the right against compulsory self-incrimination was protected").

1163 *Withrow v. Williams*, 507 U.S. 680, 113 S. Ct. 1745, 1752 (1993) (quoting *Miranda v. Arizona*, 384 U.S. 436, 457, 467, 86 S. Ct. 1602, 1618, 1624 (1966)).

In *Dickerson v. United States*,[1164] the Court, for the first time since *Miranda v. Arizona* was decided, had occasion to determine whether it should overrule *Miranda* and replace it with a test of "voluntariness" as the touchstone of a confession's admissibility, with the now-familiar warnings being just one factor in the analysis.

The *Dickerson* case addressed whether a federal statute,[1165] enacted two years after *Miranda* was decided, was an unconstitutional attempt by Congress to legislatively overrule *Miranda*. To nullify *Miranda*, the federal statute set forth a rule providing that the admissibility of an accused's confession or admission should turn only on whether or not it was voluntarily made. In a 7-to-2 opinion, the *Dickerson* Court declared:

> *Miranda*, being a constitutional decision of this Court, may not be in effect overruled by an Act of Congress, and we decline to overrule *Miranda* ourselves. We therefore hold that *Miranda* and its progeny in this Court govern the admissibility of statements made during custodial interrogation in both state and federal courts.[1166]

The *Dickerson* Court reemphasized that *Miranda* "laid down 'concrete constitutional guidelines for law enforcement agencies and courts to follow.'"[1167] Those guidelines mandate the administration of four warnings which have now "come to be known colloquially as '*Miranda* rights.'"[1168] The *Miranda* warnings, held the *Dickerson* Court, are constitutional in dimension; the warnings have "become embedded in routine police practice to the point where the warnings have become part of our national culture."[1169]

8.1.3. The *Miranda* Formula

From the foregoing discussion, it is clear that prior to any custodial interrogation, law enforcement officers are required to administer the *Miranda* warnings to the person about to be questioned. The formula should be as easy as 1 + 1 = 2; that is, "custody" + "interrogation" = the requirement that *Miranda* warnings be given. As the materials in this section will demonstrate, however, the formula is easier to recite than to apply. For law enforcement, the desired, ultimate result is the acquisition of a valid confession, fully admissible at trial. In order for that to occur, officers are at all times required to scrupulously honor each of the rights contained within the *Miranda* warnings.

Assuming that a criminal suspect is "in custody" and that law enforcement officials have administered the appropriate warnings, there are several courses that the interview may take. The first, and perhaps most straightforward, course that an interview session may take is:

1) a custodial suspect;
2) is given *Miranda* warnings;
3) thereafter voluntarily, knowingly and intelligently waives his or her rights; and
4) gives a full confession.

Second, a custodial suspect may blurt out a confession before the authorities have an opportunity to administer the *Miranda* warnings.

A third direction in which an interview session may head is illustrated by the following:

1) a custodial suspect;
2) is given *Miranda* warnings; and
3) thereafter indicates that he or she does not want to talk – the suspect invokes his or her right to remain silent.

1164 *Dickerson v. United States*, 530 U.S. 428, 120 S. Ct. 2326 (2000).
1165 18 U.S.C. § 3501.
1166 *Dickerson v. United States*, 530 U.S. 428, 120 S. Ct. 2326, 2329-30 (2000).
1167 *Dickerson v. United States*, 530 U.S. 428, 120 S. Ct. 2326, 2331 (2000) (citation omitted).
1168 *Dickerson v. United States*, 530 U.S. 428, 120 S. Ct. 2326, 2331 (2000) (citation omitted).
1169 *Dickerson v. United States*, 530 U.S. 428, 120 S. Ct. 2326, 2335-36 (2000).

Fourth, an interview session may proceed as follows:

1) a custodial suspect;
2) is given *Miranda* warnings; and
3) thereafter indicates that he or she wants a lawyer – the suspect invokes his or her right to counsel.

Fifth, the suspect may change his or her mind; in this instance:

1) a custodial suspect;
2) is given *Miranda* warnings;
3) indicates that he or she wants;
   a. to remain silent; or
   b. a lawyer; but
4) sometime thereafter changes his or her mind and indicates a desire to communicate with the authorities, to open up a dialogue about the investigation.

Sixth, outside influences may interrupt or affect an interview, for example, where

1) a custodial suspect;
2) is given *Miranda* warnings; and
3) voluntarily, knowingly and intelligently waives his or her rights, but at some time during the process;
4) an attorney, family member or close friend of the suspect;
   a. notifies the authorities of his or her pending or actual arrival at the station house; and / or
   b. advises the authorities not to question the suspect.

The following sections explore each of the above-described paths down which an interview or questioning session may travel.[1170] There are, however, several preliminary issues that need to be addressed. For example, "What constitutes custody?" "What constitutes interrogation?" "Is a validly obtained confession, by itself, sufficient to support a criminal conviction?" and, "What effect does the Texas statutory scheme have on this area of the law?'

The Texas legislature has codified the principles found in *Miranda*, and many of the cases following *Miranda*, in Texas Code of Criminal Procedure art. 38.22. The legislature has also mandated in Code of Criminal Procedure art. 2.32 that statements regarding certain enumerated offenses must be recorded by audiovisual means, or by audio means if an audiovisual recording cannot be made. In pertinent part, these statutes provide:

Art. 38.22. When Statements May Be Used.

Sec. 1. In this article, a written statement of an accused means:
(1) a statement made by the accused in his own handwriting; or
(2) a statement made in a language the accused can read or understand that:
(A) is signed by the accused; or
(B) bears the mark of the accused, if the accused is unable to write and the mark is witnessed by a person other than a peace officer.

Sec. 2. No written statement made by an accused as a result of custodial interrogation is admissible as evidence against him in any criminal proceeding unless it is shown on the face of the statement that:

[1170] Excerpts from the comprehensive discussion of the laws of arrest, search and seizure in Larry E. Holtz & Warren J Spencer, *Texas Criminal and Traffic Procedural Manual – An In-Depth Guide on How to Apply the Laws of Arrest, Search and Seizure, Confessions, & Eyewitness Identification* (Blue360° Media).

(a) the accused, prior to making the statement, either received from a magistrate the warning provided in Article 15.17 of this code or received from the person to whom the statement is made a warning that:

(1) he has the right to remain silent and not make any statement at all and that any statement he makes may be used against him at his trial;

(2) any statement he makes may be used as evidence against him in court;

(3) he has the right to have a lawyer present to advise him prior to and during any questioning;

(4) if he is unable to employ a lawyer, he has the right to have a lawyer appointed to advise him prior to and during any questioning; and

(5) he has the right to terminate the interview at any time; and

(b) the accused, prior to and during the making of the statement, knowingly, intelligently, and voluntarily waived the rights set out in the warning prescribed by Subsection (a) of this section.

Sec. 3.

(a) No oral or sign language statement of an accused made as a result of custodial interrogation shall be admissible against the accused in a criminal proceeding unless:

(1) an electronic recording, which may include motion picture, video tape, or other visual recording, is made of the statement;

(2) prior to the statement but during the recording the accused is given the warning in Subsection (a) of Section 2 above and the accused knowingly, intelligently, and voluntarily waives any rights set out in the warning;

(3) the recording device was capable of making an accurate recording, the operator was competent, and the recording is accurate and has not been altered;

(4) all voices on the recording are identified; and

(5) not later than the 20th day before the date of the proceeding, the attorney representing the defendant is provided with a true, complete, and accurate copy of all recordings of the defendant made under this article.

(b) Every electronic recording of any statement made by an accused during a custodial interrogation must be preserved until such time as the defendant's conviction for any offense relating thereto is final, all direct appeals therefrom are exhausted, or the prosecution of such offenses is barred by law.

(c) Subsection (a) of this section shall not apply to any statement which contains assertions of facts or circumstances that are found to be true and which conduce to establish the guilt of the accused, such as the finding of secreted or stolen property or the instrument with which he states the offense was committed.

(d) If the accused is a deaf person, the accused's statement under Section 2 or Section 3(a) of this article is not admissible against the accused unless the warning in Section 2 of this article is interpreted to the deaf person by an interpreter who is qualified and sworn as provided in Article 38.31 of this code.

(e) The courts of this state shall strictly construe Subsection (a) of this section and may not interpret Subsection (a) as making admissible a statement unless all requirements of the subsection have been satisfied by the state, except that:

(1) only voices that are material are identified; and

(2) the accused was given the warning in Subsection (a) of Section 2 above or its fully effective equivalent.

* * * *

Sec. 5. Nothing in this article precludes the admission of a statement made by the accused in open court at his trial, before a grand jury, or at an examining trial in compliance with Articles 16.03 and 16.04 of this code, or of a statement that is the res gestae of the arrest or of the offense, or of a statement that does not stem from custodial interrogation, or of a voluntary statement, whether or not the result of custodial interrogation, that has a bearing upon the credibility of the accused as a witness, or of any other statement that may be admissible under law.

* * * *

Sec. 8. Notwithstanding any other provision of this article, a written, oral, or sign language statement of an accused made as a result of a custodial interrogation is admissible against the accused in a criminal proceeding in this state if:

(1) the statement was obtained in another state and was obtained in compliance with the laws of that state or this state; or

(2) the statement was obtained by a federal law enforcement officer in this state or another state and was obtained in compliance with the laws of the United States.

Sec. 9. Notwithstanding any other provision of this article, no oral, sign language, or written statement that is made by a person accused of an offense listed in Article 2.32(b) and made as a result of a custodial interrogation occurring in a place of detention, as that term is defined by Article 2.32, is admissible against the accused in a criminal proceeding unless:

(1) an electronic recording was made of the statement, as required by Article 2.32(b); or

(2)the attorney representing the state offers proof satisfactory to the court that good cause, as described by Article 2.32(d), existed that made electronic recording of the custodial interrogation infeasible.

Art. 2.32. Electronic Recording of Custodial Interrogations.

(a) In this article:

(1) "Electronic recording" means an audiovisual electronic recording, or an audio recording if an audiovisual electronic recording is unavailable, that is authentic, accurate, and unaltered.

(2) "Law enforcement agency" means an agency of the state, or of a county, municipality, or other political subdivision of this state, that employs peace officers who, in the routine performance of the officers' duties, conduct custodial interrogations of persons suspected of committing criminal offenses.

(3) "Place of detention" means a police station or other building that is a place of operation for a law enforcement agency, including a municipal police department or county sheriff's department, and is owned or operated by the law enforcement agency for the purpose of detaining persons in connection with the suspected violation of a penal law. The term does not include a courthouse.

(b) Unless good cause exists that makes electronic recording infeasible, a law enforcement agency shall make a complete and contemporaneous electronic recording of any custodial interrogation that occurs in a place of detention and is of a person suspected of committing or charged with the commission of an offense under:

(1) Section 19.02, Penal Code (murder);

(2) Section 19.03, Penal Code (capital murder);

(3) Section 20.03, Penal Code (kidnapping);

(4) Section 20.04, Penal Code (aggravated kidnapping);

(5) Section 20A.02, Penal Code (trafficking of persons);

(6) Section 20A.03, Penal Code (continuous trafficking of persons);

(7) Section 21.02, Penal Code (continuous sexual abuse of young child or children);

(8) Section 21.11, Penal Code (indecency with a child);

(9) Section 21.12, Penal Code (improper relationship between educator and student);

(10) Section 22.011, Penal Code (sexual assault);

(11) Section 22.021, Penal Code (aggravated sexual assault); or

(12) Section 43.25, Penal Code (sexual performance by a child).

(c) For purposes of Subsection (b), an electronic recording of a custodial interrogation is complete only if the recording:

(1) begins at or before the time the person being interrogated enters the area of the place of detention in which the custodial interrogation will take place or receives a warning described by Section 2(a), Article 38.22, whichever is earlier; and

(2) continues until the time the interrogation ceases.

(d) For purposes of Subsection (b), good cause that makes electronic recording infeasible includes the following:

(1) the person being interrogated refused to respond or cooperate in a custodial interrogation at which an electronic recording was being made, provided that:

(A) a contemporaneous recording of the refusal was made; or

(B) the peace officer or agent of the law enforcement agency conducting the interrogation attempted, in good faith, to record the person's refusal but the person was unwilling to have the refusal recorded, and the peace officer or agent contemporaneously, in writing, documented the refusal;

(2) the statement was not made as the result of a custodial interrogation, including a statement that was made spontaneously by the accused and not in response to a question by a peace officer;

(3) the peace officer or agent of the law enforcement agency conducting the interrogation attempted, in good faith, to record the interrogation but the recording equipment did not function, the officer or agent inadvertently operated the equipment incorrectly, or the equipment malfunctioned or stopped operating without the knowledge of the officer or agent;

(4) exigent public safety concerns prevented or rendered infeasible the making of an electronic recording of the statement; or

(5) the peace officer or agent of the law enforcement agency conducting the interrogation reasonably believed at the time the interrogation commenced that the person being interrogated was not taken into custody for or being interrogated concerning the commission of an offense listed in Subsection (b).

(e) A recording of a custodial interrogation that complies with this article is exempt from public disclosure as provided by Section 552.108, Government Code.

The statutory scheme set forth above has led to some variations in the way a Texas peace officer must apply the procedures governing the questioning of criminal suspects in the obtaining of valid admissions and confessions. Indeed, in several respects, Article 38.22 has changed portions of the case law in this area.[1171]

In *Davidson v. State*,[1172] defendant's two daughters accused him of sexually abusing them. While an investigation into those allegations was pending, defendant and his wife joined a traveling carnival. "In June 1995, they went into Canada with the carnival. In July 1995, as the carnival prepared to re-enter the United States, Special Agent Chuck Mazzilli of the United States Custom Services ran a routine check on all carnival workers. His check for outstanding warrants revealed a Texas arrest warrant" for defendant.[1173] Thereafter, when defendant crossed the border into Great Falls, Montana, Agent Mazilli detained him and read him his *Miranda* rights. During the interview, defendant implicated himself in the sexual abuse of his two daughters. About three weeks later, Agent Mazilli wrote a report in which he recorded his recollection of defendant's statements. No other record of those statements was made. At defendant's Texas trial, the agent prepared to testify as to his recollections of defendant's statement, as recorded in his report. Defendant's wife and two daughters also testified about the sexual abuse.

The court held that defendant's statements to Mazilli were not electronically recorded and, therefore, were not in compliance with art. 38.22, § 3(a)(1). It is the law of the state in which the judicial proceedings will be held that determines the admissibility of the evidence. Although Agent Mazilli may have complied with both Montana and federal law in obtaining the statements, he violated Texas law by not recording the statements. Accordingly, the court declared that the statements were inadmissible.

In *Flores v. State*,[1174] the court was presented with a case involving a recorded statement that was missing approximately thirty minutes of the interview due to technical difficulties. The State contended that the court should treat the two recordings as separate statements and admit them. In rejecting that contention, the court explained that the two recordings did not qualify as two separate interviews; rather, there was "a

---

[1171] For a more comprehensive discussion of Texas interview and confession law *see* Larry E. Holtz & Warren J Spencer, *Texas Criminal and Traffic Procedural Manual – An In-Depth Guide on How to Apply the Laws of Arrest, Search and Seizure, Confessions, & Eyewitness Identification* (Blue360° Media).

[1172] *Davidson v. State*, 25 S.W.3d 183 (Tex. Crim. App. 2000).

[1173] *Davidson v. State*, 25 S.W.3d 183, 184 (Tex. Crim. App. 2000).

[1174] *Flores v. State*, No. PD-1189-15, 2018 Tex. Crim. App. Unpub. LEXIS 398 (Tex. Crim. App. May 23, 2018).

continuity of discussion" that established only one interview. After determining that there was only one interview, the court held that the recording did not comply with the requirements of art. 38.22 § 3(a) because the recording was not accurate.

8.2. Interviews and Confessions

Lawfully obtained admissions and confessions continue to play an integral role in the law enforcement scheme and are extremely persuasive at trial. The ability of law enforcement to obtain a valid, uncoerced confession has been described as "not an evil but an unmitigated good."[1175] As the Supreme Court observed in *McNeil v. Wisconsin*, "[a]dmissions of guilt resulting from valid *Miranda* waivers 'are more than merely "desirable"; they are essential to society's compelling interest in finding, convicting, and punishing those who violate the law.'"[1176] The introduction of an admission or a confession at trial "is like no other evidence. Indeed, 'the defendant's own confession is probably the most probative and damaging evidence that can be admitted against him.... The admissions of a defendant come from the actor himself, the most knowledgeable and unimpeachable source of information about his past conduct. Certainly, confessions have profound impact on the jury[.]'"[1177]

8.2.1. Preliminary issues

8.2.1.1. Uncorroborated confessions and the "*corpus delicti*" rule

As a general rule, "an accused may not be convicted on his own uncorroborated confession."[1178] This rule has been previously recognized by the U.S. Supreme Court in *Warszower v. United States*[1179] and *Isaacs v. United States*,[1180] and has been "consistently applied in the lower federal courts and in the overwhelming majority of state courts[.]"[1181] "Its purpose is to prevent 'errors in convictions based upon untrue confessions alone,' [and] its foundation lies in a long history of judicial experience with confessions and in the realization that sound law enforcement requires police investigations which extend beyond the words of the accused."[1182]

In Texas, "[t]he *corpus delicti* rule is a common law rule of evidentiary sufficiency that applies to convictions based on extrajudicial confessions."[1183] "When a conviction is based on a defendant's extrajudicial confession, that confession does not constitute legally sufficient evidence of guilt without corroborating evidence independent of that confession showing that the 'essential nature' of the offense was committed."[1184] The corroborating evidence need not prove that the crime was committed; it "need only make this conclusion more probable."[1185]

"The corroboration rule, at its inception, served an extremely limited function. In order to convict of serious crimes of violence, then capital offenses, independent proof was required that someone had indeed inflicted the violence, the so-called *corpus delicti*. Once the existence of the crime was established, however, the guilt of the accused could be based on his own otherwise uncorroborated confession."[1186]

1175 *McNeil v. Wisconsin*, 501 U.S. 171, 111 S. Ct. 2204, 2210 (1991).

1176 *McNeil v. Wisconsin*, 501 U.S. 171, 111 S. Ct. 2204, 2210 (1991) (citation omitted).

1177 *Arizona v. Fulminante*, 499 U.S. 279, 296, 111 S. Ct. 1246, 1257 (1991) (quoting *Bruton v. United States*, 391 U.S. 123, 139-40, 88 S. Ct. 1620, 1630 (1968) (White, J., dissenting)).

1178 *Smith v. United States*, 348 U.S. 147, 75 S. Ct. 194, 152 (1954).

1179 *Warszower v. United States*, 312 U.S. 342, 61 S. Ct. 603 (1941).

1180 *Isaacs v. United States*, 159 U.S. 487, 16 S. Ct. 51 (1895).

1181 *Smith v. United States*, 348 U.S. 147, 75 S. Ct. 194, 152-53 (1954).

1182 *Smith v. United States*, 348 U.S. 147, 75 S. Ct. 194, 153 (1954).

1183 *Miranda v. State*, 620 S.W.3d 923, 292 (Tex. Crim. App. 2021) (citing *Salazar v. State*, 86 S.W.3d 640, 644 (Tex. Crim. App. 2002)).

1184 *Miranda v. State*, 620 S.W.3d 923, 292 (Tex. Crim. App. 2021) (citing *Miller v. State*, 457 S.W.3d 919, 924 (Tex. Crim. App. 2015)).

1185 *Williams v. State*, 958 S.W.2d 186, 190 (Tex. Crim. App. 1997).

1186 *Smith v. United States*, 348 U.S. 147, 75 S. Ct. 194, 153-54 (1954).

While the rule requiring corroboration is well settled, the question is what is the quantum of proof independent of the confession that the prosecution must introduce before the confession may be considered evidential? "There has been considerable debate concerning the quantum of corroboration necessary to substantiate the existence of the crime charged. It is agreed that the corroborative evidence does not have to prove the offense beyond a reasonable doubt, or even by a preponderance, as long as there is substantial independent evidence that the offense has been committed, and the evidence as a whole proves beyond a reasonable doubt that defendant is guilty."[1187] The debate has centered largely about two questions: "(1) whether corroboration is necessary for all elements of the offense established by admissions alone," and "(2) whether it is sufficient if the corroboration merely fortifies the truth of the confession, without independently establishing the crime charged[.]"[1188] The Supreme Court has answered both questions in the affirmative. "All elements of the offense must be established by independent evidence or corroborated admissions, but one available mode of corroboration is for the independent evidence to bolster the confession itself and thereby prove the offense 'through' the statements of the accused."[1189]

In *Fisher v. State*,[1190] defendant was convicted of killing his girlfriend although her body was never found. The direct and circumstantial evidence against him included his statement to a friend that he had committed the crime, together with evidence of body parts and blood in his home, and his possession of the victim's personal property. The court found that the corpus delicti was proven by the circumstantial evidence and upheld the conviction.

In *Harrell v. State*,[1191] the Van Alstyne Police Department received a report at about 4:00 a.m. of a gray minivan being driven erratically. The caller, who was driving in the same direction, followed the minivan to a gas station, told police where it had been parked, relayed the vehicle's license plate information, then hung up. The caller did not describe the driver. Police found the minivan a few minutes later. The motor was off, and defendant was in the driver's seat with the seatbelt buckled. There was no evidence about where the keys were, but defendant admitted that he had been driving. There were two passengers in the back. All three people in the minivan were intoxicated. These facts, held the Court, were sufficient to establish the corpus delicti of DWI. Said the court:

> Absent [defendant's] confession, the evidence still tends to show that [he] and the passengers were traveling together in the same minivan identified by the 911 caller and that [he] was operating it. As we have noted, the minivan had the same license plate as reported by the 911 caller and was found where the caller said the driver parked it. When Officer Blair approached the minivan, he saw [defendant] in the driver's seat with the seatbelt buckled[.] . . . The evidence tends to show that someone in the minivan was operating it on the highway when 911 was called. (While the evidence indicates that Appellant was driving, we stress that proof of identity is not required in a corpus delicti analysis.)[1192]

Once the *corpus delicti* of the crime is established, the accused's confession is admissible.[1193]

The "closely-related-crimes exception." In *Miller v. State*,[1194] the Court recognized an exception to strict application of the *corpus delicti* rule when a defendant is charged with multiple, closely-related offenses, but the *corpus delicti* of only some of the offenses is shown. As established in Pennsylvania, the rule is satisfied if one of the related offenses to which the suspect confessed is corroborated. The key is whether the relationship between the crimes is sufficiently "close" to "avoid admitting a confession for a crime that did not occur."[1195] The "closeness" of offenses should be determined by examining not only the temporal proximity of the offenses but also the type of offenses, similarities in how the offenses were committed, whether the offense

---

1187 *Smith v. United States*, 348 U.S. 147, 75 S. Ct. 194, 155-56 (1954).
1188 *Smith v. United States*, 348 U.S. 147, 75 S. Ct. 194, 156 (1954).
1189 *Smith v. United States*, 348 U.S. 147, 75 S. Ct. 194, 156 (1954).
1190 *Fisher v. State*, 851 S.W.2d 298 (Tex. Crim. App. 1993).
1191 *Harrell v. State*, 620 S.W.3d 910 (Tex. Crim. App. 2021).
1192 *Harrell v. State*, 620 S.W.3d 910, 915 (Tex. Crim. App. 2021).
1193 *See Gribble v. State*, 808 S.W.2d 65 (Tex. Crim. App. 1990) (plurality opinion); *Self v. State*, 513 S.W.2d 832 (Tex. Crim. App. 1974); *Wood v. State*, 142 Tex. Crim. 282, 152 S.W.2d 335 (1941).
1194 *Miller v. State*, 457 S.W.3d 919, 927 (Tex. Crim. App. 2015).
1195 *Commonwealth v. Taylor*, 574 Pa. 390, 831 A.2d 587, 594 (Pa. 2003).

arose from a single criminal episode or a course of conduct, whether the *corpus delicti* of other offenses have been shown, and any other consideration that would logically inform the inquiry."[1196]

Thus, in *Miranda v. State*, the court held that, independent of defendant's confession regarding one student, the evidence showed that he engaged in a course of conduct, grooming his underage female students, and using his position of authority as a teacher and a coach, he convinced them to participate in a romantic relationship, then engaged in sexual intercourse with them. Given the identical nature of all the sexual offenses, the strikingly similar *modus operandi* for each offense, and the fact that the *corpus delicti* of many of the crimes were shown, the offenses were sufficiently closely related to alleviate any concern that the crimes against one student were never committed. Therefore, defendant's confession was corroborated and the corpus delicti rule satisfied.

8.2.1.2. Electronic recordings of custodial interrogations

The United States Supreme Court has yet to extend the Due Process Clause of the United States Constitution to require that electronic recordings be made of custodial interrogations.[1197] However, as discussed above, Art. 38.22 of the Texas Code of Criminal Procedure and Art. 2.32 of the Code of Criminal Procedure require that statements regarding certain enumerated offenses must be recorded by audiovisual means, or by audio means if an audiovisual recording cannot be made.[1198]

8.2.1.3. Volunteered statements

Not all admissions or confessions obtained in the absence of *Miranda* warnings are inadmissible. The formula set forth in the preceding section – *custody* + *interrogation* = the requirement that *Miranda* warnings be given – teaches that law enforcement officials may, without the administration of *Miranda* warnings, question a criminal suspect who is not in custody. Moreover, officers may utilize any admission or confession volunteered by an in-custody criminal suspect when no interrogation (express or implied) has taken place. In this respect, the Court in *Miranda* emphasized that "[a]ny statement given freely and voluntarily without any compelling influences is, of course, admissible in evidence."[1199] Law enforcement officials are by no means required to stop people from speaking when they step forward to confess to a crime. Volunteered statements of any kind are not barred by the Fifth Amendment and their admissibility has not been affected by the Court's ruling in *Miranda*.[1200]

Texas courts have also determined that Art. 38.22 does not require suppression of a statement if the statement was not the product of custodial interrogation. In this respect, art. 38.22, §5 "specifically

[1196] *Miranda v. State*, 620 S.W.3d 923, 929 (Tex. Crim. App. 2021) (quoting *Commonwealth v. Taylor*, 574 Pa. 390, 831 A.2d 587, 594 (Pa. 2003)).

[1197] *See generally California v. Trombetta*, 467 U.S. 479, 104 S. Ct. 2528 (1984). To date, however, various states and the District of Columbia now require or encourage, in one form or another, custodial interrogations to be recorded. *See Ark. R. Crim. P.* 4.7 (Arkansas); *Cal. Penal Code* § 859.5 (2017) (California); *Colo. Rev. Stat.* § 16-3-601 (2016) (Colorado); *Conn. Gen. Stat.* § 54-1o(b) (2014) (Connecticut); *D.C. Code* §§ 5-116.01-116.03 (2005) (District of Columbia); 705 *Ill. Comp. Stat.* 405/5-401.5 and 725 *Ill. Comp. Stat.* 5/103-2.1 (2017) (Illinois); *Ind. R. Evid.* 617 (Indiana); *Kan. Stat. Ann.* § 22-4620 (2017) (Kansas); *Me. Stat. tit.* 25, § 2803-B (2015) (Maine); *Md. Code Ann., Crim. Proc.* §§ 2-402 and 2-403 (2008) (Maryland); *Mich. Comp. Laws* §§ 763.7-11 (2013) (Michigan); *Mo. Rev. Stat.* § 590.700 (2017) (Missouri); *Mont. Code Ann.* §§ 46-4-406-411 (2009) (Montana); *Neb. Rev. Stat.* §§ 29-4501-4508 (2008) (Nebraska); *N.J. Court Rules* 3:17 (New Jersey); *N.M. Stat. Ann.* § 29-1-16 (2006) (New Mexico); *N.Y. Crim. Proc. Law* § 60.45 (2018) (New York); *N.C. Gen. Stat. Ann.* § 15A-211 (2011) (North Carolina); *Or. Rev. Stat. Ann.* § 133.400 (2018) (Oregon); *Tex. Crim. Proc. Code Ann. art.* 2.32 and *art.* 38.22, §3 (2017) (Texas); *Utah R. Evid.* 616 (Utah); *Vt. Stat. Ann. tit.* 13, §5585 (2015) (Vermont); *Va. Code Ann.* §19.2-390.04 (Virginia 2020); *Wis. Stat. Ann.* § 968.073 (2019) (Wisconsin); *Stephan v. State*, 711 P.2d 1156, 1159 (Alaska 1985); *Commonwealth v. DiGiambattista*, 442 Mass. 423, 813 N.E.2d 516, 533-34 (Mass. 2004); *State v. Scales*, 518 N.W.2d 587, 592 (Minn. 1994).

[1198] *See Davidson v. State*, 25 S.W.3d 183 (Tex. Crim. App. 2000). For a more comprehensive discussion of Texas interview and confession law *see* Larry E. Holtz & Warren J Spencer, *Texas Criminal and Traffic Procedural Manual – An In-Depth Guide on How to Apply the Laws of Arrest, Search and Seizure, Confessions, & Eyewitness Identification* (Blue360° Media).

[1199] *Miranda v. Arizona*, 384 U.S. 436, 478, 86 S. Ct. 1602, 1630 (1966).

[1200] *Rhode Island v. Innis*, 446 U.S. 291, 300-01, 100 S. Ct. 1682 (1980).

exempts statements which do not 'stem from custodial interrogation,' statements which are 'res gestae of the arrest or the offense,' and all voluntary statements, whether or not they result from custodial interrogation."[1201]

For example, in *Pugh v. State*,[1202] defendant was arrested pursuant to a warrant. At the time, he was the driver and sole occupant of a car registered to his wife. On the way to the police station, he volunteered to an officer that he was going to be "honest" and had "stuff" in the car. When asked what he had in the car, defendant responded that he had drugs and a handgun. Heroin and a loaded gun were found together in a shopping bag on the front passenger floorboard. According to the Court, even "assuming, without deciding," that the police officer's question about what was in the car constituted custodial interrogation in the absence of *Miranda* warnings, his initial comments were volunteered and provided probable cause for a search of the vehicle. Consequently, and error in admitting this answer was harmless.

8.2.2. What constitutes custody?

8.2.2.1. General aspects

In *Miranda v. Arizona,* the U.S. Supreme Court held that pre-interrogation warnings are required in the context of custodial interrogations, given "the compulsion inherent in custodial surroundings."[1203] The Court defined "custodial interrogation" as "questioning initiated by law enforcement officers after a person has been taken into custody or otherwise deprived of his freedom of action in any significant way."[1204]

Whether or not a suspect is in custody for purposes of *Miranda* is an objective determination, based on all of the components of the setting. It is determined on the basis of "how a reasonable person in the suspect's situation would perceive his circumstances."[1205] The "initial determination of custody depends on the objective circumstances of the interrogation, not on the subjective views harbored by either the interrogating officers or the person being questioned."[1206] In this regard, a "noncustodial setting," will not be transformed into a "custodial" one, even where the police investigation has focused on a particular suspect as a primary target.[1207]

In *Thompson v. Keohane*,[1208] the U.S. Supreme Court provided the following description of the *Miranda* custody test:

> Two discrete inquiries are essential to the determination: first, what were the circumstances surrounding the interrogation; and second, given those circumstances, would a reasonable person have felt he or she was not at liberty to terminate the interrogation and leave. Once the scene is set and the players' lines and actions are reconstructed, the court must apply an objective test to resolve the ultimate inquiry: was there a formal arrest or restraint on freedom of movement of the degree associated with a formal arrest.[1209]

[1201] *See, e.g., Pugh v. State*, 2021 Tex. Crim. App. LEXIS 566, at *6 ("[V]olunteered statements are not barred by *Miranda*, even when the accused is in custody."); *Jones v. State*, 795 S.W.2d 171, 176 (Tex. Crim. App. 1990) (*same*); *Morris v. State*, 897 S.W.2d 528, 531 (Tex. App. 1995).

[1202] *Pugh v. State*, 2021 Tex. Crim. App. LEXIS 566.

[1203] *Miranda v. Arizona*, 384 U.S. 436, 458, 86 S. Ct. 1602, 1619 (1966).

[1204] *Miranda v. Arizona*, 384 U.S. 436, 444, 86 S. Ct. 1602, 1612 (1966); *see also Stansbury v. California*, 511 U.S. 318 (1994).

[1205] *Yarborough v. Alvarado*, 541 U.S. 652, 662, 124 S. Ct. 2140, 2148 (2004).

[1206] *Stansbury v. California*, 511 U.S. 318, 323, 114 S. Ct. 1526, 1529 (1994).

[1207] *See Beckwith v. United States*, 425 U.S. 341, 347-47, 96 S. Ct. 1612, 1616 (1976); *see also Minnesota v. Murphy*, 465 U.S. 420, 431, 104 S. Ct. 1136, 1144 (1984) ("The mere fact that an investigation has focused on a suspect does not trigger the need for *Miranda* warnings in noncustodial settings."); *Stansbury v. California*, 511 U.S. 318, 323, 114 S. Ct. 1526, 1528-29 (1994) ("a police officer's subjective view that an individual under questioning is a suspect, if undisclosed, does not bear upon the question whether the individual is in custody for purposes of *Miranda*.").

[1208] *Thompson v. v. Keohane*, 516 U.S. 99, 116 S. Ct. 457 (1995).

[1209] *Thompson v. Keohane*, 516 U.S. 99, 112, 116 S. Ct. 457, 465 (1995).

Thus, in determining whether an interrogation is custodial requires an examination of all the circumstances surrounding the questioning.[1210] In *Dowthitt v.State*,[1211] the Texas Court of Criminal Appeals clarified Texas law with respect to custody and brought it in line with the federal Supreme Court's approach. Thus, in Texas,

> the custody determination is based entirely upon objective circumstances.... [It] must be made on an ad hoc basis, after considering all of the (objective) circumstances.... Stationhouse questioning does not, in and of itself, constitute custody.... Further, custody does not occur merely because the suspect submits to and fails a polygraph test.... However, the mere fact that an interrogation begins as non-custodial does not prevent custody from arising later; police conduct during the encounter may cause a consensual inquiry to escalate into custodial interrogation.[1212]

In Texas, the courts have outlined at least four general situations which may constitute custody. For *Miranda* purposes, a person is in custody: "(1) when the suspect is physically deprived of his freedom of action in any significant way, (2) when a law enforcement officer tells the suspect that he cannot leave, (3) when law enforcement officers create a situation that would lead a reasonable person to believe that his freedom of movement has been significantly restricted, [or] (4) when there is probable cause to arrest and law enforcement officers do not tell the suspect that he is free to leave."[1213] No single factor is determinative. Courts will examine and weigh these factors and then make an objective determination as to what a reasonable person would perceive if he or she were in the defendant's position.

In *Wexler v. State*,[1214] the Court concluded that defendant Wexler was not in custody and therefore her statements to the police were not the product of a custodial interrogation. Officers in *Wexler* executed a narcotics search warrant with the help of various uniformed and plainclothes officers, along with the Harris County Sheriff's Office "High Risk Operations Unit" (HROU), a SWAT-like team whose function was to secure the residence and detain any occupants. While uniformed officers in marked police cars blocked both ends of the street, 20 to 25 HROU officers surrounded the house, announced via loudspeaker from an armored vehicle that they had a search warrant, and directed occupants to exit the house. Defendant came out and was detained by HROU officers and put in the back of a patrol car. Detective Hill questioned defendant. Hill suspected that defendant was involved in distributing drugs, but he did not tell her that she was a suspect, and he did not give her any warnings. Hill told defendant, "We have a search warrant. Tell me where the narcotics are. It will save us some time doing the search. We're going to find it no matter what. Defendant told him that the drugs were "in her bedroom in a dresser drawer." Hill and other narcotics officers went into the house to conduct the search and found methamphetamine in the dresser drawer, marijuana packaged for individual sale, drug paraphernalia, scales, cash, and handgun magazines and ammunition. Hill arrested defendant for possession with intent to distribute.

Finding defendant's statement admissible, the Court said: Defendant's "detention was of short duration, it was in a public setting, and she was not told that her detention would not be temporary. There was no evidence that [she] was aware of an overwhelming police presence. Accordingly, the court of appeals correctly held that [defendant] failed in her burden of proving that she experienced the functional equivalent of a formal arrest."[1215]

1210 *See also United States v. Booth*, 669 F.2d 1231 (9th Cir. 1981), where the Ninth Circuit further explained that in order to determine whether a person is "in custody" or has been significantly deprived of his freedom of action so as to trigger the requirement that *Miranda* warnings be given, courts will analyze "the totality of circumstances," specifically examining such pertinent factors as: (1) the duration of the detention; (2) the nature and degree of the pressure applied to detain the individual; (3) the physical surroundings of the questioning; and (4) the language used by the officer.

1211 *Dowthitt v. State*, 931 S.W.2d 244 (Tex. Crim. App. 1996).

1212 *Dowthitt v. State*, 931 S.W.2d 244, 254-55 (Tex. Crim. App. 1996) (citations omitted). *See also Meek v. State*, 790 S.W.2d 618 (Tex. Crim. App. 1990) (arson suspect was not "in custody," for *Miranda* purposes, during his station house question session); *Dancy v. State*, 728 S.W.2d 772 (Tex. Crim. App.), *cert. denied*, 484 U.S. 975, 108 S. Ct. 485 (1987).

1213 *Dowthitt v. State*, 931 S.W.2d 244, 255 (Tex. Crim. App. 1996). *See also Gardner v. State*, 306 S.W.3d 274 (Tex. Crim. App. 2009).

1214 *Wexler v. State*, 2021 Tex. Crim. App. LEXIS 630.

1215 *Wexler v. State*, 2021 Tex. Crim. App. LEXIS 630, at *14.

8.2.2.2. A motor vehicle stop is not *Miranda* custody

"Custody," for purposes of *Miranda*, "is a term of art that specifies circumstances that are thought generally to present a serious danger of coercion. In determining whether a person is in custody in this sense, the initial step is to ascertain whether, in light of 'the objective circumstances of the interrogation,'... a 'reasonable person [would] have felt he or she was not at liberty to terminate the interrogation and leave.'"[1216]

"Determining whether an individual's freedom of movement was curtailed, however, is simply the first step in the analysis, not the last. Not all restraints on freedom of movement amount to custody for purposes of *Miranda*."[1217] In addition, there is the question of "whether the relevant environment presents the same inherently coercive pressures as the type of station house questioning at issue in *Miranda*."[1218]

Thus, in *Berkemer v. McCarty*,[1219] the Court held that the roadside questioning of a motorist who was pulled over in a routine traffic stop did not constitute custodial interrogation. In *Berkemer*, the Court did acknowledge that "a traffic stop significantly curtails the 'freedom of action' of the driver and the passengers," and that it is generally "a crime either to ignore a policeman's signal to stop one's car or, once having stopped, to drive away without permission." Indeed, "few motorists," noted the Court, "would feel free either to disobey a directive to pull over or to leave the scene of a traffic stop without being told they might do so."[1220] Nonetheless, the Court "held that a person detained as a result of a traffic stop is not in *Miranda* custody because such detention does not 'sufficiently impair [the detained person's] free exercise of his privilege against self-incrimination to require that he be warned of his constitutional rights.'"[1221]

Accordingly, "the temporary and relatively nonthreatening detention involved in a traffic stop or *Terry* stop ... does not constitute *Miranda* custody."[1222]

8.2.2.3. Stationhouse questioning

In *Oregon v. Mathiason*,[1223] the U.S. Supreme Court held that *Miranda* warnings *are not* required when law enforcement officers question a suspect who is not under arrest nor "in custody" when such questioning takes place within the confines of the police station house. According to the Court, "police officers are not required to administer *Miranda* warnings to everyone whom they question. Nor is the requirement of warnings to be imposed simply because the questioning takes place in the station house, or because the questioned person is one whom the police suspect. *Miranda* warnings are required only where there has been such a restriction on a person's freedom as to render him 'in custody.'"[1224]

In *California v. Beheler*,[1225] the U.S. Supreme Court similarly held that "*Miranda* warnings are not required simply because the questioning takes place in the station house, or because the questioned person is one whom the police suspect. " Rather, the police "are required to give *Miranda* warnings only where there has been such a restriction on a person's freedom as to render him *in custody*."

The Texas Court of Criminal Appeals has adopted and applied the holding and rational of *Beheler*. In *Turner v. State*,[1226] police contacted a former employee of a bakery shop in connection with a murder investigation of a baker at the shop. Police asked the former employee to accompany them to the station to look at some photos. He was not a suspect at that time. During the conversation at the station, the former employee mentioned that he had been stationed in Korea and had brought back a pair of nice

---

[1216] *Howes v. Fields*, 565 U.S. 499, 132 S. Ct. 1181, 1189 (2012) (citations omitted).

[1217] *Howes v. Fields*, 565 U.S. 499, 132 S. Ct. 1181, 1189 (2012).

[1218] *Howes v. Fields*, 565 U.S. 499, 132 S. Ct. 1181, 1189 (2012).

[1219] *Berkemer v. McCarty*, 468 U.S. 420, 104 S. Ct. 3138 (1984).

[1220] *Berkemer v. McCarty*, 468 U.S. 420, 436, 104 S. Ct. 3138, 3149 (1984).

[1221] *Howes v. Fields*, 565 U.S. 499, 132 S. Ct. 1181, 1190 (2012) (quoting *Berkemer v. McCarty*, 468 U.S. 420, 437, 104 S. Ct. 3138, 3151 (1984)).

[1222] *Maryland v. Shatzer*, 559 U.S. 98, 130 S. Ct. 1213, 1224 (2010); *see also Pennsylvania v. Bruder*, 488 U.S. 9, 109 S. Ct. 205, 206 (1988) (persons temporarily detained during an ordinary motor vehicle stop are not in custody for purposes of *Miranda*).

[1223] *Oregon v. Mathiason*, 429 U.S. 492, 97 S. Ct. 711 (1977).

[1224] *Oregon v. Mathiason*, 429 U.S. 492, 97 S. Ct. 711, 714 (1977).

[1225] *California v. Beheler*, 463 U.S. 1121, 103 S. Ct. 3517 (1983).

[1226] *Turner v. State*, 685 S.W.2d 38 (Tex. Crim. App. 1985).

boots which had a brand name of "Tong" something. As soon as the former employee said this, the officer became suspicious because he remembered boots found in a garbage can carrying the name "Tong Young." Thereafter, the officer left his office, spoke to his partner, came back, advised the former employee of his *Miranda* rights, and obtained initialed waivers on a confession form. The former employee then made a three-page confession to the crime. The court held that the former employee was not in custody at least until the officer realized the likelihood of the person's involvement after he mentioned the Korean boots.[1227]

8.2.2.4. Hospital settings

Generally, there is no *per se* rule for hospitals in a *Miranda* custody inquiry. Each case must be decided on its own facts. The majority approach, however, as stated in *State v. Pontbriand*, is that "the restraint on freedom of movement incumbent in hospitalization does not, on its own, constitute custody for *Miranda* purposes."[1228] Thus, in *Pontbriand*, the Court considered defendant's "illness and medical confinement only to the extent that, as part of the totality of the circumstances surrounding the interview, they would impact a reasonable person's belief that he or she was actually in police custody, unable to leave or refuse to answer police questioning."[1229]

8.2.2.5. When the suspect is a juvenile, age should be taken into account

In *J.D.B. v. North Carolina*,[1230] the U.S. Supreme Court held that the *Miranda* custody analysis includes consideration of a juvenile suspect's age. "[S]o long as the child's age was known to the officer at the time of police questioning, or would have been objectively apparent to a reasonable officer, its inclusion in the custody analysis is consistent with the objective nature of that test. This is not to say that a child's age will be a determinative, or even a significant, factor in every case."[1231] "Just as police officers are competent to account for other objective circumstances that are a matter of degree such as the length of questioning or the number of officers present, so too are they competent to evaluate the effect of relative age.... In short, officers and judges need no imaginative powers, knowledge of developmental psychology, training in cognitive science, or expertise in social and cultural anthropology to account for a child's age. They simply need the common sense to know that a 7-year-old is not a 13-year-old and neither is an adult."[1232]

Pursuant to Tex. Family Code § 52.02(b), when a child is taken into custody, police must notify the child's parent or guardian and the office or official designated by the juvenile board of the fact that the child has been taken into custody and the reason for this action. Failure to do so may result in suppression of the juvenile's statement.[1233] Pursuant to Tex. Family Code § 51.095, if a child is in a detention facility or other place of confinement, in the custody of an officer, or in the possession of the Department of Protective and Regulatory Services and suspected to have engaged in conduct that violates a penal law, for any statement by the child to be admissible the child must receive a warning from a magistrate outlining the *Miranda* rights

---

1227 *See also Meek v. State*, 790 S.W.2d 618 (Tex. Crim. App. 1990); *Dancy v. State*, 728 S.W.2d 772 (Tex. Crim. App.), *cert. denied*, 484 U.S. 975, 108 S. Ct. 485 (1987); *Dowthitt v. State*, 931 S.W.2d 244 (Tex. Crim. App. 1996).

1228 *State v. Pontbriand*, 2005 VT 20 ¶14, 178 Vt. 120, 126, 878 A2d 227, 231 ("[C]ustody is not established merely because a suspect is unable to leave the hospital due to his or her medical condition.") (citing *United States v. Robertson*, 19 F.3d 1318, 1321 (10th Cir. 1994) (hospitalized suspect not in custody where officers did not restrict his freedom of movement through physical restraint or display of authority); *United States v. Martin*, 781 F.2d 671, 673 (9th Cir. 1985) (hospitalized suspect not in custody where police were not responsible for hospitalization and did not unnecessarily extend it); *Commonwealth v. Ellis*, 379 Pa. Super. 337, 549 A.2d 1323, 1333 (Pa. Super. Ct. 1988) (holding that appellant was not in custody for Miranda purposes where police officer questioned him while he awaited treatment in hospital emergency room)).

1229 *State v. Pontbriand*, 2005 VT 20 ¶14, 178 Vt. 120, 126, 878 A2d 227, 232.

1230 *J.D.B. v. North Carolina*, 564 U.S. 261, 131 S. Ct. 2394 (2011).

1231 *J.D.B. v. North Carolina*, 564 U.S. 261, 131 S. Ct. 2394, 2406 (2011) (citing, for example, teenagers nearing age 18).

1232 *J.D.B. v. North Carolina*, 564 U.S. 261, 131 S. Ct. 2394, 2407 (2011).

1233 *State v. Simpson*, 51 S.W.3d 633 (Tex. App. 2000).

and the child's right to end the interview out at any time. Law-enforcement officers may be present when the magistrate's warning is given to the juvenile.[1234]

8.2.2.6. Prison custody is not *Miranda* custody

In *Howes v. Fields*,[1235] the Supreme Court rejected the idea that a prison inmate is *always* "in custody" within the meaning of *Miranda* whenever he is taken aside and questioned about events that occurred outside the prison walls.

The prisoner, Randall Fields, while serving a sentence in Michigan, "was escorted by a corrections officer to a conference room where two sheriff's deputies questioned him about allegations that, before he came to prison, he had engaged in sexual conduct with a 12-year-old boy."[1236] Fields was questioned for over five hours. "At the beginning of the interview, Fields was told that he was free to leave and return to his cell"; that he "could leave whenever he wanted." He was not handcuffed and the door to the conference room was sometimes open and sometimes shut. Fields eventually confessed to engaging in sex acts with the boy.

Ruling that Fields was not in *Miranda* custody, the Court emphasized that the questioning of a prisoner is *not always* custodial "when the prisoner is removed from the general prison population and questioned about events that occurred outside the prison."[1237] On the contrary, the Court has repeatedly declined to adopt any such categorical rule. For example, in *Maryland v. Shatzer*,[1238] the U.S. Supreme Court determined that an inmate's return to the general prison population after an actual custodial interrogation constituted a break in "*Miranda* custody." Clearly, if "a break in custody can occur while a prisoner is serving an uninterrupted term of imprisonment, it must follow that imprisonment alone is not enough to create a custodial situation within the meaning of *Miranda*."[1239]

Accordingly, when a prisoner is questioned, "the determination of custody should focus on all of the features of the interrogation. These include the language that is used in summoning the prisoner to the interview and the manner in which the interrogation is conducted." In this case, Fields was "not taken into custody for purposes of *Miranda*."

In *Herrera v. State*,[1240] the Texas Court of Criminal Appeals set out a list of factors that the court will consider in determining whether an inmate is in custody for purposes of *Miranda*. These factors include:

- the language used to summon the inmate;
- the physical surroundings of the interrogation;
- the extent to which the inmate is confronted with evidence of his or her guilt;
- the additional pressure exerted to detain the inmate or the change in the surroundings of the inmate which results in an added imposition on the inmate's freedom of movement; and
- the inmate's freedom to leave the scene and the purpose, place, and length of the questioning.[1241]

8.2.3. What constitutes interrogation?

8.2.3.1. General aspects

One of the many recurring problems in this area is the question of what particular type of police conduct constitutes "interrogation." *Miranda* suggested that "interrogation" referred only to actual "questioning initiated by law enforcement officers."[1242] But what of the concern about the coerciveness of the "interrogation environment" ? There are times that the creative and inventive officer may overpower the will of the

[1234] *Herring v. State*, 395 S.W.3d 161 (Tex. Crim. App. 2013).
[1235] *Howes v. Fields*, 565 U.S. 499, 132 S. Ct. 1181 (2012).
[1236] *Howes v. Fields*, 565 U.S. 499, 132 S. Ct. 1181, 1185 (2012).
[1237] *Howes v. Fields*, 565 U.S. 499, 132 S. Ct. 1181, 1187 (2012).
[1238] *Maryland v. Shatzer*, 559 U.S. 98, 130 S. Ct. 1213 (2010).
[1239] *Howes v. Fields*, 565 U.S. 499, 132 S. Ct. 1181, 1190 (2012).
[1240] *Herrera v. State*, 241 S.W.3d 520 (Tex. Crim. App. 2007).
[1241] *Herrera v. State*, 241 S.W.3d 520 (Tex. Crim. App. 2007).
[1242] *Miranda v. Arizona*, 384 U.S. 436, 444, 86 S. Ct. 1602, 1612 (1966).

individual questioned *without asking any questions whatsoever.* It is this type of "psychological ploy" which necessarily undermines the privilege against compulsory self-incrimination, and, such ploys may thereby be treated as the "functional equivalent" of interrogation.

Interestingly, to determine whether an interrogation has taken place, the first question to ask is not, "What did the officer say or do?" That question comes second. The first question is: "At what stage of the criminal proceedings is the officer-defendant interaction occurring?" The answer to this question is critical for it may change the definition of the term "interrogation." Indeed, under the law of some states, it may even determine whether a criminal defendant may be questioned at all.

In determining the stage of the criminal proceedings in which the officer-defendant interaction is occurring, there are two time periods with which to be concerned. The first covers those events occurring *prior* to the initiation of formal criminal charges. The second time period begins at the initiation of formal charges and continues at least through trial. Once formal criminal charges have been initiated, any confrontational law-enforcement procedure involving the defendant (for example, an in-person lineup or an interrogation) is generally called a "critical stage" in the prosecution. The term "critical stage" is used because, at the moment formal criminal charges are initiated, the defendant's Sixth Amendment right to counsel attaches. Under Texas law, the "initiation of adversary judicial criminal proceedings," for purposes of the attachment of the Sixth Amendment right to counsel, takes place when an accused is formally arrested and taken before a magistrate, or when he or she has been indicted.[1243]

Thus, any law enforcement procedures involving a particular defendant that occur prior to the initiation of formal charges take place in what the courts call the "Fifth-Amendment setting." Procedures occurring after formal charges take place in the "Sixth-Amendment setting." For purposes of defining the term "interrogation" in a Fifth-Amendment setting, the focus will be upon the perceptions of the suspect, rather than on the intent or design of the police. The critical question will be whether the police used any words or actions that they *knew or should have known* were "reasonably likely to elicit an incriminating response from the suspect."[1244] In the Sixth-Amendment setting, the focus is upon the intent or design of the police, and the critical question will be whether officers *deliberately elicited* incriminating information from a defendant in the absence of counsel after a formal charge against the defendant had been filed.[1245]

8.2.3.2. The Fifth Amendment setting

In *Miranda*, the Court defined "custodial interrogation" as "*questioning* initiated by law enforcement officers after a person has been taken into custody or otherwise deprived of his freedom of action in any significant way." Here, the concern was that the "interrogation environment" created by the interplay of interrogation and custody would "subjugate the individual to the will of his examiner" and thereby undermine the privilege against compulsory self-incrimination.

In *Rhode Island v. Innis*,[1246] the Supreme Court addressed the police use of a psychological ploy to prompt an admission from a suspect after his arrest but before any formal charges had been filed (a time period known as the "Fifth Amendment" setting). Since there was no direct questioning of the suspect, the Court examined whether the suspect's incriminating response, in this Fifth Amendment setting, was or was not the product of "any words or actions on the part of the police (other than those normally attendant to arrest and custody) that the *police should know are (or should have known were) reasonably likely to elicit an incriminating response from the suspect*."[1247] "Incriminating response" refers to "any response — whether inculpatory or exculpatory — that the prosecution may seek to introduce at trial." The *reasonably-likely-to-elicit standard* thus "focuses primarily upon the perceptions of the suspect, rather than the intent of the police." This focus reflects the fact that the *Miranda* safeguards were designed to vest a suspect in custody with an added

[1243] *See Upton v. State*, 853 S.W.2d 548 (Tex. Crim. App. 1993); *Fuller v. State*, 829 S.W.2d 191 (Tex. Crim. App. 1992); *State v. Hernandez*, 842 S.W.2d 306 (Tex. App. 1992). *See also DeBlanc v. State*, 799 S.W.2d 701 (Tex. Crim. App. 1990); *McCambridge v. State*, 778 S.W.2d 70, 76 (Tex. Crim. App. 1989) ("under Art. I, § 10 of the Texas Constitution, a critical stage in the criminal process does not occur until formal charges are brought against a suspect").

[1244] *Rhode Island v. Innis*, 446 U.S. 291, 301, 100 S. Ct. 1682, 1689-90 (1980).

[1245] *Massiah v. United States*, 377 U.S. 201, 206, 84 S. Ct. 1199, 1203 (1964).

[1246] *Rhode Island v. Innis*, 446 U.S. 291, 100 S. Ct. 1682 (1980).

[1247] *Rhode Island v. Innis*, 446 U.S. 291, 100 S. Ct. 1682, 1689-90 (1980) (emphasis added).

measure of protection against coercive police practices, without regard to objective proof of the underlying intent of the police. A practice that the police should know is reasonably likely to evoke an incriminating response from a suspect thus amounts to interrogation.

In *Innis*, the police were investigating the murder of a taxicab driver. He had died from what appeared to be a shotgun blast to the back of his head. The day after the driver's body was found, the police received a call from another taxicab driver reporting that he had just been robbed by a "man wielding a sawed-off shotgun." After the driver identified defendant from a photo line-up, the police began searching for him.

Within a few hours, defendant was spotted, arrested, and advised of his *Miranda* rights. Defendant stated that he understood his rights and wanted to speak to an attorney. The officers then placed defendant in a "caged wagon," a four-door police car with a wire screen mesh between the front and rear seats, and drove him to headquarters. During the ride to the police station, the following conversation took place among the officers:

> I frequent this area while on patrol and there's a lot of handicapped children running around in this area, and God forbid one of them might find a weapon with shells and they might hurt themselves... it would be too bad if the little girl would pick up the gun, maybe kill herself.

Defendant then interrupted the conversation and requested that the officers turn the patrol car around so he could show them where the gun was located. Defendant stated that he understood his rights, but he "wanted to get the gun out of the way because of the kids in the area in the school." Defendant then directed the police to a nearby field and pointed out the hidden shotgun.

According to the Court, because defendant's incriminating response was not the product of words or actions of the police that they *should have known were reasonably likely to elicit an incriminating response*, their actions did not constitute "interrogation" within the meaning of *Miranda*.[1248]

The definition of interrogation, as set forth in *Innis*, has been adopted by the Texas courts for determining whether *Miranda* warnings were necessary under the case law, and for determining whether any statement obtained was admissible under Art. 38.22. In *Jones v. State*,[1249] the Texas Court of Criminal Appeals explained, "the term 'interrogation' under *Miranda* refers not only to express questioning, but also to any words or actions on the part of the police (other than those normally attendant to arrest and custody) that the police should know are reasonably likely to elicit an incriminating response from the suspect."[1250]

8.2.3.2.1. Providing information about the crime

In general, an officer's statements that provide a defendant with information about the charges against him, about inculpatory evidence located by the police, or about statements made by witnesses or co-defendants, which allow a defendant to make an informed and intelligent reassessment of his decision whether to speak to the police, do not constitute interrogation.

8.2.3.2.2. Consent searches

As a general rule, a police officer's request for consent to search a particular area is not "interrogation" within the meaning of *Miranda*, and an individual's subsequent response granting or denying consent is not "testimonial" for purposes of the Fifth Amendment privilege against self-incrimination.[1251]

[1248] *Rhode Island v. Innis*, 446 U.S. 291, 100 S. Ct. 1682, 1691 (1980).

[1249] *Jones v. State*, 795 S.W.2d 171 (Tex. Crim. App. 1990).

[1250] *Jones v. State*, 795 S.W.2d 171, 174 (Tex. Crim. App. 1990) (quoting *Rhode Island v. Innis*, 446 U.S. 291, 300-02, 100 S. Ct. 1682, 1689-90 (1980)). *See also Morris v. State*, 897 S.W.2d 528 (Tex. App. 1995).

[1251] *United States v. Glenna*, 878 F.2d 967, 971 (7th Cir. 1989); *see also United States v. LeGrone*, 43 F.3d 332 (7th Cir. 1994) ("[B]ecause requesting consent to search is not likely to elicit an incriminating statement, such questioning is not interrogation, and thus *Miranda* warnings are not required."); *Cody v. Solem*, 755 F.2d 1323, 1330 (8th Cir. 1985) ("Simply put, a consent to search is not an incriminating statement."); *Smith v. Wainwright*, 581 F.2d 1149, 1152 (5th Cir. 1978) ("A consent to search is not a self-incriminating statement."); *United States v. Lemon*, 550 F.2d 467, 472 (9th Cir. 1977) ("A consent to search is not the type of incriminating statement toward which the fifth amendment is directed. It is not in itself 'evidence of a testimonial or communicative nature.'").

8.2.3.3. The Sixth Amendment setting

In this setting, the courts apply a stricter approach to define "interrogation." The question is whether the police "deliberately elicited" incriminating statements. In this respect, any statement that is: (1) "deliberately elicited" by (2) a "government agent," (3) from an accused who is in custody, (4) without the benefit of *Miranda* warnings, constitutes interrogation for Sixth Amendment purposes, and a violation of the accused's Sixth Amendment rights.[1252] This rule does not, however, apply "to situations where the government agent who elicits the incriminating response does so exclusively for some other legitimate purpose, or through luck or happenstance obtains an unsolicited incriminating response."[1253]

8.2.3.3.1. The "Christian Burial" case

In *Brewer v. Williams*,[1254] the famous "Christian Burial" case, the Supreme Court held that, in this "Sixth Amendment setting," defendant Williams was "interrogated" in violation of his Sixth Amendment right to counsel.

The facts unfolded on the afternoon of December 24, when 10-year-old Pamela Powers went with her family to the YMCA in Des Moines, Iowa, to watch a wrestling tournament in which her brother was participating. When she failed to return from a trip to the washroom, an unsuccessful search for her began.

Robert Williams, who had recently escaped from a mental hospital, was a resident of the YMCA. Soon after the girl's disappearance, Williams was seen leaving the YMCA carrying some clothing and a large bundle wrapped in a blanket. He placed the large bundle in his car and drove off. His abandoned car was found the following day in Davenport, Iowa, roughly 160 miles east of Des Moines. A warrant was then issued in Des Moines for his arrest on a charge of abduction.

On the morning of December 26, acting on the advice of an attorney, Williams turned himself in to the Davenport police, where he was booked on the charge specified in the arrest warrant. After advising Williams of his *Miranda* rights, the Davenport police telephoned representatives of the Des Moines Police Department and advised them that Williams had surrendered. At the time, Williams' attorney was still at Des Moines police headquarters. The attorney spoke with Williams on the telephone and, in the presence of a police detective named Leaming, the attorney advised Williams that Des Moines police officers would be driving to Davenport to pick him up, that the officers would not interrogate him or mistreat him, and that Williams was not to talk to the officers about Pamela Powers until after consulting with him upon his return to Des Moines. Detective Leaming and a fellow officer would be driving to Davenport to pick up Williams. Prior to the trip, Williams was arraigned before a judge in Davenport on the outstanding arrest warrant. (This started the "Sixth Amendment setting.").

Detective Leaming and his fellow officer arrived in Davenport at about noon to pick up Williams and return him to Des Moines. The two detectives, along with Williams, then set out on the 160-mile drive. Leaming knew that Williams was a former mental patient and knew also that he was deeply religious. Not long after leaving Davenport and reaching the interstate highway, Detective Leaming addressed Williams as "Reverend," and said:

> I want to give you something to think about while we're traveling down the road.... Number one, I want you to observe the weather conditions, it's raining, it's sleeting, it's freezing, driving is very treacherous, visibility is poor, it's going to be dark early this evening. They are predicting several inches of snow for tonight, and I feel that you yourself are the only person that knows where this little girl's body is, that you yourself have only been there once, and if you get a snow on top of it, you yourself may be unable to find it. And, since we will be going right past the area on the way into Des Moines, I feel that we could stop and locate the body, that the parents of this little girl should be entitled to a Christian burial for the little girl who was snatched away from them on Christmas Eve and murdered. And I feel we should stop and locate it on the way in, rather than waiting until morning and trying to come back out after a snow storm and possibly not being able to find it at all.[1255]

1252 *Watson v. State*, 885 S.W.2d 222, 234 (Tex. App. 1994) (citing *Massiah v. United States*, 377 U.S. 201, 206, 84 S. Ct. 1199, 1203 (1964)).

1253 *Watson v. State*, 885 S.W.2d 222, 234-35 (Tex. App. 1994).

1254 *Brewer v. Williams,* 430 U.S. 387, 97 S. Ct. 1232 (1977).

1255 *Brewer v. Williams,* 430 U.S. 387, 392-93, 97 S. Ct. 1232 (1977).

As they continued towards Des Moines, just as they approached Mitchellville, Williams said that he would show the officers where the body was. He then directed the police to the body of Pamela Powers.

Holding that Williams was "interrogated," the Court said: The police detective "deliberately and designedly set out to elicit information from Williams just as surely as – and perhaps more effectively than – if he had formally interrogated him." The detective's "Christian burial speech" was "tantamount to interrogation." Because the detective did not obtain from Williams a waiver of his right to counsel prior to that "interrogation," neither Williams' incriminating statements themselves nor any testimony describing his having led the police to the victim's body can constitutionally be admitted into evidence.[1256]

Once adversary judicial proceedings have been initiated against the defendant and the right to counsel has attached, it is at this point in the proceedings that "the government has committed itself to prosecute," and "the adverse positions of the government and the defendant have solidified."[1257]

8.2.3.3.2. After indictment

In *Patterson v. Illinois*,[1258] the Supreme Court held that the police are not barred from initiating communication, exchanges, or conversations with a defendant whose Sixth Amendment right to counsel has arisen with his indictment. Such a defendant should not be equated with a preindictment suspect who, while being questioned, asserts his Fifth Amendment right to counsel which would bar further questioning of such suspect unless he initiates the meeting. The mere fact that a defendant's Sixth Amendment right to counsel "came into existence with his indictment, *i.e.*, that he had such a right at the time of his questioning, does not distinguish him from the preindictment interrogatee whose right to counsel is in existence and available for his exercise while he is questioned." Like the preindictment setting, the request for an attorney in the post-indictment setting would also prohibit the police from any further questioning unless the accused himself initiates further communication. Here, the Court also held that the *Miranda* warnings were adequate, in a Sixth Amendment, post-indictment setting, to sufficiently apprise an accused of the nature of his Sixth Amendment rights and the consequences of abandoning them.

In *Michigan v. Harvey*,[1259] the Court observed:

> Although a defendant may sometimes later regret his decision to speak with police, the Sixth Amendment does not disable a criminal defendant from exercising his free will. To hold that a defendant is inherently incapable of relinquishing his right to counsel once it is invoked would be "to imprison a man in his privileges and call it the Constitution."[1260]

8.2.3.3.3. When the right to counsel attaches

The Sixth Amendment provides that, "[i]n all *prosecutions,* the accused shall enjoy the right [to] have the Assistance of Counsel for his defence."[1261] As the Supreme Court has explained, the Sixth Amendment right to counsel "is limited by its terms," and therefore, "it does not attach until a prosecution is commenced."[1262] Commencement of prosecution, for purposes of the attachment of the right to counsel, has been tied to

---

1256 *See also Fellers v. United States,* 540 U.S. 519, 524, 124 S. Ct. 1019, 1022 (2004) (reaffirming application of the "deliberate-elicitation standard" for Sixth Amendment cases) (citing *United States v. Henry*, 447 U.S. 264, 270, 100 S. Ct. 2183 (1980)) ("The question here is whether under the facts of this case a Government agent 'deliberately elicited' incriminating statements[.]"). The *Fellers* court also "expressly distinguished this standard from the Fifth Amendment custodial-interrogation standard." *See id.*, 124 S. Ct. at 1023 (citing *Rhode Island v. Innis*, 446 U.S. 291, 100 S. Ct. 1682 (1980)).

1257 *See Brewer v. Williams,* 430 U.S. 387, 97 S. Ct. 1232 (1977); *Maine v. Moulton,* 474 U.S. 159, 175, 106 S. Ct. 477 (1985).

1258 *Patterson v. Illinois*, 487 U.S. 285, 108 S. Ct. 2389 (1988).

1259 *Michigan v. Harvey*, 494 U.S. 344, 110 S. Ct. 1176 (1990).

1260 *Michigan v. Harvey*, 494 U.S. 344, 110 S. Ct. 1176, 1182 (1990) (quoting *Adams v. United States ex rel. McCann*, 317 U.S. 269, 280, 63 S. Ct. 236, 242 (1942)).

1261 U.S. Const. amend. VI (emphasis added). Note that the spelling of "defence" is from the original document. "Defence" = British English; "defense" = American English.

1262 *Rothgery v. Gillespie County, Texas,* 554 U.S. 191, 198, 128 S. Ct. 2578 (2008) (quoting *McNeil v. Wisconsin*, 501 U.S. 171, 175, 111 S. Ct. 2204 (1991)).

"the initiation of adversary judicial criminal proceedings – whether by way of formal charge, preliminary hearing, indictment, information, or arraignment."[1263] These pretrial proceedings are often considered to be "critical" stages because "the results might well settle the accused's fate and reduce the trial itself to a mere formality."[1264] Thus, at the earliest, "[a] defendant's right to rely on counsel as a 'medium' between the defendant and the State attaches upon the initiation of formal charges."[1265]

In *Rothgery v. Gillespie County, Texas*,[1266] the Court clarified that a defendant's right to counsel, guaranteed by the Sixth Amendment, attaches "at the first appearance before a judicial officer at which a defendant is told of the formal accusation against him and restrictions are imposed on his liberty."[1267] Moreover, the attachment of the right does not require that a public prosecutor be aware of that initial proceeding or involved in its conduct.[1268]

Once the right has attached for a given charge, the suspect cannot be questioned about that charge without counsel present. This rule applies not only to law enforcement officers, but also any government agents who "deliberately elicit" incriminating statements (*e.g.* jailhouse informants). A suspect can, however, be questioned regarding other offenses for which the Sixth Amendment right has not yet attached without violating that provision.[1269]

While the Texas Court of Criminal Appeals has adopted the principles set forth in *Patterson*, the court has been careful to draw a distinction between the Sixth Amendment protections that arise by operation of indictment, and the Sixth Amendment protections afforded an accused who is represented by counsel. In Texas, after the Sixth Amendment right to counsel attaches *and the accused is represented by counsel*, the police may not initiate a questioning session with the accused without notice to defense counsel.[1270] This rule does not depend on an accused's assertion of his or her right to counsel, for this rule is designed to preserve the integrity of the attorney-client relationship once it has been established,[1271] and provide a "distinct set of constitutional safeguards" to a represented defendant whose Sixth Amendment right to counsel has attached.[1272]

8.3. *Miranda*

8.3.1. Administration; when to advise

In *Duckworth v. Eagan*,[1273] the Supreme Court observed that in *Miranda v. Arizona*,[1274] "the court established certain procedural safeguards that require police to advise criminal suspects of their rights under the Fifth and Fourteenth Amendments before commencing custodial interrogation. In now familiar words, the Court reminded that

---

1263 *Rothgery v. Gillespie County, Texas,* 554 U.S. 191, 198, 128 S. Ct. 2578 (2008); *see also Kirby v. Illinois,* 406 U.S. 682, 689, 92 S. Ct. 1877, 1882 (1972).

1264 *United States v. Wade,* 388 U.S. 218, 224, 87 S. Ct. 1926 (1967); *see also Powell v. Alabama,* 287 U.S. 45, 57, 53 S. Ct. 55 (1932) (stating that the right to counsel "during perhaps the most critical period of the proceedings" – that is, from the time of a criminal defendant's arraignment until the beginning of his or her trial – is as important "as the trial itself.").

1265 *Michigan v. Harvey,* 494 U.S. 344, 353, 110 S. Ct. 1176, 1181 (1990).

1266 *Rothgery v. Gillespie County, Texas,* 554 U.S. 191, 128 S. Ct. 2578 (2008).

1267 *Rothgery v. Gillespie County, Texas,* 554 U.S. 191, 128 S. Ct. 2578, 2581 (2008).

1268 *Rothgery v. Gillespie County, Texas,* 554 U.S. 191, 128 S. Ct. 2578 (2008).

1269 *McNeil v. Wisconsin,* 501 U.S. 171, 111 S. Ct. 2204 (1991). Suspects can even be questioned regarding an offense which is "factually related" to the offense for which this right has been invoked, as long as the offenses are not the same for double jeopardy purposes. *Texas v. Cobb,* 532 U.S. 162, 173-74, 121 S. Ct. 1335, 1343 (2001).

1270 *Holloway v. State,* 780 S.W.2d 787 (Tex. Crim. App. 1989).

1271 *Holloway v. State,* 780 S.W.2d 787, 790-91, 794-95 (Tex. Crim. App. 1989).

1272 *See Patterson v. Illinois,* 487 U.S. 285, 289 n. 3, 108 S. Ct. 2389, 2393 n. 3 (1988). *See also Holloway v. State,* 780 S.W.2d 787, 795 (Tex. Crim. App. 1989) (recognizing that *Patterson* was limited to a defendant unrepresented by counsel). For a more comprehensive discussion of the distinction between the Fifth Amendment and Sixth Amendment right to counsel *see* Larry E. Holtz & Warren J Spencer, *Texas Criminal and Traffic Procedural Manual – An In-Depth Guide on How to Apply the Laws of Arrest, Search and Seizure, Confessions, & Eyewitness Identification* (Blue360° Media).

1273 *Duckworth v. Eagan,* 492 U.S. 195, 109 S. Ct. 2875 (1989).

1274 *Miranda v. Arizona,* 384 U.S. 436, 86 S. Ct. 1602 (1966).

> [A suspect] must be warned prior to any questioning [1] that he has the right to remain silent, [2] that anything he says can be used against him in a court of law, [3] that he has the right to the presence of an attorney, and [4] that if he cannot afford an attorney one will be appointed for him prior to any questioning if he so desires."[1275]

While there is no requirement that a suspect be given the *Miranda* warnings verbatim,[1276] the "crucial test is whether the words in the context used, considering the age, background and intelligence of the individual being interrogated, impart a clear, understandable warning of all of his rights."[1277] "The inquiry is simply whether the warnings reasonably convey to a suspect his rights as required by *Miranda*."[1278]

In *Florida v. Powell*,[1279] the U.S. Supreme Court emphasized that, as a matter of law, an individual held for questioning "must be clearly informed that he has the right to consult with a lawyer *and to have the lawyer with him during interrogation*."[1280]

Miranda's third warning — the only one at issue here — has been held in subsequent cases to require, "as an absolute prerequisite to interrogation, that an individual held for questioning [] be clearly informed that he has the right to consult with a lawyer and *to have the lawyer with him during interrogation*."[1281]

In *Garcia v. State*,[1282] the Texas Court of Criminal Appeals warned law enforcement personnel that, although "technical noncompliance" with art. 38.22, § 2(a) will not result in suppression of an accused's written statement, the better practice is to use the precise language of the statute.[1283] In *Garcia*, the statement form indicated that any statement the suspect makes "*will* be used against" him, as opposed to "*may* be used against him," as set forth in the statute. This variance, ruled the court, constituted only "technical noncompliance with the statute," and, by itself, would not affect the admissibility of the written statement thereafter obtained.[1284]

A fully effective equivalent. Section 3(e)(2) of Art. 38.22 provides:

> **(e)** The courts of this state shall strictly construe Subsection (a) of this section and may not interpret Subsection (a) as making admissible a statement unless all requirements of the subsection have been satisfied by the state, except that: ... (2) the accused was given the warning in Subsection (a) of Section 2 above ***or its fully effective equivalent.***

"For oral statements, the warnings given to the accused are effective even if not given verbatim, so long as they convey the 'fully effective equivalent' of the warnings contained in Section 2(a).[1285] This requirement has also been referred to as "substantial compliance."[1286] A warning substantially complies with article 38.22 when it "convey[s] on the face of the statement the exact meaning of the statute, but in slightly different language[.]"[1287]

[1275] *Duckworth v. Eagan*, 492 U.S. 195, 109 S. Ct. 2875, 2879 (1989) (quoting *Miranda v. Arizona*, 384 U.S. 436, 479, 86 S. Ct. 1602, 1630 (1966)).

[1276] *See California v. Prysock*, 453 U.S. 355, 359-60, 101 S. Ct. 2806 (stating that *Miranda* does not require a "talismanic incantation" of the warnings, but rather only the fully effective equivalent of such warnings).

[1277] *See Coyote v. United States*, 380 F.2d 305, 308 (10th Cir. 1967).

[1278] *Duckworth v. Eagan*, 492 U.S. 195, 203, 109 S. Ct. 2875, 2880 (1989) (internal quotes omitted).

[1279] *Florida v. Powell*, 559 U.S. 50, 130 S. Ct. 1195 (2010).

[1280] *Florida v. Powell*, 559 U.S. 50, 130 S. Ct. 1195, 1203 (2010) (emphasis added).

[1281] *Florida v. Powell*, 559 U.S. 50, 130 S. Ct. 1195, 1203 (2010) (emphasis added).

[1282] *Garcia v. State*, 919 S.W.2d 370 (Tex. Crim. App. 1996).

[1283] *See also Penry v. State*, 691 S.W.2d 636 (Tex. Crim. App. 1985) (advising the accused that he had a right to an attorney "prior to *or* during any questioning" when the statute required a warning of "prior to *and* during any questioning" held to be "technical noncompliance with the statute" to requiring suppression of the resulting statement); *Eddlemon v. State*, 591 S.W.2d 847 (Tex. Crim. App. 1979) ("technical noncompliance with the statute" should not result in suppression).

[1284] For a more comprehensive discussion of the administration of *Miranda* warnings in Texas *see* Larry E. Holtz & Warren J Spencer, *Texas Criminal and Traffic Procedural Manual — An In-Depth Guide on How to Apply the Laws of Arrest, Search and Seizure, Confessions, & Eyewitness Identification* (Blue360° Media).

[1285] *See Hernandez v. State*, 533 S.W.3d 472, 479 (Tex. App.—Corpus Christi 2017).

[1286] *See White v. State*, 779 S.W.2d 809, 827 (Tex. Crim. App. 1989).

[1287] *See White v. State*, 779 S.W.2d 809, 827 (Tex. Crim. App. 1989).

In *Bible v. State*,[1288] the Court also held that "[u]nder Section 3(e)(2) of the statute, it is sufficient that 'the accused was given the warning in Subsection (a) of Section 2 above or its fully effective equivalent.'" In this case, since the warnings given by the Louisiana officers were the "fully effective equivalent" of the warnings outlined in Article 38.22, § 2, it follows that "Article 38.22 does not bar admission of the statements."[1289]

In *Hernandez v. State*,[1290] the court held that defendant's motion to suppress his confession was properly denied because the warnings given to him prior to questioning complied with Art. 38.22, § 3(e)(2), as the statement that "anything that you say may be used as evidence against you in a court of justice" could be reasonably understood to include the term "trial."

8.3.1.1. When the administration of the *Miranda* warnings has become stale

Clearly, once *Miranda* warnings are given, they are "not to be accorded unlimited efficacy or perpetuity."[1291] But at the same time, a suspect need not be advised of his constitutional rights more than once unless the time of warning and the time of subsequent interrogation are too remote in time from one another. The cases do not require that the warnings be repeated after an interruption in the questioning.[1292]

The United States Supreme Court has confirmed this approach in *Wyrick v. Fields*,[1293] where the defendant was arrested on a rape charge and requested a polygraph examination. Prior to the polygraph examination, the defendant had waived his rights to have his attorney present and to remain silent. At the conclusion of the test, the examiner informed the defendant that the test revealed that the defendant had been deceitful. The examiner asked if the defendant wished to explain the results. Defendant then admitted to having sexual contact with the victim, but claimed it was consensual. Defendant sought to suppress these statements. The Supreme Court, in examining the "totality of the circumstances," noted that there was nothing to suggest that the completion of the test and the defendant's being asked to explain the results were significant enough occurrences to cause the defendant to immediately forget his rights under *Miranda* or render his statements involuntary. The Court held that the initial warning and waiver would still be valid, "unless the circumstances changed so seriously that [the suspect's] answers no longer were voluntary, or unless [the suspect] no longer was making a 'knowing and intelligent relinquishment or abandonment' of his rights."[1294]

Since the *Miranda* staleness issue involves an examination of the "totality of the circumstances," the amount of time that elapsed between the warning and subsequent interrogation is not the sole dispositive factor in determining whether there has been a violation of *Miranda*. A close examination of the issue reveals a lack of consistency across different jurisdictions. For example, some courts have required a re-advisement of *Miranda* rights after four hours,[1295] 18 hours,[1296] two days,[1297] and three days.[1298] While at the same time, other courts have held that a re-advisement was *not necessary* after several hours,[1299] three hours,[1300] five

[1288] *Bible v. State*, 162 S.W.3d 234, 240 (Tex. Crim. App. (2005).

[1289] *Bible v. State*, 162 S.W.3d 234, 240 (Tex. Crim. App. (2005).

[1290] *See Hernandez v. State*, 533 S.W.3d 472, 480 (Tex. App.—Corpus Christi 2017).

[1291] *United States v. Hopkins*, 433 F.2d 1041, 1045 (5th Cir. 1970).

[1292] *See, e.g., United States v. Edwards*, 581 F.3d 604, 606 (7th Cir. 2009); *United States v. Ferrer-Montoya*, 483 F.3d 565, 569 (8th Cir. 2007); *United States v. Rodriguez-Preciado*, 399 F.3d 1118, 1128-29 (9th Cir. 2005).

[1293] *Wyrick v. Fields*, 459 U.S. 42, 103 S. Ct. 394 (1982).

[1294] *Wyrick v. Fields*, 459 U.S. 42, 47, 103 S. Ct. 394, 396 (1982) (quoting *Edwards v. Arizona*, 451 U.S. 477, 483, 101 S. Ct. 1880, 1884 (1981)).

[1295] *People v. Sanchez*, 88 Misc. 2d 929, 391 N.Y.S.2d 513 (1977).

[1296] *United States v. Jones*, 147 F. Supp. 2d 752 (E.D. Mich. 2001).

[1297] *Franklin v. State*, 6 Md. App. 572, 252 A.2d 487 (1969).

[1298] *People v. Quirk*, 129 Cal. App. 3d 618, 181 Cal. Rptr. 301 (1982).

[1299] *United States v. Diaz*, 814 F.2d 454, 460 and n. 6 (7th Cir. 1987) (Here, the warnings were given at the hotel where Diaz was arrested, and his inculpatory statements came during the subsequent booking.).

[1300] *Jarrell v. Balkcom*, 735 F.2d 1242, 1253-54 (11th Cir. 1984).

hours,[1301] nine hours,[1302] 12 hours,[1303] 15 hours,[1304] 17 hours,[1305] two days,[1306] three days,[1307] and all the way up to a week or more if law enforcement asks if the suspect remembers his or her rights.[1308]

The analysis is dependent upon the facts of a particular situation. For example, the following factors may be useful in determining whether the *Miranda* warnings have gone stale:

> (1) the length of time between the giving of the first warnings and the subsequent interrogation[;] (2) whether the warnings and the subsequent interrogation were given in the same or different places[;] (3) whether the warnings were given and the subsequent interrogation conducted by the same or different officers[;] (4) the extent to which the subsequent statement differed from any previous statements[;and] (5) the apparent intellectual and emotional state of the suspect.[1309]

8.3.1.2. When a suspect becomes the "focus" or "target" of an investigation

In *Stansbury v. California*,[1310] the Supreme Court held that a person's right to receive *Miranda* warnings is *not* triggered when he or she becomes a suspect in, or the focus of, an officer's investigation. According to the Court, a law enforcement officer's obligation to administer *Miranda* warnings attaches *only* where there has been such a restriction on a person's freedom as to render him or her "in custody." A person's *Miranda* rights are not triggered by virtue of the fact that he or she has become the focus of an officer's suspicions. Case law "makes clear, in no uncertain terms, that any inquiry into whether the interrogating officers have focused their suspicions upon the individual being questioned (assuming those suspicions remain undisclosed) is not relevant for purposes of *Miranda*."[1311]

8.3.1.3. On the scene questioning

Miranda warnings are not required before general, on-the-scene questions intended to investigate the facts surrounding an apparent crime.[1312]

8.3.2. *Miranda* and motor vehicle offenses

There is no requirement that a law enforcement officer administer *Miranda* warnings during the course of a traffic stop where the officer temporarily detains a motorist in order to ask a few brief questions and issue a traffic citation. As held in *Berkemer v. McCarty*,[1313] an ordinary traffic stop, by its very nature "is presumptively temporary and brief," lasting "only a few minutes."[1314] It generally involves no more than a check of credentials

---

1301 *Stumes* v. Solem, 752 F.2d 317, 320 (8th Cir. 1985).

1302 *United States ex rel. Henne v. Fike*, 563 F.2d 809, 813-14 (7th Cir. 1977).

1303 *Commonwealth v. Wideman*, 460 Pa. 699, 334 A.2d 594, 598-99 (Pa. 1975).

1304 *People v. Dela Pena*, 72 F.3d 767, 769-70 (9th Cir. 1995).

1305 *State v. Myers*, 345 A.2d 500 (Me. 1975).

1306 *Babcock v. State*, 473 S.W.2d 941 (Tex. Crim. App. 1971).

1307 *Maguire v. United States*, 396 F.2d 327 (9th Cir. 1968); *Johnson v. State*, 56 Ala. App. 583, 324 So. 2d 298 (1975).

1308 *Martin v. Wainwright*, 770 F.2d 918 (11th Cir. 1985), *modified on denial of rehearing*, 781 F.2d 185 (11th Cir. 1986); *Biddy v. Diamond*, 516 F.2d 118 (5th Cir. 1975).

1309 *State v. Miah S.*, 290 Neb. 607, 618, 861 N.W.2d 406, 415 (2015) (quoting *State v. McZorn*, 288 N.C. 417, 43 4, 219 S.E.2d 201, 212 (1975)), *judgment vacated in part*, 428 U.S. 904, 96 S. Ct. 3210 (1976); *see also State v. DeWeese*, 213 W. Va. 339, 582 S.E.2d 786 (2003).

1310 *Stansbury v. California*, 511 U.S. 318, 114 S. Ct. 1526 (1994).

1311 *See also Beckwith v. United States*, 425 U.S. 341, 347-047, 96 S. Ct. 1612, 1616 (1976) (a "noncustodial setting," will not be transformed into a "custodial" one, even where the police investigation has focused on a particular suspect as a primary target); *Minnesota v. Murphy*, 465 U.S. 420, 431, 104 S. Ct. 1136, 1144 (1984) ("The mere fact that an investigation has focused on a suspect does not trigger the need for *Miranda* warnings in noncustodial settings.").

1312 *See Miranda v. Arizona*, 384 U.S. 436, 477, 86 S. Ct. 1602, 1629 (1966).

1313 *Berkemer v. McCarty*, 468 U.S. 420, 104 S. Ct. 3138 (1984).

1314 *Berkemer v. McCarty*, 468 U.S. 420, 104 S. Ct. 3138, 3149 (1984).

and issuance of citations for violations observed. Therefore, "persons temporarily detained pursuant to such stops are not 'in custody' for the purposes of *Miranda*."[1315]

Recall that officers need only administer the *Miranda* warnings prior to "custodial" interrogation. In *McCarty*, the defendant was not "in custody" until "he was formally placed under arrest and instructed to get into the police car." Here, the Court noted that a traffic stop significantly curtails the "freedom of action" of the driver and the passengers, if any, of the detained vehicle. Moreover, under the Fourth Amendment, the stopping of a motor vehicle and the detaining of its occupants is a "seizure" which requires a constitutional justification. But, this temporary stop, like the *Terry* stop, does not constitute "custody" for purposes of *Miranda*.

As in the case of the typical *Terry* stop, which is not subject to the dictates of *Miranda*, the similarly noncoercive aspect of ordinary traffic stops prompted the Court to hold that "persons temporarily detained pursuant to such stops are not 'in custody' for the purposes of *Miranda*."[1316]

The Texas Court of Criminal Appeals has held that questions associated with routine traffic stops are not violative of Texas statutory provisions addressing custodial interrogation.[1317] It also has been held that when a drunk-driving suspect slurs his speech and exhibits a lack of muscular coordination in response to custodial police questioning, those responses are not "testimonial" in nature such that, if elicited in the absence of *Miranda* warnings, they will be deemed inadmissible.[1318] In this regard, a DUI defendant's responses to custodial police questioning "are not rendered inadmissible by *Miranda* merely because the slurred nature of his speech was incriminating. The physical inability to articulate words in a clear manner due to 'the lack of muscular coordination of his tongue and mouth'... is not itself a testimonial component of [an intoxicated motorist's] responses to [an officer's] questions."[1319]

The "sixth birthday" question. During Muniz's traffic stop, he was asked, "Do you know what the date was of your sixth birthday?" The Court held that Muniz's answer constituted a "testimonial response," and "was incriminating, not just because of his delivery, but also because of his answer's *content*." One could infer from an intoxicated motorist's answer (that he did not *know* the proper date) that his mental state was confused.

Here, "the incriminating inference of impaired mental faculties stemmed, not just from the fact that Muniz slurred his response, but also from a testimonial aspect of that response."[1320] Accordingly, because "Muniz's response to the sixth birthday question was testimonial, the response should have been suppressed."[1321]

8.3.2.1. The routine "booking question" exception to *Miranda*

In *Muniz*, the Supreme Court also held that an in-custody accused's responses to routine booking questions, such as, "What is your name? Address? Height? Weight? Eye color? Date of birth? and Current age?" need not be suppressed when asked without prior administration of *Miranda* warnings. While such questions may involve "custodial interrogation," within the meaning of *Miranda*, the responses to such questions in the absence of *Miranda* "are nonetheless admissible because the questions fall within [the] 'routine booking question' exception which exempts from *Miranda's* coverage questions to secure the 'biographical

---

1315 *Berkemer v. McCarty*, 468 U.S. 420, 104 S. Ct. 3138, 3151 (1984).

1316 *See also Pennsylvania v. Bruder*, 488 U.S. 9, 109 S. Ct. 205 (1988).

1317 See *Loar v. State*, 627 S.W.2d 399, 400 (Tex. Crim. App. 1981) (use of drunk-driving motorist's pre-arrest statement admitting drinking did not violate *Miranda* or Art. 38.22); *Higgins v. State*, 473 S.W.2d 493, 494 (Tex. Crim. App. 1971) (officer's pre-arrest questioning of motorist suspected of drunk driving did not violate *Miranda* and was proper under Art. 38.22); *Galloway v. State*, 778 S.W.2d 110, 112 (Tex. App. 1989) ("A person is not 'in custody' under *Miranda* during a routine traffic stop for suspicion of DWI"); *Keaton v. State*, 755 S.W.2d 209, 210 (Tex. App. 1988) (officer's act of placing motorist "in the patrol car and asking him to produce a driver's license and proof of insurance, required by law for all Texas motorists, did not constitute custodial interrogation requiring *Miranda* warnings.").

1318 *Pennsylvania v. Muniz*, 496 U.S. 582, 110 S. Ct. 2638 (1990).

1319 *Pennsylvania v. Muniz*, 496 U.S. 582, 110 S. Ct. 2638, 2644-45 (1990).

1320 *Pennsylvania v. Muniz*, 496 U.S. 582, 110 S. Ct. 2638, 2649 (1990).

1321 *Pennsylvania v. Muniz*, 496 U.S. 582, 110 S. Ct. 2638 (1990).

data necessary to complete booking or pretrial services.'"[1322] These types of questions are asked for "record-keeping purposes only," and therefore "appear reasonably related to the police's administrative concerns."[1323]

8.3.2.2. Physical sobriety tests

Once a suspected drunk driver is in custody, the police request that he perform physical sobriety tests or submit to a breathalyzer examination does not constitute "interrogation" within the meaning of *Miranda*. In this regard, the *Muniz* Court noted that when an officer's dialogue with a drunk-driving suspect concerning physical sobriety tests consists primarily of carefully scripted instructions as to how the tests are to be performed, the request and the instructions are "not likely to be perceived as calling for any verbal response and therefore [are] not 'words or actions' constituting custodial interrogation."[1324] Similarly, "*Miranda* does not require suppression of [volunteered statements] made when [a suspected intoxicated motorist is] asked to submit to a breathalyzer examination." Requesting a suspected drunk driver to perform several balance tests, or take a breathalyzer test does not constitute interrogation within the meaning of *Miranda*.[1325]

8.3.3. The public safety exception

In *New York v. Quarles*,[1326] the Supreme Court held that the need for answers to questions in situations which pose a significant threat to the public safety justify a law enforcement officer's delay in advising an arrestee of his *Miranda* rights. In this case, the Court created a "*public safety exception*" to the requirement that *Miranda* warnings be administered before a suspect's answers may be admitted into evidence, and the availability of this exception does not depend upon the subjective motivation of the individual police officers involved.

In *Quarles*, officers were stopped while on patrol by a female who advised the officers that she was just raped. The female gave a particularized description of the suspect and further stated that he ran into a supermarket located nearby and was carrying a gun. The officers located the suspect in the supermarket and proceeded to stop and frisk him. The frisk revealed a concealed shoulder holster, which was empty. At this point, the officers placed the suspect under arrest, handcuffed him, and then asked him one question: "Where is the gun?" The arrestee motioned to the gun's location and the officers immediately recovered a loaded .38 caliber revolver from an empty carton. At this point the officers read the arrestee his rights as required by *Miranda*.

The Court determined that the circumstances in this case presented overriding considerations of public safety to justify the officers' failure to administer *Miranda* warnings before they asked a question devoted to locating the abandoned gun. "Public safety must be paramount to adherence to the literal language of the prophylactic rules enunciated in *Miranda*." Here, the police were presented with the immediate necessity of ascertaining the location of a gun which they had every reason to believe the suspect had just removed from his holster and discarded in the supermarket. So long as the gun was concealed somewhere in the supermarket, with its whereabouts unknown, it posed many significant dangers to the public safety. Administration of *Miranda* in such circumstances might deter a suspect from responding and have a result of creating a significant danger to the public – that of a concealed loaded gun in a public area.

Texas courts presently follow the public safety exception to *Miranda* as set out in *Quarles*. At least one court has ruled that the public safety exception applies not only to the federal *Miranda* issue, but to the application of the statutory *Miranda* protections found in Article 38.22 of the Code of Criminal Procedure.[1327]

[1322] *Pennsylvania v. Muniz*, 496 U.S. 582, 110 S. Ct. 2638, 2650 (1990).

[1323] *Pennsylvania v. Muniz*, 496 U.S. 582, 110 S. Ct. 2638, 2650 (1990).

[1324] *Pennsylvania v. Muniz*, 496 U.S. 582, 603, 110 S. Ct. 2638, 2651 (1990).

[1325] *Pennsylvania v. Muniz*, 496 U.S. 582, 604, 110 S. Ct. 2638, 2652 (1990); *Jones v. State*, 795 S.W.2d 171 (Tex. Crim. App. 1990).

[1326] *New York v. Quarles*, 467 U.S. 649, 104 S. Ct. 2626 (1984).

[1327] See *Bryant v. State*, 816 S.W.2d 554, 557 (Tex. App. 1991). *See also Wicker v. State*, 740 S.W.2d 779, 786 (Tex. Crim. App. 1987) ("the protection afforded by *Miranda* is inapplicable in those situations in which there is a prompt or immediate concern for public safety")(citing *Quarles* with approval).

Are the police required to give *Miranda* warnings to a suspect who is in custody before asking him the location of a kidnapped child? In *State v. Mata*,[1328] the Court said "no." The facts unfolded when a fifteen-year-old girl was kidnapped. Defendant called the girl's mother and demanded a ransom of $300 for her release. Antonio Porraz, an Investigator in the Major Crimes Unit of the Hidalgo County Sheriff's Office, posed as a friend of the mother to negotiate the trade. While he talked on the phone with defendant, Investigator Chavez had defendant's cell phone "pinged," and they were able to trace the phone's location. Surveillance was set up and when defendant left his location in a vehicle, the phone's "pinged" location matched his movements. Thereafter, the investigators had a marked police car – driven by Deputy Canales – stop defendant's vehicle. Porraz and Chavez arrived on the scene and questioned defendant regarding the kidnapped girl. They did not administer *Miranda* warnings. During "aggressive" questioning, defendant said he would help locate the girl, and ultimately revealed the child's location.

As in *New York v. Quarles*,[1329] the Court concluded that "the need for answers to questions in a situation posing a threat to the public safety outweighs the need for the prophylactic rule protecting the Fifth Amendment's privilege against self-incrimination."[1330] According to the *Mata* Court:

> [E]verything the Supreme Court said in Quarles applies with at least as much force to the kidnapping of a child. Even the kidnapping and holding of an adult is a very serious matter. When a child has been kidnapped, the State's interests are at their zenith. The State has a compelling interest in protecting the well-being of its children. We have recognized that even the slightest chance of rescuing a live, kidnapped child justifies overriding the attorney-client privilege.... Police officers need to have freedom to rely upon their instincts when it comes to rescuing kidnapping victims, especially when those victims are children. The possibility that warnings will deter a suspect from giving information leading to the rescue of a child is not worth the societal cost. In fact, saying that a suspect has a "right to remain silent" hardly makes sense when the question is, "Where is the kidnapped child?"
>
> The Supreme Court recognized that the small loss of clarity to the *Miranda* rule was justified in light of the interests underlying the "public safety" exception. We see no further loss of clarity in recognizing that the "public safety" exception extends to attempts to find a kidnapped child. The *Quarles* case involved the location of a weapon, but its rationale was broader than that, and that rationale easily applies to a situation involving a kidnapped child. We conclude that the *Miranda* rule poses no bar to the admission of the roadside statements in this case.[1331]

8.3.4. The impeachment exception

The "impeachment exception" to *Miranda*'s exclusionary rule provides the prosecution with a means to rebut a defendant's false or fabricated testimony, or attack the credibility of a defendant who offers testimony that contradicts a previously given, albeit inadmissible, statement. In *Walder v. United States*,[1332] the U.S. Supreme Court carved out an exception to the exclusionary rule for purposes of impeaching a defendant's credibility at trial. The Court explained: "It is one thing to say that the Government cannot make an affirmative use of evidence unlawfully obtained. It is quite another to say that the defendant can turn the illegal method by which evidence in the Government's possession was obtained to his own advantage, and provide himself with a shield against contradiction of his untruths."[1333]

1328 *State v. Mata*, 2021 Tex. Crim. App. LEXIS 606.

1329 *New York v. Quarles*, 467 U.S. 649, 104 S. Ct. 2626 (1984).

1330 *State v. Mata*, 2021 Tex. Crim. App. LEXIS 606, at *5 (citation omitted).

1331 *State v. Mata*, 2021 Tex. Crim. App. LEXIS 606, at *6 -*7.

1332 *Walder v. United States*, 347 U.S. 62, 74 S. Ct. 354 (1954).

1333 *Walder v. United States*, 347 U.S. 62, 65, 74 S. Ct. 354, 356 (1954); *see also Harris v. New York*, 401 U.S. 222, 91 S. Ct. 643 (1971) ("The shield provided by *Miranda* cannot be perverted into a license to use perjury by way of a defense, free from the risk of confrontation with prior inconsistent utterances."); *Oregon v. Hass*, 420 U.S. 714, 723, 95 S. Ct. 1215, 1223 (1975).

8.3.5. Physical fruits of an unwarned statement

In *United States v. Patane*,[1334] the Supreme Court declined to extend the fruit of the poisonous tree doctrine to exclude physical evidence obtained through voluntary but unwarned confessions. There, the officer attempted to read the defendant his rights, and the defendant interrupted and informed the officer that he was aware of his rights. The officer proceeded to act on information he received prior to the interaction and asked the defendant, a convicted felon, if he had a firearm in his residence. After the defendant hesitated in responding, the officer persisted, and, ultimately, the defendant informed the officer of the location of a pistol in his home, and the officer seized the firearm. Prior to trial, the defendant filed a motion to suppress the pistol, arguing in part that the officer unlawfully obtained the firearm as the fruit of an unwarned statement.

The U.S. Supreme Court held that the admission of the physical fruits of a voluntary statement into evidence will not implicate the Self-Incrimination Clause, finding "no justification for extending the *Miranda* rule to [that] context."[1335] The Court reasoned that "the *Miranda* rule is a prophylactic employed to protect against violations of the Self-Incrimination Clause."[1336] Moreover, the Supreme Court explained that "the core protection afforded by the Self-Incrimination Clause is a prohibition on compelling a criminal defendant to testify against himself at trial[,]" and "[t]he Clause cannot be violated by the introduction of nontestimonial evidence obtained as a result of voluntary statements."[1337] Finally, the Court drew an important distinction between unreasonable searches that violate the Fourth Amendment and failure to properly "Mirandize" a suspect, and concluded that the exclusion of unwarned statements at trial is a sufficient remedy for *Miranda* violations.[1338]

8.4. Events surrounding the interrogation process

8.4.1. Invocation of rights

8.4.1.1. The right to remain silent

The Supreme Court in *Miranda v. Arizona* was very clear in its command that once a suspect invokes his or her right to remain silent, "all questioning must cease." An individual who seeks to invoke his right to remain silent must do so unambiguously.[1339] *Miranda* did not discuss, however, whether, and under what circumstances, law enforcement authorities may resume questioning the suspect. In *Michigan v. Mosley*,[1340] the U.S. Supreme Court revisited this issue and noted that a strict, literal reading of the phrase "all questioning must cease" would lead to "absurd and unintended results."[1341] According to the Court, "a blanket prohibition against the taking of voluntary statements or a permanent immunity from further interrogation, regardless of the circumstances, would transform the *Miranda* safeguards into wholly irrational obstacles to legitimate police investigative activity, and deprive suspects of an opportunity to make informed and intelligent assessments of their interests."[1342]

Accordingly, the *Mosley* Court concluded that *Miranda* did not impose an absolute ban on the resumption of questioning following an invocation of the right to remain silent by a person in custody. The Court held that "the admissibility of statements obtained after the person in custody has decided to remain silent

---

[1334] *United States v. Patane*, 542 U.S. 630, 124 S. Ct. 2620 (2004).

[1335] *United States v. Patane*, 542 U.S. 630, 636-37, 124 S. Ct. 2620 (2004). *See also Pugh v. State*, 2021 Tex. Crim. App. LEXIS 566, at *6 ("[A] failure to comply with Miranda is not a valid basis for suppressing the physical fruits of a custodial statement."); *Contreras v. State*, 312 S.W.3d 566, 582-83 (Tex. Crim. App. 2010).

[1336] *United States v. Patane*, 542 U.S. 630, 636, 124 S. Ct. 2620 (2004).

[1337] *United States v. Patane*, 542 U.S. 630, 637, 124 S. Ct. 2620 (2004).

[1338] *United States v. Patane*, 542 U.S. 630, 641-42, 124 S. Ct. 2620 (2004).

[1339] *Berghuis v. Thompkins*, 560 U.S. 370, 381-82, 130 S. Ct. 2250 (2010). In *Berghuis*, the United States Supreme Court determined that defendant's prolonged silence in response to police questioning did not constitute an unambiguous invocation of the right to remain silent. The Court noted that defendant never said that "he wanted to remain silent" or that "he did not want to talk with the police" and held that if he had "made either of these simple, unambiguous statements, he would have invoked his 'right to cut off questioning.'" *Id.* at 382 (citing *Michigan v. Mosley*, 423 U.S. 96, 103, 96 S. Ct. 321 (1975)).

[1340] *Michigan v. Mosley*, 423 U.S. 96, 96 S. Ct. 321 (1975).

[1341] *Michigan v. Mosley*, 423 U.S. 96, 102, 96 S. Ct. 321, 325 (1975).

[1342] *Michigan v. Mosley*, 423 U.S. 96, 102, 96 S. Ct. 321, 325 (1975).

depends under *Miranda* on whether his 'right to cut off questioning' was 'scrupulously honored.'"[1343] Mosley's expression of his desire to remain silent was deemed "scrupulously honored" based on the facts that: (1) Mosley had been advised of his *Miranda* rights before both interrogations; (2) the officer conducting the first interrogation immediately ceased all questioning when Mosley expressed his desire to remain silent; (3) the second interrogation occurred after a significant time lapse; (4) the second interrogation was conducted in another location; (5) by another officer; and (6) it related to a different offense.

8.4.1.1.1. Booking questions

May an accused be deemed to have invoked his Fifth Amendment privilege simply by remaining silent during pedigree questioning? In *United States v. Montana*,[1344] the Second Circuit said yes. Generally, after receiving the *Miranda* warnings, an accused's silence in the face of repeated questioning "has been held sufficient to invoke the Fifth Amendment privilege,... or at least sufficient to create an ambiguity requiring the authorities either to cease interrogation or to limit themselves to clarifying questions[.]"[1345] In *Montana*, the Second Circuit could see "no basis for distinguishing silence in the face of pedigree questions from silence in the face of more substantive interrogation."[1346] "If a suspect refuses to answer even non-incriminating pedigree questions," reasoned the court, "the interrogating officer cannot reasonably conclude that he will immediately thereafter consent to answer incriminating ones."[1347] The court held, therefore, that an in-custody accused invokes his right to remain silent by declining to answer pedigree questions.[1348]

8.4.1.1.2. A suspect's silence and impeachment

A suspect's silence after being arrested and read the *Miranda* warnings cannot be used at trial to impeach the suspect.[1349] *Doyle's* rule does not apply – *i.e.*, a defendant's silence may be used to impeach his exculpatory testimony – if the silence occurred either (1) before arrest or (2) after arrest and before *Miranda* warnings were given.[1350] This is because, under the United States Constitution, use of a defendant's silence only deprives a defendant of due process when the government has given the defendant a reason to believe both that he has a right to remain silent and that his invocation of that right will not be used against him, which typically only occurs post-arrest and post-*Miranda*.

8.4.1.2. The right to counsel

When an in-custody suspect requests counsel, all questioning must stop. This was made clear by the Supreme Court in *Edwards v. Arizona*.[1351] *Edwards* held that once a suspect invokes the right to counsel, "a valid waiver of that right cannot be established by showing only that he responded to further *police initiated* custodial interrogation even if he has been advised of his rights."[1352]

Although the Fifth Amendment privilege against self-incrimination does not expressly provide for the right to counsel, courts construe that right as implicitly existing in the Fifth-Amendment setting as a "preventative measure" that protects an accused from self-incrimination. The correlative right to counsel found

---

1343 *Michigan v. Mosley*, 423 U.S. 96, 102-03, 96 S. Ct. 321, 326 (1975).
1344 *United States v. Montana*, 958 F.2d 516 (2d Cir. 1992).
1345 *United States v. Montana*, 958 F.2d 516, 518 (2d Cir. 1992) (citations omitted).
1346 *United States v. Montana*, 958 F.2d 516, 518 (2d Cir. 1992) (citations omitted).
1347 *United States v. Montana*, 958 F.2d 516, 518 (2d Cir. 1992) (citations omitted).
1348 *United States v. Montana*, 958 F.2d 516, 517 (2d Cir. 1992).
1349 *Doyle v. Ohio*, 426 U.S. 610, 619, 96 S. Ct. 2240, 2245 (1976) ("After an arrested person is formally advised by an officer of the law that he has a right to remain silent, the unfairness occurs when the prosecution, in the presence of the jury, is allowed to undertake impeachment on the basis of what may be the exercise of that right.").
1350 *See Fletcher v. Weir*, 455 U.S. 603, 605-07, 102 S. Ct. 1309 (1982); *Jenkins v. Anderson*, 447 U.S. 231, 239-40, 100 S. Ct. 2124 (1980).
1351 *Edwards v. Arizona*, 451 U.S. 477, 101 S. Ct. 1880 (1981).
1352 *Edwards v. Arizona*, 451 U.S. 477, 484-85, 101 S. Ct. 1880, 1884-85 (1981).

in the *Miranda* warnings is said to be necessary "to make the process of police interrogation conform to the dictates of the [Fifth Amendment] privilege."[1353]

The assertion of a suspect's right to an attorney while being questioned in police custody is "an invocation of his Fifth Amendment rights, requiring that all interrogation must cease."[1354] If the accused indicates in any manner that he may desire a lawyer, the police may not ask him any further questions or reinitiate questioning "until counsel has been made available to him, *unless the accused himself initiates further communication, exchanges or conversations with the police*."[1355] In these circumstances, courts will question first whether the accused invoked his right to counsel. If so, the inquiry next addresses whether the accused or the police initiated further communications or exchanges about the investigation.

If it is determined that the police initiated further questioning after a previous assertion of the right to counsel, any statements made by the accused will be inadmissible at trial unless, at the time of the second or subsequent questioning, the accused had been given an opportunity "to confer with [an] attorney and to have him present during" the second or subsequent questioning session.[1356] If, however, it is determined that the accused himself initiated further communication, exchanges or conversations about the investigation, the inquiry would then be whether, after providing the accused with a fresh set of *Miranda* warnings, the police received "a valid waiver of the right to counsel and the right to silence[,]" that is, whether the accused voluntarily, knowingly and intelligently waived his rights based on "the totality of the circumstances, including the necessary fact that the accused, not the police, reopened the dialogue with the authorities."[1357]

In *Minnick v. Mississippi*,[1358] the Supreme Court held that once an accused requests counsel during custodial interrogation and is then given the opportunity to consult with an attorney, the police may not thereafter initiate further questioning without the attorney present. According to the Court, "when counsel is requested, interrogation must cease, and officials may not reinitiate interrogation without counsel present, whether or not the accused has consulted with his attorney."[1359] Clearly, "the Fifth Amendment protection of *Edwards* is not terminated or suspended by consultation with counsel." The requirement dictates that counsel be *present* during the interrogation.

In *Smith v. Illinois*,[1360] the Court pointed out that, on occasion, an accused's asserted request for counsel may be ambiguous or equivocal. But in this case, no one has pointed to anything Smith previously had said that might have cast doubt on the meaning of his statement, "I'd like to do that," upon learning that he had the right to his counsel's presence. Nor is there anything in that statement itself which would suggest anything inherently ambiguous or equivocal. "Where nothing about the request for counsel or the circumstances leading up to the request would render it ambiguous, all questioning must cease."

However, in *Davis v. United States*,[1361] the Court held that defendant's "remark to the NIS agents – 'Maybe I should talk to a lawyer' – was not a request for counsel." Consequently, the NIS agents "were not required to stop questioning [defendant], though it was entirely proper for them to clarify whether [defendant] in fact wanted a lawyer."[1362] The Court wrote, "after a knowing and voluntary waiver of the *Miranda* rights, law enforcement officers may continue questioning until and unless the suspect *clearly requests* an attorney."[1363]

1353 *Miranda v. Arizona*, 384 U.S. 436, 466, 86 S. Ct. 1602, 1623 (1966).

1354 *Edwards v. Arizona*, 451 U.S. 477, 485, 101 S. Ct. 1880, 1885 (1981). *See also Upton v. State*, 853 S.W.2d 548 (Tex. Crim. App. 1993).

1355 *Edwards v. Arizona*, 451 U.S. 477, 485, 101 S. Ct. 1880, 1885 (1981) (emphasis added).

1356 *Edwards v. Arizona*, 451 U.S. 477, 485, 101 S. Ct. 1880, 1885 (1981); *see also Minnick v. Mississippi*, 498 U.S. 146, 111 S. Ct. 486, 491 (1990) ("when counsel is requested, interrogation must cease, and officials may not reinitiate interrogation without counsel present, whether or not the accused has consulted with his attorney").

1357 *Edwards v. Arizona*, 451 U.S. 477, 486 n.9, 101 S. Ct. 1880, 1885 n.9 (1981).

1358 *Minnick v. Mississippi*, 498 U.S. 146, 111 S. Ct. 486 (1990).

1359 *Minnick v. Mississippi*, 498 U.S. 146, 111 S. Ct. 486, 491 (1990).

1360 *Smith v. Illinois*, 469 U.S. 91, 105 S. Ct. 490 (1984).

1361 *Davis v. United States*, 512 U.S. 452, 114 S. Ct. 2350 (1994).

1362 *Davis v. United States*, 512 U.S. 452, 114 S. Ct. 2350, 2357 (1994).

1363 *See also Ledbetter v. Edwards*, 35 F.3d 1062 (6th Cir. 1994) (defendant's statement – "It would be nice [to have an attorney]" – was too ambiguous to require cessation of questioning); *Upton v. State*, 853 S.W.2d 548 (Tex. Crim. App. 1993);

8.4.1.2.1. A request for counsel during non-custodial questioning

In *McNeil v. Wisconsin*,[1364] the Supreme Court noted: "We have in fact never held that a person can invoke his *Miranda* rights anticipatorily, in a context other than 'custodial interrogation[.]' . . . If the *Miranda* right to counsel can be invoked at a preliminary hearing, it could be argued, there is no logical reason why it could not be invoked by a letter prior to arrest, or indeed even prior to identification as a suspect. Most rights must be asserted when the government seeks to take the action they protect against. The fact that we have allowed the *Miranda* right to counsel, once asserted, to be effective with respect to future custodial interrogation *does not necessarily mean that we will allow it to be asserted initially outside the context of custodial interrogation, with similar effect.*"[1365]

8.4.1.2.2. Conditional requests

May a law enforcement officer continue questioning a suspect after the suspect states that he would not give a written statement unless his attorney was present but has "no problem" talking about the incident? In *Connecticut v. Barrett*,[1366] the U.S. Supreme Court said *yes.* In this case, it was "undisputed that Barrett desired the presence of counsel before making a written statement. Had the police obtained such a statement without meeting the waiver standards of *Edwards*, it would clearly be inadmissible. Barrett's limited requests for counsel, however, were accompanied by affirmative announcements of his willingness to speak with the authorities. The fact that officials took the opportunity provided by Barrett to obtain an oral confession is quite consistent with the Fifth Amendment. *Miranda* gives the defendant a right to choose between speech and silence, and Barrett chose to speak."[1367] Accordingly, Barrett's oral confession was found to be admissible.

8.4.1.2.3. When the accused initiates further conversation

After an accused has been advised of his *Miranda* rights and requests counsel, does his subsequent question of "Well, what is going to happen to me now?" constitute a sufficient *initiation* of further conversation so as to satisfy the rule set forth in *Edwards v. Arizona*? In *Oregon v. Bradshaw*,[1368] the Court said, *yes.* Recall that in *Edwards*, the Court held that "after the right to counsel had been asserted by an accused, further interrogation should not take place 'unless the accused himself *initiates* further communication, exchanges, or conversations with the police.'" The rule was "designed to safeguard an accused in police custody from being badgered by police officers" into confessing. Once the *Edwards* rule is satisfied – that is, it is shown that the accused initiated further conversation with the law enforcement authorities – there is a second inquiry that will be made

---

Dowthitt v. State, 931 S.W.2d 244 (Tex. Crim. App. 1996); *Russell v. State*, 727 S.W.2d 573 (Tex. Crim. App.), *cert. denied*, 484 U.S. 856, 108 S. Ct. 164 (1987); *Dinkins v. State*, 894 S.W.2d 330 (Tex. Crim. App. 1995).

1364 *McNeil v. Wisconsin*, 501 U.S. 171, 111 S. Ct. 2204 (1991).

1365 *McNeil v. Wisconsin*, 501 U.S. 171, 111 S. Ct. 2204, 2211 n.3 (1991) (emphasis added). Relying on *McNeil v. Wisconsin*, an overwhelming number of federal courts have also held that a defendant cannot invoke his *Miranda* rights outside the context of custodial interrogation. *See, e.g., United States v. Bautista*, 145 F.3d 1140, 1151 (10th Cir. 1998) ("we do not suggest that a person can invoke his *Miranda* rights anticipatorily in any situation, *i.e.*, in a context other than custodial interrogation"; *United States v. Grimes*, 142 F.3d 1342, 1348 (11th Cir. 1998) ("*Miranda* rights may be invoked only during custodial interrogation or when interrogation is imminent"); *United States v. LaGrone*, 43 F.3d 332 (7th Cir. 1994); *United States v. Thompson*, 35 F.3d 100, 104 (2d Cir. 1994) (defendant's filing of the notice of appearance "did not occur in the context of custodial interrogation"); *Alston v. Redman*, 34 F.3d 1237, 1246 (3d Cir. 1994) (The *Miranda* right to counsel may not be invoked outside the context of custodial interrogation, in anticipation of a future interrogation; "to be effective, a request for *Miranda* counsel must be made within the context of custodial interrogation and no sooner."); *United States v. Wright*, 962 F.2d 953, 956 (9th Cir. 1992) ("to extend *Miranda-Edwards* protection as [the defendant] urges would, on the other hand, make it virtually impossible for any defendant charged with one crime ever to be questioned about unrelated criminal activity if, the first time in court on the first offense charged, he asked for counsel to be present at future interviews. This would not serve the prophylactic purposes of *Miranda*"); *United States v. Cooper*, 85 F. Supp. 2d 1, 23 (D.D.C. 2000) ("a request for counsel under *Miranda* must be made within the custodial context").

1366 *Connecticut v. Barrett*, 479 U.S. 523, 107 S. Ct. 828 (1987).

1367 *Connecticut v. Barrett*, 479 U.S. 523, 107 S. Ct. 828 (1987).

1368 *Oregon v. Bradshaw*, 462 U.S. 1039, 103 S. Ct. 2830 (1983).

by the courts. The courts will then require the police and the prosecution to demonstrate that the accused thereafter voluntarily, knowingly and intelligently waived his right to counsel and right to remain silent.

8.4.1.2.4. Offenses unrelated to the subject of the initial interrogation

Once a suspect has requested the assistance of counsel during custodial interrogation, may the police subject that suspect to further questioning about an offense that is wholly unrelated to the subject of their initial interrogation? In *Arizona v. Roberson*,[1369] the Supreme Court said *no*. Once a suspect has requested an attorney during custodial interrogation, the police are prohibited from subjecting that suspect to further questioning — regardless of whether that questioning concerns the offense at issue or a wholly unrelated offense — "unless the [suspect] himself initiates further communication, exchanges, or conversations with the police."[1370]

8.4.1.2.5. The *Shatzer* 14-day rule

In *Maryland v. Shatzer*,[1371] the U.S. Supreme Court held that once the suspect has been released from *Miranda* custody for *14 days*, the police may reapproach the suspect and ask whether he is now willing to answer questions. According to the Court, a 14-day period "provides plenty of time for the suspect to get reacclimated to his normal life, to consult with friends and counsel, and to shake off any residual coercive effects of his prior custody."[1372]

Recall that in *Edwards v. Arizona*, the Court created a *presumption* that once a suspect invokes the *Miranda* right to counsel, any waiver of that right in response to a subsequent police attempt at custodial interrogation is *involuntary*. The *Edwards* presumption is designed to preserve "the integrity of an accused's choice to communicate with police only through counsel," by preventing police from badgering him into waiving his previously asserted *Miranda* rights.

In the typical case, the suspect is arrested and is held in uninterrupted pretrial custody while the crime is being actively investigated. While *Edwards* did not address whether this rule survives a break in custody, lower courts have uniformly held that a break in custody ends the *Edwards* presumption. Here, in *Shatzer*, Justice Scalia, speaking for the Court, announced: "[L]aw enforcement officers need to know, with certainty and beforehand, when renewed interrogation is lawful. And while it is certainly unusual for this Court to set forth precise time limits governing police action, it is not unheard-of." Accordingly, 14 days is an appropriate period of time to avoid the consequence of the *Edwards* presumption. "That provides plenty of time for the suspect to get reacclimated to his normal life, to consult with friends and counsel, and to shake off any residual coercive effects of his prior custody."

As with the Fifth Amendment, once the accused has invoked his Sixth Amendment right to counsel after adversary proceedings have been commenced, this assertion must be scrupulously honored by law enforcement officers.

In *Montejo v. Louisiana*,[1373] the Supreme Court determined that if the police initiate interrogation after a defendant's assertion, at an arraignment or similar proceeding, of his right to counsel, any subsequent waiver of the defendant's right to counsel for that police-initiated interrogation will still be *valid*. In this case, the Court took the significant step of overruling *Michigan v. Jackson*,[1374] which had previously held that, "if police initiate interrogation after a defendant's assertion, at an arraignment or similar proceeding, of his right to counsel, any waiver of the defendant's right to counsel for that police-initiated interrogation [was] *invalid*."[1375] According to the Court, there is no reason "to assume that a defendant like Montejo, who has done *nothing at all* to express his intentions with respect to his Sixth Amendment rights, would not be perfectly amenable to speaking with the police without having counsel present. And no reason exists to prohibit the police from inquiring." The rule of *Jackson* was designed "to prevent police from badgering defendants into

---

1369 *Arizona v. Roberson*, 486 U.S. 675, 108 S. Ct. 2093 (1988).

1370 *Arizona v. Roberson*, 486 U.S. 675, 108 S. Ct. 2093, 2096 (1988).

1371 *Maryland v. Shatzer*, 559 U.S. 98, 130 S. Ct. 1213 (2010).

1372 *Maryland v. Shatzer*, 559 U.S. 98, 130 S. Ct. 1213, 1223 (2010).

1373 *Montejo v. Louisiana*, 556 U.S. 778, 129 S. Ct. 2079 (2009).

1374 *Michigan v. Jackson*, 475 U.S. 625, 106 S. Ct. 1404 (1986).

1375 *Michigan v. Jackson*, 475 U.S. 625, 636, 106 S. Ct. 1404, 1411 (1986).

changing their minds about their rights, but a defendant who never asked for counsel has not yet made up his mind in the first instance."

8.4.2. Waiver of rights

8.4.2.1. General aspects

To be valid, a criminal defendant's waiver of his or her rights must be made voluntarily, knowingly, and intelligently, and the government bears the burden of proof. Under the federal Constitution, the prosecution must prove waiver by a "preponderance of the evidence."[1376] When a court assesses the voluntariness of a waiver of rights, it considers the characteristics of the suspect and the totality of the circumstances surrounding the interrogation. Relevant factors will include, but not be limited to:

- The method and context in which the suspect's constitutional rights were read.
- The background, experience and conduct of the suspect, including the suspect's age, education and intelligence.
- The suspect's previous encounters with law enforcement.
- How and by what method the suspect was advised of his constitutional rights.
- The length of the detention.
- The nature of the questioning and whether it was repeated or prolonged.
- Whether physical or mental punishment, coerciveness, or mental exhaustion was involved.
- Whether the suspect was deprived of food, sleep or medical attention.
- Whether the suspect was injured, intoxicated or drugged, or in ill health.
- Whether law enforcement officials made an express promise of leniency or sentence.[1377]

8.4.2.1.1. Voluntariness — a two-step analysis

As a general proposition, the admissibility of a confession depends upon whether it was voluntarily made. "The ultimate issue is whether the confession was the product of an essentially free and unconstrained choice by its maker. 'If it is, if he has willed to confess, it may be used against him. If it is not, if his will has been overborne and his capacity for self-determination critically impaired, the use of his confession offends due process.'"[1378] Unlike the use of physical coercion, however, use of psychologically oriented methods during questioning are not inherently coercive. The critical inquiry in such cases is whether the person's decision to confess results from a free and self-directed choice rather than from an overbearing of the suspect's will.[1379] A court's inquiry into waiver has two distinct dimensions: (1) the relinquishment of the right must have been voluntary in the sense that it was the product of free and deliberate choice rather than intimidation, coercion or deception; and (2) the waiver must have been made with a full awareness of both the nature of the right being abandoned and the consequences of the decision to abandon it.

[1376] *Colorado v. Connelly*, 479 U.S. 157, 107 S. Ct. 515, 523 (1986).

[1377] *See Colorado v. Connelly*, 479 U.S. 157, 107 S. Ct. 515, 522 (1986); *see also Schneckloth v. Bustamonte*, 412 U.S. 218, 226, 93 S. Ct. 2041, 2047-48 (1973).

[1378] *Arizona v. Fulminante*, 499 U.S. 279, 111 S. Ct. 1246, 1261 (1991) (quoting *Culombe v. Connecticut*, 367 U.S. 568, 602, 81 S. Ct. 1860, 1879 (1961)); *see also Blackburn v. Alabama*, 361 U.S. 199, 206, 80 S. Ct. 274, 279 (1960) ("coercion can be mental as well as physical, and ... the blood of the accused is not the only hallmark of an unconstitutional inquisition").

[1379] *See Arizona v. Fulminante*, 499 U.S. 279, 111 S. Ct. 1246, 1252-53 (1991) (confession held involuntary where defendant, an alleged child murderer in danger of physical violence from other inmates, was motivated to confess when a fellow inmate (a government agent) promised to protect him in exchange for the confession); *Payne v. Arkansas*, 356 U.S. 560, 561, 78 S. Ct. 844, 846 (1958) (confession held to be coerced because the interrogating officer had promised that if the accused confessed, the officer would protect him from an angry mob outside the jailhouse door).

8.4.2.1.2. A free and unconstrained choice; inducements to confess

Police are not permitted to employ unreasonable or improper inducements which impair a suspect's decision whether to give a statement or seek legal counsel. The rule applies to those situations where the police prompt an admission or confession by suggesting a benefit if the suspect forgoes his or her rights. This reasoning was first announced in *Bram v. United States*,[1380] where the United States Supreme Court declared: "[A] confession, in order to be admissible, must be free and voluntary: that is, [it] must not be extracted by any sort of threats of violence, nor obtained by any direct or implied promises, however slight, nor by exertion of any improper influence[.]" Involuntariness may also be shown by an express promise of leniency, such as the police telling the defendant that, in return for his cooperation, his punishment would be less severe. Clearly, "threats of physical violence" will "render involuntary a confession obtained thereafter."[1381]

As a general rule, "[a] promise made by a law enforcement officer may render a confession involuntary if it was positive, made or sanctioned by someone with apparent authority, was of some benefit to the defendant and was of such a character as would likely cause a person to speak untruthfully."[1382] In order to determine whether the promise of a benefit is likely to influence a particular suspect to speak untruthfully, courts will "look to whether the circumstances of the promise made the [person] 'inclined to admit a crime he didn't commit.'"[1383]

In *Dykes v. State*,[1384] the court held that, where a police officer made a general statement that he would help the defendant if the defendant cooperated with him, the resulting confession was deemed to be voluntary and not the result of a promise of leniency or a lighter sentence.

Similarly, in *Sorola v. State*,[1385] the court determined that the mere fact that the officer advised the defendant that the officer would inform the district attorney of defendant's cooperation or lack of cooperation was not an improper inducement so as to render the defendant's confession inadmissible.

In *Garcia v. State*,[1386] a police detective told the defendant that if he knew anything about the crimes under investigation, and if he talked to the detective, then the detective would "do whatever [he] could to help him out," including "talk[ing] to the D.A."[1387] Finding that the detective's promise did not amount to an improper inducement, the court said:

> Detective Wilson did *not* promise [defendant] he would not be charged with capital murder[.] ... Detective Wilson did not make any specific promises — only that he would try to "help him out" or would "talk to the D.A." — if [defendant] furnished him information on [another suspect's] involvement in other crimes.
>
> Detective Wilson's statements were not made in the course of plea negotiations with [defendant]; nor was he promised anything or tricked into confessing against his will ... Detective Wilson's comments and questions were aimed at getting [defendant] to tell the truth, and as such, were proper].[1388]

In *Medrano v. State*,[1389] the court ruled that a discussion of religion and possible salvation did not constitute an inducement by the state. The detective told the defendant that a confession was the only way he could "break the chains and kill the demon" [driving the defendant to commit crimes]. The defendant claimed this was a promise of salvation from the detective. The court disagreed, noting that the detective had no authority to confer any religious benefit to the defendant. The court commented that "any alleged statement that

---

[1380] *Bram v. United States*, 168 U.S. 532, 542-43, 18 S. Ct. 183, 187 (1897).

[1381] *See, e.g., Lynum v. Illinois*, 372 U.S. 528, 537, 83 S. Ct. 917 (1963) (defendant's confession involuntary when police told her that her state financial aid would be cut off and her six children taken from her unless she "cooperated" with them).

[1382] *Garcia v. State*, 919 S.W.2d 370, 388 (Tex. Crim. App. 1996). *See also Freeman v. State*, 723 S.W.2d 727 (Tex. Crim. App. 1986); *Jacobs v. State*, 787 S.W.2d 397 (Tex. Crim. App. 1990).

[1383] *Garcia v. State*, 919 S.W.2d 370, 388 (Tex. Crim. App. 1996) (quoting *Sossamon v. State*, 816 S.W.2d 340, 345 (Tex. Crim. App. 1991)).

[1384] *Dykes v. State*, 657 S.W.2d 796 (Tex. Crim. App. 1983).

[1385] *Sorola v. State*, 674 S.W.2d 809 (Tex. App. 1984).

[1386] *Garcia v. State*, 919 S.W.2d 370 (Tex. Crim. App. 1996).

[1387] *Garcia v. State*, 919 S.W.2d 370, 388 (Tex. Crim. App. 1996).

[1388] *Garcia v. State*, 919 S.W.2d 370, 388 (Tex. Crim. App. 1996).

[1389] *Medrano v. State*, ___ S.W.3d ___, 2019 Tex. App. LEXIS 3882 (Tex. App. – San Antonio [4th Dist.] May 15, 2019).

there may be a possibility that God would give [defendant] a chance to put his life back together pertains to a future event. 'A prediction about future events' is not the same as a 'promise.'"[1390] Moreover, this court "has held that references to God and seeking forgiveness for mistakes do not rise to the level of a promise."[1391]

8.4.2.1.2.1. A knowing and intelligent choice

The question of whether a waiver of rights was the product of force, threat, duress, improper influence, or any other type of coercive police activity is only half the equation. The second step in the inquiry questions whether the waiver was given "knowingly and intelligently." Among other things, this requires that the administration of the *Miranda* warnings be more than a mere perfunctory exercise. This second aspect requires that the defendant comprehend the plain meaning of his basic *Miranda* rights. Here, the prosecution will be asked to show that any such waiver was not only knowing and voluntary, but that the suspect understood the right that he or she was waiving.

Knowledge of all the subjects of questioning. In *Colorado v. Spring*,[1392] the United States Supreme Court held that "a suspect's awareness of all the possible subjects of questioning in advance of interrogation is not relevant to determining whether the suspect voluntarily, knowingly, and intelligently waived his Fifth Amendment privilege." Spring had been arrested for firearms violations. Prior to his arrest, law enforcement agents received information that Spring killed a man in Colorado. Spring signed a written form stating that he understood and waived his *Miranda* rights but was not advised as to the topics of the interrogation. After being questioned about the firearms violations, law enforcement agents inquired whether Spring had shot anyone. Spring admitted, "I shot another guy once." Agents then asked Spring if he shot a man in Colorado, which he denied. In a subsequent interrogation and while still under arrest for the firearms violations, Spring was again given the *Miranda* warnings, signed a written waiver, and admitted that he killed a man in Colorado. On appeal, Spring argued that he did not waive his *Miranda* rights during the first interview because "he was not informed that he would be questioned about the Colorado murder."

Finding the *Miranda* waiver valid, the Court observed that a waiver of Fifth Amendment rights depends upon: (1) whether the decision was a deliberate choice or the product of intimidation, coercion, or deception; and (2) made with full awareness of the nature of the right being abandoned and the consequences of the decision to abandon it. According to the Court, "[t]he Constitution does not require that a criminal suspect know and understand every possible consequence of a waiver of the Fifth Amendment privilege." Nor will mere silence by law enforcement officials as to the subject matter of an interrogation constitute "trickery" sufficient to invalidate a suspect's waiver of *Miranda* rights, and we expressly decline so to hold today." Indeed, "we have never read the Constitution to require that the police supply a suspect with a flow of information to help him calibrate his self-interest in deciding whether to speak or stand by his rights."[1393]

Implied waivers. Although the State need not show that a waiver of *Miranda* rights was express," the giving of an uncoerced statement following the provision of *Miranda* warnings, may be sufficient to demonstrate a valid waiver."[1394] Thus, an "implicit waiver" of the right to remain silent may be "sufficient to admit a suspect's statement into evidence."[1395] To establish "an implied waiver of the right to remain silent," the State must show "that a *Miranda* warning was given and that it was understood by the accused."[1396] "As a general proposition, the law can presume that an individual who, with a full understanding of his or her rights, acts in a manner inconsistent with their exercise has made a deliberate choice to relinquish the protection those rights afford."[1397]

1390 *Medrano v. State*, ___ S.W.3d ___, ___, 2019 Tex. App. LEXIS 3882 (Tex. App. – San Antonio [4th Dist.] May 15, 2019) (citing *Mason v. State*, 116 S.W.3d 248, 260 (Tex. App. – Houston [14th Dist.] 2003)).

1391 *Medrano v. State*, ___ S.W.3d ___, ___, 2019 Tex. App. LEXIS 3882 (Tex. App. – San Antonio [4th Dist.] May 15, 2019).

1392 *Colorado v. Spring*, 479 U.S. 564, 577, 107 S. Ct. 851 (1987).

1393 *Colorado v. Spring*, 479 U.S. 564, 577, 107 S. Ct. 851 (1987).

1394 *See Berghuis v. Thompkins*, 560 U.S. 370, 384, 130 S. Ct. 2250 (2010).

1395 *Berghuis v. Thompkins*, 560 U.S. 370, 384, 130 S. Ct. 2250 (2010) (citing *North Carolina v. Butler*, 441 U.S. 369, 376, 99 S. Ct. 1755 (1979)).

1396 *Berghuis v. Thompkins*, 560 U.S. 370, 384, 130 S. Ct. 2250 (2010).

1397 *Berghuis v. Thompkins*, 560 U.S. 370, 385, 130 S. Ct. 2250 (2010).

8.4.2.1.3. Juveniles

A knowing and intelligent waiver of *Miranda* also means that the suspect had the ability to understand the very words used in the warnings. It need not mean the ability to understand far-reaching legal and strategic effects of waiving one's rights, or to appreciate how widely or deeply an interrogation may probe, or to withstand the influence of stress or fancy; but to waive rights intelligently and knowingly, one must at least understand basically what those rights encompass and minimally what their waiver will entail.[1398]

Under Texas law, mental illness or diminished capacity, standing alone, will not render a confession involuntary. "Evidence of mental retardation and mental impairment is a factor to be considered by the court in determining from the totality of the circumstances whether the accused voluntarily and knowingly waived his rights prior to confessing."[1399] "The main question is whether the accused's mental impairment is so severe that he is incapable of understanding the meaning and effect of his confession."[1400] Moreover, a confession "will not be considered involuntary absent police coercion 'casually related to the confession.'"[1401]

8.4.2.1.4. Intoxicated suspects

Suspects who are in pain, intoxicated or on drugs may not be able to give a knowing, intelligent and voluntary waiver. In such cases, the prosecution has the burden of showing by a preponderance of the evidence that the waiver was voluntary, knowing and intelligent.[1402]

8.4.2.1.5. Lying to a suspect

Lying to a suspect will not, by itself, render a confession involuntary. In *Frazier v. Cupp*,[1403] the United States Supreme Court held that the defendant's confession was admissible notwithstanding the fact that the police falsely told him that another person had confessed. The Court noted that the defendant was a mature person of normal intelligence and that the questioning session lasted only slightly over an hour.[1404]

In *Frazier*, the police falsely told a defendant that his co-defendant had already confessed. The court concluded that "the fact that the police misrepresented the statements [the co-defendant] had made is, while relevant, insufficient in our view to make this otherwise voluntary confession inadmissible."[1405]

In *Holland v. McGinnis*,[1406] the court stated that "of the numerous varieties of police trickery," a "lie that relates to a suspect's connection to the crime is the least likely to render a confession involuntary." The court went on to say the following:

> Such misrepresentations, of course, may cause a suspect to confess, but causation alone does not constitute coercion; if it did, all confessions following interrogations would be involuntary because "it can almost always be said that the interrogation caused the confession." ... Thus, the issue is not causation, but the degree of improper coercion, and in this instance the degree was slight. Inflating

---

1398 *See* Larry E. Holtz, *Miranda in a Juvenile Setting: A Child's Right to Silence*, 78 J. Crim. L. & Criminology 534, 536-37, 546-56 (1987) (citing evidence that most youths lack proper comprehension of rights under police interrogation; providing a simplified version of *Miranda* warnings – a "Youth Rights Form."). *Compare Reno v. Flores*, 507 U.S. 292, 113 S. Ct. 1439, 1451 (1993) ("juveniles are capable" – at least 16- and 17-year-olds – "of 'knowingly and intelligently' waiving their right against self-incrimination") (citing *Fare v. Michael C.*, 442 U.S. 707, 724-27, 99 S. Ct. 2560, 2571-73 (1979), and *United States v. Saucedo-Velasquez*, 843 F.2d 832, 835 (5th Cir. 1988) (applying *Fare* to an alien juvenile)).

1399 *Cornealius v. State*, 870 S.W.2d 169, 175 (Tex. App. 1994). *See also Bizzarri v. State*, 492 S.W.2d 944, 946 (Tex. Crim. App. 1973).

1400 *Cornealius v. State*, 870 S.W.2d 169, 175 (Tex. App. 1994).

1401 *Cornealius v. State*, 870 S.W.2d 169, 175 (Tex. App. 1994) (quoting *Walker v. State*, 842 S.W.2d 301 (Tex. App. 1992) (citing *Colorado v. Connelly*, 479 U.S. 157, 164 (1986)). *See also Smith v. State*, 779 S.W.2d 417, 428 (Tex. Crim. App. 1989).

1402 *Colorado v. Connelly*, 479 U.S. 157 (1986).

1403 *Frazier v. Cupp*, 394 U.S. 731, 89 S. Ct. 1420 (1969).

1404 *Frazier v. Cupp*, 394 U.S. 731, 739, 89 S. Ct. 1420, 1425 (1969).

1405 *Frazier v. Cupp*, 394 U.S. 731, 739, 89 S. Ct. 1420, 1425 (1969).

1406 *Holland v. McGinnis*, 963 F.2d 1044, 1051 (7th Cir. 1992).

evidence of Holland's guilt interfered little, if at all, with his "free and deliberate choice" of whether to confess, ... for it did not lead him to consider anything beyond his own beliefs regarding his actual guilt or innocence, his moral sense of right and wrong, and his judgment regarding the likelihood that the police had garnered enough valid evidence linking him to the crime. In other words, the deception did not interject the type of extrinsic considerations that would overcome Holland's will by distorting an otherwise rational choice of whether to confess or remain silent.[1407]

8.4.2.1.6. An initial failure to warn

Does an initial failure of a law enforcement officer to administer *Miranda* warnings "taint" subsequent admissions made after a suspect has been fully advised of, and has waived, his constitutional rights? In *Oregon v. Elstad*,[1408] the Supreme Court said *no*. A suspect "who has once responded to unwarned yet uncoercive questioning is not thereby disabled from waiving his rights and confessing after he has been given the requisite *Miranda* warnings."[1409] Said the Court:

> [A]bsent deliberately coercive or improper tactics in obtaining the initial statement, the mere fact that a suspect has made an unwarned admission does not warrant a presumption of compulsion. A subsequent administration of *Miranda* warnings to a suspect who has given a voluntary but unwarned statement ordinarily should suffice to remove the conditions that precluded admission of the earlier statement. In such circumstances, the finder of fact may reasonably conclude that the suspect made a rational and intelligent choice whether to waive or invoke his rights.[1410]

8.4.2.1.7. Deliberate "end runs" around *Miranda*

In *Missouri v. Seibert*,[1411] the Court addressed the technique of interrogating in successive, unwarned and warned phases. At the trial court level, one of the officers testified that the strategy of withholding *Miranda* warnings until after interrogating and drawing out a confession was promoted not only by his own department, but by a national police training organization. The object of "question first" / "warn later" is to render *Miranda* warnings ineffective by waiting for a particularly opportune time to give them, after the suspect has already confessed. Finding such a practice *improper*, the Court said:

> By any objective measure, ... it is likely that if the interrogators employ the technique of withholding warnings until after interrogation succeeds in eliciting a confession, the warnings will be ineffective in preparing the suspect for successive interrogation, close in time and similar in content. After all, the reason that question-first is catching on is as obvious as its manifest purpose, which is to get a confession the suspect would not make if he understood his rights at the outset; the sensible underlying assumption is that with one confession in hand before the warnings, the interrogator can count on getting its duplicate, with trifling additional trouble.
>
> Upon hearing warnings only in the aftermath of interrogation and just after making a confession, a suspect would hardly think he had a genuine right to remain silent, let alone persist in so believing once the police began to lead him over the same ground again. A more likely reaction on a suspect's part would be perplexity about the reason for discussing rights at that point, bewilderment being an unpromising frame of mind for knowledgeable decision. What is worse, telling a suspect that "anything you say can and will be used against you," without expressly excepting the statement just given, could lead to an entirely reasonable inference that what he has just said will be used, with subsequent silence being of no avail. Thus, when *Miranda* warnings are inserted in the midst of coordinated and continuing

---

1407 *Holland v. McGinnis*, 963 F.2d 1044, 1051 (7th Cir. 1992).

1408 *Oregon v. Elstad*, 470 U.S. 298, 105 S. Ct. 1285 (1985).

1409 *Oregon v. Elstad*, 470 U.S. 298, 105 S. Ct. 1285, 1298 (1985).

1410 *Oregon v. Elstad*, 470 U.S. 298, 314, 105 S. Ct. 1285 (1985). *See also Corwin v. State*, 870 S.W.2d 23 (Tex. Crim. App. 1993).

1411 *Missouri v. Seibert*, 542 U.S. 600, 124 S. Ct. 2601 (2004).

interrogation, they are likely to mislead and deprive a defendant of knowledge essential to his ability to understand the nature of his rights and the consequences of abandoning them.[1412]

The Court also rejected the prosecution's argument that a confession repeated at the end of an interrogation sequence envisioned in a question-first strategy is admissible on the authority of *Oregon v. Elstad.*[1413] In *Elstad*, the failure to preliminarily provide the *Miranda* warnings was, at most, an "oversight." The *Elstad* questioning session had "none of the earmarks of coercion."[1414] Thus, it is fair to read *Elstad* as treating the officer's failure to first administer the warnings as "a good-faith *Miranda* mistake, not only open to correction by careful warnings before systematic questioning in that particular case, but posing no threat to warn-first practice generally."[1415]

Here, in *Seibert*, the facts "reveal a police strategy adapted to undermine the *Miranda* warnings. The unwarned interrogation was conducted in the station house, and the questioning was systematic, exhaustive, and managed with psychological skill. When the police were finished there was little, if anything, of incriminating potential left unsaid."[1416]

Accordingly, "[b]ecause the question-first tactic effectively threatens to thwart *Miranda*'s purpose of reducing the risk that a coerced confession would be admitted, and because the facts here do not reasonably support a conclusion that the warnings given could have served their purpose," the Court held that Seibert's post-warning statements were inadmissible.[1417]

Missouri v. Seibert was a plurality opinion. Although a plurality of the justices would consider all two-stage interrogations eligible for a *Seibert* inquiry, Justice Kennedy's opinion narrowed the *Seibert* exception to those cases involving the deliberate use of the two-step procedure to weaken *Miranda*'s protections. In this regard, both the plurality and Justice Kennedy agree that where law enforcement officers deliberately employ a two-step interrogation to obtain a confession and where separations of time and circumstance and additional curative warnings are absent or fail to apprise a reasonable person in the suspect's shoes of his rights, the trial court should suppress the confession. This narrow test – that excludes confessions made after a deliberate, objectively ineffective mid-stream warning – represents most states' application of the *Seibert* holding.[1418]

Thus, when making a suppression determination, a trial court should conduct an initial inquiry into whether the prosecution has established that the police did not deliberately use a two-step interrogation procedure to obtain a confession. If the court determines that the use of the procedure was deliberate, then the court should determine whether curative measures (*e.g.*, an additional warning or a substantial break in time and circumstances between the pre- and post-warning statements) were employed, such that the suspect would understand the import and effect of the warning at the time of the later statement. If not, then the statements should be inadmissible. If, however, the trial court determines that the prosecution established that the police did not deliberately use a two-step technique to undermine *Miranda*, then it should apply the voluntariness test enunciated in *Elstad*.

In *Carter v. State*,[1419] the court expressly adopted Justice Kennedy's concurrence in *Seibert*, noting that it only applied to two-step interrogations that deliberately circumvented the *Miranda* protections. In this case, the officer engaged in "polite conversation" with defendant. During the interview, defendant made incriminating statements in response to a question and the officer immediately stopped defendant and told him he had not been informed of his rights. The officer read the *Miranda* warnings and defendant waived his rights. The interview resumed, but the officer did not ask any of the questions asked in the pre-warning interview. On appeal, defendant challenged the admission of his post-warning statements, claiming the officer deliberately engaged in a two-step process to undermine his *Miranda* protections. The court disagreed, finding no

---

[1412] *Missouri v. Seibert*, 542 U.S. 600, 124 S. Ct. 2601, 2610-11 (2004).
[1413] *Oregon v. Elstad*, 470 U.S. 298, 105 S. Ct. 1285 (1985).
[1414] *Missouri v. Seibert*, 542 U.S. 600, 124 S. Ct. 2601, 2611 (2004).
[1415] *Missouri v. Seibert*, 542 U.S. 600, 124 S. Ct. 2601, 2612 (2004).
[1416] *Missouri v. Seibert*, 542 U.S. 600, 124 S. Ct. 2601, 2612 (2004).
[1417] *Missouri v. Seibert*, 542 U.S. 600, 124 S. Ct. 2601, 2613 (2004).
[1418] *See, e.g., Verigan v. People*, 2018 CO 53, ¶ 34, 420 P.3d 247, 254 (concluding that "*Seibert* does create a precedential rule, namely, the rule set forth in Justice Kennedy's concurring opinion").
[1419] *Carter v. State*, 309 S.W.3d 31 (Tex. Crim. App. 2010).

evidence that the officer "exhibited hostile, aggressive, or threatening behavior toward [defendant] or that he intended to create a coercive environment."[1420] The pre-warning interview lasted approximately ten seconds, it was stopped as soon as the defendant made an incriminating statement, and the officer did not repeat any of the pre-warning questions. Said the court: "We think these facts do not necessarily exemplify the deliberate 'question first, warn later' gamesmanship so obvious in *Seibert*."[1421]

8.4.2.2. Illegal detention

The United States Supreme Court has held that a confession made by an accused during a period of illegal detention is inadmissible.[1422] The rule is based, in part, on the notion that an unlawful or "unwarranted detention" may lead "to tempting utilization of intensive interrogation, easily gliding into the evils of 'the third degree.'"[1423] The mandate of what is now known as "the *McNabb-Mallory* rule," was handed down by the Court in the context of its supervisory authority over the federal courts, and for the purpose of adequately enforcing "the congressional requirement of prompt arraignment."[1424] It is not, therefore, constitutionally compelled.[1425]

8.4.2.3. Outside influences

Often in the interrogation process, factors outside or extrinsic to the actual questioning session may work to undermine the integrity of the process or the voluntariness of the defendant's responses. How an officer deals with such outside influences will, in many cases, determine the admissibility of any statements the defendant may make.

In *Moran v. Burbine*,[1426] the Supreme Court held that law enforcement officers were permitted to continue to question a person who was in custody and who has properly waived his *Miranda* rights without telling him that a lawyer (who was contacted by his sister) has been trying to reach him. In this regard, the conduct of the police in failing to advise a suspect in custody that a lawyer (who was contacted by the suspect's sister) has been trying to reach him has no bearing on the validity of the waiver of his *Miranda* rights. "Events occurring outside of the presence of the suspect and entirely unknown to him surely can have no bearing on the capacity to comprehend and knowingly relinquish a constitutional right."

Be aware that the Texas Court of Criminal Appeals has never formally adopted the *Burbine* standard[1427] although intermediate Texas courts have.[1428]

A suspect's internal compulsion to confess. In *Colorado v. Connelly*,[1429] the accused, who suffered from "command hallucinations" incident to chronic schizophrenia, heard the "voice of God" telling him to confess. The United States Supreme Court held that his confession was not "coerced" within the meaning of the Fifth Amendment because it was not the product of police overreaching. Observing that the Fifth Amendment

[1420] *Carter v. State*, 309 S.W.3d 31, 40 (Tex. Crim. App. 2010).

[1421] *Carter v. State*, 309 S.W.3d 31, 41 (Tex. Crim. App. 2010).

[1422] *Mallory v. United States*, 354 U.S. 449, 455, 77 S. Ct. 1356, 1360 (1957); *McNabb v. United States*, 318 U.S. 332, 344-45, 63 S. Ct. 608, 615 (1943).

[1423] *Mallory v. United States*, 354 U.S. 449, 453, 77 S. Ct. 1356, 1358 (1957).

[1424] *Mallory v. United States*, 354 U.S. 449, 463, 77 S. Ct. 1356, 1359 (1957).

[1425] *See also Taylor v. Alabama*, 457 U.S. 687, 102 S. Ct. 2664, 2667 (1982) (A confession "obtained through custodial interrogation after an illegal arrest should be excluded unless intervening events break the causal connection between the illegal arrest and confession so that the confession is sufficiently an act of free will" to remove the initial illegality.); *Fuller v. State*, 829 S.W.2d 191 (Tex. Crim. App. 1992) (adopting the four factors set forth in *Taylor* as the appropriate test under Texas law). *See also Comer v. State*, 776 S.W.2d 191 (Tex. Crim. App. 1989); *Bell v. State*, 724 S.W.2d 780 (Tex. Crim. App. 1986).

[1426] *Moran v. Burbine*, 475 U.S. 412, 106 S. Ct. 1135 (1986).

[1427] *Goodwin v. State*, 799 S.W.2d 719 (Tex. Crim. App. 1990).

[1428] *Terrell v. State*, 891 S.W.2d 307 (Tex. App. 1994). For a more comprehensive discussion of the status of the *Burbine* issue in Texas *see* Larry E. Holtz & Warren J Spencer, *Texas Criminal and Traffic Procedural Manual – An In-Depth Guide on How to Apply the Laws of Arrest, Search and Seizure, Confessions, & Eyewitness Identification* (Blue360° Media).

[1429] *Colorado v. Connelly*, 479 U.S. 157, 107 S. Ct. 515 (1986).

simply does not address itself to "moral and psychological pressures to confess emanating from sources other than official coercion," the Court held that "coercive police activity is a necessary predicate" to the finding that a confession is not "voluntary" within the meaning of the Fifth Amendment and the Due Process Clause of the Fourteenth Amendment."[1430]

9. FOREIGN NATIONALS

9.1. Notification of Rights

The Vienna Convention on Consular Relations (VCCR) is a binding multi-lateral treaty to which about 170 nations, including the United States, are parties. It was drafted in 1963 with the purpose, evident in its preamble, of contributing "to 'the development of friendly relations among nations, irrespective of their differing constitutional and social systems.'"[1431] The VCCR addresses the functions of a consular post established by the nation sending the consul (the sending State) in the nation receiving the consul (the receiving State).

Under Article 36(1)(b) (ratified by the United States in 1969), when a foreign national (including an undocumented foreign national or foreign national with a "green card") is arrested or detained on criminal or immigration charges, he or she must be informed *without delay* of the right to have the consular officials of his or her home country notified and the right to communicate with those consular officials. This notice should be given in addition to, not instead of, the *Miranda* warnings.

Most law enforcement agencies have adopted policies and procedures consistent with the standards set forth in the *Standards for Law Enforcement Agencies*, from the Commission on Accreditation for Law Enforcement Agencies, including those for consular notification and access. "Without delay" is generally interpreted to mean that a detained foreign national must be advised of his or her Article 36 rights as soon as law enforcement realizes the person is a foreign national, or is probably a foreign national.

Brief, routine detentions, such as for a traffic violation or accident investigation, do not trigger this requirement. However, if the foreign national is required to accompany a law enforcement officer to a place of detention or is detained for a number of hours or overnight, the consular notification requirement will apply.

In addition, when a foreign national from one of the following countries is arrested or detained, the nearest consular officials *must* be notified without delay, *regardless* of the person's wishes.

These countries include the following:

Albania, Algeria, Anguilla
Antigua and Barbuda, Armenia
Azerbaijan, Bahamas, Barbados
Belarus, Belize, Bermuda
British Virgin Islands, Brunei
Bulgaria, Cayman Islands
China (including Macao and Hong Kong)
Costa Rica, Cyprus, Czech Republic
Dominica, Fiji, Gambia, Georgia
Ghana, Grenada, Guyana, Hungary
Jamaica, Kazakhstan, Kiribati, Kuwait
Kyrgyzstan, Malaysia, Malta, Mauritius
Moldova, Mongolia, Montserrat
Nigeria, Philippines
Poland (nonpermanent residents only)
Romania, Russia, St. Kitts and Nevis
St. Lucia
St. Vincent and the Grenadines
Seychelles, Sierra Leone
Singapore, Slovakia, Tajikistan
Tanzania, Tonga, Trinidad and Tobago
Tunisia, Turkmenistan
Turks and Caicos Islands
Tuvalu, Ukraine
United Kingdom (Residents' passports may bear the name "United Kingdom," or the name of the specific territory, such as Anguilla, Bermuda, British Virgin Islands, Cayman Islands, Montserrat, or the Turks and Caicos Islands)
Uzbekistan, Zambia, Zimbabwe

[1430] *Colorado v. Connelly*, 479 U.S. 157, 170, 107 S. Ct. 515, 522 (1986).
[1431] *See Sanchez-Llamas v. Oregon*, 548 U.S. 331, 337, 126 S. Ct. 2669, 2674 (2006) (quoting VCCR, 21 *U.S.T.* 77, 79 (1963)).

For all other countries, law enforcement must inform the foreign national that they may have their consular officer notified of the arrest or detention and may communicate with them. The foreign national can accept or decline the offer to notify. In all cases, consular notification should be made within 24-72 hours after the initial arrest. Law enforcement should document the response and the notification in the event that there are any questions later.

Note: Under no circumstances should any information indicating that a foreign national may have applied for asylum in the United States or elsewhere be disclosed to that person's government. The following statement is suggested by the U.S. Department of State when consular notification is at the foreign national's option:

As a non-U.S. citizen who is being arrested or detained, you are entitled to have us notify your country's consular representatives here in the United States. A consular official from your country may be able to help you obtain legal counsel and may contact your family and visit you in detention, among other things. If you want us to notify your country's consular officials, you can request this notification now or at any time in the future. After your consular officials are notified, they may call or visit you. Do you want us to notify your country's consular officials?

The following statement is suggested when consular notification is mandatory:

Because of your nationality, we are required to notify your country's consular representatives here in the United States that you have been arrested or detained. After your consular officials are notified, they may call or visit you. You are not required to accept their assistance, but they may be able to help you obtain legal counsel and may contact your family and visit you in detention, among other things. We will be notifying your country's consular officials as soon as possible.

Telephone and fax numbers of the foreign embassies and consulates in the United States and translations of the above statements into selected languages are available at the U.S. Department of State website, http://travel.state.gov.

Although law enforcement officers should make every effort to comply with these requirements, failure to do so is not necessarily a constitutional violation and should not result in the suppression of evidence.[1432]

Regarding individual rights, the Supreme Court has expressly declined to decide whether Article 36 of the Vienna Convention creates individual rights that are enforceable in domestic courts.[1433]

9.2. Waiver of Rights

In a case involving a suspect who is a citizen of another country, a court will still examine the totality of the circumstances surrounding any waiver of Fifth Amendment rights, the same as in a case involving a citizen of the United States. However, the court will pay special attention to such factors as: whether the defendant signed a written waiver; whether the advice of rights was in the defendant's native language; whether the defendant appeared to understand those rights; whether the defendant had the assistance of a

---

1432 *Sanchez-Llamas v. Oregon*, 548 U.S. 331, 126 S. Ct. 2669 (2006); *United States v. Emuegbunam*, 268 F.3d 377 (6th Cir. 2001). *See also United States v. Page*, 232 F.3d 536, 540 (6th Cir. 2000) ("[W]e join our colleagues in the First, Ninth, and Eleventh Circuits in concluding that although some judicial remedies may exist, there is no right in a criminal prosecution to have evidence excluded or an indictment dismissed due to a violation of Article 36.") (citing *United States v. Li*, 206 F.3d 56, 60 (1st Cir. 2000); *United States v. Lombera-Camorlinga*, 206 F.3d 882 (9th Cir. 2000); *United States v. Cordoba-Mosquera*, 212 F.3d 1194 (11th Cir. 2000)).

1433 *See Medellin v. Texas*, 552 U.S. 491, 506 n.4, 128 S. Ct. 1346 (2008) (We "assume, without deciding, that Article 36 grants foreign nationals an individually enforceable right to request that their consular officers be notified of their detention, and an accompanying right to be informed by authorities of the availability of consular notification."). *But see Sanchez-Llamas v. Oregon*, 548 U.S. 331, 346, 126 S. Ct. 2669, 2680 (2006) (noting that the Vienna Convention does not explicitly provide for a judicial remedy, and declining to impose one on state courts).

translator; whether the defendant's rights were explained painstakingly; and whether the defendant had any experience with the American criminal justice system.[1434]

9.3. Diplomatic Immunity

As a principle of international law, "diplomatic immunity" provides that certain foreign government officials are not subject to the jurisdiction of local courts and other authorities for both their official and, to a large extent, their personal activities.

International law requires that law enforcement authorities of the United States extend certain privileges and immunities to members of foreign diplomatic missions and consular posts. The failure of law enforcement officials to fully respect the privileges and immunities of foreign diplomatic and consular personnel may complicate diplomatic relations between the United States and other foreign nations. It also may lead to harsher treatment of U.S. personnel abroad since the principle of reciprocity is integral to diplomatic and consular relations.

Diplomatic immunity does not exempt diplomatic officers from the obligation of conforming with national and local laws and regulations. Diplomatic immunity is not intended to serve as a license for such persons to flout the law and purposely avoid liability for their actions. The purpose of these privileges and immunities is not to benefit individuals but to ensure the efficient and effective performance of their official missions. This is a crucial point for law-enforcement officers to understand in their dealings with foreign diplomatic and consular personnel. While police officers are obliged under international customary and treaty law to recognize the immunity of the envoy, they must not ignore or condone the commission of crimes. The proper performance of police procedures in such cases is often essential in order for the United States to formulate appropriate measures through diplomatic channels to deal with such offenders.[1435]

It is important that the law enforcement authorities of the United States always treat foreign diplomatic and consular personnel with respect and with due regard for the privileges and immunities to which they are entitled under international law. Any shortcomings have the potential of casting into doubt the commitment of the United States to carry out its international obligations or of negatively influencing larger foreign policy interests. Appropriate caution on the part of law enforcement authorities should never escalate into a total "hands off" attitude in connection with criminal law enforcement actions involving diplomats. Foreign diplomats who violate traffic laws should be cited. Allegations of serious crimes should be fully investigated, promptly reported to the Department of State, and procedurally developed to the maximum permissible extent. Local law enforcement authorities should never be inhibited in their efforts to protect the public welfare in extreme situations. The U.S. Department of State should be advised promptly of any serious difficulties arising in connection with diplomatic or consular personnel. It has provided offices to assist police authorities in verifying individuals who may enjoy inviolability or immunity. Police departments should feel free to contact the Department of State for general advice in any matter bearing on diplomatic or consular personnel.

For a comprehensive law enforcement guide on Diplomatic and Consular Immunity, refer to https://www.state.gov/documents/organization/150546.pdf

---

[1434] *United States v. Amano*, 229 F.3d 801 (9th Cir. 2000).

[1435] Excerpts from *Diplomatic and Consular Immunity: Guidance for Law Enforcement and Judicial Authorities*. (United States Department of State, Office of Foreign Missions).

TEXAS CRIMINAL AND TRAFFIC LAW

TABLE OF CONTENTS

PENAL CODE

TABLE OF CONTENTS

TEXAS CRIMINAL AND TRAFFIC LAW

TEXAS CRIMINAL AND TRAFFIC LAW

TABLE OF CONTENTS

TABLE OF CONTENTS

TABLE OF CONTENTS

TABLE OF CONTENTS

TABLE OF CONTENTS

Table of Contents

TABLE OF CONTENTS

TABLE OF CONTENTS

TABLE OF CONTENTS

Table of Contents

TABLE OF CONTENTS

TABLE OF CONTENTS

TABLE OF CONTENTS

TABLE OF CONTENTS

TABLE OF CONTENTS

TABLE OF CONTENTS

TABLE OF CONTENTS

TABLE OF CONTENTS

TABLE OF CONTENTS

TABLE OF CONTENTS

Table of Contents

TABLE OF CONTENTS

TABLE OF CONTENTS

TABLE OF CONTENTS

TEXAS CRIMINAL AND TRAFFIC LAW

TABLE OF CONTENTS

Table of Contents

TABLE OF CONTENTS

Table of Contents

TABLE OF CONTENTS

Table of Contents

TABLE OF CONTENTS

TABLE OF CONTENTS

TABLE OF CONTENTS

TABLE OF CONTENTS

Table of Contents

TABLE OF CONTENTS

TABLE OF CONTENTS

TABLE OF CONTENTS

PENAL CODE

TITLE 1
INTRODUCTORY PROVISIONS

CHAPTER 1
GENERAL PROVISIONS

Sec. 1.01. Short Title.

This code shall be known and may be cited as the Penal Code.

Sec. 1.02. Objectives of Code.

The general purposes of this code are to establish a system of prohibitions, penalties, and correctional measures to deal with conduct that unjustifiably and inexcusably causes or threatens harm to those individual or public interests for which state protection is appropriate. To this end, the provisions of this code are intended, and shall be construed, to achieve the following objectives:

(1) to insure the public safety through:

(A) the deterrent influence of the penalties hereinafter provided;

(B) the rehabilitation of those convicted of violations of this code; and

(C) such punishment as may be necessary to prevent likely recurrence of criminal behavior;

(2) by definition and grading of offenses to give fair warning of what is prohibited and of the consequences of violation;

(3) to prescribe penalties that are proportionate to the seriousness of offenses and that permit recognition of differences in rehabilitation possibilities among individual offenders;

(4) to safeguard conduct that is without guilt from condemnation as criminal;

(5) to guide and limit the exercise of official discretion in law enforcement to prevent arbitrary or oppressive treatment of persons suspected, accused, or convicted of offenses; and

(6) to define the scope of state interest in law enforcement against specific offenses and to systematize the exercise of state criminal jurisdiction.

Sec. 1.03. Effect of Code.

(a) Conduct does not constitute an offense unless it is defined as an offense by statute, municipal ordinance, order of a county commissioners court, or rule authorized by and lawfully adopted under a statute.

(b) The provisions of Titles 1, 2, and 3 apply to offenses defined by other laws, unless the statute defining the offense provides otherwise; however, the punishment affixed to an offense defined outside this code shall be applicable unless the punishment is classified in accordance with this code.

(c) This code does not bar, suspend, or otherwise affect a right or liability to damages, penalty, forfeiture, or other remedy authorized by law to be recovered or enforced in a civil suit for conduct this code defines as an offense, and the civil injury is not merged in the offense.

Sec. 1.04. Territorial Jurisdiction.

(a) This state has jurisdiction over an offense that a person commits by his own conduct or the conduct of another for which he is criminally responsible if:

(1) either the conduct or a result that is an element of the offense occurs inside this state;

(2) the conduct outside this state constitutes an attempt to commit an offense inside this state;

(3) the conduct outside this state constitutes a conspiracy to commit an offense inside this state, and an act in furtherance of the conspiracy occurs inside this state; or

(4) the conduct inside this state constitutes an attempt, solicitation, or conspiracy to commit, or establishes criminal responsibility for the commission of, an offense in another jurisdiction that is also an offense under the laws of this state.

(b) If the offense is criminal homicide, a "result" is either the physical impact causing death or the death itself. If the body of a criminal homicide victim is found in this state, it is presumed that the death occurred in this state. If death alone is the basis for jurisdiction, it is a defense to the exercise of jurisdiction by this state that the conduct that constitutes the offense is not made criminal in the jurisdiction where the conduct occurred.

(c) An offense based on an omission to perform a duty imposed on an actor by a statute of this state is committed inside this state regardless of the location of the actor at the time of the offense.

(d) This state includes the land and water and the air space above the land and water over which this state has power to define offenses.

Sec. 1.05. Construction of Code.

(a) The rule that a penal statute is to be strictly construed does not apply to this code. The provisions of this code shall be construed according to the fair import of their terms, to promote justice and effect the objectives of the code.

(b) Unless a different construction is required by the context, Sections 311.011, 311.012, 311.014, 311.015, and 311.021 through 311.032 of Chapter 311, Government Code (Code Construction Act), apply to the construction of this code.

(c) In this code:

(1) a reference to a title, chapter, or section without further identification is a reference to a title, chapter, or section of this code; and

(2) a reference to a subchapter, subsection, subdivision, paragraph, or other numbered or lettered unit without further identification is a reference to a unit of the next-larger unit of this code in which the reference appears.

Sec. 1.06. Computation of Age.

A person attains a specified age on the day of the anniversary of his birthdate.

Sec. 1.07. Definitions.

(a) In this code:

(1) "Act" means a bodily movement, whether voluntary or involuntary, and includes speech.

(2) "Actor" means a person whose criminal responsibility is in issue in a criminal action. Whenever the term "suspect" is used in this code, it means "actor."

(3) "Agency" includes authority, board, bureau, commission, committee, council, department, district, division, and office.

(4) "Alcoholic beverage" has the meaning assigned by Sec[illegible]holic Beverage Code.

(5) "Anot[illegible]han the actor.

(6) "Assoc[illegible] governmental subd[illegible]nership, or two or more [illegible] common economic interest.

(7) "Benefit" means anything reasonably regarded as economic gain or advantage, including benefit to any other person in whose welfare the beneficiary is interested.

(8) "Bodily injury" means physical pain, illness, or any impairment of physical condition.

(8-a) "Civil commitment facility" means a facility owned, leased, or operated by the state, or by a vendor under contract with the state, that houses only persons who have been civilly committed as sexually violent predators under Chapter 841, Health and Safety Code.

(9) "Coercion" means a threat, however communicated:

(A) to commit an offense;

(B) to inflict bodily injury in the future on the person threatened or another;

(C) to accuse a person of any offense;

(D) to expose a person to hatred, contempt, or ridicule;

(E) to harm the credit or business repute of any person; or

(F) to take or withhold action as a public servant, or to cause a public servant to take or withhold action.

(10) "Conduct" means an act or omission and its accompanying mental state.

(11) "Consent" means assent in fact, whether express or apparent.

(12) "Controlled substance" has the meaning assigned by Section 481.002, Health and Safety Code.

(13) "Corporation" includes nonprofit corporations, professional associations created pursuant to statute, and joint stock companies.

(14) "Correctional facility" means a place designated by law for the confinement of a person arrested for, charged with, or convicted of a criminal offense. The term includes:

(A) a municipal or county jail;

(B) a confinement facility operated by the Texas Department of Criminal Justice;

(C) a confinement facility operated under contract with any division of the Texas Department of Criminal Justice; and

(D) a community corrections facility operated by a community supervision and corrections department.

(15) "Criminal negligence" is defined in Section 6.03 (Culpable Mental States).

(16) "Dangerous drug" has the meaning assigned by Section 483.001, Health and Safety Code.

(17) "Deadly weapon" means:

(A) a firearm or anything manifestly designed, made, or adapted for the purpose of inflicting death or serious bodily injury; or

(B) anything that in the manner of its use or intended use is capable of causing death or serious bodily injury.

(18) "Drug" has the meaning assigned by Section 481.002, Health and Safety Code.

(19) "Effective consent" includes consent by a person legally authorized to act for the owner. Consent is not effective if:

(A) induced by force, threat, or fraud;

(B) given by a person the actor knows is not legally authorized to act for the owner;

(C) given by a person who by reason of youth, mental disease or defect, or intoxication is known by the actor to be unable to make reasonable decisions; or

(D) given solely to detect the commission of an offense.

(20) "Electric generating plant" means a facility that generates electric energy for distribution to the public.

(21) "Electric utility substation" means a facility used to switch or change voltage in connection with the transmission of electric energy for distribution to the public.

(22) "Element of offense" means:

(A) the forbidden conduct;

(B) the required culpability;

(C) any required result; and

(D) the negation of any exception to the offense.

(23) "Felony" means an offense so designated by law or punishable by death or confinement in a penitentiary.

(24) "Government" means:

(A) the state;

(B) a county, municipality, or political subdivision of the state; or

(C) any branch or agency of the state, a county, municipality, or political subdivision.

(25) "Harm" means anything reasonably regarded as loss, disadvantage, or injury, including harm to another person in whose welfare the person affected is interested.

(26) "Individual" means a human being who is alive, including an unborn child at every stage of gestation from fertilization until birth.

(27) [Repealed by Acts 2009, 81st Leg., ch. 87 (S.B. 1969), § 25.144, effective September 1, 2009.]

(28) "Intentional" is defined in Section 6.03 (Culpable Mental States).

(29) "Knowing" is defined in Section 6.03 (Culpable Mental States).

(30) "Law" means the constitution or a statute of this state or of the United States, a written opinion of a court of record, a municipal ordinance, an order of a county commissioners court, or a rule authorized by and lawfully adopted under a statute.

(31) "Misdemeanor" means an offense so designated by law or punishable by fine, by confinement in jail, or by both fine and confinement in jail.

(32) "Oath" includes affirmation.

(33) "Official proceeding" means any type of administrative, executive, legislative, or judicial proceeding that may be conducted before a public servant.

(34) "Omission" means failure to act.

(35) "Owner" means a person who:

(A) has title to the property, possession of the property, whether lawful or not, or a greater right to possession of the property than the actor; or

(B) is a holder in due course of a negotiable instrument.

(36) "Peace officer" means a person elected, employed, or appointed as a peace officer under Article 2.12, Code of Criminal Procedure, Section 51.212 or 51.214, Education Code, or other law.

(37) "Penal institution" means a place designated by law for confinement of persons arrested for, charged with, or convicted of an offense.

(38) "Person" means an individual or a corporation, association, limited liability company, or other entity or organization governed by the Business Organizations Code.

(39) "Possession" means actual care, custody, control, or management.

(40) "Public place" means any place to which the public or a substantial group of the public has access and includes, but is not limited to, streets, highways, and the common areas of schools, hospitals, apartment houses, office buildings, transport facilities, and shops.

(41) "Public servant" means a person elected, selected, appointed, employed, or otherwise designated as one of the following, even if he has not yet qualified for office or assumed his duties:

(A) an officer, employee, or agent of government;

(B) a juror or grand juror; or

(C) an arbitrator, referee, or other person who is authorized by law or private written agreement to hear or determine a cause or controversy; or

(D) an attorney at law or notary public when participating in the performance of a governmental function; or

(E) a candidate for nomination or election to public office; or

(F) a person who is performing a governmental function under a claim of right although he is not legally qualified to do so.

(42) "Reasonable belief" means a belief that would be held by an ordinary and prudent man in the same circumstances as the actor.

(43) "Reckless" is defined in Section 6.03 (Culpable Mental States).

(44) "Rule" includes regulation.

(45) "Secure correctional facility" means:

(A) a municipal or county jail; or

(B) a confinement facility operated by or under a contract with any division of the Texas Department of Criminal Justice.

(46) "Serious bodily injury" means bodily injury that creates a substantial risk of death or that

causes death, serious permanent disfigurement, or protracted loss or impairment of the function of any bodily member or organ.

(46-a) "Sight order" means a written or electronic instruction to pay money that is authorized by the person giving the instruction and that is payable on demand or at a definite time by the person being instructed to pay. The term includes a check, an electronic debit, or an automatic bank draft.

(46-b) "Federal special investigator" means a person described by Article 2.122, Code of Criminal Procedure.

(47) "Swear" includes affirm.

(48) "Unlawful" means criminal or tortious or both and includes what would be criminal or tortious but for a defense not amounting to justification or privilege.

(49) "Death" includes, for an individual who is an unborn child, the failure to be born alive.

(b) The definition of a term in this code applies to each grammatical variation of the term.

Sec. 1.08. Preemption.

No governmental subdivision or agency may enact or enforce a law that makes any conduct covered by this code an offense subject to a criminal penalty. This section shall apply only as long as the law governing the conduct proscribed by this code is legally enforceable.

Sec. 1.09. Concurrent Jurisdiction Under This Code to Prosecute Offenses That Involve State Property.

With the consent of the appropriate local county or district attorney, the attorney general has concurrent jurisdiction with that consenting local prosecutor to prosecute under this code any offense an element of which occurs on state property or any offense that involves the use, unlawful appropriation, or misapplication of state property, including state funds.

Sec. 1.10. Enforcement of Certain Federal Laws Regulating Firearms, Firearm Accessories, and Firearm Ammunition.

(a) In this section:

(1) "Ammunition" has the meaning assigned by Section 229.001, Local Government Code.

(2) "Firearm" has the meaning assigned by Section 46.01.

(3) "Firearm accessory" means an item that is used in conjunction with or mounted on a firearm but is not essential to the basic function of the firearm. The term includes a detachable firearm magazine.

(4) "State funds" means money appropriated by the legislature or money under the control or direction of a state agency.

(b) Notwithstanding any other law, an agency of this state, a political subdivision of this state, or a law enforcement officer or other person employed by an agency of this state or a political subdivision of this state may not contract with or in any other manner provide assistance to a federal agency or official with respect to the enforcement of a federal statute, order, rule, or regulation that:

(1) imposes a prohibition, restriction, or other regulation that does not exist under the laws of this state; and

(2) relates to:

(A) a registry requirement for a firearm, a firearm accessory, or ammunition;

(B) a requirement that an owner of a firearm, a firearm accessory, or ammunition possess a license as a condition of owning, possessing, or carrying the firearm, firearm accessory, or ammunition;

(C) a requirement that a background check be conducted for the private sale or transfer of a firearm, a firearm accessory, or ammunition;

(D) a program for confiscating a firearm, a firearm accessory, or ammunition from a person who is not otherwise prohibited by the laws of this state from possessing the firearm, firearm accessory, or ammunition; or

(E) a program that requires an owner of a firearm, a firearm accessory, or ammunition to sell the firearm, firearm accessory, or ammunition.

(c) Subsection (b) does not apply to a contract or agreement to provide assistance in the enforcement of a federal statute, order, rule, or regulation in effect on January 19, 2021.

(d) A political subdivision of this state may not receive state funds if the political subdivision enters into a contract or adopts a rule, order, ordinance, or policy under which the political subdivision requires or assists with the enforcement of any federal statute, order, rule, or regulation described by Subsection (b) or, by consistent actions, requires or assists with the enforcement of any federal statute, order, rule, or regulation described by Subsection (b). State funds for the political subdivision shall be denied for the fiscal year following the year in which a final judicial determination in an action brought under this section is made that the political subdivision has required or assisted with the enforcement of any federal statute, order, rule, or regulation described by Subsection (b).

(e) Any individual residing in the jurisdiction of a political subdivision of this state may file a complaint with the attorney general if the individual offers evidence to support an allegation that the political subdivision has entered into a contract or adopted a rule, order, ordinance, or policy under which the political subdivision requires or assists with the enforcement of any federal statute, order, rule, or regulation described by Subsection (b) or evidence to support an allegation that the political subdivision, by consistent actions, requires or assists with the enforcement of any federal statute, order, rule, or regulation described by Subsection (b). The individual must include with the complaint the evidence the individual has that supports the complaint.

(f) If the attorney general determines that a complaint filed under Subsection (e) against a political subdivision of this state is valid, the attorney general may file a petition for a writ of mandamus or apply for other appropriate equitable relief in a district court in Travis County or in a county in which the principal office of the political subdivision is located to compel the political subdivision to comply with Subsection (b). The attorney general may recover reasonable expenses incurred in obtaining relief under this subsection, including court costs, reasonable attorney's fees, investigative costs, witness fees, and deposition costs.

(g) An appeal of a suit brought under Subsection (f) is governed by the procedures for accelerated appeals in civil cases under the Texas Rules of Appellate Procedure. The appellate court shall render its final order or judgment with the least possible delay.

(h) The attorney general shall defend any agency of this state in a suit brought against the agency by the federal government for an action or omission consistent with the requirements of this section.

CHAPTER 2
BURDEN OF PROOF

Sec. 2.01. Proof B[illegible]e Doubt.

All person[illegible] innocent and no person m[illegible]n offense unless each elemen[illegible] proved beyond a reasonable dou[illegible]hat he has been arrested, confined, or in[illegible] for, or otherwise charged with, the offense give[illegible] rise to no inference of guilt at his trial.

Sec. 2.02. Exception.

(a) An exception to an offense in this code is so labeled by the phrase: "It is an exception to the application of . . . ."

(b) The prosecuting attorney must negate the existence of an exception in the accusation charging commission of the offense and prove beyond a reasonable doubt that the defendant or defendant's conduct does not fall within the exception.

(c) This section does not affect exceptions applicable to offenses enacted prior to the effective date of this code.

Sec. 2.03. Defense.

(a) A defense to [illegible]nse in this code is so [illegible] defense to prose[illegible]

(b) T[illegible]ey is not required to negate [illegible] a defense in the accusation charging [illegible]mission of the offense.

(c) The issue of the existence of a defense is not submitted to the jury unless evidence is admitted supporting the defense.

(d) If the issue of the existence of a defense is submitted to the jury, the court shall charge that a reasonable doubt on the issue requires that the defendant be acquitted.

(e) A ground of defense in a penal law that is not plainly labeled in accordance with this chapter has the procedural and evidenti[illegible] of a defense.

Sec. 2.04. Af[illegible]

(a) An affir[illegible] defense in this code is so labeled by the phrase: "It is an affirmative defense to prosecution . . . ."

(b) The prosecuting attorney is not required to negate the existence of an affirmative defense in the accusation charging commission of the offense.

(c) The issue of the existence of an affirmative defense is not submitted to the jury unless evidence is admitted supporting the defense.

(d) If the issue of the existence of an affirmative defense is submitted to the jury, the court shall charge that the defendant must prove the affirmative defense by a preponderance of evidence.

Sec. 2.05. Presumption.

(a) Except as provided by Subsection (b), when this code or another penal law establishes a presumption with respect to any fact, it has the following consequences:

(1) if there is sufficient evidence of the facts that give rise to the presumption, the issue of the existence of the presumed fact must be submitted

to the jury, unless the court is satisfied that the evidence as a whole clearly precludes a finding beyond a reasonable doubt of the presumed fact; and

(2) if the existence of the presumed fact is submitted to the jury, the court shall charge the jury, in terms of the presumption and the specific element to which it applies, as follows:

(A) that the facts giving rise to the presumption must be proven beyond a reasonable doubt;

(B) that if such facts are proven beyond a reasonable doubt the jury may find that the element of the offense sought to be presumed exists, but it is not bound to so find;

(C) that even though the jury may find the existence of such element, the state must prove beyond a reasonable doubt each of the other elements of the offense charged; and

(D) if the jury has a reasonable doubt as to the existence of a fact or facts giving rise to the presumption, the presumption fails and the jury shall not consider the presumption for any purpose.

(b) When this code or another penal law establishes a presumption in favor of the defendant with respect to any fact, it has the following consequences:

(1) if there is sufficient evidence of the facts that give rise to the presumption, the issue of the existence of the presumed fact must be submitted to the jury unless the court is satisfied that the evidence as a whole clearly precludes a finding beyond a reasonable doubt of the presumed fact; and

(2) if the existence of the presumed fact is submitted to the jury, the court shall charge the jury, in terms of the presumption, that:

(A) the presumption applies unless the state proves beyond a reasonable doubt that the facts giving rise to the presumption do not exist;

(B) if the state fails to prove beyond a reasonable doubt that the facts giving rise to the presumption do not exist, the jury must find that the presumed fact exists;

(C) even though the jury may find that the presumed fact does not exist, the state must prove beyond a reasonable doubt each of the elements of the offense charged; and

(D) if the jury has a reasonable doubt as to whether the presumed fact exists, the presumption applies and the jury must consider the presumed fact to exist.

Sec. 2.06. Prima Facie Case [Repealed].

Repealed by Acts 1975, 64th Leg., ch. 342 (S.B. 127), § 16, effective September 1, 1975.

[illegible] 3

[illegible]ECUTIONS

[illegible]. Definition.

In this chapter, "criminal episode" means the commission of two or more offenses, regardless of whether the harm is directed toward or inflicted upon more than one person or item of property, under the following circumstances:

(1) the offenses are committed pursuant to the same transaction or pursuant to two or more transactions that are connected or constitute a common scheme or plan; or

(2) the offenses are the repeated commission of the same or similar offenses.

Sec. 3.02. Consolidation and Joinder of Prosecutions.

(a) A defendant may be prosecuted in a single criminal action for all offenses arising out of the same criminal episode.

(b) When a single criminal [illegible] is based on more than one charging [illegible] within the jurisdiction of the tri[illegible] shall file written notice [illegible] 30 days prior to th[illegible]

(c) [illegible] reversed, set aside, or vacate[illegible] [illegible]al ordered, the state may not prosecu[illegible] single criminal action in the new trial any offense not joined in the former prosecution unless evidence to establish probable guilt for that offense was not known to the appropriate prosecuting official at the time the first prosecution commenced.

Sec. 3.03. Sentences for Offenses Arising Out of Same Criminal Episode.

(a) When the accused is foun[illegible] of more than one offense arising out of th[illegible] [illegible]inal episode prosecuted in a single [illegible], a sentence for each offense for [illegible] found guilty shall be pronoun[illegible] [illegible]ovided by Subsection (b), the se[illegible] concurrently.

(b) If the [illegible] guilty of more than one offense [illegible] the same criminal episode, the sent[illegible] run concurrently or consecutively if ea[illegible]ence is for a conviction of:

(1) an offe[illegible]:

(A) under Section 49.07 or 49.08, regardless of whether the accused is convicted of violations of the same section more than once or is convicted of violations of both sections; or

(B) for which a plea agreement was reached in a case in which the accused was charged with more than one offense listed in Paragraph (A), regardless of whether the accused is charged with violations of the same section more than once or is charged with violations of both sections;

(2) an offense:

(A) under Section 33.021 or an offense under Section 21.02, 21.11, 22.011, 22.021, 25.02, or 43.25 committed against a victim younger than 17 years of age at the time of the commission of the offense regardless of whether the accused is convicted of violations of the same section more than once or is convicted of violations of more than one section; or

(B) for which a plea agreement was reached in a case in which the accused was charged with more than one offense listed in Paragraph (A) committed against a victim younger than 17 years of age at the time of the commission of the offense regardless of whether the accused is charged with violations of the same section more than once or is charged with violations of more than one section;

(3) an offense:

(A) under Section 21.15 or 43.26, regardless of whether the accused is convicted of violations of the same section more than once or is convicted of violations of both sections; or

(B) for which a plea agreement was reached in a case in which the accused was charged with more than one offense listed in Paragraph (A), regardless of whether the accused is charged with violations of the same section more than once or is charged with violations of both sections;

(4) an offense for which the judgment in the case contains an affirmative finding under Article 42.0197, Code of Criminal Procedure;

(5) an offense:

(A) under Section 20A.02, 20A.03, or 43.05, regardless of whether the accused is convicted of violations of the same section more than once or is convicted of violations of more than one section; or

(B) for which a plea agreement was reached in a case in which the accused was charged with more than one offense listed in Paragraph (A), regardless of whether the accused is charged with violations of the same section more than once or is charged with violations of more than one section;

(6) an offense:

(A) under Section 22.04(a)(1) or (2) or Section 22.04(a-1)(1) or (2) that is punishable as a felony of the first degree, regardless of whether the accused is convicted of violations of the same section more than once or is convicted of violations of more than one section; or

(B) for which a plea agreement was reached in a case in which the accused was charged with more than one offense listed in Paragraph (A) and punishable as described by that paragraph, regardless of whether the accused is charged with violations of the same section more than once or is charged with violations of more than one section; or

(7) any combination of offenses listed in Subdivisions (1)-(6).

(b-1) Subsection (b)(4) does not apply to a defendant whose case was transferred to the court under Section 54.02, Family Code.

Sec. 3.04. Severance.

(a) Whenever two or more offenses have been consolidated or joined for trial under Section 3.02, the defendant shall have a right to a severance of the offenses.

(b) In the event of severance under this section, the provisions of Section 3.03 do not apply, and the court in its discretion may order the sentences to run either concurrently or consecutively.

(c) The right to severance under this section does not apply to a prosecution for offenses described by Section 3.03(b) unless the court determines that the defendant or the state would be unfairly prejudiced by a joinder of offenses, in which event the judge may order the offenses to be tried separately or may order other relief as justice requires.

TITLE 2
GENERAL PRINCIPLES OF CRIMINAL RESPONSIBILITY

CHAPTER 6
CULPABILITY GENERALLY

Sec. 6.01. Requirement of Voluntary Act or Omission.

(a) A person commits an offense only if he voluntarily engages in conduct, including an act, an omission, or possession.

(b) Possession is a voluntary act if the possessor knowingly obtains or receives the thing possessed or is aware of his control of the thing for a sufficient time to permit him to terminate his control.

(c) A person who omits to perform an act does not commit an offense unless a law as defined by Section 1.07 provides that the omission is an offense or otherwise provides that he has a duty to perform the act.

Sec. 6.02. Requirement of Culpability.

(a) Except as provid[illegible] Subsection (b), a person does not commi[illegible] he intentionally, knowingly, reckl[illegible] negligence engages in condu[illegible]fense requires.

(b) If the definition of an [illegible] not prescribe a culpable mental state, a [illegible] mental state is nevertheless required unless the definition plainly dispenses with any mental element.

(c) If the definition of an offense does not prescribe a culpable mental state, but one is nevertheless required under Subsection (b), intent, knowledge, or recklessness suffices to establish criminal responsibility.

(d) Culpable mental states are classified according to relative degrees, from highest to lowest, as follows:

(1) intentional;
(2) knowing;
(3) reckless;
(4) criminal negligence.

(e) Proof of a higher degree of culpability than that charged constitutes proof of the culpability charged.

(f) An offense defined by municipal ordinance or by order of a county commissioners court may not dispense with the requirement of a culpable mental state if the offense is punishable by a fine exceeding the amount authorized by Section 12.23.

Sec. 6.03. Definitions of Culpable Mental States.

(a) A person acts intentionally, or with intent, with respect to the nature of his conduct or to a result of his conduct when it is his conscious objective or desire to engage in the conduct or cause the result.

(b) A person acts knowingly, or with knowledge, with respect to the nature of his conduct or to circumstances surrounding his conduct when he is aware of the nature of his conduct or that the circumstances exist. A person acts knowingly, or with knowledge, with respect to a result of his conduct when he is aware that his conduct is reasonably certain to cause the result.

(c) A person acts recklessly, or is reckless, with respect to circumstances surrounding his conduct or the result of his conduct when he is aware of but consciously disregards a substantial and unjustifiable risk that the circumstances exist or the result will occur. The risk must be of such a nature and degree that its disregard constitutes a gross deviation from the standard of care that an ordinary person would exercise under all the circumstances as viewed from the actor's standpoint.

(d) A person acts with criminal negligence, or is criminally negligent, with respect to circumstances surrounding his conduct or the result of his conduct when he ought to be aware of a substantial and unjustifiable risk that the circumstances exist or the result will occur. The risk must be of such a nature and degree that the failure to perceive it constitutes a gross deviation from the standard of care that an ordinary person would exercise under all the circumstances as viewed from the actor's standpoint.

Sec. 6.04. Causation: Conduct and Results.

(a) A person is criminally responsible if the result would not have occurred but for his conduct, operating either alone or concurrently with another cause, unless the concurrent cause was clearly sufficient to produce the result and the conduct of the actor clearly insufficient.

(b) A person is nevertheless criminally responsible for causing a result if the only difference between what actually occurred and what he desired, contemplated, or risked is that:

(1) a different offense was committed; or
(2) a different person or property was injured, harmed, or otherwise affected.

CHAPTER 7
CRIMINAL RESPONSIBILITY FOR CONDUCT OF ANOTHER

SUBCHAPTER A
COMPLICITY

Sec. 7.01. Parties to Offenses.

(a) A person is criminally responsible as a party to an offense if the offense is committed by his own conduct, by the conduct of another for which he is criminally responsible, or by both.

(b) Each party to an offense may be charged with commission of the offense.

(c) All traditional distinctions between accomplices and principals are abolished by this section, and each party to an offense may be charged and convicted without alleging that he acted as a principal or accomplice.

Sec. 7.02. Criminal Responsibility for Conduct of Another.

(a) A person is criminally responsible for an offense committed by the conduct of another if:

(1) acting with the kind of culpability required for the offense, he causes or aids an innocent or nonresponsible person to engage in conduct prohibited by the definition of the offense;

(2) acting with intent to promote or assist the commission of the offense, he solicits, encourages, directs, aids, or attempts to aid the other person to commit the offense; or

(3) having a legal duty to prevent commission of the offense and acting with intent to promote or assist its commission, he fails to make a reasonable effort to prevent commission of the offense.

(b) If, in the attempt to carry out a conspiracy to commit one felony, another felony is committed by one of the conspirators, all conspirators are guilty of the felony actually committed, though having no intent to commit it, if the offense was committed in furtherance of the unlawful purpose and was one that should have been anticipated as a result of the carrying out of the conspiracy.

Sec. 7.03. Defenses Excluded.

In a prosecution in which an actor's criminal responsibility is based on the conduct of another, the actor may be convicted on proof of commission of the offense and that he was a party to its commission, and it is no defense:

(1) that the actor belongs to a class of persons that by definition of the offense is legally incapable of committing the offense in an individual capacity; or

(2) that the person for whose conduct the actor is criminally responsible has been acquitted, has not been prosecuted or convicted, has been convicted of a different offense or of a different type or class of offense, or is immune from prosecution.

SUBCHAPTER B CORPORATIONS, ASSOCIATIONS, LIMITED LIABILITY COMPANIES, AND OTHER BUSINESS ENTITIES

Sec. 7.21. Definitions.

In this subchapter:

(1) "Agent" means a director, officer, employee, or other person authorized to act in behalf of a corporation, an association, a limited liability company, or another business entity.

(1-a) "Business entity" means an entity or organization governed by the Business Organizations Code, other than a corporation, association, or limited liability company.

(2) "High managerial agent" means:

(A) a partner in a partnership;

(B) an officer of a corporation, an association, a limited liability company, or another business entity;

(C) an agent of a corporation, an association, a limited liability company, or another business entity who has duties of such responsibility that the agent's conduct reasonably may be assumed to represent the policy of the corporation, association, limited liability company, or other business entity.

Sec. 7.22. Criminal Responsibility of Corporation, Association, Limited Liability Company, or Other Business Entity.

(a) If conduct constituting an offense is performed by an agent acting in behalf of a corporation, an association, a limited liability company, or another business entity and within the scope of the agent's office or employment, the corporation, association, limited liability company, or other business entity is criminally responsible for an offense defined:

(1) in this code where corporations, associations, limited liability companies, and other business entities are made subject thereto;

(2) by law other than this code in which a legislative purpose to impose criminal responsibility on corporations, associations, limited liability companies, and other business entities plainly appears; or

(3) by law other than this code for which strict liability is imposed, unless a legislative purpose not to impose criminal responsibility on corporations, associations, limited liability companies, or other business entities plainly appears.

(b) A corporation, an association, a limited liability company, or another business entity is criminally responsible for a felony offense only if its commission was authorized, requested, commanded, performed, or recklessly tolerated by:

(1) a majority of the governing body acting in behalf of the corporation, association, limited liability company, or other business entity; or

(2) a high managerial agent acting in behalf of the corporation, association, limited liability company, or other business entity and within the scope of the agent's office or employment.

Sec. 7.23. Criminal Responsibility of Person for Conduct in Behalf of Corporation, Association, Limited Liability Company, or Other Business Entity.

(a) An individual is criminally responsible for conduct that the individual performs in the name of or in behalf of a corporation, an association, a limited liability company, or another business entity to the same extent as if the conduct were performed in the individual's own name or behalf.

(b) An agent having primary responsibility for the discharge of a duty to act imposed by law on a corporation, an association, a limited liability company, or another business entity is criminally responsible for omission to discharge the duty to the same extent as if the duty were imposed by law directly on the agent.

(c) If an individual is convicted of conduct constituting an offense performed in the name of or on behalf of a corporation, an association, a limited liability company, or another business entity, the individual is subject to the sentence authorized by law for an individual convicted of the offense.

Sec. 7.24. Defense to Criminal Responsibility of Corporation, Association, Limited Liability Company, or Other Business Entity.

It is an affirmative defense to prosecution of a corporation, an association, a limited liability company, or another business entity under Section 7.22(a)(1) or (a)(2) that the high managerial agent having supervisory responsibility over the subject matter of the offense employed due diligence to prevent its commission.

CHAPTER 8
GENERAL DEFENSES TO CRIMINAL RESPONSIBILITY

Sec. 8.01. Insanity.

(a) It is an affirmative defense to prosecution that, at the time of the conduct charged, the actor, as a result of severe mental disease or defect, did not know that his conduct was wrong.

(b) The term "mental disease or defect" does not include an abnormality manifested only by repeated criminal or otherwise antisocial conduct.

Sec. 8.02. Mistake of Fact.

(a) It is a defense to prosecution that the actor through mistake formed a reasonable belief about a matter of fact if his mistaken belief negated the kind of culpability required for commission of the offense.

(b) Although an actor's mistake of fact may constitute a defense to the offense charged, he may nevertheless be convicted of any lesser included offense of which he would be guilty if the fact were as he believed.

Sec. 8.03. Mistake of Law.

(a) It is no defense to prosecution that the actor was ignorant of the provisions of any law after the law has taken effect.

(b) It is an affirmative defense to prosecution that the actor reasonably believed the conduct charged did not constitute a crime and that he acted in reasonable reliance upon:

(1) an official statement of the law contained in a written order or grant of permission by an administrative agency charged by law with responsibility for interpreting the law in question; or

(2) a written interpretation of the law contained in an opinion of a court of record or made by a public official charged by law with responsibility for interpreting the law in question.

(c) Although an actor's mistake of law may constitute a defense to the offense charged, he may nevertheless be convicted of a lesser included offense of which he would be guilty if the law were as he believed.

Sec. 8.04. Intoxication.

(a) Voluntary intoxication does not constitute a defense to the commission of crime.

(b) Evidence of temporary insanity caused by intoxication may be introduced by the actor in mitigation of the penalty attached to the offense for which he is being tried.

(c) When temporary insanity is relied upon as a defense and the evidence tends to show that such insanity was caused by intoxication, the court shall charge the jury in accordance with the provisions of this section.

(d) For purposes of this section "intoxication" means disturbance of mental or physical capacity resulting from the introduction of any substance into the body.

Sec. 8.05. Duress.

(a) It is an affirmative defense to prosecution that the actor engaged in the proscribed conduct because he was compelled to do so by threat of imminent death or serious bodily injury to himself or another.

(b) In a prosecution for an offense that does not constitute a felony, it is an affirmative defense to prosecution that the actor engaged in the proscribed conduct because he was compelled to do so by force or threat of force.

(c) Compulsion within the meaning of this section exists only if the force or threat of force would render a person of reasonable firmness incapable of resisting the pressure.

(d) The defense provided by this section is unavailable if the actor intentionally, knowingly, or recklessly placed himself in a situation in which it was probable that he would be subjected to compulsion.

(e) It is no defense that a person acted at the command or persuasion of his spouse, unless he acted under compulsion that would establish a defense under this section.

Sec. 8.06. Entrapment.

(a) It is a defense to prosecution that the actor engaged in the conduct charged because he was induced to do so by a law enforcement agent using persuasion or other means likely to cause persons to commit the offense. Conduct merely affording a person an opportunity to commit an offense does not constitute entrapment.

(b) In this section "law enforcement agent" includes personnel of the state and local law enforcement agencies as well as of the United States and any person acting in accordance with instructions from such agents.

Sec. 8.07. Age Affecting Criminal Responsibility.

(a) A person may not be prosecuted for or convicted of any offense that the person committed when younger than 15 years of age except:

(1) perjury and aggravated perjury when it appears by proof that the person had sufficient discretion to understand the nature and obligation of an oath;

(2) a violation of a penal statute cognizable under Chapter 729, Transportation Code, except for conduct for which the person convicted may be sentenced to imprisonment or confinement in jail;

(3) a violation of a motor vehicle traffic ordinance of an incorporated city or town in this state;

(4) a misdemeanor punishable by fine only;

(5) a violation of a penal ordinance of a political subdivision;

(6) a violation of a penal statute that is, or is a lesser included offense of, a capital felony, an aggravated controlled substance felony, or a felony of the first degree for which the person is transferred to the court under Section 54.02, Family Code, for prosecution if the person committed the offense when 14 years of age or older; or

(7) a capital felony or an offense under Section 19.02 for which the person is transferred to the court under Section 54.02(j)(2)(A), Family Code.

(b) Unless the juvenile court waives jurisdiction under Section 54.02, Family Code, and certifies the individual for criminal prosecution or the juvenile court has previously waived jurisdiction under that section and certified the individual for criminal prosecution, a person may not be prosecuted for or convicted of any offense committed before reaching 17 years of age except an offense described by Subsections (a)(1)—(5).

(c) No person may, in any case, be punished by death for an offense committed while the person was younger than 18 years.

(d) Notwithstanding Subsection (a), a person may not be prosecuted for or convicted of an offense described by Subsection (a)(4) or (5) that the person committed when younger than 10 years of age.

(e) A person who is at least 10 years of age but younger than 15 years of age is presumed incapable of committing an offense described by Subsection (a)(4) or (5), other than an offense under a juvenile curfew ordinance or order. This presumption may be refuted if the prosecution proves to the court by a preponderance of the evidence that the actor had sufficient capacity to understand that the conduct engaged in was wrong at the time the conduct was engaged in. The prosecution is not required to prove that the actor at the time of engaging in the conduct knew that the act was a criminal offense or knew the legal consequences of the offense.

Sec. 8.08. Child with Mental Illness, Disability, or Lack of Capacity.

(a) On motion by the state, the defendant, or a person standing in parental relation to the defendant, or on the court's own motion, a court with jurisdiction of an offense described by Section 8.07(a)(4) or (5) shall determine whether probable cause exists to believe that a child, including a child with a mental illness or developmental disability:

(1) lacks the capacity to understand the proceedings in criminal court or to assist in the child's own defense and is unfit to proceed; or

(2) lacks substantial capacity either to appreciate the wrongfulness of the child's own conduct or to conform the child's conduct to the requirement of the law.

(b) If the court determines that probable cause exists for a finding under Subsection (a), after providing notice to the state, the court may dismiss the complaint.

(c) A dismissal of a complaint under Subsection (b) may be appealed as provided by Article 44.01, Code of Criminal Procedure.

(d) In this section, "child" has the meaning assigned by Article 45.058(h), Code of Criminal Procedure.

CHAPTER 9
JUSTIFICATION EXCLUDING CRIMINAL RESPONSIBILITY

SUBCHAPTER A
GENERAL PROVISIONS

Sec. 9.01. Definitions.

In this chapter:

(1) "Custody" has the meaning assigned by Section 38.01.

(2) "Escape" has the meaning assigned by Section 38.01.

(3) "Deadly force" means force that is intended or known by the actor to cause, or in the manner of its use or intended use is capable of causing, death or serious bodily injury.

(4) "Habitation" has the meaning assigned by Section 30.01.

(5) "Vehicle" has the meaning assigned by Section 30.01.

Sec. 9.02. Justification As a Defense.

It is a defense to prosecution that the conduct in question is justified under this chapter.

Sec. 9.03. Confinement As Justifiable Force.

Confinement is justified when force is justified by this chapter if the actor takes reasonable measures to terminate the confinement as soon as he knows he safely can unless the person confined has been arrested for an offense.

Sec. 9.03. Confinement As Justifiable Force.

Confinement is justified when force is justified by this chapter if the actor takes reasonable measures to terminate the confinement as soon as he knows he safely can unless the person confined has been arrested for an offense.

Sec. 9.03. Confinement As Justifiable Force.

Confinement is justified when force is justified by this chapter if the actor takes reasonable measures to terminate the confinement as soon as he knows he safely can unless the person confined has been arrested for an offense.

Sec. 9.03. Confinement As Justifiable Force.

Confinement is justified when force is justified by this chapter if the actor takes reasonable measures to terminate the confinement as soon as he knows he safely can unless the person confined has been arrested for an offense.

Sec. 9.03. Confinement As Justifiable Force.

Confinement is justified when force is justified by this chapter if the actor takes reasonable measures to terminate the confinement as soon as he knows he safely can unless the person confined has been arrested for an offense.

Sec. 9.04. Threats As Justifiable Force.

The threat of force is justified when the use of force is justified by this chapter. For purposes of this section, a threat to cause death or serious bodily injury by the production of a weapon or otherwise, as long as the actor's purpose is limited to creating an apprehension that he will use deadly force if necessary, does not constitute the use of deadly force.

Sec. 9.05. Reckless Injury of Innocent Third Person.

Even though an actor is justified under this chapter in threatening or using force or deadly force against another, if in doing so he also recklessly injures or kills an innocent third person, the justification afforded by this chapter is unavailable in a prosecution for the reckless injury or killing of the innocent third person.

Sec. 9.06. Civil Remedies Unaffected.

The fact that conduct is justified under this chapter does not abolish or impair any remedy for the conduct that is available in a civil suit.

SUBCHAPTER B
JUSTIFICATION GENERALLY

Sec. 9.21. Public Duty.

(a) Except as qualified by Subsections (b) and (c), conduct is justified if the actor reasonably believes the conduct is required or authorized by law, by the judgment or order of a competent court or other governmental tribunal, or in the execution of legal process.

(b) The other sections of this chapter control when force is used against a person to protect persons (Subchapter C), to protect property (Subchapter D), for law enforcement (Subchapter E), or by virtue of a special relationship (Subchapter F).

(c) The use of deadly force is not justified under this section unless the actor reasonably believes the deadly force is specifically required by statute or unless it occurs in the lawful conduct of war. If deadly force is so justified, there is no duty to retreat before using it.

(d) The justification afforded by this section is available if the actor reasonably believes:

(1) the court or governmental tribunal has jurisdiction or the process is lawful, even though the court or governmental tribunal lacks jurisdiction or the process is unlawful; or

(2) his conduct is required or authorized to assist a public servant in the performance of his official duty, even though the servant exceeds his lawful authority.

Sec. 9.22. Necessity.

Conduct is justified if:

(1) the actor reasonably believes the conduct is immediately necessary to avoid imminent harm;

(2) the desirability and urgency of avoiding the harm clearly outweigh, according to ordinary standards of reasonableness, the harm sought to be prevented by the law proscribing the conduct; and

(3) a legislative purpose to exclude the justification claimed for the conduct does not otherwise plainly appear.

SUBCHAPTER C
PROTECTION OF PERSONS

Sec. 9.31. Self-Defense.

(a) Except as provided in Subsection (b), a person is justified in using force against another when and to the degree the actor reasonably believes the force is immediately necessary to protect the actor against the other's use or attempted use of unlawful force. The actor's belief that the force was immediately necessary as described by this subsection is presumed to be reasonable if the actor:

(1) knew or had reason to believe that the person against whom the force was used:

(A) unlawfully and with force entered, or was attempting to enter unlawfully and with force, the actor's occupied habitation, vehicle, or place of business or employment;

(B) unlawfully and with force removed, or was attempting to remove unlawfully and with force, the actor from the actor's habitation, vehicle, or place of business or employment; or

(C) was committing or attempting to commit aggravated kidnapping, murder, sexual assault, aggravated sexual assault, robbery, or aggravated robbery;

(2) did not provoke the person against whom the force was used; and

(3) was not otherwise engaged in criminal activity, other than a Class C misdemeanor that is a violation of a law or ordinance regulating traffic at the time the force was used.

(b) The use of force against another is not justified:

(1) in response to verbal provocation alone;

(2) to resist an arrest or search that the actor knows is being made by a peace officer, or by a person acting in a peace officer's presence and at his direction, even though the arrest or search is unlawful, unless the resistance is justified under Subsection (c);

(3) if the actor consented to the exact force used or attempted by the other;

(4) if the actor provoked the other's use or attempted use of unlawful force, unless:

(A) the actor abandons the encounter, or clearly communicates to the other his intent to do so reasonably believing he cannot safely abandon the encounter; and

(B) the other nevertheless continues or attempts to use unlawful force against the actor; or

(5) if the actor sought an explanation from or discussion with the other person concerning the actor's differences with the other person while the actor was:

(A) carrying a weapon in violation of Section 46.02; or

(B) possessing or transporting a weapon in violation of Section 46.05.

(c) The use of force to resist an arrest or search is justified:

(1) if, before the actor offers any resistance, the peace officer (or person acting at his direction) uses or attempts to use greater force than necessary to make the arrest or search; and

(2) when and to the degree the actor reasonably believes the force is immediately necessary to protect himself against the peace officer's (or other person's) use or attempted use of greater force than necessary.

(d) The use of deadly force is not justified under this subchapter except as provided in Sections 9.32, 9.33, and 9.34.

(e) A person who has a right to be present at the location where the force is used, who has not provoked the person against whom the force is used, and who is not engaged in criminal activity at the time the force is used is not required to retreat before using force as described by this section.

(f) For purposes of Subsection (a), in determining whether an actor described by Subsection (e) reasonably believed that the use of force was necessary, a finder of fact may not consider whether the actor failed to retreat.

Sec. 9.32. Deadly Force in Defense of Person.

(a) A person is justified in using deadly force against another:

(1) if the actor would be justified in using force against the other under Section 9.31; and

(2) when and to the degree the actor reasonably believes the deadly force is immediately necessary:

(A) to protect the actor against the other's use or attempted use of unlawful deadly force; or

(B) to prevent the other's imminent commission of aggravated kidnapping, murder, sexual assault, aggravated sexual assault, robbery, or aggravated robbery.

(b) The actor's belief under Subsection (a)(2) that the deadly force was immediately necessary as described by that subdivision is presumed to be reasonable if the actor:

(1) knew or had reason to believe that the person against whom the deadly force was used:

(A) unlawfully and with force entered, or was attempting to enter unlawfully and with force, the actor's occupied habitation, vehicle, or place of business or employment;

(B) unlawfully and with force removed, or was attempting to remove unlawfully and with force, the actor from the actor's habitation, vehicle, or place of business or employment; or

(C) was committing or attempting to commit an offense described by Subsection (a)(2)(B);

(2) did not provoke the person against whom the force was used; and

(3) was not otherwise engaged in criminal activity, other than a Class C misdemeanor that is a violation of a law or ordinance regulating traffic at the time the force was used.

(c) A person who has a right to be present at the location where the deadly force is used, who has not provoked the person against whom the deadly force is used, and who is not engaged in criminal activity at the time the deadly force is used is not required to retreat before using deadly force as described by this section.

(d) For purposes of Subsection (a)(2), in determining whether an actor described by Subsection (c) reasonably believed that the use of deadly force was necessary, a finder of fact may not consider whether the actor failed to retreat.

Sec. 9.33. Defense of Third Person.

A person is justified in using force or deadly force against another to protect a third person if:

(1) under the circumstances as the actor reasonably believes them to be, the actor would be justified under Section 9.31 or 9.32 in using force or deadly force to protect himself against the unlawful force or unlawful deadly force he reasonably believes to be threatening the third person he seeks to protect; and

(2) the actor reasonably believes that his intervention is immediately necessary to protect the third person.

Sec. 9.34. Protection of Life or Health.

(a) A person is justified in using force, but not deadly force, against another when and to the degree he reasonably believes the force is immediately necessary to prevent the other from committing suicide or inflicting serious bodily injury to himself.

(b) A person is justified in using both force and deadly force against another when and to the degree he reasonably believes the force or deadly force is immediately necessary to preserve the other's life in an emergency.

Sec. 9.34. Protection of Life or Health.

(a) A person is justified in using force, but not deadly force, against another when and to the degree he reasonably believes the force is immediately necessary to prevent the other from committing suicide or inflicting serious bodily injury to himself.

(b) A person is justified in using both force and deadly force against another when and to the degree he reasonably believes the force or deadly force is immediately necessary to preserve the other's life in an emergency.

Sec. 9.34. Protection of Life or Health.

(a) A person is justified in using force, but not deadly force, against another when and to the degree he reasonably believes the force is immediately necessary to prevent the other from committing suicide or inflicting serious bodily injury to himself.

(b) A person is justified in using both force and deadly force against another when and to the degree he reasonably believes the force or deadly force is immediately necessary to preserve the other's life in an emergency.

Sec. 9.34. Protection of Life or Health.

(a) A person is justified in using force, but not deadly force, against another when and to the degree he reasonably believes the force is immediately necessary to prevent the other from committing suicide or inflicting serious bodily injury to himself.

(b) A person is justified in using both force and deadly force against another when and to the degree he reasonably believes the force or deadly force is immediately necessary to preserve the other's life in an emergency.

Sec. 9.34. Protection of Life or Health.

(a) A person is justified in using force, but not deadly force, against another when and to the degree he reasonably believes the force is immediately necessary to prevent the other from committing suicide or inflicting serious bodily injury to himself.

(b) A person is justified in using both force and deadly force against another when and to the degree he reasonably believes the force or deadly force is immediately necessary to preserve the other's life in an emergency.

SUBCHAPTER D
PROTECTION OF PROPERTY

Sec. 9.41. Protection of One's Own Property.

(a) A person in lawful possession of land or tangible, movable property is justified in using force against another when and to the degree the actor reasonably believes the force is immediately necessary to prevent or terminate the other's trespass on the land or unlawful interference with the property.

(b) A person unlawfully dispossessed of land or tangible, movable property by another is justified in using force against the other when and to the degree the actor reasonably believes the force is immediately necessary to reenter the land or recover the property if the actor uses the force immediately or in fresh pursuit after the dispossession and:

(1) the actor reasonably believes the other had no claim of right when he dispossessed the actor; or

(2) the other accomplished the dispossession by using force, threat, or fraud against the actor.

Sec. 9.42. Deadly Force to Protect Property.

A person is justified in using deadly force against another to protect land or tangible, movable property:

(1) if he would be justified in using force against the other under Section 9.41; and

(2) when and to the degree he reasonably believes the deadly force is immediately necessary:

(A) to prevent the other's imminent commission of arson, burglary, robbery, aggravated robbery, theft during the nighttime, or criminal mischief during the nighttime; or

(B) to prevent the other who is fleeing immediately after committing burglary, robbery, aggravated robbery, or theft during the nighttime from escaping with the property; and

(3) he reasonably believes that:

(A) the land or property cannot be protected or recovered by any other means; or

(B) the use of force other than deadly force to protect or recover the land or property would expose the actor or another to a substantial risk of death or serious bodily injury.

Sec. 9.43. Protection of Third Person's Property.

A person is justified in using force or deadly force against another to protect land or tangible, movable property of a third person if, under the circumstances as he reasonably believes them to be, the actor would be justified under Section 9.41 or 9.42 in using force or deadly force to protect his own land or property and:

(1) the actor reasonably believes the unlawful interference constitutes attempted or consummated theft of or criminal mischief to the tangible, movable property; or

(2) the actor reasonably believes that:

(A) the third person has requested his protection of the land or property;

(B) he has a legal duty to protect the third person's land or property; or

(C) the third person whose land or property he uses force or deadly force to protect is the actor's spouse, parent, or child, resides with the actor, or is under the actor's care.

Sec. 9.44. Use of Device to Protect Property.

The justification afforded by Sections 9.41 and 9.43 applies to the use of a device to protect land or tangible, movable property if:

(1) the device is not designed to cause, or known by the actor to create a substantial risk of causing, death or serious bodily injury; and

(2) use of the device is reasonable under all the circumstances as the actor reasonably believes them to be when he installs the device.

SUBCHAPTER E LAW ENFORCEMENT

Sec. 9.51. Arrest and Search.

(a) A peace officer, or a person acting in a peace officer's presence and at his direction, is justified in using force against another when and to the degree the actor reasonably believes the force is immediately necessary to make or assist in making an arrest or search, or to prevent or assist in preventing escape after arrest, if:

(1) the actor reasonably believes the arrest or search is lawful or, if the arrest or search is made under a warrant, he reasonably believes the warrant is valid; and

(2) before using force, the actor manifests his purpose to arrest or search and identifies himself as a peace officer or as one acting at a peace officer's direction, unless he reasonably believes his purpose and identity are already known by or cannot reasonably be made known to the person to be arrested.

(b) A person other than a peace officer (or one acting at his direction) is justified in using force against another when and to the degree the actor reasonably believes the force is immediately necessary to make or assist in making a lawful arrest, or to prevent or assist in preventing escape after lawful arrest if, before using force, the actor manifests his purpose to and the reason for the arrest or reasonably believes his purpose and the reason are already known by or cannot reasonably be made known to the person to be arrested.

(c) A peace officer is justified in using deadly force against another when and to the degree the peace officer reasonably believes the deadly force is immediately necessary to make an arrest, or to prevent escape after arrest, if the use of force would have been justified under Subsection (a) and:

(1) the actor reasonably believes the conduct for which arrest is authorized included the use or attempted use of deadly force; or

(2) the actor reasonably believes there is a substantial risk that the person to be arrested will cause death or serious bodily injury to the actor or another if the arrest is delayed.

(d) A person other than a peace officer acting in a peace officer's presence and at his direction is justified in using deadly force against another when and to the degree the person reasonably believes the deadly force is immediately necessary to make a lawful arrest, or to prevent escape after a lawful arrest, if the use of force would have been justified under Subsection (b) and:

(1) the actor reasonably believes the felony or offense against the public peace for which arrest is authorized included the use or attempted use of deadly force; or

(2) the actor reasonably believes there is a substantial risk that the person to be arrested will cause death or serious bodily injury to another if the arrest is delayed.

(e) There is no duty to retreat before using deadly force justified by Subsection (c) or (d).

(f) Nothing in this section relating to the actor's manifestation of purpose or identity shall be construed as conflicting with any other law relating to the issuance, service, and execution of an arrest or search warrant either under the laws of this state or the United States.

(g) Deadly force may only be used under the circumstances enumerated in Subsections (c) and (d).

Sec. 9.52. Prevention of Escape from Custody.

The use of force to prevent the escape of an arrested person from custody is justifiable when the force could have been employed to effect the arrest under which the person is in custody, except that a guard employed by a correctional facility or a peace officer is justified in using any force, including deadly force, that he reasonably believes to be immediately necessary to prevent the escape of a person from the correctional facility.

Sec. 9.53. Maintaining Security in Correctional Facility.

An officer or employee of a correctional facility is justified in using force against a person in custody when and to the degree the officer or employee reasonably believes the force is necessary to maintain the security of the correctional facility, the safety or security of other persons in custody or employed by the correctional facility, or his own safety or security.

Sec. 9.54. Limitation on Use of Force by Drone.

(a) In this section:

(1) "Autonomous drone" means a drone that operates autonomously through computer software or other programming.

(2) "Drone" and "law enforcement agency" have the meanings assigned by Article 2.33, Code of Criminal Procedure.

(b) Notwithstanding any other law, the use of force, including deadly force, involving a drone is justified under this subchapter only if:

(1) at the time the use of force occurred, the actor was employed by a law enforcement agency;

(2) the use of force:

(A) would have been justified under another provision of this subchapter; and

(B) did not involve the use of deadly force by means of an autonomous drone; and

(3) before the use of force occurred, the law enforcement agency employing the actor adopted and submitted to the Texas Commission on Law Enforcement a policy on the agency's use of force by means of a drone, as required by Article 2.33, Code of Criminal Procedure, and the use of force conformed to the requirements of that policy.

SUBCHAPTER F SPECIAL RELATIONSHIPS

Sec. 9.61. Parent — Child.

(a) The use of force, but not deadly force, against a child younger than 18 years is justified:

(1) if the actor is the child's parent or stepparent or is acting in loco parentis to the child; and

(2) when and to the degree the actor reasonably believes the force is necessary to discipline the child or to safeguard or promote his welfare.

(b) For purposes of this section, "in loco parentis" includes grandparent and guardian, any person acting by, through, or under the direction of a court with jurisdiction over the child, and anyone who has express or implied consent of the parent or parents.

Sec. 9.62. Educator — Student.

The use of force, but not deadly force, against a person is justified:

(1) if the actor is entrusted with the care, supervision, or administration of the person for a special purpose; and

(2) when and to the degree the actor reasonably believes the force is necessary to further the special purpose or to maintain discipline in a group.

Sec. 9.63. Guardian — Incompetent.

The use of force, but not deadly force, against a mental incompetent is justified:

(1) if the actor is the incompetent's guardian or someone similarly responsible for the general care and supervision of the incompetent; and

(2) when and to the degree the actor reasonably believes the force is necessary:

(A) to safeguard and promote the incompetent's welfare; or

(B) if the incompetent is in an institution for his care and custody, to maintain discipline in the institution.

TITLE 3 PUNISHMENTS

CHAPTER 12 PUNISHMENTS

SUBCHAPTER A GENERAL PROVISIONS

Sec. 12.01. Punishment in Accordance with Code.

(a) A person adjudged guilty of an offense under this code shall be punished in accordance with this chapter and the Code of Criminal Procedure.

(b) Penal laws enacted after the effective date of this code shall be classified for punishment purposes in accordance with this chapter.

(c) This chapter does not deprive a court of authority conferred by law to forfeit property, dissolve a corporation, suspend or cancel a license or permit, remove a person from office, cite for contempt, or impose any other civil penalty. The civil penalty may be included in the sentence.

Sec. 12.02. Classification of Offenses.

Offenses are designated as felonies or misdemeanors.

Sec. 12.03. Classification of Misdemeanors.

(a) Misdemeanors are classified according to the relative seriousness of the offense into three categories:

(1) Class A misdemeanors;

(2) Class B misdemeanors;
(3) Class C misdemeanors.

(b) An offense designated a misdemeanor in this code without specification as to punishment or category is a Class C misdemeanor.

(c) Conviction of a Class C misdemeanor does not impose any legal disability or disadvantage.

Sec. 12.04. Classification of Felonies.

(a) Felonies are classified according to the relative seriousness of the offense into five categories:
(1) capital felonies;
(2) felonies of the first degree;
(3) felonies of the second degree;
(4) felonies of the third degree; and
(5) state jail felonies.

(b) An offense designated a felony in this code without specification as to category is a state jail felony.

SUBCHAPTER B ORDINARY MISDEMEANOR PUNISHMENTS

Sec. 12.21. Class A Misdemeanor.

A [illegible] guilty of a Class A misde[illegible]
([illegible]
(2) [illegible] not to exceed one year; or
(3) both such fine and confinement.

Sec. 12.22. Class B Misdemeanor.

An individual adjudged guilty of a Class B misdemeanor shall be punished by:
(1) a fine not to exceed $2,000;
(2) confinement in jail for a term not to exceed 180 days; or
(3) both such fine and confinement.

Sec. 12.23. Class C Misdemeanor.

An individual adjudged guilty of a Class C misdemeanor shall be punished by a fine not to exceed $500.

SUBCHAPTER C ORDINARY FELONY PUNISHMENTS

Sec. 12.31. Capital Felony.

(a) An individual adjudged guilty of a capital felony in a case in which the state seeks the death penalty shall be punished by imprisonment in the Texas Department of Criminal Justice for life without parole or by death. An individual adjudged guilty of a capital felony in a case in which the state does not seek the death penalty shall be punished by imprisonment in the Texas Department of Criminal Justice for:
(1) life, if the individual committed the offense when younger than 18 years of age; or
(2) life without parole, if the individual committed the offense when 18 years of age or older.

(b) In a capital felony trial in which the state seeks the death penalty, prospective jurors shall be informed that a sentence of life imprisonment without parole or death is mandatory on conviction of a capital felony. In a capital felony trial in which the state does not seek the death penalty, prospective jurors shall be informed that the state is not seeking the death penalty and that:
(1) a sentence of life imprisonment is mandatory on conviction of the capital felony, if the individual committed the offense when younger than 18 years of age; or
(2) a sentence of life imprisonment without parole is mandatory on conviction of the capital felony, if the indivi[illegible] committed the offense when 18 years of age [illegible]

Sec. 12.32. [illegible] Felony Punishment.

(a) [illegible]ed guilty of a felony of the fi[illegible] punished by imprisonment in the [illegible]partment of Criminal Justice for life or [illegible] any term of not more than 99 years or less than 5 years.

(b) In addition to imprisonment, an individual adjudged guilty of a felony of the first degree may be punished by a fine not to exceed $10,000.

Sec. 12.33. Second Degree Felony Punishment.

(a) An individual adjudged guilty of a felony of the second degree shall be punished by imprisonment in the Texas Department of Criminal Justice for any term of not more than 20 years or less than 2 years.

(b) In addition to imprisonment, an individual adjudged guilty of a felony of the second degree may be punished by a fine not to exceed $10,000.

Sec. 12.34. Third Degree Felony Punishment.

(a) An individual adjudged guilty of a felony of the third degree shall be punished by imprisonment in the Texas Department of Criminal Justice for any term of not more than 10 years or less than 2 years.

(b) In addition to imprisonment, an individual adjudged guilty of a felony of the third degree may be punished by a fine not to exceed $10,000.

Sec. 12.35. State Jail Felony Punishment.

(a) Except as provided by Subsectio[illegible] vidual adjudged guilty of a stat[illegible] punished by confinement [illegible] of not more than tw[illegible]

State Jail Felony

(b) In addition to [illegible]ividual adjudged guilty of a sta[illegible] may be punished by a fine not to exceed [illegible]000.

(c) An individual adjudged guilty of a state jail felony shall be punished for a third degree felony if it is shown on the trial of the offense that:

(1) a deadly weapon as defined by Section 1.07 was used or exhibited during the commission of the offense or during immediate flight following the commission of the offense, and that the individual used or exhibited the deadly weapon or was a party to the offense and knew that a deadly weapon would be used or exhibited; or

(2) the individual has previously been finally convicted of any felony:

(A) under Section 20A.03 or 21.02 or listed in Article 42A.054(a), Code of Criminal Procedure; or

(B) for which the judgment contains an affirmative finding under Article 42A.054(c) or (d), Code of Criminal Procedure.

SUBCHAPTER D EXCEPTIONAL SENTENCES

Sec. 12.41. Classification of Offenses Outside This Code.

For purposes of this subchapter, any conviction not obtained from a prosecution under this code shall be classified as follows:

(1) "felony of the third degree" if imprisonment in the Texas Department of Criminal Justice or another penitentiary is affixed to the offense as a possible punishment;

(2) "Class B misdemeanor" if the offense is not a felony and confinement in a jail is affixed to the offense as a possible punishment;

(3) "Class C misdemeanor" if the offense is punishable by fine only.

Sec. 12.42. Penalties for Repeat and Habitual Felony Offenders on Trial for First, Second, or Third Degree Felony.

(a) Except as provided by Subsection (c)(2), if it is shown on the trial of a felony of the third degree that the defendant has previously been finally convicted of a felony other than a state jail felony punishable under Section 12.35(a), on conviction the defendant shall be punished for a felony of the second degree.

(b) Except as provided by Subsection (c)(2) or (c)(4), if it is shown on the trial of a felony of the second degree that the defendant has previously been finally convicted of a felony other than a state jail felony punishable under Section 12.35(a), on conviction the defendant shall be punished for a felony of the first degree.

(c) (1) If it is shown on the trial of a felony of the first degree that the defendant has previously been finally convicted of a felony other than a state jail felony punishable under Section 12.35(a), on conviction the defendant shall be punished by imprisonment in the Texas Department of Criminal Justice for life, or for any term of not more than 99 years or less than 15 years. In addition to imprisonment, an individual may be punished by a fine not to exceed $10,000.

(2) Notwithstanding Subdivision (1), a defendant shall be punished by imprisonment in the Texas Department of Criminal Justice for life if:

(A) the defendant is convicted of an offense:

(i) under Section 20A.02(a)(7) or (8), 21.11(a)(1), 22.021, or 22.011, Penal Code;

(ii) under Section 20.04(a)(4), Penal Code, if the defendant committed the offense with the intent to violate or abuse the victim sexually; or

(iii) under Section 30.02, Penal Code, punishable under Subsection (d) of that section, if the defendant committed the offense with the intent to commit a felony described by Subparagraph (i) or (ii) or a felony under Section 21.11, Penal Code; and

(B) the defendant has been previously convicted of an offense:

(i) under Section 43.25 or 43.26, Penal Code, or an offense under Section 43.23, Penal Code, punishable under Subsection (h) of that section;

(ii) under Section 20A.02(a)(7) or (8), 21.02, 21.11, 22.011, 22.021, or 25.02, Penal Code;

(iii) under Section 20.04(a)(4), Penal Code, if the defendant committed the offense with the intent to violate or abuse the victim sexually;

(iv) under Section 30.02, Penal Code, punishable under Subsection (d) of that section, if the defendant committed the offense with the intent to commit a felony described by Subparagraph (ii) or (iii); or

(v) under the laws of another state containing elements that are substantially similar to the elements of an offense listed in Subparagraph (i), (ii), (iii), or (iv).

(3) Notwithstanding Subdivision (1) or (2), a defendant shall be punished for a capital felony if it is shown on the trial of an offense under Section 22.021 otherwise punishable under Subsection (f) of that section that the defendant has previously been finally convicted of:

(A) an offense under Section 22.021 that was committed against a victim described by Section 22.021(f)(1) or was committed against a victim described by Section 22.021(f)(2) and in a manner described by Section 22.021(a)(2)(A); or

(B) an offense that was committed under the laws of another state that:

(i) contains elements that are substantially similar to the elements of an offense under Section 22.021; and

(ii) was committed against a victim described by Section 22.021(f)(1) or was committed against a victim described by Section 22.021(f)(2) and in a manner substantially similar to a manner described by Section 22.021(a)(2)(A).

(4) Notwithstanding Subdivision (1) or (2), and except as provided by Subdivision (3) for the trial of an offense under Section 22.021 as described by that subdivision, a defendant shall be punished by imprisonment in the Texas Department of Criminal Justice for life without parole if it is shown on the trial of an offense under Section 20A.03 or of a sexually violent offense, committed by the defendant on or after the defendant's 18th birthday, that the defendant has previously been finally convicted of:

(A) an offense under Section 20A.03 or of a sexually violent offense; or

(B) an offense that was committed under the laws of another state and that contains elements that are substantially similar to the elements of an offense under Section 20A.03 or of a sexually violent offense.

(5) A previous conviction for a state jail felony punishable under Section 12.35(a) may not be used for enhancement purposes under Subdivision (2).

(d) Except as provided by Subsection (c)(2) or (c)(4), if it is shown on the trial of a felony offense other than a state jail felony punishable under Section 12.35(a) that the defendant has previously been finally convicted of two felony offenses, and the second previous felony conviction is for an offense that occurred subsequent to the first previous conviction having become final, on conviction the defendant shall be punished by imprisonment in the Texas Department of Criminal Justice for life, or for any term of not more than 99 years or less than 25 years. A previous conviction for a state jail felony punishable under Section 12.35(a) may not be used for enhancement purposes under this subsection.

(e) [Repealed by Acts 2011, 82nd Leg., ch. 834 (H.B. 3384), § 6, effective September 1, 2011.]

(f) For the purposes of Subsections (a), (b), and (c)(1), an adjudication by a juvenile court under Section 54.03, Family Code, that a child engaged in delinquent conduct on or after January 1, 1996, constituting a felony offense for which the child is committed to the Texas Juvenile Justice Department under Section 54.04(d)(2), (d)(3), or (m), Family Code, or Section 54.05(f), Family Code, or to a post- adjudication secure correctional facility under Section 54.04011, Family Code, is a final felony conviction.

(g) For the purposes of Subsection (c)(2):

(1) a defendant has been previously convicted of an offense listed under Subsection (c)(2)(B) if the defendant was adjudged guilty of the offense or entered a plea of guilty or nolo contendere in return for a grant of deferred adjudication, regardless of whether the sentence for the offense was ever imposed or whether the sentence was probated and the defendant was subsequently discharged from community supervision; and

(2) a conviction under the laws of another state for an offense containing elements that are substantially similar to the elements of an offense listed under Subsection (c)(2)(B) is a conviction of an offense listed under Subsection (c)(2)(B).

(h) In this section, "sexually violent offense" means an offense:

(1) described by Article 62.001(6), Code of Criminal Procedure; and

(2) for which an affirmative finding has been entered under Article 42.015(b) or 42A.105(a), Code of Criminal Procedure, for an offense other than an offense under Section 21.02 or 22.021.

Sec. 12.422. Imposition of Substance Abuse Felony Punishment [Deleted].

Deleted by Acts 1993, 73rd Leg., ch. 900 (S.B. 1067), § 1.01, effective September 1, 1993.

Sec. 12.425. Penalties for Repeat and Habitual Felony Offenders on Trial for State Jail Felony.

(a) If it is shown on the trial of a state jail felony punishable under Section 12.35(a) that the defendant has previously been finally convicted of two state jail felonies punishable under Section 12.35(a), on conviction the defendant shall be punished for a felony of the third degree.

(b) If it is shown on the trial of a state jail felony punishable under Section 12.35(a) that the defendant has previously been finally convicted of two felonies other than a state jail felony punishable under Section 12.35(a), and the second previous felony conviction is for an offense that occurred subsequent to the first previous conviction having become final, on conviction the defendant shall be punished for a felony of the second degree.

(c) If it is shown on the trial of a state jail felony for which punishment may be enhanced under Section 12.35(c) that the defendant has previously been finally convicted of a felony other than a state jail felony punishable under Section 12.35(a), on conviction the defendant shall be punished for a felony of the second degree.

Sec. 12.43. Penalties for Repeat and Habitual Misdemeanor Offenders.

(a) If it is shown on the trial of a Class A misdemeanor that the defendant has been before convicted of a Class A misdemeanor or any degree of felony, on conviction he shall be punished by:

(1) a fine not to exceed $4,000;

(2) confinement in jail for any term of not more than one year or less than 90 days; or

(3) both such fine and confinement.

(b) If it is shown on the trial of a Class B misdemeanor that the defendant has been before convicted of a Class A or Class B misdemeanor or any degree of felony, on conviction he shall be punished by:

(1) a fine not to exceed $2,000;

(2) confinement in jail for any term of not more than 180 days or less than 30 days; or

(3) both such fine and confinement.

(c) If it is shown on the trial of an offense punishable as a Class C misdemeanor under Section 42.01 or 49.02 that the defendant has been before convicted under either of those sections three times or three times for any combination of those offenses and each prior offense was committed in the 24 months preceding the date of commission of the instant offense, the defendant shall be punished by:

(1) a fine not to exceed $2,000;

(2) confinement in jail for a term not to exceed 180 days; or

(3) both such fine and confinement.

(d) If the punishment scheme for an offense contains a specific enhancement provision increasing punishment for a defendant who has previously been convicted of the offense, the specific enhancement provision controls over this section.

Sec. 12.44. Reduction of State Jail Felony Punishment to Misdemeanor Punishment.

(a) A court may punish a defendant who is convicted of a state jail felony by imposing the confinement permissible as punishment for a Class A misdemeanor if, after considering the gravity and circumstances of the felony committed and the history, character, and rehabilitative needs of the defendant, the court finds that such punishment would best serve the ends of justice.

(b) At the request of the prosecuting attorney, the court may authorize the prosecuting attorney to prosecute a state jail felony as a Class A misdemeanor.

Sec. 12.45. Admission of Unadjudicated Offense.

(a) A person may, with the consent of the attorney for the state, admit during the sentencing hearing his guilt of one or more unadjudicated offenses and request the court to take each into account in determining sentence for the offense or offenses of which he stands adjudged guilty.

(b) Before a court may take into account an admitted offense over which exclusive venue lies in another county or district, the court must obtain permission from the prosecuting attorney with jurisdiction over the offense.

(c) If a court lawfully takes into account an admitted offense, prosecution is barred for that offense.

Sec. 12.46. Use of Prior Convictions.

The use of a conviction for enhancement purposes shall not preclude the subsequent use of such conviction for enhancement purposes.

Sec. 12.47. Penalty If Offense Committed Because of Bias or Prejudice.

(a) If an affirmative finding under Article 42.014, Code of Criminal Procedure, is made in the trial of an offense other than a first degree felony or a Class A misdemeanor, the punishment for the offense is increased to the punishment prescribed for the next highest category of offense. If the offense is a Class A misdemeanor, the minimum term of confinement for the offense is increased to 180 days. This section does not apply to the trial of an offense of injury to a disabled individual under Section 22.04, if the affirmative finding in the case under Article 42.014, Code of Criminal Procedure, shows that the defendant intentionally selected the victim because the victim was disabled.

(b) The attorney general, if requested to do so by a prosecuting attorney, may assist the prosecuting attorney in the investigation or prosecution of an offense committed because of bias or prejudice. The attorney general shall designate one individual in the division of the attorney general's office that assists in the prosecution of criminal cases to coordinate responses to requests made under this subsection.

Sec. 12.48. Certain Offenses Resulting in Loss to Nursing and Convalescent Homes.

If it is shown on the trial of an offense under Chapter 31 or 32 that, as a result of a loss incurred because of the conduct charged, a trustee was appointed and emergency assistance funds, other than funds used to pay the expenses of the trustee, were used for a nursing or convalescent home under Subchapter D, Chapter 242, Health and Safety Code, the punishment for the offense is increased to the punishment prescribed for the next higher category of offense except that a felony of the first degree is punished as a felony of the first degree.

Sec. 12.49. Penalty If Controlled Substance Used to Commit Offense.

If the court makes an affirmative finding under Article 42.012, Code of Criminal Procedure, in the punishment phase of the trial of an offense under Chapter 29, Chapter 31, or Title 5, other than a first degree felony or a Class A misdemeanor, the punishment for the offense is increased to the punishment prescribed for the next highest category of offense. If the offense is a Class A misdemeanor, the minimum term of confinement for the offense is increased to 180 days.

Sec. 12.50. Penalty If Offense Committed in Disaster Area or Evacuated Area.

(a) Subject to Subsection (c), the punishment for an offense described by Subsection (b) is increased to the punishment prescribed for the next higher category of offense if it is shown on the trial of the offense that the offense was committed in an area that was, at the time of the offense:

(1) subject to a declaration of a state of disaster made by:

(A) the president of the United States under the Robert T. Stafford Disaster Relief and Emergency Assistance Act (42 U.S.C. Section 5121 et seq.);

(B) the governor under Section 418.014, Government Code; or

(C) the presiding officer of the governing body of a political subdivision under Section 418.108, Government Code; or

(2) subject to an emergency evacuation order.

(b) The increase in punishment authorized by this section applies only to an offense under:

(1) Section 22.01;

(2) Section 28.02;

(3) Section 29.02;

(4) Section 30.02;

(5) Section 30.03;

(6) Section 30.04;

(7) Section 30.05; and

(8) Section 31.03.

(c) If an offense listed under Subsection (b)(1), (5), (6), (7), or (8) is punishable as a Class A misdemeanor, the minimum term of confinement for the offense is increased to 180 days. If an offense listed under Subsection (b)(2), (4), or (8) is punishable as a felony of the first degree, the punishment for that offense may not be increased under this section.

(d) [Repealed.]

(e) For purposes of this section, "emergency evacuation order" means an official statement issued by the governing body of this state or a political subdivision of this state to recommend or require the evacuation of all or part of the population of an area stricken or threatened with a disaster.

Sec. 12.501. Penalty for Certain Offenses Committed in Retaliation for or on Account of Person's Service or Status As Public Servant.

(a) In this section, "public servant" has the meaning assigned by Section 36.06.

(b) Subject to Subsection (d), the punishment for an offense described by Subsection (c) is increased to the punishment prescribed for the next higher category of offense if it is shown on the trial of the offense that:

(1) the offense:

(A) was committed against a person the actor knows is a public servant or a member of a public servant's family or household; or

(B) involves property that the actor knows belongs to, is under the control of, or is lawfully possessed by a public servant; and

(2) the offense was committed in retaliation for or on account of the service or status of the person as a public servant.

(c) The increase in punishment authorized by this section applies only to:

(1) an offense under Section 21.16, 21.18, 21.19, 22.011, 28.02, 28.03, 30.05, 33.02, 42.07, or 42.072; or

(2) an offense under Section 32.51, other than an offense punishable under Subsection (c-1) of that section.

(d) If an offense described by Subsection (c) is punishable as a Class A misdemeanor, the minimum term of confinement for the offense is increased to 180 days. If an offense described by Subsection (c) is punishable as a felony of the first degree, the punishment for that offense may not be increased under this section.

(e) For purposes of this section, "member of a public servant's family" means a person related to the public servant within the second degree of consanguinity.

SUBCHAPTER E CORPORATIONS AND ASSOCIATIONS

Sec. 12.51. Authorized Punishments for Corporations, Associations, Limited Liability Companies, and Other Business Entities.

(a) If a corporation, an association, a limited liability company, or another business entity is adjudged guilty of an offense that provides a penalty consisting of a fine only, a court may sentence the corporation, association, limited liability company, or other business entity to pay a fine in an amount fixed by the court, not to exceed the fine provided by the offense.

(b) If a corporation, an association, a limited liability company, or another business entity is adjudged guilty of an offense that provides a penalty including imprisonment, or that provides no specific penalty, a court may sentence the corporation, association, limited liability company, or other business entity to pay a fine in an amount fixed by the court, not to exceed:

(1) $20,000 if the offense is a felony of any category;

(2) $10,000 if the offense is a Class A or Class B misdemeanor;

(3) $2,000 if the offense is a Class C misdemeanor; or

(4) $50,000 if, as a result of an offense classified as a felony or Class A misdemeanor, an individual suffers serious bodily injury or death.

(c) In lieu of the fines authorized by Subsections (a), (b)(1), (b)(2), and (b)(4), if a court finds that the corporation, association, limited liability company, or other business entity gained money or property or caused personal injury or death, property damage, or other loss through the commission of a felony or Class A or Class B misdemeanor, the court may sentence the corporation, association, limited liability company, or other business entity to pay a fine in an amount fixed by the court, not to exceed double the amount gained or caused by the corporation, association, limited liability company, or business entity to be lost or damaged, whichever is greater.

(d) In addition to any sentence that may be imposed by this section, a corporation, an association, a limited liability company, or another business entity that has been adjudged guilty of an offense may be ordered by the court to give notice of the conviction to any person the court deems appropriate.

(e) On conviction of a corporation, an association, a limited liability company, or another business entity, the court shall notify the attorney general of that fact.

(f) In this section, "business entity" has the meaning assigned by Section 7.21.

TITLE 4 INCHOATE OFFENSES

CHAPTER 15 PREPARATORY OFFENSES

Sec. 15.01. Criminal Attempt.

(a) A person commits an offense if, with specific intent to commit an offense, he does an act amounting to more than mere preparation that tends but fails to effect the commission of the offense intended.

(b) If a person attempts an offense that may be aggravated, his conduct constitutes an attempt to commit the aggravated offense if an element that aggravates the offense accompanies the attempt.

(c) It is no defense to prosecution for criminal attempt that the offense attempted was actually committed.

(d) An offense under this section is one category lower than the offense attempted, and if the offense attempted is a state jail felony, the offense is a Class A misdemeanor.

Sec. 15.02. Criminal Conspiracy.

(a) A person commits criminal conspiracy if, with intent that a felony be committed:

(1) he agrees with one or more persons that they or one or more of them engage in conduct that would constitute the offense; and

(2) he or one or more of them performs an overt act in pursuance of the agreement.

(b) An agreement constituting a conspiracy may be inferred from acts of the parties.

(c) It is no defense to prosecution for criminal conspiracy that:

(1) one or more of the coconspirators is not criminally responsible for the object offense;

(2) one or more of the coconspirators has been acquitted, so long as two or more coconspirators have not been acquitted;

(3) one or more of the coconspirators has not been prosecuted or convicted, has been convicted of a different offense, or is immune from prosecution;

(4) the actor belongs to a class of persons that by definition of the object offense is legally incapable of committing the object offense in an individual capacity; or

(5) the object offense was actually committed.

(d) An offense under this section is one category lower than the most serious felony that is the object of the conspiracy, and if the most serious felony that is the object of the conspiracy is a state jail felony, the offense is a Class A misdemeanor.

Sec. 15.03. Criminal Solicitation.

(a) A person commits an offense if, with intent that a capital felony or felony of the first degree be committed, he requests, commands, or attempts to induce another to engage in specific conduct that, under the circumstances surrounding his conduct as the actor believes them to be, would constitute the felony or make the other a party to its commission.

(b) A person may not be convicted under this section on the uncorroborated testimony of the person allegedly solicited and unless the solicitation is made under circumstances strongly corroborative of both the solicitation itself and the actor's intent that the other person act on the solicitation.

(c) It is no defense to prosecution under this section that:

(1) the person solicited is not criminally responsible for the felony solicited;

(2) the person solicited has been acquitted, has not been prosecuted or convicted, has been convicted of a different offense or of a different type or class of offense, or is immune from prosecution;

(3) the actor belongs to a class of persons that by definition of the felony solicited is legally incapable of committing the offense in an individual capacity; or

(4) the felony solicited was actually committed.

(d) An offense under this section is:

(1) a felony of the first degree if the offense solicited is a capital offense; or

(2) a felony of the second degree if the offense solicited is a felony of the first degree.

Sec. 15.031. Criminal Solicitation of a Minor.

(a) A person commits an offense if, with intent that an offense listed by Article 42A.054(a), Code of Criminal Procedure, be committed, the person requests, commands, or attempts to induce a minor to engage in specific conduct that, under the circumstances surrounding the actor's conduct as the actor believes them to be, would constitute an offense listed by Article 42A.054(a) or make the minor a party to the commission of an offense listed by Article 42A.054(a).

(b) A person commits an offense if, with intent that an offense under Section 20A.02(a)(7) or (8), 21.02, 21.11, 22.011, 22.021, 43.02, 43.021, 43.05(a)(2), or 43.25 be committed, the person by any means requests, commands, or attempts to induce a minor or another whom the person believes to be a minor to engage in specific conduct that, under the circumstances surrounding the actor's conduct as the actor believes them to be, would constitute an offense under one of those sections or would make the minor or other believed by the person to be a minor a party to the commission of an offense under one of those sections.

(c) A person may not be convicted under this section on the uncorroborated testimony of the minor allegedly solicited unless the solicitation is made under circumstances strongly corroborative of both the solicitation itself and the actor's intent that the minor act on the solicitation.

(d) It is no defense to prosecution under this section that:

(1) the minor solicited is not criminally responsible for the offense solicited;

(2) the minor solicited has been acquitted, has not been prosecuted or convicted, has been convicted of a different offense or of a different type or class of offense, or is immune from prosecution;

(3) the actor belongs to a class of persons that by definition of the offense solicited is legally incapable of committing the offense in an individual capacity; or

(4) the offense solicited was actually committed.

(e) An offense under this section is one category lower than the solicited offense, except that an offense under this section is the same category as the solicited offense if it is shown on the trial of the offense that the actor:

(1) was at the time of the offense 17 years of age or older and a member of a criminal street gang, as defined by Section 71.01; and

(2) committed the offense with the intent to:

(A) further the criminal activities of the criminal street gang; or

(B) avoid detection as a member of a criminal street gang.

(f) In this section, "minor" means an individual younger than 17 years of age.

Sec. 15.04. Renunciation Defense.

(a) It is an affirmative defense to prosecution under Section 15.01 that under circumstances manifesting a voluntary and complete renunciation of his criminal objective the actor avoided commission of the offense attempted by abandoning his criminal conduct or, if abandonment was insufficient to avoid commission of the offense, by taking further affirmative action that prevented the commission.

(b) It is an affirmative defense to prosecution under Section 15.02 or 15.03 that under circumstances manifesting a voluntary and complete renunciation of his criminal objective the actor countermanded his solicitation or withdrew from the conspiracy before commission of the object offense and took further affirmative action that prevented the commission of the object offense.

(c) Renunciation is not voluntary if it is motivated in whole or in part:

(1) by circumstances not present or apparent at the inception of the actor's course of conduct that increase the probability of detection or apprehension or that make more difficult the accomplishment of the objective; or

(2) by a decision to postpone the criminal conduct until another time or to transfer the criminal act to another but similar objective or victim.

(d) Evidence that the defendant renounced his criminal objective by abandoning his criminal conduct, countermanding his solicitation, or withdrawing from the conspiracy before the criminal offense was committed and made substantial effort to prevent the commission of the object offense shall be admissible as mitigation at the hearing on punishment if he has been found guilty of criminal attempt, criminal solicitation, or criminal conspiracy; and in the event of a finding of renunciation under this subsection, the punishment shall be one grade lower than that provided for the offense committed.

Sec. 15.05. No Offense.

Attempt or conspiracy to commit, or solicitation of, a preparatory offense defined in this chapter is not an offense.

CHAPTER 16
CRIMINAL INSTRUMENTS, INTERCEPTION OF WIRE OR ORAL COMMUNICATION, AND INSTALLATION OF TRACKING DEVICE

Sec. 16.01. Unlawful Use of Criminal Instrument or Mechanical Security Device.

(a) A person commits an offense if:

(1) the person possesses a criminal instrument or mechanical security device with the intent to use the instrument or device in the commission of an offense; or

(2) with knowledge of its character and with the intent to use a criminal instrument or mechanical security device or aid or permit another to use the instrument or device in the commission of an offense, the person manufactures, adapts, sells, installs, or sets up the instrument or device.

(b) For the purpose of this section:

(1) "Criminal instrument" means anything, the possession, manufacture, or sale of which is not otherwise an offense, that is specially designed, made, or adapted for use in the commission of an offense.

(2) "Mechanical security device" means a device designed or manufactured for use by a locksmith to perform services for a customer who seeks entry to a structure, motor vehicle, or other property.

(c) An offense under Subsection (a)(1) is one category lower than the offense intended. An offense under Subsection (a)(2) is a state jail felony.

Sec. 16.02. Unlawful Interception, Use, or Disclosure of Wire, Oral, or Electronic Communications.

(a) In this section:

(1) "Communication common carrier," "computer trespasser," "contents," "covert entry," "electronic communication," "intercept," "interception device," "investigative or law enforcement officer," "oral communication," "protected computer," and "wire communication" have the meanings assigned by Article 18A.001, Code of Criminal Procedure.

(2) "Immediate life-threatening situation" and "member of a law enforcement unit specially trained to respond to and deal with life-threatening situations" have the meanings assigned by Article 18A.201, Code of Criminal Procedure.

(3) "Readily accessible to the general public" means, with respect to a radio communication, a communication that is not:

(A) scrambled or encrypted;

(B) transmitted using modulation techniques whose essential parameters have been withheld from the public with the intention of preserving the privacy of the communication;

(C) carried on a subcarrier or other signal subsidiary to a radio transmission;

(D) transmitted over a communication system provided by a common carrier, unless the communication is a tone-only paging system communication;

(E) transmitted on frequencies allocated under Part 25, Subpart D, E, or F of Part 74, or Part 94 of the rules of the Federal Communications Commission, unless, in the case of a communication transmitted on a frequency allocated under Part 74 that is not exclusively allocated to broadcast auxiliary services, the communication is a two-way voice communication by radio; or

(F) an electronic communication.

(b) A person commits an offense if the person:

(1) intentionally intercepts, endeavors to intercept, or procures another person to intercept or endeavor to intercept a wire, oral, or electronic communication;

(2) intentionally discloses or endeavors to disclose to another person the contents of a wire, oral, or electronic communication if the person knows or has reason to know the information was obtained through the interception of a wire, oral, or electronic communication in violation of this subsection;

(3) intentionally uses or endeavors to use the contents of a wire, oral, or electronic communication if the person knows or is reckless about whether the information was obtained through the interception of a wire, oral, or electronic communication in violation of this subsection;

(4) knowingly or intentionally effects a covert entry for the purpose of intercepting wire, oral, or electronic communications without court order or authorization; or

(5) intentionally uses, endeavors to use, or procures any other person to use or endeavor to use any interception device to intercept any oral communication when the device:

(A) is affixed to, or otherwise transmits a signal through a wire, cable, or other connection used in wire communications; or

(B) transmits communications by radio or interferes with the transmission of communications by radio.

(c) It is an affirmative defense to prosecution under Subsection (b) that:

(1) an operator of a switchboard or an officer, employee, or agent of a communication common carrier whose facilities are used in the transmission of a wire or electronic communication intercepts a communication or discloses or uses an intercepted communication in the normal course of employment while engaged in an activity that is a necessary incident to the rendition of service or to the protection of the rights or property of the carrier of the communication, unless the interception results from the communication common carrier's use of service observing or random monitoring for purposes other than mechanical or service quality control checks;

(2) an officer, employee, or agent of a communication common carrier provides information, facilities, or technical assistance to an investigative or law enforcement officer who is authorized as provided by this section to intercept a wire, oral, or electronic communication;

(3) a person acting under color of law intercepts:

(A) a wire, oral, or electronic communication, if the person is a party to the communication or if one of the parties to the communication has given prior consent to the interception;

(B) a wire, oral, or electronic communication, if the person is acting under the authority of Chapter 18A, Code of Criminal Procedure; or

(C) a wire or electronic communication made by a computer trespasser and transmitted to, through, or from a protected computer, if:

(i) the interception did not acquire a communication other than one transmitted to or from the computer trespasser;

(ii) the owner of the protected computer consented to the interception of the computer trespasser's communications on the protected computer; and

(iii) the actor was lawfully engaged in an ongoing criminal investigation and the actor had reasonable suspicion to believe that the contents of the computer trespasser's communications likely to be obtained would be material to the investigation;

(4) a person not acting under color of law intercepts a wire, oral, or electronic communication, if:

(A) the person is a party to the communication; or

(B) one of the parties to the communication has given prior consent to the interception, unless the communication is intercepted for the purpose of committing an unlawful act;

(5) a person acting under color of law intercepts a wire, oral, or electronic communication if:

(A) oral or written consent for the interception is given by a magistrate before the interception;

(B) an immediate life-threatening situation exists;

(C) the person is a member of a law enforcement unit specially trained to:

(i) respond to and deal with life-threatening situations; or

(ii) install interception devices; and

(D) the interception ceases immediately on termination of the life-threatening situation;

(6) an officer, employee, or agent of the Federal Communications Commission intercepts a communication transmitted by radio or discloses or uses an intercepted communication in the normal course of employment and in the discharge of the monitoring responsibilities exercised by the Federal Communications Commission in the enforcement of Chapter 5, Title 47, United States Code;

(7) a person intercepts or obtains access to an electronic communication that was made through an electronic communication system that is configured to permit the communication to be readily accessible to the general public;

(8) a person intercepts radio communication, other than a cordless telephone communication that is transmitted between a cordless telephone handset and a base unit, that is transmitted:

(A) by a station for the use of the general public;

(B) to ships, aircraft, vehicles, or persons in distress;

(C) by a governmental, law enforcement, civil defense, private land mobile, or public safety communications system that is readily accessible to the general public, unless the radio communication is transmitted by a law enforcement representative to or from a mobile data terminal;

(D) by a station operating on an authorized frequency within the bands allocated to the amateur, citizens band, or general mobile radio services; or

(E) by a marine or aeronautical communications system;

(9) a person intercepts a wire or electronic communication the transmission of which causes harmful interference to a lawfully operating station or consumer electronic equipment, to the extent necessary to identify the source of the interference;

(10) a user of the same frequency intercepts a radio communication made through a system that uses frequencies monitored by individuals engaged in the provision or the use of the system, if the communication is not scrambled or encrypted; or

(11) a provider of an electronic communications service records the fact that a wire or electronic communication was initiated or completed in order to protect the provider, another provider furnishing service towards the completion of the communication, or a user of that service from fraudulent, unlawful, or abusive use of the service.

(d) A person commits an offense if the person:

(1) intentionally manufactures, assembles, possesses, or sells an interception device knowing or having reason to know that the device is designed primarily for nonconsensual interception of wire, electronic, or oral communications and that the device or a component of the device has been or will be used for an unlawful purpose; or

(2) places in a newspaper, magazine, handbill, or other publication an advertisement of an interception device:

(A) knowing or having reason to know that the device is designed primarily for nonconsensual interception of wire, electronic, or oral communications;

(B) promoting the use of the device for the purpose of nonconsensual interception of wire, electronic, or oral communications; or

(C) knowing or having reason to know that the advertisement will promote the use of the device for the purpose of nonconsensual interception of wire, electronic, or oral communications.

(e) It is an affirmative defense to prosecution under Subsection (d) that the manufacture, assembly, possession, or sale of an interception device that is designed primarily for the purpose of nonconsensual interception of wire, electronic, or oral communication is by:

(1) a communication common carrier or a provider of wire or electronic communications service or an officer, agent, or employee of or a person under contract with a communication common carrier or service provider acting in the normal course of the provider's or carrier's business;

(2) an officer, agent, or employee of a person under contract with, bidding on contracts with, or doing business with the United States or this state acting in the normal course of the activities of the United States or this state;

(3) a member of the Department of Public Safety who is specifically trained to install wire, oral, or electronic communications intercept equipment; or

(4) a member of a local law enforcement agency that has an established unit specifically designated to respond to and deal with life-threatening situations.

(e-1) It is a defense to prosecution under Subsection (d)(1) that the interception device is possessed by a person authorized to possess the device under Section 500.008, Government Code, or Section 242.103, Human Resources Code.

(f) An offense under this section is a felony of the second degree, unless the offense is committed under Subsection (d) or (g), in which event the offense is a state jail felony.

(g) A person commits an offense if, knowing that a government attorney or an investigative or law enforcement officer has been authorized or has applied for authorization to intercept wire, electronic, or oral communications, the person obstructs, impedes, prevents, gives notice to another of, or attempts to give notice to another of the interception.

(h) [Repealed by Acts 2005, 79th Leg., ch. 889 (S.B. 1551), § 1, effective June 17, 2005.]

Sec. 16.021. Illegal Interception [Deleted].

Deleted by Acts 1993, 73rd Leg., ch. 900 (S.B. 1067), § 1.01, effective September 1, 1994.

Sec. 16.03. Unlawful Use of Pen Register or Trap and Trace Device.

(a) A person commits an offense if the person knowingly installs or uses a pen register or trap and trace device to record or decode electronic or other impulses for the purpose of identifying telephone numbers dialed or otherwise transmitted on a telephone line.

(b) In this section:

(1) "Authorized" peace officer," "pen register," and "trap and trace device" have the meanings assigned by Article 18B.001, Code of Criminal Procedure.

(2) "Communication common carrier" has the meaning assigned by Article 18A.001, Code of Criminal Procedure.

(c) It is an affirmative defense to prosecution under Subsection (a) that the actor is:

(1) an officer, employee, or agent of a communication common carrier and the actor installs or uses a device or equipment to record a number dialed from or to a telephone instrument in the normal course of business of the carrier for purposes of:

(A) protecting property or services provided by the carrier; or

(B) assisting another who the actor reasonably believes to be a peace officer authorized to install or use a pen register or trap and trace device under Chapter 18B, Code of Criminal Procedure;

(2) an officer, employee, or agent of a lawful enterprise and the actor installs or uses a device or equipment while engaged in an activity that:

(A) is a necessary incident to the rendition of service or to the protection of property of or services provided by the enterprise; and

(B) is not made for the purpose of gathering information for a law enforcement agency or private investigative agency, other than information related to the theft of communication or information services provided by the enterprise; or

(3) a person authorized to install or use a pen register or trap and trace device under Chapter 18B, Code of Criminal Procedure.

(d) An offense under this section is a state jail felony.

Sec. 16.04. Unlawful Access to Stored Communications.

(a) In this section:

(1) "Electronic communication," "user," and "wire communication" have the meanings assigned by Article 18A.001, Code of Criminal Procedure.

(2) "Electronic storage" has the meaning assigned by Article 18B.001, Code of Criminal Procedure.

(b) A person commits an offense if the person obtains, alters, or prevents authorized access to a wire or electronic communication while the communication is in electronic storage by:

(1) intentionally obtaining access without authorization to a facility through which a wire or electronic communications service is provided; or

(2) intentionally exceeding an authorization for access to a facility through which a wire or electronic communications service is provided.

(c) Except as provided by Subsection (d), an offense under Subsection (b) is a Class A misdemeanor.

(d) If committed to obtain a benefit or to harm another, an offense is a state jail felony.

(e) It is an affirmative defense to prosecution under Subsection (b) that the conduct was authorized by:

(1) the provider of the wire or electronic communications service;

(2) the user of the wire or electronic communications service;

(3) the addressee or intended recipient of the wire or electronic communication; or

(4) Chapter 18B, Code of Criminal Procedure.

Sec. 16.05. Illegal Divulgence of Public Communications.

(a) In this section, "electronic communications service" has the meaning assigned by Article 18A.001, Code of Criminal Procedure.

(b) A person who provides electronic communications service to the public commits an offense if the person knowingly divulges the contents of a communication to another who is not the intended recipient of the communication.

(c) It is an affirmative defense to prosecution under Subsection (b) that the actor divulged the contents of the communication:

(1) as authorized by federal or state law;

(2) to a person employed, authorized, or whose facilities are used to forward the communication to the communication's destination; or

(3) to a law enforcement agency if the contents reasonably appear to pertain to the commission of a crime.

(d) Except as provided by Subsection (e), an offense under Subsection (b) that involves a scrambled or encrypted radio communication is a state jail felony.

(e) If committed for a tortious or illegal purpose or to gain a benefit, an offense under Subsection (b) that involves a radio communication that is not scrambled or encrypted:

(1) is a Class A misdemeanor if the communication is not a public land mobile radio service communication or a paging service communication; or

(2) is a Class C misdemeanor if the communication is a public land mobile radio service communication or a paging service communication.

(f) [Repealed by Acts 1997, 75th Leg., ch. 1051 (S.B. 1120), § 13, effective September 1, 1997.]

Sec. 16.06. Unlawful Installation of Tracking Device.

(a) In this section:

(1) "Electronic or mechanical tracking device" means a device capable of emitting an electronic frequency or other signal that may be used by a person to identify, monitor, or record the location of another person or object.

(2) "Motor vehicle" has the meaning assigned by Section 501.002, Transportation Code.

(b) A person commits an offense if the person knowingly installs an electronic or mechanical tracking device on a motor vehicle owned or leased by another person.

(c) An offense under this section is a Class A misdemeanor.

(d) It is an affirmative defense to prosecution under this section that the person:

(1) obtained the effective consent of the owner or lessee of the motor vehicle before the electronic or mechanical tracking device was installed;

(2) assisted another whom the person reasonably believed to be a peace officer authorized to install the device in the course of a criminal investigation or pursuant to an order of a court to gather information for a law enforcement agency; or

(3) was a private investigator licensed under Chapter 1702, Occupations Code, who installed the device:

(A) with written consent:

(i) to install the device given by the owner or lessee of the motor vehicle; and

(ii) to enter private residential property, if that entry was necessary to install the device, given by the owner or lessee of the property; or

(B) pursuant to an order of or other authorization from a court to gather information.

(e) This section does not apply to a peace officer who installed the device in the course of a criminal investigation or pursuant to an order of a court to gather information for a law enforcement agency.

TITLE 5
OFFENSES AGAINST THE PERSON

CHAPTER 19
CRIMINAL HOMICIDE

Sec. 19.01. Types of Criminal Homicide.

(a) A person commits criminal homicide if he intentionally, knowingly, recklessly, or with criminal negligence causes the death of an individual.

(b) Criminal homicide is murder, capital murder, manslaughter, or criminally negligent homicide.

Sec. 19.02. Murder.

(a) In this section:

(1) "Adequate cause" means cause that would commonly produce a degree of anger, rage, resentment, or terror in a person of ordinary temper, sufficient to render the mind incapable of cool reflection.

(2) "Sudden passion" means passion directly caused by and arising out of provocation by the individual killed or another acting with the person killed which passion arises at the time of the offense and is not solely the result of former provocation.

(b) A person commits an offense if he:

(1) intentionally or knowingly causes the death of an individual;

(2) intends to cause serious bodily injury and commits an act clearly dangerous to human life that causes the death of an individual; or

(3) commits or attempts to commit a felony, other than manslaughter, and in the course of and in furtherance of the commission or attempt, or in immediate flight from the commission or attempt, he commits or attempts to commit an act clearly dangerous to human life that causes the death of an individual.

(c) Except as provided by Subsection (d), an offense under this section is a felony of the first degree.

(d) At the punishment stage of a trial, the defendant may raise the issue as to whether he caused the death under the immediate influence of sudden passion arising from an adequate cause. If the defendant proves the issue in the affirmative by a preponderance of the evidence, the offense is a felony of the second degree.

Sec. 19.03. Capital Murder.

(a) A person commits an offense if the person commits murder as defined under Section 19.02(b)(1) and:

(1) the person murders a peace officer or fireman who is acting in the lawful discharge of an official duty and who the person knows is a peace officer or fireman;

(2) the person intentionally commits the murder in the course of committing or attempting to commit kidnapping, burglary, robbery, aggravated sexual assault, arson, obstruction or retaliation, or terroristic threat under Section 22.07(a)(1), (3), (4), (5), or (6);

(3) the person commits the murder for remuneration or the promise of remuneration or employs another to commit the murder for remuneration or the promise of remuneration;

(4) the person commits the murder while escaping or attempting to escape from a penal institution;

(5) the person, while incarcerated in a penal institution, murders another:

(A) who is employed in the operation of the penal institution; or

(B) with the intent to establish, maintain, or participate in a combination or in the profits of a combination;

(6) the person:

(A) while incarcerated for an offense under this section or Section 19.02, murders another; or

(B) while serving a sentence of life imprisonment or a term of 99 years for an offense under Section 20.04, 22.021, or 29.03, murders another;

(7) the person murders more than one person:

(A) during the same criminal transaction; or

(B) during different criminal transactions but the murders are committed pursuant to the same scheme or course of conduct;

(8) the person murders an individual under 10 years of age;

(9) the person murders an individual 10 years of age or older but younger than 15 years of age; or

(10) the person murders another person in retaliation for or on account of the service or status of the other person as a judge or justice of the supreme court, the court of criminal appeals, a court of appeals, a district court, a criminal district court, a constitutional county court, a statutory county court, a justice court, or a municipal court.

(b) An offense under this section is a capital felony.

(c) If the jury or, when authorized by law, the judge does not find beyond a reasonable doubt that the defendant is guilty of an offense under this section, he may be convicted of murder or of any other lesser included offense.

Sec. 19.04. Manslaughter.

(a) A person commits an offense if he recklessly causes the death of an individual.

(b) An offense under this section is a felony of the second degree.

Sec. 19.05. Criminally Negligent Homicide.

(a) A person commits an offense if he causes the death of an individual by criminal negligence.

(b) An offense under this section is a state jail felony.

Sec. 19.06. Applicability to Certain Conduct.

This chapter does not apply to the death of an unborn child if the conduct charged is:

(1) conduct committed by the mother of the unborn child;

(2) a lawful medical procedure performed by a physician or other licensed health care provider with the requisite consent, if the death of the unborn child was the intended result of the procedure;

(3) a lawful medical procedure performed by a physician or other licensed health care provider with the requisite consent as part of an assisted reproduction as defined by Section 160.102, Family Code; or

(4) the dispensation of a drug in accordance with law or administration of a drug prescribed in accordance with law.

Sec. 19.07. Criminally Negligent Homicide [Renumbered].

Renumbered to Tex. Penal Code § 19.05 by Acts 1993, 73rd Leg., ch. 900 (S.B. 1067), § 1.01, effective September 1, 1994.

CHAPTER 20
KIDNAPPING, UNLAWFUL RESTRAINT, AND SMUGGLING OF PERSONS

Sec. 20.01. Definitions.

In this chapter:

(1) "Restrain" means to restrict a person's movements without consent, so as to interfere substantially with the person's liberty, by moving the person from one place to another or by confining the person. Restraint is "without consent" if it is accomplished by:

(A) force, intimidation, or deception; or

(B) any means, including acquiescence of the victim, if:

(i) the victim is a child who is less than 14 years of age or an incompetent person and the parent, guardian, or person or institution acting in loco parentis has not acquiesced in the movement or confinement; or

(ii) the victim is a child who is 14 years of age or older and younger than 17 years of age, the victim is taken outside of the state and outside a 120-mile radius from the victim's residence, and the parent, guardian, or person or institution acting in loco parentis has not acquiesced in the movement.

(2) "Abduct" means to restrain a person with intent to prevent his liberation by:

(A) secreting or holding him in a place where he is not likely to be found; or

(B) using or threatening to use deadly force.

(3) "Relative" means a parent or stepparent, ancestor, sibling, or uncle or aunt, including an adoptive relative of the same degree through marriage or adoption.

(4) "Person" means an individual or a corporation, association, limited liability company, or other entity or organization governed by the Business Organizations Code.

(5) Notwithstanding Section 1.07, "individual" means a human being who has been born and is alive.

(6) "Agricultural land" has the meaning assigned by Section 75.001, Civil Practice and Remedies Code.

(7) "Firearm" has the meaning assigned by Section 46.01.

(8) "Special investigator" includes an agent of the United States Department of Homeland Security.

Sec. 20.02. Unlawful Restraint.

(a) A person commits an offense if he intentionally or knowingly restrains another person.

(b) It is an affirmative defense to prosecution under this section that:

(1) the person restrained was a child younger than 14 years of age;

(2) the actor was a relative of the child; and

(3) the actor's sole intent was to assume lawful control of the child.

(c) An offense under this section is a Class A misdemeanor, except that the offense is:

(1) a state jail felony if the person restrained was a child younger than 17 years of age;

(2) a felony of the third degree if:

(A) the actor recklessly exposes the victim to a substantial risk of serious bodily injury;

(B) the actor restrains an individual the actor knows is a public servant while the public servant is lawfully discharging an official duty or in retaliation or on account of an exercise of official power or performance of an official duty as a public servant; or

(C) the actor while in custody restrains any other person; or

(3) notwithstanding Subdivision (2)(B), a felony of the second degree if the actor restrains an individual the actor knows is a peace officer or judge while the officer or judge is lawfully discharging an official duty or in retaliation or on account of an exercise of official power or performance of an official duty as a peace officer or judge.

(d) It is no offense to detain or move another under this section when it is for the purpose of effecting a lawful arrest or detaining an individual lawfully arrested.

(e) It is an affirmative defense to prosecution under this section that:

(1) the person restrained was a child who is 14 years of age or older and younger than 17 years of age;

(2) the actor does not restrain the child by force, intimidation, or deception; and

(3) the actor is not more than three years older than the child.

Sec. 20.03. Kidnapping.

(a) A person commits an offense if he intentionally or knowingly abducts another person.

(b) It is an affirmative defense to prosecution under this section that:

(1) the abduction was not coupled with intent to use or to threaten to use deadly force;

(2) the actor was a relative of the person abducted; and

(3) the actor's sole intent was to assume lawful control of the victim.

(c) An offense under this section is a felony of the third degree.

Sec. 20.04. Aggravated Kidnapping.

(a) A person commits an offense if he intentionally or knowingly abducts another person with the intent to:

(1) hold him for ransom or reward;

(2) use him as a shield or hostage;

(3) facilitate the commission of a felony or the flight after the attempt or commission of a felony;

(4) inflict bodily injury on him or violate or abuse him sexually;

(5) terrorize him or a third person; or

(6) interfere with the performance of any governmental or political function.

(b) A person commits an offense if the person intentionally or knowingly abducts another person and uses or exhibits a deadly weapon during the commission of the offense.

(c) Except as provided by Subsection (d), an offense under this section is a felony of the first degree.

(d) At the punishment stage of a trial, the defendant may raise the issue as to whether he voluntarily released the victim in a safe place. If the defendant proves the issue in the affirmative by a preponderance of the evidence, the offense is a felony of the second degree.

Sec. 20.05. Smuggling of Persons.

(a) A person commits an offense if the person knowingly:

(1) uses a motor vehicle, aircraft, watercraft, or other means of conveyance to transport an individual with the intent to:

(A) conceal the individual from a peace officer or special investigator; or

(B) flee from a person the actor knows is a peace officer or special investigator attempting to lawfully arrest or detain the actor;

(2) encourages or induces a person to enter or remain in this country in violation of federal law by concealing, harboring, or shielding that person from detection; or

(3) assists, guides, or directs two or more individuals to enter or remain on agricultural land without the effective consent of the owner.

(b) An offense under this section is a felony of the third degree, except that the offense is:

(1) a felony of the second degree if:

(A) the actor commits the offense in a manner that creates a substantial likelihood that the smuggled individual will suffer serious bodily injury or death;

(B) the smuggled individual is a child younger than 18 years of age at the time of the offense;

(C) the offense was committed with the intent to obtain a pecuniary benefit;

(D) during the commission of the offense the actor, another party to the offense, or an individual assisted, guided, or directed by the actor knowingly possessed a firearm; or

(E) the actor commits the offense under Subsection (a)(1)(B); or

(2) a felony of the first degree if:

(A) it is shown on the trial of the offense that, as a direct result of the commission of the offense, the smuggled individual became a victim of sexual assault, as defined by Section 22.011, or aggravated sexual assault, as defined by Section 22.021; or

(B) the smuggled individual suffered serious bodily injury or death.

(c) It is an affirmative defense to prosecution of an offense under this section, other than an offense punishable under Subsection (b)(1)(A) or (b)(2), that the actor is related to the smuggled individual within the second degree of consanguinity or, at the time of the offense, within the second degree of affinity.

(d) If conduct constituting an offense under this section also constitutes an offense under another section of this code, the actor may be prosecuted under either section or under both sections.

Sec. 20.06. Continuous Smuggling of Persons.

(a) A person commits an offense if, during a period that is 10 or more days in duration, the person engages two or more times in conduct that constitutes an offense under Section 20.05.

(b) If a jury is the trier of fact, members of the jury are not required to agree unanimously on which specific conduct engaged in by the defendant constituted an offense under Section 20.05 or on which exact date the defendant engaged in that conduct. The jury must agree unanimously that the defendant, during a period that is 10 or more days in duration, engaged two or more times in conduct that constitutes an offense under Section 20.05.

(c) If the victim of an offense under Subsection (a) is the same victim as a victim of an offense under Section 20.05, a defendant may not be convicted of the offense under Section 20.05 in the same criminal action as the offense under Subsection (a), unless the offense under Section 20.05:

(1) is charged in the alternative;

(2) occurred outside the period in which the offense alleged under Subsection (a) was committed; or

(3) is considered by the trier of fact to be a lesser included offense of the offense alleged under Subsection (a).

(d) A defendant may not be charged with more than one count under Subsection (a) if all of the conduct that constitutes an offense under Section 20.05 is alleged to have been committed against the same victim.

(e) Except as provided by Subsections (f) and (g), an offense under this section is a felony of the second degree.

(f) An offense under this section is a felony of the first degree if:

(1) the conduct constituting an offense under Section 20.05 is conducted in a manner that creates a substantial likelihood that the smuggled individual will suffer serious bodily injury or death; or

(2) the smuggled individual is a child younger than 18 years of age at the time of the offense.

(g) An offense under this section is a felony of the first degree, punishable by imprisonment in the Texas Department of Criminal Justice for life or for any term of not more than 99 years or less than 25 years, if:

(1) it is shown on the trial of the offense that, as a direct result of the commission of the offense, the smuggled individual became a victim of sexual assault, as defined by Section 22.011, or aggravated sexual assault, as defined by Section 22.021; or

(2) the smuggled individual suffered serious bodily injury or death.

Sec. 20.07. Operation of Stash House.

(a) A person commits an offense if the person knowingly:

(1) uses or permits another to use any real estate, building, room, tent, vehicle, boat, or other property owned by the person or under the person's control to commit an offense or to facilitate the commission of an offense under Section 20.05, 20.06, 20A.02, 20A.03, 43.04, or 43.05; or

(2) rents or leases any property to another, intending that the property be used as described by Subdivision (1).

(b) An offense under this section is a Class A misdemeanor.

(c) If conduct that constitutes an offense under this section also constitutes an offense under another law, the actor may be prosecuted under this section, the other law, or both.

CHAPTER 20A
TRAFFICKING OF PERSONS

Sec. 20A.01. Definitions.

In this chapter:

(1) "Child" means a person younger than 18 years of age.

(1-a) "Coercion" as defined by Section 1.07 includes:

(A) destroying, concealing, confiscating, or withholding from a trafficked person, or threatening to destroy, conceal, confiscate, or withhold from a trafficked person, the person's actual or purported:

(i) government records; or

(ii) identifying information or documents;

(B) causing a trafficked person, without the person's consent, to become intoxicated, as defined by Section 49.01, to a degree that impairs the person's ability to appraise the nature of or resist engaging in any conduct, including performing or providing labor or services; or

(C) withholding alcohol or a controlled substance to a degree that impairs the ability of a trafficked person with a chemical dependency, as defined by Section 462.001, Health and Safety Code, to appraise the nature of or resist engaging in any conduct, including performing or providing labor or services.

(2) "Forced labor or services" means labor or services, other than labor or services that constitute sexual conduct, that are performed or provided by another person and obtained through an actor's use of force, fraud, or coercion.

(2-a) "Premises" has the meaning assigned by Section 481.134, Health and Safety Code.

(2-b) "School" means a public or private primary or secondary school.

(3) "Sexual conduct" has the meaning assigned by Section 43.25.

(4) "Traffic" means to transport, entice, recruit, harbor, provide, or otherwise obtain another person by any means.

Sec. 20A.02. Trafficking of Persons.

(a) A person commits an offense if the person knowingly:

(1) traffics another person with the intent that the trafficked person engage in forced labor or services;

(2) receives a benefit from participating in a venture that involves an activity described by Subdivision (1), including by receiving labor or services the person knows are forced labor or services;

(3) traffics another person and, through force, fraud, or coercion, causes the trafficked person to engage in conduct prohibited by:

(A) Section 43.02 (Prostitution);

(B) Section 43.03 (Promotion of Prostitution);

(B-1) Section 43.031 (Online Promotion of Prostitution);

(C) Section 43.04 (Aggravated Promotion of Prostitution);

(C-1) Section 43.041 (Aggravated Online Promotion of Prostitution); or

(D) Section 43.05 (Compelling Prostitution);

(4) receives a benefit from participating in a venture that involves an activity described by

Subdivision (3) or engages in sexual conduct with a person trafficked in the manner described in Subdivision (3);

(5) traffics a child with the intent that the trafficked child engage in forced labor or services;

(6) receives a benefit from participating in a venture that involves an activity described by Subdivision (5), including by receiving labor or services the person knows are forced labor or services;

(7) traffics a child and by any means causes the trafficked child to engage in, or become the victim of, conduct prohibited by:

(A) Section 21.02 (Continuous Sexual Abuse of Young Child or Disabled Individual);

(B) Section 21.11 (Indecency with a Child);

(C) Section 22.011 (Sexual Assault);

(D) Section 22.021 (Aggravated Sexual Assault);

(E) Section 43.02 (Prostitution);

(E-1) Section 43.021 (Solicitation of Prostitution);

(F) Section 43.03 (Promotion of Prostitution);

(F-1) Section 43.031 (Online Promotion of Prostitution);

(G) Section 43.04 (Aggravated Promotion of Prostitution);

(G-1) Section 43.041 (Aggravated Online Promotion of Prostitution);

(H) Section 43.05 (Compelling Prostitution);

(I) Section 43.25 (Sexual Performance by a Child);

(J) Section 43.251 (Employment Harmful to Children); or

(K) Section 43.26 (Possession or Promotion of Child Pornography); or

(8) receives a benefit from participating in a venture that involves an activity described by Subdivision (7) or engages in sexual conduct with a child trafficked in the manner described in Subdivision (7).

(a-1) [Repealed.]

(b) Except as otherwise provided by this subsection and Subsection (b-1), an offense under this section is a felony of the second degree. An offense under this section is a felony of the first degree if:

(1) the applicable conduct constitutes an offense under Subsection (a)(5), (6), (7), or (8), regardless of whether the actor knows the age of the child at the time of the offense;

(2) the commission of the offense results in the death of the person who is trafficked;

(3) the commission of the offense results in the death of an unborn child of the person who is trafficked; or

(4) the actor recruited, enticed, or obtained the victim of the offense from a shelter or facility operating as a residential treatment center that serves runaway youth, foster children, the homeless, or persons subjected to human trafficking, domestic violence, or sexual assault.

(b-1) An offense under this section is a felony of the first degree punishable by imprisonment in the Texas Department of Criminal Justice for life or for a term of not more than 99 years or less than 25 years if it is shown on the trial of the offense that the actor committed the offense in a location that was:

(1) on the premises of or within 1,000 feet of the premises of a school; or

(2) on premises or within 1,000 feet of premises where:

(A) an official school function was taking place; or

(B) an event sponsored or sanctioned by the University Interscholastic League was taking place.

(c) If conduct constituting an offense under this section also constitutes an offense under another section of this code, the actor may be prosecuted under either section or under both sections.

(d) If the victim of an offense under Subsection (a)(7)(A) is the same victim as a victim of an offense under Section 21.02, a defendant may not be convicted of the offense under Section 21.02 in the same criminal action as the offense under Subsection (a)(7)(A) unless the offense under Section 21.02:

(1) is charged in the alternative;

(2) occurred outside the period in which the offense alleged under Subsection (a)(7)(A) was committed; or

(3) is considered by the trier of fact to be a lesser included offense of the offense alleged under Subsection (a)(7)(A).

Sec. 20A.03. Continuous Trafficking of Persons.

(a) A person commits an offense if, during a period that is 30 or more days in duration, the person engages two or more times in conduct that constitutes an offense under Section 20A.02 against one or more victims.

(b) If a jury is the trier of fact, members of the jury are not required to agree unanimously on which specific conduct engaged in by the defendant constituted an offense under Section 20A.02 or on which exact date the defendant engaged in that conduct. The jury must agree unanimously that the defendant, during a period that is 30 or more days in duration, engaged in conduct that constituted an offense under Section 20A.02.

(c) If the victim of an offense under Subsection (a) is the same victim as a victim of an offense under Section 20A.02, a defendant may not be convicted of the offense under Section 20A.02 in the same criminal action as the offense under Subsection (a), unless the offense under Section 20A.02:

(1) is charged in the alternative;

(2) occurred outside the period in which the offense alleged under Subsection (a) was committed; or

(3) is considered by the trier of fact to be a lesser included offense of the offense alleged under Subsection (a).

(d) A defendant may not be charged with more than one count under Subsection (a) if all of the conduct that constitutes an offense under Section 20A.02 is alleged to have been committed against the same victim.

(e) An offense under this section is a felony of the first degree, punishable by imprisonment in the Texas Department of Criminal Justice for life or for any term of not more than 99 years or less than 25 years.

Sec. 20A.04. Accomplice Witness; Testimony and Immunity.

(a) A party to an offense under this chapter may be required to provide evidence or testify about the offense.

(b) A party to an offense under this chapter may not be prosecuted for any offense about which the party is required to provide evidence or testify, and the evidence and testimony may not be used against the party in any adjudicatory proceeding except a prosecution for aggravated perjury. For purposes of this subsection, "adjudicatory proceeding" means a proceeding before a court or any other agency of government in which the legal rights, powers, duties, or privileges of specified parties are determined.

(c) A conviction under this chapter may be had on the uncorroborated testimony of a party to the offense.

CHAPTER 21
SEXUAL OFFENSES

Sec. 21.01. Definitions.

In this chapter:

(1) "Deviate sexual intercourse" means:

(A) any contact between any part of the genitals of one person and the mouth or anus of another person; or

(B) the penetration of the genitals or the anus of another person with an object.

(2) "Sexual contact" means, except as provided by Section 21.11 or 21.12, any touching of the anus, breast, or any part of the genitals of another person with intent to arouse or gratify the sexual desire of any person.

(3) "Sexual intercourse" means any penetration of the female sex organ by the male sex organ.

(4) "Spouse" means a person to whom a person is legally married under Subtitle A, Title 1, Family Code, or a comparable law of another jurisdiction.

Sec. 21.02. Continuous Sexual Abuse of Young Child or Disabled Individual.

(a) In this section:

(1) "Child" has the meaning assigned by Section 22.011(c).

(2) "Disabled individual" has the meaning assigned by Section 22.021(b).

(b) A person commits an offense if:

(1) during a period that is 30 or more days in duration, the person commits two or more acts of sexual abuse, regardless of whether the acts of sexual abuse are committed against one or more victims; and

(2) at the time of the commission of each of the acts of sexual abuse, the actor is 17 years of age or older and the victim is:

(A) a child younger than 14 years of age, regardless of whether the actor knows the age of the victim at the time of the offense; or

(B) a disabled individual.

(c) For purposes of this section, "act of sexual abuse" means any act that is a violation of one or more of the following penal laws:

(1) aggravated kidnapping under Section 20.04(a)(4), if the actor committed the offense with the intent to violate or abuse the victim sexually;

(2) indecency with a child under Section 21.11(a)(1), if the actor committed the offense in a manner other than by touching, including touching through clothing, the breast of a child;

(3) sexual assault under Section 22.011;

(4) aggravated sexual assault under Section 22.021;

(5) burglary under Section 30.02, if the offense is punishable under Subsection (d) of that section and the actor committed the offense with the intent to commit an offense listed in Subdivisions (1)-(4);

(6) sexual performance by a child under Section 43.25;

(7) trafficking of persons under Section 20A.02(a)(3), (4), (7), or (8); and

(8) compelling prostitution under Section 43.05.

(d) If a jury is the trier of fact, members of the jury are not required to agree unanimously on which specific acts of sexual abuse were committed by the defendant or the exact date when those acts were committed. The jury must agree unanimously that the defendant, during a period that is 30 or more days in duration, committed two or more acts of sexual abuse.

(e) A defendant may not be convicted in the same criminal action of an offense listed under Subsection (c) the victim of which is the same victim as a victim of the offense alleged under Subsection (b) unless the offense listed in Subsection (c):

(1) is charged in the alternative;

(2) occurred outside the period in which the offense alleged under Subsection (b) was committed; or

(3) is considered by the trier of fact to be a lesser included offense of the offense alleged under Subsection (b).

(f) A defendant may not be charged with more than one count under Subsection (b) if all of the specific acts of sexual abuse that are alleged to have been committed are alleged to have been committed against a single victim.

(g) With respect to a prosecution under this section involving only one or more victims described by Subsection (b)(2)(A), it is an affirmative defense to prosecution under this section that the actor:

(1) was not more than five years older than:

(A) the victim of the offense, if the offense is alleged to have been committed against only one victim; or

(B) the youngest victim of the offense, if the offense is alleged to have been committed against more than one victim;

(2) did not use duress, force, or a threat against a victim at the time of the commission of any of the acts of sexual abuse alleged as an element of the offense; and

(3) at the time of the commission of any of the acts of sexual abuse alleged as an element of the offense:

(A) was not required under Chapter 62, Code of Criminal Procedure, to register for life as a sex offender; or

(B) was not a person who under Chapter 62 had a reportable conviction or adjudication for an offense under this section or an act of sexual abuse as described by Subsection (c).

(h) An offense under this section is a felony of the first degree, punishable by imprisonment in the Texas Department of Criminal Justice for life, or for any term of not more than 99 years or less than 25 years.

Sec. 21.03. Aggravated Rape [Repealed].

Repealed by Acts 1983, 68th Leg., ch. 977 (H.B. 2008), § 12, effective September 1, 1983.

Sec. 21.04. Sexual Abuse [Repealed].

Repealed by Acts 1983, 68th Leg., ch. 977 (H.B. 2008), § 12, effective September 1, 1983.

Sec. 21.05. Aggravated Sexual Abuse [Repealed].

Repealed by Acts 1983, 68th Leg., ch. 977 (H.B. 2008), § 12, effective September 1, 1983.

Sec. 21.06. Homosexual Conduct.

(a) A person commits an offense if he engages in deviate sexual intercourse with another individual of the same sex.

(b) An offense under this section is a Class C misdemeanor.

Sec. 21.07. Public Lewdness.

(a) A person commits an offense if the person knowingly engages in any of the following acts in a public place or, if not in a public place, the person is reckless about whether another is present who will be offended or alarmed by the person's:

(1) act of sexual intercourse;

(2) act of deviate sexual intercourse; or

(3) act of sexual contact.

(b) An offense under this section is a Class A misdemeanor.

Sec. 21.08. Indecent Exposure.

(a) A person commits an offense if he exposes his anus or any part of his genitals with intent to arouse or gratify the sexual desire of any person, and he is reckless about whether another is present who will be offended or alarmed by his act.

(b) An offense under this section is a Class B misdemeanor.

Sec. 21.09. Bestiality.

(a) A person commits an offense if the person knowingly:

(1) engages in an act involving contact between:

(A) the person's mouth, anus, or genitals and the anus or genitals of an animal; or

(B) the person's anus or genitals and the mouth of the animal;

(2) fondles or touches the anus or genitals of an animal in a manner that is not a generally accepted and otherwise lawful animal husbandry or veterinary practice, including touching through clothing;

(3) causes an animal to contact the seminal fluid of the person;

(4) inserts any part of a person's body or any object into the anus or genitals of an animal in a manner that is not a generally accepted and otherwise lawful animal husbandry or veterinary practice;

(5) possesses, sells, transfers, purchases, or otherwise obtains an animal with the intent that the animal be used for conduct described by Subdivision (1), (2), (3), or (4);

(6) organizes, promotes, conducts, or participates as an observer of conduct described by Subdivision (1), (2), (3), or (4);

(7) causes a person to engage or aids a person in engaging in conduct described by Subdivision (1), (2), (3), or (4);

(8) permits conduct described by Subdivision (1), (2), (3), or (4) to occur on any premises under the person's control;

(9) engages in conduct described by Subdivision (1), (2), (3), or (4) in the presence of a child younger than 18 years of age; or

(10) advertises, offers, or accepts the offer of an animal with the intent that the animal be used in this state for conduct described by Subdivision (1), (2), (3), or (4).

(b) An offense under this section is a state jail felony, unless the offense is committed under Subsection (a)(9) or results in serious bodily injury or death of the animal, in which event the offense is a felony of the second degree.

(c) It is an exception to the application of this section that the conduct engaged in by the actor is a generally accepted and otherwise lawful animal husbandry or veterinary practice.

Sec. 21.10. Sexual Abuse of a Child [Repealed].

Repealed by Acts 1983, 68th Leg., ch. 977 (H.B. 2008), § 12, effective September 1, 1983.

Sec. 21.11. Indecency with a Child.

(a) A person commits an offense if, with a child younger than 17 years of age, whether the child is of the same or opposite sex and regardless of whether the person knows the age of the child at the time of the offense, the person:

(1) engages in sexual contact with the child or causes the child to engage in sexual contact; or

(2) with intent to arouse or gratify the sexual desire of any person:

(A) exposes the person's anus or any part of the person's genitals, knowing the child is present; or

(B) causes the child to expose the child's anus or any part of the child's genitals.

(b) It is an affirmative defense to prosecution under this section that the actor:

(1) was not more than three years older than the victim and of the opposite sex;

(2) did not use duress, force, or a threat against the victim at the time of the offense; and

(3) at the time of the offense:

(A) was not required under Chapter 62, Code of Criminal Procedure, to register for life as a sex offender; or

(B) was not a person who under Chapter 62 had a reportable conviction or adjudication for an offense under this section.

(b-1) It is an affirmative defense to prosecution under this section that the actor was the spouse of the child at the time of the offense.

(c) In this section, "sexual contact" means the following acts, if committed with the intent to arouse or gratify the sexual desire of any person:

(1) any touching by a person, including touching through clothing, of the anus, breast, or any part of the genitals of a child; or

(2) any touching of any part of the body of a child, including touching through clothing, with the anus, breast, or any part of the genitals of a person.

(d) An offense under Subsection (a)(1) is a felony of the second degree and an offense under Subsection (a)(2) is a felony of the third degree.

Sec. 21.12. Improper Relationship Between Educator and Student.

(a) An employee of a public or private primary or secondary school commits an offense if the employee:

(1) engages in sexual contact, sexual intercourse, or deviate sexual intercourse with a person who is enrolled in a public or private primary or secondary school at which the employee works;

(2) holds a position described by Section 21.003(a) or (b), Education Code, regardless of whether the employee holds the appropriate certificate, permit, license, or credential for the position, and engages in sexual contact, sexual intercourse, or deviate sexual intercourse with a person the employee knows is:

(A) enrolled in a public or private primary or secondary school, other than a school described by Subdivision (1); or

(B) a student participant in an educational activity that is sponsored by a school district or a public or private primary or secondary school, if students enrolled in a public or private primary or secondary school are the primary participants in the activity;

or

(3) engages in conduct described by Section 33.021, with a person described by Subdivision (1), or a person the employee knows is a person described by Subdivision (2)(A) or (B), regardless of the age of that person.

(b) An offense under this section is a felony of the second degree.

(b-1) It is an affirmative defense to prosecution under this section that:

(1) the actor was the spouse of the enrolled person at the time of the offense; or

(2) the actor was not more than three years older than the enrolled person and, at the time of the offense, the actor and the enrolled person were in a relationship that began before the actor's employment at a public or private primary or secondary school.

(c) If conduct constituting an offense under this section also constitutes an offense under another section of this code, the actor may be prosecuted under either section or both sections.

(d) The name of a person who is enrolled in a public or private primary or secondary school and involved in an improper relationship with an educator as provided by Subsection (a) may not be released to the public and is not public information under Chapter 552, Government Code.

(d-1) Except as otherwise provided by this subsection, a public or private primary or secondary school, or a person or entity that operates a public or private primary or secondary school, may not release externally to the general public the name of an employee of the school who is accused of committing an offense under this section until the employee is indicted for the offense. The school, or the person or entity that operates the school, may release the name of the accused employee regardless of whether the employee has been indicted for the offense as necessary for the school to:

(1) report the accusation:

(A) to the Texas Education Agency, another state agency, or local law enforcement or as otherwise required by law; or

(B) to the school's members or community in accordance with the school's policies or procedures or with the religious law observed by the school; or

(2) conduct an investigation of the accusation.

(e) In this section, "sexual contact" means the following acts, if committed with the intent to arouse or gratify the sexual desire of any person:

(1) any touching by an employee of a public or private primary or secondary school of the anus, breast, or any part of the genitals of:

(A) an enrolled person described by Subsection (a)(1) or (a)(2)(A); or

(B) a student participant described by Subsection (a)(2)(B); or

(2) any touching of any part of the body of the enrolled person or student participant with the anus, breast, or any part of the genitals of the employee.

Sec. 21.13. Evidence of Previous Sexual Conduct [Renumbered].

Renumbered to Tex. Penal Code § 22.065 by Acts 1983, 68th Leg., ch. 977 (H.B. 2008), § 4, effective September 1, 1983.

Sec. 21.14. Sexual Exploitation by Mental Health Services Provider [Deleted].

Deleted by Acts 1993, 73rd Leg., ch. 900 (S.B. 1067), § 1.01, effective September 1, 1994.

Sec. 21.15. Invasive Visual Recording.

(a) In this section:

(1) "Female breast" means any portion of the female breast below the top of the areola.

(2) "Intimate area" means the naked or clothed genitals, pubic area, anus, buttocks, or female breast of a person.

(3) "Changing room" means a room or portioned area provided for or primarily used for the changing of clothing and includes dressing rooms, locker rooms, and swimwear changing areas.

(4) "Promote" has the meaning assigned by Section 43.21.

(b) A person commits an offense if, without the other person's consent and with intent to invade the privacy of the other person, the person:

(1) photographs or by videotape or other electronic means records, broadcasts, or transmits a visual image of an intimate area of another person if the other person has a reasonable expectation that the intimate area is not subject to public view;

(2) photographs or by videotape or other electronic means records, broadcasts, or transmits a visual image of another in a bathroom or changing room; or

(3) knowing the character and content of the photograph, recording, broadcast, or transmission, promotes a photograph, recording, broadcast, or transmission described by Subdivision (1) or (2).

(c) An offense under this section is a state jail felony.

(d) If conduct that constitutes an offense under this section also constitutes an offense under any other law, the actor may be prosecuted under this section or the other law.

(e) For purposes of Subsection (b)(2), a sign or signs posted indicating that the person is being photographed or that a visual image of the person is being recorded, broadcast, or transmitted is not sufficient to establish the person's consent under that subdivision.

Sec. 21.16. Unlawful Disclosure or Promotion of Intimate Visual Material.

(a) In this section:

(1) "Intimate parts" means the naked genitals, pubic area, anus, buttocks, or female nipple of a person.

(2) "Promote" means to procure, manufacture, issue, sell, give, provide, lend, mail, deliver, transfer, transmit, publish, distribute, circulate, disseminate, present, exhibit, or advertise or to offer or agree to do any of the above.

(3) "Sexual conduct" means sexual contact, actual or simulated sexual intercourse, deviate sexual intercourse, sexual bestiality, masturbation, or sadomasochistic abuse.

(4) "Simulated" means the explicit depiction of sexual conduct that creates the appearance of actual sexual conduct and during which a person engaging in the conduct exhibits any uncovered portion of the breasts, genitals, or buttocks.

(5) "Visual material" means:

(A) any film, photograph, videotape, negative, or slide or any photographic reproduction that contains or incorporates in any manner any film, photograph, videotape, negative, or slide; or

(B) any disk, diskette, or other physical medium that allows an image to be displayed on a computer or other video screen and any image transmitted to a computer or other video screen by telephone line, cable, satellite transmission, or other method.

(b) A person commits an offense if:

(1) without the effective consent of the depicted person and with the intent to harm that person, the person discloses visual material depicting another person with the person's intimate parts exposed or engaged in sexual conduct;

(2) at the time of the disclosure, the person knows or has reason to believe that the visual material was obtained by the person or created under circumstances in which the depicted person had a reasonable expectation that the visual material would remain private;

(3) the disclosure of the visual material causes harm to the depicted person; and

(4) the disclosure of the visual material reveals the identity of the depicted person in any manner, including through:

(A) any accompanying or subsequent information or material related to the visual material; or

(B) information or material provided by a third party in response to the disclosure of the visual material.

(c) A person commits an offense if the person intentionally threatens to disclose, without the consent of the depicted person, visual material depicting another person with the person's intimate parts exposed or engaged in sexual conduct and the actor makes the threat to obtain a benefit:

(1) in return for not making the disclosure; or

(2) in connection with the threatened disclosure.

(d) A person commits an offense if, knowing the character and content of the visual material, the person promotes visual material described by Subsection (b) on an Internet website or other forum for publication that is owned or operated by the person.

(e) It is not a defense to prosecution under this section that the depicted person:

(1) created or consented to the creation of the visual material; or

(2) voluntarily transmitted the visual material to the actor.

(f) It is an affirmative defense to prosecution under Subsection (b) or (d) that:

(1) the disclosure or promotion is made in the course of:

(A) lawful and common practices of law enforcement or medical treatment;

(B) reporting unlawful activity; or

(C) a legal proceeding, if the disclosure or promotion is permitted or required by law;

(2) the disclosure or promotion consists of visual material depicting in a public or commercial setting only a person's voluntary exposure of:

(A) the person's intimate parts; or

(B) the person engaging in sexual conduct; or

(3) the actor is an interactive computer service, as defined by 47 U.S.C. Section 230, and the disclosure or promotion consists of visual material provided by another person.

(g) An offense under this section is a state jail felony.

(h) If conduct that constitutes an offense under this section also constitutes an offense under another law, the actor may be prosecuted under this section, the other law, or both.

Sec. 21.17. Voyeurism.

(a) A person commits an offense if the person, with the intent to arouse or gratify the sexual desire of the actor, observes another person without the other person's consent while the other person is in a dwelling or structure in which the other person has a reasonable expectation of privacy.

(b) Except as provided by Subsection (c) or (d), an offense under this section is a Class C misdemeanor.

(c) An offense under this section is a Class B misdemeanor if it is shown on the trial of the offense that the actor has previously been convicted two or more times of an offense under this section.

(d) An offense under this section is a state jail felony if the victim was a child younger than 14 years of age at the time of the offense.

(e) If conduct that constitutes an offense under this section also constitutes an offense under any other law, the actor may be prosecuted under this section, the other law, or both.

Sec. 21.18. Sexual Coercion.

(a) In this section:

(1) "Intimate visual material" means the visual material described by Section 21.16(b)(1) or (c).

(2) "Sexual conduct" has the meaning assigned by Section 43.25.

(b) A person commits an offense if the person intentionally threatens, including by coercion or extortion, to commit an offense under Chapter 43 or Section 20A.02(a)(3), (4), (7), or (8), 21.02, 21.08, 21.11, 21.12, 21.15, 21.16, 21.17, 22.011, or 22.021 to obtain, in return for not committing the threatened offense or in connection with the threatened offense, any of the following benefits:

(1) intimate visual material;

(2) an act involving sexual conduct causing arousal or gratification; or

(3) a monetary benefit or other benefit of value.

(c) A person commits an offense if the person intentionally threatens, including by coercion or extortion, to commit an offense under Chapter 19 or 20 or Section 20A.02(a)(1), (2), (5), or (6) to obtain, in return for not committing the threatened offense or in connection with the threatened offense, either of the following benefits:

(1) intimate visual material; or

(2) an act involving sexual conduct causing arousal or gratification.

(d) This section applies to a threat regardless of how that threat is communicated, including a threat transmitted through e-mail or an Internet website, social media account, or chat room and a threat made by other electronic or technological means.

(e) An offense under this section is a state jail felony, except that the offense is a felony of the third degree if it is shown on the trial of the offense that the defendant has previously been convicted of an offense under this section.

Sec. 21.19. Unlawful Electronic Transmission of Sexually Explicit Visual Material.

(a) In this section, "intimate parts," "sexual conduct," and "visual material" have the meanings assigned by Section 21.16.

(b) A person commits an offense if the person knowingly transmits by electronic means visual material that:

(1) depicts:

(A) any person engaging in sexual conduct or with the person's intimate parts exposed; or

(B) covered genitals of a male person that are in a discernibly turgid state; and

(2) is not sent at the request of or with the express consent of the recipient.

(c) An offense under this section is a Class C misdemeanor.

(d) If conduct that constitutes an offense under this section also constitutes an offense under any other law, the actor may be prosecuted under this section or the other law.

CHAPTER 22
ASSAULTIVE OFFENSES

Sec. 22.01. Assault.

(a) A person commits an offense if the person:

(1) intentionally, knowingly, or recklessly causes bodily injury to another, including the person's spouse;

(2) intentionally or knowingly threatens another with imminent bodily injury, including the person's spouse; or

(3) intentionally or knowingly causes physical contact with another when the person knows or should reasonably believe that the other will regard the contact as offensive or provocative.

(b) An offense under Subsection (a)(1) is a Class A misdemeanor, except that the offense is a felony of the third degree if the offense is committed against:

(1) a person the actor knows is a public servant while the public servant is lawfully discharging an official duty, or in retaliation or on account of an exercise of official power or performance of an official duty as a public servant;

(2) a person whose relationship to or association with the defendant is described by Section 71.0021(b), 71.003, or 71.005, Family Code, if:

(A) it is shown on the trial of the offense that the defendant has been previously convicted of an offense under this chapter, Chapter 19, or Section 20.03, 20.04, 21.11, or 25.11 against a person whose relationship to or association with the defendant is described by Section 71.0021(b), 71.003, or 71.005, Family Code; or

(B) the offense is committed by intentionally, knowingly, or recklessly impeding the normal breathing or circulation of the blood of the person by applying pressure to the person's throat or neck or by blocking the person's nose or mouth;

(3) a person who contracts with government to perform a service in a facility as defined by Section 1.07(a)(14), Penal Code, or Section 51.02(13) or (14), Family Code, or an employee of that person:

(A) while the person or employee is engaged in performing a service within the scope of the contract, if the actor knows the person or employee is authorized by government to provide the service; or

(B) in retaliation for or on account of the person's or employee's performance of a service within the scope of the contract;

(4) a person the actor knows is a security officer while the officer is performing a duty as a security officer;

(5) a person the actor knows is emergency services personnel while the person is providing emergency services;

(6) a person the actor knows is a process server while the person is performing a duty as a process server;

(7) a pregnant individual to force the individual to have an abortion; or

(8) a person the actor knows is pregnant at the time of the offense.

(b-1) Notwithstanding Subsection (b), an offense under Subsection (a)(1) is a felony of the third degree if the offense is committed:

(1) while the actor is committed to a civil commitment facility; and

(2) against:

(A) an officer or employee of the Texas Civil Commitment Office:

(i) while the officer or employee is lawfully discharging an official duty at a civil commitment facility; or

(ii) in retaliation for or on account of an exercise of official power or performance of an official duty by the officer or employee; or

(B) a person who contracts with the state to perform a service in a civil commitment facility or an employee of that person:

(i) while the person or employee is engaged in performing a service within the scope of the contract, if the actor knows the person or employee is authorized by the state to provide the service; or

(ii) in retaliation for or on account of the person's or employee's performance of a service within the scope of the contract.

(b-2) Notwithstanding Subsection (b)(1), an offense under Subsection (a)(1) is a felony of the second degree if the offense is committed against a person the actor knows is a peace officer or judge while the officer or judge is lawfully discharging an official duty or in retaliation or on account of an exercise of official power or performance of an official duty as a peace officer or judge.

(b-3) Notwithstanding Subsection (b)(2), an offense under Subsection (a)(1) is a felony of the second degree if:

(1) the offense is committed against a person whose relationship to or association with the defendant is described by Section 71.0021(b), 71.003, or 71.005, Family Code;

(2) it is shown on the trial of the offense that the defendant has been previously convicted of an offense under this chapter, Chapter 19, or Section 20.03, 20.04, or 21.11 against a person whose relationship to or association with the defendant is described by Section 71.0021(b), 71.003, or 71.005, Family Code; and

(3) the offense is committed by intentionally, knowingly, or recklessly impeding the normal breathing or circulation of the blood of the person by applying pressure to the person's throat or neck or by blocking the person's nose or mouth.

(c) An offense under Subsection (a)(2) or (3) is a Class C misdemeanor, except that the offense is:

(1) a Class A misdemeanor if the offense is committed under Subsection (a)(3) against an elderly individual or disabled individual, as those terms are defined by Section 22.04;

(2) a Class B misdemeanor if the offense is committed by a person who is not a sports participant against a person the actor knows is a sports participant either:

(A) while the participant is performing duties or responsibilities in the participant's capacity as a sports participant; or

(B) in retaliation for or on account of the participant's performance of a duty or responsibility within the participant's capacity as a sports participant; or

(3) a Class A misdemeanor if the offense is committed against a pregnant individual to force the individual to have an abortion.

(d) For purposes of Subsection (b), the actor is presumed to have known the person assaulted was a public servant, a security officer, or emergency services personnel if the person was wearing a distinctive uniform or badge indicating the person's employment as a public servant or status as a security officer or emergency services personnel.

(e) In this section:

(1) "Emergency services personnel" includes firefighters, emergency medical services personnel

as defined by Section 773.003, Health and Safety Code, emergency room personnel, and other individuals who, in the course and scope of employment or as a volunteer, provide services for the benefit of the general public during emergency situations.

(2) "Process server" has the meaning assigned by Section 156.001, Government Code.

(3) "Security officer" means a commissioned security officer as defined by Section 1702.002, Occupations Code, or a noncommissioned security officer registered under Section 1702.221, Occupations Code.

(4) "Sports participant" means a person who participates in any official capacity with respect to an interscholastic, intercollegiate, or other organized amateur or professional athletic competition and includes an athlete, referee, umpire, linesman, coach, instructor, administrator, or staff member.

(f) For the purposes of Subsections (b)(2)(A) and (b-3)(2):

(1) a defendant has been previously convicted of an offense listed in those subsections committed against a person whose relationship to or association with the defendant is described by Section 71.0021(b), 71.003, or 71.005, Family Code, if the defendant was adjudged guilty of the offense or entered a plea of guilty or nolo contendere in return for a grant of deferred adjudication, regardless of whether the sentence for the offense was ever imposed or whether the sentence was probated and the defendant was subsequently discharged from community supervision; and

(2) a conviction under the laws of another state for an offense containing elements that are substantially similar to the elements of an offense listed in those subsections is a conviction of the offense listed.

(g) If conduct constituting an offense under this section also constitutes an offense under another section of this code, the actor may be prosecuted under either section or both sections.

Sec. 22.011. Sexual Assault.

(a) A person commits an offense if:

(1) the person intentionally or knowingly:

(A) causes the penetration of the anus or sexual organ of another person by any means, without that person's consent;

(B) causes the penetration of the mouth of another person by the sexual organ of the actor, without that person's consent; or

(C) causes the sexual organ of another person, without that person's consent, to contact or penetrate the mouth, anus, or sexual organ of another person, including the actor; or

(2) regardless of whether the person knows the age of the child at the time of the offense, the person intentionally or knowingly:

(A) causes the penetration of the anus or sexual organ of a child by any means;

(B) causes the penetration of the mouth of a child by the sexual organ of the actor;

(C) causes the sexual organ of a child to contact or penetrate the mouth, anus, or sexual organ of another person, including the actor;

(D) causes the anus of a child to contact the mouth, anus, or sexual organ of another person, including the actor; or

(E) causes the mouth of a child to contact the anus or sexual organ of another person, including the actor.

(b) A sexual assault under Subsection (a)(1) is without the consent of the other person if:

(1) the actor compels the other person to submit or participate by the use of physical force, violence, or coercion;

(2) the actor compels the other person to submit or participate by threatening to use force or violence against the other person or to cause harm to the other person, and the other person believes that the actor has the present ability to execute the threat;

(3) the other person has not consented and the actor knows the other person is unconscious or physically unable to resist;

(4) the actor knows that as a result of mental disease or defect the other person is at the time of the sexual assault incapable either of appraising the nature of the act or of resisting it;

(5) the other person has not consented and the actor knows the other person is unaware that the sexual assault is occurring;

(6) the actor has intentionally impaired the other person's power to appraise or control the other person's conduct by administering any substance without the other person's knowledge;

(7) the actor compels the other person to submit or participate by threatening to use force or violence against any person, and the other person believes that the actor has the ability to execute the threat;

(8) the actor is a public servant who coerces the other person to submit or participate;

(9) the actor is a mental health services provider or a health care services provider who causes the other person, who is a patient or former patient of the actor, to submit or participate by exploiting the other person's emotional dependency on the actor;

(10) the actor is a clergyman who causes the other person to submit or participate by exploiting the other person's emotional dependency on the

clergyman in the clergyman's professional character as spiritual adviser;

(11) the actor is an employee of a facility where the other person is a resident, unless the employee and resident are formally or informally married to each other under Chapter 2, Family Code;

(12) the actor is a health care services provider who, in the course of performing an assisted reproduction procedure on the other person, uses human reproductive material from a donor knowing that the other person has not expressly consented to the use of material from that donor;

(13) the actor is a coach or tutor who causes the other person to submit or participate by using the actor's power or influence to exploit the other person's dependency on the actor; or

(14) the actor is a caregiver hired to assist the other person with activities of daily life and causes the other person to submit or participate by exploiting the other person's dependency on the actor.

(c) In this section:

(1) "Child" means a person younger than 17 years of age.

(2) "Spouse" means a person who is legally married to another.

(3) "Health care services provider" means:

(A) a physician licensed under Subtitle B, Title 3, Occupations Code;

(B) a chiropractor licensed under Chapter 201, Occupations Code;

(C) a physical therapist licensed under Chapter 453, Occupations Code;

(D) a physician assistant licensed under Chapter 204, Occupations Code; or

(E) a registered nurse, a vocational nurse, or an advanced practice nurse licensed under Chapter 301, Occupations Code.

(4) "Mental health services provider" means an individual, licensed or unlicensed, who performs or purports to perform mental health services, including a:

(A) licensed social worker as defined by Section 505.002, Occupations Code;

(B) chemical dependency counselor as defined by Section 504.001, Occupations Code;

(C) licensed professional counselor as defined by Section 503.002, Occupations Code;

(D) licensed marriage and family therapist as defined by Section 502.002, Occupations Code;

(E) member of the clergy;

(F) psychologist offering psychological services as defined by Section 501.003, Occupations Code; or

(G) special officer for mental health assignment certified under Section 1701.404, Occupations Code.

(5) "Employee of a facility" means a person who is an employee of a facility defined by Section 250.001, Health and Safety Code, or any other person who provides services for a facility for compensation, including a contract laborer.

(6) "Assisted reproduction" and "donor" have the meanings assigned by Section 160.102, Family Code.

(7) "Human reproductive material" means:

(A) a human spermatozoon or ovum; or

(B) a human organism at any stage of development from fertilized ovum to embryo.

(d) It is a defense to prosecution under Subsection (a)(2) that the conduct consisted of medical care for the child and did not include any contact between the anus or sexual organ of the child and the mouth, anus, or sexual organ of the actor or a third party.

(e) It is an affirmative defense to prosecution under Subsection (a)(2):

(1) that the actor was the spouse of the child at the time of the offense; or

(2) that:

(A) the actor was not more than three years older than the victim and at the time of the offense:

(i) was not required under Chapter 62, Code of Criminal Procedure, to register for life as a sex offender; or

(ii) was not a person who under Chapter 62, Code of Criminal Procedure, had a reportable conviction or adjudication for an offense under this section; and

(B) the victim:

(i) was a child of 14 years of age or older; and

(ii) was not:

(a) a person whom the actor was prohibited from marrying or purporting to marry or with whom the actor was prohibited from living under the appearance of being married under Section 25.01; or

(b) a person with whom the actor was prohibited from engaging in sexual intercourse or deviate sexual intercourse under Section 25.02.

(f) An offense under this section is a felony of the second degree, except that an offense under this section is:

(1) a felony of the first degree if the victim was:

(A) a person whom the actor was prohibited from marrying or purporting to marry or with whom the actor was prohibited from living under the appearance of being married under Section 25.01; or

(B) a person with whom the actor was prohibited from engaging in sexual intercourse or deviate sexual intercourse under Section 25.02; or

(2) a state jail felony if the offense is committed under Subsection (a)(1) and the actor has not received express consent as described by Subsection (b)(12).

Sec. 22.012. Indecent Assault.

(a) A person commits an offense if, without the other person's consent and with the intent to arouse or gratify the sexual desire of any person, the person:

(1) touches the anus, breast, or any part of the genitals of another person;

(2) touches another person with the anus, breast, or any part of the genitals of any person;

(3) exposes or attempts to expose another person's genitals, pubic area, anus, buttocks, or female areola; or

(4) causes another person to contact the blood, seminal fluid, vaginal fluid, saliva, urine, or feces of any person.

(b) An offense under this section is a Class A misdemeanor.

(c) If conduct that constitutes an offense under this section also constitutes an offense under another law, the actor may be prosecuted under this section, the other law, or both.

Sec. 22.015. Coercing, Soliciting, or Inducing Gang Membership [Repealed].

Repealed by Acts 2009, 81st Leg., ch. 435 (H.B. 2187), § 3, effective September 1, 2009.

Sec. 22.02. Aggravated Assault.

(a) A person commits an offense if the person commits assault as defined in Section 22.01 and the person:

(1) causes serious bodily injury to another, including the person's spouse; or

(2) uses or exhibits a deadly weapon during the commission of the assault.

(b) An offense under this section is a felony of the second degree, except that the offense is a felony of the first degree if:

(1) the actor uses a deadly weapon during the commission of the assault and causes serious bodily injury to a person whose relationship to or association with the defendant is described by Section 71.0021(b), 71.003, or 71.005, Family Code;

(2) regardless of whether the offense is committed under Subsection (a)(1) or (a)(2), the offense is committed:

(A) by a public servant acting under color of the servant's office or employment;

(B) against a person the actor knows is a public servant while the public servant is lawfully discharging an official duty, or in retaliation or on account of an exercise of official power or performance of an official duty as a public servant;

(C) in retaliation against or on account of the service of another as a witness, prospective witness, informant, or person who has reported the occurrence of a crime;

(D) against a person the actor knows is a process server while the person is performing a duty as a process server; or

(E) against a person the actor knows is a security officer while the officer is performing a duty as a security officer; or

(3) the actor is in a motor vehicle, as defined by Section 501.002, Transportation Code, and:

(A) knowingly discharges a firearm at or in the direction of a habitation, building, or vehicle;

(B) is reckless as to whether the habitation, building, or vehicle is occupied; and

(C) in discharging the firearm, causes serious bodily injury to any person.

(c) The actor is presumed to have known the person assaulted was a public servant or a security officer if the person was wearing a distinctive uniform or badge indicating the person's employment as a public servant or status as a security officer.

(d) In this section:

(1) "Process server" has the meaning assigned by Section 156.001, Government Code.

(2) "Security officer" means a commissioned security officer as defined by Section 1702.002, Occupations Code, or a noncommissioned security officer registered under Section 1702.221, Occupations Code.

Sec. 22.021. Aggravated Sexual Assault.

(a) A person commits an offense:

(1) if the person:

(A) intentionally or knowingly:

(i) causes the penetration of the anus or sexual organ of another person by any means, without that person's consent;

(ii) causes the penetration of the mouth of another person by the sexual organ of the actor, without that person's consent; or

(iii) causes the sexual organ of another person, without that person's consent, to contact or penetrate the mouth, anus, or sexual organ of another person, including the actor; or

(B) regardless of whether the person knows the age of the child at the time of the offense, intentionally or knowingly:

(i) causes the penetration of the anus or sexual organ of a child by any means;

(ii) causes the penetration of the mouth of a child by the sexual organ of the actor;

(iii) causes the sexual organ of a child to contact or penetrate the mouth, anus, or sexual organ of another person, including the actor;

(iv) causes the anus of a child to contact the mouth, anus, or sexual organ of another person, including the actor; or

(v) causes the mouth of a child to contact the anus or sexual organ of another person, including the actor; and

(2) if:

(A) the person:

(i) causes serious bodily injury or attempts to cause the death of the victim or another person in the course of the same criminal episode;

(ii) by acts or words places the victim in fear that any person will become the victim of an offense under Section 20A.02(a)(3), (4), (7), or (8) or that death, serious bodily injury, or kidnapping will be imminently inflicted on any person;

(iii) by acts or words occurring in the presence of the victim threatens to cause any person to become the victim of an offense under Section 20A.02(a)(3), (4), (7), or (8) or to cause the death, serious bodily injury, or kidnapping of any person;

(iv) uses or exhibits a deadly weapon in the course of the same criminal episode;

(v) acts in concert with another who engages in conduct described by Subdivision (1) directed toward the same victim and occurring during the course of the same criminal episode; or

(vi) with the intent of facilitating the commission of the offense, administers or provides to the victim of the offense any substance capable of impairing the victim's ability to appraise the nature of the act or to resist the act;

(B) the victim is younger than 14 years of age, regardless of whether the person knows the age of the victim at the time of the offense; or

(C) the victim is an elderly individual or a disabled individual.

(b) In this section:

(1) "Child" has the meaning assigned by Section 22.011(c).

(2) "Elderly individual" has the meaning assigned by Section 22.04(c).

(3) "Disabled individual" means a person older than 13 years of age who by reason of age or physical or mental disease, defect, or injury is substantially unable to protect the person's self from harm or to provide food, shelter, or medical care for the person's self.

(c) An aggravated sexual assault under this section is without the consent of the other person if the aggravated sexual assault occurs under the same circumstances listed in Section 22.011(b).

(d) The defense provided by Section 22.011(d) applies to this section.

(e) An offense under this section is a felony of the first degree.

(f) The minimum term of imprisonment for an offense under this section is increased to 25 years if:

(1) the victim of the offense is younger than six years of age at the time the offense is committed; or

(2) the victim of the offense is younger than 14 years of age at the time the offense is committed and the actor commits the offense in a manner described by Subsection (a)(2)(A).

Sec. 22.03. Deadly Assault on Law Enforcement or Corrections Officer, Member or Employee of Board of Pardons and Paroles, Court Participant, Probation Personnel, or Employee of Texas Youth Commission [Deleted].

Deleted by Acts 1993, 73rd Leg., ch. 900 (S.B. 1067), § 1.01, effective September 1, 1994.

Sec. 22.04. Injury to a Child, Elderly Individual, or Disabled Individual.

(a) A person commits an offense if he intentionally, knowingly, recklessly, or with criminal negligence, by act or intentionally, knowingly, or recklessly by omission, causes to a child, elderly individual, or disabled individual:

(1) serious bodily injury;

(2) serious mental deficiency, impairment, or injury; or

(3) bodily injury.

(a-1) A person commits an offense if the person is an owner, operator, or employee of a group home, nursing facility, assisted living facility, boarding home facility, intermediate care facility for persons with an intellectual or developmental disability, or other institutional care facility and the person intentionally, knowingly, recklessly, or with criminal negligence by omission causes to a child, elderly individual, or disabled individual who is a resident of that group home or facility:

(1) serious bodily injury;

(2) serious mental deficiency, impairment, or injury; or

(3) bodily injury.

(b) An omission that causes a condition described by Subsection (a)(1), (2), or (3) or (a-1)(1), (2), or (3) is conduct constituting an offense under this section if:

(1) the actor has a legal or statutory duty to act; or

(2) the actor has assumed care, custody, or control of a child, elderly individual, or disabled individual.

(c) In this section:

(1) "Child" means a person 14 years of age or younger.

(2) "Elderly individual" means a person 65 years of age or older.

(3) "Disabled individual" means a person:

(A) with one or more of the following:

(i) autism spectrum disorder, as defined by Section 1355.001, Insurance Code;

(ii) developmental disability, as defined by Section 112.042, Human Resources Code;

(iii) intellectual disability, as defined by Section 591.003, Health and Safety Code;

(iv) severe emotional disturbance, as defined by Section 261.001, Family Code;

(v) traumatic brain injury, as defined by Section 92.001, Health and Safety Code; or

(vi) mental illness, as defined by Section 571.003, Health and Safety Code; or

(B) who otherwise by reason of age or physical or mental disease, defect, or injury is substantially unable to protect the person's self from harm or to provide food, shelter, or medical care for the person's self.

(4) [Repealed by Acts 2011, 82nd Leg., ch. 620 (S.B. 688), § 11, effective September 1, 2011.]

(d) For purposes of an omission that causes a condition described by Subsection (a)(1), (2), or (3), the actor has assumed care, custody, or control if the actor has by act, words, or course of conduct acted so as to cause a reasonable person to conclude that the actor has accepted responsibility for protection, food, shelter, or medical care for a child, elderly individual, or disabled individual. For purposes of an omission that causes a condition described by Subsection (a-1)(1), (2), or (3), the actor acting during the actor's capacity as owner, operator, or employee of a group home or facility described by Subsection (a-1) is considered to have accepted responsibility for protection, food, shelter, or medical care for the child, elderly individual, or disabled individual who is a resident of the group home or facility.

(e) An offense under Subsection (a)(1) or (2) or (a-1)(1) or (2) is a felony of the first degree when the conduct is committed intentionally or knowingly. When the conduct is engaged in recklessly, the offense is a felony of the second degree.

(f) An offense under Subsection (a)(3) or (a-1)(3) is a felony of the third degree when the conduct is committed intentionally or knowingly, except that an offense under Subsection (a)(3) is a felony of the second degree when the conduct is committed intentionally or knowingly and the victim is a disabled individual residing in a center, as defined by Section 555.001, Health and Safety Code, or in a facility licensed under Chapter 252, Health and Safety Code, and the actor is an employee of the center or facility whose employment involved providing direct care for the victim. When the conduct is engaged in recklessly, the offense is a state jail felony.

(g) An offense under Subsection (a) is a state jail felony when the person acts with criminal negligence. An offense under Subsection (a-1) is a state jail felony when the person, with criminal negligence and by omission, causes a condition described by Subsection (a-1)(1), (2), or (3).

(h) A person who is subject to prosecution under both this section and another section of this code may be prosecuted under either or both sections. Section 3.04 does not apply to criminal episodes prosecuted under both this section and another section of this code. If a criminal episode is prosecuted under both this section and another section of this code and sentences are assessed for convictions under both sections, the sentences shall run concurrently.

(i) It is an affirmative defense to prosecution under Subsection (b)(2) that before the offense the actor:

(1) notified in person the child, elderly individual, or disabled individual that the actor would no longer provide the applicable care described by Subsection (d), and notified in writing the parents or a person, other than the actor, acting in loco parentis to the child, elderly individual, or disabled individual that the actor would no longer provide the applicable care described by Subsection (d); or

(2) notified in writing the Department of Family and Protective Services that the actor would no longer provide the applicable care described by Subsection (d).

(j) Written notification under Subsection (i)(2) or (i)(3) is not effective unless it contains the name and address of the actor, the name and address of the child, elderly individual, or disabled individual, the type of care provided by the actor, and the date the care was discontinued.

(k) It is a defense to prosecution under this section that the act or omission consisted of:

(1) reasonable medical care occurring under the direction of or by a licensed physician; or

(2) emergency medical care administered in good faith and with reasonable care by a person not licensed in the healing arts.

(*l*) It is an affirmative defense to prosecution under this section:

(1) that the act or omission was based on treatment in accordance with the tenets and practices of a recognized religious method of healing with a generally accepted record of efficacy;

(2) for a person charged with an act of omission causing to a child, elderly individual, or disabled individual a condition described by Subsection (a)(1), (2), or (3) that:

(A) there is no evidence that, on the date prior to the offense charged, the defendant was aware of an incident of injury to the child, elderly individual, or disabled individual and failed to report the incident; and

(B) the person:

(i) was a victim of family violence, as that term is defined by Section 71.004, Family Code, committed by a person who is also charged with an offense against the child, elderly individual, or disabled individual under this section or any other section of this title;

(ii) did not cause a condition described by Subsection (a)(1), (2), or (3); and

(iii) did not reasonably believe at the time of the omission that an effort to prevent the person also charged with an offense against the child, elderly individual, or disabled individual from committing the offense would have an effect; or

(3) that:

(A) the actor was not more than three years older than the victim at the time of the offense; and

(B) the victim was a nondisabled or disabled child at the time of the offense.

(m) It is an affirmative defense to prosecution under Subsections (a)(1), (2), and (3) for injury to a disabled individual that the person did not know and could not reasonably have known that the individual was a disabled individual, as defined by Subsection (c), at the time of the offense.

Sec. 22.041. Abandoning or Endangering Child.

(a) In this section, "abandon" means to leave a child in any place without providing reasonable and necessary care for the child, under circumstances under which no reasonable, similarly situated adult would leave a child of that age and ability.

(b) A person commits an offense if, having custody, care, or control of a child younger than 15 years, he intentionally abandons the child in any place under circumstances that expose the child to an unreasonable risk of harm.

(c) A person commits an offense if he intentionally, knowingly, recklessly, or with criminal negligence, by act or omission, engages in conduct that places a child younger than 15 years in imminent danger of death, bodily injury, or physical or mental impairment.

(c-1) For purposes of Subsection (c), it is presumed that a person engaged in conduct that places a child in imminent danger of death, bodily injury, or physical or mental impairment if:

(1) the person manufactured, possessed, or in any way introduced into the body of any person the controlled substance methamphetamine in the presence of the child;

(2) the person's conduct related to the proximity or accessibility of the controlled substance methamphetamine to the child and an analysis of a specimen of the child's blood, urine, or other bodily substance indicates the presence of methamphetamine in the child's body; or

(3) the person injected, ingested, inhaled, or otherwise introduced a controlled substance listed in Penalty Group 1, Section 481.102, Health and Safety Code, or Penalty Group 1-B, Section 481.1022, Health and Safety Code, into the human body when the person was not in lawful possession of the substance as defined by Section 481.002(24) of that code.

(d) Except as provided by Subsection (e), an offense under Subsection (b) is:

(1) a state jail felony if the actor abandoned the child with intent to return for the child; or

(2) a felony of the third degree if the actor abandoned the child without intent to return for the child.

(e) An offense under Subsection (b) is a felony of the second degree if the actor abandons the child under circumstances that a reasonable person would believe would place the child in imminent danger of death, bodily injury, or physical or mental impairment.

(f) An offense under Subsection (c) is a state jail felony.

(g) It is a defense to prosecution under Subsection (c) that the act or omission enables the child to practice for or participate in an organized athletic event and that appropriate safety equipment and procedures are employed in the event.

(h) It is an exception to the application of this section that the actor voluntarily delivered the child to a designated emergency infant care provider under Section 262.302, Family Code.

Sec. 22.05. Deadly Conduct.

(a) A person commits an offense if he recklessly engages in conduct that places another in imminent danger of serious bodily injury.

(b) A person commits an offense if he knowingly discharges a firearm at or in the direction of:

(1) one or more individuals; or

(2) a habitation, building, or vehicle and is reckless as to whether the habitation, building, or vehicle is occupied.

(c) Recklessness and danger are presumed if the actor knowingly pointed a firearm at or in the direction of another whether or not the actor believed the firearm to be loaded.

(d) For purposes of this section, "building," "habitation," and "vehicle" have the meanings assigned those terms by Section 30.01.

(e) An offense under Subsection (a) is a Class A misdemeanor. An offense under Subsection (b) is a felony of the third degree.

Sec. 22.06. Consent As Defense to Assaultive Conduct.

(a) The victim's effective consent or the actor's reasonable belief that the victim consented to the actor's conduct is a defense to prosecution under Section 22.01 (Assault), 22.02 (Aggravated Assault), or 22.05 (Deadly Conduct) if:

(1) the conduct did not threaten or inflict serious bodily injury; or

(2) the victim knew the conduct was a risk of:

(A) his occupation;

(B) recognized medical treatment; or

(C) a scientific experiment conducted by recognized methods.

(b) The defense to prosecution provided by Subsection (a) is not available to a defendant who commits an offense described by Subsection (a) as a condition of the defendant's or the victim's initiation or continued membership in a criminal street gang, as defined by Section 71.01.

Sec. 22.065. Evidence of Previous Sexual Conduct [Repealed].

Repealed by the Texas Court of Criminal Appeals pursuant to Acts 1985, 69th Leg., ch. 685 (H.B. 13), § 9.

Sec. 22.07. Terroristic Threat.

(a) A person commits an offense if he threatens to commit any offense involving violence to any person or property with intent to:

(1) cause a reaction of any type to his threat by an official or volunteer agency organized to deal with emergencies;

(2) place any person in fear of imminent serious bodily injury;

(3) prevent or interrupt the occupation or use of a building, room, place of assembly, place to which the public has access, place of employment or occupation, aircraft, automobile, or other form of conveyance, or other public place;

(4) cause impairment or interruption of public communications, public transportation, public water, gas, or power supply or other public service;

(5) place the public or a substantial group of the public in fear of serious bodily injury; or

(6) influence the conduct or activities of a branch or agency of the federal government, the state, or a political subdivision of the state.

(b) An offense under Subsection (a)(1) is a Class B misdemeanor.

(c) An offense under Subsection (a)(2) is a Class B misdemeanor, except that the offense is a Class A misdemeanor if the offense:

(1) is committed against a member of the person's family or household or otherwise constitutes family violence; or

(2) is committed against a public servant.

(c-1) Notwithstanding Subsection (c)(2), an offense under Subsection (a)(2) is a state jail felony if the offense is committed against a person the actor knows is a peace officer or judge.

(d) An offense under Subsection (a)(3) is a Class A misdemeanor, unless the actor causes pecuniary loss of $1,500 or more to the owner of the building, room, place, or conveyance, in which event the offense is a state jail felony.

(e) An offense under Subsection (a)(4), (a)(5), or (a)(6) is a felony of the third degree.

(f) In this section:

(1) "Family" has the meaning assigned by Section 71.003, Family Code.

(2) "Family violence" has the meaning assigned by Section 71.004, Family Code.

(3) "Household" has the meaning assigned by Section 71.005, Family Code.

(g) For purposes of Subsection (d), the amount of pecuniary loss is the amount of economic loss suffered by the owner of the building, room, place, or conveyance as a result of the prevention or interruption of the occupation or use of the building, room, place, or conveyance.

Sec. 22.08. Aiding Suicide.

(a) A person commits an offense if, with intent to promote or assist the commission of suicide by another, he aids or attempts to aid the other to commit or attempt to commit suicide.

(b) An offense under this section is a Class C misdemeanor unless the actor's conduct causes suicide or attempted suicide that results in serious bodily injury, in which event the offense is a state jail felony.

Sec. 22.09. Tampering with Consumer Product.

(a) In this section:

(1) "Consumer Product" means any product offered for sale to or for consumption by the public and includes "food" and "drugs" as those terms are defined in Section 431.002, Health and Safety Code.

(2) "Tamper" means to alter or add a foreign substance to a consumer product to make it probable that the consumer product will cause serious bodily injury.

(b) A person commits an offense if he knowingly or intentionally tampers with a consumer product knowing that the consumer product will be offered for sale to the public or as a gift to another.

(c) A person commits an offense if he knowingly or intentionally threatens to tamper with a consumer product with the intent to cause fear, to affect the sale of the consumer product, or to cause bodily injury to any person.

(d) An offense under Subsection (b) is a felony of the second degree unless a person suffers serious bodily injury, in which event it is a felony of the first degree. An offense under Subsection (c) is a felony of the third degree.

Sec. 22.10. Leaving a Child in a Vehicle.

(a) A person commits an offense if he intentionally or knowingly leaves a child in a motor vehicle for longer than five minutes, knowing that the child is:

(1) younger than seven years of age; and

(2) not attended by an individual in the vehicle who is 14 years of age or older.

(b) An offense under this section is a Class C misdemeanor.

Sec. 22.11. Harassment by Persons in Certain Facilities; Harassment of Public Servant.

(a) A person commits an offense if, with the intent to assault, harass, or alarm, the person:

(1) while imprisoned or confined in a correctional or detention facility, causes another person to contact the blood, seminal fluid, vaginal fluid, saliva, urine, or feces of the actor, any other person, or an animal;

(2) while committed to a civil commitment facility, causes:

(A) an officer or employee of the Texas Civil Commitment Office to contact the blood, seminal fluid, vaginal fluid, saliva, urine, or feces of the actor, any other person, or an animal:

(i) while the officer or employee is lawfully discharging an official duty at a civil commitment facility; or

(ii) in retaliation for or on account of an exercise of official power or performance of an official duty by the officer or employee; or

(B) a person who contracts with the state to perform a service in the facility or an employee of that person to contact the blood, seminal fluid, vaginal fluid, saliva, urine, or feces of the actor, any other person, or an animal:

(i) while the person or employee is engaged in performing a service within the scope of the contract, if the actor knows the person or employee is authorized by the state to provide the service; or

(ii) in retaliation for or on account of the person's or employee's performance of a service within the scope of the contract; or

(3) causes another person the actor knows to be a public servant to contact the blood, seminal fluid, vaginal fluid, saliva, urine, or feces of the actor, any other person, or an animal while the public servant is lawfully discharging an official duty or in retaliation or on account of an exercise of the public servant's official power or performance of an official duty.

(b) An offense under this section is a felony of the third degree.

(c) If conduct constituting an offense under this section also constitutes an offense under another section of this code, the actor may be prosecuted under either section.

(d) In this section, "correctional or detention facility" means:

(1) a secure correctional facility; or

(2) a "secure correctional facility" or a "secure detention facility" as defined by Section 51.02, Family Code, operated by or under contract with a juvenile board or the Texas Juvenile Justice Department or any other facility operated by or under contract with that department.

(e) For purposes of Subsection (a)(3), the actor is presumed to have known the person was a public servant if the person was wearing a distinctive uniform or badge indicating the person's employment as a public servant.

Sec. 22.12. Applicability to Certain Conduct.

This chapter does not apply to conduct charged as having been committed against an individual who is an unborn child if the conduct is:

(1) committed by the mother of the unborn child;

(2) a lawful medical procedure performed by a physician or other health care provider with the requisite consent;

(3) a lawful medical procedure performed by a physician or other licensed health care provider with the requisite consent as part of an assisted reproduction as defined by Section 160.102, Family Code; or

(4) the dispensation of a drug in accordance with law or administration of a drug prescribed in accordance with law.

TITLE 6
OFFENSES AGAINST THE FAMILY

CHAPTER 25
OFFENSES AGAINST THE FAMILY

Sec. 25.01. Bigamy.

(a) An individual commits an offense if:

(1) he is legally married and he:

(A) purports to marry or does marry a person other than his spouse in this state, or any other state or foreign country, under circumstances that would, but for the actor's prior marriage, constitute a marriage; or

(B) lives with a person other than his spouse in this state under the appearance of being married; or

(2) he knows that a married person other than his spouse is married and he:

(A) purports to marry or does marry that person in this state, or any other state or foreign country, under circumstances that would, but for the person's prior marriage, constitute a marriage; or

(B) lives with that person in this state under the appearance of being married.

(b) For purposes of this section, "under the appearance of being married" means holding out that the parties are married with cohabitation and an intent to be married by either party.

(c) It is a defense to prosecution under Subsection (a)(1) that the actor reasonably believed at the time of the commission of the offense that the actor and the person whom the actor married or purported to marry or with whom the actor lived under the appearance of being married were legally eligible to be married because the actor's prior marriage was void or had been dissolved by death, divorce, or annulment. For purposes of this subsection, an actor's belief is reasonable if the belief is substantiated by a certified copy of a death certificate or other signed document issued by a court.

(d) For the purposes of this section, the lawful wife or husband of the actor may testify both for or against the actor concerning proof of the original marriage.

(e) An offense under this section is a felony of the third degree, except that if at the time of the commission of the offense, the person whom the actor marries or purports to marry or with whom the actor lives under the appearance of being married is:

(1) 17 years of age, the offense is a felony of the second degree; or

(2) 16 years of age or younger, the offense is a felony of the first degree.

Sec. 25.02. Prohibited Sexual Conduct.

(a) A person commits an offense if the person engages in sexual intercourse or deviate sexual intercourse with another person the actor knows to be, without regard to legitimacy:

(1) the actor's ancestor or descendant by blood or adoption;

(2) the actor's current or former stepchild or stepparent;

(3) the actor's parent's brother or sister of the whole or half blood;

(4) the actor's brother or sister of the whole or half blood or by adoption;

(5) the children of the actor's brother or sister of the whole or half blood or by adoption; or

(6) the son or daughter of the actor's aunt or uncle of the whole or half blood or by adoption.

(b) For purposes of this section:

(1) "Deviate sexual intercourse" means any contact between the genitals of one person and the mouth or anus of another person with intent to arouse or gratify the sexual desire of any person.

(2) "Sexual intercourse" means any penetration of the female sex organ by the male sex organ.

(c) An offense under this section is a felony of the third degree, unless the offense is committed under Subsection (a)(1), in which event the offense is a felony of the second degree.

Sec. 25.03. Interference with Child Custody.

(a) A person commits an offense if the person takes or retains a child younger than 18 years of age:

(1) when the person knows that the person's taking or retention violates the express terms of a judgment or order, including a temporary order, of a court disposing of the child's custody;

(2) when the person has not been awarded custody of the child by a court of competent jurisdiction, knows that a suit for divorce or a civil suit or application for habeas corpus to dispose of the child's custody has been filed, and takes the child out of the geographic area of the counties composing the judicial district if the court is a district court or the county if the court is a statutory county court, without the permission of the court and with the intent to deprive the court of authority over the child; or

(3) outside of the United States with the intent to deprive a person entitled to possession of or access to the child of that possession or access and without the permission of that person.

(b) A noncustodial parent commits an offense if, with the intent to interfere with the lawful custody of a child younger than 18 years, the noncustodial parent knowingly entices or persuades the child to leave the custody of the custodial parent, guardian, or person standing in the stead of the custodial parent or guardian of the child.

(c) It is a defense to prosecution under Subsection (a)(2) that the actor returned the child to the geographic area of the counties composing the judicial district if the court is a district court or the county if the court is a statutory county court, within three days after the date of the commission of the offense.

(c-1) It is an affirmative defense to prosecution under Subsection (a)(3) that:

(1) the taking or retention of the child was pursuant to a valid order providing for possession of or access to the child; or

(2) notwithstanding any violation of a valid order providing for possession of or access to the child, the actor's retention of the child was due only to circumstances beyond the actor's control and the actor promptly provided notice or made reasonable attempts to provide notice of those circumstances to the other person entitled to possession of or access to the child.

(c-2) Subsection (a)(3) does not apply if, at the time of the offense, the person taking or retaining the child:

(1) was entitled to possession of or access to the child; and

(2) was fleeing the commission or attempted commission of family violence, as defined by Section 71.004, Family Code, against the child or the person.

(d) An offense under this section is a state jail felony.

Sec. 25.031. Agreement to Abduct from Custody.

(a) A person commits an offense if the person agrees, for remuneration or the promise of remuneration, to abduct a child younger than 18 years of age by force, threat of force, misrepresentation, stealth, or unlawful entry, knowing that the child is under the care and control of a person having custody or physical possession of the child under a court order, including a temporary order, or under the care and control of another person who is exercising care and control with the consent of a person having custody or physical possession under a court order, including a temporary order.

(b) An offense under this section is a state jail felony.

Sec. 25.04. Enticing a Child.

(a) A person commits an offense if, with the intent to interfere with the lawful custody of a child younger than 18 years, he knowingly entices, persuades, or takes the child from the custody of the parent or guardian or person standing in the stead of the parent or guardian of such child.

(b) An offense under this section is a Class B misdemeanor, unless it is shown on the trial of the offense that the actor intended to commit a felony against the child, in which event an offense under this section is a felony of the third degree.

Sec. 25.05. Criminal Nonsupport.

(a) An individual commits an offense if the individual intentionally or knowingly fails to provide support for the individual's child younger than 18 years of age, or for the individual's child who is the subject of a court order requiring the individual to support the child.

(b) For purposes of this section, "child" includes a child born out of wedlock whose paternity has either been acknowledged by the actor or has been established in a civil suit under the Family Code or the law of another state.

(c) Under this section, a conviction may be had on the uncorroborated testimony of a party to the offense.

(d) It is an affirmative defense to prosecution under this section that the actor could not provide support for the actor's child.

(e) The pendency of a prosecution under this section does not affect the power of a court to enter an order for child support under the Family Code.

(f) An offense under this section is a state jail felony.

Sec. 25.06. Harboring Runaway Child.

(a) A person commits an offense if he knowingly harbors a child and he is criminally negligent about whether the child:

(1) is younger than 18 years; and

(2) has escaped from the custody of a peace officer, a probation officer, the Texas Youth Council, or a detention facility for children, or is voluntarily absent from the child's home without the consent of the child's parent or guardian for a substantial length of time or without the intent to return.

(b) It is a defense to prosecution under this section that the actor was related to the child within the second degree by consanguinity or affinity, as determined under Chapter 573, Government Code.

(c) It is a defense to prosecution under this section that the actor notified:

(1) the person or agency from which the child escaped or a law enforcement agency of the presence of the child within 24 hours after discovering that the child had escaped from custody; or

(2) a law enforcement agency or a person at the child's home of the presence of the child within 24 hours after discovering that the child was voluntarily absent from home without the consent of the child's parent or guardian.

(d) An offense under this section is a Class A misdemeanor.

(e) On the receipt of a report from a peace officer, probation officer, the Texas Youth Council, a foster home, or a detention facility for children that a child has escaped its custody or upon receipt of a report from a parent, guardian, conservator, or legal custodian that a child is missing, a law enforcement agency shall immediately enter a record of the child into the National Crime Information Center.

Sec. 25.07. Violation of Certain Court Orders or Conditions of Bond in a Family Violence, Child Abuse or Neglect, Sexual Assault or Abuse, Indecent Assault, Stalking, or Trafficking Case.

(a) A person commits an offense if, in violation of a condition of bond set in a family violence, sexual assault or abuse, indecent assault, stalking, or trafficking case and related to the safety of a victim or the safety of the community, an order issued under Subchapter A, Chapter 7B, Code of Criminal Procedure, an order issued under Article 17.292, Code of Criminal Procedure, an order issued under Section 6.504, Family Code, Chapter 83, Family Code, if the temporary ex parte order has been served on the person, Chapter 85, Family Code, or Subchapter F, Chapter 261, Family Code, or an order issued by another jurisdiction as provided by Chapter 88, Family Code, the person knowingly or intentionally:

(1) commits family violence or an act in furtherance of an offense under Section 20A.02, 22.011, 22.012, 22.021, or 42.072;

(2) communicates:

(A) directly with a protected individual or a member of the family or household in a threatening or harassing manner;

(B) a threat through any person to a protected individual or a member of the family or household; or

(C) in any manner with the protected individual or a member of the family or household except through the person's attorney or a person appointed by the court, if the violation is of an order described by this subsection and the order prohibits any communication with a protected individual or a member of the family or household;

(3) goes to or near any of the following places as specifically described in the order or condition of bond:

(A) the residence or place of employment or business of a protected individual or a member of the family or household; or

(B) any child care facility, residence, or school where a child protected by the order or condition of bond normally resides or attends;

(4) possesses a firearm;

(5) harms, threatens, or interferes with the care, custody, or control of a pet, companion animal, or assistance animal that is possessed by a person protected by the order or condition of bond; or

(6) removes, attempts to remove, or otherwise tampers with the normal functioning of a global positioning monitoring system.

(a-1) For purposes of Subsection (a)(5), possession of a pet, companion animal, or assistance animal by a person means:

(1) actual care, custody, control, or managementm of a pet, companion animal, or assistance animal by the person; or

(2) constructive possession of a pet, companion animal, or assistance animal owned by the person or for which the person has been the primary caregiver.

(b) For the purposes of this section:

(1) "Family violence," "family," "household," and "member of a household" have the meanings assigned by Chapter 71, Family Code.

(2) "Firearm" has the meaning assigned by Chapter 46.

(2-a) "Global positioning monitoring system" has the meaning assigned by Article 17.49, Code of Criminal Procedure.

(3) "Assistance animal" has the meaning assigned by Section 121.002, Human Resources Code.

(4) "Sexual abuse" means any act as described by Section 21.02 or 21.11.

(5) "Sexual assault" means any act as described by Section 22.011 or 22.021.

(6) "Stalking" means any conduct that constitutes an offense under Section 42.072.

(7) "Trafficking" means any conduct that constitutes an offense under Section 20A.02.

(8) "Indecent assault" means any conduct that constitutes an offense under Section 22.012.

(c) If conduct constituting an offense under this section also constitutes an offense under another section of this code, the actor may be prosecuted under either section or under both sections.

(d) Reconciliatory actions or agreements made by persons affected by an order do not affect the validity of the order or the duty of a peace officer to enforce this section.

(e) A peace officer investigating conduct that may constitute an offense under this section for a violation of an order may not arrest a person protected by that order for a violation of that order.

(f) It is not a defense to prosecution under this section that certain information has been excluded, as provided by Section 85.007, Family Code, or Article 17.292, Code of Criminal Procedure, from an order to which this section applies.

(g) **As amended by Acts 2021, 87th Leg., ch. XXX (HB 39)** An offense under this section is a Class A misdemeanor, except the offense is:

(1) subject to Subdivision (2), a state jail felony if it is shown at the trial of the offense that the defendant violated an order issued under Subchapter A, Chapter 7B, Code of Criminal Procedure, following the defendant's conviction of or placement on deferred adjudication community supervision for an offense, if the order was issued with respect to a victim of that offense; or

(2) a felony of the third degree if it is shown on the trial of the offense that the defendant:

(A) has previously been convicted two or more times of an offense under this section or two or more times of an offense under Section 25.072, or has previously been convicted of an offense under this section and an offense under Section 25.072; or

(B) has violated the order or condition of bond by committing an assault or the offense of stalking.

(g) **As amended by Acts 2021, 87th Leg., ch. XXX (HB 3607)** An offense under this section is a Class A misdemeanor, except the offense is:

(1) subject to Subdivision (2), a state jail felony if it is shown at the trial of the offense that the defendant violated an order issued as a result of an application filed under Article 7B.001(a-1), Code of Criminal Procedure; or

(2) a felony of the third degree if it is shown on the trial of the offense that the defendant:

(A) has previously been convicted two or more times of an offense under this section or two or more times of an offense under Section 25.072, or has previously been convicted of an offense under this section and an offense under Section 25.072; or

(B) has violated the order or condition of bond by committing an assault or the offense of stalking.

(h) For purposes of Subsection (g), a conviction under the laws of another state for an offense containing elements that are substantially similar to the elements of an offense under this section or Section 25.072 is considered to be a conviction under this section or Section 25.072, as applicable.

Sec. 25.071. Violation of Protective Order Preventing Offense Caused by Bias or Prejudice.

(a) A person commits an offense if, in violation of an order issued under Subchapter C, Chapter 7B, Code of Criminal Procedure, the person knowingly or intentionally:

(1) commits an offense under Title 5 or Section 28.02, 28.03, or 28.08 and commits the offense because of bias or prejudice as described by Article 42.014, Code of Criminal Procedure;

(2) communicates:

(A) directly with a protected individual in a threatening or harassing manner;

(B) a threat through any person to a protected individual; or

(C) in any manner with the protected individual, if the order prohibits any communication with a protected individual; or

(3) goes to or near the residence or place of employment or business of a protected individual.

(b) If conduct constituting an offense under this section also constitutes an offense under another section of this code, the actor may be prosecuted under either section or under both sections.

(c) A peace officer investigating conduct that may constitute an offense under this section for a violation of an order may not arrest a person protected by that order for a violation of that order.

(d) An offense under this section is a Class A misdemeanor unless it is shown on the trial of the offense that the defendant has previously been convicted under this section two or more times or has violated the protective order by committing an assault, in which event the offense is a third degree felony.

Sec. 25.072. Repeated Violation of Certain Court Orders or Conditions of Bond in Family Violence, Child Abuse or Neglect, Sexual Assault or Abuse, Indecent Assault, Stalking, or Trafficking Case.

(a) A person commits an offense if, during a period that is 12 months or less in duration, the person two or more times engages in conduct that constitutes an offense under Section 25.07.

(b) If the jury is the trier of fact, members of the jury must agree unanimously that the defendant, during a period that is 12 months or less in duration, two or more times engaged in conduct that constituted an offense under Section 25.07.

(c) A defendant may not be convicted in the same criminal action of another offense an element of which is any conduct that is alleged as an element of the offense under Subsection (a) unless the other offense:

(1) is charged in the alternative;

(2) occurred outside the period in which the offense alleged under Subsection (a) was committed; or

(3) is considered by the trier of fact to be a lesser included offense of the offense alleged under Subsection (a).

(d) A defendant may not be charged with more than one count under Subsection (a) if all of the specific conduct that is alleged to have been engaged in is alleged to have been committed in violation of a single court order or single setting of bond.

(e) An offense under this section is a felony of the third degree.

Sec. 25.08. Sale or Purchase of Child.

(a) A person commits an offense if he:

(1) possesses a child younger than 18 years of age or has the custody, conservatorship, or guardianship of a child younger than 18 years of age, whether or not he has actual possession of the child, and he offers to accept, agrees to accept, or accepts a thing of value for the delivery of the child to another or for the possession of the child by another for purposes of adoption; or

(2) offers to give, agrees to give, or gives a thing of value to another for acquiring or maintaining the possession of a child for the purpose of adoption.

(b) It is an exception to the application of this section that the thing of value is:

(1) a fee or reimbursement paid to a child-placing agency as authorized by law;

(2) a fee paid to an attorney, social worker, mental health professional, or physician for services rendered in the usual course of legal or medical practice or in providing adoption counseling;

(3) a reimbursement of legal or medical expenses incurred by a person for the benefit of the child; or

(4) a necessary pregnancy-related expense paid by a child-placing agency for the benefit of the child's parent during the pregnancy or after the birth of the child as permitted by the minimum standards for child-placing agencies and Department of Protective and Regulatory Services rules.

(c) An offense under this section is a felony of the third degree, except that the offense is a felony of the second degree if the actor commits the offense with intent to commit an offense under Section 20A.02, 43.021, 43.05, or 43.25.

Sec. 25.081. Unregulated Custody Transfer of Adopted Child.

(a) In this section:

(1) "Adopted child" means a person younger than 18 years of age who was legally adopted through a governmental entity or through private means, including a person who is in foster care or from a foreign country at the time of the adoption.

(2) "Unregulated custody transfer" means the transfer of the permanent physical custody of an adopted child by the parent, managing conservator, or guardian of the child without receiving approval of the transfer by a court as required by Section 162.026, Family Code.

(b) Except as otherwise provided by this section, a person commits an offense if the person knowingly:

(1) conducts an unregulated custody transfer of an adopted child; or

(2) facilitates or participates in the unregulated custody transfer of an adopted child, including by transferring, recruiting, harboring, transporting, providing, soliciting, or obtaining an adopted child for that purpose.

(c) An offense under this section is a felony of the third degree, except that the offense is a felony of the second degree if the actor commits the offense with intent to commit an offense under Section 20A.02, 43.021, 43.05, 43.25, 43.251, or 43.26.

(d) This section does not apply to:

(1) the placement of an adopted child with a licensed child-placing agency, the Department of Family and Protective Services, or an adult relative, stepparent, or other adult with a significant and long-standing relationship to the child;

(2) the placement of an adopted child by a licensed child-placing agency or the Department of Family and Protective Services;

(3) the temporary placement of an adopted child by the child's parent, managing conservator, or guardian for a designated short-term period with a specified intent and period for return of the child due to temporary circumstances, including:

(A) a vacation;

(B) a school-sponsored function or activity; or

(C) the incarceration, military service, medical treatment, or incapacity of the parent, managing conservator, or guardian;

(4) the placement of an adopted child in another state in accordance with the requirements of Subchapter B, Chapter 162, Family Code; or

(5) the voluntary delivery of an adopted child under Subchapter D, Chapter 262, Family Code.

Sec. 25.09. Advertising for Placement of Child.

(a) A person commits an offense if the person advertises in the public media that the person will place, provide, or obtain a child for adoption or any other form of permanent physical custody of the child.

(b) This section does not apply to a licensed child-placing agency that is identified in the advertisement as a licensed child-placing agency.

(c) An offense under this section is a Class A misdemeanor unless the person has been convicted previously under this section, in which event the offense is a felony of the third degree.

(d) In this section:

(1) "Child" has the meaning assigned by Section 101.003, Family Code.

(2) "Public media" has the meaning assigned by Section 38.01. The term also includes communications through the use of the Internet or another public computer network.

Sec. 25.10. Interference with Rights of Guardian of the Person.

(a) In this section:

(1) "Possessory right" means the right of a guardian of the person to have physical possession of a ward and to establish the ward's legal domicile, as provided by Section 1151.051(c)(1), Estates Code.

(2) "Ward" has the meaning assigned by Chapter 1002, Estates Code.

(b) A person commits an offense if the person takes, retains, or conceals a ward when the person knows that the person's taking, retention, or concealment interferes with a possessory right with respect to the ward.

(c) An offense under this section is a state jail felony.

(d) This section does not apply to a governmental entity where the taking, retention, or concealment of the ward was authorized by Subtitle E, Title 5, Family Code, or Chapter 48, Human Resources Code.

Sec. 25.11. Continuous Violence Against the Family.

(a) A person commits an offense if, during a period that is 12 months or less in duration, the person two or more times engages in conduct that constitutes an offense under Section 22.01(a)(1) against another person or persons whose relationship to or association with the defendant is described by Section 71.0021(b), 71.003, or 71.005, Family Code.

(b) If the jury is the trier of fact, members of the jury are not required to agree unanimously on the specific conduct in which the defendant engaged that constituted an offense under Section 22.01(a)(1) against the person or persons described by Subsection (a), the exact date when that conduct occurred, or the county in which each instance of the conduct occurred. The jury must agree unanimously that the defendant, during a period that is 12 months or less in duration, two or more times engaged in conduct that constituted an offense under Section 22.01(a)(1) against the person or persons described by Subsection (a).

(c) A defendant may not be convicted in the same criminal action of another offense the victim of which is an alleged victim of the offense under Subsection (a) and an element of which is any conduct that is alleged as an element of the offense under Subsection (a) unless the other offense:

(1) is charged in the alternative;

(2) occurred outside the period in which the offense alleged under Subsection (a) was committed; or

(3) is considered by the trier of fact to be a lesser included offense of the offense alleged under Subsection (a).

(d) A defendant may not be charged with more than one count under Subsection (a) if all of the specific conduct that is alleged to have been engaged in is alleged to have been committed against a single victim or members of the same household, as defined by Section 71.005, Family Code.

(e) An offense under this section is a felony of the third degree.

TITLE 7 OFFENSES AGAINST PROPERTY

CHAPTER 28 ARSON, CRIMINAL MISCHIEF, AND OTHER PROPERTY DAMAGE OR DESTRUCTION

Sec. 28.01. Definitions.

In this chapter:

(1) "Habitation" means a structure or vehicle that is adapted for the overnight accommodation of persons and includes:

(A) each separately secured or occupied portion of the structure or vehicle; and

(B) each structure appurtenant to or connected with the structure or vehicle.

(2) "Building" means any structure or enclosure intended for use or occupation as a habitation or for some purpose of trade, manufacture, ornament, or use.

(3) "Property" means:

(A) real property;

(B) tangible or intangible personal property, including anything severed from land; or

(C) a document, including money, that represents or embodies anything of value.

(4) "Vehicle" includes any device in, on, or by which any person or property is or may be propelled, moved, or drawn in the normal course of commerce or transportation.

(5) "Open-space land" means real property that is undeveloped for the purpose of human habitation.

(6) "Controlled burning" means the burning of unwanted vegetation with the consent of the owner of the property on which the vegetation is located and in such a manner that the fire is controlled and limited to a designated area.

Sec. 28.02. Arson.

(a) A person commits an offense if the person starts a fire, regardless of whether the fire continues after ignition, or causes an explosion with intent to destroy or damage:

(1) any vegetation, fence, or structure on open-space land; or

(2) any building, habitation, or vehicle:

(A) knowing that it is within the limits of an incorporated city or town;

(B) knowing that it is insured against damage or destruction;

(C) knowing that it is subject to a mortgage or other security interest;

(D) knowing that it is located on property belonging to another;

(E) knowing that it has located within it property belonging to another; or

(F) when the person is reckless about whether the burning or explosion will endanger the life of some individual or the safety of the property of another.

(a-1) A person commits an offense if the person recklessly starts a fire or causes an explosion while manufacturing or attempting to manufacture a controlled substance and the fire or explosion damages any building, habitation, or vehicle.

(a-2) A person commits an offense if the person intentionally starts a fire or causes an explosion and in so doing:

(1) recklessly damages or destroys a building belonging to another; or

(2) recklessly causes another person to suffer bodily injury or death.

(b) It is an exception to the application of Subsection (a)(1) that the fire or explosion was a part of the controlled burning of open-space land.

(c) It is a defense to prosecution under Subsection (a)(2)(A) that prior to starting the fire or causing the explosion, the actor obtained a permit or other written authorization granted in accordance with a city ordinance, if any, regulating fires and explosions.

(d) An offense under Subsection (a) is a felony of the second degree, except that the offense is a felony of the first degree if it is shown on the trial of the offense that:

(1) bodily injury or death was suffered by any person by reason of the commission of the offense; or

(2) the property intended to be damaged or destroyed by the actor was a habitation or a place of assembly or worship.

(e) An offense under Subsection (a-1) is a state jail felony, except that the offense is a felony of the third degree if it is shown on the trial of the offense that bodily injury or death was suffered by any person by reason of the commission of the offense.

(f) An offense under Subsection (a-2) is a state jail felony.

(g) If conduct that constitutes an offense under Subsection (a-1) or that constitutes an offense under Subsection (a-2) also constitutes an offense under another subsection of this section or another section of this code, the actor may be prosecuted under Subsection (a-1) or Subsection (a-2), under the other subsection of this section, or under the other section of this code.

Sec. 28.03. Criminal Mischief.

(a) A person commits an offense if, without the effective consent of the owner:

(1) he intentionally or knowingly damages or destroys the tangible property of the owner;

(2) he intentionally or knowingly tampers with the tangible property of the owner and causes pecuniary loss or substantial inconvenience to the owner or a third person; or

(3) he intentionally or knowingly makes markings, including inscriptions, slogans, drawings, or paintings, on the tangible property of the owner.

(b) Except as provided by Subsections (f) and (h), an offense under this section is:

(1) a Class C misdemeanor if:

(A) the amount of pecuniary loss is less than $100; or

(B) except as provided in Subdivision (3)(A) or (3)(B), it causes substantial inconvenience to others;

(2) a Class B misdemeanor if the amount of pecuniary loss is $100 or more but less than $750;

(3) a Class A misdemeanor if:

(A) the amount of pecuniary loss is $750 or more but less than $2,500; or

(B) the actor causes in whole or in part impairment or interruption of any public water supply, or causes to be diverted in whole, in part, or in any manner, including installation or removal of any device for any such purpose, any public water supply, regardless of the amount of the pecuniary loss;

(4) a state jail felony if the amount of pecuniary loss is:

(A) $2,500 or more but less than $30,000;

(B) less than $2,500, if the property damaged or destroyed is a habitation and if the damage or destruction is caused by a firearm or explosive weapon;

(C) less than $2,500, if the property was a fence used for the production or containment of:

(i) cattle, bison, horses, sheep, swine, goats, exotic livestock, or exotic poultry; or

(ii) game animals as that term is defined by Section 63.001, Parks and Wildlife Code; or

(D) less than $30,000 and the actor:

(i) causes wholly or partly impairment or interruption of property used for flood control purposes or a dam or of public communications, public transportation, public gas or power supply, or other public service; or

(ii) causes to be diverted wholly, partly, or in any manner, including installation or removal of any device for any such purpose, any public communications or public gas or power supply;

(5) a felony of the third degree if:

(A) the amount of the pecuniary loss is $30,000 or more but less than $150,000;

(B) the actor, by discharging a firearm or other weapon or by any other means, causes the death of one or more head of cattle or bison or one or more horses; or

(C) the actor causes wholly or partly impairment or interruption of access to an automated teller machine, regardless of the amount of the pecuniary loss;

(6) a felony of the second degree if the amount of pecuniary loss is $150,000 or more but less than $300,000; or

(7) a felony of the first degree if the amount of pecuniary loss is $300,000 or more.

(c) For the purposes of this section, it shall be presumed that a person who is receiving the economic benefit of public communications, public water, gas, or power supply, has knowingly tampered with the tangible property of the owner if the communication or supply has been:

(1) diverted from passing through a metering device; or

(2) prevented from being correctly registered by a metering device; or

(3) activated by any device installed to obtain public communications, public water, gas, or power supply without a metering device.

(d) The terms "public communication, public transportation, public gas or power supply, or other public service" and "public water supply" shall mean, refer to, and include any such services subject to regulation by the Public Utility Commission of Texas, the Railroad Commission of Texas, or the Texas Natural Resource Conservation Commission or any such services enfranchised by the State of Texas or any political subdivision thereof.

(e) When more than one item of tangible property, belonging to one or more owners, is damaged, destroyed, or tampered with in violation of this section pursuant to one scheme or continuing course of conduct, the conduct may be considered as one offense, and the amounts of pecuniary loss to property resulting from the damage to, destruction of, or tampering with the property may be aggregated in determining the grade of the offense.

(f) An offense under this section is a state jail felony if the damage or destruction is inflicted on a place of worship or human burial, a public monument, or a community center that provides medical, social, or educational programs and the amount of the pecuniary loss to real property or to tangible personal property is $750 or more but less than $30,000.

(g) In this section:

(1) "Explosive weapon" means any explosive or incendiary device that is designed, made, or adapted for the purpose of inflicting serious bodily injury, death, or substantial property damage, or for the principal purpose of causing such a loud report as to cause undue public alarm or terror, and includes:

(A) an explosive or incendiary bomb, grenade, rocket, and mine;

(B) a device designed, made, or adapted for delivering or shooting an explosive weapon; and

(C) a device designed, made, or adapted to start a fire in a time-delayed manner.

(2) "Firearm" has the meaning assigned by Section 46.01.

(3) "Institution of higher education" has the meaning assigned by Section 61.003, Education Code.

(4) "Aluminum wiring" means insulated or noninsulated wire or cable that consists of at least 50 percent aluminum, including any tubing or conduit attached to the wire or cable.

(5) "Bronze wiring" means insulated or noninsulated wire or cable that consists of at least 50 percent bronze, including any tubing or conduit attached to the wire or cable.

(6) "Copper wiring" means insulated or noninsulated wire or cable that consists of at least 50 percent copper, including any tubing or conduit attached to the wire or cable.

(7) "Transportation communications equipment" means:

(A) an official traffic-control device, railroad sign or signal, or traffic-control signal, as those terms are defined by Section 541.304, Transportation Code; or

(B) a sign, signal, or device erected by a railroad, public body, or public officer to direct the movement of a railroad train, as defined by Section 541.202, Transportation Code.

(8) "Transportation communications device" means any item attached to transportation communications equipment, including aluminum wiring, bronze wiring, and copper wiring.

(9) "Automated teller machine" has the meaning assigned by Section 31.03.

(h) An offense under this section is a state jail felony if the amount of the pecuniary loss to real property or to tangible personal property is $750 or more but less than $30,000 and the damage or destruction is inflicted on a public or private elementary school, secondary school, or institution of higher education.

(i) Notwithstanding Subsection (b), an offense under this section is a felony of the first degree if the property is livestock and the damage is caused by introducing bovine spongiform encephalopathy, commonly known as mad cow disease, or a disease listed in rules adopted by the Texas Animal Health Commission under Section 161.041(a), Agriculture Code. In this subsection, "livestock" has the meaning assigned by Section 161.001, Agriculture Code.

(j) Notwithstanding Subsection (b), an offense under this section is a felony of the third degree if:

(1) the tangible property damaged, destroyed, or tampered with is transportation communications equipment or a transportation communications device; and

(2) the amount of the pecuniary loss to the tangible property is less than $150,000.

(k) Subsection (a)(1) or (2) does not apply if the tangible personal property of the owner was a head of cattle or bison killed, or a horse killed, in the course of the actor's:

(1) actual discharge of official duties as a member of the United States armed forces or the state military forces as defined by Section 437.001, Government Code; or

(2) regular agricultural labor duties and practices.

Sec. 28.04. Reckless Damage or Destruction.

(a) A person commits an offense if, without the effective consent of the owner, he recklessly damages or destroys property of the owner.

(b) An offense under this section is a Class C misdemeanor.

Sec. 28.05. Actor's Interest in Property.

It is no defense to prosecution under this chapter that the actor has an interest in the property damaged or destroyed if another person also has an interest that the actor is not entitled to infringe.

Sec. 28.06. Amount of Pecuniary Loss.

(a) The amount of pecuniary loss under this chapter, if the property is destroyed, is:

(1) the fair market value of the property at the time and place of the destruction; or

(2) if the fair market value of the property cannot be ascertained, the cost of replacing the property within a reasonable time after the destruction.

(b) The amount of pecuniary loss under this chapter, if the property is damaged, is the cost of repairing or restoring the damaged property within a reasonable time after the damage occurred.

(c) The amount of pecuniary loss under this chapter for documents, other than those having a readily ascertainable market value, is:

(1) the amount due and collectible at maturity less any part that has been satisfied, if the document constitutes evidence of a debt; or

(2) the greatest amount of economic loss that the owner might reasonably suffer by virtue of the destruction or damage if the document is other than evidence of a debt.

(d) If the amount of pecuniary loss cannot be ascertained by the criteria set forth in Subsections (a) through (c), the amount of loss is deemed to be greater than $750 but less than $2,500.

(e) If the actor proves by a preponderance of the evidence that he gave consideration for or had a legal interest in the property involved, the value of the interest so proven shall be deducted from:

(1) the amount of pecuniary loss if the property is destroyed; or

(2) the amount of pecuniary loss to the extent of an amount equal to the ratio the value of the

interest bears to the total value of the property, if the property is damaged.

Sec. 28.07. Interference with Railroad Property.

(a) In this section:

(1) "Railroad property" means:

(A) a train, locomotive, railroad car, caboose, work equipment, rolling stock, safety device, switch, or connection that is owned, leased, operated, or possessed by a railroad; or

(B) a railroad track, rail, bridge, trestle, or right-of-way owned or used by a railroad.

(2) "Tamper" means to move, alter, or interfere with railroad property.

(b) A person commits an offense if the person:

(1) throws an object or discharges a firearm or weapon at a train or rail-mounted work equipment; or

(2) without the effective consent of the owner:

(A) enters or remains on railroad property, knowing that it is railroad property;

(B) tampers with railroad property;

(C) places an obstruction on a railroad track or right-of-way; or

(D) causes in any manner the derailment of a train, railroad car, or other railroad property that moves on tracks.

(c) An offense under Subsection (b)(1) is a Class B misdemeanor unless the person causes bodily injury to another, in which event the offense is a felony of the third degree.

(d) An offense under Subsection (b)(2)(A) is a Class C misdemeanor.

(e) An offense under Subsection (b)(2)(B), (b)(2)(C), or (b)(2)(D) is a Class C misdemeanor unless the person causes pecuniary loss of $100 or more, in which event the offense is:

(1) a Class B misdemeanor if the amount of pecuniary loss is $100 or more but less than $750;

(2) a Class A misdemeanor if the amount of pecuniary loss is $750 or more but less than $2,500;

(3) a state jail felony if the amount of pecuniary loss is $2,500 or more but less than $30,000;

(4) a felony of the third degree if the amount of the pecuniary loss is $30,000 or more but less than $150,000;

(5) a felony of the second degree if the amount of pecuniary loss is $150,000 or more but less than $300,000; or

(6) a felony of the first degree if the amount of the pecuniary loss is $300,000 or more.

(f) The conduct described in Subsection (b)(2)(A) is not an offense under this section if it is undertaken by an employee of the railroad or by a representative of a labor organization which represents or is seeking to represent the employees of the railroad as long as the employee or representative has a right to engage in such conduct under the Railway Labor Act (45 U.S.C. Section 151 et seq.).

Sec. 28.08. Graffiti.

(a) A person commits an offense if, without the effective consent of the owner, the person intentionally or knowingly makes markings, including inscriptions, slogans, drawings, or paintings, on the tangible property of the owner with:

(1) paint;

(2) an indelible marker; or

(3) an etching or engraving device.

(b) Except as provided by Subsection (d), an offense under this section is:

(1) a Class C misdemeanor if the amount of pecuniary loss is less than $100;

(2) a Class B misdemeanor if the amount of pecuniary loss is $100 or more but less than $750;

(3) a Class A misdemeanor if the amount of pecuniary loss is $750 or more but less than $2,500;

(4) a state jail felony if the amount of pecuniary loss is $2,500 or more but less than $30,000;

(5) a felony of the third degree if the amount of pecuniary loss is $30,000 or more but less than $150,000;

(6) a felony of the second degree if the amount of pecuniary loss is $150,000 or more but less than $300,000; or

(7) a felony of the first degree if the amount of pecuniary loss is $300,000 or more.

(c) When more than one item of tangible property, belonging to one or more owners, is marked in violation of this section pursuant to one scheme or continuing course of conduct, the conduct may be considered as one offense, and the amounts of pecuniary loss to property resulting from the marking of the property may be aggregated in determining the grade of the offense.

(d) An offense under this section is a state jail felony if:

(1) the marking is made on a school, an institution of higher education, a place of worship or human burial, a public monument, or a community center that provides medical, social, or educational programs; and

(2) the amount of the pecuniary loss to real property or to tangible personal property is $750 or more but less than $30,000.

(e) In this section:

(1) "Aerosol paint" means an aerosolized paint product.

(2) "Etching or engraving device" means a device that makes a delineation or impression on tangible property, regardless of the manufacturer's intended use for that device.

(3) "Indelible marker" means a device that makes a mark with a paint or ink product that is specifically formulated to be more difficult to erase, wash out, or remove than ordinary paint or ink products.

(4) "Institution of higher education" has the meaning assigned by Section 481.134, Health and Safety Code.

(5) "School" means a private or public elementary or secondary school.

CHAPTER 29 ROBBERY

Sec. 29.01. Definitions.

In this chapter:

(1) "In the course of committing theft" means conduct that occurs in an attempt to commit, during the commission, or in immediate flight after the attempt or commission of theft.

(2) "Property" means:

(A) tangible or intangible personal property including anything severed from land; or

(B) a document, including money, that represents or embodies anything of value.

Sec. 29.02. Robbery.

(a) A person commits an offense if, in the course of committing theft as defined in Chapter 31 and with intent to obtain or maintain control of the property, he:

(1) intentionally, knowingly, or recklessly causes bodily injury to another; or

(2) intentionally or knowingly threatens or places another in fear of imminent bodily injury or death.

(b) An offense under this section is a felony of the second degree.

Sec. 29.03. Aggravated Robbery.

(a) A person commits an offense if he commits robbery as defined in Section 29.02, and he:

(1) causes serious bodily injury to another;

(2) uses or exhibits a deadly weapon; or

(3) causes bodily injury to another person or threatens or places another person in fear of imminent bodily injury or death, if the other person is:

(A) 65 years of age or older; or

(B) a disabled person.

(b) An offense under this section is a felony of the first degree.

(c) In this section, "disabled person" means an individual with a mental, physical, or developmental disability who is substantially unable to protect himself from harm.

CHAPTER 30 BURGLARY AND CRIMINAL TRESPASS

Sec. 30.01. Definitions.

In this chapter:

(1) "Habitation" means a structure or vehicle that is adapted for the overnight accommodation of persons, and includes:

(A) each separately secured or occupied portion of the structure or vehicle; and

(B) each structure appurtenant to or connected with the structure or vehicle.

(2) "Building" means any enclosed structure intended for use or occupation as a habitation or for some purpose of trade, manufacture, ornament, or use.

(3) "Vehicle" includes any device in, on, or by which any person or property is or may be propelled, moved, or drawn in the normal course of commerce or transportation, except such devices as are classified as "habitation."

(4) "Controlled substance" has the meaning assigned by Section 481.002, Health and Safety Code.

(5) "Wholesale distributor of prescription drugs" means a wholesale distributor, as defined by Section 431.401, Health and Safety Code.

Sec. 30.02. Burglary.

(a) A person commits an offense if, without the effective consent of the owner, the person:

(1) enters a habitation, or a building (or any portion of a building) not then open to the public, with intent to commit a felony, theft, or an assault; or

(2) remains concealed, with intent to commit a felony, theft, or an assault, in a building or habitation; or

(3) enters a building or habitation and commits or attempts to commit a felony, theft, or an assault.

(b) For purposes of this section, "enter" means to intrude:

(1) any part of the body; or

(2) any physical object connected with the body.

(c) Except as provided in Subsection (c-1) or (d), an offense under this section is a:

(1) state jail felony if committed in a building other than a habitation; or

(2) felony of the second degree if committed in a habitation.

(c-1) An offense under this section is a felony of the third degree if:

(1) the premises are a commercial building in which a controlled substance is generally stored, including a pharmacy, clinic, hospital, nursing facility, or warehouse; and

(2) the person entered or remained concealed in that building with intent to commit a theft of a controlled substance.

(d) An offense under this section is a felony of the first degree if:

(1) the premises are a habitation; and

(2) any party to the offense entered the habitation with intent to commit a felony other than felony theft or committed or attempted to commit a felony other than felony theft.

Sec. 30.03. Burglary of Coin-Operated or Coin Collection Machines.

(a) A person commits an offense if, without the effective consent of the owner, he breaks or enters into any coin-operated machine, coin collection machine, or other coin-operated or coin collection receptacle, contrivance, apparatus, or equipment used for the purpose of providing lawful amusement, sales of goods, services, or other valuable things, or telecommunications with intent to obtain property or services.

(b) For purposes of this section, "entry" includes every kind of entry except one made with the effective consent of the owner.

(c) An offense under this section is a Class A misdemeanor.

Sec. 30.04. Burglary of Vehicles.

(a) A person commits an offense if, without the effective consent of the owner, he breaks into or enters a vehicle or any part of a vehicle with intent to commit any felony or theft.

(b) For purposes of this section, "enter" means to intrude:

(1) any part of the body; or

(2) any physical object connected with the body.

(c) For purposes of this section, a container or trailer carried on a rail car is a part of the rail car.

(d) An offense under this section is a Class A misdemeanor, except that:

(1) the offense is a Class A misdemeanor with a minimum term of confinement of six months if it is shown on the trial of the offense that the defendant has been previously convicted of an offense under this section;

(2) the offense is a state jail felony if:

(A) it is shown on the trial of the offense that the defendant has been previously convicted two or more times of an offense under this section; or

(B) the vehicle or part of the vehicle broken into or entered is a rail car; and

(3) the offense is a felony of the third degree if:

(A) the vehicle broken into or entered is owned or operated by a wholesale distributor of prescription drugs; and

(B) the actor breaks into or enters that vehicle with the intent to commit theft of a controlled substance.

(d-1) For the purposes of Subsection (d), a defendant has been previously convicted under this section if the defendant was adjudged guilty of the offense or entered a plea of guilty or nolo contendere in return for a grant of deferred adjudication, regardless of whether the sentence for the offense was ever imposed or whether the sentence was probated and the defendant was subsequently discharged from community supervision.

(e) It is a defense to prosecution under this section that the actor entered a rail car or any part of a rail car and was at that time an employee or a representative of employees exercising a right under the Railway Labor Act (45 U.S.C. Section 151 et seq.).

Sec. 30.05. Criminal Trespass.

(a) A person commits an offense if the person enters or remains on or in property of another, including residential land, agricultural land, a recreational vehicle park, a building, a general residential operation operating as a residential treatment center, or an aircraft or other vehicle, without effective consent and the person:

(1) had notice that the entry was forbidden; or

(2) received notice to depart but failed to do so.

(b) For purposes of this section:

(1) "Entry" means the intrusion of the entire body.

(2) "Notice" means:

(A) oral or written communication by the owner or someone with apparent authority to act for the owner;

(B) fencing or other enclosure obviously designed to exclude intruders or to contain livestock;

(C) a sign or signs posted on the property or at the entrance to the building, reasonably likely to come to the attention of intruders, indicating that entry is forbidden;

(D) the placement of identifying purple paint marks on trees or posts on the property, provided that the marks are:

(i) vertical lines of not less than eight inches in length and not less than one inch in width;

(ii) placed so that the bottom of the mark is not less than three feet from the ground or more than five feet from the ground; and

(iii) placed at locations that are readily visible to any person approaching the property and no more than:

(a) 100 feet apart on forest land; or

(b) 1,000 feet apart on land other than forest land; or

(E) the visible presence on the property of a crop grown for human consumption that is under cultivation, in the process of being harvested, or marketable if harvested at the time of entry.

(3) "Shelter center" has the meaning assigned by Section 51.002, Human Resources Code.

(4) "Forest land" means land on which the trees are potentially valuable for timber products.

(5) "Agricultural land" has the meaning assigned by Section 75.001, Civil Practice and Remedies Code.

(6) "Superfund site" means a facility that:

(A) is on the National Priorities List established under Section 105 of the federal Comprehensive Environmental Response, Compensation, and Liability Act of 1980 (42 U.S.C. Section 9605); or

(B) is listed on the state registry established under Section 361.181, Health and Safety Code.

(7) "Critical infrastructure facility" means one of the following, if completely enclosed by a fence or other physical barrier that is obviously designed to exclude intruders:

(A) a chemical manufacturing facility;

(B) a refinery;

(C) an electrical power generating facility, substation, switching station, electrical control center, or electrical transmission or distribution facility;

(D) a water intake structure, water treatment facility, wastewater treatment plant, or pump station;

(E) a natural gas transmission compressor station;

(F) a liquid natural gas terminal or storage facility;

(G) a telecommunications central switching office;

(H) a port, railroad switching yard, trucking terminal, or other freight transportation facility;

(I) a gas processing plant, including a plant used in the processing, treatment, or fractionation of natural gas; or

(J) a transmission facility used by a federally licensed radio or television station.

(8) "Protected freshwater area" has the meaning assigned by Section 90.001, Parks and Wildlife Code.

(9) "Recognized state" means another state with which the attorney general of this state, with the approval of the governor of this state, negotiated an agreement after determining that the other state:

(A) has firearm proficiency requirements for peace officers; and

(B) fully recognizes the right of peace officers commissioned in this state to carry weapons in the other state.

(10) "Recreational vehicle park" has the meaning assigned by Section 13.087, Water Code.

(11) "Residential land" means real property improved by a dwelling and zoned for or otherwise authorized for single-family or multifamily use.

(12) "Institution of higher education" has the meaning assigned by Section 61.003, Education Code.

(13) "General residential operation" has the meaning assigned by Section 42.002, Human Resources Code.

(c) A person may provide notice that firearms are prohibited on the property by posting a sign at each entrance to the property that:

(1) includes language that is identical to or substantially similar to the following: "Pursuant to Section 30.05, Penal Code (criminal trespass), a person may not enter this property with a firearm";

(2) includes the language described by Subdivision (1) in both English and Spanish;

(3) appears in contrasting colors with block letters at least one inch in height; and

(4) is displayed in a conspicuous manner clearly visible to the public.

(d) Subject to Subsection (d-3), an offense under this section is:

(1) a Class B misdemeanor, except as provided by Subdivisions (2) and (3);

(2) a Class C misdemeanor, except as provided by Subdivision (3), if the offense is committed:

(A) on agricultural land and within 100 feet of the boundary of the land; or

(B) on residential land and within 100 feet of a protected freshwater area; and

(3) a Class A misdemeanor if:

(A) the offense is committed:

(i) in a habitation or a shelter center;

(ii) on a Superfund site; or

(iii) on or in a critical infrastructure facility;

(B) the offense is committed on or in property of an institution of higher education and it is shown on the trial of the offense that the person has previously been convicted of:

(i) an offense under this section relating to entering or remaining on or in property of an institution of higher education; or

(ii) an offense under Section 51.204(b)(1), Education Code, relating to trespassing on the grounds of an institution of higher education;

(C) the person carries a deadly weapon during the commission of the offense; or

(D) the offense is committed on the property of or within a general residential operation operating as a residential treatment center.

(d-1) For the purposes of Subsection (d)(3)(B), a person has previously been convicted of an offense described by that paragraph if the person was adjudged guilty of the offense or entered a plea of guilty or nolo contendere in return for a grant of deferred adjudication community supervision, regardless of whether the sentence for the offense was ever imposed or whether the sentence was probated and the person was subsequently discharged from deferred adjudication community supervision.

(d-2) At the punishment stage of a trial in which the attorney representing the state seeks the increase in punishment provided by Subsection (d)(3)(B), the defendant may raise the issue as to whether, at the time of the instant offense or the previous offense, the defendant was engaging in speech or expressive conduct protected by the First Amendment to the United States Constitution or Section 8, Article I, Texas Constitution. If the defendant proves the issue in the affirmative by a preponderance of the evidence, the increase in punishment provided by Subsection (d)(3)(B) does not apply.

(d-3) An offense under this section is a Class C misdemeanor punishable by a fine not to exceed $200 if the person enters the property, land, or building with a firearm or other weapon and the sole basis on which entry on the property or land or in the building was forbidden is that entry with a firearm or other weapon was forbidden, except that the offense is a Class A misdemeanor if it is shown on the trial of the offense that, after entering the property, land, or building with the firearm or other weapon, the actor:

(1) personally received from the owner of the property or another person with apparent authority to act for the owner notice that entry with a firearm or other weapon was forbidden, as given through:

(A) notice under Subsection (b)(2)(A), including oral or written communication; or

(B) if the actor is unable to reasonably understand the notice described by Paragraph (A), other personal notice that is reasonable under the circumstances; and

(2) subsequently failed to depart.

(e) It is a defense to prosecution under this section that the actor at the time of the offense was:

(1) a firefighter or emergency medical services personnel, as defined by Section 773.003, Health and Safety Code, acting in the lawful discharge of an official duty under exigent circumstances;

(2) a person who was:

(A) an employee or agent of:

(i) an electric utility, as defined by Section 31.002, Utilities Code;

(ii) a telecommunications provider, as defined by Section 51.002, Utilities Code;

(iii) a video service provider or cable service provider, as defined by Section 66.002, Utilities Code;

(iv) a gas utility, as defined by Section 101.003, Utilities Code, which for the purposes of this subsection includes a municipally owned utility as defined by that section;

(v) a gas utility, as defined by Section 121.001, Utilities Code;

(vi) a pipeline used for the transportation or sale of oil, gas, or related products; or

(vii) an electric cooperative or municipally owned utility, as defined by Section 11.003, Utilities Code; and

(B) performing a duty within the scope of that employment or agency; or

(3) a person who was:

(A) employed by or acting as agent for an entity that had, or that the person reasonably believed had, effective consent or authorization provided by law to enter the property; and

(B) performing a duty within the scope of that employment or agency.

(f) It is a defense to prosecution under this section that:

(1) the basis on which entry on the property or land or in the building was forbidden is that entry with a handgun was forbidden; and

(2) the person was carrying:

(A) a license issued under Subchapter H, Chapter 411, Government Code, to carry a handgun; and

(B) a handgun:

(i) in a concealed manner; or

(ii) in a holster.

(f-1) It is a defense to prosecution under this section that:

(1) the basis on which entry on the property was forbidden is that entry with a firearm or firearm ammunition was forbidden;

(2) the actor is:

(A) an owner of an apartment in a condominium regime governed by Chapter 81, Property Code;

(B) an owner of a condominium unit governed by Chapter 82, Property Code;

(C) a tenant or guest of an owner described by Paragraph (A) or (B); or

(D) a guest of a tenant of an owner described by Paragraph (A) or (B);

(3) the actor:

(A) carries or stores a firearm or firearm ammunition in the condominium apartment or unit owner's apartment or unit;

(B) carries a firearm or firearm ammunition directly en route to or from the condominium apartment or unit owner's apartment or unit;

(C) carries a firearm or firearm ammunition directly en route to or from the actor's vehicle located in a parking area provided for residents or guests of the condominium property; or

(D) carries or stores a firearm or firearm ammunition in the actor's vehicle located in a parking area provided for residents or guests of the condominium property; and

(4) the actor is not otherwise prohibited by law from possessing a firearm or firearm ammunition.

(f-2) It is a defense to prosecution under this section that:

(1) the basis on which entry on a leased premises governed by Chapter 92, Property Code, was forbidden is that entry with a firearm or firearm ammunition was forbidden;

(2) the actor is a tenant of the leased premises or the tenant's guest;

(3) the actor:

(A) carries or stores a firearm or firearm ammunition in the tenant's rental unit;

(B) carries a firearm or firearm ammunition directly en route to or from the tenant's rental unit;

(C) carries a firearm or firearm ammunition directly en route to or from the actor's vehicle located in a parking area provided for tenants or guests by the landlord of the leased premises; or

(D) carries or stores a firearm or firearm ammunition in the actor's vehicle located in a parking area provided for tenants or guests by the landlord of the leased premises; and

(4) the actor is not otherwise prohibited by law from possessing a firearm or firearm ammunition.

(f-3) It is a defense to prosecution under this section that:

(1) the basis on which entry on a leased premises governed by Chapter 94, Property Code, was forbidden is that entry with a firearm or firearm ammunition was forbidden;

(2) the actor is a tenant of a manufactured home lot or the tenant's guest;

(3) the actor:

(A) carries or stores a firearm or firearm ammunition in the tenant's manufactured home;

(B) carries a firearm or firearm ammunition directly en route to or from the tenant's manufactured home;

(C) carries a firearm or firearm ammunition directly en route to or from the actor's vehicle located in a parking area provided for tenants or tenants' guests by the landlord of the leased premises; or

(D) carries or stores a firearm or firearm ammunition in the actor's vehicle located in a parking area provided for tenants or tenants' guests by the landlord of the leased premises; and

(4) the actor is not otherwise prohibited by law from possessing a firearm or firearm ammunition.

(f-4) It is a defense to prosecution under this section that:

(1) the conduct occurred on hotel property, and the basis on which entry on that property was forbidden is that entry with a firearm or firearm ammunition was forbidden;

(2) the actor is a guest of a hotel, as defined by Section 2155.101, Occupations Code; and

(3) the actor:

(A) carries or stores a firearm or firearm ammunition in the actor's hotel room;

(B) carries a firearm or firearm ammunition directly en route to or from the hotel or the actor's hotel room;

(C) carries a firearm or firearm ammunition directly en route to or from the actor's vehicle located on the hotel property, including a vehicle in a parking area provided for hotel guests; or

(D) carries or stores a firearm or firearm ammunition in the actor's vehicle located on the hotel property, including a vehicle in a parking area provided for hotel guests.

(g) It is a defense to prosecution under this section that the actor entered a railroad switching yard or any part of a railroad switching yard and was at that time an employee or a representative of employees exercising a right under the Railway Labor Act (45 U.S.C. Section 151 et seq.).

(h) At the punishment stage of a trial in which the attorney representing the state seeks the increase in punishment provided by Subsection (d)(3)(A)(iii), the defendant may raise the issue as to whether the defendant entered or remained on or in a critical infrastructure facility as part of a peaceful or lawful assembly, including an attempt to exercise rights guaranteed by state or federal labor laws. If the defendant proves the issue in the affirmative by a preponderance of the evidence, the increase in punishment provided by Subsection (d)(3)(A)(iii) does not apply.

(i) This section does not apply if:

(1) the basis on which entry on the property or land or in the building was forbidden is that entry

with a handgun or other weapon was forbidden; and

(2) the actor at the time of the offense was a peace officer, including a commissioned peace officer of a recognized state, or a special investigator under Article 2.122, Code of Criminal Procedure, regardless of whether the peace officer or special investigator was engaged in the actual discharge of an official duty while carrying the weapon.

(j) [Repealed by Acts 2009, 81st Leg., ch. 1138 (H.B. 2609), § 4, effective September 1, 2009.]

Sec. 30.06. Trespass by License Holder with A Concealed Handgun.

(a) A license holder commits an offense if the license holder:

(1) carries a concealed handgun under the authority of Subchapter H, Chapter 411, Government Code, on property of another without effective consent; and

(2) received notice that entry on the property by a license holder with a concealed handgun was forbidden.

(b) For purposes of this section, a person receives notice if the owner of the property or someone with apparent authority to act for the owner provides notice to the person by oral or written communication.

(c) In this section:

(1) "Entry" has the meaning assigned by Section 30.05(b).

(2) "License holder" has the meaning assigned by Section 46.03.

(3) "Written communication" means:

(A) a card or other document on which is written language identical to the following: "Pursuant to Section 30.06, Penal Code (trespass by license holder with a concealed handgun), a person licensed under Subchapter H, Chapter 411, Government Code (handgun licensing law), may not enter this property with a concealed handgun"; or

(B) a sign posted on the property that:

(i) includes the language described by Paragraph (A) in both English and Spanish;

(ii) appears in contrasting colors with block letters at least one inch in height; and

(iii) is displayed in a conspicuous manner clearly visible to the public.

(d) An offense under this section is a Class C misdemeanor punishable by a fine not to exceed $200, except that the offense is a Class A misdemeanor if it is shown on the trial of the offense that, after entering the property, the license holder was personally given the notice by oral communication described by Subsection (b) and subsequently failed to depart.

(e) It is an exception to the application of this section that the property on which the license holder carries a handgun is owned or leased by a governmental entity and is not a premises or other place on which the license holder is prohibited from carrying the handgun under Section 46.03.

(e-1) It is a defense to prosecution under this section that:

(1) the license holder is:

(A) an owner of an apartment in a condominium regime governed by Chapter 81, Property Code;

(B) an owner of a condominium unit governed by Chapter 82, Property Code;

(C) a tenant or guest of an owner described by Paragraph (A) or (B); or

(D) a guest of a tenant of an owner described by Paragraph (A) or (B); and

(2) the license holder:

(A) carries or stores a handgun in the condominium apartment or unit owner's apartment or unit;

(B) carries a handgun directly en route to or from the condominium apartment or unit owner's apartment or unit;

(C) carries a handgun directly en route to or from the license holder's vehicle located in a parking area provided for residents or guests of the condominium property; or

(D) carries or stores a handgun in the license holder's vehicle located in a parking area provided for residents or guests of the condominium property.

(e-2) It is a defense to prosecution under this section that:

(1) the license holder is a tenant of a leased premises governed by Chapter 92, Property Code, or the tenant's guest; and

(2) the license holder:

(A) carries or stores a handgun in the tenant's rental unit;

(B) carries a handgun directly en route to or from the tenant's rental unit;

(C) carries a handgun directly en route to or from the license holder's vehicle located in a parking area provided for tenants or guests by the landlord of the leased premises; or

(D) carries or stores a handgun in the license holder's vehicle located in a parking area provided for tenants or guests by the landlord of the leased premises.

(e-3) It is a defense to prosecution under this section that:

(1) the license holder is a tenant of a manufactured home lot governed by Chapter 94, Property Code, or the tenant's guest; and

(2) the license holder:

(A) carries or stores a handgun in the tenant's manufactured home;

(B) carries a handgun directly en route to or from the tenant's manufactured home;

(C) carries a handgun directly en route to or from the license holder's vehicle located in a parking area provided for tenants or tenants' guests by the landlord of the leased premises; or

(D) carries or stores a handgun in the license holder's vehicle located in a parking area provided for tenants or tenants' guests by the landlord of the leased premises.

(e-4) It is a defense to prosecution under this section that the license holder is a guest of a hotel, as defined by Section 2155.101, Occupations Code, and the license holder:

(1) carries or stores a handgun in the license holder's hotel room;

(2) carries a handgun directly en route to or from the hotel or the license holder's hotel room;

(3) carries a handgun directly en route to or from the license holder's vehicle located on the hotel property, including a vehicle in a parking area provided for hotel guests; or

(4) carries or stores a handgun in the license holder's vehicle located on the hotel property, including a vehicle in a parking area provided for hotel guests.

(f) It is a defense to prosecution under this section that the license holder is volunteer emergency services personnel, as defined by Section 46.01.

(f-1) It is a defense to prosecution under this section that the license holder is a first responder, as defined by Section 46.01, who:

(1) holds an unexpired certificate of completion under Section 411.184, Government Code, at the time of engaging in the applicable conduct;

(2) was engaged in the actual discharge of the first responder's duties while carrying the handgun; and

(3) was employed or supervised by a municipality or county to which Chapter 179, Local Government Code, applies.

(g) It is a defense to prosecution under this section that the license holder was personally given notice by oral communication described by Subsection (b) and promptly departed from the property.

Sec. 30.07. Trespass by License Holder with an Openly Carried Handgun.

(a) A license holder commits an offense if the license holder:

(1) openly carries a handgun under the authority of Subchapter H, Chapter 411, Government Code, on property of another without effective consent; and

(2) received notice that entry on the property by a license holder openly carrying a handgun was forbidden.

(b) For purposes of this section, a person receives notice if the owner of the property or someone with apparent authority to act for the owner provides notice to the person by oral or written communication.

(c) In this section:

(1) "Entry" has the meaning assigned by Section 30.05(b).

(2) "License holder" has the meaning assigned by Section 46.03.

(3) "Written communication" means:

(A) a card or other document on which is written language identical to the following: "Pursuant to Section 30.07, Penal Code (trespass by license holder with an openly carried handgun), a person licensed under Subchapter H, Chapter 411, Government Code (handgun licensing law), may not enter this property with a handgun that is carried openly"; or

(B) a sign posted on the property that:

(i) includes the language described by Paragraph (A) in both English and Spanish;

(ii) appears in contrasting colors with block letters at least one inch in height; and

(iii) is displayed in a conspicuous manner clearly visible to the public at each entrance to the property.

(d) An offense under this section is a Class C misdemeanor punishable by a fine not to exceed $200, except that the offense is a Class A misdemeanor if it is shown on the trial of the offense that, after entering the property, the license holder was personally given the notice by oral communication described by Subsection (b) and subsequently failed to depart.

(e) It is an exception to the application of this section that the property on which the license holder openly carries the handgun is owned or leased by a governmental entity and is not a premises or other place on which the license holder is prohibited from carrying the handgun under Section 46.03.

(e-1) It is a defense to prosecution under this section that:

(1) the license holder is:

(A) an owner of an apartment in a condominium regime governed by Chapter 81, Property Code;

(B) an owner of a condominium unit governed by Chapter 82, Property Code;

(C) a tenant or guest of an owner described by Paragraph (A) or (B); or

(D) a guest of a tenant of an owner described by Paragraph (A) or (B); and

(2) the license holder is:

(A) carries or stores a handgun in the condominium apartment or unit owner's apartment or unit;

(B) carries a handgun directly en route to or from the condominium apartment or unit owner's apartment or unit;

(C) carries a handgun directly en route to or from the license holder's vehicle located in a parking area provided for residents or guests of the condominium property; or

(D) carries or stores a handgun in the license holder's vehicle located in a parking area provided for residents or guests of the condominium property.

(e-2) It is a defense to prosecution under this section that:

(1) the license holder is a tenant of a leased premises governed by Chapter 92, Property Code, or the tenant's guest; and

(2) the license holder:

(A) carries or stores a handgun in the tenant's rental unit;

(B) carries a handgun directly en route to or from the tenant's rental unit;

(C) carries a handgun directly en route to or from the license holder's vehicle located in a parking area provided for tenants or guests by the landlord of the leased premises; or

(D) carries or stores a handgun in the license holder's vehicle located in a parking area provided for tenants or guests by the landlord of the leased premises.

(e-3) It is a defense to prosecution under this section that:

(1) the license holder is a tenant of a manufactured home lot governed by Chapter 94, Property Code, or the tenant's guest; and

(2) the license holder:

(A) carries or stores a handgun in the tenant's manufactured home;

(B) carries a handgun directly en route to or from the tenant's manufactured home;

(C) carries a handgun directly en route to or from the license holder's vehicle located in a parking area provided for tenants or tenants' guests by the landlord of the leased premises; or

(D) carries or stores a handgun in the license holder's vehicle located in a parking area provided for tenants or tenants' guests by the landlord of the leased premises.

(e-4) It is a defense to prosecution under this section that the license holder is a guest of a hotel, as defined by Section 2155.101, Occupations Code, and the license holder:

(1) carries or stores a handgun in the license holder's hotel room;

(2) carries a handgun directly en route to or from the hotel or the license holder's hotel room;

(3) carries a handgun directly en route to or from the license holder's vehicle located on the hotel property, including a vehicle in a parking area provided for hotel guests; or

(4) carries or stores a handgun in the license holder's vehicle located on the hotel property, including a vehicle in a parking area provided for hotel guests.

(f) It is not a defense to prosecution under this section that the handgun was carried in a holster.

(g) It is a defense to prosecution under this section that the license holder is volunteer emergency services personnel, as defined by Section 46.01.

(g-1) It is a defense to prosecution under this section that the license holder is a first responder, as defined by Section 46.01, who:

(1) holds an unexpired certificate of completion under Section 411.184, Government Code, at the time of engaging in the applicable conduct;

(2) was engaged in the actual discharge of the first responder's duties while carrying the handgun; and

(3) was employed or supervised by a municipality or county to which Chapter 179, Local Government Code, applies.

(h) It is a defense to prosecution under this section that the license holder was personally given notice by oral communication described by Subsection (b) and promptly departed from the property.

CHAPTER 31
THEFT

Sec. 31.01. Definitions.

In this chapter:

(1) "Deception" means:

(A) creating or confirming by words or conduct a false impression of law or fact that is likely to affect the judgment of another in the transaction, and that the actor does not believe to be true;

(B) failing to correct a false impression of law or fact that is likely to affect the judgment of another in the transaction, that the actor previously created or confirmed by words or conduct, and that the actor does not now believe to be true;

(C) preventing another from acquiring information likely to affect his judgment in the transaction;

(D) selling or otherwise transferring or encumbering property without disclosing a lien, security interest, adverse claim, or other legal impediment to the enjoyment of the property, whether the lien, security interest, claim, or impediment is or is not valid, or is or is not a matter of official record; or

(E) promising performance that is likely to affect the judgment of another in the transaction and that the actor does not intend to perform or knows will not be performed, except that failure to perform the promise in issue without other evidence of intent or knowledge is not sufficient proof that the actor did not intend to perform or knew the promise would not be performed.

(2) "Deprive" means:

(A) to withhold property from the owner permanently or for so extended a period of time that a major portion of the value or enjoyment of the property is lost to the owner;

(B) to restore property only upon payment of reward or other compensation; or

(C) to dispose of property in a manner that makes recovery of the property by the owner unlikely.

(3) "Effective consent" includes consent by a person legally authorized to act for the owner. Consent is not effective if:

(A) induced by deception or coercion;

(B) given by a person the actor knows is not legally authorized to act for the owner;

(C) given by a person who by reason of youth, mental disease or defect, or intoxication is known by the actor to be unable to make reasonable property dispositions;

(D) given solely to detect the commission of an offense; or

(E) given by a person who by reason of advanced age is known by the actor to have a diminished capacity to make informed and rational decisions about the reasonable disposition of property.

(4) "Appropriate" means:

(A) to bring about a transfer or purported transfer of title to or other nonpossessory interest in property, whether to the actor or another; or

(B) to acquire or otherwise exercise control over property other than real property.

(5) "Property" means:

(A) real property;

(B) tangible or intangible personal property including anything severed from land; or

(C) a document, including money, that represents or embodies anything of value.

(6) "Service" includes:

(A) labor and professional service;

(B) telecommunication, public utility, or transportation service;

(C) lodging, restaurant service, and entertainment; and

(D) the supply of a motor vehicle or other property for use.

(7) "Steal" means to acquire property or service by theft.

(8) "Certificate of title" has the meaning assigned by Section 501.002, Transportation Code.

(9) "Used or secondhand motor vehicle" means a used motor vehicle, as that term is defined by Section 501.002, Transportation Code.

(10) "Elderly individual" has the meaning assigned by Section 22.04(c).

(11) "Retail merchandise" means one or more items of tangible personal property displayed, held, stored, or offered for sale in a retail establishment.

(12) "Retail theft detector" means an electrical, mechanical, electronic, or magnetic device used to prevent or detect shoplifting and includes any article or component part essential to the proper operation of the device.

(13) "Shielding or deactivation instrument" means any item or tool designed, made, or adapted for the purpose of preventing the detection of stolen merchandise by a retail theft detector. The term includes a metal-lined or foil-lined shopping bag and any item used to remove a security tag affixed to retail merchandise.

(14) "Fire exit alarm" has the meaning assigned by Section 793.001, Health and Safety Code.

Sec. 31.02. Consolidation of Theft Offenses.

Theft as defined in Section 31.03 constitutes a single offense superseding the separate offenses previously known as theft, theft by false pretext, conversion by a bailee, theft from the person, shoplifting, acquisition of property by threat, swindling, swindling by worthless check, embezzlement, extortion, receiving or concealing embezzled property, and receiving or concealing stolen property.

Sec. 31.03. Theft.

(a) A person commits an offense if he unlawfully appropriates property with intent to deprive the owner of property.

(b) Appropriation of property is unlawful if:

(1) it is without the owner's effective consent;

(2) the property is stolen and the actor appropriates the property knowing it was stolen by another; or

(3) property in the custody of any law enforcement agency was explicitly represented by any law enforcement agent to the actor as being stolen and the actor appropriates the property believing it was stolen by another.

(c) For purposes of Subsection (b):

(1) evidence that the actor has previously participated in recent transactions other than, but similar to, that which the prosecution is based is admissible for the purpose of showing knowledge

or intent and the issues of knowledge or intent are raised by the actor's plea of not guilty;

(2) the testimony of an accomplice shall be corroborated by proof that tends to connect the actor to the crime, but the actor's knowledge or intent may be established by the uncorroborated testimony of the accomplice;

(3) an actor engaged in the business of buying and selling used or secondhand personal property, or lending money on the security of personal property deposited with the actor, is presumed to know upon receipt by the actor of stolen property (other than a motor vehicle subject to Chapter 501, Transportation Code) that the property has been previously stolen from another if the actor pays for or loans against the property $25 or more (or consideration of equivalent value) and the actor knowingly or recklessly:

(A) fails to record the name, address, and physical description or identification number of the seller or pledgor;

(B) fails to record a complete description of the property, including the serial number, if reasonably available, or other identifying characteristics; or

(C) fails to obtain a signed warranty from the seller or pledgor that the seller or pledgor has the right to possess the property. It is the express intent of this provision that the presumption arises unless the actor complies with each of the numbered requirements;

(4) for the purposes of Subdivision (3)(A), "identification number" means driver's license number, military identification number, identification certificate, or other official number capable of identifying an individual;

(5) stolen property does not lose its character as stolen when recovered by any law enforcement agency;

(6) an actor engaged in the business of obtaining abandoned or wrecked motor vehicles or parts of an abandoned or wrecked motor vehicle for resale, disposal, scrap, repair, rebuilding, demolition, or other form of salvage is presumed to know on receipt by the actor of stolen property that the property has been previously stolen from another if the actor knowingly or recklessly:

(A) fails to maintain an accurate and legible inventory of each motor vehicle component part purchased by or delivered to the actor, including the date of purchase or delivery, the name, age, address, sex, and driver's license number of the seller or person making the delivery, the license plate number of the motor vehicle in which the part was delivered, a complete description of the part, and the vehicle identification number of the motor vehicle from which the part was removed, or in lieu of maintaining an inventory, fails to record the name and certificate of inventory number of the person who dismantled the motor vehicle from which the part was obtained;

(B) fails on receipt of a motor vehicle to obtain a certificate of authority, sales receipt, or transfer document as required by Chapter 683, Transportation Code, or a certificate of title showing that the motor vehicle is not subject to a lien or that all recorded liens on the motor vehicle have been released; or

(C) fails on receipt of a motor vehicle to immediately remove an unexpired license plate from the motor vehicle, to keep the plate in a secure and locked place, or to maintain an inventory, on forms provided by the Texas Department of Motor Vehicles, of license plates kept under this paragraph, including for each plate or set of plates the license plate number and the make, motor number, and vehicle identification number of the motor vehicle from which the plate was removed;

(7) an actor who purchases or receives a used or secondhand motor vehicle is presumed to know on receipt by the actor of the motor vehicle that the motor vehicle has been previously stolen from another if the actor knowingly or recklessly:

(A) fails to report to the Texas Department of Motor Vehicles the failure of the person who sold or delivered the motor vehicle to the actor to deliver to the actor a properly executed certificate of title to the motor vehicle at the time the motor vehicle was delivered; or

(B) fails to file with the county tax assessor-collector of the county in which the actor received the motor vehicle, not later than the 20th day after the date the actor received the motor vehicle, the registration license receipt and certificate of title or evidence of title delivered to the actor in accordance with Subchapter D, Chapter 520, Transportation Code, at the time the motor vehicle was delivered;

(8) an actor who purchases or receives from any source other than a licensed retailer or distributor of pesticides a restricted-use pesticide or a state-limited-use pesticide or a compound, mixture, or preparation containing a restricted-use or state-limited-use pesticide is presumed to know on receipt by the actor of the pesticide or compound, mixture, or preparation that the pesticide or compound, mixture, or preparation has been previously stolen from another if the actor:

(A) fails to record the name, address, and physical description of the seller or pledgor;

(B) fails to record a complete description of the amount and type of pesticide or compound, mixture, or preparation purchased or received; and

(C) fails to obtain a signed warranty from the seller or pledgor that the seller or pledgor has the right to possess the property; and

(9) an actor who is subject to Section 409, Packers and Stockyards Act (7 U.S.C. Section 228b), that obtains livestock from a commission merchant by representing that the actor will make prompt payment is presumed to have induced the commission merchant's consent by deception if the actor fails to make full payment in accordance with Section 409, Packers and Stockyards Act (7 U.S.C. Section 228b).

(d) It is not a defense to prosecution under this section that:

(1) the offense occurred as a result of a deception or strategy on the part of a law enforcement agency, including the use of an undercover operative or peace officer;

(2) the actor was provided by a law enforcement agency with a facility in which to commit the offense or an opportunity to engage in conduct constituting the offense; or

(3) the actor was solicited to commit the offense by a peace officer, and the solicitation was of a type that would encourage a person predisposed to commit the offense to actually commit the offense, but would not encourage a person not predisposed to commit the offense to actually commit the offense.

(e) Except as provided by Subsection (f), an offense under this section is:

(1) a Class C misdemeanor if the value of the property stolen is less than $100;

(2) a Class B misdemeanor if:

(A) the value of the property stolen is $100 or more but less than $750;

(B) the value of the property stolen is less than $100 and the defendant has previously been convicted of any grade of theft; or

(C) the property stolen is a driver's license, commercial driver's license, or personal identification certificate issued by this state or another state;

(3) a Class A misdemeanor if the value of the property stolen is $750 or more but less than $2,500;

(4) a state jail felony if:

(A) the value of the property stolen is $2,500 or more but less than $30,000, or the property is less than 10 head of sheep, swine, or goats or any part thereof under the value of $30,000;

(B) regardless of value, the property is stolen from the person of another or from a human corpse or grave, including property that is a military grave marker;

(C) the property stolen is a firearm, as defined by Section 46.01;

(D) the value of the property stolen is less than $2,500 and the defendant has been previously convicted two or more times of any grade of theft;

(E) the property stolen is an official ballot or official carrier envelope for an election; or

(F) the value of the property stolen is less than $20,000 and the property stolen is:

(i) aluminum;

(ii) bronze;

(iii) copper; or

(iv) brass;

(5) a felony of the third degree if the value of the property stolen is $30,000 or more but less than $150,000, or the property is:

(A) cattle, horses, or exotic livestock or exotic fowl as defined by Section 142.001, Agriculture Code, stolen during a single transaction and having an aggregate value of less than $150,000;

(B) 10 or more head of sheep, swine, or goats stolen during a single transaction and having an aggregate value of less than $150,000; or

(C) a controlled substance, having a value of less than $150,000, if stolen from:

(i) a commercial building in which a controlled substance is generally stored, including a pharmacy, clinic, hospital, nursing facility, or warehouse; or

(ii) a vehicle owned or operated by a wholesale distributor of prescription drugs;

(6) a felony of the second degree if:

(A) the value of the property stolen is $150,000 or more but less than $300,000; or

(B) the value of the property stolen is less than $300,000 and the property stolen is an automated teller machine or the contents or components of an automated teller machine; or

(7) a felony of the first degree if the value of the property stolen is $300,000 or more.

(f) An offense described for purposes of punishment by Subsections (e)(1)—(6) is increased to the next higher category of offense if it is shown on the trial of the offense that:

(1) the actor was a public servant at the time of the offense and the property appropriated came into the actor's custody, possession, or control by virtue of his status as a public servant;

(2) the actor was in a contractual relationship with government at the time of the offense and the property appropriated came into the actor's custody, possession, or control by virtue of the contractual relationship;

(3) the owner of the property appropriated was at the time of the offense:

(A) an elderly individual; or

(B) a nonprofit organization;

(4) the actor was a Medicare provider in a contractual relationship with the federal government at the time of the offense and the property appropriated came into the actor's custody, possession, or control by virtue of the contractual relationship; or

(5) during the commission of the offense, the actor intentionally, knowingly, or recklessly:

(A) caused a fire exit alarm to sound or otherwise become activated;

(B) deactivated or otherwise prevented a fire exit alarm or retail theft detector from sounding; or

(C) used a shielding or deactivation instrument to prevent or attempt to prevent detection of the offense by a retail theft detector.

(g) For the purposes of Subsection (a), a person is the owner of exotic livestock or exotic fowl as defined by Section 142.001, Agriculture Code, only if the person qualifies to claim the animal under Section 142.0021, Agriculture Code, if the animal is an estray.

(h) In this section:

(1) "Restricted-use pesticide" means a pesticide classified as a restricted-use pesticide by the administrator of the Environmental Protection Agency under 7 U.S.C. Section 136a, as that law existed on January 1, 1995, and containing an active ingredient listed in the federal regulations adopted under that law (40 C.F.R. Section 152.175) and in effect on that date.

(2) "State-limited-use pesticide" means a pesticide classified as a state-limited-use pesticide by the Department of Agriculture under Section 76.003, Agriculture Code, as that section existed on January 1, 1995, and containing an active ingredient listed in the rules adopted under that section (4 TAC Section 7.24) as that section existed on that date.

(3) "Nonprofit organization" means an organization that is exempt from federal income taxation under Section 501(a), Internal Revenue Code of 1986, by being described as an exempt organization by Section 501(c)(3) of that code.

(4) "Automated teller machine" means an unstaffed electronic information processing device that, at the request of a user, performs a financial transaction through the direct transmission of electronic impulses to a financial institution or through the recording of electronic impulses or other indicia of a transaction for delayed transmission to a financial institution. The term includes an automated banking machine.

(5) "Controlled substance" has the meaning assigned by Section 481.002, Health and Safety Code.

(6) "Wholesale distributor of prescription drugs" means a wholesale distributor, as defined by Section 431.401, Health and Safety Code.

(i) For purposes of Subsection (c)(9), "livestock" and "commission merchant" have the meanings assigned by Section 147.001, Agriculture Code.

(j) With the consent of the appropriate local county or district attorney, the attorney general has concurrent jurisdiction with that consenting local prosecutor to prosecute an offense under this section that involves the state Medicaid program.

Sec. 31.04. Theft of Service.

(a) A person commits theft of service if, with intent to avoid payment for service that the actor knows is provided only for compensation:

(1) the actor intentionally or knowingly secures performance of the service by deception, threat, or false token;

(2) having control over the disposition of services of another to which the actor is not entitled, the actor intentionally or knowingly diverts the other's services to the actor's own benefit or to the benefit of another not entitled to the services;

(3) having control of personal property under a written rental agreement, the actor holds the property beyond the expiration of the rental period without the effective consent of the owner of the property, thereby depriving the owner of the property of its use in further rentals; or

(4) the actor intentionally or knowingly secures the performance of the service by agreeing to provide compensation and, after the service is rendered, fails to make full payment after receiving notice demanding payment.

(b) For purposes of this section, intent to avoid payment is presumed if any of the following occurs:

(1) the actor absconded without paying for the service or expressly refused to pay for the service in circumstances where payment is ordinarily made immediately upon rendering of the service, as in hotels, campgrounds, recreational vehicle parks, restaurants, and comparable establishments;

(2) the actor failed to make payment under a service agreement within 10 days after receiving notice demanding payment;

(3) the actor returns property held under a rental agreement after the expiration of the rental agreement and fails to pay the applicable rental charge for the property within 10 days after the date on which the actor received notice demanding payment;

(4) the actor failed to return the property held under a rental agreement:

(A) within five days after receiving notice demanding return, if the property is valued at less than $2,500;

(B) within three days after receiving notice demanding return, if the property is valued at $2,500 or more but less than $10,000; or

(C) within two days after receiving notice demanding return, if the property is valued at $10,000 or more; or

(5) the actor:

(A) failed to return the property held under an agreement described by Subsections (d-2)(1)-(3) within five business days after receiving notice demanding return; and

(B) has made fewer than three complete payments under the agreement.

(c) For purposes of Subsections (a)(4), (b)(2), (b)(4), and (b)(5), notice must be:

(1) in writing;

(2) sent by:

(A) registered or certified mail with return receipt requested; or

(B) commercial delivery service; and

(3) sent to the actor using the actor's mailing address shown on the rental agreement or service agreement.

(d) Except as otherwise provided by this subsection, if written notice is given in accordance with Subsection (c), it is presumed that the notice was received not later than two days after the notice was sent. For purposes of Subsections (b)(4)(A) and (B) and (b)(5), if written notice is given in accordance with Subsection (c), it is presumed that the notice was received not later than five days after the notice was sent.

(d-1) For purposes of Subsection (a)(2), the diversion of services to the benefit of a person who is not entitled to those services includes the disposition of personal property by an actor having control of the property under an agreement described by Subsections (d-2)(1)-(3), if the actor disposes of the property in violation of the terms of the agreement and to the benefit of any person who is not entitled to the property.

(d-2) For purposes of Subsection (a)(3), the term "written rental agreement" does not include an agreement that:

(1) permits an individual to use personal property for personal, family, or household purposes for an initial rental period;

(2) is automatically renewable with each payment after the initial rental period; and

(3) permits the individual to become the owner of the property.

(d-3) For purposes of Subsection (a)(4):

(1) if the compensation is or was to be paid on a periodic basis, the intent to avoid payment for a service may be formed at any time during or before a pay period;

(2) the partial payment of wages alone is not sufficient evidence to negate the actor's intent to avoid payment for a service; and

(3) the term "service" does not include leasing personal property under an agreement described by Subsections (d-2)(1)-(3).

(d-4) A presumption established under Subsection (b) involving a defendant's failure to return property held under an agreement described by Subsections (d-2)(1)-(3) may be refuted if the defendant shows that the defendant:

(1) intended to return the property; and

(2) was unable to return the property.

(d-5) For purposes of Subsection (b)(5), "business day" means a day other than Sunday or a state or federal holiday.

(e) An offense under this section is:

(1) a Class C misdemeanor if the value of the service stolen is less than $100;

(2) a Class B misdemeanor if the value of the service stolen is $100 or more but less than $750;

(3) a Class A misdemeanor if the value of the service stolen is $750 or more but less than $2,500;

(4) a state jail felony if the value of the service stolen is $2,500 or more but less than $30,000;

(5) a felony of the third degree if the value of the service stolen is $30,000 or more but less than $150,000;

(6) a felony of the second degree if the value of the service stolen is $150,000 or more but less than $300,000; or

(7) a felony of the first degree if the value of the service stolen is $300,000 or more.

(f) Notwithstanding any other provision of this code, any police or other report of stolen vehicles by a political subdivision of this state shall include on the report any rental vehicles whose renters have been shown to such reporting agency to be in violation of Subsection (b)(2) and shall indicate that the renting agency has complied with the notice requirements demanding return as provided in this section.

(g) It is a defense to prosecution under this section that:

(1) the defendant secured the performance of the service by giving a post-dated check or similar sight order to the person performing the service; and

(2) the person performing the service or any other person presented the check or sight order for payment before the date on the check or sight order.

Sec. 31.05. Theft of Trade Secrets.

(a) For purposes of this section:

(1) "Article" means any object, material, device, or substance or any copy thereof, including a writing, recording, drawing, sample, specimen, prototype, model, photograph, microorganism, blueprint, or map.

(2) "Copy" means a facsimile, replica, photograph, or other reproduction of an article or a note, drawing, or sketch made of or from an article.

(3) "Representing" means describing, depicting, containing, constituting, reflecting, or recording.

(4) "Trade secret" means the whole or any part of any scientific or technical information, design, process, procedure, formula, or improvement that has value and that the owner has taken measures to prevent from becoming available to persons other than those selected by the owner to have access for limited purposes.

(b) A person commits an offense if, without the owner's effective consent, he knowingly:

(1) steals a trade secret;

(2) makes a copy of an article representing a trade secret; or

(3) communicates or transmits a trade secret.

(c) An offense under this section is a felony of the third degree.

Sec. 31.06. Presumption for Theft by Check or Similar Sight Order.

(a) If the actor obtained property or secured performance of service by issuing or passing a check or similar sight order for the payment of money, when the issuer did not have sufficient funds in or on deposit with the bank or other drawee for the payment in full of the check or order as well as all other checks or orders then outstanding, it is prima facie evidence of the issuer's intent to deprive the owner of property under Section 31.03 (Theft) including a drawee or third-party holder in due course who negotiated the check or order or to avoid payment for service under Section 31.04 (Theft of Service) (except in the case of a postdated check or order) if:

(1) the issuer had no account with the bank or other drawee at the time the issuer issued the check or sight order; or

(2) payment was refused by the bank or other drawee for lack of funds or insufficient funds, on presentation within 30 days after issue, and the issuer failed to pay the holder in full within 10 days after receiving notice of that refusal.

(b) For purposes of Subsection (a)(2) or (f)(3), notice may be actual notice or notice in writing that:

(1) is sent by:

(A) first class mail, evidenced by an affidavit of service; or

(B) registered or certified mail with return receipt requested;

(2) is addressed to the issuer at the issuer's address shown on:

(A) the check or order;

(B) the records of the bank or other drawee; or

(C) the records of the person to whom the check or order has been issued or passed; and

(3) contains the following statement:

"This is a demand for payment in full for a check or order not paid because of a lack of funds or insufficient funds. If you fail to make payment in full within 10 days after the date of receipt of this notice, the failure to pay creates a presumption for committing an offense, and this matter may be referred for criminal prosecution."

(c) If written notice is given in accordance with Subsection (b), it is presumed that the notice was received no later than five days after it was sent.

(d) Nothing in this section prevents the prosecution from establishing the requisite intent by direct evidence.

(e) Partial restitution does not preclude the presumption of the requisite intent under this section.

(f) If the actor obtained property by issuing or passing a check or similar sight order for the payment of money, the actor's intent to deprive the owner of the property under Section 31.03 (Theft) is presumed, except in the case of a postdated check or order, if:

(1) the actor ordered the bank or other drawee to stop payment on the check or order;

(2) the bank or drawee refused payment to the holder on presentation of the check or order within 30 days after issue;

(3) the owner gave the actor notice of the refusal of payment and made a demand to the actor for payment or return of the property; and

(4) the actor failed to:

(A) pay the holder within 10 days after receiving the demand for payment; or

(B) return the property to the owner within 10 days after receiving the demand for return of the property.

Sec. 31.07. Unauthorized Use of a Vehicle.

(a) A person commits an offense if he intentionally or knowingly operates another's boat, airplane, or motor-propelled vehicle without the effective consent of the owner.

(b) An offense under this section is a state jail felony.

Sec. 31.08. Value.

(a) Subject to the additional criteria of Subsections (b) and (c), value under this chapter is:

(1) the fair market value of the property or service at the time and place of the offense; or

(2) if the fair market value of the property cannot be ascertained, the cost of replacing the property within a reasonable time after the theft.

(b) The value of documents, other than those having a readily ascertainable market value, is:

(1) the amount due and collectible at maturity less that part which has been satisfied, if the document constitutes evidence of a debt; or

(2) the greatest amount of economic loss that the owner might reasonably suffer by virtue of loss of the document, if the document is other than evidence of a debt.

(c) If property or service has value that cannot be reasonably ascertained by the criteria set forth in Subsections (a) and (b), the property or service is deemed to have a value of $750 or more but less than $2,500.

(d) If the actor proves by a preponderance of the evidence that he gave consideration for or had a legal interest in the property or service stolen, the amount of the consideration or the value of the interest so proven shall be deducted from the value of the property or service ascertained under Subsection (a), (b), or (c) to determine value for purposes of this chapter.

Sec. 31.09. Aggregation of Amounts Involved in Theft.

When amounts are obtained in violation of this chapter pursuant to one scheme or continuing course of conduct, whether from the same or several sources, the conduct may be considered as one offense and the amounts aggregated in determining the grade of the offense.

Sec. 31.10. Actor's Interest in Property.

It is no defense to prosecution under this chapter that the actor has an interest in the property or service stolen if another person has the right of exclusive possession of the property.

Sec. 31.11. Tampering with Identification Numbers.

(a) A person commits an offense if the person:

(1) knowingly or intentionally removes, alters, or obliterates the serial number or other permanent identification marking on tangible personal property; or

(2) possesses, sells, or offers for sale tangible personal property and:

(A) the actor knows that the serial number or other permanent identification marking has been removed, altered, or obliterated; or

(B) a reasonable person in the position of the actor would have known that the serial number or other permanent identification marking has been removed, altered, or obliterated.

(b) It is an affirmative defense to prosecution under this section that the person was:

(1) the owner or acting with the effective consent of the owner of the property involved;

(2) a peace officer acting in the actual discharge of official duties; or

(3) acting with respect to a number assigned to a vehicle by the Texas Department of Transportation or the Texas Department of Motor Vehicles, as applicable, and the person was:

(A) in the actual discharge of official duties as an employee or agent of the department; or

(B) in full compliance with the rules of the department as an applicant for an assigned number approved by the department.

(c) Property involved in a violation of this section may be treated as stolen for purposes of custody and disposition of the property.

(d) An offense under this section is a Class A misdemeanor.

(e) In this section, "vehicle" has the meaning given by Section 541.201, Transportation Code.

Sec. 31.12. Theft of or Tampering with Multichannel Video or Information Services.

(a) A person commits an offense if, without the authorization of the multichannel video or information services provider, the person intentionally or knowingly:

(1) makes or maintains a connection, whether physically, electrically, electronically, or inductively, to:

(A) a cable, wire, or other component of or media attached to a multichannel video or information services system; or

(B) a television set, videotape recorder, or other receiver attached to a multichannel video or information system;

(2) attaches, causes to be attached, or maintains the attachment of a device to:

(A) a cable, wire, or other component of or media attached to a multichannel video or information services system; or

(B) a television set, videotape recorder, or other receiver attached to a multichannel video or information services system;

(3) tampers with, modifies, or maintains a modification to a device installed by a multichannel video or information services provider; or

(4) tampers with, modifies, or maintains a modification to an access device or uses that access device or any unauthorized access device to obtain

services from a multichannel video or information services provider.

(b) In this section:

(1) "Access device," "connection," and "device" mean an access device, connection, or device wholly or partly designed to make intelligible an encrypted, encoded, scrambled, or other nonstandard signal carried by a multichannel video or information services provider.

(2) "Encrypted, encoded, scrambled, or other nonstandard signal" means any type of signal or transmission not intended to produce an intelligible program or service without the use of a device, signal, or information provided by a multichannel video or information services provider.

(3) "Multichannel video or information services provider" means a licensed cable television system, video dialtone system, multichannel multipoint distribution services system, direct broadcast satellite system, or other system providing video or information services that are distributed by cable, wire, radio frequency, or other media.

(c) This section does not prohibit the manufacture, distribution, sale, or use of satellite receiving antennas that are otherwise permitted by state or federal law.

(d) An offense under this section is a Class C misdemeanor unless it is shown on the trial of the offense that the actor:

(1) has been previously convicted one time of an offense under this section, in which event the offense is a Class B misdemeanor, or convicted two or more times of an offense under this section, in which event the offense is a Class A misdemeanor; or

(2) committed the offense for remuneration, in which event the offense is a Class A misdemeanor, unless it is also shown on the trial of the offense that the actor has been previously convicted two or more times of an offense under this section, in which event the offense is a Class A misdemeanor with a minimum fine of $2,000 and a minimum term of confinement of 180 days.

(e) For the purposes of this section, each connection, attachment, modification, or act of tampering is a separate offense.

Sec. 31.13. Manufacture, Distribution, or Advertisement of Multichannel Video or Information Services Device.

(a) A person commits an offense if the person for remuneration intentionally or knowingly manufactures, assembles, modifies, imports into the state, exports out of the state, distributes, advertises, or offers for sale, with an intent to aid in the commission of an offense under Section 31.12, a device, a kit or part for a device, or a plan for a system of components wholly or partly designed to make intelligible an encrypted, encoded, scrambled, or other nonstandard signal carried or caused by a multichannel video or information services provider.

(b) In this section, "device," "encrypted, encoded, scrambled, or other nonstandard signal," and "multichannel video or information services provider" have the meanings assigned by Section 31.12.

(c) This section does not prohibit the manufacture, distribution, advertisement, offer for sale, or use of satellite receiving antennas that are otherwise permitted by state or federal law.

(d) An offense under this section is a Class A misdemeanor.

Sec. 31.14. Sale or Lease of Multichannel Video or Information Services Device.

(a) A person commits an offense if the person intentionally or knowingly sells or leases, with an intent to aid in the commission of an offense under Section 31.12, a device, a kit or part for a device, or a plan for a system of components wholly or partly designed to make intelligible an encrypted, encoded, scrambled, or other nonstandard signal carried or caused by a multichannel video or information services provider.

(b) In this section, "device," "encrypted, encoded, scrambled, or other nonstandard signal," and "multichannel video or information services provider" have the meanings assigned by Section 31.12.

(c) This section does not prohibit the sale or lease of satellite receiving antennas that are otherwise permitted by state or federal law without providing notice to the comptroller.

(d) An offense under this section is a Class A misdemeanor.

Sec. 31.15. Possession, Manufacture, or Distribution of Certain Instruments Used to Commit Retail Theft.

(a) [Repealed by Acts 2011, 82nd Leg., ch. 323 (H.B. 2482), § 4, effective September 1, 2011.]

(b) A person commits an offense if, with the intent to use the instrument to commit theft, the person:

(1) possesses a shielding or deactivation instrument; or

(2) knowingly manufactures, sells, offers for sale, or otherwise distributes a shielding or deactivation instrument.

(c) An offense under this section is a Class A misdemeanor.

Sec. 31.16. Organized Retail Theft.

(a) [Repealed by Acts 2011, 82nd Leg., ch. 323 (H.B. 2482), § 4, effective September 1, 2011.]

(b) A person commits an offense if the person intentionally conducts, promotes, or facilitates an activity in which the person receives, possesses, conceals, stores, barters, sells, or disposes of:

(1) stolen retail merchandise; or

(2) merchandise explicitly represented to the person as being stolen retail merchandise.

(c) An offense under this section is:

(1) a Class C misdemeanor if the total value of the merchandise involved in the activity is less than $100;

(2) a Class B misdemeanor if the total value of the merchandise involved in the activity is $100 or more but less than $750;

(3) a Class A misdemeanor if the total value of the merchandise involved in the activity is $750 or more but less than $2,500;

(4) a state jail felony if the total value of the merchandise involved in the activity is $2,500 or more but less than $30,000;

(5) a felony of the third degree if the total value of the merchandise involved in the activity is $30,000 or more but less than $150,000;

(6) a felony of the second degree if the total value of the merchandise involved in the activity is $150,000 or more but less than $300,000; or

(7) a felony of the first degree if the total value of the merchandise involved in the activity is $300,000 or more.

(d) An offense described for purposes of punishment by Subsections (c)(1)-(6) is increased to the next higher category of offense if it is shown on the trial of the offense that:

(1) the person organized, supervised, financed, or managed one or more other persons engaged in an activity described by Subsection (b); or

(2) during the commission of the offense, a person engaged in an activity described by Subsection (b) intentionally, knowingly, or recklessly:

(A) caused a fire exit alarm to sound or otherwise become activated;

(B) deactivated or otherwise prevented a fire exit alarm or retail theft detector from sounding; or

(C) used a shielding or deactivation instrument to prevent or attempt to prevent detection of the offense by a retail theft detector.

(e) [Repealed by Acts 2011, 82nd Leg., ch. 323 (H.B. 2482), § 4, effective September 1, 2011.]

Sec. 31.17. Unauthorized Acquisition or Transfer of Certain Financial Information.

(a) In this section:

(1) "Check" has the meaning assigned by Section 3.104, Business & Commerce Code.

(2) "Credit card" and "debit card" have the meanings assigned by Section 32.31.

(3) "Financial sight order or payment card information" means financial information that is:

(A) contained on either side of a check or similar sight order, check card, debit card, or credit card; or

(B) encoded on the magnetic strip or stripe of a check card, debit card, or credit card.

(b) A person commits an offense if the person, knowing that the person is not entitled to obtain or possess that financial information:

(1) obtains the financial sight order or payment card information of another by use of an electronic, photographic, visual imaging, recording, or other device capable of accessing, reading, recording, capturing, copying, imaging, scanning, reproducing, or storing in any manner the financial sight order or payment card information; or

(2) transfers to a third party information obtained as described by Subdivision (1).

(c) An offense under Subsection (b)(1) is a Class B misdemeanor. An offense under Subsection (b)(2) is a Class A misdemeanor.

(d) If conduct that constitutes an offense under this section also constitutes an offense under any other law, the actor may be prosecuted under this section or the other law.

Sec. 31.18. Cargo Theft.

(a) In this section:

(1) "Cargo" means goods, as defined by Section 7.102, Business & Commerce Code, that constitute, wholly or partly, a commercial shipment of freight moving in commerce. A shipment is considered to be moving in commerce if the shipment is located at any point between the point of origin and the final point of destination regardless of any temporary stop that is made for the purpose of transshipment or otherwise.

(2) "Vehicle" has the meaning assigned by Section 541.201, Transportation Code.

(b) A person commits an offense if the person:

(1) knowingly or intentionally conducts, promotes, or facilitates an activity in which the person receives, possesses, conceals, stores, barters, sells, abandons, or disposes of:

(A) stolen cargo; or

(B) cargo explicitly represented to the person as being stolen cargo; or

(2) is employed as a driver lawfully contracted to transport a specific cargo by vehicle from a known point of origin to a known point of destination and, with the intent to conduct, promote, or facilitate an activity described by Subdivision (1), knowingly or intentionally:

(A) fails to deliver the entire cargo to the known point of destination as contracted; or

(B) causes the seal to be broken on the vehicle or on an intermodal container containing any part of the cargo.

(c) An offense under this section is:

(1) a state jail felony if the total value of the cargo involved in the activity is $1,500 or more but less than $10,000;

(2) a felony of the third degree if the total value of the cargo involved in the activity is $10,000 or more but less than $100,000;

(3) a felony of the second degree if the total value of the cargo involved in the activity is $100,000 or more but less than $200,000; or

(4) a felony of the first degree if the total value of the cargo involved in the activity is $200,000 or more.

(d) For purposes of Subsection (c), the total value of the cargo involved in the activity includes the value of any vehicle stolen or damaged in the course of the same criminal episode as the conduct that is the subject of the prosecution.

(e) An offense described for purposes of punishment by Subsections (c)(1)-(3) is increased to the next higher category of offense if it is shown on the trial of the offense that the person organized, supervised, financed, or managed one or more other persons engaged in an activity described by Subsection (b).

(f) It is not a defense to prosecution under this section that:

(1) the offense occurred as a result of a deception or strategy on the part of a law enforcement agency, including the use of:

(A) an undercover operative or peace officer; or

(B) a bait vehicle;

(2) the actor was provided by a law enforcement agency with a facility in which to commit the offense or with an opportunity to engage in conduct constituting the offense; or

(3) the actor was solicited to commit the offense by a peace officer, and the solicitation was of a type that would encourage a person predisposed to commit the offense to actually commit the offense but would not encourage a person not predisposed to commit the offense to actually commit the offense.

Sec. 31.19. Theft of Petroleum Product.

(a) In this section, "petroleum product" means crude oil, natural gas, or condensate.

(b) A person commits an offense if the person unlawfully appropriates a petroleum product with intent to deprive the owner of the petroleum product by:

(1) possessing, removing, delivering, receiving, purchasing, selling, moving, concealing, or transporting the petroleum product; or

(2) making or causing a connection to be made with, or drilling or tapping or causing a hole to be drilled or tapped in, a pipe, pipeline, or tank used to store or transport a petroleum product.

(c) Appropriation of a petroleum product is unlawful if it is without the owner's effective consent.

(d) An offense under this section is:

(1) a state jail felony if the total value of the petroleum product appropriated is less than $10,000;

(2) a felony of the third degree if the total value of the petroleum product appropriated is $10,000 or more but less than $100,000;

(3) a felony of the second degree if the total value of the petroleum product appropriated is $100,000 or more but less than $300,000; or

(4) a felony of the first degree if the total value of the petroleum product appropriated is $300,000 or more.

Sec. 31.20. Mail Theft.

(a) In this section:

(1) "Disabled individual" and "elderly individual" have the meanings assigned by Section 22.04.

(2) "Identifying information" has the meaning assigned by Section 32.51.

(3) "Mail" means a letter, postal card, package, bag, or other sealed article that:

(A) is delivered by a common carrier or delivery service and not yet received by the addressee; or

(B) has been left to be collected for delivery by a common carrier or delivery service.

(b) A person commits an offense if the person intentionally appropriates mail from another person's mailbox or premises without the effective consent of the addressee and with the intent to deprive that addressee of the mail.

(c) Except as provided by Subsections (d) and (e), an offense under this section is:

(1) a Class A misdemeanor if the mail is appropriated from fewer than 10 addressees;

(2) a state jail felony if the mail is appropriated from at least 10 but fewer than 30 addressees; or

(3) a felony of the third degree if the mail is appropriated from 30 or more addressees.

(d) If it is shown on the trial of an offense under this section that the appropriated mail contained an item of identifying information and the actor committed the offense with the intent to facilitate an offense under Section 32.51, an offense under this section is:

(1) a state jail felony if the mail is appropriated from fewer than 10 addressees;

(2) a felony of the third degree if the mail is appropriated from at least 10 but fewer than 20 addressees;

(3) a felony of the second degree if the mail is appropriated from at least 20 but fewer than 50 addressees; or

(4) a felony of the first degree if the mail is appropriated from 50 or more addressees.

(e) An offense described for purposes of punishment by Subsection (d)(1), (2), or (3) is increased to the next higher category of offense if it is shown on the trial of the offense that at the time of the offense the actor knew or had reason to believe that an addressee from whom the actor appropriated mail was a disabled individual or an elderly individual.

(f) If conduct that constitutes an offense under this section also constitutes an offense under another law, the actor may be prosecuted under this section, the other law, or both.

CHAPTER 32 FRAUD

SUBCHAPTER A GENERAL PROVISIONS

Sec. 32.01. Definitions.

In this chapter:

(1) "Financial institution" means a bank, trust company, insurance company, credit union, building and loan association, savings and loan association, investment trust, investment company, or any other organization held out to the public as a place for deposit of funds or medium of savings or collective investment.

(2) "Property" means:

(A) real property;

(B) tangible or intangible personal property including anything severed from land; or

(C) a document, including money, that represents or embodies anything of value.

(3) "Service" includes:

(A) labor and professional service;

(B) telecommunication, public utility, and transportation service;

(C) lodging, restaurant service, and entertainment; and

(D) the supply of a motor vehicle or other property for use.

(4) "Steal" means to acquire property or service by theft.

Sec. 32.02. Value.

(a) Subject to the additional criteria of Subsections (b) and (c), value under this chapter is:

(1) the fair market value of the property or service at the time and place of the offense; or

(2) if the fair market value of the property cannot be ascertained, the cost of replacing the property within a reasonable time after the offense.

(b) The value of documents, other than those having a readily ascertainable market value, is:

(1) the amount due and collectible at maturity less any part that has been satisfied, if the document constitutes evidence of a debt; or

(2) the greatest amount of economic loss that the owner might reasonably suffer by virtue of loss of the document, if the document is other than evidence of a debt.

(c) If property or service has value that cannot be reasonably ascertained by the criteria set forth in Subsections (a) and (b), the property or service is deemed to have a value of $750 or more but less than $2,500.

(d) If the actor proves by a preponderance of the evidence that he gave consideration for or had a legal interest in the property or service stolen, the amount of the consideration or the value of the interest so proven shall be deducted from the value of the property or service ascertained under Subsection (a), (b), or (c) to determine value for purposes of this chapter.

Sec. 32.03. Aggregation of Amounts Involved in Fraud.

When amounts are obtained in violation of this chapter pursuant to one scheme or continuing course of conduct, whether from the same or several sources, the conduct may be considered as one offense and the amounts aggregated in determining the grade of offense.

SUBCHAPTER B FORGERY

Sec. 32.21. Forgery.

(a) For purposes of this section:

(1) "Forge" means:

(A) to alter, make, complete, execute, or authenticate any writing so that it purports:

(i) to be the act of another who did not authorize that act;

(ii) to have been executed at a time or place or in a numbered sequence other than was in fact the case; or

(iii) to be a copy of an original when no such original existed;

(B) to issue, transfer, register the transfer of, pass, publish, or otherwise utter a writing that is forged within the meaning of Paragraph (A); or

(C) to possess a writing that is forged within the meaning of Paragraph (A) with intent to utter it in a manner specified in Paragraph (B).

(2) "Writing" includes:

(A) printing or any other method of recording information;

(B) money, coins, tokens, stamps, seals, credit cards, badges, and trademarks; and

(C) symbols of value, right, privilege, or identification.

(b) A person commits an offense if he forges a writing with intent to defraud or harm another.

(c) Except as provided by Subsections (d), (e), and (e-1), an offense under this section is a Class A misdemeanor.

(d) Subject to Subsection (e-1), an offense under this section is a state jail felony if the writing is or purports to be a will, codicil, deed, deed of trust, mortgage, security instrument, security agreement, credit card, check, authorization to debit an account at a financial institution, or similar sight order for payment of money, contract, release, or other commercial instrument.

(e) Subject to Subsection (e-1), an offense under this section is a felony of the third degree if the writing is or purports to be:

(1) part of an issue of money, securities, postage or revenue stamps;

(2) a government record listed in Section 37.01(2)(C); or

(3) other instruments issued by a state or national government or by a subdivision of either, or part of an issue of stock, bonds, or other instruments representing interests in or claims against another person.

(e-1) If it is shown on the trial of an offense under this section that the actor engaged in the conduct to obtain or attempt to obtain a property or service, an offense under this section is:

(1) a Class C misdemeanor if the value of the property or service is less than $100;

(2) a Class B misdemeanor if the value of the property or service is $100 or more but less than $750;

(3) a Class A misdemeanor if the value of the property or service is $750 or more but less than $2,500;

(4) a state jail felony if the value of the property or service is $2,500 or more but less than $30,000;

(5) a felony of the third degree if the value of the property or service is $30,000 or more but less than $150,000;

(6) a felony of the second degree if the value of the property or service is $150,000 or more but less than $300,000; and

(7) a felony of the first degree if the value of the property or service is $300,000 or more.

(e-2) Notwithstanding any other provision of this section, an offense under this section, other than an offense described for purposes of punishment by Subsection (e-1)(7), is increased to the next higher category of offense if it is shown on the trial of the offense that the offense was committed against an elderly individual as defined by Section 22.04.

(f) A person is presumed to intend to defraud or harm another if the person acts with respect to two or more writings of the same type and if each writing is a government record listed in Section 37.01(2)(C).

(g) If conduct that constitutes an offense under this section also constitutes an offense under any other law, the actor may be prosecuted under this section or the other law.

Sec. 32.22. Criminal Simulation.

(a) A person commits an offense if, with intent to defraud or harm another:

(1) he makes or alters an object, in whole or in part, so that it appears to have value because of age, antiquity, rarity, source, or authorship that it does not have;

(2) he possesses an object so made or altered, with intent to sell, pass, or otherwise utter it; or

(3) he authenticates or certifies an object so made or altered as genuine or as different from what it is.

(b) An offense under this section is a Class A misdemeanor.

Sec. 32.23. Trademark Counterfeiting.

(a) In this section:

(1) "Counterfeit mark" means a mark that is identical to or substantially indistinguishable from a protected mark the use or production of which is not authorized by the owner of the protected mark.

(2) "Identification mark" means a data plate, serial number, or part identification number.

(3) "Protected mark" means a trademark or service mark or an identification mark that is:

(A) registered with the secretary of state;

(B) registered on the principal register of the United States Patent and Trademark Office;

(C) registered under the laws of another state; or

(D) protected by Section 16.105, Business & Commerce Code, or by 36 U.S.C. Section 371 et seq.

(4) "Retail value" means the actor's regular selling price for a counterfeit mark or an item or service that bears or is identified by a counterfeit mark, except that if an item bearing a counterfeit mark is a component of a finished product, the retail value means the actor's regular selling price of the finished product on or in which the component is used, distributed, or sold.

(5) "Service mark" has the meaning assigned by Section 16.001, Business & Commerce Code.

(6) "Trademark" has the meaning assigned by Section 16.001, Business & Commerce Code.

(b) A person commits an offense if the person intentionally manufactures, displays, advertises, distributes, offers for sale, sells, or possesses with intent to sell or distribute a counterfeit mark or an item or service that:

(1) bears or is identified by a counterfeit mark; or

(2) the person knows or should have known bears or is identified by a counterfeit mark.

(c) A state or federal certificate of registration of intellectual property is prima facie evidence of the facts stated in the certificate.

(d) For the purposes of Subsection (e), when items or services are the subject of counterfeiting in violation of this section pursuant to one scheme or continuing course of conduct, the conduct may be considered as one offense and the retail value of the items or services aggregated in determining the grade of offense.

(e) An offense under this section is a:

(1) Class C misdemeanor if the retail value of the item or service is less than $100;

(2) Class B misdemeanor if the retail value of the item or service is $100 or more but less than $750;

(3) Class A misdemeanor if the retail value of the item or service is $750 or more but less than $2,500;

(4) state jail felony if the retail value of the item or service is $2,500 or more but less than $30,000;

(5) felony of the third degree if the retail value of the item or service is $30,000 or more but less than $150,000;

(6) felony of the second degree if the retail value of the item or service is $150,000 or more but less than $300,000; or

(7) felony of the first degree if the retail value of the item or service is $300,000 or more.

Sec. 32.24. Stealing or Receiving Stolen Check or Similar Sight Order.

(a) A person commits an offense if the person steals an unsigned check or similar sight order or, with knowledge that an unsigned check or similar sight order has been stolen, receives the check or sight order with intent to use it, to sell it, or to transfer it to a person other than the person from whom the check or sight order was stolen.

(b) An offense under this section is a Class A misdemeanor.

SUBCHAPTER C CREDIT

Sec. 32.31. Credit Card or Debit Card Abuse.

(a) For purposes of this section:

(1) "Cardholder" means the person named on the face of a credit card or debit card to whom or for whose benefit the card is issued.

(2) "Credit card" means an identification card, plate, coupon, book, number, or any other device authorizing a designated person or bearer to obtain property or services on credit. The term includes the number or description of the device if the device itself is not produced at the time of ordering or obtaining the property or service.

(3) "Expired credit card" means a credit card bearing an expiration date after that date has passed.

(4) "Debit card" means an identification card, plate, coupon, book, number, or any other device authorizing a designated person or bearer to communicate a request to an unmanned teller machine or a customer convenience terminal or obtain property or services by debit to an account at a financial institution. The term includes the number or description of the device if the device itself is not produced at the time of ordering or obtaining the benefit.

(5) "Expired debit card" means a debit card bearing as its expiration date a date that has passed.

(6) "Unmanned teller machine" means a machine, other than a telephone, capable of being operated by a customer, by which a customer may communicate to a financial institution a request to withdraw a benefit for himself or for another directly from the customer's account or from the customer's account under a line of credit previously authorized by the institution for the customer.

(7) "Customer convenience terminal" means an unmanned teller machine the use of which does not involve personnel of a financial institution.

(b) A person commits an offense if:

(1) with intent to obtain a benefit fraudulently, he presents or uses a credit card or debit card with knowledge that:

(A) the card, whether or not expired, has not been issued to him and is not used with the effective consent of the cardholder; or

(B) the card has expired or has been revoked or cancelled;

(2) with intent to obtain a benefit, he uses a fictitious credit card or debit card or the pretended number or description of a fictitious card;

(3) he receives a benefit that he knows has been obtained in violation of this section;

(4) he steals a credit card or debit card or, with knowledge that it has been stolen, receives a credit card or debit card with intent to use it, to sell it, or to transfer it to a person other than the issuer or the cardholder;

(5) he buys a credit card or debit card from a person who he knows is not the issuer;

(6) not being the issuer, he sells a credit card or debit card;

(7) he uses or induces the cardholder to use the cardholder's credit card or debit card to obtain property or service for the actor's benefit for which the cardholder is financially unable to pay;

(8) not being the cardholder, and without the effective consent of the cardholder, he possesses a credit card or debit card with intent to use it;

(9) he possesses two or more incomplete credit cards or debit cards that have not been issued to him with intent to complete them without the effective consent of the issuer. For purposes of this subdivision, a card is incomplete if part of the matter that an issuer requires to appear on the card before it can be used, other than the signature of the cardholder, has not yet been stamped, embossed, imprinted, or written on it;

(10) being authorized by an issuer to furnish goods or services on presentation of a credit card or debit card, he, with intent to defraud the issuer or the cardholder, furnishes goods or services on presentation of a credit card or debit card obtained or retained in violation of this section or a credit card or debit card that is forged, expired, or revoked; or

(11) being authorized by an issuer to furnish goods or services on presentation of a credit card or debit card, he, with intent to defraud the issuer or a cardholder, fails to furnish goods or services that he represents in writing to the issuer that he has furnished.

(c) It is presumed that a person who used a revoked, cancelled, or expired credit card or debit card had knowledge that the card had been revoked, cancelled, or expired if he had received notice of revocation, cancellation, or expiration from the issuer. For purposes of this section, notice may be either notice given orally in person or by telephone, or in writing by mail or by telegram. If written notice was sent by registered or certified mail with return receipt requested, or by telegram with report of delivery requested, addressed to the cardholder at the last address shown by the records of the issuer, it is presumed that the notice was received by the cardholder no later than five days after sent.

(d) An offense under this section is a state jail felony, except that the offense is a felony of the third degree if it is shown on the trial of the offense that the offense was committed against an elderly individual as defined by Section 22.04.

Sec. 32.315. Fraudulent Use or Possession of Credit Card or Debit Card Information.

(a) In this section:

(1) "Counterfeit credit card or debit card" means a:

(A) credit card or debit card that:

(i) purports on its face to have been issued by an issuer that did not issue the card;

(ii) has been altered to contain a digital imprint other than that which was placed on the card by the issuer;

(iii) contains a digital imprint with account information or account holder information differing from that which is printed or embossed on the card; or

(iv) has been altered to change the account information or account holder information on the face of the card from that which was printed or embossed on the card by the issuer; or

(B) card, other than one issued as a credit card or debit card, that has been altered to contain the digital imprint of a credit card or debit card.

(2) "Credit card" and "debit card" have the meanings assigned by Section 32.31.

(3) "Digital imprint" means the digital data placed on a credit card or debit card or on a counterfeit credit card or debit card.

(b) A person commits an offense if the person, with the intent to harm or defraud another, obtains, possesses, transfers, or uses:

(1) a counterfeit credit card or debit card;

(2) the number and expiration date of a credit card or debit card without the consent of the account holder; or

(3) the data stored on the digital imprint of a credit card or debit card without the consent of the account holder.

(c) If an actor possessed five or more of an item described by Subsection (b)(2) or (3), a rebuttable presumption exists that the actor possessed each item without the consent of the account holder.

(d) The presumption established under Subsection (c) does not apply to a business or other commercial entity or a government agency that is engaged in a business activity or governmental function that does not violate a penal law of this state.

(e) An offense under this section is:

(1) a state jail felony if the number of items obtained, possessed, transferred, or used is less than five;

(2) a felony of the third degree if the number of items obtained, possessed, transferred, or used is five or more but less than 10;

(3) a felony of the second degree if the number of items obtained, possessed, transferred, or used is 10 or more but less than 50; or

(4) a felony of the first degree if the number of items obtained, possessed, transferred, or used is 50 or more.

(f) If a court orders a defendant convicted of an offense under this section to make restitution to a victim of the offense, the court may order the defendant to reimburse the victim for lost income or other expenses, other than attorney's fees, incurred as a result of the offense.

(g) If conduct that constitutes an offense under this section also constitutes an offense under any other law, the actor may be prosecuted under this section, the other law, or both.

Sec. 32.32. False Statement to Obtain Property or Credit or in the Provision of Certain Services.

(a) For purposes of this section, "credit" includes:

(1) a loan of money;

(2) furnishing property or service on credit;

(3) extending the due date of an obligation;

(4) comaking, endorsing, or guaranteeing a note or other instrument for obtaining credit;

(5) a line or letter of credit;

(6) a credit card, as defined in Section 32.31 (Credit Card or Debit Card Abuse); and

(7) a mortgage loan.

(b) A person commits an offense if he intentionally or knowingly makes a materially false or misleading written statement to obtain property or credit, including a mortgage loan.

(b-1) A person commits an offense if the person intentionally or knowingly makes a materially false or misleading written statement in providing an appraisal of real property for compensation.

(c) An offense under this section is:

(1) a Class C misdemeanor if the value of the property or the amount of credit is less than $100;

(2) a Class B misdemeanor if the value of the property or the amount of credit is $100 or more but less than $750;

(3) a Class A misdemeanor if the value of the property or the amount of credit is $750 or more but less than $2,500;

(4) a state jail felony if the value of the property or the amount of credit is $2,500 or more but less than $30,000;

(5) a felony of the third degree if the value of the property or the amount of credit is $30,000 or more but less than $150,000;

(6) a felony of the second degree if the value of the property or the amount of credit is $150,000 or more but less than $300,000; or

(7) a felony of the first degree if the value of the property or the amount of credit is $300,000 or more.

(d) The following agencies shall assist a prosecuting attorney of the United States or of a county or judicial district of this state, a county or state law enforcement agency of this state, or a federal law enforcement agency in the investigation of an offense under this section involving a mortgage loan:

(1) the office of the attorney general;

(2) the Department of Public Safety;

(3) the Texas Department of Insurance;

(4) the Office of Consumer Credit Commissioner;

(5) the Texas Department of Banking;

(6) the credit union department;

(7) the Department of Savings and Mortgage Lending;

(8) the Texas Real Estate Commission;

(9) the Texas Appraiser Licensing and Certification Board; and

(10) the Texas Department of Housing and Community Affairs.

(e) With the consent of the appropriate local county or district attorney, the attorney general has concurrent jurisdiction with that consenting local prosecutor to prosecute an offense under this section that involves a mortgage loan.

Sec. 32.33. Hindering Secured Creditors.

(a) For purposes of this section:

(1) "Remove" means transport, without the effective consent of the secured party, from the state in which the property was located when the security interest or lien attached.

(2) "Security interest" means an interest in personal property or fixtures that secures payment or performance of an obligation.

(b) A person who has signed a security agreement creating a security interest in property or a mortgage or deed of trust creating a lien on property commits an offense if, with intent to hinder enforcement of that interest or lien, he destroys, removes, conceals, encumbers, or otherwise harms or reduces the value of the property.

(c) For purposes of this section, a person is presumed to have intended to hinder enforcement of the security interest or lien if, when any part of the debt secured by the security interest or lien was due, he failed:

(1) to pay the part then due; and

(2) if the secured party had made demand, to deliver possession of the secured property to the secured party.

(d) An offense under Subsection (b) is a:

(1) Class C misdemeanor if the value of the property destroyed, removed, concealed, encumbered, or otherwise harmed or reduced in value is less than $100;

(2) Class B misdemeanor if the value of the property destroyed, removed, concealed, encumbered, or otherwise harmed or reduced in value is $100 or more but less than $750;

(3) Class A misdemeanor if the value of the property destroyed, removed, concealed, encumbered, or otherwise harmed or reduced in value is $750 or more but less than $2,500;

(4) state jail felony if the value of the property destroyed, removed, concealed, encumbered, or otherwise harmed or reduced in value is $2,500 or more but less than $30,000;

(5) felony of the third degree if the value of the property destroyed, removed, concealed, encumbered, or otherwise harmed or reduced in value is $30,000 or more but less than $150,000;

(6) felony of the second degree if the value of the property destroyed, removed, concealed, encumbered, or otherwise harmed or reduced in value is $150,000 or more but less than $300,000; or

(7) felony of the first degree if the value of the property destroyed, removed, concealed, encumbered, or otherwise harmed or reduced in value is $300,000 or more.

(e) A person who is a debtor under a security agreement, and who does not have a right to sell or dispose of the secured property or is required to account to the secured party for the proceeds of a permitted sale or disposition, commits an offense if the person sells or otherwise disposes of the secured property, or does not account to the secured party for the proceeds of a sale or other disposition as required, with intent to appropriate (as defined in Chapter 31) the proceeds or value of the secured property. A person is presumed to have intended to appropriate proceeds if the person does not deliver the proceeds to the secured party or account to the secured party for the proceeds before the 11th day after the day that the secured party makes a lawful demand for the proceeds or account. An offense under this subsection is:

(1) a Class C misdemeanor if the proceeds obtained from the sale or other disposition are money or goods having a value of less than $100;

(2) a Class B misdemeanor if the proceeds obtained from the sale or other disposition are money or goods having a value of $100 or more but less than $750;

(3) a Class A misdemeanor if the proceeds obtained from the sale or other disposition are money or goods having a value of $750 or more but less than $2,500;

(4) a state jail felony if the proceeds obtained from the sale or other disposition are money or goods having a value of $2,500 or more but less than $30,000;

(5) a felony of the third degree if the proceeds obtained from the sale or other disposition are money or goods having a value of $30,000 or more but less than $150,000;

(6) a felony of the second degree if the proceeds obtained from the sale or other disposition are money or goods having a value of $150,000 or more but less than $300,000; or

(7) a felony of the first degree if the proceeds obtained from the sale or other disposition are money or goods having a value of $300,000 or more.

Sec. 32.34. Fraudulent Transfer of a Motor Vehicle.

(a) In this section:

(1) "Lease" means the grant of use and possession of a motor vehicle for consideration, whether or not the grant includes an option to buy the vehicle.

(2) "Motor vehicle" means a device in, on, or by which a person or property is or may be transported or drawn on a highway, except a device used exclusively on stationary rails or tracks.

(3) "Security interest" means an interest in personal property or fixtures that secures payment or performance of an obligation.

(4) "Third party" means a person other than the actor or the owner of the vehicle.

(5) "Transfer" means to transfer possession, whether or not another right is also transferred, by means of a sale, lease, sublease, lease assignment, or other property transfer.

(b) A person commits an offense if the person acquires, accepts possession of, or exercises control over the motor vehicle of another under a written or oral agreement to arrange for the transfer of the vehicle to a third party and:

(1) knowing the vehicle is subject to a security interest, lease, or lien, the person transfers the vehicle to a third party without first obtaining written authorization from the vehicle's secured creditor, lessor, or lienholder;

(2) intending to defraud or harm the vehicle's owner, the person transfers the vehicle to a third party;

(3) intending to defraud or harm the vehicle's owner, the person disposes of the vehicle in a manner other than by transfer to a third party; or

(4) the person does not disclose the location of the vehicle on the request of the vehicle's owner, secured creditor, lessor, or lienholder.

(c) For the purposes of Subsection (b)(2), the actor is presumed to have intended to defraud or harm the motor vehicle's owner if the actor does not take reasonable steps to determine whether or not the third party is financially able to pay for the vehicle.

(d) It is a defense to prosecution under Subsection (b)(1) that the entire indebtedness secured by or owed under the security interest, lease, or lien is paid or satisfied in full not later than the 30th day after the date that the transfer was made.

(e) It is not a defense to prosecution under Subsection (b)(1) that the motor vehicle's owner has violated a contract creating a security interest, lease, or lien in the motor vehicle.

(f) An offense under Subsection (b)(1), (b)(2), or (b)(3) is:

(1) a state jail felony if the value of the motor vehicle is less than $30,000;

(2) a felony of the third degree if the value of the motor vehicle is $30,000 or more but less than $150,000;

(3) a felony of the second degree if the value of the motor vehicle is $150,000 or more but less than $300,000; or

(4) a felony of the first degree if the value of the motor vehicle is $300,000 or more.

(g) An offense under Subsection (b)(4) is a Class A misdemeanor.

Sec. 32.35. Credit Card Transaction Record Laundering.

(a) In this section:

(1) "Agent" means a person authorized to act on behalf of another and includes an employee.

(2) "Authorized vendor" means a person authorized by a creditor to furnish property, service, or anything else of value upon presentation of a credit card by a cardholder.

(3) "Cardholder" means the person named on the face of a credit card to whom or for whose benefit the credit card is issued, and includes the named person's agents.

(4) "Credit card" means an identification card, plate, coupon, book, number, or any other device authorizing a designated person or bearer to obtain property or services on credit. It includes the number or description on the device if the device itself is not produced at the time of ordering or obtaining the property or service.

(5) "Creditor" means a person licensed under Chapter 342, Finance Code, a bank, savings and loan association, credit union, or other regulated financial institution that lends money or otherwise extends credit to a cardholder through a credit card and that authorizes other persons to honor the credit card.

(b) A person commits an offense if the person is an authorized vendor who, with intent to defraud the creditor or cardholder, presents to a creditor, for payment, a credit card transaction record of a sale that was not made by the authorized vendor or the vendor's agent.

(c) A person commits an offense if, without the creditor's authorization, the person employs, solicits, or otherwise causes an authorized vendor or the vendor's agent to present to a creditor, for payment, a credit card transaction record of a sale that was not made by the authorized vendor or the vendor's agent.

(d) It is presumed that a person is not the agent of an authorized vendor if a fee is paid or offered to be paid by the person to the authorized vendor in connection with the vendor's presentment to a creditor of a credit card transaction record.

(e) An offense under this section is a:

(1) Class C misdemeanor if the amount of the record of a sale is less than $100;

(2) Class B misdemeanor if the amount of the record of a sale is $100 or more but less than $750;

(3) Class A misdemeanor if the amount of the record of a sale is $750 or more but less than $2,500;

(4) state jail felony if the amount of the record of a sale is $2,500 or more but less than $30,000;

(5) felony of the third degree if the amount of the record of a sale is $30,000 or more but less than $150,000;

(6) felony of the second degree if the amount of the record of a sale is $150,000 or more but less than $300,000; or

(7) felony of the first degree if the amount of the record of a sale is $300,000 or more.

Sec. 32.36. Fraudulent Transfer of a Motor Vehicle [Renumbered].

Renumbered to Tex. Penal Code § 32.34 by Acts 1993, 73rd Leg., ch. 900 (S.B. 1067), § 1.01, effective September 1, 1994.

Sec. 32.37. Credit Card Transaction Record Laundering [Renumbered].

Renumbered to Tex. Penal Code § 32.35 by Acts 1993, 73rd Leg., ch. 900 (S.B. 1067), § 1.01, effective September 1, 1994.

SUBCHAPTER D OTHER DECEPTIVE PRACTICES

Sec. 32.41. Issuance of Bad Check or Similar Sight Order.

(a) A person commits an offense if he issues or passes a check or similar sight order for the payment of money knowing that the issuer does not have sufficient funds in or on deposit with the bank or other drawee for the payment in full of the check or order as well as all other checks or orders outstanding at the time of issuance.

(b) This section does not prevent the prosecution from establishing the required knowledge by direct evidence; however, for purposes of this section, the issuer's knowledge of insufficient funds is presumed (except in the case of a postdated check or order) if:

(1) he had no account with the bank or other drawee at the time he issued the check or order; or

(2) payment was refused by the bank or other drawee for lack of funds or insufficient funds on presentation within 30 days after issue and the issuer failed to pay the holder in full within 10 days after receiving notice of that refusal.

(c) Notice for purposes of Subsection (b)(2) may be actual notice or notice in writing that:

(1) is sent by:

(A) first class mail, evidenced by an affidavit of service; or

(B) registered or certified mail with return receipt requested;

(2) is addressed to the issuer at the issuer's address shown on:

(A) the check or order;

(B) the records of the bank or other drawee; or

(C) the records of the person to whom the check or order has been issued or passed; and

(3) contains the following statement:

"This is a demand for payment in full for a check or order not paid because of a lack of funds or insufficient funds. If you fail to make payment in full within 10 days after the date of receipt of this notice, the failure to pay creates a presumption for committing an offense, and this matter may be referred for criminal prosecution."

(d) If notice is given in accordance with Subsection (c), it is presumed that the notice was received no later than five days after it was sent.

(e) A person charged with an offense under this section may make restitution for the bad checks or sight orders. Restitution shall be made through the prosecutor's office if collection and processing were initiated through that office. In other cases restitution may be, with the approval of the court in which the offense is filed:

(1) made through the court; or

(2) collected by a law enforcement agency if a peace officer of that agency executes a warrant against the person charged with the offense.

(f) Except as otherwise provided by this subsection, an offense under this section is a Class C misdemeanor. If the check or similar sight order that was issued or passed was for a child support payment the obligation for which is established under a court order, the offense is a Class B misdemeanor.

(g) An offense under this section is not a lesser included offense of an offense under Section 31.03 or 31.04.

Sec. 32.42. Deceptive Business Practices.

(a) For purposes of this section:

(1) "Adulterated" means varying from the standard of composition or quality prescribed by law or set by established commercial usage.

(2) "Business" includes trade and commerce and advertising, selling, and buying service or property.

(3) "Commodity" means any tangible or intangible personal property.

(4) "Contest" includes sweepstake, puzzle, and game of chance.

(5) "Deceptive sales contest" means a sales contest:

(A) that misrepresents the participant's chance of winning a prize;

(B) that fails to disclose to participants on a conspicuously displayed permanent poster (if the contest is conducted by or through a retail outlet) or on each card game piece, entry blank, or other paraphernalia required for participation in the contest (if the contest is not conducted by or through a retail outlet):

(i) the geographical area or number of outlets in which the contest is to be conducted;

(ii) an accurate description of each type of prize;

(iii) the minimum number and minimum amount of cash prizes; and

(iv) the minimum number of each other type of prize; or

(C) that is manipulated or rigged so that prizes are given to predetermined persons or retail establishments. A sales contest is not deceptive if the total value of prizes to each retail outlet is in a uniform ratio to the number of game pieces distributed to that outlet.

(6) "Mislabeled" means varying from the standard of truth or disclosure in labeling prescribed by law or set by established commercial usage.

(7) "Prize" includes gift, discount, coupon, certificate, gratuity, and any other thing of value awarded in a sales contest.

(8) "Sales contest" means a contest in connection with the sale of a commodity or service by which a person may, as determined by drawing, guessing, matching, or chance, receive a prize and which is not regulated by the rules of a federal regulatory agency.

(9) "Sell" and "sale" include offer for sale, advertise for sale, expose for sale, keep for the purpose of sale, deliver for or after sale, solicit and offer to buy, and every disposition for value.

(b) A person commits an offense if in the course of business he intentionally, knowingly, recklessly, or with criminal negligence commits one or more of the following deceptive business practices:

(1) using, selling, or possessing for use or sale a false weight or measure, or any other device for falsely determining or recording any quality or quantity;

(2) selling less than the represented quantity of a property or service;

(3) taking more than the represented quantity of property or service when as a buyer the actor furnishes the weight or measure;

(4) selling an adulterated or mislabeled commodity;

(5) passing off property or service as that of another;

(6) representing that a commodity is original or new if it is deteriorated, altered, rebuilt, reconditioned, reclaimed, used, or secondhand;

(7) representing that a commodity or service is of a particular style, grade, or model if it is of another;

(8) advertising property or service with intent:

(A) not to sell it as advertised, or

(B) not to supply reasonably expectable public demand, unless the advertising adequately discloses a time or quantity limit;

(9) representing the price of property or service falsely or in a way tending to mislead;

(10) making a materially false or misleading statement of fact concerning the reason for, existence of, or amount of a price or price reduction;

(11) conducting a deceptive sales contest; or

(12) making a materially false or misleading statement:

(A) in an advertisement for the purchase or sale of property or service; or

(B) otherwise in connection with the purchase or sale of property or service.

(c) An offense under Subsections (b)(1), (b)(2), (b)(3), (b)(4), (b)(5), and (b)(6) is:

(1) a Class C misdemeanor if the actor commits an offense with criminal negligence and if he has not previously been convicted of a deceptive business practice; or

(2) a Class A misdemeanor if the actor commits an offense intentionally, knowingly, recklessly or if he has been previously convicted of a Class B or C misdemeanor under this section.

(d) An offense under Subsections (b)(7), (b)(8), (b)(9), (b)(10), (b)(11), and (b)(12) is a Class A misdemeanor.

Sec. 32.43. Commercial Bribery.

(a) For purposes of this section:

(1) "Beneficiary" means a person for whom a fiduciary is acting.

(2) "Fiduciary" means:

(A) an agent or employee;

(B) a trustee, guardian, custodian, administrator, executor, conservator, receiver, or similar fiduciary;

(C) a lawyer, physician, accountant, appraiser, or other professional advisor; or

(D) an officer, director, partner, manager, or other participant in the direction of the affairs of a corporation or association.

(b) A person who is a fiduciary commits an offense if, without the consent of his beneficiary, he intentionally or knowingly solicits, accepts, or agrees to accept any benefit from another person on agreement or understanding that the benefit will influence the conduct of the fiduciary in relation to the affairs of his beneficiary.

(c) A person commits an offense if he offers, confers, or agrees to confer any benefit the acceptance of which is an offense under Subsection (b).

(d) An offense under this section is a state jail felony.

(e) In lieu of a fine that is authorized by Subsection (d), and in addition to the imprisonment that is authorized by that subsection, if the court finds that an individual who is a fiduciary gained a benefit through the commission of an offense under Subsection (b), the court may sentence the individual to pay a fine in an amount fixed by the court, not to exceed double the value of the benefit gained. This subsection does not affect the application of

Section 12.51(c) to an offense under this section committed by a corporation, an association, a limited liability company, or another business entity, as defined by Section 7.21.

Sec. 32.44. Rigging Publicly Exhibited Contest.

(a) A person commits an offense if, with intent to affect the outcome (including the score) of a publicly exhibited contest:

(1) he offers, confers, or agrees to confer any benefit on, or threatens harm to:

(A) a participant in the contest to induce him not to use his best efforts; or

(B) an official or other person associated with the contest; or

(2) he tampers with a person, animal, or thing in a manner contrary to the rules of the contest.

(b) A person commits an offense if he intentionally or knowingly solicits, accepts, or agrees to accept any benefit the conferring of which is an offense under Subsection (a).

(c) An offense under this section is a Class A misdemeanor.

Sec. 32.441. Illegal Recruitment of an Athlete.

(a) A person commits an offense if, without the consent of the governing body or a designee of the governing body of an institution of higher education, the person intentionally or knowingly solicits, accepts, or agrees to accept any benefit from another on an agreement or understanding that the benefit will influence the conduct of the person in enrolling in the institution and participating in intercollegiate athletics.

(b) A person commits an offense if he offers, confers, or agrees to confer any benefit the acceptance of which is an offense under Subsection (a).

(c) It is an exception to prosecution under this section that the person offering, conferring, or agreeing to confer a benefit and the person soliciting, accepting, or agreeing to accept a benefit are related within the second degree of consanguinity or affinity, as determined under Chapter 573, Government Code.

(d) It is an exception to prosecution under Subsection (a) that, not later than the 60th day after the date the person accepted or agreed to accept a benefit, the person contacted a law enforcement agency and furnished testimony or evidence about the offense.

(e) An offense under this section is a:

(1) Class C misdemeanor if the value of the benefit is less than $100;

(2) Class B misdemeanor if the value of the benefit is $100 or more but less than $750;

(3) Class A misdemeanor if the value of the benefit is $750 or more but less than $2,500;

(4) state jail felony if the value of the benefit is $2,500 or more but less than $30,000;

(5) felony of the third degree if the value of the benefit is $30,000 or more but less than $150,000;

(6) felony of the second degree if the value of the benefit is $150,000 or more but less than $300,000; or

(7) felony of the first degree if the value of the benefit is $300,000 or more.

Sec. 32.45. Misapplication of Fiduciary Property or Property of Financial Institution.

(a) For purposes of this section:

(1) "Fiduciary" includes:

(A) a trustee, guardian, administrator, executor, conservator, and receiver;

(B) an attorney in fact or agent appointed under a durable power of attorney as provided by Subtitle P, Title 2, Estates Code;

(C) any other person acting in a fiduciary capacity, but not a commercial bailee unless the commercial bailee is a party in a motor fuel sales agreement with a distributor or supplier, as those terms are defined by Section 162.001, Tax Code; and

(D) an officer, manager, employee, or agent carrying on fiduciary functions on behalf of a fiduciary.

(2) "Misapply" means deal with property contrary to:

(A) an agreement under which the fiduciary holds the property; or

(B) a law prescribing the custody or disposition of the property.

(b) A person commits an offense if he intentionally, knowingly, or recklessly misapplies property he holds as a fiduciary or property of a financial institution in a manner that involves substantial risk of loss to the owner of the property or to a person for whose benefit the property is held.

(c) An offense under this section is:

(1) a Class C misdemeanor if the value of the property misapplied is less than $100;

(2) a Class B misdemeanor if the value of the property misapplied is $100 or more but less than $750;

(3) a Class A misdemeanor if the value of the property misapplied is $750 or more but less than $2,500;

(4) a state jail felony if the value of the property misapplied is $2,500 or more but less than $30,000;

(5) a felony of the third degree if the value of the property misapplied is $30,000 or more but less than $150,000;

(6) a felony of the second degree if the value of the property misapplied is $150,000 or more but less than $300,000; or

(7) a felony of the first degree if the value of the property misapplied is $300,000 or more.

(d) An offense described for purposes of punishment by Subsections (c)(1)—(6) is increased to the next higher category of offense if it is shown on the trial of the offense that the offense was committed against an elderly individual as defined by Section 22.04.

(e) With the consent of the appropriate local county or district attorney, the attorney general has concurrent jurisdiction with that consenting local prosecutor to prosecute an offense under this section that involves the state Medicaid program.

Sec. 32.46. Fraudulent Securing of Document Execution.

(a) A person commits an offense if the person, with the intent to defraud or harm any person:

(1) causes another person, without that person's effective consent, to sign or execute any document affecting property or service or the pecuniary interest of any person; or

(2) causes a public servant, without the public servant's effective consent, to file or record any purported judgment or other document purporting to memorialize or evidence an act, an order, a directive, or process of:

(A) a purported court that is not expressly created or established under the constitution or the laws of this state or of the United States;

(B) a purported judicial entity that is not expressly created or established under the constitution or laws of this state or of the United States; or

(C) a purported judicial officer of a purported court or purported judicial entity described by Paragraph (A) or (B).

(b) An offense under Subsection (a)(1) is a:

(1) Class C misdemeanor if the value of the property, service, or pecuniary interest is less than $100;

(2) Class B misdemeanor if the value of the property, service, or pecuniary interest is $100 or more but less than $750;

(3) Class A misdemeanor if the value of the property, service, or pecuniary interest is $750 or more but less than $2,500;

(4) state jail felony if the value of the property, service, or pecuniary interest is $2,500 or more but less than $30,000;

(5) felony of the third degree if the value of the property, service, or pecuniary interest is $30,000 or more but less than $150,000;

(6) felony of the second degree if the value of the property, service, or pecuniary interest is $150,000 or more but less than $300,000; or

(7) felony of the first degree if the value of the property, service, or pecuniary interest is $300,000 or more.

(c) An offense under Subsection (a)(2) is a state jail felony.

(c-1) An offense described for purposes of punishment by Subsections (b)(1)—(6) and (c) is increased to the next higher category of offense if it is shown on the trial of the offense that the offense was committed against an elderly individual as defined by Section 22.04 or involves the state Medicaid program.

(d) In this section:

(1) "Deception" has the meaning assigned by Section 31.01.

(2) "Document" includes electronically stored data or other information that is retrievable in a readable, perceivable form.

(3) "Effective consent" includes consent by a person legally authorized to act for the owner. Consent is not effective if:

(A) induced by deception or coercion;

(B) given by a person who by reason of youth, mental disease or defect, or intoxication is known by the actor to be unable to make reasonable property dispositions; or

(C) given by a person who by reason of advanced age is known by the actor to have a diminished capacity to make informed and rational decisions about the reasonable disposition of property.

(e) With the consent of the appropriate local county or district attorney, the attorney general has concurrent jurisdiction with that consenting local prosecutor to prosecute an offense under this section that involves the state Medicaid program.

Sec. 32.47. Fraudulent Destruction, Removal, or Concealment of Writing.

(a) A person commits an offense if, with intent to defraud or harm another, he destroys, removes, conceals, alters, substitutes, or otherwise impairs the verity, legibility, or availability of a writing, other than a governmental record.

(b) For purposes of this section, "writing" includes:

(1) printing or any other method of recording information;

(2) money, coins, tokens, stamps, seals, credit cards, badges, trademarks;

(3) symbols of value, right, privilege, or identification; and

(4) universal product codes, labels, price tags, or markings on goods.

(c) Except as provided by Subsection (d), an offense under this section is a Class A misdemeanor, provided that:

(1) the writing is not attached to tangible property to indicate the price for the sale of that property; and

(2) the actor did not engage in the conduct described by Subsection (a) with respect to that writing for the purpose of obtaining the property for a lesser price indicated by a separate writing.

(d) An offense under this section is a state jail felony if the writing:

(1) is a will or codicil of another, whether or not the maker is alive or dead and whether or not it has been admitted to probate; or

(2) is a deed, mortgage, deed of trust, security instrument, security agreement, or other writing for which the law provides public recording or filing, whether or not the writing has been acknowledged.

(e) If at the time of the offense the writing was attached to tangible property to indicate the price for the sale of that property and the actor engaged in the conduct described by Subsection (a) with respect to that writing for the purpose of obtaining the property for a lesser price indicated by a separate writing, an offense under this section is:

(1) a Class C misdemeanor if the difference between the impaired writing and the lesser price indicated by the other writing is less than $100;

(2) a Class B misdemeanor if the difference between the impaired writing and the lesser price indicated by the other writing is $100 or more but less than $750;

(3) a Class A misdemeanor if the difference between the impaired writing and the lesser price indicated by the other writing is $750 or more but less than $2,500;

(4) a state jail felony if the difference between the impaired writing and the lesser price indicated by the other writing is $2,500 or more but less than $30,000;

(5) a felony of the third degree if the difference between the impaired writing and the lesser price indicated by the other writing is $30,000 or more but less than $150,000;

(6) a felony of the second degree if the difference between the impaired writing and the lesser price indicated by the other writing is $150,000 or more but less than $300,000; or

(7) a felony of the first degree if the difference between the impaired writing and the lesser price indicated by the other writing is $300,000 or more.

Sec. 32.48. Simulating Legal Process.

(a) A person commits an offense if the person recklessly causes to be delivered to another any document that simulates a summons, complaint, judgment, or other court process with the intent to:

(1) induce payment of a claim from another person; or

(2) cause another to:

(A) submit to the putative authority of the document; or

(B) take any action or refrain from taking any action in response to the document, in compliance with the document, or on the basis of the document.

(b) Proof that the document was mailed to any person with the intent that it be forwarded to the intended recipient is a sufficient showing that the document was delivered.

(c) It is not a defense to prosecution under this section that the simulating document:

(1) states that it is not legal process; or

(2) purports to have been issued or authorized by a person or entity who did not have lawful authority to issue or authorize the document.

(d) If it is shown on the trial of an offense under this section that the simulating document was filed with, presented to, or delivered to a clerk of a court or an employee of a clerk of a court created or established under the constitution or laws of this state, there is a rebuttable presumption that the document was delivered with the intent described by Subsection (a).

(e) Except as provided by Subsection (f), an offense under this section is a Class A misdemeanor.

(f) If it is shown on the trial of an offense under this section that the defendant has previously been convicted of a violation of this section, the offense is a state jail felony.

Sec. 32.49. Refusal to Execute Release of Fraudulent Lien or Claim.

(a) A person commits an offense if, with intent to defraud or harm another, the person:

(1) owns, holds, or is the beneficiary of a purported lien or claim asserted against real or personal property or an interest in real or personal property that is fraudulent, as described by Section 51.901(c), Government Code; and

(2) not later than the 21st day after the date of receipt of actual or written notice sent by either certified or registered mail, return receipt requested, to the person's last known address, or by telephonic document transfer to the recipient's current telecopier number, requesting the execution of

a release of the fraudulent lien or claim, refuses to execute the release on the request of:

(A) the obligor or debtor; or

(B) any person who owns any interest in the real or personal property described in the document or instrument that is the basis for the lien or claim.

(b) A person who fails to execute a release of the purported lien or claim within the period prescribed by Subsection (a)(2) is presumed to have had the intent to harm or defraud another.

(c) An offense under this section is a Class A misdemeanor.

Sec. 32.50. Deceptive Preparation and Marketing of Academic Product.

(a) For purposes of this section:

(1) "Academic product" means a term paper, thesis, dissertation, essay, report, recording, work of art, or other written, recorded, pictorial, or artistic product or material submitted or intended to be submitted by a person to satisfy an academic requirement of the person.

(2) "Academic requirement" means a requirement or prerequisite to receive course credit or to complete a course of study or degree, diploma, or certificate program at an institution of higher education.

(3) "Institution of higher education" means an institution of higher education or private or independent institution of higher education as those terms are defined by Section 61.003, Education Code, or a private postsecondary educational institution as that term is defined by Section 61.302, Education Code.

(b) A person commits an offense if, with intent to make a profit, the person prepares, sells, offers or advertises for sale, or delivers to another person an academic product when the person knows, or should reasonably have known, that a person intends to submit or use the academic product to satisfy an academic requirement of a person other than the person who prepared the product.

(c) A person commits an offense if, with intent to induce another person to enter into an agreement or obligation to obtain or have prepared an academic product, the person knowingly makes or disseminates a written or oral statement that the person will prepare or cause to be prepared an academic product to be sold for use in satisfying an academic requirement of a person other than the person who prepared the product.

(d) It is a defense to prosecution under this section that the actor's conduct consisted solely of action taken as an employee of an institution of higher education in providing instruction, counseling, or tutoring in research or writing to students of the institution.

(e) It is a defense to prosecution under this section that the actor's conduct consisted solely of offering or providing tutorial or editing assistance to another person in connection with the other person's preparation of an academic product to satisfy the other person's academic requirement, and the actor does not offer or provide substantial preparation, writing, or research in the production of the academic product.

(f) It is a defense to prosecution under this section that the actor's conduct consisted solely of typing, transcribing, or reproducing a manuscript for a fee, or of offering to do so.

(g) An offense under this section is a Class C misdemeanor.

Sec. 32.51. Fraudulent Use or Possession of Identifying Information.

(a) In this section:

(1) "Identifying information" means information that alone or in conjunction with other information identifies a person, including a person's:

(A) name and date of birth;

(B) unique biometric data, including the person's fingerprint, voice print, or retina or iris image;

(C) unique electronic identification number, address, routing code, or financial institution account number;

(D) telecommunication identifying information or access device; and

(E) social security number or other government-issued identification number.

(2) "Telecommunication access device" means a card, plate, code, account number, personal identification number, electronic serial number, mobile identification number, or other telecommunications service, equipment, or instrument identifier or means of account access that alone or in conjunction with another telecommunication access device may be used to:

(A) obtain money, goods, services, or other thing of value; or

(B) initiate a transfer of funds other than a transfer originated solely by paper instrument.

(b) A person commits an offense if the person, with the intent to harm or defraud another, obtains, possesses, transfers, or uses an item of:

(1) identifying information of another person without the other person's consent or effective consent;

(2) information concerning a deceased natural person, including a stillborn infant or fetus, that would be identifying information of that person were that person alive, if the item of information is obtained, possessed, transferred, or used without legal authorization; or

(3) identifying information of a child younger than 18 years of age.

(b-1) For the purposes of Subsection (b), the actor is presumed to have the intent to harm or defraud another if the actor possesses:

(1) the identifying information of three or more other persons;

(2) information described by Subsection (b)(2) concerning three or more deceased persons; or

(3) information described by Subdivision (1) or (2) concerning three or more persons or deceased persons.

(b-2) The presumption established under Subsection (b-1) does not apply to a business or other commercial entity or a government agency that is engaged in a business activity or governmental function that does not violate a penal law of this state.

(c) An offense under this section is:

(1) a state jail felony if the number of items obtained, possessed, transferred, or used is less than five;

(2) a felony of the third degree if the number of items obtained, possessed, transferred, or used is five or more but less than 10;

(3) a felony of the second degree if the number of items obtained, possessed, transferred, or used is 10 or more but less than 50; or

(4) a felony of the first degree if the number of items obtained, possessed, transferred, or used is 50 or more.

(c-1) An offense described for purposes of punishment by Subsections (c)(1)—(3) is increased to the next higher category of offense if it is shown on the trial of the offense that:

(1) the offense was committed against an elderly individual as defined by Section 22.04; or

(2) the actor fraudulently used identifying information with the intent to facilitate an offense under Article 62.102, Code of Criminal Procedure.

(d) If a court orders a defendant convicted of an offense under this section to make restitution to the victim of the offense, the court may order the defendant to reimburse the victim for lost income or other expenses, other than attorney's fees, incurred as a result of the offense.

(e) If conduct that constitutes an offense under this section also constitutes an offense under any other law, the actor may be prosecuted under this section, the other law, or both.

Sec. 32.52. Fraudulent, Substandard, or Fictitious Degree.

(a) In this section, "fraudulent or substandard degree" has the meaning assigned by Section 61.302, Education Code.

(b) A person commits an offense if the person:

(1) uses or claims to hold a postsecondary degree that the person knows:

(A) is a fraudulent or substandard degree;

(B) is fictitious or has otherwise not been granted to the person; or

(C) has been revoked; and

(2) uses or claims to hold that degree:

(A) in a written or oral advertisement or other promotion of a business; or

(B) with the intent to:

(i) obtain employment;

(ii) obtain a license or certificate to practice a trade, profession, or occupation;

(iii) obtain a promotion, a compensation or other benefit, or an increase in compensation or other benefit, in employment or in the practice of a trade, profession, or occupation;

(iv) obtain admission to an educational program in this state; or

(v) gain a position in government with authority over another person, regardless of whether the actor receives compensation for the position.

(c) An offense under this section is a Class B misdemeanor.

(d) If conduct that constitutes an offense under this section also constitutes an offense under any other law, the actor may be prosecuted under this section or the other law.

Sec. 32.53. Exploitation of Child, Elderly Individual, or Disabled Individual.

(a) In this section:

(1) "Child," "elderly individual," and "disabled individual" have the meanings assigned by Section 22.04.

(2) "Exploitation" means the illegal or improper use of a child, elderly individual, or disabled individual or of the resources of a child, elderly individual, or disabled individual for monetary or personal benefit, profit, or gain.

(b) A person commits an offense if the person intentionally, knowingly, or recklessly causes the exploitation of a child, elderly individual, or disabled individual.

(c) An offense under this section is a felony of the third degree.

(d) A person who is subject to prosecution under both this section and another section of this code may be prosecuted under either or both sections. Section 3.04 does not apply to criminal episodes prosecuted under both this section and another section of this code. If a criminal episode is prosecuted under both this section and another section of this code and sentences are assessed for convictions under both sections, the sentences shall run concurrently.

(e) With the consent of the appropriate local county or district attorney, the attorney general has concurrent jurisdiction with that consenting local prosecutor to prosecute an offense under this section that involves the Medicaid program.

Sec. 32.54. Fraudulent or Fictitious Military Record.

(a) In this section:

(1) "Military record" means an enlistment record, occupation specialty, medal, award, decoration, or certification obtained by a person through the person's service in the armed forces of the United States or the state military forces.

(2) "State military forces" has the meaning assigned by Section 437.001, Government Code.

(b) A person commits an offense if the person:

(1) uses or claims to hold a military record that the person knows:

(A) is fraudulent;

(B) is fictitious or has otherwise not been granted or assigned to the person; or

(C) has been revoked; and

(2) uses or claims to hold that military record:

(A) in a written or oral advertisement or other promotion of a business; or

(B) with the intent to:

(i) obtain priority in receiving services or resources under Subchapter G, Chapter 302, Labor Code;

(ii) qualify for a veteran's employment preference under Chapter 657, Government Code;

(iii) obtain a license or certificate to practice a trade, profession, or occupation;

(iv) obtain a promotion, compensation, or other benefit, or an increase in compensation or other benefit, in employment or in the practice of a trade, profession, or occupation;

(v) obtain a benefit, service, or donation from another person;

(vi) obtain admission to an educational program in this state; or

(vii) gain a position in state government with authority over another person, regardless of whether the actor receives compensation for the position.

(c) An offense under this section is a Class B misdemeanor.

(d) If conduct that constitutes an offense under this section also constitutes an offense under any other law, the actor may be prosecuted under this section or the other law.

Sec. 32.55. Financial Abuse of Elderly Individual.

(a) In this section:

(1) "Elderly individual" has the meaning assigned by Section 22.04.

(2) "Financial abuse" means the wrongful taking, appropriation, obtaining, retention, or use of, or assisting in the wrongful taking, appropriation, obtaining, retention, or use of, money or other property of another person by any means, including by exerting undue influence. The term includes financial exploitation.

(3) "Financial exploitation" means the wrongful taking, appropriation, obtaining, retention, or use of money or other property of another person by a person who has a relationship of confidence or trust with the other person. Financial exploitation may involve coercion, manipulation, threats, intimidation, misrepresentation, or the exerting of undue influence. The term includes:

(A) the breach of a fiduciary relationship, including the misuse of a durable power of attorney or the abuse of guardianship powers, that results in the unauthorized appropriation, sale, or transfer of another person's property;

(B) the unauthorized taking of personal assets;

(C) the misappropriation, misuse, or unauthorized transfer of another person's money from a personal or a joint account; and

(D) the knowing or intentional failure to effectively use another person's income and assets for the necessities required for the person's support and maintenance.

(b) For purposes of Subsection (a)(3), a person has a relationship of confidence or trust with another person if the person:

(1) is a parent, spouse, adult child, or other relative by blood or marriage of the other person;

(2) is a joint tenant or tenant in common with the other person;

(3) has a legal or fiduciary relationship with the other person;

(4) is a financial planner or investment professional who provides services to the other person; or

(5) is a paid or unpaid caregiver of the other person.

(c) A person commits an offense if the person knowingly engages in the financial abuse of an elderly individual.

(d) An offense under this section is:

(1) a Class B misdemeanor if the value of the property taken, appropriated, obtained, retained, or used is less than $100;

(2) a Class A misdemeanor if the value of the property taken, appropriated, obtained, retained, or used is $100 or more but less than $750;

(3) a state jail felony if the value of the property taken, appropriated, obtained, retained, or used is $750 or more but less than $2,500;

(4) a felony of the third degree if the value of the property taken, appropriated, obtained, retained, or used is $2,500 or more but less than $30,000;

(5) a felony of the second degree if the value of the property taken, appropriated, obtained, retained, or used is $30,000 or more but less than $150,000; and

(6) a felony of the first degree if the value of the property taken, appropriated, obtained, retained, or used is $150,000 or more.

(e) A person who is subject to prosecution under both this section and another section of this code may be prosecuted under either section or both sections.

SUBCHAPTER E SAVINGS AND LOAN ASSOCIATIONS [DELETED]

Sec. 32.71. Embezzlement; Unauthorized Issuance; False Entry [Deleted].

Deleted by Acts 1993, 73rd Leg., ch. 900 (S.B. 1067), § 1.01, effective September 1, 1994.

Sec. 32.72. False Information; Suppressing Evidence [Deleted].

Deleted by Acts 1993, 73rd Leg., ch. 900 (S.B. 1067), § 1.01, effective September 1, 1994.

CHAPTER 33 COMPUTER CRIMES

Sec. 33.01. Definitions.

In this chapter:

(1) "Access" means to approach, instruct, communicate with, store data in, retrieve or intercept data from, alter data or computer software in, or otherwise make use of any resource of a computer, computer network, computer program, or computer system.

(2) "Aggregate amount" means the amount of:

(A) any direct or indirect loss incurred by a victim, including the value of money, property, or service stolen, appropriated, or rendered unrecoverable by the offense; or

(B) any expenditure required by the victim to:

(i) determine whether data or a computer, computer network, computer program, or computer system was altered, acquired, appropriated, damaged, deleted, or disrupted by the offense; or

(ii) attempt to restore, recover, or replace any data altered, acquired, appropriated, damaged, deleted, or disrupted.

(3) "Communication common carrier" means a person who owns or operates a telephone system in this state that includes equipment or facilities for the conveyance, transmission, or reception of communications and who receives compensation from persons who use that system.

(4) "Computer" means an electronic, magnetic, optical, electrochemical, or other high-speed data processing device that performs logical, arithmetic, or memory functions by the manipulations of electronic or magnetic impulses and includes all input, output, processing, storage, or communication facilities that are connected or related to the device.

(5) "Computer network" means the interconnection of two or more computers or computer systems by satellite, microwave, line, or other communication medium with the capability to transmit information among the computers.

(6) "Computer program" means an ordered set of data representing coded instructions or statements that when executed by a computer cause the computer to process data or perform specific functions.

(7) "Computer services" means the product of the use of a computer, the information stored in the computer, or the personnel supporting the computer, including computer time, data processing, and storage functions.

(8) "Computer system" means any combination of a computer or computer network with the documentation, computer software, or physical facilities supporting the computer or computer network.

(9) "Computer software" means a set of computer programs, procedures, and associated documentation related to the operation of a computer, computer system, or computer network.

(10) "Computer virus" means an unwanted computer program or other set of instructions inserted into a computer's memory, operating system, or program that is specifically constructed with the ability to replicate itself or to affect the other programs or files in the computer by attaching a copy of the unwanted program or other set of instructions to one or more computer programs or files.

(10-a) "Critical infrastructure facility" means:

(A) a chemical manufacturing facility;

(B) a refinery;

(C) an electrical power generating facility, substation, switching station, electrical control center, or electrical transmission or distribution facility;

(D) a water intake structure, water treatment facility, wastewater treatment plant, or pump station;

(E) a natural gas transmission compressor station;

(F) a liquid natural gas terminal or storage facility;

(G) a telecommunications central switching office;

(H) a port, railroad switching yard, trucking terminal, or other freight transportation facility;

(I) a gas processing plant, including a plant used in the processing, treatment, or fractionation of natural gas;

(J) a transmission facility used by a federally licensed radio or television station; or

(K) a cable television or video service provider headend.

(11) "Data" means a representation of information, knowledge, facts, concepts, or instructions that is being prepared or has been prepared in a formalized manner and is intended to be stored or processed, is being stored or processed, or has been stored or processed in a computer. Data may be embodied in any form, including but not limited to computer printouts, magnetic storage media, laser storage media, and punchcards, or may be stored internally in the memory of the computer.

(11-a) "Decryption," "decrypt," or "decrypted" means the decoding of encrypted communications or information, whether by use of a decryption key, by breaking an encryption formula or algorithm, or by the interference with a person's use of an encryption service in a manner that causes information or communications to be stored or transmitted without encryption.

(12) "Effective consent" includes consent by a person legally authorized to act for the owner. Consent is not effective if:

(A) induced by deception, as defined by Section 31.01, or induced by coercion;

(B) given by a person the actor knows is not legally authorized to act for the owner;

(C) given by a person who by reason of youth, mental disease or defect, or intoxication is known by the actor to be unable to make reasonable property dispositions;

(D) given solely to detect the commission of an offense; or

(E) used for a purpose other than that for which the consent was given.

(13) "Electric utility" has the meaning assigned by Section 31.002, Utilities Code.

(13-a) "Encrypted private information" means encrypted data, documents, wire or electronic communications, or other information stored on a computer or computer system, whether in the possession of the owner or a provider of an electronic communications service or a remote computing service, and which has not been accessible to the public.

(13-b) "Encryption," "encrypt," or "encrypted" means the encoding of data, documents, wire or electronic communications, or other information, using mathematical formulas or algorithms in order to preserve the confidentiality, integrity, or authenticity of, and prevent unauthorized access to, such information.

(13-c) "Encryption service" means a computing service, a computer device, computer software, or technology with encryption capabilities, and includes any subsequent version of or update to an encryption service.

(14) "Harm" includes partial or total alteration, damage, or erasure of stored data, interruption of computer services, introduction of a computer virus, or any other loss, disadvantage, or injury that might reasonably be suffered as a result of the actor's conduct.

(14-a) "Identifying information" has the meaning assigned by Section 32.51.

(15) "Owner" means a person who:

(A) has title to the property, possession of the property, whether lawful or not, or a greater right to possession of the property than the actor;

(B) has the right to restrict access to the property; or

(C) is the licensee of data or computer software.

(15-a) "Privileged information" means:

(A) protected health information, as that term is defined by Section 182.002, Health and Safety Code;

(B) information that is subject to the attorney-client privilege; or

(C) information that is subject to the accountant-client privilege under Section 901.457, Occupations Code, or other law, if the information is on a computer, computer network, or computer system owned by a person possessing a license issued under Subchapter H, Chapter 901, Occupations Code.

(16) "Property" means:

(A) tangible or intangible personal property including a computer, computer system, computer network, computer software, or data; or

(B) the use of a computer, computer system, computer network, computer software, or data.

Sec. 33.02. Breach of Computer Security.

(a) A person commits an offense if the person knowingly accesses a computer, computer network, or computer system without the effective consent of the owner.

(b) An offense under Subsection (a) is a Class B misdemeanor, except that the offense is a state jail felony if:

(1) the defendant has been previously convicted two or more times of an offense under this chapter; or

(2) the computer, computer network, or computer system is owned by the government or a critical infrastructure facility.

(b-1) A person commits an offense if, with the intent to defraud or harm another or alter, damage, or delete property, the person knowingly accesses:

(1) a computer, computer network, or computer system without the effective consent of the owner; or

(2) a computer, computer network, or computer system:

(A) that is owned by:

(i) the government; or

(ii) a business or other commercial entity engaged in a business activity;

(B) in violation of:

(i) a clear and conspicuous prohibition by the owner of the computer, computer network, or computer system; or

(ii) a contractual agreement to which the person has expressly agreed; and

(C) with the intent to obtain or use a file, data, or proprietary information stored in the computer, network, or system to defraud or harm another or alter, damage, or delete property.

(b-2) An offense under Subsection (b-1) is:

(1) a Class C misdemeanor if the aggregate amount involved is less than $100;

(2) a Class B misdemeanor if the aggregate amount involved is $100 or more but less than $750;

(3) a Class A misdemeanor if the aggregate amount involved is $750 or more but less than $2,500;

(4) a state jail felony if the aggregate amount involved is $2,500 or more but less than $30,000;

(5) a felony of the third degree if the aggregate amount involved is $30,000 or more but less than $150,000;

(6) a felony of the second degree if:

(A) the aggregate amount involved is $150,000 or more but less than $300,000;

(B) the aggregate amount involved is any amount less than $300,000 and the computer, computer network, or computer system is owned by the government or a critical infrastructure facility; or

(C) the actor obtains the identifying information of another by accessing only one computer, computer network, or computer system; or

(7) a felony of the first degree if:

(A) the aggregate amount involved is $300,000 or more; or

(B) the actor obtains the identifying information of another by accessing more than one computer, computer network, or computer system.

(c) When benefits are obtained, a victim is defrauded or harmed, or property is altered, damaged, or deleted in violation of this section, whether or not in a single incident, the conduct may be considered as one offense and the value of the benefits obtained and of the losses incurred because of the fraud, harm, or alteration, damage, or deletion of property may be aggregated in determining the grade of the offense.

(d) A person who is subject to prosecution under this section and any other section of this code may be prosecuted under either or both sections.

(e) It is a defense to prosecution under this section that the person acted with the intent to facilitate a lawful seizure or search of, or lawful access to, a computer, computer network, or computer system for a legitimate law enforcement purpose.

(f) It is a defense to prosecution under Subsection (b-1)(2) that the actor's conduct consisted solely of action taken pursuant to a contract that was entered into with the owner of the computer, computer network, or computer system for the purpose of assessing the security of the computer, network, or system or providing other security-related services.

Sec. 33.021. Online Solicitation of a Minor.

(a) In this section:

(1) "Minor" means:

(A) an individual who is younger than 17 years of age; or

(B) an individual whom the actor believes to be younger than 17 years of age.

(2) "Sexual contact," "sexual intercourse," and "deviate sexual intercourse" have the meanings assigned by Section 21.01.

(3) "Sexually explicit" means any communication, language, or material, including a photographic or video image, that relates to or describes sexual conduct, as defined by Section 43.25.

(b) A person who is 17 years of age or older commits an offense if, with the intent to commit an offense listed in Article 62.001(5)(A), (B), or (K), Code of Criminal Procedure, the person, over the Internet, by electronic mail or text message or other electronic message service or system, or through a commercial online service, intentionally:

(1) communicates in a sexually explicit manner with a minor; or

(2) distributes sexually explicit material to a minor.

(c) A person commits an offense if the person, over the Internet, by electronic mail or text message or other electronic message service or system, or through a commercial online service, knowingly solicits a minor to meet another person, including the actor, with the intent that the minor will engage in sexual contact, sexual intercourse, or deviate sexual intercourse with the actor or another person.

(d) It is not a defense to prosecution under Subsection (c) that the meeting did not occur.

(e) It is a defense to prosecution under this section that at the time conduct described by Subsection (c) was committed:

(1) the actor was married to the minor; or

(2) the actor was not more than three years older than the minor and the minor consented to the conduct.

(f) An offense under Subsection (b) is a felony of the third degree, except that the offense is a felony of the second degree if the minor is younger than 14 years of age or is an individual whom the actor believes to be younger than 14 years of age at the time of the commission of the offense. An offense under Subsection (c) is a felony of the second degree.

(f-1) The punishment for an offense under this section is increased to the punishment prescribed for the next higher category of offense if it is shown on the trial of the offense that:

(1) the actor committed the offense during regular public or private primary or secondary school hours; and

(2) the actor knew or reasonably should have known that the minor was enrolled in a public or private primary or secondary school at the time of the offense.

(g) If conduct that constitutes an offense under this section also constitutes an offense under any other law, the actor may be prosecuted under this section, the other law, or both.

Sec. 33.022. Electronic Access Interference.

(a) A person, other than a network provider or online service provider acting for a legitimate business purpose, commits an offense if the person intentionally interrupts or suspends access to a computer system or computer network without the effective consent of the owner.

(b) An offense under this section is a third degree felony.

(c) It is a defense to prosecution under this section that the person acted with the intent to facilitate a lawful seizure or search of, or lawful access to, a computer, computer network, or computer system for a legitimate law enforcement purpose.

Sec. 33.023. Electronic Data Tampering.

(a) In this section, "ransomware" means a computer contaminant or lock that restricts access by an unauthorized person to a computer, computer system, or computer network or any data in a computer, computer system, or computer network under circumstances in which a person demands money, property, or a service to remove the computer contaminant or lock, restore access to the computer, computer system, computer network, or data, or otherwise remediate the impact of the computer contaminant or lock.

(b) A person commits an offense if the person intentionally alters data as it transmits between two computers in a computer network or computer system through deception and without a legitimate business purpose.

(c) A person commits an offense if the person intentionally introduces ransomware onto a computer, computer network, or computer system through deception and without a legitimate business purpose.

(d) Subject to Subsections (d-1) and (d-2), an offense under this section is a Class C misdemeanor.

(d-1) Subject to Subsection (d-2), if it is shown on the trial of the offense that the defendant acted with the intent to defraud or harm another, an offense under this section is:

(1) a Class C misdemeanor if the aggregate amount involved is less than $100 or cannot be determined;

(2) a Class B misdemeanor if the aggregate amount involved is $100 or more but less than $750;

(3) a Class A misdemeanor if the aggregate amount involved is $750 or more but less than $2,500;

(4) a state jail felony if the aggregate amount involved is $2,500 or more but less than $30,000;

(5) a felony of the third degree if the aggregate amount involved is $30,000 or more but less than $150,000;

(6) a felony of the second degree if the aggregate amount involved is $150,000 or more but less than $300,000; and

(7) a felony of the first degree if the aggregate amount involved is $300,000 or more.

(d-2) If it is shown on the trial of the offense that the defendant knowingly restricted a victim's access to privileged information, an offense under this section is:

(1) a state jail felony if the value of the aggregate amount involved is less than $2,500;

(2) a felony of the third degree if:

(A) the value of the aggregate amount involved is $2,500 or more but less than $30,000; or

(B) a client or patient of a victim suffered harm attributable to the offense;

(3) a felony of the second degree if:

(A) the value of the aggregate amount involved is $30,000 or more but less than $150,000; or

(B) a client or patient of a victim suffered bodily injury attributable to the offense; and

(4) a felony of the first degree if:

(A) the value of the aggregate amount involved is $150,000 or more; or

(B) a client or patient of a victim suffered serious bodily injury or death attributable to the offense.

(e) When benefits are obtained, a victim is defrauded or harmed, or property is altered, appropriated, damaged, or deleted in violation of this section, whether or not in a single incident, the conduct may be considered as one offense and the value of the benefits obtained and of the losses incurred because of the fraud, harm, or alteration, appropriation, damage, or deletion of property may be aggregated in determining the grade of the offense.

(f) A person who is subject to prosecution under this section and any other section of this code may be prosecuted under either or both sections.

(g) Software is not ransomware for the purposes of this section if the software restricts access to data because:

(1) authentication is required to upgrade or access purchased content; or

(2) access to subscription content has been blocked for nonpayment.

Sec. 33.024. Unlawful Decryption.

(a) A person commits an offense if the person intentionally decrypts encrypted private information through deception and without a legitimate business purpose.

(b) Subject to Subsections (b-1) and (b-2), an offense under this section is a Class C misdemeanor.

(b-1) Subject to Subsection (b-2), if it is shown on the trial of the offense that the defendant acted with the intent to defraud or harm another, an offense under this section is:

(1) a Class C misdemeanor if the value of the aggregate amount involved is less than $100 or cannot be determined;

(2) a Class B misdemeanor if the value of the aggregate amount involved is $100 or more but less than $750;

(3) a Class A misdemeanor if the value of the aggregate amount involved is $750 or more but less than $2,500;

(4) a state jail felony if the value of the aggregate amount involved is $2,500 or more but less than $30,000;

(5) a felony of the third degree if the value of the aggregate amount involved is $30,000 or more but less than $150,000;

(6) a felony of the second degree if the value of the aggregate amount involved is $150,000 or more but less than $300,000; and

(7) a felony of the first degree if the value of the aggregate amount involved is $300,000 or more.

(b-2) If it is shown on the trial of the offense that the defendant knowingly decrypted privileged information, an offense under this section is:

(1) a state jail felony if the value of the aggregate amount involved is less than $2,500;

(2) a felony of the third degree if:

(A) the value of the aggregate amount involved is $2,500 or more but less than $30,000; or

(B) a client or patient of a victim suffered harm attributable to the offense;

(3) a felony of the second degree if:

(A) the value of the aggregate amount involved is $30,000 or more but less than $150,000; or

(B) a client or patient of a victim suffered bodily injury attributable to the offense; and

(4) a felony of the first degree if:

(A) the value of the aggregate amount involved is $150,000 or more; or

(B) a client or patient of a victim suffered serious bodily injury or death attributable to the offense.

(c) It is a defense to prosecution under this section that the actor's conduct was pursuant to an agreement entered into with the owner for the purpose of:

(1) assessing or maintaining the security of the information or of a computer, computer network, or computer system; or

(2) providing other services related to security.

(d) A person who is subject to prosecution under this section and any other section of this code may be prosecuted under either or both sections.

Sec. 33.03. Defenses.

It is an affirmative defense to prosecution under Section 33.02 or 33.022 that the actor was an officer, employee, or agent of a communication common carrier or electric utility and committed the proscribed act or acts in the course of employment while engaged in an activity that is a necessary incident to the rendition of service or to the protection of the rights or property of the communication common carrier or electric utility.

Sec. 33.04. Assistance by Attorney General.

The attorney general, if requested to do so by a prosecuting attorney, may assist the prosecuting attorney in the investigation or prosecution of an offense under this chapter or of any other offense involving the use of a computer.

Sec. 33.05. Tampering with Direct Recording Electronic Voting Machine.

(a) In this section:

(1) "Direct recording electronic voting machine" has the meaning assigned by Section 121.003, Election Code.

(2) "Measure" has the meaning assigned by Section 1.005, Election Code.

(b) A person commits an offense if the person knowingly accesses a computer, computer network, computer program, computer software, or computer system that is a part of a voting system that uses direct recording electronic voting machines and by means of that access:

(1) prevents a person from lawfully casting a vote;

(2) changes a lawfully cast vote;

(3) prevents a lawfully cast vote from being counted; or

(4) causes a vote that was not lawfully cast to be counted.

(c) An offense under this section does not require that the votes as affected by the person's actions described by Subsection (b) actually be the votes used in the official determination of the outcome of the election.

(d) An offense under this section is a felony of the first degree.

(e) Notwithstanding Section 15.01(d), an offense under Section 15.01(a) is a felony of the third degree if the offense the actor intends to commit is an offense under this section.

(f) With the consent of the appropriate local county or district attorney, the attorney general has concurrent jurisdiction with that consenting local prosecutor to investigate or prosecute an offense under this section.

Sec. 33.07. Online Impersonation.

(a) A person commits an offense if the person, without obtaining the other person's consent and with the intent to harm, defraud, intimidate, or threaten any person, uses the name or persona of another person to:

(1) create a web page on a commercial social networking site or other Internet website; or

(2) post or send one or more messages on or through a commercial social networking site or other Internet website, other than on or through an electronic mail program or message board program.

(b) A person commits an offense if the person sends an electronic mail, instant message, text message, or similar communication that references a name, domain address, phone number, or other item of identifying information belonging to any person:

(1) without obtaining the other person's consent;

(2) with the intent to cause a recipient of the communication to reasonably believe that the other person authorized or transmitted the communication; and

(3) with the intent to harm or defraud any person.

(c) An offense under Subsection (a) is a felony of the third degree. An offense under Subsection (b) is a Class A misdemeanor, except that the offense is a felony of the third degree if the actor commits the offense with the intent to solicit a response by emergency personnel.

(d) If conduct that constitutes an offense under this section also constitutes an offense under any other law, the actor may be prosecuted under this section, the other law, or both.

(e) It is a defense to prosecution under this section that the actor is any of the following entities or that the actor's conduct consisted solely of action taken as an employee of any of the following entities:

(1) a commercial social networking site;

(2) an Internet service provider;

(3) an interactive computer service, as defined by 47 U.S.C. Section 230;

(4) a telecommunications provider, as defined by Section 51.002, Utilities Code; or

(5) a video service provider or cable service provider, as defined by Section 66.002, Utilities Code.

(f) In this section:

(1) "Commercial social networking site" means any business, organization, or other similar entity operating a website that permits persons to become registered users for the purpose of establishing personal relationships with other users through direct or real-time communication with other users or the creation of web pages or profiles available to the public or to other users. The term does not include an electronic mail program or a message board program.

(2) "Identifying information" has the meaning assigned by Section 32.51.

CHAPTER 33A TELECOMMUNICATIONS CRIMES

Sec. 33A.01. Definitions.

In this chapter:

(1) "Counterfeit telecommunications access device" means a telecommunications access device that is false, fraudulent, not issued to a legitimate telecommunications access device subscriber account, or otherwise unlawful or invalid.

(2) "Counterfeit telecommunications device" means a telecommunications device that has been altered or programmed alone or with another telecommunications device to acquire, intercept, receive, or otherwise facilitate the use of a telecommunications service without the authority or consent of the telecommunications service provider and includes a clone telephone, clone microchip, tumbler telephone, tumbler microchip, or wireless scanning device capable of acquiring, intercepting, receiving, or otherwise facilitating the use of a telecommunications service without immediate detection.

(3) "Deliver" means to actually or constructively sell, give, loan, or otherwise transfer a telecommunications device, or a counterfeit telecommunications device or any telecommunications plans, instructions, or materials, to another person.

(4) "Publish" means to communicate information or make information available to another person orally, in writing, or by means of telecommunications and includes communicating information on a computer bulletin board or similar system.

(5) "Telecommunications" means the origination, emission, transmission, or reception of data, images, signals, sounds, or other intelligence or equivalence of intelligence over a communications system by any method, including an electronic, magnetic, optical, digital, or analog method.

(6) "Telecommunications access device" means an instrument, device, card, plate, code, account number, personal identification number, electronic serial number, mobile identification number, counterfeit number, or financial transaction device that alone or with another telecommunications access device can acquire, intercept, provide, receive, use, or otherwise facilitate the use of a telecommunications device, counterfeit telecommunications device, or telecommunications service.

(7) "Telecommunications device" means any instrument, equipment, machine, or device that facilitates telecommunications and includes a computer, computer chip or circuit, telephone, pager, personal communications device, transponder, receiver, radio, modem, or device that enables use of a modem.

(8) "Telecommunications service" means the provision, facilitation, or generation of telecommunications through the use of a telecommunications device or telecommunications access device over a telecommunications system.

(9) "Value of the telecommunications service obtained or attempted to be obtained" includes the value of:

(A) a lawful charge for telecommunications service avoided or attempted to be avoided;

(B) money, property, or telecommunications service lost, stolen, or rendered unrecoverable by an offense; and

(C) an expenditure incurred by a victim to verify that a telecommunications device or telecommunications access device or telecommunications service was not altered, acquired, damaged, or disrupted as a result of an offense.

Sec. 33A.02. Unauthorized Use of Telecommunications Service.

(a) A person commits an offense if the person is an officer, shareholder, partner, employee, agent, or independent contractor of a telecommunications service provider and the person knowingly and without authority uses or diverts telecommunications service for the person's own benefit or to the benefit of another.

(b) An offense under this section is:

(1) a Class B misdemeanor if the value of the telecommunications service used or diverted is less than $500;

(2) a Class A misdemeanor if:

(A) the value of the telecommunications service used or diverted is $500 or more but less than $1,500; or

(B) the value of the telecommunications service used or diverted is less than $500 and the defendant has been previously convicted of an offense under this chapter;

(3) a state jail felony if:

(A) the value of the telecommunications service used or diverted is $1,500 or more but less than $20,000; or

(B) the value of the telecommunications service used or diverted is less than $1,500 and the defendant has been previously convicted two or more times of an offense under this chapter;

(4) a felony of the third degree if the value of the telecommunications service used or diverted is $20,000 or more but less than $100,000;

(5) a felony of the second degree if the value of the telecommunications service used or diverted is $100,000 or more but less than $200,000; or

(6) a felony of the first degree if the value of the telecommunications service used or diverted is $200,000 or more.

(c) When telecommunications service is used or diverted in violation of this section pursuant to one scheme or continuing course of conduct, whether or not in a single incident, the conduct may be considered as one offense and the values of the service used or diverted may be aggregated in determining the grade of the offense.

Sec. 33A.03. Manufacture, Possession, or Delivery of Unlawful Telecommunications Device.

(a) A person commits an offense if the person manufactures, possesses, delivers, offers to deliver, or advertises:

(1) a counterfeit telecommunications device; or

(2) a telecommunications device that is intended to be used to:

(A) commit an offense under Section 33A.04; or

(B) conceal the existence or place of origin or destination of a telecommunications service.

(b) A person commits an offense if the person delivers, offers to deliver, or advertises plans, instructions, or materials for manufacture of:

(1) a counterfeit telecommunications device; or

(2) a telecommunications device that is intended to be used to commit an offense under Subsection (a).

(c) An offense under this section is a felony of the third degree.

(d) It is a defense to prosecution under this section that the person was an officer, agent, or employee of a telecommunications service provider who engaged in the conduct for the purpose of gathering information for a law enforcement investigation related to an offense under this chapter.

Sec. 33A.04. Theft of Telecommunications Service.

(a) A person commits an offense if the person knowingly obtains or attempts to obtain telecommunications service to avoid or cause another person to avoid a lawful charge for that service by using:

(1) a telecommunications access device without the authority or consent of the subscriber or lawful holder of the device or pursuant to an agreement for an exchange of value with the subscriber or lawful holder of the device to allow another person to use the device;

(2) a counterfeit telecommunications access device;

(3) a telecommunications device or counterfeit telecommunications device; or

(4) a fraudulent or deceptive scheme, pretense, method, or conspiracy, or other device or means, including a false, altered, or stolen identification.

(b) An offense under this section is:

(1) a Class B misdemeanor if the value of the telecommunications service obtained or attempted to be obtained is less than $500;

(2) a Class A misdemeanor if:

(A) the value of the telecommunications service obtained or attempted to be obtained is $500 or more but less than $1,500; or

(B) the value of the telecommunications service obtained or attempted to be obtained is less than $500 and the defendant has been previously convicted of an offense under this chapter;

(3) a state jail felony if:

(A) the value of the telecommunications service obtained or attempted to be obtained is $1,500 or more but less than $20,000; or

(B) the value of the telecommunications service obtained or attempted to be obtained is less than $1,500 and the defendant has been previously convicted two or more times of an offense under this chapter;

(4) a felony of the third degree if the value of the telecommunications service obtained or attempted to be obtained is $20,000 or more but less than $100,000;

(5) a felony of the second degree if the value of the telecommunications service obtained or attempted to be obtained is $100,000 or more but less than $200,000; or

(6) a felony of the first degree if the value of the telecommunications service obtained or attempted to be obtained is $200,000 or more.

(c) When telecommunications service is obtained or attempted to be obtained in violation of this section pursuant to one scheme or continuing course of conduct, whether or not in a single incident, the conduct may be considered as one offense and the values of the service obtained or attempted to be obtained may be aggregated in determining the grade of the offense.

Sec. 33A.05. Publication of Telecommunications Access Device.

(a) A person commits an offense if the person with criminal negligence publishes a telecommunications access device or counterfeit telecommunications access device that is designed to be used to commit an offense under Section 33A.04.

(b) Except as otherwise provided by this subsection, an offense under this section is a Class A misdemeanor. An offense under this section is a felony of the third degree if the person has been previously convicted of an offense under this chapter.

Sec. 33A.051. False Caller Identification Information Display.

(a) A person commits an offense if the person, with the intent to defraud or cause harm, makes a call or engages in any other conduct using any type of technology that results in the display on another person's telecommunications device of data that misrepresents the actor's identity or telephone number.

(b) An offense under this section is a Class A misdemeanor.

(c) Notwithstanding any other provision of this chapter, a conviction for an offense under this section may not be used for enhancement purposes under any other section of this chapter.

(d) It is a defense to prosecution that the actor:

(1) blocked caller identification information;

(2) was a peace officer or federal law enforcement officer lawfully discharging an official duty;

(3) was an officer, agent, or employee of a federal intelligence or security agency lawfully discharging an official duty;

(4) was an officer, agent, or employee of a telecommunications service provider who was:

(A) acting in the provider's capacity as an intermediary for the transmission of telephone service, a Voice over Internet Protocol transmission, or another type of telecommunications transmission between the caller and the recipient;

(B) providing or configuring a service or service feature as requested by a customer;

(C) acting in a manner that is authorized or required by other law; or

(D) engaging in other conduct that is a necessary incident to the provision of service; or

(5) was a private investigator licensed under Chapter 1702, Occupations Code, lawfully conducting an investigation.

(e) For the purposes of this section, "telecommunications service provider" means a:

(1) telecommunications provider, as defined by Section 51.002, Utilities Code; or

(2) provider of telecommunications service, advanced communications services, or information service, as those terms are defined by 47 U.S.C. Section 153.

Sec. 33A.06. Assistance by Attorney General.

The attorney general, if requested to do so by a prosecuting attorney, may assist the prosecuting attorney in the investigation or prosecution of an offense under this chapter or of any other offense involving the use of telecommunications equipment, services, or devices.

CHAPTER 34
MONEY LAUNDERING

Sec. 34.01. Definitions.

In this chapter:

(1) "Criminal activity" means any offense, including any preparatory offense, that is:

(A) classified as a felony under the laws of this state or the United States; or

(B) punishable by confinement for more than one year under the laws of another state.

(2) "Funds" includes:

(A) coin or paper money of the United States or any other country that is designated as legal tender and that circulates and is customarily used and accepted as a medium of exchange in the country of issue;

(B) United States silver certificates, United States Treasury notes, and Federal Reserve System notes;

(C) an official foreign bank note that is customarily used and accepted as a medium of exchange in a foreign country and a foreign bank draft; and

(D) currency or its equivalent, including an electronic fund, a personal check, a bank check, a traveler's check, a money order, a bearer negotiable instrument, a bearer investment security, a bearer security, a certificate of stock in a form that allows title to pass on delivery, a stored value card as defined by Section 604.001, Business & Commerce Code, or a digital currency.

(3) "Financial institution" has the meaning assigned by Section 32.01.

(4) "Proceeds" means funds acquired or derived directly or indirectly from, produced through, realized through, or used in the commission of:

(A) an act; or

(B) conduct that constitutes an offense under Section 151.7032, Tax Code.

Sec. 34.02. Money Laundering.

(a) A person commits an offense if the person knowingly:

(1) acquires or maintains an interest in, conceals, possesses, transfers, or transports the proceeds of criminal activity;

(2) conducts, supervises, or facilitates a transaction involving the proceeds of criminal activity;

(3) invests, expends, or receives, or offers to invest, expend, or receive, the proceeds of criminal activity or funds that the person believes are the proceeds of criminal activity; or

(4) finances or invests or intends to finance or invest funds that the person believes are intended to further the commission of criminal activity.

(a-1) Knowledge of the specific nature of the criminal activity giving rise to the proceeds is not required to establish a culpable mental state under this section.

(b) For purposes of this section, a person is presumed to believe that funds are the proceeds of or are intended to further the commission of criminal activity if a peace officer or a person acting at the direction of a peace officer represents to the person that the funds are proceeds of or are intended to further the commission of criminal activity, as applicable, regardless of whether the peace officer or person acting at the peace officer's direction discloses the person's status as a peace officer or that the person is acting at the direction of a peace officer.

(c) It is a defense to prosecution under this section that the person acted with intent to facilitate the lawful seizure, forfeiture, or disposition of funds or other legitimate law enforcement purpose pursuant to the laws of this state or the United States.

(d) It is a defense to prosecution under this section that the transaction was necessary to preserve a person's right to representation as guaranteed by the Sixth Amendment of the United States Constitution and by Article 1, Section 10, of the Texas Constitution or that the funds were received as bona fide legal fees by a licensed attorney and at the time of their receipt, the attorney did not have actual knowledge that the funds were derived from criminal activity.

(e) An offense under this section is:

(1) a state jail felony if the value of the funds is $2,500 or more but less than $30,000;

(2) a felony of the third degree if the value of the funds is $30,000 or more but less than $150,000;

(3) a felony of the second degree if the value of the funds is $150,000 or more but less than $300,000; or

(4) a felony of the first degree if the value of the funds is $300,000 or more.

(f) For purposes of this section, if proceeds of criminal activity are related to one scheme or continuing course of conduct, whether from the same or several sources, the conduct may be considered as one offense and the value of the proceeds aggregated in determining the classification of the offense.

(g) For purposes of this section, funds on deposit at a branch of a financial institution are considered the property of that branch and any other branch of the financial institution.

(h) If conduct that constitutes an offense under this section also constitutes an offense under any other law, the actor may be prosecuted under this section, the other law, or both.

Sec. 34.021. Protection from Civil Liability.

Notwithstanding Section 1.03(c), a financial institution or an agent of the financial institution acting in a manner described by Section 34.02(c) is not liable for civil damages to a person who:

(1) claims an ownership interest in funds involved in an offense under Section 34.02; or

(2) conducts with the financial institution or an insurer, as defined by Article 1.02, Insurance Code, a transaction concerning funds involved in an offense under Section 34.02.

Sec. 34.03. Assistance by Attorney General.

The attorney general, if requested to do so by a prosecuting attorney, may assist in the prosecution of an offense under this chapter.

CHAPTER 35
INSURANCE FRAUD

Sec. 35.01. Definitions.

In this chapter:

(1) "Insurance policy" means a written instrument in which is provided the terms of any certificate of insurance, binder of coverage, contract of insurance, benefit plan, nonprofit hospital service plan, motor club service plan, surety bond, cash bond, or any other alternative to insurance authorized by Chapter 601, Transportation Code. The term includes any instrument authorized to be regulated by the Texas Department of Insurance.

(2) "Insurer" has the meaning assigned by Article 1.02, Insurance Code.

(3) "Statement" means an oral or written communication or a record or documented representation of fact made to an insurer. The term includes computer-generated information.

(4) "Value of the claim" means the total dollar amount of a claim for payment under an insurance policy or, as applicable, the value of the claim determined under Section 35.025.

Sec. 35.015. Materiality.

A statement is material for the purposes of this chapter, regardless of the admissibility of the statement at trial, if the statement could have affected:

(1) the eligibility for coverage or amount of the payment on a claim for payment under an insurance policy; or

(2) the decision of an insurer whether to issue an insurance policy.

Sec. 35.02. Insurance Fraud.

(a) A person commits an offense if, with intent to defraud or deceive an insurer, the person, in support of a claim for payment under an insurance policy:

(1) prepares or causes to be prepared a statement that:

(A) the person knows contains false or misleading material information; and

(B) is presented to an insurer; or

(2) presents or causes to be presented to an insurer a statement that the person knows contains false or misleading material information.

(a-1) A person commits an offense if the person, with intent to defraud or deceive an insurer and in support of an application for an insurance policy:

(1) prepares or causes to be prepared a statement that:

(A) the person knows contains false or misleading material information; and

(B) is presented to an insurer; or

(2) presents or causes to be presented to an insurer a statement that the person knows contains false or misleading material information.

(b) A person commits an offense if, with intent to defraud or deceive an insurer, the person solicits, offers, pays, or receives a benefit in connection with the furnishing of goods or services for which a claim for payment is submitted under an insurance policy.

(c) An offense under Subsection (a) or (b) is:

(1) a Class C misdemeanor if the value of the claim is less than $100;

(2) a Class B misdemeanor if the value of the claim is $100 or more but less than $750;

(3) a Class A misdemeanor if the value of the claim is $750 or more but less than $2,500;

(4) a state jail felony if the value of the claim is $2,500 or more but less than $30,000;

(5) a felony of the third degree if the value of the claim is $30,000 or more but less than $150,000;

(6) a felony of the second degree if the value of the claim is $150,000 or more but less than $300,000; or

(7) a felony of the first degree if:

(A) the value of the claim is $300,000 or more; or

(B) an act committed in connection with the commission of the offense places a person at risk of death or serious bodily injury.

(d) An offense under Subsection (a-1) is a state jail felony.

(e) The court shall order a defendant convicted of an offense under this section to pay restitution, including court costs and attorney's fees, to an affected insurer.

(f) If conduct that constitutes an offense under this section also constitutes an offense under any other law, the actor may be prosecuted under this section, the other law, or both.

(g) For purposes of this section, if the actor proves by a preponderance of the evidence that a portion of the claim for payment under an insurance policy resulted from a valid loss, injury, expense, or service covered by the policy, the value of the claim is equal to the difference between the total claim amount and the amount of the valid portion of the claim.

(h) If it is shown on the trial of an offense under this section that the actor submitted a bill for goods or services in support of a claim for payment under an insurance policy to the insurer issuing the policy, a rebuttable presumption exists that the actor caused the claim for payment to be prepared or presented.

Sec. 35.025. Value of Claim.

(a) Except as provided by Subsection (b) and subject to Subsection (c), for the purposes of Section 35.02(c), if the value of a claim is not readily ascertainable, the value of the claim is:

(1) the fair market value, at the time and place of the offense, of the goods or services that are the subject of the claim; or

(2) the cost of replacing the goods or services that are the subject of the claim within a reasonable time after the claim.

(b) If goods or services that are the subject of a claim cannot be reasonably ascertained under Subsection (a), the goods or services are considered to have a value of $750 or more but less than $2,500.

(c) If the actor proves by a preponderance of the evidence that a portion of the claim for payment under an insurance policy resulted from a valid loss, injury, expense, or service covered by the policy, the value of the claim is equal to the difference between the total claim amount and the amount of the valid portion of the claim.

Sec. 35.03. Aggregation and Multiple Offenses.

(a) When separate claims in violation of this chapter are communicated to an insurer or group of insurers pursuant to one scheme or continuing course of conduct, the conduct may be considered as one offense and the value of the claims aggregated in determining the classification of the offense. If claims are aggregated under this subsection, Subsection (b) shall not apply.

(b) When three or more separate claims in violation of this chapter are communicated to an insurer or group of insurers pursuant to one scheme or continuing course of conduct, the conduct may be considered as one offense, and the classification of the offense shall be one category higher than the most serious single offense proven from the separate claims, except that if the most serious offense is a felony of the first degree, the offense is a felony of the first degree. This subsection shall not be applied if claims are aggregated under Subsection (a).

Sec. 35.04. Jurisdiction of Attorney General.

(a) The attorney general may offer to an attorney representing the state in the prosecution of an offense under Section 35.02 the investigative, technical, and litigation assistance of the attorney general's office.

(b) The attorney general may prosecute or assist in the prosecution of an offense under Section 35.02 on the request of the attorney representing the state described by Subsection (a).

CHAPTER 35A HEALTH CARE FRAUD

Sec. 35A.01. Definitions.

In this chapter:

(1) "Claim" means a written or electronically submitted request or demand that:

(A) is submitted by a provider or the provider's agent and identifies a service or product provided or purported to have been provided to a health care recipient as reimbursable under a health care program, without regard to whether the money that is requested or demanded is paid; or

(B) states the income earned or expense incurred by a provider in providing a service or product and is used to determine a rate of payment under a health care program.

(2) "Fiscal agent" means:

(A) a person who, through a contractual relationship with a state agency or the federal government, receives, processes, and pays a claim under a health care program; or

(B) the designated agent of a person described by Paragraph (A).

(3) "Health care practitioner" means a dentist, podiatrist, psychologist, physical therapist, chiropractor, registered nurse, or other provider licensed to provide health care services in this state.

(4) "Health care program" means a program funded by this state, the federal government, or both and designed to provide health care services to health care recipients, including a program that is administered in whole or in part through a managed care delivery model.

(5) "Health care recipient" means an individual to whom a service or product is provided or purported to have been provided and with respect to whom a person claims or receives a payment for that service or product from a health care program or fiscal agent, without regard to whether the individual was eligible for benefits under the health care program.

(6) "Managed care organization" means a person who is authorized or otherwise permitted by law to arrange for or provide a managed care plan.

(7) "Physician" means a physician licensed to practice medicine in this state.

(8) "Provider" means a person who participates in or has applied to participate in a health care program as a supplier of a service or product and includes:

(A) a management company that manages, operates, or controls another provider;

(B) a person, including a medical vendor, who provides a service or product to another provider or the other provider's agent;

(C) an employee of the person who participates in or has applied to participate in the program;

(D) a managed care organization; and

(E) a manufacturer or distributor of a product for which a health care program provides reimbursement.

(9) "Service" includes care or treatment of a health care recipient.

(10) "High managerial agent" means a director, officer, or employee who is authorized to act on behalf of a provider and has duties of such responsibility that the conduct of the director, officer, or employee reasonably may be assumed to represent the policy or intent of the provider.

Sec. 35A.02. Health Care Fraud.

(a) A person commits an offense if the person:

(1) knowingly makes or causes to be made a false statement or misrepresentation of a material fact to permit a person to receive a benefit or payment under a health care program that is not authorized or that is greater than the benefit or payment that is authorized;

(2) knowingly conceals or fails to disclose information that permits a person to receive a benefit or payment under a health care program that is not authorized or that is greater than the benefit or payment that is authorized;

(3) knowingly applies for and receives a benefit or payment on behalf of another person under a health care program and converts any part of the benefit or payment to a use other than for the benefit of the person on whose behalf it was received;

(4) knowingly makes, causes to be made, induces, or seeks to induce the making of a false statement or misrepresentation of material fact concerning:

(A) the conditions or operation of a facility in order that the facility may qualify for certification or recertification under a health care program; or

(B) information required to be provided by a federal or state law, rule, regulation, or provider agreement pertaining to a health care program;

(5) except as authorized under a health care program, knowingly pays, charges, solicits, accepts, or receives, in addition to an amount paid under the health care program, a gift, money, donation, or other consideration as a condition to the provision of a service or product or the continued provision of a service or product if the cost of the service or product is paid for, in whole or in part, under a health care program;

(6) knowingly presents or causes to be presented a claim for payment under a health care program for a product provided or a service rendered by a person who:

(A) is not licensed to provide the product or render the service, if a license is required; or

(B) is not licensed in the manner claimed;

(7) knowingly makes or causes to be made a claim under a health care program for:

(A) a service or product that has not been approved or acquiesced in by a treating physician or health care practitioner;

(B) a service or product that is substantially inadequate or inappropriate when compared to generally recognized standards within the particular discipline or within the health care industry; or

(C) a product that has been adulterated, debased, mislabeled, or that is otherwise inappropriate;

(8) makes a claim under a health care program and knowingly fails to indicate the type of license and the identification number of the licensed health care practitioner who actually provided the service;

(9) knowingly enters into an agreement, combination, or conspiracy to defraud the state or federal government by obtaining or aiding another person in obtaining an unauthorized payment or benefit from a health care program or fiscal agent;

(10) is a managed care organization that contracts with the Health and Human Services Commission, another state agency, or the federal government to provide or arrange to provide health care benefits or services to individuals eligible under a health care program and knowingly:

(A) fails to provide to an individual a health care benefit or service that the organization is required to provide under the contract;

(B) fails to provide or falsifies information required to be provided by law, rule, or contractual provision; or

(C) engages in a fraudulent activity in connection with the enrollment of an individual eligible under a health care program in the organization's managed care plan or in connection with marketing the organization's services to an individual eligible under a health care program;

(11) knowingly obstructs an investigation by the attorney general of an alleged unlawful act under this section or under Section 32.039, 32.0391, or 36.002, Human Resources Code; or

(12) knowingly makes, uses, or causes the making or use of a false record or statement to conceal, avoid, or decrease an obligation to pay or transmit money or property to this state or the federal government under a health care program.

(b) An offense under this section is:

(1) a Class C misdemeanor if the amount of any payment or the value of any monetary or in-kind benefit provided or claim for payment made under a health care program, directly or indirectly, as a result of the conduct is less than $100;

(2) a Class B misdemeanor if the amount of any payment or the value of any monetary or in-kind benefit provided or claim for payment made under a health care program, directly or indirectly, as a result of the conduct is $100 or more but less than $750;

(3) a Class A misdemeanor if the amount of any payment or the value of any monetary or in-kind benefit provided or claim for payment made under a health care program, directly or indirectly, as a result of the conduct is $750 or more but less than $2,500;

(4) a state jail felony if:

(A) the amount of any payment or the value of any monetary or in-kind benefit provided or claim for payment made under a health care program, directly or indirectly, as a result of the conduct is $2,500 or more but less than $30,000;

(B) the offense is committed under Subsection (a)(11); or

(C) it is shown on the trial of the offense that the amount of the payment or value of the benefit described by this subsection cannot be reasonably ascertained;

(5) a felony of the third degree if:

(A) the amount of any payment or the value of any monetary or in-kind benefit provided or claim for payment made under a health care program, directly or indirectly, as a result of the conduct is $30,000 or more but less than $150,000; or

(B) it is shown on the trial of the offense that the defendant submitted more than 25 but fewer than 50 fraudulent claims under a health care program and the submission of each claim constitutes conduct prohibited by Subsection (a);

(6) a felony of the second degree if:

(A) the amount of any payment or the value of any monetary or in-kind benefit provided or claim for payment made under a health care program, directly or indirectly, as a result of the conduct is $150,000 or more but less than $300,000; or

(B) it is shown on the trial of the offense that the defendant submitted 50 or more fraudulent claims under a health care program and the submission of each claim constitutes conduct prohibited by Subsection (a); or

(7) a felony of the first degree if the amount of any payment or the value of any monetary or in-kind benefit provided or claim for payment made under a health care program, directly or indirectly, as a result of the conduct is $300,000 or more.

(c) If conduct constituting an offense under this section also constitutes an offense under another section of this code or another provision of law, the actor may be prosecuted under either this section or the other section or provision or both this section and the other section or provision.

(d) When multiple payments or monetary or in-kind benefits are provided under one or more health care programs as a result of one scheme or continuing course of conduct, the conduct may be considered as one offense and the amounts of the payments or monetary or in-kind benefits aggregated in determining the grade of the offense.

(e) The punishment prescribed for an offense under this section, other than the punishment prescribed by Subsection (b)(7), is increased to the punishment prescribed for the next highest category of offense if it is shown beyond a reasonable doubt on the trial of the offense that the actor was a high managerial agent at the time of the offense.

(f) With the consent of the appropriate local county or district attorney, the attorney general has concurrent jurisdiction with that consenting local prosecutor to prosecute an offense under this section that involves a health care program.

TITLE 8
OFFENSES AGAINST PUBLIC ADMINISTRATION

CHAPTER 36
BRIBERY AND CORRUPT INFLUENCE

Sec. 36.01. Definitions.

In this chapter:

(1) "Custody" means:

(A) detained or under arrest by a peace officer; or

(B) under restraint by a public servant pursuant to an order of a court.

(2) "Party official" means a person who holds any position or office in a political party, whether by election, appointment, or employment.

(3) "Benefit" means anything reasonably regarded as pecuniary gain or pecuniary advantage, including benefit to any other person in whose welfare the beneficiary has a direct and substantial interest.

(4) "Vote" means to cast a ballot in an election regulated by law.

Sec. 36.02. Bribery.

(a) A person commits an offense if he intentionally or knowingly offers, confers, or agrees to confer on another, or solicits, accepts, or agrees to accept from another:

(1) any benefit as consideration for the recipient's decision, opinion, recommendation, vote, or other exercise of discretion as a public servant, party official, or voter;

(2) any benefit as consideration for the recipient's decision, vote, recommendation, or other exercise of official discretion in a judicial or administrative proceeding;

(3) any benefit as consideration for a violation of a duty imposed by law on a public servant or party official; or

(4) any benefit that is a political contribution as defined by Title 15, Election Code, or that is an expenditure made and reported in accordance with Chapter 305, Government Code, if the benefit was offered, conferred, solicited, accepted, or agreed to pursuant to an express agreement to take or withhold a specific exercise of official discretion if such exercise of official discretion would not have been taken or withheld but for the benefit; notwithstanding any rule of evidence or jury instruction allowing factual inferences in the absence of certain evidence, direct evidence of the express agreement shall be required in any prosecution under this subdivision.

(b) It is no defense to prosecution under this section that a person whom the actor sought to influence was not qualified to act in the desired way whether because he had not yet assumed office or he lacked jurisdiction or for any other reason.

(c) It is no defense to prosecution under this section that the benefit is not offered or conferred or that the benefit is not solicited or accepted until after:

(1) the decision, opinion, recommendation, vote, or other exercise of discretion has occurred; or

(2) the public servant ceases to be a public servant.

(d) It is an exception to the application of Subdivisions (1), (2), and (3) of Subsection (a) that the benefit is a political contribution as defined by Title 15, Election Code, or an expenditure made and reported in accordance with Chapter 305, Government Code.

(e) An offense under this section is a felony of the second degree.

Sec. 36.03. Coercion of Public Servant or Voter.

(a) A person commits an offense if by means of coercion he:

(1) influences or attempts to influence a public servant in a specific exercise of his official power or a specific performance of his official duty or influences or attempts to influence a public servant to violate the public servant's known legal duty; or

(2) influences or attempts to influence a voter not to vote or to vote in a particular manner.

(b) An offense under this section is a Class A misdemeanor unless the coercion is a threat to commit a felony, in which event it is a felony of the third degree.

(c) It is an exception to the application of Subsection (a)(1) of this section that the person who influences or attempts to influence the public servant is a member of the governing body of a governmental entity, and that the action that influences or attempts to influence the public servant is an official action taken by the member of the governing body. For the purposes of this subsection, the term "official action" includes deliberations by the governing body of a governmental entity.

Sec. 36.04. Improper Influence.

(a) A person commits an offense if he privately addresses a representation, entreaty, argument, or other communication to any public servant who exercises or will exercise official discretion in an adjudicatory proceeding with an intent to influence the outcome of the proceeding on the basis of considerations other than those authorized by law.

(b) For purposes of this section, "adjudicatory proceeding" means any proceeding before a court or any other agency of government in which the legal rights, powers, duties, or privileges of specified parties are determined.

(c) An offense under this section is a Class A misdemeanor.

Sec. 36.05. Tampering with Witness.

(a) A person commits an offense if, with intent to influence the witness, he offers, confers, or agrees to confer any benefit on a witness or prospective witness in an official proceeding, or he coerces a witness or a prospective witness in an official proceeding:

(1) to testify falsely;

(2) to withhold any testimony, information, document, or thing;

(3) to elude legal process summoning him to testify or supply evidence;

(4) to absent himself from an official proceeding to which he has been legally summoned; or

(5) to abstain from, discontinue, or delay the prosecution of another.

(b) A witness or prospective witness in an official proceeding commits an offense if he knowingly solicits, accepts, or agrees to accept any benefit on the representation or understanding that he will do any of the things specified in Subsection (a).

(c) It is a defense to prosecution under Subsection (a)(5) that the benefit received was:

(1) reasonable restitution for damages suffered by the complaining witness as a result of the offense; and

(2) a result of an agreement negotiated with the assistance or acquiescence of an attorney for the state who represented the state in the case.

(d) An offense under this section is a felony of the third degree, except that if the official proceeding is part of the prosecution of a criminal case, an offense under this section is the same category of offense as the most serious offense charged in that criminal case.

(e) Notwithstanding Subsection (d), if the most serious offense charged is a capital felony, an offense under this section is a felony of the first degree.

(e-1) Notwithstanding Subsection (d), if the underlying official proceeding involves family violence, as defined by Section 71.004, Family Code, an offense under this section is the greater of:

(1) a felony of the third degree; or

(2) the most serious offense charged in the criminal case.

(e-2) Notwithstanding Subsections (d) and (e-1), if the underlying official proceeding involves family violence, as defined by Section 71.004, Family Code, and it is shown at the trial of the offense that the defendant has previously been convicted of an offense involving family violence under the laws of this state or another state, an offense under this section is the greater of:

(1) a felony of the second degree; or

(2) the most serious offense charged in the criminal case.

(e-3) For purposes of Subsection (a), a person is considered to coerce a witness or prospective witness if the person commits an act of family violence as defined by Section 71.004, Family Code, that is perpetrated, in part, with the intent to cause the witness's or prospective witness's unavailability or failure to comply and the offense is punishable under Subsection (e-1) or (e-2), as applicable.

(f) If conduct that constitutes an offense under this section also constitutes an offense under any other law, the actor may be prosecuted under this section, the other law, or both.

Sec. 36.06. Obstruction or Retaliation.

(a) A person commits an offense if the person intentionally or knowingly harms or threatens to harm another by an unlawful act:

(1) in retaliation for or on account of the service or status of another as a:

(A) public servant, witness, prospective witness, or informant; or

(B) person who has reported or who the actor knows intends to report the occurrence of a crime; or

(2) to prevent or delay the service of another as a:

(A) public servant, witness, prospective witness, or informant; or

(B) person who has reported or who the actor knows intends to report the occurrence of a crime.

(a-1) A person commits an offense if the person posts on a publicly accessible website the residence address or telephone number of an individual the actor knows is a public servant or a member of a public servant's family or household with the intent to cause harm or a threat of harm to the individual or a member of the individual's family or household in retaliation for or on account of the service or status of the individual as a public servant.

(b) In this section:

(1) "Honorably retired peace officer" means a peace officer who:

(A) did not retire in lieu of any disciplinary action;

(B) was eligible to retire from a law enforcement agency or was ineligible to retire only as a result of an injury received in the course of the officer's employment with the agency; and

(C) is entitled to receive a pension or annuity for service as a law enforcement officer or is not entitled to receive a pension or annuity only because the law enforcement agency that employed the officer does not offer a pension or annuity to its employees.

(2) "Informant" means a person who has communicated information to the government in connection with any governmental function.

(3) "Public servant" has the meaning assigned by Section 1.07, except that the term also includes an honorably retired peace officer.

(c) An offense under this section is a felony of the third degree, except that the offense is a felony of the second degree if:

(1) the victim of the offense was harmed or threatened because of the victim's service or status as a juror; or

(2) the actor's conduct is described by Subsection (a-1) and results in the bodily injury of a public servant or a member of a public servant's family or household.

(d) For purposes of Subsection (a-1), it is prima facie evidence of the intent to cause harm or a threat of harm to an individual the person knows is a public servant or a member of a public servant's family or household if the actor:

(1) receives a written demand from the individual to not disclose the address or telephone number for reasons of safety; and

(2) either:

(A) fails to remove the address or telephone number from the publicly accessible website within a period of 48 hours after receiving the demand; or

(B) reposts the address or telephone number on the same or a different publicly accessible website, or makes the information publicly available through another medium, within a period of four years after receiving the demand, regardless of whether the individual is no longer a public servant.

Sec. 36.07. Acceptance of Honorarium.

(a) A public servant commits an offense if the public servant solicits, accepts, or agrees to accept an honorarium in consideration for services that the public servant would not have been requested to provide but for the public servant's official position or duties.

(b) This section does not prohibit a public servant from accepting transportation and lodging expenses in connection with a conference or similar event in which the public servant renders services, such as addressing an audience or engaging in a seminar, to the extent that those services are more than merely perfunctory, or from accepting meals in connection with such an event.

(b-1) Transportation, lodging, and meals described by Subsection (b) are not political contributions as defined by Title 15, Election Code.

(c) An offense under this section is a Class A misdemeanor.

Sec. 36.08. Gift to Public Servant by Person Subject to His Jurisdiction.

(a) A public servant in an agency performing regulatory functions or conducting inspections or investigations commits an offense if he solicits, accepts, or agrees to accept any benefit from a person the public servant knows to be subject to regulation, inspection, or investigation by the public servant or his agency.

(b) A public servant in an agency having custody of prisoners commits an offense if he solicits, accepts, or agrees to accept any benefit from a person the public servant knows to be in his custody or the custody of his agency.

(c) A public servant in an agency carrying on civil or criminal litigation on behalf of government commits an offense if he solicits, accepts, or agrees to accept any benefit from a person against whom the public servant knows litigation is pending or contemplated by the public servant or his agency.

(d) A public servant who exercises discretion in connection with contracts, purchases, payments, claims, or other pecuniary transactions of government commits an offense if he solicits, accepts, or agrees to accept any benefit from a person the public servant knows is interested in or likely to become interested in any contract, purchase, payment, claim, or transaction involving the exercise of his discretion.

(e) A public servant who has judicial or administrative authority, who is employed by or in a tribunal having judicial or administrative authority, or who participates in the enforcement of the tribunal's decision, commits an offense if he solicits, accepts, or agrees to accept any benefit from a person the public servant knows is interested in or likely to become interested in any matter before the public servant or tribunal.

(f) A member of the legislature, the governor, the lieutenant governor, or a person employed by a member of the legislature, the governor, the lieutenant governor, or an agency of the legislature commits an offense if he solicits, accepts, or agrees to accept any benefit from any person.

(g) A public servant who is a hearing examiner employed by an agency performing regulatory functions and who conducts hearings in contested cases commits an offense if the public servant solicits, accepts, or agrees to accept any benefit from any person who is appearing before the agency in a contested case, who is doing business with the agency, or who the public servant knows is interested in any matter before the public servant. The exception provided by Section 36.10(b) does not apply to a benefit under this subsection.

(h) An offense under this section is a Class A misdemeanor.

(i) A public servant who receives an unsolicited benefit that the public servant is prohibited from accepting under this section may donate the benefit to a governmental entity that has the authority to accept the gift or may donate the benefit to a recognized tax-exempt charitable organization formed for educational, religious, or scientific purposes.

Sec. 36.09. Offering Gift to Public Servant.

(a) A person commits an offense if he offers, confers, or agrees to confer any benefit on a public servant that he knows the public servant is prohibited by law from accepting.

(b) An offense under this section is a Class A misdemeanor.

Sec. 36.10. Non-Applicable.

(a) Sections 36.08 (Gift to Public Servant) and 36.09 (Offering Gift to Public Servant) do not apply to:

(1) a fee prescribed by law to be received by a public servant or any other benefit to which the public servant is lawfully entitled or for which he gives legitimate consideration in a capacity other than as a public servant;

(2) a gift or other benefit conferred on account of kinship or a personal, professional, or business relationship independent of the official status of the recipient;

(3) a benefit to a public servant required to file a statement under Chapter 572, Government Code, or a report under Title 15, Election Code, that is derived from a function in honor or appreciation of the recipient if:

(A) the benefit and the source of any benefit in excess of $50 is reported in the statement; and

(B) the benefit is used solely to defray the expenses that accrue in the performance of duties or activities in connection with the office which are nonreimbursable by the state or political subdivision;

(4) a political contribution as defined by Title 15, Election Code;

(5) a gift, award, or memento to a member of the legislative or executive branch that is required to be reported under Chapter 305, Government Code;

(6) an item with a value of less than $50, excluding cash or a negotiable instrument as described by Section 3.104, Business & Commerce Code;

(7) an item issued by a governmental entity that allows the use of property or facilities owned, leased, or operated by the governmental entity;

(8) transportation, lodging, and meals described by Section 36.07(b); or

(9) complimentary legal advice or legal services relating to a will, power of attorney, advance directive, or other estate planning document rendered:

(A) to a public servant who is a first responder; and

(B) through a program or clinic that is:

(i) operated by a local bar association or the State Bar of Texas; and

(ii) approved by the head of the agency employing the public servant, if the public servant is employed by an agency.

(b) Section 36.08 (Gift to Public Servant) does not apply to food, lodging, transportation, or entertainment accepted as a guest and, if the donee is required by law to report those items, reported by the donee in accordance with that law.

(c) Section 36.09 (Offering Gift to Public Servant) does not apply to food, lodging, transportation, or entertainment accepted as a guest and, if the donor is required by law to report those items, reported by the donor in accordance with that law.

(d) Section 36.08 (Gift to Public Servant) does not apply to a gratuity accepted and reported in accordance with Section 11.0262, Parks and Wildlife Code. Section 36.09 (Offering Gift to Public Servant) does not apply to a gratuity that is offered in accordance with Section 11.0262, Parks and Wildlife Code.

(e) In this section, "first responder" means:

(1) a peace officer whose duties include responding rapidly to an emergency;

(2) fire protection personnel, as that term is defined by Section 419.021, Government Code;

(3) a volunteer firefighter who performs firefighting duties on behalf of a political subdivision and who is not serving as a member of the Texas Legislature or holding a statewide elected office;

(4) an ambulance driver; or

(5) an individual certified as emergency medical services personnel by the Department of State Health Services.

CHAPTER 37 PERJURY AND OTHER FALSIFICATION

Sec. 37.01. Definitions.

In this chapter:

(1) "Court record" means a decree, judgment, order, subpoena, warrant, minutes, or other document issued by a court of:

(A) this state;

(B) another state;

(C) the United States;

(D) a foreign country recognized by an act of congress or a treaty or other international convention to which the United States is a party;

(E) an Indian tribe recognized by the United States; or

(F) any other jurisdiction, territory, or protectorate entitled to full faith and credit in this state under the United States Constitution.

(2) "Governmental record" means:

(A) anything belonging to, received by, or kept by government for information, including a court record;

(B) anything required by law to be kept by others for information of government;

(C) a license, certificate, permit, seal, title, letter of patent, or similar document issued by government, by another state, or by the United States;

(D) a standard proof of motor vehicle liability insurance form described by Section 601.081, Transportation Code, a certificate of an insurance company described by Section 601.083 of that code, a document purporting to be such a form or certificate that is not issued by an insurer authorized to write motor vehicle liability insurance in this state, an electronic submission in a form described by Section 502.046(i), Transportation Code, or an evidence of financial responsibility described by Section 601.053 of that code;

(E) an official ballot or other election record; or

(F) the written documentation a mobile food unit is required to obtain under Section 437.0074, Health and Safety Code.

(3) "Statement" means any representation of fact.

Sec. 37.02. Perjury.

(a) A person commits an offense if, with intent to deceive and with knowledge of the statement's meaning:

(1) he makes a false statement under oath or swears to the truth of a false statement previously made and the statement is required or authorized by law to be made under oath; or

(2) he makes a false unsworn declaration under Chapter 132, Civil Practice and Remedies Code.

(b) An offense under this section is a Class A misdemeanor.

Sec. 37.03. Aggravated Perjury.

(a) A person commits an offense if he commits perjury as defined in Section 37.02, and the false statement:

(1) is made during or in connection with an official proceeding; and

(2) is material.

(b) An offense under this section is a felony of the third degree.

Sec. 37.04. Materiality.

(a) A statement is material, regardless of the admissibility of the statement under the rules of evidence, if it could have affected the course or outcome of the official proceeding.

(b) It is no defense to prosecution under Section 37.03 (Aggravated Perjury) that the declarant mistakenly believed the statement to be immaterial.

(c) Whether a statement is material in a given factual situation is a question of law.

Sec. 37.05. Retraction.

It is a defense to prosecution under Section 37.03 (Aggravated Perjury) that the actor retracted his false statement:

(1) before completion of the testimony at the official proceeding; and

(2) before it became manifest that the falsity of the statement would be exposed.

Sec. 37.06. Inconsistent Statements.

An information or indictment for perjury under Section 37.02 or aggravated perjury under Section 37.03 that alleges that the declarant has made statements under oath, both of which cannot be true, need not allege which statement is false. At the trial the prosecution need not prove which statement is false.

Sec. 37.07. Irregularities No Defense.

(a) It is no defense to prosecution under Section 37.02 (Perjury) or 37.03 (Aggravated Perjury) that the oath was administered or taken in an irregular manner, or that there was some irregularity in the appointment or qualification of the person who administered the oath.

(b) It is no defense to prosecution under Section 37.02 (Perjury) or 37.03 (Aggravated Perjury) that a document was not sworn to if the document contains a recital that it was made under oath, the declarant was aware of the recital when he signed the document, and the document contains the signed jurat of a public servant authorized to administer oaths.

Sec. 37.08. False Report to Peace Officer, Federal Special Investigator, Law Enforcement Employee Corrections Officer, or Jailer.

(a) A person commits an offense if, with intent to deceive, he knowingly makes a false statement that is material to a criminal investigation and makes the statement to:

(1) a peace officer or federal special investigator conducting the investigation;

(2) any employee of a law enforcement agency that is authorized by the agency to conduct the investigation and that the actor knows is conducting the investigation; or

(3) a corrections officer or jailer.

(b) In this section, "law enforcement agency" has the meaning assigned by Article 59.01, Code of Criminal Procedure.

(c) An offense under this section is a Class B misdemeanor.

Sec. 37.081. False Report Regarding Missing Child or Missing Person.

(a) A person commits an offense if, with intent to deceive, the person knowingly:

(1) files a false report of a missing child or missing person with a law enforcement officer or agency; or

(2) makes a false statement to a law enforcement officer or other employee of a law enforcement agency relating to a missing child or missing person.

(b) An offense under this section is a Class C misdemeanor.

Sec. 37.082. Misrepresenting Child As Family Member at Port of Entry.

(a) In this section:

(1) "Child" means a person younger than 18 years of age.

(2) "Family member" means a person who is related to another person by consanguinity or affinity.

(3) "Port of entry" means a place designated by executive order of the president of the United States, by order of the United States secretary of the treasury, or by act of the United States Congress at which a customs officer is authorized to enforce customs laws.

(b) A person commits an offense if the person, with intent to commit an offense under Section 20A.02, knowingly misrepresents a child as a family member of the person to a peace officer or federal special investigator at a port of entry.

(c) An offense under this section is a Class B misdemeanor.

(d) If conduct that constitutes an offense under this section also constitutes an offense under another law, the actor may be prosecuted under this section, the other law, or both.

Sec. 37.09. Tampering with or Fabricating Physical Evidence.

(a) A person commits an offense if, knowing that an investigation or official proceeding is pending or in progress, he:

(1) alters, destroys, or conceals any record, document, or thing with intent to impair its verity, legibility, or availability as evidence in the investigation or official proceeding; or

(2) makes, presents, or uses any record, document, or thing with knowledge of its falsity and with intent to affect the course or outcome of the investigation or official proceeding.

(b) This section shall not apply if the record, document, or thing concealed is privileged or is the work product of the parties to the investigation or official proceeding.

(c) An offense under Subsection (a) or Subsection (d)(1) is a felony of the third degree, unless the thing altered, destroyed, or concealed is a human corpse, in which case the offense is a felony of the second degree. An offense under Subsection (d)(2) is a Class A misdemeanor.

(c-1) It is a defense to prosecution under Subsection (a) or (d)(1) that the record, document, or thing was visual material prohibited under Section 43.261 that was destroyed as described by Subsection (f)(3) of that section.

(d) A person commits an offense if the person:

(1) knowing that an offense has been committed, alters, destroys, or conceals any record, document, or thing with intent to impair its verity, legibility, or availability as evidence in any subsequent investigation of or official proceeding related to the offense; or

(2) observes a human corpse under circumstances in which a reasonable person would believe that an offense had been committed, knows or reasonably should know that a law enforcement agency is not aware of the existence of or location of the corpse, and fails to report the existence of and location of the corpse to a law enforcement agency.

(e) In this section, "human corpse" has the meaning assigned by Section 42.08.

Sec. 37.10. Tampering with Governmental Record.

(a) A person commits an offense if he:

(1) knowingly makes a false entry in, or false alteration of, a governmental record;

(2) makes, presents, or uses any record, document, or thing with knowledge of its falsity and with intent that it be taken as a genuine governmental record;

(3) intentionally destroys, conceals, removes, or otherwise impairs the verity, legibility, or availability of a governmental record;

(4) possesses, sells, or offers to sell a governmental record or a blank governmental record form with intent that it be used unlawfully;

(5) makes, presents, or uses a governmental record with knowledge of its falsity; or

(6) possesses, sells, or offers to sell a governmental record or a blank governmental record form with knowledge that it was obtained unlawfully.

(b) It is an exception to the application of Subsection (a)(3) that the governmental record is destroyed pursuant to legal authorization or transferred under Section 441.204, Government Code. With regard to the destruction of a local government record, legal authorization includes compliance with the provisions of Subtitle C, Title 6, Local Government Code.

(c) (1) Except as provided by Subdivisions (2), (3), (4), and (5), and by Subsection (d), an offense under this section is a Class A misdemeanor unless the actor's intent is to defraud or harm another, in which event the offense is a state jail felony.

(2) An offense under this section is a felony of the third degree if it is shown on the trial of the offense that the governmental record was:

(A) a public school record, report, or assessment instrument required under Chapter 39, Education Code, data reported for a school district or open-enrollment charter school to the Texas Education Agency through the Public Education Information Management System (PEIMS) described by Sections 48.008 and 48.009, Education Code, under a law or rule requiring that reporting, or a license, certificate, permit, seal, title, letter of patent, or similar document issued by government, by another state, or by the United States, unless the actor's intent is to defraud or harm another, in which event the offense is a felony of the second degree;

(B) a written report of a medical, chemical, toxicological, ballistic, or other expert examination or test performed on physical evidence for the purpose of determining the connection or relevance of the evidence to a criminal action;

(C) a written report of the certification, inspection, or maintenance record of an instrument, apparatus, implement, machine, or other similar device used in the course of an examination or test performed on physical evidence for the purpose of determining the connection or relevance of the evidence to a criminal action; or

(D) a search warrant issued by a magistrate.

(3) An offense under this section is a Class C misdemeanor if it is shown on the trial of the offense that the governmental record is a governmental record that is required for enrollment of a student in a school district and was used by the actor to establish the residency of the student.

(4) An offense under this section is a Class B misdemeanor if it is shown on the trial of the offense that the governmental record is a written appraisal filed with an appraisal review board under Section 41.43(a-1), Tax Code, that was performed by a person who had a contingency interest in the outcome of the appraisal review board hearing.

(5) An offense under this section is a Class B misdemeanor if the governmental record is an application for a place on the ballot under Section 141.031, Election Code, and the actor knowingly provides false information under Subsection (a)(4)(G) of that section.

(d) An offense under this section, if it is shown on the trial of the offense that the governmental record is described by Section 37.01(2)(D), is:

(1) a Class B misdemeanor if the offense is committed under Subsection (a)(2) or Subsection (a)(5) and the defendant is convicted of presenting or using the record;

(2) a felony of the third degree if the offense is committed under:

(A) Subsection (a)(1), (3), (4), or (6); or

(B) Subsection (a)(2) or (5) and the defendant is convicted of making the record; and

(3) a felony of the second degree, notwithstanding Subdivisions (1) and (2), if the actor's intent in committing the offense was to defraud or harm another.

(e) It is an affirmative defense to prosecution for possession under Subsection (a)(6) that the possession occurred in the actual discharge of official duties as a public servant.

(f) It is a defense to prosecution under Subsection (a)(1), (a)(2), or (a)(5) that the false entry or false information could have no effect on the government's purpose for requiring the governmental record.

(g) A person is presumed to intend to defraud or harm another if the person acts with respect to two or more of the same type of governmental records or blank governmental record forms and if each governmental record or blank governmental record form is a license, certificate, permit, seal, title, or similar document issued by government.

(h) If conduct that constitutes an offense under this section also constitutes an offense under Section 32.48 or 37.13, the actor may be prosecuted under any of those sections.

(i) With the consent of the appropriate local county or district attorney, the attorney general has concurrent jurisdiction with that consenting local prosecutor to prosecute an offense under this section that involves the state Medicaid program.

(j) It is not a defense to prosecution under Subsection (a)(2) that the record, document, or thing made, presented, or used displays or contains the statement "NOT A GOVERNMENT DOCUMENT" or another substantially similar statement intended to alert a person to the falsity of the record, document, or thing, unless the record, document, or thing displays the statement diagonally printed clearly and indelibly on both the front and back of the record, document, or thing in solid red capital letters at least one-fourth inch in height.

Sec. 37.101. Fraudulent Filing of Financing Statement.

(a) A person commits an offense if the person knowingly presents for filing or causes to be presented for filing a financing statement that the person knows:

(1) is forged;

(2) contains a material false statement; or

(3) is groundless.

(b) An offense under Subsection (a)(1) is a felony of the third degree, unless it is shown on the trial of the offense that the person had previously been convicted under this section on two or more occasions, in which event the offense is a felony of the second degree. An offense under Subsection (a)(2) or (a)(3) is a Class A misdemeanor, unless the person commits the offense with the intent to defraud or harm another, in which event the offense is a state jail felony.

Sec. 37.11. Impersonating Public Servant.

(a) A person commits an offense if the person:

(1) impersonates a public servant with intent to induce another to submit to the person's pretended official authority or to rely on the person's pretended official acts; or

(2) knowingly purports to exercise, without legal authority, any function of a public servant or of a public office, including that of a judge and court.

(b) An offense under this section is a felony of the third degree.

Sec. 37.12. False Identification As Peace Officer; Misrepresentation of Property.

(a) A person commits an offense if:

(1) the person makes, provides to another person, or possesses a card, document, badge, insignia,

shoulder emblem, or other item, including a vehicle, bearing an insignia of a law enforcement agency that identifies a person as a peace officer or a reserve law enforcement officer; and

(2) the person who makes, provides, or possesses the item bearing the insignia knows that the person so identified by the item is not commissioned as a peace officer or reserve law enforcement officer as indicated on the item.

(b) It is a defense to prosecution under this section that:

(1) the card, document, badge, insignia, shoulder emblem, or other item bearing an insignia of a law enforcement agency clearly identifies the person as an honorary or junior peace officer or reserve law enforcement officer, or as a member of a junior posse; or

(2) the person identified as a peace officer or reserve law enforcement officer by the item bearing the insignia was commissioned in that capacity when the item was made.

(b-1) It is an exception to the application of this section that the item was used or intended for use exclusively for decorative purposes or in an artistic or dramatic presentation.

(c) In this section, "reserve law enforcement officer" has the same meaning as is given that term in Section 1701.001, Occupations Code.

(c-1) For purposes of this section, an item bearing an insignia of a law enforcement agency includes an item that contains the word "police," "sheriff," "constable," or "trooper."

(d) A person commits an offense if the person intentionally or knowingly misrepresents an object, including a vehicle, as property belonging to a law enforcement agency. For purposes of this subsection, intentionally or knowingly misrepresenting an object as property belonging to a law enforcement agency includes intentionally or knowingly displaying an item bearing an insignia of a law enforcement agency in a manner that would lead a reasonable person to interpret the item as property belonging to a law enforcement agency.

(e) An offense under this section is a Class B misdemeanor.

Sec. 37.13. Record of a Fraudulent Court.

(a) A person commits an offense if the person makes, presents, or uses any document or other record with:

(1) knowledge that the document or other record is not a record of a court created under or established by the constitution or laws of this state or of the United States; and

(2) the intent that the document or other record be given the same legal effect as a record of a court created under or established by the constitution or laws of this state or of the United States.

(b) An offense under this section is a Class A misdemeanor, except that the offense is a felony of the third degree if it is shown on the trial of the offense that the defendant has previously been convicted under this section on two or more occasions.

(c) If conduct that constitutes an offense under this section also constitutes an offense under Section 32.48 or 37.10, the actor may be prosecuted under any of those sections.

Sec. 37.14. False Statement Regarding Child Custody Determination Made in Foreign Country.

(a) For purposes of this section, "child custody determination" has the meaning assigned by Section 152.102, Family Code.

(b) A person commits an offense if the person knowingly makes or causes to be made a false statement relating to a child custody determination made in a foreign country during a hearing held under Chapter 152 or Subchapter I, Chapter 153, Family Code.

(c) An offense under this section is a felony of the third degree.

CHAPTER 38 OBSTRUCTING GOVERNMENTAL OPERATION

Sec. 38.01. Definitions.

In this chapter:

(1) "Custody" means:

(A) under arrest by a peace officer or under restraint by a public servant pursuant to an order of a court of this state or another state of the United States; or

(B) under restraint by an agent or employee of a facility that is operated by or under contract with the United States and that confines persons arrested for, charged with, or convicted of criminal offenses.

(2) "Escape" means unauthorized departure from custody or failure to return to custody following temporary leave for a specific purpose or limited period or leave that is part of an intermittent sentence, but does not include a violation of conditions of community supervision or parole other than conditions that impose a period of confinement in a secure correctional facility.

(3) "Economic benefit" means anything reasonably regarded as an economic gain or advantage,

including accepting or offering to accept employment for a fee, accepting or offering to accept a fee, entering into a fee contract, or accepting or agreeing to accept money or anything of value.

(4) "Finance" means to provide funds or capital or to furnish with necessary funds.

(5) "Fugitive from justice" means a person for whom a valid arrest warrant has been issued.

(6) "Governmental function" includes any activity that a public servant is lawfully authorized to undertake on behalf of government.

(7) "Invest funds" means to commit money to earn a financial return.

(8) "Member of the family" means anyone related within the third degree of consanguinity or affinity, as determined under Chapter 573, Government Code.

(9) "Qualified nonprofit organization" means a nonprofit organization that meets the following conditions:

(A) the primary purposes of the organization do not include the rendition of legal services or education regarding legal services;

(B) the recommending, furnishing, paying for, or educating persons regarding legal services is incidental and reasonably related to the primary purposes of the organization;

(C) the organization does not derive a financial benefit from the rendition of legal services by a lawyer; and

(D) the person for whom the legal services are rendered, and not the organization, is recognized as the client of a lawyer.

(10) "Public media" means a telephone directory or legal directory, newspaper or other periodical, billboard or other sign, radio or television broadcast, recorded message the public may access by dialing a telephone number, or a written communication not prohibited by Section 38.12(d).

(11) "Solicit employment" means to communicate in person or by telephone with a prospective client or a member of the prospective client's family concerning professional employment within the scope of a professional's license, registration, or certification arising out of a particular occurrence or event, or series of occurrences or events, or concerning an existing problem of the prospective client within the scope of the professional's license, registration, or certification, for the purpose of providing professional services to the prospective client, when neither the person receiving the communication nor anyone acting on that person's behalf has requested the communication. The term does not include a communication initiated by a family member of the person receiving a communication, a communication by a professional who has a prior or existing professional-client relationship with the person receiving the communication, or communication by an attorney for a qualified nonprofit organization with the organization's members for the purpose of educating the organization's members to understand the law, to recognize legal problems, to make intelligent selection of legal counsel, or to use available legal services. The term does not include an advertisement by a professional through public media.

(12) "Professional" means an attorney, chiropractor, physician, surgeon, private investigator, or any other person licensed, certified, or registered by a state agency that regulates a health care profession.

Sec. 38.02. Failure to Identify.

(a) A person commits an offense if he intentionally refuses to give his name, residence address, or date of birth to a peace officer who has lawfully arrested the person and requested the information.

(b) A person commits an offense if he intentionally gives a false or fictitious name, residence address, or date of birth to a peace officer who has:

(1) lawfully arrested the person;

(2) lawfully detained the person; or

(3) requested the information from a person that the peace officer has good cause to believe is a witness to a criminal offense.

(c) Except as provided by Subsections (d) and (e), an offense under this section is:

(1) a Class C misdemeanor if the offense is committed under Subsection (a); or

(2) a Class B misdemeanor if the offense is committed under Subsection (b).

(d) If it is shown on the trial of an offense under this section that the defendant was a fugitive from justice at the time of the offense, the offense is:

(1) a Class B misdemeanor if the offense is committed under Subsection (a); or

(2) a Class A misdemeanor if the offense is committed under Subsection (b).

(e) If conduct that constitutes an offense under this section also constitutes an offense under Section 106.07, Alcoholic Beverage Code, the actor may be prosecuted only under Section 106.07.

Sec. 38.03. Resisting Arrest, Search, or Transportation.

(a) A person commits an offense if he intentionally prevents or obstructs a person he knows is a peace officer or a person acting in a peace officer's presence and at his direction from effecting an arrest, search, or transportation of the actor or another by using force against the peace officer or another.

(b) It is no defense to prosecution under this section that the arrest or search was unlawful.

(c) Except as provided in Subsection (d), an offense under this section is a Class A misdemeanor.

(d) An offense under this section is a felony of the third degree if the actor uses a deadly weapon to resist the arrest or search.

Sec. 38.04. Evading Arrest or Detention.

(a) A person commits an offense if he intentionally flees from a person he knows is a peace officer or federal special investigator attempting lawfully to arrest or detain him.

(b) **[2 Versions: As amended by Acts 2011, 82nd Leg., chs. 391 and 839]** An offense under this section is a Class A misdemeanor, except that the offense is:

(1) a state jail felony if:

(A) the actor has been previously convicted under this section; or

(B) the actor uses a vehicle or watercraft while the actor is in flight and the actor has not been previously convicted under this section;

(2) a felony of the third degree if:

(A) the actor uses a vehicle or watercraft while the actor is in flight and the actor has been previously convicted under this section; or

(B) another suffers serious bodily injury as a direct result of an attempt by the officer or investigator from whom the actor is fleeing to apprehend the actor while the actor is in flight; or

(3) a felony of the second degree if another suffers death as a direct result of an attempt by the officer or investigator from whom the actor is fleeing to apprehend the actor while the actor is in flight.

(b) **[2 Versions: As amended by Acts 2011, 82nd Leg., ch. 920]** An offense under this section is a Class A misdemeanor, except that the offense is:

(1) a state jail felony if the actor has been previously convicted under this section;

(2) a felony of the third degree if:

(A) the actor uses a vehicle while the actor is in flight;

(B) another suffers serious bodily injury as a direct result of an attempt by the officer from whom the actor is fleeing to apprehend the actor while the actor is in flight; or

(C) the actor uses a tire deflation device against the officer while the actor is in flight; or

(3) a felony of the second degree if:

(A) another suffers death as a direct result of an attempt by the officer from whom the actor is fleeing to apprehend the actor while the actor is in flight; or

(B) another suffers serious bodily injury as a direct result of the actor's use of a tire deflation device while the actor is in flight.

(c) In this section:

(1) "Vehicle" has the meaning assigned by Section 541.201, Transportation Code.

(2) "Tire deflation device" has the meaning assigned by Section 46.01.

(3) "Watercraft" has the meaning assigned by Section 49.01.

(d) A person who is subject to prosecution under both this section and another law may be prosecuted under either or both this section and the other law.

Sec. 38.05. Hindering Apprehension or Prosecution.

(a) A person commits an offense if, with intent to hinder the arrest, prosecution, conviction, or punishment of another for an offense or, with intent to hinder the arrest, detention, adjudication, or disposition of a child for engaging in delinquent conduct that violates a penal law of the state, or with intent to hinder the arrest of another under the authority of a warrant or capias, he:

(1) harbors or conceals the other;

(2) provides or aids in providing the other with any means of avoiding arrest or effecting escape; or

(3) warns the other of impending discovery or apprehension.

(b) It is a defense to prosecution under Subsection (a)(3) that the warning was given in connection with an effort to bring another into compliance with the law.

(c) Except as provided by Subsection (d), an offense under this section is a Class A misdemeanor.

(d) An offense under this section is a felony of the third degree if the person who is harbored, concealed, provided with a means of avoiding arrest or effecting escape, or warned of discovery or apprehension is under arrest for, charged with, or convicted of a felony, including an offense under Section 62.102, Code of Criminal Procedure, or is in custody or detention for, is alleged in a petition to have engaged in, or has been adjudicated as having engaged in delinquent conduct that violates a penal law of the grade of felony, including an offense under Section 62.102, Code of Criminal Procedure, and the person charged under this section knew that the person they harbored, concealed, provided with a means of avoiding arrest or effecting escape, or warned of discovery or apprehension is under arrest for, charged with, or convicted of a felony, or is in custody or detention for, is alleged in a petition to have engaged in, or has been adjudicated as having engaged in delinquent conduct that violates a penal law of the grade of felony.

Sec. 38.06. Escape.

(a) A person commits an offense if the person escapes from custody when the person is:

(1) under arrest for, lawfully detained for, charged with, or convicted of an offense;

(2) in custody pursuant to a lawful order of a court;

(3) detained in a secure detention facility, as that term is defined by Section 51.02, Family Code; or

(4) in the custody of a juvenile probation officer for violating an order imposed by the juvenile court under Section 52.01, Family Code.

(b) Except as provided in Subsections (c), (d), and (e), an offense under this section is a Class A misdemeanor.

(c) An offense under this section is a felony of the third degree if the actor:

(1) is under arrest for, charged with, or convicted of a felony;

(2) is confined or lawfully detained in a secure correctional facility or law enforcement facility; or

(3) is committed to or lawfully detained in a secure correctional facility, as defined by Section 51.02, Family Code, other than a halfway house, operated by or under contract with the Texas Juvenile Justice Department.

(d) An offense under this section is a felony of the second degree if the actor to effect his escape causes bodily injury.

(e) An offense under this section is a felony of the first degree if to effect his escape the actor:

(1) causes serious bodily injury; or

(2) uses or threatens to use a deadly weapon.

Sec. 38.07. Permitting or Facilitating Escape.

(a) An official or employee of a correctional facility commits an offense if he knowingly permits or facilitates the escape of a person in custody.

(b) A person commits an offense if he knowingly causes or facilitates the escape of one who is in custody pursuant to:

(1) an allegation or adjudication of delinquency; or

(2) involuntary commitment for mental illness under Subtitle C, Title 7, Health and Safety Code, or for chemical dependency under Chapter 462, Health and Safety Code.

(c) Except as provided in Subsections (d) and (e), an offense under this section is a Class A misdemeanor.

(d) An offense under this section is a felony of the third degree if the person in custody:

(1) was under arrest for, charged with, or convicted of a felony; or

(2) was confined in a correctional facility other than a secure correctional facility after conviction of a felony.

(e) An offense under this section is a felony of the second degree if:

(1) the actor or the person in custody used or threatened to use a deadly weapon to effect the escape; or

(2) the person in custody was confined in a secure correctional facility after conviction of a felony.

(f) In this section, "correctional facility" means:

(1) any place described by Section 1.07(a)(14); or

(2) a "secure correctional facility" or "secure detention facility" as those terms are defined by Section 51.02, Family Code.

Sec. 38.08. Effect of Unlawful Custody.

It is no defense to prosecution under Section 38.06 or 38.07 that the custody was unlawful.

Sec. 38.09. Implements for Escape.

(a) A person commits an offense if, with intent to facilitate escape, he introduces into a correctional facility, or provides a person in custody or an inmate with, a deadly weapon or anything that may be useful for escape.

(b) An offense under this section is a felony of the third degree unless the actor introduced or provided a deadly weapon, in which event the offense is a felony of the second degree.

(c) In this section, "correctional facility" means:

(1) any place described by Section 1.07(a)(14); or

(2) a "secure correctional facility" or "secure detention facility" as those terms are defined by Section 51.02, Family Code.

Sec. 38.10. Bail Jumping and Failure to Appear.

(a) A person lawfully released from custody, with or without bail, on condition that he subsequently appear commits an offense if he intentionally or knowingly fails to appear in accordance with the terms of his release.

(b) It is a defense to prosecution under this section that the appearance was incident to community supervision, parole, or an intermittent sentence.

(c) It is a defense to prosecution under this section that the actor had a reasonable excuse for his failure to appear in accordance with the terms of his release.

(d) Except as provided in Subsections (e) and (f), an offense under this section is a Class A misdemeanor.

(e) An offense under this section is a Class C misdemeanor if the offense for which the actor's appearance was required is punishable by fine only.

(f) An offense under this section is a felony of the third degree if the offense for which the actor's appearance was required is classified as a felony.

Sec. 38.11. Prohibited Substances and Items in Correctional or Civil Commitment Facility.

(a) A person commits an offense if the person provides, or possesses with the intent to provide:

(1) an alcoholic beverage, controlled substance, or dangerous drug to a person in the custody of a correctional facility or civil commitment facility, except on the prescription of a practitioner;

(2) a deadly weapon to a person in the custody of a correctional facility or civil commitment facility;

(3) a cellular telephone or other wireless communications device or a component of one of those devices to a person in the custody of a correctional facility;

(4) money to a person confined in a correctional facility; or

(5) a cigarette or tobacco product to a person confined in a correctional facility, except that if the facility is a local jail regulated by the Commission on Jail Standards, the person commits an offense only if providing the cigarette or tobacco product violates a rule or regulation adopted by the sheriff or jail administrator that:

(A) prohibits the possession of a cigarette or tobacco product by a person confined in the jail; or

(B) places restrictions on:

(i) the possession of a cigarette or tobacco product by a person confined in the jail; or

(ii) the manner in which a cigarette or tobacco product may be provided to a person confined in the jail.

(b) A person commits an offense if the person takes an alcoholic beverage, controlled substance, or dangerous drug into a correctional facility or civil commitment facility.

(c) A person commits an offense if the person takes a controlled substance or dangerous drug on property owned, used, or controlled by a correctional facility or civil commitment facility.

(d) A person commits an offense if the person:

(1) possesses a controlled substance or dangerous drug while in a correctional facility or civil commitment facility or on property owned, used, or controlled by a correctional facility or civil commitment facility; or

(2) possesses a deadly weapon while in a correctional facility or civil commitment facility.

(e) It is an affirmative defense to prosecution under Subsection (b), (c), or (d)(1) that the person possessed the alcoholic beverage, controlled substance, or dangerous drug pursuant to a prescription issued by a practitioner or while delivering the beverage, substance, or drug to a warehouse, pharmacy, or practitioner on property owned, used, or controlled by the correctional facility or civil commitment facility. It is an affirmative defense to prosecution under Subsection (d)(2) that the person possessing the deadly weapon is a peace officer or is an officer or employee of the correctional facility or civil commitment facility who is authorized to possess the deadly weapon while on duty or traveling to or from the person's place of assignment.

(f) In this section:

(1) "Practitioner" has the meaning assigned by Section 481.002, Health and Safety Code.

(2) "Prescription" has the meaning assigned by Section 481.002, Health and Safety Code.

(3) "Cigarette" has the meaning assigned by Section 154.001, Tax Code.

(4) "Tobacco product" has the meaning assigned by Section 155.001, Tax Code.

(5) "Component" means any item necessary for the current, ongoing, or future operation of a cellular telephone or other wireless communications device, including a subscriber identity module card or functionally equivalent portable memory chip, a battery or battery charger, and any number of minutes that have been purchased or for which a contract has been entered into and during which a cellular telephone or other wireless communications device is capable of transmitting or receiving communications.

(6) "Correctional facility" means:

(A) any place described by Section 1.07(a)(14)(A), (B), or (C); or

(B) a secure correctional facility or secure detention facility, as defined by Section 51.02, Family Code.

(g) An offense under this section is a felony of the third degree.

(h) Notwithstanding Section 15.01(d), if a person commits the offense of criminal attempt to commit an offense under Subsection (a), (b), or (c), the offense committed under Section 15.01 is a felony of the third degree.

(i) It is an affirmative defense to prosecution under Subsection (b) that the actor:

(1) is a duly authorized member of the clergy with rights and privileges granted by an ordaining

authority that includes administration of a religious ritual or ceremony requiring the presence or consumption of an alcoholic beverage; and

(2) takes four ounces or less of an alcoholic beverage into a correctional facility and personally consumes all of the alcoholic beverage or departs from the facility with any portion of the beverage not consumed.

(j) A person commits an offense if the person, while confined in a correctional facility, possesses a cellular telephone or other wireless communications device or a component of one of those devices.

(k) A person commits an offense if, with the intent to provide to or make a cellular telephone or other wireless communications device or a component of one of those devices available for use by a person in the custody of a correctional facility, the person:

(1) acquires a cellular telephone or other wireless communications device or a component of one of those devices to be delivered to the person in custody;

(2) provides a cellular telephone or other wireless communications device or a component of one of those devices to another person for delivery to the person in custody; or

(3) makes a payment to a communication common carrier, as defined by Article 18A.001, Code of Criminal Procedure, or to any communication service that provides to its users the ability to send or receive wire or electronic communications.

Sec. 38.111. Improper Contact with Victim.

(a) A person commits an offense if the person, while confined in a correctional facility after being charged with or convicted of an offense listed in Article 62.001(5), Code of Criminal Procedure, contacts by letter, telephone, or any other means, either directly or through a third party, a victim of the offense or a member of the victim's family, if the director of the correctional facility has not, before the person makes contact with the victim:

(1) received written and dated consent to the contact from:

(A) the victim, if the victim was 17 years of age or older at the time of the commission of the offense for which the person is confined; or

(B) if the victim was younger than 17 years of age at the time of the commission of the offense for which the person is confined:

(i) a parent of the victim;

(ii) a legal guardian of the victim;

(iii) the victim, if the victim is 17 years of age or older at the time of giving the consent; or

(iv) a member of the victim's family who is 17 years of age or older; and

(2) provided the person with a copy of the consent.

(b) The person confined in a correctional facility may not give the written consent required under Subsection (a)(2)(A).

(c) It is an affirmative defense to prosecution under this section that the contact was:

(1) indirect contact made through an attorney representing the person in custody; and

(2) solely for the purpose of representing the person in a criminal proceeding.

(d) An offense under this section is a Class A misdemeanor unless the actor is confined in a correctional facility after being convicted of a felony described by Subsection (a), in which event the offense is a felony of the third degree.

(e) In this section, "correctional facility" means:

(1) any place described by Section 1.07(a)(14); or

(2) a "secure correctional facility" or "secure detention facility" as those terms are defined by Section 51.02, Family Code.

Sec. 38.112. Violation of Protective Order Issued on Basis of Sexual Assault or Abuse, Stalking, or Trafficking. [Repealed]

Sec. 38.113. Unauthorized Absence from Community Corrections Facility, County Correctional Center, or Assignment Site.

(a) A person commits an offense if the person:

(1) is sentenced to or is required as a condition of community supervision or correctional programming to submit to a period of detention or treatment in a community corrections facility or county correctional center;

(2) fails to report to or leaves the facility, the center, or a community service assignment site as directed by the court, community supervision and corrections department supervising the person, or director of the facility or center in which the person is detained or treated, as appropriate; and

(3) in failing to report or leaving acts without the approval of the court, the community supervision and corrections department supervising the person, or the director of the facility or center in which the person is detained or treated.

(b) An offense under this section is a state jail felony.

Sec. 38.114. Contraband in Correctional Facility.

(a) A person commits an offense if the person:

(1) provides contraband to an inmate of a correctional facility;

(2) otherwise introduces contraband into a correctional facility; or

(3) possesses contraband while confined in a correctional facility.

(b) In this section, "contraband":

(1) means:

(A) any item not provided by or authorized by the operator of the correctional facility; or

(B) any item provided by or authorized by the operator of the correctional facility that has been altered to accommodate a use other than the originally intended use; and

(2) does not include any item specifically prohibited under Section 38.11.

(c) An offense under this section is a Class C misdemeanor, unless the offense is committed by an employee or a volunteer of the correctional facility, in which event the offense is a Class B misdemeanor.

(d) In this section, "correctional facility" means:

(1) any place described by Section 1.07(a)(14); or

(2) a "secure correctional facility" or "secure detention facility" as those terms are defined by Section 51.02, Family Code.

Sec. 38.12. Barratry and Solicitation of Professional Employment.

(a) A person commits an offense if, with intent to obtain an economic benefit the person:

(1) knowingly institutes a suit or claim that the person has not been authorized to pursue;

(2) solicits employment, either in person or by telephone, for himself or for another;

(3) pays, gives, or advances or offers to pay, give, or advance to a prospective client money or anything of value to obtain employment as a professional from the prospective client;

(4) pays or gives or offers to pay or give a person money or anything of value to solicit employment;

(5) pays or gives or offers to pay or give a family member of a prospective client money or anything of value to solicit employment; or

(6) accepts or agrees to accept money or anything of value to solicit employment.

(b) A person commits an offense if the person:

(1) knowingly finances the commission of an offense under Subsection (a);

(2) invests funds the person knows or believes are intended to further the commission of an offense under Subsection (a); or

(3) is a professional who knowingly accepts employment within the scope of the person's license, registration, or certification that results from the solicitation of employment in violation of Subsection (a).

(c) It is an exception to prosecution under Subsection (a) or (b) that the person's conduct is authorized by the Texas Disciplinary Rules of Professional Conduct or any rule of court.

(d) A person commits an offense if the person:

(1) is an attorney, chiropractor, physician, surgeon, or private investigator licensed to practice in this state or any person licensed, certified, or registered by a health care regulatory agency of this state; and

(2) with the intent to obtain professional employment for the person or for another, provides or knowingly permits to be provided to an individual who has not sought the person's employment, legal representation, advice, or care a written communication or a solicitation, including a solicitation in person or by telephone, that:

(A) concerns an action for personal injury or wrongful death or otherwise relates to an accident or disaster involving the person to whom the communication or solicitation is provided or a relative of that person and that was provided before the 31st day after the date on which the accident or disaster occurred;

(B) concerns a specific matter and relates to legal representation and the person knows or reasonably should know that the person to whom the communication or solicitation is directed is represented by a lawyer in the matter;

(C) concerns a lawsuit of any kind, including an action for divorce, in which the person to whom the communication or solicitation is provided is a defendant or a relative of that person, unless the lawsuit in which the person is named as a defendant has been on file for more than 31 days before the date on which the communication or solicitation was provided;

(D) is provided or permitted to be provided by a person who knows or reasonably should know that the injured person or relative of the injured person has indicated a desire not to be contacted by or receive communications or solicitations concerning employment;

(E) involves coercion, duress, fraud, overreaching, harassment, intimidation, or undue influence; or

(F) contains a false, fraudulent, misleading, deceptive, or unfair statement or claim.

(e) For purposes of Subsection (d)(2)(D), a desire not to be contacted is presumed if an accident report reflects that such an indication has been made by an injured person or that person's relative.

(f) An offense under Subsection (a) or (b) is a felony of the third degree.

(g) Except as provided by Subsection (h), an offense under Subsection (d) is a Class A misdemeanor.

(h) An offense under Subsection (d) is a felony of the third degree if it is shown on the trial of the offense that the defendant has previously been convicted under Subsection (d).

(i) Final conviction of felony barratry is a serious crime for all purposes and acts, specifically including the State Bar Rules and the Texas Rules of Disciplinary Procedure.

Sec. 38.122. Falsely Holding Oneself Out As a Lawyer.

(a) A person commits an offense if, with intent to obtain an economic benefit for himself or herself, the person holds himself or herself out as a lawyer, unless he or she is currently licensed to practice law in this state, another state, or a foreign country and is in good standing with the State Bar of Texas and the state bar or licensing authority of any and all other states and foreign countries where licensed.

(b) An offense under Subsection (a) of this section is a felony of the third degree.

(c) Final conviction of falsely holding oneself out to be a lawyer is a serious crime for all purposes and acts, specifically including the State Bar Rules.

Sec. 38.123. Unauthorized Practice of Law.

(a) A person commits an offense if, with intent to obtain an economic benefit for himself or herself, the person:

(1) contracts with any person to represent that person with regard to personal causes of action for property damages or personal injury;

(2) advises any person as to the person's rights and the advisability of making claims for personal injuries or property damages;

(3) advises any person as to whether or not to accept an offered sum of money in settlement of claims for personal injuries or property damages;

(4) enters into any contract with another person to represent that person in personal injury or property damage matters on a contingent fee basis with an attempted assignment of a portion of the person's cause of action; or

(5) enters into any contract with a third person which purports to grant the exclusive right to select and retain legal counsel to represent the individual in any legal proceeding.

(b) This section does not apply to a person currently licensed to practice law in this state, another state, or a foreign country and in good standing with the State Bar of Texas and the state bar or licensing authority of any and all other states and foreign countries where licensed.

(c) Except as provided by Subsection (d) of this section, an offense under Subsection (a) of this section is a Class A misdemeanor.

(d) An offense under Subsection (a) of this section is a felony of the third degree if it is shown on the trial of the offense that the defendant has previously been convicted under Subsection (a) of this section.

Sec. 38.13. Hindering Proceedings by Disorderly Conduct.

(a) A person commits an offense if he intentionally hinders an official proceeding by noise or violent or tumultuous behavior or disturbance.

(b) A person commits an offense if he recklessly hinders an official proceeding by noise or violent or tumultuous behavior or disturbance and continues after explicit official request to desist.

(c) An offense under this section is a Class A misdemeanor.

Sec. 38.14. Taking or Attempting to Take Weapon from Peace Officer, Federal Special Investigator, Employee or Official of Correctional Facility, Parole Officer, Community Supervision and Corrections Department Officer, or Commissioned Security Officer.

(a) In this section:

(1) "Firearm" has the meanings assigned by Section 46.01.

(2) "Stun gun" means a device designed to propel darts or other projectiles attached to wires that, on contact, will deliver an electrical pulse capable of incapacitating a person.

(3) "Commissioned security officer" has the meaning assigned by Section 1702.002(5), Occupations Code.

(b) A person commits an offense if the person intentionally or knowingly and with force takes or attempts to take from a peace officer, federal special investigator, employee or official of a correctional facility, parole officer, community supervision and corrections department officer, or commissioned security officer the officer's, investigator's, employee's, or official's firearm, nightstick, stun gun, or personal protection chemical dispensing device.

(c) The actor is presumed to have known that the peace officer, federal special investigator, employee or official of a correctional facility, parole officer, community supervision and corrections department officer, or commissioned security officer was a peace officer, federal special investigator, employee or official of a correctional facility, parole officer, community supervision and corrections department officer, or commissioned security officer if:

(1) the officer, investigator, employee, or official was wearing a distinctive uniform or badge indicating his employment; or

(2) the officer, investigator, employee, or official identified himself as a peace officer, federal special investigator, employee or official of a correctional facility, parole officer, community supervision and corrections department officer, or commissioned security officer.

(d) It is a defense to prosecution under this section that the defendant took or attempted to take the weapon from a peace officer, federal special investigator, employee or official of a correctional facility, parole officer, community supervision and corrections department officer, or commissioned security officer who was using force against the defendant or another in excess of the amount of force permitted by law.

(e) An offense under this section is:

(1) a felony of the third degree, if the defendant took a weapon described by Subsection (b) from an officer, investigator, employee, or official described by that subsection; and

(2) a state jail felony, if the defendant attempted to take a weapon described by Subsection (b) from an officer, investigator, employee, or official described by that subsection.

Sec. 38.15. Interference with Public Duties.

(a) A person commits an offense if the person with criminal negligence interrupts, disrupts, impedes, or otherwise interferes with:

(1) a peace officer while the peace officer is performing a duty or exercising authority imposed or granted by law;

(2) a person who is employed to provide emergency medical services including the transportation of ill or injured persons while the person is performing that duty;

(3) a fire fighter, while the fire fighter is fighting a fire or investigating the cause of a fire;

(4) an animal under the supervision of a peace officer, corrections officer, or jailer, if the person knows the animal is being used for law enforcement, corrections, prison or jail security, or investigative purposes;

(5) the transmission of a communication over a citizen's band radio channel, the purpose of which communication is to inform or inquire about an emergency;

(6) an officer with responsibility for animal control in a county or municipality, while the officer is performing a duty or exercising authority imposed or granted under Chapter 821 or 822, Health and Safety Code; or

(7) a person who:

(A) has responsibility for assessing, enacting, or enforcing public health, environmental, radiation, or safety measures for the state or a county or municipality;

(B) is investigating a particular site as part of the person's responsibilities under Paragraph (A);

(C) is acting in accordance with policies and procedures related to the safety and security of the site described by Paragraph (B); and

(D) is performing a duty or exercising authority imposed or granted under the Agriculture Code, Health and Safety Code, Occupations Code, or Water Code.

(b) An offense under this section is a Class B misdemeanor.

(c) It is a defense to prosecution under Subsection (a)(1) that the conduct engaged in by the defendant was intended to warn a person operating a motor vehicle of the presence of a peace officer who was enforcing Subtitle C, Title 7, Transportation Code.

(d) It is a defense to prosecution under this section that the interruption, disruption, impediment, or interference alleged consisted of speech only.

(d-1) Except as provided by Subsection (d-2), in a prosecution for an offense under Subsection (a)(1), there is a rebuttable presumption that the actor interferes with a peace officer if it is shown on the trial of the offense that the actor intentionally disseminated the home address, home telephone number, emergency contact information, or social security number of the officer or a family member of the officer or any other information that is specifically described by Section 552.117(a), Government Code.

(d-2) The presumption in Subsection (d-1) does not apply to information disseminated by:

(1) a radio or television station that holds a license issued by the Federal Communications Commission; or

(2) a newspaper that is:

(A) a free newspaper of general circulation or qualified to publish legal notices;

(B) published at least once a week; and

(C) available and of interest to the general public.

(e) In this section, "emergency" means a condition or circumstance in which an individual is or is reasonably believed by the person transmitting the communication to be in imminent danger of serious bodily injury or in which property is or is reasonably believed by the person transmitting the communication to be in imminent danger of damage or destruction.

Sec. 38.151. Interference with Police Service Animals.

(a) In this section:

(1) "Area of control" includes a vehicle, trailer, kennel, pen, or yard.

(2) "Handler or rider" means a peace officer, corrections officer, or jailer who is specially trained to use a police service animal for law enforcement, corrections, prison or jail security, or investigative purposes.

(3) "Police service animal" means a dog, horse, or other domesticated animal that is specially trained for use by a handler or rider.

(b) A person commits an offense if the person recklessly:

(1) taunts, torments, or strikes a police service animal;

(2) throws an object or substance at a police service animal;

(3) interferes with or obstructs a police service animal or interferes with or obstructs the handler or rider of a police service animal in a manner that:

(A) inhibits or restricts the handler's or rider's control of the animal; or

(B) deprives the handler or rider of control of the animal;

(4) releases a police service animal from its area of control;

(5) enters the area of control of a police service animal without the effective consent of the handler or rider, including placing food or any other object or substance into that area;

(6) injures or kills a police service animal; or

(7) engages in conduct likely to injure or kill a police service animal, including administering or setting a poison, trap, or any other object or substance.

(c) An offense under this section is:

(1) a Class C misdemeanor if the person commits an offense under Subsection (b)(1);

(2) a Class B misdemeanor if the person commits an offense under Subsection (b)(2);

(3) a Class A misdemeanor if the person commits an offense under Subsection (b)(3), (4), or (5);

(4) except as provided by Subdivision (5), a state jail felony if the person commits an offense under Subsection (b)(6) or (7) by injuring a police service animal or by engaging in conduct likely to injure the animal; or

(5) a felony of the second degree if the person commits an offense under Subsection (b)(6) or (7) by:

(A) killing a police service animal or engaging in conduct likely to kill the animal;

(B) injuring a police service animal in a manner that materially and permanently affects the ability of the animal to perform as a police service animal; or

(C) engaging in conduct likely to injure a police service animal in a manner that would materially and permanently affect the ability of the animal to perform as a police service animal.

Sec. 38.152. Interference with Radio Frequency Licensed to Government Entity.

(a) A person commits an offense if, without the effective consent of the law enforcement agency, fire department, or emergency medical services provider, the person intentionally interrupts, disrupts, impedes, jams, or otherwise interferes with a radio frequency that is licensed by the Federal Communications Commission to a government entity and is used by the law enforcement agency, fire department, or emergency medical services provider.

(b) An offense under this section is a Class A misdemeanor, except that the offense is a state jail felony if the actor committed the offense with the intent to:

(1) facilitate the commission of another offense; or

(2) interfere with the ability of a law enforcement agency, a fire department, or an emergency medical services provider to respond to an emergency.

(c) In this section:

(1) "Emergency" has the meaning assigned by Section 38.15.

(2) "Emergency medical services provider" has the meaning assigned by Section 773.003, Health and Safety Code.

(3) "Law enforcement agency" has the meaning assigned by Article 59.01, Code of Criminal Procedure.

(d) If conduct constituting an offense under this section also constitutes an offense under another section of this code, the actor may be prosecuted under either section or under both sections.

Sec. 38.16. Preventing Execution of Civil Process.

(a) A person commits an offense if he intentionally or knowingly by words or physical action prevents the execution of any process in a civil cause.

(b) It is an exception to the application of this section that the actor evaded service of process by avoiding detection.

(c) An offense under this section is a Class C misdemeanor.

Sec. 38.17. Failure to Stop or Report Aggravated Sexual Assault of Child.

(a) A person, other than a person who has a relationship with a child described by Section 22.04(b), commits an offense if:

(1) the actor observes the commission or attempted commission of an offense prohibited by Section 21.02 or 22.021(a)(2)(B) under circumstances in which a reasonable person would believe that an offense of a sexual or assaultive nature was being committed or was about to be committed against the child;

(2) the actor fails to assist the child or immediately report the commission of the offense to a peace officer or law enforcement agency; and

(3) the actor could assist the child or immediately report the commission of the offense without placing the actor in danger of suffering serious bodily injury or death.

(b) An offense under this section is a Class A misdemeanor.

Sec. 38.171. Failure to Report Felony.

(a) A person commits an offense if the person:

(1) observes the commission of a felony under circumstances in which a reasonable person would believe that an offense had been committed in which serious bodily injury or death may have resulted; and

(2) fails to immediately report the commission of the offense to a peace officer or law enforcement agency under circumstances in which:

(A) a reasonable person would believe that the commission of the offense had not been reported; and

(B) the person could immediately report the commission of the offense without placing himself or herself in danger of suffering serious bodily injury or death.

(b) An offense under this section is a Class A misdemeanor.

Sec. 38.18. Use of Accident Report Information and Other Information for Pecuniary Gain.

(a) This section applies to:

(1) information described by Section 550.065(a), Transportation Code;

(2) information reported under Chapter 772, Health and Safety Code, other than information that is confidential under that chapter; and

(3) information contained in a dispatch log, a towing record, or a record of a 9-1-1 service provider, other than information that is confidential under Chapter 772, Health and Safety Code.

(b) A person commits an offense if:

(1) the person obtains information described by Subsection (a) from the Department of Public Safety of the State of Texas or other governmental entity; and

(2) the information is subsequently used for the direct solicitation of business or employment for pecuniary gain by:

(A) the person;

(B) an agent or employee of the person; or

(C) the person on whose behalf the information was requested.

(c) A person who employs or engages another to obtain information described by Subsection (a) from the Department of Public Safety or other governmental entity commits an offense if the person subsequently uses the information for direct solicitation of business or employment for pecuniary gain.

(d) An offense under this section is a Class B misdemeanor.

Sec. 38.19. Failure to Provide Notice and Report of Death of Resident of Institution.

(a) A superintendent or general manager of an institution commits an offense if, as required by Article 49.24 or 49.25, Code of Criminal Procedure, the person fails to:

(1) provide notice of the death of an individual under the care, custody, or control of or residing in the institution;

(2) submit a report on the death of the individual; or

(3) include in the report material facts known or discovered by the person at the time the report was filed.

(b) An offense under this section is a Class B misdemeanor.

CHAPTER 39
ABUSE OF OFFICE

Sec. 39.01. Definitions.

In this chapter:

(1) "Law relating to a public servant's office or employment" means a law that specifically applies to a person acting in the capacity of a public servant and that directly or indirectly:

(A) imposes a duty on the public servant; or

(B) governs the conduct of the public servant.

(2) "Misuse" means to deal with property contrary to:

(A) an agreement under which the public servant holds the property;

(B) a contract of employment or oath of office of a public servant;

(C) a law, including provisions of the General Appropriations Act specifically relating to government property, that prescribes the manner of custody or disposition of the property; or

(D) a limited purpose for which the property is delivered or received.

Sec. 39.015. Concurrent Jurisdiction to Prosecute Offenses Under This Chapter.

With the consent of the appropriate local county or district attorney, the attorney general has concurrent jurisdiction with that consenting local prosecutor to prosecute an offense under this chapter.

Sec. 39.02. Abuse of Official Capacity.

(a) A public servant commits an offense if, with intent to obtain a benefit or with intent to harm or defraud another, he intentionally or knowingly:

(1) violates a law relating to the public servant's office or employment; or

(2) misuses government property, services, personnel, or any other thing of value belonging to the government that has come into the public servant's custody or possession by virtue of the public servant's office or employment.

(b) An offense under Subsection (a)(1) is a Class A misdemeanor.

(c) An offense under Subsection (a)(2) is:

(1) a Class C misdemeanor if the value of the use of the thing misused is less than $100;

(2) a Class B misdemeanor if the value of the use of the thing misused is $100 or more but less than $750;

(3) a Class A misdemeanor if the value of the use of the thing misused is $750 or more but less than $2,500;

(4) a state jail felony if the value of the use of the thing misused is $2,500 or more but less than $30,000;

(5) a felony of the third degree if the value of the use of the thing misused is $30,000 or more but less than $150,000;

(6) a felony of the second degree if the value of the use of the thing misused is $150,000 or more but less than $300,000; or

(7) a felony of the first degree if the value of the use of the thing misused is $300,000 or more.

(d) A discount or award given for travel, such as frequent flyer miles, rental car or hotel discounts, or food coupons, are not things of value belonging to the government for purposes of this section due to the administrative difficulty and cost involved in recapturing the discount or award for a governmental entity.

(e) If separate transactions that violate Subsection (a)(2) are conducted pursuant to one scheme or continuing course of conduct, the conduct may be considered as one offense and the value of the use of the things misused in the transactions may be aggregated in determining the classification of the offense.

(f) The value of the use of a thing of value misused under Subsection (a)(2) may not exceed:

(1) the fair market value of the thing at the time of the offense; or

(2) if the fair market value of the thing cannot be ascertained, the cost of replacing the thing within a reasonable time after the offense.

Sec. 39.021. Violations of the Civil Rights of a Prisoner [Renumbered].

Renumbered to Tex. Penal Code § 39.04 by Acts 1993, 73rd Leg., ch. 900 (S.B. 1067), § 1.01, effective September 1, 1994.

Sec. 39.022. Failure to Report Death of Prisoner [Renumbered].

Renumbered to Tex. Penal Code § 39.05 by Acts 1993, 73rd Leg., ch. 900 (S.B. 1067), § 1.01, effective September 1, 1994.

Sec. 39.03. Official Oppression.

(a) A public servant acting under color of his office or employment commits an offense if he:

(1) intentionally subjects another to mistreatment or to arrest, detention, search, seizure, dispossession, assessment, or lien that he knows is unlawful;

(2) intentionally denies or impedes another in the exercise or enjoyment of any right, privilege, power, or immunity, knowing his conduct is unlawful; or

(3) intentionally subjects another to sexual harassment.

(b) For purposes of this section, a public servant acts under color of his office or employment if he acts or purports to act in an official capacity or takes advantage of such actual or purported capacity.

(c) In this section, "sexual harassment" means unwelcome sexual advances, requests for sexual favors, or other verbal or physical conduct of a sexual nature, submission to which is made a term or condition of a person's exercise or enjoyment of any right, privilege, power, or immunity, either explicitly or implicitly.

(d) An offense under this section is a Class A misdemeanor, except that an offense is a felony of the third degree if the public servant acted with the intent to impair the accuracy of data reported to the Texas Education Agency through the Public Education Information Management System (PEIMS) described by Sections 48.008 and 48.009, Education Code, under a law requiring that reporting.

Sec. 39.04. Violations of the Civil Rights of Person in Custody; Improper Sexual Activity with Person in Custody or Under Supervision.

(a) An official of a correctional facility or juvenile facility, an employee of a correctional facility or juvenile facility, a person other than an employee who works for compensation at a correctional facility or juvenile facility, a volunteer at a correctional facility or juvenile facility, or a peace officer commits an offense if the person intentionally:

(1) denies or impedes a person in custody in the exercise or enjoyment of any right, privilege, or immunity knowing his conduct is unlawful; or

(2) engages in sexual contact, sexual intercourse, or deviate sexual intercourse with an individual in custody or, in the case of an individual in the custody of the Texas Juvenile Justice Department or placed in a juvenile facility, employs, authorizes, or induces the individual to engage in sexual conduct or a sexual performance.

(b) **As amended by Acts 2021, 87th Leg., ch. XXX (HB 3157)** An offense under Subsection (a)(1) is a felony of the third degree. An offense under Subsection (a)(2) is a felony of the second degree, except that an offense under Subsection (a)(2) is a felony of the first degree if the offense is committed against:

(1) an individual in the custody of the Texas Juvenile Justice Department or placed in a juvenile facility; or

(2) a juvenile offender detained in or committed to a correctional facility.

(b) **As amended by Acts 2021, 87th Leg., ch. XXX (SB 312)** An offense under Subsection (a)(1) is a Class A misdemeanor. An offense under Subsection (a)(2) is a felony of the second degree.

(c) This section shall not preclude prosecution for any other offense set out in this code.

(d) The Attorney General of Texas shall have concurrent jurisdiction with law enforcement agencies to investigate violations of this statute involving serious bodily injury or death.

(e) In this section:

(1) **[2 Versions: As amended by Acts 2015, 84th Leg., ch. 216]** "Correctional facility" means:

(A) any place described by Section 1.07(a)(14);

(B) any place or facility designated for the detention of a person suspected of violating a provision of the Immigration and Nationality Act (8 U.S.C. Section 1101 et seq.); or

(C) a "secure correctional facility" or "secure detention facility" as defined by Section 51.02, Family Code.

(1) **[2 Versions: As amended by Acts 2015, 84th Leg., ch. 1136]** "Correctional facility" means any place described by Section 1.07(a)(14).

(2) "Custody" means the detention, arrest, or confinement of an adult offender, the detention of a juvenile offender, or the commitment of a juvenile offender to a correctional facility or juvenile facility.

(2-a) "Juvenile facility" means:

(A) a facility operated by the Texas Juvenile Justice Department or a private vendor under a contract with the Texas Juvenile Justice Department; or

(B) a facility for the detention or placement of juveniles under juvenile court jurisdiction and that is operated wholly or partly by a juvenile board or another governmental unit or by a private vendor under a contract with the juvenile board or governmental unit.

(3) "Sexual contact," "sexual intercourse," and "deviate sexual intercourse" have the meanings assigned by Section 21.01.

(4) "Sexual conduct" and "performance" have the meanings assigned by Section 43.25.

(5) "Sexual performance" means any performance or part thereof that includes sexual conduct by an individual.

(f) An employee of the Texas Department of Criminal Justice, the Texas Juvenile Justice Department, a juvenile facility, a local juvenile probation department, or a community supervision and corrections department established under Chapter 76, Government Code, a person other than an employee who works for compensation at a juvenile facility or local juvenile probation department, or a volunteer at a juvenile facility or local juvenile probation department commits an offense if the actor engages in sexual contact, sexual intercourse, or deviate sexual intercourse with an individual who the actor knows is under the supervision of the Texas Department of Criminal Justice, Texas Juvenile Justice Department, probation department, or community supervision and corrections department but not in the custody of the Texas Department of Criminal Justice, Texas Juvenile Justice Department, probation department, or community supervision and corrections department.

(g) An offense under Subsection (f) is a state jail felony.

(h) It is an affirmative defense to prosecution under Subsection (f) that the actor was the spouse of the individual at the time of the offense.

Sec. 39.05. Failure to Report Death of Prisoner.

(a) A person commits an offense if the person is required to conduct an investigation and file a report by Article 49.18, Code of Criminal Procedure, and the person fails to investigate the death, fails to file the report as required, or fails to include in a filed report facts known or discovered in the investigation.

(b) A person commits an offense if the person is required by Section 501.055, Government Code, to:

(1) give notice of the death of an inmate and the person fails to give the notice; or

(2) conduct an investigation and file a report and the person:

(A) fails to conduct the investigation or file the report; or

(B) fails to include in the report facts known to the person or discovered by the person in the investigation.

(c) An offense under this section is a Class B misdemeanor.

Sec. 39.06. Misuse of Official Information.

(a) A public servant commits an offense if, in reliance on information to which the public servant has access by virtue of the person's office or employment and that has not been made public, the person:

(1) acquires or aids another to acquire a pecuniary interest in any property, transaction, or enterprise that may be affected by the information;

(2) speculates or aids another to speculate on the basis of the information; or

(3) as a public servant, including as a school administrator, coerces another into suppressing or failing to report that information to a law enforcement agency.

(b) A public servant commits an offense if with intent to obtain a benefit or with intent to harm or defraud another, he discloses or uses information for a nongovernmental purpose that:

(1) he has access to by means of his office or employment; and

(2) has not been made public.

(c) A person commits an offense if, with intent to obtain a benefit or with intent to harm or defraud another, he solicits or receives from a public servant information that:

(1) the public servant has access to by means of his office or employment; and

(2) has not been made public.

(d) In this section, "information that has not been made public" means any information to which the public does not generally have access, and that is prohibited from disclosure under Chapter 552, Government Code.

(e) Except as provided by Subsection (f), an offense under this section is a felony of the third degree.

(f) An offense under Subsection (a)(3) is a Class C misdemeanor.

Sec. 39.07. Failure to Comply with Immigration Detainer Request.

(a) A person who is a sheriff, chief of police, or constable or a person who otherwise has primary authority for administering a jail commits an offense if the person:

(1) has custody of a person subject to an immigration detainer request issued by United States Immigration and Customs Enforcement; and

(2) knowingly fails to comply with the detainer request.

(b) An offense under this section is a Class A misdemeanor.

(c) It is an exception to the application of this section that the person who was subject to an immigration detainer request described by Subsection (a)(1) had provided proof that the person is a citizen of the United States or that the person has lawful immigration status in the United States, such as a Texas driver's license or similar government-issued identification.

TITLE 9 OFFENSES AGAINST PUBLIC ORDER AND DECENCY

CHAPTER 42 DISORDERLY CONDUCT AND RELATED OFFENSES

Sec. 42.01. Disorderly Conduct.

(a) A person commits an offense if he intentionally or knowingly:

(1) uses abusive, indecent, profane, or vulgar language in a public place, and the language by its very utterance tends to incite an immediate breach of the peace;

(2) makes an offensive gesture or display in a public place, and the gesture or display tends to incite an immediate breach of the peace;

(3) creates, by chemical means, a noxious and unreasonable odor in a public place;

(4) abuses or threatens a person in a public place in an obviously offensive manner;

(5) makes unreasonable noise in a public place other than a sport shooting range, as defined by Section 250.001, Local Government Code, or in or near a private residence that he has no right to occupy;

(6) fights with another in a public place;

(7) discharges a firearm in a public place other than a public road or a sport shooting range, as defined by Section 250.001, Local Government Code;

(8) displays a firearm or other deadly weapon in a public place in a manner calculated to alarm;

(9) discharges a firearm on or across a public road;

(10) exposes his anus or genitals in a public place and is reckless about whether another may be present who will be offended or alarmed by his act; or

(11) for a lewd or unlawful purpose:

(A) enters on the property of another and looks into a dwelling on the property through any window or other opening in the dwelling;

(B) while on the premises of a hotel or comparable establishment, looks into a guest room not the person's own through a window or other opening in the room; or

(C) while on the premises of a public place, looks into an area such as a restroom or shower stall or changing or dressing room that is designed to provide privacy to a person using the area.

(a-1) For purposes of Subsection (a), the term "public place" includes a public school campus or the school grounds on which a public school is located.

(b) It is a defense to prosecution under Subsection (a)(4) that the actor had significant provocation for his abusive or threatening conduct.

(c) For purposes of this section:

(1) an act is deemed to occur in a public place or near a private residence if it produces its offensive or proscribed consequences in the public place or near a private residence; and

(2) a noise is presumed to be unreasonable if the noise exceeds a decibel level of 85 after the person making the noise receives notice from a magistrate or peace officer that the noise is a public nuisance.

(d) An offense under this section is a Class C misdemeanor unless committed under Subsection (a)(7) or (a)(8), in which event it is a Class B misdemeanor.

(e) It is a defense to prosecution for an offense under Subsection (a)(7) or (9) that the person who discharged the firearm had a reasonable fear of bodily injury to the person or to another by a dangerous wild animal as defined by Section 822.101, Health and Safety Code.

(f) Subsections (a)(1), (2), (3), (5), and (6) do not apply to a person who, at the time the person engaged in conduct prohibited under the applicable subdivision, was a student younger than 12 years of age, and the prohibited conduct occurred at a public school campus during regular school hours.

(g) Noise arising from space flight activities, as defined by Section 100A.001, Civil Practice and Remedies Code, if lawfully conducted, does not constitute "unreasonable noise" for purposes of this section.

Sec. 42.015. Discharge of Firearm in Certain Metropolitan Areas [Deleted].

Deleted by Acts 1993, 73rd Leg., ch. 900 (S.B. 1067), § 13.02, effective September 1, 1994.

Sec. 42.02. Riot.

(a) For the purpose of this section, "riot" means the assemblage of seven or more persons resulting in conduct which:

(1) creates an immediate danger of damage to property or injury to persons;

(2) substantially obstructs law enforcement or other governmental functions or services; or

(3) by force, threat of force, or physical action deprives any person of a legal right or disturbs any person in the enjoyment of a legal right.

(b) A person commits an offense if he knowingly participates in a riot.

(c) It is a defense to prosecution under this section that the assembly was at first lawful and when one of those assembled manifested an intent to engage in conduct enumerated in Subsection (a), the actor retired from the assembly.

(d) It is no defense to prosecution under this section that another who was a party to the riot has been acquitted, has not been arrested, prosecuted, or convicted, has been convicted of a different offense or of a different type or class of offense, or is immune from prosecution.

(e) Except as provided in Subsection (f), an offense under this section is a Class B misdemeanor.

(f) An offense under this section is an offense of the same classification as any offense of a higher grade committed by anyone engaged in the riot if the offense was:

(1) in the furtherance of the purpose of the assembly; or

(2) an offense which should have been anticipated as a result of the assembly.

Sec. 42.03. Obstructing Highway or Other Passageway.

(a) A person commits an offense if, without legal privilege or authority, he intentionally, knowingly, or recklessly:

(1) obstructs a highway, street, sidewalk, railway, waterway, elevator, aisle, hallway, entrance, or exit to which the public or a substantial group of the public has access, or any other place used for the passage of persons, vehicles, or conveyances, regardless of the means of creating the obstruction and whether the obstruction arises from his acts alone or from his acts and the acts of others; or

(2) disobeys a reasonable request or order to move issued by a person the actor knows to be or is informed is a peace officer, a fireman, or a person with authority to control the use of the premises:

(A) to prevent obstruction of a highway or any of those areas mentioned in Subdivision (1); or

(B) to maintain public safety by dispersing those gathered in dangerous proximity to a fire, riot, or other hazard.

(b) For purposes of this section, "obstruct" means to render impassable or to render passage unreasonably inconvenient or hazardous.

(c) **As amended by Acts 2021, 87th Leg., ch. XXX (HB 9)** An offense under this section is a Class B misdemeanor, except that the offense is a state jail felony if, in committing the offense, the actor knowingly:

(1) prevents the passage of an authorized emergency vehicle, as defined by Section 541.201, Transportation Code, that is operating the vehicle's emergency audible or visual signals required by Section 546.003, Transportation Code; or

(2) obstructs access to a hospital licensed under Chapter 241, Health and Safety Code, or other health care facility that provides emergency medical care, as defined by Section 773.003, Health and Safety Code.

(c) **As amended by Acts 2021, 87th Leg., ch. XXX (SB 1495)** Except as otherwise provided by Subsections (d) and (e), an offense under this section is a Class B misdemeanor.

(d) Subject to Subsection (e), an offense under this section is a Class A misdemeanor if it is shown on the trial of the offense that, at the time of the offense, the person was operating a motor vehicle while engaging in a reckless driving exhibition.

(e) An offense under this section is a state jail felony if it is shown on the trial of the offense that, at the time of the offense, the person was operating a motor vehicle while engaging in a reckless driving exhibition, and:

(1) the person has previously been convicted of an offense punishable under Subsection (d);

(2) at the time of the offense, the person was operating a motor vehicle while intoxicated, as defined by Section 49.01; or

(3) a person suffered bodily injury as a result of the offense.

(f) For purposes of this section, "reckless driving exhibition" means an operator of a motor vehicle, on a highway or street and in the presence of two or more persons assembled for the purpose of spectating the conduct, intentionally:

(1) breaking the traction of the vehicle's rear tires;

(2) spinning the vehicle's rear tires continuously by pressing the accelerator and increasing the engine speed; and

(3) steering the vehicle in a manner designed to rotate the vehicle.

Sec. 42.04. Defense When Conduct Consists of Speech or Other Expression.

(a) If conduct that would otherwise violate Section 42.01(a)(5) (Unreasonable Noise), 42.03 (Obstructing Passageway), or 42.055 (Funeral Service Disruptions) consists of speech or other communication, of gathering with others to hear or observe such speech or communication, or of gathering with others to picket or otherwise express in a nonviolent manner a position on social, economic, political, or religious questions, the actor must be ordered to move, disperse, or otherwise remedy the violation prior to his arrest if he has not yet intentionally harmed the interests of others which those sections seek to protect.

(b) The order required by this section may be given by a peace officer, a fireman, a person with authority to control the use of the premises, or any person directly affected by the violation.

(c) It is a defense to prosecution under Section 42.01(a)(5), 42.03, or 42.055:

(1) that in circumstances in which this section requires an order no order was given;

(2) that an order, if given, was manifestly unreasonable in scope; or

(3) that an order, if given, was promptly obeyed.

Sec. 42.05. Disrupting Meeting or Procession.

(a) A person commits an offense if, with intent to prevent or disrupt a lawful meeting, procession, or gathering, he obstructs or interferes with the meeting, procession, or gathering by physical action or verbal utterance.

(b) An offense under this section is a Class B misdemeanor.

Sec. 42.055. Funeral Service Disruptions.

(a) In this section:

(1) "Facility" means a building at which any portion of a funeral service takes place, including a funeral parlor, mortuary, private home, or established place of worship.

(2) "Funeral service" means a ceremony, procession, or memorial service, including a wake or viewing, held in connection with the burial or cremation of the dead.

(3) "Picketing" means:

(A) standing, sitting, or repeated walking, riding, driving, or other similar action by a person displaying or carrying a banner, placard, or sign;

(B) engaging in loud singing, chanting, whistling, or yelling, with or without noise amplification through a device such as a bullhorn or microphone; or

(C) blocking access to a facility or cemetery being used for a funeral service.

(b) A person commits an offense if, during the period beginning three hours before the service begins and ending three hours after the service is completed, the person engages in picketing within 1,000 feet of a facility or cemetery being used for a funeral service.

(c) An offense under this section is a Class B misdemeanor.

Sec. 42.06. False Alarm or Report.

(a) A person commits an offense if he knowingly initiates, communicates or circulates a report of a present, past, or future bombing, fire, offense, or other emergency that he knows is false or baseless and that would ordinarily:

(1) cause action by an official or volunteer agency organized to deal with emergencies;

(2) place a person in fear of imminent serious bodily injury; or

(3) prevent or interrupt the occupation of a building, room, place of assembly, place to which the public has access, or aircraft, automobile, or other mode of conveyance.

(b) An offense under this section is a Class A misdemeanor unless the false report is of an emergency involving a public or private institution of higher education or involving a public primary or secondary school, public communications, public transportation, public water, gas, or power supply or other public service, in which event the offense is a state jail felony.

Sec. 42.0601. False Report to Induce Emergency Response.

(a) A person commits an offense if:

(1) the person makes a report of a criminal offense or an emergency or causes a report of a criminal offense or an emergency to be made to a peace officer, law enforcement agency, 9-1-1 service as defined by Section 771.001, Health and Safety Code, official or volunteer agency organized to deal with emergencies, or any other governmental employee or contractor who is authorized to receive reports of a criminal offense or emergency;

(2) the person knows that the report is false;

(3) the report causes an emergency response from a law enforcement agency or other emergency responder; and

(4) in making the report or causing the report to be made, the person is reckless with regard to whether the emergency response by a law enforcement agency or other emergency responder may directly result in bodily injury to another person.

(b) An offense under this section is a Class A misdemeanor, except that the offense is:

(1) a state jail felony if it is shown on the trial of the offense that the defendant has previously been convicted two or more times of an offense under this section; or

(2) a felony of the third degree if:

(A) the false report was of a criminal offense to which a law enforcement agency or other emergency responder responded; and

(B) a person suffered serious bodily injury or death as a direct result of lawful conduct arising out of that response.

(c) If conduct constituting an offense under this section also constitutes an offense under another section of this code, the actor may be prosecuted under either section or both sections.

(d) This section may not be construed in any manner to conflict with 47 U.S.C. Section 230 or 42 U.S.C. Section 1983.

Sec. 42.061. Silent or Abusive Calls to 9-1-1 Service.

(a) In this section "9-1-1 service" and "public safety answering point" or "PSAP" have the meanings assigned by Section 771.001, Health and Safety Code.

(b) A person commits an offense if the person makes a call to a 9-1-1 service, or requests 9-1-1 service using an electronic communications device, when there is not an emergency and knowingly or intentionally:

(1) remains silent; or

(2) makes abusive or harassing statements to a PSAP employee.

(c) A person commits an offense if the person knowingly permits an electronic communications device, including a telephone, under the person's control to be used by another person in a manner described in Subsection (b).

(d) An offense under this section is a Class B misdemeanor.

Sec. 42.062. Interference with Emergency Request for Assistance.

(a) An individual commits an offense if the individual knowingly prevents or interferes with another individual's ability to place an emergency call or to request assistance, including a request for assistance using an electronic communications device, in an emergency from a law enforcement agency, medical facility, or other agency or entity the primary purpose of which is to provide for the safety of individuals.

(b) An individual commits an offense if the individual recklessly renders unusable an electronic communications device, including a telephone, that would otherwise be used by another individual to place an emergency call or to request assistance in an emergency from a law enforcement agency, medical facility, or other agency or entity the primary purpose of which is to provide for the safety of individuals.

(c) An offense under this section is a Class A misdemeanor, except that the offense is a state jail felony if the actor has previously been convicted under this section.

(d) In this section, "emergency" means a condition or circumstance in which any individual is or is reasonably believed by the individual making a call or requesting assistance to be in fear of imminent assault or in which property is or is reasonably believed by the individual making the call or requesting assistance to be in imminent danger of damage or destruction.

Sec. 42.07. Harassment.

(a) A person commits an offense if, with intent to harass, annoy, alarm, abuse, torment, or embarrass another, the person:

(1) initiates communication and in the course of the communication makes a comment, request, suggestion, or proposal that is obscene;

(2) threatens, in a manner reasonably likely to alarm the person receiving the threat, to inflict bodily injury on the person or to commit a felony against the person, a member of the person's family or household, or the person's property;

(3) conveys, in a manner reasonably likely to alarm the person receiving the report, a false report, which is known by the conveyor to be false, that another person has suffered death or serious bodily injury;

(4) causes the telephone of another to ring repeatedly or makes repeated telephone communications anonymously or in a manner reasonably likely to harass, annoy, alarm, abuse, torment, embarrass, or offend another;

(5) makes a telephone call and intentionally fails to hang up or disengage the connection;

(6) knowingly permits a telephone under the person's control to be used by another to commit an offense under this section;

(7) sends repeated electronic communications in a manner reasonably likely to harass, annoy, alarm, abuse, torment, embarrass, or offend another; or

(8) publishes on an Internet website, including a social media platform, repeated electronic communications in a manner reasonably likely to cause emotional distress, abuse, or torment to another person, unless the communications are made in connection with a matter of public concern.

(b) In this section:

(1) "Electronic communication" means a transfer of signs, signals, writing, images, sounds, data, or intelligence of any nature transmitted in whole or in part by a wire, radio, electromagnetic, photoelectronic, or photo-optical system. The term includes:

(A) a communication initiated through the use of electronic mail, instant message, network call, a cellular or other type of telephone, a computer, a camera, text message, a social media platform or application, an Internet website, any other Internet-based communication tool, or facsimile machine; and

(B) a communication made to a pager.

(2) "Family" and "household" have the meaning assigned by Chapter 71, Family Code.

(3) "Obscene" means containing a patently offensive description of or a solicitation to commit an ultimate sex act, including sexual intercourse, masturbation, cunnilingus, fellatio, or anilingus, or a description of an excretory function.

(c) An offense under this section is a Class B misdemeanor, except that the offense is a Class A misdemeanor if:

(1) the actor has previously been convicted under this section; or

(2) the offense was committed under Subsection (a)(7) or (8) and:

(A) the offense was committed against a child under 18 years of age with the intent that the child:

(i) commit suicide; or

(ii) engage in conduct causing serious bodily injury to the child; or

(B) the actor has previously violated a temporary restraining order or injunction issued under Chapter 129A, Civil Practice and Remedies Code.

(d) In this section, "matter of public concern" has the meaning assigned by Section 27.001, Civil Practice and Remedies Code.

Sec. 42.071. Stalking [Repealed].

Repealed by Acts 1997, 75th Leg., ch. 1 (S.B. 97), § 10, effective January 28, 1997.

Sec. 42.072. Stalking.

(a) A person commits an offense if the person, on more than one occasion and pursuant to the same scheme or course of conduct that is directed specifically at another person, knowingly engages in conduct that:

(1) constitutes an offense under Section 42.07, or that the actor knows or reasonably should know the other person will regard as threatening:

(A) bodily injury or death for the other person;

(B) bodily injury or death for a member of the other person's family or household or for an individual with whom the other person has a dating relationship; or

(C) that an offense will be committed against the other person's property;

(2) causes the other person, a member of the other person's family or household, or an individual with whom the other person has a dating relationship to be placed in fear of bodily injury or death or in fear that an offense will be committed against the other person's property, or to feel harassed, annoyed, alarmed, abused, tormented, embarrassed, or offended; and

(3) would cause a reasonable person to:

(A) fear bodily injury or death for himself or herself;

(B) fear bodily injury or death for a member of the person's family or household or for an individual with whom the person has a dating relationship;

(C) fear that an offense will be committed against the person's property; or

(D) feel harassed, annoyed, alarmed, abused, tormented, embarrassed, or offended.

(b) An offense under this section is a felony of the third degree, except that the offense is a felony of the second degree if the actor has previously been convicted of an offense under this section or of an offense under any of the following laws that contains elements that are substantially similar to the elements of an offense under this section:

(1) the laws of another state;

(2) the laws of a federally recognized Indian tribe;

(3) the laws of a territory of the United States; or

(4) federal law.

(c) For purposes of this section, a trier of fact may find that different types of conduct described by Subsection (a), if engaged in on more than one occasion, constitute conduct that is engaged in pursuant to the same scheme or course of conduct.

(d) In this section:

(1) "Dating relationship," "family," "household," and "member of a household" have the meanings assigned by Chapter 71, Family Code.

(2) "Property" includes a pet, companion animal, or assistance animal, as defined by Section 121.002, Human Resources Code.

Sec. 42.075. Disclosure of Confidential Information Regarding Family Violence or Victims of Trafficking Shelter Center.

(a) In this section, "family violence shelter center" and "victims of trafficking shelter center" have the meanings assigned by Section 552.138, Government Code.

(b) A person commits an offense if the person, with the intent to threaten the safety of any inhabitant of a family violence shelter center or victims of trafficking shelter center, discloses or publicizes the location or physical layout of the center.

(c) An offense under this section is a Class A misdemeanor.

(d) If conduct constituting an offense under this section also constitutes an offense under Section 552.352, Government Code, the actor may be prosecuted under either section.

Sec. 42.08. Abuse of Corpse.

(a) A person commits an offense if the person, without legal authority, knowingly:

(1) disinters, disturbs, damages, dissects, in whole or in part, carries away, or treats in an offensive manner a human corpse;

(2) conceals a human corpse knowing it to be illegally disinterred;

(3) sells or buys a human corpse or in any way traffics in a human corpse;

(4) transmits or conveys, or procures to be transmitted or conveyed, a human corpse to a place outside the state; or

(5) vandalizes, damages, or treats in an offensive manner the space in which a human corpse has been interred or otherwise permanently laid to rest.

(b) An offense under this section is a state jail felony, except that an offense under Subsection (a)(5) is a Class A misdemeanor.

(c) In this section, "human corpse" includes:

(1) any portion of a human corpse;

(2) the cremated remains of a human corpse; or

(3) any portion of the cremated remains of a human corpse.

(d) If conduct constituting an offense under this section also constitutes an offense under another section of this code, the actor may be prosecuted under either section or both sections.

(e) It is a defense to prosecution under this section that the actor:

(1) as a member or agent of a cemetery organization, removed or damaged anything that had been placed in or on any portion of the organization's cemetery in violation of the rules of the organization; or

(2) removed anything:

(A) placed in the cemetery in violation of the rules of the cemetery organization; or

(B) placed in the cemetery by or with the cemetery organization's consent but that, in the organization's judgment, had become wrecked, unsightly, or dilapidated.

(f) In this section, "cemetery" and "cemetery organization" have the meanings assigned by Section 711.001, Health and Safety Code.

Sec. 42.09. Cruelty to Livestock Animals.

(a) A person commits an offense if the person intentionally or knowingly:

(1) tortures a livestock animal;

(2) fails unreasonably to provide necessary food, water, or care for a livestock animal in the person's custody;

(3) abandons unreasonably a livestock animal in the person's custody;

(4) transports or confines a livestock animal in a cruel and unusual manner;

(5) administers poison to a livestock animal, other than cattle, horses, sheep, swine, or goats, belonging to another without legal authority or the owner's effective consent;

(6) causes one livestock animal to fight with another livestock animal or with an animal as defined by Section 42.092;

(7) uses a live livestock animal as a lure in dog race training or in dog coursing on a racetrack;

(8) trips a horse; or

(9) seriously overworks a livestock animal.

(b) In this section:

(1) "Abandon" includes abandoning a livestock animal in the person's custody without making reasonable arrangements for assumption of custody by another person.

(2) "Cruel manner" includes a manner that causes or permits unjustified or unwarranted pain or suffering.

(3) "Custody" includes responsibility for the health, safety, and welfare of a livestock animal subject to the person's care and control, regardless of ownership of the livestock animal.

(4) "Depredation" has the meaning assigned by Section 71.001, Parks and Wildlife Code.

(5) "Livestock animal" means:

(A) cattle, sheep, swine, goats, ratites, or poultry commonly raised for human consumption;

(B) a horse, pony, mule, donkey, or hinny;

(C) native or nonnative hoofstock raised under agriculture practices; or

(D) native or nonnative fowl commonly raised under agricultural practices.

(6) "Necessary food, water, or care" includes food, water, or care provided to the extent required to maintain the livestock animal in a state of good health.

(7) "Torture" includes any act that causes unjustifiable pain or suffering.

(8) "Trip" means to use an object to cause a horse to fall or lose its balance.

(c) An offense under Subsection (a)(2), (3), (4), or (9) is a Class A misdemeanor, except that the offense is a state jail felony if the person has previously been convicted two times under this section, two times under Section 42.092, or one time under this section and one time under Section 42.092. An offense under Subsection (a)(1), (5), (6), (7), or (8) is a state jail felony, except that the offense is a felony of the third degree if the person has previously been convicted two times under this section, two times under Section 42.092, or one time under this section and one time under Section 42.092.

(d) It is a defense to prosecution under Subsection (a)(8) that the actor tripped the horse for the purpose of identifying the ownership of the horse or giving veterinary care to the horse.

(e) It is a defense to prosecution for an offense under this section that the actor was engaged in bona fide experimentation for scientific research.

(f) It is an exception to the application of this section that the conduct engaged in by the actor is a generally accepted and otherwise lawful:

(1) form of conduct occurring solely for the purpose of or in support of:

(A) fishing, hunting, or trapping; or

(B) wildlife management, wildlife or depredation control, or shooting preserve practices as regulated by state and federal law; or

(2) animal husbandry or agriculture practice involving livestock animals.

(g) This section does not create a civil cause of action for damages or enforcement of this section.

Sec. 42.091. Attack on Assistance Animal.

(a) A person commits an offense if the person intentionally, knowingly, or recklessly attacks, injures, or kills an assistance animal.

(b) A person commits an offense if the person intentionally, knowingly, or recklessly incites or permits an animal owned by or otherwise in the custody of the actor to attack, injure, or kill an assistance animal and, as a result of the person's conduct, the assistance animal is attacked, injured, or killed.

(c) An offense under this section is a:

(1) Class A misdemeanor if the actor or an animal owned by or otherwise in the custody of the actor attacks an assistance animal;

(2) state jail felony if the actor or an animal owned by or otherwise in the custody of the actor injures an assistance animal; or

(3) felony of the third degree if the actor or an animal owned by or otherwise in the custody of the actor kills an assistance animal.

(d) A court shall order a defendant convicted of an offense under Subsection (a) to make restitution to the owner of the assistance animal for:

(1) related veterinary or medical bills;

(2) the cost of:

(A) replacing the assistance animal; or

(B) retraining an injured assistance animal by an organization generally recognized by agencies involved in the rehabilitation of persons with disabilities as reputable and competent to provide special equipment for or special training to an animal to help a person with a disability; and

(3) any other expense reasonably incurred as a result of the offense.

(e) In this section:

(1) "Assistance animal" has the meaning assigned by Section 121.002, Human Resources Code.

(2) "Custody" has the meaning assigned by Section 42.09.

Sec. 42.092. Cruelty to Nonlivestock Animals.

(a) In this section:

(1) "Abandon" includes abandoning an animal in the person's custody without making reasonable arrangements for assumption of custody by another person.

(2) "Animal" means a domesticated living creature, including any stray or feral cat or dog, and a wild living creature previously captured. The term does not include an uncaptured wild living creature or a livestock animal.

(3) "Cruel manner" includes a manner that causes or permits unjustified or unwarranted pain or suffering.

(4) "Custody" includes responsibility for the health, safety, and welfare of an animal subject to the person's care and control, regardless of ownership of the animal.

(5) "Depredation" has the meaning assigned by Section 71.001, Parks and Wildlife Code.

(6) "Livestock animal" has the meaning assigned by Section 42.09.

(7) "Necessary food, water, care, or shelter" includes food, water, care, or shelter provided to the extent required to maintain the animal in a state of good health.

(8) "Torture" includes any act that causes unjustifiable pain or suffering.

(b) A person commits an offense if the person intentionally, knowingly, or recklessly:

(1) tortures an animal or in a cruel manner kills or causes serious bodily injury to an animal;

(2) without the owner's effective consent, kills, administers poison to, or causes serious bodily injury to an animal;

(3) fails unreasonably to provide necessary food, water, care, or shelter for an animal in the person's custody;

(4) abandons unreasonably an animal in the person's custody;

(5) transports or confines an animal in a cruel manner;

(6) without the owner's effective consent, causes bodily injury to an animal;

(7) causes one animal to fight with another animal, if either animal is not a dog;

(8) uses a live animal as a lure in dog race training or in dog coursing on a racetrack; or

(9) seriously overworks an animal.

(c) An offense under Subsection (b)(3), (4), (5), (6), or (9) is a Class A misdemeanor, except that the offense is a state jail felony if the person has previously been convicted two times under this section, two times under Section 42.09, or one time under this section and one time under Section 42.09.

(c-1) An offense under Subsection (b)(1) or (2) is a felony of the third degree, except that the offense is a felony of the second degree if the person has previously been convicted under Subsection (b)(1), (2), (7), or (8) or under Section 42.09.

(c-2) An offense under Subsection (b)(7) or (8) is a state jail felony, except that the offense is a felony of the third degree if the person has previously been convicted under this section or under Section 42.09.

(d) It is a defense to prosecution under this section that:

(1) the actor had a reasonable fear of bodily injury to the actor or to another person by a dangerous

wild animal as defined by Section 822.101, Health and Safety Code; or

(2) the actor was engaged in bona fide experimentation for scientific research.

(e) It is a defense to prosecution under Subsection (b)(2) or (6) that:

(1) the animal was discovered on the person's property in the act of or after injuring or killing the person's livestock animals or damaging the person's crops and that the person killed or injured the animal at the time of this discovery; or

(2) the person killed or injured the animal within the scope of the person's employment as a public servant or in furtherance of activities or operations associated with electricity transmission or distribution, electricity generation or operations associated with the generation of electricity, or natural gas delivery.

(f) It is an exception to the application of this section that the conduct engaged in by the actor is a generally accepted and otherwise lawful:

(1) form of conduct occurring solely for the purpose of or in support of:

(A) fishing, hunting, or trapping; or

(B) wildlife management, wildlife or depredation control, or shooting preserve practices as regulated by state and federal law; or

(2) animal husbandry or agriculture practice involving livestock animals.

(g) This section does not create a civil cause of action for damages or enforcement of the section.

Sec. 42.10. Dog Fighting.

(a) A person commits an offense if the person intentionally or knowingly:

(1) causes a dog to fight with another dog;

(2) participates in the earnings of or operates a facility used for dog fighting;

(3) uses or permits another to use any real estate, building, room, tent, arena, or other property for dog fighting;

(4) owns or possesses dog-fighting equipment with the intent that the equipment be used to train a dog for dog fighting or in furtherance of dog fighting;

(5) owns or trains a dog with the intent that the dog be used in an exhibition of dog fighting; or

(6) attends as a spectator an exhibition of dog fighting.

(b) In this section:

(1) "Dog fighting" means any situation in which one dog attacks or fights with another dog.

(2) "Dog-fighting equipment" has the meaning assigned by Article 18.18(g), Code of Criminal Procedure.

(c) A conviction under Subsection (a)(2) or (3) may be had upon the uncorroborated testimony of a party to the offense.

(d) It is a defense to prosecution under Subsection (a)(1) that the actor caused a dog to fight with another dog to protect livestock, other property, or a person from the other dog, and for no other purpose.

(e) An offense under Subsection (a)(4), (5), or (6) is a Class A misdemeanor. An offense under Subsection (a)(1), (2), or (3) is a state jail felony.

Sec. 42.105. Cockfighting.

(a) In this section:

(1) "Bridle" means a leather device designed to fit over the head and beak of a cock to prevent the cock from injuring another cock.

(2) "Cock" means the male of any type of domestic fowl.

(3) "Cockfighting" means any situation in which one cock attacks or fights with another cock.

(4) "Gaff" means an artificial steel spur designed to attach to the leg of a cock to replace or supplement the cock's natural spur.

(5) "Slasher" means a steel weapon resembling a curved knife blade designed to attach to the foot of a cock.

(b) A person commits an offense if the person knowingly:

(1) causes a cock to fight with another cock;

(2) participates in the earnings of a cockfight;

(3) uses or permits another to use any real estate, building, room, tent, arena, or other property for cockfighting;

(4) owns or trains a cock with the intent that the cock be used in an exhibition of cockfighting;

(5) manufactures, buys, sells, barters, exchanges, possesses, advertises, or otherwise offers a gaff, slasher, or other sharp implement designed for attachment to a cock with the intent that the implement be used in cockfighting; or

(6) attends as a spectator an exhibition of cockfighting.

(c) It is an affirmative defense to prosecution under this section that the actor's conduct:

(1) occurred solely for the purpose of or in support of breeding cocks for poultry shows in which a cock is judged by the cock's physical appearance; or

(2) was incidental to collecting bridles, gaffs, or slashers.

(d) An affirmative defense to prosecution is not available under Subsection (c) if evidence shows that the actor is also engaging in use of the cocks for cockfighting.

(e) It is a defense to prosecution for an offense under this section that:

(1) the actor was engaged in bona fide experimentation for scientific research; or

(2) the conduct engaged in by the actor is a generally accepted and otherwise lawful animal husbandry or agriculture practice involving livestock animals.

(f) It is an exception to the application of Subsection (b)(6) that the actor is 15 years of age or younger at the time of the offense.

(g) An offense under Subsection (b)(1) or (2) is a state jail felony. An offense under Subsection (b)(3), (4), or (5) is a Class A misdemeanor. An offense under Subsection (b)(6) is a Class C misdemeanor, except that the offense is a Class A misdemeanor if it is shown on the trial of the offense that the person has been previously convicted of an offense under that subdivision.

Sec. 42.11. Destruction of Flag.

(a) A person commits an offense if the person intentionally or knowingly damages, defaces, mutilates, or burns the flag of the United States or the State of Texas.

(b) In this section, "flag" means an emblem, banner, or other standard or a copy of an emblem, standard, or banner that is an official or commonly recognized depiction of the flag of the United States or of this state and is capable of being flown from a staff of any character or size. The term does not include a representation of a flag on a written or printed document, a periodical, stationery, a painting or photograph, or an article of clothing or jewelry.

(c) It is an exception to the application of this section that the act that would otherwise constitute an offense is done in conformity with statutes of the United States or of this state relating to the proper disposal of damaged flags.

(d) An offense under this section is a Class A misdemeanor.

Sec. 42.111. Dog Fighting [Renumbered].

Renumbered to Tex. Penal Code § 42.10 by Acts 1993, 73rd Leg., ch. 900 (S.B. 1067), § 1.01, effective September 1, 1994.

Sec. 42.12. Discharge of Firearm in Certain Municipalities.

(a) A person commits an offense if the person recklessly discharges a firearm inside the corporate limits of a municipality having a population of 100,000 or more.

(b) An offense under this section is a Class A misdemeanor.

(c) If conduct constituting an offense under this section also constitutes an offense under another section of this code, the person may be prosecuted under either section.

(d) Subsection (a) does not affect the authority of a municipality to enact an ordinance which prohibits the discharge of a firearm.

Sec. 42.13. Use of Laser Pointers.

(a) A person commits an offense if the person knowingly directs a light from a laser pointer at a uniformed safety officer, including a peace officer, security guard, firefighter, emergency medical service worker, or other uniformed municipal, state, or federal officer.

(b) In this section, "laser pointer" means a device that emits a visible light amplified by the stimulated emission of radiation.

(c) An offense under this section is a Class C misdemeanor, except that the offense is:

(1) a felony of the third degree if the conduct causes bodily injury to the officer; or

(2) a felony of the first degree if the conduct causes serious bodily injury to the officer.

(d) If conduct that constitutes an offense under this section also constitutes an offense under any other law, the actor may be prosecuted under this section or the other law, but not both.

Sec. 42.14. Illumination of Aircraft by Intense Light.

(a) A person commits an offense if:

(1) the person intentionally directs a light from a laser pointer or other light source at an aircraft; and

(2) the light has an intensity sufficient to impair the operator's ability to control the aircraft.

(b) It is an affirmative defense to prosecution under this section that the actor was using the light to send an emergency distress signal.

(c) An offense under this section is a Class C misdemeanor unless the intensity of the light impairs the operator's ability to control the aircraft, in which event the offense is a Class A misdemeanor.

(d) If conduct that constitutes an offense under this section also constitutes an offense under any other law, the actor may be prosecuted under this section or the other law.

(e) In this section, "laser pointer" has the meaning assigned by Section 42.13.

CHAPTER 43
PUBLIC INDECENCY

SUBCHAPTER A
PROSTITUTION

Sec. 43.01. Definitions.

In this subchapter:

(1) "Access software provider" means a provider of software, including client or server software, or enabling tools that perform one or more of the following functions:

(A) filter, screen, allow, or disallow content;

(B) select, analyze, or digest content; or

(C) transmit, receive, display, forward, cache, search, subset, organize, reorganize, or translate content.

(1-a) "Deviate sexual intercourse" means any contact between the genitals of one person and the mouth or anus of another person.

(1-b) "Fee" means the payment or offer of payment in the form of money, goods, services, or other benefit.

(1-c) "Information content provider" means any person or entity that is wholly or partly responsible for the creation or development of information provided through the Internet or any other interactive computer service.

(1-d) "Interactive computer service" means any information service, system, or access software provider that provides or enables computer access to a computer server by multiple users, including a service or system that provides access to the Internet or a system operated or service offered by a library or educational institution.

(1-e) "Internet" means the international computer network of both federal and nonfederal interoperable packet switched data networks.

(1-f) "Premises" has the meaning assigned by Section 481.134, Health and Safety Code.

(2) "Prostitution" means the offense defined in Section 43.02.

(2-a) "School" means a public or private primary or secondary school.

(3) "Sexual contact" means any touching of the anus, breast, or any part of the genitals of another person with intent to arouse or gratify the sexual desire of any person.

(4) "Sexual conduct" includes deviate sexual intercourse, sexual contact, and sexual intercourse.

(5) "Sexual intercourse" means any penetration of the female sex organ by the male sex organ.

(6) "Solicitation of prostitution" means the offense defined in Section 43.021.

Sec. 43.02. Prostitution. Class B

(a) A person commits an offense if the person knowingly offers or agrees to receive a fee from another to engage in sexual conduct.

(b) [Renumbered to Tex. Penal Code § 43.021 by Acts 2021, 87th Leg., H.B. 1540, § 29]

(b-1) [Repealed.]

(c) An offense under Subsection (a) is a Class B misdemeanor, except that the offense is:

(1) a Class A misdemeanor if the actor has previously been convicted one or two times of an offense under Subsection (a); or

(2) a state jail felony if the actor has previously been convicted three or more times of an offense under Subsection (a).

(c-1) [Renumbered to Tex. Penal Code § 43.021 by Acts 2021, 87th Leg., H.B. 1540, § 29]

(c-2) The punishment prescribed for an offense under Subsection (b) is increased to the punishment prescribed for the next highest category of offense if it is shown on the trial of the offense that the actor committed the offense in a location that was:

(1) on the premises of or within 1,000 feet of the premises of a school; or

(2) on premises or within 1,000 feet of premises where:

(A) an official school function was taking place; or

(B) an event sponsored or sanctioned by the University Interscholastic League was taking place.

(d) It is a defense to prosecution for an offense under Subsection (a) that the actor engaged in the conduct that constitutes the offense because the actor was the victim of conduct that constitutes an offense under Section 20A.02 or 43.05.

(e) A conviction may be used for purposes of enhancement under this section or enhancement under Subchapter D, Chapter 12, but not under both this section and Subchapter D, Chapter 12. For purposes of enhancement of penalties under this section or Subchapter D, Chapter 12, a defendant is previously convicted of an offense under this section if the defendant was adjudged guilty of the offense or entered a plea of guilty or nolo contendere in return for a grant of deferred adjudication, regardless of whether the sentence for the offense was ever imposed or whether the sentence was probated and the defendant was subsequently discharged from community supervision.

Sec. 43.021. Solicitation of Prostitution. [Renumbered from Tex. Penal Code § 43.02]

(a) A person commits an offense if the person knowingly offers or agrees to pay a fee to another person for the purpose of engaging in sexual conduct with that person or another.

(b) An offense under Subsection (a) is a state jail felony, except that the offense is:

(1) a felony of the third degree if the actor has previously been convicted of an offense under Subsection (a) or under Section 43.02(b), as that law existed before September 1, 2021; or

(2) a felony of the second degree if the person with whom the actor agrees to engage in sexual conduct is:

(A) younger than 18 years of age, regardless of whether the actor knows the age of the person at the time of the offense;

(B) represented to the actor as being younger than 18 years of age; or

(C) believed by the actor to be younger than 18 years of age.

Sec. 43.03. Promotion of Prostitution.

(a) A person commits an offense if, acting other than as a prostitute receiving compensation for personally rendered prostitution services, he or she knowingly:

(1) receives money or other property pursuant to an agreement to participate in the proceeds of prostitution; or

(2) solicits another to engage in sexual conduct with another person for compensation.

(b) An offense under this section is a felony of the third degree, except that the offense is:

(1) a felony of the second degree if the actor has been previously convicted of an offense under this section; or

(2) a felony of the first degree if the actor engages in conduct described by Subsection (a)(1) or (2) involving a person younger than 18 years of age engaging in prostitution, regardless of whether the actor knows the age of the person at the time of the offense.

Sec. 43.031. Online Promotion of Prostitution.

(a) A person commits an offense if the person owns, manages, or operates an interactive computer service or information content provider, or operates as an information content provider, with the intent to promote the prostitution of another person or facilitate another person to engage in prostitution or solicitation of prostitution.

(b) An offense under this section is a felony of the third degree, except that the offense is a felony of the second degree if the actor:

(1) has been previously convicted of an offense under this section or Section 43.041; or

(2) engages in conduct described by Subsection (a) involving a person younger than 18 years of age engaging in prostitution, regardless of whether the actor knows the age of the person at the time of the offense.

Sec. 43.04. Aggravated Promotion of Prostitution.

(a) A person commits an offense if he knowingly owns, invests in, finances, controls, supervises, or manages a prostitution enterprise that uses two or more prostitutes.

(b) An offense under this section is a felony of the first degree.

Sec. 43.041. Aggravated Online Promotion of Prostitution.

(a) A person commits an offense if the person owns, manages, or operates an interactive computer service or information content provider, or operates as an information content provider, with the intent to promote the prostitution of five or more persons or facilitate five or more persons to engage in prostitution or solicitation of prostitution.

(b) An offense under this section is a felony of the second degree, except that the offense is a felony of the first degree if the actor:

(1) has been previously convicted of an offense under this section; or

(2) engages in conduct described by Subsection (a) involving two or more persons younger than 18 years of age engaging in prostitution, regardless of whether the actor knows the age of the persons at the time of the offense.

Sec. 43.05. Compelling Prostitution.

(a) A person commits an offense if the person knowingly:

(1) causes another by force, threat, coercion, or fraud to commit prostitution; or

(2) causes by any means a child younger than 18 years to commit prostitution, regardless of whether the actor knows the age of the child at the time of the offense.

(b) An offense under this section is a felony of the first degree.

(c) If conduct constituting an offense under this section also constitutes an offense under another section of this code, the actor may be prosecuted under either section or under both sections.

(d) For purposes of this section, "coercion" as defined by Section 1.07 includes:

(1) destroying, concealing, confiscating, or withholding from a person, or threatening to destroy, conceal, confiscate, or withhold from a person, the person's actual or purported:

(A) government records; or

(B) identifying information or documents;

(2) causing a person, without the person's consent, to become intoxicated, as defined by Section 49.01, to a degree that impairs the person's ability to appraise the nature of the person's conduct that constitutes prostitution or to resist engaging in that conduct; or

(3) withholding alcohol or a controlled substance to a degree that impairs the ability of a person with a chemical dependency, as defined by Section 462.001, Health and Safety Code, to appraise the nature of the person's conduct that constitutes prostitution or to resist engaging in that conduct.

Sec. 43.06. Accomplice Witness: Testimony and Immunity.

(a) A party to an offense under this subchapter may be required to furnish evidence or testify about the offense.

(b) A party to an offense under this subchapter may not be prosecuted for any offense about which he is required to furnish evidence or testify, and the evidence and testimony may not be used against the party in any adjudicatory proceeding except a prosecution for aggravated perjury.

(c) For purposes of this section, "adjudicatory proceeding" means a proceeding before a court or any other agency of government in which the legal rights, powers, duties, or privileges of specified parties are determined.

(d) A conviction under this subchapter may be had upon the uncorroborated testimony of a party to the offense.

SUBCHAPTER B OBSCENITY

Sec. 43.21. Definitions.

(a) In this subchapter:

(1) "Obscene" means material or a performance that:

(A) the average person, applying contemporary community standards, would find that taken as a whole appeals to the prurient interest in sex;

(B) depicts or describes:

(i) patently offensive representations or descriptions of ultimate sexual acts, normal or perverted, actual or simulated, including sexual intercourse, sodomy, and sexual bestiality; or

(ii) patently offensive representations or descriptions of masturbation, excretory functions, sadism, masochism, lewd exhibition of the genitals, the male or female genitals in a state of sexual stimulation or arousal, covered male genitals in a discernibly turgid state or a device designed and marketed as useful primarily for stimulation of the human genital organs; and

(C) taken as a whole, lacks serious literary, artistic, political, and scientific value.

(2) "Material" means anything tangible that is capable of being used or adapted to arouse interest, whether through the medium of reading, observation, sound, or in any other manner, but does not include an actual three dimensional obscene device.

(3) "Performance" means a play, motion picture, dance, or other exhibition performed before an audience.

(4) "Patently offensive" means so offensive on its face as to affront current community standards of decency.

(5) "Promote" means to manufacture, issue, sell, give, provide, lend, mail, deliver, transfer, transmit, publish, distribute, circulate, disseminate, present, exhibit, or advertise, or to offer or agree to do the same.

(6) "Wholesale promote" means to manufacture, issue, sell, provide, mail, deliver, transfer, transmit, publish, distribute, circulate, disseminate, or to offer or agree to do the same for purpose of resale.

(7) "Obscene device" means a device including a dildo or artificial vagina, designed or marketed as useful primarily for the stimulation of human genital organs.

(b) If any of the depictions or descriptions of sexual conduct described in this section are declared by a court of competent jurisdiction to be unlawfully included herein, this declaration shall not invalidate this section as to other patently offensive sexual conduct included herein.

Sec. 43.22. Obscene Display or Distribution.

(a) A person commits an offense if he intentionally or knowingly displays or distributes an obscene photograph, drawing, or similar visual representation or other obscene material and is reckless about whether a person is present who will be offended or alarmed by the display or distribution.

(b) An offense under this section is a Class C misdemeanor.

Sec. 43.23. Obscenity.

(a) A person commits an offense if, knowing its content and character, he wholesale promotes or possesses with intent to wholesale promote any obscene material or obscene device.

(b) Except as provided by Subsection (h), an offense under Subsection (a) is a state jail felony.

(c) A person commits an offense if, knowing its content and character, he:

(1) promotes or possesses with intent to promote any obscene material or obscene device; or

(2) produces, presents, or directs an obscene performance or participates in a portion thereof that is obscene or that contributes to its obscenity.

(d) Except as provided by Subsection (h), an offense under Subsection (c) is a Class A misdemeanor.

(e) A person who promotes or wholesale promotes obscene material or an obscene device or possesses the same with intent to promote or wholesale promote it in the course of his business is presumed to do so with knowledge of its content and character.

(f) A person who possesses six or more obscene devices or identical or similar obscene articles is presumed to possess them with intent to promote the same.

(g) It is an affirmative defense to prosecution under this section that the person who possesses or promotes material or a device proscribed by this section does so for a bona fide medical, psychiatric, judicial, legislative, or law enforcement purpose.

(h) The punishment for an offense under Subsection (a) or (c) is increased to the punishment for a felony of the second degree if it is shown on the trial of the offense that obscene material that is the subject of the offense visually depicts activities described by Section 43.21(a)(1)(B) engaged in by:

(1) a child younger than 18 years of age at the time the image of the child was made;

(2) an image that to a reasonable person would be virtually indistinguishable from the image of a child younger than 18 years of age; or

(3) an image created, adapted, or modified to be the image of an identifiable child.

(i) In this section, "identifiable child" means a person, recognizable as an actual person by the person's face, likeness, or other distinguishing characteristic, such as a unique birthmark or other recognizable feature:

(1) who was younger than 18 years of age at the time the visual depiction was created, adapted, or modified; or

(2) whose image as a person younger than 18 years of age was used in creating, adapting, or modifying the visual depiction.

(j) An attorney representing the state who seeks an increase in punishment under Subsection (h)(3) is not required to prove the actual identity of an identifiable child.

Sec. 43.24. Sale, Distribution, or Display of Harmful Material to Minor.

(a) For purposes of this section:

(1) "Minor" means an individual younger than 18 years.

(2) "Harmful material" means material whose dominant theme taken as a whole:

(A) appeals to the prurient interest of a minor, in sex, nudity, or excretion;

(B) is patently offensive to prevailing standards in the adult community as a whole with respect to what is suitable for minors; and

(C) is utterly without redeeming social value for minors.

(b) A person commits an offense if, knowing that the material is harmful:

(1) and knowing the person is a minor, he sells, distributes, exhibits, or possesses for sale, distribution, or exhibition to a minor harmful material;

(2) he displays harmful material and is reckless about whether a minor is present who will be offended or alarmed by the display; or

(3) he hires, employs, or uses a minor to do or accomplish or assist in doing or accomplishing any of the acts prohibited in Subsection (b)(1) or (b)(2).

(c) It is an affirmative defense to prosecution under this section that the sale, distribution, or exhibition was by a person having scientific, educational, governmental, or other similar justification.

(c-1) It is a defense to prosecution under this section that the actor was the spouse of the minor at the time of the offense.

(d) An offense under this section is a Class A misdemeanor unless it is committed under Subsection (b)(3) in which event it is a felony of the third degree.

Sec. 43.25. Sexual Performance by a Child.

(a) In this section:

(1) "Sexual performance" means any performance or part thereof that includes sexual conduct by a child younger than 18 years of age.

(2) "Sexual conduct" means sexual contact, actual or simulated sexual intercourse, deviate sexual

intercourse, sexual bestiality, masturbation, sadomasochistic abuse, or lewd exhibition of the genitals, the anus, or any portion of the female breast below the top of the areola.

(3) "Performance" means any play, motion picture, photograph, dance, or other visual representation that can be exhibited before an audience of one or more persons.

(4) "Produce" with respect to a sexual performance includes any conduct that directly contributes to the creation or manufacture of the sexual performance.

(5) "Promote" means to procure, manufacture, issue, sell, give, provide, lend, mail, deliver, transfer, transmit, publish, distribute, circulate, disseminate, present, exhibit, or advertise or to offer or agree to do any of the above.

(6) "Simulated" means the explicit depiction of sexual conduct that creates the appearance of actual sexual conduct and during which a person engaging in the conduct exhibits any uncovered portion of the breasts, genitals, or buttocks.

(7) "Deviate sexual intercourse" and "sexual contact" have the meanings assigned by Section 43.01.

(b) A person commits an offense if, knowing the character and content thereof, he employs, authorizes, or induces a child younger than 18 years of age to engage in sexual conduct or a sexual performance. A parent or legal guardian or custodian of a child younger than 18 years of age commits an offense if he consents to the participation by the child in a sexual performance.

(c) An offense under Subsection (b) is a felony of the second degree, except that the offense is a felony of the first degree if the victim is younger than 14 years of age at the time the offense is committed, regardless of whether the actor knows the age of the victim at the time of the offense.

(d) A person commits an offense if, knowing the character and content of the material, he produces, directs, or promotes a performance that includes sexual conduct by a child younger than 18 years of age.

(e) An offense under Subsection (d) is a felony of the third degree, except that the offense is a felony of the second degree if the victim is younger than 14 years of age at the time the offense is committed, regardless of whether the actor knows the age of the victim at the time of the offense.

(f) It is an affirmative defense to a prosecution under this section that:

(1) the defendant was the spouse of the child at the time of the offense;

(2) the conduct was for a bona fide educational, medical, psychological, psychiatric, judicial, law enforcement, or legislative purpose; or

(3) the defendant is not more than two years older than the child.

(g) When it becomes necessary for the purposes of this section or Section 43.26 to determine whether a child who participated in sexual conduct was younger than 18 years of age, the court or jury may make this determination by any of the following methods:

(1) personal inspection of the child;

(2) inspection of the photograph or motion picture that shows the child engaging in the sexual performance;

(3) oral testimony by a witness to the sexual performance as to the age of the child based on the child's appearance at the time;

(4) expert medical testimony based on the appearance of the child engaging in the sexual performance; or

(5) any other method authorized by law or by the rules of evidence at common law.

(h) Conduct under this section constitutes an offense regardless of whether the actor knows the age of the victim at the time of the offense.

Sec. 43.251. Employment Harmful to Children.

(a) In this section:

(1) "Child" means a person younger than 21 years of age.

(2) "Massage" has the meaning assigned to the term "massage therapy" by Section 455.001, Occupations Code.

(3) "Massage establishment" has the meaning assigned by Section 455.001, Occupations Code.

(4) "Nude" means a child who is:

(A) entirely unclothed; or

(B) clothed in a manner that leaves uncovered or visible through less than fully opaque clothing any portion of the breasts below the top of the areola of the breasts, if the child is female, or any portion of the genitals or buttocks.

(5) "Sexually oriented commercial activity" means a massage establishment, nude studio, modeling studio, love parlor, or other similar commercial enterprise the primary business of which is the offering of a service that is intended to provide sexual stimulation or sexual gratification to the customer.

(6) "Topless" means a female child clothed in a manner that leaves uncovered or visible through less than fully opaque clothing any portion of her breasts below the top of the areola.

(b) A person commits an offense if the person employs, authorizes, or induces a child to work:

(1) in a sexually oriented commercial activity; or

(2) in any place of business permitting, requesting, or requiring a child to work nude or topless.

(c) **[2 Versions: As amended by Acts 2017, 85th Leg., ch. 685]** An offense under this section is a felony of the second degree, except that the offense is a felony of the first degree if the child is younger than 14 years of age at the time the offense is committed, regardless of whether the actor knows the age of the child at the time of the offense.

(c) **[2 Versions: As amended by Acts 2017, 85th Leg., ch. 1038]** An offense under this section is a felony of the second degree, except that the offense is a felony of the first degree if the victim is younger than 14 years of age at the time the offense is committed, regardless of whether the actor knows the age of the victim at the time of the offense.

(d) **[2 Versions: As amended by Acts 2017, 85th Leg., ch. 685]** Conduct under this section constitutes an offense regardless of whether the actor knows the age of the child at the time of the offense.

(d) **[2 Versions: As amended by Acts 2017, 85th Leg., ch. 1038]** Conduct under this section constitutes an offense regardless of whether the actor knows the age of the victim at the time of the offense.

Sec. 43.26. Possession or Promotion of Child Pornography.

(a) A person commits an offense if:

(1) the person knowingly or intentionally possesses, or knowingly or intentionally accesses with intent to view, visual material that visually depicts a child younger than 18 years of age at the time the image of the child was made who is engaging in sexual conduct, including a child who engages in sexual conduct as a victim of an offense under Section 20A.02(a)(5), (6), (7), or (8); and

(2) the person knows that the material depicts the child as described by Subdivision (1).

(b) In this section:

(1) "Promote" has the meaning assigned by Section 43.25.

(2) "Sexual conduct" has the meaning assigned by Section 43.25.

(3) "Visual material" means:

(A) any film, photograph, videotape, negative, or slide or any photographic reproduction that contains or incorporates in any manner any film, photograph, videotape, negative, or slide; or

(B) any disk, diskette, or other physical medium that allows an image to be displayed on a computer or other video screen and any image transmitted to a computer or other video screen by telephone line, cable, satellite transmission, or other method.

(c) The affirmative defenses provided by Section 43.25(f) also apply to a prosecution under this section.

(d) An offense under Subsection (a) is a felony of the third degree, except that the offense is:

(1) a felony of the second degree if it is shown on the trial of the offense that the person has been previously convicted one time of an offense under that subsection; and

(2) a felony of the first degree if it is shown on the trial of the offense that the person has been previously convicted two or more times of an offense under that subsection.

(e) A person commits an offense if:

(1) the person knowingly or intentionally promotes or possesses with intent to promote material described by Subsection (a)(1); and

(2) the person knows that the material depicts the child as described by Subsection (a)(1).

(f) A person who possesses visual material that contains six or more identical visual depictions of a child as described by Subsection (a)(1) is presumed to possess the material with the intent to promote the material.

(g) An offense under Subsection (e) is a felony of the second degree, except that the offense is a felony of the first degree if it is shown on the trial of the offense that the person has been previously convicted of an offense under that subsection.

(h) It is a defense to prosecution under Subsection (a) or (e) that the actor is a law enforcement officer or a school administrator who:

(1) possessed or accessed the visual material in good faith solely as a result of an allegation of a violation of Section 43.261;

(2) allowed other law enforcement or school administrative personnel to possess or access the material only as appropriate based on the allegation described by Subdivision (1); and

(3) took reasonable steps to destroy the material within an appropriate period following the allegation described by Subdivision (1).

Sec. 43.261. Electronic Transmission of Certain Visual Material Depicting Minor.

(a) In this section:

(1) "Dating relationship" has the meaning assigned by Section 71.0021, Family Code.

(2) "Minor" means a person younger than 18 years of age.

(3) "Produce" with respect to visual material includes any conduct that directly contributes to the creation or manufacture of the material.

(4) "Promote" has the meaning assigned by Section 43.25.

(5) "Sexual conduct" has the meaning assigned by Section 43.25.

(6) "Visual material" has the meaning assigned by Section 43.26.

(b) A person who is a minor commits an offense if the person intentionally or knowingly:

(1) by electronic means promotes to another minor visual material depicting a minor, including the actor, engaging in sexual conduct, if the actor produced the visual material or knows that another minor produced the visual material; or

(2) possesses in an electronic format visual material depicting another minor engaging in sexual conduct, if the actor produced the visual material or knows that another minor produced the visual material.

(c) An offense under Subsection (b)(1) is a Class C misdemeanor, except that the offense is:

(1) a Class B misdemeanor if it is shown on the trial of the offense that the actor:

(A) promoted the visual material with intent to harass, annoy, alarm, abuse, torment, embarrass, or offend another; or

(B) except as provided by Subdivision (2)(A), has previously been convicted one time of any offense under this section; or

(2) a Class A misdemeanor if it is shown on the trial of the offense that the actor has previously been:

(A) convicted one or more times of an offense punishable under Subdivision (1)(A); or

(B) convicted two or more times of any offense under this section.

(d) An offense under Subsection (b)(2) is a Class C misdemeanor, except that the offense is:

(1) a Class B misdemeanor if it is shown on the trial of the offense that the actor has previously been convicted one time of any offense under this section; or

(2) a Class A misdemeanor if it is shown on the trial of the offense that the actor has previously been convicted two or more times of any offense under this section.

(e) It is an affirmative defense to prosecution under this section that the visual material:

(1) depicted only the actor or another minor:

(A) who is not more than two years older or younger than the actor and with whom the actor had a dating relationship at the time of the offense; or

(B) who was the spouse of the actor at the time of the offense; and

(2) was promoted or received only to or from the actor and the other minor.

(f) It is a defense to prosecution under Subsection (b)(2) that the actor:

(1) did not produce or solicit the visual material;

(2) possessed the visual material only after receiving the material from another minor; and

(3) destroyed the visual material within a reasonable amount of time after receiving the material from another minor.

(g) If conduct that constitutes an offense under this section also constitutes an offense under another law, the defendant may be prosecuted under this section, the other law, or both.

(h) Notwithstanding Section 51.13, Family Code, a finding that a person has engaged in conduct in violation of this section is considered a conviction for the purposes of Subsections (c) and (d).

Sec. 43.262. Possession or Promotion of Lewd Visual Material Depicting Child.

(a) In this section:

(1) "Promote" and "sexual conduct" have the meanings assigned by Section 43.25.

(2) "Visual material" has the meaning assigned by Section 43.26.

(b) A person commits an offense if the person knowingly possesses, accesses with intent to view, or promotes visual material that:

(1) depicts the lewd exhibition of the genitals or pubic area of an unclothed, partially clothed, or clothed child who is younger than 18 years of age at the time the visual material was created;

(2) appeals to the prurient interest in sex; and

(3) has no serious literary, artistic, political, or scientific value.

(c) An offense under this section is a state jail felony, except that the offense is:

(1) a felony of the third degree if it is shown on the trial of the offense that the person has been previously convicted one time of an offense under this section or Section 43.26; and

(2) a felony of the second degree if it is shown on the trial of the offense that the person has been previously convicted two or more times of an offense under this section or Section 43.26.

(d) It is not a defense to prosecution under this section that the depicted child consented to the creation of the visual material.

Sec. 43.27. Duty to Report.

(a) For purposes of this section, "visual material" has the meaning assigned by Section 43.26.

(b) A business that develops or processes visual material and determines that the material may be evidence of a criminal offense under this subchapter shall report the existence of the visual material to a local law enforcement agency.

TITLE 10
OFFENSES AGAINST PUBLIC HEALTH, SAFETY, AND MORALS

CHAPTER 46
WEAPONS

Sec. 46.01. Definitions.

In this chapter:

(1) "Club" means an instrument that is specially designed, made, or adapted for the purpose of inflicting serious bodily injury or death by striking a person with the instrument, and includes but is not limited to the following:

(A) blackjack;

(B) nightstick;

(C) mace;

(D) tomahawk.

(2) "Explosive weapon" means any explosive or incendiary bomb, grenade, rocket, or mine, that is designed, made, or adapted for the purpose of inflicting serious bodily injury, death, or substantial property damage, or for the principal purpose of causing such a loud report as to cause undue public alarm or terror, and includes a device designed, made, or adapted for delivery or shooting an explosive weapon.

(3) "Firearm" means any device designed, made, or adapted to expel a projectile through a barrel by using the energy generated by an explosion or burning substance or any device readily convertible to that use. Firearm does not include a firearm that may have, as an integral part, a folding knife blade or other characteristics of weapons made illegal by this chapter and that is:

(A) an antique or curio firearm manufactured before 1899; or

(B) a replica of an antique or curio firearm manufactured before 1899, but only if the replica does not use rim fire or center fire ammunition.

(4) [Repealed.]

(5) "Handgun" means any firearm that is designed, made, or adapted to be fired with one hand.

(6) "Location-restricted knife" means a knife with a blade over five and one-half inches.

(7) "Knife" means any bladed hand instrument that is capable of inflicting serious bodily injury or death by cutting or stabbing a person with the instrument.

(8) [Repealed.]

(9) "Machine gun" means any firearm that is capable of shooting more than two shots automatically, without manual reloading, by a single function of the trigger.

(10) "Short-barrel firearm" means a rifle with a barrel length of less than 16 inches or a shotgun with a barrel length of less than 18 inches, or any weapon made from a shotgun or rifle if, as altered, it has an overall length of less than 26 inches.

(11) [Repealed.]

(12) "Armor-piercing ammunition" means handgun ammunition that is designed primarily for the purpose of penetrating metal or body armor and to be used principally in pistols and revolvers.

(13) "Hoax bomb" means a device that:

(A) reasonably appears to be an explosive or incendiary device; or

(B) by its design causes alarm or reaction of any type by an official of a public safety agency or a volunteer agency organized to deal with emergencies.

(14) "Chemical dispensing device" means a device, other than a small chemical dispenser sold commercially for personal protection, that is designed, made, or adapted for the purpose of dispensing a substance capable of causing an adverse psychological or physiological effect on a human being.

(15) "Racetrack" has the meaning assigned that term by Section 2021.003(41), Occupations Code.

(16) "Zip gun" means a device or combination of devices that was not originally a firearm and is adapted to expel a projectile through a smooth-bore or rifled-bore barrel by using the energy generated by an explosion or burning substance.

(17) "Tire deflation device" means a device, including a caltrop or spike strip, that, when driven over, impedes or stops the movement of a wheeled vehicle by puncturing one or more of the vehicle's tires. The term does not include a traffic control device that:

(A) is designed to puncture one or more of a vehicle's tires when driven over in a specific direction; and

(B) has a clearly visible sign posted in close proximity to the traffic control device that prohibits entry or warns motor vehicle operators of the traffic control device.

(18) "Volunteer emergency services personnel" includes a volunteer firefighter, an emergency medical services volunteer as defined by Section 773.003, Health and Safety Code, and any

individual who, as a volunteer, provides services for the benefit of the general public during emergency situations. The term does not include a peace officer or reserve law enforcement officer, as those terms are defined by Section 1701.001, Occupations Code, who is performing law enforcement duties.

(19) "Improvised explosive device" means a completed and operational bomb designed to cause serious bodily injury, death, or substantial property damage that is fabricated in an improvised manner using nonmilitary components. The term does not include:

(A) unassembled components that can be legally purchased and possessed without a license, permit, or other governmental approval; or

(B) an exploding target that is used for firearms practice, sold in kit form, and contains the components of a binary explosive.

(20) "First responder" means a public safety employee whose duties include responding rapidly to an emergency. The term includes fire protection personnel as defined by Section 419.021, Government Code, and emergency medical services personnel as defined by Section 773.003, Health and Safety Code. The term does not include:

(A) volunteer emergency services personnel;

(B) an emergency medical services volunteer, as defined by Section 773.003, Health and Safety Code; or

(C) a peace officer or reserve law enforcement officer, as those terms are defined by Section 1701.001, Occupations Code, who is performing law enforcement duties.

Sec. 46.02. Unlawful Carrying Weapons.

(a) A person commits an offense if the person:

(1) intentionally, knowingly, or recklessly carries on or about his or her person a handgun;

(2) at the time of the offense:

(A) is younger than 21 years of age; or

(B) has been convicted of an offense under Section 22.01(a)(1), 22.05, 22.07, or 42.01(a)(7) or (8) committed in the five-year period preceding the date the instant offense was committed; and

(3) is not:

(A) on the person's own premises or premises under the person's control; or

(B) inside of or directly en route to a motor vehicle or watercraft that is owned by the person or under the person's control.

(a-1) A person commits an offense if the person intentionally, knowingly, or recklessly carries on or about his or her person a handgun in a motor vehicle or watercraft that is owned by the person or under the person's control at any time in which:

(1) the handgun is in plain view, unless the person is 21 years of age or older or is licensed to carry a handgun under Subchapter H, Chapter 411, Government Code, and the handgun is carried in a holster; or

(2) the person is:

(A) engaged in criminal activity, other than a Class C misdemeanor that is a violation of a law or ordinance regulating traffic or boating; or

(B) prohibited by law from possessing a firearm.

(a-2) For purposes of this section, "premises" includes real property and a recreational vehicle that is being used as living quarters, regardless of whether that use is temporary or permanent. In this subsection, "recreational vehicle" means a motor vehicle primarily designed as temporary living quarters or a vehicle that contains temporary living quarters and is designed to be towed by a motor vehicle. The term includes a travel trailer, camping trailer, truck camper, motor home, and horse trailer with living quarters.

(a-3) For purposes of this section, "watercraft" means any boat, motorboat, vessel, or personal watercraft, other than a seaplane on water, used or capable of being used for transportation on water.

(a-4) A person commits an offense if the person:

(1) intentionally, knowingly, or recklessly carries on or about his or her person a location-restricted knife;

(2) is younger than 18 years of age at the time of the offense; and

(3) is not:

(A) on the person's own premises or premises under the person's control;

(B) inside of or directly en route to a motor vehicle or watercraft that is owned by the person or under the person's control; or

(C) under the direct supervision of a parent or legal guardian of the person.

(a-5) A person commits an offense if the person carries a handgun and intentionally displays the handgun in plain view of another person in a public place. It is an exception to the application of this subsection that the handgun was partially or wholly visible but was carried in a holster.

(a-6) A person commits an offense if the person:

(1) carries a handgun while the person is intoxicated; and

(2) is not:

(A) on the person's own property or property under the person's control or on private property with the consent of the owner of the property; or

(B) inside of or directly en route to a motor vehicle or watercraft:

(i) that is owned by the person or under the person's control; or

(ii) with the consent of the owner or operator of the vehicle or watercraft.

(a-7) A person commits an offense if the person:

(1) intentionally, knowingly, or recklessly carries on or about his or her person a handgun;

(2) is not:

(A) on the person's own premises or premises under the person's control; or

(B) inside of or directly en route to a motor vehicle or watercraft that is owned by the person or under the person's control; and

(3) at the time of the offense, was prohibited from possessing a firearm under Section 46.04(a), (b), or (c).

(a-8) If conduct constituting an offense under Subsection (a-7) constitutes an offense under another provision of law, the actor may be prosecuted under Subsection (a-7) or under both provisions.

(b) Except as provided by Subsection (d) or (e), an offense under this section is a Class A misdemeanor.

(c) [Repealed.]

(d) An offense under Subsection (a-4) is a Class C misdemeanor.

(e) An offense under Subsection (a-7) is:

(1) a felony of the second degree with a minimum term of imprisonment of five years, if the actor was prohibited from possessing a firearm under Section 46.04(a); or

(2) a felony of the third degree, if the actor was prohibited from possessing a firearm under Section 46.04(b) or (c).

Sec. 46.03. Places Weapons Prohibited.

(a) A person commits an offense if the person intentionally, knowingly, or recklessly possesses or goes with a firearm, location-restricted knife, club, or prohibited weapon listed in Section 46.05(a):

(1) on the physical premises of a school or educational institution, any grounds or building on which an activity sponsored by a school or educational institution is being conducted, or a passenger transportation vehicle of a school or educational institution, whether the school or educational institution is public or private, unless:

(A) pursuant to written regulations or written authorization of the institution; or

(B) the person possesses or goes with a concealed handgun that the person is licensed to carry under Subchapter H, Chapter 411, Government Code, and no other weapon to which this section applies, on the premises of an institution of higher education or private or independent institution of higher education, on any grounds or building on which an activity sponsored by the institution is being conducted, or in a passenger transportation vehicle of the institution;

(2) on the premises of a polling place on the day of an election or while early voting is in progress;

(3) on the premises of any government court or offices utilized by the court, unless pursuant to written regulations or written authorization of the court;

(4) on the premises of a racetrack;

(5) in or into a secured area of an airport;

(6) within 1,000 feet of premises the location of which is designated by the Texas Department of Criminal Justice as a place of execution under Article 43.19, Code of Criminal Procedure, on a day that a sentence of death is set to be imposed on the designated premises and the person received notice that:

(A) going within 1,000 feet of the premises with a weapon listed under this subsection was prohibited; or

(B) possessing a weapon listed under this subsection within 1,000 feet of the premises was prohibited;

(7) on the premises of a business that has a permit or license issued under Chapter 25, 28, 32, 69, or 74, Alcoholic Beverage Code, if the business derives 51 percent or more of its income from the sale or service of alcoholic beverages for on-premises consumption, as determined by the Texas Alcoholic Beverage Commission under Section 104.06, Alcoholic Beverage Code;

(8) on the premises where a high school, collegiate, or professional sporting event or interscholastic event is taking place, unless the person is a participant in the event and a firearm, location-restricted knife, club, or prohibited weapon listed in Section 46.05(a) is used in the event;

(9) on the premises of a correctional facility;

(10) on the premises of a civil commitment facility;

(11) on the premises of a hospital licensed under Chapter 241, Health and Safety Code, or on the premises of a nursing facility licensed under Chapter 242, Health and Safety Code, unless the person has written authorization of the hospital or nursing facility administration, as appropriate;

(12) on the premises of a mental hospital, as defined by Section 571.003, Health and Safety Code, unless the person has written authorization of the mental hospital administration;

(13) in an amusement park; or

(14) in the room or rooms where a meeting of a governmental entity is held, if the meeting is an open meeting subject to Chapter 551, Government Code, and if the entity provided notice as required by that chapter.

(a-1) [Repealed.]

(a-2) Notwithstanding Section 46.02(a-5), a license holder commits an offense if the license holder carries a partially or wholly visible handgun, regardless of whether the handgun is holstered, on or about the license holder's person under the authority of Subchapter H, Chapter 411, Government Code, and intentionally or knowingly displays the handgun in plain view of another person:

(1) on the premises of an institution of higher education or private or independent institution of higher education; or

(2) on any public or private driveway, street, sidewalk or walkway, parking lot, parking garage, or other parking area of an institution of higher education or private or independent institution of higher education.

(a-3) Notwithstanding Subsection (a) or Section 46.02(a-5), a license holder commits an offense if the license holder carries a handgun on the campus of a private or independent institution of higher education in this state that has established rules, regulations, or other provisions prohibiting license holders from carrying handguns pursuant to Section 411.2031(e), Government Code, or on the grounds or building on which an activity sponsored by such an institution is being conducted, or in a passenger transportation vehicle of such an institution, regardless of whether the handgun is concealed, provided the institution gives effective notice under Section 30.06.

(a-4) Notwithstanding Subsection (a) or Section 46.02(a-5), a license holder commits an offense if the license holder intentionally carries a concealed handgun on a portion of a premises located on the campus of an institution of higher education in this state on which the carrying of a concealed handgun is prohibited by rules, regulations, or other provisions established under Section 411.2031(d-1), Government Code, provided the institution gives effective notice under Section 30.06 with respect to that portion.

(b) It is a defense to prosecution under Subsections (a)(1)—(4) that the actor possessed a firearm while in the actual discharge of his official duties as a member of the armed forces or national guard or a guard employed by a penal institution, or an officer of the court.

(c) In this section:

(1) "Amusement park" means a permanent indoor or outdoor facility or park where amusement rides are available for use by the public that is located in a county with a population of more than one million, encompasses at least 75 acres in surface area, is enclosed with access only through controlled entries, is open for operation more than 120 days in each calendar year, and has security guards on the premises at all times. The term does not include any public or private driveway, street, sidewalk or walkway, parking lot, parking garage, or other parking area.

(2) "Institution of higher education" and "private or independent institution of higher education" have the meanings assigned by Section 61.003, Education Code.

(3) "License holder" means a person licensed to carry a handgun under Subchapter H, Chapter 411, Government Code.

(4) "Premises" means a building or a portion of a building. The term does not include any public or private driveway, street, sidewalk or walkway, parking lot, parking garage, or other parking area.

(5) "Secured area" means an area of an airport terminal building to which access is controlled by the inspection of persons and property under federal law, or an aircraft parking area that is used by common carriers in air transportation but not by general aviation and to which access is controlled under federal law. The term does not include a baggage claim area, a motor vehicle parking area used by passengers, employees, or persons awaiting an arrival, or an area used by the public to pick up or drop off passengers or employees.

(d) It is a defense to prosecution under Subsection (a)(5) that the actor possessed a firearm or club while traveling to or from the actor's place of assignment or in the actual discharge of duties as:

(1) a member of the armed forces or national guard;

(2) a guard employed by a penal institution; or

(3) a security officer commissioned by the Texas Private Security Board if:

(A) the actor is wearing a distinctive uniform; and

(B) the firearm or club is in plain view; or

(4) a security officer who holds a personal protection authorization under Chapter 1702, Occupations Code, provided that the officer is either:

(A) wearing the uniform of a security officer, including any uniform or apparel described by Section 1702.323(d), Occupations Code, and carrying the officer's firearm in plain view; or

(B) not wearing the uniform of a security officer and carrying the officer's firearm in a concealed manner.

(e) It is a defense to prosecution under Subsection (a)(5) that the actor:

(1) checked all firearms as baggage in accordance with federal or state law or regulations before entering a secured area; or

(2) was authorized by a federal agency or the airport operator to possess a firearm in a secured area.

(e-1) It is a defense to prosecution under Subsection (a)(5) that the actor:

(1) possessed, at the screening checkpoint for the secured area, a handgun that the actor was licensed to carry under Subchapter H, Chapter 411, Government Code; and

(2) exited the screening checkpoint for the secured area immediately upon completion of the required screening processes and notification that the actor possessed the handgun.

(e-2) A peace officer investigating conduct that may constitute an offense under Subsection (a)(5) and that consists only of an actor's possession of a handgun that the actor is licensed to carry under Subchapter H, Chapter 411, Government Code, may not arrest the actor for the offense unless:

(1) the officer advises the actor of the defense available under Subsection (e-1) and gives the actor an opportunity to exit the screening checkpoint for the secured area; and

(2) the actor does not immediately exit the checkpoint upon completion of the required screening processes.

(f) Except as provided by Subsection (e-1), it is not a defense to prosecution under this section that the actor possessed a handgun and was licensed to carry a handgun under Subchapter H, Chapter 411, Government Code.

(g) Except as provided by Subsections (g-1) and (g-2), an offense under this section is a felony of the third degree.

(g-1) If the weapon that is the subject of the offense is a location-restricted knife, an offense under this section is a Class C misdemeanor, except that the offense is a felony of the third degree if the offense is committed under Subsection (a)(1).

(g-2) An offense committed under Subsection (a)(8), (a)(10), (a)(11), (a)(13), (a-2), (a-3), or (a-4) is a Class A misdemeanor.

(h) It is a defense to prosecution under Subsection (a)(4) that the actor possessed a firearm or club while traveling to or from the actor's place of assignment or in the actual discharge of duties as a security officer commissioned by the Texas Board of Private Investigators and Private Security Agencies, if:

(1) the actor is wearing a distinctive uniform; and

(2) the firearm or club is in plain view.

(i) It is an exception to the application of Subsection (a)(6) that the actor possessed a firearm or club:

(1) while in a vehicle being driven on a public road; or

(2) at the actor's residence or place of employment.

Sec. 46.035. Unlawful Carrying of Handgun by License Holder.

(a) **As amended by Acts 2021, 87th Leg., chs. XXX (HB 2112) and XXX (SB 550)** A license holder commits an offense if the license holder carries a handgun on or about the license holder's person under the authority of Subchapter H, Chapter 411, Government Code, and intentionally displays the handgun in plain view of another person in a public place. It is an exception to the application of this subsection that the handgun was partially or wholly visible but was carried in a holster by the license holder.

(a) **As amended by Acts 2021, 87th Leg., ch. XXX (HB 1407)** A license holder commits an offense if the license holder carries a handgun on or about the license holder's person under the authority of Subchapter H, Chapter 411, Government Code, and intentionally displays the handgun in plain view of another person in a public place. It is an exception to the application of this subsection that the handgun was partially or wholly visible but was:

(1) carried in a shoulder or belt holster by the license holder; or

(2) in a holster, and the handgun and the license holder were in a motor vehicle.

(a-1) [Repealed.]

(a-1) [Repealed.]

(a-2) [Repealed.]

(a-3) [Repealed.]

(b) A license holder commits an offense if the license holder intentionally, knowingly, or recklessly carries a handgun under the authority of Subchapter H, Chapter 411, Government Code, regardless of whether the handgun is concealed or carried in a holster, on or about the license holder's person:

(1) on the premises of a business that has a permit or license issued under Chapter 25, 28, 32, 69, or 74, Alcoholic Beverage Code, if the business derives 51 percent or more of its income from the sale or service of alcoholic beverages for on-premises consumption, as determined by the Texas Alcoholic Beverage Commission under Section 104.06, Alcoholic Beverage Code;

(2) on the premises where a high school, collegiate, or professional sporting event or interscholastic event is taking place, unless the license holder is a participant in the event and a handgun is used in the event;

(3) on the premises of a correctional facility;

(4) on the premises of a hospital licensed under Chapter 241, Health and Safety Code, or on the premises of a nursing facility licensed under Chapter 242, Health and Safety Code, unless the license

holder has written authorization of the hospital or nursing facility administration, as appropriate;

(5) in an amusement park; or

(6) on the premises of a civil commitment facility.

(c) A license holder commits an offense if the license holder intentionally, knowingly, or recklessly carries a handgun under the authority of Subchapter H, Chapter 411, Government Code, regardless of whether the handgun is concealed or carried in a holster, in the room or rooms where a meeting of a governmental entity is held and if the meeting is an open meeting subject to Chapter 551, Government Code, and the entity provided notice as required by that chapter.

(d) A license holder commits an offense if, while intoxicated, the license holder carries a handgun under the authority of Subchapter H, Chapter 411, Government Code, regardless of whether the handgun is concealed or carried in a holster.

(e) [Repealed.]

(f) [Repealed.]

(g) [Repealed.]

(h) [Repealed.]

(h-1) **[2 Versions: As added by Acts 2007, 80th Leg., ch. 1214]** [Repealed.]

(h-1) **[2 Versions: As added by Acts 2007, 80th Leg., ch. 1222]** [Repealed.]

(i) [Repealed.]

(j) [Repealed.]

(k) [Repealed.]

(*l*) [Repealed.]

(m) [Repealed.]

Sec. 46.04. Unlawful Possession of Firearm.

(a) A person who has been convicted of a felony commits an offense if he possesses a firearm:

(1) after conviction and before the fifth anniversary of the person's release from confinement following conviction of the felony or the person's release from supervision under community supervision, parole, or mandatory supervision, whichever date is later; or

(2) after the period described by Subdivision (1), at any location other than the premises at which the person lives.

(a-1) A person who is a member of a criminal street gang, as defined by Section 71.01, commits an offense if the person intentionally, knowingly, or recklessly carries on or about his or her person a handgun in a motor vehicle or watercraft.

(b) A person who has been convicted of an offense under Section 22.01, punishable as a Class A misdemeanor and involving a member of the person's family or household, commits an offense if the person possesses a firearm before the fifth anniversary of the later of:

(1) the date of the person's release from confinement following conviction of the misdemeanor; or

(2) the date of the person's release from community supervision following conviction of the misdemeanor.

(c) A person, other than a peace officer, as defined by Section 1.07, actively engaged in employment as a sworn, full-time paid employee of a state agency or political subdivision, who is subject to an order issued under Section 6.504 or Chapter 85, Family Code, under Article 17.292 or Subchapter A, Chapter 7B, Code of Criminal Procedure, or by another jurisdiction as provided by Chapter 88, Family Code, commits an offense if the person possesses a firearm after receiving notice of the order and before expiration of the order.

(d) In this section, "family," "household," and "member of a household" have the meanings assigned by Chapter 71, Family Code.

(e) An offense under Subsection (a) is a felony of the third degree. An offense under Subsection (a-1), (b), or (c) is a Class A misdemeanor.

(f) For the purposes of this section, an offense under the laws of this state, another state, or the United States is, except as provided by Subsection (g), a felony if, at the time it is committed, the offense:

(1) is designated by a law of this state as a felony;

(2) contains all the elements of an offense designated by a law of this state as a felony; or

(3) is punishable by confinement for one year or more in a penitentiary.

(g) An offense is not considered a felony for purposes of Subsection (f) if, at the time the person possesses a firearm, the offense:

(1) is not designated by a law of this state as a felony; and

(2) does not contain all the elements of any offense designated by a law of this state as a felony.

Sec. 46.041. Unlawful Possession of Metal or Body Armor by Felon.

(a) In this section, "metal or body armor" means any body covering manifestly designed, made, or adapted for the purpose of protecting a person against gunfire.

(b) A person who has been convicted of a felony commits an offense if after the conviction the person possesses metal or body armor.

(c) An offense under this section is a felony of the third degree.

Sec. 46.05. Prohibited Weapons.

(a) A person commits an offense if the person intentionally or knowingly possesses, manufactures, transports, repairs, or sells:

(1) any of the following items, unless the item is registered in the National Firearms Registration and Transfer Record maintained by the Bureau of Alcohol, Tobacco, Firearms and Explosives or otherwise not subject to that registration requirement or unless the item is classified as a curio or relic by the United States Department of Justice:

(A) an explosive weapon;

(B) a machine gun; or

(C) a short-barrel firearm;

(2) armor-piercing ammunition;

(3) a chemical dispensing device;

(4) a zip gun;

(5) a tire deflation device; or

(6) an improvised explosive device.

(b) It is a defense to prosecution under this section that the actor's conduct was incidental to the performance of official duty by the armed forces or national guard, a governmental law enforcement agency, or a correctional facility.

(c) [Repealed by Acts 2015, 84th Leg., ch. 69 (S.B. 473), § 2, effective September 1, 2015.]

(d) It is an affirmative defense to prosecution under this section that the actor's conduct:

(1) was incidental to dealing with a short-barrel firearm or tire deflation device solely as an antique or curio;

(2) was incidental to dealing with armor-piercing ammunition solely for the purpose of making the ammunition available to an organization, agency, or institution listed in Subsection (b); or

(3) was incidental to dealing with a tire deflation device solely for the purpose of making the device available to an organization, agency, or institution listed in Subsection (b).

(e) **[2 Versions As amended by Acts 2019, 86th Leg., ch. 216 (H.B. 446)]** Except as otherwise provided by this subsection, an offense under this section is a felony of the third degree. An offense under Subsection (a)(5) is a state jail felony.

(e) **[2 Versions As amended by Acts 2019, 86th Leg., ch. 467 (H.B. 4170)]** An offense under Subsection (a)(1), (3), (4), (5), (7), or (8) is a felony of the third degree. An offense under Subsection (a)(6) is a state jail felony. An offense under Subsection (a)(2) is a Class A misdemeanor.

(f) It is a defense to prosecution under this section for the possession of a chemical dispensing device that the actor is a security officer and has received training on the use of the chemical dispensing device by a training program that is:

(1) provided by the Texas Commission on Law Enforcement; or

(2) approved for the purposes described by this subsection by the Texas Private Security Board of the Department of Public Safety.

(g) In Subsection (f), "security officer" means a commissioned security officer as defined by Section 1702.002, Occupations Code, or a noncommissioned security officer registered under Section 1702.221, Occupations Code.

Sec. 46.06. Unlawful Transfer of Certain Weapons.

(a) A person commits an offense if the person:

(1) sells, rents, leases, loans, or gives a handgun to any person knowing that the person to whom the handgun is to be delivered intends to use it unlawfully or in the commission of an unlawful act;

(2) intentionally or knowingly sells, rents, leases, or gives or offers to sell, rent, lease, or give to any child younger than 18 years of age any firearm, club, or location-restricted knife;

(3) intentionally, knowingly, or recklessly sells a firearm or ammunition for a firearm to any person who is intoxicated;

(4) knowingly sells a firearm or ammunition for a firearm to any person who has been convicted of a felony before the fifth anniversary of the later of the following dates:

(A) the person's release from confinement following conviction of the felony; or

(B) the person's release from supervision under community supervision, parole, or mandatory supervision following conviction of the felony;

(5) sells, rents, leases, loans, or gives a handgun to any person knowing that an active protective order is directed to the person to whom the handgun is to be delivered;

(6) knowingly purchases, rents, leases, or receives as a loan or gift from another a handgun while an active protective order is directed to the actor; or

(7) while prohibited from possessing a firearm under state or federal law, knowingly makes a material false statement on a form that is:

(A) required by state or federal law for the purchase, sale, or other transfer of a firearm; and

(B) submitted to a licensed firearms dealer, as defined by 18 U.S.C. Section 923.

(b) In this section:

(1) "Intoxicated" means substantial impairment of mental or physical capacity resulting from introduction of any substance into the body.

(2) "Active protective order" means a protective order issued under Title 4, Family Code, that is in effect. The term does not include a temporary

protective order issued before the court holds a hearing on the matter.

(c) It is an affirmative defense to prosecution under Subsection (a)(2) that the transfer was to a minor whose parent or the person having legal custody of the minor had given written permission for the sale or, if the transfer was other than a sale, the parent or person having legal custody had given effective consent.

(d) An offense under this section is a Class A misdemeanor, except that:

(1) an offense under Subsection (a)(2) is a state jail felony if the weapon that is the subject of the offense is a handgun; and

(2) an offense under Subsection (a)(7) is a state jail felony.

Sec. 46.07. Interstate Purchase.

A resident of this state may, if not otherwise precluded by law, purchase firearms, ammunition, reloading components, or firearm accessories in another state. This authorization is enacted in conformance with 18 U.S.C. Section 922(b)(3)(A).

Sec. 46.08. Hoax Bombs.

(a) A person commits an offense if the person knowingly manufactures, sells, purchases, transports, or possesses a hoax bomb with intent to use the hoax bomb to:

(1) make another believe that the hoax bomb is an explosive or incendiary device; or

(2) cause alarm or reaction of any type by an official of a public safety agency or volunteer agency organized to deal with emergencies.

(b) An offense under this section is a Class A misdemeanor.

Sec. 46.09. Components of Explosives.

(a) A person commits an offense if the person knowingly possesses components of an explosive weapon with the intent to combine the components into an explosive weapon for use in a criminal endeavor.

(b) An offense under this section is a felony of the third degree.

Sec. 46.10. Deadly Weapon in Penal Institution.

(a) A person commits an offense if, while confined in a penal institution, he intentionally, knowingly, or recklessly:

(1) carries on or about his person a deadly weapon; or

(2) possesses or conceals a deadly weapon in the penal institution.

(b) It is an affirmative defense to prosecution under this section that at the time of the offense the actor was engaged in conduct authorized by an employee of the penal institution.

(c) A person who is subject to prosecution under both this section and another section under this chapter may be prosecuted under either section.

(d) An offense under this section is a felony of the third degree.

Sec. 46.11. Penalty If Offense Committed Within Weapon-Free School Zone.

(a) Except as provided by Subsection (b), the punishment prescribed for an offense under this chapter is increased to the punishment prescribed for the next highest category of offense if it is shown beyond a reasonable doubt on the trial of the offense that the actor committed the offense in a place that the actor knew was:

(1) within 300 feet of the premises of a school; or

(2) on premises where:

(A) an official school function is taking place; or

(B) an event sponsored or sanctioned by the University Interscholastic League is taking place.

(b) This section does not apply to an offense under Section 46.03(a)(1).

(c) In this section:

(1) "Premises" has the meaning assigned by Section 481.134, Health and Safety Code.

(2) "School" means a private or public elementary or secondary school.

Sec. 46.12. Maps As Evidence of Location or Area.

(a) In a prosecution of an offense for which punishment is increased under Section 46.11, a map produced or reproduced by a municipal or county engineer for the purpose of showing the location and boundaries of weapon-free zones is admissible in evidence and is prima facie evidence of the location or boundaries of those areas if the governing body of the municipality or county adopts a resolution or ordinance approving the map as an official finding and record of the location or boundaries of those areas.

(b) A municipal or county engineer may, on request of the governing body of the municipality or county, revise a map that has been approved by the governing body of the municipality or county as provided by Subsection (a).

(c) A municipal or county engineer shall file the original or a copy of every approved or revised map approved as provided by Subsection (a) with the county clerk of each county in which the area is located.

(d) This section does not prevent the prosecution from:

(1) introducing or relying on any other evidence or testimony to establish any element of an offense for which punishment is increased under Section 46.11; or

(2) using or introducing any other map or diagram otherwise admissible under the Texas Rules of Evidence.

Sec. 46.13. Making a Firearm Accessible to a Child.

(a) In this section:

(1) "Child" means a person younger than 17 years of age.

(2) "Readily dischargeable firearm" means a firearm that is loaded with ammunition, whether or not a round is in the chamber.

(3) "Secure" means to take steps that a reasonable person would take to prevent the access to a readily dischargeable firearm by a child, including but not limited to placing a firearm in a locked container or temporarily rendering the firearm inoperable by a trigger lock or other means.

(b) A person commits an offense if a child gains access to a readily dischargeable firearm and the person with criminal negligence:

(1) failed to secure the firearm; or

(2) left the firearm in a place to which the person knew or should have known the child would gain access.

(c) It is an affirmative defense to prosecution under this section that the child's access to the firearm:

(1) was supervised by a person older than 18 years of age and was for hunting, sporting, or other lawful purposes;

(2) consisted of lawful defense by the child of people or property;

(3) was gained by entering property in violation of this code; or

(4) occurred during a time when the actor was engaged in an agricultural enterprise.

(d) Except as provided by Subsection (e), an offense under this section is a Class C misdemeanor.

(e) An offense under this section is a Class A misdemeanor if the child discharges the firearm and causes death or serious bodily injury to himself or another person.

(f) A peace officer or other person may not arrest the actor before the seventh day after the date on which the offense is committed if:

(1) the actor is a member of the family, as defined by Section 71.003, Family Code, of the child who discharged the firearm; and

(2) the child in discharging the firearm caused the death of or serious injury to the child.

(g) A dealer of firearms shall post in a conspicuous position on the premises where the dealer conducts business a sign that contains the following warning in block letters not less than one inch in height:

"IT IS UNLAWFUL TO STORE, TRANSPORT, OR ABANDON AN UNSECURED FIREARM IN A PLACE WHERE CHILDREN ARE LIKELY TO BE AND CAN OBTAIN ACCESS TO THE FIREARM."

Sec. 46.14. Firearm Smuggling.

(a) A person commits an offense if the person knowingly engages in the business of transporting or transferring a firearm that the person knows was acquired in violation of the laws of any state or of the United States. For purposes of this subsection, a person is considered to engage in the business of transporting or transferring a firearm if the person engages in that conduct:

(1) on more than one occasion; or

(2) for profit or any other form of remuneration.

(b) An offense under this section is a felony of the third degree, unless it is shown on the trial of the offense that the offense was committed with respect to three or more firearms in a single criminal episode, in which event the offense is a felony of the second degree.

(c) This section does not apply to a peace officer who is engaged in the actual discharge of an official duty.

(d) If conduct that constitutes an offense under this section also constitutes an offense under any other law, the actor may be prosecuted under this section, the other law, or both.

Sec. 46.15. Nonapplicability.

(a) Sections 46.02 and 46.03 do not apply to:

(1) peace officers or special investigators under Article 2.122, Code of Criminal Procedure, and neither section prohibits a peace officer or special investigator from carrying a weapon in this state, including in an establishment in this state serving the public, regardless of whether the peace officer or special investigator is engaged in the actual discharge of the officer's or investigator's duties while carrying the weapon;

(2) parole officers, and neither section prohibits an officer from carrying a weapon in this state if the officer is:

(A) engaged in the actual discharge of the officer's duties while carrying the weapon; and

(B) in compliance with policies and procedures adopted by the Texas Department of Criminal Justice regarding the possession of a weapon by an officer while on duty;

(3) community supervision and corrections department officers appointed or employed under Section 76.004, Government Code, and neither section prohibits an officer from carrying a weapon in this state if the officer is:

(A) engaged in the actual discharge of the officer's duties while carrying the weapon; and

(B) authorized to carry a weapon under Section 76.0051, Government Code;

(4) an active judicial officer as defined by Section 411.201, Government Code, who is licensed to carry a handgun under Subchapter H, Chapter 411, Government Code;

(5) an honorably retired peace officer or other qualified retired law enforcement officer, as defined by 18 U.S.C. Section 926C,who holds a certificate of proficiency issued under Section 1701.357, Occupations Code, and is carrying a photo identification that is issued by a federal, state, or local law enforcement agency, as applicable, and that verifies that the officer is an honorably retired peace officer or other qualified retired law enforcement officer;

(6) the attorney general or a United States attorney, district attorney, criminal district attorney, county attorney, or municipal attorney who is licensed to carry a handgun under Subchapter H, Chapter 411, Government Code;

(7) an assistant United States attorney, assistant attorney general, assistant district attorney, assistant criminal district attorney, or assistant county attorney who is licensed to carry a handgun under Subchapter H, Chapter 411, Government Code;

(8) a bailiff designated by an active judicial officer as defined by Section 411.201, Government Code, who is:

(A) licensed to carry a handgun under Subchapter H, Chapter 411, Government Code; and

(B) engaged in escorting the judicial officer;

(9) a juvenile probation officer who is authorized to carry a firearm under Section 142.006, Human Resources Code; or

(10) a person who is volunteer emergency services personnel if the person is:

(A) carrying a handgun under the authority of Subchapter H, Chapter 411, Government Code; and

(B) engaged in providing emergency services.

(b) Sections 46.02, 46.03(a)(14), and 46.04(a-1) do not apply to a person who:

(1) is in the actual discharge of official duties as a member of the armed forces or state military forces as defined by Section 437.001, Government Code, or as a guard employed by a penal institution;

(2) is traveling;

(3) is engaging in lawful hunting, fishing, or other sporting activity on the immediate premises where the activity is conducted, or is en route between the premises and the actor's residence, motor vehicle, or watercraft, if the weapon is a type commonly used in the activity;

(4) holds a security officer commission issued by the Texas Private Security Board, if the person is engaged in the performance of the person's duties as an officer commissioned under Chapter 1702, Occupations Code, or is traveling to or from the person's place of assignment and is wearing the officer's uniform and carrying the officer's weapon in plain view;

(5) acts as a personal protection officer and carries the person's security officer commission and personal protection officer authorization, if the person:

(A) is engaged in the performance of the person's duties as a personal protection officer under Chapter 1702, Occupations Code, or is traveling to or from the person's place of assignment; and

(B) is either:

(i) wearing the uniform of a security officer, including any uniform or apparel described by Section 1702.323(d), Occupations Code, and carrying the officer's weapon in plain view; or

(ii) not wearing the uniform of a security officer and carrying the officer's weapon in a concealed manner;

(6) is carrying:

(A) a license issued under Subchapter H, Chapter 411, Government Code, to carry a handgun; and

(B) a handgun:

(i) in a concealed manner; or

(ii) in a holster;

(7) holds an alcoholic beverage permit or license or is an employee of a holder of an alcoholic beverage permit or license if the person is supervising the operation of the permitted or licensed premises; or

(8) is a student in a law enforcement class engaging in an activity required as part of the class, if the weapon is a type commonly used in the activity and the person is:

(A) on the immediate premises where the activity is conducted; or

(B) en route between those premises and the person's residence and is carrying the weapon unloaded.

(c) [Repealed.]

(d) The provisions of Section 46.02 prohibiting the carrying of a firearm do not apply to a public security officer employed by the adjutant general under Section 437.053, Government Code, in performance of official duties or while traveling to or from a place of duty.

(e) Section 46.02(a-4) does not apply to an individual carrying a location-restricted knife used in a historical demonstration or in a ceremony in which the knife is significant to the performance of the ceremony.

(f) Section 46.03(a)(6) does not apply to a person who possesses a firearm or club while in the actual discharge of official duties as:

(1) a member of the armed forces or state military forces, as defined by Section 437.001, Government Code; or

(2) an employee of a penal institution.

(g) The provisions of Section 46.03 prohibiting the possession or carrying of a club do not apply to an animal control officer who holds a certificate issued under Section 829.006, Health and Safety Code, and who possesses or carries an instrument used specifically for deterring the bite of an animal while the officer is in the performance of official duties under the Health and Safety Code or is traveling to or from a place of duty.

(h) The provisions of Section 46.03 prohibiting the possession or carrying of a club do not apply to a code enforcement officer who:

(1) holds a certificate of registration issued under Chapter 1952, Occupations Code; and

(2) possesses or carries an instrument used specifically for deterring an animal bite while the officer is:

(A) performing official duties; or

(B) traveling to or from a place of duty.

(i) [Repealed by Acts 2007, 80th Leg., ch. 693 (H.B. 1815), § 3(2), effective September 1, 2007.]

(j) The provisions of Sections 46.02 and 46.03(a)(7), (a-2), (a-3), and (a-4) do not apply to an individual who carries a handgun as a participant in a historical reenactment performed in accordance with the rules of the Texas Alcoholic Beverage Commission.

(k) Section 46.02 does not apply to a person who carries a handgun if:

(1) the person carries the handgun while:

(A) evacuating from an area following the declaration of a state of disaster under Section 418.014, Government Code, or a local state of disaster under Section 418.108, Government Code, with respect to that area; or

(B) reentering that area following the person's evacuation;

(2) not more than 168 hours have elapsed since the state of disaster or local state of disaster was declared, or more than 168 hours have elapsed since the time the declaration was made and the governor has extended the period during which a person may carry a handgun under this subsection; and

(3) the person is not prohibited by state or federal law from possessing a firearm.

(l) Sections 46.02 and 46.03(a)(1), (a)(2), (a)(3), and (a)(4) do not apply to a person who carries a handgun if:

(1) the person carries the handgun on the premises, as defined by the statute providing the applicable offense, of a location operating as an emergency shelter during a state of disaster declared under Section 418.014, Government Code, or a local state of disaster declared under Section 418.108, Government Code;

(2) the owner, controller, or operator of the premises or a person acting with the apparent authority of the owner, controller, or operator, authorized the carrying of the handgun;

(3) the person carrying the handgun complies with any rules and regulations of the owner, controller, or operator of the premises that govern the carrying of a handgun on the premises; and

(4) the person is not prohibited by state or federal law from possessing a firearm.

(m) **As added by Acts 2021, 87th Leg., ch. XXX (HB 1069)** Sections 46.02, 46.03, and 46.035(b) and (c) do not apply to a first responder who:

(1) was carrying a handgun in a concealed manner or in a shoulder or belt holster;

(2) holds an unexpired certificate of completion under Section 411.184, Government Code, at the time of engaging in the applicable conduct;

(3) was engaged in the actual discharge of the first responder's duties while carrying the handgun; and

(4) was employed or supervised by a municipality or county to which Chapter 179, Local Government Code, applies.

(m) **As added by Acts 2021, 87th Leg., ch. XXX (HB 1927)** It is a defense to prosecution under Section 46.03 that the actor:

(1) carries a handgun on a premises or other property on which the carrying of a weapon is prohibited under that section;

(2) personally received from the owner of the property, or from another person with apparent authority to act for the owner, notice that carrying a firearm or other weapon on the premises or other property, as applicable, was prohibited; and

(3) promptly departed from the premises or other property.

(n) The defense provided by Subsection (m) does not apply if:

(1) a sign described by Subsection (o) was posted prominently at each entrance to the premises or other property, as applicable; or

(2) at the time of the offense, the actor knew that carrying a firearm or other weapon on the premises or other property was prohibited.

(o) A person may provide notice that firearms and other weapons are prohibited under Section 46.03 on the premises or other property, as applicable, by posting a sign at each entrance to the premises or other property that:

(1) includes language that is identical to or substantially similar to the following: "Pursuant to Section 46.03, Penal Code (places weapons prohibited), a person may not carry a firearm or other weapon on this property";

(2) includes the language described by Subdivision (1) in both English and Spanish;

(3) appears in contrasting colors with block letters at least one inch in height; and

(4) is displayed in a conspicuous manner clearly visible to the public.

(p) Sections 46.03(a)(7), (11), and (13) do not apply if the actor:

(1) carries a handgun on the premises or other property, as applicable;

(2) holds a license to carry a handgun issued under Subchapter H, Chapter 411, Government Code; and

(3) was not given effective notice under Section 30.06 or 30.07 of this code or Section 411.204, Government Code, as applicable.

(q) Section 46.03(a)(8) does not apply if the actor:

(1) carries a handgun on a premises where a collegiate sporting event is taking place;

(2) holds a license to carry a handgun issued under Subchapter H, Chapter 411, Government Code; and

(3) was not given effective notice under Section 30.06 or 30.07 of this code, as applicable.

CHAPTER 47
GAMBLING

Sec. 47.01. Definitions.

In this chapter:

(1) "Bet" means an agreement to win or lose something of value solely or partially by chance. A bet does not include:

(A) contracts of indemnity or guaranty, or life, health, property, or accident insurance;

(B) an offer of a prize, award, or compensation to the actual contestants in a bona fide contest for the determination of skill, speed, strength, or endurance or to the owners of animals, vehicles, watercraft, or aircraft entered in a contest; or

(C) an offer of merchandise, with a value not greater than $25, made by the proprietor of a bona fide carnival contest conducted at a carnival sponsored by a nonprofit religious, fraternal, school, law enforcement, youth, agricultural, or civic group, including any nonprofit agricultural or civic group incorporated by the state before 1955, if the person to receive the merchandise from the proprietor is the person who performs the carnival contest.

(2) "Bookmaking" means:

(A) to receive and record or to forward more than five bets or offers to bet in a period of 24 hours;

(B) to receive and record or to forward bets or offers to bet totaling more than $1,000 in a period of 24 hours; or

(C) a scheme by three or more persons to receive, record, or forward a bet or an offer to bet.

(3) "Gambling place" means any real estate, building, room, tent, vehicle, boat, or other property whatsoever, one of the uses of which is the making or settling of bets, bookmaking, or the conducting of a lottery or the playing of gambling devices.

(4) "Gambling device" means any electronic, electromechanical, or mechanical contrivance not excluded under Paragraph (B) that for a consideration affords the player an opportunity to obtain anything of value, the award of which is determined solely or partially by chance, even though accompanied by some skill, whether or not the prize is automatically paid by the contrivance. The term:

(A) includes, but is not limited to, gambling device versions of bingo, keno, blackjack, lottery, roulette, video poker, or similar electronic, electromechanical, or mechanical games, or facsimiles thereof, that operate by chance or partially so, that as a result of the play or operation of the game award credits or free games, and that record the number of free games or credits so awarded and the cancellation or removal of the free games or credits; and

(B) does not include any electronic, electromechanical, or mechanical contrivance designed, made, and adapted solely for bona fide amusement purposes if the contrivance rewards the player exclusively with noncash merchandise prizes, toys, or novelties, or a representation of value redeemable for those items, that have a wholesale value available from a single play of the game or device of not more than 10 times the amount charged to play the game or device once or $5, whichever is less.

(5) "Altered gambling equipment" means any contrivance that has been altered in some manner,

including, but not limited to, shaved dice, loaded dice, magnetic dice, mirror rings, electronic sensors, shaved cards, marked cards, and any other equipment altered or designed to enhance the actor's chances of winning.

(6) "Gambling paraphernalia" means any book, instrument, or apparatus by means of which bets have been or may be recorded or registered; any record, ticket, certificate, bill, slip, token, writing, scratch sheet, or other means of carrying on bookmaking, wagering pools, lotteries, numbers, policy, or similar games.

(7) "Lottery" means any scheme or procedure whereby one or more prizes are distributed by chance among persons who have paid or promised consideration for a chance to win anything of value, whether such scheme or procedure is called a pool, lottery, raffle, gift, gift enterprise, sale, policy game, or some other name.

(8) "Private place" means a place to which the public does not have access, and excludes, among other places, streets, highways, restaurants, taverns, nightclubs, schools, hospitals, and the common areas of apartment houses, hotels, motels, office buildings, transportation facilities, and shops.

(9) "Thing of value" means any benefit, but does not include an unrecorded and immediate right of replay not exchangeable for value.

Sec. 47.02. Gambling.

(a) A person commits an offense if he:

(1) makes a bet on the partial or final result of a game or contest or on the performance of a participant in a game or contest;

(2) makes a bet on the result of any political nomination, appointment, or election or on the degree of success of any nominee, appointee, or candidate; or

(3) plays and bets for money or other thing of value at any game played with cards, dice, balls, or any other gambling device.

(b) It is a defense to prosecution under this section that:

(1) the actor engaged in gambling in a private place;

(2) no person received any economic benefit other than personal winnings; and

(3) except for the advantage of skill or luck, the risks of losing and the chances of winning were the same for all participants.

(c) It is a defense to prosecution under this section that the actor reasonably believed that the conduct:

(1) was permitted under Chapter 2001, Occupations Code;

(2) was permitted under Chapter 2002, Occupations Code;

(3) was permitted under Chapter 2004, Occupations Code;

(4) consisted entirely of participation in the state lottery authorized by the State Lottery Act (Chapter 466, Government Code);

(5) was permitted under Subtitle A-1, Title 13, Occupations Code (Texas Racing Act); or

(6) consisted entirely of participation in a drawing for the opportunity to participate in a hunting, fishing, or other recreational event conducted by the Parks and Wildlife Department.

(d) An offense under this section is a Class C misdemeanor.

(e) It is a defense to prosecution under this section that a person played for something of value other than money using an electronic, electromechanical, or mechanical contrivance excluded from the definition of "gambling device" under Section 47.01(4)(B).

Sec. 47.03. Gambling Promotion.

(a) A person commits an offense if he intentionally or knowingly does any of the following acts:

(1) operates or participates in the earnings of a gambling place;

(2) engages in bookmaking;

(3) for gain, becomes a custodian of anything of value bet or offered to be bet;

(4) sells chances on the partial or final result of or on the margin of victory in any game or contest or on the performance of any participant in any game or contest or on the result of any political nomination, appointment, or election or on the degree of success of any nominee, appointee, or candidate; or

(5) for gain, sets up or promotes any lottery or sells or offers to sell or knowingly possesses for transfer, or transfers any card, stub, ticket, check, or other device designed to serve as evidence of participation in any lottery.

(b) An offense under this section is a Class A misdemeanor.

Sec. 47.04. Keeping a Gambling Place.

(a) A person commits an offense if he knowingly uses or permits another to use as a gambling place any real estate, building, room, tent, vehicle, boat, or other property whatsoever owned by him or under his control, or rents or lets any such property with a view or expectation that it be so used.

(b) It is an affirmative defense to prosecution under this section that:

(1) the gambling occurred in a private place;

(2) no person received any economic benefit other than personal winnings; and

(3) except for the advantage of skill or luck, the risks of losing and the chances of winning were the same for all participants.

(c) An offense under this section is a Class A misdemeanor.

Sec. 47.05. Communicating Gambling Information.

(a) A person commits an offense if, with the intent to further gambling, he knowingly communicates information as to bets, betting odds, or changes in betting odds or he knowingly provides, installs, or maintains equipment for the transmission or receipt of such information.

(b) It is an exception to the application of Subsection (a) that the information communicated is intended for use in placing a lawful wager under Chapter 2027, Occupations Code, and is not communicated in violation of Section 2033.013, Occupations Code.

(c) An offense under this section is a Class A misdemeanor.

Sec. 47.06. Possession of Gambling Device, Equipment, or Paraphernalia.

(a) A person commits an offense if, with the intent to further gambling, he knowingly owns, manufactures, transfers, or possesses any gambling device that he knows is designed for gambling purposes or any equipment that he knows is designed as a subassembly or essential part of a gambling device.

(b) A person commits an offense if, with the intent to further gambling, he knowingly owns, manufactures, transfers commercially, or possesses any altered gambling equipment that he knows is designed for gambling purposes or any equipment that he knows is designed as a subassembly or essential part of such device.

(c) A person commits an offense if, with the intent to further gambling, the person knowingly owns, manufactures, transfers commercially, or possesses gambling paraphernalia.

(d) It is a defense to prosecution under Subsections (a) and (c) that:

(1) the device, equipment, or paraphernalia is used for or is intended for use in gambling that is to occur entirely in a private place;

(2) a person involved in the gambling does not receive any economic benefit other than personal winnings; and

(3) except for the advantage of skill or luck, the chance of winning is the same for all participants.

(e) An offense under this section is a Class A misdemeanor.

(f) It is a defense to prosecution under Subsection (a) or (c) that the person owned, manufactured, transferred, or possessed the gambling device, equipment, or paraphernalia for the sole purpose of shipping it to another jurisdiction where the possession or use of the device, equipment, or paraphernalia was legal.

(g) A district or county attorney is not required to have a search warrant or subpoena to inspect a gambling device or gambling equipment or paraphernalia on an ocean-going vessel that enters the territorial waters of this state to call at a port in this state.

Sec. 47.07. Evidence.

In any prosecution under this chapter in which it is relevant to prove the occurrence of a sporting event, a published report of its occurrence in a daily newspaper, magazine, or other periodically printed publication of general circulation shall be admissible in evidence and is prima facie evidence that the event occurred.

Sec. 47.08. Testimonial Immunity.

(a) A party to an offense under this chapter may be required to furnish evidence or testify about the offense.

(b) A party to an offense under this chapter may not be prosecuted for any offense about which he is required to furnish evidence or testify, and the evidence and testimony may not be used against the party in any adjudicatory proceeding except a prosecution for aggravated perjury.

(c) For purposes of this section, "adjudicatory proceeding" means a proceeding before a court or any other agency of government in which the legal rights, powers, duties, or privileges of specified parties are determined.

(d) A conviction under this chapter may be had upon the uncorroborated testimony of a party to the offense.

Sec. 47.09. Other Defenses.

(a) It is a defense to prosecution under this chapter that the conduct:

(1) was authorized under:

(A) Chapter 2001, Occupations Code;

(B) Chapter 2002, Occupations Code;

(C) Chapter 2004, Occupations Code;

(D) Subtitle A-1, Title 13, Occupations Code (Texas Racing Act); or

(E) Chapter 280, Finance Code;

(2) consisted entirely of participation in the state lottery authorized by Chapter 466, Government Code; or

(3) was a necessary incident to the operation of the state lottery and was directly or indirectly authorized by:

(A) Chapter 466, Government Code;

(B) the lottery division of the Texas Lottery Commission;

(C) the Texas Lottery Commission; or

(D) the director of the lottery division of the Texas Lottery Commission.

(b) It is an affirmative defense to prosecution under Sections 47.04, 47.06(a), and 47.06(c) that the gambling device, equipment, or paraphernalia is aboard an ocean-going vessel that enters the territorial waters of this state to call at a port in this state if:

(1) before the vessel enters the territorial waters of this state, the district attorney or, if there is no district attorney, the county attorney for the county in which the port is located receives notice of the existence of the device, equipment, or paraphernalia on board the vessel and of the anticipated dates on which the vessel will enter and leave the territorial waters of this state;

(2) at all times while the vessel is in the territorial waters of this state all devices, equipment, or paraphernalia are disabled, electronically or by another method, from a remote and secured area of the vessel in a manner that allows only the master or crew of the vessel to remove any disabling device;

(3) at all times while the vessel is in the territorial waters of this state any disabling device is not removed except for the purposes of inspecting or repairing the device, equipment, or paraphernalia; and

(4) the device, equipment, or paraphernalia is not used for gambling or other gaming purposes while the vessel is in the territorial waters of this state.

Sec. 47.10. American Documentation of Vessel Required.

If 18 U.S.C. Section 1082 is repealed, the affirmative defenses provided by Section 47.09(b) apply only if the vessel is documented under the laws of the United States.

Sec. 47.11. Deposits in Certain Accounts Not Consideration.

For purposes of this chapter, opening or making a deposit in a savings account or other savings program subject to a savings promotion raffle under Chapter 280, Finance Code, does not constitute consideration.

Sec. 47.111. Public Hunting Drawing [Deleted].

Deleted by Acts 1993, 73rd Leg., ch. 900 (S.B. 1067), § 13.02, effective September 1, 1994.

Sec. 47.12. Raffle by Nonprofit Organization [Deleted].

Deleted by Acts 1993, 73rd Leg., ch. 900 (S.B. 1067), § 1.01, effective September 1, 1994.

Sec. 47.13. American Documentation of Vessel Required [Renumbered].

Renumbered to Tex. Penal Code § 47.10 by Acts 1993, 73rd Leg., ch. 900 (S.B. 1067), § 1.01, effective September 1, 1994.

Sec. 47.14. State Lottery [Deleted].

Deleted by Acts 1993, 73rd Leg., ch. 900 (S.B. 1067), § 1.01, effective September 1, 1994.

CHAPTER 48
CONDUCT AFFECTING PUBLIC HEALTH

Sec. 48.01. Smoking Tobacco.

(a) In this section, "e-cigarette" has the meaning assigned by Section 161.081, Health and Safety Code.

(a-1) A person commits an offense if the person is in possession of a burning tobacco product, smokes tobacco, or operates an e-cigarette in a facility of a public primary or secondary school or an elevator, enclosed theater or movie house, library, museum, hospital, transit system bus, intrastate bus, plane, or train which is a public place.

(b) It is a defense to prosecution under this section that the conveyance or public place in which the offense takes place does not have prominently displayed a reasonably sized notice that smoking is prohibited by state law in such conveyance or public place and that an offense is punishable by a fine not to exceed $500.

(c) All conveyances and public places set out in Subsection (a-1) shall be equipped with facilities for extinguishment of smoking materials and it shall be a defense to prosecution under this section if the conveyance or public place within which the offense takes place is not so equipped.

(d) It is an exception to the application of Subsection (a-1) if the person is in possession of the burning tobacco product, smokes tobacco, or operates the e-cigarette exclusively within an area designated for smoking tobacco or operating an e-cigarette or as a participant in an authorized theatrical performance.

(e) An area designated for smoking tobacco or operating an e-cigarette on a transit system bus or intrastate plane or train must also include the area occupied by the operator of the transit system bus, plane, or train.

(f) An offense under this section is punishable as a Class C misdemeanor.

Sec. 48.015. Prohibitions Relating to Certain Cigarettes.

(a) A person may not acquire, hold, own, possess, or transport for sale or distribution in this state or import or cause to be imported into this state for sale or distribution in this state:

(1) cigarettes that do not comply with all applicable requirements imposed by or under federal law and implementing regulations; or

(2) cigarettes to which stamps may not be affixed under Section 154.0415, Tax Code, other than cigarettes lawfully imported or brought into the state for personal use and cigarettes lawfully sold or intended to be sold as duty-free merchandise by a duty-free sales enterprise in accordance with 19 U.S.C. Section 1555(b), as amended.

(b) A person who commits an act prohibited by Subsection (a), knowing or having reason to know that the person is doing so, is guilty of a Class A misdemeanor.

Sec. 48.02. Prohibition of the Purchase and Sale of Human Organs.

(a) In this section, "human organ" means the human kidney, liver, heart, lung, pancreas, eye, bone, skin, or any other human organ or tissue, but does not include hair or blood, blood components (including plasma), blood derivatives, or blood reagents. The term does not include human fetal tissue as defined by Section 48.03.

(b) A person commits an offense if he or she knowingly or intentionally offers to buy, offers to sell, acquires, receives, sells, or otherwise transfers any human organ for valuable consideration.

(c) It is an exception to the application of this section that the valuable consideration is: (1) a fee paid to a physician or to other medical personnel for services rendered in the usual course of medical practice or a fee paid for hospital or other clinical services; (2) reimbursement of legal or medical expenses incurred for the benefit of the ultimate receiver of the organ; or (3) reimbursement of expenses of travel, housing, and lost wages incurred by the donor of a human organ in connection with the donation of the organ.

(d) A violation of this section is a Class A misdemeanor.

Sec. 48.03. Prohibition on Purchase and Sale of Human Fetal Tissue.

(a) In this section, "human fetal tissue" has the meaning assigned by Section 173.001, Health and Safety Code.

(b) A person commits an offense if the person knowingly offers to buy, offers to sell, acquires, receives, sells, or otherwise transfers any human fetal tissue for economic benefit.

(c) An offense under this section is a state jail felony.

(d) It is a defense to prosecution under this section that the actor:

(1) is an employee of or under contract with an accredited public or private institution of higher education; and

(2) acquires, receives, or transfers human fetal tissue solely for the purpose of fulfilling a donation authorized by Section 173.005, Health and Safety Code.

(e) This section does not apply to:

(1) human fetal tissue acquired, received, or transferred solely for diagnostic or pathological testing;

(2) human fetal tissue acquired, received, or transferred solely for the purposes of a criminal investigation;

(3) human fetal tissue acquired, received, or transferred solely for the purpose of disposing of the tissue in accordance with state law or rules applicable to the disposition of human fetal tissue remains;

(4) human fetal tissue or human tissue acquired during pregnancy or at delivery of a child, provided the tissue is acquired by an accredited public or private institution of higher education for use in research approved by an institutional review board or another appropriate board, committee, or body charged with oversight applicable to the research; or

(5) cell lines derived from human fetal tissue or human tissue existing on September 1, 2017, that are used by an accredited public or private

institution of higher education in research approved by an institutional review board or another appropriate board, committee, or body charged with oversight applicable to the research.

(f) With the consent of the appropriate local county or district attorney, the attorney general has concurrent jurisdiction with that consenting local prosecutor to prosecute an offense under this section.

Sec. 48.04. Prohibition on Purchase and Sale of Adult Stem Cells for Certain Investigational Treatments.

(a) In this section:

(1) "Adult stem cell" means an undifferentiated cell that is:

(A) found in differentiated tissue; and

(B) able to renew itself and differentiate to yield all or nearly all of the specialized cell types of the tissue from which the cell originated.

(2) "Investigational stem cell treatment" means an adult stem cell treatment that:

(A) is under investigation in a clinical trial and being administered to human participants in that trial; and

(B) has not yet been approved for general use by the United States Food and Drug Administration.

(b) A person commits an offense if the person knowingly offers to buy, offers to sell, acquires, receives, sells, or otherwise transfers any adult stem cells for valuable consideration for use in an investigational stem cell treatment.

(c) It is an exception to the application of this section that the valuable consideration is:

(1) a fee paid to a physician or to other medical personnel for services rendered in the usual course of medical practice or a fee paid for hospital or other clinical services;

(2) reimbursement of legal or medical expenses incurred for the benefit of the ultimate receiver of the investigational stem cell treatment; or

(3) reimbursement of expenses of travel, housing, and lost wages incurred by the donor of adult stem cells in connection with the donation of the adult stem cells.

(d) It is an exception to the application of this section that the actor engaged in conduct authorized under Chapter 162, Health and Safety Code.

(e) A violation of this section is a Class A misdemeanor.

Sec. 48.05. Prohibited Camping.

(a) In this section:

(1) "Camp" means to reside temporarily in a place, with shelter.

(2) "Shelter" includes a tent, tarpaulin, lean-to, sleeping bag, bedroll, blankets, or any form of temporary, semipermanent, or permanent shelter, other than clothing or any handheld device, designed to protect a person from weather conditions that threaten personal health and safety.

(b) A person commits an offense if the person intentionally or knowingly camps in a public place without the effective consent of the officer or agency having the legal duty or authority to manage the public place.

(c) The actor's intent or knowledge may be established through evidence of activities associated with sustaining a living accommodation that are conducted in a public place, including:

(1) cooking;

(2) making a fire;

(3) storing personal belongings for an extended period;

(4) digging; or

(5) sleeping.

(d) Consent given by an officer or agency of a political subdivision is not effective for purposes of Subsection (b), unless given to authorize the person to camp for:

(1) recreational purposes;

(2) purposes of sheltering homeless individuals, if the property on which the camping occurs is subject to a plan approved under Subchapter PP, Chapter 2306, Government Code, and the camping occurs in a manner that complies with the plan;

(3) purposes permitted by a beach access plan that has been approved under Section 61.015, Natural Resources Code, and the camping occurs in a manner that complies with the plan; or

(4) purposes related to providing emergency shelter during a disaster declared under Section 418.014, Government Code, or a local disaster declared under Section 418.108 of that code.

(e) An offense under this section is a Class C misdemeanor.

(f) This section does not preempt an ordinance, order, rule, or other regulation adopted by a state agency or political subdivision relating to prohibiting camping in a public place or affect the authority of a state agency or political subdivision to adopt or enforce an ordinance, order, rule, or other regulation relating to prohibiting camping in a public place if the ordinance, order, rule, or other regulation:

(1) is compatible with and equal to or more stringent than the offense prescribed by this section; or

(2) relates to an issue not specifically addressed by this section.

(g) Except as provided by Subsection (h), before or at the time a peace officer issues a citation to a person for an offense under this section, the peace officer must make a reasonable effort to:

(1) advise the person of an alternative place at which the person may lawfully camp; and

(2) contact, if reasonable and appropriate, an appropriate official of the political subdivision in which the public place is located, or an appropriate nonprofit organization operating within that political subdivision, and request the official or organization to provide the person with:

(A) information regarding the prevention of human trafficking; or

(B) any other services that would reduce the likelihood of the person suspected of committing the offense continuing to camp in the public place.

(h) Subsection (g) does not apply if the peace officer determines there is an imminent threat to the health or safety of any person to the extent that compliance with that subsection is impracticable.

(i) If the person is arrested or detained solely for an offense under this section, a peace officer enforcing this section shall ensure that all of the person's personal property not designated as contraband under other law is preserved by:

(1) permitting the person to remove all the property from the public place at the time of the person's departure; or

(2) taking custody of the property and allowing the person to retrieve the property after the person is released from custody.

(j) A fee may not be charged for the storage or release of property under Subsection (i)(2).

CHAPTER 49 INTOXICATION AND ALCOHOLIC BEVERAGE OFFENSES

Sec. 49.01. Definitions.

In this chapter:

(1) "Alcohol concentration" means the number of grams of alcohol per:

(A) 210 liters of breath;

(B) 100 milliliters of blood; or

(C) 67 milliliters of urine.

(2) "Intoxicated" means:

(A) not having the normal use of mental or physical faculties by reason of the introduction of alcohol, a controlled substance, a drug, a dangerous drug, a combination of two or more of those substances, or any other substance into the body; or

(B) having an alcohol concentration of 0.08 or more.

(3) "Motor vehicle" has the meaning assigned by Section 32.34(a).

(4) "Watercraft" means a vessel, one or more water skis, an aquaplane, or another device used for transporting or carrying a person on water, other than a device propelled only by the current of water.

(5) "Amusement ride" has the meaning assigned by Section 2151.002, Occupations Code.

(6) "Mobile amusement ride" has the meaning assigned by Section 2151.002, Occupations Code.

Sec. 49.02. Public Intoxication.

(a) A person commits an offense if the person appears in a public place while intoxicated to the degree that the person may endanger the person or another.

(a-1) For the purposes of this section, a premises licensed or permitted under the Alcoholic Beverage Code is a public place.

(b) It is a defense to prosecution under this section that the alcohol or other substance was administered for therapeutic purposes and as a part of the person's professional medical treatment by a licensed physician.

(c) Except as provided by Subsection (e), an offense under this section is a Class C misdemeanor.

(d) An offense under this section is not a lesser included offense under Section 49.04.

(e) An offense under this section committed by a person younger than 21 years of age is punishable in the same manner as if the minor committed an offense to which Section 106.071, Alcoholic Beverage Code, applies.

Sec. 49.03. Consumption or Possession of Alcoholic Beverage in Motor Vehicle [Repealed].

Repealed by Acts 2001, 77th Leg., ch. 969 (H.B. 5), § 10, effective September 1, 2001.

Sec. 49.031. Possession of Alcoholic Beverage in Motor Vehicle.

(a) In this section:

(1) "Open container" means a bottle, can, or other receptacle that contains any amount of alcoholic beverage and that is open, that has been opened, that has a broken seal, or the contents of which are partially removed.

(2) "Passenger area of a motor vehicle" means the area of a motor vehicle designed for the seating

of the operator and passengers of the vehicle. The term does not include:

(A) a glove compartment or similar storage container that is locked;

(B) the trunk of a vehicle; or

(C) the area behind the last upright seat of the vehicle, if the vehicle does not have a trunk.

(3) "Public highway" means the entire width between and immediately adjacent to the boundary lines of any public road, street, highway, interstate, or other publicly maintained way if any part is open for public use for the purpose of motor vehicle travel. The term includes the right-of-way of a public highway.

(b) A person commits an offense if the person knowingly possesses an open container in a passenger area of a motor vehicle that is located on a public highway, regardless of whether the vehicle is being operated or is stopped or parked. Possession by a person of one or more open containers in a single criminal episode is a single offense.

(c) It is an exception to the application of Subsection (b) that at the time of the offense the defendant was a passenger in:

(1) the passenger area of a motor vehicle designed, maintained, or used primarily for the transportation of persons for compensation, including a bus, taxicab, or limousine; or

(2) the living quarters of a motorized house coach or motorized house trailer, including a self-contained camper, a motor home, or a recreational vehicle.

(d) An offense under this section is a Class C misdemeanor.

(e) A peace officer charging a person with an offense under this section, instead of taking the person before a magistrate, shall issue to the person a written citation and notice to appear that contains the time and place the person must appear before a magistrate, the name and address of the person charged, and the offense charged. If the person makes a written promise to appear before the magistrate by signing in duplicate the citation and notice to appear issued by the officer, the officer shall release the person.

Sec. 49.04. Driving While Intoxicated.

(a) A person commits an offense if the person is intoxicated while operating a motor vehicle in a public place.

(b) Except as provided by Subsections (c) and (d) and Section 49.09, an offense under this section is a Class B misdemeanor, with a minimum term of confinement of 72 hours.

(c) If it is shown on the trial of an offense under this section that at the time of the offense the person operating the motor vehicle had an open container of alcohol in the person's immediate possession, the offense is a Class B misdemeanor, with a minimum term of confinement of six days.

(d) If it is shown on the trial of an offense under this section that an analysis of a specimen of the person's blood, breath, or urine showed an alcohol concentration level of 0.15 or more at the time the analysis was performed, the offense is a Class A misdemeanor.

Sec. 49.045. Driving While Intoxicated with Child Passenger.

(a) A person commits an offense if:

(1) the person is intoxicated while operating a motor vehicle in a public place; and

(2) the vehicle being operated by the person is occupied by a passenger who is younger than 15 years of age.

(b) An offense under this section is a state jail felony.

Sec. 49.05. Flying While Intoxicated.

(a) A person commits an offense if the person is intoxicated while operating an aircraft.

(b) Except as provided by Section 49.09, an offense under this section is a Class B misdemeanor, with a minimum term of confinement of 72 hours.

Sec. 49.06. Boating While Intoxicated.

(a) A person commits an offense if the person is intoxicated while operating a watercraft.

(b) Except as provided by Section 49.09, an offense under this section is a Class B misdemeanor, with a minimum term of confinement of 72 hours.

Sec. 49.065. Assembling or Operating an Amusement Ride While Intoxicated.

(a) A person commits an offense if the person is intoxicated while operating an amusement ride or while assembling a mobile amusement ride.

(b) Except as provided by Subsection (c) and Section 49.09, an offense under this section is a Class B misdemeanor with a minimum term of confinement of 72 hours.

(c) If it is shown on the trial of an offense under this section that at the time of the offense the person operating the amusement ride or assembling the mobile amusement ride had an open container of alcohol in the person's immediate possession, the offense is a Class B misdemeanor with a minimum term of confinement of six days.

Sec. 49.07. Intoxication Assault.

(a) A person commits an offense if the person, by accident or mistake:

(1) while operating an aircraft, watercraft, or amusement ride while intoxicated, or while operating a motor vehicle in a public place while intoxicated, by reason of that intoxication causes serious bodily injury to another; or

(2) as a result of assembling a mobile amusement ride while intoxicated causes serious bodily injury to another.

(b) In this section, "serious bodily injury" means injury that creates a substantial risk of death or that causes serious permanent disfigurement or protracted loss or impairment of the function of any bodily member or organ.

(c) Except as provided by Section 49.09, an offense under this section is a felony of the third degree.

Sec. 49.08. Intoxication Manslaughter.

(a) A person commits an offense if the person:

(1) operates a motor vehicle in a public place, operates an aircraft, a watercraft, or an amusement ride, or assembles a mobile amusement ride; and

(2) is intoxicated and by reason of that intoxication causes the death of another by accident or mistake.

(b) Except as provided by Section 49.09, an offense under this section is a felony of the second degree.

Sec. 49.09. Enhanced Offenses and Penalties.

(a) Except as provided by Subsection (b), an offense under Section 49.04, 49.05, 49.06, or 49.065 is a Class A misdemeanor, with a minimum term of confinement of 30 days, if it is shown on the trial of the offense that the person has previously been convicted one time of an offense relating to the operating of a motor vehicle while intoxicated, an offense of operating an aircraft while intoxicated, an offense of operating a watercraft while intoxicated, or an offense of operating or assembling an amusement ride while intoxicated.

(b) An offense under Section 49.04, 49.045, 49.05, 49.06, or 49.065 is a felony of the third degree if it is shown on the trial of the offense that the person has previously been convicted:

(1) one time of an offense under Section 49.08 or an offense under the laws of another state if the offense contains elements that are substantially similar to the elements of an offense under Section 49.08; or

(2) two times of any other offense relating to the operating of a motor vehicle while intoxicated, operating an aircraft while intoxicated, operating a watercraft while intoxicated, or operating or assembling an amusement ride while intoxicated.

(b-1) An offense under Section 49.07 is:

(1) a felony of the second degree if it is shown on the trial of the offense that the person caused serious bodily injury to a firefighter or emergency medical services personnel while in the actual discharge of an official duty; or

(2) a felony of the first degree if it is shown on the trial of the offense that the person caused serious bodily injury to a peace officer or judge while the officer or judge was in the actual discharge of an official duty.

(b-2) An offense under Section 49.08 is a felony of the first degree if it is shown on the trial of the offense that the person caused the death of a person described by Subsection (b-1).

(b-3) For the purposes of Subsection (b-1):

(1) "Emergency medical services personnel" has the meaning assigned by Section 773.003, Health and Safety Code.

(2) "Firefighter" means:

(A) an individual employed by this state or by a political or legal subdivision of this state who is subject to certification by the Texas Commission on Fire Protection; or

(B) a member of an organized volunteer firefighting unit that:

(i) renders fire-fighting services without remuneration; and

(ii) conducts a minimum of two drills each month, each at least two hours long.

(b-4) An offense under Section 49.07 is a felony of the second degree if it is shown on the trial of the offense that the person caused serious bodily injury to another in the nature of a traumatic brain injury that results in a persistent vegetative state.

(c) For the purposes of this section:

(1) "Offense relating to the operating of a motor vehicle while intoxicated" means:

(A) an offense under Section 49.04 or 49.045;

(B) an offense under Section 49.07 or 49.08, if the vehicle operated was a motor vehicle;

(C) an offense under Article 6701*l*-1, Revised Statutes, as that law existed before September 1, 1994;

(D) an offense under Article 6701*l*-2, Revised Statutes, as that law existed before January 1, 1984;

Penal Code

(E) an offense under Section 19.05(a)(2), as that law existed before September 1, 1994, if the vehicle operated was a motor vehicle; or

(F) an offense under the laws of another state that prohibit the operation of a motor vehicle while intoxicated.

(2) "Offense of operating an aircraft while intoxicated" means:

(A) an offense under Section 49.05;

(B) an offense under Section 49.07 or 49.08, if the vehicle operated was an aircraft;

(C) an offense under Section 1, Chapter 46, Acts of the 58th Legislature, Regular Session, 1963 (Article 46f-3, Vernon's Texas Civil Statutes), as that law existed before September 1, 1994;

(D) an offense under Section 19.05(a)(2), as that law existed before September 1, 1994, if the vehicle operated was an aircraft; or

(E) an offense under the laws of another state that prohibit the operation of an aircraft while intoxicated.

(3) "Offense of operating a watercraft while intoxicated" means:

(A) an offense under Section 49.06;

(B) an offense under Section 49.07 or 49.08, if the vehicle operated was a watercraft;

(C) an offense under Section 31.097, Parks and Wildlife Code, as that law existed before September 1, 1994;

(D) an offense under Section 19.05(a)(2), as that law existed before September 1, 1994, if the vehicle operated was a watercraft; or

(E) an offense under the laws of another state that prohibit the operation of a watercraft while intoxicated.

(4) "Offense of operating or assembling an amusement ride while intoxicated" means:

(A) an offense under Section 49.065;

(B) an offense under Section 49.07 or 49.08, if the offense involved the operation or assembly of an amusement ride; or

(C) an offense under the law of another state that prohibits the operation of an amusement ride while intoxicated or the assembly of a mobile amusement ride while intoxicated.

(d) For the purposes of this section, a conviction for an offense under Section 49.04, 49.045, 49.05, 49.06, 49.065, 49.07, or 49.08 that occurs on or after September 1, 1994, is a final conviction, whether the sentence for the conviction is imposed or probated.

(e), (f) [Repealed by Acts 2005, 79th Leg., ch. 996 (H.B. 51), § 3, effective September 1, 2005.]

(g) A conviction may be used for purposes of enhancement under this section or enhancement under Subchapter D, Chapter 12, but not under both this section and Subchapter D. For purposes of this section, a person is considered to have been convicted of an offense under Section 49.04 or 49.06 if the person was placed on deferred adjudication community supervision for the offense under Article 42A.102, Code of Criminal Procedure.

(h) This subsection applies only to a person convicted of a second or subsequent offense relating to the operating of a motor vehicle while intoxicated committed within five years of the date on which the most recent preceding offense was committed. The court shall enter an order that requires the defendant to have a device installed, on each motor vehicle owned or operated by the defendant, that uses a deep-lung breath analysis mechanism to make impractical the operation of the motor vehicle if ethyl alcohol is detected in the breath of the operator, and that requires that before the first anniversary of the ending date of the period of license suspension under Section 521.344, Transportation Code, the defendant not operate any motor vehicle that is not equipped with that device. The court shall require the defendant to obtain the device at the defendant's own cost on or before that ending date, require the defendant to provide evidence to the court on or before that ending date that the device has been installed on each appropriate vehicle, and order the device to remain installed on each vehicle until the first anniversary of that ending date. If the court determines the offender is unable to pay for the device, the court may impose a reasonable payment schedule not to extend beyond the first anniversary of the date of installation. The Department of Public Safety shall approve devices for use under this subsection. Section 521.247, Transportation Code, applies to the approval of a device under this subsection and the consequences of that approval. Failure to comply with an order entered under this subsection is punishable by contempt. For the purpose of enforcing this subsection, the court that enters an order under this subsection retains jurisdiction over the defendant until the date on which the device is no longer required to remain installed. To the extent of a conflict between this subsection and Subchapter I, Chapter 42A, Code of Criminal Procedure, this subsection controls.

Sec. 49.10. No Defense.

In a prosecution under Section 49.03, 49.04, 49.045, 49.05, 49.06, 49.065, 49.07, or 49.08, the fact that the defendant is or has been entitled to use the alcohol, controlled substance, drug, dangerous drug, or other substance is not a defense.

Sec. 49.11. Proof of Mental State Unnecessary.

(a) Notwithstanding Section 6.02(b), proof of a culpable mental state is not required for conviction of an offense under this chapter.

(b) Subsection (a) does not apply to an offense under Section 49.031.

Sec. 49.12. Applicability to Certain Conduct.

Sections 49.07 and 49.08 do not apply to injury to or the death of an unborn child if the conduct charged is conduct committed by the mother of the unborn child.

CHAPTER 50 FIREWORKS

Sec. 50.01. Definitions.

In this chapter:

(1) "Consumer firework" and "fireworks" have the meanings assigned by 49 C.F.R. Section 173.59.

(2) "Law enforcement officer" means a person who is a peace officer under Article 2.12, Code of Criminal Procedure, or a person who is a federal law enforcement officer, as defined by 5 U.S.C. Section 8331(20).

Sec. 50.02. Unlawful Use of Fireworks.

(a) A person commits an offense if the person explodes or ignites fireworks with the intent to:

(1) interfere with the lawful performance of an official duty by a law enforcement officer; or

(2) flee from a person the actor knows is a law enforcement officer attempting to lawfully arrest or detain the actor.

(b) Except as provided by Subsections (c) and (d), an offense under this section is a state jail felony.

(c) An offense under this section that involves any firework that is not a consumer firework is a second degree felony.

(d) Notwithstanding Subsection (c), an offense under this section is a felony of the first degree if the offense causes serious bodily injury to a person the actor knows is a law enforcement officer while the law enforcement officer is lawfully discharging an official duty or in retaliation or on account of an exercise of official power or performance of an official duty as a law enforcement officer.

(e) If conduct constituting an offense under this section also constitutes an offense under any other law, the actor may be prosecuted under this section, the other law, or both.

TITLE 11 ORGANIZED CRIME

CHAPTER 71 ORGANIZED CRIME

Sec. 71.01. Definitions.

In this chapter,

(a) "Combination" means three or more persons who collaborate in carrying on criminal activities, although:

(1) participants may not know each other's identity;

(2) membership in the combination may change from time to time; and

(3) participants may stand in a wholesaler-retailer or other arm's-length relationship in illicit distribution operations.

(b) "Conspires to commit" means that a person agrees with one or more persons that they or one or more of them engage in conduct that would constitute the offense and that person and one or more of them perform an overt act in pursuance of the agreement. An agreement constituting conspiring to commit may be inferred from the acts of the parties.

(c) "Profits" means property constituting or derived from any proceeds obtained, directly or indirectly, from an offense listed in Section 71.02.

(d) "Criminal street gang" means three or more persons having a common identifying sign or symbol or an identifiable leadership who continuously or regularly associate in the commission of criminal activities.

Sec. 71.02. Engaging in Organized Criminal Activity.

(a) A person commits an offense if, with the intent to establish, maintain, or participate in a combination or in the profits of a combination or as a member of a criminal street gang, the person commits or conspires to commit one or more of the following:

(1) murder, capital murder, arson, aggravated robbery, robbery, burglary, theft, aggravated kidnapping, kidnapping, aggravated assault, aggravated sexual assault, sexual assault, continuous

sexual abuse of young child or disabled individual, solicitation of a minor, forgery, deadly conduct, assault punishable as a Class A misdemeanor, burglary of a motor vehicle, or unauthorized use of a motor vehicle;

(2) any gambling offense punishable as a Class A misdemeanor;

(3) promotion of prostitution, aggravated promotion of prostitution, or compelling prostitution;

(4) unlawful manufacture, transportation, repair, or sale of firearms or prohibited weapons;

(5) unlawful manufacture, delivery, dispensation, or distribution of a controlled substance or dangerous drug, or unlawful possession of a controlled substance or dangerous drug through forgery, fraud, misrepresentation, or deception;

(5-a) causing the unlawful delivery, dispensation, or distribution of a controlled substance or dangerous drug in violation of Subtitle B, Title 3, Occupations Code;

(6) any unlawful wholesale promotion or possession of any obscene material or obscene device with the intent to wholesale promote the same;

(7) any offense under Subchapter B, Chapter 43, depicting or involving conduct by or directed toward a child younger than 18 years of age;

(8) any felony offense under Chapter 32;

(9) any offense under Chapter 36;

(10) any offense under Chapter 34, 35, or 35A;

(11) any offense under Section 37.11(a);

(12) any offense under Chapter 20A;

(13) any offense under Section 37.10;

(14) any offense under Section 38.06, 38.07, 38.09, or 38.11;

(15) any offense under Section 42.10;

(16) any offense under Section 46.06(a)(1) or 46.14;

(17) any offense under Section 20.05 or 20.06;

(18) any offense under Section 16.02; or

(19) any offense classified as a felony under the Tax Code.

(b) Except as provided in Subsections (c) and (d), an offense under this section is one category higher than the most serious offense listed in Subsection (a) that was committed, and if the most serious offense is a Class A misdemeanor, the offense is a state jail felony, except that the offense is a felony of the first degree punishable by imprisonment in the Texas Department of Criminal Justice for:

(1) life without parole, if the most serious offense is an aggravated sexual assault and if at the time of that offense the defendant is 18 years of age or older and:

(A) the victim of the offense is younger than six years of age;

(B) the victim of the offense is younger than 14 years of age and the actor commits the offense in a manner described by Section 22.021(a)(2)(A); or

(C) the victim of the offense is younger than 17 years of age and suffered serious bodily injury as a result of the offense;

(2) life or for any term of not more than 99 years or less than 30 years if the most serious offense is an offense under Section 20.06 that is punishable under Subsection (g) of that section; or

(3) life or for any term of not more than 99 years or less than 15 years if the most serious offense is an offense punishable as a felony of the first degree, other than an offense described by Subdivision (1) or (2).

(c) Conspiring to commit an offense under this section is of the same degree as the most serious offense listed in Subsection (a) that the person conspired to commit.

(d) At the punishment stage of a trial, the defendant may raise the issue as to whether in voluntary and complete renunciation of the offense he withdrew from the combination before commission of an offense listed in Subsection (a) and made substantial effort to prevent the commission of the offense. If the defendant proves the issue in the affirmative by a preponderance of the evidence the offense is the same category of offense as the most serious offense listed in Subsection (a) that is committed, unless the defendant is convicted of conspiring to commit the offense, in which event the offense is one category lower than the most serious offense that the defendant conspired to commit.

Sec. 71.021. Violation of Court Order Enjoining Organized Criminal Activity.

(a) A person commits an offense if the person knowingly violates a temporary or permanent order issued under Section 125.065(a) or (b), Civil Practice and Remedies Code.

(b) If conduct constituting an offense under this section also constitutes an offense under another section of this code, the actor may be prosecuted under either section or under both sections.

(c) An offense under this section is a Class A misdemeanor.

Sec. 71.022. Coercing, Inducing, or Soliciting Membership in a Criminal Street Gang.

(a) A person commits an offense if the person knowingly causes, enables, encourages, recruits, or solicits another person to become a member of a criminal street gang which, as a condition of initiation, admission, membership, or continued membership, requires the commission of any conduct which constitutes an offense punishable as a Class A misdemeanor or a felony.

(a-1) A person commits an offense if, with intent to coerce, induce, or solicit a child to actively participate in the activities of a criminal street gang, the person:

(1) threatens the child or a member of the child's family with imminent bodily injury; or

(2) causes bodily injury to the child or a member of the child's family.

(b) Except as provided by Subsection (c), an offense under this section is a felony of the third degree.

(c) A second or subsequent offense under this section is a felony of the second degree.

(d) In this section:

(1) "Child" means an individual younger than 17 years of age.

(2) "Family" has the meaning assigned by Section 71.003, Family Code.

Sec. 71.023. Directing Activities of Criminal Street Gangs

(a) A person commits an offense if the person, as part of the identifiable leadership of a criminal street gang, knowingly finances, directs, or supervises the commission of, or a conspiracy to commit, one or more of the following offenses by members of a criminal street gang:

(1) a felony offense that is listed in Article 42A.054(a), Code of Criminal Procedure;

(2) a felony offense for which it is shown that a deadly weapon, as defined by Section 1.07, was used or exhibited during the commission of the offense or during immediate flight from the commission of the offense; or

(3) an offense that is punishable under Section 481.112(e) or (f), 481.1121(b)(4), 481.1123(d), (e), or (f), 481.115(f), or 481.120(b)(6), Health and Safety Code.

(b) An offense under this section is a felony of the first degree punishable by imprisonment in the Texas Department of Criminal Justice for life or for any term of not more than 99 years or less than 25 years.

Sec. 71.028. Gang-Free Zones.

(a) In this section:

(1) "General residential operation" has the meaning assigned by Section 42.002, Human Resources Code.

(2) "Institution of higher education," "playground," "premises," "school," "video arcade facility," and "youth center" have the meanings assigned by Section 481.134, Health and Safety Code.

(3) "Shopping mall" means an enclosed public walkway or hall area that connects retail, service, or professional establishments.

(b) This section applies to an offense listed in Section 71.02(a)(1), (4), or (7), other than burglary, theft, burglary of a motor vehicle, or unauthorized use of a motor vehicle.

(c) Except as provided by Subsection (d), the punishment prescribed for an offense described by Subsection (b) is increased to the punishment prescribed for the next highest category of offense if the actor is 17 years of age or older and it is shown beyond a reasonable doubt on the trial of the offense that the actor committed the offense at a location that was:

(1) in, on, or within 1,000 feet of any:

(A) real property that is owned, rented, or leased by a school or school board;

(B) premises owned, rented, or leased by an institution of higher education;

(C) premises of a public or private youth center;

(D) playground; or

(E) general residential operation operating as a residential treatment center;

(2) in, on, or within 300 feet of any:

(A) shopping mall;

(B) movie theater;

(C) premises of a public swimming pool; or

(D) premises of a video arcade facility; or

(3) on a school bus.

(d) The punishment for an offense described by Subsection (b) may not be increased under this section if the offense is punishable under Section 71.02 as a felony of the first degree.

Sec. 71.029. Maps As Evidence of Location or Area.

(a) In a prosecution of an offense for which punishment is increased under Section 71.028, a map produced or reproduced by a municipal or county engineer for the purpose of showing the location and boundaries of gang-free zones is admissible in evidence and is prima facie evidence of the location or boundaries of those zones if the governing body of the municipality or county adopts a resolution or ordinance approving the map as an official finding and record of the location or boundaries of those zones.

(b) A municipal or county engineer may, on request of the governing body of the municipality or county, revise a map that has been approved by the governing body of the municipality or county as provided by Subsection (a).

(c) A municipal or county engineer shall file the original or a copy of every approved or revised map approved as provided by Subsection (a) with the county clerk of each county in which the zone is located.

(d) This section does not prevent the prosecution from:

(1) introducing or relying on any other evidence or testimony to establish any element of an offense for which punishment is increased under Section 71.028; or

(2) using or introducing any other map or diagram otherwise admissible under the Texas Rules of Evidence.

Sec. 71.03. Defenses Excluded.

It is no defense to prosecution under Section 71.02 that:

(1) one or more members of the combination are not criminally responsible for the object offense;

(2) one or more members of the combination have been acquitted, have not been prosecuted or convicted, have been convicted of a different offense, or are immune from prosecution;

(3) a person has been charged with, acquitted, or convicted of any offense listed in Subsection (a) of Section 71.02; or

(4) once the initial combination of three or more persons is formed there is a change in the number or identity of persons in the combination as long as two or more persons remain in the combination and are involved in a continuing course of conduct constituting an offense under this chapter.

Sec. 71.04. Testimonial Immunity.

(a) A party to an offense under this chapter may be required to furnish evidence or testify about the offense.

(b) No evidence or testimony required to be furnished under the provisions of this section nor any information directly or indirectly derived from such evidence or testimony may be used against the witness in any criminal case, except a prosecution for aggravated perjury or contempt.

Sec. 71.05. Renunciation Defense.

(a) It is an affirmative defense to prosecution under Section 71.02 that under circumstances manifesting a voluntary and complete renunciation of the actor's criminal objective, the actor withdrew from the combination before commission of an offense listed in Section 71.02(a) and took further affirmative action that prevented the commission of the offense.

(b) For the purposes of this section and Subsection (d) of Section 71.02, renunciation is not voluntary if it is motivated in whole or in part:

(1) by circumstances not present or apparent at the inception of the actor's course of conduct that increase the probability of detection or apprehension or that make more difficult the accomplishment of the objective; or

(2) by a decision to postpone the criminal conduct until another time or to transfer the criminal act to another but similar objective or victim.

(c) Evidence that the defendant withdrew from the combination before commission of an offense listed in Section 71.02(a) and made substantial effort to prevent the commission of an offense listed in Section 71.02(a) shall be admissible as mitigation at the hearing on punishment if the actor has been found guilty under Section 71.02, and in the event of a finding of renunciation under this subsection, the punishment shall be one grade lower than that provided under Section 71.02.

CODE OF CRIMINAL PROCEDURE

TITLE 1
CODE OF CRIMINAL PROCEDURE OF 1965

INTRODUCTORY

CHAPTER 1
GENERAL PROVISIONS

Art. 1.01. Short Title.

This Act shall be known, and may be cited, as the "Code of Criminal Procedure".

Art. 1.02. Effective Date.

This Code shall take effect and be in force on and after January 1, 1966. The procedure herein prescribed shall govern all criminal proceedings instituted after the effective date of this Act and all proceedings pending upon the effective date hereof insofar as are applicable.

Art. 1.025. Severability.

If any provision of this code or its application to any person or circumstance is held invalid, the invalidity does not affect other provisions or applications of the code that can be given effect without the invalid provision or application, and to this end the provisions of this code are severable. (Code Crim. Proc., Art. 54.01.)

Art. 1.026. Construction.

The articles contained in Chapter 722 (S.B. 107), Acts of the 59th Legislature, Regular Session, 1965, as revised, rewritten, changed, combined, and codified, may not be construed as a continuation of former laws except as otherwise provided in that Act. (Code Crim. Proc., Art. 54.02, Sec. 2(a) (part).)

Art. 1.03. Objects of this Code.

This Code is intended to embrace rules applicable to the prevention and prosecution of offenses against the laws of this State, and to make the rules of procedure in respect to the prevention and punishment of offenses intelligible to the officers who are to act under them, and to all persons whose rights are to be affected by them. It seeks:

1. To adopt measures for preventing the commission of crime;
2. To exclude the offender from all hope of escape;
3. To insure a trial with as little delay as is consistent with the ends of justice;
4. To bring to the investigation of each offense on the trial all the evidence tending to produce conviction or acquittal;
5. To insure a fair and impartial trial; and
6. The certain execution of the sentence of the law when declared.

Art. 1.04. Due Course of Law.

No citizen of this State shall be deprived of life, liberty, property, privileges or immunities, or in any manner disfranchised, except by the due course of the law of the land.

Art. 1.05. Rights of Accused.

In all criminal prosecutions the accused shall have a speedy public trial by an impartial jury. He shall have the right to demand the nature and cause of the accusation against him, and to have a copy thereof. He shall not be compelled to give evidence against himself. He shall have the right of being heard by himself, or counsel, or both; shall be confronted with the witnesses against him, and shall have compulsory process for obtaining witnesses in his favor. No person shall be held to answer for a felony unless on indictment of a grand jury.

Art. 1.051. Right to Representation by Counsel.

(a) A defendant in a criminal matter is entitled to be represented by counsel in an adversarial judicial proceeding. The right to be represented by counsel includes the right to consult in private with counsel sufficiently in advance of a proceeding to allow adequate preparation for the proceeding.

(b) For the purposes of this article and Articles 26.04 and 26.05 of this code, "indigent" means a person who is not financially able to employ counsel.

(c) An indigent defendant is entitled to have an attorney appointed to represent him in any adversary judicial proceeding that may result

Code of Criminal Procedure

in punishment by confinement and in any other criminal proceeding if the court concludes that the interests of justice require representation. Subject to Subsection (c-1), if an indigent defendant is entitled to and requests appointed counsel and if adversarial judicial proceedings have been initiated against the defendant, a court or the courts' designee authorized under Article 26.04 to appoint counsel for indigent defendants in the county in which the defendant is arrested shall appoint counsel as soon as possible, but not later than:

(1) the end of the third working day after the date on which the court or the courts' designee receives the defendant's request for appointment of counsel, if the defendant is arrested in a county with a population of less than 250,000; or

(2) the end of the first working day after the date on which the court or the courts' designee receives the defendant's request for appointment of counsel, if the defendant is arrested in a county with a population of 250,000 or more.

(c-1) If an indigent defendant is arrested under a warrant issued in a county other than the county in which the arrest was made and the defendant is entitled to and requests appointed counsel, a court or the courts' designee authorized under Article 26.04 to appoint counsel for indigent defendants in the county that issued the warrant shall appoint counsel within the periods prescribed by Subsection (c), regardless of whether the defendant is present within the county issuing the warrant and even if adversarial judicial proceedings have not yet been initiated against the defendant in the county issuing the warrant. However, if the defendant has not been transferred or released into the custody of the county issuing the warrant before the 11th day after the date of the arrest and if counsel has not otherwise been appointed for the defendant in the arresting county under this article, a court or the courts' designee authorized under Article 26.04 to appoint counsel for indigent defendants in the arresting county immediately shall appoint counsel to represent the defendant in any matter under Chapter 11 or 17, regardless of whether adversarial judicial proceedings have been initiated against the defendant in the arresting county. If counsel is appointed for the defendant in the arresting county as required by this subsection, the arresting county may seek from the county that issued the warrant reimbursement for the actual costs paid by the arresting county for the appointed counsel.

(d) An eligible indigent defendant is entitled to have the trial court appoint an attorney to represent him in the following appellate and postconviction habeas corpus matters:

(1) an appeal to a court of appeals;

(2) an appeal to the Court of Criminal Appeals if the appeal is made directly from the trial court or if a petition for discretionary review has been granted;

(3) a habeas corpus proceeding if the court concludes that the interests of justice require representation; and

(4) any other appellate proceeding if the court concludes that the interests of justice require representation.

(e) An appointed counsel is entitled to 10 days to prepare for a proceeding but may waive the preparation time with the consent of the defendant in writing or on the record in open court. If a nonindigent defendant appears without counsel at a proceeding after having been given a reasonable opportunity to retain counsel, the court, on 10 days' notice to the defendant of a dispositive setting, may proceed with the matter without securing a written waiver or appointing counsel. If an indigent defendant who has refused appointed counsel in order to retain private counsel appears without counsel after having been given an opportunity to retain counsel, the court, after giving the defendant a reasonable opportunity to request appointment of counsel or, if the defendant elects not to request appointment of counsel, after obtaining a waiver of the right to counsel pursuant to Subsections (f) and (g), may proceed with the matter on 10 days' notice to the defendant of a dispositive setting.

(f) A defendant may voluntarily and intelligently waive in writing the right to counsel. A waiver obtained in violation of Subsection (f-1) or (f-2) is presumed invalid.

(f-1) In any adversary judicial proceeding that may result in punishment by confinement, the attorney representing the state may not:

(1) initiate or encourage an attempt to obtain from a defendant who is not represented by counsel a waiver of the right to counsel; or

(2) communicate with a defendant who has requested the appointment of counsel, unless the court or the court's designee authorized under Article 26.04 to appoint counsel for indigent defendants in the county has denied the request and, subsequent to the denial, the defendant:

(A) has been given a reasonable opportunity to retain and has failed to retain private counsel; or

(B) waives or has waived the opportunity to retain private counsel.

(f-2) In any adversary judicial proceeding that may result in punishment by confinement, the court may not direct or encourage the defendant to communicate with the attorney representing the state until the court advises the defendant of the right to counsel and the procedure for requesting appointed counsel and the defendant has been given a reasonable opportunity to request appointed counsel. If the defendant has requested appointed counsel, the court may not direct or encourage the defendant to communicate with the attorney representing the state unless the court or the court's designee authorized under Article 26.04 to appoint counsel for indigent defendants in the county has denied the request and, subsequent to the denial, the defendant:

(1) has been given a reasonable opportunity to retain and has failed to retain private counsel; or

(2) waives or has waived the opportunity to retain private counsel.

(g) If a defendant wishes to waive the right to counsel for purposes of entering a guilty plea or proceeding to trial, the court shall advise the defendant of the nature of the charges against the defendant and, if the defendant is proceeding to trial, the dangers and disadvantages of self-representation. If the court determines that the waiver is voluntarily and intelligently made, the court shall provide the defendant with a statement substantially in the following form, which, if signed by the defendant, shall be filed with and become part of the record of the proceedings:

"I have been advised this __________ day of __________, 2 __________, by the (name of court) Court of my right to representation by counsel in the case pending against me. I have been further advised that if I am unable to afford counsel, one will be appointed for me free of charge. Understanding my right to have counsel appointed for me free of charge if I am not financially able to employ counsel, I wish to waive that right and request the court to proceed with my case without an attorney being appointed for me. I hereby waive my right to counsel. (signature of defendant)"

(h) A defendant may withdraw a waiver of the right to counsel at any time but is not entitled to repeat a proceeding previously held or waived solely on the grounds of the subsequent appointment or retention of counsel. If the defendant withdraws a waiver, the trial court, in its discretion, may provide the appointed counsel 10 days to prepare.

(i) Subject to Subsection (c-1), with respect to a county with a population of less than 250,000, if an indigent defendant is entitled to and requests appointed counsel and if adversarial judicial proceedings have not been initiated against the defendant, a court or the courts' designee authorized under Article 26.04 to appoint counsel for indigent defendants in the county in which the defendant is arrested shall appoint counsel immediately following the expiration of three working days after the date on which the court or the courts' designee receives the defendant's request for appointment of counsel. If adversarial judicial proceedings are initiated against the defendant before the expiration of the three working days, the court or the courts' designee shall appoint counsel as provided by Subsection (c). Subject to Subsection (c-1), in a county with a population of 250,000 or more, the court or the courts' designee shall appoint counsel as required by this subsection immediately following the expiration of one working day after the date on which the court or the courts' designee receives the defendant's request for appointment of counsel. If adversarial judicial proceedings are initiated against the defendant before the expiration of the one working day, the court or the courts' designee shall appoint counsel as provided by Subsection (c).

(j) Notwithstanding any other provision of this section, if an indigent defendant is released from custody prior to the appointment of counsel under this section, appointment of counsel is not required until the defendant's first court appearance or when adversarial judicial proceedings are initiated, whichever comes first.

(k) A court or the courts' designee may without unnecessary delay appoint new counsel to represent an indigent defendant for whom counsel is appointed under Subsection (c), (c-1), or (i) if:

(1) the defendant is subsequently charged in the case with an offense different from the offense with which the defendant was initially charged; and

(2) good cause to appoint new counsel is stated on the record as required by Article 26.04(j)(2).

Art. 1.052. Signed Pleadings of Defendant.

(a) A pleading, motion, and other paper filed for or on behalf of a defendant represented by an attorney must be signed by at least one attorney of record in the attorney's name and state the attorney's address. A defendant who is not represented by an attorney must sign any pleading, motion, or other paper filed for or on the defendant's behalf and state the defendant's address.

(b) The signature of an attorney or a defendant constitutes a certificate by the attorney or defendant that the person has read the pleading, motion, or other paper and that to the best of the person's knowledge, information, and belief formed after reasonable inquiry that the instrument is not groundless and brought in bad faith or groundless and brought for harassment, unnecessary delay, or other improper purpose.

(c) If a pleading, motion, or other paper is not signed, the court shall strike it unless it is signed promptly after the omission is called to the attention of the attorney or defendant.

(d) An attorney or defendant who files a fictitious pleading in a cause for an improper purpose described by Subsection (b) or who makes a statement in a pleading that the attorney or defendant knows to be groundless and false to obtain a delay of the trial of the cause or for the purpose of harassment shall be held guilty of contempt.

(e) If a pleading, motion, or other paper is signed in violation of this article, the court, on motion or on its own initiative, after notice and hearing, shall impose an appropriate sanction, which may include an order to pay to the other party or parties to the prosecution or to the general fund of the county in which the pleading, motion, or other paper was filed the amount of reasonable expenses incurred because of the filing of the pleading, motion, or other paper, including reasonable attorney's fees.

(f) A court shall presume that a pleading, motion, or other paper is filed in good faith. Sanctions under this article may not be imposed except for good cause stated in the sanction order.

(g) A plea of "not guilty" or "no contest" or "nolo contendere" does not constitute a violation of this article. An allegation that an event took place or occurred on or about a particular date does not constitute a violation of this article.

(h) In this article, "groundless" means without basis in law or fact and not warranted by a good faith argument for the extension, modification, or reversal of existing law.

Art. 1.053. Present Ability to Pay.

Except as otherwise specifically provided, in determining a defendant's ability to pay for any purpose, the court shall consider only the defendant's present ability to pay.

Art. 1.06. Searches and Seizures.

The people shall be secure in their persons, houses, papers and possessions from all unreasonable seizures or searches. No warrant to search any place or to seize any person or thing shall issue without describing them as near as may be, nor without probable cause supported by oath or affirmation.

Art. 1.07. Right to Bail.

All prisoners shall be bailable unless for capital offenses when the proof is evident. This provision shall not be so construed as to prevent bail after indictment found upon examination of the evidence, in such manner as may be prescribed by law.

Art. 1.08. Habeas Corpus.

The writ of habeas corpus is a writ of right and shall never be suspended.

Art. 1.09. Cruelty Forbidden.

Excessive bail shall not be required, nor excessive fines imposed, nor cruel or unusual punishment inflicted.

Art. 1.10. Jeopardy.

No person for the same offense shall be twice put in jeopardy of life or liberty; nor shall a person be again put upon trial for the same offense, after a verdict of not guilty in a court of competent jurisdiction.

Art. 1.11. Acquittal a Bar.

An acquittal of the defendant exempts him from a second trial or a second prosecution for the same offense, however irregular the proceedings may have been; but if the defendant shall have been acquitted upon trial in a court having no jurisdiction of the offense, he may be prosecuted again in a court having jurisdiction.

Art. 1.12. Right to Jury.

The right of trial by jury shall remain inviolate.

Art. 1.13. Waiver of Trial by Jury.

(a) The defendant in a criminal prosecution for any offense other than a capital felony case in which the state notifies the court and the defendant that it will seek the death penalty shall have the right, upon entering a plea, to waive the right of trial by jury, conditioned, however, that, except as provided by Article 27.19, the waiver must be made in person by the defendant in writing in open court with the consent and approval of the court, and the attorney representing the state. The consent and approval by the court shall be entered of record on the minutes of the court, and the consent and approval of the attorney representing the state shall be in writing, signed by that attorney, and filed in the papers of the cause before the defendant enters the defendant's plea.

(b) In a capital felony case in which the attorney representing the State notifies the court and the defendant that it will not seek the death penalty, the defendant may waive the right to trial by jury but only if the attorney representing the State, in writing and in open court, consents to the waiver.

(c) A defendant may agree to waive a jury trial regardless of whether the defendant is represented by an attorney at the time of making the waiver, but before a defendant charged with a felony who has no attorney can agree to waive the jury, the court must appoint an attorney to represent him.

Art. 1.14. Waiver of Rights.

(a) The defendant in a criminal prosecution for any offense may waive any rights secured him by law except that a defendant in a capital felony case may waive the right of trial by jury only in the manner permitted by Article 1.13(b) of this code.

(b) If the defendant does not object to a defect, error, or irregularity of form or substance in an indictment or information before the date on which the trial on the merits commences, he waives and forfeits the right to object to the defect, error, or irregularity and he may not raise the objection on appeal or in any other postconviction proceeding. Nothing in this article prohibits a trial court from requiring that an objection to an indictment or information be made at an earlier time in compliance with Article 28.01 of this code.

Art. 1.141. Waiver of Indictment for Noncapital Felony.

A person represented by legal counsel may in open court or by written instrument voluntarily waive the right to be accused by indictment of any offense other than a capital felony. On waiver as provided in this article, the accused shall be charged by information.

Art. 1.15. Jury in Felony.

No person can be convicted of a felony except upon the verdict of a jury duly rendered and recorded, unless the defendant, upon entering a plea, has in open court in person waived his right of trial by jury in writing in accordance with Articles 1.13 and 1.14; provided, however, that it shall be necessary for the state to introduce evidence into the record showing the guilt of the defendant and said evidence shall be accepted by the court as the basis for its judgment and in no event shall a person charged be convicted upon his plea without sufficient evidence to support the same. The evidence may be stipulated if the defendant in such case consents in writing, in open court, to waive the appearance, confrontation, and cross-examination of witnesses, and further consents either to an oral stipulation of the evidence and testimony or to the introduction of testimony by affidavits, written statements of witnesses, and any other documentary evidence in support of the judgment of the court. Such waiver and consent must be approved by the court in writing, and be filed in the file of the papers of the cause.

Art. 1.16. Liberty of Speech and Press.

Every person shall be at liberty to speak, write or publish his opinion on any subject, being liable for the abuse of that privilege; and no law shall ever be passed curtailing the liberty of speech or of the press. In prosecutions for the publication of papers investigating the conduct of officers or men in public capacity, or when the matter published is proper for public information, the truth thereof may be given in evidence. In all indictments for libels, the jury shall have the right to determine the law and the facts, under the direction of the court, as in other cases.

Art. 1.17. Religious Belief.

No person shall be disqualified to give evidence in any court of this State on account of his religious opinions, or for the want of any religious belief; but all oaths or affirmations shall be administered in the mode most binding upon the conscience, and shall be taken subject to the pains and penalties of perjury.

Art. 1.18. Outlawry and Transportation.

No citizen shall be outlawed, nor shall any person be transported out of the State for any offense committed within the same.

Art. 1.19. Corruption of Blood, Etc.

No conviction shall work corruption of blood or forfeiture of estate.

Art. 1.20. Conviction of Treason.

No person shall be convicted of treason except on the testimony of two witnesses to the same overt act, or on confession in open court.

Art. 1.21. Privilege of Legislators.

Senators and Representatives shall, except in cases of treason, felony or breach of the peace, be privileged from arrest during the session of the Legislature, and in going to and returning from the same, allowing one day for every twenty miles such member may reside from the place at which the Legislature is convened.

Art. 1.22. Privilege of Voters [Repealed].

Repealed by Acts 1985, 69th Leg., ch. 211 (S.B. 616), § 9(a)(6), effective January 1, 1986.

Art. 1.23. Dignity of State.

All justices of the Supreme Court, judges of the Court of Criminal Appeals, justices of the Courts of Appeals and judges of the District Courts, shall, by virtue of their offices, be conservators of the peace throughout the State. The style of all writs and process shall be "The State of Texas". All prosecutions shall be carried on "in the name and by authority of The State of Texas", and conclude, "against the peace and dignity of the State".

Art. 1.24. Public Trial.

The proceedings and trials in all courts shall be public.

Art. 1.25. Confronted by Witnesses.

The defendant, upon a trial, shall be confronted with the witnesses, except in certain cases provided for in this Code where depositions have been taken.

Art. 1.26. Construction of This Code.

The provisions of this Code shall be liberally construed, so as to attain the objects intended by the Legislature: The prevention, suppression and punishment of crime.

Art. 1.27. Common Law Governs.

If this Code fails to provide a rule of procedure in any particular state of case which may arise, the rules of the common law shall be applied and govern.

CHAPTER 2 GENERAL DUTIES OF OFFICERS

Art. 2.01. Duties of District Attorneys.

Each district attorney shall represent the State in all criminal cases in the district courts of his district and in appeals therefrom, except in cases where he has been, before his election, employed adversely. When any criminal proceeding is had before an examining court in his district or before a judge upon habeas corpus, and he is notified of the same, and is at the time within his district, he shall represent the State therein, unless prevented by other official duties. It shall be the primary duty of all prosecuting attorneys, including any special prosecutors, not to convict, but to see that justice is done. They shall not suppress facts or secrete witnesses capable of establishing the innocence of the accused.

Art. 2.02. Duties of County Attorneys.

The county attorney shall attend the terms of court in his county below the grade of district court, and shall represent the State in all criminal cases under examination or prosecution in said county; and in the absence of the district attorney he shall represent the State alone and, when requested, shall aid the district attorney in the prosecution of any case in behalf of the State in the district court. He shall represent the State in cases he has prosecuted which are appealed.

Art. 2.021. Duties of Attorney General.

The attorney general may offer to a county or district attorney the assistance of the attorney general's office in the prosecution of an offense described by Article 66.102(h) the victim of which is younger than 17 years of age at the time the offense is committed. On request of a county or district attorney, the attorney general shall assist in the prosecution of an offense described by Article 66.102(h) the victim of which is younger than 17 years of age at the time the offense is committed. For purposes of this article, assistance includes investigative, technical, and litigation assistance of the attorney general's office.

Art. 2.022. Assistance of Texas Rangers.

(a) The attorney representing the state may request the Texas Rangers division of the Department of Public Safety to provide assistance to a local law enforcement agency investigating an offense that:

(1) is alleged to have been committed by an elected officer of the political subdivision served by the local law enforcement agency; and

(2) on conviction or adjudication, would subject the elected officer to registration as a sex offender under Chapter 62.

(b) For purposes of this article, "assistance" includes investigative, technical, and administrative assistance.

Art. 2.023. Notification to Texas Department of Criminal Justice.

(a) This article applies only to a defendant who, in connection with a previous conviction for an offense listed in Article 42A.054(a) or for which the judgment contains an affirmative finding under Article 42A.054(c) or (d):

(1) received a sentence that included imprisonment at a facility operated by or under contract with the Texas Department of Criminal Justice; and

(2) was subsequently released from the imprisonment, including a release on parole, to mandatory supervision, or following discharge of the defendant's sentence.

(b) Not later than the 10th day after the date that a defendant described by Subsection (a) is indicted for an offense listed in Article 42A.054(a) or for which the judgment contains an affirmative finding under Article 42A.054(c) or (d), the attorney representing the state shall notify an officer designated by the Texas Department of Criminal Justice of the offense charged in the indictment.

Art. 2.024. Tracking Use of Certain Testimony.

(a) In this article:

(1) "Attorney representing the state" means a district attorney, a criminal district attorney, or a county attorney with criminal jurisdiction.

(2) "Correctional facility" has the meaning assigned by Section 1.07, Penal Code.

(b) An attorney representing the state shall track:

(1) the use of testimony of a person to whom a defendant made a statement against the defendant's interest while the person was imprisoned or confined in the same correctional facility as the defendant, if known by the attorney representing the state, regardless of whether the testimony is presented at trial; and

(2) any benefits offered or provided to a person in exchange for testimony described by Subdivision (1).

Art. 2.025. Special Duty of District or County Attorney Relating to Child Support.

If a district or county attorney receives money from a person who is required by a court order to pay child support through a local registry or the Title IV-D agency and the money is presented to the attorney as payment for the court-ordered child support, the attorney shall transfer the money to the local registry or Title IV-D agency designated as the place of payment in the child support order.

Art. 2.03. Neglect of Duty.

(a) It shall be the duty of the attorney representing the State to present by information to the court having jurisdiction, any officer for neglect or failure of any duty enjoined upon such officer, when such neglect or failure can be presented by information, whenever it shall come to the knowledge of said attorney that there has been a neglect or failure of duty upon the part of said officer; and he shall bring to the notice of the grand jury any act of violation of law or neglect or failure of duty upon the part of any officer, when such violation, neglect or failure is not presented by information, and whenever the same may come to his knowledge.

(b) It is the duty of the trial court, the attorney representing the accused, the attorney representing the state and all peace officers to so conduct themselves as to insure a fair trial for both the state and the defendant, not impair the presumption of innocence, and at the same time afford the public the benefits of a free press.

Art. 2.04. Shall Draw Complaints.

Upon complaint being made before a district or county attorney that an offense has been committed in his district or county, he shall reduce the complaint to writing and cause the same to be signed and sworn to by the complainant, and it shall be duly attested by said attorney.

Art. 2.05. When Complaint Is Made.

If the offense be a misdemeanor, the attorney shall forthwith prepare an information based upon such complaint and file the same in the court having jurisdiction; provided, that in counties having no county attorney, misdemeanor cases may be tried upon complaint alone, without an information, provided, however, in counties having one or more criminal district courts an information must be filed in each misdemeanor case. If the offense be a felony, he shall forthwith file the complaint with a magistrate of the county.

Art. 2.06. May Administer Oaths.

For the purpose mentioned in the two preceding Articles, district and county attorneys are authorized to administer oaths.

Code of Criminal Procedure

Art. 2.07. Attorney Pro Tem.

(a) Whenever an attorney for the state is disqualified to act in any case or proceeding, is absent from the county or district, or is otherwise unable to perform the duties of the attorney's office, or in any instance where there is no attorney for the state, the judge of the court in which the attorney represents the state may appoint, from any county or district, an attorney for the state or may appoint an assistant attorney general to perform the duties of the office during the absence or disqualification of the attorney for the state.

(b) Except as otherwise provided by this subsection, the duties of the appointed office are additional duties of the appointed attorney's present office, and the attorney is not entitled to additional compensation. This subsection does not prevent a commissioners court of a county from contracting with another commissioners court to pay expenses and reimburse compensation paid by a county to an attorney who is appointed to perform additional duties.

(b-1) An attorney for the state who is not disqualified to act may request the court to permit the attorney's recusal in a case for good cause, and on approval by the court, the attorney is disqualified.

(c) [Repealed.]

(d) In this article, "attorney for the state" means a county attorney with criminal jurisdiction, a district attorney, or a criminal district attorney.

(e) [Repealed.]

(f) [Repealed.]

(g) [Repealed.]

Art. 2.08. Disqualified.

(a) District and county attorneys shall not be of counsel adversely to the State in any case, in any court, nor shall they, after they cease to be such officers, be of counsel adversely to the State in any case in which they have been of counsel for the State.

(b) A judge of a court in which a district or county attorney represents the State shall declare the district or county attorney disqualified for purposes of Article 2.07 on a showing that the attorney is the subject of a criminal investigation by a law enforcement agency if that investigation is based on credible evidence of criminal misconduct for an offense that is within the attorney's authority to prosecute. A disqualification under this subsection applies only to the attorney's access to the criminal investigation pending against the attorney and to any prosecution of a criminal charge resulting from that investigation.

Art. 2.09. Who Are Magistrates.

Each of the following officers is a magistrate within the meaning of this Code: The justices of the Supreme Court, the judges of the Court of Criminal Appeals, the justices of the Courts of Appeals, the judges of the District Court, the magistrates appointed by the judges of the district courts of Bexar County, Dallas County, or Tarrant County that give preference to criminal cases, the criminal law hearing officers for Harris County appointed under Subchapter L, Chapter 54, Government Code, the criminal law hearing officers for Cameron County appointed under Subchapter BB, Chapter 54, Government Code, the magistrates or associate judges appointed by the judges of the district courts of Lubbock County, Nolan County, or Webb County, the magistrates appointed by the judges of the criminal district courts of Dallas County or Tarrant County, the associate judges appointed by the judges of the district courts and the county courts at law that give preference to criminal cases in Jefferson County, the associate judges appointed by the judges of the district courts and the statutory county courts of Brazos County, Nueces County, or Williamson County, the magistrates appointed by the judges of the district courts and statutory county courts that give preference to criminal cases in Travis County, the criminal magistrates appointed by the Brazoria County Commissioners Court, the criminal magistrates appointed by the Burnet County Commissioners Court, the magistrates appointed by the El Paso Council of Judges, the county judges, the judges of the county courts at law, judges of the county criminal courts, the judges of statutory probate courts, the associate judges appointed by the judges of the statutory probate courts under Chapter 54A, Government Code, the associate judges appointed by the judge of a district court under Chapter 54A, Government Code, the magistrates appointed under Subchapter JJ, Chapter 54, Government Code, the magistrates appointed by the Collin County Commissioners Court, the magistrates appointed by the Fort Bend County Commissioners Court, the justices of the peace, and the mayors and recorders and the judges of the municipal courts of incorporated cities or towns.

Art. 2.10. Duty of Magistrates.

It is the duty of every magistrate to preserve the peace within his jurisdiction by the use of all lawful means; to issue all process intended to aid in preventing and suppressing crime; to cause the arrest of offenders by the use of lawful means in order that they may be brought to punishment.

Art. 2.11. Examining Court.

When the magistrate sits for the purpose of inquiring into a criminal accusation against any person, this is called an examining court.

Art. 2.12. Who Are Peace Officers.

The following are peace officers:

(1) sheriffs, their deputies, and those reserve deputies who hold a permanent peace officer license issued under Chapter 1701, Occupations Code;

(2) constables, deputy constables, and those reserve deputy constables who hold a permanent peace officer license issued under Chapter 1701, Occupations Code;

(3) marshals or police officers of an incorporated city, town, or village, and those reserve municipal police officers who hold a permanent peace officer license issued under Chapter 1701, Occupations Code;

(4) rangers, officers, and members of the reserve officer corps commissioned by the Public Safety Commission and the Director of the Department of Public Safety;

(5) investigators of the district attorneys', criminal district attorneys', and county attorneys' offices;

(6) law enforcement agents of the Texas Alcoholic Beverage Commission;

(7) each member of an arson investigating unit commissioned by a city, a county, or the state;

(8) officers commissioned under Section 37.081, Education Code, or Subchapter E, Chapter 51, Education Code;

(9) officers commissioned by the General Services Commission;

(10) law enforcement officers commissioned by the Parks and Wildlife Commission;

(11) officers commissioned under Chapter 23, Transportation Code;

(12) municipal park and recreational patrolmen and security officers;

(13) security officers and investigators commissioned as peace officers by the comptroller;

(14) officers commissioned by a water control and improvement district under Section 49.216, Water Code;

(15) officers commissioned by a board of trustees under Chapter 54, Transportation Code;

(16) investigators commissioned by the Texas Medical Board;

(17) officers commissioned by:

(A) the board of managers of the Dallas County Hospital District, the Tarrant County Hospital District, the Bexar County Hospital District, or the El Paso County Hospital District under Section 281.057, Health and Safety Code;

(B) the board of directors of the Ector County Hospital District under Section 1024.117, Special District Local Laws Code;

(C) the board of directors of the Midland County Hospital District of Midland County, Texas, under Section 1061.121, Special District Local Laws Code; and

(D) the board of hospital managers of the Lubbock County Hospital District of Lubbock County, Texas, under Section 1053.113, Special District Local Laws Code;

(18) county park rangers commissioned under Subchapter E, Chapter 351, Local Government Code;

(19) investigators employed by the Texas Racing Commission;

(20) officers commissioned under Chapter 554, Occupations Code;

(21) officers commissioned by the governing body of a metropolitan rapid transit authority under Section 451.108, Transportation Code, or by a regional transportation authority under Section 452.110, Transportation Code;

(22) investigators commissioned by the attorney general under Section 402.009, Government Code;

(23) security officers and investigators commissioned as peace officers under Chapter 466, Government Code;

(24) officers appointed by an appellate court under Subchapter F, Chapter 53, Government Code;

(25) officers commissioned by the state fire marshal under Chapter 417, Government Code;

(26) an investigator commissioned by the commissioner of insurance under Section 701.104, Insurance Code;

(27) apprehension specialists and inspectors general commissioned by the Texas Juvenile Justice Department as officers under Sections 242.102 and 243.052, Human Resources Code;

(28) officers appointed by the inspector general of the Texas Department of Criminal Justice under Section 493.019, Government Code;

(29) investigators commissioned by the Texas Commission on Law Enforcement under Section 1701.160, Occupations Code;

(30) commission investigators commissioned by the Texas Private Security Board under Section 1702.061, Occupations Code;

(31) the fire marshal and any officers, inspectors, or investigators commissioned by an emergency services district under Chapter 775, Health and Safety Code;

(32) officers commissioned by the State Board of Dental Examiners under Section 254.013, Occupations Code, subject to the limitations imposed by that section;

(33) investigators commissioned by the Texas Juvenile Justice Department as officers under Section 221.011, Human Resources Code; and

(34) the fire marshal and any related officers, inspectors, or investigators commissioned by a county under Subchapter B, Chapter 352, Local Government Code.

Art. 2.121. Railroad Peace Officers.

(a) The director of the Department of Public Safety may appoint up to 250 railroad peace officers who are employed by a railroad company to aid law enforcement agencies in the protection of railroad property and the protection of the persons and property of railroad passengers and employees.

(b) Except as provided by Subsection (c) of this article, a railroad peace officer may make arrests and exercise all authority given peace officers under this code when necessary to prevent or abate the commission of an offense involving injury to passengers and employees of the railroad or damage to railroad property or to protect railroad property or property in the custody or control of the railroad.

(c) A railroad peace officer may not issue a traffic citation for a violation of Chapter 521, Transportation Code, or Subtitle C, Title 7, Transportation Code.

(d) A railroad peace officer is not entitled to state benefits normally provided by the state to a peace officer.

(e) A person may not serve as a railroad peace officer for a railroad company unless:

(1) the Texas Railroad Association submits the person's application for appointment and certification as a railroad peace officer to the director of the Department of Public Safety and to the executive director of the Texas Commission on Law Enforcement;

(2) the director of the department issues the person a certificate of authority to act as a railroad peace officer; and

(3) the executive director of the commission determines that the person meets minimum standards required of peace officers by the commission relating to competence, reliability, education, training, morality, and physical and mental health and issues the person a license as a railroad peace officer; and

(4) the person has met all standards for certification as a peace officer by the Texas Commission on Law Enforcement.

(f) For good cause, the director of the department may revoke a certificate of authority issued under this article and the executive director of the commission may revoke a license issued under this article. Termination of employment with a railroad company, or the revocation of a railroad peace officer license, shall constitute an automatic revocation of a certificate of authority to act as a railroad peace officer.

(g) A railroad company is liable for any act or omission by a person serving as a railroad peace officer for the company that is within the person's scope of employment. Neither the state nor any political subdivision or agency of the state shall be liable for any act or omission by a person appointed as a railroad peace officer. All expenses incurred by the granting or revocation of a certificate of authority to act as a railroad peace officer shall be paid by the employing railroad company.

(h) A railroad peace officer who is a member of a railroad craft may not perform the duties of a member of any other railroad craft during a strike or labor dispute.

(i) The director of the department and the executive director of the commission shall have the authority to promulgate rules necessary for the effective administration and performance of the duties and responsibilities delegated to them by this article.

Art. 2.122. Special Investigators.

(a) The following named criminal investigators of the United States shall not be deemed peace officers, but shall have the powers of arrest, search, and seizure under the laws of this state as to felony offenses only:

(1) Special Agents of the Federal Bureau of Investigation;

(2) Special Agents of the Secret Service;

(3) Special Agents of the United States Immigration and Customs Enforcement;

(4) Special Agents of the Bureau of Alcohol, Tobacco, Firearms and Explosives;

(5) Special Agents of the United States Drug Enforcement Administration;

(6) Inspectors of the United States Postal Inspection Service;

(7) Special Agents of the Criminal Investigation Division of the Internal Revenue Service;

(8) Civilian Special Agents of the United States Naval Criminal Investigative Service;

(9) Marshals and Deputy Marshals of the United States Marshals Service;

(10) Special Agents of the United States Department of State, Bureau of Diplomatic Security;

(11) Special Agents of the Treasury Inspector General for Tax Administration;

(12) Special Agents of the Office of Inspector General of the United States Social Security Administration;

(13) Special Agents of the Office of Inspector General of the United States Department of Veterans Affairs;

(14) Special Agents of the Office of Inspector General of the United States Department of Agriculture;

(15) Special Agents of the Office of Export Enforcement of the United States Department of Commerce;

(16) Special Agents of the Criminal Investigation Command of the United States Army;

(17) Special Agents of the Office of Special Investigations of the United States Air Force; and

(18) a police officer with the Office of Security and Law Enforcement of the United States Department of Veterans Affairs.

(b) An officer or agent designated by the Secretary of Homeland Security under 40 U.S.C. Section 1315 for duty in connection with the protection of property owned or occupied by the federal government and persons on the property is not a peace officer but has the powers of arrest and search and seizure as to any offense under the laws of this state.

(c) A Customs and Border Protection Officer or Border Patrol Agent of the United States Customs and Border Protection or an immigration enforcement agent or deportation officer of the Department of Homeland Security is not a peace officer under the laws of this state but, on the premises of a port facility designated by the commissioner of the United States Customs and Border Protection as a port of entry for arrival in the United States by land transportation from the United Mexican States into the State of Texas or at a permanent established border patrol traffic check point, has the authority to detain a person pending transfer without unnecessary delay to a peace officer if the agent or officer has probable cause to believe that the person has engaged in conduct that is a violation of Section 49.02, 49.04, 49.07, or 49.08, Penal Code, regardless of whether the violation may be disposed of in a criminal proceeding or a juvenile justice proceeding.

(d) A commissioned law enforcement officer of the National Park Service is not a peace officer under the laws of this state, except that the officer has the powers of arrest, search, and seizure as to any offense under the laws of this state committed within the boundaries of a national park or national recreation area. In this subsection, "national park or national recreation area" means a national park or national recreation area included in the National Park System as defined by 16 U.S.C. Section 1c(a).

(e) A Special Agent or Law Enforcement Officer of the United States Forest Service is not a peace officer under the laws of this state, except that the agent or officer has the powers of arrest, search, and seizure as to any offense under the laws of this state committed within the National Forest System. In this subsection, "National Forest System" has the meaning assigned by 16 U.S.C. Section 1609.

(f) Security personnel working at a commercial nuclear power plant, including contract security personnel, trained and qualified under a security plan approved by the United States Nuclear Regulatory Commission, are not peace officers under the laws of this state, except that such personnel have the powers of arrest, search, and seizure, including the powers under Section 9.51, Penal Code, while in the performance of their duties on the premises of a commercial nuclear power plant site or under agreements entered into with local law enforcement regarding areas surrounding the plant site.

(g) In addition to the powers of arrest, search, and seizure under Subsection (a), a Special Agent of the Secret Service protecting a person described by 18 U.S.C. Section 3056(a) or investigating a threat against a person described by 18 U.S.C. Section 3056(a) has the powers of arrest, search, and seizure as to:

(1) misdemeanor offenses under the laws of this state; and

(2) any criminal offense under federal law.

Art. 2.123. Adjunct Police Officers.

(a) Within counties under 200,000 population, the chief of police of a municipality or the sheriff of the county, if the institution is outside the corporate limits of a municipality, that has jurisdiction over the geographical area of a private institution of higher education, provided the governing board of such institution consents, may appoint up to 50 peace officers who are commissioned under Section 51.212, Education Code, and who are employed by a private institution of higher education located in the municipality or county, to serve as adjunct police officers of the municipality or county. Officers appointed under this article shall aid law enforcement agencies in the protection of the municipality or county in a geographical area that is designated by agreement on an annual basis between the appointing chief of police or sheriff and the private institution.

(b) The geographical area that is subject to designation under Subsection (a) of this article may include only the private institution's campus area and an area that:

(1) is adjacent to the campus of the private institution;

(2) does not extend further than a distance of one mile from the perimeter of the campus of the private institution; and

(3) is inhabited primarily by students or employees of the private institution.

(c) A peace officer serving as an adjunct police officer may make arrests and exercise all authority given peace officers under this code only within the geographical area designated by agreement between the appointing chief of police or sheriff and the private institution.

(d) A peace officer serving as an adjunct police officer has all the rights, privileges, and immunities of a peace officer but is not entitled to state compensation and retirement benefits normally provided by the state to a peace officer.

(e) A person may not serve as an adjunct police officer for a municipality or county unless:

(1) the institution of higher education submits the person's application for appointment and certification as an adjunct police officer to the chief of police of the municipality or, if outside a municipality, the sheriff of the county that has jurisdiction over the geographical area of the institution;

(2) the chief of police of the municipality or sheriff of the county to whom the application was made issues the person a certificate of authority to act as an adjunct police officer; and

(3) the person undergoes any additional training required for that person to meet the training standards of the municipality or county for peace officers employed by the municipality or county.

(f) For good cause, the chief of police or sheriff may revoke a certificate of authority issued under this article.

(g) A private institution of higher education is liable for any act or omission by a person while serving as an adjunct police officer outside of the campus of the institution in the same manner as the municipality or county governing that geographical area is liable for any act or omission of a peace officer employed by the municipality or county. This subsection shall not be construed to act as a limitation on the liability of a municipality or county for the acts or omissions of a person serving as an adjunct police officer.

(h) The employing institution shall pay all expenses incurred by the municipality or county in granting or revoking a certificate of authority to act as an adjunct police officer under this article.

(i) This article does not affect any duty of the municipality or county to provide law enforcement services to a geographical area designated under Subsection (a) of this article.

Art. 2.124. Peace Officers from Adjoining States.

(a) A commissioned peace officer of a state of the United States of America adjoining this state, while the officer is in this state, has under this subsection the same powers, duties, and immunities as a peace officer of this state who is acting in the discharge of an official duty, but only:

(1) during a time in which:

(A) the peace officer from the adjoining state has physical custody of an inmate or criminal defendant and is transporting the inmate or defendant from a county in the adjoining state that is on the border between the two states to a hospital or other medical facility in a county in this state that is on the border between the two states; or

(B) the peace officer has physical custody of the inmate or defendant and is returning the inmate or defendant from the hospital or facility to the county in the adjoining state; and

(2) to the extent necessary to:

(A) maintain physical custody of the inmate or defendant while transporting the inmate or defendant; or

(B) regain physical custody of the inmate or defendant if the inmate or defendant escapes while being transported.

(b) A commissioned peace officer of a state of the United States of America adjoining this state, while the officer is in this state, has under this subsection the same powers, duties, and immunities as a peace officer of this state who is acting in the discharge of an official duty, but only in a municipality some part of the municipal limits of which are within one mile of the boundary between this state and the adjoining state and only at a time the peace officer is regularly assigned to duty in a county, parish, or municipality that adjoins this state. A peace officer described by this subsection may also as part of the officer's powers in this state enforce the ordinances of a Texas municipality described by this subsection but only after the governing body of the municipality authorizes that enforcement by majority vote at an open meeting.

Art. 2.125. Special Rangers of Texas and Southwestern Cattle Raisers Association.

(a) The director of the Department of Public Safety may appoint up to 50 special rangers who are employed by the Texas and Southwestern Cattle Raisers Association to aid law enforcement agencies in the investigation of the theft of livestock or related property.

(b) Except as provided by Subsection (c) of this article, a special ranger may make arrests and exercise all authority given peace officers under this code when necessary to prevent or abate the commission of an offense involving livestock or related property.

(c) A special ranger may not issue a traffic citation for a violation of Chapter 521, Transportation Code, or Subtitle C, Title 7, Transportation Code.

(d) A special ranger is not entitled to state benefits normally provided by the state to a peace officer.

(e) A person may not serve as a special ranger unless:

(1) the Texas and Southwestern Cattle Raisers Association submits the person's application for appointment and certification as a special ranger to the director of the Department of Public Safety and to the executive director of the Texas Commission on Law Enforcement;

(2) the director of the department issues the person a certificate of authority to act as a special ranger;

(3) the executive director of the commission determines that the person meets minimum standards required of peace officers by the commission relating to competence, reliability, education, training, morality, and physical and mental health and issues the person a license as a special ranger; and

(4) the person has met all standards for certification as a peace officer by the Texas Commission on Law Enforcement.

(f) For good cause, the director of the department may revoke a certificate of authority issued under this article and the executive director of the commission may revoke a license issued under this article. Termination of employment with the association, or the revocation of a special ranger license, shall constitute an automatic revocation of a certificate of authority to act as a special ranger.

(g) The Texas and Southwestern Cattle Raisers Association is liable for any act or omission by a person serving as a special ranger for the association that is within the person's scope of employment. Neither the state nor any political subdivision or agency of the state shall be liable for any act or omission by a person appointed as a special ranger. All expenses incurred by the granting or revocation of a certificate of authority to act as a special ranger shall be paid by the association.

(h) The director of the department and the executive director of the commission shall have the authority to promulgate rules necessary for the effective administration and performance of the duties and responsibilities delegated to them by this article.

Art. 2.126. Peace Officers Commissioned by the Alabama-Coushatta Tribe of Texas and the Kickapoo Traditional Tribe of Texas.

(a) The tribal council of the Alabama-Coushatta Tribe of Texas or the tribal council of the Kickapoo Traditional Tribe of Texas is authorized to employ and commission peace officers for the purpose of enforcing state law within the boundaries of the tribe's reservation.

(b) Within the boundaries of the tribe's reservation, a peace officer commissioned under this article:

(1) is vested with all the powers, privileges, and immunities of peace officers;

(2) may, in accordance with Chapter 14, arrest without a warrant any person who violates a law of the state; and

(3) may enforce all traffic laws on streets and highways.

(c) Outside the boundaries of the tribe's reservation, a peace officer commissioned under this article is vested with all the powers, privileges, and immunities of peace officers and may arrest any person who violates any law of the state if the peace officer:

(1) is summoned by another law enforcement agency to provide assistance; or

(2) is assisting another law enforcement agency.

(d) Any officer assigned to duty and commissioned under this article shall take and file the oath required of peace officers and shall execute and file a good and sufficient bond in the sum of $1,000, payable to the governor, with two or more good and sufficient sureties, conditioned that the officer will fairly, impartially, and faithfully perform the duties as may be required of the officer by law. The bond may be sued on from time to time in the name of the person injured until the whole amount is recovered.

(e) Any person commissioned under this article must:

(1) meet the minimum standards required of peace officers by the commission relating to competence, reliability, education, training, morality, and physical and mental health; and

(2) meet all standards for certification as a peace officer by the Texas Commission on Law Enforcement.

(f) A peace officer commissioned under this article is not entitled to state benefits normally provided by the state to a peace officer.

Art. 2.127. School Marshals.

(a) Except as provided by Subsection (b), a school marshal may:

(1) make arrests and exercise all authority given peace officers under this code, subject to written regulations adopted by:

(A) the board of trustees of a school district or the governing body of an open-enrollment charter school under Section 37.0811, Education Code;

(B) the governing body of a private school under Section 37.0813, Education Code; or

(C) the governing board of a public junior college under Section 51.220, Education Code; and

(2) only act as necessary to prevent or abate the commission of an offense that threatens serious bodily injury or death of students, faculty, or visitors on school premises.

(a-1) In this section, "private school" means a school that:

(1) offers a course of instruction for students in one or more grades from prekindergarten through grade 12;

(2) is not operated by a governmental entity; and

(3) is not a school whose students meet the definition provided by Section 29.916(a)(1), Education Code.

(b) A school marshal may not issue a traffic citation for a violation of Chapter 521, Transportation Code, or Subtitle C, Title 7, Transportation Code.

(c) A school marshal is not entitled to state benefits normally provided by the state to a peace officer.

(d) A person may not serve as a school marshal unless the person is:

(1) licensed under Section 1701.260, Occupations Code; and

(2) appointed by:

(A) the board of trustees of a school district or the governing body of an open-enrollment charter school under Section 37.0811, Education Code;

(B) the governing body of a private school under Section 37.0813, Education Code; or

(C) the governing board of a public junior college under Section 51.220, Education Code.

Art. 2.13. Duties and Powers.

(a) It is the duty of every peace officer to preserve the peace within the officer's jurisdiction. To effect this purpose, the officer shall use all lawful means.

(b) The officer shall:

(1) in every case authorized by the provisions of this Code, interfere without warrant to prevent or suppress crime;

(2) execute all lawful process issued to the officer by any magistrate or court;

(3) give notice to some magistrate of all offenses committed within the officer's jurisdiction, where the officer has good reason to believe there has been a violation of the penal law; and

(4) arrest offenders without warrant in every case where the officer is authorized by law, in order that they may be taken before the proper magistrate or court and be tried.

(c) It is the duty of every officer to take possession of a child under Article 63.009(g).

(d) Subject to Subsection (e), in the course of investigating an alleged criminal offense, a peace officer may inquire as to the nationality or immigration status of a victim of or witness to the offense only if the officer determines that the inquiry is necessary to:

(1) investigate the offense; or

(2) provide the victim or witness with information about federal visas designed to protect individuals providing assistance to law enforcement.

(e) Subsection (d) does not prevent a peace officer from:

(1) conducting a separate investigation of any other alleged criminal offense; or

(2) inquiring as to the nationality or immigration status of a victim of or witness to a criminal offense if the officer has probable cause to believe that the victim or witness has engaged in specific conduct constituting a separate criminal offense.

(f) On a request made by that office, a peace officer shall execute an emergency detention order issued by the Texas Civil Commitment Office under Section 841.0837, Health and Safety Code.

Art. 2.1305. Carrying Weapon on Certain Premises.

(a) An establishment serving the public may not prohibit or otherwise restrict a peace officer or special investigator from carrying on the establishment's premises a weapon that the peace officer or special investigator is otherwise authorized to carry, regardless of whether the peace officer or special investigator is engaged in the actual discharge of the officer's or investigator's duties while carrying the weapon.

(b) For purposes of this article:

(1) "Establishment serving the public" means:

(A) a hotel, motel, or other place of lodging;

(B) a restaurant or other place where food is offered for sale to the public;

(C) a retail business or other commercial establishment or an office building to which the general public is invited;

(D) a sports venue; and

(E) any other place of public accommodation, amusement, convenience, or resort to which the general public or any classification of persons from the general public is regularly, normally, or customarily invited.

(2) "Sports venue" means an arena, coliseum, stadium, or other type of area or facility that is primarily used or is planned for primary use for one or more professional or amateur sports or athletics events and for which a fee is charged or is planned to be charged for admission to the sports or athletics events, other than occasional civic, charitable, or promotional events.

(c) An establishment serving the public that violates this article is subject to a civil penalty in the amount of $1,000 for each violation. The attorney general may sue to collect a civil penalty under this subsection. Money collected under this subsection shall be deposited in the state treasury to the credit of the general revenue fund.

Art. 2.131. Racial Profiling Prohibited.

A peace officer may not engage in racial profiling.

Art. 2.132. Law Enforcement Policy on Racial Profiling.

(a) In this article:

(1) "Law enforcement agency" means an agency of the state, or of a county, municipality, or other political subdivision of the state, that employs peace officers who make motor vehicle stops in the routine performance of the officers' official duties.

(2) "Motor vehicle stop" means an occasion in which a peace officer stops a motor vehicle for an alleged violation of a law or ordinance.

(3) "Race or ethnicity" means the following categories:

(A) Alaska native or American Indian;

(B) Asian or Pacific Islander;

(C) black;

(D) white; and

(E) Hispanic or Latino.

(b) Each law enforcement agency in this state shall adopt a detailed written policy on racial profiling. The policy must:

(1) clearly define acts constituting racial profiling;

(2) strictly prohibit peace officers employed by the agency from engaging in racial profiling;

(3) implement a process by which an individual may file a complaint with the agency if the individual believes that a peace officer employed by the agency has engaged in racial profiling with respect to the individual;

(4) provide public education relating to the agency's compliment and complaint process, including providing the telephone number, mailing address, and e-mail address to make a compliment or complaint with respect to each ticket, citation, or warning issued by a peace officer;

(5) require appropriate corrective action to be taken against a peace officer employed by the agency who, after an investigation, is shown to have engaged in racial profiling in violation of the agency's policy adopted under this article;

(6) require collection of information relating to motor vehicle stops in which a ticket, citation, or warning is issued and to arrests made as a result of those stops, including information relating to:

(A) the race or ethnicity of the individual detained;

(B) whether a search was conducted and, if so, whether the individual detained consented to the search;

(C) whether the peace officer knew the race or ethnicity of the individual detained before detaining that individual;

(D) whether the peace officer used physical force that resulted in bodily injury, as that term is defined by Section 1.07, Penal Code, during the stop;

(E) the location of the stop; and

(F) the reason for the stop; and

(7) require the chief administrator of the agency, regardless of whether the administrator is elected, employed, or appointed, to submit an annual report of the information collected under Subdivision (6) to:

(A) the Texas Commission on Law Enforcement; and

(B) the governing body of each county or municipality served by the agency, if the agency is an agency of a county, municipality, or other political subdivision of the state.

(c) The data collected as a result of the reporting requirements of this article shall not constitute prima facie evidence of racial profiling.

(d) On adoption of a policy under Subsection (b), a law enforcement agency shall examine the feasibility of installing video camera and transmitter-activated equipment in each agency law enforcement motor vehicle regularly used to make motor vehicle stops and transmitter-activated equipment in each agency law enforcement motorcycle regularly used to make motor vehicle stops. The agency also shall examine the feasibility of equipping each peace officer who regularly detains or stops motor vehicles with a body worn camera, as that term is defined by Section 1701.651, Occupations Code. If a law enforcement agency installs video or audio equipment or equips peace officers with body worn

Code of Criminal Procedure

cameras as provided by this subsection, the policy adopted by the agency under Subsection (b) must include standards for reviewing video and audio documentation.

(e) A report required under Subsection (b)(7) may not include identifying information about a peace officer who makes a motor vehicle stop or about an individual who is stopped or arrested by a peace officer. This subsection does not affect the collection of information as required by a policy under Subsection (b)(6).

(f) On the commencement of an investigation by a law enforcement agency of a complaint described by Subsection (b)(3) in which a video or audio recording of the occurrence on which the complaint is based was made, the agency shall promptly provide a copy of the recording to the peace officer who is the subject of the complaint on written request by the officer.

(g) On a finding by the Texas Commission on Law Enforcement that the chief administrator of a law enforcement agency intentionally failed to submit a report required under Subsection (b)(7), the commission shall begin disciplinary procedures against the chief administrator.

(h) A law enforcement agency shall review the data collected under Subsection (b)(6) to identify any improvements the agency could make in its practices and policies regarding motor vehicle stops.

Art. 2.133. Reports Required for Motor Vehicle Stops.

(a) In this article, "race or ethnicity" has the meaning assigned by Article 2.132(a).

(b) A peace officer who stops a motor vehicle for an alleged violation of a law or ordinance shall report to the law enforcement agency that employs the officer information relating to the stop, including:

(1) a physical description of any person operating the motor vehicle who is detained as a result of the stop, including:

(A) the person's gender; and

(B) the person's race or ethnicity, as stated by the person or, if the person does not state the person's race or ethnicity, as determined by the officer to the best of the officer's ability;

(2) the initial reason for the stop;

(3) whether the officer conducted a search as a result of the stop and, if so, whether the person detained consented to the search;

(4) whether any contraband or other evidence was discovered in the course of the search and a description of the contraband or evidence;

(5) the reason for the search, including whether:

(A) any contraband or other evidence was in plain view;

(B) any probable cause or reasonable suspicion existed to perform the search; or

(C) the search was performed as a result of the towing of the motor vehicle or the arrest of any person in the motor vehicle;

(6) whether the officer made an arrest as a result of the stop or the search, including a statement of whether the arrest was based on a violation of the Penal Code, a violation of a traffic law or ordinance, or an outstanding warrant and a statement of the offense charged;

(7) the street address or approximate location of the stop;

(8) whether the officer issued a verbal or written warning or a ticket or citation as a result of the stop; and

(9) whether the officer used physical force that resulted in bodily injury, as that term is defined by Section 1.07, Penal Code, during the stop.

(c) The chief administrator of a law enforcement agency, regardless of whether the administrator is elected, employed, or appointed, is responsible for auditing reports under Subsection (b) to ensure that the race or ethnicity of the person operating the motor vehicle is being reported.

Art. 2.134. Compilation and Analysis of Information Collected.

(a) In this article:

(1) "Motor vehicle stop" has the meaning assigned by Article 2.132(a).

(2) "Race or ethnicity" has the meaning assigned by Article 2.132(a).

(b) A law enforcement agency shall compile and analyze the information contained in each report received by the agency under Article 2.133. Not later than March 1 of each year, each law enforcement agency shall submit a report containing the incident-based data compiled during the previous calendar year to the Texas Commission on Law Enforcement and, if the law enforcement agency is a local law enforcement agency, to the governing body of each county or municipality served by the agency.

(c) A report required under Subsection (b) must be submitted by the chief administrator of the law enforcement agency, regardless of whether the administrator is elected, employed, or appointed, and must include:

(1) a comparative analysis of the information compiled under Article 2.133 to:

(A) evaluate and compare the number of motor vehicle stops, within the applicable jurisdiction, of persons who are recognized as racial or ethnic minorities and persons who are not recognized as racial or ethnic minorities;

(B) examine the disposition of motor vehicle stops made by officers employed by the agency, categorized according to the race or ethnicity of the affected persons, as appropriate, including any searches resulting from stops within the applicable jurisdiction; and

(C) evaluate and compare the number of searches resulting from motor vehicle stops within the applicable jurisdiction and whether contraband or other evidence was discovered in the course of those searches; and

(2) information relating to each complaint filed with the agency alleging that a peace officer employed by the agency has engaged in racial profiling.

(d) A report required under Subsection (b) may not include identifying information about a peace officer who makes a motor vehicle stop or about an individual who is stopped or arrested by a peace officer. This subsection does not affect the reporting of information required under Article 2.133(b)(1).

(e) The Texas Commission on Law Enforcement, in accordance with Section 1701.162, Occupations Code, shall develop guidelines for compiling and reporting information as required by this article.

(f) The data collected as a result of the reporting requirements of this article shall not constitute prima facie evidence of racial profiling.

(g) On a finding by the Texas Commission on Law Enforcement that the chief administrator of a law enforcement agency intentionally failed to submit a report required under Subsection (b), the commission shall begin disciplinary procedures against the chief administrator.

Art. 2.135. Partial Exemption for Agencies Using Video and Audio Equipment. [Repealed]

Art. 2.136. Liability.

A peace officer is not liable for damages arising from an act relating to the collection or reporting of information as required by Article 2.133 or under a policy adopted under Article 2.132.

Art. 2.137. Provision of Funding or Equipment.

(a) The Department of Public Safety shall adopt rules for providing funds or video and audio equipment to law enforcement agencies for the purpose of installing video and audio equipment in law enforcement motor vehicles and motorcycles or equipping peace officers with body worn cameras, including specifying criteria to prioritize funding or equipment provided to law enforcement agencies. The criteria may include consideration of tax effort, financial hardship, available revenue, and budget surpluses. The criteria must give priority to:

(1) law enforcement agencies that employ peace officers whose primary duty is traffic enforcement;

(2) smaller jurisdictions; and

(3) municipal and county law enforcement agencies.

(b) The Department of Public Safety shall collaborate with an institution of higher education to identify law enforcement agencies that need funds or video and audio equipment for the purpose of installing video and audio equipment in law enforcement motor vehicles and motorcycles or equipping peace officers with body worn cameras. The collaboration may include the use of a survey to assist in developing criteria to prioritize funding or equipment provided to law enforcement agencies.

(c) To receive funds or video and audio equipment from the state for the purpose of installing video and audio equipment in law enforcement motor vehicles and motorcycles or equipping peace officers with body worn cameras, the governing body of a county or municipality, in conjunction with the law enforcement agency serving the county or municipality, shall certify to the Department of Public Safety that the law enforcement agency needs funds or video and audio equipment for that purpose.

(d) On receipt of funds or video and audio equipment from the state for the purpose of installing video and audio equipment in law enforcement motor vehicles and motorcycles or equipping peace officers with body worn cameras, the governing body of a county or municipality, in conjunction with the law enforcement agency serving the county or municipality, shall certify to the Department of Public Safety that the law enforcement agency has taken the necessary actions to use and is using video and audio equipment and body worn cameras for those purposes.

Art. 2.138. Rules.

The Department of Public Safety may adopt rules to implement Articles 2.131—2.137.

Art. 2.1385. Civil Penalty.

(a) If the chief administrator of a local law enforcement agency intentionally fails to submit the incident-based data as required by Article 2.134, the agency is liable to the state for a civil penalty in an amount not to exceed $5,000 for each violation. The attorney general may sue to collect a civil penalty under this subsection.

(b) From money appropriated to the agency for the administration of the agency, the executive director of a state law enforcement agency that intentionally fails to submit the incident-based data as required by Article 2.134 shall remit to the comptroller the amount of $1,000 for each violation.

(c) Money collected under this article shall be deposited in the state treasury to the credit of the general revenue fund.

Art. 2.1386. Eyewitness Identification Protocols.

(a) In this article, "law enforcement agency" means an agency of the state or an agency of a political subdivision of the state authorized by law to employ peace officers.

(b) The Texas Commission on Law Enforcement shall establish a comprehensive education and training program on eyewitness identification, including material regarding variables that affect a witness's vision and memory, practices for minimizing contamination, and effective eyewitness identification protocols.

(c) Each law enforcement agency shall require each peace officer who is employed by the agency and who performs eyewitness identification procedures to complete the education and training described by Subsection (b).

Art. 2.1387. Intervention Required for Excessive Force; Report Required.

(a) A peace officer has a duty to intervene to stop or prevent another peace officer from using force against a person suspected of committing an offense if:

(1) the amount of force exceeds that which is reasonable under the circumstances; and

(2) the officer knows or should know that the other officer's use of force:

(A) violates state or federal law;

(B) puts a person at risk of bodily injury, as that term is defined by Section 1.07, Penal Code, and is not immediately necessary to avoid imminent bodily injury to a peace officer or other person; and

(C) is not required to apprehend the person suspected of committing an offense.

(b) A peace officer who witnesses the use of excessive force by another peace officer shall promptly make a detailed report of the incident and deliver the report to the supervisor of the peace officer making the report.

Art. 2.139. Reports Required for Officer-Involved Injuries or Deaths.

(a) In this article:

(1) "Deadly weapon" means:

(A) a firearm or any object manifestly designed, made, or adapted for the purpose of inflicting death or serious bodily injury; or

(B) any object that in the manner of its use or intended use is capable of causing death or serious bodily injury.

(2) "Officer-involved injury or death" means an incident during which a peace officer discharges a firearm causing injury or death to another.

(b) The office of the attorney general by rule shall create a written and electronic form for the reporting by law enforcement agencies of an officer-involved injury or death. The form must include spaces to report only the following information:

(1) the date on which the incident occurred;

(2) the location where the incident occurred;

(3) the age, gender, and race or ethnicity of each peace officer involved in the incident;

(4) if known, the age, gender, and race or ethnicity of each injured or deceased person involved in the incident;

(5) whether the person was injured or died as a result of the incident;

(6) whether each injured or deceased person used, exhibited, or was carrying a deadly weapon during the incident;

(7) whether each peace officer involved in the incident was on duty during the incident;

(8) whether each peace officer involved in the incident was responding to an emergency call or a request for assistance and, if so, whether the officer responded to that call or request with one or more other peace officers; and

(9) whether the incident occurred during or as a result of:

(A) the execution of a warrant; or

(B) a hostage, barricade, or other emergency situation.

(c) Not later than the 30th day after the date of an officer-involved injury or death, the law enforcement agency employing an officer involved in the incident must complete and submit a written or electronic report, using the form created under Subsection (b), to the office of the attorney general. The report must include all information described in Subsection (b).

(d) Not later than the fifth day after the date of receipt of a report submitted under Subsection (c), the office of the attorney general shall post a copy of the report on the office's Internet website.

(e) Not later than March 1 of each year, the office of the attorney general shall submit a report regarding all officer-involved injuries or deaths that occurred during the preceding year to the governor and the standing legislative committees with primary jurisdiction over criminal justice matters. The report must include:

(1) the total number of officer-involved injuries or deaths;

(2) a summary of the reports submitted to the office under this article; and

(3) a copy of each report submitted to the office under this article.

Art. 2.1395. Reports Required for Certain Injuries or Deaths of Peace Officers.

(a) The office of the attorney general by rule shall create a written and electronic form for the reporting by law enforcement agencies of incidents in which, while a peace officer is performing an official duty, a person who is not a peace officer discharges a firearm and causes injury or death to the officer. The form must include spaces to report only the following information:

(1) the date on which the incident occurred;

(2) the location where the incident occurred;

(3) the age, gender, and race or ethnicity of each injured or deceased peace officer involved in the incident;

(4) if known, the age, gender, and race or ethnicity of each person who discharged a firearm and caused injury or death to a peace officer involved in the incident; and

(5) whether the officer or any other person was injured or died as a result of the incident.

(b) Not later than the 30th day after the date of the occurrence of an incident described by Subsection (a), the law enforcement agency employing the injured or deceased officer at the time of the incident must complete and submit a written or electronic report, using the form created under that subsection, to the office of the attorney general. The report must include all information described in Subsection (a).

(c) Not later than March 1 of each year, the office of the attorney general shall submit a report regarding all incidents described by Subsection (a) that occurred during the preceding year to the governor and the standing legislative committees with primary jurisdiction over criminal justice matters. The report must include:

(1) the total number of incidents that occurred;

(2) a summary of the reports submitted to the office under this article; and

(3) a copy of each report submitted to the office under this article.

Art. 2.13951. Notice of Violation of Reporting Requirements for Certain Injuries or Deaths; Civil Penalty.

(a) The office of the attorney general shall conduct an investigation after receiving a written and signed report, on a form prescribed by the office, asserting that a law enforcement agency failed to submit a report required by Article 2.139 or 2.1395. If the office determines that the law enforcement agency failed to submit the report, the office shall provide notice of the failure to the agency. The notice must summarize the applicable reporting requirement and state that the agency may be subject to a civil penalty as provided by Subsection (b) or (c), as applicable.

(b) Except as provided by Subsection (c), a law enforcement agency that fails to submit the required report on or before the seventh day after the date of receiving notice under Subsection (a) is liable for a civil penalty in the amount of $1,000 for each day after the seventh day that the agency fails to submit the report.

(c) Beginning on the day after the date of receiving notice under Subsection (a), a law enforcement agency that, in the five-year period preceding the date the agency received the notice, has been liable for a civil penalty under Subsection (b) or this subsection is liable for a civil penalty for each day the agency fails to submit the required report. The amount of a civil penalty under this subsection is $10,000 for the first day and $1,000 for each additional day that the agency fails to submit the report.

(d) The attorney general may sue to collect a civil penalty under this article.

(e) A civil penalty collected under this article shall be deposited to the credit of the compensation to victims of crime fund established under Subchapter J, Chapter 56B.

Art. 2.1396. Video Recordings of Arrests for Intoxication Offenses.

A person stopped or arrested on suspicion of an offense under Section 49.04, 49.045, 49.07, or 49.08, Penal Code, is entitled to receive from a law enforcement agency employing the peace officer who made the stop or arrest a copy of any video made by or at the direction of the officer that contains footage of:

(1) the stop;

(2) the arrest;

(3) the conduct of the person stopped during any interaction with the officer, including during the administration of a field sobriety test; or

(4) a procedure in which a specimen of the person's breath or blood is taken.

Art. 2.1397. Duties of Law Enforcement Agency Filing Case.

(a) In this article:

(1) "Attorney representing the state" means an attorney authorized by law to represent the state in a criminal case, including a district attorney, criminal district attorney, or county attorney with criminal jurisdiction. The term does not include an attorney representing the state in a justice or municipal court under Chapter 45.

(2) "Law enforcement agency" means an agency of the state or an agency of a political subdivision of the state authorized by law to employ peace officers.

(b) A law enforcement agency filing a case with the attorney representing the state shall submit to the attorney representing the state a written statement by an agency employee with knowledge of the case acknowledging that all documents, items, and information in the possession of the agency that are required to be disclosed to the defendant in the case under Article 39.14 have been disclosed to the attorney representing the state.

(c) If at any time after the case is filed with the attorney representing the state the law enforcement agency discovers or acquires any additional document, item, or information required to be disclosed to the defendant under Article 39.14, an agency employee shall promptly disclose the document, item, or information to the attorney representing the state.

Art. 2.14. May Summon Aid.

Whenever a peace officer meets with resistance in discharging any duty imposed upon him by law, he shall summon a sufficient number of citizens of his county to overcome the resistance; and all persons summoned are bound to obey.

Art. 2.15. Person Refusing to Aid.

The peace officer who has summoned any person to assist him in performing any duty shall report such person, if he refuse to obey, to the proper district or county attorney, in order that he may be prosecuted for the offense.

Art. 2.16. Neglecting to Execute Process.

If any sheriff or other officer shall wilfully refuse or fail from neglect to execute any summons, subpoena or attachment for a witness, or any other legal process which it is made his duty by law to execute, he shall be liable to a fine for contempt not less than ten nor more than two hundred dollars, at the discretion of the court. The payment of such fine shall be enforced in the same manner as fines for contempt in civil cases.

Art. 2.17. Conservator of the Peace.

Each sheriff shall be a conservator of the peace in his county, and shall arrest all offenders against the laws of the State, in his view or hearing, and take them before the proper court for examination or trial. He shall quell and suppress all assaults and batteries, affrays, insurrections and unlawful assemblies. He shall apprehend and commit to jail all offenders, until an examination or trial can be had.

Art. 2.18. Custody of Prisoners.

When a prisoner is committed to jail by warrant from a magistrate or court, he shall be placed in jail by the sheriff. It is a violation of duty on the part of any sheriff to permit a defendant so committed to remain out of jail, except that he may, when a defendant is committed for want of bail, or when he arrests in a bailable case, give the person arrested a reasonable time to procure bail; but he shall so guard the accused as to prevent escape.

Art. 2.19. Report As to Prisoners.

On the first day of each month, the sheriff shall give notice, in writing, to the district or county attorney, where there be one, as to all prisoners in his custody, naming them, and of the authority under which he detains them.

Art. 2.195. Report of Warrant or Capias Information.

Not later than the 30th day after the date the court clerk issues the warrant or capias, the sheriff:

(1) shall report to the national crime information center each warrant or capias issued for a defendant charged with a felony who fails to appear in court when summoned; and

(2) may report to the national crime information center each warrant or capias issued for a defendant charged with a misdemeanor other than a Class C misdemeanor who fails to appear in court when summoned.

Art. 2.20. Deputy.

Wherever a duty is imposed by this Code upon the sheriff, the same duty may lawfully be performed by his deputy. When there is no sheriff in a county, the duties of that office, as to all proceedings under the criminal law, devolve upon the officer who, under the law, is empowered to discharge the duties of sheriff, in case of vacancy in the office.

Art. 2.21. Duty of Clerks.

(a) In a criminal proceeding, a clerk of the district or county court shall:

(1) receive and file all papers;

(2) receive all exhibits at the conclusion of the proceeding;

(3) issue all process;

(4) accept and file electronic documents received from the defendant, if the clerk accepts electronic documents from an attorney representing the state;

(5) accept and file digital multimedia evidence received from the defendant, if the clerk accepts digital multimedia evidence from an attorney representing the state; and

(6) perform all other duties imposed on the clerk by law.

(a-1) A district clerk is exempt from the requirements of Subsections (a)(4) and (5) if the electronic filing system used by the clerk for accepting electronic documents or electronic digital media from an attorney representing the state does not have the capability of accepting electronic filings from a defendant and the system was established or procured before June 1, 2009. If the electronic filing system described by this subsection is substantially upgraded or is replaced with a new system, the exemption provided by this subsection is no longer applicable.

(b) At any time during or after a criminal proceeding, the court reporter shall release for safekeeping any firearm or contraband received as an exhibit in that proceeding to:

(1) the sheriff; or

(2) in a county with a population of 500,000 or more, the law enforcement agency that collected, seized, or took possession of the firearm or contraband or produced the firearm or contraband at the proceeding.

(c) The sheriff or the law enforcement agency, as applicable, shall receive and hold the exhibits consisting of firearms or contraband and release them only to the person or persons authorized by the court in which such exhibits have been received or dispose of them as provided by Chapter 18.

(d) In this article, "eligible exhibit" means an exhibit filed with the clerk that:

(1) is not a firearm or contraband;

(2) has not been ordered by the court to be returned to its owner; and

(3) is not an exhibit in another pending criminal action.

(e) An eligible exhibit may be disposed of as provided by this article:

(1) on or after the first anniversary of the date on which a conviction becomes final in the case, if the case is a misdemeanor or a felony for which the sentence imposed by the court is five years or less;

(2) on or after the second anniversary of the date on which a conviction becomes final in the case, if the case is a non-capital felony for which the sentence imposed by the court is greater than five years;

(3) on or after the first anniversary of the date of the acquittal of a defendant; or

(4) on or after the first anniversary of the date of the death of a defendant.

(f) Subject to Subsections (g), (h), (i), and (j), a clerk may dispose of an eligible exhibit or may deliver the eligible exhibit to the county purchasing agent for disposal as surplus or salvage property under Section 263.152, Local Government Code, if on the date provided by Subsection (e) the clerk has not received a request for the exhibit from either the attorney representing the state in the case or the attorney representing the defendant.

(f-1) Notwithstanding Section 263.156, Local Government Code, or any other law, the commissioners court shall remit 50 percent of any proceeds of the disposal of an eligible exhibit as surplus or salvage property as described by Subsection (f), less the reasonable expense of keeping the exhibit before disposal and the costs of that disposal, to each of the following:

(1) the county treasury, to be used only to defray the costs incurred by the district clerk of the county for the management, maintenance, or destruction of eligible exhibits in the county; and

(2) the state treasury to the credit of the compensation to victims of crime fund established under Subchapter J, Chapter 56B.

(g) A clerk in a county with a population of less than two million must provide written notice by mail to the attorney representing the state in the case and the attorney representing the defendant before disposing of an eligible exhibit.

(h) The notice under Subsection (g) of this article must:

(1) describe the eligible exhibit;

(2) give the name and address of the court holding the exhibit; and

(3) state that the eligible exhibit will be disposed of unless a written request is received by the clerk before the 31st day after the date of notice.

(i) If a request is not received by a clerk covered by Subsection (g) before the 31st day after the date of notice, the clerk may dispose of the eligible exhibit in the manner permitted by this article, including the delivery of the eligible exhibit for disposal as surplus or salvage property as described by Subsection (f).

(j) If a request is timely received, the clerk shall deliver the eligible exhibit to the person making the request if the court determines the requestor is the owner of the eligible exhibit.

(k) In this article, "digital multimedia evidence" means evidence stored or transmitted in a binary form and includes data representing documents, audio, video metadata, and any other information attached to a digital file.

Art. 2.211. Hate Crime Reporting.

In addition to performing duties required by Article 2.21, a clerk of a district or county court in which an affirmative finding under Article 42.014 is requested shall report that request to the Texas Judicial Council, along with a statement as to whether the request was granted by the court and, if so, whether the affirmative finding was entered in the judgment in the case. The clerk shall make the report required by this article not later than the 30th day after the date the judgment is entered in the case.

Art. 2.212. Writ of Attachment Reporting.

Not later than the 30th day after the date a writ of attachment is issued in a district court, statutory county court, or county court, the clerk of the court shall report to the Texas Judicial Council:

(1) the date the attachment was issued;

(2) whether the attachment was issued in connection with a grand jury investigation, criminal trial, or other criminal proceeding;

(3) the names of the person requesting and the judge issuing the attachment; and

(4) the statutory authority under which the attachment was issued.

Art. 2.22. Power of Deputy Clerks.

Whenever a duty is imposed upon the clerk of the district or county court, the same may be lawfully performed by his deputy.

Art. 2.23. Report to Attorney General.

(a) The clerks of the district and county courts shall, when requested in writing by the Attorney General, report to the Attorney General not later than the 10th day after the date the request is received, and in the form prescribed by the Attorney General, information in court records that relates to a criminal matter, including information requested by the Attorney General for purposes of federal habeas review.

(b) A state agency or the office of an attorney representing the state shall, when requested in writing by the Attorney General, provide to the Attorney General any record that is needed for purposes of federal habeas review. The agency or office must provide the record not later than the 10th day after the date the request is received and in the form prescribed by the Attorney General.

(c) A district court, county court, state agency, or office of an attorney representing the state may not restrict or delay the reproduction or delivery of a record requested by the Attorney General under this article.

Art. 2.24. Authenticating Officer.

(a) The governor may appoint an authenticating officer, in accordance with Subsection (b) of this article, and delegate to that officer the power to sign for the governor or to use the governor's facsimile signature for signing any document that does not have legal effect under this code unless it is signed by the governor.

(b) To appoint an authenticating officer under this article, the governor shall file with the secretary of state a document that contains:

(1) the name of the person to be appointed as authenticating officer and a copy of the person's signature;

(2) the types of documents the authenticating officer is authorized to sign for the governor; and

(3) the types of documents on which the authenticating officer is authorized to use the governor's facsimile signature.

(c) The governor may revoke an appointment made under this article by filing with the secretary of state a document that expressly revokes the appointment of the authenticating agent.

(d) If an authenticating officer signs a document described in Subsection (a) of this article, the officer shall sign in the following manner: "______________, Authenticating Officer for Governor______________."

(e) If a provision of this code requires the governor's signature on a document before that document has legal effect, the authorized signature of the authenticating officer or an authorized facsimile signature of the governor gives the document the same legal effect as if it had been signed manually by the governor.

Art. 2.25. Reporting Certain Aliens to Federal Government.

A judge shall report to the United States Immigration and Naturalization Service a person who has been convicted in the judge's court of a crime or has been placed on deferred adjudication for a felony and is an illegal criminal alien as defined by Section 493.015(a), Government Code.

Art. 2.251. Duties Related to Immigration Detainer Requests.

(a) A law enforcement agency that has custody of a person subject to an immigration detainer request issued by United States Immigration and Customs Enforcement shall:

(1) comply with, honor, and fulfill any request made in the detainer request provided by the federal government; and

(2) inform the person that the person is being held pursuant to an immigration detainer request issued by United States Immigration and Customs Enforcement.

(b) A law enforcement agency is not required to perform a duty imposed by Subsection (a) with respect to a person who has provided proof that the person is a citizen of the United States or that the person has lawful immigration status in the United States, such as a Texas driver's license or similar government-issued identification.

Art. 2.26. Digital Signature and Electronic Documents.

(a) In this section, "digital signature" means an electronic identifier intended by the person using it to have the same force and effect as the use of a manual signature.

(b) An electronically transmitted document issued or received by a court or a clerk of the court in a criminal matter is considered signed if a digital signature is transmitted with the document.

(b-1) An electronically transmitted document is a written document for all purposes and exempt from any additional writing requirement under this code or any other law of this state.

(c) This section does not preclude any symbol from being valid as a signature under other applicable law, including Section 1.201(b)(37), Business & Commerce Code.

(d) The use of a digital signature under this section is subject to criminal laws pertaining to fraud and computer crimes, including Chapters 32 and 33, Penal Code.

Art. 2.27. Investigation of Certain Reports Alleging Abuse.

(a) On receipt of a report that is assigned the highest priority in accordance with rules adopted by the Department of Family and Protective Services under Section 261.301(d), Family Code, and that alleges an immediate risk of physical or sexual abuse of a child that could result in the death of or serious harm to the child by a person responsible for the care, custody, or welfare of the child, a peace officer from the appropriate local law enforcement agency shall investigate the report jointly with the department or with the agency responsible for conducting an investigation under Subchapter E, Chapter 261, Family Code. As soon as possible after being notified by the department of the report, but not later than 24 hours after being notified, the peace officer shall accompany the department investigator in initially responding to the report.

(b) On receipt of a report of abuse or neglect or other complaint of a resident of a nursing home, convalescent home, or other related institution under Section 242.126(c)(1), Health and Safety Code, the appropriate local law enforcement agency shall investigate the report as required by Section 242.135, Health and Safety Code.

Art. 2.271. Investigation of Certain Reports Alleging Abuse, Neglect, or Exploitation.

Notwithstanding Article 2.27, on receipt of a report of abuse, neglect, exploitation, or other complaint of a resident of a nursing home, convalescent home, or other related institution or an assisted living facility, under Section 260A.007(c)(1), Health and Safety Code, the appropriate local law enforcement agency shall investigate the report as required by Section 260A.017, Health and Safety Code.

Art. 2.272. Law Enforcement Response to Child Safety Check Alert.

(a) If a peace officer locates a child or other person listed on the Texas Crime Information Center's child safety check alert list established under Section 261.3022, Family Code, the officer shall:

(1) immediately contact the Department of Family and Protective Services on the department's dedicated law-enforcement telephone number for statewide intake;

(2) request information from the department regarding the circumstances of the case involving the child or other person; and

(3) request information from the child and the other person regarding the child's safety, well-being, and current residence.

(b) The peace officer may temporarily detain the child or other person to ensure the safety and well-being of the child.

(c) If the peace officer determines that the circumstances described by Section 262.104, Family Code, exist, the officer may take temporary possession of the child without a court order as provided by Section 262.104, Family Code. If the peace officer does not take temporary possession of the child, the officer shall obtain the child's current address and any other relevant information and report that information to the Department of Family and Protective Services.

(d) A peace officer who locates a child or other person listed on the Texas Crime Information Center's child safety check alert list and who reports the child's or other person's current address and other relevant information to the Department of Family and Protective Services shall report to the Texas Crime Information Center that the child or other person has been located and to whom the child was released, as applicable.

Art. 2.273. Release of Child by Law Enforcement Officer.

(a) A law enforcement officer who takes possession of a child under Section 262.104, Family Code, may release the child to:

(1) a residential child-care facility licensed by the Department of Family and Protective Services under Chapter 42, Human Resources Code, if the facility is authorized by the department to take possession of the child;

(2) a juvenile probation department;

(3) the Department of Family and Protective Services; or

(4) any other person authorized by law to take possession of the child.

(b) Before a law enforcement officer may release a child to a person authorized by law to take possession of the child other than a governmental entity, the officer shall:

(1) verify with the National Crime Information Center that the child is not a missing child;

(2) search the relevant databases of the National Crime Information Center system, including those pertaining to protection orders, historical protection orders, warrants, sex offender registries, and persons on supervised release to:

(A) verify that the person to whom the child is being released:

(i) does not have a protective order issued against the person; and

(ii) is not registered as a sex offender unless the person is the child's parent or guardian and there are no restrictions regarding the person's contact with the child; and

(B) obtain any other information the Department of Family and Protective Services considers:

(i) relevant to protect the welfare of the child; or

(ii) reflective of the responsibility of the person to whom the child is being released;

(3) call the Department of Family and Protective Services Texas Abuse Hotline to determine whether the person to whom the child is being released is listed in the registry as a person who abused or neglected a child;

(4) verify that the person to whom the child is being released is at least 18 years of age; and

(5) maintain a record regarding the child's placement, including:

(A) identifying information about the child, including the child's name or pseudonyms; and

(B) the name and address of the person to whom the child is being released.

Art. 2.28. Duties Regarding Misused Identity.

On receipt of information to the effect that a person's identifying information was falsely given by a person arrested as the arrested person's identifying information, the local law enforcement agency responsible for collecting identifying information on arrested persons in the county in which the arrest was made shall:

(1) notify the person that:

(A) the person's identifying information was misused by another person arrested in the county;

(B) the person may file a declaration with the Department of Public Safety under Section 411.0421, Government Code; and

(C) the person is entitled to expunction of information contained in criminal records and files under Chapter 55 of this code; and

(2) notify the Department of Public Safety regarding:

(A) the misuse of the identifying information;

(B) the actual identity of the person arrested, if known by the agency; and

(C) whether the agency was able to notify the person whose identifying information was misused.

Art. 2.29. Report Required in Connection with Fraudulent Use or Possession of Identifying Information.

(a) A peace officer to whom an alleged violation of Section 32.51, Penal Code, is reported shall make a written report to the law enforcement agency that employs the peace officer that includes the following information:

(1) the name of the victim;

(2) the name of the suspect, if known;

(3) the type of identifying information obtained, possessed, transferred, or used in violation of Section 32.51, Penal Code; and

(4) the results of any investigation.

(b) On the victim's request, the law enforcement agency shall provide the report created under Subsection (a) to the victim. In providing the report, the law enforcement agency shall redact any otherwise confidential information that is included in the report, other than the information described by Subsection (a).

Art. 2.295. Report Required in Connection with Unauthorized Acquisition or Transfer of Certain Financial Information.

(a) A peace officer to whom an alleged violation of Section 31.17, Penal Code, is reported shall make a written report to the law enforcement agency that employs the peace officer that includes the following information:

(1) the name of the victim;

(2) the name of the suspect, if known;

(3) the type of financial sight order or payment card information obtained or transferred in violation of Section 31.17, Penal Code; and

(4) the results of any investigation.

(b) On the victim's request, the law enforcement agency shall provide the report created under Subsection (a) to the victim. In providing the report, the law enforcement agency shall redact any otherwise confidential information that is included in the report, other than the information described by Subsection (a).

Art. 2.30. Report Concerning Certain Assaultive or Terroristic Offenses.

(a) This article applies only to the following offenses:

(1) assault under Section 22.01, Penal Code;

(2) aggravated assault under Section 22.02, Penal Code;

(3) sexual assault under Section 22.011, Penal Code;

(4) aggravated sexual assault under Section 22.021, Penal Code; and

(5) terroristic threat under Section 22.07, Penal Code.

(b) A peace officer who investigates the alleged commission of an offense listed under Subsection (a) shall prepare a written report that includes the information required under Article 5.05(a).

(c) On request of a victim of an offense listed under Subsection (a), the local law enforcement agency responsible for investigating the commission of the offense shall provide the victim, at no cost to the victim, with any information that is:

(1) contained in the written report prepared under Subsection (b);

(2) described by Article 5.05(a)(1) or (2); and

(3) not exempt from disclosure under Chapter 552, Government Code, or other law.

Art. 2.305. Report Required Concerning Human Trafficking Cases.

(a) This article applies only to:

(1) a municipal police department, sheriff's department, constable's office, county attorney's office, district attorney's office, and criminal district attorney's office, as applicable, in a county with a population of more than 50,000; and

(2) the Department of Public Safety.

(b) An entity described by Subsection (a) that investigates the alleged commission of an offense under Chapter 20A, Penal Code, or the alleged commission of an offense under Chapter 43, Penal Code, which may involve human trafficking, shall submit to the attorney general a report in the manner and form prescribed by the attorney general containing the following information:

(1) the offense being investigated, including a brief description of the alleged prohibited conduct;

(2) regarding each person suspected of committing the offense and each victim of the offense:

(A) the person's:

(i) age;

(ii) gender; and

(iii) race or ethnicity, as defined by Article 2.132; and

(B) the case number associated with the offense and the person suspected of committing the offense;

(3) the date, time, and location of the alleged offense;

(4) the type of human trafficking involved, including:

(A) forced labor or services, as defined by Section 20A.01, Penal Code;

(B) causing the victim by force, fraud, or coercion to engage in prohibited conduct involving one or more sexual activities, including conduct described by Section 20A.02(a)(3), Penal Code; or

(C) causing a child victim by any means to engage in, or become the victim of, prohibited conduct involving one or more sexual activities, including

Code of Criminal Procedure

conduct described by Section 20A.02(a)(7), Penal Code;

(5) if available, information regarding any victims' service organization or program to which the victim was referred as part of the investigation; and

(6) the disposition of the investigation, if any, regardless of the manner of disposition.

(c) An attorney representing the state who prosecutes the alleged commission of an offense under Chapter 20A, Penal Code, or the alleged commission of an offense under Chapter 43, Penal Code, which may involve human trafficking, shall submit to the attorney general the following information:

(1) the offense being prosecuted, including a brief description of the alleged prohibited conduct;

(2) any other charged offense that is part of the same criminal episode out of which the offense described by Subdivision (1) arose;

(3) the information described by Subsections (b)(2), (3), (4), and (5); and

(4) the disposition of the prosecution, regardless of the manner of disposition.

(d) The attorney general may enter into a contract with a university that provides for the university's assistance in the collection and analysis of information received under this article.

(e) In consultation with the entities described by Subsection (a), the attorney general shall adopt rules to administer this article, including rules prescribing:

(1) the form and manner of submission of a report required by Subsection (b) or (c); and

(2) additional information to include in a report required by Subsection (b) or (c).

Art. 2.31. [2 Versions: As added by Acts 2011, 82nd Leg., ch. 176] County Jailers.

If a jailer licensed under Chapter 1701, Occupations Code, has successfully completed a training program provided by the sheriff, the jailer may execute lawful process issued to the jailer by any magistrate or court on a person confined in the jail at which the jailer is employed to the same extent that a peace officer is authorized to execute process under Article 2.13(b)(2), including:

(1) a warrant under Chapter 15, 17, or 18;

(2) a capias under Chapter 17 or 23;

(3) a subpoena under Chapter 20A or 24; or

(4) an attachment under Chapter 20A or 24.

Art. 2.31. [2 Versions: As added by Acts 2011, 82nd Leg., ch. 1341] County Jailers.

A jailer licensed under Chapter 1701, Occupations Code, may execute lawful process issued to the jailer by any magistrate or court on a person confined in the jail at which the jailer is employed to the same extent that a peace officer is authorized to execute process under Article 2.13(b)(2), including:

(1) a warrant under Chapter 15, 17, or 18;

(2) a capias under Chapter 17 or 23;

(3) a subpoena under Chapter 20A or 24; or

(4) an attachment under Chapter 20A or 24.

Art. 2.32. Electronic Recording of Custodial Interrogations.

(a) In this article:

(1) "Electronic recording" means an audiovisual electronic recording, or an audio recording if an audiovisual electronic recording is unavailable, that is authentic, accurate, and unaltered.

(2) "Law enforcement agency" means an agency of the state, or of a county, municipality, or other political subdivision of this state, that employs peace officers who, in the routine performance of the officers' duties, conduct custodial interrogations of persons suspected of committing criminal offenses.

(3) "Place of detention" means a police station or other building that is a place of operation for a law enforcement agency, including a municipal police department or county sheriff's department, and is owned or operated by the law enforcement agency for the purpose of detaining persons in connection with the suspected violation of a penal law. The term does not include a courthouse.

(b) Unless good cause exists that makes electronic recording infeasible, a law enforcement agency shall make a complete and contemporaneous electronic recording of any custodial interrogation that occurs in a place of detention and is of a person suspected of committing or charged with the commission of an offense under:

(1) Section 19.02, Penal Code (murder);

(2) Section 19.03, Penal Code (capital murder);

(3) Section 20.03, Penal Code (kidnapping);

(4) Section 20.04, Penal Code (aggravated kidnapping);

(5) Section 20A.02, Penal Code (trafficking of persons);

(6) Section 20A.03, Penal Code (continuous trafficking of persons);

(7) Section 21.02, Penal Code (continuous sexual abuse of young child or disabled individual);

(8) Section 21.11, Penal Code (indecency with a child);

(9) Section 21.12, Penal Code (improper relationship between educator and student);

(10) Section 22.011, Penal Code (sexual assault);
(11) Section 22.021, Penal Code (aggravated sexual assault); or
(12) Section 43.25, Penal Code (sexual performance by a child).

(c) For purposes of Subsection (b), an electronic recording of a custodial interrogation is complete only if the recording:

(1) begins at or before the time the person being interrogated enters the area of the place of detention in which the custodial interrogation will take place or receives a warning described by Section 2(a), Article 38.22, whichever is earlier; and

(2) continues until the time the interrogation ceases.

(d) For purposes of Subsection (b), good cause that makes electronic recording infeasible includes the following:

(1) the person being interrogated refused to respond or cooperate in a custodial interrogation at which an electronic recording was being made, provided that:

(A) a contemporaneous recording of the refusal was made; or

(B) the peace officer or agent of the law enforcement agency conducting the interrogation attempted, in good faith, to record the person's refusal but the person was unwilling to have the refusal recorded, and the peace officer or agent contemporaneously, in writing, documented the refusal;

(2) the statement was not made as the result of a custodial interrogation, including a statement that was made spontaneously by the accused and not in response to a question by a peace officer;

(3) the peace officer or agent of the law enforcement agency conducting the interrogation attempted, in good faith, to record the interrogation but the recording equipment did not function, the officer or agent inadvertently operated the equipment incorrectly, or the equipment malfunctioned or stopped operating without the knowledge of the officer or agent;

(4) exigent public safety concerns prevented or rendered infeasible the making of an electronic recording of the statement; or

(5) the peace officer or agent of the law enforcement agency conducting the interrogation reasonably believed at the time the interrogation commenced that the person being interrogated was not taken into custody for or being interrogated concerning the commission of an offense listed in Subsection (b).

(e) A recording of a custodial interrogation that complies with this article is exempt from public disclosure as provided by Section 552.108, Government Code.

Art. 2.33. Use of Neck Restraints During Search or Arrest Prohibited.

A peace officer may not intentionally use a choke hold, carotid artery hold, or similar neck restraint in searching or arresting a person unless the restraint is necessary to prevent serious bodily injury to or the death of the officer or another person.

CHAPTER 3
DEFINITIONS

Art. 3.01. Words and Phrases.

All words, phrases and terms used in this Code are to be taken and understood in their usual acceptation in common language, except where specially defined.

Art. 3.02. Criminal Action.

A criminal action is prosecuted in the name of the State of Texas against the accused, and is conducted by some person acting under the authority of the State, in accordance with its laws.

Art. 3.03. Officers.

The general term "officers" includes both magistrates and peace officers.

Art. 3.04. Official Misconduct.

In this code:

(1) "Official misconduct" means an offense that is an intentional or knowing violation of a law committed by a public servant while acting in an official capacity as a public servant.

(2) "Public servant" has the meaning assigned by Section 1.07, Penal Code.

Art. 3.05. Racial Profiling.

In this code, "racial profiling" means a law enforcement-initiated action based on an individual's race, ethnicity, or national origin rather than on the individual's behavior or on information identifying the individual as having engaged in criminal activity.

COURTS AND CRIMINAL JURISDICTION

CHAPTER 4
COURTS AND CRIMINAL JURISDICTION

Art. 4.01. What Courts Have Criminal Jurisdiction.

The following courts have jurisdiction in criminal actions:

1. The Court of Criminal Appeals;
2. Courts of appeals;
3. The district courts;
4. The criminal district courts;
5. The magistrates appointed by the judges of the district courts of Bexar County, Dallas County, Tarrant County, or Travis County that give preference to criminal cases and the magistrates appointed by the judges of the criminal district courts of Dallas County or Tarrant County;
6. The county courts;
7. All county courts at law with criminal jurisdiction;
8. County criminal courts;
9. Justice courts;
10. Municipal courts;
11. The magistrates appointed by the judges of the district courts of Lubbock County;
12. The magistrates appointed by the El Paso Council of Judges;
13. The magistrates appointed by the Collin County Commissioners Court;
14. The magistrates appointed by the Brazoria County Commissioners Court or the local administrative judge for Brazoria County; and
15. The magistrates appointed by the judges of the district courts of Tom Green County.

Art. 4.02. Existing Courts Continued.

No existing courts shall be abolished by this Code and shall continue with the jurisdiction, organization, terms and powers currently existing unless otherwise provided by law.

Art. 4.03. Courts of Appeals.

The Courts of Appeals shall have appellate jurisdiction coextensive with the limits of their respective districts in all criminal cases except those in which the death penalty has been assessed. This Article shall not be so construed as to embrace any case which has been appealed from any inferior court to the county court, the county criminal court, or county court at law, in which the fine imposed or affirmed by the county court, the county criminal court or county court at law does not exceed one hundred dollars, unless the sole issue is the constitutionality of the statute or ordinance on which the conviction is based.

Art. 4.04. Court of Criminal Appeals.

Sec. 1. The Court of Criminal Appeals and each judge thereof shall have, and is hereby given, the power and authority to grant and issue and cause the issuance of writs of habeas corpus, and, in criminal law matters, the writs of mandamus, procedendo, prohibition, and certiorari. The court and each judge thereof shall have, and is hereby given, the power and authority to grant and issue and cause the issuance of such other writs as may be necessary to protect its jurisdiction or enforce its judgments.

Sec. 2. The Court of Criminal Appeals shall have, and is hereby given, final appellate and review jurisdiction in criminal cases coextensive with the limits of the state, and its determinations shall be final. The appeal of all cases in which the death penalty has been assessed shall be to the Court of Criminal Appeals. In addition, the Court of Criminal Appeals may, on its own motion, with or without a petition for such discretionary review being filed by one of the parties, review any decision of a court of appeals in a criminal case. Discretionary review by the Court of Criminal Appeals is not a matter of right, but of sound judicial discretion.

Art. 4.05. Jurisdiction of District Courts.

District courts and criminal district courts shall have original jurisdiction in criminal cases of the grade of felony, of all misdemeanors involving official misconduct, and of misdemeanor cases transferred to the district court under Article 4.17 of this code.

Art. 4.06. When Felony Includes Misdemeanor.

Upon the trial of a felony case, the court shall hear and determine the case as to any grade of offense included in the indictment, whether the proof shows a felony or a misdemeanor.

Art. 4.07. Jurisdiction of County Courts.

The county courts shall have original jurisdiction of all misdemeanors of which exclusive original jurisdiction is not given to the justice court, and when the fine to be imposed shall exceed five hundred dollars.

Art. 4.08. Appellate Jurisdiction of County Courts.

The county courts shall have appellate jurisdiction in criminal cases of which justice courts and other inferior courts have original jurisdiction.

Art. 4.09. Appeals from Inferior Court.

If the jurisdiction of any county court has been transferred to the district court or to a county court at law, then an appeal from a justice or other inferior court will lie to the court to which such appellate jurisdiction has been transferred.

Art. 4.10. To Forfeit Bail Bonds.

County courts and county courts at law shall have jurisdiction in the forfeiture and final judgment of all bail bonds and personal bonds taken in criminal cases of which said courts have jurisdiction.

Art. 4.11. Jurisdiction of Justice Courts.

(a) Justices of the peace shall have original jurisdiction in criminal cases:

(1) punishable by fine only or punishable by:

(A) a fine; and

(B) as authorized by statute, a sanction not consisting of confinement or imprisonment; or

(2) arising under Chapter 106, Alcoholic Beverage Code, that do not include confinement as an authorized sanction.

(b) The fact that a conviction in a justice court has as a consequence the imposition of a penalty or sanction by an agency or entity other than the court, such as a denial, suspension, or revocation of a privilege, does not affect the original jurisdiction of the justice court.

(c) A justice court has concurrent jurisdiction with a municipal court in criminal cases that arise in the municipality's extraterritorial jurisdiction and that arise under an ordinance of the municipality applicable to the extraterritorial jurisdiction under Section 216.902, Local Government Code.

Art. 4.12. Misdemeanor Cases; Precinct in Which Defendant to Be Tried in Justice Court.

(a) Except as otherwise provided by this article, a misdemeanor case to be tried in justice court shall be tried:

(1) in the precinct in which the offense was committed;

(2) in the precinct in which the defendant or any of the defendants reside;

(3) with the written consent of the state and each defendant or the defendant's attorney, in any other precinct within the county; or

(4) if the offense was committed in a county with a population of 3.3 million or more, in any precinct in the county that is adjacent to the precinct in which the offense was committed.

(b) In any misdemeanor case in which the offense was committed in a precinct where there is no qualified justice court, then trial shall be held:

(1) in the next adjacent precinct in the same county which has a duly qualified justice court; or

(2) in the precinct in which the defendant may reside.

(c) In any misdemeanor case in which each justice of the peace in the precinct where the offense was committed is disqualified for any reason, such case may be tried in the next adjoining precinct in the same county having a duly qualified justice of the peace.

(d) A defendant who is taken before a magistrate in accordance with Article 15.18 may waive trial by jury and enter a written plea of guilty or nolo contendere.

(e) The justices of the peace in each county shall, by majority vote, adopt local rules of administration regarding the transfer of a pending misdemeanor case from one precinct to a different precinct.

Art. 4.13. Justice May Forfeit Bond.

A justice of the peace shall have the power to take forfeitures of all bonds given for the appearance of any party at his court, regardless of the amount.

Art. 4.14. Jurisdiction of Municipal Court.

(a) A municipal court, including a municipal court of record, shall have exclusive original jurisdiction within the territorial limits of the municipality in all criminal cases that:

(1) arise under the ordinances of the municipality; and

(2) are punishable by a fine not to exceed:

(A) $2,000 in all cases arising under municipal ordinances that govern fire safety, zoning, or public health and sanitation, other than the dumping of refuse;

(B) $4,000 in cases arising under municipal ordinances that govern the dumping of refuse; or

(C) $500 in all other cases arising under a municipal ordinance.

(b) The municipal court shall have concurrent jurisdiction with the justice court of a precinct in which the municipality is located in all criminal cases arising under state law that:

(1) arise within the territorial limits of the municipality and are punishable by fine only, as defined in Subsection (c) of this article; or

(2) arise under Chapter 106, Alcoholic Beverage Code, and do not include confinement as an authorized sanction.

(c) In this article, an offense which is punishable by "fine only" is defined as an offense that is punishable by fine and such sanctions, if any, as authorized by statute not consisting of confinement in jail or imprisonment.

(d) The fact that a conviction in a municipal court has as a consequence the imposition of a penalty or sanction by an agency or entity other than the court, such as a denial, suspension, or revocation of a privilege, does not affect the original jurisdiction of the municipal court.

(e) The municipal court has jurisdiction in the forfeiture and final judgment of all bail bonds and personal bonds taken in criminal cases of which the court has jurisdiction.

(f) A municipality with a population of 1.19 million or more and another municipality contiguous to that municipality may enter into an agreement providing concurrent jurisdiction for the municipal courts of either jurisdiction for all criminal cases arising from offenses under state law that are:

(1) committed on the boundary of those municipalities or in one or both of the following areas:

(A) within 200 yards of that boundary; or

(B) within 2.25 miles of that boundary on a segment of highway in the state highway system that traverses a major water supply reservoir; and

(2) punishable by fine only.

(g) A municipality may enter into an agreement with a contiguous municipality or a municipality with boundaries that are within one-half mile of the municipality seeking to enter into the agreement to establish concurrent jurisdiction of the municipal courts in the municipalities and provide original jurisdiction to a municipal court in which a case is brought as if the municipal court were located in the municipality in which the case arose, for:

(1) all cases in which either municipality has jurisdiction under Subsection (a) or (b); and

(2) cases that arise under Section 821.022, Health and Safety Code.

Art. 4.15. May Sit at Any Time.

Justice courts and corporation courts may sit at any time to try criminal cases over which they have jurisdiction. Any case in which a fine may be assessed shall be tried in accordance with the rules of evidence and this Code.

Art. 4.16. Concurrent Jurisdiction.

When two or more courts have concurrent jurisdiction of any criminal offense, the court in which an indictment or a complaint shall first be filed shall retain jurisdiction except as provided in Article 4.12.

Art. 4.17. Transfer of Certain Misdemeanors.

On a plea of not guilty to a misdemeanor offense punishable by confinement in jail, entered in a county court of a judge who is not a licensed attorney, on the motion of the state or the defendant, the judge may transfer the case to a district court having jurisdiction in the county or to a county court at law in the county presided over by a judge who is a licensed attorney. The judge may make the transfer on his own motion. The attorney representing the state in the case in county court shall continue the prosecution in the court to which the case is transferred. Provided, in no case may any such case be transferred to a district court except with the written consent of the judge of the district court to which the transfer is sought.

Art. 4.18. Claim of Underage.

(a) A claim that a district court or criminal district court does not have jurisdiction over a person because jurisdiction is exclusively in the juvenile court and that the juvenile court could not waive jurisdiction under Section 8.07(a), Penal Code, or did not waive jurisdiction under Section 8.07(b), Penal Code, must be made by written motion in bar of prosecution filed with the court in which criminal charges against the person are filed.

(b) The motion must be filed and presented to the presiding judge of the court:

(1) if the defendant enters a plea of guilty or no contest, before the plea;

(2) if the defendant's guilt or punishment is tried or determined by a jury, before selection of the jury begins; or

(3) if the defendant's guilt is tried by the court, before the first witness is sworn.

(c) Unless the motion is not contested, the presiding judge shall promptly conduct a hearing without a jury and rule on the motion. The party making the motion has the burden of establishing by a preponderance of the evidence those facts necessary for the motion to prevail.

(d) A person may not contest the jurisdiction of the court on the ground that the juvenile court has exclusive jurisdiction if:

(1) the person does not file a motion within the time requirements of this article; or

(2) the presiding judge finds under Subsection (c) that a motion made under this article does not prevail.

(e) An appellate court may review a trial court's determination under this article, if otherwise authorized by law, only after conviction in the trial court.

(f) A court that finds that it lacks jurisdiction over a case because exclusive jurisdiction is in the juvenile court shall transfer the case to the juvenile court as provided by Section 51.08, Family Code.

(g) This article does not apply to a claim of a defect or error in a discretionary transfer proceeding in juvenile court. A defendant may appeal a defect or error only as provided by Chapter 56, Family Code.

Art. 4.19. Transfer of Person Certified to Stand Trial As an Adult.

(a) Notwithstanding the order of a juvenile court to detain a person under the age of 17 who has been certified to stand trial as an adult in a certified juvenile detention facility under Section 54.02(h), Family Code, the judge of the criminal court having jurisdiction over the person may order the person to be transferred to an adult facility. A child who is transferred to an adult facility must be detained under conditions meeting the requirements of Section 51.12, Family Code.

(b) On the 17th birthday of a person described by Subsection (a) who is detained in a certified juvenile detention facility under Section 54.02(h), Family Code, the judge of the criminal court having jurisdiction over the person shall order the person to be transferred to an adult facility.

PREVENTION AND SUPPRESSION OF OFFENSES

CHAPTER 5 FAMILY VIOLENCE PREVENTION

Art. 5.01. Legislative Statement.

(a) Family violence is a serious danger and threat to society and its members. Victims of family violence are entitled to the maximum protection from harm or abuse or the threat of harm or abuse as is permitted by law.

(b) In any law enforcement, prosecutorial, or judicial response to allegations of family violence, the responding law enforcement or judicial officers shall protect the victim, without regard to the relationship between the alleged offender and victim.

Art. 5.02. Definitions.

In this chapter, "family violence," "family," "household," and "member of a household" have the meanings assigned by Chapter 71, Family Code.

Art. 5.03. Family or Household Relationship Does Not Create an Exception to Official Duties.

A general duty prescribed for an officer by Chapter 2 of this code is not waived or excepted in any family violence case or investigation because of a family or household relationship between an alleged violator and the victim of family violence. A peace officer's or a magistrate's duty to prevent the commission of criminal offenses, including acts of family violence, is not waived or excepted because of a family or household relationship between the potential violator and victim.

Art. 5.04. Duties of Peace Officers.

(a) The primary duties of a peace officer who investigates a family violence allegation or who responds to a disturbance call that may involve family violence are to protect any potential victim of family violence, enforce the law of this state, enforce a protective order from another jurisdiction as provided by Chapter 88, Family Code, and make lawful arrests of violators.

(a-1) A peace officer who investigates a family violence allegation or who responds to a disturbance call that may involve family violence shall determine whether the address of the persons involved in the allegation or call matches the address of a current licensed foster home or verified agency foster home listed in the Texas Crime Information Center.

(b) A peace officer who investigates a family violence allegation or who responds to a disturbance call that may involve family violence shall advise any possible adult victim of all reasonable means to prevent further family violence, including giving written notice of a victim's legal rights and remedies and of the availability of shelter or other community services for family violence victims.

(c) A written notice required by Subsection (b) of this article is sufficient if it is in substantially the following form with the required information in English and in Spanish inserted in the notice:

Code of Criminal Procedure

"It is a crime for any person to cause you any physical injury or harm EVEN IF THAT PERSON IS A MEMBER OR FORMER MEMBER OF YOUR FAMILY OR HOUSEHOLD.

"NOTICE TO ADULT VICTIMS OF FAMILY VIOLENCE

"Please tell the investigating peace officer:

"IF you, your child, or any other household resident has been injured; or

"IF you feel you are going to be in danger when the officer leaves or later.

"You have the right to:

"ASK the local prosecutor to file a criminal complaint against the person committing family violence; and

"APPLY to a court for an order to protect you (you should consult a legal aid office, a prosecuting attorney, or a private attorney). If a family or household member assaults you and is arrested, you may request that a magistrate's order for emergency protection be issued. Please inform the investigating officer if you want an order for emergency protection. You need not be present when the order is issued. You cannot be charged a fee by a court in connection with filing, serving, or entering a protective order. For example, the court can enter an order that:

"(1) the abuser not commit further acts of violence;

"(2) the abuser not threaten, harass, or contact you at home;

"(3) directs the abuser to leave your household; and

"(4) establishes temporary custody of the children and directs the abuser not to interfere with the children or any property.

"A VIOLATION OF CERTAIN PROVISIONS OF COURT-ORDERED PROTECTION (such as (1) and (2) above) MAY BE A FELONY.

"CALL THE FOLLOWING VIOLENCE SHELTERS OR SOCIAL ORGANIZATIONS IF YOU NEED PROTECTION:

"________________

"________________."

Art. 5.045. Standby Assistance; Liability.

(a) In the discretion of a peace officer, the officer may stay with a victim of family violence to protect the victim and allow the victim to take the personal property of the victim or of a child in the care of the victim to a place of safety in an orderly manner.

(b) A peace officer who provides assistance under Subsection (a) of this article is not:

(1) civilly liable for an act or omission of the officer that arises in connection with providing the assistance or determining whether to provide the assistance; or

(2) civilly or criminally liable for the wrongful appropriation of any personal property by the victim.

Art. 5.05. Reports and Records.

(a) A peace officer who investigates a family violence incident or who responds to a disturbance call that may involve family violence shall make a written report, including but not limited to:

(1) the names of the suspect and complainant;

(2) the date, time, and location of the incident;

(3) any visible or reported injuries;

(4) a description of the incident and a statement of its disposition; and

(5) whether the suspect is a member of the state military forces or is serving in the armed forces of the United States in an active-duty status.

(a-1) In addition to the written report required under Subsection (a), a peace officer who investigates a family violence incident or who responds to a disturbance call that may involve family violence shall make a report to the Department of Family and Protective Services if the location of the incident or call, or the known address of a person involved in the incident or call, matches the address of a current licensed foster home or a verified agency foster home as listed in the Texas Crime Information Center. The report under this subsection may be made orally or electronically and must:

(1) include the information required by Subsection (a); and

(2) be filed with the Department of Family and Protective Services within 24 hours of the beginning of the investigation or receipt of the disturbance call.

(a-2) If a suspect is identified as being a member of the military, as described by Subsection (a)(5), the peace officer shall provide written notice of the incident or disturbance call to the staff judge advocate at Joint Force Headquarters or the provost marshal of the military installation to which the suspect is assigned with the intent that the commanding officer will be notified, as applicable.

(b) Each local law enforcement agency shall establish a departmental code for identifying and retrieving family violence reports as outlined in Subsection (a) of this section. A district or county attorney or an assistant district or county attorney exercising authority in the county where the law enforcement agency maintains records under this section is entitled to access to the records. The Department of Family and Protective Services is entitled to access the records relating to any person who is 14 years of age or older and who resides in a licensed foster home or a verified agency foster home.

(c) In order to ensure that officers responding to calls are aware of the existence and terms of protective orders, each municipal police department and sheriff shall establish procedures within the department or office to provide adequate information or access to information for law enforcement officers of the names of persons protected by a protective order and of persons to whom protective orders are directed.

(d) Each law enforcement officer shall accept a certified copy of an original or modified protective order as proof of the validity of the order and it is presumed the order remains valid unless:

(1) the order contains a termination date that has passed;

(2) it is more than one year after the date the order was issued; or

(3) the law enforcement officer has been notified by the clerk of the court vacating the order that the order has been vacated.

(e) A peace officer who makes a report under Subsection (a) of this article shall provide information concerning the incident or disturbance to the bureau of identification and records of the Department of Public Safety for its recordkeeping function under Section 411.042, Government Code. The bureau shall prescribe the form and nature of the information required to be reported to the bureau by this article.

(f) On request of a victim of an incident of family violence, the local law enforcement agency responsible for investigating the incident shall provide the victim, at no cost to the victim, with any information that is:

(1) contained in the written report prepared under Subsection (a);

(2) described by Subsection (a)(1) or (2); and

(3) not exempt from disclosure under Chapter 552, Government Code, or other law.

Art. 5.06. Duties of Prosecuting Attorneys and Courts.

(a) Neither a prosecuting attorney nor a court may:

(1) dismiss or delay any criminal proceeding that involves a prosecution for an offense that constitutes family violence because a civil proceeding is pending or not pending; or

(2) require proof that a complaining witness, victim, or defendant is a party to a suit for the dissolution of a marriage or a suit affecting the parent-child relationship before presenting a criminal allegation to a grand jury, filing an information, or otherwise proceeding with the prosecution of a criminal case.

(b) A prosecuting attorney's decision to file an application for a protective order under Chapter 71, Family Code, should be made without regard to whether a criminal complaint has been filed by the applicant. A prosecuting attorney may require the applicant to provide information for an offense report, relating to the facts alleged in the application, with a local law enforcement agency.

(c) The prosecuting attorney having responsibility under Section 71.04(c), Family Code, for filing applications for protective orders under Chapter 71, Family Code, shall provide notice of that responsibility to all law enforcement agencies within the jurisdiction of the prosecuting attorney for the prosecuting attorney.

Art. 5.07. Venue for Protective Order Offenses. [Renumbered]

Art. 5.08. Mediation in Family Violence Cases.

Notwithstanding Article 26.13(g) or 42A.301(b)(15), in a criminal prosecution arising from family violence, as that term is defined by Section 71.004, Family Code, a court shall not refer or order the victim or the defendant involved to mediation, dispute resolution, arbitration, or other similar procedures.

Code of Criminal Procedure

Code of Criminal Procedure

CHAPTER 6
PREVENTING OFFENSES BY THE ACT OF MAGISTRATES AND OTHER OFFICERS; EDUCATION CONCERNING CONSEQUENCES OF CERTAIN OFFENSES

Art. 6.01. When Magistrate Hears Threat.

It is the duty of every magistrate, when he may have heard, in any manner, that a threat has been made by one person to do some injury to himself or the person or property of another, including the person or property of his spouse, immediately to give notice to some peace officer, in order that such peace officer may use lawful means to prevent the injury.

Art. 6.02. Threat to Take Life.

If, within the hearing of a magistrate, one person shall threaten to take the life of another, including that of his spouse, or himself, the magistrate shall issue a warrant for the arrest of the person making the threat, or in case of emergency, he may himself immediately arrest such person.

Art. 6.03. On Attempt to Injure.

Whenever, in the presence or within the observation of a magistrate, an attempt is made by one person to inflict an injury upon himself or to the person or property of another, including the person or property of his spouse, it is his duty to use all lawful means to prevent the injury. This may be done, either by verbal order to a peace officer to interfere and prevent the injury, or by the issuance of an order of arrest against the offender, or by arresting the offender; for which purpose he may call upon all persons present to assist in making the arrest.

Art. 6.04. May Compel Offender to Give Security.

When the person making such threat is brought before a magistrate, he may compel him to give security to keep the peace, or commit him to custody.

Art. 6.05. Duty of Peace Officer As to Threats.

It is the duty of every peace officer, when he may have been informed in any manner that a threat has been made by one person to do some injury to himself or to the person or property of another, including the person or property of his spouse, to prevent the threatened injury, if within his power; and, in order to do this, he may call in aid any number of citizens in his county. He may take such measures as the person about to be injured might for the prevention of the offense.

Art. 6.06. Peace Officer to Prevent Injury.

Whenever, in the presence of a peace officer, or within his view, one person is about to commit an offense against the person or property of another, including the person or property of his spouse, or injure himself, it is his duty to prevent it; and, for this purpose the peace officer may summon any number of the citizens of his county to his aid. The peace officer must use the amount of force necessary to prevent the commission of the offense, and no greater.

Art. 6.07. Conduct of Peace Officer.

The conduct of peace officers, in preventing offenses about to be committed in their presence, or within their view, is to be regulated by the same rules as are prescribed to the action of the person about to be injured. They may use all force necessary to repel the aggression.

Art. 6.08. Protective Order Prohibiting Offense Caused by Bias or Prejudice. [Repealed]

Art. 6.09. Stalking Protective Order. [Repealed]

Art. 6.10. Educational Programs Concerning Certain Offenses Committed by Minors; Mandatory Court Attendance.

(a) In this article, "parent" means a natural or adoptive parent, managing or possessory conservator, or legal guardian. The term does not include a parent whose parental rights have been terminated.

(b) This article applies to a defendant who has not had the disabilities of minority removed and has been charged with an offense under Section 43.261, Penal Code.

(c) The judge of a county court:

(1) must take the defendant's plea in open court; and

(2) shall issue a summons to compel the defendant's parent to be present during:

(A) the taking of the defendant's plea; and

(B) all other proceedings relating to the case.

(d) If a county court finds that a defendant has committed an offense under Section 43.261, Penal Code, the court may enter an order requiring the defendant to attend and successfully complete an educational program described by Section 37.218, Education Code, or another equivalent educational program.

(e) A court that enters an order under Subsection (d) shall require the defendant or the defendant's parent to pay the cost of attending an educational program under Subsection (d) if the court determines that the defendant or the defendant's parent is financially able to make payment.

CHAPTER 7 PROCEEDINGS BEFORE MAGISTRATES TO PREVENT OFFENSES

Art. 7.01. Shall Issue Warrant.

Whenever a magistrate is informed upon oath that an offense is about to be committed against the person or property of the informant, or of another, or that any person has threatened to commit an offense, the magistrate shall immediately issue a warrant for the arrest of the accused; that he may be brought before such magistrate or before some other named in the warrant.

Art. 7.02. Appearance Bond Pending Peace Bond Hearing.

In proceedings under this Chapter, the accused shall have the right to make an appearance bond; such bond shall be conditioned as appearance bonds in other cases, and shall be further conditioned that the accused, pending the hearing, will not commit such offense and that he will keep the peace toward the person threatened or about to be injured, and toward all others, pending the hearing. Should the accused enter into such appearance bond, such fact shall not constitute any evidence of the accusation brought against him at the hearing on the merits before the magistrate.

Art. 7.03. Accused Brought Before Magistrate.

When the accused has been brought before the magistrate, he shall hear proof as to the accusation, and if he be satisfied that there is just reason to apprehend that the offense was intended to be committed, or that the threat was seriously made, he shall make an order that the accused enter into bond in such sum as he may in his discretion require, conditioned that he will not commit such offense, and that he will keep the peace toward the person threatened or about to be injured, and toward all others named in the bond for any period of time, not to exceed one year from the date of the bond. The magistrate shall admonish the accused that if the accused violates a condition of the bond, the court, in addition to ordering forfeiture of the bond, may punish the accused for contempt under Section 21.002(c), Government Code.

Art. 7.04. Form of Peace Bond.

Such bond shall be sufficient if it be payable to the State of Texas, conditioned as required in said order of the magistrate, be for some certain sum, and be signed by the defendant and his surety or sureties and dated, and the provisions of Article 17.02 permitting the deposit of current United States money in lieu of sureties is applicable to this bond. No error of form shall vitiate such bond, and no error in the proceedings prior to the execution of the bond shall be a defense in a suit thereon.

Art. 7.05. Oath of Surety; Bond Filed.

The officer taking such bond shall require the sureties of the accused to make oath as to the value of their property as pointed out with regard to bail bonds. Such officer shall forthwith deposit such bond and oaths in the office of the clerk of the county where such bond is taken.

Art. 7.06. Amount of Bail.

The magistrate, in fixing the amount of such bonds, shall be governed by the pecuniary circumstances of the accused and the nature of the offense threatened or about to be committed.

Art. 7.07. Surety May Exonerate Himself.

A surety upon any such bond may, at any time before a breach thereof, exonerate himself from the obligations of the same by delivering to any magistrate of the county where such bond was taken, the person of the defendant; and such magistrate shall in that case again require of the defendant bond, with other security in the same amount as the first bond; and the same proceeding shall be had as in the first instance, but the one year's time

Code of Criminal Procedure

shall commence to run from the date of the first order.

Art. 7.08. Failure to Give Bond.

If the defendant fail to give bond, he shall be committed to jail for one year from the date of the first order requiring such bond.

Art. 7.09. Discharge of Defendant.

A defendant committed for failing to give bond shall be discharged by the officer having him in custody, upon giving the required bond, or at the expiration of the time for which he has been committed.

Art. 7.10. May Discharge Defendant.

If the magistrate believes from the evidence that there is no good reason to apprehend that the offense was intended or will be committed, or that no serious threat was made by the defendant, he shall discharge the accused, and may, in his discretion, tax the cost of the proceeding against the party making the complaint.

Art. 7.11. Bond of Person Charged with Libel [Repealed].

Repealed by Acts 1973, 63rd Leg., ch. 399 (S.B. 34), § 3(b), effective January 1, 1974.

Art. 7.12. Destruction of Libel [Repealed].

Repealed by Acts 1973, 63rd Leg., ch. 399 (S.B. 34), § 3(b), effective January 1, 1974.

Art. 7.13. When the Defendant Has Committed a Crime.

If it appears from the evidence before the magistrate that the defendant has committed a criminal offense, the same proceedings shall be had as in other cases where parties are charged with crime.

Art. 7.14. Costs.

If the accused is found subject to the charge and required to give bond, the costs of the proceedings shall be adjudged against him.

Art. 7.15. May Order Protection.

When, from the nature of the case and the proof offered to the magistrate, it may appear necessary and proper, he shall have a right to order any peace officer to protect the person or property of any individual threatened; and such peace officer shall have the right to summon aid by requiring any number of citizens of his county to assist in giving the protection.

Art. 7.16. Suit on Bond.

A suit to forfeit any bond taken under the provisions of this Chapter shall be brought in the name of the State by the district or county attorney in the county where the bond was taken.

Art. 7.17. Limitation and Procedure.

Suits upon such bonds shall be commenced within two years from the breach of the same, and not thereafter, and shall be governed by the same rules as civil actions, except that the sureties may be sued without joining the principal. To entitle the State to recover, it shall only be necessary to prove that the accused violated any condition of said bond. The full amount of such bond may be recovered of the accused and the sureties.

Art. 7.18. Contempt.

Violation of a condition of bond imposed under this chapter is punishable by:

(1) forfeiture of the bond;

(2) imposition of the fine and confinement for contempt under Section 21.002(c), Government Code; or

(3) both forfeiture of the bond and imposition of the fine and confinement.

CHAPTER 7A
PROTECTIVE ORDER FOR VICTIMS OF SEXUAL ASSAULT OR ABUSE, INDECENT ASSAULT, STALKING, OR TRAFFICKING

Art. 7A.01. Application for Protective Order. [Repealed]

Art. 7A.02. Temporary Ex Parte Order. [Repealed]

Art. 7A.03. Required Findings; Issuance of Protective Order. [Repealed]

Art. 7A.035. Hearsay Statement of Child Victim.

In a hearing on an application for a protective order under this chapter, a statement that is made by a child younger than 14 years of age who is the victim of an offense under Section 21.02, 21.11, 22.011, or 22.021, Penal Code, and that describes the offense committed against the child is admissible as evidence in the same manner that a child's statement regarding alleged abuse against the child is admissible under Section 104.006, Family Code, in a suit affecting the parent-child relationship.

Art. 7A.04. Application of Other Law. [Repealed]

Art. 7A.05. Conditions Specified by Order. [Repealed]

Art. 7A.06. Warning on Protective Order. [Repealed]

Art. 7A.07. Duration of Protective Order. [Repealed]

CHAPTER 7B PROTECTIVE ORDER FOR VICTIM OF TRAFFICKING OF PERSONS [REPEALED]

Art. 7B.01. Application for Protective Order [Repealed].

Repealed by Acts 2013, 83rd Leg., ch. 1252 (H.B. 8), § 22, effective September 1, 2013.

Art. 7B.02. Temporary Ex Parte Order [Repealed].

Repealed by Acts 2013, 83rd Leg., ch. 1252 (H.B. 8), § 22, effective September 1, 2013.

Art. 7B.03. Required Findings; Issuance of Temporary Pretrial Protective Order [Repealed].

Repealed by Acts 2013, 83rd Leg., ch. 1252 (H.B. 8), § 22, effective September 1, 2013.

Art. 7B.04. Required Findings; Issuance of Post-Trial Protective Order [Repealed].

Repealed by Acts 2013, 83rd Leg., ch. 1252 (H.B. 8), § 22, effective September 1, 2013.

Art. 7B.05. Application of Other Law [Repealed].

Repealed by Acts 2013, 83rd Leg., ch. 1252 (H.B. 8), § 22, effective September 1, 2013.

Art. 7B.06. Conditions Specified by Order [Repealed].

Repealed by Acts 2013, 83rd Leg., ch. 1252 (H.B. 8), § 22, effective September 1, 2013.

Art. 7B.07. Warning on Protective Order [Repealed].

Repealed by Acts 2013, 83rd Leg., ch. 1252 (H.B. 8), § 22, effective September 1, 2013.

Art. 7B.08. Duration of Post-Trial Protective Order [Repealed].

Repealed by Acts 2013, 83rd Leg., ch. 1252 (H.B. 8), § 22, effective September 1, 2013.

CHAPTER 7B PROTECTIVE ORDERS

SUBCHAPTER A PROTECTIVE ORDER FOR VICTIMS OF SEXUAL ASSAULT OR ABUSE, INDECENT ASSAULT, STALKING, OR TRAFFICKING

Art. 7B.001. Application for Protective Order.

(a) The following persons may file an application for a protective order under this subchapter without regard to the relationship between the applicant and the alleged offender:

(1) a person who is the victim of an offense under Section 20A.02, 20A.03, 21.02, 21.11, 22.011, 22.012, 22.021, 42.072, or 43.05, Penal Code;

(2) any adult, including a parent or guardian, who is acting on behalf of a victim described by Subdivision (1), if the victim is younger than 18 years of age or an adult ward; or

(3) a prosecuting attorney acting on behalf of a person described by Subdivision (1) or (2).

(a-1) **[As added by Acts 2021, 87th Leg., ch. XXX (HB 39)]** Except as provided by Subsection (a-2), if an application has not yet been filed in the case under Subsection (a), the attorney representing the state shall promptly file an application for a protective order with respect to each victim of an offense listed in Subdivision (1) of that subsection following the offender's conviction of or placement on deferred adjudication community supervision for the offense.

(a-1) **[As added by Acts 2021, 87th Leg., ch. XXX (HB 3607)]** Except as provided by Subsection (a-2), if an application has not yet been filed in the case under Subsection (a), the attorney representing the state shall promptly file an application for a protective order with respect to each victim of an offense listed in Subdivision (1) or (2) of that subsection following the offender's conviction of or placement on deferred adjudication community supervision for the offense.

(a-1) **[As added by Acts 2021, 87th Leg., ch. XXX (SB 623)]** In addition to the persons having standing to file the application under Subsection (a), the state sexual offense response coordinator described by Subchapter J-1, Chapter 432, Government Code, with the consent of a person who is the victim of an offense under Section 22.011, 22.012, or 22.021, Penal Code, alleged to have been committed by a person subject to Chapter 432, Government Code, may file an application for a protective order under this subchapter on behalf of the victim.

(a-2) **[As added by Acts 2021, 87th Leg., ch. XXX (HB 39)]** The attorney representing the state may not file an application under Subsection (a-1) with respect to a victim if the victim requests that the attorney representing the state not file the application. This subsection does not apply to a victim who is younger than 18 years of age or who is an adult ward.

(a-2) **[As added by Acts 2021, 87th Leg., ch. XXX (HB 3607)]** The attorney representing the state may not file an application under Subsection (a-1) with respect to a victim who is at least 18 years of age if the victim requests that the attorney representing the state not file the application.

(b) An application for a protective order under this subchapter may be filed in:

(1) a district court, juvenile court having the jurisdiction of a district court, statutory county court, or constitutional county court in:

(A) the county in which the applicant resides;

(B) the county in which the alleged offender resides; or

(C) any county in which an element of the alleged offense occurred; or

(2) any court with jurisdiction over a protective order under Title 4, Family Code, involving the same parties named in the application. (Code Crim. Proc., Art. 7A.01.)

Art. 7B.002. Temporary Ex Parte Order.

(a) If the court finds from the information contained in an application for a protective order that there is a clear and present danger of sexual assault or abuse, indecent assault, stalking, trafficking, or other harm to the applicant, the court, without further notice to the alleged offender and without a hearing, may issue a temporary ex parte order for the protection of the applicant or any other member of the applicant's family or household.

(b) For purposes of this article, a military protective order issued to a person because the person was a reported victim of an offense under Section 22.011, 22.012, or 22.021, Penal Code, constitutes sufficient information for a court to find there is a clear and present danger of sexual assault or abuse or other harm to the applicant.

Art. 7B.003. Required Findings; Issuance of Protective Order.

(a) At the close of a hearing on an application for a protective order under this subchapter, the court shall find whether there are reasonable grounds to believe that the applicant is the victim of sexual assault or abuse, indecent assault, stalking, or trafficking.

(b) If the court finds that there are reasonable grounds to believe that the applicant is the victim of sexual assault or abuse, stalking, or trafficking, the court shall issue a protective order that includes a statement of the required findings. (Code Crim. Proc., Art. 7A.03.)

(c) **[As added by Acts 2021, 87th Leg., ch. XXX (HB 3607)]** An offender's conviction of or placement on deferred adjudication community supervision for an offense listed in Article 7B.001(a)(1) or (2) constitutes reasonable grounds under Subsection (a).

(c) **[As added by Acts 2021, 87th Leg., ch. XXX (HB 39)]** An offender's conviction of or placement on deferred adjudication community supervision for an offense listed in Article 7B.001(a)(1) constitutes reasonable grounds under Subsection (a).

Art. 7B.004. Hearsay Statement of Child Victim.

In a hearing on an application for a protective order under this subchapter, a statement that is made by a child younger than 14 years of age who is the victim of an offense under Section 21.02, 21.11, 22.011, 22.012, or 22.021, Penal Code, and that describes the offense committed against the child is admissible as evidence in the same manner that a child's statement regarding alleged abuse against the child is admissible under Section 104.006, Family Code, in a suit affecting the parent-child relationship.

Art. 7B.005. Conditions Specified by Protective Order.

(a) In a protective order issued under this subchapter, the court may:

(1) order the alleged offender to take action as specified by the court that the court determines is necessary or appropriate to prevent or reduce the likelihood of future harm to the applicant or a member of the applicant's family or household; or

(2) prohibit the alleged offender from:

(A) communicating:

(i) directly or indirectly with the applicant or any member of the applicant's family or household in a threatening or harassing manner; or

(ii) in any manner with the applicant or any member of the applicant's family or household except through the applicant's attorney or a person appointed by the court, if the court finds good cause for the prohibition;

(B) going to or near the residence, place of employment or business, or child-care facility or school of the applicant or any member of the applicant's family or household;

(C) engaging in conduct directed specifically toward the applicant or any member of the applicant's family or household, including following the person, that is reasonably likely to harass, annoy, alarm, abuse, torment, or embarrass the person; and

(D) possessing a firearm, unless the alleged offender is a peace officer, as defined by Section 1.07, Penal Code, actively engaged in employment as a sworn, full-time paid employee of a state agency or political subdivision.

(b) In a protective order that includes a condition described by Subsection (a)(2)(B), the court shall specifically describe each prohibited location and the minimum distance from the location, if any, that the alleged offender must maintain. This subsection does not apply to a protective order with respect to which the court has received a request to maintain confidentiality of information revealing the locations.

(c) In a protective order, the court may suspend a license to carry a handgun issued under Section 411.177, Government Code, that is held by the alleged offender. (Code Crim. Proc., Art. 7A.05.)

Art. 7B.006. Warning on Protective Order.

(a) Each protective order issued under this subchapter, including a temporary ex parte order, must contain the following prominently displayed statements in boldfaced type, in capital letters, or underlined:

"A PERSON WHO VIOLATES THIS ORDER MAY BE PUNISHED FOR CONTEMPT OF COURT BY A FINE OF AS MUCH AS $500 OR BY CONFINEMENT IN JAIL FOR AS LONG AS SIX MONTHS, OR BOTH."

"NO PERSON, INCLUDING A PERSON WHO IS PROTECTED BY THIS ORDER, MAY GIVE PERMISSION TO ANYONE TO IGNORE OR VIOLATE ANY PROVISION OF THIS ORDER. DURING THE TIME IN WHICH THIS ORDER IS VALID, EVERY PROVISION OF THIS ORDER IS IN FULL FORCE AND EFFECT UNLESS A COURT CHANGES THE ORDER."

"IT IS UNLAWFUL FOR ANY PERSON, OTHER THAN A PEACE OFFICER, AS DEFINED BY SECTION 1.07, PENAL CODE, ACTIVELY ENGAGED IN EMPLOYMENT AS A SWORN, FULL-TIME PAID EMPLOYEE OF A STATE AGENCY OR POLITICAL SUBDIVISION, WHO IS SUBJECT TO A PROTECTIVE ORDER TO POSSESS A FIREARM OR AMMUNITION."

(b) Each protective order issued under this subchapter, except for a temporary ex parte order, must contain the following prominently displayed statement in boldfaced type, in capital letters, or underlined:

"A VIOLATION OF THIS ORDER BY COMMISSION OF AN ACT PROHIBITED BY THE ORDER MAY BE PUNISHABLE BY A FINE OF AS MUCH AS $4,000 OR BY CONFINEMENT IN JAIL FOR AS LONG AS ONE YEAR, OR BOTH. AN ACT THAT RESULTS IN A SEPARATE OFFENSE MAY BE PROSECUTED AS A SEPARATE OFFENSE IN ADDITION TO A VIOLATION OF THIS ORDER." (Code Crim. Proc., Art. 7A.06.)

Art. 7B.007. Duration of Protective Order; Rescission.

(a) A protective order issued under Article 7B.003 may be effective for the duration of the lives of the offender and victim or for any shorter period stated in the order. If a period is not stated in the order, the order is effective until the second anniversary of the date the order was issued.

(a-1) **[As added by Acts 2021, 87th Leg., ch. XXX (HB 39)]** The court shall issue a protective order effective for the duration of the lives of the offender and victim if the offender is:

(1) convicted of or placed on deferred adjudication community supervision for an offense listed in Article 7B.001(a)(1); and

(2) required under Chapter 62 to register for life as a sex offender.

(a-1) **[As added by Acts 2021, 87th Leg., ch. XXX (HB 3607)]** The court shall issue a protective order effective for the duration of the lives of the offender and victim if the offender is:

(1) convicted of or placed on deferred adjudication community supervision for an offense listed in Article 7B.001(a)(1) or (2); and

(2) required under Chapter 62 to register for life as a sex offender.

(b) The following persons may file at any time an application with the court to rescind the protective order:

(1) a victim of an offense listed in Article 7B.001(a)(1) who is 18 years of age or older;

(2) subject to Subsection (b-1), a parent or guardian acting on behalf of a victim of an offense listed in Article 7B.001(a)(1) who is younger than 18 years of age or an adult ward; or

(3) a person not otherwise described by Subdivision (1) or (2) who filed the application for the protective order.

(b-1) A parent or guardian may not file an application to rescind the protective order under Subsection (b)(2) if the parent or guardian is the alleged offender subject to the protective order.

(c) To the extent of any conflict with Section 85.025, Family Code, this article prevails. (Code Crim. Proc., Art. 7A.07.)

Art. 7B.008. Application of Other Law.

To the extent applicable, except as otherwise provided by this subchapter, Title 4, Family Code, applies to a protective order issued under this subchapter. (Code Crim. Proc., Art. 7A.04.)

SUBCHAPTER B STALKING PROTECTIVE ORDER

Art. 7B.051. Request for Protective Order.

(a) At any proceeding related to an offense under Section 42.072, Penal Code, in which the defendant appears before the court, a person may request the court to issue a protective order under Title 4, Family Code, for the protection of the person.

(b) The request under Subsection (a) is made by filing an application for a protective order in the same manner as an application for a protective order under Title 4, Family Code. (Code Crim. Proc., Art. 6.09(a).)

Art. 7B.052. Required Findings; Issuance of Protective Order.

The court shall issue a protective order in the manner provided by Title 4, Family Code, if, in lieu of the finding that family violence occurred and is likely to occur in the future as required by Section 85.001, Family Code, the court finds that:

(1) probable cause exists to believe that an offense under Section 42.072, Penal Code, was committed; and

(2) the nature of the scheme or course of conduct engaged in by the defendant in committing the offense indicates the defendant is likely in the future to engage in conduct prohibited by Section 42.072(a)(1), (2), or (3), Penal Code. (Code Crim. Proc., Art. 6.09(b).)

Art. 7B.053. Enforcement.

The procedure for the enforcement of a protective order under Title 4, Family Code, applies to the fullest extent practicable to the enforcement of a protective order under this subchapter, including provisions relating to findings, contents, duration, warning, delivery, law enforcement duties, and modification. (Code Crim. Proc., Art. 6.09(c).)

SUBCHAPTER C PROTECTIVE ORDER PROHIBITING OFFENSE MOTIVATED BY BIAS OR PREJUDICE

Art. 7B.101. Request for Protective Order.

A person may request the court to issue a protective order under Title 4, Family Code, for the protection of the person at any proceeding:

(1) in which the defendant appears in constitutional county court, statutory county court, or district court;

(2) that is related to an offense under Title 5, Penal Code, or Section 28.02, 28.03, or 28.08, Penal Code; and

(3) in which it is alleged that the defendant committed the offense because of bias or prejudice as described by Article 42.014. (Code Crim. Proc., Art. 6.08(a).)

Art. 7B.102. Required Findings; Issuance of Protective Order.

The court shall issue a protective order in the manner provided by Title 4, Family Code, if, in lieu of the finding that family violence occurred and is likely to occur in the future as required by Section 85.001, Family Code, the court finds that:

(1) probable cause exists to believe that an offense under Title 5, Penal Code, or Section 28.02, 28.03, or 28.08, Penal Code, was committed;

(2) the defendant committed the offense because of bias or prejudice; and

(3) the nature of the scheme or course of conduct engaged in by the defendant in committing the offense indicates the defendant is likely in the future to:

(A) engage in conduct prohibited by Title 5, Penal Code, or Section 28.02, 28.03, or 28.08, Penal Code; and

(B) engage in that conduct described by Paragraph (A) because of bias or prejudice. (Code Crim. Proc., Art. 6.08(b).)

Art. 7B.103. Enforcement.

The procedure for the enforcement of a protective order under Title 4, Family Code, applies to the fullest extent practicable to the enforcement of a protective order under this subchapter, including provisions relating to findings, contents, duration, warning, delivery, law enforcement duties, and modification, except that:

(1) the printed statement on the warning must refer to the prosecution of subsequent offenses committed because of bias or prejudice;

(2) the court shall require a constable to serve a protective order issued under this subchapter; and

(3) the clerk of the court shall forward a copy of a protective order issued under this subchapter to the Department of Public Safety with a designation indicating that the order was issued to prevent offenses committed because of bias or prejudice. (Code Crim. Proc., Art. 6.08(c).)

Art. 7B.104. Reporting.

For an original or modified protective order issued under this subchapter, on receipt of the order from the clerk of the court, a law enforcement agency shall immediately, but not later than the 10th day after the date the order is received, enter the information required by Section 411.042(b)(6), Government Code, into the statewide law enforcement information system maintained by the Department of Public Safety. (Code Crim. Proc., Art. 6.08(d).)

CHAPTER 8
SUPPRESSION OF RIOTS AND OTHER DISTURBANCES

Art. 8.01. Officer May Require Aid.

When any officer authorized to execute process is resisted, or when he has sufficient reason to believe that he will meet with resistance in executing the same, he may command as many of the citizens of his county as he may think proper; and the sheriff may call any military company in the county to aid him in overcoming the resistance, and if necessary, in seizing and arresting the persons engaged in such resistance.

Art. 8.02. Military Aid in Executing Process.

If it be represented to the Governor in such manner as to satisfy him that the power of the county is not sufficient to enable the sheriff to execute process, he may, on application, order any military company of volunteers or militia company from another county to aid in overcoming such resistance.

Art. 8.03. Military Aid in Suppressing Riots.

Whenever, for the purpose of suppressing riots or unlawful assemblies, the aid of military or militia companies is called, they shall obey the orders of the civil officer who is engaged in suppressing the same.

Art. 8.04. Dispersing Riot.

Whenever a number of persons are assembled together in such a manner as to constitute a riot, according to the penal law of the State, it is the duty of every magistrate or peace officer to cause such persons to disperse. This may either be done by commanding them to disperse or by arresting the persons engaged, if necessary, either with or without warrant.

Art. 8.05. Officer May Call Aid.

In order to enable the officer to disperse a riot, he may call to his aid the power of the county in the same manner as is provided where it is necessary for the execution of process.

Art. 8.06. Means Adopted to Suppress.

The officer engaged in suppressing a riot, and those who aid him are authorized and justified in adopting such measures as are necessary to suppress the riot, but are not authorized to use any greater degree of force than is requisite to accomplish that object.

Art. 8.07. Unlawful Assembly.

The Articles of this Chapter relating to the suppression of riots apply equally to an unlawful assembly and other unlawful disturbances, as defined by the Penal Code.

Art. 8.08. Suppression at Election.

To suppress riots, unlawful assemblies and other disturbances at elections, any magistrate may appoint a sufficient number of special constables. Such appointments shall be made to each special constable, shall be in writing, dated and signed by the magistrate, and shall recite the purposes for which such appointment is made, and the length of time it is to continue. Before the same is delivered to such special constable, he shall take an oath before the magistrate to suppress, by lawful means, all riots, unlawful assemblies and breaches of the peace of which he may receive information, and to act impartially between all parties and persons interested in the result of the election.

Art. 8.09. Power of Special Constable.

Special constables so appointed shall, during the time for which they are appointed, exercise the powers and perform the duties properly belonging to peace officers.

CHAPTER 9 OFFENSES INJURIOUS TO PUBLIC HEALTH

Art. 9.01. Trade Injurious to Health.

After an indictment or information has been presented against any person for carrying on a trade, business or occupation injurious to the health of those in the neighborhood, the court shall have power, on the application of anyone interested, and after hearing proof both for and against the accused, to restrain the defendant, in such penalty as may be deemed proper, from carrying on such trade, business or occupation, or may make such order respecting the manner and place of carrying on the same as may be deemed advisable; and if upon trial, the defendant be convicted, the restraint shall be made perpetual, and the party shall be required to enter into bond, with security, not to continue such trade, business or occupation to the detriment of the health of such neighborhood, or of any other neighborhood within the county.

Art. 9.02. Refusal to Give Bond.

If the party refuses to give bond when required under the provisions of the preceding Article, the court may either commit him to jail, or make an order requiring the sheriff to seize upon the implements of such trade, business or occupation, or the goods and property used in conducting such trade, business or occupation, and destroy the same.

Art. 9.03. Requisites of Bond.

Such bond shall be payable to the State of Texas, in a reasonable amount to be fixed by the court, conditioned that the defendant will not carry on such trade, business or occupation, naming the same, at such place, naming the place, or at any other place in the county, to the detriment of the health of the neighborhood. The bond shall be signed by the defendant and his sureties and dated, and shall be approved by the court taking the same, and filed in such court.

Art. 9.04. Suit upon Bond.

Any such bond, upon the breach thereof, may be sued upon by the district or county attorney, in the name of the State of Texas, within two years after such breach, and not afterwards; and such suits shall be governed by the same rules as civil actions.

Art. 9.05. Proof.

It shall be sufficient proof of the breach of any such bond to show that the party continued after executing the same, to carry on the trade, business or occupation which he bound himself to discontinue; and the full amount of such bond may be recovered of the defendant and his sureties.

Art. 9.06. Unwholesome Food.

After conviction for selling unwholesome food or adulterated medicine, the court shall enter and issue an order to the sheriff or other proper officer to seize and destroy such as remains in the hands of the defendant.

CHAPTER 10 OBSTRUCTIONS OF PUBLIC HIGHWAYS [REPEALED]

Art. 10.01. Order to Remove. [Repealed]

Art. 10.02. Bond of Applicant. [Repealed]

Art. 10.03. Removal. [Repealed]

HABEAS CORPUS

CHAPTER 11 HABEAS CORPUS

Art. 11.01. What Writ Is.

The writ of habeas corpus is the remedy to be used when any person is restrained in his liberty. It is an order issued by a court or judge of competent jurisdiction, directed to any one having a person in his custody, or under his restraint, commanding him to produce such person, at a time and place named in the writ, and show why he is held in custody or under restraint.

Art. 11.02. To Whom Directed.

The writ runs in the name of "The State of Texas". It is addressed to a person having another under restraint, or in his custody, describing, as near as may be, the name of the office, if any, of the person to whom it is directed, and the name of the person said to be detained. It shall fix the time and place of return, and be signed by the judge, or by the clerk with his seal, where issued by a court.

Art. 11.03. Want of Form.

The writ of habeas corpus is not invalid, nor shall it be disobeyed for any want of form, if it substantially appear that it is issued by competent authority, and the writ sufficiently show the object of its issuance.

Art. 11.04. Construction.

Every provision relating to the writ of habeas corpus shall be most favorably construed in order to give effect to the remedy, and protect the rights of the person seeking relief under it.

Art. 11.05. By Whom Writ May Be Granted.

The Court of Criminal Appeals, the District Courts, the County Courts, or any Judge of said Courts, have power to issue the writ of habeas corpus; and it is their duty, upon proper motion, to grant the writ under the rules prescribed by law.

Art. 11.051. Filing Fee Prohibited.

Notwithstanding any other law, a clerk of a court may not require a filing fee from an individual who files an application or petition for a writ of habeas corpus.

Art. 11.06. Returnable to Any County.

Before indictment found, the writ may be made returnable to any county in the State.

Art. 11.07. Procedure After Conviction Without Death Penalty.

Sec. 1. This article establishes the procedures for an application for writ of habeas corpus in which the applicant seeks relief from a felony judgment imposing a penalty other than death.

Sec. 2. After indictment found in any felony case, other than a case in which the death penalty is imposed, and before conviction, the writ must be made returnable in the county where the offense has been committed.

Sec. 3. (a) After final conviction in any felony case, the writ must be made returnable to the Court of Criminal Appeals of Texas at Austin, Texas.

(b) An application for writ of habeas corpus filed after final conviction in a felony case, other than a case in which the death penalty is imposed, must be filed with the clerk of the court in which the conviction being challenged was obtained, and the clerk shall assign the application to that court. When the application is received by that court, a writ of habeas corpus, returnable to the Court of Criminal Appeals, shall issue by operation of law. The clerk of that court shall make appropriate notation thereof, assign to the case a file number (ancillary to that of the conviction being challenged), and forward a copy of the application by certified mail, return receipt requested, by secure electronic mail, or by personal service to the attorney representing the state in that court, who shall answer the application not later than the 30th day after the date the copy of the application is received. Matters alleged in the application not admitted by the state are deemed denied.

(c) Within 20 days of the expiration of the time in which the state is allowed to answer, it shall be the duty of the convicting court to decide whether there are controverted, previously unresolved facts material to the legality of the applicant's confinement. Confinement means confinement for any offense or any collateral consequence resulting from the conviction that is the basis of the instant habeas corpus. If the convicting court decides that there are no such issues, the clerk shall immediately transmit to the Court of Criminal Appeals a copy of the application, any answers filed, and a certificate reciting the date upon which that finding was made. Failure of the court to act within the allowed 20 days shall constitute such a finding.

(d) If the convicting court decides that there are controverted, previously unresolved facts which are material to the legality of the applicant's confinement, it shall enter an order within 20 days of the expiration of the time allowed for the state to reply, designating the issues of fact to be resolved. To resolve those issues the court may order affidavits, depositions, interrogatories, additional forensic testing, and hearings, as well as using personal recollection. The state shall pay the cost of additional forensic testing ordered under this subsection, except that the applicant shall pay the cost of the testing if the applicant retains counsel for purposes of filing an application under this article. The convicting court may appoint an attorney or a magistrate to hold a hearing and make findings of fact. An attorney so appointed shall be compensated as provided in Article 26.05 of this code. It shall be the duty of the reporter who is designated to transcribe a hearing held pursuant to this article to prepare a transcript within 15 days of its conclusion. On completion of the transcript, the reporter shall immediately transmit the transcript to the clerk of the convicting court. After the convicting court makes findings of fact or approves the findings of the person designated to make them, the clerk of the convicting court shall immediately transmit to the Court of Criminal Appeals, under one cover, the application, any answers filed, any motions filed, transcripts of all depositions and hearings, any affidavits, and any other matters such as official records used by the court in resolving issues of fact.

(e) For the purposes of Subsection (d), "additional forensic testing" does not include forensic DNA testing as provided for in Chapter 64.

Sec. 4. (a) If a subsequent application for writ of habeas corpus is filed after final disposition of an initial application challenging the same conviction, a court may not consider the merits of or grant relief based on the subsequent application unless the application contains sufficient specific facts establishing that:

(1) the current claims and issues have not been and could not have been presented previously in an original application or in a previously considered application filed under this article because the factual or legal basis for the claim was unavailable on the date the applicant filed the previous application; or

(2) by a preponderance of the evidence, but for a violation of the United States Constitution no rational juror could have found the applicant guilty beyond a reasonable doubt.

(b) For purposes of Subsection (a)(1), a legal basis of a claim is unavailable on or before a date described by Subsection (a)(1) if the legal basis was not recognized by and could not have been reasonably formulated from a final decision of the United States Supreme Court, a court of appeals of the United States, or a court of appellate jurisdiction of this state on or before that date.

(c) For purposes of Subsection (a)(1), a factual basis of a claim is unavailable on or before a date described by Subsection (a)(1) if the factual basis was not ascertainable through the exercise of reasonable diligence on or before that date.

Sec. 5. The Court of Criminal Appeals may deny relief upon the findings and conclusions of the hearing judge without docketing the cause, or may direct that the cause be docketed and heard as though originally presented to said court or as an appeal. Upon reviewing the record the court shall enter its judgment remanding the applicant to custody or ordering his release, as the law and facts may justify. The mandate of the court shall issue to the court issuing the writ, as in other criminal cases. After conviction the procedure outlined in this Act shall be exclusive and any other proceeding shall be void and of no force and effect in discharging the prisoner.

Sec. 6. Upon any hearing by a district judge by virtue of this Act, the attorney for applicant, and the state, shall be given at least seven full days' notice before such hearing is held.

Sec. 7. When the attorney for the state files an answer, motion, or other pleading relating to an application for a writ of habeas corpus or the court issues an order relating to an application for a writ of habeas corpus, the clerk of the court shall mail or deliver to the applicant a copy of the answer, motion, pleading, or order.

Art. 11.071. Procedure in Death Penalty Case.

Sec. 1. **Application to Death Penalty Case. —** Notwithstanding any other provision of this chapter, this article establishes the procedures for an application for a writ of habeas corpus in which the applicant seeks relief from a judgment imposing a penalty of death.

Sec. 2. **Representation by Counsel.**

(a) An applicant shall be represented by competent counsel unless the applicant has elected to proceed pro se and the convicting trial court finds, after a hearing on the record, that the applicant's election is intelligent and voluntary.

(b) If a defendant is sentenced to death the convicting court, immediately after judgment is entered under Article 42.01, shall determine if the defendant is indigent and, if so, whether the defendant desires appointment of counsel for the purpose of a writ of habeas corpus. If the defendant desires appointment of counsel for the purpose of a writ of habeas corpus, the court shall appoint the office of capital and forensic writs to represent the defendant as provided by Subsection (c).

(c) At the earliest practical time, but in no event later than 30 days, after the convicting court makes the findings required under Subsections (a) and (b), the convicting court shall appoint the office of capital and forensic writs or, if the office of capital and forensic writs does not accept or is prohibited from accepting an appointment under Section 78.054, Government Code, other competent counsel under Subsection (f), unless the applicant elects to proceed pro se or is represented by retained counsel. On appointing counsel under this section, the convicting court shall immediately notify the court of criminal appeals of the appointment, including in the notice a copy of the judgment and the name, address, and telephone number of the appointed counsel.

(d) [Repealed by Acts 2009, 81st Leg., ch. 781 (S.B. 1091), § 11, effective January 1, 2010.]

(e) If the court of criminal appeals denies an applicant relief under this article, an attorney appointed under this section to represent the applicant shall, not later than the 15th day after the date the court of criminal appeals denies relief or, if the case is filed and set for submission, the 15th day after the date the court of criminal appeals issues a mandate on the initial application for a writ of habeas corpus under this article, move for the appointment of counsel in federal habeas review under 18 U.S.C. Section 3599. The attorney shall immediately file a copy of the motion with the court of criminal appeals, and if the attorney fails to do so, the court may take any action to ensure that the applicant's right to federal habeas review is protected, including initiating contempt proceedings against the attorney.

(f) If the office of capital and forensic writs does not accept or is prohibited from accepting an appointment under Section 78.054, Government Code, the convicting court shall appoint counsel from a list of competent counsel maintained by the presiding judges of the administrative judicial regions under Section 78.056, Government Code. The convicting court shall reasonably compensate as provided by Section 2A an attorney appointed under this section, other than an attorney employed by the office of capital and forensic writs, regardless of whether the attorney is appointed by the convicting court or was appointed by the court of criminal appeals under prior law. An attorney appointed under this section who is employed by the office of capital and forensic writs shall be compensated in accordance with Subchapter B, Chapter 78, Government Code.

Sec. 2A. **State Reimbursement; County Obligation.**

(a) The state shall reimburse a county for compensation of counsel under Section 2, other than for compensation of counsel employed by the office of capital and forensic writs, and for payment of expenses under Section 3, regardless of whether counsel is employed by the office of capital and forensic writs. The total amount of reimbursement to which a county is entitled under this section for an application under this article may not exceed $25,000. Compensation and expenses in excess of the $25,000 reimbursement provided by the state are the obligation of the county.

(b) A convicting court seeking reimbursement for a county shall certify to the comptroller of public accounts the amount of compensation that the county is entitled to receive under this section. The comptroller of public accounts shall issue a warrant to the county in the amount certified by the convicting court, not to exceed $25,000.

(c) The limitation imposed by this section on the reimbursement by the state to a county for compensation of counsel and payment of reasonable expenses does not prohibit a county from compensating counsel and reimbursing expenses in an amount that is in excess of the amount the county receives from the state as reimbursement, and a county is specifically granted discretion by this subsection to make payments in excess of the state reimbursement.

(d) The comptroller shall reimburse a county for the compensation and payment of expenses of an attorney appointed by the court of criminal appeals under prior law. A convicting court seeking reimbursement for a county as permitted by this subsection shall certify the amount the county is entitled to receive under this subsection for an application filed under this article, not to exceed a total amount of $25,000.

Sec. 3. **Investigation of Grounds for Application.**

(a) On appointment, counsel shall investigate expeditiously, before and after the appellate record is filed in the court of criminal appeals, the factual and legal grounds for the filing of an application for a writ of habeas corpus.

(b) Not later than the 30th day before the date the application for a writ of habeas corpus is filed with the convicting court, counsel may file with the convicting court an ex parte, verified, and confidential request for prepayment of expenses, including expert fees, to investigate and present potential habeas corpus claims. The request for expenses must state:

(1) the claims of the application to be investigated;

(2) specific facts that suggest that a claim of possible merit may exist; and

(3) an itemized list of anticipated expenses for each claim.

(c) The court shall grant a request for expenses in whole or in part if the request for expenses is timely and reasonable. If the court denies in whole or in part the request for expenses, the court shall briefly state the reasons for the denial in a written order provided to the applicant.

(d) Counsel may incur expenses for habeas corpus investigation, including expenses for experts, without prior approval by the convicting court or the court of criminal appeals. On presentation of a claim for reimbursement, which may be presented ex parte, the convicting court shall order reimbursement of counsel for expenses, if the expenses are reasonably necessary and reasonably incurred. If the convicting court denies in whole or in part the request for expenses, the court shall briefly state the reasons for the denial in a written order provided to the applicant. The applicant may request reconsideration of the denial for reimbursement by the convicting court.

(e) Materials submitted to the court under this section are a part of the court's record.

(f) This section applies to counsel's investigation of the factual and legal grounds for the filing of an application for a writ of habeas corpus, regardless of whether counsel is employed by the office of capital and forensic writs.

Sec. 4. **Filing of Application.**

(a) An application for a writ of habeas corpus, returnable to the court of criminal appeals, must be filed in the convicting court not later than the 180th day after the date the convicting court appoints counsel under Section 2 or not later than the 45th day after the date the state's original brief is filed on direct appeal with the court of criminal appeals, whichever date is later.

(b) The convicting court, before the filing date that is applicable to the applicant under Subsection (a), may for good cause shown and after notice and an opportunity to be heard by the attorney representing the state grant one 90-day extension that begins on the filing date applicable to the defendant under Subsection (a). Either party may request that the court hold a hearing on the request. If the convicting court finds that the applicant cannot establish good cause justifying the requested extension, the court shall make a finding stating that fact and deny the request for the extension.

(c) An application filed after the filing date that is applicable to the applicant under Subsection (a) or (b) is untimely.

(d) If the convicting court receives an untimely application or determines that after the filing date that is applicable to the applicant under Subsection (a) or (b) no application has been filed, the convicting court immediately, but in any event within 10 days, shall send to the court of criminal appeals and to the attorney representing the state:

(1) a copy of the untimely application, with a statement of the convicting court that the application is untimely, or a statement of the convicting court that no application has been filed within the time periods required by Subsections (a) and (b); and

(2) any order the judge of the convicting court determines should be attached to an untimely application or statement under Subdivision (1).

(e) A failure to file an application before the filing date applicable to the applicant under Subsection (a) or (b) constitutes a waiver of all grounds for relief that were available to the applicant before the last date on which an application could be timely filed, except as provided by Section 4A.

Sec. 4A. **Untimely Application; Application Not Filed.**

(a) On command of the court of criminal appeals, a counsel who files an untimely application or fails to file an application before the filing date applicable under Section 4(a) or (b) shall show cause as to why the application was untimely filed or not filed before the filing date.

(b) At the conclusion of the counsel's presentation to the court of criminal appeals, the court may:

(1) find that good cause has not been shown and dismiss the application;

(2) permit the counsel to continue representation of the applicant and establish a new filing date for

the application, which may be not more than 180 days from the date the court permits the counsel to continue representation; or

(3) appoint new counsel to represent the applicant and establish a new filing date for the application, which may be not more than 270 days after the date the court appoints new counsel.

(c) The court of criminal appeals may hold in contempt counsel who files an untimely application or fails to file an application before the date required by Section 4(a) or (b). The court of criminal appeals may punish as a separate instance of contempt each day after the first day on which the counsel fails to timely file the application. In addition to or in lieu of holding counsel in contempt, the court of criminal appeals may enter an order denying counsel compensation under Section 2A.

(d) If the court of criminal appeals establishes a new filing date for the application, the court of criminal appeals shall notify the convicting court of that fact and the convicting court shall proceed under this article.

(e) Sections 2A and 3 apply to compensation and reimbursement of counsel appointed under Subsection (b)(3) in the same manner as if counsel had been appointed by the convicting court, unless the attorney is employed by the office of capital and forensic writs, in which case the compensation of that attorney is governed by Subchapter B, Chapter 78, Government Code.

(f) Notwithstanding any other provision of this article, the court of criminal appeals shall appoint counsel and establish a new filing date for application, which may be no later than the 270th day after the date on which counsel is appointed, for each applicant who before September 1, 1999, filed an untimely application or failed to file an application before the date required by Section 4(a) or (b). Section 2A applies to the compensation and payment of expenses of counsel appointed by the court of criminal appeals under this subsection, unless the attorney is employed by the office of capital and forensic writs, in which case the compensation of that attorney is governed by Subchapter B, Chapter 78, Government Code.

Sec. 5. **Subsequent Application.**

(a) If a subsequent application for a writ of habeas corpus is filed after filing an initial application, a court may not consider the merits of or grant relief based on the subsequent application unless the application contains sufficient specific facts establishing that:

(1) the current claims and issues have not been and could not have been presented previously in a timely initial application or in a previously considered application filed under this article or Article 11.07 because the factual or legal basis for the claim was unavailable on the date the applicant filed the previous application;

(2) by a preponderance of the evidence, but for a violation of the United States Constitution no rational juror could have found the applicant guilty beyond a reasonable doubt; or

(3) by clear and convincing evidence, but for a violation of the United States Constitution no rational juror would have answered in the state's favor one or more of the special issues that were submitted to the jury in the applicant's trial under Article 37.071, 37.0711, or 37.072.

(b) If the convicting court receives a subsequent application, the clerk of the court shall:

(1) attach a notation that the application is a subsequent application;

(2) assign to the case a file number that is ancillary to that of the conviction being challenged; and

(3) immediately send to the court of criminal appeals a copy of:

(A) the application;

(B) the notation;

(C) the order scheduling the applicant's execution, if scheduled; and

(D) any order the judge of the convicting court directs to be attached to the application.

(c) On receipt of the copies of the documents from the clerk, the court of criminal appeals shall determine whether the requirements of Subsection (a) have been satisfied. The convicting court may not take further action on the application before the court of criminal appeals issues an order finding that the requirements have been satisfied. If the court of criminal appeals determines that the requirements have not been satisfied, the court shall issue an order dismissing the application as an abuse of the writ under this section.

(d) For purposes of Subsection (a)(1), a legal basis of a claim is unavailable on or before a date described by Subsection (a)(1) if the legal basis was not recognized by or could not have been reasonably formulated from a final decision of the United States Supreme Court, a court of appeals of the United States, or a court of appellate jurisdiction of this state on or before that date.

(e) For purposes of Subsection (a)(1), a factual basis of a claim is unavailable on or before a date described by Subsection (a)(1) if the factual basis was not ascertainable through the exercise of reasonable diligence on or before that date.

(f) If an amended or supplemental application is not filed within the time specified under Section 4(a) or (b), the court shall treat the application as a subsequent application under this section.

Sec. 6. **Issuance of Writ.**

(a) If a timely application for a writ of habeas corpus is filed in the convicting court, a writ of habeas corpus, returnable to the court of criminal appeals, shall issue by operation of law.

(b) If the convicting court receives notice that the requirements of Section 5 for consideration of a subsequent application have been met, a writ of habeas corpus, returnable to the court of criminal appeals, shall issue by operation of law.

(b-1) If the convicting court receives notice that the requirements of Section 5(a) for consideration of a subsequent application have been met and if the applicant has not elected to proceed pro se and is not represented by retained counsel, the convicting court shall appoint, in order of priority:

(1) the attorney who represented the applicant in the proceedings under Section 5, if the attorney seeks the appointment;

(2) the office of capital and forensic writs, if the office represented the applicant in the proceedings under Section 5 or otherwise accepts the appointment; or

(3) counsel from a list of competent counsel maintained by the presiding judges of the administrative judicial regions under Section 78.056, Government Code, if the office of capital and forensic writs:

(A) did not represent the applicant as described by Subdivision (2); or

(B) does not accept or is prohibited from accepting the appointment under Section 78.054, Government Code.

(b-2) Regardless of whether the subsequent application is ultimately dismissed, compensation and reimbursement of expenses for counsel appointed under Subsection (b-1) shall be provided as described by Section 2, 2A, or 3, including compensation for time previously spent and reimbursement of expenses previously incurred with respect to the subsequent application.

(c) The clerk of the convicting court shall:

(1) make an appropriate notation that a writ of habeas corpus was issued;

(2) assign to the case a file number that is ancillary to that of the conviction being challenged; and

(3) send a copy of the application by certified mail, return receipt requested, or by secure electronic mail to the attorney representing the state in that court.

(d) The clerk of the convicting court shall promptly deliver copies of documents submitted to the clerk under this article to the applicant and the attorney representing the state.

Sec. 7. **Answer to Application.**

(a) The state shall file an answer to the application for a writ of habeas corpus not later than the 120th day after the date the state receives notice of issuance of the writ. The state shall serve the answer on counsel for the applicant or, if the applicant is proceeding pro se, on the applicant. The state may request from the convicting court an extension of time in which to answer the application by showing particularized justifying circumstances for the extension, but in no event may the court permit the state to file an answer later than the 180th day after the date the state receives notice of issuance of the writ.

(b) Matters alleged in the application not admitted by the state are deemed denied.

Sec. 8. **Findings of Fact Without Evidentiary Hearing.**

(a) Not later than the 20th day after the last date the state answers the application, the convicting court shall determine whether controverted, previously unresolved factual issues material to the legality of the applicant's confinement exist and shall issue a written order of the determination.

(b) If the convicting court determines the issues do not exist, the parties shall file proposed findings of fact and conclusions of law for the court to consider on or before a date set by the court that is not later than the 30th day after the date the order is issued.

(c) After argument of counsel, if requested by the court, the convicting court shall make appropriate written findings of fact and conclusions of law not later than the 15th day after the date the parties filed proposed findings or not later than the 45th day after the date the court's determination is made under Subsection (a), whichever occurs first.

(d) The clerk of the court shall immediately send to:

(1) the court of criminal appeals a copy of the:

(A) application;

(B) answer;

(C) orders entered by the convicting court;

(D) proposed findings of fact and conclusions of law; and

(E) findings of fact and conclusions of law entered by the court; and

(2) counsel for the applicant or, if the applicant is proceeding pro se, to the applicant, a copy of:

(A) orders entered by the convicting court;

(B) proposed findings of fact and conclusions of law; and

(C) findings of fact and conclusions of law entered by the court.

Sec. 9. **Hearing.**

(a) If the convicting court determines that controverted, previously unresolved factual issues material to the legality of the applicant's confinement exist, the court shall enter an order, not later than the 20th day after the last date the state answers the application, designating the issues of fact to be resolved and the manner in which the issues shall be resolved. To resolve the issues, the court may require affidavits, depositions, interrogatories, and evidentiary hearings and may use personal recollection.

(b) The convicting court shall hold the evidentiary hearing not later than the 30th day after the date on which the court enters the order designating issues under Subsection (a). The convicting court may grant a motion to postpone the hearing, but not for more than 30 days, and only if the court states, on the record, good cause for delay.

(c) The presiding judge of the convicting court shall conduct a hearing held under this section unless another judge presided over the original capital felony trial, in which event that judge, if qualified for assignment under Section 74.054 or 74.055, Government Code, may preside over the hearing.

(d) The court reporter shall prepare a transcript of the hearing not later than the 30th day after the date the hearing ends and file the transcript with the clerk of the convicting court.

(e) The parties shall file proposed findings of fact and conclusions of law for the convicting court to consider on or before a date set by the court that is not later than the 30th day after the date the transcript is filed. If the court requests argument of counsel, after argument the court shall make written findings of fact that are necessary to resolve the previously unresolved facts and make conclusions of law not later than the 15th day after the date the parties file proposed findings or not later than the 45th day after the date the court reporter files the transcript, whichever occurs first.

(f) The clerk of the convicting court shall immediately transmit to:

(1) the court of criminal appeals a copy of:

(A) the application;

(B) the answers and motions filed;

(C) the court reporter's transcript;

(D) the documentary exhibits introduced into evidence;

(E) the proposed findings of fact and conclusions of law;

(F) the findings of fact and conclusions of law entered by the court;

(G) the sealed materials such as a confidential request for investigative expenses; and

(H) any other matters used by the convicting court in resolving issues of fact; and

(2) counsel for the applicant or, if the applicant is proceeding pro se, to the applicant, a copy of:

(A) orders entered by the convicting court;

(B) proposed findings of fact and conclusions of law; and

(C) findings of fact and conclusions of law entered by the court.

(g) The clerk of the convicting court shall forward an exhibit that is not documentary to the court of criminal appeals on request of the court.

Sec. 10. **Rules of Evidence.** — The Texas Rules of Criminal Evidence apply to a hearing held under this article.

Sec. 11. **Review by Court of Criminal Appeals.** — The court of criminal appeals shall expeditiously review all applications for a writ of habeas corpus submitted under this article. The court may set the cause for oral argument and may request further briefing of the issues by the applicant or the state. After reviewing the record, the court shall enter its judgment remanding the applicant to custody or ordering the applicant's release, as the law and facts may justify.

Art. 11.072. Procedure in Community Supervision Case.

Sec. 1. This article establishes the procedures for an application for a writ of habeas corpus in a felony or misdemeanor case in which the applicant seeks relief from an order or a judgment of conviction ordering community supervision.

Sec. 2. (a) An application for a writ of habeas corpus under this article must be filed with the clerk of the court in which community supervision was imposed.

(b) At the time the application is filed, the applicant must be, or have been, on community supervision, and the application must challenge the legal validity of:

(1) the conviction for which or order in which community supervision was imposed; or

(2) the conditions of community supervision.

Sec. 3. (a) An application may not be filed under this article if the applicant could obtain the requested relief by means of an appeal under Article 44.02 and Rule 25.2, Texas Rules of Appellate Procedure.

(b) An applicant seeking to challenge a particular condition of community supervision but not the legality of the conviction for which or the order in which community supervision was imposed must first attempt to gain relief by filing a motion to amend the conditions of community supervision.

(c) An applicant may challenge a condition of community supervision under this article only on constitutional grounds.

Sec. 4. (a) When an application is filed under this article, a writ of habeas corpus issues by operation of law.

(b) At the time the application is filed, the clerk of the court shall assign the case a file number

Code of Criminal Procedure

ancillary to that of the judgment of conviction or order being challenged.

Sec. 5. (a) Immediately on filing an application, the applicant shall serve a copy of the application on the attorney representing the state by:

(1) certified mail, return receipt requested;

(2) personal service;

(3) electronic service through the electronic filing manager authorized by Rule 21, Texas Rules of Civil Procedure; or

(4) a secure electronic transmission to the attorney's e-mail address filed with the electronic filing system as required under Section 80.003, Government Code.

(b) The state may file an answer within the period established by Subsection (c), but is not required to file an answer.

(c) The state may not file an answer after the 30th day after the date of service, except that for good cause the convicting court may grant the state one 30-day extension.

(d) Any answer, motion, or other document filed by the state must be served on the applicant by certified mail, return receipt requested, or by personal service.

(e) Matters alleged in the application not admitted by the state are considered to have been denied.

Sec. 6. (a) Not later than the 60th day after the day on which the state's answer is filed, the trial court shall enter a written order granting or denying the relief sought in the application.

(b) In making its determination, the court may order affidavits, depositions, interrogatories, or a hearing, and may rely on the court's personal recollection.

(c) If a hearing is ordered, the hearing may not be held before the eighth day after the day on which the applicant and the state are provided notice of the hearing.

(d) The court may appoint an attorney or magistrate to hold a hearing ordered under this section and make findings of fact. An attorney appointed under this subsection is entitled to compensation as provided by Article 26.05.

Sec. 7. (a) If the court determines from the face of an application or documents attached to the application that the applicant is manifestly entitled to no relief, the court shall enter a written order denying the application as frivolous. In any other case, the court shall enter a written order including findings of fact and conclusions of law. The court may require the prevailing party to submit a proposed order.

(b) At the time an order is entered under this section, the clerk of the court shall immediately, by certified mail, return receipt requested, or by secure electronic mail, send a copy of the order to the applicant and to the state.

Sec. 8. If the application is denied in whole or part, the applicant may appeal under Article 44.02 and Rule 31, Texas Rules of Appellate Procedure. If the application is granted in whole or part, the state may appeal under Article 44.01 and Rule 31, Texas Rules of Appellate Procedure.

Sec. 9. (a) If a subsequent application for a writ of habeas corpus is filed after final disposition of an initial application under this article, a court may not consider the merits of or grant relief based on the subsequent application unless the application contains sufficient specific facts establishing that the current claims and issues have not been and could not have been presented previously in an original application or in a previously considered application filed under this article because the factual or legal basis for the claim was unavailable on the date the applicant filed the previous application.

(b) For purposes of Subsection (a), a legal basis of a claim is unavailable on or before a date described by that subsection if the legal basis was not recognized by and could not have been reasonably formulated from a final decision of the United States Supreme Court, a court of appeals of the United States, or a court of appellate jurisdiction of this state on or before that date.

(c) For purposes of Subsection (a), a factual basis of a claim is unavailable on or before a date described by that subsection if the factual basis was not ascertainable through the exercise of reasonable diligence on or before that date.

Art. 11.073. Procedure Related to Certain Scientific Evidence.

(a) This article applies to relevant scientific evidence that:

(1) was not available to be offered by a convicted person at the convicted person's trial; or

(2) contradicts scientific evidence relied on by the state at trial.

(b) A court may grant a convicted person relief on an application for a writ of habeas corpus if:

(1) the convicted person files an application, in the manner provided by Article 11.07, 11.071, or 11.072, containing specific facts indicating that:

(A) relevant scientific evidence is currently available and was not available at the time of the convicted person's trial because the evidence was not ascertainable through the exercise of reasonable diligence by the convicted person before the date of or during the convicted person's trial; and

(B) the scientific evidence would be admissible under the Texas Rules of Evidence at a trial held on the date of the application; and

(2) the court makes the findings described by Subdivisions (1)(A) and (B) and also finds that, had the scientific evidence been presented at trial, on the preponderance of the evidence the person would not have been convicted.

(c) For purposes of Section 4(a)(1), Article 11.07, Section 5(a)(1), Article 11.071, and Section 9(a), Article 11.072, a claim or issue could not have been presented previously in an original application or in a previously considered application if the claim or issue is based on relevant scientific evidence that was not ascertainable through the exercise of reasonable diligence by the convicted person on or before the date on which the original application or a previously considered application, as applicable, was filed.

(d) In making a finding as to whether relevant scientific evidence was not ascertainable through the exercise of reasonable diligence on or before a specific date, the court shall consider whether the field of scientific knowledge, a testifying expert's scientific knowledge, or a scientific method on which the relevant scientific evidence is based has changed since:

(1) the applicable trial date or dates, for a determination made with respect to an original application; or

(2) the date on which the original application or a previously considered application, as applicable, was filed, for a determination made with respect to a subsequent application.

Art. 11.0731. Procedures Related to Certain Previously Tested Evidence.

(a) This article applies to relevant evidence consisting of biological material described by Article 64.01(a) that was:

(1) presented by the state at the convicted person's trial; and

(2) subjected to testing:

(A) at a laboratory that ceased conducting DNA testing after an audit by the Texas Forensic Science Commission revealed the laboratory engaged in faulty testing practices; and

(B) during the period identified in the audit as involving faulty testing practices.

(b) A court may grant a convicted person relief on an application for a writ of habeas corpus if the convicted person files an application, in the manner provided by Article 11.07, 11.071, or 11.072, containing specific facts indicating that:

(1) the person previously filed a motion under Chapter 64 for forensic DNA testing of evidence described by Subsection (a) that was denied because of a negative finding under Article 64.03(a)(1)(A) or (B); and

(2) had the evidence not been presented at the person's trial, on the preponderance of the evidence the person would not have been convicted.

(c) For purposes of Section 4(a)(1), Article 11.07, Section 5(a)(1), Article 11.071, and Section 9(a), Article 11.072, a claim or issue could not have been presented previously in an original application or in a previously considered application if the claim or issue is based on evidence that has been determined by the Texas Forensic Science Commission to have been subjected to faulty DNA testing practices.

Art. 11.074. Court-Appointed Representation Required in Certain Cases.

(a) This article applies only to a felony or misdemeanor case in which the applicant seeks relief on a writ of habeas corpus from a judgment of conviction that:

(1) imposes a penalty other than death; or

(2) orders community supervision.

(b) If at any time the state represents to the convicting court that an eligible indigent defendant under Article 1.051 who was sentenced or had a sentence suspended is not guilty, is guilty of only a lesser offense, or was convicted or sentenced under a law that has been found unconstitutional by the court of criminal appeals or the United States Supreme Court, the court shall appoint an attorney to represent the indigent defendant for purposes of filing an application for a writ of habeas corpus, if an application has not been filed, or to otherwise represent the indigent defendant in a proceeding based on the application for the writ.

(c) An attorney appointed under this article shall be compensated as provided by Article 26.05.

Art. 11.08. Applicant Charged with Felony.

If a person is confined after indictment on a charge of felony, he may apply to the judge of the court in which he is indicted; or if there be no judge within the district, then to the judge of any district whose residence is nearest to the court house of the county in which the applicant is held in custody.

Art. 11.09. Applicant Charged with Misdemeanor.

If a person is confined on a charge of misdemeanor, he may apply to the county judge of the county in which the misdemeanor is charged to have been committed, or if there be no county judge in said county, then to the county judge whose residence is nearest to the courthouse of the county in which the applicant is held in custody.

Art. 11.10. Proceedings Under the Writ.

When motion has been made to a judge under the circumstances set forth in the two preceding Articles, he shall appoint a time when he will examine the cause of the applicant, and issue the writ returnable at that time, in the county where the offense is charged in the indictment or information to have been committed. He shall also specify some place in the county where he will hear the motion.

Art. 11.11. Early Hearing.

The time so appointed shall be the earliest day which the judge can devote to hearing the cause of the applicant.

Art. 11.12. Who May Present Petition.

Either the party for whose relief the writ is intended, or any person for him, may present a petition to the proper authority for the purpose of obtaining relief.

Art. 11.13. Applicant.

The word applicant, as used in this Chapter, refers to the person for whose relief the writ is asked, though the petition may be signed and presented by any other person.

Art. 11.14. Requisites of Petition.

The petition must state substantially:

1. That the person for whose benefit the application is made is illegally restrained in his liberty, and by whom, naming both parties, if their names are known, or if unknown, designating and describing them;

2. When the party is confined or restrained by virtue of any writ, order or process, or under color of either, a copy shall be annexed to the petition, or it shall be stated that a copy cannot be obtained;

3. When the confinement or restraint is not by virtue of any writ, order or process, the petition may state only that the party is illegally confined or restrained in his liberty;

4. There must be a prayer in the petition for the writ of habeas corpus; and

5. Oath must be made that the allegations of the petition are true, according to the belief of the petitioner.

Art. 11.15. Writ Granted Without Delay.

The writ of habeas corpus shall be granted without delay by the judge or court receiving the petition, unless it be manifest from the petition itself, or some documents annexed to it, that the party is entitled to no relief whatever.

Art. 11.16. Writ May Issue Without Motion.

A judge of the district or county court who has knowledge that any person is illegally confined or restrained in his liberty within his district or county may, if the case be one within his jurisdiction, issue the writ of habeas corpus, without any motion being made for the same.

Art. 11.17. Judge May Issue Warrant of Arrest.

Whenever it appears by satisfactory evidence to any judge authorized to issue such writ that any one is held in illegal confinement or custody, and there is good reason to believe that he will be carried out of the State, or suffer some irreparable injury before he can obtain relief in the usual course of law, or whenever the writ of habeas corpus has been issued and disregarded, the said judge may issue a warrant to any peace officer, or to any person specially named by said judge, directing him to take and bring such person before such judge, to be dealt with according to law.

Art. 11.18. May Arrest Detainer.

Where it appears by the proof offered, under circumstances mentioned in the preceding Article, that the person charged with having illegal custody of the prisoner is, by such act, guilty of an offense against the law, the judge may, in the warrant, order that he be arrested and brought before him; and upon examination, he may be committed, discharged, or held to bail, as the law and the nature of the case may require.

Art. 11.19. Proceedings Under the Warrant.

The officer charged with the execution of the warrant shall bring the persons therein mentioned before the judge or court issuing the same, who shall inquire into the cause of the imprisonment or restraint, and make an order thereon, as in cases of habeas corpus, either remanding into custody, discharging or admitting to bail the party so imprisoned or restrained.

Art. 11.20. Officer Executing Warrant.

The same power may be exercised by the officer executing the warrant in cases arising under the foregoing Articles as is exercised in the execution of warrants of arrest.

Art. 11.21. Constructive Custody.

The words "confined", "imprisoned", "in custody", "confinement", "imprisonment", refer not only to the actual, corporeal and forcible detention of a person, but likewise to any coercive measures by threats, menaces or the fear of injury, whereby one person exercises a control over the person of another, and detains him within certain limits.

Art. 11.22. Restraint.

By "restraint" is meant the kind of control which one person exercises over another, not to confine him within certain limits, but to subject him to the general authority and power of the person claiming such right.

Art. 11.23. Scope of Writ.

The writ of habeas corpus is intended to be applicable to all such cases of confinement and restraint, where there is no lawful right in the person exercising the power, or where, though the power in fact exists, it is exercised in a manner or degree not sanctioned by law.

Art. 11.24. One Committed in Default of Bail.

Where a person has been committed to custody for failing to enter into bond, he is entitled to the writ of habeas corpus, if it be stated in the petition that there was no sufficient cause for requiring bail, or that the bail required is excessive. If the proof sustains the petition, it will entitle the party to be discharged, or have the bail reduced.

Art. 11.25. Person Afflicted with Disease.

When a judge or court authorized to grant writs of habeas corpus shall be satisfied, upon investigation, that a person in legal custody is afflicted with a disease which will render a removal necessary for the preservation of life, an order may be made for the removal of the prisoner to some other place where his health will not be likely to suffer; or he may be admitted to bail when it appears that any species of confinement will endanger his life.

Art. 11.26. Who May Serve Writ.

The service of the writ may be made by any person competent to testify.

Art. 11.27. How Writ May Be Served and Returned.

The writ may be served by delivering a copy of the original to the person who is charged with having the party under restraint or in custody, and exhibiting the original, if demanded; if he refuse to receive it, he shall be informed verbally of the purport of the writ. If he refuses admittance to the person wishing to make the service, or conceals himself, a copy of the writ may be fixed upon some conspicuous part of the house where such person resides or conceals himself, or of the place where the prisoner is confined; and the person serving the writ of habeas corpus shall, in all cases, state fully, in his return, the manner and the time of the service of the writ.

Art. 11.28. Return Under Oath.

The return of a writ of habeas corpus, under the provisions of the preceding Article, if made by any person other than an officer, shall be under oath.

Art. 11.29. Must Make Return.

The person on whom the writ of habeas corpus is served shall immediately obey the same, and make the return required by law upon the copy of the original writ served on him, and this, whether the writ be directed to him or not.

Art. 11.30. How Return Is Made.

The return is made by stating in plain language upon the copy of the writ or some paper connected with it:

1. Whether it is true or not, according to the statement of the petition, that he has in his custody, or under his restraint, the person named or described in such petition;

2. By virtue of what authority, or for what cause, he took and detains such person;

3. If he had such person in his custody or under restraint at any time before the service of the writ, and has transferred him to the custody of another, he shall state particularly to whom, at what time, for what reason or by what authority he made such transfer;

4. He shall annex to his return the writ or warrant, if any, by virtue of which he holds the person in custody; and

5. The return must be signed and sworn to by the person making it.

Art. 11.31. Applicant Brought Before Judge.

The person on whom the writ is served shall bring before the judge the person in his custody, or under his restraint, unless it be made to appear that by reason of sickness he cannot be removed; in which case, another day may be appointed by the judge or court for hearing the cause, and for the production of the person confined; or the application may be heard and decided without the production of the person detained, by the consent of his counsel.

Art. 11.32. Custody Pending Examination.

When the return of the writ has been made, and the applicant brought before the court, he is no longer detained on the original warrant or process, but under the authority of the habeas corpus. The safekeeping of the prisoner, pending the examination or hearing, is entirely under the direction and authority of the judge or court issuing the writ, or to which the return is made. He may be bailed from day to day, or be remanded to the same jail whence he came, or to any other place of safekeeping under the control of the judge or court, till the case is finally determined.

Art. 11.33. Court Shall Allow Time.

The court or judge granting the writ of habeas corpus shall allow reasonable time for the production of the person detained in custody.

Art. 11.34. Disobeying Writ.

When service has been made upon a person charged with the illegal custody of another, if he refuses to obey the writ and make the return required by law, or, if he refuses to receive the writ, or conceals himself, the court or judge issuing the writ shall issue a warrant directed to any officer or other suitable person willing to execute the same, commanding him to arrest the person charged with the illegal custody or detention of another, and bring him before such court or judge. When such person has been arrested and brought before the court or judge, if he still refuses to return the writ, or does not produce the person in his custody, he shall be committed to jail and remain there until he is willing to obey the writ of habeas corpus, and until he pays all the costs of the proceeding.

Art. 11.35. Further Penalty for Disobeying Writ.

Any person disobeying the writ of habeas corpus shall also be liable to a civil action at the suit of the party detained, and shall pay in such suit fifty dollars for each day of illegal detention and restraint, after service of the writ. It shall be deemed that a person has disobeyed the writ who detains a prisoner a longer time than three days after service thereof, unless where further time is allowed in the writ for making the return thereto.

Art. 11.36. Applicant May Be Brought Before Court.

In case of disobedience of the writ of habeas corpus, the person for whose relief it is intended may also be brought before the court or judge having competent authority, by an order for that purpose, issued to any peace officer or other proper person specially named.

Art. 11.37. Death, Etc., Sufficient Return of Writ.

It is a sufficient return of the writ of habeas corpus that the person, once detained, has died or escaped, or that by some superior force he has been taken from the custody of the person making the return; but where any such cause shall be assigned, the court or judge shall proceed to hear testimony; and the facts stated in the return shall be proved by satisfactory evidence.

Art. 11.38. When a Prisoner Dies.

When a prisoner confined in jail, or who is in legal custody, shall die, the officer having charge of him shall forthwith report the same to a justice of the peace of the county, who shall hold an inquest to ascertain the cause of his death. All the proceedings had in such cases shall be reduced to writing, certified and returned as in other cases of inquest; a certified copy of which shall be sufficient proof of the death of the prisoner at the hearing of a motion under habeas corpus.

Art. 11.39. Who Shall Represent the State.

If neither the county nor the district attorney be present, the judge may appoint some qualified practicing attorney to represent the State, who shall be paid the same fee allowed district attorneys for like services.

Art. 11.40. Prisoner Discharged.

The judge or court before whom a person is brought by writ of habeas corpus shall examine the writ and the papers attached to it; and if no legal cause be shown for the imprisonment or restraint, or if it appear that the imprisonment or restraint, though at first legal, cannot for any cause be lawfully prolonged, the applicant shall be discharged.

Art. 11.41. Where Party Is Indicted for Capital Offense.

If it appears by the return and papers attached that the party stands indicted for a capital offense, the judge or court having jurisdiction of the case shall, nevertheless, proceed to hear such testimony as may be offered on the part of the State and the applicant, and may either remand or admit him to bail, as the law and the facts may justify.

Art. 11.42. If Court Has No Jurisdiction.

If it appear by the return and papers attached that the judge or court has no jurisdiction, such court or judge shall at once remand the applicant to the person from whose custody he has been taken.

Art. 11.43. Presumption of Innocence.

No presumption of guilt arises from the mere fact that a criminal accusation has been made before a competent authority.

Art. 11.44. Action of Court upon Examination.

The judge or court, after having examined the return and all documents attached, and heard the testimony offered on both sides, shall, according to the facts and circumstances of the case, proceed either to remand the party into custody, admit him to bail or discharge him; provided, that no defendant shall be discharged after indictment without bail.

Art. 11.45. Void or Informal.

If it appears that the applicant is detained or held under a warrant of commitment which is informal, or void; yet, if from the document on which the warrant was based, or from the proof on the hearing of the habeas corpus, it appears that there is probable cause to believe that an offense has been committed by the prisoner, he shall not be discharged, but shall be committed or held to bail.

Art. 11.46. If Proof Shows Offense.

Where, upon an examination under habeas corpus, it appears to the court or judge that there is probable cause to believe that an offense has been committed by the prisoner, he shall not be discharged, but shall be committed or admitted to bail.

Art. 11.47. May Summon Magistrate.

To ascertain the grounds on which an informal or void warrant has been issued, the judge or court may cause to be summoned the magistrate who issued the warrant, and may, by an order, require him to bring with him all the papers and proceedings touching the matter. The attendance of such magistrate and the production of such papers may be enforced by warrant of arrest.

Art. 11.48. Written Issue Not Necessary.

It shall not be necessary, on the trial of any cause arising under habeas corpus, to make up a written issue, though it may be done by the applicant for the writ. He may except to the sufficiency of, or controvert the return or any part thereof, or allege any new matter in avoidance. If written denial on his part be not made, it shall be considered, for the purpose of investigation, that the statements of said return are contested by a denial of the same; and the proof shall be heard accordingly, both for and against the applicant for relief.

Art. 11.49. Order of Argument.

The applicant shall have the right by himself or counsel to open and conclude the argument upon the trial under habeas corpus.

Art. 11.50. Costs.

The judge trying the cause under habeas corpus may make such order as is deemed right concerning the cost of bringing the defendant before him, and all other costs of the proceeding, awarding the same either against the person to whom the writ was directed, the person seeking relief, or may award no costs at all.

Art. 11.51. Record of Proceedings.

If a writ of habeas corpus be made returnable before a court in session, all the proceedings had shall be entered of record by the clerk thereof, as in any other case in such court. When the motion is heard out of the county where the offense was committed, or in the Court of Criminal Appeals, the clerk shall transmit a certified copy of all the proceedings upon the motion to the clerk of the court which has jurisdiction of the offense.

Art. 11.52. Proceedings Had in Vacation.

If the return is made and the proceedings had before a judge of a court in vacation, he shall cause all of the proceedings to be written, shall certify to the same, and cause them to be filed with the clerk of the court which has jurisdiction of the offense, who shall keep them safely.

Art. 11.53. Construing the Two Preceding Articles.

The two preceding Articles refer only to cases where an applicant is held under accusation for some offense; in all other cases the proceedings had before the judge shall be filed and kept by the clerk of the court hearing the case.

Art. 11.54. Court May Grant Necessary Orders.

The court or judge granting a writ of habeas corpus may grant all necessary orders to bring before him the testimony taken before the examining court, and may issue process to enforce the attendance of witnesses.

Art. 11.55. Meaning of "Return".

The word "return", as used in this Chapter, means the report made by the officer or person charged with serving the writ of habeas corpus, and also the answer made by the person served with such writ.

Art. 11.56. Effect of Discharge Before Indictment.

Where a person, before indictment found against him, has been discharged or held to bail on habeas corpus by order of a court or judge of competent jurisdiction, he shall not be again imprisoned or detained in custody on an accusation for the same offense, until after he shall have been indicted, unless surrendered by his bail.

Art. 11.57. Writ After Indictment.

Where a person once discharged or admitted to bail is afterward indicted for the same offense for which he has been once arrested, he may be committed on the indictment, but shall be again entitled to the writ of habeas corpus, and may be admitted to bail, if the facts of the case render it proper; but in cases where, after indictment is found, the cause of the defendant has been investigated on habeas corpus, and an order made, either remanding him to custody, or admitting him to bail, he shall neither be subject to be again placed in custody, unless when surrendered by his bail, nor shall he be again entitled to the writ of habeas corpus, except in the special cases mentioned in this Chapter.

Art. 11.58. Person Committed for a Capital Offense.

If the accusation against the defendant for a capital offense has been heard on habeas corpus before indictment found, and he shall have been committed after such examination, he shall not be entitled to the writ, unless in the special cases mentioned in Articles 11.25 and 11.59.

Art. 11.59. Obtaining Writ a Second Time.

A party may obtain the writ of habeas corpus a second time by stating in a motion therefor that since the hearing of his first motion important testimony has been obtained which it was not in his power to produce at the former hearing. He shall also set forth the testimony so newly discovered; and if it be that of a witness, the affidavit of the witness shall also accompany such motion.

Art. 11.60. Refusing to Execute Writ.

Any officer to whom a writ of habeas corpus, or other writ, warrant or process authorized by this Chapter shall be directed, delivered or tendered, who refuses to execute the same according to his directions, or who wantonly delays the service or execution of the same, shall be liable to fine as for contempt of court.

Art. 11.61. Refusal to Obey Writ.

Any one having another in his custody, or under his power, control or restraint who refuses to obey a writ of habeas corpus, or who evades the service of the same, or places the person illegally detained under the control of another, removes him, or in any other manner attempts to evade the operation of the writ, shall be dealt with as provided in Article 11.34 of this Code.

Art. 11.62. Refusal to Give Copy of Process.

Any jailer, sheriff or other officer who has a prisoner in his custody and refuses, upon demand, to furnish a copy of the process under which he holds the person, is guilty of an offense, and shall be dealt with as provided in Article 11.34 of this Code for refusal to return the writ therein required.

Art. 11.63. Held Under Federal Authority.

No person shall be discharged under the writ of habeas corpus who is in custody by virtue of a commitment for any offense exclusively cognizable by the courts of the United States, or by order or process issuing out of such courts in cases where they have jurisdiction, or who is held by virtue of any legal engagement or enlistment in the army, or who, being rightfully subject to the rules and articles of war, is confined by any one legally acting under the authority thereof, or who is held as a prisoner of war under the authority of the United States.

Art. 11.64. Application of Chapter.

This Chapter applies to all cases of habeas corpus for the enlargement of persons illegally held in custody or in any manner restrained in their personal liberty, for the admission of prisoners to bail, and for the discharge of prisoners before indictment upon a hearing of the testimony. Instead of a writ of habeas corpus in other cases heretofore used, a simple order shall be substituted.

Art. 11.65. Bond for Certain Applicants.

(a) This article applies to an applicant for a writ of habeas corpus seeking relief from the judgment in a criminal case, other than an applicant seeking relief from a judgment imposing a penalty of death.

(b) On making proposed findings of fact and conclusions of law jointly stipulated to by the applicant and the state, or on approving proposed findings of fact and conclusions of law made by an attorney or magistrate appointed by the court to perform that duty and jointly stipulated to by the applicant and the state, the convicting court may order the release of the applicant on bond, subject to conditions imposed by the convicting court, until the applicant is denied relief, remanded to custody, or ordered released.

(c) For the purposes of this chapter, an applicant released on bond under this article remains restrained in his liberty.

(d) Article 44.04(b) does not apply to the release of an applicant on bond under this article.

LIMITATION AND VENUE

CHAPTER 12
LIMITATION

Art. 12.01. Felonies.

Except as provided in Article 12.03, felony indictments may be presented within these limits, and not afterward:

(1) no limitation:

(A) murder and manslaughter;

(B) sexual assault under Section 22.011(a)(2), Penal Code, or aggravated sexual assault under Section 22.021(a)(1)(B), Penal Code;

(C) sexual assault, if:

(i) during the investigation of the offense biological matter is collected and the matter:

(a) has not yet been subjected to forensic DNA testing; or

(b) has been subjected to forensic DNA testing and the testing results show that the matter does not match the victim or any other person whose identity is readily ascertained; or

(ii) probable cause exists to believe that the defendant has committed the same or a similar sex offense against five or more victims;

(D) continuous sexual abuse of young child or disabled individual under Section 21.02, Penal Code;

(E) indecency with a child under Section 21.11, Penal Code;

(F) an offense involving leaving the scene of an accident under Section 550.021, Transportation Code, if the accident resulted in the death of a person;

(G) trafficking of persons under Section 20A.02(a)(7) or (8), Penal Code;

(H) continuous trafficking of persons under Section 20A.03, Penal Code; or

(I) compelling prostitution under Section 43.05(a)(2), Penal Code;

(2) ten years from the date of the commission of the offense:

(A) theft of any estate, real, personal or mixed, by an executor, administrator, guardian or trustee, with intent to defraud any creditor, heir, legatee, ward, distributee, beneficiary or settlor of a trust interested in such estate;

(B) theft by a public servant of government property over which the public servant exercises control in the public servant's official capacity;

(C) forgery or the uttering, using or passing of forged instruments;

(D) injury to an elderly or disabled individual punishable as a felony of the first degree under Section 22.04, Penal Code;

(E) sexual assault, except as provided by Subdivision (1) or (7);

(F) arson;

(G) trafficking of persons under Section 20A.02(a) (1), (2), (3), or (4), Penal Code; or

(H) compelling prostitution under Section 43.05(a)(1), Penal Code;

(3) seven years from the date of the commission of the offense:

(A) misapplication of fiduciary property or property of a financial institution;

(B) fraudulent securing of document execution;

(C) a felony violation under Chapter 162, Tax Code;

(D) false statement to obtain property or credit under Section 32.32, Penal Code;

(E) money laundering;

(F) credit card or debit card abuse under Section 32.31, Penal Code;

(G) fraudulent use or possession of identifying information under Section 32.51, Penal Code;

(H) exploitation of a child, elderly individual, or disabled individual under Section 32.53, Penal Code;

(I) health care fraud under Section 35A.02, Penal Code; or

(J) bigamy under Section 25.01, Penal Code, except as provided by Subdivision (6);

(4) five years from the date of the commission of the offense:

(A) theft or robbery;

(B) except as provided by Subdivision (5), kidnapping or burglary;

(C) injury to an elderly or disabled individual that is not punishable as a felony of the first degree under Section 22.04, Penal Code;

(D) abandoning or endangering a child; or

(E) insurance fraud;

(5) if the investigation of the offense shows that the victim is younger than 17 years of age at the time the offense is committed, 20 years from the 18th birthday of the victim of one of the following offenses:

(A) sexual performance by a child under Section 43.25, Penal Code;

(B) aggravated kidnapping under Section 20.04(a)(4), Penal Code, if the defendant committed the offense with the intent to violate or abuse the victim sexually; or

(C) burglary under Section 30.02, Penal Code, if the offense is punishable under Subsection (d) of that section and the defendant committed the offense with the intent to commit an offense described by Subdivision (1)(B) or (D) of this article or Paragraph (B) of this subdivision;

(6) ten years from the 18th birthday of the victim of the offense:

(A) trafficking of persons under Section 20A.02(a) (5) or (6), Penal Code;

(B) injury to a child under Section 22.04, Penal Code; or

(C) bigamy under Section 25.01, Penal Code, if the investigation of the offense shows that the person, other than the legal spouse of the defendant, whom the defendant marries or purports to marry or with whom the defendant lives under the appearance of being married is younger than 18 years of age at the time the offense is committed;

(7) two years from the date the offense was discovered: sexual assault punishable as a state jail felony under Section 22.011(f)(2), Penal Code; or

(8) three years from the date of the commission of the offense: all other felonies.

Art. 12.02. Misdemeanors.

(a) An indictment or information for any Class A or Class B misdemeanor may be presented within two years from the date of the commission of the offense, and not afterward.

(b) A complaint or information for any Class C misdemeanor may be presented within two years from the date of the commission of the offense, and not afterward.

Art. 12.03. Aggravated Offenses, Attempt, Conspiracy, Solicitation, Organized Criminal Activity.

(a) The limitation period for criminal attempt is the same as that of the offense attempted.

(b) The limitation period for criminal conspiracy or organized criminal activity is the same as that of the most serious offense that is the object of the conspiracy or the organized criminal activity.

(c) The limitation period for criminal solicitation is the same as that of the felony solicited.

(d) Except as otherwise provided by this chapter, any offense that bears the title "aggravated" shall carry the same limitation period as the primary crime.

Art. 12.04. Computation.

The day on which the offense was committed and the day on which the indictment or information is presented shall be excluded from the computation of time.

Art. 12.05. Absence from State and Time of Pendency of Indictment, Etc., Not Computed.

(a) The time during which the accused is absent from the state shall not be computed in the period of limitation.

(b) The time during the pendency of an indictment, information, or complaint shall not be computed in the period of limitation.

(c) The term "during the pendency," as used herein, means that period of time beginning with the day the indictment, information, or complaint is filed in a court of competent jurisdiction, and ending with the day such accusation is, by an order of a trial court having jurisdiction thereof, determined to be invalid for any reason.

Art. 12.06. An Indictment Is "Presented," When.

An indictment is considered as "presented" when it has been duly acted upon by the grand jury and received by the court.

Art. 12.07. An Information Is "Presented," When.

An information is considered as "presented," when it has been filed by the proper officer in the proper court.

Art. 12.08. An Indictment Is "Presented," When [Deleted].

Deleted by Acts 1973, 63rd Leg., ch. 399 (S.B. 34), § 2(B), effective January 1, 1974.

Art. 12.09. An Information Is "Presented," When [Deleted].

Deleted by Acts 1973, 63rd Leg., ch. 399 (S.B. 34), § 2(B), effective January 1, 1974.

CHAPTER 13
VENUE

Art. 13.01. Offenses Committed Outside This State.

Offenses committed wholly or in part outside this State, under circumstances that give this State jurisdiction to prosecute the offender, may be prosecuted in any county in which the offender is found or in any county in which an element of the offense occurs.

Art. 13.02. Forgery.

Forgery may be prosecuted in any county where the writing was forged, or where the same was used or passed, or attempted to be used or passed, or deposited or placed with another person, firm, association, or corporation either for collection or credit for the account of any person, firm, association or corporation. In addition, a forging and uttering, using or passing of forged instruments in writing which concern or affect the title to land in this State may be prosecuted in the county in which such land, or any part thereof, is situated.

Art. 13.03. Perjury.

Perjury and aggravated perjury may be prosecuted in the county where committed, or in the county where the false statement is used or attempted to be used.

Art. 13.04. On the Boundaries of Counties.

An offense committed on the boundaries of two or more counties, or within four hundred yards thereof, may be prosecuted and punished in any one of such counties and any offense committed on the premises of any airport operated jointly by two municipalities and situated in two counties may be prosecuted and punished in either county.

Art. 13.045. On the Boundaries of Certain Municipalities.

An offense punishable by fine only that is committed on or near the boundary of contiguous municipalities that have entered into an agreement authorized by Article 4.14(f) and Section 29.003(h), Government Code, may be prosecuted in either of those municipalities as provided in the agreement.

Art. 13.05. Criminal Homicide Committed Outside This State.

The offense of criminal homicide committed wholly or in part outside this State, under circumstances that give this State jurisdiction to prosecute the offender, may be prosecuted in the county where the injury was inflicted, or in the county where the offender was located when he inflicted the injury, or in the county where the victim died or the body was found.

Art. 13.06. Committed on a Boundary Stream.

If an offense be committed upon any river or stream, the boundary of this State, it may be prosecuted in the county the boundary of which is upon such stream or river, and the county seat of which is nearest the place where the offense was committed.

Art. 13.07. Injured in One County and Dying in Another.

If a person receives an injury in one county and dies in another by reason of such injury, the offender may be prosecuted in the county where the injury was received or where the death occurred, or in the county where the dead body is found.

Art. 13.072. Continuous Violence Against the Family Committed in More Than One County.

An offense under Section 25.11, Penal Code, may be prosecuted in any county in which the defendant engaged in the conduct constituting an offense under Section 22.01(a)(1), Penal Code, against a person described by Section 25.11(a), Penal Code.

Art. 13.075. Child Injured in One County and Residing in Another.

An offense under Title 5, Penal Code, involving a victim younger than 18 years of age, or an offense under Section 25.03, Penal Code, that results in bodily injury to a child younger than 18 years of age, may be prosecuted in the county:

(1) in which an element of the offense was committed;

(2) in which the defendant is apprehended;

(3) in which the victim resides; or

(4) in which the defendant resides.

Art. 13.08. Theft; Organized Retail Theft; Cargo Theft.

(a) Where property is stolen in one county and removed to another county, the offender may be prosecuted either in the county in which the property was stolen or in any other county through or into which the property was removed.

(b) An offense under Section 31.16 or 31.18, Penal Code, may be prosecuted in any county in which an underlying theft could have been prosecuted as a separate offense.

Art. 13.09. Hindering Secured Creditors.

If secured property is taken from one county and unlawfully disposed of in another county or state, the offender may be prosecuted either in the county in which such property was disposed of, or in the county from which it was removed, or in the county in which the security agreement is filed.

Art. 13.10. Persons Acting Under Authority of This State.

An offense committed outside this State by any officer acting under the authority of this State, under circumstances that give this state jurisdiction to prosecute the offender, may be prosecuted in the county of his residence or, if a nonresident of this State, in Travis County.

Art. 13.11. On Vessels.

An offense committed on board a vessel which is at the time upon any navigable water within the boundaries of this State, may be prosecuted in any county through which the vessel is navigated in the course of her voyage, or in the county where the voyage commences or terminates.

Art. 13.12. Trafficking of Persons, False Imprisonment, Kidnapping, and Smuggling of Persons.

Venue for trafficking of persons, false imprisonment, kidnapping, and smuggling of persons is in:

(1) the county in which the offense was committed; or

(2) any county through, into, or out of which the person trafficked, falsely imprisoned, kidnapped, or transported may have been taken.

Art. 13.13. Conspiracy.

Criminal conspiracy may be prosecuted in the county where the conspiracy was entered into, in the county where the conspiracy was agreed to be executed, or in any county in which one or more of the conspirators does any act to effect an object of the conspiracy. If the object of the conspiracy is an offense classified as a felony under the Tax Code, regardless of whether the offense was committed, the conspiracy may be prosecuted in any county in which venue is proper under the Tax Code for the offense. If a conspiracy was entered into outside this State under circumstances that give this State jurisdiction to prosecute the offender, the offender may be prosecuted in the county where the conspiracy was agreed to be executed, in the county where any one of the conspirators was found, or in Travis County.

Art. 13.14. Bigamy.

Bigamy may be prosecuted:

(1) in the county where the bigamous marriage occurred;

(2) in any county in this State in which the parties to such bigamous marriage may live or cohabit together as man and wife; or

(3) in any county in this State in which a party to the bigamous marriage not charged with the offense resides.

Art. 13.15. Sexual Assault.

Sexual assault may be prosecuted in the county in which it is committed, in the county in which the victim is abducted, or in any county through or into which the victim is transported in the course of the abduction and sexual assault. When it shall come to the knowledge of any district judge whose court has jurisdiction under this Article that sexual assault has probably been committed, he shall immediately, if his court be in session, and if not in session, then, at the first term thereafter in any county of the district, call the attention of the grand jury thereto; and if the court be in session, but the grand jury has been discharged, he shall immediately recall the grand jury to investigate the accusation. The district courts are authorized and directed to change the venue in such cases whenever it shall be necessary to secure a speedy trial.

Art. 13.16. Criminal Nonsupport.

Criminal nonsupport may be prosecuted in the county where the offended spouse or child is residing at the time the information or indictment is presented.

Art. 13.17. Proof of Venue.

In all cases mentioned in this Chapter, the indictment or information, or any pleading in the case, may allege that the offense was committed in the county where the prosecution is carried on. To sustain the allegation of venue, it shall only be necessary to prove by the preponderance of the evidence that by reason of the facts in the case, the county where such prosecution is carried on has venue.

Art. 13.18. Other Offenses.

If venue is not specifically stated, the proper county for the prosecution of offenses is that in which the offense was committed.

Art. 13.19. Where Venue Cannot Be Determined.

If an offense has been committed within the state and it cannot readily be determined within which county or counties the commission took place, trial may be held in the county in which the defendant resides, in the county in which he is apprehended, or in the county to which he is extradited.

Art. 13.20. Venue by Consent.

The trial of all felony cases, without a jury, may, with the consent of the defendant in writing, his attorney, and the attorney for the state, be held in any county within the judicial district or districts for the county where venue is otherwise authorized by law.

Art. 13.21. Organized Criminal Activity.

The offense of engaging in organized criminal activity may be prosecuted in any county in which any act is committed to effect an objective of the combination or, if the prosecution is based on a criminal offense classified as a felony under the Tax Code, in any county in which venue is proper under the Tax Code for the offense.

Art. 13.22. Possession and Delivery of Marihuana.

An offense of possession or delivery of marihuana may be prosecuted in the county where the offense was committed or with the consent of the defendant in a county that is adjacent to and in the same judicial district as the county where the offense was committed.

Art. 13.23. Unauthorized Use of a Vehicle.

An offense of unauthorized use of a vehicle may be prosecuted in any county where the unauthorized use of the vehicle occurred or in the county in which the vehicle was originally reported stolen.

Art. 13.24. Illegal Recruitment of Athletes.

An offense of illegal recruitment of an athlete may be prosecuted in any county in which the offense was committed or in the county in which is located the institution of higher education in which the athlete agreed to enroll or was influenced to enroll.

Art. 13.25. Computer Crimes.

(a) In this section "access," "computer," "computer network," "computer program," "computer system," and "owner" have the meanings assigned to those terms by Section 33.01, Penal Code.

(b) An offense under Chapter 33, Penal Code, may be prosecuted in:

(1) the county of the principal place of business of the owner or lessee of a computer, computer network, or computer system involved in the offense;

(2) any county in which a defendant had control or possession of:

(A) any proceeds of the offense; or

(B) any books, records, documents, property, negotiable instruments, computer programs, or other material used in furtherance of the offense;

(3) any county from which, to which, or through which access to a computer, computer network, computer program, or computer system was made in violation of Chapter 33, whether by wires, electromagnetic waves, microwaves, or any other means of communication; or

(4) any county in which an individual who is a victim of the offense resides.

Art. 13.26. Telecommunications Crimes.

An offense under Chapter 33A, Penal Code, may be prosecuted in the county in which the telecommunications service originated or terminated or in the county to which the bill for the telecommunications service was or would have been delivered.

Art. 13.27. Simulating Legal Process.

An offense under Section 32.46, 32.48, 32.49, or 37.13, Penal Code, may be prosecuted either in the county from which any material document was sent or in the county in which it was delivered.

Art. 13.271. Prosecution of Mortgage Fraud.

(a) In this article, "real estate transaction" means a sale, lease, trade, exchange, gift, grant, or other conveyance of a real property interest.

(b) Any offense under Chapter 32, Penal Code, that involves a real estate transaction may be prosecuted in:

(1) the county where the property is located; or

(2) any county in which part of the transaction occurred, including the generation of documentation supporting the transaction.

(c) An offense under Section 32.46, 32.48, or 32.49, Penal Code, that involves a real estate transaction may also be prosecuted in any county authorized by Article 13.27.

Art. 13.28. Escape; Unauthorized Absence.

An offense of escape under Section 38.06, Penal Code, or unauthorized absence under Section 38.113, Penal Code, may be prosecuted in:

(1) the county in which the offense of escape or unauthorized absence was committed; or

(2) the county in which the defendant committed the offense for which the defendant was placed in custody, detained, or required to submit to treatment.

Art. 13.29. Fraudulent Use or Possession of Identifying Information.

An offense under Section 32.51, Penal Code, may be prosecuted in any county in which the offense was committed or in the county of residence for the person whose identifying information was fraudulently obtained, possessed, transferred, or used.

Art. 13.291. Credit Card or Debit Card Abuse.

An offense under Section 32.31, Penal Code, may be prosecuted in any county in which the offense was committed or in the county of residence for any person whose credit card or debit card was unlawfully possessed or used by the defendant.

Art. 13.295. Unauthorized Acquisition or Transfer of Certain Financial Information.

An offense under Section 31.17, Penal Code, may be prosecuted in any county in which the offense was committed or in the county of residence of the person whose financial sight order or payment card information was unlawfully obtained or transferred.

Art. 13.30. Fraudulent, Substandard, or Fictitious Degree.

An offense under Section 32.52, Penal Code, may be prosecuted in the county in which an element of the offense occurs or in Travis County.

Art. 13.31. Failure to Comply with Sex Offender Registration Statute.

An offense under Chapter 62 may be prosecuted in:

(1) any county in which an element of the offense occurs;

(2) the county in which the person subject to Chapter 62 last registered, verified registration, or otherwise complied with a requirement of Chapter 62;

(3) the county in which the person required to register under Chapter 62 has indicated that the person intends to reside, regardless of whether the person establishes or attempts to establish residency in that county;

(4) any county in which the person required to register under Chapter 62 is placed under custodial arrest for an offense subsequent to the person's most recent reportable conviction or adjudication under Chapter 62; or

(5) the county in which the person required to register under Chapter 62 resides or is found by a peace officer, regardless of how long the person has been in the county or intends to stay in the county.

Art. 13.315. Failure to Comply with Sexually Violent Predator Civil Commitment Requirement.

An offense under Section 841.085, Health and Safety Code, may be prosecuted in the county in which any element of the offense occurs or in the court that retains jurisdiction over the civil commitment proceeding under Section 841.082, Health and Safety Code.

Art. 13.32. Misapplication of Certain Property.

(a) An offender who misapplies property held as a fiduciary or property of a financial institution in one county and removes the property to another county may be prosecuted in the county where the offender misapplied the property, in any other county through or into which the offender removed the property, or, as applicable, in the county in which the fiduciary was appointed to serve.

(b) An offense related to misapplication of construction trust funds under Chapter 162, Property Code, must be prosecuted in the county where the construction project is located.

Art. 13.34. Certain Offenses Committed Against a Child Committed to the Texas Juvenile Justice Department.

An offense described by Article 104.003(a) committed by an employee or officer of the Texas Juvenile Justice Department or a person providing services under a contract with the department against a child committed to the department may be prosecuted in:

(1) any county in which an element of the offense occurred; or

(2) Travis County.

Art. 13.35. Money Laundering.

Money laundering may be prosecuted in the county in which the offense was committed as provided by Article 13.18 or, if the prosecution is based on a criminal offense classified as a felony under the Tax Code, in any county in which venue is proper under the Tax Code for the offense.

Art. 13.36. Stalking.

The offense of stalking may be prosecuted in any county in which an element of the offense occurred.

Art. 13.37. Obstruction or Retaliation.

An offense under Section 36.06(a)(1), Penal Code, may be prosecuted in any county in which:

(1) the harm occurs; or

(2) the threat to do harm originated or was received.

Art. 13.38. Venue for Protective Order Offenses.

The venue for an offense under Section 25.07 or 25.072, Penal Code, is in the county in which the order was issued or, without regard to the identity or location of the court that issued the protective order, in the county in which the offense was committed.

Art. 13.40. False Report to Induce Emergency Response.

An offense under Section 42.0601, Penal Code, may be prosecuted in any county in which:

(1) the defendant resides;

(2) the false report was made; or

(3) a law enforcement agency or other emergency responder responded to the false report.

ARREST, COMMITMENT AND BAIL

CHAPTER 14 ARREST WITHOUT WARRANT

Art. 14.01. Offense Within View.

(a) A peace officer or any other person, may, without a warrant, arrest an offender when the offense is committed in his presence or within his view, if the offense is one classed as a felony or as an offense against the public peace.

(b) A peace officer may arrest an offender without a warrant for any offense committed in his presence or within his view.

Art. 14.02. Within View of Magistrate.

A peace officer may arrest, without warrant, when a felony or breach of the peace has been committed in the presence or within the view of a magistrate, and such magistrate verbally orders the arrest of the offender.

Art. 14.03. Authority of Peace Officers.

(a) Any peace officer may arrest, without warrant:

(1) persons found in suspicious places and under circumstances which reasonably show that such persons have been guilty of some felony, violation of Title 9, Chapter 42, Penal Code, breach of the peace, or offense under Section 49.02, Penal Code, or threaten, or are about to commit some offense against the laws;

(2) persons who the peace officer has probable cause to believe have committed an assault resulting in bodily injury to another person and the peace officer has probable cause to believe that there is danger of further bodily injury to that person;

(3) persons who the peace officer has probable cause to believe have committed an offense defined by Section 25.07, Penal Code, if the offense is not committed in the presence of the peace officer;

(4) persons who the peace officer has probable cause to believe have committed an offense involving family violence;

(5) persons who the peace officer has probable cause to believe have prevented or interfered with an individual's ability to place a telephone call in an emergency, as defined by Section 42.062(d), Penal Code, if the offense is not committed in the presence of the peace officer; or

(6) a person who makes a statement to the peace officer that would be admissible against the person under Article 38.21 and establishes probable cause to believe that the person has committed a felony.

(b) A peace officer shall arrest, without a warrant, a person the peace officer has probable cause to believe has committed an offense under Section 25.07, Penal Code, if the offense is committed in the presence of the peace officer.

(c) If reasonably necessary to verify an allegation of a violation of a protective order or of the commission of an offense involving family violence, a peace officer shall remain at the scene of the investigation to verify the allegation and to prevent the further commission of the violation or of family violence.

(d) A peace officer who is outside his jurisdiction may arrest, without warrant, a person who commits an offense within the officer's presence or view, if the offense is a felony, a violation of Chapter 42 or 49, Penal Code, or a breach of the peace. A peace officer making an arrest under this subsection shall, as soon as practicable after making the arrest, notify a law enforcement agency having jurisdiction where the arrest was made. The law enforcement agency shall then take custody of the person committing the offense and take the person before a magistrate in compliance with Article 14.06 of this code.

(e) The justification for conduct provided under Section 9.21, Penal Code, applies to a peace officer when the peace officer is performing a duty required by this article.

(f) In this article, "family violence" has the meaning assigned by Section 71.004, Family Code.

(g) (1) A peace officer listed in Subdivision (1), (2), or (5), Article 2.12, who is licensed under Chapter 1701, Occupations Code, and is outside of the officer's jurisdiction may arrest without a warrant a person who commits any offense within the officer's presence or view, other than a violation of Subtitle C, Title 7, Transportation Code.

(2) A peace officer listed in Subdivision (3), Article 2.12, who is licensed under Chapter 1701, Occupations Code, and is outside of the officer's jurisdiction may arrest without a warrant a person who commits any offense within the officer's presence or view, except that an officer described in this subdivision who is outside of that officer's jurisdiction may arrest a person for a violation of Subtitle C, Title 7, Transportation Code, only if the offense is committed in the county or counties in which the municipality employing the peace officer is located.

(3) A peace officer making an arrest under this subsection shall as soon as practicable after making the arrest notify a law enforcement agency having jurisdiction where the arrest was made. The law enforcement agency shall then take custody of:

(A) the person committing the offense and take the person before a magistrate in compliance with Article 14.06; and

(B) any property seized during or after the arrest as if the property had been seized by a peace officer of that law enforcement agency.

(h) (1) A peace officer who is acting in the lawful discharge of the officer's official duties may disarm a person at any time the officer reasonably believes it is necessary for the protection of the person, officer, or another individual. The peace officer shall return the handgun to the person before discharging the person from the scene if the officer determines that the person is not a threat to the officer, person, or another individual and if the person has not committed a violation that results in the arrest of the person.

(2) A peace officer who is acting in the lawful discharge of the officer's official duties may temporarily disarm a person when the person enters a nonpublic, secure portion of a law enforcement facility, if the law enforcement agency provides a gun locker or other secure area where the peace officer can secure the person's handgun. The peace officer shall secure the handgun in the locker or other secure area and shall return the handgun to the person immediately after the person leaves the nonpublic, secure portion of the law enforcement facility.

(3) For purposes of this subsection, "law enforcement facility" and "nonpublic, secure portion of a law enforcement facility" have the meanings assigned by Section 411.207, Government Code.

Art. 14.031. Public Intoxication.

(a) In lieu of arresting an individual who is not a child, as defined by Section 51.02, Family Code, and who commits an offense under Section 49.02, Penal Code, a peace officer may release the individual if:

(1) the officer believes detention in a penal facility is unnecessary for the protection of the individual or others; and

(2) the individual:

(A) is released to the care of an adult who agrees to assume responsibility for the individual;

(B) verbally consents to voluntary treatment for substance use in a program in a treatment facility licensed and approved by the Health and Human Services Commission, and the program admits the individual for treatment; or

(C) verbally consents to voluntary admission to a facility that provides a place for individuals to become sober under supervision, and the facility admits the individual for supervision.

(b) A magistrate may release from custody an individual who is not a child, as defined by Section 51.02, Family Code, and who is arrested under Section 49.02, Penal Code, if the magistrate determines the individual meets the conditions required for release in lieu of arrest under Subsection (a) of this article.

(c) The release of an individual under Subsection (a) or (b) of this article to a substance use treatment program or a facility that provides a place for individuals to become sober under supervision may not be considered by a peace officer or magistrate in determining whether the individual should be released to such a program or facility for a subsequent incident or arrest under Section 49.02, Penal Code.

(d) A peace officer and the agency or political subdivision that employs the peace officer may not be held liable for damage to persons or property that results from the actions of an individual released under Subsection (a) or (b) of this article.

Art. 14.035. Authority to Release in Lieu of Arrest Certain Persons with Intellectual or Developmental Disability.

(a) This article applies only to a person with an intellectual or developmental disability who resides at one of the following types of facilities operated under the home and community-based services waiver program in accordance with Section 1915(c) of the Social Security Act (42 U.S.C. Section 1396n):

(1) a group home; or

(2) an intermediate care facility for persons with an intellectual or developmental disability (ICF/IID) as defined by 40 T.A.C. Section 9.153.

(b) In lieu of arresting a person described by Subsection (a), a peace officer may release the person at the person's residence if the officer:

(1) believes confinement of the person in a correctional facility as defined by Section 1.07, Penal Code, is unnecessary to protect the person and the other persons who reside at the residence; and

(2) made reasonable efforts to consult with the staff at the person's residence and with the person regarding that decision.

(c) A peace officer and the agency or political subdivision that employs the peace officer may not be held liable for damage to persons or property that results from the actions of a person released under Subsection (b).

Art. 14.04. When Felony Has Been Committed.

Where it is shown by satisfactory proof to a peace officer, upon the representation of a credible person, that a felony has been committed, and that the offender is about to escape, so that there is no time to procure a warrant, such peace officer may, without warrant, pursue and arrest the accused.

Art. 14.05. Rights of Officer.

In each case enumerated where arrests may be lawfully made without warrant, the officer or person making the arrest is justified in adopting all the measures which he might adopt in cases of arrest under warrant, except that an officer making an arrest without a warrant may not enter a residence to make the arrest unless:

(1) a person who resides in the residence consents to the entry; or

(2) exigent circumstances require that the officer making the arrest enter the residence without the consent of a resident or without a warrant.

Art. 14.051. Arrest by Peace Officer from Other Jurisdiction.

(a) A peace officer commissioned and authorized by another state to make arrests for felonies who is in fresh pursuit of a person for the purpose of arresting that person for a felony may continue the pursuit into this state and arrest the person.

(b) In this article, "fresh pursuit" means a pursuit without unreasonable delay by a peace officer of a person the officer reasonably suspects has committed a felony.

Art. 14.055. Duty of Officer to Notify Probate Court.

(a) In this article, "ward" has the meaning assigned by Section 22.033, Estates Code.

(b) As soon as practicable, but not later than the first working day after the date a peace officer detains or arrests a person who is a ward, the peace officer or the person having custody of the ward shall notify the court having jurisdiction over the ward's guardianship of the ward's detention or arrest.

Art. 14.06. Must Take Offender Before Magistrate.

(a) Except as otherwise provided by this article, in each case enumerated in this Code, the person making the arrest or the person having custody of the person arrested shall take the person arrested or have him taken without unnecessary delay, but not later than 48 hours after the person is arrested, before the magistrate who may have ordered the arrest, before some magistrate of the county where the arrest was made without an order, or, to provide more expeditiously to the person arrested the warnings described by Article 15.17 of this Code, before a magistrate in any other county of this state. The magistrate shall immediately perform the duties described in Article 15.17 of this Code.

(b) A peace officer who is charging a person, including a child, with committing an offense that is a Class C misdemeanor, other than an offense under Section 49.02, Penal Code, may, instead of taking the person before a magistrate, issue a citation to the person that contains:

(1) written notice of the time and place the person must appear before a magistrate;

(2) the name and address of the person charged;

(3) the offense charged;

(4) information regarding the alternatives to the full payment of any fine or costs assessed against the person, if the person is convicted of the offense and is unable to pay that amount; and

(5) the following admonishment, in boldfaced or underlined type or in capital letters:

"If you are convicted of a misdemeanor offense involving violence where you are or were a spouse, intimate partner, parent, or guardian of the victim or are or were involved in another, similar relationship with the victim, it may be unlawful for you to possess or purchase a firearm, including a handgun or long gun, or ammunition, pursuant to federal law under 18 U.S.C. Section 922(g)(9) or Section 46.04(b), Texas Penal Code. If you have any questions whether these laws make it illegal for you to possess or purchase a firearm, you should consult an attorney."

(c) If the person resides in the county where the offense occurred, a peace officer who is charging a person with committing an offense that is a Class A or B misdemeanor may, instead of taking the person before a magistrate, issue a citation to the person that contains written notice of the time and place the person must appear before a magistrate of this state as described by Subsection (a), the name and address of the person charged, and the offense charged.

(d) Subsection (c) applies only to a person charged with committing an offense under:

(1) Section 481.121, Health and Safety Code, if the offense is punishable under Subsection (b)(1) or (2) of that section;

(1-a) Section 481.1161, Health and Safety Code, if the offense is punishable under Subsection (b)(1) or (2) of that section;

(2) Section 28.03, Penal Code, if the offense is punishable under Subsection (b)(2) of that section;

(3) Section 28.08, Penal Code, if the offense is punishable under Subsection (b)(2) or (3) of that section;

(4) Section 31.03, Penal Code, if the offense is punishable under Subsection (e)(2)(A) of that section;

(5) Section 31.04, Penal Code, if the offense is punishable under Subsection (e)(2) of that section;

(6) Section 38.114, Penal Code, if the offense is punishable as a Class B misdemeanor; or

(7) Section 521.457, Transportation Code.

CHAPTER 15
ARREST UNDER WARRANT

Art. 15.01. Warrant of Arrest.

A "warrant of arrest" is a written order from a magistrate, directed to a peace officer or some other person specially named, commanding him to take the body of the person accused of an offense, to be dealt with according to law.

Art. 15.02. Requisites of Warrant.

It issues in the name of "The State of Texas", and shall be sufficient, without regard to form, if it have these substantial requisites:

1. It must specify the name of the person whose arrest is ordered, if it be known, if unknown, then some reasonably definite description must be given of him.

2. It must state that the person is accused of some offense against the laws of the State, naming the offense.

3. It must be signed by the magistrate, and his office be named in the body of the warrant, or in connection with his signature.

Art. 15.03. Magistrate May Issue Warrant or Summons.

(a) A magistrate may issue a warrant of arrest or a summons:

1. In any case in which he is by law authorized to order verbally the arrest of an offender;

2. When any person shall make oath before the magistrate that another has committed some offense against the laws of the State; and

3. In any case named in this Code where he is specially authorized to issue warrants of arrest.

(b) A summons may be issued in any case where a warrant may be issued, and shall be in the same form as the warrant except that it shall summon the defendant to appear before a magistrate at a stated time and place. The summons shall be served upon a defendant by delivering a copy to him personally, or by leaving it at his dwelling house or usual place of abode with some person of suitable age and discretion then residing therein or by mailing it to the defendant's last known address. If a defendant fails to appear in response to the summons a warrant shall be issued.

(c) For purposes of Subdivision 2, Subsection (a), a person may appear before the magistrate in person or the person's image may be presented to the magistrate through an electronic broadcast system.

(d) A recording of the communication between the person and the magistrate must be made if the person's image is presented through an electronic broadcast system under Subsection (c). If the defendant is charged with the offense, the recording must be preserved until:

(1) the defendant is acquitted of the offense; or

(2) all appeals relating to the offense have been exhausted.

(e) The counsel for the defendant may obtain a copy of the recording on payment of an amount reasonably necessary to cover the costs of reproducing the recording.

(f) In this article, "electronic broadcast system" means a two-way electronic communication of image and sound between a person and magistrate and includes secure Internet videoconferencing.

Art. 15.04. Complaint.

The affidavit made before the magistrate or district or county attorney is called a "complaint" if it charges the commission of an offense.

Art. 15.05. Requisites of Complaint.

The complaint shall be sufficient, without regard to form, if it have these substantial requisites:

1. It must state the name of the accused, if known, and if not known, must give some reasonably definite description of him.

2. It must show that the accused has committed some offense against the laws of the State, either directly or that the affiant has good reason to believe, and does believe, that the accused has committed such offense.

3. It must state the time and place of the commission of the offense, as definitely as can be done by the affiant.

4. It must be signed by the affiant by writing his name or affixing his mark.

Art. 15.051. Polygraph Examination of Complainant Prohibited.

(a) A peace officer or an attorney representing the state may not require, request, or take a polygraph examination of a person who charges or seeks to charge in a complaint the commission of an offense under Section 21.02, 21.11, 22.011, 22.021, or 25.02, Penal Code.

(b) [Repealed.]

(c) [Repealed.]

(d) A complaint may not be dismissed solely:

(1) because a complainant did not take a polygraph examination; or

(2) on the basis of the results of a polygraph examination taken by the complainant.

Art. 15.06. Warrant Extends to Every Part of the State.

A warrant of arrest, issued by any county or district clerk, or by any magistrate (except mayors of an incorporated city or town), shall extend to any part of the State; and any peace officer to whom said warrant is directed, or into whose hands the same has been transferred, shall be authorized to execute the same in any county in this State.

Art. 15.07. Warrant Issued by Other Magistrate.

When a warrant of arrest is issued by any mayor of an incorporated city or town, it cannot be executed in another county than the one in which it issues, except:

1. It be endorsed by a judge of a court of record, in which case it may be executed anywhere in the State; or

2. If it be endorsed by any magistrate in the county in which the accused is found, it may be executed in such county. The endorsement may be: "Let this warrant be executed in the county of ...." Or, if the endorsement is made by a judge of a court of record, then the endorsement may be: "Let this warrant be executed in any county of the State of Texas". Any other words of the same meaning will be sufficient. The endorsement shall be dated, and signed officially by the magistrate making it.

Art. 15.08. Warrant May Be Forwarded.

A warrant of arrest may be forwarded by any method that ensures the transmission of a duplicate of the original warrant, including secure facsimile transmission or other secure electronic means. If issued by any magistrate named in Article 15.06, the peace officer receiving the same shall execute it without delay. If it be issued by any other magistrate than is named in Article 15.06, the peace officer receiving the same shall proceed with it to the nearest magistrate of the peace officer's county, who shall endorse thereon, in substance, these words:

"Let this warrant be executed in the county of ....", which endorsement shall be dated and signed officially by the magistrate making the same.

Art. 15.09. Complaint May Be Forwarded.

A complaint in accordance with Article 15.05, may be forwarded as provided by Article 15.08 to any magistrate in the State; and the magistrate who receives the same shall forthwith issue a warrant for the arrest of the accused; and the accused, when arrested, shall be dealt with as provided in this Chapter in similar cases.

Art. 15.10. Copy to Be Deposited. [Repealed]

Art. 15.11. Duty of Telegraph Manager. [Repealed]

Art. 15.12. Warrant or Complaint Must Be Under Seal. [Repealed]

Art. 15.13. Telegram Prepaid. [Repealed]

Art. 15.14. Arrest After Dismissal Because of Delay.

If a prosecution of a defendant is dismissed under Article 32.01, the defendant may be rearrested for the same criminal conduct alleged in the dismissed prosecution only upon presentation of indictment or information for the offense and the issuance of a capias subsequent to the indictment or information.

Art. 15.15. Private Person Executing Warrant [Repealed].

Repealed by Acts 1991, 72nd Leg., ch. 446 (S.B. 411), § 2, effective June 11, 1991.

Art. 15.16. How Warrant Is Executed.

(a) The officer or person executing a warrant of arrest shall without unnecessary delay take the person or have him taken before the magistrate who issued the warrant or before the magistrate named in the warrant, if the magistrate is in the same county where the person is arrested. If the issuing or named magistrate is in another county, the person arrested shall without unnecessary delay be taken before some magistrate in the county in which he was arrested.

(b) Notwithstanding Subsection (a), to provide more expeditiously to the person arrested the warnings described by Article 15.17, the officer or person executing the arrest warrant may as permitted by that article take the person arrested before a magistrate in a county other than the county of arrest.

Art. 15.17. Duties of Arresting Officer and Magistrate.

(a) In each case enumerated in this Code, the person making the arrest or the person having custody of the person arrested shall without unnecessary delay, but not later than 48 hours after the person is arrested, take the person arrested or have him taken before some magistrate of the county where the accused was arrested or, to provide more expeditiously to the person arrested the warnings described by this article, before a magistrate in any other county of this state. The arrested person may be taken before the magistrate in person or the image of the arrested person may be presented to the magistrate by means of a videoconference. The magistrate shall inform in clear language the person arrested, either in person or through a videoconference, of the accusation against him and of any affidavit filed therewith, of his right to retain counsel, of his right to remain silent, of his right to have an attorney present during any interview with peace officers or attorneys representing the state, of his right to terminate the interview at any time, and of his right to have an examining trial. The magistrate shall also inform the person arrested of the person's right to request the appointment of counsel if the person cannot afford counsel. The magistrate shall inform the person arrested of the procedures for requesting appointment of counsel. If the person does not speak and understand the English language or is deaf, the magistrate shall inform the person in a manner consistent with Articles 38.30 and 38.31, as appropriate. The magistrate shall ensure that reasonable assistance in completing the necessary forms for requesting appointment of counsel is provided to the person at the same time. If the person arrested is indigent and requests appointment of counsel and if the magistrate is authorized under Article 26.04 to appoint counsel for indigent defendants in the county, the magistrate shall appoint counsel in accordance with Article 1.051. If the magistrate is not authorized to appoint counsel, the magistrate shall without unnecessary delay, but not later than 24 hours after the person arrested requests appointment of counsel, transmit, or cause to be transmitted to the court or to the courts' designee authorized under Article 26.04 to appoint counsel in the county, the forms requesting the appointment of counsel. The magistrate shall also inform the person arrested that he is not required to make a statement and that any statement made by him may be used against him. The magistrate shall allow the person arrested reasonable time and opportunity to consult counsel and shall, after determining whether the person is currently on bail for a separate criminal offense, admit the person arrested to bail if allowed by law. A record of the communication between the arrested person and the magistrate shall be made. The record shall be preserved until the earlier of the following dates: (1) the date on which the pretrial hearing ends; or (2) the 91st day after the date on which the record is made if the person is charged with a misdemeanor or the 120th day after the date on which the record is made if the person is charged with a felony. For purposes of this subsection, "videoconference" means a two-way electronic communication of image and sound between the arrested person and the magistrate and includes secure Internet videoconferencing.

(a-1) If a magistrate is provided written or electronic notice of credible information that may establish reasonable cause to believe that a person brought before the magistrate has a mental illness or is a person with an intellectual disability, the magistrate shall conduct the proceedings described by Article 16.22 or 17.032, as appropriate.

(b) After an accused charged with a misdemeanor punishable by fine only is taken before a magistrate under Subsection (a) and the magistrate has identified the accused with certainty, the magistrate may release the accused without bond and order the accused to appear at a later date for arraignment in the applicable justice court or municipal court. The order must state in writing the time, date, and place of the arraignment, and the magistrate must sign the order. The accused shall receive a copy of the order on release. If an accused fails to appear as required by the order, the judge of the court in which the accused is required to appear shall issue a warrant for the arrest of the accused. If the accused is arrested and brought before the judge, the judge may admit the accused to bail, and in admitting the accused to bail, the judge should set as the amount of bail an amount double that generally set for the offense for which the accused was arrested. This subsection does not apply to an accused who has previously been convicted of a felony or a misdemeanor other than a misdemeanor punishable by fine only.

(c) When a deaf accused is taken before a magistrate under this article or Article 14.06 of this Code, an interpreter appointed by the magistrate qualified and sworn as provided in Article 38.31 of this Code shall interpret the warning required by those articles in a language that the accused can understand, including but not limited to sign language.

(d) If a magistrate determines that a person brought before the magistrate after an arrest authorized by Article 14.051 of this code was arrested unlawfully, the magistrate shall release the person from custody. If the magistrate determines that the arrest was lawful, the person arrested is considered a fugitive from justice for the purposes of Article 51.13 of this code, and the disposition of the person is controlled by that article.

(e) In each case in which a person arrested is taken before a magistrate as required by Subsection (a) or Article 15.18(a), a record shall be made of:

(1) the magistrate informing the person of the person's right to request appointment of counsel;

(2) the magistrate asking the person whether the person wants to request appointment of counsel; and

(3) whether the person requested appointment of counsel.

(f) A record required under Subsection (a) or (e) may consist of written forms, electronic recordings, or other documentation as authorized by procedures adopted in the county under Article 26.04(a). The counsel for the defendant may obtain a copy of the record on payment of a reasonable amount to cover the costs of reproduction or, if the defendant is indigent, the court shall provide a copy to the defendant without charging a cost for the copy.

(g) If a person charged with an offense punishable as a misdemeanor appears before a magistrate in compliance with a citation issued under Article 14.06(b) or (c), the magistrate shall perform the duties imposed by this article in the same manner as if the person had been arrested and brought before the magistrate by a peace officer. After the magistrate performs the duties imposed by this article, the magistrate except for good cause shown may release the person on personal bond. If a person who was issued a citation under Article 14.06(c) fails to appear as required by that citation, the magistrate before which the person is required to appear shall issue a warrant for the arrest of the accused.

Art. 15.171. Duty of Officer to Notify Probate Court.

(a) In this article, "ward" has the meaning assigned by Section 22.033, Estates Code.

(b) As soon as practicable, but not later than the first working day after the date a peace officer arrests a person who is a ward, the peace officer or the person having custody of the ward shall notify the court having jurisdiction over the ward's guardianship of the ward's arrest.

Art. 15.18. Arrest for Out-of-County Offense.

(a) A person arrested under a warrant issued in a county other than the one in which the person is arrested shall be taken before a magistrate of the county where the arrest takes place or, to provide more expeditiously to the arrested person the warnings described by Article 15.17, before a magistrate in any other county of this state, including the county where the warrant was issued. The magistrate shall:

(1) take bail, if allowed by law, and, if without jurisdiction, immediately transmit the bond taken to the court having jurisdiction of the offense; or

(2) in the case of a person arrested under warrant for an offense punishable by fine only, accept a written plea of guilty or nolo contendere, set a fine, determine costs, accept payment of the fine and costs, give credit for time served, determine indigency, or, on satisfaction of the judgment, discharge the defendant, as the case may indicate.

(a-1) If the arrested person is taken before a magistrate of a county other than the county that issued the warrant, the magistrate shall inform the person arrested of the procedures for requesting appointment of counsel and ensure that reasonable assistance in completing the necessary forms for requesting appointment of counsel is provided to the person at the same time. If the person requests the appointment of counsel, the magistrate shall, without unnecessary delay but not later than 24 hours after the person requested the appointment of counsel, transmit, or cause to be transmitted, the necessary request forms to a court or the courts' designee authorized under Article 26.04 to appoint counsel in the county issuing the warrant.

(b) Before the 11th business day after the date a magistrate accepts a written plea of guilty or nolo contendere in a case under Subsection (a)(2), the magistrate shall, if without jurisdiction, transmit to the court having jurisdiction of the offense:

(1) the written plea;

(2) any orders entered in the case; and

(3) any fine or costs collected in the case.

(c) The arrested person may be taken before a magistrate by means of an electronic broadcast system as provided by and subject to the requirements of Article 15.17.

(d) This article does not apply to an arrest made pursuant to a capias pro fine issued under Chapter 43 or Article 45.045.

Art. 15.19. Notice of Arrest.

(a) If the arrested person fails or refuses to give bail, as provided in Article 15.18, the arrested person shall be committed to the jail of the county where the person was arrested. The magistrate committing the arrested person shall immediately provide notice to the sheriff of the county in which the offense is alleged to have been committed regarding:

(1) the arrest and commitment, which notice may be given by mail or other written means or by secure facsimile transmission or other secure electronic means; and

(2) whether the person was also arrested under a warrant issued under Section 508.251, Government Code.

(b) If a person is arrested and taken before a magistrate in a county other than the county in which the arrest is made and if the person is remanded to custody, the person may be confined in a jail in the county in which the magistrate serves for a period of not more than 72 hours after the arrest before being transferred to the county jail of the county in which the arrest occurred.

Art. 15.20. Duty of Sheriff Receiving Notice.

(a) Subject to Subsection (b), the sheriff receiving the notice of arrest and commitment under Article 15.19 shall forthwith go or send for the arrested person and have the arrested person brought before the proper court or magistrate.

(b) A sheriff who receives notice under Article 15.19(a)(2) of a warrant issued under Section 508.251, Government Code, shall have the arrested person brought before the proper magistrate or court before the 11th day after the date the person is committed to the jail of the county in which the person was arrested.

Art. 15.21. Release on Personal Bond If Not Timely Demanded.

If the proper office of the county where the offense is alleged to have been committed does not demand an arrested person described by Article 15.19 and take charge of the arrested person before the 11th day after the date the person is committed to the jail of the county in which the person is arrested, a magistrate in the county where the person was arrested shall:

(1) release the arrested person on personal bond without sureties or other security; and

(2) forward the personal bond to:

(A) the sheriff of the county where the offense is alleged to have been committed; or

(B) the court that issued the warrant of arrest.

Art. 15.22. When a Person Is Arrested.

A person is arrested when he has been actually placed under restraint or taken into custody by an officer or person executing a warrant of arrest, or by an officer or person arresting without a warrant.

Art. 15.23. Time of Arrest.

An arrest may be made on any day or at any time of the day or night.

Art. 15.24. What Force May Be Used.

In making an arrest, all reasonable means are permitted to be used to effect it. No greater force, however, shall be resorted to than is necessary to secure the arrest and detention of the accused.

Art. 15.25. May Break Door.

In case of felony, the officer may break down the door of any house for the purpose of making an arrest, if he be refused admittance after giving notice of his authority and purpose.

Art. 15.26. Authority to Arrest Must Be Made Known.

In executing a warrant of arrest, it shall always be made known to the accused under what authority the arrest is made. The warrant shall be executed by the arrest of the defendant. The officer need not have the warrant in his possession at the time of the arrest, provided the warrant was issued under the provisions of this Code, but upon request he shall show the warrant to the defendant as soon as possible. If the officer does not have the warrant in his possession at the time of arrest he shall then inform the defendant of the offense charged and of the fact that a warrant has been issued. The arrest warrant, and any affidavit presented to the magistrate in support of the issuance of the warrant, is public information, and beginning immediately when the warrant is executed the magistrate's clerk shall make a copy of the warrant and the affidavit available for public inspection in the clerk's office during normal business hours. A person may request the clerk to provide copies of the warrant and affidavit on payment of the cost of providing the copies.

Art. 15.27. Notification to Schools Required.

(a) A law enforcement agency that arrests any person or refers a child to the office or official designated by the juvenile board who the agency believes is enrolled as a student in a public primary or secondary school, for an offense listed in Subsection (h), shall attempt to ascertain whether

Code of Criminal Procedure

the person is so enrolled. If the law enforcement agency ascertains that the individual is enrolled as a student in a public primary or secondary school, the head of the agency or a person designated by the head of the agency shall orally notify the superintendent or a person designated by the superintendent in the school district in which the student is enrolled of that arrest or referral within 24 hours after the arrest or referral is made, or before the next school day, whichever is earlier. If the law enforcement agency cannot ascertain whether the individual is enrolled as a student, the head of the agency or a person designated by the head of the agency shall orally notify the superintendent or a person designated by the superintendent in the school district in which the student is believed to be enrolled of that arrest or detention within 24 hours after the arrest or detention, or before the next school day, whichever is earlier. If the individual is a student, the superintendent or the superintendent's designee shall immediately notify all instructional and support personnel who have responsibility for supervision of the student. All personnel shall keep the information received in this subsection confidential. The State Board for Educator Certification may revoke or suspend the certification of personnel who intentionally violate this subsection. Within seven days after the date the oral notice is given, the head of the law enforcement agency or the person designated by the head of the agency shall mail written notification, marked "PERSONAL and CONFIDENTIAL" on the mailing envelope, to the superintendent or the person designated by the superintendent. The written notification must include the facts contained in the oral notification, the name of the person who was orally notified, and the date and time of the oral notification. Both the oral and written notice shall contain sufficient details of the arrest or referral and the acts allegedly committed by the student to enable the superintendent or the superintendent's designee to determine whether there is a reasonable belief that the student has engaged in conduct defined as a felony offense by the Penal Code or whether it is necessary to conduct a threat assessment or prepare a safety plan related to the student. The information contained in the notice shall be considered by the superintendent or the superintendent's designee in making such a determination.

(a-1) The superintendent or a person designated by the superintendent in the school district shall send to a school district employee having direct supervisory responsibility over the student the information contained in the confidential notice under Subsection (a).

(b) On conviction, deferred prosecution, or deferred adjudication or an adjudication of delinquent conduct of an individual enrolled as a student in a public primary or secondary school, for an offense or for any conduct listed in Subsection (h) of this article, the office of the prosecuting attorney acting in the case shall orally notify the superintendent or a person designated by the superintendent in the school district in which the student is enrolled of the conviction or adjudication and whether the student is required to register as a sex offender under Chapter 62. Oral notification must be given within 24 hours of the time of the order or before the next school day, whichever is earlier. The superintendent shall, within 24 hours of receiving notification from the office of the prosecuting attorney, or before the next school day, whichever is earlier, notify all instructional and support personnel who have regular contact with the student. Within seven days after the date the oral notice is given, the office of the prosecuting attorney shall mail written notice, which must contain a statement of the offense of which the individual is convicted or on which the adjudication, deferred adjudication, or deferred prosecution is grounded and a statement of whether the student is required to register as a sex offender under Chapter 62.

(c) A parole, probation, or community supervision office, including a community supervision and corrections department, a juvenile probation department, the paroles division of the Texas Department of Criminal Justice, and the Texas Juvenile Justice Department, having jurisdiction over a student described by Subsection (a), (b), or (e) who transfers from a school or is subsequently removed from a school and later returned to a school or school district other than the one the student was enrolled in when the arrest, referral to a juvenile court, conviction, or adjudication occurred shall within 24 hours of learning of the student's transfer or reenrollment, or before the next school day, whichever is earlier, notify the superintendent or a person designated by the superintendent of the school district to which the student transfers or is returned or, in the case of a private school, the principal or a school employee designated by the principal of the school to which the student transfers or is returned of the arrest or referral in a manner similar to that provided for by Subsection (a) or (e)(1), or of the conviction or delinquent adjudication in a manner similar to that provided for by Subsection (b) or (e)(2). The superintendent of the school district to which the student transfers or is returned or, in the case of a private school, the principal of the school to which the student transfers or is returned shall, within 24 hours of receiving notification under this subsection or before the next school day, whichever is earlier, notify all instructional and support personnel who have regular contact with the student.

(d) [Repealed by Acts 2007, 80th Leg., ch. 1240 (H.B. 2532), § 5, effective June 15, 2007 and Acts 2007, 80th Leg., ch. 1291 (S.B. 6), § 8, effective September 1, 2007.]

(e) (1) A law enforcement agency that arrests, or refers to a juvenile court under Chapter 52, Family Code, an individual who the law enforcement agency knows or believes is enrolled as a student in a private primary or secondary school shall make the oral and written notifications described by Subsection (a) to the principal or a school employee designated by the principal of the school in which the student is enrolled.

(2) On conviction, deferred prosecution, or deferred adjudication or an adjudication of delinquent conduct of an individual enrolled as a student in a private primary or secondary school, the office of prosecuting attorney shall make the oral and written notifications described by Subsection (b) of this article to the principal or a school employee designated by the principal of the school in which the student is enrolled.

(3) The principal of a private school in which the student is enrolled or a school employee designated by the principal shall send to a school employee having direct supervisory responsibility over the student the information contained in the confidential notice, for the same purposes as described by Subsection (a-1) of this article.

(f) A person who receives information under this article may not disclose the information except as specifically authorized by this article. A person who intentionally violates this article commits an offense. An offense under this subsection is a Class C misdemeanor.

(g) The office of the prosecuting attorney or the office or official designated by the juvenile board shall, within two working days, notify the school district that removed a student to a disciplinary alternative education program under Section 37.006, Education Code, if:

(1) prosecution of the student's case was refused for lack of prosecutorial merit or insufficient evidence and no formal proceedings, deferred adjudication, or deferred prosecution will be initiated; or

(2) the court or jury found the student not guilty or made a finding the child did not engage in delinquent conduct or conduct indicating a need for supervision and the case was dismissed with prejudice.

(h) This article applies to any felony offense and the following misdemeanors:

(1) an offense under Section 20.02, 21.08, 22.01, 22.05, 22.07, or 71.02, Penal Code;

(2) the unlawful use, sale, or possession of a controlled substance, drug paraphernalia, or marihuana, as defined by Chapter 481, Health and Safety Code; or

(3) the unlawful possession of any of the weapons or devices listed in Sections 46.01(1)—(14) or (16), Penal Code, or a weapon listed as a prohibited weapon under Section 46.05, Penal Code.

(i) A person may substitute electronic notification for oral notification where oral notification is required by this article. If electronic notification is substituted for oral notification, any written notification required by this article is not required.

(j) The notification provisions of this section concerning a person who is required to register as a sex offender under Chapter 62 do not lessen the requirement of a person to provide any additional notification prescribed by that chapter.

(k) Oral or written notice required under this article must include all pertinent details of the offense or conduct, including details of any:

(1) assaultive behavior or other violence;

(2) weapons used in the commission of the offense or conduct; or

(3) weapons possessed during the commission of the offense or conduct.

(k-1) In addition to the information provided under Subsection (k), the law enforcement agency shall provide to the superintendent or superintendent's designee information relating to the student that is requested for the purpose of conducting a threat assessment or preparing a safety plan relating to that student. A school board may enter into a memorandum of understanding with a law enforcement agency regarding the exchange of information relevant to conducting a threat assessment or preparing a safety plan. Absent a memorandum of understanding, the information requested by the superintendent or the superintendent's designee shall be considered relevant.

(*l*) If a school district board of trustees learns of a failure by the superintendent of the district or a district principal to provide a notice required under Subsection (a), (a-1), or (b), the board of trustees shall report the failure to the State Board for Educator Certification. If the governing body of a private primary or secondary school learns of a failure by the principal of the school to provide a notice required under Subsection (e), and the principal holds a certificate issued under Subchapter B, Chapter 21, Education Code, the governing body shall report the failure to the State Board for Educator Certification.

(m) If the superintendent of a school district in which the student is enrolled learns of a failure of the head of a law enforcement agency or a person designated by the head of the agency to provide a notification under Subsection (a), the superintendent or principal shall report the failure to notify to the Texas Commission on Law Enforcement.

(n) If a juvenile court judge or official designated by the juvenile board learns of a failure by the office of the prosecuting attorney to provide a notification required under Subsection (b) or (g), the official shall report the failure to notify to the elected prosecuting attorney responsible for the operation of the office.

(o) If the supervisor of a parole, probation, or community supervision department officer learns of a failure by the officer to provide a notification under Subsection (c), the supervisor shall report the failure to notify to the director of the entity that employs the officer.

CHAPTER 16
THE COMMITMENT OR DISCHARGE OF THE ACCUSED

Art. 16.01. Examining Trial.

When the accused has been brought before a magistrate for an examining trial that officer shall proceed to examine into the truth of the accusation made, allowing the accused, however, sufficient time to procure counsel. In a proper case, the magistrate may appoint counsel to represent an accused in such examining trial only, to be compensated as otherwise provided in this Code. The accused in any felony case shall have the right to an examining trial before indictment in the county having jurisdiction of the offense, whether he be in custody or on bail, at which time the magistrate at the hearing shall determine the amount or sufficiency of bail, if a bailable case. If the accused has been transferred for criminal prosecution after a hearing under Section 54.02, Family Code, the accused may be granted an examining trial at the discretion of the court.

Art. 16.02. Examination Postponed.

The magistrate may at the request of either party postpone the examination to procure testimony; but the accused shall in the meanwhile be detained in custody unless he give bail to be present from day to day before the magistrate until the examination is concluded, which he may do in all cases except murder and treason.

Art. 16.03. Warning to Accused.

Before the examination of the witnesses, the magistrate shall inform the accused that it is his right to make a statement relative to the accusation brought against him, but at the same time shall also inform him that he cannot be compelled to make any statement whatever, and that if he does make such statement, it may be used in evidence against him.

Art. 16.04. Voluntary Statement.

If the accused desires to make a voluntary statement, he may do so before the examination of any witness, but not afterward. His statement shall be reduced to writing by or under the direction of the magistrate, or by the accused or his counsel, and shall be signed by the accused by affixing his name or mark, but shall not be sworn to by him. The magistrate shall attest by his own certificate and signature to the execution and signing of the statement.

Art. 16.05. Witness Placed Under Rule [Repealed].

Repealed by Texas Court of Criminal Appeals pursuant to Acts 1985, 69th Leg., ch. 685 (H.B. 13), § 9.

Art. 16.06. Counsel May Examine Witness.

The counsel for the State, and the accused or his counsel may question the witnesses on direct or cross examination. If no counsel appears for the State the magistrate may examine the witnesses.

Art. 16.07. Same Rules of Evidence As on Final Trial.

The same rules of evidence shall apply to and govern a trial before an examining court that apply to and govern a final trial.

Art. 16.08. Presence of the Accused.

The examination of each witness shall be in the presence of the accused.

Art. 16.09. Testimony Reduced to Writing.

The testimony of each witness shall be reduced to writing by or under the direction of the magistrate, and shall then be read over to the witness, or he may read it over himself. Such corrections shall be made in the same as the witness may direct; and he shall then sign the same by affixing thereto his name or mark. All the testimony thus taken shall be certified to by the magistrate. In lieu of the above provision, a statement of facts authenticated by State and defense counsel and approved by the presiding magistrate may be used to preserve the testimony of witnesses.

Art. 16.10. Attachment for Witness.

The magistrate has the power in all cases, where a witness resides or is in the county where the prosecution is pending, to issue an attachment for the purpose of enforcing the attendance of such witness; this he may do without having previously issued a subpoena for that purpose.

Art. 16.11. Attachment to Another County.

The magistrate may issue an attachment for a witness to any county in the State, when affidavit is made by the party applying therefor that the testimony of the witness is material to the prosecution, or the defense, as the case may be; and the affidavit shall further state the facts which it is expected will be proved by the witness; and if the facts set forth are not considered material by the magistrate, or if they be admitted to be true by the adverse party, the attachment shall not issue.

Art. 16.12. Witness Need Not Be Tendered His Witness Fees or Expenses.

A witness attached need not be tendered his witness fees or expenses.

Art. 16.13. Attachment Executed Forthwith.

The officer receiving the attachment shall execute it forthwith by bringing before the magistrate the witness named therein, unless such witness shall give bail for his appearance before the magistrate at the time and place required by the writ.

Art. 16.14. Postponing Examination.

After examining the witness in attendance, if it appear to the magistrate that there is other important testimony which may be had by a postponement, he shall, at the request of the prosecutor or of the defendant, postpone the hearing for a reasonable time to enable such testimony to be procured; but in such case the accused shall remain in the custody of the proper officer until the day fixed for such further examination. No postponement shall take place, unless a sworn statement be made by the defendant, or the prosecutor, setting forth the name and residence of the witness, and the facts which it is expected will be proved. If it be testimony other than that of a witness, the statement made shall set forth the nature of the evidence. If the magistrate is satisfied that the testimony is not material, or if the same be admitted to be true by the adverse party, the postponement shall be refused.

Art. 16.15. Who May Discharge Capital Offense.

The examination of one accused of a capital offense shall be conducted by a justice of the peace, county judge, county court at law, or county criminal court. The judge may admit to bail, except in capital cases where the proof is evident.

Art. 16.16. If Insufficient Bail Has Been Taken.

Where it is made to appear by affidavit to a judge of the Court of Criminal Appeals, a justice of a court of appeals, or to a judge of the district or county court, that the bail taken in any case is insufficient in amount, or that the sureties are not good for the amount, or that the bond is for any reason defective or insufficient, such judge shall issue a warrant of arrest, and require of the defendant sufficient bond and security, according to the nature of the case.

Art. 16.17. Decision of Judge.

After the examining trial has been had, the judge shall make an order committing the defendant to the jail of the proper county, discharging him or admitting him to bail, as the law and facts of the case may require. Failure of the judge to make or enter an order within 48 hours after the examining trial has been completed operates as a finding of no probable cause and the accused shall be discharged.

Art. 16.18. When No Safe Jail.

If there is no safe jail in the county in which the prosecution is carried on, the magistrate may commit defendant to the nearest safe jail in any other county.

Art. 16.19. Warrant in Such Case.

The commitment in the case mentioned in the preceding Article shall be directed to the sheriff of the county to which the defendant is sent, but the sheriff of the county from which the defendant is taken shall be required to deliver the prisoner into the hands of the sheriff to whom he is sent.

Art. 16.20. "Commitment".

A "commitment" is an order signed by the proper magistrate directing a sheriff to receive and place in jail the person so committed. It will be sufficient if it have the following requisites:

1. That it run in the name of "The State of Texas";

2. That it be addressed to the sheriff of the county to the jail of which the defendant is committed;

3. That it state in plain language the offense for which the defendant is committed, and give his name, if it be known, or if unknown, contain an accurate description of the defendant;

4. That it state to what court and at what time the defendant is to be held to answer;

5. When the prisoner is sent out of the county where the prosecution arose, the warrant of commitment shall state that there is no safe jail in the proper county; and

6. If bail has been granted, the amount of bail shall be stated in the warrant of commitment.

Art. 16.21. Duty of Sheriff As to Prisoners.

Every sheriff shall keep safely a person committed to his custody. He shall use no cruel or unusual means to secure this end, but shall adopt all necessary measures to prevent the escape of a prisoner. He may summon a guard of sufficient number, in case it becomes necessary to prevent an escape from jail, or the rescue of a prisoner.

Art. 16.22. Early Identification of Defendant Suspected of Having Mental Illness or Intellectual Disability.

(a) (1) Not later than 12 hours after the sheriff or municipal jailer having custody of a defendant for an offense punishable as a Class B misdemeanor or any higher category of offense receives credible information that may establish reasonable cause to believe that the defendant has a mental illness or is a person with an intellectual disability, the sheriff or municipal jailer shall provide written or electronic notice to the magistrate. The notice must include any information related to the sheriff's or municipal jailer's determination, such as information regarding the defendant's behavior immediately before, during, and after the defendant's arrest and, if applicable, the results of any previous assessment of the defendant. On a determination that there is reasonable cause to believe that the defendant has a mental illness or is a person with an intellectual disability, the magistrate, except as provided by Subdivision (2), shall order the service provider that contracts with the jail to provide mental health or intellectual and developmental disability services, the local mental health authority, the local intellectual and developmental disability authority, or another qualified mental health or intellectual and developmental disability expert to:

(A) interview the defendant if the defendant has not previously been interviewed by a qualified mental health or intellectual and developmental disability expert on or after the date the defendant was arrested for the offense for which the defendant is in custody and otherwise collect information regarding whether the defendant has a mental illness as defined by Section 571.003, Health and Safety Code, or is a person with an intellectual disability as defined by Section 591.003, Health and Safety Code, including, if applicable, information obtained from any previous assessment of the defendant and information regarding any previously recommended treatment or service; and

(B) provide to the magistrate a written report of an interview described by Paragraph (A) and the other information collected under that paragraph on the form approved by the Texas Correctional Office on Offenders with Medical or Mental Impairments under Section 614.0032(c), Health and Safety Code.

(2) The magistrate is not required to order the interview and collection of other information under Subdivision (1) if the defendant is no longer in custody or if the defendant in the year preceding the defendant's applicable date of arrest has been determined to have a mental illness or to be a person with an intellectual disability by the service provider that contracts with the jail to provide mental health or intellectual and developmental disability services, the local mental health authority, the local intellectual and developmental disability authority, or another mental health or intellectual and developmental disability expert described by Subdivision (1). A court that elects to use the results of that previous determination may proceed under Subsection (c).

(3) If the defendant fails or refuses to submit to the interview and collection of other information regarding the defendant as required under Subdivision (1), the magistrate may order the defendant to submit to an examination in a jail, or in another place determined to be appropriate by the local mental health authority or local intellectual and developmental disability authority, for a reasonable period not to exceed 72 hours. If applicable, the county in which the committing court is located shall reimburse the local mental health authority or local intellectual and developmental disability authority for the mileage and per diem expenses of the personnel required to transport the defendant, calculated in accordance with the state travel regulations in effect at the time.

(a-1) If a magistrate orders a local mental health authority, a local intellectual and developmental disability authority, or another qualified mental health or intellectual and developmental disability expert to conduct an interview or collect information under Subsection (a)(1), the commissioners court for the county in which the magistrate is located shall reimburse the local mental health authority, local intellectual and developmental disability authority, or qualified mental health or intellectual and developmental disability expert for the cost of performing those duties in the amount provided by the fee schedule adopted under Subsection (a-2) or in the amount determined by the judge under Subsection (a-3), as applicable.

(a-2) The commissioners court for a county may adopt a fee schedule to pay for the costs to conduct an interview and collect information under Subsection (a)(1). In developing the fee schedule, the commissioners court shall consider the generally accepted reasonable cost in that county of performing the duties described by Subsection (a)(1). A fee schedule described by this subsection must be adopted in a public hearing and must be periodically reviewed by the commissioners court.

(a-3) If the cost of performing the duties described by Subsection (a)(1) exceeds the amount provided by the applicable fee schedule or if the commissioners court for the applicable county has not adopted a fee schedule, the authority or expert who performed the duties may request that the judge who has jurisdiction over the underlying offense determine the reasonable amount for which the authority or expert is entitled to be reimbursed under Subsection (a-1). The amount determined under this subsection may not be less than the amount provided by the fee schedule, if applicable. The judge shall determine the amount not later than the 45th day after the date the request is made. The judge is not required to hold a hearing before making a determination under this subsection.

(a-4) An interview under Subsection (a)(1) may be conducted in person in the jail, by telephone, or through a telemedicine medical service or telehealth service.

(b) Except as otherwise permitted by the magistrate for good cause shown, a written report of an interview described by Subsection (a)(1)(A) and the other information collected under that paragraph shall be provided to the magistrate:

(1) for a defendant held in custody, not later than 96 hours after the time an order was issued under Subsection (a); or

(2) for a defendant released from custody, not later than the 30th day after the date an order was issued under Subsection (a).

(b-1) The magistrate shall provide copies of the written report to:

(1) the defense counsel;

(2) the attorney representing the state;

(3) the trial court;

(4) the sheriff or other person responsible for the defendant's medical records while the defendant is confined in county jail; and

(5) as applicable:

(A) any personal bond office established under Article 17.42 for the county in which the defendant is being confined; or

(B) the director of the office or department that is responsible for supervising the defendant while the defendant is released on bail and receiving mental health or intellectual and developmental disability services as a condition of bail.

(b-2) The written report must include a description of the procedures used in the interview and collection of other information under Subsection (a)(1)(A) and the applicable expert's observations and findings pertaining to:

(1) whether the defendant is a person who has a mental illness or is a person with an intellectual disability;

(2) whether there is clinical evidence to support a belief that the defendant may be incompetent to stand trial and should undergo a complete competency examination under Subchapter B, Chapter 46B; and

(3) any appropriate or recommended treatment or service.

(c) After the trial court receives the applicable expert's written report relating to the defendant under Subsection (b-1) or elects to use the results of a previous determination as described by Subsection (a)(2), the trial court may, as applicable:

(1) resume criminal proceedings against the defendant, including any appropriate proceedings related to the defendant's release on personal bond under Article 17.032 if the defendant is being held in custody;

(2) resume or initiate competency proceedings, if required, as provided by Chapter 46B;

(3) consider the written report during the punishment phase after a conviction of the offense for which the defendant was arrested, as part of a presentence investigation report, or in connection with the impositions of conditions following placement on community supervision, including deferred adjudication community supervision;

(4) refer the defendant to an appropriate specialty court established or operated under Subtitle K, Title 2, Government Code; or

(5) if the offense charged does not involve an act, attempt, or threat of serious bodily injury to

another person, release the defendant on bail while charges against the defendant remain pending and enter an order transferring the defendant to the appropriate court for court-ordered outpatient mental health services under Chapter 574, Health and Safety Code.

(c-1) If an order is entered under Subsection (c)(5), an attorney representing the state shall file the application for court-ordered outpatient services under Chapter 574, Health and Safety Code.

(c-2) On the motion of an attorney representing the state, if the court determines the defendant has complied with appropriate court-ordered outpatient treatment, the court may dismiss the charges pending against the defendant and discharge the defendant.

(c-3) On the motion of an attorney representing the state, if the court determines the defendant has failed to comply with appropriate court-ordered outpatient treatment, the court shall proceed under this chapter or with the trial of the offense.

(d) This article does not prevent the applicable court from, before, during, or after the interview and collection of other information regarding the defendant as described by this article:

(1) releasing a defendant who has a mental illness or is a person with an intellectual disability from custody on personal or surety bond, including imposing as a condition of release that the defendant submit to an examination or other assessment; or

(2) ordering an examination regarding the defendant's competency to stand trial.

(e) The Texas Judicial Council shall adopt rules to require the reporting of the number of written reports provided to a court under Subsection (a)(1)(B). The rules must require submission of the reports to the Office of Court Administration of the Texas Judicial System on a monthly basis.

(f) A written report submitted to a magistrate under Subsection (a)(1)(B) is confidential and not subject to disclosure under Chapter 552, Government Code, but may be used or disclosed as provided by this article.

Art. 16.23. Diversion of Persons Suffering Mental Health Crisis or Substance Abuse Issue.

(a) Each law enforcement agency shall make a good faith effort to divert a person suffering a mental health crisis or suffering from the effects of substance abuse to a proper treatment center in the agency's jurisdiction if:

(1) there is an available and appropriate treatment center in the agency's jurisdiction to which the agency may divert the person;

(2) it is reasonable to divert the person;

(3) the offense that the person is accused of is a misdemeanor, other than a misdemeanor involving violence; and

(4) the mental health crisis or substance abuse issue is suspected to be the reason the person committed the alleged offense.

(b) Subsection (a) does not apply to a person who is accused of an offense under Section 49.04, 49.045, 49.05, 49.06, 49.065, 49.07, or 49.08, Penal Code.

CHAPTER 17
BAIL

Art. 17.01. Definition of "Bail".

"Bail" is the security given by the accused that he will appear and answer before the proper court the accusation brought against him, and includes a bail bond or a personal bond.

Art. 17.02. Definition of "Bail Bond".

A "bail bond" is a written undertaking entered into by the defendant and the defendant's sureties for the appearance of the principal therein before a court or magistrate to answer a criminal accusation; provided, however, that the defendant on execution of the bail bond may deposit with the custodian of funds of the court in which the prosecution is pending current money of the United States in the amount of the bond in lieu of having sureties signing the same. Any cash funds deposited under this article shall be receipted for by the officer receiving the funds and, on order of the court, be refunded in the amount shown on the face of the receipt less the administrative fee authorized by Section 117.055, Local Government Code, after the defendant complies with the conditions of the defendant's bond, to:

(1) any person in the name of whom a receipt was issued, including the defendant if a receipt was issued to the defendant; or

(2) the defendant, if no other person is able to produce a receipt for the funds.

Art. 17.025. Officers Taking Bail Bond.

A jailer licensed under Chapter 1701, Occupations Code, is considered to be an officer for the purposes of taking a bail bond and discharging any other related powers and duties under this chapter.

Art. 17.026. Electronic Filing of Bail Bond.

In any manner permitted by the county in which the bond is written, a bail bond may be filed electronically with the court, judge, magistrate, or other officer taking the bond.

Art. 17.03. Personal Bond.

(a) Except as provided by Subsection (b) or (b-1), a magistrate may, in the magistrate's discretion, release the defendant on personal bond without sureties or other security.

(b) Only the court before whom the case is pending may release on personal bond a defendant who:

(1) is charged with an offense under the following sections of the Penal Code:

(A) Section 19.03 (Capital Murder);

(B) Section 20.04 (Aggravated Kidnapping);

(C) Section 22.021 (Aggravated Sexual Assault);

(D) Section 22.03 (Deadly Assault on Law Enforcement or Corrections Officer, Member or Employee of Board of Pardons and Paroles, or Court Participant);

(E) Section 22.04 (Injury to a Child, Elderly Individual, or Disabled Individual);

(F) Section 29.03 (Aggravated Robbery);

(G) Section 30.02 (Burglary);

(H) Section 71.02 (Engaging in Organized Criminal Activity);

(I) Section 21.02 (Continuous Sexual Abuse of Young Child or Disabled Individual); or

(J) Section 20A.03 (Continuous Trafficking of Persons);

(2) is charged with a felony under Chapter 481, Health and Safety Code, or Section 485.033, Health and Safety Code, punishable by imprisonment for a minimum term or by a maximum fine that is more than a minimum term or maximum fine for a first degree felony; or

(3) does not submit to testing for the presence of a controlled substance in the defendant's body as requested by the court or magistrate under Subsection (c) of this article or submits to testing and the test shows evidence of the presence of a controlled substance in the defendant's body.

(b-1) A magistrate may not release on personal bond a defendant who, at the time of the commission of the charged offense, is civilly committed as a sexually violent predator under Chapter 841, Health and Safety Code.

(c) When setting a personal bond under this chapter, on reasonable belief by the investigating or arresting law enforcement agent or magistrate of the presence of a controlled substance in the defendant's body or on the finding of drug or alcohol abuse related to the offense for which the defendant is charged, the court or a magistrate shall require as a condition of personal bond that the defendant submit to testing for alcohol or a controlled substance in the defendant's body and participate in an alcohol or drug abuse treatment or education program if such a condition will serve to reasonably assure the appearance of the defendant for trial.

(d) The state may not use the results of any test conducted under this chapter in any criminal proceeding arising out of the offense for which the defendant is charged.

(e) Costs of testing may be assessed as court costs or ordered paid directly by the defendant as a condition of bond.

(f) In this article, "controlled substance" has the meaning assigned by Section 481.002, Health and Safety Code.

(g) The court may order that a personal bond fee assessed under Section 17.42 be:

(1) paid before the defendant is released;

(2) paid as a condition of bond;

(3) paid as court costs;

(4) reduced as otherwise provided for by statute; or

(5) waived.

Art. 17.031. Release on Personal Bond.

(a) Any magistrate in this state may release a defendant eligible for release on personal bond under Article 17.03 of this code on his personal bond where the complaint and warrant for arrest does not originate in the county wherein the accused is arrested if the magistrate would have had jurisdiction over the matter had the complaint arisen within the county wherein the magistrate presides. The personal bond may not be revoked by the judge of the court issuing the warrant for arrest except for good cause shown.

(b) If there is a personal bond office in the county from which the warrant for arrest was issued, the court releasing a defendant on his personal bond will forward a copy of the personal bond to the personal bond office in that county.

Art. 17.032. Release on Personal Bond of Certain Defendants with Mental Illness or Intellectual Disability.

(a) In this article, "violent offense" means an offense under the following sections of the Penal Code:

(1) Section 19.02 (murder);

(2) Section 19.03 (capital murder);

(3) Section 20.03 (kidnapping);

Code of Criminal Procedure

(4) Section 20.04 (aggravated kidnapping);
(5) Section 21.11 (indecency with a child);
(6) Section 22.01(a)(1) (assault), if the offense involved family violence as defined by Section 71.004, Family Code;
(7) Section 22.011 (sexual assault);
(8) Section 22.02 (aggravated assault);
(9) Section 22.021 (aggravated sexual assault);
(10) Section 22.04 (injury to a child, elderly individual, or disabled individual);
(11) Section 29.03 (aggravated robbery);
(12) Section 21.02 (continuous sexual abuse of young child or disabled individual); or
(13) Section 20A.03 (continuous trafficking of persons).

(b) Notwithstanding Article 17.03(b), or a bond schedule adopted or a standing order entered by a judge, a magistrate shall release a defendant on personal bond unless good cause is shown otherwise if:

(1) the defendant is not charged with and has not been previously convicted of a violent offense;

(2) the defendant is examined by the service provider that contracts with the jail to provide mental health or intellectual and developmental disability services, the local mental health authority, the local intellectual and developmental disability authority, or another qualified mental health or intellectual and developmental disability expert under Article 16.22;

(3) the applicable expert, in a written report submitted to the magistrate under Article 16.22:

(A) concludes that the defendant has a mental illness or is a person with an intellectual disability and is nonetheless competent to stand trial; and

(B) recommends mental health treatment or intellectual and developmental disability services for the defendant, as applicable;

(4) the magistrate determines, in consultation with the local mental health authority or local intellectual and developmental disability authority, that appropriate community-based mental health or intellectual and developmental disability services for the defendant are available in accordance with Section 534.053 or 534.103, Health and Safety Code, or through another mental health or intellectual and developmental disability services provider; and

(5) the magistrate finds, after considering all the circumstances, a pretrial risk assessment, if applicable, and any other credible information provided by the attorney representing the state or the defendant, that release on personal bond would reasonably ensure the defendant's appearance in court as required and the safety of the community and the victim of the alleged offense.

(c) The magistrate, unless good cause is shown for not requiring treatment or services, shall require as a condition of release on personal bond under this article that the defendant submit to outpatient or inpatient mental health treatment or intellectual and developmental disability services as recommended by the service provider that contracts with the jail to provide mental health or intellectual and developmental disability services, the local mental health authority, the local intellectual and developmental disability authority, or another qualified mental health or intellectual and developmental disability expert if the defendant's:

(1) mental illness or intellectual disability is chronic in nature; or

(2) ability to function independently will continue to deteriorate if the defendant does not receive the recommended treatment or services.

(d) In addition to a condition of release imposed under Subsection (c), the magistrate may require the defendant to comply with other conditions that are reasonably necessary to ensure the defendant's appearance in court as required and the safety of the community and the victim of the alleged offense.

(e) In this article, a person is considered to have been convicted of an offense if:

(1) a sentence is imposed;

(2) the person is placed on community supervision or receives deferred adjudication; or

(3) the court defers final disposition of the case.

Art. 17.033. Release on Bond of Certain Persons Arrested Without a Warrant.

(a) Except as provided by Subsection (c), a person who is arrested without a warrant and who is detained in jail must be released on bond, in an amount not to exceed $5,000, not later than the 24th hour after the person's arrest if the person was arrested for a misdemeanor and a magistrate has not determined whether probable cause exists to believe that the person committed the offense. If the person is unable to obtain a surety for the bond or unable to deposit money in the amount of the bond, the person must be released on personal bond.

(a-1) [Expired pursuant to Acts 2011, 82nd Leg., ch. 1350 (H.B. 1173), § 1, effective September 1, 2013.]

(b) Except as provided by Subsection (c), a person who is arrested without a warrant and who is detained in jail must be released on bond, in an amount not to exceed $10,000, not later than the 48th hour after the person's arrest if the person was arrested for a felony and a magistrate has not determined whether probable cause exists to believe that the person committed the offense. If the person is unable to obtain a surety for the bond or unable to deposit money in the amount of the bond, the person must be released on personal bond.

(c) On the filing of an application by the attorney representing the state, a magistrate may postpone the release of a person under Subsection (a) or (b) for not more than 72 hours after the person's arrest. An application filed under this subsection must state the reason a magistrate has not determined whether probable cause exists to believe that the person committed the offense for which the person was arrested.

(d) The time limits imposed by Subsections (a) and (b) do not apply to a person arrested without a warrant who is taken to a hospital, clinic, or other medical facility before being taken before a magistrate under Article 15.17. For a person described by this subsection, the time limits imposed by Subsections (a) and (b) begin to run at the time, as documented in the records of the hospital, clinic, or other medical facility, that a physician or other medical professional releases the person from the hospital, clinic, or other medical facility.

(e) [Expired pursuant to Acts 2011, 82nd Leg., ch. 1350 (H.B. 1173), § 1, effective September 1, 2013.]

Art. 17.0331. Impact Study [Expired].

Expired pursuant to Acts 2011, 82nd Leg., ch. 1350 (H.B. 1173), § 2, effective September 1, 2013.

Art. 17.04. Requisites of a Personal Bond.

(a) A personal bond is sufficient if it includes the requisites of a bail bond as set out in Article 17.08, except that no sureties are required. In addition, a personal bond shall contain:

(1) the defendant's name, address, and place of employment;

(2) identification information, including the defendant's:

(A) date and place of birth;

(B) height, weight, and color of hair and eyes;

(C) driver's license number and state of issuance, if any; and

(D) nearest relative's name and address, if any; and

(3) except as provided by Subsection (b), the following oath sworn and signed by the defendant:

"I swear that I will appear before (the court or magistrate) at (address, city, county) Texas, on the (date), at the hour of (time, a.m. or p.m.) or upon notice by the court, or pay to the court the principal sum of (amount) plus all necessary and reasonable expenses incurred in any arrest for failure to appear."

(b) A personal bond is not required to contain the oath described by Subsection (a)(3) if:

(1) the magistrate makes a determination under Article 16.22 that the defendant has a mental illness or is a person with an intellectual disability, including by using the results of a previous determination under that article;

(2) the defendant is released on personal bond under Article 17.032; or

(3) the defendant is found incompetent to stand trial in accordance with Chapter 46B.

Art. 17.045. Bail Bond Certificates.

A bail bond certificate with respect to which a fidelity and surety company has become surety as provided in the Automobile Club Services Act, or for any truck and bus association incorporated in this state, when posted by the person whose signature appears thereon, shall be accepted as bail bond in an amount not to exceed $200 to guarantee the appearance of such person in any court in this state when the person is arrested for violation of any motor vehicle law of this state or ordinance of any municipality in this state, except for the offense of driving while intoxicated or for any felony, and the alleged violation was committed prior to the date of expiration shown on such bail bond certificate.

Art. 17.05. When a Bail Bond Is Given.

A bail bond is entered into either before a magistrate, upon an examination of a criminal accusation, or before a judge upon an application under habeas corpus; or it is taken from the defendant by a peace officer or jailer if authorized by Article 17.20, 17.21, or 17.22.

Art. 17.06. Corporation As Surety.

Wherever in this Chapter, any person is required or authorized to give or execute any bail bond, such bail bond may be given or executed by such principal and any corporation authorized by law to act as surety, subject to all the provisions of this Chapter regulating and governing the giving of bail bonds by personal surety insofar as the same is applicable.

Art. 17.07. Corporation to File with County Clerk Power of Attorney Designating Agent.

(a) Any corporation authorized by the law of this State to act as a surety, shall before executing any bail bond as authorized in the preceding Article, first file in the office of the county clerk of the county where such bail bond is given, a power of attorney designating and authorizing the named agent, agents or attorney of such corporation to execute such bail bonds and thereafter the execution of such bail bonds by such agent, agents or attorney, shall be a valid and binding obligation of such corporation.

(b) A corporation may limit the authority of an agent designated under Subsection (a) by specifying the limitation in the power of attorney that is filed with the county clerk.

Art. 17.08. Requisites of a Bail Bond.

A bail bond must contain the following requisites:

1. That it be made payable to "The State of Texas";

2. That the defendant and his sureties, if any, bind themselves that the defendant will appear before the proper court or magistrate to answer the accusation against him;

3. If the defendant is charged with a felony, that it state that he is charged with a felony. If the defendant is charged with a misdemeanor, that it state that he is charged with a misdemeanor;

4. That the bond be signed by name or mark by the principal and sureties, if any, each of whom shall write thereon his mailing address;

5. That the bond state the time and place, when and where the accused binds himself to appear, and the court or magistrate before whom he is to appear. The bond shall also bind the defendant to appear before any court or magistrate before whom the cause may thereafter be pending at any time when, and place where, his presence may be required under this Code or by any court or magistrate, but in no event shall the sureties be bound after such time as the defendant receives an order of deferred adjudication or is acquitted, sentenced, placed on community supervision, or dismissed from the charge;

6. The bond shall also be conditioned that the principal and sureties, if any, will pay all necessary and reasonable expenses incurred by any and all sheriffs or other peace officers in rearresting the principal in the event he fails to appear before the court or magistrate named in the bond at the time stated therein. The amount of such expense shall be in addition to the principal amount specified in the bond. The failure of any bail bond to contain the conditions specified in this paragraph shall in no manner affect the legality of any such bond, but it is intended that the sheriff or other peace officer shall look to the defendant and his sureties, if any, for expenses incurred by him, and not to the State for any fees earned by him in connection with the rearresting of an accused who has violated the conditions of his bond.

Art. 17.081. Additional Requisites of Bail Bond Given by Certain Defendants.

In addition to the requirements of Article 17.08, a bail bond for a defendant charged with an offense under Section 20A.02, 20A.03, 43.02, 43.03, 43.031, 43.04, 43.041, or 43.05, Penal Code, must include the address, identification number, and state of issuance as shown on a valid driver's license or identification card for the defendant and any surety, including any agent executing the bail bond on behalf of a corporation acting as surety.

Art. 17.085. Notice of Appearance Date.

The clerk of a court that does not provide online Internet access to that court's criminal case records shall post in a designated public place in the courthouse notice of a prospective criminal court docket setting as soon as the court notifies the clerk of the setting.

Art. 17.09. Duration; Original and Subsequent Proceedings; New Bail.

Sec. 1. Where a defendant, in the course of a criminal action, gives bail before any court or person authorized by law to take same, for his personal appearance before a court or magistrate, to answer a charge against him, the said bond shall be valid and binding upon the defendant and his sureties, if any, thereon, for the defendant's personal appearance before the court or magistrate designated therein, as well as before any other court to which same may be transferred, and for any and all subsequent proceedings had relative to the charge, and each such bond shall be so conditioned except as hereinafter provided.

Sec. 2. When a defendant has once given bail for his appearance in answer to a criminal charge, he shall not be required to give another bond in the course of the same criminal action except as herein provided.

Sec. 3. Provided that whenever, during the course of the action, the judge or magistrate in whose court such action is pending finds that the bond is defective, excessive or insufficient in amount, or that the sureties, if any, are not acceptable, or for any other good and sufficient cause, such judge or magistrate may, either in term-time or in vacation, order the accused to be rearrested, and require the accused to give another bond in such amount as the judge or magistrate may deem proper. When such bond is so given and approved, the defendant shall be released from custody.

Sec. 4. Notwithstanding any other provision of this article, the judge or magistrate in whose court a criminal action is pending may not order the accused to be rearrested or require the accused to give another bond in a higher amount because the accused:

(1) withdraws a waiver of the right to counsel; or

(2) requests the assistance of counsel, appointed or retained.

Art. 17.091. Notice of Certain Bail Reductions Required.

Before a judge or magistrate reduces the amount of bail set for a defendant charged with an offense listed in Article 42A.054, an offense described by Article 62.001(5), or an offense under Section 20A.03, Penal Code, the judge or magistrate shall provide:

(1) to the attorney representing the state, reasonable notice of the proposed bail reduction; and

(2) on request of the attorney representing the state or the defendant or the defendant's counsel, an opportunity for a hearing concerning the proposed bail reduction.

Art. 17.10. Disqualified Sureties.

(a) A minor may not be surety on a bail bond, but the accused party may sign as principal.

(b) A person, for compensation, may not be a surety on a bail bond written in a county in which a county bail bond board regulated under Chapter 1704, Occupations Code, does not exist unless the person, within two years before the bail bond is given, completed in person at least eight hours of continuing legal education in criminal law courses or bail bond law courses that are:

(1) approved by the State Bar of Texas; and

(2) offered by an accredited institution of higher education in this state.

(c) A person, for compensation, may not act as a surety on a bail bond if the person has been finally convicted of:

(1) a misdemeanor involving moral turpitude; or

(2) a felony.

Art. 17.11. How Bail Bond Is Taken.

Sec. 1. Every court, judge, magistrate or other officer taking a bail bond shall require evidence of the sufficiency of the security offered; but in every case, one surety shall be sufficient, if it be made to appear that such surety is worth at least double the amount of the sum for which he is bound, exclusive of all property exempted by law from execution, and of debts or other encumbrances; and that he is a resident of this state, and has property therein liable to execution worth the sum for which he is bound.

Sec. 2. Provided, however, any person who has signed as a surety on a bail bond and is in default thereon shall thereafter be disqualified to sign as a surety so long as the person is in default on the bond. It shall be the duty of the clerk of the court where the surety is in default on a bail bond to notify in writing the sheriff, chief of police, or other peace officer of the default. If a bail bond is taken for an offense other than a Class C misdemeanor, the clerk of the court where the surety is in default on the bond shall send notice of the default by certified mail to the last known address of the surety.

Sec. 3. A surety is considered to be in default from the time execution may be issued on a final judgment in a bond forfeiture proceeding under the Texas Rules of Civil Procedure, unless the final judgment is superseded by the posting of a supersedeas bond.

Art. 17.12. Exempt Property.

The property secured by the Constitution and laws from forced sale shall not, in any case, be held liable for the satisfaction of bail, either as to principal or sureties, if any.

Art. 17.13. Sufficiency of Sureties Ascertained.

To test the sufficiency of the security offered to any bail bond, unless the court or officer taking the same is fully satisfied as to its sufficiency, the following oath shall be made in writing and subscribed by the sureties: "I, do swear that I am worth, in my own right, at least the sum of (here insert the amount in which the surety is bound), after deducting from my property all that which is exempt by the Constitution and Laws of the State from forced sale, and after the payment of all my debts of every description, whether individual or security debts, and after satisfying all encumbrances upon my property which are known to me; that I reside in .... County, and have property in this State liable to execution worth said amount or more.

(Dated ...., and attested by the judge of the court, clerk, magistrate or sheriff.)"

Such affidavit shall be filed with the papers of the proceedings.

Art. 17.14. Affidavit Not Conclusive.

Such affidavit shall not be conclusive as to the sufficiency of the security; and if the court or officer taking the bail bond is not fully satisfied as to the sufficiency of the security offered, further evidence shall be required before approving the same.

Art. 17.141. Eligible Bail Bond Sureties in Certain Counties.

In a county in which a county bail bond board regulated under Chapter 1704, Occupations Code, does not exist, the sheriff may post a list of eligible bail bond sureties whose security has been determined to be sufficient. Each surety listed under this article must file annually a sworn financial statement with the sheriff.

Art. 17.15. Rules for Fixing Amount of Bail.

The amount of bail to be required in any case is to be regulated by the court, judge, magistrate or officer taking the bail; they are to be governed in the exercise of this discretion by the Constitution and by the following rules:

1. The bail shall be sufficiently high to give reasonable assurance that the undertaking will be complied with.

2. The power to require bail is not to be so used as to make it an instrument of oppression.

3. The nature of the offense and the circumstances under which it was committed are to be considered.

4. The ability to make bail is to be regarded, and proof may be taken upon this point.

5. The future safety of a victim of the alleged offense and the community shall be considered.

Art. 17.151. Release Because of Delay.

Sec. 1. A defendant who is detained in jail pending trial of an accusation against him must be released either on personal bond or by reducing the amount of bail required, if the state is not ready for trial of the criminal action for which he is being detained within:

(1) 90 days from the commencement of his detention if he is accused of a felony;

(2) 30 days from the commencement of his detention if he is accused of a misdemeanor punishable by a sentence of imprisonment in jail for more than 180 days;

(3) 15 days from the commencement of his detention if he is accused of a misdemeanor punishable by a sentence of imprisonment for 180 days or less; or

(4) five days from the commencement of his detention if he is accused of a misdemeanor punishable by a fine only.

Sec. 2. The provisions of this article do not apply to a defendant who is:

(1) serving a sentence of imprisonment for another offense while the defendant is serving that sentence;

(2) being detained pending trial of another accusation against the defendant as to which the applicable period has not yet elapsed;

(3) incompetent to stand trial, during the period of the defendant's incompetence; or

(4) being detained for a violation of the conditions of a previous release related to the safety of a victim of the alleged offense or to the safety of the community under this article.

Sec. 3. [Repealed by Acts 2005, 79th Leg., ch. 110 (S.B. 599), § 2, effective September 1, 2005.]

Art. 17.152. Denial of Bail for Violation of Certain Court Orders or Conditions of Bond in a Family Violence Case.

(a) In this article, "family violence" has the meaning assigned by Section 71.004, Family Code.

(b) Except as otherwise provided by Subsection (d), a person who commits an offense under Section 25.07, Penal Code, related to a violation of a condition of bond set in a family violence case and whose bail in the case under Section 25.07, Penal Code, or in the family violence case is revoked or forfeited for a violation of a condition of bond may be taken into custody and, pending trial or other court proceedings, denied release on bail if following a hearing a judge or magistrate determines by a preponderance of the evidence that the person violated a condition of bond related to:

(1) the safety of the victim of the offense under Section 25.07, Penal Code, or the family violence case, as applicable; or

(2) the safety of the community.

(c) Except as otherwise provided by Subsection (d), a person who commits an offense under Section 25.07, Penal Code, other than an offense related to a violation of a condition of bond set in a family violence case, may be taken into custody and, pending trial or other court proceedings, denied release on bail if following a hearing a judge or magistrate determines by a preponderance of the evidence that the person committed the offense.

(d) A person who commits an offense under Section 25.07(a)(3), Penal Code, may be held without bail under Subsection (b) or (c), as applicable, only if following a hearing the judge or magistrate determines by a preponderance of the evidence that the person went to or near the place described in the order or condition of bond with the intent to commit or threaten to commit:

(1) family violence; or

(2) an act in furtherance of an offense under Section 42.072, Penal Code.

(e) In determining whether to deny release on bail under this article, the judge or magistrate may consider:

(1) the order or condition of bond;

(2) the nature and circumstances of the alleged offense;

(3) the relationship between the accused and the victim, including the history of that relationship;

(4) any criminal history of the accused; and

(5) any other facts or circumstances relevant to a determination of whether the accused poses an imminent threat of future family violence.

(f) A person arrested for committing an offense under Section 25.07, Penal Code, shall without unnecessary delay and after reasonable notice is given to the attorney representing the state, but not later than 48 hours after the person is arrested, be taken before a magistrate in accordance with Article 15.17. At that time, the magistrate shall conduct the hearing and make the determination required by this article.

Art. 17.153. Denial of Bail for Violation of Condition of Bond Where Child Alleged Victim.

(a) This article applies to a defendant charged with a felony offense under any of the following provisions of the Penal Code, if committed against a child younger than 14 years of age:

(1) Chapter 21 (Sexual Offenses);

(2) Section 25.02 (Prohibited Sexual Conduct);

(3) Section 43.25 (Sexual Performance by a Child);

(4) Section 20A.02 (Trafficking of Persons), if the defendant is alleged to have:

(A) trafficked the child with the intent or knowledge that the child would engage in sexual conduct, as defined by Section 43.25, Penal Code; or

(B) benefited from participating in a venture that involved a trafficked child engaging in sexual conduct, as defined by Section 43.25, Penal Code; or

(5) Section 43.05(a)(2)(Compelling Prostitution).

(b) A defendant described by Subsection (a) who violates a condition of bond set under Article 17.41 and whose bail in the case is revoked for the violation may be taken into custody and denied release on bail pending trial if, following a hearing, a judge or magistrate determines by a preponderance of the evidence that the defendant violated a condition of bond related to the safety of the victim of the offense or the safety of the community. If the magistrate finds that the violation occurred, the magistrate may revoke the defendant's bond and order that the defendant be immediately returned to custody. Once the defendant is placed in custody, the revocation of the defendant's bond discharges the sureties on the bond, if any, from any future liability on the bond. A discharge under this subsection from any future liability on the bond does not discharge any surety from liability for previous forfeitures on the bond.

Art. 17.16. Discharge of Liability; Surrender or Incarceration of Principal Before Forfeiture; Verification of Incarceration.

(a) A surety may before forfeiture relieve the surety of the surety's undertaking by:

(1) surrendering the accused into the custody of the sheriff of the county where the prosecution is pending; or

(2) delivering to the sheriff of the county in which the prosecution is pending and to the office of the prosecuting attorney an affidavit stating that the accused is incarcerated in:

(A) federal custody, subject to Subsection (a-1);

(B) the custody of any state; or

(C) any county of this state.

(a-1) For purposes of Subsection (a)(2), the surety may not be relieved of the surety's undertaking if the accused is in federal custody to determine whether the accused is lawfully present in the United States.

(b) On receipt of an affidavit described by Subsection (a)(2), the sheriff of the county in which the prosecution is pending shall verify whether the accused is incarcerated as stated in the affidavit. If the sheriff verifies the statement in the affidavit, the sheriff shall notify the magistrate before which the prosecution is pending of the verification.

(c) On a verification described by this article, the sheriff shall place a detainer against the accused with the appropriate officials in the jurisdiction in which the accused is incarcerated. On receipt of notice of a verification described by this article, the magistrate before which the prosecution is pending shall direct the clerk of the court to issue a capias for the arrest of the accused, except as provided by Subsection (d).

(d) A capias for the arrest of the accused is not required if:

(1) a warrant has been issued for the accused's arrest and remains outstanding; or

(2) the issuance of a capias would otherwise be unnecessary for the purpose of taking the accused into custody.

(e) For the purposes of Subsection (a)(2) of this article, the bond is discharged and the surety is absolved of liability on the bond on the verification of the incarceration of the accused.

(f) An affidavit described by Subsection (a)(2) and the documentation of any verification obtained under Subsection (b) must be:

(1) filed in the court record of the underlying criminal case in the court in which the prosecution is pending or, if the court record does not exist, in a general file maintained by the clerk of the court; and

(2) delivered to the office of the prosecuting attorney.

(g) A surety is liable for all reasonable and necessary expenses incurred in returning the accused into the custody of the sheriff of the county in which the prosecution is pending.

Art. 17.17. When Surrender Is Made During Term.

If a surrender of the accused be made during a term of the court to which he has bound himself to appear, the sheriff shall take him before the court; and if he is willing to give other bail, the court shall forthwith require him to do so. If he fails or refuses to give bail, the court shall make an order that he be committed to jail until the bail is given, and this shall be a sufficient commitment without any written order to the sheriff.

Art. 17.18. Surrender in Vacation.

When the surrender is made at any other time than during the session of the court, the sheriff may take the necessary bail bond, but if the defendant fails or refuses to give other bail, the sheriff shall take him before the nearest magistrate; and such magistrate shall issue a warrant of commitment, reciting the fact that the accused has been once admitted to bail, has been surrendered, and now fails or refuses to give other bail.

Art. 17.19. Surety May Obtain a Warrant.

(a) Any surety, desiring to surrender his principal and after notifying the principal's attorney, if the principal is represented by an attorney, in a manner provided by Rule 21a, Texas Rules of Civil Procedure, of the surety's intention to surrender the principal, may file an affidavit of such intention before the court or magistrate before which the prosecution is pending. The affidavit must state:

(1) the court and cause number of the case;

(2) the name of the defendant;

(3) the offense with which the defendant is charged;

(4) the date of the bond;

(5) the cause for the surrender; and

(6) that notice of the surety's intention to surrender the principal has been given as required by this subsection.

(b) In a prosecution pending before a court, if the court finds that there is cause for the surety to surrender the surety's principal, the court shall issue a capias for the principal. In a prosecution pending before a magistrate, if the magistrate finds that there is cause for the surety to surrender the surety's principal, the magistrate shall issue a warrant of arrest for the principal. It is an affirmative defense to any liability on the bond that:

(1) the court or magistrate refused to issue a capias or warrant of arrest for the principal; and

(2) after the refusal to issue the capias or warrant of arrest, the principal failed to appear.

(c) If the court or magistrate before whom the prosecution is pending is not available, the surety may deliver the affidavit to any other magistrate in the county and that magistrate, on a finding of cause for the surety to surrender the surety's principal, shall issue a warrant of arrest for the principal.

(d) An arrest warrant or capias issued under this article shall be issued to the sheriff of the county in which the case is pending, and a copy of the warrant or capias shall be issued to the surety or his agent.

(e) An arrest warrant or capias issued under this article may be executed by a peace officer, a security officer, or a private investigator licensed in this state.

Art. 17.20. Bail in Misdemeanor.

In cases of misdemeanor, the sheriff or other peace officer, or a jailer licensed under Chapter 1701, Occupations Code, may, whether during the term of the court or in vacation, where the officer has a defendant in custody, take of the defendant a bail bond.

Art. 17.21. Bail in Felony.

In cases of felony, when the accused is in custody of the sheriff or other officer, and the court before which the prosecution is pending is in session in the county where the accused is in custody, the court shall fix the amount of bail, if it is a bailable case and determine if the accused is eligible for a personal bond; and the sheriff or other peace officer, unless it be the police of a city, or a jailer licensed under Chapter 1701, Occupations Code, is authorized to take a bail bond of the accused in the amount as fixed by the court, to be approved by such officer taking the same, and will thereupon discharge the accused from custody. The defendant and the defendant's sureties are not required to appear in court.

Art. 17.22. May Take Bail in Felony.

In a felony case, if the court before which the same is pending is not in session in the county where the defendant is in custody, the sheriff or other peace officer, or a jailer licensed under Chapter 1701, Occupations Code, who has the defendant in custody may take the defendant's bail bond in such amount as may have been fixed by the court or magistrate, or if no amount has been fixed, then in such amount as such officer may consider reasonable.

Art. 17.23. Sureties Severally Bound.

In all bail bonds taken under any provision of this Code, the sureties shall be severally bound. Where a surrender of the principal is made by one or more of them, all the sureties shall be considered discharged.

Art. 17.24. General Rules Applicable.

All general rules in the Chapter are applicable to bail defendant before an examining court.

Art. 17.25. Proceedings When Bail Is Granted.

After a full examination of the testimony, the magistrate shall, if the case be one where bail may properly be granted and ought to be required, proceed to make an order that the accused execute a bail bond with sufficient security, conditioned for his appearance before the proper court.

Art. 17.26. Time Given to Procure Bail.

Reasonable time shall be given the accused to procure security.

Art. 17.27. When Bail Is Not Given.

If, after the allowance of a reasonable time, the security be not given, the magistrate shall make an order committing the accused to jail to be kept safely until legally discharged; and he shall issue a commitment accordingly.

Art. 17.28. When Ready to Give Bail.

If the party be ready to give bail, the magistrate shall cause to be prepared a bond, which shall be signed by the accused and his surety or sureties, if any.

Art. 17.29. Accused Liberated.

(a) When the accused has given the required bond, either to the magistrate or the officer having him in custody, he shall at once be set at liberty.

(b) Before releasing on bail a person arrested for an offense under Section 42.072, Penal Code, or a person arrested or held without warrant in the prevention of family violence, the law enforcement agency holding the person shall make a reasonable attempt to give personal notice of the imminent release to the victim of the alleged offense or to another person designated by the victim to receive the notice. An attempt by an agency to give notice to the victim or the person designated by the victim at the victim's or person's last known telephone number or address, as shown on the records of the agency, constitutes a reasonable attempt to give notice under this subsection. If possible, the arresting officer shall collect the address and telephone number of the victim at the time the arrest is made and shall communicate that information to the agency holding the person.

(c) A law enforcement agency or an employee of a law enforcement agency is not liable for damages arising from complying or failing to comply with Subsection (b) of this article.

(d) In this article, "family violence" has the meaning assigned by Section 71.004, Family Code.

Art. 17.291. Further Detention of Certain Persons.

(a) In this article:

(1) "family violence" has the meaning assigned to that phrase by Section 71.004, Family Code; and

(2) "magistrate" has the meaning assigned to it by Article 2.09 of this code.

(b) Article 17.29 does not apply when a person has been arrested or held without a warrant in the prevention of family violence if there is probable cause to believe the violence will continue if the person is immediately released. The head of the agency arresting or holding such a person may hold the person for a period of not more than four hours after bond has been posted. This detention period may be extended for an additional period not to exceed 48 hours, but only if authorized in a writing directed to the person having custody of the detained person by a magistrate who concludes that:

(1) the violence would continue if the person is released; and

(2) if the additional period exceeds 24 hours, probable cause exists to believe that the person committed the instant offense and that, during the 10-year period preceding the date of the instant offense, the person has been arrested:

(A) on more than one occasion for an offense involving family violence; or

(B) for any other offense, if a deadly weapon, as defined by Section 1.07, Penal Code, was used or exhibited during commission of the offense or during immediate flight after commission of the offense.

Art. 17.292. Magistrate's Order for Emergency Protection.

(a) At a defendant's appearance before a magistrate after arrest for an offense involving family violence or an offense under Section 20A.02, 20A.03, 22.011, 22.012, 22.021, or 42.072, Penal Code, the magistrate may issue an order for emergency protection on the magistrate's own motion or on the request of:

(1) the victim of the offense;

(2) the guardian of the victim;

(3) a peace officer; or

(4) the attorney representing the state.

(b) At a defendant's appearance before a magistrate after arrest for an offense involving family violence, the magistrate shall issue an order for emergency protection if the arrest is for an offense that also involves:

(1) serious bodily injury to the victim; or

(2) the use or exhibition of a deadly weapon during the commission of an assault.

(c) The magistrate in the order for emergency protection may prohibit the arrested party from:

(1) committing:

(A) family violence or an assault on the person protected under the order; or

(B) an act in furtherance of an offense under Section 20A.02 or 42.072, Penal Code;

(2) communicating:

(A) directly with a member of the family or household or with the person protected under the order in a threatening or harassing manner;

(B) a threat through any person to a member of the family or household or to the person protected under the order; or

(C) if the magistrate finds good cause, in any manner with a person protected under the order or a member of the family or household of a person protected under the order, except through the party's attorney or a person appointed by the court;

(3) going to or near:

(A) the residence, place of employment, or business of a member of the family or household or of the person protected under the order; or

(B) the residence, child care facility, or school where a child protected under the order resides or attends; or

(4) possessing a firearm, unless the person is a peace officer, as defined by Section 1.07, Penal Code, actively engaged in employment as a sworn, full-time paid employee of a state agency or political subdivision.

(c-1) In addition to the conditions described by Subsection (c), the magistrate in the order for emergency protection may impose a condition described by Article 17.49(b) in the manner provided by that article, including ordering a defendant's participation in a global positioning monitoring system or allowing participation in the system by an alleged victim or other person protected under the order.

(d) The victim of the offense need not be present when the order for emergency protection is issued.

(e) In the order for emergency protection the magistrate shall specifically describe the prohibited locations and the minimum distances, if any, that the party must maintain, unless the magistrate determines for the safety of the person or persons protected by the order that specific descriptions of the locations should be omitted.

(f) To the extent that a condition imposed by an order for emergency protection issued under this article conflicts with an existing court order granting possession of or access to a child, the condition imposed under this article prevails for the duration of the order for emergency protection.

(f-1) To the extent that a condition imposed by an order issued under this article conflicts with a condition imposed by an order subsequently issued under Chapter 85, Subtitle B, Title 4, Family Code, or under Title 1 or Title 5, Family Code, the condition imposed by the order issued under the Family Code prevails.

(f-2) To the extent that a condition imposed by an order issued under this article conflicts with a condition imposed by an order subsequently issued under Chapter 83, Subtitle B, Title 4, Family Code, the condition imposed by the order issued under this article prevails unless the court issuing the order under Chapter 83, Family Code:

(1) is informed of the existence of the order issued under this article; and

(2) makes a finding in the order issued under Chapter 83, Family Code, that the court is superseding the order issued under this article.

(g) An order for emergency protection issued under this article must contain the following statements printed in bold-face type or in capital letters:

A VIOLATION OF THIS ORDER BY COMMISSION OF AN ACT PROHIBITED BY THE ORDER MAY BE PUNISHABLE BY A FINE OF AS MUCH AS $4,000 OR BY CONFINEMENT IN JAIL FOR AS LONG AS ONE YEAR OR BY BOTH. AN ACT THAT RESULTS IN A SEPARATE OFFENSE MAY BE PROSECUTED AS A SEPARATE MISDEMEANOR OR FELONY OFFENSE, AS APPLICABLE, IN ADDITION TO A VIOLATION OF THIS ORDER. IF THE ACT IS PROSECUTED AS A SEPARATE FELONY OFFENSE, IT IS PUNISHABLE BY CONFINEMENT IN PRISON FOR AT LEAST TWO YEARS. THE POSSESSION OF A FIREARM BY A PERSON, OTHER THAN A PEACE OFFICER, AS DEFINED BY SECTION 1.07, PENAL CODE, ACTIVELY ENGAGED IN EMPLOYMENT AS A SWORN, FULL-TIME PAID EMPLOYEE OF A STATE AGENCY OR POLITICAL SUBDIVISION, WHO IS SUBJECT TO THIS ORDER MAY BE PROSECUTED AS A SEPARATE OFFENSE PUNISHABLE BY CONFINEMENT OR IMPRISONMENT.

"NO PERSON, INCLUDING A PERSON WHO IS PROTECTED BY THIS ORDER, MAY GIVE PERMISSION TO ANYONE TO IGNORE OR VIOLATE ANY PROVISION OF THIS ORDER. DURING THE TIME IN WHICH THIS ORDER IS VALID, EVERY PROVISION OF THIS ORDER IS IN FULL FORCE AND EFFECT UNLESS A COURT CHANGES THE ORDER."

(h) As soon as possible but not later than the next business day after the date the magistrate issues an order for emergency protection under this article, the magistrate shall send a copy of the order to the chief of police in the municipality where the member of the family or household or individual protected by the order resides, if the person resides in a municipality, or to the sheriff of the county where the person resides, if the person does not reside in a municipality. If the victim of the offense is not present when the order is issued, the magistrate issuing the order shall order an appropriate peace officer to make a good faith effort to notify, within 24 hours, the victim that the order has been issued by calling the victim's residence and place of employment. The clerk of the court shall send a copy of the order to the victim at the victim's last known address as soon as possible but not later than the next business day after the date the order is issued.

(h-1) A magistrate or clerk of the court may delay sending a copy of the order under Subsection (h) only if the magistrate or clerk lacks information necessary to ensure service and enforcement.

(i) If an order for emergency protection issued under this article prohibits a person from going to or near a child care facility or school, the magistrate shall send a copy of the order to the child care facility or school.

(i-1) The copy of the order and any related information may be sent under Subsection (h) or (i) electronically or in another manner that can be accessed by the recipient.

(j) An order for emergency protection issued under this article is effective on issuance, and the defendant shall be served a copy of the order by the magistrate or the magistrate's designee in person or electronically. The magistrate shall make a separate record of the service in written or electronic format. An order for emergency protection issued under Subsection (a) or (b)(1) of this article remains in effect up to the 61st day but not less than 31 days after the date of issuance. An order for emergency protection issued under Subsection (b)(2) of this article remains in effect up to the 91st day but not less than 61 days after the date of issuance. After notice to each affected party and a hearing, the issuing court may modify all or part of an order issued under this article if the court finds that:

(1) the order as originally issued is unworkable;

(2) the modification will not place the victim of the offense at greater risk than did the original order; and

(3) the modification will not in any way endanger a person protected under the order.

(k) To ensure that an officer responding to a call is aware of the existence and terms of an order for emergency protection issued under this article, not later than the third business day after the date of receipt of the copy of the order by the applicable law enforcement agency with jurisdiction over the municipality or county in which the victim resides, the law enforcement agency shall enter the information required under Section 411.042(b)(6), Government Code, into the statewide law enforcement information system maintained by the Department of Public Safety.

(k-1) A law enforcement agency may delay entering the information required under Subsection (k) only if the agency lacks information necessary to ensure service and enforcement.

(*l*) In the order for emergency protection, the magistrate shall suspend a license to carry a handgun issued under Subchapter H, Chapter 411, Government Code, that is held by the defendant.

(m) In this article:

(1) "Family," "family violence," and "household" have the meanings assigned by Chapter 71, Family Code.

(2) "Firearm" has the meaning assigned by Chapter 46, Penal Code.

(3) "Business day" means a day other than a Saturday, Sunday, or state or national holiday.

(n) On motion, notice, and hearing, or on agreement of the parties, an order for emergency protection issued under this article may be transferred to the court assuming jurisdiction over the criminal act giving rise to the issuance of the emergency order for protection. On transfer, the criminal court may modify all or part of an order issued under this subsection in the same manner and under the same standards as the issuing court under Subsection (j).

Art. 17.293. Delivery of Order for Emergency Protection to Other Persons.

The magistrate or the clerk of the magistrate's court issuing an order for emergency protection under Article 17.292 that suspends a license to carry a handgun shall immediately send a copy of the order to the appropriate division of the Department of Public Safety at its Austin headquarters. On receipt of the order suspending the license, the department shall:

(1) record the suspension of the license in the records of the department;

(2) report the suspension to local law enforcement agencies, as appropriate; and

(3) demand surrender of the suspended license from the license holder.

Art. 17.294. Confidentiality of Certain Information in Order for Emergency Protection.

On request by a person protected by an order for emergency protection issued under Article 17.292, or if determined necessary by the magistrate, the court issuing the order may protect the person's mailing address by rendering an order:

(1) requiring the person protected under the order to:

(A) disclose the person's mailing address to the court;

(B) designate another person to receive on behalf of the person any notice or documents filed with the court related to the order; and

(C) disclose the designated person's mailing address to the court;

(2) requiring the court clerk to:

(A) strike the mailing address of the person protected by the order from the public records of the court, if applicable; and

(B) maintain a confidential record of the mailing address for use only by:

(i) the court; or

(ii) a law enforcement agency for purposes of entering the information required by Section 411.042(b)(6), Government Code, into the statewide law enforcement information system maintained by the Department of Public Safety; and

(3) prohibiting the release of the information to the defendant.

Art. 17.30. Shall Certify Proceedings.

The magistrate, before whom an examination has taken place upon a criminal accusation, shall certify to all the proceedings had before him, as well as where he discharges, holds to bail or commits, and transmit them, sealed up, to the court before which the defendant may be tried, writing his name across the seals of the envelope. The voluntary statement of the defendant, the testimony, bail bonds, and every other proceeding in the case, shall be thus delivered to the clerk of the proper court, without delay.

Art. 17.31. Duty of Clerks Who Receive Such Proceedings.

If the proceedings be delivered to a district clerk, he shall keep them safely and deliver the same to the next grand jury. If the proceedings are delivered to a county clerk, he shall without delay deliver them to the district or county attorney of his county.

Art. 17.32. In Case of No Arrest.

Upon failure from any cause to arrest the accused the magistrate shall file with the proper clerk the complaint, warrant of arrest, and a list of the witnesses.

Art. 17.33. Request Setting of Bail.

The accused may at any time after being confined request a magistrate to review the written statements of the witnesses for the State as well as all other evidence available at that time in determining the amount of bail. This setting of the amount of bail does not waive the defendant's right to an examining trial as provided in Article 16.01.

Art. 17.34. Witnesses to Give Bond.

Witnesses for the State or defendant may be required by the magistrate, upon the examination of any criminal accusation before him, to give bail for their appearance to testify before the proper court. A personal bond may be taken of a witness by the court before whom the case is pending.

Art. 17.35. Security of Witness.

The amount of security to be required of a witness is to be regulated by his pecuniary condition, character and the nature of the offense with respect to which he is a witness.

Art. 17.36. Effect of Witness Bond.

The bond given by a witness for his appearance has the same effect as a bond of the accused and may be forfeited and recovered upon in the same manner.

Art. 17.37. Witness May Be Committed.

A witness required to give bail who fails or refuses to do so shall be committed to jail as in other cases of a failure to give bail when required, but shall be released from custody upon giving such bail.

Art. 17.38. Rules Applicable to All Cases of Bail.

The rules in this Chapter respecting bail are applicable to all such undertakings when entered into in the course of a criminal action, whether before or after an indictment, in every case where authority is given to any court, judge, magistrate, or other officer, to require bail of a person accused of an offense, or of a witness in a criminal action.

Art. 17.39. Records of Bail.

A magistrate or other officer who sets the amount of bail or who takes bail shall record in a well-bound book the name of the person whose appearance the bail secures, the amount of bail, the date bail is set, the magistrate or officer who sets bail, the offense or other cause for which the appearance is secured, the magistrate or other officer who takes bail, the date the person is released, and the name of the bondsman, if any.

Art. 17.40. Conditions Related to Victim or Community Safety.

(a) To secure a defendant's attendance at trial, a magistrate may impose any reasonable condition of bond related to the safety of a victim of the alleged offense or to the safety of the community.

(b) At a hearing limited to determining whether the defendant violated a condition of bond imposed under Subsection (a), the magistrate may revoke the defendant's bond only if the magistrate finds by a preponderance of the evidence that the violation occurred. If the magistrate finds that the violation occurred, the magistrate shall revoke the defendant's bond and order that the defendant be immediately returned to custody. Once the defendant is placed in custody, the revocation of the defendant's bond discharges the sureties on the bond, if any, from any future liability on the bond. A discharge under this subsection from any future liability on the bond does not discharge any surety from liability for previous forfeitures on the bond.

Art. 17.41. Condition Where Child Alleged Victim.

(a) This article applies to a defendant charged with an offense under any of the following provisions of the Penal Code, if committed against a child younger than 18 years of age:

(1) Chapter 20A (Trafficking of Persons), 21 (Sexual Offenses), 22 (Assaultive Offenses), or 43 (Public Indecency); or

(2) Section 25.02 (Prohibited Sexual Conduct).

(b) Subject to Subsections (c) and (d), a magistrate shall require as a condition of bond for a defendant charged with an offense described by Subsection (a) that the defendant not:

(1) directly communicate with the alleged victim of the offense; or

(2) go near a residence, school, or other location, as specifically described in the bond, frequented by the alleged victim.

(c) A magistrate who imposes a condition of bond under this article may grant the defendant supervised access to the alleged victim.

(d) To the extent that a condition imposed under this article conflicts with an existing court order granting possession of or access to a child, the condition imposed under this article prevails for a period specified by the magistrate, not to exceed 90 days.

Art. 17.42. Personal Bond Office.

Sec. 1. Any county, or any judicial district with jurisdiction in more than one county, with the approval of the commissioners court of each county in the district, may establish a personal bond office to gather and review information about an accused that may have a bearing on whether he will comply with the conditions of a personal bond and report

Code of Criminal Procedure

its findings to the court before which the case is pending.

Sec. 2. (a) The commissioners court of a county that establishes the office or the district and county judges of a judicial district that establishes the office may employ a director of the office.

(b) The director may employ the staff authorized by the commissioners court of the county or the commissioners court of each county in the judicial district.

Sec. 3. If a judicial district establishes an office, each county in the district shall pay its pro rata share of the costs of administering the office according to its population.

Sec. 4. (a) Except as otherwise provided by this subsection, if a court releases an accused on personal bond on the recommendation of a personal bond office, the court shall assess a personal bond reimbursement fee of $20 or three percent of the amount of the bail fixed for the accused, whichever is greater. The court may waive the fee or assess a lesser fee if good cause is shown. A court that requires a defendant to give a personal bond under Article 45.016 may not assess a personal bond fee under this subsection.

(b) Reimbursement fees collected under this article may be used solely to defray expenses of the personal bond office, including defraying the expenses of extradition.

(c) Reimbursement fees collected under this article shall be deposited in the county treasury, or if the office serves more than one county, the fees shall be apportioned to each county in the district according to each county's pro rata share of the costs of the office.

Sec. 5. (a) A personal bond pretrial release office established under this article shall:

(1) prepare a record containing information about any accused person identified by case number only who, after review by the office, is released by a court on personal bond before sentencing in a pending case;

(2) update the record on a monthly basis; and

(3) file a copy of the record with the district or county clerk, as applicable based on court jurisdiction over the categories of offenses addressed in the records, in any county served by the office.

(b) In preparing a record under Subsection (a), the office shall include in the record a statement of:

(1) the offense with which the person is charged;

(2) the dates of any court appearances scheduled in the matter that were previously unattended by the person;

(3) whether a warrant has been issued for the person's arrest for failure to appear in accordance with the terms of the person's release;

(4) whether the person has failed to comply with conditions of release on personal bond; and

(5) the presiding judge or magistrate who authorized the personal bond.

(c) This section does not apply to a personal bond pretrial release office that on January 1, 1995, was operated by a community corrections and supervision department.

Sec. 6. (a) Not later than April 1 of each year, a personal bond office established under this article shall submit to the commissioners court or district and county judges that established the office an annual report containing information about the operations of the office during the preceding year.

(b) In preparing an annual report under Subsection (a), the office shall include in the report a statement of:

(1) the office's operating budget;

(2) the number of positions maintained for office staff;

(3) the number of accused persons who, after review by the office, were released by a court on personal bond before sentencing in a pending case; and

(4) the number of persons described by Subdivision (3):

(A) who failed to attend a scheduled court appearance;

(B) for whom a warrant was issued for the arrest of those persons for failure to appear in accordance with the terms of their release; or

(C) who, while released on personal bond, were arrested for any other offense in the same county in which the persons were released on bond.

(c) This section does not apply to a personal bond pretrial release office that on January 1, 1995, was operated by a community corrections and supervision department.

Art. 17.43. Home Curfew and Electronic Monitoring As Condition.

(a) A magistrate may require as a condition of release on personal bond that the defendant submit to home curfew and electronic monitoring under the supervision of an agency designated by the magistrate.

(b) Cost of monitoring may be assessed as reimbursement fees or ordered paid directly by the defendant as a condition of bond.

Art. 17.44. Home Confinement, Electronic Monitoring, and Drug Testing As Condition.

(a) A magistrate may require as a condition of release on bond that the defendant submit to:

(1) home confinement and electronic monitoring under the supervision of an agency designated by the magistrate; or

(2) testing on a weekly basis for the presence of a controlled substance in the defendant's body.

(b) In this article, "controlled substance" has the meaning assigned by Section 481.002, Health and Safety Code.

(c) The magistrate may revoke the bond and order the defendant arrested if the defendant:

(1) violates a condition of home confinement and electronic monitoring;

(2) refuses to submit to a test for controlled substances or submits to a test for controlled substances and the test indicates the presence of a controlled substance in the defendant's body; or

(3) fails to pay the reimbursement fee for monitoring or testing for controlled substances, if payment is ordered under Subsection (e) as a condition of bond and the magistrate determines that the defendant is not indigent and is financially able to make the payments as ordered.

(d) The community justice assistance division of the Texas Department of Criminal Justice may provide grants to counties to implement electronic monitoring programs authorized by this article.

(e) The cost of electronic monitoring or testing for controlled substances under this article may be assessed as a reimbursement fee or ordered paid directly by the defendant as a condition of bond.

Art. 17.441. Conditions Requiring Motor Vehicle Ignition Interlock.

(a) Except as provided by Subsection (b), a magistrate shall require on release that a defendant charged with a subsequent offense under Section 49.04, 49.05, or 49.06, Penal Code, or an offense under Section 49.045, 49.07, or 49.08 of that code:

(1) have installed on the motor vehicle owned by the defendant or on the vehicle most regularly driven by the defendant, a device that uses a deep-lung breath analysis mechanism to make impractical the operation of a motor vehicle if ethyl alcohol is detected in the breath of the operator; and

(2) not operate any motor vehicle unless the vehicle is equipped with that device.

(b) The magistrate may not require the installation of the device if the magistrate finds that to require the device would not be in the best interest of justice.

(c) If the defendant is required to have the device installed, the magistrate shall require that the defendant have the device installed on the appropriate motor vehicle, at the defendant's expense, before the 30th day after the date the defendant is released on bond.

(d) The magistrate may designate an appropriate agency to verify the installation of the device and to monitor the device. If the magistrate designates an agency under this subsection, in each month during which the agency verifies the installation of the device or provides a monitoring service the defendant shall pay a reimbursement fee to the designated agency in the amount set by the magistrate. The defendant shall pay the initial reimbursement fee at the time the agency verifies the installation of the device. In each subsequent month during which the defendant is required to pay a reimbursement fee the defendant shall pay the fee on the first occasion in that month that the agency provides a monitoring service. The magistrate shall set the fee in an amount not to exceed $10 as determined by the county auditor, or by the commissioners court of the county if the county does not have a county auditor, to be sufficient to cover the cost incurred by the designated agency in conducting the verification or providing the monitoring service, as applicable in that county.

Art. 17.45. Conditions Requiring AIDS and HIV Instruction.

A magistrate may require as a condition of bond that a defendant charged with an offense under Section 43.02 or 43.021, Penal Code, receive counseling or education, or both, relating to acquired immune deficiency syndrome or human immunodeficiency virus.

Art. 17.46. Conditions for a Defendant Charged with Stalking.

(a) A magistrate may require as a condition of release on bond that a defendant charged with an offense under Section 42.072, Penal Code, may not:

(1) communicate directly or indirectly with the victim; or

(2) go to or near the residence, place of employment, or business of the victim or to or near a school, day-care facility, or similar facility where a dependent child of the victim is in attendance.

(b) If the magistrate requires the prohibition contained in Subsection (a)(2) of this article as a condition of release on bond, the magistrate shall specifically describe the prohibited locations and the minimum distances, if any, that the defendant must maintain from the locations.

Art. 17.465. Conditions for Defendant Charged with Certain Trafficking or Prostitution Related Offenses Involving Adult Victims.

(a) This article does not apply with respect to a defendant to whom Article 17.41 applies.

(b) A magistrate shall require as a condition of release on bond that a defendant charged with an offense under Section 20A.02, 20A.03, 43.03, 43.031, 43.04, 43.041, or 43.05, Penal Code, committed against a person 18 years of age or older may not:

(1) communicate directly or indirectly with the victim; or

(2) go to or near:

(A) the residence, place of employment, or business of the victim; or

(B) if applicable, a school, day-care facility, or similar facility where a dependent child of the victim is in attendance.

(c) The magistrate shall specifically describe the prohibited locations under Subsection (b)(2) and the minimum distances, if any, that the defendant must maintain from the locations.

(d) At a hearing limited to determining whether the defendant violated a condition of bond imposed under Subsection (b), the magistrate may revoke the defendant's bond only if the magistrate finds by a preponderance of the evidence that the violation occurred. If the magistrate finds that the violation occurred, the magistrate shall revoke the defendant's bond and order that the defendant be immediately returned to custody. Once the defendant is placed in custody, the revocation of the defendant's bond discharges the sureties on the bond, if any, from any future liability on the bond. A discharge under this subsection from any future liability on the bond does not discharge any surety from liability for previous forfeitures on the bond.

Art. 17.47. Conditions Requiring Submission of Specimen.

(a) A magistrate may require as a condition of release on bail or bond of a defendant that the defendant provide to a local law enforcement agency one or more specimens for the purpose of creating a DNA record under Subchapter G, Chapter 411, Government Code.

(b) A magistrate shall require as a condition of release on bail or bond of a defendant described by Section 411.1471(a), Government Code, that the defendant provide to a local law enforcement agency one or more specimens for the purpose of creating a DNA record under Subchapter G, Chapter 411, Government Code.

Art. 17.48. Posttrial Actions.

A convicting court on entering a finding favorable to a convicted person under Article 64.04, after a hearing at which the attorney representing the state and the counsel for the defendant are entitled to appear, may release the convicted person on bail under this chapter pending the conclusion of court proceedings or proceedings under Section 11, Article IV, Texas Constitution, and Article 48.01.

Art. 17.49. Conditions for Defendant Charged with Offense Involving Family Violence.

(a) In this article:

(1) "Family violence" has the meaning assigned by Section 71.004, Family Code.

(2) "Global positioning monitoring system" means a system that electronically determines and reports the location of an individual through the use of a transmitter or similar device carried or worn by the individual that transmits latitude and longitude data to a monitoring entity through global positioning satellite technology. The term does not include a system that contains or operates global positioning system technology, radio frequency identification technology, or any other similar technology that is implanted in or otherwise invades or violates the individual's body.

(b) A magistrate may require as a condition of release on bond that a defendant charged with an offense involving family violence:

(1) refrain from going to or near a residence, school, place of employment, or other location, as specifically described in the bond, frequented by an alleged victim of the offense;

(2) carry or wear a global positioning monitoring system device and, except as provided by Subsection (h), pay a reimbursement fee for the costs associated with operating that system in relation to the defendant; or

(3) except as provided by Subsection (h), if the alleged victim of the offense consents after receiving the information described by Subsection (d), pay a reimbursement fee for the costs associated with providing the victim with an electronic receptor device that:

(A) is capable of receiving the global positioning monitoring system information from the device carried or worn by the defendant; and

(B) notifies the victim if the defendant is at or near a location that the defendant has been ordered to refrain from going to or near under Subdivision (1).

(c) Before imposing a condition described by Subsection (b)(1), a magistrate must afford an alleged victim an opportunity to provide the magistrate with a list of areas from which the victim would like the defendant excluded and shall consider the victim's request, if any, in determining the locations the defendant will be ordered to refrain from going to or near. If the magistrate imposes a condition described by Subsection (b)(1), the magistrate shall specifically describe the locations that the defendant has been ordered to refrain from going to or near and the minimum distances, if any, that the defendant must maintain from those locations.

(d) Before imposing a condition described by Subsection (b)(3), a magistrate must provide to an alleged victim information regarding:

(1) the victim's right to participate in a global positioning monitoring system or to refuse to participate in that system and the procedure for requesting that the magistrate terminate the victim's participation;

(2) the manner in which the global positioning monitoring system technology functions and the risks and limitations of that technology, and the extent to which the system will track and record the victim's location and movements;

(3) any locations that the defendant is ordered to refrain from going to or near and the minimum distances, if any, that the defendant must maintain from those locations;

(4) any sanctions that the court may impose on the defendant for violating a condition of bond imposed under this article;

(5) the procedure that the victim is to follow, and support services available to assist the victim, if the defendant violates a condition of bond or if the global positioning monitoring system equipment fails;

(6) community services available to assist the victim in obtaining shelter, counseling, education, child care, legal representation, and other assistance available to address the consequences of family violence; and

(7) the fact that the victim's communications with the court concerning the global positioning monitoring system and any restrictions to be imposed on the defendant's movements are not confidential.

(e) In addition to the information described by Subsection (d), a magistrate shall provide to an alleged victim who participates in a global positioning monitoring system under this article the name and telephone number of an appropriate person employed by a local law enforcement agency whom the victim may call to request immediate assistance if the defendant violates a condition of bond imposed under this article.

(f) In determining whether to order a defendant's participation in a global positioning monitoring system under this article, the magistrate shall consider the likelihood that the defendant's participation will deter the defendant from seeking to kill, physically injure, stalk, or otherwise threaten the alleged victim before trial.

(g) An alleged victim may request that the magistrate terminate the victim's participation in a global positioning monitoring system at any time. The magistrate may not impose sanctions on the victim for requesting termination of the victim's participation in or refusing to participate in a global positioning monitoring system under this article.

(h) If the magistrate determines that a defendant is indigent, the magistrate may, based on a sliding scale established by local rule, require the defendant to pay a reimbursement fee under Subsection (b)(2) or (3) in an amount that is less than the full amount of the costs associated with operating the global positioning monitoring system in relation to the defendant or providing the victim with an electronic receptor device.

(i) If an indigent defendant pays to an entity that operates a global positioning monitoring system the partial amount ordered by a magistrate under Subsection (h), the entity shall accept the partial amount as payment in full. The county in which the magistrate who enters an order under Subsection (h) is located is not responsible for payment of any costs associated with operating the global positioning monitoring system in relation to an indigent defendant.

(j) A magistrate that imposes a condition described by Subsection (b)(1) or (2) shall order the entity that operates the global positioning monitoring system to notify the court and the appropriate local law enforcement agency if a defendant violates a condition of bond imposed under this article.

(k) A magistrate that imposes a condition described by Subsection (b) may only allow or require the defendant to execute or be released under a type of bond that is authorized by this chapter.

(*l*) This article does not limit the authority of a magistrate to impose any other reasonable conditions of bond or enter any orders of protection under other applicable statutes.

Art. 17.50. Entry Into Texas Crime Information Center of Certain Information in Cases Involving Violent Offenses; Duties of Magistrates, Sheriffs, and Department of Public Safety. [Effective January 1, 2022]

(a) In this article:

(1) "Business day" means a day other than a Saturday, Sunday, or state or national holiday.

(2) "Database" means the statewide law enforcement information system maintained by the Department of Public Safety, also known as the Texas Crime Information Center.

(3) "Violent offense" means:

(A) an offense under the following sections of the Penal Code:

(i) Section 19.02 (murder);

(ii) Section 19.03 (capital murder);

(iii) Section 20.03 (kidnapping);

(iv) Section 20.04 (aggravated kidnapping);

(v) Section 21.11 (indecency with a child);

(vi) Section 22.011 (sexual assault);

(vii) Section 22.02 (aggravated assault);

(viii) Section 22.021 (aggravated sexual assault);

(ix) Section 22.04 (injury to a child, elderly individual, or disabled individual);

(x) Section 29.03 (aggravated robbery);

(xi) Section 21.02 (continuous sexual abuse of young child or children); or

(xii) Section 20A.03 (continuous trafficking of persons); or

(B) any offense involving family violence, as defined by Section 71.004, Family Code.

(b) As soon as practicable but not later than the next day after the date a magistrate issues an order imposing a condition of bond on a defendant under this chapter for a violent offense, the magistrate shall notify the sheriff of the condition and provide to the sheriff the following information:

(1) the information listed in Section 411.042(b)(6), Government Code, as that information relates to an order described by this subsection;

(2) the name and address of any named person the condition of bond is intended to protect, and if different and applicable, the name and address of the victim of the alleged offense;

(3) the date the order releasing the defendant on bond was issued; and

(4) the court that issued the order releasing the defendant on bond.

(c) As soon as practicable but not later than the next day after the date a magistrate, in a case described by Subsection (b), revokes a bond that contains a condition, modifies the terms of or removes a condition of bond, or disposes of the underlying criminal charges, the magistrate shall notify the sheriff and provide the sheriff with information that is sufficient to enable the sheriff to modify or remove the appropriate record in the database.

(d) As soon as practicable but not later than the next business day after the date the sheriff receives the information:

(1) described by Subsection (b), the sheriff shall:

(A) enter the information into the database; and

(B) make a good faith effort to notify by telephone any named person the condition of bond is intended to protect, and if different and applicable, the victim of the alleged offense that the defendant to whom the order is directed has been released on bond; and

(2) described by Subsection (c), the sheriff shall modify or remove the appropriate record in the database.

(e) The clerk of a court that issues an order described by Subsection (b) shall send a copy of the order to any named person the condition of bond is intended to protect, and if different and applicable, the victim of the alleged offense at the person's last known address not later than the next business day after the date the court issues the order.

(f) The Department of Public Safety shall:

(1) modify the database to enable the database to accept and maintain detailed information on active conditions of bond regarding the requirements and status of a condition of bond imposed by a magistrate for a violent offense, including information described by Subsections (b) and (c); and

(2) develop and adopt a form for use by magistrates and sheriffs to facilitate the data collection and data entry required by this article.

(g) This article does not create liability for any errors or omissions of a sheriff caused by inaccurate information provided under this article to the sheriff by a magistrate.

CHAPTER 17A CORPORATIONS AND ASSOCIATIONS

Art. 17A.01. Application and Definitions.

(a) This chapter sets out some of the procedural rules applicable to the criminal responsibility of corporations and associations. Where not in conflict with this chapter, the other chapters of this code apply to corporations and associations.

(b) In this code, unless the context requires a different definition:

(1) "Agent" means a director, officer, employee, or other person authorized to act in behalf of a corporation or association.

(2) "Association" means a government or governmental subdivision or agency, trust, partnership, or two or more persons having a joint or common economic interest.

(3) "High managerial agent" means:

(A) an officer of a corporation or association;

(B) a partner in a partnership; or

(C) an agent of a corporation or association who has duties of such responsibility that his conduct may reasonably be assumed to represent the policy of the corporation or association.

(4) "Person," "he," and "him" include corporation and association.

Art. 17A.02. Allegation of Name.

(a) In alleging the name of a defendant corporation, it is sufficient to state in the complaint, indictment, or information the corporate name, or to state any name or designation by which the corporation is known or may be identified. It is not necessary to allege that the defendant was lawfully incorporated.

(b) In alleging the name of a defendant association it is sufficient to state in the complaint, indictment, or information the association's name, or to state any name or designation by which the association is known or may be identified, or to state the name or names of one or more members of the association, referring to the unnamed members as "others." It is not necessary to allege the legal form of the association.

Art. 17A.03. Summoning Corporation or Association.

(a) When a complaint is filed or an indictment or information presented against a corporation or association, the court or clerk shall issue a summons to the corporation or association. The summons shall be in the same form as a capias except that:

(1) it shall summon the corporation or association to appear before the court named at the place stated in the summons; and

(2) it shall be accompanied by a certified copy of the complaint, indictment, or information; and

(3) it shall provide that the corporation or association appear before the court named at or before 10 a.m. of the Monday next after the expiration of 20 days after it is served with summons, except when service is made upon the secretary of state or the Commissioner of Insurance, in which instance the summons shall provide that the corporation or association appear before the court named at or before 10 a.m. of the Monday next after the expiration of 30 days after the secretary of state or the Commissioner of Insurance is served with summons.

(b) No individual may be arrested upon a complaint, indictment, information, judgment, or sentence against a corporation or association.

Art. 17A.04. Service on Corporation.

(a) Except as provided in Paragraph (d) of this article, a peace officer shall serve a summons on a corporation by personally delivering a copy of it to the corporation's registered agent. However, if a registered agent has not been designated, or cannot with reasonable diligence be found at the registered office, then the peace officer shall serve the summons by personally delivering a copy of it to the president or a vice-president of the corporation.

(b) If the peace officer certifies on the return that he diligently but unsuccessfully attempted to effect service under Paragraph (a) of this article, or if the corporation is a foreign corporation that has no certificate of authority, then he shall serve the summons on the secretary of state by personally delivering a copy of it to him, or to the deputy secretary of state, or to any clerk in charge of the corporation department of his office. On receipt of the summons copy, the secretary of state shall immediately forward it by certified or registered mail, return receipt requested, addressed to the defendant corporation at its registered or principal office in the state or country under whose law it was incorporated.

(c) The secretary of state shall keep a permanent record of the date and time of receipt and his disposition of each summons served under Paragraph (b) of this article together with the return receipt.

(d) The method of service on a corporation regulated under the Insurance Code is governed by that code.

Art. 17A.05. Service on Association.

(a) Except as provided in Paragraph (b) of this article, a peace officer shall serve a summons on an association by personally delivering a copy of it:

(1) to a high managerial agent at any place where business of the association is regularly conducted; or

(2) if the peace officer certifies on the return that he diligently but unsuccessfully attempted to serve a high managerial agent, to any employee of suitable age and discretion at any place where business of the association is regularly conducted; or

(3) if the peace officer certifies on the return that he diligently but unsuccessfully attempted to serve a high managerial agent, or employee of suitable age and discretion, to any member of the association.

(b) The method of service on an association regulated under the Insurance Code is governed by that code.

Art. 17A.06. Appearance.

(a) In all criminal actions instituted against a corporation or association, in which original jurisdiction is in a district or county-level court:

(1) appearance is for the purpose of arraignment;

(2) the corporation or association has 10 full days after the day the arraignment takes place and before the day the trial begins to file written pleadings.

(b) In all criminal actions instituted against a corporation or association, in which original jurisdiction is in a justice court or corporation court:

(1) appearance is for the purpose of entering a plea; and

(2) 10 full days must elapse after the day of appearance before the corporation or association may be tried.

Art. 17A.07. Presence of Corporation or Association.

(a) A defendant corporation or association appears through counsel.

(b) If a corporation or association does not appear in response to summons, or appears but fails or refuses to plead:

(1) it is deemed to be present in person for all purposes; and

(2) the court shall enter a plea of not guilty in its behalf; and

(3) the court may proceed with trial, judgment, and sentencing.

(c) If, having appeared and entered a plea in response to summons, a corporation or association is absent without good cause at any time during later proceedings:

(1) it is deemed to be present in person for all purposes; and

(2) the court may proceed with trial, judgment, or sentencing.

Art. 17A.08. Probation.

The benefits of the adult probation laws shall not be available to corporations and associations.

Art. 17A.09. Notifying Attorney General of Corporation's Conviction.

If a corporation is convicted of an offense, or if a high managerial agent is convicted of an offense committed in the conduct of the affairs of the corporation, the court shall notify the attorney general in writing of the conviction when it becomes final and unappealable. The notice shall include:

(1) the corporation's name, and the name of the corporation's registered agent and the address of the registered office, or the high managerial agent's name and address, or both; and

(2) certified copies of the judgment and sentence and of the complaint, information, or indictment on which the judgment and sentence were based.

SEARCH WARRANTS

CHAPTER 18
SEARCH WARRANTS

Art. 18.01. Search Warrant.

(a) A "search warrant" is a written order, issued by a magistrate and directed to a peace officer, commanding him to search for any property or thing and to seize the same and bring it before such magistrate or commanding him to search for and photograph a child and to deliver to the magistrate any of the film exposed pursuant to the order.

(b) No search warrant shall issue for any purpose in this state unless sufficient facts are first presented to satisfy the issuing magistrate that probable cause does in fact exist for its issuance. A sworn affidavit setting forth substantial facts establishing probable cause shall be filed in every instance in which a search warrant is requested. Except as otherwise provided by this code, the affidavit becomes public information when the search warrant for which the affidavit was presented is executed, and the magistrate's clerk shall make a copy of the affidavit available for public inspection in the clerk's office during normal business hours.

(b-1) (1) For purposes of this article, a magistrate may consider information communicated by telephone or other reliable electronic means in determining whether to issue a search warrant. The magistrate may examine an applicant for a search warrant and any person on whose testimony the application is based. The applicant or other person must be placed under oath before the examination.

(2) If an applicant for a search warrant attests to the contents of an affidavit submitted by reliable electronic means, the magistrate must acknowledge the attestation in writing on the affidavit. If the magistrate considers additional testimony or exhibits, the magistrate must:

(A) ensure that the testimony is recorded verbatim by an electronic recording device, by a court reporter, or in writing;

(B) ensure that any recording or reporter's notes are transcribed and that the transcription is certified as accurate and is preserved;

(C) sign, certify the accuracy of, and preserve any other written record; and

(D) ensure that the exhibits are preserved.

(3) An applicant for a search warrant who submits information as authorized by this subsection must prepare a proposed duplicate original of the warrant and must read or otherwise transmit its contents verbatim to the magistrate. A magistrate must enter into an original search warrant the contents of a proposed duplicate original that are read to the magistrate. If the applicant transmits the contents by reliable electronic means, the transmission received by the magistrate may serve as the original search warrant.

(4) The magistrate may modify a search warrant that is submitted as described by Subdivision (3). If the magistrate modifies the warrant, the magistrate must:

(A) transmit the modified version to the applicant by reliable electronic means; or

(B) file the modified original and direct the applicant to modify the proposed duplicate original accordingly.

(5) A magistrate who issues a search warrant for which information is provided by telephone or reliable electronic means must:

(A) sign the original documents;

(B) enter the date and time of issuance on the warrant; and

(C) transmit the warrant by reliable electronic means to the applicant or direct the applicant to sign the judge's name and enter the date and time on the duplicate original.

(6) Evidence obtained pursuant to a search warrant for which information was provided in accordance with this subsection is not subject to suppression on the ground that issuing the warrant in compliance with this subsection was unreasonable under the circumstances, absent a finding of bad faith.

(c) A search warrant may not be issued under Article 18.02(a)(10) unless the sworn affidavit required by Subsection (b) sets forth sufficient facts to establish probable cause: (1) that a specific offense has been committed, (2) that the specifically described property or items that are to be searched for or seized constitute evidence of that offense or evidence that a particular person committed that offense, and (3) that the property or items constituting evidence to be searched for or seized are located at or on the particular person, place, or thing to be searched. Except as provided by Subsections (d), (i), and (j), only a judge of a municipal court of record or a county court who is an attorney licensed by the State of Texas, a statutory county court judge, a district court judge, a judge of the Court of Criminal Appeals, including the presiding judge, a justice of the Supreme Court of Texas, including the chief justice, or a magistrate with jurisdiction over criminal cases serving a district court may issue warrants under Article 18.02(a)(10).

(d) Only the specifically described property or items set forth in a search warrant issued under Article 18.02(a)(10) or property, items or contraband enumerated in Article 18.02(a)(1), (2), (3), (4), (5), (6), (7), (8), (9), or (12) may be seized. A subsequent search warrant may be issued pursuant to Article 18.02(a)(10) to search the same person, place, or thing subjected to a prior search under Article 18.02(a)(10) only if the subsequent search warrant is issued by a judge of a district court, a court of appeals, the court of criminal appeals, or the supreme court.

(e) A search warrant may not be issued under Article 18.02(a)(10) to search for and seize property or items that are not described in Article 18.02(a)(1), (2), (3), (4), (5), (6), (7), (8), or (9) and that are located in an office of a newspaper, news magazine, television station, or radio station, and in no event may property or items not described in Article 18.02(a)(1), (2), (3), (4), (5), (6), (7), (8), or (9) be legally seized in any search pursuant to a search warrant of an office of a newspaper, news magazine, television station, or radio station.

(f) A search warrant may not be issued pursuant to Article 18.021 of this code unless the sworn affidavit required by Subsection (b) of this article sets forth sufficient facts to establish probable cause:

(1) that a specific offense has been committed;

(2) that a specifically described person has been a victim of the offense;

(3) that evidence of the offense or evidence that a particular person committed the offense can be detected by photographic means; and

(4) that the person to be searched for and photographed is located at the particular place to be searched.

(g) A search warrant may not be issued under Article 18.02(a)(12) unless the sworn affidavit required by Subsection (b) of this article sets forth sufficient facts to establish probable cause that a specific felony offense has been committed and that the specifically described property or items that are to be searched for or seized constitute contraband as defined in Article 59.01 of this code and are located at or on the particular person, place, or thing to be searched.

Code of Criminal Procedure

(h) Except as provided by Subsection (i) of this article, a warrant under Article 18.02(a)(12) may only be issued by:

(1) a judge of a municipal court of record who is an attorney licensed by the state;

(2) a judge of a county court who is an attorney licensed by the state; or

(3) a judge of a statutory county court, district court, the court of criminal appeals, or the supreme court.

(i) In a county that does not have a municipal court of record with a courtroom located in that county and a judge who is an attorney licensed by the state, a county court judge who is an attorney licensed by the state, or a statutory county court judge, any magistrate may issue a search warrant under Article 18.02(a)(10) or (12). This subsection is not applicable to a subsequent search warrant under Article 18.02(a)(10).

(j) Any magistrate who is an attorney licensed by this state may issue a search warrant under Article 18.02(a)(10) to collect a blood specimen from a person who:

(1) is arrested for an offense under Section 49.04, 49.045, 49.05, 49.06, 49.065, 49.07, or 49.08, Penal Code; and

(2) refuses to submit to a breath or blood alcohol test.

Art. 18.011. Sealing of Affidavit.

(a) An attorney representing the state in the prosecution of felonies may request a district judge or the judge of an appellate court to seal an affidavit presented under Article 18.01(b). The judge may order the affidavit sealed if the attorney establishes a compelling state interest in that:

(1) public disclosure of the affidavit would jeopardize the safety of a victim, witness, or confidential informant or cause the destruction of evidence; or

(2) the affidavit contains information obtained from a court-ordered wiretap that has not expired at the time the attorney representing the state requests the sealing of the affidavit.

(b) An order sealing an affidavit under this section expires on the 31st day after the date on which the search warrant for which the affidavit was presented is executed. After an original order sealing an affidavit is issued under this article, an attorney representing the state in the prosecution of felonies may request, and a judge may grant, before the 31st day after the date on which the search warrant for which the affidavit was presented is executed, on a new finding of compelling state interest, one 30-day extension of the original order.

(c) On the expiration of an order issued under Subsection (b) and any extension, the affidavit must be unsealed.

(d) An order issued under this section may not:

(1) prohibit the disclosure of information relating to the contents of a search warrant, the return of a search warrant, or the inventory of property taken pursuant to a search warrant; or

(2) affect the right of a defendant to discover the contents of an affidavit.

Art. 18.02. Grounds for Issuance.

(a) A search warrant may be issued to search for and seize:

(1) property acquired by theft or in any other manner which makes its acquisition a penal offense;

(2) property specially designed, made, or adapted for or commonly used in the commission of an offense;

(3) arms and munitions kept or prepared for the purposes of insurrection or riot;

(4) weapons prohibited by the Penal Code;

(5) gambling devices or equipment, altered gambling equipment, or gambling paraphernalia;

(6) obscene materials kept or prepared for commercial distribution or exhibition, subject to the additional rules set forth by law;

(7) a drug, controlled substance, immediate precursor, chemical precursor, or other controlled substance property, including an apparatus or paraphernalia kept, prepared, or manufactured in violation of the laws of this state;

(8) any property the possession of which is prohibited by law;

(9) implements or instruments used in the commission of a crime;

(10) property or items, except the personal writings by the accused, constituting evidence of an offense or constituting evidence tending to show that a particular person committed an offense;

(11) persons;

(12) contraband subject to forfeiture under Chapter 59 of this code;

(13) electronic customer data held in electronic storage, including the contents of and records and other information related to a wire communication or electronic communication held in electronic storage; or

(14) a cellular telephone or other wireless communications device, subject to Article 18.0215.

(b) For purposes of Subsection (a)(13):

(1) "Electronic communication" and "wire communication" have the meanings assigned by Article 18A.001.

(2) Electronic customer data" and "electronic storage" have the meanings assigned by Article 18B.001.

Art. 18.021. Issuance of Search Warrant to Photograph Injured Child.

(a) A search warrant may be issued to search for and photograph a child who is alleged to be the victim of the offenses of injury to a child as prohibited by Section 22.04, Penal Code; sexual assault of a child as prohibited by Section 22.011(a), Penal Code; aggravated sexual assault of a child as prohibited by Section 22.021, Penal Code; or continuous sexual abuse of young child or disabled individual as prohibited by Section 21.02, Penal Code.

(b) The officer executing the warrant may be accompanied by a photographer who is employed by a law enforcement agency and who acts under the direction of the officer executing the warrant. The photographer is entitled to access to the child in the same manner as the officer executing the warrant.

(c) In addition to the requirements of Subdivisions (1), (4), and (5) of Article 18.04 of this code, a warrant issued under this article shall identify, as near as may be, the child to be located and photographed, shall name or describe, as near as may be, the place or thing to be searched, and shall command any peace officer of the proper county to search for and cause the child to be photographed.

(d) After having located and photographed the child, the peace officer executing the warrant shall take possession of the exposed film and deliver it forthwith to the magistrate. The child may not be removed from the premises on which he or she is located except under Subchapters A and B, Chapter 262, Family Code.

(e) A search warrant under this section shall be executed by a peace officer of the same sex as the alleged victim or, if the officer is not of the same sex as the alleged victim, the peace officer must be assisted by a person of the same sex as the alleged victim. The person assisting an officer under this subsection must be acting under the direction of the officer and must be with the alleged victim during the taking of the photographs.

Art. 18.0215. Access to Cellular Telephone or Other Wireless Communications Device.

(a) A peace officer may not search a person's cellular telephone or other wireless communications device, pursuant to a lawful arrest of the person without obtaining a warrant under this article.

(b) A warrant under this article may be issued only by a judge in the same judicial district as the site of:

(1) the law enforcement agency that employs the peace officer, if the cellular telephone or other wireless communications device is in the officer's possession; or

(2) the likely location of the telephone or device.

(c) A judge may issue a warrant under this article only on the application of a peace officer. An application must be written and signed and sworn to or affirmed before the judge. The application must:

(1) state the name, department, agency, and address of the applicant;

(2) identify the cellular telephone or other wireless communications device to be searched;

(3) state the name of the owner or possessor of the telephone or device to be searched;

(4) state the judicial district in which:

(A) the law enforcement agency that employs the peace officer is located, if the telephone or device is in the officer's possession; or

(B) the telephone or device is likely to be located; and

(5) state the facts and circumstances that provide the applicant with probable cause to believe that:

(A) criminal activity has been, is, or will be committed; and

(B) searching the telephone or device is likely to produce evidence in the investigation of the criminal activity described in Paragraph (A).

(d) Notwithstanding any other law, a peace officer may search a cellular telephone or other wireless communications device without a warrant if:

(1) the owner or possessor of the telephone or device consents to the search;

(2) the telephone or device is reported stolen by the owner or possessor; or

(3) the officer reasonably believes that:

(A) the telephone or device is in the possession of a fugitive from justice for whom an arrest warrant has been issued for committing a felony offense; or

(B) there exists an immediate life-threatening situation, as defined by Article 18A.201.

(e) A peace officer must apply for a warrant to search a cellular telephone or other wireless communications device as soon as practicable after a search is conducted under Subsection (d)(3)(A) or (B). If the judge finds that the applicable situation under Subsection (d)(3)(A) or (B) did not occur and declines to issue the warrant, any evidence obtained is not admissible in a criminal action.

Art. 18.03. Search Warrant May Order Arrest.

If the facts presented to the magistrate under Article 18.02 of this chapter also establish the existence of probable cause that a person has committed some offense under the laws of this state, the search warrant may, in addition, order the arrest of such person.

Art. 18.04. Contents of Warrant.

A search warrant issued under this chapter, Chapter 18A, or Chapter 18B shall be sufficient if it contains the following requisites:

(1) that it run in the name of "The State of Texas";

(2) that it identify, as near as may be, that which is to be seized and name or describe, as near as may be, the person, place, or thing to be searched;

(3) that it command any peace officer of the proper county to search forthwith the person, place, or thing named;

(4) that it be dated and signed by the magistrate; and

(5) that the magistrate's name appear in clearly legible handwriting or in typewritten form with the magistrate's signature.

Art. 18.05. Warrants for Fire, Health, and Code Inspections.

(a) Except as provided by Subsection (e) of this article, a search warrant may be issued to a fire marshal, health officer, or code enforcement official of the state or of any county, city, or other political subdivision for the purpose of allowing the inspection of any specified premises to determine the presence of a fire or health hazard or unsafe building condition or a violation of any fire, health, or building regulation, statute, or ordinance.

(b) A search warrant may not be issued under this article except upon the presentation of evidence of probable cause to believe that a fire or health hazard or violation or unsafe building condition is present in the premises sought to be inspected.

(c) In determining probable cause, the magistrate is not limited to evidence of specific knowledge, but may consider any of the following:

(1) the age and general condition of the premises;

(2) previous violations or hazards found present in the premises;

(3) the type of premises;

(4) the purposes for which the premises are used; and

(5) the presence of hazards or violations in and the general condition of premises near the premises sought to be inspected.

(d) Each city or county may designate one or more code enforcement officials for the purpose of being issued a search warrant as authorized by Subsection (a) of this article. A political subdivision other than a city or county may designate not more than one code enforcement official for the purpose of being issued a search warrant as authorized by Subsection (a) of this article only if the political subdivision routinely inspects premises to determine whether there is a fire or health hazard or unsafe building condition or a violation of fire, health, or building regulation, statute, or ordinance.

(e) A search warrant may not be issued under this article to a code enforcement official of a county with a population of 3.3 million or more for the purpose of allowing the inspection of specified premises to determine the presence of an unsafe building condition or a violation of a building regulation, statute, or ordinance.

Art. 18.06. Execution of Warrants.

(a) A peace officer to whom a search warrant is delivered shall execute the warrant without delay and shall return the warrant to the proper magistrate.

(b) On searching the place ordered to be searched, the officer executing the warrant shall present a copy of the warrant to the owner of the place, if he is present. If the owner of the place is not present but a person who is present is in possession of the place, the officer shall present a copy of the warrant to the person. Before the officer takes property from the place, he shall prepare a written inventory of the property to be taken. He shall legibly endorse his name on the inventory and present a copy of the inventory to the owner or other person in possession of the property. If neither the owner nor a person in possession of the property is present when the officer executes the warrant, the officer shall leave a copy of the warrant and the inventory at the place.

Art. 18.065. Execution of Warrant Issued by District Judge for DNA Specimen.

(a) A warrant issued by the judge of a district court under Article 18.02(a)(10) to collect a DNA specimen from a person for the purpose of connecting that person to an offense may be executed in any county in this state.

(b) This article does not apply to a warrant issued by a justice of the peace, judge, or other magistrate other than a judge of a district court.

Art. 18.067. Execution of Warrant for Blood Specimen in Intoxication Offense.

Notwithstanding any other law, a warrant issued under Article 18.02(a)(10) to collect a blood specimen from a person suspected of committing an intoxication offense under Section 49.04, 49.045, 49.05, 49.06, 49.065, 49.07, or 49.08, Penal Code, may be executed:

(1) in any county adjacent to the county in which the warrant was issued; and

(2) by any law enforcement officer authorized to make an arrest in the county of execution.

Art. 18.07. Days Allowed for Warrant to Run.

(a) Unless the magistrate directs in the warrant a shorter period for the execution of any search warrant issued under this chapter, Chapter 18A, or Chapter 18B, the period allowed for the execution of the warrant, exclusive of the day of its issuance and of the day of its execution, is:

(1) 15 whole days if the warrant is issued solely to search for and seize specimens from a specific person for DNA analysis and comparison, including blood and saliva samples;

(2) 10 whole days if the warrant is issued under Article 18B.354 or Subchapter G-1, Chapter 18B; or

(3) three whole days if the warrant is issued for a purpose other than that described by Subdivision (1) or (2).

(b) The magistrate issuing a search warrant under this chapter, Chapter 18A, or Chapter 18B shall endorse on the search warrant the date and hour of its issuance.

(c) If a warrant is issued to search for and seize data or information contained in or on a computer, disk drive, flash drive, cellular telephone, or other electronic, communication, or data storage device, the warrant is considered to have been executed within the time allowed under Subsection (a) if the device was seized before the expiration of the time allowed. Notwithstanding any other law, any data or information contained in or on a device seized may be recovered and analyzed after the expiration of the time allowed under Subsection (a).

Art. 18.08. Power of Officer Executing Warrant.

In the execution of a search warrant, the officer may call to his aid any number of citizens in this county, who shall be bound to aid in the execution of the same.

Art. 18.09. Shall Seize Accused and Property.

When the property which the officer is directed to search for and seize is found he shall take possession of the same and carry it before the magistrate. He shall also arrest any person whom he is directed to arrest by the warrant and immediately take such person before the magistrate. For purposes of this chapter, "seizure," in the context of property, means the restraint of property, whether by physical force or by a display of an officer's authority, and includes the collection of property or the act of taking possession of property.

Art. 18.095. Seizure of Circuit Board of Gambling Device, Equipment, or Paraphernalia.

For purposes of this chapter, an officer directed under a search warrant to search for and seize a gambling device or equipment, altered gambling equipment, or gambling paraphernalia in the discretion of the officer may:

(1) seize only the programmable main circuit board of the device, equipment, or paraphernalia if that circuit board is designed as a subassembly or essential part of the device, equipment, or paraphernalia to provide the information necessary for the device, equipment, or paraphernalia to operate as a gambling device or equipment, altered gambling equipment, or gambling paraphernalia;

(2) carry the circuit board before the magistrate; and

(3) retain custody of the circuit board as the property seized pursuant to the warrant as required under this chapter.

Art. 18.10. How Return Made.

(a) Not later than three whole days after executing a search warrant, the officer shall return the search warrant. Upon returning the search warrant, the officer shall state on the back of the same, or on some paper attached to it, the manner in which the warrant has been executed. The officer shall also deliver to the magistrate a copy of the inventory of the property taken into his possession under the warrant. The failure of an officer to make a timely return of an executed search warrant or to submit an inventory of the property taken into the officer's possession under the warrant does not bar the admission of evidence under Article 38.23. The officer who seized the property shall retain custody of it until the magistrate issues an order directing the manner of safekeeping the property. Except as otherwise provided by Subsection (b), the property may not be removed from the county in which it was seized without an order approving the removal, issued by a magistrate in the county in which the warrant was issued; provided, however, nothing herein shall prevent the officer, or his department, from forwarding any item or items seized to a laboratory for scientific analysis.

(b) For the purposes of complying with this article, property seized pursuant to a warrant executed under Article 18.067 may be removed from the county in which it was seized and returned to the county in which the warrant was issued without a court order.

Art. 18.11. Custody of Property Found.

Property seized pursuant to a search warrant shall be kept as provided by the order of a magistrate issued in accordance with Article 18.10 of this code.

Art. 18.12. Magistrate Shall Investigate.

The magistrate, upon the return of a search warrant, shall proceed to try the questions arising upon the same, and shall take testimony as in other examinations before him.

Art. 18.13. Shall Discharge Defendant.

If the magistrate be not satisfied, upon investigation, that there was good ground for the issuance of the warrant, he shall discharge the defendant and order restitution of the property taken from him, except for criminal instruments. In such case, the criminal instruments shall be kept by the sheriff subject to the order of the proper court.

Art. 18.14. Examining Trial.

The magistrate shall proceed to deal with the accused as in other cases before an examining court if he is satisfied there was good ground for issuing the warrant.

Art. 18.15. Certify Record to Proper Court.

The magistrate shall keep a record of all the proceedings had before him in cases of search warrants, and shall certify the same and deliver them to the clerk of the court having jurisdiction of the case, before the next term of said court, and accompany the same with all the original papers relating thereto, including the certified schedule of the property seized.

Art. 18.16. Preventing Consequences of Theft.

Any person has a right to prevent the consequences of theft by seizing any personal property that has been stolen and bringing it, with the person suspected of committing the theft, if that person can be taken, before a magistrate for examination, or delivering the property and the person suspected of committing the theft to a peace officer for that purpose. To justify a seizure under this article, there must be reasonable ground to believe the property is stolen, and the seizure must be openly made and the proceedings had without delay.

Art. 18.17. Disposition of Abandoned or Unclaimed Property.

(a) All unclaimed or abandoned personal property of every kind, other than contraband subject to forfeiture under Chapter 59 and whiskey, wine and malt beverages, seized by any peace officer in the State of Texas which is not held as evidence to be used in any pending case and has not been ordered destroyed or returned to the person entitled to possession of the same by a magistrate, which shall remain unclaimed for a period of 30 days shall be delivered for disposition to a person designated by the municipality or the purchasing agent of the county in which the property was seized. If a peace officer of a municipality seizes the property, the peace officer shall deliver the property to a person designated by the municipality. If any other peace officer seizes the property, the peace officer shall deliver the property to the purchasing agent of the county. If the county has no purchasing agent, then such property shall be disposed of by the sheriff of the county.

(b) The county purchasing agent, the person designated by the municipality, or the sheriff of the county, as the case may be, shall mail a notice to the last known address of the owner of such property by certified mail. Such notice shall describe the property being held, give the name and address of the officer holding such property, and shall state that if the owner does not claim such property within 90 days from the date of the notice such property will be disposed of and the proceeds, after deducting the reasonable expense of keeping such property and the costs of the disposition, placed in the treasury of the municipality or county giving the notice.

(c) If the property has a fair market value of $500 or more and the owner or the address of the owner is unknown, the person designated by the municipality, the county purchasing agent, or the sheriff, as the case may be, shall cause to be published once in a paper of general circulation in the municipality or county a notice containing a general description of the property held, the name of the owner if known, the name and address of the officer holding such property, and a statement that if the owner does not claim such property within 90 days from the date of the publication such property will be disposed of and the proceeds, after deducting the reasonable expense of keeping such property and the costs of the disposition, placed in the treasury of the municipality or county disposing of the property. If the property has a fair market value of less than $500 and the owner or the address of the owner is unknown, the person designated by the municipality, the county purchasing agent, or the sheriff may sell or donate the property. The person designated by the municipality, the purchasing agent, or the sheriff shall deposit the sale proceeds, after deducting the reasonable expense of keeping the property and costs of the sale, in the treasury of the municipality or county selling or donating the property.

(d) The sale under this article of any property that has a fair market value of $500 or more shall be preceded by a notice published once at least 14 days prior to the date of such sale in a newspaper of general circulation in the municipality or county where the sale is to take place, stating the general description of the property, the names of the owner if known, and the date and place that such sale will occur. This article does not require disposition by sale.

(d-1) Notwithstanding Subsection (a), (b), (c), or (d), if property described by Subsection (a), other than money, is seized by a peace officer at the time the owner of the property is arrested for an offense punishable as a Class C misdemeanor, the law enforcement agency may provide notice to the owner at the time the owner is taken into or released from custody. On receiving the notice, the owner must sign the notice and attach a thumbprint to the notice. The notice must include:

(1) a description of the property being held;

(2) the address where the property is being held; and

(3) a statement that if the owner does not claim the property before the 31st day after the date the owner is released from custody, the property will be disposed of and the proceeds of the property, after deducting the reasonable expense of keeping and disposing of the property, will be placed in the treasury of the municipality or county providing the notice.

(d-2) If the property for which notice is provided under Subsection (d-1) is not claimed by the owner before the 31st day after the date the owner is released from custody, the law enforcement agency holding the property shall deliver the property for disposition to a person designated by the municipality or to the purchasing agent or sheriff of the county in which the property was seized, as applicable. The person designated by the municipality, the purchasing agent, or the sheriff may sell or donate the property without mailing or publishing an additional notice as required by Subsection (b), (c), or (d). The sale proceeds, after deducting the reasonable expense of keeping and disposing of the property, must be deposited in the treasury of the municipality or county disposing of the property.

(e) The real owner of any property disposed of shall have the right to file a claim to the proceeds with the commissioners court of the county or with the governing body of the municipality in which the disposition took place. A claim by the real owner must be filed not later than the 30th day after the date of disposition. If the claim is allowed by the commissioners court or the governing body of the municipality, the municipal or county treasurer shall pay the owner such funds as were paid into the treasury of the municipality or county as proceeds of the disposition. If the claim is denied by the commissioners court or the governing body or if said court or body fails to act upon such claim within 90 days, the claimant may sue the municipal or county treasurer in a court of competent jurisdiction in the county, and upon sufficient proof of ownership, recover judgment against such municipality or county for the recovery of the proceeds of the disposition.

(f) For the purposes of this article:

(1) "Person designated by a municipality" means an officer or employee of a municipality who is designated by the municipality to be primarily responsible for the disposition of property under this article.

(2) "Property held as evidence" means property related to a charge that has been filed or to a matter that is being investigated for the filing of a charge.

(g) If the provisions of this section have been met and the property is scheduled for disposition, the municipal or county law enforcement agency that originally seized the property may request and have the property converted to agency use. The agency at any time may transfer the property to another municipal or county law enforcement agency for the use of that agency. The agency last using the property shall return the property to the person designated by the municipality, county purchasing agent, or sheriff, as the case may be, for disposition when the agency has completed the intended use of the property.

(h) If the abandoned or unclaimed personal property is money, the person designated by the municipality, the county purchasing agent, or the sheriff of the county, as appropriate, may, after giving notice under Subsection (b) or (c) of this article, deposit the money in the treasury of the municipality or county giving notice without conducting the sale as required by Subsection (d) of this article.

(i) While offering the property for sale under this article, if a person designated by a municipality, county purchasing agent, or sheriff considers any bid as insufficient, the person, agent, or sheriff may decline the bid and reoffer the property for sale.

(j) Chapters 72, 74, 75, and 76, Property Code, do not apply to unclaimed or abandoned property to which this article applies.

Art. 18.18. Disposition of Gambling Paraphernalia, Prohibited Weapon, Criminal Instrument, and Other Contraband.

(a) Following the final conviction of a person for possession of a gambling device or equipment, altered gambling equipment, or gambling paraphernalia, for an offense involving a criminal instrument, for an offense involving an obscene device or material, for an offense involving child pornography, or for an offense involving a scanning device or re-encoder, the court entering the judgment of conviction shall order that the machine, device, gambling equipment or gambling paraphernalia, instrument, obscene device or material, child pornography, or scanning device or re-encoder be destroyed or forfeited to the state. Not later than the 30th day after the final conviction of a person for an offense involving a prohibited weapon, the court entering the judgment of conviction on its own motion, on the motion of the prosecuting attorney in the case, or on the motion of the law enforcement agency initiating the complaint on notice to the prosecuting attorney in the case if the prosecutor fails to move for the order shall order that the prohibited weapon be destroyed or forfeited to the law enforcement agency that initiated the complaint. If the court fails to enter the order within the time required by this subsection, any magistrate in the county in which the offense occurred may enter the order. Following the final conviction of a person for an offense involving dog fighting, the court entering the judgment of conviction shall order that any dog-fighting equipment be destroyed or forfeited to the state. Destruction of dogs, if necessary, must be carried out by a veterinarian licensed in this state or, if one is not available, by trained personnel of a humane society or an animal shelter. If forfeited, the court shall order the contraband delivered to the state, any political subdivision of the state, or to any state institution or agency. If gambling proceeds were seized, the court shall order them forfeited to the state and shall transmit them to the grand jury of the county in which they were seized for use in investigating alleged violations of the Penal Code, or to the state, any political subdivision of the state, or to any state institution or agency.

(b) If there is no prosecution or conviction following seizure, the magistrate to whom the return was made shall notify in writing the person found in possession of the alleged gambling device or equipment, altered gambling equipment or gambling paraphernalia, gambling proceeds, prohibited weapon, obscene device or material, child pornography, scanning device or re-encoder, criminal instrument, or dog-fighting equipment to show cause why the property seized should not be destroyed or the proceeds forfeited. The magistrate, on the motion of the law enforcement agency seizing a prohibited weapon, shall order the weapon destroyed or forfeited to the law enforcement agency seizing the weapon, unless a person shows cause as to why the prohibited weapon should not be destroyed or forfeited. A law enforcement agency shall make a motion under this section in a timely manner after the time at which the agency is informed in writing by the attorney representing the state that no prosecution will arise from the seizure.

(c) The magistrate shall include in the notice a detailed description of the property seized and the total amount of alleged gambling proceeds; the name of the person found in possession; the address where the property or proceeds were seized; and the date and time of the seizure.

(d) The magistrate shall send the notice by registered or certified mail, return receipt requested, to the person found in possession at the address where the property or proceeds were seized. If no one was found in possession, or the possessor's address is unknown, the magistrate shall post the notice on the courthouse door.

(e) Any person interested in the alleged gambling device or equipment, altered gambling equipment or gambling paraphernalia, gambling proceeds, prohibited weapon, obscene device or material, child pornography, scanning device or re-encoder, criminal instrument, or dog-fighting equipment seized must appear before the magistrate on the 20th day following the date the notice was mailed or posted. Failure to timely appear forfeits any interest the person may have in the property or proceeds seized, and no person after failing to timely appear may contest destruction or forfeiture.

(f) If a person timely appears to show cause why the property or proceeds should not be destroyed or forfeited, the magistrate shall conduct a hearing on the issue and determine the nature of property or proceeds and the person's interest therein. Unless the person proves by a preponderance of the evidence that the property or proceeds is not gambling equipment, altered gambling equipment, gambling paraphernalia, gambling device, gambling proceeds, prohibited weapon, obscene device or material, child pornography, criminal instrument, scanning device or re-encoder, or dog-fighting equipment and that he is entitled to possession, the magistrate shall dispose of the property or proceeds in accordance with Paragraph (a) of this article.

(g) For purposes of this article:

(1) "criminal instrument" has the meaning defined in the Penal Code;

(2) "gambling device or equipment, altered gambling equipment or gambling paraphernalia" has the meaning defined in the Penal Code;

(3) "prohibited weapon" has the meaning defined in the Penal Code;

(4) "dog-fighting equipment" means:

(A) equipment used for training or handling a fighting dog, including a harness, treadmill, cage, decoy, pen, house for keeping a fighting dog, feeding apparatus, or training pen;

(B) equipment used for transporting a fighting dog, including any automobile, or other vehicle, and its appurtenances which are intended to be used as a vehicle for transporting a fighting dog;

(C) equipment used to promote or advertise an exhibition of dog fighting, including a printing press or similar equipment, paper, ink, or photography equipment; or

(D) a dog trained, being trained, or intended to be used to fight with another dog;

(5) "obscene device" and "obscene" have the meanings assigned by Section 43.21, Penal Code;

(6) "re-encoder" has the meaning assigned by Section 522.001, Business & Commerce Code;

(7) "scanning device" has the meaning assigned by Section 522.001, Business & Commerce Code; and

(8) "obscene material" and "child pornography" include digital images and the media and equipment on which those images are stored.

(h) No provider of an electronic communication service or of a remote computing service to the public shall be held liable for an offense involving obscene material or child pornography under this section on account of any action taken in good faith in providing that service.

Art. 18.181. Disposition of Explosive Weapons and Chemical Dispensing Devices.

(a) After seizure of an explosive weapon or chemical dispensing device, as these terms are defined in Section 46.01, Penal Code, a peace officer or a person acting at the direction of a peace officer shall:

(1) photograph the weapon in the position where it is recovered before touching or moving it;

(2) record the identification designations printed on a weapon if the markings are intact;

(3) if the weapon can be moved, move it to an isolated area in order to lessen the danger to the public;

(4) if possible, retain a portion of a wrapper or other packaging materials connected to the weapon;

(5) retain a small portion of the explosive material and submit the material to a laboratory for chemical analysis;

(6) separate and retain components associated with the weapon such as fusing and triggering mechanisms if those mechanisms are not hazardous in themselves;

(7) destroy the remainder of the weapon in a safe manner;

(8) at the time of destruction, photograph the destruction process and make careful observations of the characteristics of the destruction;

(9) after destruction, inspect the disposal site and photograph the site to record the destructive characteristics of the weapon; and

(10) retain components of the weapon and records of the destruction for use as evidence in court proceedings.

(b) Representative samples, photographs, and records made pursuant to this article are admissible in civil or criminal proceedings in the same manner and to the same extent as if the explosive weapon were offered in evidence, regardless of whether or not the remainder of the weapon has been destroyed. No inference or presumption of spoliation applies to weapons destroyed pursuant to this article.

Art. 18.182. Disposition of Item Bearing Counterfeit Mark.

(a) In this article, "counterfeit mark" and "protected mark" have the meanings assigned by Section 32.23, Penal Code.

(b) Following the conviction or placement on deferred adjudication community supervision of a person for an offense under Section 32.23, Penal Code, the court entering the judgment of conviction or order of deferred adjudication community supervision shall order that any item bearing or identified by a counterfeit mark seized in connection with the offense be:

(1) forfeited to the owner of the protected mark, if prior to an order disposing of property under this article the owner of the protected mark requests the return of the item; or

(2) destroyed.

Art. 18.183. Deposit of Money Pending Disposition.

(a) If money is seized by a law enforcement agency in connection with a violation of Chapter 47, Penal Code, the state or the political subdivision of the state that employs the law enforcement agency may deposit the money in an interest-bearing bank account in the jurisdiction of the agency that made seizure or in the county in which the money was seized until a final judgment is rendered concerning the violation.

(b) If a final judgment is rendered concerning a violation of Chapter 47, Penal Code, money seized in connection with the violation that has been placed in an interest-bearing bank account shall be distributed according to this chapter, with any interest being distributed in the same manner and used for the same purpose as the principal.

Art. 18.19. Disposition of Seized Weapons.

(a) Weapons seized in connection with an offense involving the use of a weapon or an offense under Penal Code Chapter 46 shall be held by the law enforcement agency making the seizure, subject to the following provisions, unless:

(1) the weapon is a prohibited weapon identified in Penal Code Chapter 46, in which event Article 18.18 of this code applies; or

(2) the weapon is alleged to be stolen property, in which event Chapter 47 of this code applies.

(b) When a weapon described in Paragraph (a) of this article is seized, and the seizure is not made pursuant to a search or arrest warrant, the person seizing the same shall prepare and deliver to a magistrate a written inventory of each weapon seized.

(c) If there is no prosecution or conviction for an offense involving the weapon seized, the magistrate to whom the seizure was reported shall, before the 61st day after the date the magistrate determines that there will be no prosecution or conviction, notify in writing the person found in possession of the weapon that the person is entitled to the weapon upon written request to the magistrate. The magistrate shall order the weapon returned to the person found in possession before the 61st day after the date the magistrate receives a request from the person. If the weapon is not requested before the 61st day after the date of notification, the magistrate shall, before the 121st day after the date of notification, order the weapon destroyed, sold at public sale by the law enforcement agency holding the weapon or by an auctioneer licensed under Chapter 1802, Occupations Code, or forfeited to the state for use by the law enforcement agency holding the weapon or by a county forensic laboratory designated by the magistrate. If the magistrate does not order the return, destruction, sale, or forfeiture of the weapon within the applicable period prescribed by this subsection, the law enforcement agency holding the weapon may request an order of destruction, sale, or forfeiture of the weapon from the magistrate. Only a firearms dealer licensed under 18 U.S.C. Section 923 may purchase a weapon at public sale under this subsection. Proceeds from the sale of a seized weapon under this subsection shall be transferred, after the deduction of court costs to which a district court clerk is entitled under Article 59.05(f), followed by the deduction of auction costs, to the law enforcement agency holding the weapon.

(d) A person either convicted or receiving deferred adjudication under Chapter 46, Penal Code, is entitled to the weapon seized upon request to the court in which the person was convicted or placed on deferred adjudication. However, the court entering the judgment shall order the weapon destroyed, sold at public sale by the law enforcement agency holding the weapon or by an auctioneer licensed under Chapter 1802, Occupations Code, or forfeited to the state for use by the law enforcement agency holding the weapon or by a county forensic laboratory designated by the court if:

(1) the person does not request the weapon before the 61st day after the date of the judgment of conviction or the order placing the person on deferred adjudication;

(2) the person has been previously convicted under Chapter 46, Penal Code;

(3) the weapon is one defined as a prohibited weapon under Chapter 46, Penal Code;

(4) the offense for which the person is convicted or receives deferred adjudication was committed in or on the premises of a playground, school, video arcade facility, or youth center, as those terms are defined by Section 481.134, Health and Safety Code; or

(5) the court determines based on the prior criminal history of the defendant or based on the circumstances surrounding the commission of the offense that possession of the seized weapon would pose a threat to the community or one or more individuals.

(d-1) Only a firearms dealer licensed under 18 U.S.C. Section 923 may purchase a weapon at public sale under Subsection (d). Proceeds from the sale of a seized weapon under Subsection (d) shall be transferred, after the deduction of court costs to which a district court clerk is entitled under Article 59.05(f), followed by the deduction of auction costs, to the law enforcement agency holding the weapon.

(e) If the person found in possession of a weapon is convicted of an offense involving the use of the weapon, before the 61st day after the date of conviction the court entering judgment of conviction shall order destruction of the weapon, sale at public sale by the law enforcement agency holding the weapon or by an auctioneer licensed under Chapter 1802, Occupations Code, or forfeiture to the state for use by the law enforcement agency holding the weapon or by a county forensic laboratory designated by the court. If the court entering judgment of conviction does not order the destruction, sale, or forfeiture of the weapon within the period prescribed by this subsection, the law enforcement agency holding the weapon may request an order of destruction, sale, or forfeiture of the weapon from a magistrate. Only a firearms dealer licensed under 18 U.S.C. Section 923 may purchase a weapon at public sale under this subsection. Proceeds from the sale of a seized weapon under this subsection shall be transferred, after the deduction of court costs to which a district court clerk is entitled under Article 59.05(f), followed by the deduction of auction costs, to the law enforcement agency holding the weapon.

Art. 18.191. Disposition of Firearm Seized from Certain Persons with Mental Illness.

(a) A law enforcement officer who seizes a firearm from a person taken into custody under Section 573.001, Health and Safety Code, and not in connection with an offense involving the use of a weapon or an offense under Chapter 46, Penal Code, shall immediately provide the person a written copy of the receipt for the firearm and a written notice of the procedure for the return of a firearm under this article.

(b) The law enforcement agency holding a firearm subject to disposition under this article shall, as soon as possible, but not later than the 15th day after the date the person is taken into custody under Section 573.001, Health and Safety Code, provide written notice of the procedure for the return of a firearm under this article to the last known address of the person's closest immediate family member as identified by the person or reasonably identifiable by the law enforcement agency, sent by certified mail, return receipt requested. The written notice must state the date by which a request for the return of the firearm must be submitted to the law enforcement agency as provided by Subsection (h).

(c) Not later than the 30th day after the date a firearm subject to disposition under this article is seized, the law enforcement agency holding the firearm shall contact the court in the county having jurisdiction to order commitment under Chapter 574, Health and Safety Code, and request the disposition of the case. Not later than the 30th day after the date of this request, the clerk of the court shall advise the requesting agency whether the person taken into custody was released under Section 573.023, Health and Safety Code, or was ordered to receive inpatient mental health services under Section 574.034 or 574.035, Health and Safety Code.

(d) Not later than the 30th day after the date the clerk of the court informs a law enforcement agency holding a firearm subject to disposition under this article that the person taken into custody was released under Section 573.023, Health and Safety Code, the law enforcement agency shall:

(1) conduct a check of state and national criminal history record information to verify whether the person may lawfully possess a firearm under 18 U.S.C. Section 922(g); and

(2) provide written notice to the person by certified mail that the firearm may be returned to the person on verification under Subdivision (1) that the person may lawfully possess the firearm.

(e) Not later than the 30th day after the date the clerk of the court informs a law enforcement agency holding a firearm subject to disposition under this article that the person taken into custody was ordered to receive inpatient mental health services under Section 574.034 or 574.035, Health and Safety Code, the law enforcement agency shall provide written notice to the person by certified mail that the person:

(1) is prohibited from owning, possessing, or purchasing a firearm under 18 U.S.C. Section 922(g)(4);

(2) may petition the court that entered the commitment order for relief from the firearms disability under Section 574.088, Health and Safety Code; and

(3) may dispose of the firearm in the manner provided by Subsection (f).

(f) A person who receives notice under Subsection (e) may dispose of the person's firearm by:

(1) releasing the firearm to the person's designee, if:

(A) the law enforcement agency holding the firearm conducts a check of state and national criminal history record information and verifies that the designee may lawfully possess a firearm under 18 U.S.C. Section 922(g);

(B) the person provides to the law enforcement agency a copy of a notarized statement releasing the firearm to the designee; and

(C) the designee provides to the law enforcement agency an affidavit confirming that the designee:

(i) will not allow access to the firearm by the person who was taken into custody under Section 573.001, Health and Safety Code, at any time during which the person may not lawfully possess a firearm under 18 U.S.C. Section 922(g); and

(ii) acknowledges the responsibility of the designee and no other person to verify whether the person has reestablished the person's eligibility to lawfully possess a firearm under 18 U.S.C. Section 922(g); or

(2) releasing the firearm to the law enforcement agency holding the firearm, for disposition under Subsection (h).

(g) If a firearm subject to disposition under this article is wholly or partly owned by a person other than the person taken into custody under Section 573.001, Health and Safety Code, the law enforcement agency holding the firearm shall release the firearm to the person claiming a right to or interest in the firearm after:

(1) the person provides an affidavit confirming that the person:

(A) wholly or partly owns the firearm;

(B) will not allow access to the firearm by the person who was taken into custody under Section 573.001, Health and Safety Code, at any time during which that person may not lawfully possess a firearm under 18 U.S.C. Section 922(g); and

(C) acknowledges the responsibility of the person and no other person to verify whether the person who was taken into custody under Section 573.001, Health and Safety Code, has reestablished the person's eligibility to lawfully possess a firearm under 18 U.S.C. Section 922(g); and

(2) the law enforcement agency holding the firearm conducts a check of state and national criminal history record information and verifies that the person claiming a right to or interest in the firearm may lawfully possess a firearm under 18 U.S.C. Section 922(g).

(h) If a person to whom written notice is provided under Subsection (b) or another lawful owner of a firearm subject to disposition under this article does not submit a written request to the law enforcement agency for the return of the firearm before the 121st day after the date the law enforcement agency holding the firearm provides written notice under Subsection (b), the law enforcement agency may have the firearm sold by a person who is a licensed firearms dealer under 18 U.S.C. Section 923. The proceeds from the sale of a firearm under this subsection shall be given to the owner of the seized firearm, less the cost of administering this subsection. An unclaimed firearm that was seized from a person taken into custody under Section 573.001, Health and Safety Code, may not be destroyed or forfeited to the state.

Art. 18.20. Detection, Interception, and Use of Wire, Oral, or Electronic Communications. [Repealed]

Art. 18.21. Pen Registers and Trap and Trace Devices; Access to Stored Communications; Mobile Tracking Devices. [Repealed]

Art. 18.22. Testing Certain Defendants or Confined Persons for Communicable Diseases.

(a) **[2 Versions: As amended by Acts 2015, 84th Leg., ch. 736]** A person who is arrested for a misdemeanor or felony and who during the commission of that offense or the arrest, during a judicial proceeding or initial period of confinement following the arrest, or during the person's confinement after a conviction or adjudication resulting from the arrest causes the person's bodily fluids to come into contact with a peace officer, a magistrate, or an employee of a correctional facility where the person is confined shall, at the direction of the court having jurisdiction over the arrested person, undergo a medical procedure or test designed to show or help show whether the person has a communicable disease. The court may direct the person to undergo the procedure or test on its own motion or on the request of the peace officer, magistrate, or correctional facility employee. If the person refuses to submit voluntarily to the procedure or test, the court shall require the person to submit to the procedure or test. Notwithstanding any other law, the person performing the procedure or test shall make the test results available to the local health authority, and the local health authority shall notify the peace officer, magistrate, or correctional facility employee, as appropriate, of the test result. The state may not use the fact that a medical procedure or test was performed on a person under this article, or use the results of the procedure or test, in any criminal proceeding arising out of the alleged offense.

(a) **[2 Versions: As amended by Acts 2015, 84th Leg., ch. 1278]** A person who is arrested for a misdemeanor or felony and who during the commission of that offense or an arrest following the commission of that offense causes an emergency response employee or volunteer, as defined by Section 81.003, Health and Safety Code, to come into contact with the person's bodily fluids shall, at the direction of the court having jurisdiction over the arrested person, undergo a medical procedure or test designed to show or help show whether the person has a communicable disease. The court may direct the person to undergo the procedure or test on its own motion or on the request of the emergency response employee or volunteer. If the person refuses to submit voluntarily to the procedure or test, the court shall require the person to submit to the procedure or test. Notwithstanding any other law, the person performing the procedure or test shall make the test results available to the local health authority and the designated infection control officer of the entity that employs or uses the services of the affected emergency response employee or volunteer, and the local health authority or the designated infection control officer of the affected employee or volunteer shall notify the emergency response employee or volunteer of the test result. The state may not use the fact that a medical procedure or test was performed on a person under this article, or use the results of the procedure or test, in any criminal proceeding arising out of the alleged offense.

(b) Testing under this article shall be conducted in accordance with written infectious disease control protocols adopted by the Department of State Health Services that clearly establish procedural guidelines that provide criteria for testing and that respect the rights of the arrested person and the peace officer, magistrate, or correctional facility employee.

(c) Nothing in this article authorizes a court to release a test result to a person other than a person specifically authorized by this article, and Section 81.103(d), Health and Safety Code, does not authorize that disclosure.

(d) In this article, "correctional facility" means:

(1) any place described by Section 1.07(a)(14), Penal Code; or

(2) a "secure correctional facility" or "secure detention facility" as those terms are defined by Section 51.02, Family Code.

Art. 18.23. Expenses for Motor Vehicle Towed and Stored for Certain Purposes.

(a) A law enforcement agency that directs the towing and storage of a motor vehicle for an evidentiary or examination purpose shall pay the cost of the towing and storage.

(b) Subsection (a) applies whether the motor vehicle is taken to or stored on property that is:

(1) owned or operated by the law enforcement agency; or

(2) owned or operated by another person who provides storage services to the law enforcement agency, including:

(A) a governmental entity; and

(B) a vehicle storage facility, as defined by Section 2303.002, Occupations Code.

(c) Subsection (a) does not require a law enforcement agency to pay the cost of:

(1) towing or storing a motor vehicle for a purpose that is not an evidentiary or examination purpose, including towing or storing a vehicle that has been abandoned, illegally parked, in an accident, or recovered after being stolen; or

(2) storing a motor vehicle after the date the law enforcement agency authorizes the owner or operator of the property to which the vehicle was taken or on which the vehicle is stored to release the vehicle to the vehicle's owner.

(d) This subsection applies only to a motor vehicle taken to or stored on property described by Subsection (b)(2). After a law enforcement agency authorizes the release of a motor vehicle held for an evidentiary or examination purpose, the owner or operator of the storage property may not refuse to release the vehicle to the vehicle's owner because the law enforcement agency has not paid the cost of the towing and storage.

(e) Subchapter J, Chapter 2308, Occupations Code, does not apply to a motor vehicle directed by a law enforcement agency to be towed and stored for an evidentiary or examination purpose.

Art. 18.24. Body Cavity Search During Traffic Stop.

(a) In this article, "body cavity search" means an inspection that is conducted of a person's anal or vaginal cavity in any manner, but the term does not include a pat-down.

(b) Notwithstanding any other law, a peace officer may not conduct a body cavity search of a person during a traffic stop unless the officer first obtains a search warrant pursuant to this chapter authorizing the body cavity search.

Art. 18.25. Magistrate Shall Investigate [Deleted].

Deleted by Acts 1973, 63rd Leg., ch. 399 (S.B. 34), § 2(E), effective January 1, 1974.

Art. 18.26. Shall Discharge Defendant [Deleted].

Deleted by Acts 1973, 63rd Leg., ch. 399 (S.B. 34), § 2(E), effective January 1, 1974.

Art. 18.27. Schedule [Deleted].

Deleted by Acts 1973, 63rd Leg., ch. 399 (S.B. 34), § 2(E), effective January 1, 1974.

Code of Criminal Procedure

Art. 18.28. Examining Trial [Deleted].

Deleted by Acts 1973, 63rd Leg., ch. 399 (S.B. 34), § 2(E), effective January 1, 1974.

Art. 18.29. Certify Record to Proper Court [Deleted].

Deleted by Acts 1973, 63rd Leg., ch. 399 (S.B. 34), § 2(E), effective January 1, 1974.

Art. 18.30. Sale of Unclaimed or Abandoned Property [Deleted].

Deleted by Acts 1973, 63rd Leg., ch. 399 (S.B. 34), § 2(E), effective January 1, 1974.

CHAPTER 18A. DETECTION, INTERCEPTION, AND USE OF WIRE, ORAL, AND ELECTRONIC COMMUNICATIONS

SUBCHAPTER A GENERAL PROVISIONS

Art. 18A.001. Definitions.

In this chapter:

(1) "Access," "computer," "computer network," "computer system," and "effective consent" have the meanings assigned by Section 33.01, Penal Code.

(2) "Aggrieved person" means a person who was a party to an intercepted wire, oral, or electronic communication or a person against whom the interception was directed.

(3) "Aural transfer" means a transfer containing the human voice at any point between and including the point of origin and the point of reception.

(4) "Communication common carrier" means a person engaged as a common carrier for hire in the transmission of wire or electronic communications.

(5) "Computer trespasser" means a person who accesses a protected computer without effective consent of the owner and has no reasonable expectation of privacy in a communication transmitted to, through, or from the protected computer. The term does not include a person who accesses the protected computer under an existing contractual relationship with the owner or operator of the computer.

(6) "Contents," with respect to a wire, oral, or electronic communication, includes any information concerning the substance, purport, or meaning of that communication.

(7) "Covert entry" means an entry that is made into or onto premises and that, if not authorized by a court order under this chapter, would violate the Penal Code.

(8) "Department" means the Department of Public Safety of the State of Texas.

(9) "Director" means:

(A) the public safety director of the department; or

(B) if the public safety director is absent or unable to serve, the assistant director of the department.

(10) "Electronic communication" means a transfer of any signs, signals, writing, images, sounds, data, or intelligence transmitted wholly or partly by a wire, radio, electromagnetic, photoelectronic, or photo-optical system. The term does not include:

(A) a wire or oral communication;

(B) a communication made through a tone-only paging device; or

(C) a communication from a tracking device.

(11) "Electronic communications service" means a service that provides to users of the service the ability to send or receive wire or electronic communications.

(12) "ESN reader," "pen register," and "trap and trace device" have the meanings assigned by Article 18B.001.

(13) "Intercept" means the aural or other acquisition of the contents of a wire, oral, or electronic communication through the use of an interception device.

(14) "Interception device" means an electronic, mechanical, or other device that may be used for the nonconsensual interception of wire, oral, or electronic communications. The term does not include a telephone or telegraph instrument, the equipment or a facility used for the transmission of electronic communications, or a component of the equipment or a facility used for the transmission of electronic communications if the instrument, equipment, facility, or component is:

(A) provided to a subscriber or user by a provider of a wire or electronic communications service in the ordinary course of the service provider's business and used by the subscriber or user in the ordinary course of the subscriber's or user's business;

(B) provided by a subscriber or user for connection to the facilities of a wire or electronic communications service for use in the ordinary course of the subscriber's or user's business;

(C) used by a communication common carrier in the ordinary course of the carrier's business; or

(D) used by an investigative or law enforcement officer in the ordinary course of the officer's duties.

(15) "Interception order" means an order authorizing the interception of a wire, oral, or electronic communication.

(16) "Investigative or law enforcement officer" means:

(A) an officer of this state or a political subdivision of this state who is authorized by law to investigate or make arrests for offenses described by Article 18A.101; or

(B) an attorney authorized by law to prosecute or participate in the prosecution of those offenses.

(17) "Judge of competent jurisdiction" means a judge described by Article 18A.051.

(18) "Mobile tracking device" has the meaning assigned by Article 18B.201.

(19) "Oral communication" means a communication uttered by a person exhibiting an expectation that the communication is not subject to interception under circumstances justifying that expectation. The term does not include an electronic communication.

(20) "Prosecutor" means a district attorney, criminal district attorney, or county attorney performing the duties of a district attorney, with jurisdiction in the county within an administrative judicial region described by Article 18A.053.

(21) "Protected computer" means a computer, computer network, or computer system that is:

(A) owned by a financial institution or governmental entity; or

(B) used by or for a financial institution or governmental entity, if conduct constituting an offense affects that use.

(22) "Residence" means a structure or the portion of a structure used as a person's home or fixed place of habitation to which the person indicates an intent to return after a temporary absence.

(23) "User" means a person who uses an electronic communications service and is authorized by the service provider to use the service.

(24) "Wire communication" means an aural transfer made wholly or partly through the use of facilities for the transmission of communications by the aid of wire, cable, or other similar connection between the point of origin and the point of reception, including the use of the connection in a switching station, if those facilities are provided or operated by a person authorized to provide or operate the facilities for the transmission of communications as a communication common carrier. (Code Crim. Proc., Art. 18.20, Secs. 1(1), (2), (3), (4), (5), (6), (7) (part), (8), (9), (10), (11), (12), (13), (14), (15), (16), (18), (21), (24), (25), (26); New.)

Art. 18A.002. Nonapplicability.

This chapter does not apply to conduct described as an affirmative defense under Section 16.02(c), Penal Code, except as otherwise specifically provided by that section. (Code Crim. Proc., Art. 18.20, Sec. 17.)

SUBCHAPTER B APPLICATION FOR INTERCEPTION ORDER

Art. 18A.051. Judge of Competent Jurisdiction.

(a) For purposes of this chapter, a judge of competent jurisdiction is a judge from the panel of nine active district judges with criminal jurisdiction who is appointed by the presiding judge of the court of criminal appeals under this article.

(b) The presiding judge of the court of criminal appeals, by order filed with the clerk of that court, shall appoint one district judge from each of the administrative judicial regions of this state to serve at the presiding judge's pleasure as the judge of competent jurisdiction in that administrative judicial region.

(c) The presiding judge shall fill vacancies as those vacancies occur in the same manner. (Code Crim. Proc., Art. 18.20, Secs. 1(7), 3(a).)

Art. 18A.052. Request for Filing of Interception Application.

(a) The director may, based on written affidavits, request in writing that a prosecutor apply for an interception order.

(b) The head of a local law enforcement agency or, if the head of the agency is absent or unable to serve, the acting head of the local law enforcement agency may, based on written affidavits, request in writing that a prosecutor apply for an interception order.

(c) Before making a request under Subsection (b), the head of a local law enforcement agency must submit the request and supporting affidavits to the director. The director shall make a written finding as to whether the request and supporting affidavits establish that other investigative procedures have been attempted and have failed or those procedures reasonably appear unlikely to succeed or to be too dangerous if attempted, is feasible, is justifiable, and whether the department has the necessary resources available.

(d) A prosecutor may file the application requested under Subsection (b) only after a written positive finding by the director on all of the requirements provided by Subsection (c). (Code Crim. Proc., Art. 18.20, Sec. 6.)

Code of Criminal Procedure

Art. 18A.053. Jurisdiction.

Except as provided by Article 18A.054, a judge of competent jurisdiction may act on an application for an interception order if any of the following is located in the administrative judicial region with respect to which the judge is appointed:

(1) the site of:

(A) the proposed interception; or

(B) the interception device to be installed or monitored;

(2) the communication device to be intercepted;

(3) the billing, residential, or business address of the subscriber to the electronic communications service to be intercepted;

(4) the headquarters of the law enforcement agency that makes the request for or will execute the interception order; or

(5) the headquarters of the service provider. (Code Crim. Proc., Art. 18.20, Sec. 3(b).)

Art. 18A.054. Alternate Jurisdiction.

(a) An application for an interception order may be made to the judge of competent jurisdiction in an administrative judicial region adjacent to a region described by Article 18A.053 if:

(1) the judge of competent jurisdiction for the administrative judicial region described by Article 18A.053 is absent or unable to serve; or

(2) exigent circumstances exist.

(b) Exigent circumstances under Subsection (a)(2) do not include a denial of a previous application on the same facts and circumstances. (Code Crim. Proc., Art. 18.20, Secs. 3(b) (part), (c) (part).)

Art. 18A.055. Application for Interception Order.

(a) A prosecutor applying for an interception order must make the application in writing under oath to a judge of competent jurisdiction.

(b) An application must:

(1) identify the prosecutor making the application and state the prosecutor's authority to make the application;

(2) identify the officer requesting the application;

(3) include a complete statement of the facts and circumstances relied on by the prosecutor to justify the prosecutor's belief that an order should be issued, including:

(A) details about the particular offense that has been, is being, or is about to be committed;

(B) except as otherwise provided by this chapter, a particular description of the nature and location of the facilities from which or the place where the communication is to be intercepted;

(C) a particular description of the type of communication sought to be intercepted; and

(D) the identity of the person, if known, committing the offense and whose communications are to be intercepted;

(4) include a complete statement as to whether other investigative procedures have been attempted and have failed or why those procedures reasonably appear to be unlikely to succeed or to be too dangerous if attempted;

(5) include a statement of the period for which the interception is required to be maintained and, if the nature of the investigation indicates that the interception order should not automatically terminate when the described type of communication is first obtained, a particular description of facts establishing probable cause to believe that additional communications of the same type will occur after the described type of communication is obtained;

(6) include a statement whether a covert entry will be necessary to properly and safely install wiretapping, electronic surveillance, or eavesdropping equipment and, if a covert entry is requested, a statement as to why a covert entry is necessary and proper under the facts of the particular investigation, including a complete statement as to whether other investigative techniques have been attempted and have failed or why those techniques reasonably appear to be unlikely to succeed or to be too dangerous if attempted or are not feasible under the circumstances or exigencies of time;

(7) include a complete statement of the facts concerning all applications known to the prosecutor that have been previously made to a judge for an interception order involving any persons, facilities, or places specified in the application and of the action taken by the judge on each application;

(8) if the application is for the extension of an order, include a statement providing the results already obtained from the interception or a reasonable explanation of the failure to obtain results; and

(9) if the application is made under Article 18A.054, fully explain the circumstances justifying application under that article.

(c) In an ex parte hearing in chambers, the judge may require additional testimony or documentary evidence to support the application. The testimony or documentary evidence must be preserved as part of the application. (Code Crim. Proc., Art. 18.20, Secs. 3(c) (part), 8.)

SUBCHAPTER C ISSUANCE OF INTERCEPTION ORDER AND RELATED ORDERS

Art. 18A.101. Offenses for Which Interception Order May Be Issued.

A judge of competent jurisdiction may issue an interception order only if the prosecutor applying for the order shows probable cause to believe that the interception will provide evidence of the commission of:

(1) a felony under any of the following provisions of the Health and Safety Code:

(A) Chapter 481, other than felony possession of marihuana;

(B) Chapter 483; or

(C) Section 485.032;

(2) an offense under any of the following provisions of the Penal Code:

(A) Section 19.02;

(B) Section 19.03;

(C) Section 20.03;

(D) Section 20.04;

(E) Chapter 20A;

(F) Chapter 34, if the criminal activity giving rise to the proceeds involves the commission of an offense under Title 5, Penal Code, or an offense under federal law or the laws of another state containing elements that are substantially similar to the elements of an offense under Title 5;

(G) Section 38.11;

(H) Section 43.04;

(I) Section 43.041;

(J) Section 43.05; or

(K) Section 43.26; or

(3) an attempt, conspiracy, or solicitation to commit an offense listed in Subdivision (1) or (2).

Art. 18A.102. Judicial Determinations Required for Issuance of Interception Order.

On receipt of an application under Subchapter B, the judge may issue an ex parte interception order, as requested or as modified, if the judge determines from the evidence submitted by the prosecutor that:

(1) there is probable cause to believe that a person is committing, has committed, or is about to commit a particular offense described by Article 18A.101;

(2) there is probable cause to believe that particular communications concerning that offense will be obtained through the interception;

(3) normal investigative procedures have been attempted and have failed or reasonably appear to be unlikely to succeed or to be too dangerous if attempted;

(4) there is probable cause to believe that the facilities from which or the place where the wire, oral, or electronic communications are to be intercepted is being used or is about to be used in connection with the commission of an offense or is leased to, listed in the name of, or commonly used by the person; and

(5) a covert entry is or is not necessary to properly and safely install the wiretapping, electronic surveillance, or eavesdropping equipment. (Code Crim. Proc., Art. 18.20, Sec. 9(a).)

Art. 18A.103. Contents of Interception Order.

(a) An interception order must specify:

(1) the identity of the person, if known, whose communications are to be intercepted;

(2) except as otherwise provided by this chapter, the nature and location of the communications facilities as to which or the place where authority to intercept is granted;

(3) a particular description of the type of communication sought to be intercepted and a statement of the particular offense to which the communication relates;

(4) the identity of the officer making the request and the identity of the prosecutor;

(5) the period during which the interception is authorized, including a statement of whether the interception will automatically terminate when the described communication is first obtained; and

(6) whether a covert entry or surreptitious entry is necessary to properly and safely install wiretapping, electronic surveillance, or eavesdropping equipment.

(b) Each interception order and extension of that order must provide that the authorization to intercept be executed as soon as practicable, be conducted in a way that minimizes the interception of communications not otherwise subject to interception under this chapter, and terminate on obtaining the authorized objective or within 30 days, whichever occurs sooner.

(c) For purposes of Subsection (b), if the intercepted communication is in code or a foreign language and an expert in that code or language is not reasonably available during the period of interception, minimization may be accomplished as soon as practicable after the interception. (Code Crim. Proc., Art. 18.20, Secs. 9(b), (d) (part).)

Code of Criminal Procedure

Art. 18A.104. Limitation on Covert Entry.

(a) An interception order may not authorize a covert entry for the purpose of intercepting an oral communication unless:

(1) the judge, in addition to making the determinations required under Article 18A.102, determines:

(A) that:

(i) the premises into or onto which the covert entry is authorized or the person whose communications are to be obtained has been the subject of a pen register previously authorized in connection with the same investigation;

(ii) the premises into or onto which the covert entry is authorized or the person whose communications are to be obtained has been the subject of an interception of wire or electronic communications previously authorized in connection with the same investigation; and

(iii) the procedures under Subparagraphs (i) and (ii) have failed; or

(B) that the procedures under Paragraph (A) reasonably appear to be unlikely to succeed or to be too dangerous if attempted or are not feasible under the circumstances or exigencies of time; and

(2) the interception order, in addition to the matters required to be specified under Article 18A.103(a), specifies that:

(A) the covert entry is for the purpose of intercepting oral communications of two or more persons; and

(B) there is probable cause to believe that the persons described by Paragraph (A) are committing, have committed, or are about to commit a particular offense described by Article 18A.101.

(b) An interception order may not authorize a covert entry into a residence solely for the purpose of intercepting a wire or electronic communication. (Code Crim. Proc., Art. 18.20, Secs. 9(e), (f).)

Art. 18A.105. Authority to Issue Certain Ancillary Orders.

An interception order may include an order to:

(1) install or use a pen register, ESN reader, trap and trace device, or mobile tracking device or similar equipment that combines the function of a pen register and trap and trace device; or

(2) disclose a stored communication, information subject to an administrative subpoena, or information subject to access under Chapter 18B. (Code Crim. Proc., Art. 18.20, Sec. 9(c) (part).)

Art. 18A.106. Order to Third Party to Assist with Execution of Interception Order.

(a) On request of the prosecutor applying for an interception order, the judge may issue a separate order directing a provider of a wire or electronic communications service, communication common carrier, landlord, custodian, or other person to provide to the prosecutor all information, facilities, and technical assistance necessary to accomplish the interception unobtrusively and with a minimum of interference with the services that the service provider, carrier, landlord, custodian, or other person is providing the person whose communications are to be intercepted.

(b) A provider of a wire or electronic communications service, communication common carrier, landlord, custodian, or other person that provides facilities or technical assistance under an order described by Subsection (a) is entitled to compensation, at the prevailing rates, by the prosecutor for reasonable expenses incurred in providing the facilities or assistance. (Code Crim. Proc., Art. 18.20, Sec. 9(c) (part).)

Art. 18A.107. Duration of Interception Order.

An interception order may not authorize the interception of a communication for a period that:

(1) is longer than is necessary to achieve the objective of the authorization; or

(2) exceeds 30 days. (Code Crim. Proc., Art. 18.20, Sec. 9(d) (part).)

Art. 18A.108. Extension of Interception Order.

(a) A judge who issues an interception order may grant extensions of the order.

(b) An extension of an interception order may be granted only if:

(1) an application for an extension is made in accordance with Article 18A.055; and

(2) the judge makes the findings required by Article 18A.102.

(c) The period of extension may not:

(1) be longer than the judge considers necessary to achieve the purposes for which the extension is granted; or

(2) exceed 30 days. (Code Crim. Proc., Art. 18.20, Sec. 9(d) (part).)

Art. 18A.109. Report on Need for Continued Interception.

(a) An interception order may require reports to the judge who issued the order that show any progress toward achieving the authorized objective and the need for continued interception.

(b) Reports under this article must be made at any interval the judge requires. (Code Crim. Proc., Art. 18.20, Sec. 9(g).)

Art. 18A.110. Subsequent Criminal Prosecution Related to Interception Order.

A judge who issues an interception order may not hear a criminal prosecution in which:

(1) evidence derived from the interception may be used; or

(2) the order may be an issue. (Code Crim. Proc., Art. 18.20, Sec. 9(h).)

SUBCHAPTER D INTERCEPTION ORDER FOR COMMUNICATION BY SPECIFIED PERSON

Art. 18A.151. Requirements Regarding Interception Order for Communication by Specified Person.

The requirements of Articles 18A.055(b)(3)(B) and 18A.103(a)(2) relating to the specification of the facilities from which or the place where a communication is to be intercepted do not apply if:

(1) in the case of an application for an interception order that authorizes the interception of an oral communication:

(A) the application contains a complete statement as to why the specification is not practical and identifies the person committing or believed to be committing the offense and whose communications are to be intercepted; and

(B) a judge of competent jurisdiction finds that the specification is not practical; or

(2) in the case of an application for an interception order that authorizes the interception of a wire or electronic communication:

(A) the application identifies the person committing or believed to be committing the offense and whose communications are to be intercepted;

(B) a judge of competent jurisdiction finds that the prosecutor has made an adequate showing of probable cause to believe that the actions of the person identified in the application could have the effect of preventing interception from a specified facility; and

(C) the authority to intercept a wire or electronic communication under the interception order is limited to a period in which it is reasonable to presume that the person identified in the application will be reasonably proximate to the interception device. (Code Crim. Proc., Art. 18.20, Sec. 9A(a).)

Art. 18A.152. Implementation of Interception Order.

A person implementing an interception order that authorizes the interception of an oral communication and that, as permitted by this subchapter, does not specify the facility from which or the place where a communication is to be intercepted may begin interception only after the person ascertains the place where the communication is to be intercepted. (Code Crim. Proc., Art. 18.20, Sec. 9A(b).)

Art. 18A.153. Motion to Modify or Quash Interception Order.

(a) A provider of a wire or electronic communications service that receives an interception order that authorizes the interception of a wire or electronic communication and that, as permitted by this subchapter, does not specify the facility from which or the place where a communication is to be intercepted may move the court to modify or quash the order on the ground that the service provider's assistance with respect to the interception cannot be performed in a timely or reasonable manner.

(b) On notice to the state, the court shall decide the motion expeditiously. (Code Crim. Proc., Art. 18.20, Sec. 9A(c).)

SUBCHAPTER E EMERGENCY INSTALLATION AND USE OF INTERCEPTION DEVICE

Art. 18A.201. Definitions.

In this subchapter:

(1) "Immediate life-threatening situation" means a hostage, barricade, or other emergency situation in which a person unlawfully and directly:

(A) threatens another with death; or

(B) exposes another to a substantial risk of serious bodily injury.

(2) "Member of a law enforcement unit specially trained to respond to and deal with life-threatening situations" means a peace officer who, as evidenced by the submission of appropriate documentation to the Texas Commission on Law Enforcement:

(A) receives each year a minimum of 40 hours of training in hostage and barricade suspect situations; or

(B) has received a minimum of 24 hours of training on kidnapping investigations and is:

(i) the sheriff of a county with a population of 3.3 million or more or the sheriff's designee; or

(ii) the police chief of a police department in a municipality with a population of 500,000 or more or the chief's designee. (Code Crim. Proc., Art. 18.20, Secs. 1(22), (23).)

Code of Criminal Procedure

Art. 18A.202. Possession and Use of Interception Device in Emergency Situation.

(a) The prosecutor in a county in which an interception device is to be installed or used shall designate in writing each peace officer in the county, other than a commissioned officer of the department, who is:

(1) a member of a law enforcement unit specially trained to respond to and deal with life-threatening situations; and

(2) authorized to possess an interception device and responsible for the installation, operation, and monitoring of the device in an immediate life-threatening situation.

(b) A peace officer designated under Subsection (a) or Article 18A.301(c) may possess, install, operate, or monitor an interception device if the officer:

(1) reasonably believes an immediate life-threatening situation exists that:

(A) is within the territorial jurisdiction of the officer or another officer the officer is assisting; and

(B) requires interception of communications before an interception order can, with due diligence, be obtained under this subchapter;

(2) reasonably believes there are sufficient grounds under this subchapter on which to obtain an interception order; and

(3) before beginning the interception, obtains oral or written consent to the interception from:

(A) a judge of competent jurisdiction;

(B) a district judge for the county in which the device will be installed or used; or

(C) a judge or justice of a court of appeals or of a higher court.

(c) If a peace officer installs or uses an interception device under Subsection (b), the officer shall:

(1) promptly report the installation or use to the prosecutor in the county in which the device is installed or used; and

(2) within 48 hours after the installation is complete or the interception begins, whichever occurs first, obtain a written interception order from a judge of competent jurisdiction.

(d) A peace officer may certify to a communication common carrier that the officer is acting lawfully under this subchapter. (Code Crim. Proc., Art. 18.20, Secs. 8A(a), (b), (d), (g).)

Art. 18A.203. Consent for Emergency Interception.

(a) An official described by Article 18A.202(b)(3) may give oral or written consent to the interception of communications under this subchapter to provide evidence of the commission of a felony, or of a threat, attempt, or conspiracy to commit a felony, in an immediate life-threatening situation.

(b) Oral or written consent given under this subchapter expires on the earlier of:

(1) 48 hours after the grant of consent; or

(2) the conclusion of the emergency justifying the interception. (Code Crim. Proc., Art. 18.20, Sec. 8A(c).)

Art. 18A.204. Written Order Authorizing Interception.

(a) A judge of competent jurisdiction under Article 18A.051 or under Article 18A.202(b) may issue a written interception order under this subchapter during the 48-hour period prescribed by Article 18A.202(c)(2).

(b) A written interception order under this subchapter expires on the earlier of:

(1) the 30th day after the date of execution of the order; or

(2) the conclusion of the emergency that initially justified the interception.

(c) If an interception order is denied or is not issued within the 48-hour period, the officer shall terminate use of and remove the interception device promptly on the earlier of:

(1) the denial;

(2) the end of the emergency that initially justified the interception; or

(3) the expiration of 48 hours. (Code Crim. Proc., Art. 18.20, Sec. 8A(e).)

Art. 18A.205. Certain Evidence Not Admissible.

The state may not use as evidence in a criminal proceeding information gained through the use of an interception device installed under this subchapter if authorization for the device is not sought or is sought but not obtained. (Code Crim. Proc., Art. 18.20, Secs. 8A(b) (part), (f).)

SUBCHAPTER F DETECTION OF CELLULAR TELEPHONE OR OTHER WIRELESS COMMUNICATIONS DEVICE IN CORRECTIONAL OR DETENTION FACILITY

Art. 18A.251. Definition.

In this subchapter, "correctional facility" means:

(1) a place described by Section 1.07(a)(14), Penal Code; or

(2) a "secure correctional facility" or "secure detention facility" as defined by Section 51.02, Family Code. (Code Crim. Proc., Art. 18.20, Sec. 8B(a).)

Art. 18A.252. Use of Interception Device by Inspector General.

(a) Notwithstanding any other provision of this chapter or Chapter 18B, the office of inspector general of the Texas Department of Criminal Justice may:

(1) without a warrant, use an interception device to detect the presence or use of a cellular telephone or other wireless communications device in a correctional facility;

(2) without a warrant, intercept, monitor, detect, or, as authorized by applicable federal laws and regulations, prevent the transmission of a communication through a cellular telephone or other wireless communications device in a correctional facility; and

(3) use, to the extent authorized by law, any information obtained under Subdivision (2), including the contents of an intercepted communication, in a criminal or civil proceeding before a court or other governmental agency or entity.

(b) When using an interception device under Subsection (a), the office of inspector general shall minimize the impact of the device on a communication that is not reasonably related to the detection of the presence or use of a cellular telephone or other wireless communications device in a correctional facility. (Code Crim. Proc., Art. 18.20, Secs. 8B(b), (d).)

Art. 18A.253. Reporting Use of Interception Device.

Not later than the 30th day after the date on which the office of inspector general uses an interception device under Article 18A.252(a), the inspector general shall report the use of the device to:

(1) a prosecutor with jurisdiction in the county in which the device was used; or

(2) the special prosecution unit established under Subchapter E, Chapter 41, Government Code, if that unit has jurisdiction in the county in which the device was used. (Code Crim. Proc., Art. 18.20, Sec. 8B(c).)

Art. 18A.254. No Expectation of Privacy.

(a) A person confined in a correctional facility does not have an expectation of privacy with respect to the possession or use of a cellular telephone or other wireless communications device located on the premises of the facility.

(b) A person confined in a correctional facility, and any person with whom the confined person communicates through the use of a cellular telephone or other wireless communications device, does not have an expectation of privacy with respect to the contents of a communication transmitted by the telephone or device. (Code Crim. Proc., Art. 18.20, Sec. 8B(e).)

SUBCHAPTER G AGENCIES AND PERSONNEL AUTHORIZED TO POSSESS AND USE INTERCEPTION DEVICES

Art. 18A.301. Department of Public Safety Authorized to Possess and Use Interception Device.

(a) Except as otherwise provided by this subchapter and Subchapters E and F, only the department is authorized by this chapter to own, possess, install, operate, or monitor an interception device.

(b) An investigative or law enforcement officer or other person may assist the department in the operation and monitoring of an interception of wire, oral, or electronic communications if the officer or other person:

(1) is designated by the director for that purpose; and

(2) acts in the presence and under the direction of a commissioned officer of the department.

(c) The director shall designate in writing the commissioned officers of the department who are responsible for the possession, installation, operation, and monitoring of interception devices for the department. (Code Crim. Proc., Art. 18.20, Secs. 5(a), (b).)

Art. 18A.302. Texas Department of Criminal Justice Authorized to Possess and Use Interception Device.

(a) The Texas Department of Criminal Justice may own an interception device for a use or purpose authorized by Section 500.008, Government Code.

(b) The inspector general of the Texas Department of Criminal Justice, a commissioned officer of that office, or a person acting in the presence and under the direction of the commissioned officer may possess, install, operate, or monitor the interception device as provided by Section 500.008, Government Code. (Code Crim. Proc., Art. 18.20, Sec. 5(c).)

Art. 18A.303. Texas Juvenile Justice Department Authorized to Possess and Use Interception Device.

(a) The Texas Juvenile Justice Department may own an interception device for a use or purpose authorized by Section 242.103, Human Resources Code.

(b) The inspector general of the Texas Juvenile Justice Department, a commissioned officer of that office, or a person acting in the presence and under the direction of the commissioned officer may possess, install, operate, or monitor the interception device as provided by Section 242.103, Human Resources Code. (Code Crim. Proc., Art. 18.20, Sec. 5(d).)

SUBCHAPTER H DISCLOSURE AND USE OF INTERCEPTED COMMUNICATIONS

Art. 18A.351. Disclosure or Use of Intercepted Communications.

An investigative or law enforcement officer who, by means authorized by this chapter, obtains knowledge of the contents of a wire, oral, or electronic communication or evidence derived from the communication may:

(1) use the contents or evidence to the extent the use is appropriate to the proper performance of the officer's official duties; or

(2) disclose the contents or evidence to another investigative or law enforcement officer, including a law enforcement officer or agent of the United States or of another state, to the extent that the disclosure is appropriate to the proper performance of the official duties of the officer making or receiving the disclosure. (Code Crim. Proc., Art. 18.20, Secs. 7(a), (b).)

Art. 18A.352. Disclosure Under Oath.

A person who receives, by means authorized by this chapter, information concerning a wire, oral, or electronic communication or evidence derived from a communication intercepted in accordance with this chapter may disclose the contents of that communication or evidence while giving testimony under oath in any proceeding held under the authority of the United States, this state, or a political subdivision of this state. (Code Crim. Proc., Art. 18.20, Sec. 7(c).)

Art. 18A.353. Privileged Communications.

(a) An otherwise privileged wire, oral, or electronic communication intercepted in accordance with, or in violation of, this chapter does not lose its privileged character.

(b) Evidence derived from a privileged communication described by Subsection (a) against a party to that communication is privileged. (Code Crim. Proc., Art. 18.20, Sec. 7(d).)

Art. 18A.354. Disclosure or Use of Incidentally Intercepted Communications.

(a) This article applies only to the contents of and evidence derived from wire, oral, or electronic communications that:

(1) are intercepted by an investigative or law enforcement officer while engaged in intercepting wire, oral, or electronic communications in a manner authorized by this chapter; and

(2) relate to offenses other than those specified by the interception order.

(b) The contents of and evidence derived from a communication described by Subsection (a) may be disclosed or used as provided by Article 18A.351.

(c) The contents of and evidence derived from a communication described by Subsection (a) may be used under Article 18A.352 when authorized by a judge of competent jurisdiction if the judge finds, on subsequent application, that the contents were otherwise intercepted in accordance with this chapter.

(d) An application under Subsection (c) must be made as soon as practicable. (Code Crim. Proc., Art. 18.20, Sec. 7(e).)

Art. 18A.355. Notice and Disclosure of Interception Application, Interception Order, and Intercepted Communications.

(a) Within a reasonable period but not later than the 90th day after the date an application for an interception order is denied or after the date an interception order or the last extension, if any, expires, the judge who granted or denied the application shall cause to be served on each person named in the order or application and any other party to an intercepted communication, if any, an inventory that must include notice of:

(1) the application or the issuance of the order;

(2) the date of denial of the application, or the date of the issuance of the order and the authorized interception period; and

(3) whether during any authorized interception period wire, oral, or electronic communications were intercepted.

(b) The judge may, on motion, make available for inspection to a person or the person's counsel any portion of an intercepted communication, application, or order that the judge determines to disclose to that person in the interest of justice.

(c) On an ex parte showing of good cause to the judge, the serving of the inventory required under Subsection (a) may be postponed.

(d) Evidence derived from an order under this chapter may not be disclosed in a trial until after the inventory has been served. (Code Crim. Proc., Art. 18.20, Sec. 13.)

Art. 18A.356. Notice of Interception Required.

(a) The contents of an intercepted wire, oral, or electronic communication or evidence derived from the communication may not be received in evidence or otherwise disclosed in a trial, hearing, or other proceeding in a federal or state court unless each party, not later than the 10th day before the date of the trial, hearing, or other proceeding, has been provided with a copy of the interception order and application under which the interception was authorized.

(b) The judge may waive the 10-day period described by Subsection (a) on a finding that:

(1) it is not possible to provide the party with the information 10 days before the trial, hearing, or proceeding; and

(2) the party will not be prejudiced by the delay in receiving the information. (Code Crim. Proc., Art. 18.20, Sec. 14(a).)

Art. 18A.357. Communications Received in Evidence.

(a) The contents of an intercepted communication and evidence derived from the communication may be received in evidence in any trial, hearing, or other proceeding in or before any court, grand jury, department, officer, agency, regulatory body, legislative committee, or other authority of the United States, this state, or a political subdivision of this state unless:

(1) the communication was intercepted in violation of this chapter, Section 16.02, Penal Code, or federal law; or

(2) the disclosure of the contents of the communication or evidence derived from the communication would violate a law described by Subdivision (1).

(b) The contents of an intercepted communication and evidence derived from the communication may be received in a civil trial, hearing, or other proceeding only if the civil trial, hearing, or other proceeding arises out of a violation of a penal law.

(c) This article does not prohibit the use or admissibility of the contents of an intercepted communication or evidence derived from the communication if the communication was intercepted in a jurisdiction outside this state in compliance with the law of that jurisdiction. (Code Crim. Proc., Art. 18.20, Sec. 2.)

Art. 18A.358. Suppression of Contents of Intercepted Communications.

(a) An aggrieved person charged with an offense in a trial, hearing, or proceeding in or before a court, department, officer, agency, regulatory body, or other authority of the United States, this state, or a political subdivision of this state may move to suppress the contents of an intercepted wire, oral, or electronic communication or evidence derived from the communication on the ground that:

(1) the communication was unlawfully intercepted;

(2) the interception order is insufficient on its face; or

(3) the interception was not made in conformity with the interception order.

(b) A person identified by a party to an intercepted wire, oral, or electronic communication during the course of that communication may move to suppress the contents of the communication on:

(1) a ground provided under Subsection (a); or

(2) the ground that the harm to the person resulting from the person's identification in court exceeds the value to the prosecution of the disclosure of the contents.

(c) The motion to suppress must be made before the trial, hearing, or proceeding unless:

(1) there was not an opportunity to make the motion; or

(2) the aggrieved person was not aware of the grounds of the motion.

(d) The hearing on the motion to suppress shall be held in camera on the written request of the aggrieved person.

(e) If the motion to suppress is granted, the contents of the intercepted wire, oral, or electronic communication and evidence derived from the communication shall be treated as having been obtained in violation of this chapter.

(f) The judge, on the filing of the motion to suppress by the aggrieved person, shall make available to the aggrieved person or the person's counsel for inspection any portion of the intercepted communication or evidence derived from the communication that the judge determines to make available in the interest of justice.

(g) A judge of this state, on hearing a pretrial motion regarding conversations intercepted by wire in accordance with this chapter, or who otherwise becomes informed that there exists on such an intercepted wire, oral, or electronic communication identification of a specific individual who is not a suspect or a party to the subject of interception shall:

(1) give notice and an opportunity to be heard on the matter of suppression of references to that individual if identification is sufficient to give notice; or

(2) suppress references to that individual if identification is:

(A) sufficient to potentially cause embarrassment or harm that outweighs the probative value, if any, of the mention of that individual; and

(B) insufficient to require the notice under Subdivision (1). (Code Crim. Proc., Art. 18.20, Secs. 14(b), (c), (d), (e).)

SUBCHAPTER I
USE AND DISPOSITION OF APPLICATIONS AND ORDERS

Art. 18A.401. Sealing of Application or Order.

The judge shall seal each application made and order issued under this chapter. (Code Crim. Proc., Art. 18.20, Sec. 11 (part).)

Art. 18A.402. Custody of Applications and Orders.

Custody of applications and orders issued under this chapter shall be wherever the judge directs. (Code Crim. Proc., Art. 18.20, Sec. 11 (part).)

Art. 18A.403. Disclosure of Application or Order.

An application made or order issued under this chapter may be disclosed only on a showing of good cause before a judge of competent jurisdiction. (Code Crim. Proc., Art. 18.20, Sec. 11 (part).)

Art. 18A.404. Destruction of Application or Order.

An application made or order issued under this chapter may be destroyed only on or after the 10th anniversary of the date the application or order was sealed and only if the judge of competent jurisdiction for the administrative judicial region in which the application was made or the order was issued orders the destruction. (Code Crim. Proc., Art. 18.20, Sec. 11 (part).)

SUBCHAPTER J
CREATION, USE, AND DISPOSITION OF RECORDINGS

Art. 18A.451. Creation of Recordings.

The contents of a wire, oral, or electronic communication intercepted by means authorized by this chapter shall be recorded on tape, wire, or other comparable device in a way that protects the recording from editing or other alterations. (Code Crim. Proc., Art. 18.20, Sec. 10(a).)

Art. 18A.452. Duplication of Recordings.

Recordings under Article 18A.451 may be duplicated for use or disclosure under Article 18A.351 for investigations. (Code Crim. Proc., Art. 18.20, Sec. 10(c).)

Art. 18A.453. Sealing and Custody of Recordings.

(a) Immediately on the expiration of the period of an interception order and all extensions, if any, the recordings under Article 18A.451 shall be:

(1) made available to the judge issuing the order; and

(2) sealed under the judge's directions.

(b) Custody of the recordings shall be wherever the judge orders. (Code Crim. Proc., Art. 18.20, Sec. 10(b) (part).)

Art. 18A.454. Destruction of Recordings.

A recording under Article 18A.451 may be destroyed only on or after the 10th anniversary of the date of expiration of the interception order and the last extension, if any, and only if the judge of competent jurisdiction for the administrative judicial region in which the interception was authorized orders the destruction. (Code Crim. Proc., Art. 18.20, Sec. 10(b) (part).)

Art. 18A.455. Prerequisite for Use or Disclosure of Recording in Certain Proceedings.

The presence of the seal required by Article 18A.453(a) or a satisfactory explanation of the seal's absence is a prerequisite for the use or disclosure of the contents of a wire, oral, or electronic communication or evidence derived from the communication under Article 18A.352. (Code Crim. Proc., Art. 18.20, Sec. 10(d).)

SUBCHAPTER K VIOLATION; SANCTIONS

Art. 18A.501. Contempt.

A violation of Subchapter I or J may be punished as contempt of court. (Code Crim. Proc., Art. 18.20, Sec. 12.)

Art. 18A.502. Recovery of Civil Damages by Aggrieved Person.

A person whose wire, oral, or electronic communication is intercepted, disclosed, or used in violation of this chapter or Chapter 16, Penal Code:

(1) has a civil cause of action against any person who intercepts, discloses, or uses or solicits another person to intercept, disclose, or use the communication; and

(2) is entitled to recover from the person:

(A) actual damages but not less than liquidated damages computed at a rate of $100 for each day the violation occurs or $1,000, whichever is higher;

(B) punitive damages; and

(C) reasonable attorney's fees and other litigation costs reasonably incurred. (Code Crim. Proc., Art. 18.20, Sec. 16(a).)

Art. 18A.503. Action Brought by Federal or State Government; Injunction; Penalties.

(a) A person is subject to suit by the federal or state government in a court of competent jurisdiction for appropriate injunctive relief if the person engages in conduct that:

(1) constitutes an offense under Section 16.05, Penal Code, but is not for a tortious or illegal purpose or for the purpose of direct or indirect commercial advantage or private commercial gain; and

(2) involves a radio communication that is:

(A) transmitted on frequencies allocated under Subpart D of Part 74 of the rules of the Federal Communications Commission; and

(B) not scrambled or encrypted.

(b) The attorney general or the county or district attorney of the county in which the conduct described by Subsection (a) is occurring may file suit under that subsection on behalf of the state.

(c) A defendant is liable for a civil penalty of $500 if it is shown at the trial of the civil suit brought under Subsection (a) that the defendant has been:

(1) convicted of an offense under Section 16.05, Penal Code; or

(2) found liable in a civil action brought under Article 18A.502.

(d) Each violation of an injunction ordered under Subsection (a) is punishable by a fine of $500. (Code Crim. Proc., Art. 18.20, Secs. 16(c), (d), (e), (f).)

Art. 18A.504. Good Faith Defense Available.

A good faith reliance on a court order or legislative authorization constitutes a complete defense to an action brought under Article 18A.502 or 18A.503. (Code Crim. Proc., Art. 18.20, Sec. 16(b).)

Art. 18A.505. No Cause of Action.

A computer trespasser or a user, aggrieved person, subscriber, or customer of a communication common carrier or provider of an electronic communications service does not have a cause of action against the carrier or service provider, the officers, employees, or agents of the carrier or service provider, or other specified persons for providing information, facilities, or assistance as required by a good faith reliance on:

(1) legislative authority; or

(2) a court order, warrant, subpoena, or certification under this chapter. (Code Crim. Proc., Art. 18.20, Sec. 16(g).)

SUBCHAPTER L REPORTS

Art. 18A.551. Report of Intercepted Communications by Judge.

(a) Within 30 days after the date an interception order or the last extension, if any, expires or after the denial of an interception order, the issuing or denying judge shall report to the Administrative Office of the United States Courts:

(1) the fact that an order or extension was applied for;

(2) the kind of order or extension applied for;

(3) the fact that the order or extension was granted as applied for, was modified, or was denied;

(4) the period of interceptions authorized by the order and the number and duration of any extensions of the order;

(5) the offense specified in the order or application or extension;

(6) the identity of the requesting officer and the prosecutor; and

(7) the nature of the facilities from which or the place where communications were to be intercepted.

(b) A judge required to file a report under this article shall forward a copy of the report to the director. (Code Crim. Proc., Art. 18.20, Secs. 15(a), (c) (part).)

Art. 18A.552. Report of Intercepted Communications by Prosecutor.

(a) In January of each year each prosecutor shall report to the Administrative Office of the United States Courts the following information for the preceding calendar year:

(1) the information required by Article 18A.551(a) with respect to each application for an interception order or extension made;

(2) a general description of the interceptions made under each order or extension, including:

(A) the approximate nature and frequency of incriminating communications intercepted;

(B) the approximate nature and frequency of other communications intercepted;

(C) the approximate number of persons whose communications were intercepted; and

(D) the approximate nature, amount, and cost of the personnel and other resources used in the interceptions;

(3) the number of arrests resulting from interceptions made under each order or extension and the offenses for which the arrests were made;

(4) the number of trials resulting from interceptions;

(5) the number of motions to suppress made with respect to interceptions and the number granted or denied;

(6) the number of convictions resulting from interceptions, the offenses for which the convictions were obtained, and a general assessment of the importance of the interceptions; and

(7) the information required by Subdivisions (2) through (6) with respect to orders or extensions obtained.

(b) A prosecutor required to file a report under this article shall forward a copy of the report to the director. (Code Crim. Proc., Art. 18.20, Secs. 15(b), (c) (part).)

Art. 18A.553. Report of Intercepted Communications by Department of Public Safety.

(a) On or before March 1 of each year, the director shall submit a report of all intercepts conducted under this chapter and terminated during the preceding calendar year to:

(1) the governor;

(2) the lieutenant governor;

(3) the speaker of the house of representatives;

(4) the chair of the senate jurisprudence committee; and

(5) the chair of the house of representatives criminal jurisprudence committee.

(b) The report must include:

(1) the reports of judges and prosecuting attorneys forwarded to the director as required by Articles 18A.551(b) and 18A.552(b);

(2) the number of department personnel authorized to possess, install, or operate an interception device;

(3) the number of department and other law enforcement personnel who participated or engaged in the seizure of intercepts under this chapter during the preceding calendar year; and

(4) the total cost to the department of all activities and procedures relating to the seizure of intercepts during the preceding calendar year, including costs of equipment, personnel, and expenses incurred as compensation for use of facilities or technical assistance provided to the department. (Code Crim. Proc., Art. 18.20, Sec. 15(c) (part).)

CHAPTER 18B. INSTALLATION AND USE OF TRACKING EQUIPMENT; ACCESS TO COMMUNICATIONS

SUBCHAPTER A GENERAL PROVISIONS

Art. 18B.001. Definitions.

In this chapter:

(1) "Authorized peace officer" means:

(A) a sheriff or deputy sheriff;

(B) a constable or deputy constable;

(C) a marshal or police officer of a municipality;

(D) a ranger or officer commissioned by the Public Safety Commission or the director of the department;

(E) an investigator of a prosecutor's office;

(F) a law enforcement agent of the Texas Alcoholic Beverage Commission;

(G) a law enforcement officer commissioned by the Parks and Wildlife Commission;

(H) an enforcement officer appointed by the inspector general of the Texas Department of Criminal Justice under Section 493.019, Government Code;

(I) an investigator commissioned by the attorney general under Section 402.009, Government Code; or

(J) a member of an arson investigating unit commissioned by a municipality, a county, or the state.

(2) "Communication common carrier," "electronic communication," "electronic communications service," "user," and "wire communication" have the meanings assigned by Article 18A.001.

(3) "Department" means the Department of Public Safety of the State of Texas.

(4) "Designated law enforcement office or agency" means:

(A) the sheriff's department of a county with a population of 3.3 million or more;

(B) a police department in a municipality with a population of 200,000 or more; or

(C) the office of inspector general of the Texas Department of Criminal Justice.

(5) "Domestic entity" has the meaning assigned by Section 1.002, Business Organizations Code.

(6) "Electronic communications system" means:

(A) a wire, radio, electromagnetic, photo-optical, or photoelectronic facility for the transmission of wire or electronic communications; and

(B) any computer facility or related electronic equipment for the electronic storage of wire or electronic communications.

(7) "Electronic customer data" means data or records that:

(A) are in the possession, care, custody, or control of a provider of an electronic communications service or provider of a remote computing service; and

(B) contain:

(i) information revealing the identity of customers of the applicable service;

(ii) information about a customer's use of the applicable service;

(iii) information that identifies the recipient or destination of a wire or electronic communication sent to or by a customer;

(iv) the content of a wire or electronic communication sent to or by a customer;

(v) any data stored with the applicable service provider by or on behalf of a customer; or

(vi) location information.

(8) "Electronic storage" means storage of electronic customer data in a computer, computer network, or computer system, regardless of whether the data is subject to recall, further manipulation, deletion, or transmission. The term includes storage of a wire or electronic communication by an electronic communications service or a remote computing service.

(9) "ESN reader" means a device that, without intercepting the contents of a communication, records the electronic serial number from the data track of a wireless telephone, cellular telephone, or similar communication device that transmits its operational status to a base site.

(9-a) "Immediate life-threatening situation" has the meaning assigned by Article 18A.201.

(9-b) "Location information" means data, records, or other information that is created by or accessible to a provider of an electronic communications service or a provider of a remote computing service and may be used to identify the geographic physical location of a communication device, including the current, real-time, or prospective geographic physical location of a communication device.

(10) "Pen register" means a device or process that records or decodes dialing, routing, addressing, or signaling information transmitted by an instrument or facility from which a wire or electronic communication is transmitted, if the information does not include the contents of the communication. The term does not include a device used by a provider or customer of a wire or electronic communications service in the ordinary course of the service provider's or customer's business for purposes of:

(A) billing or recording incident to billing for communications services; or

(B) cost accounting, security control, or other ordinary business purposes.

(11) "Prosecutor" means a district attorney, criminal district attorney, or county attorney performing the duties of a district attorney.

(12) "Remote computing service" means the provision of computer storage or processing services to the public by means of an electronic communications system.

(13) "Trap and trace device" means a device or process that records an incoming electronic or other impulse that identifies the originating number or other dialing, routing, addressing, or signaling information reasonably likely to identify the source of a wire or electronic communication, if the information does not include the contents of the communication. The term does not include a device or telecommunications network used in providing:

(A) a caller identification service authorized by the Public Utility Commission of Texas under Subchapter E, Chapter 55, Utilities Code;

(B) the services referenced by Section 55.102(b), Utilities Code; or

(C) a caller identification service provided by a commercial mobile radio service provider licensed by the Federal Communications Commission. (Code Crim. Proc., Art. 18.20, Secs. 1(17), (20); Art. 18.21, Secs. 1(1) (part), (2), (3), (3-a), (3-b), (3-c), (4), (6), (7), (8), (10).)

SUBCHAPTER B
APPLICATION FOR ORDER AUTHORIZING INSTALLATION AND USE OF EQUIPMENT

Art. 18B.051. Requirements Regarding Request for and Filing of Application.

(a) A prosecutor with jurisdiction in a county within a judicial district described by Article 18B.052 may file with a district judge in the judicial district an application for the installation and use of a pen register, ESN reader, trap and trace device, or similar equipment that combines the function of a pen register and a trap and trace device.

(b) A prosecutor may file an application under this subchapter or under federal law on:

(1) the prosecutor's own motion; or

(2) the request of an authorized peace officer, regardless of whether the peace officer is commissioned by the department.

(c) A prosecutor must make an application personally and may not make the application through an assistant or other person acting on the prosecutor's behalf if the prosecutor:

(1) files an application on the prosecutor's own motion; or

(2) files an application for the installation and use of a pen register, ESN reader, or similar equipment on the request of an authorized peace officer not commissioned by the department, other than an authorized peace officer employed by a designated law enforcement office or agency.

(d) A prosecutor may make an application through an assistant or other person acting on the prosecutor's behalf if the prosecutor files an application for the installation and use of:

(1) a pen register, ESN reader, or similar equipment on the request of:

(A) an authorized peace officer who is commissioned by the department; or

(B) an authorized peace officer of a designated law enforcement office or agency; or

(2) a trap and trace device or similar equipment on the request of an authorized peace officer, regardless of whether the peace officer is commissioned by the department. (Code Crim. Proc., Art. 18.21, Secs. 2(a) (part), (b).)

Art. 18B.052. Jurisdiction.

An application under this subchapter must be filed in a judicial district in which is located:

(1) the site of the proposed installation or use of the device or equipment;

(2) the site of the communication device on which the device or equipment is proposed to be installed or used;

(3) the billing, residential, or business address of the subscriber to the electronic communications service on which the device or equipment is proposed to be installed or used;

(4) the headquarters of:

(A) the office of the prosecutor filing an application under this subchapter; or

(B) a law enforcement agency that requests the prosecutor to file an application under this subchapter or that proposes to execute an order authorizing installation and use of the device or equipment; or

(5) the headquarters of a service provider ordered to install the device or equipment. (Code Crim. Proc., Art. 18.21, Sec. 2(a) (part).)

Art. 18B.053. Application Requirements.

An application under this subchapter must:

(1) be made in writing under oath;

(2) include the name of the subscriber and the telephone number and location of the communication device on which the pen register, ESN reader, trap and trace device, or similar equipment will be used, to the extent that information is known or is reasonably ascertainable; and

(3) state that the installation and use of the device or equipment will likely produce information that is material to an ongoing criminal investigation. (Code Crim. Proc., Art. 18.21, Sec. 2(c).)

SUBCHAPTER C
ORDER AUTHORIZING INSTALLATION AND USE OF EQUIPMENT

Art. 18B.101. Order Authorizing Installation and Use of Pen Register, ESN Reader, or Similar Equipment.

(a) On presentation of an application under Subchapter B, a judge may order the installation and use of a pen register, ESN reader, or similar equipment by an authorized peace officer commissioned by the department or an authorized peace officer of a designated law enforcement office or agency.

(b) On request of the applicant, the judge shall direct in the order that a communication common carrier or a provider of an electronic communications service provide all information, facilities, and technical assistance necessary to facilitate the installation and use of the device or equipment by the department or designated law enforcement office or agency unobtrusively and with a minimum of interference to the services provided by the carrier or service provider. (Code Crim. Proc., Art. 18.21, Sec. 2(d) (part).)

Art. 18B.102. Order Authorizing Installation and Use of Trap and Trace Device or Similar Equipment.

(a) On presentation of an application under Subchapter B, a judge may order the installation and use of a trap and trace device or similar equipment on the appropriate line by a communication common carrier or other person.

(b) The judge may direct the communication common carrier or other person, including any landlord or other custodian of equipment, to provide all information, facilities, and technical assistance necessary to install or use the device or equipment unobtrusively and with a minimum of interference to the services provided by the communication common carrier, landlord, custodian, or other person.

(c) Unless otherwise ordered by the court, the results of the device or equipment shall be provided to the applicant, as designated by the court, at reasonable intervals during regular business hours, for the duration of the order. (Code Crim. Proc., Art. 18.21, Sec. 2(e) (part).)

Art. 18B.103. Compensation for Carrier or Service Provider.

(a) A communication common carrier or a provider of an electronic communications service that provides facilities and assistance to the department or a designated law enforcement office or agency under Article 18B.101(b) is entitled to compensation at the prevailing rates for the facilities and assistance.

(b) A communication common carrier that provides facilities and assistance to a designated law enforcement office or agency under Article 18B.102(b) is entitled to compensation at the prevailing rates for the facilities and assistance. (Code Crim. Proc., Art. 18.21, Secs. 2(d) (part), (e) (part).)

Art. 18B.104. Duration of Order.

(a) An order for the installation and use of a device or equipment under this subchapter is valid for a period not to exceed 60 days after the earlier of the date the device or equipment is installed or the 10th day after the date the order is entered, unless the prosecutor applies for and obtains an extension of the order from the court before the order expires.

(b) Each extension granted under Subsection (a) may not exceed a period of 60 days, except that the court may extend an order for a period not to exceed one year with the consent of the subscriber or customer of the service on which the device or equipment is used. (Code Crim. Proc., Art. 18.21, Sec. 2(f).)

Art. 18B.105. Sealing Records of Application and Order.

A district court shall seal an application and order granted under this chapter. (Code Crim. Proc., Art. 18.21, Sec. 2(g).)

SUBCHAPTER D
EMERGENCY INSTALLATION AND USE OF CERTAIN EQUIPMENT

Art. 18B.151. Emergency Installation and Use of Pen Register or Trap and Trace Device.

(a) [Repealed.]

(b) A peace officer authorized to possess, install, operate, or monitor a device under Subchapter E, Chapter 18A, may install and use a pen register or trap and trace device if the peace officer reasonably believes:

(1) an immediate life-threatening situation exists that:

(A) is within the territorial jurisdiction of the peace officer or another officer the peace officer is assisting; and

(B) requires the installation of a pen register or trap and trace device before an order authorizing the installation and use can, with due diligence, be obtained under this chapter; and

(2) there are sufficient grounds under this chapter on which to obtain an order authorizing the installation and use of a pen register or trap and trace device. (Code Crim. Proc., Art. 18.21, Secs. 1(1) (part), 3(a).)

Art. 18B.152. Order Authorizing Emergency Installation and Use.

(a) A peace officer who installs or uses a pen register or trap and trace device under Article 18B.151 shall:

(1) promptly report the installation or use of the device to the prosecutor in the county in which the device is installed or used; and

(2) within 48 hours after the installation of the device is complete or the use of the device begins, whichever occurs first, obtain an order under Subchapter C authorizing the installation and use of the device.

(b) A judge may issue an order authorizing the installation and use of a device under this subchapter during the 48-hour period prescribed by Subsection (a)(2). If an order is denied or is not issued within the 48-hour period, the peace officer shall terminate use of and remove the pen register or trap and trace device promptly on the earlier of the denial or the expiration of 48 hours. (Code Crim. Proc., Art. 18.21, Secs. 3(a) (part), (b), (c).)

Art. 18B.153. Admissibility of Evidence Obtained.

The state may not use as evidence in a criminal proceeding any information gained through the use of a pen register or trap and trace device installed under this subchapter if an authorized peace officer:

(1) does not apply for authorization for the pen register or trap and trace device; or

(2) applies for but does not obtain that authorization. (Code Crim. Proc., Art. 18.21, Sec. 3(d).)

SUBCHAPTER E
MOBILE TRACKING DEVICES

Art. 18B.201. Definition.

In this subchapter, "mobile tracking device" means an electronic or mechanical device that permits tracking the movement of a person, vehicle, container, item, or object. (Code Crim. Proc., Art. 18.21, Sec. 1(5).)

Art. 18B.202. Order Authorizing Installation and Use of Mobile Tracking Device.

(a) A district judge may issue an order for the installation and use of a mobile tracking device only on the application of an authorized peace officer.

(b) An application must be written, signed, and sworn to before the judge.

(c) The affidavit must:

(1) state the name, department, agency, and address of the applicant;

(2) identify the vehicle, container, or item to which, in which, or on which the mobile tracking device is to be attached, placed, or otherwise installed;

(3) state the name of the owner or possessor of the vehicle, container, or item identified under Subdivision (2);

(4) state the judicial jurisdictional area in which the vehicle, container, or item identified under Subdivision (2) is expected to be found; and

(5) state the facts and circumstances that provide the applicant with probable cause to believe that:

(A) criminal activity has been, is, or will be committed; and

(B) the installation and use of a mobile tracking device is likely to produce information that is material to an ongoing criminal investigation of that criminal activity.

Art. 18B.203. Jurisdiction.

(a) A district judge may issue an order for the installation and use of a mobile tracking device in the same judicial district as the site of:

(1) the investigation; or

(2) the person, vehicle, container, item, or object the movement of which will be tracked by the device.

(b) The order may authorize the use of a mobile tracking device outside the judicial district but within the state, if the device is installed within the district. (Code Crim. Proc., Art. 18.21, Secs. 14(a), (b).)

Art. 18B.204. Notification of Judge Following Activation of Mobile Tracking Device.

Within 72 hours after the time a mobile tracking device is activated in place on or within a vehicle, container, or item, the applicant for whom an order was issued under this subchapter shall notify in writing the judge who issued the order. (Code Crim. Proc., Art. 18.21, Sec. 14(d).)

Art. 18B.205. Duration of Order.

(a) An order under this subchapter expires not later than the 90th day after the date that the mobile tracking device was activated in place on or within the vehicle, container, or item.

(b) For good cause shown, the judge may grant an extension for an additional 90-day period. (Code Crim. Proc., Art. 18.21, Sec. 14(e).)

Art. 18B.206. Removal of Device.

(a) The applicant shall remove or cause to be removed the mobile tracking device as soon as is practicable after the authorization period expires.

(b) If removal is not practicable, the device may not be monitored after the expiration of the order. (Code Crim. Proc., Art. 18.21, Sec. 14(f).)

Art. 18B.207. Nonapplicability.

(a) This subchapter does not apply to a global positioning or similar device installed in or on an item of property by the owner or with the consent of the owner of the property.

(b) In an emergency, a private entity may monitor a device described by Subsection (a). (Code Crim. Proc., Art. 18.21, Sec. 14(g).)

SUBCHAPTER F
LAW ENFORCEMENT POWERS AND DUTIES

Art. 18B.251. Policy Required.

Each designated law enforcement office or agency shall:

(1) adopt a written policy governing the application of this chapter to the office or agency; and

(2) submit the policy to the director of the department, or the director's designee, for approval. (Code Crim. Proc., Art. 18.21, Sec. 2(j).)

Art. 18B.252. Peace Officers Authorized to Possess, Install, Operate, or Monitor Equipment.

(a) A peace officer of a designated law enforcement office or agency is authorized to possess, install, operate, or monitor a pen register, ESN reader, or similar equipment if the peace officer's name is on the list submitted to the director of the department under Subsection (b).

(b) If the director of the department or the director's designee approves the policy submitted under Article 18B.251, the inspector general of the Texas Department of Criminal Justice or the inspector general's designee, or the sheriff or chief of a designated law enforcement agency or the sheriff's or chief's designee, as applicable, shall submit to the director a written list of all peace officers in the designated law enforcement office or agency who are authorized to possess, install, operate, or monitor pen registers, ESN readers, or similar equipment. (Code Crim. Proc., Art. 18.21, Secs. 2(i), (k).)

Art. 18B.253. Limitation: Pen Registers.

To prevent inclusion of the contents of a wire or electronic communication, a governmental agency authorized to install and use a pen register under this chapter or other law must use reasonably available technology to only record and decode electronic or other impulses used to identify the numbers dialed, routed, addressed, or otherwise processed or transmitted by the communication. (Code Crim. Proc., Art. 18.21, Sec. 16.)

Art. 18B.254. Application or Order Not Required for Certain Searches.

A peace officer is not required to file an application under Subchapter B or obtain an order under Subchapter C before the peace officer makes an otherwise lawful search, with or without a warrant, to determine the contents of a caller identification message, pager message, or voice message that is contained within the memory of an end-user's identification, paging, or answering device. (Code Crim. Proc., Art. 18.21, Sec. 2(h).)

SUBCHAPTER G
OVERSIGHT

Art. 18B.301. Compliance Audit.

(a) The department may conduct an audit of a designated law enforcement office or agency to ensure compliance with this chapter.

(b) If the department determines from the audit that the designated law enforcement office or agency is not in compliance with the policy adopted by the office or agency under Article 18B.251, the department shall notify the office or agency in writing that the office or agency, as applicable, is not in compliance.

(c) If the department determines that the office or agency still is not in compliance with the policy on the 90th day after the date the office or agency receives written notice under Subsection (b), the office or agency loses the authority granted by this chapter until:

(1) the office or agency adopts a new written policy governing the application of this chapter to the office or agency; and

(2) the department approves that policy. (Code Crim. Proc., Art. 18.21, Sec. 2(*l*).)

Art. 18B.302. Report of Expenditures.

(a) The inspector general of the Texas Department of Criminal Justice or the sheriff or chief of a designated law enforcement agency, as applicable, shall submit to the director of the department a written report of expenditures made by the designated law enforcement office or agency to purchase and maintain a pen register, ESN reader, or similar equipment authorized under this chapter.

(b) The director of the department shall report the expenditures publicly on an annual basis on the department's Internet website or by other comparable means. (Code Crim. Proc., Art. 18.21, Sec. 2(m).)

SUBCHAPTER G-1 PROSPECTIVE LOCATION INFORMATION

Art. 18B.321. Applicability.

(a) This subchapter applies only to a warrant described by Article 18B.322 for the required disclosure of location information that is:

(1) held in electronic storage in the possession, care, custody, or control of a provider of an electronic communications service or a provider of a remote computing service; and

(2) created after the issuance of the warrant.

(b) Articles 18B.355, 18B.356, and 18B.357 apply to a warrant issued under this subchapter in the same manner as those articles apply to a warrant issued under Article 18B.354.

Art. 18B.322. Warrant Required for Certain Location Information Held in Electronic Storage.

(a) A warrant is required to obtain the disclosure of location information described by Article 18B.321(a) by a provider of an electronic communications service or a provider of a remote computing service.

(b) Only a prosecutor or a prosecutor's assistant with jurisdiction in a county within a judicial district described by Article 18B.052(4) may file an application for a warrant under this subchapter. The application must be supported by the sworn affidavit required by Article 18.01(b).

(c) The application must be filed with a district judge in the applicable judicial district on:

(1) the prosecutor's or assistant's own motion; or

(2) the request of an authorized peace officer of a designated law enforcement office or agency or an authorized peace officer commissioned by the department.

Art. 18B.323. Issuance of Warrant.

(a) On the filing of an application for a warrant under this subchapter, a district judge may issue the warrant to obtain the disclosure of location information by a provider described by Article 18B.355(b), regardless of whether the location information is held at a location in this state or another state.

(b) A warrant may not be issued under this article unless the sworn affidavit required by Article 18.01(b) provides sufficient and substantial facts to establish probable cause that:

(1) the disclosure of the location information sought will:

(A) produce evidence of an offense under investigation; or

(B) result in the apprehension of a fugitive from justice; and

(2) the location information sought is held in electronic storage in the possession, care, custody, or control of the service provider on which the warrant is served.

Art. 18B.324. Duration; Sealing.

(a) A warrant issued under this subchapter is valid for a period not to exceed 60 days after the date the warrant is issued, unless the prosecutor or prosecutor's assistant applies for and obtains an extension of that period from the court before the warrant expires.

(b) Each extension granted under Subsection (a) may not exceed a period of 60 days.

(c) A district court that issues a warrant under this subchapter shall order the warrant and the application for the warrant sealed and may not unseal the warrant and application until after the warrant expires.

Art. 18B.325. Emergency Disclosure.

(a) An authorized peace officer of a designated law enforcement office or agency or an authorized peace officer commissioned by the department may, without a warrant, require the disclosure of location information described by Article 18B.321(a) if:

(1) the officer reasonably believes an immediate life-threatening situation exists that:

(A) is within the officer's territorial jurisdiction; and

(B) requires the disclosure of the location information before a warrant can, with due diligence, be obtained under this subchapter; and

(2) there are sufficient grounds under this subchapter on which to obtain a warrant requiring the disclosure of the location information.

(b) Not later than 48 hours after requiring disclosure of location information without a warrant under Subsection (a), the authorized peace officer shall obtain a warrant for that purpose in accordance with this subchapter.

Art. 18B.326. Certain Evidence Not Admissible.

The state may not use as evidence in a criminal proceeding any information obtained through the required disclosure of location information described by Article 18B.321(a), unless:

(1) a warrant is obtained before requiring the disclosure; or

(2) if the disclosure is required under Article 18B.325 before a warrant can be obtained, the authorized peace officer who required the disclosure obtains a warrant as required by Subsection (b) of that article.

SUBCHAPTER H ACCESS TO STORED COMMUNICATIONS AND OTHER STORED CUSTOMER DATA

Art. 18B.351. Government Access to Electronic Customer Data.

(a) An authorized peace officer may require a provider of an electronic communications service or a provider of a remote computing service to disclose electronic customer data that is in electronic storage by obtaining a warrant under Article 18B.354.

(b) An authorized peace officer may require a provider of an electronic communications service or a provider of a remote computing service to disclose only electronic customer data that is information revealing the identity of customers of the applicable service or information about a customer's use of the applicable service, without giving the subscriber or customer notice:

(1) by obtaining an administrative subpoena authorized by statute;

(2) by obtaining a grand jury subpoena;

(3) by obtaining a court order under Article 18B.352;

(4) by obtaining a warrant under Article 18B.354;

(5) by obtaining the consent of the subscriber or customer to the disclosure of the data; or

(6) as otherwise permitted by applicable federal law. (Code Crim. Proc., Art. 18.21, Secs. 4(a), (b).)

Art. 18B.352. Court Order for Government Access to Stored Customer Data.

(a) A court shall issue an order authorizing disclosure of contents, records, or other information of a wire or electronic communication held in electronic storage if the court determines that there is a reasonable belief that the information sought is relevant to a legitimate law enforcement inquiry.

(b) A court may grant a motion by the service provider to quash or modify the order issued under Subsection (a) if the court determines that:

(1) the information or records requested are unusually voluminous; or

(2) compliance with the order would cause an undue burden on the provider. (Code Crim. Proc., Art. 18.21, Sec. 5.)

Art. 18B.353. Warrant Issued in This State: Applicability.

Articles 18B.354–18B.357 apply to a warrant required under Article 18B.351 to obtain electronic customer data, including the contents of a wire or electronic communication. (Code Crim. Proc., Art. 18.21, Sec. 5A(a).)

Art. 18B.354. Warrant Issued in This State: Application and Issuance of Warrant.

(a) On the filing of an application by an authorized peace officer, a district judge may issue a search warrant under this article for electronic customer data held in electronic storage, including the contents of and records and other information related to a wire or electronic communication held in electronic storage, by a provider of an electronic communications service or a provider of a remote computing service described by Article 18B.355(b), regardless of whether the customer data is held at a location in this state or another state. An application made under this subsection must demonstrate probable cause for the issuance of the warrant and must be supported by the oath of the authorized peace officer.

(b) A search warrant may not be issued under this article unless the sworn affidavit required by

Article 18.01(b) provides sufficient and substantial facts to establish probable cause that:

(1) a specific offense has been committed; and

(2) the electronic customer data sought:

(A) constitutes evidence of that offense or evidence that a particular person committed that offense; and

(B) is held in electronic storage by the service provider on which the warrant is served under Article 18B.355(c).

(c) Only the electronic customer data described in the sworn affidavit required by Article 18.01(b) may be seized under the warrant.

(d) A warrant issued under this article shall run in the name of "The State of Texas."

(e) Article 18.011 applies to an affidavit presented under Article 18.01(b) for the issuance of a warrant under this article, and the affidavit may be sealed in the manner provided by that article. (Code Crim. Proc., Art. 18.21, Secs. 5A(b), (c), (d), (e), (f).)

Art. 18B.355. Warrant Issued in This State: Execution of Warrant.

(a) Not later than the 11th day after the date of issuance, an authorized peace officer shall execute a warrant issued under Article 18B.354, except that the peace officer shall execute the warrant within a shorter period if the district judge directs a shorter period in the warrant. For purposes of this subsection, a warrant is executed when the warrant is served in the manner described by Subsection (c).

(b) A warrant issued under Article 18B.354 may be served only on a provider of an electronic communications service or a provider of a remote computing service that is a domestic entity or a company or entity otherwise doing business in this state under a contract or a terms of service agreement with a resident of this state, if any part of that contract or agreement is to be performed in this state.

(c) A search warrant issued under Article 18B.354 is served when an authorized peace officer delivers the warrant by hand, by facsimile transmission, or, in a manner allowing proof of delivery, by means of the United States mail or a private delivery service to:

(1) a person specified by Section 5.255, Business Organizations Code;

(2) the secretary of state in the case of a company or entity to which Section 5.251, Business Organizations Code, applies; or

(3) any other person or entity designated to receive the service of process.

(d) The district judge shall hear and decide any motion to quash the warrant not later than the fifth business day after the date the service provider files the motion. The judge may allow the service provider to appear at the hearing by teleconference. (Code Crim. Proc., Art. 18.21, Secs. 5A(b) (part), (g), (h) (part), (i), (m).)

Art. 18B.356. Warrant Issued in This State: Compliance with Warrant.

(a) A district judge shall indicate in a warrant issued under Article 18A.354 that the deadline for compliance by the provider of an electronic communications service or the provider of a remote computing service is the 15th business day after the date the warrant is served if the warrant is to be served on a domestic entity or a company or entity otherwise doing business in this state, except that the deadline for compliance with a warrant served in accordance with Section 5.251, Business Organizations Code, may be extended to a date that is not later than the 30th day after the date the warrant is served.

(b) The judge may indicate in the warrant that the deadline for compliance is earlier than the 15th business day after the date the warrant is served if the authorized peace officer who applies for the warrant makes a showing and the judge finds that failure to comply with the warrant by the earlier deadline would cause serious jeopardy to an investigation, cause undue delay of a trial, or create a material risk of:

(1) danger to the life or physical safety of any person;

(2) flight from prosecution;

(3) the tampering with or destruction of evidence; or

(4) intimidation of potential witnesses.

(c) The service provider shall produce all electronic customer data, contents of communications, and other information sought, regardless of where the information is held and within the period allowed for compliance with the warrant, as provided by Subsection (a) or (b).

(d) A court may find any designated officer, designated director, or designated owner of a company or entity in contempt of court if the person by act or omission is responsible for the failure of the company or entity to comply with the warrant within the period allowed for compliance.

(e) The failure of a company or entity to timely deliver the information sought in the warrant does not affect the admissibility of that evidence in a criminal proceeding.

(f) On a service provider's compliance with a warrant issued under Article 18B.354, an authorized peace officer shall file a return of the warrant and a copy of the inventory of the seized property as required under Article 18.10.

(g) A provider of an electronic communications service or a provider of a remote computing service responding to a warrant issued under Article 18B.354 may request an extension of the period for compliance with the warrant if extenuating circumstances exist to justify the extension. The district judge shall grant a request for an extension based on those circumstances if:

(1) the authorized peace officer who applied for the warrant or another appropriate authorized peace officer agrees to the extension; or

(2) the district judge finds that the need for the extension outweighs the likelihood that the extension will cause an adverse circumstance described by Subsection (b). (Code Crim. Proc., Art. 18.21, Secs. 5A(b) (part), (h) (part), (j), (l), (n).)

Art. 18B.357. Warrant Issued in This State: Authentication of Records by Service Provider.

If an authorized peace officer serving a warrant under Article 18B.355 also delivers an affidavit form to the provider of an electronic communications service or the provider of a remote computing service responding to the warrant, and the peace officer also notifies the service provider in writing that an executed affidavit is required, the service provider shall verify the authenticity of the customer data, contents of communications, and other information produced in compliance with the warrant by including with the information an affidavit form that:

(1) is completed and sworn to by a person who is a custodian of the information or a person otherwise qualified to attest to the authenticity of the information; and

(2) states that the information was stored in the course of regularly conducted business of the service provider and specifies whether the regular practice of the service provider is to store that information. (Code Crim. Proc., Art. 18.21, Sec. 5A(k).)

Art. 18B.358. Warrant Issued in Another State.

Any domestic entity that provides electronic communications services or remote computing services to the public shall comply with a warrant issued in another state and seeking information described by Article 18B.354(a), if the warrant is served on the entity in a manner equivalent to the service of process requirements provided by Article 18B.355(b). (Code Crim. Proc., Art. 18.21, Sec. 5B.)

Art. 18B.359. Government Access to Certain Stored Customer Data Without Legal Process.

(a) A provider of a telephonic communications service shall disclose to an authorized peace officer, without legal process, subscriber listing information, including name, address, and telephone number or similar access code:

(1) that the service provider provides to others in the course of providing publicly available directory or similar assistance; or

(2) that is solely for use in the dispatch of emergency vehicles and personnel responding to a distress call directed to an emergency dispatch system or when the information is reasonably necessary to aid in the dispatching of emergency vehicles and personnel for the immediate prevention of death, personal injury, or destruction of property.

(b) A provider of a telephonic communications service shall provide to an authorized peace officer the name of the subscriber of record whose published telephone number is provided to the service provider by an authorized peace officer. (Code Crim. Proc., Art. 18.21, Secs. 4(c), (d).)

SUBCHAPTER I BACKUP PRESERVATION OF ELECTRONIC CUSTOMER DATA

Art. 18B.401. Backup Preservation of Electronic Customer Data.

(a) A subpoena or court order under Article 18B.351(b) for disclosure of certain electronic customer data held in electronic storage by a provider of an electronic communications service or a provider of a remote computing service may, for the purpose of preserving the customer data sought by the subpoena or court order, require that service provider to create a copy of that data.

(b) The service provider shall create the copy within a reasonable period as determined by the court issuing the subpoena or court order.

(c) On creating a copy under this article, the service provider shall immediately notify the authorized peace officer who presented the subpoena or court order requesting the copy.

(d) The service provider may not inform the subscriber or customer whose data is being sought that the subpoena or court order has been issued. (Code Crim. Proc., Art. 18.21, Secs. 6(a), (b).)

Art. 18B.402. Notice to Subscriber or Customer.

Not later than the third day after the date of the receipt of the notice under Article 18B.401(c) from the applicable service provider, the authorized peace officer who presented the subpoena or court order requesting the copy shall provide notice of the creation of the copy to the subscriber or customer whose electronic customer data is the subject of the subpoena or court order. (Code Crim. Proc., Art. 18.21, Secs. 6(b) (part), (c).)

Art. 18B.403. Release of Copy of Electronic Customer Data.

The provider of an electronic communications service or the provider of a remote computing service shall release a copy created under this subchapter to the requesting authorized peace officer not earlier than the 14th day after the date of the peace officer's notice to the subscriber or customer if the service provider has not:

(1) initiated proceedings to challenge the request of the peace officer for the copy; or

(2) received notice from the subscriber or customer that the subscriber or customer has initiated proceedings to challenge the request. (Code Crim. Proc., Art. 18.21, Sec. 6(d).)

Art. 18B.404. Destruction of Copy of Electronic Customer Data.

The provider of an electronic communications service or the provider of a remote computing service may not destroy or permit the destruction of a copy created under this subchapter until the later of:

(1) the delivery of electronic customer data to the applicable law enforcement agency; or

(2) the resolution of any court proceedings, including appeals of any proceedings, relating to the subpoena or court order requesting the creation of the copy. (Code Crim. Proc., Art. 18.21, Sec. 6(e).)

Art. 18B.405. Request for Copy of Electronic Customer Data by Authorized Peace Officer.

(a) An authorized peace officer who reasonably believes that notice to a subscriber or customer regarding a subpoena or court order would result in the destruction of or tampering with the electronic customer data sought may request the creation of a copy of the data.

(b) The peace officer's belief is not subject to challenge by the subscriber or customer or by a provider of an electronic communications service or a provider of a remote computing service. (Code Crim. Proc., Art. 18.21, Sec. 6(f).)

Art. 18B.406. Proceedings to Quash Subpoena or Vacate Court Order.

(a) Not later than the 14th day after the date a subscriber or customer receives notice under Article 18B.402, the subscriber or customer may file a written motion to quash the subpoena or vacate the court order in the court that issued the subpoena or court order. The motion must contain an affidavit or other sworn statement stating:

(1) that the applicant is a subscriber or customer of the provider of an electronic communications service or the provider of a remote computing service from which the electronic customer data held in electronic storage for the subscriber or customer has been sought; and

(2) the applicant's reasons for believing that the customer data sought is not relevant to a legitimate law enforcement inquiry or that there has not been substantial compliance with the provisions of this chapter in some other respect.

(b) The subscriber or customer shall give written notice to the applicable service provider of the challenge to the subpoena or court order. The authorized peace officer requesting the subpoena or court order must be served a copy of the filed papers by personal delivery or by registered or certified mail.

(c) The court shall order the authorized peace officer to file a sworn response to the motion filed by the subscriber or customer if the court determines that the subscriber or customer has complied with the requirements of Subsections (a) and (b). On request of the peace officer, the court may permit the response to be filed in camera. The court may conduct any additional proceedings the court considers appropriate if the court is unable to make a determination on the motion on the basis of the parties' initial allegations and response.

(d) The court shall rule on the motion as soon as practicable after the filing of the peace officer's response. The court shall deny the motion if the court finds that the applicant is not the subscriber or customer whose data is the subject of the subpoena or court order or that there is reason to believe that the peace officer's inquiry is legitimate and that the data sought is relevant to that inquiry. The court shall quash the subpoena or vacate the court order if the court finds that the applicant is the subscriber or customer whose data is the subject of the subpoena or court order and that there is not a reason to believe that the data is relevant to a legitimate law enforcement inquiry or that there has not been substantial compliance with the provisions of this chapter.

(e) A court order denying a motion or application under this article is not a final order, and an interlocutory appeal may not be taken from the denial. (Code Crim. Proc., Art. 18.21, Secs. 6(g), (h).)

SUBCHAPTER J
PRODUCTION OF CERTAIN BUSINESS RECORDS

Art. 18B.451. Subpoena Authority.

The director of the department or the director's designee, the inspector general of the Texas Department of Criminal Justice or the inspector general's designee, or the sheriff or chief of a designated law enforcement agency or the sheriff's or chief's designee may issue an administrative subpoena to a communication common carrier or a provider of an electronic communications service to compel the production of any carrier's or service provider's business records that:

(1) disclose information about:

(A) the carrier's or service provider's customers; or

(B) users of the services offered by the carrier or service provider; and

(2) are material to a criminal investigation. (Code Crim. Proc., Art. 18.21, Sec. 15(a).)

Art. 18B.452. Report of Issuance of Subpoena.

Not later than the 30th day after the date on which an administrative subpoena is issued under Article 18B.451, the inspector general of the Texas Department of Criminal Justice or the sheriff or chief of a designated law enforcement agency, as applicable, shall report to the department the issuance of the subpoena. (Code Crim. Proc., Art. 18.21, Sec. 15(b).)

Art. 18B.453. Compliance with Policy for Installation and Use of Equipment.

(a) If, based on a report received under Article 18B.452, the department determines that a designated law enforcement office or agency is not in compliance with the policy adopted by the office or agency under Article 18B.251, the department shall notify the office or agency in writing that the office or agency, as applicable, is not in compliance.

(b) If the department determines that the office or agency still is not in compliance with the policy on the 90th day after the date the office or agency receives written notice under this article, the office or agency loses the authority granted by this chapter until:

(1) the office or agency adopts a new written policy governing the application of this chapter to the office or agency; and

(2) the department approves that policy. (Code Crim. Proc., Art. 18.21, Sec. 15(c).)

SUBCHAPTER K
SERVICE PROVIDER POWERS AND DUTIES

Art. 18B.501. Preclusion of Notification.

(a) An authorized peace officer seeking electronic customer data under Article 18B.351 may apply to the court for an order commanding the service provider to whom a warrant, subpoena, or court order is directed not to disclose to any person the existence of the warrant, subpoena, or court order. The order is effective for the period the court considers appropriate.

(b) The court shall enter the order if the court determines that there is reason to believe that notification of the existence of the warrant, subpoena, or court order will have an adverse result.

(c) In this article, an "adverse result" means:

(1) endangering the life or physical safety of an individual;

(2) flight from prosecution;

(3) destruction of or tampering with evidence;

(4) intimidation of a potential witness; or

(5) otherwise seriously jeopardizing an investigation or unduly delaying a trial. (Code Crim. Proc., Art. 18.21, Sec. 8.)

Art. 18B.502. Disclosure by Service Provider Prohibited.

(a) Except as provided by Subsection (c), a provider of an electronic communications service may not knowingly divulge the contents of a communication that is in electronic storage.

(b) Except as provided by Subsection (c), a provider of a remote computing service may not knowingly divulge the contents of a communication that:

(1) is in electronic storage on behalf of a subscriber or customer of the service provider;

(2) is received by means of electronic transmission from the subscriber or customer or created by

means of computer processing of communications received by means of electronic transmission from the subscriber or customer; and

(3) is solely for the purpose of providing storage or computer processing services to the subscriber or customer, if the service provider is not authorized to obtain access to the contents of that communication for purposes of providing any service other than storage or computer processing.

(c) A provider of an electronic communications service or a provider of a remote computing service may disclose the contents of an electronically stored communication:

(1) to an intended recipient of the communication or the intended recipient's agent;

(2) to the addressee or the addressee's agent;

(3) with the consent of the originator, to the addressee or the intended recipient of the communication, or the subscriber of a remote computing service;

(4) to a person whose facilities are used to transmit the communication to its destination or the person's employee or authorized representative;

(5) as may be necessary to provide the service or to protect the property or rights of the service provider;

(6) to a law enforcement agency if the contents were obtained inadvertently by the service provider and the contents appear to pertain to the commission of an offense; or

(7) as authorized under federal or other state law. (Code Crim. Proc., Art. 18.21, Sec. 11.)

Art. 18B.503. Reimbursement of Costs.

(a) Except as provided by Subsection (c), an authorized peace officer who obtains electronic customer data under Article 18B.351 or 18B.359 or other information under this chapter shall reimburse the person assembling or providing the data or information for all costs that are reasonably necessary and that have been directly incurred in searching for, assembling, reproducing, or otherwise providing the data or information, including costs arising from necessary disruption of normal operations of a provider of an electronic communications service or a provider of a remote computing service in which the electronic customer data may be held in electronic storage or in which the other information may be stored.

(b) The authorized peace officer and the person providing the electronic customer data or other information may agree on the amount of reimbursement. If there is not an agreement, the court that issued the order for production of the data or information shall determine the amount. If a court order was not issued for production of the data or information, the court before which any criminal prosecution relating to the data or information would be brought shall determine the amount.

(c) Subsection (a) does not apply to records or other information that is maintained by a communication common carrier and that relates to telephone toll records or telephone listings obtained under Article 18B.359(a), unless the court determines that:

(1) the amount of information required was unusually voluminous; or

(2) an undue burden was imposed on the service provider. (Code Crim. Proc., Art. 18.21, Sec. 9.)

SUBCHAPTER L
REMEDIES

Art. 18B.551. Cause of Action.

(a) Except as provided by Article 18B.552, a provider of an electronic communications service or a provider of a remote computing service, or a subscriber or customer of that service provider, that is aggrieved by a violation of this chapter has a civil cause of action if the conduct constituting the violation was committed knowingly or intentionally and is entitled to:

(1) injunctive relief;

(2) reasonable attorney's fees and other litigation costs reasonably incurred; and

(3) the amount of the actual damages suffered and any profits made by the violator as a result of the violation or $1,000, whichever is more.

(b) The reliance in good faith on a court order, warrant, subpoena, or legislative authorization is a complete defense to any civil action brought under this chapter.

(c) A civil action under this article may be presented not later than the second anniversary of the date the claimant first discovered or had reasonable opportunity to discover the violation. (Code Crim. Proc., Art. 18.21, Sec. 12.)

Art. 18B.552. No Cause of Action.

A subscriber or customer of a provider of an electronic communications service or a provider of a remote computing service does not have a cause of action against a service provider or the service provider's officers, employees, or agents or against other specified persons for providing information, facilities, or assistance as required by a court order, warrant, subpoena, or certification under this chapter. (Code Crim. Proc., Art. 18.21, Sec. 10.)

Art. 18B.553. Exclusivity of Remedies.

The remedies and sanctions under this chapter are the exclusive judicial remedies and sanctions for a violation of this chapter, other than a violation that infringes on a right of a party that is guaranteed by a state or federal constitution. (Code Crim. Proc., Art. 18.21, Sec. 13.)

AFTER COMMITMENT OR BAIL AND BEFORE THE TRIAL

CHAPTER 19
ORGANIZATION OF THE GRAND JURY [REPEALED]

Art. 19.01. Selection and Summons of Prospective Grand Jurors. [Repealed]

Art. 19.02. Notified of Appointment. [Repealed]

Art. 19.03. Oath of Commissioners. [Repealed]

Art. 19.04. Instructed. [Repealed]

Art. 19.05. Kept Free from Intrusion. [Repealed]

Art. 19.06. Shall Select Grand Jurors. [Repealed]

Art. 19.07. Extension Beyond Term of Period for Which Grand Jurors Shall Sit. [Repealed]

Art. 19.08. Qualifications. [Repealed]

Art. 19.09. Names Returned. [Repealed]

Art. 19.10. List to Clerk. [Repealed]

Art. 19.11. Oath to Clerk. [Repealed]

Art. 19.12. Deputy Clerk Sworn. [Repealed]

Art. 19.13. Clerk Shall Open Lists. [Repealed]

Art. 19.14. Summoning. [Repealed]

Art. 19.15. Return of Officer. [Repealed]

Art. 19.16. Absent Juror Fined. [Repealed]

Art. 19.17. Failure to Select. [Repealed]

Art. 19.18. If Less Than Sixteen Attend. [Repealed]

Art. 19.19. Jurors to Attend Forthwith. [Repealed]

Art. 19.20. To Summon Qualified Persons. [Repealed]

Art. 19.21. To Test Qualifications. [Repealed]

Art. 19.22. Interrogated. [Repealed]

Art. 19.23. Mode of Test. [Repealed]

Art. 19.24. Qualified Juror Accepted. [Repealed]

Art. 19.25. Excuses from Service. [Repealed]

Art. 19.26. Jury Impaneled. [Repealed]

Art. 19.27. Any Person May Challenge. [Repealed]

Art. 19.28. "Array". [Repealed]

Art. 19.29. "Impaneled" and "Panel". [Repealed]

Art. 19.30. Challenge to "array". [Repealed]

Art. 19.31. Challenge to Juror. [Repealed]

Art. 19.315. Recusal of Juror. [Repealed]

Art. 19.32. Summarily Decided. [Repealed]

Art. 19.33. Other Jurors Summoned. [Repealed]

Art. 19.34. Oath of Grand Jurors. [Repealed]

Art. 19.35. To Instruct Jury. [Repealed]

Art. 19.36. Bailiffs Appointed. [Repealed]

Art. 19.37. Bailiff's Duties. [Repealed]

Art. 19.38. Bailiff Violating Duty. [Repealed]

Art. 19.39. Another Foreman Appointed. [Repealed]

Art. 19.40. Quorum. [Repealed]

Art. 19.41. Reassembled. [Repealed]

Art. 19.42. Personal Information About Grand Jurors. [Repealed]

CHAPTER 19A
GRAND JURY ORGANIZATION

SUBCHAPTER A
GENERAL PROVISIONS

Art. 19A.001. Definitions.

In this chapter:

(1) "Array" means the whole body of persons summoned to serve as grand jurors before the grand jurors have been impaneled.

(2) "Panel" means the whole body of grand jurors. (Code Crim. Proc., Arts. 19.28, 19.29 (part).)

SUBCHAPTER B
SELECTION AND SUMMONS OF PROSPECTIVE GRAND JURORS

Art. 19A.051. Selection and Summons of Prospective Grand Jurors.

(a) The district judge shall direct that the number of prospective grand jurors the judge considers necessary to ensure an adequate number of grand jurors under Article 19A.201 be selected and summoned, with return on summons.

(b) The prospective grand jurors shall be selected and summoned in the same manner as for the selection and summons of panels for the trial of civil cases in the district courts.

(c) The judge shall test the qualifications for and excuses from service as a grand juror and impanel the completed grand jury as provided by this chapter. (Code Crim. Proc., Art. 19.01.)

Art. 19A.052. Qualified Persons Summoned.

On directing the sheriff to summon grand jurors, the court shall instruct the sheriff to not summon a person to serve as a grand juror who does not possess the qualifications prescribed by law. (Code Crim. Proc., Art. 19.20.)

Art. 19A.053. Additional Qualified Persons Summoned.

(a) If fewer than 16 persons summoned to serve as grand jurors are found to be in attendance and qualified to serve, the court shall order the sheriff to summon an additional number of persons considered necessary to constitute a grand jury of 12 grand jurors and four alternate grand jurors.

(b) The sheriff shall summon the additional prospective grand jurors under Subsection (a) in person to attend before the court immediately. (Code Crim. Proc., Arts. 19.18, 19.19.)

Art. 19A.054. Failure to Attend.

The court, by an order entered on the record, may impose a fine of not less than $100 and not more than $500 on a legally summoned grand juror who fails to attend without a reasonable excuse. (Code Crim. Proc., Art. 19.16.)

SUBCHAPTER C GRAND JUROR QUALIFICATIONS; EXCUSES FROM SERVICE

Art. 19A.101. Grand Juror Qualifications.

A person may be selected or serve as a grand juror only if the person:

(1) is at least 18 years of age;

(2) is a citizen of the United States;

(3) is a resident of this state and of the county in which the person is to serve;

(4) is qualified under the constitution and other laws to vote in the county in which the grand jury is sitting, regardless of whether the person is registered to vote;

(5) is of sound mind and good moral character;

(6) is able to read and write;

(7) has not been convicted of misdemeanor theft or a felony;

(8) is not under indictment or other legal accusation for misdemeanor theft or a felony;

(9) is not related within the third degree by consanguinity or second degree by affinity, as determined under Chapter 573, Government Code, to any person selected to serve or serving on the same grand jury;

(10) has not served as a grand juror in the year before the date on which the term of court for which the person has been selected as a grand juror begins; and

(11) is not a complainant in any matter to be heard by the grand jury during the term of court for which the person has been selected as a grand juror. (Code Crim. Proc., Art. 19.08.)

Art. 19A.102. Testing Qualifications of Prospective Grand Jurors.

(a) When at least 14 persons summoned to serve as grand jurors are present, the court shall test the qualifications of the prospective grand jurors to serve as grand jurors.

(b) Before impaneling a grand juror, the court or a person under the direction of the court must interrogate under oath each person who is presented to serve as a grand juror regarding the person's qualifications.

(c) In testing the qualifications of a person to serve as a grand juror, the court or a person under the direction of the court shall ask:

(1) "Are you a citizen of this state and county, and qualified to vote in this county, under the constitution and laws of this state?";

(2) "Are you able to read and write?";

(3) "Have you ever been convicted of misdemeanor theft or any felony?"; and

(4) "Are you under indictment or other legal accusation for misdemeanor theft or for any felony?". (Code Crim. Proc., Arts. 19.21, 19.22, 19.23.)

Art. 19A.103. Qualified Grand Jurors Accepted.

If, by the person's answer, it appears to the court that the person is a qualified grand juror, the court shall accept the person as a grand juror unless it is shown that the person:

(1) is not of sound mind or of good moral character; or

(2) is in fact not qualified to serve as a grand juror. (Code Crim. Proc., Art. 19.24.)

Art. 19A.104. Personal Information Confidential.

(a) Except as provided by Subsection (c), information collected by the court, court personnel, or prosecuting attorney during the grand jury selection process about a person who serves as a grand juror is confidential and may not be disclosed by the court, court personnel, or prosecuting attorney.

(b) Information that is confidential under Subsection (a) includes a person's:

(1) home address;

(2) home telephone number;

(3) social security number;

(4) driver's license number; and

(5) other personal information.

(c) On a showing of good cause, the court shall permit disclosure of the information sought to a party to the proceeding. (Code Crim. Proc., Art. 19.42.)

Art. 19A.105. Excuses From Grand Jury Service.

(a) The court shall excuse from serving any summoned person who does not possess the requisite qualifications.

(b) The following qualified persons may be excused from grand jury service:

(1) a person older than 70 years of age;

(2) a person responsible for the care of a child younger than 18 years of age;

(3) a student of a public or private secondary school;

(4) a person enrolled in and in actual attendance at an institution of higher education; and

Code of Criminal Procedure

(5) any other person the court determines has a reasonable excuse from service. (Code Crim. Proc., Art. 19.25.)

SUBCHAPTER D CHALLENGE TO ARRAY OR GRAND JUROR

Art. 19A.151. Any Person May Challenge.

(a) Before the grand jury is impaneled, any person may challenge the array of grand jurors or any person presented as a grand juror. The court may not hear objections to the qualifications and legality of the grand jury in any other way.

(b) A person confined in jail in the county shall, on the person's request, be brought into court to make a challenge described by Subsection (a). (Code Crim. Proc., Art. 19.27.)

Art. 19A.152. Challenge to Array.

(a) A challenge to the array may be made only for the following causes:

(1) that the persons summoned as grand jurors are not in fact the persons selected by the method provided by Article 19A.051; or

(2) that the officer who summoned the grand jurors acted corruptly in summoning any grand juror.

(b) A challenge to the array must be made in writing. (Code Crim. Proc., Art. 19.30.)

Art. 19A.153. Challenge to Grand Juror.

(a) A challenge to a grand juror may be made orally for any of the following causes:

(1) that the grand juror is insane;

(2) that the grand juror has a defect in the organs of feeling or hearing, or a bodily or mental defect or disease that renders the grand juror unfit for grand jury service, or that the grand juror is legally blind and the court in its discretion is not satisfied that the grand juror is fit for grand jury service in that particular case;

(3) that the grand juror is a witness in or a target of an investigation of a grand jury;

(4) that the grand juror served on a petit jury in a former trial of the same alleged conduct or offense that the grand jury is investigating;

(5) that the grand juror has a bias or prejudice in favor of or against the person accused or suspected of committing an offense that the grand jury is investigating;

(6) that from hearsay, or otherwise, there is established in the mind of the grand juror a conclusion as to the guilt or innocence of the person accused or suspected of committing an offense that the grand jury is investigating that would influence the grand juror's vote on the presentment of an indictment;

(7) that the grand juror is related within the third degree by consanguinity or affinity, as determined under Chapter 573, Government Code, to a person accused or suspected of committing an offense that the grand jury is investigating or to a person who is a victim of an offense that the grand jury is investigating;

(8) that the grand juror has a bias or prejudice against any phase of the law on which the state is entitled to rely for an indictment;

(9) that the grand juror is not a qualified grand juror; or

(10) that the grand juror is the prosecutor on an accusation against the person making the challenge.

(b) A challenge under Subsection (a)(3) may be made ex parte. The court shall review and rule on the challenge in an in camera proceeding. The court shall seal any record of the challenge.

(c) In this article, "legally blind" has the meaning assigned by Article 35.16(a). (Code Crim. Proc., Art. 19.31.)

Art. 19A.154. Determination of Validity of Challenge.

When a person challenges the array or a grand juror, the court shall hear proof and decide in a summary manner whether the challenge is well founded. (Code Crim. Proc., Art. 19.32.)

Art. 19A.155. Additional Prospective Grand Jurors Summoned Following Challenge.

(a) If the court sustains a challenge to the array, the court shall order another grand jury to be summoned.

(b) If, because of a challenge to any particular grand juror, fewer than 12 grand jurors remain, the court shall order the panel to be completed. (Code Crim. Proc., Art. 19.33.)

SUBCHAPTER E IMPANELING OF GRAND JURY

Art. 19A.201. Grand Jury Impaneled.

(a) When at least 16 qualified grand jurors are found to be present, the court shall select 12 fair and impartial persons as grand jurors and 4 additional persons as alternate grand jurors to serve on disqualification or unavailability of a grand juror during the term of the grand jury. The grand jurors and the alternate grand jurors must be randomly selected from a fair cross section of the population of the area served by the court.

(b) The court shall impanel the grand jurors and alternate grand jurors, unless a challenge is made to the array or to a particular person presented to serve as a grand juror or an alternate grand juror.

(c) A grand juror is considered to be impaneled after the grand juror's qualifications have been tested and the grand juror has been sworn. (Code Crim. Proc., Arts. 19.26(a), (b) (part), 19.29 (part).)

Art. 19A.202. Oath of Grand Jurors.

The court or a person under the direction of the court shall administer the following oath to the grand jurors when the grand jury is completed: "You solemnly swear that you will diligently inquire into, and true presentment make, of all such matters and things as shall be given you in charge; the State's counsel, your fellows and your own, you shall keep secret, unless required to disclose the same in the course of a judicial proceeding in which the truth or falsity of evidence given in the grand jury room, in a criminal case, shall be under investigation. You shall present no person from envy, hatred or malice; neither shall you leave any person unpresented for love, fear, favor, affection or hope of reward; but you shall present things truly as they come to your knowledge, according to the best of your understanding, so help you God." (Code Crim. Proc., Art. 19.34 (part).)

Art. 19A.203. Foreperson.

(a) When the grand jury is completed, the court shall appoint one of the grand jurors as foreperson.

(b) If the foreperson is for any cause absent or unable or disqualified to act, the court shall appoint another grand juror as foreperson. (Code Crim. Proc., Arts. 19.34 (part), 19.39.)

Art. 19A.204. Court Instructions.

The court shall instruct the grand jury regarding the grand jurors' duty. (Code Crim. Proc., Art. 19.35.)

SUBCHAPTER F ORGANIZATION AND TERM OF GRAND JURY

Art. 19A.251. Quorum.

Nine grand jurors constitute a quorum for the purpose of discharging a duty or exercising a right properly belonging to the grand jury. (Code Crim. Proc., Art. 19.40.)

Art. 19A.252. Disqualification or Unavailability of Grand Juror.

(a) On learning that a grand juror has become disqualified or unavailable during the term of the grand jury, the attorney representing the state shall prepare an order for the court:

(1) identifying the disqualified or unavailable grand juror;

(2) stating the basis for the disqualification or unavailability;

(3) dismissing the disqualified or unavailable grand juror from the grand jury; and

(4) naming one of the alternate grand jurors as a member of the grand jury.

(b) The procedure established by this article may be used on disqualification or unavailability of a second or subsequent grand juror during the term of the grand jury.

(c) For purposes of this article, a grand juror is unavailable if the grand juror is unable to participate fully in the duties of the grand jury because of:

(1) the death of the grand juror;

(2) a physical or mental illness of the grand juror; or

(3) any other reason the court determines constitutes good cause for dismissing the grand juror. (Code Crim. Proc., Art. 19.26(b) (part).)

Art. 19A.253. Recusal of Grand Juror.

(a) A grand juror who, during the course of the grand juror's service on the grand jury, determines that the grand juror could be subject to a valid challenge for cause under Article 19A.153, shall recuse himself or herself from grand jury service until the cause no longer exists.

(b) A grand juror who knowingly fails to recuse himself or herself under Subsection (a) may be held in contempt of court.

(c) A person authorized to be present in the grand jury room shall report a known violation of Subsection (a) to the court.

(d) The court shall instruct the grand jury regarding the duty imposed by this article. (Code Crim. Proc., Art. 19.315.)

Art. 19A.254. Reassembly of Grand Jury.

A grand jury discharged by the court for the term may be reassembled by the court at any time during the term. (Code Crim. Proc., Art. 19.41.)

Code of Criminal Procedure

Art. 19A.255. Extension of Term.

(a) If, before the expiration of the term for which the grand jury was impaneled, the foreperson or a majority of the grand jurors declares in open court that the grand jury's investigation of the matters before the grand jury cannot be concluded before the expiration of the term, the judge of the district court in which the grand jury was impaneled may, by an order entered on the minutes of the court, extend, from time to time, the period during which the grand jury serves, for the purpose of concluding the investigation of matters then before the grand jury.

(b) The extended period during which the grand jury serves under Subsection (a) may not exceed a total of 90 days after the expiration date of the term for which the grand jury was impaneled.

(c) All indictments pertaining to the investigation for which the extension was granted returned by the grand jury during the extended period are as valid as if returned before the expiration of the term. (Code Crim. Proc., Art. 19.07.)

SUBCHAPTER G
BAILIFFS

Art. 19A.301. Bailiffs Appointed; Compensation.

(a) The court and the district attorney may each appoint one or more bailiffs to attend to the grand jury.

(b) The court, or a person under the direction of the court, shall administer the following oath to each bailiff at the time of appointment: "You solemnly swear that you will faithfully and impartially perform all the duties of bailiff of the grand jury, and that you will keep secret the proceedings of the grand jury, so help you God."

(c) Bailiffs appointed under this article shall be compensated in an amount set by the applicable county commissioners court. (Code Crim. Proc., Art. 19.36.)

Art. 19A.302. Bailiff's Duties.

(a) A bailiff shall:

(1) obey the instructions of the foreperson;

(2) summon all witnesses; and

(3) perform all duties the foreperson requires of the bailiff.

(b) One bailiff shall always be with the grand jury if two or more bailiffs are appointed. (Code Crim. Proc., Art. 19.37.)

Art. 19A.303. Bailiff's Violation of Duty.

(a) A bailiff may not:

(1) take part in the discussions or deliberations of the grand jury; or

(2) be present when the grand jury is discussing or voting on a question.

(b) The grand jury shall report to the court any violation of duty by a bailiff. The court may punish the bailiff for the violation as for contempt. (Code Crim. Proc., Art. 19.38.)

CHAPTER 20
DUTIES AND POWERS OF THE GRAND JURY [REPEALED]

Art. 20.01. Grand Jury Room. [Repealed]

Art. 20.011. Who May Be Present in Grand Jury Room. [Repealed]

Art. 20.012. Recording of Certain Testimony. [Repealed]

Art. 20.02. Proceedings Secret. [Repealed]

Art. 20.03. Attorney Representing State Entitled to Appear. [Repealed]

Art. 20.04. Attorney May Examine Witnesses. [Repealed]

Art. 20.05. May Send for Attorney. [Repealed]

Art. 20.06. Advice from Court. [Repealed]

Art. 20.07. Foreman Shall Preside. [Repealed]

Art. 20.08. Adjournments. [Repealed]

Art. 20.09. Duties of Grand Jury. [Repealed]

Art. 20.10. Attorney or Foreman May Issue Process. [Repealed]

Art. 20.11. Out-of-County Witnesses. [Repealed]

Art. 20.12. Attachment in Vacation. [Repealed]

Art. 20.13. Execution of Process. [Repealed]

Art. 20.14. Evasion of Process. [Repealed]

Art. 20.15. When Witness Refuses to Testify. [Repealed]

Art. 20.151. Certain Testimony by Video Teleconferencing. [Repealed]

Art. 20.16. Oaths to Witnesses. [Repealed]

Art. 20.17. How Suspect or Accused Questioned. [Repealed]

Art. 20.18. How Witness Questioned. [Repealed]

Art. 20.19. Grand Jury Shall Vote. [Repealed]

Art. 20.20. Indictment Prepared. [Repealed]

Art. 20.21. Indictment Presented. [Repealed]

Art. 20.22. Presentment Entered of Record. [Repealed]

CHAPTER 20A GRAND JURY PROCEEDINGS

SUBCHAPTER A GENERAL PROVISIONS

Art. 20A.001. Definitions.

In this chapter:

(1) "Attorney representing the state" means the attorney general, district attorney, criminal district attorney, or county attorney.

(2) "Foreperson" means the foreperson of the grand jury appointed under Article 19A.203. (Code Crim. Proc., Art. 20.03 (part); New.)

SUBCHAPTER B DUTIES OF GRAND JURY AND GRAND JURORS

Art. 20A.051. Duties of Grand Jury.

The grand jury shall inquire into all offenses subject to indictment of which any grand juror may have knowledge or of which the grand jury is informed by the attorney representing the state or by any other credible person. (Code Crim. Proc., Art. 20.09.)

Art. 20A.052. Duties and Powers of Foreperson.

(a) The foreperson shall:

(1) preside over the grand jury's sessions; and

(2) conduct the grand jury's business and proceedings in an orderly manner.

(b) The foreperson may appoint one or more of the grand jurors to act as clerks for the grand jury. (Code Crim. Proc., Art. 20.07.)

Art. 20A.053. Meeting and Adjournment.

The grand jury shall meet and adjourn at times agreed on by a majority of the grand jury, except that the grand jury may not adjourn for more than three consecutive days unless the court consents to the adjournment. With the court's consent, the grand jury may adjourn for a longer period and shall conform the grand jury's adjournments as closely as possible to the court's adjournments. (Code Crim. Proc., Art. 20.08.)

SUBCHAPTER C GRAND JURY ROOM; PERSONS AUTHORIZED TO BE PRESENT

Art. 20A.101. Grand Jury Room.

After the grand jury is organized, the grand jury shall discharge the grand jury's duties in a suitable place that the sheriff shall prepare for the grand jury's sessions. (Code Crim. Proc., Art. 20.01.)

Art. 20A.102. Persons Who May Be Present in Grand Jury Room.

(a) While the grand jury is conducting proceedings, only the following persons may be present in the grand jury room:

(1) a grand juror;

(2) a bailiff;
(3) the attorney representing the state;
(4) a witness:
(A) while the witness is being examined; or
(B) when the witness's presence is necessary to assist the attorney representing the state in examining another witness or presenting evidence to the grand jury;
(5) an interpreter, if necessary;
(6) a stenographer or a person operating an electronic recording device, as provided by Article 20A.201; and
(7) a person operating a video teleconferencing system for use under Article 20A.259.

(b) While the grand jury is deliberating, only a grand juror may be present in the grand jury room. (Code Crim. Proc., Art. 20.011.)

Art. 20A.103. Attorney Representing State Entitled to Appear.

The attorney representing the state is entitled to appear before the grand jury and inform the grand jury of offenses subject to indictment at any time except when the grand jury is discussing the propriety of finding an indictment or is voting on an indictment. (Code Crim. Proc., Art. 20.03 (part).)

Art. 20A.104. Persons Who May Address Grand Jury.

No person may address the grand jury about a matter before the grand jury other than the attorney representing the state, a witness, or the accused or suspected person or the attorney for the accused or suspected person if approved by the attorney representing the state. (Code Crim. Proc., Art. 20.04 (part).)

SUBCHAPTER D
ADVICE TO GRAND JURY

Art. 20A.151. Advice From Attorney Representing State.

The grand jury may send for the attorney representing the state and ask the attorney's advice on any matter of law or on any question regarding the discharge of the grand jury's duties. (Code Crim. Proc., Art. 20.05.)

Art. 20A.152. Advice From Court.

(a) The grand jury may seek and receive advice from the court regarding any matter before the grand jury. For that purpose, the grand jury shall go into court in a body.

(b) The grand jury shall ensure that the manner in which the grand jury's questions are asked does not divulge the particular accusation pending before the grand jury.

(c) The grand jury may submit questions to the court in writing. The court may respond to those questions in writing. (Code Crim. Proc., Art. 20.06.)

SUBCHAPTER E
RECORDING AND DISCLOSURE OF GRAND JURY PROCEEDINGS

Art. 20A.201. Recording of Accused or Suspected Person's Testimony; Retention of Records.

(a) The examination of an accused or suspected person before the grand jury and that person's testimony shall be recorded by a stenographer or by use of an electronic device capable of recording sound.

(b) The validity of a grand jury proceeding is not affected by an unintentional failure to record all or part of the examination or testimony under Subsection (a).

(c) The attorney representing the state shall maintain possession of all records other than stenographer's notes made under Subsection (a) and any typewritten transcription of those records, except as otherwise provided by this subchapter. (Code Crim. Proc., Art. 20.012.)

Art. 20A.202. Proceedings Secret.

(a) Grand jury proceedings are secret.

(b) A subpoena or summons relating to a grand jury proceeding or investigation must be kept secret to the extent and for as long as necessary to prevent the unauthorized disclosure of a matter before the grand jury. This subsection may not be construed to limit a disclosure permitted by Article 20A.204(b), (c), or (d) or 20A.205(a) or (b). (Code Crim. Proc., Arts. 20.02(a), (h).)

Art. 20A.203. Disclosure by Person in Proceeding Prohibited.

(a) A grand juror, bailiff, interpreter, stenographer or person operating an electronic recording device, person preparing a typewritten transcription of a stenographic or electronic recording, or person operating a video teleconferencing system for use under Article 20A.259 who discloses anything transpiring before the grand jury in the course of the grand jury's official duties, regardless of whether the thing transpiring is recorded, may be punished by a fine not to exceed $500, as for contempt of court, by a term of confinement not to exceed 30 days, or both.

(b) A witness who reveals any matter about which the witness is examined or that the witness observes during a grand jury proceeding, other than when the witness is required to give evidence on that matter in due course, may be punished by a fine not to exceed $500, as for contempt of court, and by a term of confinement not to exceed six months. (Code Crim. Proc., Arts. 20.02(b), 20.16(b).)

Art. 20A.204. Disclosure by Attorney Representing State.

(a) The attorney representing the state may not disclose anything transpiring before the grand jury except as permitted by this article or Article 20A.205(a) or (b).

(b) In performing the attorney's duties, the attorney representing the state may disclose or permit a disclosure of a record made under Article 20A.201 or a typewritten transcription of that record, or may make or permit a disclosure otherwise prohibited by Article 20A.203, to a grand juror serving on the grand jury before which the record was made, another grand jury, a law enforcement agency, or a prosecuting attorney, as the attorney representing the state determines is necessary to assist the attorney in the performance of the attorney's duties.

(c) The attorney representing the state shall warn any person authorized to receive information under Subsection (b) of the person's duty to maintain the secrecy of the information.

(d) A person who receives information under Subsection (b) and discloses that information for purposes other than those permitted by that subsection may be punished for contempt in the same manner as a person who violates Article 20A.203(a). (Code Crim. Proc., Arts. 20.02(c), (g).)

Art. 20A.205. Petition for Disclosure by Defendant.

(a) The defendant may petition a court to order the disclosure of information made secret by Article 20A.202, 20A.203(a), or 20A.204, including a recording or typewritten transcription under Article 20A.201, as a matter preliminary to or in connection with a judicial proceeding. The court may order disclosure of the information if the defendant shows a particularized need.

(b) A petition for disclosure under Subsection (a) must be filed in the district court in which the case is pending. The defendant must also file a copy of the petition with the attorney representing the state, the parties to the judicial proceeding, and any other person the court requires. Each person who receives a copy of the petition under this subsection is entitled to appear before the court. The court shall provide interested parties with an opportunity to appear and present arguments for or against the requested disclosure.

(c) A person who receives information under this article and discloses that information may be punished for contempt in the same manner as a person who violates Article 20A.203(a). (Code Crim. Proc., Arts. 20.02(d), (e), (f).)

SUBCHAPTER F WITNESSES

Art. 20A.251. In-County Witness.

(a) In term time or vacation, the foreperson or the attorney representing the state may issue a summons or attachment for any witness in the county in which the grand jury sits.

(b) A summons or attachment issued under Subsection (a) may require the witness to appear before the grand jury at a specified time, or immediately, without stating the matter under investigation. (Code Crim. Proc., Art. 20.10.)

Art. 20A.252. Out-Of-County Witness.

(a) The foreperson or the attorney representing the state may cause a subpoena or attachment for a witness to be issued to any county in the state by submitting a written application to the district court stating the name and residence of the witness and that the witness's testimony is believed to be material.

(b) A subpoena or attachment issued under this article:

(1) is returnable to the grand jury in session or to the next grand jury for the county in which the subpoena or attachment was issued, as determined by the applicant; and

(2) shall be served and returned in the manner prescribed by Chapter 24.

(c) A subpoena issued under this article may require the witness to appear and produce records and documents.

(d) A witness subpoenaed under this article shall be compensated as provided by this code.

(e) An attachment issued under this article must command the sheriff or any constable of the county in which the witness resides to serve the witness and to bring the witness before the grand jury at a time and place specified in the attachment.

(f) The attorney representing the state may cause an attachment to be issued under this article in term time or vacation. (Code Crim. Proc., Arts. 20.11, 20.12.)

Art. 20A.253. Execution of Process.

(a) A bailiff or other officer who receives process to be served from the grand jury shall immediately execute the process and return the process to:

(1) the foreperson, if the grand jury is in session; or

(2) the district clerk, if the grand jury is not in session.

(b) If the process is returned unexecuted, the return must state why the process was not executed. (Code Crim. Proc., Art. 20.13.)

Art. 20A.254. Evasion of Process.

If the court determines that a witness for whom an attachment has been issued to appear before the grand jury is in any manner wilfully evading the service of the summons or attachment, the court may fine the witness, as for contempt, in an amount not to exceed $500. (Code Crim. Proc., Art. 20.14.)

Art. 20A.255. Witness Refusal to Testify.

(a) If a witness brought in any manner before a grand jury refuses to testify, the witness's refusal shall be communicated to the attorney representing the state or to the court.

(b) The court may compel a witness described by Subsection (a) to answer a proper question by imposing a fine not to exceed $500 and by committing the witness to jail until the witness is willing to testify. (Code Crim. Proc., Art. 20.15.)

Art. 20A.256. Witness Oath.

Before each witness is examined, the foreperson or a person under the foreperson's direction shall administer the following oath to the witness: "You solemnly swear that you will not reveal, by your words or conduct, and will keep secret any matter about which you may be examined or that you have observed during the proceedings of the grand jury, and that you will answer truthfully the questions asked of you by the grand jury, or under its direction, so help you God." (Code Crim. Proc., Art. 20.16(a).)

Art. 20A.257. Examination of Witnesses.

(a) Only a grand juror or the attorney representing the state may examine a witness before the grand jury.

(b) The attorney representing the state shall advise the grand jury regarding the proper mode of examining a witness.

(c) If a felony has been committed in any county in the grand jury's jurisdiction, and the name of the offender is known or unknown or if it is uncertain when or how the felony was committed, the grand jury shall first state the subject matter under investigation to a witness called before the grand jury and may then ask questions relevant to the transaction in general terms and in a manner that enables a determination as to whether the witness has knowledge of the violation of any particular law by any person, and if so, by what person. (Code Crim. Proc., Arts. 20.04 (part), 20.18.)

Art. 20A.258. Examination of Accused or Suspected Person.

(a) Before the examination of an accused or suspected person who is subpoenaed to appear before the grand jury, the person shall be:

(1) provided the warnings described by Subsection (b) orally and in writing; and

(2) given a reasonable opportunity to:

(A) retain counsel or apply to the court for an appointed attorney; and

(B) consult with counsel before appearing before the grand jury.

(b) The warnings required under Subsection (a)(1) must consist of the following:

"Your testimony before this grand jury is under oath. Any material question that is answered falsely before this grand jury subjects you to being prosecuted for aggravated perjury. You have the right to refuse to make answers to any question, the answer to which would incriminate you in any manner. You have the right to have a lawyer present outside this chamber to advise you before making answers to questions you feel might incriminate you. Any testimony you give may be used against you at any subsequent proceeding. If you are unable to employ a lawyer, you have the right to have a lawyer appointed to advise you before making an answer to a question, the answer to which you feel might incriminate you."

(c) In examining an accused or suspected person, the grand jury shall:

(1) first state:

(A) the offense of which the person is accused or suspected;

(B) the county in which the offense is alleged to have been committed; and

(C) as closely as possible, the time the offense was committed; and

(2) direct the examination to the offense under investigation. (Code Crim. Proc., Art. 20.17.)

Art. 20A.259. Peace Officer Testimony by Video Teleconferencing.

(a) With the consent of the foreperson and the attorney representing the state, a peace officer summoned to testify before the grand jury may testify through the use of a closed circuit video teleconferencing system that provides a simultaneous, encrypted, compressed full motion video and interactive communication of image and sound between the officer, the grand jury, and the attorney representing the state.

(b) In addition to being administered the oath required under Article 20A.256, before being examined, a peace officer testifying through the use of a closed circuit video teleconferencing system under this article shall affirm that the officer's testimony:

(1) cannot be heard by any person other than a person in the grand jury room; and

(2) is not being recorded or otherwise preserved by any person at the location from which the officer is testifying.

(c) Testimony received from a peace officer under this article shall be recorded in the same manner as other testimony taken before the grand jury and shall be preserved. (Code Crim. Proc., Art. 20.151.)

SUBCHAPTER G INDICTMENT

Art. 20A.301. Voting on Indictment.

After all the testimony accessible to the grand jury has been given with respect to any criminal accusation, the grand jury shall vote on the presentment of an indictment. If at least nine grand jurors concur in finding the bill, the foreperson shall make a memorandum of the vote with any information enabling the attorney representing the state to prepare the indictment. (Code Crim. Proc., Art. 20.19.)

Art. 20A.302. Preparation of Indictment.

(a) The attorney representing the state shall prepare, with as little delay as possible, each indictment found by the grand jury and shall deliver the indictment to the foreperson. The attorney shall endorse on the indictment the name of each witness on whose testimony the indictment was found.

(b) The foreperson shall officially sign each indictment prepared and delivered under Subsection (a). (Code Crim. Proc., Art. 20.20.)

Art. 20A.303. Presentment of Indictment.

When an indictment is ready to be presented, the grand jury shall, through the foreperson, deliver the indictment to the judge or court clerk. At least nine grand jurors must be present to deliver the indictment. (Code Crim. Proc., Art. 20.21.)

Art. 20A.304. Presentment of Indictment Entered in Record.

(a) If the defendant is in custody or under bond at the time the indictment is presented, the fact of the presentment shall be entered in the court's record, noting briefly the style of the criminal action, the file number of the indictment, and the defendant's name.

(b) If the defendant is not in custody or under bond at the time the indictment is presented, the indictment may not be made public and the entry in the court's record relating to the indictment must be delayed until the capias is served and the defendant is placed in custody or under bond. (Code Crim. Proc., Art. 20.22.)

CHAPTER 21 INDICTMENT AND INFORMATION

Art. 21.01. "Indictment".

An "indictment" is the written statement of a grand jury accusing a person therein named of some act or omission which, by law, is declared to be an offense.

Art. 21.011. Filing of Charging Instrument or Related Document in Electronic Form.

(a) An indictment, information, complaint, or other charging instrument or a related document in a criminal case may be filed in electronic form with a judge or clerk of the court authorized to receive the document.

(b) A judge or clerk of the court is authorized to receive for filing purposes an information, indictment, complaint, or other charging instrument or a related document in electronic form in accordance with Subchapter I, Chapter 51, Government Code, if:

(1) the document complies with the requirements that would apply if the document were filed in hard-copy form;

(2) the clerk of the court has the means to electronically store the document for the statutory period of record retention;

(3) the judge or clerk of the court is able to reproduce the document in hard-copy form on demand; and

(4) the clerk of the court is able to display or otherwise make the document available in electronic form to the public at no charge.

(c) The person filing the document and the person receiving the document must complete the electronic filing as provided by Section 51.804, Government Code.

(d) Notwithstanding Section 51.806, Government Code, an indictment, information, complaint, or other charging instrument or a related document transmitted in electronic form is exempt from a requirement under this code that the pleading be endorsed by a natural person. The requirement of an oath under this code is satisfied if:

(1) all or part of the document was sworn to; and

(2) the electronic form states which parts of the document were sworn to and the name of the officer administering the oath.

(e) An electronically filed document described by this section may be amended or modified in compliance with Chapter 28 or other applicable law. The amended or modified document must reflect that the original document has been superseded.

(f) This section does not affect the application of Section 51.318, Government Code, Section 118.052(3), Local Government Code, or any other law permitting the collection of fees for the provision of services related to court documents.

Art. 21.02. Requisites of an Indictment.

An indictment shall be deemed sufficient if it has the following requisites:

1. It shall commence, "In the name and by authority of The State of Texas".

2. It must appear that the same was presented in the district court of the county where the grand jury is in session.

3. It must appear to be the act of a grand jury of the proper county.

4. It must contain the name of the accused, or state that his name is unknown and give a reasonably accurate description of him.

5. It must show that the place where the offense was committed is within the jurisdiction of the court in which the indictment is presented.

6. The time mentioned must be some date anterior to the presentment of the indictment, and not so remote that the prosecution of the offense is barred by limitation.

7. The offense must be set forth in plain and intelligible words.

8. The indictment must conclude, "Against the peace and dignity of the State".

9. It shall be signed officially by the foreman of the grand jury.

Art. 21.03. What Should Be Stated.

Everything should be stated in an indictment which is necessary to be proved.

Art. 21.04. The Certainty Required.

The certainty required in an indictment is such as will enable the accused to plead the judgment that may be given upon it in bar of any prosecution for the same offense.

Art. 21.05. Particular Intent; Intent to Defraud.

Where a particular intent is a material fact in the description of the offense, it must be stated in the indictment; but in any case where an intent to defraud is required to constitute an offense, it shall be sufficient to allege an intent to defraud, without naming therein the particular person intended to be defrauded.

Art. 21.06. Allegation of Venue.

When the offense may be prosecuted in either of two or more counties, the indictment may allege the offense to have been committed in the county where the same is prosecuted, or in any county or place where the offense was actually committed.

Art. 21.07. Allegation of Name.

In alleging the name of the defendant, or of any other person necessary to be stated in the indictment, it shall be sufficient to state one or more of the initials of the given name and the surname. When a person is known by two or more names, it shall be sufficient to state either name. When the name of the person is unknown to the grand jury, that fact shall be stated, and if it be the accused, a reasonably accurate description of him shall be given in the indictment.

Art. 21.08. Allegation of Ownership.

Where one person owns the property, and another person has the possession of the same, the ownership thereof may be alleged to be in either. Where property is owned in common, or jointly, by two or more persons, the ownership may be alleged to be in all or either of them. When the property belongs to the estate of a deceased person, the ownership may be alleged to be in the executor, administrator or heirs of such deceased person, or in any one of such heirs. Where the ownership of the property is unknown to the grand jury, it shall be sufficient to allege that fact.

Art. 21.09. Description of Property.

If known, personal property alleged in an indictment shall be identified by name, kind, number, and ownership. When such is unknown, that fact shall be stated, and a general classification, describing and identifying the property as near as may be, shall suffice. If the property be real estate, its general locality in the county, and the name of the owner, occupant or claimant thereof, shall be a sufficient description of the same.

Art. 21.10. "Felonious" and "Feloniously".

It is not necessary to use the words "felonious" or "feloniously" in any indictment.

Art. 21.11. Certainty; What Sufficient.

An indictment shall be deemed sufficient which charges the commission of the offense in ordinary and concise language in such a manner as to enable a person of common understanding to know what is meant, and with that degree of certainty that will give the defendant notice of the particular offense with which he is charged, and enable the court, on conviction, to pronounce the proper judgment; and in no case are the words "force and arms" or "contrary to the form of the statute" necessary.

Art. 21.12. Special and General Terms.

When a statute defining any offense uses special or particular terms, indictment on it may use the general term which, in common language, embraces the special term. To charge an unlawful sale, it is necessary to name the purchaser.

Art. 21.13. Act with Intent to Commit an Offense.

An indictment for an act done with intent to commit some other offense may charge in general terms the commission of such act with intent to commit such other offense.

Art. 21.14. Perjury and Aggravated Perjury.

(a) An indictment for perjury or aggravated perjury need not charge the precise language of the false statement, but may state the substance of the same, and no such indictment shall be held insufficient on account of any variance which does not affect the subject matter or general import of such false statement; and it is not necessary in such indictment to set forth the pleadings, records or proceeding with which the false statement is connected, nor the commission or authority of the court or person before whom the false statement was made; but it is sufficient to state the name of the court or public servant by whom the oath was administered with the allegation of the falsity of the matter on which the perjury or aggravated perjury is assigned.

(b) If an individual is charged with aggravated perjury before a grand jury, the indictment may not be entered by the grand jury before which the false statement was alleged to have been made.

Art. 21.15. Must Allege Acts of Recklessness or Criminal Negligence.

Whenever recklessness or criminal negligence enters into or is a part or element of any offense, or it is charged that the accused acted recklessly or with criminal negligence in the commission of an offense, the complaint, information, or indictment in order to be sufficient in any such case must allege, with reasonable certainty, the act or acts relied upon to constitute recklessness or criminal negligence, and in no event shall it be sufficient to allege merely that the accused, in committing the offense, acted recklessly or with criminal negligence.

Art. 21.16. Certain Forms of Indictments.

The following form of indictments is sufficient: "In the name and by authority of the State of Texas: The grand jury of .... County, State of Texas, duly organized at the .... term, A.D. ...., of the district court of said county, in said court at said term, do present that .... (defendant) on the .... day of .... A.D. ...., in said county and State, did .... (description of offense) against the peace and dignity of the State.

......................, Foreman of the grand jury."

Art. 21.17. Following Statutory Words.

Words used in a statute to define an offense need not be strictly pursued in the indictment; it is sufficient to use other words conveying the same meaning, or which include the sense of the statutory words.

Art. 21.18. Matters of Judicial Notice.

Presumptions of law and matters of which judicial notice is taken (among which are included the authority and duties of all officers elected or appointed under the General Laws of this State) need not be stated in an indictment.

Art. 21.19. Defects of Form.

An indictment shall not be held insufficient, nor shall the trial, judgment or other proceedings thereon be affected, by reason of any defect of form which does not prejudice the substantial rights of the defendant.

Art. 21.20. "Information".

An "Information" is a written statement filed and presented in behalf of the State by the district or county attorney, charging the defendant with an offense which may by law be so prosecuted.

Art. 21.21. Requisites of an Information.

An information is sufficient if it has the following requisites:

1. It shall commence, "In the name and by authority of the State of Texas";
2. That it appear to have been presented in a court having jurisdiction of the offense set forth;
3. That it appear to have been presented by the proper officer;
4. That it contain the name of the accused, or state that his name is unknown and give a reasonably accurate description of him;
5. It must appear that the place where the offense is charged to have been committed is within the jurisdiction of the court where the information is filed;
6. That the time mentioned be some date anterior to the filing of the information, and that the offense does not appear to be barred by limitation;
7. That the offense be set forth in plain and intelligible words;
8. That it conclude, "Against the peace and dignity of the State"; and
9. It must be signed by the district or county attorney, officially.

Art. 21.22. Information Based upon Complaint.

No information shall be presented until affidavit has been made by some credible person charging the defendant with an offense. The affidavit shall be filed with the information. It may be sworn to before the district or county attorney who, for that purpose, shall have power to administer the oath, or it may be made before any officer authorized by law to administer oaths.

Art. 21.23. Rules As to Indictment Apply to Information.

The rules with respect to allegations in an indictment and the certainty required apply also to an information.

Art. 21.24. Joinder of Certain Offenses.

(a) Two or more offenses may be joined in a single indictment, information, or complaint, with each offense stated in a separate count, if the offenses arise out of the same criminal episode, as defined in Chapter 3 of the Penal Code.

(b) A count may contain as many separate paragraphs charging the same offense as necessary, but no paragraph may charge more than one offense.

(c) A count is sufficient if any one of its paragraphs is sufficient. An indictment, information, or complaint is sufficient if any one of its counts is sufficient.

Art. 21.25. When Indictment Has Been Lost, Etc.

When an indictment or information has been lost, mislaid, mutilated or obliterated, the district or county attorney may suggest the fact to the court; and the same shall be entered upon the minutes of the court. In such case, another indictment or information may be substituted, upon the written statement of such attorney that it is substantially the same as that which has been lost, mislaid, mutilated, or obliterated. Or another indictment may be presented, as in the first instance; and in such case, the period for the commencement of the prosecution shall be dated from the time of making such entry.

Art. 21.26. Order Transferring Cases.

Upon the filing of an indictment in the district court which charges an offense over which such court has no jurisdiction, the judge of such court shall make an order transferring the same to such inferior court as may have jurisdiction, stating in such order the cause transferred and to what court transferred.

Art. 21.27. Causes Transferred to Justice Court.

Causes over which justices of the peace have jurisdiction may be transferred to a justice of the peace at the county seat, or in the discretion of the judge, to a justice of the precinct in which the same can be most conveniently tried, as may appear by memorandum endorsed by the grand jury on the indictment or otherwise. If it appears to the judge that the offense has been committed in any incorporated town or city, the cause shall be transferred to a justice in said town or city, if there be one therein; and any justice to whom such cause may be transferred shall have jurisdiction to try the same.

Art. 21.28. Duty on Transfer.

The clerk of the court, without delay, shall deliver the indictments in all cases transferred, together with all the papers relating to each case, to the proper court or justice, as directed in the order of transfer; and shall accompany each case with a certified copy of all the proceedings taken therein in the district court, and with a bill of the costs that have accrued therein in the district court. The said costs shall be taxed in the court in which said cause is tried, in the event of a conviction.

Art. 21.29. Proceedings of Inferior Court.

Any case so transferred shall be entered on the docket of the court to which it is transferred. All process thereon shall be issued and the defendant tried as if the case had originated in the court to which it was transferred.

Art. 21.30. Cause Improvidently Transferred.

When a cause has been improvidently transferred to a court which has no jurisdiction of the same, the court to which it has been transferred shall order it to be re-transferred to the proper court; and the same proceedings shall be had as in the case of the original transfer. In such case, the defendant and the witnesses shall be held bound to appear before the court to which the case has been re-transferred, the same as they were bound to appear before the court so transferring the same.

Art. 21.31. Testing for AIDS and Certain Other Diseases.

(a) A person who is indicted for or who waives indictment for an offense under Section 21.02, 21.11(a)(1), 22.011, or 22.021, Penal Code, shall, at the direction of the court on the court's own motion or on the request of the victim of the alleged offense, undergo a standard diagnostic test approved by the United States Food and Drug Administration for human immunodeficiency virus (HIV) infection and other sexually transmitted diseases. If the person refuses to submit voluntarily to the test, the court shall require the person to submit to the test. On request of the victim of the alleged offense, the court shall order the defendant to undergo the test not later than 48 hours after an indictment for the offense is presented against the defendant or the defendant waives indictment. Except as provided by Subsection (b-1), the court may require a defendant previously required under this article to undergo a diagnostic test on indictment for an offense to undergo a subsequent test only after conviction of the offense. A person performing a test under this subsection shall make the test results available to the local health authority, and the local health authority shall be required to make the notification of the test results to the victim of the alleged offense and to the defendant.

(a-1) If the victim requests the testing of the defendant and a law enforcement agency is unable to locate the defendant during the 48-hour period allowed for that testing under Subsection (a), the running of the 48-hour period is tolled until the law enforcement agency locates the defendant and the defendant is present in the jurisdiction.

(b) The court shall order a person who is charged with an offense under Section 22.11, Penal Code, to undergo in the manner provided by Subsection (a) a diagnostic test designed to show or help show whether the person has HIV, hepatitis A, hepatitis B, tuberculosis, or any other disease designated as a reportable disease under Section 81.048, Health and Safety Code. The person charged with the offense shall pay the costs of testing under this subsection.

(b-1) If the results of a diagnostic test conducted under Subsection (a) or (b) are positive for HIV, the court shall order the defendant to undergo any

Code of Criminal Procedure

necessary additional testing within a reasonable time after the test results are released.

(c) The state may not use the fact that a test was performed on a person under Subsection (a) or use the results of a test conducted under Subsection (a) in any criminal proceeding arising out of the alleged offense.

(d) Testing under this article shall be conducted in accordance with written infectious disease control protocols adopted by the Texas Board of Health that clearly establish procedural guidelines that provide criteria for testing and that respect the rights of the person accused and any victim of the alleged offense.

(e) This article does not permit a court to release a test result to anyone other than those authorized by law, and the provisions of Section 81.103(d), Health and Safety Code, may not be construed to allow that disclosure.

CHAPTER 22 FORFEITURE OF BAIL

Art. 22.01. Bail Forfeited, When.

When a defendant is bound by bail to appear and fails to appear in any court in which such case may be pending and at any time when his personal appearance is required under this Code, or by any court or magistrate, a forfeiture of his bail and a judicial declaration of such forfeiture shall be taken in the manner provided in Article 22.02 of this Code and entered by such court.

Art. 22.01a. Failure to Appear; Violation of Bail Bond [Repealed].

Repealed by Acts 1973, 63rd Leg., ch. 399 (S.B. 34), § 3(b), effective January 1, 1974.

Art. 22.02. Manner of Taking a Forfeiture.

Bail bonds and personal bonds are forfeited in the following manner: The name of the defendant shall be called distinctly at the courthouse door, and if the defendant does not appear within a reasonable time after such call is made, judgment shall be entered that the State of Texas recover of the defendant the amount of money in which he is bound, and of his sureties, if any, the amount of money in which they are respectively bound, which judgment shall state that the same will be made final, unless good cause be shown why the defendant did not appear.

Art. 22.021. Forfeiture After Violating Treatment Condition [Repealed].

Repealed by Acts 2007, 80th Leg., ch. 1113 (H.B. 3692), § 6, effective January 1, 2008.

Art. 22.03. Citation to Sureties.

(a) Upon entry of judgment, a citation shall issue forthwith notifying the sureties of the defendant, if any, that the bond has been forfeited, and requiring them to appear and show cause why the judgment of forfeiture should not be made final.

(b) A citation to a surety who is an individual shall be served to the individual at the address shown on the face of the bond or the last known address of the individual.

(c) A citation to a surety that is a corporation or other entity shall be served to the attorney designated for service of process by the corporation or entity under Chapter 804, Insurance Code.

(d) By filing the waiver or designation in writing with the clerk of the court, a surety may waive service of citation or may designate a person other than the surety or the surety's attorney to receive service of citation under this article. The waiver or designation is effective until a written revocation is filed with the clerk.

Art. 22.035. Citation to Defendant Posting Cash Bond.

A citation to a defendant who posted a cash bond shall be served to the defendant at the address shown on the face of the bond or the last known address of the defendant.

Art. 22.04. Requisites of Citation.

A citation shall be sufficient if it be in the form provided for citations in civil cases in such court; provided, however, that a copy of the judgment of forfeiture entered by the court, a copy of the forfeited bond, and a copy of any power of attorney attached to the forfeited bond shall be attached to the citation and the citation shall notify the parties cited to appear and show cause why the judgment of forfeiture should not be made final.

Art. 22.05. Citation As in Civil Actions.

If service of citation is not waived under Article 22.03, a surety is entitled to notice by service of citation, the length of time and in the manner required in civil actions; and the officer executing the citation shall return the same as in civil actions.

It shall not be necessary to give notice to the defendant unless he has furnished his address on the bond, in which event notice to the defendant shall be deposited in the United States mail directed to the defendant at the address shown on the bond or the last known address of the defendant.

Art. 22.06. Citation by Publication.

Where the surety is a nonresident of the State, or where he is a transient person, or where his residence is unknown, the district or county attorney may, upon application in writing to the county clerk, stating the facts, obtain a citation to be served by publication; and the same shall be served by a publication and returned as in civil actions.

Art. 22.07. Cost of Publication.

When service of citation is made by publication, the county in which the forfeiture has been taken shall pay the costs thereof, to be taxed as costs in the case.

Art. 22.08. Service out of the State.

Service of a certified copy of the citation upon any absent or non-resident surety may be made outside of the limits of this State by any person competent to make oath of the fact; and the affidavit of such person, stating the facts of such service, shall be a sufficient return.

Art. 22.09. When Surety Is Dead.

If the surety is dead at the time the forfeiture is taken, the forfeiture shall nevertheless be valid. The final judgment shall not be rendered where a surety has died, either before or after the forfeiture has been taken, unless his executor, administrator or heirs, as the case may be, have been cited to appear and show cause why the judgment should not be made final, in the same manner as provided in the case of the surety.

Art. 22.10. Scire Facias Docket.

When a forfeiture has been declared upon a bond, the court or clerk shall docket the case upon the scire facias or upon the civil docket, in the name of the State of Texas, as plaintiff, and the principal and his sureties, if any, as defendants; and, except as otherwise provided by this chapter, the proceedings had therein shall be governed by the same rules governing other civil suits.

Art. 22.11. Sureties May Answer.

After the forfeiture of the bond, if the sureties, if any, have been duly notified, the sureties, if any, may answer in writing and show cause why the defendant did not appear, which answer may be filed within the time limited for answering in other civil actions.

Art. 22.12. Proceedings Not Set Aside for Defect of Form.

The bond, the judgment declaring the forfeiture, the citation and the return thereupon, shall not be set aside because of any defect of form; but such defect of form may, at any time, be amended under the direction of the court.

Art. 22.12a. Powers of the Court [Renumbered].

Renumbered to Tex. Code Crim. Proc. art. 22.125 by Acts 1987, 70th Leg., ch. 167 (S.B. 892), § 5.02(1), effective September 1, 1987.

Art. 22.125. Powers of the Court.

After a judicial declaration of forfeiture is entered, the court may proceed with the trial required by Article 22.14 of this code. The court may exonerate the defendant and his sureties, if any, from liability on the forfeiture, remit the amount of the forfeiture, or set aside the forfeiture only as expressly provided by this chapter. The court may approve any proposed settlement of the liability on the forfeiture that is agreed to by the state and by the defendant or the defendant's sureties, if any.

Art. 22.13. Causes Which Will Exonerate.

(a) The following causes, and no other, will exonerate the defendant and his sureties, if any, from liability upon the forfeiture taken:

1. That the bond is, for any cause, not a valid and binding undertaking in law. If it be valid and binding as to the principal, and one or more of his sureties, if any, they shall not be exonerated from liability because of its being invalid and not binding as to another surety or sureties, if any. If it be invalid and not binding as to the principal, each of the sureties, if any, shall be exonerated from liability. If it be valid and binding as to the principal, but not so as to the sureties, if any, the principal shall not be exonerated, but the sureties, if any, shall be.

2. The death of the principal before the forfeiture was taken.

Code of Criminal Procedure

3. The sickness of the principal or some uncontrollable circumstance which prevented his appearance at court, and it must, in every such case, be shown that his failure to appear arose from no fault on his part. The causes mentioned in this subdivision shall not be deemed sufficient to exonerate the principal and his sureties, if any, unless such principal appear before final judgment on the bond to answer the accusation against him, or show sufficient cause for not so appearing.

4. Failure to present an indictment or information at the first term of the court which may be held after the principal has been admitted to bail, in case where the party was bound over before indictment or information, and the prosecution has not been continued by order of the court.

5. The incarceration of the principal in any jurisdiction in the United States:

(A) in the case of a misdemeanor, at the time of or not later than the 180th day after the date of the principal's failure to appear in court; or

(B) in the case of a felony, at the time of or not later than the 270th day after the date of the principal's failure to appear in court.

(b) A surety exonerated under Subdivision 5, Subsection (a), remains obligated to pay costs of court, any reasonable and necessary costs incurred by a county to secure the return of the principal, and interest accrued on the bond amount from the date of the judgment nisi to the date of the principal's incarceration.

Art. 22.14. Judgment Final.

When, upon a trial of the issues presented, no sufficient cause is shown for the failure of the principal to appear, the judgment shall be made final against him and his sureties, if any, for the amount in which they are respectively bound; and the same shall be collected by execution as in civil actions. Separate executions shall issue against each party for the amount adjudged against him. The costs shall be equally divided between the sureties, if there be more than one.

Art. 22.15. Judgment Final by Default.

When the sureties have been duly cited and fail to answer, and the principal also fails to answer within the time limited for answering in other civil actions, the court shall enter judgment final by default.

Art. 22.16. Remittitur After Forfeiture.

(a) After forfeiture of a bond and before entry of a final judgment, the court shall, on written motion, remit to the surety the amount of the bond, after deducting the costs of court and any reasonable and necessary costs to the county for the return of the principal, and the interest accrued on the bond amount as provided by Subsection (c) if the principal is released on new bail in the case or the case for which bond was given is dismissed.

(b) For other good cause shown and before the entry of a final judgment against the bond, the court in its discretion may remit to the surety all or part of the amount of the bond after deducting the costs of court and any reasonable and necessary costs to the county for the return of the principal, and the interest accrued on the bond amount as provided by Subsection (c).

(c) For the purposes of this article, interest accrues on the bond amount from the date of forfeiture in the same manner and at the same rate as provided for the accrual of prejudgment interest in civil cases.

Art. 22.17. Special Bill of Review.

(a) Not later than two years after the date a final judgment is entered in a bond forfeiture proceeding, the surety on the bond may file with the court a special bill of review. A special bill of review may include a request, on equitable grounds, that the final judgment be reformed and that all or part of the bond amount be remitted to the surety, after deducting the costs of court, any reasonable costs to the county for the return of the principal, and the interest accrued on the bond amount from the date of forfeiture. The court in its discretion may grant or deny the bill in whole or in part.

(b) For the purposes of this article, interest accrues on the bond amount from the date of:

(1) forfeiture to the date of final judgment in the same manner and at the same rate as provided for the accrual of prejudgment interest in civil cases; and

(2) final judgment to the date of the order for remittitur at the same rate as provided for the accrual of postjudgment interest in civil cases.

Art. 22.18. Limitation.

An action by the state to forfeit a bail bond under this chapter must be brought not later than the fourth anniversary of the date the principal fails to appear in court.

CHAPTER 23
THE CAPIAS

Art. 23.01. Definition of a "Capias".

In this chapter, a "capias" is a writ that is:

(1) issued by a judge of the court having jurisdiction of a case after commitment or bail and before trial, or by a clerk at the direction of the judge; and

(2) directed "To any peace officer of the State of Texas", commanding the officer to arrest a person accused of an offense and bring the arrested person before that court immediately or on a day or at a term stated in the writ.

Art. 23.02. Its Requisites.

A capias shall be held sufficient if it have the following requisites:

1. That it run in the name of "The State of Texas";
2. That it name the person whose arrest is ordered, or if unknown, describe him;
3. That it specify the offense of which the defendant is accused, and it appear thereby that he is accused of some offense against the penal laws of the State;
4. That it name the court to which and the time when it is returnable; and
5. That it be dated and attested officially by the authority issuing the same.

Art. 23.03. Capias or Summons in Felony.

(a) A capias shall be issued by the district clerk upon each indictment for felony presented, after bail has been set or denied by the judge of the court. Upon the request of the attorney representing the State, a summons shall be issued by the district clerk. The capias or summons shall be delivered by the clerk or mailed to the sheriff of the county where the defendant resides or is to be found. A capias or summons need not issue for a defendant in custody or under bond.

(b) Upon the request of the attorney representing the State a summons instead of a capias shall issue. If a defendant fails to appear in response to the summons a capias shall issue.

(c) Summons. The summons shall be in the same form as the capias except that it shall summon the defendant to appear before the proper court at a stated time and place. The summons shall be served upon a defendant by delivering a copy to him personally, or by leaving it at his dwelling house or usual place of abode with some person of suitable age and discretion then residing therein or by mailing it to the defendant's last known address.

(d) A summons issued to any person must clearly and prominently state in English and in Spanish the following:

"It is an offense for a person to intentionally influence or coerce a witness to testify falsely or to elude legal process. It is also a felony offense to harm or threaten to harm a witness or prospective witness in retaliation for or on account of the service of the person as a witness or to prevent or delay the person's service as a witness to a crime."

Art. 23.031. Issuance of Capias in Electronic Form.

A district clerk, county clerk, or court may issue in electronic form a capias for the failure of a person to appear before a court or comply with a court order.

Art. 23.04. In Misdemeanor Case.

In misdemeanor cases, the capias or summons shall issue from a court having jurisdiction of the case on the filing of an information or complaint. The summons shall be issued only upon request of the attorney representing the State and on the determination of probable cause by the judge, and shall follow the same form and procedure as in a felony case.

Art. 23.05. Capias After Surrender or Forfeiture.

(a) If a forfeiture of bail is declared by a court or a surety surrenders a defendant under Article 17.19, a capias shall be immediately issued for the arrest of the defendant, and when arrested, in its discretion, the court may require the defendant, in order to be released from custody, to deposit with the custodian of funds of the court in which the prosecution is pending current money of the United States in the amount of the new bond as set by the court, in lieu of a surety bond, unless a forfeiture is taken and set aside under the third subdivision of Article 22.13, in which case the defendant and the defendant's sureties shall remain bound under the same bail.

(b) A capias issued under this article may be executed by a peace officer or by a private investigator licensed under Chapter 1702, Occupations Code.

(c) A capias under this article must be issued not later than the 10th business day after the date of the court's issuance of the order of forfeiture or order permitting surrender of the bond.

(d) The sheriff of each county shall enter a capias issued under this article into a local warrant system not later than the 10th business day after the date of issuance of the capias by the clerk of court.

Art. 23.06. New Bail in Felony Case.

When a defendant who has been arrested for a felony under a capias has previously given bail to answer said charge, his sureties, if any, shall be released by such arrest, and he shall be required to give new bail.

Art. 23.07. Capias Does Not Lose Its Force.

A capias shall not lose its force if not executed and returned at the time fixed in the writ, but may be executed at any time afterward, and return made. All proceedings under such capias shall be as valid as if the same had been executed and returned within the time specified in the writ.

Art. 23.08. Reasons for Retaining Capias.

When the capias is not returned at the time fixed in the writ, the officer holding it shall notify the court from whence it was issued, in writing, of his reasons for retaining it.

Art. 23.09. Capias to Several Counties.

Capiases for a defendant may be issued to as many counties as the district or county attorney may direct.

Art. 23.10. Bail in Felony.

In cases of arrest for felony in the county where the prosecution is pending, during a term of court, the officer making the arrest may take bail as provided in Article 17.21.

Art. 23.11. Sheriff May Take Bail in Felony.

In cases of arrest for felony less than capital, made during vacation or made in another county than the one in which the prosecution is pending, the sheriff may take bail; in such cases the amount of the bail bond shall be the same as is endorsed upon the capias; and if no amount be endorsed on the capias, the sheriff shall require a reasonable amount of bail. If it be made to appear by affidavit, made by any district attorney, county attorney, or the sheriff approving the bail bond, to a judge of the Court of Criminal Appeals, a justice of a court of appeals, or to a judge of the district or county court, that the bail taken in any case after indictment is insufficient in amount, or that the sureties are not good for the amount, or that the bond is for any reason defective or insufficient, such judge shall issue a warrant of arrest and require of the defendant sufficient bond, according to the nature of the case.

Art. 23.12. Court Shall Fix Bail in Felony.

In felony cases which are bailable, the court shall, before adjourning, fix and enter upon the minutes the amount of the bail to be required in each case. The clerk shall endorse upon the capias the amount of bail required. In case of neglect to so comply with this Article, the arrest of the defendant, and the bail taken by the sheriff, shall be as legal as if there had been no such omission.

Art. 23.13. Who May Arrest Under Capias.

A capias may be executed by any peace officer. In felony cases, the defendant must be delivered immediately to the sheriff of the county where the arrest is made together, with the writ under which he was taken.

Art. 23.14. Bail in Misdemeanor.

Any officer making an arrest under a capias in a misdemeanor may in term time or vacation take a bail bond of the defendant.

Art. 23.15. Arrest in Capital Cases.

Where an arrest is made under a capias in a capital case, the sheriff shall confine the defendant in jail, and the capias shall, for that purpose, be a sufficient commitment. This Article is applicable when the arrest is made in the county where the prosecution is pending.

Art. 23.16. Arrest in Capital Case in Another County.

In each capital case where a defendant is arrested under a capias in a county other than that in which the case is pending, the sheriff who arrests or to whom the defendant is delivered, shall convey him immediately to the county from which the capias issued and deliver him to the sheriff of such county.

Art. 23.17. Return of Bail and Capias.

When an arrest has been made and a bail taken, such bond, together with the capias, shall be returned forthwith to the proper court.

Art. 23.18. Return of Capias.

The return of the capias shall be made to the court from which it is issued. If it has been executed, the return shall state what disposition has been made of the defendant. If it has not been executed, the cause of the failure to execute it shall be fully stated. If the defendant has not been found, the return shall further show what efforts have been made by the officer to find him, and what information he has as to the defendant's whereabouts.

CHAPTER 24
SUBPOENA AND ATTACHMENT

Art. 24.01. Issuance of Subpoenas.

(a) A subpoena may summon one or more persons to appear:

(1) before a court to testify in a criminal action at a specified term of the court or on a specified day; or

(2) on a specified day:

(A) before an examining court;

(B) at a coroner's inquest;

(C) before a grand jury;

(D) at a habeas corpus hearing; or

(E) in any other proceeding in which the person's testimony may be required in accordance with this code.

(b) The person named in the subpoena to summon the person whose appearance is sought must be:

(1) a peace officer; or

(2) a least 18 years old and, at the time the subpoena is issued, not a participant in the proceeding for which the appearance is sought.

(c) A person who is not a peace officer may not be compelled to accept the duty to execute a subpoena, but if he agrees in writing to accept that duty and neglects or refuses to serve or return the subpoena, he may be punished in accordance with Article 2.16 of this code.

(d) A court or clerk issuing a subpoena shall sign the subpoena and indicate on it the date it was issued, but the subpoena need not be under seal.

Art. 24.011. Subpoenas; Child Witnesses.

(a) If a witness is younger than 18 years, the court may issue a subpoena directing a person having custody, care, or control of the child to produce the child in court.

(b) If a person, without legal cause, fails to produce the child in court as directed by a subpoena issued under this article, the court may impose on the person penalties for contempt provided by this chapter. The court may also issue a writ of attachment for the person and the child, in the same manner as other writs of attachment are issued under this chapter.

(b-1) If the defendant or the attorney representing the state requests the issuance of an attachment under this article, other than an attachment for a witness described by Subsection (c), the request must include the applicable affidavit described by Article 24.12.

(c) If the witness is in a placement in the custody of the Texas Juvenile Justice Department, a juvenile secure detention facility, or a juvenile secure correctional facility, the court may issue a bench warrant or direct that an attachment issue to require a peace officer or probation officer to secure custody of the person at the placement and produce the person in court. When the person is no longer needed as a witness or the period prescribed by Subsection (d-1) has expired without extension, the court shall order the peace officer or probation officer to return the person to the placement from which the person was released.

(d) The court may order that the person who is the witness be detained in a certified juvenile detention facility if the person is younger than 17 years of age. If the person is at least 17 years of age, the court may order that the person be detained without bond in an appropriate county facility for the detention of adults accused of criminal offenses.

(d-1) A witness younger than 17 years of age held in custody under this article may be placed in a certified juvenile detention facility for a period not to exceed 30 days. The length of placement may be extended in increments of 30 days by the court that issued the original bench warrant. If the placement is not extended, the period under this article expires and the witness may be returned as provided by Subsection (c).

(e) In this article, "secure detention facility" and "secure correctional facility" have the meanings assigned by Section 51.02, Family Code.

Art. 24.02. Subpoena Duces Tecum.

If a witness have in his possession any instrument of writing or other thing desired as evidence, the subpoena may specify such evidence and direct that the witness bring the same with him and produce it in court.

Art. 24.03. Subpoena and Application Therefor.

(a) Before the clerk or his deputy shall be required or permitted to issue a subpoena in any

Code of Criminal Procedure

felony case pending in any district or criminal district court of this State of which he is clerk or deputy, the defendant or his attorney or the State's attorney shall make an application in writing or by electronic means to such clerk for each witness desired. Such application shall state the name of each witness desired, the location and vocation, if known, and that the testimony of said witness is material to the State or to the defense. The application must be filed with the clerk and placed with the papers in the cause or, if the application is filed electronically, placed with any other electronic information linked to the number of the cause. The application must also be made available to both the State and the defendant. Except as provided by Subsection (b), as far as is practical such clerk shall include in one subpoena the names of all witnesses for the State and for defendant, and such process shall show that the witnesses are summoned for the State or for the defendant. When a witness has been served with a subpoena, attached or placed under bail at the instance of either party in a particular case, such execution of process shall inure to the benefit of the opposite party in such case in the event such opposite party desires to use such witness on the trial of the case, provided that when a witness has once been served with a subpoena, no further subpoena shall be issued for said witness.

(b) If the defendant is a member of a combination as defined by Section 71.01, Penal Code, the clerk shall issue for each witness a subpoena that does not include a list of the names of all other witnesses for the State or the defendant.

Art. 24.04. Service and Return of Subpoena.

(a) A subpoena is served by:

(1) reading the subpoena in the hearing of the witness;

(2) delivering a copy of the subpoena to the witness;

(3) electronically transmitting a copy of the subpoena, acknowledgment of receipt requested, to the last known electronic address of the witness; or

(4) mailing a copy of the subpoena by certified mail, return receipt requested, to the last known address of the witness unless:

(A) the applicant for the subpoena requests in writing that the subpoena not be served by certified mail; or

(B) the proceeding for which the witness is being subpoenaed is set to begin within seven business days after the date the subpoena would be mailed.

(b) The officer having the subpoena shall make due return thereof, showing the time and manner of service, if served under Subsection (a)(1) or (2) of this article, the acknowledgment of receipt, if served under Subsection (a)(3) of this article, or the return receipt, if served under Subsection (a)(4) of this article. If the subpoena is not served, the officer shall show in his return the cause of his failure to serve it. If receipt of an electronically transmitted subpoena is not acknowledged within a reasonable time or a mailed subpoena is returned undelivered, the officer shall use due diligence to locate and serve the witness. If the witness could not be found, the officer shall state the diligence he has used to find him, and what information he has as to the whereabouts of the witness.

(c) A subpoena served under Subsection (a)(3) of this article must be accompanied by notice that an acknowledgment of receipt of the subpoena must be made in a manner enabling verification of the person acknowledging receipt.

Art. 24.05. Refusing to Obey.

If a witness refuses to obey a subpoena, he may be fined at the discretion of the court, as follows: In a felony case, not exceeding five hundred dollars; in a misdemeanor case, not exceeding one hundred dollars.

Art. 24.06. What Is Disobedience of a Subpoena.

It shall be held that a witness refuses to obey a subpoena:

1. If he is not in attendance on the court on the day set apart for taking up the criminal docket or on any day subsequent thereto and before the final disposition or continuance of the particular case in which he is a witness;

2. If he is not in attendance at any other time named in a writ; and

3. If he refuses without legal cause to produce evidence in his possession which he has been summoned to bring with him and produce.

Art. 24.07. Fine Against Witness Conditional.

When a fine is entered against a witness for failure to appear and testify, the judgment shall be conditional; and a citation shall issue to him to show cause, at the term of the court at which said fine is entered, or at the first term thereafter, at the discretion of the judge of said court, why the same should not be final; provided, citation shall be served upon said witness in the manner and for the length of time prescribed for citations in civil cases.

Art. 24.08. Witness May Show Cause.

A witness cited to show cause, as provided in the preceding Article, may do so under oath, in writing or verbally, at any time before judgment final is entered against him; but if he fails to show cause within the time limited for answering in civil actions, a judgment final by default shall be entered against him.

Art. 24.09. Court May Remit Fine.

It shall be within the discretion of the court to judge of the sufficiency of an excuse rendered by a witness, and upon the hearing the court shall render judgment against the witness for the whole or any part of the fine, or shall remit the fine altogether, as to the court may appear proper and right. Said fine shall be collected as fines in misdemeanor cases.

Art. 24.10. When Witness Appears and Testifies.

When a fine has been entered against a witness, but no trial of the cause takes place, and such witness afterward appears and testifies upon the trial thereof, it shall be discretionary with the judge, though no good excuse be rendered, to reduce the fine or remit it altogether; but the witness, in such case, shall, nevertheless, be adjudged to pay all the costs accruing in the proceeding against him by reason of his failure to attend.

Art. 24.11. Requisites of an "Attachment".

An "attachment" is a writ issued by a clerk of a court under seal, or by any magistrate, or by the foreman of a grand jury, in any criminal action or proceeding authorized by law, commanding some peace officer to take the body of a witness and bring him before such court, magistrate or grand jury on a day named, or forthwith, to testify in behalf of the State or of the defendant, as the case may be. It shall be dated and signed officially by the officer issuing it.

Art. 24.111. Hearing Required Before Issuance of Certain Writs of Attachment.

(a) This article applies only to an attachment that is requested to be issued under:

(1) Article 24.011, if an affidavit is required under Article 24.011(b-1); or

(2) Article 24.12, 24.14, or 24.22.

(b) Notwithstanding any other law, a writ of attachment to which this article applies may only be issued by the judge of the court in which the witness is to testify if the judge determines, after a hearing, that the issuance of the attachment is in the best interest of justice.

(c) In making a determination under Subsection (b), the judge shall consider the affidavit of the attorney representing the state or the defendant, as applicable, that was submitted with the request for the issuance of the attachment.

(d) The court shall appoint an attorney to represent the witness at the hearing under Subsection (b), including a hearing conducted outside the presence of the witness.

Art. 24.12. When Attachment May Issue.

When a witness who resides in the county of the prosecution has been duly served with a subpoena to appear and testify in any criminal action or proceeding fails to so appear, the attorney representing the state or the defendant may request that the court issue an attachment for the witness. The request must be filed with the clerk of the court and must include an affidavit of the attorney representing the state or the defendant, as applicable, stating that the affiant has good reason to believe, and does believe, that the witness is a material witness.

Art. 24.13. Attachment for Convict Witnesses.

All persons who have been or may be convicted in this state, and who are confined in an institution operated by the Texas Department of Criminal Justice or any jail in this state, shall be permitted to testify in person in any court for the state and the defendant when the presiding judge finds, after hearing, that the ends of justice require their attendance, and directs that an attachment issue to accomplish the purpose, notwithstanding any other provision of this code. Nothing in this article shall be construed as limiting the power of the courts of this state to issue bench warrants.

Art. 24.131. Notification to Department of Criminal Justice.

If after the Texas Department of Criminal Justice transfers a defendant or inmate to a county under Article 24.13 and before that person is returned to the department the person is released on bail or the charges on which the person was convicted and for which the person was transferred to the department are dismissed, the county shall immediately notify an officer designated by the department of the release on bail or the dismissal.

Code of Criminal Procedure

Art. 24.14. Attachment for Resident Witness.

(a) Regardless of whether the witness has disobeyed a subpoena, if a witness who resides in the county of the prosecution may be about to move out of the county, the defendant or the attorney representing the state may request that the court issue an attachment for the witness. The request must be filed with the clerk of the court and must include the applicable affidavit described by Article 24.12, except that the affidavit must additionally state that the affiant has good reason to believe, and does believe, that the witness is about to move out of the county.

(b) If an attachment is issued under this article in a misdemeanor case, when the witness makes oath that the witness cannot give surety, the officer executing the attachment shall take the witness's personal bond.

Art. 24.15. To Secure Attendance Before Grand Jury.

At any time before the first day of any term of the district court, the clerk, upon application of the State's attorney, shall issue a subpoena for any witness who resides in the county. If at the time such application is made, such attorney files a sworn application that he has good reason to believe and does believe that such witness is about to move out of the county, then said clerk shall issue an attachment for such witness to be and appear before said district court on the first day thereof to testify as a witness before the grand jury. Any witness so summoned, or attached, who shall fail or refuse to obey a subpoena or attachment, shall be punished by the court by a fine not exceeding five hundred dollars, to be collected as fines and costs in other criminal cases.

Art. 24.16. Application for Out-County Witness.

Where, in misdemeanor cases in which confinement in jail is a permissible punishment, or in felony cases, a witness resides out of the county in which the prosecution is pending, the State or the defendant shall be entitled, either in termtime or in vacation, to a subpoena to compel the attendance of such witness on application to the proper clerk or magistrate. Such application shall be in the manner and form as provided in Article 24.03. Witnesses in such misdemeanor cases shall be compensated in the same manner as in felony cases. This Article shall not apply to more than one character witness in a misdemeanor case.

Art. 24.17. Duty of Officer Receiving Said Subpoena.

The officer receiving said subpoena shall execute the same by delivering a copy thereof to each witness therein named. He shall make due return of said subpoena, showing therein the time and manner of executing the same, and if not executed, such return shall show why not executed, the diligence used to find said witness, and such information as the officer has as to the whereabouts of said witness.

Art. 24.18. Subpoena Returnable Forthwith.

When a subpoena is returnable forthwith, the officer shall immediately serve the witness with a copy of the same; and it shall be the duty of said witness to immediately make his appearance before the court, magistrate or other authority issuing the same. If said witness makes affidavit of his inability from lack of funds to appear in obedience to said subpoena, the officer executing the same shall provide said witness, if said subpoena be issued as provided in Article 24.16, with the necessary funds or means to appear in obedience to said subpoena, taking his receipt therefor, and showing in his return on said subpoena, under oath, the amount furnished to said witness, together with the amount of his fees for executing said subpoena.

Art. 24.19. Certificate to Officer.

The clerk, magistrate, or foreman of the grand jury issuing said process, immediately upon the return of said subpoena, if issued as provided in Article 24.16, shall issue to such officer a certificate for the amount furnished such witness, together with the amount of his fees for executing the same, showing the amount of each item; which certificate shall be approved by the district judge and recorded by the district clerk in a book kept for that purpose; and said certificate transmitted to the officer executing such subpoena, which amount shall be paid by the State, as costs are paid in other criminal matters.

Art. 24.20. Subpoena Returnable at Future Date.

If the subpoena be returnable at some future date, the officer shall have authority to take bail of such witness for his appearance under said subpoena, which bond shall be returned with such subpoena, and shall be made payable to the State of Texas, in the amount in which the witness and his surety, if any, shall be bound and conditioned for the appearance of the witness at the time and before the court, magistrate or grand jury named in said subpoena, and shall be signed by the witness and his sureties. If the witness refuses to give bond, he shall be kept in custody until such time as he starts in obedience to said subpoena, when he shall be, upon affidavit being made, provided with funds necessary to appear in obedience to said subpoena.

Art. 24.21. Stating Bail in Subpoena.

The court or magistrate issuing said subpoena may direct therein the amount of the bail to be required. The officer may fix the amount if not specified, and in either case, shall require sufficient security, to be approved by himself.

Art. 24.22. Witness Fined and Attached.

(a) If a witness summoned from outside the county refuses to obey a subpoena, the witness shall be fined by the court or magistrate not exceeding five hundred dollars, which fine and judgment shall be final, unless set aside after due notice to show cause why it should not be final, which notice may immediately issue, requiring the defaulting witness to appear at once or at the next term of the court, in the discretion of the magistrate issuing the subpoena, to answer for the default.

(b) At the time a fine is imposed under Subsection (a), on request of the defendant or the attorney representing the state, the court may cause to be issued an attachment for the witness, directed to the proper county, commanding the officer to whom the attachment is directed to take the witness into custody and have the witness before the court at the time specified in the attachment; in which case the witness shall receive no fees, unless it appears to the court that the disobedience is excusable, when the witness may receive the same pay as if the witness had not been attached.

(c) A request for the issuance of an attachment under Subsection (b) must include the applicable affidavit described by Article 24.12.

(d) The fine when made final and all related costs shall be collected in the same manner as in other criminal cases. The fine and judgment may be set aside in vacation or at the time or any subsequent term of the court for good cause shown, after the witness testifies or has been discharged.

(e) The following words shall be written or printed on the face of a subpoena for an out-of-county witness: "A disobedience of this subpoena is punishable by fine not exceeding five hundred dollars, to be collected as fines and costs in other criminal cases."

Art. 24.221. Affidavit Regarding Confinement.

As soon as practicable after the sheriff takes custody of a witness pursuant to an attachment issued as provided by Article 24.111, the sheriff shall submit an affidavit to the issuing court stating that the sheriff has taken custody of the witness.

Art. 24.222. Hearing During Confinement of Witness.

(a) A witness who has been confined for at least 24 hours pursuant to an attachment issued as provided by Article 24.111 may request a hearing in the issuing court regarding whether the continued confinement of the witness is necessary. The court shall grant the request and hold the hearing as soon as practicable.

(b) Any subsequent request for a hearing may be granted only if the court determines that holding the hearing is in the best interest of justice.

(c) The attorney appointed for the witness under Article 24.111 shall represent the witness at a hearing under this article.

Art. 24.23. Witness Released.

A witness who is in custody for failing to give bail shall be at once released upon giving bail required.

Art. 24.24. Bail for Witness.

Witnesses on behalf of the State or defendant may, at the request of either party, be required to enter into bail in an amount to be fixed by the court to appear and testify in a criminal action; but if it shall appear to the court that any witness is unable to give security upon such bail, he shall be released without security.

Art. 24.25. Personal Bond of Witness.

When it appears to the satisfaction of the court that personal bond of the witness will insure his attendance, no security need be required of him; but no bond without security shall be taken by any officer.

Art. 24.26. Enforcing Forfeiture.

The bond of a witness may be enforced against him and his sureties, if any, in the manner pointed out in this Code for enforcing the bond of a defendant in a criminal case.

Art. 24.27. No Surrender After Forfeiture.

The sureties of a witness have no right to discharge themselves by the surrender of the witness after the forfeiture of their bond.

Art. 24.28. Uniform Act to Secure Attendance of Witnesses from Without State.

Sec. 1. **Short Title.** — This Act may be cited as the "Uniform Act to Secure the Attendance of Witnesses from Without the State in Criminal Proceedings".

Sec. 2. **Definitions.** "Witness" as used in this Act shall include a person whose testimony is desired in any proceeding or investigation by a grand jury or in a criminal action, prosecution or proceeding.

The word "State" shall include any territory of the United States and the District of Columbia.

The word "summons" shall include a subpoena, order or other notice requiring the appearance of a witness.

Sec. 3. **Summoning witness in this State to testify in another State.**

(a) If a judge of a court of record in any State which by its laws has made provision for commanding persons within that State to attend and testify in this State certifies under the seal of such court that there is a criminal prosecution pending in such court, or that a grand jury investigation has commenced or is about to commence, that a person being within this State is a material witness in such prosecution, or grand jury investigation, and that his presence will be required for a specified number of days, upon presentation of such certificate to any judge of a court of record in the county in which such person is, such judge shall fix a time and place for a hearing, and shall make an order directing the witness to appear at a time and place certain for the hearing.

(b) If at a hearing the judge determines that the witness is material and necessary, that it will not cause undue hardship to the witness to be compelled to attend and testify in the prosecution or a grand jury investigation in the other State, and that the laws of the State in which the prosecution is pending, or grand jury investigation has commenced or is about to commence, (and of any other State through which the witness may be required to pass by ordinary course of travel), will give to him protection from arrest and the service of civil and criminal process, he shall issue a summons, with a copy of the certificate attached, directing the witness to attend and testify in the court where the prosecution is pending, or where a grand jury investigation has commenced or is about to commence at a time and place specified in the summons. In any such hearing the certificate shall be prima facie evidence of all the facts stated therein.

(c) If said certificate recommends that the witness be taken into immediate custody and delivered to an officer of the requesting State to assure his attendance in the requesting State, such judge may, in lieu of notification of the hearing, direct that such witness be forthwith brought before him for said hearing; and the judge at the hearing being satisfied of the desirability of such custody and delivery, for which determination the certificate shall be prima facie proof of such desirability may, in lieu of issuing subpoena or summons, order that said witness be forthwith taken into custody and delivered to an officer of the requesting State.

(d) If the witness, who is summoned as above provided, after being paid or tendered by some properly authorized person the compensation for nonresident witnesses authorized and provided for by Article 35.27 of this Code, fails without good cause to attend and testify as directed in the summons, he shall be punished in the manner provided for the punishment of any witness who disobeys a summons issued from a court of record in this State.

Sec. 4. **Witness from another State summoned to testify in this State.**

(a) If a person in any State, which by its laws has made provision for commanding persons within its borders to attend and testify in criminal prosecutions, or grand jury investigations commenced or about to commence, in this State, is a material witness in a prosecution pending in a court of record in this State, or in a grand jury investigation which has commenced or is about to commence, a judge of such court may issue a certificate under the seal of the court stating these facts and specifying the number of days the witness will be required. Said certificate may include a recommendation that the witness be taken into immediate custody and delivered to an officer of this State to assure his attendance in this State. This certificate shall be presented to a judge of a court of record in the county in which the witness is found.

(b) If the witness is summoned to attend and testify in this State he shall be tendered the compensation for nonresident witnesses authorized by Article 35.27 of this Code, together with such additional compensation, if any, required by the other State for compliance. A witness who has appeared in accordance with the provisions of the summons shall not be required to remain within this State a longer period of time than the period mentioned in the certificate, unless otherwise ordered by the court. If such witness, after coming into this State, fails without good cause to attend and testify as directed in the summons, he shall be punished in the manner provided for the punishment of any witness who disobeys a summons issued from a court of record in this State.

Sec. 5. **Exemption from arrest and service of process.** — If a person comes into this State in obedience to a summons directing him to attend and testify in this State he shall not while in this State pursuant to such summons be subject to arrest or the service of process, civil or criminal, in connection with matters which arose before his entrance into this State under the summons.

If a person passes through this State while going to another State in obedience to a summons to attend and testify in that State or while returning therefrom, he shall not while so passing through this State be subject to arrest or the service of process, civil or criminal, in connection with matters which arose before his entrance into this State under the summons.

Art. 24.29. Uniform Act to Secure Rendition of Prisoners in Criminal Proceedings.

Sec. 1. **Short title.** — This article may be cited as the "Uniform Act to Secure Rendition of Prisoners in Criminal Proceedings."

Sec. 2. **Definitions.** — In this Act:

(1) "Penal institution" means a jail, prison, penitentiary, house of correction, or other place of penal detention.

(2) "State" means a state of the United States, the District of Columbia, the Commonwealth of Puerto Rico, and any territory of the United States.

(3) "Witness" means a person who is confined in a penal institution in a state and whose testimony is desired in another state in a criminal proceeding or investigation by a grand jury or in any criminal action before a court.

Sec. 3. **Summoning witness in this state to testify in another state.**

(a) A judge of a state court of record in another state, which by its laws has made provision for commanding persons confined in penal institutions within that state to attend and testify in this state, may certify that:

(1) there is a criminal proceeding or investigation by a grand jury or a criminal action pending in the court;

(2) a person who is confined in a penal institution in this state may be a material witness in the proceeding, investigation, or action; and

(3) his presence will be required during a specified time.

(b) On presentation of the certificate to any judge having jurisdiction over the person confined and on notice to the attorney general, the judge in this state shall fix a time and place for a hearing and shall make an order directed to the person having custody of the prisoner requiring that the prisoner be produced before him at the hearing.

Sec. 4. **Court order.**

(a) A judge may issue a transfer order if at the hearing the judge determines that:

(1) the witness may be material and necessary;

(2) his attending and testifying are not adverse to the interest of this state or to the health or legal rights of the witness;

(3) the laws of the state in which he is requested to testify will give him protection from arrest and the service of civil and criminal process because of any act committed prior to his arrival in the state under the order; and

(4) as a practical matter the possibility is negligible that the witness may be subject to arrest or to the service of civil or criminal process in any state through which he will be required to pass.

(b) If a judge issues an order under Subsection (a) of this section, the judge shall attach to the order a copy of a certificate presented under Section 3 of this Act. The order shall:

(1) direct the witness to attend and testify;

(2) except as provided by Subsection (c) of this section, direct the person having custody of the witness to produce him in the court where the criminal action is pending or where the grand jury investigation is pending at a time and place specified in the order; and

(3) prescribe such conditions as the judge shall determine.

(c) The judge, in lieu of directing the person having custody of the witness to produce him in the requesting jurisdiction's court, may direct and require in his order that:

(1) an officer of the requesting jurisdiction come to the Texas penal institution in which the witness is confined to accept custody of the witness for physical transfer to the requesting jurisdiction;

(2) the requesting jurisdiction provide proper safeguards on his custody while in transit;

(3) the requesting jurisdiction be liable for and pay all expenses incurred in producing and returning the witness, including but not limited to food, lodging, clothing, and medical care; and

(4) the requesting jurisdiction promptly deliver the witness back to the same or another Texas penal institution as specified by the Texas Department of Criminal Justice at the conclusion of his testimony.

Sec. 5. **Terms and conditions.** — An order to a witness and to a person having custody of the witness shall provide for the return of the witness at the conclusion of his testimony, proper safeguards on his custody, and proper financial reimbursement or prepayment by the requesting jurisdiction for all expenses incurred in the production and return of the witness. The order may prescribe any other condition the judge thinks proper or necessary. The judge shall not require prepayment of expenses if the judge directs and requires the requesting jurisdiction to accept custody of the witness at the Texas penal institution in which the witness is confined and to deliver the witness back to the same or another Texas penal institution at the conclusion of his testimony. An order does not become effective until the judge of the state requesting the witness enters an order directing compliance with the conditions prescribed.

Sec. 6. **Exceptions. —** This Act does not apply to a person in this state who is confined as mentally ill or who is under sentence of death.

Sec. 7. **Prisoner from another state summoned to testify in this state.**

(a) If a person confined in a penal institution in any other state may be a material witness in a criminal action pending in a court of record or in a grand jury investigation in this state, a judge of the court may certify that:

(1) there is a criminal proceeding or investigation by a grand jury or a criminal action pending in the court;

(2) a person who is confined in a penal institution in the other state may be a material witness in the proceeding, investigation, or action; and

(3) his presence will be required during a specified time.

(b) The judge of the court in this state shall:

(1) present the certificate to a judge of a court of record in the other state having jurisdiction over the prisoner confined; and

(2) give notice that the prisoner's presence will be required to the attorney general of the state in which the prisoner is confined.

Sec. 8. **Compliance. —** A judge of the court in this state may enter an order directing compliance with the terms and conditions of an order specified in a certificate under Section 3 of this Act and entered by the judge of the state in which the witness is confined.

Sec. 9. **Exemption from arrest and service of process. —** If a witness from another state comes into or passes through this state under an order directing him to attend and testify in this or another state, while in this state pursuant to the order he is not subject to arrest or the service of civil or criminal process because of any act committed prior to his arrival in this state under the order.

Sec. 10. **Uniformity of interpretation. —** This Act shall be so construed as to effect its general purpose to make uniform the laws of those states which enact it.

CHAPTER 24A RESPONDING TO SUBPOENAS AND CERTAIN OTHER COURT ORDERS; PRESERVING CERTAIN INFORMATION

SUBCHAPTER A RESPONDING TO SUBPOENAS AND CERTAIN OTHER COURT ORDERS

Art. 24A.001. Applicability of Subchapter.

This subchapter applies only to a subpoena, search warrant, or other court order that:

(1) relates to the investigation or prosecution of a criminal offense under:

(A) Section 21.02, 21.11, 22.011, or 22.021, Penal Code;

(B) Chapter 20A, Penal Code;

(C) Section 33.021, Penal Code; or

(D) Chapter 43, Penal Code; and

(2) is served on or issued with respect to an online service provider that provides service in this state.

Art. 24A.0015. Definition.

In this chapter, "online service provider" means an Internet service provider, search engine, web hosting company, web browsing company, manufacturer of devices providing online application platforms, or company providing online social media platforms.

Art. 24A.002. Response Required; Deadline for Response.

(a) Except as provided by Subsection (b), not later than the 10th day after the date on which an online service provider is served with or otherwise receives a subpoena, search warrant, or other court order described by Article 24A.001, the online service provider shall:

(1) fully comply with the subpoena, warrant, or order; or

(2) petition a court to excuse the online service provider from complying with the subpoena, warrant, or order.

(b) As soon as is practicable, and in no event later than the second business day after the date the online service provider is served with or otherwise receives a subpoena, search warrant, or other court order described by Article 24A.001, the online service provider shall fully comply with the subpoena, search warrant, or order if the subpoena, search warrant, or order indicates that full compliance is necessary to address a situation that threatens a person with death or other serious bodily injury.

(c) For the purposes of Subsection (a)(1), full compliance with the subpoena, warrant, or order includes:

(1) producing or providing, to the extent permitted under federal law, all documents or information requested under the subpoena, warrant, or order; or

(2) providing, to the extent permitted under federal law, electronic access to all documents or information requested under the subpoena, warrant, or order.

Art. 24A.003. Disobeying Subpoena, Warrant, or Order.

An online service provider that disobeys a subpoena, search warrant, or other court order described by Article 24A.001 and that was not excused from complying with the subpoena, warrant, or order under Article 24A.002(a)(2) may be punished in any manner provided by law.

SUBCHAPTER B PRESERVING CERTAIN INFORMATION

Art. 24A.051. Preserving Information.

(a) On written request of a law enforcement agency in this state or a federal law enforcement agency and pending the issuance of a subpoena or other court order described by Article 24A.001, an online service provider that provides service in this state shall take all steps necessary to preserve all records or other potential evidence in a criminal trial that is in the possession of the online service provider.

(b) Subject to Subsection (c), an online service provider shall preserve information under Subsection (a) for a period of 90 days after the date the online service provider receives the written request described by Subsection (a).

(c) An online service provider shall preserve information under Subsection (a) for the 90-day period immediately following the 90-day period described by Subsection (b) if the requesting law enforcement agency in writing requests an extension of the preservation period.

CHAPTER 25 SERVICE OF A COPY OF THE INDICTMENT

Art. 25.01. In Felony.

In every case of felony, when the accused is in custody, or as soon as he may be arrested, the clerk of the court where an indictment has been presented shall immediately make a certified copy of the same, and deliver such copy to the sheriff, together with a writ directed to such sheriff, commanding him forthwith to deliver such certified copy to the accused.

Art. 25.02. Service and Return.

Upon receipt of such writ and copy, the sheriff shall immediately deliver such certified copy of the indictment to the accused and return the writ to the clerk issuing the same, with his return thereon, showing when and how the same was executed.

Art. 25.03. If on Bail in Felony.

When the accused, in case of felony, is on bail at the time the indictment is presented, the clerk shall deliver a copy of the indictment to the accused or the accused's counsel at the earliest possible time.

Art. 25.04. In Misdemeanor.

In misdemeanors, the clerk shall deliver a copy of the indictment or information to the accused or the accused's counsel at the earliest possible time before trial.

CHAPTER 26 ARRAIGNMENT

Art. 26.01. Arraignment.

In all felony cases, after indictment, and all misdemeanor cases punishable by imprisonment, there shall be an arraignment.

Art. 26.011. Waiver of Arraignment.

An attorney representing a defendant may present a waiver of arraignment, and the clerk of the court may not require the presence of the defendant as a condition of accepting the waiver.

Art. 26.02. Purpose of Arraignment.

An arraignment takes place for the purpose of fixing his identity and hearing his plea.

Art. 26.03. Time of Arraignment.

No arraignment shall take place until the expiration of at least two entire days after the day on which a copy of the indictment was served on the defendant, unless the right to such copy or to such delay be waived, or unless the defendant is on bail.

Art. 26.04. Procedures for Appointing Counsel.

(a) The judges of the county courts, statutory county courts, and district courts trying criminal cases in each county, by local rule, shall adopt and publish written countywide procedures for timely and fairly appointing counsel for an indigent defendant in the county arrested for, charged with, or taking an appeal from a conviction of a misdemeanor punishable by confinement or a felony. The procedures must be consistent with this article and Articles 1.051, 15.17, 15.18, 26.05, and 26.052 and must provide for the priority appointment of a public defender's office as described by Subsection (f). A court shall appoint an attorney from a public appointment list using a system of rotation, unless the court appoints an attorney under Subsection (f), (f-1), (h), or (i). The court shall appoint attorneys from among the next five names on the appointment list in the order in which the attorneys' names appear on the list, unless the court makes a finding of good cause on the record for appointing an attorney out of order. An attorney who is not appointed in the order in which the attorney's name appears on the list shall remain next in order on the list.

(b) Procedures adopted under Subsection (a) shall:

(1) authorize only the judges of the county courts, statutory county courts, and district courts trying criminal cases in the county, or the judges' designee, to appoint counsel for indigent defendants in the county;

(2) apply to each appointment of counsel made by a judge or the judges' designee in the county;

(3) ensure that each indigent defendant in the county who is charged with a misdemeanor punishable by confinement or with a felony and who appears in court without counsel has an opportunity to confer with appointed counsel before the commencement of judicial proceedings;

(4) require appointments for defendants in capital cases in which the death penalty is sought to comply with any applicable requirements under Articles 11.071 and 26.052;

(5) ensure that each attorney appointed from a public appointment list to represent an indigent defendant perform the attorney's duty owed to the defendant in accordance with the adopted procedures, the requirements of this code, and applicable rules of ethics; and

(6) ensure that appointments are allocated among qualified attorneys in a manner that is fair, neutral, and nondiscriminatory.

(c) Whenever a court or the courts' designee authorized under Subsection (b) to appoint counsel for indigent defendants in the county determines for purposes of a criminal proceeding that a defendant charged with or appealing a conviction of a felony or a misdemeanor punishable by confinement is indigent or that the interests of justice require representation of a defendant in the proceeding, the court or the courts' designee shall appoint one or more practicing attorneys to represent the defendant in accordance with this subsection and the procedures adopted under Subsection (a). If the court or the courts' designee determines that the defendant does not speak and understand the English language or that the defendant is deaf, the court or the courts' designee shall make an effort to appoint an attorney who is capable of communicating in a language understood by the defendant.

(d) A public appointment list from which an attorney is appointed as required by Subsection (a) shall contain the names of qualified attorneys, each of whom:

(1) applies to be included on the list;

(2) meets the objective qualifications specified by the judges under Subsection (e);

(3) meets any applicable qualifications specified by the Texas Indigent Defense Commission; and

(4) is approved by a majority of the judges who established the appointment list under Subsection (e).

(e) In a county in which a court is required under Subsection (a) to appoint an attorney from a public appointment list:

(1) the judges of the county courts and statutory county courts trying misdemeanor cases in the county, by formal action:

(A) shall:

(i) establish a public appointment list of attorneys qualified to provide representation in the county in misdemeanor cases punishable by confinement; and

(ii) specify the objective qualifications necessary for an attorney to be included on the list; and

(B) may establish, if determined by the judges to be appropriate, more than one appointment list graduated according to the degree of seriousness of the offense, the attorneys' qualifications, and whether representation will be provided in trial court proceedings, appellate proceedings, or both; and

(2) the judges of the district courts trying felony cases in the county, by formal action:

(A) shall:

(i) establish a public appointment list of attorneys qualified to provide representation in felony cases in the county; and

(ii) specify the objective qualifications necessary for an attorney to be included on the list; and

(B) may establish, if determined by the judges to be appropriate, more than one appointment list graduated according to the degree of seriousness of the offense, the attorneys' qualifications, and whether representation will be provided in trial court proceedings, appellate proceedings, or both.

(f) In a county with a public defender's office, the court or the courts' designee shall give priority in appointing that office to represent the defendant in the criminal proceeding, including a proceeding in a capital murder case. However, the court is not required to appoint the public defender's office if:

(1) the court makes a finding of good cause for appointing other counsel, provided that in a capital murder case, the court makes a finding of good cause on the record for appointing that counsel;

(2) the appointment would be contrary to the office's written plan under Article 26.044;

(3) the office is prohibited from accepting the appointment under Article 26.044(j); or

(4) a managed assigned counsel program also exists in the county and an attorney will be appointed under that program.

(f-1) In a county in which a managed assigned counsel program is operated in accordance with Article 26.047, the managed assigned counsel program may appoint counsel to represent the defendant in accordance with the guidelines established for the program.

(g) A countywide alternative program for appointing counsel for indigent defendants in criminal cases is established by a formal action in which two-thirds of the judges of the courts designated under this subsection vote to establish the alternative program. An alternative program for appointing counsel in misdemeanor and felony cases may be established in the manner provided by this subsection by the judges of the county courts, statutory county courts, and district courts trying criminal cases in the county. An alternative program for appointing counsel in misdemeanor cases may be established in the manner provided by this subsection by the judges of the county courts and statutory county courts trying criminal cases in the county. An alternative program for appointing counsel in felony cases may be established in the manner provided by this subsection by the judges of the district courts trying criminal cases in the county. In a county in which an alternative program is established:

(1) the alternative program may:

(A) use a single method for appointing counsel or a combination of methods; and

(B) use a multicounty appointment list using a system of rotation; and

(2) the procedures adopted under Subsection (a) must ensure that:

(A) attorneys appointed using the alternative program to represent defendants in misdemeanor cases punishable by confinement:

(i) meet specified objective qualifications for that representation, which may be graduated according to the degree of seriousness of the offense and whether representation will be provided in trial court proceedings, appellate proceedings, or both; and

(ii) are approved by a majority of the judges of the county courts and statutory county courts trying misdemeanor cases in the county;

(B) attorneys appointed using the alternative program to represent defendants in felony cases:

(i) meet specified objective qualifications for that representation, which may be graduated according to the degree of seriousness of the offense and whether representation will be provided in trial court proceedings, appellate proceedings, or both; and

(ii) are approved by a majority of the judges of the district courts trying felony cases in the county;

(C) appointments for defendants in capital cases in which the death penalty is sought comply with the requirements of Article 26.052; and

(D) appointments are reasonably and impartially allocated among qualified attorneys.

(h) Subject to Subsection (f), in a county in which an alternative program for appointing counsel is established as provided by Subsection (g) and is approved by the presiding judge of the administrative judicial region, a court or the courts' designee may appoint an attorney to represent an indigent defendant by using the alternative program. In establishing an alternative program under Subsection (g), the judges of the courts establishing the program may not, without the approval of the commissioners court, obligate the county by contract or by the creation of new positions that cause an increase in expenditure of county funds.

(i) Subject to Subsection (f), a court or the courts' designee required under Subsection (c) to appoint an attorney to represent a defendant accused or convicted of a felony may appoint an attorney from any county located in the court's administrative judicial region.

(j) An attorney appointed under this article shall:

(1) make every reasonable effort to contact the defendant not later than the end of the first working day after the date on which the attorney is appointed and to interview the defendant as soon as practicable after the attorney is appointed;

(2) represent the defendant until charges are dismissed, the defendant is acquitted, appeals are exhausted, or the attorney is permitted or ordered by the court to withdraw as counsel for the defendant after a finding of good cause is entered on the record;

(3) with respect to a defendant not represented by other counsel, before withdrawing as counsel for the defendant after a trial or the entry of a plea of guilty:

(A) advise the defendant of the defendant's right to file a motion for new trial and a notice of appeal;

(B) if the defendant wishes to pursue either or both remedies described by Paragraph (A), assist the defendant in requesting the prompt appointment of replacement counsel; and

(C) if replacement counsel is not appointed promptly and the defendant wishes to pursue an appeal, file a timely notice of appeal; and

(4) not later than October 15 of each year and on a form prescribed by the Texas Indigent Defense Commission, submit to the county information, for the preceding fiscal year, that describes the percentage of the attorney's practice time that was dedicated to work based on appointments accepted in the county under this article and Title 3, Family Code.

(k) A court may replace an attorney who violates Subsection (j)(1) with other counsel. A majority of the judges of the county courts and statutory county courts or the district courts, as appropriate, trying criminal cases in the county may remove from consideration for appointment an attorney who intentionally or repeatedly violates Subsection (j)(1).

(*l*) Procedures adopted under Subsection (a) must include procedures and financial standards for determining whether a defendant is indigent. The procedures and standards shall apply to each defendant in the county equally, regardless of whether the defendant is in custody or has been released on bail.

(m) In determining whether a defendant is indigent, the court or the courts' designee may consider the defendant's income, source of income, assets, property owned, outstanding obligations, necessary expenses, the number and ages of dependents, and spousal income that is available to the defendant. The court or the courts' designee may not consider whether the defendant has posted or is capable of posting bail, except to the extent that it reflects the defendant's financial circumstances as measured by the considerations listed in this subsection.

(n) A defendant who requests a determination of indigency and appointment of counsel shall:

(1) complete under oath a questionnaire concerning his financial resources;

(2) respond under oath to an examination regarding his financial resources by the judge or magistrate responsible for determining whether the defendant is indigent; or

(3) complete the questionnaire and respond to examination by the judge or magistrate.

(o) Before making a determination of whether a defendant is indigent, the court shall request the defendant to sign under oath a statement substantially in the following form: "On this ________ day of ________, 20 ________, I have been advised by the (name of the court) Court of my right to representation by counsel in connection with the charge pending against me. I am without means to employ counsel of my own choosing and I hereby request the court to appoint counsel for me. (signature of the defendant)"

(p) A defendant who is determined by the court to be indigent is presumed to remain indigent for the remainder of the proceedings in the case unless a material change in the defendant's financial circumstances occurs. If there is a material change in financial circumstances after a determination of indigency or nonindigency is made, the defendant, the defendant's counsel, or the attorney representing the state may move for reconsideration of the determination.

(q) A written or oral statement elicited under this article or evidence derived from the statement may not be used for any purpose, except to determine the defendant's indigency or to impeach the direct testimony of the defendant. This subsection does not prohibit prosecution of the defendant under Chapter 37, Penal Code.

(r) A court may not threaten to arrest or incarcerate a person solely because the person requests the assistance of counsel.

Art. 26.041. Procedures Related to Guardianships.

(a) In this article:

(1) "Guardian" has the meaning assigned by Section 1002.012, Estates Code.

(2) "Letters of guardianship" means a certificate issued under Section 1106.001(a), Estates Code.

(b) A guardian who provides a court with letters of guardianship for a defendant may:

(1) provide information relevant to the determination of indigency; and

(2) request that counsel be appointed in accordance with this chapter.

Art. 26.042. Tarrant County Public Defender [Repealed].

Repealed by Acts 2001, 77th Leg., ch. 906 (S.B. 7), § 15, effective January 1, 2002.

Art. 26.043. Public Defender in Wichita County [Repealed].

Repealed by Acts 2001, 77th Leg., ch. 906 (S.B. 7), § 15, effective January 1, 2002.

Art. 26.044. Public Defender's Office.

(a) In this chapter:

(1) "Governmental entity" includes a county, a group of counties, a department of a county, an administrative judicial region created by Section 74.042, Government Code, and any entity created under the Interlocal Cooperation Act as permitted by Chapter 791, Government Code.

(2) "Office of capital and forensic writs" means the office of capital and forensic writs established under Subchapter B, Chapter 78, Government Code.

(3) "Oversight board" means an oversight board established in accordance with Article 26.045.

(4) "Public defender's office" means an entity that:

(A) is either:

(i) a governmental entity; or

(ii) a nonprofit corporation operating under a written agreement with a governmental entity, other than an individual judge or court; and

(B) uses public funds to provide legal representation and services to indigent defendants accused of a crime or juvenile offense, as those terms are defined by Section 79.001, Government Code.

(b) The commissioners court of any county, on written approval of a judge of a county court, statutory county court, or district court trying criminal cases or cases under Title 3, Family Code, in the county, may create a department of the county or by contract may designate a nonprofit corporation to serve as a public defender's office. The commissioners courts of two or more counties may enter into a written agreement to jointly create or designate and jointly fund a regional public defender's office. In creating or designating a public defender's office under this subsection, the commissioners court shall specify or the commissioners courts shall jointly specify, if creating or designating a regional public defender's office:

(1) the duties of the public defender's office;

(2) the types of cases to which the public defender's office may be appointed under Article 26.04(f) and the courts in which an attorney employed by the public defender's office may be required to appear;

(3) if the public defender's office is a nonprofit corporation, the term during which the contract designating the public defender's office is effective and how that contract may be renewed on expiration of the term; and

(4) if an oversight board is established under Article 26.045 for the public defender's office, the powers and duties that have been delegated to the oversight board.

(b-1) The applicable commissioners court or commissioners courts shall require a written plan from a governmental entity serving as a public defender's office.

(c) Before contracting with a nonprofit corporation to serve as a public defender's office under Subsection (b), the commissioners court or commissioners courts shall solicit proposals for the public defender's office.

(c-1) A written plan under Subsection (b-1) or a proposal under Subsection (c) must include:

(1) a budget for the public defender's office, including salaries;

(2) a description of each personnel position, including the chief public defender position;

(3) the maximum allowable caseloads for each attorney employed by the public defender's office;

(4) provisions for personnel training;

(5) a description of anticipated overhead costs for the public defender's office;

(6) policies regarding the use of licensed investigators and expert witnesses by the public defender's office; and

(7) a policy to ensure that the chief public defender and other attorneys employed by the public defender's office do not provide representation to a defendant if doing so would create a conflict of interest that has not been waived by the client.

(d) After considering each proposal for the public defender's office submitted by a nonprofit

Code of Criminal Procedure

corporation under Subsection (c), the commissioners court or commissioners courts shall select a proposal that reasonably demonstrates that the public defender's office will provide adequate quality representation for indigent defendants in the county or counties.

(e) The total cost of the proposal under Subsection (c) may not be the sole consideration in selecting a proposal.

(f) A public defender's office must be directed by a chief public defender who:

(1) is a member of the State Bar of Texas;

(2) has practiced law for at least three years; and

(3) has substantial experience in the practice of criminal law.

(g) A public defender's office is entitled to receive funds for personnel costs and expenses incurred in operating as a public defender's office in amounts fixed by the commissioners court and paid out of the appropriate county fund, or jointly fixed by the commissioners courts and proportionately paid out of each appropriate county fund if the public defender's office serves more than one county.

(h) A public defender's office may employ attorneys, licensed investigators, and other personnel necessary to perform the duties of the public defender's office as specified by the commissioners court or commissioners courts under Subsection (b)(1).

(i) Except as authorized by this article, the chief public defender and other attorneys employed by a public defender's office may not:

(1) engage in the private practice of criminal law; or

(2) accept anything of value not authorized by this article for services rendered under this article.

(j) A public defender's office may not accept an appointment under Article 26.04(f) if:

(1) a conflict of interest exists that has not been waived by the client;

(2) the public defender's office has insufficient resources to provide adequate representation for the defendant;

(3) the public defender's office is incapable of providing representation for the defendant in accordance with the rules of professional conduct;

(4) the acceptance of the appointment would violate the maximum allowable caseloads established at the public defender's office; or

(5) the public defender's office shows other good cause for not accepting the appointment.

(j-1) On refusing an appointment under Subsection (j), a chief public defender shall file with the court a written statement that identifies any reason for refusing the appointment. The court shall determine whether the chief public defender has demonstrated adequate good cause for refusing the appointment and shall include the statement with the papers in the case.

(j-2) A chief public defender may not be terminated, removed, or sanctioned for refusing in good faith to accept an appointment under Subsection (j).

(k) The judge may remove from a case a person who violates a provision of Subsection (i).

(*l*) A public defender's office may investigate the financial condition of any person the public defender's office is appointed to represent. The public defender's office shall report the results of the investigation to the appointing judge. The judge may hold a hearing to determine if the person is indigent and entitled to representation under this article.

(m) If it is necessary that an attorney who is not employed by a public defender's office be appointed, the attorney is entitled to the compensation provided by Article 26.05 of this code.

(n) An attorney employed by a public defender's office may be appointed with respect to an application for a writ of habeas corpus filed under Article 11.071 only if:

(1) an attorney employed by the office of capital writs is not appointed in the case; and

(2) the attorney employed by the public defender's office is on the list of competent counsel maintained under Section 78.056, Government Code.

Art. 26.045. Public Defender Oversight Board.

(a) The commissioners court of a county or the commissioners courts of two or more counties may establish an oversight board for a public defender's office created or designated in accordance with this chapter.

(b) The commissioners court or courts that establish an oversight board under this article shall appoint members of the board. Members may include one or more of the following:

(1) an attorney;

(2) the judge of a trial court in this state;

(3) a county commissioner;

(4) a county judge;

(5) a community representative; and

(6) a former client or a family member of a former client of the public defender's office for which the oversight board was established under this article.

(c) The commissioners court or courts may delegate to the board any power or duty of the commissioners court to provide oversight of the office under Article 26.044, including:

(1) recommending selection and removal of a chief public defender;

(2) setting policy for the office; and
(3) developing a budget proposal for the office.
(d) An oversight board established under this article may not gain access to privileged or confidential information.

Art. 26.046. Public Defender in Webb County [Repealed].

Repealed by Acts 2001, 77th Leg., ch. 906 (S.B. 7), § 15, effective January 1, 2002.

Art. 26.047. Managed Assigned Counsel Program.

(a) In this article:
(1) "Governmental entity" has the meaning assigned by Article 26.044.
(2) "Managed assigned counsel program" or "program" means a program operated with public funds:
(A) by a governmental entity, nonprofit corporation, or bar association under a written agreement with a governmental entity, other than an individual judge or court; and
(B) for the purpose of appointing counsel under Article 26.04 of this code or Section 51.10, Family Code.
(b) The commissioners court of any county, on written approval of a judge of the juvenile court of a county or a county court, statutory county court, or district court trying criminal cases in the county, may appoint a governmental entity, nonprofit corporation, or bar association to operate a managed assigned counsel program. The commissioners courts of two or more counties may enter into a written agreement to jointly appoint and fund a governmental entity, nonprofit corporation, or bar association to operate a managed assigned counsel program. In appointing an entity to operate a managed assigned counsel program under this subsection, the commissioners court shall specify or the commissioners courts shall jointly specify:
(1) the types of cases in which the program may appoint counsel under Article 26.04 of this code or Section 51.10, Family Code, and the courts in which the counsel appointed by the program may be required to appear; and
(2) the term of any agreement establishing a program and how the agreement may be terminated or renewed.
(c) The commissioners court or commissioners courts shall require a written plan of operation from an entity operating a program under this article. The plan of operation must include:
(1) a budget for the program, including salaries;
(2) a description of each personnel position, including the program's director;
(3) the maximum allowable caseload for each attorney appointed by the program;
(4) provisions for training personnel of the program and attorneys appointed under the program;
(5) a description of anticipated overhead costs for the program;
(6) a policy regarding licensed investigators and expert witnesses used by attorneys appointed under the program;
(7) a policy to ensure that appointments are reasonably and impartially allocated among qualified attorneys; and
(8) a policy to ensure that an attorney appointed under the program does not accept appointment in a case that involves a conflict of interest for the attorney that has not been waived by all affected clients.
(d) A program under this article must have a director. Unless the program uses a review committee appointed under Subsection (e), a program under this article must be directed by a person who:
(1) is a member of the State Bar of Texas;
(2) has practiced law for at least three years; and
(3) has substantial experience in the practice of criminal law.
(e) The governmental entity, nonprofit corporation, or bar association operating the program may appoint a review committee of three or more individuals to approve attorneys for inclusion on the program's public appointment list described by Subsection (f). Each member of the committee:
(1) must meet the requirements described by Subsection (d);
(2) may not be employed as a prosecutor; and
(3) may not be included on or apply for inclusion on the public appointment list described by Subsection (f).
(f) The program's public appointment list from which an attorney is appointed must contain the names of qualified attorneys, each of whom:
(1) applies to be included on the list;
(2) meets any applicable requirements specified by the procedure for appointing counsel adopted under Article 26.04(a) and the Texas Indigent Defense Commission; and
(3) is approved by the program director or review committee, as applicable.
(g) A court may replace an attorney appointed by the program for the same reasons and in the same manner described by Article 26.04(k).
(h) A managed assigned counsel program is entitled to receive funds for personnel costs and expenses incurred in amounts fixed by the commissioners court and paid out of the appropriate

county fund, or jointly fixed by the commissioners courts and proportionately paid out of each appropriate county fund if the program serves more than one county.

(i) A managed assigned counsel program may employ personnel and enter into contracts necessary to perform the program's duties as specified by the commissioners court or commissioners courts under this article.

Art. 26.048. Public Defender in Cherokee County [Repealed].

Repealed by Acts 2001, 77th Leg., ch. 906 (S.B. 7), § 15, effective January 1, 2002.

Art. 26.049. Public Defender in Tom Green County [Repealed].

Repealed by Acts 2001, 77th Leg., ch. 906 (S.B. 7), § 15, effective January 1, 2002.

Art. 26.05. Compensation of Counsel Appointed to Defend.

(a) A counsel, other than an attorney with a public defender's office or an attorney employed by the office of capital and forensic writs, appointed to represent a defendant in a criminal proceeding, including a habeas corpus hearing, shall be paid a reasonable attorney's fee for performing the following services, based on the time and labor required, the complexity of the case, and the experience and ability of the appointed counsel:

(1) time spent in court making an appearance on behalf of the defendant as evidenced by a docket entry, time spent in trial, and time spent in a proceeding in which sworn oral testimony is elicited;

(2) reasonable and necessary time spent out of court on the case, supported by any documentation that the court requires;

(3) preparation of an appellate brief and preparation and presentation of oral argument to a court of appeals or the Court of Criminal Appeals; and

(4) preparation of a motion for rehearing.

(b) All payments made under this article shall be paid in accordance with a schedule of fees adopted by formal action of the judges of the county courts, statutory county courts, and district courts trying criminal cases in each county. On adoption of a schedule of fees as provided by this subsection, a copy of the schedule shall be sent to the commissioners court of the county.

(c) Each fee schedule adopted shall state reasonable fixed rates or minimum and maximum hourly rates, taking into consideration reasonable and necessary overhead costs and the availability of qualified attorneys willing to accept the stated rates, and shall provide a form for the appointed counsel to itemize the types of services performed. No payment shall be made under this article until the form for itemizing the services performed is submitted to the judge presiding over the proceedings or, if the county operates a managed assigned counsel program under Article 26.047, to the director of the program, and until the judge or director, as applicable, approves the payment. If the judge or director disapproves the requested amount of payment, the judge or director shall make written findings stating the amount of payment that the judge or director approves and each reason for approving an amount different from the requested amount. An attorney whose request for payment is disapproved or is not otherwise acted on by the 60th day after the date the request for payment is submitted may appeal the disapproval or failure to act by filing a motion with the presiding judge of the administrative judicial region. On the filing of a motion, the presiding judge of the administrative judicial region shall review the disapproval of payment or failure to act and determine the appropriate amount of payment. In reviewing the disapproval or failure to act, the presiding judge of the administrative judicial region may conduct a hearing. Not later than the 45th day after the date an application for payment of a fee is submitted under this article, the commissioners court shall pay to the appointed counsel the amount that is approved by the presiding judge of the administrative judicial region and that is in accordance with the fee schedule for that county.

(d) A counsel in a noncapital case, other than an attorney with a public defender's office, appointed to represent a defendant under this code shall be reimbursed for reasonable and necessary expenses, including expenses for investigation and for mental health and other experts. Expenses incurred with prior court approval shall be reimbursed in the same manner provided for capital cases by Articles 26.052(f) and (g), and expenses incurred without prior court approval shall be reimbursed in the manner provided for capital cases by Article 26.052(h).

(e) A majority of the judges of the county courts and statutory county courts or the district courts, as appropriate, trying criminal cases in the county may remove an attorney from consideration for appointment if, after a hearing, it is shown that the attorney submitted a claim for legal services not performed by the attorney.

(f) All payments made under this article shall be paid from the general fund of the county in which the prosecution was instituted or habeas corpus hearing held and may be included as reimbursement fees.

(g) If the judge determines that a defendant has financial resources that enable the defendant to offset in part or in whole the costs of the legal services provided to the defendant in accordance with Article 1.051(c) or (d), including any expenses and costs, the judge shall order the defendant to pay during the pendency of the charges or, if convicted, as a reimbursement fee the amount that the judge finds the defendant is able to pay. The defendant may not be ordered to pay an amount that exceeds:

(1) the actual costs, including any expenses and costs, paid by the county for the legal services provided by an appointed attorney; or

(2) if the defendant was represented by a public defender's office, the actual amount, including any expenses and costs, that would have otherwise been paid to an appointed attorney had the county not had a public defender's office.

(g-1) (1) This subsection applies only to a defendant who at the time of sentencing to confinement or placement on community supervision, including deferred adjudication community supervision, did not have the financial resources to pay the maximum amount described by Subsection (g)(1) or (2), as applicable, for legal services provided to the defendant.

(2) At any time during a defendant's sentence of confinement or period of community supervision, the judge, after providing written notice to the defendant and an opportunity for the defendant to present information relevant to the defendant's ability to pay, may order a defendant to whom this subsection applies to pay any unpaid portion of the amount described by Subsection (g)(1) or (2), as applicable, if the judge determines that the defendant has the financial resources to pay the additional portion.

(3) The judge may amend an order entered under Subdivision (2) if, subsequent to the judge's determination under that subdivision, the judge determines that the defendant is indigent or demonstrates an inability to pay the amount ordered.

(4) In making a determination under this subsection, the judge may only consider the information a court or courts' designee is authorized to consider in making an indigency determination under Article 26.04(m).

(5) Notwithstanding any other law, the judge may not revoke or extend the defendant's period of community supervision solely to collect the amount the defendant has been ordered to pay under this subsection.

(h) Reimbursement of expenses incurred for purposes of investigation or expert testimony may be paid directly to a private investigator licensed under Chapter 1702, Occupations Code, or to an expert witness in the manner designated by appointed counsel and approved by the court.

(i) [Repealed by Acts 2011, 82nd Leg., ch. 984 (H.B. 1754), § 15(1), effective September 1, 2011.]

Art. 26.05-1. Contribution from State in Certain Counties [Renumbered].

Renumbered to Tex. Code Crim. Proc. art. 26.056 by Acts 1987, 70th Leg., ch. 167 (S.B. 892), § 5.02(2), effective September 1, 1987.

Art. 26.050. Public Defender in 293rd and 365th Judicial Districts [Repealed].

Repealed by Acts 2001, 77th Leg., ch. 906 (S.B. 7), § 15, effective January 1, 2002.

Art. 26.051. Indigent Inmate Defense.

(a) In this article:

(1) "Board" means the Texas Board of Criminal Justice.

(2) "Correctional institutions division" means the correctional institutions division of the Texas Department of Criminal Justice.

(b), (c) [Repealed by Acts 2007, 80th Leg., ch. 1014 (H.B. 1267), § 7, effective September 1, 2007.]

(d) A court shall:

(1) notify the board if it determines that a defendant before the court is indigent and is an inmate charged with an offense committed while in the custody of the correctional institutions division or a correctional facility authorized by Section 495.001, Government Code; and

(2) request that the board provide legal representation for the inmate.

(e) The board shall provide legal representation for inmates described by Subsection (d) of this section. The board may employ attorneys, support staff, and any other personnel required to provide legal representation for those inmates. All personnel employed under this article are directly responsible to the board in the performance of their duties. The board shall pay all fees and costs associated with providing legal representation for those inmates.

(f) [Repealed by Acts 1993, 73rd Leg., ch. 988 (S.B. 532), § 7.02, effective September 1, 1993.]

(g) The court shall appoint an attorney other than an attorney provided by the board if the court determines for any of the following reasons that a conflict of interest could arise from the use of an attorney provided by the board under Subsection (e) of this article:

Code of Criminal Procedure

(1) the case involves more than one inmate and the representation of more than one inmate could impair the attorney's effectiveness;

(2) the case is appealed and the court is satisfied that conflict of interest would prevent the presentation of a good faith allegation of ineffective assistance of counsel by a trial attorney provided by the board; or

(3) any conflict of interest exists under the Texas Disciplinary Rules of Professional Conduct of the State Bar of Texas that precludes representation by an attorney appointed by the board.

(h) When the court appoints an attorney other than an attorney provided by the board:

(1) except as otherwise provided by this article, the inmate's legal defense is subject to Articles 1.051, 26.04, 26.05, and 26.052, as applicable; and

(2) the county in which a facility of the correctional institutions division or a correctional facility authorized by Section 495.001, Government Code, is located shall pay from its general fund the total costs of the aggregate amount allowed and awarded by the court for attorney compensation and expenses under Article 26.05 or 26.052, as applicable.

(i) The state shall reimburse a county for attorney compensation and expenses awarded under Subsection (h). A court seeking reimbursement for a county shall certify to the comptroller of public accounts the amount of compensation and expenses for which the county is entitled to be reimbursed under this article. Not later than the 60th day after the date the comptroller receives from the court the request for reimbursement, the comptroller shall issue a warrant to the county in the amount certified by the court.

Art. 26.052. Appointment of Counsel in Death Penalty Case; Reimbursement of Investigative Expenses.

(a) Notwithstanding any other provision of this chapter, this article establishes procedures in death penalty cases for appointment and payment of counsel to represent indigent defendants at trial and on direct appeal and to apply for writ of certiorari in the United States Supreme Court.

(b) If a county is served by a public defender's office, trial counsel and counsel for direct appeal or to apply for a writ of certiorari may be appointed as provided by the guidelines established by the public defender's office. In all other cases in which the death penalty is sought, counsel shall be appointed as provided by this article.

(c) A local selection committee is created in each administrative judicial region created under Section 74.042, Government Code. The administrative judge of the judicial region shall appoint the members of the committee. A committee shall have not less than four members, including:

(1) the administrative judge of the judicial region;

(2) at least one district judge;

(3) a representative from the local bar association; and

(4) at least one practitioner who is board certified by the State Bar of Texas in criminal law.

(d) (1) The committee shall adopt standards for the qualification of attorneys to be appointed to represent indigent defendants in capital cases in which the death penalty is sought.

(2) The standards must require that a trial attorney appointed as lead counsel to a capital case:

(A) be a member of the State Bar of Texas;

(B) exhibit proficiency and commitment to providing quality representation to defendants in death penalty cases;

(C) have not been found by a federal or state court to have rendered ineffective assistance of counsel during the trial or appeal of any capital case, unless the local selection committee determines under Subsection (n) that the conduct underlying the finding no longer accurately reflects the attorney's ability to provide effective representation;

(D) have at least five years of criminal law experience;

(E) have tried to a verdict as lead defense counsel a significant number of felony cases, including homicide trials and other trials for offenses punishable as second or first degree felonies or capital felonies;

(F) have trial experience in:

(i) the use of and challenges to mental health or forensic expert witnesses; and

(ii) investigating and presenting mitigating evidence at the penalty phase of a death penalty trial; and

(G) have participated in continuing legal education courses or other training relating to criminal defense in death penalty cases.

(3) The standards must require that an attorney appointed as lead appellate counsel in the direct appeal of a capital case:

(A) be a member of the State Bar of Texas;

(B) exhibit proficiency and commitment to providing quality representation to defendants in death penalty cases;

(C) have not been found by a federal or state court to have rendered ineffective assistance of counsel during the trial or appeal of any capital case, unless the local selection committee determines under Subsection (n) that the conduct underlying the finding no longer accurately reflects the attorney's ability to provide effective representation;

(D) have at least five years of criminal law experience;

(E) have authored a significant number of appellate briefs, including appellate briefs for homicide cases and other cases involving an offense punishable as a capital felony or a felony of the first degree or an offense described by Article 42A.054(a);

(F) have trial or appellate experience in:

(i) the use of and challenges to mental health or forensic expert witnesses; and

(ii) the use of mitigating evidence at the penalty phase of a death penalty trial; and

(G) have participated in continuing legal education courses or other training relating to criminal defense in appealing death penalty cases.

(4) The committee shall prominently post the standards in each district clerk's office in the region with a list of attorneys qualified for appointment.

(5) Not later than the second anniversary of the date an attorney is placed on the list of attorneys qualified for appointment in death penalty cases and each year following the second anniversary, the attorney must present proof to the committee that the attorney has successfully completed the minimum continuing legal education requirements of the State Bar of Texas, including a course or other form of training relating to criminal defense in death penalty cases or in appealing death penalty cases, as applicable. The committee shall remove the attorney's name from the list of qualified attorneys if the attorney fails to provide the committee with proof of completion of the continuing legal education requirements.

(e) The presiding judge of the district court in which a capital felony case is filed shall appoint two attorneys, at least one of whom must be qualified under this chapter, to represent an indigent defendant as soon as practicable after charges are filed, unless the state gives notice in writing that the state will not seek the death penalty.

(f) Appointed counsel may file with the trial court a pretrial ex parte confidential request for advance payment of expenses to investigate potential defenses. The request for expenses must state:

(1) the type of investigation to be conducted;

(2) specific facts that suggest the investigation will result in admissible evidence; and

(3) an itemized list of anticipated expenses for each investigation.

(g) The court shall grant the request for advance payment of expenses in whole or in part if the request is reasonable. If the court denies in whole or in part the request for expenses, the court shall:

(1) state the reasons for the denial in writing;

(2) attach the denial to the confidential request; and

(3) submit the request and denial as a sealed exhibit to the record.

(h) Counsel may incur expenses without prior approval of the court. On presentation of a claim for reimbursement, the court shall order reimbursement of counsel for the expenses, if the expenses are reasonably necessary and reasonably incurred.

(i) If the indigent defendant is convicted of a capital felony and sentenced to death, the defendant is entitled to be represented by competent counsel on appeal and to apply for a writ of certiorari to the United States Supreme Court.

(j) As soon as practicable after a death sentence is imposed in a capital felony case, the presiding judge of the convicting court shall appoint counsel to represent an indigent defendant on appeal and to apply for a writ of certiorari, if appropriate.

(k) The court may not appoint an attorney as counsel on appeal if the attorney represented the defendant at trial, unless:

(1) the defendant and the attorney request the appointment on the record; and

(2) the court finds good cause to make the appointment.

(*l*) An attorney appointed under this article to represent a defendant at trial or on direct appeal is compensated as provided by Article 26.05 from county funds. Advance payment of expenses anticipated or reimbursement of expenses incurred for purposes of investigation or expert testimony may be paid directly to a private investigator licensed under Chapter 1702, Occupations Code, or to an expert witness in the manner designated by appointed counsel and approved by the court.

(m) The local selection committee shall annually review the list of attorneys posted under Subsection (d) to ensure that each listed attorney satisfies the requirements under this chapter.

(n) At the request of an attorney, the local selection committee shall make a determination under Subsection (d)(2)(C) or (3)(C), as applicable, regarding an attorney's current ability to provide effective representation following a judicial finding that the attorney previously rendered ineffective assistance of counsel in a capital case.

Art. 26.053. Public Defender in Randall County. [Repealed]

Art. 26.054. Public Defender in Potter County [Repealed].

Repealed by Acts 2001, 77th Leg., ch. 906 (S.B. 7), § 15, effective January 1, 2002.

Art. 26.055. Contribution from State for Defense of Indigent Inmates [Repealed].

Repealed by Acts 2007, 80th Leg., ch. 1014 (H.B. 1267), § 7, effective September 1, 2007.

Art. 26.056. Contribution from State in Certain Counties.

Sec. 1. A county in which a state training school for delinquent children is located shall pay from its general fund the first $250 of fees awarded for court-appointed counsel under Article 26.05 toward defending a child committed to the school from another county who is being prosecuted for a felony or misdemeanor in the county where the training school is located.

Sec. 2. If the fees awarded for counsel compensation are in excess of $250, the court shall certify the amount in excess of $250 to the Comptroller of Public Accounts of the State of Texas. The Comptroller shall issue a warrant to the court-appointed counsel in the amount certified to the comptroller by the court.

Art. 26.057. Cost of Employment of Counsel for Certain Minors.

If a juvenile has been transferred to a criminal court under Section 54.02, Family Code, and if a court appoints counsel for the juvenile under Article 26.04 of this code, the county that pays for the counsel has a cause of action against a parent or other person who is responsible for the support of the juvenile and is financially able to employ counsel for the juvenile but refuses to do so. The county may recover its cost of payment to the appointed counsel and may recover attorney's fees necessary to prosecute the cause of action against the parent or other person.

Art. 26.058. Public Defender in Aransas County [Repealed].

Repealed by Acts 2001, 77th Leg., ch. 906 (S.B. 7), § 15, effective January 1, 2002.

Art. 26.06. Elected Officials Not to Be Appointed.

No court may appoint an elected county, district or state official to represent a person accused of crime, unless the official has notified the court of his availability for appointment. If an official has notified the court of his availability and is appointed as counsel, he may decline the appointment if he determines that it is in the best interest of his office to do so. Nothing in this Code shall modify any statutory provision for legislative continuance.

Art. 26.07. Name As Stated in Indictment.

When the defendant is arraigned, his name, as stated in the indictment, shall be distinctly called; and unless he suggest by himself or counsel that he is not indicted by his true name, it shall be taken that his name is truly set forth, and he shall not thereafter be allowed to deny the same by way of defense.

Art. 26.08. If Defendant Suggests Different Name.

If the defendant, or his counsel for him, suggests that he bears some name different from that stated in the indictment, the same shall be noted upon the minutes of the court, the indictment corrected by inserting therein the name of the defendant as suggested by himself or his counsel for him, the style of the case changed so as to give his true name, and the cause proceed as if the true name had been first recited in the indictment.

Art. 26.09. If Accused Refuses to Give His Real Name.

If the defendant alleges that he is not indicted by his true name, and refuses to say what his real name is, the cause shall proceed as if the name stated in the indictment were true; and the defendant shall not be allowed to contradict the same by way of defense.

Art. 26.10. Where Name Is Unknown.

A defendant described as a person whose name is unknown may have the indictment so corrected as to give therein his true name.

Art. 26.11. Indictment Read.

The name of the accused having been called, if no suggestion, such as is spoken of in the four preceding Articles, be made, or being made is disposed of as before directed, the indictment shall be read, and the defendant asked whether he is guilty or not, as therein charged.

Art. 26.12. Plea of Not Guilty Entered.

If the defendant answers that he is not guilty, such plea shall be entered upon the minutes of the court; if he refuses to answer, the plea of not guilty shall in like manner be entered.

Art. 26.13. Plea of Guilty.

(a) Prior to accepting a plea of guilty or a plea of nolo contendere, the court shall admonish the defendant of:

(1) the range of the punishment attached to the offense;

(2) the fact that the recommendation of the prosecuting attorney as to punishment is not binding on the court. Provided that the court shall inquire as to the existence of a plea bargain agreement between the state and the defendant and, if an agreement exists, the court shall inform the defendant whether it will follow or reject the agreement in open court and before any finding on the plea. Should the court reject the agreement, the defendant shall be permitted to withdraw the defendant's plea of guilty or nolo contendere;

(3) the fact that if the punishment assessed does not exceed the punishment recommended by the prosecutor and agreed to by the defendant and the defendant's attorney, the trial court must give its permission to the defendant before the defendant may prosecute an appeal on any matter in the case except for those matters raised by written motions filed prior to trial;

(4) the fact that if the defendant is not a citizen of the United States of America, a plea of guilty or nolo contendere for the offense charged may result in deportation, the exclusion from admission to this country, or the denial of naturalization under federal law;

(5) the fact that the defendant will be required to meet the registration requirements of Chapter 62, if the defendant is convicted of or placed on deferred adjudication for an offense for which a person is subject to registration under that chapter; and

(6) the fact that if the defendant is placed on community supervision, after satisfactorily fulfilling the conditions of community supervision and on expiration of the period of community supervision, the court is authorized to release the defendant from the penalties and disabilities resulting from the offense as provided by Article 42A.701(f).

(b) No plea of guilty or plea of nolo contendere shall be accepted by the court unless it appears that the defendant is mentally competent and the plea is free and voluntary.

(c) In admonishing the defendant as herein provided, substantial compliance by the court is sufficient, unless the defendant affirmatively shows that he was not aware of the consequences of his plea and that he was misled or harmed by the admonishment of the court.

(d) Except as provided by Subsection (d-1), the court may make the admonitions required by this article either orally or in writing. If the court makes the admonitions in writing, it must receive a statement signed by the defendant and the defendant's attorney that the defendant understands the admonitions and is aware of the consequences of the plea. If the defendant is unable or refuses to sign the statement, the court shall make the admonitions orally.

(d-1) The court shall make the admonition required by Subsection (a)(4) both orally and in writing. Unless the court has received the statement as described by Subsection (d), the court must receive a statement signed by the defendant and the defendant's attorney that the defendant understands the admonition required by Subsection (a)(4) and is aware of the consequences of the plea. If the defendant is unable or refuses to sign the statement, the court shall make a record of that fact.

(e) Before accepting a plea of guilty or a plea of nolo contendere, the court shall, as applicable in the case:

(1) inquire as to whether a victim impact statement has been returned to the attorney representing the state and ask for a copy of the statement if one has been returned; and

(2) inquire as to whether the attorney representing the state has given notice of the existence and terms of any plea bargain agreement to the victim, guardian of a victim, or close relative of a deceased victim, as those terms are defined by Article 56A.001.

(f) The court must substantially comply with Subsection (e) of this article. The failure of the court to comply with Subsection (e) of this article is not grounds for the defendant to set aside the conviction, sentence, or plea.

(g) Before accepting a plea of guilty or a plea of nolo contendere and on the request of a victim of the offense, the court may assist the victim and the defendant in participating in a victim-offender mediation program.

(h) The court must substantially comply with Subsection (a)(5). The failure of the court to comply with Subsection (a)(5) is not a ground for the defendant to set aside the conviction, sentence, or plea.

(h-1) The court must substantially comply with Subsection (a)(6). The failure of the court to comply with Subsection (a)(6) is not a ground for the defendant to set aside the conviction, sentence, or plea.

(i) Notwithstanding this article, a court shall not order the state or any of its prosecuting attorneys to participate in mediation, dispute resolution, arbitration, or other similar procedures in relation to a criminal prosecution unless upon written consent of the state.

Art. 26.14. Jury on Plea of Guilty.

Where a defendant in a case of felony persists in pleading guilty or in entering a plea of nolo contendere, if the punishment is not absolutely fixed by law, a jury shall be impaneled to assess the punishment and evidence may be heard to enable them to decide thereupon, unless the defendant in accordance with Articles 1.13 or 37.07 shall have waived his right to trial by jury.

Art. 26.15. Correcting Name.

In any case, the same proceedings shall be had with respect to the name of the defendant and the correction of the indictment or information as provided with respect to the same in capital cases.

CHAPTER 27
THE PLEADING IN CRIMINAL ACTIONS

Art. 27.01. Indictment or Information.

The primary pleading in a criminal action on the part of the State is the indictment or information.

Art. 27.02. Defendant's Pleadings.

The pleadings and motions of the defendant shall be:

(1) A motion to set aside or an exception to an indictment or information for some matter of form or substance;

(2) A special plea as provided in Article 27.05 of this code;

(3) A plea of guilty;

(4) A plea of not guilty;

(5) A plea of nolo contendere, the legal effect of which shall be the same as that of a plea of guilty, except that such plea may not be used against the defendant as an admission in any civil suit based upon or growing out of the act upon which the criminal prosecution is based;

(6) An application for probation, if any;

(7) An election, if any, to have the jury assess the punishment if he is found guilty; and

(8) Any other motions or pleadings that are by law permitted to be filed.

Art. 27.03. Motion to Set Aside Indictment.

In addition to any other grounds authorized by law, a motion to set aside an indictment or information may be based on the following:

1. That it appears by the records of the court that the indictment was not found by at least nine grand jurors, or that the information was not based upon a valid complaint;

2. That some person not authorized by law was present when the grand jury was deliberating upon the accusation against the defendant, or was voting upon the same; and

3. That the grand jury was illegally impaneled; provided, however, in order to raise such question on motion to set aside the indictment, the defendant must show that he did not have an opportunity to challenge the array at the time the grand jury was impaneled.

Art. 27.04. Motion Tried by Judge.

An issue of fact arising upon a motion to set aside an indictment or information shall be tried by the judge without a jury.

Art. 27.05. Defendant's Special Plea.

A defendant's only special plea is that he has already been prosecuted for the same or a different offense arising out of the same criminal episode that was or should have been consolidated into one trial, and that the former prosecution:

(1) resulted in acquittal;

(2) resulted in conviction;

(3) was improperly terminated; or

(4) was terminated by a final order or judgment for the defendant that has not been reversed, set aside, or vacated and that necessarily required a determination inconsistent with a fact that must be established to secure conviction in the subsequent prosecution.

Art. 27.06. Special Plea Verified.

Every special plea shall be verified by the affidavit of the defendant.

Art. 27.07. Special Plea Tried.

All issues of fact presented by a special plea shall be tried by the trier of the facts on the trial on the merits.

Art. 27.08. Exception to Substance of Indictment.

There is no exception to the substance of an indictment or information except:

1. That it does not appear therefrom that an offense against the law was committed by the defendant;

2. That it appears from the face thereof that a prosecution for the offense is barred by a lapse of time, or that the offense was committed after the finding of the indictment;

3. That it contains matter which is a legal defense or bar to the prosecution; and

4. That it shows upon its face that the court trying the case has no jurisdiction thereof.

Art. 27.09. Exception to Form of Indictment.

Exceptions to the form of an indictment or information may be taken for the following causes only:

1. That it does not appear to have been presented in the proper court as required by law;

2. The want of any requisite prescribed by Articles 21.02 and 21.21.

3. That it was not returned by a lawfully chosen or empaneled grand jury.

Art. 27.10. Written Pleadings.

All motions to set aside an indictment or information and all special pleas and exceptions shall be in writing.

Art. 27.11. Ten Days Allowed for Filing Pleadings.

In all cases the defendant shall be allowed ten entire days, exclusive of all fractions of a day after his arrest, and during the term of the court, to file written pleadings.

Art. 27.12. Time After Service.

In cases where the defendant is entitled to be served with a copy of the indictment, he shall be allowed the ten days time mentioned in the preceding Article to file written pleadings after such service.

Art. 27.13. Plea of Guilty or Nolo Contendere in Felony.

A plea of "guilty" or a plea of "nolo contendere" in a felony case must be made in open court by the defendant in person; and the proceedings shall be as provided in Articles 26.13, 26.14 and 27.02. If the plea is before the judge alone, same may be made in the same manner as is provided for by Articles 1.13 and 1.15.

Art. 27.14. Plea of Guilty or Nolo Contendere in Misdemeanor.

(a) A plea of "guilty" or a plea of "nolo contendere" in a misdemeanor case may be made either by the defendant or his counsel in open court; in such case, the defendant or his counsel may waive a jury, and the punishment may be assessed by the court either upon or without evidence, at the discretion of the court.

(b) A defendant charged with a misdemeanor for which the maximum possible punishment is by fine only may, in lieu of the method provided in Subsection (a), mail or deliver in person to the court a plea of "guilty" or a plea of "nolo contendere" and a waiver of jury trial. The defendant may also request in writing that the court notify the defendant, at the address stated in the request, of the amount of an appeal bond that the court will approve. If the court receives a plea and waiver before the time the defendant is scheduled to appear in court, the court shall dispose of the case without requiring a court appearance by the defendant. If the court receives a plea and waiver after the time the defendant is scheduled to appear in court but at least five business days before a scheduled trial date, the court shall dispose of the case without requiring a court appearance by the defendant. The court shall notify the defendant either in person or by regular mail of the amount of any fine or costs assessed in the case, information regarding the alternatives to the full payment of any fine or costs assessed against the defendant, if the defendant is unable to pay that amount, and, if requested by the defendant, the amount of an appeal bond that the court will approve. Except as otherwise provided by this code, the defendant shall pay any fine or costs assessed or give an appeal bond in the amount stated in the notice before the 31st day after receiving the notice. This subsection does not apply to a defendant charged with a misdemeanor involving family violence, as defined by Section 71.004, Family Code.

(c) In a misdemeanor case for which the maximum possible punishment is by fine only, payment of a fine or an amount accepted by the court constitutes a finding of guilty in open court as though a plea of nolo contendere had been entered by the defendant and constitutes a waiver of a jury trial in writing.

(d) If written notice of an offense for which maximum possible punishment is by fine only or of a violation relating to the manner, time, and place of parking has been prepared, delivered, and filed with the court and a legible duplicate copy has been given to the defendant, the written notice

Code of Criminal Procedure

serves as a complaint to which the defendant may plead "guilty," "not guilty," or "nolo contendere." If the defendant pleads "not guilty" to the offense or fails to appear based on the written notice, a complaint shall be filed that conforms to the requirements of Chapter 45 of this code, and that complaint serves as an original complaint. A defendant may waive the filing of a sworn complaint and elect that the prosecution proceed on the written notice of the charged offense if the defendant agrees in writing with the prosecution, signs the agreement, and files it with the court.

(e) (1) Before accepting a plea of guilty or a plea of nolo contendere by a defendant charged with a misdemeanor involving family violence, as defined by Section 71.004, Family Code, the court shall admonish the defendant by using the following statement:

"If you are convicted of a misdemeanor offense involving violence where you are or were a spouse, intimate partner, parent, or guardian of the victim or are or were involved in another, similar relationship with the victim, it may be unlawful for you to possess or purchase a firearm, including a handgun or long gun, or ammunition, pursuant to federal law under 18 U.S.C. Section 922(g)(9) or Section 46.04(b), Texas Penal Code. If you have any questions whether these laws make it illegal for you to possess or purchase a firearm, you should consult an attorney."

(2) The court may provide the admonishment under Subdivision (1) orally or in writing.

Art. 27.15. Change of Venue to Plead Guilty.

When in any county which is located in a judicial district composed of more than one county, a party is charged with a felony and the maximum punishment therefor shall not exceed fifteen years, and the district court of said county is not in session, such party may, if he desires to plead guilty, or enter a plea of nolo contendere, make application to the district judge of such district for a change of venue to the county in which said court is in session, and said district judge may enter an order changing the venue of said cause to the county in which the court is then in session, and the defendant may plead guilty or enter a plea of nolo contendere to said charge in said court to which the venue has been changed.

Art. 27.16. Plea of Not Guilty, How Made.

(a) The plea of not guilty may be made orally by the defendant or by his counsel in open court. If the defendant refuses to plead, the plea of not guilty shall be entered for him by the court.

(b) A defendant charged with a misdemeanor for which the maximum possible punishment is by fine only may, in lieu of the method provided in Subsection (a) of this article, mail to the court a plea of not guilty.

Art. 27.17. Plea of Not Guilty Construed.

The plea of not guilty shall be construed to be a denial of every material allegation in the indictment or information. Under this plea, evidence to establish the insanity of defendant, and every fact whatever tending to acquit him of the accusation may be introduced, except such facts as are proper for a special plea under Article 27.05.

Art. 27.18. Plea or Waiver of Rights by Videoconference.

(a) Notwithstanding any provision of this code requiring that a plea or a waiver of a defendant's right be made in open court, a court may accept the plea or waiver by videoconference to the court if:

(1) the defendant and the attorney representing the state file with the court written consent to the use of videoconference;

(2) the videoconference provides for a simultaneous, compressed full motion video, and interactive communication of image and sound between the judge, the attorney representing the state, the defendant, and the defendant's attorney; and

(3) on request of the defendant, the defendant and the defendant's attorney are able to communicate privately without being recorded or heard by the judge or the attorney representing the state.

(b) On motion of the defendant or the attorney representing the state or in the court's discretion, the court may terminate an appearance by videoconference at any time during the appearance and require an appearance by the defendant in open court.

(c) A record of the communication shall be made by a court reporter or by electronic recording and preserved by the court reporter or by electronic recording until all appellate proceedings have been disposed of. A court reporter or court recorder is not required to transcribe or make a duplicate electronic recording of a plea taken under this article unless an appeal is taken in the case and a party requests a transcript.

(c-1) The defendant may obtain a copy of the record, including any electronic recording, on payment of a reasonable amount to cover the costs of reproduction or, if the defendant is indigent, the court shall provide a copy to the defendant without charging a cost for the copy.

(c-2) The loss or destruction of or failure to create a court record or an electronic recording of a plea entered under this article is not alone sufficient grounds for a defendant to withdraw the defendant's plea or to request the court to set aside a conviction, sentence, or plea.

(d) A defendant who is confined in a county other than the county in which charges against the defendant are pending may use the videoconference method provided by this article or by Article 15.17 to enter a plea or waive a right in the court with jurisdiction over the case.

(e) A defendant who enters a plea or waiver under Subsection (d):

(1) consents to venue in the county in which the court receiving the plea or waiver is located; and

(2) waives any claim of error related to venue.

(f) Subsection (e) does not prohibit a court from granting a defendant's motion for a change of venue during the trial of the defendant.

(g) If a defendant enters a plea of guilty or nolo contendere under Subsection (d), the attorney representing the state may request at the time the plea is entered that the defendant submit a fingerprint of the defendant suitable for attachment to the judgment. On request for a fingerprint under this subsection, the county in which the defendant is confined shall obtain a fingerprint of the defendant and use first-class mail or other means acceptable to the attorney representing the state and the county to forward the fingerprint to the court accepting the plea.

Art. 27.19. Plea by Certain Defendants.

(a) Notwithstanding any other provision of this code, a court shall accept a plea of guilty or nolo contendere from a defendant who is confined in a penal institution if the plea is made:

(1) in accordance with the procedure established by Article 27.18; or

(2) in writing, including a writing delivered by United States mail or secure electronic or facsimile transmission, before the appropriate court having jurisdiction in the county in which the penal institution is located, provided that:

(A) the defendant is notified by the court of original jurisdiction of the right to counsel and the procedures for requesting appointment of counsel, and is provided a reasonable opportunity to request a court-appointed lawyer;

(B) if the defendant elects to proceed without counsel, the defendant must waive the right to counsel in accordance with Article 1.051;

(C) the defendant must waive the right to be present at the taking of the plea or to have counsel present, if the defendant has counsel; and

(D) if the defendant is charged with a felony, judgment and sentence are rendered in accordance with the conditions and the procedure established by Article 42.14(b).

(b) In this article, "penal institution" has the meaning assigned by Section 1.07, Penal Code.

(c) Before accepting a plea submitted under Subsection (a)(2), the court shall verify that the person submitting the plea is:

(1) the defendant named in the information or indictment; or

(2) a person with legal authority to act for the defendant named in the information or indictment.

CHAPTER 28 MOTIONS, PLEADINGS AND EXCEPTIONS

Art. 28.01. Pre-trial.

Sec. 1. The court may set any criminal case for a pre-trial hearing before it is set for trial upon its merits, and direct the defendant and his attorney, if any of record, and the State's attorney, to appear before the court at the time and place stated in the court's order for a conference and hearing. The defendant must be present at the arraignment, and his presence is required during any pre-trial proceeding. The pre-trial hearing shall be to determine any of the following matters:

(1) Arraignment of the defendant, if such be necessary; and appointment of counsel to represent the defendant, if such be necessary;

(2) Pleadings of the defendant;

(3) Special pleas, if any;

(4) Exceptions to the form or substance of the indictment or information;

(5) Motions for continuance either by the State or defendant; provided that grounds for continuance not existing or not known at the time may be presented and considered at any time before the defendant announces ready for trial;

(6) Motions to suppress evidence — When a hearing on the motion to suppress evidence is granted, the court may determine the merits of said motion on the motions themselves, or upon opposing affidavits, or upon oral testimony, subject to the discretion of the court;

(7) Motions for change of venue by the State or the defendant; provided, however, that such motions for change of venue, if overruled at the pretrial hearing, may be renewed by the State or the defendant during the voir dire examination of the jury;

(8) Discovery;

(9) Entrapment; and

(10) Motion for appointment of interpreter.

Sec. 2. When a criminal case is set for such pre-trial hearing, any such preliminary matters not raised or filed seven days before the hearing will not thereafter be allowed to be raised or filed, except by permission of the court for good cause shown; provided that the defendant shall have sufficient notice of such hearing to allow him not less than 10 days in which to raise or file such preliminary matters. The record made at such pre-trial hearing, the rulings of the court and the exceptions and objections thereto shall become a part of the trial record of the case upon its merits.

Sec. 3. The notice mentioned in Section 2 above shall be sufficient if given in any one of the following ways:

(1) By announcement made by the court in open court in the presence of the defendant or his attorney of record;

(2) By personal service upon the defendant or his attorney of record;

(3) By mail to either the defendant or his attorney of record deposited by the clerk in the mail at least six days prior to the date set for hearing. If the defendant has no attorney of record such notice shall be addressed to defendant at the address shown on his bond, if the bond shows such an address, and if not, it may be addressed to one of the sureties on his bond. If the envelope containing the notice is properly addressed, stamped and mailed, the state will not be required to show that it was received.

Art. 28.02. Order of Argument.

The counsel of the defendant has the right to open and conclude the argument upon all pleadings of the defendant presented for the decision of the judge.

Art. 28.03. Process for Testimony on Pleadings.

When the matters involved in any written pleading depend in whole or in part upon testimony, and not altogether upon the record of the court, every process known to the law may be obtained on behalf of either party to procure such testimony; but there shall be no delay on account of the want of the testimony, unless it be shown to the satisfaction of the court that all the means given by the law have been used to procure the same.

Art. 28.04. Quashing Charge in Misdemeanor.

If the motion to set aside or the exception to an indictment or information is sustained, the defendant in a misdemeanor case shall be discharged, but may be again prosecuted within the time allowed by law.

Art. 28.05. Quashing Indictment in Felony.

If the motion to set aside or the exception to the indictment in cases of felony be sustained, the defendant shall not therefor be discharged, but may immediately be recommitted by order of the court, upon motion of the State's attorney or without motion; and proceedings may afterward be had against him as if no prosecution had ever been commenced.

Art. 28.06. Shall Be Fully Discharged, When.

Where, after the motion or exception is sustained, it is made known to the court by sufficient testimony that the offense of which the defendant is accused will be barred by limitation before another indictment can be presented, he shall be fully discharged.

Art. 28.061. Discharge for Delay.

If a motion to set aside an indictment, information, or complaint for failure to provide a speedy trial is sustained, the court shall discharge the defendant. A discharge under this article is a bar to any further prosecution for the offense discharged and for any other offense arising out of the same transaction, other than an offense of a higher grade that the attorney representing the state and prosecuting the offense that was discharged does not have the primary duty to prosecute.

Art. 28.07. If Exception Is That No Offense Is Charged.

If an exception to an indictment or information is taken and sustained upon the ground that there is no offense against the law charged therein, the defendant shall be discharged, unless an affidavit be filed accusing him of the commission of a penal offense.

Art. 28.08. When Defendant Is Held by Order of Court.

If the motion to set aside the indictment or any exception thereto is sustained, but the court refuses to discharge the defendant, then at the expiration of ten days from the order sustaining such motions or exceptions, the defendant shall be discharged, unless in the meanwhile complaint has been made before a magistrate charging him with an offense, or unless another indictment has been presented against him for such offense.

Art. 28.09. Exception on Account of Form or Substance.

If the exception to an indictment or information is sustained, the information or indictment may be amended if permitted by Article 28.10 of this code, and the cause may proceed upon the amended indictment or information.

Art. 28.10. Amendment of Indictment or Information.

(a) After notice to the defendant, a matter of form or substance in an indictment or information may be amended at any time before the date the trial on the merits commences. On the request of the defendant, the court shall allow the defendant not less than 10 days, or a shorter period if requested by the defendant, to respond to the amended indictment or information.

(b) A matter of form or substance in an indictment or information may also be amended after the trial on the merits commences if the defendant does not object.

(c) An indictment or information may not be amended over the defendant's objection as to form or substance if the amended indictment or information charges the defendant with an additional or different offense or if the substantial rights of the defendant are prejudiced.

Art. 28.11. How Amended.

All amendments of an indictment or information shall be made with the leave of the court and under its direction.

Art. 28.12. Exception and Trial of Special Pleas.

When a special plea is filed by the defendant, the State may except to it for substantial defects. If the exception be sustained, the plea may be amended. If the plea be not excepted to, it shall be considered that issue has been taken upon the same. Such special pleas as set forth matter of fact proper to be tried by a jury shall be submitted and tried with a plea of not guilty.

Art. 28.13. Former Acquittal or Conviction.

A former judgment of acquittal or conviction in a court of competent jurisdiction shall be a bar to any further prosecution for the same offense, but shall not bar a prosecution for any higher grade of offense over which said court had not jurisdiction, unless such judgment was had upon indictment or information, in which case the prosecution shall be barred for all grades of the offense.

Art. 28.14. Plea Allowed.

Judgment shall, in no case, be given against the defendant where his motion, exception or plea is overruled; but in all cases the plea of not guilty may be made by or for him.

CHAPTER 29
CONTINUANCE

Art. 29.01. By Operation of Law.

Criminal actions are continued by operation of law if:

(1) The individual defendant has not been arrested;

(2) A defendant corporation or association has not been served with summons; or

(3) There is not sufficient time for trial at that term of court.

Art. 29.011. Religious Holy Day.

(a) In this article:

(1) "Religious organization" means an organization that meets the standards for qualifying as a religious organization under Section 11.20, Tax Code.

(2) "Religious holy day" means a day on which the tenets of a religious organization prohibit its members from participating in secular activities, such as court proceedings.

(b) If a defendant, an attorney representing the defendant, or an attorney representing the state in a criminal action is required to appear at a court proceeding on a religious holy day observed by the person, the court shall continue the action.

(c) A defendant or attorney seeking a continuance must file with the court an affidavit stating:

(1) the grounds for the continuance; and

(2) that the person holds religious beliefs that prohibit him from taking part in a court proceeding on the day for which the continuance is sought.

(d) An affidavit filed under Subsection (c) of this article is proof of the facts stated and need not be corroborated.

Art. 29.012. Religious Holy Day.

(a) In this article:

Code of Criminal Procedure

(1) "Religious organization" means an organization that meets the standards for qualification as a religious organization under Section 11.20, Tax Code.

(2) "Religious holy day" means a day on which the tenets of a religious organization prohibit its members from participating in secular activities, such as court proceedings.

(b) If a juror in a criminal action is required to appear at a court proceeding on a religious holy day observed by the juror, the court or the court's designee shall recess the criminal action until the next day the court is in session after the conclusion of the holy day.

(c) A juror seeking a recess must file with the court before the final selection of the jury an affidavit stating:

(1) the grounds for the recess; and

(2) that the juror holds religious beliefs that prohibit him from taking part in a court proceeding on the day for which the recess is sought.

(d) An affidavit filed under Subsection (c) of this section is proof of the facts stated and need not be corroborated.

Art. 29.02. By Agreement.

A criminal action may be continued by consent of the parties thereto, in open court, at any time on a showing of good cause, but a continuance may be only for as long as is necessary.

Art. 29.03. For Sufficient Cause Shown.

A criminal action may be continued on the written motion of the State or of the defendant, upon sufficient cause shown; which cause shall be fully set forth in the motion. A continuance may be only for as long as is necessary.

Art. 29.035. For Insufficient Notice of Hearing or Trial.

(a) Notwithstanding Article 28.01 or any other provision of this chapter, and except as otherwise provided by this article, a trial court shall grant a continuance of a criminal action on oral or written motion of the state or the defendant if the trial court sets a hearing or trial without providing to the attorney for the state and the defendant, or the defendant's attorney, notice of the hearing or trial at least three business days before the date of the hearing or trial.

(b) This article does not apply during the period between:

(1) the date the trial begins; and

(2) the date the judgment is entered.

Art. 29.04. First Motion by State.

It shall be sufficient, upon the first motion by the State for a continuance, if the same be for the want of a witness, to state:

1. The name of the witness and his residence, if known, or that his residence is unknown;

2. The diligence which has been used to procure his attendance; and it shall not be considered sufficient diligence to have caused to be issued, or to have applied for, a subpoena, in cases where the law authorized an attachment to issue; and

3. That the testimony of the witness is believed by the applicant to be material for the State.

Art. 29.05. Subsequent Motion by State.

On any subsequent motion for a continuance by the State, for the want of a witness, the motion, in addition to the requisites in the preceding Article, must show:

1. The facts which the applicant expects to establish by the witness, and it must appear to the court that they are material;

2. That the applicant expects to be able to procure the attendance of the witness at the next term of the court; and

3. That the testimony cannot be procured from any other source during the present term of the court.

Art. 29.06. First Motion by Defendant.

In the first motion by the defendant for a continuance, it shall be necessary, if the same be on account of the absence of a witness, to state:

1. The name of the witness and his residence, if known, or that his residence is not known.

2. The diligence which has been used to procure his attendance; and it shall not be considered sufficient diligence to have caused to be issued, or to have applied for, a subpoena, in cases where the law authorized an attachment to issue.

3. The facts which are expected to be proved by the witness, and it must appear to the court that they are material.

4. That the witness is not absent by the procurement or consent of the defendant.

5. That the motion is not made for delay.

6. That there is no reasonable expectation that attendance of the witness can be secured during the present term of court by a postponement of the trial to some future day of said term. The truth of the first, or any subsequent motion, as well as the merit of the ground set forth therein and its sufficiency shall be addressed to the sound discretion

of the court called to pass upon the same, and shall not be granted as a matter of right. If a motion for continuance be overruled, and the defendant convicted, if it appear upon the trial that the evidence of the witness or witnesses named in the motion was of a material character, and that the facts set forth in said motion were probably true, a new trial should be granted, and the cause continued or postponed to a future day of the same term.

Art. 29.07. Subsequent Motion by Defendant.

Subsequent motions for continuance on the part of the defendant shall, in addition to the requisites in the preceding Article, state also:

1. That the testimony cannot be procured from any other source known to the defendant; and
2. That the defendant has reasonable expectation of procuring the same at the next term of the court.

Art. 29.08. Motion Sworn To.

All motions for continuance must be sworn to by a person having personal knowledge of the facts relied on for the continuance.

Art. 29.09. Controverting Motion.

Any material fact stated, affecting diligence, in a motion for a continuance, may be denied in writing by the adverse party. The denial shall be supported by the oath of some credible person, and filed as soon as practicable after the filing of such motion.

Art. 29.10. When Denial Is Filed.

When such denial is filed, the issue shall be tried by the judge; and he shall hear testimony by affidavits, and grant or refuse continuance, according to the law and facts of the case.

Art. 29.11. Argument.

No argument shall be heard on a motion for a continuance, unless requested by the judge; and when argument is heard, the applicant shall have the right to open and conclude it.

Art. 29.12. Bail Resulting from Continuance.

If a defendant in a capital case demand a trial, and it appears that more than one continuance has been granted to the State, and that the defendant has not before applied for a continuance, he shall be entitled to be admitted to bail, unless it be made to appear to the satisfaction of the court that a material witness of the State had been prevented from attendance by the procurement of the defendant or some person acting in his behalf.

Art. 29.13. Continuance After Trial Is Begun.

A continuance or postponement may be granted on the motion of the State or defendant after the trial has begun, when it is made to appear to the satisfaction of the court that by some unexpected occurrence since the trial began, which no reasonable diligence could have anticipated, the applicant is so taken by surprise that a fair trial cannot be had.

Art. 29.14. Consideration of Impact on Certain Victims.

(a) In this article, "victim" means the victim of an assault or sexual assault who is younger than 17 years of age or whose case involves family violence as defined by Section 71.004, Family Code.

(b) On request by the attorney representing the state, a court that considers a motion for continuance on the part of the defendant shall also consider the impact of the continuance on the victim. On request by the attorney representing the state or by counsel for the defendant, the court shall state on the record the reason for granting or denying the continuance.

CHAPTER 30 DISQUALIFICATION OF THE JUDGE

Art. 30.01. Causes Which Disqualify.

No judge or justice of the peace shall sit in any case where he may be the party injured, or where he has been of counsel for the State or the accused, or where the accused or the party injured may be connected with him by consanguinity or affinity within the third degree, as determined under Chapter 573, Government Code.

Art. 30.02. District Judge Disqualified.

Whenever any case is pending in which the district judge or criminal district judge is disqualified from trying the case, no change of venue shall be made necessary thereby; but the judge presiding shall certify that fact to the presiding judge of the administrative judicial district in which the case is pending and the presiding judge of such administrative judicial district shall assign a judge to try such case in accordance with the provisions of Article 200a, V.A.C.S.

Art. 30.03. County Judge Disqualified, Absent, or Disabled [Repealed].

Repealed by Acts 1999, 76th Leg., ch. 1388 (H.B. 1606), § 14, effective September 1, 1999.

Art. 30.04. Special Judge to Take Oath [Repealed].

Repealed by Acts 1999, 76th Leg., ch. 1388 (H.B. 1606), § 14, effective September 1, 1999.

Art. 30.05. Record Made by Clerk [Repealed].

Repealed by Acts 1999, 76th Leg., ch. 1388 (H.B. 1606), § 14, effective September 1, 1999.

Art. 30.06. Compensation [Repealed].

Repealed by Acts 1999, 76th Leg., ch. 1388 (H.B. 1606), § 14, effective September 1, 1999.

Art. 30.07. Justice Disqualified.

If a justice of the peace be disqualified from sitting in any criminal action pending before him, he shall transfer the same to any justice of the peace in the county who is not disqualified to try the case.

Sec. 30.08. Adoption of Rules.

The commission shall adopt rules which it determines to be necessary to implement and administer the provisions of this chapter, including:

(1) limitations on the number of times during any calendar year a nonprofit entity may be issued a permit under this chapter, which may vary based on the type of entity and other factors the commission determines relevant;

(2) the duration for a permit issued under this chapter which may vary depending on the length of the event for which the permit is being issued; and

(3) penalties for a violation of this code or a rule adopted under this code.

CHAPTER 31
CHANGE OF VENUE

Art. 31.01. On Court's Own Motion.

Whenever in any case of felony or misdemeanor punishable by confinement, the judge presiding shall be satisfied that a trial, alike fair and impartial to the accused and to the State, cannot, from any cause, be had in the county in which the case is pending, he may, upon his own motion, after due notice to accused and the State, and after hearing evidence thereon, order a change of venue to any county in the judicial district in which such county is located or in an adjoining district, stating in his order the grounds for such change of venue. The judge, upon his own motion, after ten days notice to the parties or their counsel, may order a change of venue to any county beyond an adjoining district; provided, however, an order changing venue to a county beyond an adjoining district shall be grounds for reversal if, upon timely contest by the defendant, the record of the contest affirmatively shows that any county in his own and the adjoining district is not subject to the same conditions which required the transfer.

Art. 31.02. State May Have.

Whenever the district or county attorney shall represent in writing to the court before which any felony or misdemeanor case punishable by confinement, is pending, that, by reason of existing combinations or influences in favor of the accused, or on account of the lawless condition of affairs in the county, a fair and impartial trial as between the accused and the State cannot be safely and speedily had; or whenever he shall represent that the life of the prisoner, or of any witness, would be jeopardized by a trial in the county in which the case is pending, the judge shall hear proof in relation thereto, and if satisfied that such representation is well-founded and that the ends of public justice will be subserved thereby, he shall order a change of venue to any county in the judicial district in which such county is located or in an adjoining district.

Art. 31.03. Granted on Motion of Defendant.

(a) A change of venue may be granted in any felony or misdemeanor case punishable by confinement on the written motion of the defendant, supported by his own affidavit and the affidavit of at least two credible persons, residents of the county where the prosecution is instituted, for either of the following causes, the truth and sufficiency of which the court shall determine:

1. That there exists in the county where the prosecution is commenced so great a prejudice against him that he cannot obtain a fair and impartial trial; and

2. That there is a dangerous combination against him instigated by influential persons, by reason of which he cannot expect a fair trial.

An order changing venue to a county beyond an adjoining district shall be grounds for reversal, if upon timely contest by defendant, the record of the contest affirmatively shows that any county in his own and the adjoining district is not subject to the same conditions which required the transfer.

(b) For the convenience of parties and witnesses, and in the interest of justice, the court upon motion of the defendant and with the consent of the attorney for the state may transfer the proceeding as to him to another district.

(c) The court upon motion of the defendant and with the consent of the attorney for the state may transfer the proceedings to another district in those cases wherein the defendant stipulates that a plea of guilty will be entered.

Art. 31.04. Motion May Be Controverted.

The credibility of the persons making affidavit for change of venue, or their means of knowledge, may be attacked by the affidavit of a credible person. The issue thus formed shall be tried by the judge, and the motion granted or refused, as the law and facts shall warrant.

Art. 31.05. Clerk's Duties on Change of Venue.

Where an order for a change of venue of any court in any criminal cause in this State has been made the clerk of the court where the prosecution is pending shall make out a certified copy of the court's order directing such change of venue, together with a certified copy of the defendant's bail bond or personal bond, together with all the original papers in said cause and also a certificate of the said clerk under his official seal that such papers are the papers and all the papers on file in said court in said cause; and he shall transmit the same to the clerk of the court to which the venue has been changed.

Art. 31.06. If Defendant Be in Custody.

When the venue is changed in any criminal action if the defendant be in custody, an order shall be made for his removal to the proper county, and his delivery to the sheriff thereof before the next succeeding term of the court of the county to which the case is to be taken, and he shall be delivered by the sheriff as directed in the order.

Art. 31.07. Witness Need Not Again Be Summoned.

When the venue in a criminal action has been changed, it shall not be necessary to have the witnesses therein again subpoenaed, attached or bailed, but all the witnesses who have been subpoenaed, attached or bailed to appear and testify in the cause shall be held bound to appear before the court to which the cause has been transferred, as if there had been no such transfer.

Art. 31.08. Return to County of Original Venue.

Sec. 1. (a) On the completion of a trial in which a change of venue has been ordered and after the jury has been discharged, the court, with the consent of counsel for the state and the defendant, may return the cause to the original county in which the indictment or information was filed. Except as provided by Subsection (b) of this section, all subsequent and ancillary proceedings, including the pronouncement of sentence after appeals have been exhausted, must be heard in the county in which the indictment or information was filed.

(b) A motion for new trial alleging jury misconduct must be heard in the county in which the cause was tried. The county in which the indictment or information was filed must pay the costs of the prosecution of the motion for new trial.

Sec. 2. (a) Except as provided by Subsection (b), on an order returning venue to the original county in which the indictment or information was filed, the clerk of the county in which the cause was tried shall:

(1) make a certified copy of the court's order directing the return to the original county;

(2) make a certified copy of the defendant's bail bond, personal bond, or appeal bond;

(3) gather all the original papers in the cause and certify under official seal that the papers are all the original papers on file in the court; and

(4) transmit the items listed in this section to the clerk of the court of original venue.

(b) This article does not apply to a proceeding in which the clerk of the court of original venue was present and performed the duties as clerk for the court under Article 31.09.

Sec. 3. Except for the review of a death sentence under Section 2(h), Article 37.071, or under Section 2(h), Article 37.072, an appeal taken in a cause returned to the original county under this article must be docketed in the appellate district in which the county of original venue is located.

Art. 31.09. Change of Venue; Use of Existing Services.

(a) If a change of venue in a criminal case is ordered under this chapter, the judge ordering the change of venue may, with the written consent of the prosecuting attorney, the defense attorney, and the defendant, maintain the original case number on its own docket, preside over the case, and use the services of the court reporter, the court coordinator, and the clerk of the court of original venue. The court shall use the courtroom facilities and any other services or facilities of the district or county to which venue is changed. A jury, if required, must consist of residents of the district or county to which venue is changed.

(b) Notwithstanding Article 31.05, the clerk of the court of original venue shall:

(1) maintain the original papers of the case, including the defendant's bail bond or personal bond;

(2) make the papers available for trial; and

(3) act as the clerk in the case.

TRIAL AND ITS INCIDENTS

CHAPTER 32
DISMISSING PROSECUTIONS

Art. 32.01. Defendant in Custody and No Indictment Presented.

(a) When a defendant has been detained in custody or held to bail for the defendant's appearance to answer any criminal accusation, the prosecution, unless otherwise ordered by the court, for good cause shown, supported by affidavit, shall be dismissed and the bail discharged, if indictment or information be not presented against the defendant on or before the last day of the next term of the court which is held after the defendant's commitment or admission to bail or on or before the 180th day after the date of commitment or admission to bail, whichever date is later.

(b) A surety may file a motion under Subsection (a) for the purpose of discharging the defendant's bail only.

Art. 32.02. Dismissal by State's Attorney.

The attorney representing the State may, by permission of the court, dismiss a criminal action at any time upon filing a written statement with the papers in the case setting out his reasons for such dismissal, which shall be incorporated in the judgment of dismissal. No case shall be dismissed without the consent of the presiding judge.

CHAPTER 32A
SPEEDY TRIAL

Art. 32A.01. Trial Priorities.

(a) Insofar as is practicable, the trial of a criminal action shall be given preference over trials of civil cases, and the trial of a criminal action against a defendant who is detained in jail pending trial of the action shall be given preference over trials of other criminal actions not described by Subsection (b) or (c).

(b) Unless extraordinary circumstances require otherwise, the trial of a criminal action in which the alleged victim is younger than 14 years of age shall be given preference over other matters before the court, whether civil or criminal.

(c) Except as provided by Subsection (b), the trial of a criminal action against a defendant who has been determined to be restored to competency under Article 46B.084 shall be given preference over other matters before the court, whether civil or criminal.

Art. 32A.02. Time Limitations [Repealed].

Repealed by Acts 2005, 79th Leg., ch. 1019 (H.B. 969), § 2, effective June 18, 2005.

CHAPTER 33
THE MODE OF TRIAL

Art. 33.01. Jury Size.

(a) Except as provided by Subsection (b), in the district court, the jury shall consist of twelve qualified jurors. In the county court and inferior courts, the jury shall consist of six qualified jurors.

(b) In a trial involving a misdemeanor offense, a district court jury shall consist of six qualified jurors.

Art. 33.011. Alternate Jurors.

(a) In district courts, the judge may direct that not more than four jurors in addition to the regular jury be called and impaneled to sit as alternate jurors. In county courts, the judge may direct that not more than two jurors in addition to the regular jury be called and impaneled to sit as alternate jurors.

(b) Alternate jurors in the order in which they are called shall replace jurors who, prior to the time the jury renders a verdict on the guilt or innocence of the defendant and, if applicable, the amount of punishment, become or are found to be unable or disqualified to perform their duties or are found by the court on agreement of the parties to have good cause for not performing their duties. Alternate jurors shall be drawn and selected in the same manner, shall have the same qualifications, shall be subject to the same examination and challenges, shall take the same oath, and shall have the same functions, powers, facilities, security, and privileges as regular jurors. An alternate juror who does not replace a regular juror shall be discharged after the jury has rendered a verdict on the guilt or innocence of the defendant and, if applicable, the amount of punishment.

Art. 33.02. Failure to Register.

Failure to register to vote shall not disqualify any person from jury service.

Art. 33.03. Presence of Defendant.

In all prosecutions for felonies, the defendant must be personally present at the trial, and he must likewise be present in all cases of misdemeanor when the punishment or any part thereof is imprisonment in jail; provided, however, that in all cases, when the defendant voluntarily absents himself after pleading to the indictment or information, or after the jury has been selected when trial is before a jury, the trial may proceed to its conclusion. When the record in the appellate court shows that the defendant was present at the commencement, or any portion of the trial, it shall be presumed in the absence of all evidence in the record to the contrary that he was present during the whole trial. Provided, however, that the presence of the defendant shall not be required at the hearing on the motion for new trial in any misdemeanor case.

Art. 33.04. May Appear by Counsel.

In other misdemeanor cases, the defendant may, by consent of the State's attorney, appear by counsel, and the trial may proceed without his personal presence.

Art. 33.05. On Bail During Trial.

If the defendant is on bail when the trial commences, such bail shall be considered as discharged if he is acquitted. If a verdict of guilty is returned against him, the discharge of his bail shall be governed by other provisions of this Code.

Art. 33.06. Sureties Bound in Case of Mistrial.

If there be a mistrial in a felony case, the original sureties, if any, of the defendant shall be still held bound for his appearance until they surrender him in accordance with the provisions of this Code.

Art. 33.07. Record of Criminal Actions.

Each clerk of a court of record having criminal jurisdiction shall keep a record in which shall be set down the style and file number of each criminal action, the nature of the offense, the names of counsel, the proceedings had therein, and the date of each proceeding.

Art. 33.08. To Fix Day for Criminal Docket.

The district courts and county courts shall have control of their respective dockets as to the settings of criminal cases.

Art. 33.09. Jury Drawn.

Jury panels, including special venires, for the trial of criminal cases shall be selected and summoned (with return on summons) in the same manner as the selection of panels for the trial of civil cases except as otherwise provided in this Code.

CHAPTER 34
SPECIAL VENIRE IN CAPITAL CASES

Art. 34.01. Special Venire.

A "special venire" is a writ issued in a capital case by order of the district court, commanding the sheriff to summon either verbally or by mail such a number of persons, not less than 50, as the court may order, to appear before the court on a day named in the writ from whom the jury for the trial of such case is to be selected. Where as many as one hundred jurors have been summoned in such county for regular service for the week in which such capital case is set for trial, the judge of the court having jurisdiction of a capital case in which a motion for a special venire has been made, shall grant or refuse such motion for a special venire, and upon such refusal require the case to be tried by regular jurors summoned for service in such county for the week in which such capital case is set for trial and such additional talesmen as may be summoned by the sheriff upon order of the court as provided in Article 34.02 of this Code, but the clerk of such court shall furnish the defendant or his counsel a list of the persons summoned as provided in Article 34.04.

Art. 34.02. Additional Names Drawn.

In any criminal case in which the court deems that the veniremen theretofore drawn will be insufficient for the trial of the case, or in any criminal case in which the venire has been exhausted by challenge or otherwise, the court shall order additional veniremen in such numbers as the court may deem advisable, to be summoned as follows:

(a) In a jury wheel county, the names of those to be summoned shall be drawn from the jury wheel.

(b) In counties not using the jury wheel, the veniremen shall be summoned by the sheriff.

Art. 34.03. Instructions to Sheriff.

When the sheriff is ordered by the court to summon persons upon a special venire whose names have not been selected under the Jury Wheel Law, the court shall, in every case, caution and direct the sheriff to summon such persons as have legal qualifications to serve on juries, informing him of what those qualifications are, and shall direct him, as far as he may be able to summon persons of good character who can read and write, and such as are not prejudiced against the defendant or biased in his favor, if he knows of such bias or prejudice.

Art. 34.04. Notice of List.

No defendant in a capital case in which the state seeks the death penalty shall be brought to trial until he shall have had at least two days (including holidays) a copy of the names of the persons summoned as veniremen, for the week for which his case is set for trial except where he waives the right or is on bail. When such defendant is on bail, the clerk of the court in which the case is pending shall furnish such a list to the defendant or his counsel at least two days prior to the trial (including holidays) upon timely motion by the defendant or his counsel therefor at the office of such clerk, and the defendant shall not be brought to trial until such list has been furnished defendant or his counsel for at least two days (including holidays). Where the venire is exhausted, by challenges or otherwise, and additional names are drawn, the defendant shall not be entitled to two days service of the names additionally drawn, but the clerk shall compile a list of such names promptly after they are drawn and if the defendant is not on bail, the sheriff shall serve a copy of such list promptly upon the defendant, and if on bail, the clerk shall furnish a copy of such list to the defendant or his counsel upon request, but the proceedings shall not be delayed thereby.

Art. 34.05. Mechanical or Electronic Selection Method.

A mechanical or electronic method of jury selection as provided by Chapter 62, Government Code, may be used under this chapter.

CHAPTER 35
FORMATION OF THE JURY

Art. 35.01. Jurors Called.

When a case is called for trial and the parties have announced ready for trial, the names of those summoned as jurors in the case shall be called. Those not present may be fined not less than $100 nor more than $500. An attachment may issue on request of either party for any absent summoned juror, to have him brought forthwith before the court. A person who is summoned but not present, may upon an appearance, before the jury is qualified, be tried as to his qualifications and impaneled as a juror unless challenged, but no cause shall be unreasonably delayed on account of his absence.

Art. 35.02. Sworn to Answer Questions.

To those present the court shall cause to be administered this oath: "You, and each of you, solemnly swear that you will make true answers to such questions as may be propounded to you by the court, or under its directions, touching your service and qualifications as a juror, so help you God."

Art. 35.03. Excuses.

Sec. 1. Except as provided by Sections 2 and 3 of this article, the court shall then hear and determine excuses offered for not serving as a juror, including any claim of an exemption or a lack of qualification, and if the court considers the excuse sufficient, the court shall discharge the prospective juror or postpone the prospective juror's service to a date specified by the court, as appropriate.

Sec. 2. Under a plan approved by the commissioners court of the county in the same manner as a plan is approved for jury selection under

Section 62.011, Government Code, in a case other than a capital felony case, the court's designee may hear and determine an excuse offered for not serving as a juror, including any claim of an exemption or a lack of qualification. The court's designee may discharge the prospective juror or postpone the prospective juror's service to a date specified by the court's designee, as appropriate, if:

(1) the court's designee considers the excuse sufficient; and

(2) the juror submits to the court's designee a statement of the ground of the exemption or lack of qualification or other excuse.

Sec. 3. A court or a court's designee may discharge a juror or postpone the juror's service on the basis of the juror's observation of a religious holy day or religious beliefs only if the juror provides an affidavit as required by Article 29.012(c) of this code.

Art. 35.04. Claiming Exemption.

Any person summoned as a juror who is exempt by law from jury service may establish his exemption without appearing in person by filing a signed statement of the ground of his exemption with the clerk of the court at any time before the date upon which he is summoned to appear.

Art. 35.05. Excused by Consent.

One summoned upon a special venire may by consent of both parties be excused from attendance by the court at any time before he is impaneled.

Art. 35.06. Challenge to Array First Heard.

The court shall hear and determine a challenge to the array before interrogating those summoned as to their qualifications.

Art. 35.07. Challenge to the Array.

Each party may challenge the array only on the ground that the officer summoning the jury has wilfully summoned jurors with a view to securing a conviction or an acquittal. All such challenges must be in writing setting forth distinctly the grounds of such challenge. When made by the defendant, it must be supported by his affidavit or the affidavit of any credible person. When such challenge is made, the judge shall hear evidence and decide without delay whether or not the challenge shall be sustained.

Art. 35.08. When Challenge Is Sustained.

The array of jurors summoned shall be discharged if the challenge be sustained, and the court shall order other jurors to be summoned in their stead, and direct that the officer who summoned those so discharged, and on account of whose misconduct the challenge has been sustained shall not summon any other jurors in the case.

Art. 35.09. List of New Venire.

When a challenge to the array has been sustained, the defendant shall be entitled, as in the first instance, to service of a copy of the list of names of those summoned by order of the court.

Art. 35.10. Court to Try Qualifications.

When no challenge to the array has been made, or if made, has been over-ruled, the court shall proceed to try the qualifications of those present who have been summoned to serve as jurors.

Art. 35.11. Preparation of List.

The trial judge, on the demand of the defendant or his attorney, or of the State's counsel, shall cause a sufficient number of jurors from which a jury may be selected to try the case to be randomly selected from the members of the general panel drawn or assigned as jurors in the case. The clerk shall randomly select the jurors by a computer or other process of random selection and shall write or print the names, in the order selected, on the jury list from which the jury is to be selected to try the case. The clerk shall deliver a copy of the list to the State's counsel and to the defendant or his attorney.

Art. 35.12. Mode of Testing.

(a) In testing the qualification of a prospective juror after the juror has been sworn, the juror shall be asked by the court, or under its direction:

1. Except for failure to register, are you a qualified voter in this county and state under the Constitution and laws of this state?

2. Have you ever been convicted of theft or any felony?

3. Are you under indictment or legal accusation for theft or any felony?

(b) In testing the qualifications of a prospective juror, with respect to whether the juror has been the subject of an order of nondisclosure or has a criminal history that includes information subject

Code of Criminal Procedure

to that order, the juror may state only that the matter in question has been sealed.

Art. 35.13. Passing Juror for Challenge.

A juror in a capital case in which the state has made it known it will seek the death penalty, held to be qualified, shall be passed for acceptance or challenge first to the state and then to the defendant. Challenges to jurors are either peremptory or for cause.

Art. 35.14. A Peremptory Challenge.

A peremptory challenge is made to a juror without assigning any reason therefor.

Art. 35.15. Number of Challenges.

(a) In capital cases in which the State seeks the death penalty both the State and defendant shall be entitled to fifteen peremptory challenges. Where two or more defendants are tried together, the State shall be entitled to eight peremptory challenges for each defendant; and each defendant shall be entitled to eight peremptory challenges.

(b) In non-capital felony cases and in capital cases in which the State does not seek the death penalty, the State and defendant shall each be entitled to ten peremptory challenges. If two or more defendants are tried together each defendant shall be entitled to six peremptory challenges and the State to six for each defendant.

(c) The State and the defendant shall each be entitled to five peremptory challenges in a misdemeanor tried in the district court and to three in the county court, or county court at law. If two or more defendants are tried together, each defendant shall be entitled to three such challenges and the State to three for each defendant in either court.

(d) The State and the defendant shall each be entitled to one peremptory challenge in addition to those otherwise allowed by law if one or two alternate jurors are to be impaneled and two peremptory challenges if three or four alternate jurors are to be impaneled. The additional peremptory challenges provided by this subsection may be used against an alternate juror only, and the other peremptory challenges allowed by law may not be used against an alternate juror.

Art. 35.16. Reasons for Challenge for Cause.

(a) A challenge for cause is an objection made to a particular juror, alleging some fact which renders the juror incapable or unfit to serve on the jury. A challenge for cause may be made by either the state or the defense for any one of the following reasons:

1. That the juror is not a qualified voter in the state and county under the Constitution and laws of the state; provided, however, the failure to register to vote shall not be a disqualification;

2. That the juror has been convicted of misdemeanor theft or a felony;

3. That the juror is under indictment or other legal accusation for misdemeanor theft or a felony;

4. That the juror is insane;

5. That the juror has such defect in the organs of feeling or hearing, or such bodily or mental defect or disease as to render the juror unfit for jury service, or that the juror is legally blind and the court in its discretion is not satisfied that the juror is fit for jury service in that particular case;

6. That the juror is a witness in the case;

7. That the juror served on the grand jury which found the indictment;

8. That the juror served on a petit jury in a former trial of the same case;

9. That the juror has a bias or prejudice in favor of or against the defendant;

10. That from hearsay, or otherwise, there is established in the mind of the juror such a conclusion as to the guilt or innocence of the defendant as would influence the juror in finding a verdict. To ascertain whether this cause of challenge exists, the juror shall first be asked whether, in the juror's opinion, the conclusion so established will influence the juror's verdict. If the juror answers in the affirmative, the juror shall be discharged without further interrogation by either party or the court. If the juror answers in the negative, the juror shall be further examined as to how the juror's conclusion was formed, and the extent to which it will affect the juror's action; and, if it appears to have been formed from reading newspaper accounts, communications, statements or reports or mere rumor or hearsay, and if the juror states that the juror feels able, notwithstanding such opinion, to render an impartial verdict upon the law and the evidence, the court, if satisfied that the juror is impartial and will render such verdict, may, in its discretion, admit the juror as competent to serve in such case. If the court, in its discretion, is not satisfied that the juror is impartial, the juror shall be discharged;

11. That the juror cannot read or write.

No juror shall be impaneled when it appears that the juror is subject to the second, third or fourth grounds of challenge for cause set forth above, although both parties may consent. All other grounds for challenge may be waived by the party or parties in whose favor such grounds of challenge exist.

In this subsection "legally blind" shall mean having not more than 20/200 of visual acuity in the better eye with correcting lenses, or visual acuity greater than 20/200 but with a limitation in the field of vision such that the widest diameter of the visual field subtends an angle no greater than 20 degrees.

(b) A challenge for cause may be made by the State for any of the following reasons:

1. That the juror has conscientious scruples in regard to the infliction of the punishment of death for crime, in a capital case, where the State is seeking the death penalty;

2. That he is related within the third degree of consanguinity or affinity, as determined under Chapter 573, Government Code, to the defendant; and

3. That he has a bias or prejudice against any phase of the law upon which the State is entitled to rely for conviction or punishment.

(c) A challenge for cause may be made by the defense for any of the following reasons:

1. That he is related within the third degree of consanguinity or affinity, as determined under Chapter 573, Government Code, to the person injured by the commission of the offense, or to any prosecutor in the case; and

2. That he has a bias or prejudice against any of the law applicable to the case upon which the defense is entitled to rely, either as a defense to some phase of the offense for which the defendant is being prosecuted or as a mitigation thereof or of the punishment therefor.

Art. 35.17. Voir Dire Examination.

1. When the court in its discretion so directs, except as provided in Section 2, the state and defendant shall conduct the voir dire examination of prospective jurors in the presence of the entire panel.

2. In a capital felony case in which the State seeks the death penalty, the court shall propound to the entire panel of prospective jurors questions concerning the principles, as applicable to the case on trial, of reasonable doubt, burden of proof, return of indictment by grand jury, presumption of innocence, and opinion. Then, on demand of the State or defendant, either is entitled to examine each juror on voir dire individually and apart from the entire panel, and may further question the juror on the principles propounded by the court.

Art. 35.18. Other Evidence on Challenge.

Upon a challenge for cause, the examination is not confined to the answers of the juror, but other evidence may be heard for or against the challenge.

Art. 35.19. Absolute Disqualification.

No juror shall be impaneled when it appears that he is subject to the second, third or fourth cause of challenge in Article 35.16, though both parties may consent.

Art. 35.20. Names Called in Order.

In selecting the jury from the persons summoned, the names of such persons shall be called in the order in which they appear upon the list furnished the defendant. Each juror shall be tried and passed upon separately. A person who has been summoned, but who is not present, may, upon his appearance before the jury is completed, be tried as to his qualifications and impaneled as a juror, unless challenged, but no cause shall be unreasonably delayed on account of such absence.

Art. 35.21. Judge to Decide Qualifications.

The court is the judge, after proper examination, of the qualifications of a juror, and shall decide all challenges without delay and without argument thereupon.

Art. 35.22. Oath to Jury.

When the jury has been selected, the following oath shall be administered them by the court or under its direction: "You and each of you do solemnly swear that in the case of the State of Texas against the defendant, you will a true verdict render according to the law and the evidence, so help you God".

Art. 35.23. Jurors May Separate.

The court may adjourn veniremen to any day of the term. When jurors have been sworn in a felony case, the court may, at its discretion, permit the jurors to separate until the court has given its charge to the jury. The court on its own motion may and on the motion of either party shall, after having given its charge to the jury, order that the jury not be allowed to separate, after which the jury shall be kept together, and not permitted to separate except to the extent of housing female jurors separate and apart from male jurors, until a verdict has been rendered or the jury finally discharged. Any person who makes known to the jury which party made the motion not to allow separation of the jury shall be punished for contempt of court. If such jurors are kept overnight, facilities shall be provided for female jurors separate and apart from the facilities provided for male jurors. In misdemeanor cases the court may, at its discretion, permit the jurors to separate at any time before the verdict. In any case in which the jury is permitted to separate, the court shall first give the jurors proper instructions with regard to their conduct as jurors when so separated.

Art. 35.24. Special Pay for Veniremen [Repealed].

Repealed by Acts 1975, 64th Leg., ch. 510 (H.B. 671), § 2, effective September 1, 1975.

Art. 35.25. Making Peremptory Challenge.

In non-capital cases and in capital cases in which the State's attorney has announced that he will not qualify the jury for, or seek the death penalty, the party desiring to challenge any juror peremptorily shall strike the name of such juror from the list furnished him by the clerk.

Art. 35.26. Lists Returned to Clerk.

(a) When the parties have made or declined to make their peremptory challenges, they shall deliver their lists to the clerk. Except as provided in Subsection (b) of this section, the clerk shall, if the case be in the district court, call off the first twelve names on the lists that have not been stricken. If the case be in the county court, he shall call off the first six names on the lists that have not been stricken. Those whose names are called shall be the jury.

(b) In a capital case in which the state seeks the death penalty, the court may direct that two alternate jurors be selected and that the first fourteen names not stricken be called off by the clerk. The last two names to be called are the alternate jurors.

Art. 35.261. Peremptory Challenges Based on Race Prohibited.

(a) After the parties have delivered their lists to the clerk under Article 35.26 of this code and before the court has impanelled the jury, the defendant may request the court to dismiss the array and call a new array in the case. The court shall grant the motion of a defendant for dismissal of the array if the court determines that the defendant is a member of an identifiable racial group, that the attorney representing the state exercised peremptory challenges for the purpose of excluding persons from the jury on the basis of their race, and that the defendant has offered evidence of relevant facts that tend to show that challenges made by the attorney representing the state were made for reasons based on race. If the defendant establishes a prima facie case, the burden then shifts to the attorney representing the state to give a racially neutral explanation for the challenges. The burden of persuasion remains with the defendant to establish purposeful discrimination.

(b) If the court determines that the attorney representing the state challenged prospective jurors on the basis of race, the court shall call a new array in the case.

Art. 35.27. Reimbursement of Nonresident Witnesses.

Sec. 1. **Expenses for Nonresident Witnesses.**

(a) Every person subpoenaed by either party or otherwise required or requested in writing by the prosecuting attorney or the court to appear for the purpose of giving testimony in a criminal proceeding who resides outside the state or the county in which the prosecution is pending shall be reimbursed by the state for the reasonable and necessary transportation, meal, and lodging expenses he incurs by reason of his attendance as a witness at such proceeding.

(b) The state may reimburse a witness for transportation only if the transportation is provided by a commercial transportation company or the witness uses the witness's personally owned or leased motor vehicle. In this article, "commercial transportation company" means an entity that offers transportation of people or goods to the public in exchange for compensation.

(c) The state may reimburse a witness for lodging only if the lodging is provided by a commercial lodging establishment. In this article, "commercial lodging establishment" means a motel, hotel, inn, apartment, or similar entity that offers lodging to the public in exchange for compensation.

Sec. 2. **Amount of Reimbursement for Expenses. —** Any person seeking reimbursement as a witness shall make an affidavit setting out the transportation, meal, and lodging expenses necessitated by his travel to and from and attendance at the place he appeared to give testimony, together with the number of days that such travel and attendance made him absent from his place of residence. A reimbursement paid by the state to a witness for transportation, meal, or lodging expenses may not be paid at a rate that exceeds the maximum rates provided by law for state employees.

Sec. 2A. **Direct Payment of Transportation or Lodging Expenses. —** If this article requires the state to reimburse a witness for transportation or lodging expenses, the state may instead directly pay a commercial transportation company or commercial lodging establishment for those expenses.

Sec. 3. **Other Expenses. —** In addition to reimbursement or payment for transportation, meal, and lodging expenses, the comptroller, upon proper application by the attorney for the state, shall reimburse or pay the other expenses required by the laws of this state or the state from which the attendance of the witness is sought.

Sec. 4. **Application and Approval by Judge. —** A reimbursement to a witness as provided by this article shall be paid by the state to the witness or his assignee. Claim shall be made by sworn application to the comptroller, a copy of which shall be filed with the clerk of the court, setting out the facts showing entitlement as provided in this article to the reimbursement, which application shall be presented for approval by the judge who presided over the court or empaneled the grand jury before whom the criminal proceeding was pending. No fee shall be required of any witness for the processing of his claim for reimbursement.

Sec. 5. **Payment by State. —** The Comptroller of Public Accounts, upon receipt of a claim approved by the judge, shall examine it and, if he deems the claim in compliance with and authorized by this Article, draw his warrant on the State Treasury for the amount due the witness, or to any person to which the certificate has been assigned by the witness, but no warrant may issue to any assignee of a witness claim unless the assignment is made under oath and acknowledged before some person authorized to administer oaths, certified to by the officer, and under seal. If the appropriation for paying the account is exhausted, the Comptroller of Public Accounts shall file it away and issue a certificate in the name of the witness entitled to it, stating therein the amount of the claim. Each claim not filed in the office of the Comptroller of Public Accounts within twelve months from the date it became due and payable shall be forever barred.

Sec. 6. **Advance by State. —** Funds required to be tendered to an out-of-state witness pursuant to Article 24.28 of this Code shall be paid by the Comptroller of Public Accounts into the registry of the Court in which the case is to be tried upon certification by the Court such funds are necessary to obtain attendance of said witness. The court shall then cause to be issued checks drawn upon the registry of the Court to secure the attendance of such witness. In the event that such funds are not used pursuant to this Act, the Court shall return the funds to the Comptroller of Public Accounts.

Sec. 7. **Advance by County. —** The county in which a criminal proceeding is pending, upon request of the district attorney or other prosecutor charged with the duty of prosecution in the proceeding, may advance funds from its treasury to any witness who will be entitled to reimbursement under this article. The amount advanced may not exceed the amount that is reasonably necessary to enable the witness to attend as required or requested. However, the amount advanced may include sums in excess of the reimbursement provided for by this article if the excess is required for compliance with Section 4 of Article 24.28 in securing the attendance of a witness from another state under the Uniform Act. A county that advances funds to a witness under this section is entitled to reimbursement by the state as an assignee of the witness.

Sec. 8. **Advance for Expenses for Witnesses of Indigent Defendant. —** Upon application by a defendant shown to be indigent and a showing to the court of reasonable necessity and materiality for the testimony of a witness residing outside the State, the court shall act pursuant to Section 6 hereof to secure advance of funds necessary for the attendance of such witness.

Sec. 9. **Limitations. —** A witness, when attached and conveyed by a sheriff or other officer, is not eligible to receive reimbursement of transportation, meal, or lodging expenses incurred while in the custody of the officer. A court, in its discretion, may limit the number of character witnesses allowed reimbursement under this article to not fewer than two for each defendant and two per defendant for the state.

Art. 35.28. When No Clerk.

In each instance in Article 35.27 in which the clerk of the court is authorized or directed to perform any act, the judge of such court shall perform the same if there is no clerk of the court.

Art. 35.29. Personal Information About Jurors.

(a) Except as provided by Subsections (b) and (c), information collected by the court or by a prosecuting attorney during the jury selection process about a person who serves as a juror, including the juror's home address, home telephone number, social security number, driver's license number, and other personal information, is confidential and may not be disclosed by the court, the prosecuting attorney, the defense counsel, or any court personnel.

(b) On application by a party in the trial, or on application by a bona fide member of the news media acting in such capacity, to the court for the disclosure of information described by Subsection (a), the court shall, on a showing of good cause, permit disclosure of the information sought.

(c) The defense counsel may disclose information described by Subsection (a) to successor counsel representing the same defendant in a proceeding under Article 11.071 without application to the court or a showing of good cause.

CHAPTER 36
THE TRIAL BEFORE THE JURY

Art. 36.01. Order of Proceeding in Trial.

(a) A jury being impaneled in any criminal action, except as provided by Subsection (b) of this article, the cause shall proceed in the following order:

1. The indictment or information shall be read to the jury by the attorney prosecuting. When prior convictions are alleged for purposes of enhancement only and are not jurisdictional, that portion of the indictment or information reciting such convictions shall not be read until the hearing on punishment is held as provided in Article 37.07.
2. The special pleas, if any, shall be read by the defendant's counsel, and if the plea of not guilty is also relied upon, it shall also be stated.
3. The State's attorney shall state to the jury the nature of the accusation and the facts which are expected to be proved by the State in support thereof.
4. The testimony on the part of the State shall be offered.
5. The nature of the defenses relied upon and the facts expected to be proved in their support shall be stated by defendant's counsel.
6. The testimony on the part of the defendant shall be offered.
7. Rebutting testimony may be offered on the part of each party.
8. In the event of a finding of guilty, the trial shall then proceed as set forth in Article 37.07.

(b) The defendant's counsel may make the opening statement for the defendant immediately after the attorney representing the State makes the opening statement for the State. After the defendant's attorney concludes the defendant's opening statement, the State's testimony shall be offered. At the conclusion of the presentation of the State's testimony, the defendant's testimony shall be offered, and the order of proceedings shall continue in the manner described by Subsection (a) of this article.

Art. 36.02. Testimony at Any Time.

The court shall allow testimony to be introduced at any time before the argument of a cause is concluded, if it appears that it is necessary to a due administration of justice.

Art. 36.03. Invocation of Rule.

(a) Notwithstanding Rule 614, Texas Rules of Evidence, a court at the request of a party may order the exclusion of a witness who for the purposes of the prosecution is a victim, close relative of a deceased victim, or guardian of a victim only if the witness is to testify and the court determines that the testimony of the witness would be materially affected if the witness hears other testimony at the trial.

(b) On the objection of the opposing party, the court may require the party requesting exclusion of a witness under Subsection (a) to make an offer of proof to justify the exclusion.

(c) Subsection (a) does not limit the authority of the court on its own motion to exclude a witness or other person to maintain decorum in the courtroom.

(d) In this article:

(1) "Close relative of a deceased victim" and "guardian of a victim" have the meanings assigned by Article 56A.001.

(2) "Victim" means a victim of any criminal offense.

(e) At the commencement of a trial, the court shall admonish each witness who is to testify as to those persons whom the court determines the witness may talk to about the case before the trial ends and those persons whom the witness may not talk to about the case. The court may punish as contempt a witness who violates the admonishment provided by the court.

Art. 36.04. [Repealed].

Repealed by Texas Court of Criminal Appeals pursuant to Acts 1985, 69th Leg., ch. 685 (H.B. 13), § 9, effective September 1, 1986.

Art. 36.05. Not to Hear Testimony.

Witnesses under rule shall be attended by an officer, and all their reasonable wants provided for, unless the court, in its discretion, directs that they be allowed to go at large; but in no case where the witnesses are under rule shall they be allowed to hear any testimony in the case.

Art. 36.06. Instructed by the Court.

Witnesses, when placed under rule, shall be instructed by the court that they are not to converse with each other or with any other person about the case, except by permission of the court, and that they are not to read any report of or comment upon the testimony in the case while under rule. The officer who attends the witnesses shall report to the court at once any violation of its instructions, and the party violating the same shall be punished for contempt of court.

Art. 36.07. Order of Argument.

The order of argument may be regulated by the presiding judge; but the State's counsel shall have the right to make the concluding address to the jury.

Art. 36.08. Number of Arguments.

The court shall never restrict the argument in felony cases to a number of addresses less than two on each side.

Art. 36.09. Severance on Separate Indictments.

Two or more defendants who are jointly or separately indicted or complained against for the same offense or any offense growing out of the same transaction may be, in the discretion of the court, tried jointly or separately as to one or more defendants; provided that in any event either defendant may testify for the other or on behalf of the state; and provided further, that in cases in which, upon timely motion to sever, and evidence introduced thereon, it is made known to the court that there is a previous admissible conviction against one defendant or that a joint trial would be prejudicial to any defendant, the court shall order a severance as to the defendant whose joint trial would prejudice the other defendant or defendants.

Art. 36.10. Order of Trial.

If a severance is granted, the defendants may agree upon the order in which they are to be tried, but if they fail to agree, the court shall direct the order of the trial.

Art. 36.11. Discharge Before Verdict.

If it appears during a trial that the court has no jurisdiction of the offense, or that the facts charged in the indictment do not constitute an offense, the jury shall be discharged. The accused shall also be discharged, but such discharge shall be no bar in any case to a prosecution before the proper court for any offense unless termination of the former prosecution was improper.

Art. 36.12. Court May Commit.

If the want of jurisdiction arises from the fact that the defendant is not liable to prosecution in the county where the indictment was presented, the court may in felony cases order the accused into custody for a reasonable length of time to await a warrant for his arrest from the proper county; or if the offense be bailable, may require him to enter into recognizance to answer before the proper court; in which case a certified copy of the recognizance shall be sent forthwith to the clerk of the proper court, to be enforced by that court in case of forfeiture.

Art. 36.13. Jury Is Judge of Facts.

Unless otherwise provided in this Code, the jury is the exclusive judge of the facts, but it is bound to receive the law from the court and be governed thereby.

Art. 36.14. Charge of Court.

Subject to the provisions of Article 36.07 in each felony case and in each misdemeanor case tried in a court of record, the judge shall, before the argument begins, deliver to the jury, except in pleas of guilty, where a jury has been waived, a written charge distinctly setting forth the law applicable to the case; not expressing any opinion as to the weight of the evidence, not summing up the testimony, discussing the facts or using any argument in his charge calculated to arouse the sympathy or excite the passions of the jury. Before said charge is read to the jury, the defendant or his counsel shall have a reasonable time to examine the same and he shall present his objections thereto in writing, distinctly specifying each ground of objection. Said objections may embody errors claimed to have been committed in the charge, as well as errors claimed to have been committed by omissions therefrom or in failing to charge upon issues arising from the facts, and in no event shall it be necessary for the defendant or his counsel to present special requested charges to preserve or maintain any error assigned to the charge, as herein provided. The requirement that the objections to the court's charge be in writing will be complied with if the objections are dictated to the court reporter in the presence of the court and the state's counsel, before the reading of the court's charge to the jury. Compliance with the provisions of this Article is all that is necessary to preserve, for review, the exceptions and objections presented to the charge and any amendment or modification thereof. In no event shall it be necessary for the defendant to except to the action of the court in over-ruling defendant's exceptions or objections to the charge.

Art. 36.15. Requested Special Charges.

Before the court reads his charge to the jury, counsel on both sides shall have a reasonable time to present written instructions and ask that they be given to the jury. The requirement that the instructions be in writing is complied with if the instructions are dictated to the court reporter in the presence of the court and the state's counsel, before the reading of the court's charge to the jury. The court shall give or refuse these charges. The defendant may, by a special requested instruction, call the trial court's attention to error in the charge, as well as omissions therefrom, and no other exception or objection to the court's charge shall be necessary to preserve any error reflected by any special requested instruction which the trial court refuses.

Any special requested charge which is granted shall be incorporated in the main charge and shall be treated as a part thereof, and the jury shall not be advised that it is a special requested charge of either party. The judge shall read to the jury only such special charges as he gives.

When the defendant has leveled objections to the charge or has requested instructions or both, and the court thereafter modifies his charge and rewrites the same and in so doing does not respond to objections or requested charges, or any of them, then the objections or requested charges shall not be deemed to have been waived by the party making or requesting the same, but shall be deemed to continue to have been urged by the party making or requesting the same unless the contrary is shown by the record; no exception by the defendant to the action of the court shall be necessary or required in order to preserve for review the error claimed in the charge.

Art. 36.16. Final Charge.

After the judge shall have received the objections to his main charge, together with any special charges offered, he may make such changes in his main charge as he may deem proper, and the defendant or his counsel shall have the opportunity to present their objections thereto and in the same manner as is provided in Article 36.15, and thereupon the judge shall read his charge to the jury as finally written, together with any special charges given, and no further exception or objection shall be required of the defendant in order to preserve any objections or exceptions theretofore made. After the argument begins no further charge shall be given to the jury unless required by the improper argument of counsel or the request of the jury, or unless the judge shall, in his discretion, permit the introduction of other testimony, and in the event of such further charge, the defendant or his counsel shall have the right to present objections in the same manner as is prescribed in Article 36.15. The failure of the court to give the defendant or his counsel a reasonable time to examine the charge and specify the ground of objection shall be subject to review either in the trial court or in the appellate court.

Art. 36.17. Charge Certified by Judge.

The general charge given by the court and all special charges given or refused shall be certified by the judge and filed among the papers in the cause.

Art. 36.18. Jury May Take Charge.

The jury may take to their jury room the charges given by the court after the same have been filed. They shall not be permitted to take with them any charge or part thereof which the court has refused to give.

Art. 36.19. Review of Charge on Appeal.

Whenever it appears by the record in any criminal action upon appeal that any requirement of Articles 36.14, 36.15, 36.16, 36.17 and 36.18 has been disregarded, the judgment shall not be reversed unless the error appearing from the record was calculated to injure the rights of defendant, or unless it appears from the record that the defendant has not had a fair and impartial trial. All objections to the charge and to the refusal of special charges shall be made at the time of the trial.

Art. 36.20. [Repealed].

Repealed by Texas Court of Criminal Appeals pursuant to Acts 1985, 69th Leg., ch. 685 (H.B. 13), § 4, effective September 1, 1986.

Art. 36.21. To Provide Jury Room.

The sheriff shall provide a suitable room for the deliberation of the jury and supply them with such necessary food and lodging as he can obtain. No intoxicating liquor shall be furnished them. In all cases wherein a jury consists partly of male jurors and partly of female jurors, the sheriff shall provide facilities for the female jurors separate and apart from the facilities provided for the male jurors.

Art. 36.215. Recording of Jury Deliberations.

A person may not use any device to produce or make an audio, visual, or audio-visual broadcast, recording, or photograph of a jury while the jury is deliberating.

Art. 36.22. Conversing with Jury.

No person shall be permitted to be with a jury while it is deliberating. No person shall be permitted to converse with a juror about the case on trial except in the presence and by the permission of the court.

Art. 36.23. Violation of Preceding Article.

Any juror or other person violating the preceding Article shall be punished for contempt of court by confinement in jail not to exceed three days or by fine not to exceed one hundred dollars, or by both such fine and imprisonment.

Art. 36.24. Officer Shall Attend Jury.

The sheriff of the county shall furnish the court with a bailiff during the trial of any case to attend the wants of the jury and to act under the direction of the court. If the person furnished by the sheriff is to be called as a witness in the case he may not serve as bailiff.

Art. 36.25. Written Evidence.

There shall be furnished to the jury upon its request any exhibits admitted as evidence in the case.

Art. 36.26. Foreman of Jury.

Each jury shall appoint one of its members foreman.

Art. 36.27. Jury May Communicate with Court.

When the jury wishes to communicate with the court, it shall so notify the sheriff, who shall inform the court thereof. Any communication relative to the cause must be written, prepared by the foreman and shall be submitted to the court through the bailiff. The court shall answer any such communication in writing, and before giving such answer to the jury shall use reasonable diligence to secure the presence of the defendant and his counsel, and shall first submit the question and also submit his answer to the same to the defendant or his counsel or objections and exceptions, in the same manner as any other written instructions are submitted to such counsel, before the court gives such answer to the jury, but if he is unable to secure the presence of the defendant and his counsel, then he shall proceed to answer the same as he deems proper. The written instruction or answer to the communication shall be read in open court unless expressly waived by the defendant.

All such proceedings in felony cases shall be a part of the record and recorded by the court reporter.

Art. 36.28. Jury May Have Witness Re-Examined or Testimony Read.

In the trial of a criminal case in a court of record, if the jury disagree as to the statement of any witness they may, upon applying to the court, have read to them from the court reporter's notes that part of such witness testimony or the particular point in dispute, and no other; but if there be no such reporter, or if his notes cannot be read to the jury, the court may cause such witness to be again brought upon the stand and the judge shall direct him to repeat his testimony as to the point in dispute, and no other, as nearly as he can in the language used on the trial.

Art. 36.29. If a Juror Dies or Becomes Disabled.

(a) Not less than twelve jurors can render and return a verdict in a felony case. It must be concurred in by each juror and signed by the foreman. Except as provided in Subsection (b), however, after the trial of any felony case begins and a juror dies or, as determined by the judge, becomes disabled from sitting at any time before the charge of the court is read to the jury, the remainder of the jury shall have the power to render the verdict; but when the verdict shall be rendered by less than the whole number, it shall be signed by every member of the jury concurring in it.

(b) If alternate jurors have been selected in a capital case in which the state seeks the death penalty and a juror dies or becomes disabled from sitting at any time before the charge of the court is read to the jury, the alternate juror whose name was called first under Article 35.26 of this code shall replace the dead or disabled juror. Likewise, if another juror dies or becomes disabled from sitting before the charge of the court is read to the jury, the other alternate juror shall replace the second juror to die or become disabled.

(c) After the charge of the court is read to the jury, if a juror becomes so sick as to prevent the continuance of the juror's duty and an alternate juror is not available, or if any accident of circumstance occurs to prevent the jury from being kept together under circumstances under which the law or the instructions of the court requires that the jury be kept together, the jury shall be discharged, except that on agreement on the record by the defendant, the defendant's counsel, and the attorney representing the state 11 members of a jury may render a verdict and, if punishment is to be assessed by the jury, assess punishment. If a verdict is rendered by less than the whole number of the jury, each member of the jury shall sign the verdict.

(d) After the jury has rendered a verdict on the guilt or innocence of the defendant and, if applicable, the amount of punishment, the court shall discharge an alternate juror who has not replaced a juror.

Art. 36.30. Discharging Jury in Misdemeanor.

If nine of the jury can be kept together in a misdemeanor case in the district court, they shall not be discharged. If more than three of the twelve are discharged, the entire jury shall be discharged.

Art. 36.31. Disagreement of Jury.

After the cause is submitted to the jury, it may be discharged when it cannot agree and both parties consent to its discharge; or the court may in its discretion discharge it where it has been kept together for such time as to render it altogether improbable that it can agree.

Art. 36.32. Receipt of Verdict and Final Adjournment.

During the trial of any case, the term shall be deemed to have been extended until such time as the jury has rendered its verdict or been discharged according to law.

Art. 36.33. Discharge Without Verdict.

When a jury has been discharged, as provided in the four preceding Articles, without having rendered a verdict, the cause may be again tried at the same or another term.

CHAPTER 37
THE VERDICT

Art. 37.01. Verdict.

A "verdict" is a written declaration by a jury of its decision of the issue submitted to it in the case.

Art. 37.02. Verdict by Nine Jurors.

In misdemeanor cases in the district court, where one or more jurors have been discharged from serving after the cause has been submitted to them, if all the alternate jurors selected under Article 33.011 of this code have either been seated or discharged, and there be as many as nine of the jurors remaining, those remaining may render and return a verdict; but in such case, the verdict must be signed by each juror rendering it.

Art. 37.03. In County Court.

In the county court the verdict must be concurred in by each juror.

Art. 37.04. When Jury Has Agreed.

When the jury agrees upon a verdict, it shall be brought into court by the proper officer; and if it states that it has agreed, the verdict shall be read aloud by the judge, the foreman, or the clerk. If in proper form and no juror dissents therefrom, and neither party requests a poll of the jury, the verdict shall be entered upon the minutes of the court.

Art. 37.05. Polling the Jury.

(a) The State and the defendant each have the right to have the jury polled, which is done by calling separately the name or identification number of each juror and asking the juror if the verdict is the juror's. If all jurors, when asked, answer in the affirmative, the verdict shall be entered upon the minutes; but if any juror answers in the negative, the jury shall retire again to consider its verdict.

(b) For the purposes of polling the jury in Subsection (a), the judge may assign each juror an identification number to use in place of the juror's name.

Art. 37.06. Presence of Defendant.

In felony cases the defendant must be present when the verdict is read unless his absence is wilful or voluntary. A verdict in a misdemeanor case may be received and read in the absence of the defendant.

Art. 37.07. Verdict Must Be General; Separate Hearing on Proper Punishment.

Sec. 1. (a) The verdict in every criminal action must be general. When there are special pleas on which a jury is to find they must say in their verdict that the allegations in such pleas are true or untrue.

(b) If the plea is not guilty, they must find that the defendant is either guilty or not guilty, and, except as provided in Section 2, they shall assess the punishment in all cases where the same is not absolutely fixed by law to some particular penalty.

(c) If the charging instrument contains more than one count or if two or more offenses are consolidated for trial pursuant to Chapter 3 of the Penal Code, the jury shall be instructed to return a finding of guilty or not guilty in a separate verdict as to each count and offense submitted to them.

Sec. 2. (a) In all criminal cases, other than misdemeanor cases of which the justice court or municipal court has jurisdiction, which are tried before a jury on a plea of not guilty, the judge shall, before argument begins, first submit to the jury the issue of guilt or innocence of the defendant of the offense or offenses charged, without authorizing the jury to pass upon the punishment to be imposed. If the jury fails to agree on the issue of guilt or innocence, the judge shall declare a mistrial and discharge the jury, and jeopardy does not attach in the case.

(b) Except as provided by Article 37.071 or 37.072, if a finding of guilty is returned, it shall then be the responsibility of the judge to assess the punishment applicable to the offense; provided, however, that (1) in any criminal action where the jury may recommend community supervision and the defendant filed his sworn motion for community supervision before the trial began, and (2) in other cases where the defendant so elects in writing before the commencement of the voir dire examination of the jury panel, the punishment shall be assessed by the same jury, except as provided in Section 3(c) of this article and in Article 44.29. If a finding of guilty is returned, the defendant may, with the consent of the attorney for the state, change his election of one who assesses the punishment.

(c) Punishment shall be assessed on each count on which a finding of guilty has been returned.

Sec. 3. **Evidence of prior criminal record in all criminal cases after a finding of guilty.**

(a) (1) Regardless of the plea and whether the punishment be assessed by the judge or the jury, evidence may be offered by the state and the defendant as to any matter the court deems relevant to sentencing, including but not limited to the prior criminal record of the defendant, his general reputation, his character, an opinion regarding his character, the circumstances of the offense for which he is being tried, and, notwithstanding Rules 404 and 405, Texas Rules of Evidence, any other evidence of an extraneous crime or bad act that is shown beyond a reasonable doubt by evidence to have been committed by the defendant or for which he could be held criminally responsible, regardless of whether he has previously been charged with or finally convicted of the crime or act. A court may consider as a factor in mitigating punishment the conduct of a defendant while participating in a program under Chapter 17 as a condition of release on bail. Additionally, notwithstanding Rule 609(d), Texas Rules of Evidence, and subject to Subsection (h), evidence may be offered by the state and the defendant of an adjudication of delinquency based on a violation by the defendant of a penal law of the grade of:

(A) a felony; or

(B) a misdemeanor punishable by confinement in jail.

(2) Notwithstanding Subdivision (1), evidence may not be offered by the state to establish that the race or ethnicity of the defendant makes it likely that the defendant will engage in future criminal conduct.

(3) Regardless of the plea and whether the punishment is assessed by the judge or the jury, during the punishment phase of the trial of an offense under Section 35A.02, Penal Code, subject to the applicable rules of evidence, the state and the defendant may offer evidence not offered during the guilt or innocence phase of the trial concerning the total pecuniary loss to the affected health care program caused by the defendant's conduct or, if applicable, the scheme or continuing course of conduct of which the defendant's conduct is part. Evidence may be offered in summary form concerning the total pecuniary loss to the affected health care program. Testimony regarding the total pecuniary loss to the affected health care program is subject to cross-examination. Evidence offered under this subdivision may be considered by the judge or jury in ordering or recommending the amount of any restitution to be made to the affected health care program or the appropriate punishment for the defendant.

(b) After the introduction of such evidence has been concluded, and if the jury has the responsibility of assessing the punishment, the court shall give such additional written instructions as may be necessary and the order of procedure and the rules governing the conduct of the trial shall be the same as are applicable on the issue of guilt or innocence.

(c) If the jury finds the defendant guilty and the matter of punishment is referred to the jury, the verdict shall not be complete until a jury verdict has been rendered on both the guilt or innocence of the defendant and the amount of punishment. In the event the jury shall fail to agree on the issue of punishment, a mistrial shall be declared only in the punishment phase of the trial, the jury shall be discharged, and no jeopardy shall attach. The court shall impanel another jury as soon as practicable to determine the issue of punishment.

(d) When the judge assesses the punishment, the judge may order a presentence report as contemplated in Subchapter F, Chapter 42A, and after considering the report, and after the hearing of the evidence hereinabove provided for, the judge shall forthwith announce the judge's decision in open court as to the punishment to be assessed.

(e) Nothing herein contained shall be construed as affecting the admissibility of extraneous offenses on the question of guilt or innocence.

(f) In cases in which the matter of punishment is referred to a jury, either party may offer into evidence the availability of community corrections facilities serving the jurisdiction in which the offense was committed.

(g) On timely request of the defendant, notice of intent to introduce evidence under this article shall be given in the same manner required by Rule 404(b), Texas Rules of Evidence. If the attorney representing the state intends to introduce an extraneous crime or bad act that has not resulted in a final conviction in a court of record or a probated or suspended sentence, notice of that intent is reasonable only if the notice includes the date on which and the county in which the alleged crime or bad act occurred and the name of the alleged victim of the crime or bad act. The requirement under this subsection that the attorney representing the state give notice applies only if the defendant makes a timely request to the attorney representing the state for the notice.

(h) Regardless of whether the punishment will be assessed by the judge or the jury, neither the state nor the defendant may offer before sentencing evidence that the defendant plans to undergo an orchiectomy.

(i) Evidence of an adjudication for conduct that is a violation of a penal law of the grade of misdemeanor punishable by confinement in jail is admissible only if the conduct upon which the adjudication is based occurred on or after January 1, 1996.

Sec. 4. (a) In the penalty phase of the trial of a felony case in which the punishment is to be assessed by the jury rather than the court, if the offense of which the jury has found the defendant guilty is an offense under Section 71.02, Penal Code, other than an offense punishable as a state jail felony under that section, an offense under Section 71.023, Penal Code, or an offense listed in Article 42A.054(a), or if the judgment contains an affirmative finding under Article 42A.054(c) or (d), unless the defendant has been convicted of an offense under Section 21.02, Penal Code, an offense under Section 22.021, Penal Code, that is punishable under Subsection (f) of that section, or a capital felony, the court shall charge the jury in writing as follows:

"The length of time for which a defendant is imprisoned may be reduced by the award of parole.

"Under the law applicable in this case, if the defendant is sentenced to a term of imprisonment, the defendant will not become eligible for parole until the actual time served equals one-half of the sentence imposed or 30 years, whichever is less. If the defendant is sentenced to a term of less than four years, the defendant must serve at least two years before the defendant is eligible for parole. Eligibility for parole does not guarantee that parole will be granted.

"It cannot accurately be predicted how the parole law might be applied to this defendant if sentenced to a term of imprisonment, because the application of that law will depend on decisions made by parole authorities.

"You may consider the existence of the parole law. You are not to consider the manner in which the parole law may be applied to this particular defendant."

(b) In the penalty phase of the trial of a felony case in which the punishment is to be assessed by the jury rather than the court, if the offense is punishable as a felony of the first degree, if a prior conviction has been alleged for enhancement of punishment as provided by Section 12.42(b), (c)(1) or (2), or (d), Penal Code, or if the offense is a felony not designated as a capital felony or a felony of the first, second, or third degree and the maximum term of imprisonment that may be imposed for the offense is longer than 60 years, unless the offense of which the jury has found the defendant guilty is an offense that is punishable under Section 21.02(h), Penal Code, or is listed in Article 42A.054(a) or the judgment contains an affirmative finding under

Article 42A.054(c) or (d), the court shall charge the jury in writing as follows:

"The length of time for which a defendant is imprisoned may be reduced by the award of parole.

"Under the law applicable in this case, the defendant, if sentenced to a term of imprisonment, may earn early parole eligibility through the award of good conduct time. Prison authorities may award good conduct time to a prisoner who exhibits good behavior, diligence in carrying out prison work assignments, and attempts at rehabilitation. If a prisoner engages in misconduct, prison authorities may also take away all or part of any good conduct time earned by the prisoner.

"Under the law applicable in this case, if the defendant is sentenced to a term of imprisonment, the defendant will not become eligible for parole until the actual time served plus any good conduct time earned equals one-fourth of the sentence imposed or 15 years, whichever is less. Eligibility for parole does not guarantee that parole will be granted.

"It cannot accurately be predicted how the parole law and good conduct time might be applied to this defendant if sentenced to a term of imprisonment, because the application of these laws will depend on decisions made by prison and parole authorities.

"You may consider the existence of the parole law and good conduct time. However, you are not to consider the extent to which good conduct time may be awarded to or forfeited by this particular defendant. You are not to consider the manner in which the parole law may be applied to this particular defendant."

(c) In the penalty phase of the trial of a felony case in which the punishment is to be assessed by the jury rather than the court, if the offense is punishable as a felony of the second or third degree, if a prior conviction has been alleged for enhancement as provided by Section 12.42(a), Penal Code, or if the offense is a felony not designated as a capital felony or a felony of the first, second, or third degree and the maximum term of imprisonment that may be imposed for the offense is 60 years or less, unless the offense of which the jury has found the defendant guilty is listed in Article 42A.054(a) or the judgment contains an affirmative finding under Article 42A.054(c) or (d), the court shall charge the jury in writing as follows:

"The length of time for which a defendant is imprisoned may be reduced by the award of parole.

"Under the law applicable in this case, the defendant, if sentenced to a term of imprisonment, may earn early parole eligibility through the award of good conduct time. Prison authorities may award good conduct time to a prisoner who exhibits good behavior, diligence in carrying out prison work assignments, and attempts at rehabilitation. If a prisoner engages in misconduct, prison authorities may also take away all or part of any good conduct time earned by the prisoner.

"Under the law applicable in this case, if the defendant is sentenced to a term of imprisonment, the defendant will not become eligible for parole until the actual time served plus any good conduct time earned equals one-fourth of the sentence imposed. Eligibility for parole does not guarantee that parole will be granted.

"It cannot accurately be predicted how the parole law and good conduct time might be applied to this defendant if sentenced to a term of imprisonment, because the application of these laws will depend on decisions made by prison and parole authorities.

"You may consider the existence of the parole law and good conduct time. However, you are not to consider the extent to which good conduct time may be awarded to or forfeited by this particular defendant. You are not to consider the manner in which the parole law may be applied to this particular defendant."

(d) This section does not permit the introduction of evidence on the operation of parole and good conduct time laws.

Art. 37.071. Procedure in Capital Case.

Sec. 1. (a) If a defendant is found guilty in a capital felony case in which the state does not seek the death penalty, the judge shall sentence the defendant to life imprisonment or to life imprisonment without parole as required by Section 12.31, Penal Code.

(b) A defendant who is found guilty of an offense under Section 19.03(a)(9), Penal Code, may not be sentenced to death, and the state may not seek the death penalty in any case based solely on an offense under that subdivision.

Sec. 2. (a) (1) If a defendant is tried for a capital offense in which the state seeks the death penalty, on a finding that the defendant is guilty of a capital offense, the court shall conduct a separate sentencing proceeding to determine whether the defendant shall be sentenced to death or life imprisonment without parole. The proceeding shall be conducted in the trial court and, except as provided by Article 44.29(c) of this code, before the trial jury as soon as practicable. In the proceeding, evidence may be presented by the state and the defendant or the defendant's counsel as to any matter that the court deems relevant to sentence, including evidence of the defendant's background or character or the circumstances of the offense that mitigates against the imposition of the death penalty. This subdivision shall not be construed to authorize the introduction of any evidence secured in violation of the Constitution of the United States or of the State of Texas. The state and the defendant or the defendant's counsel shall be permitted to present argument for or against sentence of death. The introduction of evidence of extraneous conduct is governed by the notice requirements of Section 3(g), Article 37.07. The court, the attorney representing the state, the defendant, or the defendant's counsel may not inform a juror or a prospective juror of the effect of a failure of a jury to agree on issues submitted under Subsection (c) or (e).

(2) Notwithstanding Subdivision (1), evidence may not be offered by the state to establish that the race or ethnicity of the defendant makes it likely that the defendant will engage in future criminal conduct.

(b) On conclusion of the presentation of the evidence, the court shall submit the following issues to the jury:

(1) whether there is a probability that the defendant would commit criminal acts of violence that would constitute a continuing threat to society; and

(2) in cases in which the jury charge at the guilt or innocence stage permitted the jury to find the defendant guilty as a party under Sections 7.01 and 7.02, Penal Code, whether the defendant actually caused the death of the deceased or did not actually cause the death of the deceased but intended to kill the deceased or another or anticipated that a human life would be taken.

(c) The state must prove each issue submitted under Subsection (b) of this article beyond a reasonable doubt, and the jury shall return a special verdict of "yes" or "no" on each issue submitted under Subsection (b) of this Article.

(d) The court shall charge the jury that:

(1) in deliberating on the issues submitted under Subsection (b) of this article, it shall consider all evidence admitted at the guilt or innocence stage and the punishment stage, including evidence of the defendant's background or character or the circumstances of the offense that militates for or mitigates against the imposition of the death penalty;

(2) it may not answer any issue submitted under Subsection (b) of this article "yes" unless it agrees unanimously and it may not answer any issue "no" unless 10 or more jurors agree; and

(3) members of the jury need not agree on what particular evidence supports a negative answer to any issue submitted under Subsection (b) of this article.

(e) (1) The court shall instruct the jury that if the jury returns an affirmative finding to each issue submitted under Subsection (b), it shall answer the following issue:

Whether, taking into consideration all of the evidence, including the circumstances of the offense, the defendant's character and background, and the personal moral culpability of the defendant, there is a sufficient mitigating circumstance or circumstances to warrant that a sentence of life imprisonment without parole rather than a death sentence be imposed.

(2) The court shall:

(A) instruct the jury that if the jury answers that a circumstance or circumstances warrant that a sentence of life imprisonment without parole rather than a death sentence be imposed, the court will sentence the defendant to imprisonment in the Texas Department of Criminal Justice for life without parole; and

(B) charge the jury that a defendant sentenced to confinement for life without parole under this article is ineligible for release from the department on parole.

(f) The court shall charge the jury that in answering the issue submitted under Subsection (e) of this article, the jury:

(1) shall answer the issue "yes" or "no";

(2) may not answer the issue "no" unless it agrees unanimously and may not answer the issue "yes" unless 10 or more jurors agree;

(3) need not agree on what particular evidence supports an affirmative finding on the issue; and

(4) shall consider mitigating evidence to be evidence that a juror might regard as reducing the defendant's moral blameworthiness.

(g) If the jury returns an affirmative finding on each issue submitted under Subsection (b) and a negative finding on an issue submitted under Subsection (e)(1), the court shall sentence the defendant to death. If the jury returns a negative finding on any issue submitted under Subsection (b) or an affirmative finding on an issue submitted under Subsection (e)(1) or is unable to answer any issue submitted under Subsection (b) or (e), the court shall sentence the defendant to confinement in the Texas Department of Criminal Justice for life imprisonment without parole.

(h) The judgment of conviction and sentence of death shall be subject to automatic review by the Court of Criminal Appeals.

(i) This article applies to the sentencing procedure in a capital case for an offense that is committed on or after September 1, 1991. For the purposes of this section, an offense is committed on or after September 1, 1991, if any element of that offense occurs on or after that date.

Art. 37.0711. Procedure in Capital Case for Offense Committed Before September 1, 1991.

Sec. 1. This article applies to the sentencing procedure in a capital case for an offense that is committed before September 1, 1991, whether the sentencing procedure is part of the original trial of the offense, an award of a new trial for both the guilt or innocence stage and the punishment stage of the trial, or an award of a new trial only for the punishment stage of the trial. For the purposes of this section, an offense is committed before September 1, 1991, if every element of the offense occurs before that date.

Sec. 2. If a defendant is found guilty in a case in which the state does not seek the death penalty, the judge shall sentence the defendant to life imprisonment.

Sec. 3. (a) (1) If a defendant is tried for a capital offense in which the state seeks the death penalty, on a finding that the defendant is guilty of a capital offense, the court shall conduct a separate sentencing proceeding to determine whether the defendant shall be sentenced to death or life imprisonment. The proceeding shall be conducted in the trial court and, except as provided by Article 44.29(c) of this code, before the trial jury as soon as practicable. In the proceeding, evidence may be presented as to any matter that the court deems relevant to sentence. This subdivision shall not be construed to authorize the introduction of any evidence secured in violation of the Constitution of the United States or of this state. The state and the defendant or the defendant's counsel shall be permitted to present argument for or against sentence of death.

(2) Notwithstanding Subdivision (1), evidence may not be offered by the state to establish that the race or ethnicity of the defendant makes it likely that the defendant will engage in future criminal conduct.

(b) On conclusion of the presentation of the evidence, the court shall submit the following three issues to the jury:

(1) whether the conduct of the defendant that caused the death of the deceased was committed deliberately and with the reasonable expectation that the death of the deceased or another would result;

(2) whether there is a probability that the defendant would commit criminal acts of violence that would constitute a continuing threat to society; and

(3) if raised by the evidence, whether the conduct of the defendant in killing the deceased was unreasonable in response to the provocation, if any, by the deceased.

(c) The state must prove each issue submitted under Subsection (b) of this section beyond a reasonable doubt, and the jury shall return a special verdict of "yes" or "no" on each issue submitted.

(d) The court shall charge the jury that:

(1) it may not answer any issue submitted under Subsection (b) of this section "yes" unless it agrees unanimously; and

(2) it may not answer any issue submitted under Subsection (b) of this section "no" unless 10 or more jurors agree.

(e) The court shall instruct the jury that if the jury returns an affirmative finding on each issue submitted under Subsection (b) of this section, it shall answer the following issue:

Whether, taking into consideration all of the evidence, including the circumstances of the offense, the defendant's character and background, and the personal moral culpability of the defendant, there is a sufficient mitigating circumstance or circumstances to warrant that a sentence of life imprisonment rather than a death sentence be imposed.

(f) The court shall charge the jury that, in answering the issue submitted under Subsection (e) of this section, the jury:

(1) shall answer the issue "yes" or "no";

(2) may not answer the issue "no" unless it agrees unanimously and may not answer the issue "yes" unless 10 or more jurors agree; and

(3) shall consider mitigating evidence that a juror might regard as reducing the defendant's moral blameworthiness.

(g) If the jury returns an affirmative finding on each issue submitted under Subsection (b) and a negative finding on the issue submitted under Subsection (e), the court shall sentence the defendant to death. If the jury returns a negative finding on any issue submitted under Subsection (b) or an affirmative finding on the issue submitted under Subsection (e) or is unable to answer any issue submitted under Subsection (b) or (e), the court shall sentence the defendant to confinement in the Texas Department of Criminal Justice for life.

(h) If a defendant is convicted of an offense under Section 19.03(a)(7), Penal Code, the court shall submit the issues under Subsections (b) and (e) of this section only with regard to the conduct of the defendant in murdering the deceased individual first named in the indictment.

(i) The court, the attorney for the state, or the attorney for the defendant may not inform a juror or prospective juror of the effect of failure of the jury to agree on an issue submitted under this article.

(j) The Court of Criminal Appeals shall automatically review a judgment of conviction and sentence of death not later than the 60th day after the date of certification by the sentencing court of the entire record, unless the Court of Criminal Appeals extends the time for an additional period not to exceed 30 days for good cause shown. Automatic review under this subsection has priority over all other cases before the Court of Criminal Appeals, and the court shall hear automatic reviews under rules adopted by the court for that purpose.

Art. 37.072. Procedure in Repeat Sex Offender Capital Case.

Sec. 1. If a defendant is found guilty in a capital felony case punishable under Section 12.42(c)(3), Penal Code, in which the state does not seek the death penalty, the judge shall sentence the defendant to life imprisonment without parole.

Sec. 2. (a) (1) If a defendant is tried for an offense punishable under Section 12.42(c)(3), Penal Code, in which the state seeks the death penalty, on a finding that the defendant is guilty of a capital offense, the court shall conduct a separate sentencing proceeding to determine whether the defendant shall be sentenced to death or life imprisonment without parole. The proceeding shall be conducted in the trial court and, except as provided by Article 44.29(d) of this code, before the trial jury as soon as practicable. In the proceeding, evidence may be presented by the state and the defendant or the defendant's counsel as to any matter that the court considers relevant to sentence, including evidence of the defendant's background or character or the circumstances of the offense that mitigates against the imposition of the death penalty. This subdivision may not be construed to authorize the introduction of any evidence secured in violation of the Constitution of the United States or of the State of Texas. The state and the defendant or the defendant's counsel shall be permitted to present argument for or against sentence of death. The introduction of evidence of extraneous conduct is governed by the notice requirements of Section 3(g), Article 37.07. The court, the attorney representing the state, the defendant, or the defendant's counsel may not inform a juror or a prospective juror of the effect of a failure of a jury to agree on issues submitted under Subsection (b) or (e).

(2) Notwithstanding Subdivision (1), evidence may not be offered by the state to establish that the race or ethnicity of the defendant makes it likely that the defendant will engage in future criminal conduct.

(b) On conclusion of the presentation of the evidence, the court shall submit the following issues to the jury:

(1) whether there is a probability that the defendant would commit criminal acts of violence that would constitute a continuing threat to society; and

(2) in cases in which the jury charge at the guilt or innocence stage permitted the jury to find the defendant guilty as a party under Sections 7.01 and 7.02, Penal Code, whether the defendant actually engaged in the conduct prohibited by Section 22.021, Penal Code, or did not actually engage in the conduct prohibited by Section 22.021, Penal Code, but intended that the offense be committed against the victim or another intended victim.

(c) The state must prove beyond a reasonable doubt each issue submitted under Subsection (b) of this section, and the jury shall return a special verdict of "yes" or "no" on each issue submitted under Subsection (b) of this section.

(d) The court shall charge the jury that:

(1) in deliberating on the issues submitted under Subsection (b) of this section, it shall consider all evidence admitted at the guilt or innocence stage and the punishment stage, including evidence of the defendant's background or character or the circumstances of the offense that militates for or mitigates against the imposition of the death penalty;

(2) it may not answer any issue submitted under Subsection (b) of this section "yes" unless it agrees unanimously and it may not answer any issue "no" unless 10 or more jurors agree; and

(3) members of the jury need not agree on what particular evidence supports a negative answer to any issue submitted under Subsection (b) of this section.

(e) (1) The court shall instruct the jury that if the jury returns an affirmative finding to each issue submitted under Subsection (b), it shall answer the following issue:

Whether, taking into consideration all of the evidence, including the circumstances of the offense, the defendant's character and background, and the personal moral culpability of the defendant, there is a sufficient mitigating circumstance or circumstances to warrant that a sentence of life imprisonment without parole rather than a death sentence be imposed.

(2) The court shall:

(A) instruct the jury that if the jury answers that a circumstance or circumstances warrant that a sentence of life imprisonment without parole rather than a death sentence be imposed, the court will sentence the defendant to imprisonment in the Texas Department of Criminal Justice for life without parole; and

(B) charge the jury that a defendant sentenced to confinement for life without parole under this article is ineligible for release from the department on parole.

(f) The court shall charge the jury that in answering the issue submitted under Subsection (e) of this section, the jury:

(1) shall answer the issue "yes" or "no";

(2) may not answer the issue "no" unless it agrees unanimously and may not answer the issue "yes" unless 10 or more jurors agree;

(3) need not agree on what particular evidence supports an affirmative finding on the issue; and

(4) shall consider mitigating evidence to be evidence that a juror might regard as reducing the defendant's moral blameworthiness.

(g) If the jury returns an affirmative finding on each issue submitted under Subsection (b) and a negative finding on an issue submitted under Subsection (e)(1), the court shall sentence the defendant to death. If the jury returns a negative finding on any issue submitted under Subsection (b) or an affirmative finding on an issue submitted under Subsection (e)(1) or is unable to answer any issue submitted under Subsection (b) or (e), the court shall sentence the defendant to imprisonment in the Texas Department of Criminal Justice for life without parole.

(h) The judgment of conviction and sentence of death shall be subject to automatic review by the Court of Criminal Appeals.

Art. 37.073. Repayment of Rewards; Fines.

(a) After a defendant has been convicted of a felony offense, the judge may order a defendant to pay a fine repaying all or part of a reward paid by a crime stoppers organization.

(b) In determining whether the defendant must repay the reward or part of the reward, the court shall consider:

(1) the ability of the defendant to make the payment and the financial hardship on the defendant to make the required payment; and

(2) the importance of the information to the prosecution of the defendant as provided by the arresting officer or the attorney for the state with due regard for the confidentiality of the crime stoppers organization records.

(c) In this article, "crime stoppers organization" means a crime stoppers organization, as defined by Subdivision (2), Section 414.001, Government Code, that is approved by the Texas Crime Stoppers Council to receive payments of rewards under this article and Article 42.152.

Art. 37.08. Conviction of Lesser Included Offense.

In a prosecution for an offense with lesser included offenses, the jury may find the defendant not guilty of the greater offense, but guilty of any lesser included offense.

Art. 37.09. Lesser Included Offense.

An offense is a lesser included offense if:

(1) it is established by proof of the same or less than all the facts required to establish the commission of the offense charged;

(2) it differs from the offense charged only in the respect that a less serious injury or risk of injury to the same person, property, or public interest suffices to establish its commission;

(3) it differs from the offense charged only in the respect that a less culpable mental state suffices to establish its commission; or

(4) it consists of an attempt to commit the offense charged or an otherwise included offense.

Art. 37.10. Informal Verdict.

(a) If the verdict of the jury is informal, its attention shall be called to it, and with its consent the verdict may, under the direction of the court, be reduced to the proper form. If the jury refuses to have the verdict altered, it shall again retire to its room to deliberate, unless it manifestly appear that the verdict is intended as an acquittal; and in that case, the judgment shall be rendered accordingly, discharging the defendant.

(b) If the jury assesses punishment in a case and in the verdict assesses both punishment that is authorized by law for the offense and punishment that is not authorized by law for the offense, the court shall reform the verdict to show the punishment authorized by law and to omit the punishment not authorized by law. If the trial court is required to reform a verdict under this subsection and fails to do so, the appellate court shall reform the verdict as provided by this subsection.

Art. 37.11. Defendants Tried Jointly.

Where several defendants are tried together, the jury may convict each defendant it finds guilty and acquit others. If it agrees to a verdict as to one or more, it may find a verdict in accordance with such agreement, and if it cannot agree as to others, a mistrial may be entered as to them.

Art. 37.12. Judgment on Verdict.

On each verdict of acquittal or conviction, the proper judgment shall be entered immediately. If acquitted, the defendant shall be at once

Code of Criminal Procedure

discharged from all further liability upon the charge for which he was tried; provided that, in misdemeanor cases where there is returned a verdict, or a plea of guilty is entered and the punishment assessed is by fine only, the court may, on written request of the defendant and for good cause shown, defer judgment until some other day fixed by order of the court; but in no event shall the judgment be deferred for a longer period of time than six months. On expiration of the time fixed by the order of the court, the court or judge thereof, shall enter judgment on the verdict or plea and the same shall be executed as provided by Chapter 43 of this Code. Provided further, that the court or judge thereof, in the exercise of sound discretion may permit the defendant where judgment is deferred, to remain at large on his personal bond, or may require him to enter into bail bond in a sum at least double the amount of the assessed fine and costs, conditioned that the defendant and sureties, jointly and severally, will pay such fine and costs unless the defendant personally appears on the day, set in the order and discharges the judgment in the manner provided by Chapter 43 of this Code; and for the enforcement of any judgment entered, all writs, processes and remedies of this Code are made applicable so far as necessary to carry out the provisions of this Article.

Art. 37.13. If Jury Believes Accused Insane.

When a jury has been impaneled to assess the punishment upon a plea of guilty, it shall say in its verdict what the punishment is which it assesses; but if it is of the opinion that a person pleading guilty is insane, it shall so report to the court, and an issue as to that fact shall be tried before another jury; and if, upon such trial, it be found that the defendant is insane, such proceedings shall be had as directed in cases where a defendant becomes insane after conviction.

Art. 37.14. Acquittal of Higher Offense As Jeopardy.

If a defendant, prosecuted for an offense which includes within it lesser offenses, be convicted of an offense lower than that for which he is indicted, and a new trial be granted him, or the judgment be arrested for any cause other than the want of jurisdiction, the verdict upon the first trial shall be considered an acquittal of the higher offense; but he may, upon a second trial, be convicted of the same offense of which he was before convicted, or any other inferior thereto.

Art. 37.15. Texas Punishment Standards Commission [Expired].

Expired pursuant to Acts 1991, 72nd Leg., 2nd C.S., ch. 10 (H.B. 93), § 11.14, effective September 1, 1994.

CHAPTER 38
EVIDENCE IN CRIMINAL ACTIONS

Art. 38.01. Texas Forensic Science Commission.

Sec. 1. **Creation.** — The Texas Forensic Science Commission is created.

Sec. 2. **Definitions.** — In this article:

(1) "Accredited field of forensic science" means a specific forensic method or methodology validated or approved by the commission under this article.

(2) "Commission" means the Texas Forensic Science Commission.

(3) "Crime laboratory" has the meaning assigned by Article 38.35.

(4) "Forensic analysis" means a medical, chemical, toxicologic, ballistic, or other expert examination or test performed on physical evidence, including DNA evidence, for the purpose of determining the connection of the evidence to a criminal action, except that the term does not include the portion of an autopsy conducted by a medical examiner or other forensic pathologist who is a licensed physician.

(4-a) "Forensic examination or test not subject to accreditation" means an examination or test described by Article 38.35(a)(4)(A), (B), (C), or (D) that is exempt from accreditation.

(5) "Office of capital and forensic writs" means the office of capital and forensic writs established under Subchapter B, Chapter 78, Government Code.

(6) "Physical evidence" has the meaning assigned by Article 38.35.

Sec. 3. **Composition.**

(a) The commission is composed of nine members appointed by the governor as follows:

(1) two members who must have expertise in the field of forensic science;

(2) one member who must be a prosecuting attorney that the governor selects from a list of 10 names submitted by the Texas District and County Attorneys Association;

(3) one member who must be a defense attorney that the governor selects from a list of 10 names

submitted by the Texas Criminal Defense Lawyers Association;

(4) one member who must be a faculty member or staff member of The University of Texas who specializes in clinical laboratory medicine that the governor selects from a list of five names submitted by the chancellor of The University of Texas System;

(5) one member who must be a faculty member or staff member of Texas A&M University who specializes in clinical laboratory medicine that the governor selects from a list of five names submitted by the chancellor of The Texas A&M University System;

(6) one member who must be a faculty member or staff member of Texas Southern University that the governor selects from a list of five names submitted by the chancellor of Texas Southern University;

(7) one member who must be a director or division head of the University of North Texas Health Science Center at Fort Worth Missing Persons DNA Database; and

(8) one member who must be a faculty or staff member of the Sam Houston State University College of Criminal Justice and have expertise in the field of forensic science or statistical analyses that the governor selects from a list of five names submitted by the chancellor of the Texas State University System.

(b) Each member of the commission serves a two-year term. The terms expire on September 1 of:

(1) each odd-numbered year, for a member appointed under Subsection (a)(1), (2), (3), or (4); and

(2) each even-numbered year, for a member appointed under Subsection (a)(5), (6), (7), or (8).

(c) The governor shall designate a member of the commission to serve as the presiding officer.

Sec. 3-a. **Rules.** The commission shall adopt rules necessary to implement this article.

Sec. 4. **Duties.**

(a) The commission shall:

(1) develop and implement a reporting system through which a crime laboratory may report professional negligence or professional misconduct;

(2) require a crime laboratory that conducts forensic analyses to report professional negligence or professional misconduct to the commission; and

(3) investigate, in a timely manner, any allegation of professional negligence or professional misconduct that would substantially affect the integrity of the results of a forensic analysis conducted by a crime laboratory.

(a-1) The commission may initiate for educational purposes an investigation of a forensic analysis without receiving a complaint, submitted through the reporting system implemented under Subsection (a)(1), that contains an allegation of professional negligence or professional misconduct involving the forensic analysis conducted if the commission determines by a majority vote of a quorum of the members of the commission that an investigation of the forensic analysis would advance the integrity and reliability of forensic science in this state.

(b) If the commission conducts an investigation under Subsection (a)(3) of a crime laboratory that is accredited under this article pursuant to an allegation of professional negligence or professional misconduct involving an accredited field of forensic science, the investigation:

(1) must include the preparation of a written report that identifies and also describes the methods and procedures used to identify:

(A) the alleged negligence or misconduct;

(B) whether negligence or misconduct occurred;

(C) any corrective action required of the laboratory, facility, or entity;

(D) observations of the commission regarding the integrity and reliability of the forensic analysis conducted;

(E) best practices identified by the commission during the course of the investigation; and

(F) other recommendations that are relevant, as determined by the commission; and

(2) may include one or more:

(A) retrospective reexaminations of other forensic analyses conducted by the laboratory, facility, or entity that may involve the same kind of negligence or misconduct; and

(B) follow-up evaluations of the laboratory, facility, or entity to review:

(i) the implementation of any corrective action required under Subdivision (1)(C); or

(ii) the conclusion of any retrospective reexamination under Paragraph (A).

(b-1) If the commission conducts an investigation under Subsection (a)(3) of a crime laboratory that is not accredited under this article or the investigation is conducted pursuant to an allegation involving a forensic method or methodology that is not an accredited field of forensic science, the investigation may include the preparation of a written report that contains:

(1) observations of the commission regarding the integrity and reliability of the forensic analysis conducted;

(2) best practices identified by the commission during the course of the investigation; or

(3) other recommendations that are relevant, as determined by the commission.

(b-2) If the commission conducts an investigation of a forensic analysis under Subsection (a-1), the investigation must include the preparation of a written report that contains:

(1) observations of the commission regarding the integrity and reliability of the forensic analysis conducted;

(2) best practices identified by the commission during the course of the investigation; and

(3) other recommendations that are relevant, as determined by the commission.

(c) The commission by contract may delegate the duties described by Subsections (a)(1) and (3) to any person the commission determines to be qualified to assume those duties.

(d) The commission may require that a crime laboratory investigated under this section pay any costs incurred to ensure compliance with Subsection (b), (b-1), or (b-2).

(e) The commission shall make all investigation reports completed under Subsection (b), (b-1), or (b-2) available to the public. A report completed under Subsection (b), (b-1), or (b-2), in a subsequent civil or criminal proceeding, is not prima facie evidence of the information or findings contained in the report.

(f) The commission may not make a determination of whether professional negligence or professional misconduct occurred or issue a finding on that question in an investigation initiated under Subsection (a-1) or for which an investigation report may be prepared under Subsection (b-1).

(g) The commission may not issue a finding related to the guilt or innocence of a party in an underlying civil or criminal trial involving conduct investigated by the commission under this article.

(h) The commission may review and refer cases that are the subject of an investigation under Subsection (a)(3) or (a-1) to the office of capital and forensic writs in accordance with Section 78.054(b), Government Code.

Sec. 4-a. **Forensic analyst licensing.**

(a) Notwithstanding Section 2, in this section:

(1) "Forensic analysis" has the meaning assigned by Article 38.35.

(2) "Forensic analyst" means a person who on behalf of a crime laboratory accredited under this article technically reviews or performs a forensic analysis or draws conclusions from or interprets a forensic analysis for a court or crime laboratory. The term does not include a medical examiner or other forensic pathologist who is a licensed physician.

(b) A person may not act or offer to act as a forensic analyst unless the person holds a forensic analyst license. The commission by rule may establish classifications of forensic analyst licenses if the commission determines that it is necessary to ensure the availability of properly trained and qualified forensic analysts to perform activities regulated by the commission.

(c) The commission by rule may establish voluntary licensing programs for forensic disciplines that are not subject to accreditation under this article.

(d) The commission by rule shall:

(1) establish the qualifications for a license that include:

(A) successful completion of the education requirements established by the commission;

(B) specific course work and experience, including instruction in courtroom testimony and ethics in a crime laboratory;

(C) successful completion of an examination required or recognized by the commission; and

(D) successful completion of proficiency testing to the extent required for crime laboratory accreditation;

(2) set fees for the issuance and renewal of a license; and

(3) establish the term of a forensic analyst license.

(e) The commission by rule may recognize a certification issued by a national organization in an accredited field of forensic science as satisfying the requirements established under Subsection (d)(1)(C) to the extent the commission determines the content required to receive the certification is substantially equivalent to the content of the requirements under that subsection.

(f) The commission shall issue a license to an applicant who:

(1) submits an application on a form prescribed by the commission;

(2) meets the qualifications established by commission rule; and

(3) pays the required fee.

Sec. 4-b. **Advisory Committee.**

(a) The commission shall establish an advisory committee to advise the commission and make recommendations on matters related to the licensing of forensic analysts under Section 4-a.

(b) The advisory committee consists of nine members as follows:

(1) one prosecuting attorney recommended by the Texas District and County Attorneys Association;

(2) one defense attorney recommended by the Texas Criminal Defense Lawyers Association; and

(3) seven members who are forensic scientists, crime laboratory directors, or crime laboratory quality managers, selected by the commission from a list of 20 names submitted by the Texas Association of Crime Laboratory Directors.

(c) The commission shall ensure that appointments under Subsection (b)(3) include representation from municipal, county, state, and private crime laboratories that are accredited under this article.

(d) The advisory committee members serve staggered two-year terms, with the terms of four or five members, as appropriate, expiring on August 31 of each year. An advisory committee member may not serve more than two consecutive terms. A vacancy on the advisory committee is filled by appointing a member in the same manner as the original appointment to serve for the unexpired portion of the term.

(e) The advisory committee shall elect a presiding officer from among its members to serve a one-year term. A member may serve more than one term as presiding officer.

(f) The advisory committee shall meet annually and at the call of the presiding officer or the commission.

(g) An advisory committee member is not entitled to compensation. A member is entitled to reimbursement for actual and necessary expenses incurred in performing duties as a member of the advisory committee subject to the General Appropriations Act.

(h) Chapter 2110, Government Code, does not apply to the advisory committee.

Sec. 4-c. **Disciplinary Action.**

(a) On a determination by the commission that a license holder has committed professional misconduct under this article or violated this article or a rule or order of the commission under this article, the commission may:

(1) revoke or suspend the person's license;

(2) refuse to renew the person's license; or

(3) reprimand the license holder.

(b) The commission may place on probation a person whose license is suspended. If a license suspension is probated, the commission may require the license holder to:

(1) report regularly to the commission on matters that are the basis of the probation; or

(2) continue or review continuing professional education until the license holder attains a degree of skill satisfactory to the commission in those areas that are the basis of the probation.

(c) The commission shall give written notice by certified mail of a determination described by Subsection (a) to a license holder who is the subject of the determination. The notice must:

(1) include a brief summary of the alleged misconduct or violation;

(2) state the disciplinary action taken by the commission; and

(3) inform the license holder of the license holder's right to a hearing before the Judicial Branch Certification Commission on the occurrence of the misconduct or violation, the imposition of disciplinary action, or both.

(d) Not later than the 20th day after the date the license holder receives the notice under Subsection (c), the license holder may request a hearing by submitting a written request to the Judicial Branch Certification Commission. If the license holder fails to timely submit a request, the commission's disciplinary action becomes final and is not subject to review by the Judicial Branch Certification Commission.

(e) If the license holder requests a hearing, the Judicial Branch Certification Commission shall conduct a hearing to determine whether there is substantial evidence to support the determination under Subsection (a) that the license holder committed professional misconduct or violated this article or a commission rule or order under this article. If the Judicial Branch Certification Commission upholds the determination, the Judicial Branch Certification Commission shall determine the type of disciplinary action to be taken. The Judicial Branch Certification Commission shall conduct the hearing in accordance with the procedures provided by Subchapter B, Chapter 153, Government Code, as applicable, and the rules of the Judicial Branch Certification Commission.

Sec. 4-d. **Crime Laboratory Accreditation Process.**

(a) Notwithstanding Section 2, in this section "forensic analysis" has the meaning by Article 38.35.

(b) The commission by rule:

(1) shall establish an accreditation process for crime laboratories and other entities conducting forensic analyses of physical evidence for use in criminal proceedings; and

(2) may modify or remove a crime laboratory exemption under this section if the commission determines that the underlying reason for the exemption no longer applies.

(b-1) As part of the accreditation process established and implemented under Subsection (b), the commission may:

(1) establish minimum standards that relate to the timely production of a forensic analysis to the agency requesting the analysis and that are consistent with this article and applicable laws;

(2) validate or approve specific forensic methods or methodologies; and

(3) establish procedures, policies, and practices to improve the quality of forensic analyses conducted in this state.

(b-2) The commission may require that a laboratory, facility, or entity required to be accredited under this section pay any costs incurred to ensure compliance with the accreditation process.

(b-3) A laboratory, facility, or entity that must be accredited under this section shall, as part of the accreditation process, agree to consent to any request for cooperation by the commission that is made as part of the exercise of the commission's duties under this article.

(c) The commission by rule may exempt from the accreditation process established under Subsection (b) a crime laboratory conducting a forensic analysis or a type of analysis, examination, or test if the commission determines that:

(1) independent accreditation is unavailable or inappropriate for the laboratory or the type of analysis, examination, or test performed by the laboratory;

(2) the type of analysis, examination, or test performed by the laboratory is admissible under a well-established rule of evidence or a statute other than Article 38.35;

(3) the type of analysis, examination, or test performed by the laboratory is routinely conducted outside of a crime laboratory by a person other than an employee of the crime laboratory; or

(4) the laboratory:

(A) is located outside this state or, if located in this state, is operated by a governmental entity other than the state or a political subdivision of the state; and

(B) was accredited at the time of the analysis under an accreditation process with standards that meet or exceed the relevant standards of the process established under Subsection (b).

(d) The commission may at any reasonable time enter and inspect the premises or audit the records, reports, procedures, or other quality assurance matters of a crime laboratory that is accredited or seeking accreditation under this section.

(e) The commission may collect costs incurred under this section for accrediting, inspecting, or auditing a crime laboratory.

(f) If the commission provides a copy of an audit or other report made under this section, the commission may charge $6 for the copy, in addition to any other cost permitted under Chapter 552, Government Code, or a rule adopted under that chapter.

Sec. 5. **Reimbursement. —** A member of the commission may not receive compensation but is entitled to reimbursement for the member's travel expenses as provided by Chapter 660, Government Code, and the General Appropriations Act.

Sec. 6. **Assistance. —** The Texas Legislative Council, the Legislative Budget Board, and The University of Texas at Austin shall assist the commission in performing the commission's duties.

Sec. 7. **Submission. —** The commission shall submit any report received under Section 4(a)(2) and any report prepared under Section 4(b)(1) to the governor, the lieutenant governor, and the speaker of the house of representatives not later than December 1 of each even-numbered year.

Sec. 8. **Annual Report. —** Not later than December 1 of each year, the commission shall prepare and publish a report that includes:

(1) a description of each complaint filed with the commission during the preceding 12- month period, the disposition of each complaint, and the status of any complaint still pending on December 31;

(2) a description of any specific forensic method or methodology the commission designates as part of the accreditation process for crime laboratories established by rule under this article;

(3) recommendations for best practices concerning the definition of "forensic analysis" provided by statute or by rule;

(4) developments in forensic science made or used in other state or federal investigations and the activities of the commission, if any, with respect to those developments; and

(5) other information that is relevant to investigations involving forensic science, as determined by the presiding officer of the commission.

Sec. 9. **Administrative Attachment to Office of Court Administration.**

(a) The commission is administratively attached to the Office of Court Administration of the Texas Judicial System.

(b) The Office of Court Administration of the Texas Judicial System shall provide administrative support to the commission as necessary to enable the commission to carry out the purposes of this article.

(c) Only the commission may exercise the duties of the commission under this article. Except as provided by Subsection (b), the Office of Court Administration of the Texas Judicial System does not have any authority or responsibility with respect to the duties of the commission under this article.

Sec. 10. **Open Records Limitation. —** Information that is filed as part of an allegation of professional misconduct or professional negligence or that is obtained during an investigation of an allegation of professional misconduct or professional negligence is not subject to release under Chapter 552, Government Code, until the conclusion of an investigation by the commission under Section 4.

Sec. 11. **Report Inadmissible As Evidence. —** A written report prepared by the commission under this article is not admissible in a civil or criminal action.

Sec. 12. **Collection of Certain Forensic Evidence.** The commission shall establish a method for collecting DNA and other forensic evidence related to unidentified bodies located less than 120 miles from the Rio Grande River.

Sec. 13. **Texas Forensic Science Commission Operating Account.** The Texas Forensic Science Commission operating account is an account in the general revenue fund. The commission shall deposit fees collected under Section 4-a for the issuance or renewal of a forensic analyst license to the credit of the account. Money in the account may be appropriated only to the commission for the administration and enforcement of this article.

Art. 38.01. Texas Forensic Science Commission.

Sec. 1. **Creation. —** The Texas Forensic Science Commission is created.

Sec. 2. **Definitions. —** In this article:

(1) "Accredited field of forensic science" means a specific forensic method or methodology validated or approved by the commission under this article.

(2) "Commission" means the Texas Forensic Science Commission.

(3) "Crime laboratory" has the meaning assigned by Article 38.35.

(4) "Forensic analysis" means a medical, chemical, toxicologic, ballistic, or other expert examination or test performed on physical evidence, including DNA evidence, for the purpose of determining the connection of the evidence to a criminal action, except that the term does not include the portion of an autopsy conducted by a medical examiner or other forensic pathologist who is a licensed physician.

(5) "Office of capital and forensic writs" means the office of capital and forensic writs established under Subchapter B, Chapter 78, Government Code.

(6) "Physical evidence" has the meaning assigned by Article 38.35.

Sec. 3. **Composition.**

(a) The commission is composed of nine members appointed by the governor as follows:

(1) two members who must have expertise in the field of forensic science;

(2) one member who must be a prosecuting attorney that the governor selects from a list of 10 names submitted by the Texas District and County Attorneys Association;

(3) one member who must be a defense attorney that the governor selects from a list of 10 names submitted by the Texas Criminal Defense Lawyers Association;

(4) one member who must be a faculty member or staff member of The University of Texas who specializes in clinical laboratory medicine that the governor selects from a list of five names submitted by the chancellor of The University of Texas System;

(5) one member who must be a faculty member or staff member of Texas A&M University who specializes in clinical laboratory medicine that the governor selects from a list of five names submitted by the chancellor of The Texas A&M University System;

(6) one member who must be a faculty member or staff member of Texas Southern University that the governor selects from a list of five names submitted by the chancellor of Texas Southern University;

(7) one member who must be a director or division head of the University of North Texas Health Science Center at Fort Worth Missing Persons DNA Database; and

(8) one member who must be a faculty or staff member of the Sam Houston State University College of Criminal Justice and have expertise in the field of forensic science or statistical analyses that the governor selects from a list of five names submitted by the chancellor of the Texas State University System.

(b) Each member of the commission serves a two-year term. The terms expire on September 1 of:

(1) each odd-numbered year, for a member appointed under Subsection (a)(1), (2), (3), or (4); and

(2) each even-numbered year, for a member appointed under Subsection (a)(5), (6), (7), or (8).

(c) The governor shall designate a member of the commission to serve as the presiding officer.

Sec. 3-a. **Rules.** The commission shall adopt rules necessary to implement this article.

Sec. 3-b. **Code of Professional Responsibility.**

(a) The commission shall adopt a code of professional responsibility to regulate the conduct of persons, laboratories, facilities, and other entities regulated under this article.

(b) The commission shall publish the code of professional responsibility adopted under Subsection (a).

(c) The commission shall adopt rules establishing sanctions for code violations.

(d) The commission shall update the code of professional responsibility as necessary to reflect changes in science, technology, or other factors affecting the persons, laboratories, facilities, and other entities regulated under this article.

Sec. 4. **Duties.**

(a) The commission shall:

(1) develop and implement a reporting system through which a crime laboratory may report professional negligence or professional misconduct;

(2) require a crime laboratory that conducts forensic analyses to report professional negligence or professional misconduct to the commission; and

(3) investigate, in a timely manner, any allegation of professional negligence or professional misconduct that would substantially affect the integrity of:

(A) the results of a forensic analysis conducted by a crime laboratory;

(B) an examination or test that is conducted by a crime laboratory and that is a forensic examination or test not subject to accreditation; or

(C) testimony related to an analysis, examination, or test described by Paragraph (A) or (B).

(a-1) The commission may initiate an investigation of a forensic analysis or a forensic examination or test not subject to accreditation, without receiving a complaint submitted through the reporting system implemented under Subsection (a)(1), if the commission determines by a majority vote of a quorum of the members of the commission that an investigation of the analysis, examination, or test would advance the integrity and reliability of forensic science in this state.

(b) If the commission conducts an investigation under Subsection (a)(3) of a crime laboratory that is accredited under this article pursuant to an allegation of professional negligence or professional misconduct involving an accredited field of forensic science, the investigation:

(1) must include the preparation of a written report that identifies and also describes the methods and procedures used to identify:

(A) the alleged negligence or misconduct;

(B) whether negligence or misconduct occurred;

(C) any corrective action required of the laboratory, facility, or entity;

(D) observations of the commission regarding the integrity and reliability of the forensic analysis conducted;

(E) best practices identified by the commission during the course of the investigation; and

(F) other recommendations that are relevant, as determined by the commission; and

(2) may include one or more:

(A) retrospective reexaminations of other forensic analyses conducted by the laboratory, facility, or entity that may involve the same kind of negligence or misconduct; and

(B) follow-up evaluations of the laboratory, facility, or entity to review:

(i) the implementation of any corrective action required under Subdivision (1)(C); or

(ii) the conclusion of any retrospective reexamination under Paragraph (A).

(b-1) If the commission conducts an investigation under Subsection (a)(3) of a crime laboratory that is not accredited under this article or the investigation involves a forensic examination or test not subject to accreditation, the investigation may include the preparation of a written report that contains:

(1) observations of the commission regarding the integrity and reliability of the applicable analysis, examination, or test conducted;

(2) best practices identified by the commission during the course of the investigation; or

(3) other recommendations that are relevant, as determined by the commission.

(b-2) If the commission conducts an investigation of a forensic analysis under Subsection (a-1), the investigation must include the preparation of a written report that contains:

(1) observations of the commission regarding the integrity and reliability of the forensic analysis conducted;

(2) best practices identified by the commission during the course of the investigation; and

(3) other recommendations that are relevant, as determined by the commission.

(c) The commission by contract may delegate the duties described by Subsections (a)(1) and (3) and Sections 4-d(b)(1), (b-1), and (d) to any person the commission determines to be qualified to assume those duties.

(d) The commission may require that a crime laboratory investigated under this section pay any costs incurred to ensure compliance with Subsection (b), (b-1), or (b-2).

(e) The commission shall make all investigation reports completed under Subsection (b), (b-1), or (b-2) available to the public. A report completed under Subsection (b), (b-1), or (b-2), in a subsequent civil or criminal proceeding, is not prima facie evidence of the information or findings contained in the report.

(f) The commission may not make a determination of whether professional negligence or professional misconduct occurred or issue a finding on that question in an investigation initiated under Subsection (a-1) or for which an investigation report may be prepared under Subsection (b-1).

(g) The commission may not issue a finding related to the guilt or innocence of a party in an underlying civil or criminal trial involving conduct investigated by the commission under this article.

(h) The commission may review and refer cases that are the subject of an investigation under

Subsection (a)(3) or (a-1) to the office of capital and forensic writs in accordance with Section 78.054(b), Government Code.

Sec. 4-a. **Forensic analyst licensing.**

(a) Notwithstanding Section 2, in this section:

(1) "Forensic analysis" has the meaning assigned by Article 38.35.

(2) "Forensic analyst" means a person who on behalf of a crime laboratory accredited under this article technically reviews or performs a forensic analysis or draws conclusions from or interprets a forensic analysis for a court or crime laboratory. The term does not include a medical examiner or other forensic pathologist who is a licensed physician.

(b) A person may not act or offer to act as a forensic analyst unless the person holds a forensic analyst license. The commission by rule may establish classifications of forensic analyst licenses if the commission determines that it is necessary to ensure the availability of properly trained and qualified forensic analysts to perform activities regulated by the commission.

(c) The commission by rule may establish voluntary licensing programs for forensic examinations or tests not subject to accreditation.

(d) The commission by rule shall:

(1) establish the qualifications for a license that include:

(A) successful completion of the education requirements established by the commission;

(B) specific course work and experience, including instruction in courtroom testimony and ethics in a crime laboratory;

(C) successful completion of an examination required or recognized by the commission; and

(D) successful completion of proficiency testing to the extent required for crime laboratory accreditation;

(2) set fees for the issuance and renewal of a license; and

(3) establish the term of a forensic analyst license.

(e) The commission by rule may recognize a certification issued by a national organization in an accredited field of forensic science as satisfying the requirements established under Subsection (d)(1)(C) to the extent the commission determines the content required to receive the certification is substantially equivalent to the content of the requirements under that subsection.

(f) The commission shall issue a license to an applicant who:

(1) submits an application on a form prescribed by the commission;

(2) meets the qualifications established by commission rule; and

(3) pays the required fee.

Sec. 4-b. **Advisory Committee.**

(a) The commission shall establish an advisory committee to advise the commission and make recommendations on matters related to the licensing of forensic analysts under Section 4-a.

(b) The advisory committee consists of nine members as follows:

(1) one prosecuting attorney recommended by the Texas District and County Attorneys Association;

(2) one defense attorney recommended by the Texas Criminal Defense Lawyers Association; and

(3) seven members who are forensic scientists, crime laboratory directors, or crime laboratory quality managers, selected by the commission from a list of 20 names submitted by the Texas Association of Crime Laboratory Directors.

(c) The commission shall ensure that appointments under Subsection (b)(3) include representation from municipal, county, state, and private crime laboratories that are accredited under this article.

(d) The advisory committee members serve staggered two-year terms, with the terms of four or five members, as appropriate, expiring on August 31 of each year. An advisory committee member may not serve more than two consecutive terms. A vacancy on the advisory committee is filled by appointing a member in the same manner as the original appointment to serve for the unexpired portion of the term.

(e) The advisory committee shall elect a presiding officer from among its members to serve a one-year term. A member may serve more than one term as presiding officer.

(f) The advisory committee shall meet annually and at the call of the presiding officer or the commission.

(g) An advisory committee member is not entitled to compensation. A member is entitled to reimbursement for actual and necessary expenses incurred in performing duties as a member of the advisory committee subject to the General Appropriations Act.

(h) Chapter 2110, Government Code, does not apply to the advisory committee.

Sec. 4-c. **Disciplinary Action.**

(a) On a determination by the commission that a license holder has committed professional misconduct under this article or violated this article or a rule or order of the commission under this article, the commission may:

(1) revoke or suspend the person's license;

(2) refuse to renew the person's license; or

(3) reprimand the license holder.

(b) The commission may place on probation a person whose license is suspended. If a license suspension is probated, the commission may require the license holder to:

(1) report regularly to the commission on matters that are the basis of the probation; or

(2) continue or review continuing professional education until the license holder attains a degree of skill satisfactory to the commission in those areas that are the basis of the probation.

(c) The commission shall give written notice by certified mail of a determination described by Subsection (a) to a license holder who is the subject of the determination. The notice must:

(1) include a brief summary of the alleged misconduct or violation;

(2) state the disciplinary action taken by the commission; and

(3) inform the license holder of the license holder's right to a hearing before the Judicial Branch Certification Commission on the occurrence of the misconduct or violation, the imposition of disciplinary action, or both.

(d) Not later than the 20th day after the date the license holder receives the notice under Subsection (c), the license holder may request a hearing by submitting a written request to the Judicial Branch Certification Commission. If the license holder fails to timely submit a request, the commission's disciplinary action becomes final and is not subject to review by the Judicial Branch Certification Commission.

(e) If the license holder requests a hearing, the Judicial Branch Certification Commission shall conduct a hearing to determine whether there is substantial evidence to support the determination under Subsection (a) that the license holder committed professional misconduct or violated this article or a commission rule or order under this article. If the Judicial Branch Certification Commission upholds the determination, the Judicial Branch Certification Commission shall determine the type of disciplinary action to be taken. The Judicial Branch Certification Commission shall conduct the hearing in accordance with the procedures provided by Subchapter B, Chapter 153, Government Code, as applicable, and the rules of the Judicial Branch Certification Commission.

Sec. 4-d. **Crime Laboratory Accreditation Process.**

(a) Notwithstanding Section 2, in this section "forensic analysis" has the meaning by Article 38.35.

(b) The commission by rule:

(1) shall establish an accreditation process for crime laboratories and other entities conducting forensic analyses of physical evidence for use in criminal proceedings; and

(2) may modify or remove a crime laboratory exemption under this section if the commission determines that the underlying reason for the exemption no longer applies.

(b-1) As part of the accreditation process established and implemented under Subsection (b), the commission may:

(1) establish minimum standards that relate to the timely production of a forensic analysis to the agency requesting the analysis and that are consistent with this article and applicable laws;

(2) validate or approve specific forensic methods or methodologies; and

(3) establish procedures, policies, standards, and practices to improve the quality of forensic analyses conducted in this state.

(b-2) The commission may require that a laboratory, facility, or entity required to be accredited under this section pay any costs incurred to ensure compliance with the accreditation process.

(b-3) A laboratory, facility, or entity that must be accredited under this section shall, as part of the accreditation process, agree to consent to any request for cooperation by the commission that is made as part of the exercise of the commission's duties under this article.

(c) The commission by rule may exempt from the accreditation process established under Subsection (b) a crime laboratory conducting a forensic analysis or a type of analysis, examination, or test if the commission determines that:

(1) independent accreditation is unavailable or inappropriate for the laboratory or the type of analysis, examination, or test performed by the laboratory;

(2) the type of analysis, examination, or test performed by the laboratory is admissible under a well-established rule of evidence or a statute other than Article 38.35;

(3) the type of analysis, examination, or test performed by the laboratory is routinely conducted outside of a crime laboratory by a person other than an employee of the crime laboratory; or

(4) the laboratory:

(A) is located outside this state or, if located in this state, is operated by a governmental entity other than the state or a political subdivision of the state; and

(B) was accredited at the time of the analysis under an accreditation process with standards that meet or exceed the relevant standards of the process established under Subsection (b).

(d) The commission may at any reasonable time enter and inspect the premises or audit the records, reports, procedures, or other quality assurance matters of a crime laboratory that is accredited or seeking accreditation under this section.

(e) The commission may collect costs incurred under this section for accrediting, inspecting, or auditing a crime laboratory.

(f) If the commission provides a copy of an audit or other report made under this section, the commission may charge $6 for the copy, in addition to any other cost permitted under Chapter 552, Government Code, or a rule adopted under that chapter.

Sec. 5. **Reimbursement.** — A member of the commission may not receive compensation but is entitled to reimbursement for the member's travel expenses as provided by Chapter 660, Government Code, and the General Appropriations Act.

Sec. 6. **Assistance.** — The Texas Legislative Council, the Legislative Budget Board, and The University of Texas at Austin shall assist the commission in performing the commission's duties.

Sec. 7. **Submission.** — The commission shall submit any report received under Section 4(a)(2) and any report prepared under Section 4(b)(1) to the governor, the lieutenant governor, and the speaker of the house of representatives not later than December 1 of each even-numbered year.

Sec. 8. **Annual Report.** — Not later than December 1 of each year, the commission shall prepare and publish a report that includes:

(1) a description of each complaint filed with the commission during the preceding 12- month period, the disposition of each complaint, and the status of any complaint still pending on December 31;

(2) a description of any specific forensic method or methodology the commission designates as part of the accreditation process for crime laboratories established by rule under this article;

(3) recommendations for best practices concerning the definition of "forensic analysis" provided by statute or by rule;

(4) developments in forensic science made or used in other state or federal investigations and the activities of the commission, if any, with respect to those developments; and

(5) other information that is relevant to investigations involving forensic science, as determined by the presiding officer of the commission.

Sec. 9. **Administrative Attachment to Office of Court Administration.**

(a) The commission is administratively attached to the Office of Court Administration of the Texas Judicial System.

(b) The Office of Court Administration of the Texas Judicial System shall provide administrative support to the commission as necessary to enable the commission to carry out the purposes of this article.

(c) Only the commission may exercise the duties of the commission under this article. Except as provided by Subsection (b), the Office of Court Administration of the Texas Judicial System does not have any authority or responsibility with respect to the duties of the commission under this article.

Sec. 10. **Open Records Limitation.** — Information that is filed as part of an allegation of professional misconduct or professional negligence or that is obtained during an investigation of an allegation of professional misconduct or professional negligence is not subject to release under Chapter 552, Government Code, until the conclusion of an investigation by the commission under Section 4.

Sec. 11. **Report Inadmissible As Evidence.** — A written report prepared by the commission under this article is not admissible in a civil or criminal action.

Sec. 12. **Collection of Certain Forensic Evidence.** The commission shall establish a method for collecting DNA and other forensic evidence related to unidentified bodies located less than 120 miles from the Rio Grande River.

Sec. 13. **Texas Forensic Science Commission Operating Account.** The Texas Forensic Science Commission operating account is an account in the general revenue fund. The commission shall deposit fees collected under Section 4-a for the issuance or renewal of a forensic analyst license to the credit of the account. Money in the account may be appropriated only to the commission for the administration and enforcement of this article.

Sec. 14. **Funding for training and education.** The commission may use appropriated funds for the training and education of forensic analysts.

Art. 38.02. Effect Under Public Information Law of Release of Certain Information.

A release of information by an attorney representing the state to defense counsel for a purpose relating to the pending or reasonably anticipated prosecution of a criminal case is not considered a voluntary release of information to the public for purposes of Section 552.007, Government Code, and does not waive the right to assert in the future that the information is excepted from required disclosure under Chapter 552, Government Code.

Art. 38.03. Presumption of Innocence.

All persons are presumed to be innocent and no person may be convicted of an offense unless each element of the offense is proved beyond a reasonable doubt. The fact that he has been arrested, confined, or indicted for, or otherwise charged with, the offense gives rise to no inference of guilt at his trial.

Art. 38.04. Jury Are Judges of Facts.

The jury, in all cases, is the exclusive judge of the facts proved, and of the weight to be given to the testimony, except where it is provided by law that proof of any particular fact is to be taken as either conclusive or presumptive proof of the existence of another fact, or where the law directs that a certain degree of weight is to be attached to a certain species of evidence.

Art. 38.05. Judge Shall Not Discuss Evidence.

In ruling upon the admissibility of evidence, the judge shall not discuss or comment upon the weight of the same or its bearing in the case, but shall simply decide whether or not it is admissible; nor shall he, at any stage of the proceeding previous to the return of the verdict, make any remark calculated to convey to the jury his opinion of the case.

Art. 38.06. Persons Competent to Testify [Repealed].

Repealed by the Texas Court of Criminal Appeals pursuant to Acts 1985, 69th Leg., ch. 685 (H.B. 13), § 9, effective September 1, 1986.

Art. 38.07. Testimony in Corroboration of Victim of Sexual Offense.

(a) A conviction under Chapter 21, Section 20A.02(a)(3), (4), (7), or (8), Section 22.011, or Section 22.021, Penal Code, is supportable on the uncorroborated testimony of the victim of the sexual offense if the victim informed any person, other than the defendant, of the alleged offense within one year after the date on which the offense is alleged to have occurred.

(b) The requirement that the victim inform another person of an alleged offense does not apply if at the time of the alleged offense the victim was a person:

(1) 17 years of age or younger;

(2) 65 years of age or older; or

(3) 18 years of age or older who by reason of age or physical or mental disease, defect, or injury was substantially unable to satisfy the person's need for food, shelter, medical care, or protection from harm.

Art. 38.071. Testimony of Child Who Is Victim of Offense.

Sec. 1. This article applies only to a hearing or proceeding in which the court determines that a child younger than 13 years of age would be unavailable to testify in the presence of the defendant about an offense defined by any of the following sections of the Penal Code:

(1) Section 19.02 (Murder);

(2) Section 19.03 (Capital Murder);

(3) Section 19.04 (Manslaughter);

(4) Section 20.04 (Aggravated Kidnapping);

(5) Section 21.11 (Indecency with a Child);

(6) Section 22.011 (Sexual Assault);

(7) Section 22.02 (Aggravated Assault);

(8) Section 22.021 (Aggravated Sexual Assault);

(9) Section 22.04(e) (Injury to a Child, Elderly Individual, or Disabled Individual);

(10) Section 22.04(f) (Injury to a Child, Elderly Individual, or Disabled Individual), if the conduct is committed intentionally or knowingly;

(11) Section 25.02 (Prohibited Sexual Conduct);

(12) Section 29.03 (Aggravated Robbery);

(13) Section 43.25 (Sexual Performance by a Child);

(14) Section 21.02 (Continuous Sexual Abuse of Young Child or Disabled Individual);

(15) Section 43.05(a)(2) (Compelling Prostitution); or

(16) Section 20A.02(a)(7) or (8) (Trafficking of Persons).

Sec. 2. (a) The recording of an oral statement of the child made before the indictment is returned or the complaint has been filed is admissible into evidence if the court makes a determination that the factual issues of identity or actual occurrence were fully and fairly inquired into in a detached manner by a neutral individual experienced in child abuse cases that seeks to find the truth of the matter.

(b) If a recording is made under Subsection (a) of this section and after an indictment is returned or a complaint has been filed, by motion of the attorney representing the state or the attorney representing the defendant and on the approval of the court, both attorneys may propound written interrogatories that shall be presented by the same neutral individual who made the initial inquiries, if possible, and recorded under the same or similar circumstances of the original recording with the time and date of the inquiry clearly indicated in the recording.

(c) A recording made under Subsection (a) of this section is not admissible into evidence unless a recording made under Subsection (b) is admitted at the same time if a recording under Subsection (b) was requested prior to the time of the hearing or proceeding.

Sec. 3. (a) On its own motion or on the motion of the attorney representing the state or the attorney representing the defendant, the court may order that the testimony of the child be taken in a room other than the courtroom and be televised by closed circuit equipment in the courtroom to be viewed by the court and the finder of fact. To the extent practicable, only the judge, the court reporter, the attorneys for the defendant and for the state, persons necessary to operate the equipment, and any person whose presence would contribute to the welfare and well-being of the child may be present in the room with the child during his testimony. Only the attorneys and the judge may question the child. To the extent practicable, the persons necessary to operate the equipment shall be confined to an adjacent room or behind a screen or mirror that permits them to see and hear the child during his testimony, but does not permit the child to see or hear them. The court shall permit the defendant to observe and hear the testimony of the child and to communicate contemporaneously with his attorney during periods of recess or by audio contact, but the court shall attempt to ensure that the child cannot hear or see the defendant. The court shall permit the attorney for the defendant adequate opportunity to confer with the defendant during cross-examination of the child. On application of the attorney for the defendant, the court may recess the proceeding before or during cross-examination of the child for a reasonable time to allow the attorney for the defendant to confer with defendant.

(b) The court may set any other conditions and limitations on the taking of the testimony that it finds just and appropriate, taking into consideration the interests of the child, the rights of the defendant, and any other relevant factors.

Sec. 4. (a) After an indictment has been returned or a complaint filed, on its own motion or on the motion of the attorney representing the state or the attorney representing the defendant, the court may order that the testimony of the child be taken outside the courtroom and be recorded for showing in the courtroom before the court and the finder of fact. To the extent practicable, only those persons permitted to be present at the taking of testimony under Section 3 of this article may be present during the taking of the child's testimony, and the persons operating the equipment shall be confined from the child's sight and hearing as provided by Section 3. The court shall permit the defendant to observe and hear the testimony of the child and to communicate contemporaneously with his attorney during periods of recess or by audio contact but shall attempt to ensure that the child cannot hear or see the defendant.

(b) The court may set any other conditions and limitations on the taking of the testimony that it finds just and appropriate, taking into consideration the interests of the child, the rights of the defendant, and any other relevant factors. The court shall also ensure that:

(1) the recording is both visual and aural and is recorded on film or videotape or by other electronic means;

(2) the recording equipment was capable of making an accurate recording, the operator was competent, the quality of the recording is sufficient to allow the court and the finder of fact to assess the demeanor of the child and the interviewer, and the recording is accurate and is not altered;

(3) each voice on the recording is identified;

(4) the defendant, the attorneys for each party, and the expert witnesses for each party are afforded an opportunity to view the recording before it is shown in the courtroom;

(5) before giving his testimony, the child was placed under oath or was otherwise admonished in a manner appropriate to the child's age and maturity to testify truthfully;

(6) the court finds from the recording or through an in camera examination of the child that the child was competent to testify at the time the recording was made; and

(7) only one continuous recording of the child was made or the necessity for pauses in the recordings or for multiple recordings is established at the hearing or proceeding.

(c) After a complaint has been filed or an indictment returned charging the defendant, on the motion of the attorney representing the state, the court may order that the deposition of the child be taken outside of the courtroom in the same manner as a deposition may be taken in a civil matter. A deposition taken under this subsection is admissible into evidence.

Sec. 5. (a) On the motion of the attorney representing the state or the attorney representing the defendant and on a finding by the court that the following requirements have been substantially satisfied, the recording of an oral statement of the child made before a complaint has been filed or an indictment returned is admissible into evidence if:

(1) no attorney or peace officer was present when the statement was made;

(2) the recording is both visual and aural and is recorded on film or videotape or by other electronic means;

(3) the recording equipment was capable of making an accurate recording, the operator of

the equipment was competent, the quality of the recording is sufficient to allow the court and the finder of fact to assess the demeanor of the child and the interviewer, and the recording is accurate and has not been altered;

(4) the statement was not made in response to questioning calculated to lead the child to make a particular statement;

(5) every voice on the recording is identified;

(6) the person conducting the interview of the child in the recording is expert in the handling, treatment, and investigation of child abuse cases, present at the hearing or proceeding, called by the state, and subject to cross-examination;

(7) immediately after a complaint was filed or an indictment returned, the attorney representing the state notified the court, the defendant, and the attorney representing the defendant of the existence of the recording;

(8) the defendant, the attorney for the defendant, and the expert witnesses for the defendant were afforded an opportunity to view the recording before it is offered into evidence and, if a proceeding was requested as provided by Subsection (b) of this section, in a proceeding conducted before a district court judge but outside the presence of the jury were afforded an opportunity to cross-examine the child as provided by Subsection (b) of this section from any time immediately following the filing of the complaint or the returning of an indictment charging the defendant until the date the hearing or proceeding begins;

(9) the recording of the cross-examination, if there is one, is admissible under Subsection (b) of this section;

(10) before giving his testimony, the child was placed under oath or was otherwise admonished in a manner appropriate to the child's age and maturity to testify truthfully;

(11) the court finds from the recording or through an in camera examination of the child that the child was competent to testify at the time that the recording was made; and

(12) only one continuous recording of the child was made or the necessity for pauses in the recordings or for multiple recordings has been established at the hearing or proceeding.

(b) On the motion of the attorney representing the defendant, a district court may order that the cross-examination of the child be taken and be recorded before the judge of that court at any time until a recording made in accordance with Subsection (a) of this section has been introduced into evidence at the hearing or proceeding. On a finding by the court that the following requirements were satisfied, the recording of the cross-examination of the child is admissible into evidence and shall be viewed by the finder of fact only after the finder of fact has viewed the recording authorized by Subsection (a) of this section if:

(1) the recording is both visual and aural and is recorded on film or videotape or by other electronic means;

(2) the recording equipment was capable of making an accurate recording, the operator of the equipment was competent, the quality of the recording is sufficient to allow the court and the finder of fact to assess the demeanor of the child and the attorney representing the defendant, and the recording is accurate and has not been altered;

(3) every voice on the recording is identified;

(4) the defendant, the attorney representing the defendant, the attorney representing the state, and the expert witnesses for the defendant and the state were afforded an opportunity to view the recording before the hearing or proceeding began;

(5) the child was placed under oath before the cross-examination began or was otherwise admonished in a manner appropriate to the child's age and maturity to testify truthfully; and

(6) only one continuous recording of the child was made or the necessity for pauses in the recordings or for multiple recordings was established at the hearing or proceeding.

(c) During cross-examination under Subsection (b) of this section, to the extent practicable, only a district court judge, the attorney representing the defendant, the attorney representing the state, persons necessary to operate the equipment, and any other person whose presence would contribute to the welfare and well-being of the child may be present in the room with the child during his testimony. Only the attorneys and the judge may question the child. To the extent practicable, the persons operating the equipment shall be confined to an adjacent room or behind a screen or mirror that permits them to see and hear the child during his testimony but does not permit the child to see or hear them. The court shall permit the defendant to observe and hear the testimony of the child and to communicate contemporaneously with his attorney during periods of recess or by audio contact, but shall attempt to ensure that the child cannot hear or see the defendant.

(d) Under Subsection (b) of this section the district court may set any other conditions and limitations on the taking of the cross-examination of a child that it finds just and appropriate, taking into consideration the interests of the child, the rights of the defendant, and any other relevant factors.

Sec. 6. If the court orders the testimony of a child to be taken under Section 3 or 4 of this article or if the court finds the testimony of the child taken under Section 2 or 5 of this article is admissible into evidence, the child may not be required to testify in court at the proceeding for which the testimony was taken, unless the court finds there is good cause.

Sec. 7. In making any determination of good cause under this article, the court shall consider the rights of the defendant, the interests of the child, the relationship of the defendant to the child, the character and duration of the alleged offense, any court finding related to the availability of the child to testify, the age, maturity, and emotional stability of the child, the time elapsed since the alleged offense, and any other relevant factors.

Sec. 8. (a) In making a determination of unavailability under this article, the court shall consider relevant factors including the relationship of the defendant to the child, the character and duration of the alleged offense, the age, maturity, and emotional stability of the child, and the time elapsed since the alleged offense, and whether the child is more likely than not to be unavailable to testify because:

(1) of emotional or physical causes, including the confrontation with the defendant; or

(2) the child would suffer undue psychological or physical harm through his involvement at the hearing or proceeding.

(b) A determination of unavailability under this article can be made after an earlier determination of availability. A determination of availability under this article can be made after an earlier determination of unavailability.

Sec. 9. If the court finds the testimony taken under Section 2 or 5 of this article is admissible into evidence or if the court orders the testimony to be taken under Section 3 or 4 of this article and if the identity of the perpetrator is a contested issue, the child additionally must make an in-person identification of the defendant either at or before the hearing or proceeding.

Sec. 10. In ordering a child to testify under this article, the court shall take all reasonable steps necessary and available to minimize undue psychological trauma to the child and to minimize the emotional and physical stress to the child caused by relevant factors, including the confrontation with the defendant and the ordinary participation of the witness in the courtroom.

Sec. 11. In a proceeding under Section 2, 3, or 4 or Subsection (b) of Section 5 of this article, if the defendant is not represented by counsel and the court finds that the defendant is not able to obtain counsel for the purposes of the proceeding, the court shall appoint counsel to represent the defendant at the proceeding.

Sec. 12. In this article, "cross-examination" has the same meaning as in other legal proceedings in the state.

Sec. 13. The attorney representing the state shall determine whether to use the procedure provided in Section 2 of this article or the procedure provided in Section 5 of this article.

Art. 38.072. Hearsay Statement of Certain Abuse Victims.

Sec. 1. This article applies to a proceeding in the prosecution of an offense under any of the following provisions of the Penal Code, if committed against a child younger than 14 years of age or a person with a disability:

(1) Chapter 21 (Sexual Offenses) or 22 (Assaultive Offenses);

(2) Section 25.02 (Prohibited Sexual Conduct);

(3) Section 43.25 (Sexual Performance by a Child);

(4) Section 43.05(a)(2) (Compelling Prostitution);

(5) Section 20A.02(a)(7) or (8) (Trafficking of Persons); or

(6) Section 15.01 (Criminal Attempt), if the offense attempted is described by Subdivision (1), (2), (3), (4), or (5) of this section.

Sec. 2. (a) **[2 Versions: As amended by Acts 2009, 81st Leg., ch. 284]** This article applies only to statements that describe the alleged offense that:

(1) were made by the child or person with a disability against whom the offense was allegedly committed; and

(2) were made to the first person, 18 years of age or older, other than the defendant, to whom the child or person with a disability made a statement about the offense.

Sec. 2. (a) **[2 Versions: As amended by Acts 2009, 81st Leg., ch. 710]** This article applies only to statements that:

(1) describe:

(A) the alleged offense; or

(B) if the statement is offered during the punishment phase of the proceeding, a crime, wrong, or act other than the alleged offense that is:

(i) described by Section 1;

(ii) allegedly committed by the defendant against the child who is the victim of the offense or another child younger than 14 years of age; and

(iii) otherwise admissible as evidence under Article 38.37, Rule 404 or 405, Texas Rules of Evidence, or another law or rule of evidence of this state;

(2) were made by the child against whom the charged offense or extraneous crime, wrong, or act was allegedly committed; and

(3) were made to the first person, 18 years of age or older, other than the defendant, to whom the child made a statement about the offense or extraneous crime, wrong, or act.

(b) A statement that meets the requirements of Subsection (a) is not inadmissible because of the hearsay rule if:

(1) on or before the 14th day before the date the proceeding begins, the party intending to offer the statement:

(A) notifies the adverse party of its intention to do so;

(B) provides the adverse party with the name of the witness through whom it intends to offer the statement; and

(C) provides the adverse party with a written summary of the statement;

(2) the trial court finds, in a hearing conducted outside the presence of the jury, that the statement is reliable based on the time, content, and circumstances of the statement; and

(3) the child or person with a disability testifies or is available to testify at the proceeding in court or in any other manner provided by law.

Sec. 3. In this article, "person with a disability" means a person 13 years of age or older who because of age or physical or mental disease, disability, or injury is substantially unable to protect the person's self from harm or to provide food, shelter, or medical care for the person's self.

Art. 38.073. Testimony of Inmate Witnesses.

In a proceeding in the prosecution of a criminal offense in which an inmate in the custody of the Texas Department of Criminal Justice is required to testify as a witness, any deposition or testimony of the inmate witness may be conducted by a video teleconferencing system in the manner described by Article 27.18.

Art. 38.074. Testimony of Child in Prosecution of Offense.

Sec. 1. In this article:

(1) "Child" has the meaning assigned by Section 22.011(c), Penal Code.

(2) "Support person" means any person whose presence would contribute to the welfare and well-being of a child.

Sec. 2. This article applies to the testimony of a child in any hearing or proceeding in the prosecution of any offense, other than the testimony of a child in a hearing or proceeding in a criminal case in which that child is the defendant.

Sec. 3. (a) A court shall:

(1) administer an oath to a child in a manner that allows the child to fully understand the child's duty to tell the truth;

(2) ensure that questions asked of the child are stated in language appropriate to the child's age;

(3) explain to the child that the child has the right to have the court notified if the child is unable to understand any question and to have a question restated in a form that the child does understand;

(4) ensure that a child testifies only at a time of day when the child is best able to understand the questions and to undergo the proceedings without being traumatized, including:

(A) limiting the duration of the child's testimony;

(B) limiting the timing of the child's testimony to the child's normal school hours; or

(C) ordering a recess during the child's testimony when necessary for the energy, comfort, or attention span of the child; and

(5) prevent intimidation or harassment of the child by any party and, for that purpose, rephrase as appropriate any question asked of the child.

(b) On the motion of any party, or a parent, managing conservator, guardian, or guardian ad litem of a child or special advocate for a child, the court shall allow the child to have a toy, blanket, or similar comforting item in the child's possession while testifying or allow a support person to be present in close proximity to the child during the child's testimony if the court finds by a preponderance of the evidence that:

(1) the child cannot reliably testify without the possession of the item or presence of the support person, as applicable; and

(2) granting the motion is not likely to prejudice the trier of fact in evaluating the child's testimony.

(c) A support person who is present during a child's testimony may not:

(1) obscure the child from the view of the defendant or the trier of fact;

(2) provide the child with an answer to any question asked of the child; or

(3) assist or influence the testimony of the child.

(d) The court may set any other conditions and limitations on the taking of the testimony of a child that it finds just and appropriate, considering the interests of the child, the rights of the defendant, and any other relevant factors.

Art. 38.075. Corroboration of Certain Testimony Required.

(a) A defendant may not be convicted of an offense on the testimony of a person to whom the defendant made a statement against the defendant's interest during a time when the person was imprisoned or confined in the same correctional facility as the defendant unless the testimony is corroborated by other evidence tending to connect the defendant with the offense committed. In this subsection, "correctional facility" has the meaning assigned by Section 1.07, Penal Code.

(b) Corroboration is not sufficient for the purposes of this article if the corroboration only shows that the offense was committed.

(c) Evidence of a prior offense committed by a person who gives testimony described by Subsection (a) may be admitted for the purpose of impeachment if the person received a benefit described by Article 39.14(h-1)(2) with respect to the offense, regardless of whether the person was convicted of the offense.

Art. 38.076. Testimony of Forensic Analyst by Video Teleconference.

(a) In this article, "forensic analyst" has the meaning assigned by Section 4-a, Article 38.01.

(b) In a proceeding in the prosecution of a criminal offense in which a forensic analyst is required to testify as a witness, any testimony of the witness may be conducted by video teleconferencing in the manner described by Subsection (c) if:

(1) the use of video teleconferencing is approved by the court and all parties;

(2) the video teleconferencing is coordinated in advance to ensure proper scheduling and equipment compatibility and reliability; and

(3) a method of electronically transmitting documents related to the proceeding is available at both the location at which the witness is testifying and in the court.

(c) A video teleconferencing system used under this article must provide an encrypted, simultaneous, compressed full motion video and interactive communication of image and sound between the judge, the attorney representing the state, the attorney representing the defendant, and the witness.

Art. 38.08. Defendant May Testify.

Any defendant in a criminal action shall be permitted to testify in his own behalf therein, but the failure of any defendant to so testify shall not be taken as a circumstance against him, nor shall the same be alluded to or commented on by counsel in the cause.

Art. 38.09. Court May Determine Competency [Repealed].

Repealed by the Texas Court of Criminal Appeals pursuant to Acts 1985, 69th Leg., ch. 685 (H.B. 13), § 9, effective September 1, 1986.

Art. 38.10. Exceptions to the Spousal Adverse Testimony Privilege.

The privilege of a person's spouse not to be called as a witness for the state does not apply in any proceeding in which the person is charged with:

(1) a crime committed against the person's spouse, a minor child, or a member of the household of either spouse; or

(2) an offense under Section 25.01, Penal Code (Bigamy).

Art. 38.101. Communications by Drug Abusers.

A communication to any person involved in the treatment or examination of drug abusers by a person being treated voluntarily or being examined for admission to voluntary treatment for drug abuse is not admissible. However, information derived from the treatment or examination of drug abusers may be used for statistical and research purposes if the names of the patients are not revealed.

Art. 38.11. Journalist's Qualified Testimonial Privilege in Criminal Proceedings.

Sec. 1. **Definitions.** — In this article:

(1) "Communication service provider" means a person or the parent, subsidiary, division, or affiliate of a person who transmits information chosen by a customer by electronic means, including:

(A) a telecommunications carrier, as defined by Section 3, Communications Act of 1934 (47 U.S.C. Section 153);

(B) a provider of information service, as defined by Section 3, Communications Act of 1934 (47 U.S.C. Section 153);

(C) a provider of interactive computer service, as defined by Section 230, Communications Act of 1934 (47 U.S.C. Section 230); and

(D) an information content provider, as defined by Section 230, Communications Act of 1934 (47 U.S.C. Section 230).

(2) "Journalist" means a person, including a parent, subsidiary, division, or affiliate of a person, who for a substantial portion of the person's livelihood or for substantial financial gain, gathers, compiles, prepares, collects, photographs, records, writes, edits, reports, investigates, processes, or publishes news or information that is disseminated by a news medium or communication service provider and includes:

(A) a person who supervises or assists in gathering, preparing, and disseminating the news or information; or

Code of Criminal Procedure

(B) notwithstanding the foregoing, a person who is or was a journalist, scholar, or researcher employed by an institution of higher education at the time the person obtained or prepared the requested information, or a person who at the time the person obtained or prepared the requested information:

(i) is earning a significant portion of the person's livelihood by obtaining or preparing information for dissemination by a news medium or communication service provider; or

(ii) was serving as an agent, assistant, employee, or supervisor of a news medium or communication service provider.

(3) "News medium" means a newspaper, magazine or periodical, book publisher, news agency, wire service, radio or television station or network, cable, satellite, or other transmission system or carrier or channel, or a channel or programming service for a station, network, system, or carrier, or an audio or audiovisual production company or Internet company or provider, or the parent, subsidiary, division, or affiliate of that entity, that disseminates news or information to the public by any means, including:

(A) print;
(B) television;
(C) radio;
(D) photographic;
(E) mechanical;
(F) electronic; and
(G) other means, known or unknown, that are accessible to the public.

(4) "Official proceeding" means any type of administrative, executive, legislative, or judicial proceeding that may be conducted before a public servant.

(5) "Public servant" means a person elected, selected, appointed, employed, or otherwise designated as one of the following, even if the person has not yet qualified for office or assumed the person's duties:

(A) an officer, employee, or agent of government;
(B) a juror or grand juror;
(C) an arbitrator, referee, or other person who is authorized by law or private written agreement to hear or determine a cause or controversy;
(D) an attorney or notary public when participating in the performance of a governmental function; or
(E) a person who is performing a governmental function under a claim of right, although the person is not legally qualified to do so.

Sec. 2. **Purpose.** — The purpose of this article is to increase the free flow of information and preserve a free and active press and, at the same time, protect the right of the public to effective law enforcement and the fair administration of justice.

Sec. 3. **Privilege.**

(a) Except as otherwise provided by this article, a judicial, legislative, administrative, or other body with the authority to issue a subpoena or other compulsory process may not compel a journalist to testify regarding or to produce or disclose in an official proceeding:

(1) any confidential or nonconfidential unpublished information, document, or item obtained or prepared while acting as a journalist; or

(2) the source of any information, document, or item described by Subdivision (1).

(b) A subpoena or other compulsory process may not compel the parent, subsidiary, division, or affiliate of a communication service provider or news medium to disclose the unpublished information, documents, or items or the source of any information, documents, or items that are privileged from disclosure under Subsection (a).

Sec. 4. **Privilege Concerning Confidential Sources.**

(a) A journalist may be compelled to testify regarding or to disclose the confidential source of any information, document, or item obtained while acting as a journalist if the person seeking the testimony, production, or disclosure makes a clear and specific showing that the source of any information, document, or item:

(1) was observed by the journalist committing a felony criminal offense and the subpoenaing party has exhausted reasonable efforts to obtain from alternative sources the confidential source of any information, document, or item obtained or prepared while acting as a journalist;

(2) is a person who confessed or admitted to the journalist the commission of a felony criminal offense and the subpoenaing party has exhausted reasonable efforts to obtain from alternative sources the confidential source of any information, document, or item obtained or prepared while acting as a journalist;

(3) is a person for whom probable cause exists that the person participated in a felony criminal offense and the subpoenaing party has exhausted reasonable efforts to obtain from alternative sources the confidential source of any information, document, or item obtained or prepared while acting as a journalist; or

(4) disclosure of the confidential source is reasonably necessary to stop or prevent reasonably certain death or substantial bodily harm.

(b) If the alleged criminal conduct is the act of communicating, receiving, or possessing the information, document, or item, this section does not apply, and Section 5 governs the act.

(c) Notwithstanding Subsection (b), if the information, document, or item was disclosed or received in violation of a grand jury oath given to either a juror or a witness under Article 19A.202 or 20A.256, a journalist may be compelled to testify if the person seeking the testimony, production, or disclosure makes a clear and specific showing that the subpoenaing party has exhausted reasonable efforts to obtain from alternative sources the confidential source of any information, document, or item obtained. In this context, the court has the discretion to conduct an in camera hearing. The court may not order the production of the confidential source until a ruling has been made on the motion.

(d) An application for a subpoena of a journalist under Article 24.03, or a subpoena of a journalist issued by an attorney representing the state under Article 20A.251 or 20A.252, must be signed by the elected district attorney, elected criminal district attorney, or elected county attorney, as applicable. If the elected district attorney, elected criminal district attorney, or elected county attorney has been disqualified or recused or has resigned, the application for the subpoena or the subpoena must be signed by the person succeeding the elected attorney. If the elected officer is not in the jurisdiction, the highest ranking assistant to the elected officer must sign the subpoena.

Sec. 5. **Privilege Concerning Unpublished Information, Document, or Item and Nonconfidential Sources.**

(a) After service of subpoena and an opportunity to be heard, a court may compel a journalist, a journalist's employer, or a person with an independent contract with a journalist to testify regarding or to produce or disclose any unpublished information, document, or item or the source of any information, document, or item obtained while acting as a journalist, other than as described by Section 4, if the person seeking the unpublished information, document, or item or the source of any information, document, or item makes a clear and specific showing that:

(1) all reasonable efforts have been exhausted to obtain the information from alternative sources; and

(2) the unpublished information, document, or item:

(A) is relevant and material to the proper administration of the official proceeding for which the testimony, production, or disclosure is sought and is essential to the maintenance of a claim or defense of the person seeking the testimony, production, or disclosure; or

(B) is central to the investigation or prosecution of a criminal case and based on something other than the assertion of the person requesting the subpoena, reasonable grounds exist to believe that a crime has occurred.

(b) The court, when considering an order to compel testimony regarding or to produce or disclose any unpublished information, document, or item or the source of any information, document, or item obtained while acting as a journalist, should consider the following factors, including but not limited to whether:

(1) the subpoena is overbroad, unreasonable, or oppressive;

(2) reasonable and timely notice was given of the demand for the information, document, or item;

(3) in this instance, the interest of the party subpoenaing the information outweighs the public interest in gathering and dissemination of news, including the concerns of the journalist; and

(4) the subpoena or compulsory process is being used to obtain peripheral, nonessential, or speculative information.

(c) A court may not consider a single factor under Subsection (b) as outcome-determinative in the decision whether to compel the testimony or the production or disclosure of the unpublished information, document, or item, or the source of any information, document, or item.

Sec. 6. **Notice.** — An order to compel testimony, production, or disclosure to which a journalist has asserted a privilege under this article may be issued only after timely notice to the journalist, the journalist's employer, or a person who has an independent contract with the journalist and a hearing. The order must include clear and specific findings as to the showing made by the person seeking the testimony, production, or disclosure and the clear and specific evidence on which the court relied in issuing the court's order.

Sec. 7. **Publication of Privileged Information.** — Publication or dissemination by a news medium or communication service provider of information, documents, or items privileged under this article is not a waiver of the journalist's privilege regarding sources and unpublished information, documents, or items.

Sec. 8. **Published Information.** — This article does not apply to any information, document, or item that has at any time been published or broadcast by the journalist.

Sec. 9. **Reimbursement of Costs.** — The subpoenaing party shall pay a journalist a reasonable fee for the journalist's time and costs incurred in providing the information, item, or document subpoenaed, based on the fee structure provided by Subchapter F, Chapter 552, Government Code.

Art. 38.111. News Media Recordings.

Extrinsic evidence of the authenticity of evidence as a condition precedent to the admissibility of the evidence in a criminal proceeding is not required with respect to a recording that purports to be a broadcast by a radio or television station that holds a license issued by the Federal Communications Commission at the time of the recording. The court may take judicial notice of the recording license as provided by Rule 201, Texas Rules of Evidence.

Art. 38.12. Religious Opinion.

No person is incompetent to testify on account of his religious opinion or for the want of any religious belief.

Art. 38.13. Judge As a Witness [Repealed].

Repealed by the Texas Court of Criminal Appeals pursuant to Acts 1985, 69th Leg., ch. 685 (H.B. 13), § 9, effective September 1, 1986.

Art. 38.14. Testimony of Accomplice.

A conviction cannot be had upon the testimony of an accomplice unless corroborated by other evidence tending to connect the defendant with the offense committed; and the corroboration is not sufficient if it merely shows the commission of the offense.

Art. 38.141. Testimony of Undercover Peace Officer or Special Investigator.

(a) A defendant may not be convicted of an offense under Chapter 481, Health and Safety Code, on the testimony of a person who is not a licensed peace officer or a special investigator but who is acting covertly on behalf of a law enforcement agency or under the color of law enforcement unless the testimony is corroborated by other evidence tending to connect the defendant with the offense committed.

(b) Corroboration is not sufficient for the purposes of this article if the corroboration only shows the commission of the offense.

(c) In this article, "peace officer" means a person listed in Article 2.12, and "special investigator" means a person listed in Article 2.122.

Art. 38.15. Two Witnesses in Treason.

No person can be convicted of treason except upon the testimony of at least two witnesses to the same overt act, or upon his own confession in open court.

Art. 38.16. Evidence in Treason.

Evidence shall not be admitted in a prosecution for treason as to an overt act not expressly charged in the indictment; nor shall any person be convicted under an indictment for treason unless one or more overt acts are expressly charged therein.

Art. 38.17. Two Witnesses Required.

In all cases where, by law, two witnesses, or one with corroborating circumstances, are required to authorize a conviction, if the requirement be not fulfilled, the court shall instruct the jury to render a verdict of acquittal, and they are bound by the instruction.

Art. 38.18. Perjury and Aggravated Perjury.

(a) No person may be convicted of perjury or aggravated perjury if proof that his statement is false rests solely upon the testimony of one witness other than the defendant.

(b) Paragraph (a) of this article does not apply to prosecutions for perjury or aggravated perjury involving inconsistent statements.

Art. 38.19. Intent to Defraud: Certain Offenses.

(a) This article applies to the trial of an offense under any of the following sections of the Penal Code:

(1) Section 32.21 (Forgery);

(2) Section 32.31 (Credit Card or Debit Card Abuse); or

(3) Section 32.51 (Fraudulent Use or Possession of Identifying Information).

(b) In the trial of an offense to which this article applies, the attorney representing the state is not required to prove that the defendant committed the act with intent to defraud any particular person. It is sufficient to prove that the offense was, in its nature, calculated to injure or defraud any of the sovereignties, bodies corporate or politic, officers or persons, named in the definition of the offense in the Penal Code.

Art. 38.20. Photograph and Live Lineup Identification Procedures.

Sec. 1. In this article, "institute" means the Bill Blackwood Law Enforcement Management Institute of Texas located at Sam Houston State University.

Sec. 2. This article applies only to a law enforcement agency of this state or of a county, municipality, or other political subdivision of this state that employs peace officers who conduct photograph or live lineup identification procedures in the routine performance of the officers' official duties.

Sec. 3. (a) Each law enforcement agency shall adopt, implement, and as necessary amend a detailed written policy regarding the administration of photograph and live lineup identification procedures in accordance with this article. A law enforcement agency may adopt:

(1) the model policy adopted under Subsection (b); or

(2) the agency's own policy that, at a minimum, conforms to the requirements of Subsection (c).

(b) The institute, in consultation with large, medium, and small law enforcement agencies and with law enforcement associations, scientific experts in eyewitness memory research, and appropriate organizations engaged in the development of law enforcement policy, shall develop, adopt, and disseminate to all law enforcement agencies in this state a model policy and associated training materials regarding the administration of photograph and live lineup identification procedures. The institute shall provide for a period of public comment before adopting the policy and materials.

(c) The model policy or any other policy adopted by a law enforcement agency under Subsection (a) must:

(1) be based on:

(A) credible field, academic, or laboratory research on eyewitness memory;

(B) relevant policies, guidelines, and best practices designed to reduce erroneous eyewitness identifications and to enhance the reliability and objectivity of eyewitness identifications; and

(C) other relevant information as appropriate; and

(2) include the following information regarding evidence-based practices:

(A) procedures for selecting photograph and live lineup filler photographs or participants to ensure that the photographs or participants:

(i) are consistent in appearance with the description of the alleged perpetrator; and

(ii) do not make the suspect noticeably stand out;

(B) instructions given to a witness before conducting a photograph or live lineup identification procedure that must include a statement that the person who committed the offense may or may not be present in the procedure;

(C) procedures for documenting and preserving the results of a photograph or live lineup identification procedure, including the documentation of witness statements, regardless of the outcome of the procedure;

(D) procedures for administering a photograph or live lineup identification procedure to an illiterate person or a person with limited English language proficiency;

(E) for a live lineup identification procedure, if practicable, procedures for assigning an administrator who is unaware of which member of the live lineup is the suspect in the case or alternative procedures designed to prevent opportunities to influence the witness;

(F) for a photograph identification procedure, procedures for assigning an administrator who is capable of administering a photograph array in a blind manner or in a manner consistent with other proven or supported best practices designed to prevent opportunities to influence the witness; and

(G) any other procedures or best practices supported by credible research or commonly accepted as a means to reduce erroneous eyewitness identifications and to enhance the objectivity and reliability of eyewitness identifications.

(d) A witness who makes an identification based on a photograph or live lineup identification procedure shall be asked immediately after the procedure to state, in the witness's own words, how confident the witness is in making the identification. A law enforcement agency shall document in accordance with Subsection (c)(2)(C) any statement made under this subsection.

Sec. 4. (a) Not later than December 31 of each odd-numbered year, the institute shall review the model policy and training materials adopted under this article and shall modify the policy and materials as appropriate.

(b) Not later than September 1 of each even-numbered year, each law enforcement agency shall review its policy adopted under this article and shall modify that policy as appropriate.

Sec. 5. (a) Any evidence or expert testimony presented by the state or the defendant on the subject of eyewitness identification is admissible only subject to compliance with the Texas Rules of Evidence. Except as provided by Subsection (c), evidence of compliance with the model policy or any other policy adopted under this article is not a condition precedent to the admissibility of an out-of-court eyewitness identification.

(b) Notwithstanding Article 38.23 as that article relates to a violation of a state statute and except as provided by Subsection (c), a failure to conduct a photograph or live lineup identification procedure in substantial compliance with the model policy or any other policy adopted under this article does not bar the admission of eyewitness identification testimony in the courts of this state.

(c) If a witness who has previously made an out-of-court photograph or live lineup identification of the accused makes an in-court identification of the accused, the eyewitness identification is admissible into evidence against the accused only if the evidence is accompanied by the details of each prior photograph or live lineup identification made of the accused by the witness, including the manner in which the identification procedure was conducted.

Art. 38.21. Statement.

A statement of an accused may be used in evidence against him if it appears that the same was freely and voluntarily made without compulsion or persuasion, under the rules hereafter prescribed.

Art. 38.22. When Statements May Be Used.

Sec. 1. In this article, a written statement of an accused means:

(1) a statement made by the accused in his own handwriting; or

(2) a statement made in a language the accused can read or understand that:

(A) is signed by the accused; or

(B) bears the mark of the accused, if the accused is unable to write and the mark is witnessed by a person other than a peace officer.

Sec. 2. No written statement made by an accused as a result of custodial interrogation is admissible as evidence against him in any criminal proceeding unless it is shown on the face of the statement that:

(a) the accused, prior to making the statement, either received from a magistrate the warning provided in Article 15.17 of this code or received from the person to whom the statement is made a warning that:

(1) he has the right to remain silent and not make any statement at all and that any statement he makes may be used against him at his trial;

(2) any statement he makes may be used as evidence against him in court;

(3) he has the right to have a lawyer present to advise him prior to and during any questioning;

(4) if he is unable to employ a lawyer, he has the right to have a lawyer appointed to advise him prior to and during any questioning; and

(5) he has the right to terminate the interview at any time; and

(b) the accused, prior to and during the making of the statement, knowingly, intelligently, and voluntarily waived the rights set out in the warning prescribed by Subsection (a) of this section.

Sec. 3. (a) No oral or sign language statement of an accused made as a result of custodial interrogation shall be admissible against the accused in a criminal proceeding unless:

(1) an electronic recording, which may include motion picture, video tape, or other visual recording, is made of the statement;

(2) prior to the statement but during the recording the accused is given the warning in Subsection (a) of Section 2 above and the accused knowingly, intelligently, and voluntarily waives any rights set out in the warning;

(3) the recording device was capable of making an accurate recording, the operator was competent, and the recording is accurate and has not been altered;

(4) all voices on the recording are identified; and

(5) not later than the 20th day before the date of the proceeding, the attorney representing the defendant is provided with a true, complete, and accurate copy of all recordings of the defendant made under this article.

(b) Every electronic recording of any statement made by an accused during a custodial interrogation must be preserved until such time as the defendant's conviction for any offense relating thereto is final, all direct appeals therefrom are exhausted, or the prosecution of such offenses is barred by law.

(c) Subsection (a) of this section shall not apply to any statement which contains assertions of facts or circumstances that are found to be true and which conduce to establish the guilt of the accused, such as the finding of secreted or stolen property or the instrument with which he states the offense was committed.

(d) If the accused is a deaf person, the accused's statement under Section 2 or Section 3(a) of this article is not admissible against the accused unless the warning in Section 2 of this article is interpreted to the deaf person by an interpreter who is qualified and sworn as provided in Article 38.31 of this code.

(e) The courts of this state shall strictly construe Subsection (a) of this section and may not interpret Subsection (a) as making admissible a statement unless all requirements of the subsection have been satisfied by the state, except that:

(1) only voices that are material are identified; and

(2) the accused was given the warning in Subsection (a) of Section 2 above or its fully effective equivalent.

Sec. 4. When any statement, the admissibility of which is covered by this article, is sought to be used in connection with an official proceeding, any person who swears falsely to facts and circumstances which, if true, would render the statement admissible under this article is presumed to have acted with intent to deceive and with knowledge of the statement's meaning for the purpose of prosecution for aggravated perjury under Section 37.03 of the Penal Code. No person prosecuted under this subsection shall be eligible for probation.

Sec. 5. Nothing in this article precludes the admission of a statement made by the accused in open court at his trial, before a grand jury, or at an examining trial in compliance with Articles 16.03 and 16.04 of this code, or of a statement that is the res gestae of the arrest or of the offense, or of a statement that does not stem from custodial interrogation, or of a voluntary statement, whether or not the result of custodial interrogation, that has a bearing upon the credibility of the accused as a witness, or of any other statement that may be admissible under law.

Sec. 6. In all cases where a question is raised as to the voluntariness of a statement of an accused, the court must make an independent finding in the absence of the jury as to whether the statement was made under voluntary conditions. If the statement has been found to have been voluntarily made and held admissible as a matter of law and fact by the court in a hearing in the absence of the jury, the court must enter an order stating its conclusion as to whether or not the statement was voluntarily made, along with the specific finding of facts upon which the conclusion was based, which order shall be filed among the papers of the cause. Such order shall not be exhibited to the jury nor the finding thereof made known to the jury in any manner. Upon the finding by the judge as a matter of law and fact that the statement was voluntarily made, evidence pertaining to such matter may be submitted to the jury and it shall be instructed that unless the jury believes beyond a reasonable doubt that the statement was voluntarily made, the jury shall not consider such statement for any purpose nor any evidence obtained as a result thereof. In any case where a motion to suppress the statement has been filed and evidence has been submitted to the court on this issue, the court within its discretion may reconsider such evidence in his finding that the statement was voluntarily made and the same evidence submitted to the court at the hearing on the motion to suppress shall be made a part of the record the same as if it were being presented at the time of trial. However, the state or the defendant shall be entitled to present any new evidence on the issue of the voluntariness of the statement prior to the court's final ruling and order stating its findings.

Sec. 7. When the issue is raised by the evidence, the trial judge shall appropriately instruct the jury, generally, on the law pertaining to such statement.

Sec. 8. Notwithstanding any other provision of this article, a written, oral, or sign language statement of an accused made as a result of a custodial interrogation is admissible against the accused in a criminal proceeding in this state if:

(1) the statement was obtained in another state and was obtained in compliance with the laws of that state or this state; or

(2) the statement was obtained by a federal law enforcement officer in this state or another state and was obtained in compliance with the laws of the United States.

Sec. 9. Notwithstanding any other provision of this article, no oral, sign language, or written statement that is made by a person accused of an offense listed in Article 2.32(b) and made as a result of a custodial interrogation occurring in a place of detention, as that term is defined by Article 2.32, is admissible against the accused in a criminal proceeding unless:

(1) an electronic recording was made of the statement, as required by Article 2.32(b); or

(2) the attorney representing the state offers proof satisfactory to the court that good cause, as described by Article 2.32(d), existed that made electronic recording of the custodial interrogation infeasible.

Art. 38.23. Evidence Not to Be Used.

(a) No evidence obtained by an officer or other person in violation of any provisions of the Constitution or laws of the State of Texas, or of the Constitution or laws of the United States of America, shall be admitted in evidence against the accused on the trial of any criminal case.

In any case where the legal evidence raises an issue hereunder, the jury shall be instructed that if it believes, or has a reasonable doubt, that the evidence was obtained in violation of the provisions of this Article, then and in such event, the jury shall disregard any such evidence so obtained.

(b) It is an exception to the provisions of Subsection (a) of this Article that the evidence was obtained by a law enforcement officer acting in objective good faith reliance upon a warrant issued by a neutral magistrate based on probable cause.

Art. 38.24. Part of an Act, Declaration, Conversation or Writing [Repealed].

Repealed by the Texas Court of Criminal Appeals pursuant to Acts 1985, 69th Leg., ch. 685 (H.B. 13), § 9, effective September 1, 1986.

Art. 38.25. Written Part of Instrument Controls.

When an instrument is partly written and partly printed, the written shall control the printed portion when the two are inconsistent.

Art. 38.26. If Subscribing Witness Denies Execution [Repealed].

Repealed by the Texas Court of Criminal Appeals pursuant to Acts 1985, 69th Leg., ch. 685 (H.B. 13), § 9, effective September 1, 1986.

Art. 38.27. Evidence of Handwriting.

It is competent to give evidence of handwriting by comparison, made by experts or by the jury. Proof by comparison only shall not be sufficient to establish the handwriting of a witness who denies his signature under oath.

Art. 38.28. Attacking Testimony of His Own Witness [Repealed].

Repealed by the Texas Court of Criminal Appeals pursuant to Acts 1985, 69th Leg., ch. 685 (H.B. 13), § 9(b), effective September 1, 1986.

Art. 38.29. Indictment, Information or Complaint Not Admissible to Impeach Witness [Repealed].

Repealed by the Texas Court of Criminal Appeals pursuant to Acts 1985, 69th Leg., ch. 685 (H.B. 13), § 9.

Art. 38.30. Interpreter.

(a) When a motion for appointment of an interpreter is filed by any party or on motion of the court, in any criminal proceeding, it is determined that a person charged or a witness does not understand and speak the English language, an interpreter must be sworn to interpret for the person charged or the witness. Any person may be subpoenaed, attached or recognized in any criminal action or proceeding, to appear before the proper judge or court to act as interpreter therein, under the same rules and penalties as are provided for witnesses. In the event that the only available interpreter is not considered to possess adequate interpreting skills for the particular situation or the interpreter is not familiar with use of slang, the person charged or witness may be permitted by the court to nominate another person to act as intermediary between the person charged or witness and the appointed interpreter during the proceedings.

(a-1) A qualified telephone interpreter may be sworn to interpret for the person in any criminal proceeding before a judge or magistrate if an interpreter is not available to appear in person at the proceeding or if the only available interpreter is not considered to possess adequate interpreting skills for the particular situation or is unfamiliar with the use of slang. In this subsection, "qualified telephone interpreter" means a telephone service that employs:

(1) licensed court interpreters as defined by Section 157.001, Government Code; or

(2) federally certified court interpreters.

(b) Except as provided by Subsection (c) of this article, interpreters appointed under the terms of this article will receive from the general fund of the county for their services a sum not to exceed $100 a day as follows: interpreters shall be paid not less than $15 nor more than $100 a day at the discretion of the judge presiding, and when travel of the interpreter is involved all the actual expenses of travel, lodging, and meals incurred by the interpreter pertaining to the case the interpreter is appointed to serve shall be paid at the same rate applicable to state employees.

(c) A county commissioners court may set a payment schedule and expend funds for the services of interpreters in excess of the daily amount of not less than $15 or more than $100 established by Subsection (b) of this article.

Art. 38.31. Interpreters for Deaf Persons.

(a) If the court is notified by a party that the defendant is deaf and will be present at an arraignment, hearing, examining trial, or trial, or that a witness is deaf and will be called at a hearing, examining trial, or trial, the court shall appoint a qualified interpreter to interpret the proceedings in any language that the deaf person can understand, including but not limited to sign language. On the court's motion or the motion of a party, the court may order testimony of a deaf witness and the interpretation of that testimony by the interpreter visually, electronically recorded for use in verification of the transcription of the reporter's notes. The clerk of the court shall include that recording in the appellate record if requested by a party under Article 40.09 of this Code.

(b) Following the filing of an indictment, information, or complaint against a deaf defendant, the court on the motion of the defendant shall appoint a qualified interpreter to interpret in a language that the defendant can understand, including but not limited to sign language, communications concerning the case between the defendant and defense counsel. The interpreter may not disclose a communication between the defendant and defense counsel or a fact that came to the attention of the interpreter while interpreting those communications if defense counsel may not disclose that communication or fact.

(c) In all cases where the mental condition of a person is being considered and where such person may be committed to a mental institution, and where such person is deaf, all of the court proceedings pertaining to him shall be interpreted by a qualified interpreter appointed by the court.

(d) A proceeding for which an interpreter is required to be appointed under this Article may not commence until the appointed interpreter is in a position not exceeding ten feet from and in full view of the deaf person.

(e) The interpreter appointed under the terms of this Article shall be required to take an oath that he will make a true interpretation to the person accused or being examined, which person is deaf, of all the proceedings of his case in a language that he understands; and that he will repeat said deaf person's answer to questions to counsel, court, or jury, in the English language, in his best skill and judgment.

(f) Interpreters appointed under this Article are entitled to a reasonable fee determined by the court after considering the recommendations of the Texas Commission for the Deaf and Hard of Hearing. When travel of the interpreter is involved all the actual expenses of travel, lodging, and meals incurred by the interpreter pertaining to the case he is appointed to serve shall be paid at the same rate applicable to state employees.

(g) In this Code:

(1) "Deaf person" means a person who has a hearing impairment, regardless of whether the person also has a speech impairment, that inhibits the person's comprehension of the proceedings or communication with others.

(2) "Qualified interpreter" means an interpreter for the deaf who holds a current legal certificate issued by the National Registry of Interpreters for the Deaf or a current court interpreter certificate issued by the Board for Evaluation of Interpreters at the Department of Assistive and Rehabilitative Services.

Art. 38.32. Presumption of Death.

(a) Upon introduction and admission into evidence of a valid certificate of death wherein the time of death of the decedent has been entered by a licensed physician, a presumption exists that death occurred at the time stated in the certificate of death.

(b) A presumption existing pursuant to Section (a) of this Article is sufficient to support a finding as to time of death but may be rebutted through a showing by a preponderance of the evidence that death occurred at some other time.

Art. 38.33. Preservation and Use of Evidence of Certain Misdemeanor Convictions.

Sec. 1. The court shall order that a defendant who is convicted of a felony or a misdemeanor offense that is punishable by confinement in jail have a thumbprint of the defendant's right thumb rolled legibly on the judgment or the docket sheet in the case. The court shall order a defendant who is placed on deferred adjudication community supervision under Subchapter C, Chapter 42A, for an offense described by this section to have a thumbprint of the defendant's right thumb rolled legibly on the order placing the defendant on deferred adjudication community supervision. If the defendant does not have a right thumb, the defendant must have a thumbprint of the defendant's left thumb rolled legibly on the judgment, order, or docket sheet. The defendant must have a fingerprint of the defendant's index finger rolled legibly on the judgment, order, or docket sheet if the defendant does not have a right thumb or a left thumb. The judgment, order, or docket sheet must contain a statement that describes from which thumb or finger the print was taken, unless a rolled 10-finger print set was taken. A clerk or bailiff of the court or other person qualified to take fingerprints shall take the thumbprint or fingerprint, either by use of the ink-rolled print method or by use of a live-scanning device that prints the thumbprint or fingerprint image on the judgment, order, or docket sheet.

Sec. 2. This article does not prohibit a court from including in the records of the case additional information to identify the defendant.

Art. 38.34. Photographic Evidence in Theft Cases.

(a) In this article, "property" means any tangible personal property.

(b) A photograph of property that a person is alleged to have unlawfully appropriated with the intent to deprive the owner of the property is admissible into evidence under rules of law governing the admissibility of photographs. The photograph is as admissible in evidence as is the property itself.

(c) The provisions of Article 18.16 concerning the bringing of stolen property before a magistrate for examination are complied with if a photograph of the stolen property is brought before the magistrate.

(d) The defendant's rights of discovery and inspection of tangible physical evidence are satisfied if a photograph of the property is made available to the defendant by the state on order of any court having jurisdiction over the cause.

Art. 38.35. Forensic Analysis of Evidence; Admissibility.

(a) In this article:

(1) "Crime laboratory" includes a public or private laboratory or other entity that conducts a forensic analysis subject to this article.

(2) "Criminal action" includes an investigation, complaint, arrest, bail, bond, trial, appeal, punishment, or other matter related to conduct proscribed by a criminal offense.

(3) "Commission" means the Texas Forensic Science Commission established under Article 38.01.

(4) "Forensic analysis" means a medical, chemical, toxicologic, ballistic, or other expert examination or test performed on physical evidence, including DNA evidence, for the purpose of determining the connection of the evidence to a criminal action. The term includes an examination or test requested by a law enforcement agency, prosecutor, criminal suspect or defendant, or court. The term does not include:

(A) latent print examination;

(B) a test of a specimen of breath under Chapter 724, Transportation Code;

(C) digital evidence;

(D) an examination or test excluded by rule under Article 38.01;

(E) a presumptive test performed for the purpose of determining compliance with a term or condition of community supervision or parole and conducted by or under contract with a community supervision and corrections department, the parole division of the Texas Department of Criminal Justice, or the Board of Pardons and Paroles; or

(F) an expert examination or test conducted principally for the purpose of scientific research, medical practice, civil or administrative litigation, or other purpose unrelated to determining the connection of physical evidence to a criminal action.

(5) "Physical evidence" means any tangible object, thing, or substance relating to a criminal action.

(b) A law enforcement agency, prosecutor, or court may request a forensic analysis by a crime laboratory of physical evidence if the evidence was obtained in connection with the requesting entity's investigation or disposition of a criminal action and the requesting entity:

(1) controls the evidence;

(2) submits the evidence to the laboratory; or

(3) consents to the analysis.

(c) A law enforcement agency, other governmental agency, or private entity performing a forensic analysis of physical evidence may require the requesting law enforcement agency to pay a fee for such analysis.

(d) (1) Except as provided by Subsection (e), a forensic analysis of physical evidence under this article and expert testimony relating to the evidence are not admissible in a criminal action if, at the time of the analysis, the crime laboratory conducting the analysis was not accredited by the commission under Article 38.01.

(2) If before the date of the analysis the commission issues a certificate of accreditation under Article 38.01 to a crime laboratory conducting the analysis, the certificate is prima facie evidence that the laboratory was accredited by the commission at the time of the analysis.

(e) A forensic analysis of physical evidence under this article and expert testimony relating to the evidence are not inadmissible in a criminal action based solely on the accreditation status of the crime laboratory conducting the analysis if the laboratory:

(A) except for making proper application, was eligible for accreditation by the commission at the time of the examination or test; and

(B) obtains accreditation from the commission before the time of testimony about the examination or test.

(f) This article does not apply to the portion of an autopsy conducted by a medical examiner or other forensic pathologist who is a licensed physician.

Art. 38.36. Evidence in Prosecutions for Murder.

(a) In all prosecutions for murder, the state or the defendant shall be permitted to offer testimony as to all relevant facts and circumstances surrounding the killing and the previous relationship existing between the accused and the deceased, together with all relevant facts and circumstances going to show the condition of the mind of the accused at the time of the offense.

(b) In a prosecution for murder, if a defendant raises as a defense a justification provided by Section 9.31, 9.32, or 9.33, Penal Code, the defendant, in order to establish the defendant's reasonable belief that use of force or deadly force was immediately necessary, shall be permitted to offer:

(1) relevant evidence that the defendant had been the victim of acts of family violence committed by the deceased, as family violence is defined by Section 71.004, Family Code; and

(2) relevant expert testimony regarding the condition of the mind of the defendant at the time of the offense, including those relevant facts and circumstances relating to family violence that are the basis of the expert's opinion.

Art. 38.37. Evidence of Extraneous Offenses or Acts.

Sec. 1. (a) Subsection (b) applies to a proceeding in the prosecution of a defendant for an offense, or an attempt or conspiracy to commit an offense, under the following provisions of the Penal Code:

(1) if committed against a child under 17 years of age:

(A) Chapter 21 (Sexual Offenses);

(B) Chapter 22 (Assaultive Offenses); or

(C) Section 25.02 (Prohibited Sexual Conduct); or

(2) if committed against a person younger than 18 years of age:

(A) Section 43.25 (Sexual Performance by a Child);

(B) Section 20A.02(a)(7) or (8); or

(C) Section 43.05(a)(2) (Compelling Prostitution).

(b) Notwithstanding Rules 404 and 405, Texas Rules of Evidence, evidence of other crimes, wrongs, or acts committed by the defendant against the child who is the victim of the alleged offense shall be admitted for its bearing on relevant matters, including:

(1) the state of mind of the defendant and the child; and

(2) the previous and subsequent relationship between the defendant and the child.

Sec. 2. (a) Subsection (b) applies only to the trial of a defendant for:

(1) an offense under any of the following provisions of the Penal Code:

(A) Section 20A.02, if punishable as a felony of the first degree under Section 20A.02(b)(1) (Sex Trafficking of a Child);

(B) Section 21.02 (Continuous Sexual Abuse of Young Child or Disabled Individual);

(C) Section 21.11 (Indecency With a Child);

(D) Section 22.011(a)(2) (Sexual Assault of a Child);

(E) Sections 22.021(a)(1)(B) and (2) (Aggravated Sexual Assault of a Child);

(F) Section 33.021 (Online Solicitation of a Minor);

(G) Section 43.25 (Sexual Performance by a Child); or

(H) Section 43.26 (Possession or Promotion of Child Pornography), Penal Code; or

(2) an attempt or conspiracy to commit an offense described by Subdivision (1).

(b) Notwithstanding Rules 404 and 405, Texas Rules of Evidence, and subject to Section 2-a, evidence that the defendant has committed a separate offense described by Subsection (a)(1) or (2) may be admitted in the trial of an alleged offense described by Subsection (a)(1) or (2) for any bearing the evidence has on relevant matters, including the character of the defendant and acts performed in conformity with the character of the defendant.

Sec. 2-a. Before evidence described by Section 2 may be introduced, the trial judge must:

(1) determine that the evidence likely to be admitted at trial will be adequate to support a finding by the jury that the defendant committed the separate offense beyond a reasonable doubt; and

(2) conduct a hearing out of the presence of the jury for that purpose.

Sec. 3. The state shall give the defendant notice of the state's intent to introduce in the case in chief evidence described by Section 1 or 2 not later than the 30th day before the date of the defendant's trial.

Sec. 4. This article does not limit the admissibility of evidence of extraneous crimes, wrongs, or acts under any other applicable law.

Code of Criminal Procedure

Art. 38.371. Evidence in Prosecution of Offense Committed Against Member of Defendant's Family or Household or Person in Dating Relationship with Defendant

(a) This article applies to a proceeding in the prosecution of a defendant for an offense, or for an attempt or conspiracy to commit an offense, for which the alleged victim isa person whose relationship to or association with the defendant is described by Section 71.0021(b), 71.003, or 71.005, Family Code.

(b) In the prosecution of an offense described by Subsection (a), subject to the Texas Rules of Evidence or other applicable law, each party may offer testimony or other evidence of all relevant facts and circumstances that would assist the trier of fact in determining whether the actor committed the offense described by Subsection (a), including testimony or evidence regarding the nature of the relationship between the actor and the alleged victim.

(c) This article does not permit the presentation of character evidence that would otherwise be inadmissible under the Texas Rules of Evidence or other applicable law.

Art. 38.38. Evidence Relating to Retaining Attorney.

Evidence that a person has contacted or retained an attorney is not admissible on the issue of whether the person committed a criminal offense. In a criminal case, neither the judge nor the attorney representing the state may comment on the fact that the defendant has contacted or retained an attorney in the case.

Art. 38.39. Evidence in an Aggregation Prosecution with Numerous Victims.

In trials involving an allegation of a continuing scheme of fraud or theft alleged to have been committed against a large class of victims in an aggregate amount or value, it need not be proved by direct evidence that each alleged victim did not consent or did not effectively consent to the transaction in question. It shall be sufficient if the lack of consent or effective consent to a particular transaction or transactions is proven by either direct or circumstantial evidence.

Art. 38.40. Evidence of Pregnancy.

(a) In a prosecution for the death of or injury to an individual who is an unborn child, the prosecution shall provide medical or other evidence that the mother of the individual was pregnant at the time of the alleged offense.

(b) For the purpose of this section, "individual" has the meaning assigned by Section 1.07, Penal Code.

Art. 38.41. Certificate of Analysis.

Sec. 1. A certificate of analysis that complies with this article is admissible in evidence on behalf of the state or the defendant to establish the results of a laboratory analysis of physical evidence conducted by or for a law enforcement agency without the necessity of the analyst personally appearing in court.

Sec. 2. This article does not limit the right of a party to summon a witness or to introduce admissible evidence relevant to the results of the analysis.

Sec. 3. A certificate of analysis under this article must contain the following information certified under oath:

(1) the names of the analyst and the laboratory employing the analyst;

(2) a statement that the laboratory employing the analyst is accredited by a nationally recognized board or association that accredits crime laboratories;

(3) a description of the analyst's educational background, training, and experience;

(4) a statement that the analyst's duties of employment included the analysis of physical evidence for one or more law enforcement agencies;

(5) a description of the tests or procedures conducted by the analyst;

(6) a statement that the tests or procedures used were reliable and approved by the laboratory employing the analyst; and

(7) the results of the analysis.

Sec. 4. Not later than the 20th day before the trial begins in a proceeding in which a certificate of analysis under this article is to be introduced, the certificate must be filed with the clerk of the court and a copy must be provided by fax, secure electronic mail, hand delivery, or certified mail, return receipt requested, to the opposing party. The certificate is not admissible under Section 1 if, not later than the 10th day before the trial begins, the opposing party files a written objection to the use of the certificate with the clerk of the court and provides a copy of the objection by fax, secure electronic mail, hand delivery, or certified mail, return receipt requested, to the offering party.

Sec. 5. A certificate of analysis is sufficient for purposes of this article if it uses the following form or if it otherwise substantially complies with this article:

CERTIFICATE OF ANALYSIS

BEFORE ME, the undersigned authority, personally appeared ______________________, who being duly sworn, stated as follows:

My name is ______________. I am of sound mind, over the age of 18 years, capable of making this affidavit, and personally acquainted with the facts stated in this affidavit.

I am employed by the __________, which was authorized to conduct the analysis referenced in this affidavit. Part of my duties for this laboratory involved the analysis of physical evidence for one or more law enforcement agencies. This laboratory is accredited by __________.

My educational background is as follows: (description of educational background)

My training and experience that qualify me to perform the tests or procedures referred to in this affidavit and determine the results of those tests or procedures are as follows: (description of training and experience)

I received the physical evidence listed on laboratory report no. ____ (attached) on the ____ day of ________, 20____. On the date indicated in the laboratory report, I conducted the following tests or procedures on the physical evidence: (description of tests and procedures)

The tests and procedures used were reliable and approved by the laboratory. The results are as indicated on the lab report.

____

Affiant

SWORN TO AND SUBSCRIBED before me on the ____ day of ________, 20____.

____

Notary Public, State of Texas

Art. 38.42. Chain of Custody Affidavit.

Sec. 1. A chain of custody affidavit that complies with this article is admissible in evidence on behalf of the state or the defendant to establish the chain of custody of physical evidence without the necessity of any person in the chain of custody personally appearing in court.

Sec. 2. This article does not limit the right of a party to summon a witness or to introduce admissible evidence relevant to the chain of custody.

Sec. 3. A chain of custody affidavit under this article must contain the following information stated under oath:

(1) the affiant's name and address;

(2) a description of the item of evidence and its container, if any, obtained by the affiant;

(3) the name of the affiant's employer on the date the affiant obtained custody of the physical evidence;

(4) the date and method of receipt and the name of the person from whom or location from which the item of physical evidence was received;

(5) the date and method of transfer and the name of the person to whom or location to which the item of physical evidence was transferred; and

(6) a statement that the item of evidence was transferred in essentially the same condition as received except for any minor change resulting from field or laboratory testing procedures.

Sec. 4. Not later than the 20th day before the trial begins in a proceeding in which a chain of custody affidavit under this article is to be introduced, the affidavit must be filed with the clerk of the court and a copy must be provided by fax, secure electronic mail, hand delivery, or certified mail, return receipt requested, to the opposing party. The affidavit is not admissible under Section 1 if, not later than the 10th day before the trial begins, the opposing party files a written objection to the use of the affidavit with the clerk of the court and provides a copy of the objection by fax, secure electronic mail, hand delivery, or certified mail, return receipt requested, to the offering party.

Sec. 5. A chain of custody affidavit is sufficient for purposes of this article if it uses the following form or if it otherwise substantially complies with this article:

CHAIN OF CUSTODY AFFIDAVIT

BEFORE ME, the undersigned authority, personally appeared ______________________, who being by me duly sworn, stated as follows:

My name is ______________. I am of sound mind, over the age of 18 years, capable of making this affidavit, and personally acquainted with the facts stated in this affidavit.

My address is ______________.

On the ____ day of ________, 20____, I was employed by ______________.

On that date, I came into possession of the physical evidence described as follows: (description of evidence)

I received the physical evidence from ______________ (name of person or description of location) on the ____ day of ________, 20____, by ______________________ (method of receipt).

This physical evidence was in a container described and marked as follows: (description of container)

I transferred the physical evidence to ____________ (name of person or description of location) on the ____ day of ________, 20____, by ____________ (method of delivery).

During the time that the physical evidence was in my custody, I did not make any changes or alterations to the condition of the physical evidence except for those resulting from field or laboratory testing procedures, and the physical evidence or a representative sample of the physical evidence was transferred in essentially the same condition as received.

____

Affiant

SWORN TO AND SUBSCRIBED before me on the ____ day of ________, 20____.

____

Notary Public, State of Texas

Art. 38.43. Evidence Containing Biological Material.

(a) In this article, "biological evidence" means:

(1) the contents of a sexual assault examination kit; or

(2) any item that contains blood, semen, hair, saliva, skin tissue, fingernail scrapings, bone, bodily fluids, or any other identifiable biological material that was collected as part of an investigation of an alleged felony offense or conduct constituting a felony offense that might reasonably be used to:

(A) establish the identity of the person committing the offense or engaging in the conduct constituting the offense; or

(B) exclude a person from the group of persons who could have committed the offense or engaged in the conduct constituting the offense.

(b) This article applies to a governmental or public entity or an individual, including a law enforcement agency, prosecutor's office, court, public hospital, or crime laboratory, that is charged with the collection, storage, preservation, analysis, or retrieval of biological evidence.

(c) An entity or individual described by Subsection (b) shall ensure that biological evidence, other than the contents of a sexual assault examination kit subject to Subsection (c-1), collected pursuant to an investigation or prosecution of a felony offense or conduct constituting a felony offense is retained and preserved:

(1) for not less than 40 years, or until any applicable statute of limitations has expired, if there is an unapprehended actor associated with the offense; or

(2) in a case in which a defendant has been convicted, placed on deferred adjudication community supervision, or adjudicated as having engaged in delinquent conduct and there are no additional unapprehended actors associated with the offense:

(A) until the inmate is executed, dies, or is released on parole, if the defendant is convicted of a capital felony;

(B) until the defendant dies, completes the defendant's sentence, or is released on parole or mandatory supervision, if the defendant is sentenced to a term of confinement or imprisonment in the Texas Department of Criminal Justice;

(C) until the defendant completes the defendant's term of community supervision, including deferred adjudication community supervision, if the defendant is placed on community supervision;

(D) until the defendant dies, completes the defendant's sentence, or is released on parole, mandatory supervision, or juvenile probation, if the defendant is committed to the Texas Juvenile Justice Department; or

(E) until the defendant completes the defendant's term of juvenile probation, including a term of community supervision upon transfer of supervision to a criminal court, if the defendant is placed on juvenile probation.

(c-1) An entity or individual described by Subsection (b) shall ensure that the contents of a sexual assault examination kit collected pursuant to an investigation or prosecution of a felony offense or conduct constituting a felony offense is retained and preserved for not less than 40 years, or until any applicable statute of limitations has expired, whichever period is longer. This subsection applies regardless of whether a person has been apprehended for or charged with committing the offense.

(d) The attorney representing the state, clerk, or other officer in possession of biological evidence described by Subsection (a) may destroy the evidence, but only if the attorney, clerk, or officer by mail notifies the defendant, the last attorney of record for the defendant, and the convicting court of the decision to destroy the evidence and a written objection is not received by the attorney, clerk, or officer from the defendant, attorney of record, or court before the 91st day after the later of the following dates:

(1) the date on which the attorney representing the state, clerk, or other officer receives proof that

the defendant received notice of the planned destruction of evidence; or

(2) the date on which notice of the planned destruction of evidence is mailed to the last attorney of record for the defendant.

(e) To the extent of any conflict, this article controls over Article 2.21.

(f) The Department of Public Safety shall adopt standards and rules authorizing a county with a population less than 100,000 to ensure the preservation of biological evidence by promptly delivering the evidence to the Department of Public Safety for storage in accordance with Section 411.053, Government Code, and department rules.

(g) The Department of Public Safety shall adopt standards and rules, consistent with best practices, relating to a person described by Subsection (b), that specify the manner of collection, storage, preservation, and retrieval of biological evidence.

(h) A person described by Subsection (b) may solicit and accept gifts, grants, donations, and contributions to support the collection, storage, preservation, retrieval, and destruction of biological evidence.

(i) Before a defendant is tried for a capital offense in which the state is seeking the death penalty, subject to Subsection (j), the state shall require either the Department of Public Safety through one of its laboratories or a laboratory accredited under Article 38.01 to perform DNA testing, in accordance with the laboratory's capabilities at the time the testing is performed, on any biological evidence that was collected as part of an investigation of the offense and is in the possession of the state. The laboratory that performs the DNA testing shall pay for all DNA testing performed in accordance with this subsection.

(j) As soon as practicable after the defendant is charged with a capital offense, or on a motion by the state or the defendant in a capital case, unless the state has affirmatively waived the death penalty in writing, the court shall order the state and the defendant to meet and confer about which biological materials collected as part of an investigation of the offense qualify as biological evidence that is required to be tested under Subsection (i). If the state and the defendant agree on which biological materials constitute biological evidence, the biological evidence shall be tested in accordance with Subsection (i). If the state and the defendant do not agree on which biological materials qualify as biological evidence, the state or the defendant may request the court to hold a hearing to determine the issue. On receipt of a request for a hearing under this subsection, the court shall set a date for the hearing and provide written notice of the hearing date to the state and the defendant. At the hearing, there is a rebuttable presumption that the biological material that the defendant requests to be tested constitutes biological evidence that is required to be tested under Subsection (i). This subsection does not in any way prohibit the state from testing biological evidence in the state's possession.

(k) If an item of biological evidence is destroyed or lost as a result of DNA testing performed under Subsection (i), the laboratory that tested the evidence must provide to the defendant any bench notes prepared by the laboratory that are related to the testing of the evidence and the results of that testing.

(*l*) The defendant's exclusive remedy for testing that was not performed as required under Subsection (i) or (j) is to seek a writ of mandamus from the court of criminal appeals at any time on or before the date an application for a writ of habeas corpus is due to be filed in the defendant's case under Section 4(a), Article 11.071. An application for a writ of mandamus under this subsection does not toll any period of limitations applicable to a habeas petition under state or federal law. The defendant is entitled to only one application for a writ of mandamus under this subsection. At any time after the date an application for a writ of habeas corpus is filed in the defendant's case under Section 4(a), Article 11.071, the defendant may file one additional motion for forensic testing under Chapter 64.

(m) A defendant may have another laboratory accredited under Article 38.01 perform additional testing of any biological evidence required to be tested under Subsection (i). On an ex parte showing of good cause to the court, a defendant may have a laboratory accredited under Article 38.01 perform testing of any biological material that is not required to be tested under Subsection (i). The defendant is responsible for the cost of any testing performed under this subsection.

Art. 38.435. Prohibited Use of Evidence From Forensic Medical Examination Performed on Victim of Sexual Assault.

Evidence collected during a forensic medical examination conducted under Subchapter F or G, Chapter 56A, may not be used to investigate or prosecute a misdemeanor offense, or an offense under Subchapter D, Chapter 481, Health and Safety Code, alleged to have been committed by the victim from whom the evidence was collected.

Art. 38.44. Admissibility of Electronically Preserved Document.

An electronically preserved document has the same legal significance and admissibility as if the document had been maintained in hard-copy form. If a party opposes admission of the document on the grounds that the document has been materially altered, the proponent of the document must disprove the allegation by a preponderance of the evidence.

Art. 38.45. Evidence Depicting or Describing Abuse of or Sexual Conduct by Child or Minor.

(a) During the course of a criminal hearing or proceeding, the court may not make available or allow to be made available for copying or dissemination to the public property or material:

(1) that constitutes child pornography, as described by Section 43.26(a)(1), Penal Code;

(2) the promotion or possession of which is prohibited under Section 43.261, Penal Code; or

(3) that is described by Section 2 or 5, Article 38.071, of this code.

(b) The court shall place property or material described by Subsection (a) under seal of the court on conclusion of the criminal hearing or proceeding.

(c) The attorney representing the state shall be provided access to property or material described by Subsection (a). In the manner provided by Article 39.15, the defendant, the defendant's attorney, and any individual the defendant seeks to qualify to provide expert testimony at trial shall be provided access to property or material described by Subsection (a).

(d) A court that places property or material described by Subsection (a) under seal may issue an order lifting the seal on a finding that the order is in the best interest of the public.

Art. 38.451. Evidence Depicting Invasive Visual Recording of Child.

(a) During the course of a criminal hearing or proceeding concerning an offense under Section 21.15, Penal Code, that was committed against a child younger than 14 years of age, the court shall not make available or allow to be made available the copying or dissemination to the public property or material that constitutes or contains a visual image, as described by Section 21.15(b), Penal Code, of a child younger than 14 years of age and that was seized by law enforcement based on a reasonable suspicion that an offense under that subsection has been committed.

(b) The court shall place property or material described by Subsection (a) under seal of the court on the conclusion of the hearing or proceeding.

(c) The attorney representing the state shall be provided access to the property or material described by Subsection (a). In the manner provided by Article 39.151, the defendant, the defendant's attorney, and any individual the defendant seeks to qualify to provide expert testimony at trial shall be provided access to the property or material provided by Subsection (a).

(d) A court that places property or material described by Subsection (a) under seal may issue an order lifting the seal on a finding that the order is in the best interest of the public.

Art. 38.46. Evidence in Prosecutions for Stalking.

(a) In a prosecution for stalking, each party may offer testimony as to all relevant facts and circumstances that would aid the trier of fact in determining whether the actor's conduct would cause a reasonable person to experience a fear described by Section 42.072(a)(3)(A), (B), or (C), Penal Code, including the facts and circumstances surrounding any existing or previous relationship between the actor and the alleged victim, a member of the alleged victim's family or household, or an individual with whom the alleged victim has a dating relationship.

(b) This article does not permit the presentation of character evidence that would otherwise be inadmissible under the Texas Rules of Evidence or other applicable law.

Art. 38.47. Evidence in Aggregation Prosecution for Fraud or Theft Committed with Respect to Numerous Medicaid or Medicare Recipients.

In trials involving an allegation of a continuing scheme of fraud or theft that involves Medicaid or Medicare benefits and is alleged to have been committed with respect to a large class of Medicaid or Medicare recipients in an aggregate amount or value, the attorney representing the state is not required to prove by direct evidence that each Medicaid or Medicare recipient did not consent or effectively consent to a transaction in question. It is sufficient if the lack of consent or effective consent to a particular transaction or transactions is proven by either direct or circumstantial evidence.

Art. 38.471. Evidence in Prosecution for Exploitation of Child, Elderly Individual, or Disabled Individual.

(a) In the prosecution of an offense under Section 32.53, Penal Code, evidence that the defendant has engaged in other conduct that is similar to the alleged criminal conduct may be admitted for the purpose of showing the defendant's knowledge or intent regarding an element of the offense.

(b) Rule 403, Texas Rules of Evidence, applies to this article. This article does not permit the presentation of character evidence that would otherwise be inadmissible under the Texas Rules of Evidence or other applicable law.

Sec. 38.48. Evidence in Prosecution for Tampering with Witness or Prospective Witness Involving Family Violence.

(a) This article applies to the prosecution of an offense under Section 36.05, Penal Code, in which:

(1) the underlying official proceeding involved family violence, as defined by Section 71.004, Family Code; or

(2) the actor is alleged to have violated Section 36.05, Penal Code, by committing an act of family violence against a witness or prospective witness.

(b) In the prosecution of an offense described by Subsection (a), subject to the Texas Rules of Evidence or other applicable law, each party may offer testimony or other evidence of all relevant facts and circumstances that would assist the trier of fact in determining whether the actor's conduct coerced the witness or prospective witness, including the nature of the relationship between the actor and the witness or prospective witness.

Sec. 38.49. Forfeiture by Wrongdoing.

(a) A party to a criminal case who wrongfully procures the unavailability of a witness or prospective witness:

(1) may not benefit from the wrongdoing by depriving the trier of fact of relevant evidence and testimony; and

(2) forfeits the party's right to object to the admissibility of evidence or statements based on the unavailability of the witness as provided by this article through forfeiture by wrongdoing.

(b) Evidence and statements related to a party that has engaged or acquiesced in wrongdoing that was intended to, and did, procure the unavailability of a witness or prospective witness are admissible and may be used by the offering party to make a showing of forfeiture by wrongdoing under this article, subject to Subsection (c).

(c) In determining the admissibility of the evidence or statements described by Subsection (b), the court shall determine, out of the presence of the jury, whether forfeiture by wrongdoing occurred by a preponderance of the evidence. If practicable, the court shall make the determination under this subsection before trial using the procedures under Article 28.01 of this code and Rule 104, Texas Rules of Evidence.

(d) The party offering the evidence or statements described by Subsection (b) is not required to show that:

(1) the actor's sole intent was to wrongfully cause the witness's or prospective witness's unavailability;

(2) the actions of the actor constituted a criminal offense; or

(3) any statements offered are reliable.

(e) A conviction for an offense under Section 36.05 or 36.06(a), Penal Code, creates a presumption of forfeiture by wrongdoing under this article.

(f) Rule 403, Texas Rules of Evidence, applies to this article. This article does not permit the presentation of character evidence that would otherwise be inadmissible under the Texas Rules of Evidence or other applicable law.

Sec. 38.50. Retention and Preservation of Toxicological Evidence of Certain Intoxication Offenses.

(a) In this article, "toxicological evidence" means a blood or urine specimen that was collected as part of an investigation of an alleged offense under Chapter 49, Penal Code.

(b) This article applies to a governmental or public entity or an individual, including a law enforcement agency, prosecutor's office, or crime laboratory, that is charged with the collection, storage, preservation, analysis, or retrieval of toxicological evidence.

(c) An entity or individual described by Subsection (b) shall ensure that toxicological evidence collected pursuant to an investigation or prosecution of an offense under Chapter 49, Penal Code, is retained and preserved, as applicable:

(1) for the greater of two years or the period of the statute of limitations for the offense, if the indictment or information charging the defendant, or the petition in a juvenile proceeding, has not been presented or has been dismissed without prejudice;

(2) for the duration of a defendant's sentence or term of community supervision, as applicable, if the defendant is convicted or placed on community supervision, or for the duration of the commitment or supervision period applicable to the disposition of a juvenile adjudicated as having engaged in delinquent conduct or conduct indicating a need for supervision; or

(3) until the defendant is acquitted or the indictment or information is dismissed with prejudice,

or, in a juvenile proceeding, until a hearing is held and the court does not find the child engaged in delinquent conduct or conduct indicating a need for supervision.

(d) A person from whom toxicology evidence was collected and, if the person is a minor, the person's parent or guardian, shall be notified of the periods for which evidence may be retained and preserved under this article. The notice must be given by:

(1) an entity or individual described by Subsection (b) that collects the evidence, if the entity or individual collected the evidence directly from the person or collected it from a third party; or

(2) the court, if the records of the court show that the person was not given the notice described by Subdivision (1) and the toxicological evidence is subject to the retention period under Subsection (c)(2) or (3).

(e) The entity or individual charged with storing toxicological evidence may destroy the evidence on expiration of the applicable retention period:

(1) described by Subsection (c)(1); or

(2) described by Subsection (c)(2) or (c)(3), provided that:

(A) notice was given in accordance with this article; and

(B) if applicable, the prosecutor's office gives written approval for the destruction under Subsection (h).

(f) To the extent of any conflict between this article and Article 2.21 or 38.43, this article controls.

(g) Notice given under this article must be given:

(1) in writing, as soon as practicable, by hand delivery, e-mail, or first class mail to the person's last known e-mail or mailing address; or

(2) if applicable, orally and in writing on requesting the specimen under Section 724.015, Transportation Code.

(h) A prosecutor's office may require that an entity or individual charged with storing toxicological evidence seek written approval from the prosecutor's office before destroying toxicological evidence subject to the retention period under Subsection (c)(2) or (c)(3) for cases in which the prosecutor's office presented the indictment, information, or petition.

CHAPTER 39
DEPOSITIONS AND DISCOVERY

Art. 39.01. In Examining Trial.

When an examination takes place in a criminal action before a magistrate, the state or the defendant may have the deposition of any witness taken by any officer authorized by this chapter. The state or the defendant may not use the deposition for any purpose unless that party first acknowledges that the entire evidence or statement of the witness may be used for or against the defendant on the trial of the case, subject to all legal objections. The deposition of a witness duly taken before an examining trial or a jury of inquest and reduced to writing or recorded and then certified according to law, provided that the defendant and the defendant's attorney were present when that testimony was taken and that the defendant had the privilege afforded of cross-examining the witness, or taken at any prior trial of the defendant for the same offense, may be used by either the state or the defendant in the trial of the defendant's criminal case under the following circumstances:

When oath is made by the party using the deposition that the witness resides outside the state; or that since the witness's testimony was taken, the witness has died, or has removed beyond the limits of the state, or has been prevented from attending the court through the act or agency of the other party, or by the act or agency of any person whose object was to deprive the state or the defendant of the benefit of the testimony; or that by reason of age or bodily infirmity, that witness cannot attend; or that the witness is a Medicaid or Medicare recipient or a caregiver or guardian of the recipient, and the recipient's Medicaid or Medicare account was charged for a product or service that was not provided or rendered to the recipient. When the testimony is sought to be used by the state, the oath may be made by any credible person. When sought to be used by the defendant, the oath must be made by the defendant in person.

Art. 39.02. Witness Depositions.

Depositions of witnesses may be taken by either the state or the defendant. When a party desires to take the deposition of a witness, the party shall file with the clerk of the court in which the case is pending an affidavit stating the facts necessary to constitute a good reason for taking the witness's deposition and an application to take the deposition. On the filing of the affidavit and application, and after notice to the opposing party, the court shall hear the application and determine if good reason exists for taking the deposition. The court shall base its determination and shall grant or deny the application on the facts made known at the hearing. This provision is limited to the purposes stated in Article 39.01.

Art. 39.025. Depositions of Elderly or Disabled Persons.

(a) In this article:

(1) "Disabled person" means a person with a disability as defined by Section 3, Americans with Disabilities Act (42 U.S.C. 12102).

(2) "Elderly person" means a person 65 years of age or older.

(b) The court shall order the attorney representing the state to take the deposition of an elderly or disabled person who is the alleged victim of or witness to an offense not later than the 60th day after the date on which the state files an application to take the deposition under Article 39.02.

(c) The attorney representing the state and the defendant or the defendant's attorney may, by written agreement filed with the court, extend the deadline for the taking of the deposition.

(d) The court shall grant any request by the attorney representing the state to extend the deadline for the taking of the deposition if a reason for the request is the unavailability, health, or well-being of the victim or witness.

(e) The Texas Rules of Civil Procedure govern the taking of the deposition, except to the extent of any conflict with this code or applicable court rules adopted for criminal proceedings, in which event this code and the rules for criminal proceedings govern. The attorney representing the state and the defendant or defendant's attorney may agree to modify the rules applicable to the deposition by written agreement filed with the court before the taking of the deposition.

(f) If a defendant is unavailable to attend a deposition because the defendant is confined in a correctional facility, the court shall issue any orders or warrants necessary to secure the defendant's presence at the deposition. The sheriff of the county in which a deposition under this subsection is to be taken shall provide a secure location for the taking of the deposition and sufficient law enforcement personnel to ensure the deposition is taken safely. The state's application to take a deposition or notice of deposition is not required to include the identity of any law enforcement agents the sheriff assigns to the deposition and may not serve as a basis for the defendant to object to the taking of the deposition.

(g) If a defendant is unavailable to attend a deposition for any reason other than confinement in a correctional facility, the defendant or defendant's attorney shall request a continuance from the court. The court may grant the continuance if the defendant or defendant's attorney demonstrates good cause for the continuance and that the request is not brought for the purpose of delay or avoidance. A defendant's failure to attend a deposition or request a continuance in accordance with this subsection constitutes a waiver of the defendant's right to be present at the deposition.

Art. 39.026. Depositions of Medicaid or Medicare Recipients or Caregivers.

(a) In this article:

(1) "Caregiver" means a person, including a guardian, who is authorized by law, contract, or familial relationship to care for a recipient.

(2) "Medicaid" means the state Medicaid program.

(3) "Medicaid recipient" has the meaning assigned by Section 36.001, Human Resources Code.

(4) "Medicare" means the federal health insurance program that is operated under the Health Insurance for the Aged Act (42 U.S.C. Section 1395 et seq.).

(5) "Medicare recipient" means an individual on whose behalf a person claims or receives a payment under Medicare, without regard to whether the individual was eligible for benefits under Medicare.

(6) "Recipient" means a Medicaid recipient or a Medicare recipient.

(b) The court may order the attorney representing the state to take the deposition of a recipient or caregiver who is the alleged victim of or witness to an offense constituting fraud or theft that involves Medicaid or Medicare benefits. Any order under this subsection must be issued not later than the 180th day after the date on which the state files an application to take the deposition under Article 39.02.

(c) On the motion of either party, the court may order the attorney representing the state to take the deposition of a recipient or caregiver by video recording. The person operating the video recording device must be available to testify regarding the authenticity of the video recording and the taking of the deposition in order for the video recording to be admissible.

(d) If the court finds that the video recording of the deposition is properly authenticated and that requiring the jury to view the entire recording would unnecessarily prolong the trial, the court may allow a party to offer the entire video recording into evidence without requiring the jury to view the entire video recording during the trial. This subsection does not preclude the attorney representing the state, the defendant, or the defendant's attorney from offering into evidence and playing for the jury a portion of a video-recorded deposition.

(e) The attorney representing the state and the defendant or the defendant's attorney, by written

Code of Criminal Procedure

agreement filed with the court, may extend the deadline for the taking of the deposition.

(f) The court shall grant any request by the attorney representing the state to extend the deadline for the taking of the deposition if a reason for the request is the unavailability, health, or well-being of the recipient or caregiver.

(g) The Texas Rules of Civil Procedure govern the taking of the deposition, except that, to the extent of any conflict with this code or applicable court rules adopted for criminal proceedings, this code and the rules for criminal proceedings govern. The attorney representing the state and the defendant or the defendant's attorney may agree to modify the rules applicable to the deposition by written agreement filed with the court before the taking of the deposition.

(h) If a defendant is unavailable to attend a deposition because the defendant is confined in a correctional facility, the court shall issue any orders or warrants necessary to secure the defendant's presence at the deposition. The sheriff of the county in which a deposition is to be taken under this subsection shall provide a secure location for the taking of the deposition and sufficient law enforcement personnel to ensure that the deposition is taken safely. The state's application to take a deposition or notice of deposition is not required to include the identity of any law enforcement agent the sheriff assigns to the deposition under this subsection, and the defendant may not object to the taking of the deposition based solely on the state's omission of the identity of that agent.

(i) If a defendant is unavailable to attend a deposition for any reason other than confinement in a correctional facility, the defendant or the defendant's attorney shall request a continuance from the court. The court may grant the continuance if the defendant or the defendant's attorney demonstrates good cause for the continuance and that the request is not brought for the purpose of delay or avoidance. A defendant's failure to attend a deposition or request a continuance in accordance with this subsection constitutes a waiver of the defendant's right to be present at the deposition.

Art. 39.03. Officers Who May Take the Deposition.

Upon the filing of such an affidavit and application, the court shall appoint, order or designate one of the following persons before whom such deposition shall be taken:

1. A district judge.
2. A county judge.
3. A notary public.
4. A district clerk.
5. A county clerk.

Such order shall specifically name such person and the time when and place where such deposition shall be taken. Failure of a witness to respond thereto, shall be punishable by contempt by the court. Such deposition shall be oral or written, as the court shall direct.

Art. 39.04. Applicability of Civil Rules.

The rules prescribed in civil cases for issuance of commissions, subpoenaing witnesses, taking the depositions of witnesses and all other formalities governing depositions shall, as to the manner and form of taking and returning the same and other formalities to the taking of the same, govern in criminal actions, when not in conflict with this Code.

Art. 39.05. Objections.

The rules of procedure as to objections in depositions in civil actions shall govern in criminal actions when not in conflict with this Code.

Art. 39.06. Written Interrogatories.

When any such deposition is to be taken by written interrogatories, such written interrogatories shall be filed with the clerk of the court, and a copy of the same served on all other parties or their counsel for the length of time and in the manner required for service of interrogatories in civil action, and the same procedure shall also be followed with reference to cross-interrogatories as that prescribed in civil actions.

Art. 39.07. Certificate.

Where depositions are taken under commission in criminal actions, the officer or officers taking the same shall certify that the person deposing is the identical person named in the commission; or, if they cannot certify to the identity of the witness, there shall be an affidavit of some person attached to the deposition proving the identity of such witness, and the officer or officers shall certify that the person making the affidavit is known to them.

Art. 39.08. Authenticating the Deposition.

The official seal and signature of the officer taking the deposition shall be attached to the certificate authenticating the deposition.

Art. 39.09. Non-Resident Witnesses.

Depositions of a witness residing out of the State may be taken before a judge or before a commissioner of deeds and depositions for this State, who resides within the State where the deposition is to be taken, or before a notary public of the place where such deposition is to be taken, or before any commissioned officer of the armed services or before any diplomatic or consular officer. The deposition of a non-resident witness who may be temporarily within the State, may be taken under the same rules which apply to the taking of depositions of other witnesses in the State.

Art. 39.10. Return.

In all cases the return of depositions may be made as provided in civil actions.

Art. 39.11. Waiver.

The State and defense may agree upon a waiver of any formalities in the taking of a deposition other than that the taking of such deposition must be under oath.

Art. 39.12. Predicate to Read.

Depositions taken in criminal actions shall not be read unless oath be made that the witness resides out of the state; or that since the deposition was taken, the witness has died; or that the witness has removed beyond the limits of the state; or that the witness has been prevented from attending the court through the act or agency of the defendant; or by the act or agency of any person whose object was to deprive the state or the defendant of the benefit of the testimony; or that by reason of age or bodily infirmity, the witness cannot attend; or that the witness is a Medicaid or Medicare recipient or a caregiver or guardian of the recipient, and the recipient's Medicaid or Medicare account was charged for a product or service that was not provided or rendered to the recipient. When the deposition is sought to be used by the state, the oath may be made by any credible person. When sought to be used by the defendant, the oath shall be made by the defendant in person.

Art. 39.13. Impeachment.

Nothing contained in the preceding Articles shall be construed as prohibiting the use of any such evidence for impeachment purposes under the rules of evidence heretofore existing at common law.

Art. 39.14. Discovery.

(a) Subject to the restrictions provided by Section 264.408, Family Code, and Article 39.15 of this code, as soon as practicable after receiving a timely request from the defendant the state shall produce and permit the inspection and the electronic duplication, copying, and photographing, by or on behalf of the defendant, of any offense reports, any designated documents, papers, written or recorded statements of the defendant or a witness, including witness statements of law enforcement officers but not including the work product of counsel for the state in the case and their investigators and their notes or report, or any designated books, accounts, letters, photographs, or objects or other tangible things not otherwise privileged that constitute or contain evidence material to any matter involved in the action and that are in the possession, custody, or control of the state or any person under contract with the state. The state may provide to the defendant electronic duplicates of any documents or other information described by this article. The rights granted to the defendant under this article do not extend to written communications between the state and an agent, representative, or employee of the state. This article does not authorize the removal of the documents, items, or information from the possession of the state, and any inspection shall be in the presence of a representative of the state.

(b) On a party's request made not later than the 30th day before the date that jury selection in the trial is scheduled to begin or, in a trial without a jury, the presentation of evidence is scheduled to begin, the party receiving the request shall disclose to the requesting party the name and address of each person the disclosing party may use at trial to present evidence under Rules 702, 703, and 705, Texas Rules of Evidence. Except as otherwise provided by this subsection, the disclosure must be made in writing in hard copy form or by electronic means not later than the 20th day before the date that jury selection in the trial is scheduled to begin or, in a trial without a jury, the presentation of evidence is scheduled to begin. On motion of a party and on notice to the other parties, the court may order an earlier time at which one or more of the other parties must make the disclosure to the requesting party.

(c) If only a portion of the applicable document, item, or information is subject to discovery under this article, the state is not required to produce or permit the inspection of the remaining portion that is not subject to discovery and may withhold or redact that portion. The state shall inform the defendant that a portion of the document, item, or information has been withheld or redacted. On request of the defendant, the court shall conduct a hearing to determine whether withholding or redaction is justified under this article or other law.

(d) In the case of a pro se defendant, if the court orders the state to produce and permit the inspection of a document, item, or information under this subsection, the state shall permit the pro se defendant to inspect and review the document, item, or information but is not required to allow electronic duplication as described by Subsection (a).

(e) Except as provided by Subsection (f), the defendant, the attorney representing the defendant, or an investigator, expert, consulting legal counsel, or other agent of the attorney representing the defendant may not disclose to a third party any documents, evidence, materials, or witness statements received from the state under this article unless:

(1) a court orders the disclosure upon a showing of good cause after notice and hearing after considering the security and privacy interests of any victim or witness; or

(2) the documents, evidence, materials, or witness statements have already been publicly disclosed.

(f) The attorney representing the defendant, or an investigator, expert, consulting legal counsel, or agent for the attorney representing the defendant, may allow a defendant, witness, or prospective witness to view the information provided under this article, but may not allow that person to have copies of the information provided, other than a copy of the witness's own statement. Before allowing that person to view a document or the witness statement of another under this subsection, the person possessing the information shall redact the address, telephone number, driver's license number, social security number, date of birth, and any bank account or other identifying numbers contained in the document or witness statement. For purposes of this article, the defendant may not be the agent for the attorney representing the defendant.

(g) Nothing in this article shall be interpreted to limit an attorney's ability to communicate regarding his or her case within the Texas Disciplinary Rules of Professional Conduct, except for the communication of information identifying any victim or witness, including name, except as provided in Subsections (e) and (f), address, telephone number, driver's license number, social security number, date of birth, and bank account information or any information that by reference would make it possible to identify a victim or a witness. Nothing in this subsection shall prohibit the disclosure of identifying information to an administrative, law enforcement, regulatory, or licensing agency for the purposes of making a good faith complaint.

(h) Notwithstanding any other provision of this article, the state shall disclose to the defendant any exculpatory, impeachment, or mitigating document, item, or information in the possession, custody, or control of the state that tends to negate the guilt of the defendant or would tend to reduce the punishment for the offense charged.

(h-1) In this subsection, "correctional facility" has the meaning assigned by Section 1.07, Penal Code. Notwithstanding any other provision of this article, if the state intends to use at a defendant's trial testimony of a person to whom the defendant made a statement against the defendant's interest while the person was imprisoned or confined in the same correctional facility as the defendant, the state shall disclose to the defendant any information in the possession, custody, or control of the state that is relevant to the person's credibility, including:

(1) the person's complete criminal history, including any charges that were dismissed or reduced as part of a plea bargain;

(2) any grant, promise, or offer of immunity from prosecution, reduction of sentence, or other leniency or special treatment, given by the state in exchange for the person's testimony; and

(3) information concerning other criminal cases in which the person has testified, or offered to testify, against a defendant with whom the person was imprisoned or confined, including any grant, promise, or offer as described by Subdivision (2) given by the state in exchange for the testimony.

(i) The state shall electronically record or otherwise document any document, item, or other information provided to the defendant under this article.

(j) Before accepting a plea of guilty or nolo contendere, or before trial, each party shall acknowledge in writing or on the record in open court the disclosure, receipt, and list of all documents, items, and information provided to the defendant under this article.

(k) If at any time before, during, or after trial the state discovers any additional document, item, or information required to be disclosed under Subsection (h), the state shall promptly disclose the existence of the document, item, or information to the defendant or the court.

(*l*) A court may order the defendant to pay costs related to discovery under this article, provided that costs may not exceed the charges prescribed by Subchapter F, Chapter 552, Government Code.

(m) To the extent of any conflict, this article prevails over Chapter 552, Government Code.

(n) This article does not prohibit the parties from agreeing to discovery and documentation requirements equal to or greater than those required under this article.

Art. 39.15. Discovery of Evidence Depicting or Describing Abuse of or Sexual Conduct by Child or Minor.

(a) In the manner provided by this article, a court shall allow discovery under Article 39.14 of property or material:

(1) that constitutes child pornography, as described by Section 43.26(a)(1), Penal Code;

(2) the promotion or possession of which is prohibited under Section 43.261, Penal Code; or

(3) that is described by Section 2 or 5, Article 38.071, of this code.

(b) Property or material described by Subsection (a) must remain in the care, custody, or control of the court or the state as provided by Article 38.45.

(c) A court shall deny any request by a defendant to copy, photograph, duplicate, or otherwise reproduce any property or material described by Subsection (a), provided that the state makes the property or material reasonably available to the defendant.

(d) For purposes of Subsection (c), property or material is considered to be reasonably available to the defendant if, at a facility under the control of the state, the state provides ample opportunity for the inspection, viewing, and examination of the property or material by the defendant, the defendant's attorney, and any individual the defendant seeks to qualify to provide expert testimony at trial.

Art. 39.151. Discovery of Evidence Depicting Invasive Visual Recording of Child.

(a) In the manner provided by this article, a court shall allow discovery of property or material that constitutes or contains a visual image, as described by Section 21.15(b), Penal Code, of a child younger than 14 years of age and that was seized by law enforcement based on a reasonable suspicion that an offense under that subsection has been committed.

(b) Property or material described by Subsection (a) must remain in the care, custody, or control of the court or the state as provided by Article 38.451.

(c) A court shall deny any request by a defendant to copy, photograph, duplicate, or otherwise reproduce any property or material described by Subsection (a), provided that the state makes the property or material reasonably available to the defendant.

(d) For purposes of Subsection (c), property or material is considered to be reasonably available to the defendant if, at a facility under the control of the state, the state provides ample opportunity for the inspection, viewing, and examination of the property or material by the defendant, the defendant's attorney, and any individual the defendant seeks to qualify to provide expert testimony at trial.

PROCEEDINGS AFTER VERDICT

CHAPTER 40
NEW TRIALS

Art. 40.001. New Trial on Material Evidence.

A new trial shall be granted an accused where material evidence favorable to the accused has been discovered since trial.

Art. 40.01. Definition of "New Trial" [Repealed].

Repealed by the Texas Court of Criminal Appeals pursuant to Acts 1985, 69th Leg., ch. 685 (H.B. 13), § 4, effective September 1, 1986.

Art. 40.02. Granted Only to Accused [Repealed].

Repealed by the Texas Court of Criminal Appeals pursuant to Acts 1985, 69th Leg., ch. 685 (H.B. 13), § 4.

Art. 40.03. Grounds for New Trial in Felony [Repealed].

Repealed by the Texas Court of Criminal Appeals pursuant to Acts 1985, 69th Leg., ch. 685 (H.B. 13), § 4.

Art. 40.04. In Misdemeanors [Repealed].

Repealed by the Texas Court of Criminal Appeals pursuant to Acts 1985, 69th Leg., ch. 685 (H.B. 13), § 4.

Art. 40.05. Time to Apply for New Trial; Amendment [Repealed].

Repealed by the Texas Court of Criminal Appeals pursuant to Acts 1985, 69th Leg., ch. 685 (H.B. 13), § 4.

Code of Criminal Procedure

Art. 40.06. State May Controvert Motion [Repealed].

Repealed by the Texas Court of Criminal Appeals pursuant to Acts 1985, 69th Leg., ch. 685 (H.B. 13), § 4.

Art. 40.07. Judge Not to Discuss Evidence [Repealed].

Repealed by the Texas Court of Criminal Appeals pursuant to Acts 1985, 69th Leg., ch. 685 (H.B. 13), § 4.

Art. 40.08. Effect of a New Trial [Repealed].

Repealed by the Texas Court of Criminal Appeals pursuant to Acts 1985, 69th Leg., ch. 685 (H.B. 13), § 4.

Art. 40.09. Record on Appeals [Repealed].

Repealed by the Texas Court of Criminal Appeals pursuant to Acts 1985, 69th Leg., ch. 685 (H.B. 13), § 4.

Art. 40.10. Application of Civil Statutes [Repealed].

Repealed by the Texas Court of Criminal Appeals pursuant to Acts 1985, 69th Leg., ch. 685 (H.B. 13), § 4.

Art. 40.11. Requirement for Filing Court Reporter's Notes [Repealed].

Repealed by the Texas Court of Criminal Appeals pursuant to Acts 1985, 69th Leg., ch. 685 (H.B. 13), § 4.

CHAPTER 41 ARREST OF JUDGMENT [REPEALED]

Art. 41.01. Motion in Arrest of Judgment [Repealed].

Repealed by the Texas Court of Criminal Appeals pursuant to Acts 1985, 69th Leg., ch. 685 (H.B. 13), § 4.

Art. 41.02. Time to Make Motion [Repealed].

Repealed by the Texas Court of Criminal Appeals pursuant to Acts 1985, 69th Leg., ch. 685 (H.B. 13), § 4.

Art. 41.03. Granted for Substantial Defect [Repealed].

Repealed by the Texas Court of Criminal Appeals pursuant to Acts 1985, 69th Leg., ch. 685 (H.B. 13), § 4.

Art. 41.04. Want of Form [Repealed].

Repealed by the Texas Court of Criminal Appeals pursuant to Acts 1985, 69th Leg., ch. 685 (H.B. 13), § 4.

Art. 41.05. Effect of Arresting Judgment [Repealed].

Repealed by the Texas Court of Criminal Appeals pursuant to Acts 1985, 69th Leg., ch. 685 (H.B. 13), § 4.

CHAPTER 42 JUDGMENT AND SENTENCE

Art. 42.01. Judgment.

Sec. 1. A judgment is the written declaration of the court signed by the trial judge and entered of record showing the conviction or acquittal of the defendant. The sentence served shall be based on the information contained in the judgment. The judgment shall reflect:

1. The title and number of the case;
2. That the case was called and the parties appeared, naming the attorney for the state, the defendant, and the attorney for the defendant, or, where a defendant is not represented by counsel, that the defendant knowingly, intelligently, and voluntarily waived the right to representation by counsel;
3. The plea or pleas of the defendant to the offense charged;
4. Whether the case was tried before a jury or a jury was waived;
5. The submission of the evidence, if any;
6. In cases tried before a jury that the jury was charged by the court;
7. The verdict or verdicts of the jury or the finding or findings of the court;
8. In the event of a conviction that the defendant is adjudged guilty of the offense as found by the verdict of the jury or the finding of the court, and that the defendant be punished in accordance with the jury's verdict or the court's finding as to the proper punishment;

9. In the event of conviction where death or any punishment is assessed that the defendant be sentenced to death, a term of confinement or community supervision, or to pay a fine, as the case may be;

10. In the event of conviction where the imposition of sentence is suspended and the defendant is placed on community supervision, setting forth the punishment assessed, the length of community supervision, and the conditions of community supervision;

11. In the event of acquittal that the defendant be discharged;

12. The county and court in which the case was tried and, if there was a change of venue in the case, the name of the county in which the prosecution was originated;

13. The offense or offenses for which the defendant was convicted;

14. The date of the offense or offenses and degree of offense for which the defendant was convicted;

15. The term of sentence;

16. The date judgment is entered;

17. The date sentence is imposed;

18. The date sentence is to commence and any credit for time served;

19. The terms of any order entered pursuant to Article 42.08 that the defendant's sentence is to run cumulatively or concurrently with another sentence or sentences;

20. The terms of any plea bargain;

21. Affirmative findings entered pursuant to Article 42A.054(c) or (d);

22. The terms of any fee payment ordered under Article 42.151;

23. The defendant's thumbprint taken in accordance with Article 38.33;

24. In the event that the judge orders the defendant to repay a reward or part of a reward under Articles 37.073 and 42.152, a statement of the amount of the payment or payments required to be made;

25. In the event that the court orders restitution to be paid to the victim, a statement of the amount of restitution ordered and:

(A) the name and address of a person or agency that will accept and forward restitution payments to the victim; or

(B) if the court specifically elects to have payments made directly to the crime victim, the name and permanent address of the victim at the time of judgment;

26. In the event that a presentence investigation is required by Subchapter F, Chapter 42A, a statement that the presentence investigation was done according to the applicable provision;

27. In the event of conviction of an offense for which registration as a sex offender is required under Chapter 62, a statement that the registration requirement of that chapter applies to the defendant and a statement of the age of the victim of the offense;

28. The defendant's state identification number required by Article 66.152(a)(2), if that number has been assigned at the time of the judgment; and

29. The incident number required by Article 66.152(a)(4), if that number has been assigned at the time of the judgment.

Sec. 2. The judge may order the prosecuting attorney, or the attorney or attorneys representing any defendant, or the court clerk under the supervision of an attorney, to prepare the judgment, or the court may prepare the same.

Sec. 3. The provisions of this article shall apply to both felony and misdemeanor cases.

Sec. 4. The Office of Court Administration of the Texas Judicial System shall promulgate a standardized felony judgment form that conforms to the requirements of Section 1 of this article. A court entering a felony judgment shall use the form promulgated under this section.

Sec. 5. In addition to the information described by Section 1 of this article, the judgment should reflect affirmative findings entered pursuant to Article 42.013 of this code.

Sec. 6. In addition to the information described by Section 1 of this article, the judgment should reflect affirmative findings entered pursuant to Article 42.014 of this code.

Sec. 7. In addition to the information described by Section 1, the judgment should reflect affirmative findings entered pursuant to Article 42.015.

Sec. 8. In addition to the information described by Section 1, the judgment should reflect affirmative findings entered pursuant to Article 42.017.

Sec. 9. In addition to the information described by Section 1, the judgment should reflect affirmative findings entered pursuant to Article 42.0197.

Sec. 10. In addition to the information described by Section 1, the judgment should reflect affirmative findings entered pursuant to Article 42.0198.

Sec. 11. In addition to the information described by Section 1, the judgment should reflect whether a victim impact statement was returned to the attorney representing the state pursuant to Article 56A.157(a).

Sec. 12. In addition to the information described by Section 1, the judgment should reflect affirmative findings entered pursuant to Article 42.0192.

Sec. 13. In addition to the information described by Section 1, the judgment should reflect affirmative findings entered pursuant to Article 42.0196.

Sec. 14. **[2 versions: As added by Acts 2019, 86th Leg., ch. 641 (S.B. 1570)]** In addition to the information described by Section 1, the judgment should reflect affirmative findings entered pursuant to Article 42.0193.

Sec. 14. **[2 versions: As added by Acts 2019, 86th Leg., ch. 789 (H.B. 1899)]** In addition to the information described by Section 1, the judgment must reflect affirmative findings entered pursuant to Article 42.0175.

Art. 42.01. Judgment.

Sec. 1. A judgment is the written declaration of the court signed by the trial judge and entered of record showing the conviction or acquittal of the defendant. The sentence served shall be based on the information contained in the judgment. The judgment shall reflect:

1. The title and number of the case;

2. That the case was called and the parties appeared, naming the attorney for the state, the defendant, and the attorney for the defendant, or, where a defendant is not represented by counsel, that the defendant knowingly, intelligently, and voluntarily waived the right to representation by counsel;

3. The plea or pleas of the defendant to the offense charged;

4. Whether the case was tried before a jury or a jury was waived;

5. The submission of the evidence, if any;

6. In cases tried before a jury that the jury was charged by the court;

7. The verdict or verdicts of the jury or the finding or findings of the court;

8. In the event of a conviction that the defendant is adjudged guilty of the offense as found by the verdict of the jury or the finding of the court, and that the defendant be punished in accordance with the jury's verdict or the court's finding as to the proper punishment;

9. In the event of conviction where death or any punishment is assessed that the defendant be sentenced to death, a term of confinement or community supervision, or to pay a fine, as the case may be;

10. In the event of conviction where the imposition of sentence is suspended and the defendant is placed on community supervision, setting forth the punishment assessed, the length of community supervision, and the conditions of community supervision;

11. In the event of acquittal that the defendant be discharged;

12. The county and court in which the case was tried and, if there was a change of venue in the case, the name of the county in which the prosecution was originated;

13. The offense or offenses for which the defendant was convicted;

14. The date of the offense or offenses and degree of offense for which the defendant was convicted;

15. The term of sentence;

16. The date judgment is entered;

17. The date sentence is imposed;

18. The date sentence is to commence and any credit for time served;

19. The terms of any order entered pursuant to Article 42.08 that the defendant's sentence is to run cumulatively or concurrently with another sentence or sentences;

20. The terms of any plea bargain;

21. Affirmative findings entered pursuant to Article 42A.054(c) or (d);

22. The terms of any fee payment ordered under Article 42.151;

23. The defendant's thumbprint taken in accordance with Article 38.33;

24. In the event that the judge orders the defendant to repay a reward or part of a reward under Articles 37.073 and 42.152, a statement of the amount of the payment or payments required to be made;

25. In the event that the court orders restitution to be paid to the victim, a statement of the amount of restitution ordered and:

(A) the name and address of a person or agency that will accept and forward restitution payments to the victim; or

(B) if the court specifically elects to have payments made directly to the crime victim, the name and permanent address of the victim at the time of judgment;

26. In the event that a presentence investigation is required by Subchapter F, Chapter 42A, a statement that the presentence investigation was done according to the applicable provision;

27. In the event of conviction of an offense for which registration as a sex offender is required under Chapter 62, a statement that the registration requirement of that chapter applies to the defendant and a statement of the age of the victim of the offense;

28. The defendant's state identification number required by Article 66.152(a)(2), if that number has been assigned at the time of the judgment; and

29. The incident number required by Article 66.152(a)(4), if that number has been assigned at the time of the judgment.

Sec. 2. The judge may order the prosecuting attorney, or the attorney or attorneys representing any defendant, or the court clerk under the supervision of an attorney, to prepare the judgment, or the court may prepare the same.

Sec. 3. The provisions of this article shall apply to both felony and misdemeanor cases.

Sec. 4. The Office of Court Administration of the Texas Judicial System shall promulgate a standardized felony judgment form that conforms to the requirements of Section 1 of this article. A court entering a felony judgement [sic] shall use the form promulgated under this section.

Sec. 5. In addition to the information described by Section 1 of this article, the judgment should reflect affirmative findings entered pursuant to Article 42.013 of this code.

Sec. 6. In addition to the information described by Section 1 of this article, the judgment should reflect affirmative findings entered pursuant to Article 42.014 of this code.

Sec. 7. In addition to the information described by Section 1, the judgment should reflect affirmative findings entered pursuant to Article 42.015.

Sec. 8. In addition to the information described by Section 1, the judgment should reflect affirmative findings entered pursuant to Article 42.017.

Sec. 9. In addition to the information described by Section 1, the judgment should reflect affirmative findings entered pursuant to Article 42.0197.

Sec. 10. In addition to the information described by Section 1, the judgment should reflect affirmative findings entered pursuant to Article 42.0198.

Sec. 11. In addition to the information described by Section 1, the judgment should reflect whether a victim impact statement was returned to the attorney representing the state pursuant to Article 56A.157(a).

Sec. 12. In addition to the information described by Section 1, the judgment should reflect affirmative findings entered pursuant to Article 42.0192.

Sec. 13. In addition to the information described by Section 1, the judgment should reflect affirmative findings entered pursuant to Article 42.0196.

Sec. 14. **[2 versions: As added by Acts 2019, 86th Leg., ch. 789 (H.B. 1899)]** In addition to the information described by Section 1, the judgment must reflect affirmative findings entered pursuant to Article 42.0175.

Sec. 15. In addition to the information described by Section 1, the judgment should reflect affirmative findings entered pursuant to Article 42.0193.

Art. 42.011. Judgment Affecting an Officer or Jailer.

If a person licensed under Chapter 1701, Occupations Code, is charged with the commission of a felony and a court that knows the person is licensed under that chapter convicts the person or places the person on community supervision, the clerk of the court shall send the Texas Commission on Law Enforcement, by mail or electronically, the license number of the person and a certified copy of the court's judgment reflecting that the person has been convicted or placed on community supervision.

Art. 42.012. Finding That Controlled Substance Used to Commit Offense.

In the punishment phase of the trial of an offense under Chapter 29, Chapter 31, or Title 5, Penal Code, if the court determines beyond a reasonable doubt that the defendant administered or provided a controlled substance to the victim of the offense with the intent of facilitating the commission of the offense, the court shall make an affirmative finding of that fact and enter the affirmative finding in the judgment of that case.

Art. 42.013. Finding of Family Violence.

In the trial of an offense under Title 5, Penal Code, if the court determines that the offense involved family violence, as defined by Section 71.004, Family Code, the court shall make an affirmative finding of that fact and enter the affirmative finding in the judgment of the case.

Art. 42.0131. Required Notice for Persons Convicted of Misdemeanors Involving Family Violence.

If a person is convicted of a misdemeanor involving family violence, as defined by Section 71.004, Family Code, the court shall notify the person of the fact that it is unlawful for the person to possess or transfer a firearm or ammunition.

Art. 42.014. Finding That Offense Was Committed Because of Bias or Prejudice.

(a) In the trial of an offense under Title 5, Penal Code, or Section 28.02, 28.03, 28.08, or 42.0601, Penal Code, the judge shall make an affirmative finding of fact and enter the affirmative finding in the judgment of the case if at the guilt or innocence phase of the trial, the judge or the jury, whichever is the trier of fact, determines beyond a reasonable doubt that the defendant intentionally selected the person against whom the offense was committed, or intentionally selected the person's property that was damaged or affected as a result of the offense, because of the defendant's bias or prejudice against a group identified by race, color, disability, religion, national origin or ancestry, age, gender, or sexual preference or by status as a peace officer or judge.

(b) The sentencing judge may, as a condition of punishment, require attendance in an educational program to further tolerance and acceptance of others.

(c) In this article, "sexual preference" has the following meaning only: a preference for heterosexuality, homosexuality, or bisexuality.

Art. 42.015. Finding of Age of Victim.

(a) In the trial of an offense under Section 20.02, 20.03, or 20.04, Penal Code, or an attempt, conspiracy, or solicitation to commit one of those offenses, the judge shall make an affirmative finding of fact and enter the affirmative finding in the judgment in the case if the judge determines that the victim or intended victim was younger than 17 years of age at the time of the offense.

(b) In the trial of a sexually violent offense, as defined by Article 62.001, the judge shall make an affirmative finding of fact and enter the affirmative finding in the judgment in the case if the judge determines that the victim or intended victim was younger than 14 years of age at the time of the offense.

Art. 42.016. Special Driver's License or Identification Requirements for Certain Sex Offenders.

If a person is convicted of, receives a grant of deferred adjudication for, or is adjudicated as having engaged in delinquent conduct based on a violation of an offense for which a conviction or adjudication requires registration as a sex offender under Chapter 62, the court shall:

(1) issue an order requiring the Texas Department of Public Safety to include in any driver's license record or personal identification certificate record maintained by the department for the person an indication that the person is subject to the registration requirements of Chapter 62;

(2) require the person to apply to the Texas Department of Public Safety in person for an original or renewal driver's license or personal identification certificate not later than the 30th day after the date the person is released or the date the department sends written notice to the person of the requirements of Article 62.060, as applicable, and to annually renew the license or certificate;

(3) notify the person of the consequence of the conviction or order of deferred adjudication as it relates to the order issued under this article; and

(4) send to the Texas Department of Public Safety a copy of the record of conviction, a copy of the order granting deferred adjudication, or a copy of the juvenile adjudication, as applicable, and a copy of the order issued under this article.

Art. 42.017. Finding Regarding Age-Based Offense.

In the trial of an offense under Section 21.11 or 22.011, Penal Code, the judge shall make an affirmative finding of fact and enter the affirmative finding in the judgment in the case if the judge determines that:

(1) at the time of the offense, the defendant was not more than four years older than the victim or intended victim and the victim or intended victim was at least 15 years of age; and

(2) the conviction is based solely on the ages of the defendant and the victim or intended victim at the time of the offense.

Art. 42.0175. Finding Regarding Certain Health Care Professionals; Notification.

(a) In this article, "health care professional," "license," and "licensing authority" have the meanings assigned by Section 108.051, Occupations Code.

(b) In the trial of an offense, the judge shall make an affirmative finding of fact and enter the affirmative finding in the judgment in the case if the judge determines that at the time of the offense the defendant held a license as a health care professional and the offense is:

(1) an offense for which the defendant is required to register as a sex offender under Chapter 62;

(2) a felony offense and the defendant used force or threat of force in the commission of the offense; or

(3) an offense under Section 22.011, 22.02, 22.021, or 22.04, Penal Code, and:

(A) the victim of the offense was a patient of the defendant; and

(B) the offense was committed in the course of providing services within the scope of the defendant's license.

(c) Not later than the fifth day after the date the defendant is convicted or granted deferred adjudication on the basis of an offense described by Subsection (b)(1), (2), or (3), the clerk of the court in which the conviction or deferred adjudication is entered shall provide written notice of the conviction or deferred adjudication, including the offense on which the conviction or deferred adjudication was based, to:

(1) the licensing authority that issued the defendant's license as a health care professional; and

(2) the Department of Public Safety.

Art. 42.018. Notice Provided by Clerk of Court.

(a) This article applies only to:

(1) conviction or deferred adjudication community supervision granted on the basis of an offense for which a conviction or grant of deferred adjudication community supervision requires the defendant to register as a sex offender under Chapter 62; or

(2) conviction of an offense under Title 5, Penal Code, if the victim of the offense was under 18 years of age at the time the offense was committed.

(b) Not later than the fifth day after the date a person who holds a certificate issued under Subchapter B, Chapter 21, Education Code, is convicted or granted deferred adjudication on the basis of an offense, the clerk of the court in which the conviction or deferred adjudication is entered shall provide to the State Board for Educator Certification written notice of the person's conviction or deferred adjudication, including the offense on which the conviction or deferred adjudication was based.

(c) Not later than the fifth day after the date a person who is employed by a private school is convicted or granted deferred adjudication on the basis of an offense, the clerk of the court in which the conviction or deferred adjudication is entered shall provide to the chief administrative officer of the private school at which the person is employed written notice of the person's conviction or deferred adjudication, including the offense on which the conviction or deferred adjudication was based.

(d) In this article, "private school" has the meaning assigned by Section 5.001, Education Code.

Art. 42.0181. Notice of Theft, Fraud, Money Laundering, or Insurance Fraud Provided by Clerk of Court.

Not later than the fifth day after the date a person who holds a certificate of authority, license, or other authority issued by the Texas Department of Insurance is convicted of or granted deferred adjudication for an offense under Chapter 31, 32, 34, or 35, Penal Code, the clerk of the court in which the conviction or order of deferred adjudication is entered shall provide to the Texas Department of Insurance written notice of the person's conviction or deferred adjudication, including the offense on which the conviction or deferred adjudication was based.

Art. 42.0182. Findings Regarding Tax Fraud.

(a) In the trial of an offense under the Tax Code or an offense under the Penal Code related to the administration of taxes, the state may file a written request with the court in which the indictment or information is pending for the court to make affirmative findings regarding the commission of tax fraud as described by Subsection (b). The state must provide a copy of the written request to the defendant before the date the trial begins.

(b) If the state requests affirmative findings in the manner required by Subsection (a), the court shall make the requested affirmative findings and enter the findings in the papers in the case if the court finds by clear and convincing evidence that:

(1) the defendant's failure to pay a tax or file a report when due, as required by Title 2 or 3, Tax Code, was a result of fraud or an intent to evade the tax;

(2) the defendant altered, destroyed, or concealed any record, document, or thing, or presented to the comptroller any altered or fraudulent record, document, or thing, or otherwise engaged in fraudulent conduct for the apparent purpose of affecting the course or outcome of an audit, investigation, redetermination, or other proceeding before the comptroller; or

(3) the defendant's failure to file a report under Chapter 162, Tax Code, or to pay a tax under that chapter when the tax became due is attributable to fraud or an intent to evade the application of Chapter 162, Tax Code, or a rule adopted under Chapter 111 or 162, Tax Code.

Art. 42.0183. Notice of Family Violence Offenses Provided by Clerk of Court.

(a) This article applies only:

(1) to conviction or deferred adjudication granted on the basis of:

(A) an offense that constitutes family violence, as defined by Section 71.004, Family Code; or

(B) an offense under Title 5, Penal Code; and

(2) if the defendant is a member of the state military forces or is serving in the armed forces of the United States in an active-duty status.

(b) As soon as possible after the date on which the defendant is convicted or granted deferred adjudication on the basis of an offense, the clerk of the court in which the conviction or deferred adjudication is entered shall provide written notice of the conviction or deferred adjudication to the staff judge advocate general or the provost marshal of the military installation to which the defendant is assigned with the intent that the commanding officer will be notified, as applicable.

Art. 42.019. Motor Fuel Theft.

(a) A judge shall enter an affirmative finding in the judgment in a case if the judge or jury, whichever is the finder of fact, determines beyond a reasonable doubt in the guilt or innocence phase of the trial of an offense under Section 31.03, Penal Code, that the defendant, in committing the offense:

(1) dispensed motor fuel into the fuel tank of a motor vehicle on the premises of an establishment at which motor fuel is offered for retail sale; and

(2) after dispensing the motor fuel, left the premises of the establishment without paying the establishment for the motor fuel.

(b) If a judge enters an affirmative finding as required by Subsection (a) and determines that the defendant has previously been convicted of an offense the judgment for which contains an affirmative finding under Subsection (a), the judge shall enter a special affirmative finding in the judgment in the case.

Art. 42.0191. Finding Regarding Victims of Trafficking or Other Abuse.

(a) In the trial of an offense, on the motion of the attorney representing the state the judge shall make an affirmative finding of fact and enter the affirmative finding in the papers in the case if the judge determines that, regardless of whether the conduct at issue is the subject of the prosecution or part of the same criminal episode as the conduct that is the subject of the prosecution, a victim in the trial:

(1) is or has been a victim of a severe form of trafficking in persons, as defined by 22 U.S.C. Section 7102(8); or

(2) has suffered substantial physical or mental abuse as a result of having been a victim of criminal activity described by 8 U.S.C. Section 1101(a)(15)(U)(iii).

(b) That part of the papers in the case containing an affirmative finding under this article:

(1) must include specific information identifying the victim, as available;

(2) may not include information identifying the victim's location; and

(3) is confidential, unless written consent for the release of the affirmative finding is obtained from the victim or, if the victim is younger than 18 years of age, the victim's parent or guardian.

Art. 42.0192. Finding Regarding Offense Related to Performance of Public Service.

(a) In the trial of an offense described by Section 824.009, Government Code, the judge shall make an affirmative finding of fact and enter the affirmative finding in the judgment in the case if the judge determines that the offense committed was related to the defendant's employment described by Section 824.009(b), Government Code, while a member of the Teacher Retirement System of Texas.

(b) A judge who makes the affirmative finding described by this article shall make the determination and provide the notice required by Section 824.009(l), Government Code, as applicable.

Art. 42.0193. Finding Regarding Offense Related to Conduct of Certain Corrections Employees.

(a) In the trial of an offense described by Section 810.004, Government Code, the judge shall make an affirmative finding of fact and enter the affirmative finding in the judgment in the case if the judge determines that the defendant is:

(1) a member of the employee class described by Section 810.004(b)(1), Government Code, while a member of the Employees Retirement System of Texas because the person serves as a corrections officer for the Texas Department of Criminal Justice or the Texas Juvenile Justice Department; or

(2) otherwise eligible for membership in a public retirement system wholly or partly because the person served as a corrections officer for the Texas Department of Criminal Justice or the Texas Juvenile Justice Department.

(b) A judge who makes the affirmative finding described by this article shall make the determination and provide the notice required by Section 810.004(j), Government Code.

Art. 42.0193 to 42.0195. [Reserved for expansion].

Art. 42.0196. Finding Regarding Offense Related to Performance of Public Service.

(a) In the trial of an offense described by Section 810.003, Government Code, the judge shall make an affirmative finding of fact and enter the affirmative finding in the judgment in the case if the judge determines that the defendant is:

(1) a member of the elected class described by Section 810.003(b)(1), Government Code, while a member of the Employees Retirement System of Texas; or

(2) a holder of an elected office for which the defendant wholly or partly became eligible for membership in a public retirement system.

(b) A judge who makes the affirmative finding described by this article shall make the determination and provide the notice required by Section 810.003(k), Government Code.

Art. 42.0197. Finding Regarding Gang-Related Conduct.

In the trial of an offense, on the motion of the attorney representing the state the judge shall make an affirmative finding of fact and enter the affirmative finding in the judgment in the case if the judge determines that the applicable conduct was engaged in as part of the activities of a criminal street gang as defined by Section 71.01, Penal Code.

Art. 42.0198. Finding Regarding Delay in Arrest of Defendant.

In the trial of an offense under Section 19.02, 22.011, or 22.021, Penal Code, on the motion of the attorney representing the state the judge shall make an affirmative finding of fact regarding the number of months that elapsed, if any, between the date an arrest warrant was issued for the defendant following an indictment for the offense and the date the defendant was arrested for the offense. The judge shall enter the affirmative finding in the judgment in the case.

Art. 42.0199. Finding Regarding Diligent Participation Credit.

If a person is convicted of a state jail felony, the judge shall make a finding and enter the finding in the judgment of the case regarding whether the person is presumptively entitled to diligent participation credit in accordance with Article 42A.559.

Art. 42.01991. Finding Regarding Agreement on Parole Eligibility for Certain Defendants.

(a) This article applies only in the trial of an offense under Section 20A.02(a)(5), (6), (7), or (8), Penal Code, in which:

(1) the defendant enters a plea of guilty; and

(2) the attorney representing the state, the attorney representing the defendant, and the defendant agree in writing that the defendant will become eligible for release on parole as described by Section 508.145(c-1)(2), Government Code.

(b) In the trial of an offense to which this article applies, on the motion of the attorney representing the state, the judge shall make an affirmative finding of fact that the parties have entered into the agreement described by Subsection (a)(2) and shall enter the affirmative finding in the judgment in the case.

Art. 42.02. Sentence.

The sentence is that part of the judgment, or order revoking a suspension of the imposition of a sentence, that orders that the punishment be carried into execution in the manner prescribed by law.

Art. 42.023. Judge May Consider Alternative Sentencing.

Before pronouncing sentence on a defendant convicted of a criminal offense, the judge may consider whether the defendant should be committed for care and treatment under Section 462.081, Health and Safety Code.

Art. 42.025. Sentencing Hearing at Secondary School.

(a) A judge may order the sentencing hearing of a defendant convicted of an offense involving possession, manufacture, or delivery of a controlled substance under Chapter 481, Health and Safety Code, to be held at a secondary school if:

(1) the judge determines that the sentencing hearing would have educational value to students due to the nature of the offense and its consequences;

(2) the defendant agrees;

(3) the school administration agrees; and

(4) appropriate measures are taken to ensure:

(A) the safety of the students; and

(B) a fair hearing for the defendant that complies with all applicable laws and rules.

(b) A judge may, at a secondary school, receive a plea of guilty or nolo contendere from a defendant charged with an offense described by Subsection (a) and place the defendant on deferred adjudication under Subchapter C, Chapter 42A, if:

(1) the judge makes the determination that the proceeding would have educational value, as provided by Subsection (a)(1);

(2) the defendant and the school agree to the location of the proceeding, as provided by Subsections (a)(2) and (3); and

(3) appropriate measures are taken in regard to the safety of students and the rights of the defendant, as described by Subsection (a)(4).

Art. 42.03. Pronouncing Sentence; Time; Credit for Time Spent in Jail Between Arrest and Sentence or Pending Appeal.

Sec. 1. (a) Except as provided in Article 42.14, sentence shall be pronounced in the defendant's presence.

Code of Criminal Procedure

(b) The court shall permit a victim, close relative of a deceased victim, or guardian of a victim, as defined by Article 56A.001, to appear in person to present to the court and to the defendant a statement of the person's views about the offense, the defendant, and the effect of the offense on the victim. The victim, relative, or guardian may not direct questions to the defendant while making the statement. The court reporter may not transcribe the statement. The statement must be made:

(1) after punishment has been assessed and the court has determined whether or not to grant community supervision in the case;

(2) after the court has announced the terms and conditions of the sentence; and

(3) after sentence is pronounced.

(c) The court may not impose a limit on the number of victims, close relatives, or guardians who may appear and present statements under Subsection (b) unless the court finds that additional statements would unreasonably delay the proceeding.

Sec. 2. (a) In all criminal cases the judge of the court in which the defendant is convicted shall give the defendant credit on the defendant's sentence for the time that the defendant has spent:

(1) in jail for the case, including confinement served as described by Article 46B.009 and excluding confinement served as a condition of community supervision, from the time of his arrest and confinement until his sentence by the trial court;

(2) in a substance abuse treatment facility operated by the Texas Department of Criminal Justice under Section 493.009, Government Code, or another court-ordered residential program or facility as a condition of deferred adjudication community supervision granted in the case if the defendant successfully completes the treatment program at that facility; or

(3) confined in a mental health facility or residential care facility as described by Article 46B.009.

(b) In all revocations of a suspension of the imposition of a sentence the judge shall enter the restitution due and owing on the date of the revocation.

Sec. 3. If a defendant appeals his conviction, is not released on bail, and is retained in a jail as provided in Section 7, Article 42.09, pending his appeal, the judge of the court in which the defendant was convicted shall give the defendant credit on his sentence for the time that the defendant has spent in jail pending disposition of his appeal. The court shall endorse on both the commitment and the mandate from the appellate court all credit given the defendant under this section, and the Texas Department of Criminal Justice shall grant the credit in computing the defendant's eligibility for parole and discharge.

Sec. 4. When a defendant who has been sentenced to imprisonment in the Texas Department of Criminal Justice has spent time in jail pending trial and sentence or pending appeal, the judge of the sentencing court shall direct the sheriff to attach to the commitment papers a statement assessing the defendant's conduct while in jail.

Sec. 5. Except as otherwise provided by Article 42A.106(b), the court after pronouncing the sentence shall inform the defendant of the defendant's right to petition the court for an order of nondisclosure of criminal history record information under Subchapter E-1, Chapter 411, Government Code, unless the defendant is ineligible to pursue that right because of the requirements that apply to obtaining the order in the defendant's circumstances, such as:

(1) the nature of the offense for which the defendant is convicted; or

(2) the defendant's criminal history.

Sec. 6. [Repealed by Acts 1989, 71st Leg., ch. 785 (H.B. 2335), § 4.24, effective September 1, 1989.]

Secs. 7,7A,and 8. [Deleted by Acts 1993, 73rd Leg., ch. 900 (S.B. 1067), § 5.03, effective September 1, 1993.]

Art. 42.031. Work Release Program.

Sec. 1. (a) The sheriff of each county may attempt to secure employment for each defendant sentenced to the county jail work release program under Article 42.034 and each defendant confined in the county jail awaiting transfer to the Texas Department of Criminal Justice.

(b) The employer of a defendant participating in a program under this article shall pay the defendant's salary to the sheriff. The sheriff shall deposit the salary into a special fund to be given to the defendant on his release after deducting:

(1) the cost to the county for the defendant's confinement during the pay period based on the average daily cost of confining defendants in the county jail, as determined by the commissioners court of the county;

(2) support of the defendant's dependents; and

(3) restitution to the victims of an offense committed by the defendant.

(c) At the time of sentencing or at a later date, the court sentencing a defendant may direct the sheriff not to deduct the cost described under Subdivision (1) of Subsection (b) of this section or to deduct only a specified portion of the cost if the court determines that the full deduction would cause a significant financial hardship to the defendant's dependents.

(d) If the sheriff does not find employment for a defendant who would otherwise be sentenced to imprisonment in the department, the sheriff shall:

(1) transfer the defendant to the sheriff of a county who agrees to accept the defendant as a participant in the county jail work release program; or

(2) retain the defendant in the county jail for employment as soon as possible in a jail work release program.

Sec. 2. A defendant participating in a program under this article shall be confined in the county jail or in another facility designated by the sheriff at all times except for:

(1) time spent at work and traveling to or from work; and

(2) time spent attending or traveling to or from an education or rehabilitation program approved by the sheriff.

Sec. 3. (a) The sheriff of each county shall classify each felon serving a sentence in the county jail work release program for the purpose of awarding good conduct time credit in the same manner as inmates of the Texas Department of Criminal Justice are classified under Chapter 498, Government Code, and shall award good conduct time in the same manner as the director of the department does in that chapter.

(b) If the sheriff determines that the defendant is conducting himself in a manner that is dangerous to inmates in the county jail or to society as a whole, the sheriff may remove the defendant from participation in the program pending a hearing before the sentencing court. At the hearing, if the court determines that the sheriff's assessment of the defendant's conduct is correct, the court may terminate the defendant's participation in the program and order the defendant to the term of imprisonment that the defendant would have received had he not entered the program. If the court determines that the sheriff's assessment is incorrect, the court shall order the sheriff to readmit the defendant to the program. A defendant shall receive as credit toward his sentence any time served as a participant in the program.

Art. 42.032. Good Conduct.

Sec. 1. To encourage county jail discipline, a distinction may be made to give orderly, industrious, and obedient defendants the comforts and privileges they deserve. The reward for good conduct may consist of a relaxation of strict county jail rules and extension of social privileges consistent with proper discipline.

Sec. 2. The sheriff in charge of each county jail may grant commutation of time for good conduct, industry, and obedience. A deduction not to exceed one day for each day of the original sentence actually served may be made for the term or terms of sentences if a charge of misconduct has not been sustained against the defendant.

Sec. 3. This article applies whether or not the judgment of conviction is a fine or jail sentence or both, but the deduction in time may not exceed one-third of the original sentence as to fines and court costs assessed in the judgment of conviction.

Sec. 4. A defendant serving two or more cumulative sentences shall be allowed commutation as if the sentences were one sentence.

Sec. 5. Any part or all of the commutation accrued under this article may be forfeited and taken away by the sheriff:

(1) for a sustained charge of misconduct in violation of any rule known to the defendant, including escape or attempt to escape, if the sheriff has complied with discipline proceedings as approved by the Commission on Jail Standards;

(2) on receipt by the sheriff of a certified copy of a final order of a state or federal court that dismisses as frivolous or malicious a lawsuit brought by a defendant while the defendant was in the custody of the sheriff; or

(3) if the defendant, in violation of an order entered under Article 42.24, contacts the victim of the offense for which the defendant is serving a sentence or a member of the victim's family.

Sec. 6. [Repealed by Acts 2009, 81st Leg., ch. 854 (S.B. 2340), § 7, effective June 19, 2009.]

Sec. 7. The sheriff shall keep a conduct record in card or ledger form and a calendar card on each defendant showing all forfeitures of commutation time and the reasons for the forfeitures.

Art. 42.033. Sentence to Serve Time During Off-Work Hours.

(a) Where jail time has been awarded to a person sentenced for a misdemeanor or sentenced to confinement in the county jail for a felony or when a defendant is serving a period of confinement as a condition of community supervision, the trial judge, at the time of the pronouncement of sentence or at any time while the defendant is serving the sentence or period of confinement, when in the judge's discretion the ends of justice would best be served, may permit the defendant to serve the defendant's sentence or period of confinement intermittently during his off-work hours or on weekends. The judge may require bail of the defendant to ensure the faithful performance of the sentence or period of confinement. The judge may attach conditions regarding the employment, travel, and

Code of Criminal Procedure

other conduct of the defendant during the performance of such a sentence or period of confinement.

(b) The court may impose as a condition to permitting a defendant to serve the jail time assessed or period of confinement intermittently an additional requirement that the defendant make any of the following payments to the court, agencies, or persons, or that the defendant execute a letter and direct it to the defendant's employer directing the employer to deduct from the defendant's salary an amount directed by the court, which is to be sent by the employer to the clerk of the court. The money received by the court under this section may be used to pay the following expenses as directed by the court:

(1) the support of the defendant's dependents, if necessary;

(2) the defendant's documented personal, business, and travel expenses;

(3) reimbursement of the general fund of the county for the maintenance of the defendant in jail; and

(4) installment payments on restitution, fines, and court costs ordered by the court.

(c) The condition imposed under Subsection (b) of this article is not binding on an employer, except that income withheld for child support is governed by Chapter 158, Family Code.

(d) The court may permit the defendant to serve the defendant's sentence or period of confinement intermittently in order for the defendant to continue employment if the court imposes confinement for failure to pay a fine or court costs, as punishment for criminal nonsupport under Section 25.05, Penal Code, or for contempt of a court order for periodic payments for the support of a child.

(e) The court may permit the defendant to seek employment or obtain medical, psychological, or substance abuse treatment or counseling or obtain training or needed education under the same terms and conditions that apply to employment under this article.

Art. 42.034. County Jail Work Release Program.

(a) If jail time has been awarded to a person sentenced for a misdemeanor or sentenced to confinement in the county jail for a felony, the trial judge at the time of pronouncement of sentence or at any time while the defendant is serving the sentence, when in the judge's discretion the ends of justice would best be served, may require the defendant to serve an alternate term for the same period of time in the county jail work release program of the county in which the offense occurred, if the person is classified by the sheriff as a low-risk offender under the classification system developed by the Commission on Jail Standards under Section 511.009, Government Code.

(b) The sheriff shall provide a classification report for a defendant to a judge as necessary so that the judge can determine whether to require the defendant to participate in the work release program under this article.

(c) A defendant sentenced under this article who would otherwise be sentenced to confinement in jail may earn good conduct credit in the same manner as provided by Article 42.032 of this code, but only while actually confined.

Art. 42.035. Electronic Monitoring; House Arrest.

(a) A court may require a defendant to serve all or part of a sentence of confinement in county jail by participating in an electronic monitoring program rather than being confined in the county jail, if the program:

(1) is operated by a community supervision and corrections department that serves the county in which the court is located and has been approved by the community justice assistance division of the Texas Department of Criminal Justice; or

(2) is operated by the commissioners court of the county, or by a private vendor under contract with the commissioners court, under Section 351.904, Local Government Code, if the defendant has not been placed on community supervision.

(b) A judge, at the time of the pronouncement of a sentence of confinement or at any time while the defendant is serving the sentence, on the judge's own motion or on the written motion of the defendant, may permit the defendant to serve the sentence under house arrest, including electronic monitoring and any other conditions the court chooses to impose, during the person's off-work hours. The judge may require bail of the defendant to ensure the faithful performance of the sentence.

(c) The court may require the defendant to pay to the community supervision and corrections department or the county any reasonable cost incurred because of the defendant's participation in the house arrest program, including the cost of electronic monitoring.

(d) A defendant who submits to electronic monitoring or participates in the house arrest program under this article discharges a sentence of confinement in the same manner as if the defendant were confined in county jail.

(e) A court may revoke a defendant's participation in an electronic monitoring program and require the defendant to serve the remainder of the defendant's sentence of confinement in county jail if the defendant violates a condition imposed by a court under this article, including a condition requiring the defendant to pay for participating in the program under Subsection (c).

Art. 42.036. Community Service.

(a) A court may require a defendant, other than a defendant convicted of an offense under Sections 49.04—49.08, Penal Code, to serve all or part of a sentence of confinement or period of confinement required as a condition of community supervision in county jail by performing community service rather than by being confined in county jail unless the sentence of confinement was imposed by the jury in the case.

(b) In its order requiring a defendant to participate in community service work, the court must specify:

(1) the number of hours the defendant is required to work; and

(2) the entity or organization for which the defendant is required to work.

(c) The court may order the defendant to perform community service work under this article only for a governmental entity or a nonprofit organization that provides services to the general public that enhance social welfare and the general well-being of the community. A governmental entity or nonprofit organization that accepts a defendant under this section to perform community service must agree to supervise the defendant in the performance of the defendant's work and report on the defendant's work to the community supervision and corrections department or court-related services office.

(d) The court may require bail of a defendant to ensure the defendant's faithful performance of community service and may attach conditions to the bail as it determines are proper.

(e) A court may not order a defendant who is employed to perform more than 16 hours per week of community service under this article unless the court determines that requiring the defendant to work additional hours does not work a hardship on the defendant or the defendant's dependents. A court may not order a defendant who is unemployed to perform more than 32 hours per week of community service under this article, but may direct the defendant to use the remaining hours of the week to seek employment.

(f) A defendant is considered to have served one day in jail for each eight hours of community service performed under this article.

(g) [Deleted by Acts 1993, 73rd Leg., ch. 900, § 5.03, effective September 1, 1993.]

(h) [Repealed by Acts 1995, 74th Leg., ch. 76, § 3.14, effective September 1, 1995.]

Art. 42.037. Restitution.

(a) In addition to any fine authorized by law, the court that sentences a defendant convicted of an offense may order the defendant to make restitution to any victim of the offense or to the compensation to victims of crime fund established under Subchapter J, Chapter 56B, to the extent that fund has paid compensation to or on behalf of the victim. If the court does not order restitution or orders partial restitution under this subsection, the court shall state on the record the reasons for not making the order or for the limited order.

(b) (1) If the offense results in damage to or loss or destruction of property of a victim of the offense, the court may order the defendant:

(A) to return the property to the owner of the property or someone designated by the owner; or

(B) if return of the property is impossible or impractical or is an inadequate remedy, to pay an amount equal to the greater of:

(i) the value of the property on the date of the damage, loss, or destruction; or

(ii) the value of the property on the date of sentencing, less the value of any part of the property that is returned on the date the property is returned.

(2) If the offense results in personal injury to a victim, the court may order the defendant to make restitution to:

(A) the victim for any expenses incurred by the victim as a result of the offense; or

(B) the compensation to victims of crime fund to the extent that fund has paid compensation to or on behalf of the victim.

(3) If the victim or the victim's estate consents, the court may, in addition to an order under Subdivision (2), order the defendant to make restitution by performing services instead of by paying money or make restitution to a person or organization, other than the compensation to victims of crime fund, designated by the victim or the estate.

(c) The court, in determining whether to order restitution and the amount of restitution, shall consider:

(1) the amount of the loss sustained by any victim and the amount paid to or on behalf of the victim by the compensation to victims of crime fund as a result of the offense; and

(2) other factors the court deems appropriate.

(d) If the court orders restitution under this article and the victim is deceased the court shall order the defendant to make restitution to the victim's estate.

Code of Criminal Procedure

(e) The court shall impose an order of restitution that is as fair as possible to the victim or to the compensation to victims of crime fund, as applicable. The imposition of the order may not unduly complicate or prolong the sentencing process.

(f) (1) The court may not order restitution for a loss for which the victim has received or will receive compensation only from a source other than the compensation to victims of crime fund. The court may, in the interest of justice, order restitution to any person who has compensated the victim for the loss to the extent the person paid compensation. An order of restitution shall require that all restitution to a victim or to the compensation to victims of crime fund be made before any restitution to any other person is made under the order.

(2) Any amount recovered by a victim from a person ordered to pay restitution in a federal or state civil proceeding is reduced by any amount previously paid to the victim by the person under an order of restitution.

(g) The court may require a defendant to make restitution under this article within a specified period or in specified installments. The end of the period or the last installment may not be later than:

(1) the end of the period of probation, if probation is ordered;

(2) five years after the end of the term of imprisonment imposed, if the court does not order probation; or

(3) five years after the date of sentencing in any other case.

(g-1) If the court does not provide otherwise, the defendant shall make restitution immediately.

(g-2) Except as provided by Subsection (n), the order of restitution must require the defendant to:

(1) make restitution directly to the person or agency that will accept and forward restitution payments to the victim or other person eligible for restitution under this article, including the compensation to victims of crime fund;

(2) make restitution directly to the victim or other person eligible for restitution under this article, including the compensation to victims of crime fund; or

(3) deliver the amount or property due as restitution to a community supervision and corrections department for transfer to the victim or person.

(h) If a defendant is placed on community supervision or is paroled or released on mandatory supervision, the court or the parole panel shall order the payment of restitution ordered under this article as a condition of community supervision, parole, or mandatory supervision. The court may revoke community supervision and the parole panel may revoke parole or mandatory supervision if the defendant fails to comply with the order. In determining whether to revoke community supervision, parole, or mandatory supervision, the court or parole panel shall consider:

(1) the defendant's employment status;

(2) the defendant's current and future earning ability;

(3) the defendant's current and future financial resources;

(4) the willfulness of the defendant's failure to pay;

(5) any other special circumstances that may affect the defendant's ability to pay; and

(6) the victim's financial resources or ability to pay expenses incurred by the victim as a result of the offense.

(i) In addition to any other terms and conditions of community supervision imposed under Chapter 42A, the court may require a defendant to reimburse the compensation to victims of crime fund created under Subchapter J, Chapter 56B, for any amounts paid from that fund to or on behalf of a victim of the defendant's offense. In this subsection, "victim" has the meaning assigned by Article 56B.003.

(j) The court may order a community supervision and corrections department to obtain information pertaining to the factors listed in Subsection (c). The supervision officer shall include the information in the report required under Article 42A.252(a) or a separate report, as the court directs. The court shall permit the defendant and the prosecuting attorney to read the report.

(k) The court shall resolve any dispute relating to the proper amount or type of restitution. The standard of proof is a preponderance of the evidence. The burden of demonstrating the amount of the loss sustained by a victim as a result of the offense is on the prosecuting attorney. The burden of demonstrating the financial resources of the defendant and the financial needs of the defendant and the defendant's dependents is on the defendant. The burden of demonstrating other matters as the court deems appropriate is on the party designated by the court as justice requires.

(*l*) Conviction of a defendant for an offense involving the act giving rise to restitution under this article estops the defendant from denying the essential allegations of that offense in any subsequent federal civil proceeding or state civil proceeding brought by the victim, to the extent consistent with state law.

(m) An order of restitution may be enforced by the state or a victim named in the order to receive the restitution in the same manner as a judgment in a civil action.

(n) If a defendant is convicted of or receives deferred adjudication for an offense under Section 25.05, Penal Code, if the child support order on which prosecution of the offense was based required the defendant to pay the support to a local registry or the Title IV-D agency, and if the court orders restitution under this article, the order of restitution must require the defendant to pay the child support in the following manner:

(1) during any period in which the defendant is under the supervision of a community supervision and corrections department, to the department for transfer to the local registry or Title IV-D agency designated as the place of payment in the child support order; and

(2) during any period in which the defendant is not under the supervision of a department, directly to the registry or agency described by Subdivision (1).

(o) The department may waive a supervision fee or an administrative fee imposed on an inmate under Section 508.182, Government Code, during any period in which the inmate is required to pay restitution under this article.

(p) (1) A court shall order a defendant convicted of an offense under Section 28.03(f), Penal Code, involving damage or destruction inflicted on a place of human burial or under Section 42.08, Penal Code, to make restitution in the amount described by Subsection (b)(1)(B) to a cemetery organization operating a cemetery affected by the commission of the offense.

(2) If a court orders an unemancipated minor to make restitution under Subsection (a) and the minor is financially unable to make the restitution, the court may order:

(A) the minor to perform a specific number of hours of community service to satisfy the restitution; or

(B) the parents or other person responsible for the minor's support to make the restitution in the amount described by Subsection (b)(1)(B).

(3) In this subsection, "cemetery" and "cemetery organization" have the meanings assigned by Section 711.001, Health and Safety Code.

(q) The court shall order a defendant convicted of an offense under Section 22.11, Penal Code, to make restitution to the victim of the offense or the victim's employer in an amount equal to the sum of any expenses incurred by the victim or employer to:

(1) test the victim for HIV, hepatitis A, hepatitis B, tuberculosis, or any other disease designated as a reportable disease under Section 81.048, Health and Safety Code; or

(2) treat the victim for HIV, hepatitis A, hepatitis B, tuberculosis, or any other disease designated as a reportable disease under Section 81.048, Health and Safety Code, the victim contracts as a result of the offense.

(r) The court may order a defendant convicted of an offense under Section 43.26, Penal Code, to make restitution to an individual who as a child younger than 18 years of age was depicted in the visual material, in an amount equal to the expenses incurred by the individual as a result of the offense, including:

(1) medical services relating to physical, psychiatric, or psychological care;

(2) physical and occupational therapy or rehabilitation;

(3) necessary transportation, temporary housing, and child care expenses;

(4) lost income; and

(5) attorney's fees.

(s) (1) A court shall order a defendant convicted of an offense under Section 28.08, Penal Code, to make restitution by:

(A) reimbursing the owner of the property for the cost of restoring the property; or

(B) with the consent of the owner of the property, personally restoring the property by removing or painting over any markings the defendant made.

(2) A court shall order a defendant convicted of an offense under Section 28.08, Penal Code, to make restitution to a political subdivision that owns public property or erects a street sign or official traffic-control device on which the defendant makes markings in violation of Section 28.08, Penal Code, by:

(A) paying an amount equal to the lesser of the cost to the political subdivision of replacing or restoring the public property, street sign, or official traffic-control device; or

(B) with the consent of the political subdivision, restoring the public property, street sign, or official traffic-control device by removing or painting over any markings made by the defendant on the property, sign, or device.

(3) If the court orders a defendant to make restitution under this subsection and the defendant is financially unable to make the restitution, the court may order the defendant to perform a specific number of hours of community service to satisfy the restitution.

(4) Notwithstanding Subsection (g)(4), a court shall direct a defendant ordered to make restitution under this subsection as a condition of community supervision to deliver the amount or property due as restitution to the defendant's supervising officer for transfer to the owner. A parole panel shall direct a defendant ordered to make restitution under this subsection as a condition of parole

or mandatory supervision to deliver the amount or property due as restitution to the defendant's supervising officer. The defendant's supervising officer shall notify the court when the defendant has delivered the full amount of restitution ordered.

(5) For purposes of this subsection, "official traffic-control device" has the meaning assigned by Section 541.304, Transportation Code.

(t) If a person is convicted of an offense under Section 641.054, Business & Commerce Code, the court shall order the person to make restitution to an owner or lawful producer of a master recording that has suffered financial loss as a result of the offense or to a trade association that represents that owner or lawful producer. The amount of restitution ordered shall be:

(1) the greater of:

(A) the aggregate wholesale value of the lawfully manufactured and authorized recordings corresponding to the number of nonconforming recordings involved in the offense; or

(B) the actual financial loss to the owner, lawful producer, or trade association; and

(2) the costs associated with investigating the offense.

(u) For purposes of Subsection (t)(1)(A):

(1) the calculation of the aggregate wholesale value is based on the average wholesale value of the lawfully manufactured and authorized recordings; and

(2) the specific wholesale value of each nonconforming recording is not relevant to the calculation.

(v) For purposes of Subsection (t)(1)(B), the possession of a nonconforming recording intended for sale constitutes an actual financial loss to an owner or lawful producer equal to the actual value of the legitimate wholesale purchases displaced by the nonconforming recordings.

(w) If a defendant is convicted of an offense under Section 42.0601, Penal Code, the court may order the defendant to make restitution to an entity for the reasonable costs of the emergency response by that entity resulting from the false report.

Art. 42.0371. Mandatory Restitution for Kidnapped or Abducted Children.

(a) The court shall order a defendant convicted of an offense under Chapter 20, Penal Code, or Section 25.03, 25.031, or 25.04, Penal Code, to pay restitution in an amount equal to the cost of necessary rehabilitation, including medical, psychiatric, and psychological care and treatment, for the victim of the offense if the victim is younger than 17 years of age.

(b) The court shall, after considering the financial circumstances of the defendant, specify in a restitution order issued under Subsection (a) the manner in which the defendant must pay the restitution.

(c) A restitution order issued under Subsection (a) may be enforced by the state or a victim named in the order to receive the restitution in the same manner as a judgment in a civil action.

(d) The court may hold a hearing, make findings of fact, and amend a restitution order issued under Subsection (a) if the defendant fails to pay the victim named in the order in the manner specified by the court.

Art. 42.0372. Mandatory Restitution for Child Victims of Trafficking of Persons or Compelling Prostitution.

(a) The court shall order a defendant convicted of an offense under Section 20A.02 or 43.05(a)(2), Penal Code, to pay restitution in an amount equal to the cost of necessary rehabilitation, including medical, psychiatric, and psychological care and treatment, for any victim of the offense who is younger than 18 years of age.

(b) The court shall, after considering the financial circumstances of the defendant, specify in a restitution order issued under Subsection (a) the manner in which the defendant must pay the restitution.

(c) A restitution order issued under Subsection (a) may be enforced by the state, or by a victim named in the order to receive the restitution, in the same manner as a judgment in a civil action.

(d) The court may hold a hearing, make findings of fact, and amend a restitution order issued under Subsection (a) if the defendant fails to pay the victim named in the order in the manner specified by the court.

Art. 42.0373. Mandatory Restitution for Child Witness of Family Violence.

(a) If after a conviction or a grant of deferred adjudication a court places a defendant on community supervision for an offense involving family violence, as defined by Section 71.004, Family Code, the court shall determine from the complaint, information, indictment, or other charging instrument, the presentence report, or other evidence before the court whether:

(1) the offense was committed in the physical presence of, or in the same habitation or vehicle occupied by, a person younger than 15 years of age; and

(2) at the time of the offense, the defendant had knowledge or reason to know that the person younger than 15 years of age was physically present or occupied the same habitation or vehicle.

(b) If the court determines both issues described by Subsection (a) in the affirmative, the court shall order the defendant to pay restitution in an amount equal to the cost of necessary rehabilitation, including medical, psychiatric, and psychological care and treatment, for a person described by Subsection (a)(1).

(c) The court shall, after considering the financial circumstances of the defendant, specify in a restitution order issued under Subsection (b) the manner in which the defendant must pay the restitution. The order must require restitution payments to be delivered in the manner described by Article 42.037(g-2)(3).

(d) A restitution order issued under Subsection (b) may be enforced by the state, or by a person or a parent or guardian of the person named in the order to receive the restitution, in the same manner as a judgment in a civil action.

(e) The court may hold a hearing, make findings of fact, and amend a restitution order issued under Subsection (b) if the defendant fails to pay the person named in the order in the manner specified by the court.

(f) A determination under this article may not be entered as an affirmative finding in the judgment for the offense for which the defendant was placed on community supervision.

Art. 42.038. Reimbursement for Confinement Expenses.

(a) In addition to any fine, cost, or fee authorized by law, a court that sentences a defendant convicted of a misdemeanor to serve a term of confinement in county jail and orders execution of the sentence may require the defendant to reimburse the county for the defendant's confinement at a rate of $25 a day.

(b) A court that requires a defendant convicted of a misdemeanor or placed on deferred adjudication for a misdemeanor to submit to a period of confinement in county jail as a condition of community supervision may also require as a condition of community supervision that the defendant reimburse the county for the defendant's confinement, with the amount of reimbursement determined as if the defendant were serving an executed sentence.

(c) A judge may not require reimbursement under this article if the judge determines the defendant is indigent based on the defendant's sworn statement or affidavit filed with the court. A court that requires reimbursement under this article may require the defendant to reimburse the county only for those days the defendant is confined after the date of conviction or on which a plea of guilty or nolo contendere was entered. The court may not require a defendant to reimburse the county for those days the defendant was confined after arrest and before the date of conviction or on which the plea of guilty or nolo contendere was entered.

(d) The court, in determining whether to order reimbursement under this article, shall consider:

(1) the defendant's employment status, earning ability, and financial resources; and

(2) any other special circumstances that may affect the defendant's ability to pay, including child support obligations and including any financial responsibilities owed by the defendant to dependents or restitution payments owed by the defendant to a victim.

(e) On the day on which a defendant who is required to reimburse the county under this article discharges an executed sentence of confinement or completes the period of confinement required as a condition of community supervision, the sheriff shall present to the defendant a bill computed by multiplying the daily rate of $25 times the number of days the defendant was confined in the county jail, not counting the day on which the execution of the sentence or the period of confinement began. For purposes of this subsection, a defendant who is confined in county jail for only a portion of a day is nonetheless considered to have been confined for the whole day.

(f) The court may require a defendant to reimburse the county under this article by paying to the sheriff the bill presented by the sheriff within a specified period or in specified installments. The end of the period or the last installment may not be later than:

(1) the end of the period of community supervision, if community supervision is ordered; or

(2) the fifth anniversary of the last day of the term of confinement, if the court does not order community supervision.

Art. 42.039. Completion of Sentence in Federal Custody.

(a) This article applies only to a criminal case in which:

(1) the judgment requires the defendant to be confined in a secure correctional facility; and

(2) the defendant is subject to an immigration detainer request.

(b) In a criminal case described by Subsection (a), the judge shall, at the time of pronouncement of a sentence of confinement, issue an order requiring the secure correctional facility in which the defendant is to be confined and all appropriate government officers, including a sheriff, a warden, or members of the Board of Pardons and Paroles, as appropriate, to require the defendant to serve in federal custody the final portion of the defendant's sentence, not to exceed a period of seven days, following the facility's or officer's determination that the change in the place of confinement will facilitate the seamless transfer of the defendant into federal custody. In the absence of an order issued under this subsection, a facility or officer acting under exigent circumstances may perform the transfer after making the determination described by this subsection. This subsection applies only if appropriate officers of the federal government consent to the transfer of the defendant into federal custody under the circumstances described by this subsection.

(c) If the applicable information described by Subsection (a)(2) is not available at the time sentence is pronounced in the case, the judge shall issue the order described by Subsection (b) as soon as the information becomes available. The judge retains jurisdiction for the purpose of issuing an order under this article.

(d) For purposes of this article, "secure correctional facility" has the meaning assigned by Section 1.07, Penal Code.

Art. 42.04. Sentence When Appeal Is Taken.

When a defendant is sentenced to death, no date shall be set for the execution of sentence until after the receipt by the clerk of the trial court of the mandate of affirmance of the court of criminal appeals.

Art. 42.05. If Court Is About to Adjourn.

The time limit within which any act is to be done within the meaning of this Code shall not be affected by the expiration of the term of the court.

Art. 42.07. Reasons to Prevent Sentence.

Before pronouncing sentence, the defendant shall be asked whether he has anything to say why the sentence should not be pronounced against him. The only reasons which can be shown, on account of which sentence cannot be pronounced, are:

1. That the defendant has received a pardon from the proper authority, on the presentation of which, legally authenticated, he shall be discharged.

2. That the defendant is incompetent to stand trial; and if evidence be shown to support a finding of incompetency to stand trial, no sentence shall be pronounced, and the court shall proceed under Chapter 46B; and

3. When a person who has been convicted escapes after conviction and before sentence and an individual supposed to be the same has been arrested he may before sentence is pronounced, deny that he is the person convicted, and an issue be accordingly tried before a jury, or before the court if a jury is waived, as to his identity.

Art. 42.08. Cumulative or Concurrent Sentence.

(a) When the same defendant has been convicted in two or more cases, judgment and sentence shall be pronounced in each case in the same manner as if there had been but one conviction. Except as provided by Subsections (b) and (c), in the discretion of the court, the judgment in the second and subsequent convictions may either be that the sentence imposed or suspended shall begin when the judgment and the sentence imposed or suspended in the preceding conviction has ceased to operate, or that the sentence imposed or suspended shall run concurrently with the other case or cases, and sentence and execution shall be accordingly; provided, however, that the cumulative total of suspended sentences in felony cases shall not exceed 10 years, and the cumulative total of suspended sentences in misdemeanor cases shall not exceed the maximum period of confinement in jail applicable to the misdemeanor offenses, though in no event more than three years, including extensions of periods of community supervision under Article 42A.752(a)(2), if none of the offenses are offenses under Chapter 49, Penal Code, or four years, including extensions, if any of the offenses are offenses under Chapter 49, Penal Code.

(b) If a defendant is sentenced for an offense committed while the defendant was an inmate in the Texas Department of Criminal Justice and serving a sentence for an offense other than a state jail felony and the defendant has not completed the sentence he was serving at the time of the offense, the judge shall order the sentence for the subsequent offense to commence immediately on completion of the sentence for the original offense.

(c) If a defendant has been convicted in two or more cases and the court suspends the imposition of the sentence in one of the cases, the court may not order a sentence of confinement to commence on the completion of a suspended sentence for an offense.

Art. 42.09. Commencement of Sentence; Status During Appeal; Pen Packet.

Sec. 1. Except as provided in Sections 2 and 3, a defendant shall be delivered to a jail or to the

Texas Department of Criminal Justice when his sentence is pronounced, or his sentence to death is announced, by the court. The defendant's sentence begins to run on the day it is pronounced, but with all credits, if any, allowed by Article 42.03.

Sec. 2. If a defendant appeals his conviction and is released on bail pending disposition of his appeal, when his conviction is affirmed, the clerk of the trial court, on receipt of the mandate from the appellate court, shall issue a commitment against the defendant. The officer executing the commitment shall endorse thereon the date he takes the defendant into custody and the defendant's sentence begins to run from the date endorsed on the commitment. The Texas Department of Criminal Justice shall admit the defendant named in the commitment on the basis of the commitment.

Sec. 3. If a defendant convicted of a felony is sentenced to death or to life in the Texas Department of Criminal Justice or is ineligible for release on bail pending appeal under Article 44.04(b) and gives notice of appeal, the defendant shall be transferred to the department on a commitment pending a mandate from the court of appeals or the Court of Criminal Appeals.

Sec. 4. If a defendant is convicted of a felony, is eligible for release on bail pending appeal under Article 44.04(b), and gives notice of appeal, he shall be transferred to the Texas Department of Criminal Justice on a commitment pending a mandate from the Court of Appeals or the Court of Criminal Appeals upon request in open court or upon written request to the sentencing court. Upon a valid transfer to the department under this section, the defendant may not thereafter be released on bail pending his appeal.

Sec. 5. If a defendant is transferred to the Texas Department of Criminal Justice pending appeal under Section 3 or 4, his sentence shall be computed as if no appeal had been taken if the appeal is affirmed.

Sec. 6. All defendants who have been transferred to the Texas Department of Criminal Justice pending the appeal of their convictions under this article shall be under the control and authority of the department for all purposes as if no appeal were pending.

Sec. 7. If a defendant is sentenced to a term of imprisonment in the Texas Department of Criminal Justice but is not transferred to the department under Section 3 or 4, the court, before the date on which it would lose jurisdiction under Article 42A.202(a), shall send to the department a document containing a statement of the date on which the defendant's sentence was pronounced and credits earned by the defendant under Article 42.03 as of the date of the statement.

Sec. 8. (a) A county that transfers a defendant to the Texas Department of Criminal Justice under this article shall deliver to an officer designated by the department:

(1) a copy of the judgment entered pursuant to Article 42.01, completed on a standardized felony judgment form described by Section 4 of that article;

(2) a copy of any order revoking community supervision and imposing sentence pursuant to Article 42A.755, including:

(A) any amounts owed for restitution, fines, and court costs, completed on a standardized felony judgment form described by Section 4, Article 42.01; and

(B) a copy of the client supervision plan prepared for the defendant by the community supervision and corrections department supervising the defendant, if such a plan was prepared;

(3) a written report that states the nature and the seriousness of each offense and that states the citation to the provision or provisions of the Penal Code or other law under which the defendant was convicted;

(4) a copy of the victim impact statement, if one has been prepared in the case under Subchapter D, Chapter 56A;

(5) a statement as to whether there was a change in venue in the case and, if so, the names of the county prosecuting the offense and the county in which the case was tried;

(6) if requested, information regarding the criminal history of the defendant, including the defendant's state identification number if the number has been issued;

(7) a copy of the indictment or information for each offense;

(8) a checklist sent by the department to the county and completed by the county in a manner indicating that the documents required by this subsection and Subsection (c) accompany the defendant;

(9) if prepared, a copy of a presentence or postsentence report prepared under Subchapter F, Chapter 42A;

(10) a copy of any detainer, issued by an agency of the federal government, that is in the possession of the county and that has been placed on the defendant;

(11) if prepared, a copy of the defendant's Texas Uniform Health Status Update Form;

(12) a written description of a hold or warrant, issued by any other jurisdiction, that the county is aware of and that has been placed on or issued for the defendant; and

(13) a copy of any mental health records, mental health screening reports, or similar information regarding the mental health of the defendant.

(b) The Texas Department of Criminal Justice shall not take a defendant into custody under this article until the designated officer receives the documents required by Subsections (a) and (c) of this section. The designated officer shall certify under the seal of the department the documents received under Subsections (a) and (c) of this section. A document certified under this subsection is self-authenticated for the purposes of Rules 901 and 902, Texas Rules of Evidence.

(c) A county that transfers a defendant to the Texas Department of Criminal Justice under this article shall also deliver to the designated officer any presentence or postsentence investigation report, revocation report, psychological or psychiatric evaluation of the defendant, including a written report provided to a court under Article 16.22(a)(1)(B) or an evaluation prepared for the juvenile court before transferring the defendant to criminal court and contained in the criminal prosecutor's file, and available social or psychological background information relating to the defendant and may deliver to the designated officer any additional information upon which the judge or jury bases the punishment decision.

(d) The correctional institutions division of the Texas Department of Criminal Justice shall make documents received under Subsections (a) and (c) available to the parole division on the request of the parole division and shall, on release of a defendant on parole or to mandatory supervision, immediately provide the parole division with copies of documents received under Subsection (a). The parole division shall provide to the parole officer appointed to supervise the defendant a comprehensive summary of the information contained in the documents referenced in this section not later than the 14th day after the date of the defendant's release. The summary shall include a current photograph of the defendant and a complete set of the defendant's fingerprints. Upon written request from the county sheriff, the photograph and fingerprints shall be filed with the sheriff of the county to which the parolee is assigned if that county is not the county from which the parolee was sentenced.

(e) A county is not required to deliver separate documents containing information relating to citations to provisions of the Penal Code or other law and to changes of venue, as otherwise required by Subsections (a)(3) and (a)(5) of this article, if the standardized felony judgment form described by Section 4, Article 42.01, of this code is modified to require that information.

(f) Except as provided by Subsection (g) of this section, the county sheriff is responsible for ensuring that documents and information required by this section accompany defendants sentenced by district courts in the county to the Texas Department of Criminal Justice.

(g) If the presiding judge of the administrative judicial region in which the county is located determines that the county sheriff is unable to perform the duties required by Subsection (f) of this section, the presiding judge may impose those duties on:

(1) the district clerk; or

(2) the prosecutor of each district court in the county.

(h) If a parole panel releases on parole a person who is confined in a jail in this state, a federal correctional institution, or a correctional institution in another state, the Texas Department of Criminal Justice shall request the sheriff who would otherwise be required to transfer the person to the department to forward to the department the information described by Subsections (a) and (c) of this section. The sheriff shall comply with the request of the department. The department shall determine whether the information forwarded by the sheriff under this subsection contains a thumbprint taken from the person in the manner provided by Article 38.33 of this code and, if not, the department shall obtain a thumbprint taken in the manner provided by that article and shall forward the thumbprint to the department for inclusion with the information sent by the sheriff.

(i) A county may deliver the documents required under Subsections (a) and (c) of this section to the Texas Department of Criminal Justice by electronic means. For purposes of this subsection, "electronic means" means the transmission of data between word processors, data processors, or similar automated information equipment over dedicated cables, commercial lines, or other similar methods of transmission.

(j) If after a county transfers a defendant or inmate to the Texas Department of Criminal Justice the charges on which the defendant or inmate was convicted and for which the defendant or inmate was transferred are dismissed, the county shall immediately notify an officer designated by the department of the dismissal.

Sec. 9. A county that transfers a defendant to the Texas Department of Criminal Justice under this article may deliver to an officer designated by the department a certified copy of a final order of a state or federal court that dismisses as frivolous or malicious a lawsuit brought by the inmate while the inmate was confined in the county jail awaiting transfer to the department following conviction of a felony or revocation of community supervision, parole, or mandatory supervision. The county may deliver the copy to the department at the time of the transfer of the inmate or at any time after the transfer of the inmate.

Art. 42.10. Satisfaction of Judgment As in Misdemeanor Convictions.

When a person is convicted of a felony, and the punishment assessed is only a fine or a term in jail, or both, the judgment may be satisfied in the same manner as a conviction for a misdemeanor is by law satisfied.

Art. 42.11. Uniform Act for Out-of-State Probationer and Parolee Supervision [Repealed].

Repealed by Acts 2001, 77th Leg., ch. 543 (H.B. 2494), § 2, effective June 19, 2003.

Art. 42.111. Deferral of Proceedings in Cases Appealed to County Court.

If a defendant convicted of a misdemeanor punishable by fine only appeals the conviction to a county court, on the trial in county court the defendant may enter a plea of guilty or nolo contendere to the offense. If the defendant enters a plea of guilty or nolo contendere, the court may defer further proceedings without entering an adjudication of guilt in the same manner as provided for the deferral of proceedings in justice court or municipal court under Article 45.051 of this code. This article does not apply to a misdemeanor case disposed of under Subchapter B, Chapter 543, Transportation Code, or a serious traffic violation as defined by Section 522.003, Transportation Code.

Art. 42.12. Community Supervision. [Repealed]

Art. 42.122. Adult Probation Officers of the 222nd Judicial District; Salary and Allowances.

The adult probation officer of the 222nd Judicial District receives a salary of not less than $15,000 per annum. Also, the probation officer receives allowances, not to exceed the amount allowed by the federal government for traveling the most practical route to and from the place where the duties are discharged, for his necessary travel and hotel expenses. Upon the sworn statement of the officer, approved by the judge, the respective counties of the judicial district pay the expenses incurred for their regular or special term of court out of the general county fund. In lieu of travel allowances the commissioners court of each county, by agreement, may provide transportation under the same terms and conditions as provided for sheriffs.

Art. 42.13. [Repealed].

Repealed by Acts 1995, 74th Leg., ch. 76 (S.B. 959), § 7.10, effective September 1, 1995.

Art. 42.131. [Repealed].

Repealed by Acts 1995, 74th Leg., ch. 76 (S.B. 959), § 7.12, effective September 1, 1995.

Art. 42.14. In Absence of Defendant.

(a) In a misdemeanor case, the judgment and sentence may be rendered in the absence of the defendant.

(b) In a felony case, the judgment and sentence may be rendered in the absence of the defendant only if:

(1) the defendant is confined in a penal institution;

(2) the defendant is not charged with a felony offense:

(A) that is listed in Article 42A.054(a); or

(B) for which it is alleged that:

(i) a deadly weapon was used or exhibited during the commission of the offense or during immediate flight from the commission of the offense; and

(ii) the defendant used or exhibited the deadly weapon or was a party to the offense and knew that a deadly weapon would be used or exhibited;

(3) the defendant in writing before the appropriate court having jurisdiction in the county in which the penal institution is located:

(A) waives the right to be present at the rendering of the judgment and sentence or to have counsel present;

(B) affirms that the defendant does not have anything to say as to why the sentence should not be pronounced and that there is no reason to prevent the sentence under Article 42.07;

(C) states that the defendant has entered into a written plea agreement with the attorney representing the state in the prosecution of the case; and

(D) requests the court to pronounce sentence in the case in accordance with the plea agreement;

(4) the defendant and the attorney representing the state in the prosecution of the case have entered into a written plea agreement that is made a part of the record in the case; and

Code of Criminal Procedure

(5) sentence is pronounced in accordance with the plea agreement.

(c) A judgment and sentence may be rendered under this article in the absence of the defendant only after the defendant is notified by the court of original jurisdiction of the right to counsel and the defendant requests counsel or waives the right to counsel in accordance with Article 1.051.

(d) In this article, "deadly weapon" and "penal institution" have the meanings assigned by Section 1.07, Penal Code.

(e) If a defendant enters a plea of guilty or nolo contendere under Article 27.19, the attorney representing the state may request at the time the plea is entered that the defendant submit a fingerprint of the defendant suitable for attachment to the judgment. On request for a fingerprint under this subsection, the county in which the defendant is confined shall obtain a fingerprint of the defendant and use first-class mail or other means acceptable to the attorney representing the state and the county to forward the fingerprint to the court accepting the plea.

Art. 42.141. Battering Intervention and Prevention Program.

Sec. 1. **Definitions.** — In this article:

(1) "Batterer" means a person who commits repeated acts of violence or who repeatedly threatens violence against another who is:

(A) related to the actor by affinity or consanguinity, as determined under Chapter 573, Government Code;

(B) is a former spouse of the actor; or

(C) resides or has resided in the same household with the actor.

(2) "Division" means the community justice assistance division of the Texas Department of Criminal Justice.

(3) "Family" has the meaning assigned by Section 71.003, Family Code.

(4) "Family violence" has the meaning assigned by Section 71.004, Family Code.

(5) "Shelter center" has the meaning assigned by Section 51.002, Human Resources Code.

(6) "Household" has the meaning assigned by Section 71.005, Family Code.

(7) "Program" means a battering intervention and prevention program that:

(A) meets:

(i) the guidelines adopted by the community justice assistance division of the Texas Department of Criminal Justice with the assistance of the statewide nonprofit organization described by Section 3(1); and

(ii) any other eligibility requirements adopted by the Texas Department of Criminal Justice; and

(B) provides, on a local basis to batterers referred by the courts for intervention, educational services and intervention designed to help the batterers stop their abusive behavior.

(8) "Project" means the statewide activities for the funding of battering intervention and prevention programs, the related community educational campaign, and education and research regarding such programs.

(9) "Responsive law enforcement climate" means an area where, in cases of family violence:

(A) the local law enforcement agency has a policy or record of arresting batterers; and

(B) the local criminal justice system:

(i) cooperates with the victim in filing protective orders; and

(ii) takes appropriate action against a person who violates protective orders.

Sec. 2. **Establishment.** — The battering intervention and prevention program is established in the division.

Sec. 3. **Duties of the Division.** — The division shall:

(1) contract with a nonprofit organization that for the five-year period before the date on which a contract is to be signed has been involved in providing to shelter centers, law enforcement agencies, and the legal community statewide advocacy and technical assistance relating to family violence, with the contract requiring the nonprofit organization to perform the duties described in Section (4) of this article;

(2) seek the input of the statewide nonprofit organization described in Subdivision (1) in the development of standards for selection of programs for inclusion in the project and the review of proposals submitted by programs;

(3) issue requests for proposals for the programs and an educational campaign not later than January 1, 1990;

(4) award contracts for programs that are operated by nonprofit organizations and that take into consideration:

(A) a balanced geographical distribution of urban, rural, and suburban models; and

(B) the presence of a responsive law enforcement climate in the community;

(5) develop and monitor the project in cooperation with the nonprofit organization described by Subdivision (1);

(6) monitor the development of a community educational campaign in cooperation with the nonprofit organization described by Subdivision (1);

(7) assist the nonprofit organization described by Subdivision (1) in designing program evaluations and research activities;

(8) facilitate training of probation officers and other criminal justice professionals by the nonprofit organization described by Subdivision (1) and by programs;

(9) seek the assistance of the nonprofit organization described by Subdivision (1) in developing program guidelines and in accrediting programs and providers providing battering intervention and prevention services as conforming to those guidelines; and

(10) before adopting program guidelines under Section 4A:

(A) notify the licensing authorities described by Chapters 152, 501, 502, 503, and 505, Occupations Code, that the division is considering adopting program guidelines; and

(B) invite the licensing authorities to comment on the program guidelines.

Sec. 4. **Duties of the Nonprofit Organization.** — The nonprofit organization with which the division contracts under Section 3(1) shall:

(1) assist the division in developing and issuing requests for proposals for the programs and the educational campaign;

(2) assist the division in reviewing the submitted proposals and making recommendations for proposals to be selected for funding;

(3) develop and monitor the project in cooperation with the division;

(4) provide technical assistance to programs to:

(A) develop appropriate services for batterers;

(B) train staff;

(C) improve coordination with shelter centers, the criminal justice system, the judiciary, law enforcement agencies, prosecutors, and other appropriate officials and support services;

(D) implement the community educational campaign; and

(E) participate in project administered program evaluation and research activities;

(5) provide technical assistance to the division to:

(A) develop and implement standards for selection of programs for inclusion in the project; and

(B) develop standards for selection of the community educational campaign described in Section 6 of this article;

(6) submit an annual written report to the division and to the legislature with recommendations for continuation, elimination, or changes in the project;

(7) evaluate the programs and the community educational campaign, including an analysis of the effectiveness of the project and the level of public awareness relating to family violence; and

(8) assist the division in developing program guidelines and in accrediting programs and providers providing battering intervention and prevention services as conforming to those guidelines.

Sec. 4A. **Adoption of Program Guidelines; Accreditation Process.** — With the assistance of the statewide nonprofit organization described by Section 3(1) and after notifying the licensing authorities described by Section 3(10), the division shall adopt guidelines for programs and shall accredit programs and providers providing battering intervention and prevention services as conforming to those guidelines. The division shall collect from each program or provider that applies for accreditation under this section a one-time application fee in an amount set by the Texas Department of Criminal Justice.

Sec. 5. **Programs.**

(a) A program proposal must:

(1) describe the counseling or treatment the program will offer;

(2) include letters from a local law enforcement agency or agencies, courts, probation officers, and other community resources describing the community's commitment to improve the criminal justice system's response to victims and batterers and to cooperate with and interact in the programs' activities;

(3) include a letter from the local shelter center describing the support services available to victims of family violence in the community and the shelter's commitment to cooperate and work with the program; and

(4) describe the public education and local community outreach activities relating to family violence currently available in the community and a statement of commitment to participate on the local level in the public educational campaign described in Section 6 of this article.

(b) A program must:

(1) be situated in a county in which a shelter center is located;

(2) offer counseling or treatment in which the primary approach is direct intervention with the batterer, on an individual or group basis, but that does not require the victim of the family violence to participate in the counseling or treatment;

(3) offer training to law enforcement prosecutors, judges, probation officers, and others on the dynamics of family violence, treatment options, and program activities; and

(4) have a system for receiving referrals from the courts and for reporting to the court regarding batterers' compliance with the treatment program.

(c) This section does not preclude a program from serving a batterer other than one who was ordered by a court to participate in the program established under this subchapter.

Sec. 6. **Community Educational Campaign.**

(a) The division, with assistance from the nonprofit organization, shall select the community educational campaign relating to family violence after the commission has selected the programs. The campaign is to be implemented in the areas covered by the programs.

(b) The campaign shall use a variety of media, including newspapers, radio, television, and billboards, and shall focus on:

(1) the criminality of acts of violence toward family members;

(2) the consequences of family violence crimes to the batterer; and

(3) eradicating public misconceptions of family violence.

Sec. 7. **Use of Legislative Appropriation. —** Of a legislative appropriation for the project established under this article:

(1) not more than six percent may be used by the division for management and administration of the project;

(2) not more than 14 percent may be applied to the contract between the division and the nonprofit organization; and

(3) not more than three percent may be applied to the contract for the community educational campaign.

Sec. 8. **Contract Date. —** The contract required under Section 3(a) of this article shall be signed not later than November 1, 1989.

Art. 42.15. Fines and Costs.

(a) When the defendant is fined, the judgment shall be that the defendant pay the amount of the fine and all costs to the state.

(a-1) Notwithstanding any other provision of this article, during or immediately after imposing a sentence in a case in which the defendant entered a plea in open court as provided by Article 27.13, 27.14(a), or 27.16(a), a court shall inquire on the record whether the defendant has sufficient resources or income to immediately pay all or part of the fine and costs. If the court determines that the defendant does not have sufficient resources or income to immediately pay all or part of the fine and costs, the court shall determine whether the fine and costs should be:

(1) subject to Subsection (c), required to be paid at some later date or in a specified portion at designated intervals;

(2) discharged by performing community service under, as applicable, Article 43.09(f), Article 45.049, Article 45.0492, as added by Chapter 227 (H.B. 350), Acts of the 82nd Legislature, Regular Session, 2011, or Article 45.0492, as added by Chapter 777 (H.B. 1964), Acts of the 82nd Legislature, Regular Session, 2011;

(3) waived in full or in part under Article 43.091 or 45.0491; or

(4) satisfied through any combination of methods under Subdivisions (1)—(3).

(b) Subject to Subsections (c) and (d) and Article 43.091, when imposing a fine and costs, a court may direct a defendant:

(1) to pay the entire fine and costs when sentence is pronounced;

(2) to pay the entire fine and costs at some later date; or

(3) to pay a specified portion of the fine and costs at designated intervals.

(c) When imposing a fine and costs in a misdemeanor case, if the court determines that the defendant is unable to immediately pay the fine and costs, the court shall allow the defendant to pay the fine and costs in specified portions at designated intervals.

(d) A judge may allow a defendant who is a child, as defined by Article 45.058(h), to elect at the time of conviction, as defined by Section 133.101, Local Government Code, to discharge the fine and costs by:

(1) performing community service or receiving tutoring under Article 45.0492, as added by Chapter 227 (H.B. 350), Acts of the 82nd Legislature, Regular Session, 2011; or

(2) paying the fine and costs in a manner described by Subsection (b).

(e) The election under Subsection (d) must be made in writing, signed by the defendant, and, if present, signed by the defendant's parent, guardian, or managing conservator. The court shall maintain the written election as a record of the court and provide a copy to the defendant.

(f) The requirement under Article 45.0492(a), as added by Chapter 227 (H.B. 350), Acts of the 82nd Legislature, Regular Session, 2011, that an offense occur in a building or on the grounds of the primary or secondary school at which the defendant was enrolled at the time of the offense does not apply to the performance of community service or the receipt of tutoring to discharge a fine or costs under Subsection (d)(1).

Art. 42.151. Fees for Abused Children's Counseling.

If a court orders a defendant to pay a fee under Article 37.072 of this code, the court shall assess the fee against the defendant in the same manner as other costs of prosecution are assessed against a defendant. The court may direct a defendant:

(1) to pay the entire fee when sentence is pronounced;

(2) to pay the entire fee at some later date; or

(3) to pay a specified portion of the fee at designated intervals.

Art. 42.152. Repayment of Reward.

(a) If a judge orders a defendant to pay a fine repaying a reward or part of a reward under Article 37.073, the court shall assess this fine against the defendant in the same manner as other fines are assessed against a defendant. The court may order the defendant to:

(1) pay the entire amount required when sentence is pronounced;

(2) pay the entire amount required at a later date specified by the court; or

(3) pay specified portions of the required amount at designated intervals.

(b) After receiving a payment of a fine from a person ordered to make the payment under this article, the clerk of the court or fee officer shall:

(1) make a record of the payment;

(2) deduct a one-time $7 reimbursement fee from the payment for deposit in the general fund of the county;

(3) forward the payment to the designated crime stoppers organization; and

(4) make a record of the forwarding of the payment.

Art. 42.16. On Other Judgment.

If the punishment is any other than a fine, the judgment shall specify it, and order it enforced by the proper process. It shall also adjudge the costs against the defendant, and order the collection thereof as in other cases.

Art. 42.17. Transfer Under Treaty.

When a treaty is in effect between the United States and a foreign country providing for the transfer of convicted offenders who are citizens or nationals of foreign countries to the foreign countries of which they are citizens or nationals, the governor is authorized, subject to the terms of such treaty, to act on behalf of the State of Texas and to consent to the transfer of such convicted offenders under the provisions of Article IV, Section 11 of the Constitution of the State of Texas.

Art. 42.18. [Repealed].

Repealed by Acts 1997, 75th Leg., ch. 165 (S.B. 898), § 12.22, effective September 1, 1997.

Art. 42.19. Interstate Corrections Compact.

Article I. Purpose and Policy

The party states, desiring by common action to fully utilize and improve their institutional facilities and provide adequate programs for the confinement, treatment, and rehabilitation of various types of offenders, declare that it is the policy of each of the party states to provide such facilities and programs on a basis of cooperation with one another, thereby serving the best interests of such offenders and of society and effecting economies in capital expenditures and operational costs. The purpose of this compact is to provide for the mutual development and execution of such programs of cooperation for the confinement, treatment, and rehabilitation of offenders with the most economical use of human and material resources.

Article II. Definitions

As used in this compact, unless the context clearly requires otherwise:

(a) "State" means a state of the United States; the United States of America; a territory or possession of the United States; the District of Columbia; the commonwealth of Puerto Rico.

(b) "Sending state" means a state party to this compact in which conviction or court commitment was had.

(c) "Receiving state" means a state party to this compact to which an inmate is sent for confinement other than a state in which conviction or court commitment was had.

(d) "Inmate" means a male or female offender who is committed, under sentence to or confined in a penal or correctional institution.

(e) "Institution" means any penal or correctional facility, including but not limited to a facility for the mentally ill or mentally defective, in which inmates as defined in (d) above may lawfully be confined.

Article III. Contracts

(a) Each party state may make one or more contracts with any one or more of the other party states for the confinement of inmates on behalf of a sending state in institutions situated within receiving states. Any such contract shall provide for:

1. Its duration.

2. Payments to be made to the receiving state by the sending state for inmate maintenance, extraordinary medical and dental expenses, and any

participation in or receipt by inmates of rehabilitative or correctional services, facilities, programs, or treatment not reasonably included as part of normal maintenance.

3. Participation in programs of inmate employment, if any; the disposition or crediting of any payments received by inmates on account thereof; and the crediting of proceeds from or disposal of any products resulting therefrom.

4. Delivery and retaking of inmates.

5. Such other matters as may be necessary and appropriate to fix the obligations, responsibilities, and rights of the sending and receiving states.

(b) The terms and provisions of this compact shall be a part of any contract entered into by the authority of or pursuant thereto, and nothing in any such contract shall be inconsistent therewith.

Article IV. Procedures and Rights

(a) Whenever the duly constituted authorities in a state party to this compact, and which has entered into a contract pursuant to Article III, shall decide that confinement in, or transfer of an inmate to, an institution within the territory of another party state is necessary or desirable in order to provide adequate quarters and care or an appropriate program of rehabilitation or treatment, such official may direct that the confinement be within an institution within the territory of such other party state, the receiving state to act in that regard solely as agent for the sending state.

(b) The appropriate officials of any state party to this compact shall have access, at all reasonable times, to any institution in which it has a contractual right to confine inmates for the purpose of inspecting the facilities thereof and visiting such of its inmates as may be confined in the institution.

(c) Inmates confined in an institution pursuant to this compact shall at all times be subject to the jurisdiction of the sending state and may at any time be removed therefrom for transfer to a prison or other institution within the sending state, for transfer to another institution in which the sending state may have a contractual or other right to confine inmates, for release on probation or parole, for discharge, or for any other purpose permitted by the laws of the sending state. However, the sending state shall continue to be obligated to such payments as may be required pursuant to the terms of any contract entered into under the terms of Article III.

(d) Each receiving state shall provide regular reports to each sending state on the inmates of that sending state who are in institutions pursuant to this compact including a conduct record of each inmate and shall certify such record to the official designated by the sending state, in order that each inmate may have official review of his or her record in determining and altering the disposition of the inmate in accordance with the law which may obtain in the sending state and in order that the same may be a source of information for the sending state.

(e) All inmates who may be confined in an institution pursuant to this compact shall be treated in a reasonable and humane manner and shall be treated equally with such similar inmates of the receiving state as may be confined in the same institution. The fact of confinement in a receiving state shall not deprive any inmate so confined of any legal rights which the inmate would have had if confined in an appropriate institution of the sending state.

(f) Any hearing or hearings to which an inmate confined pursuant to this compact may be entitled by the laws of the sending state may be had before the appropriate authorities of the sending state, or of the receiving state if authorized by the sending state. The receiving state shall provide adequate facilities for such hearing as may be conducted by the appropriate officials of a sending state. In the event such hearing or hearings are had before officials of the receiving state, the governing law shall be that of the sending state and a record of the hearing or hearings as prescribed by the sending state shall be made. The record together with any recommendations of the hearing officials shall be transmitted forthwith to the official or officials before whom the hearing would have been had if it had taken place in the sending state. In any and all proceedings had pursuant to the provisions of this paragraph (f), the officials of the receiving state shall act solely as agents of the sending state and no final determination shall be made in any matter except by the appropriate officials of the sending state.

(g) Any inmate confined pursuant to this compact shall be released within the territory of the sending state unless the inmate and the sending and receiving states shall agree upon release in some other place. The sending state shall bear the cost of such return to its territory.

(h) Any inmate confined pursuant to this compact shall have any rights and all rights to participate in and derive any benefits or incur or be relieved of any obligations or have such obligations modified or his status changed on account of any action or proceeding in which he could have participated if confined in any appropriate institution of the sending state located within such state.

(i) The parent, guardian, trustee, or other person or persons entitled under the laws of the sending state to act for, advise, or otherwise function with respect to any inmate shall not be deprived of or restricted in his exercise of any power in respect of any inmate confined pursuant to the terms of this compact.

Article V. Act Not Reviewable in Receiving State: Extradition

(a) Any decision of the sending state in respect of any matter over which it retains jurisdiction pursuant to this compact shall be conclusive upon and not reviewable within the receiving state, but if at the time the sending state seeks to remove an inmate from an institution in the receiving state there is pending against the inmate within such state any criminal charge or if the inmate is formally accused of having committed within such state a criminal offense, the inmate shall not be returned without the consent of the receiving state until discharged from prosecution or other form of proceeding, imprisonment, or detention for such offense. The duly accredited officer of the sending state shall be permitted to transport inmates pursuant to this compact through any and all states party to this compact without interference.

(b) An inmate who escapes from an institution in which he is confined pursuant to this compact shall be deemed a fugitive from the sending state and from the state in which the institution escaped from is situated. In the case of an escape to a jurisdiction other than the sending or receiving state, the responsibility for institution of extradition or rendition proceedings shall be that of the sending state, but nothing contained herein shall be construed to prevent or affect the activities of officers and agencies of any jurisdiction directed toward the apprehension and return of an escapee.

Article VI. Federal Aid

Any state party to this compact may accept federal aid for use in connection with any institution or program, the use of which is or may be affected by this compact or any contract pursuant thereto. Any inmate in a receiving state pursuant to this compact may participate in any such federally aided program or activity for which the sending and receiving states have made contractual provision. However, if such program or activity is not part of the customary correctional regimen, the express consent of the appropriate official of the sending state shall be required therefor.

Article VII. Entry into Force

This compact shall enter into force and become effective and binding upon the states so acting when it has been enacted into law by any two states. Thereafter, this compact shall enter into force and become effective and binding as to any other of such states upon similar action by such state.

Article VIII. Withdrawal and Termination

This compact shall continue in force and remain binding upon a party state until it shall have enacted a statute repealing the compact and providing for the sending of formal written notice of withdrawal from the compact to the appropriate officials of all other party states. An actual withdrawal shall not take effect until one year after the notices provided in the statute have been sent. Such withdrawal shall not relieve the withdrawing state from its obligations assumed hereunder prior to the effective date of withdrawal. Before the effective date of withdrawal, a withdrawal state shall remove to its territory, at its own expense, such inmates as it may have confined pursuant to the provisions of this compact.

Article IX. Other Arrangements Unaffected

Nothing contained in this compact shall be construed to abrogate or impair an agreement or other arrangement which a party state may have with a nonparty state for the confinement, rehabilitation, or treatment of inmates, nor to repeal any other laws of a party state authorizing the making of cooperative institutional arrangements.

Article X. Construction and Severability

(a) The provisions of this compact shall be liberally construed and shall be severable. If any phrase, clause, sentence, or provision of this compact is declared to be contrary to the constitution of any participating state or of the United States or the applicability thereof to any government, agency, person, or circumstance is held invalid, the validity of the remainder of this compact and the applicability thereof to any government, agency, person, or circumstance shall not be affected thereby. If this compact shall be held contrary to the constitution of any state participating therein, the compact shall remain in full force and effect as to the remaining states and in full force and effect as to the state affected as to all severable matters.

(b) Powers. The director of the Texas Department of Criminal Justice is authorized and directed to do all things necessary or incidental to the carrying out of the compact in every particular.

Art. 42.20. Immunities.

(a) An individual listed in Subsection (c) of this article and the governmental entity that the individual serves as an officer or employee are not liable for damages arising from an act or failure to act by the individual or governmental entity in connection with a community service program or work program established under this chapter or in connection with an inmate, offender, or releasee programmatic or nonprogrammatic activity, including work, educational, and treatment activities, if the act or failure to act:

(1) was performed pursuant to a court order or was otherwise performed in an official capacity; and

(2) was not performed with conscious indifference for the safety of others.

(b) Chapter 101, Civil Practice and Remedies Code, does not apply to a claim based on an act or a failure to act of an individual listed in Subsection (c) of this article or a governmental entity the officer serves as an officer or employee if the act or failure to act is in connection with a program described by Subsection (a) of this article.

(c) This article applies to:

(1) a director or employee of a community supervision and corrections department or a community corrections facility;

(2) a sheriff or employee of a sheriff's department;

(3) a county judge, county attorney, county commissioner, or county employee;

(4) a district judge, district attorney, or criminal district attorney;

(5) an officer or employee of a state agency; or

(6) an officer or employee of a political subdivision other than a county.

Art. 42.21. Notice of Release of Family Violence Offenders.

(a) Before releasing a person convicted of a family violence offense, the entity holding the person shall make a reasonable attempt to give personal notice of the imminent release to the victim of the offense or to another person designated by the victim to receive the notice. An attempt by an entity to give notice to the victim or person designated by the victim at the victim's or person's last known telephone number or address, as shown on the records of the entity, constitutes a reasonable attempt to give notice under this subsection.

(b) An entity or an employee of an entity is not liable for damages arising from complying or failing to comply with Subsection (a) of this article.

(c) In this article, "family violence" has the meaning assigned by Section 71.004, Family Code.

Art. 42.22. Restitution Liens.

Sec. 1. **Definitions. —** In this article:

(1) "Department" means the Texas Department of Motor Vehicles.

(2) "Motor vehicle" has the meaning assigned by Chapter 501, Transportation Code.

(3) "State" means the State of Texas and all political subdivisions thereof.

(4) "Victim" means:

(A) a "close relative of a deceased victim," "guardian of a victim," or "victim," as those terms are defined by Article 56A.001; or

(B) an individual who suffers damages as a result of another committing an offense under Section 38.04, Penal Code, in which the defendant used a motor vehicle while the defendant was in flight.

(5) "Personal property" means any property other than real property including all tangible and intangible types of property and including but not limited to copyrights, book rights, movie rights, patents, and trademarks acquired by the defendant prior to, during, and after conviction.

Sec. 2. **Lien Established.**

(a) The victim of a criminal offense has a restitution lien to secure the amount of restitution to which the victim is entitled under the order of a court in a criminal case.

(b) The state also has a restitution lien to secure the:

(1) amount of fines or costs entered against a defendant in the judgment in a felony criminal case;

(2) amount of reimbursement for costs of:

(A) confinement ordered under Article 42.038; or

(B) notice provided under Article 62.056 or 62.201; and

(3) amount of damages incurred by the state as a result of the commission of an offense under Section 38.04, Penal Code, in which the defendant used a motor vehicle while the defendant was in flight.

Sec. 3. **Perfection.**

(a) Except as provided by this section, a restitution lien attaches and is perfected when an affidavit to perfect the lien is filed in accordance with this article.

(b) If a lien established under this article is attached to a motor vehicle, the lien must be perfected in the manner provided by Chapter 501, Transportation Code, and the court that entered the order of restitution giving rise to the lien shall include in the order a requirement that the defendant surrender to the court evidence of current legal ownership of the motor vehicle and the title, if applicable, against which the lien attaches. A lien against a motor vehicle as provided by this article is not perfected until the defendant's title to the vehicle has been surrendered to the court and the department has issued a subsequent title that discloses on its face the fact that the vehicle is subject to a restitution lien established as provided by this article.

Sec. 4. **Judgment Required.** — An affidavit to perfect a restitution lien may not be filed under this article until a court has ordered restitution or entered a judgment requiring the defendant to pay a fine or costs.

Sec. 5. **Persons Who May File.** — The following persons may file an affidavit to perfect a restitution lien:

(1) the attorney representing the state in a criminal case in which a victim is determined by the court to be entitled to restitution or in which a defendant is ordered to pay fines or costs; or

(2) a victim in a criminal case determined by the court to be entitled to restitution.

Sec. 6. **Affidavit.** — An affidavit to perfect a restitution lien must be signed by the attorney representing the state or a magistrate and must contain:

(1) the name and date of birth of the defendant whose property or other interests are subject to the lien;

(2) the residence or principal place of business of the person named in the lien, if known;

(3) the criminal proceeding giving rise to the lien, including the name of the court, the name of the case, and the court's file number for the case;

(4) the name and address of the attorney representing the state and the name of the person entitled to restitution;

(5) a statement that the notice is being filed under this article;

(6) the amount of restitution and the amount of fines and costs the defendant has been ordered to pay by the court;

(7) a statement that the amount of restitution owed at any one time may be less than the original balance and that the outstanding balance is reflected in the records of the clerk of the court hearing the criminal proceeding giving rise to the lien; and

(8) the vehicle description and vehicle identification number.

Sec. 7. **Filing.**

(a) An affidavit to perfect a restitution lien may be filed with:

(1) the secretary of state;

(2) the department in the manner provided by Chapter 501, Transportation Code; or

(3) the county clerk of the county in which:

(A) the crime was committed;

(B) the defendant resides; or

(C) the property is located.

(b) The uniform fee for filing and indexing and for stamping a copy furnished by the state or victim to show the date and place of filing is $5.

(c) The secretary of state shall deposit the filing fee in the state treasury to the credit of the statutory filing fund solely to defray the costs of administration of this section. The department shall deposit the filing fee in the state treasury to the credit of the state highway fund to be used solely to defray the costs of administering this section.

(d) The county clerk shall immediately record the restitution lien in the judgment records of the county. The clerk shall note in the records the date and hour the lien is received.

(e) The secretary of state shall immediately file the restitution lien in the security interest and financing statement records of the secretary of state. The secretary of state shall note in the records the date and hour the lien is received.

(f) The department shall immediately file the restitution lien in the motor vehicle records of the department. The department shall note in the records the date and hour the lien is received.

(g) When a restitution lien is filed, the county clerk or secretary of state shall enter the restitution lien in an alphabetical index to the records in which the lien is filed showing:

(1) the name of the person entitled to restitution;

(2) the name of the defendant obligated to pay restitution, fines, or costs;

(3) the amount of the lien; and

(4) the name of the court that ordered restitution.

(h) A person who files an affidavit to perfect a restitution lien under this article shall notify in writing the clerk of the court entering the judgment creating the lien of all officers or entities with which the affidavit was filed.

Sec. 8. **Subject Property.** — A restitution lien extends to:

(1) any interest of the defendant in real property whether then owned or after-acquired located in a county in which the lien is perfected by the filing of an affidavit with the county clerk;

(2) any interest of the defendant in tangible or intangible personal property whether then owned or after-acquired other than a motor vehicle if the lien is perfected by the filing of the affidavit with the secretary of state; or

(3) any interest of the defendant in a motor vehicle whether then owned or after-acquired if the lien is perfected by the filing of the affidavit with the department.

Sec. 9. **Priority.** — The perfection of a restitution lien under this article is notice of the claim to all persons dealing with the defendant or the property identified in the affidavit perfecting the lien. Without regard to whether perfected before or after the perfection of a restitution lien filed and perfected under this article, a perfected real estate mortgage lien, a vendor's lien, a purchase money security interest, a chattel paper security interest, a lien on a motor vehicle perfected as provided by Chapter 501, Transportation Code, or a worker's lien perfected in the manner provided by law is superior and prior to a restitution lien filed and perfected under this article. Except as provided by this article, a perfected lien in favor of a victim is superior and prior to a lien perfected by the state under this article, and the perfected lien in favor of the state is superior and prior to the claim or interest of any other person, other than:

(1) a person who acquires a valid lien or security interest perfected before the perfection of the restitution lien;

(2) a bona fide purchaser who acquires an interest in the property, if personal property, before the filing of the restitution lien, to the extent that the purchaser gives value; or

(3) a bona fide purchaser for value who acquires and files for record an interest in the property, if real property, before the perfection of the restitution lien.

Sec. 10. **Payment.** — The clerk receiving a payment from a defendant ordered to pay restitution shall make payments to the person having an interest in the restitution lien on a schedule of not less than quarterly payments as determined by the clerk or agency.

Sec. 11. **Foreclosure.** — If a defendant fails to timely make a payment required by the order of the court entering the judgment creating the restitution lien, the person having an interest in the lien may file suit in a court of competent jurisdiction to foreclose the lien. If the defendant cures the default on or before the 20th day after the date the suit is filed and pays the person who files the suit costs of court and reasonable attorney's fees, the court may dismiss the suit without prejudice to the person. The person may refile the suit against the defendant if the defendant subsequently defaults.

Sec. 12. **Expiration; Records.**

(a) A restitution lien expires on the 10th anniversary of the date the lien was filed or on the date the defendant satisfies the judgment creating the lien, whichever occurs first. The person having an interest in the lien may refile the lien before the date the lien expires. A lien that is refiled expires on the 10th anniversary of the date the lien was refiled or the date the defendant satisfies the judgment creating the lien, whichever occurs first.

(b) Failure to execute or foreclose the restitution lien does not cause dormancy of the lien.

(c) The clerk of the court entering the judgment creating the restitution lien shall maintain a record of the outstanding balance of restitution, fines, or costs owed. If the defendant satisfies the judgment, the clerk shall immediately execute and file for record a release of the restitution lien with all officers or entities with which the affidavit perfecting the lien was filed, as indicated by the notice received by the clerk under Section 7(h) of this article, unless a release was executed and filed by the person who filed the affidavit to perfect the lien.

(d) A partial release of a lien as to specific property may be executed by the attorney representing the state or a magistrate who signs an affidavit described by Section 6 of this article on payment of a sum determined to represent the defendant's interest in any property to which the lien may attach.

Art. 42.23. Notification of Court of Family Violence Conviction.

(a) In this article, "family violence" has the meaning assigned by Section 71.004, Family Code.

(b) If the attorney representing the state in a criminal case involving family violence learns that the defendant is subject to the jurisdiction of another court relating to an order that provides for the appointment of a conservator or that sets the terms and conditions of conservatorship or for possession of or access to a child, the attorney representing the state shall notify the court in which the defendant is being tried of the existence of the order and the identity of the court of continuing jurisdiction.

(c) On the conviction or entry of an order deferring adjudication of a defendant for an offense involving family violence, the convicting court or the court entering the order shall notify the court of continuing jurisdiction of the conviction or deferred adjudication.

Art. 42.24. Prohibiting Contact with Victim.

If a defendant's sentence includes a term of confinement or imprisonment, the convicting court may, as part of the sentence, prohibit the defendant from contacting, during the term of the defendant's confinement or imprisonment, the victim of the offense of which the defendant is convicted or a member of the victim's family.

Sec. Art. 42.25. Filing of Reporter Notes.

A court reporter may comply with Rule 13.6, Texas Rules of Appellate Procedure, by electronically filing with the trial court clerk not later than the 20th day after the expiration of the time the defendant is allotted to perfect the appeal the untranscribed notes created by the court reporter using computer-aided software.

CHAPTER 42A COMMUNITY SUPERVISION

SUBCHAPTER A GENERAL PROVISIONS

Art. 42A.001. Definitions.

In this chapter:

(1) "Community supervision" means the placement of a defendant by a court under a continuum of programs and sanctions, with conditions imposed by the court for a specified period during which:

(A) criminal proceedings are deferred without an adjudication of guilt; or

(B) a sentence of imprisonment or confinement, imprisonment and fine, or confinement and fine, is probated and the imposition of sentence is suspended in whole or in part.

(2) "Court" means a court of record having original criminal jurisdiction.

(3) "Electronic monitoring" includes voice tracking systems, position tracking systems, position location systems, biometric tracking systems, and any other electronic or telecommunications system that may be used to assist in the supervision of defendants under this chapter.

(4) "Supervision officer" means a person appointed or employed under Section 76.004, Government Code, to supervise defendants placed on community supervision.

Art. 42A.002. Reference in Law.

A reference in a law to a statute or a part of a statute revised in this chapter by Chapter 770 (H.B. 2299), Acts of the 84th Legislature, Regular Session, 2015, is considered to be a reference to the part of this chapter that revises that statute or part of that statute.

SUBCHAPTER B PLACEMENT ON COMMUNITY SUPERVISION

Art. 42A.051. Authority to Grant Community Supervision, Impose or Modify Conditions, or Discharge Defendant.

(a) Unless the judge has transferred jurisdiction of the case to another court under Article 42A.151, only the court in which the defendant was tried may:

(1) grant community supervision;

(2) impose conditions; or

(3) discharge the defendant.

(b) The judge of the court having jurisdiction of the case may, at any time during the period of community supervision, modify the conditions of community supervision. Except as provided by Article 42A.052(a), only the judge may modify the conditions.

Art. 42A.052. Modification of Conditions by Supervision Officer or Magistrate.

(a) A judge who places a defendant on community supervision may authorize the supervision officer supervising the defendant or a magistrate appointed by the district courts in the county that give preference to criminal cases to modify the conditions of community supervision for the limited purposes of:

(1) transferring the defendant to different programs within the community supervision continuum of programs and sanctions; or

(2) prioritizing the conditions ordered by the court according to the defendant's progress under supervision.

(b) A supervision officer or magistrate who modifies the conditions of community supervision shall:

(1) deliver a copy of the modified conditions to the defendant;

(2) file a copy of the modified conditions with the sentencing court; and

(3) note the date of delivery of the copy in the defendant's file.

(c) If the defendant agrees to the modification in writing, the officer or magistrate shall file a copy of the modified conditions with the district clerk and the conditions shall be enforced as modified. If the defendant does not agree to the modification in writing, the supervision officer or magistrate shall refer the case to the judge for modification in the manner provided by Article 42A.752.

Art. 42A.053. Judge-Ordered Community Supervision.

(a) A judge, in the best interest of justice, the public, and the defendant, after conviction or a plea of guilty or nolo contendere, may:

(1) suspend the imposition of the sentence and place the defendant on community supervision; or

(2) impose a fine applicable to the offense and place the defendant on community supervision.

(b) A judge may not deny community supervision to a defendant based solely on the defendant's inability to speak, read, write, hear, or understand English.

(c) A defendant is not eligible for community supervision under this article if the defendant is sentenced to serve:

(1) a term of imprisonment that exceeds 10 years; or

(2) a term of confinement under Section 12.35, Penal Code.

(d) In a felony case:

(1) the minimum period of community supervision is the same as the minimum term of imprisonment applicable to the offense; and

(2) the maximum period of community supervision is:

(A) 10 years, for a felony other than a third degree felony described by Paragraph (B); and

(B) five years, for any of the following third degree felonies:

(i) a third degree felony under Title 7, Penal Code; and

(ii) a third degree felony under Chapter 481, Health and Safety Code.

(e) Notwithstanding Subsection (d), the minimum period of community supervision under this article for a felony described by Article 42A.453(b) is five years.

(f) The maximum period of community supervision in a misdemeanor case is two years.

(g) Notwithstanding Subsection (d)(2) or (f), a judge may extend the maximum period of community supervision in the manner provided by Article 42A.753 or 42A.757.

Art. 42A.054. Limitation on Judge-Ordered Community Supervision.

(a) Article 42A.053 does not apply to a defendant adjudged guilty of an offense under:

(1) Section 15.03, Penal Code, if the offense is punishable as a felony of the first degree;

(2) Section 19.02, Penal Code (Murder);

(3) Section 19.03, Penal Code (Capital Murder);

(4) Section 20.04, Penal Code (Aggravated Kidnapping);

(5) Section 20A.02, Penal Code (Trafficking of Persons);

(6) Section 20A.03, Penal Code (Continuous Trafficking of Persons);

(7) Section 21.11, Penal Code (Indecency with a Child);

(8) Section 22.011, Penal Code (Sexual Assault);

(9) Section 22.021, Penal Code (Aggravated Sexual Assault);

(10) Section 22.04(a)(1), Penal Code (Injury to a Child, Elderly Individual, or Disabled Individual), if:

(A) the offense is punishable as a felony of the first degree; and

(B) the victim of the offense is a child;

(11) Section 29.03, Penal Code (Aggravated Robbery);

(12) Section 30.02, Penal Code (Burglary), if:

(A) the offense is punishable under Subsection (d) of that section; and

(B) the actor committed the offense with the intent to commit a felony under Section 21.02, 21.11, 22.011, 22.021, or 25.02, Penal Code;

(13) Section 43.04, Penal Code (Aggravated Promotion of Prostitution);

(14) Section 43.05, Penal Code (Compelling Prostitution);

(15) Section 43.25, Penal Code (Sexual Performance by a Child);

(16) Chapter 481, Health and Safety Code, for which punishment is increased under:

(A) Section 481.140 of that code (Use of Child in Commission of Offense); or

(B) Section 481.134(c), (d), (e), or (f) of that code (Drug-free Zones) if it is shown that the defendant has been previously convicted of an offense for which punishment was increased under any of those subsections; or

(17) Section 481.1123, Health and Safety Code (Manufacture or Delivery of Substance in Penalty Group 1-B), if the offense is punishable under Subsection (d), (e), or (f) of that section.

(b) Article 42A.053 does not apply to a defendant when it is shown that:

(1) a deadly weapon as defined by Section 1.07, Penal Code, was used or exhibited during the:

(A) commission of a felony offense; or

(B) immediate flight from the commission of a felony offense; and

(2) the defendant:

(A) used or exhibited the deadly weapon; or

(B) was a party to the offense and knew that a deadly weapon would be used or exhibited.

(c) On an affirmative finding regarding the use or exhibition of a deadly weapon as described by Subsection (b), the trial court shall enter the finding in the judgment of the court.

(d) On an affirmative finding that the deadly weapon under Subsection (c) was a firearm, the court shall enter that finding in its judgment.

(e) Notwithstanding Subsection (a), with respect to an offense committed by a defendant under Section 43.04 or 43.05, Penal Code, a judge may place the defendant on community supervision as permitted by Article 42A.053 if the judge makes a finding that the defendant committed the offense solely as a victim of an offense under Section 20A.02, 20A.03, 43.03, 43.04, or 43.05, Penal Code.

Art. 42A.055. Jury-Recommended Community Supervision.

(a) A jury that imposes confinement as punishment for an offense may recommend to the judge that the judge suspend the imposition of the sentence and place the defendant on community supervision. A judge shall suspend the imposition of the sentence and place the defendant on community supervision if the jury makes that recommendation in the verdict.

(b) A defendant is eligible for community supervision under this article only if:

(1) before the trial begins, the defendant files a written sworn motion with the judge that the defendant has not previously been convicted of a felony in this or any other state; and

(2) the jury enters in the verdict a finding that the information contained in the defendant's motion is true.

(c) If the jury recommends to the judge that the judge place the defendant on community supervision, the judge shall place the defendant on community supervision for any period permitted under Articles 42A.053(d) and (f), as appropriate.

(d) A judge may extend the maximum period of community supervision in the manner provided by Article 42A.753 or 42A.757.

Art. 42A.056. Limitation on Jury-Recommended Community Supervision.

A defendant is not eligible for community supervision under Article 42A.055 if the defendant:

(1) is sentenced to a term of imprisonment that exceeds 10 years;

(2) is convicted of a state jail felony for which suspension of the imposition of the sentence occurs automatically under Article 42A.551;

(3) is adjudged guilty of an offense under Section 19.02, Penal Code;

(4) is convicted of an offense under Section 21.11, 22.011, or 22.021, Penal Code, if the victim of the offense was younger than 14 years of age at the time the offense was committed;

(5) is convicted of an offense under Section 20.04, Penal Code, if:

(A) the victim of the offense was younger than 14 years of age at the time the offense was committed; and

(B) the actor committed the offense with the intent to violate or abuse the victim sexually;

(6) is convicted of an offense under Section 20A.02, 20A.03, 43.04, 43.05, or 43.25, Penal Code;

(7) is convicted of an offense for which punishment is increased under Section 481.134(c), (d), (e), or (f), Health and Safety Code, if it is shown that the defendant has been previously convicted of an offense for which punishment was increased under any of those subsections; or

(8) is convicted of an offense under Section 481.1123, Health and Safety Code, if the offense is punishable under Subsection (d), (e), or (f) of that section.

Art. 42A.057. Minimum Period of Community Supervision for Certain Burglaries of Vehicles.

The minimum period of community supervision for an offense under Section 30.04, Penal Code, punishable as a Class A misdemeanor with a minimum term of confinement of six months is one year.

Art. 42A.058. Information Provided to Defendant Placed on Community Supervision.

A judge placing a defendant on community supervision shall inform the defendant in writing and on a form prescribed by the Office of Court Administration of the Texas Judicial System that, after satisfactorily fulfilling the conditions of community supervision and on expiration of the period of community supervision, the judge is authorized to release the defendant from the penalties and disabilities resulting from the offense as provided by Article 42A.701(f).

SUBCHAPTER C DEFERRED ADJUDICATION COMMUNITY SUPERVISION

Art. 42A.101. Placement on Deferred Adjudication Community Supervision.

(a) Except as provided by Article 42A.102(b), if in the judge's opinion the best interest of society and the defendant will be served, the judge may, after receiving a plea of guilty or nolo contendere, hearing the evidence, and finding that it substantiates the defendant's guilt, defer further proceedings without entering an adjudication of guilt and place the defendant on deferred adjudication community supervision.

(b) After placing the defendant on deferred adjudication community supervision under Subsection (a), the judge shall inform the defendant orally or in writing of the possible consequences under Articles 42A.108 and 42A.110 of a violation of a condition of deferred adjudication community supervision. If the information is provided orally, the judge must record and maintain the judge's statement to the defendant. The failure of a judge to inform a defendant of possible consequences under Articles 42A.108 and 42A.110 is not a ground for reversal unless the defendant shows that the defendant was harmed by the failure of the judge to provide the information.

Art. 42A.102. Eligibility for Deferred Adjudication Community Supervision.

(a) Subject to Subsection (b), a judge may place on deferred adjudication community supervision a defendant charged with an offense under Section 21.11, 22.011, or 22.021, Penal Code, regardless of the age of the victim, or a defendant charged with a felony described by Article 42A.453(b) only if the judge makes a finding in open court that placing the defendant on deferred adjudication community supervision is in the best interest of the victim. The failure of the judge to make a finding under this subsection is not grounds for the defendant to set aside the plea, deferred adjudication, or any subsequent conviction or sentence.

(b) In all other cases, the judge may grant deferred adjudication community supervision unless:

(1) the defendant is charged with an offense:

(A) under Section 20A.02, 20A.03, 49.045, 49.05, 49.065, 49.07, or 49.08, Penal Code;

(B) under Section 49.04 or 49.06, Penal Code, and, at the time of the offense:

(i) the defendant held a commercial driver's license or a commercial learner's permit; or

(ii) the defendant's alcohol concentration, as defined by Section 49.01, Penal Code, was 0.15 or more;

(C) for which punishment may be increased under Section 49.09, Penal Code;

(D) for which punishment may be increased under Section 481.134(c), (d), (e), or (f), Health and Safety Code, if it is shown that the defendant has been previously convicted of an offense for which punishment was increased under any one of those subsections; or

(E) under Section 481.1123, Health and Safety Code, that is punishable under Subsection (d), (e), or (f) of that section;

(2) the defendant:

(A) is charged with an offense under Section 21.11, 22.011, 22.021, 43.04, or 43.05, Penal Code, regardless of the age of the victim, or a felony described by Article 42A.453(b), other than a felony described by Subdivision (1)(A) or (3)(B) of this subsection; and

(B) has previously been placed on community supervision for an offense under Paragraph (A);

(3) the defendant is charged with an offense under:

(A) Section 21.02, Penal Code; or

(B) Section 22.021, Penal Code, that is punishable under Subsection (f) of that section or under Section 12.42(c)(3) or (4), Penal Code; or

(4) the defendant is charged with an offense under Section 19.02, Penal Code, except that the judge may grant deferred adjudication community supervision on determining that the defendant did not cause the death of the deceased, did not intend to kill the deceased or another, and did not anticipate that a human life would be taken.

Art. 42A.103. Period of Deferred Adjudication Community Supervision.

(a) In a felony case, the period of deferred adjudication community supervision may not exceed 10 years. For a defendant charged with a felony under Section 21.11, 22.011, or 22.021, Penal Code, regardless of the age of the victim, and for a defendant charged with a felony described by Article 42A.453(b), the period of deferred adjudication community supervision may not be less than five years.

(b) In a misdemeanor case, the period of deferred adjudication community supervision may not exceed two years.

(c) A judge may extend the maximum period of deferred adjudication community supervision in the manner provided by Article 42A.753 or 42A.757.

Art. 42A.104. Conditions of Deferred Adjudication Community Supervision; Imposition of Fine.

(a) The judge may impose a fine applicable to the offense and require any reasonable condition of deferred adjudication community supervision that a judge could impose on a defendant placed on community supervision for a conviction that was probated and suspended, including:

(1) confinement; and

(2) mental health treatment under Article 42A.506.

(b) The provisions of Subchapter L specifying whether a defendant convicted of a state jail felony is to be confined in a county jail or state jail felony facility and establishing the minimum and maximum terms of confinement as a condition of community supervision apply in the same manner to a defendant placed on deferred adjudication community supervision after pleading guilty or nolo contendere to a state jail felony.

Art. 42A.105. Affirmative Findings.

(a) If a judge places on deferred adjudication community supervision a defendant charged with a sexually violent offense, as defined by Article 62.001, the judge shall make an affirmative finding of fact and file a statement of that affirmative finding with the papers in the case if the judge determines that the victim or intended victim was younger than 14 years of age at the time of the offense.

(b) If a judge places on deferred adjudication community supervision a defendant charged with an offense under Section 20.02, 20.03, or 20.04, Penal Code, or an attempt, conspiracy, or solicitation to commit one of those offenses, the judge shall make an affirmative finding of fact and file a statement of that affirmative finding with the papers in the case if the judge determines that the victim or intended victim was younger than 17 years of age at the time of the offense.

(c) If a judge places on deferred adjudication community supervision a defendant charged with an offense under Section 21.11 or 22.011, Penal Code, the judge shall make an affirmative finding of fact and file a statement of that affirmative finding with the papers in the case if the judge determines that:

(1) at the time of the offense, the defendant was not more than four years older than the victim or intended victim and the victim or intended victim was at least 15 years of age; and

(2) the charge to which the plea is entered under this subchapter is based solely on the ages of the defendant and the victim or intended victim at the time of the offense.

(d) If a judge places a defendant on deferred adjudication community supervision, on the motion of the attorney representing the state the judge shall make an affirmative finding of fact and file a statement of that affirmative finding with the papers in the case if the judge determines that, regardless of whether the conduct at issue is the subject of the prosecution or part of the same criminal episode as the conduct that is the subject of the prosecution, a victim in the trial:

(1) is or has been a victim of a severe form of trafficking in persons, as defined by 22 U.S.C. Section 7102(9); or

(2) has suffered substantial physical or mental abuse as a result of having been a victim of criminal activity described by 8 U.S.C. Section 1101(a)(15)(U)(iii).

(e) The part of the papers in the case containing an affirmative finding under Subsection (d):

(1) must include specific information identifying the victim, as available;

(2) may not include information identifying the victim's location; and

(3) is confidential, unless written consent for the release of the affirmative finding is obtained from the victim or, if the victim is younger than 18 years of age, the victim's parent or guardian.

(f) If a judge places on deferred adjudication community supervision a defendant charged with a misdemeanor other than a misdemeanor under Chapter 20, 21, 22, 25, 42, 43, 46, or 71, Penal Code, the judge shall make an affirmative finding of fact and file a statement of that affirmative finding with the papers in the case if the judge determines that it is not in the best interest of justice that the defendant receive an automatic order of nondisclosure under Section 411.072, Government Code.

Art. 42A.106. Record Not Confidential; Right to Petition for Order of Nondisclosure.

(a) Except as provided by Section 552.142, Government Code, a record in the custody of the court clerk regarding a case in which a defendant is granted deferred adjudication community supervision is not confidential.

(b) Before placing a defendant on deferred adjudication community supervision, the court shall inform the defendant of the defendant's right to receive or petition the court for an order of nondisclosure of criminal history record information under Subchapter E-1, Chapter 411, Government Code, as applicable, unless the defendant is ineligible for an order because of:

(1) the nature of the offense for which the defendant is placed on deferred adjudication community supervision; or

(2) the defendant's criminal history.

Art. 42A.107. Request for Final Adjudication.

On written motion of the defendant requesting final adjudication that is filed within 30 days after the entry of the defendant's plea and the deferment of adjudication, the judge shall proceed to final adjudication as in all other cases.

Art. 42A.108. Violation of Condition of Deferred Adjudication Community Supervision; Hearing.

(a) On violation of a condition of deferred adjudication community supervision imposed under

Code of Criminal Procedure

Article 42A.104, the defendant may be arrested and detained as provided in Article 42A.751.

(b) The defendant is entitled to a hearing limited to a determination by the court of whether the court will proceed with an adjudication of guilt on the original charge. The court may not proceed with an adjudication of guilt on the original charge if the court finds that the only evidence supporting the alleged violation of a condition of deferred adjudication community supervision is the uncorroborated results of a polygraph examination. The determination to proceed with an adjudication of guilt on the original charge is reviewable in the same manner as a revocation hearing conducted under Article 42A.751(d) in a case in which the adjudication of guilt was not deferred.

(c) A court retains jurisdiction to hold a hearing under Subsection (b) and to proceed with an adjudication of guilt, regardless of whether the period of deferred adjudication community supervision imposed on the defendant has expired, if before the expiration of the supervision period:

(1) the attorney representing the state files a motion to proceed with the adjudication; and

(2) a capias is issued for the arrest of the defendant.

Art. 42A.109. Due Diligence Defense.

For the purposes of a hearing under Article 42A.108, it is an affirmative defense to revocation for an alleged violation based on a failure to report to a supervision officer as directed or to remain within a specified place that no supervision officer, peace officer, or other officer with the power of arrest under a warrant issued by a judge for that alleged violation contacted or attempted to contact the defendant in person at the defendant's last known residence address or last known employment address, as reflected in the files of the department serving the county in which the order of deferred adjudication community supervision was entered.

Art. 42A.110. Proceedings After Adjudication.

(a) After an adjudication of guilt, all proceedings, including assessment of punishment, pronouncement of sentence, granting of community supervision, and defendant's appeal, continue as if the adjudication of guilt had not been deferred.

(b) A court assessing punishment after an adjudication of guilt of a defendant charged with a state jail felony may suspend the imposition of the sentence and place the defendant on community supervision or may order the sentence to be executed, regardless of whether the defendant has previously been convicted of a felony.

Art. 42A.111. Dismissal and Discharge.

(a) On expiration of a period of deferred adjudication community supervision imposed under this subchapter, if the judge has not proceeded to an adjudication of guilt, the judge shall dismiss the proceedings against the defendant and discharge the defendant.

(b) The judge may dismiss the proceedings and discharge a defendant before the expiration of the period of deferred adjudication community supervision if, in the judge's opinion, the best interest of society and the defendant will be served, except that the judge may not dismiss the proceedings and discharge a defendant charged with an offense requiring the defendant to register as a sex offender under Chapter 62.

(c) Except as provided by Section 12.42(g), Penal Code, a dismissal and discharge under this article may not be considered a conviction for the purposes of disqualifications or disabilities imposed by law for conviction of an offense.

(c-1) Subject to Subsection (d), an offense for which the defendant received a dismissal and discharge under this article may not be used as grounds for denying issuance of a professional or occupational license or certificate to, or suspending or revoking the professional or occupational license or certificate of, an individual otherwise entitled to or qualified for the license or certificate.

(d) For any defendant who receives a dismissal and discharge under this article:

(1) on conviction of a subsequent offense, the fact that the defendant previously has received deferred adjudication community supervision is admissible before the court or jury for consideration on the issue of penalty;

(2) if the defendant is an applicant for or the holder of a license under Chapter 42, Human Resources Code, the Department of Family and Protective Services may consider the fact that the defendant previously has received deferred adjudication community supervision in issuing, renewing, denying, or revoking a license under that chapter;

(3) if the defendant is an applicant for or the holder of a license to provide mental health or medical services for the rehabilitation of sex offenders, the Council on Sex Offender Treatment may consider the fact that the defendant previously has received deferred adjudication community supervision in issuing, renewing, denying, or revoking a license issued by that council; and

(4) if the defendant is an applicant for or the holder of a professional or occupational license or certificate, the licensing agency may consider the fact that the defendant previously has received

deferred adjudication community supervision in issuing, renewing, denying, or revoking a license or certificate if:

(A) the defendant was placed on deferred adjudication community supervision for an offense:

(i) listed in Article 42A.054(a);

(ii) described by Article 62.001(5) or (6);

(iii) committed under Chapter 21 or 43, Penal Code; or

(iv) related to the activity or conduct for which the person seeks or holds the license;

(B) the profession for which the defendant holds or seeks a license or certificate involves direct contact with children in the normal course of official duties or duties for which the license or certification is required; or

(C) the defendant is an applicant for or the holder of a license or certificate issued under Chapter 1701, Occupations Code.

(e) A judge who dismisses the proceedings against a defendant and discharges the defendant under this article:

(1) shall provide the defendant with a copy of the order of dismissal and discharge; and

(2) if the judge determines that the defendant is or may become eligible for an order of nondisclosure of criminal history record information under Subchapter E-1, Chapter 411, Government Code, shall, as applicable:

(A) grant an order of nondisclosure of criminal history record information to the defendant;

(B) inform the defendant of the defendant's eligibility to receive an order of nondisclosure of criminal history record information without a petition and the earliest date on which the defendant is eligible to receive the order; or

(C) inform the defendant of the defendant's eligibility to petition the court for an order of nondisclosure of criminal history record information and the earliest date the defendant is eligible to file the petition for the order.

SUBCHAPTER D JURISDICTION OVER CASE; GEOGRAPHICAL JURISDICTION

Art. 42A.151. Transfer of Jurisdiction.

(a) After a defendant has been placed on community supervision, jurisdiction of the case may be transferred to a court of the same rank in this state that:

(1) has geographical jurisdiction where the defendant:

(A) resides; or

(B) violates a condition of community supervision; and

(2) consents to the transfer.

(b) On transfer, the clerk of the court of original jurisdiction shall forward to the court accepting jurisdiction a transcript of any portion of the record as the transferring judge shall direct. The court accepting jurisdiction subsequently shall proceed as if the defendant's trial and conviction had occurred in that court.

Art. 42A.152. Issuance of Warrant by Court Having Geographical Jurisdiction.

(a) A judge of a court having geographical jurisdiction where a defendant resides or where the defendant violates a condition of community supervision may issue a warrant for the defendant's arrest.

(b) Notwithstanding Subsection (a), the determination of the action to be taken after the defendant's arrest may be made only by the judge of the court having jurisdiction of the case at the time the action is taken.

Art. 42A.153. Change of Residence Within the State.

(a) If, for good and sufficient reasons, a defendant desires to change the defendant's residence within the state, the change may be effected by application to the supervising supervision officer.

(b) The change of residence is subject to:

(1) the judge's consent; and

(2) any regulations the judge may require in the absence of a supervision officer in the locality to which the defendant is transferred.

Art. 42A.154. Leaving the State.

A defendant who leaves the state without permission of the judge having jurisdiction of the case is:

(1) considered a fugitive from justice; and

(2) subject to extradition as provided by law.

SUBCHAPTER E PARTIAL EXECUTION OF SENTENCE; CONTINUING JURISDICTION

Art. 42A.201. Continuing Jurisdiction in Misdemeanor Cases.

(a) For the purposes of this article, the jurisdiction of the courts in this state in which a sentence requiring confinement in a jail is imposed for conviction of a misdemeanor continues for 180 days from the date the execution of the sentence actually begins.

(b) The judge of a court that imposed a sentence requiring confinement in a jail for conviction of a misdemeanor may, on the judge's own motion, on the motion of the attorney representing the state, or on the written motion of the defendant, suspend further execution of the sentence and place the defendant on community supervision under the terms and conditions of this chapter if, in the opinion of the judge, the defendant would not benefit from further confinement.

(c) When the defendant files a written motion with the court requesting suspension of further execution of the sentence and placement on community supervision or when requested to do so by the judge, the clerk of the court shall request a copy of the defendant's record while confined from the agency operating the jail in which the defendant is confined. On receipt of the request, the agency shall forward a copy of the record to the court as soon as possible.

(d) The judge may deny the motion without holding a hearing but may not grant a motion without holding a hearing and allowing the attorney representing the state and the defendant to present evidence in the case.

Art. 42A.202. Continuing Jurisdiction in Felony Cases.

(a) For the purposes of this article, the jurisdiction of a court imposing a sentence requiring imprisonment in the Texas Department of Criminal Justice for an offense other than a state jail felony continues for 180 days from the date the execution of the sentence actually begins.

(b) Before the expiration of the 180-day period described by Subsection (a), the judge of the court that imposed the sentence described by that subsection may, on the judge's own motion, on the motion of the attorney representing the state, or on the written motion of the defendant, suspend further execution of the sentence and place the defendant on community supervision under the terms and conditions of this chapter if:

(1) in the opinion of the judge, the defendant would not benefit from further imprisonment;

(2) the defendant is otherwise eligible for community supervision under this chapter; and

(3) the defendant had never before been incarcerated in a penitentiary serving a sentence for a felony.

(c) When the defendant files a written motion requesting the judge to suspend further execution of the sentence and place the defendant on community supervision, the defendant shall immediately deliver or cause to be delivered a copy of the motion to the office of the attorney representing the state.

(d) When the defendant or the attorney representing the state files a written motion requesting the judge to suspend further execution of the sentence and place the defendant on community supervision, and when requested to do so by the judge, the clerk of the court shall request a copy of the defendant's record while imprisoned from the Texas Department of Criminal Justice or, if the defendant is confined in county jail, from the sheriff. On receipt of the request, the Texas Department of Criminal Justice or the sheriff shall forward a copy of the record to the judge as soon as possible.

(e) The judge may deny the motion without holding a hearing but may not grant the motion without holding a hearing and providing the attorney representing the state and the defendant the opportunity to present evidence on the motion.

Art. 42A.203. Authority to Suspend Execution of Sentence in Felony Cases.

(a) Except as otherwise provided by Subsection (b), only the judge who originally sentenced the defendant may suspend execution of the sentence and place the defendant on community supervision under Article 42A.202.

(b) If the judge who originally sentenced the defendant is deceased or disabled or the office is vacant, and if a motion is filed in accordance with Article 42A.202, the clerk of the court shall promptly forward a copy of the motion to the presiding judge of the administrative judicial district for that court. The presiding judge may deny the motion without holding a hearing or may appoint a judge to hold a hearing on the motion.

Art. 42A.204. Partial Execution of Sentence: Firearm Used or Exhibited.

(a) If in the trial of a felony of the second degree or higher there is an affirmative finding described by Article 42A.054(d) and the jury recommends that the court place the defendant on community supervision, the court may order the defendant imprisoned in the Texas Department of Criminal Justice for not less than 60 and not more than 120 days.

(b) At any time after the defendant has served 60 days in the custody of the Texas Department of Criminal Justice, the sentencing judge, on the judge's own motion or on motion of the defendant, may order the defendant released to community supervision.

(c) The department shall release the defendant to community supervision after the defendant has served 120 days.

SUBCHAPTER F PRESENTENCE AND POSTSENTENCE REPORTS AND EVALUATIONS

Art. 42A.251. Definitions.

In this subchapter:

(1) "Council" means the Council on Sex Offender Treatment.

(2) "Sex offender" means a person who has been convicted of, or has entered a plea of guilty or nolo contendere for, an offense under any one of the following provisions of the Penal Code:

(A) Section 20.04(a)(4) (Aggravated Kidnapping), if the person committed the offense with the intent to violate or abuse the victim sexually;

(B) Section 21.08 (Indecent Exposure);

(C) Section 21.11 (Indecency with a Child);

(D) Section 22.011 (Sexual Assault);

(E) Section 22.021 (Aggravated Sexual Assault);

(F) Section 25.02 (Prohibited Sexual Conduct);

(G) Section 30.02 (Burglary), if:

(i) the offense is punishable under Subsection (d) of that section; and

(ii) the person committed the offense with the intent to commit a felony listed in this subdivision;

(H) Section 43.25 (Sexual Performance by a Child); or

(I) Section 43.26 (Possession or Promotion of Child Pornography).

Art. 42A.252. Presentence Report Required.

(a) Except as provided by Subsections (b) and (c), before the imposition of the sentence by a judge, the judge shall direct a supervision officer to prepare a presentence report for the judge.

(b) The judge is not required to direct a supervision officer to prepare a presentence report in a misdemeanor case if:

(1) the defendant requests that a report not be made and the judge agrees to the request; or

(2) the judge:

(A) finds that there is sufficient information in the record to permit the meaningful exercise of sentencing discretion; and

(B) explains that finding on the record.

(c) The judge is not required to direct a supervision officer to prepare a presentence report in a felony case if:

(1) punishment is to be assessed by a jury;

(2) the defendant is convicted of or enters a plea of guilty or nolo contendere to capital murder;

(3) the only available punishment is imprisonment; or

(4) the judge is informed that a plea bargain agreement exists, under which the defendant agrees to a punishment of imprisonment, and the judge intends to follow that agreement.

Art. 42A.253. Contents of Presentence Report.

(a) A presentence report must be in writing and include:

(1) the circumstances of the offense with which the defendant is charged;

(2) the amount of restitution necessary to adequately compensate a victim of the offense;

(3) the criminal and social history of the defendant;

(4) a proposed supervision plan describing programs and sanctions that the community supervision and corrections department will provide the defendant if the judge suspends the imposition of the sentence or grants deferred adjudication community supervision;

(5) if the defendant is charged with a state jail felony, recommendations for conditions of community supervision that the community supervision and corrections department considers advisable or appropriate based on the circumstances of the offense and other factors addressed in the report;

(6) the results of a psychological evaluation of the defendant that determines, at a minimum, the defendant's IQ and adaptive behavior score if the defendant:

(A) is convicted of a felony offense; and

(B) appears to the judge, through the judge's own observation or on the suggestion of a party, to have a mental impairment;

(7) information regarding whether the defendant is a current or former member of the state military forces or whether the defendant currently serves or has previously served in the armed forces of the United States in an active-duty status and, if available, a copy of the defendant's military discharge papers and military records;

(8) if the defendant has served in the armed forces of the United States in an active-duty status, a determination as to whether the defendant was deployed to a combat zone and whether the defendant may suffer from post-traumatic stress disorder or a traumatic brain injury; and

(9) any other information relating to the defendant or the offense as requested by the judge.

(b) A presentence report is not required to contain a sentencing recommendation.

Art. 42A.254. Inspection by Judge; Disclosure of Contents.

The judge may not inspect a presentence report and the contents of the report may not be disclosed to any person unless:

(1) the defendant pleads guilty or nolo contendere or is convicted of the offense; or

(2) the defendant, in writing, authorizes the judge to inspect the report.

Art. 42A.255. Inspection and Comment by Defendant; Access to Information by State.

(a) Unless waived by the defendant, at least 48 hours before sentencing a defendant, the judge shall permit the defendant or the defendant's attorney to read the presentence report.

(b) The judge shall allow the defendant or the defendant's attorney to comment on a presentence investigation or a postsentence report and, with the approval of the judge, introduce testimony or other information alleging a factual inaccuracy in the investigation or report.

(c) The judge shall allow the attorney representing the state access to any information made available to the defendant under this article.

Art. 42A.256. Release of Information to Supervision Officer; Confidentiality of Report.

(a) The judge by order may direct that any information and records that are not privileged and that are relevant to a presentence or postsentence report be released to a supervision officer conducting a presentence investigation under this subchapter or preparing a postsentence report under Article 42A.259. The judge may also issue a subpoena to obtain that information.

(b) A presentence or postsentence report and all information obtained in connection with a presentence investigation or postsentence report are confidential and may be released only as:

(1) provided by:

(A) Subsection (c);

(B) Article 42A.255;

(C) Article 42A.257;

(D) Article 42A.259; or

(E) Section 614.017, Health and Safety Code; or

(2) directed by the judge for the effective supervision of the defendant.

(c) If the defendant is a sex offender, a supervision officer may release information in a presentence or postsentence report concerning the social and criminal history of the defendant to a person who:

(1) is licensed or certified in this state to provide mental health or medical services, including a:

(A) physician;

(B) psychiatrist;

(C) psychologist;

(D) licensed professional counselor;

(E) licensed marriage and family therapist; or

(F) certified social worker; and

(2) provides mental health or medical services for the rehabilitation of the defendant.

Art. 42A.257. Evaluation for Purposes of Alcohol or Drug Rehabilitation.

(a) The judge shall direct a supervision officer approved by the community supervision and corrections department or the judge, or a person, program, or other agency approved by the Department of State Health Services, to conduct an evaluation to determine the appropriateness of, and a course of conduct necessary for, alcohol or drug rehabilitation for a defendant and to report the results of that evaluation to the judge, if:

(1) the judge determines that alcohol or drug abuse may have contributed to the commission of the offense; or

(2) the case involves a second or subsequent offense under:

(A) Section 49.04, Penal Code, if the offense was committed within five years of the date on which the most recent preceding offense was committed; or

(B) Section 49.07 or 49.08, Penal Code, if the offense involved the operation of a motor vehicle and was committed within five years of the date on which the most recent preceding offense was committed.

(b) The evaluation must be made:

(1) after arrest and before conviction, if requested by the defendant;

(2) after conviction and before sentencing, if the judge assesses punishment in the case;

(3) after sentencing and before the entry of a final judgment, if the jury assesses punishment in the case; or

(4) after community supervision is granted, if the evaluation is required as a condition of community supervision under Article 42A.402.

Art. 42A.258. Evaluation for Purposes of Sex Offender Treatment, Specialized Supervision, or Rehabilitation.

(a) If the defendant is a sex offender, the judge shall direct a supervision officer approved by the community supervision and corrections department or the judge, or a person, program, or other agency approved by the council, to:

(1) evaluate the appropriateness of, and a course of conduct necessary for, treatment, specialized supervision, or rehabilitation of the defendant; and

(2) report the results of the evaluation to the judge.

(b) The judge may require the evaluation to use offense-specific standards of practice adopted by the council and may require the report to reflect those standards.

(c) The evaluation must be made:

(1) after arrest and before conviction, if requested by the defendant; or

(2) after conviction and before the entry of a final judgment.

Art. 42A.259. Postsentence Report.

(a) If a presentence report in a felony case is not required under Article 42A.252(c), the judge may direct a supervision officer to prepare a postsentence report containing the same information that would have been required for the presentence report, other than a proposed supervision plan and any information that is reflected in the judgment.

(b) If a postsentence report is ordered, the supervision officer shall send the report to the clerk of the court not later than the 30th day after the date on which sentence is pronounced or deferred adjudication community supervision is granted. The clerk shall deliver the postsentence report with the papers in the case to a designated officer of the Texas Department of Criminal Justice, to the extent required by Section 8(a), Article 42.09.

SUBCHAPTER G DISCRETIONARY CONDITIONS GENERALLY

Art. 42A.301. Basic Discretionary Conditions.

(a) The judge of the court having jurisdiction of the case shall determine the conditions of community supervision after considering the results of a risk and needs assessment conducted with respect to the defendant. The assessment must be conducted using an instrument that is validated for the purpose of assessing the risks and needs of a defendant placed on community supervision. The judge may impose any reasonable condition that is not duplicative of another condition and that is designed to protect or restore the community, protect or restore the victim, or punish, rehabilitate, or reform the defendant. In determining the conditions, the judge shall consider the extent to which the conditions impact the defendant's:

(1) work, education, and community service schedule or obligations; and

(2) ability to meet financial obligations.

(b) Conditions of community supervision may include conditions requiring the defendant to:

(1) commit no offense against the laws of this state or of any other state or of the United States;

(2) avoid injurious or vicious habits;

(3) report to the supervision officer as directed by the judge or supervision officer and obey all rules and regulations of the community supervision and corrections department;

(4) permit the supervision officer to visit the defendant at the defendant's home or elsewhere;

(5) work faithfully at suitable employment to the extent possible;

(6) remain within a specified place;

(7) pay in one or more amounts:

(A) the defendant's fine, if one is assessed; and

(B) all court costs, regardless of whether a fine is assessed;

(8) support the defendant's dependents;

(9) participate, for a period specified by the judge, in any community-based program, including a community service project under Article 42A.304;

(10) if the judge determines that the defendant has financial resources that enable the defendant to offset in part or in whole the costs of the legal services provided to the defendant in accordance with Article 1.051(c) or (d), including any expenses and costs, reimburse the county in which the prosecution was instituted for the costs of the legal services in an amount that the judge finds the defendant is able to pay, except that the defendant may not be ordered to pay an amount that exceeds:

(A) the actual costs, including any expenses and costs, paid by the county for the legal services provided by an appointed attorney; or

(B) if the defendant was represented by a public defender's office, the actual amount, including any expenses and costs, that would have otherwise been paid to an appointed attorney had the county not had a public defender's office;

(11) if under custodial supervision in a community corrections facility:

(A) remain under that supervision;

Code of Criminal Procedure

(B) obey all rules and regulations of the facility; and

(C) pay a percentage of the defendant's income to the facility for room and board;

(12) submit to testing for alcohol or controlled substances;

(13) attend counseling sessions for substance abusers or participate in substance abuse treatment services in a program or facility approved or licensed by the Department of State Health Services;

(14) with the consent of the victim of a misdemeanor offense or of any offense under Title 7, Penal Code, participate in victim-defendant mediation;

(15) submit to electronic monitoring;

(16) reimburse the compensation to victims of crime fund for any amounts paid from that fund to or on behalf of a victim, as defined by Article 56B.003, of the offense or if no reimbursement is required, make one payment to the compensation to victims of crime fund in an amount not to exceed $50 if the offense is a misdemeanor or not to exceed $100 if the offense is a felony;

(17) reimburse a law enforcement agency for the analysis, storage, or disposal of raw materials, controlled substances, chemical precursors, drug paraphernalia, or other materials seized in connection with the offense;

(18) reimburse all or part of the reasonable and necessary costs incurred by the victim for psychological counseling made necessary by the offense or for counseling and education relating to acquired immune deficiency syndrome or human immunodeficiency virus made necessary by the offense;

(19) pay a fine in an amount not to exceed $50 to a crime stoppers organization, as defined by Section 414.001, Government Code, and as certified by the Texas Crime Stoppers Council;

(20) submit a DNA sample to the Department of Public Safety under Subchapter G, Chapter 411, Government Code, for the purpose of creating a DNA record of the defendant; and

(21) in any manner required by the judge, provide in the county in which the offense was committed public notice of the offense for which the defendant was placed on community supervision.

(c) Before the judge may require as a condition of community supervision that the defendant receive treatment in a state-funded substance abuse treatment program, including an inpatient or outpatient program, a substance abuse felony program under Article 42A.303, or a program provided to the defendant while confined in a community corrections facility as defined by Article 42A.601, the judge must consider the results of an evaluation conducted to determine the appropriate type and level of treatment necessary to address the defendant's alcohol or drug dependency.

Art. 42A.302. Confinement.

(a) If a judge having jurisdiction of a case requires as a condition of community supervision that the defendant submit to a term of confinement in a county jail, the term of confinement may not exceed:

(1) 30 days, in a misdemeanor case; or

(2) 180 days, in a felony case.

(b) A judge who requires as a condition of community supervision that the defendant serve a term of confinement in a community corrections facility under Subchapter M may not impose a term of confinement under this article that, if added to the term imposed under Subchapter M, exceeds 24 months.

(c) A judge may impose a term of confinement as a condition of community supervision under this article on placing the defendant on supervision or at any time during the supervision period. The judge may impose terms of confinement as a condition of community supervision in increments smaller than the maximum terms provided by Subsection (a), except that the judge may not impose terms of confinement that, if added together, exceed the maximum terms provided by Subsection (a).

Art. 42A.303. Substance Abuse Felony Program.

(a) If a court places a defendant on community supervision under any provision of this chapter as an alternative to imprisonment, the judge may require as a condition of community supervision that the defendant serve a term of confinement and treatment in a substance abuse felony punishment facility operated by the Texas Department of Criminal Justice under Section 493.009, Government Code.

(b) A term of confinement and treatment imposed under this article must be an indeterminate term of not more than one year or less than 90 days.

(c) The judge may impose the condition of community supervision described by this article if:

(1) the defendant is charged with or convicted of a felony other than:

(A) a felony under Section 21.11, 22.011, or 22.021, Penal Code; or

(B) criminal attempt of a felony under Section 21.11, 22.011, or 22.021, Penal Code; and

(2) the judge makes an affirmative finding that:

(A) drug or alcohol abuse significantly contributed to the commission of the offense or violation of a condition of community supervision, as applicable; and

(B) the defendant is a suitable candidate for treatment, as determined by the suitability criteria established by the Texas Board of Criminal Justice under Section 493.009(b), Government Code.

(d) If a judge requires as a condition of community supervision that the defendant serve a term of confinement and treatment in a substance abuse felony punishment facility under this article, the judge shall also require as a condition of community supervision that on release from the facility the defendant:

(1) participate in a drug or alcohol abuse continuum of care treatment plan; and

(2) pay a reimbursement fee in an amount established by the judge for residential aftercare required as part of the treatment plan.

(e) The Department of State Health Services or the community supervision and corrections department supervising the defendant shall develop the continuum of care treatment plan described by Subsection (d)(1).

(f) The clerk of a court that collects a reimbursement fee imposed under Subsection (d)(2) shall deposit the reimbursement fee to be sent to the comptroller as provided by Subchapter B, Chapter 133, Local Government Code, and the comptroller shall deposit the reimbursement fee into the general revenue fund. If the clerk does not collect a reimbursement fee imposed under Subsection (d)(2), the clerk is not required to file any report required by the comptroller that relates to the collection of the reimbursement fee. In establishing the amount of a reimbursement fee under Subsection (d)(2), the judge shall consider fines, fees, and other necessary expenses for which the defendant is obligated. The judge may not:

(1) establish the reimbursement fee in an amount that is greater than 25 percent of the defendant's gross income while the defendant is a participant in residential aftercare; or

(2) require the defendant to pay the reimbursement fee at any time other than a time at which the defendant is both employed and a participant in residential aftercare.

Art. 42A.304. Community Service.

(a) A judge may require as a condition of community supervision that the defendant work a specified number of hours at one or more community service projects for one or more organizations approved by the judge and designated by the department. The judge may not require the defendant to work at a community service project if, as determined and noted on the community supervision order by the judge:

(1) the defendant is physically or mentally incapable of participating in the project;

(2) participating in the project will cause a hardship to the defendant or to the defendant's dependents;

(3) the defendant is to be confined in a substance abuse felony punishment facility as a condition of community supervision; or

(4) there is other good cause shown.

(b) The amount of community service work ordered by the judge may not exceed:

(1) 1,000 hours for an offense classified as a first degree felony;

(2) 800 hours for an offense classified as a second degree felony;

(3) 600 hours for:

(A) an offense classified as a third degree felony; or

(B) an offense under Section 30.04, Penal Code, classified as a Class A misdemeanor;

(4) 400 hours for an offense classified as a state jail felony;

(5) 200 hours for:

(A) an offense classified as a Class A misdemeanor, other than an offense described by Subdivision (3)(B); or

(B) a misdemeanor for which the maximum permissible confinement, if any, exceeds six months or the maximum permissible fine, if any, exceeds $4,000; and

(6) 100 hours for:

(A) an offense classified as a Class B misdemeanor; or

(B) a misdemeanor for which the maximum permissible confinement, if any, does not exceed six months and the maximum permissible fine, if any, does not exceed $4,000.

(c) A defendant required to perform community service under this article is not a state employee for the purposes of Chapter 501 or 504, Labor Code.

(d) If the court makes an affirmative finding under Article 42.014, the judge may order the defendant to perform community service under this article at a project designated by the judge that primarily serves the person or group who was the target of the defendant. If the judge orders community service under this subsection, the judge shall order the defendant to perform not less than:

(1) 300 hours of service if the offense is classified as a felony; or

(2) 100 hours of service if the offense is classified as a misdemeanor.

(e) A defendant required to perform community service under this article after conviction of an offense under Section 352.082, Local Government Code, or Section 365.012, 365.013, or 365.016, Health and Safety Code, shall perform the amount of service ordered by the court, which may not exceed 60 hours. The community service must consist of picking up litter in the county in which the defendant resides or working at a recycling facility if a program for performing that type of service is available in the community in which the court is located. A court may credit the amount of community service performed by a defendant under this subsection toward any amount of community service the defendant is ordered to perform under another provision of this code as a result of the defendant's inability to pay a fine or cost imposed in the judgment for the applicable offense.

(f) Instead of requiring the defendant to work a specified number of hours at one or more community service projects under Subsection (a), the judge may order a defendant to make a specified donation to:

(1) a nonprofit food bank or food pantry in the community in which the defendant resides;

(2) a charitable organization engaged primarily in performing charitable functions for veterans in the community in which the defendant resides; or

(3) in a county with a population of less than 50,000, another nonprofit organization that:

(A) is exempt from taxation under Section 501(a) of the Internal Revenue Code of 1986 because it is listed in Section 501(c)(3) of that code; and

(B) provides services or assistance to needy individuals and families in the community in which the defendant resides.

(g) In this article:

(1) "Charitable organization" has the meaning assigned by Section 2252.906, Government Code.

(2) "Veteran" has the meaning assigned by Section 434.022, Government Code.

Art. 42A.305. Community Outreach.

(a) This article applies only to a defendant placed on community supervision for an offense involving the possession, manufacture, or delivery of a controlled substance under Chapter 481, Health and Safety Code.

(b) If a judge orders a defendant to whom this article applies to perform community service, the judge may authorize the defendant to perform not more than 30 hours of community outreach under this article instead of performing hours of community service.

(c) Community outreach under this article must consist of working with a secondary school at the direction of the judge to educate students on the dangers and legal consequences of possessing, manufacturing, or delivering a controlled substance.

(d) A secondary school is not required to allow a defendant to perform community outreach at that school.

(e) The judge may not authorize the defendant to perform hours of community outreach under this article instead of performing hours of community service if:

(1) the defendant is physically or mentally incapable of participating in community outreach; or

(2) the defendant is subject to registration as a sex offender under Chapter 62.

Art. 42A.306. Supervision of Defendant From Out of State.

A judge who receives a defendant for supervision as authorized by Section 510.017, Government Code, may impose on the defendant any term of community supervision authorized by this chapter.

Art. 42A.307. Orchiectomy Prohibited.

A judge may not require a defendant to undergo an orchiectomy as a condition of community supervision.

SUBCHAPTER H MANDATORY CONDITIONS GENERALLY

Art. 42A.351. Educational Skill Level.

(a) If the judge or jury places a defendant on community supervision, the judge shall require the defendant to demonstrate to the court whether the defendant has an educational skill level that is equal to or greater than the average educational skill level of students who have completed the sixth grade in public schools in this state.

(b) If the judge determines that the defendant has not attained the educational skill level described by Subsection (a), the judge shall require as a condition of community supervision that the defendant attain that level of educational skill, unless the judge also determines that the defendant lacks the intellectual capacity or the learning ability to ever achieve that level of educational skill.

Art. 42A.352. DNA Sample.

A judge granting community supervision to a defendant convicted of a felony shall require as a condition of community supervision that the defendant provide a DNA sample under Subchapter G, Chapter 411, Government Code, for the purpose of creating a DNA record of the defendant, unless the defendant has already submitted the required sample under Section 411.1471, Government Code, or other law.

SUBCHAPTER H-1 VETERANS REEMPLOYMENT PROGRAM

Art. 42A.381. Veterans Reemployment Program.

In this subchapter, "veterans reemployment program" means a program that provides education and training to veterans with the goal that the veterans obtain workforce skills and become gainfully employed.

Art. 42A.382. Eligibility.

(a) A defendant placed on community supervision, including deferred adjudication community supervision, for a misdemeanor offense is eligible to participate in a veterans reemployment program under this subchapter if the defendant is a veteran of the United States armed forces, including a member of the reserves, national guard, or state guard.

(b) The judge granting community supervision to a defendant described by Subsection (a) shall inform the defendant of the defendant's eligibility for participation in a veterans reemployment program but may not require the defendant to participate in the program.

(c) A judge may impose any condition of community supervision that the judge is authorized to impose under this chapter on a defendant who chooses to participate in the program under this subchapter, except that the judge may not impose a condition related to the program or the defendant's participation in the program.

Art. 42A.383. Education and Training Courses.

(a) The program shall provide program participants with access to workforce development education and training courses developed or approved by the Texas Workforce Commission under Chapter 316, Labor Code.

(b) The education and training courses under this article must focus on providing a participant with useful workplace skills most likely to lead to gainful employment by the participant.

(c) The education and training courses may be individualized based on any physical or intellectual limitations of the participant.

Art. 42A.384. Completion of Program.

A participant successfully completes the veterans reemployment program if the participant diligently attends and successfully completes the education and training courses under Article 42A.383 and:

(1) obtains employment and retains that employment for a continuous period of three months;

(2) diligently searches for employment for a continuous period of six months; or

(3) is determined by the court to be unemployable because of a disability.

Art. 42A.385. Extended Period Allowed for Completion of Program.

A defendant is not required to successfully complete a program under this subchapter before the defendant completes the applicable period of community supervision. The defendant may continue to participate in a program following the defendant's completion of that period.

Art. 42A.386. Failure to Complete Program.

The judge may not revoke the community supervision of a defendant solely because the defendant fails to successfully complete a program under this subchapter.

SUBCHAPTER I CONDITIONS APPLICABLE TO CERTAIN INTOXICATION OFFENSES

Art. 42A.401. Confinement As Condition of Community Supervision for Certain Intoxication Offenses.

(a) A judge granting community supervision to a defendant convicted of an offense under Chapter 49, Penal Code, shall require as a condition of community supervision that the defendant submit to:

(1) not less than 72 hours of continuous confinement in county jail if the defendant was punished under Section 49.09(a), Penal Code;

Code of Criminal Procedure

(2) not less than five days of confinement in county jail if the defendant was punished under Section 49.09(a), Penal Code, and was subject to Section 49.09(h), Penal Code;

(3) not less than 10 days of confinement in county jail if the defendant was punished under Section 49.09(b), Penal Code;

(4) not less than 30 days of confinement in county jail if the defendant was convicted of an offense under Section 49.07, Penal Code; or

(5) a term of confinement of not less than 120 days if the defendant was convicted of an offense under Section 49.08, Penal Code.

(b) If a sentence of confinement is imposed on the revocation of community supervision, the term of confinement served under Subsection (a) may not be credited toward completion of the sentence imposed.

Art. 42A.402. Drug or Alcohol Dependence Evaluation and Rehabilitation.

(a) A judge granting community supervision to a defendant convicted of an offense under Chapter 49, Penal Code, shall require as a condition of community supervision that the defendant submit to an evaluation by a supervision officer or by a person, program, or facility approved by the Department of State Health Services for the purpose of having the facility prescribe and carry out a course of conduct necessary for the rehabilitation of the defendant's drug or alcohol dependence condition.

(b) If the director of a facility to which a defendant is referred under Subsection (a) determines that the defendant is not making a good faith effort to participate in a program of rehabilitation, the director shall notify the judge who referred the defendant to the facility of that determination.

(c) If a judge requires as a condition of community supervision that the defendant participate in a prescribed course of conduct necessary for the rehabilitation of the defendant's drug or alcohol dependence condition, the judge shall require that the defendant pay for all or part of the cost of the rehabilitation based on the defendant's ability to pay. The judge, in the judge's discretion, may credit against the fine assessed the cost paid by the defendant. In determining a defendant's ability to pay the cost of rehabilitation under this subsection, the judge shall consider whether the defendant has insurance coverage that will pay for rehabilitation.

(d) A judge who grants community supervision to a defendant convicted of an offense under Sections 49.04-49.08, Penal Code, shall require, if the defendant has not submitted to an evaluation under Article 42A.257 before receiving community supervision, that the defendant submit to the evaluation as a condition of community supervision. If the evaluation indicates to the judge that the defendant needs treatment for drug or alcohol dependency, the judge shall require the defendant to submit to that treatment as a condition of community supervision in a program or facility that:

(1) is approved or licensed by the Department of State Health Services; or

(2) complies with standards established by the community justice assistance division of the Texas Department of Criminal Justice, after consultation by the division with the Department of State Health Services.

(e) If, based on the evaluation conducted under Subsection (d), the judge determines that the defendant would likely benefit from medication-assisted treatment approved by the United States Food and Drug Administration for alcohol dependence, the judge may require as a condition of community supervision that the defendant submit to an evaluation by a licensed physician to determine whether the defendant would benefit from medication-assisted treatment. Only a licensed physician may recommend that a defendant participate in medication-assisted treatment. A defendant is entitled to refuse to participate in medication-assisted treatment, and a judge may not require as a condition of community supervision that the defendant participate in medication-assisted treatment.

Art. 42A.403. Educational Program for Certain Intoxication Offenses; Waiver or Extension of Time.

(a) A judge who places on community supervision a defendant convicted of an offense under Sections 49.04-49.08, Penal Code, shall require as a condition of community supervision that the defendant successfully complete, before the 181st day after the date community supervision is granted, an educational program designed to rehabilitate persons who have driven while intoxicated that is regulated by the Texas Department of Licensing and Regulation under Chapter 171, Government Code.

(b) This article does not apply to a defendant if a jury recommends community supervision for the defendant and also recommends that the defendant's driver's license not be suspended.

(c) If the defendant by a motion in writing shows good cause, the judge may:

(1) waive the educational program requirement; or

(2) to enable the defendant to successfully complete the program, grant an extension of time that

expires not later than the first anniversary of the beginning date of the defendant's community supervision.

(d) In determining good cause, the judge may consider but is not limited to:

(1) the defendant's school and work schedule;

(2) the defendant's health;

(3) the distance that the defendant must travel to attend an in-person educational program;

(4) the fact that the defendant resides out of state, does not have a valid driver's license, or does not have access to transportation; and

(5) whether the defendant has access to reliable Internet service sufficient to successfully complete an educational program offered online.

(d-1) The judge shall waive the educational program requirement if the defendant successfully completes education at a residential treatment facility under Article 42A.4045.

(e) The judge shall set out in the judgment, as applicable:

(1) the finding of good cause for waiver; or

(2) the finding that the defendant has successfully completed education as provided by Article 42A.4045.

Art. 42A.404. Educational Program for Certain Repeat Intoxication Offenses; Waiver.

(a) The judge shall require a defendant who is punished under Section 49.09, Penal Code, to attend and successfully complete as a condition of community supervision an educational program for repeat offenders that is regulated by the Texas Department of Licensing and Regulation under Chapter 171, Government Code.

(b) The judge may waive the educational program requirement if the defendant by a motion in writing shows good cause. In determining good cause, the judge may consider:

(1) the defendant's school and work schedule;

(2) the defendant's health;

(3) the distance that the defendant must travel to attend an in-person educational program;

(4) whether the defendant resides out of state or does not have access to transportation; and

(5) whether the defendant has access to reliable Internet service sufficient to successfully complete an educational program offered online.

(b-1) The judge shall waive the educational program requirement if the defendant successfully completes education at a residential treatment facility under Article 42A.4045.

(c) The judge shall set out in the judgment, as applicable:

(1) the finding of good cause for waiver; or

(2) the finding that the defendant has successfully completed education as provided by Article 42A.4045.

Art. 42A.4045. Alternative to Educational Program: Substance Abuse Treatment Facility.

(a) A judge shall waive the educational requirement under Article 42A.403 or 42A.404 for a defendant who is required to receive treatment as a resident of a substance abuse treatment facility as a condition of community supervision if the defendant successfully completes education while the defendant is confined to the residential treatment facility.

(b) The Department of State Health Services shall approve education provided at substance abuse treatment facilities.

(c) The executive commissioner of the Health and Human Services Commission shall adopt rules to implement this article.

(d) For purposes of this article, a substance abuse treatment facility includes:

(1) a substance abuse felony punishment facility operated by the Texas Department of Criminal Justice under Section 493.009, Government Code;

(2) a community corrections facility, as defined by Section 509.001, Government Code; or

(3) a chemical dependency treatment facility licensed under Chapter 464, Health and Safety Code.

Art. 42A.405. Rules for and Administration of Educational Programs. [Repealed]

Art. 42A.406. Effect of Educational Program Requirements on Driving Record and License.

(a) If a defendant is required as a condition of community supervision to successfully complete an educational program under Article 42A.403 or 42A.404, or if the court waives the educational program requirement under Article 42A.403 or the defendant successfully completes education under Article 42A.4045, the court clerk shall immediately report that fact to the Department of Public Safety, on a form prescribed by the department, for inclusion in the defendant's driving record. If the court grants an extension of time in which the defendant may complete the educational program under Article 42A.403, the court clerk shall immediately report that fact to the Department of Public Safety on a form prescribed by the department. The clerk's report under this subsection must include the beginning date of the defendant's community supervision.

(b) On the defendant's successful completion of an educational program under Article 42A.403 or 42A.404, the defendant's instructor shall give notice to the Department of Public Safety for inclusion in the defendant's driving record and to the community supervision and corrections department. The community supervision and corrections department shall forward the notice to the court clerk for filing.

(b-1) Upon release from a residential treatment facility at which the person successfully completed education under Article 42A.4045, at the request of the court clerk, the director of the residential treatment facility shall give notice to the Department of Public Safety for inclusion in the person's driving record.

(c) If the Department of Public Safety does not receive notice that a defendant required to complete an educational program has successfully completed the program within the period required by the judge under this subchapter, as shown on department records, the department, as provided by Sections 521.344(e) and (f), Transportation Code, shall:

(1) revoke the defendant's driver's license; or

(2) prohibit the defendant from obtaining a license.

(d) The Department of Public Safety may not reinstate a license revoked under Subsection (c) as the result of an educational program requirement imposed under Article 42A.403 unless the defendant whose license was revoked applies to the department for reinstatement of the license and pays to the department a reinstatement fee of $100. The Department of Public Safety shall remit all fees collected under this subsection to the comptroller for deposit in the general revenue fund.

Art. 42A.407. Suspension of Driver's License.

(a) A jury that recommends community supervision for a defendant convicted of an offense under Sections 49.04-49.08, Penal Code, may recommend that any driver's license issued to the defendant under Chapter 521, Transportation Code, not be suspended. This subsection does not apply to a defendant punished under Section 49.09(a) or (b), Penal Code, and subject to Section 49.09(h), Penal Code.

(b) Notwithstanding Sections 521.344(d)-(i), Transportation Code, if under Article 42A.404 the judge requires a defendant punished under Section 49.09, Penal Code, to successfully complete an educational program as a condition of community supervision, or waives the required completion of the program, and the defendant has previously been required to successfully complete such an educational program, or the required completion of the program had been waived, the judge shall order the suspension of the defendant's driver's license for a period determined by the judge according to the following schedule:

(1) not less than 90 days or more than one year, if the defendant is convicted under Sections 49.04-49.08, Penal Code;

(2) not less than 180 days or more than two years, if the defendant is punished under Section 49.09(a) or (b), Penal Code; or

(3) not less than one year or more than two years, if the defendant is convicted of a second or subsequent offense under Sections 49.04-49.08, Penal Code, committed within five years of the date on which the most recent preceding offense was committed.

(c) If the Department of Public Safety receives notice that a defendant has been required to successfully complete a subsequent educational program under Article 42A.403 or 42A.404, although the previously required completion had been waived, but the judge has not ordered a period of suspension, the department shall:

(1) suspend the defendant's driver's license; or

(2) issue an order prohibiting the defendant from obtaining a license for a period of one year.

(d) The judge shall suspend the defendant's driver's license for a period provided under Subchapter O, Chapter 521, Transportation Code, if:

(1) a judge revokes the community supervision of the defendant for:

(A) an offense under Section 49.04, Penal Code; or

(B) an offense involving the operation of a motor vehicle under Section 49.07, Penal Code; and

(2) the license has not previously been ordered by the judge to be suspended, or the suspension was previously probated.

(e) The suspension of a defendant's driver's license under Subsection (d) shall be reported to the Department of Public Safety as provided under Section 521.347, Transportation Code.

(f) Notwithstanding any other provision of this subchapter or other law, a judge who places on community supervision a defendant who was younger than 21 years of age at the time of the offense and was convicted for an offense under Sections 49.04-49.08, Penal Code, shall order that the defendant's driver's license be suspended for 90 days beginning on the date the defendant is placed on community supervision.

(g) Notwithstanding any other provision of this subchapter, a defendant whose license is suspended for an offense under Sections 49.04-49.08, Penal Code, may operate a motor vehicle during the period of suspension if the defendant:

(1) obtains and uses an ignition interlock device as provided by Article 42A.408 for the entire period of the suspension; and

(2) applies for and receives an occupational driver's license with an ignition interlock designation under Section 521.2465, Transportation Code.

Art. 42A.408. Use of Ignition Interlock Device.

(a) In this article, "ignition interlock device" means a device that uses a deep-lung breath analysis mechanism to make impractical the operation of the motor vehicle if ethyl alcohol is detected in the breath of the operator.

(b) The court may require as a condition of community supervision that a defendant placed on community supervision after conviction of an offense under Sections 49.04-49.08, Penal Code, have an ignition interlock device installed on the motor vehicle owned by the defendant or on the vehicle most regularly driven by the defendant and that the defendant not operate any motor vehicle that is not equipped with that device.

(c) The court shall require as a condition of community supervision that a defendant described by Subsection (b) have an ignition interlock device installed on the motor vehicle owned by the defendant or on the vehicle most regularly driven by the defendant and that the defendant not operate any motor vehicle unless the vehicle is equipped with that device if:

(1) it is shown on the trial of the offense that an analysis of a specimen of the defendant's blood, breath, or urine showed an alcohol concentration level of 0.15 or more at the time the analysis was performed;

(2) the defendant is placed on community supervision after conviction of an offense under Sections 49.04-49.06, Penal Code, for which the defendant is punished under Section 49.09(a) or (b), Penal Code; or

(3) the court determines under Subsection (d) that the defendant has one or more previous convictions under Sections 49.04-49.08, Penal Code.

(d) Before placing on community supervision a defendant convicted of an offense under Sections 49.04-49.08, Penal Code, the court shall determine from criminal history record information maintained by the Department of Public Safety whether the defendant has one or more previous convictions under any of those sections. A previous conviction may not be used for purposes of restricting a defendant to the operation of a motor vehicle equipped with an ignition interlock device under Subsection (c) if:

(1) the previous conviction was a final conviction under Section 49.04, 49.045, 49.05, 49.06, 49.07, or 49.08, Penal Code, and was for an offense committed before the beginning of the 10-year period preceding the date of the instant offense for which the defendant was convicted and placed on community supervision; and

(2) the defendant has not been convicted of an offense under Section 49.04, 49.045, 49.05, 49.06, 49.07, or 49.08, Penal Code, committed within the 10-year period preceding the date of the instant offense for which the defendant was convicted and placed on community supervision.

(e) Notwithstanding any other provision of this subchapter or other law, a judge who places on community supervision a defendant who was younger than 21 years of age at the time of the offense and was convicted for an offense under Sections 49.04-49.08, Penal Code, shall require as a condition of community supervision that the defendant not operate any motor vehicle unless the vehicle is equipped with an ignition interlock device.

(e-1) Except as provided by Subsection (e-2), a judge granting deferred adjudication community supervision to a defendant for an offense under Section 49.04 or 49.06, Penal Code, shall require that the defendant as a condition of community supervision have an ignition interlock device installed on the motor vehicle owned by the defendant or on the vehicle most regularly driven by the defendant and that the defendant not operate any motor vehicle that is not equipped with that device. If the judge determines that the defendant is unable to pay for the ignition interlock device, the judge may impose a reasonable payment schedule, as provided by Subsection (f). If the defendant provides the court evidence under Section 709.001, Transportation Code, sufficient to establish that the defendant is indigent for purposes of that section, the judge may enter in the record a finding that the defendant is indigent and reduce the costs to the defendant by ordering a waiver of the installation charge for the ignition interlock device and a 50 percent reduction of the monthly device monitoring fee. A reduction in costs ordered under this subsection does not apply to any fees that may be assessed against the defendant if the ignition interlock device detects ethyl alcohol on the breath of the person attempting to operate the motor vehicle.

(e-2) A judge may waive the ignition interlock requirement under Subsection (e-1) for a defendant if, based on a controlled substance and alcohol evaluation of the defendant, the judge determines and enters in the record that restricting the defendant to the use of an ignition interlock is not necessary for the safety of the community.

(f) The court shall require the defendant to obtain an ignition interlock device at the defendant's own cost before the 30th day after the date of conviction unless the court finds that to do so would not be in the best interest of justice and enters its findings on record. The court shall require the defendant to provide evidence to the court within the 30-day period that the device has been installed on the appropriate vehicle and order the device to remain installed on that vehicle for a period the length of which is not less than 50 percent of the supervision period. If the court determines the defendant is unable to pay for the ignition interlock device, the court may impose a reasonable payment schedule not to exceed twice the length of the period of the court's order.

(g) The Department of Public Safety shall approve ignition interlock devices for use under this article. Section 521.247, Transportation Code, applies to the approval of a device under this article and the consequences of that approval.

(h) Notwithstanding any other provision of this subchapter, if a defendant is required to operate a motor vehicle in the course and scope of the defendant's employment and if the vehicle is owned by the employer, the defendant may operate that vehicle without installation of an approved ignition interlock device if the employer has been notified of that driving privilege restriction and if proof of that notification is with the vehicle. The employment exemption does not apply if the business entity that owns the vehicle is owned or controlled by the defendant.

Art. 42A.409. Community Supervision for Enhanced Public Intoxication Offense.

(a) On conviction of an offense punishable as a Class C misdemeanor under Section 49.02, Penal Code, for which punishment is enhanced under Section 12.43(c), Penal Code, based on previous convictions under Section 49.02 or 42.01, Penal Code, the court may suspend the imposition of the sentence and place the defendant on community supervision if the court finds that the defendant would benefit from community supervision and enters its finding on the record. The judge may suspend in whole or in part the imposition of any fine imposed on conviction.

(b) All provisions of this chapter applying to a defendant placed on community supervision for a misdemeanor apply to a defendant placed on community supervision under Subsection (a), except that the court shall require the defendant as a condition of community supervision to:

(1) submit to diagnostic testing for addiction to alcohol or a controlled substance or drug;

(2) submit to a psychological assessment;

(3) if indicated as necessary by testing and assessment, participate in an alcohol or drug abuse treatment or education program; and

(4) pay the costs of testing, assessment, and treatment or education, either directly or as a court cost.

SUBCHAPTER J CONDITIONS APPLICABLE TO SEX OFFENDERS

Art. 42A.451. Sex Offender Registration; DNA Sample.

A judge granting community supervision to a defendant required to register as a sex offender under Chapter 62 shall require that the defendant, as a condition of community supervision:

(1) register under that chapter; and

(2) submit a DNA sample to the Department of Public Safety under Subchapter G, Chapter 411, Government Code, for the purpose of creating a DNA record of the defendant, unless the defendant has already submitted the required sample under other state law.

Art. 42A.452. Treatment, Specialized Supervision, or Rehabilitation.

A judge who grants community supervision to a sex offender evaluated under Article 42A.258 may require the sex offender as a condition of community supervision to submit to treatment, specialized supervision, or rehabilitation according to offense-specific standards of practice adopted by the Council on Sex Offender Treatment. On a finding that the defendant is financially able to make payment, the judge shall require the defendant to pay a reimbursement fee for all or part of the reasonable and necessary costs of the treatment, supervision, or rehabilitation.

Art. 42A.453. Child Safety Zone.

(a) In this article, "playground," "premises," "school," "video arcade facility," and "youth center" have the meanings assigned by Section 481.134,

Health and Safety Code, and "general residential operation" has the meaning assigned by Section 42.002, Human Resources Code.

(b) This article applies to a defendant placed on community supervision for an offense under:

(1) Section 20.04(a)(4), Penal Code, if the defendant committed the offense with the intent to violate or abuse the victim sexually;

(2) Section 20A.02, Penal Code, if the defendant:

(A) trafficked the victim with the intent or knowledge that the victim would engage in sexual conduct, as defined by Section 43.25, Penal Code; or

(B) benefited from participating in a venture that involved a trafficked victim engaging in sexual conduct, as defined by Section 43.25, Penal Code;

(3) Section 21.08, 21.11, 22.011, 22.021, or 25.02, Penal Code;

(4) Section 30.02, Penal Code, punishable under Subsection (d) of that section, if the defendant committed the offense with the intent to commit a felony listed in Subdivision (1) or (3); or

(5) Section 43.05(a)(2), 43.25, or 43.26, Penal Code.

(c) If a judge grants community supervision to a defendant described by Subsection (b) and the judge determines that a child as defined by Section 22.011(c), Penal Code, was the victim of the offense, the judge shall establish a child safety zone applicable to the defendant by requiring as a condition of community supervision that the defendant:

(1) not:

(A) supervise or participate in any program that:

(i) includes as participants or recipients persons who are 17 years of age or younger; and

(ii) regularly provides athletic, civic, or cultural activities; or

(B) go in, on, or within 1,000 feet of a premises where children commonly gather, including a school, day-care facility, playground, public or private youth center, public swimming pool, video arcade facility, or general residential operation operating as a residential treatment center; and

(2) attend psychological counseling sessions for sex offenders with an individual or organization that provides sex offender treatment or counseling as specified or approved by the judge or the defendant's supervision officer.

(d) Notwithstanding Subsection (c)(1), a judge is not required to impose the conditions described by Subsection (c)(1) if the defendant is a student at a primary or secondary school.

(e) At any time after the imposition of a condition under Subsection (c)(1), the defendant may request the court to modify the child safety zone applicable to the defendant because the zone as created by the court:

(1) interferes with the defendant's ability to attend school or hold a job and consequently constitutes an undue hardship for the defendant; or

(2) is broader than is necessary to protect the public, given the nature and circumstances of the offense.

(f) A supervision officer for a defendant described by Subsection (b) may permit the defendant to enter on an event-by-event basis into the child safety zone from which the defendant is otherwise prohibited from entering if:

(1) the defendant has served at least two years of the period of community supervision;

(2) the defendant enters the zone as part of a program to reunite with the defendant's family;

(3) the defendant presents to the supervision officer a written proposal specifying where the defendant intends to go within the zone, why and with whom the defendant is going, and how the defendant intends to cope with any stressful situations that occur;

(4) the sex offender treatment provider treating the defendant agrees with the supervision officer that the defendant should be allowed to attend the event; and

(5) the supervision officer and the treatment provider agree on a chaperon to accompany the defendant and the chaperon agrees to perform that duty.

(g) Article 42A.051(b) does not prohibit a supervision officer from modifying a condition of community supervision by permitting a defendant to enter a child safety zone under Subsection (f).

(h) Notwithstanding Subsection (c)(1)(B), a requirement that a defendant not go in, on, or within 1,000 feet of certain premises does not apply to a defendant while the defendant is in or going immediately to or from a:

(1) community supervision and corrections department office;

(2) premises at which the defendant is participating in a program or activity required as a condition of community supervision;

(3) residential facility in which the defendant is required to reside as a condition of community supervision, if the facility was in operation as a residence for defendants on community supervision on June 1, 2003; or

(4) private residence at which the defendant is required to reside as a condition of community supervision.

(i) A supervision officer who under Subsection (c)(2) specifies a sex offender treatment provider to provide counseling to a defendant shall:

(1) contact the provider before the defendant is released;

(2) establish the date, time, and place of the first session between the defendant and the provider; and

(3) request the provider to immediately notify the supervision officer if the defendant fails to attend the first session or any subsequent scheduled session.

Art. 42A.454. Certain Internet Activity Prohibited.

(a) This article applies only to a defendant who is required to register as a sex offender under Chapter 62, by court order or otherwise, and:

(1) is convicted of or receives a grant of deferred adjudication community supervision for a violation of Section 21.11, 22.011(a)(2), 22.021(a)(1)(B), 33.021, or 43.25, Penal Code;

(2) used the Internet or any other type of electronic device used for Internet access to commit the offense or engage in the conduct for which the person is required to register under Chapter 62; or

(3) is assigned a numeric risk level of two or three based on an assessment conducted under Article 62.007.

(b) If the court grants community supervision to a defendant described by Subsection (a), the court as a condition of community supervision shall:

(1) prohibit the defendant from using the Internet to:

(A) access material that is obscene, as defined by Section 43.21, Penal Code;

(B) access a commercial social networking site, as defined by Article 62.0061(f);

(C) communicate with any individual concerning sexual relations with an individual who is younger than 17 years of age; or

(D) communicate with another individual the defendant knows is younger than 17 years of age; and

(2) to ensure the defendant's compliance with Subdivision (1), require the defendant to submit to regular inspection or monitoring of each electronic device used by the defendant to access the Internet.

(c) The court may modify at any time the condition described by Subsection (b)(1)(D) if:

(1) the condition interferes with the defendant's ability to attend school or become or remain employed and consequently constitutes an undue hardship for the defendant; or

(2) the defendant is the parent or guardian of an individual who is younger than 17 years of age and the defendant is not otherwise prohibited from communicating with that individual.

Art. 42A.455. Payment to Children's Advocacy Center.

A judge who grants community supervision to a defendant charged with or convicted of an offense under Section 21.11 or 22.011(a)(2), Penal Code, may require the defendant to pay a fine in an amount not to exceed $50 to a children's advocacy center established under Subchapter E, Chapter 264, Family Code.

SUBCHAPTER K
CONDITIONS APPLICABLE TO CERTAIN OTHER OFFENSES AND OFFENDERS

Art. 42A.501. Community Supervision for Offense Committed Because of Bias or Prejudice.

(a) A court granting community supervision to a defendant convicted of an offense for which the court has made an affirmative finding under Article 42.014 shall require as a term of community supervision that the defendant:

(1) serve a term of not more than one year imprisonment in the Texas Department of Criminal Justice if the offense is a felony other than an offense under Section 19.02, Penal Code; or

(2) serve a term of not more than 90 days confinement in jail if the offense is a misdemeanor.

(b) The court may not grant community supervision on its own motion or on the recommendation of the jury to a defendant convicted of an offense for which the court has made an affirmative finding under Article 42.014 if:

(1) the offense for which the court has made the affirmative finding is an offense under Section 19.02, Penal Code; or

(2) the defendant has been previously convicted of an offense for which the court made an affirmative finding under Article 42.014.

Art. 42A.502. Community Supervision for Certain Violent Offenses; Child Safety Zone.

(a) In this article, "playground," "premises," "school," "video arcade facility," and "youth center" have the meanings assigned by Section 481.134, Health and Safety Code.

(b) A judge granting community supervision to a defendant convicted of an offense listed in Article 42A.054(a) or for which the judgment contains an affirmative finding under Article 42A.054(c) or (d) may establish a child safety zone applicable to the defendant, if the nature of the offense for which the defendant is convicted warrants the establishment of a child safety zone, by requiring as a condition of community supervision that the defendant not:

Code of Criminal Procedure

(1) supervise or participate in any program that:

(A) includes as participants or recipients persons who are 17 years of age or younger; and

(B) regularly provides athletic, civic, or cultural activities; or

(2) go in or on, or within a distance specified by the judge of, a premises where children commonly gather, including a school, day-care facility, playground, public or private youth center, public swimming pool, or video arcade facility.

(c) At any time after the imposition of a condition under Subsection (b), the defendant may request the judge to modify the child safety zone applicable to the defendant because the zone as created by the judge:

(1) interferes with the defendant's ability to attend school or hold a job and consequently constitutes an undue hardship for the defendant; or

(2) is broader than is necessary to protect the public, given the nature and circumstances of the offense.

(d) This article does not apply to a defendant described by Article 42A.453.

Art. 42A.503. Community Supervision for Certain Child Abuse Offenses; Prohibited Contact with Victim.

(a) If the court grants community supervision to a defendant convicted of an offense described by Article 17.41(a), the court may require as a condition of community supervision that the defendant not:

(1) directly communicate with the victim of the offense; or

(2) go near a residence, school, or other location, as specifically described in the copy of terms and conditions, that is frequented by the victim.

(b) In imposing the condition under Subsection (a), the court may grant the defendant supervised access to the victim.

(c) To the extent that a condition imposed under this article conflicts with an existing court order granting possession of or access to a child, the condition imposed under this article prevails for a period specified by the court granting community supervision, not to exceed 90 days.

Art. 42A.504. Community Supervision for Certain Offenses Involving Family Violence; Special Conditions.

(a) In this article:

(1) "Family violence" has the meaning assigned by Section 71.004, Family Code.

(2) "Family violence center" has the meaning assigned by Section 51.002, Human Resources Code.

(b) If a judge grants community supervision to a defendant convicted of an offense under Title 5, Penal Code, that the court determines involves family violence, the judge shall require the defendant to pay a fine of $100 to a family violence center that:

(1) receives state or federal funds; and

(2) serves the county in which the court is located.

(c) If the court grants community supervision to a defendant convicted of an offense involving family violence, the court may require the defendant, at the direction of the supervision officer, to:

(1) attend a battering intervention and prevention program or counsel with a provider of battering intervention and prevention services if the program or provider has been accredited under Section 4A, Article 42.141, as conforming to program guidelines under that article; or

(2) if the referral option under Subdivision (1) is not available, attend counseling sessions for the elimination of violent behavior with a licensed counselor, social worker, or other professional who has completed family violence intervention training that the community justice assistance division of the Texas Department of Criminal Justice has approved, after consultation with the licensing authorities described by Chapters 152, 501, 502, 503, and 505, Occupations Code, and experts in the field of family violence.

(d) If the court requires the defendant to attend counseling or a program, the court shall require the defendant to begin attendance not later than the 60th day after the date the court grants community supervision, notify the supervision officer of the name, address, and phone number of the counselor or program, and report the defendant's attendance to the supervision officer. The court shall require the defendant to pay all the reasonable costs of the counseling sessions or attendance in the program on a finding that the defendant is financially able to make payment. If the court finds the defendant is unable to make payment, the court shall make the counseling sessions or enrollment in the program available without cost to the defendant. The court may also require the defendant to pay all or a part of the reasonable costs incurred by the victim for counseling made necessary by the offense, on a finding that the defendant is financially able to make payment. The court may order the defendant to make payments under this subsection for a period not to exceed one year after the date on which the order is entered.

Art. 42A.505. Community Supervision for Stalking Offense; Prohibited Contact with Victim.

(a) If the court grants community supervision to a defendant convicted of an offense under

Section 42.072, Penal Code, the court may require as a condition of community supervision that the defendant not:

(1) communicate directly or indirectly with the victim; or

(2) go to or near:

(A) the residence, place of employment, or business of the victim; or

(B) a school, day-care facility, or similar facility where a dependent child of the victim is in attendance.

(b) If the court requires the prohibition contained in Subsection (a)(2) as a condition of community supervision, the court shall specifically describe the prohibited locations and the minimum distances, if any, that the defendant must maintain from the locations.

Art. 42A.506. Community Supervision for Defendant with Mental Impairment.

If the judge places a defendant on community supervision and the defendant is determined to be a person with mental illness or a person with an intellectual disability, as provided by Article 16.22 or Chapter 46B or in a psychological evaluation conducted under Article 42A.253(a)(6), the judge may require the defendant as a condition of community supervision to submit to outpatient or inpatient mental health or intellectual disability treatment if:

(1) the defendant's:

(A) mental impairment is chronic in nature; or

(B) ability to function independently will continue to deteriorate if the defendant does not receive mental health or intellectual disability services; and

(2) the judge determines, in consultation with a local mental health or intellectual disability services provider, that mental health or intellectual disability services, as appropriate, are available for the defendant through:

(A) the Department of State Health Services or the Department of Aging and Disability Services under Section 534.053, Health and Safety Code; or

(B) another mental health or intellectual disability services provider.

Art. 42A.507. Community Supervision for Certain Defendants Identified As Members of Criminal Street Gangs; Electronic Monitoring.

(a) This article applies only to a defendant who:

(1) is identified as a member of a criminal street gang in an intelligence database established under Chapter 67; and

(2) has two or more times been previously convicted of, or received a grant of deferred adjudication community supervision or another functionally equivalent form of community supervision or probation for, a felony offense under the laws of this state, another state, or the United States.

(b) A court granting community supervision to a defendant described by Subsection (a) may, on the defendant's conviction of a felony offense, require as a condition of community supervision that the defendant submit to tracking under an electronic monitoring service or other appropriate technological service designed to track a person's location.

Art. 42A.508. Community Supervision for Certain Organized Crime Offenses; Restrictions on Operation of Motor Vehicle.

A court granting community supervision to a defendant convicted of an offense under Chapter 71, Penal Code, may impose as a condition of community supervision restrictions on the defendant's operation of a motor vehicle, including specifying:

(1) hours during which the defendant may not operate a motor vehicle; and

(2) locations at or in which the defendant may not operate a motor vehicle.

Art. 42A.509. Community Supervision for Graffiti Offense.

A court granting community supervision to a defendant convicted of an offense under Section 28.08, Penal Code, shall require as a condition of community supervision that the defendant perform:

(1) at least 15 hours of community service if the amount of pecuniary loss resulting from the commission of the offense is $50 or more but less than $500; or

(2) at least 30 hours of community service if the amount of pecuniary loss resulting from the commission of the offense is $500 or more.

Art. 42A.510. Community Supervision for Enhanced Disorderly Conduct Offense.

(a) On conviction of an offense punishable as a Class C misdemeanor under Section 42.01, Penal Code, for which punishment is enhanced under Section 12.43(c), Penal Code, based on previous convictions under Section 42.01 or 49.02, Penal Code, the court may suspend the imposition of the sentence and place the defendant on community supervision if the court finds that the defendant would benefit from community supervision and enters its finding on the record. The judge may suspend in whole or in part the imposition of any fine imposed on conviction.

(b) All provisions of this chapter applying to a defendant placed on community supervision for a misdemeanor apply to a defendant placed on community supervision under this article, except that the court shall require the defendant as a condition of community supervision to:

(1) submit to diagnostic testing for addiction to alcohol or a controlled substance or drug;

(2) submit to a psychological assessment;

(3) if indicated as necessary by testing and assessment, participate in an alcohol or drug abuse treatment or education program; and

(4) pay the costs of testing, assessment, and treatment or education, either directly or as a court cost.

Art. 42A.511. Community Supervision for Certain Offenses Involving Animals.

(a) If a judge grants community supervision to a defendant convicted of an offense under Section 42.09, 42.091, 42.092, or 42.10, Penal Code, the judge may require the defendant to attend a responsible pet owner course sponsored by a municipal animal shelter, as defined by Section 823.001, Health and Safety Code, that:

(1) receives federal, state, county, or municipal funds; and

(2) serves the county in which the court is located.

(b) For purposes of the online responsible pet owner course described by Subsection (a)(1), the Texas Department of Licensing and Regulation or the Texas Commission of Licensing and Regulation, as appropriate:

(1) is responsible for the approval, certification, and administration of the course and course providers;

(2) may charge fees for:

(A) initial and renewal course certifications;

(B) initial and renewal course provider certifications;

(C) course participant completion certificates; and

(D) other fees necessary for the administration of the course and course providers;

(3) shall adopt rules regarding the administration of the course and course providers, including rules regarding:

(A) the criteria for course approval and certification;

(B) the criteria for course provider approval and certification;

(C) curriculum development;

(D) course length and content;

(E) criteria for a participant to complete the course; and

(F) a course completion certificate that is acceptable to a court;

(4) is authorized to monitor and audit the provision of the course by the course providers; and

(5) may take enforcement actions as appropriate to enforce this subsection.

(c) If a judge grants community supervision to a defendant convicted of an offense under Section 21.09, 42.091, 42.092, 42.10, or 42.105, Penal Code, the judge may:

(1) require the defendant to relinquish custody of any animals in the defendant's possession;

(2) prohibit the defendant from possessing or exercising control over any animals or residing in a household where animals are present; or

(3) require the defendant to participate in a psychological counseling or other appropriate treatment program for a period to be determined by the court.

Art. 42A.512. Community Supervision for Electronic Transmission of Certain Visual Material.

(a) In this article, "parent" means a natural or adoptive parent, managing or possessory conservator, or legal guardian. The term does not include a parent whose parental rights have been terminated.

(b) If a judge grants community supervision to a defendant who is convicted of or charged with an offense under Section 43.261, Penal Code, the judge may require as a condition of community supervision that the defendant attend and successfully complete an educational program described by Section 37.218, Education Code, or another equivalent educational program.

(c) The court shall require the defendant or the defendant's parent to pay the cost of attending an educational program under Subsection (b) if the court determines that the defendant or the defendant's parent is financially able to make payment.

Art. 42A.513. Community Supervision for Making Firearm Accessible to Child.

(a) A court granting community supervision to a defendant convicted of an offense under Section 46.13, Penal Code, may require as a condition of community supervision that the defendant:

(1) provide an appropriate public service activity designated by the court; or

(2) attend a firearms safety course that meets or exceeds the requirements set by the National Rifle Association as of January 1, 1995, for a firearms

safety course that requires not more than 17 hours of instruction.

(b) The court shall require the defendant to pay the cost of attending the firearms safety course under Subsection (a)(2).

Art. 42A.514. Community Supervision for Certain Alcohol or Drug Related Offenses.

(a) If a judge grants community supervision to a defendant younger than 18 years of age convicted of an alcohol-related offense under Section 106.02, 106.025, 106.04, 106.041, 106.05, or 106.07, Alcoholic Beverage Code, or Section 49.02, Penal Code, or an offense involving possession of a controlled substance or marihuana under Section 481.115, 481.1151, 481.116, 481.1161, 481.117, 481.118, or 481.121, Health and Safety Code, the judge may require the defendant as a condition of community supervision to successfully complete, as appropriate:

(1) an alcohol awareness program under Section 106.115, Alcoholic Beverage Code, that is regulated by the Texas Department of Licensing and Regulation under Chapter 171, Government Code; or

(2) a drug education program that is designed to educate persons on the dangers of drug abuse in accordance with Section 521.374(a)(1), Transportation Code, and that is regulated by the Texas Department of Licensing and Regulation under Chapter 171, Government Code.

(b) If a judge requires a defendant as a condition of community supervision to attend an alcohol awareness program or drug education program described by Subsection (a), unless the judge determines that the defendant is indigent and unable to pay the cost, the judge shall require the defendant to pay the cost of attending the program. The judge may allow the defendant to pay the cost of attending the program in installments during the term of community supervision.

Art. 42A.515. Community Supervision for Certain Prostitution Offenses.

(a) Except as provided by Subsection (e), on a defendant's conviction of a Class B misdemeanor under Section 43.02(a), Penal Code, the judge shall suspend imposition of the sentence and place the defendant on community supervision.

(b) Except as provided by Subsection (e), on a defendant's conviction of a state jail felony under Section 43.02(c)(2), Penal Code, that is punished under Section 12.35(a), Penal Code, the judge shall suspend the imposition of the sentence and place the defendant on community supervision. This subsection does not apply to a defendant who has previously been convicted of any other state jail felony under Section 43.02(c)(2), Penal Code, that is punished under Section 12.35, Penal Code.

(c) A judge who places a defendant on community supervision under Subsection (a) or (b) shall require as a condition of community supervision that the defendant participate in a commercially sexually exploited persons court program established under Chapter 126, Government Code, if a program has been established for the county or municipality where the defendant resides. Sections 126.002(b) and (c), Government Code, do not apply with respect to a defendant required to participate in the court program under this subsection.

(d) A judge who requires a defendant to participate in a commercially sexually exploited persons court program under Subsection (c) may suspend in whole or in part the imposition of the program fee described by Section 126.006, Government Code.

(e) In any case in which the jury assesses punishment, the judge must follow the recommendations of the jury in suspending the imposition of a sentence or ordering a sentence to be executed. If a jury assessing punishment does not recommend community supervision, the judge must order the sentence to be executed in whole.

(f) The judge may suspend in whole or in part the imposition of any fine imposed on conviction.

Art. 42A.515. Community Supervision for Leaving Scene of Motor Vehicle Accident Resulting in Death of Person. [Renumbered to § Tex. Code Crim. Proc. Art. 42A.516]

Sec. 42A.516. Community Supervision for Leaving Scene of Motor Vehicle Accident Resulting in Death of Person. [Renumbered from § Tex. Code Crim. Proc. Art. 42A.515]

(a) A judge granting community supervision to a defendant convicted of an offense punishable under Section 550.021(c)(1)(A), Transportation Code, shall require as a condition of community supervision that the defendant submit to a term of confinement of not less than 120 days.

(b) If a sentence of confinement is imposed on the revocation of community supervision, the term of confinement served under Subsection (a) may not be credited toward completion of the sentence imposed.

Sec. Art. 42A.517. Community Supervision for Certain Offenses Involving Obstruction of Highway or Other Passageway.

A court granting community supervision to a defendant convicted of an offense punishable as a state jail felony under Section 42.03, Penal Code, shall require as a condition of community supervision that the defendant submit to not less than 10 days of confinement in a county jail.

SUBCHAPTER L
STATE JAIL FELONY COMMUNITY SUPERVISION

Art. 42A.551. Placement on Community Supervision; Execution of Sentence.

(a) Except as otherwise provided by Subsection (b) or (c), on conviction of a state jail felony under Section 481.115(b), 481.1151(b)(1), 481.116(b), 481.1161(b)(3), 481.121(b)(3), or 481.129(g)(1), Health and Safety Code, that is punished under Section 12.35(a), Penal Code, the judge shall suspend the imposition of the sentence and place the defendant on community supervision.

(b) If the defendant has been previously convicted of a felony, other than a felony punished under Section 12.44(a), Penal Code, or if the conviction resulted from an adjudication of the guilt of a defendant previously placed on deferred adjudication community supervision for the offense, the judge may:

(1) suspend the imposition of the sentence and place the defendant on community supervision; or

(2) order the sentence to be executed.

(c) Subsection (a) does not apply to a defendant who:

(1) under Section 481.1151(b)(1), Health and Safety Code, possessed more than five abuse units of the controlled substance;

(2) under Section 481.1161(b)(3), Health and Safety Code, possessed more than one pound, by aggregate weight, including adulterants or dilutants, of the controlled substance; or

(3) under Section 481.121(b)(3), Health and Safety Code, possessed more than one pound of marihuana.

(d) On conviction of a state jail felony punished under Section 12.35(a), Penal Code, other than a state jail felony listed in Subsection (a) or to which Article 42A.515 applies, subject to Subsection (e), the judge may:

(1) suspend the imposition of the sentence and place the defendant on community supervision; or

(2) order the sentence to be executed:

(A) in whole; or

(B) in part, with a period of community supervision to begin immediately on release of the defendant from confinement.

(e) In any case in which the jury assesses punishment, the judge must follow the recommendations of the jury in suspending the imposition of a sentence or ordering a sentence to be executed. If a jury assessing punishment does not recommend community supervision, the judge must order the sentence to be executed in whole.

(f) A defendant is considered to be finally convicted if the judge orders the sentence to be executed under Subsection (d)(2), regardless of whether the judge orders the sentence to be executed in whole or only in part.

(g) The judge may suspend in whole or in part the imposition of any fine imposed on conviction.

Art. 42A.552. Review of Presentence Report.

Before imposing a sentence in a state jail felony case in which the judge assesses punishment, the judge shall:

(1) review the presentence report prepared for the defendant under Subchapter F; and

(2) determine whether the best interests of justice require the judge to:

(A) suspend the imposition of the sentence and place the defendant on community supervision; or

(B) order the sentence to be executed in whole or in part as provided by Article 42A.551(d).

Art. 42A.553. Minimum and Maximum Periods of Community Supervision; Extension.

(a) The minimum period of community supervision a judge may impose under this subchapter is two years. The maximum period of community supervision a judge may impose under this subchapter is five years, except that the judge may extend the maximum period of community supervision under this subchapter to not more than 10 years.

(b) A judge may extend a period of community supervision under this subchapter:

(1) at any time during the period of community supervision; or

(2) before the first anniversary of the date the period of community supervision ends, if a motion for revocation of community supervision is filed before the date the period of community supervision ends.

Art. 42A.554. Conditions of Community Supervision.

(a) A judge assessing punishment in a state jail felony case may impose any condition of community supervision on the defendant that the judge

Code of Criminal Procedure

could impose on a defendant placed on supervision for an offense other than a state jail felony.

(b) If the judge suspends the execution of the sentence or orders the execution of the sentence only in part as provided by Article 42A.551(d), the judge shall impose conditions of community supervision consistent with the recommendations contained in the presentence report prepared for the defendant under Subchapter F.

(c) Except as otherwise provided by this subsection, a judge who places a defendant on community supervision for an offense listed in Article 42A.551(a) shall require the defendant to comply with substance abuse treatment conditions that are consistent with standards adopted by the Texas Board of Criminal Justice under Section 509.015, Government Code. A judge is not required to impose the substance abuse treatment conditions if the judge makes an affirmative finding that the defendant does not require imposition of the conditions to successfully complete the period of community supervision.

Art. 42A.555. Confinement As a Condition of Community Supervision.

(a) A judge assessing punishment in a state jail felony case may impose as a condition of community supervision that a defendant submit at the beginning of the period of community supervision to a term of confinement in a state jail felony facility for a term of:

(1) not less than 90 days or more than 180 days; or

(2) not less than 90 days or more than one year, if the defendant is convicted of an offense punishable as a state jail felony under Section 481.112, 481.1121, 481.113, or 481.120, Health and Safety Code.

(b) A judge may not require a defendant to submit to both the term of confinement authorized by this article and a term of confinement under Subchapter C or Article 42A.302.

Art. 42A.556. Sanctions Imposed on Modification of Community Supervision.

If in a state jail felony case a defendant violates a condition of community supervision imposed under this chapter and after a hearing under Article 42A.751(d) the judge modifies the defendant's community supervision, the judge may impose any sanction permitted by Article 42A.752, except that if the judge requires a defendant to serve a term of confinement in a state jail felony facility as a modification of the defendant's community supervision, the minimum term of confinement is 90 days and the maximum term of confinement is 180 days.

Art. 42A.557. Report by Director of Facility.

The facility director of a state jail felony facility shall report to a judge who orders a defendant confined in the facility as a condition of community supervision or as a sanction imposed on a modification of community supervision under Article 42A.556 not less than every 90 days on the defendant's programmatic progress, conduct, and conformity to the rules of the facility.

Art. 42A.558. Revocation; Options Regarding Execution of Sentence.

(a) If in a state jail felony case a defendant violates a condition of community supervision imposed under this chapter and after a hearing under Article 42A.751(d) the judge revokes the defendant's community supervision, the judge shall dispose of the case in the manner provided by Article 42A.755.

(b) The court retains jurisdiction over the defendant for the period during which the defendant is confined in a state jail felony facility. At any time after the 75th day after the date the defendant is received into the custody of a state jail felony facility, the judge on the judge's own motion, on the motion of the attorney representing the state, or on the motion of the defendant may suspend further execution of the sentence and place the defendant on community supervision under the conditions of this subchapter.

(c) When the defendant or the attorney representing the state files a written motion requesting the judge to suspend further execution of the sentence and place the defendant on community supervision, the clerk of the court, if requested to do so by the judge, shall request a copy of the defendant's record while confined from the facility director of the state jail felony facility in which the defendant is confined or, if the defendant is confined in county jail, from the sheriff. On receipt of the request, the facility director or the sheriff shall forward a copy of the record to the judge as soon as possible.

(d) When the defendant files a written motion requesting the judge to suspend further execution of the sentence and place the defendant on community supervision, the defendant shall immediately deliver or cause to be delivered a copy of the motion to the office of the attorney representing the state. The judge may deny the motion without holding a hearing but may not grant the motion without holding a hearing and providing the attorney representing the state and the defendant the opportunity to present evidence on the motion.

Art. 42A.559. Credits for Time Served.

(a) For purposes of this article, "diligent participation" includes:

(1) successful completion of an educational, vocational, or treatment program;

(2) progress toward successful completion of an educational, vocational, or treatment program that was interrupted by illness, injury, or another circumstance outside the control of the defendant; and

(3) active involvement in a work program.

(b) A defendant confined in a state jail felony facility does not earn good conduct time for time served in the facility but may be awarded diligent participation credit in accordance with Subsection (f) or (g).

(c) A judge:

(1) may credit against any time a defendant is required to serve in a state jail felony facility time served in a county jail from the time of the defendant's arrest and confinement until sentencing by the trial court; and

(2) shall credit against any time a defendant is required to serve in a state jail felony facility time served before sentencing in a substance abuse felony punishment facility operated by the Texas Department of Criminal Justice under Section 493.009, Government Code, or other court-ordered residential program or facility as a condition of deferred adjudication community supervision, but only if the defendant successfully completes the treatment program in that facility.

(d) A judge shall credit against any time a defendant is subsequently required to serve in a state jail felony facility after revocation of community supervision time served after sentencing:

(1) in a state jail felony facility; or

(2) in a substance abuse felony punishment facility operated by the Texas Department of Criminal Justice under Section 493.009, Government Code, or other court-ordered residential program or facility if the defendant successfully completes the treatment program in that facility.

(e) For a defendant who has participated in an educational, vocational, treatment, or work program while confined in a state jail felony facility, the Texas Department of Criminal Justice shall record the number of days during which the defendant diligently participated in any educational, vocational, treatment, or work program.

(f) For a defendant with a judgment that contains a finding under Article 42.0199 that the defendant is presumptively entitled to diligent participation credit and who has not been the subject of disciplinary action while confined in the state jail felony facility, the department shall credit against any time the defendant is required to serve in a state jail felony facility additional time for each day the defendant actually served in the facility while diligently participating in an educational, vocational, treatment, or work program.

(g) For a defendant with a judgment that contains a finding under Article 42.0199 that the defendant is not presumptively entitled to diligent participation credit or who has been the subject of disciplinary action while confined in the state jail felony facility, the department shall, not later than the 30th day before the date on which the defendant will have served 80 percent of the defendant's sentence, report to the sentencing court the record of the number of days under Subsection (e). The contents of a report submitted under this subsection are not subject to challenge by a defendant. A judge, based on the report, may credit against any time a defendant is required to serve in a state jail felony facility additional time for each day the defendant actually served in the facility while diligently participating in an educational, vocational, treatment, or work program.

(h) A time credit under Subsection (f) or (g) may not exceed one-fifth of the amount of time the defendant is originally required to serve in the facility. A defendant may not be awarded a time credit under Subsection (f) or (g) for any period during which the defendant is subject to disciplinary status. A time credit under Subsection (f) or (g) is a privilege and not a right.

Art. 42A.560. Medical Release.

(a) If a defendant is convicted of a state jail felony and the sentence is executed, the judge sentencing the defendant may release the defendant to a medically suitable placement if the judge determines that the defendant does not constitute a threat to public safety and the Texas Correctional Office on Offenders with Medical or Mental Impairments:

(1) in coordination with the Correctional Managed Health Care Committee, prepares a case summary and medical report that identifies the defendant as:

(A) being a person who is elderly or terminally ill or a person with a physical disability;

(B) being a person with mental illness or an intellectual disability; or

(C) having a condition requiring long-term care; and

(2) in cooperation with the community supervision and corrections department serving the sentencing court, prepares for the defendant a medically recommended intensive supervision and continuity of care plan that:

(A) ensures appropriate supervision of the defendant by the community supervision and corrections department; and

(B) requires the defendant to remain under the care of a physician at and reside in a medically suitable placement.

(b) The Texas Correctional Office on Offenders with Medical or Mental Impairments shall submit to a judge who releases a defendant to an appropriate medical care facility under Subsection (a) a quarterly status report concerning the defendant's medical and treatment status.

(c) If a defendant released to a medically suitable placement under Subsection (a) violates the terms of that release, the judge may dispose of the matter as provided by Articles 42A.556 and 42A.558(a).

Art. 42A.561. Medical Release.

(a) If a defendant is convicted of a state jail felony and the sentence is executed, the judge sentencing the defendant may release the defendant to a medical care facility or medical treatment program if the Texas Correctional Office on Offenders with Medical or Mental Impairments:

(1) identifies the defendant as:

(A) being a person who is elderly or terminally ill or a person with a physical disability;

(B) being a person with mental illness or an intellectual disability; or

(C) having a condition requiring long-term care; and

(2) in cooperation with the community supervision and corrections department serving the sentencing court, prepares for the defendant a medically recommended intensive supervision plan that:

(A) ensures appropriate supervision of the defendant; and

(B) requires the defendant to remain under the care of a physician at the facility or in the program.

(b) If a defendant released to a medical care facility or medical treatment program under Subsection (a) violates the terms of that release, the judge may dispose of the matter as provided by Articles 42A.556 and 42A.558(a).

Art. 42A.562. Placement on Community Supervision; Educational and Vocational Training Pilot Program.

(a) Except as provided by Subsection (b), a judge assessing punishment in a state jail felony case may suspend the imposition of the sentence and place the defendant on community supervision with the condition that the defendant participate in a program operated under Section 493.034, Government Code.

(b) A judge may not place a defendant on community supervision under this article if the defendant is or has previously been convicted of an offense under Title 5, Penal Code.

(c) Before a judge may place a defendant on community supervision under this article, the defendant must be assessed using the risk and needs assessment instrument adopted under Section 501.0921, Government Code, or a similar instrument that takes into consideration the defendant's prior criminal history.

(d) [Repealed.]

(e) Notwithstanding the minimum period of community supervision provided by Article 42A.553(a), a judge placing a defendant on community supervision under this article shall impose a period of community supervision not to exceed 270 days.

(f) A defendant placed on community supervision under this article must participate fully in the program described by Subsection (a). The provisions of Subchapter P authorizing the judge to revoke a defendant's community supervision or otherwise sanction the defendant apply with respect to a defendant who violates the requirement of this subsection.

SUBCHAPTER M COMMUNITY CORRECTIONS FACILITIES

Art. 42A.601. Definition.

In this subchapter, "community corrections facility" has the meaning assigned by Section 509.001, Government Code.

Art. 42A.602. Maximum Term or Terms of Confinement.

(a) If a judge requires as a condition of community supervision or participation in a pretrial intervention program operated under Section 76.011, Government Code, or a drug court program established under Chapter 123, Government Code, or former law that the defendant serve a term of confinement in a community corrections facility, the term may not exceed 24 months.

(b) A judge who requires as a condition of community supervision that the defendant serve a term of confinement in a community corrections facility may not impose a subsequent term of confinement in a community corrections facility or jail during the same supervision period that, if added to the terms previously imposed, exceeds 36 months.

Art. 42A.603. Effect of Revocation on Credit for Time Spent in Facility.

A defendant granted community supervision under this chapter and required as a condition of community supervision to serve a term of confinement under this subchapter may not earn good conduct credit for time spent in a community corrections facility or apply time spent in the facility toward completion of a prison sentence if the community supervision is revoked.

Art. 42A.604. Evaluation of Defendant's Behavior and Attitude.

(a) As directed by the judge, the community corrections facility director shall file with the community supervision and corrections department director or administrator of a drug court program, as applicable, a copy of an evaluation made by the facility director of the defendant's behavior and attitude at the facility. The community supervision and corrections department director or program administrator shall examine the evaluation, make written comments on the evaluation that the director or administrator considers relevant, and file the evaluation and comments with the judge who granted community supervision to the defendant or placed the defendant in a pretrial intervention program or drug court program. If the evaluation indicates that the defendant has made significant progress toward compliance with court-ordered conditions of community supervision or objectives of placement in the program, as applicable, the judge may release the defendant from the community corrections facility. A defendant who served a term in the facility as a condition of community supervision shall serve the remainder of the defendant's community supervision under any terms and conditions the court imposes under this chapter.

(b) Not later than 18 months after the date on which a defendant is granted community supervision under this chapter and required as a condition of community supervision to serve a term of confinement under this subchapter, the community corrections facility director shall file with the community supervision and corrections department director a copy of an evaluation made by the facility director of the defendant's behavior and attitude at the facility. The community supervision and corrections department director shall examine the evaluation, make written comments on the evaluation that the director considers relevant, and file the evaluation and comments with the judge who granted community supervision to the defendant. If the report indicates that the defendant has made significant progress toward court-ordered conditions of community supervision, the judge shall modify the judge's sentence and release the defendant in the same manner as provided by Subsection (a). If the report indicates that the defendant would benefit from continued participation in the community corrections facility program, the judge may order the defendant to remain at the community corrections facility for a period determined by the judge. If the report indicates that the defendant has not made significant progress toward rehabilitation, the judge may revoke community supervision and order the defendant to serve the term of confinement specified in the defendant's sentence.

Art. 42A.605. Placement in Community Service Project.

If ordered by the judge who placed the defendant on community supervision, a community corrections facility director shall attempt to place a defendant as a worker in a community service project of a type described by Article 42A.304.

Art. 42A.606. Confinement Required; Exceptions.

A defendant participating in a program under this subchapter must be confined in the community corrections facility at all times except for time spent:

(1) attending and traveling to and from:

(A) an education or rehabilitation program as ordered by the court; or

(B) a community service project;

(2) away from the facility for purposes described by this subchapter; and

(3) traveling to and from work, if applicable.

Art. 42A.607. Disposition of Salary.

If a defendant who is required as a condition of community supervision to serve a term of confinement under this subchapter is not required by the judge to deliver the defendant's salary to the restitution center director, the employer of the defendant shall deliver the salary to the director. The director shall deposit the salary into a fund to be given to the defendant on release after the director deducts:

(1) the cost to the center for the defendant's food, housing, and supervision;

(2) the necessary expense for the defendant's travel to and from work and community service projects, and other incidental expenses of the defendant;

(3) support of the defendant's dependents; and

(4) restitution to the victims of an offense committed by the defendant.

SUBCHAPTER N PAYMENTS; FEES

Art. 42A.651. Payment As Condition of Community Supervision.

(a) A judge may not order a defendant to make a payment as a term or condition of community supervision, except for:

(1) the payment of fines, court costs, or restitution to the victim;

(2) reimbursement of a county as described by Article 42A.301(b)(11); or

(3) a payment ordered as a condition that relates personally to the rehabilitation of the defendant or that is otherwise expressly authorized by law.

(b) A defendant's obligation to pay a fine or court cost as ordered by a judge is independent of any requirement to pay the fine or court cost as a condition of the defendant's community supervision. A defendant remains obligated to pay any unpaid fine or court cost after the expiration of the defendant's period of community supervision.

(c) A judge may not impose a condition of community supervision requiring a defendant to reimburse a county for the costs of legal services as described by Article 42A.301(b)(11) if the defendant has already satisfied that obligation under Article 26.05(g).

Art. 42A.652. Monthly Reimbursement Fee.

(a) Except as otherwise provided by this article, a judge who grants community supervision to a defendant shall set a reimbursement fee of not less than $25 and not more than $60 to be paid each month during the period of community supervision by the defendant to:

(1) the court of original jurisdiction; or

(2) the court accepting jurisdiction of the defendant's case, if jurisdiction is transferred under Article 42A.151.

(b) The judge may make payment of the monthly reimbursement fee a condition of granting or continuing the community supervision. The judge may waive or reduce the reimbursement fee or suspend a monthly payment of the fee if the judge determines that payment of the reimbursement fee would cause the defendant a significant financial hardship.

(c) A court accepting jurisdiction of a defendant's case under Article 42A.151 shall enter an order directing the defendant to pay the monthly reimbursement fee to that court instead of to the court of original jurisdiction. To the extent of any conflict between an order issued under this subsection and an order issued by a court of original jurisdiction, the order entered under this subsection prevails.

(d) A judge who receives a defendant for supervision as authorized by Section 510.017, Government Code, may require the defendant to pay the reimbursement fee authorized by this article.

(e) A judge may not require a defendant to pay the reimbursement fee under this article for any month after the period of community supervision has been terminated by the judge under Article 42A.701.

(f) A judge shall deposit any reimbursement fee received under this article in the special fund of the county treasury, to be used for the same purposes for which state aid may be used under Chapter 76, Government Code.

Art. 42A.653. Additional Monthly Fine for Certain Sex Offenders.

(a) A judge who grants community supervision to a defendant convicted of an offense under Section 21.08, 21.11, 22.011, 22.021, 25.02, 43.25, or 43.26, Penal Code, shall require as a condition of community supervision that the defendant pay to the defendant's supervision officer a community supervision fine of $5 each month during the period of community supervision.

(b) A fine imposed under this article is in addition to court costs or any other fee or fine imposed on the defendant.

(c) A community supervision and corrections department shall deposit a fine collected under this article to be sent to the comptroller as provided by Subchapter B, Chapter 133, Local Government Code. The comptroller shall deposit the fine in the sexual assault program fund under Section 420.008, Government Code.

(d) If a community supervision and corrections department does not collect a fine imposed under this article, the department is not required to file any report required by the comptroller that relates to the collection of the fine.

Art. 42A.654. Fees Due on Conviction.

For the purpose of determining when fees due on conviction are to be paid to any officer, the placement of a defendant on community supervision is considered a final disposition of the case, without the necessity of waiting for the termination of the period of community supervision.

Art. 42A.655. Ability to Pay.

(a) The court shall consider the defendant's ability to pay before ordering the defendant to make any payments under this chapter.

(b) Notwithstanding any other law and subject to Subsection (c), the court shall consider whether the defendant has sufficient resources or income to make any payments under this chapter, excluding restitution but including any fee, fine, reimbursement cost, court cost, rehabilitation cost, program cost, service cost, counseling cost, ignition interlock cost, assessment cost, testing cost, education cost, treatment cost, payment required under Article 42A.652, or any other payment or cost authorized or required under this chapter. The court shall consider under this subsection whether a defendant has sufficient resources or income:

(1) before or immediately after placing the defendant on community supervision, including deferred adjudication community supervision; and

(2) during the period of community supervision, before or immediately after the court orders or requires the defendant to make any payments under this chapter.

(c) Subsection (b) does not apply to consideration of a defendant's ability to pay restitution.

(d) Notwithstanding any other law, if a defendant is ordered to make a payment included under Subsection (b), the court shall reconsider whether the defendant has sufficient resources or income to make the payment at any hearing held under Article 42A.751(d).

(e) A defendant who is ordered to make a payment included under Subsection (b) may, at any time during the defendant's period of community supervision, including deferred adjudication community supervision, but not more than once in any six-month period unless the defendant shows a substantial and compelling reason for making an additional request during that period, file a written statement with the clerk of the court requesting reconsideration of the defendant's ability to make the payment and requesting that the payment be satisfied by an alternative method provided under Subsection (f). On receipt of the statement, the court shall consider whether the defendant's financial status or required payments have changed in such a way that the defendant's ability to make a payment previously ordered by the court is substantially hindered. If after conducting a review under this subsection the court finds that the defendant's ability to make a payment previously ordered by the court is substantially hindered, the court shall determine whether all or a portion of the payment should be satisfied by an alternative method provided under Subsection (f). The court shall notify the defendant and the attorney representing the state of the court's decision regarding whether to allow all or a portion of the payment to be satisfied by an alternative method.

(f) Notwithstanding any other law, if the court determines under this article at any time during a defendant's period of community supervision, including deferred adjudication community supervision, that the defendant does not have sufficient resources or income to make a payment included under Subsection (b), the court shall determine whether all or a portion of the payment should be:

(1) required to be paid at a later date or in a specified portion at designated intervals;

(2) waived completely or partially under Article 43.091 or 45.0491;

(3) discharged by performing community service under Article 42A.304 or 45.049, as applicable; or

(4) satisfied through any combination of methods under Subdivisions (1)-(3).

(g) In making a determination under Subsection (f), a court may waive completely or partially a payment required under Article 42A.652 only if, after waiving all other applicable payments included under Subsection (b), the court determines that the defendant does not have sufficient resources or income to make the payment.

(h) The Office of Court Administration of the Texas Judicial System shall adopt a standardized form that a defendant may use to make a request under Subsection (e) for the reconsideration of the defendant's ability to pay. The form must include:

(1) detailed and clear instructions for how to fill out the form and submit a request to the court; and

(2) the following statement at the top of the form, in bold type and in any language in which the form is produced: "If at any time while you are on community supervision your ability to pay any fine, fee, program cost, or other payment ordered by the court, other than restitution, changes and you cannot afford to pay, you have the right to request that the court review your payments and consider changing or waiving your payments. You can use this form to make a request for a change in your payments. You cannot use this form to request a change in restitution payments."

Code of Criminal Procedure

(i) A supervision officer or the court shall promptly provide a defendant a copy of the form adopted under Subsection (h) on the defendant's request for the form.

(j) This subsection applies only to a defendant whose payments are wholly or partly waived under this article. At any time during the defendant's period of community supervision, including deferred adjudication community supervision, the court, on the court's own motion or by motion of the attorney representing the state, may reconsider the waiver of the payment. After providing written notice to the defendant and an opportunity for the defendant to present information relevant to the defendant's ability to pay, the court may order the defendant to pay all or part of the waived amount of the payment only if the court determines that the defendant has sufficient resources or income to pay the amount.

SUBCHAPTER O REDUCTION OR TERMINATION OF COMMUNITY SUPERVISION PERIOD

Art. 42A.701. Reduction or Termination of Community Supervision Period.

(a) At any time after the defendant has satisfactorily completed one-third of the original community supervision period or two years of community supervision, whichever is less, the judge may reduce or terminate the period of community supervision.

(b) On completion of one-half of the original community supervision period or two years of community supervision, whichever is more, the judge shall review the defendant's record and consider whether to reduce or terminate the period of community supervision, unless the defendant:

(1) is delinquent in paying required restitution that the defendant has the ability to pay; or

(2) has not completed court-ordered counseling or treatment.

(b-1) The supervision officer shall notify the judge as soon as practicable after the date a defendant, who at the time of the review required by Subsection (b) was delinquent in paying restitution or had not completed court-ordered counseling or treatment, completes the remaining court-ordered counseling or treatment and makes the delinquent restitution payments, as applicable, and is otherwise compliant with the conditions of community supervision. On receipt of the notice the judge shall review the defendant's record and consider whether to reduce or terminate the period of community supervision.

(b-2) Following a review conducted under Subsection (b) or (b-1), the judge may reduce or terminate the period of community supervision or decide not to reduce or terminate the period of community supervision. In making the determination, the judge may consider any factors the judge considers relevant, including whether the defendant is delinquent in paying court-ordered costs, fines, or fees that the defendant has the ability to pay as provided by Article 42A.655.

(c) Before reducing or terminating a period of community supervision or conducting a review under this article, the judge shall notify the attorney representing the state and the defendant or, if the defendant has an attorney, the defendant's attorney.

(d) If the judge determines that the defendant has failed to satisfactorily fulfill the conditions of community supervision, the judge shall advise the defendant in writing of the requirements for satisfactorily fulfilling those conditions.

(d-1) If the judge does not terminate the defendant's period of community supervision after conducting a review under this article:

(1) the judge shall promptly advise the defendant's supervision officer of the reasons the judge did not terminate the defendant's period of community supervision; and

(2) the supervision officer shall promptly advise the defendant in writing of the reasons provided under Subdivision (1).

(e) On the satisfactory fulfillment of the conditions of community supervision and the expiration of the period of community supervision, the judge by order shall:

(1) amend or modify the original sentence imposed, if necessary, to conform to the community supervision period; and

(2) discharge the defendant.

(f) If the judge discharges the defendant under this article, the judge may set aside the verdict or permit the defendant to withdraw the defendant's plea. A judge acting under this subsection shall dismiss the accusation, complaint, information, or indictment against the defendant. A defendant who receives a discharge and dismissal under this subsection is released from all penalties and disabilities resulting from the offense of which the defendant has been convicted or to which the defendant has pleaded guilty, except that:

(1) proof of the conviction or plea of guilty shall be made known to the judge if the defendant is convicted of any subsequent offense; and

(2) if the defendant is an applicant for or the holder of a license under Chapter 42, Human Resources Code, the Department of Family and Protective Services may consider the fact that the defendant previously has received community supervision under this chapter in issuing, renewing, denying, or revoking a license under Chapter 42, Human Resources Code.

(f-1) The Office of Court Administration of the Texas Judicial System shall adopt a standardized form for use in discharging a defendant under this article. A judge discharging a defendant under this article must use the form adopted under this subsection. The form must provide for the judge to:

(1) discharge the defendant; or

(2) discharge the defendant, set aside the verdict or permit the defendant to withdraw the defendant's plea, and dismiss the accusation, complaint, information, or indictment against the defendant.

(f-2) The form adopted under Subsection (f-1) must state that a defendant who receives a discharge described by Subsection (f-1)(2) is released from the penalties and disabilities resulting from the offense as provided by Subsection (f).

(g) This article does not apply to a defendant convicted of:

(1) an offense under Sections 49.04-49.08, Penal Code;

(2) an offense the conviction of which requires registration as a sex offender under Chapter 62; or

(3) a felony described by Article 42A.054.

Art. 42A.702. Time Credits for Completion of Certain Conditions of Community Supervision.

(a) This article applies only to a defendant who:

(1) is granted community supervision, including deferred adjudication community supervision, for an offense punishable as a state jail felony or a felony of the third degree, other than an offense:

(A) included as a "reportable conviction or adjudication" under Article 62.001(5);

(B) involving family violence as defined by Section 71.004, Family Code;

(C) under Section 20.03 or 28.02, Penal Code; or

(D) under Chapter 49, Penal Code; and

(2) has fully satisfied any order to pay restitution to a victim.

(b) A defendant described by Subsection (a) is entitled to receive any combination of time credits toward the completion of the defendant's period of community supervision in accordance with this article if the court ordered the defendant as a condition of community supervision to:

(1) make a payment described by Subsection (c);

(2) complete a treatment or rehabilitation program described by Subsection (d); or

(3) earn a diploma, certificate, or degree described by Subsection (e).

(c) A defendant is entitled to time credits toward the completion of the defendant's period of community supervision for the full payment of court costs, fines, attorney's fees, and restitution as follows:

(1) court costs: 15 days;

(2) fines: 30 days;

(3) attorney's fees: 30 days; and

(4) restitution: 60 days.

(d) A defendant is entitled to time credits toward the completion of the defendant's period of community supervision for the successful completion of treatment or rehabilitation programs as follows:

(1) parenting class or parental responsibility program: 30 days;

(2) anger management program: 30 days;

(3) life skills training program: 30 days;

(4) vocational, technical, or career education or training program: 60 days;

(5) alcohol or substance abuse counseling or treatment: 90 days; and

(6) any other faith-based, volunteer, or community-based program ordered or approved by the court: 30 days.

(e) A defendant is entitled to time credits toward the completion of the defendant's period of community supervision for earning the following diplomas, certificates, or degrees:

(1) a high school diploma or high school equivalency certificate: 90 days; and

(2) an associate's degree: 120 days.

(f) A defendant's supervision officer shall notify the court if one or more time credits under this article, cumulated with the amount of the original community supervision period the defendant has completed, allow or require the court to conduct a review of the defendant's community supervision under Article 42A.701. On receipt of the notice from the supervision officer, the court shall conduct the review of the defendant's community supervision to determine if the defendant is eligible for a reduction or termination of community supervision under Article 42A.701, taking into account any time credits to which the defendant is entitled under this article in determining if the defendant has completed, as applicable:

(1) the lesser of one-third of the original community supervision period or two years of community supervision; or

(2) the greater of one-half of the original community supervision period or two years of community supervision.

(g) A court may order that some or all of the time credits to which a defendant is entitled under this article be forfeited if, before the expiration of the original period or a reduced period of community supervision, the court:

(1) after a hearing under Article 42A.751(d), finds that a defendant violated one or more conditions of community supervision; and

(2) modifies or continues the defendant's period of community supervision under Article 42A.752 or revokes the defendant's community supervision under Article 42A.755.

SUBCHAPTER P REVOCATION AND OTHER SANCTIONS

Art. 42A.751. Violation of Conditions of Community Supervision; Detention and Hearing.

(a) At any time during the period of community supervision, the judge may issue a warrant for a violation of any condition of community supervision and cause a defendant convicted under Section 43.02 or 43.021, Penal Code, Chapter 481, Health and Safety Code, or Sections 485.031 through 485.035, Health and Safety Code, or placed on deferred adjudication community supervision after being charged with one of those offenses, to be subject to:

(1) the control measures of Section 81.083, Health and Safety Code; and

(2) the court-ordered-management provisions of Subchapter G, Chapter 81, Health and Safety Code.

(b) At any time during the period of community supervision, the judge may issue a warrant for a violation of any condition of community supervision and cause the defendant to be arrested. Any supervision officer, police officer, or other officer with the power of arrest may arrest the defendant with or without a warrant on the order of the judge to be noted on the docket of the court. Subject to Subsection (c), a defendant arrested under this subsection may be detained in the county jail or other appropriate place of confinement until the defendant can be taken before the judge for a determination regarding the alleged violation. The arresting officer shall immediately report the arrest and detention to the judge.

(c) Without any unnecessary delay, but not later than 48 hours after the defendant is arrested, the arresting officer or the person with custody of the defendant shall take the defendant before the judge who ordered the arrest for the alleged violation of a condition of community supervision or, if the judge is unavailable, before a magistrate of the county in which the defendant was arrested. The judge or magistrate shall perform all appropriate duties and may exercise all appropriate powers as provided by Article 15.17 with respect to an arrest for a new offense, except that only the judge who ordered the arrest for the alleged violation may authorize the defendant's release on bail. The defendant may be taken before the judge or magistrate under this subsection by means of an electronic broadcast system as provided by and subject to the requirements of Article 15.17.

(d) If the defendant has not been released on bail as permitted under Subsection (c), on motion by the defendant, the judge who ordered the arrest for the alleged violation of a condition of community supervision shall cause the defendant to be brought before the judge for a hearing on the alleged violation within 20 days of the date the motion is filed. After a hearing without a jury, the judge may continue, extend, modify, or revoke the community supervision.

(e) A judge may revoke without a hearing the community supervision of a defendant who is imprisoned in a penal institution if the defendant in writing before a court of record or a notary public in the jurisdiction where the defendant is imprisoned:

(1) waives the defendant's right to a hearing and to counsel;

(2) affirms that the defendant has nothing to say as to why sentence should not be pronounced against the defendant; and

(3) requests the judge to revoke community supervision and to pronounce sentence.

(f) In a felony case, the state may amend the motion to revoke community supervision at any time before the seventh day before the date of the revocation hearing, after which time the motion may not be amended except for good cause shown. The state may not amend the motion after the commencement of taking evidence at the revocation hearing.

(g) The judge may continue the revocation hearing for good cause shown by either the defendant or the state.

(h) The court may not revoke the community supervision of a defendant if, at the revocation hearing, the court finds that the only evidence supporting the alleged violation of a condition of community supervision is the uncorroborated results of a polygraph examination.

(i) In a revocation hearing at which it is alleged only that the defendant violated the conditions of community supervision by failing to pay community supervision fees or court costs or by failing to pay the costs of legal services as described by Article 42A.301(b)(11), the state must prove by a preponderance of the evidence that the defendant was able to pay and did not pay as ordered by the judge.

(j) The court may order a community supervision and corrections department to obtain information pertaining to the factors listed under Article 42.037(h) and include that information in the presentence report required under Article 42A.252(a) or a separate report, as the court directs.

(k) A defendant has a right to counsel at a hearing under this article. The court shall appoint counsel for an indigent defendant in accordance with the procedures adopted under Article 26.04.

(l) A court retains jurisdiction to hold a hearing under Subsection (d) and to revoke, continue, or modify community supervision, regardless of whether the period of community supervision imposed on the defendant has expired, if before the expiration of the supervision period:

(1) the attorney representing the state files a motion to revoke, continue, or modify community supervision; and

(2) a capias is issued for the arrest of the defendant.

Art. 42A.752. Continuation or Modification of Community Supervision After Violation.

(a) If after a hearing under Article 42A.751(d) a judge continues or modifies community supervision after determining that the defendant violated a condition of community supervision, the judge may impose any other conditions the judge determines are appropriate, including:

(1) a requirement that the defendant perform community service for a number of hours specified by the court under Article 42A.304, or an increase in the number of hours that the defendant has previously been required to perform under that article in an amount not to exceed double the number of hours permitted by that article;

(2) an extension of the period of community supervision, in the manner described by Article 42A.753;

(3) an increase in the defendant's fine, in the manner described by Subsection (b); or

(4) the placement of the defendant in a substance abuse felony punishment program operated under Section 493.009, Government Code, if:

(A) the defendant is convicted of a felony other than:

(i) a felony under Section 21.11, 22.011, or 22.021, Penal Code; or

(ii) criminal attempt of a felony under Section 21.11, 22.011, or 22.021, Penal Code; and

(B) the judge makes an affirmative finding that:

(i) drug or alcohol abuse significantly contributed to the commission of the offense or violation of a condition of community supervision, as applicable; and

(ii) the defendant is a suitable candidate for treatment, as determined by the suitability criteria established by the Texas Board of Criminal Justice under Section 493.009(b), Government Code.

(b) A judge may impose a sanction on a defendant described by Subsection (a)(3) by increasing the fine imposed on the defendant. The original fine imposed on the defendant and an increase in the fine imposed under this subsection may not exceed the maximum fine for the offense for which the defendant was sentenced. The judge shall deposit money received from an increase in the defendant's fine under this subsection in the special fund of the county treasury to be used for the same purposes for which state aid may be used under Chapter 76, Government Code.

(c) If the judge imposes a sanction under Subsection (a)(4), the judge shall also impose a condition requiring the defendant on successful completion of the program to participate in a drug or alcohol abuse continuum of care treatment plan.

Art. 42A.753. Extension of Community Supervision After Violation.

(a) On a showing of good cause, the judge may extend a period of community supervision under Article 42A.752(a)(2) as frequently as the judge determines is necessary, but the period of community supervision in a first, second, or third degree felony case may not exceed 10 years and, except as otherwise provided by Subsection (b), the period of community supervision in a misdemeanor case may not exceed three years.

(b) The judge may extend the period of community supervision in a misdemeanor case for any period the judge determines is necessary, not to exceed an additional two years beyond the three-year limit provided by Subsection (a), if:

(1) the defendant fails to pay a previously assessed fine, cost, or restitution; and

(2) the judge determines that extending the supervision period increases the likelihood that the defendant will fully pay the fine, cost, or restitution.

(c) A court may extend a period of community supervision under Article 42A.752(a)(2):

(1) at any time during the supervision period; or

(2) before the first anniversary of the date the supervision period ends, if a motion for revocation of

community supervision is filed before the date the supervision period ends.

Art. 42A.754. Authority to Revoke Community Supervision.

Only the court in which the defendant was tried may revoke the defendant's community supervision unless the judge has transferred jurisdiction of the case to another court under Article 42A.151.

Art. 42A.755. Revocation of Community Supervision.

(a) If community supervision is revoked after a hearing under Article 42A.751(d), the judge may:

(1) proceed to dispose of the case as if there had been no community supervision; or

(2) if the judge determines that the best interests of society and the defendant would be served by a shorter term of confinement, reduce the term of confinement originally assessed to any term of confinement not less than the minimum prescribed for the offense of which the defendant was convicted.

(b) The judge shall enter in the judgment in the case the amount of restitution owed by the defendant on the date of revocation.

(c) Except as otherwise provided by Subsection (d), no part of the period that the defendant is on community supervision may be considered as any part of the term that the defendant is sentenced to serve.

(d) On revocation, the judge shall credit to the defendant time served as a condition of community supervision in a substance abuse felony punishment facility operated by the Texas Department of Criminal Justice under Section 493.009, Government Code, or other court-ordered residential program or facility, but only if the defendant successfully completes the treatment program in that facility.

(e) The right of the defendant to appeal for a review of the conviction and punishment, as provided by law, shall be accorded the defendant at the time the defendant is placed on community supervision. When the defendant is notified that the defendant's community supervision is revoked for a violation of the conditions of community supervision and the defendant is called on to serve a sentence in a jail or in the Texas Department of Criminal Justice, the defendant may appeal the revocation.

Art. 42A.756. Due Diligence Defense.

For the purposes of a hearing under Article 42A.751(d), it is an affirmative defense to revocation for an alleged violation based on a failure to report to a supervision officer as directed or to remain within a specified place that no supervision officer, peace officer, or other officer with the power of arrest under a warrant issued by a judge for that alleged violation contacted or attempted to contact the defendant in person at the defendant's last known residence address or last known employment address, as reflected in the files of the department serving the county in which the order of community supervision was entered.

Art. 42A.757. Extension of Community Supervision for Certain Sex Offenders.

(a) If a defendant is placed on community supervision after receiving a grant of deferred adjudication community supervision for or being convicted of an offense under Section 21.11, 22.011, or 22.021, Penal Code, at any time during the period of community supervision, the judge may extend the period of community supervision as provided by this article.

(b) At a hearing at which the defendant is provided the same rights as are provided to a defendant at a hearing under Article 42A.751(d), the judge may extend the defendant's supervision period for a period not to exceed 10 additional years if the judge determines that:

(1) the defendant has not sufficiently demonstrated a commitment to avoid future criminal behavior; and

(2) the release of the defendant from supervision would endanger the public.

(c) A judge may extend a period of community supervision under this article only once.

(d) A judge may extend a period of community supervision for a defendant under both Article 42A.752(a)(2) and this article.

(e) The prohibition in Article 42A.753(a) against a period of community supervision in a felony case exceeding 10 years does not apply to a defendant for whom community supervision is increased under this article or under both Article 42A.752(a)(2) and this article.

CHAPTER 43 EXECUTION OF JUDGMENT

Art. 43.01. Discharging Judgment for Fine.

(a) When the sentence against an individual defendant is for fine and costs, he shall be discharged from the same:

(1) when the amount thereof has been fully paid;
(2) when remitted by the proper authority;
(3) when he has remained in custody for the time required by law to satisfy the amount thereof; or
(4) when the defendant has discharged the amount of fines and costs in any other manner permitted by this code.

(b) When the sentence against a defendant corporation or association is for fine and costs, it shall be discharged from same:
(1) when the amount thereof has been fully paid;
(2) when the execution against the corporation or association has been fully satisfied; or
(3) when the judgment has been fully satisfied in any other manner.

Art. 43.015. Definitions.

In this chapter:
(1) "Capias" means a writ that is:
(A) issued by a court having jurisdiction of a case after judgment and sentence; and
(B) directed "To any peace officer of the State of Texas" and commanding the officer to arrest a person convicted of an offense and bring the arrested person before that court immediately or on a day or at a term stated in the writ.
(2) "Capias pro fine" means a writ that is:
(A) issued by a court having jurisdiction of a case after judgment and sentence for unpaid fines and costs; and
(B) directed "To any peace officer of the State of Texas" and commanding the officer to arrest a person convicted of an offense and bring the arrested person before that court immediately.
(3) "Cost" includes any fee, including a reimbursement fee, imposed on a defendant by the court.

Art. 43.02. Payable in Money.

All recognizances, bail bonds, and undertakings of any kind, whereby a party becomes bound to pay money to the State, and all fines and forfeitures of a pecuniary character, shall be collected in the lawful money of the United States only.

Art. 43.021. Capias or Capias Pro Fine in Electronic Form.

A capias or capias pro fine may be issued in electronic form.

Art. 43.03. Payment of Fine.

(a) If a defendant is sentenced to pay a fine or costs or both and the defendant defaults in payment, the court after a hearing under Subsection (d) of this article may order the defendant confined in jail until discharged as provided by law, may order the defendant to discharge the fines and costs in any other manner provided by Article 43.09 of this code, or may waive payment of the fines and costs as provided by Article 43.091. A certified copy of the judgment, sentence, and order is sufficient to authorize confinement under this subsection.

(b) A term of confinement for default in payment of fine or costs or both may not exceed the maximum term of confinement authorized for the offense for which the defendant was sentenced to pay the fine or costs or both. If a court orders a term of confinement for default in payment of fines or costs under this article at a time during which a defendant is serving another term of confinement for default or is serving a term of confinement for conviction of an offense, the term of confinement for default runs concurrently with the other term of confinement, unless the court orders the terms to run consecutively under Article 42.08 of this code.

(c) If a defendant is sentenced both to confinement and to pay a fine or costs or both, and he defaults in payment of either, a term of confinement for the default, when combined with the term of confinement already assessed, may not exceed the maximum term of confinement authorized for the offense for which the defendant was sentenced.

(d) A court may not order a defendant confined under Subsection (a) of this article unless the court at a hearing makes a written determination that:
(1) the defendant is not indigent and has failed to make a good faith effort to discharge the fines and costs; or
(2) the defendant is indigent and:
(A) has failed to make a good faith effort to discharge the fines and costs under Article 43.09(f); and
(B) could have discharged the fines and costs under Article 43.09 without experiencing any undue hardship.

(e) This article does not apply to a court governed by Chapter 45.

(f) For purposes of a hearing described by Subsection (d), a defendant may be brought before the court in person or by means of an electronic broadcast system through which an image of the defendant is presented to the court. For purposes of this subsection, "electronic broadcast system" means a two-way electronic communication of image and sound between the defendant and the court and includes secure Internet videoconferencing.

Art. 43.035. Reconsideration of Fine or Costs.

(a) If a defendant notifies the court that the defendant has difficulty paying the fine and costs in compliance with the judgment, the court shall hold a hearing to determine whether that portion of the judgment imposes an undue hardship on the defendant.

(b) For purposes of Subsection (a), a defendant may notify the court by:

(1) voluntarily appearing and informing the court or the clerk of the court in the manner established by the court for that purpose;

(2) filing a motion with the court;

(3) mailing a letter to the court; or

(4) any other method established by the court for that purpose.

(c) If the court determines at the hearing under Subsection (a) that the portion of the judgment regarding the fine and costs imposes an undue hardship on the defendant, the court shall consider whether the fine and costs should be satisfied through one or more methods listed under Article 42.15(a-1).

(d) The court may decline to hold a hearing under Subsection (a) if the court:

(1) previously held a hearing under that subsection with respect to the case and is able to determine without holding a hearing that the portion of the judgment regarding the fine and costs does not impose an undue hardship on the defendant; or

(2) is able to determine without holding a hearing that:

(A) the applicable portion of the judgment imposes an undue hardship on the defendant; and

(B) the fine and costs should be satisfied through one or more methods listed under Article 42.15(a-1).

(e) The court retains jurisdiction for the purpose of making a determination under this article.

Art. 43.04. If Defendant Is Absent.

When a judgment and sentence have been rendered against a defendant in the defendant's absence, the court may order a capias issued for the defendant's arrest. The sheriff shall execute the capias by bringing the defendant before the court or by placing the defendant in jail until the defendant can be brought before the court.

Art. 43.05. Issuance and Recall of Capias Pro Fine.

(a) A capias pro fine issued for the arrest and commitment of a defendant convicted of a misdemeanor or felony, or found in contempt, the penalty for which includes a fine, shall recite the judgment and sentence and command a peace officer to immediately bring the defendant before the court.

(a-1) A court may not issue a capias pro fine for the defendant's failure to satisfy the judgment according to its terms unless the court holds a hearing to determine whether the judgment imposes an undue hardship on the defendant and the defendant fails to:

(1) appear at the hearing; or

(2) comply with an order issued under Subsection (a-3) as a result of the hearing.

(a-2) If the court determines at the hearing under Subsection (a-1) that the judgment imposes an undue hardship on the defendant, the court shall determine whether the fine and costs should be satisfied through one or more methods listed under Article 42.15(a-1). The court retains jurisdiction for the purpose of making a determination under this subsection.

(a-3) If the court determines at the hearing under Subsection (a-1) that the judgment does not impose an undue hardship on the defendant, the court shall order the defendant to comply with the judgment not later than the 30th day after the date the determination is made.

(a-4) The court shall recall a capias pro fine if, before the capias pro fine is executed, the defendant:

(1) provides notice to the court under Article 43.035 and a hearing is set under that article; or

(2) voluntarily appears and makes a good faith effort to resolve the capias pro fine.

(b) A capias pro fine authorizes a peace officer to place the defendant in jail until the business day following the date of the defendant's arrest if the defendant cannot be brought before the court immediately.

(c) **[2 Versions: As added by Acts 2015, 84th Leg., ch. 1171]** If the court that issued the capias pro fine is unavailable, the arresting officer may, in lieu of placing the defendant in jail, take the defendant to:

(1) another court in the same county with jurisdiction over Class A and Class B misdemeanors or a county criminal law magistrate court in the same county, if the court that issued the capias pro fine was a county court or a statutory county court with Class A and Class B misdemeanor jurisdiction; or

(2) another court in the same county with jurisdiction over felony cases or a county criminal law magistrate court in the same county, if the court that issued the capias pro fine was a district court with felony jurisdiction.

(c) **[2 Versions: As added by Acts 2015, 84th Leg., ch. 1182]** If the court that issued the capias pro fine is unavailable, the arresting officer may take the defendant to one of the following locations in lieu of placing the defendant in jail:

(1) if the court that issued the capias pro fine was a county court or a statutory county court with Class A and Class B misdemeanor jurisdiction, to another court in the same county with concurrent jurisdiction over Class A and Class B misdemeanors or to a county criminal law magistrate in the same county; or

(2) if the court that issued the capias pro fine was a district court with felony jurisdiction, to another court in the same county with concurrent jurisdiction over felony cases or to a county criminal law magistrate in the same county.

Art. 43.06. Capias or Capias Pro Fine May Issue to Any County.

A capias or capias pro fine may be issued to any county in the State, and shall be executed and returned as in other cases, but no bail shall be taken in such cases.

Art. 43.07. Execution for Fine and Costs.

In each case of pecuniary fine, an execution may issue for the fine and costs, though a capias pro fine was issued for the defendant; and a capias pro fine may issue for the defendant though an execution was issued against the defendant's property. The execution shall be collected and returned as in civil actions. When the execution has been collected, the defendant shall be at once discharged; and whenever the fine and costs have been legally discharged in any way, the execution shall be returned satisfied.

Art. 43.08. Further Enforcement of Judgment.

When a defendant has been committed to jail in default of the fine and costs adjudged against him, the further enforcement of such judgment and sentence shall be in accordance with the provisions of this Code.

Art. 43.09. Fine Discharged.

(a) When a defendant is convicted of a misdemeanor and the defendant's punishment is assessed at a pecuniary fine or is confined in a jail after conviction of a felony for which a fine is imposed, if the defendant is unable to pay the fine and costs adjudged against the defendant, the defendant may for such time as will satisfy the judgment be put to work in the county jail industries program, in the workhouse, or on the county farm, or public improvements and maintenance projects of the county or a political subdivision located in whole or in part in the county, as provided in Article 43.10; or if there is no such county jail industries program, workhouse, farm, or improvements and maintenance projects, the defendant shall be confined in jail for a sufficient length of time to discharge the full amount of fine and costs adjudged against the defendant; rating such confinement at $100 for each day and rating such labor at $100 for each day; provided, however, that the defendant may pay the pecuniary fine assessed against the defendant at any time while the defendant is serving at work in the county jail industries program, in the workhouse, or on the county farm, or on the public improvements and maintenance projects of the county or a political subdivision located in whole or in part in the county, or while the defendant is serving the defendant's jail sentence, and in such instances the defendant is entitled to the credit earned under this subsection during the time that the defendant has served and the defendant shall only be required to pay the balance of the pecuniary fine assessed against the defendant. A defendant who performs labor under this article during a day in which the defendant is confined is entitled to both the credit for confinement and the credit for labor provided by this article.

(b) In its discretion, the court may order that for each day's confinement served by a defendant under this article, the defendant receive credit toward payment of the pecuniary fine and credit toward payment of costs adjudged against the defendant. Additionally, the court may order that the defendant receive credit under this article for each day's confinement served by the defendant as punishment for the offense.

(c) In its discretion, the court may order that a defendant serving concurrent, but not consecutive, sentences for two or more misdemeanors may, for each day served, receive credit toward the satisfaction of costs and fines imposed for each separate offense.

(d) Notwithstanding any other provision of this article, in its discretion, the court or the sheriff of the county may grant an additional two days credit for each day served to any inmate participating in an approved work program under this article or a rehabilitation, restitution, or education program.

(e) A court in a county that operates an electronic monitoring program or contracts with a private vendor to operate an electronic monitoring program under Section 351.904, Local Government Code, or that is served by a community supervision and corrections department that operates an electronic monitoring program approved by the community justice assistance division of the Texas Department of Criminal Justice, may require a defendant who is unable to pay a fine or costs to discharge all or part of the fine or costs by participating in the program. A defendant who participates in an electronic monitoring program under this subsection discharges fines and costs in the same manner as if the defendant were confined in county jail.

(f) A court may require a defendant who is unable to pay a fine or costs to discharge all or part of the fine or costs by performing community service.

(g) In the court's order requiring a defendant to perform community service under Subsection (f), the court must specify:

(1) the number of hours of community service the defendant is required to perform;

(2) whether the community supervision and corrections department or a court-related services office will perform the administrative duties required by the placement of the defendant in the community service program; and

(3) the date by which the defendant must submit to the court documentation verifying the defendant's completion of the community service.

(h) The court may order the defendant to perform community service under Subsection (f):

(1) by attending:

(A) a work and job skills training program;

(B) a preparatory class for the high school equivalency examination administered under Section 7.111, Education Code;

(C) an alcohol or drug abuse program;

(D) a rehabilitation program;

(E) a counseling program, including a self-improvement program;

(F) a mentoring program; or

(G) any similar activity; or

(2) for:

(A) a governmental entity;

(B) a nonprofit organization or another organization that provides services to the general public that enhance social welfare and the general well-being of the community, as determined by the court; or

(C) an educational institution.

(h-1) An entity that accepts a defendant under Subsection (f) to perform community service must agree to supervise, either on-site or remotely, the defendant in the performance of the defendant's community service and report on the defendant's community service to the district probation department or court-related services office.

(i) The court may require bail of a defendant to ensure the defendant's faithful performance of community service under Subsection (f) of this article and may attach conditions to the bail as it determines are proper.

(j) A court may not order a defendant to perform more than 16 hours per week of community service under Subsection (f) unless the court determines that requiring the defendant to perform additional hours does not impose an undue hardship on the defendant or the defendant's dependents.

(k) A defendant is considered to have discharged $100 of fines or costs for each eight hours of community service performed under Subsection (f) of this article.

(*l*) A sheriff, employee of a sheriff's department, county commissioner, county employee, county judge, an employee of a community corrections and supervision department, restitution center, or officer or employee of a political subdivision other than a county or an entity that accepts a defendant under this article to perform community service is not liable for damages arising from an act or failure to act in connection with manual labor performed by an inmate or community service performed by a defendant under this article if the act or failure to act:

(1) was performed pursuant to confinement or other court order; and

(2) was not intentional, wilfully or wantonly negligent, or performed with conscious indifference or reckless disregard for the safety of others.

(m) [Repealed by Acts 2007, 80th Leg., ch. 1263 (H.B. 3060), § 22, effective September 1, 2007.]

(n) This article does not apply to a court governed by Chapter 45.

Art. 43.091. Waiver of Payment of Fines and Costs for Certain Defendants and for Children.

(a) A court may waive payment of all or part of a fine imposed on a defendant if the court determines that:

(1) the defendant is indigent or does not have sufficient resources or income to pay all or part of the fine or was, at the time the offense was committed, a child as defined by Article 45.058(h); and

(2) each alternative method of discharging the fine under Article 43.09 or 42.15 would impose an undue hardship on the defendant.

(b) A determination of undue hardship made under Subsection (a)(2) is in the court's discretion. In making that determination, the court may consider, as applicable, the defendant's:

(1) significant physical or mental impairment or disability;

(2) pregnancy and childbirth;

(3) substantial family commitments or responsibilities, including child or dependent care;

(4) work responsibilities and hours;
(5) transportation limitations;
(6) homelessness or housing insecurity; and
(7) any other factor the court determines relevant.

(c) A court may waive payment of all or part of the costs imposed on a defendant if the court determines that the defendant:

(1) is indigent or does not have sufficient resources or income to pay all or part of the costs; or

(2) was, at the time the offense was committed, a child as defined by Article 45.058(h).

(d) This subsection applies only to a defendant placed on community supervision, including deferred adjudication community supervision, whose fine or costs are wholly or partly waived under this article. At any time during the defendant's period of community supervision, the court, on the court's own motion or by motion of the attorney representing the state, may reconsider the waiver of the fine or costs. After providing written notice to the defendant and an opportunity for the defendant to present information relevant to the defendant's ability to pay, the court may order the defendant to pay all or part of the waived amount of the fine or costs only if the court determines that the defendant has sufficient resources or income to pay that amount.

Art. 43.10. Manual Labor.

Where the punishment assessed in a conviction for a misdemeanor is confinement in jail for more than one day or is only a pecuniary fine and the defendant is unable to pay the fine and costs adjudged against the defendant, or where the defendant is sentenced to jail for a felony or is confined in jail after conviction of a felony, the defendant shall be required to work in the county jail industries program or shall be required to do manual labor in accordance with the following rules and regulations:

1. Each commissioners court may provide for the erection of a workhouse and the establishment of a county farm in connection therewith for the purpose of utilizing the labor of defendants under this article;

2. Such farms and workhouses shall be under the control and management of the sheriff, and the sheriff may adopt such rules and regulations not inconsistent with the rules and regulations of the Commission on Jail Standards and with the laws as the sheriff deems necessary;

3. Such overseers and guards may be employed by the sheriff under the authority of the commissioners court as may be necessary to prevent escapes and to enforce such labor, and they shall be paid out of the county treasury such compensation as the commissioners court may prescribe;

4. They shall be put to labor upon public works and maintenance projects, including public works and maintenance projects for a political subdivision located in whole or in part in the county. They may be put to labor upon maintenance projects for a cemetery that the commissioners court uses public funds, county employees, or county equipment to maintain under Section 713.028, Health and Safety Code. They may also be put to labor providing maintenance and related services to a nonprofit organization that qualifies for a tax exemption under Section 501(a), Internal Revenue Code of 1986, as an organization described by Section 501(c)(3) of that code, and is organized as a nonprofit corporation under the Texas Non-Profit Corporation Act (Article 1396-1.01 et seq., Vernon's Texas Civil Statutes), provided that, at the sheriff's request, the commissioners court determines that the nonprofit organization provides a public service to the county or to a political subdivision located in whole or in part in the county;

5. A defendant who from age, disease, or other physical or mental disability is unable to do manual labor shall not be required to work. The defendant's inability to do manual labor may be determined by a physician appointed for that purpose by the county judge or the commissioners court, who shall be paid for such service such compensation as said court may allow; and

6. For each day of manual labor, in addition to any other credits allowed by law, a defendant is entitled to have one day deducted from each sentence the defendant is serving.

Art. 43.101. Voluntary Work.

(a) A defendant who is confined in county jail before trial, after conviction of a misdemeanor, or after conviction of a felony or revocation of community supervision, parole, or mandatory supervision and awaiting transfer to the Texas Department of Criminal Justice may volunteer to participate in any work program operated by the sheriff that uses the labor of convicted defendants.

(b) The sheriff may accept a defendant as a volunteer under Subsection (a) if the defendant is not awaiting trial for an offense involving violence or is not awaiting transfer to the Texas Department of Criminal Justice after conviction of a felony involving violence, and if the sheriff determines that the inmate has not engaged previously in violent conduct and does not pose a security risk to the general public if allowed to participate in the work program.

(c) A defendant participating in a work program under this section is not an employee for the purposes of Chapter 501 or 504, Labor Code.

(d) For each day of volunteer work, in addition to any other credits allowed by law, the court or sheriff may deduct one day from each sentence imposed on the defendant in relation to the offense or violation of the terms of release for which the defendant was confined in county jail.

Art. 43.11. Authority for Confinement.

When, by the judgment and sentence of the court, a defendant is to be confined in jail, a certified copy of such judgment and sentence shall be sufficient authority for the sheriff to place such defendant in jail.

Art. 43.12. Capias for Confinement [Repealed].

Repealed by Acts 2007, 80th Leg., ch. 1263 (H.B. 3060), § 22, effective September 1, 2007.

Art. 43.13. Discharge of Defendant.

(a) A defendant who has remained in jail the length of time required by the judgment and sentence shall be discharged. The sheriff shall return the copy of the judgment and sentence, or the capias under which the defendant was imprisoned, to the proper court, stating how it was executed.

(b) A defendant convicted of a misdemeanor and sentenced to a term of confinement discharges the defendant's sentence at any time beginning at 6 a.m. and ending at 5 p.m. on the day of discharge.

(c) Except as provided by Subsections (d) and (e), the sheriff or other county jail administrator shall release a defendant at any time beginning at 6 a.m. and ending at 5 p.m. on the day the defendant discharges the defendant's sentence.

(d) The sheriff or other county jail administrator may:

(1) credit a defendant with not more than 18 hours of time served; and

(2) release the defendant at any time beginning at 6 a.m. and ending at 5 p.m. on the day preceding the day on which the defendant discharges the defendant's sentence.

(e) A sheriff or other county jail administrator may release a defendant from county jail after 5 p.m. and before 6 a.m. if the defendant:

(1) agrees to or requests a release after 5 p.m. and before 6 a.m.;

(2) is subject to an arrest warrant issued by another county and is being released for purposes of executing that arrest warrant;

(3) is being transferred to the custody of another state, a unit of the federal government, or a facility operated by or under contract with the Texas Department of Criminal Justice; or

(4) is being admitted to an inpatient mental health facility or a state supported living center for court-ordered mental health or intellectual disability services.

Art. 43.131. Immunities.

(a) An individual listed in Subsection (c) of this article and the governmental entity that the individual serves as an officer or employee are not liable for damages arising from an act or failure to act by the individual or governmental entity in connection with a community service program or work program established under this chapter if the act or failure to act:

(1) was performed pursuant to a court order or was otherwise performed in an official capacity; and

(2) was not performed with conscious indifference for the safety of others.

(b) Chapter 101, Civil Practice and Remedies Code, does not apply to a claim based on an act or a failure to act of an individual listed in Subsection (c) of this article or a governmental entity the officer serves as an officer or employee if the act or failure to act is in connection with a program described by Subsection (a) of this article.

(c) This article applies to:

(1) a director or employee of a community supervision and corrections department or a community corrections facility;

(2) a sheriff or employee of a sheriff's department;

(3) a county judge, county commissioner, or county employee;

(4) an officer or employee of a state agency; or

(5) an officer or employee of a political subdivision other than a county.

Art. 43.14. Execution of Convict: Confidential Information.

(a) Whenever the sentence of death is pronounced against a convict, the sentence shall be executed at any time after the hour of 6 p.m. on the day set for the execution, by intravenous injection of a substance or substances in a lethal quantity sufficient to cause death and until such convict is dead, such execution procedure to be determined and supervised by the director of the correctional institutions division of the Texas Department of Criminal Justice.

(b) The name, address, and other identifying information of the following is confidential and excepted from disclosure under Section 552.021, Government Code:

(1) any person who participates in an execution procedure described by Subsection (a), including a person who uses, supplies, or administers a substance during the execution; and

(2) any person or entity that manufactures, transports, tests, procures, compounds, prescribes, dispenses, or provides a substance or supplies used in an execution.

Art. 43.141. Scheduling of Execution Date; Withdrawal; Modification.

(a) If an initial application under Article 11.071 is timely filed, the convicting court may not set an execution date before:

(1) the court of criminal appeals denies relief; or

(2) if the case is filed and set for submission, the court of criminal appeals issues a mandate.

(b) If an original application is not timely filed under Article 11.071 or good cause is not shown for an untimely application under Article 11.071, the convicting court may set an execution date.

(b-1) Not later than the second business day after the date on which the convicting court enters an order setting the execution date, a copy of the order must be sent by first-class mail, e-mail, or fax to:

(1) the attorney who represented the condemned person in the most recently concluded stage of a state or federal postconviction proceeding; and

(2) the office of capital writs established under Subchapter B, Chapter 78, Government Code.

(b-2) The exclusive remedy for a failure to comply with Subsection (b-1) is the resetting of the execution date under this article.

(c) An execution date may not be earlier than the 91st day after the date the convicting court enters the order setting the execution date.

(d) The convicting court may modify or withdraw the order of the court setting a date for execution in a death penalty case if the court determines that additional proceedings are necessary on:

(1) a subsequent or untimely application for a writ of habeas corpus filed under Article 11.071; or

(2) a motion for forensic testing of DNA evidence submitted under Chapter 64.

(e) If the convicting court withdraws the order of the court setting the execution date, the court shall recall the warrant of execution. If the court modifies the order of the court setting the execution date, the court shall recall the previous warrant of execution, and the clerk of the court shall issue a new warrant.

Art. 43.15. Warrant of Execution.

(a) Whenever any person is sentenced to death, the clerk of the court in which the sentence is pronounced shall, not later than the 10th day after the court enters its order setting the date for execution, issue a warrant under the seal of the court for the execution of the sentence of death, which shall recite the fact of conviction, setting forth specifically the offense, the judgment of the court, and the time fixed for the execution, and which shall be directed to the director of the correctional institutions division of the Texas Department of Criminal Justice at Huntsville, Texas, commanding the director to proceed, at the time and place named in the order of execution, to carry the same into execution, as provided in Article 43.14, and shall deliver such warrant to the sheriff of the county in which such judgment of conviction was had, to be delivered by the sheriff to the director, together with the condemned person if the person has not previously been so delivered.

(b) At the time the warrant is issued under Subsection (a), the clerk of the court shall send a copy of the warrant to:

(1) the attorney who represented the condemned person in the most recently concluded stage of a state or federal postconviction proceeding;

(2) the attorney representing the state; and

(3) the office of capital writs established under Subchapter B, Chapter 78, Government Code.

Art. 43.16. Taken to Department of Corrections.

Immediately upon the receipt of such warrant, the sheriff shall transport such condemned person to the Director of the Department of Corrections, if he has not already been so delivered, and shall deliver him and the warrant aforesaid into the hands of the Director of the Department of Corrections and shall take from the Director of the Department of Corrections his receipt for such person and such warrant, which receipt the sheriff shall return to the office of the clerk of the court where the judgment of death was rendered. For his services, the sheriff shall be entitled to the same compensation as is now allowed by law to sheriffs for removing or conveying prisoners under the provisions of Section 4 of Article 1029 or 1030 of the Code of Criminal Procedure of 1925, as amended.

Art. 43.17. Visitors.

Upon the receipt of such condemned person by the Director of the Department of Corrections, the condemned person shall be confined therein until the time for his or her execution arrives, and while so confined, all persons outside of said prison shall be denied access to him or her, except his or her physician, lawyer, and clergyperson, who shall be admitted to see him or her when necessary for his or her health or for the transaction of business, and the relatives and friends of the condemned person, who shall be admitted to see and converse with him or her at all proper times, under such reasonable rules and regulations as may be made by the Board of Directors of the Department of Corrections.

Art. 43.18. Executioner.

The director of the Texas Department of Criminal Justice shall designate an executioner to carry out the death penalty provided by law.

Art. 43.19. Place of Execution.

The execution shall take place at a location designated by the Texas Department of Criminal Justice in a room arranged for that purpose.

Art. 43.20. Present at Execution.

The following persons may be present at the execution: the executioner, and such persons as may be necessary to assist him in conducting the execution; the Board of Directors of the Department of Corrections, two physicians, including the prison physician, the spiritual advisor of the condemned, the chaplains of the Department of Corrections, the county judge and sheriff of the county in which the Department of Corrections is situated, and any of the relatives or friends of the condemned person that he may request, not exceeding five in number, shall be admitted. No convict shall be permitted by the prison authorities to witness the execution.

Art. 43.21. Escape After Sentence.

If the condemned escape after sentence and before his delivery to the Director of the Department of Corrections, and be not rearrested until after the time fixed for execution, any person may arrest and commit him to the jail of the county in which he was sentenced; and thereupon the court by whom the condemned was sentenced; either in term-time or vacation, on notice of such arrest being given by the sheriff, shall again appoint a time for the execution, not less than thirty days from such appointment, which appointment shall be by the clerk of said court immediately certified to the Director of the Department of Corrections and such clerk shall place such certificate in the hands of the sheriff, who shall deliver the same, together with the warrant aforesaid and the condemned person to the Director of the Department of Corrections, who shall receipt to the sheriff for the same and proceed at the appointed time to carry the sentence of death into execution as hereinabove provided.

Art. 43.22. Escape from Department of Corrections.

If the condemned person escapes after his delivery to the Director of the Department of Corrections, and is not retaken before the time appointed for his execution, any person may arrest and commit him to the Director of the Department of Corrections whereupon the Director of the Department of Corrections shall certify the fact of his escape and recapture to the court in which sentence was passed; and the court, either in term-time or vacation, shall again appoint a time for the execution which shall not be less than thirty days from the date of such appointment; and thereupon the clerk of such court shall certify such appointment to the Director of the Department of Corrections, who shall proceed at the time so appointed to execute the condemned, as hereinabove provided. The sheriff or other officer or other person performing any service under this and the preceding Article shall receive the same compensation as is provided for similar services under the provisions of Articles 1029 or 1030 of the Code of Criminal Procedure of 1925, as amended. If for any reason execution is delayed beyond the date set, then the court which originally sentenced the defendant may set a later date for execution.

Art. 43.23. Return of Director.

When the execution of sentence is suspended or respited to another date, same shall be noted on the warrant and on the arrival of such date, the Director of the Department of Corrections shall proceed with such execution; and in case of death of any condemned person before the time for his execution arrives, or if he should be pardoned or his sentence commuted by the Governor, no execution shall be had; but in such cases, as well as when the sentence is executed, the Director of the Department of Corrections shall return the warrant and certificate with a statement of any such act and his proceedings endorsed thereon, together with a statement showing what disposition was made of the dead body of the convict, to the clerk of the court in which the sentence was passed, who shall record the warrant and return in the minutes of the court.

Art. 43.24. Treatment of Condemned.

No torture, or ill treatment, or unnecessary pain, shall be inflicted upon a prisoner to be executed under the sentence of the law.

Art. 43.25. Body of Convict.

The body of a convict who has been legally executed shall be embalmed immediately and so directed by the Director of the Department of Corrections. If the body is not demanded or requested by a relative or bona fide friend within forty-eight hours after execution then it shall be delivered to the Anatomical Board of the State of Texas, if requested by the Board. If the body is requested by a relative, bona fide friend, or the Anatomical Board of the State of Texas, such recipient shall pay a fee of not to exceed twenty-five dollars to the mortician for his services in embalming the body for which the mortician shall issue to the recipient a written receipt. When such receipt is delivered to the Director of the Department of Corrections, the body of the deceased shall be delivered to the party named in the receipt or his authorized agent. If the body is not delivered to a relative, bona fide friend, or the Anatomical Board of the State of Texas, the Director of the Department of Corrections shall cause the body to be decently buried, and the fee for embalming shall be paid by the county in which the indictment which resulted in conviction was found.

Art. 43.26. Preventing Rescue.

The sheriff may, when he supposes there will be a necessity, order such number of citizens of his county, or request any military or militia company, to aid in preventing the rescue of a prisoner.

Art. 43.27. Timothy Cole Exoneration Review Commission. [Expired]

APPEAL AND WRIT OF ERROR

CHAPTER 44
APPEAL AND WRIT OF ERROR

Art. 44.01. Appeal by State.

(a) The state is entitled to appeal an order of a court in a criminal case if the order:

(1) dismisses an indictment, information, or complaint or any portion of an indictment, information, or complaint;

(2) arrests or modifies a judgment;

(3) grants a new trial;

(4) sustains a claim of former jeopardy;

(5) grants a motion to suppress evidence, a confession, or an admission, if jeopardy has not attached in the case and if the prosecuting attorney certifies to the trial court that the appeal is not taken for the purpose of delay and that the evidence, confession, or admission is of substantial importance in the case; or

(6) is issued under Chapter 64.

(b) The state is entitled to appeal a sentence in a case on the ground that the sentence is illegal.

(c) The state is entitled to appeal a ruling on a question of law if the defendant is convicted in the case and appeals the judgment.

(d) The prosecuting attorney may not make an appeal under Subsection (a) or (b) of this article later than the 20th day after the date on which the order, ruling, or sentence to be appealed is entered by the court.

(e) The state is entitled to a stay in the proceedings pending the disposition of an appeal under Subsection (a) or (b) of this article.

(f) The court of appeals shall give precedence in its docket to an appeal filed under Subsection (a) or (b) of this article. The state shall pay all costs of appeal under Subsection (a) or (b) of this article, other than the cost of attorney's fees for the defendant.

(g) If the state appeals pursuant to this article and the defendant is on bail, he shall be permitted to remain at large on the existing bail. If the defendant is in custody, he is entitled to reasonable bail, as provided by law, unless the appeal is from an order which would terminate the prosecution, in which event the defendant is entitled to release on personal bond.

(h) The Texas Rules of Appellate Procedure apply to a petition by the state to the Court of Criminal Appeals for review of a decision of a court of appeals in a criminal case.

(i) In this article, "prosecuting attorney" means the county attorney, district attorney, or criminal district attorney who has the primary responsibility of prosecuting cases in the court hearing the case and does not include an assistant prosecuting attorney.

(j) Nothing in this article is to interfere with the defendant's right to appeal under the procedures of Article 44.02. The defendant's right to appeal under Article 44.02 may be prosecuted by the defendant where the punishment assessed is in accordance with Subchapter C, Chapter 42A, as well as any other punishment assessed in compliance with Article 44.02.

(k) The state is entitled to appeal an order granting relief to an applicant for a writ of habeas corpus under Article 11.072.

(*l*) The state is entitled to appeal an order entered under:

(1) Subchapter G or H, Chapter 62, that exempts a person from complying with the requirements of Chapter 62; and

(2) Subchapter I, Chapter 62, that terminates a person's obligation to register under Chapter 62.

Art. 44.02. Defendant May Appeal.

A defendant in any criminal action has the right of appeal under the rules hereinafter prescribed, provided, however, before the defendant who has been convicted upon either his plea of guilty or plea of nolo contendere before the court and the court, upon the election of the defendant, assesses punishment and the punishment does not exceed the punishment recommended by the prosecutor and agreed to by the defendant and his attorney may prosecute his appeal, he must have permission of the trial court, except on those matters which have been raised by written motion filed prior to trial. This article in no way affects appeals pursuant to Article 44.17 of this chapter.

Art. 44.03. [Blank].

Art. 44.04. Bond Pending Appeal.

(a) Pending the determination of any motion for new trial or the appeal from any misdemeanor conviction, the defendant is entitled to be released on reasonable bail.

(b) The defendant may not be released on bail pending the appeal from any felony conviction where the punishment equals or exceeds 10 years confinement or where the defendant has been convicted of an offense listed under Article 42A.054(a), but shall immediately be placed in custody and the bail discharged.

(c) Pending the appeal from any felony conviction other than a conviction described in Subsection (b) of this section, the trial court may deny bail and commit the defendant to custody if there then exists good cause to believe that the defendant would not appear when his conviction became final or is likely to commit another offense while on bail, permit the defendant to remain at large on the existing bail, or, if not then on bail, admit him to reasonable bail until his conviction becomes final. The court may impose reasonable conditions on bail pending the finality of his conviction. On a finding by the court on a preponderance of the evidence of a violation of a condition, the court may revoke the bail.

(d) After conviction, either pending determination of any motion for new trial or pending final determination of the appeal, the court in which trial was had may increase or decrease the amount of bail, as it deems proper, either upon its own motion or the motion of the State or of the defendant.

(e) Any bail entered into after conviction and the sureties on the bail must be approved by the court where trial was had. Bail is sufficient if it substantially meets the requirements of this code and may be entered into and given at any term of court.

(f) In no event shall the defendant and the sureties on his bond be released from their liability on such bond or bonds until the defendant is placed in the custody of the sheriff.

(g) The right of appeal to the Court of Appeals of this state is expressly accorded the defendant for a review of any judgment or order made hereunder, and said appeal shall be given preference by the appellate court.

(h) If a conviction is reversed by a decision of a Court of Appeals, the defendant, if in custody, is entitled to release on reasonable bail, regardless of the length of term of imprisonment, pending final determination of an appeal by the state or the defendant on a motion for discretionary review. If the defendant requests bail before a petition for discretionary review has been filed, the Court of Appeals shall determine the amount of bail. If the defendant requests bail after a petition for discretionary review has been filed, the Court of Criminal Appeals shall determine the amount of bail. The sureties on the bail must be approved by the court where the trial was had. The defendant's right to release under this subsection attaches immediately on the issuance of the Court of Appeals' final ruling as defined by Tex.Cr.App.R. 209(c).

(i) Notwithstanding any other law, pending the determination of a defendant's motion for new trial or the defendant's appeal from a misdemeanor conviction, the defendant is entitled to be released after completion of a sentence of confinement imposed for the conviction. The trial court may require the defendant to give a personal bond but may not, either instead of or in addition to the personal bond, require:

(1) any condition of the personal bond;

(2) another type of bail bond; or

(3) a surety or other security.

Art. 44.041. Conditions in Lieu of Bond.

(a) If a defendant is confined in county jail pending appeal and is eligible for release on bond pending appeal but is financially unable to make bond, the court may release the defendant without bond pending the conclusion of the appeal only if the court determines that release under this article is reasonable given the circumstances of the defendant's offense and the sentence imposed.

(b) A court that releases a defendant under this article must require the defendant to participate in a program under Article 42.033, 42.034, 42.035, or 42.036 during the pendency of the appeal. A defendant required to participate in a program may receive credit toward completion of the defendant's sentence while participating in the program in the same manner and to the same extent provided by Article 42.033, 42.034, 42.035, or 42.036, as applicable.

Art. 44.05. Receipt of Mandate [Repealed].

Repealed by Acts 1985, 69th Leg., ch. 685 (H.B. 13), § 4, effective September 1, 1986.

Art. 44.06. Capias May Issue to Any County [Repealed].

Repealed by Acts 1985, 69th Leg., ch. 685 (H.B. 13), § 4, effective September 1, 1986.

Art. 44.07. Right of Appeal Not Abridged.

The right of appeal, as otherwise provided by law, shall in no wise be abridged by any provision of this Chapter.

Arts. 44.08 to 44.09. [Blank].

Art. 44.10. Sheriff to Report Escape.

When any such escape occurs, the sheriff who had the prisoner in custody shall immediately report the fact under oath to the district or county attorney of the county in which the conviction was had, who shall forthwith forward such report to the State prosecuting attorney. Such report shall be sufficient evidence of the fact of such escape to authorize the dismissal of the appeal.

Art. 44.11. [Blank].

Art. 44.12. Procedure As to Bail Pending Appeal.

The amount of any bail given in any felony or misdemeanor case to perfect an appeal from any court to the Court of Appeals shall be fixed by the court in which the judgment or order appealed from was rendered. The sufficiency of the security thereon shall be tested, and the same proceedings had in case of forfeiture, as in other cases regarding bail.

Art. 44.13. [Repealed].

Repealed by Acts 1999, 76th Leg., ch. 1545 (S.B. 1230), § 75(a), effective September 1, 1999.

Art. 44.14. [Renumbered].

Renumbered to Tex. Code Crim Proc. art. 45.0426 by Acts 1999, 76th Leg., ch. 1545 (S.B. 1230), § 42, effective September 1, 1999.

Art. 44.15. Appellate Court May Allow New Bond.

When an appeal is taken from any court of this State, by filing a bond within the time prescribed by law in such cases, and the court to which appeal is taken determines that such bond is defective in form or substance, such appellate court may allow the appellant to amend such bond by filing a new bond, on such terms as the court may prescribe.

Art. 44.16. Appeal Bond Given Within What Time.

If the defendant is not in custody, a notice of appeal as provided in Article 44.13 shall have no effect whatever until the required appeal bond has been given and approved. The appeal bond shall be given within ten days after the sentence of the court has been rendered, except as provided in Article 27.14 of this code.

Art. 44.17. Appeal to County Court, How Conducted.

In all appeals to a county court from justice courts and municipal courts other than municipal courts of record, the trial shall be de novo in the trial in the county court, the same as if the prosecution had been originally commenced in that court. An appeal to the county court from a municipal court of record may be based only on errors reflected in the record.

Art. 44.18. Original Papers Sent Up.

In appeals from justice and corporation courts, all the original papers in the case, together with the appeal bond, if any, and together, with a certified transcript of all the proceedings had in the case before such court shall be delivered without delay to the clerk of the court to which the appeal was taken, who shall file the same and docket the case.

Art. 44.181. Defect in Complaint.

(a) A court conducting a trial de novo based on an appeal from a justice or municipal court may dismiss the case because of a defect in the complaint only if the defendant objected to the defect before the trial began in the justice or municipal court.

(b) The attorney representing the state may move to amend a defective complaint before the trial de novo begins.

Art. 44.19. Witnesses Not Again Summoned.

In the cases mentioned in the preceding Article, the witnesses who have been summoned or attached to appear in the case before the court below, shall appear before the court to which the appeal is taken without further process. In case of their failure to do so, the same proceedings may be had as if they had been originally summoned or attached to appear before such court.

Art. 44.20. Rules Governing Appeal Bonds.

The rules governing the taking and forfeiture of bail shall govern appeal bonds, and the forfeiture and collection of such appeal bonds shall be in the court to which such appeal is taken.

Arts. 44.21 to 44.24. [Repealed].

Art. 44.25. Cases Remanded.

The courts of appeals or the Court of Criminal Appeals may reverse the judgment in a criminal action, as well upon the law as upon the facts.

Art. 44.251. Reformation of Sentence in Capital Case.

(a) The court of criminal appeals shall reform a sentence of death to a sentence of confinement in the Texas Department of Criminal Justice for life without parole if the court finds that there is legally insufficient evidence to support an affirmative answer to an issue submitted to the jury under Section 2(b), Article 37.071, or Section 2(b), Article 37.072.

(b) The court of criminal appeals shall reform a sentence of death to a sentence of confinement in the Texas Department of Criminal Justice for life without parole if:

(1) the court finds reversible error that affects the punishment stage of the trial other than a finding of insufficient evidence under Subsection (a); and

(2) within 30 days after the date on which the opinion is handed down, the date the court disposes of a timely request for rehearing, or the date that the United States Supreme Court disposes of a timely filed petition for writ of certiorari, whichever date is later, the prosecuting attorney files a motion requesting that the sentence be reformed to confinement for life without parole.

(c) If the court of criminal appeals finds reversible error that affects the punishment stage of the trial only, as described by Subsection (b) of this article, and the prosecuting attorney does not file a motion for reformation of sentence in the period described by that subsection, the defendant shall receive a new sentencing trial in the manner required by Article 44.29(c) or (d), as applicable.

(d) The court of criminal appeals shall reform a sentence of death imposed under Section 12.42(c)(3), Penal Code, to a sentence of imprisonment in the Texas Department of Criminal Justice for life without parole if the United States Supreme Court:

(1) finds that the imposition of the death penalty under Section 12.42(c)(3), Penal Code, violates the United States Constitution; and

(2) issues an order that is not inconsistent with this article.

Art. 44.2511. Reformation of Sentence in Capital Case for Offense Committed Before September 1, 1991.

(a) This article applies to the reformation of a sentence of death in a capital case for an offense committed before September 1, 1991. For purposes of this subsection, an offense is committed before September 1, 1991, if every element of the offense occurred before that date.

(b) The court of criminal appeals shall reform a sentence of death to a sentence of confinement in the Texas Department of Criminal Justice for life if the court finds that there is legally insufficient evidence to support an affirmative answer to an issue submitted to the jury under Section 3(b), Article 37.0711.

(c) The court of criminal appeals shall reform a sentence of death to a sentence of confinement in the Texas Department of Criminal Justice for life if:

(1) the court finds reversible error that affects the punishment stage of the trial other than a finding of insufficient evidence under Subsection (b); and

(2) within 30 days after the date on which the opinion is handed down, the date the court disposes of a timely request for rehearing, or the date that the United States Supreme Court disposes of a timely filed petition for writ of certiorari, whichever date is later, the prosecuting attorney files a motion requesting that the sentence be reformed to confinement for life.

(d) If the court of criminal appeals finds reversible error that affects the punishment stage of the trial only, as described by Subsection (c), and the prosecuting attorney does not file a motion for reformation of sentence in the period described by that subsection, the defendant shall receive a new sentencing trial in the manner required by Article 44.29(c).

Arts. 44.26 to 44.27. [Blank].

Art. 44.28. When Misdemeanor Is Affirmed.

In misdemeanor cases where there has been an affirmance, no proceedings need be had after filing the mandate, except to forfeit the bond of the defendant, or to issue a capias for the defendant, or an execution against his property, to enforce the judgment of the court, as if no appeal had been taken.

Art. 44.281. Disposition of Fines and Costs When Misdemeanor Affirmed.

In misdemeanor cases affirmed on appeal from a municipal court, the fine imposed on appeal and the costs imposed on appeal shall be collected from the defendant, and the fine of the municipal court when collected shall be paid into the municipal treasury.

Art. 44.2811. [2 Versions: As amended by Acts 2013, 83rd Leg., ch. 1257] Records Relating to Certain Fine-Only Misdemeanors Committed by a Child.

All records and files and information stored by electronic means or otherwise, from which a record or file could be generated, relating to a criminal case for a fine-only misdemeanor, other than a traffic offense, that is committed by a child and that is appealed are confidential and may not be disclosed to the public except as provided under Article 45.0217(b).

Art. 44.2811. Records Relating to Certain Fine-Only Misdemeanors Committed by a Child.

All records and files and information stored by electronic means or otherwise, from which a record or file could be generated, relating to a criminal case for a fine-only misdemeanor, other than a traffic offense, that is committed by a child and that is appealed are confidential and may not be disclosed to the public except as provided under Article 45.0217(b).

Art. 44.2812. Confidential Records Related to Fine-Only Misdemeanor.

(a) Except as provided by Subsection (b) and Article 45.0218(b), following the fifth anniversary of the date of a final conviction of, or of a dismissal after deferral of disposition for, a misdemeanor offense punishable by fine only, all records and files and information stored by electronic means or otherwise, from which a record or file could be generated, that are held or stored by or for an appellate court and relate to the person who was convicted of, or who received a dismissal after deferral of disposition for, the offense are confidential and may not be disclosed to the public.

(b) This article does not apply to:

(1) an opinion issued by an appellate court; or

(2) records, files, and information described by Subsection (a) that relate to an offense that is sexual in nature, as determined by the holder of the records, files, or information.

Art. 44.29. Effect of Reversal.

(a) Where the court of appeals or the Court of Criminal Appeals awards a new trial to the defendant on the basis of an error in the guilt or innocence stage of the trial or on the basis of errors in both the guilt or innocence stage of the trial and the punishment stage of the trial, the cause shall stand as it would have stood in case the new trial had been granted by the court below.

(b) If the court of appeals or the Court of Criminal Appeals awards a new trial to a defendant other than a defendant convicted of an offense under Section 19.03, Penal Code, only on the basis of an error or errors made in the punishment stage of the trial, the cause shall stand as it would have stood in case the new trial had been granted by the court below, except that the court shall commence the new trial as if a finding of guilt had been returned and proceed to the punishment stage of the trial under Subsection (b), Section 2, Article 37.07, of this code. If the defendant elects, the court shall empanel a jury for the sentencing stage of the trial in the same manner as a jury is empaneled by the court for other trials before the court. At the new trial, the court shall allow both the state and the defendant to introduce evidence to show the circumstances of the offense and other evidence as permitted by Section 3 of Article 37.07 of this code.

(c) If any court sets aside or invalidates the sentence of a defendant convicted of an offense under Section 19.03, Penal Code, and sentenced to death on the basis of any error affecting punishment only, the court shall not set the conviction aside but rather shall commence a new punishment hearing under Article 37.071 or Article 37.0711 of this code, as appropriate, as if a finding of guilt had been returned. The court shall empanel a jury for the sentencing stage of the trial in the same manner as a jury is to be empaneled by the court in other trials before the court for offenses under Section 19.03, Penal Code. At the new punishment hearing, the court shall permit both the state and the defendant to introduce evidence as permitted by Article 37.071 or Article 37.0711 of this code.

(d) If any court sets aside or invalidates the sentence of a defendant convicted of an offense punishable as a capital felony under Section 12.42(c)(3), Penal Code, and sentenced to death on the basis of any error affecting punishment only, the court shall not set the conviction aside but rather shall commence a new punishment hearing under Article 37.072, as if a finding of guilt had been returned. The court shall empanel a jury for the sentencing stage of the trial in the same manner as a jury is to be empaneled by the court in other trials before the court for the offense of which the defendant was convicted. At the new punishment hearing, the court shall permit both the state and the defendant to introduce evidence as permitted by Article 37.072.

Arts. 44.30 to 44.32. [Blank].

Art. 44.33. Hearing in Appellate Court.

(a) The Court of Criminal Appeals shall make rules of posttrial and appellate procedure as to the hearing of criminal actions not inconsistent with this Code. After the record is filed in the Court of Appeals or the Court of Criminal Appeals the parties may file such supplemental briefs as they may desire before the case is submitted to the court. Each party, upon filing any such supplemental brief, shall promptly cause true copy thereof to be delivered to the opposing party or to the latter's counsel. In every case at least two counsel for the defendant shall be heard in the Court of Appeals if such be desired by defendant. In every case heard by the Court of Criminal Appeals at least two counsel for the defendant shall be permitted oral argument if desired by the appellant.

(b) Appellant's failure to file his brief in the time prescribed shall not authorize a dismissal of the appeal by the Court of Appeals or the Court of Criminal Appeals, nor shall the Court of Appeals or the Court of Criminal Appeals, for such reason, refuse to consider appellant's case on appeal.

Art. 44.34. [Blank].

Art. 44.35. Bail Pending Habeas Corpus Appeal.

In any habeas corpus proceeding in any court or before any judge in this State where the defendant is remanded to the custody of an officer and an appeal is taken to an appellate court, the defendant shall be allowed bail by the court or judge so remanding the defendant, except in capital cases where the proof is evident. The fact that such defendant is released on bail shall not be grounds for a dismissal of the appeal except in capital cases where the proof is evident.

Arts. 44.36 to 44.38. [Blank].

Art. 44.39. Appellant Detained by Other Than Officer.

If the appellant in a case of habeas corpus be detained by any person other than an officer, the sheriff receiving the mandate of the appellate court, shall immediately cause the person so held to be discharged; and the mandate shall be sufficient authority therefor.

Art. 44.40. [Blank].

Art. 44.41. Who Shall Take Bail Bond.

When, by the judgment of the appellate court upon cases of habeas corpus, the applicant is ordered to give bail, such judgment shall be certified to the officer holding him in custody; and if such officer be the sheriff, the bail bond may be executed before him; if any other officer, he shall take the person detained before some magistrate, who may receive a bail bond, and shall file the same in the proper court of the proper county; and such bond may be forfeited and enforced as provided by law.

Art. 44.42. Appeal on Forfeitures.

An appeal may be taken by the defendant from every final judgment rendered upon a personal bond, bail bond or bond taken for the prevention or suppression of offenses, where such judgment is for twenty dollars or more, exclusive of costs, but not otherwise.

Art. 44.43. Writ of Error.

The defendant may also have any such judgment as is mentioned in the preceding Article, and which may have been rendered in courts other than the justice and corporation courts, reviewed upon writ of error.

Art. 44.44. Rules in Forfeitures.

In the cases provided for in the two preceding Articles, the proceeding shall be regulated by the same rules that govern civil actions where an appeal is taken or a writ of error sued out.

Art. 44.45. Review by Court of Criminal Appeals.

(a) The Court of Criminal Appeals may review decisions of the court of appeals on its own motion. An order for review must be filed before the decision of the court of appeals becomes final as determined by Article 42.045.

(b) The Court of Criminal Appeals may review decisions of the court of appeals upon a petition for review.

(1) The state or a defendant in a case may petition the Court of Criminal Appeals for review of the decision of a court of appeals in that case.

(2) The petition shall be filed with the clerk of the court of appeals which rendered the decision within 30 days after the final ruling of the court of appeals.

(3) The petition for review shall be addressed to "The Court of Criminal Appeals of Texas," and shall state the name of the petitioning party and shall include a statement of the case and authorities and arguments in support of each ground for review.

(4) Upon filing a petition for review, the petitioning party shall cause a true copy to be delivered to the attorney representing the opposing party. The opposing party may file a reply to the petition with the Court of Criminal Appeals within 30 days after receipt of the petition from the petitioning party.

(5) Within 15 days after the filing of a petition for review, the clerk of the court of appeals shall note the filing on the record and forward the petition together with the original record and the opinion of the court of appeals to the Court of Criminal Appeals.

(6) The Court of Criminal Appeals shall either grant the petition and review the case or refuse the petition.

(7) Subsequent to granting the petition for review, the Court of Criminal Appeals may reconsider, set aside the order granting the petition, and refuse the petition as though the petition had never been granted.

(c) The Court of Criminal Appeals may promulgate rules pursuant to this article.

(d) Extensions of time for meeting the limits prescribed in Subdivisions (2) and (4) of Subsection (b) of this article may be granted by the Court of Criminal Appeals or a judge thereof for good cause shown on timely application to the Court of Criminal Appeals.

Art. 44.46. Reversal of Conviction on the Basis of Service on Jury by a Disqualified Juror.

A conviction in a criminal case may be reversed on appeal on the ground that a juror in the case was absolutely disqualified from service under Article 35.19 of this code only if:

(1) the defendant raises the disqualification before the verdict is entered; or

(2) the disqualification was not discovered or brought to the attention of the trial court until after the verdict was entered and the defendant makes a showing of significant harm by the service of the disqualified juror.

Art. 44.47. Appeal of Transfer from Juvenile Court. [Repealed]

JUSTICE AND CORPORATION COURTS

CHAPTER 45
JUSTICE AND MUNICIPAL COURTS

SUBCHAPTER A
GENERAL PROVISIONS

Art. 45.001. Objectives of Chapter.

The purpose of this chapter is to establish procedures for processing cases that come within the criminal jurisdiction of the justice courts and municipal courts. This chapter is intended and shall be construed to achieve the following objectives:

(1) to provide fair notice to a person appearing in a criminal proceeding before a justice or municipal court and a meaningful opportunity for that person to be heard;

(2) to ensure appropriate dignity in court procedure without undue formalism;

(3) to promote adherence to rules with sufficient flexibility to serve the ends of justice; and

(4) to process cases without unnecessary expense or delay.

Art. 45.002. Application of Chapter.

Criminal proceedings in the justice and municipal courts shall be conducted in accordance with this chapter, including any other rules of procedure specifically made applicable to those proceedings by this chapter. If this chapter does not provide a rule of procedure governing any aspect of a case, the justice or judge shall apply the other general provisions of this code to the extent necessary to achieve the objectives of this chapter.

Art. 45.003. Definition for Certain Prosecutions.

For purposes of dismissing a charge under Section 502.407, Transportation Code, "day" does not include Saturday, Sunday, or a legal holiday.

Art. 45.004. General Definition.

Unless the context clearly indicates otherwise, in this chapter, "cost" includes any fee, including a reimbursement fee, imposed on a defendant by the justice or judge.

Art. 45.01. Complaint [Repealed].

Repealed by Acts 1999, 76th Leg., ch. 1545 (S.B. 1230), § 75(a), effective September 1, 1999.

SUBCHAPTER B
PROCEDURES FOR JUSTICE AND MUNICIPAL COURTS

Art. 45.011. Rules of Evidence.

The rules of evidence that govern the trials of criminal actions in the district court apply to a criminal proceeding in a justice or municipal court.

Art. 45.012. Electronically Created Records.

(a) Notwithstanding any other provision of law, a document that is issued or maintained by a justice or municipal court or a notice or a citation issued by a law enforcement officer may be created by electronic means, including optical imaging, optical disk, digital imaging, or other electronic reproduction technique that does not permit changes, additions, or deletions to the originally created document.

(b) The court may use electronic means to:

(1) produce a document required by law to be written;

(2) record an instrument, paper, or notice that is permitted or required by law to be recorded or filed; or

(3) maintain a docket.

(c) The court shall maintain original documents as provided by law.

(d) An electronically recorded judgment has the same force and effect as a written signed judgment.

(e) A record created by electronic means is an original record or a certification of the original record.

(f) A printed copy of an optical image of the original record printed from an optical disk system is an accurate copy of the original record.

(g) A justice or municipal court shall have a court seal, the impression of which must be attached to all papers issued out of the court except subpoenas, and which must be used to authenticate the official acts of the clerk and of the recorder. A court seal may be created by electronic means, including optical imaging, optical disk, or other electronic reproduction technique that does not permit changes, additions, or deletions to an original document created by the same type of system.

(h) A statutory requirement that a document contain the signature of any person, including a judge, clerk of the court, or defendant, is satisfied if the document contains that signature as captured on an electronic device.

Art. 45.013. Filing with Clerk by Mail.

(a) Notwithstanding any other law, for the purposes of this chapter a document is considered timely filed with the clerk of a court if:

(1) the document is deposited with the United States Postal Service in a first class postage prepaid envelope properly addressed to the clerk on or before the date the document is required to be filed with the clerk; and

(2) the clerk receives the document not later than the 10th day after the date the document is required to be filed with the clerk.

(b) A legible postmark affixed by the United States Postal Service is prima facie evidence of the date the document is deposited with the United States Postal Service.

(c) In this article, "day" does not include Saturday, Sunday, or a legal holiday.

Art. 45.014. Warrant of Arrest.

(a) When a sworn complaint or affidavit based on probable cause has been filed before the justice or municipal court, the justice or judge may issue a warrant for the arrest of the accused and deliver the same to the proper officer to be executed.

(b) The warrant is sufficient if:

(1) it is issued in the name of "The State of Texas";

(2) it is directed to the proper peace officer or some other person specifically named in the warrant;

(3) it includes a command that the body of the accused be taken, and brought before the authority issuing the warrant, at the time and place stated in the warrant;

(4) it states the name of the person whose arrest is ordered, if known, or if not known, it describes the person as in the complaint;

(5) it states that the person is accused of some offense against the laws of this state, naming the offense; and

(6) it is signed by the justice or judge, naming the office of the justice or judge in the body of the warrant or in connection with the signature of the justice or judge.

(c) Chapter 15 applies to a warrant of arrest issued under this article, except as inconsistent or in conflict with this chapter.

(d) In a county with a population of more than two million that does not have a county attorney, a justice or judge may not issue a warrant under this section for an offense under Section 32.41, Penal Code, unless the district attorney has approved the complaint or affidavit on which the warrant is based.

(e) **[2 Versions; as added by Acts 2017, 85th R.S. Ch. 977 (H.B. 351)]** [Repealed.]

(e) **[2 Versions; as added by Acts 2017, 85th R.S. Ch. 1127 (S.B. 1913)]** A justice or judge may not issue an arrest warrant for the defendant's failure to appear at the initial court setting, including failure to appear as required by a citation issued under Article 14.06(b), unless:

(1) the justice or judge provides by telephone or regular mail to the defendant notice that includes:

(A) a date and time, occurring within the 30-day period following the date that notice is provided, when the defendant must appear before the justice or judge;

(B) the name and address of the court with jurisdiction in the case;

(C) information regarding alternatives to the full payment of any fine or costs owed by the defendant, if the defendant is unable to pay that amount; and

(D) a statement that the defendant may be entitled to a credit toward any fine or costs owed by the defendant if the defendant was confined in jail or prison after the commission of the offense for which the notice is given; and

(E) an explanation of the consequences if the defendant fails to appear before the justice or judge as required by this article; and

(2) the defendant fails to appear before the justice or judge as required by this article.

(f) A defendant who receives notice under Subsection (e) may request an alternative date or time to appear before the justice or judge if the defendant is unable to appear on the date and time included in the notice.

(g) **[2 Versions; as added by Acts 2017, 85th R.S. Ch. 977 (H.B. 351)]** A justice or judge shall recall an arrest warrant for the defendant's failure to appear if, before the arrest warrant is executed:

(1) the defendant voluntarily appears to resolve the arrest warrant; and

(2) the arrest warrant is resolved in any manner authorized by this code.

(g) **[2 Versions; as added by Acts 2017, 85th R.S. Ch. 1127 (S.B.1913)]** A justice or judge shall recall an arrest warrant for the defendant's failure to appear if the defendant voluntarily appears and makes a good faith effort to resolve the arrest warrant before the warrant is executed.

Art. 45.015. Defendant Placed in Jail.

Whenever, by the provisions of this title, the peace officer is authorized to retain a defendant in custody, the peace officer may place the defendant in jail in accordance with this code or other law.

Art. 45.016. Personal Bond; Bail Bond.

(a) The justice or judge may require the defendant to give a personal bond to secure the defendant's appearance in accordance with this code.

(b) The justice or judge may not, either instead of or in addition to the personal bond, require a defendant to give a bail bond unless:

(1) the defendant fails to appear in accordance with this code with respect to the applicable offense; and

(2) the justice or judge determines that:

(A) the defendant has sufficient resources or income to give a bail bond; and

(B) a bail bond is necessary to secure the defendant's appearance in accordance with this code.

(c) **[2 Versions; As Added by Acts 2017, 85th R.S. Ch. 977 (H.B. 351)]** If a defendant required to give a bail bond under Subsection (b) remains in custody, without giving the bond, for more than 48 hours after the issuance of the applicable order, the justice or judge shall reconsider the requirement for the defendant to give the bond.

(c) **[2 Versions; As Added by Acts 2017, 85th R.S. Ch. 1127 (S.B. 1913)]** If before the expiration of a 48-hour period following the issuance of the applicable order a defendant described by Subsections (b)(1) and (2) does not give a required bail bond, the justice or judge:

(1) shall reconsider the requirement for the defendant to give the bail bond and presume that the defendant does not have sufficient resources or income to give the bond; and

(2) may require the defendant to give a personal bond.

(d) If the defendant refuses to give a personal bond or, except as provided by Subsection (c), refuses or otherwise fails to give a bail bond, the defendant may be held in custody.

Art. 45.017. Criminal Docket.

(a) The justice or judge of each court, or, if directed by the justice or judge, the clerk of the court, shall keep a docket containing the following information:

(1) the style and file number of each criminal action;

(2) the nature of the offense charged;

(3) the plea offered by the defendant and the date the plea was entered;

(4) the date the warrant, if any, was issued and the return made thereon;

(5) the date the examination or trial was held, and if a trial was held, whether it was by a jury or by the justice or judge;

(6) the verdict of the jury, if any, and the date of the verdict;

(7) the judgment and sentence of the court, and the date each was given;

(8) the motion for new trial, if any, and the decision thereon; and

(9) whether an appeal was taken and the date of that action.

(b) The information in the docket may be processed and stored by the use of electronic data processing equipment, at the discretion of the justice of the peace or the municipal court judge.

Art. 45.018. Complaint.

(a) For purposes of this chapter, a complaint is a sworn allegation charging the accused with the commission of an offense.

(b) A defendant is entitled to notice of a complaint against the defendant not later than the day before the date of any proceeding in the prosecution of the defendant under the complaint. The defendant may waive the right to notice granted by this subsection.

Art. 45.019. Requisites of Complaint.

(a) A complaint is sufficient, without regard to its form, if it substantially satisfies the following requisites:

(1) it must be in writing;

(2) it must commence "In the name and by the authority of the State of Texas";

(3) it must state the name of the accused, if known, or if unknown, must include a reasonably definite description of the accused;

(4) it must show that the accused has committed an offense against the law of this state, or state that the affiant has good reason to believe and does believe that the accused has committed an offense against the law of this state;

(5) it must state the date the offense was committed as definitely as the affiant is able to provide;

(6) it must bear the signature or mark of the affiant; and

(7) it must conclude with the words "Against the peace and dignity of the State" and, if the offense charged is an offense only under a municipal ordinance, it may also conclude with the words "Contrary to the said ordinance".

(b) A complaint filed in justice court must allege that the offense was committed in the county in which the complaint is made.

(c) A complaint filed in municipal court must allege that the offense was committed in the territorial limits of the municipality in which the complaint is made.

(d) A complaint may be sworn to before any officer authorized to administer oaths.

(e) A complaint in municipal court may be sworn to before:

(1) the municipal judge;

(2) the clerk of the court or a deputy clerk;

(3) the city secretary; or

(4) the city attorney or a deputy city attorney.

(f) If the defendant does not object to a defect, error, or irregularity of form or substance in a charging instrument before the date on which the trial on the merits commences, the defendant waives and forfeits the right to object to the defect, error, or irregularity. Nothing in this article prohibits a trial court from requiring that an objection to a charging instrument be made at an earlier time.

(g) In a county with a population of more than two million that does not have a county attorney, a complaint for an offense under Section 32.41, Penal Code, must be approved by the district attorney, regardless of whether a collection proceeding is initiated by the district attorney under Section 32.41(e), Penal Code.

Art. 45.02. Seal [Repealed].

Repealed by Acts 1999, 76th Leg., ch. 1545 (S.B. 1230), § 75(a), effective September 1, 1999.

Art. 45.020. Appearance by Counsel.

(a) The defendant has a right to appear by counsel as in all other cases.

(b) State's counsel may open and conclude the argument in the case.

Art. 45.0201. Appearance by Telephone or Videoconference.

If the justice or judge determines that requiring a defendant to appear before the justice or judge in person for a hearing under Article 45.0445 or 45.045 would impose an undue hardship on the defendant, the justice or judge may allow the defendant to appear by telephone or videoconference.

Art. 45.021. Pleadings.

All pleading of the defendant in justice or municipal court may be oral or in writing as the court may direct.

Art. 45.0211. Plea by Defendant Charged with Family Violence Offense.

(a) In this article, "family violence" has the meaning assigned by Section 71.004, Family Code.

(b) If a defendant is charged with an offense involving family violence, the judge or justice must take the defendant's plea in open court.

Art. 45.0215. Plea by Minor and Appearance of Parent.

(a) This article applies to a defendant who has not had the disabilities of minority removed and has been:

(1) charged with an offense other than an offense under Section 43.261, Penal Code, if the defendant is younger than 17 years of age; or

(2) charged with an offense under Section 43.261, Penal Code, if the defendant is younger than 18 years of age.

(a-1) The judge or justice:

(1) must take the defendant's plea in open court; and

(2) shall issue a summons to compel the defendant's parent, guardian, or managing conservator to be present during:

(A) the taking of the defendant's plea; and

(B) all other proceedings relating to the case.

(b) If the court is unable to secure the appearance of the defendant's parent, guardian, or managing conservator by issuance of a summons, the court may, without the defendant's parent, guardian, or managing conservator present, take the defendant's plea and proceed against the defendant.

(c) If the defendant resides in a county other than the county in which the alleged offense occurred, the defendant may, with leave of the judge of the court of original jurisdiction, enter the plea, including a plea under Article 45.052, before a judge in the county in which the defendant resides.

(d) A justice or municipal court shall endorse on the summons issued to a parent an order to appear personally at a hearing with the child. The summons must include a warning that the failure of the parent to appear may result in arrest and is a Class C misdemeanor.

Art. 45.0216. Expunction of Certain Conviction Records.

(a) In this article, "child" has the meaning assigned by Section 51.02, Family Code.

(b) A person may apply to the court in which the person was convicted to have the conviction expunged as provided by this article on or after the person's 17th birthday if:

(1) the person was convicted of not more than one offense described by Section 8.07(a)(4) or (5), Penal Code, while the person was a child; or

(2) the person was convicted only once of an offense under Section 43.261, Penal Code.

(c) The person must make a written request to have the records expunged. The request must be under oath.

(d) The request must contain the person's statement that the person was not convicted of any additional offense or found to have engaged in conduct indicating a need for supervision as described by Subsection (f)(1) or (2), as applicable.

Code of Criminal Procedure

(e) The judge shall inform the person and any parent in open court of the person's expunction rights and provide them with a copy of this article.

(f) The court shall order the conviction, together with all complaints, verdicts, sentences, and prosecutorial and law enforcement records, and any other documents relating to the offense, expunged from the person's record if the court finds that:

(1) for a person applying for the expunction of a conviction for an offense described by Section 8.07(a)(4) or (5), Penal Code, the person was not convicted of any other offense described by Section 8.07(a)(4) or (5), Penal Code, while the person was a child; and

(2) for a person applying for the expunction of a conviction for an offense described by Section 43.261, Penal Code, the person was not found to have engaged in conduct indicating a need for supervision described by Section 51.03(b)(6), Family Code, while the person was a child.

(f-1) After entry of an order under Subsection (f), the person is released from all disabilities resulting from the conviction and the conviction may not be shown or made known for any purpose.

(g) This article does not apply to any offense otherwise covered by:

(1) Chapter 106, Alcoholic Beverage Code; or

(2) Chapter 161, Health and Safety Code.

(h) Records of a person under 17 years of age relating to a complaint may be expunged under this article if:

(1) the complaint was dismissed under Article 45.051 or 45.052 or other law; or

(2) the person was acquitted of the offense.

(i) The justice or municipal court shall require a person who requests expungement under this article to pay a reimbursement fee in the amount of $30 to defray the cost of notifying state agencies of orders of expungement under this article.

(j) The procedures for expunction provided under this article are separate and distinct from the expunction procedures under Chapter 55.

Art. 45.0217. [2 Versions: As amended by Acts 2013, 83rd Leg., ch. 1257] Confidential Records Related to Charges Against or the Conviction of a Child.

(a) Except as provided by Article 15.27 and Subsection (b), all records and files, including those held by law enforcement, and information stored by electronic means or otherwise, from which a record or file could be generated, relating to a child who is charged with, is convicted of, is found not guilty of, had a charge dismissed for, or is granted deferred disposition for a fine-only misdemeanor offense other than a traffic offense are confidential and may not be disclosed to the public.

(b) Information subject to Subsection (a) may be open to inspection only by:

(1) judges or court staff;

(2) a criminal justice agency for a criminal justice purpose, as those terms are defined by Section 411.082, Government Code;

(3) the Department of Public Safety;

(4) an attorney for a party to the proceeding;

(5) the child defendant; or

(6) the defendant's parent, guardian, or managing conservator.

Art. 45.0217. Confidential Records Related to Charges Against or Conviction of a Child.

(a) Except as provided by Article 15.27 and Subsection (b), all records and files, including those held by law enforcement, and information stored by electronic means or otherwise, from which a record or file could be generated, relating to a child who is charged with, is convicted of, is found not guilty of, had a charge dismissed for, or is granted deferred disposition for a fine-only misdemeanor offense other than a traffic offense are confidential and may not be disclosed to the public.

(b) Information subject to Subsection (a) may be open to inspection only by:

(1) judges or court staff;

(2) a criminal justice agency for a criminal justice purpose, as those terms are defined by Section 411.082, Government Code;

(3) the Department of Public Safety;

(4) an attorney for a party to the proceeding;

(5) the child defendant; or

(6) the defendant's parent, guardian, or managing conservator.

(c) In this article, "child" has the meaning assigned by Article 45.058(h).

Art. 45.0218. Confidential Records Related to Fine-Only Misdemeanor.

(a) Except as provided by Subsections (b) and (c), following the fifth anniversary of the date of a final conviction of, or of a dismissal after deferral of disposition for, a misdemeanor offense punishable by fine only, all records and files and information stored by electronic means or otherwise, from which a record or file could be generated, that are held or stored by or for a municipal or justice court and relate to the person who was convicted of, or who received a dismissal after deferral of disposition for, the offense are confidential and may not be disclosed to the public.

(b) Records, files, and information subject to Subsection (a) may be open to inspection only:

(1) by judges or court staff;

(2) by a criminal justice agency for a criminal justice purpose, as those terms are defined by Section 411.082, Government Code;

(3) by the Department of Public Safety;

(4) by the attorney representing the state;

(5) by the defendant or the defendant's counsel;

(6) if the offense is a traffic offense, an insurance company or surety company authorized to write motor vehicle liability insurance in this state; or

(7) for the purpose of complying with a requirement under federal law or if federal law requires the disclosure as a condition of receiving federal highway funds.

(c) This article does not apply to records, files, and information described by Subsection (a) that relate to an offense that is sexual in nature, as determined by the holder of the records, files, or information.

Art. 45.022. Plea of Guilty or Nolo Contendere.

Proof as to the offense may be heard upon a plea of guilty or a plea of nolo contendere and the punishment assessed by the court.

Art. 45.023. Defendant's Plea.

(a) After the jury is impaneled, or after the defendant has waived trial by jury, the defendant may:

(1) plead guilty or not guilty;

(2) enter a plea of nolo contendere; or

(3) enter the special plea of double jeopardy as described by Article 27.05.

(b) If a defendant is detained in jail before trial, the justice or judge may permit the defendant to enter any of the pleas described by Subsection (a).

(c) If a defendant who is detained in jail enters a plea of guilty or nolo contendere, the justice or judge may, after complying with Article 15.17 and advising the defendant of the defendant's right to trial by jury, as appropriate:

(1) accept the defendant's plea;

(2) assess a fine, determine costs, and accept payment of the fine and costs;

(3) give the defendant credit for time served;

(4) determine whether the defendant is indigent; or

(5) discharge the defendant.

(d) Notwithstanding Article 45.037, following a plea of guilty or nolo contendere entered under Subsection (b), a motion for new trial must be made not later than 10 days after the rendition of judgment and sentence, and not afterward. The justice or judge shall grant a motion for new trial made under this subsection.

Art. 45.024. Defendant's Refusal to Plead.

The justice or judge shall enter a plea of not guilty if the defendant refuses to plead.

Art. 45.0241. Acceptance of Defendant's Plea.

A justice or judge may not accept a plea of guilty or plea of nolo contendere from a defendant in open court unless it appears to the justice or judge that the defendant is mentally competent and the plea is free and voluntary.

Art. 45.025. Defendant May Waive Jury.

The accused may waive a trial by jury in writing. If the defendant waives a trial by jury, the justice or judge shall hear and determine the cause without a jury.

Art. 45.026. Jury Trial; Failure to Appear.

(a) A justice or municipal court may order a party who does not waive a jury trial in a justice or municipal court and who fails to appear for the trial to pay a reimbursement fee for the costs incurred for impaneling the jury.

(b) The justice or municipal court may release a party from the obligation to pay the reimbursement fee under this section for good cause.

(c) An order issued by a justice or municipal court under this section may be enforced by contempt as prescribed by Section 21.002(c), Government Code.

Art. 45.027. Jury Summoned.

(a) If the accused does not waive a trial by jury, the justice or judge shall issue a writ commanding the proper officer to summon a venire from which six qualified persons shall be selected to serve as jurors in the case.

(b) The jurors when so summoned shall remain in attendance as jurors in all cases that may come up for hearing until discharged by the court.

(c) Any person so summoned who fails to attend may be fined an amount not to exceed $100 for contempt.

Art. 45.028. Other Jurors Summoned.

If, from challenges or any other cause, a sufficient number of jurors are not in attendance, the justice or judge shall order the proper officer to summon a sufficient number of qualified persons to form the jury.

Art. 45.029. Peremptory Challenges.

In all jury trials in a justice or municipal court, the state and each defendant in the case is entitled to three peremptory challenges.

Art. 45.03. Prosecutions [Renumbered].

Renumbered to Tex. Code Crim Proc. art. 45.201 by Acts 1999, 76th Leg., ch. 1545 (S.B. 1230), § 59, effective September 1, 1999.

Art. 45.030. Formation of Jury.

The justice or judge shall form the jury and administer the appropriate oath in accordance with Chapter 35.

Art. 45.031. Counsel for State Not Present.

If the state is not represented by counsel when the case is called for trial, the justice or judge may:

(1) postpone the trial to a date certain;

(2) appoint an attorney pro tem as provided by this code to represent the state; or

(3) proceed to trial.

Art. 45.032. Directed Verdict.

If, upon the trial of a case in a justice or municipal court, the state fails to prove a prima facie case of the offense alleged in the complaint, the defendant is entitled to a directed verdict of "not guilty."

Art. 45.033. Jury Charge.

The judge shall charge the jury. The charge may be made orally or in writing, except that the charge shall be made in writing if required by law.

Art. 45.034. Jury Kept Together.

The jury shall retire in charge of an officer when the cause is submitted to them, and be kept together until they agree to a verdict, are discharged, or the court recesses.

Art. 45.035. Mistrial.

A jury shall be discharged if it fails to agree to a verdict after being kept together a reasonable time. If a jury is discharged because it fails to agree to a verdict, the justice or judge may impanel another jury as soon as practicable to try such cause.

Art. 45.036. Verdict.

(a) When the jury has agreed on a verdict, the jury shall bring the verdict into court.

(b) The justice or judge shall see that the verdict is in proper form and shall render the proper judgment and sentence on the verdict.

Art. 45.037. Motion for New Trial.

A motion for a new trial must be made within five days after the rendition of judgment and sentence, and not afterward.

Art. 45.038. New Trial Granted.

(a) Not later than the 10th day after the date that the judgment is entered, a justice or judge may, for good cause shown, grant the defendant a new trial, whenever the justice or judge considers that justice has not been done the defendant in the trial of the case.

(b) If a motion for a new trial is not granted before the 11th day after the date that the judgment is entered, the motion shall be considered denied.

Art. 45.039. Only One New Trial Granted.

Not more than one new trial shall be granted the defendant in the same case. When a new trial has been granted, the justice or judge shall proceed, as soon as practicable, to try the case again.

Art. 45.04. Service of Process [Renumbered].

Renumbered to Tex. Code Crim Proc. art. 45.202 by Acts 1999, 76th Leg., ch. 1545 (S.B. 1230), § 60, effective September 1, 1999.

Art. 45.040. State Not Entitled to New Trial.

In no case shall the state be entitled to a new trial.

Art. 45.041. Judgment.

(a) The judgment and sentence, in case of conviction in a criminal action before a justice of the peace or municipal court judge, shall be that the defendant pay the amount of the fine and costs to the state.

(a-1) Notwithstanding any other provision of this article, during or immediately after imposing a sentence in a case in which the defendant entered a plea in open court as provided by Article 27.14(a) or 27.16(a), the justice or judge shall inquire whether the defendant has sufficient resources or income to immediately pay all or part of the fine and costs. If the justice or judge determines that the defendant does not have sufficient resources or income to immediately pay all or part of the fine and costs, the justice or judge shall determine whether the fine and costs should be:

(1) subject to Subsection (b-2), required to be paid at some later date or in a specified portion at designated intervals;

(2) discharged by performing community service under, as applicable, Article 45.049, Article 45.0492, as added by Chapter 227 (H.B. 350), Acts of the 82nd Legislature, Regular Session, 2011, or Article 45.0492, as added by Chapter 777 (H.B. 1964), Acts of the 82nd Legislature, Regular Session, 2011;

(3) waived in full or in part under Article 45.0491; or

(4) satisfied through any combination of methods under Subdivisions (1)-(3).

(b) Subject to Subsections (b-2) and (b-3) and Article 45.0491, the justice or judge may direct the defendant:

(1) to pay:

(A) the entire fine and costs when sentence is pronounced;

(B) the entire fine and costs at some later date; or

(C) a specified portion of the fine and costs at designated intervals;

(2) if applicable, to make restitution to any victim of the offense; and

(3) to satisfy any other sanction authorized by law.

(b-1) Restitution made under Subsection (b)(2) may not exceed $5,000 for an offense under Section 32.41, Penal Code.

(b-2) When imposing a fine and costs, if the justice or judge determines that the defendant is unable to immediately pay the fine and costs, the justice or judge shall allow the defendant to pay the fine and costs in specified portions at designated intervals.

(b-3) A judge may allow a defendant who is a child, as defined by Article 45.058(h), to elect at the time of conviction, as defined by Section 133.101, Local Government Code, to discharge the fine and costs by:

(1) performing community service or receiving tutoring under Article 45.0492, as added by Chapter 227 (H.B. 350), Acts of the 82nd Legislature, Regular Session, 2011; or

(2) paying the fine and costs in a manner described by Subsection (b).

(b-4) The election under Subsection (b-3) must be made in writing, signed by the defendant, and, if present, signed by the defendant's parent, guardian, or managing conservator. The court shall maintain the written election as a record of the court and provide a copy to the defendant.

(b-5) The requirement under Article 45.0492(a), as added by Chapter 227 (H.B. 350), Acts of the 82nd Legislature, Regular Session, 2011, that an offense occur in a building or on the grounds of the primary or secondary school at which the defendant was enrolled at the time of the offense does not apply to the performance of community service or the receipt of tutoring to discharge a fine or costs under Subsection (b-3)(1).

(b-6) Notwithstanding Subsection (a-1) or any other provision of this chapter, when imposing a fine and costs, the justice or judge may not require a defendant who is under the conservatorship of the Department of Family and Protective Services or in extended foster care as provided by Subchapter G, Chapter 263, Family Code, to pay any amount of the fine and costs. In lieu of the payment of fine and costs, the justice or judge may require the defendant to perform community service as provided by Article 45.049, 45.0492, as added by Chapter 227 (H.B. 350), Acts of the 82nd Legislature, Regular Session, 2011, or 45.0492, as added by Chapter 777 (H.B. 1964), Acts of the 82nd Legislature, Regular Session, 2011, as appropriate.

(c) The justice or judge shall credit the defendant for time served in jail as provided by Article 42.03. The credit under this subsection shall be applied to the amount of the fine and costs at the rate provided by Article 45.048.

(c-1) In addition to credit under Subsection (c), in imposing a fine and costs in a case involving a misdemeanor punishable by a fine only, the justice or judge shall credit the defendant for any time the defendant was confined in jail or prison while serving a sentence for another offense if that confinement occurred after the commission of the misdemeanor. The credit under this subsection shall be applied to the amount of the fine and costs at the rate of not less than $150 for each day of confinement.

(d) All judgments, sentences, and final orders of the justice or judge shall be rendered in open court.

Art. 45.042. Appeal.

(a) Appeals from a justice or municipal court, including appeals from final judgments in bond forfeiture proceedings, shall be heard by the county court except in cases where the county court has no jurisdiction, in which counties such appeals shall be heard by the proper court.

(b) Unless the appeal is taken from a municipal court of record and the appeal is based on error reflected in the record, the trial shall be de novo.

(c) In an appeal from the judgment and sentence of a justice or municipal court, if the defendant is in custody, the defendant is to be committed to jail unless the defendant gives bail.

Art. 45.0425. Appeal Bond.

(a) If the court from whose judgment and sentence the appeal is taken is in session, the court must approve the bail. The amount of an appeal bond may not be less than two times the amount of the fine and costs adjudged against the defendant, payable to the State of Texas. The appeal bond may not in any case be for an amount less than $50. If the appeal bond otherwise meets the requirements of this code, the court without requiring a court appearance by the defendant shall approve the appeal bond in the amount the court under Article 27.14(b) notified the defendant would be approved.

(b) An appeal bond shall recite that in the cause the defendant was convicted and has appealed and be conditioned that the defendant shall make the defendant's personal appearance before the court to which the appeal is taken instanter, if the court is in session, or, if the court is not in session, at its next regular term, stating the time and place of that session, and there remain from day to day and term to term, and answer in the cause in the court.

Art. 45.0426. Filing Bond Perfects Appeal.

(a) When the appeal bond has been filed with the justice or judge who tried the case not later than the 10th day after the date the judgment was entered, the appeal in such case shall be held to be perfected.

(b) If an appeal bond is not timely filed, the appellate court does not have jurisdiction over the case and shall remand the case to the justice or municipal court for execution of the sentence.

(c) An appeal may not be dismissed because the defendant failed to give notice of appeal in open court. An appeal by the defendant or the state may not be dismissed on account of any defect in the transcript.

Art. 45.043. Effect of Appeal.

When a defendant files the appeal bond required by law with the justice or municipal court, all further proceedings in the case in the justice or municipal court shall cease.

Art. 45.044. Forfeiture of Cash Bond in Satisfaction of Fine.

(a) A justice or judge may enter a judgment of conviction and forfeit a cash bond posted by the defendant in satisfaction of the defendant's fine and cost if the defendant:

(1) has entered a written and signed plea of nolo contendere and a waiver of jury trial; and

(2) fails to appear according to the terms of the defendant's release.

(b) A justice or judge who enters a judgment of conviction and forfeiture under Subsection (a) of this article shall immediately notify the defendant in writing, by regular mail addressed to the defendant at the defendant's last known address, that:

(1) a judgment of conviction and forfeiture of bond was entered against the defendant on a date certain and the forfeiture satisfies the defendant's fine and costs in the case; and

(2) the defendant has a right to a new trial in the case if the defendant applies for the new trial not later than the 10th day after the date of judgment and forfeiture.

(c) Notwithstanding Article 45.037 of this code, the defendant may file a motion for a new trial within the period provided by Subsection (b) of this article, and the court shall grant the motion if the motion is made within that period. On the new trial, the court shall permit the defendant to withdraw the previously entered plea of nolo contendere and waiver of jury trial.

Art. 45.0445. Reconsideration of Satisfaction of Fine or Costs.

(a) If the defendant notifies the justice or judge that the defendant has difficulty paying the fine and costs in compliance with the judgment, the justice or judge shall hold a hearing to determine whether the judgment imposes an undue hardship on the defendant.

(b) For purposes of Subsection (a), a defendant may notify the justice or judge by:

(1) voluntarily appearing and informing the justice or judge or the clerk of the court in the manner established by the justice or judge for that purpose;

(2) filing a motion with the justice or judge;

(3) mailing a letter to the justice or judge; or

(4) any other method established by the justice or judge for that purpose.

(c) If the justice or judge determines at the hearing under Subsection (a) that the judgment imposes an undue hardship on the defendant, the justice or judge shall consider whether to allow the defendant to satisfy the fine and costs through one or more methods listed under Article 45.041(a-1).

(d) The justice or judge may decline to hold a hearing under Subsection (a) if the justice or judge:

(1) previously held a hearing under that subsection with respect to the case and is able to determine without holding a hearing that the judgment does not impose an undue hardship on the defendant; or

(2) is able to determine without holding a hearing that:

(A) the judgment imposes an undue hardship on the defendant; and

(B) the fine and costs should be satisfied through one or more methods listed under Article 45.041(a-1).

(e) The justice or judge retains jurisdiction for the purpose of making a determination under this article.

Art. 45.045. Capias Pro Fine.

(a) If the defendant is not in custody when the judgment is rendered or if the defendant fails to satisfy the judgment according to its terms, the court may order a capias pro fine, as defined by Article 43.015, issued for the defendant's arrest. The capias pro fine shall state the amount of the judgment and sentence, and command the appropriate peace officer to bring the defendant before the court immediately or place the defendant in jail until the business day following the date of the defendant's arrest if the defendant cannot be brought before the court immediately.

(a-1) **[2 Versions: As added by Acts 2015, 84th Leg., ch. 1171]** If the court that issued the capias pro fine is unavailable, the arresting officer may, in lieu of placing the defendant in jail, take the defendant to:

(1) a justice of the peace court or county criminal law magistrate court with jurisdiction over Class C misdemeanors that is located in the same county, if the court that issued the capias pro fine was a justice of the peace court; or

(2) a municipal court that is located in the same municipality, if the court that issued the capias pro fine was a municipal court.

(a-1) **[2 Versions: As added by Acts 2015, 84th Leg., ch. 1182]** If the court that issued the capias pro fine is unavailable, the arresting officer may take the defendant to one of the following locations in lieu of placing the defendant in jail:

(1) if the court that issued the capias pro fine was a justice of the peace, to a justice of the peace or county criminal law magistrate court with jurisdiction over Class C misdemeanors that is located within the same county; or

(2) if the court that issued the capias pro fine was a municipal court, to a municipal court judge that is located within the same city.

(a-2) The court may not issue a capias pro fine for the defendant's failure to satisfy the judgment according to its terms unless the court holds a hearing to determine whether the judgment imposes an undue hardship on the defendant and the defendant fails to:

(1) appear at the hearing; or

(2) comply with an order issued under Subsection (a-4) as a result of the hearing.

(a-3) If the justice or judge determines at the hearing under Subsection (a-2) that the judgment imposes an undue hardship on the defendant, the justice or judge shall determine whether the fine and costs should be satisfied through one or more methods listed under Article 45.041(a-1). The justice or judge retains jurisdiction for the purpose of making a determination under this subsection.

(a-4) If the justice or judge determines at the hearing under Subsection (a-2) that the judgment does not impose an undue hardship on the defendant, the justice or judge shall order the defendant to comply with the judgment not later than the 30th day after the date the determination is made.

(a-5) The court shall recall a capias pro fine if, before the capias pro fine is executed, the defendant:

(1) provides notice to the justice or judge under Article 45.0445 and a hearing is set under that article; or

(2) voluntarily appears and makes a good faith effort to resolve the capias pro fine.

(b) A capias pro fine may not be issued for an individual convicted for an offense committed before the individual's 17th birthday unless:

(1) the individual is 17 years of age or older;

(2) the court finds that the issuance of the capias pro fine is justified after considering:

(A) the sophistication and maturity of the individual;

(B) the criminal record and history of the individual; and

(C) the reasonable likelihood of bringing about the discharge of the judgment through the use of procedures and services currently available to the court; and

(3) the court has proceeded under Article 45.050 to compel the individual to discharge the judgment.

(c) This article does not limit the authority of a court to order a child taken into custody under Article 45.058 or 45.059.

Code of Criminal Procedure

Art. 45.046. Commitment.

(a) When a judgment and sentence have been entered against a defendant and the defendant defaults in the discharge of the judgment, the judge may order the defendant confined in jail until discharged by law if the judge at a hearing makes a written determination that:

(1) the defendant is not indigent and has failed to make a good faith effort to discharge the fine or costs; or

(2) the defendant is indigent and:

(A) has failed to make a good faith effort to discharge the fine or costs under Article 45.049; and

(B) could have discharged the fine or costs under Article 45.049 without experiencing any undue hardship.

(b) A certified copy of the judgment, sentence, and order is sufficient to authorize such confinement.

(c) For purposes of a hearing described by Subsection (a), a defendant may be brought before the court in person or by means of an electronic broadcast system through which an image of the defendant is presented to the court. For purposes of this subsection, "electronic broadcast system" means a two-way electronic communication of image and sound between the defendant and the court and includes secure Internet videoconferencing.

(d) **[2 Versions: As added by Acts 2015, 84th Leg., ch. 1171]** For purposes of a hearing described by Subsection (a), if the court that issued the capias pro fine is unavailable, the following judicial officers may conduct the hearing:

(1) a justice of the peace or county criminal law magistrate with jurisdiction over Class C misdemeanors who is located in the same county as the issuing court, if the issuing court was a justice of the peace court; or

(2) a municipal court judge who is located in the same municipality as the issuing court, if the issuing court was a municipal court.

(d) **[2 Versions: As added by Acts 2015, 84th Leg., ch. 1182]** For purposes of a hearing described by Subsection (a), if the court that issued the capias pro fine is unavailable, the following judicial officers may conduct the hearing:

(1) if the court that issued the capias pro fine was a justice of the peace, a justice of the peace or a county criminal law magistrate with jurisdiction over Class C misdemeanors that is located within the same county as the issuing court; or

(2) if the court that issued the capias pro fine was a municipal court, a municipal court judge that is located within the same city as the issuing municipal court.

Art. 45.047. Civil Collection of Fines After Judgment.

If after a judgment and sentence is entered the defendant defaults in payment of a fine, the justice or judge may order the fine and costs collected by execution against the defendant's property in the same manner as a judgment in a civil suit.

Art. 45.048. Discharged From Jail.

(a) A defendant placed in jail on account of failure to pay the fine and costs shall be discharged on habeas corpus by showing that the defendant:

(1) is too poor to pay the fine and costs; or

(2) has remained in jail a sufficient length of time to satisfy the fine and costs, at the rate of not less than $150 for each period served, as specified by the convicting court in the judgment in the case.

(b) A convicting court may specify a period that is not less than eight hours or more than 24 hours as the period for which a defendant who fails to pay the fine and costs in the case must remain in jail to satisfy $150 of the fine and costs.

Art. 45.049. Community Service in Satisfaction of Fine or Costs.

(a) A justice or judge may require a defendant who fails to pay a previously assessed fine or costs, or who is determined by the court to have insufficient resources or income to pay a fine or costs, to discharge all or part of the fine or costs by performing community service. A defendant may discharge an obligation to perform community service under this article by paying at any time the fine and costs assessed.

(b) In the justice's or judge's order requiring a defendant to perform community service under this article, the justice or judge must specify:

(1) the number of hours of community service the defendant is required to perform; and

(2) the date by which the defendant must submit to the court documentation verifying the defendant's completion of the community service.

(c) The justice or judge may order the defendant to perform community service under this article:

(1) by attending:

(A) a work and job skills training program;

(B) a preparatory class for the high school equivalency examination administered under Section 7.111, Education Code;

(C) an alcohol or drug abuse program;

(D) a rehabilitation program;

(E) a counseling program, including a self-improvement program;

(F) a mentoring program; or
(G) any similar activity; or
(2) for:
(A) a governmental entity;
(B) a nonprofit organization or another organization that provides services to the general public that enhance social welfare and the general well-being of the community, as determined by the justice or judge; or
(C) an educational institution.

(c-1) An entity that accepts a defendant under this article to perform community service must agree to supervise, either on-site or remotely, the defendant in the performance of the defendant's community service and report on the defendant's community service to the justice or judge who ordered the service.

(d) A justice or judge may not order a defendant to perform more than 16 hours per week of community service under this article unless the justice or judge determines that requiring the defendant to perform additional hours does not impose an undue hardship on the defendant or the defendant's dependents.

(e) A defendant is considered to have discharged not less than $100 of fines or costs for each eight hours of community service performed under this article.

(f) A sheriff, employee of a sheriff's department, county commissioner, county employee, county judge, justice of the peace, municipal court judge, or officer or employee of a political subdivision other than a county or an entity that accepts a defendant under this article to perform community service is not liable for damages arising from an act or failure to act in connection with community service performed by a defendant under this article if the act or failure to act:
(1) was performed pursuant to court order; and
(2) was not intentional, wilfully or wantonly negligent, or performed with conscious indifference or reckless disregard for the safety of others.

(g) This subsection applies only to a defendant who is charged with a traffic offense or an offense under Section 106.05, Alcoholic Beverage Code, and is a resident of this state. If under Article 45.051(b)(10), Code of Criminal Procedure, the judge requires the defendant to perform community service as a condition of the deferral, the defendant is entitled to elect whether to perform the required service in:
(1) the county in which the court is located; or
(2) the county in which the defendant resides, but only if the applicable entity agrees to:
(A) supervise, either on-site or remotely, the defendant in the performance of the defendant's community service; and
(B) report to the court on the defendant's community service.

(h) This subsection applies only to a defendant charged with an offense under Section 106.05, Alcoholic Beverage Code, who, under Subsection (g), elects to perform the required community service in the county in which the defendant resides. The community service must comply with Sections 106.071(d) and (e), Alcoholic Beverage Code, except that if the educational programs or services described by Section 106.071(e) are not available in the county of the defendant's residence, the court may order community service that it considers appropriate for rehabilitative purposes.

(i) A community supervision and corrections department or a court-related services office may provide the administrative and other services necessary for supervision of a defendant required to perform community service under this article.

Art. 45.0491. Waiver of Payment of Fines and Costs for Certain Defendants and for Children.

(a) A municipal court, regardless of whether the court is a court of record, or a justice court may waive payment of all or part of a fine imposed on a defendant if the court determines that:
(1) the defendant is indigent or does not have sufficient resources or income to pay all or part of the fine or was, at the time the offense was committed, a child as defined by Article 45.058(h); and
(2) discharging the fine under Article 45.049 or as otherwise authorized by this chapter would impose an undue hardship on the defendant.

(b) A defendant is presumed to be indigent or to not have sufficient resources or income to pay all or part of the fine or costs for purposes of Subsection (a) or (d) if the defendant:
(1) is in the conservatorship of the Department of Family and Protective Services, or was in the conservatorship of that department at the time of the offense; or
(2) is designated as a homeless child or youth or an unaccompanied youth, as those terms are defined by 42 U.S.C. Section 11434a, or was so designated at the time of the offense.

(c) A determination of undue hardship made under Subsection (a)(2) is in the court's discretion. In making that determination, the court may consider, as applicable, the defendant's:
(1) significant physical or mental impairment or disability;
(2) pregnancy and childbirth;
(3) substantial family commitments or responsibilities, including child or dependent care;

Code of Criminal Procedure

(4) work responsibilities and hours;
(5) transportation limitations;
(6) homelessness or housing insecurity; and
(7) any other factors the court determines relevant.

(d) A municipal court, regardless of whether the court is a court of record, or a justice court may waive payment of all or part of the costs imposed on a defendant if the court determines that the defendant:

(1) is indigent or does not have sufficient resources or income to pay all or part of the costs; or

(2) was, at the time the offense was committed, a child as defined by Article 45.058(h).

Art. 45.0492. Community Service in Satisfaction of Fine or Costs for Certain Juvenile Defendants.

(a) This article applies only to a defendant younger than 17 years of age who is assessed a fine or costs for a Class C misdemeanor occurring in a building or on the grounds of the primary or secondary school at which the defendant was enrolled at the time of the offense.

(b) A justice or judge may require a defendant described by Subsection (a) to discharge all or part of the fine or costs by performing community service. A defendant may discharge an obligation to perform community service under this article by paying at any time the fine and costs assessed.

(c) In the justice's or judge's order requiring a defendant to perform community service under this article, the justice or judge must specify:

(1) the number of hours of community service the defendant is required to perform; and

(2) the date by which the defendant must submit to the court documentation verifying the defendant's completion of the community service.

(d) The justice or judge may order the defendant to perform community service under this article:

(1) by attending:

(A) a work and job skills training program;

(B) a preparatory class for the high school equivalency examination administered under Section 7.111, Education Code;

(C) an alcohol or drug abuse program;

(D) a rehabilitation program;

(E) a counseling program, including a self-improvement program;

(F) a mentoring program;

(G) a tutoring program; or

(H) any similar activity; or

(2) for:

(A) a governmental entity;

(B) a nonprofit organization or another organization that provides services to the general public that enhance social welfare and the general well-being of the community, as determined by the justice or judge; or

(C) an educational institution.

(d-1) An entity that accepts a defendant under this article to perform community service must agree to supervise, either on-site or remotely, the defendant in the performance of the defendant's community service and report on the defendant's community service to the justice or judge who ordered the service.

(e) [Repealed by Acts 2017, 85th Leg., ch. 977 (H.B. 351), § 31 and ch. 1127 (S.B. 1913), § 27, effective September 1, 2017.]

(f) A justice or judge may not order a defendant to perform more than 16 hours of community service per week under this article unless the justice or judge determines that requiring the defendant to perform additional hours does not impose an undue hardship on the defendant or the defendant's family. For purposes of this subsection, "family" has the meaning assigned by Section 71.003, Family Code.

(g) A defendant is considered to have discharged not less than $100 of fines or costs for each eight hours of community service performed under this article.

(h) A sheriff, employee of a sheriff's department, county commissioner, county employee, county judge, justice of the peace, municipal court judge, or officer or employee of a political subdivision other than a county or an entity that accepts a defendant under this article to perform community service is not liable for damages arising from an act or failure to act in connection with community service performed by a defendant under this article if the act or failure to act:

(1) was performed pursuant to court order; and

(2) was not intentional, grossly negligent, or performed with conscious indifference or reckless disregard for the safety of others.

(i) A local juvenile probation department or a court-related services office may provide the administrative and other services necessary for supervision of a defendant required to perform community service under this article.

Art. 45.05. Commitment [Repealed].

Repealed by Acts 1999, 76th Leg., ch. 1545 (S.B. 1230), § 75(a), effective September 1, 1999.

Art. 45.050. Failure to Pay Fine; Failure to Appear; Contempt: Juveniles.

(a) In this article, "child" has the meaning assigned by Article 45.058(h).

(b) A justice or municipal court may not order the confinement of a child for:

(1) the failure to pay all or any part of a fine or costs imposed for the conviction of an offense punishable by fine only;

(2) the failure to appear for an offense committed by the child; or

(3) contempt of another order of a justice or municipal court.

(c) If a child fails to obey an order of a justice or municipal court under circumstances that would constitute contempt of court, the justice or municipal court, after providing notice and an opportunity to be heard, may:

(1) refer the child to the appropriate juvenile court for delinquent conduct for contempt of the justice or municipal court order; or

(2) retain jurisdiction of the case, hold the child in contempt of the justice or municipal court, and order either or both of the following:

(A) that the contemnor pay a fine not to exceed $500; or

(B) that the Department of Public Safety suspend the contemnor's driver's license or permit or, if the contemnor does not have a license or permit, to deny the issuance of a license or permit to the contemnor until the contemnor fully complies with the orders of the court.

(d) A justice or municipal court may hold a person in contempt and impose a remedy authorized by Subsection (c)(2) if:

(1) the person was convicted for an offense committed before the person's 17th birthday;

(2) the person failed to obey the order while the person was 17 years of age or older; and

(3) the failure to obey occurred under circumstances that constitute contempt of court.

(e) A justice or municipal court may hold a person in contempt and impose a remedy authorized by Subsection (c)(2) if the person, while younger than 17 years of age, engaged in conduct in contempt of an order issued by the justice or municipal court, but contempt proceedings could not be held before the person's 17th birthday.

(f) A court that orders suspension or denial of a driver's license or permit under Subsection (c)(2)(B) shall notify the Department of Public Safety on receiving proof of compliance with the orders of the court.

(g) A justice or municipal court may not refer a child who violates a court order while 17 years of age or older to a juvenile court for delinquency proceedings for contempt of court.

Art. 45.051. Suspension of Sentence and Deferral of Final Disposition.

(a) On a plea of guilty or nolo contendere by a defendant or on a finding of guilt in a misdemeanor case punishable by fine only and payment of all court costs, the judge may defer further proceedings without entering an adjudication of guilt and place the defendant on probation for a period not to exceed 180 days. In issuing the order of deferral, the judge may impose a fine on the defendant in an amount not to exceed the amount of the fine that could be imposed on the defendant as punishment for the offense. The fine may be collected at any time before the date on which the period of probation ends. The judge may elect not to impose the fine for good cause shown by the defendant. If the judge orders the collection of a fine under this subsection, the judge shall require that the amount of the fine be credited toward the payment of the amount of any fine imposed by the judge as punishment for the offense. An order of deferral under this subsection terminates any liability under a bond given for the charge.

(a-1) Notwithstanding any other provision of law, as an alternative to requiring a defendant charged with one or more offenses to make payment of all fines and court costs as required by Subsection (a), the judge may:

(1) allow the defendant to enter into an agreement for payment of those fines and costs in installments during the defendant's period of probation;

(2) require an eligible defendant to discharge all or part of those fines and costs by performing community service or attending a tutoring program under Article 45.049 or under Article 45.0492, as added by Chapter 227 (H.B. 350), Acts of the 82nd Legislature, Regular Session, 2011;

(3) waive all or part of those fines and costs under Article 45.0491; or

(4) take any combination of actions authorized by Subdivision (1), (2), or (3).

(b) During the deferral period, the judge may require the defendant to:

(1) post a bond in the amount of the fine assessed as punishment for the offense to secure payment of the fine;

(2) pay restitution to the victim of the offense in an amount not to exceed the fine assessed as punishment for the offense;

(3) submit to professional counseling;

(4) submit to diagnostic testing for alcohol or a controlled substance or drug;

(5) submit to a psychosocial assessment;

(6) successfully complete an alcohol or drug abuse treatment or education program, such as:

(A) a drug education program that is designed to educate persons on the dangers of drug abuse in accordance with Section 521.374(a)(1), Transportation Code, and that is regulated by the Texas

Department of Licensing and Regulation under Chapter 171, Government Code; or

(B) an alcohol awareness program described by Section 106.115, Alcoholic Beverage Code, that is regulated by the Texas Department of Licensing and Regulation under Chapter 171, Government Code;

(7) pay as reimbursement fees the costs of any diagnostic testing, psychosocial assessment, or participation in a treatment or education program either directly or through the court as court costs;

(8) complete a driving safety course approved under Chapter 1001, Education Code, or another course as directed by the judge;

(9) present to the court satisfactory evidence that the defendant has complied with each requirement imposed by the judge under this article; and

(10) comply with any other reasonable condition.

(b-1) If the defendant is younger than 25 years of age and the offense committed by the defendant is a traffic offense classified as a moving violation:

(1) Subsection (b)(8) does not apply;

(2) during the deferral period, the judge shall require the defendant to complete a driving safety course approved under Chapter 1001, Education Code; and

(3) if the defendant holds a provisional license, during the deferral period the judge shall require that the defendant be examined by the Department of Public Safety as required by Section 521.161(b)(2), Transportation Code; a defendant is not exempt from the examination regardless of whether the defendant was examined previously.

(b-2) A person examined as required by Subsection (b-1)(3) must pay a $10 reimbursement fee for the examination.

(b-3) The reimbursement fee collected under Subsection (b-2) must be deposited to the credit of a special account in the general revenue fund and may be used only by the Department of Public Safety for the administration of Chapter 521, Transportation Code.

(c) On determining that the defendant has complied with the requirements imposed by the judge under this article, the judge shall dismiss the complaint, and it shall be clearly noted in the docket that the complaint is dismissed and that there is not a final conviction.

(c-1) If the defendant fails to present within the deferral period satisfactory evidence of compliance with the requirements imposed by the judge under this article, the court shall:

(1) notify the defendant in writing, mailed to the address on file with the court or appearing on the notice to appear, of that failure; and

(2) require the defendant to appear at the time and place stated in the notice to show cause why the order of deferral should not be revoked.

(c-2) On the defendant's showing of good cause for failure to present satisfactory evidence of compliance with the requirements imposed by the judge under this article, the court may allow an additional period during which the defendant may present evidence of the defendant's compliance with the requirements.

(d) If on the date of a show cause hearing under Subsection (c-1) or, if applicable, by the conclusion of an additional period provided under Subsection (c-2) the defendant does not present satisfactory evidence that the defendant complied with the requirements imposed, the judge may impose the fine assessed or impose a lesser fine. The imposition of the fine or lesser fine constitutes a final conviction of the defendant. This subsection does not apply to a defendant required under Subsection (b-1) to complete a driving safety course approved under Chapter 1001, Education Code, or an examination under Section 521.161(b)(2), Transportation Code.

(d-1) If the defendant was required to complete a driving safety course or an examination under Subsection (b-1) and on the date of a show cause hearing under Subsection (c-1) or, if applicable, by the conclusion of an additional period provided under Subsection (c-2) the defendant does not present satisfactory evidence that the defendant completed that course or examination, the judge shall impose the fine assessed. The imposition of the fine constitutes a final conviction of the defendant.

(e) Records relating to a complaint dismissed as provided by this article may be expunged under Article 55.01. If a complaint is dismissed under this article, there is not a final conviction and the complaint may not be used against the person for any purpose.

(f) This article does not apply to:

(1) an offense to which Section 542.404, Transportation Code, applies; or

(2) a violation of a state law or local ordinance relating to motor vehicle control, other than a parking violation, committed by a person who:

(A) holds a commercial driver's license; or

(B) held a commercial driver's license when the offense was committed.

(g) If a judge requires a defendant under Subsection (b) to successfully complete an alcohol awareness program or drug education program as described by Subdivision (6) of that subsection, unless the judge determines that the defendant is indigent and unable to pay the cost, the judge shall require the defendant to pay a reimbursement fee for the cost of the program. The judge may allow the defendant to pay the fee in installments during the deferral period.

Art. 45.0511. Driving Safety Course or Motorcycle Operator Course Dismissal Procedures.

(a) Except as provided by Subsection (a-1), this article applies only to an alleged offense that:

(1) is within the jurisdiction of a justice court or a municipal court;

(2) involves the operation of a motor vehicle; and

(3) is defined by:

(A) Section 472.022, Transportation Code;

(B) Subtitle C, Title 7, Transportation Code; or

(C) Section 729.001(a)(3), Transportation Code.

(a-1) If the defendant is younger than 25 years of age, this article applies to any alleged offense that:

(1) is within the jurisdiction of a justice court or a municipal court;

(2) involves the operation of a motor vehicle; and

(3) is classified as a moving violation.

(b) The judge shall require the defendant to successfully complete a driving safety course approved by the Texas Department of Licensing and Regulation or a course under the motorcycle operator training and safety program approved by the designated state agency under Chapter 662, Transportation Code, if:

(1) the defendant elects driving safety course or motorcycle operator training course dismissal under this article;

(2) the defendant:

(A) has not completed an approved driving safety course or motorcycle operator training course, as appropriate, within the 12 months preceding the date of the offense; or

(B) does not have a valid Texas driver's license or permit, is a member, or the spouse or dependent child of a member, of the United States military forces serving on active duty, and has not completed a driving safety course or motorcycle operator training course, as appropriate, in another state within the 12 months preceding the date of the offense;

(3) the defendant enters a plea under Article 45.021 in person or in writing of no contest or guilty on or before the answer date on the notice to appear and:

(A) presents in person or by counsel to the court a request to take a course; or

(B) sends to the court by certified mail, return receipt requested, postmarked on or before the answer date on the notice to appear, a written request to take a course;

(4) the defendant:

(A) has a valid Texas driver's license or permit; or

(B) is a member, or the spouse or dependent child of a member, of the United States military forces serving on active duty;

(5) the defendant is charged with an offense to which this article applies, other than speeding at a speed of:

(A) 95 miles per hour or more; or

(B) 25 miles per hour or more over the posted speed limit; and

(6) the defendant provides evidence of financial responsibility as required by Chapter 601, Transportation Code.

(c) The court shall enter judgment on the defendant's plea of no contest or guilty at the time the plea is made, defer imposition of the judgment, and allow the defendant 90 days to successfully complete the approved driving safety course or motorcycle operator training course and present to the court:

(1) a uniform certificate of completion of the driving safety course or a verification of completion of the motorcycle operator training course;

(2) unless the judge proceeds under Subsection (c-1), the defendant's driving record as maintained by the Department of Public Safety, if any, showing that the defendant had not completed an approved driving safety course or motorcycle operator training course, as applicable, within the 12 months preceding the date of the offense;

(3) an affidavit stating that the defendant was not taking a driving safety course or motorcycle operator training course, as applicable, under this article on the date the request to take the course was made and had not completed such a course that is not shown on the defendant's driving record within the 12 months preceding the date of the offense; and

(4) if the defendant does not have a valid Texas driver's license or permit and is a member, or the spouse or dependent child of a member, of the United States military forces serving on active duty, an affidavit stating that the defendant was not taking a driving safety course or motorcycle operator training course, as appropriate, in another state on the date the request to take the course was made and had not completed such a course within the 12 months preceding the date of the offense.

(c-1) In this subsection, "state electronic Internet portal" has the meaning assigned by Section 2054.003, Government Code. As an alternative to receiving the defendant's driving record under Subsection (c)(2), the judge, at the time the defendant requests a driving safety course or motorcycle operator training course dismissal under this article, may require the defendant to pay a reimbursemen fee in an amount equal to the sum of the amount of the fee established by Section 521.048, Transportation Code, and the state electronic Internet portal fee and, using the state electronic Internet portal, may request the Texas Department of Public Safety to provide the judge with a copy of the defendant's driving record that shows the information described by Section 521.047(b), Transportation Code. As soon as practicable and using the state electronic Internet portal, the Texas Department of Public Safety shall provide the judge with the requested copy of the defendant's driving record. The reimbursemen fee authorized by this subsection is in addition to any other fee required under this article. If the copy of the defendant's driving record provided to the judge under this subsection shows that the defendant has not completed an approved driving safety course or motorcycle operator training course, as appropriate, within the 12 months preceding the date of the offense, the judge shall allow the defendant to complete the appropriate course as provided by this article. The custodian of a municipal or county treasury who receives reimbursemen fees collected under this subsection shall keep a record of the fees and, without deduction or proration, forward the fees to the comptroller, with and in the manner required for other fees and costs received in connection with criminal cases. The comptroller shall credit fees received under this subsection to the Texas Department of Public Safety.

(d) Notwithstanding Subsections (b)(2) and (3), before the final disposition of the case, the court may grant a request to take a driving safety course or a motorcycle operator training course under this article.

(e) A request to take a driving safety course or motorcycle operator training course made at or before the time and at the place at which a defendant is required to appear in court is an appearance in compliance with the defendant's promise to appear.

(f) In addition to court costs and fees authorized or imposed by a law of this state and applicable to the offense, the court may:

(1) require a defendant requesting a course under Subsection (b) to pay a reimbursement fee to cover the cost of administering this article in an amount of not more than $10; or

(2) require a defendant requesting a course under Subsection (d) to pay a fine set by the court at an amount not to exceed the maximum amount of the fine for the offense committed by the defendant.

(g) A defendant who requests but does not take a course is not entitled to a refund of the reimbursement fee or fine assessed under Subsection (f).

(h) Money collected by a municipal court shall be deposited in the municipal treasury. Money collected by another court shall be deposited in the county treasury of the county in which the court is located.

(i) If a defendant requesting a course under this article fails to comply with Subsection (c), the court shall:

(1) notify the defendant in writing, mailed to the address on file with the court or appearing on the notice to appear, of that failure; and

(2) require the defendant to appear at the time and place stated in the notice to show cause why the evidence was not timely submitted to the court.

(j) If the defendant fails to appear at the time and place stated in the notice under Subsection (i), or appears at the time and place stated in the notice but does not show good cause for the defendant's failure to comply with Subsection (c), the court shall enter an adjudication of guilt and impose sentence.

(k) On a defendant's showing of good cause for failure to furnish evidence to the court, the court may allow an extension of time during which the defendant may present:

(1) a uniform certificate of course completion as evidence that the defendant successfully completed the driving safety course; or

(2) a verification of course completion as evidence that the defendant successfully completed the motorcycle operator training course.

(*l*) When a defendant complies with Subsection (c), the court shall:

(1) remove the judgment and dismiss the charge;

(2) report the fact that the defendant successfully completed a driving safety course or a motorcycle operator training course and the date of completion to the Texas Department of Public Safety for inclusion in the person's driving record; and

(3) state in that report whether the course was taken under this article to provide information necessary to determine eligibility to take a subsequent course under Subsection (b).

(m) The court may dismiss only one charge for each completion of a course.

(n) A charge that is dismissed under this article may not be part of a person's driving record or used for any purpose.

(o) An insurer delivering or issuing for delivery a motor vehicle insurance policy in this state may not cancel or increase the premium charged an insured under the policy because the insured completed a driving safety course or a motorcycle operator training course, or had a charge dismissed under this article.

(p) The court shall advise a defendant charged with a misdemeanor under Section 472.022,

Transportation Code, Subtitle C, Title 7, Transportation Code, or Section 729.001(a)(3), Transportation Code, committed while operating a motor vehicle of the defendant's right under this article to successfully complete a driving safety course or, if the offense was committed while operating a motorcycle, a motorcycle operator training course. The right to complete a course does not apply to a defendant charged with:

(1) a violation of Section 545.066, 550.022, or 550.023, Transportation Code;

(2) a serious traffic violation; or

(3) an offense to which Section 542.404, Transportation Code, applies.

(q) A notice to appear issued for an offense to which this article applies must inform a defendant charged with an offense under Section 472.022, Transportation Code, an offense under Subtitle C, Title 7, Transportation Code, or an offense under Section 729.001(a)(3), Transportation Code, committed while operating a motor vehicle of the defendant's right to complete a driving safety course or, if the offense was committed while operating a motorcycle, of the defendant's right to complete a motorcycle operator training course. The notice required by this subsection must read substantially as follows:

"You may be able to require that this charge be dismissed by successfully completing a driving safety course or a motorcycle operator training course. You will lose that right if, on or before your appearance date, you do not provide the court with notice of your request to take the course."

(r) If the notice required by Subsection (q) is not provided to the defendant charged with the offense, the defendant may continue to exercise the defendant's right to take a driving safety course or a motorcycle operator training course until the notice required by Subsection (q) is provided to the defendant or there is a final disposition of the case.

(s) This article does not apply to an offense committed by a person who:

(1) holds a commercial driver's license; or

(2) held a commercial driver's license when the offense was committed.

(t) An order of deferral under Subsection (c) terminates any liability under a bond given for the charge.

(u) **[Repealed effective June 1, 2023]** The requirement of Subsection (b)(2) does not apply to a defendant charged with an offense under Section 545.412, Transportation Code, if the judge requires the defendant to attend and present proof that the defendant has successfully completed a specialized driving safety course that includes four hours of instruction that encourages the use of child passenger safety seat systems, and any driving safety course taken by the defendant under this section within the 12 months preceding the date of the offense did not include that training. The person's driving record under Subsection (c)(2) and the affidavit of the defendant under Subsection (c)(3) is required to include only previous or concurrent courses that included that training.

Art. 45.052. Dismissal of Misdemeanor Charge on Completion of Teen Court Program.

(a) A justice or municipal court may defer proceedings against a defendant who is under the age of 18 or enrolled full time in an accredited secondary school in a program leading toward a high school diploma for not more than 180 days if the defendant:

(1) is charged with an offense that the court has jurisdiction of under Article 4.11 or 4.14;

(2) pleads nolo contendere or guilty to the offense in open court with the defendant's parent, guardian, or managing conservator present;

(3) presents to the court an oral or written request to attend a teen court program or is recommended to attend the program by a school employee under Section 37.146, Education Code; and

(4) has not successfully completed a teen court program in the year preceding the date that the alleged offense occurred.

(b) The teen court program must be approved by the court.

(c) A defendant for whom proceedings are deferred under Subsection (a) shall complete the teen court program not later than the 90th day after the date the teen court hearing to determine punishment is held or the last day of the deferral period, whichever date is earlier. The justice or municipal court shall dismiss the charge at the time the defendant presents satisfactory evidence that the defendant has successfully completed the teen court program.

(d) A charge dismissed under this article may not be part of the defendant's criminal record or driving record or used for any purpose. However, if the charge was for a traffic offense, the court shall report to the Department of Public Safety that the defendant successfully completed the teen court program and the date of completion for inclusion in the defendant's driving record.

(e) The justice or municipal court may require a person who requests a teen court program to pay a reimbursement fee not to exceed $10 that is set by the court to cover the costs of administering this article. Reimbursement fees collected by a

Code of Criminal Procedure

municipal court shall be deposited in the municipal treasury. Reimbursement fees collected by a justice court shall be deposited in the county treasury of the county in which the court is located. A person who requests a teen court program and fails to complete the program is not entitled to a refund of the fee.

(f) A court may transfer a case in which proceedings have been deferred under this section to a court in another county if the court to which the case is transferred consents. A case may not be transferred unless it is within the jurisdiction of the court to which it is transferred.

(g) In addition to the reimbursement fee authorized by Subsection (e), the court may require a child who requests a teen court program to pay a $10 reimbursement fee to cover the cost to the teen court for performing its duties under this article. The court shall pay the fee to the teen court program, and the teen court program must account to the court for the receipt and disbursal of the fee. A child who pays a fee under this subsection is not entitled to a refund of the fee, regardless of whether the child successfully completes the teen court program.

(h) A justice or municipal court may exempt a defendant for whom proceedings are deferred under this article from the requirement to pay a court cost or fee that is imposed by another statute.

(i) Notwithstanding Subsection (e) or (g), a justice or municipal court that is located in the Texas-Louisiana border region, as defined by Section 2056.002, Government Code, may charge a reimbursement fee of $20 under those subsections.

Art. 45.053. Dismissal of Misdemeanor Charge on Commitment of Chemically Dependent Person.

(a) On a plea of guilty or nolo contendere by a defendant or on a finding of guilt in a misdemeanor case punishable by a fine only, a justice or municipal court may defer further proceedings for 90 days without entering an adjudication of guilt if:

(1) the court finds that the offense resulted from or was related to the defendant's chemical dependency; and

(2) an application for court-ordered treatment of the defendant is filed in accordance with Chapter 462, Health and Safety Code.

(b) At the end of the deferral period, the justice or municipal court shall dismiss the charge if satisfactory evidence is presented that the defendant was committed for and completed court-ordered treatment in accordance with Chapter 462, Health and Safety Code, and it shall be clearly noted in the docket that the complaint is dismissed and that there is not a final conviction.

(c) If at the conclusion of the deferral period satisfactory evidence that the defendant was committed for and completed court-ordered treatment in accordance with Chapter 462, Health and Safety Code, is not presented, the justice or municipal court may impose the fine assessed or impose a lesser fine. The imposition of a fine constitutes a final conviction of the defendant.

(d) Records relating to a complaint dismissed under this article may be expunged under Article 55.01 of this code. If a complaint is dismissed under this article, there is not a final conviction and the complaint may not be used against the person for any purpose.

Art. 45.0531. Dismissal of Parent Contributing to Nonattendance Charge.

Notwithstanding any other law, a county, justice, or municipal court, at the court's discretion, may dismiss a charge against a defendant alleging the defendant committed an offense under Section 25.093, Education Code, if the court finds that a dismissal would be in the interest of justice because:

(1) there is a low likelihood of recidivism by the defendant; or

(2) sufficient justification exists for the failure to attend school.

Art. 45.054. Failure to Attend School Proceedings. [Repealed]

Art. 45.0541. Expunction of Failure to Attend School Records.

(a) In this article, "truancy offense" means an offense committed under the former Section 25.094, Education Code.

(b) An individual who has been convicted of a truancy offense or has had a complaint for a truancy offense dismissed is entitled to have the conviction or complaint and records relating to the conviction or complaint expunged.

(c) Regardless of whether the individual has filed a petition for expunction, the court in which the individual was convicted or a complaint for a truancy offense was filed shall order the conviction, complaints, verdicts, sentences, and other documents relating to the offense, including any documents in the possession of a school district or law enforcement agency, to be expunged from the individual's record. After entry of the order, the individual is released from all disabilities resulting from the conviction or complaint, and the conviction or complaint may not be shown or made known for any purpose.

Art. 45.055. Expunction of Conviction and Records in Failure to Attend School Cases. [Repealed]

Art. 45.056. Juvenile Case Managers.

(a) On approval of the commissioners court, city council, school district board of trustees, juvenile board, or other appropriate authority, a county court, justice court, municipal court, school district, juvenile probation department, or other appropriate governmental entity may:

(1) employ a case manager to provide services in cases involving juvenile offenders who are before a court consistent with the court's statutory powers or referred to a court by a school administrator or designee for misconduct that would otherwise be within the court's statutory powers prior to a case being filed, with the consent of the juvenile and the juvenile's parents or guardians;

(2) employ one or more juvenile case managers who:

(A) shall assist the court in administering the court's juvenile docket and in supervising the court's orders in juvenile cases; and

(B) may provide:

(i) prevention services to a child considered at risk of entering the juvenile justice system; and

(ii) intervention services to juveniles engaged in misconduct before cases are filed, excluding traffic offenses; or

(3) agree in accordance with Chapter 791, Government Code, with any appropriate governmental entity to jointly employ a case manager or to jointly contribute to the costs of a case manager employed by one governmental entity to provide services described by Subdivisions (1) and (2).

(b) A local entity may apply or more than one local entity may jointly apply to the criminal justice division of the governor's office for reimbursement of all or part of the costs of employing one or more juvenile case managers from funds appropriated to the governor's office or otherwise available for that purpose. To be eligible for reimbursement, the entity applying must present to the governor's office a comprehensive plan to reduce juvenile crimes in the entity's jurisdiction that addresses the role of the case manager in that effort.

(c) **[2 Versions: As amended by Acts 2013, 83rd Leg., ch. 1213]** An entity that jointly employs a case manager under Subsection (a)(3) employs a juvenile case manager for purposes of Chapter 102 of this code and Chapter 102, Government Code.

(c) **[2 Versions: As amended by Acts 2013, 83rd Leg., ch. 1407]** A county or justice court on approval of the commissioners court or a municipality or municipal court on approval of the city council may employ one or more juvenile case managers who:

(1) shall assist the court in administering the court's juvenile docket and in supervising its court orders in juvenile cases; and

(2) may provide:

(A) prevention services to a child considered at-risk of entering the juvenile justice system; and

(B) intervention services to juveniles engaged in misconduct prior to cases being filed, excluding traffic offenses.

(d) The court or governing body may pay the salary and benefits of a juvenile case manager and the costs of training, travel, office supplies, and other necessary expenses relating to the position of the juvenile case manager from the local truancy prevention and diversion fund established under Section 134.156, Local Government Code.

(e) A juvenile case manager employed under Subsection (c) shall give priority to cases brought under Sections 25.093 and 25.094, Education Code.

(f) The governing body of the employing governmental entity under Subsection (a) shall adopt reasonable rules for juvenile case managers that provide:

(1) a code of ethics, and for the enforcement of the code of ethics;

(2) appropriate educational preservice and in-service training standards for juvenile case managers; and

(3) training in:

(A) the role of the juvenile case manager;

(B) case planning and management;

(C) applicable procedural and substantive law;

(D) courtroom proceedings and presentation;

(E) services to at-risk youth under Subchapter D, Chapter 264, Family Code;

(F) local programs and services for juveniles and methods by which juveniles may access those programs and services; and

(G) detecting and preventing abuse, exploitation, and neglect of juveniles.

(g) The employing court or governmental entity under this article shall implement the rules adopted under Subsection (f).

(h) The commissioners court or governing body of the municipality that administers a local truancy prevention and diversion fund under Section 134.156, Local Government Code, shall require periodic review of juvenile case managers to ensure the implementation of the rules adopted under Subsection (f).

(i) The juvenile case manager shall timely report to the judge who signed the order or judgment and, on request, to the judge assigned to the case or the presiding judge any information or recommendations relevant to assisting the judge in making decisions that are in the best interest of the child.

(j) The judge who is assigned to the case shall consult with the juvenile case manager who is supervising the case regarding:

(1) the child's home environment;

(2) the child's developmental, psychological, and educational status;

(3) the child's previous interaction with the justice system; and

(4) any sanctions available to the court that would be in the best interest of the child.

(k) Subsections (i) and (j) do not apply to:

(1) a part-time judge; or

(2) a county judge of a county court that has one or more appointed full-time magistrates under Section 54.1172, Government Code.

Art. 45.057. Offenses Committed by Juveniles.

(a) In this article:

(1) "Child" has the meaning assigned by Article 45.058(h).

(2) "Residence" means any place where the child lives or resides for a period of at least 30 days.

(3) "Parent" includes a person standing in parental relation, a managing conservator, or a custodian.

(b) On a finding by a justice or municipal court that a child committed an offense that the court has jurisdiction of under Article 4.11 or 4.14, the court has jurisdiction to enter an order:

(1) referring the child or the child's parent for services under Section 264.302, Family Code;

(2) requiring that the child attend a special program that the court determines to be in the best interest of the child and, if the program involves the expenditure of municipal or county funds, that is approved by the governing body of the municipality or county commissioners court, as applicable, including a rehabilitation, counseling, self-esteem and leadership, work and job skills training, job interviewing and work preparation, self-improvement, parenting, manners, violence avoidance, tutoring, sensitivity training, parental responsibility, community service, restitution, advocacy, or mentoring program; or

(3) requiring that the child's parent do any act or refrain from doing any act that the court determines will increase the likelihood that the child will comply with the orders of the court and that is reasonable and necessary for the welfare of the child, including:

(A) attend a parenting class or parental responsibility program; and

(B) attend the child's school classes or functions.

(c) The justice or municipal court may order the parent, managing conservator, or guardian of a child required to attend a program under Subsection (b) to pay an amount not greater than $100 to pay for the costs of the program.

(d) A justice or municipal court may require a child, parent, managing conservator, or guardian required to attend a program, class, or function under this article to submit proof of attendance to the court.

(e) A justice or municipal court shall endorse on the summons issued to a parent an order to appear personally at the hearing with the child. The summons must include a warning that the failure of the parent to appear may result in arrest and is a Class C misdemeanor.

(f) An order under this article involving a child is enforceable under Article 45.050.

(g) A person commits an offense if the person is a parent, managing conservator, or guardian who fails to attend a hearing under this article after receiving an order under Subsection (e). An offense under this subsection is a Class C misdemeanor.

(h) A child and parent required to appear before the court have an obligation to provide the court in writing with the current address and residence of the child. The obligation does not end when the child reaches age 17. On or before the seventh day after the date the child or parent changes residence, the child or parent shall notify the court of the current address in the manner directed by the court. A violation of this subsection may result in arrest and is a Class C misdemeanor. The obligation to provide notice terminates on discharge and satisfaction of the judgment or final disposition not requiring a finding of guilt.

(i) If an appellate court accepts an appeal for a trial de novo, the child and parent shall provide the notice under Subsection (h) to the appellate court.

(j) The child and parent are entitled to written notice of their obligation under Subsections (h) and (i), which may be satisfied by being given a copy of those subsections by:

(1) the court during their initial appearance before the court;

(2) a peace officer arresting and releasing a child under Article 45.058(a) on release; and

(3) a peace officer that issues a citation under Section 543.003, Transportation Code, or Article 14.06(b) of this code.

(k) It is an affirmative defense to prosecution under Subsection (h) that the child and parent were not informed of their obligation under this article.

(*l*) Any order under this article is enforceable by the justice or municipal court by contempt.

Art. 45.058. Children Taken into Custody.

(a) A child may be released to the child's parent, guardian, custodian, or other responsible adult as provided by Section 52.02(a)(1), Family Code, if the child is taken into custody for an offense that a justice or municipal court has jurisdiction of under Article 4.11 or 4.14.

(b) A child described by Subsection (a) must be taken only to a place previously designated by the head of the law enforcement agency with custody of the child as an appropriate place of nonsecure custody for children unless the child:

(1) is released under Section 52.02(a)(1), Family Code; or

(2) is taken before a justice or municipal court.

(c) A place of nonsecure custody for children must be an unlocked, multipurpose area. A lobby, office, or interrogation room is suitable if the area is not designated, set aside, or used as a secure detention area and is not part of a secure detention area. A place of nonsecure custody may be a juvenile processing office designated under Section 52.025, Family Code, if the area is not locked when it is used as a place of nonsecure custody.

(d) The following procedures shall be followed in a place of nonsecure custody for children:

(1) a child may not be secured physically to a cuffing rail, chair, desk, or other stationary object;

(2) the child may be held in the nonsecure facility only long enough to accomplish the purpose of identification, investigation, processing, release to parents, or the arranging of transportation to the appropriate juvenile court, juvenile detention facility, secure detention facility, justice court, or municipal court;

(3) residential use of the area is prohibited; and

(4) the child shall be under continuous visual supervision by a law enforcement officer or facility staff person during the time the child is in nonsecure custody.

(e) Notwithstanding any other provision of this article, a child may not, under any circumstances, be detained in a place of nonsecure custody for more than six hours.

(f) A child taken into custody for an offense that a justice or municipal court has jurisdiction of under Article 4.11 or 4.14 may be presented or detained in a detention facility designated by the juvenile court under Section 52.02(a)(3), Family Code, only if:

(1) the child's non-traffic case is transferred to the juvenile court by a justice or municipal court under Section 51.08(b), Family Code; or

(2) the child is referred to the juvenile court by a justice or municipal court for contempt of court under Article 45.050.

(g) Except as provided by Subsection (g-1) and Section 37.143(a), Education Code, a law enforcement officer may issue a field release citation as provided by Article 14.06 in place of taking a child into custody for a traffic offense or an offense punishable by fine only.

(g-1) A law enforcement officer may issue a field release citation as provided by Article 14.06 in place of taking a child into custody for conduct constituting a violation of Section 49.02, Penal Code, only if the officer releases the child to the child's parent, guardian, custodian, or other responsible adult.

(h) In this article, "child" means a person who is:

(1) at least 10 years of age and younger than 17 years of age; and

(2) charged with or convicted of an offense that a justice or municipal court has jurisdiction of under Article 4.11 or 4.14.

(i) If a law enforcement officer issues a citation or files a complaint in the manner provided by Article 45.018 for conduct by a child 12 years of age or older that is alleged to have occurred on school property or on a vehicle owned or operated by a county or independent school district, the officer shall submit to the court the offense report, a statement by a witness to the alleged conduct, and a statement by a victim of the alleged conduct, if any. An attorney representing the state may not proceed in a trial of an offense unless the law enforcement officer complied with the requirements of this subsection.

(j) Notwithstanding Subsection (g) or (g-1), a law enforcement officer may not issue a citation or file a complaint in the manner provided by Article 45.018 for conduct by a child younger than 12 years of age that is alleged to have occurred on school property or on a vehicle owned or operated by a county or independent school district.

Art. 45.059. Children Taken into Custody for Violation of Juvenile Curfew or Order.

(a) A peace officer taking into custody a person younger than 17 years of age for violation of a juvenile curfew ordinance of a municipality or order of the commissioners court of a county shall, without unnecessary delay:

(1) release the person to the person's parent, guardian, or custodian;

(2) take the person before a justice or municipal court to answer the charge; or

(3) take the person to a place designated as a juvenile curfew processing office by the head of the law enforcement agency having custody of the person.

(b) A juvenile curfew processing office must observe the following procedures:

(1) the office must be an unlocked, multipurpose area that is not designated, set aside, or used as a secure detention area or part of a secure detention area;

(2) the person may not be secured physically to a cuffing rail, chair, desk, or stationary object;

(3) the person may not be held longer than necessary to accomplish the purposes of identification, investigation, processing, release to a parent, guardian, or custodian, or arrangement of transportation to school or court;

(4) a juvenile curfew processing office may not be designated or intended for residential purposes;

(5) the person must be under continuous visual supervision by a peace officer or other person during the time the person is in the juvenile curfew processing office; and

(6) a person may not be held in a juvenile curfew processing office for more than six hours.

(c) A place designated under this article as a juvenile curfew processing office is not subject to the approval of the juvenile board having jurisdiction where the governmental entity is located.

Art. 45.06. Fines and Special Expenses [Renumbered].

Renumbered to Tex. Code Crim. Proc. art. 45.203 by Acts 1999, 76th Leg., ch. 1545 (S.B. 1230), § 61, effective September 1, 1999.

Art. 45.060. Unadjudicated Children, Now Adults; Notice on Reaching Age of Majority; Offense.

(a) Except as provided by Articles 45.058 and 45.059, an individual may not be taken into secured custody for offenses alleged to have occurred before the individual's 17th birthday.

(b) On or after an individual's 17th birthday, if the court has used all available procedures under this chapter to secure the individual's appearance to answer allegations made before the individual's 17th birthday, the court may issue a notice of continuing obligation to appear by personal service or by mail to the last known address and residence of the individual. The notice must order the individual to appear at a designated time, place, and date to answer the allegations detailed in the notice.

(c) Failure to appear as ordered by the notice under Subsection (b) is a Class C misdemeanor independent of Section 38.10, Penal Code, and Section 543.003, Transportation Code.

(d) It is an affirmative defense to prosecution under Subsection (c) that the individual was not informed of the individual's obligation under Articles 45.057(h) and (i) or did not receive notice as required by Subsection (b).

(e) A notice of continuing obligation to appear issued under this article must contain the following statement provided in boldfaced type or capital letters:

"WARNING: COURT RECORDS REVEAL THAT BEFORE YOUR 17TH BIRTHDAY YOU WERE ACCUSED OF A CRIMINAL OFFENSE AND HAVE FAILED TO MAKE AN APPEARANCE OR ENTER A PLEA IN THIS MATTER. AS AN ADULT, YOU ARE NOTIFIED THAT YOU HAVE A CONTINUING OBLIGATION TO APPEAR IN THIS CASE. FAILURE TO APPEAR AS REQUIRED BY THIS NOTICE MAY BE AN ADDITIONAL CRIMINAL OFFENSE AND RESULT IN A WARRANT BEING ISSUED FOR YOUR ARREST."

Art. 45.061. Proceedings Concerning Electronic Transmission of Certain Visual Material Depicting Minor.

(a) In this article, "parent" means a natural or adoptive parent, managing or possessory conservator, or legal guardian. The term does not include a parent whose parental rights have been terminated.

(b) If a justice or municipal court finds that a defendant has committed an offense under Section 43.261, Penal Code, the court may enter an order requiring the defendant to attend and successfully complete an educational program described by Section 37.218, Education Code, or another equivalent educational program.

(c) A court that enters an order under Subsection (b) shall require the defendant or the defendant's parent to pay the cost of attending an educational program under Subsection (b) if the court determines that the defendant or the defendant's parent is financially able to make payment.

Art. 45.07. Collection of Costs [Repealed].

Repealed by Acts 1999, 76th Leg., ch. 1545 (S.B. 1230), § 75(a), effective September 1, 1999.

Art. 45.08. Jury Fees [Repealed].

Repealed by Acts 1999, 76th Leg., ch. 1545 (S.B. 1230), § 75(a), effective September 1, 1999.

Art. 45.09. Officers' Fees [Repealed].

Repealed by Acts 1999, 76th Leg., ch. 1545 (S.B. 1230), § 75(a), effective September 1, 1999.

Art. 45.10. Appeal [Renumbered].

Renumbered to Tex. Code Crim Proc. art. 45.042 by Acts 1999, 76th Leg., ch. 1545 (S.B. 1230), § 40, effective September 1, 1999.

SUBCHAPTER C PROCEDURES IN JUSTICE COURT

Art. 45.101. Justice Court Prosecutions.

(a) All prosecutions in a justice court shall be conducted by the county or district attorney or a deputy county or district attorney.

(b) Except as otherwise provided by law, appeals from justice court may be prosecuted by the district attorney or a deputy district attorney with the consent of the county attorney.

Art. 45.102. Offenses Committed in Another County.

Whenever complaint is made before any justice of the peace that a felony has been committed in any other than a county in which the complaint is made, the justice shall issue a warrant for the arrest of the accused, directed as in other cases, commanding that the accused be arrested and taken before any magistrate of the county where such felony is alleged to have been committed, forthwith, for examination as in other cases.

Art. 45.103. Warrant Without Complaint.

If a criminal offense that a justice of the peace has jurisdiction to try is committed within the view of the justice, the justice may issue a warrant for the arrest of the offender.

Art. 45.11. Disposition of Fees [Renumbered].

Renumbered to Tex. Code Crim. Proc. art. 44.281 by Acts 1999, 76th Leg., ch. 1545 (S.B. 1230), § 65, effective September 1, 1999.

Art. 45.12. Contempt and Bail [Repealed].

Repealed by Acts 1999, 76th Leg., ch. 1545 (S.B. 1230), § 75(a), effective September 1, 1999.

Art. 45.13. Criminal Docket [Renumbered].

Renumbered to Tex. Code Crim. Proc. art. 45.017 by Acts 1999, 76th Leg., ch. 1545 (S.B. 1230), § 14, effective September 1, 1999.

Art. 45.14. To File Transcript of Docket [Repealed].

Repealed by Acts 1989, 71st Leg., ch. 499 (H.B. 1101), § 2, effective August 28, 1989.

Art. 45.15. Warrant Without Complaint [Renumbered].

Renumbered to Tex. Code Crim. Proc. art. 45.103 by Acts 1999, 76th Leg., ch. 1545 (S.B. 1230), § 57, effective September 1, 1999.

Art. 45.16. Complaint Shall Be Written [Repealed].

Repealed by Acts 1999, 76th Leg., ch. 1545 (S.B. 1230), § 75(a), effective September 1, 1999.

Art. 45.17. What Complaint Must State [Renumbered].

Renumbered to Tex. Code Crim. Proc. art. 45.019 by Acts 1999, 76th Leg., ch. 1545 (S.B. 1230), § 16, effective September 1, 1999.

Art. 45.18. Warrant Shall Issue [Renumbered].

Renumbered to Tex. Code Crim. Proc. art. 45.014 by Acts 1999, 76th Leg., ch. 1545 (S.B. 1230), § 11, effective September 1, 1999.

Art. 45.19. Requisites of Warrant [Repealed].

Repealed by Acts 1999, 76th Leg., ch. 1545 (S.B. 1230), § 75(a), effective September 1, 1999.

SUBCHAPTER D PROCEDURES IN MUNICIPAL COURT

Art. 45.20. [Repealed].

Repealed by Acts 1991, 72nd Leg., ch. 446 (S.B. 411), § 2, effective June 11, 1991.

Art. 45.201. Municipal Prosecutions.

(a) All prosecutions in a municipal court shall be conducted by the city attorney of the municipality or by a deputy city attorney.

(b) The county attorney of the county in which the municipality is situated may, if the county attorney so desires, also represent the state in such prosecutions. In such cases, the county attorney is not entitled to receive any fees or other compensation for those services.

(c) With the consent of the county attorney, appeals from municipal court to a county court, county court at law, or any appellate court may be prosecuted by the city attorney or a deputy city attorney.

(d) It is the primary duty of a municipal prosecutor not to convict, but to see that justice is done.

Art. 45.202. Service of Process.

(a) All process issuing out of a municipal court may be served and shall be served when directed by the court, by a peace officer or marshal of the municipality within which it is situated, under the same rules as are provided by law for the service by sheriffs and constables of process issuing out of the justice court, so far as applicable.

(b) The peace officer or marshal may serve all process issuing out of a municipal court anywhere in the county in which the municipality is situated. If the municipality is situated in more than one county, the peace officer or marshal may serve the process throughout those counties.

Art. 45.203. Collection of Fines and Costs.

(a) The governing body of each municipality shall by ordinance prescribe rules, not inconsistent with any law of this state, as may be proper to enforce the collection of fines imposed by a municipal court. In addition to any other method of enforcement, the municipality may enforce the collection of fines by:

(1) execution against the property of the defendant; or

(2) imprisonment of the defendant.

(b) The governing body of a municipality may adopt such rules and regulations, not inconsistent with any law of this state, concerning the practice and procedure in the municipal court as the governing body may consider proper.

(c) The governing body of each municipality may prescribe by ordinance the collection, after due notice, of a fine not to exceed $25 for an offense under Section 38.10(e), Penal Code, or Section 543.009, Transportation Code. Money collected from the fine shall be paid into the municipal treasury for the use and benefit of the municipality.

(d) Costs may not be imposed or collected in criminal cases in municipal court by municipal ordinance.

Art. 45.21. [Renumbered].

Renumbered to Tex. Code Crim. Proc. art. 45.102 by Acts 1999, 76th Leg., ch. 1545 (S.B. 1230), § 56, effective September 1, 1999.

Art. 45.22. [Repealed].

Repealed by Acts 1999, 76th Leg., ch. 1545 (S.B. 1230), § 75(a), effective September 1, 1999.

Art. 45.23. [Repealed].

Repealed by Acts 1999, 76th Leg., ch. 1545 (S.B. 1230), § 75(a), effective September 1, 1999.

Art. 45.231. [Renumbered].

Art. 45.24. [Renumbered].

Renumbered to Tex. Code Crim. Proc. art. 45.025 by Acts 1999, 76th Leg., ch. 1545 (S.B. 1230), § 23, effective September 1, 1999.

Art. 45.25. [Renumbered].

Renumbered to Tex. Code Crim. Proc. art. 45.027 by Acts 1999, 76th Leg., ch. 1545 (S.B. 1230), § 25, effective September 1, 1999.

Art. 45.251. [Renumbered].

Renumbered to Tex. Code Crim. Proc. art. 45.026 by Acts 1999, 76th Leg., ch. 1545 (S.B. 1230), § 24, effective September 1, 1999.

Art. 45.26. [Repealed].

Repealed by Acts 1999, 76th Leg., ch. 1545 (S.B. 1230), § 75(a), effective September 1, 1999.

Art. 45.27. [Repealed].

Repealed by Acts 1999, 76th Leg., ch. 1545 (S.B. 1230), § 75(a), effective September 1, 1999.

Art. 45.28. [Renumbered].

Renumbered to Tex. Code Crim. Proc. art. 45.029 by Acts 1999, 76th Leg., ch. 1545 (S.B. 1230), § 27, effective September 1, 1999.

Art. 45.29. [Renumbered].

Renumbered to Tex. Code Crim. Proc. art. 45.028 by Acts 1999, 76th Leg., ch. 1545 (S.B. 1230), § 26, effective September 1, 1999.

Art. 45.30. [Renumbered].

Renumbered to Tex. Code Crim. Proc. art. 45.030 by Acts 1999, 76th Leg., ch. 1545 (S.B. 1230), § 28, effective September 1, 1999.

Art. 45.31. [Renumbered].

Renumbered to Tex. Code Crim. Proc. art. 45.023 by Acts 1999, 76th Leg., ch. 1545 (S.B. 1230), § 21, effective September 1, 1999.

Art. 45.32. [Repealed].

Repealed by Acts 1999, 76th Leg., ch. 1545 (S.B. 1230), § 75(a), effective September 1, 1999.

Art. 45.33. [Renumbered].

Renumbered to Tex. Code Crim. Proc. art. 45.021 by Acts 1999, 76th Leg., ch. 1545 (S.B. 1230), § 18, effective September 1, 1999.

Art. 45.331. [Renumbered].

Renumbered to Tex. Code Crim. Proc. art. 45.0215 by Acts 1999, 76th Leg., ch. 1545 (S.B. 1230), § 19, effective September 1, 1999.

Art. 45.34. [Renumbered].

Renumbered to Tex. Code Crim. Proc. art. 45.022 by Acts 1999, 76th Leg., ch. 1545 (S.B. 1230), § 20, effective September 1, 1999.

Art. 45.35. [Renumbered].

Renumbered to Tex. Code Crim. Proc. art. 45.024 by Acts 1999, 76th Leg., ch. 1545 (S.B. 1230), § 22, effective September 1, 1999.

Art. 45.36. [Renumbered].

Renumbered to Tex. Code Crim. Proc. art. 45.031 by Acts 1999, 76th Leg., ch. 1545 (S.B. 1230), § 29, effective September 1, 1999.

Art. 45.37. [Renumbered].

Renumbered to Tex. Code Crim. Proc. art. 45.020 by Acts 1999, 76th Leg., ch. 1545 (S.B. 1230), § 17, effective September 1, 1999.

Art. 45.38. [Renumbered].

Renumbered to Tex. Code Crim. Proc. art. 45.011 by Acts 1999, 76th Leg., ch. 1545 (S.B. 1230), § 8, effective September 1, 1999.

Art. 45.39. [Renumbered].

Renumbered to Tex. Code Crim. Proc. art. 45.034 by Acts 1999, 76th Leg., ch. 1545 (S.B. 1230), § 32, effective September 1, 1999.

Art. 45.40. [Renumbered].

Renumbered to Tex. Code Crim. Proc. art. 45.035 by Acts 1999, 76th Leg., ch. 1545 (S.B. 1230), § 33, effective September 1, 1999.

Art. 45.41. [Renumbered].

Renumbered to Tex. Code Crim. Proc. art. 45.016 by Acts 1999, 76th Leg., ch. 1545 (S.B. 1230), § 13, effective September 1, 1999.

Art. 45.42. [Renumbered].

Renumbered to Tex. Code Crim. Proc. art. 45.036 by Acts 1999, 76th Leg., ch. 1545 (S.B. 1230), § 34, effective September 1, 1999.

Art. 45.43. [Renumbered].

Renumbered to Tex. Code Crim. Proc. art. 45.015 by Acts 1999, 76th Leg., ch. 1545 (S.B. 1230), § 12, effective September 1, 1999.

Art. 45.44. [Renumbered].

Renumbered to Tex. Code Crim. Proc. art. 45.038 by Acts 1999, 76th Leg., ch. 1545 (S.B. 1230), § 36, effective September 1, 1999.

Art. 45.45. [Renumbered].

Renumbered to Tex. Code Crim. Proc. art. 45.037 by Acts 1999, 76th Leg., ch. 1545 (S.B. 1230), § 35, effective September 1, 1999.

Art. 45.46. [Renumbered].

Renumbered to Tex. Code Crim. Proc. art. 45.039 by Acts 1999, 76th Leg., ch. 1545 (S.B. 1230), § 37, effective September 1, 1999.

Art. 45.47. [Renumbered].

Renumbered to Tex. Code Crim. Proc. art. 45.040 by Acts 1999, 76th Leg., ch. 1545 (S.B. 1230), § 38, effective September 1, 1999.

Art. 45.48. [Renumbered].

Renumbered to Tex. Code Crim. Proc. art. 45.043 by Acts 1999, 76th Leg., ch. 1545 (S.B. 1230), § 43, effective September 1, 1999.

Art. 45.49. [Repealed].

Repealed by Acts 1999, 76th Leg., ch. 1545 (s.B. 1230), § 75(a), effective September 1, 1999.

Art. 45.50. [Renumbered].

Renumbered to Article 45.041 by Acts 1999, 76th Leg., ch. 1545 (S.B. 1230), § 39, effective September 1, 1999.

Art. 45.51. [Renumbered].

Renumbered to Article 45.045 by Acts 1999, 76th Leg., ch. 1545 (S.B. 1230), § 45, effective September 1, 1999.

Art. 45.52. [Renumbered].

Renumbered to Article 45.046 by Acts 1999, 76th Leg., ch. 1545 (S.B. 1230), § 46, effective September 1, 1999.

Art. 45.521. [Renumbered].

Renumbered to Article 45.049 by Acts 1999, 76th Leg., ch. 1545 (S.B. 1230), § 49, effective September 1, 1999.

Art. 45.522. [Renumbered].

Renumbered to Article 45.050 by Acts 1999, 76th Leg., ch. 1545 (S.B. 1230), § 49, effective September 1, 1999.

Art. 45.53. [Renumbered].

Renumbered to Article 45.048 by Acts 1999, 76th Leg., ch. 1545 (S.B. 1230), § 48, effective September 1, 1999.

Art. 45.54. [Renumbered].

Renumbered to Article 45.051 by Acts 1999, 76th Leg., ch. 1545 (S.B. 1230), § 50, effective September 1, 1999.

Art. 45.541. [Repealed].

Repealed by Acts 2001, 77th Leg., ch. 1420 (H.B. 2812), § 3.0021(b), effective September 1, 2001.

Art. 45.55. [Renumbered].

Renumbered to Article 45.052 by Acts 1999, 76th Leg., ch, 1545 (S.B. 1230), § 52, effective September 1, 1999.

Art. 45.56. [Renumbered].

Renumbered to Article 45.053 by Acts 1999, 76th Leg., ch. 1545 (S.B. 1230), § 53, effective September 1, 1999.

MISCELLANEOUS PROCEEDINGS

CHAPTER 46
MISCELLANEOUS PROVISIONS RELATING TO MENTAL ILLNESS AND INTELLECTUAL DISABILITY

Art. 46.01. [Repealed].

Repealed by Acts 1999, 76th Leg., ch. 561 (S.B. 421), § 8, effective September 1, 1999.

Art. 46.02. Incompetency to Stand Trial [Repealed].

Repealed by Acts 2003, 78th Leg., ch. 35 (S.B. 1057), § 15, effective January 1, 2004.

Art. 46.03. Insanity Defense [Repealed in Part; Renumbered in Part].

Secs. 1 to 3. [Repealed by Acts 2005, 79th Leg., ch. 831 (H.B. 837), § 1, effective September 1, 2005.]

Sec. 4. (a) to (c) [Repealed by Acts 2005, 79th Leg., ch. 831 (H.B. 837), § 1, effective September 1, 2005.]

(d) (1) to (7) [Repealed by Acts 2005, 79th Leg., ch. 831 (H.B. 837), § 1, effective September 1, 2005.]

(8) [Renumbered to Tex.Code Crim. Proc § 46C.003 by Acts 2011, 82nd Leg., ch. 787 (H.B. 2124), § 1, effective June 17, 2011.]

Art. 46.04. Transportation to a Mental Health Facility or Residential Care Facility.

Sec. 1. **Persons Accompanying Transport.**

(a) A patient transported from a jail or detention facility to a mental health facility or a residential care facility shall be transported by a special officer for mental health assignment certified under Section 1701.404, Occupations Code, or by a sheriff or constable.

(b) The court ordering the transport shall require appropriate medical personnel to accompany the person transporting the patient, at the expense of the county from which the patient is transported, if there is reasonable cause to believe the patient will require medical assistance or will require the administration of medication during the transportation.

(c) A female patient must be accompanied by a female attendant.

Sec. 2. **Requirements for Transport. —** The transportation of a patient from a jail or detention facility to a mental health facility or residential care facility must meet the following requirements:

(1) the patient must be transported directly to the facility within a reasonable amount of time and without undue delay;

(2) a vehicle used to transport the patient must be adequately heated in cold weather and adequately ventilated in warm weather;

(3) a special diet or other medical precautions recommended by the patient's physician must be followed;

(4) the person transporting the patient shall give the patient reasonable opportunities to get food and water and to use a bathroom; and

(5) the patient may not be transported with a state prisoner.

Art. 46.05. Competency to Be Executed.

(a) A person who is incompetent to be executed may not be executed.

(b) The trial court retains jurisdiction over motions filed by or for a defendant under this article.

(c) A motion filed under this article must identify the proceeding in which the defendant was convicted, give the date of the final judgment, set forth the fact that an execution date has been set if the date has been set, and clearly set forth alleged facts in support of the assertion that the defendant is presently incompetent to be executed. The defendant shall attach affidavits, records, or other evidence supporting the defendant's allegations or shall state why those items are not attached. The defendant shall identify any previous proceedings in which the defendant challenged the defendant's competency in relation to the conviction and sentence in question, including any challenge to the defendant's competency to be executed, competency to stand trial, or sanity at the time of the offense. The motion must be verified by the oath of some person on the defendant's behalf.

(d) On receipt of a motion filed under this article, the trial court shall determine whether the defendant has raised a substantial doubt of the defendant's competency to be executed on the basis of:

(1) the motion, any attached documents, and any responsive pleadings; and

(2) if applicable, the presumption of competency under Subsection (e).

(e) If a defendant is determined to have previously filed a motion under this article, and has previously been determined to be competent to be executed, the previous adjudication creates a presumption of competency and the defendant is not entitled to a hearing on the subsequent motion filed under this article, unless the defendant makes a prima facie showing of a substantial change in circumstances sufficient to raise a significant question as to the defendant's competency to be executed at the time of filing the subsequent motion under this article.

(f) If the trial court determines that the defendant has made a substantial showing of incompetency, the court shall order at least two mental health experts to examine the defendant using the standard described by Subsection (h) to determine whether the defendant is incompetent to be executed.

(g) If the trial court does not determine that the defendant has made a substantial showing of incompetency, the court shall deny the motion and may set an execution date as otherwise provided by law.

(h) A defendant is incompetent to be executed if the defendant does not understand:

(1) that he or she is to be executed and that the execution is imminent; and

(2) the reason he or she is being executed.

(i) Mental health experts who examine a defendant under this article shall provide within a time ordered by the trial court copies of their reports to the attorney representing the state, the attorney representing the defendant, and the court.

(j) By filing a motion under this article, the defendant waives any claim of privilege with respect to, and consents to the release of, all mental health and medical records relevant to whether the defendant is incompetent to be executed.

(k) The trial court shall determine whether, on the basis of reports provided under Subsection (i), the motion, any attached documents, any responsive pleadings, and any evidence introduced in the final competency hearing, the defendant has established by a preponderance of the evidence that the defendant is incompetent to be executed. If the court makes a finding that the defendant is not incompetent to be executed, the court may set an execution date as otherwise provided by law.

(*l*) Following the trial court's determination under Subsection (k) and on motion of a party, the clerk shall send immediately to the court of criminal appeals in accordance with Section 8(d), Article 11.071, the appropriate documents for that court's review and entry of a judgment of whether to adopt the trial court's order, findings, or recommendations issued under Subsection (g) or (k). The court of criminal appeals also shall determine whether any existing execution date should be withdrawn and a stay of execution issued while that court is conducting its review or, if a stay is not issued during the review, after entry of its judgment.

(*l*-1) Notwithstanding Subsection (*l*), the court of criminal appeals may not review any finding of the defendant's competency made by a trial court as a result of a motion filed under this article if the motion is filed on or after the 20th day before the defendant's scheduled execution date.

(m) If a stay of execution is issued by the court of criminal appeals, the trial court periodically shall order that the defendant be reexamined by mental health experts to determine whether the defendant is no longer incompetent to be executed.

(n) If the court of criminal appeals enters a judgment that a defendant is not incompetent to be executed, the court may withdraw any stay of execution issued under Subsection (*l*), and the trial court may set an execution date as otherwise provided by law.

CHAPTER 46A AIDS AND HIV TESTING IN COUNTY AND MUNICIPAL JAILS [EFFECTIVE UNTIL SEPTEMBER 1, 2019]

Art. 46A.01. Testing; Segregation; Disclosure. [Renumbered, effective September 1, 2019]

CHAPTER 46B INCOMPETENCY TO STAND TRIAL

SUBCHAPTER A GENERAL PROVISIONS

Art. 46B.001. Definitions.

In this chapter:

(1) "Adaptive behavior" means the effectiveness with or degree to which a person meets the standards of personal independence and social responsibility expected of the person's age and cultural group.

(2) "Commission" means the Health and Human Services Commission.

(3) "Competency restoration" means the treatment or education process for restoring a person's ability to consult with the person's attorney with a reasonable degree of rational understanding, including a rational and factual understanding of the court proceedings and charges against the person.

(4) "Developmental period" means the period of a person's life from birth through 17 years of age.

(5) "Electronic broadcast system" means a two-way electronic communication of image and sound between the defendant and the court and includes secure Internet videoconferencing.

(6) "Executive commissioner" means the executive commissioner of the Health and Human Services Commission.

(7) "Inpatient mental health facility" has the meaning assigned by Section 571.003, Health and Safety Code.

(8) "Intellectual disability" means significantly subaverage general intellectual functioning that is concurrent with deficits in adaptive behavior and originates during the developmental period.

(9) "Local mental health authority" has the meaning assigned by Section 571.003, Health and Safety Code.

(10) "Local intellectual and developmental disability authority" has the meaning assigned by Section 531.002, Health and Safety Code.

(11) "Mental health facility" has the meaning assigned by Section 571.003, Health and Safety Code.

(12) "Mental illness" means an illness, disease, or condition, other than epilepsy, dementia, substance abuse, or intellectual disability, that grossly impairs:

(A) a person's thought, perception of reality, emotional process, or judgment; or

(B) behavior as demonstrated by recent disturbed behavior.

(13) "Residential care facility" has the meaning assigned by Section 591.003, Health and Safety Code.

(14) "Subaverage general intellectual functioning" means a measured intelligence two or more standard deviations below the age-group mean, using a standardized psychometric instrument.

Art. 46B.002. Applicability.

This chapter applies to a defendant charged with a felony or with a misdemeanor punishable by confinement.

Art. 46B.0021. Facility Designation.

The commission may designate for the commitment of a defendant under this chapter only a facility operated by the commission or under a contract with the commission for that purpose.

Art. 46B.003. Incompetency; Presumptions.

(a) A person is incompetent to stand trial if the person does not have:

(1) sufficient present ability to consult with the person's lawyer with a reasonable degree of rational understanding; or

(2) a rational as well as factual understanding of the proceedings against the person.

(b) A defendant is presumed competent to stand trial and shall be found competent to stand trial unless proved incompetent by a preponderance of the evidence.

Art. 46B.004. Raising Issue of Incompetency to Stand Trial.

(a) Either party may suggest by motion, or the trial court may suggest on its own motion, that the defendant may be incompetent to stand trial. A motion suggesting that the defendant may be incompetent to stand trial may be supported by affidavits setting out the facts on which the suggestion is made.

(b) If evidence suggesting the defendant may be incompetent to stand trial comes to the attention of the court, the court on its own motion shall suggest that the defendant may be incompetent to stand trial.

(c) On suggestion that the defendant may be incompetent to stand trial, the court shall determine by informal inquiry whether there is some evidence from any source that would support a finding that the defendant may be incompetent to stand trial.

(c-1) A suggestion of incompetency is the threshold requirement for an informal inquiry under Subsection (c) and may consist solely of a representation from any credible source that the defendant may be incompetent. A further evidentiary showing is not required to initiate the inquiry, and the court is not required to have a bona fide doubt about the competency of the defendant. Evidence suggesting the need for an informal inquiry may be based on observations made in relation to one or more of the factors described by Article 46B.024 or on any other indication that the defendant is incompetent within the meaning of Article 46B.003.

(d) If the court determines there is evidence to support a finding of incompetency, the court, except as provided by Subsection (e) and Article 46B.005(d), shall stay all other proceedings in the case.

(e) At any time during the proceedings under this chapter after the issue of the defendant's incompetency to stand trial is first raised, the court on the motion of the attorney representing the state may dismiss all charges pending against the defendant, regardless of whether there is any evidence to support a finding of the defendant's incompetency under Subsection (d) or whether the court has made a finding of incompetency under this chapter. If the court dismisses the charges against the defendant, the court may not continue the proceedings under this chapter, except that, if there is evidence to support a finding of the defendant's incompetency under Subsection (d), the court may proceed under Subchapter F. If the court does not elect to proceed under Subchapter F, the court shall discharge the defendant.

Art. 46B.005. Determining Incompetency to Stand Trial.

(a) If after an informal inquiry the court determines that evidence exists to support a finding of incompetency, the court shall order an examination under Subchapter B to determine whether the defendant is incompetent to stand trial in a criminal case.

(b) Except as provided by Subsection (c), the court shall hold a trial under Subchapter C before determining whether the defendant is incompetent to stand trial on the merits.

(c) A trial under this chapter is not required if:

(1) neither party's counsel requests a trial on the issue of incompetency;

(2) neither party's counsel opposes a finding of incompetency; and

(3) the court does not, on its own motion, determine that a trial is necessary to determine incompetency.

(d) If the issue of the defendant's incompetency to stand trial is raised after the trial on the merits begins, the court may determine the issue at any time before the sentence is pronounced. If the determination is delayed until after the return of a verdict, the court shall make the determination as soon as reasonably possible after the return. If a verdict of not guilty is returned, the court may not determine the issue of incompetency.

Art. 46B.006. Appointment of and Representation by Counsel.

(a) A defendant is entitled to representation by counsel before any court-ordered competency evaluation and during any proceeding at which it is suggested that the defendant may be incompetent to stand trial.

(b) If the defendant is indigent and the court has not appointed counsel to represent the defendant, the court shall appoint counsel as necessary to comply with Subsection (a).

Art. 46B.007. Admissibility of Statements and Certain Other Evidence.

A statement made by a defendant during an examination or trial on the defendant's incompetency, the testimony of an expert based on that statement, and evidence obtained as a result of that statement may not be admitted in evidence against the defendant in any criminal proceeding, other than at:

(1) a trial on the defendant's incompetency; or

(2) any proceeding at which the defendant first introduces into evidence a statement, testimony, or evidence described by this article.

Art. 46B.008. Rules of Evidence.

Notwithstanding Rule 101, Texas Rules of Evidence, the Texas Rules of Evidence apply to a trial under Subchapter C or other proceeding under this chapter whether the proceeding is before a jury or before the court.

Art. 46B.009. Time Credits.

A court sentencing a person convicted of a criminal offense shall credit to the term of the person's sentence each of the following periods for which the person may be confined in a mental health facility, residential care facility, or jail:

(1) any period of confinement that occurs pending a determination under Subchapter C as to the defendant's competency to stand trial; and

(2) any period of confinement that occurs between the date of any initial determination of the defendant's incompetency under that subchapter and the date the person is transported to jail following a final judicial determination that the person has been restored to competency.

Art. 46B.0095. Maximum Period of Commitment or Program Participation Determined by Maximum Term for Offense.

(a) A defendant may not, under Subchapter D or E or any other provision of this chapter, be committed to a mental hospital or other inpatient or residential facility or to a jail-based competency restoration program, ordered to participate in an outpatient competency restoration or treatment program, or subjected to any combination of inpatient treatment, outpatient competency restoration or treatment program participation, or jail-based competency restoration under this chapter for a cumulative period that exceeds the maximum term provided by law for the offense for which the defendant was to be tried, except that if the defendant is charged with a misdemeanor and has been ordered only to participate in an outpatient competency restoration or treatment program under Subchapter D or E, the maximum period of restoration is two years.

(b) On expiration of the maximum restoration period under Subsection (a), the mental hospital, facility, or program provider identified in the most recent order of commitment or order of outpatient competency restoration or treatment program participation under this chapter shall assess the defendant to determine if civil proceedings under Subtitle C or D, Title 7, Health and Safety Code, are appropriate. The defendant may be confined for an additional period in a mental hospital or other facility or may be ordered to participate for an additional period in an outpatient treatment program, as appropriate, only pursuant to civil proceedings conducted under Subtitle C or D, Title 7, Health and Safety Code, by a court with probate jurisdiction.

(c) The cumulative period described by Subsection (a):

(1) begins on the date the initial order of commitment or initial order for outpatient competency restoration or treatment program participation is entered under this chapter; and

(2) in addition to any inpatient or outpatient competency restoration periods or program participation periods described by Subsection (a), includes any time that, following the entry of an order described by Subdivision (1), the defendant is confined in a correctional facility, as defined by Section 1.07, Penal Code, or is otherwise in the custody of the sheriff during or while awaiting, as applicable:

(A) the defendant's transfer to:

(i) a mental hospital or other inpatient or residential facility; or

(ii) a jail-based competency restoration program;

(B) the defendant's release on bail to participate in an outpatient competency restoration or treatment program; or

(C) a criminal trial following any temporary restoration of the defendant's competency to stand trial.

(d) The court shall credit to the cumulative period described by Subsection (a) any time that a defendant, following arrest for the offense for which the defendant was to be tried, is confined in a correctional facility, as defined by Section 1.07, Penal Code, before the initial order of commitment or initial order for outpatient competency restoration or treatment program participation is entered under this chapter.

(e) In addition to the time credit awarded under Subsection (d), the court may credit to the cumulative period described by Subsection (a) any good conduct time the defendant may have been granted under Article 42.032 in relation to the defendant's confinement as described by Subsection (d).

Art. 46B.010. Mandatory Dismissal of Misdemeanor Charges.

If a court orders that a defendant charged with a misdemeanor punishable by confinement be committed to a mental hospital or other inpatient or residential facility or to a jail-based competency restoration program, that the defendant participate in an outpatient competency restoration or treatment program, or that the defendant be subjected to any combination of inpatient treatment, outpatient competency restoration or treatment program participation, or jail-based competency restoration under this chapter, and the defendant is not tried before the expiration of the maximum period of restoration described by Article 46B.0095:

(1) on the motion of the attorney representing the state, the court shall dismiss the charge; or

(2) on the motion of the attorney representing the defendant and notice to the attorney representing the state, the court:

(A) shall set the matter to be heard not later than the 10th day after the date of filing of the motion; and

(B) may dismiss the charge on a finding that the defendant was not tried before the expiration of the maximum period of restoration.

Art. 46B.011. Appeals.

Neither the state nor the defendant is entitled to make an interlocutory appeal relating to a determination or ruling under Article 46B.005.

Art. 46B.012. Compliance with Chapter.

The failure of a person to comply with this chapter does not provide a defendant with a right to dismissal of charges.

Art. 46B.013. Use of Electronic Broadcast System in Certain Proceedings Under This Chapter.

(a) A hearing may be conducted using an electronic broadcast system as permitted by this chapter and in accordance with the other provisions of this code if:

(1) written consent to the use of an electronic broadcast system is filed with the court by:

(A) the defendant or the attorney representing the defendant; and

(B) the attorney representing the state;

(2) the electronic broadcast system provides for a simultaneous, compressed full motion video, and interactive communication of image and sound between the judge, the attorney representing the state, the attorney representing the defendant, and the defendant; and

(3) on request of the defendant or the attorney representing the defendant, the defendant and the attorney representing the defendant are able to communicate privately without being recorded or heard by the judge or the attorney representing the state.

(b) On the motion of the defendant, the attorney representing the defendant, or the attorney representing the state or on the court's own motion, the court may terminate an appearance made through an electronic broadcast system at any time during the appearance and require an appearance by the defendant in open court.

(c) A recording of the communication shall be made and preserved until any appellate proceedings have been concluded. The defendant may obtain a copy of the recording on payment of a reasonable amount to cover the costs of reproduction or, if the defendant is indigent, the court shall provide a copy to the defendant without charging a cost for the copy.

SUBCHAPTER B EXAMINATION

Art. 46B.021. Appointment of Experts.

(a) On a suggestion that the defendant may be incompetent to stand trial, the court may appoint one or more disinterested experts to:

(1) examine the defendant and report to the court on the competency or incompetency of the defendant; and

(2) testify as to the issue of competency or incompetency of the defendant at any trial or hearing involving that issue.

(b) On a determination that evidence exists to support a finding of incompetency to stand trial, the court shall appoint one or more experts to perform the duties described by Subsection (a).

(c) An expert involved in the treatment of the defendant may not be appointed to examine the defendant under this article.

(d) The movant or other party as directed by the court shall provide to experts appointed under this article information relevant to a determination of the defendant's competency, including copies of the indictment or information, any supporting documents used to establish probable cause in the case, and previous mental health evaluation and treatment records.

(e) The court may appoint as experts under this chapter qualified psychiatrists or psychologists employed by the local mental health authority or local intellectual and developmental disability authority. The local mental health authority or local intellectual and developmental disability authority is entitled to compensation and reimbursement as provided by Article 46B.027.

(f) If a defendant wishes to be examined by an expert of the defendant's own choice, the court on timely request shall provide the expert with reasonable opportunity to examine the defendant.

Art. 46B.022. Experts: Qualifications.

(a) To qualify for appointment under this subchapter as an expert, a psychiatrist or psychologist must:

(1) as appropriate, be a physician licensed in this state or be a psychologist licensed in this state who has a doctoral degree in psychology; and

(2) have the following certification or training:

(A) as appropriate, certification by:

(i) the American Board of Psychiatry and Neurology with added or special qualifications in forensic psychiatry; or

(ii) the American Board of Professional Psychology in forensic psychology; or

(B) training consisting of:

(i) at least 24 hours of specialized forensic training relating to incompetency or insanity evaluations; and

(ii) at least eight hours of continuing education relating to forensic evaluations, completed in the 12 months preceding the appointment.

(b) In addition to meeting qualifications required by Subsection (a), to be appointed as an expert a psychiatrist or psychologist must have completed six hours of required continuing education in courses in forensic psychiatry or psychology, as appropriate, in either of the reporting periods in the 24 months preceding the appointment.

(c) A court may appoint as an expert a psychiatrist or psychologist who does not meet the requirements of Subsections (a) and (b) only if exigent circumstances require the court to base the appointment on professional training or experience of the expert that directly provides the expert with a specialized expertise to examine the defendant that would not ordinarily be possessed by a psychiatrist or psychologist who meets the requirements of Subsections (a) and (b).

Art. 46B.023. Custody Status.

During an examination under this subchapter, except as otherwise ordered by the court, the defendant shall be maintained under the same custody or status as the defendant was maintained under immediately before the examination began.

Art. 46B.024. Factors Considered in Examination.

During an examination under this subchapter and in any report based on that examination, an expert shall consider, in addition to other issues determined relevant by the expert, the following:

(1) the capacity of the defendant during criminal proceedings to:

(A) rationally understand the charges against the defendant and the potential consequences of the pending criminal proceedings;

(B) disclose to counsel pertinent facts, events, and states of mind;

(C) engage in a reasoned choice of legal strategies and options;

(D) understand the adversarial nature of criminal proceedings;

(E) exhibit appropriate courtroom behavior; and

(F) testify;

(2) as supported by current indications and the defendant's personal history, whether the defendant:

(A) is a person with mental illness; or

(B) is a person with an intellectual disability ;

(3) whether the identified condition has lasted or is expected to last continuously for at least one year;

(4) the degree of impairment resulting from the mental illness or intellectual disability , if existent, and the specific impact on the defendant's capacity to engage with counsel in a reasonable and rational manner; and

(5) if the defendant is taking psychoactive or other medication:

(A) whether the medication is necessary to maintain the defendant's competency; and

(B) the effect, if any, of the medication on the defendant's appearance, demeanor, or ability to participate in the proceedings.

Art. 46B.025. Expert's Report.

(a) An expert's report to the court must state an opinion on a defendant's competency or incompetency to stand trial or explain why the expert is unable to state such an opinion and must also:

(1) identify and address specific issues referred to the expert for evaluation;

(2) document that the expert explained to the defendant the purpose of the evaluation, the persons to whom a report on the evaluation is provided, and the limits on rules of confidentiality applying to the relationship between the expert and the defendant;

(3) in specific terms, describe procedures, techniques, and tests used in the examination, the purpose of each procedure, technique, or test, and the conclusions reached; and

(4) state the expert's clinical observations, findings, and opinions on each specific issue referred to the expert by the court, state the specific criteria supporting the expert's diagnosis, and state specifically any issues on which the expert could not provide an opinion.

(a-1) The expert's opinion on the defendant's competency or incompetency may not be based solely on the defendant's refusal to communicate during the examination.

(b) If in the opinion of an expert appointed under Article 46B.021 the defendant is incompetent to proceed, the expert shall state in the report:

(1) the symptoms, exact nature, severity, and expected duration of the deficits resulting from the defendant's mental illness or intellectual disability, if any, and the impact of the identified condition on the factors listed in Article 46B.024;

(2) an estimate of the period needed to restore the defendant's competency, including whether the defendant is likely to be restored to competency in the foreseeable future; and

(3) prospective treatment options, if any, appropriate for the defendant.

(c) An expert's report may not state the expert's opinion on the defendant's sanity at the time of the alleged offense, if in the opinion of the expert the defendant is incompetent to proceed.

(d) The court shall direct an expert to provide the expert's report to the court and the appropriate parties in the form approved by the Texas Correctional Office on Offenders with Medical or Mental Impairments under Section 614.0032(b), Health and Safety Code.

Art. 46B.026. Report Deadline.

(a) Except as provided by Subsection (b), an expert examining the defendant shall provide the report on the defendant's competency or incompetency to stand trial to the court, the attorney representing the state, and the attorney representing the defendant not later than the 30th day after the date on which the expert was ordered to examine the defendant and prepare the report.

(b) For good cause shown, the court may permit an expert to complete the examination and report and provide the report to the court and attorneys at a date later than the date required by Subsection (a).

(c) [Repealed by Acts 2017, 85th Leg., ch. 748 (S.B. 1326), § 35(1), effective September 1, 2017.]

(d) The court shall submit to the Office of Court Administration of the Texas Judicial System on a monthly basis the number of reports provided to the court under this article.

Art. 46B.027. Compensation of Experts; Reimbursement of Facilities.

(a) For any appointment under this chapter, the county in which the indictment was returned or information was filed shall pay for services described by Articles 46B.021(a)(1) and (2). If those services are provided by an expert who is an employee of the local mental health authority or local intellectual and developmental disability authority, the county shall pay the authority for the services.

(b) The county in which the indictment was returned or information was filed shall reimburse a facility that accepts a defendant for examination under this chapter for expenses incurred that are reasonably necessary and incidental to the proper examination of the defendant.

SUBCHAPTER C INCOMPETENCY TRIAL

Art. 46B.051. Trial Before Judge or Jury.

(a) If a court holds a trial to determine whether the defendant is incompetent to stand trial, on the request of either party or the motion of the court, a jury shall make the determination.

(b) The court shall make the determination of incompetency if a jury determination is not required by Subsection (a).

(c) If a jury determination is required by Subsection (a), a jury that has not been selected to determine the guilt or innocence of the defendant must determine the issue of incompetency.

Art. 46B.052. Jury Verdict.

(a) If a jury determination of the issue of incompetency to stand trial is required by Article

46B.051(a), the court shall require the jury to state in its verdict whether the defendant is incompetent to stand trial.

(b) The verdict must be concurred in by each juror.

Art. 46B.053. Procedure After Finding of Competency.

If the court or jury determines that the defendant is competent to stand trial, the court shall continue the trial on the merits. If a jury determines that the defendant is competent and the trial on the merits is to be held before a jury, the court shall continue the trial with another jury selected for that purpose.

Art. 46B.054. Uncontested Incompetency.

If the court finds that evidence exists to support a finding of incompetency to stand trial and the court and the counsel for each party agree that the defendant is incompetent to stand trial, the court shall proceed in the same manner as if a jury had been impaneled and had found the defendant incompetent to stand trial.

Art. 46B.055. Procedure After Finding of Incompetency.

If the defendant is found incompetent to stand trial, the court shall proceed under Subchapter D.

SUBCHAPTER D PROCEDURES AFTER DETERMINATION OF INCOMPETENCY

Art. 46B.071. Options on Determination of Incompetency.

(a) Except as provided by Subsection (b), on a determination that a defendant is incompetent to stand trial, the court shall:

(1) if the defendant is charged with an offense punishable as a Class B misdemeanor:

(A) release the defendant on bail under Article 46B.0711; or

(B) commit the defendant to:

(i) a jail-based competency restoration program under Article 46B.073(e); or

(ii) a mental health facility or residential care facility under Article 46B.073(f); or

(2) if the defendant is charged with an offense punishable as a Class A misdemeanor or any higher category of offense:

(A) release the defendant on bail under Article 46B.072; or

(B) commit the defendant to a facility or a jail-based competency restoration program under Article 46B.073(c) or (d).

(b) On a determination that a defendant is incompetent to stand trial and is unlikely to be restored to competency in the foreseeable future, the court shall:

(1) proceed under Subchapter E or F; or

(2) release the defendant on bail as permitted under Chapter 17.

Art. 46B.0711. Release on Bail for Class B Misdemeanor.

(a) This article applies only to a defendant who is subject to an initial restoration period based on Article 46B.071.

(b) Subject to conditions reasonably related to ensuring public safety and the effectiveness of the defendant's treatment, if the court determines that a defendant charged with an offense punishable as a Class B misdemeanor and found incompetent to stand trial is not a danger to others and may be safely treated on an outpatient basis with the specific objective of attaining competency to stand trial, and an appropriate outpatient competency restoration program is available for the defendant, the court shall:

(1) release the defendant on bail or continue the defendant's release on bail; and

(2) order the defendant to participate in an outpatient competency restoration program for a period not to exceed 60 days.

(c) Notwithstanding Subsection (b), the court may order a defendant to participate in an outpatient competency restoration program under this article only if:

(1) the court receives and approves a comprehensive plan that:

(A) provides for the treatment of the defendant for purposes of competency restoration; and

(B) identifies the person who will be responsible for providing that treatment to the defendant; and

(2) the court finds that the treatment proposed by the plan will be available to and will be provided to the defendant.

(d) An order issued under this article may require the defendant to participate in:

(1) as appropriate, an outpatient competency restoration program administered by a community center or an outpatient competency restoration

Code of Criminal Procedure

program administered by any other entity that provides competency restoration services; and

(2) an appropriate prescribed regimen of medical, psychiatric, or psychological care or treatment.

Art. 46B.072. Release on Bail for Felony or Class A Misdemeanor.

(a) This article applies only to a defendant who is subject to an initial restoration period based on Article 46B.071.

(a-1) Subject to conditions reasonably related to ensuring public safety and the effectiveness of the defendant's treatment, if the court determines that a defendant charged with an offense punishable as a felony or a Class A misdemeanor and found incompetent to stand trial is not a danger to others and may be safely treated on an outpatient basis with the specific objective of attaining competency to stand trial, and an appropriate outpatient competency restoration program is available for the defendant, the court:

(1) may release on bail a defendant found incompetent to stand trial with respect to an offense punishable as a felony or may continue the defendant's release on bail; and

(2) shall release on bail a defendant found incompetent to stand trial with respect to an offense punishable as a Class A misdemeanor or shall continue the defendant's release on bail.

(b) The court shall order a defendant released on bail under Subsection (a-1) to participate in an outpatient competency restoration program for a period not to exceed 120 days.

(c) Notwithstanding Subsection (a-1), the court may order a defendant to participate in an outpatient competency restoration program under this article only if:

(1) the court receives and approves a comprehensive plan that:

(A) provides for the treatment of the defendant for purposes of competency restoration; and

(B) identifies the person who will be responsible for providing that treatment to the defendant; and

(2) the court finds that the treatment proposed by the plan will be available to and will be provided to the defendant.

(d) An order issued under this article may require the defendant to participate in:

(1) as appropriate, an outpatient competency restoration program administered by a community center or an outpatient competency restoration program administered by any other entity that provides outpatient competency restoration services; and

(2) an appropriate prescribed regimen of medical, psychiatric, or psychological care or treatment, including care or treatment involving the administration of psychoactive medication, including those required under Article 46B.086.

Art. 46B.073. Commitment for Restoration to Competency.

(a) This article applies only to a defendant not released on bail who is subject to an initial restoration period based on Article 46B.071.

(b) For purposes of further examination and competency restoration services with the specific objective of the defendant attaining competency to stand trial, the court shall commit a defendant described by Subsection (a) to a mental health facility, residential care facility, or jail-based competency restoration program for the applicable period as follows:

(1) a period of not more than 60 days, if the defendant is charged with an offense punishable as a misdemeanor; or

(2) a period of not more than 120 days, if the defendant is charged with an offense punishable as a felony.

(c) If the defendant is charged with an offense listed in Article 17.032(a) or if the indictment alleges an affirmative finding under Article 42A.054(c) or (d), the court shall enter an order committing the defendant for competency restoration services to a facility designated by the commission.

(d) If the defendant is not charged with an offense described by Subsection (c) and the indictment does not allege an affirmative finding under Article 42A.054(c) or (d), the court shall enter an order committing the defendant to a mental health facility or residential care facility determined to be appropriate by the local mental health authority or local intellectual and developmental disability authority or to a jail-based competency restoration program. A defendant may be committed to a jail-based competency restoration program only if the program provider determines the defendant will begin to receive competency restoration services within 72 hours of arriving at the program.

(e) Except as provided by Subsection (f), a defendant charged with an offense punishable as a Class B misdemeanor may be committed under this subchapter only to a jail-based competency restoration program.

(f) A defendant charged with an offense punishable as a Class B misdemeanor may be committed to a mental health facility or residential care facility described by Subsection (d) only if a jail-based competency restoration program is not available or a licensed or qualified mental health professional determines that a jail-based competency restoration program is not appropriate.

Code of Criminal Procedure

Art. 46B.0735. Date Competency Restoration Period Begins.

The initial restoration period for a defendant under Article 46B.0711, 46B.072, or 46B.073 begins on the later of:

(1) the date the defendant is:

(A) ordered to participate in an outpatient competency restoration program; or

(B) committed to a mental health facility, residential care facility, or jail-based competency restoration program; or

(2) the date competency restoration services actually begin.

Art. 46B.074. Competent Testimony Required.

(a) A defendant may be committed to a jail-based competency restoration program, mental health facility, or residential care facility under this subchapter only on competent medical or psychiatric testimony provided by an expert qualified under Article 46B.022.

(b) The court may allow an expert to substitute the expert's report under Article 46B.025 for any testimony by the expert that may be required under this article.

Art. 46B.075. Transfer of Defendant to Facility or Program.

An order issued under Article 46B.0711, 46B.072, or 46B.073 must place the defendant in the custody of the sheriff or sheriff's deputy for transportation to the facility or program, as applicable, in which the defendant is to receive competency restoration services.

Art. 46B.0755. Procedures on Credible Evidence of Immediate Restoration.

(a) Notwithstanding any other provision of this subchapter, if the court receives credible evidence indicating that the defendant has been restored to competency at any time after the defendant's incompetency trial under Subchapter C but before the defendant is transported under Article 46B.075 to the facility or program, as applicable, the court may appoint disinterested experts to reexamine the defendant in accordance with Subchapter B. The court is not required to appoint the same expert or experts who performed the initial examination of the defendant under that subchapter.

(b) If after a reexamination of the defendant the applicable expert's report states an opinion that the defendant remains incompetent, the court's order under Article 46B.0711, 46B.072, or 46B.073 remains in effect, and the defendant shall be transported to the facility or program as required by Article 46B.075. If after a reexamination of the defendant the applicable expert's report states an opinion that the defendant has been restored to competency, the court shall withdraw its order under Article 46B.0711, 46B.072, or 46B.073 and proceed under Subsection (c) or (d).

(c) The court shall find the defendant competent to stand trial and proceed in the same manner as if the defendant had been found restored to competency at a hearing if:

(1) both parties agree that the defendant is competent to stand trial; and

(2) the court concurs.

(d) The court shall hold a hearing to determine whether the defendant has been restored to competency if any party fails to agree or if the court fails to concur that the defendant is competent to stand trial. If a court holds a hearing under this subsection, on the request of the counsel for either party or the motion of the court, a jury shall make the competency determination. For purposes of the hearing, incompetency is presumed, and the defendant's competency must be proved by a preponderance of the evidence. If after the hearing the defendant is again found to be incompetent to stand trial, the court shall issue a new order under Article 46B.0711, 46B.072, or 46B.073, as appropriate based on the defendant's current condition.

Art. 46B.076. Court's Order.

(a) If the defendant is found incompetent to stand trial, not later than the date of the order of commitment or of release on bail, as applicable, the court shall send a copy of the order to the applicable facility or program. The court shall also provide to the facility or program copies of the following made available to the court during the incompetency trial:

(1) reports of each expert;

(2) psychiatric, psychological, or social work reports that relate to the mental condition of the defendant;

(3) documents provided by the attorney representing the state or the attorney representing the defendant that relate to the defendant's current or past mental condition;

(4) copies of the indictment or information and any supporting documents used to establish probable cause in the case;

(5) the defendant's criminal history record; and

(6) the addresses of the attorney representing the state and the attorney representing the defendant.

(b) The court shall order that the transcript of all medical testimony received by the jury or court be promptly prepared by the court reporter and forwarded to the applicable facility or program.

Art. 46B.077. Individual Treatment Program.

(a) The facility or jail-based competency restoration program to which the defendant is committed or the outpatient competency restoration program to which the defendant is released on bail shall:

(1) develop an individual program of treatment;

(2) assess and evaluate whether the defendant is likely to be restored to competency in the foreseeable future; and

(3) report to the court and to the local mental health authority or to the local intellectual and developmental disability authority on the defendant's progress toward achieving competency.

(b) If the defendant is committed to an inpatient mental health facility, residential care facility, or jail-based competency restoration program, the facility or program shall report to the court at least once during the commitment period.

(c) If the defendant is released to an outpatient competency restoration program, the program shall report to the court:

(1) not later than the 14th day after the date on which the defendant's competency restoration services begin; and

(2) until the defendant is no longer released to the program, at least once during each 30-day period following the date of the report required by Subdivision (1).

Art. 46B.078. Charges Subsequently Dismissed.

If the charges pending against a defendant are dismissed, the court that issued the order under Article 46B.0711, 46B.072, or 46B.073 shall send a copy of the order of dismissal to the sheriff of the county in which the court is located and to the head of the facility, the provider of the jail-based competency restoration program, or the provider of the outpatient competency restoration program, as appropriate. On receipt of the copy of the order, the facility or program shall discharge the defendant into the care of the sheriff or sheriff's deputy for transportation in the manner described by Article 46B.082.

Art. 46B.079. Notice and Report to Court.

(a) The head of the facility, the provider of the jail-based competency restoration program, or the provider of the outpatient competency restoration program, as appropriate, not later than the 15th day before the date on which the initial restoration period is to expire according to the terms of the order or under Article 46B.0095 or other applicable provisions of this chapter, shall notify the applicable court that the period is about to expire.

(b) The head of the facility or jail-based competency restoration program provider shall promptly notify the court when the head of the facility or program provider believes that:

(1) the defendant is clinically ready and can be safely transferred to a competency restoration program for education services but has not yet attained competency to stand trial;

(2) the defendant has attained competency to stand trial; or

(3) the defendant is not likely to attain competency in the foreseeable future.

(b-1) The outpatient competency restoration program provider shall promptly notify the court when the program provider believes that:

(1) the defendant has attained competency to stand trial; or

(2) the defendant is not likely to attain competency in the foreseeable future.

(c) When the head of the facility or program provider gives notice to the court under Subsection (a), (b), or (b-1), the head of the facility or program provider also shall file a final report with the court stating the reason for the proposed discharge or transfer under this chapter and including a list of the types and dosages of medications prescribed for the defendant while the defendant was receiving competency restoration services in the facility or through the program. The court shall provide to the attorney representing the defendant and the attorney representing the state copies of a report based on notice under this article, other than notice under Subsection (b)(1), to enable any objection to the findings of the report to be made in a timely manner as required under Article 46B.084(a-1).

(d) If the head of the facility or program provider notifies the court that the initial restoration period is about to expire, the notice may contain a request for an extension of the period for an additional period of 60 days and an explanation for the basis of the request. An explanation provided under this subsection must include a description of any evidence indicating a reduction in the severity of the defendant's symptoms or impairment.

Art. 46B.080. Extension of Order.

(a) On a request of the head of a facility or a program provider that is made under Article 46B.079(d) and notwithstanding any other

Code of Criminal Procedure

provision of this subchapter, the court may enter an order extending the initial restoration period for an additional period of 60 days.

(b) The court may enter an order under Subsection (a) only if the court determines that:

(1) the defendant has not attained competency; and

(2) an extension of the initial restoration period will likely enable the facility or program to restore the defendant to competency within the period of the extension.

(c) The court may grant only one 60-day extension under this article in connection with the specific offense with which the defendant is charged.

(d) An extension under this article begins on the later of:

(1) the date the court enters the order under Subsection (a); or

(2) the date competency restoration services actually begin pursuant to the order entered under Subsection (a).

Art. 46B.0805. Competency Restoration Education Services.

(a) On notification from the head of a facility or a jail-based competency restoration program provider under Article 46B.079(b)(1), the court shall order the defendant to receive competency restoration education services in a jail-based competency restoration program or an outpatient competency restoration program, as appropriate and if available.

(b) If a defendant for whom an order is entered under Subsection (a) was committed for competency restoration to a facility other than a jail-based competency restoration program, the court shall send a copy of that order to:

(1) the sheriff of the county in which the court is located;

(2) the head of the facility to which the defendant was committed for competency restoration; and

(3) the local mental health authority or local intellectual and developmental disability authority, as appropriate.

(c) As soon as practicable but not later than the 10th day after the date of receipt of a copy of an order under Subsection (b)(2), the applicable facility shall discharge the defendant into the care of the sheriff of the county in which the court is located or into the care of the sheriff's deputy. The sheriff or sheriff's deputy shall transport the defendant to the jail-based competency restoration program or outpatient competency restoration program, as appropriate.

(d) A jail-based competency restoration program or outpatient competency restoration program that receives a defendant under this article shall give to the court:

(1) notice regarding the defendant's entry into the program for purposes of receiving competency restoration education services; and

(2) subsequent notice as otherwise required under Article 46B.079.

Art. 46B.081. Return to Court.

Subject to Article 46B.082(b), a defendant committed or released on bail under this subchapter shall be returned to the applicable court as soon as practicable after notice to the court is provided under Article 46B.079(a), (b)(2), (b)(3), or (b-1), but not later than the date of expiration of the period for restoration specified by the court under Article 46B.0711, 46B.072, or 46B.073.

Art. 46B.082. Transportation of Defendant to Court.

(a) On notification from the court under Article 46B.078, the sheriff of the county in which the court is located or the sheriff's deputy shall transport the defendant to the court.

(b) If before the 15th day after the date on which the court received notification under Article 46B.079(a), (b)(2), (b)(3), or (b-1) a defendant committed to a facility or jail-based competency restoration program or ordered to participate in an outpatient competency restoration program has not been transported to the court that issued the order under Article 46B.0711, 46B.072, or 46B.073, as applicable, the head of the facility or provider of the jail-based competency restoration program to which the defendant is committed or the provider of the outpatient competency restoration program in which the defendant is participating shall cause the defendant to be promptly transported to the court and placed in the custody of the sheriff of the county in which the court is located. The county in which the court is located shall reimburse the Health and Human Services Commission or program provider, as appropriate, for the mileage and per diem expenses of the personnel required to transport the defendant, calculated in accordance with rates provided in the General Appropriations Act for state employees.

Art. 46B.0825. Administration of Medication While in Custody of Sheriff.

(a) A sheriff or sheriff's deputy having custody of a defendant for transportation as required by Article 46B.0805 or 46B.082 or during proceedings described by Article 46B.084 shall, according to information available at the time and unless directed otherwise by a physician treating the defendant, ensure that the defendant is provided with the types and dosages of medication prescribed for the defendant.

(b) To the extent funds are appropriated for that purpose, a sheriff is entitled to reimbursement from the state for providing the medication required by Subsection (a).

(c) If the sheriff determines that funds are not available from the state to reimburse the sheriff as provided by Subsection (b), the sheriff is not required to comply with Subsection (a).

Art. 46B.083. Supporting Commitment Information Provided by Facility or Program.

(a) If the head of the facility, the jail-based competency restoration program provider, or the outpatient competency restoration program provider believes that the defendant is a person with mental illness and meets the criteria for court-ordered mental health services under Subtitle C, Title 7, Health and Safety Code, the head of the facility or the program provider shall have submitted to the court a certificate of medical examination for mental illness.

(b) If the head of the facility, the jail-based competency restoration program provider, or the outpatient competency restoration program provider believes that the defendant is a person with an intellectual disability, the head of the facility or the program provider shall have submitted to the court an affidavit stating the conclusions reached as a result of the examination.

Art. 46B.0831. Determination Whether Defendant Is Manifestly Dangerous.

A defendant committed to a maximum security unit by the commission may be assessed, at any time before the defendant is restored to competency, by the review board established under Section 46B.105 to determine whether the defendant is manifestly dangerous. If the review board determines the defendant is not manifestly dangerous, the commission shall transfer the defendant to a non-maximum security facility designated by the commission.

Art. 46B.084. Proceedings on Return of Defendant to Court.

(a) (1) Not later than the next business day following the return of a defendant to the court, the court shall notify the attorney representing the state and the attorney for the defendant regarding the return. Within three business days of the date that notice is received under this subsection or, on a showing of good cause, a later date specified by the court, the attorney for the defendant shall meet and confer with the defendant to evaluate whether there is any suggestion that the defendant has not yet regained competency.

(2) Notwithstanding Subdivision (1), in a county with a population of less than one million or in a county with a population of four million or more, as soon as practicable following the date of the defendant's return to the court, the court shall provide the notice required by that subdivision to the attorney representing the state and the attorney for the defendant, and the attorney for the defendant shall meet and confer with the defendant as soon as practicable after the date of receipt of that notice.

(a-1) (1) Following the defendant's return to the court, the court shall make a determination with regard to the defendant's competency to stand trial. The court may make the determination based only on the most recent report that is filed under Article 46B.079(c) and based on notice under that article, other than notice under Subsection (b)(1) of that article, and on other medical information or personal history information relating to the defendant. A party may object in writing or in open court to the findings of the most recent report not later than the 15th day after the date on which the court received the applicable notice under Article 46B.079. The court shall make the determination not later than the 20th day after the date on which the court received the applicable notice under Article 46B.079, or not later than the fifth day after the date of the defendant's return to court, whichever occurs first, regardless of whether a party objects to the report as described by this subsection and the issue is set for hearing under Subsection (b).

(2) Notwithstanding Subdivision (1), in a county with a population of less than one million or in a county with a population of four million or more, the court shall make the determination described by that subdivision not later than the 20th day after the date on which the court received notification under Article 46B.079, regardless of whether a party objects to the report as described by that subdivision and the issue is set for a hearing under Subsection (b).

(b) If a party objects under Subsection (a-1), the issue shall be set for a hearing. The hearing is before the court, except that on motion by the defendant, the defense counsel, the prosecuting attorney, or the court, the hearing shall be held before a jury.

Code of Criminal Procedure

(b-1) If the hearing is before the court, the hearing may be conducted by means of an electronic broadcast system as provided by Article 46B.013. Notwithstanding any other provision of this chapter, the defendant is not required to be returned to the court with respect to any hearing that is conducted under this article in the manner described by this subsection.

(c) [Repealed by Acts 2007, 80th Leg., ch. 1307 (S.B. 867), § 21, effective September 1, 2007.]

(d) (1) If the defendant is found competent to stand trial, on the court's own motion criminal proceedings in the case against the defendant shall be resumed not later than the 14th day after the date of the court's determination under this article that the defendant's competency has been restored.

(2) Notwithstanding Subdivision (1), in a county with a population of less than one million or in a county with a population of four million or more, on the court's own motion criminal proceedings in the case against the defendant shall be resumed as soon as practicable after the date of the court's determination under this article that the defendant's competency has been restored.

(d-1) This article does not require the criminal case to be finally resolved within any specific period.

(e) If the defendant is found incompetent to stand trial and if all charges pending against the defendant are not dismissed, the court shall proceed under Subchapter E.

(f) If the defendant is found incompetent to stand trial and if all charges pending against the defendant are dismissed, the court shall proceed under Subchapter F.

Art. 46B.085. Subsequent Restoration Periods and Extensions of Those Periods Prohibited.

(a) The court may order only one initial period of restoration and one extension under this subchapter in connection with the same offense.

(b) After an initial restoration period and an extension are ordered as described by Subsection (a), any subsequent court orders for treatment must be issued under Subchapter E or F.

Art. 46B.086. Court-Ordered Medications.

(a) This article applies only to a defendant:

(1) who is determined under this chapter to be incompetent to stand trial;

(2) who either:

(A) remains confined in a correctional facility, as defined by Section 1.07, Penal Code, for a period exceeding 72 hours while awaiting transfer to an inpatient mental health facility, a residential care facility, or an outpatient competency restoration program;

(B) is committed to an inpatient mental health facility, a residential care facility, or a jail-based competency restoration program for the purpose of competency restoration;

(C) is confined in a correctional facility while awaiting further criminal proceedings following competency restoration; or

(D) is subject to Article 46B.072, if the court has made the determinations required by Subsection (a-1) of that article;

(3) for whom a correctional facility or jail-based competency restoration program that employs or contracts with a licensed psychiatrist, an inpatient mental health facility, a residential care facility, or an outpatient competency restoration program provider has prepared a continuity of care plan that requires the defendant to take psychoactive medications; and

(4) who, after a hearing held under Section 574.106 or 592.156, Health and Safety Code, if applicable, has been found to not meet the criteria prescribed by Sections 574.106(a) and (a-1) or 592.156(a) and (b), Health and Safety Code, for court-ordered administration of psychoactive medications.

(b) If a defendant described by Subsection (a) refuses to take psychoactive medications as required by the defendant's continuity of care plan, the director of the facility or the program provider, as applicable, shall notify the court in which the criminal proceedings are pending of that fact not later than the end of the next business day following the refusal. The court shall promptly notify the attorney representing the state and the attorney representing the defendant of the defendant's refusal. The attorney representing the state may file a written motion to compel medication. The motion to compel medication must be filed not later than the 15th day after the date a judge issues an order stating that the defendant does not meet the criteria for court-ordered administration of psychoactive medications under Section 574.106 or 592.156, Health and Safety Code, except that, for a defendant in an outpatient competency restoration program, the motion may be filed at any time.

(c) The court, after notice and after a hearing held not later than the 10th day after the motion to compel medication is filed, may authorize the director of the facility or the program provider, as applicable, to have the medication administered to the defendant, by reasonable force if necessary. A hearing under this subsection may be conducted using an electronic broadcast system as provided by Article 46B.013.

(d) The court may issue an order under this article only if the order is supported by the testimony of two physicians, one of whom is the physician at or with the applicable facility or program who is prescribing the medication as a component of the defendant's continuity of care plan and another who is not otherwise involved in proceedings against the defendant. The court may require either or both physicians to examine the defendant and report on the examination to the court.

(e) The court may issue an order under this article if the court finds by clear and convincing evidence that:

(1) the prescribed medication is medically appropriate, is in the best medical interest of the defendant, and does not present side effects that cause harm to the defendant that is greater than the medical benefit to the defendant;

(2) the state has a clear and compelling interest in the defendant obtaining and maintaining competency to stand trial;

(3) no other less invasive means of obtaining and maintaining the defendant's competency exists; and

(4) the prescribed medication will not unduly prejudice the defendant's rights or use of defensive theories at trial.

(f) A statement made by a defendant to a physician during an examination under Subsection (d) may not be admitted against the defendant in any criminal proceeding, other than at:

(1) a hearing on the defendant's incompetency; or

(2) any proceeding at which the defendant first introduces into evidence the contents of the statement.

(g) For a defendant described by Subsection (a)(2)(A), an order issued under this article:

(1) authorizes the initiation of any appropriate mental health treatment for the defendant awaiting transfer; and

(2) does not constitute authorization to retain the defendant in a correctional facility for competency restoration treatment.

Art. 46B.090. Jail-Based Restoration of Competency Pilot Program.

(a) [Repealed.]

(a-1) If the legislature appropriates to the commission the funding necessary for the commission to operate a jail-based restoration of competency pilot program as described by this article, the commission shall develop and implement the pilot program in one or two counties in this state that choose to participate in the pilot program. In developing the pilot program, the commission shall coordinate and allow for input from each participating county.

(b) The commission shall contract with a provider of jail-based competency restoration services to provide services under the pilot program if the commission develops a pilot program under this article.

(c) The executive commissioner shall adopt rules as necessary to implement the pilot program.

(d), (e) [Repealed by Acts 2015, 84th Leg., ch. 946 (S.B. 277), § 1.15(d), effective September 1, 2015.]

(f) To contract with the commission under Subsection (b), a provider of jail-based competency restoration services must:

(1) be a local mental health authority or local behavioral health authority that is in good standing with the commission, which may include an authority that is in good standing with the commission and subcontracts with a provider of jail-based competency restoration services; and

(2) contract with a county or counties to develop and implement a jail-based competency restoration program.

(f-1) The provider's jail-based competency restoration program must:

(1) through the use of a multidisciplinary treatment team, provide jail-based competency restoration services that are:

(A) directed toward the specific objective of restoring the defendant's competency to stand trial; and

(B) similar to other competency restoration programs;

(2) employ or contract for the services of at least one psychiatrist;

(3) provide jail-based competency restoration services through licensed or qualified mental health professionals;

(4) provide weekly competency restoration hours commensurate to the hours provided as part of other competency restoration programs;

(5) operate in the jail in a designated space that is separate from the space used for the general population of the jail;

(6) ensure coordination of general health care;

(7) provide mental health treatment and substance use disorder treatment to defendants, as necessary, for competency restoration; and

(8) supply clinically appropriate psychoactive medications for purposes of administering court-ordered medication to defendants as applicable and in accordance with Article 46B.086 of this code or Section 574.106, Health and Safety Code.

(g) A contract under Subsection (b) must require the designated provider to collect and submit to the commission the information specified by rules adopted under Subsection (c).

(h) [Repealed.]

(i) A psychiatrist or psychologist for the provider who has the qualifications described by Article 46B.022 shall evaluate the defendant's competency and report to the court as required by Article 46B.079.

(j) If at any time during a defendant's participation in the jail-based restoration of competency pilot program the psychiatrist or psychologist for the provider determines that the defendant has attained competency to stand trial:

(1) the psychiatrist or psychologist for the provider shall promptly issue and send to the court a report demonstrating that fact; and

(2) the court shall consider that report as the report of an expert stating an opinion that the defendant has been restored to competency for purposes of Article 46B.0755(a) or (b).

(k) If at any time during a defendant's participation in the jail-based restoration of competency pilot program the psychiatrist or psychologist for the provider determines that the defendant's competency to stand trial is unlikely to be restored in the foreseeable future:

(1) the psychiatrist or psychologist for the provider shall promptly issue and send to the court a report demonstrating that fact; and

(2) the court shall:

(A) proceed under Subchapter E or F and order the transfer of the defendant, without unnecessary delay, to the first available facility that is appropriate for that defendant, as provided under Subchapter E or F, as applicable; or

(B) release the defendant on bail as permitted under Chapter 17.

(*l*) If the psychiatrist or psychologist for the provider determines that a defendant ordered to participate in the pilot program has not been restored to competency by the end of the 60th day after the date the defendant began to receive services in the pilot program, the jail-based competency restoration program shall continue to provide competency restoration services to the defendant for the period authorized by this subchapter, including any extension ordered under Article 46B.080, unless the jail-based competency restoration program is notified that space at a facility or outpatient competency restoration program appropriate for the defendant is available and, as applicable:

(1) for a defendant charged with a felony, not less than 45 days are remaining in the initial restoration period; or

(2) for a defendant charged with a felony or a misdemeanor, an extension has been ordered under Article 46B.080 and not less than 45 days are remaining under the extension order.

(l-1) After receipt of a notice under Subsection (l), the defendant shall be transferred without unnecessary delay to the appropriate mental health facility, residential care facility, or outpatient competency restoration program for the remainder of the period permitted by this subchapter, including any extension that may be ordered under Article 46B.080 if an extension has not previously been ordered under that article. If the defendant is not transferred, and if the psychiatrist or psychologist for the provider determines that the defendant has not been restored to competency by the end of the period authorized by this subchapter, the defendant shall be returned to the court for further proceedings. For a defendant charged with a misdemeanor, the court may:

(1) proceed under Subchapter E or F;

(2) release the defendant on bail as permitted under Chapter 17; or

(3) dismiss the charges in accordance with Article 46B.010.

(l-2) The court retains authority to order the transfer of a defendant who is subject to an order for jail-based competency restoration services to an outpatient competency restoration program if:

(1) the court determines that the defendant is not a danger to others and may be safely treated on an outpatient basis with the specific objective of attaining competency to stand trial; and

(2) the other requirements of this subchapter relating to an order for outpatient competency restoration services are met.

(m) Unless otherwise provided by this article, the provisions of this chapter, including the maximum periods prescribed by Article 46B.0095, apply to a defendant receiving competency restoration services, including competency restoration education services, under the pilot program in the same manner as those provisions apply to any other defendant who is subject to proceedings under this chapter.

(n) If the commission develops and implements a jail-based restoration of competency pilot program under this article, not later than December 1, 2021, the executive commissioner shall submit a report concerning the pilot program to the presiding officers of the standing committees of the senate and house of representatives having primary jurisdiction over health and human services issues and over criminal justice issues. The report must include the information collected by the commission during the pilot program and the executive commissioner's evaluation of the outcome of the program as of the date the report is submitted.

(o) This article expires September 1, 2022. After the expiration of this article, a pilot program established under this article may continue to operate subject to the requirements of Article 46B.091.

Art. 46B.091. Jail-Based Competency Restoration Program Implemented by County.

(a) [Repealed.]

(b) A county or counties jointly may develop and implement a jail-based competency restoration program.

(c) A county that implements a program under this article shall contract with a provider of jail-based competency restoration services that is a local mental health authority or local behavioral health authority that is in good standing with the commission, which may include an authority that is in good standing with the commission and subcontracts with a provider of jail-based competency restoration services.

(d) A jail-based competency restoration program must:

(1) provide jail-based competency restoration services through the use of a multidisciplinary treatment team that are:

(A) directed toward the specific objective of restoring the defendant's competency to stand trial; and

(B) similar to other competency restoration programs;

(2) employ or contract for the services of at least one psychiatrist;

(3) provide jail-based competency restoration services through licensed or qualified mental health professionals;

(4) provide weekly competency restoration hours commensurate to the hours provided as part of a competency restoration program at an inpatient mental health facility;

(5) operate in the jail in a designated space that is separate from the space used for the general population of the jail;

(6) ensure coordination of general health care;

(7) provide mental health treatment and substance use disorder treatment to defendants, as necessary, for competency restoration; and

(8) supply clinically appropriate psychoactive medications for purposes of administering court-ordered medication to defendants as applicable and in accordance with Article 46B.086 of this code or Section 574.106, Health and Safety Code.

(e) The executive commissioner shall adopt rules as necessary for a county to develop and implement a program under this article. The commission shall, as part of the rulemaking process, establish contract monitoring and oversight requirements for a local mental health authority or local behavioral health authority that contracts with a county to provide jail-based competency restoration services under this article. The contract monitoring and oversight requirements must be consistent with local mental health authority or local behavioral health authority performance contract monitoring and oversight requirements, as applicable.

(f) The commission may inspect on behalf of the state any aspect of a program implemented under this article.

(g) A psychiatrist or psychologist for the provider who has the qualifications described by Article 46B.022 shall evaluate the defendant's competency and report to the court as required by Article 46B.079.

(h) If at any time during a defendant's commitment to a program implemented under this article the psychiatrist or psychologist for the provider determines that the defendant has attained competency to stand trial:

(1) the psychiatrist or psychologist for the provider shall promptly issue and send to the court a report demonstrating that fact; and

(2) the court shall consider that report as the report of an expert stating an opinion that the defendant has been restored to competency for purposes of Article 46B.0755(a) or (b).

(i) If at any time during a defendant's commitment to a program implemented under this article the psychiatrist or psychologist for the provider determines that the defendant's competency to stand trial is unlikely to be restored in the foreseeable future:

(1) the psychiatrist or psychologist for the provider shall promptly issue and send to the court a report demonstrating that fact; and

(2) the court shall:

(A) proceed under Subchapter E or F and order the transfer of the defendant, without unnecessary delay, to the first available facility that is appropriate for that defendant, as provided under Subchapter E or F, as applicable; or

(B) release the defendant on bail as permitted under Chapter 17.

(j) If the psychiatrist or psychologist for the provider determines that a defendant committed to a program implemented under this article has not been restored to competency by the end of the 60th day after the date the defendant began to receive services in the program, the jail-based competency restoration program shall continue to provide competency restoration services to the defendant for the period authorized by this

Code of Criminal Procedure

subchapter, including any extension ordered under Article 46B.080, unless the jail-based competency restoration program is notified that space at a facility or outpatient competency restoration program appropriate for the defendant is available and, as applicable:

(1) for a defendant charged with a felony, not less than 45 days are remaining in the initial restoration period; or

(2) for a defendant charged with a felony or a misdemeanor, an extension has been ordered under Article 46B.080 and not less than 45 days are remaining under the extension order.

(j-1) After receipt of a notice under Subsection (j), the defendant shall be transferred without unnecessary delay to the appropriate mental health facility, residential care facility, or outpatient competency restoration program for the remainder of the period permitted by this subchapter, including any extension that may be ordered under Article 46B.080 if an extension has not previously been ordered under that article. If the defendant is not transferred, and if the psychiatrist or psychologist for the provider determines that the defendant has not been restored to competency by the end of the period authorized by this subchapter, the defendant shall be returned to the court for further proceedings. For a defendant charged with a misdemeanor, the court may:

(1) proceed under Subchapter E or F;

(2) release the defendant on bail as permitted under Chapter 17; or

(3) dismiss the charges in accordance with Article 46B.010.

(k) Unless otherwise provided by this article, the provisions of this chapter, including the maximum periods prescribed by Article 46B.0095, apply to a defendant receiving competency restoration services, including competency restoration education services, under a program implemented under this article in the same manner as those provisions apply to any other defendant who is subject to proceedings under this chapter.

(*l*) This article does not affect the responsibility of a county to ensure the safety of a defendant who is committed to the program and to provide the same adequate care to the defendant as is provided to other inmates of the jail in which the defendant is located.

(m) The court retains authority to order the transfer of a defendant who is subject to an order for jail-based competency restoration services to an outpatient competency restoration program if:

(1) the court determines that the defendant is not a danger to others and may be safely treated on an outpatient basis with the specific objective of attaining competency to stand trial; and

(2) the other requirements of this subchapter relating to an order for outpatient competency restoration services are met.

SUBCHAPTER E
CIVIL COMMITMENT: CHARGES PENDING

Art. 46B.101. Applicability.

This subchapter applies to a defendant against whom a court is required to proceed according to Article 46B.084(e) or according to the court's appropriate determination under Article 46B.071.

Art. 46B.102. Civil Commitment Hearing: Mental Illness.

(a) If it appears to the court that the defendant may be a person with mental illness, the court shall hold a hearing to determine whether the defendant should be court-ordered to mental health services under Subtitle C, Title 7, Health and Safety Code.

(b) Proceedings for commitment of the defendant to court-ordered mental health services are governed by Subtitle C, Title 7, Health and Safety Code, to the extent that Subtitle C applies and does not conflict with this chapter, except that the criminal court shall conduct the proceedings whether or not the criminal court is also the county court.

(c) If the court enters an order committing the defendant to a mental health facility, the defendant shall be:

(1) treated in conformity with Subtitle C, Title 7, Health and Safety Code, except as otherwise provided by this chapter; and

(2) released in conformity with Article 46B.107.

(d) In proceedings conducted under this subchapter for a defendant described by Subsection (a):

(1) an application for court-ordered temporary or extended mental health services may not be required;

(2) the provisions of Subtitle C, Title 7, Health and Safety Code, relating to notice of hearing do not apply; and

(3) appeals from the criminal court proceedings are to the court of appeals as in the proceedings for court-ordered inpatient mental health services under Subtitle C, Title 7, Health and Safety Code.

Art. 46B.103. Civil Commitment Hearing: Intellectual Disability.

(a) If it appears to the court that the defendant may be a person with an intellectual disability, the court shall hold a hearing to determine whether the defendant is a person with an intellectual disability.

(b) Proceedings for commitment of the defendant to a residential care facility are governed by Subtitle D, Title 7, Health and Safety Code, to the extent that Subtitle D applies and does not conflict with this chapter, except that the criminal court shall conduct the proceedings whether or not the criminal court is also a county court.

(c) If the court enters an order committing the defendant to a residential care facility, the defendant shall be:

(1) treated and released in accordance with Subtitle D, Title 7, Health and Safety Code, except as otherwise provided by this chapter; and

(2) released in conformity with Article 46B.107.

(d) In the proceedings conducted under this subchapter for a defendant described by Subsection (a):

(1) an application to have the defendant declared a person with an intellectual disability may not be required;

(2) the provisions of Subtitle D, Title 7, Health and Safety Code, relating to notice of hearing do not apply; and

(3) appeals from the criminal court proceedings are to the court of appeals as in the proceedings for commitment to a residential care facility under Subtitle D, Title 7, Health and Safety Code.

Art. 46B.104. Civil Commitment Placement: Finding of Violence.

A defendant committed to a facility as a result of proceedings initiated under this chapter shall be committed to the facility designated by the commission if:

(1) the defendant is charged with an offense listed in Article 17.032(a); or

(2) the indictment charging the offense alleges an affirmative finding under Article 42A.054(c) or (d).

Art. 46B.105. Transfer Following Civil Commitment Placement.

(a) Unless a defendant committed to a maximum security unit by the commission is determined to be manifestly dangerous by a review board established under Subsection (b), not later than the 60th day after the date the defendant arrives at the maximum security unit, the defendant shall be transferred to:

(1) a unit of an inpatient mental health facility other than a maximum security unit;

(2) a residential care facility; or

(3) a program designated by a local mental health authority or a local intellectual and developmental disability authority.

(b) The executive commissioner shall appoint a review board of five members, including one psychiatrist licensed to practice medicine in this state and two persons who work directly with persons with mental illness or an intellectual disability, to determine whether the defendant is manifestly dangerous and, as a result of the danger the defendant presents, requires continued placement in a maximum security unit.

(c) The review board may not make a determination as to the defendant's need for treatment.

(d) A finding that the defendant is not manifestly dangerous is not a medical determination that the defendant no longer meets the criteria for involuntary civil commitment under Subtitle C or D, Title 7, Health and Safety Code.

(e) If the superintendent of the facility at which the maximum security unit is located disagrees with the determination, the matter shall be referred to the executive commissioner. The executive commissioner shall decide whether the defendant is manifestly dangerous.

Art. 46B.1055. Modification of Order Following Inpatient Civil Commitment Placement.

(a) This article applies to a defendant who has been transferred under Article 46B.105 from a maximum security unit to any facility other than a maximum security unit.

(b) The defendant, the head of the facility to which the defendant is committed, or the attorney representing the state may request that the court modify an order for inpatient treatment or residential care to order the defendant to participate in an outpatient treatment program.

(c) If the head of the facility to which the defendant is committed makes a request under Subsection (b), not later than the 14th day after the date of the request the court shall hold a hearing to determine whether the court should modify the order for inpatient treatment or residential care in accordance with Subtitle C, Title 7, Health and Safety Code.

(d) If the defendant or the attorney representing the state makes a request under Subsection (b), not later than the 14th day after the date of the request the court shall grant the request, deny the request, or hold a hearing on the request to determine whether the court should modify the order for inpatient treatment or residential care. A court is not required to hold a hearing under this subsection unless the request and any supporting materials provided to the court provide a basis for believing modification of the order may be appropriate.

(e) On receipt of a request to modify an order under Subsection (b), the court shall require the local mental health authority or local behavioral health authority to submit to the court, before any hearing is held under this article, a statement regarding whether treatment and supervision for the defendant can be safely and effectively provided on an outpatient basis and whether appropriate outpatient mental health services are available to the defendant.

(f) If the head of the facility to which the defendant is committed believes that the defendant is a person with mental illness who meets the criteria for court-ordered outpatient mental health services under Subtitle C, Title 7, Health and Safety Code, the head of the facility shall submit to the court before the hearing a certificate of medical examination for mental illness stating that the defendant meets the criteria for court-ordered outpatient mental health services.

(g) If a request under Subsection (b) is made by a defendant before the 91st day after the date the court makes a determination on a previous request under that subsection, the court is not required to act on the request until the earlier of:

(1) the expiration of the current order for inpatient treatment or residential care; or

(2) the 91st day after the date of the court's previous determination.

(h) Proceedings for commitment of the defendant to a court-ordered outpatient treatment program are governed by Subtitle C, Title 7, Health and Safety Code, to the extent that Subtitle C applies and does not conflict with this chapter, except that the criminal court shall conduct the proceedings regardless of whether the criminal court is also the county court.

(i) The court shall rule on a request made under Subsection (b) as soon as practicable after a hearing on the request, but not later than the 14th day after the date of the request.

(j) An outpatient treatment program may not refuse to accept a placement ordered under this article on the grounds that criminal charges against the defendant are pending.

Art. 46B.106. Civil Commitment Placement: No Finding of Violence.

(a) A defendant committed to a facility as a result of the proceedings initiated under this chapter, other than a defendant described by Article 46B.104, shall be committed to:

(1) a facility designated by the commission; or

(2) an outpatient treatment program.

(b) A facility or outpatient treatment program may not refuse to accept a placement ordered under this article on the grounds that criminal charges against the defendant are pending.

Art. 46B.107. Release of Defendant After Civil Commitment.

(a) The release of a defendant committed under this chapter from the commission, an outpatient treatment program, or another facility is subject to disapproval by the committing court if the court or the attorney representing the state has notified the head of the facility or outpatient treatment provider, as applicable, to which the defendant has been committed that a criminal charge remains pending against the defendant.

(b) If the head of the facility or outpatient treatment provider to which a defendant has been committed under this chapter determines that the defendant should be released from the facility, the head of the facility or outpatient treatment provider shall notify the committing court and the sheriff of the county from which the defendant was committed in writing of the release not later than the 14th day before the date on which the facility or outpatient treatment provider intends to release the defendant.

(c) The head of the facility or outpatient treatment provider shall provide with the notice a written statement that states an opinion as to whether the defendant to be released has attained competency to stand trial.

(d) The court shall, on receiving notice from the head of a facility or outpatient treatment provider of intent to release the defendant under Subsection (b), hold a hearing to determine whether release is appropriate under the applicable criteria in Subtitle C or D, Title 7, Health and Safety Code. The court may, on motion of the attorney representing the state or on its own motion, hold a hearing to determine whether release is appropriate under the applicable criteria in Subtitle C or D, Title 7, Health and Safety Code, regardless of whether the court receives notice that the head of a facility or outpatient treatment provider provides notice of intent to release the defendant under Subsection (b). The court may conduct the hearing:

(1) at the facility; or

(2) by means of an electronic broadcast system as provided by Article 46B.013.

(e) If the court determines that release is not appropriate, the court shall enter an order directing the head of the facility or the outpatient treatment provider to not release the defendant.

(f) If an order is entered under Subsection (e), any subsequent proceeding to release the defendant is subject to this article.

Art. 46B.108. Redetermination of Competency.

(a) If criminal charges against a defendant found incompetent to stand trial have not been dismissed, the trial court at any time may determine whether the defendant has been restored to competency.

(b) An inquiry into restoration of competency under this subchapter may be made at the request of the head of the mental health facility, outpatient treatment provider, or residential care facility to which the defendant has been committed, the defendant, the attorney representing the defendant, or the attorney representing the state, or may be made on the court's own motion.

Art. 46B.109. Request by Head of Facility or Outpatient Treatment Provider.

(a) The head of a facility or outpatient treatment provider to which a defendant has been committed as a result of a finding of incompetency to stand trial may request the court to determine that the defendant has been restored to competency.

(b) The head of the facility or outpatient treatment provider shall provide with the request a written statement that in their opinion the defendant is competent to stand trial.

Art. 46B.110. Motion by Defendant, Attorney Representing Defendant, or Attorney Representing State.

(a) The defendant, the attorney representing the defendant, or the attorney representing the state may move that the court determine that the defendant has been restored to competency.

(b) A motion for a determination of competency may be accompanied by affidavits supporting the moving party's assertion that the defendant is competent.

Art. 46B.111. Appointment of Examiners.

On the filing of a request or motion to determine that the defendant has been restored to competency or on the court's decision on its own motion to inquire into restoration of competency, the court may appoint disinterested experts to examine the defendant in accordance with Subchapter B.

Art. 46B.112. Determination of Restoration with Agreement.

On the filing of a request or motion to determine that the defendant has been restored to competency or on the court's decision on its own motion to inquire into restoration of competency, the court shall find the defendant competent to stand trial and proceed in the same manner as if the defendant had been found restored to competency at a hearing if:

(1) both parties agree that the defendant is competent to stand trial; and

(2) the court concurs.

Art. 46B.113. Determination of Restoration Without Agreement.

(a) The court shall hold a hearing on a request by the head of a facility or outpatient treatment provider to which a defendant has been committed as a result of a finding of incompetency to stand trial to determine whether the defendant has been restored to competency.

(b) The court may hold a hearing on a motion to determine whether the defendant has been restored to competency or on the court's decision on its own motion to inquire into restoration of competency, and shall hold a hearing if a motion and any supporting material establish good reason to believe the defendant may have been restored to competency.

(c) If a court holds a hearing under this article, on the request of the counsel for either party or the motion of the court, a jury shall make the competency determination. If the competency determination will be made by the court rather than a jury, the court may conduct the hearing:

(1) at the facility; or

(2) by means of an electronic broadcast system as provided by Article 46B.013.

(d) If the head of a facility or outpatient treatment provider to which the defendant was committed as a result of a finding of incompetency to stand trial has provided an opinion that the defendant has regained competency, competency is presumed at a hearing under this subchapter and continuing incompetency must be proved by a preponderance of the evidence.

(e) If the head of a facility or outpatient treatment provider has not provided an opinion described by Subsection (d), incompetency is presumed at a hearing under this subchapter and the defendant's competency must be proved by a preponderance of the evidence.

Art. 46B.114. Transportation of Defendant to Court.

If the hearing is not conducted at the facility to which the defendant has been committed under this chapter or conducted by means of an electronic broadcast system as described by this subchapter, an order setting a hearing to determine whether the defendant has been restored to competency shall direct that, as soon as practicable but not earlier than 72 hours before the date the hearing is scheduled, the defendant be placed in the custody of the sheriff of the county in which the committing court is located or the sheriff's designee for transportation to the court. The sheriff or the sheriff's designee may not take custody of the defendant under this article until 72 hours before the date the hearing is scheduled.

Art. 46B.115. Subsequent Redeterminations of Competency.

(a) If the court has made a determination that a defendant has not been restored to competency under this subchapter, a subsequent request or motion for a redetermination of competency filed before the 91st day after the date of that determination must:

(1) explain why the person making the request or motion believes another inquiry into restoration is appropriate; and

(2) provide support for the belief.

(b) The court may hold a hearing on a request or motion under this article only if the court first finds reason to believe the defendant's condition has materially changed since the prior determination that the defendant was not restored to competency.

(c) If the competency determination will be made by the court, the court may conduct the hearing at the facility to which the defendant has been committed under this chapter or may conduct the hearing by means of an electronic broadcast system as provided by Article 46B.013.

Art. 46B.116. Disposition on Determination of Competency.

If the defendant is found competent to stand trial, the proceedings on the criminal charge may proceed.

Art. 46B.117. Disposition on Determination of Incompetency.

If a defendant under order of commitment to a facility or outpatient treatment program is found to not have been restored to competency to stand trial, the court shall remand the defendant pursuant to that order of commitment, and, if applicable, order the defendant placed in the custody of the sheriff or the sheriff's designee for transportation back to the facility or outpatient treatment program.

SUBCHAPTER F CIVIL COMMITMENT: CHARGES DISMISSED

Art. 46B.151. Court Determination Related to Civil Commitment.

(a) If a court is required by Article 46B.084(f) or by its appropriate determination under Article 46B.071 to proceed under this subchapter, or if the court is permitted by Article 46B.004(e) to proceed under this subchapter, the court shall determine whether there is evidence to support a finding that the defendant is either a person with mental illness or a person with an intellectual disability.

(b) If it appears to the court that there is evidence to support a finding of mental illness or an intellectual disability, the court shall enter an order transferring the defendant to the appropriate court for civil commitment proceedings and stating that all charges pending against the defendant in that court have been dismissed. The court may order the defendant:

(1) detained in jail or any other suitable place pending the prompt initiation and prosecution by the attorney for the state or other person designated by the court of appropriate civil proceedings to determine whether the defendant will be committed to a mental health facility or residential care facility; or

(2) placed in the care of a responsible person on satisfactory security being given for the defendant's proper care and protection.

(c) Notwithstanding Subsection (b), a defendant placed in a facility of the commission pending civil hearing under this article may be detained in that facility only with the consent of the head of the facility and pursuant to an order of protective custody issued under Subtitle C, Title 7, Health and Safety Code.

(d) If the court does not detain or place the defendant under Subsection (b), the court shall release the defendant.

SUBCHAPTER G PROVISIONS APPLICABLE TO SUBCHAPTERS E AND F

Art. 46B.171. Transcripts and Other Records.

(a) The court shall order that:

(1) a transcript of all medical testimony received in both the criminal proceedings and the civil commitment proceedings under Subchapter E or F be prepared as soon as possible by the court reporters; and

(2) copies of documents listed in Article 46B.076 accompany the defendant to the mental health facility, outpatient treatment program, or residential care facility.

(b) On the request of the defendant or the attorney representing the defendant, a mental health facility, an outpatient treatment program, or a residential care facility shall provide to the defendant or the attorney copies of the facility's records regarding the defendant.

CHAPTER 46C INSANITY DEFENSE

SUBCHAPTER A GENERAL PROVISIONS

Art. 46C.001. Definitions.

In this chapter:

(1) "Commission" means the Health and Human Services Commission.

(2) "Executive commissioner" means the executive commissioner of the Health and Human Services Commission.

(3) "Mental illness" has the meaning assigned by Section 571.003, Health and Safety Code.

(4) "Mental retardation" has the meaning assigned by Section 591.003, Health and Safety Code.

(5) "Residential care facility" has the meaning assigned by Section 591.003, Health and Safety Code.

Art. 46C.0011. Facility Designation.

The commission may designate for the commitment of a defendant under this chapter only a facility operated by the commission or under a contract with the commission for that purpose.

Art. 46C.002. Maximum Period of Commitment Determined by Maximum Term for Offense.

(a) A person acquitted by reason of insanity may not be committed to a mental hospital or other inpatient or residential care facility or ordered to receive outpatient or community-based treatment and supervision under Subchapter F for a cumulative period that exceeds the maximum term provided by law for the offense for which the acquitted person was tried.

(b) On expiration of that maximum term, the acquitted person may be further confined in a mental hospital or other inpatient or residential care facility or ordered to receive outpatient or community-based treatment and supervision only under civil commitment proceedings.

Art. 46C.003. Victim Notification of Release.

If the court issues an order that requires the release of an acquitted person on discharge or on a regimen of outpatient care, the clerk of the court issuing the order, using the information provided on any victim impact statement received by the court under Subchapter D, Chapter 56A or other information made available to the court, shall notify the victim or the victim's guardian or close relative of the release. Notwithstanding Article 56A.156, the clerk of the court may inspect a victim impact statement for the purpose of notification under this article. On request, a victim assistance coordinator may provide the clerk of the court with information or other assistance necessary for the clerk to comply with this article.

SUBCHAPTER B RAISING THE INSANITY DEFENSE

Art. 46C.051. Notice of Intent to Raise Insanity Defense.

(a) A defendant planning to offer evidence of the insanity defense must file with the court a notice of the defendant's intention to offer that evidence.

(b) The notice must:

(1) contain a certification that a copy of the notice has been served on the attorney representing the state; and

(2) be filed at least 20 days before the date the case is set for trial, except as described by Subsection (c).

(c) If before the 20-day period the court sets a pretrial hearing, the defendant shall give notice at the hearing.

Art. 46C.052. Effect of Failure to Give Notice.

Unless notice is timely filed under Article 46C.051, evidence on the insanity defense is not admissible unless the court finds that good cause exists for failure to give notice.

SUBCHAPTER C COURT-ORDERED EXAMINATION AND REPORT

Art. 46C.101. Appointment of Experts.

(a) If notice of intention to raise the insanity defense is filed under Article 46C.051, the court may, on its own motion or motion by the defendant, the defendant's counsel, or the attorney representing the state, appoint one or more disinterested experts to:

(1) examine the defendant with regard to the insanity defense; and

(2) testify as to the issue of insanity at any trial or hearing involving that issue.

(b) The court shall advise an expert appointed under this article of the facts and circumstances of the offense with which the defendant is charged and the elements of the insanity defense.

Art. 46C.102. Experts: Qualifications.

(a) The court may appoint qualified psychiatrists or psychologists as experts under this chapter. To qualify for appointment under this subchapter as an expert, a psychiatrist or psychologist must:

(1) as appropriate, be a physician licensed in this state or be a psychologist licensed in this state who has a doctoral degree in psychology; and

(2) have the following certification or training:

(A) as appropriate, certification by:

(i) the American Board of Psychiatry and Neurology with added or special qualifications in forensic psychiatry; or

(ii) the American Board of Professional Psychology in forensic psychology; or

(B) training consisting of:

(i) at least 24 hours of specialized forensic training relating to incompetency or insanity evaluations; and

(ii) at least eight hours of continuing education relating to forensic evaluations, completed in the 12 months preceding the appointment.

(b) In addition to meeting qualifications required by Subsection (a), to be appointed as an expert a psychiatrist or psychologist must have completed six hours of required continuing education in courses in forensic psychiatry or psychology, as appropriate, in the 24 months preceding the appointment.

(c) A court may appoint as an expert a psychiatrist or psychologist who does not meet the requirements of Subsections (a) and (b) only if exigent circumstances require the court to base the appointment on professional training or experience of the expert that directly provides the expert with a specialized expertise to examine the defendant that would not ordinarily be possessed by a psychiatrist or psychologist who meets the requirements of Subsections (a) and (b).

Art. 46C.103. Competency to Stand Trial: Concurrent Appointment.

(a) An expert appointed under this subchapter to examine the defendant with regard to the insanity defense also may be appointed by the court to examine the defendant with regard to the defendant's competency to stand trial under Chapter 46B, if the expert files with the court separate written reports concerning the defendant's competency to stand trial and the insanity defense.

(b) Notwithstanding Subsection (a), an expert may not examine the defendant for purposes of determining the defendant's sanity and may not file a report regarding the defendant's sanity if in the opinion of the expert the defendant is incompetent to proceed.

Art. 46C.104. Order Compelling Defendant to Submit to Examination.

(a) For the purposes described by this chapter, the court may order any defendant to submit to examination, including a defendant who is free on bail. If the defendant fails or refuses to submit to examination, the court may order the defendant to custody for examination for a reasonable period not to exceed 21 days. Custody ordered by the court under this subsection may include custody at a facility operated by the commission.

(b) If a defendant who has been ordered to a facility operated by the commission for examination remains in the facility for a period that exceeds 21 days, the head of that facility shall cause the defendant to be immediately transported to the committing court and placed in the custody of the sheriff of the county in which the committing court is located. That county shall reimburse the facility for the mileage and per diem expenses of the personnel required to transport the defendant, calculated in accordance with the state travel rules in effect at that time.

(c) The court may not order a defendant to a facility operated by the commission for examination without the consent of the head of that facility.

Art. 46C.105. Reports Submitted by Experts.

(a) A written report of the examination shall be submitted to the court not later than the 30th day after the date of the order of examination. The court shall provide copies of the report to the defense counsel and the attorney representing the state.

(b) The report must include a description of the procedures used in the examination and the examiner's observations and findings pertaining to the insanity defense.

(c) The examiner shall submit a separate report stating the examiner's observations and findings concerning:

(1) whether the defendant is presently a person with a mental illness and requires court-ordered mental health services under Subtitle C, Title 7, Health and Safety Code; or

(2) whether the defendant is presently a person with mental retardation.

Art. 46C.106. Compensation of Experts.

(a) The appointed experts shall be paid by the county in which the indictment was returned or information was filed.

(b) The county in which the indictment was returned or information was filed shall reimburse a facility operated by the commission that accepts a defendant for examination under this subchapter for expenses incurred that are determined by the commission to be reasonably necessary and incidental to the proper examination of the defendant.

Art. 46C.107. Examination by Expert of Defendant's Choice.

If a defendant wishes to be examined by an expert of the defendant's own choice, the court on timely request shall provide the examiner with reasonable opportunity to examine the defendant.

SUBCHAPTER D
DETERMINATION OF ISSUE OF DEFENDANT'S SANITY

Art. 46C.151. Determination of Sanity Issue by Jury.

(a) In a case tried to a jury, the issue of the defendant's sanity shall be submitted to the jury only if the issue is supported by competent evidence. The jury shall determine the issue.

(b) If the issue of the defendant's sanity is submitted to the jury, the jury shall determine and specify in the verdict whether the defendant is guilty, not guilty, or not guilty by reason of insanity.

Art. 46C.152. Determination of Sanity Issue by Judge.

(a) If a jury trial is waived and if the issue is supported by competent evidence, the judge as trier of fact shall determine the issue of the defendant's sanity.

(b) The parties may, with the consent of the judge, agree to have the judge determine the issue of the defendant's sanity on the basis of introduced or stipulated competent evidence, or both.

(c) If the judge determines the issue of the defendant's sanity, the judge shall enter a finding of guilty, not guilty, or not guilty by reason of insanity.

Art. 46C.153. General Provisions Relating to Determination of Sanity Issue by Judge or Jury.

(a) The judge or jury shall determine that a defendant is not guilty by reason of insanity if:

(1) the prosecution has established beyond a reasonable doubt that the alleged conduct constituting the offense was committed; and

(2) the defense has established by a preponderance of the evidence that the defendant was insane at the time of the alleged conduct.

(b) The parties may, with the consent of the judge, agree to both:

(1) dismissal of the indictment or information on the ground that the defendant was insane; and

(2) entry of a judgment of dismissal due to the defendant's insanity.

(c) An entry of judgment under Subsection (b)(2) has the same effect as a judgment stating that the defendant has been found not guilty by reason of insanity.

Art. 46C.154. Informing Jury Regarding Consequences of Acquittal.

The court, the attorney representing the state, or the attorney for the defendant may not inform a juror or a prospective juror of the consequences to the defendant if a verdict of not guilty by reason of insanity is returned.

Art. 46C.155. Finding of Not Guilty by Reason of Insanity Considered Acquittal.

(a) Except as provided by Subsection (b), a defendant who is found not guilty by reason of insanity

Code of Criminal Procedure

stands acquitted of the offense charged and may not be considered a person charged with an offense.

(b) A defendant who is found not guilty by reason of insanity is not considered to be acquitted for purposes of Chapter 55.

Art. 46C.156. Judgment.

(a) In each case in which the insanity defense is raised, the judgment must reflect whether the defendant was found guilty, not guilty, or not guilty by reason of insanity.

(b) If the defendant was found not guilty by reason of insanity, the judgment must specify the offense of which the defendant was found not guilty.

(c) If the defendant was found not guilty by reason of insanity, the judgment must reflect the finding made under Article 46C.157.

Art. 46C.157. Determination Regarding Dangerous Conduct of Acquitted Person.

If a defendant is found not guilty by reason of insanity, the court immediately shall determine whether the offense of which the person was acquitted involved conduct that:

(1) caused serious bodily injury to another person;

(2) placed another person in imminent danger of serious bodily injury; or

(3) consisted of a threat of serious bodily injury to another person through the use of a deadly weapon.

Art. 46C.158. Continuing Jurisdiction of Dangerous Acquitted Person.

If the court finds that the offense of which the person was acquitted involved conduct that caused serious bodily injury to another person, placed another person in imminent danger of serious bodily injury, or consisted of a threat of serious bodily injury to another person through the use of a deadly weapon, the court retains jurisdiction over the acquitted person until either:

(1) the court discharges the person and terminates its jurisdiction under Article 46C.268; or

(2) the cumulative total period of institutionalization and outpatient or community-based treatment and supervision under the court's jurisdiction equals the maximum term provided by law for the offense of which the person was acquitted by reason of insanity and the court's jurisdiction is automatically terminated under Article 46C.269.

Art. 46C.159. Proceedings Regarding Nondangerous Acquitted Person.

If the court finds that the offense of which the person was acquitted did not involve conduct that caused serious bodily injury to another person, placed another person in imminent danger of serious bodily injury, or consisted of a threat of serious bodily injury to another person through the use of a deadly weapon, the court shall proceed under Subchapter E.

Art. 46C.160. Detention Pending Further Proceedings.

(a) On a determination by the judge or jury that the defendant is not guilty by reason of insanity, pending further proceedings under this chapter, the court may order the defendant detained in jail or any other suitable place for a period not to exceed 14 days.

(b) The court may order a defendant detained in a facility of the commission under this article only with the consent of the head of the facility.

SUBCHAPTER E DISPOSITION FOLLOWING ACQUITTAL BY REASON OF INSANITY: NO FINDING OF DANGEROUS CONDUCT

Art. 46C.201. Disposition: Nondangerous Conduct.

(a) If the court determines that the offense of which the person was acquitted did not involve conduct that caused serious bodily injury to another person, placed another person in imminent danger of serious bodily injury, or consisted of a threat of serious bodily injury to another person through the use of a deadly weapon, the court shall determine whether there is evidence to support a finding that the person is a person with a mental illness or with mental retardation.

(b) If the court determines that there is evidence to support a finding of mental illness or mental retardation, the court shall enter an order transferring the person to the appropriate court for civil commitment proceedings to determine whether the person should receive court-ordered mental health services under Subtitle C, Title 7, Health and Safety Code, or be committed to a residential care facility to receive mental retardation services under Subtitle D, Title 7, Health and Safety Code. The court may also order the person:

(1) detained in jail or any other suitable place pending the prompt initiation and prosecution of appropriate civil proceedings by the attorney representing the state or other person designated by the court; or

(2) placed in the care of a responsible person on satisfactory security being given for the acquitted person's proper care and protection.

Art. 46C.202. Detention or Release.

(a) Notwithstanding Article 46C.201(b), a person placed in a commission facility pending civil hearing as described by that subsection may be detained only with the consent of the head of the facility and under an Order of Protective Custody issued under Subtitle C or D, Title 7, Health and Safety Code.

(b) If the court does not detain or place the person under Article 46C.201(b), the court shall release the person.

SUBCHAPTER F DISPOSITION FOLLOWING ACQUITTAL BY REASON OF INSANITY: FINDING OF DANGEROUS CONDUCT

Art. 46C.251. Commitment for Evaluation and Treatment; Report.

(a) The court shall order the acquitted person to be committed for evaluation of the person's present mental condition and for treatment to the facility designated by the commission. The period of commitment under this article may not exceed 30 days.

(b) The court shall order that:

(1) a transcript of all medical testimony received in the criminal proceeding be prepared as soon as possible by the court reporter and the transcript be forwarded to the facility to which the acquitted person is committed; and

(2) the following information be forwarded to the facility and to the commission:

(A) the complete name, race, and gender of the person;

(B) any known identifying number of the person, including social security number, driver's license number, or state identification number;

(C) the person's date of birth; and

(D) the offense of which the person was found not guilty by reason of insanity and a statement of the facts and circumstances surrounding the alleged offense.

(c) The court shall order that a report be filed with the court under Article 46C.252.

(d) To determine the proper disposition of the acquitted person, the court shall hold a hearing on disposition not later than the 30th day after the date of acquittal.

Art. 46C.252. Report After Evaluation.

(a) The report ordered under Article 46C.251 must be filed with the court as soon as practicable before the hearing on disposition but not later than the fourth day before that hearing.

(b) The report in general terms must describe and explain the procedure, techniques, and tests used in the examination of the person.

(c) The report must address:

(1) whether the acquitted person has a mental illness or mental retardation and, if so, whether the mental illness or mental retardation is severe;

(2) whether as a result of any severe mental illness or mental retardation the acquitted person is likely to cause serious harm to another;

(3) whether as a result of any impairment the acquitted person is subject to commitment under Subtitle C or D, Title 7, Health and Safety Code;

(4) prospective treatment and supervision options, if any, appropriate for the acquitted person; and

(5) whether any required treatment and supervision can be safely and effectively provided as outpatient or community-based treatment and supervision.

Art. 46C.253. Hearing on Disposition.

(a) The hearing on disposition shall be conducted in the same manner as a hearing on an application for involuntary commitment under Subtitle C or D, Title 7, Health and Safety Code, except that the use of a jury is governed by Article 46C.255.

(b) At the hearing, the court shall address:

(1) whether the person acquitted by reason of insanity has a severe mental illness or mental retardation;

(2) whether as a result of any mental illness or mental retardation the person is likely to cause serious harm to another; and

(3) whether appropriate treatment and supervision for any mental illness or mental retardation rendering the person dangerous to another can be safely and effectively provided as outpatient or community-based treatment and supervision.

(c) The court shall order the acquitted person committed for inpatient treatment or residential care under Article 46C.256 if the grounds required for that order are established.

(d) The court shall order the acquitted person to receive outpatient or community-based treatment and supervision under Article 46C.257 if the grounds required for that order are established.

(e) The court shall order the acquitted person transferred to an appropriate court for proceedings under Subtitle C or D, Title 7, Health and Safety Code, if the state fails to establish the grounds required for an order under Article 46C.256 or 46C.257 but the evidence provides a reasonable basis for believing the acquitted person is a proper subject for those proceedings.

(f) The court shall order the acquitted person discharged and immediately released if the evidence fails to establish that disposition under Subsection (c), (d), or (e) is appropriate.

Art. 46C.254. Effect of Stabilization on Treatment Regimen.

If an acquitted person is stabilized on a treatment regimen, including medication and other treatment modalities, rendering the person no longer likely to cause serious harm to another, inpatient treatment or residential care may be found necessary to protect the safety of others only if:

(1) the person would become likely to cause serious harm to another if the person fails to follow the treatment regimen on an Order to Receive Outpatient or Community-Based Treatment and Supervision; and

(2) under an Order to Receive Outpatient or Community-Based Treatment and Supervision either:

(A) the person is likely to fail to comply with an available regimen of outpatient or community-based treatment, as determined by the person's insight into the need for medication, the number, severity, and controllability of side effects, the availability of support and treatment programs for the person from community members, and other appropriate considerations; or

(B) a regimen of outpatient or community-based treatment will not be available to the person.

Art. 46C.255. Trial by Jury.

(a) The following proceedings under this chapter must be before the court, and the underlying matter determined by the court, unless the acquitted person or the state requests a jury trial or the court on its own motion sets the matter for jury trial:

(1) a hearing under Article 46C.253;

(2) a proceeding for renewal of an order under Article 46C.261;

(3) a proceeding on a request for modification or revocation of an order under Article 46C.266; and

(4) a proceeding seeking discharge of an acquitted person under Article 46C.268.

(b) The following proceedings may not be held before a jury:

(1) a proceeding to determine outpatient or community-based treatment and supervision under Article 46C.262; or

(2) a proceeding to determine modification or revocation of outpatient or community-based treatment and supervision under Article 46C.267.

(c) If a hearing is held before a jury and the jury determines that the person has a mental illness or mental retardation and is likely to cause serious harm to another, the court shall determine whether inpatient treatment or residential care is necessary to protect the safety of others.

Art. 46C.256. Order of Commitment to Inpatient Treatment or Residential Care.

(a) The court shall order the acquitted person committed to a mental hospital or other appropriate facility for inpatient treatment or residential care if the state establishes by clear and convincing evidence that:

(1) the person has a severe mental illness or mental retardation;

(2) the person, as a result of that mental illness or mental retardation, is likely to cause serious bodily injury to another if the person is not provided with treatment and supervision; and

(3) inpatient treatment or residential care is necessary to protect the safety of others.

(b) In determining whether inpatient treatment or residential care has been proved necessary, the court shall consider whether the evidence shows both that:

(1) an adequate regimen of outpatient or community-based treatment will be available to the person; and

(2) the person will follow that regimen.

(c) The order of commitment to inpatient treatment or residential care expires on the 181st day following the date the order is issued but is subject to renewal as provided by Article 46C.261.

Art. 46C.257. Order to Receive Outpatient or Community-Based Treatment and Supervision.

(a) The court shall order the acquitted person to receive outpatient or community-based treatment and supervision if:

(1) the state establishes by clear and convincing evidence that the person:

(A) has a severe mental illness or mental retardation; and

(B) as a result of that mental illness or mental retardation is likely to cause serious bodily injury to another if the person is not provided with treatment and supervision; and

(2) the state fails to establish by clear and convincing evidence that inpatient treatment or residential care is necessary to protect the safety of others.

(b) The order of commitment to outpatient or community-based treatment and supervision expires on the first anniversary of the date the order is issued but is subject to renewal as provided by Article 46C.261.

Art. 46C.258. Responsibility of Inpatient or Residential Care Facility.

(a) The head of the facility to which an acquitted person is committed has, during the commitment period, a continuing responsibility to determine:

(1) whether the acquitted person continues to have a severe mental illness or mental retardation and is likely to cause serious harm to another because of any severe mental illness or mental retardation; and

(2) if so, whether treatment and supervision cannot be safely and effectively provided as outpatient or community-based treatment and supervision.

(b) The head of the facility must notify the committing court and seek modification of the order of commitment if the head of the facility determines that an acquitted person no longer has a severe mental illness or mental retardation, is no longer likely to cause serious harm to another, or that treatment and supervision can be safely and effectively provided as outpatient or community-based treatment and supervision.

(c) Not later than the 60th day before the date of expiration of the order, the head of the facility shall transmit to the committing court a psychological evaluation of the acquitted person, a certificate of medical examination of the person, and any recommendation for further treatment of the person. The committing court shall make the documents available to the attorneys representing the state and the acquitted person.

Art. 46C.259. Status of Committed Person.

If an acquitted person is committed under this subchapter, the person's status as a patient or resident is governed by Subtitle C or D, Title 7, Health and Safety Code, except that:

(1) transfer to a nonsecure unit is governed by Article 46C.260;

(2) modification of the order to direct outpatient or community-based treatment and supervision is governed by Article 46C.262; and

(3) discharge is governed by Article 46C.268.

Art. 46C.260. Transfer of Committed Person to Non-Maximum Security Facility.

(a) A person committed to a facility under this subchapter shall be committed to a facility designated by the commission.

(b) A person committed under this subchapter shall be transferred to the designated facility immediately on the entry of the order of commitment.

(c) Unless a person committed to a maximum security unit by the commission is determined to be manifestly dangerous by a review board under this article, not later than the 60th day following the date of the person's arrival at the maximum security unit the person shall be transferred to a non-maximum security unit of a facility designated by the commission.

(d) The executive commissioner shall appoint a review board of five members, including one psychiatrist licensed to practice medicine in this state and two persons who work directly with persons with mental illnesses or with mental retardation, to determine whether the person is manifestly dangerous and, as a result of the danger the person presents, requires continued placement in a maximum security unit.

(e) If the head of the facility at which the maximum security unit is located disagrees with the determination, then the matter shall be referred to the executive commissioner. The executive commissioner shall decide whether the person is manifestly dangerous.

Art. 46C.261. Renewal of Orders for Inpatient Commitment or Outpatient or Community-Based Treatment and Supervision.

(a) A court that orders an acquitted person committed to inpatient treatment or orders outpatient or community-based treatment and supervision annually shall determine whether to renew the order.

(b) Not later than the 30th day before the date an order is scheduled to expire, the institution to which a person is committed, the person responsible for providing outpatient or community-based treatment and supervision, or the attorney representing the state may file a request that the order be renewed. The request must explain in detail the

Code of Criminal Procedure

reasons why the person requests renewal under this article. A request to renew an order committing the person to inpatient treatment must also explain in detail why outpatient or community-based treatment and supervision is not appropriate.

(c) The request for renewal must be accompanied by a certificate of medical examination for mental illness signed by a physician who examined the person during the 30-day period preceding the date on which the request is filed.

(d) On the filing of a request for renewal under this article, the court shall:

(1) set the matter for a hearing; and

(2) appoint an attorney to represent the person.

(e) The court shall act on the request for renewal before the order expires.

(f) If a hearing is held, the person may be transferred from the facility to which the acquitted person was committed to a jail for purposes of participating in the hearing only if necessary but not earlier than 72 hours before the hearing begins. If the order is renewed, the person shall be transferred back to the facility immediately on renewal of the order.

(g) If no objection is made, the court may admit into evidence the certificate of medical examination for mental illness. Admitted certificates constitute competent medical or psychiatric testimony, and the court may make its findings solely from the certificate and the detailed request for renewal.

(h) A court shall renew the order only if the court finds that the party who requested the renewal has established by clear and convincing evidence that continued mandatory supervision and treatment are appropriate. A renewed order authorizes continued inpatient commitment or outpatient or community-based treatment and supervision for not more than one year.

(i) The court, on application for renewal of an order for inpatient or residential care services, may modify the order to provide for outpatient or community-based treatment and supervision if the court finds the acquitted person has established by a preponderance of the evidence that treatment and supervision can be safely and effectively provided as outpatient or community-based treatment and supervision.

Art. 46C.262. Court-Ordered Outpatient or Community-Based Treatment and Supervision After Inpatient Commitment.

(a) An acquitted person, the head of the facility to which the acquitted person is committed, or the attorney representing the state may request that the court modify an order for inpatient treatment or residential care to order outpatient or community-based treatment and supervision.

(b) The court shall hold a hearing on a request made by the head of the facility to which the acquitted person is committed. A hearing under this subsection must be held not later than the 14th day after the date of the request.

(c) If a request is made by an acquitted person or the attorney representing the state, the court must act on the request not later than the 14th day after the date of the request. A hearing under this subsection is at the discretion of the court, except that the court shall hold a hearing if the request and any accompanying material provide a basis for believing modification of the order may be appropriate.

(d) If a request is made by an acquitted person not later than the 90th day after the date of a hearing on a previous request, the court is not required to act on the request except on the expiration of the order or on the expiration of the 90-day period following the date of the hearing on the previous request.

(e) The court shall rule on the request during or as soon as practicable after any hearing on the request but not later than the 14th day after the date of the request.

(f) The court shall modify the commitment order to direct outpatient or community-based treatment and supervision if at the hearing the acquitted person establishes by a preponderance of the evidence that treatment and supervision can be safely and effectively provided as outpatient or community-based treatment and supervision.

Art. 46C.263. Court-Ordered Outpatient or Community-Based Treatment and Supervision.

(a) The court may order an acquitted person to participate in an outpatient or community-based regimen of treatment and supervision:

(1) as an initial matter under Article 46C.253;

(2) on renewal of an order of commitment under Article 46C.261; or

(3) after a period of inpatient treatment or residential care under Article 46C.262.

(b) An acquitted person may be ordered to participate in an outpatient or community-based regimen of treatment and supervision only if:

(1) the court receives and approves an outpatient or community-based treatment plan that comprehensively provides for the outpatient or community-based treatment and supervision; and

(2) the court finds that the outpatient or community-based treatment and supervision

provided for by the plan will be available to and provided to the acquitted person.

(c) The order may require the person to participate in a prescribed regimen of medical, psychiatric, or psychological care or treatment, and the regimen may include treatment with psychoactive medication.

(d) The court may order that supervision of the acquitted person be provided by the appropriate community supervision and corrections department or the facility administrator of a community center that provides mental health or mental retardation services.

(e) The court may order the acquitted person to participate in a supervision program funded by the Texas Correctional Office on Offenders with Medical or Mental Impairments.

(f) An order under this article must identify the person responsible for administering an ordered regimen of outpatient or community-based treatment and supervision.

(g) In determining whether an acquitted person should be ordered to receive outpatient or community-based treatment and supervision rather than inpatient care or residential treatment, the court shall have as its primary concern the protection of society.

Art. 46C.264. Location of Court-Ordered Outpatient or Community-Based Treatment and Supervision.

(a) The court may order the outpatient or community-based treatment and supervision to be provided in any appropriate county where the necessary resources are available.

(b) This article does not supersede any requirement under the other provisions of this subchapter to obtain the consent of a treatment and supervision provider to administer the court-ordered outpatient or community-based treatment and supervision.

Art. 46C.265. Supervisory Responsibility for Outpatient or Community-Based Treatment and Supervision.

(a) The person responsible for administering a regimen of outpatient or community-based treatment and supervision shall:

(1) monitor the condition of the acquitted person; and

(2) determine whether the acquitted person is complying with the regimen of treatment and supervision.

(b) The person responsible for administering a regimen of outpatient or community-based treatment and supervision shall notify the court ordering that treatment and supervision and the attorney representing the state if the person:

(1) fails to comply with the regimen; and

(2) becomes likely to cause serious harm to another.

Art. 46C.266. Modification or Revocation of Order for Outpatient or Community-Based Treatment and Supervision.

(a) The court, on its own motion or the motion of any interested person and after notice to the acquitted person and a hearing, may modify or revoke court-ordered outpatient or community-based treatment and supervision.

(b) At the hearing, the court without a jury shall determine whether the state has established clear and convincing evidence that:

(1) the acquitted person failed to comply with the regimen in a manner or under circumstances indicating the person will become likely to cause serious harm to another if the person is provided continued outpatient or community-based treatment and supervision; or

(2) the acquitted person has become likely to cause serious harm to another if provided continued outpatient or community-based treatment and supervision.

(c) On a determination under Subsection (b), the court may take any appropriate action, including:

(1) revoking court-ordered outpatient or community-based treatment and supervision and ordering the person committed for inpatient or residential care; or

(2) imposing additional or more stringent terms on continued outpatient or community-based treatment.

(d) An acquitted person who is the subject of a proceeding under this article is entitled to representation by counsel in the proceeding.

(e) The court shall set a date for a hearing under this article that is not later than the seventh day after the applicable motion was filed. The court may grant one or more continuances of the hearing on the motion of a party or of the court and for good cause shown.

Art. 46C.267. Detention Pending Proceedings to Modify or Revoke Order for Outpatient or Community-Based Treatment and Supervision.

(a) The state or the head of the facility or other person responsible for administering a regimen of outpatient or community-based treatment and supervision may file a sworn application with the court for the detention of an acquitted person receiving court-ordered outpatient or community-based treatment and supervision. The application must state that the person meets the criteria of Article 46C.266 and provide a detailed explanation of that statement.

(b) If the court determines that the application establishes probable cause to believe the order for outpatient or community-based treatment and supervision should be revoked, the court shall issue an order to an on-duty peace officer authorizing the acquitted person to be taken into custody and brought before the court.

(c) An acquitted person taken into custody under an order of detention shall be brought before the court without unnecessary delay.

(d) When an acquitted person is brought before the court, the court shall determine whether there is probable cause to believe that the order for outpatient or community-based treatment and supervision should be revoked. On a finding that probable cause for revocation exists, the court shall order the person held in protective custody pending a determination of whether the order should be revoked.

(e) An acquitted person may be detained under an order for protective custody for a period not to exceed 72 hours, excluding Saturdays, Sundays, legal holidays, and the period prescribed by Section 574.025(b), Health and Safety Code, for an extreme emergency.

(f) This subchapter does not affect the power of a peace officer to take an acquitted person into custody under Section 573.001, Health and Safety Code.

Art. 46C.268. Advance Discharge of Acquitted Person and Termination of Jurisdiction.

(a) An acquitted person, the head of the facility to which the acquitted person is committed, the person responsible for providing the outpatient or community-based treatment and supervision, or the state may request that the court discharge an acquitted person from inpatient commitment or outpatient or community-based treatment and supervision.

(b) Not later than the 14th day after the date of the request, the court shall hold a hearing on a request made by the head of the facility to which the acquitted person is committed or the person responsible for providing the outpatient or community-based treatment and supervision.

(c) If a request is made by an acquitted person, the court must act on the request not later than the 14th day after the date of the request. A hearing under this subsection is at the discretion of the court, except that the court shall hold a hearing if the request and any accompanying material indicate that modification of the order may be appropriate.

(d) If a request is made by an acquitted person not later than the 90th day after the date of a hearing on a previous request, the court is not required to act on the request except on the expiration of the order or on the expiration of the 90-day period following the date of the hearing on the previous request.

(e) The court shall rule on the request during or shortly after any hearing that is held and in any case not later than the 14th day after the date of the request.

(f) The court shall discharge the acquitted person from all court-ordered commitment and treatment and supervision and terminate the court's jurisdiction over the person if the court finds that the acquitted person has established by a preponderance of the evidence that:

(1) the acquitted person does not have a severe mental illness or mental retardation; or

(2) the acquitted person is not likely to cause serious harm to another because of any severe mental illness or mental retardation.

Art. 46C.269. Termination of Court's Jurisdiction.

(a) The jurisdiction of the court over a person covered by this subchapter automatically terminates on the date when the cumulative total period of institutionalization and outpatient or community-based treatment and supervision imposed under this subchapter equals the maximum term of imprisonment provided by law for the offense of which the person was acquitted by reason of insanity.

(b) On the termination of the court's jurisdiction under this article, the person must be discharged from any inpatient treatment or residential care or outpatient or community-based treatment and supervision ordered under this subchapter.

(c) An inpatient or residential care facility to which a person has been committed under this subchapter or a person responsible for administering a regimen of outpatient or community-based treatment and supervision under this subchapter must notify the court not later than the 30th day before the court's jurisdiction over the person ends under this article.

(d) This subchapter does not affect whether a person may be ordered to receive care or treatment under Subtitle C or D, Title 7, Health and Safety Code.

Art. 46C.270. Appeals.

(a) An acquitted person may appeal a judgment reflecting an acquittal by reason of insanity on the basis of the following:

(1) a finding that the acquitted person committed the offense; or

(2) a finding that the offense on which the prosecution was based involved conduct that:

(A) caused serious bodily injury to another person;

(B) placed another person in imminent danger of serious bodily injury; or

(C) consisted of a threat of serious bodily injury to another person through the use of a deadly weapon.

(b) Either the acquitted person or the state may appeal from:

(1) an Order of Commitment to Inpatient Treatment or Residential Care entered under Article 46C.256;

(2) an Order to Receive Outpatient or Community-Based Treatment and Supervision entered under Article 46C.257 or 46C.262;

(3) an order renewing or refusing to renew an Order for Inpatient Commitment or Outpatient or Community-Based Treatment and Supervision entered under Article 46C.261;

(4) an order modifying or revoking an Order for Outpatient or Community-Based Treatment and Supervision entered under Article 46C.266 or refusing a request to modify or revoke that order; or

(5) an order discharging an acquitted person under Article 46C.268 or denying a request for discharge of an acquitted person.

(c) An appeal under this subchapter may not be considered moot solely due to the expiration of an order on which the appeal is based.

CHAPTER 47 DISPOSITION OF STOLEN PROPERTY

Art. 47.01. Subject to Order of Court.

(a) Except as provided by Subsection (b), an officer who comes into custody of property alleged to have been stolen shall hold it subject to the order of the proper court only if the ownership of the property is contested or disputed.

(b) An officer who comes into custody of property governed by Chapter 371, Finance Code, that is alleged to have been stolen shall hold the property subject to the order of the proper court regardless of whether the ownership of the property is contested or disputed.

Art. 47.01a. Restoration When No Trial Is Pending.

(a) If a criminal action relating to allegedly stolen property is not pending, a district judge, county court judge, statutory county court judge, or justice of the peace having jurisdiction as a magistrate in the county in which the property is held or in which the property was alleged to have been stolen or a municipal judge having jurisdiction as a magistrate in the municipality in which the property is being held or in which the property was alleged to have been stolen may hold a hearing to determine the right to possession of the property, upon the petition of an interested person, a county, a city, or the state. Jurisdiction under this article is based solely on jurisdiction as a criminal magistrate under this code and not jurisdiction as a civil court. The court shall:

(1) order the property delivered to whoever has the superior right to possession, without conditions;

(2) on the filing of a written motion before trial by an attorney representing the state, order the property delivered to whoever has the superior right to possession, subject to the condition that the property be made available to the prosecuting authority should it be needed in future prosecutions; or

(3) order the property awarded to the custody of the peace officer, pending resolution of criminal investigations regarding the property.

(b) If it is shown in a hearing that probable cause exists to believe that the property was acquired by theft or by another manner that makes its acquisition an offense and that the identity of the actual owner of the property cannot be determined, the court shall order the peace officer to:

(1) deliver the property to a government agency for official purposes;

(2) deliver the property to a person authorized by Article 18.17 of this code to receive and dispose of the property; or

(3) destroy the property.

(c) At a hearing under Subsection (a) of this article, any interested person may present evidence showing that the property was not acquired by theft or another offense or that the person is entitled to possess the property. At the hearing, hearsay evidence is admissible.

(d) Venue for a hearing under this article is in any justice, county, statutory county, or district court in the county in which the property is seized or in which the property was alleged to have been stolen or in any municipal court in any municipality in which the property is seized or in which the property was alleged to have been stolen, except that the court may transfer venue to a court in another county on the motion of any interested party.

(e) The person who has the superior right to possession of the property, as determined in a hearing under Subsection (a), is responsible for any transportation necessary to deliver the property to the person as ordered under that subsection.

Art. 47.02. Restored on Trial.

(a) On the trial of any criminal action for theft or any other offense involving the illegal acquisition of property, the court trying the case shall order the property to be restored to the person appearing by the proof to be the owner of the property.

(b) On written consent of the prosecuting attorney and following an order described by Subsection (a), any magistrate having jurisdiction in the county in which the property was alleged to have been stolen or, if the criminal action for theft or any other offense involving the illegal acquisition of property is pending in another county, the county in which the action is pending may hold a hearing to determine the right to possession of the property. If it is proved to the satisfaction of the magistrate that any person is a true owner of the property alleged to have been stolen, and the property is under the control of a peace officer, the magistrate may, by written order, direct the property to be restored to that person.

(c) The owner of the property is responsible for any transportation necessary to restore the property to the owner as ordered under this article.

Art. 47.03. Schedule.

When an officer seizes property alleged to have been stolen, he shall immediately file a schedule of the same, and its value, with the court having jurisdiction of the case, certifying that the property has been seized by him, and the reason therefor. The officer shall notify the court of the names and addresses of each party known to the officer who has a claim to possession of the seized property.

Art. 47.04. Restored to Owner.

Upon an examining trial, if it is proven to the satisfaction of the court that any person is the true owner of property alleged to have been stolen, and which is in possession of a peace officer, the court may upon motion by the state, by written order direct the property to be restored to such owner subject to the conditions that such property shall be made available to the state or by order of any court having jurisdiction over the offense to be used for evidentiary purposes.

Art. 47.05. Bond Required.

If the court has any doubt as to the ownership of the property, the court may require a bond of the claimant for its re-delivery in case it should thereafter be shown not to belong to such claimant; or the court may, in its discretion, direct the property to be retained by the sheriff until further orders as to its possession. Such bond shall be in a sum equal to the value of the property, with sufficient security, payable to and approved by the county judge of the county in which the property is in custody. Such bond shall be filed in the office of the county clerk of such county, and in case of a breach thereof may be sued upon in such county by any claimant of the property; or by the county treasurer of such county.

Art. 47.06. Property Sold.

If the property is not claimed within 30 days from the conviction of the person accused of illegally acquiring it, the same procedure for its disposition as set out in Article 18.17 of this Code shall be followed.

Art. 47.07. Owner May Recover.

The real owner of the property sold under the provisions of Article 47.06 may recover such property under the same terms as prescribed in Subsection (e) of Article 18.17 of this Code.

Art. 47.08. Written Instrument.

If the property is a written instrument, it shall be deposited with the county clerk of the county where the proceedings are had, subject to the claim of any person who may establish his right thereto. The claimant of any such written instrument shall file his written sworn claim thereto with the county judge. If such judge be satisfied that such claimant is the real owner of the written instrument, the same shall be delivered to him. The county judge may, in his discretion, require a bond of such claimant, as in other cases of property claimed under any provision of this Chapter, and may also before such delivery require the written instrument to be recorded in the minutes of his court.

Art. 47.09. Claimant to Pay Charges.

The claimant of the property, before he shall be entitled to have the same delivered to him, shall pay all reasonable charges for the safekeeping of the same while in the custody of the law, which charges shall be verified by the affidavit of the officer claiming the same, and determined by the court having jurisdiction thereof. If said charges are not paid, the property shall be sold as under execution; and the proceeds of sale, after the payment of said charges and costs of sale, paid to the owner of such property.

Art. 47.10. Charges of Officer.

When property is sold, and the proceeds of sale are ready to be paid into the county treasury, the amount of expenses for keeping the same and the costs of sale shall be determined by the county judge. The account thereof shall be in writing and verified by the officer claiming the same, with the approval of the county judge thereto for the amount allowed and shall be filed in the office of the county treasurer at the time of paying into his hands the balance of the proceeds of such sale.

Art. 47.11. Scope of Chapter.

Each provision of this Chapter relating to stolen property applies as well to property acquired in any manner which makes the acquisition a penal offense.

Art. 47.12. Appeal.

(a) Appeals from a hearing in a district court, county court, or statutory county court under Article 47.01a of this code shall be heard by a court of appeals. The appeal is governed by the applicable rules of procedure for appeals of civil cases to a court of appeals.

(b) Appeals from a hearing in a municipal court or justice court under Article 47.01a of this code shall be heard by a county court or statutory county court. The appeal is governed by the applicable rules of procedure for appeals for civil cases in justice courts to a county court or statutory county court.

(c) Only an interested person who appears at a hearing under this article may appeal, and such person must give an oral notice of appeal at the conclusion of the hearing and must post an appeal bond by the end of the next business day, exclusive of Saturdays, Sundays, and legal holidays.

(d) The court may require an appeal bond, in an amount determined appropriate by the court, but not to exceed twice the value of the property. The bond shall be made payable to the party who was awarded possession at the hearing, with sufficient sureties approved by the court, and conditioned that appellant will prosecute his appeal to conclusion.

CHAPTER 48
PARDON AND PAROLE

Art. 48.01. Governor May Pardon.

(a) In all criminal cases, except treason and impeachment, the Governor shall have power, after conviction or successful completion of a term of deferred adjudication community supervision, on the written signed recommendation and advice of the Board of Pardons and Paroles, or a majority thereof, to grant reprieves and commutations of punishments and pardons; and upon the written recommendation and advice of a majority of the Board of Pardons and Paroles, he shall have the power to remit fines and forfeitures. The Governor shall have the power to grant one reprieve in any capital case for a period not to exceed 30 days; and he shall have power to revoke conditional pardons. With the advice and consent of the Legislature, the Governor may grant reprieves, commutations of punishment and pardons in cases of treason.

(b) The Board of Pardons and Paroles may recommend that the Governor grant a pardon to a person who:

(1) is placed on deferred adjudication community supervision under Subchapter C, Chapter 42A, and subsequently receives a discharge and dismissal under Article 42A.111; and

(2) on or after the 10th anniversary of the date of discharge and dismissal, submits a written request to the board for a recommendation under this subsection.

Art. 48.02. Shall File Reasons.

When the Governor remits fines or forfeitures, or grants reprieves, commutation of punishment or pardons, he shall file in the office of Secretary of State his reasons therefor.

Art. 48.03. Governor's Acts Under Seal.

All remissions of fines and forfeitures, and all reprieves, commutations of punishment and pardons, shall be signed by the Governor, and certified by the Secretary of State, under the state seal, and shall be forthwith obeyed by any officer to whom the same may be presented.

Art. 48.04. Power to Remit Fines and Forfeitures.

The Governor shall have the power to remit forfeitures of bail bonds.

Art. 48.05. Restoration of Civil Rights.

(a) (1) An individual convicted of an offense described by Subdivision (2) of this subsection may, except as provided by Subsection (b) of this article, submit an application for restoration of any civil rights forfeited under the laws of this state as a result of the conviction.

(2) This article applies to:

(A) a federal offense, other than an offense involving:

(i) violence or the threat of violence;

(ii) drugs; or

(iii) firearms; and

(B) an offense under the laws of another country, other than an offense involving:

(i) violence or the threat of violence;

(ii) drugs; or

(iii) firearms, if the elements of the offense are substantially similar to elements of an offense under the laws of this state punishable as a felony.

(b) An individual may not apply for restoration of civil rights under this article unless:

(1) the individual has completed the sentence for the offense;

(2) the conviction occurred:

(A) three or more years before the date of application, if the offense is a federal offense; or

(B) two or more years before the date of application, if the offense is an offense under the laws of another country; and

(3) the individual has not been convicted at any other time of an offense under the laws of this state, another state, or the United States.

(c) An application for restoration of civil rights must contain:

(1) a completed application on a form adopted by the Board of Pardons and Paroles;

(2) three or more affidavits attesting to the good character of the applicant; and

(3) proof that the applicant has completed the sentence for the offense.

(d) The applicant must submit the application to:

(1) the sheriff of the county in which the applicant resides at the time of application or resided at the time of conviction of the offense, if the individual resided in this state at that time; or

(2) the Board of Pardons and Paroles.

(e) If an application is submitted to a sheriff, the sheriff shall review the application and recommend to the Board of Pardons and Paroles whether the individual's civil rights should be restored. If the sheriff recommends restoration of the individual's civil rights, the board may either:

(1) concur in the recommendation and forward the recommendation to the governor; or

(2) independently review the application to determine whether to recommend to the governor the restoration of the individual's civil rights.

(f) If the sheriff does not recommend the restoration of the individual's civil rights, the individual may apply directly to the Board of Pardons and Paroles.

(g) If an application is submitted to the Board of Pardons and Paroles without first being submitted to a sheriff, the board shall review the application and recommend to the governor as to whether the individual's civil rights should be restored.

(h) The Board of Pardons and Paroles may require or obtain additional information as necessary to perform a review under Subsection (e)(2) or Subsection (g) of this article.

(i) On receipt from the Board of Pardons and Paroles of a recommendation to restore the civil rights of an individual, the governor may either grant or deny the restoration of civil rights to the individual. If the governor grants the restoration of civil rights to the individual, the governor shall issue a certificate of restoration of civil rights.

(j) If an application under this article is denied by the Board of Pardons and Paroles or the governor, the individual may not file another application under this article before the first anniversary of the date of the denial.

(k) A restoration of civil rights under this article is a form of pardon that restores all civil rights under the laws of this state that an individual forfeits as a result of the individual's conviction of an offense, except as specifically provided in the certificate of restoration.

Sec. 48.06. Educational Materials Concerning Pardons for Certain Victims of Trafficking of Persons.

(a) The Board of Pardons and Paroles shall develop educational materials specifically for persons convicted of or placed on deferred adjudication community supervision for an offense the person committed solely as a victim of trafficking of persons under Section 20A.02, Penal Code. The board shall include in the educational materials a detailed description of the process by which the person may submit a request to the board for a written signed recommendation advising the governor to grant the person a pardon.

(b) The Board of Pardons and Paroles shall post educational materials described by Subsection (a) on the board's Internet website.

CHAPTER 49 INQUESTS UPON DEAD BODIES

SUBCHAPTER A DUTIES PERFORMED BY JUSTICES OF THE PEACE

Art. 49.01. Definitions.

In this article:

(1) "Autopsy" means a post mortem examination of the body of a person, including X-rays and an examination of the internal organs and structures after dissection, to determine the cause of death or the nature of any pathological changes that may have contributed to the death.

(2) "Inquest" means an investigation into the cause and circumstances of the death of a person, and a determination, made with or without a formal court hearing, as to whether the death was caused by an unlawful act or omission.

(3) "Inquest hearing" means a formal court hearing held to determine whether the death of a person was caused by an unlawful act or omission and, if the death was caused by an unlawful act or omission, to obtain evidence to form the basis of a criminal prosecution.

(4) "Institution" means any place where health care services are rendered, including a hospital, clinic, health facility, nursing home, extended-care facility, out-patient facility, foster-care facility, and retirement home.

(5) "Physician" means a practicing doctor of medicine or doctor of osteopathic medicine who is licensed by the Texas State Board of Medical Examiners under Subtitle B, Title 3, Occupations Code.

Art. 49.02. Applicability.

This subchapter applies to the inquest into a death occurring in a county that does not have a medical examiner's office or that is not part of a medical examiner's district.

Art. 49.03. Powers and Duties.

The powers granted and duties imposed on a justice of the peace under this article are independent of the powers and duties of a law enforcement agency investigating a death.

Art. 49.04. Deaths Requiring an Inquest.

(a) A justice of the peace shall conduct an inquest into the death of a person who dies in the county served by the justice if:

(1) the person dies in prison under circumstances other than those described by Section 501.055(b), Government Code, or in jail;

(2) the person dies an unnatural death from a cause other than a legal execution;

(3) the body or a body part of a person is found, the cause or circumstances of death are unknown, and:

(A) the person is identified; or

(B) the person is unidentified;

(4) the circumstances of the death indicate that the death may have been caused by unlawful means;

(5) the person commits suicide or the circumstances of the death indicate that the death may have been caused by suicide;

(6) the person dies without having been attended by a physician;

(7) the person dies while attended by a physician who is unable to certify the cause of death and who requests the justice of the peace to conduct an inquest; or

(8) the person is a child younger than six years of age and an inquest is required by Chapter 264, Family Code.

(b) Except as provided by Subsection (c) of this section, a physician who attends the death of a person and who is unable to certify the cause of death shall report the death to the justice of the peace of the precinct where the death occurred and request that the justice conduct an inquest.

(c) If a person dies in a hospital or other institution and an attending physician is unable to certify the cause of death, the superintendent or general manager of the hospital or institution shall report the death to the justice of the peace of the precinct where the hospital or institution is located.

(d) A justice of the peace investigating a death described by Subsection (a)(3)(B) shall report the death to the missing children and missing persons information clearinghouse of the Department of Public Safety and the national crime information center not later than the 10th working day after the date the investigation began.

(e) A justice of the peace investigating a death described by Subsection (a)(3)(B), or the justice's designee, shall, not later than the 10th working day after the date that one or more identifying features of the unidentified body are determined or the 60th day after the date the investigation began, whichever is earlier, enter all available identifying features of the unidentified body (fingerprints, dental records, any unusual physical characteristics, and a description of the clothing found on the body) into the National Missing and Unidentified Persons System.

Art. 49.041. Reopening an Inquest.

A justice of the peace may reopen an inquest if, based on information provided by a credible person or facts within the knowledge of the justice of the peace, the justice of the peace determines that reopening the inquest may reveal a different cause or different circumstances of death.

Art. 49.05. Time and Place of Inquest; Removal of Property and Body from Place of Death.

(a) A justice of the peace shall conduct an inquest immediately or as soon as practicable after the justice receives notification of the death.

(b) A justice of the peace may conduct an inquest:

(1) at the place where the death occurred;

(2) where the body was found; or

(3) at any other place determined to be reasonable by the justice.

(c) A justice of the peace may direct the removal of a body from the scene of death or move any part of the physical surroundings of a body only after a law enforcement agency is notified of the death and a peace officer has conducted an investigation or, if a law enforcement agency has not begun an investigation, a reasonable time has elapsed from the time the law enforcement agency was notified.

(d) A law enforcement agency that is notified of a death requiring an inquest under Article 49.04 of this code shall begin its investigation immediately or as soon as practicable after the law enforcement agency receives notification of the death.

(e) Except in emergency circumstances, a peace officer or other person conducting a death investigation for a law enforcement agency may not move the body or any part of the physical surroundings of the place of death without authorization from a justice of the peace.

(f) A person not authorized by law to move the body of a decedent or any part of the physical surroundings of the body commits an offense if the person tampers with a body that is subject to an inquest under Article 49.04 of this code or any part of the physical surroundings of the body. An offense under this section is punishable by a fine in an amount not to exceed $500.

Art. 49.06. Hindering an Inquest.

(a) A person commits an offense if the person intentionally or knowingly hinders the entrance of a justice of the peace to a premises where a death occurred or a body is found.

(b) An offense under this article is a Class B misdemeanor.

Art. 49.07. Notification of Investigating Official.

(a) A physician or other person who has possession of a body or body part of a person whose death requires an inquest under Article 49.04 of this code shall immediately notify the justice of the peace who serves the precinct in which the body or body part was found.

(b) A peace officer who has been notified of the death of a person whose death requires an inquest under Article 49.04 of this code shall immediately notify the justice of the peace who serves the precinct in which the body or body part was found.

(c) (1) If the justice of the peace who serves the precinct in which the body or body part was found is not available to conduct an inquest, a person required to give notice under this article shall notify the nearest available justice of the peace serving the county in which the body or body part was found, and that justice of the peace shall conduct the inquest.

(2) If no justice of the peace serving the county in which the body or body part was found is available to conduct an inquest, a person required to give notice under this article shall notify the county judge, and the county judge shall initiate the inquest. The county judge may exercise any power and perform any duty otherwise granted to or imposed under this subchapter on the justice of the peace serving the county in which the body or body part was found, except that not later than the fifth day after the day on which the inquest is initiated, the county judge shall transfer all information obtained by the judge to the justice of the peace in whose precinct the body or body part was found for final disposition of the matter.

(3) If a justice of the peace or the county judge serving the county in which the body or body part was found is not available to conduct an inquest, a person required to give notice under this article

may ask the justice of the peace of the precinct in which the body or body part was found or the county judge to request a justice of the peace of another county to which this subchapter applies to conduct the inquest. The justice of the peace that conducts the inquest shall, not later than the fifth day after the date the inquest is initiated, transfer all information related to the inquest to the justice of the peace of the precinct in which the body or body part was found for final disposition of the matter. All expenses related to the inquest must be paid as provided by this chapter.

(d) A person commits an offense if the person is required by this article to give notice and intentionally or knowingly fails to give the notice. An offense under this subsection is a Class C misdemeanor.

Art. 49.08. Information Leading to an Inquest.

A justice of the peace conducting an inquest may act on information the justice receives from any credible person or on facts within his knowledge.

Art. 49.09. Body Disinterred or Cremated.

(a) If a body or body part subject to investigation under Article 49.04 of this code is interred and an authorized person has not conducted an inquest required under this subchapter, a justice of the peace may direct the disinterment of the body or body part in order to conduct an inquest.

(b) A person may not cremate or direct the cremation of a body subject to investigation under Article 49.04 unless the body is identified and the person has received from the justice of the peace a certificate signed by the justice stating that:

(1) an autopsy was performed on the body under Article 49.10 of this code; or

(2) no autopsy was necessary.

(c) An owner or operator of a crematory shall retain a certificate received under Subsection (b) of this article for a period of 10 years from the date of cremation of the body named on the certificate.

(d) A person commits an offense if the person cremates or directs the cremation of a body without obtaining a certificate from a justice of the peace as required by Subsection (b) of this article. An offense under this section is a Class B misdemeanor.

(e) If the body of a deceased person is unidentified, a person may not cremate or direct the cremation of the body under this article. If the body is buried, the justice of the peace shall record and maintain for not less than 10 years all information pertaining to the body and the location of burial.

Art. 49.10. Autopsies and Tests.

(a) At his discretion, a justice of the peace may obtain the opinion of a county health officer or a physician concerning the necessity of obtaining an autopsy in order to determine or confirm the nature and cause of a death.

(b) The commissioners court of the county shall pay a reasonable fee for a consultation obtained by a justice of the peace under Subsection (a) of this article.

(c) Except as required by Section 264.514, Family Code, for each body that is the subject of an inquest by a justice of the peace, the justice, in the justice's discretion, shall:

(1) direct a physician to perform an autopsy; or

(2) certify that no autopsy is necessary.

(d) A justice of the peace may not order a person to perform an autopsy on the body of a deceased person whose death was caused by Asiatic cholera, bubonic plague, typhus fever, or smallpox. A justice of the peace may not order a person to perform an autopsy on the body of a deceased person whose death was caused by a communicable disease during a public health disaster.

(e) A justice of the peace shall order an autopsy performed on a body if:

(1) the justice determines that an autopsy is necessary to determine or confirm the nature and cause of death;

(2) the deceased was a child younger than six years of age and the death is determined under Section 264.514, Family Code, to be unexpected or the result of abuse or neglect; or

(3) directed to do so by the district attorney, criminal district attorney, or, if there is no district or criminal district attorney, the county attorney.

(f) A justice of the peace shall request a physician to perform the autopsy.

(g) The commissioners court shall pay a reasonable fee to a physician performing an autopsy on the order of a justice of the peace, if a fee is assessed.

(h) The commissioners court shall pay a reasonable fee for the transportation of a body to a place where an autopsy can be performed under this article if a justice of the peace orders the body to be transported to the place.

(i) If a justice of the peace determines that a complete autopsy is unnecessary to confirm or determine the cause of death, the justice may order a physician to take or remove from a body a sample of body fluids, tissues, or organs in order to determine the nature and cause of death. Except as provided by Subsection (j) of this article, a justice may not order any person other than a physician to take samples from the body of a deceased person.

Code of Criminal Procedure

(j) A justice of the peace may order a physician, qualified technician, paramedic, chemist, registered professional nurse, or licensed vocational nurse to take a specimen of blood from the body of a person who died as the result of a motor vehicle accident if the justice determines that circumstances indicate that the person may have been driving while intoxicated.

(k) A justice of the peace may order an investigative or laboratory test to determine the identity of a deceased person. After proper removal of a sample from a body, a justice may order any person specially trained in identification work to complete any tests necessary to determine the identity of the deceased person.

(*l*) A medical examination on an unidentified person shall include the following information to enable a timely and accurate identification of the person:

(1) all available fingerprints and palm prints;

(2) dental charts and radiographs (X-rays) of the person's teeth;

(3) frontal and lateral facial photographs with scale indicated;

(4) notation and photographs, with scale indicated, of a significant scar, mark, tattoo, or item of clothing or other personal effect found with or near the body;

(5) notation of antemortem medical conditions;

(6) notation of observations pertinent to the estimation of time of death; and

(7) precise documentation of the location of burial of the remains.

(m) A medical examination on an unidentified person may include the following information to enable a timely and accurate identification of the person:

(1) full body radiographs (X-rays); and

(2) hair specimens with roots.

(n) On discovering the body or body part of a deceased person in the circumstances described by Article 49.04(a)(3)(B), the justice of the peace may request the aid of a forensic anthropologist in the examination of the body or body part. The forensic anthropologist must hold a doctoral degree in anthropology with an emphasis in physical anthropology. The forensic anthropologist shall attempt to establish whether the body or body part is of a human or animal, whether evidence of childbirth, injury, or disease exists, and the sex, race, age, stature, and physical anomalies of the body or body part. The forensic anthropologist may also attempt to establish the cause, manner, and time of death.

(o) If a person is injured in one county and dies as a result of those injuries, with the death occurring in another county, the attorney representing the state in the prosecution of felonies in the county in which the injury occurred may request a justice of the peace in the county in which the death occurred to order an autopsy be performed on the body of the deceased person. If the justice of the peace orders that the autopsy be performed, the county in which the injury occurred shall reimburse the county in which the death occurred.

Art. 49.11. Chemical Analysis.

(a) A justice of the peace may obtain a chemical analysis of a sample taken from a body in order to determine whether death was caused, in whole or in part, by the ingestion, injection, or introduction into the body of a poison or other chemical substance. A justice may obtain a chemical analysis under this article from a chemist, toxicologist, pathologist, or other medical expert.

(b) A justice of the peace shall obtain a chemical analysis under Subsection (a) of this article if requested to do so by the physician who performed an autopsy on the body.

(c) The commissioners court shall pay a reasonable fee to a person who conducts a chemical analysis at the request of a justice of the peace.

Art. 49.12. Liability of Person Performing Autopsy or Test.

A person who performs an autopsy or makes a test on a body on the order of a justice of the peace in the good faith belief that the order is valid is not liable for damages if the order is invalid.

Art. 49.13. Consent to Autopsy [Repealed].

Repealed by Acts 2011, 82nd Leg., ch. 950 (H.B. 1009), § 4, effective January 1, 2012.

Art. 49.14. Inquest Hearing.

(a) A justice of the peace conducting an inquest may hold an inquest hearing if the justice determines that the circumstances warrant the hearing. The justice shall hold an inquest hearing if requested to do so by a district attorney or a criminal district attorney who serves the county in which the body was found.

(b) An inquest hearing may be held with or without a jury unless the district attorney or criminal district attorney requests that the hearing be held with a jury.

(c) A jury in an inquest hearing is composed of six persons. Jurors shall be summoned in the same manner as are jurors for county court. A juror who is properly summoned and fails to appear, other than a juror exempted by law, commits an offense. An offense under this subsection is punishable by a fine not to exceed $100.

(d) A justice of the peace may hold a public or a private inquest hearing. If a person has been arrested and charged with causing the death of the deceased, the defendant and the defendant's counsel are entitled to be present at the inquest hearing, examine witnesses, and introduce evidence.

(e) A justice of the peace may issue a subpoena to enforce the attendance of a witness at an inquest hearing and may issue an attachment for a person who is subpoenaed and fails to appear at the time and place cited on the subpoena.

(f) A justice of the peace may require bail of a witness to secure the appearance of the witness at an inquest hearing or before a grand jury, examining court, or other court investigating a death.

(g) The justice of the peace shall swear witnesses appearing at an inquest hearing. The justice and an attorney representing the state may examine witnesses at an inquest hearing. The justice shall direct that all sworn testimony be reduced to writing and the justice shall subscribe the transcription.

(h) Only the justice of the peace, a person charged in the death under investigation, the counsel for the person charged, and an attorney representing the state may question a witness at an inquest hearing.

(i) A justice of the peace may hold a person who disrupts the proceedings of an inquest hearing in contempt of court. A person who is found in contempt of court under this subsection may be fined in an amount not to exceed $100 and removed from court by a peace officer.

Art. 49.15. Inquest Record.

(a) A justice of the peace or other person authorized under this subchapter to conduct an inquest shall make an inquest record for each inquest he conducts. The inquest record must include a report of the events, proceedings, findings, and conclusions of the inquest. The record must also include any autopsy prepared in the case and all other papers of the case. All papers of the inquest record must be marked with the case number and be clearly indexed and be maintained in the office of the justice of the peace and be made available to the appropriate officials upon request.

(b) As part of the inquest record, the justice of the peace shall make and keep complete and permanent records of all inquest hearings. The inquest hearing records must include:

(1) the name of the deceased person or, if the person is unidentified, a description of the body;

(2) the time, date, and place where the body was found;

(3) the time, date, and place where the inquest was held;

(4) the name of every witness who testified at the inquest;

(5) the name of every person who provided to the justice information pertinent to the inquest;

(6) the amount of bail set for each witness and person charged in the death;

(7) a transcript of the testimony given by each witness at the inquest hearing;

(8) the autopsy report, if an autopsy was performed; and

(9) the name of every person arrested as a suspect in the death who appeared at the inquest and the details of that person's arrest.

(c) The commissioners court shall pay a reasonable fee to a person who records or transcribes sworn testimony during an inquest hearing.

(d) [Repealed.]

Art. 49.16. Orders and Death Certificates.

The justice of the peace or other person who conducts an inquest under this subchapter shall sign the death certificate and all orders made as a necessary part of the inquest.

Art. 49.17. Evidence.

A justice of the peace shall preserve all tangible evidence that the justice accumulates in the course of an inquest that tends to show the real cause of death or identify the person who caused the death. The justice shall deposit the evidence with the appropriate law enforcement agency to be stored in the agency's property room for safekeeping.

Art. 49.18. Death in Custody.

(a) If a person confined in a penal institution dies, the sheriff or other person in charge of the penal institution shall as soon as practicable inform the justice of the peace of the precinct where the penal institution is located of the death.

(b) If a person dies while in the custody of a peace officer or as a result of a peace officer's use of force or if a person incarcerated in a jail, correctional facility, or state juvenile facility dies, the director of the law enforcement agency of which the officer is a member or of the facility in which the person was incarcerated shall investigate the death and file a written report of the cause of death with the attorney general no later than the 30th day after the date on which the person in custody or the incarcerated person died. The director shall make a good faith effort to obtain all facts relevant to the death and include those facts in the report. The attorney general shall make the report, with the exception of any portion of the report that the attorney general determines is privileged, available to any interested person.

(c) Subsection (a) does not apply to a death that occurs in a facility operated by or under contract with the Texas Department of Criminal Justice. Subsection (b) does not apply to a death that occurs in a facility operated by or under contract with the Texas Department of Criminal Justice if the death occurs under circumstances described by Section 501.055(b)(2), Government Code.

(d) In this article:

(1) "Correctional facility" means a confinement facility or halfway house operated by or under contract with any division of the Texas Department of Criminal Justice.

(2) "In the custody of a peace officer" means:

(A) under arrest by a peace officer; or

(B) under the physical control or restraint of a peace officer.

(3) "State juvenile facility" means any facility or halfway house:

(A) operated by or under contract with the Texas Juvenile Justice Department; or

(B) described by Section 51.02(13) or (14), Family Code.

Art. 49.19. Warrant of Arrest.

(a) A justice of the peace who is conducting an inquest of a death under this subchapter may issue a warrant for the arrest of a person suspected of causing the death if:

(1) the justice has knowledge that the person caused the death of the deceased;

(2) the justice receives an affidavit stating that the person caused the death; or

(3) evidence is adduced at an inquest hearing that shows probable cause to believe the person caused the death.

(b) A peace officer who receives an arrest warrant issued by a justice of the peace shall:

(1) execute the warrant without delay; and

(2) detain the person arrested until the person's discharge is ordered by the justice of the peace or other proper authority.

(c) A person who is charged in a death and arrested under a warrant of a justice of the peace shall remain in the custody of the arresting peace officer and may not be removed from the peace officer's custody on the authority of a warrant from another magistrate. A person charged in a death who has not been arrested under a warrant of a justice of the peace may be arrested on the order of a magistrate other than the justice of the peace and examined by that magistrate while an inquest is pending.

Art. 49.20. Requisites of Warrant.

A warrant of arrest issued under Article 49.19 of this code is sufficient if it:

(1) is issued in the name of "The State of Texas";

(2) specifies the name of the person whose arrest is ordered or, if the person's name is unknown, reasonably describes the person;

(3) recites in plain language the offense with which the person is charged; and

(4) is signed and dated by a justice of the peace.

Art. 49.21. Commitment of Homicide Suspect.

At the conclusion of an inquest, if a justice of the peace finds that a person who has been arrested in the case caused or contributed to the death of the deceased, the justice may:

(1) commit the person to jail; or

(2) require the person to execute a bail bond with security for the person's appearance before the proper court to answer for the offense.

Art. 49.22. Sealing Premises of Deceased.

(a) If a body or body part that is subject to an inquest under Article 49.04 of this code is found on premises that were under the sole control of the deceased, a justice of the peace or other person authorized under this subchapter to conduct an inquest may direct that the premises be locked and sealed to prohibit entrance by any person other than a peace officer conducting an investigation of the death.

(b) Rent, utility charges, taxes, and all other reasonable expenses accruing against the property of the deceased during the time the premises of the deceased are locked and sealed under this article may be charged against the estate of the deceased.

(c) A person other than a peace officer commits an offense if the person tampers with or removes a lock or seal placed on premises under this article.

(d) An offense under this article is a Class B misdemeanor.

Art. 49.23. Office of Death Investigator.

(a) The commissioners court of a county may establish an office of death investigator and employ one or more death investigators to provide assistance to those persons in the county who conduct inquests. A death investigator employed under this article is entitled to receive compensation from the county in an amount set by the commissioners court. A death investigator serves at the will of the commissioners court and on terms and conditions set by the commissioners court.

(b) To be eligible for employment as a death investigator, a person must have experience or training in investigative procedures concerning the circumstances, manner, and cause of the death of a deceased person.

(c) At the request of and under the supervision of a justice of the peace or other person conducting an inquest, a death investigator may assist the person conducting the inquest to investigate the time, place, and manner of death and lock and seal the premises of the deceased. A death investigator who assists in an inquest under this subsection shall make a complete report of the death investigator's activities, findings, and conclusions to the justice of the peace or other person conducting the inquest not later than eight hours after the death investigator completes the investigation.

Art. 49.24. Notification and Report of Death of Resident of Institution.

(a) A superintendent or general manager of an institution who is required by Article 49.04 to report to a justice of the peace the death of an individual under the care, custody, or control of or residing in the institution shall:

(1) notify the office of the attorney general of the individual's death within 24 hours of the death; and

(2) prepare and submit to the office of the attorney general a report containing all facts relevant to the individual's death within 72 hours of the death.

(b) The superintendent or general manager of the institution shall make a good faith effort to obtain all facts relevant to an individual's death and to include those facts in the report submitted under Subsection (a)(2).

(c) The office of the attorney general may investigate each death reported to the office by an institution that receives payments through the medical assistance program under Chapter 32, Human Resources Code.

(d) Except as provided by Subsection (e), the office of the attorney general shall make a report submitted under Subsection (a)(2) available to any interested person who submits a written request for access to the report.

(e) The office of the attorney general may deny a person access to a report or a portion of a report filed under Subsection (a)(2) if the office determines that the report or a portion of the report is:

(1) privileged from discovery; or

(2) exempt from required public disclosure under Chapter 552, Government Code.

(f) This article does not relieve a superintendent or general manager of an institution of the duty of making any other notification or report of an individual's death as required by law.

(g) For the purposes of this article, the definition of "institution" excludes hospitals.

SUBCHAPTER B DUTIES PERFORMED BY MEDICAL EXAMINERS

Art. 49.25. Medical Examiners.

Sec. 1. **Office Authorized.** — Subject to the provisions of this article, the commissioners court of any county having a population of more than two million shall establish and maintain the office of medical examiner, and the commissioners court of any county may establish and provide for the maintenance of the office of medical examiner. Population shall be according to the last preceding federal census.

Sec. 1-a. **Multi-County District; Joint Office.**

(a) The commissioners courts of two or more counties may enter into an agreement to create a medical examiners district and to jointly operate and maintain the office of medical examiner of the district. The district must include the entire area of all counties involved. The counties within the district must, when taken together, form a continuous area.

(b) There may be only one medical examiner in a medical examiners district, although he may employ, within the district, necessary staff personnel. When a county becomes a part of a medical examiners district, the effect is the same within the county as if the office of medical examiner had been established in that county alone. The district medical examiner has all the powers and duties within the district that a medical examiner who serves in a single county has within that county.

(c) The commissioners court of any county which has become a part of a medical examiners district may withdraw the county from the district, but twelve months' notice of withdrawal must be given to the commissioners courts of all other counties in the district.

Sec. 2. **Appointments and Qualifications.**

(a) The commissioners court shall appoint the medical examiner, who serves at the pleasure of

Code of Criminal Procedure

the commissioners court. A person appointed as the medical examiner must be:

(1) a physician licensed by the Texas Medical Board; or

(2) a person who:

(A) is licensed and in good standing as a physician in another state;

(B) has applied to the Texas Medical Board for a license to practice medicine in this state; and

(C) has been granted a provisional license under Section 155.101, Occupations Code.

(b) To the greatest extent possible, the medical examiner shall be appointed from persons having training and experience in pathology, toxicology, histology and other medico-legal sciences.

(c) The medical examiner shall devote the time and energy necessary to perform the duties conferred by this Article.

Sec. 3. **Assistants.** — The medical examiner may, subject to the approval of the commissioners court, employ such deputy examiners, scientific experts, trained technicians, officers and employees as may be necessary to the proper performance of the duties imposed by this Article upon the medical examiner.

Sec. 4. **Salaries.** — The commissioners court shall establish and pay the salaries and compensations of the medical examiner and his staff.

Sec. 5. **Offices.** — The commissioners court shall provide the medical examiner and his staff with adequate office space and shall provide laboratory facilities or make arrangements for the use of existing laboratory facilities in the county, if so requested by the medical examiner.

Sec. 6. **Death Investigations.**

(a) Any medical examiner, or his duly authorized deputy, shall be authorized, and it shall be his duty, to hold inquests with or without a jury within his county, in the following cases:

1. When a person shall die within twenty-four hours after admission to a hospital or institution or in prison or in jail;

2. When any person is killed; or from any cause dies an unnatural death, except under sentence of the law; or dies in the absence of one or more good witnesses;

3. When the body or a body part of a person is found, the cause or circumstances of death are unknown, and:

(A) the person is identified; or

(B) the person is unidentified;

4. When the circumstances of the death of any person are such as to lead to suspicion that he came to his death by unlawful means;

5. When any person commits suicide, or the circumstances of his death are such as to lead to suspicion that he committed suicide;

6. When a person dies without having been attended by a duly licensed and practicing physician, and the local health officer or registrar required to report the cause of death under Section 193.005, Health and Safety Code, does not know the cause of death. When the local health officer or registrar of vital statistics whose duty it is to certify the cause of death does not know the cause of death, he shall so notify the medical examiner of the county in which the death occurred and request an inquest;

7. When the person is a child who is younger than six years of age and the death is reported under Chapter 264, Family Code; and

8. When a person dies who has been attended immediately preceding his death by a duly licensed and practicing physician or physicians, and such physician or physicians are not certain as to the cause of death and are unable to certify with certainty the cause of death as required by Section 193.004, Health and Safety Code. In case of such uncertainty the attending physician or physicians, or the superintendent or general manager of the hospital or institution in which the deceased shall have died, shall so report to the medical examiner of the county in which the death occurred, and request an inquest.

(b) The inquests authorized and required by this Article shall be held by the medical examiner of the county in which the death occurred.

(c) In making such investigations and holding such inquests, the medical examiner or an authorized deputy may administer oaths and take affidavits. In the absence of next of kin or legal representatives of the deceased, the medical examiner or authorized deputy shall take charge of the body and all property found with it.

Sec. 6a. **Organ Transplant Donors; Notice; Inquests.**

(a) When death occurs to an individual designated a prospective organ donor for transplantation by a licensed physician under circumstances requiring the medical examiner of the county in which death occurred, or the medical examiner's authorized deputy, to hold an inquest, the medical examiner, or a member of his staff will be so notified by the administrative head of the facility in which the transplantation is to be performed.

(b) When notified pursuant to Subsection (a) of this Section, the medical examiner or the medical examiner's deputy shall perform an inquest on the deceased prospective organ donor.

Sec. 7. **Reports of Death.**

(a) Any police officer, superintendent or general manager of an institution, physician, or private citizen who shall become aware of a death under any of the circumstances set out in Section 6(a) of this Article, shall immediately report such death to the office of the medical examiner or to the city or county police departments; any such report to a city or county police department shall be immediately transmitted to the office of the medical examiner.

(b) A person investigating a death described by Subdivision 3(B) of Section 6(a) shall report the death to the missing children and missing persons information clearinghouse of the Department of Public Safety and the national crime information center not later than the 10th working day after the date the investigation began.

(c) A superintendent or general manager of an institution who reports a death under Subsection (a) must comply with the notice and reporting requirements of Article 49.24. The office of the attorney general has the same powers and duties provided the office under that article regarding the dissemination and investigation of the report.

(d) A person investigating a death described by Section 6(a)(3)(B), or the person's designee, shall, not later than the 10th working day after the date that one or more identifying features of the unidentified body are determined or the 60th day after the date the investigation began, whichever is earlier, enter all available identifying features of the unidentified body (fingerprints, dental records, any unusual physical characteristics, and a description of the clothing found on the body) into the National Missing and Unidentified Persons System.

Sec. 8. **Removal of Bodies.** — When any death under circumstances set out in Section 6 shall have occurred, the body shall not be disturbed or removed from the position in which it is found by any person without authorization from the medical examiner or authorized deputy, except for the purpose of preserving such body from loss or destruction or maintaining the flow of traffic on a highway, railroad or airport.

Sec. 9. **Autopsy.**

(a) If the cause of death shall be determined beyond a reasonable doubt as a result of the investigation, the medical examiner shall file a report thereof setting forth specifically the cause of death with the district attorney or criminal district attorney, or in a county in which there is no district attorney or criminal district attorney with the county attorney, of the county in which the death occurred. If in the opinion of the medical examiner an autopsy is necessary, or if such is requested by the district attorney or criminal district attorney, or county attorney where there is no district attorney or criminal district attorney, the autopsy shall be immediately performed by the medical examiner or a duly authorized deputy. In those cases where a complete autopsy is deemed unnecessary by the medical examiner to ascertain the cause of death, the medical examiner may perform a limited autopsy involving the taking of blood samples or any other samples of body fluids, tissues or organs, in order to ascertain the cause of death or whether a crime has been committed. In the case of a body of a human being whose identity is unknown, the medical examiner may authorize such investigative and laboratory tests and processes as are required to determine its identity as well as the cause of death. In performing an autopsy the medical examiner or authorized deputy may use the facilities of any city or county hospital within the county or such other facilities as are made available. Upon completion of the autopsy, the medical examiner shall file a report setting forth the findings in detail with the office of the district attorney or criminal district attorney of the county, or if there is no district attorney or criminal district attorney, with the county attorney of the county.

(b) A medical examination on an unidentified person shall include the following information to enable a timely and accurate identification of the person:

(1) all available fingerprints and palm prints;

(2) dental charts and radiographs (X-rays) of the person's teeth;

(3) frontal and lateral facial photographs with scale indicated;

(4) notation and photographs, with scale indicated, of a significant scar, mark, tattoo, or item of clothing or other personal effect found with or near the body;

(5) notation of antemortem medical conditions;

(6) notation of observations pertinent to the estimation of time of death; and

(7) precise documentation of the location of burial of the remains.

(c) A medical examination on an unidentified person may include the following information to enable a timely and accurate identification of the person:

(1) full body radiographs (X-rays); and

(2) hair specimens with roots.

Sec. 10. **Disinterments and Cremations.** — When a body upon which an inquest ought to have been held has been interred, the medical examiner may cause it to be disinterred for the purpose of holding such inquest.

Before any body, upon which an inquest is authorized by the provisions of this Article, can be lawfully cremated, an autopsy shall be performed thereon as provided in this Article, or a certificate that no autopsy was necessary shall be furnished by the medical examiner. Before any dead body can be lawfully cremated, the owner or operator

Code of Criminal Procedure

of the crematory shall demand and be furnished with a certificate, signed by the medical examiner of the county in which the death occurred showing that an autopsy was performed on said body or that no autopsy thereon was necessary. It shall be the duty of the medical examiner to determine whether or not, from all the circumstances surrounding the death, an autopsy is necessary prior to issuing a certificate under the provisions of this section. No autopsy shall be required by the medical examiner as a prerequisite to cremation in case death is caused by the pestilential diseases of Asiatic cholera, bubonic plague, typhus fever, or smallpox. All certificates furnished to the owner or operator of a crematory by any medical examiner, under the terms of this Article, shall be preserved by such owner or operator of such crematory for a period of two years from the date of the cremation of said body. A medical examiner is not required to perform an autopsy on the body of a deceased person whose death was caused by a communicable disease during a public health disaster.

Sec. 10a. **Waiting Period Between Death and Cremation. —** The body of a deceased person shall not be cremated within 48 hours after the time of death as indicated on the regular death certificate, unless the death certificate indicates death was caused by the pestilential diseases of Asiatic cholera, bubonic plague, typhus fever, or smallpox, or unless the time requirement is waived in writing by the county medical examiner or, in counties not having a county medical examiner, a justice of the peace. In a public health disaster, the commissioner of public health may designate other communicable diseases for which cremation within 48 hours of the time of death is authorized.

Sec. 10b. **Disposal of Unidentified Body. —** If the body of a deceased person is unidentified, a person may not cremate or direct the cremation of the body under this article. If the body is buried, the investigating agency responsible for the burial shall record and maintain for not less than 10 years all information pertaining to the body and the location of burial.

Sec. 11. **Records.**

(a) The medical examiner shall keep full and complete records properly indexed, giving the name if known of every person whose death is investigated, the place where the body was found, the date, the cause and manner of death, and shall issue a death certificate. The full report and detailed findings of the autopsy, if any, shall be a part of the record. Copies of all records shall promptly be delivered to the proper district, county, or criminal district attorney in any case where further investigation is advisable. The records may not be withheld, subject to a discretionary exception under Chapter 552, Government Code, except that a photograph or x-ray of a body taken during an autopsy is excepted from required public disclosure in accordance with Chapter 552, Government Code, but is subject to disclosure:

(1) under a subpoena or authority of other law; or

(2) if the photograph or x-ray is of the body of a person who died while in the custody of law enforcement.

(b) Under the exception to public disclosure provided by Subsection (a), a governmental body as defined by Section 552.003, Government Code, may withhold a photograph or x-ray described by Subsection (a) without requesting a decision from the attorney general under Subchapter G, Chapter 552, Government Code. This subsection does not affect the required disclosure of a photograph or x-ray under Subsection (a)(1) or (2).

(c) The medical examiner may release a copy of an autopsy report of a deceased person to any organ and tissue procurement organization, hospital, or other covered entity as defined by Section 181.001, Health and Safety Code, that treated the deceased person before death or procured any anatomical gift from the body of the deceased person. The release of a report under this subsection is not considered a disclosure under Chapter 552, Government Code. A report obtained under this subsection is confidential and not subject to disclosure under Chapter 552, Government Code.

Sec. 12. **Transfer of Duties of Justice of Peace. —** When the commissioners court of any county shall establish the office of medical examiner, all powers and duties of justices of the peace in such county relating to the investigation of deaths and inquests shall vest in the office of the medical examiner. Any subsequent General Law pertaining to the duties of justices of the peace in death investigations and inquests shall apply to the medical examiner in such counties as to the extent not inconsistent with this Article, and all laws or parts of laws otherwise in conflict herewith are hereby declared to be inapplicable to this Article.

Sec. 13. **Use of Forensic Anthropologist. —** On discovering the body or body part of a deceased person in the circumstances described by Subdivision 3(B) of Section 6(a), the medical examiner may request the aid of a forensic anthropologist in the examination of the body or body part. The forensic anthropologist must hold a doctoral degree in anthropology with an emphasis in physical anthropology. The forensic anthropologist shall attempt to establish whether the body or body part is of a human or animal, whether evidence of childbirth, injury, or disease exists, and the sex, race, age, stature, and physical anomalies of the body or body part. The forensic anthropologist may also attempt to establish the cause, manner, and time of death.

Sec. 13A. **Fees.**

(a) A medical examiner may charge reasonable fees for services provided by the office of medical examiner under this article, including cremation approvals, court testimonies, consultations, and depositions.

(b) The commissioners court must approve the amount of the fee before the fee may be assessed. The fee may not exceed the amount necessary to provide the services described by Subsection (a).

(c) The fee may not be assessed against the county's district attorney or a county office.

Sec. 14. **Penalty.**

(a) A person commits an offense if the person knowingly violates this article.

(b) An offense under this section is a Class B misdemeanor.

SUBCHAPTER C INFORMED CONSENT FOR POSTMORTEM EXAMINATION OR AUTOPSY

Art. 49.31. Applicability.

This subchapter does not apply to an autopsy that:

(1) is ordered by the Texas Department of Criminal Justice or an authorized official of the department in accordance with Section 501.055, Government Code; or

(2) a justice of the peace or medical examiner determines is required under this chapter or other law.

Art. 49.32. Consent to Postmortem Examination or Autopsy.

(a) Except as provided by Subsection (b) of this article, a physician may not perform, or assist in the performance of, a postmortem examination or autopsy on the body of a deceased person unless the physician obtains the written informed consent of a person authorized to provide consent under Article 49.33 of this code. The consent must be provided on the form prescribed under Article 49.34 of this code.

(b) If, after due diligence, a physician is unable to identify or contact a person authorized to give consent under Article 49.33 of this code, the physician may, as authorized by a medical examiner, justice of the peace, or county judge, as appropriate, perform a postmortem examination or autopsy on the body of a deceased person not less than 24 hours and not more than 48 hours from the time of the decedent's death or the time the physician or other person took possession of the body.

Art. 49.33. Persons Authorized to Consent to Postmortem Examination or Autopsy.

(a) Subject to Subsections (b) and (c) of this article, consent for a postmortem examination or autopsy may be given by any member of the following classes of persons who is reasonably available, in the order of priority listed:

(1) the spouse of the decedent;

(2) the person acting as guardian of the person of the decedent at the time of death or the executor or administrator of the decedent's estate;

(3) the adult children of the decedent;

(4) the parents of the decedent; and

(5) the adult siblings of the decedent.

(b) If there is more than one member of a class listed in Subsection (a)(2), (3), (4), or (5) of this article entitled to give consent to a postmortem examination or autopsy, consent may be given by a member of the class unless another member of the class files an objection with the physician, medical examiner, justice of the peace, or county judge. If an objection is filed, the consent may be given only by a majority of the members of the class who are reasonably available.

(c) A person may not give consent under this article if, at the time of the decedent's death, a person in a class granted higher priority under Subsection (a) of this article is reasonably available to give consent or to file an objection to a postmortem examination or autopsy.

Art. 49.34. Postmortem Examination or Autopsy Consent Form.

The commissioner of state health services, in consultation with the Texas Medical Board, shall prescribe a standard written consent form for a postmortem examination or autopsy. The form must:

(1) include the name of the hospital or other institution and the department that will perform the examination or autopsy;

(2) include a statement that the removal from the deceased person's body and retention by the

physician of organs, fluids, prosthetic devices, or tissue may be required for purposes of comprehensive evaluation or accurate determination of a cause of death;

(3) provide the family of the deceased person with an opportunity to place restrictions or special limitations on the examination or autopsy;

(4) include a separate section regarding the disposition of organs, fluids, prosthetic devices, or tissue after the examination or autopsy, including a prioritized list of the persons authorized to control that disposition, as provided by Chapter 692A, Health and Safety Code;

(5) provide for documented and witnessed consent;

(6) allow authorization for the release of human remains to a funeral home or individual designated by the person giving consent for the postmortem examination or autopsy;

(7) include information regarding the rights described by Article 49.35 of this code;

(8) list the circumstances under which a medical examiner is required by law to conduct an investigation, inquest, or autopsy under Article 49.25 of this code;

(9) include a statement that the form is required by state law; and

(10) be written in plain language designed to be easily understood by the average person.

Art. 49.35. Right to Nonaffiliated Physician.

(a) A person authorized to consent to a postmortem examination or autopsy under Article 49.33 of this code may request that a physician who is not affiliated with the hospital or other institution where the deceased person died:

(1) perform the postmortem examination or autopsy at another hospital or institution; or

(2) review the postmortem examination or autopsy conducted by a physician affiliated with the hospital or other institution where the deceased person died.

(b) A representative of the hospital or other institution shall inform the person of the person's right to request the performance or review of a postmortem examination or autopsy by a nonaffiliated physician under Subsection (a) before the person consents to the postmortem examination or autopsy.

(c) A person requesting a nonaffiliated physician to perform or review a postmortem examination or autopsy shall bear the additional costs incurred as a result of the nonaffiliated physician's performance or review of the examination or autopsy under Subsection (a) of this article.

SUBCHAPTER D
RIGHT OF PARENT OF DECEASED PERSON TO VIEW PERSON'S BODY

Art. 49.51. Definitions.

In this subchapter:

(1) [Repealed.]

(2) "Parent" has the meaning assigned by Section 160.102(11), Family Code.

Art. 49.52. Right of Parent of Deceased Person to View Person's Body.

(a) Except as provided by Subsection (b) or (c), a parent of a deceased person is entitled to view the person's body before a justice of the peace or the medical examiner, as applicable, for the county in which the death occurred assumes control over the body under Subchapter A or B, as applicable. If the person's death occurred at a hospital or other health care facility, the viewing may be conducted at the hospital or facility.

(b) A parent of a deceased person may not view the person's body after a justice of the peace or medical examiner described by Subsection (a) assumes control over the body under Subchapter A or B, as applicable, unless the parent first obtains the consent of the justice of the peace or medical examiner or a person acting on behalf of the justice of the peace or medical examiner.

(c) A viewing of the body of a deceased person under this article whose death is determined to be subject to an inquest under Article 49.04 or 49.25, as applicable, must be conducted in compliance with the following conditions:

(1) the viewing must be supervised by:

(A) if law enforcement has assumed control over the body at the time of the viewing, an appropriate peace officer or, with the officer's consent, a person described by Paragraph (B); or

(B) a physician, registered nurse, or licensed vocational nurse or the justice of the peace or the medical examiner or a person acting on behalf of the justice of the peace or medical examiner;

(2) a parent of the deceased person may not have contact with the person's body unless the parent first obtains the consent of the justice of the peace or medical examiner or a person acting on behalf of the justice of the peace or medical examiner; and

(3) a person may not remove a medical device from the deceased person's body or otherwise alter the condition of the body for purposes of conducting

the viewing unless the person first obtains the consent of the justice of the peace or medical examiner or a person acting on behalf of the justice of the peace or medical examiner.

(d) A person is not entitled to compensation for performing duties on behalf of a justice of the peace or medical examiner under this article unless the commissioners court of the applicable county approves the compensation.

CHAPTER 50
FIRE INQUESTS

Art. 50.01. Investigations.

When an affidavit is made by a credible person before any justice of the peace that there is ground to believe that any building has been unlawfully set or attempted to be set on fire, such justice shall cause the truth of such complaint to be investigated.

Art. 50.02. Proceedings.

The proceedings in such case shall be governed by the laws relating to inquests upon dead bodies. The officer conducting such investigations shall have the same powers as are conferred upon justices of the peace in the preceding Articles of this Chapter.

Art. 50.03. Verdict in Fire Inquest.

The jury after inspecting the place in question and after hearing the testimony, shall deliver to the justice holding such inquest its written signed verdict in which it shall find and certify how and in what manner such fire happened or was attempted, and all the circumstances attending the same, and who are guilty thereof, and in what manner. If such a jury is unable to so ascertain, it shall find and certify accordingly.

Art. 50.04. Witnesses Bound Over.

If the jury finds that any building has been unlawfully set on fire or has been attempted so to be, the justice holding such inquest shall bind over the witnesses to appear and testify before the next grand jury of the county in which such offense was committed.

Art. 50.05. Warrant for Accused.

If the person charged with the offense, if any, be not in custody, the justice of the peace shall issue a warrant for his arrest, and when arrested, such person shall be dealt with as in other like cases.

Art. 50.06. Testimony Written Down.

In all such investigations, the testimony of all witnesses examined before the jury shall be reduced to writing by or under the direction of the justice and signed by each witness. Such testimony together with the verdict and all bail bonds taken in the case shall be certified to and returned by the justice to the next district or criminal district court of his county.

Art. 50.07. Compensation.

The pay of the officers and jury making such investigation shall be the same as that allowed for the holding of an inquest upon a dead body, so far as applicable, and shall be paid in like manner.

CHAPTER 51
FUGITIVES FROM JUSTICE

Art. 51.01. Delivered Up.

A person in any other State of the United States charged with treason or any felony who shall flee from justice and be found in this State, shall on demand of the executive authority of the State from which he fled, be delivered up, to be removed to the State having jurisdiction of the crime.

Art. 51.02. To Aid in Arrest.

All peace officers of the State shall give aid in the arrest and detention of a fugitive from any other State that he may be held subject to a requisition by the Governor of the State from which he fled.

Art. 51.03. Magistrate's Warrant.

When a complaint is made to a magistrate that any person within his jurisdiction is a fugitive from justice from another State, he shall issue a warrant of arrest directing a peace officer to apprehend and bring the accused before him.

Art. 51.04. Complaint.

The complaint shall be sufficient if it recites:
1. The name of the person accused;
2. The State from which he has fled;
3. The offense committed by the accused;

4. That he has fled to this State from the State where the offense was committed; and

5. That the act alleged to have been committed by the accused is a violation of the penal law of the State from which he fled.

Art. 51.05. Bail or Commitment.

When the accused is brought before the magistrate, he shall hear proof, and if satisfied that the accused is charged in another State with the offense named in the complaint, he shall require of him bail with sufficient security, in such amount as the magistrate deems reasonable, to appear before such magistrate at a specified time. In default of such bail, he may commit the defendant to jail to await a requisition from the Governor of the State from which he fled. A properly certified transcript of an indictment against the accused is sufficient to show that he is charged with the crime alleged. One arrested under the provisions of this title shall not be committed or held to bail for a longer time than ninety days.

Art. 51.06. Notice of Arrest.

The magistrate who held or committed such fugitive shall immediately notify the Secretary of State and the district or county attorney of his county of such fact and the date thereof, stating the name of such fugitive, the State from which he fled, and the crime with which he is charged; and such officers so notified shall in turn notify the Governor of the proper State.

Art. 51.07. Discharge.

A fugitive not arrested under a warrant from the Governor of this State before the expiration of ninety days from the day of his commitment or the date of the bail shall be discharged.

Art. 51.08. Second Arrest.

A person who has once been arrested under the provisions of this title and discharged under the provisions of the preceding Article or by habeas corpus shall not be again arrested upon a charge of the same offense, except by a warrant from the Governor of this State.

Art. 51.09. Governor May Demand Fugitive.

When the Governor deems it proper to demand a person who has committed an offense in this State and has fled to another State, he may commission any suitable person to take such requisition. The accused, if brought back to the State, shall be delivered up to the sheriff of the county in which it is alleged he has committed the offense.

Art. 51.10. Pay of Agent; Traveling Expenses.

Sec. 1. The officer or person so commissioned shall receive as compensation the actual and necessary traveling expenses upon requisition of the Governor to be allowed by such Governor and to be paid out of the State Treasury upon a certificate of the Governor reciting the services rendered and the allowance therefor.

Sec. 2. The commissioners court of the county where an offense is committed may in its discretion, on the request of the sheriff and the recommendation of the district attorney, pay the actual and necessary traveling expenses of the officer or person so commissioned out of any fund or funds not otherwise pledged.

Art. 51.11. Reward.

The Governor may offer a reward for the apprehension of one accused of a felony in this State who is evading arrest, by causing such offer to be published in such manner as he deems most likely to effect the arrest. The reward shall be paid out of the State Treasury to the person who becomes entitled to it upon a certificate of the Governor reciting the facts which entitle such person to receive it.

Art. 51.12. Sheriff to Report.

Each sheriff upon the close of any regular term of the district or criminal district court in his county, or within thirty days thereafter, shall make out and mail to the Director of the Department of Public Safety a certified list of all persons, who, after indictment for a felony, have fled from said county. Such lists shall contain the full name of each such fugitive, the offense with which he is charged, and a description giving his age, height, weight, color and occupation, the complexion of the skin and the color of eyes and hair, and any peculiarity in person, speech, manner or gait that may serve to identify such person so far as the sheriff may be able to give them. The Director of the Department of Public Safety shall prescribe and forward to all sheriffs the necessary blanks upon which are to be made the lists herein required.

Art. 51.13. Uniform Criminal Extradition Act.

Sec. 1. **Definitions. —** Where appearing in this Article, the term "Governor" includes any person performing the functions of Governor by authority of the laws of this State. The term "Executive Authority" includes the Governor, and any person performing the functions of Governor in a State other than this State, and the term "State", referring to a State other than this State, includes any other State organized or unorganized of the United States of America.

Sec. 2. **Fugitives from Justice; Duty of Governor.** — Subject to the provisions of this Article, the provisions of the Constitution of the United States controlling, and any and all Acts of Congress enacted in pursuance thereof, it is the duty of the Governor of this State to have arrested and delivered up to the Executive Authority of any other State of the United States any person charged in that State with treason, felony, or other crime, who has fled from justice and is found in this State.

Sec. 3. **Form of Demand.** — No demand for the extradition of a person charged with crime in another State shall be recognized by the Governor unless in writing, alleging, except in cases arising under Section 6, that the accused was present in the demanding State at the time of the commission of the alleged crime, and that thereafter he fled from the State, and accompanied by a copy of an indictment found or by information supported by affidavit in the State having jurisdiction of the crime, or by a copy of an affidavit before a magistrate there, together with a copy of any warrant which issued thereupon; or by a copy of a judgment of conviction or of a sentence imposed in execution thereof, together with a statement by the Executive Authority of the demanding State that the person claimed has escaped from confinement or has broken the terms of his bail, probation or parole. The indictment, information, or affidavit made before the magistrate must substantially charge the person demanded with having committed a crime under the law of that State; and the copy of indictment, information, affidavit, judgment of conviction or sentence must be authenticated by the Executive Authority making the demand; provided, however, that all such copies of the aforesaid instruments shall be in duplicate, one complete set of such instruments to be delivered to the defendant or to his attorney.

Sec. 4. **Governor May Investigate Case.** — When a demand shall be made upon the Governor of this State by the Executive Authority of another State for the surrender of a person so charged with crime, the Governor may call upon the Secretary of State, Attorney General or any prosecuting officer in this State to investigate or assist in investigating the demand, and to report to him the situation and circumstances of the person so demanded, and whether he ought to be surrendered.

Sec. 5. **Extradition of Persons Imprisoned or Awaiting Trial in Another State or Who Have Left the Demanding State Under Compulsion.** — When it is desired to have returned to this State a person charged in this State with a crime, and such person is imprisoned or is held under criminal proceedings then pending against him in another State, the Governor of this State may agree with the Executive Authority of such other State for the extradition of such person before the conclusion of such proceedings or his term of sentence in such other State, upon condition that such person be returned to such other State at the expense of this State as soon as the prosecution in this State is terminated.

The Governor of this State may also surrender on demand of the Executive Authority of any other State any person in this State who is charged in the manner provided in Section 23 of this Act with having violated the laws of the State whose Executive Authority is making the demand, even though such person left the demanding State involuntarily.

Sec. 6. **Extradition of Persons Not Present in Demanding State at Time of Commission of Crime.** — The Governor of this State may also surrender, on demand of the Executive Authority of any other State, any person in this State charged in such other State in the manner provided in Section 3 with committing an act in this State, or in a third State, intentionally resulting in a crime in the State whose Executive Authority is making the demand, and the provisions of this Article not otherwise inconsistent, shall apply to such cases, even though the accused was not in that State at the time of the commission of the crime, and has not fled therefrom.

Sec. 7. **Issue of Governor's Warrant of Arrest; Its Recitals.** — If the Governor decides that the demand should be complied with, he shall sign a warrant of arrest, which shall be sealed with the state seal and be directed to any peace officer or other person whom he may think fit to entrust with the execution thereof. The warrant must substantially recite the facts necessary to the validity of its issuance.

Sec. 8. **Manner and Place of Execution.** — Such warrant shall authorize the peace officer or other person to whom directed to arrest the accused at any time and any place where he may be found within the State and to command the aid of all peace officers and other persons in the execution of the warrant, and to deliver the accused, subject to the provisions of this Article to the duly authorized agent of the demanding State.

Sec. 9. **Authority of Arresting Officer.** — Every such peace officer or other person empowered

Code of Criminal Procedure

to make the arrest, shall have the same authority, in arresting the accused, to command assistance therein, as peace officers have by law in the execution of any criminal process directed to them, with like penalties against those who refuse their assistance.

Sec. 10. **Rights of Accused Person; Application for Writ of Habeas Corpus.**

(a) No person arrested upon such warrant shall be delivered over to the agent whom the Executive Authority demanding him shall have appointed to receive him unless he shall first be taken forthwith before a judge of a court of record in this State, or before a justice of the peace serving a precinct that is located in a county bordering another state, who shall inform him of the demand made for his surrender and of the crime with which he is charged, and that he has the right to demand and procure legal counsel; and if the prisoner or his counsel shall state that he or they desire to test the legality of his arrest, the judge of the court of record shall fix a reasonable time to be allowed the prisoner in which to apply for a writ of habeas corpus, or the justice of the peace shall direct the prisoner to a court of record for purposes of obtaining such a writ. When the writ is applied for, notice thereof, and of the time and place of hearing thereon, shall be given to the prosecuting officer of the county in which the arrest is made and in which the accused is in custody, and to the said agent of the demanding State.

(b) Before a justice of the peace who is not an attorney may perform a duty or function permitted by Subsection (a), the justice must take, through the Texas Justice Court Training Center, a training course that focuses on extradition law. The center shall develop a course to satisfy the requirements of this subsection.

(c) Each justice of the peace who performs a duty or function permitted by Subsection (a) shall ensure that the applicable proceeding is transcribed or videotaped and that the record of the proceeding is retained in the records of the court for at least 270 days.

Sec. 11. **Penalty for Non-Compliance with Preceding Section.** — Any officer who shall deliver to the agent for extradition of the demanding State a person in his custody under the Governor's warrant, in wilful disobedience to Section 10 of this Act, shall be guilty of a misdemeanor and, on conviction, shall be fined not more than one thousand dollars or be imprisoned not more than six months, or both.

Sec. 12. **Confinement in Jail, When Necessary.** — The officer or persons executing the Governor's warrant of arrest, or the agent of the demanding State to whom the prisoner may have been delivered may, when necessary, confine the prisoner in the jail of any county or city through which he may pass; and the keeper of such jail must receive and safely keep the prisoner until the officer or person having charge of him is ready to proceed on his route, such officer or person being chargeable with the expense of keeping.

The officer or agent of a demanding State to whom a prisoner may have been delivered following extradition proceedings in another State, or to whom a prisoner may have been delivered after waiving extradition in such other State, and who is passing through this State with such a prisoner for the purpose of immediately returning such prisoner to the demanding State may, when necessary, confine the prisoner in the jail of any county or city through which he may pass; and the keeper of such jail must receive and safely keep the prisoner until the officer or agent having charge of him is ready to proceed on his route, such officer or agent, however, being chargeable with the expense of keeping; provided, however, that such officer or agent shall produce and show to the keeper of such jail satisfactory written evidence of the fact that he is actually transporting such prisoner to the demanding State after a requisition by the Executive Authority of such demanding State. Such prisoner shall not be entitled to demand a new requisition while in this State.

Sec. 13. **Arrest Prior to Requisition.** — Whenever any person within this State shall be charged on the oath of any credible person before any judge or magistrate of this State with the commission of any crime in any other State and except in cases arising under Section 6, with having fled from justice, or with having been convicted of a crime in that State and having escaped from confinement, or having broken the terms of his bail, probation or parole, or whenever complaint shall have been made before any judge or magistrate in this State setting forth on the affidavit of any credible person in another State that a crime has been committed in such other State and that the accused has been charged in such State with the commission of the crime, and except in cases arising under Section 6, has fled from justice, or with having been convicted of a crime in that State and having escaped from confinement, or having broken the terms of his bail, probation or parole and is believed to be in this State, the judge or magistrate shall issue a warrant directed to any peace officer commanding him to apprehend the person named therein, wherever he may be found in this State, and to bring him before the same or any other judge, magistrate or court who or which may be available in or convenient of access to the place where the arrest may be made, to answer the charge or complaint and affidavit, and a certified copy of the sworn charge or complaint and affidavit upon which the warrant is issued shall be attached to the warrant.

Sec. 14. **Arrest Without a Warrant. —** The arrest of a person may be lawfully made also by any peace officer or private person, without a warrant upon reasonable information that the accused stands charged in the courts of a State with a crime punishable by death or imprisonment for a term exceeding one year, but when so arrested the accused must be taken before a judge or magistrate with all practicable speed and complaint must be made against him under oath setting forth the ground for the arrest as in the preceding section; and thereafter his answer shall be heard as if he had been arrested on a warrant.

Sec. 15. **Commitment to Await Requisition; Bail. —** If from the examination before the judge or magistrate it appears that the person held is the person charged with having committed the crime alleged and except in cases arising under Section 6, that he has fled from justice, the judge or magistrate must, by warrant reciting the accusation, commit him to the county jail for such time not exceeding thirty days and specified in the warrant, as will enable the arrest of the accused to be made under a warrant of the Governor on a requisition of the Executive Authority of the State having jurisdiction of the offense, unless the accused give bail as provided in the next section, or until he shall be legally discharged.

Sec. 16. **Bail; in What Cases; Conditions of Bond. —** Unless the offense with which the prisoner is charged is shown to be an offense punishable by death or life imprisonment under the laws of the State in which it was committed, a judge or magistrate in this State may admit the person arrested to bail by bond, with sufficient sureties and in such sum as he deems proper, conditioned for his appearance before him at a time specified in such bond, and for his surrender, to be arrested upon the warrant of the Governor in this State.

Sec. 17. **Extension of Time of Commitment; Adjournment. —** If the accused is not arrested under warrant of the Governor by the expiration of the time specified in the warrant or bond, a judge or magistrate may discharge him or may recommit him for a further period not to exceed sixty days, or a judge or magistrate may again take bail for his appearance and surrender, as provided in Section 16, but within a period not to exceed sixty days after the date of such new bond.

Sec. 18. **Forfeiture of Bail. —** If the prisoner is admitted to bail and fails to appear and surrender himself according to the conditions of his bond, the judge, or magistrate by proper order, shall declare the bond forfeited and order his immediate arrest without warrant if he be within this State. Recovery may be had on such bond in the name of the State as in the case of other bonds given by the accused in criminal proceedings within this State.

Sec. 19. **Persons Under Criminal Prosecution in This State at the Time of Requisition. —** If a criminal prosecution has been instituted against such person under the laws of this State and is still pending, the Governor, in his discretion, either may surrender him on demand of the Executive Authority of another State or hold him until he has been tried and discharged or convicted and punished in this State.

Sec. 20. **Guilt or Innocence of Accused, When Inquired into. —** The guilt or innocence of the accused as to the crime of which he is charged may not be inquired into by the Governor or in any proceeding after the demand for extradition accompanied by a charge of crime in legal form as above provided shall have been presented to the Governor, except as it may be involved in identifying the person held as the person charged with the crime.

Sec. 21. **Governor May Recall Warrant or Issue Alias. —** The governor may recall his warrant of the arrest or may issue another warrant whenever he deems proper. Each warrant issued by the Governor shall expire and be of no force and effect when not executed within one year from the date thereof.

Sec. 22. **Fugitives from This State; Duty of Governor. —** Whenever the Governor of this State shall demand a person charged with crime or with escaping from confinement or breaking the terms of his bail, probation or parole in this State, from the Executive Authority of any other State, or from the Chief Justice or an Associate Justice of the Supreme Court of the District of Columbia authorized to receive such demand under the laws of the United States, he shall issue a warrant under the state seal, to some agent, commanding him to receive the person so charged if delivered to him and convey him to the proper officer of the county in this State in which the offense was committed, or in which the prosecution for such offense is then pending.

Sec. 23. **Application for Issuance of Requisition; by Whom Made; Contents.**

1. When the return to this State of a person charged with crime in this State is required, the State's attorney shall present to the Governor his written motion for a requisition for the return of the person charged, in which motion shall be stated the name of the person so charged, the crime

Code of Criminal Procedure

charged against him, the approximate time, place and circumstances of its commission, the State in which he is believed to be, including the location of the accused therein at the time the motion is made and certifying that, in the opinion of the said State's attorney the ends of justice require the arrest and return of the accused to this State for trial and that the proceeding is not instituted to enforce a private claim.

2. When the return to this State is required of a person who has been convicted of a crime in this State and has escaped from confinement, or broken the terms of his bail, probation or parole, the prosecuting attorney of the county in which the offense was committed, the parole board, or the warden of the institution or sheriff of the county, from which escape was made, shall present to the Governor a written application for a requisition for the return of such person, in which application shall be stated the name of the person, the crime of which he was convicted, the circumstances of his escape from confinement, or the circumstances of the breach of the terms of his bail, probation or parole, the State in which he is believed to be, including the location of the person therein at the time application is made.

3. The application shall be verified by affidavit, shall be executed in duplicate and shall be accompanied by two certified copies of the indictment returned, or information and affidavit filed, or of the complaint made to the judge or magistrate, stating the offense with which the accused is charged, or of the judgment of conviction or of the sentence. The prosecuting officer, parole board, warden or sheriff may also attach such further affidavits and other documents in duplicate as he shall deem proper to be submitted with such application. One copy of the application, with the action of the Governor indicated by endorsement thereon, and one of the certified copies of the indictment, complaint, information, and affidavits, or of the judgment of conviction or of the sentence shall be filed in the office of the Governor. The other copies of all papers shall be forwarded with the Governor's requisition.

Sec. 24. **Costs and Expenses. —** In all cases of extradition, the commissioners court of the county where an offense is alleged to have been committed, or in which the prosecution is then pending may in its discretion, on request of the sheriff and the recommendation of the prosecuting attorney, pay the actual and necessary expenses of the officer or person commissioned to receive the person charged, out of any county fund or funds not otherwise pledged.

Sec. 25. **Immunity from Service of Process in Certain Civil Cases. —** A person brought into this State by, or after waiver of, extradition based on a criminal charge shall not be subject to service of personal process in civil actions arising out of the same facts as the criminal proceeding to answer which he is being or has been returned, until he has been convicted in the criminal proceeding, or if acquitted, until he has had reasonable opportunity to return to the State from which he was extradited.

Sec. 25a. **Written Waiver of Extradition Proceedings.**

(a) Any person arrested in this State charged with having committed any crime in another State or alleged to have escaped from confinement, or broken the terms of his bail, probation, or parole may waive the issuance and service of the warrant provided for in Sections 7 and 8 and all other procedure incidental to extradition proceedings, by executing or subscribing in the presence of a judge or any court of record within this State, or in the presence of a justice of the peace serving a precinct that is located in a county bordering another state, a writing which states that the arrested person consents to return to the demanding State; provided, however, that before such waiver shall be executed or subscribed by such person the judge or justice of the peace shall inform such person of his:

(1) right to the issuance and service of a warrant of extradition; and

(2) right to obtain a writ of habeas corpus as provided for in Section 10.

If and when such consent has been duly executed it shall forthwith be forwarded to the office of the Governor of this State and filed therein. The judge or justice of the peace shall direct the officer having such person in custody to deliver forthwith such person to the duly accredited agent or agents of the demanding State, and shall deliver or cause to be delivered to such agent or agents a copy of such consent; provided, however, that nothing in this section shall be deemed to limit the rights of the accused person to return voluntarily and without formality to the demanding State, nor shall this waiver procedure be deemed to be an exclusive procedure or to limit the powers, rights or duties of the officers of the demanding State or of this State.

(b) Before a justice of the peace who is not an attorney may perform a duty or function permitted by Subsection (a), the justice must take, through the Texas Justice Court Training Center, a training course that focuses on extradition law. The center shall develop a course to satisfy the requirements of this subsection.

(c) Each justice of the peace who performs a duty or function permitted by Subsection (a) shall ensure that the applicable proceeding is transcribed or videotaped and that the record of the proceeding is retained in the records of the court for at least 270 days.

Sec. 25b. **Non-Waiver by This State.** — Nothing in this Act contained shall be deemed to constitute a waiver by this State of its right, power or privilege to try such demanded person for crime committed within this State, or of its right, power or privilege to regain custody of such person by extradition proceedings or otherwise for the purpose of trial, sentence or punishment for any crime committed within this State, nor shall any proceedings had under this Article which result, or fail to result in, extradition to be deemed a waiver by this State of any of its rights, privileges or jurisdiction in any way whatsoever.

Sec. 26. **No Right of Asylum, No Immunity from Other Criminal Prosecutions While in This State.** — After a person has been brought back to this State by, or after waiver of extradition proceedings, he may be tried in this State for other crimes which he may be charged with having committed here as well as that specified in the requisition for his extradition.

Sec. 27. **Interpretation.** — The provisions of this Article shall be interpreted and construed as to effectuate its general purposes to make uniform the law of those States which enact it.

Art. 51.14. Interstate Agreement on Detainers.

This article may be cited as the "Interstate Agreement on Detainers Act." This agreement on detainers is hereby enacted into law and entered into by this state with all other jurisdictions legally joined therein in the form substantially as follows:

The contracting states solemnly agree that:

ARTICLE I.

The party states find that charges outstanding against a prisoner, detainers based on untried indictments, informations, or complaints, and difficulties in securing speedy trial of persons already incarcerated in other jurisdictions, produce uncertainties which obstruct programs of prisoner treatment and rehabilitation. Accordingly, it is the policy of the party states and the purpose of this agreement to encourage the expeditious and orderly disposition of such charges and determination of the proper status of any and all detainers based on untried indictments, informations, or complaints. The party states also find that proceedings with reference to such charges and detainers, when emanating from another jurisdiction, cannot properly be had in the absence of cooperative procedures. It is the further purpose of this agreement to provide such cooperative procedures.

ARTICLE II.

As used is this agreement:

(a) "State" shall mean a state of the United States; the United States of America; a territory or possession of the United States; the District of Columbia; the Commonwealth of Puerto Rico.

(b) "Sending state" shall mean a state in which a prisoner is incarcerated at the time that he initiates a request for final disposition pursuant to Article III hereof or at the time that a request for custody or availability is initiated pursuant to Article IV hereof.

ARTICLE III.

(a) Whenever a person has entered upon a term of imprisonment in a penal or correctional institution of a party state, and whenever during the continuance of the term of imprisonment there is pending in any other party state any untried indictment, information, or complaint on the basis of which a detainer has been lodged against the prisoner, he shall be brought to trial within 180 days after he shall have caused to be delivered to the prosecuting officer and the appropriate court of the prosecuting officer's jurisdiction written notice of the place of his imprisonment and his request for a final disposition to be made of the indictment, information, or complaint; provided that for good cause shown in open court, the prisoner or his counsel being present, the court having jurisdiction of the matter may grant any necessary or reasonable continuance. The request of the prisoner shall be accompanied by a certificate of the appropriate official having custody of the prisoner, stating the term of commitment under which the prisoner is being held, the time already served, the time remaining to be served on the sentence, the amount of good time earned, the time of parole eligibility of the prisoner, and any decision of the state parole agency relating to the prisoner.

(b) The written notice and request for final disposition referred to in Paragraph (a) hereof shall be given or sent by the prisoner to the warden, commissioner of corrections, or other official having custody of him, who shall promptly forward it together with the certificate to the appropriate prosecuting official and court by registered or certified mail, return receipt requested.

(c) The warden, commissioner of corrections, or other official having custody of the prisoner shall promptly inform him of the source and contents of any detainer lodged against him and shall also inform him of his right to make a request for final disposition of the indictment, information, or complaint on which the detainer is based.

(d) Any request for final disposition made by a prisoner pursuant to Paragraph (a) hereof shall operate as a request for final disposition of all untried indictments, informations, or complaints on the basis of which detainers have been lodged against the prisoner from the state to whose prosecuting official the request for final disposition is specifically directed. The warden, commissioner of corrections, or other official having custody of the prisoner shall forthwith notify all appropriate prosecuting officers and courts in the several jurisdictions within the state to which the prisoner's request for final disposition is being sent of the proceeding being initiated by the prisoner. Any notification sent pursuant to this paragraph shall be accompanied by copies of the prisoner's written notice, request, and the certificate. If trial is not had on any indictment, information, or complaint contemplated hereby prior to the return of the prisoner to the original place of imprisonment, such indictment, information, or complaint shall not be of any further force or effect, and the court shall enter an order dismissing the same with prejudice.

(e) Any request for final disposition made by a prisoner pursuant to Paragraph (a) hereof shall also be deemed to be a waiver of extradition with respect to any charge or proceeding contemplated thereby or included therein by reason of Paragraph (d) hereof, and a waiver of extradition to the receiving state to serve any sentence there imposed upon him after completion of his term of imprisonment in the sending state. The request for final disposition shall also constitute a consent by the prisoner to the production of his body in any court where his presence may be required in order to effectuate the purposes of this agreement and a further consent voluntarily to be returned to the original place of imprisonment in accordance with the provisions of this agreement. Nothing in this paragraph shall prevent the imposition of a concurrent sentence if otherwise permitted by law.

(f) Escape from custody by the prisoner subsequent to his execution of the request for final disposition referred to in Paragraph (a) hereof shall void the request.

ARTICLE IV.

(a) The appropriate officer of the jurisdiction in which an untried indictment, information, or complaint is pending shall be entitled to have a prisoner against whom he has lodged a detainer and who is serving a term of imprisonment in any party state made available in accordance with Paragraph (a) of Article V hereof upon presentation of a written request for temporary custody or availability to the appropriate authorities of the state in which the prisoner is incarcerated; provided that the court having jurisdiction of such indictment, information, or complaint shall have duly approved, recorded, and transmitted the request; and provided further that there shall be a period of 30 days after receipt by the appropriate authorities before the request be honored, within which period the governor of the sending state may disapprove the request for temporary custody or availability, either upon his own motion or upon motion of the prisoner.

(b) Upon receipt of the officer's written request as provided in Paragraph (a) hereof, the appropriate authorities having the prisoner in custody shall furnish the officer with a certificate stating the term of commitment under which the prisoner is being held, the time already served, the time remaining to be served on the sentence, the amount of good time earned, the time of parole eligibility of the prisoner, and any decisions of the state parole agency relating to the prisoner. Said authorities simultaneously shall furnish all other officers and appropriate courts in the receiving state who have lodged detainers against the prisoner with similar certificates and with notices informing them of the request for custody or availability and of the reasons therefor.

(c) In respect of any proceeding made possible by this article, trial shall be commenced within 120 days of the arrival of the prisoner in the receiving state, but for good cause shown in open court, the prisoner or his counsel being present, the court having jurisdiction of the matter may grant any necessary or reasonable continuance.

(d) Nothing contained in this article shall be construed to deprive any prisoner of any right which he may have to contest the legality of his delivery as provided in Paragraph (a) hereof, but such delivery may not be opposed or denied on the ground that the executing authority of the sending state has not affirmatively consented to or ordered such delivery.

(e) If trial is not had on any indictment, information, or complaint contemplated hereby prior to the prisoner's being returned to the original place of imprisonment pursuant to Paragraph (e) of Article V hereof, such indictment, information, or complaint shall not be of any further force or effect, and the court shall enter an order dismissing the same with prejudice.

ARTICLE V.

(a) In response to a request made under Article III or Article IV hereof, the appropriate authority in a sending state shall offer to deliver temporary custody of such prisoner to the appropriate authority in the state where such indictment, information, or complaint is pending against such person in order that speedy and efficient prosecution may be had. If the request for final disposition is made by the prisoner, the offer of temporary custody shall accompany the written notice provided for in Article III of this agreement. In the case of a federal prisoner, the appropriate authority in the receiving state shall be entitled to temporary custody as provided by this agreement or to the prisoner's presence in federal custody at the place of trial, whichever custodial arrangement may be approved by the custodian.

(b) The officer or other representative of a state accepting an offer of temporary custody shall present the following upon demand:

(1) proper identification and evidence of his authority to act for the state into whose temporary custody this prisoner is to be given;

(2) a duly certified copy of the indictment, information, or complaint on the basis of which the detainer has been lodged and on the basis of which the request for temporary custody of the prisoner has been made.

(c) If the appropriate authority shall refuse or fail to accept temporary custody of said person, or in the event that an action on the indictment, information, or complaint on the basis of which the detainer has been lodged is not brought to trial within the period provided in Article III or Article IV hereof, the appropriate court of the jurisdiction where the indictment, information, or complaint has been pending shall enter an order dismissing the same with prejudice, and any detainer based thereon shall cease to be of any force or effect.

(d) The temporary custody referred to in this agreement shall be only for the purpose of permitting prosecution on the charge or charges contained in one or more untried indictments, informations, or complaints which form the basis of the detainer or detainers or for prosecution on any other charge or charges arising out of the same transaction. Except for his attendance at court and while being transported to or from any place at which his presence may be required, the prisoner shall be held in a suitable jail or other facility regularly used for persons awaiting prosecution.

(e) At the earliest practicable time consonant with the purposes of this agreement, the prisoner shall be returned to the sending state.

(f) During the continuance of temporary custody or while the prisoner is otherwise being made available for trial as required by this agreement, time being served on the sentence shall continue to run but good time shall be earned by the prisoner only if, and to the extent that, the law and practice of the jurisdiction which imposed the sentence may allow.

(g) For all purposes other than that for which temporary custody as provided in this agreement is exercised, the prisoner shall be deemed to remain in the custody of and subject to the jurisdiction of the sending state and any escape from temporary custody may be dealt with in the same manner as an escape from the original place of imprisonment or in any other manner permitted by law.

(h) From the time that a party state receives custody of a prisoner pursuant to this agreement until such prisoner is returned to the territory and custody of the sending state, the state in which the one or more untried indictments, informations, or complaints are pending or in which trial is being had shall be responsible for the prisoner and shall also pay all costs of transporting, caring for, keeping, and returning the prisoner. The provisions of this paragraph shall govern unless the states concerned shall have entered into a supplementary agreement providing for a different allocation of costs and responsibilities as between or among themselves. Nothing herein contained shall be construed to alter or affect any internal relationship among the departments, agencies, and officers of and in the government of a party state, or between a party state and its subdivisions, as to the payment of costs, or responsibilities therefor.

ARTICLE VI.

(a) In determining the duration and expiration dates of the time periods provided in Articles III and IV of this agreement, the running of said time periods shall be tolled whenever and for as long as the prisoner is unable to stand trial, as determined by the court having jurisdiction of the matter.

(b) No provision of this agreement, and no remedy made available by this agreement shall apply to any person who is adjudged to be mentally ill.

ARTICLE VII.

Each state party to this agreement shall designate an officer who, acting jointly with like officers of other party states, shall promulgate rules and regulations to carry out more effectively the terms and provisions of this agreement, and who shall provide, within and without the state, information necessary to the effective operation of this agreement.

ARTICLE VIII.

This agreement shall enter into full force and effect as to a party state when such state has enacted the same into law. A state party to this agreement may withdraw herefrom by enacting a statute repealing the same. However, the withdrawal of any state shall not affect the status of any proceedings already initiated by inmates or by state officers at the time such withdrawal takes effect, nor shall it affect their rights in respect thereof.

ARTICLE IX.

(a) This agreement shall be liberally construed so as to effectuate its purposes. The provisions of this agreement shall be severable and if any phrase, clause, sentence, or provision of this agreement is declared to be contrary to the constitution of any party state or of the United States or the applicability thereof to any government, agency, person, or circumstance is held invalid, the validity of the remainder of this agreement and the applicability thereof to any government, agency, person, or circumstance shall not be affected thereby. If this agreement shall be held contrary to the constitution of any state party hereto, the agreement shall remain in full force and effect as to the remaining states and in full force and effect as to the state affected as to all severable matters.

(b) As used in this article, "appropriate court" means a court of record with criminal jurisdiction.

(c) All courts, departments, agencies, officers, and employees of this state and its political subdivisions are hereby directed to enforce this article and to cooperate with one another and with other party states in enforcing the agreement and effectuating its purpose.

(d) Any prisoner escapes from lawful custody while in another state as a result of the application of this article shall be punished as though such escape had occurred within this state.

(e) The governor is empowered to designate the officer who will serve as central administrator of and information agent for the agreement on detainers pursuant to the provisions of Article VII hereof.

(f) Copies of this article, upon its enactment, shall be transmitted to the governor of each state, the Attorney General and the Secretary of State of the United States, and the council of state governments.

CHAPTER 52
COURT OF INQUIRY

Art. 52.01. Courts of Inquiry Conducted by District Judges.

(a) When a judge of any district court of this state, acting in his capacity as magistrate, has probable cause to believe that an offense has been committed against the laws of this state, he may request that the presiding judge of the administrative judicial district appoint a district judge to commence a Court of Inquiry. The judge, who shall be appointed in accordance with Subsection (b), may summon and examine any witness in relation to the offense in accordance with the rules hereinafter provided, which procedure is defined as a "Court of Inquiry".

(b) (1) Before requesting the presiding judge to appoint a district judge to commence a Court of Inquiry, a judge must enter into the minutes of his court a sworn affidavit stating the substantial facts establishing probable cause that a specific offense has been committed against the laws of this state.

(2) After the affidavit has been entered into the minutes of his court and a copy filed with the district clerk, the judge shall request the presiding judge of the administrative judicial district in which the affidavit is filed to appoint a judge to commence the Court of Inquiry. The judge appointed to commence the Court of Inquiry shall issue a written order commencing the Court of Inquiry and stating its scope. The presiding judge shall not name the judge who requests the Court of Inquiry to preside over the Court of Inquiry.

(c) The district or county attorney of the district or county in which the Court of Inquiry is held shall assist the district judge in conducting the Court of Inquiry. The attorney shall examine witnesses and evidence admitted before the court to determine if an offense has been committed and shall render other assistance to the judge as is necessary in the proceeding.

(d) If the Court of Inquiry pertains to the activities of the district or county attorney or to the attorney's office, deputies, or employees, or if the attorney is otherwise disqualified in the proceeding, the judge shall appoint one attorney pro tem to assist in the proceeding. In any other circumstance, the judge may appoint an attorney pro tem to assist in the proceeding.

(e) If more than one Court of Inquiry is commenced which pertains to the activities of a state governmental entity or public servant thereof, then, upon motion of the state governmental entity or public servant, made to the presiding judge or judges of the administrative judicial region or regions where the Courts of Inquiry have been commenced, the presiding judge or judges shall transfer the Courts of Inquiry to the presiding administrative judge of Travis County. The presiding administrative judge of Travis County shall consolidate the Courts of Inquiry for further proceedings and shall assign a district judge to preside over the consolidated Courts of Inquiry.

Art. 52.02. Evidence; Deposition; Affidavits.

At the hearing at a Court of Inquiry, evidence may be taken orally or by deposition, or, in the discretion of the judge, by affidavit. If affidavits are admitted, any witness against whom they may bear has the right to propound written interrogatories to the affiants or to file answering affidavits. The judge in hearing such evidence, at his discretion, may conclude not to sustain objections to all or to any portion of the evidence taken nor exclude same; but any of the witnesses or attorneys engaged in taking the testimony may have any objections they make recorded with the testimony and reserved for the action of any court in which such evidence is thereafter sought to be admitted, but such court is not confined to objections made at the taking of the testimony at the Court of Inquiry. Without restricting the foregoing, the judge may allow the introduction of any documentary or real evidence which he deems reliable, and the testimony adduced before any grand jury.

Art. 52.03. Subpoenas.

The judge or his clerk has power to issue subpoenas which may be served within the same territorial limits as subpoenas issued in felony prosecutions or to summon witnesses before grand juries in this state.

Art. 52.04. Rights of Witnesses.

(a) All witnesses testifying in any Court of Inquiry have the same rights as to testifying as do defendants in felony prosecutions in this state. Before any witness is sworn to testify in any Court of Inquiry, he shall be instructed by the judge that he is entitled to counsel; that he cannot be forced to testify against himself; and that such testimony may be taken down and used against him in a later trial or trials ensuing from the instant Court of Inquiry. Any witness or his counsel has the right to fully cross-examine any of the witnesses whose testimony bears in any manner against him.

(b) If the Court of Inquiry pertains to the activities of a state governmental entity or its officers or employees, the officers and employees of that state governmental entity shall be indemnified for attorney's fees incurred as a result of exercising the employees' or officers' right to counsel under Subsection (a) if:

(1) the officer or employee is found not guilty after a trial or appeal or the complaint, information, or indictment is dismissed without a plea of guilty or nolo contendere being entered; and

(2) the judge commencing the Court of Inquiry, or the judge to whom the Court of Inquiry was transferred pursuant to Article 52.01(e), determines that the complaint, information, or indictment presented against the person was dismissed because:

(A) the presentment was made on mistake, false information, or other similar basis, indicating absence of probable cause to believe, at the time of dismissal, the person committed the offense; or

(B) the complaint, information, or indictment was void.

(c) The county in which the affidavit under Article 52.01 was filed shall be responsible for any attorney's fees awarded under Subsection (b).

Art. 52.05. Witness Must Testify.

A person may be compelled to give testimony or produce evidence when legally called upon to do so at any Court of Inquiry; however, if any person refuses or declines to testify or produce evidence on the ground that it may incriminate him under laws of this state, then the judge may, in his discretion, compel such person to testify or produce evidence but the person shall not be prosecuted or subjected to any penalty or forfeiture for, or on account of, any transaction, matter or thing concerning which he may be compelled to testify or produce evidence at such Court of Inquiry.

Art. 52.06. Contempt.

Contempt of court in a Court of Inquiry may be punished by a fine not exceeding One Hundred Dollars ($100.00) and any witness refusing to testify may be attached and imprisoned until he does testify.

Art. 52.07. Stenographic Record; Public Hearing.

All evidence taken at a Court of Inquiry shall be transcribed by the court reporter and all proceedings shall be open to the public.

Art. 52.08. Criminal Prosecutions.

If it appear from a Court of Inquiry or any testimony adduced therein, that an offense has been committed, the Judge shall issue a warrant for the arrest of the offender as if complaint had been made and filed.

Art. 52.09. Costs and Attorney's Fees.

(a) All costs incurred in conducting a Court of Inquiry, including compensation of an attorney pro tem, shall be borne by the county in which said Court of Inquiry is conducted; provided, however, that where the Attorney General of Texas has submitted a request in writing to the judge for the holding of such Court of Inquiry, then and in that event the costs shall be borne by the State of Texas and shall be taxed to the attorney general and paid in the same manner and from the same funds as other court costs.

(b) Assistance by a county or district attorney to a Court of Inquiry is a duty of the attorney's office, and the attorney may not receive a fee for the service. A county is not liable for attorney's fees claimed for assistance in a Court of Inquiry by any attorney other than an attorney pro tem appointed under Article 52.01(d) of this code.

(c) An attorney pro tem appointed under Article 52.01(d) is entitled to compensation in the same amount and manner as an attorney appointed to represent an indigent person. The district judge shall set the compensation of the attorney pro tem based on the sworn testimony of the attorney or other evidence that is given in open court.

CHAPTER 53 COSTS AND FEES [REPEALED]

Art. 53.01. Peace Officers [Repealed].

Repealed by Acts 1987, 70th Leg., ch. 167 (S.B. 892), § 4.01(b) effective September 1, 1987.

Art. 53.02. Fees of Peace Officers [Repealed].

Repealed by Acts 1985, 69th Leg., ch. 269 (S.B. 854), § 5(1) effective September 1, 1985.

Art. 53.03. Fee of State's Attorney [Repealed].

Repealed by Acts 1987, 70th Leg., ch. 167 (S.B. 892), § 4.01(b) effective September 1, 1987.

Art. 53.04. Officers in Examining Court [Repealed].

Repealed by Acts 1987, 70th Leg., ch. 167 (S.B. 892), § 4.01(b) effective September 1, 1987.

Art. 53.05. In District and County Courts [Repealed].

Repealed by Acts 1987, 70th Leg., ch. 167 (S.B. 892), § 4.01(b) effective September 1, 1987.

Art. 53.06. Trial Fee [Repealed].

Repealed by Acts 1987, 70th Leg., ch. 167 (S.B. 892), § 4.01(b) effective September 1, 1987.

Art. 53.07. Justice of Peace Salary [Repealed].

Repealed by Acts 1985, 69th Leg., ch. 269 (S.B. 854), § 5(1) effective September 1, 1985.

Art. 53.08. Fee for Collecting and Processing Sight Order [Repealed].

Repealed by Acts 1987, 70th Leg., ch. 167 (S.B. 892), § 4.01(b) effective September 1, 1987.

Art. 53.09. Justice of Peace Costs in Counties over Two Million [Repealed].

Repealed by Acts 1987, 70th Leg., ch. 167 (S.B. 892), § 4.01(b) effective September 1, 1987.

Art. 53.10. [Blank].

Art. 53.11. Fees in Proceedings for Expunction of Criminal Records [Repealed].

Repealed by Acts 1987, 70th Leg., ch. 167 (S.B. 892), § 4.01(b) effective September 1, 1987.

CHAPTER 54 MISCELLANEOUS PROVISIONS [REPEALED]

Art. 54.01. Severability Clause. [Repealed]

Art. 54.02. Repealing Clause. [Repealed]

Art. 54.03. Emergency Clause. [Repealed]

CHAPTER 55 EXPUNCTION OF CRIMINAL RECORDS

Art. 55.01. Right to Expunction.

(a) A person who has been placed under a custodial or noncustodial arrest for commission of either a felony or misdemeanor is entitled to have all records and files relating to the arrest expunged if:

(1) the person is tried for the offense for which the person was arrested and is:

(A) acquitted by the trial court, except as provided by Subsection (c);

(B) convicted and subsequently:

(i) pardoned for a reason other than that described by Subparagraph (ii); or

(ii) pardoned or otherwise granted relief on the basis of actual innocence with respect to that offense, if the applicable pardon or court order clearly indicates on its face that the pardon or order was granted or rendered on the basis of the person's actual innocence; or

(C) convicted of an offense committed before September 1, 2021, under Section 46.02(a), Penal Code, as that section existed before that date; or

(2) the person has been released and the charge, if any, has not resulted in a final conviction and is no longer pending and there was no court-ordered community supervision under Chapter 42A for the offense, unless the offense is a Class C misdemeanor, provided that:

(A) regardless of whether any statute of limitations exists for the offense and whether any limitations period for the offense has expired, an indictment or information charging the person with the commission of a misdemeanor offense based on the person's arrest or charging the person with the commission of any felony offense arising out of the same transaction for which the person was arrested:

(i) has not been presented against the person at any time following the arrest, and:

(a) at least 180 days have elapsed from the date of arrest if the arrest for which the expunction was sought was for an offense punishable as a Class C misdemeanor and if there was no felony charge arising out of the same transaction for which the person was arrested;

(b) at least one year has elapsed from the date of arrest if the arrest for which the expunction was sought was for an offense punishable as a Class B or A misdemeanor and if there was no felony charge arising out of the same transaction for which the person was arrested;

(c) at least three years have elapsed from the date of arrest if the arrest for which the expunction was sought was for an offense punishable as a felony or if there was a felony charge arising out of the same transaction for which the person was arrested; or

(d) the attorney representing the state certifies that the applicable arrest records and files are not needed for use in any criminal investigation or prosecution, including an investigation or prosecution of another person; or

(ii) if presented at any time following the arrest, was dismissed or quashed, and the court finds that the indictment or information was dismissed or quashed because:

(a) the person completed a veterans treatment court program created under Chapter 124, Government Code, or former law, subject to Subsection (a-3);

(b) the person completed a mental health court program created under Chapter 125, Government Code, or former law, subject to Subsection (a-4);

(c) the person completed a pretrial intervention program authorized under Section 76.011, Government Code, other than a veterans treatment court program created under Chapter 124, Government Code, or former law, or a mental health court program created under Chapter 125, Government Code, or former law;

(d) the presentment had been made because of mistake, false information, or other similar reason indicating absence of probable cause at the time of the dismissal to believe the person committed the offense; or

(e) the indictment or information was void; or

(B) prosecution of the person for the offense for which the person was arrested is no longer possible because the limitations period has expired.

(a-1) Notwithstanding any other provision of this article, a person may not expunge records and files relating to an arrest that occurs pursuant to a warrant issued under Article 42A.751(b).

(a-2) Notwithstanding any other provision of this article, a person who intentionally or knowingly absconds from the jurisdiction after being released under Chapter 17 following an arrest is not eligible under Subsection (a)(2)(A)(i)(a), (b), or (c) or Subsection (a)(2)(B) for an expunction of the records and files relating to that arrest.

(a-3) A person is eligible under Subsection (a)(2)(A)(ii)(a) for an expunction of arrest records and files only if:

(1) the person has not previously received an expunction of arrest records and files under that subsubparagraph; and

(2) the person submits to the court an affidavit attesting to that fact.

(a-4) A person is eligible under Subsection (a)(2)(A)(ii)(b) for an expunction of arrest records and files only if:

(1) the person has not previously received an expunction of arrest records and files under that subsubparagraph; and

(2) the person submits to the court an affidavit attesting to that fact.

Code of Criminal Procedure

(b) Except as provided by Subsection (c) and subject to Subsection (b-1), a district court, a justice court, or a municipal court of record may expunge all records and files relating to the arrest of a person under the procedure established under Article 55.02 if:

(1) the person is:

(A) tried for the offense for which the person was arrested;

(B) convicted of the offense; and

(C) acquitted by the court of criminal appeals or, if the period for granting a petition for discretionary review has expired, by a court of appeals; or

(2) an office of the attorney representing the state authorized by law to prosecute the offense for which the person was arrested recommends the expunction to the court before the person is tried for the offense, regardless of whether an indictment or information has been presented against the person in relation to the offense.

(b-1) A justice court or a municipal court of record may only expunge records and files under Subsection (b) that relate to the arrest of a person for an offense punishable by fine only.

(c) A court may not order the expunction of records and files relating to an arrest for an offense for which a person is subsequently acquitted, whether by the trial court, a court of appeals, or the court of criminal appeals, if the offense for which the person was acquitted arose out of a criminal episode, as defined by Section 3.01, Penal Code, and the person was convicted of or remains subject to prosecution for at least one other offense occurring during the criminal episode.

(d) A person is entitled to obtain the expunction of any information that identifies the person, including the person's name, address, date of birth, driver's license number, and social security number, contained in records and files relating to the person's arrest or the arrest of another person if:

(1) the expunction of identifying information is sought with respect to the arrest of the person asserting the entitlement and the person was arrested solely as a result of identifying information that was inaccurate due to a clerical error; or

(2) the expunction of identifying information is sought with respect to the arrest of a person other than the person asserting the entitlement and:

(A) the information identifying the person asserting the entitlement was falsely given by the arrested person as the arrested person's identifying information without the consent of the person asserting the entitlement; and

(B) the only reason why the identifying information of the person asserting the entitlement is contained in the applicable arrest records and files is because of the deception of the arrested person.

Art. 55.011. Right of Close Relative to Seek Expunction on Behalf of Deceased Person.

(a) In this article, "close relative of a deceased person" means the grandparent, parent, spouse, or adult brother, sister, or child of a deceased person.

(b) A close relative of a deceased person who, if not deceased, would be entitled to expunction of records and files under Article 55.01 may file on behalf of the deceased person an ex parte petition for expunction under Section 2 or 2a, Article 55.02. If the court finds that the deceased person would be entitled to expunction of any record or file that is the subject of the petition, the court shall enter an order directing expunction.

Art. 55.02. Procedure for Expunction.

Sec. 1. At the request of the acquitted person and after notice to the state, or at the request of the attorney for the state with the consent of the acquitted person, the trial court presiding over the case in which the person was acquitted, if the trial court is a district court, a justice court, or a municipal court of record, or a district court in the county in which the trial court is located shall enter an order of expunction for a person entitled to expunction under Article 55.01(a)(1)(A) not later than the 30th day after the date of the acquittal. On acquittal, the trial court shall advise the acquitted person of the right to expunction. The party requesting the order of expunction shall provide to the court all of the information required in a petition for expunction under Section 2(b). The attorney for the acquitted person in the case in which the person was acquitted, if the person was represented by counsel, or the attorney for the state, if the person was not represented by counsel or if the attorney for the state requested the order of expunction, shall prepare the order for the court's signature.

Sec. 1a. (a) The trial court presiding over a case in which a person is convicted and subsequently granted relief or pardoned on the basis of actual innocence of the offense of which the person was convicted, if the trial court is a district court, a justice court, or a municipal court of record, or a district court in the county in which the trial court is located shall enter an order of expunction for a person entitled to expunction under Article 55.01(a)(1)(B)(ii) not later than the 30th day after the date the court receives notice of the pardon or other grant of relief. The person shall provide to the court all of the information required in a petition for expunction under Section 2(b).

(a-1) A trial court dismissing a case following a person's successful completion of a veterans treatment court program created under Chapter 124, Government Code, or former law, if the trial court is a district court, or a district court in the county in which the trial court is located may, with the consent of the attorney representing the state, enter an order of expunction for a person entitled to expunction under Article 55.01(a)(2)(A)(ii)(a) not later than the 30th day after the date the court dismisses the case or receives the information regarding that dismissal, as applicable. Notwithstanding any other law, a court that enters an order for expunction under this subsection may not charge any fee or assess any cost for the expunction.

(a-2) A trial court dismissing a case following a person's successful completion of a mental health court program created under Chapter 125, Government Code, or former law, if the trial court is a district court, or a district court in the county in which the trial court is located may, with the consent of the attorney representing the state, enter an order of expunction for a person entitled to expunction under Article 55.01(a)(2)(A)(ii)(b) not later than the 30th day after the date the court dismisses the case or receives the information regarding that dismissal, as applicable. Notwithstanding any other law, a court that enters an order for expunction under this subsection may not charge any fee or assess any cost for the expunction.

(b) The attorney for the state shall:

(1) prepare an expunction order under this section for the court's signature; and

(2) notify the Texas Department of Criminal Justice if the person is in the custody of the department.

(c) The court shall include in an expunction order under this section a listing of each official, agency, or other entity of this state or political subdivision of this state and each private entity that there is reason to believe has any record or file that is subject to the order. The court shall also provide in an expunction order under this section that:

(1) the Texas Department of Criminal Justice shall send to the court the documents delivered to the department under Section 8(a), Article 42.09; and

(2) the Department of Public Safety and the Texas Department of Criminal Justice shall delete or redact, as appropriate, from their public records all index references to the records and files that are subject to the expunction order.

(d) The court shall retain all documents sent to the court under Subsection (c)(1) until the statute of limitations has run for any civil case or proceeding relating to the wrongful imprisonment of the person subject to the expunction order.

Sec. 2. (a) A person who is entitled to expunction of records and files under Article 55.01(a)(1)(A), 55.01(a)(1)(B)(i), 55.01(a)(1)(C), or 55.01(a)(2) or a person who is eligible for expunction of records and files under Article 55.01(b) may file an ex parte petition for expunction in a district court for the county in which:

(1) the petitioner was arrested; or

(2) the offense was alleged to have occurred.

(a-1) If the arrest for which expunction is sought is for an offense punishable by fine only, a person who is entitled to expunction of records and files under Article 55.01(a) or a person who is eligible for expunction of records and files under Article 55.01(b) may file an ex parte petition for expunction in a justice court or a municipal court of record in the county in which:

(1) the petitioner was arrested; or

(2) the offense was alleged to have occurred.

(b) A petition filed under Subsection (a) or (a-1) must be verified and must include the following or an explanation for why one or more of the following is not included:

(1) the petitioner's:

(A) full name;

(B) sex;

(C) race;

(D) date of birth;

(E) driver's license number;

(F) social security number; and

(G) address at the time of the arrest;

(2) the offense charged against the petitioner;

(3) the date the offense charged against the petitioner was alleged to have been committed;

(4) the date the petitioner was arrested;

(5) the name of the county where the petitioner was arrested and if the arrest occurred in a municipality, the name of the municipality;

(6) the name of the agency that arrested the petitioner;

(7) the case number and court of offense; and

(8) together with the applicable physical or email addresses, a list of all:

(A) law enforcement agencies, jails or other detention facilities, magistrates, courts, prosecuting attorneys, correctional facilities, central state depositories of criminal records, and other officials or agencies or other entities of this state or of any political subdivision of this state;

(B) central federal depositories of criminal records that the petitioner has reason to believe have records or files that are subject to expunction; and

(C) private entities that compile and disseminate for compensation criminal history record information that the petitioner has reason to believe have information related to records or files that are subject to expunction.

(c) The court shall set a hearing on the matter no sooner than thirty days from the filing of the petition and shall give to each official or agency or other governmental entity named in the petition reasonable notice of the hearing by:

(1) certified mail, return receipt requested; or

(2) secure electronic mail, electronic transmission, or facsimile transmission.

(c-1) An entity described by Subsection (c) may be represented by the attorney responsible for providing the entity with legal representation in other matters.

(d) If the court finds that the petitioner, or a person for whom an ex parte petition is filed under Subsection (e), is entitled to expunction of any records and files that are the subject of the petition, it shall enter an order directing expunction.

(e) The director of the Department of Public Safety or the director's authorized representative may file on behalf of a person described by Subsection (a) of this section or by Section 2a an ex parte petition for expunction in a district court for the county in which:

(1) the person was arrested; or

(2) the offense was alleged to have occurred.

(f) An ex parte petition filed under Subsection (e) must be verified and must include the following or an explanation for why one or more of the following is not included:

(1) the person's:

(A) full name;

(B) sex;

(C) race;

(D) date of birth;

(E) driver's license number;

(F) social security number; and

(G) address at the time of the arrest;

(2) the offense charged against the person;

(3) the date the offense charged against the person was alleged to have been committed;

(4) the date the person was arrested;

(5) the name of the county where the person was arrested and if the arrest occurred in a municipality, the name of the municipality;

(6) the name of the agency that arrested the person;

(7) the case number and court of offense; and

(8) together with the applicable physical or e-mail addresses, a list of all:

(A) law enforcement agencies, jails or other detention facilities, magistrates, courts, prosecuting attorneys, correctional facilities, central state depositories of criminal records, and other officials or agencies or other entities of this state or of any political subdivision of this state;

(B) central federal depositories of criminal records that the person has reason to believe have records or files that are subject to expunction; and

(C) private entities that compile and disseminate for compensation criminal history record information that the person has reason to believe have information relating to records or files that are subject to expunction.

Sec. 2a. (a) A person who is entitled to expunction of information contained in records and files under Article 55.01(d) may file an application for expunction with the attorney representing the state in the prosecution of felonies in the county in which the person resides.

(b) The application must be verified, include authenticated fingerprint records of the applicant, and include the following or an explanation for why one or more of the following is not included:

(1) the applicant's full name, sex, race, date of birth, driver's license number, social security number, and address at the time of the applicable arrest;

(2) the following information regarding the arrest:

(A) the date of arrest;

(B) the offense charged against the person arrested;

(C) the name of the county or municipality in which the arrest occurred; and

(D) the name of the arresting agency; and

(3) a statement, as appropriate, that the applicant:

(A) was arrested solely as a result of identifying information that was inaccurate due to a clerical error; or

(B) is not the person arrested and for whom the arrest records and files were created and

did not give the arrested person consent to falsely identify himself or herself as the applicant.

(c) After verifying the allegations in an application received under Subsection (a), the attorney representing the state shall:

(1) include on the application information regarding the arrest that was requested of the applicant but was unknown by the applicant;

(2) forward a copy of the application to the district court for the county;

(3) together with the applicable physical or e-mail addresses, attach to the copy a list of all:

(A) law enforcement agencies, jails or other detention facilities, magistrates, courts, prosecuting attorneys, correctional facilities, central state depositories of criminal records, and other officials or agencies or other entities of this state or of any political subdivision of this state;

(B) central federal depositories of criminal records that are reasonably likely to have records or files containing information that is subject to expunction; and

(C) private entities that compile and disseminate for compensation criminal history record information that are reasonably likely to have records or files containing information that is subject to expunction; and

(4) request the court to enter an order directing expunction based on an entitlement to expunction under Article 55.01(d).

(d) On receipt of a request under Subsection (c), the court shall, without holding a hearing on the matter, enter a final order directing expunction.

Sec. 3. (a) In an order of expunction issued under this article, the court shall require any state agency that sent information concerning the arrest to a central federal depository to request the depository to return all records and files subject to the order of expunction. The person who is the subject of the expunction order or an agency protesting the expunction may appeal the court's decision in the same manner as in other civil cases.

(b) The order of expunction entered by the court shall have attached and incorporate by reference a copy of the judgment of acquittal and shall include:

(1) the following information on the person who is the subject of the expunction order:

(A) full name;

(B) sex;

(C) race;

(D) date of birth;

(E) driver's license number; and

(F) social security number;

(2) the offense charged against the person who is the subject of the expunction order;

(3) the date the person who is the subject of the expunction order was arrested;

(4) the case number and court of offense; and

(5) the tracking incident number (TRN) assigned to the individual incident of arrest under Article 66.251(b)(1) by the Department of Public Safety.

(c) When the order of expunction is final, the clerk of the court shall send a certified copy of the order to the Crime Records Service of the Department of Public Safety and to each official or agency or other governmental entity of this state or of any political subdivision of this state named in the order. The certified copy of the order must be sent by secure electronic mail, electronic transmission, or facsimile transmission or otherwise by certified mail, return receipt requested. In sending the order to a governmental entity named in the order, the clerk may elect to substitute hand delivery for certified mail under this subsection, but the clerk must receive a receipt for that hand-delivered order.

(c-1) The Department of Public Safety shall notify any central federal depository of criminal records by any means, including secure electronic mail, electronic transmission, or facsimile transmission, of the order with an explanation of the effect of the order and a request that the depository, as appropriate, either:

(1) destroy or return to the court the records in possession of the depository that are subject to the order, including any information with respect to the order; or

(2) comply with Section 5(f) pertaining to information contained in records and files of a person entitled to expunction under Article 55.01(d).

(c-2) The Department of Public Safety shall also provide, by secure electronic mail, electronic transmission, or facsimile transmission, notice of the order to any private entity that is named in the order or that purchases criminal history record information from the department. The notice must include an explanation of the effect of the order and a request that the entity destroy any information in the possession of the entity that is subject to the order. The department may charge to a private entity that purchases criminal history record information from the department a fee in an amount sufficient to recover costs incurred by the department in providing notice under this subsection to the entity.

(d) Any returned receipts received by the clerk from notices of the hearing and copies of the order shall be maintained in the file on the proceedings under this chapter.

Sec. 4. (a) If the state establishes that the person who is the subject of an expunction order is still subject to conviction for an offense arising out of the transaction for which the person was arrested because the statute of limitations has not run and there is reasonable cause to believe that the state may proceed against the person for the offense, the court may provide in its expunction order that the law enforcement agency and the prosecuting attorney responsible for investigating the offense may retain any records and files that are necessary to the investigation.

(a-1) The court shall provide in its expunction order that the applicable law enforcement agency and prosecuting attorney may retain the arrest records and files of any person who becomes entitled to an expunction of those records and files based on the expiration of a period described by Article 55.01(a)(2)(A)(i)(a), (b), or (c), but without the certification of the prosecuting attorney as described by Article 55.01(a)(2)(A)(i)(d).

(a-2) In the case of a person who is the subject of an expunction order on the basis of an acquittal, the court may provide in the expunction order that the law enforcement agency and the prosecuting attorney retain records and files if:

(1) the records and files are necessary to conduct a subsequent investigation and prosecution of a person other than the person who is the subject of the expunction order; or

(2) the state establishes that the records and files are necessary for use in:

(A) another criminal case, including a prosecution, motion to adjudicate or revoke community supervision, parole revocation hearing, mandatory supervision revocation hearing, punishment hearing, or bond hearing; or

(B) a civil case, including a civil suit or suit for possession of or access to a child.

(b) Unless the person who is the subject of the expunction order is again arrested for or charged with an offense arising out of the transaction for which the person was arrested or unless the court provides for the retention of records and files under Subsection (a-1) or (a-2), the provisions of Articles 55.03 and 55.04 apply to files and records retained under this section.

Sec. 5. (a) Except as provided by Subsections (f) and (g), on receipt of the order, each official or agency or other governmental entity named in the order shall:

(1) return all records and files that are subject to the expunction order to the court or in cases other than those described by Section 1a, if removal is impracticable, obliterate all portions of the record or file that identify the person who is the subject of the order and notify the court of its action; and

(2) delete from its public records all index references to the records and files that are subject to the expunction order.

(b) Except in the case of a person who is the subject of an expunction order on the basis of an acquittal or an expunction order based on an entitlement under Article 55.01(d), the court may give the person who is the subject of the order all records and files returned to it pursuant to its order.

(c) Except in the case of a person who is the subject of an expunction order based on an entitlement under Article 55.01(d) and except as provided by Subsection (g), if an order of expunction is issued under this article, the court records concerning expunction proceedings are not open for inspection by anyone except the person who is the subject of the order unless the order permits retention of a record under Section 4 of this article and the person is again arrested for or charged with an offense arising out of the transaction for which the person was arrested or unless the court provides for the retention of records and files under Section 4(a) of this article. The clerk of the court issuing the order shall obliterate all public references to the proceeding and maintain the files or other records in an area not open to inspection.

(d) Except in the case of a person who is the subject of an expunction order on the basis of an acquittal or an expunction order based on an entitlement under Article 55.01(d) and except as provided by Subsection (g), the clerk of the court shall destroy all the files or other records maintained under Subsection (c) not earlier than the 60th day after the date the order of expunction is issued or later than the first anniversary of that date unless the records or files were released under Subsection (b).

(d-1) Not later than the 30th day before the date on which the clerk destroys files or other records under Subsection (d), the clerk shall provide notice by mail, electronic mail, or facsimile transmission to the attorney representing the state in the expunction proceeding. If the attorney representing the state in the expunction proceeding objects to the destruction not later than the 20th day after receiving notice under this subsection, the clerk may not destroy the files or other records until the first anniversary of the date the order of expunction is issued or the first business day after that date.

(e) The clerk shall certify to the court the destruction of files or other records under Subsection (d) of this section.

(f) On receipt of an order granting expunction to a person entitled to expunction under Article 55.01(d), each official, agency, or other governmental entity named in the order:

(1) shall:

(A) obliterate all portions of the record or file that identify the petitioner; and

(B) substitute for all obliterated portions of the record or file any available information that identifies the person arrested; and

(2) may not return the record or file or delete index references to the record or file.

(g) Notwithstanding any other provision in this section, an official, agency, court, or other entity may retain receipts, invoices, vouchers, or similar records of financial transactions that arose from the expunction proceeding or prosecution of the underlying criminal cause in accordance with internal financial control procedures. An official, agency, court, or other entity that retains records under this subsection shall obliterate all portions of the record or the file that identify the person who is the subject of the expunction order.

Art. 55.03. Effect of Expunction.

When the order of expunction is final:

(1) the release, maintenance, dissemination, or use of the expunged records and files for any purpose is prohibited;

(2) except as provided in Subdivision (3) of this article, the person arrested may deny the occurrence of the arrest and the existence of the expunction order; and

(3) the person arrested or any other person, when questioned under oath in a criminal proceeding about an arrest for which the records have been expunged, may state only that the matter in question has been expunged.

Art. 55.04. Violation of Expunction Order.

Sec. 1. A person who acquires knowledge of an arrest while an officer or employee of the state or of any agency or other entity of the state or any political subdivision of the state and who knows of an order expunging the records and files relating to that arrest commits an offense if he knowingly releases, disseminates, or otherwise uses the records or files.

Sec. 2. A person who knowingly fails to return or to obliterate identifying portions of a record or file ordered expunged under this chapter commits an offense.

Sec. 3. An offense under this article is a Class B misdemeanor.

Art. 55.05. Notice of Right to Expunction.

On release or discharge of an arrested person, the person responsible for the release or discharge shall give him a written explanation of his rights under this chapter and a copy of the provisions of this chapter.

Art. 55.06. License Suspensions and Revocations.

Records relating to the suspension or revocation of a driver's license, permit, or privilege to operate a motor vehicle may not be expunged under this chapter except as provided in Section 524.015, Transportation Code, or Section 724.048 of that code.

CHAPTER 56
RIGHTS OF CRIME VICTIMS
[REPEALED]

SUBCHAPTER A
CRIME VICTIMS' RIGHTS
[REPEALED]

Art. 56.01. Definitions. [Repealed]

Art. 56.02. Crime Victims' Rights. [Repealed]

Art. 56.021. Rights of Victim of Sexual Assault or Abuse, Indecent Assault, Stalking, or Trafficking. [Repealed]

Art. 56.03. Victim Impact Statement. [Repealed]

Art. 56.04. Victim Assistance Coordinator; Crime Victim Liaison. [Repealed]

Art. 56.045. Presence of Advocate or Representative During Forensic Medical Examination. [Repealed]

Art. 56.05. Reports Required. [Repealed]

Art. 56.06. Forensic Medical Examination for Sexual Assault Victim Who Has Reported Assault; Costs. [Repealed]

Art. 56.065. Medical Examination for Sexual Assault Victim Who Has Not Reported Assault; Costs. [Repealed]

Art. 56.07. Notification. [Repealed]

Art. 56.08. Notification of Rights by Attorney Representing the State. [Repealed]

Art. 56.09. Victim's Right to Privacy. [Repealed]

Art. 56.10. Victim's Discovery Attendance. [Repealed]

Art. 56.11. Notification to Victim or Witness of Release or Escape of Defendant. [Repealed]

Art. 56.12. Notification of Escape or Transfer. [Repealed]

Art. 56.13. Victim-Offender Mediation. [Repealed]

Art. 56.14. Clearinghouse Annual Conference. [Repealed]

Art. 56.15. Computerized Database; Defendant Release Information. [Repealed]

SUBCHAPTER B CRIME VICTIMS' COMPENSATION [REPEALED]

Art. 56.31. Short Title. [Repealed]

Art. 56.311. Legislative Findings and Intent. [Repealed]

Art. 56.32. Definitions. [Repealed]

Art. 56.33. Administration; Rules. [Repealed]

Art. 56.34. Compensation. [Repealed]

Art. 56.35. Types of Assistance. [Repealed]

Art. 56.36. Application. [Repealed]

Art. 56.37. Time for Filing. [Repealed]

Art. 56.38. Review; Verification. [Repealed]

Art. 56.385. Review of Health Care Services. [Repealed]

Art. 56.39. Mental or Physical Examination; Autopsy. [Repealed]

Art. 56.40. Hearings. [Repealed]

Art. 56.41. Approval of Claim. [Repealed]

Art. 56.42. Limits on Compensation. [Repealed]

Art. 56.43. Attorney Fees. [Repealed]

Art. 56.44. Payments. [Repealed]

Art. 56.45. Denial or Reduction of Award. [Repealed]

Art. 56.46. Reporting of Crime. [Repealed]

Art. 56.47. Reconsideration. [Repealed]

Art. 56.48. Judicial Review. [Repealed]

Art. 56.49. Exemption; Assignability. [Repealed]

Art. 56.50. Emergency Award. [Repealed]

Art. 56.51. Subrogation. [Repealed]

Art. 56.52. Notice of Private Action. [Repealed]

Art. 56.53. Annual Report. [Repealed]

Art. 56.54. Funds. [Repealed]

Art. 56.541. Appropriation of Excess Money for Other Crime Victim Assistance. [Repealed]

Art. 56.542. Payments for Certain Disabled Peace Officers. [Repealed]

Art. 56.55. Court Costs [Repealed].

Repealed by Acts 2003, 78th Leg., ch. 209 (H.B. 2424), § 85(a)(1), effective January 1, 2004.

Art. 56.56. Deposit and Remittance of Court Costs [Repealed].

Repealed by Acts 2003, 78th Leg., ch. 209 (H.B. 2424), § 85(a)(2), effective January 1, 2004.

Art. 56.57. Deposit by Comptroller; Audit [Repealed].

Repealed by Acts 2003, 78th Leg., ch. 209 (H.B. 2424), § 85(a)(3), effective January 1, 2004.

Art. 56.58. Adjustment of Awards and Payments. [Repealed]

Art. 56.59. Attorney General Supervision of Collection of Costs; Failure to Comply [Repealed].

Repealed by Acts 2003, 78th Leg., ch. 209 (H.B. 2424), § 85(a)(4), effective January 1, 2004.

Art. 56.60. Public Notice. [Repealed]

Art. 56.61. Compensation for Certain Criminally Injurious Conduct Prohibited; Exception. [Repealed]

Art. 56.62. Public Letter of Reprimand. [Repealed]

Art. 56.63. Civil Penalty. [Repealed]

Art. 56.64. Administrative Penalty. [Repealed]

Art. 56.65. Disclosure and Use of Information. [Repealed]

SUBCHAPTER C ADDRESS CONFIDENTIALITY PROGRAM FOR VICTIMS OF FAMILY VIOLENCE, SEXUAL ASSAULT OR ABUSE, STALKING, OR TRAFFICKING OF PERSONS [REPEALED]

Art. 56.81. Definitions. [Repealed]

Art. 56.82. Address Confidentiality Program. [Repealed]

Art. 56.83. Eligibility to Participate in Program. [Repealed]

Art. 56.84. Certification; Expiration. [Repealed]

Art. 56.85. Renewal. [Repealed]

Art. 56.86. Ineligibility and Cancellation. [Repealed]

Art. 56.87. Withdrawal. [Repealed]

Art. 56.88. Confidentiality; Destruction of Information. [Repealed]

Art. 56.89. Acceptance of Substitute Address; Exemptions. [Repealed]

Art. 56.90. Exceptions. [Repealed]

Art. 56.91. Liability. [Repealed]

Art. 56.92. Program Information and Application Materials. [Repealed]

Art. 56.93. Rules. [Repealed]

CHAPTER 56A
RIGHTS OF CRIME VICTIMS

SUBCHAPTER A
GENERAL PROVISIONS

Art. 56A.001. Definitions.

Except as otherwise provided by this chapter, in this chapter:

(1) "Board" means the Board of Pardons and Paroles.

(2) "Clearinghouse" means the Texas Crime Victim Clearinghouse.

(3) "Close relative of a deceased victim" means a person who:

(A) was the spouse of a deceased victim at the time of the victim's death; or

(B) is a parent or adult brother, sister, or child of a deceased victim.

(4) "Department" means the Texas Department of Criminal Justice.

(5) "Guardian of a victim" means a person who is the legal guardian of the victim, regardless of whether the legal relationship between the guardian and victim exists because of the age of the victim or the physical or mental incompetency of the victim.

(6) "Sexual assault" means an offense under the following provisions of the Penal Code:

(A) Section 21.02;

(B) Section 21.11(a)(1);

(C) Section 22.011; or

(D) Section 22.021.

(6-a) "Sexual assault examiner" and "sexual assault nurse examiner" have the meanings assigned by Section 420.003, Government Code.

(7) "Victim" means a person who:

(A) is the victim of the offense of:

(i) sexual assault;

(ii) kidnapping;

(iii) aggravated robbery;

(iv) trafficking of persons; or

(v) injury to a child, elderly individual, or disabled individual; or

(B) has suffered personal injury or death as a result of the criminal conduct of another. (Code Crim. Proc., Art. 56.01; New.)

SUBCHAPTER B
CRIME VICTIMS' RIGHTS

Art. 56A.051. General Rights.

(a) A victim, guardian of a victim, or close relative of a deceased victim is entitled to the following rights within the criminal justice system:

(1) the right to receive from a law enforcement agency adequate protection from harm and threats of harm arising from cooperation with prosecution efforts;

(2) the right to have the magistrate consider the safety of the victim or the victim's family in setting the amount of bail for the defendant;

(3) if requested, the right to be informed:

(A) by the attorney representing the state of relevant court proceedings, including appellate proceedings, and to be informed if those proceedings have been canceled or rescheduled before the event; and

(B) by an appellate court of the court's decisions, after the decisions are entered but before the decisions are made public;

(4) when requested, the right to be informed:

(A) by a peace officer concerning the defendant's right to bail and the procedures in criminal investigations; and

(B) by the office of the attorney representing the state concerning the general procedures in the criminal justice system, including general procedures in guilty plea negotiations and arrangements, restitution, and the appeals and parole process;

(5) the right to provide pertinent information to a community supervision and corrections department conducting a presentencing investigation concerning the impact of the offense on the victim and the victim's family by testimony, written statement, or any other manner before any sentencing of the defendant;

(6) the right to receive information regarding compensation to victims of crime as provided by Chapter 56B, including information related to the costs that may be compensated under that chapter and the amount of compensation, eligibility for compensation, and procedures for application for compensation under that chapter, the payment for a forensic medical examination under Article 56A.252 for a victim of an alleged sexual assault, and when requested, to referral to available social service agencies that may offer additional assistance;

(7) the right to:

(A) be informed, on request, of parole procedures;

(B) participate in the parole process;

(C) provide to the board for inclusion in the defendant's file information to be considered by the board before the parole of any defendant convicted of any offense subject to this chapter; and

(D) be notified, if requested, of parole proceedings concerning a defendant in the victim's case and of the defendant's release;

(8) the right to be provided with a waiting area, separate or secure from other witnesses, including the defendant and relatives of the defendant, before testifying in any proceeding concerning the defendant; if a separate waiting area is not available, other safeguards should be taken to minimize the victim's contact with the defendant and the defendant's relatives and witnesses, before and during court proceedings;

(9) the right to the prompt return of any of the victim's property that is held by a law enforcement agency or the attorney representing the state as evidence when the property is no longer required for that purpose;

(10) the right to have the attorney representing the state notify the victim's employer, if requested, that the victim's cooperation and testimony is necessary in a proceeding that may require the victim to be absent from work for good cause;

(11) the right to request victim-offender mediation coordinated by the victim services division of the department;

(12) the right to be informed of the uses of a victim impact statement and the statement's purpose in the criminal justice system as described by Subchapter D, to complete the victim impact statement, and to have the victim impact statement considered:

(A) by the attorney representing the state and the judge before sentencing or before a plea bargain agreement is accepted; and

(B) by the board before a defendant is released on parole;

(13) for a victim of an assault or sexual assault who is younger than 17 years of age or whose case involves family violence, as defined by Section 71.004, Family Code, the right to have the court consider the impact on the victim of a continuance requested by the defendant; if requested by the attorney representing the state or by the defendant's attorney, the court shall state on the record the reason for granting or denying the continuance; and

(14) if the offense is a capital felony, the right to:

(A) receive by mail from the court a written explanation of defense-initiated victim outreach if the court has authorized expenditures for a defense-initiated victim outreach specialist;

(B) not be contacted by the victim outreach specialist unless the victim, guardian, or relative has consented to the contact by providing a written notice to the court; and

(C) designate a victim service provider to receive all communications from a victim outreach specialist acting on behalf of any person.

(b) A victim, guardian of a victim, or close relative of a deceased victim is entitled to the right to be present at all public court proceedings related to the offense, subject to the approval of the judge in the case.

(c) The office of the attorney representing the state and the sheriff, police, and other law enforcement agencies shall ensure to the extent practicable that a victim, guardian of a victim, or close relative of a deceased victim is provided the rights granted by this subchapter and, on request, an explanation of those rights. (Code Crim. Proc., Arts. 56.02(a), (b), (c).)

Art. 56A.052. Additional Rights of Victims of Sexual Assault, Indecent Assault, Stalking, or Trafficking.

(a) If the offense is a sexual assault, a victim, guardian of a victim, or close relative of a deceased victim is entitled to the following rights within the criminal justice system:

(1) if requested, the right to a disclosure of information regarding:

(A) any evidence that was collected during the investigation of the offense, unless disclosing the information would interfere with the investigation or prosecution of the offense, in which event the victim, guardian, or relative shall be informed of the estimated date on which that information is expected to be disclosed; and

(B) the status of any analysis being performed of any evidence described by Paragraph (A);

(2) if requested, the right to be notified:

(A) at the time a request is submitted to a crime laboratory to process and analyze any evidence that was collected during the investigation of the offense;

(B) at the time of the submission of a request to compare any biological evidence collected during the investigation of the offense with DNA profiles maintained in a state or federal DNA database; and

(C) of the results of the comparison described by Paragraph (B), unless disclosing the results would interfere with the investigation or prosecution of the offense, in which event the victim, guardian, or relative shall be informed of the estimated date on which those results are expected to be disclosed;

(3) if requested, the right to counseling regarding acquired immune deficiency syndrome (AIDS) and human immunodeficiency virus (HIV) infection; and

Code of Criminal Procedure

(4) for the victim, the right to:

(A) testing for acquired immune deficiency syndrome (AIDS), human immunodeficiency virus (HIV) infection, antibodies to HIV, or infection with any other probable causative agent of AIDS; and

(B) a forensic medical examination to the extent provided by Subchapters F and G if, within 120 hours of the offense:

(i) the offense is reported to a law enforcement agency; or

(ii) a forensic medical examination is otherwise conducted at a health care provider.

(b) A victim, guardian of a victim, or close relative of a deceased victim who requests to be notified under Subsection (a)(2) must provide a current address and phone number to the attorney representing the state and the law enforcement agency that is investigating the offense. The victim, guardian, or relative must inform the attorney representing the state and the law enforcement agency of any change in the address or phone number.

(c) A victim, guardian of a victim, or close relative of a deceased victim may designate a person, including an entity that provides services to victims of sexual assault, to receive any notice requested under Subsection (a)(2).

(d) This subsection applies only to a victim of an offense under Section 20A.02, 20A.03, 21.02, 21.11, 22.011, 22.012, 22.021, 42.072, or 43.05, Penal Code. A victim described by this subsection or a parent or guardian of the victim, if the victim is younger than 18 years of age or an adult ward, is entitled to the following rights within the criminal justice system:

(1) the right to be informed:

(A) that the victim or, if the victim is younger than 18 years of age or an adult ward, the victim's parent or guardian or another adult acting on the victim's behalf may file an application for a protective order under Article 7B.001;

(B) of the court in which the application for a protective order may be filed;

(C) that, on request of the victim or, if the victim is younger than 18 years of age or an adult ward, on request of the victim's parent or guardian or another adult acting on the victim's behalf, the attorney representing the state may, subject to the Texas Disciplinary Rules of Professional Conduct, file the application for a protective order on behalf of the requestor; and

(D) that, subject to the Texas Disciplinary Rules of Professional Conduct, the attorney representing the state generally is required to file the application for a protective order with respect to the victim if the defendant is convicted of or placed on deferred adjudication community supervision for the offense;

(2) the right to:

(A) request that the attorney representing the state, subject to the Texas Disciplinary Rules of Professional Conduct, file an application for a protective order described by Subdivision (1); and

(B) be notified when the attorney representing the state files an application for a protective order under Article 7B.001;

(3) if the victim or the victim's parent or guardian, as applicable, is present when the defendant is convicted or placed on deferred adjudication community supervision, the right to:

(A) be given by the court the information described by Subdivision (1); and

(B) file an application for a protective order under Article 7B.001 immediately following the defendant's conviction or placement on deferred adjudication community supervision if the court has jurisdiction over the application; and

(4) if the victim or the victim's parent or guardian, as applicable, is not present when the defendant is convicted or placed on deferred adjudication community supervision, the right to be given by the attorney representing the state the information described by Subdivision (1).

(e) A victim of an offense under Section 20A.02, 20A.03, or 43.05, Penal Code, is entitled to be informed that the victim may petition for an order of nondisclosure of criminal history record information under Section 411.0728, Government Code, if the victim:

(1) has been convicted of or placed on deferred adjudication community supervision for an offense described by Subsection (a)(1) of that section; and

(2) committed that offense solely as a victim of an offense under Section 20A.02, 20A.03, or 43.05, Penal Code.

Art. 56A.053. Failure to Provide Right or Service.

(a) A judge, attorney representing the state, peace officer, or law enforcement agency is not liable for a failure or inability to provide a right granted by this subchapter.

(b) The failure or inability of any person to provide a right or service granted by this subchapter may not be used by a defendant in a criminal case as a ground for appeal, a ground to set aside the conviction or sentence, or a ground in a habeas corpus petition. (Code Crim. Proc., Art. 56.02(d) (part).)

Art. 56A.054. Standing.

A victim, guardian of a victim, or close relative of a deceased victim does not have standing to:

(1) participate as a party in a criminal proceeding; or

(2) contest the disposition of any charge. (Code Crim. Proc., Art. 56.02(d) (part).)

SUBCHAPTER C
ADDITIONAL PROTECTIONS FOR VICTIMS AND WITNESSES

Art. 56A.101. Victim Privacy.

(a) As far as reasonably practical, the address of the victim may not be a part of the court file except as necessary to identify the place of the offense.

(b) The phone number of the victim may not be a part of the court file. (Code Crim. Proc., Art. 56.09.)

Art. 56A.102. Victim or Witness Discovery Attendance.

Unless absolutely necessary, a victim or witness who is not confined may not be required to attend a deposition in a correctional facility. (Code Crim. Proc., Art. 56.10.)

SUBCHAPTER D
VICTIM IMPACT STATEMENT

Art. 56A.151. Victim Impact Statement; Information Booklet.

(a) The clearinghouse, with the participation of the board and the community justice assistance division of the department, shall develop a form to be used by law enforcement agencies, attorneys representing the state, and other participants in the criminal justice system to record the impact of an offense on a victim of the offense, guardian of a victim, or close relative of a deceased victim and to provide the agencies, attorneys, and participants with information needed to contact the victim, guardian, or relative if needed at any stage of a prosecution of a person charged with the offense. The clearinghouse, with the participation of the board and the community justice assistance division of the department, shall also develop a victims' information booklet that provides a general explanation of the criminal justice system to victims of an offense, guardians of victims, and relatives of deceased victims.

(b) The victim impact statement must be in a form designed to:

(1) inform a victim, guardian of a victim, or close relative of a deceased victim with a clear statement of rights granted by Subchapter B; and

(2) collect the following information:

(A) the name of the victim of the offense or, if the victim has a legal guardian or is deceased, the name of a guardian or close relative of the victim;

(B) the address and telephone number of the victim, guardian, or relative through which the victim, guardian, or relative may be contacted;

(C) a statement of economic loss suffered by the victim, guardian, or relative as a result of the offense;

(D) a statement of any physical or psychological injury suffered by the victim, guardian, or relative as a result of the offense, as described by the victim, guardian, or relative or by a physician or counselor;

(E) a statement of any psychological services requested as a result of the offense;

(F) a statement of any change in the victim's, guardian's, or relative's personal welfare or familial relationship as a result of the offense;

(G) a statement regarding whether the victim, guardian, or relative wants to be notified of any parole hearing for the defendant;

(H) if the victim is a child, whether there is an existing court order granting to the defendant possession of or access to the victim; and

(I) any other information related to the impact of the offense on the victim, guardian, or relative, other than facts related to the commission of the offense.

(c) The victim impact statement must include an explanation regarding the procedures by which a victim, guardian of a victim, or close relative of a deceased victim may obtain information concerning the release of the defendant from the department.

(d) Not later than December 1 of each odd-numbered year, the clearinghouse, with the participation of the board and the community justice assistance division of the department, shall update the victim impact statement form and any other information provided by the community justice assistance division to victims, guardians of victims, and relatives of deceased victims, if necessary, to reflect changes in law relating to criminal justice and the rights of victims and guardians and relatives of victims. (Code Crim. Proc., Arts. 56.03(a), (b), (h), (i) (part).)

Art. 56A.152. Recommendations to Ensure Submission of Statement.

The victim services division of the department, in consultation with the board, law enforcement agencies, offices of attorneys representing the state, and other participants in the criminal justice system, shall develop recommendations to ensure that completed victim impact statements are submitted to the department as provided by Article 56A.159(b). (Code Crim. Proc., Art. 56.04(d-1).)

Art. 56A.153. Notification to Court Regarding Release of Defendant with Access to Child Victim.

If information collected under Article 56A.151(b)(2)(H) indicates the defendant is granted possession of or access to a child victim under court order and the department subsequently imprisons the defendant as a result of the defendant's commission of the offense, the victim services division of the department shall contact the court that issued the order before the department releases the defendant on parole or to mandatory supervision. (Code Crim. Proc., Art. 56.03(i) (part).)

Art. 56A.154. Change of Address.

If a victim, guardian of a victim, or close relative of a deceased victim states on a victim impact statement that the victim, guardian, or relative wants to be notified of parole proceedings, the victim, guardian, or relative must notify the board of any change of address. (Code Crim. Proc., Art. 56.03(d).)

Art. 56A.155. Discovery of Statement.

A victim impact statement is subject to discovery under Article 39.14 before the testimony of the victim is taken only if the court determines that the statement contains exculpatory material. (Code Crim. Proc., Art. 56.03(g).)

Art. 56A.156. Inspection of Statement by Court; Disclosure of Contents.

The court may not inspect a victim impact statement until after a finding of guilt or until deferred adjudication community supervision is ordered and the contents of the statement may not be disclosed to any person unless:

(1) the defendant pleads guilty or nolo contendere or is convicted of the offense; or

(2) the defendant authorizes the court in writing to inspect the statement. (Code Crim. Proc., Art. 56.03(f).)

Art. 56A.157. Consideration of Statement by Court.

(a) Before imposing a sentence, a court shall, as applicable, inquire as to whether a victim impact statement has been returned to the attorney representing the state and, if a statement has been returned to the attorney, consider the information provided in the statement.

(b) On inquiry by the sentencing court, the attorney representing the state shall make a copy of the statement available for consideration by the court. (Code Crim. Proc., Arts. 56.03(e) (part), 56.04(e) (part).)

Art. 56A.158. Defendant Response to Statement.

Before sentencing a defendant, a court shall permit the defendant or the defendant's attorney a reasonable period to:

(1) read the victim impact statement, excluding the victim's name, address, and telephone number;

(2) comment on the statement; and

(3) with the approval of the court, introduce testimony or other information alleging a factual inaccuracy in the statement. (Code Crim. Proc., Art. 56.03(e) (part).)

Art. 56A.159. Transfer of Statement After Sentencing.

(a) If a court sentences a defendant to a period of community supervision, the attorney representing the state shall forward any victim impact statement received in the case to the community supervision and corrections department supervising the defendant.

(b) If a court sentences a defendant to imprisonment in the department, the court shall attach to the commitment papers the copy of the victim impact statement provided to the court under Article 56A.157(b). (Code Crim. Proc., Arts. 56.03(e) (part), 56.04(e) (part).)

Art. 56A.160. Survey Plan Regarding Statements.

(a) In this article, "planning body" means the board, the clearinghouse, and the community justice assistance division of the department.

(b) The planning body shall develop a survey plan to maintain statistics on the numbers and types of persons to whom state and local agencies provide victim impact statements during each year.

(c) At intervals specified in the survey plan, the planning body may require any state or local agency to submit the following, in a form prescribed for the reporting of the information:

(1) statistical data on the numbers and types of persons to whom the agency provides victim impact statements; and

(2) any other information required by the planning body.

(d) The form described by Subsection (c) must be designed to:

(1) protect the privacy of persons provided rights under Subchapter B; and

(2) determine whether the selected agency is making a good faith effort to protect the rights of the persons served. (Code Crim. Proc., Arts. 56.05(a), (b).)

SUBCHAPTER E VICTIM ASSISTANCE COORDINATOR; CRIME VICTIM LIAISON

Art. 56A.201. Designation of Victim Assistance Coordinator.

The district attorney, criminal district attorney, or county attorney who prosecutes criminal cases shall designate a person to serve as victim assistance coordinator in that jurisdiction. (Code Crim. Proc., Art. 56.04(a).)

Art. 56A.202. Duties of Victim Assistance Coordinator.

(a) The victim assistance coordinator designated under Article 56A.201 shall:

(1) ensure that a victim, guardian of a victim, or close relative of a deceased victim is provided the rights granted to victims, guardians, or relatives by Subchapter B; and

(2) work closely with appropriate law enforcement agencies, attorneys representing the state, the board, and the judiciary in carrying out the duty described by Subdivision (1).

(b) The victim assistance coordinator shall send to a victim, guardian of a victim, or close relative of a deceased victim a victim impact statement and victims' information booklet described by Article 56A.151 and an application for compensation under Chapter 56B. The victim assistance coordinator shall include an offer to assist in completing the statement and application on request.

(c) The victim assistance coordinator, on request, shall explain the possible use and consideration of the victim impact statement at any sentencing or parole hearing of the defendant. (Code Crim. Proc., Arts. 56.03(c), 56.04(b).)

Art. 56A.203. Designation of Crime Victim Liaison.

Each local law enforcement agency shall designate one person to serve as the agency's crime victim liaison. (Code Crim. Proc., Art. 56.04(c) (part).)

Art. 56A.204. Duties of Crime Victim Liaison.

(a) The crime victim liaison designated under Article 56A.203 shall ensure that a victim, guardian of a victim, or close relative of a deceased victim is provided the rights granted to victims, guardians, or relatives by Articles 56A.051(a)(4), (6), and (9).

(b) Each local law enforcement agency shall consult with the victim assistance coordinator in the office of the attorney representing the state to determine the most effective manner in which the crime victim liaison can perform the duties imposed on the crime victim liaison under this article and, if applicable, Article 56A.205. (Code Crim. Proc., Arts. 56.04(c) (part), (d).)

Art. 56A.205. Psychological Counseling for Certain Jurors.

(a) A commissioners court may approve a program in which a crime victim liaison or victim assistance coordinator may offer not more than 10 hours of post-investigation or posttrial psychological counseling for a person who:

(1) serves as a grand juror, alternate grand juror, juror, or alternate juror in a grand jury investigation or criminal trial involving graphic evidence or testimony; and

(2) requests the counseling not later than the 180th day after the date on which the grand jury or jury is dismissed.

(b) The crime victim liaison or victim assistance coordinator may provide the counseling using a provider that assists local criminal justice agencies in providing similar services to victims. (Code Crim. Proc., Art. 56.04(f).)

SUBCHAPTER F FORENSIC MEDICAL EXAMINATION OF SEXUAL ASSAULT VICTIM REPORTING ASSAULT

Art. 56A.2505. Applicability.

This subchapter applies to health care providers described by Article 56A.302.

Art. 56A.2506. Definition.

In this subchapter, "reported sexual assault" means a sexual assault that has been reported to a law enforcement agency.

Code of Criminal Procedure

Art. 56A.251. Request for Forensic Medical Examination.

(a) If a sexual assault is reported to a law enforcement agency within 120 hours after the assault, the law enforcement agency, with the consent of the victim of the reported assault, a person authorized to act on behalf of the victim, or an employee of the Department of Family and Protective Services, shall request a forensic medical examination of the victim for use in the investigation or prosecution of the offense.

(b) If a sexual assault is not reported within the period described by Subsection (a) and the victim is a minor as defined by Section 101.003, Family Code, on receiving the consent described by Subsection (a) or the consent described by Section 32.003 or 32.005, Family Code, a law enforcement agency shall request a forensic medical examination of the victim for use in the investigation or prosecution of the offense.

(c) If a sexual assault is not reported within the period described by Subsection (a) and the victim is not a minor as defined by Section 101.003, Family Code, on receiving the consent described by Subsection (a), a law enforcement agency may request a forensic medical examination of a victim of a reported sexual assault for use in the investigation or prosecution of the offense if:

(1) based on the circumstances of the reported assault, the agency believes a forensic medical examination would further that investigation or prosecution; or

(2) after a medical evaluation by a physician, sexual assault examiner, or sexual assault nurse examiner, the physician or examiner notifies the agency that a forensic medical examination should be conducted.

(d) **As amended by Acts 2021, 87th Leg., ch. XXX (HB 2462)** If a sexual assault is reported to a law enforcement agency as provided by Subsection (a), (b), or (c), the law enforcement agency shall document, in the form and manner required by the attorney general, whether the agency requested a forensic medical examination. The law enforcement agency shall:

(1) provide the documentation of the agency's decision regarding a request for a forensic medical examination to:

(A) the health care provider and the physician, sexual assault examiner, or sexual assault nurse examiner, as applicable, who provides services to the victim that are related to the sexual assault; and

(B) the victim or the person who consented to the forensic medical examination on behalf of the victim; and

(2) maintain the documentation of the agency's decision in accordance with the agency's record retention policies.

(d) **As amended by Acts 2021, 87th Leg., ch. XXX (HB 3607)** If a sexual assault is reported to a law enforcement agency as provided by Subsection (a) or (c), the law enforcement agency shall document, in the form and manner required by the attorney general, whether the agency requested a forensic medical examination. The law enforcement agency shall:

(1) provide the documentation of the agency's decision regarding a request for a forensic medical examination to:

(A) the health care facility and the sexual assault examiner or sexual assault nurse examiner, as applicable, who provides services to the victim that are related to the sexual assault; and

(B) the victim or the person who consented to the forensic medical examination on behalf of the victim; and

(2) maintain the documentation of the agency's decision in accordance with the agency's record retention policies.

Art. 56A.252. [As amended by Acts 2021, 87th Leg., ch. XXX (HB 2706)] Payment of Costs of Examination.

(a) On application to the attorney general, a health care provider that provides a forensic medical examination to a sexual assault survivor in accordance with this subchapter, or the sexual assault examiner or sexual assault nurse examiner who conducts the examination, as applicable, is entitled to be reimbursed in an amount set by attorney general rule for:

(1) the reasonable costs of the forensic portion of that examination; and

(2) the evidence collection kit.

(b) The application under Subsection (a) must be in the form and manner prescribed by the attorney general and must include:

(1) the documentation of the law enforcement agency's request for the forensic medical examination, as required under Article 56A.251(d); and

(2) a complete and itemized bill of the reasonable costs of the forensic portion of the examination.

(c) A health care provider or a sexual assault examiner or sexual assault nurse examiner, as applicable, who applies for reimbursement under Subsection (a) shall accept reimbursement from the attorney general as payment for the costs unless:

(1) the health care provider or sexual assault examiner or sexual assault nurse examiner, as applicable:

(A) requests, in writing, additional reimbursement from the attorney general; and

(B) provides documentation in support of the additional reimbursement, as reasonably requested by the attorney general; and

(2) the attorney general determines that there is a reasonable justification for additional reimbursement.

(d) A health care provider is not entitled to reimbursement under this article unless the forensic medical examination is conducted on the premises of the provider by a sexual assault examiner or sexual assault nurse examiner.

(e) On request, the attorney general may provide training to a health care provider regarding the process for applying for reimbursement under this article.

Art. 56A.252. [As amended by Acts 2021, 87th Leg., ch. XXX (HB 2462)] Payment of Costs of Examination.

(a) On application to the attorney general, a health care provider that provides a forensic medical examination to a sexual assault survivor in accordance with this subchapter, or the sexual assault examiner or sexual assault nurse examiner who conducts that examination, as applicable, is entitled to be reimbursed in an amount set by attorney general rule for:

(1) the reasonable costs of the forensic portion of that examination; and

(2) the evidence collection kit.

(b) The application under Subsection (a) must be in the form and manner prescribed by the attorney general and must include:

(1) the documentation that the law enforcement agency requested the forensic medical examination, as required under Article 56A.251(d); and

(2) a complete and itemized bill of the reasonable costs of the forensic portion of the examination.

(c) A health care provider or a sexual assault examiner or sexual assault nurse examiner, as applicable, who applies for reimbursement under Subsection (a) shall accept reimbursement from the attorney general as payment for the costs unless:

(1) the health care provider or the sexual assault examiner or sexual assault nurse examiner, as applicable:

(A) requests, in writing, additional reimbursement from the attorney general; and

(B) provides documentation in support of the additional reimbursement, as reasonably requested by the attorney general; and

(2) the attorney general determines that there is a reasonable justification for additional reimbursement.

(d) A health care provider is not entitled to reimbursement under this article unless the forensic medical examination was conducted by a physician, sexual assault examiner, or sexual assault nurse examiner.

(e) On request, the attorney general may provide training to a health care provider regarding the process for applying for reimbursement under this article.

Art. 56A.252. [As amended by Acts 2021, 87th Leg., ch. XXX (HB 3607)] Payment of Costs of Examination.

(a) On application to the attorney general, a health care facility that provides a forensic medical examination to a sexual assault survivor in accordance with this subchapter, or the sexual assault examiner or sexual assault nurse examiner who conducts that examination, as applicable, is entitled to be reimbursed in an amount set by attorney general rule for:

(1) the reasonable costs of the forensic portion of that examination; and

(2) the evidence collection kit.

(b) The application under Subsection (a) must be in the form and manner prescribed by the attorney general and must include:

(1) the documentation that the law enforcement agency requested the forensic medical examination, as required under Article 56A.251(d); and

(2) a complete and itemized bill of the reasonable costs of the forensic portion of the examination.

(c) A health care facility or a sexual assault examiner or sexual assault nurse examiner, as applicable, who applies for reimbursement under Subsection (a) shall accept reimbursement from the attorney general as payment for the costs unless:

(1) the health care facility or sexual assault examiner or sexual assault nurse examiner, as applicable:

(A) requests, in writing, additional reimbursement from the attorney general; and

(B) provides documentation in support of the additional reimbursement, as reasonably requested by the attorney general; and

(2) the attorney general determines that there is a reasonable justification for additional reimbursement.

(d) A health care facility is not entitled to reimbursement under this article unless the forensic medical examination was conducted at the facility by a physician, sexual assault examiner, or sexual assault nurse examiner.

(e) On request, the attorney general may provide training to a health care facility regarding the process for applying for reimbursement under this article.

Art. 56A.253. Payment of Costs Related to Testimony.

A law enforcement agency or office of the attorney representing the state may pay all costs related to the testimony of a licensed health care professional in a criminal proceeding regarding the results of a forensic medical examination described by Article 56A.251 or the manner in which the examination was performed. (Code Crim. Proc., Art. 56.06(d).)

Art. 56A.254. Payment of Costs for Certain Medical Care.

The attorney general may make a payment to or on behalf of an individual for the reasonable costs incurred for medical care provided in accordance with Sections 323.004, 323.053, and 323.054, Health and Safety Code.

Art. 56A.255. Payment of Costs of Treatment Not Required.

This subchapter does not require a law enforcement agency to pay any costs of treatment for injuries. (Code Crim. Proc., Art. 56.06(e).)

Art. 56A.256. Rules.

The attorney general shall adopt rules necessary to implement this subchapter.

SUBCHAPTER G
FORENSIC MEDICAL EXAMINATION OF SEXUAL ASSAULT VICTIM NOT REPORTING ASSAULT

Art. 56A.301. Definitions.

In this subchapter:

(1) "Crime laboratory" has the meaning assigned by Article 38.35.

(2) "Department" means the Department of Public Safety of the State of Texas.

(3) [Repealed.]

Art. 56A.302. Applicability.

This subchapter applies to the following health care providers that provide diagnosis or treatment services to victims of sexual assault:

(1) a general or special hospital licensed under Chapter 241, Health and Safety Code;

(2) a general or special hospital owned by this state;

(3) an outpatient clinic;

(4) a private physician's office; and

(5) a SAFE program as defined by Section 323.051, Health and Safety Code.

Art. 56A.303. Forensic Medical Examination.

(a) In accordance with Subchapter B, Chapter 420, Government Code, and except as provided by Subsection (b), a health care provider shall conduct a forensic medical examination of a victim of a sexual assault if:

(1) the victim arrives at the provider within 120 hours after the assault occurred;

(2) the victim consents to the examination; and

(3) at the time of the examination the victim has not reported the assault to a law enforcement agency.

(b) If a health care provider does not provide diagnosis or treatment services to victims of sexual assault, the provider shall refer a victim of a sexual assault who seeks a forensic medical examination under Subsection (a) to a health care provider that provides services to those victims.

(c) A victim of a sexual assault may not be required to participate in the investigation or prosecution of an offense as a condition of receiving a forensic medical examination under this article.

Art. 56A.304. Payment of Fees Related to Examination.

(a) On application to the attorney general, a health care provider that provides a forensic medical examination to a sexual assault survivor in accordance with this subchapter, or the sexual assault examiner or sexual assault nurse examiner who conducts that examination, as applicable, within 120 hours after the sexual assault occurred is entitled to be reimbursed in an amount set by attorney general rule for:

(1) the reasonable costs of the forensic portion of that examination; and

(2) the evidence collection kit.

(b) The application under Subsection (a) must be in the form and manner prescribed by the attorney general and must include:

(1) certification that the examination was conducted in accordance with the requirements of Article 56A.303(a); and

(2) a complete and itemized bill of the reasonable costs of the forensic portion of the examination.

(c) **As amended by Acts 2021, 87th Leg., chs. XXX (HB 2706) and XXX (HB 2462)** A health care provider or a sexual assault examiner or sexual assault nurse examiner, as applicable, who applies for reimbursement under Subsection (a) shall accept reimbursement from the attorney general as payment for the costs unless:

(1) the health care provider or sexual assault examiner or sexual assault nurse examiner, as applicable:

(A) requests, in writing, additional reimbursement from the attorney general; and

(B) provides documentation in support of the additional reimbursement, as reasonably requested by the attorney general; and

(2) the attorney general determines that there is a reasonable justification for additional reimbursement.

(c) **[As amended by Acts 2021, 87th Leg., ch. XXX (HB 3607)]** A health care facility or a sexual assault examiner or sexual assault nurse examiner, as applicable, who applies for reimbursement under Subsection (a) shall accept reimbursement from the attorney general as payment for the costs unless:

(1) the health care facility or sexual assault examiner or sexual assault nurse examiner, as applicable:

(A) requests, in writing, additional reimbursement from the attorney general; and

(B) provides documentation in support of the additional reimbursement, as reasonably requested by the attorney general; and

(2) the attorney general determines that there is a reasonable justification for additional reimbursement.

(d) **As amended by Acts 2021, 87th Leg., chs. XXX (HB 2706) and XXX (HB 2462)** A health care provider is not entitled to reimbursement under this article unless the forensic medical examination was conducted at the provider by a physician, sexual assault examiner, or sexual assault nurse examiner.

(d) **[As amended by Acts 2021, 87th Leg., ch. XXX (HB 3607)]** A health care facility is not entitled to reimbursement under this article unless the forensic medical examination was conducted at the facility by a physician, sexual assault examiner, or sexual assault nurse examiner.

(e) **As amended by Acts 2021, 87th Leg., chs. XXX (HB 2706) and XXX (HB 2462)** On request, the attorney general may provide training to a health care provider regarding the process for applying for reimbursement under this article.

(e) **[As amended by Acts 2021, 87th Leg., ch. XXX (HB 3607)]** On request, the attorney general may provide training to a health care facility regarding the process for applying for reimbursement under this article.

(f) A victim of a sexual assault may not be required to pay for:

(1) the forensic portion of the forensic medical examination; or

(2) the evidence collection kit.

Art. 56A.305. Payment of Costs for Certain Medical Care.

The attorney general may make a payment to or on behalf of an individual for the reasonable costs incurred for medical care provided in accordance with Sections 323.004, 323.053, and 323.054, Health and Safety Code.

Art. 56A.306. Procedures for Transfer and Preservation of Evidence.

(a) The department, consistent with Chapter 420, Government Code, shall develop procedures for:

(1) the transfer of evidence collected under this subchapter to a crime laboratory or other suitable location designated by the public safety director of the department;

(2) the preservation of the evidence by the entity receiving the evidence; and

(3) the notification of the victim of the offense before a planned destruction of evidence under this article.

(b) Subject to Subsection (c), an entity receiving evidence described by Subsection (a) shall preserve the evidence until the earlier of:

(1) the fifth anniversary of the date on which the evidence was collected; or

(2) the date on which written consent to release the evidence is obtained as provided by Section 420.0735, Government Code.

(c) An entity receiving evidence described by Subsection (a) may destroy the evidence on the expiration of the entity's duty to preserve the evidence under Subsection (b)(1) only if:

(1) the entity provides written notification to the victim of the offense, in a trauma-informed manner, of the decision to destroy the evidence that includes:

(A) detailed instructions on how the victim may make a written objection to the decision, including contact information for the entity; or

(B) a standard form for the victim to complete and return to the entity to make a written objection to the decision; and

(2) a written objection is not received by the entity from the victim before the 91st day after the date on which the entity notifies the victim of the planned destruction of the evidence.

(d) The entity shall document the entity's attempt to notify the victim under Subsection (c).

Art. 56A.307. Procedures for Submission or Collection of Additional Evidence.

The department, consistent with Chapter 420, Government Code, may develop procedures regarding the submission or collection of additional evidence of a sexual assault other than through a forensic medical examination as described by Article 56A.303(a).

Art. 56A.308. Confidentiality of Certain Records.

(a) In this article, "identifying information" includes information that:

(1) reveals the identity, personal history, or background of a person; or

(2) concerns the victimization of a person.

(b) A communication or record is confidential for purposes of Section 552.101, Government Code, if the communication or record:

(1) contains identifying information regarding a victim who receives a forensic medical examination under Article 56A.303(a); and

(2) is created by, provided to, or in the control or possession of the department. (Code Crim. Proc., Art. 56.065(j).)

Art. 56A.309. Rules.

The attorney general and the department shall each adopt rules as necessary to implement this subchapter. (Code Crim. Proc., Art. 56.065(i).)

SUBCHAPTER H PRESENCE OF ADVOCATE OR REPRESENTATIVE DURING FORENSIC MEDICAL EXAMINATION

Art. 56A.351. Presence of Sexual Assault Program Advocate.

(a) Before conducting a forensic medical examination of a victim who consents to the examination for the collection of evidence for an alleged sexual assault, the physician or other medical services personnel conducting the examination shall offer the victim the opportunity to have an advocate from a sexual assault program as defined by Section 420.003, Government Code, be present with the victim during the examination, if the advocate is available at the time of the examination. The advocate must have completed a sexual assault training program described by Section 420.011(b), Government Code.

(b) An advocate may only provide the victim with:

(1) counseling and other support services; and

(2) information regarding the rights of crime victims under Subchapter B.

(c) Notwithstanding Subsection (a), an advocate and a sexual assault program providing the advocate may not delay or otherwise impede the screening or stabilization of an emergency medical condition.

(d) A sexual assault program providing an advocate shall pay all costs associated with providing the advocate.

(e) Any individual or entity, including a health care facility, that provides an advocate with access under Subsection (a) to a victim consenting to a forensic medical examination is not subject to civil or criminal liability for providing that access. In this article, "health care facility" includes a hospital licensed under Chapter 241, Health and Safety Code. (Code Crim. Proc., Arts. 56.045(a), (b), (c), (d), (e).)

SUBCHAPTER H PRESENCE OF ADVOCATE OR REPRESENTATIVE DURING FORENSIC MEDICAL EXAMINATION OR LAW ENFORCEMENT INTERVIEW

Art. 56A.3515. Presence of Sexual Assault Program Advocate or Other Victim's Representative During Law Enforcement Interview.

(a) Before conducting an investigative interview with a victim reporting a sexual assault, other than a victim who is a minor as defined by Section 101.003, Family Code, the peace officer conducting the interview shall offer the victim the opportunity to have an advocate from a sexual assault program, as defined by Section 420.003,

Government Code, be present with the victim during the interview, if the advocate is available at the time of the interview. The advocate must have completed a sexual assault training program described by Section 420.011(b), Government Code.

(b) If an advocate described by Subsection (a) is not available at the time of the interview, the peace officer conducting the interview shall offer the victim the opportunity to have a crime victim liaison from the law enforcement agency, a peace officer who has completed a sexual assault training program described by Section 420.011(b), Government Code, or a victim's assistance counselor from a state or local agency or other entity be present with the victim during the interview.

(b-1) The peace officer conducting an investigative interview described by Subsection (a) shall make a good faith effort to comply with Subsections (a) and (b), except that the officer's compliance with those subsections may not unreasonably delay or otherwise impede the interview process.

(c) An advocate, liaison, officer, or counselor authorized to be present during an interview under this article may only provide the victim reporting the sexual assault with:

(1) counseling and other support services; and

(2) information regarding the rights of crime victims under Subchapter B.

(d) The advocate, liaison, officer, or counselor and the sexual assault program or other entity providing the advocate, liaison, officer, or counselor may not delay or otherwise impede the interview process.

(e) A sexual assault program providing an advocate under Subsection (a) shall pay all costs associated with providing the advocate. An entity providing a victim's assistance counselor under Subsection (b) shall pay all costs associated with providing the counselor.

(f) A peace officer or law enforcement agency that provides an advocate, liaison, officer, or counselor with access to a victim reporting a sexual assault is not subject to civil or criminal liability for providing that access.

Art. 56A.352. Representative Provided by Penal Institution.

(a) In this article, "penal institution" has the meaning assigned by Section 1.07, Penal Code.

(b) If a victim alleging to have sustained injuries as the victim of a sexual assault was confined in a penal institution at the time of the alleged assault, the penal institution shall provide, at the victim's request, a representative to be present with the victim:

(1) at any forensic medical examination conducted for the purpose of collecting and preserving evidence related to the investigation or prosecution of the alleged assault; and

(2) during an investigative interview conducted by a peace officer in relation to the investigation of the alleged assault.

(b-1) The representative provided by the penal institution under Subsection (b) must:

(1) be approved by the penal institution; and

(2) be a:

(A) psychologist;

(B) sociologist;

(C) chaplain;

(D) social worker;

(E) case manager; or

(F) volunteer who has completed a sexual assault training program described by Section 420.011(b), Government Code.

(c) A representative may only provide the victim with:

(1) counseling and other support services; and

(2) information regarding the rights of crime victims under Subchapter B.

(d) A representative may not delay or otherwise impede:

(1) the screening or stabilization of an emergency medical condition; or

(2) the interview process.

SUBCHAPTER I
REQUIRED NOTIFICATIONS BY LAW ENFORCEMENT AGENCY

Art. 56A.401. Notification of Rights.

At the initial contact or at the earliest possible time after the initial contact between a victim of a reported offense and the law enforcement agency having the responsibility for investigating the offense, the agency shall provide the victim a written notice containing:

(1) information about the availability of emergency and medical services, if applicable;

(2) information about the rights of crime victims under Subchapter B;

(3) notice that the victim has the right to receive information regarding compensation to victims of crime as provided by Chapter 56B, including information about:

(A) the costs that may be compensated under that chapter and the amount of compensation, eligibility for compensation, and procedures for application for compensation under that chapter;

Code of Criminal Procedure

(B) the payment for a forensic medical examination under Article 56A.252 for a victim of an alleged sexual assault; and

(C) referral to available social service agencies that may offer additional assistance;

(4) the name, address, and phone number of the law enforcement agency's crime victim liaison;

(5) the name, address, and phone number of the victim assistance coordinator of the office of the attorney representing the state; and

(6) the following statement:

"You may call the law enforcement agency's telephone number for the status of the case and information about victims' rights." (Code Crim. Proc., Art. 56.07(a).)

Art. 56A.402. Referral to Sexual Assault Program.

(a) At the time a law enforcement agency provides notice under Article 56A.401, the agency shall provide, if the agency possesses the relevant information:

(1) a referral to a sexual assault program as defined by Section 420.003, Government Code; and

(2) a written description of the services provided by the program.

(b) A sexual assault program may provide a written description of the program's services to a law enforcement agency. (Code Crim. Proc., Art. 56.07(b).)

SUBCHAPTER J REQUIRED NOTIFICATIONS BY ATTORNEY REPRESENTING THE STATE

Art. 56A.451. Notification of Rights.

(a) Not later than the 10th day after the date that an indictment or information is returned against a defendant for an offense, the attorney representing the state shall give to each victim of the offense a written notice containing:

(1) the case number and assigned court for the case;

(2) a brief general statement of each procedural stage in the processing of a criminal case, including bail, plea bargaining, parole restitution, and appeal;

(3) suggested steps the victim may take if the victim is subjected to threats or intimidation;

(4) the name, address, and phone number of the local victim assistance coordinator; and

(5) notification of:

(A) the rights and procedures under this chapter, Chapter 56B, and Subchapter B, Chapter 58;

(B) the right to file a victim impact statement with the office of the attorney representing the state and the department;

(C) the right to receive information regarding compensation to victims of crime as provided by Chapter 56B, including information about:

(i) the costs that may be compensated under that chapter, eligibility for compensation, and procedures for application for compensation under that chapter;

(ii) the payment for a forensic medical examination under Article 56A.252 for a victim of an alleged sexual assault; and

(iii) referral to available social service agencies that may offer additional assistance; and

(D) the right of a victim, guardian of a victim, or close relative of a deceased victim, as defined by Section 508.117, Government Code, to appear in person before a member of the board as provided by Section 508.153, Government Code.

(b) The brief general statement required by Subsection (a)(2) that describes the plea bargaining stage in a criminal trial must include a statement that:

(1) a victim impact statement provided by a victim, guardian of a victim, or close relative of a deceased victim will be considered by the attorney representing the state in entering into a plea bargain agreement; and

(2) the judge before accepting a plea bargain agreement is required under Article 26.13(e) to ask:

(A) whether a victim impact statement has been returned to the attorney representing the state;

(B) if a victim impact statement has been returned, for a copy of the statement; and

(C) whether the attorney representing the state has given the victim, guardian of a victim, or close relative of a deceased victim notice of the existence and terms of the plea bargain agreement. (Code Crim. Proc., Arts. 56.08(a), (e).)

Art. 56A.452. Notification of Scheduled Court Proceedings.

If requested by the victim, the attorney representing the state, as far as reasonably practical, shall give the victim notice of:

(1) any scheduled court proceedings and changes in that schedule; and

(2) the filing of a request for continuance of a trial setting. (Code Crim. Proc., Art. 56.08(b).)

Art. 56A.453. Notification of Plea Bargain Agreement.

The attorney representing the state, as far as reasonably practical, shall give a victim, guardian of a victim, or close relative of a deceased victim notice of the existence and terms of any plea bargain agreement to be presented to the court. (Code Crim. Proc., Art. 56.08(b-1).)

Art. 56A.454. Victim Contact Information.

(a) A victim who receives a notice under Article 56A.451(a) and who chooses to receive other notice under law about the same case must keep the following persons informed of the victim's current address and phone number:

(1) the attorney representing the state; and

(2) the department if the defendant is imprisoned in the department after sentencing.

(b) An attorney representing the state who receives information concerning a victim's current address and phone number shall immediately provide that information to the community supervision and corrections department supervising the defendant, if the defendant is placed on community supervision. (Code Crim. Proc., Arts. 56.08(c), (d).)

SUBCHAPTER K
NOTIFICATION BY CERTAIN ENTITIES OF RELEASE OR ESCAPE

Art. 56A.501. Definitions.

In this subchapter:

(1) "Correctional facility" has the meaning assigned by Section 1.07, Penal Code.

(2) "Family violence" has the meaning assigned by Section 71.004, Family Code. (Code Crim. Proc., Art. 56.11(h).)

Art. 56A.502. Applicability.

This subchapter applies to a defendant convicted of:

(1) an offense under Title 5, Penal Code, that is punishable as a felony;

(2) an offense described by Section 508.187(a), Government Code, other than an offense described by Subdivision (1); or

(3) an offense involving family violence, stalking, or violation of a protective order or magistrate's order. (Code Crim. Proc., Art. 56.11(c).)

Art. 56A.503. Notification of Release or Escape.

(a) The department or sheriff, whichever has custody of a defendant in the case of a felony, or the sheriff in the case of a misdemeanor, shall notify a victim of the offense or a witness who testified against the defendant at the trial for the offense, other than a witness who testified in the course and scope of the witness's official or professional duties, when a defendant convicted of an offense described by Article 56A.502:

(1) completes the defendant's sentence and is released; or

(2) escapes from a correctional facility.

(b) If the department is required by Subsection (a) to give notice to a victim or witness, the department shall also give notice to local law enforcement officials in the county in which the victim or witness resides. (Code Crim. Proc., Arts. 56.11(a), (b).)

Art. 56A.504. Notification Regarding Defendant Subject to Electronic Monitoring.

The department, in the case of a defendant released on parole or to mandatory supervision following a term of imprisonment for an offense described by Article 56A.502, or a community supervision and corrections department supervising a defendant convicted of an offense described by Article 56A.502 and subsequently released on community supervision, shall notify a victim or witness described by Article 56A.503(a) when the defendant, if subject to electronic monitoring as a condition of release, ceases to be electronically monitored. (Code Crim. Proc., Art. 56.11(a-1).)

Art. 56A.505. Notification of Right to Notice.

Not later than immediately following the conviction of a defendant for an offense described by Article 56A.502, the attorney who represented the state in the prosecution of the case shall notify in writing a victim or witness described by Article 56A.503(a) of the victim's or witness's right to receive notice under this subchapter. (Code Crim. Proc., Art. 56.11(g).)

Art. 56A.506. Victim or Witness Contact Information; Confidentiality.

(a) A victim or witness who wants notification under this subchapter must:

(1) provide the department, the sheriff, or the community supervision and corrections department supervising the defendant, as appropriate,

Code of Criminal Procedure

with the e-mail address, mailing address, and telephone number of the victim, witness, or other person through whom the victim or witness may be contacted; and

(2) notify the appropriate department or the sheriff of any change of address or telephone number of the victim, witness, or other person.

(b) Information obtained and maintained by the department, a sheriff, or a community supervision and corrections department under this article is privileged and confidential. (Code Crim. Proc., Art. 56.11(d).)

Art. 56A.507. Time for Notice.

(a) The department, the sheriff, or the community supervision and corrections department supervising the defendant, as appropriate:

(1) shall make a reasonable attempt to give any notice required by Article 56A.503(a) or 56A.504:

(A) not later than the 30th day before the date the defendant:

(i) completes the sentence and is released; or

(ii) ceases to be electronically monitored as a condition of release; or

(B) immediately if the defendant escapes from the correctional facility; and

(2) may give the notice by e-mail, if possible.

(b) An attempt by the department, the sheriff, or the community supervision and corrections department supervising the defendant to give notice to a victim or witness at the victim's or witness's last known mailing address or, if notice by e-mail is possible, last known e-mail address, as shown on the records of the appropriate department or agency, constitutes a reasonable attempt to give notice under this subchapter. (Code Crim. Proc., Arts. 56.11(e), (f).)

SUBCHAPTER L NOTIFICATION BY DEPARTMENT OF ESCAPE OR TRANSFER

Art. 56A.551. Definition.

In this subchapter, "witness's close relative" means a person who:

(1) was the spouse of a deceased witness at the time of the witness's death; or

(2) is a parent or adult brother, sister, or child of a deceased witness. (Code Crim. Proc., Art. 56.12(d).)

Art. 56A.552. Notification of Victim.

The department shall immediately notify the victim of an offense, the victim's guardian, or the victim's close relative if the victim is deceased, if the victim, victim's guardian, or victim's close relative has notified the department as provided by Article 56A.554, when the defendant:

(1) escapes from a facility operated by the department for the imprisonment of individuals convicted of felonies other than state jail felonies; or

(2) is transferred from the custody of a facility described by Subdivision (1) to the custody of a peace officer under a writ of attachment or a bench warrant. (Code Crim. Proc., Art. 56.12(a).)

Art. 56A.553. Notification of Witness.

The department shall immediately notify a witness who testified against a defendant at the trial for the offense for which the defendant is imprisoned, the witness's guardian, or the witness's close relative, if the witness, witness's guardian, or witness's close relative has notified the department as provided by Article 56A.554, when the defendant:

(1) escapes from a facility operated by the department for the imprisonment of individuals convicted of felonies other than state jail felonies; or

(2) is transferred from the custody of a facility described by Subdivision (1) to the custody of a peace officer under a writ of attachment or a bench warrant. (Code Crim. Proc., Art. 56.12(a-1).)

Art. 56A.554. Request for Notification; Change of Address.

A victim, witness, guardian, or close relative who wants notification of a defendant's escape or transfer from custody under a writ of attachment or bench warrant must notify the department of that fact and of any change of address. (Code Crim. Proc., Art. 56.12(b).)

Art. 56A.555. Notice of Transfer From or Return to Custody.

The department shall include in a notice provided under Article 56A.552(2) or 56A.553(2) the name, address, and telephone number of the peace officer receiving the defendant into custody. On returning the defendant to the custody of the department, the victim services division of the department shall notify the victim, witness, guardian, or close relative, as applicable, of the return. (Code Crim. Proc., Art. 56.12(c).)

SUBCHAPTER M
OTHER POWERS AND DUTIES OF DEPARTMENT AND CLEARINGHOUSE

Art. 56A.601. Database for Defendant Release Information.

The department shall:

(1) create and maintain a computerized database containing the release information and release date of a defendant convicted of an offense described by Article 56A.502; and

(2) allow a victim or witness entitled to notice under Subchapter K or L to access through the Internet the computerized database maintained under Subdivision (1). (Code Crim. Proc., Art. 56.15.)

Art. 56A.602. Victim-Offender Mediation.

The victim services division of the department shall:

(1) train volunteers to act as mediators between victims, guardians of victims, and close relatives of deceased victims and offenders whose criminal conduct caused bodily injury or death to victims; and

(2) provide mediation services through referral of a trained volunteer, if requested by a victim, guardian of a victim, or close relative of a deceased victim. (Code Crim. Proc., Art. 56.13.)

Art. 56A.603. Clearinghouse Annual Conference.

The clearinghouse may:

(1) conduct an annual conference to provide to participants in the criminal justice system training containing information on crime victims' rights; and

(2) charge a fee to a person attending the conference described by Subdivision (1). (Code Crim. Proc., Art. 56.14.)

Art. 56A.604. Crime Victim Assistance Standards.

The clearinghouse shall develop crime victim assistance standards and distribute those standards to law enforcement officers and attorneys representing the state to aid those officers and attorneys in performing duties imposed by this chapter, Chapter 56B, and Subchapter B, Chapter 58. (Code Crim. Proc., Art. 56.05(c).)

CHAPTER 56B
CRIME VICTIMS' COMPENSATION

SUBCHAPTER A
GENERAL PROVISIONS

Art. 56B.001. Short Title.

This chapter may be cited as the Crime Victims' Compensation Act. (Code Crim. Proc., Art. 56.31.)

Art. 56B.002. Legislative Findings and Intent.

(a) The legislature recognizes that many innocent individuals suffer personal injury or death as a result of criminal acts. Crime victims and persons who intervene to prevent criminal acts often suffer disabilities, incur financial burdens, or become dependent on public assistance. The legislature finds that there is a need to compensate crime victims and those who suffer personal injury or death in the prevention of crime or in the apprehension of criminals.

(b) It is the legislature's intent that the compensation of innocent victims of violent crime encourage greater public cooperation in the successful apprehension and prosecution of criminals. (Code Crim. Proc., Art. 56.311.)

Art. 56B.003. Definitions.

In this chapter:

(1) "Child" means an individual younger than 18 years of age who:

(A) is not married; or

(B) has not had the disabilities of minority removed for general purposes under Chapter 31, Family Code.

(2) "Claimant" means any of the following individuals, other than a service provider, who is entitled to file or has filed a claim for compensation under this chapter:

(A) an authorized individual acting on behalf of a victim;

(B) an individual who legally assumes the obligation or who voluntarily pays medical or burial expenses of a victim incurred as a result of the criminally injurious conduct of another;

(C) a dependent of a victim who died as a result of the criminally injurious conduct;

Code of Criminal Procedure

(D) an immediate family member or a household member of a victim who, as a result of the criminally injurious conduct:

(i) requires psychiatric care or counseling;

(ii) incurs expenses for traveling to and attending a deceased victim's funeral; or

(iii) suffers wage loss from bereavement leave taken in connection with the death of the victim; or

(E) an authorized individual acting on behalf of a child described by Paragraph (C) or (D).

(3) "Collateral source" means any of the following sources of benefits or advantages for pecuniary loss that a claimant or victim has received or that is readily available to the claimant or victim from:

(A) the offender under an order of restitution to the claimant or victim that is imposed by a court as a condition of community supervision;

(B) the United States, a federal agency, a state or any of its political subdivisions, or an instrumentality of two or more states, unless the law providing for the benefits or advantages makes those benefits or advantages in addition to or secondary to benefits under this chapter;

(C) social security, Medicare, or Medicaid;

(D) another state's or another country's crime victims' compensation program;

(E) workers' compensation;

(F) an employer's wage continuation program, not including vacation and sick leave benefits;

(G) proceeds of an insurance contract payable to or on behalf of the claimant or victim for loss that the claimant or victim sustained because of the criminally injurious conduct;

(H) a contract or self-funded program providing hospital and other health care services or benefits; or

(I) proceeds awarded to the claimant or victim as a result of third-party litigation.

(4) "Criminally injurious conduct" means conduct that:

(A) occurs or is attempted;

(B) poses a substantial threat of personal injury or death;

(C) is punishable by fine, imprisonment, or death, or would be punishable by fine, imprisonment, or death if the person engaging in the conduct possessed the capacity to commit the conduct; and

(D) does not arise out of the ownership, maintenance, or use of a motor vehicle, aircraft, or water vehicle, unless the conduct is:

(i) intended to cause personal injury or death;

(ii) in violation of Section 545.157 or 545.401, Transportation Code, if the conduct results in bodily injury or death;

(iii) in violation of Section 550.021, Transportation Code; or

(iv) in violation of one or more of the following sections of the Penal Code:

(a) Section 19.04 (manslaughter);

(b) Section 19.05 (criminally negligent homicide);

(c) Section 22.02 (aggravated assault);

(d) Section 22.05 (deadly conduct);

(e) Section 49.04 (driving while intoxicated);

(f) Section 49.05 (flying while intoxicated);

(g) Section 49.06 (boating while intoxicated);

(h) Section 49.07 (intoxication assault); or

(i) Section 49.08 (intoxication manslaughter).

(5) "Dependent" means:

(A) a surviving spouse;

(B) a person who is a dependent, within the meaning of the Internal Revenue Code of 1986, of a victim; and

(C) a posthumous child of a deceased victim.

(6) "Family violence" has the meaning assigned by Section 71.004(1), Family Code.

(7) "Household member" means an individual who:

(A) is related by consanguinity or affinity to the victim; and

(B) resided in the same permanent household as the victim at the time that the criminally injurious conduct occurred.

(8) "Immediate family member" means an individual who is related to a victim within the second degree by consanguinity or affinity.

(9) "Intervenor" means an individual who goes to the aid of another and is killed or injured in a good faith effort to:

(A) prevent criminally injurious conduct;

(B) apprehend a person reasonably suspected of having engaged in criminally injurious conduct; or

(C) aid a peace officer.

(10) "Pecuniary loss" means the amount of the expense reasonably and necessarily incurred as a result of personal injury or death for:

(A) medical, hospital, nursing, or psychiatric care or counseling, or physical therapy;

(B) actual loss of past earnings and anticipated loss of future earnings and necessary travel expenses because of:

(i) a disability resulting from the personal injury;

(ii) the receipt of medically indicated services related to the disability; or

(iii) participation in or attendance at investigative, prosecutorial, or judicial processes or any postconviction or postadjudication proceeding relating to criminally injurious conduct;

(C) care of a child or dependent, including specialized care for a child who is a victim;

(D) funeral and burial expenses, including, for an immediate family member or a household member of the victim, the necessary expenses of traveling to and attending the funeral;

(E) loss of support to a dependent, consistent with Article 56B.057(b)(5);

(F) reasonable and necessary costs of cleaning the crime scene;

(G) reasonable replacement costs for clothing, bedding, or property of the victim seized as evidence or rendered unusable as a result of the criminal investigation;

(H) reasonable and necessary costs for relocation and housing rental assistance payments as provided by Article 56B.106(c);

(I) for an immediate family member or a household member of a deceased victim, bereavement leave of not more than 10 work days; and

(J) reasonable and necessary costs of traveling to and from a place of execution to witness the execution, including one night's lodging near the place where the execution is conducted.

(11) "Personal injury" means physical or mental harm.

(12) "Sexual assault" means an offense under Section 21.02, 21.11(a)(1), 22.011, or 22.021, Penal Code.

(13) "Trafficking of persons" means any offense that results in a person engaging in forced labor or services, including sexual conduct, and that may be prosecuted under Section 20A.02, 20A.03, 43.03, 43.031, 43.04, 43.041, 43.05, 43.25, 43.251, or 43.26, Penal Code.

(14) "Victim" means:

(A) an individual who:

(i) suffers personal injury or death as a result of criminally injurious conduct or as a result of actions taken by the individual as an intervenor, if the conduct or actions occurred in this state; and

(ii) is a resident of this state or another state of the United States;

(B) an individual who:

(i) suffers personal injury or death as a result of criminally injurious conduct or as a result of actions taken by the individual as an intervenor, if the conduct or actions occurred in a state or country that does not have a crime victims' compensation program that meets the requirements of Section 1403(b), Victims of Crime Act of 1984 (34 U.S.C. Section 20102(b));

(ii) is a resident of this state; and

(iii) would be entitled to compensation under this chapter if the criminally injurious conduct or actions had occurred in this state; or

(C) an individual who:

(i) suffers personal injury or death as a result of criminally injurious conduct caused by an act of international terrorism as defined by 18 U.S.C. Section 2331 committed outside of the United States; and

(ii) is a resident of this state.

(15) "Victim-related services or assistance" means compensation, services, or assistance provided directly to a victim or claimant to support or assist in the recovery of the victim or claimant from the consequences of criminally injurious conduct. (Code Crim. Proc., Arts. 56.01(2-a), 56.32.)

Art. 56B.004. Administration; Rules.

(a) The attorney general shall adopt rules consistent with this chapter governing its administration, including rules relating to the method of filing claims and the proof of entitlement to compensation and the review of health care services subject to compensation under this chapter, Chapter 56A, and Subchapter B, Chapter 58.

(b) Subchapters A and B, Chapter 2001, Government Code, except Sections 2001.004(3) and 2001.005, apply to the attorney general.

(c) The attorney general may delegate to a person in the attorney general's office a power or duty given to the attorney general under this chapter. (Code Crim. Proc., Art. 56.33.)

Art. 56B.005. Annual Report.

Not later than the 100th day after the end of each state fiscal year, the attorney general shall submit to the governor and the legislature a report on the attorney general's activities during the preceding fiscal year, including a statistical summary of claims and awards made and denied. (Code Crim. Proc., Art. 56.53.)

Art. 56B.006. Public Notice.

(a) A hospital licensed under the laws of this state shall display prominently in its emergency room posters giving notice of the existence and general provisions of this chapter.

(b) The attorney general shall:

(1) set standards for the location of the posters described by Subsection (a); and

(2) provide posters, application forms, and general information regarding this chapter to each hospital and physician licensed to practice in this state. (Code Crim. Proc., Art. 56.60(a).)

Art. 56B.007. Notice by Local Law Enforcement Agency.

(a) Each local law enforcement agency shall inform a claimant or victim of the provisions of this chapter and make application forms available.

(b) The attorney general:

(1) shall:

(A) provide application forms and all other documents that a local law enforcement agency may require to comply with this article; and

(B) set standards to be followed by a local law enforcement agency to comply with this article; and

(2) may require a local law enforcement agency to file with the attorney general a description of the procedures adopted by the agency to comply with this article. (Code Crim. Proc., Art. 56.60(b).)

SUBCHAPTER B APPLICATION AND REVIEW

Art. 56B.051. Application for Compensation.

(a) An applicant for compensation under this chapter must apply in writing on a form prescribed by the attorney general.

(b) An application for compensation under this chapter must be verified and contain:

(1) the date on which the criminally injurious conduct occurred;

(2) a description of the nature and circumstances of the criminally injurious conduct;

(3) a complete financial statement, including:

(A) the cost of medical care or burial expenses and the loss of wages or support the claimant or victim has incurred or will incur; and

(B) the extent to which the claimant or victim has been indemnified for the expenses under Paragraph (A) from a collateral source;

(4) a statement indicating the extent of any disability resulting from the injury incurred;

(5) an authorization permitting the attorney general to verify the contents of the application; and

(6) any other information the attorney general requires. (Code Crim. Proc., Art. 56.36.)

Art. 56B.052. Period for Filing Application.

(a) Except as otherwise provided by this article, a claimant or victim must file an application not later than the third anniversary of the date of the criminally injurious conduct.

(b) The attorney general may extend the time for filing for good cause shown by the claimant or victim.

(c) If the victim is a child, the application must be filed not later than the third anniversary of the date the claimant or victim is made aware of the offense, but not after the child attains 21 years of age.

(d) If a claimant or victim presents medically documented evidence of a physical or mental incapacity that was incurred by the claimant or victim as a result of the criminally injurious conduct and that reasonably prevented the claimant or victim from filing the application within the limitations period under Subsection (a), the period of the incapacity is not included.

(e) For a claim that is based on criminally injurious conduct in violation of Chapter 19, Penal Code, the claimant must file an application not later than the third anniversary of the date the identity of the victim is established by a law enforcement agency. (Code Crim. Proc., Art. 56.37.)

Art. 56B.053. Reporting of Offense Required.

(a) Except as otherwise provided by this article, a claimant or victim may not file an application unless the victim reports the criminally injurious conduct to the appropriate state or local public safety or law enforcement agency within a reasonable period, but not so late as to interfere with or hamper the investigation and prosecution of the offense after the criminally injurious conduct is committed.

(b) The attorney general may extend the time for reporting the criminally injurious conduct if the attorney general determines that the extension is justified by extraordinary circumstances.

(c) Subsection (a) does not apply if the victim is a child. (Code Crim. Proc., Art. 56.46.)

Art. 56B.054. Review and Investigation of Application.

(a) The attorney general shall appoint a clerk to review each application for compensation described by Article 56B.051 to ensure the application is complete.

(b) The attorney general may review the actual or proposed health care services for which a claimant or victim seeks compensation in an application filed under Article 56B.051.

(c) The clerk shall return to the claimant or victim any application that is incomplete and shall provide a brief statement showing the additional information required. Not later than the 30th day after the date of receiving a returned application, a claimant or victim may:

(1) provide the additional information; or

(2) appeal the action to the attorney general, who shall review the application to determine whether the application is complete.

(d) The attorney general may investigate an application.

(e) As part of the attorney general's review, verification, and hearing duties under this chapter, the attorney general may:

(1) subpoena witnesses and administer oaths to determine whether and the extent to which a claimant or victim qualifies for an award; and

(2) as provided by Article 56B.055 and if the mental, physical, or emotional condition of a claimant or victim is material to the claim, order:

(A) a claimant or victim to submit to a mental or physical examination by a physician or psychologist; or

(B) an autopsy of a deceased victim.

(f) On request by the attorney general and not later than the 14th business day after the date of the request, a law enforcement agency shall release to the attorney general all reports, including witness statements and criminal history record information, to allow the attorney general to determine whether a claimant or victim qualifies for an award and the extent of the qualification. (Code Crim. Proc., Arts. 56.38, 56.385(a).)

Art. 56B.055. Mental or Physical Examination; Autopsy.

(a) For good cause shown, an order for a mental or physical examination or an autopsy as provided by Article 56B.054(e)(2) may be made on notice to the individual to be examined and, if applicable, to each person who has appeared at a hearing under Article 56B.056.

(b) An order under Subsection (a) must:

(1) specify the time, place, manner, conditions, and scope of the examination or autopsy;

(2) specify the person who is to perform the examination or autopsy; and

(3) require the person performing the examination or autopsy to file with the attorney general a detailed written report of the examination or autopsy.

(c) A report must set out the findings of the person performing the examination or autopsy, including:

(1) the results of any test performed; and

(2) any diagnosis, prognosis, or other conclusion or report of an earlier examination of the same condition.

(d) On request of the individual examined, the attorney general shall provide to the individual a copy of the report. If the victim is deceased, the attorney general on request shall provide to the claimant a copy of the report.

(e) A physician or psychologist performing an examination or autopsy under this article shall be compensated from money appropriated for the administration of this chapter. (Code Crim. Proc., Art. 56.39.)

Art. 56B.056. Hearings and Prehearing Conferences.

(a) The attorney general shall determine whether a hearing on an application for compensation under this chapter is necessary.

(b) On determining that a hearing is not necessary, the attorney general may approve the application in accordance with Article 56B.057.

(c) On determining that a hearing is necessary or on request for a hearing by the claimant or victim, the attorney general shall consider the application at a hearing at a time and place of the attorney general's choosing. The attorney general shall notify all interested persons not later than the 10th day before the date of the hearing.

(d) At the hearing the attorney general shall:

(1) review the application for compensation and any report prepared under Article 56B.055 and any other evidence obtained as a result of the attorney general's investigation; and

(2) receive other evidence that the attorney general finds necessary or desirable to evaluate the application properly.

(e) The attorney general may appoint hearing officers to conduct hearings or prehearing conferences under this chapter.

(f) A hearing or prehearing conference is open to the public unless the hearing officer or attorney general determines in a particular case that all or part of the hearing or conference should be held in private because a criminal suspect has not been apprehended or because a private hearing or conference is in the interest of the claimant or victim.

(g) The attorney general may suspend the proceedings pending disposition of a criminal prosecution that has been commenced or is imminent, except that the attorney general may make an emergency award under Article 56B.102.

(h) Subchapters C through H, Chapter 2001, Government Code, do not apply to the attorney general or the attorney general's orders and decisions. (Code Crim. Proc., Art. 56.40.)

Art. 56B.057. Approval of Application.

(a) The attorney general shall approve an application for compensation under this chapter if the attorney general finds by a preponderance of the evidence that grounds for compensation under this chapter exist.

(b) The attorney general shall deny an application for compensation under this chapter if:

(1) the criminally injurious conduct is not reported as provided by Article 56B.053;

Code of Criminal Procedure

(2) the application is not made in the manner provided by Articles 56B.051 and 56B.052;

(3) the claimant or victim knowingly and willingly participated in the criminally injurious conduct;

(4) the claimant or victim is the offender or an accomplice of the offender;

(5) an award of compensation to the claimant or victim would benefit the offender or an accomplice of the offender;

(6) the claimant or victim was incarcerated in a penal institution, as defined by Section 1.07, Penal Code, at the time the offense was committed; or

(7) the claimant or victim knowingly or intentionally submits false or forged information to the attorney general.

(c) Subsection (b)(3) does not apply to a claimant or victim who seeks compensation for criminally injurious conduct that is:

(1) in violation of Section 20A.02(a)(7), Penal Code; or

(2) trafficking of persons, other than an offense described by Subdivision (1), if the criminally injurious conduct the claimant or victim participated in was the result of force, fraud, or coercion.

(d) Except as provided by rules adopted by the attorney general to prevent the unjust enrichment of an offender, the attorney general may not deny an award otherwise payable to a claimant or victim because the claimant or victim:

(1) is an immediate family member of the offender; or

(2) resides in the same household as the offender. (Code Crim. Proc., Art. 56.41.)

Art. 56B.058. Disclosure and Use of Information.

(a) This article does not apply to information made confidential by law.

(b) An application for compensation under this chapter and any information, document, summary, or other record provided to or received, maintained, or created by the attorney general under this chapter is:

(1) except as provided by Section 552.132(c), Government Code, not subject to disclosure under Chapter 552 of that code; and

(2) except as provided by Subsection (c), not subject to disclosure, discovery, subpoena, or other means of legal compulsion for release.

(c) The attorney general may not release or disclose an application for compensation under this chapter, or any information, document, summary, or other record provided to or received, maintained, or created by the attorney general under this chapter, except:

(1) by court order for good cause shown, if the order includes a finding that the information is not available from any other source;

(2) with the consent of:

(A) the claimant or victim; or

(B) the person that provided the information to the attorney general;

(3) to an employee or other person under the direction of the attorney general;

(4) to another crime victims' compensation program that meets the requirements of 34 U.S.C. Section 20102(b);

(5) to a person authorized by the attorney general to receive the information to:

(A) conduct an audit as required by state or federal law;

(B) provide a review or examination under Article 56B.054 or 56B.055 or under another provision of this chapter to determine the appropriateness of an award under this chapter;

(C) prevent, deter, or punish fraud related to this chapter; or

(D) assert subrogation or restitution rights;

(6) as the attorney general determines necessary to enforce this chapter, including presenting the application, information, document, summary, or record in court; or

(7) in response to a subpoena that is issued in a criminal proceeding and that requests an application for compensation under this chapter, subject to Subsection (d).

(d) In responding to a subpoena described by Subsection (c)(7), the attorney general shall release only the victim's completed application form as described by Article 56B.051(a) after redacting any confidential information described by Section 552.132(b), Government Code. The release of a victim's completed application form under this subsection does not affect the authority of the court to order the release or disclosure of additional information under this article. (Code Crim. Proc., Art. 56.65.)

SUBCHAPTER C AWARD OF COMPENSATION

Art. 56B.101. Types of Assistance.

(a) On approving an application for compensation under Article 56B.057, the attorney general shall determine the type of state assistance that will best aid the claimant or victim.

(b) The attorney general may:

(1) authorize a cash payment to or on behalf of a claimant or victim for pecuniary loss;

(2) refer a claimant or victim to a state agency for vocational or other rehabilitative services; or

(3) provide counseling services for a claimant or victim or contract with a private entity to provide counseling services. (Code Crim. Proc., Art. 56.35.)

Art. 56B.102. Emergency Award.

(a) Before acting on an application for compensation under this chapter, the attorney general may make an emergency award if it appears likely that:

(1) a final award will be made; and

(2) the claimant or victim will suffer undue hardship if immediate economic relief is not obtained.

(b) An emergency award may not exceed $1,500.

(c) The amount of an emergency award must be:

(1) deducted from the final award; or

(2) repaid by and recoverable from the claimant or victim to the extent the emergency award exceeds the final award. (Code Crim. Proc., Art. 56.50.)

Art. 56B.103. Compensation for Pecuniary Loss.

(a) The attorney general shall award compensation for pecuniary loss arising from criminally injurious conduct if the attorney general is satisfied by a preponderance of the evidence that the requirements of this chapter are met.

(b) The attorney general shall establish whether, as a direct result of criminally injurious conduct, a claimant or victim suffered personal injury or death that resulted in a pecuniary loss for which the claimant or victim is not compensated from a collateral source. (Code Crim. Proc., Arts. 56.34(a), (b).)

Art. 56B.104. Compensation for Health Care Services.

(a) The attorney general shall award compensation for health care services according to the medical fee guidelines prescribed by Subtitle A, Title 5, Labor Code.

(b) The attorney general, a claimant, or a victim is not liable for health care service charges that exceed the medical fee guidelines. A health care provider shall accept compensation from the attorney general as payment in full for the charges unless an investigation of the charges by the attorney general determines that there is a reasonable health care justification for the deviation from the guidelines.

(c) The attorney general may not compensate a claimant or victim for health care services that the attorney general determines are not medically necessary.

(d) The attorney general, a claimant, or a victim is not liable for a charge that is not medically necessary. (Code Crim. Proc., Arts. 56.34(c), (d), 56.385(b), (c).)

Art. 56B.105. Compensation for Certain Criminally Injurious Conduct Prohibited.

(a) Except as provided by Subsection (b), the attorney general may not award compensation for pecuniary loss arising from criminally injurious conduct that occurred before January 1, 1980.

(b) The attorney general may award compensation for pecuniary loss arising from criminally injurious conduct that occurred before January 1, 1980, if:

(1) the conduct was in violation of Chapter 19, Penal Code;

(2) the identity of the victim is established by a law enforcement agency on or after January 1, 2009; and

(3) the claimant files the application for compensation within the limitations period provided by Article 56B.052(e). (Code Crim. Proc., Art. 56.61.)

Art. 56B.106. Limits on Compensation.

(a) Except as otherwise provided by this article, awards payable to a victim and any other claimant sustaining pecuniary loss because of injury or death of that victim may not exceed $50,000 in the aggregate.

(b) In addition to an award payable under Subsection (a), the attorney general may award not more than $75,000 for extraordinary pecuniary loss if the personal injury to a victim is catastrophic and results in a total and permanent disability to the victim. An award described by this subsection may be made for lost wages and the reasonable and necessary costs of:

(1) making a home or motor vehicle accessible;

(2) obtaining job training and vocational rehabilitation;

(3) training in the use of a special appliance;

(4) receiving home health care;

(5) durable medical equipment;

(6) rehabilitation technology; and

(7) long-term medical expenses incurred as a result of medically indicated treatment for the personal injury.

(c) A victim of stalking, family violence, or trafficking of persons, a victim of sexual assault who is assaulted in the victim's place of residence, or a child who is a victim of a murder attempt in the child's place of residence may receive a one-time assistance payment in an amount not to exceed:

(1) $2,000 to be used for relocation expenses, including expenses for rental deposit, utility connections, expenses relating to moving belongings, motor vehicle mileage expenses, and for an out-of-state move, transportation, lodging, and meals; and

(2) $1,800 to be used for housing rental expenses.

(d) An immediate family member or household member of a deceased victim may not receive more than $1,000 in lost wages as a result of bereavement leave taken by the family or household member.

(e) The attorney general by rule may establish a limitation on any other pecuniary loss compensated under this chapter, including a limitation on pecuniary loss incurred as a result of a claimant's travel to and attendance of a deceased victim's funeral. (Code Crim. Proc., Art. 56.42.)

Art. 56B.107. Denial or Reduction of Award.

(a) Except as otherwise provided by this article, the attorney general may deny or reduce an award otherwise payable:

(1) if the claimant or victim has not substantially cooperated with an appropriate law enforcement agency;

(2) if, as a result of the claimant's or victim's behavior, the claimant or victim bears a share of the responsibility for the act or omission giving rise to the claim;

(3) to the extent that pecuniary loss is recouped from a collateral source; or

(4) if the claimant or victim was engaging in an activity that at the time of the criminally injurious conduct was prohibited by law, including a rule.

(b) Subsection (a)(4) does not apply to a claimant or victim who seeks compensation for criminally injurious conduct that is:

(1) in violation of Section 20A.02(a)(7), Penal Code; or

(2) trafficking of persons, other than an offense described by Subdivision (1), if the activity the claimant or victim engaged in was the result of force, fraud, or coercion. (Code Crim. Proc., Art. 56.45.)

(c) The attorney general may not deny or reduce an award under Subsection (a)(1) based on the interactions of the claimant or victim with a law enforcement agency at the crime scene or hospital unless the attorney general finds that the claimant or victim, subsequent to the claimant's or victim's interactions at the crime scene or hospital, failed or refused to substantially cooperate with the law enforcement agency.

Art. 56B.108. Reconsideration.

(a) On the attorney general's own motion or on request of a claimant or victim, the attorney general may reconsider:

(1) a decision to make or deny an award; or

(2) the amount of an award.

(b) At least annually, the attorney general shall reconsider each award being paid in installments.

(c) On reconsideration, the attorney general may order the refund of an award if:

(1) the award was obtained by fraud or mistake; or

(2) newly discovered evidence shows the claimant or victim to be ineligible for the award under Article 56B.057 or 56B.107. (Code Crim. Proc., Art. 56.47.)

SUBCHAPTER D PAYMENT OF AWARD

Art. 56B.151. Method of Payment.

The attorney general may pay an award in a lump sum or in installments as provided by this subchapter. (Code Crim. Proc., Art. 56.44(a) (part).)

Art. 56B.152. Payment for Pecuniary Loss Accrued at Time of Award.

The attorney general shall pay in a lump sum the part of an award equal to the amount of pecuniary loss accrued to the date of the award. (Code Crim. Proc., Art. 56.44(a) (part).)

Art. 56B.153. Payment for Pecuniary Loss Accrued After Time of Award.

(a) Except as provided by Subsection (b), the attorney general shall pay in installments the part of an award for allowable expenses that accrue after the award is made.

(b) At the request of the claimant or victim, the attorney general may pay in a lump sum an award for future pecuniary loss if the attorney general finds that:

(1) paying the award in a lump sum will promote the interests of the claimant or victim; or

(2) the present value of all future pecuniary loss does not exceed $1,000.

(c) The attorney general may not pay in installments an award for future pecuniary loss for a period for which the attorney general cannot reasonably determine the future pecuniary loss. (Code Crim. Proc., Arts. 56.44(a) (part), (b), (c).)

Art. 56B.154. Recipient of Payment.

The attorney general may make payments only to an individual who is a claimant or a victim or to a provider on the individual's behalf. (Code Crim. Proc., Art. 56.44(d).)

SUBCHAPTER E
GENERAL PROVISIONS RELATING TO PAYMENT

Art. 56B.201. Adjustment of Awards and Payments.

(a) The attorney general shall establish a policy to adjust awards and payments so that the total amount of awards granted in each calendar year does not exceed the amount of money credited to the compensation to victims of crime fund during that year.

(b) On the establishment of a policy under Subsection (a), the attorney general, the claimant, or the victim is not liable for the amount of incurred charges exceeding the adjusted amount for the service on which the adjusted payment is determined.

(c) A service provider who accepts a payment that has been adjusted by a policy established under Subsection (a) agrees to accept the adjusted payment as payment in full for the service and is barred from legal action against the claimant or victim for collection. (Code Crim. Proc., Arts. 56.34(e), 56.58.)

Art. 56B.202. Subrogation.

If compensation is awarded under this chapter, the state is subrogated to all the claimant's or victim's rights to receive or recover benefits for pecuniary loss to the extent compensation is awarded from a collateral source. (Code Crim. Proc., Art. 56.51.)

Art. 56B.203. Award Not Subject to Execution.

(a) Except as provided by Subsection (b), an award is not subject to execution, attachment, garnishment, or other process.

(b) An award is not exempt from a claim of a creditor to the extent that the creditor provided a product, service, or accommodation, the cost of which is included in the award. (Code Crim. Proc., Art. 56.49(a).)

Art. 56B.204. Assignment of Benefits for Loss Accruing in Future.

(a) Except as provided by Subsections (b) and (c), an assignment of or agreement to assign a right to benefits for loss accruing in the future is unenforceable.

(b) An assignment of a right to benefits for loss of earnings is enforceable to secure payment of alimony, maintenance, or child support.

(c) An assignment of a right to benefits is enforceable to the extent that the benefits are for the cost of a product, service, or accommodation:

(1) made necessary by the injury or death on which the claim is based; and

(2) provided or to be provided by the assignee. (Code Crim. Proc., Art. 56.49(b).)

SUBCHAPTER F
PAYMENTS FOR CERTAIN DISABLED PEACE OFFICERS

Art. 56B.251. Definition.

In this subchapter, "peace officer" means an individual elected, appointed, or employed to serve as a peace officer for a governmental entity under Article 2.12 or other law. The term includes a former peace officer who is entitled to receive payments under this subchapter because of an injury suffered while performing duties as a peace officer. (Code Crim. Proc., Art. 56.542(a).)

Art. 56B.252. Applicability.

This subchapter applies only to a peace officer who is employed by this state or a local governmental entity in this state and who sustains an injury in the performance of the officer's duties as a peace officer as a result of criminally injurious conduct on or after September 1, 1989. (Code Crim. Proc., Art. 56.542(b) (part).)

Art. 56B.253. Payment Entitlement.

A peace officer to whom this subchapter applies is entitled to an annual payment in the amount described by Article 56B.254 if the officer presents evidence satisfactory to the attorney general that:

(1) the officer's condition is a total disability resulting in permanent incapacity for work; and

(2) the total disability has persisted for more than 12 months. (Code Crim. Proc., Art. 56.542(b) (part).)

Art. 56B.254. Amount of Payment.

The amount of an annual payment under this subchapter is equal to the difference between:

(1) any amount received by the peace officer for the injury or disability from another source of income, including settlements related to the injury or disability, insurance benefits, federal disability benefits, workers' compensation benefits, and benefits from another governmental entity, if those amounts do not exceed the amount described by Subdivision (2); and

(2) an amount equal to the officer's average annual salary during the officer's final three years as a peace officer. (Code Crim. Proc., Art. 56.542(b) (part).)

Art. 56B.255. Method of Payment.

A peace officer who is entitled to an annual payment under Article 56B.253 may elect to receive the payment in:

(1) a single payment paid each year; or

(2) equal monthly installments. (Code Crim. Proc., Art. 56.542(l).)

Art. 56B.256. Cost-Of-Living Adjustment.

(a) The amount of a payment under Article 56B.254 is subject to an annual cost-of-living adjustment calculated by the attorney general.

(b) The attorney general shall calculate the amount of the cost-of-living adjustment by multiplying the amount of the annual payment received by the peace officer under this subchapter during the preceding year by the percentage by which the Consumer Price Index for All Urban Consumers published by the Bureau of Labor Statistics of the United States Department of Labor, or its successor index, increased during the preceding calendar year. (Code Crim. Proc., Art. 56.542(c).)

Art. 56B.257. Calculation of Initial Payment.

The attorney general shall calculate the amount of an initial payment based on an injury suffered after September 1, 1989, by:

(1) calculating the amount to which the peace officer is entitled under Article 56B.254; and

(2) adding to that amount the cumulative successive cost-of-living adjustments for the intervening years calculated from the date of the injury. (Code Crim. Proc., Art. 56.542(d).)

Art. 56B.258. Proof Required for Payment.

To receive a payment under this subchapter, a peace officer must provide to the attorney general:

(1) proof that the injury:

(A) was sustained in the performance of the applicant's duties as a peace officer; and

(B) is a total disability resulting in permanent incapacity for work; and

(2) any other information or evidence the attorney general requires. (Code Crim. Proc., Art. 56.542(e).)

Art. 56B.259. Hearing.

The attorney general may approve the application without a hearing or may conduct a hearing under Article 56B.056. (Code Crim. Proc., Art. 56.542(f) (part).)

Art. 56B.260. Judicial Review.

The decision of the attorney general is subject to judicial review under Subchapter H. (Code Crim. Proc., Art. 56.542(f) (part).)

Art. 56B.261. Periodic Review.

The attorney general may appoint a panel of physicians to periodically review each application for assistance under this subchapter to ensure the validity of the application and the necessity of continued assistance to the peace officer. (Code Crim. Proc., Art. 56.542(g).)

Art. 56B.262. Issuance of Warrant for Payment.

(a) The attorney general shall notify the comptroller of the attorney general's determination that a claim under this subchapter is valid and justifies payment. On receipt of the notice, the comptroller shall issue a warrant to or on behalf of the peace officer in the proper amount from amounts in the compensation to victims of crime fund. A payment under this subchapter to or on behalf of a peace officer is payable as soon as possible after the attorney general notifies the comptroller.

(b) The attorney general and the comptroller by rule shall adopt a memorandum of understanding to establish procedures under which annual payments continue to a peace officer until continued assistance is no longer necessary. (Code Crim. Proc., Arts. 56.542(h), (i).)

Art. 56B.263. Limits on Compensation.

The total aggregate amount of all annual payments made to an individual peace officer under this subchapter may not exceed $200,000. The limits on compensation imposed by Article 56B.106 do not apply to payments made under this subchapter. (Code Crim. Proc., Art. 56.542(k).)

Art. 56B.264. Application of Other Law.

(a) Article 56B.052 does not apply to the filing of an application under this subchapter.

(b) Other provisions of this chapter apply to this subchapter to the extent applicable and consistent with this subchapter. (Code Crim. Proc., Art. 56.542(j).)

SUBCHAPTER G ATTORNEY'S FEES

Art. 56B.301. Award of Attorney's Fees.

(a) As part of an order, the attorney general shall determine and award reasonable attorney's fees commensurate with legal services rendered, to be paid by the state to the attorney representing the claimant or victim.

(b) Attorney's fees may be denied on a finding that the claim or appeal is frivolous.

(c) An award of attorney's fees is in addition to an award of compensation.

(d) Attorney's fees may not be paid to an attorney of a claimant or victim unless an award is made to the claimant or victim. (Code Crim. Proc., Arts. 56.43(a) (part), (b), (c), (e).)

Art. 56B.302. Amount of Attorney's Fees.

(a) Attorney's fees may not exceed 25 percent of the amount of the award the attorney assisted the claimant or victim in obtaining.

(b) If there is no dispute of the attorney general's determination of the amount due to the claimant or victim and a hearing is not held, the attorney's fee shall be the lesser of:

(1) 25 percent of the amount the attorney assisted the claimant or victim in obtaining; or

(2) $300.

(c) An attorney may not contract for or receive an amount that exceeds the amount allowed under this article. (Code Crim. Proc., Arts. 56.43(a) (part), (d).)

SUBCHAPTER H JUDICIAL REVIEW

Art. 56B.351. Notice of Dissatisfaction.

Not later than the 40th day after the date the attorney general renders a final decision, a claimant or victim may file with the attorney general a notice of dissatisfaction with the decision. (Code Crim. Proc., Art. 56.48(a) (part).)

Art. 56B.352. Suit; Venue.

Not later than the 40th day after the date the claimant or victim gives notice of dissatisfaction under Article 56B.351, the claimant or victim must bring suit in:

(1) the district court having jurisdiction in the county in which:

(A) the injury or death occurred; or

(B) the victim resided at the time of the injury or death; or

(2) if the victim resided out of state at the time of the injury or death:

(A) the district court having jurisdiction in the county in which the injury or death occurred; or

(B) a district court in Travis County. (Code Crim. Proc., Art. 56.48(a) (part).)

Art. 56B.353. Restrictions on Attorney General During Judicial Review.

While judicial review of a decision by the attorney general is pending, the attorney general:

(1) shall suspend payments to the claimant or victim; and

(2) may not reconsider the award. (Code Crim. Proc., Art. 56.48(b).)

Art. 56B.354. Standard of Review.

The court shall determine the issues by trial de novo. (Code Crim. Proc., Art. 56.48(c) (part).)

Art. 56B.355. Burden of Proof.

The burden of proof is on the claimant or victim filing the notice of dissatisfaction. (Code Crim. Proc., Art. 56.48(c) (part).)

Art. 56B.356. Attorney's Fees.

In the event of judicial review, a court may award as attorney's fees an amount not to exceed 25 percent of the total recovery by the claimant or victim. (Code Crim. Proc., Art. 56.48(d).)

Art. 56B.357. Calculation of Time.

In calculating a period under Article 56B.351 or 56B.352, if the last day is a legal holiday or Sunday, the last day is not counted, and the time is extended to include the next business day. (Code Crim. Proc., Art. 56.48(e).)

SUBCHAPTER I PRIVATE ACTION

Art. 56B.401. Notice of Proposed Private Action.

Before a claimant or victim may bring an action to recover damages related to criminally injurious conduct for which compensation under this chapter is claimed or awarded, the claimant or victim must give the attorney general written notice of the proposed action. (Code Crim. Proc., Art. 56.52(a) (part).)

Art. 56B.402. Receipt of Notice.

After receiving notice under Article 56B.401, the attorney general shall promptly:

(1) join in the action as a party plaintiff to recover benefits awarded;

(2) require the claimant or victim to bring the action in the claimant's or victim's name as a trustee on behalf of the state to recover benefits awarded; or

(3) reserve the attorney general's rights and take neither action described by Subdivision (1) or (2). (Code Crim. Proc., Art. 56.52(a) (part).)

Art. 56B.403. Deduction for Reasonable Expenses.

(a) A claimant or victim who brings an action as a trustee as described by Article 56B.402(2) and recovers compensation awarded by the attorney general may deduct from the benefits recovered on behalf of the state the reasonable expenses of the suit, including attorney's fees, expended in pursuing the recovery for the state.

(b) The claimant or victim must justify a deduction under Subsection (a) to the attorney general in writing on a form provided by the attorney general. (Code Crim. Proc., Art. 56.52(b).)

Art. 56B.404. Limitations on Resolution of Action.

(a) A claimant or victim may not settle or otherwise resolve any such action without the attorney general's written authorization.

(b) A third party or agent, insurer, or attorney of a third party may not participate in the settlement or other resolution of such an action if the third party, agent, insurer, or attorney actually knows, or should know, that the claimant or victim has received money from the compensation to victims of crime fund and is subject to the subrogation provisions of this subchapter.

(c) Any attempt by a third party or agent, insurer, or attorney of a third party to settle an action is void and does not result in a release from liability to the compensation to victims of crime fund for any rights subrogated under this subchapter.

(d) An agent, insurer, or attorney described by this article is personally liable to the compensation to victims of crime fund for any money paid to a claimant or victim in violation of this article, in an amount not to exceed the full amount of the fund's right to reimbursement. (Code Crim. Proc., Art. 56.52(c) (part).)

Art. 56B.405. Criminal Penalty.

(a) A claimant, victim, or third party, or an agent, insurer, or attorney of a third party, commits an offense if the person knowingly fails to comply with the requirements of this chapter, Chapter 56A, or Subchapter B, Chapter 58.

(b) An offense under Subsection (a) is a Class B misdemeanor, except that any fine imposed may not exceed $500. (Code Crim. Proc., Arts. 56.52(c) (part), (d).)

SUBCHAPTER J FUNDS

Art. 56B.451. Definition.

In this subchapter, "fund" means the compensation to victims of crime fund. (New.)

Art. 56B.452. Establishment.

(a) The compensation to victims of crime fund is in the state treasury.

(b) Section 403.095, Government Code, does not apply to the fund. (Code Crim. Proc., Arts. 56.54(a), (g) (part).)

Art. 56B.453. Use of Money.

(a) Money in the fund may be used only as provided by this chapter and is not available for any other purpose.

(b) Except as provided by Subsection (d) and Articles 56B.455, 56B.458, 56B.459, and 56B.460, the fund may be used only by the attorney general to pay compensation to claimants or victims under this chapter.

(c) For purposes of Subsection (b), compensation to claimants or victims includes money allocated from the fund to the Crime Victims' Institute created by Section 96.65, Education Code, for the operation of the institute and for other expenses in administering this chapter. The institute shall use money allocated from the fund only for the purposes of Sections 96.65, 96.651, and 96.652, Education Code.

(d) **[As amended by Acts 2021, 87th Leg., ch. XXX (HB 3607)]** The attorney general may use the fund to:

(1) reimburse a health care facility or a sexual assault examiner or sexual assault nurse examiner for certain costs of a forensic medical examination that are incurred by the facility or the examiner under Subchapter F or G, Chapter 56A, as provided by those subchapters; and

(2) make a payment to or on behalf of an individual for the reasonable costs incurred for medical care provided under Subchapter F or G, Chapter 56A, in accordance with Section 323.004, Health and Safety Code.

(d) **[As amended by Acts 2021, 87th Leg., ch. XXX (HB 2462)]** The attorney general may use the fund to:

(1) reimburse a health care provider or a sexual assault examiner or sexual assault nurse examiner for certain costs of a forensic medical examination that are incurred by the provider or the examiner under Subchapter F or G, Chapter 56A, as provided by those subchapters; and

(2) make a payment to or on behalf of an individual for the reasonable costs incurred for medical care provided under Subchapter F or G, Chapter 56A, in accordance with Section 323.004, Health and Safety Code.

Art. 56B.454. Limitations on Payments.

(a) The attorney general may not make compensation payments that exceed the amount of money available in the fund.

(b) General revenue funds may not be used for payments under this chapter. (Code Crim. Proc., Arts. 56.54(d), (e).)

Art. 56B.455. Amount Carried Forward.

An amount of money deposited to the credit of the fund not to exceed one-quarter of the amount disbursed from that fund in the form of compensation payments during a state fiscal year shall be carried forward into the next succeeding state fiscal year and applied toward the amount listed in that fiscal year's method of financing. (Code Crim. Proc., Art. 56.54(h).)

Art. 56B.456. Transfer of Money From Auxiliary Fund.

(a) Not later than September 15 of each year, the attorney general, after consulting with the comptroller, shall certify the amount of money remaining in the compensation to victims of crime auxiliary fund at the end of the preceding state fiscal year.

(b) If the amount remaining in the compensation to victims of crime auxiliary fund as certified under Subsection (a) exceeds $5 million, as soon as practicable after the date of certification, the attorney general may transfer to the fund an amount that is not more than 50 percent of the excess amount in the auxiliary fund. Money transferred under this subsection may be used only to make compensation payments during the state fiscal year in which the amount is transferred. (Code Crim. Proc., Art. 56.54(m).)

Art. 56B.457. Gifts, Grants, and Donations.

(a) The attorney general may accept gifts, grants, and donations to be credited to the fund.

(b) The attorney general shall file annually with the governor and the presiding officer of each house of the legislature a complete and detailed written report accounting for all gifts, grants, and donations received and disbursed, used, or maintained by the attorney general that are credited to the fund. (Code Crim. Proc., Art. 56.54(f).)

Art. 56B.458. Emergency Reserve.

(a) If the amount available in the fund is sufficient in a state fiscal year to make all compensation payments, the attorney general may retain any portion of the fund that was deposited during the fiscal year that exceeded compensation payments made during that fiscal year as an emergency reserve for the next fiscal year. The emergency reserve may not exceed $10,000,000.

(b) The emergency reserve may be used only:

(1) to make compensation awards in claims; and

(2) to provide emergency relief and assistance, including crisis intervention, emergency housing, travel, food, or expenses and technical assistance expenses incurred in implementing this article in

incidents resulting from an act of mass violence or from an act of international terrorism as defined by 18 U.S.C. Section 2331, occurring in this state or for Texas residents injured or killed in an act of terrorism outside of the United States. (Code Crim. Proc., Art. 56.54(i).)

Art. 56B.459. Appropriation for Associate Judge Program.

The legislature may appropriate money in the fund to administer the associate judge program under Subchapter C, Chapter 201, Family Code. (Code Crim. Proc., Art. 56.54(j).)

Art. 56B.460. Appropriation for Other Crime Victim Assistance.

(a) Not later than December 15 of each even-numbered year, the attorney general, after consulting with the comptroller, shall prepare forecasts and certify estimates of:

(1) the amount of money in the fund that the attorney general anticipates will remain unexpended at the end of the current state fiscal year and that is available for appropriation in the next state fiscal biennium;

(2) the amount of money that the attorney general anticipates will be received from deposits made to the credit of the fund during the next state fiscal biennium, other than deposits of:

(A) gifts, grants, and donations; and

(B) money received from the United States; and

(3) the amount of money from the fund that the attorney general anticipates will be obligated during the next state fiscal biennium to comply with this chapter, Chapter 56A, and Subchapter B, Chapter 58.

(b) At the time the attorney general certifies the estimates made under Subsection (a), the attorney general shall also certify for the next state fiscal biennium the amount of excess money in the fund available for the purposes of Subsection (c), calculated by multiplying the amount estimated under Subsection (a)(3) by 105 percent and subtracting that product from the sum of the amounts estimated under Subsections (a)(1) and (2).

(c) For a state fiscal biennium, the legislature may appropriate from the fund the amount of excess money in the fund certified for the biennium under Subsection (b) to state agencies that deliver or fund victim-related services or assistance.

(d) The attorney general and the comptroller shall cooperate in determining the proper allocation of the various sources of revenue deposited to the credit of the fund for purposes of this article.

(e) The attorney general may use money appropriated from the fund for grants or contracts supporting victim-related services or assistance, including support for private Texas nonprofit corporations that provide victim-related civil legal services directly to victims, immediate family members of victims, or claimants. A grant supporting victim-related services or assistance is governed by Chapter 783, Government Code.

(f) The attorney general shall adopt rules necessary to implement this article. (Code Crim. Proc., Art. 56.541.)

Art. 56B.461. Use of Auxiliary Fund.

As appropriated by the legislature, the attorney general may use the compensation to victims of crime auxiliary fund to cover costs incurred by the attorney general in administering the address confidentiality program established under Subchapter B, Chapter 58. (Code Crim. Proc., Art. 56.54(l).)

Art. 56B.462. Payers of Last Resort.

The fund and the compensation to victims of crime auxiliary fund are the payers of last resort. (Code Crim. Proc., Art. 56.34(f).)

SUBCHAPTER K ADMINISTRATIVE PENALTY

Art. 56B.501. Conduct Subject to Penalty; Amount of Penalty.

(a) A person who presents to the attorney general, or engages in conduct that results in the presentation to the attorney general of, an application for compensation under this chapter that contains a statement or representation the person knows to be false is liable to the attorney general for:

(1) the amount paid in reliance on the application, plus interest on that amount determined at the rate provided by law for legal judgments and accruing from the date on which the payment was made;

(2) payment of an administrative penalty in an amount not to exceed twice the amount paid as a result of the false application for benefits or claim for pecuniary loss; and

(3) payment of an administrative penalty in an amount not to exceed $10,000 for each item or service for which payment was claimed.

(b) In determining the amount of the penalty to be assessed under Subsection (a)(3), the attorney general shall consider:

(1) the seriousness of the violation;

(2) whether the person has previously submitted a false application for benefits or a claim for pecuniary loss; and

(3) the amount necessary to deter the person from submitting future false applications for benefits or claims for pecuniary loss. (Code Crim. Proc., Arts. 56.64(a), (b).)

Art. 56B.502. Report and Notice of Violation and Penalty.

(a) On determining that a violation has occurred, the attorney general may issue a report stating:

(1) the facts on which the determination is made; and

(2) the attorney general's recommendation on the imposition of an administrative penalty, including a recommendation on the amount of the penalty.

(b) The attorney general shall give written notice of the report to the person described by Article 56B.501. The notice may be given by certified mail and must:

(1) include a brief summary of the alleged violation;

(2) state the amount of the recommended penalty; and

(3) inform the person of the right to a hearing on the occurrence of the violation, the amount of the penalty, or both. (Code Crim. Proc., Arts. 56.64(c), (d).)

Art. 56B.503. Penalty to Be Paid or Hearing Requested.

(a) Not later than the 20th day after the date the person receives the notice, the person in writing may:

(1) accept the attorney general's determination and recommended administrative penalty; or

(2) request a hearing on the occurrence of the violation, the amount of the penalty, or both.

(b) If the person accepts the attorney general's determination and recommended penalty, the attorney general by order shall approve the determination and impose the recommended penalty. (Code Crim. Proc., Arts. 56.64(e), (f).)

Art. 56B.504. Hearing.

(a) If the person requests a hearing as provided by Article 56B.503(a) or fails to respond to the notice in a timely manner, the attorney general shall set a contested case hearing under Chapter 2001, Government Code, and notify the person of the hearing.

(b) The administrative law judge shall make findings of fact and conclusions of law and promptly issue to the attorney general a proposal for a decision regarding the occurrence of the violation and the amount of a proposed administrative penalty. (Code Crim. Proc., Art. 56.64(g) (part).)

Art. 56B.505. Decision by Attorney General.

(a) Based on the findings of fact, conclusions of law, and proposal for a decision, the attorney general by order may find that:

(1) a violation occurred and impose an administrative penalty; or

(2) a violation did not occur.

(b) Notice of the attorney general's order given to the person under Chapter 2001, Government Code, must include a statement of the person's right to judicial review of the order. (Code Crim. Proc., Arts. 56.64(g) (part), (h).)

Art. 56B.506. Options Following Decision: Pay or Appeal.

(a) Not later than the 30th day after the date the attorney general's order becomes final under Section 2001.144, Government Code, the person shall:

(1) pay the administrative penalty;

(2) pay the penalty and file a petition for judicial review contesting the occurrence of the violation, the amount of the penalty, or both; or

(3) without paying the penalty, file a petition for judicial review contesting the occurrence of the violation, the amount of the penalty, or both.

(b) Within the 30-day period, a person who acts under Subsection (a)(3) may:

(1) stay enforcement of the penalty by:

(A) paying the penalty to the court for placement in an escrow account; or

(B) giving to the court a supersedeas bond that is approved by the court and that is:

(i) for the amount of the penalty; and

(ii) effective until judicial review of the attorney general's order is final; or

(2) request the court to stay enforcement of the penalty by:

(A) filing with the court a sworn affidavit of the person stating that the person is financially unable to pay the penalty or give the supersedeas bond; and

(B) delivering a copy of the affidavit to the attorney general by certified mail.

Code of Criminal Procedure

(c) On receipt by the attorney general of a copy of an affidavit under Subsection (b)(2), the attorney general may file with the court a contest to the affidavit not later than the fifth day after the date the copy is received.

(d) The court shall hold a hearing on the facts alleged in the affidavit as soon as practicable and shall stay the enforcement of the penalty on finding that the alleged facts are true. A person who files an affidavit under Subsection (b)(2) has the burden of proving that the person is financially unable to pay the penalty or give a supersedeas bond. (Code Crim. Proc., Arts. 56.64(i), (j), (k).)

Art. 56B.507. Collection of Penalty.

If the person does not pay the administrative penalty and the enforcement of the penalty is not stayed, the attorney general may file suit to collect the penalty. (Code Crim. Proc., Art. 56.64(l).)

Art. 56B.508. Decision by Court.

(a) If the court sustains the finding that a violation occurred, the court may order the person to pay the full or a reduced administrative penalty.

(b) If the court does not sustain the finding that a violation occurred, the court shall order that a penalty is not owed. (Code Crim. Proc., Art. 56.64(n).)

Art. 56B.509. Remittance of Penalty and Interest.

(a) If the person paid the administrative penalty and the amount is reduced or is not upheld by the court, the court shall order that the appropriate amount plus accrued interest be remitted to the person.

(b) The interest accrues at the rate charged on loans to depository institutions by the New York Federal Reserve Bank. The interest shall be paid for the period beginning on the date the penalty was paid and ending on the date the penalty is remitted. (Code Crim. Proc., Art. 56.64(o) (part).)

Art. 56B.510. Release of Bond.

(a) If the person gave a supersedeas bond and the administrative penalty is not upheld by the court, the court shall order the release of the bond.

(b) If the person gave a supersedeas bond and the amount of the penalty is reduced, the court shall order the release of the bond after the person pays the amount. (Code Crim. Proc., Art. 56.64(o) (part).)

Art. 56B.511. Disposition of Penalty.

An administrative penalty collected under this subchapter shall be sent to the comptroller and deposited to the credit of the compensation to victims of crime fund. (Code Crim. Proc., Art. 56.64(p).)

Art. 56B.512. Recovery of Expenses.

In addition to the administrative penalty authorized by this subchapter, the attorney general may recover all expenses incurred by the attorney general in the investigation, institution, and prosecution of the suit, including investigative costs, witness fees, attorney's fees, and deposition expenses. (Code Crim. Proc., Art. 56.64(r).)

Art. 56B.513. Administrative Procedure.

A proceeding under this subchapter is subject to Chapter 2001, Government Code. (Code Crim. Proc., Art. 56.64(q).)

SUBCHAPTER L
OTHER PENALTIES AND SANCTIONS

Art. 56B.551. Letter of Reprimand.

(a) The attorney general may issue a letter of reprimand against an individual who the attorney general finds has filed or has caused to be filed under this chapter an application for benefits or claim for pecuniary loss that contains a statement or representation that the individual knows is false.

(b) The attorney general must give the individual notice of the proposed action before issuing the letter.

(c) An individual may challenge the denial of compensation and the issuance of a letter of reprimand in a contested case hearing under Chapter 2001, Government Code.

(d) A letter of reprimand issued under this article is public information. (Code Crim. Proc., Art. 56.62.)

Art. 56B.552. Civil Penalty.

(a) A person is subject to a civil penalty of not less than $2,500 or more than $25,000 for each application for compensation that:

(1) is filed under this chapter by the person or as a result of the person's conduct; and

(2) contains a material statement or representation that the person knows is false.

(b) The attorney general shall institute and conduct a suit to collect on behalf of the state the civil penalty authorized by this article.

(c) A civil penalty recovered under this article shall be deposited to the credit of the compensation to victims of crime fund.

(d) The civil penalty authorized by this article is in addition to any other civil, administrative, or criminal penalty provided by law.

(e) In addition to the civil penalty authorized by this article, the attorney general may recover expenses incurred by the attorney general in the investigation, institution, and prosecution of the suit, including investigative costs, witness fees, attorney's fees, and deposition expenses. (Code Crim. Proc., Art. 56.63.)

CHAPTER 57 CONFIDENTIALITY OF IDENTIFYING INFORMATION OF SEX OFFENSE VICTIMS [REPEALED]

Art. 57.01. Definitions. [Repealed]

Art. 57.02. Confidentiality of Files and Records. [Repealed]

Art. 57.03. Offense. [Repealed]

CHAPTER 57A CONFIDENTIALITY OF IDENTIFYING INFORMATION OF VICTIMS OF STALKING [REPEALED]

Art. 57A.01. Definitions. [Repealed]

Art. 57A.02. Confidentiality of Files and Records. [Repealed]

Art. 57A.03. Offense. [Repealed]

Art. 57A.04. Effect on Other Law. [Repealed]

CHAPTER 57B CONFIDENTIALITY OF IDENTIFYING INFORMATION OF FAMILY VIOLENCE VICTIMS [REPEALED]

Art. 57B.01. Definitions. [Repealed]

Art. 57B.02. Confidentiality of Files and Records. [Repealed]

Art. 57B.03. Offense. [Repealed]

Art. 57B.04. Applicability of Chapter to Department of Family and Protective Services. [Repealed]

Art. 57B.05. Applicability of Chapter to Political Subdivisions. [Repealed]

CHAPTER 57C SEALING OF COURT RECORDS CONTAINING MEDICAL INFORMATION FOR CERTAIN CHILD VICTIMS [REPEALED]

Art. 57C.01. Definitions. [Repealed]

Art. 57C.02. Sealing of Records. [Repealed]

CHAPTER 57D CONFIDENTIALITY OF IDENTIFYING INFORMATION OF VICTIMS OF TRAFFICKING OF PERSONS [REPEALED]

Art. 57D.01. Definitions. [Repealed]

Code of Criminal Procedure

Art. 57D.02. Confidentiality of Files and Records. [Repealed]

Art. 57D.03. Offense. [Repealed]

CHAPTER 58 CONFIDENTIALITY OF IDENTIFYING INFORMATION AND MEDICAL RECORDS OF CERTAIN CRIME VICTIMS

SUBCHAPTER A GENERAL PROVISIONS

Art. 58.001. General Definitions.

In this chapter:

(1) "Name" means the legal name of a person.

(2) "Pseudonym" means a set of initials or a fictitious name chosen by a victim to designate the victim in all public files and records concerning the offense, including police summary reports, press releases, and records of judicial proceedings.

(3) "Public servant" has the meaning assigned by Section 1.07(a), Penal Code. (Code Crim. Proc., Arts. 57.01(1), (2), (3), 57A.01(1), (2), (3), 57B.01(1), (2), (3), 57D.01(1), (2), (3).)

SUBCHAPTER B ADDRESS CONFIDENTIALITY PROGRAM FOR CERTAIN CRIME VICTIMS

Art. 58.051. Definitions.

In this subchapter:

(1) "Applicant" means a person who applies to participate in the program.

(2) "Family violence" has the meaning assigned by Section 71.004, Family Code.

(3) "Family violence shelter center" has the meaning assigned by Section 51.002, Human Resources Code.

(4) "Household" has the meaning assigned by Section 71.005, Family Code.

(5) "Mail" means first class mail and any mail sent by a government agency. The term does not include a package, regardless of size or type of mailing.

(6) "Participant" means an applicant who is certified for participation in the program.

(7) "Program" means the address confidentiality program created under this subchapter.

(8) "Sexual abuse" means any conduct that constitutes an offense under Section 21.02, 21.11, or 25.02, Penal Code.

(9) "Sexual assault" means any conduct that constitutes an offense under Section 22.011 or 22.021, Penal Code.

(10) "Stalking" means any conduct that constitutes an offense under Section 42.072, Penal Code.

(11) "Trafficking of persons" means any conduct that:

(A) constitutes an offense under Section 20A.02, 20A.03, 43.03, 43.031, 43.04, 43.041, 43.05, 43.25, 43.251, or 43.26, Penal Code; and

(B) results in a person:

(i) engaging in forced labor or services; or

(ii) otherwise becoming a victim of the offense.

Art. 58.052. Address Confidentiality Program.

(a) The attorney general shall establish an address confidentiality program, as provided by this subchapter, to assist a victim of family violence, sexual assault or abuse, stalking, or trafficking of persons in maintaining a confidential address.

(b) The attorney general shall:

(1) designate a substitute post office box address that a participant may use in place of the participant's true residential, business, or school address;

(2) act as agent to receive service of process and mail on behalf of the participant; and

(3) forward to the participant mail received by the office of the attorney general on behalf of the participant.

(c) A summons, writ, notice, demand, or process may be served on the attorney general on behalf of the participant by delivery of two copies of the document to the office of the attorney general. The attorney general shall retain a copy of the summons, writ, notice, demand, or process and forward the original to the participant not later than the third day after the date of service on the attorney general.

(d) The attorney general shall make and retain a copy of the envelope in which certified mail is received on behalf of the participant.

(e) The attorney general shall adopt rules to administer the program. (Code Crim. Proc., Arts. 56.82, 56.93.)

Art. 58.053. Agency Acceptance of Substitute Address Required; Exemptions.

(a) Except as provided by Subsection (b), a state or local agency must accept the substitute post office box address designated by the attorney general if the substitute address is presented to the agency by a participant in place of the participant's true residential, business, or school address.

(b) The attorney general by rule may permit an agency to require a participant to provide the participant's true residential, business, or school address, if necessary for the agency to perform a duty or function that is imposed by law or administrative requirement. (Code Crim. Proc., Art. 56.89.)

Art. 58.054. Eligibility.

To be eligible to participate in the program:

(1) an applicant must:

(A) meet with a victim's assistance counselor from a state or local agency or other for-profit or nonprofit entity that is identified by the attorney general as an entity that provides shelter or civil legal services or counseling to victims of family violence, sexual assault or abuse, stalking, or trafficking of persons;

(B) be protected under, or be filing an application on behalf of a victim who is the applicant's child or another person in the applicant's household and who is protected under:

(i) a temporary injunction issued under Subchapter F, Chapter 6, Family Code;

(ii) a temporary ex parte order issued under Chapter 83, Family Code;

(iii) an order issued under Subchapter A or B, Chapter 7B, of this code or Chapter 85, Family Code; or

(iv) a magistrate's order for emergency protection issued under Article 17.292; or

(C) possess documentation of family violence, as identified by the rules adopted under Article 58.056, or of sexual assault or abuse or stalking, as described by Section 92.0161, Property Code; and

(2) an applicant must:

(A) file an application for participation with the attorney general or a state or local agency or other entity identified by the attorney general under Subdivision (1);

(B) file an affirmation that the applicant has discussed safety planning with a victim's assistance counselor described by Subdivision (1)(A);

(C) designate the attorney general as agent to receive service of process and mail on behalf of the applicant; and

(D) live at a residential address, or relocate to a residential address, that is unknown to the person who committed or is alleged to have committed the family violence, sexual assault or abuse, stalking, or trafficking of persons. (Code Crim. Proc., Art. 56.83(a).)

Art. 58.055. Application.

(a) An application under Article 58.054(2)(A) must contain:

(1) a signed, sworn statement by the applicant stating that the applicant fears for the safety of the applicant, the applicant's child, or another person in the applicant's household because of a threat of immediate or future harm caused by the person who committed or is alleged to have committed the family violence, sexual assault or abuse, stalking, or trafficking of persons;

(2) the applicant's true residential address and, if applicable, the applicant's business and school addresses; and

(3) a statement by the applicant of whether there is an existing court order or a pending court case for child support or child custody or visitation that involves the applicant, the applicant's child, or another person in the applicant's household and, if so, the name and address of:

(A) the legal counsel of record; and

(B) each parent involved in the court order or pending case.

(b) An application under Article 58.054(2)(A) must be completed by the applicant in person at the state or local agency or other entity with which the application is filed.

(c) A state or local agency or other entity with which an application is filed under Article 58.054(2)(A) shall forward the application to the office of the attorney general.

(d) Any assistance or counseling provided by the attorney general or an employee or agent of the attorney general to an applicant does not constitute legal advice.

(e) The attorney general shall make program information and application materials available online. (Code Crim. Proc., Arts. 56.83(b), (c) (part), (d), (f), 56.92.)

Art. 58.056. Application and Eligibility Rules and Procedures.

(a) The attorney general may establish procedures for requiring an applicant, in appropriate circumstances, to submit with the application under Article 58.054(2)(A) independent documentary

Code of Criminal Procedure

evidence of family violence, sexual assault or abuse, stalking, or trafficking of persons in the form of:

(1) an active or recently issued order described by Article 58.054(1)(B);

(2) an incident report or other record maintained by a law enforcement agency or official;

(3) a statement of a physician or other health care provider regarding the medical condition of the applicant, applicant's child, or other person in the applicant's household as a result of the family violence, sexual assault or abuse, stalking, or trafficking of persons;

(4) a statement of a mental health professional, a member of the clergy, an attorney or other legal advocate, a trained staff member of a family violence center, or another professional who has assisted the applicant, applicant's child, or other person in the applicant's household in addressing the effects of the family violence, sexual assault or abuse, stalking, or trafficking of persons; or

(5) any other independent documentary evidence necessary to show the applicant's eligibility to participate in the program.

(b) The attorney general by rule may establish additional eligibility requirements for participation in the program that are consistent with the purpose of the program as stated in Article 58.052(a). (Code Crim. Proc., Arts. 56.83(e), (e-1).)

Art. 58.057. False Statement on Application.

(a) An applicant who knowingly or intentionally makes a false statement in an application under Article 58.054(2)(A) is subject to prosecution under Chapter 37, Penal Code.

(b) An applicant is ineligible for, and a participant may be excluded from, participation in the program if the applicant or participant knowingly makes a false statement on an application filed under Article 58.054(2)(A). (Code Crim. Proc., Arts. 56.83(c) (part), 56.86(a).)

Art. 58.058. Exclusion From Participation in Program; Withdrawal.

(a) A participant may be excluded from participation in the program if:

(1) mail forwarded to the participant by the attorney general is returned undeliverable on at least four occasions;

(2) the participant changes the participant's true residential address as provided in the application filed under Article 58.054(2)(A) and does not notify the attorney general of the change at least 10 days before the date of the change; or

(3) the participant changes the participant's name.

(b) A participant may withdraw from the program by notifying the attorney general in writing of the withdrawal. (Code Crim. Proc., Arts. 56.86(b), 56.87.)

Art. 58.059. Certification of Participation in Program.

(a) The attorney general shall certify for participation in the program an applicant who satisfies the eligibility requirements under Articles 58.054 and 58.056(b).

(b) A certification under this article expires on the third anniversary of the date of certification.

(c) To renew a certification under this article, a participant must satisfy the eligibility requirements under Articles 58.054 and 58.056(b) as if the participant were originally applying for participation in the program. (Code Crim. Proc., Arts. 56.84, 56.85.)

Art. 58.060. Confidentiality of Participant Information; Destruction of Information.

(a) Information relating to a participant:

(1) is confidential, except as provided by Article 58.061; and

(2) may not be disclosed under Chapter 552, Government Code.

(b) Except as provided by Article 58.052(d), the attorney general may not make a copy of any mail received by the office of the attorney general on behalf of the participant.

(c) The attorney general shall destroy all information relating to a participant on the third anniversary of the date the participant's participation in the program ends. (Code Crim. Proc., Art. 56.88.)

Art. 58.061. Exceptions.

(a) The attorney general shall disclose a participant's true residential, business, or school address if:

(1) requested by:

(A) a law enforcement agency for the purpose of conducting an investigation;

(B) the Department of Family and Protective Services for the purpose of conducting a child protective services investigation under Chapter 261, Family Code; or

(C) the Department of State Health Services or a local health authority for the purpose of making a notification described by Article 21.31 of this code, Section 54.033, Family Code, or Section 81.051, Health and Safety Code; or

(2) required by court order.

(b) The attorney general may disclose a participant's true residential, business, or school address if:

(1) the participant consents to the disclosure; and

(2) the disclosure is necessary to administer the program.

(c) A person to whom a participant's true residential, business, or school address is disclosed under this article shall maintain the requested information in a manner that protects the confidentiality of the participant's true residential, business, or school address. (Code Crim. Proc., Art. 56.90.)

Art. 58.062. Liability.

(a) The attorney general or an agent or employee of the attorney general is immune from liability for any act or omission by the agent or employee in administering the program if the agent or employee was acting in good faith and in the course and scope of assigned responsibilities and duties.

(b) An agent or employee of the attorney general who does not act in good faith and in the course and scope of assigned responsibilities and duties in disclosing a participant's true residential, business, or school address is subject to prosecution under Chapter 39, Penal Code. (Code Crim. Proc., Art. 56.91.)

SUBCHAPTER C CONFIDENTIALITY OF IDENTIFYING INFORMATION OF SEX OFFENSE VICTIMS

Art. 58.101. Definition.

In this subchapter, "victim" means a person who was the subject of:

(1) an offense the commission of which leads to a reportable conviction or adjudication under Chapter 62; or

(2) an offense that is part of the same criminal episode, as defined by Section 3.01, Penal Code, as an offense described by Subdivision (1). (Code Crim. Proc., Art. 57.01(4).)

Art. 58.102. Designation of Pseudonym; Pseudonym Form.

(a) A victim may choose a pseudonym to be used instead of the victim's name to designate the victim in all public files and records concerning the offense, including police summary reports, press releases, and records of judicial proceedings. A victim who elects to use a pseudonym as provided by this subchapter must complete a pseudonym form developed under Subsection (b) and return the form to the law enforcement agency investigating the offense.

(b) The Sexual Assault Prevention and Crisis Services Program of the office of the attorney general shall develop and distribute to all law enforcement agencies of the state a pseudonym form to record the name, address, telephone number, and pseudonym of a victim. (Code Crim. Proc., Arts. 57.02(a), (b).)

Art. 58.103. Victim Information Confidential.

(a) A victim who completes a pseudonym form and returns the form to the law enforcement agency investigating the offense may not be required to disclose the victim's name, address, and telephone number in connection with the investigation or prosecution of the offense.

(b) A completed and returned pseudonym form is confidential and may not be disclosed to any person other than a defendant in the case or the defendant's attorney, except on an order of a court. The court finding required by Article 58.104 is not required to disclose the confidential pseudonym form to the defendant in the case or to the defendant's attorney.

(c) If a victim completes a pseudonym form and returns the form to a law enforcement agency under Article 58.102(a), the law enforcement agency receiving the form shall:

(1) remove the victim's name and substitute the pseudonym for the name on all reports, files, and records in the agency's possession;

(2) notify the attorney representing the state of the pseudonym and that the victim has elected to be designated by the pseudonym; and

(3) maintain the form in a manner that protects the confidentiality of the information contained on the form.

(d) An attorney representing the state who receives notice that a victim has elected to be designated by a pseudonym shall ensure that the victim is designated by the pseudonym in all legal proceedings concerning the offense. (Code Crim. Proc., Arts. 57.02(c), (d), (e), (f).)

Art. 58.104. Court-Ordered Disclosure of Victim Information.

A court may order the disclosure of a victim's name, address, and telephone number only if the court finds that the information is essential in the trial of the defendant for the offense or the identity of the victim is in issue. (Code Crim. Proc., Art. 57.02(g).)

Art. 58.105. Disclosure of Certain Child Victim Information Prohibited.

Except as required or permitted by other law or by court order, a public servant or other person who has access to or obtains the name, address, telephone number, or other identifying information of a victim younger than 17 years of age may not release or disclose the identifying information to any person who is not assisting in the investigation, prosecution, or defense of the case. This article does not apply to the release or disclosure of a victim's identifying information by:

(1) the victim; or

(2) the victim's parent, conservator, or guardian, unless the parent, conservator, or guardian is a defendant in the case. (Code Crim. Proc., Art. 57.02(h).)

Art. 58.106. Disclosure of Information of Confined Victim.

This subchapter does not prohibit the inspector general of the Texas Department of Criminal Justice from disclosing a victim's identifying information to an employee of the department or the department's ombudsperson if the victim is an inmate or state jail defendant confined in a facility operated by or under contract with the department. (Code Crim. Proc., Art. 57.02(i) as added Acts 80th Leg., R.S., Chs. 619, 1217.)

Art. 58.107. Offense.

(a) A public servant commits an offense if the public servant:

(1) has access to the name, address, or telephone number of a victim 17 years of age or older who has chosen a pseudonym under this subchapter; and

(2) knowingly discloses the name, address, or telephone number of the victim to:

(A) a person who is not assisting in the investigation or prosecution of the offense; or

(B) a person other than:

(i) the defendant;

(ii) the defendant's attorney; or

(iii) the person specified in the order of a court.

(b) Unless the disclosure is required or permitted by other law, a public servant or other person commits an offense if the person:

(1) has access to or obtains the name, address, or telephone number of a victim younger than 17 years of age; and

(2) knowingly discloses the name, address, or telephone number of the victim to:

(A) a person who is not assisting in the investigation or prosecution of the offense; or

(B) a person other than:

(i) the defendant;

(ii) the defendant's attorney; or

(iii) a person specified in an order of a court.

(c) It is an affirmative defense to prosecution under Subsection (b) that the actor is:

(1) the victim; or

(2) the victim's parent, conservator, or guardian, unless the actor is a defendant in the case.

(d) It is an exception to the application of this article that:

(1) the person who discloses the name, address, or telephone number of a victim is the inspector general of the Texas Department of Criminal Justice;

(2) the victim is an inmate or state jail defendant confined in a facility operated by or under contract with the department; and

(3) the person to whom the disclosure is made is an employee of the department or the department's ombudsperson.

(e) An offense under this article is a Class C misdemeanor. (Code Crim. Proc., Art. 57.03.)

SUBCHAPTER D CONFIDENTIALITY OF IDENTIFYING INFORMATION OF VICTIMS OF STALKING

Art. 58.151. Definition.

In this subchapter, "victim" means a person who is the subject of:

(1) an offense that allegedly constitutes stalking under Section 42.072, Penal Code; or

(2) an offense that is part of the same criminal episode, as defined by Section 3.01, Penal Code, as an offense under Section 42.072, Penal Code. (Code Crim. Proc., Art. 57A.01(4).)

Art. 58.152. Designation of Pseudonym; Pseudonym Form.

(a) A victim may choose a pseudonym to be used instead of the victim's name to designate the victim in all public files and records concerning the offense, including police summary reports, press releases, and records of judicial proceedings. A victim who elects to use a pseudonym as provided by this subchapter must complete a pseudonym form developed under Subsection (b) and return the form to the law enforcement agency investigating the offense.

(b) The office of the attorney general shall develop and distribute to all law enforcement agencies of the state a pseudonym form to record the name, address, telephone number, and pseudonym of a victim. (Code Crim. Proc., Arts. 57A.02(a), (b).)

Art. 58.153. Victim Information Confidential.

(a) A victim who completes a pseudonym form and returns the form to the law enforcement agency investigating the offense may not be required to disclose the victim's name, address, and telephone number in connection with the investigation or prosecution of the offense.

(b) A completed and returned pseudonym form is confidential and may not be disclosed to any person other than the victim identified by the pseudonym form, a defendant in the case, or the defendant's attorney, except on an order of a court. The court finding required by Article 58.154 is not required to disclose the confidential pseudonym form to the victim identified by the pseudonym form, the defendant in the case, or the defendant's attorney.

(c) If a victim completes a pseudonym form and returns the form to a law enforcement agency under Article 58.152(a), the law enforcement agency receiving the form shall:

(1) remove the victim's name and substitute the pseudonym for the name on all reports, files, and records in the agency's possession;

(2) notify the attorney representing the state of the pseudonym and that the victim has elected to be designated by the pseudonym;

(3) provide to the victim a copy of the completed pseudonym form showing that the form was returned to the law enforcement agency; and

(4) maintain the form in a manner that protects the confidentiality of the information contained on the form.

(d) An attorney representing the state who receives notice that a victim has elected to be designated by a pseudonym shall ensure that the victim is designated by the pseudonym in all legal proceedings concerning the offense. (Code Crim. Proc., Arts. 57A.02(c), (d), (e), (f).)

Art. 58.154. Court-Ordered Disclosure of Victim Information.

A court may order the disclosure of a victim's name, address, and telephone number only if the court finds that:

(1) the information is essential in the trial of the defendant for the offense;

(2) the identity of the victim is in issue; or

(3) the disclosure is in the best interest of the victim. (Code Crim. Proc., Art. 57A.02(g).)

Art. 58.155. Disclosure of Certain Child Victim Information Prohibited.

Except as required or permitted by other law or by court order, a public servant or other person who has access to or obtains the name, address, telephone number, or other identifying information of a victim younger than 17 years of age may not release or disclose the identifying information to any person who is not assisting in the investigation, prosecution, or defense of the case. This article does not apply to the release or disclosure of a victim's identifying information by:

(1) the victim; or

(2) the victim's parent, conservator, or guardian, unless the victim's parent, conservator, or guardian allegedly committed the offense described by Article 58.151. (Code Crim. Proc., Art. 57A.02(h).)

Art. 58.156. Offense.

(a) A public servant commits an offense if the public servant:

(1) has access to the name, address, or telephone number of a victim 17 years of age or older who has chosen a pseudonym under this subchapter; and

(2) knowingly discloses the name, address, or telephone number of the victim to:

(A) a person who is not assisting in the investigation or prosecution of the offense; or

(B) a person other than:

(i) the defendant;

(ii) the defendant's attorney; or

(iii) the person specified in the order of a court.

(b) Unless the disclosure is required or permitted by other law, a public servant or other person commits an offense if the person:

(1) has access to or obtains the name, address, or telephone number of a victim younger than 17 years of age; and

(2) knowingly discloses the name, address, or telephone number of the victim to:

(A) a person who is not assisting in the investigation or prosecution of the offense; or

(B) a person other than:

(i) the defendant;

(ii) the defendant's attorney; or

(iii) a person specified in an order of a court.

(c) It is an affirmative defense to prosecution under Subsection (b) that the actor is:

(1) the victim; or

(2) the victim's parent, conservator, or guardian, unless the victim's parent, conservator, or guardian allegedly committed the offense described by Article 58.151.

(d) An offense under this article is a Class C misdemeanor. (Code Crim. Proc., Art. 57A.03.)

Art. 58.157. Effect on Other Law.

This subchapter does not affect:

(1) a victim's responsibility to provide documentation of stalking under Section 92.0161, Property Code; or

(2) a person's power or duty to disclose the documented information as provided by Subsection (j) of that section. (Code Crim. Proc., Art. 57A.04.)

SUBCHAPTER E CONFIDENTIALITY OF IDENTIFYING INFORMATION OF VICTIMS OF FAMILY VIOLENCE

Art. 58.201. Definition.

In this subchapter, "victim" means a person who is the subject of:

(1) an offense that allegedly constitutes family violence, as defined by Section 71.004, Family Code; or

(2) an offense that is part of the same criminal episode, as defined by Section 3.01, Penal Code, as an offense described by Subdivision (1). (Code Crim. Proc., Art. 57B.01(4).)

Art. 58.202. Designation of Pseudonym; Pseudonym Form.

(a) A victim may choose a pseudonym to be used instead of the victim's name to designate the victim in all public files and records concerning the offense, including police summary reports, press releases, and records of judicial proceedings. A victim who elects to use a pseudonym as provided by this subchapter must complete a pseudonym form developed under Subsection (b) and return the form to the law enforcement agency investigating the offense.

(b) The office of the attorney general shall develop and distribute to all law enforcement agencies of the state a pseudonym form to record the name, address, telephone number, and pseudonym of a victim. (Code Crim. Proc., Arts. 57B.02(a), (b).)

Art. 58.203. Victim Information Confidential.

(a) A victim who completes a pseudonym form and returns the form to the law enforcement agency investigating the offense may not be required to disclose the victim's name, address, and telephone number in connection with the investigation or prosecution of the offense.

(b) A completed and returned pseudonym form is confidential and may not be disclosed to any person other than a defendant in the case or the defendant's attorney, except on an order of a court. The court finding required by Article 58.204 is not required to disclose the confidential pseudonym form to the defendant in the case or to the defendant's attorney.

(c) If a victim completes a pseudonym form and returns the form to a law enforcement agency under Article 58.202(a), the law enforcement agency receiving the form shall:

(1) remove the victim's name and substitute the pseudonym for the name on all reports, files, and records in the agency's possession;

(2) notify the attorney representing the state of the pseudonym and that the victim has elected to be designated by the pseudonym; and

(3) maintain the form in a manner that protects the confidentiality of the information contained on the form.

(d) An attorney representing the state who receives notice that a victim has elected to be designated by a pseudonym shall ensure that the victim is designated by the pseudonym in all legal proceedings concerning the offense. (Code Crim. Proc., Arts. 57B.02(c), (d), (e), (f).)

Art. 58.204. Court-Ordered Disclosure of Victim Information.

A court may order the disclosure of a victim's name, address, and telephone number only if the court finds that the information is essential in the trial of the defendant for the offense or the identity of the victim is in issue. (Code Crim. Proc., Art. 57B.02(g).)

Art. 58.205. Disclosure of Certain Child Victim Information Prohibited.

Except as required or permitted by other law or by court order, a public servant or other person who has access to or obtains the name, address, telephone number, or other identifying information of a victim younger than 17 years of age may not release or disclose the identifying information to any person who is not assisting in the investigation, prosecution, or defense of the case. This article does not apply to the release or disclosure of a victim's identifying information by:

(1) the victim; or

(2) the victim's parent, conservator, or guardian, unless the victim's parent, conservator, or guardian allegedly committed the offense described by Article 58.201. (Code Crim. Proc., Art. 57B.02(h).)

Art. 58.206. Offense.

(a) A public servant commits an offense if the public servant:

(1) has access to the name, address, or telephone number of a victim 17 years of age or older who has chosen a pseudonym under this subchapter; and

(2) knowingly discloses the name, address, or telephone number of the victim to:

(A) a person who is not assisting in the investigation or prosecution of the offense; or

(B) a person other than:

(i) the defendant;

(ii) the defendant's attorney; or

(iii) the person specified in the order of a court.

(b) Unless the disclosure is required or permitted by other law, a public servant or other person commits an offense if the person:

(1) has access to or obtains the name, address, or telephone number of a victim younger than 17 years of age; and

(2) knowingly discloses the name, address, or telephone number of the victim to:

(A) a person who is not assisting in the investigation or prosecution of the offense; or

(B) a person other than:

(i) the defendant;

(ii) the defendant's attorney; or

(iii) a person specified in an order of a court.

(c) It is an affirmative defense to prosecution under Subsection (b) that the actor is:

(1) the victim; or

(2) the victim's parent, conservator, or guardian, unless the victim's parent, conservator, or guardian allegedly committed the offense described by Article 58.201.

(d) An offense under this article is a Class C misdemeanor. (Code Crim. Proc., Art. 57B.03.)

Art. 58.207. Applicability of Subchapter to Department of Family and Protective Services.

(a) This subchapter does not require the Department of Family and Protective Services to use a pseudonym in a department report, file, or record relating to the abuse, neglect, or exploitation of a child or adult who may also be the subject of an offense described by Article 58.201.

(b) To the extent permitted by law, the Department of Family and Protective Services and a department employee, as necessary in performing department duties, may disclose the name of a victim who elects to use a pseudonym under this subchapter. (Code Crim. Proc., Art. 57B.04.)

Art. 58.208. Applicability of Subchapter to Political Subdivisions.

This subchapter does not require a political subdivision to use a pseudonym in a report, file, or record that:

(1) is not intended for distribution to the public; or

(2) is not the subject of an open records request under Chapter 552, Government Code. (Code Crim. Proc., Art. 57B.05.)

SUBCHAPTER F
CONFIDENTIALITY OF IDENTIFYING INFORMATION OF VICTIMS OF TRAFFICKING OF PERSONS

Art. 58.251. Definition.

In this subchapter, "victim" means a person who is the subject of:

(1) an offense under Section 20A.02, Penal Code; or

(2) an offense that is part of the same criminal episode, as defined by Section 3.01, Penal Code, as an offense under Section 20A.02, Penal Code. (Code Crim. Proc., Art. 57D.01(4).)

Art. 58.252. Designation of Pseudonym; Pseudonym Form.

(a) A victim may choose a pseudonym to be used instead of the victim's name to designate the victim in all public files and records concerning the offense, including police summary reports, press releases, and records of judicial proceedings. A victim who elects to use a pseudonym as provided by this subchapter must complete a pseudonym form developed under Subsection (b) and return the form to the law enforcement agency investigating the offense.

(b) The office of the attorney general shall develop and distribute to all law enforcement agencies of the state a pseudonym form to record the name, address, telephone number, and pseudonym of a victim. (Code Crim. Proc., Arts. 57D.02(a), (b).)

Art. 58.253. Victim Information Confidential.

(a) A victim who completes a pseudonym form and returns the form to the law enforcement agency investigating the offense may not be required to disclose the victim's name, address, and telephone number in connection with the investigation or prosecution of the offense.

(b) A completed and returned pseudonym form is confidential and may not be disclosed to any person other than a defendant in the case or the defendant's attorney, except on an order of a court. The court finding required by Article 58.254 is not required to disclose the confidential pseudonym form to the defendant in the case or to the defendant's attorney.

(c) If a victim completes a pseudonym form and returns the form to a law enforcement agency under Article 58.252(a), the law enforcement agency receiving the form shall:

(1) remove the victim's name and substitute the pseudonym for the name on all reports, files, and records in the agency's possession;

(2) notify the attorney representing the state of the pseudonym and that the victim has elected to be designated by the pseudonym; and

(3) maintain the form in a manner that protects the confidentiality of the information contained on the form.

(d) An attorney representing the state who receives notice that a victim has elected to be designated by a pseudonym shall ensure that the victim is designated by the pseudonym in all legal proceedings concerning the offense. (Code Crim. Proc., Arts. 57D.02(c), (d), (e), (f).)

Art. 58.254. Court-Ordered Disclosure of Victim Information.

A court may order the disclosure of a victim's name, address, and telephone number only if the court finds that the information is essential in the trial of the defendant for the offense or the identity of the victim is in issue. (Code Crim. Proc., Art. 57D.02(g).)

Art. 58.255. Disclosure of Child Victim Information Prohibited.

Except as required or permitted by other law or by court order, a public servant or other person who has access to or obtains the name, address, telephone number, or other identifying information of a victim younger than 18 years of age may not release or disclose the identifying information to any person who is not assisting in the investigation, prosecution, or defense of the case. This article does not apply to the release or disclosure of a victim's identifying information by:

(1) the victim; or

(2) the victim's parent, conservator, or guardian, unless the victim's parent, conservator, or guardian allegedly committed the offense described by Article 58.251. (Code Crim. Proc., Art. 57D.02(h).)

Art. 58.256. Offense.

(a) A public servant commits an offense if the public servant:

(1) has access to the name, address, or telephone number of a victim 18 years of age or older who has chosen a pseudonym under this subchapter; and

(2) knowingly discloses the name, address, or telephone number of the victim to:

(A) a person who is not assisting in the investigation or prosecution of the offense; or

(B) a person other than:

(i) the defendant;

(ii) the defendant's attorney; or

(iii) the person specified in the order of a court.

(b) Unless the disclosure is required or permitted by other law, a public servant or other person commits an offense if the person:

(1) has access to or obtains the name, address, or telephone number of a victim younger than 18 years of age; and

(2) knowingly discloses the name, address, or telephone number of the victim to:

(A) a person who is not assisting in the investigation or prosecution of the offense; or

(B) a person other than:

(i) the defendant;

(ii) the defendant's attorney; or

(iii) a person specified in an order of a court.

(c) It is an affirmative defense to prosecution under Subsection (b) that the actor is:

(1) the victim; or

(2) the victim's parent, conservator, or guardian, unless the victim's parent, conservator, or guardian allegedly committed the offense described by Article 58.251.

(d) An offense under this article is a Class C misdemeanor. (Code Crim. Proc., Art. 57D.03.)

SUBCHAPTER G SEALING OF MEDICAL RECORDS OF CERTAIN CHILD VICTIMS

Art. 58.301. Definitions.

In this subchapter:

(1) "Child" means a person who is younger than 18 years of age.

(2) "Medical records" means any information used or generated by health care providers, including records relating to emergency room treatment, rehabilitation therapy, or counseling. (Code Crim. Proc., Art. 57C.01.)

Art. 58.302. Sealing of Medical Records.

(a) Except as provided by Subsection (c), on a motion filed by a person described by Subsection (b), the court shall seal the medical records of a child who is a victim of an offense described by Section 1, Article 38.071.

(b) A motion under this article may be filed on the court's own motion or by:

(1) the attorney representing the state;

(2) the defendant; or

(3) the parent or guardian of the victim or, if the victim is no longer a child, the victim.

(c) The court is not required to seal the records described by this article on a finding of good cause after a hearing held under Subsection (d).

(d) The court shall grant the motion without a hearing unless the motion is contested not later than the seventh day after the date the motion is filed. (Code Crim. Proc., Arts. 57C.02(a), (b), (c), (d).)

Art. 58.303. Access to Sealed Medical Records.

Medical records sealed under this subchapter are not open for inspection by any person except:

(1) on further order of the court after:

(A) notice to a parent or guardian of the victim whose information is sealed or, if the victim is no longer a child, notice to the victim; and

(B) a finding of good cause;

(2) in connection with a criminal or civil proceeding as otherwise provided by law; or

(3) on request of a parent or legal guardian of the victim whose information is sealed or, if the victim is no longer a child, on request of the victim. (Code Crim. Proc., Art. 57C.02(e).)

Art. 58.304. Liability.

Except on a showing of bad faith, a clerk of the court is not liable for any failure to seal medical records after the court grants a motion under this subchapter. (Code Crim. Proc., Art. 57C.02(f).)

CHAPTER 58 SEALING FILES AND RECORDS OF CHILDREN [REPEALED]

Art. 58.01. Sealing Files and Records of Children [Repealed].

Repealed by Acts 2001, 77th Leg., ch. 1297 (H.B. 1118), § 71(3), effective September 1, 2001.

CHAPTER 59 FORFEITURE OF CONTRABAND

Art. 59.01. Definitions.

In this chapter:

(1) "Attorney representing the state" means the prosecutor with felony jurisdiction in the county in which a forfeiture proceeding is held under this chapter or, in a proceeding for forfeiture of contraband as defined under Subdivision (2)(B)(v) of this article, the city attorney of a municipality if the property is seized in that municipality by a peace officer employed by that municipality and the governing body of the municipality has approved procedures for the city attorney acting in a forfeiture proceeding. In a proceeding for forfeiture of contraband as defined under Subdivision (2)(B)(vi) of this article, the term includes the attorney general.

(2) "Contraband" means property of any nature, including real, personal, tangible, or intangible, that is:

(A) used in the commission of:

(i) any first or second degree felony under the Penal Code;

(ii) any felony under Section 15.031(b), 21.11, or 38.04 or Chapter 29, 30, 31, 32, 33, 33A, or 35, Penal Code;

(iii) any felony under Chapter 43, Penal Code, except as provided by Paragraph (B);

(iv) any felony under The Securities Act (Article 581-1 et seq., Vernon's Texas Civil Statutes); or

(v) any offense under Chapter 49, Penal Code, that is punishable as a felony of the third degree or state jail felony, if the defendant has been previously convicted three times of an offense under that chapter;

(B) used or intended to be used in the commission of:

(i) any felony under Chapter 481, Health and Safety Code (Texas Controlled Substances Act);

(ii) any felony under Chapter 483, Health and Safety Code;

(iii) a felony under Chapter 151, Finance Code;

(iv) any felony under Chapter 20A or 34, Penal Code;

(v) a Class A misdemeanor under Subchapter B, Chapter 365, Health and Safety Code, if the defendant has been previously convicted twice of an offense under that subchapter;

(vi) any felony under Chapter 32, Human Resources Code, or Chapter 31, 32, 35A, or 37, Penal Code, that involves a health care program, as defined by Section 35A.01, Penal Code;

(vii) a Class B misdemeanor under Chapter 522, Business & Commerce Code;

(viii) a Class A misdemeanor under Section 306.051, Business & Commerce Code;

(ix) any offense under Section 42.10, Penal Code;

(x) any offense under Section 46.06(a)(1) or 46.14, Penal Code;

(xi) any offense under Chapter 71, Penal Code;

(xii) any offense under Section 20.05, 20.06, 20.07, 43.04, or 43.05, Penal Code;

(xiii) an offense under Section 326.002, Business & Commerce Code; or

(xiv) a Class A misdemeanor or any felony under Section 545.420, Transportation Code, other than a Class A misdemeanor that is classified as a Class A misdemeanor based solely on conduct constituting a violation of Subsection (e)(2)(B) of that section;

(C) the proceeds gained from the commission of a felony listed in Paragraph (A) or (B) of this subdivision, a misdemeanor listed in Paragraph (B)(vii), (ix), (x), (xi), or (xii) of this subdivision, or a crime of violence;

(D) acquired with proceeds gained from the commission of a felony listed in Paragraph (A) or (B) of this subdivision, a misdemeanor listed in Paragraph (B)(vii), (ix), (x), (xi), or (xii) of this subdivision, or a crime of violence;

(E) used to facilitate or intended to be used to facilitate the commission of a felony under Section 15.031 or Chapter 43, Penal Code; or

(F) used to facilitate or intended to be used to facilitate the commission of an offense under Section 20.05, 20.06, or 20.07 or Chapter 20A, Penal Code.

(3) "Crime of violence" means:

(A) any criminal offense defined in the Penal Code or in a federal criminal law that results in a personal injury to a victim; or

(B) an act that is not an offense under the Penal Code involving the operation of a motor vehicle, aircraft, or water vehicle that results in injury or death sustained in an accident caused by a driver in violation of Section 550.021, Transportation Code.

(4) "Interest holder" means the bona fide holder of a perfected lien or a perfected security interest in property.

(5) "Law enforcement agency" means an agency of the state or an agency of a political subdivision of the state authorized by law to employ peace officers.

(6) "Owner" means a person who claims an equitable or legal ownership interest in property.

(7) "Proceeds" includes income a person accused or convicted of a crime or the person's representative or assignee receives from:

(A) a movie, book, magazine article, tape recording, phonographic record, radio or television presentation, telephone service, electronic media format, including an Internet website, or live entertainment in which the crime was reenacted; or

(B) the sale of tangible property the value of which is increased by the notoriety gained from the conviction of an offense by the person accused or convicted of the crime.

(8) "Seizure" means the restraint of property by a peace officer under Article 59.03(a) or (b) of this code, whether the officer restrains the property by physical force or by a display of the officer's authority, and includes the collection of property or the act of taking possession of property.

(9) "Depository account" means the obligation of a regulated financial institution to pay the account owner under a written agreement, including a checking account, savings account, money market account, time deposit, NOW account, or certificate of deposit.

(10) "Primary state or federal financial institution regulator" means the state or federal regulatory agency that chartered and comprehensively regulates a regulated financial institution.

(11) "Regulated financial institution" means a depository institution chartered by a state or federal government, the deposits of which are insured by the Federal Deposit Insurance Corporation or the National Credit Union Administration.

Art. 59.01. Definitions.

In this chapter:

(1) "Attorney representing the state" means the prosecutor with felony jurisdiction in the county in which a forfeiture proceeding is held under this chapter or, in a proceeding for forfeiture of contraband as defined under Subdivision (2)(B)(v) of this article, the city attorney of a municipality if the property is seized in that municipality by a peace officer employed by that municipality and the governing body of the municipality has approved procedures for the city attorney acting in a forfeiture proceeding. In a proceeding for forfeiture of contraband as defined under Subdivision (2)(B)(vi) of this article, the term includes the attorney general.

(2) "Contraband" means property of any nature, including real, personal, tangible, or intangible, that is:

(A) used in the commission of:

(i) any first or second degree felony under the Penal Code;

(ii) any felony under Section 15.031(b), 21.11, or 38.04 or Chapter 29, 30, 31, 32, 33, 33A, or 35, Penal Code;

(iii) any felony under Chapter 43, Penal Code, except as provided by Paragraph (B);

(iv) any felony under The Securities Act (Title 12, Government Code); or

(v) any offense under Chapter 49, Penal Code, that is punishable as a felony of the third degree or state jail felony, if the defendant has been previously convicted three times of an offense under that chapter;

(B) used or intended to be used in the commission of:

(i) any felony under Chapter 481, Health and Safety Code (Texas Controlled Substances Act);

(ii) any felony under Chapter 483, Health and Safety Code;

(iii) a felony under Chapter 151, Finance Code;

(iv) any felony under Chapter 20A or 34, Penal Code;

(v) a Class A misdemeanor under Subchapter B, Chapter 365, Health and Safety Code, if the defendant has been previously convicted twice of an offense under that subchapter;

(vi) any felony under Chapter 32, Human Resources Code, or Chapter 31, 32, 35A, or 37, Penal Code, that involves a health care program, as defined by Section 35A.01, Penal Code;

(vii) a Class B misdemeanor under Chapter 522, Business & Commerce Code;

(viii) a Class A misdemeanor under Section 306.051, Business & Commerce Code;

(ix) any offense under Section 42.10, Penal Code;

(x) any offense under Section 46.06(a)(1) or 46.14, Penal Code;

(xi) any offense under Chapter 71, Penal Code;

(xii) any offense under Section 20.05, 20.06, 20.07, 43.04, or 43.05, Penal Code;

(xiii) an offense under Section 326.002, Business & Commerce Code; or

(xiv) a Class A misdemeanor or any felony under Section 545.420, Transportation Code, other than a Class A misdemeanor that is classified as a Class A misdemeanor based solely on conduct constituting a violation of Subsection (e)(2)(B) of that section;

(C) the proceeds gained from the commission of a felony listed in Paragraph (A) or (B) of this subdivision, a misdemeanor listed in Paragraph (B)(vii), (ix), (x), (xi), or (xii) of this subdivision, or a crime of violence;

(D) acquired with proceeds gained from the commission of a felony listed in Paragraph (A) or (B) of this subdivision, a misdemeanor listed in Paragraph (B)(vii), (ix), (x), (xi), or (xii) of this subdivision, or a crime of violence;

(E) used to facilitate or intended to be used to facilitate the commission of a felony under Section 15.031 or Chapter 43, Penal Code; or

(F) used to facilitate or intended to be used to facilitate the commission of an offense under Section 20.05, 20.06, or 20.07 or Chapter 20A, Penal Code.

(3) "Crime of violence" means:

(A) any criminal offense defined in the Penal Code or in a federal criminal law that results in a personal injury to a victim; or

(B) an act that is not an offense under the Penal Code involving the operation of a motor vehicle, aircraft, or water vehicle that results in injury or death sustained in an accident caused by a driver in violation of Section 550.021, Transportation Code.

(4) "Interest holder" means the bona fide holder of a perfected lien or a perfected security interest in property.

(5) "Law enforcement agency" means an agency of the state or an agency of a political subdivision of the state authorized by law to employ peace officers.

(6) "Owner" means a person who claims an equitable or legal ownership interest in property.

Code of Criminal Procedure

(7) "Proceeds" includes income a person accused or convicted of a crime or the person's representative or assignee receives from:

(A) a movie, book, magazine article, tape recording, phonographic record, radio or television presentation, telephone service, electronic media format, including an Internet website, or live entertainment in which the crime was reenacted; or

(B) the sale of tangible property the value of which is increased by the notoriety gained from the conviction of an offense by the person accused or convicted of the crime.

(8) "Seizure" means the restraint of property by a peace officer under Article 59.03(a) or (b) of this code, whether the officer restrains the property by physical force or by a display of the officer's authority, and includes the collection of property or the act of taking possession of property.

(9) "Depository account" means the obligation of a regulated financial institution to pay the account owner under a written agreement, including a checking account, savings account, money market account, time deposit, NOW account, or certificate of deposit.

(10) "Primary state or federal financial institution regulator" means the state or federal regulatory agency that chartered and comprehensively regulates a regulated financial institution.

(11) "Regulated financial institution" means a depository institution chartered by a state or federal government, the deposits of which are insured by the Federal Deposit Insurance Corporation or the National Credit Union Administration.

Art. 59.01. Definitions.

In this chapter:

(1) "Attorney representing the state" means the prosecutor with felony jurisdiction in the county in which a forfeiture proceeding is held under this chapter or, in a proceeding for forfeiture of contraband as defined under Subdivision (2)(B)(v) of this article, the city attorney of a municipality if the property is seized in that municipality by a peace officer employed by that municipality and the governing body of the municipality has approved procedures for the city attorney acting in a forfeiture proceeding. In a proceeding for forfeiture of contraband as defined under Subdivision (2)(B)(vi) of this article, the term includes the attorney general.

(2) "Contraband" means property of any nature, including real, personal, tangible, or intangible, that is:

(A) used in the commission of:

(i) any first or second degree felony under the Penal Code;

(ii) any felony under Section 15.031(b), 21.11, or 38.04 or Chapter 29, 30, 31, 32, 33, 33A, or 35, Penal Code;

(iii) any felony under Chapter 43, Penal Code, except as provided by Paragraph (B);

(iv) any felony under The Securities Act (Title 12, Government Code); or

(v) any offense under Chapter 49, Penal Code, that is punishable as a felony of the third degree or state jail felony, if the defendant has been previously convicted three times of an offense under that chapter;

(B) used or intended to be used in the commission of:

(i) any felony under Chapter 481, Health and Safety Code (Texas Controlled Substances Act);

(ii) any felony under Chapter 483, Health and Safety Code;

(iii) a felony under Chapter 151, Finance Code;

(iv) any felony under Chapter 20A or 34, Penal Code;

(v) a Class A misdemeanor under Subchapter B, Chapter 365, Health and Safety Code, if the defendant has been previously convicted twice of an offense under that subchapter;

(vi) any felony under Chapter 32, Human Resources Code, or Chapter 31, 32, 35A, or 37, Penal Code, that involves a health care program, as defined by Section 35A.01, Penal Code;

(vii) a Class B misdemeanor under Chapter 522, Business & Commerce Code;

(viii) a Class A misdemeanor under Section 306.051, Business & Commerce Code;

(ix) any offense under Section 42.10, Penal Code;

(x) any offense under Section 46.06(a)(1) or 46.14, Penal Code;

(xi) any offense under Chapter 71, Penal Code;

(xii) any offense under Section 20.05, 20.06, 20.07, 43.04, or 43.05, Penal Code; or

(xiii) an offense under Section 326.002, Business & Commerce Code;

(C) the proceeds gained from the commission of a felony listed in Paragraph (A) or (B) of this subdivision, a misdemeanor listed in Paragraph (B)(vii), (ix), (x), (xi), or (xii) of this subdivision, or a crime of violence;

(D) acquired with proceeds gained from the commission of a felony listed in Paragraph (A) or (B) of this subdivision, a misdemeanor listed in Paragraph (B)(vii), (ix), (x), (xi), or (xii) of this subdivision, or a crime of violence;

(E) used to facilitate or intended to be used to facilitate the commission of a felony under Section 15.031 or Chapter 43, Penal Code; or

(F) used to facilitate or intended to be used to facilitate the commission of an offense under Section 20.05, 20.06, or 20.07 or Chapter 20A, Penal Code.

(3) "Crime of violence" means:

(A) any criminal offense defined in the Penal Code or in a federal criminal law that results in a personal injury to a victim; or

(B) an act that is not an offense under the Penal Code involving the operation of a motor vehicle, aircraft, or water vehicle that results in injury or death sustained in an accident caused by a driver in violation of Section 550.021, Transportation Code.

(4) "Interest holder" means the bona fide holder of a perfected lien or a perfected security interest in property.

(5) "Law enforcement agency" means an agency of the state or an agency of a political subdivision of the state authorized by law to employ peace officers.

(6) "Owner" means a person who claims an equitable or legal ownership interest in property.

(7) "Proceeds" includes income a person accused or convicted of a crime or the person's representative or assignee receives from:

(A) a movie, book, magazine article, tape recording, phonographic record, radio or television presentation, telephone service, electronic media format, including an Internet website, or live entertainment in which the crime was reenacted; or

(B) the sale of tangible property the value of which is increased by the notoriety gained from the conviction of an offense by the person accused or convicted of the crime.

(8) "Seizure" means the restraint of property by a peace officer under Article 59.03(a) or (b) of this code, whether the officer restrains the property by physical force or by a display of the officer's authority, and includes the collection of property or the act of taking possession of property.

(9) "Depository account" means the obligation of a regulated financial institution to pay the account owner under a written agreement, including a checking account, savings account, money market account, time deposit, NOW account, or certificate of deposit.

(10) "Primary state or federal financial institution regulator" means the state or federal regulatory agency that chartered and comprehensively regulates a regulated financial institution.

(11) "Regulated financial institution" means a depository institution chartered by a state or federal government, the deposits of which are insured by the Federal Deposit Insurance Corporation or the National Credit Union Administration.

Art. 59.011. Election of Forfeiture Proceeding.

If property described by Article 59.01(2)(B)(ix), (x), or (xi) is subject to forfeiture under this chapter and Article 18.18, the attorney representing the state may proceed under either this chapter or that article.

Art. 59.02. Forfeiture of Contraband.

(a) Property that is contraband is subject to seizure and forfeiture under this chapter.

(b) Any property that is contraband other than property held as evidence in a criminal investigation or a pending criminal case, money, a negotiable instrument, or a security that is seized under this chapter may be replevied by the owner or interest holder of the property, on execution of a good and valid bond with sufficient surety in a sum equal to the appraised value of the property replevied. The bond may be approved as to form and substance by the court after the court gives notice of the bond to the authority holding the seized property. The bond must be conditioned:

(1) on return of the property to the custody of the state on the day of hearing of the forfeiture proceedings; and

(2) that the interest holder or owner of the property will abide by the decision that may be made in the cause.

(c) An owner or interest holder's interest in property may not be forfeited under this chapter if the owner or interest holder proves by a preponderance of the evidence that the owner or interest holder acquired and perfected the interest:

(1) before or during the act or omission giving rise to forfeiture or, if the property is real property, he acquired an ownership interest, security interest, or lien interest before a lis pendens notice was filed under Article 59.04(g) of this code and did not know or should not reasonably have known of the act or omission giving rise to the forfeiture or that it was likely to occur at or before the time of acquiring and perfecting the interest or, if the property is real property, at or before the time of acquiring the ownership interest, security interest, or lien interest; or

(2) after the act or omission giving rise to the forfeiture, but before the seizure of the property, and only if the owner or interest holder:

(A) was, at the time that the interest in the property was acquired, an owner or interest holder for value; and

(B) was without reasonable cause to believe that the property was contraband and did not

Code of Criminal Procedure

purposefully avoid learning that the property was contraband.

(d) Notwithstanding any other law, if property is seized from the possession of an owner or interest holder who asserts an ownership interest, security interest, or lien interest in the property under applicable law, the owner or interest holder's rights remain in effect during the pendency of proceedings under this chapter as if possession of the property had remained with the owner or interest holder.

(e) On motion by any party or on the motion of the court, after notice in the manner provided by Article 59.04 of this code to all known owners and interest holders of property subject to forfeiture under this chapter, and after a hearing on the matter, the court may make appropriate orders to preserve and maintain the value of the property until a final disposition of the property is made under this chapter, including the sale of the property if that is the only method by which the value of the property may be preserved until final disposition.

(f) Any property that is contraband and has been seized by the Texas Department of Criminal Justice shall be forfeited to the department under the same rules and conditions as for other forfeitures.

(g) An individual, firm, corporation, or other entity insured under a policy of title insurance may not assert a claim or cause of action on or because of the policy if the claim or cause of action is based on forfeiture under this chapter and, at or before the time of acquiring the ownership of real property, security interest in real property, or lien interest against real property, the insured knew or reasonably should have known of the act or omission giving rise to the forfeiture or that the act or omission was likely to occur.

(h) (1) An owner or interest holder's interest in property may not be forfeited under this chapter if at the forfeiture hearing the owner or interest holder proves by a preponderance of the evidence that the owner or interest holder was not a party to the offense giving rise to the forfeiture and that the contraband:

(A) was stolen from the owner or interest holder before being used in the commission of the offense giving rise to the forfeiture;

(B) was purchased with:

(i) money stolen from the owner or interest holder; or

(ii) proceeds from the sale of property stolen from the owner or interest holder; or

(C) was used or intended to be used without the effective consent of the owner or interest holder in the commission of the offense giving rise to the forfeiture.

(2) An attorney representing the state who has a reasonable belief that property subject to forfeiture is described by Subdivision (1) and who has a reasonable belief as to the identity of the rightful owner or interest holder of the property shall notify the owner or interest holder as provided by Article 59.04.

(3) An attorney representing the state is not liable in an action for damages resulting from an act or omission in the performance of the duties imposed by Subdivision (2).

(4) The exclusive remedy for failure by the attorney representing the state to provide the notice required under Subdivision (2) is submission of that failure as a ground for new trial in a motion for new trial or bill of review.

(i) The forfeiture provisions of this chapter apply to contraband as defined by Article 59.01(2)(B)(v) of this code only in a municipality with a population of 250,000 or more.

Sec. 59.021. Forfeiture of Substitute Property.

(a) In this article, "substitute property" means property:

(1) that is not contraband; and

(2) that is owned by a person who is or was the owner of, or has or had an interest in, contraband with an aggregate value of $200,000 or more.

(b) Substitute property may be seized under authority of a search warrant issued under Subsection (c) if property that is contraband:

(1) can no longer be located after the exercise of reasonable diligence;

(2) has been transferred, conveyed, sold to, or deposited with a person other than the owner or interest holder;

(3) is not within the jurisdiction of the court;

(4) has substantially diminished in value;

(5) has been commingled with other property and cannot be readily distinguished or separated; or

(6) is proceeds described by Article 59.01(2)(C) and was used to acquire other property that is not within the jurisdiction of the court.

(c) A district court may issue a search warrant authorizing a peace officer to seize substitute property if the officer submits an affidavit that states:

(1) probable cause for the commission of an offense giving rise to forfeiture of contraband;

(2) a description of the contraband involved and the estimated current fair market value of the substitute property to be seized;

(3) the reasons the contraband is unavailable for forfeiture;

(4) probable cause to believe that the owner of the substitute property owned or had an interest

in contraband with an aggregate value of $200,000 or more in connection with the commission of an underlying offense giving rise to the forfeiture; and

(5) that due diligence has been exercised in identifying the minimum amount of substitute property necessary to approximate the estimated highest fair market value of the contraband during the period in which the owner of the substitute property owned, or had an interest in, the contraband.

(d) After seizure of the substitute property, the disposition shall proceed as other cases in this chapter except that the attorney representing the state must prove by a preponderance of the evidence:

(1) that the contraband described by Subsection (b) was subject to seizure and forfeiture under this chapter;

(2) the highest fair market value of that contraband during the period in which the owner of the substitute property owned, or had an interest in, the contraband;

(3) the fair market value of the substitute property at the time it was seized; and

(4) that the owner of the substitute property owned or had an interest in contraband with an aggregate value of $200,000 or more in connection with the commission of an underlying offense giving rise to the forfeiture.

(e) For purposes of determining the aggregate value of contraband under Subsection (c) or (d), the owner or interest holder is not required to have simultaneously owned or had an interest in all of the property constituting contraband.

(f) If the fair market value of the substitute property seized exceeds the highest fair market value of the contraband described by Subsection (b) during the period in which the owner of the substitute property owned, or had an interest in, the contraband, the court shall make appropriate orders to ensure that property equal in value to the excess is returned to the person or persons from whom the substitute property was seized.

Sec. 59.022. Property Removed from This State.

(a) This article applies to contraband, other than real property, that is determined to be located outside of this state.

(b) A peace officer who identifies contraband described by Subsection (a) shall provide the attorney representing the state a sworn statement that identifies the contraband and the reasons the contraband is subject to seizure. On receiving the sworn statement, the attorney representing the state may file, in the name of the state, a notice of intended forfeiture in a district court in:

(1) the county in which the contraband, or proceeds used to acquire the contraband, was known to be situated before its removal out of this state;

(2) the county in which any owner or possessor of the contraband was prosecuted for an underlying offense for which the property is subject to forfeiture;

(3) the county in which venue existed for prosecution of an underlying offense for which the property is subject to forfeiture; or

(4) Travis County.

(c) The attorney representing the state shall request that citation be served on any person who owns or is in possession or control of the contraband to which this article applies and, on service in accordance with the Texas Rules of Civil Procedure, may move to have the court order that the contraband be:

(1) returned or brought to the jurisdiction of the court; or

(2) delivered to an agent of this state for transportation to the jurisdiction of the court.

(d) The attorney representing the state is entitled to all reasonable discovery in accordance with the Texas Rules of Civil Procedure to assist in identifying and locating contraband described by Subsection (a).

(e) If the court orders the return of contraband under this article, the contraband, after return, is subject to seizure and forfeiture as otherwise provided by this chapter.

(f) If it is found that any person after being served with a citation under Subsection (c) has transported, concealed, disposed of, or otherwise acted to prevent the seizure and forfeiture of contraband described by Subsection (a), the court may:

(1) order the payment to the attorney representing the state of costs incurred in investigating and identifying the location of the contraband, including discovery costs, reasonable attorney's fees, expert fees, other professional fees incurred by the attorney, and travel expenses;

(2) enter a judgment for civil contempt and impose:

(A) a fine of not more than $10,000 or less than $1,000;

(B) confinement in jail for a term of not more than 30 days or less than 10 days; or

(C) both fine and confinement;

(3) enter a judgment of forfeiture of the person's interest in the contraband;

(4) enter a judgment in the amount of the fair market value of the contraband;

(5) impose a civil penalty of not more than $25,000 or less than $1,000 for each item of contraband, or each separate fund, of which the

person transported, concealed, disposed, or otherwise acted to prevent the seizure and forfeiture; or

(6) order any combination of Subdivisions (1) through (5).

Sec. 59.023. Suit for Proceeds.

(a) A peace officer who identifies proceeds that are gained from the commission of an offense listed in Article 59.01(2)(A) or (B) shall provide the attorney representing the state with an affidavit that identifies the amount of the proceeds and that states probable cause that the proceeds are contraband subject to forfeiture. On receiving the affidavit, the attorney representing the state may file for a judgment in the amount of the proceeds in a district court in:

(1) the county in which the proceeds were gained;

(2) the county in which any owner or possessor of the property was prosecuted for an underlying offense for which the property is subject to forfeiture;

(3) the county in which venue existed for prosecution of an underlying offense for which the property is subject to forfeiture;

(4) the county in which the proceeds were seized; or

(5) Travis County.

(b) If the court determines that, based on an examination of the affidavit described by Subsection (a), probable cause exists for the suit to proceed, the court shall order that citation be served on all defendants named in the suit in accordance with the Texas Rules of Civil Procedure.

(c) Each person who is shown to have been a party to an underlying offense for which the proceeds are subject to forfeiture is jointly and severally liable in a suit under this article, regardless of whether the person has been charged for the offense.

Sec. 59.024. Multiple Recovery Prohibited.

The attorney representing the state may proceed under Article 59.02, 59.021, 59.022, or 59.023, or any combination of those articles. If property or proceeds are awarded or forfeited to the state under this chapter for an underlying offense, a court may not award or forfeit additional property or proceeds that would exceed the highest fair market value of the contraband subject to forfeiture for that offense. For purposes of this article, the highest fair market value may be calculated at any time during the period in which the applicable person owned, possessed, or had an interest in the contraband.

Art. 59.03. Seizure of Contraband.

(a) Property subject to forfeiture under this chapter, other than property described by Article 59.12, may be seized by any peace officer under authority of a search warrant.

(b) Seizure of property subject to forfeiture may be made without warrant if:

(1) the owner, operator, or agent in charge of the property knowingly consents;

(2) the seizure is incident to a search to which the owner, operator, or agent in charge of the property knowingly consents;

(3) the property subject to seizure has been the subject of a prior judgment in favor of the state in a forfeiture proceeding under this chapter; or

(4) the seizure was incident to a lawful arrest, lawful search, or lawful search incident to arrest.

(c) A peace officer who seizes property under this chapter has custody of the property, subject only to replevy under Article 59.02 of this code or an order of a court. A peace officer who has custody of property shall provide the attorney representing the state with a sworn statement that contains a schedule of the property seized, an acknowledgment that the officer has seized the property, and a list of the officer's reasons for the seizure. Not later than 72 hours after the seizure, the peace officer shall:

(1) place the property under seal;

(2) remove the property to a place ordered by the court; or

(3) require a law enforcement agency of the state or a political subdivision to take custody of the property and move it to a proper location.

(d) A person in the possession of property at the time a peace officer seizes the property under this chapter may at the time of seizure assert the person's interest in or right to the property. A peace officer, including the peace officer who seizes the property, may not request, require, or in any manner induce any person, including a person who asserts an interest in or right to the property, to execute a document purporting to waive the person's interest in or rights to property seized under this chapter.

(e) At any time before notice is filed under Article 59.04(b), an attorney representing the state may not request, require, or in any manner induce any person, including a person who asserts an interest in or right to property seized under this chapter, to execute a document purporting to waive the person's interest in or rights to the property.

Art. 59.04. Notification of Forfeiture Proceeding.

(a) If a peace officer seizes property under this chapter, the attorney representing the state shall commence proceedings under this section not later than the 30th day after the date of the seizure.

(b) A forfeiture proceeding commences under this chapter when the attorney representing the state files a notice of the seizure and intended forfeiture in the name of the state with the clerk of the district court in the county in which the seizure is made. The attorney representing the state must attach to the notice the peace officer's sworn statement under Article 59.03 of this code or, if the property has been seized under Article 59.12(b), the statement of the terms and amount of the depository account or inventory of assets provided by the regulated financial institution to the peace officer executing the warrant in the manner described by Article 59.12(b). Except as provided by Subsection (c) of this article, the attorney representing the state shall cause certified copies of the notice to be served on the following persons in the same manner as provided for the service of process by citation in civil cases:

(1) the owner of the property; and

(2) any interest holder in the property.

(c) If the property is a motor vehicle, and if there is reasonable cause to believe that the vehicle has been registered under the laws of this state, the attorney representing the state shall ask the Texas Department of Motor Vehicles to identify from its records the record owner of the vehicle and any interest holder. If the addresses of the owner and interest holder are not otherwise known, the attorney representing the state shall request citation be served on such persons at the address listed with the Texas Department of Motor Vehicles. If the citation issued to such address is returned unserved, the attorney representing the state shall cause a copy of the notice of the seizure and intended forfeiture to be posted at the courthouse door, to remain there for a period of not less than 30 days. If the owner or interest holder does not answer or appear after the notice has been so posted, the court shall enter a judgment by default as to the owner or interest holder, provided that the attorney representing the state files a written motion supported by affidavit setting forth the attempted service. An owner or interest holder whose interest is forfeited in this manner shall not be liable for court costs. If the person in possession of the vehicle at the time of the seizure is not the owner or the interest holder of the vehicle, notification shall be provided to the possessor in the same manner specified for notification to an owner or interest holder.

(d) If the property is a motor vehicle and is not registered in this state, the attorney representing the state shall attempt to ascertain the name and address of the person in whose name the vehicle is licensed in another state. If the vehicle is licensed in a state that has a certificate of title law, the attorney representing the state shall request the appropriate agency of that state to identify the record owner of the vehicle and any interest holder.

(e) If a financing statement is required by law to be filed to perfect a security interest affecting the property, and if there is reasonable cause to believe that a financing statement has been filed, the attorney representing the state who commences the proceedings shall ask the appropriate official designated by Chapter 9, Business & Commerce Code, to identify the record owner of the property and the person who is an interest holder.

(f) If the property is an aircraft or a part of an aircraft, and if there is reasonable cause to believe that a perfected security instrument affects the property, the attorney representing the state shall request an administrator of the Federal Aviation Administration to identify from the records of that agency the record owner of the property and the holder of the perfected security instrument. The attorney representing the state shall also notify the Department of Public Safety in writing of the fact that an aircraft has been seized and shall provide the department with a description of the aircraft.

(g) If the property is real property, the attorney representing the state, not later than the third day after the date proceedings are commenced, shall file a lis pendens notice describing the property with the county clerk of each county in which the property is located.

(h) For all other property subject to forfeiture, if there is reasonable cause to believe that a perfected security instrument affects the property, the attorney representing the state shall make a good faith inquiry to identify the holder of the perfected security instrument.

(i) Except as provided by Section (c) of this article, the attorney representing the state who commences the proceedings shall cause the owner and any interest holder to be named as a party and to be served with citation as provided by the Texas Rules of Civil Procedure.

(j) A person who was in possession of the property at the time it was seized shall be made a party to the proceeding.

(k) If no person was in possession of the property at the time it was seized, and if the owner of the property is unknown, the attorney representing the state shall file with the clerk of the court in which the proceedings are pending an affidavit stating that no person was in possession of the property at the time it was seized and that the owner of the property is unknown. The clerk of the court shall issue a citation for service by publication addressed to "The Unknown Owner of ___," filling in the blank space with a reasonably detailed description of the property subject to forfeiture. The citation must contain the other requisites prescribed by and be served as provided by Rules 114, 115, and 116, Texas Rules of Civil Procedure.

(*l*) Proceedings commenced under this chapter may not proceed to hearing unless the judge who is to conduct the hearing is satisfied that this article has been complied with and that the attorney representing the state will introduce into evidence at the hearing any answer received from an inquiry required by Subsections (c)—(h) of this article.

Art. 59.05. Forfeiture Hearing.

(a) All parties must comply with the rules of pleading as required in civil suits.

(b) All cases under this chapter shall proceed to trial in the same manner as in other civil cases. The state has the burden of proving by a preponderance of the evidence that property is subject to forfeiture.

(c) It is an affirmative defense to forfeiture under this chapter of property belonging to the spouse of a person whose acts gave rise to the seizure of community property that, because of an act of family violence, as defined by Section 71.004, Family Code, the spouse was unable to prevent the act giving rise to the seizure.

(d) A final conviction for an underlying offense is not a requirement for forfeiture under this chapter. An owner or interest holder may present evidence of a dismissal or acquittal of an underlying offense in a forfeiture proceeding, and evidence of an acquittal raises a presumption that the property or interest that is the subject of the hearing is nonforfeitable. This presumption can be rebutted by evidence that the owner or interest holder knew or should have known that the property was contraband.

(e) It is the intention of the legislature that asset forfeiture is remedial in nature and not a form of punishment. If the court finds that all or any part of the property is subject to forfeiture, the judge shall forfeit the property to the state, with the attorney representing the state as the agent for the state, except that if the court finds that the nonforfeitable interest of an interest holder in the property is valued in an amount greater than or substantially equal to the present value of the property, the court shall order the property released to the interest holder. If the court finds that the nonforfeitable interest of an interest holder is valued in an amount substantially less than the present value of the property and that the property is subject to forfeiture, the court shall order the property forfeited to the state with the attorney representing the state acting as the agent of the state, and making necessary orders to protect the nonforfeitable interest of the interest holder. On final judgment of forfeiture, the attorney representing the state shall dispose of the property in the manner required by Article 59.06 of this code.

(f) On forfeiture to the state of an amount greater than $2,500, the clerk of the court in which the forfeiture proceeding was held is entitled to court costs in that proceeding as in other civil proceedings unless the forfeiture violates federal requirements for multijurisdictional task force cases authorized under Chapter 362, Local Government Code. The procedure for collecting the costs is the procedure established under Subsections (a) and (c), Article 59.06.

(g) If property is seized at a federal checkpoint, the notice of seizure and intended forfeiture may be filed in and the proceeding may be held in:

(1) the county in which the seizure occurred; or

(2) with the consent of the owner, operator, or agent in charge of the property, a county that is adjacent to the county in which the seizure occurred, if both counties are in the same judicial district.

Art. 59.06. Disposition of Forfeited Property.

(a) Except as provided by Subsection (k), all forfeited property shall be administered by the attorney representing the state, acting as the agent of the state, in accordance with accepted accounting practices and with the provisions of any local agreement entered into between the attorney representing the state and law enforcement agencies. If a local agreement has not been executed, the property shall be sold on the 75th day after the date of the final judgment of forfeiture at public auction under the direction of the county sheriff, after notice of public auction as provided by law for other sheriff's sales. The proceeds of the sale shall be distributed as follows:

(1) to any interest holder to the extent of the interest holder's nonforfeitable interest;

(2) after any distributions under Subdivision (1), if the Title IV-D agency has filed a child support lien in the forfeiture proceeding, to the Title IV-D agency in an amount not to exceed the amount of child support arrearages identified in the lien; and

(3) the balance, if any, after the deduction of court costs to which a district court clerk is entitled under Article 59.05(f) and, after that deduction, the deduction of storage and disposal costs, to be deposited not later than the 30th day after the date

of the sale in the state treasury to the credit of the general revenue fund.

(b) If a local agreement exists between the attorney representing the state and law enforcement agencies, the attorney representing the state may transfer the property to law enforcement agencies to maintain, repair, use, and operate the property for official purposes if the property is free of any interest of an interest holder. The agency receiving the forfeited property may purchase the interest of an interest holder so that the property can be released for use by the agency. The agency receiving the forfeited property may maintain, repair, use, and operate the property with money appropriated for current operations. If the property is a motor vehicle subject to registration under the motor vehicle registration laws of this state, the agency receiving the forfeited vehicle is considered to be the purchaser and the certificate of title shall issue to the agency. A law enforcement agency to which property is transferred under this subsection at any time may transfer or loan the property to any other municipal or county agency, a groundwater conservation district governed by Chapter 36, Water Code, or a school district for the use of that agency or district. A municipal or county agency, a groundwater conservation district, or a school district to which a law enforcement agency loans a motor vehicle under this subsection shall maintain any automobile insurance coverage for the vehicle that is required by law.

(b-1) If a loan is made by a sheriff's office or by a municipal police department, the commissioners court of the county in which the sheriff has jurisdiction or the governing body of the municipality in which the department has jurisdiction, as applicable, may revoke the loan at any time by notifying the receiving agency or district, by mail, that the receiving agency or district must return the loaned vehicle to the loaning agency before the seventh day after the date the receiving agency or district receives the notice.

(b-2) An agency that loans property under this article shall:

(1) keep a record of the loan, including the name of the agency or district to which the vehicle was loaned, the fair market value of the vehicle, and where the receiving agency or district will use the vehicle; and

(2) update the record when the information relating to the vehicle changes.

(c) If a local agreement exists between the attorney representing the state and law enforcement agencies, all money, securities, negotiable instruments, stocks or bonds, or things of value, or proceeds from the sale of those items, shall be deposited, after the deduction of court costs to which a district court clerk is entitled under Article 59.05(f), according to the terms of the agreement into one or more of the following funds:

(1) a special fund in the county treasury for the benefit of the office of the attorney representing the state, to be used by the attorney solely for the official purposes of his office;

(2) a special fund in the municipal treasury if distributed to a municipal law enforcement agency, to be used solely for law enforcement purposes;

(3) a special fund in the county treasury if distributed to a county law enforcement agency, to be used solely for law enforcement purposes; or

(4) a special fund in the state law enforcement agency if distributed to a state law enforcement agency, to be used solely for law enforcement purposes.

(c-1) Notwithstanding Subsection (a), the attorney representing the state and special rangers of the Texas and Southwestern Cattle Raisers Association who meet the requirements of Article 2.125 may enter into a local agreement that allows the attorney representing the state to transfer proceeds from the sale of forfeited property described by Subsection (c), after the deduction of court costs as described by that subsection, to a special fund established for the special rangers. Proceeds transferred under this subsection must be used by the special rangers solely for law enforcement purposes. Any expenditures of the proceeds are subject to the audit provisions established under this article.

(c-2) Any postjudgment interest from money, securities, negotiable instruments, stocks or bonds, or things of value, or proceeds from the sale of those items, that are deposited in an interest-bearing bank account under Subsection (c) shall be used for the same purpose as the principal.

(c-3) Notwithstanding Subsection (a), with respect to forfeited property seized in connection with a violation of Chapter 481, Health and Safety Code (Texas Controlled Substances Act), by a peace officer employed by the Department of Public Safety, in a proceeding under Article 59.05 in which a default judgment is rendered in favor of the state, the attorney representing the state shall enter into a local agreement with the department that allows the attorney representing the state either to:

(1) transfer forfeited property to the department to maintain, repair, use, and operate for official purposes in the manner provided by Subsection (b); or

(2) allocate proceeds from the sale of forfeited property described by Subsection (c), after the deduction of court costs as described by that subsection, in the following proportions:

Code of Criminal Procedure

(A) 40 percent to a special fund in the department to be used solely for law enforcement purposes;

(B) 30 percent to a special fund in the county treasury for the benefit of the office of the attorney representing the state, to be used by the attorney solely for the official purposes of the attorney's office; and

(C) 30 percent to the general revenue fund.

(c-4) Notwithstanding Subsections (a) and (c-3), with respect to forfeited property seized in connection with a violation of Chapter 481, Health and Safety Code (Texas Controlled Substances Act), by the Department of Public Safety concurrently with any other law enforcement agency, in a proceeding under Article 59.05 in which a default judgment is rendered in favor of the state, the attorney representing the state may allocate property or proceeds in accordance with a memorandum of understanding between the law enforcement agencies and the attorney representing the state.

(d) Proceeds awarded under this chapter to a law enforcement agency or to the attorney representing the state may be spent by the agency or the attorney after a budget for the expenditure of the proceeds has been submitted to the commissioners court or governing body of the municipality. The budget must be detailed and clearly list and define the categories of expenditures, but may not list details that would endanger the security of an investigation or prosecution. Expenditures are subject to the audit and enforcement provisions established under this chapter. A commissioners court or governing body of a municipality may not use the existence of an award to offset or decrease total salaries, expenses, and allowances that the agency or the attorney receives from the commissioners court or governing body at or after the time the proceeds are awarded.

(d-1) The head of a law enforcement agency or an attorney representing the state may not use proceeds or property received under this chapter to:

(1) contribute to a political campaign;

(2) make a donation to any entity, except as provided by Subsection (d-2);

(3) pay expenses related to the training or education of any member of the judiciary;

(4) pay any travel expenses related to attendance at training or education seminars if the expenses violate generally applicable restrictions established by the commissioners court or governing body of the municipality, as applicable;

(5) purchase alcoholic beverages;

(6) make any expenditure not approved by the commissioners court or governing body of the municipality, as applicable, if the head of a law enforcement agency or attorney representing the state holds an elective office and:

(A) the deadline for filing an application for a place on the ballot as a candidate for reelection to that office in the general primary election has passed and the person did not file an application for a place on that ballot; or

(B) during the person's current term of office, the person was a candidate in a primary, general, or runoff election for reelection to that office and was not the prevailing candidate in that election; or

(7) increase a salary, expense, or allowance for an employee of the law enforcement agency or attorney representing the state who is budgeted by the commissioners court or governing body of the municipality unless the commissioners court or governing body first approves the increase.

(d-2) The head of a law enforcement agency or an attorney representing the state may use as an official purpose of the agency or attorney proceeds or property received under this chapter to make a donation to an entity that assists in:

(1) the detection, investigation, or prosecution of:

(A) criminal offenses; or

(B) instances of abuse, as defined by Section 261.001, Family Code;

(2) the provision of:

(A) mental health, drug, or rehabilitation services; or

(B) services for victims or witnesses of criminal offenses or instances of abuse described by Subdivision (1); or

(3) the provision of training or education related to duties or services described by Subdivision (1) or (2).

(d-3) Except as otherwise provided by this article, an expenditure of proceeds or property received under this chapter is considered to be for a law enforcement purpose if the expenditure is made for an activity of a law enforcement agency that relates to the criminal and civil enforcement of the laws of this state, including an expenditure made for:

(1) equipment, including vehicles, computers, firearms, protective body armor, furniture, software, uniforms, and maintenance equipment;

(2) supplies, including office supplies, mobile phone and data account fees for employees, and Internet services;

(3) investigative and training-related travel expenses, including payment for hotel rooms, airfare, meals, rental of and fuel for a motor vehicle, and parking;

(4) conferences and training expenses, including fees and materials;

(5) investigative costs, including payments to informants and lab expenses;

(6) crime prevention and treatment programs;

(7) facility costs, including building purchase, lease payments, remodeling and renovating, maintenance, and utilities;

(8) witness-related costs, including travel and security; and

(9) audit costs and fees, including audit preparation and professional fees.

(d-4) Except as otherwise provided by this article, an expenditure of proceeds or property received under this chapter is considered to be for an official purpose of an attorney's office if the expenditure is made for an activity of an attorney or office of an attorney representing the state that relates to the preservation, enforcement, or administration of the laws of this state, including an expenditure made for:

(1) equipment, including vehicles, computers, visual aid equipment for litigation, firearms, body armor, furniture, software, and uniforms;

(2) supplies, including office supplies, legal library supplies and access fees, mobile phone and data account fees for employees, and Internet services;

(3) prosecution and training-related travel expenses, including payment for hotel rooms, airfare, meals, rental of and fuel for a motor vehicle, and parking;

(4) conferences and training expenses, including fees and materials;

(5) investigative costs, including payments to informants and lab expenses;

(6) crime prevention and treatment programs;

(7) facility costs, including building purchase, lease payments, remodeling and renovating, maintenance, and utilities;

(8) legal fees, including court costs, witness fees, and related costs, including travel and security, audit costs, and professional fees; and

(9) state bar and legal association dues.

(e) On the sale of contraband under this article, the appropriate state agency shall issue a certificate of title to the recipient if a certificate of title is required for the property by other law.

(f) A final judgment of forfeiture under this chapter perfects the title of the state to the property as of the date that the contraband was seized or the date the forfeiture action was filed, whichever occurred first, except that if the property forfeited is real property, the title is perfected as of the date a notice of lis pendens is filed on the property.

(g) (1) All law enforcement agencies and attorneys representing the state who receive proceeds or property under this chapter shall account for the seizure, forfeiture, receipt, and specific expenditure of all the proceeds and property in an audit, which is to be performed annually by the commissioners court or governing body of a municipality, as appropriate. The annual period of the audit for a law enforcement agency is the fiscal year of the appropriate county or municipality and the annual period for an attorney representing the state is the state fiscal year. The audit must be completed on a form provided by the attorney general and must include a detailed report and explanation of all expenditures, including salaries and overtime pay, officer training, investigative equipment and supplies, and other items. Certified copies of the audit shall be delivered by the law enforcement agency or attorney representing the state to the attorney general not later than the 60th day after the date on which the annual period that is the subject of the audit ends.

(2) If a copy of the audit is not delivered to the attorney general within the period required by Subdivision (1), within five days after the end of the period the attorney general shall notify the law enforcement agency or the attorney representing the state of that fact. On a showing of good cause, the attorney general may grant an extension permitting the agency or attorney to deliver a copy of the audit after the period required by Subdivision (1) and before the 76th day after the date on which the annual period that is the subject of the audit ends. If the law enforcement agency or the attorney representing the state fails to establish good cause for not delivering the copy of the audit within the period required by Subdivision (1) or fails to deliver a copy of an audit within the extension period, the attorney general shall notify the comptroller of that fact.

(3) On notice under Subdivision (2), the comptroller shall perform the audit otherwise required by Subdivision (1). At the conclusion of the audit, the comptroller shall forward a copy of the audit to the attorney general. The law enforcement agency or attorney representing the state is liable to the comptroller for the costs of the comptroller in performing the audit.

(h) As a specific exception to the requirement of Subdivisions (1)—(3) of Subsection (c) of this article that the funds described by those subdivisions be used only for the official purposes of the attorney representing the state or for law enforcement purposes, on agreement between the attorney representing the state or the head of a law enforcement agency and the governing body of a political subdivision, the attorney representing the state or the head of the law enforcement agency shall comply with the request of the governing body to deposit not more than a total of 10 percent of the gross amount credited to the attorney's or agency's fund into the treasury of the political subdivision. The governing body of the political subdivision shall, by ordinance, order, or resolution, use funds received under this subsection for:

(1) nonprofit programs for the prevention of drug abuse;

(2) nonprofit chemical dependency treatment facilities licensed under Chapter 464, Health and Safety Code;

(3) nonprofit drug and alcohol rehabilitation or prevention programs administered or staffed by professionals designated as qualified and credentialed by the Texas Commission on Alcohol and Drug Abuse; or

(4) financial assistance as described by Subsection (o).

(i) The governing body of a political subdivision may not use funds received under this subchapter for programs or facilities listed under Subsections (h)(1)—(3) if an officer of or member of the Board of Directors of the entity providing the program or facility is related to a member of the governing body, the attorney representing the state, or the head of the law enforcement agency within the third degree by consanguinity or the second degree by affinity.

(j) As a specific exception to Subdivision (4) of Subsection (c) of this article, the director of a state law enforcement agency may use not more than 10 percent of the amount credited to the special fund of the agency under that subdivision for the prevention of drug abuse and the treatment of persons with drug-related problems.

(k) (1) The attorney for the state shall transfer all forfeited property that is income from, or acquired with the income from, a movie, book, magazine article, tape recording, phonographic record, radio or television presentation, telephone service, electronic media format, including an Internet website, or live entertainment in which a crime is reenacted to the attorney general.

(2) The attorney for the state shall transfer to the attorney general all income from the sale of tangible property the value of which is increased by the notoriety gained from the conviction of an offense by the person accused or convicted of the crime, minus the deduction authorized by this subdivision. The attorney for the state shall determine the fair market value of property that is substantially similar to the property that was sold but that has not been increased in value by notoriety and deduct that amount from the proceeds of the sale. After transferring income to the attorney general, the attorney for the state shall transfer the remainder of the proceeds of the sale to the owner of the property. The attorney for the state, the attorney general, or a person who may be entitled to claim money from the escrow account described by Subdivision (3) in satisfaction of a claim may at any time bring an action to enjoin the waste of income described by this subdivision.

(3) The attorney general shall deposit the money or proceeds from the sale of the property into an escrow account. The money in the account is available to satisfy a judgment against the person who committed the crime in favor of a victim of the crime if the judgment is for damages incurred by the victim caused by the commission of the crime. The attorney general shall transfer the money in the account that has not been ordered paid to a victim in satisfaction of a judgment to the compensation to victims of crime fund on the fifth anniversary of the date the account was established. In this subsection, "victim" has the meaning assigned by Article 56B.003.

(*l*) A law enforcement agency that, or an attorney representing the state who, does not receive proceeds or property under this chapter during an annual period as described by Subsection (g) shall, not later than the 30th day after the date on which the annual period ends, report to the attorney general that the agency or attorney, as appropriate, did not receive proceeds or property under this chapter during the annual period.

(m) As a specific exception to Subdivisions (1)—(3) of Subsection (c), a law enforcement agency or attorney representing the state may use proceeds received under this chapter to contract with a person or entity to prepare an audit as required by Subsection (g).

(n) As a specific exception to Subsection (c)(2) or (3), a local law enforcement agency may transfer not more than a total of 10 percent of the gross amount credited to the agency's fund to a separate special fund in the treasury of the political subdivision. The agency shall administer the separate special fund, and expenditures from the fund are at the sole discretion of the agency and may be used only for financial assistance as described by Subsection (o).

(o) The governing body of a political subdivision or a local law enforcement agency may provide financial assistance under Subsection (h)(4) or (n) only to a person who is a Texas resident, who plans to enroll or is enrolled at an institution of higher education in an undergraduate degree or certificate program in a field related to law enforcement, and who plans to return to that locality to work for the political subdivision or the agency in a field related to law enforcement. To ensure the promotion of a law enforcement purpose of the political subdivision or the agency, the governing body of the political subdivision or the agency shall impose other reasonable criteria related to the provision of this financial assistance, including a requirement that a recipient of the financial assistance work for a certain period of time for the political subdivision or the agency in a field related to law enforcement and including a requirement that the recipient sign an agreement to perform that work for that period of time. In this subsection, "institution of higher education" has the meaning assigned by Section 61.003, Education Code.

(p) Notwithstanding Subsection (a), and to the extent necessary to protect the state's ability to recover amounts wrongfully obtained by the owner of the property and associated damages and penalties to which the affected health care program may otherwise be entitled by law, the attorney representing the state shall transfer to the governmental entity administering the affected health care program all forfeited property defined as contraband under Article 59.01(2)(B)(vi). If the forfeited property consists of property other than money or negotiable instruments, the attorney representing the state may, with the consent of the governmental entity administering the affected health care program, sell the property and deliver to the governmental entity administering the affected health care program the proceeds from the sale, minus costs attributable to the sale. The sale must be conducted in a manner that is reasonably expected to result in receiving the fair market value for the property.

(q) (1) Notwithstanding any other provision of this article, a multicounty drug task force, or a county or municipality participating in the task force, that is not established in accordance with Section 362.004, Local Government Code, or that fails to comply with the policies and procedures established by the Department of Public Safety under that section, and that participates in the seizure of contraband shall forward to the comptroller all proceeds received by the task force from the forfeiture of the contraband. The comptroller shall deposit the proceeds in the state treasury to the credit of the general revenue fund.

(2) The attorney general shall ensure the enforcement of Subdivision (1) by filing any necessary legal proceedings in the county in which the contraband is forfeited or in Travis County.

(r) As a specific exception to Subsection (c)(2), (3), or (4), a law enforcement agency may transfer not more than 10 percent of the gross amount credited to the agency's fund to a separate special fund established in the treasury of the political subdivision or maintained by the state law enforcement agency, as applicable. The law enforcement agency shall administer the separate special fund. Interest received from the investment of money in the fund shall be credited to the fund. The agency may use money in the fund only to provide scholarships to children of peace officers who were employed by the agency or by another law enforcement agency with which the agency has overlapping geographic jurisdiction and who were killed in the line of duty. Scholarships under this subsection may be used only to pay the costs of attendance at an institution of higher education or private or independent institution of higher education, including tuition and fees and costs for housing, books, supplies, transportation, and other related personal expenses. In this subsection, "institution of higher education" and "private or independent institution of higher education" have the meanings assigned by Section 61.003, Education Code.

(s) Not later than April 30 of each year, the attorney general shall develop a report based on information submitted by law enforcement agencies and attorneys representing the state under Subsection (g) detailing the total amount of funds forfeited, or credited after the sale of forfeited property, in this state in the preceding calendar year. The attorney general shall maintain in a prominent location on the attorney general's publicly accessible Internet website a link to the most recent annual report developed under this subsection.

(t) (1) This subsection applies only to contraband for which forfeiture is authorized with respect to an offense under Section 20.05, 20.06, 20.07, 43.04, or 43.05 or Chapter 20A, Penal Code.

(2) Notwithstanding any other provision of this article, the gross amount credited to the special fund of the office of the attorney representing the state or of a law enforcement agency under Subsection (c) from the forfeiture of contraband described by Subdivision (1) shall be:

(A) used to provide direct victim services by the victim services division or other similar division of the office of the attorney representing the state or of a law enforcement agency, as applicable; or

(B) used by the office of the attorney representing the state or of the law enforcement agency to cover the costs of a contract with a local nonprofit organization to provide direct services to crime victims.

(3) An expenditure of money in the manner required by this subsection is considered to be for an official purpose of the office of the attorney representing the state or for a law enforcement purpose, as applicable.

(u) As a specific exception to Subsection (c) that the funds described by that subsection be used only for the official purposes of the attorney representing the state or for law enforcement purposes, to cover the costs of a contract with a municipal or county program to provide services to domestic victims of trafficking, the attorney representing the state or the head of a law enforcement agency, as applicable, may use any portion of the gross amount credited to the attorney's or agency's special fund under Subsection (c) from the forfeiture of contraband that:

(1) is used in the commission of, or used to facilitate or intended to be used to facilitate the commission of, an offense under Chapter 20A, Penal Code; or

(2) consists of proceeds gained from the commission of, or property acquired with proceeds gained from the commission of, an offense under Chapter 20A, Penal Code.

Art. 59.061. Audits and Investigations.

(a) The state auditor may at any time perform an audit or conduct an investigation, in accordance with this article and Chapter 321, Government Code, related to the seizure, forfeiture, receipt, and specific expenditure of proceeds and property received under this chapter.

(b) The state auditor is entitled at any time to access any book, account, voucher, confidential or nonconfidential report, or other record of information, including electronic data, maintained under Article 59.06, except that if the release of the applicable information is restricted under state or federal law, the state auditor may access the information only with the approval of a court or federal administrative agency, as appropriate.

(c) If the results of an audit or investigation under this article indicate that a law enforcement agency or attorney representing the state has knowingly violated or is knowingly violating a provision of this chapter relating to the disposition of proceeds or property received under this chapter, the state auditor shall promptly notify the attorney general for the purpose of initiating appropriate enforcement proceedings under Article 59.062.

(d) The law enforcement agency or attorney representing the state shall reimburse the state auditor for costs incurred by the state auditor in performing an audit under this article.

Art. 59.062. Enforcement.

(a) In the name of the state, the attorney general may institute in a district court in Travis County or in a county served by the law enforcement agency or attorney representing the state, as applicable, a suit for injunctive relief, to recover a civil penalty, or for both injunctive relief and a civil penalty if the results of an audit or investigation under Article 59.061 indicate that the law enforcement agency or attorney representing the state has knowingly violated or is knowingly violating a provision of this chapter relating to the disposition of proceeds or property received under this chapter.

(b) On application for injunctive relief and a finding that the law enforcement agency or attorney representing the state is knowingly violating a provision of this chapter relating to the disposition of proceeds or property received under this chapter, the district court shall grant the injunctive relief the facts may warrant, without requirement for bond.

(c) A law enforcement agency or attorney representing the state who knowingly commits a violation described by Subsection (a) is liable to the state for a civil penalty in an amount not to exceed $100,000 as determined by the district court to be appropriate for the nature and seriousness of the violation. In determining an appropriate penalty for the violation, the court shall consider:

(1) any previous violations committed by the agency or attorney;

(2) the seriousness of the violation, including the nature, circumstances, extent, and gravity of the violation;

(3) the demonstrated good faith of the agency or attorney; and

(4) the amount necessary to deter future violations.

(d) If the attorney general brings a suit under this article and an injunction is granted or a civil penalty is imposed, the attorney general may recover reasonable expenses, court costs, investigative costs, and attorney's fees.

(e) Notwithstanding any other provision of this article, a law enforcement agency or attorney representing the state ordered to pay a civil penalty, expense, cost, or fee under this article shall make the payment out of money available in any fund established by the agency or attorney, as applicable, for the purpose of administering proceeds or property received under this chapter. If sufficient money is not available to make payment in full at the time the court enters an order requiring payment, the agency or attorney shall continue to make payments out of money available in any fund described by this subsection until the payment is made in full.

(f) A civil penalty collected under this article shall be deposited to the credit of the drug court account in the general revenue fund to help fund specialty court programs established under Chapter 122, 123, 124, 125, or 129, Government Code, or former law.

(g) A law enforcement agency or attorney representing the state is immune from liability under this article if the agency or attorney reasonably relied on:

(1) the advice, consent, or approval of an entity that conducts an audit of the agency or attorney under this chapter; or

(2) a written opinion of the attorney general relating to:

(A) the statute or other provision of law the agency or attorney is alleged to have knowingly violated; or

(B) a fact situation that is substantially similar to the fact situation in which the agency or attorney is involved.

Art. 59.07. Immunity.

This chapter does not impose any additional liability on any authorized state, county, or municipal officer engaged in the lawful performance of the officer's duties.

Art. 59.08. Deposit of Money Pending Disposition.

(a) If money that is contraband is seized, the attorney representing the state may deposit the money in an interest-bearing bank account in the jurisdiction of the attorney representing the state until a final judgment is rendered concerning the contraband.

(b) If a final judgment is rendered concerning contraband, money that has been placed in an interest-bearing bank account under Subsection (a) of this article shall be distributed in the same manner as proceeds are distributed under Article 59.06 of this code, with any interest being distributed in the same manner and used for the same purpose as the principal.

Art. 59.09. Right to Attorney Not to Be Abridged.

This chapter is not intended to abridge an accused person's right to counsel in a criminal case.

Art. 59.10. Election of Laws.

If property is subject to forfeiture under this chapter and under any other law of this state, the attorney representing the state may bring forfeiture proceedings under either law.

Art. 59.11. Report of Seized and Forfeited Aircraft. [Repealed]

Art. 59.12. Seizure of Accounts and Assets at Regulated Financial Institution.

(a) This article applies to property consisting of a depository account or assets in a regulated financial institution.

(b) A regulated financial institution, at the time a seizure warrant issued under Chapter 18 is served on the institution, may either:

(1) pay an account or tender assets held as security for an obligation owed to the institution at the time of the service of the seizure warrant; or

(2) transfer the depository account or assets to a segregated interest-bearing account in the name of the attorney representing the state as trustee, to remain in the account until the time has expired for an appeal from a decision of the court relating to the forfeiture of accounts or assets under Article 59.05.

(c) Immediately on service of the seizure warrant, the regulated financial institution shall take action as necessary to segregate the account or assets and shall provide evidence, certified by an officer of the institution, of the terms and amount of the account or a detailed inventory of the assets to the peace officer serving the warrant. Except as otherwise provided by this article, a transaction involving an account or assets, other than the deposit or reinvestment of interest, dividends, or other normally recurring payments on the account or assets that do not involve distribution of proceeds to the owner, is not authorized unless approved by the court that issued the seizure warrant or, if a forfeiture action has been instituted, the court in which that action is pending.

(d) Any accrual to the value of the account or assets during the pendency of the forfeiture proceedings is subject to the procedures for the disbursement of interest under Article 59.08.

(e) If the regulated financial institution fails to release the depository account or assets to a peace officer pursuant to a seizure warrant or transfer the account or assets as required by Subsection (b), and as a result cannot comply with the court's forfeiture order, the court:

(1) shall order the regulated financial institution and its culpable officers, agents, or employees to pay actual damages, attorney's fees, and court costs incurred as a result of the institution's failure to comply; and

(2) may find the regulated financial institution and its culpable officers, agents, or employees in contempt.

(f) A regulated financial institution that complies with this article is not liable in damages because of the compliance.

(g) This article does not:

(1) impair the right of the state to obtain possession of physical evidence or to seize a depository account or other assets for purposes other than forfeiture under this chapter; or

(2) waive criminal or civil remedies available under other law.

Art. 59.13. Disclosure of Information Relating to Accounts and Assets at Regulated Financial Institution.

(a) The attorney representing the state may disclose information to the primary state or federal financial institution regulator, including grand jury information or otherwise confidential information, relating to any action contemplated or brought under this chapter that involves property consisting of a depository account in a regulated financial institution or assets held by a regulated financial institution as security for an obligation owed to a regulated financial institution. An attorney representing the state who discloses information as permitted by this subsection is not subject to contempt under Subchapter E, Chapter 20A, for that disclosure.

(b) A primary state or federal financial institution regulator shall keep confidential any information provided by the attorney representing the state under Subsection (a). The sharing of information under Subsection (a) by a representative of the state is not considered a waiver by the state of any privilege or claim of confidentiality.

(c) A regulator described by Subsection (b) commits an offense if the regulator knowingly discloses information in violation of this article. An offense under this subsection is punishable by confinement in jail for a period not to exceed 30 days, a fine not to exceed $500, or both such confinement and fine.

Art. 59.14. Notice to Primary State and Federal Financial Institution Regulators.

(a) Before taking any action under this chapter that implicates a potentially culpable officer or director of a regulated financial institution, the attorney representing the state shall notify the banking commissioner, who shall notify the appropriate state or federal financial institution regulator.

(b) A state or federal financial institution regulator shall keep confidential any information provided by the attorney representing the state under Subsection (a).

(c) A regulator described by Subsection (b) commits an offense if the regulator knowingly discloses information in violation of this article. An offense under this subsection is punishable by confinement in jail for a period not to exceed 30 days, a fine not to exceed $500, or both such confinement and fine.

(d) The provision of notice under Subsection (a) is not considered a waiver by the state of any privilege or claim of confidentiality.

CHAPTER 60 CRIMINAL HISTORY RECORD SYSTEM [REPEALED]

Art. 60.01. Definitions. [Repealed]

Art. 60.02. Information Systems. [Repealed]

Art. 60.03. Interagency Cooperation; Confidentiality. [Repealed]

Art. 60.04. Compatibility of Data. [Repealed]

Art. 60.05. Types of Information Collected. [Repealed]

Art. 60.051. Information in Computerized Criminal History System. [Repealed]

Art. 60.052. Information in Corrections Tracking System. [Repealed]

Art. 60.06. Duties of Agencies. [Repealed]

Art. 60.061. Information on Persons Licensed by Certain Agencies. [Repealed]

Art. 60.07. Uniform Incident Fingerprint Card. [Repealed]

Art. 60.08. Reporting. [Repealed]

Art. 60.09. Local Data Advisory Boards. [Repealed]

Art. 60.10. Data Reporting Improvement Plan [Expired].

Expired pursuant to Acts 2009, 81st Leg., ch. 1146 (H.B. 2730), § 21.001, effective September 1, 2013.

Art. 60.11. Operation Date [Repealed].

Repealed by Acts 2005, 79th Leg., ch. 1218 (H.B. 967), § 6(2), effective September 1, 2005.

Art. 60.12. Fingerprint and Arrest Information in Computerized System. [Repealed]

Art. 60.13. Contracts for Software Development [Repealed].

Repealed by Acts 2005, 79th Leg., ch. 1218 (H.B. 967), § 6(3), effective September 1, 2005.

Art. 60.14. Allocation of Grant Program Money for Criminal Justice Programs. [Repealed]

Art. 60.15. Timetable for System Records [Repealed].

Repealed by Acts 2005, 79th Leg., ch. 1218 (H.B. 967), § 6(4), effective September 1, 2005.

Art. 60.16. Report [Repealed].

Repealed by Acts 2005, 79th Leg., ch. 1218 (H.B. 967), § 6(5), effective September 1, 2005.

Art. 60.17. Coordination of Implementation Process [Repealed].

Repealed by Acts 2005, 79th Leg., ch. 1218 (H.B. 967), § 6(6), effective September 1, 2005.

Art. 60.18. Information on Subsequent Arrest of Certain Individuals. [Repealed]

Art. 60.19. Information Related to Misused Identity. [Repealed]

Art. 60.20. Information Related to Non-Fingerprint Supported Actions. [Repealed]

Art. 60.21. Monitoring Tracking; Information Submission. [Repealed]

CHAPTER 61 COMPILATION OF INFORMATION PERTAINING TO CRIMINAL COMBINATIONS AND CRIMINAL STREET GANGS [REPEALED]

Art. 61.01. Definitions. [Repealed]

Art. 61.02. Criminal Combination and Criminal Street Gang Intelligence Database; Submission Criteria. [Repealed]

Art. 61.03. Release of Information. [Repealed]

Art. 61.04. Criminal Information Relating to Child. [Repealed]

Art. 61.05. Unauthorized Use or Release of Criminal Information. [Repealed]

Art. 61.06. Removal of Records Relating to an Individual Other Than a Child. [Repealed]

Art. 61.07. Removal of Records Relating to a Child. [Repealed]

Art. 61.075. Right to Request Existence of Criminal Information. [Repealed]

Art. 61.08. Right to Request Review of Criminal Information. [Repealed]

Art. 61.09. Judicial Review. [Repealed]

Art. 61.10. Texas Violent Gang Task Force. [Repealed]

Art. 61.11. Gang Resource System. [Repealed]

Art. 61.12. Database User Training. [Repealed]

CHAPTER 62 SEX OFFENDER REGISTRATION PROGRAM

SUBCHAPTER A GENERAL PROVISIONS

Art. 62.001. Definitions.

In this chapter:

(1) "Department" means the Department of Public Safety.

(2) "Local law enforcement authority" means, as applicable, the office of the chief of police of a municipality, the office of the sheriff of a county in this state, or a centralized registration authority.

(3) "Penal institution" means a confinement facility operated by or under a contract with any division of the Texas Department of Criminal Justice, a confinement facility operated by or under contract with the Texas Juvenile Justice Department, or a juvenile secure pre-adjudication or post-adjudication facility operated by or under a local juvenile probation department, or a county jail.

(4) "Released" means discharged, paroled, placed in a nonsecure community program for juvenile offenders, or placed on juvenile probation, community supervision, or mandatory supervision.

(5) "Reportable conviction or adjudication" means a conviction or adjudication, including an adjudication of delinquent conduct or a deferred adjudication, that, regardless of the pendency of an appeal, is a conviction for or an adjudication for or based on:

(A) a violation of Section 21.02 (Continuous sexual abuse of young child or disabled individual), 21.09 (Bestiality), 21.11 (Indecency with a child), 22.011 (Sexual assault), 22.021 (Aggravated sexual assault), or 25.02 (Prohibited sexual conduct), Penal Code;

(B) a violation of Section 43.04 (Aggravated promotion of prostitution), 43.05 (Compelling prostitution), 43.25 (Sexual performance by a child), or 43.26 (Possession or promotion of child pornography), Penal Code;

(B-1) a violation of Section 43.021 (Solicitation of Prostitution), Penal Code, if the offense is punishable as a felony of the second degree;

(C) a violation of Section 20.04(a)(4) (Aggravated kidnapping), Penal Code, if the actor committed the offense or engaged in the conduct with intent to violate or abuse the victim sexually;

(D) a violation of Section 30.02 (Burglary), Penal Code, if the offense or conduct is punishable under Subsection (d) of that section and the actor committed the offense or engaged in the conduct with intent to commit a felony listed in Paragraph (A) or (C);

(E) a violation of Section 20.02 (Unlawful restraint), 20.03 (Kidnapping), or 20.04 (Aggravated kidnapping), Penal Code, if, as applicable:

(i) the judgment in the case contains an affirmative finding under Article 42.015; or

(ii) the order in the hearing or the papers in the case contain an affirmative finding that the victim or intended victim was younger than 17 years of age;

(F) the second violation of Section 21.08 (Indecent exposure), Penal Code, but not if the second violation results in a deferred adjudication;

(G) an attempt, conspiracy, or solicitation, as defined by Chapter 15, Penal Code, to commit an offense or engage in conduct listed in Paragraph (A), (B), (C), (D), (E), (K), or (L);

(H) a violation of the laws of another state, federal law, the laws of a foreign country, or the Uniform Code of Military Justice for or based on the violation of an offense containing elements that are substantially similar to the elements of an offense listed under Paragraph (A), (B), (B-1), (C), (D), (E), (G), (J), (K), or (L), but not if the violation results in a deferred adjudication;

(I) the second violation of the laws of another state, federal law, the laws of a foreign country, or the Uniform Code of Military Justice for or based on the violation of an offense containing elements that are substantially similar to the elements of the offense of indecent exposure, but not if the second violation results in a deferred adjudication;

(J) a violation of Section 33.021 (Online solicitation of a minor), Penal Code;

(K) a violation of Section 20A.02(a)(3), (4), (7), or (8) (Trafficking of persons), Penal Code; or

(L) a violation of Section 20A.03 (Continuous trafficking of persons), Penal Code, if the offense is based partly or wholly on conduct that constitutes an offense under Section 20A.02(a)(3), (4), (7), or (8) of that code.

(6) "Sexually violent offense" means any of the following offenses committed by a person 17 years of age or older:

(A) an offense under Section 21.02 (Continuous sexual abuse of young child or children), 21.11(a)(1) (Indecency with a child), 22.011 (Sexual assault), or 22.021 (Aggravated sexual assault), Penal Code;

(B) an offense under Section 43.25 (Sexual performance by a child), Penal Code;

(C) an offense under Section 20.04(a)(4) (Aggravated kidnapping), Penal Code, if the defendant committed the offense with intent to violate or abuse the victim sexually;

(D) an offense under Section 30.02 (Burglary), Penal Code, if the offense is punishable under Subsection (d) of that section and the defendant committed the offense with intent to commit a felony listed in Paragraph (A) or (C) of Subdivision (5); or

(E) an offense under the laws of another state, federal law, the laws of a foreign country, or the Uniform Code of Military Justice if the offense contains elements that are substantially similar to the elements of an offense listed under Paragraph (A), (B), (C), or (D).

(7) "Residence" includes a residence established in this state by a person described by Article 62.152(e).

(8) "Public or private institution of higher education" includes a college, university, community college, or technical or trade institute.

(9) "Authority for campus security" means the authority with primary law enforcement jurisdiction over property under the control of a public or private institution of higher education, other than a local law enforcement authority.

(10) "Extrajurisdictional registrant" means a person who:

(A) is required to register as a sex offender under:

(i) the laws of another state with which the department has entered into a reciprocal registration agreement;

(ii) federal law or the Uniform Code of Military Justice; or

(iii) the laws of a foreign country; and

(B) is not otherwise required to register under this chapter because:

(i) the person does not have a reportable conviction for an offense under the laws of the other state, federal law, the laws of the foreign country, or the Uniform Code of Military Justice containing elements that are substantially similar to the elements of an offense requiring registration under this chapter; or

(ii) the person does not have a reportable adjudication of delinquent conduct based on a violation of an offense under the laws of the other state, federal law, or the laws of the foreign country containing elements that are substantially similar to the elements of an offense requiring registration under this chapter.

(11) "Centralized registration authority" means a mandatory countywide registration location designated under Article 62.0045.

(12) "Online identifier" means electronic mail address information or a name used by a person when sending or receiving an instant message, social networking communication, or similar Internet communication or when participating in an Internet chat. The term includes an assumed name, nickname, pseudonym, moniker, or user name established by a person for use in connection with an electronic mail address, chat or instant chat room platform, commercial social networking site, or online picture-sharing service.

Art. 62.0015. Presumption Regarding Parentage [Renumbered].

Renumbered to Tex. Code of Crim. Proc. art. 63.0015 by Acts 2009, 81st Leg., ch. 87 (S.B. 1969), § 27.001(3), effective September 1, 2009.

Art. 62.002. Applicability of Chapter.

(a) This chapter applies only to a reportable conviction or adjudication occurring on or after September 1, 1970.

(b) Except as provided by Subsection (c), the duties imposed on a person required to register under this chapter on the basis of a reportable conviction or adjudication, and the corresponding duties and powers of other entities in relation to the person required to register on the basis of that conviction or adjudication, are not affected by:

(1) an appeal of the conviction or adjudication; or

(2) a pardon of the conviction or adjudication.

(c) If a conviction or adjudication that is the basis of a duty to register under this chapter is set aside on appeal by a court or if the person required to register under this chapter on the basis of a conviction or adjudication receives a pardon on the basis of subsequent proof of innocence, the duties imposed on the person by this chapter and the corresponding duties and powers of other entities in relation to the person are terminated.

Art. 62.003. Determination Regarding Substantially Similar Elements of Offense.

(a) For the purposes of this chapter, the department is responsible for determining whether an offense under the laws of another state, federal law, the laws of a foreign country, or the Uniform Code of Military Justice contains elements that are substantially similar to the elements of an offense under the laws of this state.

(b) The department annually shall provide or make available to each prosecuting attorney's office in this state:

(1) the criteria used in making a determination under Subsection (a); and

(2) any existing record or compilation of offenses under the laws of another state, federal law, the laws of a foreign country, and the Uniform Code of Military Justice that the department has already determined to contain elements that are substantially similar to the elements of offenses under the laws of this state.

(c) An appeal of a determination made under this article shall be brought in a district court in Travis County.

Art. 62.004. Determination Regarding Primary Registration Authority.

(a) Except as provided by Subsection (a-1), for each person subject to registration under this chapter, the department shall determine which local law enforcement authority serves as the person's primary registration authority based on the municipality or county in which the person resides or, as provided by Article 62.152, the municipality or county in which the person works or attends school.

(a-1) Notwithstanding any other provision of this chapter, if a person resides or, as described by Article 62.152, works or attends school in a county with a centralized registration authority, the centralized registration authority serves as the person's primary registration authority under this chapter, regardless of whether the person resides, works, or attends school, as applicable, in any municipality located in that county.

(b) The department shall notify each person subject to registration under this chapter of the person's primary registration authority in a timely manner.

Art. 62.0045. Centralized Registration Authority.

(a) The commissioners court of a county may designate the office of the sheriff of the county or may, through interlocal agreement, designate the office of a chief of police of a municipality in that county to serve as a mandatory countywide registration location for persons subject to this chapter.

(b) Notwithstanding any other provision of this chapter, a person subject to this chapter is required to perform the registration and verification requirements of Articles 62.051 and 62.058 and the change of address requirements of Article 62.055 only with respect to the centralized registration authority for the county, regardless of whether the person resides in any municipality located in that county. If the person resides in a municipality, and the local law enforcement authority in the municipality does not serve as the person's centralized registration authority, the centralized registration authority, not later than the third day after the date the person registers or verifies registration or changes address with that authority, shall provide to the local law enforcement authority in that municipality notice of the person's registration, verification of registration, or change of address, as applicable, with the centralized registration authority.

(c) This section does not affect a person's duty to register with secondary sex offender registries under this chapter, such as those described by Articles 62.059 and 62.153.

Art. 62.005. Central Database; Public Information.

(a) The department shall maintain a computerized central database containing the information required for registration under this chapter. The department may include in the computerized central database the numeric risk level assigned to a person under this chapter.

(b) The information contained in the database, including the numeric risk level assigned to a person under this chapter, is public information, with the exception of any information:

(1) regarding the person's social security number or driver's license number, or any home, work, or cellular telephone number of the person;

(2) that is described by Article 62.051(c)(7) or required by the department under Article 62.051(c)(9), including any information regarding an employer's name, address, or telephone number; or

(3) that would identify the victim of the offense for which the person is subject to registration.

(c) Notwithstanding Chapter 730, Transportation Code, the department shall maintain in the database, and shall post on any department website related to the database, any photograph of the person that is available through the process for obtaining or renewing a personal identification certificate or driver's license under Section 521.103 or 521.272, Transportation Code. The department shall update the photograph in the database and on the website annually or as the photograph otherwise becomes available through the renewal process for the certificate or license.

(d) A local law enforcement authority shall release public information described under

Subsection (b) to any person who requests the information from the authority. The authority may charge the person a fee not to exceed the amount reasonably necessary to cover the administrative costs associated with the authority's release of information to the person under this subsection.

(e) The department shall provide a licensing authority with notice of any person required to register under this chapter who holds or seeks a license that is issued by the authority. The department shall provide the notice required by this subsection as the applicable licensing information becomes available through notification by a court clerk under Article 42.0175, a parole panel under Section 508.1864, Government Code, or the person's registration or verification of registration.

(f) On the written request of a licensing authority that identifies an individual and states that the individual is an applicant for or a holder of a license issued by the authority, the department shall release any information described by Subsection (a) to the licensing authority.

(g) For the purposes of Subsections (e) and (f):

(1) "License" means a license, certificate, registration, permit, or other authorization that:

(A) is issued by a licensing authority; and

(B) a person must obtain to practice or engage in a particular business, occupation, or profession.

(2) "Licensing authority" means a department, commission, board, office, or other agency of the state or a political subdivision of the state that issues a license.

(h) Not later than the third day after the date on which the applicable information becomes available through the person's registration or verification of registration or under Article 62.058, the department shall send notice of any person required to register under this chapter who is or will be employed, carrying on a vocation, or a student at a public or private institution of higher education in this state to:

(1) for an institution in this state:

(A) the authority for campus security for that institution; or

(B) if an authority for campus security for that institution does not exist, the local law enforcement authority of:

(i) the municipality in which the institution is located; or

(ii) the county in which the institution is located, if the institution is not located in a municipality; or

(2) for an institution in another state, any existing authority for campus security at that institution.

(i) On the written request of an institution of higher education described by Subsection (h) that identifies an individual and states that the individual has applied to work or study at the institution, the department shall release any information described by Subsection (a) to the institution.

(j) The department, for law enforcement purposes, shall release all relevant information described by Subsection (a), including information that is not public information under Subsection (b), to a peace officer, an employee of a local law enforcement authority, or the attorney general on the request of the applicable person or entity.

Art. 62.006. Information Provided to Peace Officer on Request.

The department shall establish a procedure by which a peace officer or employee of a law enforcement agency who provides the department with a driver's license number, personal identification certificate number, or license plate number is automatically provided information as to whether the person to whom the driver's license or personal identification certificate is issued is required to register under this chapter or whether the license plate number is entered in the computerized central database under Article 62.005 as assigned to a vehicle owned or driven by a person required to register under this chapter.

Art. 62.0061. Request for Online Identifiers by Social Networking Sites.

(a) On request by a commercial social networking site, the department may provide to the commercial social networking site:

(1) all public information that is contained in the database maintained under Article 62.005; and

(2) notwithstanding Article 62.005(b)(2), any online identifier established or used by a person who uses the site, is seeking to use the site, or is precluded from using the site.

(b) The department by rule shall establish a procedure through which a commercial social networking site may request information under Subsection (a), including rules regarding the eligibility of commercial social networking sites to request information under Subsection (a). The department shall consult with the attorney general, other appropriate state agencies, and other appropriate entities in adopting rules under this subsection.

(c) A commercial social networking site or the site's agent:

(1) may use information received under Subsection (a) only to:

(A) prescreen persons seeking to use the site; or

(B) preclude persons registered under this chapter from using the site; and

(2) may not use any information received under Subsection (a) that the networking site obtained solely under Subsection (a) in any manner not described by Subdivision (1).

(d) A commercial social networking site that uses information received under Subsection (a) in any manner not described by Subsection (c)(1) or that violates a rule adopted by the department under Subsection (b) is subject to a civil penalty of $1,000 for each misuse of information or rule violation. A commercial social networking site that is assessed a civil penalty under this article shall pay, in addition to the civil penalty, all court costs, investigative costs, and attorney's fees associated with the assessment of the penalty. A civil penalty assessed under this subsection shall be deposited to the compensation to victims of crime fund established under Subchapter J, Chapter 56B.

(e) This article does not create a private cause of action against a commercial social networking site, including a cause of action that is based on the site:

(1) identifying, removing, disabling, blocking, or otherwise affecting the user of a commercial social networking site, based on a good faith belief that the person is required to register as a sex offender under this chapter or federal law; or

(2) failing to identify, remove, disable, block, or otherwise affect the user of a commercial social networking site who is required to register as a sex offender under this chapter or federal law.

(f) In this article, "commercial social networking site":

(1) means an Internet website that:

(A) allows users, through the creation of Internet web pages or profiles or other similar means, to provide personal information to the public or other users of the Internet website;

(B) offers a mechanism for communication with other users of the Internet website; and

(C) has the primary purpose of facilitating online social interactions; and

(2) does not include an Internet service provider, unless the Internet service provider separately operates and directly derives revenue from an Internet website described by Subdivision (1).

Art. 62.007. Risk Assessment Review Committee; Sex Offender Screening Tool.

(a) The Texas Department of Criminal Justice shall establish a risk assessment review committee composed of at least seven members, each of whom serves on the review committee in addition to the member's other employment-related duties. The review committee, to the extent feasible, must include at least:

(1) one member having experience in law enforcement;

(2) one member having experience working with juvenile sex offenders;

(3) one member having experience as a sex offender treatment provider;

(4) one member having experience working with victims of sex offenses;

(5) the executive director of the Council on Sex Offender Treatment; and

(6) one sex offender treatment provider registered under Chapter 110, Occupations Code, and selected by the executive director of the Council on Sex Offender Treatment to serve on the review committee.

(b) The risk assessment review committee functions in an oversight capacity. The committee shall:

(1) develop or select, from among existing tools or from any tool recommended by the Council on Sex Offender Treatment, a sex offender screening tool to be used in determining the level of risk of a person subject to registration under this chapter;

(2) ensure that staff is trained on the use of the screening tool;

(3) monitor the use of the screening tool in the state; and

(4) analyze other screening tools as they become available and revise or replace the existing screening tool if warranted.

(c) The sex offender screening tool must use an objective point system under which a person is assigned a designated number of points for each of various factors. In developing or selecting the sex offender screening tool, the risk assessment review committee shall use or shall select a screening tool that may be adapted to use the following general guidelines:

(1) level one (low): a designated range of points on the sex offender screening tool indicating that the person poses a low danger to the community and will not likely engage in criminal sexual conduct;

(2) level two (moderate): a designated range of points on the sex offender screening tool indicating that the person poses a moderate danger to the community and might continue to engage in criminal sexual conduct; and

(3) level three (high): a designated range of points on the sex offender screening tool indicating that the person poses a serious danger to the community and will continue to engage in criminal sexual conduct.

(d) The risk assessment review committee, the Texas Department of Criminal Justice, the Texas

Juvenile Justice Department, or a court may override a risk level only if the entity:

(1) believes that the risk level assessed is not an accurate prediction of the risk the offender poses to the community; and

(2) documents the reason for the override in the offender's case file.

(e) Records and files, including records that have been sealed under Chapter 58, Family Code, relating to a person for whom a court, the Texas Department of Criminal Justice, or the Texas Juvenile Justice Department is required under this article to determine a level of risk shall be released to the court, the Texas Department of Criminal Justice, or the Texas Juvenile Justice Department, as appropriate, for the purpose of determining the person's risk level.

(f) Chapter 551, Government Code, does not apply to a meeting of the risk assessment review committee.

(g) The numeric risk level assigned to a person using the sex offender screening tool described by this article is not confidential and is subject to disclosure under Chapter 552, Government Code.

Art. 62.008. General Immunity.

The following persons are immune from liability for good faith conduct under this chapter:

(1) an employee or officer of the Texas Department of Criminal Justice, the Texas Juvenile Justice Department, the Department of Public Safety, the Board of Pardons and Paroles, or a local law enforcement authority;

(2) an employee or officer of a community supervision and corrections department or a juvenile probation department;

(3) a member of the judiciary; and

(4) a member of the risk assessment review committee established under Article 62.007.

Art. 62.009. Immunity for Release of Public Information.

(a) The department, a penal institution, a local law enforcement authority, or an authority for campus security may release to the public information regarding a person required to register under this chapter only if the information is public information under this chapter.

(b) An individual, agency, entity, or authority is not liable under Chapter 101, Civil Practice and Remedies Code, or any other law for damages arising from conduct authorized by Subsection (a).

(c) For purposes of determining liability, the release or withholding of information by an appointed or elected officer of an agency, entity, or authority is a discretionary act.

(d) A private primary or secondary school, public or private institution of higher education, or administrator of a private primary or secondary school or public or private institution of higher education may release to the public information regarding a person required to register under this chapter only if the information is public information under this chapter and is released to the administrator under Article 62.005, 62.053, 62.054, 62.055, or 62.153. A private primary or secondary school, public or private institution of higher education, or administrator of a private primary or secondary school or public or private institution of higher education is not liable under any law for damages arising from conduct authorized by this subsection.

Art. 62.01. Definitions [Renumbered].

Renumbered to Tex. Code Crim. Proc. art. 62.001 by Acts 2005, 79th Leg., ch. 1008 (H.B. 867), § 1.01, effective September 1, 2005.

Art. 62.010. Rulemaking Authority.

The Texas Department of Criminal Justice, the Texas Juvenile Justice Department, and the department may adopt any rule necessary to implement this chapter.

Art. 62.0101. Determination Regarding Substantially Similar Elements of Offense [Renumbered].

Renumbered to Tex. Code Crim. Proc. art. 62.003 by Acts 2005, 79th Leg., ch. 1008 (H.B. 867), § 1.01, effective September 1, 2005.

Art. 62.0102. Determination Regarding Primary Registration Authority [Renumbered].

Renumbered to Tex. Code Crim. Proc. art. 62.004 by Acts 2005, 79th Leg., ch. 1008 (H.B. 867), § 1.01, effective September 1, 2005.

Art. 62.0105. Exemption from Registration for Certain Sex Offenders [Deleted].

Deleted by Acts 2005, 79th Leg., ch. 1008 (H.B. 867), § 1.01, effective September 1, 2005.

Art. 62.011. Workers or Students [Deleted].

Deleted by Acts 2005, 79th Leg., ch. 1008 (H.B. 867), § 1.01, effective September 1, 2005.

Art. 62.012. Report of Inquiry [Renumbered].

Renumbered to Tex. Code Crim. Proc. art. 63.012 by Acts 1999, 76th Leg., ch. 62 (S.B. 1368), § 19.01(8)(A), effective September 1, 1999.

Art. 62.013. Information to Clearinghouse [Renumbered].

Renumbered to Tex. Code Crim. Proc. art. 63.013 by Acts 1999, 76th Leg., ch. 62 (S.B. 1368), § 19.01(8)(A), effective September 1, 1999.

Art. 62.014. Cross-Checking and Matching [Renumbered].

Renumbered to Tex. Code Crim. Proc. art. 63.014 by Acts 1999, 76th Leg., ch. 62 (S.B. 1368), § 19.01(8)(A), effective September 1, 1999.

Art. 62.015. Availability of Information Through Other Agencies [Renumbered].

Renumbered to Tex. Code Crim. Proc. art. 63.015 by Acts 1999, 76th Leg., ch. 62 (S.B. 1368), § 19.01(8)(A), effective September 1, 1999.

Art. 62.016. Donations [Renumbered].

Renumbered to Tex. Code Crim. Proc. art. 63.016 by Acts 1999, 76th Leg., ch. 62 (S.B. 1368), § 19.01(8)(A), effective September 1, 1999.

Art. 62.017. Confidentiality of Certain Records [Renumbered].

Renumbered to Tex. Code Crim. Proc. art. 63.017 by Acts 1999, 76th Leg., ch. 62 (S.B. 1368), § 19.01(8)(A), effective September 1, 1999.

Art. 62.018. Death Certificates [Renumbered].

Renumbered to Tex. Code Crim. Proc. art. 63.018 by Acts 1999, 76th Leg., ch. 62 (S.B. 1368), § 19.01(8)(A), effective September 1, 1999.

Art. 62.02. Registration [Renumbered].

Renumbered to Tex. Code Crim. Proc. art. 62.051 by Acts 2005, 79th Leg., ch. 1008 (H.B. 867), § 1.01, effective September 1, 2005.

Art. 62.021. Out of State Registrants [Renumbered].

Renumbered to Tex. Code Crim. Proc. art. 62.052 by Acts 2005, 79th Leg., ch. 1008 (H.B. 867), § 1.01, effective September 1, 2005.

Art. 62.023. Receivership for Certain Missing Persons [Repealed].

Repealed by Acts 1999, 76th Leg., ch. 1081 (H.B. 3343), § 8, effective September 1, 1999.

Art. 62.024. Notice and Citation for Receivership for Certain Missing Persons [Repealed].

Repealed by Acts 1999, 76th Leg., ch. 1081 (H.B. 3343), § 8, effective September 1, 1999.

Art. 62.03. Prerelease Notification [Renumbered].

Renumbered to Tex. Code Crim. Proc. art. 62.053 by Acts 2005, 79th Leg., ch. 1008 (H.B. 867), § 1.01, effective September 1, 2005.

Art. 62.031. Limitations on Newspaper Publication [Deleted].

Deleted by Acts 2005, 79th Leg., ch. 1008 (H.B. 867), § 1.01, effective September 1, 2005.

Art. 62.032. Circumstances Requiring Notice to Superintendent or School Administrator [Renumbered].

Renumbered to Tex. Code Crim. Proc. art. 62.054 by Acts 2005, 79th Leg., ch. 1008 (H.B. 867), § 1.01, effective September 1, 2005.

Art. 62.035. Risk Assessment Review Committee; Sex Offender Screening Tool [Deleted].

Deleted by Acts 2005, 79th Leg., ch. 1008 (H.B. 867), § 1.01, effective September 1, 2005.

Art. 62.04. Change of Address [Renumbered].

Renumbered to Tex. Code Crim. Proc. art. 62.055 by Acts 2005, 79th Leg., ch. 1008 (H.B. 867), § 1.01, effective September 1, 2005.

Art. 62.041. Authority of Political Subdivision to Collect Costs of Certain Notice [Deleted].

Deleted by Acts 2005, 79th Leg., ch. 1008 (H.B. 867), § 1.01, effective September 1, 2005.

Art. 62.045. Additional Public Notice for Certain Offenders [Renumbered].

Renumbered to Tex. Code Crim. Proc. art. 62.056 by Acts 2005, 79th Leg., ch. 1008 (H.B. 867), § 1.01, effective September 1, 2005.

Art. 62.0451. Additional Public Notice for Individuals Subject to Civil Commitment [Deleted].

Deleted by Acts 2005, 79th Leg., ch. 1008 (H.B. 867), § 1.01, effective September 1, 2005.

Art. 62.05. Status Report by Supervising Officer or Local Law Enforcement Agency [Renumbered].

Renumbered to Tex. Code Crim. Proc. art. 62.057 by Acts 2005, 79th Leg., ch. 1008 (H.B. 867), § 1.01, effective September 1, 2005.

SUBCHAPTER B REGISTRATION AND VERIFICATION REQUIREMENTS; RELATED NOTICE

Art. 62.051. Registration: General.

(a) A person who has a reportable conviction or adjudication or who is required to register as a condition of parole, release to mandatory supervision, or community supervision shall register or, if the person is a person for whom registration is completed under this chapter, verify registration as provided by Subsection (f), with the local law enforcement authority in any municipality where the person resides or intends to reside for more than seven days. If the person does not reside or intend to reside in a municipality, the person shall register or verify registration in any county where the person resides or intends to reside for more than seven days. The person shall satisfy the requirements of this subsection not later than the later of:

(1) the seventh day after the person's arrival in the municipality or county; or

(2) the first date the local law enforcement authority of the municipality or county by policy allows the person to register or verify registration, as applicable.

(b) The department shall provide the Texas Department of Criminal Justice, the Texas Juvenile Justice Department, and each local law enforcement authority, authority for campus security, county jail, and court with a form for registering persons required by this chapter to register.

(c) The registration form shall require:

(1) the person's full name, date of birth, sex, race, height, weight, eye color, hair color, social security number, driver's license number, and shoe size;

(1-a) the address at which the person resides or intends to reside or, if the person does not reside or intend to reside at a physical address, a detailed description of each geographical location at which the person resides or intends to reside;

(1-b) each alias used by the person and any home, work, or cellular telephone number of the person;

(2) a recent color photograph or, if possible, an electronic digital image of the person and a complete set of the person's fingerprints;

(3) the type of offense the person was convicted of, the age of the victim, the date of conviction, and the punishment received;

(4) an indication as to whether the person is discharged, paroled, or released on juvenile probation, community supervision, or mandatory supervision;

(5) an indication of each license, as defined by Article 62.005(g), that is held or sought by the person;

(6) an indication as to whether the person is or will be employed, carrying on a vocation, or a student at a particular public or private institution of higher education in this state or another state, and the name and address of that institution;

(7) the identification of any online identifier established or used by the person;

(8) the vehicle registration information, including the make, model, vehicle identification number, color, and license plate number, of any vehicle owned by the person, if the person has a reportable conviction or adjudication for an offense under:

(A) Section 20A.02(a)(3), (4), (7), or (8), Penal Code; or

(B) Section 20A.03, Penal Code, if based partly or wholly on conduct that constitutes an offense under Section 20A.02(a)(3), (4), (7), or (8) of that code; and

(9) any other information required by the department.

(d) The registration form must contain a statement and description of any registration duties the person has or may have under this chapter.

(e) Not later than the third day after a person's registering, the local law enforcement authority with whom the person registered shall send a copy of the registration form to the department and, if the person resides on the campus of a public or private institution of higher education, to any authority for campus security for that institution.

Code of Criminal Procedure

(f) Not later than the seventh day after the date on which the person is released, a person for whom registration is completed under this chapter shall report to the applicable local law enforcement authority to verify the information in the registration form received by the authority under this chapter. The authority shall require the person to produce proof of the person's identity and residence before the authority gives the registration form to the person for verification. If the information in the registration form is complete and accurate, the person shall verify registration by signing the form. If the information is not complete or not accurate, the person shall make any necessary additions or corrections before signing the form.

(g) A person who is required to register or verify registration under this chapter shall ensure that the person's registration form is complete and accurate with respect to each item of information required by the form in accordance with Subsection (c).

(h) If a person subject to registration under this chapter does not move to an intended residence by the end of the seventh day after the date on which the person is released or the date on which the person leaves a previous residence, the person shall:

(1) report to the juvenile probation officer, community supervision and corrections department officer, or parole officer supervising the person by not later than the seventh day after the date on which the person is released or the date on which the person leaves a previous residence, as applicable, and provide the officer with the address of the person's temporary residence; and

(2) continue to report to the person's supervising officer not less than weekly during any period of time in which the person has not moved to an intended residence and provide the officer with the address of the person's temporary residence.

(i) If the other state has a registration requirement for sex offenders, a person who has a reportable conviction or adjudication, who resides in this state, and who is employed, carries on a vocation, or is a student in another state shall, not later than the 10th day after the date on which the person begins to work or attend school in the other state, register with the law enforcement authority that is identified by the department as the authority designated by that state to receive registration information. If the person is employed, carries on a vocation, or is a student at a public or private institution of higher education in the other state and if an authority for campus security exists at the institution, the person shall also register with that authority not later than the 10th day after the date on which the person begins to work or attend school.

(j) If a person subject to registration under this chapter is released from a penal institution without being released to parole or placed on any other form of supervision and the person does not move to the address indicated on the registration form as the person's intended residence or does not indicate an address on the registration form, the person shall, not later than the seventh day after the date on which the person is released:

(1) report in person to the local law enforcement authority for the municipality or county, as applicable, in which the person is residing and provide that authority with the address at which the person is residing or, if the person's residence does not have a physical address, a detailed description of the geographical location of the person's residence; and

(2) until the person indicates the person's current address as the person's intended residence on the registration form or otherwise complies with the requirements of Article 62.055, as appropriate, continue to report, in the manner required by Subdivision (1), to that authority not less than once in each succeeding 30-day period and provide that authority with the address at which the person is residing or, if applicable, a detailed description of the geographical location of the person's residence.

(k) A person required to register under this chapter may not refuse or otherwise fail to provide any information required for the accurate completion of the registration form.

Art. 62.052. Registration: Extrajurisdictional Registrants.

(a) An extrajurisdictional registrant is required to comply with the annual verification requirements of Article 62.058 in the same manner as a person who is required to verify registration on the basis of a reportable conviction or adjudication.

(b) The duty to register for an extrajurisdictional registrant expires on the date the person's duty to register would expire under the laws of the other state or foreign country had the person remained in that state or foreign country, under federal law, or under the Uniform Code of Military Justice, as applicable.

(c) The department may negotiate and enter into a reciprocal registration agreement with any other state to prevent residents of this state and residents of the other state from frustrating the public purpose of the registration of sex offenders by moving from one state to the other.

Art. 62.053. Prerelease Notification.

(a) Before a person who will be subject to registration under this chapter is due to be released from a penal institution, the Texas Department of Criminal Justice or the Texas Juvenile Justice Department shall determine the person's level of risk to the community using the sex offender screening tool developed or selected under Article 62.007 and assign to the person a numeric risk level of one, two, or three. Before releasing the person, an official of the penal institution shall:

(1) inform the person that:

(A) not later than the later of the seventh day after the date on which the person is released or after the date on which the person moves from a previous residence to a new residence in this state or not later than the first date the applicable local law enforcement authority by policy allows the person to register or verify registration, the person must register or verify registration with the local law enforcement authority in the municipality or county in which the person intends to reside;

(B) not later than the seventh day after the date on which the person is released or the date on which the person moves from a previous residence to a new residence in this state, the person must, if the person has not moved to an intended residence, report to the applicable entity or entities as required by Article 62.051(h) or (j) or 62.055(e);

(C) not later than the seventh day before the date on which the person moves to a new residence in this state or another state, the person must report in person to the local law enforcement authority designated as the person's primary registration authority by the department and to the juvenile probation officer, community supervision and corrections department officer, or parole officer supervising the person;

(D) not later than the 10th day after the date on which the person arrives in another state in which the person intends to reside, the person must register with the law enforcement agency that is identified by the department as the agency designated by that state to receive registration information, if the other state has a registration requirement for sex offenders;

(E) not later than the 30th day after the date on which the person is released, the person must apply to the department in person for the issuance of an original or renewal driver's license or personal identification certificate and a failure to apply to the department as required by this paragraph results in the automatic revocation of any driver's license or personal identification certificate issued by the department to the person;

(F) the person must notify appropriate entities of any change in status as described by Article 62.057;

(G) certain types of employment are prohibited under Article 62.063 for a person with a reportable conviction or adjudication for a sexually violent offense involving a victim younger than 14 years of age and occurring on or after September 1, 2013;

(H) certain locations of residence are prohibited under Article 62.064 for a person with a reportable conviction or adjudication for an offense occurring on or after September 1, 2017, except as otherwise provided by that article; and

(I) if the person enters the premises of a school as described by Article 62.065 and is subject to the requirements of that article, the person must immediately notify the administrative office of the school of the person's presence and the person's registration status under this chapter;

(2) require the person to sign a written statement that the person was informed of the person's duties as described by Subdivision (1) or Subsection (g) or, if the person refuses to sign the statement, certify that the person was so informed;

(3) obtain the address or, if applicable, a detailed description of each geographical location where the person expects to reside on the person's release and other registration information, including a photograph and complete set of fingerprints; and

(4) complete the registration form for the person.

(b) On the seventh day before the date on which a person who will be subject to registration under this chapter is due to be released from a penal institution, or on receipt of notice by a penal institution that a person who will be subject to registration under this chapter is due to be released in less than seven days, an official of the penal institution shall send the person's completed registration form and numeric risk level to the department and to:

(1) the applicable local law enforcement authority in the municipality or county in which the person expects to reside, if the person expects to reside in this state; or

(2) the law enforcement agency that is identified by the department as the agency designated by another state to receive registration information, if the person expects to reside in that other state and that other state has a registration requirement for sex offenders.

(c) If a person who is subject to registration under this chapter receives an order deferring adjudication, placing the person on community supervision or juvenile probation, or imposing only a fine, the court pronouncing the order or sentence shall make a determination of the person's numeric risk level using the sex offender screening tool developed or selected under Article 62.007, assign to the

Code of Criminal Procedure

person a numeric risk level of one, two, or three, and ensure that the prerelease notification and registration requirements specified in this article are conducted on the day of entering the order or sentencing. If a community supervision and corrections department representative is available in court at the time a court pronounces a sentence of deferred adjudication or community supervision, the representative shall immediately obtain the person's numeric risk level from the court and conduct the prerelease notification and registration requirements specified in this article. In any other case in which the court pronounces a sentence under this subsection, the court shall designate another appropriate individual to obtain the person's numeric risk level from the court and conduct the prerelease notification and registration requirements specified in this article.

(d) If a person who has a reportable conviction described by Article 62.001(5)(H) or (I) is placed under the supervision of the parole division of the Texas Department of Criminal Justice or a community supervision and corrections department under Section 510.017, Government Code, the division or community supervision and corrections department shall conduct the prerelease notification and registration requirements specified in this article on the date the person is placed under the supervision of the division or community supervision and corrections department. If a person who has a reportable adjudication of delinquent conduct described by Article 62.001(5)(H) or (I) is, as permitted by Section 60.002, Family Code, placed under the supervision of the Texas Youth Commission, a public or private vendor operating under contract with the Texas Youth Commission, a local juvenile probation department, or a juvenile secure pre-adjudication or post-adjudication facility, the commission, vendor, probation department, or facility shall conduct the prerelease notification and registration requirements specified in this article on the date the person is placed under the supervision of the commission, vendor, probation department, or facility.

(e) Not later than the eighth day after receiving a registration form under Subsection (b), (c), or (d), the local law enforcement authority shall verify the age of the victim, the basis on which the person is subject to registration under this chapter, and the person's numeric risk level. The local law enforcement authority shall immediately provide notice to the superintendent of the public school district and to the administrator of any private primary or secondary school located in the public school district in which the person subject to registration intends to reside by mail to the office of the superintendent or administrator, as appropriate, in accordance with Article 62.054. On receipt of a notice under this subsection, the superintendent shall release the information contained in the notice to appropriate school district personnel, including peace officers and security personnel, principals, nurses, and counselors.

(f) The local law enforcement authority shall include in the notice to the superintendent of the public school district and to the administrator of any private primary or secondary school located in the public school district any information the authority determines is necessary to protect the public, except:

(1) the person's social security number or driver's license number, or any home, work, or cellular telephone number of the person; and

(2) any information that would identify the victim of the offense for which the person is subject to registration.

(g) Before a person who will be subject to registration under this chapter is due to be released from a penal institution in this state, an official of the penal institution shall inform the person that:

(1) if the person intends to reside in another state and to work or attend school in this state, the person must, not later than the later of the seventh day after the date on which the person begins to work or attend school or the first date the applicable local law enforcement authority by policy allows the person to register or verify registration, register or verify registration with the local law enforcement authority in the municipality or county in which the person intends to work or attend school;

(2) if the person intends to reside in this state and to work or attend school in another state and if the other state has a registration requirement for sex offenders, the person must:

(A) not later than the 10th day after the date on which the person begins to work or attend school in the other state, register with the law enforcement authority that is identified by the department as the authority designated by that state to receive registration information; and

(B) if the person intends to be employed, carry on a vocation, or be a student at a public or private institution of higher education in the other state and if an authority for campus security exists at the institution, register with that authority not later than the 10th day after the date on which the person begins to work or attend school; and

(3) regardless of the state in which the person intends to reside, if the person intends to be employed, carry on a vocation, or be a student at a public or private institution of higher education in this state, the person must:

(A) not later than the later of the seventh day after the date on which the person begins to work or attend school or the first date the applicable authority by policy allows the person to register, register with:

(i) the authority for campus security for that institution; or

(ii) except as provided by Article 62.153(e), if an authority for campus security for that institution does not exist, the local law enforcement authority of:

(a) the municipality in which the institution is located; or

(b) the county in which the institution is located, if the institution is not located in a municipality; and

(B) not later than the seventh day after the date the person stops working or attending school, notify the appropriate authority for campus security or local law enforcement authority of the termination of the person's status as a worker or student.

Art. 62.054. Circumstances Requiring Notice to Superintendent or School Administrator.

(a) A local law enforcement authority shall provide notice to the superintendent and each administrator under Article 62.053(e) or 62.055(f) only if:

(1) the victim was at the time of the offense a child younger than 17 years of age or a student enrolled in a public or private secondary school;

(2) the person subject to registration is a student enrolled in a public or private secondary school; or

(3) the basis on which the person is subject to registration is a conviction, a deferred adjudication, or an adjudication of delinquent conduct for an offense under Section 43.25 or 43.26, Penal Code, or an offense under the laws of another state, federal law, or the Uniform Code of Military Justice that contains elements substantially similar to the elements of an offense under either of those sections.

(b) A local law enforcement authority may not provide notice to the superintendent or any administrator under Article 62.053(e) or 62.055(f) if the basis on which the person is subject to registration is a conviction, a deferred adjudication, or an adjudication of delinquent conduct for an offense under Section 25.02, Penal Code, or an offense under the laws of another state, federal law, or the Uniform Code of Military Justice that contains elements substantially similar to the elements of an offense under that section.

Art. 62.055. Change of Address; Lack of Address.

(a) If a person, other than a person described by Subsection (j), required to register under this chapter intends to change address, regardless of whether the person intends to move to another state, the person shall, not later than the seventh day before the intended change, report in person to the local law enforcement authority designated as the person's primary registration authority by the department and to the juvenile probation officer, community supervision and corrections department officer, or parole officer supervising the person and provide the authority and the officer with the person's anticipated move date and new address. If a person, other than a person described by Subsection (j), required to register changes address, the person shall, not later than the later of the seventh day after changing the address or the first date the applicable local law enforcement authority by policy allows the person to report, report in person to the local law enforcement authority in the municipality or county in which the person's new residence is located and provide the authority with proof of identity and proof of residence.

(b) Not later than the third day after receipt of notice under Subsection (a), the person's juvenile probation officer, community supervision and corrections department officer, or parole officer shall forward the information provided under Subsection (a) to the local law enforcement authority designated as the person's primary registration authority by the department and, if the person intends to move to another municipality or county in this state, to the applicable local law enforcement authority in that municipality or county.

(c) If the person moves to another state that has a registration requirement for sex offenders, the person shall, not later than the 10th day after the date on which the person arrives in the other state, register with the law enforcement agency that is identified by the department as the agency designated by that state to receive registration information.

(d) Not later than the third day after receipt of information under Subsection (a) or (b), whichever is earlier, the local law enforcement authority shall forward this information to the department and, if the person intends to move to another municipality or county in this state, to the applicable local law enforcement authority in that municipality or county.

(e) If a person who reports to a local law enforcement authority under Subsection (a) does not move on or before the anticipated move date or does not move to the new address provided to the authority, the person shall:

(1) not later than the seventh day after the anticipated move date, and not less than weekly after that seventh day, report to the local law

Code of Criminal Procedure

enforcement authority designated as the person's primary registration authority by the department and provide an explanation to the authority regarding any changes in the anticipated move date and intended residence; and

(2) report to the juvenile probation officer, community supervision and corrections department officer, or parole officer supervising the person not less than weekly during any period in which the person has not moved to an intended residence.

(f) If the person moves to another municipality or county in this state, the department shall inform the applicable local law enforcement authority in the new area of the person's residence not later than the third day after the date on which the department receives information under Subsection (a). Not later than the eighth day after the date on which the local law enforcement authority is informed under Subsection (a) or under this subsection, the authority shall verify the age of the victim, the basis on which the person is subject to registration under this chapter, and the person's numeric risk level. The local law enforcement authority shall immediately provide notice to the superintendent of the public school district and to the administrator of any private primary or secondary school located in the public school district in which the person subject to registration intends to reside by mail to the office of the superintendent or administrator, as appropriate, in accordance with Article 62.054. On receipt of a notice under this subsection, the superintendent shall release the information contained in the notice to appropriate school district personnel, including peace officers and security personnel, principals, nurses, and counselors.

(g) The local law enforcement authority shall include in the notice to the superintendent of the public school district and the administrator of any private primary or secondary school located in the public school district any information the authority determines is necessary to protect the public, except:

(1) the person's social security number or driver's license number, or any home, work, or cellular telephone number of the person; and

(2) any information that would identify the victim of the offense for which the person is subject to registration.

(h) If the person moves to another state, the department shall, immediately on receiving information under Subsection (d):

(1) inform the agency that is designated by the other state to receive registration information, if that state has a registration requirement for sex offenders; and

(2) send to the Federal Bureau of Investigation a copy of the person's registration form, including the record of conviction and a complete set of fingerprints.

(i) If a person required to register under this chapter resides for more than seven days at a location or locations to which a physical address has not been assigned by a governmental entity, the person, not less than once in each 30-day period, shall confirm the person's location or locations by:

(1) reporting to the local law enforcement authority in the municipality where the person resides or, if the person does not reside in a municipality, the local law enforcement authority in the county in which the person resides; and

(2) providing a detailed description of the applicable location or locations.

(j) The Texas Civil Commitment Office shall report a change in address to each local law enforcement authority serving as the current or proposed primary registration authority for a person required to register under this chapter who is:

(1) civilly committed as a sexually violent predator under Chapter 841, Health and Safety Code; and

(2) required to reside in a location other than a civil commitment center by:

(A) a court under Chapter 574, Health and Safety Code; or

(B) the Texas Civil Commitment Office.

Art. 62.0551. Change in Online Identifiers.

(a) If a person required to register under this chapter changes any online identifier included on the person's registration form or establishes any new online identifier not already included on the person's registration form, the person, not later than the later of the seventh day after the change or establishment or the first date the applicable authority by policy allows the person to report, shall report the change or establishment to the person's primary registration authority in the manner prescribed by the authority.

(b) A primary registration authority that receives information under this article shall forward information in the same manner as information received by the authority under Article 62.055.

Art. 62.056. Additional Public Notice for Certain Offenders.

(a) On receipt of notice under this chapter that a person subject to registration is due to be released from a penal institution, has been placed on community supervision or juvenile probation, or intends to move to a new residence in this state, the department shall verify the person's numeric risk level assigned under this chapter. If the person is assigned a numeric risk level of three, the department shall, not later than the seventh day after the date on which the person is released or the 10th day after the date on which the person moves, provide written notice mailed or delivered to at least each address, other than a post office box, within a one-mile radius, in an area that has not been subdivided, or a three-block area, in an area that has been subdivided, of the place where the person intends to reside. In providing written notice under this subsection, the department shall use employees of the department whose duties in providing the notice are in addition to the employees' regular duties.

(b) The department shall provide the notice in English and Spanish and shall include in the notice any information that is public information under this chapter. The department may not include any information that is not public information under this chapter.

(c) The department shall establish procedures for a person with respect to whom notice is provided under Subsection (a), other than a person subject to registration on the basis of an adjudication of delinquent conduct, to pay to the department all costs incurred by the department in providing the notice. The person shall pay those costs in accordance with the procedures established under this subsection.

(d) On receipt of notice under this chapter that a person subject to registration under this chapter is required to register or verify registration with a local law enforcement authority and has been assigned a numeric risk level of three, the local law enforcement authority may provide notice to the public in any manner determined appropriate by the local law enforcement authority, including publishing notice in a newspaper or other periodical or circular in circulation in the area where the person intends to reside, holding a neighborhood meeting, posting notices in the area where the person intends to reside, distributing printed notices to area residents, or establishing a specialized local website. The local law enforcement authority may include in the notice only information that is public information under this chapter.

(e) An owner, builder, seller, or lessor of a single-family residential real property or any improvement to residential real property or that person's broker, salesperson, or other agent or representative in a residential real estate transaction does not have a duty to make a disclosure to a prospective buyer or lessee about registrants under this chapter. To the extent of any conflict between this subsection and another law imposing a duty to disclose information about registered sex offenders, this subsection controls.

Art. 62.057. Status Report by Supervising Officer or Local Law Enforcement Authority.

(a) If the juvenile probation officer, community supervision and corrections department officer, or parole officer supervising a person subject to registration under this chapter receives information to the effect that the person's status has changed in any manner that affects proper supervision of the person, including a change in the person's name, online identifiers, physical health, job or educational status, including higher educational status, incarceration, or terms of release, the supervising officer shall promptly notify the appropriate local law enforcement authority or authorities of that change. If the person required to register intends to change address, the supervising officer shall notify the local law enforcement authorities designated by Article 62.055(b). Not later than the seventh day after the date the supervising officer receives the relevant information, the supervising officer shall notify the local law enforcement authority of any change in the person's job or educational status in which the person:

(1) becomes employed, begins to carry on a vocation, or becomes a student at a particular public or private institution of higher education; or

(2) terminates the person's status in that capacity.

(b) Not later than the later of the seventh day after the date of the change or the first date the applicable authority by policy allows the person to report, a person subject to registration under this chapter shall report to the local law enforcement authority designated as the person's primary registration authority by the department any change in the person's name, online identifiers, physical health, or job or educational status, including higher educational status.

(c) For purposes of Subsection (b):

(1) a person's job status changes if the person leaves employment for any reason, remains employed by an employer but changes the location at which the person works, or begins employment with a new employer;

(2) a person's health status changes if the person is hospitalized as a result of an illness;

(3) a change in a person's educational status includes the person's transfer from one educational facility to another; and

(4) regarding a change of name, notice of the proposed name provided to a local law enforcement

Code of Criminal Procedure

authority as described by Sections 45.004 and 45.103, Family Code, is sufficient, except that the person shall promptly notify the authority of any denial of the person's petition for a change of name.

(d) Not later than the seventh day after the date the local law enforcement authority receives the relevant information, the local law enforcement authority shall notify the department of any change in the person's job or educational status in which the person:

(1) becomes employed, begins to carry on a vocation, or becomes a student at a particular public or private institution of higher education; or

(2) terminates the person's status in that capacity.

Art. 62.058. Law Enforcement Verification of Registration Information.

(a) A person subject to registration under this chapter who has for a sexually violent offense been convicted two or more times, received an order of deferred adjudication two or more times, or been convicted and received an order of deferred adjudication shall report to the local law enforcement authority designated as the person's primary registration authority by the department not less than once in each 90-day period following the date the person first registered under this chapter to verify the information in the registration form maintained by the authority for that person. A person subject to registration under this chapter who is not subject to the 90-day reporting requirement described by this subsection shall report to the local law enforcement authority designated as the person's primary registration authority by the department once each year not earlier than the 30th day before and not later than the 30th day after the anniversary of the person's date of birth to verify the information in the registration form maintained by the authority for that person. For purposes of this subsection, a person complies with a requirement that the person register within a 90-day period following a date if the person registers at any time on or after the 83rd day following that date but before the 98th day after that date.

(b) A local law enforcement authority designated as a person's primary registration authority by the department may direct the person to report to the authority to verify the information in the registration form maintained by the authority for that person. The authority may direct the person to report under this subsection once in each 90-day period following the date the person first registered under this chapter, if the person is required to report not less than once in each 90-day period under Subsection (a) or once in each year not earlier than the 30th day before and not later than the 30th day after the anniversary of the person's date of birth, if the person is required to report once each year under Subsection (a). A local law enforcement authority may not direct a person to report to the authority under this subsection if the person is required to report under Subsection (a) and is in compliance with the reporting requirements of that subsection.

(c) A local law enforcement authority with whom a person reports under this article shall require the person to produce proof of the person's identity and residence before the authority gives the registration form to the person for verification. If the information in the registration form is complete and accurate, the person shall verify registration by signing the form. If the information is not complete or not accurate, the person shall make any necessary additions or corrections before signing the form.

(d) A local law enforcement authority designated as a person's primary registration authority by the department may at any time mail a nonforwardable verification form to the last reported address of the person. Not later than the 21st day after receipt of a verification form under this subsection, the person shall:

(1) indicate on the form whether the person still resides at the last reported address and, if not, provide on the form the person's new address;

(2) complete any other information required by the form;

(3) sign the form; and

(4) return the form to the authority.

(e) For purposes of this article, a person receives multiple convictions or orders of deferred adjudication regardless of whether:

(1) the judgments or orders are entered on different dates; or

(2) the offenses for which the person was convicted or placed on deferred adjudication arose out of different criminal transactions.

(f) A local law enforcement authority that provides to a person subject to the prohibitions described by Article 62.063 a registration form for verification as required by this chapter shall include with the form a statement summarizing the types of employment that are prohibited for that person.

(g) A local law enforcement authority that provides to a person a registration form for verification as required by this chapter shall include with the form a statement describing the prohibition under Article 62.064.

(h) A local law enforcement authority who provides a person with a registration form for verification as required by this chapter shall include with the form a statement and, if applicable, a description of the person's duty to provide notice under Article 62.065.

Art. 62.059. Registration of Persons Regularly Visiting Location.

(a) A person subject to this chapter who on at least three occasions during any month spends more than 48 consecutive hours in a municipality or county in this state, other than the municipality or county in which the person is registered under this chapter, before the last day of that month shall report that fact to:

(1) the local law enforcement authority of the municipality in which the person is a visitor; or

(2) if the person is a visitor in a location that is not a municipality, the local law enforcement authority of the county in which the person is a visitor.

(b) A person described by Subsection (a) shall provide the local law enforcement authority with:

(1) all information the person is required to provide under Article 62.051(c);

(2) the address of any location in the municipality or county, as appropriate, at which the person was lodged during the month; and

(3) a statement as to whether the person intends to return to the municipality or county during the succeeding month.

(c) This article does not impose on a local law enforcement authority requirements of public notification or notification to schools relating to a person about whom the authority is not otherwise required by this chapter to make notifications.

Art. 62.06. Law Enforcement Verification of Registration Information [Renumbered].

Renumbered to Tex. Code Crim. Proc. art. 62.058 by Acts 2005, 79th Leg., ch. 1008 (H.B. 867), § 1.01, effective September 1, 2005.

Art. 62.060. Requirements Relating to Driver's License or Personal Identification Certificate.

(a) A person subject to registration under this chapter shall apply to the department in person for the issuance of, as applicable, an original or renewal driver's license under Section 521.272, Transportation Code, an original or renewal personal identification certificate under Section 521.103, Transportation Code, or an original or renewal commercial driver's license or commercial learner's permit under Section 522.033, Transportation Code, not later than the 30th day after the date:

(1) the person is released from a penal institution or is released by a court on community supervision or juvenile probation; or

(2) the department sends written notice to the person of the requirements of this article.

(b) The person shall annually renew in person each driver's license or personal identification certificate issued by the department to the person, including each renewal, duplicate, or corrected license or certificate, until the person's duty to register under this chapter expires.

Art. 62.061. DNA Specimen.

A person required to register under this chapter shall comply with a request for a DNA specimen made by a law enforcement agency under Section 411.1473, Government Code.

Art. 62.062. Limitation on Newspaper Publication.

(a) Except as provided by Subsection (b), a local law enforcement authority may not publish notice in a newspaper or other periodical or circular concerning a person's registration under this chapter if the only basis on which the person is subject to registration is one or more adjudications of delinquent conduct.

(b) This article does not apply to a publication of notice under Article 62.056.

Art. 62.063. Prohibited Employment.

(a) In this article:

(1) "Amusement ride" has the meaning assigned by Section 2151.002, Occupations Code.

(2) "Bus" has the meaning assigned by Section 541.201, Transportation Code.

(b) A person subject to registration under this chapter because of a reportable conviction or adjudication for which an affirmative finding is entered under Article 42.015(b) or 42A.105(a), as appropriate, may not, for compensation:

(1) operate or offer to operate a bus;

(2) provide or offer to provide a passenger taxicab or limousine transportation service;

(3) provide or offer to provide any type of service in the residence of another person unless the provision of service will be supervised; or

(4) operate or offer to operate any amusement ride.

Art. 62.064. Prohibited Location of Residence.

A person subject to registration under this chapter may not reside on the campus of a public or private institution of higher education unless:

(1) the person is assigned a numeric risk level of one based on an assessment conducted using the sex offender screening tool developed or selected under Article 62.007; and

(2) the institution approves the person to reside on the institution's campus.

Art. 62.065. Entry Onto School Premises; Notice Required.

(a) In this article:

(1) "Premises" means a building or portion of a building and the grounds on which the building is located, including any public or private driveway, street, sidewalk or walkway, parking lot, or parking garage on the grounds.

(2) "School" has the meaning assigned by Section 481.134, Health and Safety Code.

(b) A person subject to registration under this chapter who enters the premises of any school in this state during the standard operating hours of the school shall immediately notify the administrative office of the school of the person's presence on the premises of the school and the person's registration status under this chapter. The office may provide a chaperon to accompany the person while the person is on the premises of the school.

(c) The requirements of this article:

(1) are in addition to any requirement associated with the imposition of a child safety zone on the person under Section 508.187, Government Code, or Article 42A.453 of this code; and

(2) do not apply to:

(A) a student enrolled at the school;

(B) a student from another school participating at an event at the school; or

(C) a person who has entered into a written agreement with the school that exempts the person from those requirements.

Art. 62.07. Remedies Related to Public Notice [Deleted].

Deleted by Acts 2005, 79th Leg., ch. 1008 (H.B. 867), § 1.01, effective September 1, 2005.

Art. 62.08. Central Database; Public Information [Deleted].

Deleted by Acts 2005, 79th Leg., ch. 1008 (H.B. 867), § 1.01, effective September 1, 2005.

Art. 62.085. Information Provided to Peace Officer [Deleted].

Deleted by Acts 2005, 79th Leg., ch. 1008 (H.B. 867), § 1.01, effective September 1, 2005.

Art. 62.09. Immunity for Release of Public Information [Deleted].

Deleted by Acts 2005, 79th Leg., ch. 1008 (H.B. 867), § 1.01, effective September 1, 2005.

Art. 62.091. General Immunity [Deleted].

Deleted by Acts 2005, 79th Leg., ch. 1008 (H.B. 867), § 1.01, effective September 1, 2005.

Art. 62.10. Failure to Comply with Registration Requirements [Renumbered].

Renumbered to Tex. Code Crim. Proc. art. 62.102 by Acts 2005, 79th Leg., ch. 1008 (H.B. 867), § 1.01, effective September 1, 2005.

SUBCHAPTER C EXPIRATION OF DUTY TO REGISTER; GENERAL PENALTIES FOR NONCOMPLIANCE

Art. 62.101. Expiration of Duty to Register.

(a) Except as provided by Subsection (b) and Subchapter I, the duty to register for a person ends when the person dies if the person has a reportable conviction or adjudication, other than an adjudication of delinquent conduct, for:

(1) a sexually violent offense;

(2) an offense under Section 20A.02(a)(3), (4), (7), or (8), 25.02, 43.05(a)(2), or 43.26, Penal Code;

(3) an offense under Section 20A.03, Penal Code, if based partly or wholly on conduct that constitutes an offense under Section 20A.02(a)(3), (4), (7), or (8) of that code;

(4) an offense under Section 21.11(a)(2), Penal Code, if before or after the person is convicted or adjudicated for the offense under Section 21.11(a)(2), Penal Code, the person receives or has received another reportable conviction or adjudication, other than an adjudication of delinquent conduct, for an offense or conduct that requires registration under this chapter;

(5) an offense under Section 20.02, 20.03, or 20.04, Penal Code, if:

(A) the judgment in the case contains an affirmative finding under Article 42.015 or, for a deferred adjudication, the papers in the case contain an affirmative finding that the victim or intended victim was younger than 17 years of age; and

(B) before or after the person is convicted or adjudicated for the offense under Section 20.02, 20.03, or 20.04, Penal Code, the person receives or has received another reportable conviction or adjudication, other than an adjudication of delinquent conduct, for an offense or conduct that requires registration under this chapter; or

(6) an offense under Section 43.23, Penal Code, that is punishable under Subsection (h) of that section.

(b) Except as provided by Subchapter I, the duty to register for a person otherwise subject to Subsection (a) ends on the 10th anniversary of the date on which the person is released from a penal institution or discharges community supervision or the court dismisses the criminal proceedings against the person and discharges the person, whichever date is later, if the person's duty to register is based on a conviction or an order of deferred adjudication in a cause that was transferred to a district court or criminal district court under Section 54.02, Family Code.

(c) Except as provided by Subchapter I, the duty to register for a person with a reportable conviction or adjudication for an offense other than an offense described by Subsection (a) ends:

(1) if the person's duty to register is based on an adjudication of delinquent conduct, on the 10th anniversary of the date on which the disposition is made or the person completes the terms of the disposition, whichever date is later; or

(2) if the person's duty to register is based on a conviction or on an order of deferred adjudication, on the 10th anniversary of the date on which the court dismisses the criminal proceedings against the person and discharges the person, the person is released from a penal institution, or the person discharges community supervision, whichever date is later.

Art. 62.102. Failure to Comply with Registration Requirements.

(a) A person commits an offense if the person is required to register and fails to comply with any requirement of this chapter.

(b) An offense under this article is:

(1) a state jail felony if the actor is a person whose duty to register expires under Article 62.101(b) or (c);

(2) a felony of the third degree if the actor is a person whose duty to register expires under Article 62.101(a) and who is required to verify registration once each year under Article 62.058; and

(3) a felony of the second degree if the actor is a person whose duty to register expires under Article 62.101(a) and who is required to verify registration once each 90-day period under Article 62.058.

(c) If it is shown at the trial of a person for an offense or an attempt to commit an offense under this article that the person has previously been convicted of an offense or an attempt to commit an offense under this article, the punishment for the offense or the attempt to commit the offense is increased to the punishment for the next highest degree of felony.

(d) If it is shown at the trial of a person for an offense under this article or an attempt to commit an offense under this article that the person fraudulently used identifying information in violation of Section 32.51, Penal Code, during the commission or attempted commission of the offense, the punishment for the offense or the attempt to commit the offense is increased to the punishment for the next highest degree of felony.

Art. 62.11. Applicability [Deleted].

Deleted by Acts 2005, 79th Leg., ch. 1008 (H.B. 867), § 1.01, effective September 1, 2005.

Art. 62.12. Expiration of Duty to Register [Deleted].

Deleted by Acts 2005, 79th Leg., ch. 1008 (H.B. 867), § 1.01, effective September 1, 2005.

Art. 62.13. Hearing to Determine Need for Registration of a Juvenile [Deleted].

Deleted by Acts 2005, 79th Leg., ch. 1008 (H.B. 867), § 1.01, effective September 1, 2005.

Art. 62.14. Removing Juvenile Registration Information When Duty to Register Expires [Renumbered].

Renumbered to Tex.Code Crim. Proc. art. 62.251 by Acts 2005, 79th Leg., ch. 1008 (H.B. 867), § 1.01, effective September 1, 2005.

SUBCHAPTER D PROVISIONS APPLICABLE TO CERTAIN WORKERS AND STUDENTS

Art. 62.151. Definitions.

For purposes of this subchapter, a person:

(1) is employed or carries on a vocation if the person works or volunteers on a full-time or part-time

basis for a consecutive period exceeding 14 days or for an aggregate period exceeding 30 days in a calendar year;

(2) works regardless of whether the person works for compensation or for governmental or educational benefit; and

(3) is a student if the person enrolls on a full-time or part-time basis in any educational facility, including:

(A) a public or private primary or secondary school, including a high school or alternative learning center; or

(B) a public or private institution of higher education.

Art. 62.152. Registration of Certain Workers or Students.

(a) A person is subject to this subchapter and, except as otherwise provided by this article, to the other subchapters of this chapter if the person:

(1) has a reportable conviction or adjudication;

(2) resides in another state; and

(3) is employed, carries on a vocation, or is a student in this state.

(b) A person described by Subsection (a) is subject to the registration and verification requirements of Articles 62.051 and 62.058 and to the change of address requirements of Article 62.055, except that the registration and verification and the reporting of a change of address are based on the municipality or county in which the person works or attends school. The person is subject to the school notification requirements of Articles 62.053—62.055, except that notice provided to the superintendent and any administrator is based on the public school district in which the person works or attends school.

(c) A person described by Subsection (a) is not subject to Article 62.101.

(d) The duty to register for a person described by Subsection (a) ends when the person no longer works or studies in this state, provides notice of that fact to the local law enforcement authority in the municipality or county in which the person works or attends school, and receives notice of verification of that fact from the authority. The authority must verify that the person no longer works or studies in this state and must provide to the person notice of that verification within a reasonable time.

(e) Notwithstanding Subsection (a), this article does not apply to a person who has a reportable conviction or adjudication, who resides in another state, and who is employed, carries on a vocation, or is a student in this state if the person establishes another residence in this state to work or attend school in this state. However, that person remains subject to the other articles of this chapter based on that person's residence in this state.

Art. 62.153. Registration of Workers or Students at Institutions of Higher Education.

(a) Not later than the later of the seventh day after the date on which the person begins to work or attend school or the first date the applicable authority by policy allows the person to register, a person required to register under Article 62.152 or any other provision of this chapter who is employed, carries on a vocation, or is a student at a public or private institution of higher education in this state shall report that fact to:

(1) the authority for campus security for that institution; or

(2) if an authority for campus security for that institution does not exist, the local law enforcement authority of:

(A) the municipality in which the institution is located; or

(B) the county in which the institution is located, if the institution is not located in a municipality.

(b) A person described by Subsection (a) shall provide the authority for campus security or the local law enforcement authority with all information the person is required to provide under Article 62.051(c).

(c) A person described by Subsection (a) shall notify the authority for campus security or the local law enforcement authority not later than the seventh day after the date of termination of the person's status as a worker or student at the institution.

(d) The authority for campus security or the local law enforcement authority shall promptly forward to the administrative office of the institution any information received from the person under this article and any information received from the department under Article 62.005.

(e) Subsection (a)(2) does not require a person to register with a local law enforcement authority if the person is otherwise required by this chapter to register with that authority.

(f) This article does not impose the requirements of public notification or notification to public or private primary or secondary schools on:

(1) an authority for campus security; or

(2) a local law enforcement authority, if those requirements relate to a person about whom the authority is not otherwise required by this chapter to make notifications.

(g) Notwithstanding Article 62.059, the requirements of this article supersede those of Article

62.059 for a person required to register under both this article and Article 62.059.

SUBCHAPTER E PROVISIONS APPLICABLE TO PERSONS SUBJECT TO CIVIL COMMITMENT

Art. 62.201. Additional Public Notice for Individuals Subject to Civil Commitment.

(a) On receipt of notice under this chapter that a person subject to registration who is civilly committed as a sexually violent predator is due to be released from a penal institution or intends to move to a new residence in this state, the department shall, not later than the seventh day after the date on which the person is released or the seventh day after the date on which the person moves, provide written notice mailed or delivered to at least each address, other than a post office box, within a one-mile radius, in an area that has not been subdivided, or a three-block area, in an area that has been subdivided, of the place where the person intends to reside.

(b) The department shall provide the notice in English and Spanish and shall include in the notice any information that is public information under this chapter. The department may not include any information that is not public information under this chapter.

(c) The department shall establish procedures for a person with respect to whom notice is provided under this article to pay to the department all costs incurred by the department in providing the notice. The person shall pay those costs in accordance with the procedures established under this subsection.

(d) The department's duty to provide notice under this article in regard to a particular person ends on the date on which a court releases the person from all requirements of the civil commitment process.

Art. 62.202. Verification of Individuals Subject to Commitment.

(a) Notwithstanding Article 62.058, if an individual subject to registration under this chapter is civilly committed as a sexually violent predator, the person shall report to the local law enforcement authority designated as the person's primary registration authority by the department to verify the information in the registration form maintained by the authority for that person as follows:

(1) if the person resides at a civil commitment center, not less than once each year; or

(2) if the person does not reside at a civil commitment center, not less than once in each 30-day period following:

(A) the date the person first registered under this chapter; or

(B) if applicable, the date the person moved from the center.

(a-1) For purposes of Subsection (a)(2), a person complies with a requirement that the person register within a 30-day period following a date if the person registers at any time on or after the 27th day following that date but before the 33rd day after that date.

(b) On the date a court releases a person described by Subsection (a) from all requirements of the civil commitment process:

(1) the person's duty to verify registration as a sex offender is no longer imposed by this article; and

(2) the person is required to verify registration as provided by Article 62.058.

Art. 62.2021. Requirements Relating to Driver's License or Personal Identification Certificate: Individuals Residing at Civil Commitment Center.

(a) Notwithstanding Article 62.060(b), a person subject to registration who is civilly committed as a sexually violent predator and resides at a civil commitment center shall renew the person's department-issued driver's license or personal identification certificate as prescribed by Section 521.103, 521.272, or 522.033, Transportation Code, as applicable.

(b) On the date that a person described by Subsection (a) no longer resides at a civil commitment center, the person is required to renew a driver's license or personal identification certificate only as provided by Article 62.060(b).

Art. 62.203. Failure to Comply: Individuals Subject to Commitment.

(a) A person commits an offense if the person, after commitment as a sexually violent predator but before the person is released from all requirements of the civil commitment process, fails to comply with any requirement of this chapter.

(b) An offense under this article is a felony of the second degree.

SUBCHAPTER F REMOVAL OF REGISTRATION INFORMATION

Art. 62.251. Removing Registration Information When Duty to Register Expires.

(a) When a person is no longer required to register as a sex offender under this chapter, the department shall remove all information about the person from the sex offender registry.

(b) The duty to remove information under Subsection (a) arises if:

(1) the department has received notice from a local law enforcement authority under Subsection (c) or (d) that the person is no longer required to register or will no longer be required to renew registration and the department verifies the correctness of that information;

(2) the court having jurisdiction over the case for which registration is required requests removal and the department determines that the duty to register has expired; or

(3) the person or the person's representative requests removal and the department determines that the duty to register has expired.

(c) When a person required to register under this chapter appears before a local law enforcement authority to renew or modify registration information, the authority shall determine whether the duty to register has expired. If the authority determines that the duty to register has expired, the authority shall remove all information about the person from the sex offender registry and notify the department that the person's duty to register has expired.

(d) When a person required to register under this chapter appears before a local law enforcement authority to renew registration information, the authority shall determine whether the renewal is the final annual renewal of registration required by law. If the authority determines that the person's duty to register will expire before the next annual renewal is scheduled, the authority shall automatically remove all information about the person from the sex offender registry on expiration of the duty to register and notify the department that the information about the person has been removed from the registry.

(e) When the department has removed information under Subsection (a), the department shall notify all local law enforcement authorities that have provided registration information to the department about the person of the removal. A local law enforcement authority that receives notice from the department under this subsection shall remove all registration information about the person from its registry.

(f) When the department has removed information under Subsection (a), the department shall notify all public and private agencies or organizations to which it has provided registration information about the person of the removal. On receiving notice, the public or private agency or organization shall remove all registration information about the person from any registry the agency or organization maintains that is accessible to the public with or without charge.

SUBCHAPTER G EXEMPTION FROM REGISTRATION FOR CERTAIN YOUNG ADULT SEX OFFENDERS

Art. 62.301. Exemption from Registration for Certain Young Adult Sex Offenders.

(a) If eligible under Subsection (b) or (c), a person required to register under this chapter may petition the court having jurisdiction over the case for an order exempting the person from registration under this chapter at any time on or after the date of the person's sentencing or the date the person is placed on deferred adjudication community supervision, as applicable.

(b) A person is eligible to petition the court as described by Subsection (a) if:

(1) the person is required to register only as a result of a single reportable conviction or adjudication, other than an adjudication of delinquent conduct; and

(2) the court has entered in the appropriate judgment or has filed with the appropriate papers a statement of an affirmative finding described by Article 42.017 or 42A.105(c).

(c) A defendant who before September 1, 2011, is convicted of or placed on deferred adjudication community supervision for an offense under Section 21.11 or 22.011, Penal Code, is eligible to petition the court as described by Subsection (a). The court may consider the petition only if the petition states and the court finds that the defendant would have been entitled to the entry of an affirmative finding under Article 42.017 or 42A.105(c), as appropriate, had the conviction or placement on deferred adjudication community supervision occurred after September 1, 2011.

(c-1) At a hearing on the petition described by Subsection (a), the court may consider:

(1) testimony from the victim or intended victim, or a member of the victim's or intended victim's family, concerning the requested exemption;

(2) the relationship between the victim or intended victim and the petitioner at the time of the hearing; and

(3) any other evidence that the court determines is relevant and admissible.

(d) After a hearing on the petition described by Subsection (a), the court may issue an order exempting the person from registration under this chapter if it appears by a preponderance of the evidence that:

(1) the exemption does not threaten public safety;

(2) the person's conduct did not occur without the consent of the victim or intended victim as described by Section 22.011(b), Penal Code;

(3) the exemption is in the best interest of the victim or intended victim; and

(4) the exemption is in the best interest of justice.

(e) An order exempting the person from registration under this chapter does not expire, but the court shall withdraw the order if after the order is issued the person receives a reportable conviction or adjudication under this chapter.

SUBCHAPTER H EXEMPTIONS FROM REGISTRATION FOR CERTAIN JUVENILES

Art. 62.351. Motion and Hearing Generally.

(a) During or after disposition of a case under Section 54.04, Family Code, for adjudication of an offense for which registration is required under this chapter, the juvenile court on motion of the respondent shall conduct a hearing to determine whether the interests of the public require registration under this chapter. The motion may be filed and the hearing held regardless of whether the respondent is under 18 years of age. Notice of the motion and hearing shall be provided to the prosecuting attorney.

(b) The hearing is without a jury and the burden of persuasion is on the respondent to show by a preponderance of evidence that the criteria of Article 62.352(a) have been met. The court at the hearing may make its determination based on:

(1) the receipt of exhibits;

(2) the testimony of witnesses;

(3) representations of counsel for the parties; or

(4) the contents of a social history report prepared by the juvenile probation department that may include the results of testing and examination of the respondent by a psychologist, psychiatrist, or counselor.

(c) All written matter considered by the court shall be disclosed to all parties as provided by Section 54.04(b), Family Code.

(d) If a respondent, as part of a plea agreement, promises not to file a motion seeking an order exempting the respondent from registration under this chapter, the court may not recognize a motion filed by a respondent under this article.

Art. 62.352. Order Generally.

(a) The court shall enter an order exempting a respondent from registration under this chapter if the court determines:

(1) that the protection of the public would not be increased by registration of the respondent under this chapter; or

(2) that any potential increase in protection of the public resulting from registration of the respondent is clearly outweighed by the anticipated substantial harm to the respondent and the respondent's family that would result from registration under this chapter.

(b) After a hearing under Article 62.351 or under a plea agreement described by Article 62.355(b), the juvenile court may enter an order:

(1) deferring decision on requiring registration under this chapter until the respondent has completed treatment for the respondent's sexual offense as a condition of probation or while committed to the Texas Juvenile Justice Department; or

(2) requiring the respondent to register as a sex offender but providing that the registration information is not public information and is restricted to use by law enforcement and criminal justice agencies, the Council on Sex Offender Treatment, and public or private institutions of higher education.

(c) If the court enters an order described by Subsection (b)(1), the court retains discretion and jurisdiction to require, or exempt the respondent from, registration under this chapter at any time during the treatment or on the successful or unsuccessful completion of treatment, except that during the period of deferral, registration may not be required. Following successful completion of treatment, the respondent is exempted from registration under this chapter unless a hearing under this subchapter is held on motion of the prosecuting attorney, regardless of whether the respondent is 18 years of age or older, and the court determines the interests

Code of Criminal Procedure

of the public require registration. Not later than the 10th day after the date of the respondent's successful completion of treatment, the treatment provider shall notify the juvenile court and prosecuting attorney of the completion.

(d) Information that is the subject of an order described by Subsection (b)(2) may not be posted on the Internet or released to the public.

Art. 62.353. Motion, Hearing, and Order Concerning Person Already Registered.

(a) A person who has registered as a sex offender for an adjudication of delinquent conduct, regardless of when the delinquent conduct or the adjudication for the conduct occurred, may file a motion in the adjudicating juvenile court for a hearing seeking:

(1) exemption from registration under this chapter as provided by Article 62.351; or

(2) an order under Article 62.352(b)(2) that the registration become nonpublic.

(b) The person may file a motion under Subsection (a) in the original juvenile case regardless of whether the person, at the time of filing the motion, is 18 years of age or older. Notice of the motion shall be provided to the prosecuting attorney. A hearing on the motion shall be provided as in other cases under this subchapter.

(c) Only one subsequent motion may be filed under Subsection (a) if a previous motion under this article has been filed concerning the case.

(d) To the extent feasible, the motion under Subsection (a) shall identify those public and private agencies and organizations, including public or private institutions of higher education, that possess sex offender registration information about the case.

(e) The juvenile court, after a hearing, may:

(1) deny a motion filed under Subsection (a);

(2) grant a motion described by Subsection (a)(1); or

(3) grant a motion described by Subsection (a)(2).

(f) If the court grants a motion filed under Subsection (a), the clerk of the court shall by certified mail, return receipt requested, send a copy of the order to the department, to each local law enforcement authority that the person has proved to the juvenile court has registration information about the person, and to each public or private agency or organization that the person has proved to the juvenile court has information about the person that is currently available to the public with or without payment of a fee. The clerk of the court shall by certified mail, return receipt requested, send a copy of the order to any other agency or organization designated by the person. The person shall identify the agency or organization and its address and pay a fee of $20 to the court for each agency or organization the person designates.

(g) In addition to disseminating the order under Subsection (f), at the request of the person, the clerk of the court shall by certified mail, return receipt requested, send a copy of the order to each public or private agency or organization that at any time following the initial dissemination of the order under Subsection (f) gains possession of sex offender registration information pertaining to that person, if the agency or organization did not otherwise receive a copy of the order under Subsection (f).

(h) An order under Subsection (f) must require the recipient to conform its records to the court's order either by deleting the sex offender registration information or changing its status to nonpublic, as applicable. A public or private institution of higher education may not be required to delete the sex offender registration information under this subsection.

(i) A private agency or organization that possesses sex offender registration information the agency or organization obtained from a state, county, or local governmental entity is required to conform the agency's or organization's records to the court's order on or before the 30th day after the date of the entry of the order. Unless the agency or organization is a public or private institution of higher education, failure to comply in that period automatically bars the agency or organization from obtaining sex offender registration information from any state, county, or local governmental entity in this state in the future.

Art. 62.354. Motion, Hearing, and Order Concerning Person Required to Register Because of Out-of-State Adjudication.

(a) A person required to register as a sex offender in this state because of an out-of-state adjudication of delinquent conduct may file in the juvenile court of the person's county of residence a petition under Article 62.351 for an order exempting the person from registration under this chapter.

(b) If the person is already registered as a sex offender in this state because of an out-of-state adjudication of delinquent conduct, the person may file in the juvenile court of the person's county of residence a petition under Article 62.353 for an order removing the person from sex offender registries in this state.

(c) On receipt of a petition under this article, the juvenile court shall conduct a hearing and make rulings as in other cases under this subchapter.

(d) An order entered under this article requiring removal of registration information applies only to registration information derived from registration in this state.

Art. 62.355. Waiver of Hearing.

(a) The prosecuting attorney may waive the state's right to a hearing under this subchapter and agree that registration under this chapter is not required. A waiver under this subsection must state whether the waiver is entered under a plea agreement.

(b) If the waiver is entered under a plea agreement, the court, without a hearing, shall:

(1) enter an order exempting the respondent from registration under this chapter; or

(2) under Section 54.03(j), Family Code, inform the respondent that the court believes a hearing under this article is required and give the respondent the opportunity to:

(A) withdraw the respondent's plea of guilty, nolo contendere, or true; or

(B) affirm the respondent's plea and participate in the hearing.

(c) If the waiver is entered other than under a plea agreement, the court, without a hearing, shall enter an order exempting the respondent from registration under this chapter.

Art. 62.356. Effect of Certain Orders.

(a) A person who has an adjudication of delinquent conduct that would otherwise be reportable under Article 62.001(5) does not have a reportable adjudication of delinquent conduct for purposes of this chapter if the juvenile court enters an order under this subchapter exempting the person from the registration requirements of this chapter.

(b) If the juvenile court enters an order exempting a person from registration under this chapter, the respondent may not be required to register in this or any other state for the offense for which registration was exempted.

Art. 62.357. Appeal of Certain Orders.

(a) Notwithstanding Section 56.01, Family Code, on entry by a juvenile court of an order under Article 62.352(a) exempting a respondent from registration under this chapter, the prosecuting attorney may appeal that order by giving notice of appeal within the time required under Rule 26.2(b), Texas Rules of Appellate Procedure. The appeal is civil and the standard of review in the appellate court is whether the juvenile court committed procedural error or abused its discretion in exempting the respondent from registration under this chapter. The appeal is limited to review of the order exempting the respondent from registration under this chapter and may not include any other issues in the case.

(b) A respondent may under Section 56.01, Family Code, appeal a juvenile court's order under Article 62.352(a) requiring registration in the same manner as the appeal of any other legal issue in the case. The standard of review in the appellate court is whether the juvenile court committed procedural error or abused its discretion in requiring registration.

SUBCHAPTER I EARLY TERMINATION OF CERTAIN PERSONS' OBLIGATION TO REGISTER

Art. 62.401. Definition.

In this subchapter, "council" means the Council on Sex Offender Treatment.

Art. 62.402. Determination of Minimum Required Registration Period.

(a) The department by rule shall determine the minimum required registration period under federal law for each reportable conviction or adjudication under this chapter.

(b) After determining the minimum required registration period for each reportable conviction or adjudication under Subsection (a), the department shall compile and publish a list of reportable convictions or adjudications for which a person must register under this chapter for a period that exceeds the minimum required registration period under federal law.

(c) To the extent possible, the department shall periodically verify with the United States Department of Justice's Office of Sex Offender Sentencing, Monitoring, Apprehending, Registering, and Tracking or another appropriate federal agency or office the accuracy of the list of reportable convictions or adjudications described by Subsection (b).

Art. 62.403. Individual Risk Assessment.

(a) The council by rule shall establish, develop, or adopt an individual risk assessment tool or a group of individual risk assessment tools that:

(1) evaluates the criminal history of a person required to register under this chapter; and

(2) seeks to predict:

(A) the likelihood that the person will engage in criminal activity that may result in the person receiving a second or subsequent reportable adjudication or conviction; and

(B) the continuing danger, if any, that the person poses to the community.

(b) On the written request of a person with a single reportable adjudication or conviction that appears on the list published under Article 62.402(b), the council shall:

(1) evaluate the person using the individual risk assessment tool or group of individual risk assessment tools established, developed, or adopted under Subsection (a); and

(2) provide to the person a written report detailing the outcome of an evaluation conducted under Subdivision (1).

(c) An individual risk assessment provided to a person under this subchapter is confidential and is not subject to disclosure under Chapter 552, Government Code.

Art. 62.404. Motion for Early Termination.

(a) A person required to register under this chapter who has requested and received an individual risk assessment under Article 62.403 may file with the trial court that sentenced the person for the reportable conviction or adjudication a motion for early termination of the person's obligation to register under this chapter.

(b) A motion filed under this article must be accompanied by:

(1) a written explanation of how the reportable conviction or adjudication giving rise to the movant's registration under this chapter qualifies as a reportable conviction or adjudication that appears on the list published under Article 62.402(b); and

(2) a certified copy of a written report detailing the outcome of an individual risk assessment evaluation conducted under Article 62.403(b)(1).

Art. 62.405. Hearing on Petition.

(a) After reviewing a motion filed with the court under Article 62.404, the court may:

(1) deny without a hearing the movant's request for early termination; or

(2) hold a hearing on the motion to determine whether to grant or deny the motion.

(b) The court may not grant a motion filed under Article 62.404 if:

(1) the motion is not accompanied by the documents required under Article 62.404(b); or

(2) the court determines that the reportable conviction or adjudication for which the movant is required to register under this chapter is not a reportable conviction or adjudication for which the movant is required to register for a period that exceeds the minimum required registration period under federal law.

Art. 62.406. Costs of Individual Risk Assessment and Court.

A person required to register under this chapter who files a motion for early termination of the person's registration obligation under this chapter is responsible for and shall remit to the council and to the court, as applicable, all costs associated with and incurred by the council in providing the individual risk assessment or by the court in holding a hearing under this subchapter.

Art. 62.407. Effect of Order Granting Early Termination.

(a) If, after notice to the person and to the prosecuting attorney and a hearing, the court grants a motion filed under Article 62.404 for the early termination of a person's obligation to register under this chapter, notwithstanding Article 62.101, the person's obligation to register under this chapter ends on the later of:

(1) the date the court enters the order of early termination; or

(2) the date the person has paid each cost described by Section 62.406.

(b) If the court grants a motion filed under Article 62.404 for the early termination of a person's obligation to register under this chapter, all conditions of the person's parole, release to mandatory supervision, or community supervision shall be modified in accordance with the court's order.

Art. 62.408. Nonapplicability.

This subchapter does not apply to a person without a reportable conviction or adjudication who is required to register as a condition of parole, release to mandatory supervision, or community supervision.

CHAPTER 63
MISSING CHILDREN AND MISSING PERSONS

SUBCHAPTER A
GENERAL PROVISIONS

Art. 63.001. Definitions.

In this chapter:

(1) "Abduct" has the meaning assigned by Section 20.01, Penal Code.

(1-a) "Child" means a person under 18 years of age.

(2) "Missing person" means a person 18 years old or older whose disappearance is possibly not voluntary.

(3) "Missing child" means a child whose whereabouts are unknown to the child's legal custodian, the circumstances of whose absence indicate that:

(A) the child did not voluntarily leave the care and control of the custodian, and the taking of the child was not authorized by law;

(B) the child voluntarily left the care and control of the custodian without the custodian's consent and without intent to return;

(C) the child was taken or retained in violation of the terms of a court order for possession of or access to the child; or

(D) the child was taken or retained without the permission of the custodian and with the effect of depriving the custodian of possession of or access to the child unless the taking or retention of the child was prompted by the commission or attempted commission of family violence, as defined by Section 71.004, Family Code, against the child or the actor.

(4) "Missing child" or "missing person" also includes a person of any age who is missing and:

(A) is under proven physical or mental disability or is senile, and because of one or more of these conditions is subject to immediate danger or is a danger to others;

(B) is in the company of another person or is in a situation the circumstances of which indicate that the missing child's or missing person's safety is in doubt; or

(C) is unemancipated as defined by the law of this state.

(5) "Missing child or missing person report" means information that is:

(A) given to a law enforcement agency on a form used for sending information to the national crime information center; and

(B) about a child or missing person whose whereabouts are unknown to the reporter and who is alleged in the form by the reporter to be missing.

(6) "Legal custodian of a child" means a parent of a child if no managing conservator or guardian of the person of the child has been appointed, the managing conservator of a child or a guardian of a child if a managing conservator or guardian has been appointed for the child, a possessory conservator of a child if the child is absent from the possessory conservator of the child at a time when the possessory conservator is entitled to possession of the child and the child is not believed to be with the managing conservator, or any other person who has assumed temporary care and control of a child if at the time of disappearance the child was not living with his parent, guardian, managing conservator, or possessory conservator.

(7) "Clearinghouse" means the missing children and missing persons information clearinghouse.

(8) "Law enforcement agency" means a police department of a city in this state, a sheriff of a county in this state, or the Department of Public Safety.

(9) "Possible match" occurs if the similarities between an unidentified body and a missing child or person would lead one to believe they are the same person.

(10) "City or state agency" means an employment commission, the Texas Department of Human Services, the Texas Department of Transportation, and any other agency that is funded or supported by the state or a city government.

(11) "Birth certificate agency" means a municipal or county official that records and maintains birth certificates and the bureau of vital statistics.

(12) "Bureau of vital statistics" means the bureau of vital statistics of the Texas Department of Health.

(13) "School" means a public primary school or private primary school that charges a fee for tuition and has more than 25 students enrolled and attending courses at a single location.

Art. 63.0015. Presumption Regarding Parentage.

For purposes of this chapter, a person named as a child's mother or father in the child's birth certificate is presumed to be the child's parent.

Sec. 63.0016. Attempted Child Abduction by Relative.

For purposes of this chapter, "attempted child abduction" does not include an attempted abduction in which the actor was a relative, as defined by Section 20.01, Penal Code, of the person intended to be abducted.

Art. 63.002. Missing Children and Missing Persons Information Clearinghouse.

(a) The missing children and missing persons information clearinghouse is established within the Department of Public Safety.

(b) The clearinghouse is under the administrative direction of the director of the department.

(c) The clearinghouse shall be used by all law enforcement agencies of the state.

Art. 63.003. Function of Clearinghouse.

(a) The clearinghouse is a central repository of information on missing children, missing persons, and attempted child abductions.

(b) The clearinghouse shall:

(1) establish a system of intrastate communication of information relating to missing children and missing persons;

(2) provide a centralized file for the exchange of information on missing children, missing persons, and unidentified dead bodies within the state;

(3) communicate with the national crime information center for the exchange of information on missing children and missing persons suspected of interstate travel;

(4) collect, process, maintain, and disseminate accurate and complete information on missing children and missing persons;

(5) provide a statewide toll-free telephone line for the reporting of missing children and missing persons and for receiving information on missing children and missing persons;

(6) provide and disseminate to legal custodians, law enforcement agencies, and the Texas Education Agency information that explains how to prevent child abduction and what to do if a child becomes missing; and

(7) receive and maintain information on attempted child abductions in this state.

Art. 63.004. Report Forms.

(a) The Department of Public Safety shall distribute missing children and missing person report forms.

(b) A missing child or missing person report may be made to a law enforcement officer authorized by that department to receive reports in person or by telephone or other indirect method of communication and the officer may enter the information on the form for the reporting person. A report form may also be completed by the reporting person and delivered to a law enforcement officer.

Sec. 63.0041. Reporting of Attempted Child Abduction.

(a) A local law enforcement agency, on receiving a report of an attempted child abduction, shall as soon as practicable, but not later than eight hours after receiving the report, provide any relevant information regarding the attempted child abduction to the clearinghouse. Information not immediately available shall be obtained by the agency and entered into the clearinghouse as a supplement to the original entry as soon as possible.

(b) A law enforcement officer or local law enforcement agency reporting an attempted child abduction to the clearinghouse shall make the report by use of the Texas Law Enforcement Telecommunications System or a successor system of telecommunication used by law enforcement agencies and operated by the Department of Public Safety.

Art. 63.005. Distribution of Information.

(a) The clearinghouse shall print and distribute posters, flyers, and other forms of information containing descriptions of missing children.

(b) The clearinghouse shall also provide to the Texas Education Agency information about missing children who may be located in the school systems.

(c) The clearinghouse may also receive information about missing children from the Public Education Information Management System of the Texas Education Agency and from school districts.

Art. 63.006. Release of Dental Records.

(a) At the time a report is made for a missing child, the person to whom the report is given shall give or mail to the reporter a dental record release form. The officer receiving the report shall endorse the form with the notation that a missing child report has been made in compliance with this chapter. When the form is properly completed by the reporter, and contains the endorsement, the form is sufficient to permit any dentist or physician in this state to release dental records relating to the child reported missing.

(b) At any time a report is made for a missing person the law enforcement officer taking the report shall complete a dental release form that states that the person is missing and that there is reason to believe that the person has not voluntarily relocated or removed himself from communications with others and that authorizes the bearer of the release to obtain dental information records from any dentist or physician in this state.

(c) Any person who obtains dental records through the use of the form authorized by this article shall send the records to the clearinghouse.

(d) The judge of any court of record of this state may for good cause shown authorize the release of dental records of a missing child or missing person.

(e) A dentist or physician who releases dental records to a person presenting a proper release executed or ordered under this article is immune from civil liability or criminal prosecution for the release of those records.

Art. 63.007. Release of Medical Records.

(a) At the time a report is made for a missing child or adult, the law enforcement officer taking the report shall give a medical record release form to the parent, spouse, adult child, or legal guardian who is making the report. The officer receiving the report shall endorse the form with the notation that a missing child or missing adult report has been made in compliance with this chapter. When the form is properly completed by the parent, spouse, adult child, or legal guardian, and contains the endorsement, the form is sufficient to permit any physician, health care facility, or other licensed health care provider in this state to release to the law enforcement officer presenting the release dental records, blood type, height, weight, X rays, and information regarding scars, allergies, or any unusual illnesses suffered by the person who is reported missing. Except as provided by Subsection (d), a medical record of a missing child may be released only if the medical record release form is signed by a parent or legal guardian.

(b) At any time a report is made for an adult missing person, the law enforcement officer taking the report shall complete a medical release form that states that the person is missing and that there is reason to believe that the person has not voluntarily relocated or removed himself or herself from communications with others. A release under this subsection is not valid unless it is signed by the adult missing person's:

(1) spouse;
(2) adult child who is reasonably available;
(3) parent; or
(4) legal guardian.

(c) A law enforcement officer who obtains medical records under this article shall send a copy of the records to the clearinghouse. A law enforcement officer who obtains records under this article, a law enforcement agency using the records, and the clearinghouse are prohibited from disclosing the information contained in or obtained through the medical records unless permitted by law. Information contained in or obtained through medical records may be used only for purposes directly related to locating the missing person.

(d) The judge of any court of record of this state may for good cause shown authorize the release of pertinent medical records of a missing child or missing adult.

(e) A physician, health care facility, or other licensed health care provider releasing a medical record to a person presenting a proper release executed or ordered under this article is immune from civil liability or criminal prosecution for the release of the record.

Art. 63.008. Missing Children Program.

(a) The Texas Education Agency shall develop and administer a program for the location of missing children who may be enrolled within the Texas school system, including nonpublic schools, and for the reporting of children who may be missing or who may be unlawfully removed from schools.

(b) The program shall include the use of information received from the missing children and missing persons information clearinghouse and shall be coordinated with the operations of that information clearinghouse.

(c) The State Board of Education may adopt rules for the operation of the program and shall require the participation of all school districts and accredited private schools in this state.

Art. 63.009. Law Enforcement Requirements.

(a) A law enforcement agency, on receiving a report of a missing child or missing person, shall:

(1) if the subject of the report is a child and the child is at a high risk of harm or is otherwise in danger or if the subject of the report is a person who is known by the agency to have or is reported to have chronic dementia, including Alzheimer's dementia, whether caused by illness, brain defect, or brain injury, immediately start an investigation in order to determine the present location of the child or person;

(2) if the subject of the report is a child or person other than a child or person described by Subdivision (1), start an investigation with due diligence in order to determine the present location of the child or person;

(3) immediately, but not later than two hours after receiving the report, enter the name of the child or person into the clearinghouse and the national crime information center missing person file if the child or person meets the center's criteria, and report that name to the Alzheimer's Association Safe Return emergency response center if applicable, with all available identifying features such as dental records, fingerprints, other physical characteristics, and a description of the clothing worn when last seen, and all available information describing

any person reasonably believed to have taken or retained the missing child or missing person;

(4) not later than the 60th day after the date the agency receives the report, enter the name of the child or person into the National Missing and Unidentified Persons System, with all available identifying features such as dental records, fingerprints, other physical characteristics, and a description of the clothing worn when last seen, and all available information describing any person reasonably believed to have taken or retained the missing child or missing person; and

(5) inform the person who filed the report of the missing child or missing person that the information will be:

(A) entered into the clearinghouse, the national crime information center missing person file, and the National Missing and Unidentified Persons System; and

(B) reported to the Alzheimer's Association Safe Return emergency response center if applicable.

(a-1) A local law enforcement agency, on receiving a report of a child missing under the circumstances described by Article 63.001(3)(D) for a period of not less than 48 hours, shall immediately make a reasonable effort to locate the child and determine the well-being of the child. On determining the location of the child, if the agency has reason to believe that the child is a victim of abuse or neglect as defined by Section 261.001, Family Code, the agency:

(1) shall notify the Department of Family and Protective Services; and

(2) may take possession of the child under Subchapter B, Chapter 262, Family Code.

(a-2) The Department of Family and Protective Services, on receiving notice under Subsection (a-1), may initiate an investigation into the allegation of abuse or neglect under Section 261.301, Family Code, and take possession of the child under Chapter 262, Family Code.

(a-3) [Repealed.]

(b) Information not immediately available when the original entry is made shall be entered into the clearinghouse, the national crime information center file, and the National Missing and Unidentified Persons System as a supplement to the original entry as soon as possible.

(c) All Texas law enforcement agencies are required to enter information about all unidentified bodies into the clearinghouse and the national crime information center unidentified person file. A law enforcement agency shall, not later than the 10th working day after the date the death is reported to the agency, enter all available identifying features of the unidentified body (fingerprints, dental records, any unusual physical characteristics, and a description of the clothing found on the body) into the clearinghouse and the national crime information center file. If an information entry into the national crime information center file results in an automatic entry of the information into the clearinghouse, the law enforcement agency is not required to make a direct entry of that information into the clearinghouse.

(d) If a local law enforcement agency investigating a report of a missing child or missing person obtains a warrant for the arrest of a person for taking or retaining the missing child or missing person, the local law enforcement agency shall immediately enter the name and other descriptive information of the person into the national crime information center wanted person file if the person meets the center's criteria. The local law enforcement agency shall also enter all available identifying features, including dental records, fingerprints, and other physical characteristics of the missing child or missing person. The information shall be cross-referenced with the information in the national crime information center missing person file.

(e) A local law enforcement agency that has access to the national crime information center database shall cooperate with other law enforcement agencies in entering or retrieving information from the national crime information center database.

(f) Immediately after the return of a missing child or missing person or the identification of an unidentified body, the local law enforcement agency having jurisdiction of the investigation shall:

(1) clear the entry in the national crime information center database; and

(2) notify the National Missing and Unidentified Persons System.

(g) On determining the location of a child under Subsection (a)(1) or (2), other than a child who is subject to the continuing jurisdiction of a district court, an officer shall take possession of the child and shall deliver or arrange for the delivery of the child to a person entitled to possession of the child. If the person entitled to possession of the child is not immediately available, the law enforcement officer shall deliver the child to the Department of Protective and Regulatory Services.

Sec. 63.0091. Law Enforcement Requirements Regarding Reports of Certain Missing Children.

(a) The public safety director of the Department of Public Safety shall adopt rules regarding the procedures for a local law enforcement agency on receiving a report of a missing child who:

(1) had been reported missing on four or more occasions in the 24-month period preceding the date of the current report;

(2) is in foster care or in the conservatorship of the Department of Family and Protective Services and had been reported missing on two or more occasions in the 24-month period preceding the date of the current report; or

(3) is under 14 years of age and otherwise determined by the local law enforcement agency or the Department of Public Safety to be at a high risk of human trafficking, sexual assault, exploitation, abuse, or neglectful supervision.

(b) The rules adopted under this article must require that in entering information regarding the report into the national crime information center missing person file as required by Article 63.009(a)(3) for a missing child described by Subsection (a), the local law enforcement agency shall indicate, in the manner specified in the rules, that the child is at a high risk of harm and include relevant information regarding any prior occasions on which the child was reported missing.

(c) If, at the time the initial entry into the national crime information center missing person file is made, the local law enforcement agency has not determined that the requirements of this article apply to the report of the missing child, the information required by Subsection (b) must be added to the entry promptly after the agency investigating the report or the Department of Public Safety determines that the missing child is described by Subsection (a).

Art. 63.0092. Option to Designate Missing Child As High Risk.

(a) This article applies to a report of a missing child who is at least 14 years of age and who a local law enforcement agency or the Department of Public Safety determines is at a high risk of human trafficking, sexual assault, exploitation, abuse, or neglectful supervision.

(b) In entering information regarding a report described by Subsection (a) into the national crime information center missing person file as required by Article 63.009(a)(3), the local law enforcement agency may indicate that the child is at a high risk of harm and may include any other relevant information.

Art. 63.010. Attorney General to Require Compliance.

The attorney general shall require each law enforcement agency to comply with this chapter and may seek writs of mandamus or other appropriate remedies to enforce this chapter.

Art. 63.011. Missing Children Investigations.

On the written request made to a law enforcement agency by a parent, foster parent, managing or possessory conservator, guardian of the person or the estate, or other court-appointed custodian of a child whose whereabouts are unknown, the law enforcement agency shall request from the missing children and missing persons information clearinghouse information concerning the child that may aid the person making the request in the identification or location of the child.

Art. 63.012. Report of Inquiry.

A law enforcement agency to which a request has been made under Article 63.011 of this code shall report to the parent on the results of its inquiry within 14 days after the day that the written request is filed with the law enforcement agency.

Art. 63.013. Information to Clearinghouse.

Each law enforcement agency shall provide to the missing children and missing persons information clearinghouse:

(1) any information that would assist in the location or identification of any missing child who has been reported to the agency as missing; and

(2) any information regarding an attempted child abduction that has been reported to the agency or that the agency has received from any person or another agency.

Art. 63.014. Cross-Checking and Matching.

(a) The clearinghouse shall cross-check and attempt to match unidentified bodies with missing children or missing persons. When the clearinghouse discovers a possible match between an unidentified body and a missing child or missing person, the Department of Public Safety shall notify the appropriate law enforcement agencies.

(b) Those law enforcement agencies that receive notice of a possible match shall make arrangements for positive identification and complete and close out the investigation with notification to the clearinghouse.

Art. 63.015. Availability of Information Through Other Agencies.

(a) On the request of any law enforcement agency, a city or state agency shall furnish the law enforcement agency with any information about a

Code of Criminal Procedure

missing child or missing person that will assist in completing the investigation.

(b) The information given under Subsection (a) of this article is confidential and may not be released to any other person outside of the law enforcement agency.

Art. 63.016. Donations.

The Department of Public Safety may accept money donated from any source to assist in financing the activities and purposes of the missing children and missing persons information clearinghouse.

Art. 63.017. Confidentiality of Certain Records.

Clearinghouse records that relate to the investigation by a law enforcement agency of a missing child, a missing person, or an unidentified body and records or notations that the clearinghouse maintains for internal use in matters relating to missing children, missing persons, or unidentified bodies are confidential.

Art. 63.018. Death Certificates.

A physician who performs a postmortem examination on the body of an unidentified person shall complete and file a death certificate in accordance with Chapter 193, Health and Safety Code. The physician shall note on the certificate the name of the law enforcement agency that submitted the body for examination and shall send a copy of the certificate to the clearinghouse not later than the 10th working day after the date the physician files the certificate.

Art. 63.019. School Records System.

(a) On enrollment of a child under 11 years of age in a school for the first time at the school, the school shall:

(1) request from the person enrolling the child the name of each previous school attended by the child;

(2) request from each school identified in Subdivision (1), the school records for the child and, if the person enrolling the child provides copies of previous school records, request verification from the school of the child's name, address, birth date, and grades and dates attended; and

(3) notify the person enrolling the student that not later than the 30th day after enrollment, or the 90th day if the child was not born in the United States, the person must provide:

(A) a certified copy of the child's birth certificate; or

(B) other reliable proof of the child's identity and age and a signed statement explaining the person's inability to produce a copy of the child's birth certificate.

(b) If a person enrolls a child under 11 years of age in school and does not provide the valid prior school information or documentation required by this section, the school shall notify the appropriate law enforcement agency before the 31st day after the person fails to comply with this section. On receipt of notification, the law enforcement agency shall immediately check the clearinghouse to determine if the child has been reported missing. If the child has been reported missing, the law enforcement agency shall immediately notify other appropriate law enforcement agencies that the missing child has been located.

Art. 63.020. Duty of Schools and Other Entities to Flag Missing Children's Records.

(a) When a report that a child under 11 years of age is missing is received by a law enforcement agency, the agency shall immediately notify each school and day care facility that the child attended or in which the child was enrolled as well as the bureau of vital statistics, if the child was born in the state, that the child is missing.

(b) On receipt of notice that a child under 11 years of age is missing, the bureau of vital statistics shall notify the appropriate municipal or county birth certificate agency that the child is missing.

(c) A school, day care facility, or birth certificate agency that receives notice concerning a child under this section shall flag the child's records that are maintained by the school, facility, or agency.

(d) The law enforcement agency shall notify the clearinghouse that the notification required under this section has been made. The clearinghouse shall provide the notice required under this section if the clearinghouse determines that the notification has not been made by the law enforcement agency.

(e) If a missing child under 11 years of age, who was the subject of a missing child report made in this state, was born in or attended a school or licensed day care facility in another state, the law enforcement agency shall notify law enforcement or the missing and exploited children clearinghouse in each appropriate state regarding the missing child and request the law enforcement agency or clearinghouse to contact the state birth certificate agency and each school or licensed day care facility the missing child attended to flag the missing child's records.

Code of Criminal Procedure

Art. 63.021. System for Flagging Records.

(a) On receipt of notification by a law enforcement agency or the clearinghouse regarding a missing child under 11 years of age, the school, day care facility, or birth certificate agency shall maintain the child's records in its possession so that on receipt of a request regarding the child, the school, day care facility, or agency will be able to notify law enforcement or the clearinghouse that a request for a flagged record has been made.

(b) When a request concerning a flagged record is made in person, the school, day care facility, or agency may not advise the requesting party that the request concerns a missing child and shall:

(1) require the person requesting the flagged record to complete a form stating the person's name, address, telephone number, and relationship to the child for whom a request is made and the name, address, and birth date of the child;

(2) obtain a copy of the requesting party's driver's license or other photographic identification, if possible;

(3) if the request is for a birth certificate, inform the requesting party that a copy of a certificate will be sent by mail; and

(4) immediately notify the appropriate law enforcement agency that a request has been made concerning a flagged record and include a physical description of the requesting party, the identity and address of the requesting party, and a copy of the requesting party's driver's license or other photographic identification.

(c) After providing the notification required under Subsection (a)(4), the school, day care facility, or agency shall mail a copy of the requested record to the requesting party on or after the 21st day after the date of the request.

(d) When a request concerning a flagged record is made in writing, the school, day care facility, or agency may not advise the party that the request concerns a missing child and shall immediately notify the appropriate law enforcement agency that a request has been made concerning a flagged record and provide to the law enforcement agency a copy of the written request. After providing the notification under this subsection, the school, day care facility, or agency shall mail a copy of the requested record to the requesting party on or after the 21st day after the date of the request.

Art. 63.022. Removal of Flag from Records.

(a) On the return of a missing child under 11 years of age, the law enforcement agency shall notify each school or day care facility that has maintained flagged records for the child and the bureau of vital statistics that the child is no longer missing. The law enforcement agency shall notify the clearinghouse that notification under this section has been made. The bureau of vital statistics shall notify the appropriate municipal or county birth certificate agency. The clearinghouse shall notify the school, day care facility, or bureau of vital statistics that the missing child is no longer missing if the clearinghouse determines that the notification was not provided by the law enforcement agency.

(b) On notification by the law enforcement agency or the clearinghouse that a missing child has been recovered, the school, day care facility, or birth certificate agency that maintained flagged records shall remove the flag from the records.

(c) A school, day care facility, or birth certificate agency that has reason to believe a missing child has been recovered may request confirmation that the missing child has been recovered from the appropriate law enforcement agency or the clearinghouse. If a response is not received after the 45th day after the date of the request for confirmation, the school, day care facility, or birth certificate agency may remove the flag from the record and shall inform the law enforcement agency or the clearinghouse that the flag has been removed.

SUBCHAPTER B
UNIVERSITY OF NORTH TEXAS HEALTH SCIENCE CENTER AT FORT WORTH MISSING PERSONS DNA DATABASE

Art. 63.051. Definitions.

In this subchapter:

(1) "Board" means the board of regents of the University of North Texas System.

(2) "Center" means the University of North Texas Health Science Center at Fort Worth.

(3) "DNA" means deoxyribonucleic acid.

(4) "DNA database" means the database containing forensic DNA analysis results, including any known name of the person who is the subject of the forensic DNA analysis, that is maintained by the center.

(5) "High-risk missing person" means:

(A) a person missing as a result of an abduction by a stranger;

(B) a person missing under suspicious or unknown circumstances; or

(C) a person who has been missing more than 30 days, or less than 30 days at the discretion of the investigating agency, if there is reason to believe that the person is in danger or deceased.

(6) "Law enforcement agency" means the law enforcement agency primarily responsible for investigating a report of a high-risk missing person.

Art. 63.0515. Criminal Justice Agency.

For purposes of this subchapter, the center is a criminal justice agency that performs forensic DNA analyses on evidence, including evidence related to a case involving unidentified human remains or a high-risk missing person. The center shall comply with 42 U.S.C. Section 14132.

Art. 63.052. Establishment of DNA Database for Missing or Unidentified Persons.

(a) The board shall develop at the University of North Texas Health Science Center at Fort Worth a DNA database for any case based on the report of unidentified human remains or a report of a high-risk missing person.

(b) The database may be used to identify unidentified human remains and high-risk missing persons.

(c) [Repealed by Acts 2011, 82nd Leg., ch. 320 (H.B. 2385), § 3, effective June 17, 2011.]

Art. 63.053. Information Stored in Database.

(a) The database required in Article 63.052 may contain only DNA genetic markers that are commonly recognized as appropriate for human identification. Except to the extent that those markers are appropriate for human identification, the database may not contain DNA genetic markers that predict biological function. The center shall select the DNA genetic markers for inclusion in the DNA database based on existing technology for forensic DNA analysis.

(b) The results of the forensic DNA analysis must be compatible with the CODIS DNA database established by the Federal Bureau of Investigation and the center must make the results available for inclusion in that database.

Art. 63.054. Comparison of Samples.

The center shall compare DNA samples taken from unidentified human remains with DNA samples taken from personal articles belonging to high-risk missing persons or from parents of high-risk missing persons or other appropriate persons.

Art. 63.055. Standards Collection; Storage.

In consultation with the center, the board by rule shall develop standards and guidelines for the collection of DNA samples submitted to the center and the center's storage of DNA samples.

Art. 63.056. Collection of Samples from Unidentified Human Remains.

(a) A physician acting on the request of a justice of the peace under Subchapter A, Chapter 49, a county coroner, a county medical examiner, or other law enforcement entity, as appropriate, shall collect samples from unidentified human remains. The justice of the peace, coroner, medical examiner, or other law enforcement entity shall submit those samples to the center for forensic DNA analysis and inclusion of the results in the DNA database.

(b) After the center has performed the forensic DNA analysis, the center shall return the remaining sample to the entity that submitted the sample under Subsection (a).

Art. 63.057. Duty of Law Enforcement Agency to Notify Appropriate Persons Regarding Provision of Voluntary Sample.

Not later than the 30th day after the date a report of a high-risk missing person is filed, the law enforcement agency shall inform a parent or any other person considered appropriate by the agency that the person may provide:

(1) a DNA sample for forensic DNA analysis; or

(2) for purposes of DNA sampling, a personal article belonging to the high-risk missing person.

Art. 63.058. Release Form.

(a) The center shall develop a standard release form that authorizes a parent or other appropriate person to voluntarily provide under Article 63.057 a DNA sample or a personal article for purposes of DNA sampling. The release must explain that the DNA sample is to be used only to identify the high-risk missing person.

(b) A law enforcement agency may not use any form of incentive or coercion to compel the parent or other appropriate person to provide a sample or article under this subchapter.

Art. 63.059. Protocol for Obtaining Samples Relating to High-Risk Missing Persons.

(a) The law enforcement agency shall take DNA samples from parents or other appropriate persons under Article 63.057 in any manner prescribed by the center.

(b) The center shall develop a model kit to be used by a law enforcement agency to take DNA samples from parents or other appropriate persons.

Art. 63.060. Submission of Sample to Center.

(a) Before submitting to the center a DNA sample obtained under Article 63.057, the law enforcement agency shall reverify the status of a high-risk missing person.

(b) As soon as practicable after a DNA sample is obtained, the law enforcement agency shall submit the DNA sample, a copy of the missing person's report, and any supplemental information to the center.

Art. 63.061. Destruction of Samples.

All DNA samples extracted from a living person shall be destroyed after a positive identification is made and a report is issued.

Art. 63.062. Confidentiality.

(a) Except as provided by Subsection (b), the results of a forensic DNA analysis performed by the center are confidential.

(b) The center may disclose the results of a forensic DNA analysis only to:

(1) personnel of the center;

(2) law enforcement agencies;

(3) justices of the peace, coroners, medical examiners, or other law enforcement entities submitting a sample to the center under Article 63.056;

(4) attorneys representing the state; and

(5) a parent or other appropriate person voluntarily providing a DNA sample or an article under Article 63.057.

Art. 63.063. Criminal Penalty.

(a) A person who collects, processes, or stores a DNA sample from a living person for forensic DNA analysis under this subchapter commits an offense if the person intentionally violates Article 63.061 or 63.062.

(b) An offense under this section is a Class B misdemeanor.

Art. 63.064. Civil Penalty.

A person who collects, processes, or stores a DNA sample from a living person for forensic DNA analysis under this subchapter and who intentionally violates Article 63.061 or 63.062 is liable in civil damages to the donor of the DNA in the amount of $5,000 for each violation, plus reasonable attorney's fees and court costs.

Art. 63.065. Missing Persons DNA Database Fund.

(a) The missing persons DNA database fund is a separate account in the general revenue fund.

(b) Notwithstanding Article 56B.453(a), the legislature may appropriate money in the compensation to victims of crime fund and the compensation to victims of crime auxiliary fund to fund the University of North Texas Health Science Center at Fort Worth missing persons DNA database. Legislative appropriations under this subsection shall be deposited to the credit of the account created under Subsection (a).

(c) Money in the account may be used only for purposes of developing and maintaining the DNA database as described by this section.

(d) The center may use money in the account only to:

(1) establish and maintain center infrastructure;

(2) pay the costs of DNA sample storage, forensic DNA analysis, and labor costs for cases of high-risk missing persons and unidentified human remains;

(3) reimburse counties for the purposes of pathology and exhumation as considered necessary by the center;

(4) publicize the DNA database for the purpose of contacting parents and other appropriate persons so that they may provide a DNA sample or a personal article for DNA sampling;

(5) educate law enforcement officers about the DNA database and DNA sampling; and

(6) provide outreach programs related to the purposes of this chapter.

(e) Section 403.095(b), Government Code, does not apply to the account established under Subsection (a).

Art. 63.066. Backlog of Unidentified Human Remains: Advisory Committee and Outsourcing.

(a) The center shall create an advisory committee, consisting of medical examiners, law enforcement officials, and other interested persons as determined appropriate by the center, to impose priorities regarding the identification of the backlog of high-risk missing person cases and unidentified human remains.

(b) The center shall use any available federal funding to assist in reducing the backlog of

Code of Criminal Procedure

high-risk missing person cases and unidentified human remains.

(c) The reduction of the backlog may be outsourced to other appropriate laboratories at the center's discretion.

Art. 63.067. Initial Operations [Expired].

Expired pursuant to Acts 2001, 77th Leg., ch. 1496 (S.B. 1304), § 1, effective January 1, 2006.

CHAPTER 64
MOTION FOR FORENSIC DNA TESTING

Art. 64.01. Motion.

(a) In this section, "biological material":

(1) means an item that is in possession of the state and that contains blood, semen, hair, saliva, skin tissue or cells, fingernail scrapings, bone, bodily fluids, or other identifiable biological evidence that may be suitable for forensic DNA testing; and

(2) includes the contents of a sexual assault evidence collection kit.

(a-1) A convicted person may submit to the convicting court a motion for forensic DNA testing of evidence that has a reasonable likelihood of containing biological material. The motion must be accompanied by an affidavit, sworn to by the convicted person, containing statements of fact in support of the motion.

(b) The motion may request forensic DNA testing only of evidence described by Subsection (a-1) that was secured in relation to the offense that is the basis of the challenged conviction and was in the possession of the state during the trial of the offense, but:

(1) was not previously subjected to DNA testing; or

(2) although previously subjected to DNA testing:

(A) can be subjected to testing with newer testing techniques that provide a reasonable likelihood of results that are more accurate and probative than the results of the previous test; or

(B) was tested:

(i) at a laboratory that ceased conducting DNA testing after an audit by the Texas Forensic Science Commission revealed the laboratory engaged in faulty testing practices; and

(ii) during the period identified in the audit as involving faulty testing practices.

(c) A convicted person is entitled to counsel during a proceeding under this chapter. The convicting court shall appoint counsel for the convicted person if the person informs the court that the person wishes to submit a motion under this chapter, the court finds reasonable grounds for a motion to be filed, and the court determines that the person is indigent. Counsel must be appointed under this subsection not later than the 45th day after the date the court finds reasonable grounds or the date the court determines that the person is indigent, whichever is later. Compensation of counsel is provided in the same manner as is required by:

(1) Article 11.071 for the representation of a petitioner convicted of a capital felony; and

(2) Chapter 26 for the representation in a habeas corpus hearing of an indigent defendant convicted of a felony other than a capital felony.

Art. 64.011. Guardians and Other Representatives.

(a) In this chapter, "guardian of a convicted person" means a person who is the legal guardian of the convicted person, whether the legal relationship between the guardian and convicted person exists because of the age of the convicted person or because of the physical or mental incompetency of the convicted person.

(b) A guardian of a convicted person may submit motions for the convicted person under this chapter and is entitled to counsel otherwise provided to a convicted person under this chapter.

Art. 64.02. Notice to State; Response.

(a) On receipt of the motion, the convicting court shall:

(1) provide the attorney representing the state with a copy of the motion; and

(2) require the attorney representing the state to take one of the following actions in response to the motion not later than the 60th day after the date the motion is served on the attorney representing the state:

(A) deliver the evidence to the court, along with a description of the condition of the evidence; or

(B) explain in writing to the court why the state cannot deliver the evidence to the court.

(b) The convicting court may proceed under Article 64.03 after the response period described by Subsection (a)(2) has expired, regardless of whether the attorney representing the state submitted a response under that subsection.

Art. 64.03. Requirements; Testing.

(a) A convicting court may order forensic DNA testing under this chapter only if:

(1) the court finds that:
(A) the evidence:
(i) still exists and is in a condition making DNA testing possible; and
(ii) has been subjected to a chain of custody sufficient to establish that it has not been substituted, tampered with, replaced, or altered in any material respect;
(B) there is a reasonable likelihood that the evidence contains biological material suitable for DNA testing; and
(C) identity was or is an issue in the case; and
(2) the convicted person establishes by a preponderance of the evidence that:
(A) the person would not have been convicted if exculpatory results had been obtained through DNA testing; and
(B) the request for the proposed DNA testing is not made to unreasonably delay the execution of sentence or administration of justice.

(b) A convicted person who pleaded guilty or nolo contendere or, whether before or after conviction, made a confession or similar admission in the case may submit a motion under this chapter, and the convicting court is prohibited from finding that identity was not an issue in the case solely on the basis of that plea, confession, or admission, as applicable.

(b-1) Notwithstanding Subsection (c), a convicting court shall order that the requested DNA testing be done with respect to evidence described by Article 64.01(b)(2)(B) if the court finds in the affirmative the issues listed in Subsection (a)(1), regardless of whether the convicted person meets the requirements of Subsection (a)(2). The court may order the test to be conducted by any laboratory that the court may order to conduct a test under Subsection (c).

(c) If the convicting court finds in the affirmative the issues listed in Subsection (a)(1) and the convicted person meets the requirements of Subsection (a)(2), the court shall order that the requested forensic DNA testing be conducted. The court may order the test to be conducted by:
(1) the Department of Public Safety;
(2) a laboratory operating under a contract with the department; or
(3) on the request of the convicted person, another laboratory if that laboratory is accredited under Article 38.01.

(d) If the convicting court orders that the forensic DNA testing be conducted by a laboratory other than a Department of Public Safety laboratory or a laboratory under contract with the department, the State of Texas is not liable for the cost of testing under this subsection unless good cause for payment of that cost has been shown. A political subdivision of the state is not liable for the cost of testing under this subsection, regardless of whether good cause for payment of that cost has been shown. If the court orders that the testing be conducted by a laboratory described by this subsection, the court shall include in the order requirements that:
(1) the DNA testing be conducted in a timely and efficient manner under reasonable conditions designed to protect the integrity of the evidence and the testing process;
(2) the DNA testing employ a scientific method sufficiently reliable and relevant to be admissible under Rule 702, Texas Rules of Evidence; and
(3) on completion of the DNA testing, the results of the testing and all data related to the testing required for an evaluation of the test results be immediately filed with the court and copies of the results and data be served on the convicted person and the attorney representing the state.

(e) The convicting court, not later than the 30th day after the conclusion of a proceeding under this chapter, shall forward the results to the Department of Public Safety.

Art. 64.035. Unidentified DNA Profiles.

If an analyzed sample meets the applicable requirements of state or federal submission policies, on completion of the testing under Article 64.03, the convicting court shall order any unidentified DNA profile to be compared with the DNA profiles in:
(1) the DNA database established by the Federal Bureau of Investigation; and
(2) the DNA database maintained by the Department of Public Safety under Subchapter G, Chapter 411, Government Code.

Art. 64.04. Finding.

After examining the results of testing under Article 64.03 and any comparison of a DNA profile under Article 64.035, the convicting court shall hold a hearing and make a finding as to whether, had the results been available during the trial of the offense, it is reasonably probable that the person would not have been convicted.

Art. 64.05. Appeals.

An appeal under this chapter is to a court of appeals in the same manner as an appeal of any other criminal matter, except that if the convicted person was convicted in a capital case and was sentenced to death, the appeal is a direct appeal to the court of criminal appeals.

CHAPTER 66. CRIMINAL HISTORY RECORD SYSTEM

SUBCHAPTER A. GENERAL PROVISIONS

Art. 66.001. Definitions.

In this chapter:

(1) "Administration of criminal justice" means the detection, apprehension, detention, pretrial release, post-trial release, prosecution, adjudication, correctional supervision, or rehabilitation of an offender. The term includes criminal identification activities and the collection, storage, and dissemination of criminal history record information.

(2) "Computerized criminal history system" means the database containing arrest, disposition, and other criminal history maintained by the Department of Public Safety.

(3) "Corrections tracking system" means the database maintained by the Texas Department of Criminal Justice on all offenders under the department's supervision.

(4) "Council" means the Criminal Justice Policy Council.

(5) "Criminal justice agency" means a federal or state agency that is engaged in the administration of criminal justice under a statute or executive order and allocates a substantial part of the agency's annual budget to the administration of criminal justice.

(6) "Criminal justice information system" means the computerized criminal history system and the corrections tracking system.

(7) "Disposition" means an action that results in the termination, transfer to another jurisdiction, or indeterminate suspension of the prosecution of a criminal charge.

(8) "Electronic means" means the transmission of data between word processors, data processors, or similar automated information equipment over dedicated cables, commercial lines, or other similar methods of transmission.

(9) "Incident number" means the unique number assigned to a specific person during a specific arrest.

(10) "Offender" means any person who is assigned an incident number.

(11) "Offense code" means the numeric code for each offense category.

(12) "Release" means the termination of jurisdiction over an individual by the criminal justice system.

(13) "State identification number" means the unique number assigned by the Department of Public Safety to each person whose name appears in the criminal justice information system. (Code Crim. Proc., Arts. 60.01(1), (3), (4), (5), (6), (7), (8), (9), (10), (11), (13), (14), (16).)

SUBCHAPTER B. CRIMINAL JUSTICE INFORMATION SYSTEM

Art. 66.051. Purpose and Functions.

The criminal justice information system shall be maintained to supply the state with a system:

(1) that provides an accurate criminal history record depository to:

(A) law enforcement officers; and

(B) criminal justice agencies for operational decision making;

(2) from which accurate criminal justice system modeling can be conducted; and

(3) that improves:

(A) the quality of data used to conduct impact analyses of proposed legislative changes in the criminal justice system; and

(B) the ability of interested parties to analyze the functioning of the criminal justice system. (Code Crim. Proc., Art. 60.02(c).)

Art. 66.052. Implementation and Operation of Criminal Justice Information System.

(a) The Department of Public Safety shall designate offense codes and has the sole responsibility for designating the state identification number for each person whose name appears in the criminal justice information system.

(b) The Department of Public Safety and the Texas Department of Criminal Justice shall implement a system to link the computerized criminal history system and the corrections tracking system. (Code Crim. Proc., Arts. 60.02(e), (f) (part).)

Art. 66.053. Information Collected.

For each arrest for a felony or misdemeanor other than a misdemeanor punishable by fine only, the criminal justice information system must include information relating to:

(1) offenders;

(2) arrests;
(3) prosecutions;
(4) the disposition of cases by courts;
(5) sentencing; and
(6) the handling of offenders received by a correctional agency, facility, or other institution. (Code Crim. Proc., Art. 60.05.)

Art. 66.054. Fingerprint and Arrest Information in Criminal Justice Information System.

(a) When a jurisdiction transmits fingerprints and arrest information by a remote terminal accessing the statewide automated fingerprint identification system, the Department of Public Safety shall use that transmission to create:

(1) a permanent record in the criminal justice information system; or

(2) a temporary arrest record in the criminal justice information system to be maintained by the department until the department receives and processes the physical copy of the arrest information.

(b) The Department of Public Safety shall make available to a criminal justice agency making a background criminal inquiry any information contained in a temporary arrest record maintained by the department, including a statement that a physical copy of the arrest information was not available at the time the information was entered in the criminal justice information system. (Code Crim. Proc., Art. 60.12.)

SUBCHAPTER C COMPUTERIZED CRIMINAL HISTORY SYSTEM

Art. 66.101. Computerized Criminal History System Database.

(a) The Department of Public Safety shall record data and maintain the computerized criminal history system that serves as the record creation point for criminal history information maintained by the state.

(b) The computerized criminal history system must contain the information required by this chapter.

(c) The Department of Public Safety shall operate the computerized criminal history system and develop the necessary interfaces in the system to accommodate inquiries from the statewide automated fingerprint identification system implemented by the department. (Code Crim. Proc., Arts. 60.02(b), (d), (g).)

Art. 66.102. Information Contained in Computerized Criminal History System.

(a) In this article:

(1) "Appeal" means the review of a decision of a lower court by a superior court other than by collateral attack.

(2) "Rejected case" means:

(A) a charge that, after the arrest of the offender, the prosecutor declines to include in an information or present to a grand jury; or

(B) an information or indictment that, after the arrest of the offender, the prosecutor refuses to prosecute.

(b) Information in the computerized criminal history system relating to an offender must include the offender's:

(1) name, including other names by which the offender is known;
(2) date of birth;
(3) physical description, including sex, weight, height, race, ethnicity, eye color, hair color, scars, marks, and tattoos; and
(4) state identification number.

(c) Information in the computerized criminal history system relating to an arrest must include:

(1) the offender's name;
(2) the offender's state identification number;
(3) the arresting law enforcement agency;
(4) the arrest charge, by offense code and incident number;
(5) whether the arrest charge is a misdemeanor or felony;
(6) the date of the arrest;
(7) the exact disposition of the case by a law enforcement agency following the arrest; and
(8) the date of disposition of the case by the law enforcement agency.

(d) Information in the computerized criminal history system relating to a prosecution must include:

(1) each charged offense, by offense code and incident number;
(2) the level of the offense charged or the degree of the offense charged for each offense in Subdivision (1); and
(3) for a rejected case:
(A) the date of rejection;
(B) the offense code;
(C) the incident number; and
(D) whether the rejection is a result of a successful pretrial diversion program.

(e) Information in the computerized criminal history system relating to the disposition of a case other than a rejected case must include:

(1) the final pleading to each charged offense and the level of the offense;

(2) a listing of each charged offense disposed of by the court and:

(A) the date of disposition;

(B) the offense code for the disposed charge and incident number; and

(C) the type of disposition; and

(3) for a conviction that is appealed, the final court decision and the final disposition of the offender's case on appeal.

(f) Information in the computerized criminal history system relating to sentencing must include for each sentence:

(1) the sentencing date;

(2) the sentence for each offense, by offense code and incident number;

(3) if the offender was sentenced to confinement:

(A) the agency that receives custody of the offender;

(B) the length of the sentence for each offense; and

(C) if multiple sentences were ordered, whether the sentences were ordered to be served consecutively or concurrently;

(4) if the offender was sentenced to pay a fine, the amount of the fine;

(5) if a sentence to pay a fine or to confinement was ordered but was deferred, probated, suspended, or otherwise not imposed:

(A) the length of the sentence or the amount of the fine that was deferred, probated, suspended, or otherwise not imposed; and

(B) the offender's name, offense code, and incident number;

(6) if a sentence other than a fine or confinement was ordered, a description of the sentence ordered; and

(7) whether the judgment imposing the sentence reflects an affirmative finding entered under Article 42.013 (Finding of Family Violence).

(g) The Department of Public Safety shall maintain in the computerized criminal history system any information the department maintains in the central database under Article 62.005.

(h) In addition to the information described by this article, information in the computerized criminal history system must include the age of the victim of the offense if the offender was arrested for or charged with an offense under the following provisions of the Penal Code:

(1) Section 20.04(a)(4) (Aggravated Kidnapping), if the offender committed the offense with the intent to violate or abuse the victim sexually;

(2) Section 20A.02 (Trafficking of Persons), if the offender:

(A) trafficked a person with the intent or knowledge that the person would engage in sexual conduct, as defined by Section 43.25, Penal Code; or

(B) benefited from participating in a venture that involved a trafficked person engaging in sexual conduct, as defined by Section 43.25, Penal Code;

(3) Section 21.02 (Continuous Sexual Abuse of Young Child or Disabled Individual);

(4) Section 21.11 (Indecency with a Child);

(5) Section 22.011 (Sexual Assault) or 22.021 (Aggravated Sexual Assault);

(6) Section 30.02 (Burglary), if the offense is punishable under Subsection (d) of that section and the offender committed the offense with the intent to commit an offense described by Subdivision (1), (4), or (5);

(7) Section 43.05(a)(2) (Compelling Prostitution); or

(8) Section 43.25 (Sexual Performance by a Child).

Art. 66.103. Duties of Texas Department of Criminal Justice Regarding Criminal Justice Information System.

Data received by the Texas Department of Criminal Justice that is required by the Department of Public Safety for the preparation of a criminal history record shall be made available to the computerized criminal history system not later than the seventh day after the date on which the Texas Department of Criminal Justice receives the request for the data from the Department of Public Safety. (Code Crim. Proc., Art. 60.02(f) (part).)

Art. 66.104. Duties of Licensing Agencies to Provide Information Regarding License Holders.

(a) The Texas Medical Board, the Texas Department of Licensing and Regulation, only with respect to a person licensed under Chapter 202, Occupations Code, the State Board of Dental Examiners, the Texas State Board of Pharmacy, the Texas Behavioral Health Executive Council, only with respect to a person licensed under Chapter 501, Occupations Code, and the State Board of Veterinary Medical Examiners shall provide to the Department of Public Safety through electronic means, magnetic tape, or disk, as specified by the department, a list of each person licensed by the respective agency, including the person's name and date of birth and any other personal descriptive information required by the department. Each agency shall update the information and submit the updated information quarterly to the department.

(b) The Department of Public Safety shall:

(1) perform at least quarterly a computer match of the licensing list against the convictions maintained in the computerized criminal history system; and

(2) report to the appropriate licensing agency for verification and administrative action, as considered appropriate by the licensing agency, the name of any person found to have a record of conviction, other than a defendant whose prosecution is deferred during a period of community supervision without an adjudication of guilt or a plea of guilty.

(c) The Department of Public Safety may charge a licensing agency a fee not to exceed the actual direct cost incurred by the department in performing a computer match and reporting to the agency under Subsection (b).

(d) The transmission of information by electronic means under Subsection (a) does not affect whether the information is subject to disclosure under Chapter 552, Government Code. (Code Crim. Proc., Art. 60.061.)

Art. 66.105. Information Related to Misused Identity.

(a) On receipt of information from a local law enforcement agency under Article 2.28, the Department of Public Safety shall:

(1) provide the notice described by Article 2.28(1) to the person whose identity was misused, if the local law enforcement agency was unable to notify the person under that subdivision;

(2) take action to ensure that the information maintained in the computerized criminal history system reflects the use of the person's identity as a stolen alias; and

(3) notify the Texas Department of Criminal Justice that the person's identifying information may have been falsely used by an inmate in the custody of the Texas Department of Criminal Justice.

(b) On receipt of a declaration under Section 411.0421, Government Code, or on receipt of information similar to that contained in a declaration filed under that section, the Department of Public Safety shall separate information maintained in the computerized criminal history system regarding an individual whose identity has been misused from information maintained in that system regarding the person who misused the identity. (Code Crim. Proc., Art. 60.19.)

Art. 66.106. Information Related to Non-Fingerprint Supported Actions.

(a) On receipt of a report of prosecution or court disposition information from a jurisdiction for which corresponding arrest data does not exist in the computerized criminal history system, the Department of Public Safety shall enter the report into a non-fingerprint supported file that is separate from the computerized criminal history system.

(b) The Department of Public Safety shall grant access to records in a non-fingerprint supported file created under Subsection (a) that include the subject's name or other identifier in the same manner as the department is required to grant access to criminal history record information under Subchapter F, Chapter 411, Government Code.

(c) On receipt of a report of arrest information that corresponds to a record in a non-fingerprint supported file created under Subsection (a), the Department of Public Safety shall transfer the record from the non-fingerprint supported file to the computerized criminal history system. (Code Crim. Proc., Art. 60.20.)

SUBCHAPTER D CORRECTIONS TRACKING SYSTEM

Art. 66.151. Corrections Tracking System Database.

(a) The Texas Department of Criminal Justice shall record data and establish and maintain the corrections tracking system.

(b) The corrections tracking system must contain the information required by this chapter. (Code Crim. Proc., Arts. 60.02(a), (d).)

Art. 66.152. Information Contained in Corrections Tracking System.

(a) Information in the corrections tracking system relating to a sentence to be served under the jurisdiction of the Texas Department of Criminal Justice must include:

(1) the offender's name;

(2) the offender's state identification number;

(3) the sentencing date;

(4) the sentence for each offense, by offense code and incident number;

(5) if the offender was sentenced to imprisonment:

(A) the unit of imprisonment;

(B) the length of the sentence for each offense; and

(C) if multiple sentences were ordered, whether the sentences were ordered to be served consecutively or concurrently; and

(6) if a sentence other than a fine or imprisonment was ordered, a description of the sentence ordered.

Code of Criminal Procedure

(b) Sentencing information in the corrections tracking system must also include the following information about each community supervision, including deferred adjudication community supervision, or other alternative to imprisonment ordered:

(1) each conviction for which a sentence was ordered but was deferred, probated, suspended, or otherwise not imposed, by offense code and incident number; and

(2) if a sentence or portion of a sentence of imprisonment was deferred, probated, suspended, or otherwise not imposed:

(A) the offense, the sentence, and the amount of the sentence deferred, probated, suspended, or otherwise not imposed;

(B) a statement of whether any return to imprisonment or confinement was a condition of community supervision or an alternative sentence;

(C) the community supervision and corrections department exercising jurisdiction over the offender;

(D) the date the offender was received by a community supervision and corrections department;

(E) any program in which the offender is placed or has previously been placed and the level of supervision on which the offender is placed while under the jurisdiction of a community supervision and corrections department;

(F) the date a program described by Paragraph (E) begins, the date the program ends, and whether the program was completed successfully;

(G) the date a level of supervision described by Paragraph (E) begins and the date the level of supervision ends;

(H) if the offender's community supervision is revoked:

(i) the reason for the revocation and the date of revocation, by offense code and incident number; and

(ii) other current sentences of community supervision or other alternatives to confinement that have not been revoked, by offense code and incident number; and

(I) the date of the offender's release from the community supervision and corrections department.

(c) Information in the corrections tracking system relating to the handling of offenders must include the following information about each imprisonment, confinement, or execution of an offender:

(1) the date of the imprisonment or confinement;

(2) if the offender was sentenced to death:

(A) the date of execution; and

(B) if the death sentence was commuted, the sentence to which the sentence of death was commuted and the date of commutation;

(3) the date the offender was released from imprisonment or confinement and whether the release was a discharge or a release on parole or to mandatory supervision;

(4) if the offender is released on parole or to mandatory supervision:

(A) the offense for which the offender was convicted, by offense code and incident number;

(B) the date the offender was received by an office of the parole division of the Texas Department of Criminal Justice;

(C) the county in which the offender resides while under supervision;

(D) any program in which the offender is placed or has previously been placed and the level of supervision on which the offender is placed while under the jurisdiction of the parole division;

(E) the date a program described by Paragraph (D) begins, the date the program ends, and whether the program was completed successfully;

(F) the date a level of supervision described by Paragraph (D) begins and the date the level of supervision ends;

(G) if the offender's release status is revoked, the reason for the revocation and the date of revocation;

(H) the expiration date of the sentence; and

(I) the date on which the offender is:

(i) released from the parole division; or

(ii) granted clemency; and

(5) if the offender is released under Article 42A.202(b), the date of the offender's release. (Code Crim. Proc., Art. 60.052.)

SUBCHAPTER E
ACCESS TO INFORMATION IN CRIMINAL JUSTICE INFORMATION SYSTEM

Art. 66.201. Access to Databases by Criminal Justice Agencies and Other Entities.

(a) Criminal justice agencies, the Legislative Budget Board, and the council are entitled to access the databases of the Department of Public Safety, the Texas Juvenile Justice Department, and the Texas Department of Criminal Justice in accordance with applicable state or federal law or regulations.

(b) The access granted by this article does not entitle a criminal justice agency, the Legislative Budget Board, or the council to add, delete, or alter data maintained by another agency. (Code Crim. Proc., Art. 60.03(a).)

Art. 66.202. Request for Data File From Databases.

(a) The council or the Legislative Budget Board may submit to the Department of Public Safety, the Texas Juvenile Justice Department, and the Texas Department of Criminal Justice an annual request for a data file containing data elements from the departments' systems.

(b) The Department of Public Safety, the Texas Juvenile Justice Department, and the Texas Department of Criminal Justice shall provide the council and the Legislative Budget Board with the data file for the period requested, in accordance with state and federal law and regulations.

(c) If the council submits a data file request other than the annual data file request, the director of the agency maintaining the requested records must approve the request.

(d) The Legislative Budget Board may submit a data file request other than the annual data file request without the approval of the director of the agency maintaining the requested records. (Code Crim. Proc., Art. 60.03(b).)

Art. 66.203. Public Disclosure of Data Prohibited.

A criminal justice agency, the council, and the Legislative Budget Board may not disclose to the public information in an individual's criminal history record if the record is protected by state or federal law or regulation. (Code Crim. Proc., Art. 60.03(c).)

SUBCHAPTER F
DATA COLLECTION AND SUBMISSION

Art. 66.251. Uniform Incident Fingerprint Card.

(a) The Department of Public Safety, in consultation with the council, shall design, print, and distribute a uniform incident fingerprint card to each law enforcement agency in this state.

(b) The uniform incident fingerprint card must be:

(1) serially numbered with an incident number in such a manner that the individual incident of arrest may be readily ascertained; and

(2) a multiple-part form that:

(A) has space for information relating to each charge for which a person is arrested, the person's fingerprints, and other information relevant to the arrest;

(B) can be transmitted with the offender through the criminal justice process; and

(C) allows each law enforcement agency to report required data to the Department of Public Safety or the Texas Department of Criminal Justice.

(c) Subject to available telecommunications capacity, the Department of Public Safety shall develop the capability to receive the information on the uniform incident fingerprint card by electronic means from a law enforcement agency. The information must be in a form that is compatible with the form required for data supplied to the criminal justice information system. (Code Crim. Proc., Arts. 60.01(15), 60.07.)

Art. 66.252. Reporting of Information by Local Entities.

(a) The Department of Public Safety and the Texas Department of Criminal Justice by rule shall develop reporting procedures that:

(1) ensure that the offender processing data is reported from the time an offender is arrested until the time an offender is released; and

(2) provide measures and policies designed to identify and eliminate redundant reporting of information to the criminal justice information system.

(b) The arresting law enforcement agency shall prepare a uniform incident fingerprint card described by Article 66.251 and initiate the reporting process for each offender charged with:

(1) a felony;

(2) a misdemeanor for which a term of confinement may be imposed; or

(3) a misdemeanor punishable by fine only that involves family violence, as defined by Section 71.004, Family Code.

(b-1) At any time before final disposition of the case, the justice or judge of a court having jurisdiction of the case of a misdemeanor described by Subsection (b)(3) may order a law enforcement officer to use the uniform incident fingerprint card to take the fingerprints of an offender who is charged with the misdemeanor, but was not placed under custodial arrest at the time of the offense.

(c) The clerk of the court exercising jurisdiction over a case shall report the disposition of the case to the Department of Public Safety.

(d) Except as provided by Subsection (e) or as otherwise required by applicable state law or rule, information or data required by this chapter to be reported to the Department of Public Safety or the Texas Department of Criminal Justice shall be reported promptly but not later than the 30th day after the date on which the information or data is received by the agency responsible for reporting it.

Code of Criminal Procedure

(e) An offender's arrest shall be reported to the Department of Public Safety not later than the seventh day after the date of the arrest.

(f) A court that orders the release of an offender under Article 42A.202(b) when the offender is under a bench warrant and not physically imprisoned in the Texas Department of Criminal Justice shall report the release to the department not later than the seventh day after the date of the release. (Code Crim. Proc., Art. 60.08.)

(g) On disposition of a case in which an offender is charged with a misdemeanor described by Subsection (b)(3), the clerk of the court exercising jurisdiction over the case shall report the applicable information regarding the person's citation or arrest and the disposition of the case to the Department of Public Safety using a uniform incident fingerprint card described by Article 66.251 or an electronic methodology approved by the Department of Public Safety.

Art. 66.253. Compatibility of Data.

(a) Data supplied to the criminal justice information system must:

(1) be compatible with the system; and

(2) contain both incident numbers and state identification numbers.

(b) A discrete submission of information under this chapter must contain, in conjunction with the required information, the person's name and state identification number. (Code Crim. Proc., Art. 60.04.)

Art. 66.254. Electronic Reporting of Information.

Whenever possible, information relating to dispositions and subsequent offender processing data shall be reported electronically. (Code Crim. Proc., Art. 60.02(h).)

Art. 66.255. Information on Subsequent Arrests.

The Department of Public Safety and the Texas Department of Criminal Justice shall develop the capability to send by electronic means information about the subsequent arrest of a person under supervision to:

(1) the community supervision and corrections department serving the court of original jurisdiction; or

(2) the district parole office supervising the person. (Code Crim. Proc., Art. 60.18.)

SUBCHAPTER G
DUTIES OF CRIMINAL JUSTICE AGENCIES AND CERTAIN COURT CLERKS

Art. 66.301. Duties of Criminal Justice Agencies.

(a) Each criminal justice agency shall:

(1) compile and maintain records needed for reporting data required by the Department of Public Safety and the Texas Department of Criminal Justice;

(2) transmit to the Department of Public Safety and the Texas Department of Criminal Justice, when and in the manner each department directs, all data required by the appropriate department;

(3) give the Department of Public Safety and the Texas Department of Criminal Justice, or the departments' accredited agents, access to the agency for the purpose of inspection to determine the completeness and accuracy of data reported;

(4) cooperate with the Department of Public Safety and the Texas Department of Criminal Justice so that each department may properly and efficiently perform the department's duties under this chapter; and

(5) cooperate with the Department of Public Safety and the Texas Department of Criminal Justice to identify and eliminate redundant reporting of information to the criminal justice information system.

(b) An optical disk or other technology may be used instead of microfilm as a medium to store information if allowed by the applicable state laws or rules relating to the archiving of state agency information. (Code Crim. Proc., Arts. 60.06(a), (d).)

Art. 66.302. Public Disclosure Not Authorized.

(a) An individual's identifiable description or a notation of an individual's arrest, detention, indictment, information, or other formal criminal charge and of any disposition of the charge, including sentencing, correctional supervision, and release, that is collected and compiled by the Department of Public Safety or the Texas Department of Criminal Justice from criminal justice agencies and maintained in a central location is not subject to public disclosure except as authorized by federal or state law or regulation.

(b) Subsection (a) does not apply to a document maintained by a criminal justice agency that is the source of information collected by the Department of Public Safety or the Texas Department of Criminal Justice. Each criminal justice agency shall retain the documents described by this subsection. (Code Crim. Proc., Arts. 60.06(b), (c).)

Art. 66.303. Prohibited Acts.

An agency official may not intentionally conceal or destroy any record with the intent to violate this subchapter. (Code Crim. Proc., Art. 60.06(e).)

Art. 66.304. Applicability to District Court and County Court Clerks.

The duties imposed on a criminal justice agency under this subchapter are also imposed on district court and county court clerks. (Code Crim. Proc., Art. 60.06(f).)

SUBCHAPTER H OVERSIGHT AND REPORTING

Art. 66.351. Biennial Plans.

The Department of Public Safety and the Texas Department of Criminal Justice, with advice from the council and the Department of Information Resources, shall develop biennial plans to:

(1) improve the reporting and accuracy of the criminal justice information system; and

(2) develop and maintain monitoring systems capable of identifying missing information. (Code Crim. Proc., Art. 60.02(i).)

Art. 66.352. Examination of Records and Operations.

(a) At least once during each five-year period, the council shall coordinate an examination of the records and operations of the criminal justice information system to ensure:

(1) the accuracy and completeness of information in the system; and

(2) the promptness of information reporting.

(b) The state auditor or other appropriate entity selected by the council shall conduct the examination under Subsection (a) with the cooperation of the council, the Department of Public Safety, and the Texas Department of Criminal Justice.

(c) The council, the Department of Public Safety, and the Texas Department of Criminal Justice may examine the records of the agencies required to report information to the Department of Public Safety or the Texas Department of Criminal Justice.

(d) The examining entity under Subsection (b) shall submit to the legislature and the council a report that summarizes the findings of each examination and contains recommendations for improving the criminal justice information system.

(e) Not later than the first anniversary of the date the examining entity under Subsection (b) submits a report under Subsection (d), the Department of Public Safety shall report to the Legislative Budget Board, the governor, and the council the department's progress in implementing the examining entity's recommendations, including the reason for not implementing any recommendation.

(f) Each year following the submission of the report described by Subsection (e), the Department of Public Safety shall submit a similar report until each of the examining entity's recommendations is implemented.

(g) Notwithstanding any other provision of this article, work performed under this article by the state auditor is subject to approval by the legislative audit committee for inclusion in the audit plan under Section 321.013(c), Government Code. (Code Crim. Proc., Arts. 60.02(j), (m).)

Art. 66.353. Monitoring and Reporting Duties of Department of Public Safety.

(a) The Department of Public Safety shall:

(1) monitor the submission of arrest and disposition information by local jurisdictions;

(2) annually submit to the Legislative Budget Board, the governor, the lieutenant governor, the state auditor, and the standing committees in the senate and house of representatives with primary jurisdiction over criminal justice and the department a report regarding the level of reporting by local jurisdictions;

(3) identify local jurisdictions that do not report arrest or disposition information or that partially report information; and

(4) for use in determining the status of outstanding dispositions, publish monthly on the department's Internet website or in another electronic publication a report listing by local jurisdiction each arrest for which there is no corresponding final court disposition.

(b) The report described by Subsection (a)(2) must contain a disposition completeness percentage for each county in this state. For purposes of this subsection, "disposition completeness percentage" means the percentage of arrest charges a county reports to the Department of Public Safety, to be entered in the computerized criminal history system under this chapter, that were brought against a person in the county and for which a disposition has been subsequently reported and entered in the computerized criminal history system. (Code Crim. Proc., Arts. 60.21(b), (c).)

Art. 66.354. Local Data Advisory Boards.

(a) The commissioners court of each county may create a local data advisory board to:

(1) analyze the structure of local automated and manual data systems to identify redundant data entry and data storage;

(2) develop recommendations for the commissioners to improve the local data systems;

(3) develop recommendations, when appropriate, for the effective electronic transfer of required data from local agencies to state agencies; and

(4) perform any related duties to be determined by the commissioners court.

(b) Local officials responsible for collecting, storing, reporting, and using data may be appointed to a local data advisory board.

(c) The council and the Department of Public Safety shall, to the extent that resources allow, provide technical assistance and advice on the request of a local data advisory board. (Code Crim. Proc., Art. 60.09.)

SUBCHAPTER I. GRANTS

Art. 66.401. Grants for Criminal Justice Programs.

The council, the Department of Public Safety, the criminal justice division of the governor's office, and the Department of Information Resources cooperatively shall develop and adopt a grant program, to be implemented by the criminal justice division at a time and in a manner determined by the division, to aid local law enforcement agencies, prosecutors, and court personnel in obtaining equipment and training necessary to operate a telecommunications network capable of:

(1) making inquiries to and receiving responses from the statewide automated fingerprint identification system and from the computerized criminal history system; and

(2) transmitting information to those systems. (Code Crim. Proc., Art. 60.02(k).)

Art. 66.402. Certification Required.

Before allocating money to a county from any federal or state grant program for the enhancement of criminal justice programs, an agency of the state must certify that, using all or part of the allocated money, the county has taken or will take all action necessary to provide the Department of Public Safety and the Texas Department of Criminal Justice any criminal history records maintained by the county in the manner specified for purposes of those departments. (Code Crim. Proc., Art. 60.14.)

CHAPTER 67. COMPILATION OF INFORMATION PERTAINING TO COMBINATIONS AND CRIMINAL STREET GANGS

SUBCHAPTER A GENERAL PROVISIONS

Art. 67.001. Definitions.

In this chapter:

(1) "Administration of criminal justice" has the meaning assigned by Article 66.001.

(2) "Child" has the meaning assigned by Section 51.02, Family Code.

(3) "Combination" has the meaning assigned by Section 71.01, Penal Code.

(4) "Criminal activity" means conduct that is subject to prosecution.

(5) "Criminal information" means facts, material, photographs, or data reasonably related to the investigation or prosecution of criminal activity.

(6) "Criminal justice agency" means:

(A) an entity defined as a criminal justice agency under Article 66.001; or

(B) a municipal or county agency, or school district law enforcement agency, that is engaged in the administration of criminal justice under a statute or executive order.

(7) "Criminal street gang" has the meaning assigned by Section 71.01, Penal Code.

(8) "Department" means the Department of Public Safety of the State of Texas.

(9) "Intelligence database" means a collection or compilation of data organized for search and retrieval to evaluate, analyze, disseminate, or use intelligence information relating to a combination or criminal street gang for the purpose of investigating or prosecuting a criminal offense.

(10) "Juvenile justice agency" has the meaning assigned by Section 58.101, Family Code.

(11) "Law enforcement agency" does not include the Texas Department of Criminal Justice, the Texas Juvenile Justice Department, or a local juvenile probation department. (Code Crim. Proc., Art. 61.01.)

SUBCHAPTER B INTELLIGENCE DATABASES

Art. 67.051. Intelligence Databases Required.

(a) Subject to Subsection (b), a criminal justice agency or juvenile justice agency shall compile criminal information into an intelligence database for the purpose of investigating or prosecuting the criminal activities of combinations or criminal street gangs.

(b) A law enforcement agency in a municipality with a population of 50,000 or more or in a county with a population of 100,000 or more shall compile and maintain in a local or regional intelligence database criminal information relating to a criminal street gang as provided by Subsection (a). The agency must compile and maintain the information in accordance with the criminal intelligence systems operating policies established under 28 C.F.R. Section 23.1 et seq. and the submission criteria established under Article 67.054(b).

(c) Information described by this article may be compiled on paper, by computer, or in any other useful manner by a criminal justice agency, juvenile justice agency, or law enforcement agency.

(d) A local law enforcement agency described by Subsection (b) shall send to the department information the agency compiles and maintains under this chapter. (Code Crim. Proc., Arts. 61.02(a), (b), (b-1), 61.03(c).)

Art. 67.052. Department Intelligence Database.

(a) The department shall establish an intelligence database and shall maintain information received from an agency under Article 67.051(d) in the database in accordance with the criminal intelligence systems operating policies established under 28 C.F.R. Section 23.1 et seq. and the submission criteria under Article 67.054(b).

(b) The department shall designate a code to distinguish criminal information relating to a child and contained in the department's intelligence database from criminal information relating to an adult offender and contained in the database. (Code Crim. Proc., Arts. 61.02(b) (part), 61.03(d), (e).)

Art. 67.053. Intelligence Database User Training; Rules.

(a) The department shall enter into a memorandum of understanding with the United States Department of Justice or other appropriate federal department or agency to provide any person in this state who enters information into or retrieves information from an intelligence database described by this chapter with training regarding the operating principles described by 28 C.F.R. Part 23, as those principles relate to an intelligence database established or maintained under this chapter.

(b) A person in this state who enters information into or retrieves information from an intelligence database described by this chapter shall complete continuing education training on the material described by Subsection (a) at least once for each continuous two-year period the person has primary responsibility for performing a function described by this subsection.

(c) The department shall adopt rules necessary to implement this article. (Code Crim. Proc., Art. 61.12.)

Art. 67.054. Submission Criteria.

(a) In this article:

(1) "Family member" means a person related to another person within the third degree by consanguinity or affinity, as described by Subchapter B, Chapter 573, Government Code, except that the term does not include a person who is considered to be related to another person by affinity only as described by Section 573.024(b), Government Code.

(2) "Penal institution" means:

(A) a confinement facility operated by or under contract with any division of the Texas Department of Criminal Justice;

(B) a confinement facility operated by or under contract with the Texas Juvenile Justice Department;

(C) a juvenile secure pre-adjudication or post-adjudication facility operated by or under a local juvenile probation department; or

(D) a county jail.

(b) Criminal information collected under this chapter relating to a criminal street gang must:

(1) be relevant to the identification of an organization that is reasonably suspected of involvement in criminal activity; and

(2) consist of:

(A) a judgment under any law that includes, as a finding or as an element of a criminal offense, participation in a criminal street gang;

(B) a self-admission by an individual of criminal street gang membership that is made during a judicial proceeding; or

(C) except as provided by Subsection (c), any two of the following:

(i) a self-admission by the individual of criminal street gang membership that is not made during a judicial proceeding, including the use of the Internet or other electronic format or medium to post photographs or other documentation identifying the individual as a member of a criminal street gang;

(ii) an identification of the individual as a criminal street gang member by a reliable informant or other individual;

(iii) a corroborated identification of the individual as a criminal street gang member by an informant or other individual of unknown reliability;

(iv) evidence that the individual frequents a documented area of a criminal street gang and associates with known criminal street gang members;

(v) evidence that the individual uses, in more than an incidental manner, criminal street gang dress, hand signals, tattoos, or symbols, including expressions of letters, numbers, words, or marks, regardless of how or the means by which the symbols are displayed, that are associated with a criminal street gang that operates in an area frequented by the individual and described by Subparagraph (iv);

(vi) evidence that the individual has been arrested or taken into custody with known criminal street gang members for an offense or conduct consistent with criminal street gang activity;

(vii) evidence that the individual has visited a known criminal street gang member, other than a family member of the individual, while the gang member is confined in or committed to a penal institution; or

(viii) evidence of the individual's use of technology, including the Internet, to recruit new criminal street gang members.

(c) Evidence described by Subsections (b)(2)(C)(iv) and (vii) is not sufficient to create the eligibility of a person's information to be included in an intelligence database described by this chapter unless the evidence is combined with information described by another subparagraph of Subsection (b)(2)(C). (Code Crim. Proc., Arts. 61.02(c), (d), (e).)

SUBCHAPTER C. RELEASE AND USE OF INFORMATION

Art. 67.101. Release and Use of Information.

(a) On request, a criminal justice agency may release information maintained under this chapter to:

(1) another criminal justice agency;

(2) a court; or

(3) a defendant in a criminal proceeding who is entitled to the discovery of the information under Chapter 39.

(b) A criminal justice agency or court may use information received under this article or Article 67.051(d) or 67.052 only for the administration of criminal justice.

(c) A defendant may use information received under this article or Article 67.051(d) or 67.052 only for a defense in a criminal proceeding. (Code Crim. Proc., Arts. 61.03(a), (b).)

Art. 67.102. Criminal Information Relating to Child.

(a) Notwithstanding Chapter 58, Family Code, criminal information relating to a child associated with a combination or criminal street gang may be compiled and released under this chapter regardless of the age of the child.

(b) A criminal justice agency or juvenile justice agency may release information maintained under this chapter to an attorney representing a child who is a party to a proceeding under Title 3, Family Code, if the juvenile court determines the information:

(1) is material to the proceeding; and

(2) is not privileged under law.

(c) An attorney may use information received under this article only for a child's defense in a proceeding under Title 3, Family Code.

(d) The governing body of a county or municipality served by a law enforcement agency described by Article 67.051(b) may adopt a policy to notify the parent or guardian of a child of the agency's observations relating to the child's association with a criminal street gang. (Code Crim. Proc., Art. 61.04.)

Art. 67.103. Unauthorized Release or Use of Criminal Information; Penalty.

(a) A person commits an offense if the person knowingly:

(1) uses criminal information obtained under this chapter for an unauthorized purpose; or

(2) releases the information to a person who is not entitled to the information.

(b) An offense under this article is a Class A misdemeanor. (Code Crim. Proc., Art. 61.05.)

SUBCHAPTER D. REMOVAL OF INFORMATION

Art. 67.151. Removal of Information Relating to Individual Other Than Child.

(a) This article does not apply to information collected under this chapter by the Texas Department of Criminal Justice or the Texas Juvenile Justice Department.

(b) Subject to Subsection (c), information collected under this chapter relating to a criminal street gang must be removed after five years from an intelligence database established under Article 67.051 and the intelligence database maintained by the department under Article 67.052 if:

(1) the information relates to the investigation or prosecution of criminal activity engaged in by an individual other than a child; and

(2) the individual who is the subject of the information has not been arrested for criminal activity reported to the department under Chapter 66.

(c) The five-year period described by Subsection (b) does not include any period during which the individual who is the subject of the information is:

(1) confined in a correctional facility operated by or under contract with the Texas Department of Criminal Justice;

(2) committed to a secure correctional facility, as defined by Section 51.02, Family Code, operated by or under contract with the Texas Juvenile Justice Department; or

(3) confined in a county jail or confined in or committed to a facility operated by a juvenile board in lieu of being confined in a correctional facility described by Subdivision (1) or committed to a secure correctional facility described by Subdivision (2). (Code Crim. Proc., Art. 61.06.)

Art. 67.152. Removal of Information Relating to Child.

(a) This article does not apply to information collected under this chapter by the Texas Department of Criminal Justice or the Texas Juvenile Justice Department.

(b) Subject to Subsection (c), information collected under this chapter relating to a criminal street gang must be removed after two years from an intelligence database established under Article 67.051 and the intelligence database maintained by the department under Article 67.052 if:

(1) the information relates to the investigation or prosecution of criminal activity engaged in by a child; and

(2) the child who is the subject of the information has not been:

(A) arrested for criminal activity reported to the department under Chapter 66; or

(B) taken into custody for delinquent conduct reported to the department under Chapter 58, Family Code.

(c) The two-year period described by Subsection (b) does not include any period during which the child who is the subject of the information is:

(1) committed to the Texas Juvenile Justice Department for conduct that violates a penal law of the grade of felony; or

(2) confined in the Texas Department of Criminal Justice. (Code Crim. Proc., Art. 61.07.)

SUBCHAPTER E. RIGHTS OF SUBJECT OF CRIMINAL INFORMATION

Art. 67.201. Right to Request Existence of Criminal Information.

(a) A person or the parent or guardian of a child may request that a law enforcement agency determine whether the agency has collected or is maintaining, under submission criteria established under Article 67.054(b), criminal information relating solely to the person or child. The law enforcement agency shall respond to the request not later than the 10th business day after the date the agency receives the request.

(b) Before responding to a request under Subsection (a), a law enforcement agency may require reasonable written verification of the identity of the person making the request and the relationship between the parent or guardian and the child, if applicable, including written verification of an address, date of birth, driver's license number, state identification card number, or social security number. (Code Crim. Proc., Art. 61.075.)

Art. 67.202. Right to Request Review of Criminal Information.

(a) On receipt of a written request of a person or the parent or guardian of a child that includes a showing by the person or the parent or guardian that a law enforcement agency may have collected criminal information under this chapter relating to the person or child that is inaccurate or does not comply with the submission criteria under Article 67.054(b), the head of the agency or the designee of the agency head shall review criminal information

Code of Criminal Procedure

collected by the agency under this chapter relating to the person or child to determine if:

(1) reasonable suspicion exists to believe that the information is accurate; and

(2) the information complies with the submission criteria established under Article 67.054(b).

(b) If, after conducting a review of criminal information under Subsection (a), the agency head or designee determines that reasonable suspicion does not exist to believe that the information is accurate, or determines that the information does not comply with the submission criteria, the agency shall:

(1) destroy all records containing the information; and

(2) notify the department and the person who requested the review of the agency's determination and the destruction of the records.

(c) If, after conducting a review of criminal information under Subsection (a), the agency head or designee determines that reasonable suspicion exists to believe that the information is accurate, and determines that the information complies with the submission criteria, the agency shall notify the person who requested the review:

(1) of the agency's determination; and

(2) that the person is entitled to seek judicial review of the agency's determination under Article 67.203.

(d) On receipt of notice under Subsection (b)(2), the department immediately shall destroy all records containing the information that is the subject of the notice in the intelligence database maintained by the department under Article 67.052.

(e) A person who is committed to the Texas Juvenile Justice Department or confined in the Texas Department of Criminal Justice does not, while committed or confined, have the right to request review of criminal information under this article. (Code Crim. Proc., Art. 61.08.)

Art. 67.203. Judicial Review.

(a) A person who is entitled to seek judicial review of a determination made under Article 67.202(c) may file a petition for review in district court in the county in which the person resides.

(b) On the filing of a petition for review under Subsection (a), the district court shall conduct an in camera review of the criminal information that is the subject of the determination to determine if:

(1) reasonable suspicion exists to believe that the information is accurate; and

(2) the information complies with the submission criteria under Article 67.054(b).

(c) If, after conducting an in camera review of criminal information under Subsection (b), the court finds that reasonable suspicion does not exist to believe that the information is accurate, or finds that the information does not comply with the submission criteria, the court shall:

(1) order the law enforcement agency that collected the information to destroy all records containing the information; and

(2) notify the department of the court's determination and the destruction of the records.

(d) A petitioner may appeal a final judgment of a district court conducting an in camera review under this article.

(e) Information that is the subject of an in camera review under this article is confidential and may not be disclosed. (Code Crim. Proc., Art. 61.09.)

SUBCHAPTER F. GANG RESOURCE SYSTEM

Art. 67.251. Establishment of Gang Resource System.

The office of the attorney general shall establish an electronic gang resource system to provide criminal justice agencies and juvenile justice agencies with information about criminal street gangs in this state. (Code Crim. Proc., Art. 61.11(a) (part).)

Art. 67.252. Information Included in Gang Resource System.

(a) The gang resource system established under Article 67.251 may include the following information with regard to any gang:

(1) gang name;

(2) gang identifiers, such as colors used, tattoos, and clothing preferences;

(3) criminal activities;

(4) migration trends;

(5) recruitment activities; and

(6) a local law enforcement contact.

(b) Information in the gang resource system shall be accessible according to:

(1) municipality or county; and

(2) gang name.

(c) The office of the attorney general may coordinate with the Texas Department of Criminal Justice to include information in the gang resource system regarding groups that have been identified by the Security Threat Group Management Office of the Texas Department of Criminal Justice. (Code Crim. Proc., Arts. 61.11(a) (part), (g), (h).)

Art. 67.253. Inclusion of Certain Information Prohibited.

Information relating to the identity of a specific offender or alleged offender may not be maintained in the gang resource system. (Code Crim. Proc., Art. 61.11(d).)

Art. 67.254. Collection of Information.

(a) On request by the office of the attorney general, a criminal justice agency or juvenile justice agency shall make a reasonable attempt to provide gang information to the office of the attorney general for the purpose of maintaining an updated, comprehensive gang resource system.

(b) The office of the attorney general shall cooperate with criminal justice agencies and juvenile justice agencies in collecting and maintaining the accuracy of the information included in the gang resource system. (Code Crim. Proc., Arts. 61.11(b), (c).)

Art. 67.255. Use of Information.

Information in the gang resource system may be used in investigating gang-related crimes. Information from the system may be included in an affidavit or subpoena or used in connection with any other legal or judicial proceeding only if the information is corroborated by information not provided by or maintained in the system. (Code Crim. Proc., Art. 61.11(e).)

Art. 67.256. Access to Information.

Access to the gang resource system shall be limited to criminal justice agency personnel and juvenile justice agency personnel. (Code Crim. Proc., Art. 61.11(f).)

SUBCHAPTER G. TEXAS VIOLENT GANG TASK FORCE

Art. 67.301. Definition.

In this subchapter, "task force" means the Texas Violent Gang Task Force. (Code Crim. Proc., Art. 61.10(a).)

Art. 67.302. Purpose.

The purpose of the task force is to form a strategic partnership among local, state, and federal criminal justice, juvenile justice, and correctional agencies to better enable those agencies to take a proactive stance toward tracking gang activity and the growth and spread of gangs statewide. (Code Crim. Proc., Art. 61.10(b).)

Art. 67.303. Task Force Members.

The task force shall consist of:

(1) a representative of the department designated by the director of the department;

(2) two representatives of the Texas Department of Criminal Justice, including a representative of the parole division, designated by the executive director of that agency;

(3) a representative of the office of the inspector general of the Texas Department of Criminal Justice designated by the inspector general;

(4) two representatives of the Texas Juvenile Justice Department designated by the executive director of that agency;

(5) a representative of the office of the attorney general designated by the attorney general;

(6) six representatives who are local law enforcement officers or local community supervision personnel, including juvenile probation personnel, designated by the governor;

(7) two representatives who are local prosecutors designated by the governor; and

(8) a representative of the Texas Alcoholic Beverage Commission designated by the executive director of that agency. (Code Crim. Proc., Art. 61.10(f).)

Art. 67.304. Duties of Task Force.

(a) The task force shall focus its efforts on:

(1) developing, through regional task force meetings, a statewide networking system that will provide timely access to gang information;

(2) establishing communication between different criminal justice, juvenile justice, and correctional agencies, combining independent agency resources, and joining agencies together in a cooperative effort to focus on gang membership, gang activity, and gang migration trends; and

(3) forming a working group of criminal justice, juvenile justice, and correctional representatives from throughout this state to discuss specific cases and investigations involving gangs and other related gang activities.

(b) The task force may take any other actions necessary to accomplish the purposes of this subchapter.

(c) If practicable, the task force shall consult with representatives from one or more United States attorneys' offices in this state and with

Code of Criminal Procedure

representatives from the following federal agencies who are available and assigned to a duty station in this state:

(1) the Federal Bureau of Investigation;

(2) the Federal Bureau of Prisons;

(3) the United States Drug Enforcement Administration;

(4) United States Immigration and Customs Enforcement;

(5) United States Customs and Border Protection;

(6) the Bureau of Alcohol, Tobacco, Firearms and Explosives;

(7) the United States Marshals Service; and

(8) the United States Probation and Pretrial Services System. (Code Crim. Proc., Arts. 61.10(c), (d), (g).)

Art. 67.305. Duties of Department Regarding Task Force.

The department shall support the task force to assist in coordinating statewide antigang initiatives. (Code Crim. Proc., Art. 61.10(e).)

TITLE 2
CODE OF CRIMINAL PROCEDURE

CHAPTER 101
GENERAL PROVISIONS

Art. 101.001. Purpose of Title.

(a) This title is enacted as a part of the state's continuing statutory revision program, begun by the Texas Legislative Council in 1963 as directed by the legislature in Chapter 448, Acts of the 58th Legislature, Regular Session, 1963 (Article 5429b-1, Vernon's Texas Civil Statutes). The program contemplates a topic-by-topic revision of the state's general and permanent statute law without substantive change.

(b) Consistent with the objectives of the statutory revision program, the purpose of this title is to make the law encompassed by this title more accessible and understandable by:

(1) rearranging the statutes into a more logical order;

(2) employing a format and numbering system designed to facilitate citation of the law and to accommodate future expansion of the law;

(3) eliminating repealed, duplicative, unconstitutional, expired, executed, and other ineffective provisions; and

(4) restating the law in modern American English to the greatest extent possible.

Art. 101.002. Construction of Title.

The Code Construction Act (Article 5429b-2, Vernon's Texas Civil Statutes) applies to the construction of each provision in this title, except as otherwise expressly provided by this title.

Art. 101.003. Internal References.

In this title:

(1) a reference to a chapter or article without further identification is a reference to a chapter or article of this title; and

(2) a reference to a subchapter, article, subsection, subdivision, paragraph, or other numbered or lettered unit without further identification is a reference to a unit of the next larger unit of this title in which the reference appears.

Sec. Art. 101.004. Meaning of Conviction.

In this title, a person is considered to have been convicted in a case if:

(1) a judgment, a sentence, or both a judgment and a sentence are imposed on the person;

(2) the person receives community supervision, deferred adjudication, or deferred disposition; or

(3) the court defers final disposition of the case or imposition of the judgment and sentence.

CHAPTER 102
COSTS, FEES AND FINES PAID BY DEFENDANTS

SUBCHAPTER A
COSTS; REIMBURSEMENT FEES; FINES

Art. 102.001. Reimbursement Fees for Services of Peace Officers.

(a) [Repealed by Acts 1989, 71st Leg., ch. 826 (S.B. 356), § 2, effective September 1, 1989.]

(b) A defendant required to pay reimbursement fees under this article shall pay 15 cents per mile for mileage required of an officer to perform a service listed in this subsection and to return from performing that service. If the service provided is the execution of a writ and the writ is directed to two or more persons or the officer executes more than one writ in a case, the defendant is required to pay only mileage actually and necessarily traveled. In calculating mileage, the officer must use the railroad or the most practical route by private conveyance. This subsection applies to:

(1) conveying a prisoner after conviction to the county jail;

(2) conveying a prisoner arrested on a warrant or capias issued in another county to the court or jail of the county in which the warrant or capias was issued; and

(3) traveling to execute criminal process, to summon or attach a witness, and to execute process not otherwise described by this article.

(c) to (e) [Repealed by Acts 1989, 71st Leg., ch. 826 (S.B. 356), § 2, effective September 1, 1989.]

(f) [Repealed.]

(g) [Repealed by Acts 1989, 71st Leg., ch. 826 (S.B. 356), § 2, effective September 1, 1989.]

(h) [Repealed.]

Art. 102.002. Witness Fees.

(a) [Repealed by Acts 1999, 76th Leg., ch. 580 (S.B. 577), § 11(a), effective September 1, 1999.]

(b) The justices of the peace and municipal courts shall maintain a record of and the clerks of district and county courts and county courts at law shall keep a book and record in the book:

(1) the number and style of each criminal action before the court;

(2) the name of each witness subpoenaed, attached, or recognized to testify in the action; and

(3) whether the witness was a witness for the state or for the defendant.

(c) Except as otherwise provided by this subsection, a defendant is liable on conviction for the fees provided by this article for witnesses in the defendant's case. If a defendant convicted of a misdemeanor does not pay the defendant's fines and costs, the county or municipality, as appropriate, is liable for the fees provided by this article for witnesses in the defendant's case.

(d) If a person is subpoenaed as a witness in a criminal case and fails to appear, the person is liable for the costs of an attachment, unless he shows good cause to the court why he did not appear.

Art. 102.003. Trial Fee [Repealed].

Repealed by Acts 1995, 74th Leg., ch. 122 (S.B. 1060), § 4, effective September 1, 1995.

Art. 102.004. Jury Fee. [Repealed]

Art. 102.0045. Fee for Jury Reimbursement to Counties. [Repealed]

Art. 102.005. Fees to Clerks. [Repealed]

Art. 102.006. Fees in Expunction Proceedings.

(a) In addition to any other fees required by other law and except as provided by Subsections (b) and (b-1), a petitioner seeking expunction of a criminal record in a district court shall pay the following fees:

(1) the fee charged for filing an ex parte petition in a civil action in district court;

(2) $1 plus postage for each certified mailing of notice of the hearing date; and

(3) $2 plus postage for each certified mailing of certified copies of an order of expunction.

(a-1) In addition to any other fees required by other law and except as provided by Subsection (b), a petitioner seeking expunction of a criminal record in a justice court or a municipal court of record under Chapter 55 shall pay a fee of $100 for filing an ex parte petition for expunction to defray the cost of notifying state agencies of orders of expunction under that chapter.

(b) The fees under Subsection (a) or the fee under Subsection (a-1), as applicable, shall be waived if the petitioner seeks expunction of a criminal record that relates to an arrest for an offense of which the person was acquitted, other than an acquittal for an offense described by Article 55.01(c), and the petition for expunction is filed not later than the 30th day after the date of the acquittal.

(b-1) The fees under Subsection (a) shall be waived if the petitioner is entitled to expunction:

(1) under Article 55.01(a)(2)(A)(ii)(a) after successful completion of a veterans treatment court program created under Chapter 124, Government Code, or former law; or

(2) under Article 55.01(a)(2)(A)(ii)(b) after successful completion of a mental health court program created under Chapter 125, Government Code, or former law.

(c) A court that grants a petition for expunction of a criminal record may order that any fee, or portion of a fee, required to be paid under Subsection (a) be returned to the petitioner.

Art. 102.007. Reimbursement Fee for Collecting and Processing Check or Similar Sight Order.

(a) A county attorney, district attorney, or criminal district attorney may collect a reimbursement fee if the attorney's office collects and processes a check or similar sight order, as defined by Section 1.07, Penal Code, and the check or similar sight order:

(1) has been issued or passed in a manner that makes the issuance or passing an offense under:

(A) Section 31.03, Penal Code;

(B) Section 31.04, Penal Code; or

(C) Section 32.41, Penal Code; or

(2) has been forged, as defined by Section 32.21, Penal Code.

(b) The county attorney, district attorney, or criminal district attorney may collect the reimbursement fee from any person who is a party to the offense described in Subsection (a).

(c) The amount of the reimbursement fee may not exceed:

(1) $10 if the face amount of the check or sight order does not exceed $10;

(2) $15 if the face amount of the check or sight order is greater than $10 but does not exceed $100;

(3) $30 if the face amount of the check or sight order is greater than $100 but does not exceed $300;

(4) $50 if the face amount of the check or sight order is greater than $300 but does not exceed $500; and

(5) $75 if the face amount of the check or sight order is greater than $500.

(d) If the person from whom the reimbursement fee is collected was a party to the offense of forgery, as defined by Section 32.21, Penal Code, committed by altering the face amount of the check or sight order, the face amount as altered governs for the purposes of determining the amount of the fee.

(e) In addition to the reimbursement fee specified in Subsection (c), the county attorney, district attorney, or criminal district attorney may collect the fee authorized by Section 3.506, Business & Commerce Code, for the benefit of the holder of a check or similar sight order or the holder's assignee, agent, representative, or any other person retained by the holder to seek collection of the check or order.

(f) Reimbursement fees collected under Subsection (c) shall be deposited in the county treasury in a special fund to be administered by the county attorney, district attorney, or criminal district attorney. Expenditures from this fund shall be at the sole discretion of the attorney and may be used only to defray the salaries and expenses of the prosecutor's office, but in no event may the county attorney, district attorney, or criminal district attorney supplement his or her own salary from this fund.

(g) In addition to the reimbursement fee specified in Subsections (b) and (c), the issuer of a check or similar sight order that has been issued or passed as described by Subsection (a)(1) is liable for a reimbursement fee in an amount equal to the costs of delivering notification by registered or certified mail with return receipt requested. The reimbursement fee under this subsection must be collected in all cases described by Subsection (a)(1), and on receipt of proof of the actual costs expended, the fee shall be remitted to the holder of the check or similar sight order.

Art. 102.0071. Justice Court Dishonored Check or Similar Sight Order. [Repealed]

Art. 102.008. Fees for Services of Prosecutors.

(a) [Repealed.]

(b) No fee for the trying of a case may be charged against a defendant prosecuted in a justice court for violation of a penal statute or of the Uniform Act Regulating Traffic on Highways.

(c) [Repealed.]

(d) [Repealed.]

Art. 102.009. Court Costs in Certain Counties. [Repealed]

Art. 102.011. Reimbursement Fees for Services of Peace Officers.

(a) A defendant convicted of a felony or a misdemeanor shall pay the following reimbursement fees to defray the cost of the services provided in the case by a peace officer:

(1) $5 for issuing a written notice to appear in court following the defendant's violation of a traffic law, municipal ordinance, or penal law of this state, or for making an arrest without a warrant;

(2) $50 for executing or processing an issued arrest warrant, capias, or capias pro fine, with the fee imposed for the services of:

(A) the law enforcement agency that executed the arrest warrant or capias, if the agency requests of the court, not later than the 15th day after the date of the execution of the arrest warrant or capias, the imposition of the fee on conviction; or

(B) the law enforcement agency that processed the arrest warrant or capias, if:

(i) the arrest warrant or capias was not executed; or

(ii) the executing law enforcement agency failed to request the fee within the period required by Paragraph (A);

(3) $5 for summoning a witness;

(4) $35 for serving a writ not otherwise listed in this article;

(5) $10 for taking and approving a bond and, if necessary, returning the bond to the courthouse;

(6) $5 for commitment or release;

(7) $5 for summoning a jury, if a jury is summoned; and

(8) $8 for each day's attendance of a prisoner in a habeas corpus case if the prisoner has been remanded to custody or held to bail.

(b) In addition to the reimbursement fees provided by Subsection (a), a defendant required to pay reimbursement fees under this article shall also pay 29 cents per mile for mileage required of an officer to perform a service listed in this subsection and to return from performing that service. If the service provided is the execution of a writ and the writ is directed to two or more persons or the officer executes more than one writ in a case, the defendant is required to pay only mileage actually and necessarily traveled. In calculating mileage, the officer must use the railroad or the most practical route by private conveyance. The defendant shall also pay all necessary and reasonable expenses for meals and lodging incurred by the officer in the performance of services under this subsection, to the extent such expenses meet the requirements of Section 611.001, Government Code. This subsection applies to:

(1) conveying a prisoner after conviction to the county jail;

(2) conveying a prisoner arrested on a warrant or capias issued in another county to the court or jail of the county; and

(3) traveling to execute criminal process, to summon or attach a witness, and to execute process not otherwise described by this article.

(c) If an officer attaches a witness on the order of a court outside the county, the defendant shall pay a reimbursement fee of $10 per day or part of a day spent by the officer conveying the witness and actual necessary expenses for travel by the most practical public conveyance. In order to receive expenses under this subsection, the officer must make a sworn statement of the expenses and the judge issuing the attachment must approve the statement.

(d) A defendant shall pay for the services of a sheriff or constable who serves process and attends an examining trial in a felony or a misdemeanor case the same reimbursement fees allowed for those services in the trial of a felony or a misdemeanor, not to exceed $5.

(e) A reimbursement fee under Subsection (a)(1) or (2) shall be assessed on conviction, regardless of whether the defendant was also arrested at the same time for another offense, and shall be assessed for each arrest made of a defendant arising out of the offense for which the defendant has been convicted.

(f) to (h) [Repealed by Acts 2003, 78th Leg., ch. 209 (H.B. 2424), § 85(a)(5), effective January 1, 2004.]

(i) In addition to reimbursement fees provided by Subsections (a) through (e), a defendant required to pay reimbursement fees under this article shall also pay the costs of overtime paid to a peace officer for time spent testifying in the trial of the case or for traveling to or from testifying in the trial of the case.

(j) [Repealed.]

Art. 102.012. Reimbursement Fees for Pretrial Intervention Programs.

(a) A court that authorizes a defendant to participate in a pretrial intervention program established under Section 76.011, Government Code, may order the defendant to pay to the court a supervision reimbursement fee in an amount not more than $60 per month as a condition of participating in the program.

(b) In addition to or in lieu of the supervision reimbursement fee authorized by Subsection (a), the court may order the defendant to pay or reimburse a community supervision and corrections department for any other expense that is:

(1) incurred as a result of the defendant's participation in the pretrial intervention program, other than an expense described by Article 102.0121; or

(2) necessary to the defendant's successful completion of the program.

Art. 102.0121. Reimbursement Fees for Certain Expenses Related to Pretrial Intervention Programs.

(a) A district attorney, criminal district attorney, or county attorney may collect a reimbursement fee in an amount not to exceed $500 to be used to reimburse a county for expenses, including expenses of the district attorney's, criminal district attorney's, or county attorney's office, related to a defendant's participation in a pretrial intervention program offered in that county.

(b) The district attorney, criminal district attorney, or county attorney may collect the reimbursement fee from any defendant who participates in a pretrial intervention program administered in any part by the attorney's office.

(c) Reimbursement fees collected under this article shall be deposited in the county treasury in a special fund to be used solely to administer the pretrial intervention program. An expenditure from the fund may be made only in accordance with a budget approved by the commissioners court.

Art. 102.013. Court Costs; Crime Stoppers Assistance Account.

(a) The legislature shall appropriate funds from the crime stoppers assistance account to the Criminal Justice Division of the Governor's Office. The Criminal Justice Division may use 10 percent of the funds for the operation of the free statewide telephone service or other appropriate systems for the reporting of crime under Section 414.012, Government Code, and shall distribute the remainder of the funds only to crime stoppers organizations. The Criminal Justice Division may adopt a budget and rules to implement the distribution of these funds.

(b) All funds distributed by the Criminal Justice Division under Subsection (a) of this article are subject to audit by the state auditor. All funds collected or distributed are subject to audit by the Governor's Division of Planning Coordination.

(c) In this article, "crime stoppers organization" has the meaning assigned by Section 414.001, Government Code.

Art. 102.014. Fines for Child Safety Fund in Municipalities.

(a) The governing body of a municipality with a population greater than 850,000 according to the most recent federal decennial census that has adopted an ordinance, regulation, or order regulating the stopping, standing, or parking of vehicles as allowed by Section 542.202, Transportation Code, or Chapter 682, Transportation Code, shall by order assess on each parking violation a fine of not less than $2 and not to exceed $5.

(b) The governing body of a municipality with a population less than 850,000 according to the most recent federal decennial census that has adopted an ordinance, regulation, or order regulating the stopping, standing, or parking of vehicles as allowed by Section 542.202, Transportation Code, or Chapter 682, Transportation Code, may by order assess on each parking violation a fine not to exceed $5.

(c) A person convicted of an offense under Subtitle C, Title 7, Transportation Code, when the offense occurs within a school crossing zone as defined by Section 541.302 of that code, shall pay a fine of $25. A person convicted of an offense under Section 545.066, Transportation Code, shall pay a fine of $25 in addition to other taxable court costs. A fine under this subsection shall be assessed only in a municipality.

(d) A person convicted of an offense under Section 25.093, Education Code, shall pay a fine of $20.

(e) [Repealed.]

(f) In a municipality with a population greater than 850,000 according to the most recent federal decennial census, the officer collecting a fine in a municipal court case shall deposit money collected under this article in the municipal child safety trust fund established as required by Chapter 106, Local Government Code.

(g) In a municipality with a population less than 850,000 according to the most recent federal decennial census, the money collected under this article in a municipal court case must be used for a school crossing guard program if the municipality operates one. If the municipality does not operate a school crossing guard program or if the money received from fines from municipal court cases exceeds the amount necessary to fund the school crossing guard program, the municipality may:

(1) deposit the additional money in an interest-bearing account;

(2) expend the additional money for programs designed to enhance child safety, health, or nutrition, including child abuse prevention and intervention and drug and alcohol abuse prevention; or

(3) expend the additional money for programs designed to enhance public safety and security.

(h) Money collected under this article in a justice, county, or district court shall be used to fund school crossing guard programs in the county where they are collected. If the county does not operate a school crossing guard program, the county may:

(1) remit fine revenues to school districts in its jurisdiction for the purpose of providing school crossing guard services;

(2) fund programs the county is authorized by law to provide which are designed to enhance child safety, health, or nutrition, including child abuse prevention and intervention and drug and alcohol abuse prevention;

(3) provide funding to the sheriff's department for school-related activities;

(4) provide funding to the county juvenile probation department; or

(5) deposit the money in the general fund of the county.

(i) Each collecting officer shall keep separate records of money collected under this article.

Art. 102.015. Court Costs: Truancy Prevention and Diversion Fund. [Renumbered]

Art. 102.016. Costs for Breath Alcohol Testing Program.

(a) The custodians of municipal and county treasuries may deposit funds collected under this article in interest-bearing accounts and retain for the municipality or county interest earned on the funds. The custodians shall keep records of funds received and disbursed under this article and shall provide a yearly report of all funds received and disbursed under this article to the comptroller, the Department of Public Safety, and to each agency in the county served by the court that participates in or maintains a certified breath alcohol testing program. The comptroller shall approve the form of the report.

(b) The custodian of a municipal or county treasury in a county that maintains a certified breath alcohol testing program but does not use the services of a certified technical supervisor employed by the department may, to defray the costs of maintaining and supporting a certified breath alcohol testing program, retain $22.50 of each court cost collected under Section 133.102, Local Government Code, on conviction of an offense under Chapter 49, Penal Code, other than an offense that is a Class C misdemeanor.

(c) The legislature may appropriate money deposited to the credit of the breath alcohol testing account in the general revenue fund under this subsection to the Department of Public Safety for use by the department in the implementation, administration, and maintenance of the statewide certified breath alcohol testing program.

(d) The Department of Public Safety shall maintain a list of counties that do not use the services of a certified technical supervisor employed by the department.

Art. 102.0169. County and District Court Technology Fund.

(a) The county and district court technology fund is a fund in the county treasury. The fund consists of money allocated to the fund under Sections 134.101 and 134.102, Local Government Code.

(b) Money in the county and district court technology fund may be used only to finance:

(1) the cost of continuing education and training for county court, statutory county court, or district court judges and clerks regarding technological enhancements for those courts; and

(2) the purchase and maintenance of technological enhancements for a county court, statutory county court, or district court, including:

(A) computer systems;

(B) computer networks;

(C) computer hardware;

(D) computer software;

(E) imaging systems;

(F) electronic kiosks; and

(G) docket management systems.

(c) The county and district court technology fund shall be administered by or under the direction of the commissioners court of the county.

Art. 102.017. Courthouse Security Fund; Municipal Court Building Security Fund; Justice Court Building Security Fund.

(a) The courthouse security fund is a fund in the county treasury, and the municipal court building security fund is a fund in the municipal treasury. The funds consist of money allocated to the funds under Sections 134.101, 134.102, 134.103, 135.101, and 135.102, Local Government Code.

(b) Money deposited in a courthouse security fund may be used only for security personnel, services, and items related to buildings that house the operations of district, county, or justice courts, and money deposited in a municipal court building security fund may be used only for security personnel, services, and items related to buildings that house the operations of municipal courts. For purposes of this subsection, operations of a district, county, or justice court include the activities of associate judges, masters, magistrates, referees, hearing officers, criminal law magistrate court judges, and masters in chancery appointed under:

(1) Section 61.311, Alcoholic Beverage Code;

(2) Section 51.04(g) or Chapter 201, Family Code;

(3) Section 574.0085, Health and Safety Code;

(4) Section 33.71, Tax Code;

(5) Chapter 54A, Government Code; or

(6) Rule 171, Texas Rules of Civil Procedure.

(c) For purposes of this article, the term "security personnel, services, and items" includes:

(1) the purchase or repair of X-ray machines and conveying systems;

(2) handheld metal detectors;

(3) walkthrough metal detectors;

(4) identification cards and systems;

(5) electronic locking and surveillance equipment;

(6) video teleconferencing systems;

(7) bailiffs, deputy sheriffs, deputy constables, or contract security personnel during times when they are providing appropriate security services;

(8) signage;

(9) confiscated weapon inventory and tracking systems;

(10) locks, chains, alarms, or similar security devices;

(11) the purchase or repair of bullet-proof glass;

(12) continuing education on security issues for court personnel and security personnel; and

(13) warrant officers and related equipment.

(d) This subsection applies only to a justice court located in a county in which one or more justice courts are located in a building that is not the county courthouse. The county treasurer shall deposit one-fourth of the money allocated to the courthouse security fund under Section 134.103, Local Government Code, in a fund to be known as the justice court building security fund. A fund designated by this subsection may be used only for the purpose of providing security personnel, services, and items for a justice court located in a building that is not the county courthouse.

(e) The courthouse security fund and the justice court building security fund shall be administered by or under the direction of the commissioners court. The municipal court building security fund shall be administered by or under the direction of the governing body of the municipality.

(f) The sheriff, constable, or other law enforcement agency or entity that provides security for a court shall provide to the Office of Court Administration of the Texas Judicial System a written report regarding any security incident involving court security that occurs in or around a building housing a court for which the sheriff, constable, agency, or entity provides security not later than the third business day after the date the incident occurred. A copy of the report must be provided to the presiding judge of the court in which the incident occurred. The report is confidential and exempt from disclosure under Chapter 552, Government Code.

Art. 102.0171. Fines: Juvenile Delinquency Prevention Funds.

(a) A defendant convicted of an offense under Section 28.08, Penal Code, in a county court, county court at law, or district court shall pay a fine of $50 for juvenile delinquency prevention and graffiti eradication.

(b) In this article, a person is considered convicted if:

(1) a sentence is imposed on the person;

(2) the person receives community supervision, including deferred adjudication; or

(3) the court defers final disposition of the person's case.

(c) The clerks of the respective courts shall collect the fines and pay the fines to the county treasurer or to any other official who discharges the duties commonly delegated to the county treasurer for deposit in a fund to be known as the county juvenile delinquency prevention fund. A fund designated by this subsection may be used only to:

(1) repair damage caused by the commission of offenses under Section 28.08, Penal Code;

(2) provide educational and intervention programs and materials, including printed educational materials for distribution to primary and secondary school students, designed to prevent individuals from committing offenses under Section 28.08, Penal Code;

(3) provide to the public rewards for identifying and aiding in the apprehension and prosecution of offenders who commit offenses under Section 28.08, Penal Code;

(4) provide funding for teen recognition and teen recreation programs;

(5) provide funding for local teen court programs;

(6) provide funding for the local juvenile probation department; and

(7) provide educational and intervention programs designed to prevent juveniles from engaging in delinquent conduct.

(d) The county juvenile delinquency prevention fund shall be administered by or under the direction of the commissioners court.

Art. 102.0172. Municipal Court Technology Fund.

(a) The municipal court technology fund is a fund in the municipal treasury. The fund consists of money allocated to the fund under Section 134.103, Local Government Code.

(b) Money in a municipal court technology fund may be used only to finance the purchase of or to maintain technological enhancements for a municipal court or municipal court of record, including:

(1) computer systems;

(2) computer networks;

(3) computer hardware;

(4) computer software;

(5) imaging systems;

(6) electronic kiosks;

(7) electronic ticket writers; and

(8) docket management systems.

(c) The municipal court technology fund shall be administered by or under the direction of the governing body of the municipality.

Art. 102.0173. Justice Court Assistance and Technology Fund.

(a) The justice court assistance and technology fund is a fund in the county treasury. The fund consists of money allocated to the fund under Section 134.103, Local Government Code.

(b) Money in the justice court assistance and technology fund may be used only to finance:

(1) the cost of providing court personnel, including salaries and benefits for the court personnel;

(2) the cost of continuing education and training for justice court judges and court personnel; and

(3) the purchase and maintenance of technological enhancements for a justice court, including:

(A) computer systems;

(B) computer networks;

(C) computer hardware;

(D) computer software;

(E) imaging systems;

(F) electronic kiosks;

(G) electronic ticket writers; and

(H) docket management systems.

(c) The justice court assistance and technology fund shall be administered by or under the direction of the commissioners court of the county.

(d) A justice court may, subject to the approval of the commissioners court, use a fund designated by this article to assist a constable's office or other county department with a technological enhancement, or cost related to the enhancement, described by Subsection (b)(3) if the enhancement directly relates to the operation or efficiency of the justice court.

Art. 102.0174. Court Costs; Juvenile Case Manager Fund. [Repealed]

Art. 102.0178. Costs Attendant to Certain Intoxication and Drug Convictions. [Repealed]

Art. 102.0179. Fine for Certain Drug and Texas Controlled Substance Act Convictions. [Contingently enacted]

(a) In this article, "convicted" includes an adjudication under juvenile proceedings.

(b) In addition to any other fees and fines imposed under this subchapter, a defendant convicted of a misdemeanor drug offense as defined by Section 521.371, Transportation Code, whose driver's license is not suspended under Section 521.372, Transportation Code, as a result of that conviction, shall pay a fine of $100.

(c) The court shall waive imposition of a fine under this article if the defendant's driver's license is suspended under Section 521.372, Transportation Code, or under another provision of that code as a result of the conviction of:

(1) an offense described by Section 521.372(a), Transportation Code; or

(2) another offense arising from the same criminal episode.

(d) A fine imposed under this article is due regardless of whether the defendant is granted community supervision in the case. The court shall collect the fine under this article in the same manner as court costs are collected in the case.

(e) A fine collected under this article shall be deposited to the credit of the Texas mobility fund.

Art. 102.018. Reimbursement Fees and Expenses Attendant to Intoxication Convictions.

(a) Except as provided by Subsection (d), on conviction of an offense relating to the driving or operating of a motor vehicle under Section 49.04, Penal Code, the court shall impose a reimbursement fee of $15 on a defendant if, subsequent to the arrest of the defendant, a law enforcement agency visually recorded the defendant with an electronic device. Reimbursement fees imposed under this subsection are in addition to other court costs or fees and are due whether or not the defendant is granted probation in the case. The court shall collect the reimbursement fees in the same manner as other fees are collected in the case.

(b) Except as provided by Subsection (d), on conviction of an offense relating to the driving or operating of a motor vehicle punishable under Section 49.04(b), Penal Code, the court shall impose as a reimbursement fee on the defendant an amount that is equal to the reimbursement fee of an evaluation of the defendant performed under Article 42A.402(a). Reimbursement fees imposed under this subsection are in addition to other court costs and are due whether or not the defendant is granted community supervision in the case, except that if the court determines that the defendant is indigent and unable to pay the fee, the court may waive the imposition of the fee.

(c) (1) Except as provided by Subsection (d) of this article, if a person commits an offense under Chapter 49, Penal Code, and as a direct result of the offense the person causes an incident resulting in an accident response by a public agency, the person is liable on conviction for the offense for the reasonable expense to the agency of the accident response.

(2) The liability authorized by this subsection may be established by civil suit; however, if a determination is made during a criminal trial that a person committed an offense under Chapter 49, Penal Code, and as a direct result of the offense the person caused an incident resulting in an accident response by a public agency, the court may include

the obligation for the liability as part of the judgment. A judgment that includes such an obligation is enforceable as any other judgment.

(3) The liability is a debt of the person to the public agency, and the public agency may collect the debt in the same manner as the public agency collects an express or implied contractual obligation to the agency.

(4) A person's liability under this subsection for the reasonable expense of an accident response may not exceed $1,000 for a particular incident. For the purposes of this subdivision, a reasonable expense for an accident response includes only those costs to the public agency arising directly from an accident response to a particular incident, such as the cost of providing police, fire-fighting, rescue, ambulance, and emergency medical services at the scene of the incident and the salaries of the personnel of the public agency responding to the incident.

(5) A bill for the expense of an accident response sent to a person by a public agency under this subsection must contain an itemized accounting of the components of the total charge. A bill that complies with this subdivision is prima facie evidence of the reasonableness of the costs incurred in the accident response to which the bill applies.

(6) A policy of motor vehicle insurance delivered, issued for delivery, or renewed in this state may not cover payment of expenses charged to a person under this subsection.

(7) In this subsection, "public agency" means the state, a county, a municipality district, or a public authority located in whole or in part in this state that provides police, fire-fighting, rescue, ambulance, or emergency medical services.

(d) Subsections (a), (b), and (c) of this article do not apply to an offense under Section 49.02 or 49.03, Penal Code.

Art. 102.0185. Fine For Intoxication Convictions: Emergency Medical Services, Trauma Facilities, and Trauma Care Systems.

(a) In addition to the reimbursement fee imposed by Article 102.018, a person convicted of an offense under Chapter 49, Penal Code, except for Sections 49.02 and 49.031 of that code, shall pay a fine of $100 on conviction of the offense.

(b) Fines imposed under this article are imposed without regard to whether the defendant is placed on community supervision after being convicted of the offense or receives deferred disposition or deferred adjudication for the offense.

(c) Fines imposed under this article are collected in the manner provided for the collection of court costs by Subchapter B, Chapter 133, Local Government Code.

(d) The officer collecting the fines under this article shall keep separate records of the money collected and shall pay the money to the custodian of the municipal or county treasury.

(e) The custodian of the municipal or county treasury shall:

(1) keep records of the amount of money collected under this article that is deposited with the treasury under this article; and

(2) not later than the last day of the first month following each calendar quarter:

(A) pay the money collected under this article during the preceding calendar quarter to the comptroller; or

(B) if, in the calendar quarter, the custodian of the municipal or county treasury did not receive any money attributable to fines paid under this article, file a report with the comptroller stating that fact.

(f) The comptroller shall deposit the funds received under this article to the credit of the account established under Section 773.006, Health and Safety Code.

Art. 102.0186. Fine for Certain Child Sexual Assault and Related Convictions.

(a) A person convicted of an offense under Section 21.02, 21.11, 22.011(a)(2), 22.021(a)(1)(B), 43.25, 43.251, or 43.26, Penal Code, shall pay a fine of $100 on conviction of the offense.

(b) A fine imposed under this article is imposed without regard to whether the defendant is placed on community supervision after being convicted of the offense or receives deferred adjudication for the offense.

(c) The clerks of the respective courts shall collect the fines and pay the fines to the county treasurer or to any other official who discharges the duties commonly delegated to the county treasurer for deposit in a fund to be known as the county child abuse prevention fund. A fund designated by this subsection may be used only to fund child abuse prevention programs in the county where the court is located.

(d) The county child abuse prevention fund shall be administered by or under the direction of the commissioners court.

Art. 102.019. Costs on Conviction for Fugitive Apprehension [Repealed].

Repealed by Acts 2003, 78th Leg., ch. 209 (H.B. 2424), § 85(6), effective January 1, 2004.

Art. 102.020. Costs Related to DNA Testing.

(a) [Repealed.]

(b) The court shall assess and make a reasonable effort to collect the cost due under this article whether or not any other court cost is assessed or collected.

(c) For purposes of this article, a person is considered to have been convicted if:

(1) a sentence is imposed; or

(2) the defendant receives community supervision or deferred adjudication.

(d) Court costs under this article are collected in the same manner as other fines or costs. An officer collecting the costs shall keep separate records of the funds collected as costs under this article and shall deposit the funds in the county treasury.

(e) The custodian of a county treasury shall:

(1) keep records of the amount of funds on deposit collected under this article; and

(2) send to the comptroller before the last day of the first month following each calendar quarter the funds collected under this article during the preceding quarter.

(f) A county may retain 10 percent of the funds collected under this article by an officer of the county as a collection fee if the custodian of the county treasury complies with Subsection (e).

(g) If no funds due as costs under this article are deposited in a county treasury in a calendar quarter, the custodian of the treasury shall file the report required for the quarter in the regular manner and must state that no funds were collected.

(h) Except as provided by Subsection (h-1), the comptroller shall deposit 35 percent of the funds received under this article in the state treasury to the credit of the state highway fund and 65 percent of the funds received under this article to the credit of the criminal justice planning account in the general revenue fund.

(h-1) The clerk of the court shall transfer to the comptroller any funds received under Subsection (a)(2) or (3). The comptroller shall credit the funds to the Department of Public Safety to help defray the cost of collecting or analyzing DNA samples provided by defendants who are required to pay a court cost under this article.

(i) Funds collected under this article are subject to audit by the comptroller.

(j) The court may waive the imposition of a court cost under this article if the court determines that the defendant is indigent and unable to pay the cost.

Art. 102.021. [Blank].

Art. 102.022. Costs on Conviction to Fund Statewide Repository for Data Related to Civil Justice.

(a) [Repealed.]

(b) A defendant convicted of a moving violation in a justice court, county court, county court at law, or municipal court shall pay a fee of 10 cents as a cost of court.

(c) In this article, a person is considered convicted if:

(1) a sentence is imposed on the person;

(2) the person receives community supervision, including deferred adjudication; or

(3) the court defers final disposition of the person's case.

(d) The clerks of the respective courts shall collect the costs described by this article. The clerk shall keep separate records of the funds collected as costs under this article and shall deposit the funds in the county or municipal treasury, as appropriate.

(e) The custodian of a county or municipal treasury shall:

(1) keep records of the amount of funds on deposit collected under this article; and

(2) send to the comptroller before the last day of the first month following each calendar quarter the funds collected under this article during the preceding quarter.

(f) A county or municipality may retain 10 percent of the funds collected under this article by an officer of the county or municipality as a collection fee if the custodian of the county or municipal treasury complies with Subsection (e).

(g) If no funds due as costs under this article are deposited in a county or municipal treasury in a calendar quarter, the custodian of the treasury shall file the report required for the quarter in the regular manner and must state that no funds were collected.

(h) The comptroller shall deposit the funds received under this article to the credit of the Civil Justice Data Repository fund in the general revenue fund, to be used only by the Texas Commission on Law Enforcement to implement duties under Section 1701.162, Occupations Code.

(i) Funds collected under this article are subject to audit by the comptroller.

Art. 102.030. Time Payment Reimbursement Fee.

(a) A person convicted of an offense shall pay a reimbursement fee of $15 if the person:

(1) has been convicted of a felony or misdemeanor; and

(2) pays any part of a fine, court costs, or restitution, or another reimbursement fee, on or after the 31st day after the date on which a judgment is entered assessing the fine, court costs, restitution, or other reimbursement fee.

(b) The treasurer shall deposit the reimbursement fees collected under this article in a separate account in the general fund of the county or municipality to be used for the purpose of improving the collection of outstanding court costs, fines, reimbursement fees, or restitution or improving the efficiency of the administration of justice in the county or municipality. The county or municipality shall prioritize the needs of the judicial officer who collected the fees when making expenditures under this subsection and use the money deposited to provide for those needs.

SUBCHAPTER B CRIMINAL JUSTICE PLANNING FUND

Art. 102.051. Misdemeanor and Felony Costs [Repealed].

Repealed by Acts 1997, 75th Leg., ch. 1100 (H.B. 2272), § 6(3), effective September 1, 1997.

Art. 102.052. Record of Collection [Repealed].

Repealed by Acts 1997, 75th Leg., ch. 1100 (H.B. 2272), § 6(3), effective September 1, 1997.

Art. 102.053. Reports Required [Repealed].

Repealed by Acts 1997, 75th Leg., ch. 1100 (H.B. 2272), § 6(3), effective September 1, 1997.

Art. 102.054. Transfer of Funds to Comptroller [Repealed].

Repealed by Acts 1997, 75th Leg., ch. 1100 (H.B. 2272), § 6(3), effective September 1, 1997.

Art. 102.055. Special Fund [Repealed].

Repealed by Acts 1997, 75th Leg., ch. 1100 (H.B. 2272), § 6(3), effective September 1, 1997.

Art. 102.056. Distribution of Funds.

(a) The legislature shall determine and appropriate the necessary amount from the criminal justice planning fund to the criminal justice division of the governor's office for expenditure for state and local criminal justice projects and for costs of administering the funds for the projects. The criminal justice division shall allocate not less than 20 percent of these funds to juvenile justice programs. The distribution of the funds to local units of government shall be in an amount equal at least to the same percentage as local expenditures for criminal justice activities are to total state and local expenditures for criminal justice activities for the preceding state fiscal year. Funds shall be allocated among combinations of local units of government taking into consideration the population of the combination of local units of government as compared to the population of the state and the incidence of crime in the jurisdiction of the combination of local units of government as compared to the incidence of crime in the state. All funds collected are subject to audit by the comptroller of public accounts. All funds expended are subject to audit by the State Auditor. All funds collected or expended are subject to audit by the governor's division of planning coordination.

(b) The legislature may appropriate any unobligated balance of the criminal justice planning fund for any court-related purpose.

(c) Notwithstanding any other provision of this article, the criminal justice division shall allocate to a local unit of government or combination of local units of government located in an impacted region occurring as the result of the establishment of a significant new naval military facility an amount that exceeds by 10 percent the amount it would otherwise receive under this article.

(d) In this article, "significant new naval military facility" and "impacted region" have the meanings assigned by Section 4, Article 1, National Defense Impacted Region Assistance Act of 1985.

(e) The legislature shall determine and appropriate the necessary amount from the criminal justice planning account to the criminal justice division of the governor's office for reimbursement in the form of grants to the Department of Public Safety of the State of Texas and other law enforcement agencies for expenses incurred in performing duties imposed on those agencies under Section 411.1471 or Subchapter B-1, Chapter 420, Government Code, as applicable. On the first day after the end of a calendar quarter, a law enforcement agency incurring expenses described by this subsection in the previous calendar quarter shall send a certified statement of the costs incurred to the criminal justice division. The criminal justice division through a grant shall reimburse the law enforcement agency for the costs not later than the 30th day after the date the certified statement is received. If the criminal justice division does not reimburse the law enforcement agency before the 90th day after the date the certified statement is received, the agency is not required to perform duties imposed under Section 411.1471 or Subchapter B-1, Chapter 420, Government Code, as applicable, until the agency has been compensated for all costs for which the agency has submitted a certified statement under this subsection.

SUBCHAPTER C COURT COSTS AND FEES

Art. 102.071. Collection, Allocation, and Administration.

The comptroller of public accounts may require state court costs and fees in criminal cases to be reported in lump-sum amounts. The comptroller shall allocate the amounts received to the appropriate fund, with each fund receiving the same amount of money the fund would have received if the costs and fees had been reported individually.

Art. 102.072. Administrative Fee.

An officer listed in Article 103.003 or a community supervision and corrections department may assess an administrative fee for each transaction made by the officer or department relating to the collection of fines, fees, restitution, or other costs imposed by a court. The fee may not exceed $2 for each transaction. This article does not apply to a transaction relating to the collection of child support.

Art. 102.073. Assessment of Court Costs and Fees in a Single Criminal Action.

(a) In a single criminal action in which a defendant is convicted of two or more offenses or of multiple counts of the same offense, the court may assess each court cost or fee only once against the defendant.

(b) In a criminal action described by Subsection (a), each court cost or fee the amount of which is determined according to the category of offense must be assessed using the highest category of offense that is possible based on the defendant's convictions.

(c) This article does not apply to a single criminal action alleging only the commission of two or more offenses punishable by fine only.

Art. 102.075. Court Costs for Special Services [Repealed].

Repealed by Acts 2003, 78th Leg., ch. 209 (H.B. 2424), § 85(7), effective January 1, 2004.

SUBCHAPTER D COMPREHENSIVE REHABILITATION FUND [REPEALED]

Art. 102.081. Traffic Conviction Costs [Repealed].

Repealed by Acts 1997, 75th Leg., ch. 1100 (H.B. 2272), § 6(4), effective September 1, 1997.

Art. 102.082. Record of Collection [Repealed].

Repealed by Acts 1997, 75th Leg., ch. 1100 (H.B. 2272), § 6(4), effective September 1, 1997.

Art. 102.083. Reports Required [Repealed].

Repealed by Acts 1997, 75th Leg., ch. 1100 (H.B. 2272), § 6(4), effective September 1, 1997.

Art. 102.084. Transfer of Funds to Comptroller [Repealed].

Repealed by Acts 1997, 75th Leg., ch. 1100 (H.B. 2272), § 6(4), effective September 1, 1997.

Art. 102.085. Special Fund [Repealed].

Repealed by Acts 1997, 75th Leg., ch. 1100 (H.B. 2272), § 6(4), effective September 1, 1997.

CHAPTER 103 PAYMENT, COLLECTION, AND RECORDKEEPING

Art. 103.001. Costs Payable.

(a) In a justice or municipal court, a cost is not payable by the person charged with the cost until a written bill is:

(1) produced or ready to be produced, containing the items of cost; and

(2) signed by the officer who charged the cost or the officer who is entitled to receive payment for the cost.

(b) In a court other than a justice or municipal court, a cost is not payable by the person charged with the cost until a written bill containing the items of cost is:

(1) produced;

(2) signed by the officer who charged the cost or the officer who is entitled to receive payment for the cost; and

(3) provided to the person charged with the cost.

Art. 103.002. Certain Costs Barred.

An officer may not impose a cost for a service not performed or for a service for which a cost is not expressly provided by law.

Art. 103.0025. Alternative Payment Procedure for Certain Past Due Fines and Costs.

(a) This article applies to a defendant's past due payment on a judgment for a fine and related court costs if a capias pro fine has been issued in the case.

(b) Notwithstanding any other provision of law, the court may adopt an alternative procedure for collecting a past due payment described by Subsection (a). Under the procedure, a peace officer who executes a capias pro fine or who is authorized to arrest a defendant on other grounds and knows that the defendant owes a past due payment described by Subsection (a):

(1) shall inform the defendant of:

(A) the possibility of making an immediate payment of the fine and related court costs by use of a credit or debit card; and

(B) the defendant's available alternatives to making an immediate payment; and

(2) may accept, on behalf of the court, the defendant's immediate payment of the fine and related court costs by use of a credit or debit card, after which the peace officer may release the defendant as appropriate based on the officer's authority for the arrest.

(c) A peace officer accepting a payment under Subsection (b)(2) may also accept payment for fees for the issuance and execution of the capias pro fine.

Art. 103.003. Collection.

(a) District and county attorneys, clerks of district and county courts, sheriffs, constables, and justices of the peace may collect money payable under this title.

(a-1) The clerk of a municipal court may collect money payable to the municipal court under this title.

(b) A community supervision and corrections department and a county treasurer may collect money payable under this title with the written approval of the clerk of the court or fee officer, and may collect money payable as otherwise provided by law.

(b-1) [Repealed.]

(c) This article does not limit the authority of a commissioners court to contract with a private vendor or private attorney for the provision of collection services under Article 103.0031.

Art. 103.0031. Collection Contracts.

(a) The commissioners court of a county or the governing body of a municipality may enter into a contract with a private attorney or a public or private vendor for the provision of collection services for one or more of the following items:

(1) debts and accounts receivable such as unpaid fines, fees, court costs, forfeited bonds, and restitution ordered paid by:

(A) a court serving the county or a court serving the municipality, as applicable; or

(B) a hearing officer serving the municipality under Chapter 682, Transportation Code;

(2) amounts in cases in which the accused has failed to appear:

(A) as promised under Subchapter A, Chapter 543, Transportation Code, or other law;

(B) in compliance with a lawful written notice to appear issued under Article 14.06(b) or other law;

(C) in compliance with a lawful summons issued under Article 15.03(b) or other law;

(D) in compliance with a lawful order of a court serving the county or municipality; or

(E) as specified in a citation, summons, or other notice authorized by Section 682.002, Transportation Code, that charges the accused with a parking or stopping offense; and

(3) false alarm penalties or fees imposed by a county under Chapter 118 or 233, Local Government Code, or by a municipality under a municipal ordinance.

(b) A commissioners court or governing body of a municipality that enters into a contract with a private attorney or private vendor under this article may authorize the addition of a collection fee in the amount of 30 percent on each item described in Subsection (a) that is more than 60 days past due and has been referred to the attorney or vendor for collection. The collection fee does not apply to a case that has been dismissed by a court of competent jurisdiction or to any amount that has been satisfied through time-served credit or community service. The collection fee may be applied to any balance remaining after a partial credit for time served or community service if the balance is more than 60 days past due. Unless the contract provides otherwise, the court shall calculate the amount of any collection fee due to the governmental entity or to the private attorney or private vendor performing the collection services and shall receive all fees, including the collection fee. With respect to cases described by Subsection (a)(2), the amount to which the 30 percent collection fee applies is:

(1) the amount to be paid that is communicated to the accused as acceptable to the court under its standard policy for resolution of the case, if the accused voluntarily agrees to pay that amount; or

(2) the amount ordered paid by the court after plea or trial.

(c) The governing body of a municipality with a population of more than 1.9 million may authorize the addition of collection fees under Subsection (b) for a collection program performed by employees of the governing body.

(d) A defendant is not liable for the collection fees authorized under Subsection (b) if the court of original jurisdiction has determined the defendant is indigent, or has insufficient resources or income, or is otherwise unable to pay all or part of the underlying fine or costs.

(e) If a county or municipality has entered into a contract under Subsection (a) and a person pays an amount that is less than the aggregate total to be collected under Subsections (a) and (b), the allocation to the comptroller, the county or municipality, and the private attorney or vendor shall be reduced proportionately.

(f) An item subject to collection services under Subsection (a) and to the additional collection fee authorized by Subsection (b) is considered more than 60 days past due under Subsection (b) if it remains unpaid on the 61st day after the following appropriate date:

(1) with respect to an item described by Subsection (a)(1), the date on which the debt, fine, fee, forfeited bond, or court cost must be paid in full as determined by the court or hearing officer;

(2) with respect to an item described by Subsection (a)(2), the date by which the accused promised to appear or was notified, summoned, or ordered to appear; or

(3) with respect to an item described by Subsection (a)(3), the date on which a penalty or fee is due under a rule or order adopted under Chapter 233, Local Government Code, or an ordinance, policy, procedure, or rule of a municipality.

(g) A county or municipality that enters into a contract under Subsection (a) may not use the additional 30 percent collection fee authorized by Subsection (b) for any purpose other than compensating the private attorney or private vendor who earns the fee.

(h) This section does not apply to the collection of commercial bail bonds.

(i) The commissioners court of a county or the governing body of a municipality may enter into a contract as described in this article to collect a debt incurred as a result of the commission of a criminal or civil offense committed before the effective date of this subsection. The collection fee does not apply to a debt collected pursuant to a contract entered into under this subsection.

(j) A communication to the accused person regarding the amount of payment that is acceptable to the court under the court's standard policy for resolution of a case must include:

(1) a notice of the person's right to enter a plea or go to trial on any offense charged; and

(2) a statement that, if the person is unable to pay the full amount of payment that is acceptable to the court, the person should contact the court regarding the alternatives to full payment that are available to resolve the case.

Art. 103.0032. Collection Improvement Plans.

Not later than January 1 of each even-numbered year, the Office of Court Administration of the Texas Judicial System may award grants to counties and municipalities to prepare a collection plan. The grants shall reimburse the county or municipality for the cost of preparing the plan. The plan shall provide methods to improve the collection of court costs, fees, and fines imposed in criminal cases. The Office of Court Administration of the Texas Judicial System may require that the county or municipality reimburse the state from the additional collections as a condition of the grant.

Art. 103.0033. Collection Improvement Program. [Repealed]

Art. 103.004. Disposition of Collected Money.

(a) Except as provided by Subsection (c), an officer who collects recognizances, bail bonds, fines, forfeitures, judgments, jury fees, and other obligations recovered in the name of the state under any provision of this title shall deposit the money in the county treasury not later than the next regular business day after the date that the money is collected. If it is not possible for the officer to deposit the money in the county treasury by that date, the officer shall deposit the money in the county treasury as soon as possible, but not later than the fifth regular business day after the date that the money is collected.

(b) [Repealed by Acts 2011, 82nd Leg., ch. 606 (S.B. 373), § 31(a), effective September 1, 2011.]

(c) The commissioners court of a county with a population of less than 50,000 may authorize an officer who is required to deposit money under Subsection (a) to deposit the money in the county treasury not later than the 15th day after the date that the money is collected.

(d) The custodian of the county treasury shall deposit money received from fees imposed under Article 102.012 in the special fund of the county treasury for the community supervision and corrections department serving the county.

Art. 103.005. Report Required.

(a) An officer listed in Article 103.003 who collects money other than taxes for a county shall report to the commissioners court of the county for which the money was collected during each term of the court.

(b) An officer listed in Article 103.003 who collects money other than taxes for the state shall report to the district court having jurisdiction in the county the officer serves on the first day of each term of the court.

(c) The report must state for the reporting period:

(1) the amount of money collected by the officer;

(2) when and from whom the money was collected;

(3) the process by which the money was collected; and

(4) the disposition of the money.

(d) The report must be in writing and under the oath of the officer.

(e) If an officer has not collected money since the last report required to be filed with the court or the commissioners court, the officer shall report that fact to the court or commissioners court.

Art. 103.006. Transfer of Bill of Costs.

If a criminal action or proceeding is transferred from one court to another or is appealed, an officer of the court shall certify and sign a bill of costs stating the costs that have accrued and send the bill of costs to the court to which the action or proceeding is transferred or appealed.

Art. 103.007. Additional Costs After Payment.

After a defendant has paid costs, no more costs may be charged against the defendant unless the court rules on a motion presented to the court that additional costs are due.

Art. 103.008. Correction of Costs.

(a) On the filing of a motion by a defendant not later than one year after the date of the final disposition of a case in which costs were imposed, the court in which the case is pending or was last pending shall correct any error in the costs.

(b) The defendant must notify each person affected by the correction of costs in the same manner as notice of a similar motion is given in a civil action.

Art. 103.0081. [As amended by Acts 2021, 87th Leg., ch. 106 (SB 1373)] Uncollectible Fines and Fees.

(a) Any officer authorized by this chapter to collect a fine, reimbursement or other fee, or item of cost may request the trial court in which a criminal action or proceeding was held to make a finding that a fine, reimbursement or other fee, or item of cost imposed in the action or proceeding is uncollectible if the officer believes:

(1) the defendant is deceased;

(2) the defendant is serving a sentence for imprisonment for life or life without parole; or

(3) the fine, reimbursement or other fee, or item of cost has been unpaid for at least 15 years.

(b) On a finding by a court that any condition described by Subsection (a) is true, the court may order the officer to designate the fine, reimbursement or other fee, or item of cost as uncollectible in the fee record. The officer shall attach a copy of the court's order to the fee record.

Art. 103.0081. [As amended by Acts 2021, 87th Leg., ch. XXX (HB 3774)] Uncollectible Fines and Fees.

(a) Any officer authorized by this chapter to collect a fine, fee, or item of cost may request the trial court in which a criminal action or proceeding was held to make a finding that a fine, fee, or item of cost imposed in the action or proceeding is uncollectible if the officer believes:

(1) the defendant is deceased;

(2) the defendant is serving a sentence for imprisonment for life or life without parole; or

(3) the fine, fee, or item of cost has been unpaid for at least 15 years.

(b) On a finding by a court that any condition described by Subsections (a)(1)-(3) is true, the court may order the officer to designate the fine, fee, or item of cost as uncollectible in the fee record. The officer shall attach a copy of the court's order to the fee record.

Art. 103.009. Fee Records.

(a) Each clerk of a court, county judge, justice of the peace, sheriff, constable, and marshal shall keep a fee record. The record must contain:

(1) a statement of each fee or item of cost charged for a service rendered in a criminal action or proceeding;

(2) the number and style of the action or proceeding; and

(3) the name of the officer or person who is entitled to receive the fee.

(b) Any person may inspect a fee record described by Subsection (a).

(c) A statement of an item of cost in a fee record is prima facie evidence of the correctness of the statement.

(d) The county shall provide to officers required to keep a fee record by this article equipment and supplies necessary to keep the record.

Art. 103.010. Receipt Book.

(a) Each county shall provide a receipt book to each officer collecting fines and fees in criminal cases for the county. The book must contain duplicate official receipts. Each receipt must bear a distinct number and a facsimile of the official seal of the county.

(b) An officer who collects fines or fees in a criminal case shall give the person paying the money a receipt from the receipt book. The receipt must show:

(1) the amount of money paid;

(2) the date the money was paid;

(3) the style and number of the case in which the costs were accrued;

(4) the item of costs;

(5) the name of the person paying the money; and

(6) the official signature of the officer receiving the money.

(c) Instead of a receipt book, each officer collecting fines or fees in criminal cases for the county may maintain the information listed in Subsections (b)(1)—(5) in a computer database. The officer shall provide a receipt to each person paying a fine or fee.

Art. 103.011. Audit.

An officer shall deliver the receipt book or a copy of any receipt records contained in a computer database to the county auditor at the end of each month's business or at the end of each month shall allow the county auditor electronic access to receipt records contained in the computer database. The county auditor shall examine the receipt book or computer records and determine whether the money collected has been properly disposed of. If each receipt in a receipt book has been used, the county auditor shall keep the book. If any receipt in the book has not been used, the auditor shall return the book to the officer. The county auditor may keep a copy of computer generated receipt records delivered to the county auditor. Any person may inspect a receipt book or a computer generated receipt record kept by the county auditor.

Art. 103.012. Penalty.

(a) An officer commits an offense if the officer violates a provision of Article 103.010 or Article 103.011.

(b) An offense under this article is a Class C misdemeanor.

(c) An officer who violates a provision of Article 103.010 or Article 103.011 or whose deputy violates a provision of those articles may be removed from office on the petition of the county or district attorney.

Art. 103.013. Collection of Fees for Delinquent Traffic Fines [Repealed].

Repealed by Acts 2003, 78th Leg., ch. 1276 (H.B. 3507), § 5.004, effective September 1, 2003.

CHAPTER 104
CERTAIN EXPENSES PAID BY STATE OR COUNTY

Art. 104.001. Jury Pay and Expenses for Jurors.

(a) The sheriff of a county shall, with the approval of the commissioners court, provide food and lodging for jurors impaneled in a felony case tried in the county. A juror may pay his own expenses and draw his script.

(b) A juror in a felony case is entitled to receive as jury pay the amount authorized by Article 2122, Revised Statutes.

(c) The county treasurer shall pay a juror the amount due the juror for expenses under this article after receiving a certificate from a clerk of a court or justice of the peace stating the amount due the juror.

(d) A draft or certificate issued under this article may be transferred by delivery and, without further action of any authority except registration by the county treasurer, may be used at par to pay county taxes owed by the holder of the draft or certificate.

(e) If a defendant is indicted in one county and tried in another county after a change of venue, the county in which the defendant was indicted is liable for jury pay and expenses paid to jurors by the county trying the case.

(f) At each regular meeting of the commissioners court of a county, the court shall determine whether, since the last regular meeting of the court, a defendant described by Subsection (e) has been tried in the county. The commissioners court shall prepare an account against another county liable for jury pay and expenses under this article. The account must show the number of days the jury was impaneled in the case and the jury pay and expenses incurred by the county in the case.

(g) The county judge of the county in which the defendant was tried shall certify the correctness of the account and send the account to the county judge of the county in which the defendant was indicted. The county in which the defendant was indicted shall pay the account in the same manner required for payment of the expenses of transferred prisoners under Article 104.002.

Art. 104.002. Expenses for Prisoners.

(a) Except as otherwise provided by this article, a county is liable for all expenses incurred in the safekeeping of prisoners confined in the county jail or kept under guard by the county. If a prisoner is transferred to a county from another county on a change of venue, for safekeeping, or for a habeas corpus hearing, the county transferring the prisoner is liable for the expenses described by this article.

(b) If a county incurs expenses for the safekeeping of a prisoner from another county, the sheriff shall submit to the county judge an account of expenses incurred by the county for the prisoner. The county judge shall approve the amount he determines is a correct statement of the expenses and sign and date the account.

(c) The county judge shall submit to the commissioners court of the county for which the prisoner was kept, at a regular term of the court, his signed statement of the account described by Subsection (b). If the commissioners court determines that the account is in accordance with the law, it shall order the county treasurer to issue to the sheriff of the county submitting the statement a draft in an amount approved by the court.

(d) A person who is or was a prisoner in a county jail and received medical, dental, or health related services from a county or a hospital district shall be required to pay a reimbursement fee for such services when they are rendered. If such prisoner is an eligible county resident as defined in Section 61.002, Health and Safety Code, the county or hospital district providing the services has a right of subrogation to the prisoner's right of recovery from any source, limited to the cost of services provided. A prisoner, unless the prisoner fully pays for the cost of services received, shall remain obligated to reimburse the county or hospital district for any medical, dental, or health services provided, and the county or hospital district may apply for reimbursement in the manner provided by Chapter 61, Health and Safety Code. A county or hospital district shall have authority to recover the amount expended in a civil action.

Art. 104.003. State Payment of Certain Prosecution Costs.

(a) In a prosecution of a criminal offense or delinquent conduct committed on property owned or operated by or under contract with the Texas Department of Criminal Justice or the Texas Juvenile Justice Department, or committed by or against a person in the custody of the Texas Department of Criminal Justice or the Texas Juvenile Justice Department while the person is performing a duty away from Texas Department of Criminal Justice or Texas Juvenile Justice Department property, the state shall reimburse the county for expenses incurred by the county, in an amount that the court determines to be reasonable, for payment of:

(1) salaries and expenses of foreign language interpreters and interpreters for deaf persons whose services are necessary to the prosecution;

(2) consultation fees of experts whose assistance is directly related to the prosecution;

(3) travel expenses for witnesses;

(4) expenses for the food, lodging, and compensation of jurors;

(5) compensation of witnesses;

(6) the cost of preparation of a statement of facts and a transcript of the trial for purposes of appeal;

(7) if the death of a person is an element of the offense, expenses of an inquest relating to the death;

(8) food, lodging, and travel expenses incurred by the prosecutor's staff during travel essential to the prosecution of the offense;

(9) court reporter's fees; and

(10) the cost of special security officers.

(b) If there is a change of venue, the court may, in its discretion, determine that a special prosecutor should be hired for the prosecution of an offense described in Section (a), and the state shall reimburse the county for the salary and expenses of the special prosecutor if the court determines that the hiring of the special prosecutor was reasonable and necessary for effective prosecution. The amount of reimbursement may not exceed an amount that the court determines to be reasonable.

(c) The court shall certify the amount of reimbursement for expenses under Sections (a) and (b) on presentation by the county of an itemized and verified receipt for those expenses.

(d) The state shall reimburse the county for expenses incurred by the county for the investigation of an offense described in Section (a), whether or not the investigation results in the prosecution of an offense, and shall reimburse the county for reasonable operational expenses of the special prison prosecution unit, including educational activities for the staff and general expenses relating to its investigative and prosecutorial duties.

(e) The court shall certify the amount of reimbursement for expenses under Sections (a) and (b) to the comptroller. The comptroller shall issue a warrant in that amount to the commissioners court of the county or, if the comptroller determines that the amount certified by the court is unreasonable, in an amount that the comptroller determines to be reasonable.

(f) The commissioners court of the county shall certify the amount of reimbursement for expenses under Section (d) to the comptroller. The comptroller shall issue a warrant in that amount to the commissioners court or, if the comptroller determines that the amount certified by the commissioners court is unreasonable, in an amount that the comptroller determines to be reasonable.

(g) Notwithstanding any other provision of this article, the expenses submitted by the county for reimbursement may not exceed the amount the county would pay for the same activity or service, if that activity or service was not reimbursed by the state. The county judge shall certify compliance with this section on request by the comptroller.

Art. 104.004. Extraordinary Costs of Prosecution.

(a) The criminal justice division of the governor's office may distribute money appropriated by the legislature for the purposes of this article to a county for the reimbursement of expenses incurred by the county during the fiscal year during which application is made or the fiscal year preceding the year during which application is made for the investigation or prosecution of an offense under Section 19.03, Penal Code, or an offense under the Penal Code alleged by the attorney representing the state to have been committed for a purpose or reason described by Article 42.014.

(b) For each fiscal year, the division shall distribute at least 50 percent of the money distributed under this article during that year to counties with a population of less than 50,000, except that if the total distributions applied for by those counties is less than 50 percent of the money distributed during that year, the division is only required to distribute to those counties the amount of money for which applications have been made.

(c) The division may adopt a budget and rules for the distribution of money under this article.

(d) All money distributed to a county under this article and its expenditure by the county are subject to audit by the state auditor.

TRANSPORTATION CODE

TITLE 3
AVIATION

CHAPTER 24
OPERATION OF AIRCRAFT

SUBCHAPTER B
OTHER FEDERAL REQUIREMENTS REGARDING AIRCRAFT

Sec. 24.011. Failure to Register Aircraft; Offense.

(a) A person commits an offense if the person operates or navigates an aircraft that the person knows is not properly registered under Federal Aviation Administration aircraft registration regulations, 14 C.F.R. Part 47, as those regulations existed on September 1, 1985.

(b) An offense under Subsection (a) is a felony of the third degree.

Sec. 24.012. Aircraft Identification Numbers; Offense.

(a) The failure to have the aircraft identification numbers clearly displayed on an aircraft in compliance with federal aviation regulations is probable cause for a peace officer to further inspect the aircraft to determine the identity of the owner of the aircraft.

(b) A peace officer may inspect an aircraft under Subsection (a) if the aircraft is located on public property or on private property if the officer has the consent of the property owner.

(c) A person commits an offense if the person operates an aircraft that the person knows does not have aircraft identification numbers that comply with federal aviation regulations.

(d) An offense under Subsection (c) is a felony of the third degree.

(e) In this section, "federal aviation regulations" means the regulations adopted by the Federal Aviation Administration regarding identification and registration marking, 14 C.F.R. Part 45, as those regulations existed on September 1, 1985, except a regulation in existence on September 1, 1985, that is inconsistent with a regulation adopted after that date.

Sec. 24.013. Aircraft Fuel Containers; Offense.

(a) A person commits an offense if the person operates or intends to operate an aircraft equipped with:

(1) a fuel container that the person knows does not conform to federal aviation regulations or that has not been approved by the Federal Aviation Administration by inspection or special permit; or

(2) a pipe, hose, or auxiliary pump that is used or intended for transferring fuel to the primary fuel system of an aircraft from a fuel container that the person knows does not conform to federal aviation regulations or that has not been approved by the Federal Aviation Administration by inspection or special permit.

(b) An offense under Subsection (a) is a felony of the third degree.

(c) A peace officer may seize an aircraft equipped with a fuel container that is the subject of an offense under Subsection (a).

(d) An aircraft seized under Subsection (c) may be forfeited to the Department of Public Safety in the same manner as property subject to forfeiture under Article 18.18, Code of Criminal Procedure.

(e) An aircraft forfeited under Subsection (d) is subject to Chapter 2205, Government Code.

(f) In this section:

(1) "Federal aviation regulations" means the following regulations adopted by the Federal Aviation Administration as those regulations existed on September 1, 1985, except a regulation in existence on September 1, 1985, that is inconsistent with a regulation adopted after that date:

(A) certification procedures for products and parts, 14 C.F.R. Part 21;

(B) maintenance, preventive maintenance, rebuilding, and alteration regulations, 14 C.F.R. Part 43; and

(C) general operating and flight rules, 14 C.F.R. Part 91.

(2) "Operate" means to use, cause to use, or authorize to use an aircraft for air navigation and includes:

(A) the piloting of an aircraft, with or without the right of legal control;

(B) the taxiing of an aircraft before takeoff or after landing; and

(C) the postflight or preflight inspection or starting of the engine of an aircraft.

SUBCHAPTER C
USE OF PUBLIC ROADS BY AIRCRAFT

Sec. 24.021. Taking Off, Landing, or Maneuvering Aircraft on Highways, Roads, or Streets; Offense.

(a) A person commits an offense if the person takes off, lands, or maneuvers an aircraft, whether heavier or lighter than air, on a public highway, road, or street except:

(1) when necessary to prevent serious injury to a person or property;

(2) during or within a reasonable time after an emergency; or

(3) as provided by Section 24.022.

(b) An offense under Subsection (a) is a misdemeanor punishable by a fine of not less than $25 and not more than $200.

(c) The procedure prescribed by Section 543.003 applies to a violation of this section.

Sec. 24.022. Use of Aircraft on County Roads.

(a) A commissioners court of a county may enact ordinances to ensure the safe use of county roads by aircraft. An ordinance may:

(1) limit the kinds of aircraft that may use the roads;

(2) establish the procedure that a pilot shall follow before using a road, including requiring the pilot to furnish persons with flags at both ends of the road to be used; or

(3) establish other requirements considered necessary for the safe use of the roads by aircraft.

(b) A pilot who follows the ordinances adopted under Subsection (a):

(1) may land or take off in the aircraft on a county road; and

(2) is not subject to the traffic laws of this state during the landing or takeoff.

TITLE 5
RAILROADS

SUBTITLE Z
MISCELLANEOUS PROVISIONS

CHAPTER 192
ENGINEER'S OPERATOR PERMIT AND TRAIN OPERATOR PERMIT

Sec. 192.001. Issuance of Permit.

(a) A railroad company shall issue an engineer's operator permit to each person whom the company employs to operate or permits to operate a railroad locomotive in this state.

(b) A railroad company shall issue a train operator permit to each person:

(1) whom the company employs to operate or permits to operate a train in this state; and

(2) who has not been issued an engineer's operator permit.

Sec. 192.002. Permit Required.

(a) A person operating a railroad locomotive in this state shall have in the person's immediate possession an engineer's operator permit issued under this chapter.

(b) A person operating a train in this state, other than a person issued a permit under Section 192.001(a), shall have in the person's immediate possession a train operator permit issued under this chapter.

Sec. 192.003. Form of Permit.

A permit issued under this chapter must include the permit holder's name, address, physical description, photograph, and date of birth.

Sec. 192.004. Proof of Identification.

If a peace officer requires a person to show proof of identification in connection with the person's operation of a railroad locomotive or train, the person:

(1) shall display the person's permit issued under this chapter; and

(2) may not be required to display a driver's license issued under Chapter 521 or commercial driver's license issued under Chapter 522.

Sec. 192.005. Record of Accident or Violation.

If a person operating a railroad locomotive or train is involved in an accident with another train or a motor vehicle or is arrested for violation of a law relating to the person's operation of a railroad locomotive or train:

Transportation Code

(1) the number of or other identifying information on the person's driver's license or commercial driver's license may not be included in any report of the accident or violation; and

(2) the person's involvement in the accident or violation may not be recorded in the person's individual driving record maintained by the Department of Public Safety.

TITLE 6 ROADWAYS

SUBTITLE A TEXAS DEPARTMENT OF TRANSPORTATION

CHAPTER 201 GENERAL PROVISIONS AND ADMINISTRATION

SUBCHAPTER K ROAD AND HIGHWAY USE; SIGNS

Sec. 201.901. Prohibiting Use of Highway or Road.

(a) The commission may prohibit the use of any part of a highway or road under the control of the department by any vehicle that will unduly damage the highway or road when:

(1) because of wet weather or recent construction or repairs, the highway or road cannot be safely used without probable serious damage to it; or

(2) a bridge or culvert on the highway or road is unsafe.

(b) Before prohibiting the use of a highway or road under this section, the commission shall post notices that state the maximum load permitted and the time the use of the highway or road is prohibited. The notices must be posted at locations that enable drivers to detour to avoid the restricted highway or road.

(c) The commission may not prohibit the use of a highway or road under this section until a detour has been provided.

(d) If the owner or operator of a vehicle that is prohibited from using a highway or road under this section is aggrieved by the prohibition, the person may file with the county judge of the county in which the restricted highway or road is located a written complaint that sets forth the nature of the grievance. On the filing of the complaint the county judge immediately shall set the issue for a hearing to be held not later than the third day after the date on which the complaint is filed. The county judge shall give to the commission written notice of the day and purpose of each hearing.

(e) The county judge shall hear testimony offered by the parties. On conclusion of the hearing, the county judge shall sustain, revoke, or modify the commission's decision on the restriction. The county judge's judgment is final as to the issues raised.

(f) A person who violates a prohibition established under this section before or after it is approved by the county judge under Subsection (e) commits an offense. An offense under this section is a misdemeanor punishable by a fine not to exceed $200.

Sec. 201.902. Road Use by Bicyclists.

(a) The department shall designate:

(1) a statewide bicycle coordinator; and

(2) a bicycle coordinator in each regional office.

(b) A bicycle coordinator shall assist the department in developing rules and plans to enhance the use of the state highway system by bicyclists.

(c) The commission shall adopt rules relating to use of roads in the state highway system by bicyclists, including provisions for:

(1) the specific duties of the statewide bicycle coordinator and the regional bicycle coordinators;

(2) obtaining comments from bicyclists on:

(A) a highway project that might affect bicycle use;

(B) the use of a highway for bicycling events; and

(C) department policies affecting bicycle use of state highways;

(3) the consideration of acceptable national bicycle design, construction, and maintenance standards on a project in an area with significant bicycle use; and

(4) any other matter the commission determines necessary to enhance the use of the state highway system by bicyclists.

(d) A rule adopted under this section may not be inconsistent with Chapter 551.

Sec. 201.903. Classification, Designation, and Marking of Highways.

(a) The department may classify, designate, and mark state highways in this state.

Transportation Code

(b) The department may provide a uniform system of marking and signing state highways under the control of the state. The system must correlate with and, to the extent possible, conform to the system adopted in other states.

Sec. 201.904. Speed Signs.

The department shall erect and maintain on the highways and roads of this state appropriate signs that show the maximum lawful speed for commercial motor vehicles, truck tractors, truck trailers, truck semitrailers, and motor vehicles engaged in the business of transporting passengers for compensation or hire (buses).

SUBCHAPTER L
ELECTRONIC ISSUANCE OF OUTDOOR ADVERTISING LICENSES

Sec. 201.931. Definitions.

In this subchapter:

(1) "Digital signature" means an electronic identifier intended by the person using it to have the same force and effect as the use of a manual signature.

(2) "License" means a license or permit for a commercial sign issued under Chapter 391 or for an off-premise sign issued under Chapter 394.

Sec. 201.932. Application for and Issuance of License.

(a) The commission may by rule provide for the filing of a license application and the issuance of a license by electronic means.

(b) The commission may limit applicant eligibility under Subsection (a) if the rules include reasonable eligibility criteria.

Sec. 201.933. Digital Signature.

(a) A license application received by the department is considered signed if a digital signature is transmitted with the application and intended by the applicant to authenticate the license in accordance with Subsection (b).

(b) The department may only accept a digital signature used to authenticate a license application under procedures that:

(1) comply with any applicable rules of another state agency having jurisdiction over department use or acceptance of a digital signature; and

(2) provide for consideration of factors that may affect a digital signature's reliability, including whether a digital signature is:

(A) unique to the person using it;

(B) capable of independent verification;

(C) under the sole control of the person using it; and

(D) transmitted in a manner that will make it infeasible to change the data in the communication or digital signature without invalidating the digital signature.

Sec. 201.934. Payment of Fees.

The commission may adopt rules regarding the method of payment of a fee for a license issued under this subchapter. The rules may authorize the use of electronic funds transfer or a valid credit card issued by a financial institution chartered by a state or the federal government or by a nationally recognized credit organization approved by the department. The rules may require the payment of a discount or service charge for a credit card payment in addition to the fee.

SUBTITLE B
STATE HIGHWAY SYSTEM

CHAPTER 224
ACQUISITION, CONSTRUCTION, AND MAINTENANCE

SUBCHAPTER F
CONGESTION MITIGATION PROJECTS AND FACILITIES

Sec. 224.155. Failure or Refusal to Pay Toll; Offense [Repealed].

Repealed by Acts 2005, 79th Leg., ch. 281 (H.B. 2702), § 2.101(3), effective June 14, 2005.

Sec. 224.156. Collection Fee; Notice; Offense [Repealed].

Repealed by Acts 2005, 79th Leg., ch. 281 (H.B. 2702), § 2.101(3), effective June 14, 2005.

Sec. 224.158. Use and Return of Transponders [Repealed].

Repealed by Acts 2005, 79th Leg., ch. 281 (H.B. 2702), § 2.101(3), effective June 14, 2005.

Sec. 224.160. Automated Enforcement Technology [Repealed].

Repealed by Acts 2005, 79th Leg., ch. 281 (H.B. 2702), § 2.101(3), effective June 14, 2005.

CHAPTER 228
STATE HIGHWAY TOLL PROJECTS

SUBCHAPTER B
USE AND OPERATION OF TOLL PROJECTS OR SYSTEMS.

Sec. 228.054. Toll Payment Required; Emergency Vehicles Exempt.

(a) Except as provided by Subsection (e), the operator of a vehicle, other than an authorized emergency vehicle, as defined by Section 541.201, that is driven or towed through a toll collection facility shall pay the proper toll. The exemption from payment of a toll for an authorized emergency vehicle applies regardless of whether the vehicle is:

(1) responding to an emergency;

(2) displaying a flashing light; or

(3) marked as an emergency vehicle.

(b) [Repealed.]

(c) [Repealed.]

(d) In this section, "authorized emergency vehicle" has the meaning assigned by Section 541.201.

(e) Notwithstanding Subsection (a), the department may waive the requirement of the payment of a toll or may authorize the payment of a reduced toll for any vehicle or class of vehicles.

Sec. 228.0545. Toll Not Paid at Time of Use; Invoice.

(a) As an alternative to requiring payment of a toll at the time a vehicle is driven or towed through a toll collection facility, the department may use video billing or other tolling methods to permit the registered owner of the vehicle to pay the toll at a later date.

(b) The department may use automated enforcement technology authorized under Section 228.058 to identify the registered owner of the vehicle for purposes of billing, collection, and enforcement activities.

(c) The department shall send by first class mail to the registered owner of a vehicle a written invoice containing an assessment for tolls incurred by the vehicle.

(d) The department shall send the invoice required under Subsection (c) and related communications to:

(1) the registered owner's address as shown in the vehicle registration records of the Texas Department of Motor Vehicles or the analogous department or agency of another state or country; or

(2) an alternate address provided by the owner or derived through other reliable means.

(e) The department may provide that the invoice under Subsection (c), instead of being sent by first class mail, be sent as an electronic record to a registered owner that agrees to the terms of the electronic record transmission of the information.

SUBTITLE C
COUNTY ROADS AND BRIDGES

CHAPTER 251
GENERAL COUNTY AUTHORITY RELATING TO ROADS AND BRIDGES

SUBCHAPTER A
GENERAL PROVISIONS

Sec. 251.011. Detour Roads.

(a) The commissioners court of a county shall establish detour roads for the convenience of the public when a county road that is not part of the state highway system must be closed to traffic for road construction. When a county detour road is in use, the county has the same authority over the road as over an established public road.

(b) The commissioners court shall:

(1) post all signs necessary for the convenience and guidance of the public at each end of a county detour road; and

(2) maintain a county detour road so that it is reasonably adequate for normal traffic requirements.

Sec. 251.013. Road Names and Address Numbers.

(a) The commissioners court of a county by order may adopt uniform standards for naming public roads located wholly or partly in unincorporated

Transportation Code

areas of the county and for assigning address numbers to property located in unincorporated areas of the county. The standards apply to any new public road that is established.

(b) The commissioners court of a county by order may adopt a name for a public road located wholly or partly in an unincorporated area of the county and may assign address numbers to property located in an unincorporated area of the county for which there is no established address system.

(b-1) The commissioners court of a county by order may:

(1) adopt standards and specifications for the design and installation of address number signs to identify properties located in unincorporated areas of the county, including standards or specifications as to sign size, material, longevity, ability to be seen and to reflect light, and any other factor the commissioners court considers necessary or appropriate; and

(2) require the owners or occupants of properties in unincorporated areas of the county to:

(A) obtain address number signs that comply with the standards and specifications adopted under Subdivision (1); and

(B) install and maintain those signs at the locations and in the manner required by those standards and specifications.

(c) If an order adopted under this section conflicts with a municipal ordinance, the municipal ordinance prevails in the territory in which it is effective.

(d) A commissioners court may adopt an order under this section only after conducting a public hearing on the proposed order. The court shall give public notice of the hearing at least two weeks before the date of the hearing.

(e) A person who knowingly fails or refuses to comply with an order of a commissioners court under Subsection (b-1)(2) commits an offense. An offense under this subsection is a Class C misdemeanor.

Sec. 251.016. General County Authority over Roads, Highways, and Bridges.

The commissioners court of a county may exercise general control over all roads, highways, and bridges in the county.

Sec. 251.0165. Control of Access Within Certain Counties.

(a) Except as limited by Section 203.032, a county with a population of 3.3 million or more or a county adjacent to a county with a population of 3.3 million or more, by resolution or order, may:

(1) deny access to or from a controlled access highway within the county and outside the limits of a municipality, including a state highway, from or to adjoining public or private real property and from or to a public or private way intersecting the highway, except at specific locations designated by the county; and

(2) designate locations on a controlled access highway within the county and outside the limits of a municipality, including a state highway, at which access to or from the highway is permitted and determine the type and extent of access permitted at each location.

(b) This section does not apply to the placement of or access to a utility facility in or near a highway right-of-way.

SUBCHAPTER E COUNTY TRAFFIC REGULATIONS

Sec. 251.151. Authority of Commissioners Court to Regulate Certain Roads.

(a) The commissioners court of a county may regulate traffic on a county road or on real property owned by the county that is under the jurisdiction of the commissioners court.

(b) Under the terms of an interlocal contract under Section 791.036, Government Code, the commissioners court of a county may:

(1) by order apply the county's traffic regulations to a public road in the county that is owned, operated, and maintained by a special district and located wholly or partly in the county; and

(2) provide for the enforcement of the regulations.

(c) A public road that is subject to an order under Subsection (b) is considered to be a county road for purposes of applying a traffic regulation to the public road.

Sec. 251.152. Public Hearing Required.

(a) Except as provided by Section 251.159, before the commissioners court may issue a traffic regulation under this subchapter, the commissioners court must hold a public hearing on the proposed regulation.

(b) The commissioners court shall publish notice of the hearing in a newspaper of general circulation in the county. The notice must be published not later than the seventh or earlier than the 30th day before the date of the hearing.

Transportation Code

Sec. 251.153. Load Limits on County Roads and Bridges.

(a) The commissioners court of a county may establish load limits for any county road or bridge in the manner prescribed by Section 621.301.

(b) The commissioners court may authorize a county traffic officer, sheriff, deputy sheriff, constable, or deputy constable to weigh a vehicle to ascertain whether the vehicle's load exceeds the limit prescribed by the commissioners court.

Sec. 251.154. Maximum Reasonable and Prudent Speeds on County Roads.

(a) The commissioners court of a county, by order entered on the minutes of the court, may determine and set a maximum reasonable and prudent speed for a vehicle travelling on any segment of a county road, including a road or highway intersection, railroad grade crossing, curve, or hill.

(b) In determining the maximum reasonable and prudent speed, the commissioners court shall consider all circumstances on the affected segment of the road, including the width and condition of the road surface and the usual traffic on the road.

(c) The maximum reasonable and prudent speed set by the commissioners court under this section may be lower than the maximum speed set by law for a vehicle travelling on a public highway.

(d) A speed limit set by the commissioners court under this section is effective when appropriate signs giving notice of the speed limit are installed on the affected segment of the county road.

Sec. 251.155. Restricted Traffic Zones.

(a) The commissioners court of a county may adopt regulations establishing a system of traffic control devices in restricted traffic zones on:

(1) property described by Section 251.151(a); and

(2) property abutting a public road that is the subject of an order under Section 251.151(b) if the property is owned by the district that is subject to the order or is a public right-of-way.

(b) A system of traffic control devices adopted under this section must conform to the manual and specifications of the Texas Department of Transportation.

(c) The commissioners court by order entered on its minutes may install and maintain on property to which this section applies any traffic signal light, stop sign, or no-parking sign that the court considers necessary for public safety.

Sec. 251.156. Parking Restrictions.

(a) The commissioners court of a county by order may have signs installed that prohibit or restrict the stopping, standing, or parking of a vehicle in a restricted traffic zone on property described by Section 251.151, if in the opinion of the court the stopping, standing, or parking:

(1) is dangerous to those using the road or property; or

(2) will unduly interfere with:

(A) the free movement of traffic; or

(B) the necessary control or use of the property.

(b) The commissioners court of a county by order may provide that in a prosecution for an offense involving the stopping, standing, or parking of an unattended motor vehicle in a restricted traffic zone on property described by Section 251.151 it is presumed that the registered owner of the vehicle is the person who stopped, stood, or parked the vehicle at the time and place the offense occurred.

Sec. 251.157. Prohibiting or Restricting Use of Road.

(a) In this section, "road supervisor" means a person authorized to supervise roads in a county or in a district or precinct of a county.

(b) A road supervisor may prohibit or restrict, if an alternative, more suitable road is available within the county at the time, the use of a road or a section of a road under the supervisor's control by any vehicle that will unduly damage the road when:

(1) because of wet weather or recent construction or repairs, the road cannot be safely used without probable serious damage to it; or

(2) a bridge or culvert on the road is unsafe.

(c) Before prohibiting or restricting the use of a road under this section, the road supervisor shall post notices that state the road and the expected duration of the prohibition or restriction, and identify the alternate route. The notices must be posted at locations that enable drivers to detour to avoid the restricted road.

(d) The road supervisor may not prohibit the use of a road under this section until a detour has been provided.

(e) If the owner or operator of a vehicle that is prohibited or restricted from using a road under this section is aggrieved by the prohibition or restriction, the person may file with the county judge of the county in which the restricted road is located a written complaint that sets forth the nature of the grievance. On the filing of the complaint the county judge promptly shall set the issue for a hearing to be held not later than the third day after

Transportation Code

the date on which the complaint is filed. The county judge shall give the road supervisor, the county engineer, and the commissioners court written notice of the date and purpose of each hearing.

(f) The county judge shall hear testimony offered by the parties. On conclusion of the hearing, the county judge shall sustain, revoke, or modify the road supervisor's decision on the prohibition or restriction. The county judge's judgment is final as to the issues raised.

Sec. 251.1575. Prohibiting Use of Road for Certain Vehicles.

(a) A commissioners court may identify an alternate route to a road and require heavy vehicles having a gross weight of more than 60,000 pounds to travel the alternate route in order to prevent excessive damage to the road due to the volume of traffic by such heavy vehicles. An alternate route identified under this subsection must be:

(1) of sufficient strength and design to withstand the weight of the vehicles traveling the alternate route, including any bridges or culverts along the road; and

(2) located within the same county as the road described by this subsection.

(b) Notice of the prohibition must be provided in the same manner as for a prohibition or restriction under Section 251.157.

(c) A person who is required to operate or move a vehicle or other object on an alternate route identified under this section is not liable for damage sustained by the road, including a bridge, as a result of the operation or movement of the vehicle or other object, unless the act, error, or omission resulting in the damage constitutes:

(1) wanton, wilful, and intentional misconduct; or

(2) gross negligence.

Sec. 251.158. Temporary Use of County Road for Festival or Civic Event.

(a) The commissioners court of a county by order may permit the temporary use of a county road located in an unincorporated area of the county for a civic event, including a festival.

(b) The court by order shall establish procedures for the temporary diversion of traffic from the road being used for the event.

Sec. 251.159. Delegation of Commissioners' Authority.

(a) This section applies only to a county with a population of more than 78,000.

(b) The commissioners court of a county may delegate to the county engineer or other county employee any function of the commissioners court under this subchapter, except as provided by Subsection (e). An action of the county engineer or other county employee under this section has the same effect as if the action were an action of the commissioners court.

(c) Before issuing a traffic regulation under this subchapter, the commissioners court, in lieu of publishing notice required by a law other than this subchapter, may give notice of the proposed regulation by posting a conspicuous sign in any location to be affected by the regulation.

(d) The commissioners court is not required to hold a public hearing on the proposed traffic regulation unless a resident of the county requests a public hearing. The request must be in writing and made before the eighth day after the later of:

(1) the date that the sign is posted; or

(2) the date that the notice under Section 251.152 is published.

(e) If a public hearing is requested, the commissioners court may not delegate the duty to hold the hearing.

Sec. 251.160. Liability of Owner or Operator for Road Damage.

(a) A person who operates or moves a vehicle or other object on a public road or bridge and the owner of the vehicle or other object are jointly and severally liable for damage sustained by the road or bridge as a result of the negligent operation or moving of the vehicle or other object or as a result of the operation or movement of the vehicle at a time prohibited by the officials with authority over the road.

(b) The county judge by appropriate legal action may recover damages for which liability is provided by this section. The county attorney shall represent the county in an action under this subsection. Damages collected under this subsection are for the use of the county to benefit the damaged road or bridge.

Sec. 251.161. Violations of Subchapter; Offense.

(a) A person commits a misdemeanor offense if the person:

(1) stops, stands, or parks a vehicle in violation of a restriction stated on a sign installed under Section 251.156;

(2) defaces, injures, knocks down, or removes a sign or traffic control device installed under an

Transportation Code

order of the commissioners court of a county issued under this subchapter;

(3) operates a motor vehicle in violation of an order of the commissioners court entered under this subchapter; or

(4) otherwise violates this subchapter.

(b) An offense under this section is punishable by a fine not to exceed $200.

(c) If conduct that constitutes an offense under this section also constitutes an offense under any other law, the actor may be prosecuted under this section or the other law.

(d) [Repealed by Acts 2007, 80th Leg., ch. 806 (S.B. 1127), § 2, effective September 1, 2007.]

SUBTITLE D
ROAD LAWS RELATING TO PARTICULAR COUNTIES

CHAPTER 284
CAUSEWAYS, BRIDGES, TUNNELS, TURNPIKES, FERRIES, AND HIGHWAYS IN CERTAIN COUNTIES

SUBCHAPTER C
CONSTRUCTION AND OPERATION

Sec. 284.069. Tolls and Charges.

If bonds under this chapter are payable in whole or in part from project revenue, the county shall impose tolls and charges that are, together with other money or revenues available for the project, including ad valorem tax, sufficient to:

(1) pay the maintenance and operating expenses of the project;

(2) pay the principal of, premium of, if any, and interest on the bonds when due;

(3) establish a reserve for payment of bond principal, premium, and interest; and

(4) establish an adequate fund for project depreciation and replacement.

Sec. 284.070. Nonpayment of Toll; Offense.

(a) A person commits an offense if the person:

(1) operates a vehicle on a county project; and

(2) fails or refuses to pay a toll imposed under Section 284.069.

(b) An offense under this section is a misdemeanor punishable by a fine not to exceed $100.

(c) The county may take and retain possession of a vehicle operated in violation of Subsection (a) until the amount of the toll and all charges in connection with the toll are paid.

(d) In a county with a population over 2.8 million, an offense under this section may be prosecuted in any precinct in the county in which the offense was committed.

(e) An authorized emergency vehicle, as defined by Section 541.201, is exempt from payment of a toll imposed under this chapter regardless of whether the vehicle is:

(1) responding to an emergency;

(2) displaying a flashing light; or

(3) marked as an emergency vehicle.

Sec. 284.0701. Administrative Costs; Notice; Offense.

(a) In the event of an offense committed under Section 284.070, on issuance of a written notice of nonpayment, the registered owner of the nonpaying vehicle is liable for the payment of both the proper toll and an administrative cost.

(b) The county may impose and collect the administrative cost so as to recover the expense of collecting the unpaid toll, not to exceed $100. The county shall send a written notice of nonpayment to the registered owner of the vehicle at that owner's address as shown in the vehicle registration records of the Texas Department of Motor Vehicles by first-class mail not later than the 30th day after the date of the alleged failure to pay and may require payment not sooner than the 30th day after the date the notice was mailed. The registered owner shall pay a separate toll and administrative cost for each event of nonpayment under Section 284.070.

(c) The registered owner of a vehicle for which the proper toll was not paid who is mailed a written notice of nonpayment under Subsection (b) and fails to pay the proper toll and administrative cost within the time specified by the notice of nonpayment commits an offense. Each failure to pay a toll or administrative cost under this subsection is a separate offense.

(d) It is an exception to the application of Subsection (a) or (c) if the registered owner of the vehicle is a lessor of the vehicle and not later than the 30th day after the date the notice of nonpayment is mailed provides to the authority:

(1) a copy of the rental, lease, or other contract document covering the vehicle on the date of the

nonpayment under Section 284.070, with the name and address of the lessee clearly legible; or

(2) electronic data, other than a photocopy or scan of a rental or lease contract, that contains the information required under Sections 521.460(c)(1), (2), and (3) covering the vehicle on the date of the nonpayment under Section 284.070.

(d-1) If the lessor provides the required information within the period prescribed under Subsection (d), the authority may send a notice of nonpayment to the lessee at the address provided under Subsection (d) by first class mail before the 30th day after the date of receipt of the required information from the lessor. The lessee of the vehicle for which the proper toll was not paid who is mailed a written notice of nonpayment under this subsection and fails to pay the proper toll and administrative cost within the time specified by the notice of nonpayment commits an offense. The lessee shall pay a separate toll and administrative cost for each event of nonpayment. Each failure to pay a toll or administrative cost under this subsection is a separate offense.

(e) It is an exception to the application of Subsection (a) or (c) if the registered owner of the vehicle transferred ownership of the vehicle to another person before the event of nonpayment under Section 284.070 occurred, submitted written notice of the transfer to the Texas Department of Motor Vehicles in accordance with Section 501.147, and before the 30th day after the date the notice of nonpayment is mailed, provides to the county the name and address of the person to whom the vehicle was transferred. If the former owner of the vehicle provides the required information within the period prescribed, the county may send a notice of nonpayment to the person to whom ownership of the vehicle was transferred at the address provided by the former owner by first-class mail before the 30th day after the date of receipt of the required information from the former owner. The subsequent owner of the vehicle for which the proper toll was not paid who is mailed a written notice of nonpayment under this subsection and fails to pay the proper toll and administrative cost within the time specified by the notice of nonpayment commits an offense. The subsequent owner shall pay a separate toll and administrative cost for each event of nonpayment under Section 284.070. Each failure to pay a toll or administrative cost under this subsection is a separate offense.

(f) An offense under this section is a misdemeanor punishable by a fine not to exceed $250.

(g) The court in which a person is convicted of an offense under this section shall also collect the proper toll and administrative cost and forward the toll and cost to the county.

(h) In this section, "registered owner" means the owner of a vehicle as shown on the vehicle registration records of the Texas Department of Motor Vehicles or the analogous department or agency of another state or country.

Sec. 284.0702. Prima Facie Evidence; Defense.

(a) In the prosecution of an offense under Section 284.070 or 284.0701, proof that the vehicle was driven or towed through the toll collection facility without payment of the proper toll may be shown by a video recording, photograph, electronic recording, or other appropriate evidence, including evidence obtained by automated enforcement technology.

(b) In the prosecution of an offense under Section 284.0701(c), (d-1), or (e):

(1) a computer record of the department of the registered owner of the vehicle is prima facie evidence of its contents and that the defendant was the registered owner of the vehicle when the underlying event of nonpayment under Section 284.070 occurred; and

(2) a copy of the rental, lease, or other contract document, or the electronic data provided to the authority under Section 284.0701(d), covering the vehicle on the date of the underlying event of nonpayment under Section 284.070 is prima facie evidence of its contents and that the defendant was the lessee of the vehicle when the underlying event of nonpayment under Section 284.070 occurred.

(c) It is a defense to prosecution under Section 284.0701(c), (d-1), or (e) that the vehicle in question was stolen before the failure to pay the proper toll occurred and had not been recovered before the failure to pay occurred, but only if the theft was reported to the appropriate law enforcement authority before the earlier of:

(1) the occurrence of the failure to pay; or

(2) eight hours after the discovery of the theft.

Sec. 284.0703. Method of Sending Invoice or Notice.

As authorized under Section 322.008(d)(2), Business & Commerce Code, a county may provide an invoice or notice required under this chapter to be sent by first class mail instead as an electronic record:

(1) if the recipient of the information agrees to the transmission of the information as an electronic record; and

(2) on terms acceptable to the recipient.

SUBCHAPTER D
UNAUTHORIZED USE OF TOLL ROADS IN CERTAIN COUNTIES

Sec. 284.201. Applicability of Subchapter.

This subchapter applies only to:

(1) a county with a population of more than 3.3 million; or

(2) a county adjacent to a county with a population of more than 3.3 million.

Sec. 284.202. Order Prohibiting Operation of Motor Vehicle on Toll Project.

(a) The commissioners court of a county by order may prohibit the operation of a motor vehicle on a county project described by Section 284.001(3) if:

(1) an operator of the vehicle has failed to pay a required toll or charge; and

(2) the county provides the registered owner of the vehicle with notice of the unpaid toll or charge.

(b) The notice required by Subsection (a)(2) must be mailed to the registered owner of the vehicle at least 10 days before the date the prohibition takes effect.

(c) If the registered owner of the vehicle fails to pay a toll or charge not later than the 10th day after the notice under Subsection (b) is mailed, the commissioners court by order may impose a reasonable cost for expenses associated with collecting the unpaid toll or charge.

Sec. 284.203. Violation of Order; Offense.

(a) A person commits an offense if the person operates a motor vehicle or causes or allows the operation of a motor vehicle in violation of an order adopted under Section 284.202(a).

(b) An offense under this section is a Class C misdemeanor.

Sec. 284.2031. Civil and Criminal Enforcement: Fine.

(a) A county may impose, in addition to other costs, a fine of $1 on conviction to a defendant convicted of an offense under Section 284.070, 284.0701, or 284.203 in an action brought by the county or district attorney.

(b) In this section, a person is considered convicted if:

(1) a sentence is imposed on the person; or

(2) the court defers final disposition of the person's case.

(c) In a county with a population of 3.3 million or more, money collected under Subsection (a) shall be deposited in the county treasury in a special fund to be administered by the county attorney or district attorney. Expenditures from this fund shall be at the sole discretion of the attorney and may be used only to defray the salaries and expenses of the prosecutor's office, but in no event may the county attorney or district attorney supplement his or her own salary from this fund.

(d) In a county with a population of less than 3.3 million, money collected under Subsection (a) shall be deposited in the general fund of the county.

Sec. 284.2032. Fine in Certain Counties.

(a) A county with a population of 3.3 million or more may impose a fine of $1 for each event of nonpayment of a required toll or charge imposed under Section 284.069.

(b) Money collected under Subsection (a) shall be deposited in the county treasury in a special fund to be administered by the county attorney. Expenditures from the fund shall be at the sole discretion of the attorney and may be used only to defray the salaries and expenses of the attorney's office, but in no event may the county attorney supplement his or her own salary from the fund.

Sec. 284.204. Administrative Adjudication Hearing Procedure.

(a) The commissioners court of a county may adopt an administrative adjudication hearing procedure for a person who is suspected of having violated an order adopted under Section 284.202(a) on at least two separate occasions within a 12-month period.

(b) A hearing procedure adopted under Subsection (a) must provide:

(1) a period for a person charged with violating the order:

(A) to pay the toll or charge plus administrative costs authorized by Sections 284.202 and 284.2031; or

(B) to request a hearing;

(2) for appointment of one or more hearing officers with authority to administer oaths and issue orders compelling the attendance of witnesses and the production of documents; and

(3) for the amount and disposition of civil fines, costs, and fees.

(c) An order issued under Subsection (b)(2) may be enforced by a justice of the peace.

Sec. 284.205. Citation or Summons.

(a) A citation or summons issued under this subchapter must:

(1) inform the recipient of the time and place of the hearing; and

(2) notify the person charged with a violation that the person has the right of a hearing without delay.

(b) The original or any copy of the summons or citation is a record kept in the ordinary course of business of the county and is rebuttable proof of the facts it contains.

Sec. 284.206. Administrative Hearing: Presumption; Evidence of Ownership.

(a) In an administrative adjudication hearing under this subchapter it is presumed that the registered owner of the motor vehicle that is the subject of the hearing is the person who operated or allowed the operation of the motor vehicle in violation of the order.

(b) A computer record of the department of the registered vehicle owner is prima facie evidence of its contents and that the defendant was the registered owner of the vehicle at the time the violation occurred.

(c) Proof of the violation of the order may be shown by a video recording, photograph, electronic recording, or other appropriate evidence, including evidence obtained by automated enforcement technology.

(d) It is a defense to prosecution under this subchapter that the vehicle in question was stolen before the failure to pay the proper toll occurred and had not been recovered before the failure to pay occurred, but only if the theft was reported to the appropriate law enforcement authority before the earlier of:

(1) the occurrence of the failure to pay; or

(2) eight hours after the discovery of the theft.

Sec. 284.207. Attendance on Hearing.

(a) The peace officer or toll road agent who alleges a violation is not required to attend the hearing.

(b) The failure of a person charged with an offense to appear at the hearing is considered an admission of liability for the violation.

Sec. 284.208. Decision of Hearing Officer.

(a) The hearing officer shall issue a decision stating:

(1) whether the person charged is liable for a violation of the order; and

(2) the amount of the fine and costs to be assessed against the person.

(b) The hearing officer shall file the decision with the county clerk.

(c) A decision of a hearing officer filed under Subsection (b) must be kept in a separate index and file. The decision may be recorded using a computer printout, microfilm, microfiche, or a similar data processing technique.

(d), (e) [Repealed by Acts 2005, 79th Leg., ch. 963 (H.B. 1672), § 2(b), effective September 1, 2005.]

Sec. 284.209. Enforcement of Decision.

A decision issued under Section 284.208(a) may be enforced by:

(1) placing a device that prohibits movement of a motor vehicle on the vehicle that is the subject of the decision;

(2) imposing an additional fine if the fine for the offense is not paid within a specified time; or

(3) refusing to allow the registration of the vehicle.

Sec. 284.210. Appeal of Hearing Officer Decision.

(a) A person determined by a hearing officer to be in violation of an order may appeal the determination to a county court at law.

(b) To appeal, the person must file a petition with the court not later than the 30th day after the date the hearing officer's decision is filed with the county clerk. The petition must be accompanied by payment of the costs required by law for the court.

Sec. 284.211. Hearing on Appeal.

The court in which an appeal petition is filed shall:

(1) schedule a hearing; and

(2) notify all parties of the date, time, and place of the hearing.

Sec. 284.212. Effect of Appeal.

Service of notice of appeal does not stay the enforcement and collection of the decision of the hearing officer unless the person who files the appeal posts a bond with an agency designated by the county to accept payment for a violation.

Transportation Code

Sec. 284.213. Seizure of Transponders.

(a) For purposes of this section, "transponder" means a device, placed on or within a motor vehicle, that is capable of transmitting information used to assess or to collect tolls. A transponder is insufficiently funded when there are no remaining funds in the account in connection with which the transponder was issued.

(b) Any peace officer of this state may seize a stolen or insufficiently funded transponder and return it to the county, except that an insufficiently funded transponder may not be seized sooner than the 30th day after the date the county has sent a notice of delinquency to the holder of the account.

CHAPTER 285 COUNTY REGULATION OF ROADSIDE VENDOR AND SOLICITOR IN CERTAIN COUNTIES

Sec. 285.001. Regulation of Roadside Vendor and Solicitor.

(a) To promote the public safety, the commissioners court of a county with a population of more than 1.3 million by order may regulate the following in the unincorporated area of the county if they occur on a public highway or road, in the right-of-way of a public highway or road, or in a parking lot:

(1) the sale of items by a vendor of food or merchandise, including live animals;

(2) the erection, maintenance, or placement of a structure by a vendor of food or merchandise, including live animals; and

(3) the solicitation of money.

(b) The commissioners court of a county with a population of more than 700,000 and less than 800,000 that borders the United Mexican States by order may regulate the activities described by Subsection (a) in the manner described by that subsection, except that:

(1) the regulation of activities on or in the right-of-way of a public highway or road is limited to public highways and roads with a speed limit of 40 miles per hour or faster; and

(2) the county may not prohibit the sale of livestock.

(c) A county regulating vendors under Subsection (b) may require that a vendor be located not closer to the edge of the public highway or road than a distance that is equal to one-half the width of the right-of-way adjacent to the highway or road.

Sec. 285.002. Permit; Removal of Structure.

The commissioners court may:

(1) require a vendor or a person soliciting money to obtain a permit to sell the food or merchandise or to solicit money;

(2) charge a reasonable fee for the permit; and

(3) provide for the removal of a structure that is in violation of the regulations.

Sec. 285.003. Conflict with Statute or State Agency Rule.

If a regulation adopted under this chapter conflicts with a statute or state agency rule, the statute or rule prevails to the extent of the conflict.

Sec. 285.004. Violation of Regulation; Offense.

(a) A person commits an offense if the person knowingly:

(1) violates a regulation adopted under this chapter; or

(2) obstructs or threatens to obstruct the removal of a structure that is in violation of a regulation adopted under this chapter.

(b) Each day a violation continues is a separate offense.

(c) An offense under this section is a Class C misdemeanor.

SUBTITLE E MUNICIPAL STREETS

CHAPTER 311 GENERAL PROVISIONS RELATING TO MUNICIPAL STREETS

SUBCHAPTER A GENERAL AUTHORITY

Sec. 311.001. General Authority of Home-Rule Municipality.

(a) A home-rule municipality has exclusive control over and under the public highways, streets, and alleys of the municipality.

(b) The municipality may:

(1) control, regulate, or remove an encroachment or obstruction on a public street or alley of the municipality;

(2) open or change a public street or alley of the municipality; or

(3) improve a public highway, street, or alley of the municipality.

(c) Notwithstanding Subsection (a) or (b) or Section 311.007, before a municipality with a population of 1.9 million or more may install traffic calming measures within the municipality, the governing body of the municipality must:

(1) publish standards and criteria, which must include sufficient notice to allow the governing body to receive and consider public comments from residents within one-half mile of the proposed traffic calming measure;

(2) on request of affected residents, schedule and hold a public meeting before implementation of the measure; and

(3) if the measure involves the closure of a street to motor vehicular traffic, before the closure:

(A) hold a public hearing on the issue of the closure; and

(B) approve the closure by a majority vote.

Sec. 311.002. General Authority of General-Law Municipality.

(a) A general-law municipality has exclusive control over the highways, streets, and alleys of the municipality.

(b) The municipality may:

(1) abate or remove an encroachment or obstruction on a highway, street, or alley;

(2) open, change, regulate, or improve a street; or

(3) put a drain or sewer in a street, prevent the obstruction of the drain or sewer, or protect the drain or sewer from encroachment or damage.

(c) To carry out its powers under this section, the municipality may:

(1) regulate or change the grade of land; and

(2) require that the grade of land be raised by filling an area.

Sec. 311.003. Additional Authority of Type A General-Law Municipality.

The governing body of a Type A general-law municipality may:

(1) prevent an encroachment or obstruction on a sidewalk in the municipality;

(2) abate an encroachment or obstruction on a bridge, culvert, sidewalk, or crossway in the municipality;

(3) construct, regulate, or maintain a bridge, culvert, sidewalk, or crossway in the municipality;

(4) regulate the construction of a bridge, culvert, sewer, sidewalk, or crossway in the municipality;

(5) require a person to keep weeds, unclean matter, or trash from the street, sidewalk, or gutter in front of the person's premises; or

(6) require the owner of land to improve the sidewalk in front of the person's land.

Sec. 311.004. Authority over Sidewalk in Home-Rule Municipality.

A home-rule municipality may:

(1) construct a sidewalk;

(2) provide for the improvement of a sidewalk or the construction of a curb under an ordinance enforced by a penal provision; or

(3) declare a defective sidewalk to be a public nuisance.

Sec. 311.005. Movement of Structure on Street in Home-Rule Municipality.

A home-rule municipality may regulate the movement of a structure over or on a street of the municipality.

Sec. 311.006. Authority of County to Improve Street in Type B General-Law Municipality.

To facilitate travel on a street in a Type B general-law municipality, the commissioners court of a county may construct a bridge for or otherwise improve the street if:

(1) the street is a continuation of a public road of the county; and

(2) the governing body of the municipality consents.

Sec. 311.007. Closing of Street or Alley by Home-Rule Municipality.

A home-rule municipality may vacate, abandon, or close a street or alley.

Sec. 311.008. Closing of Street or Alley by General-Law Municipality.

The governing body of a general-law municipality by ordinance may vacate, abandon, or close a street or alley of the municipality if a petition signed by all the owners of real property abutting the street or alley is submitted to the governing body.

SUBCHAPTER B MUNICIPAL FREEWAYS

Sec. 311.031. Definition.

In this subchapter, "freeway" means a municipal street for which the right of access to or from adjoining land has been acquired in whole or in part from the owners of the adjoining land by the governing body of a municipality.

Sec. 311.032. Establishment of Freeway.

(a) The governing body of a municipality may establish, maintain, and operate a freeway.

(b) To establish a freeway by using a street that exists at the time of the establishment, the municipality must have the consent of the owners of lands abutting the freeway or must purchase or condemn the right of access to the abutting lands. This subsection does not require consent to establish a freeway for the first time as a new way for vehicular and pedestrian traffic.

Sec. 311.033. Acquisition of Land.

For the purposes of this subchapter, the governing body may acquire necessary property or property rights by gift, devise, purchase, or condemnation in the same manner that the governing body may acquire property for a municipal street.

Sec. 311.034. Control of Intersecting Street.

The governing body of a municipality may:

(1) close a street in the municipality at or near the place the street intersects a freeway;

(2) provide for the construction of a street over or under a freeway;

(3) connect a street with a freeway; or

(4) perform other actions on a street as necessary to carry out a power granted by this section.

Sec. 311.035. Lease of Land Under Freeway.

(a) A governmental agency that holds the title and property rights to land on which a freeway is located may lease for parking purposes the part of the land beneath an elevated section of the freeway.

(b) Revenue from the parking lease shall be used only for general governmental purposes.

SUBCHAPTER C AUTHORITY RELATING TO RAIL TRANSPORTATION

Sec. 311.051. Regulation of Street Railway by Type A General-Law Municipality.

(a) The governing body of a Type A general-law municipality may:

(1) require a street railway company to:

(A) keep the company's roads in repair;

(B) conform the area in which the company's tracks lie to the grade of the street on which they lie, if the municipality has graded the street; or

(C) take measures to provide for the safe and convenient travel of people on the street on which the company's tracks lie; or

(2) regulate the speed of vehicles that use the company's tracks.

(b) The governing body by ordinance may establish penalties to enforce a regulation adopted under this section.

Sec. 311.052. Regulation of Railroad by Type A General-Law Municipality.

The governing body of a Type A general-law municipality may:

(1) direct and control the location and construction of railroad tracks, turnouts, and switches and prohibit the construction of those facilities in a street or alley, unless that action has been authorized by law;

(2) require that railroad tracks, turnouts, and switches be constructed in a way that interferes as little as possible with the ordinary use of a street or alley and that leaves sufficient space on each side of the tracks for the safe and convenient passage of vehicles and people;

(3) require a railroad company to keep in repair the street or alley on which their tracks are located;

(4) order a railroad company to construct and keep in repair a crossing at the place where the company's tracks intersect a street or alley;

(5) require a railroad company to construct and keep in repair a ditch, sewer, or culvert;

(6) direct or prohibit the use of or regulate the speed of a locomotive in the municipality; or

(7) direct and control the location of railroad depots in the municipality.

Sec. 311.053. Closing Street for Certain Purposes in General-Law or Special-Law Municipality.

The governing body of a general-law municipality or special-law municipality may close temporarily or permanently any part of a street or alley for the exclusive use by a railroad company or other corporation having the right of eminent domain or may ratify an ordinance closing a street or alley for that purpose if:

(1) the municipality operates under a municipal charter that authorizes the governing body to take that action; or

(2) a majority of the qualified voters of the municipality voting at an election on the question approve the grant of authority to the governing body.

Sec. 311.054. Railroad Quiet Zone Located Outside Type A General-Law Municipality.

(a) This section applies only to a Type A general-law municipality that is an enclave surrounded entirely by a municipality with a population of 1.1 million or more.

(b) The governing body of the general-law municipality may enter into an interlocal contract with the surrounding municipality for the establishment of a railroad quiet zone located outside the boundaries of the general-law municipality that the governing body determines will benefit the general-law municipality.

(c) A general-law municipality may expend municipal funds and may issue certificates of obligation or bonds to pay for expenses associated with a railroad quiet zone under Subsection (b), including expenses related to feasibility, engineering, and traffic studies and improvements related to the railroad quiet zone.

SUBCHAPTER D
FRANCHISE TO USE STREETS IN HOME-RULE MUNICIPALITY

Sec. 311.071. Authority to Grant Franchise.

(a) The governing body of a home-rule municipality by ordinance may grant to a person a franchise to use or occupy a public street or alley of the municipality.

(b) The authority to grant a franchise is the exclusive authority of the governing body.

Sec. 311.072. Prohibition of Grant by Charter.

The charter of the municipality may not grant to a person a franchise described by Section 311.071.

Sec. 311.073. Election After Petition.

(a) The governing body shall submit to the voters of the municipality the question of granting a franchise to a person if, before the effective date of the ordinance granting the franchise, the governing body receives a petition that requests the election and is signed by 10 percent of the registered voters of the municipality.

(b) In a municipality with a population of more than 1.9 million, the number of registered voters who must sign the petition may be set at a lower number by the municipal charter.

Sec. 311.074. Election Date.

After receipt of a petition under Section 311.073, the election shall be held on the first uniform election date prescribed by Section 41.001, Election Code, that allows sufficient time to comply with other requirements of law.

Sec. 311.075. Election Notice.

(a) Notice of the election must be published in a daily newspaper in the municipality for at least 20 successive days before the date of the election.

(b) This notice requirement supersedes the notice requirements prescribed by Section 4.003, Election Code, except as provided by that section.

Sec. 311.076. Ballot Proposition.

The ballot at the election shall be printed to provide for voting for or against the proposition: "Granting of a franchise (brief description of the franchise and its terms)."

Sec. 311.077. Effective Date of Franchise.

If a majority of the votes cast at the election favor the proposition:

(1) the governing body shall declare that result on canvassing the election returns; and

(2) the franchise takes effect according to its terms.

Sec. 311.078. Duration of Franchise.

A franchise under this subchapter may not extend beyond the period set for its termination.

SUBCHAPTER E
FINANCING IMPROVEMENTS

Sec. 311.091. Assessment for Street Improvement in Home-Rule Municipality.

(a) A home-rule municipality may assess a landowner for the cost of improving a public highway, street, or alley abutting the owner's land, if the municipal charter provides for apportioning the cost between the municipality and the landowner. The assessment may not exceed the amount by which the improvement specially benefits the owner's abutting land by enhancing the land's value.

(b) The municipality may issue assignable certificates for the payment of the assessed cost.

(c) The assessment creates a lien on the owner's abutting land for the assessed cost.

(d) Regardless of Subsection (a), a railway company shall pay the cost of a street improvement made between the rails or tracks of the company or made in the area extending two feet from a rail or track of the company.

Sec. 311.092. Assessment for Opening, Extending, or Widening of Street or Alley in Home-Rule Municipality.

(a) A home-rule municipality may:

(1) acquire land necessary for opening, extending, or widening a public street or alley by the exercise of the right of eminent domain under Section 251.001, Local Government Code; and

(2) assess the owners of land located in the territory of the improvement and specially benefitted by the improvement for the cost of the improvement.

(b) The special commissioners appointed under Chapter 21, Property Code, as part of the eminent domain proceeding shall apportion the cost of the improvement between the municipality and the landowners. The municipality's share of the cost may not exceed one-third of the cost. The municipality shall pay its share of the cost, and the landowners shall pay the balance.

(c) The special commissioners shall determine the land that is located in the territory of the improvement and is specially benefitted in enhanced value.

(d) The assessment creates a lien on the owner's land for the assessed cost.

(e) The municipality may issue assignable certificates for the payment of the assessed cost and may provide for the payment of the cost in deferred payments, which bear interest at a rate determined by the municipal charter but not to exceed eight percent.

Sec. 311.093. Assessment for Sidewalk in Home-Rule Municipality.

(a) A home-rule municipality may assess a landowner for the entire cost of constructing a sidewalk, including a curb, abutting the owner's land.

(b) The assessment creates a lien on the owner's abutting land for the assessed cost.

Sec. 311.094. Other Financing Methods in Charter of Home-Rule Municipality.

(a) A home-rule municipality by charter may adopt any other method of financing an improvement described by Section 311.091, 311.092, or 311.093.

(b) Another method adopted by charter for financing an improvement described by Section 311.092 must:

(1) charge the cost of the improvement to the property and to the owner of the property specially benefitted in enhanced value by the improvement and located in the territory in which the improvement is made; and

(2) describe the manner of:

(A) appointing commissioners;

(B) giving notice; and

(C) fixing assessments or otherwise providing for the payment of the improvement.

Sec. 311.095. Assessment for Street Improvement in Type A General-Law Municipality.

(a) The governing body of a Type A general-law municipality, by a two-thirds vote of the aldermen present, may improve a street or alley under this section.

(b) The governing body shall assess the land abutting the street or alley improved under this section for two-thirds of the cost of the improvement. The municipality shall pay the other one-third of the cost. The municipality shall pay the entire cost of an improvement at the intersection of streets.

(c) The landowner shall pay the assessment in not fewer than five equal annual payments. A collected assessment shall be appropriated for the payment of the bonds issued to finance the cost of the improvement.

(d) After the governing body determines to make an improvement, the governing body shall require the municipal engineer, another municipal officer, or a committee of three aldermen to prepare a report. The report must:

(1) contain an estimate of the cost of the improvement;

(2) list each lot or part of a lot abutting the street or alley to be improved and list the number and size of the lot, the number of the block in which the lot is located, the owner of the lot or a statement

that the owner is unknown, and other information required by the governing body; and

(3) state, opposite a lot's listing, one-third the estimated cost of the improvement of the street or alley abutting the lot.

(e) On the acceptance and approval of the report, the governing body shall impose the assessment as taxes. After the assessment is imposed, the individual or committee that prepared the report shall give, as may be required by ordinance, notice of the time in which the payment of the assessment is due and shall begin to collect the payment.

(f) The assessment is a lien on the land until it is paid. After an assessment on the land becomes delinquent, the individual or committee that prepared the report on the assessments may seize any part of the land that is sufficient to pay the assessment. The individual or committee shall sell the seized land if the assessment is not paid before the day of the sale. The municipality shall give the same notice of the sale that is required to be given in other sales to collect delinquent taxes. The sale is subject to the same ordinance provisions that govern the name, circumstances, and conditions under which a sale of land may be made and the extent to which a sale may be made to collect delinquent taxes owed the municipality. The individual or committee shall execute a deed to the purchaser at the sale. The deed used in the sale is subject to another statute that governs a deed prepared by an assessor or collector of taxes for a general-law municipality.

(g) The governing body may initiate a suit in the municipality's corporate name to recover from a landowner an assessment.

(h) The governing body may adopt resolutions, ordinances, or regulations necessary to carry out the authority granted by this section.

Sec. 311.096. Cost of Sidewalk in Type A General-Law Municipality.

(a) The governing body of a Type A general-law municipality may require the owner of a lot, or part of a lot or block, in front of which the municipality constructs a sidewalk to pay the cost of the construction.

(b) If necessary to collect the cost of the construction, the municipality shall sell the lot, or the part of the lot or block, in the manner the governing body of the municipality by ordinance provides. The municipality may keep an amount of the sale proceeds that covers the cost of the construction and the cost of collection. The municipality shall pay to the owner the balance of the sale proceeds.

(c) The sale of the lot, or the part of the lot or block, under this section conveys a good title to the purchaser.

SUBCHAPTER Z MISCELLANEOUS PROVISIONS

Sec. 311.901. Regulation of Animals on Street of Type A General-Law Municipality.

The governing body of a Type A general-law municipality may:

(1) prohibit or suppress horse racing on a street or immoderate riding or driving of an animal on a street; or

(2) require a person to fasten in place the person's horse or other animal remaining in a street.

Sec. 311.902. Street Lighting in Type A General-Law Municipality.

The governing body of a Type A general-law municipality may:

(1) provide for and regulate the lighting of a street;

(2) create or change lamp districts; or

(3) exclusively regulate or direct the laying or repairing of gas pipes and gas fixtures in a street, alley, sidewalk, or other place.

Sec. 311.903. Street Work Required of Inhabitant in Type B General-Law Municipality.

(a) The governing body of a Type B general-law municipality may require the male inhabitants of the municipality who are at least 18 years of age but younger than 46 years of age to work on the streets and public alleys. The period of work may not exceed five days in a year.

(b) Instead of performing the work, a person may furnish a substitute to perform the work or may pay a sum not to exceed $1 for each day of work demanded so that a substitute may be employed.

(c) The requirement does not apply to a minister of the gospel actually engaged in the discharge of the minister's duties.

Sec. 311.904. Former President's Street in Home-Rule Municipality.

A home-rule municipality, alone or in conjunction with another person, may regulate or restrict access to a street or alley in the municipality on which the dwelling of a former president of the United States is located. This authority includes the authority to install and maintain a fence, gate, or other structure.

SUBTITLE G
TURNPIKES AND TOLL PROJECTS

CHAPTER 370
REGIONAL MOBILITY AUTHORITIES

SUBCHAPTER E
ACQUISITION, CONSTRUCTION, AND OPERATION OF TRANSPORTATION PROJECTS

Sec. 370.177. Failure or Refusal to Pay Turnpike Project Toll; Offense; Administrative Penalty.

(a) Except as provided by Subsection (a-1), the operator of a vehicle, other than an authorized emergency vehicle as defined by Section 541.201, that is driven or towed through a toll collection facility of a turnpike project shall pay the proper toll. The operator of a vehicle who drives or tows a vehicle through a toll collection facility and does not pay the proper toll commits an offense. An offense under this subsection is a misdemeanor punishable by a fine not to exceed $250. The exemption from payment of a toll for an authorized emergency vehicle applies regardless of whether the vehicle is:

(1) responding to an emergency;

(2) displaying a flashing light; or

(3) marked as an emergency vehicle.

(a-1) Notwithstanding Subsection (a), the board may waive the requirement of the payment of a toll or may authorize the payment of a reduced toll for any vehicle or class of vehicles.

(b) In the event of nonpayment of the proper toll as required by Subsection (a), on issuance of a written notice of nonpayment, the registered owner of the nonpaying vehicle is liable for the payment of both the proper toll and an administrative fee.

(c) The authority may impose and collect the administrative fee to recover the cost of collecting the unpaid toll, not to exceed $100. The authority shall send a written notice of nonpayment to the registered owner of the vehicle at that owner's address as shown in the vehicle registration records of the department by first class mail not later than the 30th day after the date of the alleged failure to pay and may require payment not sooner than the 30th day after the date the notice was mailed. The registered owner shall pay a separate toll and administrative fee for each event of nonpayment under Subsection (a).

(d) The registered owner of a vehicle for which the proper toll was not paid who is mailed a written notice of nonpayment under Subsection (c) and fails to pay the proper toll and administrative fee within the time specified by the notice of nonpayment commits an offense. Each failure to pay a toll or administrative fee under this subsection is a separate offense.

(e) It is an exception to the application of Subsection (b) or (d) that the registered owner of the vehicle is a lessor of the vehicle and not later than the 30th day after the date the notice of nonpayment is mailed provides to the authority:

(1) a copy of the rental, lease, or other contract document covering the vehicle on the date of the nonpayment under Subsection (a), with the name and address of the lessee clearly legible; or

(2) electronic data, other than a photocopy or scan of a rental or lease contract, that contains the information required under Sections 521.460(c)(1), (2), and (3) covering the vehicle on the date of the nonpayment under Subsection (a).

(e-1) If the lessor provides the required information within the period prescribed under Subsection (e), the authority may send a notice of nonpayment to the lessee at the address provided under Subsection (e) by first class mail before the 30th day after the date of receipt of the required information from the lessor. The lessee of the vehicle for which the proper toll was not paid who is mailed a written notice of nonpayment under this subsection and fails to pay the proper toll and administrative fee within the time specified by the notice of nonpayment commits an offense. The lessee shall pay a separate toll and administrative fee for each event of nonpayment. Each failure to pay a toll or administrative fee under this subsection is a separate offense.

(f) It is an exception to the application of Subsection (b) or (d) that the registered owner of the vehicle transferred ownership of the vehicle to another person before the event of nonpayment under Subsection (a) occurred, submitted written notice of the transfer to the department in accordance with Section 501.147, and before the 30th day after the date the notice of nonpayment is mailed, provides to the authority the name and address of the person to whom the vehicle was transferred. If the former owner of the vehicle provides the required information within the period prescribed, the authority may send a notice of nonpayment to the person to whom ownership of the vehicle was transferred at the address provided by the former owner by first class mail before the 30th day after the date of receipt of the required information from the former owner. The subsequent owner of the vehicle for which the proper toll was not paid who is mailed a written notice of nonpayment under this subsection and fails to pay the proper toll and administrative fee within the time specified by the notice of nonpayment commits an offense. The subsequent owner shall pay a separate toll and administrative fee for each event of nonpayment under Subsection (a). Each failure to pay a toll or administrative fee under this subsection is a separate offense.

(g) An offense under Subsection (d), (e-1), or (f) is a misdemeanor punishable by a fine not to exceed $250.

(h) The court in which a person is convicted of an offense under this section shall also collect the proper toll and administrative fee and forward the toll and fee to the authority.

(i) In the prosecution of an offense under this section, proof that the vehicle passed through a toll collection facility without payment of the proper toll together with proof that the defendant was the registered owner or the driver of the vehicle when the failure to pay occurred, establishes the nonpayment of the registered owner. The proof may be by testimony of a peace officer or authority employee, video surveillance, or any other reasonable evidence, including:

(1) evidence obtained by automated enforcement technology that the authority determines is necessary, including automated enforcement technology described by Sections 228.058(a) and (b); or

(2) a copy of the rental, lease, or other contract document or the electronic data provided to the authority under Subsection (e) that shows the defendant was the lessee of the vehicle when the underlying event of nonpayment occurred.

(j) It is a defense to prosecution under this section that the motor vehicle in question was stolen before the failure to pay the proper toll occurred and was not recovered by the time of the failure to pay, but only if the theft was reported to the appropriate law enforcement authority before the earlier of:

(1) the occurrence of the failure to pay; or

(2) eight hours after the discovery of the theft.

(k) In this section, "registered owner" means the owner of a vehicle as shown on the vehicle registration records of the department or the analogous department or agency of another state or country.

(*l*) In addition to the other powers and duties provided by this chapter, with regard to its toll collection and enforcement powers for its turnpike projects or other toll projects developed, financed, constructed, and operated under an agreement with the authority or another entity, an authority has the same powers and duties as the department under Chapter 228, a county under Chapter 284, and a regional tollway authority under Chapter 366.

(m) Information collected for the purposes of this section, including contact, payment, and other account information and trip data, is confidential and not subject to disclosure under Chapter 552, Government Code.

(n) As authorized under Section 322.008(d)(2), Business & Commerce Code, an authority may provide an invoice or notice required under this section to be sent by first class mail instead as an electronic record:

(1) if the recipient of the information agrees to the transmission of the information as an electronic record; and

(2) on terms acceptable to the recipient.

Sec. 370.178. Use and Return of Transponders.

(a) For purposes of this section, "transponder" means a device placed on or within a motor vehicle that is capable of transmitting or receiving information used to assess or collect tolls or provide toll exemptions. A transponder is insufficiently funded if there is no money in the account for which the transponder was issued.

(b) Any law enforcement or peace officer of an entity with which an authority has contracted under Section 370.181(c) may seize a stolen or insufficiently funded transponder and return it to the authority that issued the transponder. An insufficiently funded transponder may not be seized before the 30th day after the date that an authority has sent a notice of delinquency to the holder of the account.

(c) The following entities shall consider offering motor vehicle operators the option of using a transponder to pay tolls without stopping, to mitigate congestion at toll locations, to enhance traffic flow, and to otherwise increase the efficiency of operations:

(1) the authority;

(2) an entity to which a project authorized by this chapter is transferred; or

(3) a third-party service provider under contract with an entity described by Subdivision (1) or (2).

Transportation Code

(d) Transponder account information, including contact and payment information and trip data, is confidential and not subject to disclosure under Chapter 552, Government Code.

Sec. 370.179. Controlled Access to Turnpike Projects.

(a) An authority by order may designate a turnpike project or a portion of a project as a controlled-access toll road.

(b) An authority by order may:

(1) prohibit the use of or access to or from a turnpike project by a motor vehicle, bicycle, another classification or type of vehicle, or a pedestrian;

(2) deny access to or from:

(A) a turnpike project;

(B) real property adjacent to a turnpike project; or

(C) a street, road, alley, highway, or other public or private way intersecting a turnpike project;

(3) designate locations on a turnpike project at which access to or from the toll road is permitted;

(4) control, restrict, and determine the type and extent of access permitted at a designated location of access to a turnpike project; or

(5) erect appropriate protective devices to preserve the utility, integrity, and use of a turnpike project.

(c) Denial of access to or from a segment of the state highway system is subject to the approval of the commission.

Sec. 370.180. Promotion of Transportation Project.

An authority may promote the use of a transportation project, including a project that it operates on behalf of another entity, by appropriate means, including advertising or marketing as the authority determines appropriate.

Sec. 370.181. Operation of Transportation Project.

(a) An authority shall operate a transportation project with employees of the authority or by using services contracted under Subsection (b) or (c).

(b) An authority may enter into an agreement with one or more persons to provide, on terms and conditions approved by the authority, personnel and services to design, construct, operate, maintain, expand, enlarge, or extend a transportation project owned or operated by the authority.

(c) An authority may contract with any state or local government for the services of peace officers of that agency.

(d) An authority may not directly provide water, wastewater, natural gas, petroleum pipeline, electric transmission, electric distribution, telecommunications, information, or cable television services.

(e) Nothing in this chapter, or any contractual right obtained under a contract with an authority authorized by this chapter, supersedes or renders ineffective any provision of another law applicable to the owner or operator of a public utility facility, including any provision of the Utilities Code regarding licensing, certification, and regulatory jurisdiction of the Public Utility Commission of Texas or Railroad Commission of Texas.

Sec. 370.186. Contracts with Governmental Entities.

(a) Except as provided by Subsection (c), an authority may not construct, maintain, or operate a turnpike or toll project in an area having a governmental entity established under Chapter 284 or 366 unless the governmental entity and the authority enter into a written agreement specifying the terms and conditions under which the project shall be undertaken. An authority may not construct, maintain, or operate a transportation project that another governmental entity has determined to be a project under Chapter 451, 452, or 460 unless the governmental entity and the authority enter into a written agreement specifying the terms and conditions under which the project shall be undertaken.

(b) An authority may not receive or be paid revenue derived by another governmental entity operating under Chapter 284, 366, 451, 452, or 460 unless the governmental entity and the authority enter into a written agreement specifying the terms and conditions under which the revenue shall be received by or paid to the authority.

(c) Subsection (a) does not apply to a turnpike or toll project located in a county in which a regional tollway authority has transferred under Section 366.036 or 366.172:

(1) all turnpike projects of the regional tollway authority that are located in the county; and

(2) all work product developed by the regional tollway authority in determining the feasibility of the construction, improvement, extension, or expansion of a turnpike project to be located in the county.

(d) An authority may not construct, maintain, or operate a passenger rail facility within the boundaries of an intermunicipal commuter rail district created under former Article 6550c-1, Vernon's Texas Civil Statutes, as those boundaries existed on September 1, 2005, unless the district and the authority enter into a written agreement specifying

Transportation Code

the terms and conditions under which the project will be undertaken.

Sec. 370.187. Project Approval.

(a) An authority may not begin construction of a transportation project that will connect to the state highway system or to a department rail facility without the approval of the commission.

(b) The commission by rule shall establish procedures and criteria for an approval under this section. The rules must require the commission to consider a request for project approval not later than the 60th day after the date the department receives all information reasonably necessary to review the request.

Sec. 370.191. Commercial Transportation Processing Systems.

(a) In this section, "port of entry" means a place designated by executive order of the president of the United States, by order of the United States secretary of the treasury, or by act of the United States Congress at which a customs officer is authorized to accept entries of merchandise, to collect duties, and to enforce the various provisions of the customs and navigation laws.

(b) This section applies only to a port of entry for land traffic from the United Mexican States and does not apply to a port of entry for marine traffic.

(c) To the extent an authority considers appropriate to expedite commerce and based on the Texas ITS/CVO Business Plan prepared by the department, the Department of Public Safety, and the comptroller, the authority shall provide for implementation by the appropriate agencies of the use of Intelligent Transportation Systems for Commercial Vehicle Operations (ITS/CVO) in any new commercial motor vehicle inspection facility constructed by the authority and in any existing facility located at a port of entry to which this section applies. The authority shall coordinate with other state and federal transportation officials to develop interoperability standards for the systems.

(d) If an authority constructs a facility at which commercial vehicle safety inspections are conducted, the facility may not be used solely for the purpose of conducting commercial motor vehicle inspections by the Department of Public Safety and the facility must include implementation of ITS/CVO technology by the appropriate agencies to support all commercial motor vehicle regulation and enforcement functions.

(e) As part of its implementation of technology under this section, an authority shall to the greatest extent possible as a requirement of the construction of the facility:

(1) enhance efficiency and reduce complexity for motor carriers by providing a single point of contact between carriers and regulating state and federal government officials and providing a single point of information, available to wireless access, about federal and state regulatory and enforcement requirements;

(2) prevent duplication of state and federal procedures and locations for regulatory and enforcement activities, including consolidation of collection of applicable fees;

(3) link information systems of the authority, the department, the Department of Public Safety, the comptroller, and, to the extent possible, the United States Department of Transportation and other appropriate regulatory and enforcement entities; and

(4) take other necessary action to:

(A) facilitate the flow of commerce;

(B) assist federal interdiction efforts;

(C) protect the environment by reducing idling time of commercial motor vehicles at the facilities;

(D) prevent highway damage caused by overweight commercial motor vehicles; and

(E) seek federal funds to assist in the implementation of this section.

(f) Construction of a facility to which this section applies is subject to the availability of federal funding for that purpose.

SUBTITLE H HIGHWAY BEAUTIFICATION

CHAPTER 391 HIGHWAY BEAUTIFICATION ON INTERSTATE AND PRIMARY SYSTEMS AND CERTAIN ROADS

SUBCHAPTER A GENERAL PROVISIONS

Sec. 391.001. Definitions.

In this chapter:

(1) "Automobile graveyard" means an establishment that is maintained, used, or operated for storing, buying, or selling wrecked, scrapped, ruined, or dismantled motor vehicles or motor vehicle parts.

Transportation Code

(1-a) "Commercial sign" means a sign that is:

(A) intended to be leased, or for which payment of any type is intended to be or is received, for the display of any good, service, brand, slogan, message, product, or company, except that the term does not include a sign that is leased to a business entity and located on the same property on which the business is located; or

(B) located on property owned or leased for the primary purpose of displaying a sign.

(2) "Eligible highway" means a highway along which an information logo sign may be located as determined by the commission under Section 391.092(d).

(3) [Repealed by Acts 2007, 80th Leg., ch. 935 (H.B. 3441), § 4, effective June 15, 2007.]

(4) "Information logo sign" means a specific information logo sign or a major shopping area guide sign.

(5) "Interstate system" means that portion of the national system of interstate and defense highways that is located in this state and is designated officially by the commission and approved under Title 23, United States Code.

(6) "Junk" means:

(A) old or scrap copper, brass, rope, rags, batteries, paper, trash, rubber, debris, or waste;

(B) junked, dismantled, or wrecked automobiles or automobile parts; or

(C) iron, steel, and other old or scrap ferrous or nonferrous material.

(7) "Junkyard" means:

(A) an automobile graveyard;

(B) an establishment maintained, used, or operated for storing, buying, or selling junk or processing scrap metal; or

(C) a garbage dump or sanitary fill.

(8) [Repealed by Acts 2007, 80th Leg., ch. 935 (H.B. 3441), § 4, effective June 15, 2007.]

(9) "Major shopping area guide sign" means a rectangular guide sign panel imprinted with the name of a major shopping area eligible to have its name displayed as determined by the commission under Section 391.0935 and containing directional information to the major shopping area.

(10) [Repealed.]

(11) "Primary system" means that portion of connected main highways located in this state that is designated officially by the commission and approved under Title 23, United States Code.

(11-a) "Sign" means any structure, display, light, device, figure, painting, drawing, message, plaque, placard, poster, billboard, logo, or symbol that is designed, intended, or used to advertise or inform.

(12) "Specific information logo sign" means a rectangular sign imprinted with the words "GAS," "FOOD," "LODGING," "CAMPING," or "24 HOUR Rx," or with a combination of those words, and the specific brand names of commercial establishments offering those services.

(13) "Urban area" means an area defined by the commission in cooperation with local officials, subject to approval by the secretary of the United States Department of Transportation, that as a minimum includes an urban place as designated by the United States Bureau of the Census having a population of 5,000 or more and not located within an urbanized area.

(14) "Urbanized area" means an area defined by the commission in cooperation with local officials, subject to approval by the secretary of the United States Department of Transportation, that as a minimum includes an urbanized area as defined by the United States Bureau of the Census or that part of a multistate urbanized area located in this state.

Sec. 391.003. Violation of Rule; Offense.

(a) A person commits an offense if the person wilfully violates a rule adopted by the commission under this chapter.

(b) An offense under this section is a misdemeanor punishable by a fine of not less than $500 or more than $1,000.

(c) Each day of a rule violation is a separate offense.

SUBCHAPTER E REGULATION OF JUNKYARDS AND AUTOMOBILE GRAVEYARDS

Sec. 391.121. Prohibited Junkyard; Offense.

(a) A person commits an offense if:

(1) the person wilfully establishes, operates, or maintains a junkyard any portion of which is within 1,000 feet of the nearest edge of a right-of-way of a highway in the interstate or primary system; and

(2) the junkyard is not:

(A) screened by appropriate means, including natural objects, plantings, or fences, so that it is not visible from the main-traveled way of the interstate or primary highway; or

(B) located in an area that is a zoned or unzoned industrial area.

(b) The determination of whether an area is industrial must be made under criteria established by commission rule and according to actual land use.

(c) An offense under this section is a misdemeanor punishable by a fine of not less than $500 or more than $1,000. Each day of the proscribed conduct is a separate offense.

Sec. 391.122. Authority of Commission to Screen Junkyard.

(a) The commission may screen with appropriate means, including natural objects, plantings, or fences, a lawfully existing junkyard that is within 1,000 feet of the nearest edge of a right-of-way of a highway in the interstate or primary system.

(b) The commission may acquire an area outside of a highway right-of-way so that a junkyard may be screened from the main-traveled way of a highway in the interstate or primary system.

Sec. 391.123. Rules Relating to Screening of Junkyards.

The commission may adopt rules governing the location, planting, construction, and maintenance of the materials used in screening junkyards.

Sec. 391.124. Compensation to Owner of Junkyard.

If the commission determines that the screening of a lawfully existing junkyard that is within 1,000 feet of the nearest edge of a right-of-way of a highway in the interstate or primary system is not feasible, the commission shall pay just compensation to:

(1) the owner of the junkyard for its relocation, removal, or disposal; and

(2) the owner or, if appropriate, the lessee of the real property on which the junkyard is located for the taking of the right to erect and maintain a junkyard.

Sec. 391.125. Injunction to Require Screening.

(a) On written notice by certified mail from the department, an owner of a junkyard that is established, operated, or maintained in violation of this subchapter or a rule adopted under this subchapter shall screen the junkyard in accordance with Section 391.121. If the owner does not screen the junkyard within 45 days of the date of the notice, the department may request the attorney general to apply for an injunction to require the screening of the junkyard.

(b) Under an action brought under Subsection (a), the state is entitled to recover from the owner of a junkyard all administrative and legal costs and expenses incurred to require the screening of the junkyard, including court costs and reasonable attorney's fees.

Sec. 391.126. Civil Penalty.

(a) In addition to being subject to a criminal penalty or injunctive action, a person who intentionally violates this subchapter is liable to the state for a civil penalty. The attorney general may sue to collect the penalty.

(b) The amount of a civil penalty under this section is not less than $500 or more than $1,000 for each violation, depending on the seriousness of the violation. A separate penalty may be collected for each day a continuing violation occurs.

Sec. 391.127. Salvage Vehicle Dealer License.

The commission may revoke or suspend a license issued under Chapter 2302, Occupations Code, or place on probation a license holder whose license is suspended, if the license holder violates this chapter or a rule adopted under this chapter.

SUBCHAPTER I PROHIBITION OF SIGNS ON CERTAIN HIGHWAYS

Sec. 391.251. Definitions. [Repealed]

Sec. 391.252. Prohibited Commercial Signs.

(a) A person may not erect a commercial sign that is adjacent to and visible from:

(1) U.S. Highway 290 between the western city limits of the city of Austin and the eastern city limits of the city of Fredericksburg;

(2) State Highway 317 between the northern city limits of the city of Belton to the southern city limits of the city of Valley Mills;

(3) State Highway 16 between the northern city limits of the city of Kerrville and Interstate Highway 20;

(4) U.S. Highway 77 between State Highway 186 and State Highway 44;

(5) U.S. Highway 281 between:

(A) State Highway 186 and Interstate Highway 37, exclusive of the segment of U.S. Highway 281 located in the city limits of Three Rivers; and

(B) the southern boundary line of Comal County and State Highway 306;

(6) State Highway 17 between State Highway 118 and U.S. Highway 90;

(7) State Highway 67 between U.S. Highway 90 and Farm-to-Market Road 170;

(8) Farm-to-Market Road 170 between State Highway 67 and State Highway 118;

(9) State Highway 118 between Farm-to-Market Road 170 and State Highway 17;

(10) State Highway 105 between the western city limits of the city of Sour Lake to the eastern city limits of the city of Cleveland;

(11) State Highway 73 between the eastern city limits of the city of Winnie to the western city limits of the city of Port Arthur;

(12) State Highway 21 between the southern city limits of the city of College Station and U.S. Highway 290;

(13) a highway located in:

(A) the Sabine National Forest;

(B) the Davy Crockett National Forest; or

(C) the Sam Houston National Forest;

(14) Segments 1 through 4 of State Highway 130;

(15) a highway in Bandera County that is part of the state highway system;

(16) Farm-to-Market Road 3238 beginning at State Highway 71 and any extension of that road through Hays and Blanco Counties;

(17) Farm-to-Market Road 2978 between Farm-to-Market Road 1488 and the boundary line between Harris and Montgomery Counties;

(18) U.S. Highway 90 between the western city limits of the city of San Antonio and the eastern city limits of the city of Hondo; or

(19) the following highways in Austin County:

(A) State Highway 159;

(B) Farm-to-Market Road 331;

(C) Farm-to-Market Road 529;

(D) Farm-to-Market Road 1094; and

(E) Farm-to-Market Road 2502.

(b) This section does not affect the ability of a municipality to regulate a sign located on the portion of a roadway listed in Subsection (a) that is within the corporate limits or extraterritorial jurisdiction of the municipality in accordance with Chapter 216, Local Government Code.

(c) This section does not prohibit a person from erecting a commercial sign permitted by other law, rule, or regulation that is adjacent to and visible from a roadway not listed in this section and is visible from a roadway listed under this section if the intended purpose of the sign is to be visible only from the roadway not listed under this section.

Sec. 391.253. Reerection, Reconstruction, Repair, or Rebuilding of Commercial Signs.

(a) A commercial sign that is adjacent to and visible from a highway listed in Section 391.252 that is blown down, destroyed, taken down, or removed for a purpose other than maintenance or to change a letter, symbol, or other matter on the sign may be reerected, reconstructed, repaired, or rebuilt only if the cost of reerecting, reconstructing, repairing, or rebuilding the sign is not more than 60 percent of the cost of erecting a new commercial sign of the same size, type, and construction at the same location.

(b) The department shall permit the relocation of a commercial sign adjacent to and visible from a highway listed in Section 391.252 to another location that is adjacent to and visible from the same highway if:

(1) the construction, reconstruction, or expansion of a highway requires the removal of the sign;

(2) the sign is not modified to increase the above-grade height, the area of each sign face, the dimensions of the sign face, the number of sign faces, or the illumination of the sign; and

(3) the department identifies an alternate site for the relocation of the sign adjacent to and visible from the highway listed in Section 391.252.

(c) For purposes of this section, the department shall specify, within 30 days of receipt of a request for a relocation site, a minimum of three alternate sites that meet permitting requirements for a commercial sign to be reerected, reconstructed, repaired, or rebuilt adjacent to and visible from a highway listed in Section 391.252.

(d) The owner of a commercial sign that is reerected, reconstructed, repaired, or rebuilt according to Subsection (a) or relocated according to Subsection (b) may alter the materials and design of the sign to reduce the number of upright supports, subject to other restrictions in this section, in a manner that meets or exceeds the pre-existing structural specifications of the sign.

Sec. 391.254. Civil Penalty.

(a) A person who violates Section 391.252 is liable to the state for a civil penalty of not less than $500 or more than $1,000 for each violation, depending on the seriousness of the violation. A separate penalty may be imposed for each day a continuing violation occurs.

(b) The attorney general, the district or county attorney for the county, or the municipal attorney of the municipality in which the violation is alleged to have occurred may bring suit to collect the penalty.

Transportation Code

(c) A civil penalty collected by the attorney general under this section shall be deposited to the credit of the state highway fund.

(d) Before a suit may be brought for a violation of Section 391.252, the attorney general, the district or county attorney for the county, or the municipal attorney of the municipality in which the violation is alleged to have occurred shall give the owner of the commercial sign a written notice that:

(1) describes the violation and specific location of the sign found to be in violation;

(2) states the amount of the proposed penalty for the violation; and

(3) gives the owner 30 days from receipt to remove the sign and cure the violation to avoid the penalty unless the sign owner was given notice and opportunity to cure a similar violation within the preceding 12 months.

Sec. 391.255. Applicability of Subchapter.

The restrictions imposed by this subchapter are in addition to those imposed by the remainder of this chapter.

Sec. 391.256. Scenic Byways Program.

(a) The department shall plan, design, and establish a program for designating highways as State Scenic Byways.

(b) The program must include a process by which the department:

(1) receives proposals from political subdivisions or other community groups approved by the department for funding projects in accordance with 23 U.S.C. Section 162;

(2) applies for grants under 23 U.S.C. Section 162 for the projects; and

(3) allows an applicant who consents to pay for the costs of the projects that are not covered by grants made under 23 U.S.C. Section 162.

(c) A highway must be designated as a State Scenic Byway under the program established by this section before the department applies for a grant under Subsection (b)(2) for a project related to the highway.

(d) The department may use money from the state highway fund for a project that receives a grant made under 23 U.S.C. Section 162 only for the purpose of satisfying matching funds requirements for the grant.

(e) The department may only designate a highway described by Section 391.252 as a State Scenic Byway.

(f) The commission by rule shall prohibit outdoor advertising in a manner consistent with 23 U.S.C. Section 131(s) on a State Scenic Byway designated under this section.

CHAPTER 392 HIGHWAY BEAUTIFICATION ON STATE HIGHWAY RIGHT-OF-WAY

SUBCHAPTER B SIGNS ON STATE HIGHWAY RIGHT-OF-WAY

Sec. 392.032. Offense.

(a) A person may not place or maintain a sign on a state highway right-of-way unless authorized by state law.

(b) A person commits an offense if the person violates this section.

(c) An offense under this section is a Class C misdemeanor.

Sec. 392.0325. Exception.

(a) A person may submit a request to the department for an exception to this subchapter for a sign that is attached to a building located on property other than a state highway right-of-way and that refers to a commercial activity or business located in the building if the sign:

(1) consists solely of the name of the establishment;

(2) identifies the establishment's principal product or services; or

(3) advertises the sale or lease of the property on which the sign is located.

(b) The department shall approve a request submitted under Subsection (a) if the department:

(1) determines that the sign will not constitute a safety hazard;

(2) determines that the sign will not interfere with the construction, reconstruction, operation, or maintenance of the highway facility; and

(3) obtains the approval of the Federal Highway Administration if approval is required under federal law.

(c) This subchapter does not apply to a temporary directional sign or kiosk erected by a political subdivision as part of a program approved by the department and administered by the political subdivision on a highway within the boundaries of the political subdivision.

Transportation Code

(d) This subchapter does not apply to a sign placed in the right-of-way by a public utility or its contractor for purposes of the utility.

Sec. 392.036. Defense.

It is a defense to prosecution or suit for a violation under this chapter if at the time of the alleged violation the defendant is a candidate for elective public office and the sign is placed:

(1) by a person other than the defendant; and

(2) in connection with a campaign for an elective public office by the defendant.

SUBTITLE K MASS TRANSPORTATION

CHAPTER 451 METROPOLITAN RAPID TRANSIT AUTHORITIES

SUBCHAPTER B POWERS OF AUTHORITIES

Sec. 451.0611. Enforcement of Fares and Other Charges; Penalties.

(a) A board by resolution may prohibit the use of the public transportation system by a person who fails to possess evidence showing that the appropriate fare for the use of the system has been paid and may establish reasonable and appropriate methods to ensure that persons using the public transportation system pay the appropriate fare for that use.

(b) A board by resolution may provide that a fare for or charge for the use of the public transportation system that is not paid incurs a penalty, not to exceed $100.

(c) The authority shall post signs designating each area in which a person is prohibited from using the transportation system without possession of evidence showing that the appropriate fare has been paid.

(d) A person commits an offense if:

(1) the person or another for whom the person is criminally responsible under Section 7.02, Penal Code, uses the public transportation system and does not possess evidence showing that the appropriate fare has been paid; and

(2) the person fails to pay the appropriate fare or other charge for the use of the public transportation system and any penalty on the fare on or before the 30th day after the date the authority notifies the person that the person is required to pay the amount of the fare or charge and the penalty.

(e) The notice required by Subsection (d)(2) may be included in a citation issued to the person under Article 14.06, Code of Criminal Procedure, or under Section 451.0612, in connection with an offense relating to the nonpayment of the appropriate fare or charge for the use of the public transportation system.

(f) An offense under Subsection (d) is:

(1) a Class C misdemeanor; and

(2) not a crime of moral turpitude.

(g) An authority created before 1980 in which the principal municipality has a population of less than 1.9 million may allow peace officers of another political subdivision serving under a contract with the authority to enforce a resolution passed by a board under this section.

Sec. 451.0612. Fare Enforcement Officers.

(a) An authority may employ persons to serve as fare enforcement officers to enforce the payment of fares for use of the public transportation system by:

(1) requesting and inspecting evidence showing payment of the appropriate fare from a person using the public transportation system; and

(2) issuing a citation to a person described by Section 451.0611(d)(1).

(b) Before commencing duties as a fare enforcement officer, a person must complete a 40-hour training course approved by the authority that is appropriate to the duties required of a fare enforcement officer.

(c) While performing duties, a fare enforcement officer shall:

(1) wear a distinctive uniform that identifies the officer as a fare enforcement officer; and

(2) work under the direction of the authority's manager of safety and security.

(d) A fare enforcement officer may:

(1) request evidence showing payment of the appropriate fare from passengers of the public transportation system;

(2) request personal identification from a passenger who does not produce evidence showing payment of the appropriate fare on request by the officer;

(3) request that a passenger leave the public transportation system if the passenger does not possess evidence of payment of the appropriate fare; and

(4) file a complaint in the appropriate court that charges the person with an offense under Section 451.0611(d).

(e) A fare enforcement officer may not carry a weapon while performing duties under this section.

(f) A fare enforcement officer is not a peace officer and has no authority to enforce a criminal law, other than the authority possessed by any other person who is not a peace officer.

SUBTITLE Z MISCELLANEOUS ROADWAY PROVISIONS

CHAPTER 471 RAILROAD AND ROADWAY CROSSINGS

Sec. 471.001. Duty to Maintain Crossings.

(a) A railway company shall maintain the part of its roadbed and right-of-way that is crossed by a public street of a Type B general-law municipality in proper condition for use by travelers.

(b) A railway company that does not make needed repairs before the 31st day after the date the municipal marshal gives written notice to the section boss of the section where repairs are needed is liable to the municipality for a penalty of $25 for each week the railway company does not make needed repairs. The municipality may sue to recover the penalty.

Sec. 471.002. Signs at Crossings.

(a) A railway company shall place at each place where its railroad crosses a first or second class public road a sign with large and distinct letters giving notice that the railroad is near and warning persons to watch for railroad cars. The sign must be high enough above the road to permit the free passage of vehicles.

(b) A railway company that does not erect a sign required by Subsection (a) is liable for a resulting injury to a person or resulting damage to property.

Sec. 471.003. Telephone Service to Report Malfunctions of Mechanical Safety Devices at Crossings. [Repealed]

Sec. 471.004. Warning Sign Visibility at Railroad Grade Crossings.

(a) The department shall develop guidelines and specifications for the installation and maintenance of reflecting material at each unsignaled crossing. The material shall be affixed to the back and support post of each crossbuck in a manner that reflects light from vehicle headlights to focus attention on the presence of the unsignaled crossing.

(b) The department shall pay the cost of initial installation of reflecting material from money appropriated to the department to maintain grade crossing warning devices. The department or the local jurisdiction responsible for maintaining the roadway at each grade crossing shall pay the maintenance costs of the material.

(c) The state, an agency or political subdivision of the state, or a railway company is not liable for damages caused by an action taken under this section or failure to perform a duty imposed by this section. Evidence may not be introduced in a judicial proceeding that reflecting material exists or that the state or railway company relies on the material.

(d) The department shall adopt rules governing the installation and maintenance of reflecting material at grade crossings.

(e) A railway company shall permit department personnel to affix the reflecting material on the company's property.

(f) In this section:

(1) "Active warning device" means an automatically activated warning device, including a bell, flashing light, gate, or wigwag.

(2) "Crossbuck" means a standard grade crossing warning sign designated as Number R 15-1 and described in the Manual of Uniform Traffic Control Devices issued by the United States Department of Transportation, Federal Highway Administration.

(3) "Department" means the Texas Department of Transportation.

(4) "Grade crossing" means the intersection at grade of a railroad and a roadway constructed and maintained with public money.

(5) "Reflecting material" means material that reflects light so that the paths of the reflected light rays are parallel to those of the incident rays.

(6) "Unsignaled crossing" means a grade crossing not protected by active warning devices.

(7) "Warning device" means a traffic control sign, including an active warning device or crossbuck, the purpose of which is to alert motorists of a grade crossing.

Sec. 471.005. Dismantling of Warning Signals at Railroad Grade Crossings; Offense.

(a) A person may not dismantle a warning signal at a grade crossing on an active rail line, as defined by rule of the Texas Department of Transportation, if the cost of the warning signal was originally paid entirely or partly from public money unless the person:

(1) obtains a permit from the governmental entity that maintains the road or highway that intersects the rail line at the grade crossing; and

(2) pays that governmental entity an amount equal to the present salvage value of the warning signal, as determined by the governmental entity.

(b) The governmental entity shall grant the permit if:

(1) payment is received; and

(2) the entity finds that removal of the warning signal will not adversely affect public safety.

(c) Money received under Subsection (a)(2) shall be deposited in the state treasury.

(d) This section does not apply to a Class I or Class II railroad, as defined by Interstate Commerce Commission regulations.

(e) A person commits an offense if the person violates this section. An offense under this section is a Class C misdemeanor.

(f) The Texas Department of Transportation may adopt rules necessary to administer this section.

(g) In this section:

(1) "Grade crossing" has the meaning assigned by Section 472.004(f).

(2) "Warning signal" means a traffic control device that is activated by the approach or presence of a train, including a flashing light signal, an automatic gate, or a similar device that displays to motorists a warning of the approach or presence of a train.

Sec. 471.006. Use of Bell and Whistle or Siren at Crossings; Offense. [Repealed]

Sec. 471.007. Obstructing Railroad Crossings; Offense. [Repealed]

Sec. 471.008. Franchise to Obstruct Street Crossing. [Repealed]

Sec. 471.009. Enhanced Pavement Marking Visibility at Certain Grade Crossings.

(a) In this section:

(1) "Grade crossing" and "reflecting material" have the meanings assigned by Section 471.004.

(2) "Pavement markings" means markings applied or attached to the surface of a roadway to regulate, warn, or guide traffic.

(3) "Stop bar" means the marking that is applied or attached to the surface of a roadway on either side of a grade crossing and that indicates that a vehicle must stop at the grade crossing.

(b) A county or municipality shall use standards developed by the department in applying pavement markings or a stop bar at a grade crossing if the cost of the markings or stop bar is paid either entirely or partly from state or federal funds. In developing its standards, the department shall follow the standards in the Manual on Uniform Traffic Control Devices issued by the United States Department of Transportation Federal Highway Administration and, where appropriate, require the use of reflecting materials.

CHAPTER 472
MISCELLANEOUS PROVISIONS

SUBCHAPTER B
DEPARTMENT AUTHORITY TO REMOVE PROPERTY FROM STATE HIGHWAYS

Sec. 472.011. Definition.

In this subchapter, "personal property" includes personal property of any kind or character, including:

(1) a vehicle, as defined by Section 502.001, that is damaged or disabled;

(2) spilled cargo;

(3) a hazardous material as defined by 49 U.S.C. App. Section 1802; and

(4) a hazardous substance as defined by Section 26.263, Water Code.

Sec. 472.012. Department Authority Generally.

(a) The department may remove personal property from the right-of-way or roadway of the state highway system if the department determines the property blocks the roadway or endangers public safety.

(b) The department may remove the personal property without the consent of the owner or carrier of the property.

Sec. 472.013. Owner and Carrier Responsible for Costs of Removal and Disposition.

The owner and the carrier of personal property removed under this subchapter shall reimburse the department for the costs of removal and disposition.

Sec. 472.014. Department Not Liable for Damages.

Notwithstanding any other provision of law, the department and its officers and employees are not liable for:

(1) any damage to personal property resulting from its removal or disposal by the department unless the removal or disposal is carried out recklessly or in a grossly negligent manner; or

(2) any damage resulting from the failure to exercise authority granted under this subchapter.

Sec. 472.015. Contracts for Removal of Property.

In contracting with a private business or businesses for the removal of personal property from the right-of-way or roadway of the state highway system, the department may:

(1) use a purchasing method described in Chapter 2156, Government Code;

(2) include the removal work in a contract entered into under Chapter 223; or

(3) select a business or businesses based on an evaluation of the experience of the business and the price and quality of the business's equipment and services.

SUBCHAPTER C CRIMINAL OFFENSES AND PENALTIES REGARDING WARNING SIGNS AND BARRICADES

Sec. 472.021. Tampering with Warning Devices.

(a) A person commits an offense if the person tampers with, damages, or removes a barricade, flare pot, sign, flasher signal, or other device warning of construction, repair, or detour on or adjacent to a highway set out by the state, a political subdivision, a contractor, or a public utility.

(b) This section does not apply to a person acting within the scope and duty of employment if the person is:

(1) an officer, agent, independent contractor, employee, or trustee of the state or a political subdivision;

(2) a contractor; or

(3) a public utility.

(c) An offense under this section is a misdemeanor punishable by:

(1) a fine of not less than $25 or more than $1,000;

(2) confinement in a county jail for a term not to exceed two years; or

(3) both the fine and the confinement.

(d) In this section:

(1) "Contractor" means a person engaged in highway construction or repair under contract with this state or a political subdivision of this state.

(2) "Highway" means the entire width between the boundary lines of a publicly maintained way, any part of which is open to the public for vehicular travel or any part of which is under construction or repair and intended for public vehicular travel on completion. The term includes the space above or below the highway surface.

(3) "Person" means an individual, firm, association, or corporation and includes an officer, agent, independent contractor, employee, or trustee of that individual or entity.

(4) "Political subdivision" includes a county, municipality, local board, or other body of this state having authority to authorize highway construction or repair.

(5) "Public utility" means:

(A) a telegraph, telephone, water, gas, light, or sewage company or cooperative;

(B) a contractor of a company or cooperative described by Subdivision (A); or

(C) another business recognized by the legislature as a public utility.

Sec. 472.022. Obeying Warning Signs and Barricades.

(a) A person commits an offense if the person:

(1) disobeys the instructions, signals, warnings, or markings of a warning sign; or

(2) drives around a barricade.

(b) This section does not apply to:

(1) a person who is following the directions of a police officer; or

(2) a person, including an employee of the department, a political subdivision of this state, or a contractor or subcontractor, whose duties require the person to go beyond or around a barricade.

(c) Each violation of this section is a separate offense.

(d) An offense under this section is a misdemeanor punishable by a fine of not less than $1 or more than $200, except that:

(1) if the offense is committed in a construction or maintenance work zone when workers are present and any written notice to appear issued for the offense states on its face that workers were present when the offense was committed, the offense is a misdemeanor punishable by a fine of not less than $2 or more than $400; or

(2) if a person commits an offense under Subsection (a) where a warning sign or barricade has been placed because water is over any portion of a road, street, or highway, the offense is a Class B misdemeanor.

(e) In this section:

(1) "Barricade" means an obstruction:

(A) placed on or across a road, street, or highway of this state by the department, a political subdivision of this state, or a contractor or subcontractor constructing or repairing the road, street, or highway under authorization of the department or a political subdivision of this state; and

(B) placed to prevent the passage of motor vehicles over the road, street, or highway during construction, repair, or dangerous conditions.

(2) "Construction or maintenance work zone" means a portion of a highway or street:

(A) where highway construction or maintenance is being undertaken, other than mobile operations as defined by the Texas Manual on Uniform Traffic Control Devices; and

(B) that is marked by signs:

(i) indicating that it is a construction or maintenance work zone;

(ii) indicating where the zone begins and ends; and

(iii) stating: "Fines double when workers present."

(3) "Warning sign" means a signal, marking, or device placed on a barricade or on a road, street, or highway during construction, repair, or dangerous conditions by the department, a political subdivision of this state, or a contractor or subcontractor to warn or regulate motor vehicular traffic. The term includes a flagger deployed on a road, street, or highway by the department, a political subdivision of this state, or a contractor or subcontractor to direct traffic around or on the road, street, or highway during construction, repair, or dangerous conditions.

(f) Articles 45.051 and 45.0511, Code of Criminal Procedure, do not apply to an offense under this section committed in a construction or maintenance work zone when workers are present.

TITLE 7 VEHICLES AND TRAFFIC

SUBTITLE A CERTIFICATES OF TITLE AND REGISTRATION OF VEHICLES

CHAPTER 501 CERTIFICATE OF TITLE ACT

SUBCHAPTER A GENERAL PROVISIONS

Sec. 501.001. Short Title.

This chapter may be cited as the Certificate of Title Act.

Sec. 501.002. Definitions.

In this chapter:

(1) "Assembled vehicle" has the meaning assigned by Section 731.001.

(1-a) "Certificate of title" means a printed record of title issued under Section 501.021.

(2) "Credit card" means a card, plate, or similar device used to make a purchase or to borrow money.

(3) "Dealer" has the meaning assigned by Section 503.001.

(4) "Debit card" means a card that enables the holder to withdraw money or to have the cost of a purchase charged directly to the holder's bank account.

(5) "Department" means the Texas Department of Motor Vehicles.

(6) "Distributor" has the meaning assigned by Section 2301.002, Occupations Code.

(7) [Repealed.]

(8) "First sale" means:

(A) the bargain, sale, transfer, or delivery of a motor vehicle, other than an assembled vehicle, that has not been previously registered or titled, with intent to pass an interest in the motor vehicle, other than a lien, regardless of where the bargain, sale, transfer, or delivery occurred; and

(B) the registration or titling of that vehicle.

(9) "House trailer" means a trailer designed for human habitation. The term does not include manufactured housing.

(10) "Importer" means a person, other than a manufacturer, that brings a used motor vehicle into this state for sale in this state.

(11) "Importer's certificate" means a certificate for a used motor vehicle brought into this state for sale in this state.

(12) "Lien" means:

(A) a lien provided for by the constitution or statute in a motor vehicle;

(B) a security interest, as defined by Section 1.201, Business & Commerce Code, in a motor

Transportation Code

vehicle, other than an absolute title, created by any written security agreement, as defined by Section 9.102, Business & Commerce Code, including a lease, conditional sales contract, deed of trust, chattel mortgage, trust receipt, or reservation of title; or

(C) a child support lien under Chapter 157, Family Code.

(13) "Manufactured housing" has the meaning assigned by Chapter 1201, Occupations Code.

(14) "Manufacturer" has the meaning assigned by Section 503.001.

(15) "Manufacturer's permanent vehicle identification number" means the number affixed by the manufacturer to a motor vehicle in a manner and place easily accessible for physical examination and die-stamped or otherwise permanently affixed on one or more removable parts of the vehicle.

(16) "Motorcycle" has the meaning assigned by Section 521.001 or 541.201, as applicable.

(17) "Motor vehicle" means:

(A) any motor driven or propelled vehicle required to be registered under the laws of this state;

(B) a trailer or semitrailer, other than manufactured housing, that has a gross vehicle weight that exceeds 4,000 pounds;

(C) a travel trailer;

(D) an off-highway vehicle, as defined by Section 551A.001; or

(E) a motorcycle or moped that is not required to be registered under the laws of this state.

(18) "New motor vehicle" has the meaning assigned by Section 2301.002, Occupations Code.

(19) "Owner" means a person, other than a manufacturer, importer, distributor, or dealer, claiming title to or having a right to operate under a lien a motor vehicle that has been subject to a first sale.

(20) "Purchaser" means a person or entity to which a motor vehicle is donated, given, sold, or otherwise transferred.

(21) "Record of title" means an electronic record of motor vehicle ownership in the department's motor vehicle database that is created under Subchapter I.

(22) "Seller" means a person or entity that donates, gives, sells, or otherwise transfers ownership of a motor vehicle.

(23) "Semitrailer" means a vehicle that is designed or used with a motor vehicle so that part of the weight of the vehicle and its load rests on or is carried by another vehicle.

(24) "Serial number" means a vehicle identification number that is affixed to a part of a motor vehicle and that is:

(A) the manufacturer's permanent vehicle identification number;

(B) a derivative number of the manufacturer's permanent vehicle identification number;

(C) the motor number;

(D) the vehicle identification number assigned by the department; or

(E) the vehicle identification number assigned by the maker of a kit, if the vehicle is an assembled vehicle that is assembled from a kit.

(25) "Steal" has the meaning assigned by Section 31.01, Penal Code.

(26) "Subsequent sale" means:

(A) the bargain, sale, transfer, or delivery of a used motor vehicle, with intent to pass an interest in the vehicle, other than a lien; and

(B) the registration of the vehicle if registration is required under the laws of this state.

(27) "Title" means a certificate or record of title that is issued under Section 501.021.

(28) "Title receipt" means a document issued under Section 501.024.

(29) "Trailer" means a vehicle that:

(A) is designed or used to carry a load wholly on the trailer's own structure; and

(B) is drawn or designed to be drawn by a motor vehicle.

(30) "Travel trailer" means a house trailer-type vehicle or a camper trailer:

(A) that is a recreational vehicle defined under 24 C.F.R. Section 3282.8(g); or

(B) that:

(i) is less than eight feet six inches in width or 45 feet in length, exclusive of any hitch installed on the vehicle;

(ii) is designed primarily for use as temporary living quarters in connection with recreational, camping, travel, or seasonal use;

(iii) is not used as a permanent dwelling; and

(iv) is not a utility trailer, enclosed trailer, or other trailer that does not have human habitation as its primary function.

(31) "Used motor vehicle" means:

(A) a motor vehicle that has been the subject of a first sale; or

(B) an assembled vehicle that has been issued a title.

(32) "Vehicle identification number" means:

(A) the manufacturer's permanent vehicle identification number affixed by the manufacturer to the motor vehicle that is easily accessible for physical examination and permanently affixed on one or more removable parts of the vehicle; or

(B) a serial number affixed to a part of a motor vehicle that is:

(i) a derivative number of the manufacturer's permanent vehicle identification number;

(ii) the motor number;

(iii) a vehicle identification number assigned by the department; or

(iv) the vehicle identification number assigned by the maker of a kit, if the vehicle is an assembled vehicle that is assembled from a kit.

Sec. 501.003. Purpose.

This chapter shall be liberally construed to lessen and prevent:

(1) the theft of motor vehicles;

(2) the importation into this state of and traffic in motor vehicles that are stolen; and

(3) the sale of an encumbered motor vehicle without the enforced disclosure to the purchaser of a lien secured by the vehicle.

Sec. 501.004. Applicability.

(a) Except as provided by this section, this chapter applies to all motor vehicles, including a motor vehicle owned by the state or a political subdivision of the state.

(b) This chapter does not apply to:

(1) a farm trailer or farm semitrailer with a gross vehicle weight of not more than 34,000 pounds used only for the transportation of farm products if the products are not transported for hire;

(2) the filing or recording of a lien that is created only on an automobile accessory, including a tire, radio, or heater;

(3) a motor vehicle while it is owned or operated by the United States; or

(4) a new motor vehicle on loan to a political subdivision of the state for use only in a driver education course conducted by an entity exempt from licensure under Section 1001.002, Education Code.

Sec. 501.0041. Rules; Forms.

(a) The department may adopt rules to administer this chapter.

(b) The department shall post forms on the Internet and provide each county assessor-collector with a sufficient supply of any necessary forms on request.

Sec. 501.005. Conflicts with Business & Commerce Code.

Chapters 1—9, Business & Commerce Code, control over a conflicting provision of this chapter.

Sec. 501.006. Alias Title.

On receipt of a verified request approved by the executive administrator of a law enforcement agency, the department may issue a title in the form requested by the executive administrator for a vehicle in an alias for the law enforcement agency's use in a covert criminal investigation.

Sec. 501.007. [Expired August 31, 2015] Study on Feasibility of Title Being Obtained for All Trailers, Semitrailers, and Travel Trailers That Are Not Manufactured Housing.

Sec. 501.008. Title for Autocycle.

(a) In this section, "autocycle" means a motor vehicle, other than a tractor, that is:

(1) designed to have when propelled not more than three wheels on the ground;

(2) equipped with a steering wheel;

(3) equipped with seating that does not require the operator to straddle or sit astride the seat; and

(4) manufactured and certified to comply with federal safety requirements for a motorcycle.

(b) For purposes of issuing a title under this chapter, an autocycle is considered to be a motorcycle.

SUBCHAPTER B CERTIFICATE OF TITLE REQUIREMENTS

Sec. 501.021. Title for Motor Vehicle.

(a) A motor vehicle title issued by the department must include:

(1) the legal name and address of each purchaser;

(2) the legal name of the seller and the municipality and state in which the seller is located or resides;

(3) the year, make, and body style of the vehicle;

(4) the vehicle identification number of the vehicle;

(5) if the vehicle is subject to odometer disclosure under Section 501.072, the odometer reading and odometer brand as recorded on the last title assignment for the vehicle;

(6) the name and address of each lienholder and the date of each lien on the vehicle, listed in the chronological order in which the lien was recorded;

(7) a statement indicating rights of survivorship under Section 501.031; and

(8) any other information required by the department.

(b) A printed certificate of title must bear the following statement on its face:

"UNLESS OTHERWISE AUTHORIZED BY LAW, IT IS A VIOLATION OF STATE LAW TO SIGN THE NAME OF ANOTHER PERSON ON A CERTIFICATE OF TITLE OR OTHERWISE GIVE FALSE INFORMATION ON A CERTIFICATE OF TITLE."

(c) A title for a motor vehicle that has been the subject of an ordered repurchase or replacement under Chapter 2301, Occupations Code, must contain on its face a notice sufficient to inform a purchaser that the motor vehicle has been the subject of an ordered repurchase or replacement.

Sec. 501.022. Motor Vehicle Title Required.

(a) The owner of a motor vehicle registered in this state:

(1) except as provided by Section 501.029, shall apply for title to the vehicle; and

(2) may not operate or permit the operation of the vehicle on a public highway until the owner:

(A) applies for title and registration for the vehicle; or

(B) obtains a receipt evidencing title for registration purposes only under Section 501.029.

(b) A person may not operate a motor vehicle registered in this state on a public highway if the person knows or has reason to believe that the owner has not applied for a title for the vehicle.

(c) The owner of a motor vehicle that is required to be titled and registered in this state must obtain a title to the vehicle before selling or disposing of the vehicle.

(d) Subsection (c) does not apply to a motor vehicle operated on a public highway in this state with a metal dealer's license plate or a dealer's or buyer's temporary tag attached to the vehicle as provided by Chapter 503.

Sec. 501.023. Application for Title. [Effective until March 1, 2022]

(a) The owner of a motor vehicle must present identification and apply for a title as prescribed by the department, unless otherwise exempted by law. To obtain a title, the owner must apply:

(1) to the county assessor-collector in the county in which:

(A) the owner is domiciled; or

(B) the motor vehicle is purchased or encumbered; or

(2) to the county assessor-collector of a county who is willing to accept the application if the county assessor-collector's office of the county in which the owner resides is closed or may be closed for a protracted period of time as defined by the department.

(b) The assessor-collector shall send the application to the department or enter it into the department's titling system within 72 hours after receipt of the application.

(c) The owner or a lessee of a commercial motor vehicle operating under the International Registration Plan or other agreement described by Section 502.091 that is applying for a title for purposes of registration only may apply directly to the department. Notwithstanding Section 501.138(a), an applicant for registration under this subsection shall pay the fee imposed by that section. The fee shall be distributed to the appropriate county assessor-collector in the manner provided by Section 501.138.

(d) An application filed by the owner or lessee of a foreign commercial motor vehicle, as defined by Section 648.001, must be accompanied by a copy of the applicable federal declaration form required by the Federal Motor Carrier Safety Administration or its successor in connection with the importation of a motor vehicle or motor vehicle equipment subject to the federal motor vehicle safety, bumper, and theft prevention standards.

(e) Applications submitted to the department electronically must request the purchaser's choice of county as stated in Subsection (a) as the recipient of all taxes, fees, and other revenue collected as a result of the transaction.

Sec. 501.023. Application for Title. [Effective March 1, 2022]

(a) The owner of a motor vehicle must present identification and apply for a title as prescribed by the department, unless otherwise exempted by law. To obtain a title, the owner must apply:

(1) to the county assessor-collector in the county in which:

(A) the owner is domiciled; or

(B) the motor vehicle is purchased or encumbered; or

(2) to any county assessor-collector who is willing to accept the application.

(b) The assessor-collector shall send the application to the department or enter it into the department's titling system within 72 hours after receipt of the application.

(c) The owner or a lessee of a commercial motor vehicle operating under the International Registration Plan or other agreement described by Section 502.091 that is applying for a title for purposes of registration only may apply directly to the department. Notwithstanding Section 501.138(a), an applicant for registration under this subsection shall pay the fee imposed by that section. The fee shall be distributed to the appropriate county assessor-collector in the manner provided by Section 501.138.

(d) An application filed by the owner or lessee of a foreign commercial motor vehicle, as defined by Section 648.001, must be accompanied by a copy of the applicable federal declaration form required by the Federal Motor Carrier Safety Administration or its successor in connection with the importation of a motor vehicle or motor vehicle equipment subject to the federal motor vehicle safety, bumper, and theft prevention standards.

(e) [Repealed.]

Sec. 501.0234. Duty of Vehicle Dealer on Sale of Certain Vehicles. [Effective until March 1, 2022]

(a) A person who sells at the first or a subsequent sale a motor vehicle and who holds a general distinguishing number issued under Chapter 503 of this code or Chapter 2301, Occupations Code, shall:

(1) except as provided by this section, in the time and manner provided by law, apply, in the name of the purchaser of the vehicle, for the registration of the vehicle, if the vehicle is to be registered, and a title for the vehicle and file with the appropriate designated agent each document necessary to transfer title to or register the vehicle; and at the same time

(2) remit any required motor vehicle sales tax.

(b) This section does not apply to a motor vehicle:

(1) that has been declared a total loss by an insurance company in the settlement or adjustment of a claim;

(2) for which the title has been surrendered in exchange for:

(A) a salvage vehicle title or salvage record of title issued under this chapter;

(B) a nonrepairable vehicle title or nonrepairable vehicle record of title issued under this chapter or Subchapter D, Chapter 683; or

(C) an ownership document issued by another state that is comparable to a document described by Paragraph (A) or (B);

(3) with a gross weight in excess of 11,000 pounds; or

(4) purchased by a commercial fleet buyer who:

(A) is a deputy authorized by rules adopted under Section 520.0071;

(B) utilizes the dealer title application process developed to provide a method to submit title transactions to the county in which the commercial fleet buyer is a deputy; and

(C) has authority to accept an application for registration and application for title transfer that the county assessor-collector may accept.

(c) Each duty imposed by this section on the seller of a motor vehicle is solely that of the seller.

(d) A seller who applies for the registration or a title for a motor vehicle under Subsection (a)(1) shall apply in the county as directed by the purchaser from the counties set forth in Section 501.023.

(e) The department shall develop a form or electronic process in which the purchaser of a motor vehicle shall designate the purchaser's choice as set out in Section 501.023 as the recipient of all taxes, fees, and other revenue collected as a result of the transaction, which the tax assessor-collector is authorized by law to retain. A seller shall make that form or electronic process available to the purchaser of a vehicle at the time of purchase.

(f) A seller has a reasonable time to comply with the terms of Subsection (a)(1) and is not in violation of that provision during the time the seller is making a good faith effort to comply. Notwithstanding compliance with this chapter, equitable title to a vehicle passes to the purchaser of the vehicle at the time the vehicle is the subject of a sale that is enforceable by either party.

Sec. 501.0234. Duty of Vehicle Dealer on Sale of Certain Vehicles. [Effective March 1, 2022]

(a) A person who sells at the first or a subsequent sale a motor vehicle and who holds a general distinguishing number issued under Chapter 503 of this code or Chapter 2301, Occupations Code, shall:

(1) except as provided by this section, in the time and manner provided by law, apply, in the name of the purchaser of the vehicle, for the registration of the vehicle, if the vehicle is to be registered, and a title for the vehicle and file with the appropriate designated agent each document necessary to transfer title to or register the vehicle; and at the same time

(2) remit any required motor vehicle sales tax.

(b) This section does not apply to a motor vehicle:

(1) that has been declared a total loss by an insurance company in the settlement or adjustment of a claim;

(2) for which the title has been surrendered in exchange for:

(A) a salvage vehicle title or salvage record of title issued under this chapter;

(B) a nonrepairable vehicle title or nonrepairable vehicle record of title issued under this chapter or Subchapter D, Chapter 683; or

(C) an ownership document issued by another state that is comparable to a document described by Paragraph (A) or (B);

(3) with a gross weight in excess of 11,000 pounds; or

(4) purchased by a commercial fleet buyer who:

(A) is a deputy authorized by rules adopted under Section 520.0071;

(B) utilizes the dealer title application process developed to provide a method to submit title transactions to the county in which the commercial fleet buyer is a deputy; and

(C) has authority to accept an application for registration and application for title transfer that the county assessor-collector may accept.

(c) Each duty imposed by this section on the seller of a motor vehicle is solely that of the seller.

(d) A seller who applies for the registration or a title for a motor vehicle under Subsection (a)(1) may apply:

(1) to the county assessor-collector of the county in which:

(A) the owner is domiciled; or

(B) the motor vehicle is purchased or encumbered; or

(2) to any county assessor-collector who is willing to accept the application.

(e) [Repealed.]

(f) A seller has a reasonable time to comply with the terms of Subsection (a)(1) and is not in violation of that provision during the time the seller is making a good faith effort to comply. Notwithstanding compliance with this chapter, equitable title to a vehicle passes to the purchaser of the vehicle at the time the vehicle is the subject of a sale that is enforceable by either party.

Sec. 501.0235. Personal Identification Information for Obtaining Title.

(a) The department may require an applicant for a title to provide current personal identification as determined by department rule.

(b) Any identification number required by the department under this section may be entered in the department's electronic titling system but may not be printed on the title.

Sec. 501.0236. Issuance of Title and Permits When Dealer Goes Out of Business.

(a) This section applies only to a person who is the purchaser of a motor vehicle for which the dealer:

(1) is required to apply for a title for the vehicle under Section 501.0234; and

(2) does not apply for the title because the dealer has gone out of business.

(b) A purchaser to whom this section applies may apply for:

(1) a title in the manner prescribed by the department by rule; and

(2) on expiration of the buyer's tag issued to the purchaser under Section 503.063, a 30-day permit under Section 502.095.

(c) An application for a title under this section must include a release of any recorded lien on the motor vehicle unless the only recorded lienholder is a dealer described by Subsection (a).

(d) The department shall waive the payment of fees for:

(1) a title issued to a purchaser described by this section, if the purchaser can show that fees for a title were paid to the dealer; and

(2) one 30-day permit issued to a purchaser described by this section.

(e) Notwithstanding Section 503.033(e), the department may recover against the surety bond executed by the dealer under Section 503.033 the amount of any fee waived for a title or permit issued under this section.

(f) The department shall adopt the rules necessary to implement this section.

Sec. 501.024. Title Receipt.

(a) A county assessor-collector who receives an application for a title shall issue a title receipt to the applicant containing the information concerning the motor vehicle required for issuance of a title under Section 501.021 or Subchapter I after:

(1) the requirements of this chapter are met, including the payment of the fees required under Section 501.138; and

(2) the information is entered into the department's titling system.

(b) If a lien is not disclosed on the application for a title, the assessor-collector shall issue a title receipt to the applicant.

(c) If a lien is disclosed on the application for a title, the assessor-collector shall issue a duplicate title receipt to the lienholder.

(d) A title receipt with registration or permit authorizes the operation of the motor vehicle on a public highway in this state until the title is issued.

Sec. 501.025. Manufacturer's Certificate Required on First Sale.

A county assessor-collector may not issue a title receipt on the first sale of a motor vehicle unless the applicant for the title provides the application for a title and a manufacturer's certificate in a manner prescribed by the department.

Sec. 501.026. Importer's Certificate [Repealed].

Repealed by Acts 2011, 82nd Leg., ch. 1296 (H.B. 2357), § 247(1), effective January 1, 2012.

Sec. 501.027. Issuance of Title.

(a) On the day that a county assessor-collector issues a title receipt, a copy of the title receipt and all evidence of title shall be submitted to the department in the period specified in Section 501.023(b).

(b) Not later than the fifth day after the date the department receives an application for a title and the department determines the requirements of this chapter are met:

(1) the title shall be issued to the first lienholder or to the applicant if a lien is not disclosed on the application; or

(2) the department shall notify the applicant that the department's titling system has established a record of title of the motor vehicle in the applicant's name if a lien is not disclosed. If a lien is disclosed on the application, the department shall notify the lienholder that the lien has been recorded.

Sec. 501.0275. Issuance of Title for Unregistered Vehicle.

(a) The department shall issue a title for a motor vehicle that complies with the other requirements under this chapter unless:

(1) the vehicle is not registered for a reason other than a reason provided by Section 501.051(a)(6); and

(2) the applicant does not provide evidence of financial responsibility that complies with Section 502.046.

(b) On application for a title under this section, the applicant must surrender any license plates issued for the motor vehicle if the plates are not being transferred to another vehicle and any registration insignia for validation of those plates to the department.

Sec. 501.0276. Denial of Title Receipt, Title, or Record of Title for Failure to Provide Proof of Emissions Testing.

A county assessor-collector may not issue a title receipt and the department may not issue a certificate of title for a vehicle subject to Section 548.3011 unless proof that the vehicle has passed a vehicle emissions test as required by that section, in a manner authorized by that section, is presented to the county assessor-collector with the application for a title.

Sec. 501.028. Signatures.

(a) On receipt of a certificate of title, the owner of a motor vehicle shall write the owner's name in ink in the space provided on the certificate.

(b) Upon transfer of ownership, the seller shall complete assignment of title by signing and printing the seller's name, printing the date of transfer, and printing the purchaser's name and address on the title.

Sec. 501.029. Acceptable Proof of Ownership.

The board by rule may provide a list of the documents required for the issuance of a receipt that evidences title to a motor vehicle for registration purposes only. The fee for application for the receipt is the fee applicable to application for a title. The title receipt may not be used to transfer an interest in or establish a lien on the vehicle.

Sec. 501.030. Motor Vehicles Brought into State. [Effective until March 1, 2022]

(a) Before a motor vehicle that was last registered or titled in another state or country may be titled in this state, the county assessor-collector shall verify that the vehicle has passed the inspections required by Chapter 548, as indicated in the Department of Public Safety's inspection database under Section 548.251, or that the owner has obtained an identification number inspection in accordance with department rule.

(b) Before a motor vehicle that was not manufactured for sale or distribution in the United States may be titled in this state, the applicant must:

(1) provide to the assessor-collector:

(A) a bond release letter, with all attachments, issued by the United States Department of Transportation acknowledging:

(i) receipt of a statement of compliance submitted by the importer of the vehicle; and

(ii) that the statement meets the safety requirements of 19 C.F.R. Section 12.80(e);

(B) a bond release letter, with all attachments, issued by the United States Environmental Protection Agency stating that the vehicle has been tested and shown to conform to federal emission requirements; and

(C) a receipt or certificate issued by the United States Department of the Treasury showing that all gas guzzler taxes due on the vehicle under 26 U.S.C. Section 4064(a) have been paid; or

(2) provide to the assessor-collector proof, satisfactory to the department, that the vehicle was not brought into the United States from outside the country.

(c) Subsections (a) and (b) do not apply to a motor vehicle lawfully imported into the United States by a distributor or dealer from the vehicle's manufacturer.

Transportation Code

(d) If a motor vehicle has not been titled or registered in the United States, the application for title must be accompanied by:

(1) a manufacturer's certificate of origin written in English issued by the vehicle manufacturer;

(2) the original documents that constitute valid proof of ownership in the country where the vehicle was originally purchased, with an English translation of the documents verified as to the accuracy of the translation by an affidavit of the translator; or

(3) if the vehicle was imported from a country that cancels the vehicle registration and title for export, the documents assigned to the vehicle after the registration and title were canceled, with an English translation of the documents verified as to the accuracy of the translation by an affidavit of the translator.

(e) Before a motor vehicle that is required to be registered in this state and that is brought into this state by a person other than a manufacturer or importer may be bargained, sold, transferred, or delivered with an intent to pass an interest in the vehicle or encumbered by a lien, the owner must apply for a title in a manner prescribed by the department to the county assessor-collector for the county in which the transaction is to take place. The assessor-collector may not issue a title receipt unless the applicant delivers to the assessor-collector satisfactory evidence showing that the applicant is the owner of the vehicle and that the vehicle is free of any undisclosed liens.

(f) A county assessor-collector may not be held liable for civil damages arising out of the assessor-collector's failure to reflect on the title receipt a lien or encumbrance on a motor vehicle to which Subsection (e) applies unless the failure constitutes wilful or wanton negligence.

(g) Until an applicant has complied with this section:

(1) a county assessor-collector may not accept an application for title; and

(2) the applicant is not entitled to an appeal as provided by Sections 501.052 and 501.053.

Sec. 501.030. Motor Vehicles Brought into State. [Effective March 1, 2022]

(a) Before a motor vehicle that was last registered or titled in another state or country may be titled in this state, the county assessor-collector shall verify that the vehicle has passed the inspections required by Chapter 548, as indicated in the Department of Public Safety's inspection database under Section 548.251, or that the owner has obtained an identification number inspection in accordance with department rule.

(b) Before a motor vehicle that was not manufactured for sale or distribution in the United States may be titled in this state, the applicant must:

(1) provide to the assessor-collector:

(A) a bond release letter, with all attachments, issued by the United States Department of Transportation acknowledging:

(i) receipt of a statement of compliance submitted by the importer of the vehicle; and

(ii) that the statement meets the safety requirements of 19 C.F.R. Section 12.80(e);

(B) a bond release letter, with all attachments, issued by the United States Environmental Protection Agency stating that the vehicle has been tested and shown to conform to federal emission requirements; and

(C) a receipt or certificate issued by the United States Department of the Treasury showing that all gas guzzler taxes due on the vehicle under 26 U.S.C. Section 4064(a) have been paid; or

(2) provide to the assessor-collector proof, satisfactory to the department, that the vehicle was not brought into the United States from outside the country.

(c) Subsections (a) and (b) do not apply to a motor vehicle lawfully imported into the United States by a distributor or dealer from the vehicle's manufacturer.

(d) If a motor vehicle has not been titled or registered in the United States, the application for title must be accompanied by:

(1) a manufacturer's certificate of origin written in English issued by the vehicle manufacturer;

(2) the original documents that constitute valid proof of ownership in the country where the vehicle was originally purchased, with an English translation of the documents verified as to the accuracy of the translation by an affidavit of the translator; or

(3) if the vehicle was imported from a country that cancels the vehicle registration and title for export, the documents assigned to the vehicle after the registration and title were canceled, with an English translation of the documents verified as to the accuracy of the translation by an affidavit of the translator.

(e) Before a motor vehicle that is required to be registered in this state and that is brought into this state by a person other than a manufacturer or importer may be bargained, sold, transferred, or delivered with an intent to pass an interest in the vehicle or encumbered by a lien, the owner must apply for a title in a manner prescribed by the department to the county assessor-collector for the county in which the transaction is to take place or to any assessor-collector who is willing to accept the application. The assessor-collector may not issue a title receipt unless the applicant delivers to the assessor-collector satisfactory evidence showing that the applicant is the owner of the vehicle and that the vehicle is free of any undisclosed liens.

(f) A county assessor-collector may not be held liable for civil damages arising out of the assessor-collector's failure to reflect on the title receipt a lien or encumbrance on a motor vehicle to which Subsection (e) applies unless the failure constitutes wilful or wanton negligence.

(g) Until an applicant has complied with this section:

(1) a county assessor-collector may not accept an application for title; and

(2) the applicant is not entitled to an appeal as provided by Sections 501.052 and 501.053.

Sec. 501.0301. Certain Off-Highway Vehicles Purchased Outside This State.

(a) In this section:

(1) "Off-highway vehicle" means:

(A) an all-terrain vehicle or recreational off-highway vehicle, as those terms are defined by Section 551A.001;

(B) a motorcycle, as that term is defined by Section 541.201, other than a motorcycle described by Section 521.001, that is designed by the manufacturer for off-highway use only; or

(C) a utility vehicle, as that term is defined by Section 551A.001.

(2) "Retailer" has the meaning assigned by Section 151.008, Tax Code.

(b) A county assessor-collector may not issue a title receipt and the department may not issue a certificate of title for an off-highway vehicle purchased from a retailer located outside this state and designated by the manufacturer as a model year that is not more than one year before the year in which the application for title is made unless the applicant for the title delivers to the assessor-collector or the department, as applicable, satisfactory evidence showing that the applicant:

(1) has paid to the comptroller the applicable use tax imposed on the vehicle under Subchapter D, Chapter 151, Tax Code; or

(2) is not required to pay any taxes described by Subdivision (1).

(c) The comptroller shall promulgate forms to be used by each county assessor-collector for purposes of implementing this section.

(d) The comptroller may adopt rules as necessary to implement this section, including rules that define "satisfactory evidence" for purposes of this section.

Sec. 501.031. Rights of Survivorship Agreement.

(a) The department shall include on each title an optional rights of survivorship agreement that:

(1) provides that if the agreement is between two or more eligible persons, the motor vehicle will be owned by the surviving owners when one or more of the owners die; and

(2) provides for the acknowledgment by signature, either electronically or by hand, of the persons.

(b) If the vehicle is registered in the name of one or more of the persons who acknowledged the agreement, the title may contain a:

(1) rights of survivorship agreement acknowledged by all the persons; or

(2) remark if a rights of survivorship agreement is on file with the department.

(c) Ownership of the vehicle may be transferred only:

(1) by all the persons acting jointly, if all the persons are alive; or

(2) on the death of one of the persons, by the surviving person or persons by transferring ownership of the vehicle, in the manner otherwise required by law, with a copy of the death certificate of the deceased person.

(d) A rights of survivorship agreement under this section may be revoked only if the persons named in the agreement file a joint application for a new title in the name of the person or persons designated in the application.

(e) A person is eligible to file a rights of survivorship agreement under this section if the person:

(1) is married and the spouse of the person is the only other party to the agreement;

(2) is unmarried and attests to that unmarried status by affidavit; or

(3) is married and provides the department with an affidavit from the person's spouse that attests that the person's interest in the vehicle is the person's separate property.

(f) The department may develop an optional electronic rights of survivorship agreement for public use.

Sec. 501.0315. Beneficiary Designation.

(a) The owner of a motor vehicle may designate a sole beneficiary to whom the owner's interest in the vehicle transfers on the owner's death as provided by Chapter 115, Estates Code, by submitting an application for title under Section 501.023 with the designation. To be effective, the designation must state that the transfer of an interest in the vehicle to the designated beneficiary is to occur at the transferor's death.

(b) The legal name of a beneficiary designated under this section must be included on the title.

(c) The department shall transfer title of a motor vehicle to a beneficiary designated under this section for the vehicle if the beneficiary submits:

(1) an application for title under Section 501.023 not later than the 180th day after the date of the owner's death or, if the vehicle is owned by joint owners, the last surviving owner's death, as applicable; and

(2) satisfactory proof of the death of the owner or owners, as applicable.

(d) A beneficiary designation may be changed or revoked by submitting a new application for title under Section 501.023.

(e) A beneficiary designation or a change or revocation of a beneficiary designation made on an application for title of a motor vehicle that has not been submitted to the department before the death of a vehicle's owner or owners who made, changed, or revoked the designation, as applicable, is invalid.

(f) The department may adopt rules to administer this section.

Sec. 501.032. Identification Number Inspection Required.

(a) In addition to any requirement established by department rule, a motor vehicle, trailer, or semitrailer must have an identification number inspection under Section 501.0321 if:

(1) the department does not have a motor vehicle record for the motor vehicle, trailer, or semitrailer in the department's registration and title system, and the owner of the motor vehicle, trailer, or semitrailer is filing a bond with the department under Section 501.053;

(2) the motor vehicle, trailer, or semitrailer was last titled or registered outside of the United States and imported into the United States; or

(3) the owner or person claiming ownership requires an assigned or reassigned identification number under Section 501.033.

(b) An active duty member of a branch of the United States armed forces, or an immediate family member of such a member, returning to Texas with acceptable proof of the active duty status is exempt from an identification number inspection required under Subsection (a)(2).

(c) [Repealed.]

(d) [Repealed.]

Sec. 501.0321. Identification Number Inspection.

(a) An inspection required under Section 501.032 must verify, as applicable, the identity of:

(1) a motor vehicle;

(2) a trailer or semitrailer;

(3) a frame, body, or motor of a motor vehicle; or

(4) an item of equipment not required to be titled but that may be registered under Chapter 502 or issued licensed plates under Chapter 504.

(b) An inspection under this section may not rely solely on the public identification number to verify the identity.

(c) An inspection under this section may be performed only by a person who has successfully completed an appropriate training program as determined by department rule and is:

(1) an auto theft investigator who is a law enforcement officer of this state or a political subdivision of this state;

(2) a person working under the direct supervision of a person described by Subdivision (1);

(3) an employee of the department authorized by the department to perform an inspection under this section; or

(4) an employee of the National Insurance Crime Bureau authorized by the department to perform an inspection under this section.

(d) The department shall prescribe a form on which the identification number inspection is to be recorded. The department may provide the form only to a person described by Subsection (c).

(e) The department or another entity that provides an inspection under this section may impose a fee of not more than $40 for the inspection. The county or municipal treasurer of a county or municipal entity that provides an inspection under this section shall credit the fee to the general fund of the county or municipality, as applicable, to defray the entity's cost associated with the inspection. If the department provides an inspection under this section, the fee shall be deposited to the credit of the Texas Department of Motor Vehicles fund.

(f) The department may not impose a fee for an inspection requested by the department. The department shall include a notification of the waiver to the owner at the time the department requests the identification number inspection.

Sec. 501.0322. Alternative Identification Number Inspection.

The department by rule may establish a process for verifying the identity of an item listed in Section 501.0321(a) as an alternative to an identification number inspection under Section 501.0321. The rules may include the persons authorized to perform the inspection, when an alternative inspection under this section is required, and any fees that may be assessed. Any fee authorized must comply with Sections 501.0321(e) and (f).

Sec. 501.033. Assignment and Reassignment of Identification Number by Department.

(a) If the permanent identification number affixed by the manufacturer has been removed, altered, or obliterated, or a permanent identification number was never assigned, the department shall assign an identification number to a motor vehicle, semitrailer, trailer, motor, frame, or body of a motor vehicle, or an item of equipment not required to be titled but that may be registered under Chapter 502 or issued license plates under Chapter 504 on inspection under Section 501.0321 and application to the department.

(b) An application under this section must be in a manner prescribed by the department and accompanied by valid evidence of ownership in the name of, or properly assigned to, the applicant as required by the department.

(c) A fee of $2 must accompany each application under this section to be deposited in the Texas Department of Motor Vehicles fund.

(d) The assigned identification number shall be die-stamped or otherwise affixed in the manner and location designated by the department.

(e) The department shall reassign an original manufacturer's identification number only if the person who conducts the inspection under Section 501.0321 determines that the permanent identification number affixed by the manufacturer has been removed, altered, or obliterated.

(f) If the department reassigns a manufacturer's identification number, a representative of the department shall affix the number in a manner and location designated by the department.

(g) On affixing an assigned identification number or witnessing the affixing of a reassigned identification number, the owner or the owner's representative shall certify on a form prescribed by the department that the identification number has been affixed in the manner and location designated by the department and shall submit the form in a manner prescribed by the department.

(h) Only the department may issue an identification number to a motor vehicle, trailer, semitrailer, motor, frame, or body of a motor vehicle, or an item of equipment not required to be titled but that may be registered under Chapter 502 or issued license plates under Chapter 504. The department may not recognize an identification number assigned by any other agency or political subdivision of this state.

Sec. 501.0331. Motor Number Required for Registration.

A person may not apply to the county assessor-collector for the registration of a motor vehicle from which the original motor number has been removed, erased, or destroyed until the motor vehicle bears the motor number assigned by the department.

Sec. 501.0332. Application for Motor Number Record.

(a) To obtain a motor number assigned by the department, the owner of a motor vehicle that has had the original motor number removed, erased, or destroyed must file a sworn application with the department.

(b) The department shall maintain a record of each motor number assigned by the department that includes:

(1) the motor number assigned by the department;

(2) the name and address of the owner of the motor vehicle; and

(3) the make, model, and year of manufacture of the motor vehicle.

Sec. 501.034. Issuance of Title to Government Agency.

The department may issue a title to a government agency if a vehicle or part of a vehicle is:

(1) forfeited to the government agency;

(2) delivered by court order under the Code of Criminal Procedure to a government agency for official purposes; or

(3) sold as abandoned or unclaimed property under the Code of Criminal Procedure.

Sec. 501.0341. Issuance of Title to Government Agency for Travel Trailer.

(a) The department by rule shall establish a process to automatically issue a title to a government agency for a travel trailer used by the government agency to provide temporary housing in response to a natural disaster or other declared emergency.

(b) Notwithstanding Section 501.004(b)(3), rules adopted under this section may provide for the issuance of a title for a travel trailer described by Subsection (a) that is owned or operated by the United States or transferred to a state agency from the United States.

Sec. 501.035. Title for Former Military Vehicle.

(a) Notwithstanding any other law, the department shall issue a title for a former military vehicle if all requirements for issuance of a title are met.

(b) In this section, "former military vehicle" has the meaning assigned by Section 502.001.

Sec. 501.036. Title for Farm Trailer or Farm Semitrailer.

(a) Notwithstanding any other provision of this chapter, the department may issue a title for a farm trailer or farm semitrailer with a gross vehicle weight of not more than 34,000 pounds if all requirements for issuance of a title are met.

(b) To obtain a title under this section, the owner must:

(1) apply for the title in the manner required by Section 501.023; and

(2) pay the fee required by Section 501.138.

(c) A subsequent purchaser of a farm trailer or farm semitrailer titled previously under this section or in another jurisdiction must obtain a title under this section.

Sec. 501.037. Title for Trailers or Semitrailers.

(a) Notwithstanding any other provision of this chapter, the department may issue a title for a trailer or semitrailer that has a gross vehicle weight of 4,000 pounds or less if all other requirements for issuance of a title are met.

(b) To obtain a title under this section, the owner of the trailer or semitrailer must:

(1) apply for the title in the manner required by Section 501.023; and

(2) pay the fee required by Section 501.138.

(c) A subsequent purchaser of a trailer or semitrailer titled previously under this section or in another jurisdiction must obtain a title under this section.

Sec. 501.038. Certificate of Title for Custom Vehicle or Street Rod.

(a) In this section, "custom vehicle" and "street rod" have the meanings assigned by Section 504.501.

(b) Notwithstanding any other provision of this chapter, if the department issues a certificate of title for a custom vehicle or street rod, the model year and make of the vehicle must be listed on the certificate of title and must be the model year and make that the body of the vehicle resembles. The certificate of title must also include the word "replica."

(c) The owner of the custom vehicle or street rod shall provide the department with documentation identifying the model year and make that the body of the vehicle resembles.

SUBCHAPTER C REFUSAL TO ISSUE, REVOCATION, SUSPENSION, OR ALTERATION OF CERTIFICATE

Sec. 501.051. Grounds for Refusal to Issue or for Revocation or Suspension of Title.

(a) A title may be refused, canceled, suspended, or revoked by the department if:

(1) the application contains a false or fraudulent statement;

(2) the applicant failed to furnish required information requested by the department;

(3) the applicant is not entitled to a title;

(4) the department has reason to believe that the motor vehicle is stolen;

(5) the department has reason to believe that the issuance of a title would defraud the owner or a lienholder of the motor vehicle;

(6) the registration for the motor vehicle is suspended or revoked; or

(7) the required fee has not been paid.

(b) The department may rescind, cancel, or revoke an application for a title if a notarized or county-stamped affidavit is presented containing:

(1) a statement that the vehicle involved was a new motor vehicle in the process of a first sale;

(2) a statement that the dealer, the applicant, and any lienholder have canceled the sale;

(3) a statement that the vehicle:

(A) was never in the possession of the title applicant; or

(B) was in the possession of the title applicant; and

(4) the signatures of the dealer, the applicant, and any lienholder.

(c) A rescission, cancellation, or revocation containing the statement authorized under Subsection (b)(3)(B) does not negate the fact that the vehicle has been the subject of a previous retail sale.

(d) The department shall place a hold on processing a title application for a motor vehicle if the department receives a request for a hold accompanied by evidence of a legal action regarding ownership of or a lien interest in the motor vehicle. The hold shall continue until a final, nonappealable judgment is entered in the action or the party requesting the hold requests that the hold be removed.

Sec. 501.052. Hearing on Refusal to Issue or Revocation or Suspension of Title; Appeal.

(a) An interested person aggrieved by a refusal, rescission, cancellation, suspension, or

Transportation Code

revocation under Section 501.051 may apply for a hearing to the county assessor-collector for the county in which the person is a resident. On the day an assessor-collector receives the application, the assessor-collector shall notify the department of the date of the hearing.

(b) The assessor-collector shall hold the hearing not earlier than the 11th day and not later than the 15th day after the date the assessor-collector receives the application for a hearing.

(c) At the hearing, the applicant and the department may submit evidence.

(d) A determination of the assessor-collector is binding on the applicant and the department as to whether the department correctly refused to issue or correctly rescinded, canceled, revoked, or suspended the title.

(e) An applicant aggrieved by the determination under Subsection (d) may appeal only to the county or district court of the county of the applicant's residence. An applicant must file an appeal not later than the fifth day after receipt of the assessor-collector's determination. The judge shall try the appeal in the manner of other civil cases. All rights and immunities granted in the trial of a civil case are available to the interested parties. If the department's action is not sustained, the department shall promptly issue a title for the vehicle.

(f) A person may not apply for a hearing under this section if the department's decision under Section 501.051 is related to a title for a salvage motor vehicle or a nonrepairable motor vehicle, as defined by Section 501.091.

Sec. 501.0521. Court Ordered Title Changes.

(a) A justice of the peace or municipal court judge may not issue an order related to a title except as provided by Chapter 47, Code of Criminal Procedure, or Section 27.031(a)(3), Government Code.

(b) A county or district court judge may not order the department to change the type of title for:

(1) a nonrepairable vehicle titled after September 1, 2003; or

(2) a vehicle for which the department has issued a certificate of authority under Section 683.054.

Sec. 501.053. Filing of Bond As Alternative to Hearing.

(a) As an alternative to the procedure provided by Section 501.052, the person may obtain a title by filing a bond with the department if the vehicle is in the possession of the applicant and:

(1) there is no security interest on the vehicle;

(2) any lien on the vehicle is at least 10 years old; or

(3) the person provides a release of all liens with bond.

(b) The bond must be:

(1) in the manner prescribed by the department;

(2) executed by the applicant;

(3) issued by a person authorized to conduct a surety business in this state;

(4) in an amount equal to one and one-half times the value of the vehicle as determined by the department, which may set an appraisal system by rule if it is unable to determine that value; and

(5) conditioned to indemnify all prior owners and lienholders and all subsequent purchasers of the vehicle or persons who acquire a security interest in the vehicle, and their successors in interest, against any expense, loss, or damage, including reasonable attorney's fees, occurring because of the issuance of the title for the vehicle or for a defect in or undisclosed security interest on the right, title, or interest of the applicant to the vehicle.

(c) An interested person has a right of action to recover on the bond for a breach of the bond's condition. The aggregate liability of the surety to all persons may not exceed the amount of the bond.

(d) A bond under this section expires on the third anniversary of the date the bond became effective.

(e) The board by rule may establish a fee to cover the cost of administering this section.

(f) A person may not obtain a title under this section for a salvage motor vehicle or a nonrepairable motor vehicle, as defined by Section 501.091.

SUBCHAPTER D SALES OF MOTOR VEHICLES AND TRANSFERS OF TITLE

Sec. 501.071. Sale of Vehicle; Transfer of Title.

(a) Except as provided by Sections 503.036 and 503.039, a motor vehicle may not be the subject of a subsequent sale unless the owner designated on the title submits a transfer of ownership of the title.

(b) The transfer of the title must be in a manner prescribed by the department that:

(1) certifies the purchaser is the owner of the vehicle; and

(2) certifies there are no liens on the vehicle or provides a release of each lien on the vehicle.

Sec. 501.072. Odometer Disclosure Statement.

(a) Except as provided by Subsection (c), the transferor of a motor vehicle transferred in this state shall provide to the transferee a disclosure of the vehicle's odometer reading at the time of the transfer in compliance with 49 U.S.C. Section 32705.

(b) When application for a title is made, the transferee shall record the odometer reading on the application. The disclosure required by Subsection (a) must accompany the application.

(c) An odometer disclosure statement is not required for the transfer of a motor vehicle that is exempt from odometer disclosure requirements under 49 C.F.R. Part 580.

(d) The department shall provide for use consistent with 49 C.F.R. Part 580:

(1) a secure power of attorney form; and

(2) a secure reassignment form for licensed motor vehicle dealers.

(e) In this section, "transferee" and "transferor" have the meanings assigned by 49 C.F.R. Section 580.3.

Sec. 501.0721. Delivery of Receipt and Title to Purchaser of Used Motor Vehicle.

A person, whether acting for that person or another, who sells, trades, or otherwise transfers a used motor vehicle shall deliver to the purchaser at the time of delivery of the vehicle a properly assigned title or other evidence of title as required under this chapter.

Sec. 501.073. Sales in Violation of Chapter.

A sale made in violation of this chapter is void and title may not pass until the requirements of this chapter are satisfied.

Sec. 501.074. Transfer of Vehicle by Operation of Law.

(a) The department shall issue a new title for a motor vehicle registered in this state for which the ownership is transferred by operation of law or other involuntary divestiture of ownership after receiving:

(1) a certified copy of an order appointing a temporary administrator or of the probate proceedings;

(2) letters testamentary or letters of administration;

(3) if administration of an estate is not necessary, an affidavit showing that administration is not necessary, identifying all heirs, and including a statement by the heirs of the name in which the certificate shall be issued;

(4) a court order; or

(5) the bill of sale from an officer making a judicial sale.

(b) If a lien is foreclosed by nonjudicial means, the department may issue a new title in the name of the purchaser at the foreclosure sale on receiving the affidavit of the lienholder of the fact of the nonjudicial foreclosure.

(c) If a constitutional or statutory lien is foreclosed, the department may issue a new title in the name of the purchaser at the foreclosure sale on receiving:

(1) the affidavit of the lienholder of the fact of the creation of the lien and of the divestiture of title according to law; and

(2) proof of notice as required by Sections 70.004 and 70.006, Property Code, or by Section 59.0445, Property Code.

(d) Notwithstanding the terms of Section 501.005, in the event of a conflict between this section and other law, this section controls.

Sec. 501.075. Validity of Documents Not Notarized [Repealed].

Repealed by Acts 2011, 82nd Leg., ch. 1296 (H.B. 2357), § 247(1), effective January 1, 2012.

Sec. 501.076. Limited Power of Attorney.

(a) An owner who has a contractual option to transfer ownership of a vehicle in full or partial satisfaction of the balance owed on the vehicle, as provided in Section 348.123(b)(5), Finance Code, may execute a written limited power of attorney that authorizes an agent to complete and sign for the owner, and provide to the transferee, the form to transfer the title under Section 501.071 and the odometer disclosure under Section 501.072, and the other documents necessary to transfer title.

(b) The owner may execute the limited power of attorney at the time the owner enters the contract giving the owner the option to transfer the vehicle or at any time after that date. The limited power of attorney may only be used if an owner elects to transfer the vehicle in full or partial satisfaction of the contract and may not be used by the holder of the contract as part of the holder's exercise of a remedy for a default by the owner under the contract.

(c) The person named as the agent in the limited power of attorney must meet the following requirements:

(1) the person may be a person who has been deputized to perform vehicle registration functions as authorized by rules adopted under Section 520.0071, a licensed vehicle auction company holding a wholesale general distinguishing number under Section 503.022, a person who has a permit similar to one of the foregoing that is issued by the state in which the owner is located, or another person authorized by law to execute title documents in the state in which the owner executes the documents; and

(2) the person may not be the transferee or an employee of the transferee. The person may not act as the agent of both the transferor and transferee in the transaction. For the purposes of this section, a person is not the agent of both the transferor and transferee in a transaction unless the person has the authority to sign the documents pertaining to the transfer of title on behalf of both the transferor and the transferee.

(d) If a limited power of attorney is used under Subsection (a), the holder of the contract shall accompany the power of attorney with a written statement that the vehicle was returned at the election of the owner in full or partial satisfaction of the owner's obligations under the contract and not as the result of the exercise by the holder of the contract of its remedies for default.

(e) A signed and dated written odometer disclosure containing the information described in this subsection may be included on or with the power of attorney if the power of attorney is executed within 120 days before the date of the transfer and is accompanied by the conspicuous written notification described in this subsection. If an odometer disclosure is not obtained in that manner, the transferee or agent or the person to whom the vehicle is delivered at the time of the transfer shall request an odometer disclosure as provided in this subsection. Not more than 120 days before the transfer of the vehicle by the owner, the transferee or agent under the power of attorney or person receiving delivery of the vehicle shall in writing request the owner to provide a signed and dated written statement stating the odometer reading (not to include tenths of a mile) as of the date of the statement, and further stating words to the effect that either: (i) to the best of the owner's knowledge, the odometer reading reflects the actual mileage of the vehicle; (ii) the actual mileage has gone over the odometer's mechanical limits and the odometer reading reflects the amount of mileage in excess of the mechanical limits of the odometer, if the owner knows that to be the case; or (iii) the odometer reading is not the actual mileage, if the owner knows that to be the case. The statement may consist of a form in which the agent or transferee or person receiving the vehicle includes the identification of the vehicle and owner and which allows the owner to fill in the odometer reading and mark an applicable box to indicate which of condition (i), (ii), or (iii) is applicable and to date and sign the statement. With the request for the owner's statement, the transferee or agent or person receiving the vehicle shall provide a written notification to the owner to the effect that the owner has a duty under law to state the odometer reading, state which of conditions (i), (ii), or (iii) is applicable, and sign, date, and return the statement and that failing to do so or providing false information may result in fines or imprisonment. Unless the written notification is delivered to the owner at substantially the same time that the owner is delivering the signed and dated owner's statement, the written notification must also state a date by which the owner must provide this information and an address to which it may be delivered. This written notification to the owner must be in bold letters, underlined, or otherwise conspicuous and may be in a separate document or included as part of a form to be used for the owner's statement or in another document relating to the potential transfer. The transferee or agent or the person receiving delivery of the vehicle may mail the request and notification to the last known address of the owner or may otherwise send or deliver it to the owner. If there are multiple owners of the same vehicle, the request and notification may be sent to one or more of them and it shall be sufficient for one owner to sign the statement. The owner has a duty to return the signed and dated statement as directed in the notification. In completing the odometer disclosure on the owner's behalf, the agent shall identify the same condition (i), (ii), or (iii) provided in the owner's statement, unless the agent knows that the condition identified in the owner's statement is not correct. The agent will not indicate in the odometer disclosure it completes on the owner's behalf that the odometer reading is not the actual mileage unless either the owner has so indicated in the owner's statement or the agent knows that the owner's statement is not correct. The agent shall transmit the owner's statement it receives to the transferee after the title transfer is completed. The owner's statement received by the transferee under this subsection need not be filed with the filing office for the other title documents, but the transferee shall retain the owner's statement for a time period and in a similar manner to the retention methods used by a lessor to retain statements under 49 C.F.R. Section 580.8(b), as it may from time to time be amended. The transferee may rely upon the agent's odometer disclosure and the owner's statement unless it knows that they are not correct. A failure by an owner to comply with an obligation under this subsection subjects the owner to the penalties and enforcement provisions of Subchapter H but does not affect the validity of the transfer of title.

(f) This section does not in any way impair or impede any transfers made through use of a power of attorney prior to the effective date of this section, and such transfers shall continue to be valid if they comply with the provisions of this section or would otherwise comply with the law in effect prior to the effective date of this section. This section does not apply to powers of attorney authorized under federal law or regulation that authorize a transferee to act as the agent of the transferor under certain circumstances or to powers of attorney otherwise authorized by the law of this state. This section does not affect the use of powers of attorney to sign, complete, and deliver the form to transfer title and other documents necessary to transfer title, including the odometer disclosure, in title transfers other than those described in Subsection (a).

(g) The power of attorney created in this section shall be limited for the purposes and duration specified in this section.

SUBCHAPTER E NONREPAIRABLE AND SALVAGE MOTOR VEHICLES

Sec. 501.091. Definitions.

In this subchapter:

(1) "Actual cash value" means the market value of a motor vehicle.

(2) "Casual sale" means the sale by a salvage vehicle dealer or an insurance company of five or fewer nonrepairable motor vehicles or salvage motor vehicles to the same person during a calendar year, but does not include:

(A) a sale at auction to a salvage vehicle dealer;

(B) a sale to an insurance company, out-of-state buyer, or governmental entity; or

(C) the sale of an export-only motor vehicle to a person who is not a resident of the United States.

(3) "Damage" means sudden damage to a motor vehicle caused by the motor vehicle being wrecked, burned, flooded, or stripped of major component parts. The term does not include:

(A) gradual damage from any cause;

(B) sudden damage caused by hail;

(C) any damage caused only to the exterior paint of the motor vehicle; or

(D) theft, unless the motor vehicle was damaged during the theft and before recovery.

(4) "Export-only motor vehicle" means a motor vehicle described by Section 501.099.

(5) "Insurance company" means:

(A) a person authorized to write automobile insurance in this state; or

(B) an out-of-state insurance company that pays a loss claim for a motor vehicle in this state.

(6) "Major component part" means one of the following parts of a motor vehicle:

(A) the engine;

(B) the transmission;

(C) the frame;

(D) a fender;

(E) the hood;

(F) a door allowing entrance to or egress from the passenger compartment of the motor vehicle;

(G) a bumper;

(H) a quarter panel;

(I) a deck lid, tailgate, or hatchback;

(J) the cargo box of a vehicle with a gross vehicle weight of 10,000 pounds or less, including a pickup truck;

(K) the cab of a truck;

(L) the body of a passenger motor vehicle;

(M) the roof or floor pan of a passenger motor vehicle, if separate from the body of the motor vehicle.

(7) "Metal recycler" means a person who:

(A) is engaged in the business of obtaining, converting, or selling ferrous or nonferrous metal for conversion into raw material products consisting of prepared grades and having an existing or potential economic value;

(B) has a facility to convert ferrous or nonferrous metal into raw material products by method other than the exclusive use of hand tools, including the processing, sorting, cutting, classifying, cleaning, baling, wrapping, shredding, shearing, or changing the physical form or chemical content of the metal; and

(C) sells or purchases the ferrous or nonferrous metal solely for use as raw material in the production of new products.

(8) "Motor vehicle" has the meaning assigned by Section 501.002.

(9) "Nonrepairable motor vehicle" means a motor vehicle:

(A) that is damaged, wrecked, or burned to the extent that the only residual value of the vehicle is as a source of parts or scrap metal;

(B) that comes into this state under a comparable ownership document that indicates that the vehicle is nonrepairable;

(C) that a salvage vehicle dealer has reported to the department under Section 501.1003;

(D) for which an owner has surrendered evidence of ownership for the purpose of dismantling, scrapping, or destroying the motor vehicle; or

(E) that is sold for export only under Section 501.099.

(10) "Nonrepairable vehicle title" means a printed document issued by the department that evidences ownership of a nonrepairable motor vehicle.

(10-a) "Nonrepairable record of title" means an electronic record of ownership of a nonrepairable motor vehicle.

(11) "Out-of-state buyer" means a person licensed in an automotive business by another state or jurisdiction if the department has listed the holders of such a license as permitted purchasers of salvage motor vehicles or nonrepairable motor vehicles based on substantially similar licensing requirements and on whether salvage vehicle dealers licensed in Texas are permitted to purchase salvage motor vehicles or nonrepairable motor vehicles in the other state or jurisdiction.

(12) "Out-of-state ownership document" means a negotiable document issued by another state or jurisdiction that the department considers sufficient to prove ownership of a nonrepairable motor vehicle or salvage motor vehicle and to support the issuance of a comparable Texas title for the motor vehicle. The term does not include any title or certificate issued by the department.

(13) "Public highway" has the meaning assigned by Section 502.001.

(14) "Rebuilder" means a person who acquires and repairs, rebuilds, or reconstructs for operation on a public highway, more than five salvage motor vehicles in a calendar year.

(15) "Salvage motor vehicle" means a motor vehicle that:

(A) has damage to or is missing a major component part to the extent that the cost of repairs, including parts and labor other than the cost of materials and labor for repainting the motor vehicle and excluding sales tax on the total cost of repairs, exceeds the actual cash value of the motor vehicle immediately before the damage; or

(B) comes into this state under an out-of-state salvage motor vehicle title or similar out-of-state ownership document.

(16) "Salvage vehicle title" means a printed document issued by the department that evidences ownership of a salvage motor vehicle.

(16-a) "Salvage record of title" means an electronic record of ownership of a salvage motor vehicle.

(17) "Salvage vehicle dealer" means a person engaged in this state in the business of acquiring, selling, repairing, rebuilding, reconstructing, or otherwise dealing in nonrepairable motor vehicles, salvage motor vehicles, or, if incidental to a salvage motor vehicle dealer's primary business, used automotive parts regardless of whether the person holds a license issued by the department to engage in that business. The term does not include an unlicensed person who:

(A) casually repairs, rebuilds, or reconstructs not more than five nonrepairable motor vehicles or salvage motor vehicles in the same calendar year;

(B) buys not more than five nonrepairable motor vehicles or salvage motor vehicles in the same calendar year; or

(C) is a licensed used automotive parts recycler if the sale of repaired, rebuilt, or reconstructed nonrepairable motor vehicles or salvage motor vehicles is more than an incidental part of the used automotive parts recycler's business.

(18) "Self-insured motor vehicle" means a motor vehicle for which the owner or a governmental entity assumes full financial responsibility for motor vehicle loss claims without regard to the number of motor vehicles they own or operate. The term does not include a motor vehicle that is insured by an insurance company.

(19) "Used part" means a part that is salvaged, dismantled, or removed from a motor vehicle for resale as is or as repaired. The term includes a major component part but does not include a rebuildable or rebuilt core, including an engine, block, crankshaft, transmission, or other core part that is acquired, possessed, or transferred in the ordinary course of business.

(20) "Used parts dealer" and "used automotive parts recycler" have the meaning assigned to "used automotive parts recycler" by Section 2309.002, Occupations Code.

Sec. 501.0911. Definitions [Renumbered].

Renumbered to Tex. Transp. Code § 501.091 by Acts 2003, 78th Leg., ch. 1325 (H.B. 3588), § 17.02, effective September 1, 2003.

Sec. 501.09111. Rights and Limitations of Nonrepairable Vehicle Title, Nonrepairable Record of Title, Salvage Vehicle Title, or Salvage Record of Title.

(a) A person who owns a nonrepairable motor vehicle:

(1) is entitled to possess, transport, dismantle, scrap, destroy, record a lien as provided for in Section 501.097(a)(3)(A), and sell, transfer, or release ownership of the motor vehicle or a used part from the motor vehicle; and

(2) may not:

(A) operate or permit the operation of the motor vehicle on a public highway, in addition to any other requirement of law;

(B) repair, rebuild, or reconstruct the motor vehicle; or

(C) register the motor vehicle.

(b) A person who holds a nonrepairable certificate of title issued prior to September 1, 2003, is entitled to the same rights listed in Subsection (a) and may repair, rebuild, or reconstruct the motor vehicle.

(c) A person who owns a salvage motor vehicle:

(1) is entitled to possess, transport, dismantle, scrap, destroy, repair, rebuild, reconstruct, record a lien on, and sell, transfer, or release ownership of the motor vehicle or a used part from the motor vehicle; and

(2) may not operate, register, or permit the operation of the motor vehicle on a public highway, in addition to any other requirement of law.

Sec. 501.09112. Appearance of Nonrepairable Vehicle Title or Salvage Vehicle Title.

(a) The department's printed nonrepairable vehicle title must clearly indicate that it is the negotiable ownership document for a nonrepairable motor vehicle.

(b) A nonrepairable vehicle title must clearly indicate that the motor vehicle:

(1) may not be:

(A) issued a regular title;

(B) registered in this state; or

(C) repaired, rebuilt, or reconstructed; and

(2) may be used only as a source for used parts or scrap metal.

(c) The department's printed salvage vehicle title must clearly show that it is the ownership document for a salvage motor vehicle.

(d) A salvage vehicle title or a salvage record of title for a vehicle that is a salvage motor vehicle because of damage caused exclusively by flood must bear a notation that the department considers appropriate. If the title for a motor vehicle reflects the notation required by this subsection, the owner may sell, transfer, or release the motor vehicle only as provided by this subchapter.

(d-1) The department and the Texas Division of Emergency Management shall coordinate with the Federal Emergency Management Agency to ensure that the department has information, including a vehicle identification number, necessary to apply the notation under Subsection (d) to the title of a vehicle:

(1) to which that subsection applies; and

(2) that has been repaired or salvaged using financial assistance designated for that purpose and administered by the Federal Emergency Management Agency.

(e) An electronic application for a nonrepairable vehicle title, nonrepairable record of title, salvage vehicle title, or salvage record of title must clearly advise the applicant of the same provisions required on a printed title.

(f) A nonrepairable vehicle title, nonrepairable record of title, salvage vehicle title, or salvage record of title in the department's electronic database must include appropriate remarks so that the vehicle record clearly shows the status of the vehicle.

Sec. 501.09113. Out-of-State Salvage or Rebuilt Salvage Vehicle.

(a) On receipt of a proper application from the owner of a motor vehicle, the department shall issue the applicant the appropriate title with any notations determined by the department as necessary to describe or disclose the motor vehicle's current or former condition if the motor vehicle was brought into this state from another state or jurisdiction and has on any title or comparable out-of-state ownership document issued by the other state or jurisdiction or record in the National Motor Vehicle Title Information System reported by another state or jurisdiction:

(1) a "rebuilt," "repaired," "reconstructed," "flood damage," "fire damage," "owner retained," "salvage," or similar notation; or

(2) a "nonrepairable," "dismantle only," "parts only," "junked," "scrapped," "crushed," or similar notation.

(b) [Repealed.]

Sec. 501.0912. Insurance Company to Surrender Certificates of Title to Certain Late Model Salvage Motor Vehicles [Renumbered].

Renumbered to Tex. Transp. Code § 501.092 by Acts 2003, 78th Leg., ch. 1325 (H.B. 3588), § 17.02, effective September 1, 2003.

Sec. 501.0913. Insurance Company to Deliver Certificates of Title to Certain Motor Vehicles [Repealed].

Repealed by Acts 2003, 78th Leg., ch. 1325 (H.B. 3588), § 17.09(1), effective September 1, 2003.

Sec. 501.0914. Nonapplicability [Repealed].

Repealed by Acts 2003, 78th Leg., ch. 1325 (H.B. 3588), § 17.09(1), effective September 1, 2003.

Sec. 501.0915. Insurance Company to Submit Report to Department [Renumbered].

Renumbered to Tex. Transp. Code § 501.093 by Acts 2003, 78th Leg., ch. 1325 (H.B. 3588), § 17.02, effective September 1, 2003.

Sec. 501.0916. Sale, Transfer, or Release of Late Model Salvage or Nonrepairable Motor Vehicle [Renumbered].

Renumbered to Tex. Transp. Code § 501.095 by Acts 2003, 78th Leg., ch. 1325 (H.B. 3588), § 17.02, effective September 1, 2003.

Sec. 501.0917. Salvage Vehicle Dealer to Submit Report to Department [Renumbered].

Renumbered to Tex. Transp. Code § 501.096 by Acts 2003, 78th Leg., ch. 1325 (H.B. 3588), § 17.02, effective September 1, 2003.

Sec. 501.0918. Person Acquiring Late Model Salvage Motor Vehicle to Surrender Certificate of Title [Repealed].

Repealed by Acts 2003, 78th Leg., ch. 1325 (H.B. 3588), § 17.09(1), effective September 1, 2003.

Sec. 501.0919. Sale of Certain Late Model Salvage Motor Vehicles [Repealed].

Repealed by Acts 2003, 78th Leg., ch. 1325 (H.B. 3588), § 17.09(1), effective September 1, 2003.

Sec. 501.092. Insurance Company to Surrender Certificates of Title to Certain Salvage Motor Vehicles or Nonrepairable Motor Vehicles [Renumbered].

Renumbered to Tex. Transp. Code § 501.1001 by Acts 2011, 82nd Leg., ch. 1296 (H.B. 2357), § 44, effective January 1, 2012.

Sec. 501.0920. Application for Salvage Motor Vehicle Certificate of Title [Renumbered].

Renumbered to Tex. Transp. Code § 501.097 by Acts 2003, 78th Leg., ch. 1325 (H.B. 3588), § 17.02, effective September 1, 2003.

Sec. 501.0921. Possession and Operation of Salvage Motor Vehicle [Renumbered].

Renumbered to Tex. Transp. Code § 501.098 by Acts 2003, 78th Leg., ch. 1325 (H.B. 3588), § 17.02, effective September 1, 2003.

Sec. 501.0922. Application for Regular Certificate of Title for Salvage Motor Vehicle [Renumbered].

Renumbered to Tex. Transp. Code § 501.100(a) by Acts 2003, 78th Leg., ch. 1325 (H.B. 3588), § 17.02, effective September 1, 2003.

Sec. 501.0923. Issuance of Certificate of Title for Rebuilt Salvage Motor Vehicle [Renumbered].

Renumbered to Tex. Transp. Code § 501.100(b) and (c) by Acts 2003, 78th Leg., ch. 1325 (H.B. 3588), § 17.02, effective September 1, 2003.

Sec. 501.0924. Issuance of Certificate of Title to Certain Vehicles Brought into State [Renumbered].

Renumbered to Tex. Transp. Code § 501.101 by Acts 2003, 78th Leg., ch. 1325 (H.B. 3588), § 17.02, effective September 1, 2003.

Sec. 501.0925. Insurance Company Not Required to Surrender Certificates of Title in Certain Situations.

(a) An insurance company that acquires, through payment of a claim, ownership or possession of a motor vehicle covered by a certificate of title that the company is unable to obtain may obtain from the department not earlier than the 30th day after the date of payment of the claim:

(1) a salvage vehicle title for a salvage motor vehicle;

(2) a nonrepairable vehicle title for a nonrepairable motor vehicle; or

(3) a regular certificate of title for a motor vehicle other than a salvage motor vehicle or a nonrepairable motor vehicle.

(b) An application for a title under Subsection (a) must be submitted to the department on a form prescribed by the department and include:

(1) a statement that the insurance company has provided at least two written notices attempting to obtain the certificate of title for the motor vehicle; and

(2) evidence acceptable to the department that the insurance company has made payment of a claim involving the motor vehicle.

(c) An insurance company that acquires, through payment of a claim, ownership or possession of a motor vehicle covered by a certificate of title for which the company is unable to obtain proper assignment of the certificate may obtain from the

Transportation Code

department not earlier than the 30th day after the date of payment of the claim:

(1) a salvage vehicle title for a salvage motor vehicle;

(2) a nonrepairable vehicle title for a nonrepairable motor vehicle; or

(3) a regular certificate of title for a motor vehicle other than a salvage motor vehicle or a nonrepairable motor vehicle.

(d) An application for a title under Subsection (c) must be submitted to the department on a form prescribed by the department and include:

(1) a statement that the insurance company has provided at least two written notices attempting to obtain a proper assignment of the certificate of title; and

(2) the certificate of title.

(e) A title issued under Subsection (a) or (c) must be issued in the name of the insurance company.

(f) An insurance company that acquires, through payment of a claim, ownership or possession of a salvage motor vehicle or nonrepairable motor vehicle covered by an out-of-state ownership document may obtain from the department a salvage vehicle title or nonrepairable vehicle title if:

(1) the motor vehicle was damaged, stolen, or recovered in this state;

(2) the motor vehicle owner from whom the company acquired ownership resides in this state; or

(3) otherwise allowed by department rule.

(g) A title may be issued under Subsection (f) if the insurance company:

(1) surrenders a properly assigned title on a form prescribed by the department; or

(2) complies with the application process for a title issued under Subsection (a) or (c).

(h) The department shall issue the appropriate title to a person authorized to apply for the title under this section if the department determines that the application is complete and complies with applicable law.

(i) The department by rule may provide that a person required by this section to provide notice may provide the notice electronically, including through the use of e-mail or an interactive website established by the department for that purpose.

(j) Section 501.1001(c) applies to a motor vehicle acquired by an insurance company as described in Subsection (a), (c), or (f).

(k) The department may adopt rules to implement this section.

Transportation Code

Sec. 501.0926. Offense [Renumbered].

Renumbered to Tex. Transp. Code § 501.102 by Acts 2003, 78th Leg., ch. 1325 (H.B. 3588), § 17.02, effective September 1, 2003.

Sec. 501.0927. Application for Certificate of Title by Rebuilder of Nonrepairable Motor Vehicle [Repealed].

Repealed by Acts 2003, 78th Leg., ch. 1325 (H.B. 3588), § 17.09(1), effective September 1, 2003.

Sec. 501.0928. Department to Print Salvage and Nonrepairable Motor Vehicle Certificates of Title [Renumbered].

Renumbered to Tex. Transp. Code § 501.103 by Acts 2003, 78th Leg., ch. 1325 (H.B. 3588), § 17.02, effective September 1, 2003.

Sec. 501.0929. Rebuilder to Possess Certificate of Title [Renumbered].

Renumbered to Tex. Transp. Code § 501.104 by Acts 2003, 78th Leg., ch. 1325 (H.B. 3588), § 17.02, effective September 1, 2003.

Sec. 501.093. Insurance Company Report on Certain Vehicles [Renumbered].

Renumbered to Tex. Transp. Code § 501.1002 by Acts 2011, 82nd Leg., ch. 1296 (H.B. 2357), § 45, effective January 1, 2012.

Sec. 501.0930. Enforcement of Subchapter [Renumbered].

Renumbered to Tex. Transp. Code § 501.106 by Acts 2003, 78th Leg., ch. 1325 (H.B. 3588), § 17.02, effective September 1, 2003.

Sec. 501.0931. Applicability of Subchapter [Renumbered].

Renumbered to Tex. Transp. Code § 501.107 by Acts 2003, 78th Leg., ch. 1325 (H.B. 3588), § 17.02, effective September 1, 2003.

Sec. 501.0935. Issuance of Title to Salvage Pool Operator.

(a) In this section, "salvage pool operator" has the meaning assigned by Section 2302.001, Occupations Code.

(b) This section applies only to a salvage pool operator who, on request of an insurance company, takes possession of a motor vehicle that is the subject of an insurance claim and the insurance company subsequently:

(1) denies coverage with respect to the motor vehicle; or

(2) does not otherwise take ownership of the motor vehicle.

(b-1) An insurance company described by Subsection (b) shall notify the salvage pool operator of the denial of the claim regarding the motor vehicle or other disposition of the motor vehicle. The insurance company must include in the notice the name and address of the owner of the motor vehicle and the lienholder, if any.

(c) Before the 31st day after receiving notice under Subsection (b-1), a salvage pool operator shall notify the owner of the motor vehicle and any lienholder that:

(1) the owner or lienholder must remove the motor vehicle from the salvage pool operator's possession at the location specified in the notice to the owner and any lienholder not later than the 30th day after the date the notice is mailed; and

(2) if the motor vehicle is not removed within the time specified in the notice, the salvage pool operator will sell the motor vehicle and retain from the proceeds any costs actually incurred by the operator in obtaining, handling, and disposing of the motor vehicle as described by Subsection (d).

(d) The salvage pool operator may include in the costs described by Subsection (c)(2) only costs actually incurred by the salvage pool operator that have not been reimbursed by a third party or are not subject to being reimbursed by a third party, such as costs of notices, title searches, and towing and other costs incurred with respect to the motor vehicle. The costs described by Subsection (c)(2):

(1) may not include charges for storage or impoundment of the motor vehicle; and

(2) may be deducted only from the proceeds of a sale of the motor vehicle.

(e) The notice required of a salvage pool operator under this section must be sent by registered or certified mail, return receipt requested.

(f) If a motor vehicle is not removed from a salvage pool operator's possession before the 31st day after the date notice is mailed to the motor vehicle's owner and any lienholder under Subsection (c), the salvage pool operator may obtain from the department:

(1) a salvage vehicle title for a salvage motor vehicle; or

(2) a nonrepairable vehicle title for a nonrepairable motor vehicle.

(g) An application for a title under Subsection (f) must:

(1) be submitted to the department on a form prescribed by the department; and

(2) include evidence that the notice was mailed as required by Subsection (c) to the motor vehicle owner and any lienholder.

(h) A title issued under this section must be issued in the name of the salvage pool operator.

(i) The department shall issue the appropriate title to a person authorized to apply for the title under this section if the department determines that the application is complete and complies with applicable law.

(j) On receipt of a title under this section, the salvage pool operator shall sell the motor vehicle and retain from the proceeds of the sale the costs incurred by the salvage pool operator as permitted by Subsection (d) along with the cost of titling and selling the motor vehicle. The salvage pool operator shall pay any excess proceeds from the sale to the previous owner of the motor vehicle and the lienholder, if any. The excess proceeds must be mailed to the lienholder.

(k) If the previous owner of the motor vehicle and the lienholder, if any, cannot be identified or located, any excess proceeds from the sale of the motor vehicle under Subsection (j) shall escheat to the State of Texas. The proceeds shall be administered by the comptroller and shall be disposed of in the manner provided by Chapter 74, Property Code.

Sec. 501.094. Self-Insured Motor Vehicle [Repealed].

Repealed by Acts 2011, 82nd Leg., ch. 1296 (H.B. 2357), § 247(2), effective January 1, 2012.

Sec. 501.095. Sale, Transfer, or Release.

(a) If the department has not issued a nonrepairable vehicle title, nonrepairable record of title, salvage vehicle title, or salvage record of title for the motor vehicle and a comparable out-of-state ownership document for the motor vehicle has not been issued by another state or jurisdiction, a business or governmental entity described by Subdivisions (1)—(3) may sell, transfer, or release a nonrepairable motor vehicle or salvage motor vehicle only to a person who is:

(1) a licensed salvage vehicle dealer, a used automotive parts recycler under Chapter 2309, Occupations Code, or a metal recycler under Chapter 2302, Occupations Code;

(2) an insurance company that has paid a claim on the nonrepairable or salvage motor vehicle; or

(3) a governmental entity.

(b) A person, other than a salvage vehicle dealer, a used automotive parts recycler, or an insurance company licensed to do business in this state, who acquired ownership of a nonrepairable or salvage motor vehicle that has not been issued a nonrepairable vehicle title, nonrepairable record of title,

Transportation Code

salvage vehicle title, salvage record of title, or a comparable ownership document issued by another state or jurisdiction shall, before selling the motor vehicle, surrender the properly assigned title for the motor vehicle to the department and apply to the department for the appropriate ownership document.

(c) If the department has issued a nonrepairable vehicle title or salvage vehicle title for the motor vehicle or another state or jurisdiction has issued a comparable out-of-state ownership document for the motor vehicle, a person may sell, transfer, or release a nonrepairable motor vehicle or salvage motor vehicle to any person.

Sec. 501.096. Nonrepairable Motor Vehicle or Salvage Motor Vehicle Dismantled, Scrapped, or Destroyed [Renumbered].

Renumbered to Tex. Transp. Code § 501.1003 by Acts 2011, 82nd Leg., ch. 1296 (H.B. 2357), § 46, effective January 1, 2012.

Sec. 501.097. Application for Nonrepairable Vehicle Title or Salvage Vehicle Title.

(a) An application for a nonrepairable vehicle title, nonrepairable record of title, salvage vehicle title, or salvage record of title must:

(1) be made in a manner prescribed by the department and accompanied by a $8 application fee;

(2) include, in addition to any other information required by the department:

(A) the name and current address of the owner; and

(B) a description of the motor vehicle, including the make, style of body, model year, and vehicle identification number; and

(3) include the name and address of:

(A) any currently recorded lienholder, if the motor vehicle is a nonrepairable motor vehicle; or

(B) any currently recorded lienholder or a new lienholder, if the motor vehicle is a salvage motor vehicle.

(b) Except as provided by Sections 501.0925 and 501.0935, on receipt of a complete application, the properly assigned title or manufacturer's certificate of origin, and the application fee, the department shall, before the sixth business day after the date the department receives the application, issue the applicant the appropriate title for the motor vehicle.

(c) A printed nonrepairable vehicle title must state on its face that the motor vehicle:

(1) may not:

(A) be repaired, rebuilt, or reconstructed;

(B) be issued a title or registered in this state;

(C) be operated on a public highway, in addition to any other requirement of law; and

(2) may only be used as a source for used parts or scrap metal.

(c-1) The department's titling system must include a remark that clearly identifies the vehicle as a salvage or nonrepairable motor vehicle.

(d) The fee collected under Subsection (a)(1) shall be credited to the Texas Department of Motor Vehicles fund to defray the costs of administering this subchapter and the costs to the department for issuing the title.

Sec. 501.098. Rights of Holder of Nonrepairable Vehicle Title or Salvage Vehicle Title [Renumbered].

Renumbered to Tex. Transp. Code § 501.09111 by Acts 2011, 82nd Leg., ch. 1296 (H.B. 2357), § 37, effective January 1, 2012.

Sec. 501.099. Sale of Export-Only Motor Vehicles.

(a) This section applies to a nonrepairable motor vehicle or a salvage motor vehicle that is offered for sale in this state to a person who resides in a jurisdiction outside the United States.

(b) A person may purchase a nonrepairable motor vehicle or a salvage motor vehicle only if:

(1) the person purchases the motor vehicle from a licensed salvage vehicle dealer or a governmental entity;

(2) the motor vehicle has been issued a nonrepairable vehicle title or a salvage vehicle title; and

(3) the purchaser certifies to the seller on a form provided by the department that the purchaser will:

(A) remove the motor vehicle from the United States; and

(B) not return the motor vehicle to any state of the United States as a motor vehicle titled or registered under its manufacturer's vehicle identification number.

(c) A salvage vehicle dealer or a governmental entity that sells a nonrepairable motor vehicle or a salvage motor vehicle to a person who is not a resident of the United States shall, before the sale of the motor vehicle, obtain a copy, photocopy, or other accurate reproduction of a valid identification card, identification certificate, or an equivalent document issued to the purchaser by the appropriate authority of the jurisdiction in which the purchaser resides that bears a photograph of the purchaser and is capable of being verified using identification

Transportation Code

standards adopted by the United States or the international community.

(d) The department by rule shall establish a list of identification documents that are valid under Subsection (c) and provide a copy of the list to each holder of a salvage vehicle dealer license and to each appropriate governmental entity.

(e) A salvage vehicle dealer or a governmental entity that sells a nonrepairable motor vehicle or a salvage motor vehicle to a person who is not a resident of the United States shall:

(1) stamp on the face of the title so as not to obscure any name, date, or mileage statement on the title the words "FOR EXPORT ONLY" in capital letters that are black; and

(2) stamp in each unused reassignment space on the back of the title the words "FOR EXPORT ONLY" and print the number of the dealer's salvage vehicle license or the name of the governmental entity, as applicable.

(f) The words "FOR EXPORT ONLY" required by Subsection (e) must be at least two inches wide and clearly legible.

(g) A salvage vehicle dealer or governmental entity who sells a nonrepairable motor vehicle or a salvage motor vehicle under this section to a person who is not a resident of the United States shall keep on the business premises of the dealer or entity until the third anniversary of the date of the sale:

(1) a copy of each document related to the sale of the vehicle; and

(2) a list of all vehicles sold under this section that contains:

(A) the date of the sale;

(B) the name of the purchaser;

(C) the name of the country that issued the identification document provided by the purchaser, as shown on the document; and

(D) the vehicle identification number.

(h) This section does not prevent a person from exporting or importing a used part obtained from an export-only motor vehicle.

Sec. 501.100. Application for Regular Certificate of Title for Salvage Vehicle.

(a) The owner of a motor vehicle for which a nonrepairable vehicle title issued prior to September 1, 2003, or for which a salvage vehicle title or salvage record of title has been issued may apply for a title after the motor vehicle has been repaired, rebuilt, or reconstructed and, in addition to any other requirement of law, only if the application:

(1) describes each major component part used to repair the motor vehicle;

(2) states the name of each person from whom the parts used in assembling the vehicle were obtained; and

(3) shows the identification number required by federal law to be affixed to or inscribed on the part.

(b) On receipt of a complete application under this section accompanied by the fee for the title, the department shall issue the applicant a title.

(c) A title issued under this section must describe or disclose the motor vehicle's former condition in a manner reasonably understandable to a potential purchaser of the motor vehicle.

(d) In addition to the fee described by Subsection (b), the applicant shall pay a $65 rebuilder fee. The applicant shall include the fee with the statement submitted under Section 502.156 for the vehicle.

(e) On or after the 31st day after the date the department receives a rebuilder fee under Subsection (d), the department shall deposit $50 of the fee to the credit of the state highway fund to be used only by the Department of Public Safety to enforce this chapter and $15 to the credit of the general revenue fund.

(f) The department may not issue a regular title for a motor vehicle based on a:

(1) nonrepairable vehicle title or comparable out-of-state ownership document;

(2) receipt issued under Section 501.1003(b); or

(3) certificate of authority.

Sec. 501.1001. Salvage Motor Vehicles or Nonrepairable Motor Vehicles for Insurance Companies or Self-Insured Persons.

(a) Except as provided by Section 501.0925, an insurance company that is licensed to conduct business in this state and that acquires, through payment of a claim, ownership or possession of a salvage motor vehicle or nonrepairable motor vehicle shall surrender the properly assigned evidence of ownership and apply for the appropriate title under Section 501.097 .

(b) For a salvage motor vehicle, the insurance company shall apply for a salvage vehicle title or salvage record of title. For a nonrepairable motor vehicle, the insurance company shall apply for a nonrepairable vehicle title or nonrepairable record of title.

(c) An insurance company or other person who acquires ownership of a motor vehicle other than a nonrepairable or salvage motor vehicle may voluntarily and on proper application obtain a salvage vehicle title, salvage record of title, nonrepairable vehicle title, or nonrepairable record of title for the vehicle.

Transportation Code

(d) This subsection applies only to a motor vehicle in this state that is a self-insured motor vehicle and that is damaged to the extent it becomes a nonrepairable or salvage motor vehicle. The owner of a motor vehicle to which this subsection applies shall submit to the department before the 31st business day after the date of the damage, in a manner prescribed by the department, a statement that the motor vehicle was self-insured and damaged. When the owner submits a report, the owner shall surrender the ownership document and apply for a nonrepairable vehicle title, nonrepairable record of title, salvage vehicle title, or salvage record of title.

Sec. 501.1002. Owner-Retained Vehicles.

(a) If an insurance company pays a claim on a nonrepairable motor vehicle or salvage motor vehicle and the insurance company does not acquire ownership of the motor vehicle, the insurance company shall:

(1) submit to the department, before the 31st day after the date of the payment of the claim, on the form prescribed by the department, a report stating that the insurance company:

(A) has paid a claim on the motor vehicle; and

(B) has not acquired ownership of the motor vehicle; and

(2) provide notice to the owner of the motor vehicle of:

(A) the report required under Subdivision (1); and

(B) the requirements for operation or transfer of ownership of the motor vehicle under Subsection (b).

(b) The owner of a salvage or nonrepairable motor vehicle may not transfer ownership of the motor vehicle by sale or otherwise unless the department has issued a salvage vehicle title, salvage record of title, nonrepairable vehicle title, or nonrepairable record of title for the motor vehicle or a comparable ownership document has been issued by another state or jurisdiction for the motor vehicle in the name of the owner.

Sec. 501.1003. Salvage Dealer Responsibilities.

(a) If a salvage vehicle dealer acquires ownership of a nonrepairable motor vehicle or salvage motor vehicle for the purpose of dismantling, scrapping, or destroying the motor vehicle, the dealer shall, before the 31st day after the date the dealer acquires the motor vehicle, submit to the department a report stating that the motor vehicle will be dismantled, scrapped, or destroyed. The dealer shall:

(1) make the report in a manner prescribed by the department; and

(2) submit with the report a properly assigned manufacturer's certificate of origin, regular certificate of title, nonrepairable vehicle title, salvage vehicle title, or comparable out-of-state ownership document for the motor vehicle.

(b) After receiving the report and title or document, the department shall issue the salvage vehicle dealer a receipt for the manufacturer's certificate of origin, regular certificate of title, nonrepairable vehicle title, salvage vehicle title, or comparable out-of-state ownership document.

(c) The department shall adopt rules to notify the salvage dealer if the vehicle was not issued a printed title, but has a record of title in the department's titling system.

Sec. 501.101. Issuance of Title to Motor Vehicle Brought into State [Renumbered].

Renumbered to Tex. Transp. Code § 501.09113 by Acts 2011, 82nd Leg., ch. 1296 (H.B. 2357), § 39, effective January 1, 2012.

Sec. 501.102. Offenses [Renumbered].

Renumbered to Tex. Transp. Code § 501.109 by Acts 2011, 82nd Leg., ch. 1296 (H.B. 2357), § 49, effective January 1, 2012.

Sec. 501.103. Color of Nonrepairable Vehicle Title or Salvage Vehicle Title [Renumbered].

Renumbered to Tex. Transp. Code § 501.09112 by Acts 2011, 82nd Leg., ch. 1296 (H.B. 2357), § 38, effective January 1, 2012.

Sec. 501.104. Rebuilder to Possess Title or Other Documentation.

(a) This section applies to a person engaged in repairing, rebuilding, or reconstructing more than five motor vehicles, regardless of whether the person is licensed to engage in that business.

(b) A person described by Subsection (a) must possess:

(1) an acceptable ownership document or proof of ownership for any motor vehicle that is:

(A) owned by the person;

(B) in the person's inventory; and

(C) being offered for resale; or

(2) a contract entered into with the owner, a work order, or another document that shows the authority for the person to possess any motor vehicle that is:

(A) owned by another person;
(B) on the person's business or casual premises; and
(C) being repaired, rebuilt, or reconstructed for the other person.

Sec. 501.105. Retention of Records Relating to Certain Casual Sales [Renumbered].

Renumbered to Tex. Transp. Code § 501.108 by Acts 2011, 82nd Leg., ch. 1296 (H.B. 2357), § 48, effective January 1, 2012.

Sec. 501.106. Enforcement of Subchapter [Renumbered].

Renumbered to Tex. Transp. Code § 501.110 by Acts 2011, 82nd Leg., ch. 1296 (H.B. 2357), § 50, effective January 1, 2012.

Sec. 501.107. Applicability of Subchapter to Recycler.

(a) This subchapter does not apply to a sale to, purchase by, or other transaction by or with, a metal recycler except as provided by Subsections (b) and (c).

(b) A metal recycler shall submit to the department the properly assigned manufacturer's certificate of origin, regular certificate of title, nonrepairable vehicle title, salvage vehicle title, or comparable out-of-state ownership document that the person receives in conjunction with the purchase of a motor vehicle not later than the 60th day after the date the metal recycler receives the title or out-of-state ownership document.

(c) This subchapter applies to a transaction with a metal recycler in which a motor vehicle:
(1) is sold or delivered to the metal recycler for the purpose of reuse or resale as a motor vehicle or as a source of used parts; and
(2) is used for that purpose.

Sec. 501.108. Record Retention.

(a) Each licensed salvage vehicle dealer, used automotive parts recycler, or insurance company that sells a nonrepairable motor vehicle or a salvage motor vehicle at a casual sale shall keep on the business premises of the dealer or the insurance company a list of all casual sales made during the preceding 36-month period that contains:
(1) the date of the sale;
(2) the name of the purchaser;
(3) the name of the jurisdiction that issued the identification document provided by the purchaser, as shown on the document; and
(4) the vehicle identification number.

(b) A salvage vehicle dealer or used automotive parts recycler shall keep on the business premises of the dealer or recycler, until the third anniversary of the date the report on the motor vehicle is submitted to the department, a record of the vehicle, its ownership, and its condition as dismantled, scrapped, or destroyed as required by Section 501.1003.

Sec. 501.109. Offenses.

(a) A person commits an offense if the person:
(1) applies to the department for a title for a motor vehicle; and
(2) knows or reasonably should know that:
(A) the vehicle is a nonrepairable motor vehicle that has been repaired, rebuilt, or reconstructed;
(B) the vehicle identification number assigned to the motor vehicle belongs to a nonrepairable motor vehicle that has been repaired, rebuilt, or reconstructed;
(C) the title issued to the motor vehicle belongs to a nonrepairable motor vehicle that has been repaired, rebuilt, or reconstructed;
(D) the vehicle identification number assigned to the motor vehicle belongs to an export-only motor vehicle;
(E) the motor vehicle is an export-only motor vehicle; or
(F) the motor vehicle is a nonrepairable motor vehicle or salvage motor vehicle for which a nonrepairable vehicle title, salvage vehicle title, or comparable ownership document issued by another state or jurisdiction has not been issued.

(b) A person commits an offense if the person knowingly sells, transfers, or releases a salvage motor vehicle in violation of this subchapter.

(c) A person commits an offense if the person knowingly fails or refuses to surrender a regular certificate of title after the person:
(1) receives a notice from an insurance company that the motor vehicle is a nonrepairable or salvage motor vehicle; or
(2) knows the vehicle has become a nonrepairable motor vehicle or salvage motor vehicle under Section 501.1001.

(d) Except as provided by Subsection (e), an offense under Subsection (a), (b), or (c) is a Class C misdemeanor.

(e) If it is shown on the trial of an offense under Subsection (a), (b), or (c) that the defendant has been previously convicted of:

(1) one offense under Subsection (a), (b), or (c), the offense is a Class B misdemeanor; or

(2) two or more offenses under Subsection (a), (b), or (c), the offense is a state jail felony.

(f) Subsection (c) does not apply to an applicant for a title under Sections 501.0925 and 501.0935.

(g) A person commits an offense if the person knowingly provides false or incorrect information or without legal authority signs the name of another person on:

(1) an application for a title to a nonrepairable motor vehicle or salvage motor vehicle;

(2) an application for a certified copy of an original title to a nonrepairable motor vehicle or salvage motor vehicle;

(3) an assignment of title for a nonrepairable motor vehicle or salvage motor vehicle;

(4) a discharge of a lien on a title for a nonrepairable motor vehicle or salvage motor vehicle; or

(5) any other document required by the department or necessary for the transfer of ownership of a nonrepairable motor vehicle or salvage motor vehicle.

(h) An offense under Subsection (g) is a felony of the third degree.

Sec. 501.110. Enforcement of Subchapter.

(a) This subchapter shall be enforced by the department and any other governmental or law enforcement entity, including the Department of Public Safety, and the personnel of the entity as provided by this subchapter.

(b) The department, an agent, officer, or employee of the department, or another person enforcing this subchapter is not liable to a person damaged or injured by an act or omission relating to the issuance or revocation of a title, nonrepairable vehicle title, nonrepairable record of title, salvage vehicle title, or salvage record of title under this subchapter.

SUBCHAPTER F SECURITY INTERESTS

Sec. 501.111. Perfection of Security Interest.

(a) Except as provided by Subsection (b), a person may perfect a security interest in a motor vehicle that is the subject of a first or subsequent sale only by recording the security interest on the title as provided by this chapter.

(b) A person may perfect a security interest in a motor vehicle held as inventory by a person in the business of selling motor vehicles only by complying with Chapter 9, Business & Commerce Code.

Sec. 501.112. Sale or Security Interest Not Created by Certain Vehicle Leases.

Notwithstanding any other law, an agreement for the lease of a motor vehicle does not create a sale or security interest by merely providing that the rental price is permitted or required to be adjusted under the agreement as determined by the amount realized on the sale or other disposition of the vehicle.

Sec. 501.113. Recordation of Security Interest.

(a) Recordation of a lien under this chapter is considered to occur when:

(1) the department's titling system is updated; or

(2) the county assessor-collector accepts the application of title that discloses the lien with the filing fee.

(b) For purposes of Chapter 9, Business & Commerce Code, the time of recording a lien under this chapter is considered to be the time of filing the security interest, and on such recordation, the recorded lienholder and assignees under Section 501.114 obtain priority over the rights of a lien creditor, as defined by Section 9.102, Business & Commerce Code, for so long as the lien is recorded on the title.

Sec. 501.114. Assignment of Lien.

(a) A lienholder may assign a lien recorded under Section 501.113 without making any filing or giving any notice under this chapter. The lien assigned remains valid and perfected and retains its priority, securing the obligation assigned to the assignee, against transferees from and creditors of the debtor, including lien creditors, as defined by Section 9.102, Business & Commerce Code.

(b) An assignee or assignor may, but need not to retain the validity, perfection, and priority of the lien assigned, as evidence of the assignment of a lien recorded under Section 501.113:

(1) apply to the county assessor-collector for the assignee to be named as lienholder on the title; and

(2) notify the debtor of the assignment.

(c) Failure to make application under Subsection (b) or notify a debtor of an assignment does not create a cause of action against the recorded lienholder, the assignor, or the assignee or affect the continuation of the perfected status of the assigned lien in favor of the assignee against transferees from and creditors of the debtor, including lien creditors, as defined by Section 9.102, Business & Commerce Code.

(d) An application under Subsection (b) must be acknowledged by the assignee.

(e) On receipt of the completed application and fee, the department may:

(1) amend the department's records to substitute the assignee for the recorded lienholder; and

(2) issue a new title as provided by this chapter.

(f) The issuance of a title under Subsection (e) is recordation of the assignment.

(g) Regardless of whether application is made for the assignee to be named as lienholder on the title, the time of the recordation of a lien assigned under this section is considered to be the time the lien was initially recorded under Section 501.113.

(h) Notwithstanding Subsections (a)—(g) and procedures that may be conducted under those subsections, the assignment of a lien does not affect the procedures applicable to the foreclosure of a worker's lien under Chapter 70, Property Code, or the rights of the holder of a worker's lien. Notice given to the last known lienholder of record, as provided by that chapter, is adequate to allow foreclosure under that chapter.

(i) Notwithstanding Subsections (a)—(g) and the procedures that may be conducted under those subsections, the assignment of a lien does not affect the procedures applicable to the release of a holder's lien under Section 348.408, Finance Code.

Sec. 501.115. Discharge of Lien.

(a) **[2 Versions: As amended by Acts 2011, 82nd Leg., ch. 117]** When a debt or claim secured by a lien has been satisfied, the lienholder shall, within a reasonable time not to exceed the maximum time allowed by Section 348.408 or 353.405(b), Finance Code, as applicable, execute and deliver to the owner, or the owner's designee, a discharge of the lien on a form prescribed by the department.

(a) **[2 Versions: As amended by Acts 2011, 82nd Leg., ch. 1296]** When a debt or claim secured by a lien has been satisfied, the lienholder shall, within a reasonable time not to exceed the maximum time allowed by Section 348.408, Finance Code, execute and deliver to the owner, or the owner's designee, a discharge of the lien in a manner prescribed by the department.

(b) The owner may submit the discharge and title to the department for a new title.

Sec. 501.116. Cancellation of Discharged Lien.

The department may cancel a discharged lien that has been recorded on a title for 10 years or more if the recorded lienholder:

(1) does not exist; or

(2) cannot be located for the owner to obtain a release of the lien.

Sec. 501.117. Electronic Lien System.

(a) The department by rule shall develop a system under which a security interest in a motor vehicle may be perfected, assigned, discharged, and canceled electronically instead of by record maintained on a certificate of title. The department may establish categories of lienholders that may participate in the system and, except as provided by this section, may require a lienholder to participate in the system.

(b) The department shall publish and distribute procedures for using the system to county assessor-collectors and to financial institutions and other potential motor vehicle lienholders.

(c) The provisions of this chapter relating to perfecting, assigning, discharging, and canceling a security interest in a motor vehicle by record maintained on a certificate of title do not apply to the extent the security interest is governed by rules adopted under this section.

(d) The department may not require a depository institution, as defined by Section 180.002, Finance Code, to participate in the system if the department has issued fewer than 100 notifications of security interests in motor vehicles to the depository institution during a calendar year.

(d-1) [Expired pursuant to Acts 2011, 82nd Leg., ch. 813 (H.B. 2575), § 1, effective January 1, 2013.]

(d-2) [Expired pursuant to Acts 2011, 82nd Leg., ch. 813 (H.B. 2575), § 1, effective January 1, 2013.]

(e) The department by rule shall establish a reasonable schedule for compliance with the requirements of Subsection (a) for each category of lienholder that the department requires to participate in the system.

(f) The department may not:

(1) prohibit a lienholder from using an intermediary to access the system; or

(2) require a lienholder to use an intermediary to access the system.

SUBCHAPTER G ADMINISTRATIVE PROVISIONS

Sec. 501.131. Rules; Forms [Renumbered].

Renumbered to Tex. Transp. Code § 501.0041 by Acts 2011, 82nd Leg., ch. 1296 (H.B. 2357), § 4, effective January 1, 2012.

Transportation Code

Sec. 501.132. Duplicate Title Receipt.

Except as otherwise provided by department rule, the department may not issue a duplicate title receipt unless the original title receipt or certificate of title is surrendered.

Sec. 501.133. Issuance of New Certificate of Title Because of Subsequent Sales [Repealed].

Repealed by Acts 2011, 82nd Leg., ch. 1296 (H.B. 2357), § 247(2), effective January 1, 2012.

Sec. 501.134. Certified Copy of Lost or Destroyed Certificate of Title.

(a) If a printed title is lost or destroyed, the owner or lienholder disclosed on the title may obtain, in the manner provided by this section and department rule, a certified copy of the lost or destroyed title directly from the department by applying in a manner prescribed by the department and paying a fee of $2. A fee collected under this subsection shall be deposited to the credit of the Texas Department of Motor Vehicles fund.

(b) If a lien is disclosed on a title, the department may issue a certified copy of the title only to the first lienholder or the lienholder's verified agent unless the owner has original proof from the lienholder of lien satisfaction.

(c) The department must plainly mark "certified copy" on the face of a certified copy issued under this section.

(d) A certified copy of the title that is lawfully obtained under this section supersedes and invalidates any previously issued title or certified copy. If the certified copy of the title is later rescinded, canceled, or revoked under Section 501.051, the department may revalidate a previously superseded or invalidated title or certified copy of title.

(e),(f) [Repealed by Acts 2011, 82nd Leg., ch. 1296 (H.B. 2357), § 247(3), effective January 1, 2012.]

(g) The department may issue a certified copy of a title only if the applicant:

(1) is the registered owner of the vehicle, the holder of a recorded lien against the vehicle, or a verified agent of the owner or lienholder; and

(2) submits personal identification as required by department rule.

(h) If the applicant is the agent of the owner or lienholder of the vehicle and is applying on behalf of the owner or lienholder, the applicant must submit verifiable proof that the person is the agent of the owner or lienholder.

(i) [Repealed by Acts 2011, 82nd Leg., ch. 1296 (H.B. 2357), § 247(3), effective January 1, 2012.]

Sec. 501.135. Record of Stolen or Concealed Motor Vehicle.

(a) The department shall:

(1) make a record of each report to the department that a motor vehicle registered in this state has been stolen or concealed in violation of Section 32.33, Penal Code; and

(2) note the fact of the report in the department's records.

(b) A person who reports a motor vehicle as stolen or concealed under Subsection (a) shall notify the department promptly if the vehicle is recovered, and the department shall change its records accordingly.

Sec. 501.136. Acts by Deputy County Assessor-Collector [Renumbered].

Renumbered to Tex. Transp. Code § 520.0092 by Acts 2011, 82nd Leg., ch. 1296 (H.B. 2357), § 231, effective January 1, 2012.

Sec. 501.137. Duty of County Assessor-Collector [Renumbered].

Renumbered to Tex. Transp. Code § 520.005 by Acts 2011, 82nd Leg., ch. 1290 (H.B. 2017), § 31, effective September 1, 2011 and by Acts 2011, 82nd Leg., ch. 1296 (H.B. 2237), § 225, effective January 1, 2012.

Sec. 501.138. Collection and Disposition of Fees.

(a) An applicant for a title, other than the state or a political subdivision of the state, must pay a fee of:

(1) $33 if the applicant's residence is a county located within a nonattainment area as defined under Section 107(d) of the federal Clean Air Act (42 U.S.C. Section 7407), as amended, or is an affected county, as defined by Section 386.001, Health and Safety Code; or

(2) $28 if the applicant's residence is any other county.

(b) The fees shall be distributed as follows:

(1) $5 of the fee to the county treasurer for deposit in the officers' salary fund;

(2) $8 of the fee to the department:

(A) together with the application within the time prescribed by Section 501.023; or

(B) if the fee is deposited in an interest-bearing account or certificate in the county depository or invested in an investment authorized by Subchapter A, Chapter 2256, Government Code, not later than the 35th day after the date on which the fee is received; and

(3) the following amount to the comptroller at the time and in the manner prescribed by the comptroller:

(A) $20 of the fee if the applicant's residence is a county located within a nonattainment area as defined under Section 107(d) of the federal Clean Air Act (42 U.S.C. Section 7407), as amended, or is an affected county, as defined by Section 386.001, Health and Safety Code; or

(B) $15 of the fee if the applicant's residence is any other county.

(b-1) Except as provided by Subsection (b-4), fees collected under Subsection (b) to be sent to the comptroller shall be deposited to the credit of the Texas emissions reduction plan fund.

(b-2) The comptroller shall establish a record of the amount of the fees deposited to the credit of the Texas emissions reduction plan fund under Subsection (b-1). On or before the fifth workday of each month, the Texas Department of Transportation shall remit to the comptroller for deposit to the credit of the Texas Mobility Fund an amount of money equal to the amount of the fees deposited by the comptroller to the credit of the Texas emissions reduction plan fund under Subsection (b-1) in the preceding month. The Texas Department of Transportation shall use for remittance to the comptroller as required by this subsection money in the state highway fund that is not required to be used for a purpose specified by Section 7-a, Article VIII, Texas Constitution, and may not use for that remittance money received by this state under the congestion mitigation and air quality improvement program established under 23 U.S.C. Section 149.

(b-3) This subsection and Subsections (b-1) and (b-2) expire on the last day of the state fiscal biennium during which the Texas Commission on Environmental Quality publishes in the Texas Register the notice required by Section 382.037, Health and Safety Code.

(b-4) Fees collected under Subsection (b) to be sent to the comptroller shall be deposited to the credit of the Texas Mobility Fund if the fees are collected on or after the last day of the state fiscal biennium during which the Texas Commission on Environmental Quality publishes in the Texas Register the notice required by Section 382.037, Health and Safety Code.

(c) Of the amount received under Subsection (b)(2), the department shall deposit:

(1) $5 in the general revenue fund; and

(2) $3 to the credit of the Texas Department of Motor Vehicles fund to recover the expenses necessary to administer this chapter.

(d) The county owns all interest earned on fees deposited or invested under Subsection (b)(2)(B). The county treasurer shall credit that interest to the county general fund.

Sec. 501.139. Electronic Funds Transfer.

A county assessor-collector that transfers money to the department under this chapter shall transfer the money electronically.

SUBCHAPTER H PENALTIES AND OTHER ENFORCEMENT PROVISIONS

Sec. 501.145. Filing by Purchaser; Application for Transfer of Title.

(a) Not later than the later of the 30th day after the date of assignment on the documents or the date provided by Section 152.069, Tax Code, the purchaser of the used motor vehicle shall file with the county assessor-collector:

(1) the certificate of title or other evidence of title; or

(2) if appropriate, a document described by Section 502.457 and the title or other evidence of ownership.

(b) The filing under Subsection (a) is an application for transfer of title as required under this chapter and an application for transfer of the registration of the motor vehicle.

(c) Notwithstanding Subsection (a), if the purchaser is a member of the armed forces of the United States, a member of the Texas National Guard or of the National Guard of another state serving on active duty under an order of the president of the United States, or a member of a reserve component of the armed forces of the United States serving on active duty under an order of the president of the United States, the documents described by Subsection (a) must be filed with the county assessor-collector not later than the 60th day after the date of assignment of ownership.

Sec. 501.146. Title Transfer; Late Fee.

(a) If the application for the transfer of title is not filed during the period provided by Section 501.145, the late fee is to be paid to the county assessor-collector when the application is filed. If the seller

Transportation Code

holds a general distinguishing number issued under Chapter 503 of this code or Chapter 2301, Occupations Code, the seller is liable for the late fee in the amount of $10. If the seller does not hold a general distinguishing number, subject to Subsection (b) the applicant's late fee is $25.

(b) If the application is filed after the 60th day after the date the purchaser was assigned ownership of the documents under Section 501.0721, the late fee imposed under Subsection (a) accrues an additional penalty in the amount of $25 for each subsequent 30-day period, or portion of a 30-day period, in which the application is not filed.

(c) Subsections (a) and (b) do not apply if the motor vehicle is eligible to be issued:

(1) classic vehicle license plates under Section 504.501; or

(2) antique vehicle license plates under Section 504.502.

(d) A late fee imposed under this section may not exceed $250.

Sec. 501.147. Vehicle Transfer Notification.

(a) On receipt of a written notice of transfer from the seller of a motor vehicle, the department shall indicate the transfer on the motor vehicle records maintained by the department. As an alternative to a written notice of transfer, the department shall establish procedures that permit the seller of a motor vehicle to electronically submit a notice of transfer to the department through the department's Internet website. A notice of transfer provided through the department's Internet website is not required to bear the signature of the seller or include the date of signing.

(b) The notice of transfer shall be provided by the department and must include a place for the seller to state:

(1) a complete description of the vehicle as prescribed by the department;

(2) the full name and address of the seller;

(3) the full name and address of the purchaser;

(4) the date the seller delivered possession of the vehicle to the purchaser;

(5) the signature of the seller; and

(6) the date the seller signed the form.

(c) This subsection applies only if the department receives notice under Subsection (a) before the 30th day after the date the seller delivered possession of the vehicle to the purchaser or in accordance with Section 152.069, Tax Code. After the date of the transfer of the vehicle shown on the records of the department, the purchaser of the vehicle shown on the records is rebuttably presumed to be:

(1) the owner of the vehicle; and

(2) subject to civil and criminal liability arising out of the use, operation, or abandonment of the vehicle, to the extent that ownership of the vehicle subjects the owner of the vehicle to criminal or civil liability under another provision of law.

(d) The department may adopt rules to implement this section.

(e) This section does not impose or establish civil or criminal liability on the owner of a motor vehicle who transfers ownership of the vehicle but does not disclose the transfer to the department.

(f) The department may not issue a title or register the vehicle until the purchaser applies for a title to the county assessor-collector as provided by this chapter.

(g) A transferor who files the appropriate form with the department as provided by, and in accordance with, this section, whether that form is a part of a title or a form otherwise promulgated by the department to comply with the terms of this section, has no vicarious civil or criminal liability arising out of the use, operation, or abandonment of the vehicle by another person. Proof by the transferor that the transferor filed a form under this section is a complete defense to an action brought against the transferor for an act or omission, civil or criminal, arising out of the use, operation, or abandonment of the vehicle by another person after the transferor filed the form. A copy of the form filed under this section is proof of the filing of the form.

Sec. 501.148. Allocation of Fees.

(a) The county assessor-collector may retain as commission for services provided under this subchapter half of each late fee.

(b) The county assessor-collector shall report and remit the balance of the fees collected to the department on Monday of each week as other fees are required to be reported and remitted. The department shall deposit the remitted fees in the state treasury to the credit of the Texas Department of Motor Vehicles fund.

(c) Of each late fee collected from a person who does not hold a general distinguishing number by the department under Subsection (b), $10 may be used only to fund a statewide public awareness campaign designed to inform and educate the public about the provisions of this chapter.

Sec. 501.151. Placement of Serial Number with Intent to Change Identity.

(a) A person commits an offense if the person stamps or places a serial number on a vehicle or part of a vehicle with the intent of changing the identity of the vehicle.

(b) It is an affirmative defense to prosecution of an offense under this section that the person acted with respect to a number assigned by:

(1) a vehicle manufacturer and the person was an employee of the manufacturer acting within the course and scope of employment; or

(2) the department, and the person was:

(A) discharging official duties as an agent of the department; or

(B) complying with department rule as an applicant for a serial number assigned by the department.

(c) An offense under this section is a felony of the third degree.

Sec. 501.152. Sale or Offer Without Title Receipt or Title.

(a) Except as provided by this section, a person commits an offense if the person:

(1) sells, offers to sell, or offers as security for an obligation a motor vehicle registered in this state; and

(2) does not possess the title receipt or certificate of title for the vehicle.

(b) It is not a violation of this section for the beneficial owner of a vehicle to sell or offer to sell a vehicle without having possession of the title to the vehicle if the sole reason he or she does not have possession of the title is that the title is in the possession of a lienholder who has not complied with the terms of Section 501.115(a).

Sec. 501.153. Application for Title for Stolen or Concealed Vehicle.

A person commits an offense if the person applies for a title for a motor vehicle that the person knows is stolen or concealed in violation of Section 32.33, Penal Code.

Sec. 501.154. Alteration of Certificate or Receipt.

A person commits an offense if the person alters a manufacturer's certificate, a title receipt, or a title.

Sec. 501.155. False Name, False Information, and Forgery.

(a) A person commits an offense if the person knowingly provides false or incorrect information or without legal authority signs the name of another person on:

(1) an application for a title;

(2) an application for a certified copy of an original title;

(3) an assignment of title for a motor vehicle;

(4) a discharge of a lien on a title for a motor vehicle; or

(5) any other document required by the department or necessary to the transfer of ownership of a motor vehicle.

(b) An offense under this section is a felony of the third degree.

Sec. 501.156. Duty of Transporters to Determine Right of Possession; Offense.

(a) The master or captain of a ship or airplane or a person who owns or controls the operation of a ship or airplane, in whole or part:

(1) may not take on board or allow to be taken on board the ship or airplane in this state for transport a motor vehicle without inquiring of the motor vehicle titles and registration division of the department as to the recorded ownership of the motor vehicle; and

(2) must make a reasonable inquiry as to the right of possession of a motor vehicle by the person delivering the vehicle for transport if the recorded owner of the vehicle is a person other than the person delivering the vehicle for transport.

(b) A person who violates this section commits an offense. An offense under this section is a misdemeanor punishable by a fine of not less than $50 or more than $500 for a first offense and, at the jury's discretion, not less than $100 or more than $1,000 for a subsequent offense.

Sec. 501.157. Penalties.

(a) Unless otherwise provided by this chapter, an offense under this chapter is a misdemeanor punishable by a fine of not less than $1 or more than $100 for the first offense. If a person is subsequently convicted of the same offense, at the jury's discretion, a person may be fined not less than $2 or more than $200.

(b) A person commits an offense if the person violates Subchapter E or a rule adopted under that subchapter. An offense under this subsection is a Class A misdemeanor.

Sec. 501.158. Seizure of Stolen Vehicle or Vehicle with Altered Vehicle Identification Number.

(a) A peace officer may seize a vehicle or part of a vehicle without a warrant if the officer has probable cause to believe that the vehicle or part:

(1) is stolen; or

(2) has had the serial number removed, altered, or obliterated.

(b) A vehicle or part seized under this section may be treated as stolen property for purposes of custody and disposition of the vehicle or part.

Sec. 501.159. Alias Certificate of Title [Renumbered].

Renumbered to Tex. Transp. Code § 501.006 by Acts 2011, 82nd Leg., ch. 1296 (H.B. 2357), § 5, effective January 1, 2012.

Sec. 501.161. Execution of Transfer Documents; Penalty.

(a) A person who transfers a motor vehicle in this state shall complete in full and date as of the date of the transfer all documents relating to the transfer of registration or title. A person who transfers a vehicle commits an offense if the person fails to execute the documents in full.

(b) A person commits an offense if the person:

(1) accepts a document described by Subsection (a) that does not contain all of the required information; or

(2) alters or mutilates such a document.

(c) An offense under this section is a misdemeanor punishable by a fine of not less than $50 and not more than $200.

Sec. 501.162. Motor Number Required for Registration; Penalty.

A person commits an offense if the person violates Section 501.0331. An offense under this section is a misdemeanor punishable by a fine of not less than $50 and not more than $100.

Sec. 501.163. Application for Motor Number Record; Penalty.

A person who fails to comply with Section 501.0332 commits an offense. An offense under this section is a misdemeanor punishable by a fine of not less than $10 and not more than $100.

SUBCHAPTER I ELECTRONIC TITLING SYSTEM

Sec. 501.171. Application of Subchapter.

This subchapter applies only if the department implements a titling system under Section 501.173.

Sec. 501.172. Definitions.

In this subchapter:

(1) "Document" means information that is inscribed on a tangible medium or that is stored in an electronic or other medium and is retrievable in perceivable form.

(2) "Electronic" means relating to technology having electrical, digital, magnetic, wireless, optical, electromagnetic, or similar capabilities.

(3) "Electronic document" means a document that is in an electronic form.

(4) "Electronic signature" means an electronic sound, symbol, or process attached to or logically associated with a document and executed or adopted by a person with the intent to sign the document.

(5) "Paper document" means a document that is in printed form.

Sec. 501.173. Electronic Titling System.

(a) The board by rule may implement an electronic titling system.

(b) A record of title maintained electronically by the department in the titling system is the official record of vehicle ownership unless the owner requests that the department issue a printed title.

(c) In addition to other title fees, the board by rule may set a fee to be assessed for the issuance of a paper title to cover the cost of administering the electronic titling system.

Sec. 501.174. Validity of Electronic Documents.

(a) If this chapter requires that a document be an original, be on paper or another tangible medium, or be in writing, the requirement is met by an electronic document that complies with this subchapter.

(b) Except as otherwise provided by this section, if a law requires that a document be signed, the requirement is satisfied by an electronic signature.

(c) A requirement that a document or a signature associated with a document be notarized, acknowledged, verified, witnessed, or made under oath is satisfied if the electronic signature of the person authorized to perform that act, and all other information required to be included, is attached to or logically associated with the document or signature. A physical or electronic image of a stamp, impression, or seal is not required to accompany an electronic signature.

(d) The department by rule shall establish a process to accept electronic signatures on secure documents that have been electronically signed through a system not controlled by the department.

(e) A system used for submitting electronic signatures to the department must verify the identity of the person electronically signing a document and submit the document through the electronic titling system.

(f) This section does not require the department to certify an electronic signature process or an electronic signature vendor before accepting a document that is executed with an electronic signature.

Sec. 501.175. Recording of Documents.

(a) Under the titling system, the department may:

(1) receive, index, store, archive, and transmit electronic documents;

(2) provide for access to, and for search and retrieval of, documents and information by electronic means; and

(3) convert into electronic form:

(A) paper documents that it accepts for the titling of a motor vehicle; and

(B) information recorded and documents that were accepted for the titling of a motor vehicle before the titling system was implemented.

(b) The department shall continue to accept paper documents after the titling system is implemented.

Sec. 501.176. [2 Versions: As added by Acts 2011, 82nd Leg., ch. 1296] Payment of Fees by Electronic Funds Transfer or Credit Card.

(a) The department may accept payment by electronic funds transfer, credit card, or debit card of any title or registration fee that the department is required or authorized to collect under this chapter.

(b) The department may collect a fee for processing a title or registration payment by electronic funds transfer, credit card, or debit card in an amount not to exceed the amount of the charges incurred by the department to process the payment.

(c) The department may collect the fee set under Section 2054.2591, Government Code, from a person making a payment by electronic funds transfer, credit card, or debit card through the online project implemented under Section 2054.252, Government Code.

Sec. 501.176. [2 Versions: As added by Acts 2011, 82nd Leg., ch. 1290] Payment of Fees by Electronic Funds Transfer or Credit Card.

(a) The department may accept payment by electronic funds transfer, credit card, or debit card of any title or registration fee that the department is required or authorized to collect under this chapter.

(b) The department may collect a fee for processing a title or registration payment by electronic funds transfer, credit card, or debit card. The amount of the fee must not exceed the charges incurred by the state because of the use of the electronic funds transfer, credit card, or debit card.

(c) For online transactions the department may collect from a person making payment by electronic funds transfer, credit card, or debit card an amount equal to any fee charged in accordance with Section 2054.2591, Government Code.

Sec. 501.177. Service Charge.

If, for any reason, the payment of a fee under this chapter by electronic funds transfer, credit card, or debit card is not honored by the funding institution, or by the electronic funds transfer, credit card, or debit card company on which the funds are drawn, the department may collect from the person who owes the fee being collected a service charge that is for the collection of that original amount and is in addition to the original fee. The amount of the service charge must be reasonably related to the expense incurred by the department in collecting the original amount.

Sec. 501.178. Disposition of Fees.

All fees collected under this subchapter shall be deposited to the credit of the Texas Department of Motor Vehicles fund.

Sec. 501.179. Relation to Electronic Signatures in Global and National Commerce Act.

This subchapter modifies, limits, and supersedes the federal Electronic Signatures in Global and National Commerce Act (15 U.S.C. Section 7001 et seq.) but does not modify, limit, or supersede Section 101(c) of that Act (15 U.S.C. Section 7001(c)) or authorize electronic delivery of any of the notices described in Section 103(b) of that Act (15 U.S.C. Section 7003(b)).

CHAPTER 502
REGISTRATION OF VEHICLES

SUBCHAPTER A
GENERAL PROVISIONS

Sec. 502.001. Definitions.

In this chapter:

(1) [Repealed.]

(2) "Apportioned license plate" means a license plate issued in lieu of a truck, motor bus, or combination license plate to a motor carrier in this state who proportionally registers a vehicle owned or leased by the carrier in one or more other states.

(3) "Board" means the board of the Texas Department of Motor Vehicles.

(4) "Combination license plate" means a license plate issued for a truck or truck-tractor that is used or intended to be used in combination with a semitrailer that has a gross weight of more than 6,000 pounds.

(5) "Combined gross weight" means the empty weight of the truck-tractor or commercial motor vehicle combined with the empty weight of the heaviest semitrailer used or to be used in combination with the truck-tractor or commercial motor vehicle plus the heaviest net load to be carried on the combination during the registration year.

(6) "Commercial fleet" means a group of at least 25 nonapportioned motor vehicles, semitrailers, or trailers owned, operated, or leased by a corporation, limited or general partnership, limited liability company, or other business entity and used for the business purposes of that entity.

(7) "Commercial motor vehicle" means a motor vehicle, other than a motorcycle or moped, designed or used primarily to transport property. The term includes a passenger car reconstructed and used primarily for delivery purposes. The term does not include a passenger car used to deliver the United States mail.

(8) "Construction machinery" means a vehicle that:

(A) is used for construction;

(B) is built from the ground up;

(C) is not mounted or affixed to another vehicle such as a trailer;

(D) was originally and permanently designed as machinery;

(E) was not in any way originally designed to transport persons or property; and

(F) does not carry a load, including fuel.

(9) "Credit card" has the meaning assigned by Section 501.002.

(10) "Debit card" has the meaning assigned by Section 501.002.

(11) "Department" means the Texas Department of Motor Vehicles.

(12) [Repealed.]

(13) "Electric personal assistive mobility device" has the meaning assigned by Section 551.201.

(14) "Empty weight" means the unladen weight of a truck-tractor or commercial motor vehicle and semitrailer combination fully equipped, as certified by a public weigher or license and weight inspector of the Department of Public Safety.

(15) "Farm semitrailer" or "farm trailer" means a vehicle designed and used primarily as a farm vehicle.

(16) "Farm tractor" has the meaning assigned by Section 541.201.

(17) "Forestry vehicle" means a vehicle designed and used exclusively for transporting forest products in their natural state, including logs, debarked logs, untreated ties, stave bolts, plywood bolts, pulpwood billets, wood chips, stumps, sawdust, moss, bark, and wood shavings, and property used in production of those products.

(17-a) "Former military vehicle" means a vehicle, including a trailer, that:

(A) was manufactured for use in any country's military forces; and

(B) is not operated on continuous tracks.

(18) [Repealed.]

(19) "Gross vehicle weight" has the meaning assigned by Section 541.401.

(20) "Implements of husbandry" has the meaning assigned by Section 541.201.

(21) "Light truck" has the meaning assigned by Section 541.201.

(22) "Moped" has the meaning assigned by Section 541.201.

(23) "Motor bus" includes every vehicle used to transport persons on the public highways for compensation, other than:

(A) a vehicle operated by muscular power; or

(B) a municipal bus.

(24) "Motorcycle" has the meaning assigned by Section 521.001 or 541.201, as applicable.

(25) "Motor vehicle" means a vehicle that is self-propelled.

(26) "Motorized mobility device" has the meaning assigned by Section 552A.0101.

(27) "Municipal bus" includes every vehicle, other than a passenger car, used to transport persons for compensation exclusively within the limits of a municipality or a suburban addition to the municipality.

(28) "Net carrying capacity" means the heaviest net load that is able to be carried on a vehicle, but not less than the manufacturer's rated carrying capacity.

(29) "Oil well servicing, cleanout, or drilling machinery":

(A) has the meaning assigned by Section 623.149; or

(B) means a mobile crane:

(i) that is an unladen, self-propelled vehicle constructed as a machine and used solely to raise, shift, or lower heavy weights by means of a projecting, swinging mast with an engine for power on a chassis permanently constructed or assembled for that purpose; and

(ii) for which the owner has secured a permit from the department under Section 623.142.

(30) "Operate temporarily on the highways" means to travel between:

(A) different farms;

(B) a place of supply or storage and a farm; or

(C) an owner's farm and the place at which the owner's farm produce is prepared for market or is marketed.

(31) "Owner" means a person who:

(A) holds the legal title of a vehicle;

(B) has the legal right of possession of a vehicle; or

(C) has the legal right of control of a vehicle.

(32) "Passenger car" has the meaning assigned by Section 541.201.

(33) "Power sweeper" means an implement, with or without motive power, designed for the removal by a broom, vacuum, or regenerative air system of debris, dirt, gravel, litter, or sand from asphaltic concrete or cement concrete surfaces, including surfaces of parking lots, roads, streets, highways, and warehouse floors. The term includes a vehicle on which the implement is permanently mounted if the vehicle is used only as a power sweeper.

(34) "Private bus" means a bus that:

(A) is not operated for hire; and

(B) is not a municipal bus or a motor bus.

(35) "Public highway" includes a road, street, way, thoroughfare, or bridge:

(A) that is in this state;

(B) that is for the use of vehicles;

(C) that is not privately owned or controlled; and

(D) over which the state has legislative jurisdiction under its police power.

(36) "Public property" means property owned or leased by this state or a political subdivision of this state.

(37) [Repealed.]

(38) "Road tractor" means a vehicle designed for the purpose of mowing the right-of-way of a public highway or a motor vehicle designed or used for drawing another vehicle or a load and not constructed to carry:

(A) an independent load; or

(B) a part of the weight of the vehicle and load to be drawn.

(39) "Semitrailer" means a vehicle designed or used with a motor vehicle so that part of the weight of the vehicle and its load rests on or is carried by another vehicle.

(39-a) "Shipping weight" means the weight generally accepted as the empty weight of a vehicle.

(40) "Token trailer" means a semitrailer that:

(A) has a gross weight of more than 6,000 pounds; and

(B) is operated in combination with a truck or a truck-tractor that has been issued:

(i) an apportioned license plate;

(ii) a combination license plate; or

(iii) a forestry vehicle license plate.

(41) "Tow truck" means a motor vehicle adapted or used to tow, winch, or otherwise move another motor vehicle.

(42) "Trailer" means a vehicle that:

(A) is designed or used to carry a load wholly on its own structure; and

(B) is drawn or designed to be drawn by a motor vehicle.

(43) "Travel trailer" has the meaning assigned by Section 501.002.

(44) "Truck-tractor" means a motor vehicle:

(A) designed and used primarily for drawing another vehicle; and

(B) not constructed to carry a load other than a part of the weight of the vehicle and load to be drawn.

(45) "Vehicle" means a device in or by which a person or property is or may be transported or drawn on a public highway, other than a device used exclusively on stationary rails or tracks.

Sec. 502.002. Registration Required; General Rule [Renumbered].

Renumbered to Tex. Transp. Code § 502.040 by Acts 2011, 82nd Leg., ch. 1296 (H.B. 2357), § 78, effective January 1, 2012.

Sec. 502.0021. Rules and Forms.

(a) The department may adopt rules to administer this chapter.

(b) The department shall post forms on the Internet and provide each county assessor-collector with a sufficient supply of any necessary forms on request.

Sec. 502.00211. Design of Registration Insignia.

The department shall prepare the designs and specifications to be used as the registration insignia.

Sec. 502.0022. Consolidated Registration of Fleet Vehicles [Repealed].

Repealed by Acts 2009, 81st Leg., ch. 1173 (H.B. 3433), § 4, effective September 1, 2009 and Acts

Transportation Code

2009, 81st Leg., ch. 1232 (S.B. 1759), § 7, effective September 1, 2009.

Sec. 502.0023. Extended Registration of Commercial Fleet Vehicles. [Effective until March 1, 2022]

(a) Notwithstanding Section 502.044(c), the department shall develop and implement a system of registration to allow an owner of a commercial fleet to register the motor vehicles, semitrailers, and trailers in the commercial fleet for an extended registration period of not less than one year or more than eight years. The owner may select the number of years for registration under this section within that range and register the commercial fleet for that period. Payment for all registration fees for the entire registration period selected is due at the time of registration.

(b) A system of extended registration under this section must allow the owner of a commercial fleet to register:

(1) an entire commercial fleet in the county of the owner's residence or principal place of business; or

(2) the motor vehicles in a commercial fleet that are operated most regularly in the same county.

(c) In addition to the registration fees prescribed by this chapter, an owner registering a commercial fleet under this section shall pay:

(1) a one-time fee of $10 per motor vehicle, semitrailer, or trailer in the fleet; and

(2) except as provided by Subsection (e), a one-time license plate manufacturing fee of $1.50 for each fleet motor vehicle, semitrailer, or trailer license plate.

(c-1) A fee collected under Subsection (c) shall be deposited to the credit of the Texas Department of Motor Vehicles fund.

(d) A license plate issued under this section:

(1) may, on request of the owner, include the name or logo of the business entity that owns the vehicle;

(2) except as provided by Subsection (d-1), must include the expiration date of the registration period; and

(3) does not require an annual registration insignia to be valid.

(d-1) The department shall issue a license plate for a token trailer registered under this section that does not expire. The alphanumeric pattern for a license plate issued under this subsection may remain on a token trailer for as long as the registration of the token trailer is renewed or until the token trailer is removed from service or sold. The registration receipt required under Section 621.002 is not required for a vehicle that displays a license plate issued under this subsection.

(e) In addition to all other applicable registration fees, an owner registering a commercial fleet under this section shall pay a one-time license plate manufacturing fee of $8 for each set of plates issued that includes on the legend the name or logo of the business entity that owns the vehicle instead of the fee imposed by Subsection (c)(2). A license plate manufacturing fee collected under this section shall be deposited to the credit of the Texas Department of Motor Vehicles fund.

(f) If a motor vehicle registered under this section has a gross weight in excess of 10,000 pounds, the department shall also issue a registration card for the vehicle that is valid for the selected registration period.

(g) The department shall adopt rules to implement this section, including rules on suspension from the commercial fleet program for failure to comply with this section or rules adopted under this section.

(h) The department and the counties in their budgeting processes shall consider any temporary increases and resulting decreases in revenue that will result from the use of the process provided under this section.

(i) The department may provide for credits for fleet registration.

(j) A motor vehicle, semitrailer, or trailer registered under this section is subject to the inspection requirements of Chapter 548 as if the vehicle, semitrailer, or trailer were registered without extended registration. The department and the Department of Public Safety shall by rule establish a method to enforce the inspection requirements of Chapter 548 for motor vehicles, semitrailers, and trailers registered under this section. The department may assess a fee to cover the department's administrative costs of implementing this subsection.

Sec. 502.0023. Extended Registration of Commercial Fleet Vehicles. [Effective March 1, 2022]

(a) Notwithstanding Section 502.044(c), the department shall develop and implement a system of registration to allow an owner of a commercial fleet to register the motor vehicles, semitrailers, and trailers in the commercial fleet for an extended registration period of not less than one year or more than eight years. The owner may select the number of years for registration under this section within that range and register the commercial fleet for that period. Payment for all registration fees for the entire registration period selected is due at the time of registration.

(b) A system of extended registration under this section must allow the owner of a commercial fleet

Transportation Code

to register an entire commercial fleet in the county of the owner's residence or principal place of business or in any county in which the county assessor-collector is willing to accept the registration.

(c) In addition to the registration fees prescribed by this chapter, an owner registering a commercial fleet under this section shall pay:

(1) a one-time fee of $10 per motor vehicle, semitrailer, or trailer in the fleet; and

(2) except as provided by Subsection (e), a one-time license plate manufacturing fee of $1.50 for each fleet motor vehicle, semitrailer, or trailer license plate.

(c-1) A fee collected under Subsection (c) shall be deposited to the credit of the Texas Department of Motor Vehicles fund.

(d) A license plate issued under this section:

(1) may, on request of the owner, include the name or logo of the business entity that owns the vehicle;

(2) except as provided by Subsection (d-1), must include the expiration date of the registration period; and

(3) does not require an annual registration insignia to be valid.

(d-1) The department shall issue a license plate for a token trailer registered under this section that does not expire. The alphanumeric pattern for a license plate issued under this subsection may remain on a token trailer for as long as the registration of the token trailer is renewed or until the token trailer is removed from service or sold. The registration receipt required under Section 621.002 is not required for a vehicle that displays a license plate issued under this subsection.

(e) In addition to all other applicable registration fees, an owner registering a commercial fleet under this section shall pay a one-time license plate manufacturing fee of $8 for each set of plates issued that includes on the legend the name or logo of the business entity that owns the vehicle instead of the fee imposed by Subsection (c)(2). A license plate manufacturing fee collected under this section shall be deposited to the credit of the Texas Department of Motor Vehicles fund.

(f) If a motor vehicle registered under this section has a gross weight in excess of 10,000 pounds, the department shall also issue a registration card for the vehicle that is valid for the selected registration period.

(g) The department shall adopt rules to implement this section, including rules on suspension from the commercial fleet program for failure to comply with this section or rules adopted under this section.

(h) The department and the counties in their budgeting processes shall consider any temporary increases and resulting decreases in revenue that will result from the use of the process provided under this section.

(i) The department may provide for credits for fleet registration.

(j) A motor vehicle, semitrailer, or trailer registered under this section is subject to the inspection requirements of Chapter 548 as if the vehicle, semitrailer, or trailer were registered without extended registration. The department and the Department of Public Safety shall by rule establish a method to enforce the inspection requirements of Chapter 548 for motor vehicles, semitrailers, and trailers registered under this section. The department may assess a fee to cover the department's administrative costs of implementing this subsection.

Sec. 502.0024. Extended Registration of Certain Vehicles Not Subject to Inspection.

(a) Notwithstanding Section 502.044(c), the department shall develop and implement a system of registration to allow an owner of a vehicle described by Section 548.052(3) other than a mobile home to register the vehicle for an extended registration period of not more than five years. The owner may select the number of years for registration under this section within that range and register the vehicle for that period. Payment for all applicable fees, including any optional fee imposed under Subchapter H and other registration fees and the fee required by Section 548.510, for the entire registration period selected is due at the time of registration.

(b) The fee required by Section 548.510 shall be remitted to the comptroller for deposit in the Texas mobility fund, the general revenue fund, and the clean air account in amounts proportionate to the allocation prescribed by Subsection (b) of that section.

(c) The fees imposed under Subchapter H shall be collected and remitted as prescribed by that subchapter.

Sec. 502.0025. Extended Registration of Certain County Fleet Vehicles.

(a) In this section, "exempt county fleet" means a group of two or more nonapportioned motor vehicles, semitrailers, or trailers described by Section 502.453(a) that is owned by and used exclusively in the service of a county with a population of 3.3 million or more.

(b) Notwithstanding the annual registration requirements of Sections 502.044(c) and 502.453(a), the department shall develop and implement a system of registration to allow an owner of an exempt

Transportation Code

county fleet to register vehicles in the fleet for an extended registration period of not less than one year or more than eight years.

(c) A system of extended registration under this section must allow the owner of an exempt county fleet to:

(1) select the number of years for registration under this section;

(2) register the entire fleet in the county of the owner's principal place of business;

(3) register the motor vehicles in the fleet that are operated most regularly in the same county; or

(4) register the entire fleet directly with the department.

(d) A motor vehicle, semitrailer, or trailer registered under this section is subject to the inspection requirements of Chapter 548 as if the vehicle, semitrailer, or trailer were registered without an extended registration period.

(e) The department shall adopt rules to implement this section, including rules:

(1) regarding the suspension of an exempt county fleet's registration under this section if the owner of the exempt county fleet fails to comply with this section or rules adopted under this section; and

(2) establishing a method to enforce the inspection requirements of Chapter 548 for motor vehicles, semitrailers, and trailers registered under this section.

Sec. 502.003. Registration by Political Subdivision Prohibited.

(a) Except as provided by Subsection (b), a political subdivision of this state may not require an owner of a motor vehicle to:

(1) register the vehicle;

(2) pay a motor vehicle registration fee; or

(3) pay an occupation tax or license fee in connection with a motor vehicle.

(b) This section does not affect the authority of a municipality to:

(1) license and regulate the use of motor vehicles for compensation within the municipal limits; and

(2) impose a permit fee or street rental charge for the operation of each motor vehicle used to transport passengers for compensation, other than a motor vehicle operating under a registration certificate from the department or a permit from the federal Surface Transportation Board.

(c) A fee or charge under Subsection (b) may not exceed two percent of the annual gross receipts from the vehicle.

(d) This section does not impair the payment provisions of an agreement or franchise between a municipality and the owners or operators of motor vehicles used to transport passengers for compensation.

Sec. 502.004. Information on Alternatively Fueled Vehicles.

(a) In this section, "alternatively fueled vehicle" means a motor vehicle that is capable of using a fuel other than gasoline or diesel fuel.

(b) The department by rule shall establish a program to collect information about the number of alternatively fueled vehicles registered in this state.

(c) The department shall submit an annual report to the legislature that includes the information collected under this section. The report must, at a minimum, show the number of vehicles registered in this state that use:

(1) electric plug-in drives;

(2) hybrid electric drives;

(3) compressed natural gas drives; and

(4) liquefied natural gas drives.

Sec. 502.005. Registration of Autocycle.

(a) In this section, "autocycle" means a motor vehicle, other than a tractor, that is:

(1) designed to have when propelled not more than three wheels on the ground;

(2) equipped with a steering wheel;

(3) equipped with seating that does not require the operator to straddle or sit astride the seat; and

(4) manufactured and certified to comply with federal safety requirements for a motorcycle.

(b) For purposes of registering a vehicle under this chapter, an autocycle is considered to be a motorcycle.

Sec. 502.006. Certain Off-Highway Vehicles [Renumbered].

Renumbered to Tex. Transp. Code § 502.140 by Acts 2011, 82nd Leg., ch. 1296 (H.B. 2357), § 100, effective January 1, 2012.

Sec. 502.007. Mopeds [Repealed].

Repealed by Acts 2009, 81st Leg., ch. 1136 (H.B. 2553), § 39(1), effective September 1, 2011.

Sec. 502.0071. Golf Carts [Repealed].

Repealed by Acts 2009, 81st Leg., ch. 1136 (H.B. 2553), § 12(1), effective September 1, 2009.

Sec. 502.0072. Manufactured Housing [Renumbered].

Renumbered to Tex. Transp. Code § 502.142 by Acts 2011, 82nd Leg., ch. 1296 (H.B. 2357), § 101, effective January 1, 2012.

Sec. 502.0073. Power Sweepers [Renumbered].

Renumbered to Tex. Transp. Code § 502.143 by Acts 2011, 82nd Leg., ch. 1296 (H.B. 2357), § 102, effective January 1, 2012.

Sec. 502.0074. Motorized Mobility Device [Repealed].

Repealed by Acts 2011, 82nd Leg., ch. 1296 (H.B. 2357), § 247(4), effective January 1, 2012.

Sec. 502.0075. Electric Bicycles [Repealed].

Repealed by Acts 2011, 82nd Leg., ch. 1296 (H.B. 2357), § 247(4), effective January 1, 2012.

Sec. 502.0078. Vehicles Operated on Public Highway Separating Real Property Under Vehicle Owner's Control [Renumbered].

Renumbered to Tex. Transp. Code § 502.144 by Acts 2011, 82nd Leg., ch. 1296 (H.B. 2357), § 103, effective January 1, 2012.

Sec. 502.0079. Vehicles Operated by Certain Nonresidents [Renumbered].

Renumbered to Tex. Transp. Code § 502.145 by Acts 2011, 82nd Leg., ch. 1296 (H.B. 2357), § 104, effective January 1, 2012.

Sec. 502.008. Release of Information in Vehicle Registration Records [Repealed].

Repealed by Acts 2011, 82nd Leg., ch. 1296 (H.B. 2357), § 247(4), effective January 1, 2012.

Sec. 502.009. Motor Vehicle Emissions Inspection and Maintenance Requirements [Renumbered].

Renumbered to Tex. Transp. Code § 502.047 by Acts 2011, 82nd Leg., ch. 1296 (H.B. 2357), § 85, effective January 1, 2012.

Sec. 502.010. County Scofflaw.

(a) Except as otherwise provided by this section, a county assessor-collector or the department may refuse to register a motor vehicle if the assessor-collector or the department receives information that the owner of the vehicle:

(1) owes the county money for a fine, fee, or tax that is past due; or

(2) failed to appear in connection with a complaint, citation, information, or indictment in a court in the county in which a criminal proceeding is pending against the owner.

(b) A county may contract with the department to provide information to the department necessary to make a determination under Subsection (a).

(b-1) Information that is provided to make a determination under Subsection (a)(1) and that concerns the past due status of a fine or fee imposed for a criminal offense and owed to the county expires on the second anniversary of the date the information was provided and may not be used to refuse registration after that date. Once information about a past due fine or fee is provided under Subsection (b), subsequent information about other fines or fees that are imposed for a criminal offense and that become past due before the second anniversary of the date the initial information was provided may not be used, either before or after the second anniversary of that date, to refuse registration under this section unless the motor vehicle is no longer subject to refusal of registration because of notice received under Subsection (c).

(c) A county that has a contract under Subsection (b) shall notify the department regarding a person for whom the county assessor-collector or the department has refused to register a motor vehicle on:

(1) the person's payment or other means of discharge, including a waiver, of the past due fine, fee, or tax; or

(2) perfection of an appeal of the case contesting payment of the fine, fee, or tax.

(d) After notice is received under Subsection (c), the county assessor-collector or the department may not refuse to register the motor vehicle under Subsection (a).

(e) A contract under Subsection (b) must be entered into in accordance with Chapter 791, Government Code, and is subject to the ability of the parties to provide or pay for the services required under the contract.

(f) Except as otherwise provided by this section, a county that has a contract under Subsection (b) may impose an additional reimbursement fee of $20 to:

(1) a person who fails to pay a fine, fee, or tax to the county by the date on which the fine, fee, or tax is due; or

(2) a person who fails to appear in connection with a complaint, citation, information, or indictment in a court in which a criminal proceeding is pending against the owner.

(f-1) The additional reimbursement fee may be used only to reimburse the department or the

Transportation Code

county assessor-collector for its expenses for providing services under the contract, or another county department for expenses related to services under the contract.

(g) In this section:

(1) a fine, fee, or tax is considered past due if it is unpaid 90 or more days after the date it is due; and

(2) registration of a motor vehicle includes renewal of the registration of the vehicle.

(h) This section does not apply to the registration of a motor vehicle under Section 501.0234, unless the vehicle is titled and registered in the name of a person who holds a general distinguishing number.

(i) A municipal court judge or justice of the peace who has jurisdiction over the underlying offense may waive an additional reimbursement fee imposed under Subsection (f) if the judge or justice makes a finding that the defendant is economically unable to pay the fee or that good cause exists for the waiver.

(j) If a county assessor-collector is notified that the court having jurisdiction over the underlying offense has waived the past due fine or fee, including a reimbursement fee, due to the defendant's indigency, the county may not impose an additional reimbursement fee on the defendant under Subsection (f).

Sec. 502.011. Refusal to Register Vehicle for Nonpayment of Toll or Administrative Fee.

(a) A county assessor-collector or the department may refuse to register or renew the registration of a motor vehicle if it has received written notice from a toll project entity that the owner of the vehicle has been finally determined to be a habitual violator under Subchapter C, Chapter 372.

(b) A toll project entity shall notify a county assessor-collector or the department, as applicable, that:

(1) a person for whom the assessor-collector or the department has refused to register a vehicle is no longer determined to be a habitual violator; or

(2) an appeal has been perfected and the appellant has posted any bond required to stay the toll project entity's exercise of habitual violator remedies pending the appeal.

(c) This section does not apply to the registration of a motor vehicle under Section 501.0234.

Sec. 502.012. Notice Regarding Whether Certain Trailers Are Subject to Inspection.

The department shall include in each registration renewal notice for a vehicle that is a trailer, semitrailer, or pole trailer a statement regarding whether the vehicle is subject to inspection under Chapter 548.

SUBCHAPTER B REGISTRATION REQUIREMENTS

Sec. 502.040. Registration Required; General Rule. [Effective until March 1, 2022]

(a) Not more than 30 days after purchasing a vehicle or becoming a resident of this state, the owner of a motor vehicle, trailer, or semitrailer shall apply for the registration of the vehicle for:

(1) each registration year in which the vehicle is used or to be used on a public highway; and

(2) if the vehicle is unregistered for a registration year that has begun and that applies to the vehicle and if the vehicle is used or to be used on a public highway, the remaining portion of that registration year.

(b) The application must be accompanied by personal identification as determined by department rule and made in a manner prescribed by the department:

(1) through the county assessor-collector of the county in which the owner resides; or

(2) if the office of that assessor-collector is closed, or may be closed for a protracted period of time, as defined by department rule, through a county assessor-collector who is willing to accept the application.

(c) A provision of this chapter that conflicts with this section prevails over this section to the extent of the conflict.

(d) A county assessor-collector, a deputy county assessor-collector, or a person acting on behalf of a county assessor-collector is not liable to any person for:

(1) refusing to register a vehicle because of the person's failure to submit evidence of residency that complies with the department's rules; or

(2) registering a vehicle under this section.

Sec. 502.040. Registration Required; General Rule. [Effective March 1, 2022]

(a) Not more than 30 days after purchasing a vehicle or becoming a resident of this state, the owner of a motor vehicle, trailer, or semitrailer shall apply for the registration of the vehicle for:

(1) each registration year in which the vehicle is used or to be used on a public highway; and

(2) if the vehicle is unregistered for a registration year that has begun and that applies to the vehicle and if the vehicle is used or to be used on a public highway, the remaining portion of that registration year.

(b) The application must be accompanied by personal identification as determined by department rule and made in a manner prescribed by the department through:

(1) the county assessor-collector of the county in which the owner resides; or

(2) any county assessor-collector who is willing to accept the application.

(c) A provision of this chapter that conflicts with this section prevails over this section to the extent of the conflict.

(d) A county assessor-collector, a deputy county assessor-collector, or a person acting on behalf of a county assessor-collector is not liable to any person for:

(1) refusing to register a vehicle because of the person's failure to submit evidence of residency that complies with the department's rules; or

(2) registering a vehicle under this section.

Sec. 502.041. Initial Registration. [Effective until March 1, 2022]

(a) Notwithstanding Section 502.040, the owner of a vehicle may concurrently apply for a title and for registration through the county assessor-collector of the county in which:

(1) the owner resides; or

(2) the vehicle is purchased or encumbered.

(b) The first time an owner applies for registration of a vehicle, the owner may demonstrate compliance with Section 502.046(a) as to the vehicle by showing proof of financial responsibility in any manner specified in Section 502.046(c) as to:

(1) any vehicle of the owner; or

(2) any vehicle used as part of the consideration for the purchase of the vehicle the owner applies to register.

Sec. 502.041. Initial Registration. [Effective March 1, 2022]

(a) Notwithstanding Section 502.040, the owner of a vehicle may concurrently apply for a title and for registration through the county assessor-collector of the county in which:

(1) the owner resides;

(2) the vehicle is purchased or encumbered; or

(3) the county assessor-collector is willing to accept the application.

(b) The first time an owner applies for registration of a vehicle, the owner may demonstrate compliance with Section 502.046(a) as to the vehicle by showing proof of financial responsibility in any manner specified in Section 502.046(c) as to:

(1) any vehicle of the owner; or

(2) any vehicle used as part of the consideration for the purchase of the vehicle the owner applies to register.

Sec. 502.042. Title Required for Registration.

The department may not register or renew the registration of a motor vehicle for which a title is required under Chapter 501 unless the owner:

(1) obtains a title for the vehicle; or

(2) presents satisfactory evidence that a title was previously issued to the owner by the department or another jurisdiction.

Sec. 502.043. Application for Registration and Certain Permits.

(a) An application for vehicle registration or a permit described by Section 502.094 or 502.095 must:

(1) be made in a manner prescribed and include the information required by the department by rule; and

(2) contain a full description of the vehicle as required by department rule.

(b) The department shall deny the registration of or permitting under Section 502.094 or 502.095 of a commercial motor vehicle, truck-tractor, trailer, or semitrailer if the applicant:

(1) has a business operated, managed, or otherwise controlled or affiliated with a person who is ineligible for registration or whose privilege to operate has been suspended, including the applicant entity, a relative, family member, corporate officer, or shareholder;

(2) has a vehicle that has been prohibited from operating by the Federal Motor Carrier Safety Administration for safety-related reasons;

(3) is a carrier whose business is operated, managed, or otherwise controlled or affiliated with a person who is ineligible for registration, including the owner, a relative, a family member, a corporate officer, or a shareholder; or

(4) fails to deliver to the county assessor-collector proof of the weight of the vehicle, the maximum load to be carried on the vehicle, and the gross weight for which the vehicle is to be registered.

(c) In lieu of filing an application during a year as provided by Subsection (a), the owner of a vehicle

Transportation Code

registered in any state for that year or the preceding year may present:

(1) the registration receipt and transfer receipt for the vehicle; or

(2) other evidence satisfactory to the county assessor-collector that the person owns the vehicle.

(c-1) A county assessor-collector shall accept a receipt or evidence provided under Subsection (c) as an application for renewal of the registration if the receipt or evidence indicates the applicant owns the vehicle. This section allows issuance for registration purposes only but does not authorize the department to issue a title.

(d) The department may require an applicant for registration to provide current personal identification as determined by department rule. Any identification number required by the department under this subsection may be entered into the department's electronic titling system but may not be printed on the title.

Sec. 502.0435. Online Registration Renewal.

If a person is otherwise eligible to renew a vehicle registration under this chapter, the person may renew the vehicle registration through an online registration system maintained by the department.

Sec. 502.044. Registration Period.

(a) The department shall designate a vehicle registration year of 12 consecutive months to begin on the first day of a calendar month and end on the last day of the 12th calendar month.

(b) The department shall designate vehicle registration years so as to distribute the work of the department and the county assessor-collectors as uniformly as possible throughout the year. The department may establish separate registration years for any vehicle or classification of vehicle and may adopt rules to administer the year-round registration system.

(c) The department may designate a registration period of less than 12 months to be computed at a rate of one-twelfth the annual registration fee multiplied by the number of months in the registration period. The board by rule may allow payment of registration fees for a designated period not to exceed the amount of time determined by department rule.

(d) The department shall issue a registration receipt and registration insignia that are valid until the expiration of the designated period.

(e) The department shall use the date of sale of the vehicle in designating the registration year for a vehicle for which registration is applied for under Section 501.0234.

Sec. 502.045. Delinquent Registration.

(a) A registration fee for a vehicle becomes delinquent immediately if the vehicle is used on a public highway without the fee having been paid in accordance with this chapter.

(b) An applicant for registration who provides evidence to establish good reason for delinquent registration and who complies with the other requirements for registration under this chapter may register the vehicle for a 12-month period that ends on the last day of the 11th month after the month in which the registration occurs under this subsection.

(c) An applicant for registration who is delinquent and has not provided evidence acceptable to establish good reason for delinquent registration but who complies with the other requirements for registration under this chapter shall register the vehicle for a 12-month period without changing the initial month of registration.

(d) A person who has been arrested or received a citation for a violation of Section 502.472 may register the vehicle being operated at the time of the offense for a 12-month period without change to the initial month of registration only if the person:

(1) meets the other requirements for registration under this chapter; and

(2) pays an additional charge equal to 20 percent of the prescribed fee.

(e) The board by rule shall adopt a list of evidentiary items sufficient to establish good reason for delinquent registration under Subsection (b) and provide for the evidence that may be used to establish good reason under that subsection.

(f) The board by rule shall adopt procedures to implement this section in connection with the delinquent registration of a vehicle registered directly with the department or through other means.

Sec. 502.046. Evidence of Financial Responsibility.

(a) Evidence of financial responsibility as required by Section 601.051 other than for a trailer or semitrailer shall be submitted with the application for registration under Section 502.043. A county assessor-collector may not register the motor vehicle unless the owner or the owner's representative submits the evidence of financial responsibility.

(b) The county assessor-collector shall examine the evidence of financial responsibility to determine whether it complies with Subsection (c). After examination, the evidence shall be returned unless it is in the form of a photocopy or an electronic submission.

(c) In this section, evidence of financial responsibility may be:

(1) a document listed under Section 601.053(a) or verified in compliance with Section 601.452;

(2) a liability self-insurance or pool coverage document issued by a political subdivision or governmental pool under the authority of Chapter 791, Government Code, Chapter 119, Local Government Code, or other applicable law in at least the minimum amounts required by Chapter 601;

(3) a photocopy of a document described by Subdivision (1) or (2); or

(4) an electronic submission of a document or the information contained in a document described by Subdivision (1) or (2).

(d) A personal automobile policy used as evidence of financial responsibility under this section must comply with Section 1952.052 et seq. and Sections 2301.051 through 2301.055, Insurance Code.

(e) At the time of registration, the county assessor-collector shall provide to a person registering a motor vehicle a statement that the motor vehicle may not be operated in this state unless:

(1) liability insurance coverage for the motor vehicle in at least the minimum amounts required by law remains in effect to insure against potential losses; or

(2) the motor vehicle is exempt from the insurance requirement because the person has established financial responsibility in a manner described by Sections 601.051(2)—(5) or is exempt under Section 601.052.

(f) A county assessor-collector is not liable to any person for refusing to register a motor vehicle to which this section applies because of the person's failure to submit evidence of financial responsibility that complies with Subsection (c).

(g) A county, a county assessor-collector, a deputy county assessor-collector, a person acting for or on behalf of a county or a county assessor-collector, or a person acting on behalf of an owner for purposes of registering a motor vehicle is not liable to any person for registering a motor vehicle under this section.

(h) This section does not prevent a person from registering a motor vehicle by mail or through an electronic submission.

(i) To be valid under this section, an electronic submission must be in a format that is:

(1) submitted by electronic means, including a telephone, facsimile machine, or computer;

(2) approved by the department; and

(3) authorized by the commissioners court for use in the county.

(j) This section does not apply to a vehicle registered pursuant to Section 501.0234.

Sec. 502.047. Registration-Based Enforcement of Motor Vehicle Inspection Requirements.

(a) Except as provided by Chapter 548, the department and the Department of Public Safety shall ensure compliance with the motor vehicle inspection requirements under Chapter 548, including compliance with the motor vehicle emissions inspection and maintenance program under Subchapter F of that chapter, through a vehicle registration-based enforcement system.

(b) A motor vehicle may not be registered if the department receives from the Texas Commission on Environmental Quality or the Department of Public Safety notification that the registered owner of the vehicle has not complied with Chapter 548.

(c) A motor vehicle may not be registered if the vehicle was denied registration under Subsection (b) unless verification is received that the registered vehicle owner is in compliance with Chapter 548.

(d) The department and the Department of Public Safety shall enter into an agreement regarding the timely submission by the Department of Public Safety of inspection compliance information to the department.

(d-1) The department, the Texas Commission on Environmental Quality, and the Department of Public Safety shall enter an agreement regarding the responsibilities for costs associated with implementing this section.

(e) A county tax assessor-collector is not liable to any person for refusing to register a motor vehicle because of the person's failure to provide verification of the person's compliance with Chapter 548.

Sec. 502.048. Refusal to Register Unsafe Vehicle.

The department may refuse to register a motor vehicle and may cancel, suspend, or revoke a registration if the department determines that a motor vehicle is unsafe, improperly equipped, or otherwise unfit to be operated on a public highway.

Sec. 502.051. Deposit of Registration Fees in State Highway Fund [Renumbered].

Renumbered to Tex. Transp. Code § 502.196 by Acts 2011, 82nd Leg., ch. 1296 (H.B. 2357), § 113, effective January 1, 2012.

Sec. 502.052. License Plates and Registration Insignia; Reflectorized Material [Renumbered].

Transportation Code

Renumbered to Tex. Transp. Code § 502.00211 by Acts 2011, 82nd Leg., ch. 1296 (H.B. 2357), § 73, effective January 1, 2012.

Sec. 502.053. Cost of Manufacturing License Plates or Registration Insignia [Renumbered].

Renumbered to Tex. Transp. Code § 504.006 by Acts 2011, 82nd Leg., ch. 1296 (H.B. 2357), § 171, effective January 1, 2012.

Sec. 502.054. Agreements with Other Jurisdictions; Offense [Renumbered].

Renumbered to Tex. Transp. Code § 502.091 by Acts 2011, 82nd Leg., ch. 1296 (H.B. 2357), § 94, effective January 1, 2012.

Sec. 502.055. Determination of Weight and Seating Capacity.

(a) The weight, net weight, or gross weight of a vehicle, as determined by the department, is the correct weight for registration purposes, regardless of any other purported weight of the vehicle.

(b) The department may require an applicant for registration under this chapter to provide the department with evidence of:

(1) the manufacturer's rated carrying capacity for the vehicle; or

(2) the gross vehicle weight rating.

(c) For the purposes of this section, the seating capacity of a bus is:

(1) the manufacturer's rated seating capacity, excluding the operator's seat; or

(2) if the manufacturer has not rated the vehicle for seating capacity, a number computed by allowing one passenger for each 16 inches of seating on the bus, excluding the operator's seat.

(d) For registration purposes:

(1) the weight of a passenger car is the shipping weight of the car plus 100 pounds; and

(2) the weight of a municipal bus or private bus is calculated by adding the following and rounding to the next highest 100 pounds:

(A) the shipping weight of the bus; and

(B) the seating capacity multiplied by 150 pounds.

Sec. 502.056. Disputed Classification of Vehicle.

In a disputed case, the department may determine:

(1) the classification to which a vehicle belongs; and

(2) the amount of the registration fee for the vehicle.

Sec. 502.057. Registration Receipt.

(a) The department shall issue or require to be issued to the owner of a vehicle registered under this chapter a registration receipt showing the information required by rule.

(b) A receipt for the renewed registration of a vehicle generated by an online registration system approved by the department is proof of the vehicle's registration until the 31st day after the date of renewal on the receipt.

Sec. 502.058. Duplicate Registration Receipt.

(a) The owner of a vehicle for which the registration receipt has been lost or destroyed may obtain a duplicate receipt from the department or the county assessor-collector who issued the original receipt by paying a fee of $2.

(b) The office issuing a duplicate receipt shall retain the fee received.

(c) A fee collected by the department under Subsection (a) shall be deposited to the credit of the Texas Department of Motor Vehicles fund.

Sec. 502.059. Issuance of Registration Insignia.

(a) On payment of the prescribed fee an applicant for motor vehicle registration shall be issued a registration insignia.

(b) On application and payment of the prescribed fee for a renewal of the registration of a vehicle through the period set by rule, the department shall issue a registration insignia for the validation of the license plate or plates to be attached as provided by Subsection (c).

(c) Except as provided by Subsection (f), the registration insignia for validation of a license plate shall be attached to the inside of the vehicle's windshield, if the vehicle has a windshield, in the lower left corner in a manner that will not obstruct the vision of the driver. If the vehicle does not have a windshield, the owner, when applying for registration or renewal of registration, shall notify the department, and the department shall issue a distinctive device for attachment to the rear license plate of the vehicle.

(d) Department rules may provide for the use of an automated registration process, including:

(1) the automated on-site production of registration insignia; and

(2) automated on-premises and off-premises self-service registration.

(e) Subsection (c) does not apply to:

(1) the issuance of specialized license plates as designated by the department, including state official license plates, exempt plates for governmental entities, and temporary registration plates; or

(2) the issuance or validation of replacement license plates, except as provided by Chapter 504.

(f) The registration insignia shall be attached to the rear license plate of the vehicle, if the vehicle is:

(1) a motorcycle;

(2) machinery used exclusively to drill water wells or construction machinery for which a distinguishing license plate has been issued under Section 502.146; or

(3) oil well servicing, oil clean out, or oil well drilling machinery or equipment for which a distinguishing license plate has been issued under Subchapter G, Chapter 623.

Sec. 502.060. Replacement of Registration Insignia.

(a) The owner of a registered motor vehicle may obtain a replacement registration insignia by:

(1) certifying that the replacement registration insignia will not be used on any other vehicle owned or operated by the person making the statement;

(2) paying a fee of $6 plus the fees required by Section 502.356(a) for each replacement registration insignia, except as provided by other law; and

(3) returning each replaced registration insignia in the owner's possession.

(b) **[2 Versions: As amended by Acts 2017, 85th Leg., ch. 490]** No fee is required under this section if:

(1) the replacement fee for a license plate has been paid under Section 504.007; or

(2) a county assessor-collector determines that the owner of a registered motor vehicle did not receive a registration insignia that was issued to the owner by mail.

(b) **[2 Versions: As amended by Acts 2017, 85th Leg., ch. 968]** No fee is required under this section if:

(1) the replacement fee for a license plate has been paid under Section 504.007; or

(2) the county assessor-collector determines that the owner paid for a registration insignia for the same registration period that was mailed to the owner but not received by the owner.

(c) A county assessor-collector may not issue a replacement registration insignia without complying with this section.

(d) A county assessor-collector shall retain $2.50 of each fee collected under this section and shall report and send the remainder to the department.

(e) The portion of the fee sent to the department under Subsection (d) shall be deposited to the credit of the Texas Department of Motor Vehicles fund.

Sec. 502.061. Registration by Owner with Condition That Impedes Effective Communication.

(a) An application for registration must provide space for the applicant to voluntarily indicate that the applicant has a health condition or disability that may impede effective communication with a peace officer. The department may request from a person who makes an indication under this subsection verification of a condition in the form of:

(1) for a physical health condition, a written statement from a licensed physician; or

(2) for a mental health condition, a written statement from a licensed physician, a licensed psychologist, or a non-physician mental health professional, as defined by Section 571.003, Health and Safety Code.

(b) The department shall provide to the Department of Public Safety the vehicle registration information of a person who voluntarily indicated on an application under Subsection (a) that the person has a health condition or disability that may impede effective communication. The department may not provide to the Department of Public Safety information that shows the type of health condition or disability a person has.

(c) The Department of Public Safety shall establish a system to include information received under Subsection (b) in the Texas Law Enforcement Telecommunications System for the purpose of alerting a peace officer who makes a traffic stop that the operator of the stopped vehicle may have a health condition or disability that may impede effective communication.

(d) The Department of Public Safety may not make information received under Subsection (b) available in the Texas Law Enforcement Telecommunications System to a person who has access to the system under a contract unless the contract prohibits the person from disclosing that information to a person who is not subject to the contract.

(e) The department may not issue to a person without the person's consent a license plate with a visible marking that indicates to the general public that the person voluntarily indicated on an application under Subsection (a) that the person has a health condition or disability that may impede effective communication.

(f) Except as provided by Subsection (d), information supplied to the department relating to an applicant's health condition or disability is for the confidential use of the department and the Department of Public Safety and may not be disclosed to any person.

SUBCHAPTER C SPECIAL REGISTRATIONS

Sec. 502.090. Effect of Certain Military Service on Registration Requirement.

(a) This section applies only to a motor vehicle that is owned by a person who:

(1) is a resident of this state;

(2) is on active duty in the armed forces of the United States;

(3) is stationed in or has been assigned to another nation under military orders; and

(4) has registered the vehicle or been issued a license for the vehicle under the applicable status of forces agreement by:

(A) the appropriate branch of the armed forces of the United States; or

(B) the nation in which the person is stationed or to which the person has been assigned.

(b) Unless the registration or license issued for a vehicle described by Subsection (a) is suspended, canceled, or revoked by this state as provided by law:

(1) Section 502.040(a) does not apply; and

(2) the registration or license issued by the armed forces or host nation remains valid and the motor vehicle may be operated in this state under that registration or license for a period of not more than 90 days after the date on which the vehicle returns to this state.

Sec. 502.091. International Registration Plan.

(a) The department, through its director, may enter into an agreement with an authorized officer of another jurisdiction, including another state of the United States, a foreign country or a state, province, territory, or possession of a foreign country, to provide for:

(1) the registration of vehicles by residents of this state and nonresidents on an allocation or mileage apportionment plan, as under the International Registration Plan; and

(2) the exemption from payment of registration fees by nonresidents if residents of this state are granted reciprocal exemptions.

(b) The department may adopt and enforce rules to carry out the International Registration Plan or other agreement under this section. The rules may require an applicant to register under the unified carrier registration system as defined by Section 643.001 before the applicant applies for registration under the International Registration Plan.

(c) To carry out the International Registration Plan or other agreement under this section, the department shall direct that fees collected for other jurisdictions under the agreement be deposited to the credit of the proportional registration distributive fund in the state treasury and distributed to the appropriate jurisdiction through that fund. The department is not required to refund any amount less than $10 unless required by the plan.

(d) This section prevails to the extent of conflict with another law relating to the subject of this section.

(e) A person commits an offense if the person owns or operates a vehicle not registered in this state in violation of:

(1) an agreement under this section; or

(2) the applicable registration laws of this state, in the absence of an agreement under this section.

(f) An offense under Subsection (e) is a misdemeanor punishable by a fine not to exceed $200.

Sec. 502.092. Nonresident-Owned Vehicles Used to Transport Farm Products.

(a) The department may issue to a nonresident owner a permit for a truck, truck-tractor, trailer, or semitrailer that:

(1) is registered in the owner's home state or country; and

(2) will be used to transport:

(A) farm products produced in this state from the place of production to a place of market or storage or a railhead that is not more than 75 miles from the place of production;

(B) machinery used to harvest farm products produced in this state; or

(C) farm products produced outside this state from the point of entry into this state to a place of market, storage, or processing or a railhead or seaport that is not more than 80 miles from the point of entry.

(b) The department shall issue a receipt for a permit issued under this section in a manner provided by the department. The permit receipt must contain the information required by this section and be carried in the vehicle for which it is issued at all times during which it is valid. A permit issued under this section is valid until the earlier of:

Transportation Code

(1) the date the vehicle's registration in the owner's home state or country expires; or

(2) the 30th day after the date the permit is issued.

(c) A person may obtain a permit under this section by:

(1) applying to the department in a manner prescribed by the department;

(2) paying a fee equal to 1/12 the registration fee prescribed by this chapter for the vehicle;

(3) furnishing satisfactory evidence that the motor vehicle is insured under an insurance policy that complies with Section 601.072 and that is written by:

(A) an insurance company or surety company authorized to write motor vehicle liability insurance in this state; or

(B) with the department's approval, a surplus lines insurer that meets the requirements of Chapter 981, Insurance Code, and rules adopted by the commissioner of insurance under that chapter, if the applicant is unable to obtain insurance from an insurer described by Paragraph (A); and

(4) furnishing evidence that the vehicle has been inspected as required under Chapter 548.

(d) A nonresident owner may not obtain more than three permits under this section during a registration year.

(e) A vehicle for which a permit is issued under this section may not be operated in this state after the permit expires unless the owner:

(1) obtains another temporary permit; or

(2) registers the vehicle under Section 502.253, 502.254, 502.255, or 502.256, as appropriate, for the remainder of the registration year.

(f) A vehicle for which a permit is issued under this section may not be registered under Section 502.433.

(g) A mileage referred to in this section is a state highway mileage.

Sec. 502.093. Annual Permits.

(a) The department may issue an annual permit in lieu of registration to a foreign commercial motor vehicle, trailer, or semitrailer that is subject to registration in this state and is not authorized to travel on a public highway because of the lack of registration in this state or the lack of reciprocity with the state or country in which the vehicle is registered.

(b) A permit issued under this section is valid for a vehicle registration year to begin on the first day of a calendar month designated by the department and end on the last day of the last calendar month of the registration year.

(c) A permit may not be issued under this section for the importation of citrus fruit into this state from a foreign country except for foreign export or processing for foreign export.

(d) A person may obtain a permit under this section by:

(1) applying in the manner prescribed by the department;

(2) paying a fee in the amount required by Subsection (e) in the manner prescribed by the department, including a service charge for a credit card payment or escrow account; and

(3) furnishing evidence of financial responsibility for the motor vehicle that complies with Sections 502.046(c) and 601.168(a), the policies to be written by an insurance company or surety company authorized to write motor vehicle liability insurance in this state.

(e) The fee for a permit under this section is the fee that would be required for registering the vehicle under Section 502.253 or 502.255, except as provided by Subsection (f).

(f) A vehicle registered under this section is exempt from the token fee and is not required to display the associated distinguishing license plate if the vehicle:

(1) is a semitrailer that has a gross weight of more than 6,000 pounds; and

(2) is used or intended to be used in combination with a truck tractor or commercial motor vehicle with a gross vehicle weight of more than 10,000 pounds.

(g) A vehicle registered under this section is not subject to the fee required by Section 502.401 or 502.403.

Sec. 502.094. 72- or 144-Hour Permits.

(a) The department may issue a temporary registration permit in lieu of registration for a commercial motor vehicle, trailer, semitrailer, or motor bus that:

(1) is owned by a resident of the United States, Canada, or the United Mexican States;

(2) is subject to registration in this state; and

(3) is not authorized to travel on a public highway because of the lack of registration in this state or the lack of reciprocity with the state or province in which the vehicle is registered.

(b) A permit issued under this section is valid for the period stated on the permit, effective from the date and time shown on the receipt issued as evidence of registration under this section.

(c) A person may obtain a permit under this section by:

Transportation Code

(1) applying to the county assessor-collector or the department;

(2) paying a fee of $25 for a 72-hour permit or $50 for a 144-hour permit in the manner prescribed by the department that may include a service charge for a credit card payment or escrow account;

(3) furnishing to the county assessor-collector or the department evidence of financial responsibility for the vehicle that complies with Sections 502.046(c) and 601.168(a); and

(4) submitting a copy of the applicable federal declaration form required by the Federal Motor Carrier Safety Administration or its successor in connection with the importation of a motor vehicle or motor vehicle equipment subject to the federal motor vehicle safety, bumper, and theft prevention standards.

(d) A county assessor-collector shall report and send a fee collected under this section in the manner provided by Section 502.198. The board by rule shall prescribe the format and content of a report required by this subsection.

(e) A vehicle issued a permit under this section is subject to Subchapters B and F, Chapter 548, unless the vehicle:

(1) is registered in another state of the United States, in a province of Canada, or in a state of the United Mexican States; or

(2) is mobile drilling or servicing equipment used in the production of gas, crude petroleum, or oil, including a mobile crane or hoisting equipment, mobile lift equipment, forklift, or tug.

(f) A commercial motor vehicle, trailer, semitrailer, or motor bus apprehended for violating a registration law of this state:

(1) may not be issued a permit under this section; and

(2) is immediately subject to registration in this state.

(g) A person who operates a commercial motor vehicle, trailer, or semitrailer with an expired permit issued under this section is considered to be operating an unregistered vehicle subject to each penalty prescribed by law.

(h) The department may establish one or more escrow accounts in the Texas Department of Motor Vehicles fund for the prepayment of a 72-hour permit or a 144-hour permit. Any fee established by the department for the administration of this subsection shall be administered as required by an agreement entered into by the department.

Sec. 502.095. One-Trip or 30-Day Trip Permits.

(a) The department may issue a temporary permit in lieu of registration for a vehicle subject to registration in this state that is not authorized to travel on a public highway because of the lack of registration in this state or the lack of reciprocity with the state or country in which the vehicle is registered.

(b) A permit issued under this section is valid for:

(1) one trip, as provided by Subsection (c); or

(2) 30 days, as provided by Subsection (d).

(c) A one-trip permit is valid for one trip between the points of origin and destination and those intermediate points specified in the application and registration receipt. Unless the vehicle is a bus operating under charter that is not covered by a reciprocity agreement with the state or country in which the bus is registered, a one-trip permit is for the transit of the vehicle only, and the vehicle may not be used for the transportation of any passenger or property. A one-trip permit may not be valid for longer than 15 days from the effective date of registration.

(d) A 30-day permit may be issued only to a passenger vehicle, a private bus, a trailer or semitrailer with a gross weight of not more than 10,000 pounds, a light truck, or a light commercial vehicle with a gross vehicle weight of more than 10,000 pounds that will operate unladen. A person may obtain multiple 30-day permits. The department may issue a single registration receipt to apply to all of the periods for which the vehicle is registered.

(e) A person may obtain a permit under this section by:

(1) applying as provided by the department to:

(A) the county assessor-collector of the county in which the vehicle will first be operated on a public highway; or

(B) the department in Austin or at one of the department's vehicle title and registration regional offices;

(2) paying a fee, in the manner prescribed by the department including a registration service charge for a credit card payment or escrow account of:

(A) $5 for a one-trip permit; or

(B) $25 for each 30-day period; and

(3) furnishing evidence of financial responsibility for the vehicle in a form listed under Section 502.046(c).

(f) A registration receipt shall be carried in the vehicle at all times during the period in which it is valid. The temporary tag must contain all pertinent information required by this section and must be displayed in the rear window of the vehicle so that the tag is clearly visible and legible when viewed from the rear of the vehicle. If the vehicle does not have a rear window, the temporary tag must be attached on or carried in the vehicle to allow ready inspection. The registration receipt must be carried in the vehicle at all times during the period in which it is valid.

Transportation Code

(g) The department may refuse and may instruct a county assessor-collector to refuse to issue a temporary registration for any vehicle if, in the department's opinion, the vehicle or the owner of the vehicle has been involved in operations that constitute an abuse of the privilege granted by this section. A registration issued after notice to a county assessor-collector under this subsection is void.

Sec. 502.101. Registration by Mail or Electronic Means; Service Charge [Renumbered].

Renumbered to Tex. Transp. Code § 502.197 by Acts 2011, 82nd Leg., ch. 1296 (H.B. 2357), § 114, effective January 1, 2012.

Sec. 502.102. Disposition of Fees Generally [Renumbered].

Renumbered to Tex. Transp. Code § 502.198 by Acts 2011, 82nd Leg., ch. 1296 (H.B. 2357), § 115, effective January 1, 2012.

Sec. 502.1025. Calculation of Additional Fee Amounts Retained by a County [Renumbered].

Renumbered to Tex. Transp. Code § 502.1981 by Acts 2011, 82nd Leg., ch. 1296 (H.B. 2357), § 116, effective January 1, 2012.

Sec. 502.103. Disposition of Optional County Road and Bridge Fee [Renumbered].

Renumbered to Tex. Transp. Code § 502.1982 by Acts 2011, 82nd Leg., ch. 1296 (H.B. 2357), § 117, effective January 1, 2012.

Sec. 502.104. Disposition of Certain Special Fees [Repealed].

Repealed by Acts 2011, 82nd Leg., ch. 1296 (H.B. 2357), § 247(4), effective January 1, 2012.

Sec. 502.105. Report of Fees Collected [Repealed].

Repealed by Acts 2011, 82nd Leg., ch. 1296 (H.B. 2357), § 247(4), effective January 1, 2012.

Sec. 502.106. Deposit of Fees in Interest-Bearing Account [Renumbered].

Renumbered to Tex. Transp. Code § 502.1983 by Acts 2011, 82nd Leg., ch. 1296 (H.B. 2357), § 118, effective January 1, 2012.

Sec. 502.107. Interest on Fees [Renumbered].

Renumbered to Tex. Transp. Code § 502.1984 by Acts 2011, 82nd Leg., ch. 1296 (H.B. 2357), § 119, effective January 1, 2012.

Sec. 502.108. Use of Registration Fees Retained by County [Renumbered].

Renumbered to Tex. Transp. Code § 502.1985 by Acts 2011, 82nd Leg., ch. 1296 (H.B. 2357), § 120, effective January 1, 2012.

Sec. 502.109. Compensation of Assessor-Collector [Renumbered].

Renumbered to Transportation Code § 520.006 by Acts 2011, 82nd Leg., ch. 1290 (H.B. 2017), § 32, effective September 1, 2011 and Acts 2011, 82nd Leg., ch. 1296 (H.B. 2357), § 226, effective January 1, 2012.

Sec. 502.110. Contingent Provision for Distribution of Fees Between State and Counties [Renumbered].

Renumbered to Tex. Transp. Code § 502.1986 by Acts 2011, 82nd Leg., ch. 1296 (H.B. 2357), § 121, effective January 1, 2012.

Sec. 502.111. Branch Offices [Renumbered].

Renumbered to Tex. Transp. Code § 520.007 by Acts 2011, 82nd Leg., ch. 1296 (H.B. 2357), § 227, effective January 1, 2012.

Sec. 502.112. Deputy Assessor-Collectors [Renumbered].

Renumbered to Tex. Transp. Code § 520.0091 by Acts 2011, 82nd Leg., ch. 1296 (H.B. 2357), § 230, effective January 1, 2012.

Sec. 502.113. Limited-Service Deputies [Renumbered].

Renumbered to Tex. Transp. Code § 520.009 by Acts 2011, 82nd Leg., ch. 1296 (H.B. 2357), § 229, effective January 1, 2012.

Sec. 502.114. Full-Service Deputies [Renumbered].

Renumbered to Tex. Transp. Code § 520.008 by Acts 2011, 82nd Leg., ch. 1296 (H.B. 2357), § 228, effective January 1, 2012.

SUBCHAPTER D VEHICLES NOT ISSUED REGISTRATION

Sec. 502.140. Certain Off-Highway Vehicles.

(a) In this section, "off-highway vehicle" has the meaning assigned by Section 551A.001.

(b) Except as provided by Subsection (c), the department may not register an off-highway vehicle, with or without design alterations, for operation on a public highway.

(c) The department may register an off-highway vehicle that is owned by the state, county, or municipality for operation on a public beach or highway to maintain public safety and welfare.

(d) Section 504.401 does not apply to an off-highway vehicle.

(e) An off-highway vehicle that is registered under this section:

(1) is not subject to the requirements of Subchapter D, Chapter 551A; and

(2) is subject to the requirements of Subchapter E, Chapter 551A.

Sec. 502.141. Off-Highway Former Military Vehicles.

(a) Except as provided by Subsections (b) and (c), a person may not register a former military vehicle designated for off-highway use, with or without design alterations, for operation on a public highway.

(b) A former military vehicle may be registered for on-road use if the vehicle:

(1) is a high mobility multipurpose wheeled vehicle designated for off-highway use; and

(2) has a gross vehicle weight rating of less than 10,000 pounds.

(c) A former military vehicle issued specialty license plates under Section 504.502 may be operated on a public highway in accordance with that section.

Sec. 502.142. Manufactured Housing.

Manufactured housing, as defined by Section 1201.003, Occupations Code, is not a vehicle subject to this chapter.

Sec. 502.143. Other Vehicles.

An owner may not register the following vehicles for operation on a public highway:

(1) power sweepers;

(2) motorized mobility devices;

(3) electric personal assistive mobility devices; and

(4) electric bicycles, as defined by Section 664.001.

Sec. 502.144. Vehicles Operated on Public Highway Separating Real Property Under Vehicle Owner's Control.

Where a public highway separates real property under the control of the owner of a motor vehicle, the operation of the motor vehicle by the owner or the owner's agent or employee across the highway is not a use of the motor vehicle on the public highway.

Sec. 502.145. Vehicles Operated by Certain Nonresidents.

(a) A nonresident owner of a privately owned passenger car that is registered in the state or country in which the person resides and that is not operated for compensation may operate the car in this state for the period in which the car's license plates are valid. In this subsection, "nonresident" means a resident of a state or country other than this state whose presence in this state is as a visitor and who does not engage in gainful employment or enter into business or an occupation, except as may otherwise be provided by any reciprocal agreement with another state or country.

(b) This section does not prevent:

(1) a nonresident owner of a motor vehicle from operating the vehicle in this state for the sole purpose of marketing farm products raised exclusively by the person; or

(2) a resident of an adjoining state or country from operating in this state a privately owned and registered vehicle to go to and from the person's place of regular employment and to make trips to purchase merchandise, if the vehicle is not operated for compensation.

(c) The privileges provided by this section may be allowed only if, under the laws of the appropriate state or country, similar privileges are granted to vehicles registered under the laws of this state and owned by residents of this state.

(d) This section does not affect the right or status of a vehicle owner under any reciprocal agreement between this state and another state or country.

Sec. 502.146. Certain Farm Vehicles and Drilling and Construction Equipment.

(a) The department shall issue distinguishing license plates to a vehicle described by Subsection

Transportation Code

(b) or (c). The fee for the license plates is $5 and shall be deposited to the credit of the Texas Department of Motor Vehicles fund.

(b) An owner is not required to register a vehicle that is used only temporarily on the highways if the vehicle is:

(1) a farm trailer or farm semitrailer with a gross weight of more than 4,000 pounds but not more than 34,000 pounds that is used exclusively:

(A) to transport seasonally harvested agricultural products or livestock from the place of production to the place of processing, market, or storage;

(B) to transport farm supplies from the place of loading to the farm; or

(C) for the purpose of participating in equine activities or attending livestock shows, as defined by Section 87.001, Civil Practice and Remedies Code;

(2) machinery used exclusively for the purpose of drilling water wells;

(3) oil well servicing or drilling machinery and if at the time of obtaining the license plates, the applicant submits proof that the applicant has a permit under Section 623.142; or

(4) construction machinery.

(c) An owner is not required to register a vehicle that is:

(1) a farm trailer or farm semitrailer owned by a cotton gin and used exclusively to transport agricultural products without charge from the place of production to the place of processing, market, or storage;

(2) a trailer used exclusively to transport fertilizer without charge from a place of supply or storage to a farm; or

(3) a trailer used exclusively to transport cottonseed without charge from a place of supply or storage to a farm or place of processing.

(c-1) An exemption provided by this section applies to a vehicle owned by a farmers' cooperative society incorporated under Chapter 51, Agriculture Code, or a marketing association organized under Chapter 52, Agriculture Code, and used by members of the society or association for a fee if the vehicle otherwise meets the requirements for the exemption.

(d) A vehicle described by Subsection (b) is exempt from the inspection requirements of Subchapters B and F, Chapter 548.

(e) Except as provided by Subsection (c-1), this section does not apply to a farm trailer or farm semitrailer that:

(1) is used for hire;

(2) has metal tires operating in contact with the highway;

(3) is not equipped with an adequate hitch pinned or locked so that it will remain securely engaged to the towing vehicle while in motion; or

(4) is not operated and equipped in compliance with all other law.

(f) A vehicle to which this section applies that is operated on a public highway in violation of this section is considered to be operated while unregistered and is immediately subject to the applicable registration fees and penalties prescribed by this chapter.

(g) In this section, the gross weight of a trailer or semitrailer is the combined weight of the vehicle and the load carried on the highway.

(h) A distinguishing license plate may not be issued or renewed under Subsection (a) to an owner of a vehicle described by Subsection (b)(1) unless the vehicle's owner provides a registration number issued by the comptroller under Section 151.1551, Tax Code, or the vehicle is owned by a farmers' cooperative society incorporated under Chapter 51, Agriculture Code, or a marketing association organized under Chapter 52, Agriculture Code. The comptroller shall allow access to the online system established under Section 151.1551(l), Tax Code, to verify a registration number provided under this subsection.

Sec. 502.151. Application for Registration [Renumbered].

Renumbered to Tex. Transp. Code § 502.043 by Acts 2011, 82nd Leg., ch. 1296 (H.B. 2357), § 81, effective January 1, 2012.

Sec. 502.1515. Outsourcing Production of Renewal Notices; Paid Advertising.

The board may authorize the department to enter into a contract with a private vendor to produce and distribute motor vehicle registration renewal notices. The contract may provide for the inclusion of paid advertising in the registration renewal notice packet.

Sec. 502.152. Certificate of Title Required for Registration [Renumbered].

Renumbered to Tex. Transp. Code § 502.042 by Acts 2011, 82nd Leg., ch. 1296 (H.B. 2357), § 80, effective January 1, 2012.

Sec. 502.153. Evidence of Financial Responsibility [Renumbered].

Renumbered to Tex. Transp. Code § 502.046 by Acts 2011, 82nd Leg., ch. 1296 (H.B. 2357), § 84, effective January 1, 2012.

Transportation Code

Sec. 502.1535. Evidence of Vehicle Emissions Inspection [Repealed].

Repealed by Acts 2011, 82nd Leg., ch. 1296 (H.B. 2357), § 247(4), effective January 1, 2012.

Sec. 502.154. Report by County Assessor-Collector [Repealed].

Repealed by Acts 2011, 82nd Leg., ch. 1296 (H.B. 2357), § 247(4), effective January 1, 2012.

Sec. 502.155. Proof of Residency Required in Certain Counties [Repealed].

Repealed by Acts 1997, 75th Leg., ch. 165 (S.B. 898), § 30.44(d), effective September 1, 1997.

Sec. 502.156. Statement Required for Rebuilt Vehicles.

A county assessor-collector shall require an applicant for registration of a rebuilt vehicle to provide a statement that the vehicle is rebuilt and that states the name of each person from whom the parts used in assembling the vehicle were obtained.

Sec. 502.157. Initial Registration [Renumbered].

Renumbered to Tex. Transp. Code § 502.041 by Acts 2011, 82nd Leg., ch. 1296 (H.B. 2357), § 79, effective January 1, 2012.

Sec. 502.158. Registration Year [Renumbered].

Renumbered to Tex. Transp. Code § 502.044 by Acts 2011, 82nd Leg., ch. 1296 (H.B. 2357), § 82, effective January 1, 2012.

Sec. 502.1585. Designation of Registration Period by Owner. [Repealed]

Sec. 502.1586. Registration Period for Truck-Tractor or Commercial Motor Vehicle Transporting Seasonal Agricultural Products [Renumbered].

Renumbered to Tex. Transp. Code § 502.432 by Acts 2011, 82nd Leg., ch. 1296 (H.B. 2357), § 142, effective January 1, 2012.

Sec. 502.159. Schedule of Fees [Renumbered].

Renumbered to Tex. Transp. Code § 502.190 by Acts 2011, 82nd Leg., ch. 1296 (H.B. 2357), § 107, effective January 1, 2012.

Sec. 502.160. Fee: Motorcycle or Moped [Renumbered].

Renumbered to Tex. Transp. Code § 502.251 by Acts 2011, 82nd Leg., ch. 1296 (H.B. 2357), § 123, effective January 1, 2012.

Sec. 502.161. Fee: Vehicles That Weigh 6,000 Pounds or Less [Renumbered].

Renumbered to Tex. Transp. Code § 502.252 by Acts 2011, 82nd Leg., ch. 1296 (H.B. 2357), § 124, effective January 1, 2012.

Sec. 502.162. Fee: Vehicles That Weigh More Than 6,000 pounds [Renumbered].

Renumbered to Tex. Transp. Code § 502.253 by Acts 2011, 82nd Leg., ch. 1296 (H.B. 2357), § 125, effective January 1, 2012.

Sec. 502.163. Fee: Commercial Motor Vehicle Used Primarily for Farm Purposes; Offense [Renumbered].

Renumbered to Tex. Transp. Code § 502.433 by Acts 2011, 82nd Leg., ch. 1296 (H.B. 2357), § 143, effective January 1, 2012.

Sec. 502.164. Fee: Motor Vehicle Used Exclusively to Transport and Spread Fertilizer [Renumbered].

Renumbered to Tex. Transp. Code § 502.431 by Acts 2011, 82nd Leg., ch. 1296 (H.B. 2357), § 141, effective January 1, 2012.

Sec. 502.165. Fee: Road Tractor [Renumbered].

Renumbered to Tex. Transp. Code § 502.256 by Acts 2011, 82nd Leg., ch. 1296 (H.B. 2357), § 128, effective January 1, 2012.

Sec. 502.166. Fee: Trailer, Travel Trailer, or Semitrailer [Renumbered].

Renumbered to Tex. Transp. Code § 502.254 by Acts 2011, 82nd Leg., ch. 1296 (H.B. 2357), § 126, effective January 1, 2012.

Sec. 502.167. Truck-Tractor or Commercial Motor Vehicle Combination Fee; Semitrailer Token Fee [Renumbered].

Renumbered to Tex. Transp. Code § 502.255 by Acts 2011, 82nd Leg., ch. 1296 (H.B. 2357), § 127, effective January 1, 2012.

Sec. 502.1675. Texas Emissions Reduction Plan Surcharge [Renumbered].

Renumbered to Tex. Transp. Code § 502.358 by Acts 2011, 82nd Leg., ch. 1296 (H.B. 2357), § 132, effective January 1, 2012.

Sec. 502.168. Fee: Motor Bus.

The fee for a registration year for registration of a motor bus is the fee prescribed by Section 502.252 or 502.253, as applicable.

Sec. 502.169. Fee: All-Terrain Vehicle [Repealed].

Repealed by Acts 2007, 80th Leg., ch. 1280 (H.B. 3849), § 6, effective June 15, 2007.

Sec. 502.170. Additional Fee for Reflectorized License Plates [Repealed].

Repealed by Acts 2009, 81st Leg., ch. 1136 (H.B. 2553), § 39(3), effective September 1, 2011.

Sec. 502.1705. Additional Fee for Automated Registration and Title System [Renumbered].

Renumbered to Tex. Transp. Code § 502.356 by Acts 2011, 82nd Leg., ch. 1296 (H.B. 2357), § 130, effective January 1, 2012.

Sec. 502.171. Additional Fee for Certain Vehicles Using Diesel Motor [Renumbered].

Renumbered to Tex. Transp. Code § 502.359 by Acts 2011, 82nd Leg., ch. 1296 (H.B. 2357), § 133, effective January 1, 2012.

Sec. 502.1715. Additional Fee for Certain Department Programs [Renumbered].

Renumbered to Tex. Transp. Code § 502.357 by Acts 2011, 82nd Leg., ch. 1296 (H.B. 2357), § 131, effective January 1, 2012.

Sec. 502.172. Optional County Fee for Road and Bridge Fund [Renumbered].

Renumbered to Tex. Transp. Code § 502.401 by Acts 2011, 82nd Leg., ch. 1296 (H.B. 2357), § 135, effective January 1, 2012.

Sec. 502.1725. Optional County Fee for Transportation Projects [Renumbered].

Renumbered to Tex. Transp. Code § 502.402 by Acts 2011, 82nd Leg., ch. 1296 (H.B. 2357), § 136, effective January 1, 2012.

Sec. 502.173. Optional County Fee for Child Safety [Renumbered].

Renumbered to Tex. Transp. Code § 502.403 by Acts 2011, 82nd Leg., ch. 1296 (H.B. 2357), § 137, effective January 1, 2012.

Sec. 502.174. Voluntary Assessment for Young Farmer Loan Guarantees [Renumbered].

Renumbered to Tex. Transp. Code § 502.404 by Acts 2011, 82nd Leg., ch. 1296 (H.B. 2357), § 138, effective January 1, 2012.

Sec. 502.1745. Voluntary Fee [Renumbered].

Renumbered to Tex. Transp. Code § 502.405 by Acts 2011, 82nd Leg., ch. 1296 (H.B. 2357), § 139, effective January 1, 2012.

Sec. 502.1746. Voluntary Contribution to Veterans' Assistance Fund.

(a) When a person registers a motor vehicle under this chapter, the person is entitled to make a voluntary contribution in any amount to the fund for veterans' assistance established by Section 434.017, Government Code, as redesignated and amended by Chapter 1418 (H.B. 3107), Acts of the 80th Legislature, Regular Session, 2007.

(b) The county assessor-collector shall send any contribution made under this section to the comptroller for deposit in the state treasury to the credit of the fund for veterans' assistance before the 31st day after the date the contribution is made. A contribution made under this section may be used only for the purposes of the fund for veterans' assistance.

(c) The department shall:

(1) include space on each motor vehicle registration renewal notice, on the page that states the total fee for registration renewal, that allows a person renewing a registration to indicate the amount

Transportation Code

that the person is voluntarily contributing to the fund for veterans' assistance;

(2) provide an opportunity to contribute to the fund for veterans' assistance similar to the opportunity described by Subsection (a) and in the manner described by Subdivision (1) in any registration renewal system that succeeds the system in place on September 1, 2011; and

(3) provide an opportunity for a person to contribute to the fund for veterans' assistance during the registration renewal process on the department's Internet website.

(d) If a person makes a contribution under this section and does not pay the full amount of a registration fee, the county assessor-collector may credit all or a portion of the contribution to the person's registration fee.

(e) The department shall consult with the Texas Veterans Commission in performing the department's duties under this section.

Sec. 502.1747. Voluntary Contribution to Parks and Wildlife Department.

(a) When a person registers or renews the registration of a motor vehicle under this chapter, the person may contribute $5 or more to the Parks and Wildlife Department.

(b) The department shall:

(1) include space on each motor vehicle registration renewal notice, on the page that states the total fee for registration renewal, that allows a person renewing a registration to indicate the amount that the person is voluntarily contributing to the state parks account;

(2) provide an opportunity to contribute to the state parks account similar to the opportunity described by Subsection (a) and in the manner described by Subdivision (1) in any registration renewal system that succeeds the system in place on September 1, 2011; and

(3) provide an opportunity for a person to contribute to the state parks account during the registration renewal process on the department's Internet website.

(c) If a person makes a contribution under this section and does not pay the full amount of a registration fee, the county assessor-collector may credit all or a portion of the contribution to the person's registration fee.

(d) The county assessor-collector shall send any contribution made under this section to the comptroller for deposit to the credit of the state parks account under Section 11.035, Parks and Wildlife Code. Money received by the Parks and Wildlife Department under this section may be used only for the operation and maintenance of state parks, historic sites, or natural areas under the jurisdiction of the Parks and Wildlife Department.

(e) The department shall consult with the Parks and Wildlife Department in performing the department's duties under this section.

Sec. 502.1748. Disposition of Certain Voluntary Contributions.

If a person makes a voluntary contribution under Section 502.1746 or 502.1747 at the time the person registers or renews the registration of a motor vehicle under this chapter but the person does not clearly specify the entity to which the person intends to contribute, the county assessor-collector shall divide the contribution between the entities authorized to receive contributions under those sections.

Sec. 502.175. Transfer Fee [Repealed].

Repealed by Acts 2011, 82nd Leg., ch. 1296 (H.B. 2357), § 247(4), effective January 1, 2012.

Sec. 502.176. Delinquent Registration [Renumbered].

Renumbered to Tex. Transp. Code § 502.045 by Acts 2011, 82nd Leg., ch. 1296 (H.B. 2357), § 83, effective January 1, 2012.

Sec. 502.177. Minimum Registration Fee [Repealed].

Repealed by Acts 2011, 82nd Leg., ch. 1296 (H.B. 2357), § 247(4), effective January 1, 2012.

Sec. 502.178. Registration Receipt [Renumbered].

Renumbered to Tex. Transp. Code § 502.057 by Acts 2011, 82nd Leg., ch. 1296 (H.B. 2357), § 88, effective January 1, 2012.

Sec. 502.179. Duplicate Registration Receipt [Renumbered].

Renumbered to Tex. Transp. Code § 502.058 by Acts 2011, 82nd Leg., ch. 1296 (H.B. 2357), § 89, effective January 1, 2012.

Sec. 502.180. Issuance of License Plate or Registration Insignia [Renumbered].

Renumbered to Tex. Transp. Code § 502.059 by Acts 2011, 82nd Leg., ch. 1296 (H.B. 2357), § 90, effective January 1, 2012.

Sec. 502.181. Payment of Registration Fee by Check Drawn Against Insufficient Funds [Renumbered].

Renumbered to Tex. Transp. Code § 502.193 by Acts 2011, 82nd Leg., ch. 1296 (H.B. 2357), § 110, effective January 1, 2012.

Sec. 502.182. Credit for Registration Fee Paid on Motor Vehicle Subsequently Destroyed [Renumbered].

Renumbered to Tex. Transp. Code § 502.194 by Acts 2011, 82nd Leg., ch. 1296 (H.B. 2357), § 111, effective January 1, 2012.

Sec. 502.183. Refund of Overcharged Registration Fee [Renumbered].

Renumbered to Tex. Transp. Code § 502.195 by Acts 2011, 82nd Leg., ch. 1296 (H.B. 2357), § 112, effective January 1, 2012.

Sec. 502.184. Replacement of Registration Insignia [Renumbered].

Renumbered to Tex. Transp. Code § 502.060 by Acts 2011, 82nd Leg., ch. 1296 (H.B. 2357), § 91, effective January 1, 2012.

Sec. 502.1841. Replacement License Plates [Renumbered].

Renumbered to Tex. Transp. Code § 504.007 by Acts 2011, 82nd Leg., ch. 1296 (H.B. 2357), § 172, effective January 1, 2012.

Sec. 502.185. Refusal to Register Vehicle in Certain Counties [Renumbered].

Renumbered to Tex. Transp. Code § 502.010 by Acts 2011, 82nd Leg., ch. 1296 (H.B. 2357), § 76, effective January 1, 2012.

Sec. 502.186. "Low-Emissions Vehicle" Insignia for Certain Motor Vehicles [Expired].

Expired pursuant to Acts 2001, 77th Leg., ch. 967 (S.B. 5), § 8, effective August 31, 2008.

Sec. 502.187. Parade Vehicles Owned by Nonprofit Service Organizations [Repealed].

Repealed by Acts 2009, 81st Leg., ch. 1136 (H.B. 2553), § 39(5), effective September 1, 2011.

Sec. 502.188. Certain Soil Conservation Equipment [Renumbered].

Renumbered to Tex. Transp. Code § 502.435 by Acts 2011, 82nd Leg., ch. 1296 (H.B. 2357), § 145, effective January 1, 2012.

Sec. 502.189. Donor Registry Information.

(a) The department, with expert input and support from the nonprofit organization administering the Glenda Dawson Donate Life-Texas Registry under Chapter 692A, Health and Safety Code, shall:

(1) add a link from the department's Internet website to the Glenda Dawson Donate Life-Texas Registry operated under Chapter 692A, Health and Safety Code; and

(2) provide a method to distribute donor registry information to interested individuals in each office authorized to issue motor vehicle registrations.

(b) The department shall make available for distribution to each office authorized to issue motor vehicle registrations Donate Life brochures that provide basic donor information in English and Spanish and a contact phone number and e-mail address. The department shall ensure that the question provided in Section 521.401(c)(1)(B) and information on the donor registry Internet website is included with registration renewal notices.

SUBCHAPTER E
ADMINISTRATION OF FEES

Sec. 502.190. Schedule of Registration Fees.

The department shall post a complete schedule of registration fees on the Internet.

Sec. 502.191. Collection of Fees.

(a) A person may not collect a registration fee under this chapter unless the person is:

(1) an officer or employee of the department; or

(2) a county assessor-collector or a deputy county assessor-collector.

(b) The department may accept electronic payment by electronic funds transfer, credit card, or debit card of any fee that the department is authorized to collect under this chapter.

(c) The department may collect a fee for processing a payment by electronic funds transfer, credit card, or debit card in an amount not to exceed the amount of the charges incurred by the department to process the payment.

Transportation Code

(d) The department may collect the fee set under Section 2054.2591, Government Code, from a person making a payment by electronic funds transfer, credit card, or debit card through the online project implemented under Section 2054.252, Government Code.

(e) If, for any reason, the payment of a fee under this chapter by electronic funds transfer, credit card, or debit card is not honored by the funding institution or by the electronic funds transfer, credit card, or debit card company on which the funds are drawn, the department may collect from the person who owes the fee being collected a service charge that is for the collection of that original amount and is in addition to the original fee. The amount of the service charge must be reasonably related to the expense incurred by the department in collecting the original amount.

(f) The department may not collect a fee under Subsection (c) or (d) if the department collects a fee under Section 502.1911.

Sec. 502.1911. Registration Processing and Handling Fee.

(a) The department may collect a fee, in addition to other registration fees for the issuance of a license plate, a set of license plates, or another device used as the registration insignia, to cover the expenses of collecting those registration fees, including a service charge for registration by mail.

(b) The board by rule shall set the fee in an amount that:

(1) includes the fee established under Section 502.356(a); and

(2) is sufficient to cover the expenses associated with collecting registration fees by:

(A) the department;

(B) a county tax assessor-collector;

(C) a private entity with which a county tax assessor-collector contracts under Section 502.197; or

(D) a deputy assessor-collector that is deputized in accordance with board rule under Section 520.0071.

(c) The county tax assessor-collector, a private entity with which a county tax assessor-collector contracts under Section 502.197, or a deputy assessor-collector may retain a portion of the fee collected under Subsection (b) as provided by board rule. Remaining amounts collected under this section shall be deposited to the credit of the Texas Department of Motor Vehicles fund.

Sec. 502.192. Transfer Fee.

The purchaser of a used motor vehicle shall pay, in addition to any fee required under Chapter 501 for the transfer of title, a transfer fee of $2.50 for the transfer of the registration of the motor vehicle. The county assessor-collector may retain as commission for services provided under this subchapter half of each transfer fee collected. The portion of each transfer fee not retained by the county assessor-collector shall be deposited to the credit of the Texas Department of Motor Vehicles fund.

Sec. 502.193. Payment by Check Drawn Against Insufficient Funds.

(a) A county assessor-collector who receives from any person a check or draft for payment of a registration fee for a registration year that has not ended that is returned unpaid because of insufficient funds or no funds in the bank or trust company to the credit of the drawer of the check or draft shall certify the fact to the sheriff or a constable or highway patrol officer in the county after attempts to contact the person fail to result in the collection of payment. The certification must be made before the 30th day after the date the check or draft is returned unpaid and:

(1) be under the assessor-collector's official seal;

(2) include the name and address of the person who gave the check or draft;

(3) include the license plate number and make of the vehicle;

(4) be accompanied by the check or draft; and

(5) be accompanied by documentation of any attempt to contact the person and collect payment.

(b) On receiving a complaint under Subsection (a) from the county assessor-collector, the sheriff, constable, or highway patrol officer shall find the person who gave the check or draft, if the person is in the county, and demand immediate redemption of the check or draft from the person. If the person fails or refuses to redeem the check or draft, the sheriff, constable, or highway patrol officer shall:

(1) seize and remove the license plates and registration insignia from the vehicle; and

(2) return the license plates and registration insignia to the county assessor-collector.

Sec. 502.1931. Disputed Payment by Credit Card or Debit Card.

(a) A county assessor-collector who receives from any person a payment by credit card or debit card for a registration fee for a registration year that has not ended that is returned unpaid because the payment by the credit card or debit card has been disputed by the credit card or debit card company shall certify the fact to the sheriff or a constable or highway patrol officer in the county after attempts to contact the person fail to result in the collection of payment. The certification must be made before the 30th day after the date the assessor-collector is made aware that the credit card or debit card payment has been disputed and:

(1) be under the assessor-collector's official seal;

(2) include the name and address of the person who authorized the credit card or debit card payment;

(3) include the license plate number and make of the vehicle;

(4) be accompanied by evidence from the credit card or debit card company that the company has determined that it will not make payment on the disputed credit card or debit card charge; and

(5) be accompanied by documentation of any attempt to contact the person and collect payment.

(b) On receiving a complaint under Subsection (a) from the county assessor-collector, the sheriff, constable, or highway patrol officer shall find the person who authorized the credit card or debit card payment, if the person is in the county, and demand immediate redemption of payment from the person. If the person fails or refuses to redeem the payment, the sheriff, constable, or highway patrol officer shall:

(1) seize and remove the license plates and registration insignia from the vehicle; and

(2) return the license plates and registration insignia to the assessor-collector.

Sec. 502.194. Credit for Registration Fee Paid on Motor Vehicle Subsequently Destroyed.

(a) The owner of a motor vehicle that is destroyed to the extent that it cannot afterwards be operated on a public highway is entitled to a registration fee credit if the prorated portion of the registration fee for the remainder of the registration year is more than $15. The owner must claim the credit by sending the registration fee receipt for the vehicle to the department.

(b) The department, on satisfactory proof that the vehicle is destroyed, shall issue a registration fee credit slip to the owner in an amount equal to the prorated portion of the registration fee for the remainder of the registration year. The owner, during the same or the next registration year, may use the registration fee credit slip as payment or part payment for the registration of another vehicle to the extent of the credit.

Sec. 502.195. Refund of Overcharged Registration Fee.

(a) The owner of a motor vehicle who pays an annual registration fee in excess of the statutory amount is entitled to a refund of the overcharge.

(b) The county assessor-collector who collects the excessive fee shall refund an overcharge on presentation to the assessor-collector of satisfactory evidence of the overcharge not later than the first anniversary of the date the excessive registration fee was paid.

(c) A refund shall be paid from the fund in which the county's share of registration fees is deposited.

Sec. 502.196. Deposit of Registration Fees in State Highway Fund.

Except as otherwise provided by this chapter, the board and the department shall deposit all money received from registration fees in the state treasury to the credit of the state highway fund.

Sec. 502.197. Registration by Mail or Electronic Means; Service Charge.

(a) A county assessor-collector may retain a service charge in the amount determined by the board under Section 502.1911 from each applicant registering a vehicle by mail. The service charge shall be used to pay the costs of handling and postage to mail the registration receipt and insignia to the applicant.

(b) With the approval of the commissioners court of a county, a county assessor-collector may contract with a private entity to enable an applicant for registration to use an electronic off-premises location. A private entity may retain an amount determined by the board under Section 502.1911 for the service provided.

(c) The department may adopt rules to cover the timely application for and issuance of registration receipts and insignia by mail or through an electronic off-premises location.

Sec. 502.198. Disposition of Fees Generally.

(a) Except as provided by Sections 502.058, 502.060, 502.1911, 502.192, 502.356, and 502.357 and Subchapter H, this section applies to all fees collected by a county assessor-collector under this chapter.

(b) Each Tuesday, a county assessor-collector shall credit to the county road and bridge fund an amount equal to the net collections made during the preceding week until the amount so credited for the calendar year equals the total of:

(1) $60,000; and

(2) $350 for each mile of county road maintained by the county, according to the most recent information available from the department, not to exceed 500 miles.

Transportation Code

(c) After the credits to the county road and bridge fund equal the total computed under Subsection (b), each Tuesday the county assessor-collector shall:

(1) credit to the county road and bridge fund an amount equal to 50 percent of the net collections made during the preceding week, until the amount so credited for the calendar year equals $125,000; and

(2) send to the department an amount equal to 50 percent of those collections for deposit to the credit of the state highway fund.

(d) After the credits to the county road and bridge fund equal the total amounts computed under Subsections (b) and (c)(1), each Tuesday the county assessor-collector shall send to the department all collections made during the preceding week for deposit to the credit of the state highway fund.

Sec. 502.1981. Calculation of Additional Fee Amounts Retained by a County. [Repealed]

Sec. 502.1982. Disposition of Optional County Road and Bridge Fee [Repealed].

Repealed by Acts 2013, 83rd Leg., ch. 1287 (H.B. 2202), § 72, effective September 1, 2013.

Sec. 502.1983. Deposit of Fees in Interest-Bearing Account.

(a) A county assessor-collector may:

(1) deposit the fees subject to Section 502.198 in an interest-bearing account or certificate in the county depository; and

(2) send the fees to the department not later than the 34th day after the date the fees are due under Section 502.198.

(b) The county owns all interest earned on fees deposited under this section. The county treasurer shall credit the interest to the county general fund.

Sec. 502.1984. Interest on Fees.

(a) A fee required to be sent to the department under this chapter bears interest for the benefit of the state highway fund or the Texas Department of Motor Vehicles fund, as applicable, at an annual rate of 10 percent beginning on the 60th day after the date the county assessor-collector collects the fee.

(b) The department shall audit the registration and transfer fees collected and disbursed by each county assessor-collector and shall determine the exact amount of interest due on any fee not sent to the department.

(c) The state has a claim against a county assessor-collector and the sureties on the assessor-collector's official bond for the amount of interest due on a fee.

Sec. 502.1985. Use of Registration Fees Retained by County.

(a) Money credited to the county road and bridge fund under Section 502.198 may not be used to pay the compensation of the county judge or a county commissioner. The money may be used only for the construction and maintenance of lateral roads in the county, under the supervision of the county engineer.

(b) If there is not a county engineer, the commissioners court of the county may require the services of the department's district engineer or resident engineer to supervise the construction and surveying of lateral roads in the county.

(c) A county may use money allocated to it under this chapter to:

(1) pay obligations issued in the construction or improvement of any roads, including state highways in the county;

(2) improve the roads in the county road system; or

(3) construct new roads.

(d) To the maximum extent possible, contracts for roads constructed by a county using funds provided under this chapter should be awarded by competitive bids.

Sec. 502.1986. Contingent Provision for Distribution of Fees Between State and Counties.

If the method of distributing vehicle registration fees collected under this chapter between the state and counties is declared invalid because of inequality of collection or distribution of those fees, 60 percent of each fee shall be distributed to the county collecting the fee and 40 percent shall be sent to the state in the manner provided by this chapter.

Sec. 502.199. Electronic Funds Transfer.

A county assessor-collector that transfers money to the department under this chapter shall transfer the money electronically.

Sec. 502.201. License Plates for Exempt Vehicles [Renumbered].

Renumbered to Tex. Transp. Code § 502.451 by Acts 2011, 82nd Leg., ch. 1296 (H.B. 2357), § 147, effective January 1, 2012.

Sec. 502.2015. Limitation on Issuance of Exempt License Plates; Seizure of Certain Vehicles [Renumbered].

Renumbered to Tex. Transp. Code § 502.452 by Acts 2011, 82nd Leg., ch. 1296 (H.B. 2357), § 148, effective January 1, 2012.

Sec. 502.202. Government-Owned Vehicles; Public School Buses; Fire-Fighting Vehicles; County Marine Law Enforcement Vehicles [Renumbered].

Renumbered to Tex. Transp. Code § 502.453 by Acts 2011, 82nd Leg., ch. 1296 (H.B. 2357), § 149, effective January 1, 2012.

Sec. 502.203. Vehicles Used by Nonprofit Disaster Relief Organizations [Renumbered].

Renumbered to Tex. Transp. Code § 502.454 by Acts 2011, 82nd Leg., ch. 1296 (H.B. 2357), § 150, effective January 1, 2012.

Sec. 502.2035. Trailers and Semitrailers Owned by Religious Organizations [Renumbered].

Renumbered to Tex. Transp. Code § 502.455 by Acts 2011, 82nd Leg., ch. 1296 (H.B. 2357), § 151, effective January 1, 2012.

Sec. 502.204. Emergency Services Vehicles [Renumbered].

Renumbered to Tex. Transp. Code § 502.456 by Acts 2011, 82nd Leg., ch. 1296 (H.B. 2357), § 152, effective January 1, 2012.

Sec. 502.205. All-Terrain Vehicles [Repealed].

Repealed by Acts 2007, 80th Leg., ch. 1280 (H.B. 3849), § 6, effective June 15, 2007.

Sec. 502.206. Registration of Certain Law Enforcement Vehicles Under Alias [Repealed].

Repealed by Acts 2011, 82nd Leg., ch. 1296 (H.B. 2357), § 247(4), effective January 1, 2012.

SUBCHAPTER F REGULAR REGISTRATION FEES

Sec. 502.251. Fee: Motorcycle or Moped.

The fee for a registration year for registration of a motorcycle or moped is $30.

Sec. 502.252. Fee: Vehicles That Weigh 6,000 Pounds or Less.

(a) The fee for a registration year for registration of a vehicle with a gross weight of 6,000 pounds or less is $50.75, unless otherwise provided in this chapter.

(b) [Repealed by Acts 2013, 83rd Leg., ch. 1135 (H.B. 2741), § 140(2), effective September 1, 2013.]

Sec. 502.2525. Discontinuance of Certain Specialized License Plates [Repealed].

Repealed by Acts 2003, 78th Leg., ch. 1320 (H.B. 2971), § 10(a), effective September 1, 2003.

Sec. 502.2526. Specialized License Plates Authorized After January 1, 1999 [Repealed].

Repealed by Acts 2003, 78th Leg., ch. 1320 (H.B. 2971), § 10(a), effective September 1, 2003.

Sec. 502.253. Fee: Vehicles That Weigh More Than 6,000 Pounds.

The fee for a registration year for registration of a vehicle with a gross weight of more than 6,000 pounds is as follows unless otherwise provided in this chapter:

Weight Classification in pounds	Fee Schedule
6,001—10,000	$54.00
10,001—18,000	$110.00
18,001—25,999	$205.00
26,000—40,000	$340.00
40,001—54,999	$535.00
55,000—70,000	$740.00
70,001—80,000	$840.00

Sec. 502.2531. Issuance of Disabled Plates to Certain Institutions [Repealed].

Repealed by Acts 2003, 78th Leg., ch. 1320 (H.B. 2971), § 10(a), effective September 1, 2003.

Sec. 502.254. Fee: Trailer, Travel Trailer, or Semitrailer.

(a) The fee for a registration year for registration of a trailer, travel trailer, or semitrailer with a gross weight of 6,000 pounds or less is $45.00.

Transportation Code

(b) The fee for a registration year for registration of a trailer, travel trailer, or semitrailer with a gross weight of more than 6,000 pounds is calculated by gross weight according to Section 502.253.

Sec. 502.255. Truck-Tractor or Commercial Motor Vehicle Combination Fee; Semitrailer Token Fee.

(a) This section applies only to a truck-tractor or commercial motor vehicle with a gross weight of more than 10,000 pounds that is used or is to be used in combination with a semitrailer that has a gross weight of more than 6,000 pounds.

(b) The fee for a registration year for registration of a truck-tractor or commercial motor vehicle is calculated by gross weight according to Section 502.253.

(c) The fee for registration of a semitrailer used in the manner described by Subsection (a), regardless of the date the semitrailer is registered, is $15 for a registration year.

(d) A registration made under Subsection (c) is valid only when the semitrailer is used in the manner described by Subsection (a).

(e) For registration purposes, a semitrailer converted to a trailer by means of an auxiliary axle assembly retains its status as a semitrailer.

(f) A combination of vehicles may not be registered under this section for a combined gross weight of less than 18,000 pounds.

(g) This section does not apply to:

(1) a combination of vehicles that includes a vehicle that has a distinguishing license plate under Section 502.146;

(2) a truck-tractor or commercial motor vehicle registered or to be registered with $5 distinguishing license plates for which the vehicle is eligible under this chapter;

(3) a truck-tractor or commercial motor vehicle used exclusively in combination with a semitrailer of the travel trailer type; or

(4) a vehicle registered or to be registered:

(A) with a temporary registration permit;

(B) under Section 502.433; or

(C) under Section 502.435.

(h) The department may adopt rules to administer this section.

(i) The department shall issue a license plate for a token trailer registered under this section that does not expire or require an annual registration insignia to be valid. The alphanumeric pattern for a license plate issued under this subsection may remain on a token trailer for as long as the registration of the token trailer is renewed or until the token trailer is removed from service or sold. The registration receipt required under Section 621.002 is not required for a vehicle that displays a license plate issued under this subsection.

(j) A person may register a semitrailer under this section if the person:

(1) applies to the department for registration;

(2) provides proof of the person's eligibility to register the vehicle under this subsection as required by the department; and

(3) pays a fee of $15, plus any applicable fee under Section 502.401, for each year included in the registration period.

Sec. 502.2555. Air Force Cross or Distinguished Service Cross, Army Distinguished Service Cross, Navy Cross, or Medal of Honor Recipients [Repealed].

Repealed by Acts 2003, 78th Leg., ch. 1320 (H.B. 2971), § 10(a), effective September 1, 2003.

Sec. 502.256. Fee: Road Tractor.

The fee for a registration year for registration of a road tractor is the fee prescribed by weight as certified by a public weigher or a license and weight inspector of the Department of Public Safety under Section 502.252 or 502.253, as applicable.

Sec. 502.257. Former Prisoners of War [Repealed].

Repealed by Acts 2003, 78th Leg., ch. 1320 (H.B. 2971), § 10(a), effective September 1, 2003.

Sec. 502.258. Members or Former Members of United States Armed Forces [Repealed].

Repealed by Acts 2003, 78th Leg., ch. 1320 (H.B. 2971), § 10(a), effective September 1, 2003.

Sec. 502.2585. Persons Retired from Service in Merchant Marine of the United States [Repealed].

Repealed by Acts 2003, 78th Leg., ch. 1320 (H.B. 2971), § 10(a), effective September 1, 2003.

Sec. 502.259. Pearl Harbor Survivors [Repealed].

Repealed by Acts 2003, 78th Leg., ch. 1320 (H.B. 2971), § 10(a), effective September 1, 2003.

Sec. 502.260. Purple Heart Recipients [Repealed].

Repealed by Acts 2003, 78th Leg., ch. 1320 (H.B. 2971), § 10(a), effective September 1, 2003.

Sec. 502.261. Members of United States Armed Forces Auxiliaries [Repealed].

Repealed by Acts 2003, 78th Leg., ch. 1320 (H.B. 2971), § 10(a), effective September 1, 2003.

Sec. 502.262. World War II Veterans [Repealed].

Repealed by Acts 2003, 78th Leg., ch. 1320 (H.B. 2971), § 10(a), effective September 1, 2003.

Sec. 502.263. Korean Conflict Veterans [Repealed].

Repealed by Acts 2003, 78th Leg., ch. 1320 (H.B. 2971), § 10(a), effective September 1, 2003.

Sec. 502.264. Vietnam Veterans [Repealed].

Repealed by Acts 2003, 78th Leg., ch. 1320 (H.B. 2971), § 10(a), effective September 1, 2003.

Sec. 502.265. Desert Shield or Desert Storm Veterans [Repealed].

Repealed by Acts 2003, 78th Leg., ch. 1320 (H.B. 2971), § 10(a), effective September 1, 2003.

Sec. 502.266. Surviving Spouses of Certain Military Veterans [Repealed].

Repealed by Acts 2003, 78th Leg., ch. 1320 (H.B. 2971), § 10(a), effective September 1, 2003.

Sec. 502.2661. Gold Star Mothers [Repealed].

Repealed by Acts 2003, 78th Leg., ch. 1320 (H.B. 2971), § 10(a), effective September 1, 2003.

Sec. 502.2663. New Millenium License Plates [Repealed].

Repealed by Acts 2003, 78th Leg., ch. 1320 (H.B. 2971), § 10(a), effective September 1, 2003.

Sec. 502.267. Honorary Consuls [Repealed].

Repealed by Acts 2003, 78th Leg., ch. 1320 (H.B. 2971), § 10(a), effective September 1, 2003.

Sec. 502.268. Volunteer Firefighters [Repealed].

Repealed by Acts 2003, 78th Leg., ch. 1320 (H.B. 2971), § 10(a), effective September 1, 2003.

Sec. 502.269. Texas Capitol License Plates [Repealed].

Repealed by Acts 2003, 78th Leg., ch. 1320 (H.B. 2971), § 10(a), effective September 1, 2003.

Sec. 502.270. Collegiate License Plates [Repealed].

Repealed by Acts 2003, 78th Leg., ch. 1320 (H.B. 2971), § 10(a), effective September 1, 2003.

Sec. 502.2703. Professional Sports Team License Plates [Repealed].

Repealed by Acts 2003, 78th Leg., ch. 1320 (H.B. 2971), § 10(a), effective September 1, 2003.

Sec. 502.2704. United States Olympic Committee License Plates [Repealed].

Repealed by Acts 2003, 78th Leg., ch. 1320 (H.B. 2971), § 10(a), effective September 1, 2003.

Sec. 502.271. Texas Aerospace and Aviation License Plates [Repealed].

Repealed by Acts 2011, 82nd Leg., ch. 1296 (H.B. 2357), § 247(4), effective January 1, 2012.

Sec. 502.272. Texas Commission on the Arts License Plates [Repealed].

Repealed by Acts 2003, 78th Leg., ch. 1320 (H.B. 2971), § 10(a), effective September 1, 2003.

Sec. 502.2721. Texas Commission on Alcohol and Drug Abuse License Plates [Repealed].

Repealed by Acts 2003, 78th Leg., ch. 1320 (H.B. 2971), § 10(a), effective September 1, 2003.

Sec. 502.2722. Texas Commission for the Deaf and Hard of Hearing License Plates [Repealed].

Repealed by Acts 2003, 78th Leg., ch. 1320 (H.B. 2971), § 10(a), effective September 1, 2003.

Sec. 502.273. Private Nonprofit Organizations [Repealed].

Repealed by Acts 2003, 78th Leg., ch. 1320 (H.B. 2971), § 10(a), effective September 1, 2003.

Sec. 502.2731. Keep Texas Beautiful License Plates [Repealed].

Repealed by Acts 2003, 78th Leg., ch. 1320 (H.B. 2971), § 10(a), effective September 1, 2003.

Sec. 502.2732. Big Bend National Park License Plates [Repealed].

Repealed by Acts 2003, 78th Leg., ch. 1320 (H.B. 2971), § 10(a), effective September 1, 2003.

Sec. 502.2733. Texas. It's Like a Whole Other Country License Plates [Repealed].

Repealed by Acts 2003, 78th Leg., ch. 1320 (H.B. 2971), § 10(a), effective September 1, 2003.

Sec. 502.2734. Conservation License Plates [Repealed].

Repealed by Acts 2003, 78th Leg., ch. 1320 (H.B. 2971), § 10(a), effective September 1, 2003.

Sec. 502.2735. Texans Conquer Cancer License Plates [Repealed].

Repealed by Acts 2003, 78th Leg., ch. 1320 (H.B. 2971), § 10(a), effective September 1, 2003.

Sec. 502.274. Classic Motor Vehicles [Repealed].

Repealed by Acts 2003, 78th Leg., ch. 1320 (H.B. 2971), § 10(a), effective September 1, 2003.

Sec. 502.275. Certain Exhibition Vehicles; Offense [Repealed].

Repealed by Acts 2003, 78th Leg., ch. 1320 (H.B. 2971), § 10(a), effective September 1, 2003.

Sec. 502.276. Certain Farm Vehicles and Drilling and Construction Equipment [Repealed].

Repealed by Acts 2003, 78th Leg., ch. 1320 (H.B. 2971), § 10(a), effective September 1, 2003.

Sec. 502.2761. Texas Agricultural Products License Plates [Repealed].

Repealed by Acts 2003, 78th Leg., ch. 1320 (H.B. 2971), § 10(a), effective September 1, 2003.

Sec. 502.277. Cotton Vehicles [Repealed].

Repealed by Acts 2003, 78th Leg., ch. 1320 (H.B. 2971), § 10(a), effective September 1, 2003.

Sec. 502.278. Certain Soil Conservation Equipment [Repealed].

Repealed by Acts 2003, 78th Leg., ch. 1320 (H.B. 2971), § 10(a), effective September 1, 2003.

Sec. 502.279. Certain Log-Loader Vehicles [Repealed].

Repealed by Acts 2003, 78th Leg., ch. 1320 (H.B. 2971), § 10(a), effective September 1, 2003.

Sec. 502.280. Forestry Vehicles [Repealed].

Repealed by Acts 2003, 78th Leg., ch. 1320 (H.B. 2971), § 10(a), effective September 1, 2003.

Sec. 502.281. Tow Trucks [Repealed].

Repealed by Acts 2003, 78th Leg., ch. 1320 (H.B. 2971), § 10(a), effective September 1, 2003.

Sec. 502.282. Vehicles Carrying Mobile Amateur Radio Equipment [Repealed].

Repealed by Acts 2003, 78th Leg., ch. 1320 (H.B. 2971), § 10(a), effective September 1, 2003.

Sec. 502.283. Parade Vehicles Owned by Nonprofit Service Organizations [Repealed].

Repealed by Acts 2003, 78th Leg., ch. 1320 (H.B. 2971), § 10(a), effective September 1, 2003.

Sec. 502.284. Golf Carts [Repealed].

Repealed by Acts 2003, 78th Leg., ch. 1320 (H.B. 2971), § 10(a), effective September 1, 2003.

Sec. 502.285. Manufactured Housing [Repealed].

Repealed by Acts 2003, 78th Leg., ch. 1320 (H.B. 2971), § 10(a), effective September 1, 2003.

Sec. 502.286. Power Sweepers [Repealed].

Repealed by Acts 2003, 78th Leg., ch. 1320 (H.B. 2971), § 10(a), effective September 1, 2003.

Sec. 502.2861. [Motorized Mobility Device] [Repealed].

Repealed by Acts 2003, 78th Leg., ch. 1320 (H.B. 2971), § 10(a), effective September 1, 2003.

Sec. 502.2862. Electric Personal Assistive Mobility Devices [Repealed].

Repealed by Acts 2011, 82nd Leg., ch. 1296 (H.B. 2357), § 247(4), effective January 1, 2012.

Sec. 502.287. Vehicles Operated on Public Highway Separating Real Property Under Vehicle Owner's Control [Repealed].

Repealed by Acts 2003, 78th Leg., ch. 1320 (H.B. 2971), § 10(a), effective September 1, 2003.

Sec. 502.288. Vehicles Operated by Certain Nonresidents [Repealed].

Repealed by Acts 2003, 78th Leg., ch. 1320 (H.B. 2971), § 10(a), effective September 1, 2003.

Sec. 502.289. Peace Officers Wounded or Killed in Line of Duty [Repealed].

Repealed by Acts 2003, 78th Leg., ch. 1320 (H.B. 2971), § 10(a), effective September 1, 2003.

Sec. 502.290. Foreign Organization Vehicles [Repealed].

Repealed by Acts 2003, 78th Leg., ch. 1320 (H.B. 2971), § 10(a), effective September 1, 2003.

Sec. 502.291. Animal Friendly License Plates [Repealed].

Repealed by Acts 2003, 78th Leg., ch. 1320 (H.B. 2971), § 10(a), effective September 1, 2003.

Sec. 502.292. Read to Succeed [Repealed].

Repealed by Acts 2003, 78th Leg., ch. 1320 (H.B. 2971), § 10(a), effective September 1, 2003.

Sec. 502.2921. Volunteer Advocate Program License Plates [Repealed].

Repealed by Acts 2003, 78th Leg., ch. 1320 (H.B. 2971), § 10(a), effective September 1, 2003.

Sec. 502.2922. Special Olympics Texas License Plates [Repealed].

Repealed by Acts 2003, 78th Leg., ch. 1320 (H.B. 2971), § 10(a), effective September 1, 2003.

Sec. 502.293. Houston Livestock Show and Rodeo License Plates [Repealed].

Repealed by Acts 2003, 78th Leg., ch. 1320 (H.B. 2971), § 10(a), effective September 1, 2003.

Sec. 502.2931. Girl Scout License Plates [Repealed].

Repealed by Acts 2003, 78th Leg., ch. 1320 (H.B. 2971), § 10(a), effective September 1, 2003.

Sec. 502.2932. TexasYMCA [Repealed].

Repealed by Acts 2003, 78th Leg., ch. 1320 (H.B. 2971), § 10(a), effective September 1, 2003.

Sec. 502.2933. Texas Young Lawyers Association License Plates [Repealed].

Repealed by Acts 2003, 78th Leg., ch. 1320 (H.B. 2971), § 10(a), effective September 1, 2003.

Sec. 502.294. Municipal and Private Buses [Repealed].

Repealed by Acts 2003, 78th Leg., ch. 1320 (H.B. 2971), § 10(a), effective September 1, 2003.

Sec. 502.295. State Officials [Repealed].

Repealed by Acts 2003, 78th Leg., ch. 1320 (H.B. 2971), § 10(a), effective September 1, 2003.

Sec. 502.2951. County Judges [Repealed].

Repealed by Acts 2003, 78th Leg., ch. 1320 (H.B. 2971), § 10(a), effective September 1, 2003.

Sec. 502.296. Members of Congress [Repealed].

Repealed by Acts 2003, 78th Leg., ch. 1320 (H.B. 2971), § 10(a), effective September 1, 2003.

Sec. 502.297. State and Federal Judges [Repealed].

Repealed by Acts 2003, 78th Leg., ch. 1320 (H.B. 2971), § 10(a), effective September 1, 2003.

Sec. 502.2971. Federal Administrative Law Judges [Repealed].

Repealed by Acts 2011, 82nd Leg., ch. 1296 (H.B. 2357), § 247(4), effective January 1, 2012.

Sec. 502.298. 100th Football Season of Stephen F. Austin High School [Repealed].

Repealed by Acts 2003, 78th Leg., ch. 1320 (H.B. 2971), § 10(a), effective September 1, 2003.

Sec. 502.299. Texas Citrus Industry [Repealed].

Repealed by Acts 2003, 78th Leg., ch. 1320 (H.B. 2971), § 10(a), effective September 1, 2003.

Sec. 502.303. Waterfowl and Wetland Conservation License Plates [Repealed].

Repealed by Acts 2003, 78th Leg., ch. 1320 (H.B. 2971), § 10(a), effective September 1, 2003.

SUBCHAPTER G
ADDITIONAL FEES

Sec. 502.351. Farm Vehicles: Excess Weight [Renumbered].

Renumbered to Tex. Transp. Code § 502.434 by Acts 2011, 82nd Leg., ch. 1296 (H.B. 2357), § 144, effective January 1, 2012.

Sec. 502.352. Foreign Commercial Vehicles [Renumbered].

Renumbered to Tex. Transp. Code § 502.094 by Acts 2011, 82nd Leg., ch. 1296 (H.B. 2357), § 97, effective January 1, 2012.

Sec. 502.353. Foreign Commercial Vehicles; Annual Permits; Offense [Renumbered].

Renumbered to Tex. Transp. Code § 502.093 by Acts 2011, 82nd Leg., ch. 1296 (H.B. 2357), § 96, effective January 1, 2012.

Sec. 502.354. Single or 30-Day Trip Permits; Offense [Renumbered].

Renumbered to Tex. Transp. Code § 502.095 by Acts 2011, 82nd Leg., ch. 1296 (H.B. 2357), § 98, effective January 1, 2012.

Sec. 502.355. Nonresident-Owned Vehicles Used to Transport Farm Products; Offense [Renumbered].

Renumbered to Tex. Transp. Code § 502.092 by Acts 2011, 82nd Leg., ch. 1296 (H.B. 2357), § 95, effective January 1, 2012.

Sec. 502.356. Automated Registration and Titling System.

(a) In addition to other registration fees for a license plate or set of license plates or other device used as the registration insignia, the board by rule shall adopt a fee of not less than 50 cents and not more than $1. The fee shall be collected and deposited into a subaccount in the Texas Department of Motor Vehicles fund.

(b) The department may use money collected under this section to provide for or enhance the automation of and the necessary infrastructure for:

(1) on-premises and off-premises registration and permitting, including permitting under Subtitle E;

(2) services related to the titling of vehicles; and

(3) licensing and enforcement procedures.

Sec. 502.357. Financial Responsibility Programs.

(a) In addition to other fees imposed for registration of a motor vehicle, at the time of application for registration or renewal of registration of a motor vehicle for which the owner is required to submit evidence of financial responsibility under Section 502.046, the applicant shall pay a fee of $1. In addition to other fees imposed for registration of a motor vehicle, at the time of application for registration of a motor vehicle that is subject to Section 501.0234, the applicant shall pay a fee of $1. Fees collected under this section shall be remitted weekly to the department.

(b) Fees collected under this section shall be deposited to the credit of the state highway fund except that the comptroller shall provide for a portion of the fees to be deposited first to the credit of a special fund in the state treasury outside the general revenue fund to be known as the TexasSure Fund in a total amount that is necessary to cover the total amount appropriated to the Texas Department of Insurance from that fund and for the remaining fees to be deposited to the state highway fund. Subject to appropriations, the money deposited to the credit of the state highway fund under this section may be used by the Department of Public Safety to:

(1) support the Department of Public Safety's reengineering of the driver's license system to

provide for the issuance by the Department of Public Safety of a driver's license or personal identification certificate, to include use of image comparison technology; and

(2) make lease payments to the master lease purchase program for the financing of the driver's license reengineering project.

(c) Subject to appropriation, fees collected under this section may be used by the Department of Public Safety, the Texas Department of Insurance, the Department of Information Resources, and the department to carry out Subchapter N, Chapter 601.

(d) The Department of Public Safety, the Texas Department of Insurance, the Department of Information Resources, and the department shall jointly adopt rules and develop forms necessary to administer this section.

Sec. 502.358. [Contingent Expiration – See editor's note] Texas Emissions Reduction Plan Surcharge.

(a) In addition to the registration fees charged under Section 502.255, a surcharge is imposed on the registration of a truck-tractor or commercial motor vehicle under that section in an amount equal to 10 percent of the total fees due for the registration of the truck-tractor or commercial motor vehicle under that section.

(b) The county tax assessor-collector shall remit the surcharge collected under this section to the comptroller at the time and in the manner prescribed by the comptroller for deposit in the Texas emissions reduction plan fund.

(c) This section expires on the last day of the state fiscal biennium during which the Texas Commission on Environmental Quality publishes in the Texas Register the notice required by Section 382.037, Health and Safety Code.

Sec. 502.359. Additional Fee for Certain Vehicles Using Diesel Motor.

(a) The registration fee under this chapter for a motor vehicle other than a passenger car, a truck with a gross vehicle weight of 18,000 pounds or less, or a vehicle registered in combination under Section 502.255 is increased by 11 percent if the vehicle has a diesel motor.

(b) The registration receipt for a motor vehicle, other than a passenger car or a truck with a gross vehicle weight of 18,000 pounds or less, must show that the vehicle has a diesel motor.

(c) The department may adopt rules to administer this section.

SUBCHAPTER H OPTIONAL FEES

Sec. 502.401. Optional County Fee for Road and Bridge Fund.

(a) The commissioners court of a county by order may impose an additional fee, not to exceed $10, for registering a vehicle in the county.

(b) A vehicle that may be registered under this chapter without payment of a registration fee may be registered in a county imposing a fee under this section without payment of the additional fee.

(c) A fee imposed under this section may take effect only on January 1 of a year. The county must adopt the order and notify the department not later than September 1 of the year preceding the year in which the fee takes effect.

(d) A fee imposed under this section may be removed. The removal may take effect only on January 1 of a year. A county may remove the fee only by:

(1) rescinding the order imposing the fee; and

(2) notifying the department not later than September 1 of the year preceding the year in which the removal takes effect.

(e) The county assessor-collector of a county imposing a fee under this section shall collect the additional fee for a vehicle when other fees imposed under this chapter are collected.

(f) The department shall collect the additional fee on a vehicle that is owned by a resident of a county imposing a fee under this section that must be registered directly with the department. The department shall send all fees collected for a county under this subsection to the county treasurer to be credited to the county road and bridge fund.

(g) The department shall adopt rules necessary to administer registration for a vehicle being registered in a county imposing a fee under this section.

Sec. 502.402. Optional County Fee for Transportation Projects.

(a) This section applies only to:

(1) a county that:

(A) borders the United Mexican States; and

(B) has a population of more than 250,000;

(2) a county that has a population of more than 1.5 million that is coterminous with a regional mobility authority; and

(3) a county that has a population of more than 190,000 and not more than 1.5 million that is coterminous with a regional mobility authority.

(b) The commissioners court of a county by order may impose an additional fee for a vehicle registered in the county. Except as provided by Subsection (b-1), the fee may not exceed $10. In a county described by Subsection (a)(3), the fee must be approved by a majority of the qualified voters of the county voting on the issue at a referendum election, which the commissioners court may order and hold for that purpose.

(b-1) The commissioners court of a county described by Subsection (a) with a population of less than 700,000 may increase the additional fee to an amount that does not exceed $20 if approved by a majority of the qualified voters of the county voting on the issue at a referendum election, which the commissioners court may order and hold for that purpose.

(c) A vehicle that may be registered under this chapter without payment of a registration fee may be registered under this section without payment of the additional fee.

(d) A fee imposed under this section may take effect and be removed in accordance with the requirements of Section 502.401.

(e) The additional fee shall be collected for a vehicle when other fees imposed under this chapter are collected. The fee revenue collected shall be sent to a regional mobility authority located in the county to fund long-term transportation projects in the county that are consistent with the purposes specified by Section 7-a, Article VIII, Texas Constitution.

(f) The department shall adopt rules necessary to administer registration for a vehicle being registered in a county imposing a fee under this section.

Sec. 502.403. Optional County Fee for Child Safety.

(a) The commissioners court of a county that has a population greater than 1.3 million and in which a municipality with a population of more than one million is primarily located may impose by order an additional fee of not less than 50 cents or more than $1.50 for a vehicle registered in the county. The commissioners court of any other county may impose by order an additional fee of not more than $1.50 for registering a vehicle in the county.

(b) A vehicle that may be registered under this chapter without payment of a registration fee may be registered without payment of the additional fee.

(c) A fee imposed under this section may take effect and be removed in accordance with the provisions of Section 502.401.

(d) The additional fee shall be collected for a vehicle when other fees imposed under this chapter are collected.

(e) A county imposing a fee under this section may deduct for administrative costs an amount of not more than 10 percent of the revenue it receives from the fee. The county may also deduct from the fee revenue an amount proportional to the percentage of county residents who live in unincorporated areas of the county. After making the deductions provided for by this subsection, the county shall send the remainder of the fee revenue to the municipalities in the county according to their population.

(f) A municipality with a population greater than 850,000 shall deposit revenue from a fee imposed under this subsection to the credit of the child safety trust fund created under Section 106.001, Local Government Code. A municipality with a population less than 850,000 shall use revenue from a fee imposed under this section in accordance with Article 102.014(g), Code of Criminal Procedure.

(g) After deducting administrative costs, a county may use revenue from a fee imposed under this section only for a purpose permitted by Article 102.014(g), Code of Criminal Procedure.

Sec. 502.404. Voluntary Assessment for Texas Agricultural Finance Authority.

(a) When a person registers a commercial motor vehicle under Section 502.433, the person shall pay a voluntary assessment of $5.

(b) The county assessor-collector shall send an assessment collected under this section to the comptroller, at the time and in the manner prescribed by the Texas Agricultural Finance Authority, for deposit in the Texas agricultural fund.

(c) The Texas Agricultural Finance Authority shall prescribe procedures under which an assessment collected under this section may be refunded. The county assessor-collector of the county in which an assessment is collected shall:

(1) implement the refund procedures; and

(2) provide notice of those procedures to a person paying an assessment at the time of payment.

Sec. 502.405. Voluntary Contribution to Donor Registry.

(a) The department shall provide to each county assessor-collector the educational materials for prospective donors provided under Section 502.189.

(b) When a person applies for the registration or renewal of registration of a motor vehicle, the person may elect to contribute $1 or more to the nonprofit organization administering the Glenda Dawson Donate Life-Texas Registry established under Chapter 692A, Health and Safety Code. The department shall remit any contribution paid under this subsection to the comptroller for deposit to the credit of the Glenda Dawson Donate Life-Texas Registry fund created under Section 692A.020, Health and Safety Code. Money received under this subsection by the organization may be used only for the purposes described by Section 692A.020(i), Health and Safety Code. The organization shall submit an annual report to the legislature and the comptroller that includes the total dollar amount of money received by the organization under this subsection. If a person makes a contribution under this section and does not pay the full amount of the registration fee, the department may credit all or a portion of the contribution to the person's registration fee. The department shall:

(1) include space on each motor vehicle registration renewal notice, on the page that states the total fee for registration renewal, that allows a person renewing a registration to voluntarily contribute $1 or more to the organization;

(2) provide an opportunity for a person to contribute $1 or more to the organization during the registration renewal process on the department's Internet website; and

(3) provide an opportunity to contribute $1 or more to the organization in any registration renewal system that succeeds the registration renewal system in place on September 1, 2015.

(c) Three percent of all money collected under this section shall be credited to the Texas Department of Motor Vehicles fund and may be appropriated only to the department to administer this section.

Sec. 502.406. Operation of All-Terrain Vehicle Without Sticker [Repealed].

Repealed by Acts 2007, 80th Leg., ch. 1280 (H.B. 3849), § 6, effective June 15, 2007.

Sec. 502.407. Operation of Vehicle with Expired License Plate. [Effective until March 1, 2022]

(a) A person commits an offense if, after the fifth working day after the date the registration for the vehicle expires:

(1) the person operates on a public highway during a registration period a motor vehicle, trailer, or semitrailer that has attached to it a license plate for the preceding period; and

(2) the license plate has not been validated by the attachment of a registration insignia for the registration period in effect.

(b) A justice of the peace or municipal court judge having jurisdiction of the offense may:

(1) dismiss a charge of driving with an expired motor vehicle registration if the defendant:

(A) remedies the defect not later than the 20th working day after the date of the offense or before the defendant's first court appearance date, whichever is later; and

(B) establishes that the fee prescribed by Section 502.045 has been paid; and

(2) assess a reimbursement fee not to exceed $20 when the charge is dismissed.

(c) It is a defense to prosecution under this section that at the time of the offense:

(1) the office of the county assessor-collector for the county in which the owner of the vehicle resided was closed for a protracted period of time in accordance with Section 502.040(b)(2); and

(2) the vehicle's registration was expired for 30 working days or less.

Sec. 502.407. Operation of Vehicle with Expired License Plate. [Effective March 1, 2022]

(a) A person commits an offense if, after the fifth working day after the date the registration for the vehicle expires:

(1) the person operates on a public highway during a registration period a motor vehicle, trailer, or semitrailer that has attached to it a license plate for the preceding period; and

(2) the license plate has not been validated by the attachment of a registration insignia for the registration period in effect.

(b) A justice of the peace or municipal court judge having jurisdiction of the offense may:

(1) dismiss a charge of driving with an expired motor vehicle registration if the defendant:

(A) remedies the defect not later than the 20th working day after the date of the offense or before the defendant's first court appearance date, whichever is later; and

(B) establishes that the fee prescribed by Section 502.045 has been paid; and

(2) assess a reimbursement fee not to exceed $20 when the charge is dismissed.

(c) It is a defense to prosecution under this section that at the time of the offense:

(1) the office of the county assessor-collector for the county in which the owner of the vehicle resided was closed for a protracted period of time in accordance with department rules; and

(2) the vehicle's registration was expired for 30 working days or less.

Sec. 502.408. Operation of Vehicle with Wrong License Plate [Renumbered].

Renumbered to Tex. Transp. Code § 504.944 by Acts 2011, 82nd Leg., ch. 1296 (H.B. 2357), § 222, effective January 1, 2012.

Sec. 502.409. Wrong, Fictitious, Altered, or Obscured License Plate [Renumbered].

Renumbered to Tex. Transp. Code § 502.475 by Acts 2011, 82nd Leg., ch. 1296 (H.B. 2357), § 159, effective January 1, 2012.

Sec. 502.410. Falsification or Forgery. [Effective until January 1, 2022]

(a) A person commits an offense if the person knowingly provides false or incorrect information or without legal authority signs the name of another person on a statement or application filed or given as required by this chapter.

(b) Subsection (a) does not apply to a statement or application filed or given under Section 502.060, 502.092, 502.093, 502.094, 502.095, 504.201, 504.508, or 504.515.

(c) An offense under this section is a felony of the third degree.

Sec. 502.410. Falsification or Forgery. [Effective January 1, 2022]

(a) A person commits an offense if the person knowingly provides false or incorrect information or without legal authority signs the name of another person on a statement or application filed or given as required by this chapter.

(b) Subsection (a) does not apply to a statement or application filed or given under Section 502.060, 502.092, 502.093, 502.094, 502.095, 504.201, 504.202(b-1), 504.508, or 504.515.

(c) An offense under this section is a felony of the third degree.

Sec. 502.411. Bribery of County Officer or Agent.

(a) A person commits an offense if the person directly or indirectly agrees with the commissioners court of a county or an officer or agent of the commissioners court or county that the person will register or cause to be registered a motor vehicle, trailer, or semitrailer in that county in consideration of:

(1) the use by the county of the funds derived from the registration in the purchase of property; or

(2) an act to be performed by the commissioners court or an agent or officer of the commissioners court or the county.

(b) The registration of each separate vehicle in violation of Subsection (a) is a separate offense. The agreement or conspiracy to register is a separate offense.

(c) A person who makes or seeks to make an agreement prohibited by Subsection (a) shall be restrained by injunction on application by the district or county attorney of the county in which the vehicle is registered or the attorney general.

(d) An offense under this section is punishable in the same manner as an offense under Section 36.02, Penal Code.

Sec. 502.412. Operation of Vehicle at Weight Greater Than Stated in Registration Application.

(a) A person commits an offense if the person operates, or permits to be operated, a motor vehicle registered under this chapter that has a weight greater than that stated in the person's application for registration. Each use of the vehicle is a separate offense.

(b) Venue for a prosecution under this section is in any county in which the motor vehicle is operated with a gross weight greater than that stated in the person's application for registration.

(c) [Repealed by Acts 2011, 82nd Leg., ch. 1296 (H.B. 2357), § 247(7), effective January 1, 2012.]

Sec. 502.413. Voluntary Contribution to Special Olympics Texas Fund.

(a) When a person registers or renews the registration of a motor vehicle under this chapter, the person may contribute any amount to the Special Olympics Texas fund under Subsection (f).

(b) The department shall provide, in a conspicuous manner, an opportunity to contribute to the Special Olympics Texas fund in any registration renewal system used by the department.

(c) If a person makes a contribution under this section and does not pay the full amount of a registration fee, the county assessor-collector may credit all or a portion of the contribution to the person's registration fee.

(d) The county assessor-collector shall send any contribution made under this section to the comptroller for deposit to the Special Olympics Texas fund before the 31st day after the date the contribution is made.

(e) The department shall consult with the Department of Aging and Disability Services in performing the department's duties under this section.

(f) The Special Olympics Texas fund is created as a trust fund outside the state treasury to be held by the comptroller and administered by the Department of Aging and Disability Services as trustee on behalf of Special Olympics Texas. The fund is composed of money deposited to the credit of the fund under this section. Money in the fund shall be disbursed at least monthly, without appropriation, to Special Olympics Texas to provide training and athletic competitions for persons with mental illness and intellectual disabilities.

Sec. 502.414. Voluntary Contribution for Evidence Testing Grant Program.

(a) When a person registers or renews the registration of a motor vehicle under this chapter, the person may contribute any amount to the evidence testing grant program established under Section 772.00715, Government Code.

(b) The department shall provide, in a conspicuous manner, an opportunity to contribute to the evidence testing grant program in any registration renewal system used by the department.

(c) If a person makes a contribution under this section and does not pay the full amount of a registration fee, the county assessor-collector may credit all or a portion of the contribution to the person's registration fee.

(d) The county assessor-collector shall send any contribution made under this section to the comptroller for deposit to the credit of the evidence testing account established under Section 772.00716, Government Code, at least once every three months. Before sending the money to the comptroller, the department may deduct money equal to the amount of reasonable expenses for administering this section.

Sec. 502.415. Voluntary Contribution to Ending Homelessness Fund.

(a) When a person registers or renews the registration of a motor vehicle under this chapter, the person may contribute any amount to the Ending Homelessness fund under Subsection (f).

(b) The department shall provide, in a conspicuous manner, an opportunity to contribute to the Ending Homelessness fund in any registration renewal system used by the department.

(c) If a person makes a contribution under this section and does not pay the full amount of a registration fee, the county assessor-collector may credit all or a portion of the contribution to the person's registration fee.

(d) The county assessor-collector shall send any contribution made under this section to the comptroller for deposit to the Ending Homelessness fund before the 31st day after the date the contribution is made.

(e) The department shall consult with the Texas Department of Housing and Community Affairs in performing the department's duties under this section.

(f) The Ending Homelessness fund is created as a trust fund outside the state treasury to be held by the comptroller and administered by the Texas Department of Housing and Community Affairs as trustee. The fund is composed of money deposited to the credit of the fund under this section. Money in the fund shall be used to provide grants to counties and municipalities to combat homelessness.

(g) The Texas Department of Housing and Community Affairs shall adopt rules governing application for grants from the Ending Homelessness fund and the issuance of those grants.

Sec. 502.416. Voluntary Contribution for Trafficked Persons Program Account.

(a) When a person registers or renews the registration of a motor vehicle under this chapter, the department shall, in a conspicuous manner, direct that person to the opportunity to donate to the trafficked persons program account established under Section 50.0153, Health and Safety Code, through the state's electronic Internet portal described by Section 2054.252(h), Government Code.

(b) If a person makes a contribution under this section and does not pay the full amount of a registration fee, the county assessor-collector may credit all or a portion of the contribution to the person's registration fee.

(c) The department may deduct from the donations made under this section an amount equal to the department's reasonable expenses associated with administering this section.

SUBCHAPTER I ALTERNATE REGISTRATION FEES

Sec. 502.431. Fee: Motor Vehicle Used Exclusively to Transport and Spread Fertilizer.

The fee for a registration year for registration of a motor vehicle designed or modified and used exclusively to transport to the field and spread fertilizer, including agricultural limestone, is $75.

Sec. 502.432. Vehicle Transporting Seasonal Agricultural Products.

(a) The department shall provide for a monthly registration period for a truck-tractor or a commercial motor vehicle:

(1) that is used exclusively to transport a seasonal agricultural product;

(2) that would otherwise be registered for a vehicle registration year; and

(3) for which the owner can show proof of payment of the heavy vehicle use tax or exemption.

(b) The department shall prescribe a registration receipt that is valid until the expiration of the designated registration period.

(c) The registration fee for a registration under this section is computed at a rate of one-twelfth the annual registration fee under Section 502.253, 502.255, or 502.433, as applicable, multiplied by the number of months in the registration period specified in the application for the registration, which may not be less than one month or longer than six months.

(d) For purposes of this section, "to transport a seasonal agricultural product" includes any transportation activity necessary for the production, harvest, or delivery of an agricultural product that is produced seasonally.

Transportation Code

Sec. 502.433. Fee: Commercial Farm Motor Vehicle.

(a) The registration fee for a commercial motor vehicle as a farm vehicle is 50 percent of the applicable fee under Section 502.252 or 502.253, as applicable, if the vehicle's owner will use the vehicle for commercial purposes only to transport:

(1) the person's own poultry, dairy, livestock, livestock products, timber in its natural state, or farm products to market or another place for sale or processing;

(2) laborers from their place of residence to the owner's farm or ranch; or

(3) without charge, materials, tools, equipment, or supplies from the place of purchase or storage to the owner's farm or ranch exclusively for the owner's use or for use on the farm or ranch.

(a-1) A commercial motor vehicle registration may not be issued or renewed under this section unless the vehicle's owner provides a registration number issued by the comptroller under Section 151.1551, Tax Code. The comptroller shall allow access to the online system established under Section 151.1551(l), Tax Code, to verify a registration number provided under this subsection.

(b) A commercial motor vehicle may be registered under this section despite its use for transporting without charge the owner or a member of the owner's family:

(1) to attend church or school;

(2) to visit a doctor for medical treatment or supplies;

(3) for other necessities of the home or family; or

(4) for the purpose of participating in equine activities or attending livestock shows, as defined by Section 87.001, Civil Practice and Remedies Code.

(c) Subsection (b) does not permit the use of a vehicle registered under this section in connection with gainful employment other than farming or ranching.

(d) The department shall provide distinguishing license plates for a vehicle registered under this section.

Sec. 502.434. Farm Vehicles: Excess Weight.

(a) The owner of a registered commercial motor vehicle, truck-tractor, trailer, or semitrailer may obtain a short-term permit to haul loads of a weight more than that for which the vehicle is registered by paying an additional fee before the additional weight is hauled to transport:

(1) the person's own seasonal agricultural products to market or another point for sale or processing;

(2) seasonal laborers from their place of residence to a farm or ranch; or

(3) materials, tools, equipment, or supplies, without charge, from the place of purchase or storage to a farm or ranch exclusively for use on the farm or ranch.

(a-1) A permit may not be issued under this section unless the vehicle's owner provides a registration number issued by the comptroller under Section 151.1551, Tax Code. The comptroller shall allow access to the online system established under Section 151.1551 (*l*), Tax Code, to verify a registration number provided under this subsection. This subsection does not apply to a permit issued to a retail dealer of tools or equipment that is transporting the tools or equipment from the place of purchase or storage to the customer's farm or ranch.

(b) A permit may not be issued under this section for a period that is less than one month or that:

(1) is greater than one year; or

(2) extends beyond the expiration of the registration year for the vehicle.

(c) A permit issued under this section for a quarter must be for a calendar quarter.

(d) The fee for a permit under this section is a percentage of the difference between the registration fee otherwise prescribed for the vehicle and the annual fee for the desired weight, as follows:

One month (30 consecutive days)	10 percent
One quarter	30 percent
Two quarters	60 percent
Three quarters	90 percent

(e) The department shall design, prescribe, and furnish a sticker, plate, or other means of indicating the additional weight and the registration period for each vehicle registered under this section.

Sec. 502.435. Certain Soil Conservation Equipment.

(a) The owner of a truck-tractor, semitrailer, or low-boy trailer used on a highway exclusively to transport the owner's soil conservation machinery or equipment used in clearing real property, terracing, or building farm ponds, levees, or ditches may register the vehicle for a fee equal to 50 percent of the fee otherwise prescribed by this chapter for the vehicle.

(b) An owner may register only one truck-tractor and only one semitrailer or low-boy trailer under this section.

(c) An owner must certify that the vehicle is to be used only as provided by Subsection (a).

(d) The registration receipt issued for a vehicle registered under this section must be carried in or on the vehicle and state the nature of the operation for which the vehicle may be used.

(e) A vehicle to which this section applies that is operated on a public highway in violation of this section is considered to be operated while unregistered and is immediately subject to the applicable registration fees and penalties prescribed by this chapter.

SUBCHAPTER J
REGISTRATIONS EXEMPT FROM FEES

Sec. 502.451. Exempt Vehicles.

(a) Before license plates are issued or delivered to the owner of a vehicle that is exempt by law from payment of registration fees, the department must approve the application for registration. The department may not approve an application if there is the appearance that:

(1) the vehicle was transferred to the owner or purported owner:

(A) for the sole purpose of evading the payment of registration fees; or

(B) in bad faith; or

(2) the vehicle is not being used in accordance with the exemption requirements.

(b) The department shall revoke the registration of a vehicle issued license plates under this section and may recall the plates if the vehicle is no longer:

(1) owned and operated by the person whose ownership of the vehicle qualified the vehicle for the exemption; or

(2) used in accordance with the exemption requirements.

(c) The department shall provide by rule for the issuance of specially designated license plates for vehicles that are exempt by law. Except as provided by Subsection (f), the license plates must bear the word "exempt."

(d) A license plate under Subsection (c) is not issued annually, but remains on the vehicle until:

(1) the registration is revoked as provided by Subsection (b); or

(2) the plate is lost, stolen, or mutilated.

(e) A person who operates on a public highway a vehicle after the registration has been revoked is liable for the penalties for failing to register a vehicle.

(f) The department shall provide by rule for the issuance of regularly designed license plates not bearing the word "exempt" for a vehicle that is exempt by law and that is:

(1) a law enforcement vehicle, if the agency certifies to the department that the vehicle will be dedicated to law enforcement activities;

(2) a vehicle exempt from inscription requirements under a rule adopted as provided by Section 721.003; or

(3) a vehicle exempt from inscription requirements under an order or ordinance adopted by a governing body of a municipality or commissioners court of a county as provided by Section 721.005, if the applicant presents a copy of the order or ordinance.

Sec. 502.452. Limitation on Issuance of Exempt License Plates; Seizure of Certain Vehicles.

(a) The department may not issue exempt license plates for a vehicle owned by the United States, this state, or a political subdivision of this state unless when application is made for registration of the vehicle, the person who under Section 502.453 has authority to certify to the department that the vehicle qualifies for registration under that section also certifies in writing to the department that there is printed on each side of the vehicle, in letters that

Transportation Code

are at least two inches high or in an emblem that is at least 100 square inches in size, the name of the agency, department, bureau, board, commission, or officer of the United States, this state, or the political subdivision of this state that has custody of the vehicle. The letters or emblem must be of a color sufficiently different from the body of the vehicle to be clearly legible from a distance of 100 feet.

(b) The department may not issue exempt license plates for a vehicle owned by a person other than the United States, this state, or a political subdivision of this state unless, when application is made for registration of the vehicle, the person who under Section 502.453 has authority to certify to the department that the vehicle qualifies for registration under that section also certifies in writing to the department that the name of the owner of the vehicle is printed on the vehicle in the manner prescribed by Subsection (a).

(c) A peace officer listed in Article 2.12, Code of Criminal Procedure, may seize a motor vehicle displaying exempt license plates if the vehicle is:

(1) operated on a public highway; and

(2) not identified in the manner prescribed by Subsection (a) or (b), unless the vehicle is covered by Subsection (f).

(d) A peace officer who seizes a motor vehicle under Subsection (c) may require that the vehicle be:

(1) moved to the nearest place of safety off the main-traveled part of the highway; or

(2) removed and placed in the nearest vehicle storage facility designated or maintained by the law enforcement agency that employs the peace officer.

(e) To obtain the release of the vehicle, in addition to any other requirement of law, the owner of a vehicle seized under Subsection (c) must:

(1) remedy the defect by identifying the vehicle as required by Subsection (a) or (b); or

(2) agree in writing with the law enforcement agency to provide evidence to that agency, before the 10th day after the date the vehicle is released, that the defect has been remedied by identifying the vehicle as required by Subsection (a) or (b).

(f) Subsections (a) and (b) do not apply to a vehicle to which Section 502.451(f) applies.

(g) For purposes of this section, an exempt license plate is a license plate issued by the department that is plainly marked with the word "exempt."

Sec. 502.453. Government-Owned Vehicles; Public School Buses; Fire-Fighting Vehicles; County Marine Law Enforcement Vehicles; U.S. Coast Guard Auxiliary Vehicles.

(a) The owner of a motor vehicle, trailer, or semitrailer may apply for registration under Section 502.0025 or 502.451 and is exempt from the payment of a registration fee under this chapter if the vehicle is:

(1) owned by and used exclusively in the service of:

(A) the United States;

(B) this state;

(C) a county, municipality, or school district in this state; or

(D) an open-enrollment charter school;

(2) owned by a commercial transportation company and used exclusively to provide public school transportation services to a school district under Section 34.008, Education Code;

(3) designed and used exclusively for fire fighting;

(4) owned by a volunteer fire department and used exclusively in the conduct of department business;

(5) privately owned and used by a volunteer exclusively in county marine law enforcement activities, including rescue operations, under the direction of the sheriff's department;

(6) used by law enforcement under an alias for covert criminal investigations; or

(7) owned by units of the United States Coast Guard Auxiliary headquartered in Texas and used exclusively for conduct of United States Coast Guard or Coast Guard Auxiliary business and operations, including search and rescue, emergency communications, and disaster operations.

(b) An application for registration under this section or Section 502.0025 must be made by a person having the authority to certify that the vehicle meets the exemption requirements prescribed by Subsection (a). An application for registration under this section of a fire-fighting vehicle described by Subsection (a)(3) must include a reasonable description of the vehicle and of any fire-fighting equipment mounted on the vehicle. An application for registration under this section of a vehicle described by Subsection (a)(5) must include a statement signed by a person having the authority to act for a sheriff's department that the vehicle is used exclusively in marine law enforcement activities under the direction of the sheriff's department. An application for registration under this section of a vehicle described by Subsection (a)(7) must include a statement signed by a person having authority to act for the United States Coast Guard Auxiliary that the vehicle or trailer is used exclusively in fulfillment of an authorized mission of the United States Coast Guard or Coast Guard Auxiliary, including search and rescue, patrol, emergency communications, or disaster operations.

Sec. 502.454. Vehicles Used by Nonprofit Disaster Relief Organizations.

(a) The owner of a commercial motor vehicle, trailer, or semitrailer may apply for registration under Section 502.451 and is exempt from the payment of the registration fee that would otherwise be required by this chapter if the vehicle is owned and used exclusively for emergencies by a nonprofit disaster relief organization.

(b) An application for registration under this section must include:

(1) a statement by the owner of the vehicle that the vehicle is used exclusively for emergencies and has not been used for any other purpose;

(2) a statement signed by an officer of the nonprofit disaster relief organization that the vehicle has not been used for any purpose other than emergencies and qualifies for registration under this section; and

(3) a reasonable description of the vehicle and the emergency equipment included in the vehicle.

(c) An applicant for registration under this section must pay a fee of $5.

(d) A commercial motor vehicle registered under this section must display the name of the organization that owns it on each front door.

(e) A vehicle registered under this section must display at all times an appropriate license plate showing the vehicle's status.

(f) A vehicle registered under this section that is used for any purpose other than an emergency may not again be registered under this section.

Sec. 502.455. Trailers and Semitrailers Owned by Religious Organizations.

(a) A trailer or semitrailer may be registered without payment if the trailer or semitrailer is:

(1) owned by an organization that qualifies as a religious organization under Section 11.20, Tax Code; and

(2) used primarily for the purpose of transporting property in connection with the charitable activities and functions of the organization.

(b) An application for registration under this section must include a statement signed by an officer of the religious organization stating that the trailer or semitrailer qualifies for registration under this section.

Sec. 502.456. Emergency Services Vehicles.

(a) A vehicle may be registered without payment if:

(1) the vehicle is owned or leased by an emergency medical services provider that:

(A) is a nonprofit entity; or

(B) is created and operated by:

(i) a county;

(ii) a municipality; or

(iii) any combination of counties and municipalities through a contract, joint agreement, or other method provided by Chapter 791, Government Code, or other law authorizing counties and municipalities to provide joint programs; and

(2) the vehicle:

(A) is authorized under an emergency medical services provider license issued by the Department of State Health Services under Chapter 773, Health and Safety Code, and is used exclusively as an emergency medical services vehicle; or

(B) is an emergency medical services chief or supervisor vehicle and is used exclusively as an emergency services vehicle.

(b) A vehicle may be registered without payment of a registration fee if the vehicle:

(1) is owned by the Civil Air Patrol, Texas Wing; and

(2) is used exclusively as an emergency services vehicle by members of the Civil Air Patrol, Texas Wing.

(c) An application for registration under Subsection (a) must be accompanied by a copy of the license issued by the Department of State Health Services. An application for registration of an emergency medical services vehicle must include a statement signed by an officer of the emergency medical services provider that the vehicle is used exclusively as an emergency response vehicle and qualifies for registration under this section. An application for registration of an emergency medical services chief or supervisor vehicle must include a statement signed by an officer of the emergency medical services provider stating that the vehicle qualifies for registration under this section.

(d) An application for registration under Subsection (b) must include a statement signed by an officer of the Civil Air Patrol, Texas Wing, that the vehicle is used exclusively as an emergency services vehicle by members of the Civil Air Patrol, Texas Wing.

(e) The department must approve an application for registration under this section as provided by Section 502.451.

Sec. 502.457. Persons on Active Duty in Armed Forces of United States.

(a) This section applies only to a used motor vehicle that is owned by a person who:

(1) is on active duty in the armed forces of the United States;

Transportation Code

(2) is stationed in or has been assigned to another nation under military orders; and

(3) has registered the vehicle or been issued a license for the vehicle under the applicable status of forces agreement by:

(A) the appropriate branch of the armed forces of the United States; or

(B) the nation in which the person is stationed or to which the person has been assigned.

(b) The requirement that a used vehicle be registered under the law of this state does not apply to a vehicle described by Subsection (a). In lieu of delivering the license receipt to the transferee of the vehicle, as required by Section 501.0721, the person selling, trading, or otherwise transferring a used motor vehicle described by Subsection (a) shall deliver to the transferee:

(1) a letter written on official letterhead by the owner's unit commander attesting to the registration of the vehicle under Subsection (a)(3); or

(2) the registration receipt issued by the appropriate branch of the armed forces or host nation.

(c) A registration receipt issued by a host nation that is not written in the English language must be accompanied by:

(1) a written translation of the registration receipt in English; and

(2) an affidavit, in English and signed by the person translating the registration receipt, attesting to the person's ability to translate the registration receipt into English.

SUBCHAPTER K OFFENSES AND PENALTIES

Sec. 502.471. General Penalty.

(a) A person commits an offense if the person violates a provision of this chapter and no other penalty is prescribed for the violation.

(b) This section does not apply to a violation of Section 502.003, 502.042, 502.197, or 502.431.

(c) Unless otherwise specified, an offense under this section is a misdemeanor punishable by a fine not to exceed $200.

Sec. 502.472. Operation of Vehicle Under Improper Registration.

A person commits an offense if the person operates a motor vehicle that has not been registered or registered for a class other than that to which the vehicle belongs as required by law.

Sec. 502.473. Operation of Vehicle Without Registration Insignia.

(a) A person commits an offense if the person operates on a public highway during a registration period a motor vehicle that does not properly display the registration insignia issued by the department that establishes that the license plates have been validated for the period.

(b) A person commits an offense if the person operates on a public highway during a registration period a road tractor, motorcycle, trailer, or semitrailer that does not display a registration insignia issued by the department that establishes that the vehicle is registered for the period.

(c) This section does not apply to a dealer operating a vehicle as provided by law.

(d) A court may dismiss a charge brought under Subsection (a) if the defendant pays a reimbursement fee not to exceed $10 and:

(1) remedies the defect before the defendant's first court appearance; or

(2) shows that the motor vehicle was issued a registration insignia by the department that was attached to the motor vehicle, establishing that the vehicle was registered for the period during which the offense was committed.

Sec. 502.474. Operation of One-Trip Permit Vehicle.

A person commits an offense if the person operates a vehicle for which a one-trip permit is required without the registration receipt and properly displayed temporary tag.

Sec. 502.475. Wrong, Fictitious, Altered, or Obscured Insignia.

(a) A person commits an offense if the person attaches to or displays on a motor vehicle a registration insignia that:

(1) is assigned to a different motor vehicle;

(2) is assigned to the vehicle under any other motor vehicle law other than by the department;

(3) is assigned for a registration period other than the registration period in effect; or

(4) is fictitious.

(b) Except as provided by Subsection (d), an offense under Subsection (a) is a misdemeanor punishable by a fine of not more than $200, unless it is shown at the trial of the offense that the owner knowingly altered or made illegible the letters, numbers, and other identification marks, in which case the offense is a Class B misdemeanor.

(c) A court may dismiss a charge brought under Subsection (a)(3) if the defendant:

(1) remedies the defect before the defendant's first court appearance; and

(2) pays a reimbursement fee not to exceed $10.

(d) An offense under Subsection (a)(4) is a Class B misdemeanor.

Sec. 502.4755. Deceptively Similar Insignia.

(a) A person commits an offense if the person:

(1) manufactures, sells, or possesses a registration insignia deceptively similar to the registration insignia of the department; or

(2) makes a copy or likeness of an insignia deceptively similar to the registration insignia of the department with intent to sell the copy or likeness.

(b) For the purposes of this section, an insignia is deceptively similar to the registration insignia of the department if the insignia is not prescribed by the department but a reasonable person would presume that it was prescribed by the department.

(c) A district or county court, on application of the attorney general or of the district attorney or prosecuting attorney performing the duties of the district attorney for the district in which the court is located, may enjoin a violation or threatened violation of this section on a showing that a violation has occurred or is likely to occur.

(d) It is an affirmative defense to a prosecution under this section that the insignia was produced pursuant to a licensing agreement with the department.

(e) An offense under this section is:

(1) a felony of the third degree if the person manufactures or sells a deceptively similar registration insignia; or

(2) a Class C misdemeanor if the person possesses a deceptively similar registration insignia, except that the offense is a Class B misdemeanor if the person has previously been convicted of an offense under this subdivision.

Sec. 502.476. Annual Permits; Offense.

A person who violates Section 502.093 commits an offense.

Sec. 502.477. Nonresident-Owned Vehicles Used to Transport Agricultural Product; Offense.

(a) A person operating a vehicle under a permit issued under Section 502.092 commits an offense if the person transports farm products to a place of market, storage, or processing or a railhead or seaport that is farther from the place of production or point of entry, as appropriate, than the distance provided for in the permit.

(b) An offense under this section is a misdemeanor punishable by a fine of not less than $25 or more than $200.

Sec. 502.478. Commercial Motor Vehicle Used Primarily for Agricultural Purposes; Offense.

(a) The owner of a commercial motor vehicle registered under Section 502.433 commits an offense if the person uses or permits the use of the vehicle for a purpose other than one allowed under Section 502.433. Each use or permission of use in violation of this section is a separate offense.

(b) An offense under this section is a misdemeanor punishable by a fine of not less than $25 or more than $200.

Sec. 502.479. Seasonal Agricultural Vehicle; Offense.

A person issued a registration under Section 502.432 commits an offense if the person, during the registration period, uses the truck-tractor or commercial motor vehicle for a purpose other than to transport a seasonal agricultural product.

Sec. 502.480. Violation by County Assessor-Collector; Penalty.

(a) A county assessor-collector commits an offense if the county assessor-collector knowingly accepts an application for the registration of a motor vehicle that:

(1) has had the original motor number or vehicle identification number removed, erased, or destroyed; and

(2) does not bear a motor number or vehicle identification number assigned by the department.

(b) An offense under this section is a misdemeanor punishable by a fine of not less than $10 and not more than $50.

SUBCHAPTER L REGISTRATION AND TRANSFER OF USED VEHICLES

Sec. 502.491. Transfer of Vehicle Registration.

(a) On the sale or transfer of a vehicle, the registration insignia issued for the vehicle shall be removed. The registration period remaining at the time of sale or transfer expires at the time of sale or transfer.

(b) On a sale or transfer of a vehicle in which neither party holds a general distinguishing number issued under Chapter 503, the part of the registration period remaining at the time of the sale or transfer shall continue with the vehicle being sold or transferred and does not transfer with the license plates or registration validation insignia. To continue the remainder of the registration period, the purchaser or transferee must file the documents required under Section 501.145.

(c) On the sale or transfer of a vehicle to a dealer, as defined by Section 503.001, who holds a general distinguishing number issued under Chapter 503, the registration period remaining at the time of the sale or transfer expires at the time of the sale or transfer. On the sale of a used vehicle by a dealer, the dealer shall issue to the buyer new registration documents for an entire registration year.

(d) If the transferor has paid for more than one year of registration, the department may credit the transferor for any time remaining on the registration in annual increments.

Sec. 502.492. Temporary Transit Permit for a Vehicle Purchased.

(a) A purchaser may obtain from the department a temporary transit permit to operate a motor vehicle:

(1) that is subject to registration in this state;

(2) from which the license plates and the registration insignia have been removed as authorized by Section 502.491 or 504.901; and

(3) that is not authorized to travel on a public roadway because the required license plates and the registration insignia are not attached to the vehicle.

(b) The department may issue the permit in accordance with this section.

(c) A permit issued under this section is valid for one trip between the point of origin and the destination and those intermediate points specified in the permit.

(d) A permit issued under this section may not be valid for longer than a five-day period.

(e) A person may obtain a permit under this section by applying, as provided by the department, to the department. Application may be made using the department's Internet website.

(f) A person is eligible to receive only one permit under this section for a motor vehicle.

(g) A permit receipt issued under this section must be in a manner provided by the department. The receipt must contain the information required by this section and shall be carried in the vehicle at all times during which it is valid.

(h) The department may refuse to issue a permit under this section for any vehicle if in the department's opinion the applicant has been involved in operations that constitute an abuse of the privilege granted under this section.

CHAPTER 503
DEALER'S AND MANUFACTURER'S VEHICLE LICENSE PLATES

SUBCHAPTER A
GENERAL PROVISIONS

Sec. 503.001. Definitions.

In this chapter:

(1) "Board" has the meaning assigned by Chapter 2301, Occupations Code.

(2) "Commission" means the board of the Texas Department of Motor Vehicles.

(3) "Converter" has the meaning assigned by Chapter 2301, Occupations Code.

(4) "Dealer" means a person who regularly and actively buys, sells, or exchanges vehicles at an established and permanent location. The term includes a franchised motor vehicle dealer, an independent motor vehicle dealer, an independent mobility motor vehicle dealer, and a wholesale motor vehicle dealer.

(5) "Department" means the Texas Department of Motor Vehicles.

(6) "Drive-a-way operator" means a person who transports and delivers a vehicle in this state from the manufacturer or another point of origin to a location in this state using the vehicle's own power or using the full-mount method, the saddle-mount method, the tow-bar method, or a combination of those methods.

(7) "Franchise" has the meaning assigned by Chapter 2301, Occupations Code.

(8) "Franchised motor vehicle dealer" means a person engaged in the business of buying, selling, or exchanging new motor vehicles at an established and permanent place of business under a franchise in effect with a motor vehicle manufacturer or distributor.

(8-a) "Independent mobility motor vehicle dealer" has the meaning assigned by Section 2301.002, Occupations Code.

(9) "Independent motor vehicle dealer" means a dealer other than a franchised motor vehicle dealer, an independent mobility motor vehicle dealer, or a wholesale motor vehicle dealer.

(10) "Manufacturer" means a person who manufactures, distributes, or assembles new vehicles.

(11) "Motorcycle" has the meaning assigned by Section 502.001.

(12) "Motor vehicle" has the meaning assigned by Section 502.001.

(13) "Semitrailer" has the meaning assigned by Section 502.001.

(14) "Trailer" has the meaning assigned by Section 502.001.

(15) "Vehicle" means a motor vehicle, motorcycle, house trailer, trailer, or semitrailer.

(16) "Wholesale motor vehicle auction" means the offering of a motor vehicle for sale to the highest bidder during a transaction that is one of a series of regular periodic transactions that occur at a permanent location.

(17) "Wholesale motor vehicle dealer" means a dealer who sells motor vehicles only to a person who is:

(A) the holder of a dealer's general distinguishing number; or

(B) a foreign dealer authorized by a law of this state or interstate reciprocity agreement to purchase a vehicle in this state without remitting the motor vehicle sales tax.

Sec. 503.002. Rules.

The board may adopt rules for the administration of this chapter.

Sec. 503.003. Display or Sale of Nonmotorized Vehicle or Trailer.

This chapter does not prohibit the display or sale of a nonmotorized vehicle or trailer at a regularly scheduled vehicle or boat show involving multiple dealers conducted in accordance with board rules.

Sec. 503.004. Buying, Selling, Exchanging, or Manufacturing Vehicles.

This chapter does not prohibit a person from entering into the business of buying, selling, or exchanging new or used vehicles at wholesale or retail or from manufacturing vehicles.

Sec. 503.005. Notice of Sale or Transfer.

(a) A manufacturer or dealer shall immediately notify the department if the manufacturer or dealer transfers, including by sale or lease, a motor vehicle, trailer, or semitrailer to a person other than a manufacturer or dealer.

(b) The notice must be in writing using the form provided by the department and must include:

(1) the date of the transfer;

(2) the names and addresses of the transferrer and transferee; and

(3) a description of the vehicle.

(c) A dealer who submits information to the database under Section 503.0631 satisfies the requirement for the dealer to notify the department of the sale or transfer of a motor vehicle, trailer, or semitrailer under this section.

(d) The notice required under this section is in addition to the application for vehicle registration and certificate of title a dealer is required to submit under Section 501.0234.

Sec. 503.006. Notice of Change of Address.

A dealer or manufacturer who has been issued dealer's, converter's, or manufacturer's license plates shall notify the department of a change to the dealer's, converter's, or manufacturer's address not later than the 10th day after the date the change occurs.

Sec. 503.007. Fees for General Distinguishing Number.

(a) The fee for an original general distinguishing number is $500 for the first year and $200 for each subsequent year for which the number is valid.

(b) The fee for the renewal of a general distinguishing number is $200 a year.

(c) The registration fee for a drive-a-way in-transit license is $50 a year.

(d) A fee collected under this section shall be deposited to the credit of the Texas Department of Motor Vehicles fund.

Sec. 503.008. Fees for License Plates.

(a) The fee for a metal dealer's license plate is $20 a year.

(b) The fee for a manufacturer's license plate is $40 a year.

(c) The fee for an additional set of drive-a-way in-transit license plates is $5 a year.

(d) A fee collected under this section shall be deposited to the credit of the Texas Department of Motor Vehicles fund.

Sec. 503.009. Procedure for Certain Contested Cases.

(a) The board may conduct hearings in contested cases brought under this chapter as provided by this chapter and Chapter 2301, Occupations Code.

(b) The procedures applicable to a hearing conducted under this section are those applicable to a hearing conducted under Chapter 2301, Occupations Code, or Chapter 2001, Government Code.

(c) A decision or final order issued under this section is final and may not be appealed, as a matter of right, to the board.

(d) The board may adopt rules for the procedure, a hearing, or an enforcement proceeding for an action brought under this section.

Sec. 503.010. Term of General Distinguishing Number, License, or License Plate.

Each general distinguishing number, license, or license plate issued under this chapter is valid for the period prescribed by the commission.

Sec. 503.011. Prorating Fees.

If the board prescribes the term of a general distinguishing number, license, or license plate under this chapter for a period other than one year, the board shall prorate the applicable annual fee required under this chapter as necessary to reflect the term of the number, license, or license plate.

Sec. 503.012. Collected Money.

Section 403.095, Government Code, does not apply to money received by the department and deposited to the credit of the Texas Department of Motor Vehicles fund in accordance with this chapter.

Sec. 503.013. Dealer Transfer of Certain Assembled Vehicles Prohibited.

(a) In this section, "assembled vehicle" and "replica" have the meanings assigned by Section 731.001.

(b) Ownership of an assembled vehicle, other than a replica, may not be transferred to or by a dealer under this chapter.

SUBCHAPTER B GENERAL DISTINGUISHING NUMBER

Sec. 503.021. Dealer General Distinguishing Number.

A person may not engage in business as a dealer, directly or indirectly, including by consignment, without a dealer general distinguishing number in one of the categories described by Section 503.029(a)(6) for each location from which the person conducts business as a dealer.

Sec. 503.022. Wholesale Motor Vehicle Auction General Distinguishing Number.

A person may not engage in the business of conducting a wholesale motor vehicle auction without a wholesale motor vehicle auction general distinguishing number for each location from which the person conducts business.

Sec. 503.023. Drive-a-Way Operator License.

A person may not engage in business as a drive-a-way operator without a drive-a-way in-transit license.

Sec. 503.024. Exclusions for Dealer.

(a) A person is not required to obtain a dealer general distinguishing number if the person:

(1) sells or offers to sell during a calendar year fewer than five vehicles of the same type that are owned and registered in that person's name; or

(2) is a federal, state, or local governmental agency.

(b) For the purposes of Section 503.021, a person is not engaging in business as a dealer by:

(1) selling or offering to sell, if the sale or offer is not made to avoid a requirement of this chapter, a vehicle the person acquired for personal or business use to:

(A) a person other than a retail buyer if not sold or offered through a licensed auctioneer; or

(B) any person if the sale or offer is made through a licensed auctioneer;

(2) selling, in a manner provided by law for the forced sale of vehicles, a vehicle in which the person holds a security interest;

(3) acting under a court order as a receiver, trustee, administrator, executor, guardian, or other appointed person;

(4) selling a vehicle the person acquired from the vehicle's owner as a result of paying an insurance claim if the person is an insurance company;

(5) selling an antique passenger car or truck that is at least 25 years of age; or

(6) selling a special interest vehicle that is at least 12 years of age if the person is a collector.

(c) For the purposes of Section 503.021, a domiciliary of another state who holds a dealer license

Transportation Code

and bond, if applicable, issued by the other state is not engaging in business as a dealer by:

(1) buying a vehicle from, selling a vehicle to, or exchanging a vehicle with a person who:

(A) holds a general distinguishing number issued by the department, if the transaction is not intended to avoid a requirement of this chapter; or

(B) is a domiciliary of another state who holds a dealer license and bond, if applicable, issued by the other state and the transaction is not intended to avoid a requirement of this chapter; or

(2) buying, selling, including by consignment, or exchanging at a public auction:

(A) an antique vehicle that is at least 25 years of age; or

(B) a special interest vehicle that:

(i) is at least 12 years of age; or

(ii) has been the subject of a retail sale.

(d) For the purposes of Section 503.021, a licensed auctioneer is not engaging in business as a dealer by, as a bid caller, selling or offering to sell property, including a business that holds the title to any number of vehicles, to the highest bidder at a bona fide auction if:

(1) legal or equitable title does not pass to the auctioneer;

(2) the auction is not held to avoid a requirement of this chapter; and

(3) for an auction of vehicles owned legally or equitably by a person who holds a general distinguishing number, the auction is conducted at the location for which the general distinguishing number was issued.

(e) In this section, "special interest vehicle" has the meaning assigned by Section 683.077(b).

Sec. 503.025. Wholesale Motor Vehicle Auction Exception.

A person exempt under Section 503.024(d) is not required to obtain a wholesale motor vehicle auction general distinguishing number.

Sec. 503.026. Requirement for Each Type of Dealer Vehicle.

A person must obtain a dealer general distinguishing number for each type of vehicle the person intends to sell.

Sec. 503.027. Requirements Relating to Dealer Location.

(a) A dealer must hold a general distinguishing number for a consignment location unless the consignment location is a wholesale motor vehicle auction.

(b) If a person is not otherwise prohibited from doing business as a dealer at more than one location in the territory of a municipality, a person may buy, sell, or exchange a vehicle of the type for which the person holds a dealer general distinguishing number from more than one location in the territory of the municipality without obtaining an additional dealer general distinguishing number. Each location must comply with the requirements prescribed by this chapter and board rules relating to an established and permanent place of business.

Sec. 503.028. Requirements Relating to Wholesale Motor Vehicle Auction Location.

(a) Except as provided by Subsection (b), the department may not issue more than one general distinguishing number for a location for which the wholesale motor vehicle auction general distinguishing number has been issued.

(b) The department may issue to a person who holds a wholesale motor vehicle auction general distinguishing number a dealer general distinguishing number for the location for which the wholesale motor vehicle auction general distinguishing number is issued. The provisions of this subchapter relating to the application for and issuance of a dealer general distinguishing number apply to an application for and issuance of a dealer general distinguishing number issued under this subsection.

Sec. 503.029. Application for Dealer General Distinguishing Number.

(a) An applicant for an original or renewal dealer general distinguishing number must submit to the department a written application on a form that:

(1) is provided by the department;

(2) contains the information required by the department;

(3) contains information that demonstrates the person meets the requirements prescribed by Section 503.032;

(4) contains information that demonstrates the applicant has complied with all applicable state laws and municipal ordinances;

(5) states that the applicant agrees to allow the department to examine during working hours the ownership papers for each registered or unregistered vehicle in the applicant's possession or control; and

(6) specifies whether the applicant proposes to be a:

(A) franchised motor vehicle dealer;
(B) independent motor vehicle dealer;
(C) wholesale motor vehicle dealer;
(D) motorcycle dealer;
(E) house trailer dealer;
(F) trailer or semitrailer dealer; or
(G) independent mobility motor vehicle dealer.

(b) [Repealed by Acts 2013, 83rd Leg., ch. 1135 (H.B. 2741), § 140(2), effective September 1, 2013.]

(c) A renewal application must be:

(1) submitted before the date the general distinguishing number expires; and

(2) accompanied by the appropriate fee prescribed by Section 503.007.

Sec. 503.0295. Independent Mobility Motor Vehicle Dealers.

A person who seeks to act as an independent mobility motor vehicle dealer shall provide with each application for a general distinguishing number and each renewal application:

(1) a written statement that the dealer:

(A) shall maintain written records until at least the third anniversary of the date that adaptive work is performed; and

(B) agrees to comply with Chapter 469, Government Code; and

(2) proof that the person:

(A) maintains a garagekeeper's insurance policy in an amount of at least $50,000 and a products-completed operations insurance policy in an amount of at least $1 million per occurrence and in the aggregate;

(B) holds a welder's certification, or that the person's approved subcontractor holds a certificate, that complies with the standards of the American Welding Society Sections D1.1 and D1.3, if the person or subcontractor will perform any structural modifications; and

(C) is registered with the National Highway Traffic and Safety Administration.

Sec. 503.0296. Independent Motor Vehicle Dealer Education and Training Requirement.

(a) The department by rule shall require that an applicant for an original or renewal general distinguishing number who proposes to be an independent motor vehicle dealer complete web-based education and training developed or approved by the department. The education and training must include information on the laws and board rules applicable to an independent motor vehicle dealer, including the consequences of violating those laws and rules.

(b) An applicant described by Subsection (a) who satisfies the education and training required under this section is not required to complete additional education and training under this section for the subsequent renewal of the applicant's general distinguishing number.

Sec. 503.030. Application for Wholesale Motor Vehicle Auction General Distinguishing Number.

(a) An applicant for an original or renewal wholesale motor vehicle auction general distinguishing number must submit to the department an application that contains:

(1) the information required by the department;

(2) information that demonstrates the person meets the requirements prescribed by Section 503.032; and

(3) information that demonstrates the applicant has complied with all applicable state laws and municipal ordinances.

(b) [Repealed by Acts 2013, 83rd Leg., ch. 1135 (H.B. 2741), § 140(2), effective September 1, 2013.]

Sec. 503.031. Application for Drive-a-Way In-Transit License.

(a) An applicant for a drive-a-way in-transit license must submit to the commission an application containing the information required by the commission.

(b) The license application must be accompanied by the registration fee prescribed by Section 503.007(c).

Sec. 503.032. Established and Permanent Place of Business.

(a) An applicant for a dealer general distinguishing number or wholesale motor vehicle auction general distinguishing number must demonstrate that the location for which the applicant requests the number is an established and permanent place of business. A location is considered to be an established and permanent place of business if the applicant:

(1) owns the real property on which the business is situated or has a written lease for the property that has a term of not less than the term of the general distinguishing number;

(2) maintains on the location:

(A) a permanent furnished office that is equipped as required by the department for the sale of the vehicles of the type specified in the application; and

(B) a conspicuous sign with letters at least six inches high showing the name of the applicant's business; and

(3) has sufficient space on the location to display at least five vehicles of the type specified in the application.

(b) An applicant for a general distinguishing number as a wholesale motor vehicle dealer is not required to maintain display space in accordance with Subsection (a)(3).

(c) The applicant must demonstrate that:

(1) the applicant intends to remain regularly and actively engaged in the business specified in the application for a time equal to at least the term of the general distinguishing number at the location specified in the application; and

(2) the applicant or a bona fide employee of the applicant will be:

(A) at the location to buy, sell, lease, or exchange vehicles; and

(B) available to the public or the department at that location during reasonable and lawful business hours.

Sec. 503.033. Security Requirement.

(a) The department may not issue or renew a motor vehicle dealer general distinguishing number or a wholesale motor vehicle auction general distinguishing number unless the applicant provides to the department satisfactory proof that the applicant has purchased a properly executed surety bond in the amount of $50,000 with a good and sufficient surety approved by the department.

(b) The surety bond must be:

(1) in a form approved by the attorney general;

(2) conditioned on:

(A) the payment by the applicant of all valid bank drafts, including checks, drawn by the applicant to buy motor vehicles; and

(B) the transfer by the applicant of good title to each motor vehicle the applicant offers for sale.

(c) [Repealed by Acts 2011, 82nd Leg., ch. 1290 (H.B. 2017), § 44(a)(3), effective September 1, 2011.]

(d) A person may recover against a surety bond if the person obtains against a person issued a motor vehicle dealer general distinguishing number or a wholesale motor vehicle auction general distinguishing number a judgment assessing damages and reasonable attorney's fees based on an act or omission on which the bond is conditioned that occurred during the term for which the general distinguishing number was valid.

(e) The liability imposed on a surety is limited to:

(1) the amount:

(A) of the valid bank drafts, including checks, drawn by the applicant to buy motor vehicles; or

(B) paid to the applicant for a motor vehicle for which the applicant did not deliver good title; and

(2) attorney's fees that are incurred in the recovery of the judgment and that are reasonable in relation to the work performed.

(f) The liability of a surety may not exceed the face value of the surety bond. A surety is not liable for successive claims in excess of the bond amount regardless of the number of claims made against the bond or the number of years the bond remains in force.

(g) A dealer shall post, adjacent to and in the same manner as the dealer's general distinguishing number is posted, notice of the surety bond and the procedure by which a claimant may recover against the surety bond. The department by rule may prescribe the form of the notice required under this subsection.

(h) The department shall publish on the department's Internet website:

(1) the procedure by which a claimant may recover against a surety bond; and

(2) the department's contact information.

(i) This section does not apply to a person licensed as a franchised motor vehicle dealer by the department.

Sec. 503.034. Issuance and Renewal or Denial of Dealer or Wholesale Motor Vehicle Auction General Distinguishing Number.

(a) The department shall deny an application for the issuance or renewal of a dealer general distinguishing number or a wholesale motor vehicle auction general distinguishing number if the department is satisfied from the application or from other information before it that:

(1) information in the application is not true; or

(2) the applicant is guilty of conduct that would result in the cancellation of the general distinguishing number under Section 503.038.

(b) The department may not issue a dealer general distinguishing number until the applicant complies with the requirements of this chapter.

(c) [Repealed by Acts 2001, 77th Leg., ch. 76 (H.B. 1664), § 8, effective May 14, 2001.]

Sec. 503.035. Issuance and Renewal of Drive-a-Way In-Transit License.

The department shall issue to an applicant on the filing of the application and the payment of the fee a drive-a-way in-transit license and in-transit license plates.

Sec. 503.036. Reassignment of Evidence of Ownership; Dealer Categories.

(a) The holder of a franchised motor vehicle dealer's general distinguishing number may buy, sell, or exchange new or used motor vehicles and reassign a manufacturer's certificate of origin, certificate of title, or other basic evidence of ownership of any type of vehicle owned by the dealer that the dealer is not otherwise prohibited by law from selling or offering for sale.

(b) The holder of an independent motor vehicle dealer's general distinguishing number or an independent mobility motor vehicle dealer's general distinguishing number may reassign a certificate of title or other basic evidence of ownership of any type of vehicle owned by the dealer that the dealer is not otherwise prohibited by law from selling or offering for sale.

(c) The holder of a wholesale motor vehicle dealer's general distinguishing number may sell or offer to sell motor vehicles to no person except:

(1) a person who holds a general distinguishing number; or

(2) a person who is legally recognized as and duly licensed or otherwise qualified as a dealer under the laws of another state or foreign jurisdiction.

Sec. 503.037. Rights of Wholesale Motor Vehicle Auction.

(a) A person who holds a wholesale motor vehicle auction general distinguishing number may accept on consignment one or more motor vehicles to auction. The person may offer a motor vehicle for sale only at the location for which the general distinguishing number is issued and only by bid to the highest bidder. The title to a motor vehicle may be in the name in which the general distinguishing number is issued.

(b) Except as provided by Subsection (d), a person who holds a wholesale motor vehicle auction general distinguishing number may not sell a motor vehicle to a person other than a person who:

(1) is a dealer; or

(2) has a license and, if applicable, a bond issued by the appropriate authority of another state or nation.

(c) A person who holds a wholesale motor vehicle auction general distinguishing number may not allow another person to use the auction's facilities or general distinguishing number to sell or auction a motor vehicle.

(d) Subsection (b) does not prohibit a person who holds a wholesale motor vehicle auction general distinguishing number from offering for sale a motor vehicle to a person who is not a dealer or who does not have a license issued by the appropriate authority of another state, if the motor vehicle is owned by:

(1) this state or a department, agency, or subdivision of this state; or

(2) the United States.

Sec. 503.038. Cancellation of General Distinguishing Number.

(a) The department may cancel a dealer's general distinguishing number if the dealer:

(1) falsifies or forges a title document, including an affidavit making application for a certified copy of a title;

(2) files a false or forged tax document, including a sales tax affidavit;

(3) fails to take assignment of any basic evidence of ownership, including a certificate of title or manufacturer's certificate, for a vehicle the dealer acquires;

(4) fails to assign any basic evidence of ownership, including a certificate of title or manufacturer's certificate, for a vehicle the dealer sells;

(5) uses or permits the use of a metal dealer's license plate or a dealer's temporary tag on a vehicle that the dealer does not own or control or that is not in stock and offered for sale;

(6) makes a material misrepresentation in an application or other information filed with the department;

(7) fails to maintain the qualifications for a general distinguishing number;

(8) fails to provide to the department within 30 days after the date of demand by the department satisfactory and reasonable evidence that the person is regularly and actively engaged in business as a wholesale or retail dealer;

(9) has been licensed for at least 12 months and has not assigned at least five vehicles during the previous 12-month period;

(10) has failed to demonstrate compliance with Sections 23.12, 23.121, and 23.122, Tax Code;

(11) uses or allows the use of the dealer's general distinguishing number or the location for which the general distinguishing number is issued to avoid the requirements of this chapter;

(12) misuses or allows the misuse of a temporary tag authorized under this chapter;

(13) refuses to show on a buyer's temporary tag the date of sale or other reasonable information required by the department; or

(14) otherwise violates this chapter or a rule adopted under this chapter.

(b) The department shall cancel a dealer's general distinguishing number if the dealer obtains the number by submitting false or misleading information.

(c) A person whose general distinguishing number is canceled under this chapter shall surrender to a representative of the department each license, license plate, temporary tag, sticker, and receipt issued under this chapter not later than the 10th day after the date the general distinguishing number is canceled. The department shall direct any peace officer to secure and return to the department any plate, tag, sticker, or receipt of a person who does not comply with this subsection.

(d) A person whose general distinguishing number is canceled automatically loses any benefits and privileges afforded under Chapter 501 to the person as a dealer.

Sec. 503.039. Public Motor Vehicle Auctions.

(a) A motor vehicle may not be the subject of a subsequent sale at a public auction by a holder of a dealer's general distinguishing number unless equitable or legal title has passed to the selling dealer before the transfer of title to the subsequent buyer.

(b) The holder of a dealer's general distinguishing number who sells a motor vehicle at a public auction must transfer the certificate of title for that vehicle to the buyer before the 21st day after the date of the sale.

Sec. 503.040. Sales of Certain Used Motor Vehicles Constitute Private Disposition.

(a) This section applies only to the sale of a used motor vehicle that constitutes collateral by a secured party acting under Chapter 9, Business & Commerce Code, and occurs at an auction conducted by an independent motor vehicle dealer:

(1) at which neither the debtor nor the secured party is permitted to bid; and

(2) for which there has been no advertisement or public notice before the sale that specifically describes the collateral to be sold, other than the inclusion of the motor vehicle in a list of the vehicles to be offered at the auction made available to potential bidders at the auction.

(b) The sale of the used motor vehicle constitutes a private disposition for purposes of Chapter 9, Business & Commerce Code.

SUBCHAPTER C LICENSE PLATES AND TAGS

Sec. 503.061. Dealer's License Plates.

(a) Instead of registering under Chapter 502 a vehicle that the dealer owns, operates, or permits to be operated on a public street or highway, the dealer may apply for, receive, and attach metal dealer's license plates to the vehicle if it is the type of vehicle:

(1) that the dealer sells; and

(2) for which the dealer has been issued a general distinguishing number.

(b) The board may adopt rules regulating the issuance and use of a license plate issued pursuant to the terms of this section.

Sec. 503.0615. Personalized Prestige Dealer's License Plates.

(a) The department shall establish and issue personalized prestige dealer's license plates. The department may not issue identically lettered or numbered dealer's plates to more than one dealer.

(b) The department shall establish procedures for continuous application for and issuance of personalized prestige dealer's license plates. A dealer must make a new application and pay a new fee for each registration period for which the dealer seeks to obtain personalized prestige dealer's license plates. A dealer who obtains personalized prestige dealer's license plates has first priority on those plates for each subsequent registration period for which the dealer applies.

(c) The annual fee for personalized prestige dealer's license plates is $40, in addition to any fee otherwise prescribed by this chapter.

(d) The department may issue to an applicant only one set of personalized prestige dealer's license plates for a vehicle for a six-year period. The department may issue a new set of personalized prestige dealer's license plates within the six-year period if the applicant pays a fee of $50 in addition to the fees required by Subsection (c).

(e) On application and payment of the required fee for a registration period following the issuance of the plates, the department shall issue a registration insignia.

(f) Of each fee collected by the department under this section:

(1) $1.25 shall be deposited to the credit of the Texas Department of Motor Vehicles fund to defray the cost of administering this section; and

(2) the remainder shall be deposited to the credit of the general revenue fund.

Sec. 503.0618. Converter's License Plates.

(a) In this section, "converter" means a person who holds a converter's license issued under Chapter 2301, Occupations Code.

(b) Instead of registering under Chapter 502 a vehicle that a converter operates or permits to be operated on a public street or highway, the converter may apply for, receive, and attach metal converter's license plates to the vehicle if it is the type of vehicle that the converter is engaged in the business of assembling or modifying.

(c) The fee for a metal converter's license plate is $20 a year.

(d) The department shall prescribe the form of an application under this section.

(e) A fee collected under this section shall be deposited to the credit of the Texas Department of Motor Vehicles fund.

Sec. 503.062. Dealer's Temporary Tags.

(a) A dealer may issue a temporary tag for use on an unregistered vehicle by the dealer or the dealer's employees only to:

(1) demonstrate or cause to be demonstrated to a prospective buyer the vehicle for sale purposes only;

(2) convey or cause to be conveyed the vehicle:

(A) from one of the dealer's places of business in this state to another of the dealer's places of business in this state;

(B) from the dealer's place of business to a place the vehicle is to be repaired, reconditioned, or serviced;

(C) from the state line or a location in this state where the vehicle is unloaded to the dealer's place of business;

(D) from the dealer's place of business to a place of business of another dealer;

(E) from the point of purchase by the dealer to the dealer's place of business; or

(F) to road test the vehicle; or

(3) use the vehicle for or allow its use by a charitable organization.

(b) Subsection (a)(1) does not prohibit a dealer from permitting:

(1) a prospective buyer to operate a vehicle while the vehicle is being demonstrated; or

(2) a customer to operate a vehicle temporarily while the customer's vehicle is being repaired.

(c) A vehicle being conveyed under this section is exempt from the inspection requirements of Chapter 548.

(d) The department may not issue a dealer temporary tag or contract for the issuance of a dealer temporary tag but shall prescribe:

(1) the specifications, form, and color of a dealer temporary tag;

(2) procedures for a dealer to generate a vehicle-specific number using the database developed under Section 503.0626 and assign it to each tag;

(3) procedures to clearly display the vehicle-specific number on the tag; and

(4) the period for which a tag may be used for or by a charitable organization.

(e) For purposes of this section, "charitable organization" means an organization organized to relieve poverty, to advance education, religion, or science, to promote health, governmental, or municipal purposes, or for other purposes beneficial to the community without financial gain.

Sec. 503.0625. Converter's Temporary Tags.

(a) In this section, "converter" means a person who holds a converter's license issued under Chapter 2301, Occupations Code.

(b) A converter may issue a temporary tag for use on an unregistered vehicle by the converter or the converter's employees only to:

(1) demonstrate or cause to be demonstrated to a prospective buyer who is an employee of a franchised motor vehicle dealer the vehicle; or

(2) convey or cause to be conveyed the vehicle:

(A) from one of the converter's places of business in this state to another of the converter's places of business in this state;

(B) from the converter's place of business to a place the vehicle is to be assembled, repaired, reconditioned, modified, or serviced;

(C) from the state line or a location in this state where the vehicle is unloaded to the converter's place of business;

(D) from the converter's place of business to a place of business of a franchised motor vehicle dealer; or

(E) to road test the vehicle.

(c) Subsection (b)(1) does not prohibit a converter from permitting a prospective buyer who is an employee of a franchised motor vehicle dealer to operate a vehicle while the vehicle is being demonstrated.

(d) A vehicle being conveyed while displaying a temporary tag issued under this section is exempt from the inspection requirements of Chapter 548.

(e) The department may not issue a converter temporary tag or contract for the issuance of a converter temporary tag but shall prescribe:

(1) the specifications, form, and color of a converter temporary tag;

(2) procedures for a converter to generate a vehicle-specific number using the database developed under Section 503.0626 and assign it to each tag; and

(3) procedures to clearly display the vehicle-specific number on the tag.

(f) A converter or employee of a converter may not use a temporary tag issued under this section as authorization to operate a vehicle for the converter's or the employee's personal use.

Transportation Code

Sec. 503.0626. Dealer's and Converter's Temporary Tag Database.

(a) The department shall develop, manage, and maintain a secure, real-time database of information on vehicles to which dealers and converters have affixed temporary tags.

(b) The database must allow law enforcement agencies to use the vehicle-specific number assigned to and displayed on the tag as required by Section 503.062(d) or Section 503.0625(e) to obtain information about the dealer or converter that owns the vehicle.

(c) Before a dealer's or converter's temporary tag may be displayed on a vehicle, the dealer or converter must enter into the database through the Internet information on the vehicle and information about the dealer or converter as prescribed by the department. Except as provided by Section 506.0632(f), the department may not deny access to the database to any dealer who holds a general distinguishing number issued under this chapter or who is licensed under Chapter 2301, Occupations Code, or to any converter licensed under Chapter 2301, Occupations Code.

(d) The department shall adopt rules and prescribe procedures as necessary to implement this section.

Sec. 503.063. Buyer's Temporary Tags.

(a) Except as provided by this section, a dealer shall issue to a person who buys a vehicle one temporary buyer's tag for the vehicle.

(b) Except as provided by this section, the buyer's tag is valid for the operation of the vehicle until the earlier of:

(1) the date on which the vehicle is registered; or

(2) the 60th day after the date of purchase.

(c) The dealer:

(1) must show in ink on the buyer's tag the actual date of sale and any other required information; and

(2) is responsible for displaying the tag.

(d) The dealer is responsible for the safekeeping and distribution of each buyer's tag the dealer obtains.

(e) The department may not issue a buyer's tag or contract for the issuance of a buyer's tag but shall prescribe:

(1) the specifications, color, and form of a buyer's tag; and

(2) procedures for a dealer to:

(A) generate a vehicle-specific number using the database developed under Section 503.0631 and assign it to each tag;

(B) generate a vehicle-specific number using the database developed under Section 503.0631 for future use for when a dealer is unable to access the Internet at the time of sale; and

(C) clearly display the vehicle-specific number on the tag.

(f) The department shall ensure that a dealer may generate in advance a sufficient amount of vehicle-specific numbers under Subsection (e)(2)(B) in order to continue selling vehicles for a period of up to one week in which a dealer is unable to access the Internet due to an emergency. The department shall establish an expedited procedure to allow affected dealers to apply for additional vehicle-specific numbers so they may remain in business during an emergency.

(g) For each buyer's temporary tag, a dealer shall charge the buyer a registration fee of not more than $5 as prescribed by the department to be sent to the comptroller for deposit to the credit of the Texas Department of Motor Vehicles fund.

(h) A federal, state, or local governmental agency that is exempt under Section 503.024 from the requirement to obtain a dealer general distinguishing number may issue one temporary buyer's tag in accordance with this section for a vehicle sold or otherwise disposed of by the governmental agency under Chapter 2175, Government Code, or other law that authorizes the governmental agency to sell or otherwise dispose of the vehicle. A governmental agency that issues a temporary buyer's tag under this subsection:

(1) is subject to the provisions of Sections 503.0631 and 503.067 applicable to a dealer; and

(2) is not required to charge the registration fee under Subsection (g).

(i) A vehicle may be issued and display a buyer's tag without satisfying the inspection requirements of Chapter 548 if:

(1) the buyer of the vehicle is not a resident of this state; and

(2) the vehicle:

(A) at the time of purchase, is not located or required to be titled or registered in this state;

(B) will be titled and registered in accordance with the laws of the buyer's state of residence; and

(C) will be inspected in accordance with the laws of the buyer's state of residence, if the laws of that state require inspection.

(j) A vehicle may be issued and display a buyer's tag without satisfying the inspection requirements of Chapter 548 if the vehicle is purchased at public auction in this state and is:

(1) an antique vehicle as defined by Section 683.077(b); or

(2) a special interest vehicle as defined by Section 683.077(b) that:

(A) is at least 12 years of age; and

(B) has been the subject of a retail sale.

Sec. 503.0631. Buyer's Temporary Tag Database.

(a) The department shall develop, manage, and maintain a secure, real-time database of information on persons to whom temporary buyer's tags are issued that may be used by a law enforcement agency in the same manner that the agency uses vehicle registration information.

(b) The database must allow law enforcement agencies to use a vehicle-specific number assigned to and displayed on the tag as required by Section 503.063(e)(2) to obtain information about the person to whom the tag was issued.

(c) Except as provided by Subsection (d), before a buyer's temporary tag may be displayed on a vehicle, a dealer must enter into the database through the Internet information about the buyer of the vehicle for which the tag was issued as prescribed by the department and generate a vehicle-specific number for the tag as required by Section 503.063(e). Except as provided by Section 506.0632(f), the department may not deny access to the database to any dealer who holds a general distinguishing number issued under this chapter or who is licensed under Chapter 2301, Occupations Code.

(d) A dealer shall obtain 24-hour Internet access at its place of business, but if the dealer is unable to access the Internet at the time of the sale of a vehicle, the dealer shall complete and sign a form, as prescribed by the department, that states the dealer has Internet access, but was unable to access the Internet at the time of sale. The buyer shall keep the original copy of the form in the vehicle until the vehicle is registered to the buyer. Not later than the next business day after the time of sale, the dealer shall submit the information required under Subsection (c).

(e) The department shall adopt rules and prescribe procedures as necessary to implement this section.

(f) The dealer may charge a reasonable fee not to exceed $20 for costs associated with complying with this section.

Sec. 503.0632. Department Regulation of Temporary Tags and Access to Temporary Tag Databases.

(a) The department by rule may establish the maximum number of temporary tags that a dealer or converter may obtain in a calendar year under Section 503.062, 503.0625, or 503.063.

(b) The maximum number of temporary tags that the department determines a dealer or converter may obtain under this section must be based on the dealer's or converter's anticipated need for temporary tags, taking into consideration:

(1) the dealer's or converter's:

(A) time in operation;

(B) sales data; and

(C) expected growth;

(2) expected changes in the dealer's or converter's market;

(3) temporary conditions that may affect sales by the dealer or converter; and

(4) any other information the department considers relevant.

(c) At the request of a dealer or converter, the department may authorize additional temporary tags of any type for the dealer or converter if the dealer or converter demonstrates a need for additional temporary tags resulting from business operations, including anticipated need.

(d) The department's denial of a request under Subsection (c) may be overturned if a dealer or converter shows by a preponderance of the evidence the need for additional temporary tags.

(e) The department shall monitor the number of temporary tags obtained by a dealer or converter.

(f) If the department determines that a dealer or converter is fraudulently obtaining temporary tags from the temporary tag database, the department may, after giving notice electronically and by certified mail to the dealer or converter, deny access to a temporary tag database to the dealer or converter. A dealer or converter denied access to a temporary tag database under this subsection may request a hearing on the denial as provided by Subchapter O, Chapter 2301, Occupations Code.

Sec. 503.064. Manufacturer's License Plates.

(a) Instead of registering a new vehicle that a manufacturer intends to test on a public street or highway or to loan to a consumer for the purpose described by Section 2301.605, Occupations Code, the manufacturer may apply for, receive, and attach manufacturer's license plates to the vehicle.

(b) If the vehicle to which the manufacturer's license plates are attached is a commercial motor vehicle, the vehicle may not carry a load.

Sec. 503.065. Buyer's Out-of-State License Plates.

(a) The department may issue or cause to be issued to a person a temporary license plate authorizing the person to operate a new unregistered vehicle on a public highway of this state if the person:

(1) buys the vehicle from a dealer outside this state and intends to drive the vehicle from the dealer's place of business; or

(2) buys the vehicle from a dealer in this state but intends to drive the vehicle from the manufacturer's place of business outside this state.

(b) The department may not issue a temporary license plate under this section to a manufacturer or dealer of a motor vehicle, trailer, or semitrailer or to a representative of such a dealer.

(c) A person may not use a temporary license plate issued under this section on a vehicle transporting property.

(d) A temporary license plate issued under this section expires not later than the 30th day after the date on which it is issued. The department shall place or cause to be placed on the license plate at the time of issuance the date of expiration and the type of vehicle for which the license plate is issued.

(e) The fee for a temporary license plate issued under this section is $3. Only one license plate may be issued for each vehicle.

(f) A fee collected under this section shall be deposited to the credit of the Texas Department of Motor Vehicles fund.

Sec. 503.066. Application for Dealer's or Manufacturer's License Plates.

(a) An applicant for one or more original or renewal dealer's or manufacturer's license plates must submit to the department a written application on a form that:

(1) is provided by the department; and

(2) contains a statement that the applicant agrees to allow the department to examine during working hours the ownership papers for each registered or unregistered vehicle in the applicant's possession or control.

(b) [Repealed by Acts 2013, 83rd Leg., ch. 1135 (H.B. 2741), § 140(2), effective September 1, 2013.]

(c) An application must be:

(1) submitted before the date the plate expires; and

(2) accompanied by the appropriate fee prescribed by Section 503.008.

(d) A metal license plate issued under this chapter expires on the same date as the expiration of the license under which it is issued.

Sec. 503.067. Unauthorized Reproduction, Purchase, Use, or Sale of Temporary Tags.

(a) A person may not produce or reproduce a temporary tag or an item represented to be a temporary tag for the purpose of distributing the tag to someone other than a dealer or converter.

(b) A person may not operate a vehicle that displays:

(1) a temporary tag in violation of this chapter or Chapter 502; or

(2) any other unauthorized temporary tag.

(c) A person other than a dealer or converter may not purchase a temporary tag.

(d) A person may not sell or distribute a temporary tag or an item represented to be a temporary tag unless the person is a dealer issuing the tag in connection with the sale of a vehicle.

Sec. 503.068. Limitation on Use of Dealer's License Plates and Tags.

(a) A dealer or an employee of a dealer may not use a dealer's temporary tag as authorization to operate a vehicle for the dealer's or the employee's personal use.

(b) A person may not use a metal dealer's license plate or dealer's temporary tag on:

(1) a service or work vehicle, except as provided by Subsection (b-1); or

(2) a commercial vehicle that is carrying a load.

(b-1) An independent motor vehicle dealer or an employee of an independent motor vehicle dealer may use a metal dealer's license plate on a service or work vehicle used to transport a vehicle in the dealer's inventory to or from a point of sale. This subsection does not authorize a person to operate a service or work vehicle as a tow truck, as defined by Section 2308.002, Occupations Code, without a license or permit required by Chapter 2308, Occupations Code.

(c) For purposes of this section, a boat trailer carrying a boat is not a commercial vehicle carrying a load. A dealer complying with this chapter may affix to the rear of a boat trailer the dealer owns or sells a metal dealer's license plate or temporary tag issued under Section 503.061, 503.062, or 503.063.

(d) This section does not prohibit the operation or conveyance of an unregistered vehicle using the full-mount method, saddle-mount method, tow-bar method, or a combination of those methods in accordance with Section 503.062 or 503.063.

Sec. 503.069. Display of License Plates and Tags.

(a) A license plate, other than an in-transit license plate, or a temporary tag issued under this chapter shall be displayed in accordance with commission rules.

(b) A drive-a-way operator who has been issued a drive-a-way in-transit license shall display the operator's in-transit license plates on each transported motor vehicle from the vehicle's point of origin to its point of destination in this state in accordance with the laws relating to the operation of a vehicle on a public highway.

Sec. 503.070. Removal of Out-of-State License Plates.

(a) A dealer who purchases a vehicle that displays an out-of-state license plate must remove the plate within a reasonable time.

(b) A dealer who purchases a vehicle for resale may not operate the vehicle on a public street or highway in this state while the vehicle displays an out-of-state license plate.

Sec. 503.071. Notice of Driving or Towing from Out of State.

(a) A motor vehicle that is manufactured outside this state and is driven or towed from the place of manufacture to this state for sale in this state must have affixed to it a sticker stating that the vehicle is being driven or towed from the place it was manufactured.

(b) The sticker must be at least three inches in diameter and must be affixed to the windshield or front of the motor vehicle in plain view.

(c) The sticker must remain on the motor vehicle until the vehicle is sold by a dealer.

SUBCHAPTER D ENFORCEMENT

Sec. 503.091. Enforcement Agreement.

The department may agree with an authorized official of another jurisdiction to regulate activities and exchange information relating to the wholesale operations of nonresident vehicle dealers.

Sec. 503.092. Action to Enforce Chapter.

(a) The attorney general or a district, county, or city attorney may enforce this chapter and bring an enforcement action in the county in which a violation of this chapter is alleged to have occurred.

(b) A justice or municipal court has concurrent original jurisdiction with the county court or a county court at law over an action to enforce this chapter.

Sec. 503.093. Action to Enforce Subchapter.

(a) The department or any interested person may bring an action, including an action for an injunction, to:

(1) enforce a provision of Subchapter B; or

(2) prohibit a person from operating in violation of the person's application for a general distinguishing number.

(b) A plaintiff other than the department may recover the plaintiff's attorney's fees.

Sec. 503.094. Criminal Penalty.

(a) A person commits an offense if the person violates this chapter.

(b) Except as otherwise provided by this section, an offense under this section is a misdemeanor punishable by a fine of not less than $50 or more than $5,000.

(c) If the trier of fact finds that the person committed the violation wilfully or with conscious indifference to law, the court may treble the fine otherwise due as a penalty for the violation.

(d) An offense involving a violation of:

(1) Section 503.067(b) or (c) is a Class C misdemeanor;

(2) Section 503.067(d) is a Class A misdemeanor;

(3) Section 503.067(a) is a state jail felony; and

(4) Section 503.067(b), (c), or (d) is a state jail felony if the person who committed the offense criminally conspired to engage in organized criminal activity.

Sec. 503.095. Civil Penalty.

(a) In addition to any other penalty prescribed by this chapter, a person who violates this chapter or a rule adopted under this chapter is subject to a civil penalty of not less than $50 or more than $1,000.

(b) For purposes of this section, each act in violation of this chapter and each day of a continuing violation is a separate violation.

Sec. 503.096. Towing of Vehicles.

(a) If a person is engaged in business as a dealer in violation of Section 503.021, a peace officer may cause a vehicle that is being offered for sale by the person to be towed from the location where the vehicle is being offered for sale and stored at a vehicle storage facility, as defined by Section 2308.002, Occupations Code.

(b) A peace officer may cause the vehicle to be towed under Subsection (a) only if:

(1) the peace officer has a probable cause that the vehicle is being offered for sale by a person engaged in business as a dealer in violation of Section 503.021;

(2) the peace officer has complied with the notice requirements under Subsection (c); and

Transportation Code

(3) the notice under Subsection (c) was attached to the vehicle not less than two hours before the vehicle is caused to be towed.

(c) Before a vehicle may be towed under Subsection (a), a peace officer, an appropriate local government employee, or an investigator employed by the department must attach a conspicuous notice to the vehicle's front windshield or, if the vehicle has no front windshield, to a conspicuous part of the vehicle stating:

(1) the make and model of the vehicle and the license plate number and vehicle identification number of the vehicle, if any;

(2) the date and time that the notice was affixed to the vehicle;

(3) that the vehicle is being offered for sale in violation of Section 503.021;

(4) that the vehicle and any property on or in the vehicle may be towed and stored at the expense of the owner of the vehicle not less than two hours after the notice is attached to the vehicle if the vehicle remains parked at the location; and

(5) the name, address, and telephone number of the vehicle storage facility where the vehicle will be towed.

(d) Once notice has been attached to a vehicle under Subsection (c), a peace officer may prevent the vehicle from being removed by a person unless the person provides evidence of ownership in the person's name or written authorization from the owner of the vehicle for the person to offer the vehicle for sale in a manner other than by consignment.

CHAPTER 504 LICENSE PLATES

SUBCHAPTER A GENERAL PROVISIONS

Sec. 504.001. Definitions.

(a) In this chapter:

(1) "Board" means the board of the Texas Department of Motor Vehicles.

(2) "Department" means the Texas Department of Motor Vehicles.

(3) "Purchaser" and "seller" have the meanings assigned by Section 501.002.

(b) A word or phrase that is not defined by this chapter but is defined by Section 502.001 has the meaning in this chapter that is assigned by that section.

Sec. 504.0011. Rules.

The board may adopt rules to implement and administer this chapter.

Sec. 504.002. General Provisions.

(a) Unless expressly provided by this chapter or by department rule:

(1) except for license plates specified as exempt, the fee for issuance of a license plate, including replacement plates, is in addition to each other fee that is paid for at the time of the registration of the motor vehicle and shall be deposited to the credit of the Texas Department of Motor Vehicles fund;

(2) if the registration period is greater than 12 months, the expiration date of a specialty license plate, symbol, tab, or other device shall be aligned with the registration period, and the specialty plate fee shall be adjusted pro rata, except that if the statutory annual fee for a specialty license plate is $5 or less, it may not be prorated;

(3) the department is the exclusive owner of the design of each license plate;

(4) if a license plate is lost, stolen, or mutilated, an application for a replacement plate must be accompanied by the fee prescribed by Section 502.060; and

(5) the department shall prepare the designs and specifications of license plates.

(b) If necessary to cover the costs of issuing license plates for golf carts under Section 551.402 or off-highway vehicles under Section 551A.052, the department may charge an administrative fee, in an amount established by the department by rule, for the issuance of a golf cart or off-highway vehicle license plate.

Sec. 504.003. Souvenir License Plates [Renumbered].

Renumbered to Tex. Transp. Code § 504.009 by Acts 2011, 82nd Leg., ch. 1296 (H.B. 2357), § 174, effective January 1, 2012.

Sec. 504.004. Rules and Forms [Renumbered].

Renumbered to Tex. Transp. Code § 504.0011 by Acts 2011, 82nd Leg., ch. 1296 (H.B. 2357), § 167, effective January 1, 2012.

Sec. 504.005. Design and Alphanumeric Pattern.

(a) The department has sole control over the design, typeface, color, and alphanumeric pattern for all license plates.

(b) The department shall prepare the designs and specifications of license plates and devices selected by the board to be used as a unique identifier.

(c) The department shall design each license plate to include a design at least one-half inch wide that represents in silhouette the shape of Texas and that appears between letters and numerals. The department may omit the silhouette of Texas from specially designed license plates.

(d) To promote highway safety, each license plate shall be made with a reflectorized material that provides effective and dependable brightness for the period for which the plate is issued.

Sec. 504.0051. Personalized License Plates.

(a) The department shall issue personalized license plates, including those issued in accordance with the marketing vendor as provided in Subchapter J. The department may not issue more than one set of license plates with the same alphanumeric pattern.

(b) The department may not issue a replacement set of personalized plates to the same person before the period set by rule unless the applicant for issuance of replacement plates pays the fee required by Section 504.007.

Sec. 504.006. Cost of Manufacturing.

(a) The department shall reimburse the Texas Department of Criminal Justice for the cost of manufacturing license plates as the invoices for the license plates are delivered to the department.

(b) When manufacturing is started, the Texas Department of Criminal Justice and the department, after negotiation, shall set the price to be paid for each license plate. The price must be determined from:

(1) the cost of metal, paint, and other materials purchased;

(2) the inmate maintenance cost per shift;

(3) overhead expenses;

(4) miscellaneous charges; and

(5) a previously agreed upon amount of profit for the work.

Sec. 504.007. Replacement License Plates.

(a) The owner of a registered motor vehicle may obtain replacement license plates for the vehicle by:

(1) certifying that the replacement plates will not be used on any other vehicle owned or operated by the person making the statement;

(2) paying a fee of $6 plus the fee required by Section 502.356(a) for each set of replacement license plates, unless otherwise specified by law; and

(3) returning to the department each license plate in the owner's possession for which a replacement license plate is obtained.

(b) Replacement license plates may not be issued except as provided by this section.

(c) A county assessor-collector shall retain $2.50 of each fee collected under this section and forward the remainder of the fee to the department for deposit to the credit of the Texas Department of Motor Vehicles fund.

(d) The fee required by this section applies to the issuance of license plates for a transferred used vehicle for which the registration and license plates were not transferred under Section 504.901.

(e) Replacement license plates may be used in the registration year in which the plates are issued and during each succeeding year of the registration period as set by rule if the registration insignia is properly displayed on the vehicle.

(f) Subsection (e) does not apply to the issuance of specialized license plates for limited distribution, including exempt plates for governmental entities and temporary registration plates.

(g) **[2 Versions: As added by Acts 2017, 85th Leg., ch. 490]** No fee is required under this section if a county assessor-collector determines that the owner of a registered motor vehicle did not receive license plates that were issued to the owner by mail.

(g) **[2 Versions: As added by Acts 2017, 85th Leg., ch. 968]** No fee is required under this section if the county assessor-collector determines that the owner paid for license plates for the same vehicle that were mailed to the owner but not received by the owner.

Sec. 504.008. Specialty License Plates.

(a) The department shall prepare the designs and specifications of specialty license plates.

(b) Any motor vehicle other than a vehicle manufactured for off-highway use only is eligible to be issued specialty license plates, provided that the department may vary the design of a license plate to accommodate or reflect its use on a motor vehicle other than a passenger car or light truck.

(c) An application for specialty license plates must be submitted in the manner specified by the department, provided that if issuance of a specialty license plate is limited to particular persons or motor vehicles, the application must be accompanied by evidence satisfactory to the department that the applicant or the applicant's vehicle is eligible.

(d) Each fee described by this chapter is an annual fee, provided that the department may prorate the fee for a specialty license plate fee on a monthly basis to align the license plate fee to the registration month for the motor vehicle for which the license plate was issued, and if a fee is prorated the allocation of the fee by this chapter to an account or fund shall be prorated in proportion.

(e) The director or the director's designee may refuse to issue a specialty license plate with a design or alphanumeric pattern that the director or designee considers potentially objectionable to one or more members of the public and the director or designee's refusal may not be overturned in the absence of an abuse of discretion.

(f) For each specialty license plate that is issued by a county assessor-collector and for which the department is allocated a portion of the fee for administrative costs, the department shall credit 50 cents from its administrative costs to the county treasurer of the applicable county, who shall credit the money to the general fund of the county to defray the costs to the county of administering this chapter.

(g) If the owner of a motor vehicle for which a specialty license plate is issued disposes of the vehicle or for any reason ceases to be eligible for that specialty license plate, the owner shall return the specialty license plate to the department.

(h) A person who is issued a specialty license plate may not transfer the plate to another person or vehicle unless the department approves the transfer.

Sec. 504.009. Souvenir License Plates.

(a) The department may issue a souvenir version of any specialty license plate for any vehicle.

(a-1) On request, the Texas Military Department, as defined by Section 437.001, Government Code, shall issue a souvenir version of the specialty license plate described by Section 504.322.

(b) The fee for a single souvenir license plate is $20. The fee shall be deposited to the credit of the Texas Department of Motor Vehicles fund unless the souvenir license plate is a replica of a specialty license plate issued under Subchapter G or I for which the fee is deposited to an account other than the Texas Department of Motor Vehicles fund, in which case:

(1) $10 of the fee for the souvenir license plate shall be deposited to the credit of the designated account; and

(2) $10 of the fee for the souvenir license plate shall be deposited to the credit of the Texas Department of Motor Vehicles fund.

(c) If a souvenir license plate issued before November 19, 2009, is personalized, the fee for the plate is $40. Of the fee:

(1) $20 shall be deposited to the credit of the Texas Department of Motor Vehicles fund;

(2) $10 shall be deposited to the credit of the designated account if the souvenir license plate is a replica of a specialty license plate issued under Subchapter G or I for which the fee is deposited to a designated account other than the Texas Department of Motor Vehicles fund; and

(3) the remainder shall be deposited to the credit of the general revenue fund.

(c-1) The fee for a souvenir license plate issued on or after November 19, 2009, is the amount established under Section 504.851(c).

(d) A souvenir license plate may not be used on a motor vehicle and is not an insignia of registration for a motor vehicle. Each souvenir license plate must be identified by the department in a way that identifies it to law enforcement officers and others as a souvenir license plate.

(e) A beneficiary of a specialty license plate issued under Subchapter G or I, as designated by the applicable section of those subchapters, may purchase the specialty license plates, in minimum amounts determined by the department, for use or resale by the beneficiary. The beneficiary shall pay the required fee per plate, less the amount of the fee that would be deposited to the credit of the designated account.

Sec. 504.010. Issuance and Placement of License Plate.

(a) On payment of the prescribed fee, an applicant for motor vehicle registration shall be issued a license plate or set of plates.

(b) Subject to Section 504.901, the department shall issue only one license plate or set of plates for a vehicle during the registration period set by rule.

(c) The board may adopt rules regarding the placement of license plates for a motor vehicle, road tractor, motorcycle, trailer, or semitrailer.

SUBCHAPTER B PERSONALIZED LICENSE PLATES

Sec. 504.101. Personalized License Plates.

The department shall issue personalized license plates, including those sold by the private vendor under a contract with the department as provided by Section 504.851.

Sec. 504.102. Personalization of Specialty License Plate.

Unless expressly prohibited by this chapter or department rule, any specialty license plate issued under this chapter may be personalized. If a specialty license plate is personalized, the fee for personalization of the specialty license plate shall be added to the fee for issuance of that specialty license plate.

Sec. 504.103. Design and Alphanumeric Pattern [Renumbered].

Renumbered to Tex. Transp. Code § 504.005 by Acts 2011, 82nd Leg., ch. 1296 (H.B. 2357), § 169, effective January 1, 2012.

SUBCHAPTER B-1. DIGITAL LICENSE PLATES

Sec. 504.151. Definitions.

In this subchapter:

(1) "Digital license plate" means an electronic display that is designed to:

(A) display the information required to be included on a physical license plate; and

(B) be placed on the rear of a vehicle in lieu of a physical license plate issued under this chapter.

(2) "Digital license plate provider" means a person engaged in the business of providing digital license plate hardware and services to vehicle owners, including the sale or lease of and issuance of digital license plates.

Sec. 504.152. Applicability of Other Law.

Except as otherwise provided by this subchapter or a rule adopted under this subchapter, a digital license plate issued under this subchapter is subject to the laws of this state applicable to a physical license plate.

Sec. 504.153. Rules.

The board shall adopt rules as necessary to implement and administer this subchapter.

Sec. 504.154. Digital License Plates Authorized.

(a) The board by rule shall allow a vehicle described by Subsection (b) to be equipped with a digital license plate that is placed on the rear of the vehicle in lieu of a physical license plate issued under this chapter. The rule must require the owner of a vehicle issued a digital license plate to obtain a physical license plate to be placed on the front of the vehicle unless the vehicle is of a class of vehicles that is not required to display two license plates, as provided by other law.

(b) A vehicle registered under Chapter 502 may be equipped with a digital license plate only if the vehicle:

(1) is part of a commercial fleet, as defined by Section 502.001;

(2) is owned or operated by a governmental entity; or

(3) is not a passenger vehicle.

(c) The department may contract with digital license plate providers for the issuance of digital license plates, including any services related to the issuance of digital license plates.

(d) Notwithstanding any other law, a rule adopted under this subchapter may:

(1) authorize the display of the vehicle's registration insignia on a digital license plate issued for the vehicle in lieu of attaching the registration insignia to the inside of the vehicle's windshield as required by Section 502.059;

(2) establish a fee in an amount necessary to cover any administrative costs incurred that relate to the issuance of a digital license plate and exceed the administrative costs incurred for the issuance of a physical license plate; or

(3) prohibit a digital license plate provider from contracting with the department under Subchapter J.

Sec. 504.155. Digital License Plates Requirements and Permissive Functionality.

(a) The board by rule shall set the specifications and requirements for digital license plates, including requirements for the placement of digital license plates. The design of and information displayed on a digital license plate must be approved by the department.

(b) A digital license plate issued under this subchapter must:

(1) meet the specifications and requirements adopted under Subsection (a);

(2) include the information required to be included on a physical license plate and legibly display that information at all times and in all light conditions, provided that the license plate may display the information in a smaller typeface when the vehicle is parked;

(3) have wireless connectivity capability; and

(4) provide benefits to law enforcement that meet or exceed the benefits provided by physical license plates as of the time of enactment of this subchapter and as determined by the Department of Public Safety.

Transportation Code

(c) In adopting rules under Subsection (a), the board shall consult with the Department of Public Safety. Except as otherwise provided by this subsection and Section 2001.036, Government Code, a rule adopted under Subsection (a) takes effect on the 31st day after the date on which the rule is filed in the office of the secretary of state. A rule adopted under Subsection (a) does not take effect if, not later than the 30th day after the date on which the rule is filed in the office of the secretary of state, the public safety director of the Department of Public Safety submits to the office of the secretary of state written notification invalidating the rule.

(d) A rule adopted under this subchapter may:

(1) authorize the use of a digital license plate for electronic toll collection or to display a parking permit; or

(2) establish procedures for displaying on a digital license plate:

(A) an emergency alert or other public safety alert issued by a governmental entity, including an alert authorized under Subchapter L, M, or P, Chapter 411, Government Code;

(B) vehicle manufacturer safety recall notices;

(C) static logo displays, including unique displays for fleet vehicles; or

(D) advertising approved by the department.

Sec. 504.156. Digital License Plate Provider Powers and Duties.

A digital license plate provider with whom the department contracts under Section 504.154:

(1) shall maintain an inventory of the digital license plates issued by the provider in this state;

(2) shall make available a digital version of each specialty license plate authorized by this chapter, other than personalized license plates authorized for marketing and sale under Subchapter J, provided that:

(A) each issuance of a specialty license plate with restricted distribution, including a license plate authorized under Subchapter C, D, E, or F, must be approved by the department; and

(B) the provider shall remit to the department in the manner prescribed by the department all money:

(i) payable to the department; or

(ii) required to be used or deposited in the manner prescribed by the law establishing the license plate;

(3) may contract with the private vendor under Subchapter J to make available a digital version of a personalized license plate authorized for marketing and sale under that subchapter, provided that the contract shall conform with any applicable requirements of Subchapter J and the terms of the private vendor's contract with the department;

(4) shall, if a digital license plate displays a registration insignia as authorized by a rule adopted under Section 504.154(d)(1), promptly update the display of the registration insignia to reflect the current registration period for the vehicle and, on request of the department, suspend the display of the registration insignia or indicate on the license plate that the registration insignia for the vehicle is expired;

(5) may provide any service related to the issuance of a digital license plate that is authorized by board rule, including the sale, lease, and installation of and customer service for a digital license plate; and

(6) may charge a fee, payable in installments, for the issuance of a digital license plate or any additional services provided by the provider for that license plate.

Sec. 504.157. Defense to Prosecution of Certain Offenses.

It is a defense to prosecution of an offense involving the operation of a motor vehicle and relating to the placement of a license plate or the display of a registration insignia that the vehicle was operated in compliance with rules issued under this subchapter governing the placement of a digital license plate or the display of a registration insignia on a digital license plate, as applicable.

SUBCHAPTER C LICENSE PLATES FOR VEHICLES USED BY PERSONS WITH DISABILITIES

Sec. 504.201. Persons with Disabilities.

(a) In this section:

(1) "Disability" and "mobility problem that substantially impairs a person's ability to ambulate" have the meanings assigned by Section 681.001.

(2) "Legally blind" means a condition described by Section 681.001(2)(B) or (C).

(3) "Practice of optometry" and "practice of therapeutic optometry" have the meanings assigned by Section 351.002, Occupations Code.

(b) The department shall issue specialty license plates for a motor vehicle that:

(1) has a gross vehicle weight of 18,000 pounds or less; and

(2) is regularly operated for noncommercial use by or for the transportation of a person with a permanent disability.

(c) An owner of a motor vehicle regularly operated by or for the transportation of a person described by Subsection (a) may apply to the department for registration under this section.

(d) Except as provided by Subsection (d-1), the initial application for specialty license plates under this section must be accompanied by a written statement from a physician who is licensed to practice medicine in this state or in a state adjacent to this state or who is authorized by applicable law to practice medicine in a hospital or other health facility of the Department of Veterans Affairs. If the applicant has a mobility problem caused by a disorder of the foot, the written statement may be issued by a person licensed to practice podiatry in this state or a state adjacent to this state. In this subsection, "podiatry" has the meaning assigned by Section 681.001. The statement must certify that the person making the application or on whose behalf the application is made is legally blind or has a mobility problem that substantially impairs the person's ability to ambulate. The statement must also certify whether a mobility problem is temporary or permanent. A written statement is not required as acceptable medical proof if:

(1) the person with a disability:

(A) has had a limb, hand, or foot amputated; or

(B) must use a wheelchair; and

(2) the applicant executes a statement attesting to the person's disability before the county assessor-collector.

(d-1) If the initial application for specialty license plates under this section is made by or on behalf of a person who is legally blind, the written statement required by Subsection (d) may be issued by a person licensed to engage in the practice of optometry or the practice of therapeutic optometry in this state or a state adjacent to this state.

(e) A person with a disability may receive:

(1) one disabled parking placard under Section 681.002 if the person receives a set of license plates under this section; or

(2) two disabled parking placards under Section 681.002 if the person does not receive a set of license plates under this section.

(f) A license plate issued under this section must include the symbol of access adopted by Rehabilitation International in 1969 at its Eleventh World Congress on Rehabilitation of the Disabled. The symbol must be the same size as the numbers on the license plate.

(g) In addition to a license plate issued under this section, an eligible person is entitled to be issued a set of the license plates for each motor vehicle owned by the person that has a gross vehicle weight of 18,000 pounds or less and is equipped with special equipment that:

(1) is designed to allow a person who has lost the use of one or both of the person's legs to operate the vehicle; and

(2) is not standard equipment on that type of vehicle for use by a person who has use of both legs.

(h) [Repealed by Acts 2011, 82nd Leg., ch. 1296 (H.B. 2357), § 247(9), effective January 1, 2012.]

Sec. 504.202. Veterans with Disabilities. [Expires December 31, 2022]

(a) A person entitled to specialty license plates under this section may register, for the person's own use, one vehicle without payment of any fee paid for or at the time of registration except the fee for the license plates. Registration under this section is valid for one year.

(b) A veteran of the United States armed forces is entitled to register, for the person's own use, motor vehicles under this section if:

(1) the person has suffered, as a result of military service:

(A) at least a 50 percent service-connected disability; or

(B) a 40 percent service-connected disability because of the amputation of a lower extremity;

(2) the person receives compensation from the United States because of the disability; and

(3) the motor vehicle:

(A) is owned by the person; and

(B) has a gross vehicle weight of 18,000 pounds or less or is a motor home.

(c) An organization may register a motor vehicle under this section if:

(1) the vehicle is used exclusively to transport veterans of the United States armed forces who have suffered, as a result of military service, a service-connected disability; and

(2) the veterans are not charged for the transportation.

(d) A statement by the veterans county service officer of the county in which a vehicle described by Subsection (c) is registered or by the Department of Veterans Affairs that a vehicle is used exclusively to transport veterans with disabilities without charge is satisfactory proof of eligibility for an organization.

(e) Other than license plates issued under Subsection (h), license plates issued under this section must include:

(1) the letters "DV" on the plate if the plate is issued for a vehicle other than a motorcycle; and

Transportation Code

(2) the words "Disabled Veteran" and "U.S. Armed Forces" at the bottom of each license plate.

(e-1) Other than license plates issued under Subsection (h), license plates issued under this section may include, on request:

(1) the emblem of the veteran's branch of service; or

(2) one emblem from another license plate to which the person is entitled under Section 504.308, 504.309, 504.310(b), 504.311, 504.312, 504.313, 504.3135, 504.314, 504.315, 504.316, 504.3161, 504.318, 504.319, 504.320, 504.323, 504.325, or 504.327.

(f) The fee for the first set of license plates is $3. There is no fee for each additional set of license plates.

(g) A person who receives license plates under this section may receive a disabled parking placard under Section 681.004 for each set of license plates without providing additional documentation.

(h) A person entitled to license plates under this section may elect to receive license plates issued under Chapter 502 under the same conditions for the issuance of license plates under this section.

(i) A license plate with the letters "DV" may be personalized with up to four characters.

(j) A person entitled to license plates under this section may instead use, for a vehicle that meets the requirements of Section 504.501 or 504.502, disabled veteran license plates issued by this state that are:

(1) embossed with an alphanumeric pattern;

(2) of a plate design that was issued in the same year as the model year of the vehicle; and

(3) approved for use by the department.

Sec. 504.202. Veterans with Disabilities. [Effective January 1, 2022]

(a) A person entitled to specialty license plates under this section may register, for the person's own use, one vehicle without payment of any fee paid for or at the time of registration except the fee for the license plates. Registration under this section is valid for one year.

(b) A veteran of the United States armed forces is entitled to register, for the person's own use, motor vehicles under this section if:

(1) the person has suffered, as a result of military service:

(A) at least a 50 percent service-connected disability; or

(B) a 40 percent service-connected disability because of the amputation of a lower extremity;

(2) the person receives compensation from the United States because of the disability; and

(3) the motor vehicle:

(A) is owned by the person; and

(B) has a gross vehicle weight of 18,000 pounds or less or is a motor home.

(b-1) A person described by Subsection (b) who is eligible to receive license plates under Section 504.201 may elect to receive license plates under this section that include the symbol described by Section 504.201(f). The initial application for license plates under this subsection must be accompanied by:

(1) the written statement required by Section 504.201(d), unless the applicant is an organization described by Subsection (b-2); and

(2) any other information required for an application under this section.

(b-2) An organization that registers a motor vehicle under Subsection (c) may elect to receive license plates under Subsection (b-1) if the vehicle regularly transports veterans who are eligible to receive license plates under Subsection (b-1). The department shall adopt rules prescribing satisfactory proof of eligibility under this subsection.

(c) An organization may register a motor vehicle under this section if:

(1) the vehicle is used exclusively to transport veterans of the United States armed forces who have suffered, as a result of military service, a service-connected disability; and

(2) the veterans are not charged for the transportation.

(d) A statement by the veterans county service officer of the county in which a vehicle described by Subsection (c) is registered or by the Department of Veterans Affairs that a vehicle is used exclusively to transport veterans with disabilities without charge is satisfactory proof of eligibility for an organization.

(e) Other than license plates issued under Subsection (h), license plates issued under this section must include:

(1) the letters "DV" on the plate if the plate is issued for a vehicle other than a motorcycle; and

(2) the words "Disabled Veteran" and "U.S. Armed Forces" at the bottom of each license plate.

(e-1) Other than license plates issued under Subsection (h), license plates issued under this section may include, on request:

(1) the emblem of the veteran's branch of service; or

(2) one emblem from another license plate to which the person is entitled under Section 504.308, 504.309, 504.310(b), 504.311, 504.312, 504.313, 504.3135, 504.314, 504.315, 504.316, 504.3161, 504.318, 504.319, 504.320, 504.323, 504.325, or 504.327.

(f) The fee for the first set of license plates is $3. There is no fee for each additional set of license plates.

(g) A person who receives license plates under Subsection (b-1) may receive a disabled parking placard under Section 681.004 for each set of license plates.

(h) A person entitled to license plates under this section may elect to receive license plates issued under Chapter 502 under the same conditions for the issuance of license plates under this section.

(i) A license plate with the letters "DV" may be personalized with up to four characters.

(j) A person entitled to license plates under this section may instead use, for a vehicle that meets the requirements of Section 504.501 or 504.502, disabled veteran license plates issued by this state that:

(1) are embossed with an alphanumeric pattern;

(2) are of a plate design that was issued in the same year as the model year of the vehicle;

(3) are approved for use by the department; and

(4) include the symbol described by Section 504.201(f), if the person satisfies the requirements for the issuance of license plates under Subsection (b-1) and elects to include the symbol on the plates.

(k) A reference in law to license plates issued under Subsection (b-1) includes disabled veteran license plates described by Subsection (j)(4).

Sec. 504.203. Issuance of Disabled License Plates to Certain Institutions.

(a) The department shall issue specialty license plates under this subchapter for a van or bus operated by an institution, facility, or residential retirement community for the elderly or for veterans in which an eligible person resides, including:

(1) an institution that holds a license issued under Chapter 242, Health and Safety Code; or

(2) a facility that holds a license issued under Chapter 246 or 247 of that code.

(b) An application for license plates under this section must be accompanied by a written statement acknowledged by the administrator or manager of the institution, facility, or retirement community certifying that the institution, facility, or retirement community regularly transports, as a part of the services that the institution, facility, or retirement community provides, one or more eligible persons who reside in the institution, facility, or retirement community. The department shall determine the eligibility of the institution, facility, or retirement community on the evidence the applicant provides.

(c) The application and eligibility requirements for a license plate under this section are the same as those provided by Sections 504.201 and 504.202, as applicable.

Sec. 504.204. Persons Who Are Deaf or Hard of Hearing.

(a) In this section, "deaf" and "hard of hearing" have the meanings assigned by Section 81.001, Human Resources Code.

(b) The department shall design and issue specialty license plates for a motor vehicle that is regularly operated by a person who is deaf or hard of hearing. A license plate issued under this section must include an emblem indicating that the person operating the vehicle is deaf or hard of hearing.

(c) The initial application for specialty license plates under this section must be accompanied by a written statement from a physician who is licensed to practice medicine in this state or in a state adjacent to this state or who is authorized by applicable law to practice medicine in a hospital or other health facility of the Department of Veterans Affairs. The statement must certify that the person making the application is deaf or hard of hearing.

(d) The fee for a set of license plates issued under this section is $8.

Sec. 504.205. Information Provided with Plates.

The department shall include with each set of specialty license plates issued under this subchapter a document that provides:

(1) information on laws governing parking for persons with disabilities; and

(2) instructions for reporting alleged violations of Chapter 681.

SUBCHAPTER D SPECIALTY LICENSE PLATES FOR THE MILITARY

Sec. 504.301. Provisions Generally Applicable to Military Specialty License Plates.

(a) Unless expressly provided by this subchapter or department rule:

(1) the department shall design specialty license plates for the military; and

(2) a person is not eligible to be issued a specialty license plate under this subchapter if the person

was discharged from the armed forces under conditions less than honorable.

(b) Notwithstanding any other provision of this subchapter, the department may design the wording on a specialty license plate authorized by this subchapter to enhance the legibility and reflectivity of the license plate.

(c) Section 504.702 does not apply to a specialty license plate issued under this subchapter.

Sec. 504.3011. Design of Certain License Plates for the Military.

The department shall design military license plates that:

(1) bear a color depiction of the emblem of the appropriate branch of the United States armed forces or a color depiction of the appropriate medal as provided by the United States Department of Defense; and

(2) include the words "Honorably Discharged" for license plates issued to former members of the United States armed forces.

Sec. 504.3015. Fees for Military Specialty License Plates.

(a) A person applying for a set of license plates under this subchapter shall pay the registration fee required under Chapter 502 and the applicable special plate fee required under this section, except that one set of license plates shall be issued without the payment of the registration fee under:

(1) Section 504.308;

(2) Section 504.310(b);

(3) Section 504.315, other than Subsections (c) and (q) of that section; and

(4) Section 504.319.

(b) The fee for the issuance of one set of specialty license plates issued under Section 504.315(d) or (g) is $3. There is no additional fee for a specialty license plate issued under another provision of this subchapter.

(c) A surviving spouse applying for a set of license plates under Section 504.302 shall pay the fees required for the type of license plate for which the surviving spouse is eligible.

Sec. 504.302. Surviving Spouses of Certain Military Veterans.

(a) The surviving spouse of a person who would be eligible for a specialty license plate under this subchapter is entitled to continue to register one vehicle under the applicable section as long as the spouse remains unmarried.

(a-1) The surviving spouse of a person who would be eligible for a specialty license plate under Section 504.308, 504.310, 504.315, 504.316, or 504.319 is entitled to register one vehicle under the applicable section as long as the spouse remains unmarried.

(b) An applicant under this section must submit proof of the eligibility of the applicant's deceased spouse for the applicable specialty license plate.

(c) A surviving spouse applying for specialty license plates under this section must submit a written statement that the spouse is unmarried. If the surviving spouse is applying for Former Prisoner of War, Pearl Harbor Survivor, or Purple Heart specialty license plates, the statement must be sworn to by the surviving spouse.

Sec. 504.303. Members or Former Members of United States Armed Forces.

(a) The department shall issue specialty license plates for active or former members of the United States armed forces. The license plates must designate the appropriate branch of the United States armed forces.

(b) The department shall include the word "Retired" for license plates issued to retired members of the United States armed forces.

(c) Satisfactory proof of eligibility for a license plate issued under this section to a retired member of the United States armed forces may be demonstrated by:

(1) a letter from any branch of the military under the jurisdiction of the United States Department of Defense or the United States Department of Homeland Security stating that a retired member has 20 or more years of satisfactory federal service; or

(2) an identification card issued by any branch of the military under the jurisdiction of the United States Department of Defense or the United States Department of Homeland Security indicating that the member is retired.

Sec. 504.304. Members of United States Armed Forces Auxiliaries.

(a) The department shall issue specialty license plates for members of:

(1) the United States Air Force Auxiliary, Civil Air Patrol;

(2) the United States Coast Guard Auxiliary; and

(3) the Marine Corps League or its auxiliary.

(b) The license plates must include the words "Texas Wing Civil Air Patrol," the words "Coast Guard Auxiliary," or the emblem of the Marine Corps League and the words "Marine Corps League," as applicable.

Transportation Code

(c) [Repealed by Acts 2007, 80th Leg., ch. 1166 (H.B. 191), § 13, effective September 1, 2007.]

Sec. 504.305. Members of Texas National Guard, State Guard, or United States Armed Forces Reserves.

(a) The department shall issue specialty license plates for:

(1) active members of the Texas National Guard or Texas State Guard;

(2) retired members of the Texas National Guard or Texas State Guard; and

(3) members of a reserve component of the United States armed forces.

(b) The department shall design the license plates in consultation with the adjutant general. The license plates must include the words "Texas Guard" or "Armed Forces Reserve," as applicable.

(c) Satisfactory proof of eligibility for a license plate issued under this section to a retired member of the Texas National Guard or Texas State Guard may be demonstrated by:

(1) a letter from the United States Department of Defense, the Department of the Army, or the Department of the Air Force stating that a retired guard member has 20 or more years of satisfactory federal service; or

(2) an identification card issued by the United States Department of Defense, the Department of the Army, or the Department of the Air Force indicating that the member is retired.

Transportation Code

Sec. 504.306. Members and Former Members of Merchant Marine of the United States.

The department shall issue specialty license plates for members and former members of the merchant marine of the United States. The license plates must include the words "Merchant Marine."

Sec. 504.307. United States Paratroopers.

(a) The department shall issue specialty license plates for active and former members of the United States armed services who have:

(1) satisfactorily completed the prescribed proficiency tests while assigned or attached to an airborne unit or the Airborne Department of the United States Army Infantry School; or

(2) participated in at least one combat parachute jump.

(b) The license plates must include:

(1) a likeness of the parachutist badge authorized by the Department of the Army; and

(2) the words "U.S. Paratrooper."

Sec. 504.308. Distinguished Flying Cross Medal Recipients.

The department shall issue specialty license plates for persons who have received the Distinguished Flying Cross medal and Distinguished Flying Cross medal with Valor. The license plates must bear a depiction of the Distinguished Flying Cross medal and the words "Distinguished Flying Cross" at the bottom of each license plate. License plates issued under this section to recipients of the Distinguished Flying Cross medal with Valor that are not personalized must also include the letter "V" as a prefix or suffix to the numerals on each plate.

Sec. 504.309. Military Academy License Plates.

The department shall issue specialty license plates for persons who:

(1) are graduates of:

(A) the United States Military Academy;

(B) the United States Naval Academy;

(C) the United States Air Force Academy;

(D) the United States Merchant Marine Academy; or

(E) the United States Coast Guard Academy; and

(2) are current or former commissioned officers of the United States armed forces.

Sec. 504.310. World War II Veterans and Certain Medal Recipients.

(a) The department shall issue specialty license plates for persons who served in the United States or Allied armed forces during World War II. License plates issued under this subsection must include the words "WWII Veteran."

(b) The department shall issue specialty license plates for recipients of the Army of Occupation Medal. License plates issued under this subsection must include the Army of Occupation Medal emblem and must include the words "Army of Occupation Medal" at the bottom of the plate.

Sec. 504.311. Service in Korea.

(a) The department shall issue specialty license plates for persons who served in the United States armed forces:

(1) during the period beginning on June 27, 1950, and ending on July 27, 1954, and who received the National Defense Service Medal;

(2) in a combat zone in Korea during the period beginning on June 27, 1950, and ending on July 27,

1954, and who received the Korean Service Medal; or

(3) in the Korean Demilitarized Zone beginning on July 28, 1954, and who received the Korean Defense Service Medal.

(b) License plates issued under this section must include the words "Korea Veteran" and bear a depiction of the appropriate medal.

Sec. 504.312. Vietnam Veterans.

(a) The department shall issue specialty license plates for persons who served in the United States armed forces:

(1) during the period beginning on January 1, 1961, and ending on August 14, 1974, and who received the National Defense Service Medal; or

(2) in a combat zone in the Republic of Vietnam during the period beginning on July 1, 1958, and ending on March 28, 1973, and who received the Vietnam Service Medal.

(b) License plates issued under this section must include the words "Vietnam Veteran" and bear a depiction of the appropriate medal.

Sec. 504.313. Desert Shield or Desert Storm Veterans.

(a) The department shall issue specialty license plates for persons who served in the United States armed forces:

(1) during the period beginning on August 2, 1990, and ending on November 30, 1995, and who received the National Defense Service Medal; or

(2) in a combat zone in support of Operation Desert Shield or Desert Storm during the period beginning on August 2, 1990, and ending on November 30, 1995, and who received the Southwest Asia Service Medal.

(b) License plates issued under this section must include the words "Desert Shield/Storm/Provide Comfort" and bear a depiction of the appropriate medal.

Sec. 504.3135. Operation Iraqi Freedom.

The department shall issue specialty license plates for persons who served in the United States armed forces and participated in Operation Iraqi Freedom. License plates issued under this section must include the words "Operation Iraqi Freedom."

Sec. 504.314. Enduring Freedom Veterans.

(a) The department shall issue specialty license plates for persons who served in the United States armed services and participated in Operation Enduring Freedom. The license plates must include the words "Enduring Freedom."

(b) The department shall issue specialty license plates for persons who served in the United States armed services and participated in Operation Enduring Freedom in Afghanistan. The license plates must include the words "Enduring Freedom Afghanistan."

Sec. 504.315. Military Specialty License Plates for Extraordinary Service.

(a) The department shall issue specialty license plates for recipients of the Bronze Star Medal and Bronze Star Medal with Valor. License plates issued under this subsection must include the Bronze Star Medal emblem and must include the words "Bronze Star Medal" at the bottom of each plate. License plates issued under this subsection to recipients of the Bronze Star Medal with Valor that are not personalized must also include the letter "V" as a prefix or suffix to the numerals on each plate.

(a-1) The department shall issue specialty license plates for recipients of the Air Medal and Air Medal with Valor. License plates issued under this subsection must include the Air Medal emblem and must include the words "Air Medal" at the bottom of each plate. License plates issued under this subsection to recipients of the Air Medal with Valor that are not personalized must also include the letter "V" as a prefix or suffix to the numerals on each plate. Section 504.702 does not apply to license plates authorized by this subsection.

(b) The department shall issue specialty license plates for recipients of the Distinguished Service Medal. License plates issued under this subsection must include the Distinguished Service Medal emblem and the words "Distinguished Service Medal" at the bottom of each plate.

(c) The department shall issue specialty license plates for recipients of the Commendation Medal with Valor for each branch of the military and for joint service. License plates issued under this subsection must include the appropriate Commendation Medal emblem and must include the name of the medal at the bottom of each plate. License plates issued under this subsection that are not personalized must also include the letter "V" as a prefix or suffix to the numerals on each plate.

(d) The department shall issue specialty license plates for survivors of the attack on Pearl Harbor on December 7, 1941. The license plates must include the words "Pearl Harbor Survivor." A person is eligible if the person:

(1) served in the United States armed forces;

(2) was stationed in the Hawaiian Islands on December 7, 1941; and

(3) survived the attack on Pearl Harbor on December 7, 1941.

(e) The department shall issue specialty license plates to a recipient of a Congressional Medal of Honor awarded under Title 10, United States Code. The department shall assign the license plate number, and the plates may not be personalized.

(f) The department shall issue specialty license plates for recipients of the Air Force Cross or Distinguished Service Cross, the Army Distinguished Service Cross, the Navy Cross, or the Medal of Honor. The license plates must include the words "Legion of Valor."

(g) The department shall issue specialty license plates for recipients of the Purple Heart. License plates issued under this subsection must include:

(1) the Purple Heart emblem;

(2) the words "Purple Heart" at the bottom of each plate; and

(3) the letters "PH" as a prefix or suffix to the numerals on the plate if the plate is not personalized.

(h) The department shall issue special license plates for recipients of the Silver Star Medal. License plates issued under this subsection must include the Silver Star Medal emblem and must include the words "Silver Star Medal" at the bottom of each plate.

(i) A vehicle registered under this section must be for the use of the applicant who qualifies under this section.

(j) The department shall issue specialty license plates for recipients of the Defense Meritorious Service Medal. License plates issued under this subsection must include the Defense Meritorious Service Medal emblem and must include the words "Defense Meritorious Service Medal" at the bottom of each plate.

(k) The department shall issue specialty license plates for recipients of the Meritorious Service Medal. License plates issued under this subsection must include the Meritorious Service Medal emblem and must include the words "Meritorious Service Medal" at the bottom of each plate.

(*l*) The department shall issue specialty license plates for recipients of the Coast Guard Medal. License plates issued under this subsection must include the Coast Guard Medal emblem and must include the words "Coast Guard Medal" at the bottom of each plate.

(m) The department shall issue specialty license plates for recipients of the Airman's Medal. License plates issued under this subsection must include the Airman's Medal emblem and must include the words "Airman's Medal" at the bottom of each plate.

(n) The department shall issue specialty license plates for recipients of the Soldier's Medal. License plates issued under this subsection must include the Soldier's Medal emblem and must include the words "Soldier's Medal" at the bottom of each plate.

(o) The department shall issue specialty license plates for recipients of the Navy and Marine Corps Medal. License plates issued under this subsection must include the Navy and Marine Corps Medal emblem and must include the words "Navy and Marine Corps Medal" at the bottom of each plate.

(p) The department shall issue specialty license plates for recipients of the Prisoner of War Medal. License plates issued under this subsection must include the Prisoner of War Medal emblem and must include the words "Prisoner of War Medal" at the bottom of each plate.

(q) The department shall issue specialty license plates for recipients of the Military Outstanding Volunteer Service Medal. License plates issued under this subsection must include the Military Outstanding Volunteer Service Medal emblem and must include the words "Military Outstanding Volunteer Service Medal" at the bottom of each plate.

(r) The department shall issue specialty license plates for recipients of the Borinqueneers Congressional Gold Medal. License plates issued under this subsection must include the Borinqueneers Congressional Gold Medal emblem and must include the words "Borinqueneers Congressional Gold Medal" at the bottom of each plate. License plates issued under this subsection that are not personalized must also include the letter "B" as a prefix or suffix to the numerals on each plate.

Sec. 504.316. Legion of Merit Medal Recipients.

(a) The department shall issue specialty license plates for persons who have received the Legion of Merit medal. The license plates must include the words "Legion of Merit."

(b) [Repealed by Acts 2011, 82nd Leg., ch. 1296 (H.B. 2357), § 247(10), effective January 1, 2012.]

Sec. 504.3161. Military Specialty License Plates for Recipients of Certain Military Campaign and Service Awards.

The department shall issue specialty license plates for recipients of the following military awards that include the name of the award:

(1) the Armed Forces Expeditionary Medal;

(2) the Armed Forces Service Medal;

(3) the Navy Expeditionary Medal;

(4) the Global War on Terrorism Expeditionary Medal;
(5) the Global War on Terrorism Service Medal;
(6) the Marine Corps Expeditionary Medal;
(7) the Merchant Marine Expeditionary Medal;
(8) the Kosovo Campaign Medal;
(9) the Inherent Resolve Campaign Medal;
(10) the China Service Medal; and
(11) the Nuclear Deterrence Operations Service Medal.

Sec. 504.317. Surviving Spouses of Disabled Veterans Specialty License Plates.

(a) In this section, "surviving spouse" means the individual married to a disabled veteran at the time of the veteran's death.

(b) The department shall issue specialty license plates for surviving spouses of disabled veterans of the United States armed forces.

(b-1) A person is eligible to receive specialty license plates under this section if the person is the surviving spouse of a person who had been entitled to specialty plates for veterans with disabilities under Section 504.202, regardless of whether the deceased spouse was issued plates under that section.

(c) A person entitled to specialty license plates under this section may register, for the person's own use, one vehicle without payment of any fee other than the fee for the license plates under Subsection (d).

(d) The fee for the first set of license plates is $3. There is no fee for each additional set of license plates.

Sec. 504.318. Women Veterans.

The department shall issue specialty license plates for female active or former members of the United States armed forces, Texas National Guard, or Texas State Guard. The license plates must include the words "Woman Veteran" in red.

Sec. 504.319. Defense Superior Service Medal Recipients.

The department shall issue specialty license plates for recipients of the Defense Superior Service Medal. License plates issued under this section must include the words "Defense Superior Service Medal" at the bottom of each plate.

Sec. 504.320. Recipients of Certain Combat Badges, Medals, or Ribbons.

(a) The department shall issue specialty license plates for recipients of the Combat Action Badge. License plates issued under this subsection must include the Combat Action Badge emblem and must include the words "Combat Action Badge" at the bottom of each plate.

(b) The department shall issue specialty license plates for recipients of the Combat Action Medal. License plates issued under this subsection must include the Combat Action Medal emblem and must include the words "Combat Action Medal" at the bottom of each plate.

(c) The department shall issue specialty license plates for recipients of the Combat Action Ribbon. License plates issued under this subsection must include the Combat Action Ribbon emblem and must include the words "Combat Action Ribbon" at the bottom of each plate.

(c-1) The department shall issue specialty license plates for recipients of the Combat Medical Badge. License plates issued under this subsection must include the Combat Medical Badge emblem and must include the words "Combat Medical Badge" at the bottom of each plate.

(c-2) The department shall issue specialty license plates for recipients of the Combat Infantryman Badge. License plates issued under this subsection must include the Combat Infantryman Badge emblem and must include the words "Combat Infantryman Badge" at the bottom of each plate.

(d) A specialty license plate issued under this section for a badge or ribbon that may be awarded more than once shall include only the emblem of the first award badge or ribbon.

Sec. 504.321. Commendation Medal Recipients.

The department shall issue specialty license plates for recipients of the Commendation Medal for each branch of the military and for joint service. License plates issued under this section must include the emblem of the appropriate medal and must include the name of the medal at the bottom of each plate.

Sec. 504.322. 36th Infantry Division.

The department shall issue specialty license plates for persons who have served in the 36th Infantry Division of the Texas Army National Guard. The license plates must include the 36th Infantry Division emblem and must include the words "36th Infantry Division" at the bottom of each plate.

Sec. 504.323. Tomb Guard. [Renumbered]

Sec. 504.323. 11th Armored Cavalry Regiment.

The department shall issue specialty license plates for persons who have served in the 11th Armored Cavalry Regiment of the United States Army. The license plates must include the 11th Armored Cavalry Regiment emblem and must include the words "11th Armored Cavalry Regiment" at the bottom of each plate.

Sec. 504.324. Tomb Guard.

The department shall issue specialty license plates for persons who serve or have served in the Third United States Infantry Regiment as a guard for the Tomb of the Unknown Soldier and are awarded the Guard, Tomb of the Unknown Soldier Identification Badge. The license plates must include a likeness of the Guard, Tomb of the Unknown Soldier Identification Badge and must include the words "Tomb Guard" at the bottom of each plate.

Transportation Code

Sec. 504.325. 173rd Airborne Brigade.

The department shall issue specialty license plates for persons who have served in the 173rd Airborne Brigade of the United States Army. The license plates must include the 173rd Airborne Brigade emblem and must include the words "173rd Airborne Brigade" at the bottom of each plate.

Sec. 504.325. Master Army Aviator.

The department shall issue specialty license plates for persons awarded the Master Army Aviator Badge. The license plates must include:

(1) the words "Master Army Aviator"; and

(2) a depiction of the Master Army Aviator Badge.

Sec. 504.327. Presidential Service Badge.

The department shall issue specialty license plates for persons awarded the Presidential Service Badge. The license plates must include:

(1) the words "Presidential Service Badge"; and

(2) a depiction of the Presidential Service Badge.

Sec. 504.327. United States Navy Submarine Service.

The department shall issue specialty license plates for persons who served on a submarine while in the United States Navy. The license plates must include:

(1) the words "U.S. Navy Submarine Service" in red letters at the bottom of each plate; and

(2) a depiction of the Submarine Warfare insignia on the left side of the plate.

Sec. 504.327. United States Navy Seals.

The department shall issue specialty license plates for members of the United States armed services who have been awarded the Special Warfare Insignia. The license plates must include:

(1) the words "Navy SEALs"; and

(2) a depiction of the United States Navy Special Warfare Insignia.

Sec. 504.327. United States Army Special Forces.

The department shall issue specialty license plates for persons who serve or have served in the United States armed services and have earned Special Forces qualifications. The license plates must include:

(1) the words "Army Special Forces"; and

(2) a depiction of the United States Army Special Forces shoulder sleeve insignia with the Special Forces Tab.

SUBCHAPTER E SPECIALTY LICENSE PLATES WITH RESTRICTED DISTRIBUTION

Sec. 504.400. Fees for Certain Restricted Plates.

The department shall issue, without charge, not more than three sets of specialty license plates under this subchapter.

Sec. 504.401. State Officials.

(a) The department shall issue specialty license plates to a state official.

(b) [Repealed by Acts 2011, 82nd Leg., ch. 1296 (H.B. 2357), § 247(11), effective January 1, 2012.]

(c) The registration remains valid until December 31 of each year.

(d) In this section, "state official" means:

(1) a member of the legislature;

(2) the governor;

(3) the lieutenant governor;

(4) a justice of the supreme court;

(5) a judge of the court of criminal appeals;

(6) the attorney general;

(7) the commissioner of the General Land Office;

(8) the comptroller;
(9) a member of the Railroad Commission of Texas;
(10) the commissioner of agriculture;
(11) the secretary of state; or
(12) a member of the State Board of Education.

Sec. 504.402. Members of Congress.

(a) The department shall issue specialty license plates to members of congress, which must include the words "U.S. Congress."

(b) [Repealed by Acts 2011, 82nd Leg., ch. 1296 (H.B. 2357), § 247(12), effective January 1, 2012.]

(c) The license plates remain valid until December 31 of each year.

Sec. 504.403. State and Federal Judges.

(a) The department shall issue specialty license plates for a current or visiting state or federal judge. The license plates must include the words "State Judge" or "U.S. Judge," as appropriate.

(b) [Repealed by Acts 2011, 82nd Leg., ch. 1290 (H.B. 2017), § 44(4), effective September 1, 2011 and by Acts 2011, 82nd Leg., ch. 1296 (H.B. 2357), § 247(13), effective January 1, 2012.]

(c) [Repealed by Acts 2011, 82nd Leg., ch. 1290 (H.B. 2017), § 44(4), effective September 1, 2011.]

(d) In this section:

(1) [Repealed by Acts 2011, 82nd Leg., ch. 1290 (H.B. 2017), § 44(4), effective September 1, 2011.]

(2) "State judge" means:

(A) a justice of the supreme court;

(B) a judge of the court of criminal appeals;

(C) a judge of a court of appeals of this state;

(D) a district court judge;

(E) a presiding judge of an administrative judicial district; or

(F) a statutory county court judge.

Sec. 504.404. Federal Administrative Law Judges.

(a) The department shall issue specialty license plates to current federal administrative law judges that bear the words "U.S. A. L. Judge."

(b) [Repealed by Acts 2011, 82nd Leg., ch. 1290 (H.B. 2017), § 44(4), effective September 1, 2011.]

Sec. 504.405. County Judges.

(a) The department shall issue specialty license plates for current county judges of this state that bear the words "County Judge."

(b) [Repealed by Acts 2011, 82nd Leg., ch. 1296 (H.B. 2357), § 247(15), effective January 1, 2012.]

(c) In this section, "county judge" means the judge of the county court established by Section 15, Article V, Texas Constitution.

Sec. 504.406. Texas Constables.

The department shall issue specialty license plates for Texas constables that bear the words "Texas Constable."

Sec. 504.4061. Foreign Organization Vehicles.

(a) The department shall issue specialty license plates for an instrumentality established by a foreign government recognized by the United States before January 1, 1979, that is without official representation or diplomatic relations with the United States. The license plates must include the words "Foreign Organization" and shall remain valid for seven years.

(b) A person entitled to specialty license plates under this section may register the vehicle without payment of any fee paid for or at the time of registration.

Sec. 504.407. Peace Officers Wounded or Killed in Line of Duty [Renumbered].

Renumbered to Tex. Transp. Code § 504.511 by Acts 2011, 82nd Leg., ch. 1296 (H.B. 2357), § 199, effective January 1, 2012.

Sec. 504.408. Gold Star Mother, Father, Spouse, or Family Member [Renumbered].

Renumbered to Tex. Transp. Code § 504.512 by Acts 2011, 82nd Leg., ch. 1296 (H.B. 2357), § 199, effective January 1, 2012.

Sec. 504.409. Firefighters [Renumbered].

Renumbered to Tex. Transp. Code § 504.513 by Acts 2011, 82nd Leg., ch. 1296 (H.B. 2357), § 200, effective January 1, 2012.

Sec. 504.410. Emergency Medical Services Personnel [Renumbered].

Renumbered to Tex. Transp. Code § 504.514 by Acts 2011, 82nd Leg., ch. 1296 (H.B. 2357), § 201, effective January 1, 2012.

Sec. 504.411. Honorary Consuls [Renumbered].

Renumbered to Tex. Transp. Code § 504.515 by Acts 2011, 82nd Leg., ch. 1296 (H.B. 2357), § 201, effective January 1, 2012.

Sec. 504.412. Foreign Organization Vehicles [Renumbered].

Renumbered to Tex. Transp. Code § 504.4061 by Acts 2011, 82nd Leg., ch. 1296 (H.B. 2357), § 192, effective January 1, 2012.

Sec. 504.413. Members of American Legion [Renumbered].

Renumbered to Tex. Transp. Code § 504.659 by Acts 2011, 82nd Leg., ch. 1296 (H.B. 2357), § 210, effective January 1, 2012.

Sec. 504.414. Professional Firefighter Plates.

(a) The professional firefighter plate may be issued to qualified firefighters. The sponsor of the plate may nominate a state agency for receipt of funds under Section 504.801(e)(2)(A).

(b) After deduction of the department's administrative costs in accordance with Section 504.801, the remainder of the fees from the sale of professional firefighter plates shall be deposited to the credit of an account in the state treasury to be used by the nominated state agency for the purpose of making grants to support the activities of an organization of professional firefighters located in this state that provides emergency relief and college scholarship funds to the professional firefighters and their dependents.

Transportation Code

Sec. 504.415. Vehicles Carrying Mobile Amateur Radio Equipment.

The department shall issue specialty license plates for a person who holds an amateur radio station license issued by the Federal Communications Commission and who operates receiving and transmitting mobile amateur radio equipment. The license plates shall include the person's amateur call letters as assigned by the Federal Communications Commission. A person may register more than one vehicle equipped with mobile amateur radio equipment under this section, and the department shall issue license plates that include the same amateur call letters for each vehicle.

Sec. 504.416. Star of Texas Award Recipients.

The department shall issue specialty license plates for persons who are recipients of a Star of Texas Award under Chapter 3106, Government Code. The license plates must include the Star of Texas Award emblem and the words "Star of Texas."

SUBCHAPTER F SPECIALTY LICENSE PLATES WITH RESTRICTED DISTRIBUTION AND REGULAR LICENSE PLATE FEES

Sec. 504.501. Classic Motor Vehicles and Travel Trailers; Custom Vehicles; Street Rods.

(a) The department shall issue specialty license plates for a motor vehicle that is at least 25 years old or is a custom vehicle or street rod. The license plates must include the word or words "Classic," "Custom Vehicle," or "Street Rod," or a similar designation, as appropriate.

(b) A person eligible for the license plates may instead use license plates that are:

(1) embossed with an alphanumeric pattern;

(2) of a plate design that was issued by this state in the same year as the model year of the vehicle; and

(3) approved for use by the department.

(b-1) The department may require the attachment of a registration insignia to a license plate described by Subsection (b) in a manner that does not affect the display of information originally on the license plate.

(c) There is no fee for issuance or approval of license plates under this section.

(d) Notwithstanding Chapter 547, a custom vehicle or street rod eligible to receive license plates under this section is not required to be equipped with a specific piece of equipment unless the specific piece of equipment was required by statute as a condition of sale during the year listed as the model year on the certificate of title.

(e) On initial registration of a custom vehicle or street rod, the owner must provide proof, acceptable to the department, that the custom vehicle or street rod passed a safety inspection that has been approved by the department. The department shall create a safety inspection process for inspecting custom vehicles and street rods.

(f) In this section:

(1) "Custom vehicle" means a vehicle:

(A) that is:

(i) at least 25 years old and of a model year after 1948; or

(ii) manufactured to resemble a vehicle that is at least 25 years old and of a model year after 1948; and

(B) that:

(i) has been altered from the manufacturer's original design; or

(ii) has a body constructed from materials not original to the vehicle.

(2) "Street rod" means a vehicle:

(A) that was manufactured:

(i) before 1949; or

(ii) after 1948 to resemble a vehicle manufactured before 1949; and

(B) that:

(i) has been altered from the manufacturer's original design; or

(ii) has a body constructed from materials not original to the vehicle.

Sec. 504.5011. Classic Travel Trailers [Repealed].

Repealed by Acts 2009, 81st Leg., ch. 1136 (H.B. 2553), § 39(9), effective September 1, 2011.

Sec. 504.502. Certain Exhibition Vehicles.

(a) The department shall issue specialty license plates for a passenger car, truck, motorcycle, bus, or former military vehicle that:

(1) is at least 25 years old, if the vehicle is a passenger car, truck, motorcycle, or bus;

(2) is a collector's item;

(3) is used exclusively for exhibitions, club activities, parades, and other functions of public interest and is not used for regular transportation; and

(4) does not carry advertising.

(b) The license plates must include the words "Antique Auto," "Antique Truck," "Antique Motorcycle," "Antique Bus," or "Military Vehicle," as appropriate.

(c) A person eligible for the license plates may instead use license plates that are:

(1) embossed with an alphanumeric pattern;

(2) of a plate design that was issued by this state in the same year as the model year of the vehicle, provided that a passenger car must bear passenger car or truck license plates and a truck must bear passenger car or truck license plates; and

(3) approved for use by the department.

(c-1) The department may require attachment of a registration insignia to a license plate described by Subsection (c) in a manner that does not affect the display of information originally on the license plate.

(d) License plates issued or approved under this section expire on the fifth anniversary of the date of issuance or approval.

(e) The fee for issuance or approval of license plates under this section is:

(1) $10 for each year or portion of a year remaining in the five-year registration period if the vehicle was manufactured in 1921 or later; or

(2) $8 for each year or portion of a year remaining in the five-year registration period if the vehicle was manufactured before 1921.

(f) The department may exempt a former military vehicle from the requirement to display a license plate or registration insignia if the exemption is necessary to maintain the vehicle's accurate military markings. The department may approve an alternative registration insignia that is compatible with the vehicle's original markings.

(g) A person entitled to specialty license plates or to department approval under this section may register the vehicle without payment of any fees paid for or at the time of registration except the fee for the license plate.

(h) Notwithstanding any other provision of law, a vehicle issued license plates under Subsection (a) shall be required to attach and display only one license plate on the rear of the vehicle.

(i) In this section, "former military vehicle" means a vehicle, including a trailer, regardless of the vehicle's size, weight, or year of manufacture, that:

(1) was manufactured for use in any country's military forces;

(2) is maintained to represent its military design and markings accurately; and

(3) is not operated on continuous tracks.

(j) [Repealed by Acts 2011, 82nd Leg., ch. 1296 (H.B. 2357), § 247(16), effective January 1, 2012.]

Sec. 504.503. Municipal, Motor, and Private Buses.

The department shall issue without charge specialty license plates for municipal buses, motor buses, and private buses. The license plates must include the words "City Bus," "Motor Bus," or "Private Bus," as appropriate.

Sec. 504.504. Certain Farm Vehicles and Drilling and Construction Equipment [Renumbered].

Renumbered to Tex. Transp. Code § 502.146 by Acts 2011, 82nd Leg., ch. 1296 (H.B. 2357), § 105, effective January 1, 2012.

Sec. 504.505. Cotton Vehicles.

(a) The department shall issue specialty license plates for a single motor vehicle that is:

(1) used only to transport chile pepper modules, seed cotton, cotton, cotton burrs, or equipment used in transporting or processing chile peppers or cotton; and

(2) not more than 10 feet in width.

(b) The license plates must include the words "Cotton Vehicle."

(c) There is no fee for issuance of the license plates. The license plates may be renewed without payment of a fee.

Sec. 504.506. Log Loader Vehicles.

(a) The department shall issue specialty license plates for a vehicle that is temporarily operated on public highways, during daylight hours only, and on which machinery is mounted solely to load logs on other vehicles.

(b) The fee for issuance of the license plates is $62.50.

(c) A person entitled to specialty license plates under this section may register the vehicle without payment of any fee paid for or at the time of registration other than the fee for the license plates.

(d) A vehicle having a license plate issued under this section is exempt from the inspection requirements of Chapter 548.

(e) This section does not apply to a vehicle used to haul logs.

(f) [Repealed by Acts 2011, 82nd Leg., ch. 1296 (H.B. 2357), § 247(17), effective January 1, 2012.]

Sec. 504.507. Forestry Vehicles.

(a) The department shall issue specialty license plates for forestry vehicles. License plates issued under this section must include the words "Forestry Vehicle."

(b) There is no fee for issuance of the license plates. The department shall:

(1) collect any fee that a county imposes under this chapter for registration of a forestry vehicle; and

(2) send the fee to the appropriate county for disposition.

(c) [Repealed by Acts 2011, 82nd Leg., ch. 1296 (H.B. 2357), § 247(18), effective January 1, 2012.]

Sec. 504.508. Tow Trucks.

(a) The department shall issue specialty license plates for a commercial motor vehicle used as a tow truck. The license plates must include the words "Tow Truck." A vehicle used commercially as a tow truck shall display license plates issued under this section.

(b) There is no fee for issuance of the license plates.

(c) Proof of eligibility for license plates under this section must include a copy of the permit certificate issued by the Texas Department of Licensing and Regulation for the tow truck.

(d) [Repealed by Acts 2011, 82nd Leg., ch. 1296 (H.B. 2357), § 247(19), effective January 1, 2012.]

Sec. 504.509. Vehicles Carrying Mobile Amateur Radio Equipment [Renumbered].

Renumbered to Tex. Transp. Code § 504.415 by Acts 2011, 82nd Leg., ch. 1296 (H.B. 2357), § 193, effective January 1, 2012.

Sec. 504.510. Golf Cart License Plates [Repealed].

Repealed by Acts 2013, 83rd Leg., ch. 877 (H.B. 719), § 3, effective June 14, 2013.

Sec. 504.511. Peace Officers Wounded or Killed in Line of Duty.

(a) The department shall issue specialty license plates for:

(1) a person wounded in the line of duty as a peace officer; or

(2) a surviving spouse, parent, brother, sister, or adult child, including an adopted child or stepchild, of a person killed in the line of duty as a peace officer.

(b) License plates issued under this section must include the words "To Protect and Serve" above an insignia depicting a yellow rose superimposed over the outline of a badge.

(c) The fee for issuance of the license plates is $20.

(d) In this section, "peace officer" has the meaning assigned by Section 1.07, Penal Code.

Sec. 504.5115. Certain Purple Heart Recipients.

(a) The department shall issue specialty license plates for recipients of a Purple Heart awarded by the Department of Public Safety or another law enforcement agency in this state.

(b) The fee for issuance of one set of the license plates is $3.

(c) A person issued specialty license plates under this section shall be issued one set of the license plates without payment of the registration fee required under Chapter 502.

Sec. 504.512. Gold Star Mother, Father, Spouse, or Family Member.

(a) The department shall issue a specialty license plate for the mother, father, or surviving spouse or

Transportation Code

an immediate family member of a person who died while serving in the United States armed forces. License plates issued under this section must include the words "Gold Star Mother," "Gold Star Father," "Gold Star Spouse," or "Gold Star Family" and a gold star. A person may not be issued more than one set of the license plates at a time.

(a-1) In this section "immediate family member" means the parent, child, or sibling of a person who died while serving in the United States armed forces.

(b) [Repeal by Acts 2015, 84th Leg., ch. 741 (H.B. 1702) § 1 effective January 1, 2016.]

Sec. 504.513. Firefighters.

(a) The department shall issue specialty license plates for:

(1) volunteer firefighters certified by:

(A) the Texas Commission on Fire Protection; or

(B) the State Firemen's and Fire Marshals' Association of Texas; and

(2) fire protection personnel as that term is defined by Section 419.021, Government Code.

(b) A person may be issued not more than three sets of license plates.

Sec. 504.514. Emergency Medical Services Personnel.

(a) The department shall issue specialty license plates for emergency medical services personnel certified by the Department of State Health Services under Subchapter C, Chapter 773, Health and Safety Code.

(b) The fee for issuance of the license plates is $8.

(c) A person may be issued only one set of the license plates.

Sec. 504.515. Honorary Consuls.

(a) The department shall issue specialty license plates for a person who is an honorary consul authorized by the United States to perform consular duties. License plates issued under this section must include the words "Honorary Consul."

(b) The fee for issuance of the license plates is $40.

Sec. 504.516. Rental Trailer or Travel Trailer Fee: Trailer or Semitrailer.

(a) The department may issue specially designed license plates for rental trailers and travel trailers that include, as appropriate, the words "rental trailer" or "travel trailer."

(b) In this section:

(1) "Rental fleet" means vehicles that are designated in the manner prescribed by the department as a rental fleet.

(2) "Rental trailer" means a utility trailer.

(3) "Travel trailer" has the meaning assigned by Section 501.002.

SUBCHAPTER G SPECIALTY LICENSE PLATES FOR GENERAL DISTRIBUTION

Sec. 504.601. General Provisions Applicable to Specialty License Plates for General Distribution.

(a) Unless expressly provided by this subchapter or department rule:

(1) the fee for issuance of a license plate under this subchapter is $30; and

(2) of each fee received under this subchapter, the department shall use $8 to defray its administrative costs in complying with this subchapter.

(b) This section does not apply to a specialty license plate marketed and sold by a private vendor at the request of the specialty license plate sponsor under Section 504.6011.

Sec. 504.6011. General Provisions Applicable to Specialty License Plates for General Distribution Sold Through Private Vendor.

(a) The sponsor of a specialty license plate may contract with the private vendor authorized under Subchapter J for the marketing and sale of the specialty license plate.

(b) The fee for issuance of a specialty license plate described by Subsection (a) is the amount established under Section 504.851.

(c) Notwithstanding any other law, from each fee received for the issuance of a specialty license plate described by Subsection (a), the department shall:

(1) deduct the administrative costs described by Section 504.601(a)(2);

(2) deposit to the credit of the account designated by the law authorizing the specialty license plate the portion of the fee for the sale of the plate that the state would ordinarily receive under the contract described by Section 504.851(a); and

(3) pay to the private vendor the remainder of the fee.

(d) A sponsor of a specialty license plate authorized to be issued under this subchapter before November 19, 2009, may reestablish its specialty

Transportation Code

license plate under Sections 504.601 and 504.702 and be credited its previous deposit with the department if a contract entered into by the sponsor under Subsection (a) terminates.

Sec. 504.6012. Elimination of Dedicated Revenue Accounts; Revenues in Trust.

(a) Notwithstanding any other law, not later than September 30, 2021, the comptroller shall eliminate all dedicated accounts established for specialty license plates and shall set aside the balances of those dedicated accounts so that the balances may be appropriated only for the purposes intended as provided by the dedications.

(b) On and after September 1, 2021, the portion of a fee payable that is designated for deposit to a dedicated account shall be paid instead to the credit of an account in a trust fund created by the comptroller outside the general revenue fund. The comptroller shall administer the trust fund and accounts and may allocate the corpus and earnings on each account only in accordance with the dedications of the revenue deposited to the trust fund accounts.

Sec. 504.602. Keep Texas Beautiful License Plates.

(a) The department shall issue specialty license plates including the words "Keep Texas Beautiful." The department shall design the license plates in consultation with Keep Texas Beautiful, Inc.

(b) After deduction of the department's administrative costs, the remainder of the fee for issuance of the license plates shall be used in connection with the department's litter prevention and community beautification programs.

Sec. 504.603. Texas Capitol License Plates.

(a) The department shall design and issue specialty license plates relating to the State Capitol. The department may design the license plates in consultation with the State Preservation Board.

(b) After deduction of the department's administrative costs, the remainder of the fee for issuance of the license plates shall be deposited to the credit of the Capitol fund established under Section 443.0101, Government Code.

Sec. 504.604. Texas Commission on the Arts License Plates.

(a) The department shall issue specialty license plates including the words "State of the Arts." The department shall design the license plates in consultation with the Texas Commission on the Arts.

(b) After deduction of the department's administrative costs, the remainder of the fee for issuance of the license plates shall be deposited to the credit of the Texas Commission on the Arts operating fund established under Section 444.027, Government Code.

Sec. 504.605. Animal Friendly License Plates.

(a) The department shall issue specialty license plates including the words "Animal Friendly." The department shall design the license plates.

(b) After deduction of the department's administrative costs, the remainder of the fee for issuance of the license plates shall be deposited to the credit of the animal friendly account established by Section 828.014, Health and Safety Code.

Sec. 504.606. Big Bend National Park License Plates.

(a) The department shall issue specialty license plates that include one or more graphic images of a significant feature of Big Bend National Park. The department shall design the license plates in consultation with the Parks and Wildlife Department and any organization designated by it.

(b) After deduction of the department's administrative costs, the remainder of the fee for issuance of the license plates shall be deposited to the credit of the Big Bend National Park account in the state treasury. Money in the account may be used only by the Parks and Wildlife Department to support the activities of a designated nonprofit organization whose primary purpose is the improvement or preservation of Big Bend National Park.

Sec. 504.607. Read to Succeed.

(a) The department shall issue specialty license plates including the words "Read to Succeed." The department shall design the license plates.

(b) After deduction of the department's administrative costs, the remainder of the fee shall be deposited to the credit of the "Read to Succeed" account in the general revenue fund. Money in the account may be used only to provide educational materials for public school libraries. The account is composed of:

(1) money required to be deposited to the credit of the account under this subsection; and

(2) donations made to the account.

Sec. 504.608. Mothers Against Drunk Driving License Plates.

(a) The department shall issue specialty license plates that include the words "Mothers Against Drunk Driving." The department shall design the license plates in consultation with Mothers Against Drunk Driving.

(b) After deduction of the department's administrative costs, the remainder of the fee for issuance of the license plates shall be deposited to the credit of the general revenue fund and may be appropriated only to the Texas Higher Education Coordinating Board in making grants to benefit drug-abuse prevention and education programs sponsored by Mothers Against Drunk Driving.

Sec. 504.609. United States Olympic Committee License Plates.

The department shall issue specialty license plates including the words "United States Olympic Committee." The department shall design the license plates in consultation with the United States Olympic Committee.

Sec. 504.610. Texas Aerospace Commission License Plates.

(a) The department may issue specialty license plates in recognition of the Texas Aerospace Commission. The department shall design the license plates in consultation with the Texas Aerospace Commission.

(b) After deduction of the department's administrative costs, the remainder of the fee for issuance of the license plates shall be deposited to the credit of the general revenue fund.

Sec. 504.611. Volunteer Advocate Program License Plates.

(a) The department shall issue specialty license plates in recognition of children. The department shall design the license plates in consultation with the Health and Human Services Commission.

(b) After deduction of the department's administrative costs, the remainder of the fee for issuance of the license plates shall be deposited to the credit of the volunteer advocate program account in the general revenue fund. Money deposited to the credit of the volunteer advocate program account may be used only by the Health and Human Services Commission to fund a contract entered into by the commission under Section 264.602, Family Code.

Sec. 504.612. Texas Young Lawyers Association License Plates.

(a) The department shall issue specialty license plates including the words "And Justice for All." The department shall design the license plates in consultation with the Texas Young Lawyers Association.

(b) After deduction of the department's administrative costs, the remainder of the fee for issuance of the license plates shall be deposited to the credit of the basic civil legal services account established by Section 51.943, Government Code.

Sec. 504.613. Houston Livestock Show and Rodeo License Plates.

(a) The department shall issue specialty license plates including the words "Houston Livestock Show and Rodeo." The department shall design the license plates in consultation with the Houston Livestock Show and Rodeo.

(b) After deduction of the department's administrative costs, the remainder of the fee for issuance of the license plates shall be deposited to the credit of the Houston Livestock Show and Rodeo scholarship account in the state treasury. Money in the account may be used only by the Texas Higher Education Coordinating Board in making grants to benefit the Houston Livestock Show and Rodeo.

Sec. 504.614. Professional Sports Team License Plates.

(a) The department may issue specialty license plates that include the name and insignia of a professional sports team located in this state. The department shall design the license plates in consultation with the professional sports team and may enter a trademark license with the professional sports team or its league to implement this section. A license plate may be issued under this section only for a professional sports team that:

(1) certifies to the department that the requirements of Section 504.702 are met; and

(2) plays its home games in a facility constructed or operated, in whole or in part, with public funds.

(b) After deduction of the department's administrative costs, the remainder of the fee for issuance of the license plates shall be sent to the public entity that provided public funds for the construction or renovation of the facility in which the professional sports team plays its home games or that provides public funds for the operation of that facility. The funds shall be deposited to the credit of the venue project fund, if the public entity has created a venue project fund under Section 334.042 or 335.072, Local Government Code. If the public entity has not created a venue project fund, funds distributed to a public entity under this section must first be used to retire any public debt incurred by the public entity in the construction or acquisition of the facility in which the professional sports team plays its home games. After that debt is retired, funds distributed to the public entity may be spent only for maintenance or improvement of the facility.

(b-1) A public entity that receives money under Subsection (b) may contract with the private vendor under Section 504.6011 to distribute the entity's portion of the money in a manner other than that described by Subsection (b).

(c) In this section:

(1) "Public entity" includes a municipality, county, industrial development corporation, or special district that is authorized to plan, acquire, establish, develop, construct, or renovate a facility in which a professional sports team plays its home games.

(2) "Professional sports team" means a sports team that is a member or an affiliate of a member of the National Football League, National Basketball Association, or National Hockey League or a major league baseball team.

Sec. 504.615. Collegiate License Plates.

(a) The department shall issue specialty license plates that include the name and insignia of a college. The department shall design the license plates in consultation with the applicable college. The department may issue a license plate under this section only for a college that certifies to the department that the requirements of Section 504.702 are met.

(b) After deduction of the department's administrative costs, the remainder of the fee for issuance of the license plates shall be deposited to the credit of the general revenue fund. The money may be used only for:

(1) scholarships to students who demonstrate a need for financial assistance under Texas Higher Education Coordinating Board rule; or

(2) Texas Public Educational Grants awarded under Subchapter C, Chapter 56, Education Code, if the fee is for the issuance of a license plate for a college described by Subsection (e)(1).

(c) If the fee is for the issuance of license plates for a college described by Subsection (e)(1), the money:

(1) shall be deposited to the credit of the institution of higher education designated on the license plates; and

(2) is supplementary and is not income for purposes of reducing general revenue appropriations to that institution of higher education.

(d) If the fee is for the issuance of license plates for a college described by Subsection (e)(2), the money shall be deposited to the credit of the Texas Higher Education Coordinating Board. The money:

(1) shall be allocated to students at the college designated on the plates; and

(2) is in addition to other money that the board may allocate to that college.

(d-1) If the fee is for the issuance of license plates for a college described by Subsection (e)(3), the money:

(1) shall be deposited to the credit of the Texas Higher Education Coordinating Board; and

(2) is supplementary and is not income for purposes of reducing general revenue appropriations to that board.

(e) In this section, "college" means:

(1) an institution of higher education as defined by Section 61.003, Education Code;

(2) a private college or university described by Section 61.222, Education Code; or

(3) a college or university that is not located in this state.

Sec. 504.616. Texas Reads License Plates.

(a) The department shall issue specialty license plates including the words "Texas Reads" that incorporate one or more submissions from middle school students in a competition conducted by the department.

(b) After deduction of the department's administrative costs, the remainder of the fee shall be deposited to the credit of the Texas Reads account in the general revenue fund. Money from the account may be used only to make grants under Section 441.0092, Government Code. The account is composed of:

(1) money required to be deposited to the credit of the account under this subsection; and

(2) donations made to the account.

Sec. 504.617. Texas. It's Like a Whole Other Country License Plates.

(a) The department shall issue specialty license plates that include the trademarked Texas patch and the words "Texas. It's Like A Whole Other Country." The department shall design the license plates in consultation with the Texas Department of Economic Development.

(b) After deduction of the department's administrative costs, the remainder of the fee for issuance of the license plates shall be deposited to the credit of the tourism account in the general revenue fund to finance the Texas Department of Economic Development's tourism activities.

Sec. 504.618. Conservation License Plates.

(a) The department shall issue specialty license plates to support Parks and Wildlife Department activities. The department shall design the license plates in consultation with the Parks and Wildlife Department.

(b) After deduction of the department's administrative costs, the remainder of the fee for issuance of the license plates shall be deposited to the credit of the Texas parks and wildlife conservation and capital account established by Section 11.043, Parks and Wildlife Code. Money deposited in the Texas parks and wildlife conservation and capital account under this section is supplementary and is not income for the purposes of reducing general revenue appropriations to the Parks and Wildlife Department.

Sec. 504.619. Texas Commission for the Deaf and Hard of Hearing License Plates.

(a) The department shall issue specialty license plates in support of the Texas Commission for the Deaf and Hard of Hearing. The department shall design the license plates in consultation with the Texas Commission for the Deaf and Hard of Hearing.

(b) After deduction of the department's administrative costs, the remainder of the fee for issuance of the license plates:

(1) shall be deposited to the credit of the general revenue fund; and

(2) may be appropriated only to the Texas Commission for the Deaf and Hard of Hearing for direct services programs, training, and education.

Sec. 504.620. Texans Conquer Cancer License Plates.

(a) The department shall issue specialty license plates that include the words "Texans Conquer Cancer." The department shall design the license plates in consultation with the Cancer Prevention and Research Institute of Texas.

(b) After deduction of the department's administrative costs, the remainder of the fee for issuance of the license plates shall be deposited to the credit of the cancer prevention and research fund established by Section 102.201, Health and Safety Code.

Sec. 504.6201. Cancer of Unknown Primary Origin Awareness License Plates.

(a) The department shall issue specialty license plates to raise awareness of cancer of unknown primary origin. The license plates must include the words "A Fine Cause for Unknown Cancer." The department shall design the license plates in consultation with the Orange Grove Family Career and Community Leaders of America.

(b) After deduction of the department's administrative costs, the remainder of the fee for issuance of the license plates shall be deposited to the credit of the cancer prevention and research fund established by Section 102.201, Health and Safety Code.

Sec. 504.621. Special Olympics Texas License Plates.

(a) The department shall issue specialty license plates that include the words "Special Olympics Texas." The department shall design the license plates in consultation with Special Olympics Texas.

(b) After deduction of the department's administrative costs, the remainder of the fee for issuance of the license plates shall be deposited to the credit of the Special Olympics Texas account established by Section 533.018, Health and Safety Code.

Sec. 504.622. Girl Scout License Plates.

(a) The department shall issue specialty license plates that include the words "Girl Scouts." The department shall design the license plates in consultation with the Girl Scout Councils of Texas.

(b) After deduction of the department's administrative costs, the remainder of the fee for issuance of the license plates shall be deposited to the credit of the Girl Scout account in the state treasury. Money in the account may be used by the Texas Higher Education Coordinating Board in making grants to benefit educational projects sponsored by the Girl Scout Councils of Texas.

Sec. 504.623. TexasYMCA.

(a) The department shall issue specialty license plates in honor of the Young Men's Christian Association. The department shall design the license plates.

(b) After deduction of the department's administrative costs, the remainder of the fee for issuance of the license plates shall be deposited to the credit of the YMCA account established by Section 7.025, Education Code, as added by Chapter 869, Acts of the 77th Legislature, Regular Session, 2001.

Sec. 504.624. 100th Football Season of Stephen F. Austin High School [Repealed].

Repealed by Acts 2011, 82nd Leg., ch. 1296 (H.B. 2357), § 247(20), effective January 1, 2012.

Sec. 504.625. Texas Agricultural Products License Plates.

(a) The department shall issue specialty license plates that include the words "Go Texan" and the "Go Texan" logo of the Department of Agriculture. The department shall design the license plates in consultation with the commissioner of agriculture.

(b) After deduction of the department's administrative costs, the department shall deposit the remainder of the proceeds to the credit of the "Go Texan" partner program account established by Section 46.008, Agriculture Code.

Sec. 504.626. Texas Citrus Industry.

(a) The department shall issue specialty license plates in honor of the citrus industry in this state. The department shall design the license plates.

(b) After deduction of the department's administrative costs, the remainder of the fee for issuance of the license plates shall be deposited to the credit of an account in the general revenue fund that may be appropriated only to Texas A&M University—Kingsville to provide financial assistance to graduate students in the College of Agriculture and Human Sciences.

Sec. 504.627. Waterfowl and Wetland Conservation License Plates.

(a) The department shall issue specialty license plates including one or more graphic images supplied by the Parks and Wildlife Department. The department shall design the license plates in consultation with the Parks and Wildlife Department and any organization designated by it.

(b) After deducting the department's administrative costs, the remainder of the fee for issuance of the license plates shall be deposited to the credit of an account in the state treasury. Money in the account may be used only by the Parks and Wildlife Department to support the activities of a designated nonprofit organization whose primary purpose is the conservation of waterfowl and wetland.

Sec. 504.6275. Save Our Beaches License Plates.

(a) The department shall issue specialty license plates to support the coastal protection and improvement program.

(b) After deduction of the department's administrative costs, the remainder of the fee for issuance of the license plates shall be deposited to the credit of the coastal protection and improvement fund established by Section 33.653, Natural Resources Code, to fund the cleaning, maintaining, nourishing, and protecting of state beaches.

Sec. 504.628. United We Stand License Plates.

(a) The department shall issue specialty license plates that include the words "United We Stand" and include only the colors red, white, blue, and black.

(b) After deduction of the department's administrative costs, the remainder of the fee for issuance of the license plates shall be deposited to the credit of the Texas mobility fund.

Sec. 504.629. TexasPGA Junior Golf License Plates [Repealed].

Repealed by Acts 2011, 82nd Leg., ch. 1296 (H.B. 2357), § 247(20), effective January 1, 2012.

Sec. 504.630. Air Force Association License Plates.

(a) The department shall issue specialty license plates that include the words "Air Force Association." The department shall design the license plates in consultation with the Air Force Association of Texas.

(b) After deduction of the department's administrative costs, the remainder of the fee shall be deposited to the credit of the Air Force Association of Texas account in the state treasury. Money in the account may be used by the Texas Veterans Commission in making grants to benefit projects sponsored by the Air Force Association of Texas.

Sec. 504.631. Texas State Rifle Association License Plates.

(a) The department shall issue specialty license plates to honor the Texas State Rifle Association.

(b) After deduction of the department's administrative costs, the remainder of the fee shall be deposited to the credit of an account in the general revenue fund that may be appropriated only to the Texas Cooperative Extension of The Texas A&M University System as follows:

(1) 50 percent to supplement existing and future scholarship programs supported by the Texas State Rifle Association; and

(2) 50 percent to support the 4-H Shooting Sports Program for youth.

Sec. 504.632. Urban Forestry License Plates.

(a) The department shall issue specialty license plates to benefit urban forestry. The department shall design the license plates in consultation with an organization described in Subsection (b).

(b) After deduction of the department's administrative costs, the remainder of the fee shall be deposited to the credit of the urban forestry account in the state treasury. Money in the account may be used by the Texas Forest Service in making grants to support the activities of a nonprofit organization located in Texas whose primary purpose is to sponsor projects involving urban and community:

(1) tree planting;

(2) tree preservation; and

(3) tree education programs.

Sec. 504.633. Share the Road License Plates.

(a) The department shall issue specialty license plates that include the words "Share the Road" and the image of a bicycle or a bicycle with a rider. The department shall design the plates in consultation with the Texas Bicycle Coalition Education Fund.

(b) After deduction of the department's administrative costs, the remainder of the fee shall be deposited to the credit of the share the road account in the state treasury to be used only by the Texas Education Agency to support the activities of a designated nonprofit organization whose primary purpose is to promote bicyclist safety, education, and access through:

(1) education and awareness programs; and

(2) training, workshops, educational materials, and media events.

(c) Up to 25 percent of the amount in Subsection (b) may be used to support the activities of the nonprofit organization in marketing and promoting the share the road concept and license plates.

Sec. 504.634. San Antonio Missions National Historical Park License Plates [Repealed].

Repealed by Acts 2011, 82nd Leg., ch. 1296 (H.B. 2357), § 247(20), effective January 1, 2012.

Sec. 504.635. El Paso Mission Valley License Plates.

(a) The department shall issue El Paso Mission Valley specialty license plates. The department shall design the license plates in consultation with the Socorro Mission Restoration Effort.

(b) After deduction of the department's administrative costs, the remainder of the fee shall be deposited to the credit of the El Paso Mission Restoration account in the state treasury. Money in the account may be used only by the Texas Historical Commission in making grants to be used for the purpose of the preservation and rehabilitation of the Socorro, San Elizario, and Ysleta Missions.

Sec. 504.636. Cotton Boll License Plates.

(a) The department shall issue specialty license plates depicting a graphic image of a cotton boll. The department shall design the license plates in consultation with Texas Cotton Producers, Inc.

(b) After deduction of the department's administrative costs, the remainder of the fee shall be deposited to the credit of the general revenue fund for use only by the Texas Higher Education Coordinating Board in making grants to benefit Texas Cotton Producers, Inc., for the sole purpose of providing scholarships to students who are pursuing a degree in an agricultural field related to the cotton industry while enrolled in an institution of higher education, as defined by Section 61.003, Education Code.

Sec. 504.637. Daughters of the Republic of Texas License Plates.

(a) The department shall issue specialty license plates that include the words "Native Texan." The department shall design the license plates in consultation with the Daughters of the Republic of Texas.

(b) After deduction of the department's administrative costs, the remainder of the fee shall be deposited to the credit of the Daughters of the Republic of Texas account in the state treasury. Money in the account may be used only by the Texas Department of Economic Development or its successor agency in making grants to the Daughters of the Republic of Texas to be used only for the purpose of:

(1) preserving Texas historic sites; or

(2) funding educational programs that teach Texas history.

Sec. 504.638. Knights of Columbus License Plates.

(a) The department shall issue specialty license plates that include the words "Knights of Columbus" and the emblem of the Order of the Knights of Columbus. The department shall design the license plates in consultation with the Knights of Columbus.

(b) After deduction of the department's administrative costs, the remainder of the fee for issuance of the license plates shall be deposited to the credit of the State Council Charities account in the general revenue fund. Money in the account may be used only by the Texas Education Agency to make grants to State Council Charities to carry out the purposes of that organization.

Sec. 504.639. Texas Music License Plates.

(a) The department shall issue specialty license plates that include the words "Texas Music." The department shall design the license plates in consultation with the governor's office.

(b) After deduction of the department's administrative costs, the remainder of the fee for issuance of the license plates shall be deposited to the credit of the Texas Music Foundation account established by Section 7.027, Education Code.

Sec. 504.640. Space Shuttle Columbia License Plates.

(a) The department shall issue Space Shuttle Columbia specialty license plates. The department shall design the license plates in consultation with the Aviation and Space Foundation of Texas.

(b) After deduction of the department's administrative costs, the remainder of the fee for issuance of the license plates shall be deposited to the credit of the general revenue fund and may be used only by the Texas Aerospace Commission or its successor agency in making grants to benefit the Aviation and Space Foundation of Texas for the purposes of furthering aviation and space activities in Texas and providing Columbia Crew memorial scholarships to students.

Sec. 504.641. Be a Blood Donor License Plates.

(a) The department shall issue Be a Blood Donor specialty license plates. The department shall design the license plates in consultation with the Gulf Coast Regional Blood Center in Houston.

(b) After deduction of the department's administrative costs, the remainder of the fee for issuance of the license plates shall be deposited to the credit of the be a blood donor account under Section 162.016, Health and Safety Code.

Sec. 504.642. Texas Council of Child Welfare Boards License Plates.

(a) The department shall issue Texas Council of Child Welfare Boards specialty license plates. The department shall design the license plates in consultation with the Texas Council of Child Welfare Boards, Inc.

(b) After deduction of the department's administrative costs, the remainder of the fee for issuance of the license plates shall be deposited to the credit of a special account for abused and neglected children established at the Department of Protective and Regulatory Services. Money in the account may be used only by the Department of Protective and Regulatory Services to fund programs and services supporting abused and neglected children under Section 264.004, Family Code.

Sec. 504.643. STAR Day School Library Readers Are Leaders License Plates [Repealed].

Repealed by Acts 2011, 82nd Leg., ch. 1296 (H.B. 2357), § 247(20), effective January 1, 2012.

Sec. 504.644. Marine Mammal Recovery License Plates.

(a) The department shall issue Marine Mammal Recovery specialty license plates. The department shall design the license plates in consultation with the Parks and Wildlife Department and the Texas Marine Mammal Stranding Network.

(b) After deduction of the department's administrative costs, the remainder of the fee for issuance of the license plates shall be deposited to the credit of an account in the state treasury. Money in the account may be used only by the Parks and Wildlife Department to support the activities of the Texas Marine Mammal Stranding Network in the recovery, rehabilitation, and release of stranded marine mammals. The Parks and Wildlife Department shall establish reporting and other mechanisms necessary to ensure that the money is spent for purposes for which it is dedicated.

Sec. 504.645. 4-H License Plates.

(a) The department shall issue specialty license plates that include the words "To Make the Best Better," the words "Texas 4-H," and the 4-H symbol of the four-leaf clover. The department shall design the license plates in consultation with the Texas 4-H and Youth Development Program.

(b) After deduction of the department's administrative costs, the remainder of the fee for issuance of the license plates shall be deposited to the credit of the general revenue fund and shall be used only by the Texas Cooperative Extension of the Texas A&M University System for 4-H and Youth Development Programs and to support the Texas

Cooperative Extension's activities related to 4-H and Youth Development Programs.

Sec. 504.646. Smile Texas Style License Plates.

(a) The department shall issue specialty license plates that include the words "Smile Texas Style." The department shall design the license plates in consultation with the Texas Dental Association.

(b) After deduction of the department's administrative costs, the remainder of the fee for issuance of the license plates shall be deposited to the credit of the general revenue fund to be used only by the Texas Department of Health in making grants to benefit the Texas Dental Association Financial Services for the sole use of providing charitable dental care.

Sec. 504.647. Fight Terrorism License Plates.

(a) The department shall issue Fight Terrorism specialty license plates that include a pentagon-shaped border surrounding:

(1) the date "9-11-01" with the likeness of the World Trade Center towers forming the "11";

(2) the likeness of the United States flag; and

(3) the words "Fight Terrorism."

(b) The fee shall be deposited to the credit of the Texas Department of Motor Vehicles fund.

Sec. 504.648. God Bless Texas and God Bless America License Plates.

(a) The department shall issue specialty license plates that include the words "God Bless Texas" and "God Bless America."

(b) After deduction of the department's administrative costs, the remainder of the fee shall be deposited to the credit of the share the road account in the state treasury and may only be used by the Texas Education Agency to support the Safe Routes to School Program of a designated statewide nonprofit organization whose primary purpose is to promote bicyclist safety, education, and access through:

(1) education and awareness programs; and

(2) training, workshops, educational materials, and media events.

(c) The fee for the license plates is $40.

(d) Up to 25 percent of the amount in Subsection (b) may be used to support the activities of the nonprofit organization in marketing and promoting the Safe Routes to School Program and the God Bless Texas and God Bless America license plates.

(e) The Texas Education Agency may use money received under this section to secure funds available under federal matching programs for safe routes to school and obesity prevention.

Sec. 504.649. Texas Juneteenth License Plates.

(a) The department shall issue Texas Juneteenth specialty license plates. The department shall design the license plates in consultation with Unity Unlimited Inc.

(b) After deduction of the department's administrative costs, the remainder of the fee for issuance of the license plates shall be deposited to the credit of the general revenue fund to be used only by the Texas Historical Commission in making grants to Unity Unlimited Inc. for the purpose of promoting the celebration of Juneteenth in this state, provided that verification is submitted to the Texas Historical Commission demonstrating that Unity Unlimited Inc. continues to maintain its nonprofit status. If Unity Unlimited Inc. does not have nonprofit status at the time of the distribution of a grant, the grant shall be distributed to another nonprofit organization for the purpose of promoting the celebration of Juneteenth in this state.

Sec. 504.650. Keeping Texas Strong License Plates [Repealed].

Repealed by Acts 2011, 82nd Leg., ch. 1296 (H.B. 2357), § 247(20), effective January 1, 2012.

Sec. 504.651. March of Dimes License Plates.

(a) The department shall issue specialty license plates that include the words "March of Dimes." The department shall design the license plates in consultation with the March of Dimes Texas Chapter.

(b) After deduction of the department's administrative costs, the remainder of the fee for issuance of the license plates shall be deposited to the credit of the Texas Department of Health for use in the Birth Defects Registry.

Sec. 504.652. Master Gardener License Plates.

(a) The department shall issue specialty license plates that include the seal of the Texas Master Gardener program of Texas Cooperative Extension.

(b) After deduction of the department's administrative costs, the remainder of the fee for issuance of the license plates shall be deposited to the credit of an account in the general revenue fund. Money in the account may be used only by Texas A&M AgriLife Extension for graduate student assistantships within the Texas Master Gardener program and to support Texas A&M AgriLife Extension's activities related to the Texas Master Gardener program.

Sec. 504.653. Mother-Child Survivors Educational Scholarship Fund License Plates [Repealed].

Repealed by Acts 2011, 82nd Leg., ch. 1296 (H.B. 2357), § 247(20), effective January 1, 2012.

Sec. 504.654. Eagle Scout License Plates.

(a) The department shall issue specialty license plates that bear a depiction of the Eagle Scout medal.

(b) After deduction of the department's administrative costs, the remainder of the fee for issuance of the license plates shall be deposited to the credit of the Eagle Scout account in the general revenue fund. Money in the account may be used only by the Texas Higher Education Coordinating Board in making grants to support projects sponsored by Boy Scout councils in this state. The Texas Higher Education Coordinating Board shall distribute grants under this section geographically as nearly as possible in proportion to the number of license plates issued under this section in each region of the state.

Sec. 504.6545. Boy Scout License Plates.

(a) The department shall issue specialty license plates that include the words "Boy Scouts of America." The department shall design the license plates in consultation with the Boy Scouts of America.

(b) After deduction of the department's administrative costs, the remainder of the fee for issuance of the license plates shall be deposited to the credit of the Boy Scout account in the general revenue fund. Money in the account may be used only by the Texas Higher Education Coordinating Board in making grants to benefit educational projects sponsored by Boy Scout councils in this state.

Sec. 504.655. Childhood Cancer Awareness Plates.

(a) The department shall issue specialty license plates to raise awareness of childhood cancer. The department shall design the license plates in consultation with an organization that seeks to raise awareness of childhood cancer in this state.

(b) After deduction of the department's administrative costs, the remainder of the fee for issuance of the license plates shall be deposited to the credit of an account created by the comptroller in the manner provided by Section 504.6012(b). Money deposited to that account may be used by the General Land Office only to provide grants to benefit organizations operating in this state that raise awareness of, conduct research on, or provide services for persons diagnosed with childhood cancer.

(c) The General Land Office and an organization that receives a grant under Subsection (b) may enter into a memorandum of understanding establishing the respective duties of the General Land Office and the organization in relation to carrying out the purposes of that subsection.

(d) Section 504.702 does not apply to a specialty license plate issued under this section.

Sec. 504.6551. Pediatric Cancer Research License Plates.

(a) The department shall issue specialty license plates that include the words "Kids Shouldn't Have Cancer." The department shall design the plates in consultation with the Kids Shouldn't Have Cancer Foundation.

(b) After deduction of the department's administrative costs, the remainder of the fee for issuance of the license plates shall be deposited to the credit of the cancer prevention and research fund established by Section 102.201, Health and Safety Code. Money deposited to that account may be used only to fund pediatric cancer research.

Sec. 504.656. Texas Lions Camp License Plates.

(a) The department shall issue Texas Lions Camp specialty license plates. The department shall design the license plates in consultation with the Texas Lions League for Crippled Children.

(b) After deduction of the department's administrative costs, the remainder of the fee for issuance of the license plates shall be deposited to the credit of the Texas Lions Camp account in the state treasury. Money in the account may be used only by the Parks and Wildlife Department to support the activities of a designated nonprofit organization that is accredited by the American Camping Association and is licensed by the Texas Department of Health and whose primary purpose is to provide, without charge, a camp for physically disabled, hearing or vision impaired, and diabetic children who reside in this state, regardless of race, religion, or national origin. The Parks and Wildlife Department shall establish reporting and other mechanisms necessary to ensure that the money is spent only for the purposes for which it is dedicated.

Sec. 504.657. Higher Education Coordinating Board License Plates.

(a) The department shall issue specialty license plates for the Texas Higher Education Coordinating Board. The department shall design the license plates in consultation with the coordinating board.

(b) After deduction of the department's administrative costs, the remainder of the fee shall be deposited to the credit of the "College For Texans" campaign account in the general revenue fund for use only by the Texas Higher Education Coordinating Board for purposes of the campaign.

Sec. 504.658. Insure Texas Kids License Plates.

(a) The department shall issue specialty license plates that include the words "Insure Texas Kids."

(b) After deduction of the department's administrative costs, the remainder of the fee for issuance of the license plates shall be deposited to the credit of the general revenue fund and may be appropriated only to the Health and Human Services Commission to fund outreach efforts for public and private health benefit plans available for children.

Sec. 504.659. Members of American Legion.

(a) The department shall issue specialty license plates for members of the American Legion. The license plates shall include the words "Still Serving America" and the emblem of the American Legion. The department shall design the license plates in consultation with the American Legion.

(b) The fee for the license plates is $30.

(c) After deduction of $8 to reimburse the department for its administrative costs, the remainder of the fee for issuance of the license plates shall be deposited to the credit of the American Legion, Department of Texas account in the state treasury. Money in the account may be used only by the Texas Veterans Commission in making grants to the American Legion Endowment Fund for scholarships and youth programs sponsored by the American Legion, Department of Texas.

Sec. 504.660. Sexual Assault Awareness License Plates.

(a) The department shall design and issue specialty license plates to support victims of sexual assault.

(b) [Repealed by Acts 2013, 83rd Leg., ch. 1135 (H.B. 2741), § 140(3), effective September 1, 2013.]

(c) After deduction of the department's administrative costs, the remainder of the fee for issuance of the license plates shall be deposited to the credit of the sexual assault program fund established by Section 420.008, Government Code.

Sec. 504.661. Marine Conservation License Plates.

(a) After deduction of the department's administrative costs in accordance with Section 504.801, the remainder of the fees allocated under Section 504.801(e)(2)(A) from the sale of Marine Conservation plates shall be deposited to the credit of an account in the state treasury to be used by the Texas Parks and Wildlife Department to support the activities of Coastal Conservation Association Texas in the conservation of marine resources.

(b) The Texas Parks and Wildlife Department shall establish reporting and other mechanisms necessary to ensure that the money is spent for the purpose for which it is dedicated.

Sec. 504.662. Choose Life License Plates.

(a) The department shall issue specially designed license plates that include the words "Choose Life." The department shall design the license plates in consultation with the attorney general.

(b) After deduction of the department's administrative costs, the department shall deposit the remainder of the fee for issuance of license plates under this section in the state treasury to the credit of the Choose Life account established by Section 402.036, Government Code.

Sec. 504.663. Big Brothers Big Sisters License Plates.

(a) The department shall issue specialty license plates in recognition of the mentoring efforts of Big Brothers Big Sisters of America organizations operating in this state. The department shall design the license plates in consultation with a representative from a Big Brothers Big Sisters of America organization operating in this state and the attorney general.

(b) After deduction of the department's administrative costs, the remainder of the fee for issuance of the license plates shall be deposited to the credit of the Specialty License Plates General Account in the general revenue fund. Money deposited to the credit of the Specialty License Plates General Account under this section may be used only by the attorney general to provide grants to benefit Big Brothers Big Sisters of America organizations operating in this state.

Sec. 504.664. Foundation School Program License Plates.

(a) The department shall issue specially designed license plates to benefit the Foundation School Program. The department shall design the license plates in consultation with the Texas Education Agency.

(b) After deduction of the department's administrative costs, the department shall deposit the remainder of the fee for issuance of license plates under this section to the credit of the foundation school fund.

Sec. 504.665. Alamo License Plates.

(a) The department shall issue specialty license plates that include the image of the Alamo and the word "Remember" at the bottom of each plate.

(b) After deduction of the department's administrative costs, the remainder of the fee for issuance of the license plates shall be deposited to the credit of an account created by the comptroller in the manner provided by Section 504.6012(b). Money deposited to that account may be used only by the General Land Office as follows:

(1) 75 percent of the money shall be used for the preservation of the Alamo; and

(2) 25 percent of the money shall be used to enhance the Alamo visitor experience or to fund education programs about the Alamo.

Sec. 504.666. K9s4COPs License Plates.

(a) The department shall issue K9s4COPs specialty license plates. The department shall design the license plates in consultation with K9s4COPs.

(b) After deduction of the department's administrative costs, the remainder of the fee for issuance of the license plates shall be deposited to the credit of the general revenue fund to be used only by the office of the governor in making grants to nonprofit organizations for the purpose of funding the purchase of police dogs by law enforcement agencies.

Sec. 504.667. Texas Medical Center License Plates.

(a) The department shall issue Texas Medical Center specialty license plates. The department shall design the license plates in consultation with Texas Medical Center.

(b) After deduction of the department's administrative costs, the remainder of the fee for issuance of the license plates shall be deposited to the credit of an account created by the comptroller in the manner provided by Section 504.6012(b). Money deposited to that account may be used only by the comptroller to provide grants to benefit Texas Medical Center and member institutions of Texas Medical Center.

Sec. 504.668. [3 Versions: As renumbered from Tex. Transp. Code § 504.665 by Acts 2017, 85th Leg., ch. 324] In God We Trust License Plates.

(a) The department shall issue specially designed license plates that include the words "In God We Trust."

(b) After deduction of the department's administrative costs, the remainder of the fee for issuance of the license plates shall be deposited to the credit of the general revenue fund and may be appropriated only to the Texas Veterans Commission.

Sec. 504.668. [3 Versions: As added by Acts 2017, 85th Leg., ch. 1003] Blessed Are the Peacemakers License Plates. [Renumbered]

Sec. 504.668. [3 Versions: As added by Acts 2017, 85th Leg., ch. 116] Back the Blue License Plates. [Renumbered]

Sec. 504.669. Back the Blue License Plates.

(a) The department shall issue specialty license plates that include a thin blue line and the words "Back the Blue."

(b) After deduction of the department's administrative costs, the remainder of the fee for issuance of the license plates shall be deposited to the credit of an account created by the comptroller in the manner provided by Section 504.6012(b). Money deposited to that account may be used only by the Employees Retirement System of Texas to provide financial assistance to survivors of peace officers under Chapter 615, Government Code.

Sec. 504.670. Blessed Are the Peacemakers License Plates.

(a) The department shall issue specialty license plates that include the image of the United States flag printed in black and white with a blue stripe crossing beneath the field of stars and the words

Transportation Code

"Blessed are the Peacemakers" at the bottom of each plate.

(b) After deduction of the department's administrative costs, the remainder of the fee for issuance of the license plates shall be deposited to the credit of an account created by the comptroller in the manner provided by Section 504.6012(b). Money deposited to that account may be used only by the State Preservation Board to maintain the Texas Peace Officers' Memorial Monument under Section 3105.004, Government Code.

Sec. 504.671. Register to Vote License Plates. [Renumbered to Tex. Transp. Code § 504.672]

Sec. 504.671. Keep Austin Weird License Plates. [Renumbered to Tex. Transp. Code § 504.674]

Sec. 504.671. Sickle Cell Disease Awareness License Plates. [Renumbered to Tex. Transp. Code § 504.673]

Sec. 504.672. Register to Vote License Plates. [Renumbered from Tex. Transp. Code § 504.671]

(a) The department shall issue specialty license plates that include the words "Register to Vote."

(b) After deduction of the department's administrative costs, the remainder of the fee for issuance of the license plates shall be deposited to the credit of an account created by the comptroller in the manner provided by Section 504.6012(b). Money deposited to that account may be used only by the secretary of state for Project V.O.T.E. or a successor voter education program administered by the office of the secretary of state.

Sec. 504.673. Sickle Cell Disease Awareness License Plates. [Renumbered from Tex. Transp. Code § 504.671]

(a) The department shall issue specialty license plates that include the words "Sickle Cell Matters" and an image of the burgundy sickle cell ribbon. The department shall design the plates in consultation with the Sickle Cell Association of Houston.

(b) After deduction of the department's administrative costs, the remainder of the fee for issuance of the license plates shall be deposited to the credit of an account created by the comptroller in the manner provided by Section 504.6012(b). Money deposited to that account may be used only by Texas Southern University to make grants to a nonprofit organization that has a history of providing services to persons with sickle cell disease for the purpose of providing those services.

Sec. 504.674. Keep Austin Weird License Plates. [Renumbered from Tex. Transp. Code § 504.671]

(a) The department shall issue specialty license plates that include the words "Keep Austin Weird."

(b) After deduction of the department's administrative costs, the remainder of the fee for issuance of the license plates shall be deposited to the credit of the general revenue fund.

Sec. 504.675. Autism Awareness License Plates.

(a) The department shall issue specialty license plates that include the words "Autism Awareness." The department shall design the plates in consultation with a representative of the Hope for Three nonprofit organization.

(b) After deduction of the department's administrative costs, the remainder of the fee for issuance of the license plates shall be deposited to the credit of an account created by the comptroller in the manner provided by Section 504.6012(b). Money deposited to that account may be used only by the trusteed programs within the office of the governor to make grants to a nonprofit organization whose primary purpose is to create awareness about and provide support to families living with autism spectrum disorder, to be used by that organization for that purpose.

Sec. 504.675. Make-A-Wish License Plates.

(a) The department shall issue specialty license plates that include the words "Make-A-Wish" and an image of the blue Make-A-Wish logo. The department shall design the plates in consultation with the Central and South Texas chapter of Make-A-Wish.

(b) After deduction of the department's administrative costs, the remainder of the fee for issuance of the license plates shall be deposited to the credit of an account created by the comptroller in the manner provided by Section 504.6012(b). Money deposited to that account may be used only by the Health and Human Services Commission to make grants to a nonprofit organization that has a history of providing services to children diagnosed with a critical illness for the purpose of providing those services.

Sec. 504.675. Stop Human Trafficking License Plates.

(a) The department shall issue specialty license plates to support the trafficked persons program account established under Section 50.0153, Health and Safety Code. The department shall design the license plates in consultation with an organization involved in the support and recovery of human trafficking victims.

(b) After deduction of the department's administrative costs the remainder of the fee for issuance of the license plates shall be deposited to the credit of the trafficked persons program account established under Section 50.0153, Health and Safety Code.

Sec. 504.675. Family First License Plates.

(a) The department shall issue specialty license plates that include the words "Family First." The department shall design the plates in consultation with a representative of the Family First nonprofit organization.

(b) After deduction of the department's administrative costs, the remainder of the fee for issuance of the license plates shall be deposited to the credit of an account created by the comptroller in the manner provided by Section 504.6012(b). Money deposited to that account may be used only by the Texas Education Agency to make grants to a nonprofit organization with chapters operating in schools in this state whose primary purpose is promoting the importance of fatherhood.

SUBCHAPTER H ADMINISTRATIVE PROVISIONS RELATING TO SPECIALTY LICENSE PLATES FOR GENERAL DISTRIBUTION

Sec. 504.701. Discontinuance of Certain Specialty License Plates [Repealed].

Repealed by Acts 2011, 82nd Leg., ch. 1296 (H.B. 2357), § 247(20), effective January 1, 2012.

Sec. 504.702. Specialty License Plates Authorized After January 1, 1999.

(a) This section applies only to specialty license plates that are authorized to be issued by a law that takes effect on or after January 1, 1999.

(b) The department may manufacture the specialty license plates only if a request for manufacture of the license plates is filed with the department. The request must be:

(1) made in a manner prescribed by the department;

(2) filed before the fifth anniversary of the effective date of the law that authorizes the issuance of the specialty license plates; and

(3) accompanied by a deposit of $8,000.

(c) [Repealed by Acts 2011, 82nd Leg., ch. 1296 (H.B. 2357), § 247(21), effective January 1, 2012.]

(d) If a request is not filed with the department before the date specified by Subsection (b)(2), the law that authorizes the issuance of the specialty license plates expires on that date.

(e) The department may issue license plates under:

(1) Section 504.614 for a particular professional sports team only if $8,000 has been deposited with the department for that sports team; or

(2) Section 504.615 for a particular institution of higher education or private college or university only if $8,000 has been deposited with the department for that institution, college, or university.

(f) Money deposited with the department under Subsection (b)(3) or (e) shall be returned by the department to the person who made the deposit after 800 sets of plates have been issued.

SUBCHAPTER I DEVELOPMENT OF NEW SPECIALTY LICENSE PLATES

Sec. 504.801. Creation of New Specialty License Plates by the Department.

(a) The department may create new specialty license plates on its own initiative or on receipt of an application from a potential sponsor. A new specialty license plate created under this section must comply with each requirement of Section 504.702 unless the license is created by the department on its own initiative. The department may permit a specialty license plate created under this section to be personalized. The redesign of an existing specialty license plate at the request of a sponsor shall be treated like the issuance of a new specialty license plate.

(b) Any nonprofit entity may submit an application to the department to sponsor a new specialty license plate. An application may nominate a state agency to receive funds derived from the issuance of the license plates. The application may also identify uses to which those funds should be appropriated.

(c) The department shall design each new specialty license plate in consultation with the sponsor, if any, that applied for creation of that specialty license plate. The department may refuse to create a new specialty license plate if the design might be offensive to any member of the public, if the nominated state agency does not consent to receipt of the funds derived from issuance of the license plate, if the uses identified for those funds might violate a statute or constitutional provision, or for any other reason established by rule. At the request of the sponsor, distribution of the license plate may be limited by the department.

(d) The fee for issuance of license plates created under this subchapter before November 19, 2009, is $30 unless the department sets a higher fee. This subsection does not apply to a specialty license plate marketed and sold by a private vendor at the request of the specialty license plate sponsor.

(d-1) The fee for issuance of license plates created under this subchapter on or after November 19, 2009, is the amount established under Section 504.851.

(e) For each fee collected for a license plate issued by the department under this section:

(1) $8 shall be used to reimburse the department for its administrative costs; and

(2) the remainder shall be deposited to the credit of:

(A) the specialty license plate fund, which is an account in the general revenue fund, if the sponsor nominated a state agency to receive the funds; or

(B) the Texas Department of Motor Vehicles fund if the sponsor did not nominate a state agency to receive the funds or if there is no sponsor.

(f) Subchapter D, Chapter 316, Government Code, and Section 403.095, Government Code, do not apply to fees collected under this subchapter.

(g) The department may report to the legislature at any time concerning implementation of this section. The report may include recommendations concerning the appropriations, by amount, state agency, and uses, that are necessary to implement the requests of sponsors.

(h) The department may vary the design of a license plate created under this section to accommodate or reflect its use on a motor vehicle other than a passenger car or light truck.

(i) The sponsor of a new specialty plate may not be a for-profit enterprise.

Sec. 504.802. Marketing and Sale by Private Vendor of Specialty License Plates.

(a) A sponsor of a specialty license plate created under this subchapter may contract with the private vendor authorized under Subchapter J for the marketing and sale of the specialty license plate.

(b) The fee for issuance of a specialty license plate described by Subsection (a) is the amount established under Section 504.851(c).

(c) Notwithstanding any other law, from each fee received from the issuance of a specialty license plate marketed and sold by the private vendor under this section, the department shall:

(1) deduct the administrative costs described by Section 504.801(e)(1);

(2) deposit the portion of the fee for the sale of the plate that the state would ordinarily receive under the contract described by Section 504.851(a) to the credit of:

(A) the specialty license plate fund, if the sponsor nominated a state agency to receive the funds;

(B) the general revenue fund, if the sponsor did not nominate a state agency to receive the funds or if there is no sponsor; or

(C) for a license plate issued under Section 504.614, the public entity that provides or provided funds for the professional sports team's facility; and

(3) pay to the private vendor the remainder of the fee.

(d) A sponsor of a specialty license plate may reestablish its specialty license plate under Sections 504.601 and 504.702 and be credited its previous deposit with the department if a contract entered into by the sponsor under Subsection (a) terminates.

SUBCHAPTER J MARKETING OF SPECIALTY PLATES THROUGH PRIVATE VENDOR

Sec. 504.851. Contract with Private Vendor.

(a) The department may enter into a contract with the private vendor whose proposal is most advantageous to the state, as determined from competitive sealed proposals that satisfy the requirements of this section, for the marketing and sale of:

(1) personalized license plates; or

(2) with the agreement of the private vendor, other specialty license plates authorized by Subchapters G and I.

(a-1) The department may not issue specialty, personalized, or souvenir license plates with background colors other than white, unless the plates are marketed and sold by the private vendor.

Transportation Code

(a-2) Specialty license plates authorized for marketing and sale under Subsection (a) may be personalized and must include:

(1) specialty license plates created under Subchapters G and I on or after November 19, 2009; and

(2) at the request of the specialty license plate sponsor, an existing specialty license plate created under Subchapters G and I before November 19, 2009.

(a-3) The department may contract with the private vendor for the vendor to:

(1) host all or some of the specialty license plates on the vendor's website;

(2) process the purchase of specialty license plates hosted on the vendor's website and pay any additional transaction cost; and

(3) share in the personalization fee for the license plates hosted on the vendor's website.

(b) **[2 Versions: As amended by Acts 2009, 81st Leg., ch. 933]** Instead of the fees established by Section 504.101(c), the board by rule shall establish fees for the issuance or renewal of personalized license plates that are marketed and sold by the private vendor. Fees must be reasonable and not less than the greater of:

(1) the amounts necessary to allow the department to recover all reasonable costs to the department associated with the evaluation of the competitive sealed proposals received by the department and with the implementation and enforcement of the contract, including direct, indirect, and administrative costs; or

(2) the amount established by Section 504.101(c).

(b) **[2 Versions: As amended by Acts 2009, 81st Leg., ch. 1381]** The commission by rule shall establish fees for the issuance or renewal of personalized license plates that are marketed and sold by the private vendor. Fees must be reasonable and not less than the greater of:

(1) the amounts necessary to allow the department to recover all reasonable costs to the department associated with the evaluation of the competitive sealed proposals received by the department and with the implementation and enforcement of the contract, including direct, indirect, and administrative costs; or

(2) the amount established by Section 504.853(b).

(c) The board by rule shall establish the fees for the issuance or renewal of souvenir license plates, specialty license plates, or souvenir or specialty license plates that are personalized that are marketed and sold by the private vendor or hosted on the private vendor's website. The state's portion of the personalization fee may not be less than $40 for each year issued. Other fees must be reasonable and not less than the amounts necessary to allow the department to recover all reasonable costs to the department associated with the evaluation of the competitive sealed proposals received by the department and with the implementation and enforcement of the contract, including direct, indirect, and administrative costs. A fee established under this subsection is in addition to:

(1) the registration fee and any optional registration fee prescribed by this chapter for the vehicle for which specialty license plates are issued;

(2) any additional fee prescribed by this subchapter for the issuance of specialty license plates for that vehicle; and

(3) any additional fee prescribed by this subchapter for the issuance of personalized license plates for that vehicle.

(c-1) Subsections (b) and (c) do not apply to the sale at auction of a specialty plate or personalized specialty plate that is not used on a motor vehicle.

(d) At any time as necessary to comply with Subsection (b) or (c), the board may increase or decrease the amount of a fee established under the applicable subsection.

(e) The portion of a contract with a private vendor regarding the marketing and sale of personalized license plates is payable only from amounts derived from the collection of the fee established under Subsection (b). The portion of a contract with a private vendor regarding the marketing, hosting, and sale of souvenir license plates, specialty license plates, or souvenir or specialty license plates that are personalized under Section 504.102 is payable only from amounts derived from the collection of the fee established under Subsection (c).

(f) The department may approve new design and color combinations for personalized or specialty license plates that are marketed and sold by a private vendor under a contract entered into with the private vendor. Each approved license plate design and color combination remains the property of the department.

(g) The department may approve new design and color combinations for specialty license plates authorized by this chapter, including specialty license plates that may be personalized, that are marketed and sold by a private vendor under a contract entered into with the private vendor. Each approved license plate design and color combination remains the property of the department. Except as otherwise provided by this chapter, this subsection does not authorize:

(1) the department to approve a design or color combination for a specialty license plate that is inconsistent with the design or color combination specified for the license plate by the section of this

chapter that authorizes the issuance of the specialty license plate; or

(2) the private vendor to market and sell a specialty license plate with a design or color combination that is inconsistent with the design or color combination specified by that section.

(g-1) The department may not:

(1) publish a proposed design or color combination for a specialty license plate for public comment in the Texas Register or otherwise, except on the department's website for a period not to exceed 10 days; or

(2) restrict the background color, color combinations, or color alphanumeric license plate numbers of a specialty license plate, except as determined by the Department of Public Safety as necessary for law enforcement purposes.

(h) Subject to the limitations provided by Subsections (g) and (g-1), the department may disapprove a design, cancel a license plate, or require the discontinuation of a license plate design or color combination that is marketed, hosted, or sold by a private vendor under contract at any time if the department determines that the disapproval, cancellation, or discontinuation is in the best interest of this state or the motoring public.

(i) A contract entered into by the department with a private vendor under this section:

(1) must comply with any law generally applicable to a contract for services entered into by the department;

(2) must require the private vendor to render at least quarterly to the department periodic accounts that accurately detail all material transactions, including information reasonably required by the department to support fees that are collected by the vendor, and to regularly remit all money payable to the department under the contract; and

(3) may allow or require the private vendor to establish an electronic infrastructure coordinated and compatible with the department's registration system, by which motor vehicle owners may electronically send and receive applications, other documents, or required payments, and that, when secure access is necessary, can be electronically validated by the department.

(j) From amounts received by the department under the contract described by Subsection (a), the department shall deposit to the credit of the Texas Department of Motor Vehicles fund an amount sufficient to enable the department to recover its administrative costs for all license plates issued under this section, any payments to the vendor under the contract, and any other amounts allocated by law to the Texas Department of Motor Vehicles fund. To the extent that the disposition of other amounts received by the department is governed by another law, those amounts shall be deposited in accordance with the other law. Any additional amount received by the department under the contract shall be deposited to the credit of the general revenue fund.

(k) [Repealed by Acts 2011, 82nd Leg., ch. 1296 (H.B. 2357), § 247(22), effective January 1, 2012.]

(*l*) A contract entered into with the private vendor shall provide for the department to recover all costs incurred by the department in implementing this section. Under the contract, the department may require the private vendor to reimburse the department in advance for:

(1) not more than one-half of the department's anticipated costs in connection with the contract; and

(2) the department's anticipated costs in connection with the introduction of a new specialty license plate.

(m) If the private vendor ceases operation:

(1) the program may be operated temporarily by the department under new agreements with the license plate sponsors until another vendor is selected and begins operation; and

(2) the private vendor's share of the revenue is deposited to the credit of the general revenue fund.

Sec. 504.852. Contract Limitations.

(a) In a contract under Section 504.851, the department may not:

(1) unreasonably disapprove or limit any aspect of a private vendor's marketing and sales plan;

(2) unreasonably interfere with the selection, assignment, or management by the private vendor of the private vendor's employees, agents, or subcontractors; or

(3) require a private vendor to market and sell souvenir license plates, specialty license plates, or souvenir or specialty license plates personalized under Section 504.102.

(b) If a private vendor contracts to market and sell souvenir license plates, specialty license plates, or souvenir or specialty license plates personalized under Section 504.102, the initial term of the contract shall be for at least five years from the effective date of the contract. The contract may provide, with the agreement of the department and the private vendor, a second term at least equal in length to the initial term of the contract.

(c) Notwithstanding Subsection (b), a private vendor may not market and sell souvenir license plates, specialty license plates, or souvenir or specialty license plates personalized under Section 504.102 that compete directly for sales with

Transportation Code

another specialty license plate issued under this chapter unless the department and the sponsoring agency or organization of the other license plate approve.

Sec. 504.853. Specialty and Personalized License Plates Issued Before November 19, 2009.

(a) A specialty or personalized license plate issued before November 19, 2009, may be issued for a subsequent registration period only if the applicant submits an application and pays the required fee for the applicable registration period. A person who is issued a personalized license plate has first priority on that license plate for each subsequent registration period for which the person submits a new application for that plate.

(b) Unless the board by rule adopts a higher fee or the license plate is not renewed annually, the fee for issuance of a license plate issued before November 19, 2009, is:

(1) the fee provided for in Section 504.601 for a specialty license plate; and

(2) $40 for a personalized license plate.

(c) A person who is issued a specialty or personalized license plate by the department before November 19, 2009, may:

(1) submit an application for the plate under Subsection (a) and pay the required fee for each subsequent registration period under Subsection (b); or

(2) purchase through the private vendor a license to display the alphanumeric pattern on a license plate for any term allowed by law.

(d) The department may not issue a replacement set of personalized license plates to the same person before the period set by rule unless the applicant for issuance of replacement plates pays an additional fee of $30.

(e) Of each fee collected by the department under Subsection (b)(2):

(1) $1.25 shall be used by the department to defray the cost of administering this section; and

(2) the remainder shall be deposited to the credit of the general revenue fund.

Sec. 504.854. Auction.

(a) The board by rule may provide for the private vendor to:

(1) sell at auction a license to display a unique alphanumeric pattern on a license plate for a period set by board rule;

(2) reserve an unissued alphanumeric pattern from the department for purposes of auctioning a license to display the pattern for a period set by board rule; and

(3) purchase from a customer an unexpired license to display an alphanumeric pattern for purposes of auction by the vendor.

(b) A license to display an alphanumeric pattern purchased under this section may be transferred to another person without payment of the fee provided by Section 504.855.

(c) [Repealed by Acts 2011, 82nd Leg., ch. 1296 (H.B. 2357), § 247(23), effective January 1, 2012].

Sec. 504.855. Transferability of Certain Patterns.

The board by rule may:

(1) authorize a person who purchases a license to display an alphanumeric pattern for a period of five years or more to transfer the license; and

(2) establish a transfer fee to be distributed in accordance with the contract with the private vendor.

SUBCHAPTER K TRANSFER AND REMOVAL OF LICENSE PLATES

Sec. 504.901. Transfer and Removal of License Plates.

(a) On the sale or transfer of a motor vehicle to a dealer who holds a general distinguishing number issued under Chapter 503, the dealer shall remove each license plate issued for the motor vehicle. A person may use the license plates removed from a motor vehicle on a new motor vehicle purchased from a dealer after the person obtains the department's approval of a title and registration application.

(b) On the sale or transfer of a motor vehicle to a person who does not hold a general distinguishing number issued under Chapter 503, the seller may remove each license plate issued for the motor vehicle. The license plates may be transferred to another vehicle titled in the seller's name if the seller obtains:

(1) the department's approval of an application to transfer the license plates; and

(2) a new registration insignia for the motor vehicle.

(c) A license plate removed from a motor vehicle that is not transferred to another motor vehicle must be disposed of in a manner specified by the department.

Transportation Code

(d) To be eligible for transfer, license plates must be appropriate for the class of vehicle to which the plates are being transferred.

(e) This section applies only to:

(1) a passenger vehicle with a gross weight of 6,000 pounds or less; and

(2) a light truck with a gross weight of 10,000 pounds or less.

SUBCHAPTER L OFFENSES AND PENALTIES

Sec. 504.941. Antique Vehicles; Offense.

(a) A person who violates Section 504.502 commits an offense. An offense under this section is a misdemeanor punishable by a fine of not less than $5 or more than $200.

(b) It is an affirmative defense to prosecution under this section that at the time of the offense the vehicle was en route to or from a location for the purpose of routine maintenance of the vehicle.

Sec. 504.942. Log Loader Vehicles; Penalties.

A vehicle operated in violation of Section 504.506 is considered to be operated or moved while unregistered and is immediately subject to the applicable fees and penalties prescribed by this chapter.

Sec. 504.943. Operation of Vehicle Without License Plate.

(a) Except as provided by Subsection (b), a person commits an offense if the person operates on a public highway, during a registration period, a motor vehicle that does not display two license plates that:

(1) have been assigned by the department for the period; and

(2) comply with department rules regarding the placement of license plates.

(b) A person commits an offense if the person operates on a public highway during a registration period a road tractor, motorcycle, trailer, or semitrailer that does not display a license plate that:

(1) has been assigned by the department for the period; and

(2) complies with department rules regarding the placement of license plates.

(c) This section does not apply to a dealer operating a vehicle as provided by law.

(d) A court may dismiss a charge brought under Subsection (a)(1) if the defendant:

(1) remedies the defect before the defendant's first court appearance; and

(2) pays a reimbursement fee not to exceed $10.

(e) An offense under this section is a misdemeanor punishable by a fine not to exceed $200.

Sec. 504.944. Operation of Vehicle with Wrong License Plate.

A person commits an offense if the person operates, or as the owner permits another to operate, on a public highway a motor vehicle that has attached to it a number plate or registration insignia issued for a different vehicle. An offense under this section is a misdemeanor punishable by a fine not to exceed $200.

Sec. 504.945. Wrong, Fictitious, Altered, or Obscured License Plate.

(a) A person commits an offense if the person attaches to or displays on a motor vehicle a license plate that:

(1) is issued for a different motor vehicle;

(2) is issued for the vehicle under any other motor vehicle law other than by the department;

(3) is assigned for a registration period other than the registration period in effect;

(4) is fictitious;

(5) has blurring or reflective matter that significantly impairs the readability of the name of the state in which the vehicle is registered or the letters or numbers of the license plate number at any time;

(6) has an attached illuminated device or sticker, decal, emblem, or other insignia that is not authorized by law and that interferes with the readability of the letters or numbers of the license plate number or the name of the state in which the vehicle is registered; or

(7) has a coating, covering, protective substance, or other material that:

(A) distorts angular visibility or detectability;

(B) alters or obscures one-half or more of the name of the state in which the vehicle is registered; or

(C) alters or obscures the letters or numbers of the license plate number or the color of the plate.

(b) Except as provided by Subsection (e), an offense under Subsection (a) is a misdemeanor punishable by a fine of not more than $200, unless it is shown at the trial of the offense that the owner knowingly altered or made illegible the letters, numbers, and other identification marks, in which case the offense is a Class B misdemeanor.

(c) Subsection (a)(7) may not be construed to apply to:

Transportation Code

(1) a trailer hitch installed on a vehicle in a normal or customary manner;

(2) a transponder, as defined by Section 228.057, that is attached to a vehicle in the manner required by the issuing authority;

(3) a wheelchair lift or wheelchair carrier that is attached to a vehicle in a normal or customary manner;

(4) a trailer being towed by a vehicle; or

(5) a bicycle or motorcycle rack that is attached to a vehicle in a normal or customary manner.

(d) A court may dismiss a charge brought under Subsection (a)(3), (5), (6), or (7) if the defendant:

(1) remedies the defect before the defendant's first court appearance;

(2) pays a reimbursement fee not to exceed $10; and

(3) shows that the vehicle was issued a plate by the department that was attached to the vehicle, establishing that the vehicle was registered for the period during which the offense was committed.

(e) An offense under Subsection (a)(4) is a Class B misdemeanor.

Sec. 504.946. Deceptively Similar License Plate.

(a) A person commits an offense if the person:

(1) manufactures, sells, or possesses a license plate deceptively similar to a license plate issued by the department; or

(2) makes a copy or likeness of a license plate deceptively similar to a license plate issued by the department with intent to sell the copy or likeness.

(b) For the purposes of this section, a license plate is deceptively similar to a license plate issued by the department if it is not prescribed by the department but a reasonable person would presume that it was prescribed by the department.

(c) A district or county court, on application of the attorney general or of the district attorney or prosecuting attorney performing the duties of the district attorney for the district in which the court is located, may enjoin a violation or threatened violation of this section on a showing that a violation has occurred or is likely to occur.

(d) It is an affirmative defense to a prosecution under this section that the license plate was produced pursuant to a licensing agreement with the department.

(e) An offense under this section is:

(1) a felony of the third degree if the person manufactures or sells a deceptively similar license plate; or

(2) a Class C misdemeanor if the person possesses a deceptively similar license plate, except that the offense is a Class B misdemeanor if the person has previously been convicted of an offense under this subdivision.

Sec. 504.9465. License Plate Flipper; Offense.

(a) In this section, "license plate flipper" means a manual, electronic, or mechanical device designed or adapted to be installed on a motor vehicle and:

(1) switch between two or more license plates for the purpose of allowing a motor vehicle operator to change the license plate displayed on the operator's vehicle; or

(2) hide a license plate from view by flipping the license plate so that the license plate number is not visible.

(b) A person commits an offense if the person with criminal negligence purchases or possesses a license plate flipper. An offense under this subsection is a Class B misdemeanor.

(c) A person commits an offense if the person with criminal negligence manufactures, sells, offers to sell, or otherwise distributes a license plate flipper. An offense under this subsection is a Class A misdemeanor.

Sec. 504.947. License Plate Flipper; Offense. [Repealed]

Sec. 504.948. General Penalty.

(a) A person commits an offense if the person violates a provision of this chapter and no other penalty is prescribed for the violation.

(b) An offense under Subsection (a) is a misdemeanor punishable by a fine of not less than $5 or more than $200.

CHAPTER 520 MISCELLANEOUS PROVISIONS

SUBCHAPTER A GENERAL PROVISIONS

Sec. 520.001. Definitions.

In this chapter:

(1) "Board" means the board of the Texas Department of Motor Vehicles.

(2) "Department" means the Texas Department of Motor Vehicles.

Sec. 520.002. Lease of Additional Computer Equipment [Renumbered].

Renumbered to Tex. Transp. Code § 520.0093 by Acts 2011, 82nd Leg., ch. 1296 (H.B. 2357), § 232, effective January 1, 2012.

Sec. 520.003. Rules; Fees; Refunds.

(a) The department may adopt rules to administer this chapter, including rules that:

(1) waive the payment of fees if a dealer has gone out of business and the applicant can show that fees were paid to the dealer; and

(2) allow full and partial refunds for rejected titling and registration transactions.

(b) The department may collect from a person making a transaction with the department using the state electronic Internet portal project a fee set under Section 2054.2591, Government Code. All fees collected under this subsection shall be allocated to the department to provide for the department's costs associated with administering Section 2054.2591, Government Code.

Sec. 520.004. Department Responsibilities.

The department has jurisdiction over the registration and titling of, and the issuance of license plates to, motor vehicles in compliance with the applicable statutes. The department by rule:

(1) shall provide services that are reasonable, adequate, and efficient;

(2) shall establish standards for uniformity and service quality for counties and dealers licensed under Section 520.005;

(3) may conduct public service education campaigns related to the department's functions; and

(4) shall establish a risk-based system of monitoring and preventing fraudulent activity related to vehicle registration and titling in order to efficiently allocate resources and personnel.

Sec. 520.005. Duty and Responsibilities of County Assessor-Collector.

(a) Each county assessor-collector shall comply with Chapter 501.

(b) An assessor-collector who fails or refuses to comply with Chapter 501 is liable on the assessor-collector's official bond for resulting damages suffered by any person.

(c) Notwithstanding the requirements of Section 520.0071, the assessor-collector may license franchised and non-franchised motor vehicle dealers to title and register motor vehicles in accordance with rules adopted under Section 520.004. The county assessor-collector may pay a fee to a motor vehicle dealer independent of or as part of the portion of the fees that would be collected by the county for each title and registration receipt issued.

(d) Each county assessor-collector shall process a registration renewal through an online system designated by the department.

(e) Each county assessor-collector shall make available to motor vehicle dealers the electronic system designed by the department that allows a motor vehicle dealer to submit a title and registration application online in the name of the purchaser of a motor vehicle.

Sec. 520.006. Compensation of Assessor-Collector. [Effective until March 1, 2022]

(a) A county assessor-collector shall retain an amount determined by the board under Section 502.1911 for each receipt issued under Chapter 502.

(a-1) A county assessor-collector collecting fees on behalf of a county assessor-collector whose office is closed or may be closed for a protracted period of time as defined by the department for purposes of Section 501.023 or 502.040 may retain the commission for fees collected, but shall allocate the fees to the county that is closed or may be closed for a protracted period of time.

(b) A county assessor-collector who is compensated under this section shall pay the entire expense of issuing registration receipts and license plates under Chapter 501 or 502 from the compensation allowed under this section.

Sec. 520.006. Collection of Fees on Behalf of Another Assessor-Collector; Compensation of Assessor-Collector. [Effective March 1, 2022]

(a) A county assessor-collector shall retain an amount determined by the board under Section 502.1911 for each receipt issued under Chapter 502.

(a-1) A county assessor-collector collecting fees on behalf of another county assessor-collector for purposes of Section 501.023, 501.0234, 501.030, 502.0023, 502.040, or 502.041 shall collect all taxes, fees, and other revenue based on the vehicle owner's county of residence. The vehicle owner's county of residence shall be the recipient of all taxes, fees, and other revenue collected as a result of the transaction, except that the county processing the application may retain the portion of the title application fee under Section 501.138 and the processing and handling fee under Section 502.1911 that the tax assessor-collector is authorized to retain.

(b) A county assessor-collector who is compensated under this section for processing a transaction shall pay the entire expense of issuing registration receipts and license plates under Chapter 501 or 502 from the compensation allowed under this section.

Sec. 520.0061. Contracts Between Counties.

(a) A county tax assessor-collector, with approval of the commissioners court of the county by order, may enter into an agreement with one or more counties to perform mail-in or online registration or titling duties.

(b) A contract entered into under Subsection (a) may be terminated by a county that is a party to the contract.

Sec. 520.007. County Branch Offices.

(a) The commissioners court of a county may authorize the county assessor-collector to:

(1) establish a suboffice or branch office for vehicle registration at one or more locations in the county other than the county courthouse; or

(2) appoint a deputy to register vehicles in the same manner and with the same authority as though done in the office of the assessor-collector.

(b) The report of vehicles registered through a suboffice or branch office shall be made through the office of the county assessor-collector.

Sec. 520.0071. Deputies.

(a) The board by rule shall prescribe:

(1) the classification types of deputies performing titling and registration duties;

(2) the duties and obligations of deputies;

(3) the type and amount of any bonds that may be required by a county assessor-collector for a deputy to perform titling and registration duties; and

(4) the fees that may be charged or retained by deputies.

(b) A county assessor-collector, with the approval of the commissioners court of the county, may deputize an individual or business entity to perform titling and registration services in accordance with rules adopted under Subsection (a).

Sec. 520.0075. Contracting Standards for Tax Assessor-Collector.

(a) In this section, "deputy" means a deputy classified as a full service deputy by a board rule adopted under Section 520.0071.

(b) Notwithstanding Section 262.023, Local Government Code, a county tax assessor-collector who awards a contract to a deputy for the performance of registration and titling services must comply with standard state contracting practices as if the county tax assessor-collector were a state agency, including requirements related to:

(1) purchase methods and competitive bidding under Sections 2155.062 and 2155.063, Government Code;

(2) determining the best value for the county under Sections 2155.074, 2155.075, and 2155.0755, Government Code;

(3) contracting standards and oversight under Chapter 2261, Government Code; and

(4) contract management under Chapter 2262, Government Code.

(c) A contract described by Subsection (b) must:

(1) specify an expiration date and renewal or extension terms for the contract; and

(2) include performance criteria and measures necessary to evaluate the performance of the deputy under the contract.

(d) A county tax assessor-collector shall monitor and evaluate the performance of a deputy awarded a contract described by this section and use that information in determining whether to renew or extend the contract or award a new contract.

Sec. 520.008. Full-Service Deputies [Repealed].

Repealed by Acts 2013, 83rd Leg., ch. 1135 (H.B. 2741), § 140(2), and by Acts 2013, 83rd Leg., ch. 1287 (H.B. 2202), § 72, effective September 1, 2013.

Sec. 520.009. Limited-Service Deputies [Repealed].

Repealed by Acts 2013, 83rd Leg., ch. 1135 (H.B. 2741), § 140(2), and by Acts 2013, 83rd Leg., ch. 1287 (H.B. 2202), § 72, effective September 1, 2013.

Sec. 520.0091. Deputy Assessor-Collectors [Repealed].

Repealed by Acts 2013, 83rd Leg., ch. 1135 (H.B. 2741), § 140(2), and by Acts 2013, 83rd Leg., ch. 1287 (H.B. 2202), § 72, effective September 1, 2013.

Sec. 520.0092. Acts by Deputy County Assessor-Collector [Repealed].

Repealed by Acts 2013, 83rd Leg., ch. 1135 (H.B. 2741), § 140(2), and by Acts 2013, 83rd Leg., ch. 1287 (H.B. 2202), § 72, effective September 1, 2013.

Transportation Code

Sec. 520.0093. Lease of Computer Equipment.

(a) The department may lease equipment and provide related services to a:

(1) county for the operation of the automated registration and titling system in addition to the equipment provided by the department at no cost to the county under a formula prescribed by the department; and

(2) deputy appointed under Section 520.0071.

(b) On the request of the tax assessor-collector of a county, the department may enter into an agreement with the commissioners court of that county under which the department leases additional equipment to the county for the use of the tax assessor-collector in operating the automated registration and titling system in that county.

(b-1) On the request of a deputy appointed under Section 520.0071, the department may enter into an agreement under which the department leases equipment to the deputy for the use of the deputy in operating the automated registration and titling system. The department may require the deputy to post a bond in an amount equal to the value of the equipment.

(c) A county may install equipment leased under this section at offices of the county or of an agent of the county. A deputy appointed under Section 520.0071 may install equipment leased under this section on the premises described in the agreement.

(d) Equipment leased under this section:

(1) remains the property of the department; and

(2) must be used primarily for the automated registration and titling system.

(e) Under the agreement, the department shall charge an amount not less than the amount of the cost to the department to provide the equipment and any related services under the lease. All money collected under the lease shall be deposited to the credit of the Texas Department of Motor Vehicles fund.

Sec. 520.010. [Reserved].

Sec. 520.010. Audit and Investigation Related to Registration and Titling Services.

(a) The department may:

(1) audit or perform a compliance review of a person performing registration or titling services;

(2) investigate any provision of state functions related to registration or titling; and

(3) access any records needed to conduct the audit, compliance review, or investigation.

(b) A county tax assessor-collector may:

(1) audit, perform a compliance review of, or investigate a person providing registration or titling services in the county in which the assessor-collector is located; and

(2) access any records needed to conduct the audit, compliance review, or investigation.

(c) The department's authority under Subsection (a) is not limited by a similar audit, compliance review, or investigation conducted by a county tax assessor-collector under Subsection (b).

Sec. 520.011. Audit of County Tax Assessor-Collector.

The comptroller, in coordination with the department, may include, as part of the comptroller's regular audits of state revenue collection by county tax assessor-collector offices, the review of processes relating to a county's collection and remittance of revenue included in an audit.

SUBCHAPTER B ADMINISTRATIVE PROVISIONS

Sec. 520.011. Motor Number Required for Vehicle Registration; Penalty [Renumbered].

Renumbered to Tex. Transp. Code § 501.0331 by Acts 2011, 82nd Leg., ch. 1296 (H.B. 2357), § 23, effective January 1, 2012.

Sec. 520.012. Application for Motor Number Record; Record; Penalty [Renumbered].

Renumbered to Tex. Transp. Code § 501.0332 by Acts 2011, 82nd Leg., ch. 1296 (H.B. 2357), § 24, effective January 1, 2012.

Sec. 520.013. Presentation of Motor Number Receipt Required; Penalty [Repealed].

Repealed by Acts 2011, 82nd Leg., ch. 1296 (H.B. 2357), § 247(24), effective January 1, 2012.

Sec. 520.014. Violation by County Assessor-Collector; Penalty [Renumbered].

Renumbered to Tex. Transp. Code § 502.480 by Acts 2011, 82nd Leg., ch. 1296 (H.B. 2357), § 161, effective January 1, 2012.

Sec. 520.015. Information Consolidation Study.

(a) In consultation with the Department of Public Safety, the department shall conduct a study on the consolidation of similar information that is collected separately by each agency. The study should include recommendations that sufficiently protect the privacy of the public and the security and integrity of information provided.

(b) The study must be completed not later than September 1, 2012.

Sec. 520.016. General Penalty.

(a) A person commits an offense if the person violates this subchapter in a manner for which a specific penalty is not provided.

(b) An offense under this section is a misdemeanor punishable by a fine of not less than $50 and not more than $200.

(c) This section does not apply to a violation of Section 520.006 or a rule adopted under Section 520.0071.

SUBCHAPTER C GENERAL REQUIREMENTS RELATING TO TRANSFERS OF USED MOTOR VEHICLES [REPEALED]

Transportation Code

Sec. 520.021. Current Registration Required [Repealed].

Repealed by Acts 2007, 80th Leg., ch. 101 (H.B. 310), § 3, effective January 1, 2008.

Sec. 520.022. Delivery of Receipt and Title to Transferee; Penalty [Renumbered].

Renumbered to Tex. Transp. Code § 501.0721 by Acts 2011, 82nd Leg., ch. 1296 (H.B. 2357), § 33, effective January 1, 2012.

SUBCHAPTER C AUTOMATED REGISTRATION AND TITLING SYSTEM

Sec. 520.022. Access to System.

The department has the sole authority to determine access to the department's automated registration and titling system.

Sec. 520.023. Powers and Duties of Department on Transfer of Used Vehicle [Renumbered].

Renumbered to Tex. Transp. Code § 501.147 by Acts 2011, 82nd Leg., ch. 1296 (H.B. 2357), § 61, effective January 1, 2012.

Sec. 520.023. Training.

(a) The department shall implement a training program providing information on the:

(1) department's automated registration and titling system; and

(2) identification of fraudulent activity related to vehicle registration and titling.

(b) The department shall require a person performing registration or titling services to complete the training under Subsection (a).

Sec. 520.0225. Persons on Active Duty in Armed Forces of United States [Renumbered].

Renumbered to Tex. Transp. Code § 502.457 by Acts 2011, 82nd Leg., ch. 1296 (H.B. 2357), § 153, effective January 1, 2012.

SUBCHAPTER D TRANSFER OF TITLE AND REGISTRATION OF USED VEHICLE [REPEALED]

Sec. 520.031. Filing by Transferee; Application for Transfer of Title and Registration [Renumbered].

Renumbered to Tex. Transp. Code § 501.145 by Acts 2011, 82nd Leg., ch. 1296 (H.B. 2357), § 59, effective January 1, 2012.

Sec. 520.032. Transfer Fee; Late Fee [Renumbered].

Renumbered to Tex. Transp. Code § 501.146 by Acts 2011, 82nd Leg., ch. 1296 (H.B. 2357), § 60, effective January 1, 2012.

Sec. 520.033. Allocation of Fees [Renumbered].

Renumbered to Tex. Transp. Code § 501.148 by Acts 2011, 82nd Leg., ch. 1296 (H.B. 2357), § 62, effective January 1, 2012.

Sec. 520.034. Processing of Application; Rules [Repealed].

Repealed by Acts 2011, 82nd Leg., ch. 1296 (H.B. 2357), § 247(24), effective January 1, 2012.

Sec. 520.035. Execution of Transfer Documents; Penalty [Renumbered].

Renumbered to Tex. Transp. Code § 501.161 by Acts 2011, 82nd Leg., ch. 1296 (H.B. 2357), § 68, effective January 1, 2012.

Sec. 520.036. General Penalty [Renumbered].

Renumbered to Tex. Transp. Code § 520.016 by Acts 2011, 82nd Leg., ch. 1296 (H.B. 2357), § 235, effective January 1, 2012.

SUBCHAPTER E
MOTOR VEHICLE TITLE SERVICES

Sec. 520.051. Definitions.

In this subchapter:

(1) "Motor vehicle" has the meaning assigned by Section 501.002.

(2) "Motor vehicle title service" means any person that for compensation directly or indirectly assists other persons in obtaining title documents by submitting, transmitting, or sending applications for title documents to the appropriate government agencies.

(3) "Title documents" means motor vehicle title applications, motor vehicle registration renewal applications, motor vehicle mechanic's lien title applications, motor vehicle storage lien title applications, motor vehicle temporary registration permits, motor vehicle title application transfers occasioned by the death of the title holder, or notifications under Chapter 683 of this code or Chapter 70, Property Code.

(4) "Title service license holder" means a person who holds a motor vehicle title service license or a title service runner's license.

(5) "Title service record" means the written or electronic record for each transaction in which a motor vehicle title service receives compensation.

(6) "Title service runner" means any person employed by a licensed motor vehicle title service to submit or present title documents to the county tax assessor-collector.

Sec. 520.052. Applicability.

This subchapter applies to any motor vehicle title service operating in a county:

(1) that has a population of more than 500,000; or

(2) in which the commissioners court by order has adopted this subchapter.

Sec. 520.053. License Required.

A person may not act as a motor vehicle title service or act as an agent for that business unless that person holds a license issued under this subchapter.

Sec. 520.054. General License Application Requirements.

(a) An applicant for a motor vehicle title service license must apply on a form prescribed by the county tax assessor-collector. The application form must be signed by the applicant and accompanied by the application fee.

(b) An application must include:

(1) the applicant's name, business address, and business telephone number;

(2) the name under which the applicant will do business;

(3) the physical address of each office from which the applicant will conduct business;

(4) a statement indicating whether the applicant has previously applied for a license under this subchapter, the result of the previous application, and whether the applicant has ever been the holder of a license under this subchapter that was revoked or suspended;

(5) information from the applicant as required by the county tax assessor-collector to establish the business reputation and character of the applicant;

(6) the applicant's federal tax identification number;

(7) the applicant's state sales tax number; and

(8) any other information required by rules adopted under this subchapter.

Sec. 520.055. Application Requirements: Corporation.

In addition to the information required in Section 520.054, an applicant for a motor vehicle title service license that intends to engage in business as a corporation shall submit the following information:

(1) the state of incorporation;

Transportation Code

(2) the name, address, date of birth, and social security number of each of the principal owners and directors of the corporation;

(3) information about each officer and director as required by the county tax assessor-collector to establish the business reputation and character of the applicant; and

(4) a statement indicating whether an employee, officer, or director has been refused a motor vehicle title service license or a title service runner's license or has been the holder of a license that was revoked or suspended.

Sec. 520.056. Application Requirements: Partnership.

In addition to the information required in Section 520.054, a motor vehicle title service license applicant that intends to engage in business as a partnership shall submit an application that includes the following information:

(1) the name, address, date of birth, and social security number of each partner;

(2) information about each partner as required by the county tax assessor-collector to establish the business reputation and character of the applicant; and

(3) a statement indicating whether a partner or employee has been refused a motor vehicle title service license or a title service runner's license or has been the holder of a license that was revoked or suspended.

Sec. 520.057. Records.

(a) A holder of a motor vehicle title service license shall maintain records as required by this section on a form prescribed and made available by the county tax assessor-collector for each transaction in which the license holder receives compensation. The records shall include:

(1) the date of the transaction;

(2) the name, age, address, sex, driver's license number, and a legible photocopy of the driver's license for each customer; and

(3) the license plate number, vehicle identification number, and a legible photocopy of proof of financial responsibility for the motor vehicle involved.

(b) A motor vehicle title service shall keep:

(1) two copies of all records required under this section for at least two years after the date of the transaction;

(2) legible photocopies of any documents submitted by a customer; and

(3) legible photocopies of any documents submitted to the county tax assessor-collector.

Sec. 520.058. Inspection of Records.

A motor vehicle title service license holder or any of its employees shall allow an inspection of records required under Section 520.057 by a peace officer on the premises of the motor vehicle title service at any reasonable time to verify, check, or audit the records.

Sec. 520.059. Denial, Suspension, or Revocation of License.

(a) The county tax assessor-collector may deny, suspend, revoke, or reinstate a license issued under this subchapter.

(b) The county tax assessor-collector shall adopt rules that establish grounds for the denial, suspension, revocation, or reinstatement of a license and rules that establish procedures for disciplinary action. Procedures issued under this subchapter are subject to Chapter 2001, Government Code.

(c) A person whose license is revoked may not apply for a new license before the first anniversary of the date of the revocation.

(d) A license may not be issued under a fictitious name that is similar to or may be confused with the name of a governmental entity or that is deceptive or misleading to the public.

Sec. 520.060. License Renewal.

(a) A license issued under this subchapter expires on the first anniversary of the date of issuance and may be renewed annually on or before the expiration date on payment of the required renewal fee.

(b) A person who is otherwise eligible to renew a license may renew an unexpired license by paying to the county tax assessor-collector before the expiration date of the license the required renewal fee. A person whose license has expired may not engage in activities that require a license until the license has been renewed under this section.

(c) If a person's license has been expired for 90 days or less, the person may renew the license by paying to the county tax assessor-collector 1-½ times the required renewal fee.

(d) If a person's license has been expired for longer than 90 days but less than one year, the person may renew the license by paying to the county tax assessor-collector two times the required renewal fee.

(e) If a person's license has been expired for one year or longer, the person may not renew the license. The person may obtain a new license by complying with the requirements and procedures for obtaining an original license.

(f) Notwithstanding Subsection (e), if a person was licensed in this state, moved to another state, and has been doing business in the other state for the two years preceding application, the person may renew an expired license. The person must pay to the county tax assessor-collector a fee that is equal to two times the required renewal fee for the license.

(g) Before the 30th day preceding the date on which a person's license expires, the county tax assessor-collector shall notify the person of the impending expiration. The notice must be in writing and sent to the person's last known address according to the records of the county tax assessor-collector.

Sec. 520.061. Criminal Penalty.

(a) A person commits an offense if the person violates this subchapter or a rule adopted by the county tax assessor-collector under this subchapter.

(b) An offense under this section is a Class A misdemeanor.

Sec. 520.062. Injunction.

(a) A district attorney of the county in which the motor vehicle title service is located may bring an action to enjoin the operation of a motor vehicle title service if the motor vehicle title service license holder or a runner of the motor vehicle title service while in the scope of the runner's employment is convicted of more than one offense under this subchapter.

(b) If the court grants relief under Subsection (a), the court may:

(1) enjoin the person from maintaining or participating in the business of a motor vehicle title service for a period of time as determined by the court; or

(2) declare the place where the person's business is located to be closed for any use relating to the business of the motor vehicle title service for as long as the person is enjoined from participating in that business.

Sec. 520.063. Exemptions.

The following persons and their agents are exempt from the licensing and other requirements established by this subchapter:

(1) a franchised motor vehicle dealer or independent motor vehicle dealer who holds a general distinguishing number issued by the department under Chapter 503;

(2) a vehicle lessor holding a license issued by the department under Chapter 2301, Occupations Code, or a trust or other entity that is specifically not required to obtain a lessor license under Section 2301.254(a) of that code; and

(3) a vehicle lease facilitator holding a license issued by the department under Chapter 2301, Occupations Code.

SUBTITLE B DRIVER'S LICENSES AND PERSONAL IDENTIFICATION CARDS

CHAPTER 521 DRIVER'S LICENSES AND CERTIFICATES

SUBCHAPTER A GENERAL PROVISIONS

Sec. 521.001. Definitions.

(a) In this chapter:

(1) "Correctional facility" means:

(A) a place described by Section 1.07(a)(14), Penal Code; or

(B) a secure correctional facility or secure detention facility, as defined by Section 51.02, Family Code.

(1-a) "Department" means the Texas Department of Motor Vehicles.

(2) "Director" means the executive director of the department.

(3) "Driver's license" means an authorization issued by the department for the operation of a motor vehicle. The term includes:

(A) a temporary license or learner license; and

(B) an occupational license.

(3-a) "Federal judge" means:

(A) a judge of a United States court of appeals;

(B) a judge of a United States district court;

(C) a judge of a United States bankruptcy court; or

(D) a magistrate judge of a United States district court.

(4) "Gross combination weight rating" has the meaning assigned by Section 522.003.

(5) "Gross vehicle weight rating" has the meaning assigned by Section 522.003.

(6) "License" means an authorization to operate a motor vehicle that is issued under or granted by the laws of this state. The term includes:

(A) a driver's license;

(B) the privilege of a person to operate a motor vehicle regardless of whether the person holds a driver's license; and

(C) a nonresident's operating privilege.

(6-a) "Motorcycle" includes an enclosed three-wheeled passenger vehicle that:

(A) is designed to operate with three wheels in contact with the ground;

(B) has a single, completely enclosed, occupant compartment; and

(C) at a minimum, is equipped with:

(i) seats that are certified by the vehicle manufacturer to meet the requirements of Federal Motor Vehicle Safety Standard No. 207, 49 C.F.R. Section 571.207;

(ii) a steering wheel used to maneuver the vehicle;

(iii) a propulsion unit located in front of or behind the enclosed occupant compartment;

(iv) a seat belt for each vehicle occupant certified by the manufacturer to meet the requirements of Federal Motor Vehicle Safety Standard No. 209, 49 C.F.R. Section 571.209;

(v) a windshield and one or more windshield wipers certified by the manufacturer to meet the requirements of Federal Motor Vehicle Safety Standard No. 205, 49 C.F.R. Section 571.205, and Federal Motor Vehicle Safety Standard No. 104, 49 C.F.R. Section 571.104;

(vi) a vehicle structure certified by the vehicle manufacturer to meet the requirements of Federal Motor Vehicle Safety Standard No. 216, 49 C.F.R. Section 571.216, if:

(a) the unladen weight of the vehicle is more than 900 pounds; or

(b) the unladen weight of the vehicle is not more than 900 pounds and the vehicle has a maximum speed capability of more than 40 miles per hour; and

(vii) an active tilt control system if the unladen weight of the vehicle is not more than 900 pounds and the vehicle has a maximum speed capability of 40 miles per hour or less.

(7) "Nonresident" means a person who is not a resident of this state.

(7-a) "Parole facility" means a place described by Section 508.118 or 508.119, Government Code.

(8) "State" means a state, territory, or possession of the United States, the District of Columbia, or the Commonwealth of Puerto Rico.

(8-a) "State judge" means:

(A) the judge of an appellate court, a district court, a county court at law, or a statutory probate court of this state; or

(B) an associate judge appointed under Chapter 201, Family Code, Chapter 54A, Government Code, or Chapter 574, Health and Safety Code.

(9) "Image comparison technology" means any technology that is used to compare facial images, thumbprints, or fingerprints.

(b) A word or phrase that is not defined by this chapter but is defined by Subtitle C has the meaning in this chapter that is assigned by that subtitle.

(c) The department by rule may define types of vehicles that are "motorcycles" for the purposes of this chapter, in addition to those defined under Subsection (a)(6-a), and for the purposes of Chapters 501, 502, and 503. This subsection applies only to vehicles manufactured by a manufacturer licensed under Chapter 2301, Occupations Code.

Sec. 521.0015. Statutory References.

A statutory reference to the Department of Public Safety means the Texas Department of Motor Vehicles if the statutory reference concerns:

(1) the administration of the programs established by this chapter, Chapter 522, and other law that license a person to operate a motor vehicle, as defined by Section 501.002, or a commercial motor vehicle, as defined by Section 522.003, in this state; or

(2) the administration of Chapter 521A.

Sec. 521.002. Convenience to Public.

The department shall implement its duties under this chapter in the manner that provides the greatest convenience to the public.

Sec. 521.003. Enrollment and Attendance Verification.

The Texas Education Agency shall design a standard form for use by public and private schools to verify a student's enrollment and attendance for purposes of this chapter. The form must be approved by the department.

Sec. 521.004. Penal Code References.

In this chapter:

(1) a reference to an offense under Section 49.04, Penal Code, includes an offense under Article 6701*l*–1, Revised Statutes, as that law existed immediately before September 1, 1994;

(2) a reference to an offense under Section 49.07, Penal Code:

Transportation Code

(A) means only an offense under that section involving the operation of a motor vehicle; and

(B) includes an offense under Section 6701*l*–1, Revised Statutes, as that law existed immediately before September 1, 1994; and

(3) a reference to an offense under Section 49.08, Penal Code:

(A) means only an offense under that section involving the operation of a motor vehicle; and

(B) includes an offense under Section 19.05(a)(2), Penal Code, as that law existed immediately before September 1, 1994.

Sec. 521.005. Rulemaking Authority.

The department may adopt rules necessary to administer this chapter.

Sec. 521.006. Advertising in Driver's Handbook and Driver's License Mailings.

(a) Except as provided by Subsection (c), the department may sell advertising for inclusion in:

(1) any driver's handbook that the department publishes; and

(2) any mailing the department makes in connection with a driver's license.

(b) The department shall deposit the proceeds from the advertising to the credit of the driver's license administration advertising account. The driver's license administration advertising account is an account in the general revenue fund that may be appropriated only for the purpose of administration of this chapter.

(c) The department may not include in the driver's handbook or a driver's license mailing advertising for an alcoholic beverage or a product promoting alcoholic beverages.

Sec. 521.0061. Advertising Inside Driver's License Offices.

The department may enter into an agreement with a public or private entity for a digital message display system to promote department information or news items of general interest in a publicly accessible area of a driver's license office. For the purpose of funding the system, a portion of the information displayed on the system may consist of digital advertisements. The department may review and has the right to reject any proposed advertising to be displayed on a system.

Sec. 521.0062. Information on Driving with Autism.

The department may make available, in a publicly accessible area of a driver's license office, informational materials and videos on driving with autism that are developed by an appropriate entity, as determined by the department.

Sec. 521.0062. Information on Bone Marrow Donation. [Renumbered]

Sec. 521.0063. Information on Bone Marrow Donation.

The department may make available, in a publicly accessible area of a driver's license office, informational materials and videos on bone marrow donation that are developed by an appropriate entity, as determined by the department.

Sec. 521.007. Temporary Visitor Stations.

(a) The department shall designate as temporary visitor stations certain driver's license offices.

(b) A driver's license office designated as a temporary visitor station under this section must have at least two staff members who have completed specialized training on the temporary visitor issuance guide published by the department.

(c) A driver's license office designated as a temporary visitor station shall provide information and assistance to other driver's license offices in the state.

Sec. 521.008. Voluntary Contribution to Donor Registry.

(a) When a person applies for an original or renewal driver's license under this chapter, the person may contribute $1 or more to the nonprofit organization administering the Glenda Dawson Donate Life-Texas Registry under Chapter 692A, Health and Safety Code.

(b) The department shall:

(1) include space on each application for a new or renewal driver's license that allows a person applying for a new or renewal driver's license to indicate that the person is voluntarily contributing $1 to the organization; and

(2) provide an opportunity for the person to contribute $1 to the organization during the application process for a new or renewal driver's license on the department's Internet website.

(c) The department shall remit any contribution made under this section to the comptroller for deposit to the credit of the Glenda Dawson Donate Life-Texas Registry fund created under Section 692A.020, Health and Safety Code. Before sending the money to the comptroller, the department may deduct money equal to the amount of reasonable expenses for administering this section,

Transportation Code

not to exceed five percent of the money collected under this section.

(d) The organization shall submit an annual report to the director of the department that includes the total dollar amount of contributions received by the organization under this section.

Sec. 521.009. Program Regarding the Provision of Renewal and Duplicate Driver's License and Other Identification Certificate Services.

(a) The department may establish a program for the provision of renewal and duplicate driver's license, election identification certificate, and personal identification certificate services in counties and municipalities that enter into an agreement with the department under Subsection (a-1).

(a-1) Under the program, the department may enter into an agreement with the commissioners court of a county or the governing body of a municipality to permit county or municipal employees to provide services at a county or municipal office relating to the issuance of renewal and duplicate driver's licenses, election identification certificates, and personal identification certificates, including:

(1) taking photographs;

(2) administering vision tests;

(3) updating a driver's license, election identification certificate, or personal identification certificate to change a name, address, or photograph;

(4) distributing and collecting information relating to donations under Section 521.401;

(5) collecting fees; and

(6) performing other basic ministerial functions and tasks necessary to issue renewal and duplicate driver's licenses, election identification certificates, and personal identification certificates.

(b) An agreement under Subsection (a-1) may not include training to administer an examination for driver's license applicants under Subchapter H.

(c) A participating county or municipality must remit to the department for deposit as required by this chapter fees collected for the issuance of a renewal or duplicate driver's license or personal identification certificate.

(d) The commissioners court of a county may provide services through any consenting county office. A county office may decline or consent to provide services under this section by providing written notice to the commissioners court.

(e) The department shall provide all equipment and supplies necessary to perform the services described by Subsection (a-1), including network connectivity.

(f) The department shall adopt rules to administer this section.

Sec. 521.010. Voluntary Contribution to Fund for Veterans' Assistance.

(a) When a person applies for an original or renewal driver's license or personal identification certificate under this chapter, the person may make a voluntary contribution in any amount to the fund for veterans' assistance established by Section 434.017, Government Code.

(b) The department shall:

(1) include space on the first page of each application for an original or renewal driver's license or personal identification certificate that allows a person applying for an original or renewal driver's license or personal identification certificate to indicate the amount that the person is voluntarily contributing to the fund; and

(2) provide an opportunity for the person to contribute to the fund during the application process for an original or renewal driver's license or personal identification certificate on the department's Internet website.

(c) The department shall send any contribution made under this section to the comptroller for deposit in the state treasury to the credit of the fund for veterans' assistance not later than the 14th day of each month. Before sending the money to the fund, the department may deduct money equal to the amount of reasonable expenses for administering this section.

Sec. 521.011. Services Information for Veterans.

The department and the Texas Veterans Commission shall jointly develop a one-page informational paper about veterans services provided by this state for veterans who receive:

(1) a driver's license with a designation under Section 521.1235; or

(2) a personal identification certificate with a designation under Section 521.102.

Sec. 521.012. Voluntary Contribution for Evidence Testing Grant Program.

(a) When a person applies for an original, renewal, corrected, or duplicate driver's license or personal identification certificate under this chapter, the person may contribute $1 or more to the evidence testing grant program established under Section 772.00715, Government Code.

(b) The department shall:

(1) include space on the first page of each application for an original, renewal, corrected, or duplicate driver's license or personal identification certificate that allows a person applying for an original, renewal, corrected, or duplicate driver's license or

personal identification certificate to indicate the amount that the person is voluntarily contributing to the grant program; and

(2) provide an opportunity for the person to contribute to the grant program during the application process for an original, renewal, corrected, or duplicate driver's license or personal identification certificate on the department's Internet website.

(c) The department shall send any contribution made under this section to the comptroller for deposit to the credit of the evidence testing account established under Section 772.00716, Government Code, not later than the 14th day of each month. Before sending the money to the comptroller, the department may deduct money equal to the amount of reasonable expenses for administering this section.

Sec. 521.013. Texas 1836 Project Pamphlet.

(a) The department shall provide the pamphlet described by Section 451.005, Government Code, to persons who receive a driver's license:

(1) after applying under Section 521.144; or

(2) with an expiration provided by Section 521.271(a-2) or (a-3).

(b) The department shall make the pamphlet described by Section 451.005, Government Code, available to the public on the department's Internet website.

Sec. 521.013. Voluntary Contribution for Trafficked Persons Program Account.

(a) When a person applies for an original, renewal, corrected, or duplicate driver's license or personal identification certificate under this chapter, the department shall, in a conspicuous manner, direct that person to the opportunity to donate to the trafficked persons program account established under Section 50.0153, Health and Safety Code, through the state's electronic Internet portal described by Section 2054.252(h), Government Code.

(b) The department may deduct from the donations made under this section an amount equal to the department's reasonable expenses associated with administering this section.

SUBCHAPTER B GENERAL LICENSE REQUIREMENTS

Sec. 521.021. License Required.

A person, other than a person expressly exempted under this chapter, may not operate a motor vehicle on a highway in this state unless the person holds a driver's license issued under this chapter.

Sec. 521.022. Restrictions on Operators of Certain School Buses.

(a) A person under 18 years of age may not operate a school bus for the transportation of students.

(b) A person who is 18 years of age or older may not operate a school bus unless the person holds an appropriate class of driver's license for the vehicle being operated.

(c) A person may not operate a school bus for the transportation of students unless the person meets the mental and physical capability requirements the department establishes by rule and has passed an examination approved by the department to determine the person's mental and physical capabilities to operate a school bus safely. A physician, advanced practice nurse, or physician assistant may conduct the examination. An ophthalmologist, optometrist, or therapeutic optometrist may conduct the part of the examination relating to the person's vision. Each school bus operator must pass the examination annually.

(d) A person may not operate a school bus for the transportation of students unless the person's driving record is acceptable according to minimum standards adopted by the department. A check of the person's driving record shall be made with the department annually. The minimum standards adopted by the department must provide that a person's driving record is not acceptable if the person has been convicted of an offense under Section 49.04, 49.045, 49.07, or 49.08, Penal Code, within the 10-year period preceding the date of the check of the person's driving record.

(e) A person may not operate a school bus for the transportation of students unless the person is certified in school bus safety education or has enrolled in a school bus safety education class under provisions adopted by the department. Effective on the date and under provisions determined by the department, a school bus operator must hold a card that states that the operator is enrolled in or has completed a driver training course approved by the department in school bus safety education. The card is valid for three years.

(f) Before a person is employed to operate a school bus to transport students, the employer must obtain a criminal history record check. A school district, school, service center, or shared services arrangement, or a commercial transportation company under contract with a school district, that obtains information that a person has been convicted of a felony or misdemeanor involving moral turpitude

Transportation Code

may not employ the person to drive a school bus on which students are transported unless the employment is approved by the board of trustees of the school district or the board's designee.

(g) This section does not affect the right of an otherwise qualified person with a hearing disability to be licensed, certified, and employed as a bus operator for vehicles used to transport hearing-impaired students.

(h) This section does not apply to the operation of a vehicle owned by a public institution of higher education to transport students of a school district that operates within that institution if:

(1) the person operating the vehicle is approved by the institution to operate the vehicle; and

(2) the transportation is for a special event, including a field trip.

(i) For purposes of this section, "school bus" includes a school activity bus as defined by Section 541.201.

Sec. 521.023. Junior College Buses.

(a) A person who is 18 years of age or older and who is licensed by the department to operate a motor vehicle as a school bus may operate the motor vehicle for the transportation of junior college students and employees to and from school or official school activities.

(b) A school bus operated by a junior college may also be used to transport public school students if it is convenient. If students of a local public school district are transported to and from school on a bus operated by a junior college and the operator is under 21 years of age, the selection of the operator must be approved by the principal of the public school whose students are transported on that bus.

(c) This section does not apply to the operator of a vehicle operated under a registration certificate issued under Chapter 643.

Sec. 521.024. Restrictions on Certain Common Carriers.

(a) A person under 18 years of age may not operate a motor vehicle while that vehicle is in use as a public or common carrier of persons unless the person is licensed to operate the vehicle.

(b) A person may not operate a taxicab unless the person is at least 18 years of age.

Sec. 521.025. License to Be Carried and Exhibited on Demand; Criminal Penalty.

(a) A person required to hold a license under Section 521.021 shall:

(1) have in the person's possession while operating a motor vehicle the class of driver's license appropriate for the type of vehicle operated; and

(2) display the license on the demand of a magistrate, court officer, or peace officer.

(b) A peace officer may stop and detain a person operating a motor vehicle to determine if the person has a driver's license as required by this section.

(c) A person who violates this section commits an offense. An offense under this subsection is a misdemeanor punishable by a fine not to exceed $200, except that:

(1) for a second conviction within one year after the date of the first conviction, the offense is a misdemeanor punishable by a fine of not less than $25 or more than $200;

(2) for a third or subsequent conviction within one year after the date of the second conviction the offense is a misdemeanor punishable by:

(A) a fine of not less than $25 or more than $500;

(B) confinement in the county jail for not less than 72 hours or more than six months; or

(C) both the fine and confinement; and

(3) if it is shown on the trial of the offense that at the time of the offense the person was operating the motor vehicle in violation of Section 601.191 and caused or was at fault in a motor vehicle accident that resulted in serious bodily injury to or the death of another person, an offense under this section is a Class A misdemeanor.

(d) It is a defense to prosecution under this section if the person charged produces in court a driver's license:

(1) issued to that person;

(2) appropriate for the type of vehicle operated; and

(3) valid at the time of the arrest for the offense.

(e) The judge of each court shall report promptly to the department each conviction obtained in the court under this section.

(f) The court may assess a defendant an administrative fee not to exceed $10 if a charge under this section is dismissed because of the defense listed under Subsection (d).

Sec. 521.026. Dismissal of Expired License Charge.

(a) A judge may dismiss a charge of driving with an expired license if the defendant remedies this defect within 20 working days or before the defendant's first court appearance date, whichever is later.

(b) The judge may assess the defendant a reimbursement fee not to exceed $20 when the charge of driving with an expired driver's license is dismissed under Subsection (a).

Sec. 521.027. Persons Exempt from License Requirement.

The following persons are exempt from the license requirement imposed under this chapter:

(1) a person in the service of the state military forces or the United States while the person is operating an official motor vehicle in the scope of that service;

(2) a person while the person is operating a road machine, farm tractor, or implement of husbandry on a highway, unless the vehicle is a commercial motor vehicle under Section 522.003;

(3) a nonresident on active duty in the armed forces of the United States who holds a license issued by the person's state or Canadian province of residence; and

(4) a person who is the spouse or dependent child of a nonresident exempt under Subdivision (3) and who holds a license issued by the person's state or Canadian province of residence.

Sec. 521.028. Effect of Military Service on License Requirement.

(a) Unless the license is suspended, canceled, or revoked as provided by law, a driver's license issued by this state that is held by a person who is on active duty in the armed forces of the United States and is absent from this state, notwithstanding the expiration date of the license, remains valid while the person is absent from this state. If the person is honorably discharged from active duty, the license remains valid until the earlier of:

(1) the 91st day after the date of the discharge; or

(2) the date on which the person returns to this state.

(b) A person on active duty in the armed forces of the United States who has in the person's possession a license issued in a foreign country by the armed forces of the United States may operate a motor vehicle in this state for a period of not more than 90 days after the date on which the person returns to the United States.

Sec. 521.029. Operation of Motor Vehicle by New State Residents.

(a) A person who enters this state as a new resident may operate a motor vehicle in this state for no more than 90 days after the date on which the person enters this state if the person:

(1) is 16 years of age or older; and

(2) has in the person's possession a driver's license issued to the person by the person's state or country of previous residence.

(b) If a person subject to this section is prosecuted for operating a motor vehicle without a driver's license, the prosecution alleges that the person has resided in this state for more than 90 days, and the person claims to have been covered by Subsection (a), the person must prove by the preponderance of the evidence that the person has not resided in this state for more than 90 days.

Sec. 521.030. Reciprocal License.

(a) A nonresident who is 18 years of age or older and who has in the person's possession a license issued to the person by the person's state or country of residence that is similar to a Class A or Class B driver's license issued under this chapter is not required to hold a Class A or Class B driver's license issued under this chapter if that state or country of residence recognizes such a license issued by this state and exempts the holder from securing a license issued by the state or foreign country.

(b) A nonresident who is 16 years of age or older and who has in the person's possession a driver's license issued to the person by the person's state or Canadian province of residence may operate a type of motor vehicle that is permitted to be operated with a Class C or Class M driver's license in this state if the license held by the nonresident permits operation of that type of vehicle in the person's state or province of residence.

Sec. 521.0305. Agreements with Foreign Countries.

(a) The department may enter into an agreement with a foreign country under which:

(1) a person who is 18 years of age or older and who has in the person's possession a license issued to the person by that country that is similar to a Class C driver's license issued under this chapter may receive a Class C driver's license issued in a priority manner under this chapter; and

(2) a person who is 18 years of age or older and who has in the person's possession a Class C driver's license issued under this chapter may receive a license similar to a Class C driver's license issued in a priority manner from the foreign country.

(b) The department may only enter into an agreement with a country under Subsection (a) if:

(1) the foreign country and this state are both parties to a reciprocity agreement in driver licensing; and

Transportation Code

(2) the foreign country's motor vehicle laws, ordinances, and administrative rules and regulations are similar to those of this state, as determined by the department.

(c) A person who is not a citizen of the United States must present to the department documentation issued by the United States agency responsible for citizenship and immigration authorizing the person to be in the United States before the person may be issued a driver's license under an agreement under this section.

Sec. 521.031. License from Other Authority.

A person holding a driver's license under this chapter is not required to obtain a license for the operation of a motor vehicle from another state authority or department.

Sec. 521.032. Enhanced Driver's License or Personal Identification Certificate.

(a) The department may issue an enhanced driver's license or personal identification certificate for the purposes of crossing the border between this state and Mexico to an applicant who provides the department with proof of United States citizenship, identity, and state residency. If the department issues an enhanced driver's license or personal identification certificate, the department shall continue to issue a standard driver's license and personal identification certificate and offer each applicant the option of receiving the standard or enhanced driver's license or personal identification certificate.

(b) The department shall implement a one-to-many biometric matching system for the enhanced driver's license or personal identification certificate. An applicant for an enhanced driver's license or personal identification certificate must submit a biometric identifier as designated by the department, which, notwithstanding any other law, may be used only to verify the identity of the applicant for purposes relating to implementation of the border crossing initiative established by this section. An applicant must sign a declaration acknowledging the applicant's understanding of the one-to-many biometric match.

(c) The enhanced driver's license or personal identification certificate must include reasonable security measures to protect the privacy of the license or certificate holders, including reasonable safeguards to protect against the unauthorized disclosure of information about the holders. If the enhanced driver's license or personal identification certificate includes a radio frequency identification chip or similar technology, the department shall ensure that the technology is encrypted or otherwise secure from unauthorized information access.

(d) The requirements of this section are in addition to any other requirements imposed on applicants for a driver's license or personal identification certificate. The department shall adopt rules necessary to implement this section. The department shall periodically review technological innovations related to the security of driver's licenses and personal identification certificates and amend the rules as appropriate, consistent with this section, to protect the privacy of driver's license and personal identification certificate holders.

(e) The department may set a fee for issuance of an enhanced driver's license or personal identification certificate in a reasonable amount necessary to implement and administer this section.

(f) The department may enter into a memorandum of understanding with any federal agency for the purposes of facilitating the crossing of the border between this state and Mexico. The department may enter into an agreement with Mexico, to the extent permitted by federal law, to implement a border crossing initiative authorized by this section. The department shall implement a statewide education campaign to educate residents of this state about the border crossing initiative. The campaign must include information on:

(1) the forms of travel for which the existing and enhanced driver's license and personal identification certificate can be used; and

(2) relevant dates for implementation of laws that affect identification requirements at the border with Mexico.

(g) A person may not sell or otherwise disclose biometric information accessed from an enhanced driver's license or any information from an enhanced driver's license radio frequency identification chip or similar technology to another person or an affiliate of the person. This subsection does not apply to a financial institution described by Section 521.126(e).

SUBCHAPTER C DEPARTMENT LICENSE RECORDS

Sec. 521.041. Application Records; Records of Denial, Suspension, Cancellation, or Revocation.

(a) The department shall record each driver's license application received by the department.

(b) The department shall maintain suitable indexes, in alphabetical or numerical order, that contain:

(1) each denied application and the reasons for the denial;

(2) each application that is granted;

(3) the name of each license holder whose license has been suspended, canceled, or revoked and the reasons for that action; and

(4) the citizenship status of each holder of a license or personal identification certificate.

(c) The department shall maintain the application records for personal identification certificates in the manner required for license applications under this section.

Sec. 521.042. Accident and Conviction Reports; Individual Records.

(a) Except as provided by this section, the department shall record each accident report and abstract of the court record of a conviction received by the department under a law of this state.

(b) The records must enable the department to consider, on receipt of a renewal application and at other suitable times, the record of each license holder that shows any:

(1) conviction of that license holder; and

(2) traffic accident in which the license holder has been involved.

(c) The record of a license holder who is employed as a peace officer, fire fighter, or emergency medical services employee of this state, a political subdivision of this state, or a special purpose district may not include information relating to a traffic accident that occurs while the peace officer, fire fighter, or emergency medical services employee is driving an official vehicle in the course and scope of the license holder's official duties if:

(1) the traffic accident resulted in damages to property of less than $1,000; or

(2) an investigation of the accident by a peace officer, other than a peace officer involved in the accident, determines that the peace officer, fire fighter, or emergency medical services employee involved in the accident was not at fault.

(d) Before issuing or renewing a license, the department shall examine the record of the applicant for information relating to a conviction of a traffic violation or involvement in a traffic accident. The department may not issue or renew a license if the department determines that the issuance or renewal of the license would be inimical to the public safety.

(e) The director may maintain records required under this subchapter on microfilm or computer.

Sec. 521.043. Elimination of Certain Unnecessary Records.

The department is not required to maintain records relating to a person if the director decides that the records are no longer necessary, except that the department shall maintain a record of a conviction as long as the record may be used:

(1) as grounds for a license cancellation, suspension, revocation, or denial; or

(2) in conjunction with other records of convictions, to establish that a person is a frequent violator of traffic laws.

Sec. 521.044. Use or Disclosure of Social Security Number Information.

(a) Information provided on a driver's license or personal identification certificate application that relates to the applicant's social security number may be used only by the department or disclosed only to:

(1) the child support enforcement division of the attorney general's office;

(2) another state entity responsible for enforcing the payment of child support;

(3) the United States Selective Service System as provided by Section 521.147;

(4) the unclaimed property division of the comptroller's office;

(5) the Health and Human Services Commission;

(6) the secretary of state for the purposes of voter registration or the administration of elections; or

(7) an agency of another state responsible for issuing driver's licenses or identification documents.

(b) The department shall enter an applicant's social security number in the department's electronic database but may not print the number on the applicant's driver's license or personal identification certificate.

(c) (1) On the request of a state entity responsible for investigating or enforcing the payment of child support or the secretary of state, the department shall disclose information regarding an applicant's social security number.

(2) On the request of the Health and Human Services Commission and for the purpose of assisting the commission in determining an applicant's eligibility for any program administered by the commission, the department shall disclose information regarding an applicant's social security number.

(d) Information disclosed under this section may be used by a state entity responsible for enforcing the payment of child support only to implement the duties of the state entity.

(e) The department shall include in the department's legislative appropriations requests and

Transportation Code

budgets, in quarterly performance reports, and in audits of the department's local offices performance measures on the percentage of complete and correct social security numbers on driver's licenses and personal identification certificates.

(f) This section does not prohibit the department from requiring an applicant for a driver's license to provide the applicant's social security number.

Sec. 521.0445. Notice Regarding Suspension of License for Nonpayment of Child Support.

The department shall include in each notice sent to a driver's license holder a statement advising a holder who is delinquent in the payment of child support to make satisfactory arrangements with the office of the attorney general to correct the delinquency and that failure to contact the attorney general or to make satisfactory arrangements may result in the commencement by the attorney general of procedures to suspend the holder's driver's license.

Sec. 521.045. Disclosure of Certain Information Relating to Individual Operator.

On receipt of a written request and payment of a $4 fee, the department may disclose information relating to an individual's date of birth, current license status, and most recent address, as shown in the department's records, to a person who:

(1) is eligible to receive the information under Chapter 730; and

(2) submits to the department the individual's driver's license number or the individual's full name and date of birth.

Sec. 521.046. Disclosure of Accident and Conviction Information.

(a) In addition to the information authorized to be released under Section 521.045, on receipt of a written request and payment of a $6 fee, the department may disclose that information and information regarding each reported motor vehicle moving violation, as defined by department rule, resulting in a traffic law conviction and each motor vehicle accident in which the individual received a citation, by date and location, within the three years preceding the date of the request, to a person who:

(1) is eligible to receive the information under Chapter 730; and

(2) submits to the department the individual's driver's license number or the individual's full name and date of birth.

(b) If the department receives requests for information under this section in quantities of 100 or more from a single person at one time and on data processing request forms acceptable to the department, the department may reduce the fee to $5 for each individual request.

Sec. 521.047. Disclosure of Information to License Holder.

(a) The department may disclose information relating to a license holder to that license holder on receipt of a written request that includes the individual's driver's license number or the individual's full name and date of birth, and payment of a $7 fee.

(b) The department may disclose information as recorded in department records that relates to:

(1) the individual's date of birth;

(2) the current license status of the individual;

(3) the individual's most recent address;

(4) the completion of an approved driver education course by the individual;

(5) the fact of, but not the reason for, completion of a driver safety course by the individual; and

(6) each of the individual's reported traffic law violations and motor vehicle accidents, by date and location.

Sec. 521.0475. Disclosure of Abstract Record.

(a) Except as provided by Subsection (b), the department shall provide a certified abstract of a complete driving record of a license holder, for a fee of $20, to the license holder or a person eligible to receive the information under Sections 730.007(a)(2)(A), (D), and (I).

(b) If an abstract of a complete driving record does not exist for a license holder, the department shall provide a person making a request under Subsection (a) a certified statement to that effect.

(c) [Repealed.]

Sec. 521.048. Certified Information.

The department may disclose information under Section 521.046 or 521.047 that is certified by the custodian of records on payment of a $10 fee for each individual request.

Sec. 521.0485. Requests for Information by Mail or Electronic Means.

(a) The department by rule may provide that the holder of a driver's license issued by the department may submit a request for information under

Sections 521.045—521.048 by mail, by telephone, over the Internet, or by other electronic means.

(b) A rule adopted under Subsection (a):

(1) may prescribe eligibility standards for release of the requested information; and

(2) may not conflict with any provision of this chapter or another law that relates to the release of the information by the department.

Sec. 521.049. Information Supplied to Certain Governmental Entities.

(a) The department shall disclose information relating to the name, date of birth, and most recent address as shown in department records to the Texas Department of Health during an emergency or epidemic declared by the commissioner of health to notify individuals of the need to receive certain immunizations.

(b) The department may not charge a fee for information disclosed to a law enforcement agency or other governmental agency for an official purpose, except that the department may charge its regular fees for information provided to those governmental agencies in bulk for research projects.

(c) The department may make information from driver's license record files, including class-type listings, available to an official of the United States, the state, or a political subdivision of this state for government purposes only.

(d) To assist chief appraisers in determining the eligibility of individuals for residence homestead exemptions from ad valorem taxation under Section 11.13, Tax Code, and the applicability to certain individuals of additional notice provisions under Subchapters C and D, Chapter 23, Tax Code, the department shall provide, without charge, to the chief appraiser of each appraisal district in this state:

(1) a copy of each driver's license record or personal identification certificate record held by the department; or

(2) information relating to the name, date of birth, driver's license or personal identification certificate number, and most recent address as shown in the records of individuals included in the department's driver's license or personal identification certificate records.

(e) A driver's license record or personal identification certificate record provided under Subsection (d)(1) may not include information relating to an individual's social security number or any accident or conviction information about an individual.

(f) The department shall respond to a request for a driving record check received from another state under 49 C.F.R. Section 384.206 within 30 days of the date of the request.

Sec. 521.050. Sale of License Information.

(a) In addition to the provisions of this subchapter relating to the disclosure of driver's license information on an individual, the department may provide a purchaser, in a format prescribed by the department and acceptable to the purchaser, the names, addresses, and dates of birth of all license holders that are contained in the department's basic driver's license record file if the purchaser certifies in writing that the purchaser is eligible to receive the information under Chapter 730.

(b) The department may also periodically provide to the purchaser of the information any addition to that file.

(c) The department shall impose and collect a fee of:

(1) $2,000 for the initial driver's license information provided under Subsection (a); and

(2) if the department provides a weekly update of the information, $75 for each update.

Sec. 521.051. Disclosure of Certain Information Prohibited.

The department may not disclose class-type listings from the basic driver's license record file to any person except as provided by Section 521.049(c), regardless of whether the requestor is eligible to receive the information under Chapter 730.

Sec. 521.052. Disclosure of Individual Information Prohibited.

Except as provided by Sections 521.045, 521.046, 521.0475, 521.049(c), and 521.050, and by Chapter 730, the department may not disclose information from the department's files that relates to personal information, as that term is defined by Section 730.003.

Sec. 521.053. Commercial Driver's License Information.

(a) The department may provide to any person the information specified by Section 521.045, 521.046, 521.0475, or 521.047, for the fee required by those sections, that relate to the holder of or applicant for a commercial driver's license under Chapter 522 if the person is eligible to receive the information under Chapter 730.

(b) If the information is provided through the commercial driver license information system, the fee for this service is the fee specified in the applicable section plus $2.

(c) The department may provide information under Subsection (a) through the system described by Section 521.055.

Transportation Code

(d) The department may provide information maintained under Section 644.252 that relates to a holder of a commercial driver's license under Chapter 522 to the holder, the holder's current employer, or a person acting on behalf of the employer if the department receives the holder's specific written consent to the release of information.

Sec. 521.054. Notice of Change of Address or Name.

(a) This section applies to a person who:

(1) after applying for or being issued a license or certificate moves to a new residence address;

(2) has used the procedure under Section 521.121(c) and whose status as a federal judge, including a federal bankruptcy judge, a marshal of the United States Marshals Service, a United States attorney, a state judge, or a family member of a federal judge, including a federal bankruptcy judge, a marshal of the United States Marshals Service, a United States attorney, or a state judge becomes inapplicable; or

(3) changes the person's name by marriage or otherwise.

(b) A person subject to this section shall notify the department of the change not later than the 30th day after the date on which the change takes effect and apply for a duplicate license or certificate as provided by Section 521.146. The duplicate license must include the person's current residence address.

(c) A person changing the person's address shall notify the department of the old and new addresses and the number of the license or certificate held by the person. A person changing the person's name shall notify the department of the former and new names and the number of the license or certificate held by the person.

(d) A court may dismiss a charge for a violation of this section if the defendant remedies the defect not later than the 20th working day after the date of the offense and pays a reimbursement fee not to exceed $20. The court may waive the reimbursement fee if the waiver is in the interest of justice.

(e) In this section, "family member" has the meaning assigned by Section 31.006, Finance Code.

(f) [Repealed by Acts 2005, 79th Leg., ch. 1249 (H.B. 1789), § 3(1), effective September 1, 2005.]

Sec. 521.055. Establishment of Interactive System.

(a) The department may establish a system, separate from the department's mainframe computer, that will allow interactive access to certain driver's license record information.

(b) The system may provide for the release of driving records described in:

(1) Section 521.045;

(2) Section 521.046;

(3) Section 521.047; and

(4) Section 521.0475.

(c) The fee for a driving record under Subsection (b)(1) is $2.50. The fee for a driving record under Subsection (b)(2) is $4.50. The fee for a driving record under Subsection (b)(3) is $5.50. The fee for a driving record under Subsection (b)(4) is $20.

(d) [Repealed by Acts 2003, 78th Leg., ch. 1325 (H.B. 3588), § 11.10, effective September 1, 2003.]

(e) The department may contract with private vendors as necessary to implement this section.

(f) The department may adopt rules as necessary to administer this section.

(g) For purposes of this section, a release of information to persons eligible to receive the information under Chapter 730 occurs each time a query is made of the system.

Sec. 521.056. National Driver Register.

(a) The department may process file check requests under the National Driver Register on behalf of current or prospective employers of individuals employed or seeking employment as operators of motor vehicles or railway locomotive operators if the individual:

(1) has given written consent to the release of the information; and

(2) has a license in this state.

(b) The fee for a request under Subsection (a) is $4.

(c) The department shall forward a request made under Subsection (a) directly to the current or prospective employer.

(d) The department shall assist and provide procedures for an individual to obtain information from the National Driver Register on the individual's own driving record. The department may by rule establish a reasonable fee for this service, in conformity with the policies of the National Driver Register.

(e) The department may adopt forms and rules as necessary to carry out the purposes of this section and comply with the policies of the National Driver Register.

Sec. 521.057. Information Regarding Certain Sex Offenders.

(a) On receipt of a court order issued under Article 42.016, Code of Criminal Procedure, the department shall ensure that any driver's license

Transportation Code

record or personal identification certificate record maintained by the department for the person includes an indication that the person is subject to the registration requirements of Chapter 62, Code of Criminal Procedure.

(b) The department shall include the indication required by Subsection (a) in any driver's license record or personal identification certificate record maintained by the department for the person until the expiration of the person's duty to register under Chapter 62, Code of Criminal Procedure.

Sec. 521.058. Disposition of Fees.

Each fee collected under this subchapter shall be deposited to the credit of the Texas mobility fund.

Sec. 521.059. Image Verification System.

(a) The department shall establish an image verification system based on the following identifiers collected by the department under Section 521.142(b):

(1) an applicant's facial image; and

(2) an applicant's thumbprints or, if thumbprints cannot be taken, the index fingerprints of the applicant.

(b) The department shall authenticate the facial image and thumbprints or fingerprints provided by an applicant for a personal identification certificate, driver's license, or commercial driver's license or permit using image comparison technology to ensure that the applicant:

(1) is issued only one original license, permit, or certificate;

(2) does not fraudulently obtain a duplicate license, permit, or certificate; and

(3) does not commit other fraud in connection with the application for a license, permit, or certificate.

(c) The department shall use the image verification system established under this section only to the extent allowed by Chapter 730, Transportation Code, to aid other law enforcement agencies in:

(1) establishing the identity of a victim of a disaster or crime that a local law enforcement agency is unable to establish; or

(2) conducting an investigation of criminal conduct.

(d) [Expired pursuant to Acts 2005, 79th Leg., ch. 1108 (H.B. 2337), § 4, effective September 1, 2010.]

Sec. 521.060. Emergency Contact and Medical Information Databases.

(a) The department shall maintain in its files a record of the name, address, and telephone number of each individual identified by the holder of a driver's license or personal identification certificate as an individual the holder authorizes to be contacted in the event that the holder is injured or dies in or as a result of a vehicular accident or another emergency situation. In addition, the department shall maintain in its files a record of any medical information described by Section 521.125(a) that is provided to the department under Subsection (c) or any health condition information that is voluntarily provided to the department under Section 521.142(h).

(b) A record maintained by the department under Subsection (a) is confidential and, on request, may be disclosed:

(1) only to a peace officer in this or another state;

(2) only if the peace officer is otherwise authorized to obtain information in the driver's license or personal identification certificate files of the department; and

(3) only for the purpose, as applicable, of making contact with a named individual to report the injury to or death of the holder of the driver's license or personal identification certificate, learning the nature of any medical information reported by the person who holds the driver's license or identification certificate, or learning whether the person who holds the driver's license or identification certificate has a health condition that may impede communications with the peace officer.

(c) An application for an original, renewal, or duplicate driver's license or personal identification certificate must:

(1) be designed to allow, but not require, the applicant to provide:

(A) the name, address, and telephone number of not more than two individuals to be contacted if the applicant is injured or dies in a circumstance described by Subsection (a); and

(B) in addition to health condition information voluntarily provided under Section 521.142(h), medical information described by Section 521.125(a); and

(2) include a statement that:

(A) describes the confidential nature of the information; and

(B) states that by providing the department with the information, the applicant consents to the limited disclosure and use of the information.

(d) The department shall establish and maintain on the department's Internet website forms and procedures by which the holder of a driver's license or personal identification certificate may request that the department:

(1) add specific emergency contact or medical information described by Subsection (a) to the appropriate file maintained by the department; or

Transportation Code

(2) amend or delete emergency contact or medical information the holder previously provided to the department.

(e) The forms and procedures established and maintained under Subsection (d) must:

(1) comply with Subsection (c); and

(2) allow the holder of a driver's license or personal identification certificate or an authorized agent of the holder to add, amend, or delete information described by Subsection (d) by submitting an electronic form on the department's Internet website.

(f) Subsection (b) does not prohibit the department from disclosing information to the holder of a driver's license or personal identification certificate who provided the information or to an authorized agent of the holder.

Sec. 521.061. Internal Verification System.

(a) The department by rule shall establish a system for identifying unique addresses that are submitted in license or certificate applications under this chapter or Chapter 522 in a frequency or number that, in the department's determination, casts doubt on whether the addresses are the actual addresses where the applicants reside.

(b) The department may contract with a third-party personal data verification service to assist the department in implementing this section.

(c) The department shall investigate the validity of addresses identified under Subsection (a).

(d) The department may disclose the results of an investigation under Subsection (c) to a criminal justice agency for the purposes of enforcing Section 521.4565 or other provisions of this chapter or Chapter 522.

(e) In this section, "criminal justice agency" has the meaning assigned by Article 66.001, Code of Criminal Procedure.

Sec. 521.062. Driver Record Monitoring Pilot Program.

(a) The department by rule may establish a driver record monitoring pilot program. The term of the pilot program may not exceed one year.

(b) Under the pilot program, the department shall:

(1) enter into a contract with any person qualified to provide driver record monitoring services, as described by Subsection (c); and

(2) provide certain information from the department's driver's license records to the person as provided by this section.

(b-1) A person is qualified to provide driver record monitoring services if the person:

(1) has submitted an application to the department;

(2) is an employer, an insurer, an insurance support organization, an employer support organization, or an entity that self-insures its motor vehicles; and

(3) is eligible to receive the information under Chapter 730.

(b-2) The department may not limit the number of qualified persons participating in the pilot program.

(c) A contract entered into by the department must require:

(1) the department, during the term of the contract, to:

(A) monitor the driver record of each holder of a driver's license issued by the department that is requested by the person with whom the department has contracted;

(B) identify any change in the status of a driver's license or any conviction for a traffic offense reported to the department during the monitoring period; and

(C) periodically, as specified in the contract, provide reports of those individuals identified as having a change in status or convictions to the person with whom the department has contracted; and

(2) the person with whom the department has contracted:

(A) to purchase under Section 521.046 a copy of the driver record of each individual identified in a report provided under Subdivision (1)(C);

(B) to warrant that:

(i) the person will not directly or indirectly disclose information received from the department under the contract to a third party without the express written consent of the department, except as required by law or legal process; and

(ii) if a disclosure is required by law or legal process, the person will immediately notify the department so that the department may seek to oppose, limit, or restrict the required disclosure; and

(C) if the person is an insurance support organization, to warrant that the person will not seek to obtain information about a holder of a driver's license under the contract unless the license holder is insured by a client of the organization, and that the person will provide the department with the name of each client to whom the insurance support organization provides information received from the department under the contract.

(d) The attorney general may file a suit against a person with whom the department has contracted under this section for:

(1) injunctive relief to prevent or restrain the person from violating a term of the contract or from

Transportation Code

directly or indirectly disclosing information received from the department under the contract in a manner that violates the terms of the contract; or

(2) a civil penalty in an amount not to exceed $2,000 for each disclosure in violation of those terms.

(e) If the attorney general brings an action against a person under Subsection (d) and an injunction is granted against the person or the person is found liable for a civil penalty, the attorney general may recover reasonable expenses, court costs, investigative costs, and attorney's fees. Each day a violation continues or occurs is a separate violation for purposes of imposing a penalty under Subsection (d).

(f) A violation of the terms of a contract entered into with the department by the person with whom the department has contracted is a false, misleading, or deceptive act or practice under Subchapter E, Chapter 17, Business & Commerce Code.

(g) A civil action brought under this section shall be filed in a district court:

(1) in Travis County; or

(2) in any county in which the violation occurred.

(h) A person with whom the department has contracted under this section commits an offense if the person directly or indirectly discloses information received from the department under the contract in a manner that violates the terms of the contract. An offense under this subsection is a Class B misdemeanor. If conduct constituting an offense under this subsection also constitutes an offense under another law, the actor may be prosecuted under this subsection, the other law, or both.

(i) The department shall impose a fee on each person with whom the department contracts under this section for the services provided by the department under the contract. The fee must be reasonable and be not less than the amount necessary to allow the department to recover all reasonable costs to the department associated with entering into the contract and providing services to the person under the contract, including direct, indirect, and administrative costs and costs related to the development and deployment of the pilot program.

(j) The department shall accept and consider applications to enter into a contract with the department under this section until the conclusion of the term of the pilot program .

(k) To the fullest extent practicable, the services of the department under a contract entered into under this section shall be provided by, through, or in conjunction with the interactive system established under Section 521.055.

(*l*) At the conclusion of the term of the pilot program, and on the recommendation of the department, the commission may authorize the department to implement the pilot program as a permanent program.

(m) Before the department recommends that the pilot program be implemented as a permanent program, the department shall submit to the lieutenant governor, the speaker of the house of representatives, and each member of the legislature a report that contains an analysis of the scope, effectiveness, and cost benefits of the pilot program. The report must include:

(1) a list of each insurance support organization with which the department has contracted under this section; and

(2) a list of each client to whom the insurance support organization has provided information received from the department under this section.

Sec. 521.063. Mailing Address Verification System.

The department by rule shall establish a system to ensure that addresses of driver's license holders are verified and matched to United States Postal Service delivery addresses by use of address-matching software. The software must meet certification standards under the Coding Accuracy Support System adopted by the United States Postal Service or a subsequent standard adopted by the United States Postal Service to replace Coding Accuracy Support System standards for preparation of bulk mailings. If the department contracts with a provider for bulk mailing services, the contract must require that the provider use address-matching software that meets or exceeds certification standards under the Coding Accuracy Support System or subsequent standards adopted by the United States Postal Service.

SUBCHAPTER D CLASSIFICATION OF DRIVER'S LICENSES

Sec. 521.081. Class A License.

A Class A driver's license authorizes the holder of the license to operate:

(1) a vehicle with a gross vehicle weight rating of 26,001 pounds or more; or

(2) a combination of vehicles that has a gross combination weight rating of 26,001 pounds or more, if the gross vehicle weight rating of any

vehicle or vehicles in tow is more than 10,000 pounds.

Sec. 521.082. Class B License.

(a) A Class B driver's license authorizes the holder of the license to operate:

(1) a vehicle with a gross vehicle weight rating that is more than 26,000 pounds;

(2) a vehicle with a gross vehicle weight rating of 26,000 pounds or more towing:

(A) a vehicle, other than a farm trailer, with a gross vehicle weight rating that is not more than 10,000 pounds; or

(B) a farm trailer with a gross vehicle weight rating that is not more than 20,000 pounds; and

(3) a bus with a seating capacity of 24 passengers or more.

(b) For the purposes of Subsection (a)(3), seating capacity is computed in accordance with Section 502.253, except that the operator's seat is included in the computation.

Sec. 521.083. Class C License.

A Class C driver's license authorizes the holder of the license to operate:

(1) a vehicle or combination of vehicles not described by Section 521.081 or 521.082; and

(2) a vehicle with a gross vehicle weight rating of less than 26,001 pounds towing a farm trailer with a gross vehicle weight rating that is not more than 20,000 pounds.

Sec. 521.084. Class M License.

A Class M driver's license authorizes the holder of the license to operate a motorcycle as defined by Section 541.201.

Sec. 521.085. Type of Vehicle Authorized.

(a) Unless prohibited by Chapter 522, and except as provided by Subsection (b), the license holder may operate any vehicle of the type for which that class of license is issued and any lesser type of vehicle other than a motorcycle.

(b) Subsection (a) does not prohibit a license holder from operating a lesser type of vehicle that is:

(1) a motorcycle described by Section 521.001(a)(6-a) or an autocycle as defined by Section 501.008; or

(2) a type of motorcycle defined by the department under Section 521.001(c) and designated by the department as qualifying for operation under this section.

SUBCHAPTER E CLASSIFICATION OF CERTIFICATES

Sec. 521.101. Personal Identification Certificate.

(a) The department shall issue personal identification certificates.

(b) A personal identification certificate must be similar in form to, but distinguishable in color from, a driver's license.

(c) The department shall indicate "UNDER 21" on the face of a personal identification certificate issued to a person under 21 years of age.

(d) The department may require each applicant for an original, renewal, or duplicate personal identification certificate to furnish to the department the information required by Section 521.142.

(d-1) Unless the information has been previously provided to the department, the department shall require each applicant for an original, renewal, or duplicate personal identification certificate to furnish to the department:

(1) proof of the applicant's United States citizenship; or

(2) documentation described by Subsection (f-2).

(e) The department may cancel and require surrender of a personal identification certificate after determining that the holder was not entitled to the certificate or gave incorrect or incomplete information in the application for the certificate.

(f) A personal identification certificate:

(1) for an applicant who is a citizen, national, or legal permanent resident of the United States or a refugee or asylee lawfully admitted into the United States, expires on a date specified by the department; or

(2) for an applicant not described by Subdivision (1), expires on:

(A) the earlier of:

(i) a date specified by the department; or

(ii) the expiration date of the applicant's authorized stay in the United States; or

(B) the first anniversary of the date of issuance, if there is no definite expiration date for the applicant's authorized stay in the United States.

(f-1) A personal identification certificate issued to a person whose residence or domicile is a correctional facility or a parole facility expires on the first birthday of the license holder occurring after the first anniversary of the date of issuance.

(f-2) An applicant who is not a citizen of the United States must present to the department

Transportation Code

documentation issued by the appropriate United States agency that authorizes the applicant to be in the United States.

(f-3) The department may not issue a personal identification certificate to an applicant who fails or refuses to comply with Subsection (f-2).

(f-4) The department may not deny a personal identification certificate to an applicant who complies with Subsection (f-2) based on the duration of the person's authorized stay in the United States, as indicated by the documentation presented under Subsection (f-2).

(g) An individual, corporation, or association may not deny the holder of a personal identification certificate access to goods, services, or facilities, except as provided by Section 521.460 or in regard to the operation of a motor vehicle, because the holder has a personal identification certificate rather than a driver's license.

(h) The department shall automatically revoke each personal identification certificate issued by the department to a person who:

(1) is subject to the registration requirements of Chapter 62, Code of Criminal Procedure; and

(2) fails to apply to the department for renewal of the personal identification certificate as required by Article 62.060 or 62.2021, Code of Criminal Procedure, as applicable.

(i) The department may issue a personal identification certificate to a person whose certificate is revoked under Subsection (h) only if the person applies for an original or renewal certificate under Section 521.103.

(j) The department may not issue a personal identification certificate to a person who has not established a domicile in this state.

(k) Except as provided by this section, a personal identification certificate issued under this chapter:

(1) must:

(A) be in the same format;

(B) have the same appearance and orientation; and

(C) contain the same type of information; and

(2) may not include any information that this chapter does not reference or require.

(*l*) The application for the personal identification certificate must provide space for the applicant:

(1) to voluntarily list any information that may qualify the applicant to receive a personal identification certificate with a designation under Section 521.102; and

(2) to include proof required by the department to determine the applicant's eligibility to receive that designation.

(m) The department shall adopt procedures for the issuance of a personal identification certificate to a person who surrenders the person's driver's license at the time of applying for the certificate. The procedures:

(1) must be in compliance with federal guidelines governing the issuance of identification documents;

(2) may require the person issued a personal identification certificate to update information previously provided to the department under Section 521.142; and

(3) except as provided by Subdivision (2), may not require a person to provide additional identification documents unless required for compliance with federal guidelines described by Subdivision (1).

Sec. 521.1015. Personal Identification Certificate Issued to Foster Child or Youth or Homeless Child or Youth.

(a) In this section:

(1) "Foster child or youth" means:

(A) a child in the managing conservatorship of the Department of Family and Protective Services; or

(B) a young adult who:

(i) is at least 18 years of age, but younger than 21 years of age; and

(ii) resides in a foster care placement, the cost of which is paid by the Department of Family and Protective Services.

(2) "Homeless child or youth" has the meaning assigned by 42 U.S.C. Section 11434a.

(b) This section applies to the application for a personal identification certificate only for a foster child or youth or a homeless child or youth.

(c) Notwithstanding Section 521.101, Section 521.1426, or any other provision of this chapter, a child or youth described by Subsection (b) may, in applying for a personal identification certificate:

(1) provide a copy of the child's or youth's birth certificate as proof of the child's or youth's identity and United States citizenship, as applicable; and

(2) if the child or youth does not have a residence or domicile:

(A) provide a letter certifying the child or youth is a homeless child or youth issued by:

(i) the school district in which the child or youth is enrolled;

(ii) the director of an emergency shelter or transitional housing program funded by the United States Department of Housing and Urban Development; or

(iii) the director of:

(a) a basic center for runaway and homeless youth; or

(b) a transitional living program; or

(B) use the address of the regional office where the Department of Family and Protective Services caseworker for the child or youth is based.

(d) A child or youth described by Subsection (b) may apply for and the department may issue a personal identification certificate without the signature or presence of or permission from a parent or guardian of the child or youth.

(e) The department shall exempt a child or youth described by Subsection (b) from the payment of any fee for the issuance of a personal identification certificate under this chapter, subject to Section 521.4265.

Sec. 521.1016. Personal Identification Certificate Issued to Victims and Children of Victims of Dating or Family Violence.

(a) In this section:

(1) "Advocate" has the meaning assigned by Section 93.001, Family Code.

(2) "Victim of dating violence" means the victim of violence described by Section 71.0021, Family Code.

(3) "Victim of family violence" has the meaning assigned by Section 51.002, Human Resources Code.

(b) This section applies to the application for a personal identification certificate only for a victim of dating violence, a victim of family violence, or the child of a victim of dating or family violence.

(c) Notwithstanding Section 521.101, Section 521.1426, or any other provision of this chapter, an individual described by Subsection (b) may, in applying for a personal identification certificate:

(1) provide a copy of the individual's birth certificate as proof of the individual's identity and United States citizenship, as applicable; and

(2) if the individual does not have a residence or domicile, provide a letter certifying the individual is homeless issued by:

(A) an advocate;

(B) a licensed mental health services provider who examined and evaluated the individual; or

(C) the director of an emergency shelter or transitional housing program funded by the United States Department of Housing and Urban Development or through the Victims of Crime Act of 1984 (Title II, Pub. L. No. 98-473).

(d) The department shall exempt an individual described by Subsection (b) from the payment of any fee for the issuance of a personal identification certificate under this chapter, subject to Section 521.4265.

Sec. 521.102. Designator on Personal Identification Certificate Issued to Veteran.

(a) In this section:

(1) "Disability rating" has the meaning assigned by Section 11.22, Tax Code.

(2) "Disabled veteran" and "veteran" have the meanings assigned by Section 521.1235.

(b) The department shall include the designation "VETERAN" on a personal identification certificate issued to a veteran in an available space on the face of the personal identification certificate or on the reverse side of the personal identification certificate if:

(1) the veteran requests the designation; and

(2) the veteran provides proof sufficient to the department of the veteran's military service and honorable discharge.

(b-1) If a disabled veteran provides proof sufficient to the department, the department, on request of the disabled veteran, shall include on a personal identification certificate issued to the disabled veteran in any available space on the face of the personal identification certificate or on the reverse side of the personal identification certificate:

(1) a disabled veteran designation; and

(2) the branch of the service in which the disabled veteran served.

(c) The department shall provide to the recipient of a personal identification certificate with a designation under this section the informational paper described by Section 521.011 at the time the certificate is issued.

(d) Notwithstanding any other law and except as provided by Subsection (e), for purposes of obtaining a service or benefit available for disabled veterans in this state, a disabled veteran may use a personal identification certificate described by Subsection (b-1) as satisfactory proof:

(1) that the disabled veteran has a disability rating described by Section 521.1235(a)(2)(A) or (B), as applicable; and

(2) of branch of service and honorable discharge.

(e) A personal identification certificate described by Subsection (b-1) is not satisfactory proof of the disabled veteran's disability rating for purposes of obtaining a property tax exemption provided by Chapter 11, Tax Code.

(f) A disabled veteran who renews a personal identification certificate described by Subsection (b-1) shall provide proof sufficient to the department of the disabled veteran's disability rating.

(g) The department shall establish and maintain on the department's Internet website forms and procedures by which a veteran or disabled veteran may request and provide the proof required for a

Transportation Code

designation on a personal identification certificate or renewal of a personal identification certificate with a designation under this section by submitting a form and the required proof electronically on the department's Internet website.

Sec. 521.103. Expiration and Renewal Requirements for Certain Sex Offenders.

(a) The department may issue an original or renewal personal identification certificate to a person whose driver's license or personal identification certificate record indicates that the person is subject to the registration requirements of Chapter 62, Code of Criminal Procedure, only if the person:

(1) applies in person for the issuance of a certificate under this section; and

(2) pays a fee of $20.

(b) A personal identification certificate issued under this section, including a renewal, duplicate, or corrected certificate, expires on the first birthday of the certificate holder occurring after the date of application, except that:

(1) the initial certificate issued under this section expires on the second birthday of the certificate holder occurring after the date of application, subject to Subdivision (2); and

(2) a certificate issued under this section to a person described by Article 62.2021, Code of Criminal Procedure, expires on the sixth anniversary of the date on which the certificate was issued.

(c) Sections 521.101(f-2), (f-3), and (f-4) apply to a personal identification certificate for which application is made under this section.

Sec. 521.104. Renewal by Mail or Electronic Means.

The department by rule may provide that the holder of a personal identification certificate may renew the certificate by mail, by telephone, over the Internet, or by other electronic means. A rule adopted under this section may prescribe eligibility standards for renewal under this section.

SUBCHAPTER F APPEARANCE OF DRIVER'S LICENSE

Sec. 521.121. General Information on Driver's License.

(a) The driver's license must include:

(1) a distinguishing number assigned by the department to the license holder;

(2) a photograph of the entire face of the holder;

(3) the full name and date of birth of the holder;

(4) a brief description of the holder; and

(5) the license holder's residence address or, for a license holder using the procedure under Subsection (c), the street address of the courthouse in which the license holder or license holder's spouse or parent serves as a federal judge, including a federal bankruptcy judge, a marshal of the United States Marshals Service, a United States attorney, or a state judge.

(b) The driver's license must include a facsimile of the license holder's signature or a space on which the holder shall write the holder's usual signature in ink immediately on receipt of the license. A license is not valid until it complies with this subsection.

(c) The department shall establish a procedure, on a license holder's qualification for or appointment to office as a federal or state judge as defined by Section 1.005, Election Code, or as a federal bankruptcy judge, a marshal of the United States Marshals Service, or a United States attorney, to omit the residence address of the judge or official and any family member of the judge or official on the license holder's license and to include, in lieu of that address, the street address of the courthouse or office building in which the license holder or license holder's spouse or parent serves as a federal or state judge or official.

(d) [Repealed by Acts 2011, 82nd Leg., ch. 91 (S.B. 1303), § 24.010, effective September 1, 2011.]

(e) Except as provided by this section, a driver's license issued under this chapter:

(1) must:

(A) be in the same format;

(B) have the same appearance and orientation; and

(C) contain the same type of information; and

(2) may not include any information that this chapter does not reference or require.

(f) In this section, "family member" has the meaning assigned by Section 31.006, Finance Code.

Sec. 521.1211. Driver's License for Peace Officers and Prosecutors.

(a) In this section:

(1) "Peace officer" has the meaning assigned by Article 2.12, Code of Criminal Procedure, except that the term includes a special investigator as defined by Article 2.122, Code of Criminal Procedure.

(2) "Prosecutor" means a county attorney, district attorney, criminal district attorney, assistant

county attorney, assistant district attorney, or assistant criminal district attorney.

(a-1) This section applies only to a peace officer and a prosecutor.

(b) Notwithstanding Section 521.121(a), the department by rule shall adopt procedures for the issuance of a driver's license to an applicant that omits the license holder's actual residence address and includes, as an alternative, an address described under Subsection (f).

(c) To be issued a driver's license under this section, an applicant must apply to the department and provide sufficient evidence acceptable to the department to establish the applicant's status as a person described under Subsection (a-1). On issuance of the license, the license holder shall surrender any other driver's license issued to the holder by the department.

(d) If the holder of a driver's license that includes an alternative address moves to a new residence, or, for a prosecutor, to a new office address, or if the name of the person is changed by marriage or otherwise, the license holder shall, not later than the 30th day after the date of the address or name change, notify the department and provide the department with the number of the person's driver's license and, as applicable, the person's:

(1) former and new addresses; or

(2) former and new names.

(e) If the holder of a driver's license that includes an alternative address ceases to be a person described by Subsection (a-1), the license holder shall, not later than the 30th day after the date of the status change, apply to the department for issuance of a duplicate license. The duplicate license must include the person's actual current residence address.

(f) The department shall accept as an alternative address:

(1) for a peace officer, an address that is in the:

(A) municipality or county of the peace officer's residence; or

(B) county of the peace officer's place of employment; and

(2) for a prosecutor, the address of an office of the prosecutor.

Sec. 521.122. Type of Vehicle Required to Be Indicated on License.

(a) The department shall show on each driver's license the general type of vehicle that the license holder is authorized to operate.

(b) The department may include on the driver's license an authorization to operate a motorcycle if the license holder has met all requirements for a Class M license.

Sec. 521.123. Designator on License Issued to Person Under 21 Years of Age.

The department shall:

(1) designate and clearly mark as a provisional license each original driver's license issued by the department to a person who is under 18 years of age; and

(2) for each original, renewed, or duplicate license issued to a person who is under 21 years of age:

(A) indicate "UNDER 21" on the face of the license; and

(B) orient the information on the license to clearly distinguish the license from a license that is issued to a person who is 21 years of age or older.

Sec. 521.1235. Designator on License Issued to Veteran.

(a) In this section:

(1) "Disability rating" has the meaning assigned by Section 11.22, Tax Code.

(2) "Disabled veteran" means a veteran who has suffered a service-connected disability with a disability rating of:

(A) at least 50 percent; or

(B) 40 percent if the rating is due to the amputation of a lower extremity.

(3) "Veteran" means a person who:

(A) has served in:

(i) the army, navy, air force, coast guard, or marine corps of the United States; or

(ii) the Texas National Guard as defined by Section 437.001, Government Code; and

(B) has been honorably discharged from the branch of the service in which the person served.

(b) The department shall include the designation "VETERAN" on a driver's license issued to a veteran in an available space either on the face of the driver's license or on the reverse side of the driver's license if:

(1) the veteran requests the designation; and

(2) the veteran provides proof of the veteran's military service and honorable discharge.

(b-1) If a disabled veteran provides proof sufficient to the department, the department, on request of the disabled veteran, shall include on a driver's license issued to the disabled veteran in any available space on the face of the driver's license or on the reverse side of the driver's license:

(1) a disabled veteran designation; and

(2) the branch of the service in which the disabled veteran served.

(c) The department shall provide to the recipient of a driver's license with a designation under this section the informational paper described by Section 521.011 at the time the license is issued.

(d) Notwithstanding any other law and except as provided by Subsection (e), for purposes of obtaining a service or benefit available for disabled veterans in this state, a disabled veteran may use a driver's license described by Subsection (b-1) as satisfactory proof:

(1) that the disabled veteran has a disability rating described by Subsection (a)(2)(A) or (B), as applicable; and

(2) of branch of service and honorable discharge.

(e) A driver's license described by Subsection (b-1) is not satisfactory proof of the disabled veteran's disability rating for purposes of obtaining a property tax exemption provided by Chapter 11, Tax Code.

(f) A disabled veteran who renews a driver's license described by Subsection (b-1) shall provide proof sufficient to the department of the disabled veteran's disability rating.

(g) The department shall establish and maintain on the department's Internet website forms and procedures by which a veteran or disabled veteran may request and provide the proof required for a designation on a driver's license or renewal of a driver's license with a designation under this section by submitting a form and the required proof electronically on the department's Internet website.

Sec. 521.124. Temporary License; Issued Without Photograph.

(a) The department may issue a temporary license without a photograph of the license holder:

(1) to an applicant who is out of state or a member of the armed forces of the United States; or

(2) if the department otherwise determines that a temporary license is necessary.

(b) A temporary license is valid only until the applicant has time to appear and be photographed and a license with a photograph is issued.

Sec. 521.125. Medical and Emergency Information on License.

(a) On the reverse side of a driver's license, the department shall:

(1) print:

(A) "Allergic Reaction to Drugs: ____________";

(B) "Directive to physician has been filed at tel. #";

(C) "Emergency contact tel. #"; and

(D) if space allows, any medical information provided by the license holder under Section 521.142(h);

(2) include to the right of the statements under Subdivisions (1)(B) and (C) a surface on which the license holder may write the appropriate telephone number; and

(3) include to the left of each of the statements under Subdivisions (1)(B) and (C) a box that the license holder may use to indicate for what purpose the telephone number applies.

(b) In addition to the requirements of Subsection (a)(1)(D), if space allows, the department shall indicate any medical information by a uniform symbol or code on the face of the license in the space where the department indicates a restriction or endorsement.

Sec. 521.126. Electronically Readable Information.

(a) The department may not include any information on a driver's license, commercial driver's license, or personal identification certificate in an electronically readable form other than the information printed on the license and a physical description of the licensee.

(b) Except as provided by Subsections (d), (e), (e-1), (g), (i), (j), and (n), and Section 501.101, Business & Commerce Code, a person commits an offense if the person:

(1) accesses or uses electronically readable information derived from a driver's license, commercial driver's license, or personal identification certificate; or

(2) compiles or maintains a database of electronically readable information derived from driver's licenses, commercial driver's licenses, or personal identification certificates.

(c) An offense under Subsection (b) is a Class A misdemeanor.

(d) The prohibition provided by Subsection (b) does not apply to a person who accesses, uses, compiles, or maintains a database of the information for a law enforcement or governmental purpose, including:

(1) an officer or employee of the department carrying out law enforcement or government purposes;

(2) a peace officer, as defined by Article 2.12, Code of Criminal Procedure, acting in the officer's official capacity;

(3) a license deputy, as defined by Section 12.702, Parks and Wildlife Code, issuing a license, stamp, tag, permit, or other similar item through use of a point-of-sale system under Section 12.703, Parks and Wildlife Code;

(4) a person acting as authorized by Section 109.61, Alcoholic Beverage Code;

(5) a person establishing the identity of a voter under Chapter 63, Election Code;

Transportation Code

(6) a person acting as authorized by Section 161.0825, Health and Safety Code; or

(7) a person screening an individual who will work with or have access to children if the person is an employee or an agent of an employee of a public school district or an organization exempt from federal income tax under Section 501(c)(3), Internal Revenue Code of 1986, as amended, that sponsors a program for youth.

(e) The prohibition provided by Subsection (b)(1) does not apply to a financial institution or a business that:

(1) accesses or uses electronically readable information for purposes of identification verification of an individual or check verification at the point of sale for a purchase of a good or service by check; or

(2) accesses or uses as electronically readable information a driver's license number or a name printed on a driver's license as part of a transaction initiated by the license or certificate holder to provide information encrypted in a manner:

(A) consistent with PCI DSS Standard 3.4 to a check services company or fraud prevention services company governed by the Fair Credit Reporting Act (15 U.S.C. Section 1681 et seq.) for the purpose of effecting, administering, or enforcing the transaction; and

(B) that does not involve the sale, transfer, or other dissemination of a name or driver's license number to a third party for any purpose, including any marketing, advertising, or promotional activities.

(e-1) The prohibition provided by Subsection (b) does not apply to:

(1) a check services company or a fraud prevention services company governed by the Fair Credit Reporting Act (15 U.S.C. Section 1681 et seq.) that, for the purpose of preventing fraud when effecting, administering, or enforcing the transaction:

(A) accesses or uses as electronically readable information a driver's license number or a name printed on a driver's license; or

(B) compiles or maintains a database of electronically readable driver's license numbers or names printed on driver's licenses and periodically removes the numbers or names from the database that are at least four years old; or

(2) a financial institution that compiles or maintains a database of electronically readable information, if each license or certificate holder whose information is included in the compilation or database consents to the inclusion of the person's information in the compilation or database on a separate document, signed by the license or certificate holder, that explains in at least 14-point bold type the information that will be included in the compilation or database.

(f) A person may not use information derived from electronically readable information from a driver's license, commercial driver's license, or personal identification certificate to engage in telephone solicitation to encourage the purchase or rental of, or investment in, goods, other property, or services.

(g) If authorized by the executive or administrative head of a maritime facility as defined in the Maritime Transportation Security Act of 2002 (46 U.S.C. Section 70101 et seq.), or of a port, port authority, or navigation district created or operating under Section 52, Article III, or Section 59, Article XVI, Texas Constitution, a person may access, use, compile, or maintain in a database electronically readable information derived from a driver's license, commercial driver's license, or personal identification certificate to secure the facility or port. The information may be used only to:

(1) identify an individual;

(2) provide official credentials for an individual;

(3) track or limit the movement of an individual on facility property;

(4) establish a secure database of visitors to the facility;

(5) access the information at terminal and gate operations of the facility; or

(6) conduct other security or operational activities as determined by the executive or administrative head.

(h) Except as provided by Section 418.183, Government Code, the electronically readable information derived from a driver's license, commercial driver's license, or personal identification certificate for the purposes of Subsection (g) is confidential and not subject to disclosure, inspection, or copying under Chapter 552, Government Code.

(i) The prohibition provided by Subsection (b) does not apply to a health care provider or hospital that accesses, uses, compiles, or maintains a database of the information to provide health care services to the individual who holds the driver's license, commercial driver's license, or personal identification certificate. If an individual objects to the collection of information under this subsection, the health care provider or hospital must use an alternative method to collect the individual's information.

(j) Except as otherwise provided by this subsection, a health care provider or hospital may not sell, transfer, or otherwise disseminate the information described by Subsection (i) to a third party for any purpose, including any marketing, advertising, or promotional activities. A health care provider or hospital that obtains information described by Subsection (i) may transfer the information only in

Transportation Code

accordance with the rules implementing the federal Health Insurance Portability and Accountability Act of 1996 (Pub. L. No. 104-191). A business associate, and any subcontractor of the business associate who receives the transferred information, may use the information only to service or maintain the health care provider's or hospital's database of the information.

(k) [Repealed by Acts 2015, 84th Leg., ch. 1261 (H.B. 3283), § 8, effective January 1, 2016.]

(*l*) For the purposes of this section, "financial institution" has the meaning assigned by 31 U.S.C. Section 5312(a)(2).

(m) In this section, "health care provider" means an individual or facility licensed, certified, or otherwise authorized by the law of this state to provide or administer health care, for profit or otherwise, in the ordinary course of business or professional practice, including a physician, nurse, dentist, podiatrist, pharmacist, chiropractor, therapeutic optometrist, ambulatory surgical center, urgent care facility, nursing home, home and community support services agency, and emergency medical services personnel as defined by Section 773.003, Health and Safety Code.

(n) The prohibition provided by Subsection (b) does not apply to the nonprofit organization administering the Glenda Dawson Donate Life-Texas Registry under Section 692A.020, Health and Safety Code, or an organ procurement organization, tissue bank, or eye bank, as those terms are defined by Section 692A.002, Health and Safety Code, for the purpose of scanning the individual's information on the individual's driver's license, commercial driver's license, or personal identification certificate to register the individual as an anatomical gift donor. Before transmitting information scanned under this subsection, the nonprofit organization, organ procurement organization, tissue bank, or eye bank shall:

(1) notify the individual of the registry's purpose and the purposes for which the information will be used;

(2) require the individual to verify the accuracy of the information; and

(3) require the individual to affirm consent to make an anatomical gift through the individual's use of the individual's electronic signature.

Sec. 521.127. Use of Diacritical Marks.

(a) In this section, "diacritical mark" means a mark used in Latin script to change the sound of a letter to which it is added or used to distinguish the meaning of the word in which the letter appears. The term includes accents, tildes, graves, umlauts, and cedillas.

(b) The department shall ensure that an original or renewal driver's license or personal identification certificate issued under this chapter properly records any diacritical mark used in a person's name.

SUBCHAPTER G LICENSE APPLICATION REQUIREMENTS

Sec. 521.141. General Application Requirements.

(a) An applicant for an original or renewal of a driver's license must apply in a manner prescribed by the department.

(b) An application for an original license must be verified by the applicant before a person authorized to administer oaths. An officer or employee of the department may administer the oath. An officer or employee of this state may not charge for the administration of the oath.

(c) The application must be accompanied by the required fee and must be submitted to the department before the department may administer an examination.

Sec. 521.142. Application for Original License.

(a) An application for an original license must state the applicant's full name and place and date of birth. This information must be verified by presentation of proof of identity satisfactory to the department. An applicant who is not a citizen of the United States must present to the department documentation issued by the appropriate United States agency that authorizes the applicant to be in the United States before the applicant may be issued a driver's license. The department must accept as satisfactory proof of identity under this subsection an offender identification card or similar form of identification issued to an inmate by the Texas Department of Criminal Justice if the applicant also provides supplemental verifiable records or documents that aid in establishing identity.

(b) The application must include:

(1) the thumbprints of the applicant or, if thumbprints cannot be taken, the index fingerprints of the applicant;

(2) a photograph of the applicant;

(3) the signature of the applicant; and

(4) a brief description of the applicant.

(c) The application must state:

Transportation Code

(1) the sex of the applicant;

(2) the residence address of the applicant, or if the applicant is a federal judge, including a federal bankruptcy judge, a marshal of the United States Marshals Service, a United States attorney, or a state judge, or a family member of a federal judge, including a federal bankruptcy judge, a marshal of the United States Marshals Service, a United States attorney, or a state judge using the procedure developed under Section 521.121(c), the street address of the courthouse or office building in which the applicant or the applicant's spouse or parent serves as a federal judge, including a federal bankruptcy judge, a marshal of the United States Marshals Service, a United States attorney, or a state judge;

(3) whether the applicant has been licensed to drive a motor vehicle before;

(4) if previously licensed, when and by what state or country;

(5) whether that license has been suspended or revoked or a license application denied;

(6) the date and reason for the suspension, revocation, or denial;

(7) whether the applicant is a citizen of the United States; and

(8) the county of residence of the applicant.

(d) **[2 Versions: As amended by Acts 2009, 81st Leg., ch. 1253]** If the applicant is under 21 years of age, the application must state whether the applicant has completed a driver education course required by Section 521.1601.

(d) **[2 Versions: As amended by Acts 2009, 81st Leg., ch, 1413]** If the applicant is under 25 years of age, the application must state whether the applicant has completed a driver education course required by Section 521.1601.

(e) Subject to Subsection (e-1), the application must include any other information the department requires to determine the applicant's identity, residency, competency, and eligibility as required by the department or state law.

(e-1) Other than a general inquiry as to whether the applicant has a mental condition that may affect the applicant's ability to safely operate a motor vehicle, an application may not include an inquiry regarding the mental health of the applicant, including an inquiry as to whether the applicant has been diagnosed with, treated for, or hospitalized for a psychiatric disorder.

(f) Information supplied to the department relating to an applicant's medical history is for the confidential use of the department and may not be disclosed to any person or used as evidence in a legal proceeding other than a proceeding under Subchapter N. This subsection does not apply to information provided by an applicant under Subsection (h).

(g) The department shall require an applicant to provide the applicant's social security number or proof that the applicant is not eligible for a social security number.

(h) The application must provide space for the applicant to voluntarily list any health condition that may impede communication with a peace officer as evidenced by a written statement from a licensed physician.

(i) The application must provide space for the applicant:

(1) to voluntarily list any information that may qualify the applicant to receive a license with a designation under Section 521.1235; and

(2) to include proof required by the department to determine the applicant's eligibility to receive that designation.

(j) In this section, "family member" has the meaning assigned by Section 31.006, Finance Code.

Sec. 521.1421. Inmate Identification Verification Pilot Program.

(a) The department shall participate in an inmate identification verification pilot program for the purpose of issuing driver's licenses and personal identification certificates to inmates of the Texas Department of Criminal Justice.

(b) Under the pilot program, the department may:

(1) enter into a contract with the Texas Department of Criminal Justice and the Department of State Health Services to establish an identification verification process for inmates of the Texas Department of Criminal Justice; and

(2) issue a driver's license or a personal identification certificate to an inmate whose identity has been confirmed through the verification process and who otherwise meets the requirements for the issuance of the driver's license or personal identification certificate.

(c) At the conclusion of the pilot program the governing bodies of the participating agencies may agree to continue the pilot program on a permanent basis.

(d) Not later than December 1, 2010, the department and the Texas Department of Criminal Justice shall jointly issue a report to the standing committees of the legislature with jurisdiction over issues related to criminal justice and homeland security addressing:

(1) the status of the pilot program;

(2) the effectiveness of the pilot program; and

(3) an analysis of the feasibility of implementing a statewide program based on the pilot program.

Sec. 521.1425. Information Required to Be Furnished to Department.

(a) Except as provided by Subsections (b) and (c), the department may require each applicant for an original, renewal, or duplicate driver's license to furnish to the department the information required by Section 521.142.

(b) The department shall require each applicant for an original, renewal, or duplicate driver's license to furnish to the department the information required by Sections 521.142(c)(7) and (8).

(c) Unless the information has been previously provided to the department, the department shall require each applicant for an original, renewal, or duplicate driver's license to furnish to the department:

(1) proof of the applicant's United States citizenship; or

(2) documentation described by Section 521.142(a).

(d) The department may not deny a driver's license to an applicant who provides documentation described by Section 521.142(a) based on the duration of the person's authorized stay in the United States, as indicated by the documentation presented under Section 521.142(a).

Sec. 521.1426. Domicile Requirement; Verification.

(a) The department may not issue a driver's license or a personal identification certificate to a person who has not established a domicile in this state.

(b) The department shall adopt rules for determining whether a domicile has been established, including rules prescribing the types of documentation the department may require from the applicant to verify the validity of the claimed domicile.

(c) The department may contract with a third-party personal data verification service to assist the department in verifying a claim of domicile, including whether the physical address provided by the applicant is the applicant's actual residence.

Sec. 521.1427. Post Office Box Not Valid As Address.

(a) In this section, "post office box address" means a United States Postal Service post office box address or a private mailbox address.

(b) Unless an exception exists under state or federal law, an applicant may receive delivery of a license or a personal identification certificate at a post office box address only if the applicant has provided the department the physical address where the applicant resides.

(c) The department may require the applicant to provide documentation that the department determines necessary to verify the validity of the physical address provided under Subsection (b).

(d) The department may contract with a third-party personal data verification service to assist the department in verifying whether the physical address provided by the applicant is the applicant's actual residence.

Sec. 521.143. Evidence of Financial Responsibility Required.

(a) An application for an original driver's license must be accompanied by evidence of financial responsibility or a statement that the applicant does not own a motor vehicle for which evidence of financial responsibility is required under Chapter 601. The department may require an application for a renewal of a driver's license to be accompanied by evidence of financial responsibility or a statement that the applicant does not own a motor vehicle for which evidence of financial responsibility is required under Chapter 601.

(b) Evidence of financial responsibility presented under this section must be in at least the minimum amounts required by Section 601.072 and must cover each motor vehicle owned by the applicant for which the applicant is required to maintain evidence of financial responsibility. The evidence may be shown in the manner provided by Section 601.053(a).

(c) A personal automobile insurance policy used as evidence of financial responsibility under this section must comply with Article 5.06 or 5.145, Insurance Code.

(d) A statement that an applicant does not own a motor vehicle to which the evidence of financial responsibility requirement applies must be sworn to and signed by the applicant.

Sec. 521.144. Application by New State Resident. [Effective until March 1, 2022]

(a) A new resident of this state who applies for a driver's license must submit with the application:

(1) evidence that each motor vehicle owned by the person is registered under Chapter 502; or

(2) an affidavit that the applicant does not own a motor vehicle required to be registered under Chapter 502.

(b) The department may not issue a driver's license to a new resident who fails to comply with Subsection (a).

(c) A registration receipt issued by the county assessor-collector of the county in which the new resident resides is satisfactory evidence that a motor vehicle is registered under Chapter 502.

Sec. 521.144. Application by New State Resident. [Effective March 1, 2022]

(a) A new resident of this state who applies for a driver's license must submit with the application:

(1) evidence that each motor vehicle owned by the person is registered under Chapter 502; or

(2) an affidavit that the applicant does not own a motor vehicle required to be registered under Chapter 502.

(b) The department may not issue a driver's license to a new resident who fails to comply with Subsection (a).

(c) A registration receipt issued by a county assessor-collector in this state is satisfactory evidence that a motor vehicle is registered under Chapter 502.

Transportation Code

Sec. 521.145. Application by Person Under 18 Years of Age.

(a) The application of an applicant under 18 years of age must be signed by:

(1) the parent or guardian who has custody of the applicant or the agent under a power of attorney for the parent who has custody of the applicant; or

(2) if the applicant has no parent or guardian:

(A) the applicant's employer; or

(B) the county judge of the county in which the applicant resides.

(b) The department shall provide the applicant and the cosigner with information concerning state laws relating to distracted driving, driving while intoxicated, driving by a minor with alcohol in the minor's system, and implied consent. The applicant and cosigner must acknowledge receipt of this information.

Sec. 521.146. Application for Duplicate License or Certificate.

(a) If a driver's license or certificate issued under this chapter is lost or destroyed, or there is a change in pertinent information, the person to whom the license or certificate was issued may obtain a duplicate or corrected version.

(b) An applicant for a corrected driver's license or certificate must submit to the department the required fee, accompanied by the required information that has changed with proof satisfactory to the department that supports the change.

(c) The department by rule may provide that the holder of a driver's license or identification certificate issued by the department may apply for the issuance of a duplicate license or certificate by mail, by telephone, over the Internet, or by other electronic means.

(d) A rule adopted under Subsection (c) may prescribe eligibility standards for issuance of a duplicate driver's license or identification certificate under this section.

Sec. 521.147. Registration with Selective Service System.

(a) After an application for an original, renewal, or duplicate driver's license or personal identification certificate is submitted by a male applicant who on the date of the application is at least 18 years of age but younger than 26 years of age, the department shall send in an electronic format to the United States Selective Service System the information from the application necessary to register the applicant under the Military Selective Service Act (50 U.S.C. App. Section 451 et seq.).

(b) An application under this section must give written notice to an applicant that the application also constitutes registration with the United States Selective Service System for persons who are subject to registration and have not previously registered. The notice must be conspicuous on the application and state: "By submitting this application, I am consenting to registration with the United States Selective Service System if my registration is required by federal law."

(c) An application under this section must give written notice to an applicant that information regarding alternative service options for applicants who object to conventional military service for religious or other conscientious reasons is available from the department upon request.

(d) The applicant's submission of the application following this notification constitutes the applicant's consent to the sending of the information and the registration.

(e) In addition to the notifications required by Subsections (b) and (c), the department may conspicuously post at each location where applications for driver's licenses and personal identification certificates are accepted one or more signs, in English and Spanish, providing the information contained in the notifications.

(f) Subsections (a) and (d) do not apply to an applicant concerning whom the department has previously sent information to the Selective Service System.

Sec. 521.148. Application for Class M License or Authorization to Operate Motorcycle.

(a) An applicant for an original Class M license or Class A, B, or C driver's license that includes an authorization to operate a motorcycle must furnish to the department evidence satisfactory to the department that the applicant has successfully completed a motorcycle operator training course approved by the department under Chapter 662. The department shall issue a Class M license that is restricted to the operation of a three-wheeled motorcycle if the motorcycle operator training course completed by the applicant is specific to the operation of a three-wheeled motorcycle.

(b) The department may not issue an original Class M license or Class A, B, or C driver's license that includes an authorization to operate a motorcycle to an applicant who fails to comply with Subsection (a).

(c) When the department issues a license to which this section applies, the department shall provide the person to whom the license is issued with written information about the Glenda Dawson Donate Life-Texas Registry operated under Chapter 692A, Health and Safety Code.

SUBCHAPTER H EDUCATION AND EXAMINATION REQUIREMENTS

Sec. 521.1601. [2 Versions: As added by Acts 2009, 81st Leg., ch. 1253] Driver Education Required.

The department may not issue a driver's license to a person who is younger than 21 years of age unless the person submits to the department a driver education certificate issued under Chapter 1001, Education Code, that states that the person has completed and passed:

(1) a driver education and traffic safety course conducted by an entity exempt from licensure under Section 1001.002, Education Code, or a driver education course approved by the Texas Department of Licensing and Regulation under Chapter 1001, Education Code; or

(2) if the person is 18 years of age or older, a driver education course approved by the Texas Department of Licensing and Regulation under Section 1001.101 or 1001.1015, Education Code.

Sec. 521.161. Examination of License Applicants.

(a) Except as otherwise provided by this subchapter, the department shall examine each applicant for a driver's license. The examination shall be held in the county in which the applicant resides or applies not later than the 10th day after the date on which the application is made.

(b) The examination must include:

(1) a test of the applicant's:

(A) vision;

(B) ability to identify and understand highway signs in English that regulate, warn, or direct traffic;

(C) knowledge of the traffic laws of this state;

(D) knowledge of motorists' rights and responsibilities in relation to bicyclists; and

(E) knowledge of the effect of using a wireless communication device, or engaging in other actions that may distract a driver, on the safe or effective operation of a motor vehicle;

(2) a demonstration of the applicant's ability to exercise ordinary and reasonable control in the operation of a motor vehicle of the type that the applicant will be licensed to operate; and

(3) any additional examination the department finds necessary to determine the applicant's fitness to operate a motor vehicle safely.

(c) The department shall give each applicant the option of taking the parts of the examination under Subsections (b)(1)(B), (C), (D), and (E) in writing in addition to or instead of through a mechanical, electronic, or other testing method. If the applicant takes that part of the examination in writing in addition to another testing method, the applicant is considered to have passed that part of the examination if the applicant passes either version of the examination. The department shall inform each person taking the examination of the person's rights under this subsection.

(d) On payment of the required fee, an applicant is entitled to three examinations of each element under Subsection (b) for each application to qualify for a driver's license. If the applicant has not qualified after the third examination, the applicant must submit a new application accompanied by the required fee.

(e) The department may not issue a driver's license to a person who has not passed each examination required under this chapter.

Sec. 521.162. Alternate Examination in Spanish.

(a) The department shall design and administer in each county of this state an alternate examination for Spanish-speaking applicants who are unable to take the regular examination in English.

Transportation Code

(b) The alternate examination must be identical to the examination administered to other applicants under Section 521.161 except that all directions and written material, other than the text of highway signs, must be in Spanish. The text of highway signs must be in English.

Sec. 521.163. Reexamination.

(a) The director may require the holder of a license to be reexamined if the director determines that the holder is incapable of safely operating a motor vehicle.

(b) The reexamination shall be conducted in the license holder's county of residence unless the holder and the director agree to a different location.

Sec. 521.164. Exemption from Certain Examination Requirements for Licensed Nonresidents.

(a) The department by rule may provide that a holder of a driver's license issued to the person by another state or Canadian province and who is otherwise qualified may, after passing the vision test and paying the required fees, be issued a driver's license without the complete examination required under Section 521.161.

(b) A license issued under this section must be of the class of license equivalent to the license issued by the other jurisdiction.

Sec. 521.165. Testing by Other Entities.

(a) The director may certify and set standards for the certification of certain employers, government agencies, and other appropriate organizations to allow those persons to train and test for the ability to operate certain types of vehicles.

(b) The department shall set the standards for the training and testing of driver's license applicants under Subsection (a).

(c) Except as provided by Subsection (d), in issuing a driver's license for certain types of vehicles, the director may waive a driving test for an applicant who has successfully completed and passed the training and testing conducted by a person certified under Subsection (a).

(d) The director may not waive the driving test required by Section 521.161 for an applicant who is under 18 years of age.

(e) The department may authorize an entity described by Subsection (a), including a driver education provider described by Section 521.1655, to administer the examination required by Section 521.161(b)(2).

Sec. 521.1655. Testing by Driver Education School and Certain Driver Education Course Providers.

(a) An in-person driver education provider or online driver education provider licensed under Chapter 1001, Education Code, may administer to a student of that provider the vision, highway sign, and traffic law parts of the examination required by Section 521.161.

(a-1) A parent-taught driver education provider licensed under Chapter 1001, Education Code, may administer to a student of that course the highway sign and traffic law parts of the examination required by Section 521.161.

(b) An examination administered under this section complies with the examination requirements of this subchapter as to the parts of the examination administered.

Sec. 521.166. Motorcycle Road Test Requirements.

(a) An applicant required to submit to a motorcycle road test must provide a passenger vehicle and a licensed driver to convey the license examiner during the road test.

(b) The department may refuse to administer any part of the road test to an applicant who fails to comply with Subsection (a).

Sec. 521.167. Waiver of Certain Education and Examination Requirements.

A person who has completed and passed a driver education course approved by the Texas Department of Licensing and Regulation under Section 1001.1015, Education Code, is not required to take the highway sign and traffic law parts of the examination required under Section 521.161 if those parts have been successfully completed as determined by a licensed driver education instructor.

Sec. 521.168. Payment of Fees for Certain Foster and Homeless Children and Youths.

(a) Unless prohibited under Section 521.4265(c), the Texas Workforce Commission shall on request pay the fees associated with meeting a requirement imposed under this subchapter or Chapter 1001, Education Code, for a person who is:

(1) eligible for a driver's license fee exemption under Section 521.1811; or

(2) younger than 26 years of age and:

(A) was in the managing conservatorship of the Department of Family and Protective Services on the day before the person's 18th birthday; or

(B) is a homeless child or youth as defined by 42 U.S.C. Section 11434a.

(b) The Texas Workforce Commission by rule shall establish a process by which:

(1) a person described by Subsection (a) may apply to that commission for the payment of fees under this section; and

(2) that commission pays fees associated with meeting a requirement imposed under this subchapter or Chapter 1001, Education Code, to appropriate entities on behalf of the person described by Subsection (a).

SUBCHAPTER I ISSUANCE OF DRIVER'S LICENSE

Sec. 521.181. Issuance of Driver's License.

On payment of the required fee, the department shall issue to each qualifying applicant a driver's license of the class for which the applicant has applied.

Sec. 521.1811. Waiver of Fees for Foster Child or Youth, Homeless Child or Youth, or Victim or Child of Victim of Dating or Family Violence.

A person is exempt from the payment of any fee for the issuance of a driver's license, as provided under this chapter, if that person is:

(1) younger than 18 years of age and in the managing conservatorship of the Department of Family and Protective Services;

(2) at least 18 years of age, but younger than 21 years of age, and resides in a foster care placement, the cost of which is paid by the Department of Family and Protective Services;

(3) a homeless child or youth as defined by 42 U.S.C. Section 11434a;

(4) a victim of dating violence as defined by Section 71.0021, Family Code;

(5) a victim of family violence as defined by Section 51.002, Human Resources Code; or

(6) a child of a victim described by Subdivision (4) or (5).

Sec. 521.1812. Waiver of Certain Fees for Certain Applicants Who Hold Cardiopulmonary Resuscitation Certification.

(a) A person is exempt from the payment of any fee for the issuance of an original or renewal driver's license, as provided under this chapter, if at the time of the application for an original or renewal driver's license the person submits to the department satisfactory evidence that the person:

(1) holds a current certification in cardiopulmonary resuscitation issued by the American Heart Association, the American Red Cross, or another nationally recognized association; and

(2) is not required to hold the certification described by Subdivision (1) as a condition of obtaining or maintaining employment or an occupational license.

(b) For purposes of Subsection (a)(2), "occupational license" means a license, certificate, registration, permit, or other form of authorization that a person must obtain to practice or engage in a particular business, occupation, or profession.

(c) The department shall establish a record of the amount of the fees waived under this section that would otherwise be deposited to the credit of the Texas mobility fund.

(d) On or before the fifth workday of each month, the department, using available funds, shall remit to the comptroller for deposit to the credit of the Texas mobility fund general revenue in an amount equal to the amount of the fees described by Subsection (c) in the preceding month.

Sec. 521.182. Surrender of License Issued by Other Jurisdiction.

(a) A person is not entitled to receive a driver's license until the person surrenders to the department each driver's license in the person's possession that was issued by this state or another state or Canadian province.

(b) The department shall send to the state or province that issued the license:

(1) the surrendered license or a notification that the license has been surrendered; and

(2) a statement that the person holds a driver's license issued by this state.

Sec. 521.183. Surrender of Driver's License or Personal Identification Certificate.

(a) A person is not entitled to receive a driver's license until the person surrenders to the department each personal identification certificate in the person's possession that was issued by this state.

(b) A person is not entitled to receive a personal identification certificate until the person surrenders to the department each driver's license in the person's possession that was issued by this state.

SUBCHAPTER J PERSONS INELIGIBLE FOR LICENSE

Sec. 521.201. License Ineligibility in General.

The department may not issue any license to a person who:

(1) is under 15 years of age;

(2) is under 18 years of age unless the person complies with the requirements imposed by Section 521.204;

(3) is shown to be addicted to the use of alcohol, a controlled substance, or another drug that renders a person incapable of driving;

(4) holds a driver's license issued by this state or another state or country that is revoked, canceled, or under suspension;

(5) has been determined by a judgment of a court to be totally incapacitated or incapacitated to act as the operator of a motor vehicle unless the person has, by the date of the license application, been:

(A) restored to capacity by judicial decree; or

(B) released from a hospital for the mentally incapacitated on a certificate by the superintendent or administrator of the hospital that the person has regained capacity;

(6) the department determines to be afflicted with a mental or physical disability or disease that prevents the person from exercising reasonable and ordinary control over a motor vehicle while operating the vehicle on a highway, except that a person may not be refused a license because of a physical defect if common experience shows that the defect does not incapacitate a person from safely operating a motor vehicle;

(7) has been reported by a court under Section 521.3452 for failure to appear unless the court has filed an additional report on final disposition of the case; or

(8) has been reported by a court for failure to appear or default in payment of a fine for a misdemeanor that is not covered under Subdivision (7) and that is punishable by a fine only, including a misdemeanor under a municipal ordinance, committed by a person who was under 17 years of age at the time of the alleged offense, unless the court has filed an additional report on final disposition of the case.

Sec. 521.202. Ineligibility for License Based on Certain Convictions.

(a) Unless the period of suspension that would have applied if the person held a license at the time of the conviction has expired, the department may not issue a license to a person convicted of an offense:

(1) described by Section 49.04, 49.07, or 49.08, Penal Code; or

(2) to which Section 521.342(a) applies.

(b) Until the period specified in the juvenile court order has expired, the department may not issue a license to a person if the department has been ordered by a juvenile court under Section 54.042, Family Code, to deny the person a license.

(c) A person does not have a privilege to operate a vehicle in this state during a period of suspension under Subsection (a) or (b) if the department is prohibited from issuing a license to that person.

Sec. 521.203. Restrictions on Class a and B Licenses.

The department may not issue a Class A or Class B driver's license to a person who:

(1) is under 17 years of age;

(2) is under 18 years of age unless the person has completed a driver training course approved by the Texas Department of Licensing and Regulation; or

(3) has not provided the department with an affidavit, on a form prescribed by the department, that states that no vehicle that the person will drive that requires a Class A or Class B license is a commercial motor vehicle as defined by Section 522.003.

Sec. 521.204. Restrictions on Minor.

(a) The department may issue a Class C driver's license to an applicant under 18 years of age only if the applicant:

(1) is 16 years of age or older;

(2) has submitted to the department a driver education certificate issued under Section 1001.055, Education Code, that states that the person has completed and passed a driver education course approved by the Texas Department of Licensing and Regulation;

(3) has obtained a high school diploma or its equivalent or is a student:

(A) enrolled in a public school, home school, or private school who attended school for at least 80 days in the fall or spring semester preceding the date of the driver's license application; or

(B) who has been enrolled for at least 45 days, and is enrolled as of the date of the application, in a program to prepare persons to pass the high school equivalency exam;

(4) has submitted to the department written parental or guardian permission:

(A) for the department to access the applicant's school enrollment records maintained by the Texas Education Agency; and

(B) for a school administrator or law enforcement officer to notify the department in the event that the person has been absent from school for at least 20 consecutive instructional days; and

(5) has passed the examination required by Section 521.161.

(b) The department may not issue a Class A, B, or C driver's license other than a hardship license to an applicant under 18 years of age unless the applicant has held a learner license or hardship license for at least six months preceding the date of the application.

Sec. 521.205. Department-Approved Courses.

(a) [Repealed.]

(b) to (d) [Repealed by Acts 2015, 84th Leg., ch. 1044 (H.B. 1786),§ 70(b), effective September 1, 2015.]

Sec. 521.206. Collision Rate Statistics Publication.

(a) The department shall collect data regarding collisions of students taught by public schools, driver education providers licensed under Chapter 1001, Education Code, and other entities that offer driver education courses to students for which a uniform certificate of course completion is issued. The collision rate is computed by determining the number of an entity's students who complete a driver education course during a state fiscal year, dividing that number by the number of collisions that involved students who completed such a course and that occurred in the 12-month period following their licensure, and expressing the quotient as a percentage.

(b) The department shall collect data regarding the collision rate of students taught by course instructors approved under Section 1001.112, Education Code. The collision rate is computed by determining the number of students who completed a course taught under that section during a state fiscal year, dividing that number by the number of collisions that involved students who completed such a course and that occurred in the 12-month period following their licensure, and expressing the quotient as a percentage.

(c) Not later than October 1 of each year, the department shall issue a publication listing the collision rate for students taught by each driver education entity and the collision rate for students taught by a course instructor approved under Section 1001.112, Education Code, noting the severity of collisions involving students of each entity and each type of course.

SUBCHAPTER K RESTRICTED LICENSES

Sec. 521.221. Imposition of Special Restrictions and Endorsements.

(a) For good cause the department may impose a restriction or require an endorsement suitable to the driver's license holder's driving ability. The restriction or endorsement may relate to:

(1) the type of motor vehicle that the holder may operate;

(2) a special mechanical control device required on a motor vehicle that the holder may operate;

(3) mechanical attachments, including glasses or an artificial limb, required on the person of the holder;

(4) an area, location, road, or highway in this state on which the holder is permitted to drive a motor vehicle;

(5) the time of day that the holder is permitted to operate a motor vehicle; and

(6) any other condition the department determines to be appropriate to ensure the safe operation of a motor vehicle by the holder.

(b) The department may issue a special restricted license or state the applicable restriction on the regular license.

(c) A person commits an offense if the person operates a motor vehicle in violation of a restriction imposed or without the endorsement required on the license issued to that person. An offense under this subsection is a misdemeanor punishable under Section 521.461.

(d) A court may dismiss a charge for a violation of this section if:

(1) the restriction or endorsement was imposed:

(A) because of a physical condition that was surgically or otherwise medically corrected before the date of the offense; or

(B) in error and that fact is established by the defendant;

(2) the department removes the restriction or endorsement before the defendant's first court appearance; and

(3) the defendant pays a reimbursement fee not to exceed $10.

Transportation Code

Sec. 521.222. Learner License.

(a) The department may issue a learner license, including a Class A or Class B driver's learner license, to a person who:

(1) is 15 years of age or older but under 18 years of age;

(2) has satisfactorily completed and passed the classroom phase of an approved driver education course, which may be a course taught under Section 1001.112, Education Code;

(3) meets the requirements imposed under Section 521.204(a)(3); and

(4) has passed each examination required under Section 521.161 other than the driving test.

(b) [Repealed.]

(c) [Repealed.]

(d) A learner license entitles the holder to operate a type of motor vehicle on a highway while:

(1) the license is in the holder's possession; and

(2) the holder is accompanied by a person occupying the seat by the operator who:

(A) holds a license that qualifies the operator to operate that type of vehicle;

(B) is 21 years of age or older; and

(C) has at least one year of driving experience.

(e) [Repealed.]

(f) The department may issue a learner license under this section to a person who is subject to the registration requirements under Chapter 62, Code of Criminal Procedure, and is otherwise eligible for the license. A learner license issued under this subsection must include a photograph of the person.

(g) A person who occupies the seat in a vehicle by a holder of a learner license commits an offense if, while the holder is operating the vehicle, the person:

(1) sleeps;

(2) is intoxicated, as defined by Section 49.01, Penal Code; or

(3) is engaged in an activity that prevents the person from observing and responding to the actions of the operator.

(h) It is a defense to prosecution of a violation under Subsection (g) that at the time of the violation another person in addition to the defendant:

(1) occupied the seat by the operator;

(2) complied with the requirements of Subsections (d)(2)(A)—(C); and

(3) was not in violation of Subsection (g).

Sec. 521.223. Hardship License.

(a) The department may issue a license to a person who complies with the requirements of Subsection (b) if the department finds that:

(1) the failure to issue the license will result in an unusual economic hardship for the family of the applicant;

(2) the license is necessary because of the illness of a member of the applicant's family; or

(3) the license is necessary because the applicant is enrolled in a vocational education program and requires a driver's license to participate in the program.

(b) An applicant for a license under Subsection (a) must be 15 years of age or older and must:

(1) have passed a driver education course approved by the department, which may be a course approved under Chapter 1001, Education Code; and

(2) pass the examination required by Section 521.161.

(c) To be eligible to take the driver training course, the person must be at least 14 years of age.

(d) [Repealed by Acts 2011, ch. 1121 (H.B. 90), § 3, effective September 1, 2011.]

(e) A person who is refused a driver's license under this section may appeal to the county court of the county in which the person resides. The court may try the matter on the request of the petitioner or respondent.

(f) In the manner provided by Subchapter N, the department shall suspend a license issued under this section if the holder of the license is convicted of two or more moving violations committed within a 12-month period.

(g) The department may issue a hardship license to a person who is subject to the registration requirements under Chapter 62, Code of Criminal Procedure, and is otherwise eligible for the license. A hardship license issued under this section must include a photograph of the person.

Sec. 521.224. Restricted Class M License.

(a) [Repealed.]

(b) The department may issue a special restricted Class M license that authorizes the holder to operate only a motorcycle that has not more than a 250 cubic centimeter piston displacement.

(c) A person is eligible for a restricted motorcycle license if the person:

(1) is 15 years of age or older but under 18 years of age;

(2) has completed and passed a motorcycle operator training course approved by the department; and

(3) has met the requirements imposed under Section 521.145.

(d) The department shall make the motorcycle operator training course available.

(e) On the 16th birthday of a holder of a special restricted Class M license, the department shall remove the 250 cubic centimeter restriction from the license without completion by the holder of an additional motorcycle operator training course.

(f) An applicant for the special restricted license must apply in accordance with Subchapter G. The applicant is subject to the requirements of Section 521.161 and to other provisions of this chapter in the same manner as an applicant for another license. The department shall prescribe the form of the license.

Sec. 521.225. Moped License. [Repealed]

Sec. 521.226. Certification [Repealed].

Repealed by Acts 1999, 76th Leg., ch. 797 (H.B. 1492), § 4, effective September 1, 1999.

Sec. 521.227. Inspection by Peace Officer [Repealed].

Repealed by Acts 2013, 83rd Leg., ch. 1336 (S.B. 763), § 5, effective September 1, 2013.

SUBCHAPTER L OCCUPATIONAL LICENSE

Sec. 521.241. Definitions.

In this subchapter:

(1) "Essential need" means a need of a person for the operation of a motor vehicle:

(A) in the performance of an occupation or trade or for transportation to and from the place at which the person practices the person's occupation or trade;

(B) for transportation to and from an educational facility in which the person is enrolled; or

(C) in the performance of essential household duties.

(2) "Ignition interlock device" means a device that uses a deep-lung breath analysis mechanism to make impractical the operation of a motor vehicle if ethyl alcohol is detected in the breath of the operator of the vehicle.

Sec. 521.242. Petition.

(a) A person whose license has been suspended for a cause other than a physical or mental disability or impairment or a conviction of an offense under Sections 49.04-49.08, Penal Code, may apply for an occupational license by filing a verified petition with the clerk of a justice, county, or district court with jurisdiction that includes the precinct or county in which:

(1) the person resides; or

(2) the offense occurred for which the license was suspended.

(b) A person may apply for an occupational license by filing a verified petition only with the clerk of the court in which the person was convicted if:

(1) the person's license has been automatically suspended or canceled under this chapter for a conviction of an offense under the laws of this state; and

(2) the person has not been issued, in the 10 years preceding the date of the filing of the petition, more than one occupational license after a conviction under the laws of this state.

(c) A petition filed under this section must set forth in detail the person's essential need.

(d) A petition filed under Subsection (b) must state that the petitioner was convicted in that court for an offense under the laws of this state.

(e) The clerk of the court shall file the petition as in any other matter.

(f) A court may not grant an occupational license for the operation of a commercial motor vehicle to which Chapter 522 applies.

Sec. 521.243. Notice to State; Presentation of Evidence.

(a) The clerk of the court shall send by certified mail to the attorney representing the state a copy of the petition and notice of the hearing if the petitioner's license was suspended following a conviction for:

(1) an offense under Section 19.05 or Sections 49.04-49.08, Penal Code; or

(2) an offense to which Section 521.342 applies.

(b) A person who receives a copy of a petition under Subsection (a) may attend the hearing and may present evidence at the hearing against granting the petition.

Sec. 521.244. Hearing; Order; Determination of Essential Need.

(a) The judge who hears the petition shall sign an order finding whether an essential need exists.

(b) In determining whether an essential need exists, the judge shall consider:

(1) the petitioner's driving record; and

(2) any evidence presented by a person under Section 521.243(b).

(c) If the judge finds that there is an essential need, the judge also, as part of the order, shall:

Transportation Code

(1) determine the actual need of the petitioner to operate a motor vehicle; and

(2) require the petitioner to provide evidence of financial responsibility in accordance with Chapter 601.

(d) Except as provided by Section 521.243(b), the hearing on the petition may be ex parte.

(e) A person convicted of an offense under Sections 49.04-49.08, Penal Code, who is restricted to the operation of a motor vehicle equipped with an ignition interlock device is entitled to receive an occupational license without a finding that an essential need exists for that person, provided that the person shows:

(1) evidence of financial responsibility under Chapter 601; and

(2) proof the person has had an ignition interlock device installed on each motor vehicle owned or operated by the person.

Sec. 521.245. Required Counseling.

(a) If the petitioner's license has been suspended under Chapter 524 or 724, the court shall require the petitioner to attend a program approved by the court that is designed to provide counseling and rehabilitation services to persons for alcohol dependence. This requirement shall be stated in the order granting the occupational license.

(b) The program required under Subsection (a) may not be the program provided by Section 521.344 or by Article 42A.403 or 42A.404, Code of Criminal Procedure.

(c) The court may require the person to report periodically to the court to verify that the person is attending the required program.

(d) On finding that the person is not attending the program as required, the court may revoke the order granting the occupational license. The court shall send a certified copy of the order revoking the license to the department.

(e) On receipt of the copy under Subsection (d), the department shall suspend the person's occupational license for:

(1) 60 days, if the original driver's license suspension was under Chapter 524; or

(2) 120 days, if the original driver's license suspension was under Chapter 724.

(f) A suspension under Subsection (e):

(1) takes effect on the date on which the court signs the order revoking the occupational license; and

(2) is cumulative of the original suspension.

(g) A person is not eligible for an occupational license during a period of suspension under Subsection (e).

Sec. 521.246. Ignition Interlock Device Requirement.

(a) If the person's license has been suspended after a conviction of an offense under Sections 49.04-49.08, Penal Code, the judge shall restrict the person to the operation of a motor vehicle equipped with an ignition interlock device.

(b) [Blank]

(c) The person shall obtain the ignition interlock device at the person's own expense unless the court finds that to do so is not in the best interest of justice and enters that finding in the record. If the court determines that the person is unable to pay for the device, the court may impose a reasonable payment schedule for a term not to exceed twice the period of the court's order.

(d) The court shall order the ignition interlock device to remain installed for the duration of the period of suspension.

(e) A person to whom this section applies may operate a motor vehicle without the installation of an approved ignition interlock device if:

(1) the person is required to operate a motor vehicle in the course and scope of the person's employment;

(2) the vehicle is owned by the person's employer;

(3) the employer is not owned or controlled by the person whose driving privilege is restricted;

(4) the employer is notified of the driving privilege restriction; and

(5) proof of that notification is with the vehicle.

(f) A previous conviction may not be used for purposes of restricting a person to the operation of a motor vehicle equipped with an interlock ignition device under this section if:

(1) the previous conviction was a final conviction for an offense under Sections 49.04-49.08, Penal Code, and was for an offense committed more than 10 years before the instant offense for which the person was convicted; and

(2) the person has not been convicted of an offense under Sections 49.04-49.08 of that code committed within 10 years before the date on which the instant offense for which the person was convicted.

Sec. 521.2461. Testing for Alcohol or Controlled Substances.

The court granting an occupational license under this subchapter may require as a condition of the license that the person submit to periodic testing for alcohol or controlled substances, to be conducted by an entity specified by the court, if the person's license has been suspended under Chapter 524 or 724 or as a result of the person's conviction of an

Transportation Code

offense involving the operation of a motor vehicle while intoxicated.

Sec. 521.2462. Supervision of Person Issued Occupational Driver's License.

(a) The court granting an occupational license under this subchapter may order the person receiving the license to submit to supervision for the purpose of verifying the person's compliance with the conditions specified by the order granting the license, including the conditions specified in accordance with Section 521.248.

(a-1) The court may order the supervision of the person to be conducted by:

(1) the local community supervision and corrections department; or

(2) a personal bond office established under Article 17.42, Code of Criminal Procedure.

(a-2) If the court orders the person's supervision to be conducted by the local community supervision and corrections department, the court shall order the person to pay a monthly administrative fee under Section 76.015, Government Code.

(a-3) If the court orders the person's supervision to be conducted by a personal bond office, the office may collect from the person a reasonable administrative fee of not less than $25 and not more than $60 per month.

(b) The court may order the supervision to continue until the end of the period of suspension of the person's driver's license, including any extensions of that period.

(c) The court for good cause may modify or terminate supervision before the end of the period of license suspension.

Sec. 521.2465. Restricted License.

(a) On receipt of notice that a person has been restricted to the use of a motor vehicle equipped with an ignition interlock device, the department shall notify that person that the person's driver's license expires on the 30th day after the date of the notice. On application by the person and payment of a fee of $10, the department shall issue a special restricted license that conspicuously indicates that the person is authorized to operate only a motor vehicle equipped with an ignition interlock device.

(a-1) The notice provided to the person by the department under Subsection (a) may be provided by:

(1) first class mail; or

(2) e-mail if the person has provided an e-mail address to the department and has elected to receive notice electronically.

(b) On receipt of a copy of a court order removing the restriction or at the end of the period of suspension, as applicable, the department shall issue the person a driver's license without the restriction.

Sec. 521.247. Approval of Ignition Interlock Devices by Department.

(a) The department shall adopt rules for the approval of ignition interlock devices used under this subchapter.

(b) The department by rule shall establish general standards for the calibration and maintenance of the devices. The manufacturer or an authorized representative of the manufacturer is responsible for calibrating and maintaining the device.

(c) If the department approves a device, the department shall notify the manufacturer of that approval in writing. Written notice from the department to a manufacturer is admissible in a civil or criminal proceeding in this state. The manufacturer shall reimburse the department for any cost incurred by the department in approving the device.

(d) The department is not liable in a civil or criminal proceeding that arises from the use of an approved device.

Sec. 521.2475. Ignition Interlock Device Evaluation.

(a) On January 1 of each year, the department shall issue an evaluation of each ignition interlock device approved under Section 521.247 using guidelines established by the National Highway Traffic Safety Administration, including:

(1) whether the device provides accurate detection of alveolar air;

(2) the moving retest abilities of the device;

(3) the use of tamper-proof blood alcohol content level software by the device;

(4) the anticircumvention design of the device;

(5) the recalibration requirements of the device; and

(6) the breath action required by the operator.

(b) The department shall assess the cost of preparing the evaluation equally against each manufacturer of an approved device.

Sec. 521.2476. Minimum Standards for Vendors of Ignition Interlock Devices.

(a) The department by rule shall establish:

(1) minimum standards for vendors of ignition interlock devices who conduct business in this state; and

Transportation Code

(2) procedures to ensure compliance with those standards, including procedures for the inspection of a vendor's facilities.

(b) The minimum standards shall require each vendor to:

(1) be authorized by the department to do business in this state;

(2) install a device only if the device is approved under Section 521.247;

(3) obtain liability insurance providing coverage for damages arising out of the operation or use of devices in amounts and under the terms specified by the department;

(4) install the device and activate any anticircumvention feature of the device within a reasonable time after the vendor receives notice that installation is ordered by a court;

(5) install and inspect the device in accordance with any applicable court order;

(6) repair or replace a device not later than 48 hours after receiving notice of a complaint regarding the operation of the device;

(7) submit a written report of any violation of a court order to that court and to the person's supervising officer, if any, not later than 48 hours after the vendor discovers the violation;

(8) maintain a record of each action taken by the vendor with respect to each device installed by the vendor, including each action taken as a result of an attempt to circumvent the device, until at least the fifth anniversary after the date of installation;

(9) make a copy of the record available for inspection by or send a copy of the record to any court, supervising officer, or the department on request; and

(10) annually provide to the department a written report of each service and ignition interlock device feature made available by the vendor.

(c) The department may revoke the department's authorization for a vendor to do business in this state if the vendor or an officer or employee of the vendor violates:

(1) any law of this state that applies to the vendor; or

(2) any rule adopted by the department under this section or another law that applies to the vendor.

(d) A vendor shall reimburse the department for the reasonable cost of conducting each inspection of the vendor's facilities under this section.

(e) In this section, "offense relating to the operating of a motor vehicle while intoxicated" has the meaning assigned by Section 49.09, Penal Code.

Sec. 521.248. Order Requirements.

(a) An order granting an occupational license must specify:

(1) the hours of the day and days of the week during which the person may operate a motor vehicle;

(2) the reasons for which the person may operate a motor vehicle;

(3) areas or routes of travel permitted;

(4) that the person is restricted to the operation of a motor vehicle equipped with an ignition interlock device, if applicable; and

(5) that the person must submit to periodic testing for alcohol or controlled substances, if applicable.

(b) The person may not operate a motor vehicle for more than four hours in any 24-hour period, except that on a showing of necessity the court may allow the person to drive for any period determined by the court that does not exceed 12 hours in any 24-hour period.

(c) An order granting an occupational license remains valid until the end of the period of suspension of the person's regular driver's license.

(d) A person who is restricted to the operation of a motor vehicle equipped with an ignition interlock device may not be subject to any time of travel, reason for travel, or location of travel restrictions described by Subsection (a)(1), (2), or (3) or (b).

Sec. 521.249. Notice to Department; Issuance of Occupational License.

(a) The court shall send a certified copy of the petition and the court order setting out the judge's findings and restrictions to the department. The person may use a copy of the order as a restricted license until the 45th day after the date on which the order takes effect.

(b) On receipt of the copy under this section and after compliance with Chapter 601, the department shall issue an occupational license to the person. The license must refer on its face to the court order.

Sec. 521.250. Court Order in Operator's Possession.

A person who is issued an occupational license shall have in the person's possession a certified copy of the court order granting the license while operating a motor vehicle. The person shall allow a peace officer to examine the order on request.

Sec. 521.251. Effective Date of Occupational License.

(a) If a person's license is suspended under Chapter 524 or 724 and the person has not had a prior suspension arising from an alcohol-related or drug-related enforcement contact in the five years preceding the date of the person's arrest, an order under this subchapter granting the person an occupational license takes effect immediately. However, the court shall order the person to comply with the counseling and rehabilitation program required under Section 521.245.

(b) If the person's driver's license has been suspended as a result of an alcohol-related or drug-related enforcement contact during the five years preceding the date of the person's arrest, the order may not take effect before the 91st day after the effective date of the suspension.

(c) If the person's driver's license has been suspended as a result of a conviction of an offense under Sections 49.04-49.08, Penal Code, during the five years preceding the date of the person's arrest, the order may not take effect before the 181st day after the effective date of the suspension.

(d) Notwithstanding any other provision in this section, if the person's driver's license has been suspended as a result of a second or subsequent conviction under Sections 49.04-49.08, Penal Code, committed within five years of the date on which the most recent preceding offense was committed, an order granting the person an occupational license may not take effect before the first anniversary of the effective date of the suspension.

(d-1) Notwithstanding Subsections (b), (c), and (d), the court may issue an occupational license to a person if the person submits proof the person has an ignition interlock device installed on each motor vehicle owned or operated by the person. If a person issued an occupational license under this subsection fails to maintain an installed ignition interlock device on each motor vehicle owned or operated by the person, the court shall revoke the occupational license under Section 521.252 and reinstate the suspension of the person's driver's license. A person granted an occupational license under this subsection may not be ordered, under Section 521.2462, to submit to the supervision of the local community supervision and corrections department or a personal bond office established under Article 17.42, Code of Criminal Procedure, unless the order is entered by a court of record.

(e) For the purposes of this section, "alcohol-related or drug-related enforcement contact" has the meaning assigned by Section 524.001.

Sec. 521.252. License Revocation.

(a) The court that signs an order granting an occupational license may issue at any time an order revoking the license for good cause.

(b) The court shall send a certified copy of the order to the department.

Sec. 521.253. Criminal Penalty.

(a) A person who holds an occupational license commits an offense if the person:

(1) operates a motor vehicle in violation of a restriction imposed on the license; or

(2) fails to have in the person's possession a certified copy of the court order as required under Section 521.250.

(b) An offense under this section is a Class B misdemeanor.

(c) On conviction of an offense under this section, the occupational license and the order granting that license are revoked.

SUBCHAPTER M
LICENSE EXPIRATION, RENEWAL, AND NUMBER CHANGE

Sec. 521.271. License Expiration.

(a) Each original driver's license, provisional license, learner license, or occupational driver's license issued to an applicant who is a citizen, national, or legal permanent resident of the United States or a refugee or asylee lawfully admitted into the United States expires as follows:

(1) except as provided by Section 521.2711, a driver's license expires on the first birthday of the license holder occurring after the eighth anniversary of the date of the application;

(2) a provisional license expires on the 18th birthday of the license holder;

(3) a learner license expires on the 18th birthday of the license holder;

(4) an occupational driver's license expires on the first anniversary of the court order granting the license; and

(5) unless an earlier date is otherwise provided, a driver's license issued to a person whose residence or domicile is a correctional facility or a parole facility expires on the first birthday of the license holder occurring after the first anniversary of the date of issuance.

(a-1) [Repealed by Acts 2011, ch. 1160 (H.B. 2466), § 5, effective September 1, 2011.]

(a-2) Each original driver's license issued to an applicant who is not a citizen, national, or legal permanent resident of the United States or a refugee or asylee lawfully admitted into the United States expires on:

Transportation Code

(1) the earlier of:

(A) the first birthday of the license holder occurring after the sixth anniversary of the date of the application; or

(B) the expiration date of the license holder's lawful presence in the United States as determined by the appropriate United States agency in compliance with federal law; or

(2) the first anniversary of the date of issuance, if there is no definite expiration date for the applicant's authorized stay in the United States.

(a-3) Each original provisional license or learner license issued to an applicant who is not a citizen, national, or legal permanent resident of the United States or a refugee or asylee lawfully admitted into the United States expires on the earliest of:

(1) the 18th birthday of the license holder;

(2) the first birthday of the license holder occurring after the date of the application; or

(3) the expiration of the license holder's lawful presence in the United States as determined by the United States agency responsible for citizenship and immigration in compliance with federal law.

(a-4) Each original occupational driver's license issued to an applicant who is not a citizen, national, or legal permanent resident of the United States or a refugee or asylee lawfully admitted into the United States expires on the earlier of:

(1) the first anniversary of the date of issuance; or

(2) the expiration of the license holder's lawful presence in the United States as determined by the appropriate United States agency in compliance with federal law.

(b) Except as provided by Section 521.2711, a driver's license that is renewed expires on the earlier of:

(1) the eighth anniversary of the expiration date before renewal if the applicant is a citizen, national, or legal permanent resident of the United States or a refugee or asylee lawfully admitted into the United States;

(1-a) for an applicant not described by Subdivision (1):

(A) the earlier of:

(i) the eighth anniversary of the expiration date before renewal; or

(ii) the expiration date of the applicant's authorized stay in the United States; or

(B) the first anniversary of the date of issuance, if there is no definite expiration date for the applicant's authorized stay in the United States; or

(2) for a renewal driver's license issued to a person whose residence or domicile is a correctional facility or a parole facility, the first birthday of the license holder occurring after the first anniversary of the date of issuance unless an earlier date is otherwise provided.

Sec. 521.2711. License Expiration: Person at Least 85 Years of Age.

(a) Each original driver's license of a person 85 years of age or older expires on the license holder's second birthday after the date of the license application.

(b) A driver's license of a person 85 years of age or older that is renewed expires on the second anniversary of the expiration date before renewal.

(c) Notwithstanding Subsections (a) and (b), an original or renewal driver's license issued to an applicant who is 85 years of age or older and not a citizen, national, or legal permanent resident of the United States or a refugee or asylee lawfully admitted into the United States expires on:

(1) the earlier of:

(A) the second anniversary of the expiration date before renewal; or

(B) the expiration date of the applicant's authorized stay in the United States; or

(2) the first anniversary of the date of issuance if there is no definite expiration date for the applicant's authorized stay in the United States.

Sec. 521.272. Renewal of License Issued to Certain Sex Offenders.

(a) The department may issue an original or renewal driver's license to a person whose driver's license or personal identification certificate record indicates that the person is subject to the registration requirements of Chapter 62, Code of Criminal Procedure, only if the person:

(1) applies in person for the issuance of a license under this section; and

(2) pays the fee required by Section 521.421(h).

(b) Notwithstanding Section 521.143, a person is not required to provide proof of financial responsibility to receive the person's initial driver's license under this section.

(c) Notwithstanding Sections 521.271 and 521.2711, a driver's license issued under this section, including a renewal, duplicate, or corrected license, expires:

(1) if the license holder is a citizen, national, or legal permanent resident of the United States or a refugee or asylee lawfully admitted into the United States, on the first birthday of the license holder occurring after the date of application, except that:

(A) the initial license issued under this section expires on the second birthday of the license holder occurring after the date of application, subject to Paragraph (B); and

(B) a license issued under this section to a person described by Article 62.2021, Code of Criminal Procedure, expires on the sixth anniversary of the date on which the license was issued; or

(2) if the applicant is not described by Subdivision (1), on the earlier of:

(A) the expiration date of the applicant's authorized stay in the United States; or

(B) as applicable:

(i) the first birthday of the license holder occurring after the date of application;

(ii) if the license holder holds an initial license issued under this section, the second birthday of the license holder occurring after the date of application; or

(iii) if the license holder is a person described by Article 62.2021, Code of Criminal Procedure, the sixth anniversary of the date on which the license was issued.

(d) Subsection (c) does not apply to a:

(1) provisional license;

(2) learner license issued under Section 521.222; or

(3) hardship license issued under Section 521.223.

Sec. 521.273. Renewal Examinations.

(a) The department may require and prescribe the procedure and standards for an examination for the renewal of a driver's license.

(b) A license holder who fails to obtain a renewal license as provided by this subchapter may be required to take any examination required for the original license.

Sec. 521.274. Renewal by Mail or Electronic Means.

(a) The department by rule may provide that the holder of a driver's license may renew the license by mail, by telephone, over the Internet, or by other electronic means.

(b) A rule adopted under this section:

(1) may prescribe eligibility standards for renewal under this section;

(2) may not permit a person subject to the registration requirements under Chapter 62, Code of Criminal Procedure, to register by mail or electronic means;

(3) may not permit renewal by mail or electronic means of a driver's license of a person who is 79 years of age or older; and

(4) must allow for the renewal of a driver's license by electronic means, regardless of when the license expires, of:

(A) a person who:

(i) is on active duty in the armed forces of the United States; and

(ii) is absent from the state; and

(B) the spouse or dependent child of a person described by Paragraph (A).

Sec. 521.275. Change of Driver's License or Personal Identification Certificate Number.

(a) The department shall issue to a person a new driver's license number or personal identification certificate number on the person's showing a court order stating that the person has been the victim of domestic violence.

(b) The department may require each applicant to furnish the information required by Section 521.142. If the applicant's name has changed, the department may require evidence identifying the applicant by both the former and new name.

(c) Except as provided by Sections 521.049(c), 730.005, and 730.006, the department may not disclose:

(1) the changed license or certificate number; or

(2) the person's name or any former name.

SUBCHAPTER N GENERAL PROVISIONS RELATING TO LICENSE DENIAL, SUSPENSION, OR REVOCATION

Sec. 521.291. Rules.

The department shall adopt rules to administer this subchapter.

Sec. 521.292. Department's Determination for License Suspension.

(a) The department shall suspend the person's license if the department determines that the person:

(1) has operated a motor vehicle on a highway while the person's license was suspended, canceled, disqualified, or revoked, or without a license after an application for a license was denied;

(2) is a habitually reckless or negligent operator of a motor vehicle;

(3) is a habitual violator of the traffic laws;

(4) has permitted the unlawful or fraudulent use of the person's license;

(5) has committed an offense in another state or Canadian province that, if committed in this state, would be grounds for suspension;

(6) has been convicted of two or more separate offenses of a violation of a restriction imposed on the use of the license;

(7) has been responsible as a driver for any accident resulting in serious personal injury or serious property damage;

(8) is under 18 years of age and has been convicted of two or more moving violations committed within a 12-month period; or

(9) has committed an offense under Section 545.421.

(b) For purposes of Subsection (a)(3), a person is a "habitual violator" if the person has four or more convictions that arise out of different transactions in 12 consecutive months, or seven or more convictions that arise out of different transactions in 24 months, if the convictions are for moving violations of the traffic laws of any state, Canadian province, or political subdivision, other than a violation under:

(1) Section 621.101, 621.201, or 621.203–621.207;

(2) Subchapter B or C, Chapter 623; or

(3) Section 545.413.

Sec. 521.293. Period of Suspension Under Section 521.292.

If the person does not request a hearing, the period of license suspension under Section 521.292 is 90 days.

Sec. 521.294. Department's Determination for License Revocation.

The department shall revoke the person's license if the department determines that the person:

(1) is incapable of safely operating a motor vehicle;

(2) has not complied with the terms of a citation issued by a jurisdiction that is a party to the Nonresident Violator Compact of 1977 for a traffic violation to which that compact applies;

(3) has failed to provide medical records or has failed to undergo medical or other examinations as required by a panel of the medical advisory board;

(4) has failed to pass an examination required by the director under this chapter; or

(5) has committed an offense in another state or Canadian province that, if committed in this state, would be grounds for revocation.

Sec. 521.295. Notice of Department's Determination.

(a) If the department suspends a person's license under Section 521.292 or revokes a person's license under Section 521.294, the department shall send a notice of suspension or revocation by:

(1) first class mail to the person's address in the records of the department; or

(2) e-mail if the person has provided an e-mail address to the department and has elected to receive notice electronically.

(b) Notice is considered received on the fifth day after the date the notice is sent.

Sec. 521.296. Notice of Suspension or Revocation.

A notice of suspension under Section 521.292 or revocation under Section 521.294 must state:

(1) the reason and statutory grounds for the suspension or revocation;

(2) the effective date of the suspension or revocation;

(3) the right of the person to a hearing;

(4) how to request a hearing; and

(5) the period in which the person must request a hearing.

Sec. 521.297. Suspension, Revocation, or Disqualification Effective Date.

(a) A license suspension under Section 521.292 or revocation under Section 521.294 takes effect on the 40th day after the date the person is considered to have received notice of the suspension or revocation under Section 521.295(b).

(b) A license disqualification under Section 522.081(a) takes effect on the 40th day after the date the person is considered to have received notice of the disqualification under Section 521.295(b), unless a disqualification is currently in effect. If a disqualification is currently in effect, the periods of disqualifications run consecutively.

Sec. 521.298. Hearing Request.

If, not later than the 15th day after the date on which the person is considered to have received notice of the suspension or revocation under Section 521.295(b), the department receives at its headquarters in Austin, in writing, including a facsimile transmission, or by another manner prescribed by the department, a request that a hearing be held, a hearing shall be held as provided by Sections 521.295–521.303.

Sec. 521.299. Hearing Date; Rescheduling.

(a) A hearing requested under Section 521.298 shall be held not earlier than the 11th day after the date on which the person requesting the hearing is notified of the hearing. The hearing shall be set for the earliest practical date.

(b) A hearing may be continued on a motion of the person, the department, both parties, or as necessary to accommodate the docket of the presiding officer.

(c) A request for a hearing stays suspension or revocation of a person's license until the date of the final decision of the presiding officer.

Sec. 521.300. Hearing: Location; Presiding Officer.

(a) A hearing under this subchapter shall be conducted in a municipal court or a justice court in the county in which the person resides. The judge of the municipal court or the justice is designated as the presiding officer.

(a-1) A hearing under this subchapter may be conducted by telephone or video conference call if the presiding officer provides notice to the affected parties.

(b) The presiding officer is entitled to receive a fee for hearing the case if a fee is approved and set by the commissioners court of the county in which the person resides. The fee may not exceed $5 and shall be paid from the general revenue fund of the county.

(c) The presiding officer may administer oaths and issue subpoenas to compel the attendance of witnesses and the production of relevant books and documents.

Sec. 521.301. Issue at Hearing.

(a) The issue that must be proved at the hearing by a preponderance of the evidence is whether the grounds for suspension or revocation stated in the notice are true.

(b) If the presiding officer finds in the affirmative on that issue, the suspension or revocation is sustained.

(c) If the presiding officer sustains a suspension, the department shall suspend the person's license for the period specified by the presiding officer, which may not be less than 30 days or more than one year.

(d) If the presiding officer does not find in the affirmative on that issue, the department may not suspend or revoke the person's license.

(e) The decision of the presiding officer is final when issued and signed.

Sec. 521.302. Failure to Appear.

A person who requests a hearing under this subchapter and fails to appear without just cause waives the right to a hearing and the department's determination is final.

Sec. 521.303. Continuance.

A continuance under Section 521.299 stays the suspension or revocation of a license until the date of the final decision of the presiding officer.

Sec. 521.304. Cancellation of Minor's License on Cosigner's Request; Release from Liability.

(a) The person who cosigned a minor's application for a driver's license under Section 521.145 may file with the department a request that the department cancel the license. The request must be in writing and acknowledged.

(b) On receipt of a request under Subsection (a), the department shall cancel the minor's license. On cancellation, the person who cosigned the application is released from liability based on the person's signing of the application for any subsequent negligence or wilful misconduct of the minor in operating a motor vehicle.

Sec. 521.305. Cancellation of Minor's License on Death of Cosigner.

On receipt of information satisfactory to the department of the death of a person who cosigned a minor's application for a driver's license under Section 521.145, the department shall cancel the license if the license holder is under 18 years of age and the department may not issue a new license until the minor files a new application that complies with this chapter.

Sec. 521.306. Effect of Conduct in Other Jurisdiction; Suspension Under Driver's License Compact.

(a) The department may suspend or revoke the license of a resident or the operating privilege of a nonresident to operate a motor vehicle in this state on receipt of notice of a conviction of the individual in another state or a Canadian province of an offense that, if committed in this state, would be grounds for the suspension or revocation of a driver's license.

(b) The department may give the same effect to the conduct of a resident of this state that occurs in another state or Canadian province that the

Transportation Code

department may give to conduct that occurs in this state under state law.

(c) The department may seek the suspension of the license of a person who has failed to comply with the terms of a citation to which Chapter 523 applies.

Sec. 521.307. Suspension of Certain Provisional Licenses.

(a) On the recommendation of a juvenile court with jurisdiction over the holder of a provisional license, the department shall suspend a provisional license if it is found by the juvenile court that the provisional license holder has committed:

(1) an offense that would be classified as a felony if the license holder were an adult; or

(2) a misdemeanor in which a motor vehicle was used to travel to or from the scene of the offense, other than an offense specified by Chapter 729.

(b) The department shall suspend the license for the period set by the juvenile court but not to exceed one year.

(c) The court shall report its recommendation promptly to the department in the manner and form prescribed by the department.

Sec. 521.308. Appeal; Judicial Review.

(a) A person whose driver's license suspension or revocation has been sustained by a presiding officer under this subchapter may appeal the decision of the presiding officer.

(b) To appeal the decision of the presiding officer, the person must file a petition not later than the 30th day after the date on which the department order was entered in the county court at law of the county in which the person resides, or, if there is no county court at law, in the county court. The person must send a file-stamped copy of the petition, certified by the clerk of the court in which the petition is filed, to the department by certified mail.

(c) The court shall notify the department of the hearing not later than the 31st day before the date the court sets for the hearing.

(d) The court shall take testimony, examine the facts of the case, and determine whether the petitioner is subject to the suspension or revocation of a license under this subchapter.

(e) A trial on appeal is a trial de novo, and the person has the right to trial by jury.

(f) The filing of a petition of appeal as provided by this section stays an order of suspension, probated suspension, or revocation until the earlier of the 91st day after the date the appeal petition is filed or the date the trial is completed and final judgment is rendered.

(g) On expiration of the stay, the department shall impose the suspension, probated suspension, or revocation. The stay may not be extended, and an additional stay may not be granted.

Sec. 521.309. Probation of Suspension.

(a) On determining that a license shall be suspended, the presiding officer who conducts a hearing under this subchapter, or the court that tries an appeal under this subchapter, may recommend that the suspension be probated on any terms and conditions considered necessary or proper by the presiding officer or court, if it appears that justice and the best interests of the public and the person will be served by the probation.

(b) The revocation of a license may not be probated.

(c) The report to the department of the results of the hearing must include any terms and conditions of the probation.

(d) If probation is recommended, the department shall probate the suspension.

(e) If a presiding officer or a court probates a suspension of a license under this section, the probationary period shall be for a term of not less than 90 days or more than two years.

Sec. 521.310. Probation Violation.

(a) If the director believes that a person who has been placed on probation under Section 521.309 has violated a term or condition of the probation, the director shall notify the person and summon the person to appear at a hearing in the court or before the presiding officer or judge who recommended that the person be placed on probation after notice as provided by Sections 521.295 and 521.296.

(b) The issue at the hearing under this section is whether a term or condition of the probation has been violated. The presiding officer or judge presiding at the hearing shall report the finding to the department. If the finding is that a term or condition of the probation has been violated, the department shall take the action as determined in the original hearing.

Sec. 521.311. Effective Date of Order.

Except as provided by another section of this subchapter to the contrary, a decision under this subchapter takes effect on the 11th day after the date on which an order is rendered.

Sec. 521.312. Period of Suspension or Revocation; Reinstatement of License.

Transportation Code

(a) Revocation of a license is for an indefinite period.

(b) Except as provided by Subsection (c) or Subchapter O, the department may not suspend a license for a period that exceeds one year.

(c) The department may not reinstate a license revoked under Section 521.294(5) until the court that filed the report for which the license was revoked files an additional report on final disposition of the case.

Sec. 521.313. Reinstatement and Reissuance; Fee.

(a) A license suspended or revoked under this subchapter may not be reinstated or another license issued to the person until the person pays the department a fee of $100 in addition to any other fee required by law.

(b) The payment of a reinstatement fee is not required if a suspension or revocation under this subchapter is:

(1) rescinded by the department; or

(2) not sustained by a presiding officer or a court.

(c) Each fee collected under this section shall be deposited to the credit of the Texas mobility fund.

Sec. 521.314. Cancellation Authority.

The department may cancel a license or certificate if it determines that the holder:

(1) is not entitled to the license or certificate;

(2) failed to give required information in the application for the license or certificate; or

(3) paid the required fee for the license or certificate by check or credit card that was returned to the department or not honored by the funding institution or credit card company due to insufficient funds, a closed account, or any other reason.

Sec. 521.315. Surrender of License; Return.

(a) On the suspension, cancellation, disqualification, or revocation of a license by the department, the department may require the holder to surrender the license to the department.

(b) The department shall return a suspended license to the holder on the expiration of the suspension period.

(c) A person commits an offense if the person's license has been demanded in accordance with Subsection (a) and the person fails or refuses to surrender the license to the department.

(d) An offense under this section is a Class B misdemeanor.

Sec. 521.316. Suspended Foreign License.

A person whose driver's license or privilege to operate a vehicle in this state is suspended or revoked under this chapter may not operate a motor vehicle in this state under a license, permit, or registration certificate issued by any other state or Canadian province during the suspension period or after the revocation until a new license is obtained as provided by this chapter.

Sec. 521.317. Denial of License Renewal After Warning.

The department may deny the renewal of the driver's license of a person about whom the department has received information under Section 706.004 until the date the department receives a notification from the political subdivision under Section 706.005 that there is no cause to deny the renewal based on the person's previous failure to appear for a complaint, citation, or court order to pay a fine involving a violation of a traffic law.

Sec. 521.318. Nonresidents.

(a) The department may suspend or revoke a nonresident's operating privilege in the same manner and for the same causes as a driver's license issued under this chapter.

(b) On receipt of a record of conviction of a nonresident in this state under the motor vehicle laws of this state, the department may forward a certified copy of the record to the motor vehicle administrator of the state or Canadian province of which the convicted person is a resident.

Sec. 521.319. Revocation for Medical Reasons.

(a) A person may not operate a motor vehicle if the person:

(1) is a chemically dependent person who:

(A) is likely to cause serious harm to the person or to others; or

(B) will, if not treated, continue to suffer abnormal mental, emotional, or physical distress, or to deteriorate in ability to function independently; or

(2) has been determined by a judgment of a court to be totally incapacitated or incapacitated to act as the operator of a motor vehicle.

(b) The driver's license of a person is revoked on:

(1) the judgment of a court that the person is totally incapacitated or incapacitated to act as the operator of a motor vehicle; or

(2) the order of a court of involuntary treatment of the person under Subchapter D, Chapter 462, Health and Safety Code.

(c) If the person has not been issued a driver's license, the judgment or order of a court under Subsection (b) automatically prohibits the department from issuing a driver's license to the person.

(d) The clerk of the court that renders a judgment or enters an order under Subsection (b) shall notify the department of the court's judgment or order before the 10th day after the date the court renders the judgment or enters the order.

(e) The revocation of a driver's license under Subsection (b) or the prohibition against the issuance of a driver's license under Subsection (c) expires on the date on which:

(1) the person is:

(A) restored to capacity by judicial decree; or

(B) released from a hospital for the mentally incapacitated on a certificate of the superintendent or administrator that the person has regained capacity; or

(2) the order of involuntary treatment of the chemically dependent person expires.

(f) Before the 10th day after the date under Subsection (e)(1)(A) or (2), the clerk of the appropriate court shall notify the department that:

(1) the person has been restored to capacity by judicial decree; or

(2) the order of involuntary treatment has expired or has been terminated under Section 462.080(d), Health and Safety Code.

(g) Before the 10th day after the date under Subsection (e)(1)(B), the superintendent or administrator of the hospital shall notify the department that the person has been released from the hospital on a certificate that the person has regained capacity.

(h) In this section:

(1) "Chemically dependent person" means a person with chemical dependency.

(2) "Chemical dependency" and "treatment" have the meanings assigned by Section 462.001, Health and Safety Code.

Transportation Code

Sec. 521.320. Suspension for Certain Criminal Mischief; License Denial.

(a) A court may order the department to suspend a person's driver's license on conviction of an offense under Section 28.08, Penal Code.

(b) A court may order the department to deny an application for reinstatement or issuance of a driver's license to a person convicted of an offense under Section 28.08, Penal Code, who, on the date of the conviction, did not hold a driver's license.

(c) The period of suspension under this section is one year after the date of a final conviction. The period of license denial is one year after the date the person applies to the department for reinstatement or issuance of a driver's license.

(d) The department may not reinstate a driver's license suspended under Subsection (a) unless the person whose license was suspended applies to the department for reinstatement.

(e) A person whose license is suspended under Subsection (a) remains eligible to receive an occupational license under Subchapter L.

(f) For the purposes of this section, a person is convicted of an offense regardless of whether sentence is imposed or the person is placed on community supervision for the offense under Chapter 42A, Code of Criminal Procedure.

SUBCHAPTER O AUTOMATIC SUSPENSION

Sec. 521.341. Requirements for Automatic License Suspension.

Except as provided by Sections 521.344(d)-(i), a license is automatically suspended on final conviction of the license holder of:

(1) an offense under Section 19.05, Penal Code, committed as a result of the holder's criminally negligent operation of a motor vehicle;

(2) an offense under Section 38.04, Penal Code, if the holder used a motor vehicle in the commission of the offense;

(3) an offense under Section 49.04, 49.045, or 49.08, Penal Code;

(4) an offense under Section 49.07, Penal Code, if the holder used a motor vehicle in the commission of the offense;

(5) an offense punishable as a felony under the motor vehicle laws of this state;

(6) an offense under Section 550.021;

(7) an offense under Section 521.451 or 521.453; or

(8) an offense under Section 19.04, Penal Code, if the holder used a motor vehicle in the commission of the offense.

Sec. 521.342. Person Under 21 Years of Age.

(a) Except as provided by Section 521.344, the license of a person who was under 21 years of age at the time of the offense, other than an offense classified as a misdemeanor punishable by fine only, is automatically suspended on conviction of:

(1) an offense under Section 49.04, 49.045, or 49.07, Penal Code, committed as a result of the introduction of alcohol into the body;

(2) an offense under the Alcoholic Beverage Code, other than an offense to which Section 106.071 of that code applies, involving the manufacture, delivery, possession, transportation, or use of an alcoholic beverage;

(3) a misdemeanor offense under Chapter 481, Health and Safety Code, for which Subchapter P does not require the automatic suspension of the license;

(4) an offense under Chapter 483, Health and Safety Code, involving the manufacture, delivery, possession, transportation, or use of a dangerous drug; or

(5) an offense under Chapter 485, Health and Safety Code, involving the manufacture, delivery, possession, transportation, or use of an abusable volatile chemical.

(b) The department shall suspend for one year the license of a person who is under 21 years of age and is convicted of an offense under Section 49.04, 49.045, 49.07, or 49.08, Penal Code, regardless of whether the person is required to attend an educational program under Article 42A.403, Code of Criminal Procedure, that is designed to rehabilitate persons who have operated motor vehicles while intoxicated, unless the person is placed under community supervision under Chapter 42A, Code of Criminal Procedure, and is required as a condition of the community supervision to not operate a motor vehicle unless the vehicle is equipped with the device described by Article 42A.408 of that chapter. If the person is required to attend such a program and does not complete the program before the end of the person's suspension, the department shall suspend the person's license or continue the suspension, as appropriate, until the department receives proof that the person has successfully completed the program. On the person's successful completion of the program, the person's instructor shall give notice to the department and to the community supervision and corrections department in the manner provided by Article 42A.406(b), Code of Criminal Procedure.

(c) A person whose license is suspended under Subsection (a) remains eligible to receive an occupational license under Subchapter L. Suspension under Subsection (a) is not a suspension for physical or mental disability or impairment for purposes of eligibility to apply for an occupational license under Subchapter L.

Sec. 521.343. Period of Suspension; Extension.

(a) Except as provided by Sections 521.342(b), 521.344(a), (b), (d), (e), (f), (g), (h), and (i), 521.345, 521.346, 521.3465, and 521.351, a suspension under this subchapter is for one year.

(b) If a license is suspended under this subchapter for a subsequent period, the subsequent suspension is for 18 months except as otherwise provided by a section listed in Subsection (a).

(c) If the license holder is convicted of operating a motor vehicle while the license to operate a motor vehicle is cancelled, disqualified, suspended, revoked, or denied, the period is extended for the same term as the original suspension or disqualification, in addition to any penalty assessed under this chapter or Chapter 522.

Sec. 521.344. Suspension for Offenses Involving Intoxication.

(a) Except as provided by Sections 521.342(b) and 521.345, and by Subsections (d)-(i), if a person is convicted of an offense under Section 49.04, 49.045, or 49.07, Penal Code, the license suspension:

(1) begins on a date set by the court that is not earlier than the date of the conviction or later than the 30th day after the date of the conviction, as determined by the court; and

(2) continues for a period set by the court according to the following schedule:

(A) not less than 90 days or more than one year, if the person is punished under Section 49.04, 49.045, or 49.07, Penal Code, except that if the person's license is suspended for a second or subsequent offense under Section 49.07 committed within five years of the date on which the most recent preceding offense was committed, the suspension continues for a period of one year;

(B) not less than 180 days or more than two years, if the person is punished under Section 49.09(a) or (b), Penal Code; or

(C) not less than one year or more than two years, if the person is punished under Section 49.09(a) or (b), Penal Code, and is subject to Section 49.09(h) of that code.

(b) Except as provided by Section 521.342(b), if a person is convicted of an offense under Section 49.08, Penal Code, the license suspension:

(1) begins on a date set by the court that is not earlier than the date of the conviction or later than the 30th day after the date of the conviction, as determined by the court; and

(2) continues for a period set by the court of not less than 180 days or more than two years, except

Transportation Code

that if the person's license is suspended for a second or subsequent offense under Section 49.08, Penal Code, committed within 10 years of the date on which the most recent preceding offense was committed, the suspension continues for a period set by the court of not less than one year or more than two years.

(c) The court shall credit toward the period of suspension a suspension imposed on the person for refusal to give a specimen under Chapter 724 if the refusal followed an arrest for the same offense for which the court is suspending the person's license under this chapter. The court may not extend the credit to a person:

(1) who has been previously convicted of an offense under Section 49.04, 49.045, 49.07, or 49.08, Penal Code; or

(2) whose period of suspension is governed by Section 521.342(b).

(d) Except as provided by Subsection (e) and Section 521.342(b), during a period of probation the department may not revoke the person's license if the person is required under Article 42A.403 or 42A.404, Code of Criminal Procedure, to successfully complete an educational program designed to rehabilitate persons who have operated motor vehicles while intoxicated, unless the person was punished under Section 49.09(a) or (b), Penal Code, and was subject to Section 49.09(h) of that code. The department may not revoke the license of a person:

(1) for whom the jury has recommended that the license not be revoked under Article 42A.407(a), Code of Criminal Procedure; or

(2) who is placed under community supervision under Chapter 42A, Code of Criminal Procedure, and is required as a condition of community supervision to not operate a motor vehicle unless the vehicle is equipped with the device described by Article 42A.408 of that chapter, unless the person was punished under Section 49.09(a) or (b), Penal Code, and was subject to Section 49.09(g) of that code.

(e) After the date has passed, according to department records, for successful completion of the educational program designed to rehabilitate persons who operated motor vehicles while intoxicated, the director shall revoke the license of a person who does not successfully complete the program or, if the person is a resident without a license to operate a motor vehicle in this state, shall issue an order prohibiting the person from obtaining a license.

(f) After the date has passed, according to department records, for successful completion of an educational program for repeat offenders as required by Article 42A.404, Code of Criminal Procedure, the director shall suspend the license of a person who does not successfully complete the program or, if the person is a resident without a license, shall issue an order prohibiting the person from obtaining a license.

(g) A revocation, suspension, or prohibition order under Subsection (e) or (f) remains in effect until the department receives notice of successful completion of the educational program. The director shall promptly send notice of a revocation or prohibition order issued under Subsection (e) or (f) by:

(1) first class mail to the person at the person's most recent address as shown in the records of the department; or

(2) e-mail if the person has provided an e-mail address to the department and has elected to receive notice electronically.

(g-1) The notice provided under Subsection (g) must include the date of the revocation or prohibition order, the reason for the revocation or prohibition, and a statement that the person has the right to request in writing that a hearing be held on the revocation or prohibition. Notice is considered received on the fifth day after the date the notice is sent. A revocation or prohibition under Subsection (e) or (f) takes effect on the 30th day after the date the notice is sent. The person may request a hearing not later than the 20th day after the date the notice is sent. If the department receives a request under this subsection, the department shall set the hearing for the earliest practical time and the revocation or prohibition does not take effect until resolution of the hearing.

(h) The hearing shall be held in a municipal or justice court in the county of the person's residence in the manner provided for a suspension hearing under Subchapter N. The issues to be determined at the hearing are whether the person has successfully completed a required educational program and whether the period for completion of the program has passed. If the presiding officer determines that the educational program has not been completed and the period for completion has passed, the officer shall confirm the revocation or prohibition and shall notify the department of that fact. The director may not revoke or prohibit the license if the officer finds that the program has been completed, that, before the hearing, the court that originally imposed the requirement to attend an educational program has granted an extension that has not expired, or that the period for completion has not passed. If the person or the person's agent fails to appear at the hearing, the department shall revoke the person's license until the department receives notice of successful completion of the educational program.

(i) On the date that a suspension order under Section 521.343(c) is to expire, the period of suspension or the corresponding period in which the department is prohibited from issuing a license is automatically increased to two years unless the department receives notice of successful completion of the educational program as required by Article 42A.406, Code of Criminal Procedure. At the time a person is convicted of an offense under Section 49.04 or 49.045, Penal Code, the court shall warn the person of the effect of this subsection. On the person's successful completion of the program, the person's instructor shall give notice to the department and to the community supervision and corrections department in the manner required by Article 42A.406(b), Code of Criminal Procedure. If the department receives proof of completion after a period has been extended under this subsection, the department shall immediately end the suspension or prohibition.

Sec. 521.345. Suspension on Order of Juvenile Court or on Order of Court Based on Alcoholic Beverage Violation by Minor.

(a) The department shall suspend the license of a person on receipt of an order to suspend the license that is issued by:

(1) a juvenile court under Section 54.042, Family Code; or

(2) a court under Section 106.115, Alcoholic Beverage Code.

(b) The period of suspension is for the period specified in the order.

Sec. 521.3451. Suspension or Denial on Order of Justice or Municipal Court for Contempt of Court; Reinstatement.

(a) The department shall suspend or deny the issuance of a driver's license or learner license on receipt of an order to suspend or deny the issuance of either license from a justice or municipal court under Article 45.050, Code of Criminal Procedure.

(b) The department shall reinstate a license suspended or reconsider a license denied under Subsection (a) on receiving notice from the justice or municipal court that ordered the suspension or denial that the contemnor has fully complied with the court's order.

Sec. 521.3452. Procedure in Cases Involving Minors.

(a) A court shall report to the department a person charged with a traffic offense under this chapter who does not appear before the court as required by law.

(b) In addition to any other action or remedy provided by law, the department may deny renewal of the person's driver's license under Section 521.317 or Chapter 706.

(c) The court shall also report to the department on final disposition of the case.

Sec. 521.346. Suspension on Conviction of Certain Fraudulent Activities.

(a) If an individual is convicted of an offense under Section 521.451 or 521.453, the period of suspension shall be for the period set by the court of not less than 90 days or more than one year.

(b) If the court does not set the period, the department shall suspend the license for one year.

Sec. 521.3465. Automatic Suspension on Conviction of Certain Offenses Involving Fictitious Motor Vehicle License Plates, Registration Insignia, or Vehicle Inspection Reports.

(a) A license is automatically suspended on final conviction of the license holder of:

(1) an offense under Section 502.475(a)(4); or

(2) an offense under Section 548.603(a)(1) that involves a fictitious vehicle inspection report.

(b) A suspension under this section is for 180 days.

(c) If the person is a resident of this state without a driver's license to operate a motor vehicle, the director shall issue an order prohibiting the person from being issued a driver's license before the 181st day after the date of the conviction.

Sec. 521.3466. Automatic Revocation for Offense Involving Certain Fraudulent Governmental Records.

(a) A license is automatically revoked on final conviction of the license holder of an offense under Section 37.10, Penal Code, if the governmental record was a motor vehicle license plate or registration insignia, within the meaning of Chapter 502, or a vehicle inspection report, within the meaning of Chapter 548.

(b) If the person is a resident of this state without a driver's license to operate a motor vehicle, the director shall issue an order prohibiting the person from being issued a driver's license until the second anniversary of the date of the conviction.

(c) Section 521.347 applies to a conviction under Section 37.10, Penal Code, in the same manner

Transportation Code

that section applies to a conviction of an offense that requires automatic suspension of a person's driver's license.

(d) The department may not issue a driver's license to the person before the second anniversary of the date of the conviction. The department may issue a driver's license to the person only if the person:

(1) applies to the department for the license;

(2) is otherwise qualified for the license; and

(3) pays, in addition to the fee required by Section 521.421, a fee of $100.

(e) Each fee collected under this section shall be deposited to the credit of the Texas mobility fund.

Sec. 521.347. Reports; Recommended Suspension.

(a) The court in which a person is convicted of an offense for which this chapter or Chapter 522 requires automatic suspension of the person's driver's license may require the person to surrender to the court each driver's license held by the person. Not later than the 10th day after the date on which the license is surrendered to the court, the clerk of the court shall send to the department:

(1) the license; and

(2) a record of the conviction that states whether the vehicle involved in the offense was a commercial motor vehicle as defined by Chapter 522 or was involved in the transport of hazardous materials.

(b) Each court with jurisdiction of an offense under this chapter or another law of this state regulating the operation of a motor vehicle on a highway shall send to the department a record of conviction of any person convicted in the court of such a violation. The court may recommend the suspension of the person's driver's license as provided by Subchapter N.

(c) For purposes of this section, "conviction" means a final conviction. A conviction is a final conviction regardless of whether any portion of the sentence for the conviction was suspended or probated but is not a final conviction if the defendant receives a deferred adjudication in the case or if the court defers final disposition of the case, unless the court subsequently proceeds with an adjudication of guilt and imposes a sentence on the defendant. For purposes of this section, a final judgment of forfeiture of bail or collateral deposited to secure a defendant's appearance in court is a conviction if the forfeiture is not vacated.

Sec. 521.348. Automatic Revocation for Certain Sex Offenders.

(a) A driver's license is automatically revoked if the holder of the license:

(1) is subject to the registration requirements of Chapter 62, Code of Criminal Procedure; and

(2) fails to apply to the department for renewal of the license as required by Article 62.060 or 62.2021, Code of Criminal Procedure, as applicable.

(b) The department may issue a driver's license to a person whose license is revoked under this section only if the person:

(1) applies for an original or renewal license under Section 521.272; and

(2) is otherwise qualified for the license.

Sec. 521.349. Acquiring Motor Fuel Without Payment: Automatic Suspension; License Denial.

(a) A person's driver's license is automatically suspended on final conviction of an offense under Section 31.03, Penal Code, if the judgment in the case contains a special affirmative finding under Article 42.019, Code of Criminal Procedure.

(b) The department may not issue a driver's license to a person convicted of an offense specified in Subsection (a) who, on the date of the conviction, did not hold a driver's license.

(c) The period of suspension under this section is the 180 days after the date of a final conviction, and the period of license denial is the 180 days after the date the person applies to the department for reinstatement or issuance of a driver's license, unless the person has previously been denied a license under this section or had a license suspended, in which event the period of suspension is one year after the date of a final conviction, and the period of license denial is one year after the date the person applies to the department for reinstatement or issuance of a driver's license.

Sec. 521.350. Suspension for Offense Relating to Racing of Motor Vehicle on Public Highway or Street.

(a) A license is automatically suspended on conviction of an offense under Section 545.420(a).

(b) A suspension under this section is for one year, except as provided by this section.

(c) A person whose license is suspended under Subsection (a) remains eligible to receive an occupational license under Subchapter L, except that an occupational license issued to a person younger than 18 years of age whose license is suspended under this section may permit the operation of a motor vehicle only for transportation to and from an educational facility in which the person is enrolled and the place where the person resides.

Transportation Code

(d) A person whose license is suspended under Subsection (a) shall be required by the court in which the person was convicted to perform at least 10 hours of community service as ordered by the court. If the person is a resident of this state without a driver's license to operate a motor vehicle, the court shall issue an order prohibiting the department from issuing the person a driver's license before the person completes the community service. Community service required under this subsection is in addition to any community service required of the person as a condition of community supervision under Article 42A.304, Code of Criminal Procedure.

(e) If a person who is required to perform community service under Subsection (d) completes that community service before the end of the person's license suspension, the person may apply to the department for reinstatement of the person's license or the issuance of a new license. The application must include proof satisfactory to the department that the person has performed the community service.

(f) If a person whose license is suspended under this section is subsequently convicted of an offense under Section 521.457(a) during the period of license suspension, in addition to the penalties provided by Section 521.457, the department shall revoke the person's license until the first anniversary of the date of conviction and may not reinstate the person's license or issue the person a new license before that date.

Sec. 521.351. Purchase of Alcohol for Minor or Furnishing Alcohol to Minor: Automatic Suspension; License Denial.

(a) A person's driver's license is automatically suspended on final conviction of an offense under Section 106.06, Alcoholic Beverage Code.

(b) The department may not issue a driver's license to a person convicted of an offense under Section 106.06, Alcoholic Beverage Code, who, on the date of the conviction, did not hold a driver's license.

(c) The period of suspension under this section is the 180 days after the date of a final conviction, and the period of license denial is the 180 days after the date the person applies to the department for reinstatement or issuance of a driver's license, unless the person has previously been denied a license under this section or had a license suspended, in which event the period of suspension is one year after the date of a final conviction, and the period of license denial is one year after the date the person applies to the department for reinstatement or issuance of a driver's license.

SUBCHAPTER P
AUTOMATIC SUSPENSION FOR CERTAIN DRUG OFFENSES.

Sec. 521.371. Definitions.

In this subchapter:

(1) "Controlled Substances Act" means the federal Controlled Substances Act (21 U.S.C. Sec. 801 et seq.).

(2) "Convicted" includes an adjudication under juvenile proceedings.

(3) "Drug offense" has the meaning assigned under 23 U.S.C. Section 159(c) and includes an offense under Section 49.04, 49.07, or 49.08, Penal Code, that is committed as a result of the introduction into the body of any substance the possession of which is prohibited under the Controlled Substances Act.

Sec. 521.372. Automatic Suspension; License Denial. [Effective until contingency met]

(a) A person's driver's license is automatically suspended on final conviction of:

(1) an offense under the Controlled Substances Act;

(2) a drug offense; or

(3) a felony under Chapter 481, Health and Safety Code, that is not a drug offense.

(b) The department may not issue a driver's license to a person convicted of an offense specified in Subsection (a) who, on the date of the conviction, did not hold a driver's license.

(c) Except as provided by Section 521.374(b), the period of suspension under this section is the 180 days after the date of a final conviction, and the period of license denial is the 180 days after the date the person applies to the department for reinstatement or issuance of a driver's license.

Sec. 521.372. Suspension Or License Denial. [Effective upon contingency being met]

(a) A person's driver's license is automatically suspended on final conviction of:

(1) an offense under the Controlled Substances Act;

(2) a felony drug offense;

(3) a misdemeanor drug offense, if the person has been previously convicted of a drug offense committed less than 36 months before the commission of the instant offense; or

(4) a felony under Chapter 481, Health and Safety Code, that is not a drug offense.

Transportation Code

(b) The department may not issue a driver's license to a person convicted of an offense specified in Subsection (a) who, on the date of the conviction, did not hold a driver's license.

(b-1) Except as provided by Subsection (a)(3), the court may order that the department suspend the license of a person who holds a license at the time of final conviction of a misdemeanor drug offense if the court makes a written determination that the suspension is in the interest of public safety.

(c) Except as provided by Section 521.374(b), the period of suspension or license denial under this section is 90 days after the date of a final conviction.

Sec. 521.373. Reinstatement Requirements.

(a) The department may not reinstate a driver's license suspended under Section 521.372 unless the person whose license was suspended applies to the department for reinstatement.

(b) The department may not reinstate the driver's license of a person convicted of an offense specified by Section 521.372(a) if the driver's license was under suspension on the date of the conviction.

SUBCHAPTER P AUTOMATIC SUSPENSION FOR CERTAIN DRUG OFFENSES. [EFFECTIVE UNTIL CONTINGENCY MET]

Sec. 521.374. Educational Program or Equivalent Education.

(a) **[As amended by Acts 2021, 87th Leg., ch. XXX (SB 181)]** A person whose license is suspended under Section 521.372 may:

(1) successfully complete an in-person or online educational program, approved by the Texas Department of Licensing and Regulation under rules adopted by the Texas Commission of Licensing and Regulation and the department, that is designed to educate persons on the dangers of drug abuse; or

(2) successfully complete education on the dangers of drug abuse approved by the Department of State Health Services as equivalent to the educational program described by Subdivision (1), while the person is a resident of a facility for the treatment of drug abuse or chemical dependency, including:

(A) a substance abuse treatment facility or substance abuse felony punishment facility operated by the Texas Department of Criminal Justice under Section 493.009, Government Code;

(B) a community corrections facility, as defined by Section 509.001, Government Code; or

(C) a chemical dependency treatment facility licensed under Chapter 464, Health and Safety Code.

(a) **[As amended by Acts 2021, 87th Leg., ch. XXX (SB 1480)** A person whose license is suspended under Section 521.372 may:

(1) successfully complete an in-person or online educational program, approved by the Texas Department of Licensing and Regulation under Chapter 171, Government Code, that is designed to educate persons on the dangers of drug abuse; or

(2) successfully complete education on the dangers of drug abuse approved by the Department of State Health Services as equivalent to the educational program described by Subdivision (1), while the person is a resident of a facility for the treatment of drug abuse or chemical dependency, including:

(A) a substance abuse treatment facility or substance abuse felony punishment facility operated by the Texas Department of Criminal Justice under Section 493.009, Government Code;

(B) a community corrections facility, as defined by Section 509.001, Government Code; or

(C) a chemical dependency treatment facility licensed under Chapter 464, Health and Safety Code.

(b) **[As amended by Acts 2021, 87th Leg., ch. XXX (SB 181)]** The period of suspension or prohibition under Section 521.372(c) continues until the earlier of:

(1) the date the individual successfully completes the in-person or online educational program under Subsection (a)(1) or is released from the residential treatment facility at which the individual successfully completed equivalent education under Subsection (a)(2), as applicable; or

(2) the second anniversary of the date the suspension or prohibition was imposed.

(b) **[As amended by Acts 2021, 87th Leg., ch. XXX (SB 1480)** The period of suspension or prohibition under Section 521.372(c) continues for an indefinite period until the individual successfully completes the in-person or online educational program under Subsection (a)(1) or is released from the residential treatment facility at which the individual successfully completed equivalent education under Subsection (a)(2), as applicable.

Sec. 521.375. Joint Adoption of Rules. [2 Versions: As amended by Acts 2015, 84th Leg., ch. 851]

(a) The executive commissioner of the Health and Human Services Commission and the department shall jointly adopt rules for the qualification and approval of:

(1) providers of educational programs under Section 521.374(a)(1); and

(2) equivalent education provided in a residential treatment facility described by Section 521.374(a)(2).

(b) The Department of State Health Services shall publish the jointly adopted rules.

Sec. 521.375. Joint Adoption of Rules. [2 Versions: As amended by Acts 2015, 84th Leg., ch. 838]

(a) The Texas Commission of Licensing and Regulation and the department shall jointly adopt rules for the qualification and approval of providers of in-person and online educational programs under Section 521.374(a)(1).

(a-1) The executive commissioner of the Health and Human Services Commission and the department shall jointly adopt rules for the qualification and approval of equivalent education provided in a residential treatment facility described by Section 521.374(a)(2).

(b) The Texas Department of Licensing and Regulation shall publish the jointly adopted rules under Subsection (a).

(c) The Department of State Health Services shall publish the jointly adopted rules under Subsection (a-1).

Sec. 521.376. Duties of Department of State Health Services; Application and Renewal Fees. [2 Versions: As amended by Acts 2015, 84th Leg., ch. 851]

The Department of State Health Services:

(1) shall monitor, coordinate, and provide training to:

(A) persons who provide educational programs under Section 521.374(a)(1); and

(B) residential treatment facilities described by Section 521.374(a)(2) providing equivalent education;

(2) shall administer the approval of the educational programs and the equivalent education provided in a residential treatment facility; and

(3) may charge a nonrefundable application fee to the provider of an educational program under Section 521.374(a)(1) for:

(A) initial certification of approval; and

(B) renewal of the certification.

Sec. 521.376. Duties of Texas Department of Licensing and Regulation and Department of State Health Services; Application and Renewal Fees. [2 Versions: As amended by Acts 2015, 84th Leg., ch. 838]

(a) The Texas Department of Licensing and Regulation:

(1) shall monitor, coordinate, and provide training to persons who provide in-person and online educational programs under Section 521.374(a)(1);

(2) shall administer the approval of those in-person and online educational programs; and

(3) may charge a nonrefundable application fee to the provider of an in-person or online educational program under Section 521.374(a)(1) for:

(A) initial certification of approval; and

(B) renewal of the certification.

(b) The Department of State Health Services:

(1) shall monitor, coordinate, and provide training to residential treatment facilities described by Section 521.374(a)(2) providing equivalent education; and

(2) shall administer the approval of the equivalent education provided in a residential treatment facility.

Sec. 521.377. License Reinstatement.

(a) The department, on payment of the applicable fee, shall reinstate a person's license or, if the person otherwise qualifies for a license, issue the license, if:

(1) the department receives notification from the clerk of the court in which the person was convicted that the person has successfully completed an educational program under Section 521.374(a)(1) or equivalent education in a residential treatment facility under Section 521.374(a)(2); and

(2) the person's driver's license has been suspended or license application denied for at least the period provided by Section 521.372(c).

(b) A person whose license is suspended under Section 521.372 remains eligible to receive an occupational license under Subchapter L. Suspension under Section 521.372 is not a suspension for physical or mental disability or impairment for purposes of eligibility to apply for an occupational license under Subchapter L.

SUBCHAPTER Q
ANATOMICAL GIFTS

Sec. 521.401. Statement of Gift.

(a) A person who wishes to be an eye, tissue, or organ donor may execute a statement of gift.

(b) The statement of gift may be shown on a donor's driver's license or personal identification certificate or by a card designed to be carried by the donor to evidence the donor's intentions with respect to organ, tissue, and eye donation. A donor

Transportation Code

card signed by the donor shall be given effect as if executed pursuant to Section 692A.005, Health and Safety Code.

(c) Donor registry information shall be provided to the department and the Texas Department of Transportation by organ procurement organizations, tissue banks, or eye banks, as those terms are defined in Section 692A.002, Health and Safety Code, or by the Glenda Dawson Donate Life-Texas Registry operated under Chapter 692A, Health and Safety Code. The department, with expert input and support from the nonprofit organization administering the Glenda Dawson Donate Life-Texas Registry, shall:

(1) provide to each applicant for the issuance of an original, renewal, corrected, or duplicate driver's license or personal identification certificate who applies in person, by mail, over the Internet, or by other electronic means:

(A) the opportunity to indicate on the person's driver's license or personal identification certificate that the person is willing to make an anatomical gift, in the event of death, in accordance with Section 692A.005, Health and Safety Code; and

(B) an opportunity for the person to consent to inclusion in the statewide Internet-based registry of organ, tissue, and eye donors and release to procurement organizations in the manner provided by Subsection (c-1); and

(2) provide a means to distribute donor registry information to interested individuals in each office authorized to issue driver's licenses or personal identification certificates.

(c-1) The department shall:

(1) specifically ask each applicant only the question, "Would you like to register as an organ donor?"; and

(2) if the applicant responds affirmatively to the question asked under Subdivision (1), provide the person's name, date of birth, driver's license number, most recent address, and other information needed for identification purposes at the time of donation to the nonprofit organization contracted to maintain the statewide donor registry under Section 692A.020, Health and Safety Code, for inclusion in the registry.

(d) An affirmative statement of gift on a person's driver's license or personal identification certificate executed after August 31, 2005, shall be conclusive evidence of a decedent's status as a donor and serve as consent for organ, tissue, and eye removal.

(e) The department shall distribute at all field offices Donate Life brochures that provide basic donation information in English and Spanish and include a contact phone number and e-mail address. The department shall include the question required under Subsection (c)(1)(B) and information on the donor registry Internet website in renewal notices.

Sec. 521.402. Revocation of Statement of Gift.

(a) To revoke an affirmative statement of gift on a person's driver's license or personal identification certificate, a person must apply to the department for an amendment to the license or certificate.

(b) The fee for an amendment is the same as the fee for a duplicate license.

(c) To have a person's name deleted from the statewide Internet-based registry of organ, tissue, and eye donors maintained as provided by Chapter 692A, Health and Safety Code, a person must provide written notice to the nonprofit organization selected under that chapter to maintain the registry directing the deletion of the person's name from the registry. On receipt of a written notice under this subsection, the organization shall promptly remove the person's name and information from the registry.

Sec. 521.403. Information Provided to Hospital [Repealed].

Repealed by Acts 2009, 81st Leg., ch. 186 (H.B. 2027), § 11(4), effective September 1, 2009.

Sec. 521.404. Notification to Procurement Organization [Repealed].

Repealed by Acts 2009, 81st Leg., ch. 186 (H.B. 2027), § 11(5), effective September 1, 2009.

Sec. 521.405. Determination; Request; Removal of Certain Organs [Repealed].

Repealed by Acts 2005, 79th Leg., ch. 1069 (H.B. 1544), § 3, effective September 1, 2005.

SUBCHAPTER R FEES

Sec. 521.421. License Fees; Examination Fees.

(a) The fee for issuance or renewal of a license not otherwise provided for by this section is $32.

(a-1) The fee for a personal identification certificate issued under Section 501.0165, Government Code, Section 841.153, Health and Safety Code, or Section 245.0536, Human Resources Code, is $5.

(a-2) Except as provided by Subsection (a-1), the department by rule shall establish the fee for a personal identification certificate or driver's license issued to a person whose residence or domicile is a correctional facility or a parole facility.

(a-3) Except as provided by Subsections (a-1) and (a-2), the fee for a driver's license or personal identification certificate that is issued to a person who is not a citizen, national, or legal permanent resident of the United States or a refugee or asylee lawfully admitted into the United States and that is valid for not more than one year is $24.

(b) The fee for renewal of a Class M license or for renewal of a license that includes authorization to operate a motorcycle is $43.

(c) The fee for issuance of a provisional license or learner license is $15.

(d) The fee for issuance or renewal of an occupational license is $10.

(e) An applicant who changes from a lower to a higher class of license or who adds a type of vehicle other than a motorcycle to the license shall pay a $10 fee for the required examination.

(f) An applicant applying for additional authorization to operate a motorcycle shall pay a $15 fee for the required application.

(g) If a Class A, B, or C driver's license includes an authorization to operate a motorcycle, the fee for the driver's license is increased by $11.

(h) The fee for issuance or renewal of a driver's license, a provisional license, a learner license, or a hardship license issued to a person subject to the registration requirements under Chapter 62, Code of Criminal Procedure, is $20.

(i) The fee for issuance or renewal of a driver's license is $8 for a license with an expiration date established under Section 521.2711.

(j) The department shall collect an additional fee of $1 for the issuance or renewal of a license to fund the Blindness Education, Screening, and Treatment Program established under Section 91.027, Human Resources Code, if the person applying for or renewing a license opts to pay the additional fee.

(k) A person applying for the issuance or renewal of a license, including a duplicate license or a license issued or renewed over the Internet or by other electronic means, may elect to contribute $1 or more to the identification fee exemption account established under Section 521.4265.

Sec. 521.422. Personal Identification Certificate Fee.

(a) The fee for a personal identification certificate is:

(1) $15 for a person under 60 years of age;

(2) $5 for a person 60 years of age or older; and

(3) $20 for a person subject to the registration requirements under Chapter 62, Code of Criminal Procedure.

(b) The department shall collect an additional fee of $1 for the issuance or renewal of a personal identification card to fund the Blindness Education, Screening, and Treatment Program established under Section 91.027, Human Resources Code, if the person applying for or renewing a personal identification card opts to pay the additional fee.

(c) When a person applies for the issuance or renewal of a personal identification card, including a duplicate personal identification card or a personal identification card issued or renewed over the Internet or by other electronic means, the person may elect to contribute $1 or more to the nonprofit organization administering the Glenda Dawson Donate Life-Texas Registry established under Chapter 692A, Health and Safety Code. The department shall remit any contribution paid under this subsection to the comptroller for deposit to the credit of the Glenda Dawson Donate Life-Texas Registry fund created under Section 692A.020, Health and Safety Code. Before sending the money to the comptroller, the department may deduct money equal to the amount of reasonable expenses for administering this subsection, not to exceed five percent of the money collected under this subsection. The organization shall submit an annual report to the director of the department that includes the total dollar amount of money received by the organization under this subsection.

(d) A person applying for the issuance or renewal of a personal identification card, including a duplicate personal identification card or a personal identification card issued or renewed over the Internet or by other electronic means, may elect to contribute $1 or more to the identification fee exemption account established under Section 521.4265.

Sec. 521.423. Fee for Disability Certificate or Health Condition Certificate [Repealed].

Repealed by Acts 2005, 79th Leg., ch. 1249 (H.B. 1789), § 3(3), effective September 1, 2005.

Sec. 521.424. Duplicate License or Certificate Fee.

The fee for a duplicate driver's license or duplicate personal identification certificate is $10.

Sec. 521.425. Remittance of Fees and Charges.

Each fee or charge required by this chapter and collected by an officer or agent of the department shall be sent without deduction to the department in Austin.

Sec. 521.426. Disabled Veteran Exemption.

(a) Except as provided by Subsection (c), a veteran of service in the armed forces of the United States is exempt from the payment of fees under this chapter for the issuance of a driver's license or personal identification certificate if the veteran:

(1) was honorably discharged;

(2) has a service-related disability of at least 60 percent; and

(3) receives compensation from the United States because of the disability.

(b) The department shall adopt rules relating to the proof of entitlement to this exemption.

(c) Subsection (a) does not apply to a person subject to the registration requirements of Chapter 62, Code of Criminal Procedure.

Sec. 521.4265. Identification Fee Exemption Account.

(a) The identification fee exemption account is created as an account in the general revenue fund of the state treasury. The fund consists of grants and donations made to the department for the purposes of this section, including donations received under Sections 521.421(k) and 521.422(d). The department shall administer the account. Money in the account may be appropriated for the purposes of Subsection (b).

(b) **[As amended by Acts 2021, 87th Leg., ch. XXX (SB 2054)]** From the money in the identification fee exemption account the department shall:

(1) request that the comptroller transfer to the Texas Workforce Commission amounts sufficient to cover the cost of implementing the program under Section 521.168, including amounts sufficient for the payment by the Texas Workforce Commission of:

(A) fees to entities other than the department; and

(B) the Texas Workforce Commission's implementation costs; and

(2) for each exemption granted under Section 521.1015 or 521.1811, deposit to the credit of the Texas mobility fund an amount that is equal to the amount of the waived fee that would otherwise be deposited to the mobility fund.

(b) **[As amended by Acts 2021, 87th Leg., ch. XXX (SB 798)]** For each exemption granted under Section 521.1015, 521.1016, or 521.1811, the department shall deposit to the credit of the Texas mobility fund an amount from the identification fee exemption account under Subsection (a) that is equal to the amount of the waived fee that would otherwise be deposited to the mobility fund.

(c) **[As amended by Acts 2021, 87th Leg., ch. XXX (SB 2054)]** The department may not:

(1) request a transfer under Subsection (b)(1) if the balance of the account for the fiscal year is less than three times the amount expended in the previous fiscal year for the waivers provided by Sections 521.1015(e) and 521.1811; or

(2) grant an exemption under Section 521.1015 or 521.1811 if money is not available in the identification fee exemption account to meet the requirements of Subsection (b)(2).

(c) **[As amended by Acts 2021, 87th Leg., ch. XXX (SB 798)]** The department may not grant an exemption under Section 521.1015, 521.1016, or 521.1811 if money is not available in the identification fee exemption account to meet the requirements of Subsection (b).

(d) The department, in consultation with the Texas Workforce Commission, by rule shall establish a process by which transfers are made under Subsection (b).

Sec. 521.427. Disposition of Fees.

(a) Except as provided by Subsections (b) and (c), each fee collected under this subchapter shall be deposited to the credit of the Texas mobility fund.

(b) Subsection (a) does not apply to:

(1) the portion of a fee collected under Section 521.421(b) or Section 521.421(f), as added by Chapter 1156, Acts of the 75th Legislature, Regular Session, 1997, that is required by Section 662.011 to be deposited to the credit of the motorcycle education fund account;

(2) a fee collected under Section 521.421(j); or

(3) a fee collected under Section 521.422(b) or (c).

(c) [Repealed by Acts 2003, 78th Leg., 3rd C.S., ch. 8 (H.B. 2), § 6.02(1), effective January 11, 2004.]

Sec. 521.428. County or Municipal Fee.

A county or municipality that provides services under an agreement described by Section 521.009 may collect an additional fee of up to $5 for each transaction provided that relates to driver's license and personal identification certificate services only.

SUBCHAPTER S MISCELLANEOUS OFFENSES

Sec. 521.451. General Violation.

(a) Except as provided by Section 521.452, a person may not:

(1) display, cause or permit to be displayed, or have in the person's possession a driver's license or certificate that the person knows is fictitious or has been altered;

(2) lend the person's driver's license or certificate to another person or knowingly permit another person to use the person's driver's license or certificate;

(3) display or represent as the person's own a driver's license or certificate not issued to the person;

(4) possess more than one currently valid driver's license or more than one currently valid certificate; or

(5) in an application for an original, renewal, or duplicate driver's license or certificate:

(A) provide a false name, false address, or a counterfeit document; or

(B) knowingly make a false statement, conceal a material fact, or otherwise commit fraud.

(b) An offense under this section is a Class A misdemeanor.

(c) If conduct that constitutes an offense under Subsection (a) also constitutes an offense under Section 106.07, Alcoholic Beverage Code, the actor may be prosecuted only under Section 106.07, Alcoholic Beverage Code.

Sec. 521.452. Alias Driver's License for Law Enforcement Purposes.

(a) After written approval by the director, the department may issue to a law enforcement officer an alias driver's license to be used in supervised activities involving a criminal investigation.

(b) An application for, or possession or use of, an alias driver's license for a purpose described by this section by the officer to whom the license is issued is not a violation of this subchapter unless the department has canceled, suspended, or revoked the license.

Sec. 521.453. Fictitious License or Certificate.

(a) Except as provided by Subsection (f), a person under the age of 21 years commits an offense if the person possesses, with the intent to represent that the person is 21 years of age or older, a document that is deceptively similar to a driver's license or a personal identification certificate unless the document displays the statement "NOT A GOVERNMENT DOCUMENT" diagonally printed clearly and indelibly on both the front and back of the document in solid red capital letters at least one-fourth inch in height.

(b) For purposes of this section, a document is deceptively similar to a driver's license or personal identification certificate if a reasonable person would assume that it was issued by the department, another agency of this state, another state, or the United States.

(c) A peace officer listed in Article 2.12, Code of Criminal Procedure, may confiscate a document that:

(1) is deceptively similar to a driver's license or personal identification certificate; and

(2) does not display the statement required under Subsection (a).

(d) For purposes of this section, an offense under Subsection (a) is a Class C misdemeanor.

(e) The attorney general, district attorney, or prosecuting attorney performing the duties of the district attorney may bring an action to enjoin a violation or threatened violation of this section. The action must be brought in a court in the county in which the violation or threatened violation occurs.

(f) Subsection (a) does not apply to:

(1) a government agency, office, or political subdivision that is authorized to produce or sell personal identification certificates; or

(2) a person that provides a document similar to a personal identification certificate to an employee of the person for a business purpose.

(g) In this section:

(1) "Driver's license" includes a driver's license issued by another state or by the United States.

(2) "Personal identification certificate" means a personal identification certificate issued by the department, by another agency of this state, by another state, or by the United States.

(h) In addition to the punishment provided by Subsection (d), a court, if the court is located in a municipality or county that has established a community service program, may order a person younger than 21 years of age who commits an offense under this section to perform eight hours of community service unless the person is shown to have previously committed an offense under this section, in which case the court may order the person to perform 12 hours of community service.

(i) If the person ordered to perform community service under Subsection (h) is younger than 17 years of age, the community service shall be performed as if ordered by a juvenile court under Section 54.044(a), Family Code, as a condition of probation under Section 54.04(d), Family Code.

Sec. 521.454. False Application.

(a) A person commits an offense if the person knowingly swears to or affirms falsely before a person authorized to take statements under oath any matter, information, or statement required by the department in an application for an original, renewal, or duplicate driver's license or certificate issued under this chapter.

(b) An information or indictment for a violation of Subsection (a) that alleges that the declarant has made inconsistent statements under oath, both of which cannot be true, need not allege which statement is false and the prosecution is not required to prove which statement is false.

(c) An offense under this section is a Class A misdemeanor.

(d) If conduct constituting an offense under this section also constitutes an offense under another law, the actor may be prosecuted under this section, the other law, or both.

Sec. 521.455. Use of Illegal License or Certificate.

(a) A person commits an offense if the person intentionally or knowingly uses a driver's license or certificate obtained in violation of Section 521.451 or 521.454 to harm or defraud another.

(b) An offense under this section is a Class A misdemeanor.

(c) If conduct constituting an offense under this section also constitutes an offense under another law, the actor may be prosecuted under this section, the other law, or both.

Sec. 521.456. Delivery or Manufacture of Counterfeit Instrument.

(a) A person commits an offense if the person possesses with the intent to sell, distribute, or deliver a forged or counterfeit instrument that is not printed, manufactured, or made by or under the direction of, or issued, sold, or circulated by or under the direction of, a person, board, agency, or authority authorized to do so under this chapter or under the laws of the United States, another state, or a Canadian province. An offense under this subsection is a Class A misdemeanor.

(b) A person commits an offense if the person manufactures or produces with the intent to sell, distribute, or deliver a forged or counterfeit instrument that the person knows is not printed, manufactured, or made by or under the direction of, or issued, sold, or circulated by or under the direction of, a person, board, agency, or authority authorized to do so under this chapter or under the laws of the United States, another state, or a Canadian province. An offense under this subsection is a felony of the third degree.

(c) A person commits an offense if the person possesses with the intent to use, circulate, or pass a forged or counterfeit instrument that is not printed, manufactured, or made by or under the direction of, or issued, sold, or circulated by or under the direction of, a person, board, agency, or authority authorized to do so under this chapter or under the laws of the United States, another state, or a Canadian province. An offense under this subsection is a Class C misdemeanor.

(d) For purposes of this section, "instrument" means a driver's license, driver's license form, personal identification certificate, stamp, permit, license, official signature, certificate, evidence of fee payment, or any other instrument.

(e) If conduct constituting an offense under this section also constitutes an offense under another law, the actor may be prosecuted under this section, the other law, or both.

Sec. 521.4565. Conspiring to Manufacture Counterfeit License or Certificate.

(a) In this section:

(1) "Combination," "conspires to commit," "profits," and "criminal street gang" have the meanings assigned by Section 71.01, Penal Code.

(2) "Conspires to manufacture or produce" means that:

(A) a person agrees with one or more other persons to engage in the manufacture or production of a forged or counterfeit instrument; and

(B) the person and one or more of the other persons perform an overt act in pursuance of the agreement.

(3) "Instrument" means a driver's license, commercial driver's license, or personal identification certificate.

(4) "Public servant" has the meaning assigned by Section 1.07, Penal Code.

(b) A person commits an offense if the person establishes, maintains, or participates in or conspires to establish, maintain, or participate in a combination or criminal street gang, or participates in the profits of a combination or criminal street gang, with the intent to manufacture or produce a forged or counterfeit instrument for the purpose of selling, distributing, or delivering such instrument. An agreement constituting conspiring to manufacture or produce may be inferred from the acts of the parties.

(c) An offense under this section is a state jail felony, except that an offense committed by a public servant is a felony of the third degree.

Sec. 521.457. Driving While License Invalid.

(a) A person commits an offense if the person operates a motor vehicle on a highway:

(1) after the person's driver's license has been canceled under this chapter if the person does not have a license that was subsequently issued under this chapter;

(2) during a period that the person's driver's license or privilege is suspended or revoked under any law of this state;

(3) while the person's driver's license is expired if the license expired during a period of suspension; or

(4) after renewal of the person's driver's license has been denied under any law of this state, if the person does not have a driver's license subsequently issued under this chapter.

(b) A person commits an offense if the person is the subject of an order issued under any law of this state that prohibits the person from obtaining a driver's license and the person operates a motor vehicle on a highway.

(c) It is not a defense to prosecution under this section that the person did not receive actual notice of a suspension imposed as a result of a conviction for an offense under Section 521.341.

(d) Except as provided by Subsection (c), it is an affirmative defense to prosecution of an offense, other than an offense under Section 521.341, that the person did not receive actual notice of a cancellation, suspension, revocation, or prohibition order relating to the person's license. For purposes of this section, actual notice is presumed if the notice was sent in accordance with law.

(e) Except as provided by Subsections (f), (f-1), and (f-2), an offense under this section is a Class C misdemeanor.

(f) An offense under this section is a Class B misdemeanor if it is shown on the trial of the offense that the person:

(1) has previously been convicted of an offense under this section or an offense under Section 601.371(a), as that law existed before September 1, 2003; or

(2) at the time of the offense, was operating the motor vehicle in violation of Section 601.191.

(f-1) If it is shown on the trial of an offense under this section that the license of the person has previously been suspended as the result of an offense involving the operation of a motor vehicle while intoxicated, the offense is a Class B misdemeanor.

(f-2) An offense under this section is a Class A misdemeanor if it is shown on the trial of the offense that at the time of the offense the person was operating the motor vehicle in violation of Section 601.191 and caused or was at fault in a motor vehicle accident that resulted in serious bodily injury to or the death of another person.

(g) For purposes of this section, a conviction for an offense that involves operation of a motor vehicle after August 31, 1987, is a final conviction, regardless of whether the sentence for the conviction is probated.

Sec. 521.458. Permitting Unauthorized Person to Drive.

(a) A person may not knowingly permit or cause the person's child or ward who is under 18 years of age to operate a motor vehicle on a highway in violation of this chapter.

(b) A person may not authorize or knowingly permit a motor vehicle owned by or under the control of the person to be operated on a highway by any person in violation of this chapter.

Sec. 521.459. Employment of Unlicensed Driver.

(a) Before employing a person as an operator of a motor vehicle used to transport persons or property, an employer shall request from the department:

(1) a list of convictions for traffic violations contained in the department records on the potential employee; and

(2) a verification that the person has a license.

(b) A person may not employ a person as an operator of a motor vehicle used to transport persons or property who does not hold the appropriate driver's license to operate the vehicle as provided by this chapter.

Sec. 521.460. Motor Vehicle Rentals.

(a) A person may not rent a motor vehicle to any other person unless the other person holds a driver's license under this chapter or, if a nonresident, holds a license issued under the laws of the state or Canadian province in which the person resides, unless that state or province does not require that the operator of a motor vehicle hold a license.

(b) A person may not rent a motor vehicle to a renter until the person has inspected the renter's driver's license.

(c) Each person who rents a motor vehicle to another shall maintain a record of:

(1) the number of the license plate issued for the motor vehicle;

(2) the name and address of the person to whom the vehicle is rented;

(3) the license number of the person to whom the vehicle is rented;

(4) the date the license was issued; and

(5) the place where the license was issued.

(d) The record maintained under Subsection (c) may be inspected by any police officer or officer or employee of the department.

Sec. 521.461. General Criminal Penalty.

(a) A person who violates a provision of this chapter for which a specific penalty is not provided commits an offense.

(b) An offense under this section is a misdemeanor punishable by a fine not to exceed $200.

CHAPTER 521A ELECTION IDENTIFICATION CERTIFICATE

Sec. 521A.001. Election Identification Certificate.

(a) The department shall issue an election identification certificate to a person who states that the person is obtaining the certificate for the purpose of satisfying Section 63.001(b), Election Code, and does not have another form of identification described by Section 63.0101(a), Election Code, and:

(1) who is a registered voter in this state and presents a valid voter registration certificate; or

(2) who is eligible for registration under Section 13.001, Election Code, and submits a registration application to the department.

(b) The department may not collect a fee for an election identification certificate or a duplicate election identification certificate issued under this section.

(c) An election identification certificate may not be used or accepted as a personal identification certificate.

(d) An election officer may not deny the holder of an election identification certificate the ability to vote because the holder has an election identification certificate rather than a driver's license or personal identification certificate issued under this subtitle.

(e) An election identification certificate must be similar in form to, but distinguishable in color from, a driver's license and a personal identification certificate. The department may cooperate with the secretary of state in developing the form and appearance of an election identification certificate.

(f) The department may require each applicant for an original or renewal election identification certificate to furnish to the department the information required by Section 521.142.

(g) The department may cancel and require surrender of an election identification certificate after determining that the holder was not entitled to the certificate or gave incorrect or incomplete information in the application for the certificate.

(h) A certificate expires on a date specified by the department, except that a certificate issued to a person 70 years of age or older does not expire.

CHAPTER 522 COMMERCIAL DRIVER'S LICENSES

SUBCHAPTER A GENERAL PROVISIONS

Sec. 522.001. Short Title.

This chapter may be cited as the Texas Commercial Driver's License Act.

Sec. 522.002. Construction.

This chapter is a remedial law that shall be liberally construed to promote the public health, safety, and welfare.

Sec. 522.003. Definitions.

In this chapter:

(1) "Alcohol" means:

(A) malt beverages or any other similar fermented beverages or products containing one-half of one percent or more of alcohol by volume, brewed or produced wholly or in part from malt or a malt substitute;

(B) wine, including sake, containing one-half of one percent or more of alcohol by volume; or

(C) distilled spirits, including ethyl alcohol, ethanol, and spirits of wine in any form, and all dilutions and mixtures of distilled spirits from whatever source or by whatever process produced.

(2) "Alcohol concentration" means the number of grams of alcohol for each:

(A) 100 milliliters of blood;

(B) 210 liters of breath; or

(C) 67 milliliters of urine.

(3) "Commercial driver's license" means a license issued to an individual that authorizes the individual to drive a class of commercial motor vehicle.

(4) "Commercial learner's permit" means a permit that restricts the holder to driving a commercial

Transportation Code

motor vehicle as provided by Section 522.011(a)(2)(B).

(5) "Commercial motor vehicle" means a motor vehicle or combination of motor vehicles used to transport passengers or property that:

(A) has a gross combination weight or a gross combination weight rating of 26,001 or more pounds, including a towed unit with a gross vehicle weight or a gross vehicle weight rating of more than 10,000 pounds;

(B) has a gross vehicle weight or a gross vehicle weight rating of 26,001 or more pounds;

(C) is designed to transport 16 or more passengers, including the driver; or

(D) is transporting hazardous materials and is required to be placarded under 49 C.F.R. Part 172, Subpart F.

(6) "Controlled substance" means a substance classified as a controlled substance under:

(A) Section 102(6), Controlled Substances Act (21 U.S.C. Section 802(6)), including Schedules I—V of 21 C.F.R. Part 1308; or

(B) Chapter 481, Health and Safety Code.

(7) "Conviction" means:

(A) an adjudication of guilt, an unvacated forfeiture of bail or collateral deposited to secure the person's appearance in court, a plea of guilty or nolo contendere accepted by the court, the payment of a fine or court costs, or the violation of a condition of release without bail, in a court, regardless of whether the penalty is suspended, probated, or rebated; or

(B) a determination by a court, an authorized administrative tribunal or officer, or the department as authorized by this chapter that:

(i) the person has refused to give a specimen to determine the person's alcohol concentration or the presence in the person's body of a controlled substance or drug while driving a commercial motor vehicle; or

(ii) the person has driven a commercial motor vehicle while the person's alcohol concentration was 0.04 or more.

(8) "Department" means the Department of Public Safety.

(9) "Disqualify" means to withdraw the privilege to drive a commercial motor vehicle, including to suspend, cancel, or revoke that privilege under a state or federal law.

(10) "Domicile" means the place where a person has the person's true, fixed, and permanent home and principal residence and to which the person intends to return whenever absent.

(11) "Drive" means to operate or be in physical control of a motor vehicle.

(12) "Driver's license" has the meaning assigned by Section 521.001, except the term does not include a commercial learner's permit unless otherwise provided by this chapter.

(13) "Drug" has the meaning assigned by Section 481.002, Health and Safety Code.

(14) "Employer" means a person who owns or leases a commercial motor vehicle or assigns a person to drive a commercial motor vehicle.

(15) "Federal act" means the Commercial Motor Vehicle Safety Act of 1986 (49 U.S.C. App. Section 2701 et seq.).

(16) "Foreign jurisdiction" means a jurisdiction other than a state.

(17) "Gross combination weight rating" means the value specified by the manufacturer as the loaded weight of a combination or articulated vehicle or, if the manufacturer has not specified a value, the sum of the gross vehicle weight rating of the power unit and the total weight of the towed unit or units and any load on a towed unit.

(18) "Gross vehicle weight rating" means the value specified by the manufacturer as the loaded weight of a single vehicle.

(19) "Hazardous materials" has the meaning assigned by 49 C.F.R. Section 383.5.

(20) [Repealed by Acts 2001, 77th Leg., ch. 941 (S.B. 866), § 43, effective September 1, 2001.]

(21) "Motor vehicle" means a vehicle, machine, tractor, trailer, or semitrailer propelled or drawn by mechanical power and used on a highway. The term does not include a vehicle, machine, tractor, trailer, or semitrailer operated exclusively on a rail.

(22) "Non-domiciled commercial driver's license" means a commercial driver's license issued by a state to an individual who is domiciled in a foreign jurisdiction.

(22-a) "Non-domiciled commercial learner's permit" means a commercial learner's permit issued by a state to an individual who is domiciled in a foreign jurisdiction.

(23) "Out-of-service order" means:

(A) a temporary prohibition against driving a commercial motor vehicle issued under Section 522.101, the law of another state, 49 C.F.R. Section 383.5, 386.72, 392.5, 392.9a, 395.13, or 396.9, a law compatible with those federal regulations, or the North American Standard Out-of-Service Criteria; or

(B) a declaration by the Federal Motor Carrier Safety Administration or an authorized enforcement officer of a state or local jurisdiction that a driver, commercial motor vehicle, or motor carrier operation is out of service under 49 C.F.R. Section 383.5, 386.72, 392.5, 392.9a, 395.13, or 396.9, a law compatible with those federal regulations, or the North American Standard Out-of-Service Criteria.

(23-a) "Person" includes the United States, a state, or a political subdivision of a state.

(24) "Secretary" means the United States secretary of transportation.

(24-a) "Seed cotton module" means compacted seed cotton in any form.

(25) "Serious traffic violation" means:

(A) a conviction arising from the driving of a motor vehicle, other than a parking, vehicle weight, or vehicle defect violation, for:

(i) excessive speeding, involving a single charge of driving 15 miles per hour or more above the posted speed limit;

(ii) reckless driving, as defined by state or local law;

(iii) a violation of a state or local law related to motor vehicle traffic control, including a law regulating the operation of vehicles on highways, arising in connection with a fatal accident;

(iv) improper or erratic traffic lane change;

(v) following the vehicle ahead too closely; or

(vi) a violation of Sections 522.011 or 522.042; or

(B) a violation of Section 522.015.

(26) "State" means a state of the United States or the District of Columbia.

Sec. 522.004. Applicability.

(a) This chapter does not apply to:

(1) a vehicle that is controlled and operated by a farmer and:

(A) used to transport agricultural products, farm machinery, or farm supplies to or from a farm;

(B) used within 150 miles of the person's farm; and

(C) not used in the operations of a common or contract motor carrier;

(2) a fire-fighting or emergency vehicle necessary to the preservation of life or property or the execution of emergency governmental functions, whether operated by an employee of a political subdivision or by a volunteer fire fighter;

(3) a military vehicle or a commercial motor vehicle, when operated for military purposes by military personnel, including:

(A) active duty military personnel, including personnel serving in the United States Coast Guard; and

(B) members of the reserves and national guard on active duty, including personnel on full-time national guard duty, personnel engaged in part-time training, and national guard military technicians;

(4) a recreational vehicle that is driven for personal use;

(5) a vehicle that is owned, leased, or controlled by an air carrier, as defined by Section 21.155, and that is driven or operated exclusively by an employee of the air carrier only on the premises of an airport, as defined by Section 22.001, on service roads to which the public does not have access;

(6) a vehicle used exclusively to transport seed cotton modules or cotton burrs;

(7) a vehicle, including a vehicle described by Section 504.502(i), that is:

(A) operated intrastate; and

(B) driven by an individual not for compensation and not in the furtherance of a commercial enterprise; or

(8) a covered farm vehicle as defined by 49 C.F.R. Section 390.5.

(b) In this section, "recreational vehicle" means a motor vehicle primarily designed as temporary living quarters for recreational camping or travel use. The term includes a travel trailer, camping trailer, truck camper, and motor home.

Sec. 522.005. Rulemaking Authority.

The department may adopt rules necessary to carry out this chapter and the federal act and to maintain compliance with 49 C.F.R. Parts 383 and 384.

Sec. 522.006. Contracting Authority.

The department may enter into a contract to carry out this chapter, including a contract with an agency of another state or with another organization.

Sec. 522.007. Exemption for Neighboring States.

(a) The public safety director shall enter negotiations with an appropriate person or entity of a state bordering this state for the purpose of applying the exemption contained in Section 522.004(a)(1) to residents of that state.

(b) The public safety director may enter an agreement to apply the exemption contained in Section 522.004(a)(1) to residents of a bordering state only if that state extends a similar exemption to residents of this state.

SUBCHAPTER B LICENSE OR PERMIT REQUIRED

Sec. 522.011. License or Permit Required; Offense.

(a) A person may not drive a commercial motor vehicle unless:

(1) the person:

(A) has in the person's immediate possession a commercial driver's license issued by the department appropriate for the class of vehicle being driven; and

(B) is not disqualified or subject to an out-of-service order;

(2) the person:

(A) has in the person's immediate possession a commercial learner's permit and driver's license issued by the department; and

(B) is accompanied by the holder of a commercial driver's license issued by the department with any necessary endorsements appropriate for the class of vehicle being driven, and the license holder:

(i) for the purpose of giving instruction in driving the vehicle, at all times occupies a seat beside the permit holder or, in the case of a passenger vehicle, directly behind the driver in a location that allows for direct observation and supervision of the permit holder; and

(ii) is not disqualified or subject to an out-of-service order; or

(3) the person is authorized to drive the vehicle under Section 522.015.

(b) A person commits an offense if the person violates Subsection (a).

(c) An offense under this section is a misdemeanor punishable by a fine not to exceed $500, except that the offense is a misdemeanor punishable by a fine not to exceed $1,000 if it is shown on the trial of the offense that the defendant was convicted of an offense under this section in the year preceding the date of the offense that is the subject of the trial.

(d) It is a defense to prosecution under Subsection (a)(1)(A) if the person charged produces in court a commercial driver's license that:

(1) was issued to the person;

(2) is appropriate for the class of vehicle being driven; and

(3) was valid when the offense was committed.

(e) It is a defense to prosecution for a violation of Subsection (a)(2)(A) if the person charged produces in court a commercial learner's permit or driver's license, as appropriate, that:

(1) was issued to the person; and

(2) was valid when the offense was committed.

(f) The court may assess a defendant an administrative fee not to exceed $10 if a charge under this section is dismissed because of the defense listed under Subsection (e).

Sec. 522.012. Restricted License.

(a) If the department is authorized under the federal act to grant the waiver, the department by rule may waive the knowledge and skills tests required by Section 522.022 and issue a restricted commercial driver's license to an employee of a farm-related service industry.

(b) In granting a waiver under this section, the department is subject to any condition or requirement established for the waiver by the secretary or the Federal Motor Carrier Safety Administration.

(c) In addition to any restriction or limitation imposed by this chapter or the department, a restricted commercial driver's license issued under this section is subject to any restriction or limitation imposed by the secretary or the Federal Motor Carrier Safety Administration.

(d) In this section, "farm-related service industry" has the meaning assigned by the secretary or the Federal Motor Carrier Safety Administration under the federal act.

Sec. 522.013. Non-Domiciled License or Permit.

(a) The department may issue a non-domiciled commercial driver's license or commercial learner's permit to a person domiciled in a foreign jurisdiction if the secretary has determined that the commercial motor vehicle testing and licensing standards in the foreign jurisdiction do not meet the testing standards established by 49 C.F.R. Part 383.

(b) An applicant for a non-domiciled commercial driver's license must surrender any non-domiciled commercial driver's license issued by another state.

(c) Before issuing a non-domiciled commercial driver's license, the department must establish the practical capability of disqualifying the person under the conditions applicable to a commercial driver's license issued to a resident of this state. Before issuing a non-domiciled commercial learner's permit, the department must establish the practical capability of disqualifying the person under the conditions applicable to a commercial learner's permit issued to a resident of this state.

(d) "Non-domiciled" must appear on the face of a license or permit issued under this section.

(e) The department may issue a temporary non-domiciled commercial driver's license to a person who does not present a social security card as required by Section 522.021(a-1)(1) but who otherwise meets the requirements for a non-domiciled commercial driver's license, including the requirement that the commercial motor vehicle testing and licensing standards of the country of which the applicant is domiciled not meet the testing and licensing standards established by 49 C.F.R. Part 383. A license issued under this subsection:

Transportation Code

(1) expires on the earlier of:

(A) the 60th day after the date the license is issued; or

(B) the expiration date of any Form I-94 Arrival/Departure record, or a successor document, presented under Section 522.021(a-1); and

(2) may not be renewed.

(f) The department may not issue more than one temporary non-domiciled commercial driver's license to a person.

Sec. 522.014. Permit.

(a) The department may issue a commercial learner's permit to an individual who:

(1) has been issued a driver's license by the department; and

(2) has passed the vision and written tests required for the class of vehicle to be driven.

(b) A commercial learner's permit must be a separate document from a driver's license or a commercial driver's license.

(c) The issuance of a commercial learner's permit is required for:

(1) the initial issuance of a commercial driver's license; or

(2) the upgrade in classification of a commercial driver's license that requires a skills test.

(d) A commercial learner's permit holder may not take a commercial driver's license skills test before the 15th day after the date of the issuance of the permit.

Sec. 522.015. License or Permit Issued by Other Jurisdiction.

A person may drive a commercial motor vehicle in this state if:

(1) the person has a commercial driver's license or a commercial learner's permit issued by:

(A) another state in accordance with the minimum federal standards for the issuance of a commercial motor vehicle driver's license; or

(B) a foreign jurisdiction the testing and licensing standards of which the United States Department of Transportation has determined meet the requirements of the federal act;

(2) the person's license or permit is appropriate for the class of vehicle being driven;

(3) the person is not disqualified from driving a commercial motor vehicle and is not subject to an out-of-service order;

(4) the person has not had a domicile in this state for more than 30 days; and

(5) if the person has a permit, the person also has a driver's license issued by the same jurisdiction that issued the permit.

SUBCHAPTER C LICENSE OR PERMIT APPLICATION AND ISSUANCE

Sec. 522.021. Application; Offense.

(a) An application for a commercial driver's license or commercial learner's permit must include:

(1) the full name and current residence and mailing address of the applicant;

(2) a physical description of the applicant, including sex, height, and eye color;

(3) the applicant's date of birth;

(4) the applicant's social security number, unless the application is for a non-domiciled commercial driver's license and the applicant is domiciled in a foreign jurisdiction;

(5) certifications, including those required by 49 C.F.R. Section 383.71(a); and

(6) any other information required by the department.

(a-1) If the application is for a non-domiciled commercial driver's license and the applicant is domiciled in a foreign jurisdiction that does not meet the testing and licensing standards established by 49 C.F.R. Part 383, the applicant must present:

(1) a social security card issued to the applicant;

(2) an unexpired foreign passport issued to the applicant;

(3) either:

(A) a Form I-94 Arrival/Departure record or a successor document; or

(B) an unexpired employment authorization document; and

(4) documentation demonstrating proof of Texas residence as provided by Section 522.0225 .

(b) The application must be sworn to and signed by the applicant. An officer or employee of the department may administer the oath. An officer or employee of this state may not charge for administering the oath.

(c) The application must meet the requirements of an application under Section 521.141 and must be accompanied by the fee required under Section 522.029. The department may require documentary evidence to verify the information required by Subsection (a).

(c-1) If the department requires proof of an applicant's identity as part of an application under this section, the department must accept as satisfactory proof of identity an offender identification card or similar form of identification issued to an inmate by the Texas Department of Criminal Justice if the applicant also provides supplemental verifiable records or documents that aid in establishing identity.

(d) A person who knowingly falsifies information or a certification required by Subsection (a) commits an offense and is subject to a 60-day disqualification of the person's commercial driver's license, commercial learner's permit, or application. An offense under this subsection is a Class C misdemeanor.

(e) When the department issues a license to which this section applies, the department shall provide the person to whom the license is issued with written information about the Glenda Dawson Donate Life-Texas Registry operated under Chapter 692A, Health and Safety Code.

Sec. 522.022. License Requirements.

The department may not issue a commercial driver's license other than a non-domiciled license to a person unless the person:

(1) has a domicile:

(A) in this state; or

(B) in another state and is a member of the United States armed forces, including a member of the National Guard or a reserve or auxiliary unit of any branch of the armed forces, whose temporary or permanent duty station is located in this state;

(2) has passed knowledge and skills tests for driving a commercial motor vehicle that comply with minimal federal standards established by 49 C.F.R. Part 383, Subparts G and H; and

(3) has satisfied the requirements imposed by the federal act, federal regulation, or state law.

Sec. 522.0225. Verification of Domicile.

(a) The department shall adopt rules for determining whether a domicile has been established under Section 522.022, including rules prescribing the types of documentation the department may require from the applicant to determine the validity of the claimed domicile.

(b) The department may contract with a third-party personal data verification service to assist the department in verifying a claim of domicile, including whether the physical address provided by the applicant is the applicant's actual residence.

Sec. 522.0226. Post Office Box Not Valid As Address.

(a) In this section, "post office box address" means a United States Postal Service post office box address or a private mailbox address.

(b) Unless an exception exists under state or federal law, an applicant may receive delivery of a commercial driver's license at a post office box address only if the applicant has provided the department the physical address where the applicant resides.

(c) The department may require the applicant to provide documentation that the department determines necessary to verify the validity of the physical address provided under Subsection (b).

(d) The department may contract with a third-party personal data verification service to assist the department in verifying whether the physical address provided by the applicant is the applicant's actual residence.

Sec. 522.023. Tests.

(a) The tests required by Section 522.022 must be prescribed by the department.

(b) Except as provided by Subsection (d), the knowledge test must be conducted by the department. The department shall provide each applicant who has a reading impairment an opportunity to take the knowledge test orally or, at the applicant's option, the applicant may have the questions read to the applicant and may answer in writing.

(c) Except as provided by Subsection (d), the department must conduct the skills test.

(d) The department may authorize a person, including an agency of this or another state, an employer, a private driver training facility or other private institution, or a department, agency, or instrumentality of local government, to:

(1) administer the skills test specified by this section if:

(A) the test is the same that would be administered by the department; and

(B) the person has entered into an agreement with the department that complies with 49 C.F.R. Section 383.75; or

(2) administer the knowledge test specified by this section if:

(A) the test is the same that would be administered by the department;

(B) the administration of the test is authorized by federal law; and

(C) the person provides each applicant who has a reading impairment an opportunity to, at the applicant's option:

(i) take the knowledge test orally; or

(ii) have the questions read to the applicant and answer in writing.

(e) The skills test must be taken in a commercial motor vehicle that is representative of the type of vehicle the person drives or expects to drive.

(f) The department may waive the skills test for an applicant who meets the requirements of 49 C.F.R. Section 383.77.

(g) The department shall test the applicant's ability to understand highway traffic signs and signals that are written in English.

(h) An applicant who pays the applicable fee required by Section 522.029 is entitled to three examinations of each element under Section 522.022. If the applicant has not qualified after the third examination, the applicant must submit a new application accompanied by the required fee.

(i) The department may not issue a commercial driver's license to a person who has not passed each examination required under this chapter.

(j) The department may administer a skills test to a person who holds a commercial learner's permit issued by another state or jurisdiction.

Sec. 522.0235. Waiver of Visual Standards for Intrastate Driver.

(a) Except as provided by Subsection (b), the department by rule may provide for a waiver of the visual standards for a commercial driver's license in 49 C.F.R. Part 391, Subpart E, if the person who is applying for a commercial driver's license or who has been issued a commercial driver's license is a person who drives a commercial motor vehicle only in this state.

(b) Subsection (a) does not apply to standards for distant binocular acuity.

Sec. 522.024. Additional Testing.

To ensure compliance with the federal act and to promote the systematic conversion to commercial driver's licenses, the department may require the commercial driver's license testing of a person to whom the department has previously issued a driver's license that authorizes the driving of a vehicle that may be subject to this chapter. The testing may be required before the expiration of an existing license.

Sec. 522.025. Limitations on Issuance of License or Permit.

(a) The department may not issue a commercial driver's license or commercial learner's permit to a person who is disqualified from driving a commercial motor vehicle or while the person's driver's license or driving privilege is suspended, revoked, or canceled in any state.

(b) The department may not issue a commercial driver's license to a person who has a driver's license, commercial driver's license, or commercial learner's permit issued by another state unless the person surrenders the license or permit. The department shall notify the issuing state of the surrendered license or permit.

Sec. 522.026. Limitation on Number of Driver's Licenses; Offense.

(a) A person commits an offense if the person drives a commercial motor vehicle and has more than one driver's license.

(b) It is an affirmative defense to prosecution of an offense under this section that the offense occurred during the 10-day period beginning on the date the person was issued a driver's license.

(c) An offense under this section is a Class C misdemeanor.

Sec. 522.027. Minimum Age.

The department may not issue a commercial driver's license or a commercial learner's permit to a person who is younger than 18 years of age.

Sec. 522.028. Check of Driving Record.

Before issuing a commercial driver's license or commercial learner's permit, the department shall check the applicant's driving record as required by 49 C.F.R. Section 383.73.

Sec. 522.029. Fees.

(a) The fee for a commercial driver's license issued by the department is $96, except as provided by Subsections (f), (h), (j), (k), and (m).

(b) The fee for a commercial driver's license shall be reduced by $4 for each remaining year of validity of a driver's license, other than a commercial driver's license issued by the department to the applicant.

(c) The fee for a duplicate commercial driver's license or commercial learner's permit is $10.

(d) An applicant who is changing a class of license, endorsement, or restriction or who is adding a class of vehicle other than a motorcycle to the license must pay a fee of $10 for the examination, except for a renewal or original issuance of a commercial driver's license.

(e) The fees required by this chapter and collected by an officer or agent of the department shall be remitted without deduction to the department.

(f) If a commercial driver's license includes an authorization to operate a motorcycle, the fee for the driver's license is increased by $8.

(g) An applicant who is applying for additional authorization to operate a motorcycle shall pay a fee of $15 for the examination.

(h) The fee for a commercial driver's license issued under Section 522.033 is $20.

(h-1) The fee for the issuance or renewal of a commercial learner's permit is $24.

(i) Except as provided by Section 662.011, each fee collected under this section shall be deposited to the credit of the Texas mobility fund.

(j) The fee for issuance or renewal of a commercial driver's license is $25 for a license with an expiration date established under Section 522.054.

(k) The fee for a non-domiciled commercial driver's license or a non-domiciled commercial learner's permit is $120. The fee for a temporary non-domiciled commercial driver's license is $20.

(*l*) The fee for the administration of a skills test to a person who is not domiciled in this state is $60.

(m) The fee for a commercial driver's license with a hazardous materials endorsement issued by the department is $60, except as provided by Subsections (h), (j), and (k).

Sec. 522.0295. Voluntary Contribution for Evidence Testing Grant Program.

(a) When a person applies for an original, renewal, corrected, or duplicate commercial driver's license under this chapter, the person may contribute $1 or more to the evidence testing grant program established under Section 772.00715, Government Code.

(b) The department shall:

(1) include space on the first page of each application for an original, renewal, corrected, or duplicate commercial driver's license that allows a person applying for an original, renewal, corrected, or duplicate commercial driver's license to indicate the amount that the person is voluntarily contributing to the grant program; and

(2) provide an opportunity for the person to contribute to the grant program during the application process for an original, renewal, corrected, or duplicate commercial driver's license on the department's Internet website.

(c) The department shall send any contribution made under this section to the comptroller for deposit to the credit of the evidence testing account established under Section 772.00716, Government Code, not later than the 14th day of each month. Before sending the money to the comptroller, the department may deduct money equal to the amount of reasonable expenses for administering this section.

Sec. 522.0296. Voluntary Contribution for Trafficked Persons Program Account.

(a) When a person applies for an original, renewal, corrected, or duplicate commercial driver's license under this chapter, the department shall, in a conspicuous manner, direct that person to the opportunity to donate to the trafficked persons program account established under Section 50.0153, Health and Safety Code, through the state's electronic Internet portal described by Section 2054.252(h), Government Code.

(b) The department may deduct from the donations made under this section an amount equal to the department's reasonable expenses associated with administering this section.

Sec. 522.030. Content of License.

(a) A commercial driver's license or commercial learner's permit must:

(1) be marked:

(A) "Commercial Driver License" or "CDL" for a commercial driver's license; or

(B) "Commercial Learner's Permit" or "CLP" for a commercial learner's permit;

(2) be, to the extent practicable, tamper-proof; and

(3) include:

(A) the name and domicile address of the person to whom it is issued;

(B) the person's photograph;

(C) a physical description of the person, including sex, height, and eye color;

(D) the person's date of birth;

(E) a number or identifier the department considers appropriate;

(F) the person's signature;

(G) each class of commercial motor vehicle that the person is authorized to drive, with any endorsements or restrictions;

(H) the name of this state; and

(I) the dates between which the license is valid.

(b) Except as provided by this section, a commercial driver's license issued under this chapter:

(1) must:

(A) be in the same format;

(B) have the same appearance and orientation; and

(C) contain the same type of information; and

(2) may not include any information that this chapter does not reference or require.

(c) To the extent of a conflict or inconsistency between this section and Section 522.013 or 522.051, Section 522.013 or 522.051 controls.

(d) The department shall ensure that an original or renewal commercial driver's license or

Transportation Code

commercial learner's permit issued under this chapter properly records any diacritical mark used in a person's name. In this subsection, "diacritical mark" means a mark used in Latin script to change the sound of a letter to which it is added or used to distinguish the meaning of the word in which the letter appears. The term includes accents, tildes, graves, umlauts, and cedillas.

Sec. 522.031. Notification of License Issuance.

(a) After issuing a commercial driver's license, the department shall notify the commercial driver's license information system of that fact and provide the information required to ensure identification of the person.

(b) In this section, "commercial driver's license information system" means the information system established under the federal act as a clearinghouse for locating information related to the licensing and identification of commercial motor vehicle drivers.

Sec. 522.032. Change of Name or Address of License or Permit Holder; Offense.

(a) The holder of a commercial driver's license or commercial learner's permit who changes the holder's name or mailing address must apply for a duplicate license or permit not later than the 30th day after the date of the change in the manner provided by Section 521.054.

(b) The holder of a commercial driver's license or commercial learner's permit who changes the holder's residence address shall notify the department not later than the 30th day after the date of the change.

(c) A person commits an offense if the person violates this section. An offense under this section is a Class C misdemeanor.

Sec. 522.033. Commercial Driver's License Issued to Certain Sex Offenders.

(a) The department may issue an original or renewal commercial driver's license or commercial learner's permit to a person whose driver's license or personal identification certificate record indicates that the person is subject to the registration requirements of Chapter 62, Code of Criminal Procedure, only if the person is otherwise eligible for the commercial driver's license or commercial learner's permit and:

(1) applies in person for the issuance of a license or permit under this section; and

(2) pays a fee of:

(A) $20 for a commercial driver's license; or

(B) $24 for a commercial learner's permit.

(b) Notwithstanding Sections 522.013 and 522.051, a commercial driver's license issued under this section, including a renewal, duplicate, or corrected license, expires on the first birthday of the license holder occurring after the date of application, except that:

(1) the initial license issued under this section expires on the second birthday of the license holder occurring after the date of application, subject to Subdivision (2); and

(2) a license issued under this section to a person described by Article 62.2021, Code of Criminal Procedure, expires on the fifth anniversary of the date on which the license was issued.

Sec. 522.034. Application for Authorization to Operate Motorcycle.

(a) An applicant for an original commercial driver's license that includes an authorization to operate a motorcycle must furnish to the department evidence satisfactory to the department that the applicant has successfully completed a basic motorcycle operator training course approved by the department under Chapter 662.

(b) The department may not issue an original commercial driver's license that includes an authorization to operate a motorcycle to an applicant who fails to comply with Subsection (a).

(c) When the department issues a license or permit to which this section applies, the department shall provide the person to whom the license is issued with written information about the Glenda Dawson Donate Life-Texas Registry program established under Chapter 692A, Health and Safety Code.

Sec. 522.035. Recognition and Prevention of Human Trafficking. [Repealed]

SUBCHAPTER D CLASSIFICATION, ENDORSEMENT, OR RESTRICTION OF LICENSE

Sec. 522.041. Classifications.

(a) The department may issue a Class A, Class B, or Class C commercial driver's license or commercial learner's permit.

(b) Class A covers a combination of vehicles with a gross combination weight rating of 26,001 pounds or more, if the gross vehicle weight rating of the towed vehicle or vehicles exceeds 10,000 pounds.

(c) Class B covers:

(1) a single vehicle with a gross vehicle weight rating of 26,001 pounds or more;

(2) a single vehicle with a gross vehicle weight rating of 26,001 pounds or more towing a vehicle with a gross vehicle weight rating of 10,000 pounds or less; and

(3) a vehicle designed to transport 24 passengers or more, including the driver.

(d) Class C covers a single vehicle or combination of vehicles not described by Subsection (b) or (c) that is:

(1) designed to transport 16—23 passengers, including the driver; or

(2) used in the transportation of hazardous materials that require the vehicle to be placarded under 49 C.F.R. Part 172, Subpart F.

(e) The holder of a commercial driver's license or commercial learner's permit may drive any vehicle in the class for which the license or permit is issued and lesser classes of vehicles except a motorcycle. The holder may drive a motorcycle only if authorization to drive a motorcycle is shown on the commercial driver's license and the requirements for issuance of a motorcycle license have been met.

Sec. 522.042. Endorsements; Offense.

(a) The department may issue a commercial driver's license with endorsements:

(1) authorizing the driving of a vehicle transporting hazardous materials, subject to the requirements of Title 49 C.F.R. Part 1572;

(2) authorizing the towing of a double or triple trailer or a trailer over a specified weight;

(3) authorizing the driving of a vehicle carrying passengers;

(4) authorizing the driving of a tank vehicle;

(5) representing a combination of hazardous materials and tank vehicle endorsements; or

(6) authorizing the driving of a school bus, as defined by Section 541.201.

(b) The department may issue a commercial learner's permit with endorsements authorizing the driving of a passenger vehicle, a school bus, or a tank vehicle.

(c) An endorsement under Subsection (b) for a passenger vehicle or a school bus allows a permit holder to operate a vehicle with only the following passengers:

(1) federal or state auditors and inspectors, test examiners, or other permit holders; and

(2) the commercial driver's license holder required under Section 522.011(a)(2)(B).

(d) An endorsement under Subsection (b) for a tank vehicle allows a permit holder to operate only an empty tank vehicle that has been purged of any hazardous materials.

(e) The holder of a commercial driver's license or commercial learner's permit may not drive a vehicle that requires an endorsement unless the proper endorsement appears on the license or permit.

(f) A person commits an offense if the person violates Subsection (c), (d), or (e). An offense under this section is a Class C misdemeanor.

Sec. 522.0425. Hazardous Materials Endorsement; Cancellation.

(a) The department shall cancel or deny the issuance of a hazardous materials endorsement of a person's commercial driver's license within 15 days of the date the department receives notification from a federal agency authorized to make a final determination of threat assessment under 49 C.F.R. Section 1572.13.

(b) On receipt of a notification from a federal agency authorized to make an initial determination of threat assessment under 49 C.F.R. Section 1572.13, the department shall immediately cancel or deny the person the issuance of a hazardous materials endorsement of a commercial driver's license.

(c) The cancellation or denial of a hazardous materials endorsement under this section shall be reported to the commercial driver's license information system before the 16th day after the date of cancellation or denial.

Sec. 522.043. Restrictions; Offense.

(a) On issuing a commercial driver's license, the department for good cause may impose one or more restrictions suitable to the license holder's driving ability and limitations, including restrictions:

(1) prohibiting the license holder from driving a vehicle equipped with air brakes; and

(2) as provided by 49 C.F.R. Part 391, prohibiting driving a commercial vehicle in interstate commerce by a person who:

(A) is under 21 years of age;

(B) does not meet applicable physical guidelines; or

(C) cannot sufficiently read and speak the English language.

(b) For purposes of this section, the department may not administer examinations or tests relating to the applicant's proficiency in the English language, but if an applicant cannot speak English sufficiently to communicate to department personnel the applicant's need for a commercial driver's license, the department may issue to the person a commercial driver's license restricted to operation in intrastate commerce.

(c) A person commits an offense if the person drives a commercial motor vehicle in violation of a restriction. An offense under this section is a Class C misdemeanor.

SUBCHAPTER E EXPIRATION AND RENEWAL OF LICENSE OR PERMIT

Sec. 522.051. Expiration of License or Permit.

(a) Except as provided by Subsections (f) and (i) and Sections 522.013(e), 522.033, and 522.054, an original commercial driver's license expires eight years after the applicant's next birthday.

(b) Except as provided by Subsection (j) and Section 522.054, a commercial driver's license issued to a person holding a Texas Class A, B, C, or M license that would expire one year or more after the date of issuance of the commercial driver's license expires eight years after the applicant's next birthday.

(c) Except as provided by Subsection (k) and Section 522.054, a commercial driver's license issued to a person holding a Texas Class A, B, C, or M license that would expire less than one year after the date of issuance of the commercial driver's license or that has been expired for less than one year expires eight years after the expiration date shown on the Class A, B, C, or M license.

(d) Except as provided by Subsection (l) and Section 522.054, a commercial driver's license issued to a person holding a Texas Class A, B, C, or M license that has been expired for at least one year but not more than two years expires eight years after the applicant's last birthday.

(e) For purposes of this section, a person's "last birthday" is the birthday that occurs on or before the date of issuance, and a person's "next birthday" is the birthday that occurs on or after the date of issuance.

(f) Except as provided by Section 522.013, a non-domiciled commercial driver's license other than a temporary non-domiciled commercial driver's license under Section 522.013(e) expires on:

(1) the earlier of:

(A) the first birthday of the license holder occurring after the eighth anniversary of the date of the application; or

(B) the expiration date of the license holder's lawful presence in the United States as determined by the appropriate United States agency in compliance with federal law; or

(2) the first anniversary of the date of issuance, if there is no definitive expiration date for the applicant's authorized stay in the United States.

(g) A commercial driver's license issued to a person whose residence or domicile is a correctional facility or a parole facility expires on the first birthday of the license holder occurring after the first anniversary of the date of issuance. The department by rule shall establish the fee for a commercial driver's license issued to a person whose residence or domicile is a correctional facility or a parole facility.

(h) A commercial learner's permit expires on the earlier of:

(1) the expiration date of the driver's license or commercial driver's license; or

(2) the 181st day after the date of issuance.

(i) Except as provided by Subsection (f) and Sections 522.013(e), 522.033, and 522.054, an original commercial driver's license with a hazardous materials endorsement expires five years after the applicant's next birthday.

(j) Except as provided by Section 522.054, a commercial driver's license with a hazardous materials endorsement issued to a person holding a Texas Class A, B, C, or M license that would expire one year or more after the date of issuance of the commercial driver's license expires five years after the applicant's next birthday.

(k) Except as provided by Section 522.054, a commercial driver's license with a hazardous materials endorsement issued to a person holding a Texas Class A, B, C, or M license that would expire less than one year after the date of issuance of the commercial driver's license or that has been expired for less than one year expires five years after the expiration date shown on the Class A, B, C, or M license.

(l) Except as provided by Section 522.054, a commercial driver's license with a hazardous materials endorsement issued to a person holding a Texas Class A, B, C, or M license that has been expired for at least one year but not more than two years expires five years after the applicant's last birthday.

Sec. 522.052. Renewal of License.

(a) Except as provided by Subsection (g), a commercial driver's license issued by the department may be renewed in the year preceding the expiration date.

Transportation Code

(b) Except as provided by Section 522.054, a renewal of a commercial driver's license that has been expired for less than one year expires eight years after the expiration date shown on the commercial driver's license.

(c) Except as provided by Section 522.054, a renewal of a commercial driver's license that has been expired for at least one year but not more than two years expires seven years after the applicant's last birthday.

(d) If a commercial driver's license has been expired for more than two years, the person must make an application and meet the requirements for original issuance of a commercial driver's license.

(e) A commercial learner's permit may be renewed once for an additional 180 days without requiring the applicant to retake the general and endorsement knowledge tests.

(f) For purposes of this section, a person's "last birthday" is the birthday that occurs on or before the date of issuance.

(g) A commercial driver's license issued under Section 522.033 or to which Section 522.054 applies may not be renewed before the 60th day preceding the expiration date.

(h) A renewal commercial driver's license issued to a person whose residence or domicile is a correctional facility or a parole facility expires on the first birthday of the license holder occurring after the first anniversary of the date of issuance.

(i) Unless the information has been previously provided to the department, the department shall require each applicant for a renewal or duplicate commercial driver's license to furnish to the department:

(1) proof of the applicant's United States citizenship; or

(2) documentation described by Section 521.142(a).

(j) The department may not deny a renewal or duplicate commercial driver's license to an applicant who provides documentation described by Section 521.142(a) based on the duration of the person's authorized stay in the United States, as indicated by the documentation presented under Section 521.142(a).

(k) Except as provided by Section 522.054, a renewal of a commercial driver's license with a hazardous materials endorsement that has been expired for less than one year expires five years after the expiration date shown on the commercial driver's license.

(l) Except as provided by Section 522.054, a renewal of a commercial driver's license with a hazardous materials endorsement that has been expired for at least one year but not more than two years expires five years after the applicant's last birthday.

Sec. 522.053. License Renewal Procedures.

(a) A person applying for renewal of a commercial driver's license must complete the application form required by the department, including updated information and required certifications.

(b) To retain a hazardous materials endorsement, an applicant must pass the written test for that endorsement.

(c) The department may require an examination, including a vision test, for the renewal of a commercial driver's license.

(d) Before renewing a commercial driver's license, the department shall check the applicant's driving record as required by 49 C.F.R. Section 383.73.

Sec. 522.054. License Expiration: Person at Least 85 Years of Age.

(a) Each original commercial driver's license of a person 85 years of age or older expires on the license holder's second birthday after the date of the license application.

(b) A commercial driver's license of a person 85 years of age or older that is renewed expires on the second anniversary of the expiration date before renewal.

Sec. 522.0541. Denial of Renewal of Commercial Driver License or Learner Permit.

(a) In the manner ordered by a court in another state in connection with a matter involving the violation of a state law or local ordinance relating to motor vehicle traffic control and on receipt of the necessary information from the other state, the department may deny renewal of the commercial driver's license or commercial learner's permit issued to a person by the department for the person's:

(1) failure to appear in connection with a complaint or citation;

(2) failure to pay or satisfy a judgment ordering the payment of a fine and costs; or

(3) failure to answer a citation or to pay fines, penalties, or costs related to the original violation.

(b) The information necessary under Subsection (a) may be transmitted through the commercial driver's license information system and must include:

(1) the name, date of birth, and the commercial driver's license number of the license held by the person;

Transportation Code

(2) notice that the person failed to appear as required by law or failed to satisfy a judgment that ordered the payment of a fine and costs in the manner ordered by the court;

(3) the nature of the violation; and

(4) any other information required by the department.

(c) The department shall apply any notification received under Subsection (a) as a conviction to the person's driving record.

Sec. 522.055. Clearance Notice to Department.

On receipt of notice from the other state that the grounds for denial of the renewal of the commercial driver's license or commercial learner's permit based on the holder's previous failure to appear or failure to pay a fine and costs previously reported by that state under Section 522.0541 have ceased to exist, the department shall renew the person's commercial driver's license or commercial learner's permit.

SUBCHAPTER F NOTIFICATION OF CONVICTION, ADMINISTRATIVE ACTION, OR PREVIOUS EMPLOYMENT

Sec. 522.061. Notification of Conviction to Department or Employer.

(a) A person who holds or is required to hold a commercial driver's license or a commercial learner's permit under this chapter and who is convicted in another state of violating a state law or local ordinance relating to motor vehicle traffic control shall notify the department in the manner specified by the department not later than the seventh day after the date of conviction.

(b) A person who holds or is required to hold a commercial driver's license or commercial learner's permit under this chapter and who is convicted in this state or another state of violating a state law or local ordinance relating to motor vehicle traffic control, including a law regulating the operation of vehicles on highways, shall notify the person's employer in writing of the conviction not later than the seventh day after the date of conviction.

(c) A notification to the department or an employer must be in writing and must contain:

(1) the driver's full name;

(2) the driver's license or permit number;

(3) the date of conviction;

(4) the nature of the violation;

(5) a notation of whether the violation was committed in a commercial motor vehicle;

(6) the location where the offense was committed; and

(7) the driver's signature.

(d) This section does not apply to a parking violation.

Sec. 522.062. Notification of Conviction to Licensing Authority in Other State.

(a) If a person holds a driver's license, commercial driver's license, or commercial learner's permit issued by another state and is finally convicted of a violation of a state traffic law or local traffic ordinance that was committed in a commercial motor vehicle, the department shall notify the driver's licensing authority in the issuing state of that conviction, in the time and manner required by 49 U.S.C. Section 31311.

(b) This section does not apply to a parking violation.

Sec. 522.063. Notification of Disqualification.

A person who is denied the privilege of driving a commercial motor vehicle in a state for any period, who is disqualified from driving a commercial motor vehicle, or who is subject to an out-of-service order shall notify the person's employer of that fact before the end of the first business day after the date the person receives notice of that fact.

Sec. 522.064. Notification of Previous Employment and Offenses.

(a) A person who applies for employment as a commercial motor vehicle driver shall provide the employer, at the time of the application, with the following information for the 10 years preceding the date of application:

(1) a list of the names and addresses of the applicant's previous employers for which the applicant drove a commercial motor vehicle;

(2) the dates between which the applicant drove for each employer;

(3) the reason for leaving the employment of each employer; and

(4) each specific criminal offense or serious traffic violation of which the applicant has been convicted and each suspension, revocation, or cancellation of driving privileges that resulted from the conviction.

(b) The applicant must certify that the information furnished is true and complete. An employer may require an applicant to provide additional information. Before an application is submitted, the employer shall inform the applicant that the information provided by the applicant under this section may be used, and the applicant's previous employers may be contacted, to investigate the applicant's work history.

(c) An employer shall require each applicant to provide the information specified by Subsections (a) and (b).

SUBCHAPTER G UNAUTHORIZED DRIVING

Sec. 522.071. Driving While Disqualified Prohibited.

(a) A person commits an offense if the person drives a commercial motor vehicle on a highway:

(1) after the person has been denied the issuance of a license or permit, unless the person has a driver's license appropriate for the class of vehicle being driven that was subsequently issued;

(2) during a period that a disqualification of the person's driver's license, permit, or privilege is in effect;

(3) while the person's driver's license or permit is expired, if the license or permit expired during a period of disqualification;

(4) during a period that the person was subject to an order prohibiting the person from obtaining a driver's license or permit; or

(5) during a period in which the person, the person's employer, or the vehicle being operated is subject to an out-of-service order.

(b) It is not a defense to prosecution that the person had not received notice of a disqualification imposed as a result of a conviction that results in an automatic disqualification of the person's driver's license, permit, or privilege.

(c) Except as provided by Subsection (b), it is an affirmative defense to prosecution of an offense under this section that the person had not received notice of a denial, disqualification, prohibition order, or out-of-service order concerning the person's driver's license, permit, or privilege to operate a motor vehicle. For purposes of this subsection, notice is presumed if the notice was sent by first class mail to the last known address of the person as shown by the records of the department or licensing authority of another state.

(d) An offense under this section is a misdemeanor punishable as provided for an offense under Section 521.457.

(e) For the purposes of Subsection (a)(5), "commercial motor vehicle" has the meaning assigned by Section 644.001.

Sec. 522.072. Employer Responsibilities.

(a) An employer may not knowingly permit a person to drive a commercial motor vehicle during a period in which:

(1) the person has been denied the privilege of driving a commercial motor vehicle;

(2) the person is disqualified from driving a commercial motor vehicle;

(3) the person, the person's employer, or the vehicle being operated is subject to an out-of-service order in a state; or

(4) the person has more than one commercial driver's license, except during the 10-day period beginning on the date the person is issued a driver's license.

(b) An employer may not knowingly require a driver to operate a commercial motor vehicle in violation of a federal, state, or local law that regulates the operation of a motor vehicle at a railroad grade crossing.

(b-1) An employer who violates Subsection (a) or (b) commits an offense. An offense under this subsection is a Class B misdemeanor.

(c) In addition to any penalty imposed under this chapter, an employer who violates this section may be penalized or disqualified under 49 C.F.R. Part 383.

(d) For purposes of Subsections (a)(1)(C) and (a)(2), "commercial motor vehicle" has the meaning assigned by Section 644.001.

SUBCHAPTER H DISQUALIFICATION FROM DRIVING COMMERCIAL MOTOR VEHICLE

Sec. 522.081. Disqualification.

(a) This subsection applies to a violation committed while operating any motor vehicle, including a commercial motor vehicle. A person who holds a commercial driver's license or commercial learner's permit is disqualified from driving a commercial motor vehicle for:

(1) 60 days if convicted of:

(A) two serious traffic violations that occur within a three-year period; or

(B) one violation of a law that regulates the operation of a motor vehicle at a railroad grade crossing; or

Transportation Code

(2) 120 days if convicted of:

(A) three serious traffic violations arising from separate incidents occurring within a three-year period; or

(B) two violations of a law that regulates the operation of a motor vehicle at a railroad grade crossing that occur within a three-year period.

(b) Except as provided by this subsection, this subsection applies to a violation committed while operating any type of motor vehicle, including a commercial motor vehicle. A person who holds a commercial driver's license or commercial learner's permit is disqualified from driving a commercial motor vehicle for one year:

(1) if convicted of three violations of a law that regulates the operation of a motor vehicle at a railroad grade crossing that occur within a three-year period;

(2) on first conviction of:

(A) driving a motor vehicle under the influence of alcohol or a controlled substance, including a violation of Section 49.04, 49.045, or 49.07, Penal Code;

(B) leaving the scene of an accident involving a motor vehicle driven by the person;

(C) using a motor vehicle in the commission of a felony, other than a felony described by Subsection (d)(2);

(D) causing the death of another person through the negligent or criminal operation of a motor vehicle; or

(E) driving a commercial motor vehicle while the person's commercial driver's license or commercial learner's permit is revoked, suspended, or canceled, or while the person is disqualified from driving a commercial motor vehicle, for an action or conduct that occurred while operating a commercial motor vehicle;

(3) for refusing to submit to a test under Chapter 724 to determine the person's alcohol concentration or the presence in the person's body of a controlled substance or drug while operating a motor vehicle in a public place; or

(4) if an analysis of the person's blood, breath, or urine under Chapter 522, 524, or 724 determines that the person:

(A) had an alcohol concentration of 0.04 or more, or that a controlled substance or drug was present in the person's body, while operating a commercial motor vehicle in a public place; or

(B) had an alcohol concentration of 0.08 or more while operating a motor vehicle, other than a commercial motor vehicle, in a public place.

(c) A person who holds a commercial driver's license is disqualified from operating a commercial motor vehicle for three years if:

(1) the person:

(A) is convicted of an offense listed in Subsection (b)(2) and the vehicle being operated by the person was transporting a hazardous material required to be placarded; or

(B) refuses to submit to a test under Chapter 724 to determine the person's alcohol concentration or the presence in the person's body of a controlled substance or drug while operating a motor vehicle in a public place and the vehicle being operated by the person was transporting a hazardous material required to be placarded; or

(2) an analysis of the person's blood, breath, or urine under Chapter 522, 524, or 724 determines that while transporting a hazardous material required to be placarded the person:

(A) while operating a commercial motor vehicle in a public place had an alcohol concentration of 0.04 or more, or a controlled substance or drug present in the person's body; or

(B) while operating a motor vehicle, other than a commercial motor vehicle, in a public place had an alcohol concentration of 0.08 or more.

(d) A person is disqualified from driving a commercial motor vehicle for life:

(1) if the person is convicted two or more times of an offense specified by Subsection (b)(2), or a combination of those offenses, arising from two or more separate incidents;

(2) if the person uses a motor vehicle in the commission of a felony involving:

(A) the manufacture, distribution, or dispensing of a controlled substance; or

(B) possession with intent to manufacture, distribute, or dispense a controlled substance;

(3) for any combination of two or more of the following, arising from two or more separate incidents:

(A) a conviction of the person for an offense described by Subsection (b)(2);

(B) a refusal by the person described by Subsection (b)(3); and

(C) an analysis of the person's blood, breath, or urine described by Subsection (b)(4); or

(4) if the person uses a motor vehicle in the commission of an offense under 8 U.S.C. Section 1324 that involves the transportation, concealment, or harboring of an alien.

(e) A person may not be issued a commercial driver's license or a commercial learner's permit and is disqualified from operating a commercial motor vehicle if, in connection with the person's operation of a commercial motor vehicle, the person commits an offense or engages in conduct that would disqualify the holder of a commercial driver's license from operating a commercial motor vehicle, or is determined to have had an alcohol concentration of 0.04 or more or to have had a controlled substance or drug present in the person's body. The period of prohibition under this subsection is equal to the appropriate period of disqualification required by Subsections (a)-(d).

(f) In this section, "felony" means an offense under state or federal law that is punishable by death or imprisonment for a term of more than one year.

(g) A person who holds a commercial driver's license or commercial learner's permit is disqualified from operating a commercial motor vehicle if the person's driving is determined to constitute an imminent hazard under 49 C.F.R. Section 383.52. The disqualification is for the disqualification period imposed under that section and shall be noted on the person's driving record.

(h) A disqualification imposed under Subsection (g) must run concurrently with any imminent hazard disqualification that is then currently in effect.

Sec. 522.082. Reinstatement Following Disqualification for Life.

(a) The department may adopt rules establishing guidelines, including conditions, under which a person disqualified for life under Section 522.081(d)(1) may apply to the department for reinstatement of the person's commercial driver's license, if authorized under federal law.

(b) A person is not eligible for reinstatement unless the person has been disqualified for at least 10 years and meets the department's conditions for reinstatement.

(c) If a reinstated driver is subsequently convicted of another disqualifying offense as specified by Section 522.081(b), the person is permanently disqualified and is not eligible for reinstatement.

Sec. 522.083. Update of Records.

After disqualifying a person, the department shall update its records to reflect that action.

Sec. 522.084. Notification to Other Jurisdiction.

After disqualifying a person who has a domicile in another state or in a foreign jurisdiction, the department shall give notice of that fact to the licensing authority of the state that issued the person's driver's license, commercial driver's license, or commercial learner's permit.

Sec. 522.085. Probation of Disqualification Prohibited.

Notwithstanding Section 521.303, if a person is disqualified under this chapter, the disqualification may not be probated.

Sec. 522.086. Issuance of Essential Need or Occupational Driver's License Prohibited.

A person who is disqualified from operating a commercial motor vehicle may not be granted an essential need or occupational driver's license that would authorize operation of a commercial motor vehicle.

Sec. 522.087. Procedures Applicable to Disqualification.

(a) A person is automatically disqualified under Section 522.081(a)(1)(B), Section 522.081(b)(2), or Section 522.081(d)(2). An appeal may not be taken from the disqualification.

(b) Disqualifying a person under Section 522.081(a), other than under Subdivision (1)(B) of that subsection, Section 522.081(b)(1), or Section 522.081(d)(1) or (3) is subject to the notice and hearing procedures of Sections 521.295–521.303. An appeal of the disqualification is subject to Section 521.308.

(c) A disqualification imposed under Section 522.081(a) must run consecutively to any other disqualification that is then currently in effect.

(d) A disqualification imposed under Section 522.081(a)(1)(B) or 522.081(b)(2) or (d)(2) takes effect on the 10th day after the date the department issues the order of disqualification.

Sec. 522.088. Applicability of Other Law.

Section 521.344 of this code and Subchapter I, Chapter 42A, Code of Criminal Procedure, except Article 42A.409 of that subchapter, do not apply to a person disqualified under this chapter.

Sec. 522.089. Effect of Suspension, Revocation, Cancellation, or Denial of License or Permit Under Other Law.

(a) A suspension, revocation, cancellation, or denial of a driver's license, permit, or privilege under Chapter 521 or another law of this state disqualifies the person under this chapter.

(b) If the department disqualifies a person under this chapter for a longer period than the other law, the person is disqualified for the longer period.

Sec. 522.090. Additional Penalty.

In addition to any penalty imposed under this chapter, a person convicted of an offense under Section 522.071(a)(5) may be penalized or disqualified under 49 C.F.R. Part 383.

Sec. 522.091. Recognition of Action Taken by Other State.

(a) The department shall give an out-of-state conviction, disqualification, or denial full faith and credit and treat it for sanctioning purposes under this chapter as if it occurred in this state.

(b) The department may include the conviction, disqualification, or denial on the person's driving record.

Sec. 522.092. Suspension, Revocation, Cancellation, or Denial of Driver's License Under Other Laws.

A person subject to disqualification under this chapter may also have the person's driver's license suspended, revoked, canceled, or denied under one or more of the following, if the conduct that is a ground for disqualification is also a ground for the suspension, revocation, cancellation, or denial of a driver's license suspension under:

(1) Chapter 521;

(2) Chapter 524;

(3) Chapter 601; or

(4) Chapter 724.

Sec. 522.093. Self-Certification of Medical Status.

The department shall remove the commercial driver's license privilege from the holder of a commercial driver's license or a commercial learner's permit if the holder:

(1) fails to provide the department a self-certification of operating status; or

(2) fails to provide and maintain with the department a current medical examiner's certificate that is required based on the self-certification.

SUBCHAPTER I

DRIVING WHILE HAVING ALCOHOL, CONTROLLED SUBSTANCE, OR DRUG IN SYSTEM

Sec. 522.101. Driving While Having Alcohol in System Prohibited.

(a) Notwithstanding any other law of this state, a person may not drive a commercial motor vehicle in this state while having a measurable or detectable amount of alcohol in the person's system.

(b) A person who violates Subsection (a) or who refuses to submit to an alcohol test under Section 522.102 shall be placed out of service for 24 hours.

(c) A peace officer may issue an out-of-service order based on probable cause that the person has violated this section. The order must be on a form approved by the department. The peace officer shall submit the order to the department.

Sec. 522.102. Implied Consent to Taking of Specimen.

(a) A person who drives a commercial motor vehicle in this state is considered to have consented, subject to Chapter 724, to the taking of one or more specimens of the person's breath, blood, or urine for the purpose of analysis to determine the person's alcohol concentration or the presence in the person's body of a controlled substance or drug.

(b) Notwithstanding Chapter 724, one or more specimens may be taken at the request of a peace officer who, after stopping or detaining a person driving a commercial motor vehicle, has probable cause to believe that the person was driving the vehicle while having alcohol, a controlled substance, or a drug in the person's system.

(c) This section and Section 522.103 apply only to a person who is stopped or detained while driving a commercial motor vehicle.

Sec. 522.103. Warning by Peace Officer.

(a) A peace officer requesting a person to submit a specimen under Section 522.102 shall warn the person that a refusal to submit a specimen will result in the person's being immediately placed out of service for 24 hours and being disqualified from driving a commercial motor vehicle for at least one year under Section 522.081.

(b) A peace officer requesting a person to submit a specimen under Section 522.102 is not required to comply with Section 724.015.

Sec. 522.104. Submission of Report to Department.

If a person driving a commercial motor vehicle refuses to give a specimen or submits a specimen that discloses an alcohol concentration of 0.04 or more, the peace officer shall submit to the department a sworn report, on a form approved by the department, certifying that the specimen was requested under Section 522.102 and that the person refused to submit a specimen or submitted a specimen that disclosed an alcohol concentration of 0.04 or more.

Sec. 522.105. Disqualification of Driver.

(a) On receipt of a report under Section 522.104, the department shall disqualify the person from driving a commercial motor vehicle under Section 522.081 beginning on the 45th day after the date the report is received unless a hearing is granted.

(b) Except as provided by Subsection (c), the procedure for notice and disqualification under this section is that specified by Subchapters C and D, Chapter 724, or Chapter 524.

(c) The department shall disqualify the person from driving a commercial motor vehicle for the period authorized by this chapter if, in a hearing held under this section, the court finds that:

(1) probable cause existed that the person was driving a commercial motor vehicle while having alcohol, a controlled substance, or a drug in the person's system;

(2) the person was offered an opportunity to give a specimen under this chapter; and

(3) the person submitted a specimen that disclosed an alcohol concentration of 0.04 or more or refused to submit a specimen.

(d) An appeal of a disqualification under this section is subject to Sections 524.041–524.044.

Sec. 522.106. Affidavit by Certified Breath Test Technical Supervisor.

(a) In a proceeding under this chapter, the certified breath test technical supervisor responsible for maintaining and directing the operation of the breath test instruments in compliance with department rules, in lieu of appearing in court, may attest by affidavit to:

(1) the reliability of the instrument used to take or analyze a specimen of a person's breath to determine alcohol concentration; and

(2) the validity of the results of the analysis.

(b) An affidavit submitted under this section must contain statements regarding:

(1) the reliability of the instrument and the analytical results; and

(2) compliance with state law in the administration of the program.

(c) A certified copy of an affidavit prepared in accordance with this section is admissible only if the department serves a copy of the affidavit on the person or the person's attorney not later than the seventh day before the date on which the hearing begins.

SUBCHAPTER J. ANATOMICAL GIFTS

Sec. 522.151. Definition.

In this subchapter, "registry" means the Glenda Dawson Donate Life-Texas Registry established under Section 692A.020, Health and Safety Code.

Sec. 522.152. Voluntary Contribution to Donor Registry.

(a) When an individual applies for an original or renewal commercial driver's license under this chapter, the individual may contribute $1 or more to the nonprofit organization administering the registry.

(b) The department shall:

(1) include space on each application for a new or renewal commercial driver's license that allows an individual applying for a new or renewal commercial driver's license to indicate that the individual is voluntarily contributing $1 or more to the organization; and

(2) provide an opportunity for the individual to contribute $1 or more to the organization during the application process for a new or renewal commercial driver's license on the department's Internet website.

(c) The department shall remit any contribution made under this section to the comptroller for deposit to the credit of the Glenda Dawson Donate Life-Texas Registry fund created under Section 692A.020, Health and Safety Code. Before sending the money to the comptroller, the department may deduct an amount, not to exceed five percent of the money collected under this section, for the reasonable expenses incurred by the department in administering this section.

(d) The organization shall submit an annual report to the director of the department that includes the total dollar amount of contributions received by the organization under this section.

Sec. 522.153. Statement of Gift; Provision of Registry Information.

(a) An individual who wishes to be an organ, tissue, or eye donor may execute a statement of gift.

(b) The statement of gift may be shown on a donor's commercial driver's license or by a card designed to be carried by the donor to evidence the donor's consent with respect to organ, tissue, and eye donation. A donor card signed by the donor shall be

Transportation Code

given effect as if executed under Section 692A.005, Health and Safety Code.

(c) The donor registry or organ procurement organizations, tissue banks, or eye banks, as those terms are defined by Section 692A.002, Health and Safety Code, shall provide donor registry information to the department and the Texas Department of Transportation. The department, with expert input and support from the nonprofit organization administering the registry, shall:

(1) provide to each applicant for the issuance of an original, renewal, corrected, or duplicate commercial driver's license who applies in person, by mail, over the Internet, or by other electronic means:

(A) the opportunity to indicate on the person's commercial driver's license or personal identification certificate that the person is willing to make an anatomical gift, in the event of death, in accordance with Section 692A.005, Health and Safety Code; and

(B) an opportunity for the individual to consent to inclusion in the registry and release to procurement organizations in the manner provided by Subsection (d); and

(2) provide a means to distribute registry information to interested individuals in each office authorized to issue commercial driver's licenses.

(d) The department shall:

(1) specifically ask each applicant only the question, "Would you like to register as an organ donor?"; and

(2) if the applicant responds affirmatively to the question asked under Subdivision (1), provide the individual's name, date of birth, commercial driver's license number, most recent address, and other information needed for identification purposes at the time of donation to the nonprofit organization contracted to maintain the registry for inclusion in the registry.

(e) An affirmative statement of gift on an individual's commercial driver's license executed after August 31, 2015, shall be conclusive evidence of a decedent's status as a donor and serve as consent for organ, tissue, and eye removal.

(f) The department shall distribute at all field offices Donate Life brochures that provide basic donation information in English and Spanish and include a contact phone number and e-mail address. The department shall include the question required under Subsection (d)(1) and information on the donor registry Internet website in renewal notices.

Sec. 522.154. Revocation of Statement of Gift.

(a) To revoke an affirmative statement of gift on an individual's commercial driver's license, the individual must apply to the department for an amendment to the license.

(b) The fee for an amendment is the same as the fee for a duplicate license.

(c) To have an individual's name removed from the registry, the individual must provide written notice to the nonprofit organization selected under Chapter 692A, Health and Safety Code, to maintain the registry directing the removal of the individual's name from the registry. On receipt of a written notice under this subsection, the organization shall promptly remove the individual's name and information from the registry.

CHAPTER 523
DRIVER'S LICENSE COMPACT OF 1993

Sec. 523.001. Enactment.

The Driver's License Compact of 1993 is enacted and entered into.

Sec. 523.002. Findings and Declaration of Policy.

(a) The states find that:

(1) the safety of their streets and highways is materially affected by the degree of compliance with state laws and local ordinances relating to the operation of motor vehicles;

(2) violation of such a law or ordinance is evidence that the violator engages in conduct which is likely to endanger the safety of persons and property; and

(3) the continuance in force of a license to drive is predicated on compliance with laws and ordinances relating to the operation of motor vehicles in whichever jurisdiction the vehicle is operated.

(b) It is the policy of each of the states to:

(1) promote compliance with the laws, ordinances, and administrative rules and regulations relating to the operation of motor vehicles by their operators in each of the jurisdictions where the operators drive motor vehicles; and

(2) make the reciprocal recognition of licenses to drive and eligibility therefor more just and equitable by considering the overall compliance with motor vehicle laws, ordinances, and administrative rules and regulations as a condition precedent to the continuance or issuance of any license by reason of which the licensee is authorized or permitted to operate a motor vehicle in any of the states.

Sec. 523.003. Definitions.

In this compact:

(1) "Conviction" has the same meaning as provided in Section 522.003.

(2) "Executive director" means the director of the Department of Public Safety or the equivalent officer of another state.

(3) "Home state" means the state which has issued a license or permit and has the power to suspend or revoke use of the license or permit to operate a motor vehicle.

(4) "License" means a license or permit to operate a motor vehicle issued by a state.

(5) "Licensing authority" means the Department of Public Safety or the equivalent agency of another state.

(6) "State" means a state, territory, or possession of the United States, the District of Columbia, or the commonwealth of Puerto Rico.

(7) "Violation" means the commission of an offense related to the use or operation of a motor vehicle, even if there has been no conviction. A suspension by reason of a violation includes a suspension for failure to appear in court or comply with a court order or suspension for violating an implied consent law.

Sec. 523.004. Reports of Convictions.

The licensing authority of a state shall report each conviction of a person from another state occurring within its jurisdiction to the licensing authority of the home state of the licensee. Such report shall clearly identify the person convicted; describe the violation specifying the section of the statute, code, or ordinance violated; identify the court in which action was taken; indicate whether a plea of guilty or not guilty was entered or the conviction was a result of the forfeiture of bail, bond, or other security; and include any special findings made in connection with the conviction. A conviction or judicial or administrative action of a federal or military court or tribunal may be reported to this state subject to this chapter.

Sec. 523.005. Effect of Conviction.

(a) The licensing authority in the home state, for the purpose of suspension, revocation, cancellation, denial, disqualification, or limitation of the privilege to operate a motor vehicle, shall give the same effect to the conduct reported pursuant to Section 523.004 as it would if such conduct had occurred in the home state in the case of conviction for:

(1) manslaughter or negligent homicide resulting from the operation of a motor vehicle;

(2) driving a motor vehicle while under the influence of alcoholic beverages or a narcotic to a degree which renders the driver incapable of safely driving a motor vehicle;

(3) any felony in the commission of which a motor vehicle is used; or

(4) failure to stop and render aid or information in the event of a motor vehicle accident resulting in the death or personal injury of another.

(b) As to other convictions reported pursuant to this compact, the licensing authority in the home state shall give such effect to the conduct as is provided by the laws of the home state.

(c) If the laws of a state do not provide for offenses or violations denominated or described in precisely the words employed in Subsection (a), those offenses or violations of a substantially similar nature and the laws of that state shall be understood to contain such provisions as may be necessary to ensure that full force and effect is given to this compact.

Sec. 523.006. Applications for New Licenses.

On receiving an application for a license to drive, the licensing authority in a state shall ascertain whether the applicant has ever held or is the holder of a license to drive issued by any other state. The licensing authority in the state where application is made shall not issue a license to the applicant if the applicant:

(1) has held a license but the license has been suspended by reason, in whole or in part, of a violation and the suspension period has not terminated;

(2) has held a license but the license has been revoked by reason, in whole or in part, of a violation and the revocation has not terminated, except that after the expiration of one year from the date the license was revoked the person may apply for a new license if permitted by law; the licensing authority may refuse to issue a license to any such applicant if, after investigation, the licensing authority determines that it will not be safe to grant the person the privilege of driving a motor vehicle on the public highways; or

(3) is the holder of a license issued by another state currently in force unless the applicant surrenders such license or provides an affidavit prescribed by the licensing authority that such license is no longer in the person's possession.

Sec. 523.007. Applicability of Other Laws.

Except as expressly required by provisions of this compact, nothing contained herein shall be construed to affect the right of any state to apply any of its other laws relating to licenses to drive to any person or circumstance nor to invalidate or prevent any driver's license agreement or other cooperative arrangement between a member state and a nonmember state.

Sec. 523.008. Compact Administrator and Interchange of Information and Compensation of Expenses.

(a) The compact administrator shall be appointed by the executive director of the licensing authority. A compact administrator may provide for the discharge of his duties and the performance of his position by an alternate. The administrators, acting jointly, shall have the power to formulate all necessary and proper procedures for the exchange of information under this compact.

(b) The administrator of each state shall furnish to the administrator of each other state any information or documents reasonably necessary to facilitate the administration of this compact.

(c) The compact administrator provided for in this compact shall not be entitled to any additional compensation on account of his service as such administrator but shall be entitled to expenses incurred in connection with his duties and responsibilities as such administrator in the same manner as for expenses incurred in connection with any other duties or responsibilities of his office or employment.

Sec. 523.009. Effective Date; Withdrawal from Compact.

(a) This compact shall enter into force and become effective as to any state when it has enacted the compact into law.

(b) Any member state may withdraw from this compact by enacting a statute repealing the compact, but no such withdrawal shall take effect until six months after the executive director of the withdrawing state has given notice of the withdrawal to the executive directors of all other member states. No withdrawal shall affect the validity or applicability by the licensing authorities of states remaining party to the compact of any report of conviction occurring prior to the withdrawal.

Sec. 523.010. Rulemaking Authority.

The licensing authority may adopt any rules and regulations deemed necessary by the executive director to administer and enforce the provisions of this compact.

Sec. 523.011. Construction and Severability.

This compact shall be liberally construed so as to effectuate the purposes thereof. The provisions of this compact shall be severable; if any phrase, clause, sentence, or provision of this compact is declared to be contrary to the constitution of any state or of the United States or the applicability thereof to any government, agency, person, or circumstance is held invalid, the validity of the remainder of this compact and the applicability thereof to any government, agency, person, or circumstance shall not be affected thereby. If this compact is held contrary to the constitution of any state party thereto, the compact shall remain in full force and effect in the remaining states and in full force and effect in the state affected with regard to all severable matters.

CHAPTER 524
ADMINISTRATIVE SUSPENSION OF DRIVER'S LICENSE FOR FAILURE TO PASS TEST FOR INTOXICATION

SUBCHAPTER A
GENERAL PROVISIONS

Sec. 524.001. Definitions.

In this chapter:

(1) "Adult" means an individual 21 years of age or older.

(2) "Alcohol concentration" has the meaning assigned by Section 49.01, Penal Code.

(3) "Alcohol-related or drug-related enforcement contact" means a driver's license suspension, disqualification, or prohibition order under the laws of this state or another state resulting from:

(A) a conviction of an offense prohibiting the operation of a motor vehicle or watercraft while:

(i) intoxicated;

(ii) under the influence of alcohol; or

(iii) under the influence of a controlled substance;

(B) a refusal to submit to the taking of a breath or blood specimen following an arrest for an offense prohibiting the operation of a motor vehicle or an offense prohibiting the operation of a watercraft, if the watercraft was powered with an engine having a manufacturer's rating of 50 horsepower or more, while:

(i) intoxicated;

(ii) under the influence of alcohol; or

(iii) under the influence of a controlled substance; or

(C) an analysis of a breath or blood specimen showing an alcohol concentration of a level specified by Section 49.01, Penal Code, following an arrest for an offense prohibiting the operation of a motor vehicle or watercraft while intoxicated.

(4) "Arrest" includes the taking into custody of a child, as defined by Section 51.02, Family Code.

(5) "Conviction" includes an adjudication under Title 3, Family Code.

(6) "Criminal charge" includes a charge that may result in a proceeding under Title 3, Family Code.

(7) "Criminal prosecution" includes a proceeding under Title 3, Family Code.

(8) "Department" means the Department of Public Safety.

(9) "Director" means the public safety director of the department.

(10) "Driver's license" has the meaning assigned by Section 521.001. The term includes a commercial driver's license or a commercial learner's permit issued under Chapter 522.

(11) "Minor" means an individual under 21 years of age.

(12) "Public place" has the meaning assigned by Section 1.07(a), Penal Code.

Sec. 524.002. Rules; Application of Administrative Procedure Act.

(a) The department and the State Office of Administrative Hearings shall adopt rules to administer this chapter.

(b) Chapter 2001, Government Code, applies to a proceeding under this chapter to the extent consistent with this chapter.

(c) The State Office of Administrative Hearings may adopt a rule that conflicts with Chapter 2001, Government Code, if a conflict is necessary to expedite the hearings process within the time required by this chapter and applicable federal funding guidelines.

SUBCHAPTER B SUSPENSION DETERMINATION AND NOTICE

Sec. 524.011. Officer's Duties for Driver's License Suspension.

(a) An officer arresting a person shall comply with Subsection (b) if:

(1) the person is arrested for an offense under Section 49.04, 49.045, or 49.06, Penal Code, or an offense under Section 49.07 or 49.08 of that code involving the operation of a motor vehicle or watercraft, submits to the taking of a specimen of breath or blood and an analysis of the specimen shows the person had an alcohol concentration of a level specified by Section 49.01(2)(B), Penal Code; or

(2) the person is a minor arrested for an offense under Section 106.041, Alcoholic Beverage Code, or Section 49.04, 49.045, or 49.06, Penal Code, or an offense under Section 49.07 or 49.08, Penal Code, involving the operation of a motor vehicle or watercraft and:

(A) the minor is not requested to submit to the taking of a specimen; or

(B) the minor submits to the taking of a specimen and an analysis of the specimen shows that the minor had an alcohol concentration of greater than .00 but less than the level specified by Section 49.01(2)(B), Penal Code.

(b) A peace officer shall:

(1) serve or, if a specimen is taken and the analysis of the specimen is not returned to the arresting officer before the person is admitted to bail, released from custody, delivered as provided by Title 3, Family Code, or committed to jail, attempt to serve notice of driver's license suspension by delivering the notice to the arrested person;

(2) take possession of any driver's license issued by this state and held by the person arrested;

(3) issue a temporary driving permit to the person unless department records show or the officer otherwise determines that the person does not hold a driver's license to operate a motor vehicle in this state; and

(4) send to the department not later than the fifth business day after the date of the arrest:

(A) a copy of the driver's license suspension notice;

(B) any driver's license taken by the officer under this subsection;

(C) a copy of any temporary driving permit issued under this subsection; and

(D) a sworn report of information relevant to the arrest.

(c) The report required under Subsection (b)(4)(D) must:

(1) identify the arrested person;

(2) state the arresting officer's grounds for believing the person committed the offense;

(3) give the analysis of the specimen if any; and

(4) include a copy of the criminal complaint filed in the case, if any.

(d) A peace officer shall make the report on a form approved by the department and in the manner specified by the department.

Transportation Code

(e) The department shall develop forms for the notice of driver's license suspension and temporary driving permits to be used by all state and local law enforcement agencies.

(f) A temporary driving permit issued under this section expires on the 41st day after the date of issuance. If the person was driving a commercial motor vehicle, as defined by Section 522.003, a temporary driving permit that authorizes the person to drive a commercial motor vehicle is not effective until 24 hours after the time of arrest.

Sec. 524.012. Department's Determination for Driver's License Suspension.

(a) On receipt of a report under Section 524.011, if the officer did not serve a notice of suspension of driver's license at the time the results of the analysis of a breath or blood specimen were obtained, the department shall determine from the information in the report whether to suspend the person's driver's license.

(b) The department shall suspend the person's driver's license if the department determines that:

(1) the person had an alcohol concentration of a level specified by Section 49.01(2)(B), Penal Code, while operating a motor vehicle in a public place or while operating a watercraft; or

(2) the person was a minor on the date that the breath or blood specimen was obtained and had any detectable amount of alcohol in the minor's system while operating a motor vehicle in a public place or while operating a watercraft.

(c) The department may not suspend a person's driver's license if:

(1) the person is an adult and the analysis of the person's breath or blood specimen determined that the person had an alcohol concentration of a level below that specified by Section 49.01(2)(B), Penal Code, at the time the specimen was taken; or

(2) the person is a minor and the department does not determine that the minor had any detectable amount of alcohol in the minor's system when the minor was arrested.

(d) A determination under this section is final unless a hearing is requested under Section 524.031.

(e) A determination under this section:

(1) is a civil matter;

(2) is independent of and is not an estoppel to any matter in issue in an adjudication of a criminal charge arising from the occurrence that is the basis for the suspension; and

(3) does not preclude litigation of the same or similar facts in a criminal prosecution.

Sec. 524.013. Notice of Department's Determination.

(a) If the department suspends a person's driver's license, the department shall send a notice of suspension by first class mail to the person's address:

(1) in the records of the department; or

(2) in the peace officer's report if it is different from the address in the department's records.

(b) Notice is considered received on the fifth day after the date the notice is mailed.

(c) If the department determines not to suspend a person's driver's license, the department shall notify the person of that determination and shall rescind any notice of driver's license suspension served on the person.

Sec. 524.014. Notice of Suspension.

A notice of suspension under Section 524.013 must state:

(1) the reason and statutory grounds for the suspension;

(2) the effective date of the suspension;

(3) the right of the person to a hearing;

(4) how to request a hearing; and

(5) the period in which the person must request a hearing.

Sec. 524.015. Effect of Disposition of Criminal Charge on Driver's License Suspension.

(a) Except as provided by Subsection (b), the disposition of a criminal charge does not affect a driver's license suspension under this chapter and does not bar any matter in issue in a driver's license suspension proceeding under this chapter.

(b) A suspension may not be imposed under this chapter on a person who is acquitted of a criminal charge under Section 49.04, 49.045, 49.06, 49.07, or 49.08, Penal Code, or Section 106.041, Alcoholic Beverage Code, arising from the occurrence that was the basis for the suspension. If a suspension was imposed before the acquittal, the department shall rescind the suspension and shall remove any reference to the suspension from the person's computerized driving record.

SUBCHAPTER C SUSPENSION PROVISIONS

Sec. 524.021. Suspension Effective Date.

(a) A driver's license suspension under this chapter takes effect on the 40th day after the date the person:

(1) receives a notice of suspension under Section 524.011; or

(2) is presumed to have received notice of suspension under Section 524.013.

(b) A suspension under this chapter may not be probated.

Sec. 524.022. Period of Suspension.

(a) A period of suspension under this chapter for an adult is:

(1) 90 days if the person's driving record shows no alcohol-related or drug-related enforcement contact during the 10 years preceding the date of the person's arrest; or

(2) one year if the person's driving record shows one or more alcohol-related or drug-related enforcement contacts during the 10 years preceding the date of the person's arrest.

(b) A period of suspension under this chapter for a minor is:

(1) 60 days if the minor has not been previously convicted of an offense under Section 106.041, Alcoholic Beverage Code, or Section 49.04, 49.045, or 49.06, Penal Code, or an offense under Section 49.07 or 49.08, Penal Code, involving the operation of a motor vehicle or a watercraft;

(2) 120 days if the minor has been previously convicted once of an offense listed by Subdivision (1); or

(3) 180 days if the minor has been previously convicted twice or more of an offense listed by Subdivision (1).

(c) For the purposes of determining whether a minor has been previously convicted of an offense described by Subsection (b)(1):

(1) an adjudication under Title 3, Family Code, that the minor engaged in conduct described by Subsection (b)(1) is considered a conviction under that provision; and

(2) an order of deferred adjudication for an offense alleged under a provision described by Subsection (b)(1) is considered a conviction of an offense under that provision.

(d) A minor whose driver's license is suspended under this chapter is not eligible for an occupational license under Subchapter L, Chapter 521, for:

(1) the first 30 days of a suspension under Subsection (b)(1);

(2) the first 90 days of a suspension under Subsection (b)(2); or

(3) the entire period of a suspension under Subsection (b)(3).

Sec. 524.023. Application of Suspension Under Other Laws.

(a) If a person is convicted of an offense under Section 106.041, Alcoholic Beverage Code, or Section 49.04, 49.045, 49.06, 49.07, or 49.08, Penal Code, and if any conduct on which that conviction is based is a ground for a driver's license suspension under this chapter and Section 106.041, Alcoholic Beverage Code, Subchapter O, Chapter 521, or Subchapter H, Chapter 522, each of the suspensions shall be imposed.

(b) The court imposing a driver's license suspension under Section 106.041, Alcoholic Beverage Code, or Chapter 521 or 522 as required by Subsection (a) shall credit a period of suspension imposed under this chapter toward the period of suspension required under Section 106.041, Alcoholic Beverage Code, or Subchapter O, Chapter 521, or Subchapter H, Chapter 522, unless the person was convicted of an offense under Article 6701*l*–1, Revised Statutes, as that law existed before September 1, 1994, Section 19.05(a)(2), Penal Code, as that law existed before September 1, 1994, Section 49.04, 49.045, 49.06, 49.07, or 49.08, Penal Code, or Section 106.041, Alcoholic Beverage Code, before the date of the conviction on which the suspension is based, in which event credit may not be given.

SUBCHAPTER D HEARING AND APPEAL

Sec. 524.031. Hearing Request.

If, not later than the 15th day after the date on which the person receives notice of suspension under Section 524.011 or is presumed to have received notice under Section 524.013, the department receives at its headquarters in Austin, in writing, including a facsimile transmission, or by another manner prescribed by the department, a request that a hearing be held, a hearing shall be held as provided by this subchapter.

Sec. 524.032. Hearing Date; Rescheduling.

(a) A hearing requested under this subchapter shall be held not earlier than the 11th day after the date on which the person requesting the hearing is notified of the hearing unless the parties agree to waive this requirement. The hearing shall be held before the effective date of the suspension.

(b) A hearing shall be rescheduled if, before the fifth day before the date scheduled for the hearing, a request for a continuance from the person who requested the hearing is received in accordance with the memorandum of understanding adopted under

Section 524.033(c). Unless both parties agree otherwise, the hearing shall be rescheduled for a date not earlier than the fifth day after the date the request for continuance is received.

(c) A person who requests a hearing under this chapter may obtain only one continuance under this section unless the person shows that a medical condition prevents the person from attending the rescheduled hearing, in which event one additional continuance may be granted for a period not to exceed 10 days.

(d) A request for a hearing stays suspension of a person's driver's license until the date of the final decision of the administrative law judge. If the person's driver's license was taken by a peace officer under Section 524.011(b), the department shall notify the person of the effect of the request on the suspension of the person's license before the expiration of any temporary driving permit issued to the person, if the person is otherwise eligible, in a manner that will permit the person to establish to a peace officer that the person's driver's license is not suspended.

Sec. 524.033. State Office of Administrative Hearings.

(a) A hearing under this subchapter shall be heard by an administrative law judge employed by the State Office of Administrative Hearings.

(b) The State Office of Administrative Hearings shall provide for the stenographic or electronic recording of the hearing.

(c) The department and chief administrative law judge of the State Office of Administrative Hearings shall adopt and at least biennially update a memorandum of understanding establishing that the State Office of Administrative Hearings has primary scheduling responsibility for a hearing under this subchapter. The memorandum of understanding must, at a minimum:

(1) set out the roles and responsibilities of the State Office of Administrative Hearings and the department in scheduling a hearing under this subchapter, including which agency is responsible for scheduling each stage of a hearing;

(2) ensure that the State Office of Administrative Hearings and the department have timely access to scheduling and continuance information; and

(3) provide for the transfer of funding for department employees responsible for scheduling hearings under this subchapter from the department to the State Office of Administrative Hearings when the State Office of Administrative Hearings assumes responsibility for initial scheduling of hearings under this subchapter.

(d) The State Office of Administrative Hearings and the department shall consult with the Department of Information Resources and the Office of Court Administration of the Texas Judicial System in developing any information technology solutions needed to complete the transfer of scheduling responsibilities, as outlined in the memorandum of understanding adopted under Subsection (c).

Sec. 524.034. Hearing Location.

A hearing under this subchapter shall be held:

(1) at a location designated by the State Office of Administrative Hearings:

(A) in the county of arrest if the arrest occurred in a county with a population of 300,000 or more; or

(B) in the county in which the person is alleged to have committed the offense for which the person was arrested or not more than 75 miles from the county seat of the county in which the person was arrested; or

(2) with the consent of the person and the department, by telephone conference call.

Sec. 524.035. Hearing.

(a) The issues that must be proved at a hearing by a preponderance of the evidence are:

(1) whether:

(A) the person had an alcohol concentration of a level specified by Section 49.01(2)(B), Penal Code, while operating a motor vehicle in a public place or while operating a watercraft; or

(B) the person was a minor on the date that the breath or blood specimen was obtained and had any detectable amount of alcohol in the minor's system while operating a motor vehicle in a public place or while operating a watercraft; and

(2) whether reasonable suspicion to stop or probable cause to arrest the person existed.

(b) If the administrative law judge finds in the affirmative on each issue in Subsection (a), the suspension is sustained.

(c) If the administrative law judge does not find in the affirmative on each issue in Subsection (a), the department shall:

(1) return the person's driver's license to the person, if the license was taken by a peace officer under Section 524.011(b);

(2) reinstate the person's driver's license; and

(3) rescind an order prohibiting the issuance of a driver's license to the person.

(d) An administrative law judge may not find in the affirmative on the issue in Subsection (a)(1) if:

(1) the person is an adult and the analysis of the person's breath or blood determined that the

person had an alcohol concentration of a level below that specified by Section 49.01, Penal Code, at the time the specimen was taken; or

(2) the person was a minor on the date that the breath or blood specimen was obtained and the administrative law judge does not find that the minor had any detectable amount of alcohol in the minor's system when the minor was arrested.

(e) The decision of the administrative law judge is final when issued and signed.

Sec. 524.036. Failure to Appear.

A person who requests a hearing and fails to appear without just cause waives the right to a hearing and the department's determination is final.

Sec. 524.037. Continuance.

(a) A continuance under Section 524.032 stays the suspension of a driver's license until the date of the final decision of the administrative law judge.

(b) A suspension order may not go into effect pending a final decision of the administrative law judge as a result of a continuance granted under Section 524.039.

(c) If the person's driver's license was taken by a peace officer under Section 524.011(b), the department shall notify the person of the effect of the continuance on the suspension of the person's license before the expiration of any temporary driving permit issued to the person, if the person is otherwise eligible, in a manner that will permit the person to establish to a peace officer that the person's driver's license is not suspended.

Sec. 524.038. Instrument Reliability and Analysis Validity.

(a) The reliability of an instrument used to take or analyze a specimen of a person's breath to determine alcohol concentration and the validity of the results of the analysis may be attested to in a proceeding under this subchapter by affidavit from the certified breath test technical supervisor responsible for maintaining and directing the operation of breath test instruments in compliance with department rule.

(b) An affidavit submitted under Subsection (a) must contain statements on:

(1) the reliability of the instrument and the analytical results; and

(2) compliance with state law in the administration of the program.

(c) An affidavit of an expert witness contesting the reliability of the instrument or the results is admissible.

(d) An affidavit from a person whose presence is timely requested under this section is inadmissible if the person fails to appear at a hearing without a showing of good cause. Otherwise, an affidavit under this section may be submitted in lieu of an appearance at the hearing by the breath test operator, breath test technical supervisor, or expert witness.

Sec. 524.039. Appearance of Technicians at Hearing.

(a) Not later than the fifth day before the date of a scheduled hearing, the person who requested a hearing may apply to the State Office of Administrative Hearings to issue a subpoena for the attendance of the breath test operator who took the specimen of the person's breath to determine alcohol concentration or the certified breath test technical supervisor responsible for maintaining and directing the operation of the breath test instrument used to analyze the specimen of the person's breath, or both. The State Office of Administrative Hearings shall issue the subpoena only on a showing of good cause.

(b) The department may reschedule a hearing once not less than 48 hours before the hearing if a person subpoenaed under Subsection (a) is unavailable. The department may also reschedule the hearing on showing good cause that a person subpoenaed under Subsection (a) is not available at the time of the hearing.

Sec. 524.040. Notice Requirements.

(a) Notice required to be provided by the department under this subchapter may be given by telephone or other electronic means. If notice is given by telephone or other electronic means, written notice must also be provided.

(b) Notice by mail is considered received on the fifth day after the date the notice is deposited with the United States Postal Service.

Sec. 524.041. Appeal from Administrative Hearing.

(a) A person whose driver's license suspension is sustained may appeal the decision by filing a petition not later than the 30th day after the date the administrative law judge's decision is final. The administrative law judge's final decision is immediately appealable without the requirement of a motion for rehearing.

(b) A petition under Subsection (a) must be filed in a county court at law in the county in which the person was arrested or, if there is not a county court at law in the county, in the county court. If the county judge is not a licensed attorney, the county judge shall transfer the case to a district court for the county on the motion of either party or of the judge.

(c) A person who files an appeal under this section shall send a copy of the petition by certified mail to the department and to the State Office of Administrative Hearings at each agency's headquarters in Austin. The copy must be certified by the clerk of the court in which the petition is filed.

(d) The department's right to appeal is limited to issues of law.

(e) A district or county attorney may represent the department in an appeal.

Sec. 524.042. Stay of Suspension on Appeal.

(a) A suspension of a driver's license under this chapter is stayed on the filing of an appeal petition only if:

(1) the person's driver's license has not been suspended as a result of an alcohol-related or drug-related enforcement contact during the five years preceding the date of the person's arrest; and

(2) the person has not been convicted during the 10 years preceding the date of the person's arrest of an offense under:

(A) Article 6701*l*–1, Revised Statutes, as that law existed before September 1, 1994;

(B) Section 19.05(a)(2), Penal Code, as that law existed before September 1, 1994;

(C) Section 49.04, 49.045, or 49.06, Penal Code;

(D) Section 49.07 or 49.08, Penal Code, if the offense involved the operation of a motor vehicle or a watercraft; or

(E) Section 106.041, Alcoholic Beverage Code.

(b) A stay under this section is effective for not more than 90 days after the date the appeal petition is filed. On the expiration of the stay, the department shall impose the suspension. The department or court may not grant an extension of the stay or an additional stay.

Sec. 524.043. Review; Additional Evidence.

(a) Review on appeal is on the record certified by the State Office of Administrative Hearings with no additional testimony.

(b) On appeal, a party may apply to the court to present additional evidence. If the court is satisfied that the additional evidence is material and that there were good reasons for the failure to present it in the proceeding before the administrative law judge, the court may order that the additional evidence be taken before an administrative law judge on conditions determined by the court.

(c) There is no right to a jury trial in an appeal under this section.

(d) An administrative law judge may change a finding or decision as to whether the person had an alcohol concentration of a level specified in Section 49.01, Penal Code, or whether a minor had any detectable amount of alcohol in the minor's system because of the additional evidence and shall file the additional evidence and any changes, new findings, or decisions with the reviewing court.

(e) A remand under this section does not stay the suspension of a driver's license.

Sec. 524.044. Transcript of Administrative Hearing.

(a) To obtain a transcript of an administrative hearing, the party who appeals the administrative law judge's decision must apply to the State Office of Administrative Hearings.

(b) On payment of a fee not to exceed the actual cost of preparing the transcript, the State Office of Administrative Hearings shall promptly furnish both parties with a transcript of the administrative hearing.

SUBCHAPTER E REINSTATEMENT AND REISSUANCE OF DRIVER'S LICENSE

Sec. 524.051. Reinstatement and Reissuance.

(a) A driver's license suspended under this chapter may not be reinstated or another driver's license issued to the person until the person pays the department a fee of $125 in addition to any other fee required by law.

(b) The payment of a reinstatement fee is not required if a suspension under this chapter is:

(1) rescinded by the department; or

(2) not sustained by an administrative law judge, or a court.

(c) Each fee collected under this section shall be deposited to the credit of the Texas mobility fund.

CHAPTER 525 MOTORCYCLE AND BICYCLE AWARENESS

Transportation Code

Sec. 525.001. Motorcycle and Bicycle Awareness.

(a) In this section, "motorcycle" has the meaning assigned that term by Section 502.001, and includes a motorcycle equipped with a sidecar.

(b) The Department of Public Safety shall include motorcycle and bicycle awareness information in any edition of the Texas driver's handbook published after the department exhausts the supply of the handbook that the department had on September 1, 1993.

SUBTITLE C RULES OF THE ROAD

CHAPTER 541 DEFINITIONS

SUBCHAPTER A PERSONS AND GOVERNMENTAL AUTHORITIES

Sec. 541.001. Persons.

In this subtitle:

(1) "Escort flagger" has the meaning assigned by Section 623.008.

(1-a) "Operator" means, as used in reference to a vehicle, a person who drives or has physical control of a vehicle.

(2) "Owner" means, as used in reference to a vehicle, a person who has a property interest in or title to a vehicle. The term:

(A) includes a person entitled to use and possess a vehicle subject to a security interest; and

(B) excludes a lienholder and a lessee whose lease is not intended as security.

(3) "Pedestrian" means a person on foot.

(4) "Person" means an individual, firm, partnership, association, or corporation.

(5) "School crossing guard" means a responsible person who is at least 18 years of age and is designated by a local authority to direct traffic in a school crossing zone for the protection of children going to or leaving a school.

Sec. 541.002. Governmental Authorities.

In this subtitle:

(1) "Department" means the Department of Public Safety acting directly or through its authorized officers and agents.

(2) "Director" means the public safety director.

(3) "Local authority" means:

(A) a county, municipality, or other local entity authorized to enact traffic laws under the laws of this state; or

(B) a school district created under the laws of this state only when it is designating school crossing guards for schools operated by the district.

(4) "Police officer" means an officer authorized to direct traffic or arrest persons who violate traffic regulations.

(5) "State" has the meaning assigned by Section 311.005, Government Code, and includes a province of Canada.

SUBCHAPTER B PROPERTY AREAS

Sec. 541.101. Metropolitan Area.

In this subtitle, "metropolitan area" means an area that:

(1) contains at least one municipality with a population of at least 100,000; and

(2) includes the adjacent municipalities and unincorporated urban districts.

Sec. 541.102. Restricted Districts.

In this subtitle:

(1) "Business district" means the territory adjacent to and including a highway if buildings used for business or industrial purposes, including a building used as a hotel, bank, office building, public building, or railroad station:

(A) are located within a 600-foot segment along the highway; and

(B) within that segment the buildings occupy at least 300 feet of frontage:

(i) on one side of the highway; or

(ii) collectively on both sides of the highway.

(2) "Residence district" means the territory, other than a business district, adjacent to and including a highway, if at least 300 feet of the highway frontage is primarily improved with:

(A) residences; or

(B) buildings used for business purposes and residences.

(3) "Urban district" means the territory adjacent to and including a highway, if the territory:

(A) is not in a municipality; and

Transportation Code

(B) is improved with structures that are used for business, industry, or dwelling houses and located at intervals of less than 100 feet for a distance of at least one-quarter mile on either side of the highway.

SUBCHAPTER C VEHICLES, RAIL TRANSPORTATION, AND EQUIPMENT

Sec. 541.201. Vehicles.

In this subtitle:

(1) "Authorized emergency vehicle" means:

(A) a fire department or police vehicle;

(B) a public or private ambulance operated by a person who has been issued a license by the Department of State Health Services;

(C) an emergency medical services vehicle:

(i) authorized under an emergency medical services provider license issued by the Department of State Health Services under Chapter 773, Health and Safety Code; and

(ii) operating under a contract with an emergency services district that requires the emergency medical services provider to respond to emergency calls with the vehicle;

(D) a municipal department or public service corporation emergency vehicle that has been designated or authorized by the governing body of a municipality;

(E) a county-owned or county-leased emergency management vehicle that has been designated or authorized by the commissioners court;

(F) a vehicle that has been designated by the department under Section 546.0065;

(G) a private vehicle of a volunteer firefighter or a certified emergency medical services employee or volunteer when responding to a fire alarm or medical emergency;

(H) an industrial emergency response vehicle, including an industrial ambulance, when responding to an emergency, but only if the vehicle is operated in compliance with criteria in effect September 1, 1989, and established by the predecessor of the Texas Industrial Emergency Services Board of the State Firemen's and Fire Marshals' Association of Texas;

(I) a vehicle of a blood bank or tissue bank, accredited or approved under the laws of this state or the United States, when making emergency deliveries of blood, drugs, medicines, or organs;

(J) a vehicle used for law enforcement purposes that is owned or leased by a federal governmental entity; or

(K) a private vehicle of an employee or volunteer of a county emergency management division in a county with a population of more than 46,500 and less than 48,000 that is designated as an authorized emergency vehicle by the commissioners court of that county.

(2) "Bicycle" means a device, excluding a moped, that is capable of being ridden solely using human power and has either:

(A) two tandem wheels at least one of which is more than 14 inches in diameter;

(B) three wheels, two of which are in parallel, and at least one of the three wheels is more than 14 inches in diameter; or

(C) any number of wheels and adaptive technology that allows the device to be ridden by a person with a disability.

(3) "Bus" means:

(A) a motor vehicle used to transport persons and designed to accommodate more than 10 passengers, including the operator; or

(B) a motor vehicle, other than a taxicab, designed and used to transport persons for compensation.

(4) "Farm tractor" means a motor vehicle designed and used primarily as a farm implement to draw an implement of husbandry, including a plow or a mowing machine.

(5) "House trailer" means a trailer or semitrailer, other than a towable recreational vehicle, that:

(A) is transportable on a highway in one or more sections;

(B) is less than 45 feet in length, excluding tow bar, while in the traveling mode;

(C) is built on a permanent chassis;

(D) is designed to be used as a dwelling or for commercial purposes if connected to required utilities; and

(E) includes plumbing, heating, air-conditioning, and electrical systems.

(6) "Implement of husbandry" means:

(A) a vehicle, other than a passenger car or truck, that is designed and adapted for use as a farm implement, machinery, or tool for tilling the soil;

(B) a towed vehicle that transports to the field and spreads fertilizer or agricultural chemicals; or

(C) a motor vehicle designed and adapted to deliver feed to livestock.

(7) "Light truck" means a truck, including a pickup truck, panel delivery truck, or carryall truck, that has a manufacturer's rated carrying capacity of 2,000 pounds or less.

Transportation Code

(8) "Moped" means a motor vehicle that is equipped with a rider's saddle and designed to have when propelled not more than three wheels on the ground, that cannot attain a speed in one mile of more than 30 miles per hour, and the engine of which:

(A) cannot produce more than five-brake horsepower; and

(B) if an internal combustion engine, has a piston displacement of 50 cubic centimeters or less and connects to a power drive system that does not require the operator to shift gears.

(9) "Motorcycle" means a motor vehicle, other than a tractor or moped, that is equipped with a rider's saddle and designed to have when propelled not more than three wheels on the ground.

(10) [Repealed.]

(11) "Motor vehicle" means a self-propelled vehicle or a vehicle that is propelled by electric power from overhead trolley wires. The term does not include an electric bicycle or an electric personal assistive mobility device, as defined by Section 551.201.

(11-a) "Multifunction school activity bus" means a motor vehicle that was manufactured in compliance with the federal motor vehicle safety standards for school buses in effect on the date of manufacture other than the standards requiring the bus to display alternately flashing red lights and to be equipped with movable stop arms, and that is used to transport preprimary, primary, or secondary students on a school-related activity trip other than on routes to and from school. The term does not include a school bus, a school activity bus, a school-chartered bus, or a bus operated by a mass transit authority.

(12) "Passenger car" means a motor vehicle, other than a motorcycle, used to transport persons and designed to accommodate 10 or fewer passengers, including the operator.

(13) "Pole trailer" means a vehicle without motive power:

(A) designed to be drawn by another vehicle and secured to the other vehicle by pole, reach, boom, or other security device; and

(B) ordinarily used to transport a long or irregularly shaped load, including poles, pipes, or structural members, generally capable of sustaining themselves as beams between the supporting connections.

(13-a) "Police vehicle" means a vehicle used by a peace officer, as defined by Article 2.12, Code of Criminal Procedure, for law enforcement purposes that:

(A) is owned or leased by a governmental entity;

(B) is owned or leased by the police department of a private institution of higher education that commissions peace officers under Section 51.212, Education Code; or

(C) is:

(i) a private vehicle owned or leased by the peace officer; and

(ii) approved for use for law enforcement purposes by the head of the law enforcement agency that employs the peace officer, or by that person's designee, provided that use of the private vehicle must, if applicable, comply with any rule adopted by the commissioners court of a county under Section 170.001, Local Government Code, and that the private vehicle may not be considered an authorized emergency vehicle for exemption purposes under Section 228.054, 284.070, 366.178, or 370.177, Transportation Code, unless the vehicle is marked.

(14) "Road tractor" means a motor vehicle designed and used to draw another vehicle but not constructed to carry a load independently or a part of the weight of the other vehicle or its load.

(15) "School activity bus" means a bus designed to accommodate more than 15 passengers, including the operator, that is owned, operated, rented, or leased by a school district, county school, open-enrollment charter school, regional education service center, or shared services arrangement and that is used to transport public school students on a school-related activity trip, other than on routes to and from school. The term does not include a chartered bus, a bus operated by a mass transit authority, a school bus, or a multifunction school activity bus.

(16) "School bus" means a motor vehicle that was manufactured in compliance with the federal motor vehicle safety standards for school buses in effect on the date of manufacture and that is used to transport pre-primary, primary, or secondary students on a route to or from school or on a school-related activity trip other than on routes to and from school. The term does not include a school-chartered bus or a bus operated by a mass transit authority.

(17) "Semitrailer" means a vehicle with or without motive power, other than a pole trailer:

(A) designed to be drawn by a motor vehicle and to transport persons or property; and

(B) constructed so that part of the vehicle's weight and load rests on or is carried by another vehicle.

(18) "Special mobile equipment" means a vehicle that is not designed or used primarily to transport persons or property and that is only incidentally operated on a highway. The term:

(A) includes ditchdigging apparatus, well boring apparatus, and road construction and maintenance machinery, including an asphalt spreader, bituminous mixer, bucket loader, tractor other than a truck tractor, ditcher, levelling grader, finishing machine, motor grader, road roller, scarifier, earth-moving carryall and scraper, power shovel or dragline, or self-propelled crane and earth-moving equipment; and

(B) excludes a vehicle that is designed to transport persons or property and that has machinery attached, including a house trailer, dump truck, truck-mounted transit mixer, crane, and shovel.

(19) "Towable recreational vehicle" means a nonmotorized vehicle that:

(A) is designed:

(i) to be towable by a motor vehicle; and

(ii) for temporary human habitation for uses including recreational camping or seasonal use;

(B) is permanently built on a single chassis;

(C) may contain one or more life-support systems; and

(D) may be used permanently or temporarily for advertising, selling, displaying, or promoting merchandise or services, but is not used for transporting property for hire or for distribution by a private carrier.

(20) "Trailer" means a vehicle, other than a pole trailer, with or without motive power:

(A) designed to be drawn by a motor vehicle and to transport persons or property; and

(B) constructed so that no part of the vehicle's weight and load rests on the motor vehicle.

(21) "Truck" means a motor vehicle designed, used, or maintained primarily to transport property.

(22) "Truck tractor" means a motor vehicle designed and used primarily to draw another vehicle but not constructed to carry a load other than a part of the weight of the other vehicle and its load.

(23) "Vehicle" means a device that can be used to transport or draw persons or property on a highway. The term does not include:

(A) a device exclusively used on stationary rails or tracks; or

(B) manufactured housing as that term is defined by Chapter 1201, Occupations Code.

(24) "Electric bicycle" has the meaning assigned by Section 664.001.

Sec. 541.202. Rail Transportation.

In this subtitle:

(1) "Railroad" means a carrier that operates cars, other than streetcars, on stationary rails to transport persons or property.

(2) "Railroad train" means a steam engine or electric or other motor with or without an attached car operated on rails, other than a streetcar.

(3) "Streetcar" means a car, other than a railroad train, used to transport persons or property and operated on rails located primarily within a municipality.

Sec. 541.203. Equipment.

In this subtitle:

(1) "Exhaust emission system" means a motor vehicle engine modification designed to control or reduce the emission of substances from a motor vehicle or motor vehicle engine, of a model year of 1968 or later, and installed on or incorporated in a motor vehicle or motor vehicle engine in compliance with requirements imposed by the Motor Vehicle Air Pollution Control Act (42 U.S.C. Section 1857 et seq.) or other applicable law.

(2) "Metal tire" includes a tire the surface of which in contact with the highway is wholly or partly made of metal or other hard, nonresilient material.

(3) "Muffler" means a device that reduces noise using:

(A) a mechanical design, including a series of chambers or baffle plates, to receive exhaust gas from an internal combustion engine; or

(B) turbine wheels to receive exhaust gas from a diesel engine.

(4) "Solid tire" includes only a tire that:

(A) is made of rubber or another resilient material; and

(B) does not use compressed air to support its load.

SUBCHAPTER D

TRAFFIC, TRAFFIC AREAS, AND TRAFFIC CONTROL

Sec. 541.301. Traffic.

In this subtitle "traffic" means pedestrians, ridden or herded animals, and conveyances, including vehicles and streetcars, singly or together while using a highway for the purposes of travel.

Sec. 541.302. Traffic Areas.

In this subtitle:

(1) "Alley" means a street that:

(A) is not used primarily for through traffic; and

(B) provides access to rear entrances of buildings or lots along a street.

(2) "Crosswalk" means:

(A) the portion of a roadway, including an intersection, designated as a pedestrian crossing by surface markings, including lines; or

(B) the portion of a roadway at an intersection that is within the connections of the lateral lines of the sidewalks on opposite sides of the highway measured from the curbs or, in the absence of curbs, from the edges of the traversable roadway.

(3) "Freeway" means a divided, controlled-access highway for through traffic.

(4) "Freeway main lane" means a freeway lane having an uninterrupted flow of through traffic.

(5) "Highway or street" means the width between the boundary lines of a publicly maintained way any part of which is open to the public for vehicular travel.

(6) "Improved shoulder" means a paved shoulder.

(7) "Laned roadway" means a roadway that is divided into at least two clearly marked lanes for vehicular travel.

(8) "Limited-access or controlled-access highway" means a highway or roadway to which:

(A) persons, including owners or occupants of abutting real property, have no right of access; and

(B) access by persons to enter or exit the highway or roadway is restricted under law except at a place and in the manner determined by the authority that has jurisdiction over the highway or roadway.

(9) "Private road or driveway" means a privately owned way or place used for vehicular travel and used only by the owner and persons who have the owner's express or implied permission.

(10) "Ramp" means an interconnecting roadway of a traffic interchange, or a connecting roadway between highways at different levels or between parallel highways, that allows a vehicle to enter or exit a roadway.

(11) "Roadway" means the portion of a highway, other than the berm or shoulder, that is improved, designed, or ordinarily used for vehicular travel. If a highway includes at least two separate roadways, the term applies to each roadway separately.

(12) "Safety zone" means the area in a roadway officially designated for exclusive pedestrian use and that is protected or so marked or indicated by adequate signs as to be plainly visible at all times while so designated.

(13) "School crossing zone" means a reduced-speed zone designated on a street by a local authority to facilitate safe crossing of the street by children going to or leaving a public or private elementary or secondary school during the time the reduced speed limit applies.

(14) "School crosswalk" means a crosswalk designated on a street by a local authority to facilitate safe crossing of the street by children going to or leaving a public or private elementary or secondary school.

(15) "Shoulder" means the portion of a highway that is:

(A) adjacent to the roadway;

(B) designed or ordinarily used for parking;

(C) distinguished from the roadway by different design, construction, or marking; and

(D) not intended for normal vehicular travel.

(16) "Sidewalk" means the portion of a street that is:

(A) between a curb or lateral line of a roadway and the adjacent property line; and

(B) intended for pedestrian use.

Sec. 541.303. Intersection.

(a) In this subtitle, "intersection" means the common area at the junction of two highways, other than the junction of an alley and a highway.

(b) The dimensions of an intersection include only the common area:

(1) within the connection of the lateral curb lines or, in the absence of curb lines, the lateral boundary lines of the roadways of intersecting highways that join at approximate right angles; or

(2) at the place where vehicles could collide if traveling on roadways of intersecting highways that join at any angle other than an approximate right angle.

(c) Each junction of each roadway of a highway that includes two roadways at least 30 feet apart with the roadway of an intersecting highway, including each roadway of an intersecting highway that includes two roadways at least 30 feet apart, is a separate intersection.

Sec. 541.304. Traffic Control.

In this subtitle:

(1) "Official traffic-control device" means a sign, signal, marking, or device that is:

(A) consistent with this subtitle;

(B) placed or erected by a public body or officer having jurisdiction; and

(C) used to regulate, warn, or guide traffic.

(2) "Railroad sign or signal" means a sign, signal, or device erected by a railroad, public body, or public officer to notify traffic of railroad tracks or an approaching railroad train.

(3) "Traffic-control signal" means a manual, electric, or mechanical device that alternately directs traffic to stop and to proceed.

SUBCHAPTER E MISCELLANEOUS TERMS

Sec. 541.401. Miscellaneous Terms.

In this subtitle:

(1) "Daytime" means the period beginning one-half hour before sunrise and ending one-half hour after sunset.

(2) "Explosive" means a chemical compound or mechanical mixture that:

(A) is commonly intended for use or used to produce an explosion; and

(B) contains ingredients, which may include oxidizing or combustive units, in packing, proportions, or quantities that, if ignited by fire, friction, concussion, percussion, or detonator, could suddenly generate highly heated gases that could damage surrounding objects or destroy life or limb.

(3) "Flammable liquid" means a liquid that has a flash point of not more than 70 degrees Fahrenheit as determined by a tagliabue or equivalent closed-cup test device.

(4) "Gross vehicle weight" means the weight of a vehicle and the weight of its load.

(5) "Nighttime" means the period beginning one-half hour after sunset and ending one-half hour before sunrise.

(6) "Park" or "parking" means to stand an occupied or unoccupied vehicle, other than temporarily while loading or unloading merchandise or passengers.

(7) "Personal injury" means an injury to any part of the human body and that requires treatment.

(8) "Right-of-way" means the right of one vehicle or pedestrian to proceed in a lawful manner in preference to another vehicle or pedestrian that is approaching from a direction, at a speed, and within a proximity that could cause a collision unless one grants precedence to the other.

(9) "Stand" or "standing" means to halt an occupied or unoccupied vehicle, other than temporarily while receiving or discharging passengers.

(10) "Stop" or "stopping" means:

(A) when required, to completely cease movement; and

(B) when prohibited, to halt, including momentarily halting, an occupied or unoccupied vehicle, unless necessary to avoid conflict with other traffic or to comply with the directions of a police officer or a traffic-control sign or signal.

CHAPTER 542 GENERAL PROVISIONS

SUBCHAPTER A APPLICABILITY

Sec. 542.001. Vehicles on Highways.

A provision of this subtitle relating to the operation of a vehicle applies only to the operation of a vehicle on a highway unless the provision specifically applies to a different place.

Sec. 542.002. Government Vehicles.

A provision of this subtitle applicable to an operator of a vehicle applies to the operator of a vehicle owned or operated by the United States, this state, or a political subdivision of this state, except as specifically provided otherwise by this subtitle for an authorized emergency vehicle.

Sec. 542.003. Animals and Animal-Drawn Vehicles.

A person riding an animal on a roadway or operating a vehicle drawn by an animal on a roadway has the rights and duties applicable to the operator of a vehicle under this subtitle, except a right or duty that by its nature cannot apply to a person riding an animal or operating a vehicle drawn by an animal.

Sec. 542.004. Persons and Equipment Engaged in Work on Highway Surface.

This subtitle does not apply to a person, team, motor vehicle, or other equipment engaged in work on a highway unless the provision is specifically made applicable, but does apply to those persons and vehicles while traveling to or from that work.

Sec. 542.005. Rules on Private Property.

This subtitle does not prevent an owner of private property that is a private road from:

(1) regulating or prohibiting use of the property by the public for vehicular travel; or

(2) requiring conditions different from or in addition to those specified by this subtitle.

Sec. 542.006. Speed Restrictions on Private Roads.

(a) The owners of a majority of the parcels of real property abutting a private road may petition the

Texas Transportation Commission to extend the speed restrictions of this subtitle to the portion of the road in a subdivision or across adjacent subdivisions if:

(1) the road is not in a municipality;

(2) the total number of residents in the subdivision and subdivisions adjacent to the subdivision is at least 400; and

(3) a plat for the subdivision and each adjacent subdivision included to determine the number of residents under Subdivision (2) has been filed in the deed records of the county.

(b) After the commission receives a petition and verifies the property ownership of its signers, the commission may issue an order extending the speed restrictions to the private road if the commission finds the order is in the interests of the area residents and the public generally.

(c) If the commission rejects the petition, the commission shall hold a public hearing on the advisability of making the speed restrictions applicable. The hearing must be held in the county in which the portion of the road that is the subject of the petition is located. The commission shall publish notice of the hearing in a newspaper of general circulation in that county at least 10 days before the date of the hearing.

(d) At the hearing, if the commission finds that it would be in the interests of the area residents and the public generally, the commission shall issue an order extending the speed restrictions to the private road.

(e) After the commission issues an order under this section, the private road is a public highway for purposes of setting and enforcing speed restrictions under this subtitle, and the commission shall post speed limit signs on property abutting the private road with the consent of the owner of the property on which a sign is placed.

Sec. 542.007. Traffic Regulations: Private Subdivision in Certain Counties.

(a) This section applies only to a subdivision that is located in the unincorporated area of a county with a population of 500,000 or less.

(b) On petition of 25 percent of the property owners residing in a subdivision in which the roads are privately maintained or on the request of the governing body of the entity that maintains those roads, the commissioners court of the county by order may extend any traffic rules that apply to a county road to the roads of the subdivision if the commissioners court finds the order in the interest of the county generally. The petition must specify the traffic rules that are sought to be extended. The court order may extend any or all of the requested traffic rules.

(c) As a condition of extending a traffic rule under Subsection (b), the commissioners court may require that owners of the property in the subdivision pay all or part of the cost of extending and enforcing the traffic rules in the subdivision. The commissioners court shall consult with the sheriff to determine the cost of enforcing traffic rules in the subdivision.

(d) On issuance of an order under this section, the private roads in the subdivision are considered to be county roads for purposes of the application and enforcement of the specified traffic rules. The commissioners court may place official traffic control devices on property abutting the private roads if:

(1) those devices relate to the specified traffic rule; and

(2) the consent of the owner of that property is obtained.

Sec. 542.008. Traffic Regulations: Private Subdivisions in Certain Municipalities.

(a) This section applies only to a subdivision in which the roads are privately owned or maintained that is located in a municipality with a population of 300 or more.

(b) On petition of 25 percent of the property owners residing in the subdivision or on the request of the governing body of the entity that maintains the roads, the governing body of the municipality may extend by ordinance any traffic rules that apply to a road owned by the municipality, or by the county in which the municipality is located, to the roads in the subdivision so that the roads of the subdivision are under the same traffic rules, if the governing body of the municipality finds the ordinance in the interest of the municipality generally. A petition under this subsection must specify the traffic rules that are sought to be extended. The ordinance may extend any or all of the requested rules.

(c) As a condition of extending a traffic rule under Subsection (b), the governing body of the municipality may require that owners of property in the subdivision pay all or part of the cost of extending and enforcing the traffic rules in the subdivision, including the costs associated with the placement of necessary official traffic control devices. The governing body of the municipality shall consult with the appropriate law enforcement entity to determine the cost of enforcing traffic rules in the subdivision.

(d) On issuance of an order under this section, the private roads in the subdivision are considered to be public highways or streets for purposes of the application and enforcement of the specified traffic rules. The governing body of the municipality may place official traffic control devices on property abutting the private roads if:

(1) those devices relate to the specified traffic rule; and

(2) the consent of the owner of that property is obtained or an easement is available for the placement.

Sec. 542.0081. Traffic Regulations: Special District in Certain Counties.

(a) This section applies only to a road owned or maintained by a special district that is located in the unincorporated area of a county with a population of less than one million.

(b) The residents of all or any portion of a special district may file a petition with the commissioners court of the county in which the roads are located requesting that county enforcement of traffic rules on county roads be extended to the roads of the district. The petition must:

(1) specify the roads over which county enforcement is sought;

(2) specify the traffic rules for which county enforcement is sought; and

(3) be signed by 50 percent of the property owners residing in the area that is served by the roads of the district over which county enforcement is sought.

(c) If the commissioners court finds that granting the request is in the interest of the county generally, the commissioners court shall by order extend the enforcement of traffic rules by the county to the roads of the district specified in the petition. The order may grant enforcement of some or all traffic rules requested in the petition.

(d) As a condition of extending a traffic rule under Subsection (c), the commissioners court may require the special district to pay for all or a part of the costs of extending enforcement to the roads of the district. The commissioners court shall consult with the sheriff to determine the cost of extending enforcement.

(e) On issuance of an order under this section, the roads specified in the order are considered to be county roads for the purposes of the application and enforcement of the specified traffic rules. The commissioners court may place official traffic control devices on the right-of-way of the roads of the district if those devices relate to the specified traffic rules.

Sec. 542.009. Operators of Certain Mobility Devices. [Renumbered]

SUBCHAPTER B UNIFORMITY AND INTERPRETATION OF TRAFFIC LAWS

Sec. 542.201. General Rule of Uniformity.

This subtitle applies uniformly throughout this state. A local authority may not enact or enforce an ordinance or rule that conflicts with this subtitle unless expressly authorized by this subtitle. However, a local authority may regulate traffic in a manner that does not conflict with this subtitle.

Sec. 542.202. Powers of Local Authorities.

(a) This subtitle does not prevent a local authority, with respect to a highway under its jurisdiction and in the reasonable exercise of the police power, from:

(1) regulating traffic by police officers or traffic-control devices;

(2) regulating the stopping, standing, or parking of a vehicle;

(3) regulating or prohibiting a procession or assemblage on a highway;

(4) regulating the operation and requiring registration and licensing of a bicycle or electric bicycle, including payment of a registration fee, except as provided by Section 551.106;

(5) regulating the time, place, and manner in which a roller skater may use a highway;

(6) regulating the speed of a vehicle in a public park;

(7) regulating or prohibiting the turning of a vehicle or specified type of vehicle at an intersection;

(8) designating an intersection as a stop intersection or a yield intersection and requiring each vehicle to stop or yield at one or more entrances to the intersection;

(9) designating a highway as a through highway;

(10) designating a highway as a one-way highway and requiring each vehicle on the highway to move in one specific direction;

(11) designating school crossing guards and school crossing zones;

(12) altering a speed limit as authorized by this subtitle; or

(13) adopting other traffic rules specifically authorized by this subtitle.

(b) In this section:

(1) "Roller skater" means a person wearing footwear with a set of wheels attached.

(2) "Through highway" means a highway or a portion of a highway on which:

(A) vehicular traffic is given preferential right-of-way; and

(B) vehicular traffic entering from an intersecting highway is required by law to yield right-of-way in compliance with an official traffic-control device.

(3) "Regulating" means criminal, civil, and administrative enforcement against a person, including the owner or operator of a motor vehicle, in accordance with a state law or a municipal ordinance.

Sec. 542.203. Limitation on Local Authorities.

(a) A local authority may not erect or maintain a traffic-control device to direct the traffic on a state highway, including a farm-to-market or ranch-to-market road, to stop or yield before entering or crossing an intersecting highway unless permitted by agreement between the local authority and the Texas Department of Transportation under Section 221.002.

(b) An ordinance or rule of a local authority is not effective until signs giving notice are posted on or at the entrance to the highway or part of the highway, as may be most appropriate. This subsection applies only to an ordinance or rule that:

(1) regulates the speed of a vehicle in a public park;

(2) alters a speed limit as authorized by this subtitle;

(3) designates an intersection as a stop intersection or a yield intersection; or

(4) designates a highway as a one-way highway or a through highway.

(c) An ordinance or rule of a local authority regulating the time, place, and manner in which a roller skater may use a highway may not alter the local authority's standard of care or liability with regard to construction, design, or maintenance of a highway.

Sec. 542.2035. Limitation on Municipalities.

(a) A municipality may not implement or operate an automated traffic control system with respect to a highway or street under its jurisdiction for the purpose of enforcing compliance with posted speed limits. The attorney general shall enforce this subsection.

(b) In this section, "automated traffic control system" means a photographic device, radar device, laser device, or other electrical or mechanical device designed to:

(1) record the speed of a motor vehicle; and

(2) obtain one or more photographs or other recorded images of:

(A) the vehicle;

(B) the license plate attached to the vehicle; or

(C) the operator of the vehicle.

Sec. 542.204. Powers Related to Intersections.

The Texas Transportation Commission and a local authority may, in a matter of highway or traffic engineering design, consider the separate intersections of divided highways with medians at least 30 feet apart as components of a single intersection.

Sec. 542.205. Conflict Between This Subtitle and an Order, Rule, or Regulation of Certain Agencies.

(a) If this subtitle conflicts with an order, rule, regulation, or requirement of the federal Surface Transportation Board or the department relating to a vehicle safety requirement, including a requirement relating to vehicle equipment, compliance by the owner or operator of the vehicle with the order, rule, regulation, or requirement of the federal Surface Transportation Board or the department is compliance with this subtitle.

(b) The owner or operator of a vehicle shall comply with any requirement of this subtitle that is in addition to, but not in conflict with, a requirement of the federal Surface Transportation Board or the department.

Sec. 542.206. Effect of Speed Limits in a Civil Action.

A provision of this subtitle declaring a maximum or minimum speed limit does not relieve the plaintiff in a civil action from the burden of proving negligence of the defendant as the proximate cause of an accident.

SUBCHAPTER C
OFFENSES

Sec. 542.301. General Offense.

(a) A person commits an offense if the person performs an act prohibited or fails to perform an act required by this subtitle.

(b) Except as otherwise provided, an offense under this subtitle is a misdemeanor.

Sec. 542.302. Offense by Person Owning or Controlling Vehicle.

A person who owns a vehicle or employs or otherwise directs the operator of a vehicle commits an offense if the person requires or knowingly permits the operator of the vehicle to operate the vehicle in a manner that violates law.

Sec. 542.303. Inchoate Offense.

(a) A person who attempts to commit or conspires to commit an act declared by this subtitle to be an offense is guilty of the offense.

(b) A person who falsely, fraudulently, or wilfully permits another to violate this subtitle is guilty of the violation.

Sec. 542.304. Moving Violations for Certain Purposes.

(a) **[As amended by Acts 2021, 87th Leg., ch. XXX (HB 1560)]** The department by rule shall designate the offenses involving the operation of a motor vehicle that constitute a moving violation of the traffic law for the purposes of:

(1) Section 1001.112(b)(4), Education Code;

(2) Section 411.110(f), Government Code; and

(3) Sections 773.0614(b) and 773.06141(a), Health and Safety Code.

(a) **[As amended by Acts 2021, 87th Leg., ch, XXX (HB 3607)]** The department by rule shall designate the offenses involving the operation of a motor vehicle that constitute a moving violation of the traffic law for the purposes of:

(1) Section 1001.112(a-2), Education Code;

(2) Section 411.110(f), Government Code; and

(3) Sections 773.0614(b) and 773.06141(a), Health and Safety Code.

(b) The rules must provide that for the purposes of the provisions described in Subsection (a), moving violations:

(1) include:

(A) a violation of the traffic law of this state, another state, or a political subdivision of this or another state; and

(B) an offense under Section 545.412; and

(2) do not include:

(A) an offense committed before September 1, 2003;

(B) the offense of speeding when the person convicted was at the time of the offense driving less than 10 percent faster than the posted speed limit, unless the person committed the offense in a school crossing zone;

(C) an offense adjudicated under Article 45.051 or 45.0511, Code of Criminal Procedure; or

(D) an offense under Section 545.4251.

SUBCHAPTER D PENALTIES AND COSTS OF COURT

Sec. 542.401. General Penalty.

A person convicted of an offense that is a misdemeanor under this subtitle for which another penalty is not provided shall be punished by a fine of not less than $1 or more than $200.

Sec. 542.402. Disposition of Fines.

(a) Except as provided by Subsection (b-1), a municipality or county shall use a fine collected for a violation of a highway law in this title to:

(1) construct and maintain roads, bridges, and culverts in the municipality or county;

(2) enforce laws regulating the use of highways by motor vehicles; and

(3) defray the expense of county traffic officers.

(b) In each fiscal year, a municipality having a population of less than 5,000 may retain, from fines collected for violations of this title and fines collected under Article 45.051(a), Code of Criminal Procedure, in cases in which a violation of this title is alleged, an amount equal to 30 percent of the municipality's revenue for the preceding fiscal year from all sources, other than federal funds and bond proceeds, as shown by the audit performed under Section 103.001, Local Government Code. After a municipality has retained that amount, the municipality shall send to the comptroller any portion of a fine collected that exceeds $1.

(b-1) Subject to Subsection (b-2), a county may use a fine collected for a violation of a highway law as the county determines appropriate if:

(1) the county has a population of less than 5,000; and

(2) the commissioners court of the county by resolution elects to spend the revenue in a manner other than as provided by Subsection (a).

(b-2) In each fiscal year, a county described by Subsection (b-1) may retain, from fines collected for violations of this title and from fines collected under Article 45.051(a), Code of Criminal Procedure, in cases in which a violation of this title is alleged, an amount equal to 30 percent of the county's revenue for the preceding fiscal year from all sources, other than federal funds and bond proceeds, as shown by an audit performed under Chapter 115, Local Government Code. After a county has retained that amount, the county shall send to the comptroller any portion of a fine collected that exceeds $1.

(c) The comptroller shall enforce Subsections (b) and (b-2).

(d) In a fiscal year in which a municipality retains from fines and special expenses collected for violations of this title an amount equal to at least 20 percent of the municipality's revenue for the preceding fiscal year from all sources other than federal funds and bond proceeds, not later than the 120th day after the last day of the municipality's fiscal year, the municipality shall send to the comptroller:

(1) a copy of the municipality's financial statement for that fiscal year filed under Chapter 103, Local Government Code; and

(2) a report that shows the total amount collected for that fiscal year from fines under Subsection (b).

(d-1) In a fiscal year in which a county retains from fines and special expenses collected for violations of this title an amount equal to at least 20 percent of the county's revenue for the preceding fiscal year from all sources other than federal funds and bond proceeds, not later than the 120th day after the last day of the county's fiscal year, the county shall send to the comptroller:

(1) a copy of the county's financial statement; and

(2) a report that shows the total amount collected for that fiscal year from fines under Subsection (b-1).

(e) If an audit is conducted by the comptroller under Subsection (c) and it is determined that the municipality or county is retaining more than 20 percent of the amounts under Subsection (b) or (b-2), as applicable, and has not complied with Subsection (d) or (d-1), as applicable, the municipality or county shall pay the costs incurred by the comptroller in conducting the audit.

(f) **[Expires September 1, 2021]** A municipality may include the revenue generated from services provided in the municipality by a utility company operating within the municipality as municipal revenue for a fiscal year under Subsection (b) if:

(1) the municipality has a population of more than 1,000 but less than 1,200; and

(2) part of the municipality's boundary is a river that forms part of the boundary between two counties.

(g) **[Expires September 1, 2021]** This subsection and Subsection (f) expire on September 1, 2021.

Sec. 542.403. Fines.

(a) In addition to other costs, the court shall order a person convicted of a misdemeanor under this subtitle to pay a fine of $3.

(b) The officer who collects a fine under this section shall:

(1) deposit in the municipal treasury a fine collected in a municipal court case; and

(2) deposit in the county treasury a fine collected in a justice court case or in a county court case, including a case appealed from a justice or municipal court.

(c) In this section, "conviction" has the meaning assigned by Section 133.101, Local Government Code.

Sec. 542.4031. State Traffic Fine.

(a) In addition to the fine prescribed by Section 542.401 or another section of this subtitle, as applicable, a person who enters a plea of guilty or nolo contendere to or is convicted of an offense under this subtitle shall pay $50 as a state traffic fine. The person shall pay the state traffic fine when the person enters the person's plea of guilty or nolo contendere, or on the date of conviction, whichever is earlier. The state traffic fine shall be paid regardless of whether:

(1) a sentence is imposed on the person;

(2) the court defers final disposition of the person's case; or

(3) the person is placed on community supervision, including deferred adjudication community supervision.

(b) An officer collecting a state traffic fine under this section in a case in municipal court shall keep separate records of the money collected and shall deposit the money in the municipal treasury.

(c) An officer collecting a state traffic fine under this section in a justice, county, or district court shall keep separate records of the money collected and shall deposit the money in the county treasury.

(d) Each calendar quarter, an officer collecting a state traffic fine under this section shall submit a report to the comptroller. The report must comply with Articles 103.005(c) and (d), Code of Criminal Procedure.

(e) The custodian of money in a municipal or county treasury may deposit money collected under this section in an interest-bearing account. The custodian shall:

(1) keep records of the amount of money collected under this section that is on deposit in the treasury; and

(2) not later than the last day of the month following each calendar quarter, remit to the comptroller money collected under this section during the preceding quarter, as required by the comptroller.

(f) A municipality or county may retain four percent of the money collected under this section as a service fee for the collection if the municipality or county remits the funds to the comptroller within

Transportation Code

the period prescribed in Subsection (e). The municipality or county may retain any interest accrued on the money if the custodian of the money deposited in the treasury keeps records of the amount of money collected under this section that is on deposit in the treasury and remits the funds to the comptroller within the period prescribed in Subsection (e).

(g) Of the money received by the comptroller under this section, the comptroller shall deposit:

(1) 70 percent to the credit of the undedicated portion of the general revenue fund; and

(2) 30 percent to the credit of the designated trauma facility and emergency medical services account under Section 780.003, Health and Safety Code.

(h) Notwithstanding Subsection (g)(1), in any state fiscal year the comptroller shall deposit 70 percent of the money received under Subsection (e)(2) to the credit of the general revenue fund only until the total amount of the money deposited to the credit of the general revenue fund under Subsection (g)(1) equals $250 million for that year. If in any state fiscal year the amount received by the comptroller under Subsection (e)(2) for deposit to the credit of the general revenue fund under Subsection (g)(1) exceeds $250 million, the comptroller shall deposit the additional amount to the credit of the Texas mobility fund.

(i) Money collected under this section is subject to audit by the comptroller. Money spent is subject to audit by the state auditor.

(j) [Repealed by Acts 2003, 78th Leg., 3rd C.S., ch. 8 (H.B. 2), § 6.02(2), effective January 11, 2004.]

(k) [Repealed by Acts 2005, 79th Leg., ch. 1123 (H.B. 2470), § 6(2), effective September 1, 2005.]

Sec. 542.404. Fine for Offense in Construction or Maintenance Work Zone.

(a) Except as provided by Subsection (c), if an offense under this subtitle, other than an offense under Chapter 548 or 552 or Section 545.412 or 545.413, is committed in a construction or maintenance work zone when workers are present and any written notice to appear issued for the offense states on its face that workers were present when the offense was committed:

(1) the minimum fine applicable to the offense is twice the minimum fine that would be applicable to the offense if it were committed outside a construction or maintenance work zone; and

(2) the maximum fine applicable to the offense is twice the maximum fine that would be applicable to the offense if it were committed outside a construction or maintenance work zone.

(b) In this section, "construction or maintenance work zone" has the meaning assigned by Section 472.022.

(c) The fine prescribed by Subsection (a) applies to a violation of a prima facie speed limit authorized by Subchapter H, Chapter 545, only if the construction or maintenance work zone is marked by a sign indicating the applicable maximum lawful speed.

Sec. 542.4045. Penalties for Failure to Yield Right-of-Way Offense Resulting in Accident.

If it is shown on the trial of an offense under this subtitle in which an element is the failure by the operator of a vehicle to yield the right-of-way to another vehicle that an accident resulted from the operator's failure to yield the right-of-way:

(1) the offense is punishable by a fine of not less than $500 or more than $2,000, if a person other than the operator of the vehicle suffered bodily injury, as defined by Section 1.07, Penal Code, in the accident; and

(2) the offense is punishable by a fine of not less than $1,000 or more than $4,000, if a person other than the operator of the vehicle suffered serious bodily injury, as defined by Section 1.07, Penal Code, in the accident.

Sec. 542.405. Amount of Civil Penalty; Late Payment Penalty. [Repealed]

Sec. 542.406. Deposit of Revenue from Certain Traffic Penalties. [Repealed]

SUBCHAPTER E MISCELLANEOUS

Sec. 542.501. Obedience Required to Police Officers, School Crossing Guards, and Escort Flaggers.

A person may not wilfully fail or refuse to comply with a lawful order or direction of:

(1) a police officer;

(2) a school crossing guard who:

(A) is performing crossing guard duties in a school crosswalk to stop and yield to a pedestrian; or

(B) has been trained under Section 600.004 and is directing traffic in a school crossing zone; or

(3) an escort flagger who is directing or controlling the flow of traffic in accordance with a permit

Transportation Code

issued by the Texas Department of Motor Vehicles under Subtitle E for the movement of an oversize or overweight vehicle.

CHAPTER 543 ARREST AND PROSECUTION OF VIOLATORS

SUBCHAPTER A ARREST AND CHARGING PROCEDURES; NOTICES AND PROMISES TO APPEAR

Sec. 543.001. Arrest Without Warrant Authorized.

Any peace officer may arrest without warrant a person found committing a violation of this subtitle.

Sec. 543.002. Person Arrested to Be Taken Before Magistrate.

(a) A person arrested for a violation of this subtitle punishable as a misdemeanor shall be immediately taken before a magistrate if:

(1) the person is arrested on a charge of failure to stop in the event of an accident causing damage to property; or

(2) the person demands an immediate appearance before a magistrate or refuses to make a written promise to appear in court as provided by this subchapter.

(b) The person must be taken before a magistrate who:

(1) has jurisdiction of the offense;

(2) is in the county in which the offense charged is alleged to have been committed; and

(3) is nearest or most accessible to the place of arrest.

Sec. 543.003. Notice to Appear Required: Person Not Taken Before Magistrate.

An officer who arrests a person for a violation of this subtitle punishable as a misdemeanor and who does not take the person before a magistrate shall issue a written notice to appear in court showing the time and place the person is to appear, the offense charged, the name and address of the person charged, and, if applicable, the license number of the person's vehicle.

Sec. 543.004. Notice to Appear Required: Certain Offenses.

(a) An officer shall issue a written notice to appear if:

(1) the offense charged is:

(A) speeding;

(B) the use of a wireless communication device under Section 545.4251; or

(C) a violation of the open container law, Section 49.031, Penal Code; and

(2) the person makes a written promise to appear in court as provided by Section 543.005.

(b) If the person is a resident of or is operating a vehicle licensed in a state or country other than this state, Subsection (a) applies only as provided by Chapter 703.

(c) The offenses specified by Subsection (a) are the only offenses for which issuance of a written notice to appear is mandatory.

Sec. 543.005. Promise to Appear; Release.

To secure release, the person arrested must make a written promise to appear in court by signing the written notice prepared by the arresting officer. The signature may be obtained on a duplicate form or on an electronic device capable of creating a copy of the signed notice. The arresting officer shall retain the paper or electronic original of the notice and deliver the copy of the notice to the person arrested. The officer shall then promptly release the person from custody.

Sec. 543.006. Time and Place of Appearance.

(a) The time specified in the notice to appear must be at least 10 days after the date of arrest unless the person arrested demands an earlier hearing.

(b) The place specified in the notice to appear must be before a magistrate having jurisdiction of the offense who is in the municipality or county in which the offense is alleged to have been committed.

Sec. 543.007. Notice to Appear: Commercial Vehicle or License.

A notice to appear issued to the operator of a commercial motor vehicle or holder of a commercial driver's license or commercial learner's permit, for the violation of a law regulating the operation of vehicles on highways, must contain the information required by department rule, to comply with Chapter 522 and the federal Commercial Motor

Vehicle Safety Act of 1986 (Title 49, U.S.C. Section 2701 et seq.).

Sec. 543.008. Violation by Officer.

A violation by an officer of a provision of Sections 543.003–543.007 is misconduct in office and the officer is subject to removal from the officer's position.

Sec. 543.009. Compliance with or Violation of Promise to Appear.

(a) A person may comply with a written promise to appear in court by an appearance by counsel.

(b) A person who wilfully violates a written promise to appear in court, given as provided by this subchapter, commits a misdemeanor regardless of the disposition of the charge on which the person was arrested.

Sec. 543.010. Specifications of Speeding Charge.

The complaint and the summons or notice to appear on a charge of speeding under this subtitle must specify:

(1) the maximum or minimum speed limit applicable in the district or at the location; and

(2) the speed at which the defendant is alleged to have driven.

Sec. 543.011. Persons Licensed by State Department or Claiming Diplomatic or Consular Immunity.

(a) This section applies to a person who:

(1) is stopped or issued a notice to appear by a peace officer in connection with a violation of:

(A) this subtitle;

(B) Section 49.03 or 49.04, Penal Code; or

(C) Section 49.07 or 49.08, Penal Code, involving operation of a motor vehicle; and

(2) presents to the peace officer a driver's license issued by the United States Department of State or claims immunities or privileges under 22 U.S.C. Chapter 6.

(b) A peace officer who stops or issues a notice to appear to a person to whom this section applies shall record all relevant information from any driver's license or identification card presented by the person or any statement made by the person relating to immunities or privileges and promptly deliver the record to the law enforcement agency that employs the peace officer.

(c) The law enforcement agency shall:

(1) as soon as practicable contact the United States Department of State to verify the person's status and immunity, if any; and

(2) not later than the fifth working day after the date of the stop or issuance of the notice to appear, send to the Bureau of Diplomatic Security Office of Foreign Missions of the United States Department of State the following:

(A) a copy of any notice to appear issued to the person and any accident report prepared; or

(B) if a notice to appear was not issued and an accident report was not prepared, a written report of the incident.

(d) This section does not affect application of a law described by Subsection (a)(1) to a person to whom this section applies.

SUBCHAPTER B DISMISSAL OF CERTAIN MISDEMEANOR CHARGES ON COMPLETING DRIVING SAFETY COURSE

Sec. 543.101. Statement of Right Provided on Notice to Appear [Repealed].

Repealed by Acts 2003, 78th Leg., ch. 991 (S.B. 1904), § 14(1), effective September 1, 2003 and by Acts 2003, 78th Leg., ch. 1182 (S.B. 631), § 4(1), effective September 1, 2003.

Sec. 543.102. Notice of Right to Complete Course [Repealed].

Repealed by Acts 1999, 76th Leg., ch. 1387 (H.B. 1603), § 3, effective September 1, 1999 and by Acts 1999, 76th Leg., ch. 1545 (S.B. 1230), § 75(b), effective September 1, 1999.

Sec. 543.103. Mandatory Deferral [Repealed].

Repealed by Acts 1999, 76th Leg., ch. 1387 (H.B. 1603), § 3, effective September 1, 1999 and by Acts 1999, 76th Leg., ch. 1545 (S.B. 1230), § 75(b), effective September 1, 1999.

Sec. 543.104. Permissive Deferral [Repealed].

Repealed by Acts 1999, 76th Leg., ch. 1387 (H.B. 1603), § 3, effective September 1, 1999 and by Acts 1999, 76th Leg., ch. 1545 (S.B. 1230), § 75(b), effective September 1, 1999.

Sec. 543.105. Timely Request Constitutes Appearance [Repealed].

Repealed by Acts 1999, 76th Leg., ch. 1387 (H.B. 1603), § 3, effective September 1, 1999 and by Acts 1999, 76th Leg., ch. 1545 (S.B. 1230), § 75(b), effective September 1, 1999.

Sec. 543.106. Fee for Request [Repealed].

Repealed by Acts 1999, 76th Leg., ch. 1387 (H.B. 1603), § 3, effective September 1, 1999 and by Acts 1999, 76th Leg., ch. 1545 (S.B. 1230), § 75(b), effective September 1, 1999.

Sec. 543.107. Failure to Present Evidence of Course Completion [Repealed].

Repealed by Acts 1999, 76th Leg., ch. 1387 (H.B. 1603), § 3, effective September 1, 1999 and by Acts 1999, 76th Leg., ch. 1545 (S.B. 1230), § 75(b), effective September 1, 1999.

Sec. 543.108. Court Procedures on Successful Course Completion [Repealed].

Repealed by Acts 1999, 76th Leg., ch. 1387 (H.B. 1603), § 3, effective September 1, 1999 and by Acts 1999, 76th Leg., ch. 1545 (S.B. 1230), § 75(b), effective September 1, 1999.

Sec. 543.109. Dismissal Limited to One Charge [Repealed].

Repealed by Acts 1999, 76th Leg., ch. 1387 (H.B. 1603), § 3, effective September 1, 1999 and by Acts 1999, 76th Leg., ch. 1545 (S.B. 1230), § 75(b), effective September 1, 1999.

Sec. 543.110. Use of Information Regarding Dismissed Charge on Completed Course [Repealed].

Repealed by Acts 1999, 76th Leg., ch. 1387 (H.B. 1603), § 3, effective September 1, 1999 and by Acts 1999, 76th Leg., ch. 1545 (S.B. 1230), § 75(b), effective September 1, 1999.

Sec. 543.111. Regulation by Certain State Agencies.

(a) The Texas Commission of Licensing and Regulation shall enter into a memorandum of understanding with the Texas Department of Insurance for the interagency development of a curriculum for driving safety courses.

(b) The Texas Commission of Licensing and Regulation and Texas Department of Licensing and Regulation, as appropriate, shall:

(1) adopt and administer comprehensive rules governing driving safety courses; and

(2) investigate options to develop and implement procedures to electronically transmit information pertaining to driving safety courses to municipal and justice courts.

Sec. 543.112. Standards for Uniform Certificate of Course Completion.

(a) The Texas Commission of Licensing and Regulation by rule shall provide for the design and distribution of uniform certificates of course completion so as to prevent to the greatest extent possible the unauthorized production or misuse of the certificates.

(b) The uniform certificate of course completion must include an identifying number by which the Texas Department of Licensing and Regulation, the court, or the department may verify its authenticity with the course provider and must be in a form adopted by the Texas Department of Licensing and Regulation.

(c) The Texas Commission of Licensing and Regulation by rule shall determine the amount of the fee to be charged for issuance of a duplicate certificate by persons who are licensed providers of courses approved under Chapter 1001, Education Code.

(d) A driving safety course provider shall electronically submit data identified by the Texas Department of Licensing and Regulation pertaining to issued uniform certificates of course completion to the Texas Department of Licensing and Regulation as directed by the Texas Department of Licensing and Regulation.

Sec. 543.113. Fees for Printing and Supplying Certificate.

(a) The Texas Department of Licensing and Regulation shall issue course completion certificate numbers and supply them to persons who are licensed providers of courses approved under Chapter 1001, Education Code. The Texas Commission of Licensing and Regulation by rule shall establish a fee for each certificate.

(b) A course provider shall charge an operator a fee equal to the fee paid to the agency for a certificate.

(c) Money collected by the Texas Department of Licensing and Regulation under this section may be used to pay monetary awards for information relating to abuse of uniform certificates that leads to

Transportation Code

the conviction or removal of an approval, license, or authorization.

Sec. 543.114. Distribution of Written Information on Provider.

(a) A person may not distribute written information to advertise a provider of a driving safety course within 500 feet of a court having jurisdiction over an offense to which this subchapter applies. A violation of this section by a provider or a provider's agent, employee, or representative results in loss of the provider's status as a provider of a course approved under Chapter 1001, Education Code.

(b) This section does not apply to distribution of information:

(1) by a court;

(2) to a court to obtain approval of the course; or

(3) to a court to advise the court of the availability of the course.

Sec. 543.115. Fees for Driving Safety Course.

(a) A driving safety course may not be provided to a student for less than $25.

(b) A course provider shall charge each student a fee for course materials and for overseeing and administering the course. The fee may not be less than $3.

Sec. 543.116. Delivery of Uniform Certificate of Course Completion.

(a) A driving safety course provider shall mail an issued uniform certificate of course completion to a person who successfully completes the course.

(b) The certificate must be mailed not later than the 15th working day after the date a person successfully completes the course.

Sec. 543.117. Offense in Construction or Maintenance Work Zone [Repealed].

Repealed by Acts 2003, 78th Leg., ch. 991 (S.B. 1904), § 14(2), effective September 1, 2003 and by Acts 2003, 78th Leg., ch. 1182 (S.B. 631), § 4(2), effective September 1, 2003.

SUBCHAPTER C
RECORDS AND INFORMATION MAINTAINED BY DEPARTMENT

Sec. 543.201. Conviction Reported to Department.

Each magistrate or judge of a court not of record and each clerk of a court of record shall keep a record of each case in which a person is charged with a violation of law regulating the operation of vehicles on highways.

Sec. 543.202. Form of Record.

(a) In this section, "race or ethnicity" means the following categories:

(1) Alaska native or American Indian;

(2) Asian or Pacific Islander;

(3) black;

(4) white; and

(5) Hispanic or Latino.

(b) The record must be made on a form or by a data processing method acceptable to the department and must include:

(1) the name, address, physical description, including race or ethnicity, date of birth, and driver's license number of the person charged;

(2) the registration number of the vehicle involved;

(3) whether the vehicle was a commercial motor vehicle as defined by Chapter 522 or was involved in transporting hazardous materials;

(4) the person's social security number, if the person was operating a commercial motor vehicle or was the holder of a commercial driver's license or commercial learner's permit;

(5) the date and nature of the offense, including whether the offense was a serious traffic violation as defined by Chapter 522;

(6) whether a search of the vehicle was conducted and whether consent for the search was obtained;

(7) the plea, the judgment, whether the individual was adjudicated under Article 45.0511, Code of Criminal Procedure, and whether bail was forfeited;

(8) the date of conviction; and

(9) the amount of the fine or forfeiture.

Sec. 543.203. Submitting Record to Department.

Not later than the seventh day after the date of conviction or forfeiture of bail of a person on a charge of violating a law regulating the operation of a vehicle on a highway or conviction of a person of negligent homicide or a felony in the commission of which a vehicle was used, the magistrate, judge, or clerk of the court in which the conviction was had or bail was forfeited shall immediately submit to the department a written record of the case containing the information required by Section 543.202.

Sec. 543.204. Submission of Record Prohibited.

(a) A justice of the peace or municipal judge who defers further proceedings, suspends all or part of the imposition of the fine, and places a defendant on probation under Article 45.051, Code of Criminal Procedure, or a county court judge who follows that procedure under Article 42.111, Code of Criminal Procedure, may not submit a written record to the department, except that if the justice or judge subsequently adjudicates the defendant's guilt, the justice or judge shall submit the record not later than the seventh day after the date on which the justice or judge adjudicates guilt.

(b) The department may not keep a record for which submission is prohibited by this section.

(c) The department may receive a record prepared by a department employee from court records.

Sec. 543.205. Record Received at Main Office.

The department shall receive all records under Section 543.204(a) at its main office.

Sec. 543.206. Violation.

A violation by a judicial officer of this subchapter may constitute misconduct in office and may be grounds for removal from the officer's position.

CHAPTER 544 TRAFFIC SIGNS, SIGNALS, AND MARKINGS

Sec. 544.001. Adoption of Sign Manual for State Highways.

The Texas Transportation Commission shall adopt a manual and specifications for a uniform system of traffic-control devices consistent with this chapter that correlates with and to the extent possible conforms to the system approved by the American Association of State Highway and Transportation Officials.

Sec. 544.002. Placing and Maintaining Traffic-Control Device.

(a) To implement this subtitle, the Texas Department of Transportation may place and maintain a traffic-control device on a state highway as provided by the manual and specifications adopted under Section 544.001. The Texas Department of Transportation may provide for the placement and maintenance of the device under Section 221.002.

(b) To implement this subtitle or a local traffic ordinance, a local authority may place and maintain a traffic-control device on a highway under the authority's jurisdiction. The traffic-control device must conform to the manual and specifications adopted under Section 544.001.

(c) A local authority may not place or maintain a traffic-control device on a highway under the jurisdiction of the Texas Department of Transportation without that department's permission, except as authorized under Section 545.3561.

Sec. 544.003. Authority to Designate Through Highway and Stop and Yield Intersections.

(a) The Texas Transportation Commission may:

(1) designate a state or county highway as a through highway and place a stop or yield sign at a specified entrance; or

(2) designate an intersection on a state or county highway as a stop intersection or a yield intersection and place a sign at one or more entrances to the intersection.

(b) A local authority may:

(1) designate a highway under its jurisdiction as a through highway and place a stop or yield sign at a specified entrance; or

(2) designate an intersection on a highway under its jurisdiction as a stop intersection or a yield intersection and place a sign at one or more entrances to the intersection.

(c) The stop or yield sign indicating the preferential right-of-way must:

(1) conform to the manual and specifications adopted under Section 544.001; and

(2) be located:

(A) as near as practicable to the nearest line of the crosswalk; or

(B) in the absence of a crosswalk, at the nearest line of the roadway.

Sec. 544.004. Compliance with Traffic-Control Device.

(a) The operator of a vehicle or streetcar shall comply with an applicable official traffic-control device placed as provided by this subtitle unless the person is:

(1) otherwise directed by a traffic officer, police officer, or escort flagger; or

(2) operating an authorized emergency vehicle and is subject to exceptions under this subtitle.

(b) A provision of this subtitle requiring an official traffic-control device may not be enforced against an alleged violator if at the time and place of the alleged violation the device is not in proper position and sufficiently legible to an ordinarily observant person. A provision of this subtitle that does not require an official traffic-control device is effective regardless of whether a device is in place.

Sec. 544.005. Interference with Traffic-Control Device or Railroad Sign or Signal.

A person may not, without lawful authority, alter, injure, knock down, or remove or attempt to alter, injure, knock down, or remove:

(1) an official traffic-control device or railroad sign or signal;

(2) an inscription, shield, or insignia on an official traffic-control device or railroad sign or signal; or

(3) another part of an official traffic-control device or railroad sign or signal.

Sec. 544.0055. Traffic-Control Signal Preemption Device; Offense.

(a) In this section, "traffic-control signal preemption device" means a device designed, intended, or used to interfere with or alter the operation of a traffic-control signal.

(b) Except as provided by Subsection (e), a person commits an offense if the person uses, sells, offers for sale, purchases, or possesses for use or sale a traffic-control signal preemption device.

(c) The possession of a traffic-control signal preemption device creates the presumption that the person possessed the device for use or sale.

(d) An offense under this section is a Class C misdemeanor.

(e) This section does not apply to:

(1) a person who provides fire-fighting, law enforcement, ambulance, medical, or other emergency services in the course of providing those services;

(2) a manufacturer, wholesaler, or retailer of traffic-control signal preemption devices in the course of manufacturing, selling, providing, or transporting a traffic-control signal preemption device to a person described by Subdivision (1); or

(3) a transit vehicle operated by an authority under Chapter 451 or 452 or a transit department under Chapter 453.

Sec. 544.006. Display of Unauthorized Signs, Signals, or Markings.

(a) A person may not place, maintain, or display on or in view of a highway an unauthorized sign, signal, marking, or device that:

(1) imitates or resembles an official traffic-control device or railroad sign or signal;

(2) attempts to direct the movement of traffic; or

(3) hides from view or hinders the effectiveness of an official traffic-control device or railroad sign or signal.

(b) A person may not place or maintain on a highway, and a public authority may not permit on a highway, a traffic sign or signal bearing commercial advertising.

(c) A person may not place or maintain a flashing light or flashing electric sign within 1,000 feet of an intersection except under a permit issued by the Texas Transportation Commission.

(d) This section does not prohibit a person from placing on private property adjacent to a highway a sign that gives useful directional information and that cannot be mistaken for an official sign.

(e) A sign, signal, light, or marking prohibited under this section is a public nuisance. The authority with jurisdiction over the highway may remove that sign, signal, light, or marking without notice.

Sec. 544.007. Traffic-Control Signals in General.

(a) A traffic-control signal displaying different colored lights or colored lighted arrows successively or in combination may display only green, yellow, or red and applies to operators of vehicles as provided by this section.

(b) An operator of a vehicle facing a circular green signal may proceed straight or turn right or left unless a sign prohibits the turn. The operator shall, while the signal is exhibited:

(1) yield the right-of-way to other vehicles lawfully in the intersection when the signal is exhibited; and

(2) stop and yield the right-of-way to pedestrians lawfully in the intersection or an adjacent crosswalk.

(c) An operator of a vehicle facing a green arrow signal, displayed alone or with another signal, may cautiously enter the intersection to move in the direction permitted by the arrow or other indication shown simultaneously. The operator shall stop and yield the right-of-way to a pedestrian lawfully in an adjacent crosswalk and shall yield the right-of-way to other traffic lawfully using the intersection.

(d) An operator of a vehicle facing only a steady red signal shall stop at a clearly marked stop line. In the absence of a stop line, the operator shall stop before entering the crosswalk on the near side of the intersection. A vehicle that is not turning shall remain standing until an indication to proceed is shown. After stopping, standing until the intersection may be entered safely, and yielding right-of-way to pedestrians lawfully in an adjacent crosswalk and other traffic lawfully using the intersection, the operator may:

(1) turn right; or

(2) turn left, if the intersecting streets are both one-way streets and a left turn is permissible.

(e) An operator of a vehicle facing a steady yellow signal is warned by that signal that:

(1) movement authorized by a green signal is being terminated; or

(2) a red signal is to be given.

(f) The Texas Transportation Commission, a municipal authority, or the commissioners court of a county may prohibit within the entity's jurisdiction a turn by an operator of a vehicle facing a steady red signal by posting notice at the intersection that the turn is prohibited.

(g) This section applies to an official traffic-control signal placed and maintained at a place other than an intersection, except for a provision that by its nature cannot apply. A required stop shall be made at a sign or marking on the pavement indicating where the stop shall be made. In the absence of such a sign or marking, the stop shall be made at the signal.

(h) The obligations imposed by this section apply to an operator of a streetcar in the same manner they apply to the operator of a vehicle.

(i) An operator of a vehicle facing a traffic-control signal, other than a freeway entrance ramp control signal or a pedestrian hybrid beacon, that does not display an indication in any of the signal heads shall stop as provided by Section 544.010 as if the intersection had a stop sign.

(j) In this section:

(1) "Freeway entrance ramp control signal" means a traffic-control signal that controls the flow of traffic entering a freeway.

(2) "Pedestrian hybrid beacon" means a pedestrian-controlled traffic-control signal that displays different colored lights successively only when activated by a pedestrian.

Sec. 544.0075. Certain Traffic-Actuated Electric Traffic-Control Signals.

(a) This section applies only to a traffic-actuated electric traffic-control signal that consists of a traffic-control signal for which the intervals vary according to the demands of vehicular traffic as registered by a detector and that is installed and operating at an intersection.

(b) In addition to any other type of vehicle the presence of which the detector for the traffic-actuated electric traffic-control signal may register, the detector for a traffic-actuated electric traffic-control device to which this section applies must be capable of registering the presence of a motorcycle or moped.

Sec. 544.008. Flashing Signals.

(a) The operator of a vehicle facing a flashing red signal shall stop at a clearly marked stop line. In the absence of a stop line, the operator shall stop before entering the crosswalk on the near side of the intersection. In the absence of a crosswalk, the operator shall stop at the place nearest the intersecting roadway where the operator has a view of approaching traffic on the intersecting roadway. The right to proceed is subject to the rules applicable after stopping at a stop sign.

(b) The operator of a vehicle facing a flashing yellow signal may proceed through an intersection or past the signal only with caution.

(c) This section does not apply at a railroad crossing.

Sec. 544.009. Lane-Direction-Control Signals.

If a lane-direction-control signal is placed over an individual lane of a highway, a vehicle may travel in a lane over which a green signal is shown but may not enter or travel in a lane over which a red signal is shown.

Sec. 544.010. Stop Signs and Yield Signs.

(a) Unless directed to proceed by a police officer or traffic-control signal, the operator of a vehicle or streetcar approaching an intersection with a stop sign shall stop as provided by Subsection (c).

(b) If safety requires, the operator of a vehicle approaching a yield sign shall stop as provided by Subsection (c).

(c) An operator required to stop by this section shall stop before entering the crosswalk on the near side of the intersection. In the absence of a crosswalk, the operator shall stop at a clearly marked stop line. In the absence of a stop line, the operator shall stop at the place nearest the intersecting roadway where the operator has a view of approaching traffic on the intersecting roadway.

Sec. 544.011. Lane Use Signs.

If, on a highway having more than one lane with vehicles traveling in the same direction, the Texas Department of Transportation or a local authority places a sign that directs slower traffic to travel in a lane other than the farthest left lane, the sign must read "left lane for passing only."

Sec. 544.012. Notification of Photographic Traffic Monitoring System. [Repealed]

Sec. 544.013. Changeable Message Sign System.

(a) In this section, "changeable message sign" means a sign that conforms to the manual and specifications adopted under Section 544.001. The term includes a dynamic message sign.

(b) The Texas Department of Transportation in cooperation with local governments shall actively manage a system of changeable message signs located on highways under the jurisdiction of the department to mitigate traffic congestion by providing current information to the traveling public, including information about traffic incidents, weather conditions, road construction, and alternative routes when applicable.

CHAPTER 545 OPERATION AND MOVEMENT OF VEHICLES

SUBCHAPTER A GENERAL PROVISIONS

Transportation Code

Sec. 545.001. Definitions.

In this chapter:

(1) "On-track equipment" means any car, rolling stock, equipment, or other device that, alone or coupled to another device, is operated on a railroad track.

(2) "Pass" or "passing" used in reference to a vehicle means to overtake and proceed past another vehicle moving in the same direction as the passing vehicle or to attempt that maneuver.

(3) "School bus" includes a multifunction school activity bus.

Sec. 545.002. Operator.

In this chapter, a reference to an operator includes a reference to the vehicle operated by the operator if the reference imposes a duty or provides a limitation on the movement or other operation of that vehicle.

SUBCHAPTER B DRIVING ON RIGHT SIDE OF ROADWAY AND PASSING

Sec. 545.051. Driving on Right Side of Roadway.

(a) An operator on a roadway of sufficient width shall drive on the right half of the roadway, unless:

(1) the operator is passing another vehicle;

(2) an obstruction necessitates moving the vehicle left of the center of the roadway and the operator yields the right-of-way to a vehicle that:

(A) is moving in the proper direction on the unobstructed portion of the roadway; and

(B) is an immediate hazard;

(3) the operator is on a roadway divided into three marked lanes for traffic; or

(4) the operator is on a roadway restricted to one-way traffic.

(b) An operator of a vehicle on a roadway moving more slowly than the normal speed of other vehicles at the time and place under the existing conditions shall drive in the right-hand lane available for vehicles, or as close as practicable to the right-hand curb or edge of the roadway, unless the operator is:

(1) passing another vehicle; or

(2) preparing for a left turn at an intersection or into a private road or driveway.

(c) An operator on a roadway having four or more lanes for moving vehicles and providing for two-way movement of vehicles may not drive left of the center line of the roadway except:

(1) as authorized by an official traffic-control device designating a specified lane to the left side of the center of the roadway for use by a vehicle not otherwise permitted to use the lane;

(2) under the conditions described by Subsection (a)(2); or

(3) in crossing the center line to make a left turn into or out of an alley, private road, or driveway.

Sec. 545.052. Driving Past Vehicle Moving in Opposite Direction.

An operator moving in the opposite direction of the movement of another operator shall:

(1) move to or remain to the right; and

(2) on a roadway wide enough for not more than one line of vehicle movement in each direction, give the other operator:

(A) at least one-half of the main traveled portion of the roadway; or

(B) if complying with Paragraph (A) is not possible, as much of the roadway as possible.

Sec. 545.053. Passing to the Left; Return; Being Passed.

(a) An operator passing another vehicle:

(1) shall pass to the left of the other vehicle at a safe distance; and

(2) may not move back to the right side of the roadway until safely clear of the passed vehicle.

(b) An operator being passed by another vehicle:

(1) shall, on audible signal, move or remain to the right in favor of the passing vehicle; and

(2) may not accelerate until completely passed by the passing vehicle.

(c) Subsection (b) does not apply when passing to the right is permitted.

Sec. 545.054. Passing to the Left: Safe Distance.

(a) An operator may not drive on the left side of the center of the roadway in passing another vehicle unless:

(1) driving on the left side of the center of the roadway is authorized by this subtitle; and

(2) the left side is clearly visible and free of approaching traffic for a distance sufficient to permit passing without interfering with the operation of the passed vehicle or a vehicle approaching from the opposite direction.

(b) An operator passing another vehicle shall return to an authorized lane of travel:

(1) before coming within 200 feet of an approaching vehicle, if a lane authorized for vehicles approaching from the opposite direction is used in passing; or otherwise

(2) as soon as practicable.

Sec. 545.055. Passing to the Left: Passing Zones.

(a) An operator shall obey the directions of a sign or marking in Subsection (c) or (d) if the sign or marking is in place and clearly visible to an ordinarily observant person.

(b) An operator may not drive on the left side of the roadway in a no-passing zone or on the left side of any pavement striping designed to mark a no-passing zone. This subsection does not prohibit a driver from crossing pavement striping, or the center line in a no-passing zone marked by signs only, to make a left turn into or out of an alley or private road or driveway.

(c) The Texas Transportation Commission, on a state highway under the jurisdiction of the commission, may:

(1) determine those portions of the highway where passing or driving to the left of the roadway would be especially hazardous; and

(2) show the beginning and end of each no-passing zone by appropriate signs or markings on the roadway.

(d) A local authority, on a highway under the jurisdiction of the local authority, may:

(1) determine those portions of the highway where passing or driving to the left of the roadway would be especially hazardous; and

(2) show the beginning and end of each no-passing zone by appropriate signs or markings on the roadway.

Sec. 545.056. Driving to Left of Center of Roadway: Limitations Other Than Passing.

(a) An operator may not drive to the left side of the roadway if the operator is:

(1) approaching within 100 feet of an intersection or railroad grade crossing in a municipality;

(2) approaching within 100 feet of an intersection or railroad grade crossing outside a municipality and the intersection or crossing is shown by a sign or marking in accordance with Section 545.055;

(3) approaching within 100 feet of a bridge, viaduct, or tunnel; or

(4) awaiting access to a ferry operated by the Texas Transportation Commission.

(b) The limitations in Subsection (a) do not apply:

(1) on a one-way roadway; or

(2) to an operator turning left into or from an alley or private road or driveway.

(c) The Texas Transportation Commission shall post signs along the approach to a ferry operated by the commission notifying operators that passing is prohibited if there is a standing line of vehicles awaiting access to the ferry.

Sec. 545.057. Passing to the Right.

(a) An operator may pass to the right of another vehicle only if conditions permit safely passing to the right and:

(1) the vehicle being passed is making or about to make a left turn; and

(2) the operator is:

(A) on a highway having unobstructed pavement not occupied by parked vehicles and sufficient width for two or more lines of moving vehicles in each direction; or

(B) on a one-way street or on a roadway having traffic restricted to one direction of movement and the roadway is free from obstructions and wide enough for two or more lines of moving vehicles.

(b) An operator may not pass to the right by leaving the main traveled portion of a roadway except as provided by Section 545.058.

Sec. 545.058. Driving on Improved Shoulder.

(a) An operator may drive on an improved shoulder to the right of the main traveled portion of a

Transportation Code

roadway if that operation is necessary and may be done safely, but only:

(1) to stop, stand, or park;

(2) to accelerate before entering the main traveled lane of traffic;

(3) to decelerate before making a right turn;

(4) to pass another vehicle that is slowing or stopped on the main traveled portion of the highway, disabled, or preparing to make a left turn;

(5) to allow another vehicle traveling faster to pass;

(6) as permitted or required by an official traffic-control device; or

(7) to avoid a collision.

(b) An operator may drive on an improved shoulder to the left of the main traveled portion of a divided or limited-access or controlled-access highway if that operation may be done safely, but only:

(1) to slow or stop when the vehicle is disabled and traffic or other circumstances prohibit the safe movement of the vehicle to the shoulder to the right of the main traveled portion of the roadway;

(2) as permitted or required by an official traffic-control device; or

(3) to avoid a collision.

(c) A limitation in this section on driving on an improved shoulder does not apply to:

(1) an authorized emergency vehicle responding to a call;

(2) a police patrol;

(3) a bicycle; or

(4) a slow-moving vehicle, as defined by Section 547.001.

Sec. 545.059. One-Way Roadways and Rotary Traffic Islands.

(a) The Texas Transportation Commission may designate a highway or separate roadway under the jurisdiction of the commission for one-way traffic and shall erect appropriate signs giving notice of the designation.

(b) On a roadway that is designated and on which signs are erected for one-way traffic, an operator shall drive only in the direction indicated.

(c) An operator moving around a rotary traffic island shall drive only to the right of the island.

Sec. 545.060. Driving on Roadway Laned for Traffic.

(a) An operator on a roadway divided into two or more clearly marked lanes for traffic:

(1) shall drive as nearly as practical entirely within a single lane; and

(2) may not move from the lane unless that movement can be made safely.

(b) If a roadway is divided into three lanes and provides for two-way movement of traffic, an operator on the roadway may not drive in the center lane except:

(1) if passing another vehicle and the center lane is clear of traffic within a safe distance;

(2) in preparing to make a left turn; or

(3) where the center lane is designated by an official traffic-control device for movement in the direction in which the operator is moving.

(c) Without regard to the center of the roadway, an official traffic-control device may be erected directing slow-moving traffic to use a designated lane or designating lanes to be used by traffic moving in a particular direction.

(d) Official traffic-control devices prohibiting the changing of lanes on sections of roadway may be installed.

Sec. 545.061. Driving on Multiple-Lane Roadway.

On a roadway divided into three or more lanes and providing for one-way movement of traffic, an operator entering a lane of traffic from a lane to the right shall yield the right-of-way to a vehicle entering the same lane of traffic from a lane to the left.

Sec. 545.062. Following Distance.

(a) An operator shall, if following another vehicle, maintain an assured clear distance between the two vehicles so that, considering the speed of the vehicles, traffic, and the conditions of the highway, the operator can safely stop without colliding with the preceding vehicle or veering into another vehicle, object, or person on or near the highway.

(b) An operator of a truck or of a motor vehicle drawing another vehicle who is on a roadway outside a business or residential district and who is following another truck or motor vehicle drawing another vehicle shall, if conditions permit, leave sufficient space between the vehicles so that a vehicle passing the operator can safely enter and occupy the space. This subsection does not prohibit a truck or a motor vehicle drawing another vehicle from passing another vehicle.

(c) An operator on a roadway outside a business or residential district driving in a caravan of other vehicles or a motorcade shall allow sufficient space between the operator and the vehicle preceding the operator so that another vehicle can safely enter and occupy the space. This subsection does not apply to a funeral procession.

(d) An operator of a vehicle equipped with a connected braking system that is following another vehicle equipped with that system may be assisted by the system to maintain an assured clear distance or sufficient space as required by this section. In this subsection, "connected braking system" means a system by which the braking of one vehicle is electronically coordinated with the braking system of a following vehicle.

Sec. 545.063. Driving on Divided Highway.

(a) On a highway having two or more roadways separated by a space, physical barrier, or clearly indicated dividing section constructed to impede vehicular traffic, an operator shall drive on the right roadway unless directed or permitted to use another roadway by an official traffic-control device or police officer.

(b) An operator may not drive over, across, or in a dividing space, physical barrier, or section constructed to impede vehicular traffic except:

(1) through an opening in the physical barrier or dividing section or space; or

(2) at a crossover or intersection established by a public authority.

Sec. 545.064. Restricted Access.

An operator may not drive on or from a limited-access or controlled-access roadway except at an entrance or exit that is established by a public authority.

Sec. 545.065. State and Local Regulation of Limited-Access or Controlled-Access Highways.

(a) The Texas Transportation Commission by resolution or order recorded in its minutes may prohibit the use of a limited-access or controlled-access highway under the jurisdiction of the commission by a parade, funeral procession, pedestrian, bicycle, electric bicycle, motorcycle equipped with a motor that has an engine piston displacement of 250 cubic centimeters or less, or nonmotorized traffic.

(b) If the commission adopts a rule under Subsection (a), the commission shall erect and maintain official traffic-control devices on the portions of the limited-access or controlled-access highway to which the rule applies.

(c) A local authority by ordinance may prohibit the use of a limited-access or controlled-access roadway under the jurisdiction of the authority by a parade, funeral procession, pedestrian, bicycle, electric bicycle, motorcycle equipped with a motor that has an engine piston displacement of 250 cubic centimeters or less, or nonmotorized traffic.

(d) If a local authority adopts an ordinance under Subsection (c), the authority shall erect and maintain official traffic-control devices on the portions of the limited-access or controlled-access roadway to which the ordinance applies.

Sec. 545.0651. Restriction on Use of Highway.

(a) In this section:

(1) "Commission" means the Texas Transportation Commission.

(1-a) "Department" means the Texas Department of Transportation.

(2) "Highway" means a public highway that:

(A) is in the designated state highway system;

(B) is designated a controlled access facility; and

(C) has a minimum of three travel lanes, excluding access or frontage roads, in each direction of traffic that may be part of a single roadway or may be separate roadways that are constructed as an upper and lower deck.

(b) The commission by order may restrict, by class of vehicle, through traffic to two or more designated lanes of a highway. If the lanes to be restricted by the commission are located within a municipality, the commission shall consult with the municipality before adopting an order under this section. A municipality by ordinance may restrict, by class of vehicle, through traffic to two or more designated lanes of a highway in the municipality.

(c) An order or ordinance under Subsection (b) must allow a restricted vehicle to use any lane of the highway to pass another vehicle and to enter and exit the highway.

(d) Before adopting an ordinance, a municipality shall submit to the department a description of the proposed restriction. The municipality may not enforce the restrictions unless the department's executive director or the executive director's designee has approved the restrictions.

(e) Department approval under Subsection (d) must:

(1) be based on a traffic study performed by the department to evaluate the effect of the proposed restriction; and

(2) to the greatest extent practicable, ensure a systems approach to preclude the designation of inconsistent lane restrictions among adjacent municipalities.

(f) The department's executive director or the executive director's designee may suspend or rescind approval of any restrictions approved under Subsection (d) for one or more of the following reasons:

(1) a change in pavement conditions;

(2) a change in traffic conditions;
(3) a geometric change in roadway configuration;
(4) construction or maintenance activity; or
(5) emergency or incident management.

(g) The department shall erect and maintain official traffic control devices necessary to implement and enforce an order adopted or an ordinance adopted and approved under this section. A restriction approved under this section may not be enforced until the appropriate traffic control devices are in place.

Sec. 545.0652. County Restriction on Use of Highway.

(a) In this section:
(1) "Department" means the Texas Department of Transportation.
(2) "Highway" means a public roadway that:
(A) is in the designated state highway system;
(B) is designated a controlled access facility; and
(C) has a minimum of three travel lanes, excluding access or frontage roads, in each direction of traffic.

(b) A county commissioners court by order may restrict, by class of vehicle, through traffic to two or more designated lanes of a highway located in the county and outside the jurisdiction of a municipality.

(c) An order under Subsection (b) must allow a restricted vehicle to use any lane of the highway to pass another vehicle and to enter and exit the highway.

(d) Before issuing an order under this section, the commissioners court shall submit to the department a description of the proposed restriction. The commissioners court may not enforce the restrictions unless:
(1) the department's executive director or the executive director's designee has approved the restrictions; and
(2) the appropriate traffic-control devices are in place.

(e) Department approval under Subsection (d) must to the greatest extent practicable ensure a systems approach to preclude the designation of inconsistent lane restrictions among adjacent counties or municipalities.

(f) The department's executive director or the executive director's designee may suspend or rescind approval under this section for one or more of the following reasons:
(1) a change in pavement conditions;
(2) a change in traffic conditions;
(3) a geometric change in roadway configuration;
(4) construction or maintenance activity; or
(5) emergency or incident management.

(g) The department shall erect and maintain official traffic-control devices necessary to implement and enforce an order issued and approved under this section.

Sec. 545.0653. Restriction on Use of Highway in Maintenance or Construction Work Zone.

(a) In this section:
(1) "Commercial motor vehicle" has the meaning assigned by Section 548.001.
(2) "Construction or maintenance work zone" has the meaning assigned by Section 472.022.
(3) "Department" means the Texas Department of Transportation.
(4) "Executive director" means the executive director of the department.

(b) The executive director or the executive director's designee may restrict a commercial motor vehicle to a specific lane of traffic in a construction or maintenance work zone for a highway that is part of the state highway system if the executive director or the executive director's designee determines that, based on a traffic study performed by the department to evaluate the effect of the restriction, the restriction is necessary to improve safety.

(c) The department shall erect and maintain official traffic control devices necessary to implement and enforce a lane restriction imposed under this section. A lane restriction may not be enforced until the appropriate traffic control devices are in place.

(d) The executive director or the executive director's designee may rescind a lane restriction imposed under this section at any time that the executive director or the executive director's designee determines that the restriction is no longer necessary to improve safety.

(e) A lane restriction imposed under this section expires when the lane that is subject to the restriction is no longer in a construction or maintenance work zone.

(f) The department shall remove traffic control devices erected under this section if the lane restriction is rescinded under Subsection (d) or expires under Subsection (e).

Sec. 545.066. Passing a School Bus; Offense.

(a) An operator on a highway, when approaching from either direction a school bus stopped on the highway to receive or discharge a student:
(1) shall stop before reaching the school bus when the bus is operating a visual signal as required by Section 547.701; and
(2) may not proceed until:

Transportation Code

(A) the school bus resumes motion;

(B) the operator is signaled by the bus driver to proceed; or

(C) the visual signal is no longer actuated.

(b) An operator on a highway having separate roadways is not required to stop:

(1) for a school bus that is on a different roadway; or

(2) if on a controlled-access highway, for a school bus that is stopped:

(A) in a loading zone that is a part of or adjacent to the highway; and

(B) where pedestrians are not permitted to cross the roadway.

(c) An offense under this section is a misdemeanor punishable by a fine of not less than $500 or more than $1,250, except that the offense is:

(1) a misdemeanor punishable by a fine of not less than $1,000 or more than $2,000 if the person is convicted of a second or subsequent offense under this section committed within five years of the date on which the most recent preceding offense was committed;

(2) a Class A misdemeanor if the person causes serious bodily injury to another; or

(3) a state jail felony if the person has been previously convicted under Subdivision (2).

(d) The court may order that the driver's license of a person convicted of a second or subsequent offense under this section be suspended for not longer than six months beginning on the date of conviction. In this subsection, "driver's license" has the meaning assigned by Chapter 521.

(e) If a person does not pay the previously assessed fine or costs on a conviction under this section, or is determined by the court to have insufficient resources or income to pay a fine or costs on a conviction under this section, the court may order the person to perform community service. The court shall set the number of hours of service under this subsection.

(f) For the purposes of this section:

(1) a highway is considered to have separate roadways only if the highway has roadways separated by an intervening space on which operation of vehicles is not permitted, a physical barrier, or a clearly indicated dividing section constructed to impede vehicular traffic; and

(2) a highway is not considered to have separate roadways if the highway has roadways separated only by a left turn lane.

SUBCHAPTER C
TURNING AND SIGNALS FOR STOPPING AND TURNING

Sec. 545.101. Turning at Intersection.

(a) To make a right turn at an intersection, an operator shall make both the approach and the turn as closely as practicable to the right-hand curb or edge of the roadway.

(b) To make a left turn at an intersection, an operator shall:

(1) approach the intersection in the extreme left-hand lane lawfully available to a vehicle moving in the direction of the vehicle; and

(2) after entering the intersection, turn left, leaving the intersection so as to arrive in a lane lawfully available to traffic moving in the direction of the vehicle on the roadway being entered.

(c) On a street or roadway designated for two-way traffic, the operator turning left shall, to the extent practicable, turn in the portion of the intersection to the left of the center of the intersection.

(d) To turn left, an operator who is approaching an intersection having a roadway designated for one-way traffic and for which signs are posted from a roadway designated for one-way traffic and for which signs are posted shall make the turn as closely as practicable to the left-hand curb or edge of the roadway.

(e) The Texas Transportation Commission or a local authority, with respect to a highway in its jurisdiction, may:

(1) authorize the placement of an official traffic-control device in or adjacent to an intersection; and

(2) require a course different from that specified in this section for movement by vehicles turning at an intersection.

Sec. 545.102. Turning on Curve or Crest of Grade.

An operator may not turn the vehicle to move in the opposite direction when approaching a curve or the crest of a grade if the vehicle is not visible to the operator of another vehicle approaching from either direction within 500 feet.

Sec. 545.103. Safely Turning.

An operator may not turn the vehicle to enter a private road or driveway, otherwise turn the vehicle from a direct course, or move right or left on a roadway unless movement can be made safely.

Sec. 545.104. Signaling Turns; Use of Turn Signals.

(a) An operator shall use the signal authorized by Section 545.106 to indicate an intention to turn, change lanes, or start from a parked position.

(b) An operator intending to turn a vehicle right or left shall signal continuously for not less than the last 100 feet of movement of the vehicle before the turn.

(c) An operator may not light the signals on only one side of the vehicle on a parked or disabled vehicle or use the signals as a courtesy or "do pass" signal to the operator of another vehicle approaching from the rear.

Sec. 545.105. Signaling Stops.

An operator may not stop or suddenly decrease the speed of the vehicle without first giving a stop signal as provided by this subchapter to the operator of a vehicle immediately to the rear when there is an opportunity to give the signal.

Sec. 545.106. Signals by Hand and Arm or by Signal Lamp.

(a) Except as provided by Subsection (b), an operator required to give a stop or turn signal shall do so by:

(1) using the hand and arm; or

(2) lighting signal lamps approved by the department.

(b) A motor vehicle in use on a highway shall be equipped with signal lamps, and the required signal shall be given by lighting the lamps, if:

(1) the distance from the center of the top of the steering post to the left outside limit of the body, cab, or load of the motor vehicle is more than two feet; or

(2) the distance from the center of the top of the steering post to the rear limit of the body or load, including the body or load of a combination of vehicles, is more than 14 feet.

Sec. 545.107. Method of Giving Hand and Arm Signals.

An operator who is permitted to give a hand and arm signal shall give the signal from the left side of the vehicle as follows:

(1) to make a left turn signal, extend hand and arm horizontally;

(2) to make a right turn signal, extend hand and arm upward, except that a bicycle operator may signal from the right side of the vehicle with the hand and arm extended horizontally; and

(3) to stop or decrease speed, extend hand and arm downward.

SUBCHAPTER D RIGHT-OF-WAY

Sec. 545.151. Vehicle Approaching or Entering Intersection.

(a) An operator approaching an intersection:

(1) shall stop, yield, and grant immediate use of the intersection:

(A) in obedience to an official traffic-control device, including a stop sign or yield right-of-way sign; or

(B) if a traffic-control signal is present but does not display an indication in any of the signal heads; and

(2) after stopping, may proceed when the intersection can be safely entered without interference or collision with traffic using a different street or roadway.

(b) An operator on a single-lane or two-lane street or roadway who approaches an intersection that is not controlled by an official traffic-control device and that is located on a divided highway or on a street or roadway divided into three or more marked traffic lanes:

(1) shall stop, yield, and grant immediate use of the intersection to a vehicle on the other street or roadway that is within the intersection or approaching the intersection in such proximity as to be a hazard; and

(2) after stopping, may proceed when the intersection can be safely entered without interference or collision with traffic using a different street or roadway.

(c) An operator on an unpaved street or roadway approaching an intersection of a paved street or roadway:

(1) shall stop, yield, and grant immediate use of the intersection to a vehicle on the paved street or roadway that is within the intersection or approaching the intersection in such proximity as to be a hazard; and

(2) after stopping, may proceed when the intersection can be safely entered without interference or collision with traffic using the paved street or roadway.

(d) Except as provided in Subsection (e), an operator approaching an intersection of a street or roadway that is not controlled by an official traffic-control device:

(1) shall stop, yield, and grant immediate use of the intersection to a vehicle that has entered the intersection from the operator's right or is approaching the intersection from the operator's right in a proximity that is a hazard; and

(2) after stopping, may proceed when the intersection can be safely entered without interference or collision with traffic using a different street or roadway.

Transportation Code

(e) An operator approaching an intersection of a street or roadway from a street or roadway that terminates at the intersection and that is not controlled by an official traffic-control device or controlled as provided by Subsection (b) or (c):

(1) shall stop, yield, and grant immediate use of the intersection to another vehicle that has entered the intersection from the other street or roadway or is approaching the intersection on the other street or roadway in a proximity that is a hazard; and

(2) after stopping, may proceed when the intersection can be safely entered without interference or collision with the traffic using the other street or roadway.

(f) An operator who is required by this section to stop and yield the right-of-way at an intersection to another vehicle and who is involved in a collision or interferes with other traffic at the intersection to whom right-of-way is to be given is presumed not to have yielded the right-of-way.

Sec. 545.152. Vehicle Turning Left.

To turn left at an intersection or into an alley or private road or driveway, an operator shall yield the right-of-way to a vehicle that is approaching from the opposite direction and that is in the intersection or in such proximity to the intersection as to be an immediate hazard.

Sec. 545.153. Vehicle Entering Stop or Yield Intersection.

(a) Preferential right-of-way at an intersection may be indicated by a stop sign or yield sign as authorized in Section 544.003.

(b) Unless directed to proceed by a police officer or official traffic-control device, an operator approaching an intersection on a roadway controlled by a stop sign, after stopping as required by Section 544.010, shall yield the right-of-way to a vehicle that has entered the intersection from another highway or that is approaching so closely as to be an immediate hazard to the operator's movement in or across the intersection.

(c) An operator approaching an intersection on a roadway controlled by a yield sign shall:

(1) slow to a speed that is reasonable under the existing conditions; and

(2) yield the right-of-way to a vehicle in the intersection or approaching on another highway so closely as to be an immediate hazard to the operator's movement in or across the intersection.

(d) If an operator is required by Subsection (c) to yield and is involved in a collision with a vehicle in an intersection after the operator drove past a yield sign without stopping, the collision is prima facie evidence that the operator failed to yield the right-of-way.

Sec. 545.154. Vehicle Entering or Leaving Limited-Access or Controlled-Access Highway.

An operator on an access or feeder road of a limited-access or controlled-access highway shall yield the right-of-way to a vehicle entering or about to enter the access or feeder road from the highway or leaving or about to leave the access or feeder road to enter the highway.

Sec. 545.155. Vehicle Entering Highway from Private Road or Driveway.

An operator about to enter or cross a highway from an alley, building, or private road or driveway shall yield the right-of-way to a vehicle approaching on the highway to be entered.

Sec. 545.156. Vehicle Approached by Authorized Emergency Vehicle.

(a) On the immediate approach of an authorized emergency vehicle using audible and visual signals that meet the requirements of Sections 547.305 and 547.702, or of a police vehicle lawfully using only an audible or visual signal, an operator, unless otherwise directed by a police officer, shall:

(1) yield the right-of-way;

(2) immediately drive to a position parallel to and as close as possible to the right-hand edge or curb of the roadway clear of any intersection; and

(3) stop and remain standing until the authorized emergency vehicle has passed.

(b) This section does not exempt the operator of an authorized emergency vehicle from the duty to drive with due regard for the safety of all persons using the highway.

Sec. 545.157. Passing Certain Vehicles.

(a) This section applies only to the following vehicles:

(1) a stationary authorized emergency vehicle using visual signals that meet the requirements of Sections 547.305 and 547.702;

(2) a stationary tow truck using equipment authorized by Section 547.305(d);

(3) a Texas Department of Transportation vehicle or a highway maintenance or construction vehicle operated pursuant to a contract awarded under Subchapter A, Chapter 223, not separated from

Transportation Code

the roadway by a traffic control channelizing device and using visual signals that comply with the standards and specifications adopted under Section 547.105;

(4) a service vehicle used by or for a utility, as defined by Section 203.091, and using visual signals that comply with the standards and specifications adopted under Section 547.105;

(5) a stationary vehicle used exclusively to transport municipal solid waste, as defined by Section 361.003, Health and Safety Code, or recyclable material, as defined by Section 361.421, Health and Safety Code, while being operated in connection with the removal or transportation of municipal solid waste or recyclable material from a location adjacent to the highway; and

(6) a vehicle operated by or pursuant to a contract with a toll project entity, as defined by Section 372.001, using visual signals that comply with the standards and specifications adopted under Section 547.105.

(b) On approaching a vehicle described by Subsection (a), an operator, unless otherwise directed by a police officer, shall:

(1) vacate the lane closest to the vehicle when driving on a highway with two or more lanes traveling in the direction of the vehicle; or

(2) slow to a speed not to exceed:

(A) 20 miles per hour less than the posted speed limit when the posted speed limit is 25 miles per hour or more; or

(B) five miles per hour when the posted speed limit is less than 25 miles per hour.

(c) A violation of this section is:

(1) a misdemeanor punishable under Section 542.401;

(2) a misdemeanor punishable by a fine of $500 if the violation results in property damage; or

(3) a Class B misdemeanor if the violation results in bodily injury.

(d) If conduct constituting an offense under this section also constitutes an offense under another section of this code or the Penal Code, the actor may be prosecuted under either section or under both sections.

(e) In this section:

(1) "Tow truck" means a vehicle that:

(A) has been issued a permit under Subchapter C, Chapter 2308, Occupations Code; and

(B) is operated by a person licensed under Subchapter D, Chapter 2308, Occupations Code.

(2) "Traffic control channelizing device" means equipment used to warn and alert drivers of conditions created by work activities in or near the traveled way, to protect workers in a temporary traffic control zone, and to guide drivers and pedestrians safely. The term includes a traffic cone, tubular marker, vertical panel, drum, barricade, temporary raised island, concrete or cable barrier, guardrail, or channelizer.

SUBCHAPTER E STREETCARS

Sec. 545.201. Passing Streetcar to Left.

(a) An operator may not pass to the left or drive on the left side of a streetcar moving in the same direction, even if the streetcar is temporarily at rest, unless the operator:

(1) is directed to do so by a police officer;

(2) is on a one-way street; or

(3) is on a street on which the location of the tracks prevents compliance with this section.

(b) An operator when lawfully passing to the left of a streetcar that has stopped to receive or discharge a passenger:

(1) shall reduce speed;

(2) may proceed only on exercising due caution for pedestrians; and

(3) shall accord a pedestrian the right-of-way as required by this subtitle.

Sec. 545.202. Passing Streetcar to Right.

(a) An operator passing to the right of a streetcar stopped or about to stop to receive or discharge a passenger shall:

(1) stop the vehicle at least five feet to the rear of the nearest running board or door of the streetcar; and

(2) remain standing until all passengers have entered the streetcar or, on leaving, have reached a place of safety.

(b) An operator is not required to stop before passing a streetcar to the right if a safety zone has been established and may proceed past the streetcar at a reasonable speed and with due caution for the safety of pedestrians.

Sec. 545.203. Driving on Streetcar Tracks.

(a) An operator on a streetcar track in front of a streetcar shall move the operator's vehicle off the track as soon as possible after a signal from the operator of the streetcar.

(b) An operator may not drive on or cross a streetcar track in an intersection in front of a streetcar crossing the intersection.

Transportation Code

(c) An operator who is passing a streetcar may not turn in front of the streetcar so as to interfere with or impede its movement.

Sec. 545.204. Streetcar Approached by Authorized Emergency Vehicle.

(a) On the immediate approach of an authorized emergency vehicle using audible and visual signals that meet the requirements of Sections 547.305 and 547.702, or of a police vehicle lawfully using only an audible signal, the operator of a streetcar shall immediately stop the streetcar clear of any intersection and remain there until the authorized emergency vehicle has passed, unless otherwise directed by a police officer.

(b) This section does not exempt the operator of an authorized emergency vehicle from the duty to drive with due regard for the safety of all persons using the highway.

Sec. 545.205. Crossing Fire Hose.

An operator of a streetcar may not, without the consent of the fire department official in command, drive over an unprotected hose of a fire department when the hose is on a streetcar track and intended for use at a fire or alarm of fire.

Sec. 545.206. Obstruction of Operator's View or Driving Mechanism.

A passenger in a streetcar may not ride in a position that interferes with the operator's view ahead or to the side or with control over the driving mechanism of the streetcar.

SUBCHAPTER F
SPECIAL STOPS AND SPEED RESTRICTIONS

Sec. 545.251. Obedience to Signal Indicating Approach of Train or Other On-Track Equipment.

(a) An operator approaching a railroad grade crossing shall stop not closer than 15 feet or farther than 50 feet from the nearest rail if:

(1) a clearly visible railroad signal warns of the approach of a railroad train or other on-track equipment;

(2) a crossing gate is lowered, or a flagger warns of the approach or passage of a train or other on-track equipment;

(3) a railroad engine or other on-track equipment approaching within approximately 1,500 feet of the highway crossing emits a signal audible from that distance and the engine or other equipment is an immediate hazard because of its speed or proximity to the crossing;

(4) an approaching railroad train or other on-track equipment is plainly visible to the operator and is in hazardous proximity to the crossing; or

(5) the operator is required to stop by:

(A) other law;

(B) a rule adopted under a statute;

(C) an official traffic-control device; or

(D) a traffic-control signal.

(b) An operator of a vehicle required by Subsection (a) to stop shall remain stopped until permitted to proceed and it is safe to proceed.

(c) An operator of a vehicle who approaches a railroad grade crossing equipped with railroad crossbuck signs without automatic, electric, or mechanical signal devices, crossing gates, or a flagger warning of the approach or passage of a train or other on-track equipment shall yield the right-of-way to a train or other on-track equipment in hazardous proximity to the crossing, and proceed at a speed that is reasonable for the existing conditions. If required for safety, the operator shall stop at a clearly marked stop line before the grade crossing or, if no stop line exists, not closer than 15 feet or farther than 50 feet from the nearest rail.

(d) An operator commits an offense if the operator drives around, under, or through a crossing gate or a barrier at a railroad crossing while the gate or barrier is closed, being closed, or being opened.

(e) In a prosecution under this section, proof that at the time of the offense a train or other on-track equipment was in hazardous proximity to the crossing and that the train or other equipment was plainly visible to the operator is prima facie evidence that it was not safe for the operator to proceed.

(f) An offense under this section is punishable by a fine of not less than $50 or more than $200.

Sec. 545.252. All Vehicles to Stop at Certain Railroad Grade Crossings.

(a) The Texas Department of Transportation or a local authority, with respect to a highway in its jurisdiction, may:

(1) designate a railroad grade crossing as particularly dangerous; and

(2) erect a stop sign or other official traffic-control device at the grade crossing.

(b) An operator approaching a stop sign or other official traffic-control device that requires a stop and that is erected under Subsection (a) shall stop not closer than 15 feet or farther than 50 feet from the nearest rail of the railroad and may proceed only with due care.

(c) The costs of installing and maintaining a mechanically operated grade crossing safety device, gate, sign, or signal erected under this section shall be apportioned and paid on the same percentage ratio and in the same proportionate amounts by this state and all participating political subdivisions of this state as costs are apportioned and paid between the state and the United States.

(d) An offense under this section is punishable by a fine of not less than $50 or more than $200.

Sec. 545.253. Buses to Stop at All Railroad Grade Crossings.

(a) Except as provided by Subsection (c), the operator of a motor bus carrying passengers for hire, before crossing a railroad grade crossing:

(1) shall stop the vehicle not closer than 15 feet or farther than 50 feet from the nearest rail of the railroad;

(2) while stopped, shall listen and look in both directions along the track for an approaching train or other on-track equipment and signals indicating the approach of a train or other on-track equipment; and

(3) may not proceed until it is safe to do so.

(b) After stopping as required by Subsection (a), an operator described by Subsection (a) shall proceed without manually shifting gears while crossing the track.

(c) A vehicle is not required to stop at the crossing if a police officer or a traffic-control signal directs traffic to proceed.

(d) This section does not apply at a railway grade crossing in a business or residence district.

(e) An offense under this section is punishable by a fine of not less than $50 or more than $200.

Sec. 545.2535. School Buses to Stop at All Railroad Grade Crossings.

(a) Except as provided by Subsection (c), the operator of a school bus, before crossing a track at a railroad grade crossing:

(1) shall stop the vehicle not closer than 15 feet or farther than 50 feet from the track;

(2) while stopped, shall listen and look in both directions along the track for an approaching train or other on-track equipment and signals indicating the approach of a train or other on-track equipment; and

(3) may not proceed until it is safe to do so.

(b) After stopping as required by Subsection (a), the operator may proceed in a gear that permits the vehicle to complete the crossing without a change of gears. The operator may not shift gears while crossing the track.

(c) An operator is not required to stop at:

(1) an abandoned railroad grade crossing that is marked with a sign reading "tracks out of service"; or

(2) an industrial or spur line railroad grade crossing that is marked with a sign reading "exempt."

(d) A sign under Subsection (c) may be erected only by or with the consent of the appropriate state or local governmental official.

Sec. 545.254. Vehicles Carrying Explosive Substances or Flammable Liquids.

(a) Before crossing a railroad grade crossing, an operator of a vehicle that has an explosive substance or flammable liquid as the vehicle's principal cargo and that is moving at a speed of more than 20 miles per hour:

(1) shall reduce the speed of the vehicle to 20 miles per hour or less before coming within 200 feet of the nearest rail of the railroad;

(2) shall listen and look in both directions along the track for an approaching train or other on-track equipment and for signals indicating the approach of a train or other on-track equipment; and

(3) may not proceed until the operator determines that the course is clear.

(b) The operator of a vehicle that has an explosive substance or flammable liquid as the vehicle's principal cargo, before crossing a railroad grade crossing on a highway in a municipality:

(1) shall stop the vehicle not closer than 15 feet or farther than 50 feet from the nearest rail of the railroad;

(2) while stopped, shall listen and look in both directions along the track for an approaching train or other on-track equipment and for signals indicating the approach of a train or other on-track equipment; and

(3) may not proceed until the operator determines that the course is clear.

(c) Subsections (a) and (b) do not apply:

(1) if a police officer, crossing flagger, or traffic-control signal directs traffic to proceed;

(2) where a railroad flashing signal is installed and does not indicate an approaching train or other on-track equipment;

(3) to an abandoned or exempted grade crossing that is clearly marked by or with the consent of the state, if the markings can be read from the operator's location;

(4) at a streetcar crossing in a business or residential district of a municipality; or

Transportation Code

(5) to a railroad track used exclusively for industrial switching purposes in a business district.

(d) This section does not exempt the operator from compliance with Section 545.251 or 545.252.

(e) An offense under this section is punishable by a fine of not less than $50 or more than $200.

Sec. 545.255. Moving Heavy Equipment at Railroad Grade Crossings.

(a) This section applies only to:

(1) a crawler-type tractor, steam shovel, derrick, or roller; and

(2) any other equipment or structure with:

(A) a normal operating speed of 10 miles per hour or less; or

(B) a vertical body or load clearance of less than one-half inch per foot of the distance between two adjacent axles or less than nine inches measured above the level surface of a roadway.

(b) An operator of a vehicle or equipment may not move on or across a track at a railroad grade crossing unless the operator has given notice to a station agent of the railroad and given the railroad reasonable time to provide proper protection at the crossing.

(c) To move a vehicle or equipment on or across a track at a railroad grade crossing, the operator:

(1) shall stop the vehicle or equipment not closer than 15 feet or farther than 50 feet from the nearest rail of the railroad;

(2) while stopped, shall listen and look in both directions along the track for an approaching train or other on-track equipment and for signals indicating the approach of a train or other on-track equipment; and

(3) may not proceed until it is safe to cross the track.

(d) An operator of a vehicle or equipment may not cross a railroad grade crossing when warning of the immediate approach of a railroad car, train, or other on-track equipment is given by automatic signal, crossing gates, a flagger, or otherwise. If a flagger is provided by the railroad, the operator shall move the vehicle or equipment over the crossing at the flagger's direction.

(e) An offense under this section is punishable by a fine of not less than $50 or more than $200.

Sec. 545.2555. Report and Investigation of Certain Railroad Crossing Violations.

(a) A person who on site observes a violation of Section 545.251, 545.252, 545.253, 545.254, or 545.255 may file a report of the violation if the person:

(1) is an on-engine employee of a railroad; and

(2) observes the violation while on a moving engine.

(b) A report under this section must:

(1) be made:

(A) on a form approved by the department; and

(B) not later than 72 hours after the violation;

(2) be filed with:

(A) an office of the department located in the county in which the violation occurred;

(B) the sheriff of the county in which the violation occurred, if the violation occurred in the unincorporated area of the county; or

(C) the police department of a municipality, if the violation occurred in the municipality; and

(3) contain, in addition, to any other required information:

(A) the date, time, and location of the violation;

(B) the license plate number and a description of the vehicle involved in the violation;

(C) a description of the operator of the vehicle involved in the violation; and

(D) the name, address, and telephone number of the person filing the report.

(c) A peace officer may:

(1) before the seventh day after the date a report under this section is filed, initiate an investigation of the alleged violation; and

(2) request the owner of the reported vehicle, as shown by the vehicle registration records of the Texas Department of Transportation, to disclose the name and address of the individual operating that vehicle at the time of the violation alleged in the report.

(d) Unless the owner of the reported vehicle believes that to provide the peace officer with the name and address of the individual operating the vehicle at the time of the violation alleged would incriminate the owner, the owner shall, to the best of the owner's ability, disclose that individual's name and address.

(e) An investigating peace officer who has probable cause to believe that a charge against an individual for a violation of Section 545.251, 545.252, 545.253, 545.254, or 545.255 is justified may:

(1) prepare a written notice to appear in court that complies with Sections 543.003, 543.006, and 543.007; and

(2) deliver the notice to the individual named in the notice in person or by certified mail.

Sec. 545.256. Emerging from an Alley, Driveway, or Building.

An operator emerging from an alley, driveway, or building in a business or residence district shall:

(1) stop the vehicle before moving on a sidewalk or the sidewalk area extending across an alley or driveway;

(2) yield the right-of-way to a pedestrian to avoid collision; and

(3) on entering the roadway, yield the right-of-way to an approaching vehicle.

SUBCHAPTER G STOPPING, STANDING, AND PARKING

Sec. 545.301. Stopping, Standing, or Parking Outside a Business or Residence District.

(a) An operator may not stop, park, or leave standing an attended or unattended vehicle on the main traveled part of a highway outside a business or residence district unless:

(1) stopping, parking, or leaving the vehicle off the main traveled part of the highway is not practicable;

(2) a width of highway beside the vehicle is unobstructed and open for the passage of other vehicles; and

(3) the vehicle is in clear view for at least 200 feet in each direction on the highway.

(b) This section does not apply to an operator of:

(1) a vehicle that is disabled while on the paved or main traveled part of a highway if it is impossible to avoid stopping and temporarily leaving the vehicle on the highway;

(2) a vehicle used exclusively to transport solid, semisolid, or liquid waste operated at the time in connection with the removal or transportation of solid, semisolid, or liquid waste from a location adjacent to the highway; or

(3) a tow truck, as defined by Section 545.157(e), that is performing towing duties under Chapter 2308, Occupations Code.

Sec. 545.302. Stopping, Standing, or Parking Prohibited in Certain Places.

(a) An operator may not stop, stand, or park a vehicle:

(1) on the roadway side of a vehicle stopped or parked at the edge or curb of a street;

(2) on a sidewalk;

(3) in an intersection;

(4) on a crosswalk;

(5) between a safety zone and the adjacent curb or within 30 feet of a place on the curb immediately opposite the ends of a safety zone, unless the governing body of a municipality designates a different length by signs or markings;

(6) alongside or opposite a street excavation or obstruction if stopping, standing, or parking the vehicle would obstruct traffic;

(7) on a bridge or other elevated structure on a highway or in a highway tunnel;

(8) on a railroad track; or

(9) where an official sign prohibits stopping.

(b) An operator may not, except momentarily to pick up or discharge a passenger, stand or park an occupied or unoccupied vehicle:

(1) in front of a public or private driveway;

(2) within 15 feet of a fire hydrant;

(3) within 20 feet of a crosswalk at an intersection;

(4) within 30 feet on the approach to a flashing signal, stop sign, yield sign, or traffic-control signal located at the side of a roadway;

(5) within 20 feet of the driveway entrance to a fire station and on the side of a street opposite the entrance to a fire station within 75 feet of the entrance, if the entrance is properly marked with a sign; or

(6) where an official sign prohibits standing.

(c) An operator may not, except temporarily to load or unload merchandise or passengers, park an occupied or unoccupied vehicle:

(1) within 50 feet of the nearest rail of a railroad crossing; or

(2) where an official sign prohibits parking.

(d) A person may stop, stand, or park a bicycle on a sidewalk if the bicycle does not impede the normal and reasonable movement of pedestrian or other traffic on the sidewalk.

(e) A municipality may adopt an ordinance exempting a private vehicle operated by an elevator constructor responding to an elevator emergency from Subsections (a)(1), (a)(5), (a)(6), (a)(9), (b), and (c).

(f) Subsections (a), (b), and (c) do not apply if the avoidance of conflict with other traffic is necessary or if the operator is complying with the law or the directions of a police officer or official traffic-control device.

(g) If the governing body of a municipality determines that it is necessary to improve the economic development of the municipality's central business district and that it will not adversely affect public safety, the governing body may adopt an ordinance regulating the standing, stopping, or parking of a vehicle at a place described by Subsection (a)(1), other than a road or highway in the state highway system, in the central business district of the municipality as defined in the ordinance. To the extent of any conflict between the ordinance and Subsection (a)(1), the ordinance controls.

Sec. 545.303. Additional Parking Regulations.

(a) An operator who stops or parks on a two-way roadway shall do so with the right-hand wheels of the vehicle parallel to and within 18 inches of the right-hand curb or edge of the roadway.

(b) An operator who stops or parks on a one-way roadway shall stop or park the vehicle parallel to the curb or edge of the roadway in the direction of authorized traffic movement with the right-hand wheels within 18 inches of the right-hand curb or edge of the roadway or the left-hand wheels within 18 inches of the left-hand curb or edge of the roadway. This subsection does not apply where a local ordinance otherwise regulates stopping or parking on the one-way roadway.

(c) A local authority by ordinance may permit angle parking on a roadway. This subsection does not apply to a federal-aid or state highway unless the director of the Texas Department of Transportation determines that the roadway is wide enough to permit angle parking without interfering with the free movement of traffic.

(d) The Texas Department of Transportation, on a highway under the jurisdiction of that department, may place signs prohibiting or restricting the stopping, standing, or parking of a vehicle on the highway where the director of the Texas Department of Transportation determines that stopping, standing, or parking is dangerous to, or would unduly interfere with, the free movement of traffic on the highway.

(e) To the extent of any conflict between Subsection (a) or (b) and a municipal ordinance adopted under Section 545.302(g), the ordinance controls.

Sec. 545.304. Moving the Vehicle of Another; Unlawful Parking.

A person may not move a vehicle that is not lawfully under the person's control:

(1) into an area where a vehicle is prohibited under Section 545.302; or

(2) away from a curb a distance that is unlawful under Section 545.303.

Sec. 545.305. Removal of Unlawfully Stopped Vehicle.

(a) A peace officer listed under Article 2.12, Code of Criminal Procedure, or a license and weight inspector of the department may remove or require the operator or a person in charge of a vehicle to move a vehicle from a highway if the vehicle:

(1) is unattended on a bridge, viaduct, or causeway or in a tube or tunnel and the vehicle is obstructing traffic;

(2) is unlawfully parked and blocking the entrance to a private driveway;

(3) has been reported as stolen;

(4) is identified as having been stolen in a warrant issued on the filing of a complaint;

(5) is unattended and the officer has reasonable grounds to believe that the vehicle has been abandoned for longer than 48 hours;

(6) is disabled so that normal operation is impossible or impractical and the owner or person in charge of the vehicle is:

(A) incapacitated and unable to provide for the vehicle's removal or custody; or

(B) not in the immediate vicinity of the vehicle;

(7) is disabled so that normal operation is impossible or impractical and the owner or person in charge of the vehicle does not designate a particular towing or storage company;

(8) is operated by a person an officer arrests for an alleged offense and the officer is required by law to take the person into custody; or

(9) is, in the opinion of the officer, a hazard, interferes with a normal function of a governmental agency, or because of a catastrophe, emergency, or unusual circumstance is imperiled.

(b) An officer acting under Subsection (a) may require that the vehicle be taken to:

(1) the nearest garage or other place of safety;

(2) a garage designated or maintained by the governmental agency that employs the officer; or

(3) a position off the paved or main traveled part of the highway.

(c) A law enforcement agency other than the department that removes an abandoned vehicle in an unincorporated area shall notify the sheriff.

(d) The owner of a vehicle that is removed or stored under this section is liable for all reasonable towing and storage fees incurred.

(e) In this section:

(1) "Towing company" means an individual, corporation, partnership, or other association engaged in the business of towing vehicles on a highway for compensation or with the expectation of compensation for the towing or storage of the vehicles and includes the owner, operator, employee, or agent of a towing company.

(2) "Storage company" means an individual, corporation, partnership, or other association engaged in the business of storing or repairing vehicles for compensation or with the expectation of compensation for the storage or repair of vehicles and

Transportation Code

includes the owner, operator, employee, or agent of a storage company.

Sec. 545.3051. Removal of Personal Property from Roadway or Right-of-Way.

(a) In this section:

(1) "Authority" means:

(A) a metropolitan rapid transit authority operating under Chapter 451; or

(B) a regional transportation authority operating under Chapter 452.

(2) "Law enforcement agency" means:

(A) the department;

(B) the police department of a municipality;

(C) the sheriff's office of a county; or

(D) a constable's office of a county.

(3) "Personal property" means:

(A) a vehicle described by Section 545.305;

(B) spilled cargo;

(C) a hazardous material as defined by 49 U.S.C. Section 5102 and its subsequent amendments;

(D) a hazardous substance as defined by Section 26.263, Water Code; or

(E) an unattended manufactured home as defined by Section 1201.003, Occupations Code.

(b) An authority or a law enforcement agency may remove personal property from a roadway or right-of-way if the authority or law enforcement agency determines that the property blocks the roadway or endangers public safety.

(c) Personal property may be removed under this section without the consent of the owner or carrier of the property.

(d) The owner and any carrier of personal property removed under this section shall reimburse the authority or law enforcement agency for any reasonable cost of removal and disposition of the property.

(e) Notwithstanding any other provision of law, an authority or a law enforcement agency is not liable for:

(1) any damage to personal property removed from a roadway or right-of-way under this section, unless the removal is carried out recklessly or in a grossly negligent manner; or

(2) any damage resulting from the failure to exercise the authority granted by this section.

Sec. 545.306. Regulation of Towing Companies in Certain Counties.

(a) The commissioners court of a county with a population of 3.3 million or more shall by ordinance provide for the licensing of or the granting of a permit to a person to remove or store a vehicle authorized by Section 545.305 to be removed in an unincorporated area of the county. The ordinance must include rules to ensure the protection of the public and the safe and efficient operation of towing and storage services in the county and may not regulate or restrict the use of lighting equipment more than the extent allowed by state and federal law. The sheriff shall determine the rules included in the ordinance with the review and consent of the commissioners court.

(b) The commissioners court shall set the fee for the license or permit in an amount that reasonably offsets the costs of enforcing the ordinance. The commissioners court shall use each license or permit fee to pay salaries and expenses of the sheriff's office for conducting inspections to determine compliance with the ordinance and laws relating to dealers in scrap metal and salvage.

Sec. 545.307. Overnight Parking of Commercial Motor Vehicle in or Near Residential Subdivision.

(a) In this section:

(1) "Commercial motor vehicle" means:

(A) a commercial motor vehicle, as defined by Section 522.003, and includes a vehicle meeting that definition regardless of whether the vehicle is used for a commercial purpose; or

(B) a road tractor, truck tractor, pole trailer, or semitrailer, as those terms are defined by Section 541.201.

(2) "Residential subdivision" means a subdivision in a county with a population greater than 220,000:

(A) for which a plat is recorded in the county real property records; and

(B) in which the majority of lots are subject to deed restrictions limiting the lots to residential use.

(b) Except as provided by Subsection (b-1), after 10 p.m. and before 6 a.m., a person may not park a commercial motor vehicle or leave the vehicle parked on a street that is maintained by a county or municipality and for which signs are posted as provided by Subsection (c) if the street:

(1) is located within a residential subdivision; or

(2) is adjacent to a residential subdivision and within 1,000 feet of the property line of a residence, school, place of worship, or park.

(b-1) A person may park a commercial motor vehicle or leave the vehicle parked on a street for which signs are posted as provided by Subsection (c) if the commercial motor vehicle:

(1) is transporting persons or property to or from the residential subdivision or performing work in the subdivision; and

(2) remains parked in or adjacent to the subdivision only for the period necessary to complete the transportation or work.

(c) The residents of a residential subdivision may petition a county or municipality in which the subdivision is located for the posting of signs prohibiting the overnight parking of a commercial motor vehicle in the subdivision or on a street adjacent to the subdivision and within 1,000 feet of the property line of a residence, school, place of worship, or park. The petition must be signed by at least 25 percent of the owners or tenants of residences in the subdivision. Not more than one person for each residence may sign the petition, and each person signing must be at least 18 years of age. Promptly after the filing of a petition meeting the requirements of this subsection and subject to Subsection (d), the county or municipality receiving the petition shall post the signs. The signs must:

(1) be posted:

(A) at each entrance of the subdivision through which a commercial motor vehicle may enter the subdivision or within the subdivision if there is not defined entrance to the subdivision; or

(B) on a street adjacent to the subdivision; and

(2) state, in letters at least two inches in height, that overnight parking of a commercial motor vehicle is prohibited in the subdivision or on a street adjacent to the subdivision.

(d) A county or municipality receiving a petition under Subsection (c) may condition the posting of the signs on payment by the residents of the residential subdivision of the cost of providing the signs.

(e) A person commits an offense if the person parks a commercial motor vehicle in violation of Subsection (b).

(f) This section does not limit the power of a municipality to regulate the parking of commercial motor vehicles.

(g) For the purposes of this section, contiguous subdivisions that are developed by the same entity or a successor to that entity and that are given the same public name or a variation of the same public name are considered one subdivision. Separation of one of the subdivisions from another by a road, stream, greenbelt, or similar barrier does not make the subdivisions noncontiguous.

(h) This section does not apply to:

(1) a vehicle owned by a utility that an employee of the utility who is on call 24 hours a day parks at the employee's residence; or

(2) a vehicle owned by a commercial establishment that is parked on the street adjacent to where the establishment is located.

Sec. 545.3075. Overnight Parking of Commercial Motor Vehicle Near Certain Apartment Complexes.

(a) In this section:

(1) "Apartment complex" means two or more dwellings in one or more buildings that are owned by the same owner, located on the same lot or tract, and managed by the same owner, agent, or management company.

(2) "Commercial motor vehicle" has the meaning assigned by Section 545.307.

(b) This section applies only to the unincorporated area of a county with a population of more than 3.3 million.

(c) The owner or manager of an apartment complex may make a request to the county in which the apartment complex is located for the posting of official signs prohibiting the parking of a commercial motor vehicle in a public right-of-way adjacent to the complex after 10 p.m. and before 6 a.m. A request under this subsection must be signed and in writing.

(d) A county receiving a request under Subsection (c) may post one or more signs as requested or as the county determines to be necessary.

(e) A sign posted under Subsection (d) must:

(1) be posted in the public right-of-way:

(A) not more than 10 feet from the property line of the apartment complex; and

(B) facing the roadway; and

(2) include:

(A) a statement, in letters at least two inches in height, that parking of a commercial motor vehicle is prohibited from 10 p.m. to 6 a.m. in the public right-of-way or portion of the public right-of-way; and

(B) arrows clearly indicating the area of the public right-of-way subject to the parking restriction.

(f) This section does not apply to a vehicle owned by a commercial establishment that is parked in the public right-of-way adjacent to the property where the establishment is located.

(g) This section does not apply to public rights-of-way that are part of the state highway system.

Sec. 545.308. Presumption.

The governing body of a local authority, by ordinance, order, or other official action, may provide that in a prosecution for an offense under this subchapter involving the stopping, standing, or parking of an unattended motor vehicle it is presumed that the registered owner of the vehicle is the person who stopped, stood, or parked the vehicle at the time and place the offense occurred.

SUBCHAPTER H SPEED RESTRICTIONS

Sec. 545.351. Maximum Speed Requirement.

(a) An operator may not drive at a speed greater than is reasonable and prudent under the circumstances then existing.

(b) An operator:

(1) may not drive a vehicle at a speed greater than is reasonable and prudent under the conditions and having regard for actual and potential hazards then existing; and

(2) shall control the speed of the vehicle as necessary to avoid colliding with another person or vehicle that is on or entering the highway in compliance with law and the duty of each person to use due care.

(c) An operator shall, consistent with Subsections (a) and (b), drive at an appropriate reduced speed if:

(1) the operator is approaching and crossing an intersection or railroad grade crossing;

(2) the operator is approaching and going around a curve;

(3) the operator is approaching a hill crest;

(4) the operator is traveling on a narrow or winding roadway; and

(5) a special hazard exists with regard to traffic, including pedestrians, or weather or highway conditions.

Sec. 545.352. Prima Facie Speed Limits.

(a) A speed in excess of the limits established by Subsection (b) or under another provision of this subchapter is prima facie evidence that the speed is not reasonable and prudent and that the speed is unlawful.

(b) Unless a special hazard exists that requires a slower speed for compliance with Section 545.351(b), the following speeds are lawful:

(1) 30 miles per hour in an urban district on a street other than an alley and 15 miles per hour in an alley;

(2) except as provided by Subdivision (4), 70 miles per hour on a highway numbered by this state or the United States outside an urban district, including a farm-to-market or ranch-to-market road;

(3) except as provided by Subdivision (4), 60 miles per hour on a highway that is outside an urban district and not a highway numbered by this state or the United States;

(4) outside an urban district:

(A) 60 miles per hour if the vehicle is a school bus that has passed a commercial motor vehicle inspection under Section 548.201 and is on a highway numbered by the United States or this state, including a farm-to-market road; or

(B) 50 miles per hour if the vehicle is a school bus that:

(i) has not passed a commercial motor vehicle inspection under Section 548.201; or

(ii) is traveling on a highway not numbered by the United States or this state;

(5) on a beach, 15 miles per hour; or

(6) on a county road adjacent to a public beach, 15 miles per hour, if declared by the commissioners court of the county.

(c) The speed limits for a bus or other vehicle engaged in the business of transporting passengers for compensation or hire, for a commercial vehicle used as a highway post office vehicle for highway post office service in the transportation of United States mail, for a light truck, and for a school activity bus are the same as required for a passenger car at the same time and location.

(d) In this section:

(1) "Interstate highway" means a segment of the national system of interstate and defense highways that is:

(A) located in this state;

(B) officially designated by the Texas Transportation Commission; and

(C) approved under Title 23, United States Code.

(2) "Light truck" means a truck with a manufacturer's rated carrying capacity of not more than 2,000 pounds, including a pick-up truck, panel delivery truck, and carry-all truck.

(3) "Urban district" means the territory adjacent to and including a highway, if the territory is improved with structures that are used for business, industry, or dwelling houses and are located at intervals of less than 100 feet for a distance of at least one-quarter mile on either side of the highway.

(e) An entity that establishes or alters a speed limit under this subchapter shall establish the same speed limit for daytime and nighttime.

Sec. 545.353. Authority of Texas Transportation Commission to Alter Speed Limits.

(a) If the Texas Transportation Commission determines from the results of an engineering and traffic investigation that a prima facie speed limit in this subchapter is unreasonable or unsafe on a part of the highway system, the commission, by order recorded in its minutes, and except as provided in Subsection (d), may determine and declare:

(1) a reasonable and safe prima facie speed limit; and

(2) another reasonable and safe speed because of wet or inclement weather.

(b) In determining whether a prima facie speed limit on a part of the highway system is reasonable and safe, the commission shall consider the width and condition of the pavement, the usual traffic at the affected area, and other circumstances.

(c) A prima facie speed limit that is declared by the commission under this section is effective when the commission erects signs giving notice of the new limit. A new limit that is enacted for a highway under this section is effective at all times or at other times as determined.

(d) Except as provided by Subsection (h-1), the commission may not:

(1) modify the rules established by Section 545.351(b);

(2) establish a speed limit of more than 75 miles per hour; or

(3) increase the speed limit for a vehicle described by Section 545.352(b)(4).

(e) The commission, in conducting the engineering and traffic investigation specified by Subsection (a), shall follow the "Procedure for Establishing Speed Zones" as adopted by the commission. The commission may revise the procedure to accommodate technological advancement in traffic operation, the design and construction of highways and motor vehicles, and the safety of the motoring public.

(f) The commission's authority to alter speed limits applies:

(1) to any part of a highway officially designated or marked by the commission as part of the state highway system; and

(2) both inside and outside the limits of a municipality, including a home-rule municipality, for a limited-access or controlled-access highway.

(g) For purposes of this section, "wet or inclement weather" means a condition of the roadway that makes driving on the roadway unsafe and hazardous and that is caused by precipitation, including water, ice, and snow.

(h) Notwithstanding Section 545.352(b), the commission may establish a speed limit of 75 miles per hour on a part of the highway system if the commission determines that 75 miles per hour is a reasonable and safe speed for that part of the highway system.

(h-1) Notwithstanding Section 545.352(b), the commission may establish a speed limit of 80 miles per hour on a part of Interstate Highway 10 or Interstate Highway 20 in Crockett, Culberson, Hudspeth, Jeff Davis, Kerr, Kimble, Pecos, Reeves, Sutton, or Ward County if the commission determines that 80 miles per hour is a reasonable and safe speed for that part of the highway.

(h-2) Notwithstanding Section 545.352(b), the commission may establish a speed limit not to exceed 85 miles per hour on a part of the state highway system if:

(1) that part of the highway system is designed to accommodate travel at that established speed or a higher speed; and

(2) the commission determines, after an engineering and traffic investigation, that the established speed limit is reasonable and safe for that part of the highway system.

(i) [Repealed by Acts 2011, 82nd Leg., ch. 265 (H.B. 1353), § 9, effective September 1, 2011.]

(j) The commission may not determine or declare, or agree to determine or declare, a prima facie speed limit for environmental purposes on a part of the highway system.

Sec. 545.3531. Authority of District Engineer to Temporarily Lower Speed Limit at Highway Maintenance Activity Site.

(a) A district engineer of the Texas Department of Transportation may temporarily lower a prima facie speed limit for a highway or part of a highway in a district if the district engineer determines that the prima facie speed limit for the highway or part of highway is unreasonable or unsafe because of highway maintenance activities at the site.

(b) A district engineer may temporarily lower a prima facie speed limit under this section without the approval of or permission from the Texas Transportation Commission.

(c) A temporary speed limit established under this section:

(1) is a prima facie prudent and reasonable speed limit enforceable in the same manner as other prima facie speed limits established under other provisions of this subchapter; and

(2) supersedes any other established speed limit that would permit a person to operate a motor vehicle at a higher rate of speed.

(d) After a district engineer temporarily lowers a speed limit under this section, the Texas Department of Transportation shall:

(1) place and maintain at the maintenance activity site temporary speed limit signs that conform to the manual and specifications adopted under Section 544.001;

(2) temporarily conceal all other signs on the highway or part of a highway affected by the maintenance activity that give notice of a speed limit that would permit a person to operate a motor vehicle at a higher rate of speed; and

Transportation Code

(3) remove all temporary speed limit signs placed under Subdivision (1) and concealments of other signs placed under Subdivision (2) when the temporary speed limit expires under Subsection (f).

(e) A temporary speed limit established under this section is effective when the Texas Department of Transportation, as required under Subsection (d), places temporary speed limit signs and conceals other signs that would permit a person to operate a motor vehicle at a higher rate of speed.

(f) A temporary speed limit established under this section:

(1) is effective until the earlier of:

(A) the 45th day after the date the limit becomes effective; or

(B) the date on which the district engineer determines that the maintenance activity has been completed and all equipment has been removed from the maintenance activity site; and

(2) may not be extended unless established by the Texas Transportation Commission under Section 545.353.

Sec. 545.3535. Authority of Texas Transportation Commission to Alter Speed Limits on Certain Roads.

(a) The commissioners court of a county by resolution may request the Texas Transportation Commission to determine and declare a reasonable and safe prima facie speed limit that is lower than a speed limit established by Section 545.352 on any part of a farm-to-market or a ranch-to-market road of the highway system that is located in that county and is without improved shoulders.

(b) The commission shall give consideration to local public opinion and may determine and declare a lower speed limit on any part of the road without an engineering and traffic investigation, but the commission must use sound and generally accepted traffic engineering practices in determining and declaring the lower speed limit.

(c) The commission by rule shall establish standards for determining lower speed limits within a set range.

Sec. 545.354. Authority of Regional Tollway Authorities to Alter Speed Limits on Turnpike Projects.

(a) (1) In this section, "authority" means a regional tollway authority governed by Chapter 366.

(2) If an authority determines from the results of an engineering and traffic investigation that a prima facie speed limit described in this subchapter is unreasonable or unsafe on a part of a turnpike constructed and maintained by the authority, the authority by order recorded in its minutes shall determine and declare a reasonable and safe prima facie speed limit for vehicles or classes of vehicles on the turnpike.

(b) In determining whether a prima facie speed limit on a part of a turnpike constructed and maintained by the authority is reasonable or safe, the authority shall consider the width and condition of the pavement, the usual traffic on the turnpike, and other circumstances.

(c) A prima facie speed limit that is declared by the authority in accordance with this section is effective when the authority erects signs giving notice of the new limit. A new limit that is adopted for a turnpike project constructed and maintained by the authority in accordance with this section is effective at all times or at other times as determined.

(d) The authority's power to alter prima facie speed limits is effective and exclusive on any part of a turnpike project constructed and maintained by the authority inside and outside the limits of a municipality, including a home-rule municipality.

(e) The authority may not:

(1) alter the general rule established by Section 545.351(a); or

(2) establish a speed limit of more than 75 miles per hour.

(f) The authority, in conducting the engineering and traffic investigation specified by Subsection (a), shall follow the procedure for establishing speed zones adopted by the Texas Department of Transportation.

Sec. 545.355. Authority of County Commissioners Court to Alter Speed Limits.

(a) The commissioners court of a county, for a county road or highway outside the limits of the right-of-way of an officially designated or marked highway or road of the state highway system and outside a municipality, has the same authority to increase prima facie speed limits from the results of an engineering and traffic investigation as the Texas Transportation Commission on an officially designated or marked highway of the state highway system.

(b) The commissioners court of a county may declare a lower speed limit of not less than:

(1) 30 miles per hour on a county road or highway to which this section applies, if the commissioners court determines that the prima facie speed limit on the road or highway is unreasonable or unsafe; or

(2) 20 miles per hour:

(A) in a residence district, unless the roadway has been designated as a major thoroughfare by a city planning commission; or

(B) on a county road or highway to which this section applies that is located within 500 feet of an elementary, secondary, or open-enrollment charter school or an institution of higher education, if approved under Section 545.357.

(c) The commissioners court may not modify the rule established by Section 545.351(a) or establish a speed limit of more than 70 miles per hour.

(d) The commissioners court may modify a prima facie speed limit in accordance with this section only by an order entered on its records.

(e) The commissioners court of a county with a population of more than 2.8 million may establish from the results of an engineering and traffic investigation a speed limit of not more than 75 miles per hour on any part of a highway of that county that is a limited-access or controlled-access highway, regardless of the location of the part of the highway.

Sec. 545.356. Authority of Municipality to Alter Speed Limits.

(a) The governing body of a municipality, for a highway or part of a highway in the municipality, including a highway of the state highway system, has the same authority to alter by ordinance prima facie speed limits from the results of an engineering and traffic investigation as the Texas Transportation Commission on an officially designated or marked highway of the state highway system. The governing body of a municipality may not modify the rule established by Section 545.351(a) or establish a speed limit of more than 75 miles per hour.

(b) The governing body of a municipality, for a highway or part of a highway in the municipality, including a highway of the state highway system, has the same authority to alter prima facie speed limits from the results of an engineering and traffic investigation as the commission for an officially designated or marked highway of the state highway system, when the highway or part of the highway is under repair, construction, or maintenance. A municipality may not modify the rule established by Section 545.351(a) or establish a speed limit of more than 75 miles per hour.

(b-1) Except as provided by Subsection (b-3), the governing body of a municipality, for a highway or a part of a highway in the municipality that is not an officially designated or marked highway or road of the state highway system, may declare a lower speed limit of not less than 25 miles per hour, if the governing body determines that the prima facie speed limit on the highway is unreasonable or unsafe.

(b-2) Subsection (b-1) applies only to a two-lane, undivided highway or part of a highway.

(b-3) The governing body of a municipality with a population of 2,000 or less, for a highway or a part of a highway in the municipality that is a one-lane highway used for two-way access and that is not an officially designated or marked highway or road of the state highway system, may declare a lower speed limit of not less than 10 miles per hour, if the governing body determines that the prima facie speed limit on the highway is unreasonable or unsafe.

(c) A prima facie speed limit that is altered by the governing body of a municipality under Subsection (b), (b-1), or (b-3) is effective when the governing body erects signs giving notice of the new limit and at all times or at other times as determined.

(d) The governing body of a municipality that declares a lower speed limit on a highway or part of a highway under Subsection (b-1) or (b-3), not later than February 1 of each year, shall publish on its Internet website and submit to the department a report that compares for each of the two previous calendar years:

(1) the number of traffic citations issued by peace officers of the municipality and the alleged speed of the vehicles, for speed limit violations on the highway or part of the highway;

(2) the number of warning citations issued by peace officers of the municipality on the highway or part of the highway; and

(3) the number of vehicular accidents that resulted in injury or death and were attributable to speed limit violations on the highway or part of the highway.

Sec. 545.3561. Authority of Municipality or County to Temporarily Lower Speed Limit at Vehicular Accident Reconstruction Site.

(a) The governing body of a municipality by ordinance may give a designated official with transportation engineering experience establishing speed limits discretion to temporarily lower a prima facie speed limit for a highway or part of a highway in the municipality, including a highway of the state highway system, at the site of an investigation using vehicular accident reconstruction.

(b) A county commissioners court by order may give a designated official with transportation engineering experience establishing speed limits discretion to temporarily lower prima facie speed limits for a county road or highway outside the boundaries of a municipality at the site of an investigation using vehicular accident reconstruction. The authority granted under this subsection does not include a road or highway in the state highway system.

(c) The Texas Department of Transportation shall develop safety guidelines for the use of vehicular accident reconstruction in investigations. A municipality, county, or designated official shall comply with the guidelines.

(d) A designated official may temporarily lower prima facie speed limits without the approval of or permission from the Texas Department of Transportation. A designated official who intends to temporarily lower a prima facie speed limit at the site of an investigation using vehicular accident reconstruction shall, at least 48 hours before temporary speed limit signs are posted for the vehicular accident reconstruction site, provide to the Texas Department of Transportation notice that includes:

(1) the date and time of the accident reconstruction;

(2) the location of the accident reconstruction site;

(3) the entities involved at the site;

(4) the general size of the area affected by the site; and

(5) an estimate of how long the site will be used for the accident reconstruction.

(e) A temporary speed limit established under this section:

(1) is a prima facie prudent and reasonable speed limit enforceable in the same manner as other prima facie speed limits established under other provisions of this subchapter; and

(2) supersedes any other established speed limit that would permit a person to operate a motor vehicle at a higher rate of speed.

(f) A designated official who temporarily lowers a speed limit shall:

(1) place and maintain at the vehicular accident reconstruction site temporary speed limit signs that conform to the manual and specifications adopted under Section 544.001;

(2) temporarily conceal all other signs on the highway segment affected by the vehicular accident reconstruction site that give notice of a speed limit that would permit a person to operate a motor vehicle at a higher rate of speed; and

(3) remove all temporary speed limit signs placed under Subdivision (1) and concealments of other signs placed under Subdivision (2) when the official finds that the vehicular accident reconstruction is complete and all equipment is removed from the vehicular accident reconstruction site.

(g) A temporary speed limit established under this section is effective when a designated official places temporary speed limit signs and conceals other signs that would permit a person to operate a motor vehicle at a higher rate of speed as required under Subsection (f).

(h) A temporary speed limit established under this section is effective until the designated official under Subsection (a) or (b):

(1) finds that the vehicular accident reconstruction is complete; and

(2) removes all temporary signs, concealments, and equipment used at the vehicular accident reconstruction site.

(i) If a designated official does not comply with the requirements of Subsection (f)(3) for a vehicular accident reconstruction on a state highway associated with the reconstruction, the Texas Department of Transportation may remove signs and concealments.

Sec. 545.357. Consideration of Speed Limits Where Certain Schools Are Located.

(a) The governing body of a municipality in which a public or private elementary or secondary school, an open-enrollment charter school, or an institution of higher education is located shall, on request of the governing body of a school or institution of higher education, hold a public hearing at least once each calendar year to consider prima facie speed limits on a highway in the municipality, including a highway of the state highway system, near the school or institution of higher education.

(b) If a county road outside the state highway system is located within 500 feet of a public or private elementary or secondary school, an open-enrollment charter school, or an institution of higher education that is not in a municipality, the commissioners court of the county, on request of the governing body of a school or institution of higher education, shall hold a public hearing at least once each calendar year to consider the prima facie speed limit on the road near the school or institution of higher education.

(c) A municipal governing body or commissioners court, on request of the governing body of a school or institution of higher education, may hold one public hearing for all public and private elementary and secondary schools, open-enrollment charter schools, and institutions of higher education in its jurisdiction.

(d) The Texas Transportation Commission, on request of the governing body of a school or institution of higher education, shall hold a public hearing at least once each calendar year to consider prima facie speed limits on highways in the state highway system that are near public or private elementary or secondary schools, open-enrollment charter schools, or institutions of higher education.

(e) On request of the governing body of a school or institution of higher education following a public hearing held under this section, the commissioners court, municipal governing body, or Texas Transportation Commission, as applicable, shall conduct an engineering and traffic investigation for the highway or road that is the subject of the request. On review of the results of the investigation, the commissioners court, municipal governing body, or Texas Transportation Commission has the same authority and discretion to alter prima facie speed limits as provided by Section 545.353, 545.355, or 545.356, as applicable. Following each public hearing held under this section, the governing body of a school or institution of higher education may make only one request under this subsection for an engineering and traffic investigation.

(f) In this section:

(1) "Governing body of a school or institution of higher education" means:

(A) the board of trustees of the school district in which a public elementary or secondary school is located;

(B) the governing body of a private elementary or secondary school;

(C) the governing body of an open-enrollment charter school; or

(D) the governing board of an institution of higher education.

(2) "Institution of higher education" means an institution of higher education or a private or independent institution of higher education, as those terms are defined by Section 61.003, Education Code.

(3) "Open-enrollment charter school" has the meaning assigned by Section 5.001, Education Code.

Sec. 545.358. Authority of Commanding Officer of United States Military Reservation to Alter Speed Limits.

The commanding officer of a United States military reservation, for a highway or part of a highway in the military reservation, including a highway of the state highway system, has the same authority by order to alter prima facie speed limits from the results of an engineering and traffic investigation as the Texas Transportation Commission for an officially designated or marked highway of the state highway system. A commanding officer may not modify the rule established by Section 545.351(a) or establish a speed limit of more than 75 miles per hour.

Sec. 545.359. Conflicting Designated Speed Limits.

An order of the Texas Transportation Commission declaring a speed limit on a part of a designated or marked route of the state highway system made under Section 545.353 or 545.362 supersedes any conflicting designated speed established under Sections 545.356 and 545.358.

Sec. 545.360. Duty of Texas Transportation Commission and State Board of Education to Provide Information and Assistance.

The chairman of the Texas Transportation Commission and the chairman of the State Board of Education shall provide assistance and information relevant to consideration of speed limits to commissioners courts, municipal governing bodies, and other interested persons.

Sec. 545.361. Special Speed Limitations.

(a) An operator of a moped or a motorcycle equipped with a motor that has an engine piston displacement of 250 cubic centimeters or less may not drive at a speed of more than 35 miles per hour during the time specified by Section 547.302(a) unless the motorcycle or moped is equipped with a headlamp or lamps that reveal a person or vehicle 300 feet ahead.

(b) An operator of a vehicle equipped with solid rubber or cushion tires may not drive at a speed of more than 10 miles per hour.

(c) An operator driving over a bridge or other elevated structure that is a part of a highway may not drive at a speed of more than the maximum speed that can be maintained with safety to the bridge or structure, when signs are posted as provided by this section.

(d) An operator of self-propelled machinery designed or adapted for applying plant food materials or agricultural chemicals and not designed or adapted for the sole purpose of transporting the materials or chemicals may not drive at a speed of more than 30 miles per hour unless the machinery is registered under Chapter 502.

(e) The Texas Transportation Commission, for a state highway, the Texas Turnpike Authority, for any part of a turnpike constructed and maintained by the authority, and a local authority for a highway under the jurisdiction of the local authority, may investigate a bridge or other elevated structure that is a part of a highway. If after conducting the investigation the commission, turnpike authority, or local authority finds that the structure cannot safely withstand vehicles traveling at a speed otherwise permissible under this subtitle, the commission, turnpike authority, or local authority shall:

(1) determine and declare the maximum speed of vehicles that the structure can safely withstand; and

(2) post and maintain signs before each end of the structure stating the maximum speed.

Sec. 545.362. Temporary Speed Limits.

(a) Subject to Subsection (c), the Texas Transportation Commission may enter an order establishing prima facie speed limits of not more than 75 miles per hour applicable to all highways, including a turnpike under the authority of the Texas Turnpike Authority or a highway under the control of a municipality or county. An order entered under this section does not have the effect of increasing a speed limit on any highway.

(b) The limits established under this section:

(1) are prima facie prudent and reasonable speed limits enforceable in the same manner as prima facie limits established under other provisions of this subchapter; and

(2) supersede any other established speed limit that would permit a person to operate a motor vehicle at a higher rate of speed.

(c) An order may be issued under Subsection (a) only if the commission finds and states in the order that:

(1) a severe shortage of motor fuel or other petroleum product exists, the shortage was caused by war, national emergency, or other circumstances, and a reduction of speed limits will foster conservation and safety; or

(2) the failure to alter state speed limits will prevent the state from receiving money from the United States for highway purposes.

(d) Unless a specific speed limit is required by federal law or directive under threat of loss of highway money of the United States, the commission may not set prima facie speed limits under this section of all vehicles at less than 60 miles per hour, except on a divided highway of at least four lanes, for which the commission may not set prima facie speed limits of all vehicles at less than 65 miles per hour.

(e) Before the commission may enter an order establishing a prima facie speed limit, it must hold a public hearing preceded by the publication in at least three newspapers of general circulation in the state of a notice of the date, time, and place of the hearing and of the action proposed to be taken. The notice must be published at least 12 days before the date of the hearing. At the hearing, all interested persons may present oral or written testimony regarding the proposed order.

(f) If the commission enters an order under this section, it shall file the order in the office of the governor. The governor shall then make an independent finding of fact and determine the existence of the facts in Subsection (c). Before the 13th day after the date the order is filed in the governor's office, the governor shall conclude the finding of fact, issue a proclamation stating whether the necessary facts exist to support the issuance of the commission's order, and file copies of the order and the proclamation in the office of the secretary of state.

(g) If the governor's proclamation states that the facts necessary to support the issuance of the commission's order exist, the order takes effect according to Subsection (h). Otherwise, the order has no effect.

(h) In an order issued under this section, the commission may specify the date the order takes effect, but that date may not be sooner than the eighth day after the date the order is filed with the governor. If the order does not have an effective date, it takes effect on the 21st day after the date it is filed with the governor. Unless the order by its own terms expires earlier, it remains in effect until a subsequent order adopted by the procedure prescribed by this section amends or repeals it, except that an order adopted under this section expires when this section expires. The procedure for repealing an order is the same as for adopting an order, except that the commission and the governor must find that the facts required to support the issuance of an order under Subsection (c) no longer exist.

(i) If an order is adopted in accordance with this section, the commission and all governmental authorities responsible for the maintenance of highway speed limit signs shall take appropriate action to conceal or remove all signs that give notice of a speed limit of more than the one contained in the order and to erect appropriate signs. All governmental entities responsible for administering traffic safety programs and enforcing traffic laws shall use all available resources to notify the public of the effect of the order. To accomplish this purpose, the governmental entities shall request the cooperation of all news media in the state.

(j) A change in speed limits under this section is effective until the commission makes a finding that the conditions in Subsection (c) require or authorize an additional change in those speed limits or in the highway or sections of highway to which those speed limits apply.

(k) This section expires when the national maximum speed limits are repealed.

Sec. 545.3625. Confidentiality of Violation Information: Fuel Conservation Speed Limit.

(a) If a person violates a maximum prima facie speed limit imposed under Section 545.362, as that

Transportation Code

law existed immediately before December 8, 1995, and the person was not traveling at a speed, as alleged in the citation, if not contested by the person, or, if contested by the person, as alleged in the complaint and found by the court, that is greater than the maximum prima facie speed limit for the location that has been established under this chapter, other than under Section 545.362, information in the custody of the department concerning the violation is confidential.

(b) The department may not release the information to any person or to another state governmental entity.

Sec. 545.363. Minimum Speed Regulations.

(a) An operator may not drive so slowly as to impede the normal and reasonable movement of traffic, except when reduced speed is necessary for safe operation or in compliance with law.

(b) When the Texas Transportation Commission, the Texas Turnpike Authority, the commissioners court of a county, or the governing body of a municipality, within the jurisdiction of each, as applicable, as specified in Sections 545.353–545.357, determines from the results of an engineering and traffic investigation that slow speeds on a part of a highway consistently impede the normal and reasonable movement of traffic, the commission, authority, county commissioners court, or governing body may determine and declare a minimum speed limit on the highway.

(c) If appropriate signs are erected giving notice of a minimum speed limit adopted under this section, an operator may not drive a vehicle more slowly than that limit except as necessary for safe operation or in compliance with law.

Sec. 545.364. Speed Limits on Beaches [Repealed].

Repealed by Acts 1999, 76th Leg., ch. 1346 (H.B. 676), § 3, effective September 1, 1999.

Sec. 545.364. Speed Limit Signs After Construction or Maintenance Work Zone.

(a) In this section, "construction or maintenance work zone" has the meaning assigned by Section 472.022.

(b) An entity that sets a lower speed limit on a road or highway in the state highway system for a construction or maintenance work zone shall place or require to be placed a sign at the end of the zone that indicates the speed limit after the zone ends.

Sec. 545.365. Speed Limit Exception for Emergencies; Municipal Regulation.

(a) The regulation of the speed of a vehicle under this subchapter does not apply to:

(1) an authorized emergency vehicle responding to a call;

(2) a police patrol; or

(3) a physician or ambulance responding to an emergency call.

(b) A municipality by ordinance may regulate the speed of:

(1) an ambulance;

(2) an emergency medical services vehicle; or

(3) an authorized vehicle operated by a blood or tissue bank.

SUBCHAPTER I MISCELLANEOUS RULES

Sec. 545.401. Reckless Driving; Offense.

(a) A person commits an offense if the person drives a vehicle in wilful or wanton disregard for the safety of persons or property.

(b) An offense under this section is a misdemeanor punishable by:

(1) a fine not to exceed $200;

(2) confinement in county jail for not more than 30 days; or

(3) both the fine and the confinement.

(c) Notwithstanding Section 542.001, this section applies to:

(1) a private access way or parking area provided for a client or patron by a business, other than a private residential property or the property of a garage or parking lot for which a charge is made for the storing or parking of motor vehicles; and

(2) a highway or other public place.

(d) Notwithstanding Section 542.004, this section applies to a person, a team, or motor vehicles and other equipment engaged in work on a highway surface.

Sec. 545.402. Moving a Parked Vehicle.

An operator may not begin movement of a stopped, standing, or parked vehicle unless the movement can be made safely.

Sec. 545.403. Driving Through Safety Zone.

An operator may not drive through or in a safety zone.

Sec. 545.404. Unattended Motor Vehicle.

(a) Except as provided by Subsection (b), an operator may not leave a vehicle unattended without:

(1) stopping the engine;

(2) locking the ignition;

(3) removing the key from the ignition;

(4) setting the parking brake effectively; and

(5) if standing on a grade, turning the front wheels to the curb or side of the highway.

(b) The requirements of Subsections (a)(1), (2), and (3) do not apply to an operator who starts the engine of a vehicle by using a remote starter or other similar device that:

(1) remotely starts the vehicle's engine without placing the key in the ignition; and

(2) requires the key to be placed in the ignition or physically present in the vehicle before the vehicle can be operated.

Sec. 545.405. Driving on Mountain Highway.

An operator moving through a defile or canyon or on a mountain highway shall:

(1) hold the vehicle under control and as near the right-hand edge of the highway as possible; and

(2) on approaching a curve that obstructs the view of the highway for 200 feet, give warning with the horn of the motor vehicle.

Sec. 545.406. Coasting.

(a) An operator moving on a downgrade may not coast with the gears or transmission of the vehicle in neutral.

(b) An operator of a truck, tractor, or bus moving on a downgrade may not coast with the clutch disengaged.

Sec. 545.407. Following or Obstructing Fire Apparatus or Ambulance.

(a) An operator, unless on official business, may not follow closer than 500 feet a fire apparatus responding to a fire alarm or drive into or park the vehicle in the block where the fire apparatus has stopped to answer a fire alarm.

(b) An operator may not:

(1) follow closer than 500 feet an ambulance that is flashing red lights unless the operator is on official business; or

(2) drive or park the vehicle where an ambulance has been summoned for an emergency call in a manner intended to interfere with the arrival or departure of the ambulance.

Sec. 545.408. Crossing Fire Hose.

An operator may not, without the consent of the fire department official in command, drive over an unprotected hose of a fire department if the hose is on a street or private driveway and is intended for use at a fire or alarm of fire.

Sec. 545.409. Drawbars and Trailer Hitches; Saddle-Mount Towing.

(a) The drawbar or other connection between a vehicle drawing another vehicle and the drawn vehicle:

(1) must be strong enough to pull all weight drawn; and

(2) may not exceed 15 feet between the vehicles except for a connection between two vehicles transporting poles, pipe, machinery, or other objects of structural nature that cannot readily be dismembered.

(b) An operator drawing another vehicle and using a chain, rope, or cable to connect the vehicles shall display on the connection a white flag or cloth not less than 12 inches square.

(c) A motor vehicle may not draw more than three motor vehicles attached to it by the triple saddle-mount method. In this subsection, "triple saddle-mount method" means the mounting of the front wheels of trailing vehicles on the bed of another vehicle while leaving the rear wheels only of the trailing vehicles in contact with the roadway.

Sec. 545.410. Towing Safety Chains.

(a) An operator of a passenger car or light truck may not draw a trailer, semitrailer, house trailer, or another motor vehicle unless safety chains of a type approved by the department are attached in a manner approved by the department from the trailer, semitrailer, house trailer, or drawn motor vehicle to the drawing vehicle. This subsection does not apply to the drawing of a trailer or semitrailer used for agricultural purposes.

(b) The department shall adopt rules prescribing the type of safety chains required to be used according to the weight of the trailer, semitrailer, house trailer, or motor vehicle being drawn. The rules shall:

(1) require safety chains to be strong enough to maintain the connection between the trailer, semitrailer, house trailer, or drawn motor vehicle and the drawing vehicle; and

(2) show the proper method to attach safety chains between the trailer, semitrailer, house trailer, or drawn motor vehicle and the drawing vehicle.

Transportation Code

(c) Subsection (b) does not apply to trailers, semitrailers, or house trailers that are equipped with safety chains installed by the original manufacturer before the effective date of the rules.

(d) This section does not apply to a trailer, semitrailer, house trailer, or drawn motor vehicle that is operated in compliance with the federal motor carrier safety regulations.

(e) In this section, "safety chains" means flexible tension members connected from the front of a drawn vehicle to the rear of the drawing vehicle to maintain connection between the vehicles if the primary connecting system fails.

Sec. 545.411. Use of Rest Area: Offense.

(a) A person commits an offense if the person remains at a rest area for longer than 24 hours or erects a tent, shelter, booth, or structure at the rest area and the person:

(1) has notice while conducting the activity that the activity is prohibited; or

(2) receives notice that the activity is prohibited but does not depart or remove the structure within eight hours after receiving notice.

(b) For purposes of this section, a person:

(1) has notice if a sign stating the prohibited activity and penalty is posted on the premises; or

(2) receives notice if a peace officer orally communicates to the person the prohibited activity and penalty for the offense.

(c) It is an exception to Subsection (a) if a nonprofit organization erects a temporary structure at a rest area to provide food services, food, or beverages to travelers and the Texas Department of Transportation:

(1) finds that the services would constitute a public service for the benefit of the traveling public; and

(2) issues a permit to the organization.

(d) In this section, "rest area" means public real property designated as a rest area, comfort station, picnic area, roadside park, or scenic overlook by the Texas Department of Transportation.

Sec. 545.412. Child Passenger Safety Seat Systems; Offense.

(a) A person commits an offense if the person operates a passenger vehicle, transports a child who is younger than eight years of age, unless the child is taller than four feet, nine inches, and does not keep the child secured during the operation of the vehicle in a child passenger safety seat system according to the instructions of the manufacturer of the safety seat system.

(b) An offense under this section is a misdemeanor punishable by a fine of not less than $25 and not more than $250.

(b-1) [Repealed by Acts 2011, 82nd Leg., 1st C.S., ch. 4 (S.B. 1), § 69.01(1), effective September 28, 2011.]

(c) It is a defense to prosecution under this section that the person was operating the vehicle in an emergency or for a law enforcement purpose.

(d) [Repealed by Acts 2003, 78th Leg., ch. 204 (H.B. 4), § 8.01, effective September 1, 2003.]

(e) This section does not apply to a person:

(1) operating a vehicle transporting passengers for hire, excluding third-party transport service providers when transporting clients pursuant to a contract to provide nonemergency Medicaid transportation; or

(2) transporting a child in a vehicle in which all seating positions equipped with child passenger safety seat systems or safety belts are occupied.

(f) In this section:

(1) "Child passenger safety seat system" means an infant or child passenger restraint system that meets the federal standards for crash-tested restraint systems as set by the National Highway Traffic Safety Administration.

(2) "Passenger vehicle" means a passenger car, light truck, sport utility vehicle, passenger van designed to transport 15 or fewer passengers, including the driver, truck, or truck tractor.

(3) "Safety belt" means a lap belt and any shoulder straps included as original equipment on or added to a vehicle.

(4) "Secured," in connection with use of a safety belt, means using the lap belt and any shoulder straps according to the instructions of:

(A) the manufacturer of the vehicle, if the safety belt is original equipment; or

(B) the manufacturer of the safety belt, if the safety belt has been added to the vehicle.

(g) **[Repealed effective June 1, 2023]** A judge, acting under Article 45.0511, Code of Criminal Procedure, who elects to defer further proceedings and to place a defendant accused of a violation of this section on probation under that article, in lieu of requiring the defendant to complete a driving safety course approved by the Texas Department of Licensing and Regulation, shall require the defendant to attend and present proof that the defendant has successfully completed a specialized driving safety course approved by the Texas Department of Licensing and Regulation Education Agency under Chapter 1001, Education Code, that includes four hours of instruction that encourages the use of child passenger safety seat systems and the wearing of seat belts and emphasizes:

(h) Notwithstanding Section 542.402(a), a municipality or county, at the end of the municipality's or county's fiscal year, shall send to the comptroller an amount equal to 50 percent of the fines collected by the municipality or the county for violations of this section. The comptroller shall deposit the amount received to the credit of the tertiary care fund for use by trauma centers.

Sec. 545.4121. Dismissal; Obtaining Child Passenger Safety Seat System.

(a) This section applies to an offense committed under Section 545.412.

(b) It is a defense to prosecution of an offense to which this section applies that the defendant provides to the court evidence satisfactory to the court that:

(1) at the time of the offense:

(A) the defendant was not arrested or issued a citation for violation of any other offense;

(B) the defendant did not possess a child passenger safety seat system in the vehicle; and

(C) the vehicle the defendant was operating was not involved in an accident; and

(2) subsequent to the time of the offense, the defendant obtained an appropriate child passenger safety seat system for each child required to be secured in a child passenger safety seat system under Section 545.412(a).

Sec. 545.413. Safety Belts; Offense.

(a) A person commits an offense if:

(1) the person:

(A) is at least 15 years of age;

(B) is riding in a passenger vehicle while the vehicle is being operated;

(C) is occupying a seat that is equipped with a safety belt; and

(D) is not secured by a safety belt; or

(2) as the operator of a school bus equipped with a safety belt for the operator's seat, the person is not secured by the safety belt.

(b) A person commits an offense if the person:

(1) operates a passenger vehicle that is equipped with safety belts; and

(2) allows a child who is younger than 17 years of age and who is not required to be secured in a child passenger safety seat system under Section 545.412(a) to ride in the vehicle without requiring the child to be secured by a safety belt, provided the child is occupying a seat that is equipped with a safety belt.

(b-1) A person commits an offense if the person allows a child who is younger than 17 years of age and who is not required to be secured in a child passenger safety seat system under Section 545.412(a) to ride in a passenger van designed to transport 15 or fewer passengers, including the driver, without securing the child individually by a safety belt, if the child is occupying a seat that is equipped with a safety belt.

(c) A passenger vehicle or a seat in a passenger vehicle is considered to be equipped with a safety belt if the vehicle is required under Section 547.601 to be equipped with safety belts.

(d) An offense under Subsection (a) is a misdemeanor punishable by a fine of not less than $25 or more than $50. An offense under Subsection (b) is a misdemeanor punishable by a fine of not less than $100 or more than $200.

(e) It is a defense to prosecution under this section that:

(1) the person possesses a written statement from a licensed physician stating that for a medical reason the person should not wear a safety belt;

(2) the person presents to the court, not later than the 10th day after the date of the offense, a statement from a licensed physician stating that for a medical reason the person should not wear a safety belt;

(3) the person is employed by the United States Postal Service and performing a duty for that agency that requires the operator to service postal boxes from a vehicle or that requires frequent entry into and exit from a vehicle;

(4) the person is engaged in the actual delivery of newspapers from a vehicle or is performing newspaper delivery duties that require frequent entry into and exit from a vehicle;

(5) the person is employed by a public or private utility company and is engaged in the reading of meters or performing a similar duty for that company requiring the operator to frequently enter into and exit from a vehicle;

(6) the person is operating a commercial vehicle registered as a farm vehicle under the provisions of Section 502.433 that does not have a gross weight, registered weight, or gross weight rating of 48,000 pounds or more; or

(7) the person is the operator of or a passenger in a vehicle used exclusively to transport solid waste and performing duties that require frequent entry into and exit from the vehicle.

(f) The department shall develop and implement an educational program to encourage the wearing of safety belts and to emphasize:

(1) the effectiveness of safety belts and other restraint devices in reducing the risk of harm to passengers in motor vehicles; and

Transportation Code

(2) the requirements of this section and the penalty for noncompliance.

(g) [Repealed by Acts 2003, 78th Leg., ch. 204 (H.B. 4), § 8.01, effective September 1, 2003.]

(h) In this section, "passenger vehicle," "safety belt," and "secured" have the meanings assigned by Section 545.412.

(i) **[Repealed effective June 1, 2023]** A judge, acting under Article 45.0511, Code of Criminal Procedure, who elects to defer further proceedings and to place a defendant accused of a violation of Subsection (b) on probation under that article, in lieu of requiring the defendant to complete a driving safety course approved by the Texas Department of Licensing and Regulation, shall require the defendant to attend and present proof that the defendant has successfully completed a specialized driving safety course approved by the Texas Department of Licensing and Regulation under Chapter 1001, Education Code, that includes four hours of instruction that encourages the use of child passenger safety seat systems and the wearing of seat belts and emphasizes:

(1) the effectiveness of child passenger safety seat systems and seat belts in reducing the harm to children being transported in motor vehicles; and

(2) the requirements of this section and the penalty for noncompliance.

(j) Notwithstanding Section 542.402(a), a municipality or county, at the end of the municipality's or county's fiscal year, shall send to the comptroller an amount equal to 50 percent of the fines collected by the municipality or the county for violations of Subsection (b) of this section. The comptroller shall deposit the amount received to the credit of the tertiary care fund for use by trauma centers.

Sec. 545.414. Riding in Open Beds; Offense.

(a) A person commits an offense if the person operates an open-bed pickup truck or an open flatbed truck or draws an open flatbed trailer when a child younger than 18 years of age is occupying the bed of the truck or trailer.

(b) An offense under this section is a misdemeanor punishable by a fine of not less than $25 or more than $200.

(c) It is a defense to prosecution under this section that the person was:

(1) operating or towing the vehicle in a parade or in an emergency;

(2) operating the vehicle to transport farmworkers from one field to another field on a farm-to-market road, ranch-to-market road, or county road outside a municipality;

(3) operating the vehicle on a beach;

(4) operating a vehicle that is the only vehicle owned or operated by the members of a household; or

(5) operating the vehicle in a hayride permitted by the governing body of or a law enforcement agency of each county or municipality in which the hayride will occur.

(d) Compliance or noncompliance with Subsection (a) is not admissible evidence in a civil trial.

(e) In this section, "household" has the meaning assigned by Section 71.005, Family Code.

Sec. 545.4145. Riding in or on Boat or Personal Watercraft Drawn by Vehicle; Offense.

(a) A person commits an offense if the person operates a motor vehicle on a highway or street when a child younger than 18 years of age is occupying a boat or personal watercraft being drawn by the motor vehicle.

(b) It is a defense to prosecution under this section that the person was:

(1) operating the motor vehicle in a parade or in an emergency; or

(2) operating the motor vehicle on a beach.

(c) In this section, "boat" and "personal watercraft" have the meanings assigned by Section 31.003, Parks and Wildlife Code.

Sec. 545.415. Backing a Vehicle.

(a) An operator may not back the vehicle unless the movement can be made safely and without interference with other traffic.

(b) An operator may not back the vehicle on a shoulder or roadway of a limited-access or controlled-access highway.

Sec. 545.416. Riding on Motorcycle or Moped.

(a) An operator of a motorcycle or moped shall ride on the permanent and regular seat attached to the motorcycle or moped.

(b) An operator may not carry another person on the motorcycle or moped, and a person who is not operating the motorcycle or moped may not ride on the motorcycle or moped, unless the motorcycle or moped is:

(1) designed to carry more than one person; and

(2) equipped with footrests and handholds for use by the passenger.

(c) If the motorcycle or moped is designed to carry more than one person, a passenger may ride only on the permanent and regular seat, if designed for two persons, or on another seat firmly attached to the motorcycle or moped behind or to the side of the operator.

(d) Except as provided by Subsection (e), an operator may not carry another person on a motorcycle or moped unless the other person is at least five years of age. An offense under this subsection is a misdemeanor punishable by a fine of not less than $100 or more than $200. It is a defense to prosecution under this subsection that the operator was operating the motorcycle or moped in an emergency or for a law enforcement purpose.

(e) Subsection (d) does not prohibit an operator from carrying on a motorcycle or moped a person younger than five years of age who is seated in a sidecar attached to the motorcycle or moped.

(f) For purposes of Subsections (c) and (d), an autocycle as defined by Section 501.008 is considered to be a motorcycle.

Sec. 545.4165. Operation of Certain Motorcycles.

A person may not operate a motorcycle described by Section 521.001(a)(6-a)(C)(vii) on a public highway for which the posted speed limit is more than 45 miles per hour, except that the operator may cross an intersection with a public highway that has a posted speed limit of more than 45 miles per hour.

Transportation Code

Sec. 545.417. Obstruction of Operator's View or Driving Mechanism.

(a) An operator may not drive a vehicle when it is loaded so that, or when the front seat has a number of persons, exceeding three, so that:

(1) the view of the operator to the front or sides of the vehicle is obstructed; or

(2) there is interference with the operator's control over the driving mechanism of the vehicle.

(b) A passenger in a vehicle may not ride in a position that interferes with the operator's view to the front or sides or control over the driving mechanism of the vehicle.

Sec. 545.418. Opening Vehicle Doors.

A person may not:

(1) open the door of a motor vehicle on the side available to moving traffic, unless the door may be opened in reasonable safety without interfering with the movement of other traffic; or

(2) leave a door on the side of a vehicle next to moving traffic open for longer than is necessary to load or unload a passenger.

Sec. 545.419. Riding in House Trailer.

A person may not occupy a house trailer while it is being moved.

Sec. 545.4191. Person Riding in Trailer or Semitrailer Drawn by Truck, Road Tractor, or Truck Tractor.

(a) A person may not operate a truck, road tractor, or truck tractor when another person occupies a trailer or semitrailer being drawn by the truck, road tractor, or truck tractor.

(b) It is a defense to prosecution under this section that:

(1) the person was operating or towing the vehicle:

(A) in a parade or in an emergency;

(B) to transport farmworkers from one field to another field on a farm-to-market road, ranch-to-market road, or county road outside a municipality; or

(C) in a hayride permitted by the governing body of or a law enforcement agency of each county or municipality in which the hayride will occur;

(2) the person operating or towing the vehicle did not know that another person occupied the trailer or semitrailer; or

(3) the person occupying the trailer or semitrailer was in a part of the trailer or semitrailer designed for human habitation.

(c) An offense under this section is a Class B misdemeanor.

Sec. 545.420. Racing on Highway.

(a) A person may not participate in any manner in:

(1) a race;

(2) a vehicle speed competition or contest;

(3) a drag race or acceleration contest;

(4) a test of physical endurance of the operator of a vehicle; or

(5) in connection with a drag race, an exhibition of vehicle speed or acceleration or to make a vehicle speed record.

(b) In this section:

(1) "Drag race" means the operation of:

(A) two or more vehicles from a point side by side at accelerating speeds in a competitive attempt to outdistance each other; or

(B) one or more vehicles over a common selected course, from the same place to the same place, for the purpose of comparing the relative speeds or power of acceleration of the vehicle or vehicles in a specified distance or time.

(2) "Race" means the use of one or more vehicles in an attempt to:

(A) outgain or outdistance another vehicle or prevent another vehicle from passing;

(B) arrive at a given destination ahead of another vehicle or vehicles; or

(C) test the physical stamina or endurance of an operator over a long-distance driving route.

(c) [Blank]

(d) Except as provided by Subsections (e)-(h), an offense under Subsection (a) is a Class B misdemeanor.

(e) An offense under Subsection (a) is a Class A misdemeanor if it is shown on the trial of the offense that:

(1) the person has previously been convicted one time of an offense under that subsection; or

(2) the person, at the time of the offense:

(A) was operating the vehicle while intoxicated, as defined by Section 49.01, Penal Code; or

(B) was in possession of an open container, as defined by Section 49.031, Penal Code.

(f) An offense under Subsection (a) is a state jail felony if it is shown on the trial of the offense that the person has previously been convicted two times of an offense under that subsection.

(g) An offense under Subsection (a) is a felony of the third degree if it is shown on the trial of the offense that as a result of the offense, an individual suffered bodily injury.

(h) An offense under Subsection (a) is a felony of the second degree if it is shown on the trial of the offense that as a result of the offense, an individual suffered serious bodily injury or death.

(i) This subsection applies only to a motor vehicle used in the commission of an offense under this section that results in an accident with property damage or personal injury. A peace officer shall require the vehicle to be taken to the nearest licensed vehicle storage facility unless the vehicle is seized as evidence, in which case the vehicle may be taken to a storage facility as designated by the peace officer involved. Notwithstanding Article 18.23, Code of Criminal Procedure, the owner of a motor vehicle that is removed or stored under this subsection is liable for all removal and storage fees incurred and is not entitled to take possession of the vehicle until those fees are paid.

Sec. 545.4205. Interference with Peace Officer Investigation of Highway Racing or Reckless Driving Exhibition; Criminal Offense.

(a) A person commits an offense if the person uses the person's body, a car, or a barricade to knowingly impede or otherwise interfere with a peace officer's investigation of conduct prohibited under Section 545.420 or a reckless driving exhibition, as defined by Section 42.03, Penal Code.

(b) An offense under this section is a Class B misdemeanor.

(c) If conduct constituting an offense under this section also constitutes an offense under any other law, the actor may be prosecuted under this section, the other law, or both.

Sec. 545.421. Fleeing or Attempting to Elude Police Officer; Offense.

(a) A person commits an offense if the person operates a motor vehicle and wilfully fails or refuses to bring the vehicle to a stop or flees, or attempts to elude, a pursuing police vehicle when given a visual or audible signal to bring the vehicle to a stop.

(b) A signal under this section that is given by a police officer pursuing a vehicle may be by hand, voice, emergency light, or siren. The officer giving the signal must be in uniform and prominently display the officer's badge of office. The officer's vehicle must bear the insignia of a law enforcement agency, regardless of whether the vehicle displays an emergency light.

(c) Except as provided by Subsection (d), an offense under this section is a Class B misdemeanor.

(d) An offense under this section is a Class A misdemeanor if the person, during the commission of the offense, recklessly engages in conduct that places another in imminent danger of serious bodily injury.

(e) A person is presumed to have recklessly engaged in conduct placing another in imminent danger of serious bodily injury under Subsection (d) if the person while intoxicated knowingly operated a motor vehicle during the commission of the offense. In this subsection, "intoxicated" has the meaning assigned by Section 49.01, Penal Code.

Sec. 545.422. Crossing Sidewalk or Hike and Bike Trail.

(a) A person may not drive a motor vehicle on a sidewalk, sidewalk area, or hike and bike trail except on a permanent or authorized temporary driveway.

(b) Subsection (a) does not prohibit the operation of a motor vehicle on a hike and bike trail in connection with maintenance of the trail.

(c) In this section, "hike and bike trail" means a trail designed for the exclusive use of pedestrians, bicyclists, or both.

Transportation Code

Sec. 545.423. Crossing Property.

(a) An operator may not cross a sidewalk or drive through a driveway, parking lot, or business or residential entrance without stopping the vehicle.

(b) An operator may not cross or drive in or on a sidewalk, driveway, parking lot, or business or residential entrance at an intersection to turn right or left from one highway to another highway.

Sec. 545.424. Operation of Vehicle by Person Under 18 Years of Age.

(a) A person under 18 years of age may not operate a motor vehicle while using a wireless communication device, except in case of emergency. This subsection does not apply to a person licensed by the Federal Communications Commission while operating a radio frequency device other than a wireless communication device.

(a-1) A person under 18 years of age may not operate a motor vehicle:

(1) after midnight and before 5 a.m. unless the operation of the vehicle is necessary for the operator to attend or participate in employment or a school-related activity or because of a medical emergency; or

(2) with more than one passenger in the vehicle under 21 years of age who is not a family member.

(a-2) Notwithstanding Subsection (a-1), a person under 18 years of age may operate a moped after midnight and before 5 a.m. if the person is in sight of the person's parent or guardian.

(b) A person under 17 years of age who holds a restricted motorcycle license may not operate a motorcycle while using a wireless communication device, except in case of emergency. This subsection does not apply to a person licensed by the Federal Communications Commission while operating a radio frequency device other than a wireless communication device.

(b-1) A person under 17 years of age who holds a restricted motorcycle license, during the 12-month period following the issuance of an original motorcycle license to the person, may not operate a motorcycle after midnight and before 5 a.m. unless:

(1) the person is in sight of the person's parent or guardian; or

(2) the operation of the vehicle is necessary for the operator to attend or participate in employment or a school-related activity or because of a medical emergency.

(c) Subsection (a-1) does not apply to a person operating a motor vehicle while accompanied in the manner required by Section 521.222(d)(2) for the holder of a learner license.

(d) For the purposes of this section, employment includes work on a family farm by a member of the family that owns or operates the farm.

(e) A peace officer may not stop a vehicle or detain the operator of a vehicle for the sole purpose of determining whether the operator of the vehicle has violated this section.

(f) In this section, "wireless communication device" means a handheld or hands-free device that uses commercial mobile service, as defined by 47 U.S.C. Section 332.

(g) An offense under Subsection (a) or (b) is a misdemeanor punishable by a fine of at least $25 and not more than $99 unless it is shown on the trial of the offense that the defendant has been previously convicted at least one time of an offense under either subsection, in which event the offense is punishable by a fine of at least $100 and not more than $200.

Sec. 545.425. Use of Wireless Communication Device in a School Crossing Zone or While Operating a Bus with a Minor Passenger; Local Authority Sign Requirements; Offense.

(a) In this section:

(1) "Hands-free device" means speakerphone capability, a telephone attachment, or another function or other piece of equipment, regardless of whether permanently installed in or on a wireless communication device or in a motor vehicle, that allows use of the wireless communication device without use of either of the operator's hands, except to activate or deactivate a function of the wireless communication device or hands-free device. The term includes voice-operated technology and a push-to-talk function.

(2) "Wireless communication device" means a device that uses a commercial mobile service, as defined by 47 U.S.C. Section 332.

(b) Except as provided by Subsection (c), an operator may not use a wireless communication device while operating a motor vehicle within a school crossing zone, as defined by Section 541.302, Transportation Code, unless:

(1) the vehicle is stopped; or

(2) the wireless communication device is used with a hands-free device.

(b-1) Except as provided by Subsection (b-2), a local authority that enforces this section in a school crossing zone in the local authority's jurisdiction shall post a sign, or approve the posting of a sign by a school or school district, that complies with the standards described by this subsection at each entrance to the school crossing zone. The Texas

Transportation Code

Department of Transportation shall adopt standards that:

(1) allow for a sign required to be posted under this subsection to be attached to an existing sign at a minimal cost; and

(2) require that a sign required to be posted under this subsection inform an operator that:

(A) the use of a wireless communication device is prohibited in the school crossing zone; and

(B) the operator is subject to a fine if the operator uses a wireless communication device in the school crossing zone.

(b-2) A local authority that by ordinance or rule prohibits the use of a wireless communication device while operating a motor vehicle, including a prohibition that contains an exception for the use of a wireless communication device with a hands-free device, throughout the jurisdiction of the local authority is not required to post a sign as required by Subsection (b-1) and shall:

(1) post signs that are located at each point at which a state highway, U.S. highway, or interstate highway enters the jurisdiction of the local authority and that state:

(A) that an operator is prohibited from using a wireless communication device while operating a motor vehicle in the jurisdiction of the local authority, and whether use of a wireless communication device with a hands-free device is allowed in the jurisdiction of the local authority; and

(B) that the operator is subject to a fine if the operator uses a wireless communication device while operating a motor vehicle in the jurisdiction of the local authority; and

(2) subject to all applicable United States Department of Transportation Federal Highway Administration rules, post a message that complies with Subdivision (1) on any dynamic message sign operated by the local authority located on a state highway, U.S. highway, or interstate highway in the jurisdiction of the local authority.

(b-3) A sign posted under Subsection (b-2)(1) must be readable to an operator traveling at the applicable speed limit.

(b-4) The local authority shall pay the costs associated with the posting of signs under Subsections (b-1) and (b-2), unless the authority enters an agreement providing otherwise.

(c) An operator may not use a wireless communication device while operating a school bus or passenger bus with a minor passenger on the bus unless the bus is stopped.

(d) It is an affirmative defense to prosecution of an offense under this section that:

(1) the wireless communication device was used to make an emergency call to:

(A) an emergency response service, including a rescue, emergency medical, or hazardous material response service;

(B) a hospital;

(C) a fire department;

(D) a health clinic;

(E) a medical doctor's office;

(F) an individual to administer first aid treatment; or

(G) a police department; or

(2) a sign required by Subsection (b-1) was not posted at the entrance to the school crossing zone at the time of an offense committed in the school crossing zone.

(d-1) The affirmative defense available in Subsection (d)(2) is not available for an offense under Subsection (b) committed in a school crossing zone located in the jurisdiction of a local authority that is in compliance with Subsection (b-2).

(e) This section does not apply to:

(1) an operator of an authorized emergency vehicle using a wireless communication device while acting in an official capacity; or

(2) an operator who is licensed by the Federal Communications Commission while operating a radio frequency device other than a wireless communication device.

(e-1) Subsection (c) does not apply to an operator of a school bus or passenger bus using a wireless communication device:

(1) in the performance of the operator's duties as a bus driver; and

(2) in a manner similar to using a two-way radio.

(f) Except as provided by Subsection (b-2), this section preempts all local ordinances, rules, or regulations that are inconsistent with specific provisions of this section adopted by a political subdivision of this state relating to the use of a wireless communication device by the operator of a motor vehicle.

Sec. 545.4251. Use of Portable Wireless Communication Device for Electronic Messaging; Offense.

(a) In this section:

(1) "Electronic message" means data that is read from or entered into a wireless communication device for the purpose of communicating with another person.

(2) "Wireless communication device" has the meaning assigned by Section 545.425.

(b) An operator commits an offense if the operator uses a portable wireless communication device to read, write, or send an electronic message while operating a motor vehicle unless the vehicle

Transportation Code

is stopped. To be prosecuted, the behavior must be committed in the presence of or within the view of a peace officer or established by other evidence.

(c) It is an affirmative defense to prosecution of an offense under this section that the operator used a portable wireless communication device:

(1) in conjunction with a hands-free device, as defined by Section 545.425;

(2) to navigate using a global positioning system or navigation system;

(3) to report illegal activity, summon emergency help, or enter information into a software application that provides information relating to traffic and road conditions to users of the application;

(4) to read an electronic message that the person reasonably believed concerned an emergency;

(5) that was permanently or temporarily affixed to the vehicle to relay information in the course of the operator's occupational duties between the operator and:

(A) a dispatcher; or

(B) a digital network or software application service; or

(6) to activate a function that plays music.

(d) Subsection (b) does not apply to:

(1) an operator of an authorized emergency or law enforcement vehicle using a portable wireless communication device while acting in an official capacity; or

(2) an operator who is licensed by the Federal Communications Commission while operating a radio frequency device other than a portable wireless communication device.

(e) An offense under this section is a misdemeanor punishable by a fine of at least $25 and not more than $99 unless it is shown on the trial of the offense that the defendant has been previously convicted at least one time of an offense under this section, in which event the offense is punishable by a fine of at least $100 and not more than $200.

(f) Notwithstanding Subsection (e), an offense under this section is a Class A misdemeanor punishable by a fine not to exceed $4,000 and confinement in jail for a term not to exceed one year if it is shown on the trial of the offense that the defendant caused the death or serious bodily injury of another person.

(g) If conduct constituting an offense under this section also constitutes an offense under any other law, the person may be prosecuted under this section, the other law, or both.

(h) The Texas Department of Transportation shall post a sign at each point at which an interstate highway or United States highway enters this state that informs an operator that:

(1) the use of a portable wireless communication device for electronic messaging while operating a motor vehicle is prohibited in this state; and

(2) the operator is subject to a fine if the operator uses a portable wireless communication device for electronic messaging while operating a motor vehicle in this state.

(i) A peace officer who stops a motor vehicle for an alleged violation of this section may not take possession of or otherwise inspect a portable wireless communication device in the possession of the operator unless authorized by the Code of Criminal Procedure, the Penal Code, or other law.

(j) This section preempts all local ordinances, rules, or other regulations adopted by a political subdivision relating to the use of a portable wireless communication device by the operator of a motor vehicle to read, write, or send an electronic message.

Sec. 545.4252. Use of Wireless Communication Device on School Property; Offense.

(a) In this section:

(1) "Hands-free device" has the meaning assigned by Section 545.425.

(2) "Wireless communication device" has the meaning assigned by Section 545.425.

(b) Except as provided by Section 545.425(c), an operator may not use a wireless communication device while operating a motor vehicle on the property of a public elementary, middle, junior high, or high school for which a local authority has designated a school crossing zone, during the time a reduced speed limit is in effect for the school crossing zone, unless:

(1) the vehicle is stopped; or

(2) the wireless communication device is used with a hands-free device.

(c) It is an affirmative defense to prosecution of an offense under this section that the wireless communication device was used to make an emergency call to:

(1) an emergency response service, including a rescue, emergency medical, or hazardous material response service;

(2) a hospital;

(3) a fire department;

(4) a health clinic;

(5) a medical doctor's office;

(6) an individual to administer first aid treatment; or

(7) a police department.

(d) This section does not apply to:

(1) an operator of an authorized emergency vehicle using a wireless communication device while acting in an official capacity; or

(2) an operator who is licensed by the Federal Communications Commission while operating a radio frequency device other than a wireless communication device.

(e) This section preempts all local ordinances, rules, or regulations that are inconsistent with specific provisions of this section adopted by a political subdivision of this state relating to the use of a wireless communication device by the operator of a motor vehicle, except that a political subdivision may by ordinance or rule prohibit the use of a wireless communication device while operating a motor vehicle throughout the jurisdiction of the political subdivision.

Sec. 545.426. Operation of School Bus.

(a) A person may not operate a school bus if:

(1) the door of the school bus is open; or

(2) the number of passengers on the bus is greater than the manufacturer's design capacity for the bus.

(b) An operator of a school bus, while operating the bus, shall prohibit a passenger from:

(1) standing in the bus; or

(2) sitting:

(A) on the floor of the bus; or

(B) in any location on the bus that is not designed as a seat.

(c) The department may adopt rules necessary to administer and enforce this section.

Sec. 545.427. Operation of Vehicle with Insufficient Undercarriage Clearance.

(a) An operator may not drive on or cross a railroad grade crossing unless the vehicle being operated has sufficient undercarriage clearance.

(b) An offense under this section is a misdemeanor punishable by a fine of not less than $50 or more than $200.

Sec. 545.428. Motor Vehicle Accident Involving Pedestrian or Other Vulnerable Road User Within Area of Crosswalk; Offense.

(a) In this section:

(1) "Electric personal assistive mobility device" has the meaning assigned by Section 551.201.

(2) "Golf cart" has the meaning assigned by Section 551.401.

(3) "Motor-assisted scooter" has the meaning assigned by Section 551.351.

(4) "Neighborhood electric vehicle" has the meaning assigned by Section 551.301.

(b) A person commits an offense if the person with criminal negligence:

(1) operates a motor vehicle within the area of a crosswalk; and

(2) causes bodily injury to a pedestrian or a person operating a bicycle, motor-assisted scooter, electronic personal assistive mobility device, neighborhood electric vehicle, or golf cart.

(c) An offense under this section is a Class A misdemeanor, except that the offense is a state jail felony if the person described by Subsection (b)(2) suffered serious bodily injury.

(d) It is an affirmative defense to prosecution under this section that, at the time of the offense, the person described by Subsection (b)(2) was violating a provision of this subtitle relating to walking, movement, or operation in a crosswalk or on a roadway.

(e) If conduct that constitutes an offense under this section also constitutes an offense under any other law, the actor may be prosecuted under this section, the other law, or both.

SUBCHAPTER J. OPERATION OF AUTOMATED MOTOR VEHICLES

Sec. 545.451. Definitions.

In this subchapter:

(1) "Automated driving system" means hardware and software that, when installed on a motor vehicle and engaged, are collectively capable of performing, without any intervention or supervision by a human operator:

(A) all aspects of the entire dynamic driving task for the vehicle on a sustained basis; and

(B) any fallback maneuvers necessary to respond to a failure of the system.

(2) "Automated motor vehicle" means a motor vehicle on which an automated driving system is installed.

(3) "Entire dynamic driving task" means the operational and tactical aspects of operating a vehicle. The term:

(A) includes:

(i) operational aspects, including steering, braking, accelerating, and monitoring the vehicle and the roadway; and

(ii) tactical aspects, including responding to events, determining when to change lanes, turning, using signals, and other related actions; and

(B) does not include strategic aspects, including determining destinations or waypoints.

(4) "Human operator" means a natural person in an automated motor vehicle who controls the entire dynamic driving task.

(5) "Owner" has the meaning assigned by Section 502.001.

Sec. 545.452. Exclusive Regulation of the Operation of Automated Motor Vehicles and Automated Driving Systems.

(a) Unless otherwise provided by this subchapter, the operation of automated motor vehicles, including any commercial use, and automated driving systems are governed exclusively by:

(1) this subchapter; and

(2) Section 547.618.

(b) A political subdivision of this state or a state agency may not impose a franchise or other regulation related to the operation of an automated motor vehicle or automated driving system.

Sec. 545.453. Operator of Automated Motor Vehicle.

(a) When an automated driving system installed on a motor vehicle is engaged:

(1) the owner of the automated driving system is considered the operator of the automated motor vehicle solely for the purpose of assessing compliance with applicable traffic or motor vehicle laws, regardless of whether the person is physically present in the vehicle while the vehicle is operating; and

(2) the automated driving system is considered to be licensed to operate the vehicle.

(b) Notwithstanding any other law, a licensed human operator is not required to operate a motor vehicle if an automated driving system installed on the vehicle is engaged.

Sec. 545.454. Automated Motor Vehicle Operation.

(a) An automated motor vehicle may operate in this state with the automated driving system engaged, regardless of whether a human operator is physically present in the vehicle.

(b) An automated motor vehicle may not operate on a highway in this state with the automated driving system engaged unless the vehicle is:

(1) capable of operating in compliance with applicable traffic and motor vehicle laws of this state, subject to this subchapter;

(2) equipped with a recording device, as defined by Section 547.615(a), installed by the manufacturer of the automated motor vehicle or automated driving system;

(3) equipped with an automated driving system in compliance with applicable federal law and federal motor vehicle safety standards;

(4) registered and titled in accordance with the laws of this state; and

(5) covered by motor vehicle liability coverage or self-insurance in an amount equal to the amount of coverage that is required under the laws of this state.

Sec. 545.455. Duties Following Accident Involving Automated Motor Vehicle.

In the event of an accident involving an automated motor vehicle, the automated motor vehicle or any human operator of the automated motor vehicle shall comply with Chapter 550.

Sec. 545.456. Vehicle Classification.

An owner as defined by Section 502.001(31) may identify the vehicle to the department as an automated motor vehicle or an automated driving system.

CHAPTER 546
OPERATION OF AUTHORIZED EMERGENCY VEHICLES AND CERTAIN OTHER VEHICLES

SUBCHAPTER A
AUTHORIZED EMERGENCY VEHICLES

Sec. 546.001. Permissible Conduct.

In operating an authorized emergency vehicle the operator may:

(1) park or stand, irrespective of another provision of this subtitle;

(2) proceed past a red or stop signal or stop sign, after slowing as necessary for safe operation;

(3) exceed a maximum speed limit, except as provided by an ordinance adopted under Section 545.365, as long as the operator does not endanger life or property; and

Transportation Code

(4) disregard a regulation governing the direction of movement or turning in specified directions.

Sec. 546.002. When Conduct Permissible.

(a) In this section, "police escort" means facilitating the movement of a funeral, oversized or hazardous load, or other traffic disruption for public safety purposes by a peace officer described by Articles 2.12(1)—(4), (8), (12), and (22), Code of Criminal Procedure.

(b) Sections 546.001(2), (3), and (4) apply only when the operator is:

(1) responding to an emergency call;

(2) pursuing an actual or suspected violator of the law;

(3) responding to but not returning from a fire alarm;

(4) directing or diverting traffic for public safety purposes; or

(5) conducting a police escort.

Sec. 546.003. Audible or Visual Signals Required.

Except as provided by Section 546.004, the operator of an authorized emergency vehicle engaging in conduct permitted by Section 546.001 shall use, at the discretion of the operator in accordance with policies of the department or the local government that employs the operator, audible or visual signals that meet the pertinent requirements of Sections 547.305 and 547.702.

Sec. 546.004. Exceptions to Signal Requirement.

(a) A volunteer fire fighter who operates a private vehicle as an authorized emergency vehicle may engage in conduct permitted by Section 546.001 only when the fire fighter is using visual signals meeting the pertinent requirements of Sections 547.305 and 547.702.

(b) An authorized emergency vehicle that is operated as a police vehicle is not required to be equipped with or display a red light visible from the front of the vehicle.

(c) A police officer may operate an authorized emergency vehicle for a law enforcement purpose without using the audible or visual signals required by Section 546.003 if the officer is:

(1) responding to an emergency call or pursuing a suspected violator of the law with probable cause to believe that:

(A) knowledge of the presence of the officer will cause the suspect to:

(i) destroy or lose evidence of a suspected felony;

(ii) end a suspected continuing felony before the officer has obtained sufficient evidence to establish grounds for arrest; or

(iii) evade apprehension or identification of the suspect or the suspect's vehicle; or

(B) because of traffic conditions on a multilaned roadway, vehicles moving in response to the audible or visual signals may:

(i) increase the potential for a collision; or

(ii) unreasonably extend the duration of the pursuit; or

(2) complying with a written regulation relating to the use of audible or visible signals adopted by the local government that employs the officer or by the department.

Sec. 546.005. Duty of Care.

This chapter does not relieve the operator of an authorized emergency vehicle from:

(1) the duty to operate the vehicle with appropriate regard for the safety of all persons; or

(2) the consequences of reckless disregard for the safety of others.

Sec. 546.006. Designated Emergency Vehicle During Declared Disasters.

(a) From recommendations made under Section 418.013(c), Government Code, the department shall designate which vehicles may be operated by which designated organizations as emergency vehicles during declared disasters.

(b) A vehicle designated under Subsection (a) may be operated by a designated organization as if the vehicle were an authorized emergency vehicle under this subtitle if:

(1) the governor declares a state of disaster under Section 418.014, Government Code;

(2) the department requests assistance from the designated organization; and

(3) the vehicle is operated by the designated organization or a member of the designated organization in response to the state of disaster.

(c) The department shall adopt rules as necessary to implement this section.

Sec. 546.0065. Authorized Emergency Vehicles of the Texas Division of Emergency Management.

The department shall designate vehicles of the Texas Division of Emergency Management that may be operated as authorized emergency vehicles.

Sec. 546.007. Closure of Road or Highway by Firefighter.

(a) This section applies only to a firefighter who is employed by or a member of:

(1) a fire department operated by an emergency services district;

(2) a volunteer fire department; or

(3) a fire department of a general-law municipality.

(b) A firefighter, when performing the firefighter's official duties, may close one or more lanes of a road or highway to protect the safety of persons or property.

(c) The closure shall be limited to the affected lane or lanes and one additional lane unless the safety of emergency personnel operating on the road or highway requires more lanes to be closed.

(d) In making a closure under this section, the firefighter shall deploy one or more authorized emergency vehicles with audible and visual signals that meet the requirements of Sections 547.305 and 547.702.

SUBCHAPTER B OPERATION OF CERTAIN FIRE-FIGHTING EQUIPMENT

Sec. 546.021. Mutual Aid Organizations.

(a) Two or more businesses whose activities require the maintenance of fire-fighting equipment may form a mutual aid organization in which the member businesses agree to assist each other during an emergency by supplying fire-fighting equipment or services.

(b) The presiding officer or director of an organization formed under this section shall deliver a list to the county fire marshal, or to the commissioners court of a county if the county does not have a fire marshal, in each county in which a member business is located. The list must contain the name of the registered owner and license plate number of each motor vehicle that each member intends to use in supplying fire-fighting equipment or services.

(c) If the county fire marshal or commissioners court determines that the operation of the vehicles on the list is in the public interest and not a threat to public safety, the marshal or court shall approve the list.

(d) On approval of the list by the county fire marshal or commissioners court, a person operating a listed motor vehicle in response to a call for emergency fire-fighting assistance from a member has the rights and restrictions placed by this subtitle on the operator of an authorized emergency vehicle.

(e) A county is not liable for damage to a person or property caused by a person approved by the county under this section to operate a motor vehicle for emergency fire-fighting assistance.

SUBCHAPTER C. OPERATION OF MEDICAL SUPPLY TRANSPORT VEHICLES

Sec. 546.051. Definitions.

In this subchapter:

(1) "Emergency care facility" means a health care facility, including a freestanding emergency medical care facility, hospital, temporary emergency clinic, and trauma facility, that provides emergency medical care.

(2) "Freestanding emergency medical care facility" means a facility licensed under Chapter 254, Health and Safety Code.

(3) "Medical supply distributor" means a person authorized to transport prescription drugs and other medical supplies to emergency care facilities or pharmacies.

(4) "Nursing home" means a facility licensed under Chapter 242, Health and Safety Code.

(5) "Pharmacy" has the meaning assigned by Section 551.003, Occupations Code.

(6) "Trauma facility" has the meaning assigned by Section 773.003, Health and Safety Code.

Sec. 546.052. Medical Supply Transport Vehicles During Declared Disaster.

(a) A vehicle used by a medical supply distributor to transport prescription drugs and other medical supplies to an emergency care facility, pharmacy, or nursing home located in an area declared a disaster area by the governor under Chapter 418, Government Code, may have access to highways, streets, and bridges as if the transport vehicle were an emergency vehicle if the transport vehicle will not negatively impact evacuation activities or any response or recovery activities in the disaster area.

(b) The Texas Division of Emergency Management shall establish procedures to assist medical supply distributors in accessing highways, streets, and bridges as authorized by Subsection (a).

(c) This section does not create a cause of action against a law enforcement officer involved in assisting a medical supply distributor under this section for any harm done to the distributor resulting from that assistance.

CHAPTER 547 VEHICLE EQUIPMENT

SUBCHAPTER A GENERAL PROVISIONS

Sec. 547.001. Definitions.

In this chapter:

(1) "Air-conditioning equipment" means mechanical vapor compression refrigeration equipment used to cool a motor vehicle passenger or operator compartment.

(2) "Explosive cargo vehicle" means a motor vehicle used to transport explosives or a cargo tank truck used to transport a flammable liquid or compressed gas.

(2-a) "Golf cart" has the meaning assigned by Section 551.401.

(2-b) "Highway maintenance or construction vehicle" means a highway or traffic maintenance or construction vehicle designated by the Texas Department of Transportation. The term includes equipment for:

(A) road maintenance or construction, including:

(i) equipment for snow removal, line striping, skid resistance testing, sweeping, spraying, guardrail repair, sign maintenance, and temporary traffic-control device placement or removal;

(ii) aerial platform lift machines; and

(iii) road profiler machines; and

(B) road construction or off-road use, including motor graders, road rollers, excavators, pneumatic tire equipment, movers, and tractors.

(3) "Light transmission" means the ratio of the amount of light that passes through a material to the amount of light that falls on the material and the glazing.

(4) "Luminous reflectance" means the ratio of the amount of light that is reflected by a material to the amount of light that falls on the material.

(5) "Multipurpose vehicle" means a motor vehicle that is:

(A) designed to carry 10 or fewer persons; and

(B) constructed on a truck chassis or with special features for occasional off-road use.

(5-a) "Road machinery" means a self-propelled vehicle that:

(A) was originally and permanently designed as machinery;

(B) is not designed or used primarily to transport persons or property; and

(C) is only incidentally operated on a highway.

(6) "Safety glazing material" includes only a glazing material that is constructed, treated, or combined with another material to reduce substantially, as compared to ordinary sheet or plate glass, the likelihood of injury to persons by an external object or by cracked or broken glazing material.

(6-a) "Service vehicle" means a highway or traffic maintenance vehicle that:

(A) is owned and operated on a highway by or for a governmental agency and performs a function requiring the use of a lamp or illuminating device in accordance with the standards and specifications adopted under Section 547.105; or

(B) has a public service function, including public utility vehicles, tow trucks, and any vehicle designated as a service vehicle by the Texas Department of Transportation or as an escort flag vehicle under Section 623.099.

(7) "Slow-moving vehicle" means:

(A) a motor vehicle designed to operate at a maximum speed of 25 miles per hour or less, not including an electric personal assistive mobility device, as defined by Section 551.201; or

(B) a vehicle, implement of husbandry, or machinery, including road construction machinery, that is towed by:

(i) an animal; or

(ii) a motor vehicle designed to operate at a maximum speed of 25 miles per hour or less.

(8) "Slow-moving-vehicle emblem" means a triangular emblem that conforms to standards and specifications adopted by the director under Section 547.104.

(9) "Sunscreening device" means a film, material, or device that meets the department's standards for reducing effects of the sun.

(10) "Vehicle equipment" means:

(A) a system, part, or device that is manufactured or sold as original or replacement equipment or as a vehicle accessory; or

(B) a device or apparel manufactured or sold to protect a vehicle operator or passenger.

Transportation Code

(11) "Neighborhood electric vehicle" has the meaning assigned by Section 551.301.

(12) "Off-highway vehicle" has the meaning assigned by Section 551A.001.

Sec. 547.002. Applicability.

Unless a provision is specifically made applicable, this chapter and the rules of the department adopted under this chapter do not apply to:

(1) an implement of husbandry;

(2) road machinery;

(3) a road roller;

(4) a farm tractor;

(5) a bicycle, a bicyclist, or bicycle equipment;

(6) an electric bicycle, an electric bicyclist, or electric bicycle equipment;

(7) a golf cart;

(8) a neighborhood electric vehicle; or

(9) an off-highway vehicle.

Sec. 547.003. Equipment Not Affected.

This chapter does not prohibit and the department by rule may not prohibit the use of:

(1) equipment required by an agency of the United States; or

(2) a part or accessory not inconsistent with this chapter or a rule adopted under this chapter.

Sec. 547.004. General Offenses.

(a) A person commits an offense that is a misdemeanor if the person operates or moves or, as an owner, knowingly permits another to operate or move, a vehicle that:

(1) is unsafe so as to endanger a person;

(2) is not equipped in a manner that complies with the vehicle equipment standards and requirements established by this chapter; or

(3) is equipped in a manner prohibited by this chapter.

(b) A person commits an offense that is a misdemeanor if the person operates a vehicle equipped with an item of vehicle equipment that the person knows has been determined in a compliance proceeding under Section 547.206 to not comply with a department standard.

(c) A court may dismiss a charge brought under this section if the defendant:

(1) remedies the defect before the defendant's first court appearance; and

(2) pays a reimbursement fee not to exceed $10.

(d) Subsection (c) does not apply to an offense involving a commercial motor vehicle.

Sec. 547.005. Offense Relating to Violation of Special-Use Provisions.

(a) A person may not use a slow-moving-vehicle emblem on a stationary object or a vehicle other than a slow-moving vehicle.

(b) A person may not operate a motor vehicle bearing the words "school bus" unless the vehicle is used primarily to transport persons to or from school or a school-related activity. In this subsection, "school" means a privately or publicly supported elementary or secondary school, day-care center, preschool, or institution of higher education and includes a church if the church is engaged in providing formal education.

SUBCHAPTER B ADOPTION OF RULES AND STANDARDS

Sec. 547.101. Rules and Standards in General.

(a) The department may adopt rules necessary to administer this chapter.

(b) The department may adopt standards for vehicle equipment to:

(1) protect the public from unreasonable risk of death or injury; and

(2) enforce safety standards of the United States as permitted under the federal motor vehicle act.

(c) A department standard must:

(1) duplicate a standard of the United States that applies to the same aspect of vehicle equipment performance as the department standard; or

(2) if there is no standard of the United States for the same aspect of vehicle equipment performance as the department standard, conform as closely as possible to a relevant standard of the United States, similar standards established by other states, and a standard issued or endorsed by recognized national standard-setting organizations or agencies.

(d) The department may not adopt a vehicle equipment standard inconsistent with a standard provided by this chapter.

Sec. 547.102. School Bus Equipment Standards.

The department may adopt standards and specifications that:

(1) supplement the standards and specifications provided by this chapter;

(2) apply to lighting and warning device equipment required for a school bus; and

(3) at the time adopted, correlate with and conform as closely as possible to specifications approved by the Society of Automotive Engineers.

Sec. 547.103. Air-Conditioning Equipment Standards.

The department may adopt safety requirements, rules, and specifications that:

(1) apply to air-conditioning equipment; and

(2) correlate with and conform as closely as possible to recommended practices or standards approved by the Society of Automotive Engineers.

Sec. 547.104. Slow-Moving-Vehicle Emblem Standards.

The director shall adopt standards and specifications that:

(1) apply to the color, size, and mounting position of a slow-moving-vehicle emblem; and

(2) at the time adopted, correlate with and conform as closely as practicable to the standards and specifications adopted or approved by the American Society of Agricultural Engineers for a uniform emblem to identify a slow-moving vehicle.

Sec. 547.105. Lighting Standards for Certain Vehicles.

(a) The Texas Department of Transportation shall adopt standards and specifications that:

(1) apply to lamps on highway maintenance or construction vehicles and service vehicles; and

(2) correlate with and conform as closely as possible to standards and specifications approved by the American Association of State Highway and Transportation Officials.

(b) The Texas Department of Transportation may adopt standards and specifications for lighting that permit the use of flashing lights for identification purposes on highway maintenance or construction vehicles and service vehicles.

(c) The standards and specifications adopted under this section are in lieu of the standards and specifications otherwise provided by this chapter for lamps on vehicles.

SUBCHAPTER C
PROVISIONS RELATING TO THE OFFER, DISTRIBUTION, AND SALE OF VEHICLE EQUIPMENT

Sec. 547.201. Offenses Relating to the Offer, Distribution, and Sale of Vehicle Equipment.

(a) A person may not offer or distribute for sale or sell an item of vehicle equipment for which a standard is prescribed by this chapter or the department and that does not comply with the standard. It is an affirmative defense to prosecution under this subsection that the person did not have reason to know in the exercise of due care that the item did not comply with the applicable standard.

(b) A person may not offer or distribute for sale or sell an item of vehicle equipment for which a standard is prescribed by this chapter or the department, unless the item or its package:

(1) bears the manufacturer's trademark or brand name; or

(2) complies with each applicable identification requirement established by an agency of the United States or the department.

Sec. 547.202. Department Certification or Approval of Vehicle Equipment.

(a) When or after an item of vehicle equipment is sold in this state, the department shall determine whether a department standard is prescribed for the item. If a department standard is prescribed, the department shall determine whether the item complies with the standard.

(b) If a standard of an agency of the United States or of the department is not prescribed, the department by rule may require departmental approval before the sale of the item.

Sec. 547.203. Vehicle Equipment Testing: Department Standards.

(a) The department shall prescribe standards for and approve testing facilities to:

(1) review test data submitted by a manufacturer to show compliance with a department standard; and

(2) test an item of vehicle equipment independently in connection with a proceeding to determine compliance with a department standard.

(b) The department may not impose a product certification or approval fee, including a fee for testing facility approval.

(c) The department may:

(1) by rule, require a manufacturer of an item of vehicle equipment sold in this state to submit adequate test data to show that the item complies with department standards;

Transportation Code

(2) periodically require a manufacturer to submit revised test data to demonstrate continuing compliance;

(3) purchase an item of vehicle equipment at retail for the purpose of review and testing under Subsection (a); and

(4) enter into cooperative arrangements with other states and interstate agencies to reduce duplication of testing and to facilitate compliance with rules under Subsection (c)(1).

Sec. 547.204. Vehicle Equipment Testing: Federal Standards.

(a) For a vehicle or item of vehicle equipment subject to a motor vehicle safety standard of the United States, the department may, on or after the first sale of the vehicle or item of vehicle equipment:

(1) require the manufacturer to submit adequate test data to show that the vehicle or item of vehicle equipment complies with standards of the United States;

(2) review the manufacturer's laboratory test data and the qualifications of the laboratory; and

(3) independently test the vehicle or item of vehicle equipment.

(b) The department may not require certification or approval of an item of vehicle equipment subject to a motor vehicle safety standard of the United States.

(c) The department may not require a manufacturer of a vehicle or of an item of vehicle equipment subject to a motor vehicle safety standard of the United States to use an outside laboratory or a specified laboratory.

Sec. 547.205. Initiation of Compliance Proceeding.

(a) The department may initiate a proceeding to determine whether an item of vehicle equipment complies with a department standard if the department reasonably believes that the item is being offered or distributed for sale or sold in violation of the standard.

(b) The department shall send written notice of the proceeding to the manufacturer of the item by certified mail, return receipt requested.

(c) The notice required by Subsection (b) must:

(1) cite the standard that the item allegedly violates; and

(2) state that the manufacturer must file a written request with the department for a hearing not later than the 30th day after the date the notice is received to obtain a hearing on the issue of compliance.

(d) When the department sends notice under Subsection (b), the department shall require the manufacturer to submit to the department, not later than the 30th day after the date the notice is received, the names and addresses of the persons the manufacturer knows to be offering the item for sale to retail merchants.

(e) On receipt under Subsection (d) of the names and addresses, the department shall send by certified mail, return receipt requested, written notice of the compliance proceeding to those persons.

(f) The notice must:

(1) cite the standard that the item allegedly violates;

(2) state that the manufacturer of the item has been notified and may request a hearing on the issue of compliance before a stated date;

(3) state that if the manufacturer or another person requests a hearing, the person may appear at the hearing;

(4) state that if the manufacturer does not request a hearing, the person may request a hearing by filing a written request with the department not later than the 30th day after the date notice is received; and

(5) state that the person may determine from the department whether a hearing will be held and the time and place of the hearing.

Sec. 547.206. Compliance Proceeding Hearing.

The department shall conduct a hearing on the issue of compliance if a person required by Section 547.205 to be notified requests a hearing in the manner and within the time specified by that section.

Sec. 547.207. Compliance Proceeding Issues.

(a) In a hearing under Section 547.206 or in the absence of a request for a hearing, the department may make a determination of the following issues only:

(1) whether an item of vehicle equipment has been offered, distributed, or sold in violation of a department standard;

(2) whether the manufacturer did not submit test data required by the department under Section 547.203; and

(3) whether an item of vehicle equipment has been offered, distributed, or sold without the identification required by Section 547.201.

(b) The department by order shall prohibit the manufacture, offer for sale, distribution for sale, or sale of the item if the department finds affirmatively on at least one of the issues.

(c) After entering its order, the department shall send written notice by certified mail, return receipt requested, to each person the department notified under Section 547.205.

Sec. 547.208. Judicial Review and Judicial Enforcement.

(a) A person may appeal an order entered under Section 547.207 to a district court in Travis County only if a hearing was held by the department and the person:

(1) is aggrieved by the order; and

(2) appeared at the hearing on compliance.

(b) The department may bring suit in a district court of Travis County for an injunction to prohibit the manufacture, offer, distribution, or sale of an item of vehicle equipment that is the subject of a department order entered under Section 547.207. The attorney general shall represent the department in the suit.

SUBCHAPTER D
GENERAL PROVISIONS REGARDING LIGHTING REQUIREMENTS

Sec. 547.301. General Provisions Relating to Measurements.

(a) Unless expressly stated otherwise, a visibility distance requirement imposed by this chapter for a lamp or device applies when a lighted lamp or device is required and is measured as if the vehicle were unloaded and on a straight, level, unlighted highway under normal atmospheric conditions.

(b) A mounted height requirement imposed by this chapter for a lamp or device is measured as if the vehicle were unloaded and on level ground and is measured from the center of the lamp or device to the ground.

Sec. 547.302. Duty to Display Lights.

(a) A vehicle shall display each lighted lamp and illuminating device required by this chapter to be on the vehicle:

(1) at nighttime; and

(2) when light is insufficient or atmospheric conditions are unfavorable so that a person or vehicle on the highway is not clearly discernible at a distance of 1,000 feet ahead.

(b) A signaling device, including a stoplamp or a turn signal lamp, shall be lighted as prescribed by this chapter.

(c) At least one lighted lamp shall be displayed on each side of the front of a motor vehicle.

(d) Not more than four of the following may be lighted at one time on the front of a motor vehicle:

(1) a headlamp required by this chapter; or

(2) a lamp, including an auxiliary lamp or spotlamp, that projects a beam with an intensity brighter than 300 candlepower.

Sec. 547.303. Color Requirements.

(a) Unless expressly provided otherwise, a lighting device or reflector mounted on the rear of a vehicle must be or reflect red.

(b) A signaling device mounted on the rear of a vehicle may be red, amber, or yellow.

Sec. 547.304. Applicability.

(a) A provision of this chapter that requires a vehicle to be equipped with fixed electric lights does not apply to a farm trailer or fertilizer trailer registered under Section 502.146 or a boat trailer with a gross weight of 3,000 pounds or less if the trailer is not operated at a time or under a condition specified by Section 547.302(a).

(b) Except for Sections 547.323 and 547.324, a provision of this chapter that requires a vehicle to be equipped with fixed electric lights does not apply to a boat trailer with a gross weight of less than 4,500 pounds if the trailer is not operated at a time or under a condition specified by Section 547.302(a).

(c) Except for Sections 547.323 and 547.324, a provision of this chapter that requires a vehicle to be equipped with lamps, reflectors, and lighting equipment does not apply to a mobile home if the mobile home:

(1) is moved under a permit issued by the Texas Department of Motor Vehicles under Subchapter D, Chapter 623; and

(2) is not moved at a time or under a condition specified by Section 547.302(a).

(d) A mobile home lighted as provided by this section may be moved only during daytime.

Transportation Code

Sec. 547.305. Restrictions on Use of Lights.

(a) A motor vehicle lamp or illuminating device, other than a headlamp, spotlamp, auxiliary lamp, turn signal lamp, or emergency vehicle, tow truck, or school bus warning lamp, that projects a beam with an intensity brighter than 300 candlepower shall be directed so that no part of the high-intensity portion of the beam strikes the roadway at a distance of more than 75 feet from the vehicle.

(b) Except as expressly authorized by law, a person may not operate or move equipment or a vehicle, other than a police vehicle, with a lamp or device that displays a red light visible from directly in front of the center of the equipment or vehicle.

(c) A person may not operate a motor vehicle equipped with a red, white, or blue beacon, flashing, or alternating light unless the equipment is:

(1) used as specifically authorized by this chapter; or

(2) a running lamp, headlamp, taillamp, backup lamp, or turn signal lamp that is used as authorized by law.

(d) A vehicle may be equipped with alternately flashing lighting equipment described by Section 547.701 or 547.702 only if the vehicle is:

(1) a school bus;

(2) an authorized emergency vehicle;

(3) a church bus that has the words "church bus" printed on the front and rear of the bus so as to be clearly discernable to other vehicle operators;

(4) a tow truck while under the direction of a law enforcement officer at the scene of an accident or while hooking up to a disabled vehicle on a roadway; or

(5) a tow truck with a mounted light bar which has turn signals and stop lamps in addition to those required by Sections 547.322, 547.323, and 547.324, Transportation Code.

(e) A person may not operate a highway maintenance or construction vehicle or service vehicle that is not equipped with lamps or that does not display lighted lamps as required by the standards and specifications adopted by the Texas Department of Transportation.

(e-1) A security patrol vehicle may only be equipped with green, amber, or white lights.

(e-2) A motor vehicle is equipped with a lamp or illuminating device under this section regardless of whether the lamp or illuminating device is:

(1) attached to the motor vehicle temporarily or permanently; or

(2) activated.

(e-3) An escort flag vehicle may be equipped with alternating or flashing blue and amber lights.

(e-4) A vehicle described by Section 545.157(a) may be equipped with flashing blue lights.

(f) In this section:

(1) "Escort flag vehicle" means a vehicle that precedes or follows an oversize or overweight vehicle described by Subtitle E for the purpose of facilitating the safe movement of the oversize or overweight vehicle over roads.

(2) "Security patrol vehicle" means a motor vehicle being used for the purpose of providing security services by:

(A) a guard company described by Section 1702.108, Occupations Code; or

(B) a security officer as defined by Section 1702.002, Occupations Code.

(3) "Tow truck" means a motor vehicle or mechanical device that is adapted or used to tow, winch, or move a disabled vehicle.

Sec. 547.306. Led Ground Effect Lighting Equipment on Motorcycle or Moped.

(a) In this section, "LED ground effect lighting equipment" means light emitting diode (LED) technology that is attached to the underbody of a motorcycle or moped for the purpose of illuminating:

(1) the body of the motorcycle or moped; or

(2) the ground below the motorcycle or moped.

(b) A person may operate a motorcycle or moped equipped with LED ground effect lighting that emits a non-flashing amber or white light.

Secs. 547.307 to 547.320. [Reserved for expansion].

SUBCHAPTER E GENERAL LIGHTING REQUIREMENTS FOR VEHICLES

Sec. 547.321. Headlamps Required.

(a) A motor vehicle shall be equipped with at least two headlamps.

(b) At least one headlamp shall be mounted on each side of the front of the vehicle.

(c) Each headlamp shall be mounted at a height from 24 to 54 inches.

Sec. 547.3215. Use of Federal Standard.

Unless specifically prohibited by this chapter, lighting, reflective devices, and associated equipment on a vehicle or motor vehicle must comply with:

(1) the current federal standards in 49 C.F.R. Section 571.108; or

(2) the federal standards in that section in effect, if any, at the time the vehicle or motor vehicle was manufactured.

Sec. 547.322. Taillamps Required.

(a) Except as provided by Subsection (b), a motor vehicle, trailer, semitrailer, pole trailer, or vehicle that is towed at the end of a combination of vehicles shall be equipped with at least two taillamps.

(b) A passenger car or truck that was manufactured or assembled before the model year 1960 shall be equipped with at least one taillamp.

(c) Taillamps shall be mounted on the rear of the vehicle:

(1) at a height from 15 to 72 inches; and

(2) at the same level and spaced as widely apart as practicable if a vehicle is equipped with more than one lamp.

(d) A taillamp shall emit a red light plainly visible at a distance of 1,000 feet from the rear of the vehicle.

(e) If vehicles are traveling in combination, only the taillamps on the rearmost vehicle are required to emit a light for the distance specified in Subsection (d).

(f) A taillamp or a separate lamp shall be constructed and mounted to emit a white light that:

(1) illuminates the rear license plate; and

(2) makes the plate clearly legible at a distance of 50 feet from the rear.

(g) A taillamp, including a separate lamp used to illuminate a rear license plate, must emit a light when a headlamp or auxiliary driving lamp is lighted.

Sec. 547.323. Stoplamps Required.

(a) Except as provided by Subsection (b), a motor vehicle, trailer, semitrailer, or pole trailer shall be equipped with at least two stoplamps.

(b) A passenger car manufactured or assembled before the model year 1960 shall be equipped with at least one stoplamp.

(c) A stoplamp shall be mounted on the rear of the vehicle.

(d) A stoplamp shall emit a red or amber light, or a color between red and amber, that is:

(1) visible in normal sunlight at a distance of at least 300 feet from the rear of the vehicle; and

(2) displayed when the vehicle service brake is applied.

(e) If vehicles are traveling in combination, only the stoplamps on the rearmost vehicle are required to emit a light for the distance specified in Subsection (d).

(f) A stoplamp may be included as a part of another rear lamp.

Sec. 547.324. Turn Signal Lamps Required.

(a) Except as provided by Subsection (b), a motor vehicle, trailer, semitrailer, or pole trailer shall be equipped with electric turn signal lamps that indicate the operator's intent to turn by displaying flashing lights to the front and rear of a vehicle or combination of vehicles and on that side of the vehicle or combination toward which the turn is to be made.

(b) Subsection (a) does not apply to a passenger car or truck less than 80 inches wide manufactured or assembled before the model year 1960.

(c) Turn signal lamps:

(1) shall be mounted at the same level and spaced as widely apart as practicable on the front and on the rear of the vehicle; and

(2) may be included as a part of another lamp on the vehicle.

(d) A turn signal lamp shall emit:

(1) a white or amber light, or a color between white and amber, if the lamp is mounted on the front of the vehicle; or

(2) a red or amber light, or a color between red and amber, if the lamp is mounted on the rear of the vehicle.

(e) A turn signal lamp must be visible in normal sunlight at a distance of:

(1) at least 500 feet from the front and rear of the vehicle if the vehicle is at least 80 inches wide; and

(2) at least 300 feet from the front and rear of the vehicle if the vehicle is less than 80 inches wide.

Sec. 547.325. Reflectors Required.

(a) Except as provided by Subchapter F, a motor vehicle, trailer, semitrailer, or pole trailer shall be equipped with at least two red reflectors on the rear of the vehicle. A red reflector may be included as a part of a taillamp.

(b) A reflector shall be:

(1) mounted at a height from 15 to 60 inches; and

(2) visible at night at all distances:

(A) from 100 to 600 feet when directly in front of lawful lower beams of headlamps; or

(B) from 100 to 350 feet when directly in front of lawful upper beams of headlamps if the vehicle was manufactured or assembled before January 1, 1972.

Sec. 547.326. Minimum Lighting Equipment Required.

(a) A vehicle that is not specifically required to be equipped with lamps or other lighting devices shall be equipped at the times specified in Section 547.302(a) with at least one lamp that emits a white light visible at a distance of at least 1,000 feet from the front and:

(1) two lamps that emit a red light visible at a distance of at least 1,000 feet from the rear; or

(2) one lamp that emits a red light visible at a distance of at least 1,000 feet from the rear and two red reflectors visible when illuminated by the lawful lower beams of headlamps at all distances from 100 to 600 feet to the rear.

(b) This section also applies to an animal-drawn vehicle and a vehicle exempted from this chapter by Section 547.002.

Sec. 547.327. Spotlamps Permitted.

(a) A motor vehicle may be equipped with not more than two spotlamps.

(b) A spotlamp shall be aimed so that no part of the high-intensity portion of the beam strikes the windshield, window, mirror, or occupant of another vehicle in use.

Sec. 547.328. Fog Lamps Permitted.

(a) A motor vehicle may be equipped with not more than two fog lamps.

(b) A fog lamp shall be:

(1) mounted on the front of the vehicle at a height from 12 to 30 inches; and

(2) aimed so that no part of the high-intensity portion of the beam from a lamp mounted to the left of center on a vehicle projects a beam of light at a distance of 25 feet that is higher than four inches below the level of the center of the lamp.

(c) Lighted fog lamps may be used with lower headlamp beams as specified by Section 547.333.

Sec. 547.329. Auxiliary Passing Lamps Permitted.

(a) A motor vehicle may be equipped with no more than two auxiliary passing lamps.

(b) An auxiliary passing lamp shall be mounted on the front of the vehicle at a height from 24 to 42 inches.

(c) An auxiliary passing lamp may be used with headlamps as specified by Section 547.333.

Sec. 547.330. Auxiliary Driving Lamps Permitted.

(a) A motor vehicle may be equipped with no more than two auxiliary driving lamps.

(b) An auxiliary driving lamp shall be mounted on the front of the vehicle at a height from 16 to 42 inches.

(c) Auxiliary driving lamps may be used with headlamps as specified by Section 547.333.

Sec. 547.331. Hazard Lamps Permitted.

(a) A vehicle may be equipped with lamps to warn other vehicle operators of a vehicular traffic hazard that requires unusual care in approaching, overtaking, or passing.

(b) The lamps shall be:

(1) mounted at the same level and spaced as widely apart as practicable on the front and on the rear of the vehicle; and

(2) visible at a distance of at least 500 feet in normal sunlight.

(c) The lamps shall display simultaneously flashing lights that emit:

(1) a white or amber light, or a color between white and amber, if the lamp is mounted on the front of the vehicle; or

(2) a red or amber light, or a color between red and amber, if the lamp is mounted on the rear of the vehicle.

Sec. 547.332. Other Lamps Permitted.

A motor vehicle may be equipped with:

(1) not more than two side cowl or fender lamps that emit an amber or white light without glare;

(2) not more than two running board courtesy lamps, one on each side of the vehicle, that emit an amber or white light without glare; and

(3) one or more backup lamps that:

(A) emit an amber or white light only when the vehicle is not moving forward; and

(B) may be displayed separately or in combination with another lamp.

Sec. 547.333. Multiple-Beam Lighting Equipment Required.

(a) Unless provided otherwise, a headlamp, auxiliary driving lamp, auxiliary passing lamp, or combination of those lamps mounted on a motor vehicle, other than a motorcycle or moped:

(1) shall be arranged so that the operator can select at will between distributions of light projected at different elevations; and

(2) may be arranged so that the operator can select the distribution automatically.

(b) A lamp identified by Subsection (a) shall produce:

(1) an uppermost distribution of light or composite beam that is aimed and emits light sufficient to reveal a person or vehicle at a distance of at least 450 feet ahead during all conditions of loading; and

(2) a lowermost distribution of light or composite beam that:

(A) is aimed and emits light sufficient to reveal a person or vehicle at a distance of at least 150 feet ahead; and

(B) is aimed so that no part of the high-intensity portion of the beam on a vehicle that is operated on a straight, level road under any condition of loading projects into the eyes of an approaching vehicle operator.

(c) A person who operates a vehicle on a roadway or shoulder shall select a distribution of light or composite beam that is aimed and emits light sufficient to reveal a person or vehicle at a safe distance ahead of the vehicle, except that:

(1) an operator approaching an oncoming vehicle within 500 feet shall select:

(A) the lowermost distribution of light or composite beam, regardless of road contour or condition of loading; or

(B) a distribution aimed so that no part of the high-intensity portion of the lamp projects into the eyes of an approaching vehicle operator; and

(2) an operator approaching a vehicle from the rear within 300 feet may not select the uppermost distribution of light.

(d) A motor vehicle of a model year of 1948 or later, other than a motorcycle or moped, that has multiple-beam lighting equipment shall be equipped with a beam indicator that is:

(1) designed and located so that the lighted indicator is visible without glare to the vehicle operator; and

(2) lighted only when the uppermost distribution of light is in use.

Sec. 547.334. Single-Beam Lighting Equipment Permitted.

(a) In lieu of the multiple-beam lighting equipment required by Section 547.333, a headlamp system that provides a single distribution of light and meets the requirements of Subsection (b) is permitted for:

(1) a farm tractor; or

(2) a motor vehicle manufactured and sold before September 4, 1948.

(b) The headlamp system specified by Subsection (a) shall:

(1) emit a light sufficient to reveal a person or vehicle at a distance of at least 200 feet; and

(2) be aimed so that no part of the high-intensity portion of the lamp projects a beam:

(A) higher than five inches below the level of the center of the lamp at a distance of 25 feet ahead; or

(B) higher than 42 inches above the ground at a distance of 75 feet ahead.

Sec. 547.335. Alternative Road Lighting Equipment Permitted.

In lieu of the multiple-beam or single-beam lighting equipment otherwise required by this subchapter, a motor vehicle that is operated at a speed of not more than 20 miles per hour under the conditions specified in Section 547.302(a) may be equipped with two lighted lamps:

(1) mounted on the front of the vehicle; and

(2) capable of revealing a person or vehicle 100 feet ahead.

SUBCHAPTER F ADDITIONAL LIGHTING REQUIREMENTS FOR CERTAIN LARGE VEHICLES

Sec. 547.351. Applicability.

The color, mounting, and visibility requirements in this subchapter apply only to equipment on a vehicle described by Section 547.352.

Sec. 547.352. Additional Lighting Equipment Requirements.

In addition to other equipment required by this chapter:

(1) a bus, truck, trailer, or semitrailer that is at least 80 inches wide shall be equipped with:

(A) two clearance lamps on the front, one at each side;

(B) two clearance lamps on the rear, one at each side;

(C) four side marker lamps, one on each side at or near the front and one on each side at or near the rear;

(D) four reflectors, one on each side at or near the front and one on each side at or near the rear; and

(E) hazard lamps that meet the requirements of Section 547.331;

(2) a bus or truck that is at least 30 feet long shall be equipped with hazard lamps that meet the requirements of Section 547.331;

(3) a trailer or semitrailer that is at least 30 feet long shall be equipped with:

(A) two side marker lamps, one centrally mounted on each side with respect to the length of the vehicle;

(B) two reflectors, one centrally mounted on each side with respect to the length of the vehicle; and

(C) hazard lamps that meet the requirements of Section 547.331;

(4) a pole trailer shall be equipped with:

(A) two side marker lamps, one at each side at or near the front of the load;

(B) one reflector at or near the front of the load;

(C) one combination marker lamp that:

(i) emits an amber light to the front and a red light to the rear and side; and

(ii) is mounted on the rearmost support for the load to indicate the maximum width of the trailer; and

(D) hazard lamps that meet the requirements of Section 547.331, if the pole trailer is at least 30 feet long or at least 80 inches wide;

(5) a truck-tractor shall be equipped with:

(A) two clearance lamps, one at each side on the front of the cab; and

(B) hazard lamps that meet the requirements of Section 547.331, if the truck-tractor is at least 30 feet long or at least 80 inches wide; and

(6) a vehicle at least 80 inches wide may be equipped with:

(A) not more than three front identification lamps without glare; and

(B) not more than three rear identification lamps without glare.

Sec. 547.353. Color Requirements.

(a) A clearance lamp, identification lamp, side marker lamp, or reflector mounted on the front, on the side near the front, or in the center of the vehicle must be or reflect amber.

(b) A clearance lamp, identification lamp, side marker lamp, or reflector mounted on the rear or the side near the rear of the vehicle must be or reflect red.

Sec. 547.354. Mounting Requirements.

(a) A reflector shall be mounted:

(1) at a height from 24 to 60 inches; or

(2) as high as practicable on the permanent structure of the vehicle if the highest part of the permanent structure is less than 24 inches.

(b) A rear reflector may be:

(1) included as a part of a taillamp if the reflector meets each other requirement of this subchapter; and

(2) mounted on each side of the bolster or load, if the vehicle is a pole trailer.

(c) A clearance lamp shall be mounted, if practicable, on the permanent structure of the vehicle to indicate the extreme height and width of the vehicle, except that:

(1) a clearance lamp on a truck-tractor shall be mounted to indicate the extreme width of the cab; and

(2) a front clearance lamp may be mounted at a height that indicates, as near as practicable, the extreme width of the trailer if mounting of the lamp as otherwise provided by this section would not indicate the extreme width of the trailer.

(d) A clearance lamp and side marker lamp may be mounted in combination if each lamp complies with the visibility requirements of Section 547.355.

Sec. 547.355. Visibility Requirements.

(a) A clearance lamp, identification lamp, or side marker lamp shall be visible and recognizable under normal atmospheric conditions at all distances from 50 to 500 feet from the vehicle on the side, front, or rear where the lamp is mounted.

(b) A reflector required by this chapter mounted on a vehicle subject to this subchapter shall be visible from the rear, if a rear reflector, or from the applicable side, if a side reflector, at nighttime at all distances from 100 to 600 feet from the vehicle when the reflector is directly in front of:

(1) lawful lower beams of headlamps; or

(2) lawful upper beams of headlamps on a vehicle manufactured or assembled before January 1, 1972.

SUBCHAPTER G
ALTERNATIVE LIGHTING REQUIREMENTS FOR FARM TRACTORS, FARM EQUIPMENT, AND IMPLEMENTS OF HUSBANDRY

Sec. 547.371. General Lighting Equipment Requirements.

(a) Except as provided by Subsection (b), a farm tractor, self-propelled unit of farm equipment, or implement of husbandry shall be equipped with:

(1) at least two headlamps that comply with Section 547.333, 547.334, or 547.335;

Transportation Code

(2) at least one red lamp visible at a distance of at least 1,000 feet from the rear and mounted as far to the left of the center of the vehicle as practicable;

(3) at least two red reflectors visible at all distances from 100 to 600 feet from the rear when directly in front of lawful lower beams of headlamps; and

(4) hazard lamps as described in Section 547.331, which shall be lighted and visible in normal sunlight at a distance of at least 1,000 feet from the front and rear.

(b) A farm tractor, self-propelled unit of farm equipment, or implement of husbandry manufactured or assembled on or before January 1, 1972, is required to be equipped as provided by Subsection (a) only at the times specified by Section 547.302(a), and hazard lamps are not required.

Sec. 547.372. Lighting Requirements for Combination Vehicles.

(a) If a unit of farm equipment or implement of husbandry is towed by a farm tractor and the towed object or its load extends more than four feet to the rear of the tractor or obscures a light on the tractor, the towed object shall be equipped at the times specified by Section 547.302(a) with at least two rear red reflectors that are:

(1) visible at all distances from 100 to 600 feet when directly in front of lawful lower beams of headlamps; and

(2) mounted to indicate, as nearly as practicable, the extreme width of the vehicle or combination of vehicles.

(b) If a unit of farm equipment or implement of husbandry is towed by a farm tractor and extends more than four feet to the left of the centerline of the tractor, the towed object shall be equipped at the times specified by Section 547.302(a) with a front amber reflector that is:

(1) visible at all distances from 100 to 600 feet when directly in front of lawful lower beams of headlamps; and

(2) mounted to indicate, as nearly as practicable, the extreme left projection of the towed object.

(c) Reflective tape or paint may be used as an alternative to the reflectors required by this section if the alternative complies with the other requirements of this section.

SUBCHAPTER H
LIGHTING REQUIREMENTS IN SPECIAL CIRCUMSTANCES

Sec. 547.381. Obstructed Lights on Combination Vehicles.

(a) A motor vehicle when operated in combination with another vehicle is not required to display a lighted lamp, other than a taillamp, if the lamp is obscured because of its location by another vehicle in the combination of vehicles.

(b) Subsection (a) is not an exception for the lighting as provided by this chapter of:

(1) front clearance lamps on the frontmost vehicle in the combination; or

(2) rear lamps on the rearmost vehicle in the combination.

Sec. 547.382. Lighting Equipment on Projecting Loads.

(a) A vehicle transporting a load that extends to the rear at least four feet beyond the bed or body of the vehicle shall display on the extreme end of the load at the times specified in Section 547.302(a):

(1) two red lamps visible at a distance of at least 500 feet from the rear;

(2) two red reflectors that indicate the maximum width and are visible at nighttime at all distances from 100 to 600 feet from the rear when directly in front of lawful lower beams of headlamps; and

(3) two red lamps, one on each side, that indicate the maximum overhang and are visible at a distance of at least 500 feet from the side.

(b) At all other times, a vehicle transporting a load that extends beyond the vehicle's sides or more than four feet beyond the vehicle's rear shall display red flags that:

(1) are at least 12 inches square;

(2) mark the extremities of the load; and

(3) are placed where a lamp is required by this section.

Sec. 547.383. Lighting Requirements on Parked Vehicles.

(a) A vehicle, other than a moped or a motorcycle equipped with a motor that has an engine piston displacement of 250 cubic centimeters or less, shall be equipped with at least one lamp, or a combination of lamps, that:

(1) emits a white or amber light visible at a distance of 1,000 feet from the front and a red light visible at a distance of 1,000 feet from the rear; and

(2) is mounted so that at least one lamp is installed as near as practicable to the side of the vehicle that is closest to passing traffic.

(b) A vehicle, other than a moped or a motorcycle equipped with a motor that has an engine piston

Transportation Code

displacement of 250 cubic centimeters or less, that is parked or stopped on a roadway or shoulder at a time specified in Section 547.302(a) shall display a lamp that complies with Subsection (a).

(c) A vehicle that is lawfully parked on a highway is not required to display lights at night-time if there is sufficient light to reveal a person or vehicle on the highway at a distance of 1,000 feet.

(d) A lighted headlamp on a parked vehicle shall be dimmed.

SUBCHAPTER I PROVISIONS RELATING TO BRAKE REQUIREMENTS ON VEHICLES

Sec. 547.401. Brakes Required.

(a) Except as provided by Subsection (b), a motor vehicle, trailer, semitrailer, pole trailer, or combination of those vehicles shall be equipped with brakes that comply with this chapter.

(b) A trailer, semitrailer, or pole trailer is not required to have brakes if:

(1) its gross weight is 4,500 pounds or less; or

(2) its gross weight is heavier than 4,500 pounds but not heavier than 15,000 pounds, and it is drawn at a speed of not more than 30 miles per hour.

Sec. 547.402. Operation and Maintenance of Brakes.

(a) Required brakes shall operate on each wheel of a vehicle except:

(1) special mobile equipment;

(2) a vehicle that is towed as a commodity when at least one set of the towed vehicle's wheels is on the roadway, if the combination of vehicles complies with the performance requirements of this chapter; and

(3) a trailer, semitrailer, or pole trailer with a gross weight heavier than 4,500 pounds but not heavier than 15,000 pounds drawn at a speed of more than 30 miles per hour, if the brakes operate on both wheels of the rear axle.

(b) A truck or truck-tractor that has at least three axles is not required to have brakes on the front wheels, but must have brakes that:

(1) operate on the wheels of one steerable axle if the vehicle is equipped with at least two steerable axles; and

(2) comply with the performance requirements of this chapter.

(c) A trailer or semitrailer that has a gross weight of 15,000 pounds or less may use surge or inertia brake systems to satisfy the requirements of Subsection (a).

(d) Brakes shall be maintained in good working order and adjusted to operate on wheels on each side of the vehicle as equally as practicable.

Sec. 547.403. Service Brakes Required.

(a) A vehicle required to have brakes by this subchapter, other than special mobile equipment, shall be equipped with service brakes that:

(1) comply with the performance requirements of this subchapter; and

(2) are adequate to control the movement of the vehicle, including stopping and holding, under all loading conditions and when on any grade on which the vehicle is operated.

(b) A vehicle required to have brakes by this subchapter shall be equipped so that one control device operates the service brakes. This subsection does not prohibit an additional control device that may be used to operate brakes on a towed vehicle. A vehicle that tows another vehicle as a commodity when at least one set of the towed vehicle's wheels is on the roadway is not required to comply with this requirement unless the brakes on the towing and towed vehicles are designed to be operated by a single control on the towing vehicle.

Sec. 547.404. Parking Brakes Required.

(a) A vehicle required to have brakes by this subchapter, other than a motorcycle or moped, shall be equipped with parking brakes adequate to hold the vehicle:

(1) on any grade on which the vehicle is operated;

(2) under all loading conditions; and

(3) on a surface free from snow, ice, or loose material.

(b) The parking brakes shall be:

(1) designed to operate continuously as required once applied, despite a leakage or an exhaustion of power source; and

(2) activated by the vehicle operator's muscular effort, by spring action, or by equivalent means.

(c) The parking brakes may be assisted by the service brakes or by another power source, unless a failure in the power source would prevent the parking brakes from operating as required by this section.

(d) The same brake drums, brake shoes and lining assemblies, brake shoe anchors, and mechanical brake shoe actuation mechanism normally

Transportation Code

associated with wheel brake assemblies may be used for the parking brakes and service brakes.

(e) If the means of applying the parking brakes and service brakes are connected, the brake system shall be constructed so that the failure of one part will not cause the vehicle to be without operative brakes.

Sec. 547.405. Emergency Brakes Required.

(a) A vehicle used to tow another vehicle equipped with air-controlled brakes shall be equipped with the following means, together or separate, for applying the trailer brakes in an emergency:

(1) an automatic device that applies the brakes to a fixed pressure from 20 to 45 pounds per square inch if the towing vehicle's air supply is reduced; and

(2) a manual device to apply and release the brakes that is readily operable by a person seated in the operator's seat and arranged so that:

(A) its emergency position or method of operation is clearly indicated; and

(B) its use does not prevent operation of the automatic brakes.

(b) In addition to the single control device required by Section 547.403, a vehicle used to tow another vehicle equipped with vacuum brakes shall be equipped with a second control device that:

(1) is used to operate the brakes on a towed vehicle in an emergency;

(2) is independent of brake air, hydraulic, or other pressure and independent of other controls, unless the braking system is arranged to automatically apply the towed vehicle's brakes if the pressure for the second control device on the towing vehicle fails; and

(3) is not required to provide modulated braking.

(c) Subsections (a) and (b) do not apply to a vehicle that tows another vehicle as a commodity when at least one set of wheels of the towed vehicle is on the roadway.

(d) A trailer, semitrailer, or pole trailer that is equipped with air or vacuum brakes or that has a gross weight heavier than 4,500 pounds shall be equipped with brakes that:

(1) operate on all wheels required to have brakes under Section 547.402; and

(2) are promptly applied automatically and remain applied for at least 15 minutes in case of a breakaway from the towing vehicle.

(e) A motor vehicle used to tow a trailer, semitrailer, or pole trailer equipped with brakes shall be equipped with service brakes arranged so that, in case of a breakaway of the towed vehicle, the towing vehicle is capable of stopping by use of its service brakes.

Sec. 547.406. Brake Reservoir or Reserve Capacity Required.

(a) A bus, truck, or truck-tractor equipped with air brakes shall be equipped with at least one reservoir that:

(1) is sufficient to ensure that the service brakes can be fully applied without lowering the reservoir pressure, if fully charged to the maximum pressure as regulated by the air compressor governor cut-out setting, by more than 20 percent; and

(2) has a means for readily draining accumulated oil or water.

(b) A truck with at least three axles that is equipped with vacuum brakes or a truck-tractor or truck used to tow a vehicle equipped with vacuum brakes shall be equipped with a reserve capacity or a vacuum reservoir sufficient to ensure that, with the reserve capacity or vacuum reservoir fully charged and with the engine stopped, the service brakes can be fully applied without depleting the vacuum supply by more than 40 percent.

(c) A motor vehicle, trailer, semitrailer, or pole trailer that is equipped with an air or vacuum reservoir or reserve capacity shall be equipped with a check valve or equivalent device to prevent depletion of the air or vacuum supply by failure or leakage.

(d) An air brake system installed on a trailer shall be designed to prevent a backflow of air from the supply reservoir through the supply line.

Sec. 547.407. Brake Warning Devices Required.

(a) A bus, truck, or truck-tractor that uses air to operate its brakes or the brakes of a towed vehicle shall be equipped with:

(1) a warning signal, other than a pressure gauge, that is readily audible or visible to the vehicle operator and that shows when the air reservoir pressure is below 50 percent of the air compressor governor cut-out pressure; and

(2) a pressure gauge visible to the vehicle operator that shows in pounds per square inch the pressure available for braking.

(b) A truck-tractor or truck used to tow a vehicle equipped with vacuum brakes, or a truck with at least three axles that is equipped with vacuum brakes, shall be equipped with a warning signal, other than a gauge showing vacuum, that is readily audible or visible to the vehicle operator and that shows when the vacuum in the reservoir or reserve capacity is less than eight inches of mercury. This subsection does not apply to an operation in which a motor vehicle, trailer, or semitrailer is

Transportation Code

transported as a commodity when at least one set of the vehicle's wheels is on the roadway.

(c) If a vehicle required to be equipped with a warning device is equipped with air and vacuum power to operate its brakes or the brakes on a towed vehicle, the warning devices required may be combined into a single device that is not a pressure or vacuum gauge.

Sec. 547.408. Performance Requirements for Brakes.

(a) A motor vehicle or combination of vehicles shall be equipped with service brakes capable of:

(1) developing a braking force that is not less than:

(A) 52.8 percent of the gross weight of the vehicle for a passenger vehicle; or

(B) 43.5 percent of the gross weight of the vehicle for a vehicle other than a passenger vehicle;

(2) decelerating to a stop from 20 miles per hour or less at not less than:

(A) 17 feet per second per second for a passenger vehicle; or

(B) 14 feet per second per second for other vehicles; and

(3) stopping from a speed of 20 miles per hour in a distance, measured from the location where the service brake pedal or control is activated, of not more than:

(A) 25 feet for a passenger vehicle;

(B) 30 feet for a motorcycle, moped, or single unit vehicle with a manufacturer's gross vehicle weight rating of 10,000 pounds or less;

(C) 40 feet for:

(i) a single unit vehicle with a manufacturer's gross weight rating of more than 10,000 pounds;

(ii) a two-axle towing vehicle and trailer combination with a weight of 3,000 pounds or less;

(iii) a bus that does not have a manufacturer's gross weight rating; and

(iv) the combination of vehicles in an operation exempted by Section 547.407(b); and

(D) 50 feet for other vehicles.

(b) A test for deceleration or stopping distance shall be performed on a dry, smooth, hard surface that:

(1) is free of loose material; and

(2) does not exceed plus or minus one percent grade.

(c) In this section, "passenger vehicle" means a vehicle that has a maximum seating capacity of 10 persons, including the operator, and that does not have a manufacturer's gross vehicle weight rating.

SUBCHAPTER J PROVISIONS RELATING TO WARNING DEVICE REQUIREMENTS ON VEHICLES

Sec. 547.501. Audible Warning Devices.

(a) A motor vehicle shall be equipped with a horn in good working condition that emits a sound audible under normal conditions at a distance of at least 200 feet.

(b) A vehicle may not be equipped with and a person may not use on a vehicle a siren, whistle, or bell unless the vehicle is:

(1) a commercial vehicle that is equipped with a theft alarm signal device arranged so that the device cannot be used as an ordinary warning signal; or

(2) an authorized emergency vehicle that is equipped with a siren, whistle, or bell that complies with Section 547.702.

(c) A motor vehicle operator shall use a horn to provide audible warning only when necessary to insure safe operation.

(d) A warning device, including a horn, may not emit an unreasonably loud or harsh sound or a whistle.

Sec. 547.502. Visible Warning Devices Required.

(a) Except as provided by Subsection (b), a person who operates, outside an urban district or on a divided highway, a truck, bus, or truck-tractor or a motor vehicle towing a house trailer shall carry in the vehicle:

(1) at daytime:

(A) at least two red flags at least 12 inches square; and

(B) standards to support the flags; and

(2) at nighttime:

(A) at least three flares and at least three red-burning fusees;

(B) at least three red electric lanterns; or

(C) at least three portable red emergency reflectors.

(b) A person who operates an explosive cargo vehicle at nighttime:

(1) shall carry in the vehicle three red electric lanterns or three portable red emergency reflectors; and

(2) may not carry in the vehicle a flare, fusee, or signal produced by flame.

(c) A flare, electric lantern, or portable reflector must be visible and distinguishable at a distance

Transportation Code

of at least 600 feet at night under normal atmospheric conditions.

(d) A portable reflector unit must be designed and constructed to reflect a red light clearly visible at all distances from 100 to 600 feet under normal atmospheric conditions at night when directly in front of lawful lower beams of headlamps.

(e) A flare, fusee, electric lantern, portable reflector, or warning flag must be a type approved by the department.

Sec. 547.503. Display of Hazard Lamps.

(a) The operator of a vehicle that is described by Subsection (b) and that is stopped on a roadway or shoulder shall immediately display vehicular hazard warning lamps that comply with Section 547.331, unless the vehicle:

(1) is parked lawfully in an urban district;

(2) is stopped lawfully to receive or discharge a passenger;

(3) is stopped to avoid conflict with other traffic;

(4) is stopped to comply with a direction of a police officer or an official traffic-control device; or

(5) displays other warning devices as required by Sections 547.504—547.507.

(b) This section applies to a truck, bus, truck-tractor, trailer, semitrailer, or pole trailer at least 80 inches wide or at least 30 feet long.

Sec. 547.504. Display of Devices When Lighted Lamps Required.

(a) Unless sufficient light exists to reveal a person or vehicle at a distance of 1,000 feet, the operator of a vehicle described by Section 547.503(b) or an explosive cargo vehicle shall display warning devices that comply with the requirements of Section 547.502:

(1) when lighted lamps are required; and

(2) under the conditions stated in this section.

(b) Except as provided by Section 547.506 and Subsection (d), the operator of a vehicle described by Section 547.503(b) or an explosive cargo vehicle that is disabled, or stopped for more than 10 minutes, on a roadway outside an urban district shall:

(1) immediately place a lighted red electric lantern or a portable red emergency reflector at the traffic side of the vehicle in the direction of the nearest approaching traffic; and

(2) place in the following order and as soon as practicable within 15 minutes one lighted red electric lamp or portable red emergency reflector:

(A) in the center of the lane occupied by the vehicle toward approaching traffic approximately 100 feet from the vehicle; and

(B) in the center of the lane occupied by the vehicle in the opposite direction approximately 100 feet from the vehicle.

(c) Except as provided by Section 547.506 and Subsection (d), the operator of a vehicle described by Section 547.503(b) or an explosive cargo vehicle that is disabled, or stopped for more than 10 minutes, on a roadway of a divided highway shall place the warning devices described by Subsection (b):

(1) in the center of the lane occupied by the vehicle toward approaching traffic approximately 200 feet from the vehicle;

(2) in the center of the lane occupied by the vehicle toward approaching traffic approximately 100 feet from the vehicle; and

(3) at the traffic side approximately 10 feet from the vehicle in the direction of the nearest approaching traffic.

(d) As an alternative to the use of electric lamps or red reflectors and except as provided by Subsection (e), the operator of a vehicle described by Section 547.503(b) may display a lighted fusee to comply with the requirements of Subsection (b)(1) or liquid-burning flares to comply with the requirements of Subsections (b)(2) and (c). If the operator uses liquid-burning flares to comply with Subsection (b)(2), the operator shall also, after complying with Subsection (b)(2)(B), place a liquid-burning flare at the traffic side of the vehicle at least 10 feet in the direction of the nearest approaching traffic. If a fusee is used to comply with Subsection (b)(1), the operator shall comply with Subsection (b)(2) within the burning period of the fusee.

(e) The operator of an explosive cargo vehicle may not display as a warning device a flare, fusee, or signal produced by flame.

Sec. 547.505. Display of Devices When Lighted Lamps Are Not Required.

(a) The operator of a vehicle described by Section 547.503(b) or an explosive cargo vehicle that is disabled, or stopped for more than 10 minutes, on a roadway outside an urban district or on a roadway of a divided highway when lighted lamps are not required shall display two red flags that comply with Section 547.502.

(b) If traffic on the roadway moves in two directions, one flag shall be placed approximately 100 feet to the rear and one approximately 100 feet ahead of the vehicle in the center of the lane occupied by the vehicle.

(c) If traffic on the roadway moves in one direction, one flag shall be placed approximately 100 feet and one approximately 200 feet to the rear of the vehicle in the center of the lane occupied by the vehicle.

Transportation Code

Sec. 547.506. Display of Devices: Vehicles Off Roadway.

The operator of a vehicle described by Section 547.503(b) or an explosive cargo vehicle that is stopped entirely on the shoulder at a time and in a place referred to in this subchapter shall place required warning devices on the shoulder as close as practicable to the edge of the roadway.

Sec. 547.507. Display of Devices When View of Vehicle Obstructed.

Unless sufficient light exists to reveal a person or vehicle at a distance of 1,000 feet, the operator of a vehicle described by Section 547.503(b) or an explosive cargo vehicle that is disabled, or stopped for more than 10 minutes, within 500 feet of a curve, hillcrest, or other obstruction to view shall place the required warning device for the direction of the obstruction from 100 to 500 feet from the vehicle so as to provide ample warning to other traffic.

Sec. 547.508. Offense Relating to Warning Devices.

(a) Except as provided by Subsection (b), a person may not remove, damage, destroy, misplace, or extinguish a warning device required under Sections 547.502—547.507 when the device is being displayed or used as required.

(b) This section does not apply to:

(1) an owner of a vehicle or the owner's authorized agent or employee; or

(2) a peace officer acting in an official capacity.

SUBCHAPTER K
PROVISIONS RELATING TO OTHER VEHICLE EQUIPMENT

Sec. 547.601. Safety Belts Required.

A motor vehicle required by Chapter 548 to be inspected shall be equipped with front safety belts if safety belt anchorages were part of the manufacturer's original equipment on the vehicle.

Sec. 547.602. Mirrors Required.

A motor vehicle, including a motor vehicle used to tow another vehicle, shall be equipped with a mirror located to reflect to the operator a view of the highway for a distance of at least 200 feet from the rear of the vehicle.

Sec. 547.603. Windshield Wipers Required.

A motor vehicle shall be equipped with a device that is operated or controlled by the operator of the vehicle and that cleans moisture from the windshield. The device shall be maintained in good working condition.

Sec. 547.604. Muffler Required.

(a) A motor vehicle shall be equipped with a muffler in good working condition that continually operates to prevent excessive or unusual noise.

(b) A person may not use a muffler cutout, bypass, or similar device on a motor vehicle.

Sec. 547.605. Emission Systems Required.

(a) The engine and power mechanism of a motor vehicle shall be equipped and adjusted to prevent the escape of excessive smoke or fumes.

(b) A motor vehicle or motor vehicle engine, of a model year after 1967, shall be equipped to prevent the discharge of crankcase emissions into the ambient atmosphere.

(c) The owner or operator of a motor vehicle or motor vehicle engine, of a model year after 1967, that is equipped with an exhaust emission system:

(1) shall maintain the system in good working condition;

(2) shall use the system when the motor vehicle or motor vehicle engine is operated; and

(3) may not remove the system or a part of the system or intentionally make the system inoperable in this state, unless the owner or operator removes the system or part to install another system or part intended to be equally effective in reducing atmospheric emissions.

(d) Except when travel conditions require the downshifting or use of lower gears to maintain reasonable momentum, a person commits an offense if the person operates, or as an owner knowingly permits another person to operate, a vehicle that emits:

(1) visible smoke for 10 seconds or longer; or

(2) visible smoke that remains suspended in the air for 10 seconds or longer before fully dissipating.

(e) An offense under this section is a misdemeanor punishable by a fine of not less than $1 and not more than $350 for each violation. If a person has previously been convicted of an offense under this section, an offense under this section is a misdemeanor punishable by a fine of not less than $200 and not more than $1,000 for each violation.

Sec. 547.606. Safety Guards or Flaps Required.

(a) A road tractor, truck, trailer, truck-tractor in combination with a semitrailer, or semitrailer in combination with a towing vehicle that has at least four tires or at least two super single tires on the rearmost axle of the vehicle or the rearmost vehicle in the combination shall be equipped with safety guards or flaps that:

(1) are of a type prescribed by the department; and

(2) are located and suspended behind the rearmost wheels of the vehicle or the rearmost vehicle in the combination within eight inches of the surface of the highway.

(b) This section does not apply to a truck-tractor operated alone or a pole trailer.

(c) In this section, "super single tire" means a wide-base, single tire that may be used in place of two standard tires on the same axle.

Sec. 547.607. Fire Extinguisher Required.

A school bus or a motor vehicle that transports passengers for hire or lease shall be equipped with at least one quart of chemical-type fire extinguisher in good condition and located for immediate use.

Sec. 547.608. Safety Glazing Material Required.

(a) Except as provided by Subsection (b), a person who sells or registers a new passenger-type motor vehicle, including a passenger bus and school bus, shall equip the vehicle doors, windows, and windshield with safety glazing material of a type approved by the department.

(b) The requirements of Subsection (a) do not apply to a glazing material in a compartment of a truck, including a truck-tractor, that is not designed and equipped for a person to ride in.

(c) A person may not replace or require the replacement of glass in a door, window, or windshield of any motor vehicle if the replacement is not made with safety glazing material.

(d) A person who sells or attaches to a motor vehicle a camper manufactured or assembled after January 1, 1972, shall equip the camper doors and windows with safety glazing material of a type approved by the department. In this subsection "camper" means a structure designed to:

(1) be loaded on or attached to a motor vehicle; and

(2) provide temporary living quarters for recreation, travel, or other use.

(e) A person who sells imperfect safety glass for a door, window, or windshield of a motor vehicle shall:

(1) label the glass "second," "imperfect," or by a similar term in red letters at least one inch in size to indicate to the consumer the quality of the glass;

(2) orally notify the consumer of each imperfection and the possible result of using imperfect glass; and

(3) deliver written notice at the time of purchase notifying the consumer of each imperfection and the possible result of using imperfect glass.

Sec. 547.609. Required Label for Sunscreening Devices.

A sunscreening device must have a label that:

(1) is legible;

(2) contains information required by the department on light transmission and luminous reflectance of the device;

(3) if the device is placed on or attached to a windshield or a side or rear window, states that the light transmission of the device is consistent with Section 547.613(b)(1) or (2), as applicable; and

(4) is permanently installed between the material and the surface to which the material is applied.

Sec. 547.610. Safe Air-Conditioning Equipment Required; Sale of Noncomplying Vehicle.

(a) Air-conditioning equipment:

(1) shall be manufactured, installed, and maintained to ensure the safety of the vehicle occupants and the public; and

(2) may not contain any refrigerant that is flammable or is toxic to persons unless the refrigerant is included in the list published by the United States Environmental Protection Agency as a safe alternative motor vehicle air conditioning substitute for chlorofluorocarbon-12, pursuant to 42 U.S.C. Section 7671k(c).

(b) A person may not possess or offer for sale, sell, or equip a motor vehicle with air-conditioning equipment that does not comply with the requirements of this section and Section 547.103.

Sec. 547.611. Use of Certain Video Equipment and Television Receivers.

(a) A motor vehicle may be equipped with video receiving equipment, including a television, a digital video disc player, a videocassette player, or similar equipment, only if the equipment is located so that the video display is not visible from the

Transportation Code

operator's seat unless the vehicle's transmission is in park or the vehicle's parking brake is applied.

(b) A motor vehicle specially designed as a mobile unit used by a licensed television station may have video receiving equipment located so that the video display is visible from the operator's side, but the receiver may be used only when the vehicle is stopped.

(c) This section does not prohibit the use of:

(1) equipment used:

(A) exclusively for receiving digital information for commercial purposes;

(B) exclusively for a safety or law enforcement purpose, if each installation is approved by the department;

(C) in a remote television transmission truck; or

(D) exclusively for monitoring the performance of equipment installed on a vehicle used for safety purposes in connection with the operations of a natural gas, water, or electric utility; or

(2) a monitoring device that:

(A) produces an electronic display; and

(B) is used exclusively in conjunction with a mobile navigation system installed in the vehicle.

Sec. 547.612. Restrictions on Use and Sale of Tires.

(a) A solid rubber tire used on a vehicle must have rubber on the traction surface that extends above the edge of the flange of the periphery.

(b) A person may not operate or move a motor vehicle, trailer, or semitrailer that has a metal tire in contact with the roadway, unless:

(1) the vehicle is a farm wagon or farm trailer that has a gross weight of less than 5,000 pounds; and

(2) the owner is transporting farm products to market, for processing, or from farm to farm.

(c) A tire used on a moving vehicle may not have on its periphery a block, stud, flange, cleat, or spike or other protuberance of a material other than rubber that projects beyond the tread of the traction surface, unless the protuberance:

(1) does not injure the highway; or

(2) is a tire chain of reasonable proportion that is used as required for safety because of a condition that might cause the vehicle to skid.

(d) The Texas Transportation Commission and a local authority within its jurisdiction may issue a special permit that authorizes a person to operate a tractor or traction engine that has movable tracks with transverse corrugations on the periphery or a farm tractor or other farm machinery.

(e) A person commits an offense if the person offers for sale or sells a private passenger automobile tire that is regrooved. An offense under this section is a misdemeanor punishable by a fine of not less than $500 or more than $2,000.

Sec. 547.613. Restrictions on Windows.

(a) Except as provided by Subsection (b), a person commits an offense that is a misdemeanor:

(1) if the person operates a motor vehicle that has an object or material that is placed on or attached to the windshield or side or rear window and that obstructs or reduces the operator's clear view; or

(2) if a person, including an installer or manufacturer, places on or attaches to the windshield or side or rear window of a motor vehicle a transparent material that alters the color or reduces the light transmission.

(a-1) A person in the business of placing or attaching transparent material that alters the color or reduces the light transmission to the windshield or side or rear window of a motor vehicle commits a misdemeanor punishable by a fine not to exceed $1,000 if the person:

(1) places or attaches such transparent material to the windshield or side or rear window of a motor vehicle; and

(2) does not install a label that complies with Section 547.609 between the transparent material and the windshield or side or rear window of the vehicle, as applicable.

(b) Subsection (a) does not apply to:

(1) a windshield that has a sunscreening device that:

(A) in combination with the windshield has a light transmission of 25 percent or more;

(B) in combination with the windshield has a luminous reflectance of 25 percent or less;

(C) is not red, blue, or amber; and

(D) does not extend downward beyond the AS-1 line or more than five inches from the top of the windshield, whichever is closer to the top of the windshield;

(2) a wing vent or a window that is to the left or right of the vehicle operator if the vent or window has a sunscreening device that in combination with the vent or window has:

(A) a light transmission of 25 percent or more; and

(B) a luminous reflectance of 25 percent or less;

(2-a) a side window that is to the rear of the vehicle operator;

(3) a rear window, if the motor vehicle is equipped with an outside mirror on each side of the vehicle that reflects to the vehicle operator a view of the highway for a distance of at least 200 feet from the rear;

(4) a rearview mirror;

(5) an adjustable nontransparent sun visor that is mounted in front of a side window and not attached to the glass;

(6) a direction, destination, or termination sign on a passenger common carrier motor vehicle, if the sign does not interfere with the vehicle operator's view of approaching traffic;

(7) a rear window wiper motor;

(8) a rear trunk lid handle or hinge;

(9) a luggage rack attached to the rear trunk;

(10) a side window that is to the rear of the vehicle operator on a multipurpose vehicle;

(11) a window that has a United States, state, or local certificate placed on or attached to it as required by law;

(12) a motor vehicle that is not registered in this state;

(13) a window that complies with federal standards for window materials, including a factory-tinted or a pretinted window installed by the vehicle manufacturer, or a replacement window meeting the specifications required by the vehicle manufacturer;

(14) a vehicle that is:

(A) used regularly to transport passengers for a fee; and

(B) authorized to operate under license or permit by a local authority;

(15) a vehicle that is maintained by a law enforcement agency and used for law enforcement purposes; or

(16) a commercial motor vehicle as defined by Section 644.001.

(c) A manufacturer shall certify to the department that the sunscreening device made or assembled by the manufacturer complies with the light transmission and luminous reflectance specifications established by Subsection (b) for sunscreening devices in combination with a window.

(d) The department may determine that a window that has a sunscreening device is exempt under Subsection (b)(2) if the light transmission or luminous reflectance varies by no more than three percent from the standard established in that subsection.

(e) It is a defense to prosecution under Subsection (a) that the defendant or a passenger in the vehicle at the time of the violation is required for a medical reason to be shielded from direct rays of the sun.

(f) It is not an offense under this section for a person to offer for sale or sell a motor vehicle with a windshield or window that does not comply with this section.

(g) In this section:

(1) "Installer" means a person who fabricates, laminates, or tempers a safety glazing material to incorporate, during the installation process, the capacity to reflect light or reduce light transmission.

(2) "Manufacturer" means a person who:

(A) manufactures or assembles a sunscreening device; or

(B) fabricates, laminates, or tempers safety glazing material to incorporate, during the manufacturing process, the capacity to reflect light or reduce light transmission.

Sec. 547.614. Restrictions on Airbags.

(a) In this section, "counterfeit airbag" means an airbag that does not meet all applicable federal safety regulations for an airbag designed to be installed in a vehicle of a particular make, model, and year.

(a-1) A person commits an offense if the person knowingly:

(1) installs or purports to install an airbag in a vehicle; and

(2) does not install an airbag or installs a counterfeit airbag.

(a-2) A person commits an offense if the person:

(1) makes or sells a counterfeit airbag to be installed in a motor vehicle;

(2) intentionally alters an airbag that is not counterfeit in a manner that causes the airbag to not meet all applicable federal safety regulations for an airbag designed to be installed in a vehicle of a particular make, model, and year;

(3) represents to another person that a counterfeit airbag installed in a motor vehicle is not counterfeit; or

(4) causes another person to violate Subsection (a-1) or Subdivision (1), (2), or (3) or assists a person in violating Subsection (a-1) or Subdivision (1), (2), or (3).

(b) Except as provided by Subsections (c), (d), and (e), an offense under this section is a state jail felony.

(c) An offense under this section is a felony of the third degree if it is shown on the trial of the offense that the defendant has been previously convicted of an offense under this section.

(d) An offense under this section is a felony of the second degree if it is shown on the trial of the offense that as a result of the offense an individual suffered bodily injury.

(e) An offense under this section is a felony of the first degree if it is shown on the trial of the offense that the offense resulted in the death of a person.

Sec. 547.615. Recording Devices.

(a) In this section:

(1) "Owner" means a person who:

(A) has all the incidents of ownership of a motor vehicle, including legal title, regardless of whether the person lends, rents, or creates a security interest in the vehicle;

(B) is entitled to possession of a motor vehicle as a purchaser under a security agreement; or

(C) is entitled to possession of a motor vehicle as a lessee under a written lease agreement if the agreement is for a period of not less than three months.

(2) "Recording device" means a feature that is installed by the manufacturer in a motor vehicle and that does any of the following for the purpose of retrieving information from the vehicle after an accident in which the vehicle has been involved:

(A) records the speed and direction the vehicle is traveling;

(B) records vehicle location data;

(C) records steering performance;

(D) records brake performance, including information on whether brakes were applied before an accident;

(E) records the driver's safety belt status; or

(F) transmits information concerning the accident to a central communications system when the accident occurs.

(b) A manufacturer of a new motor vehicle that is sold or leased in this state and that is equipped with a recording device shall disclose that fact in the owner's manual of the vehicle.

(c) Information recorded or transmitted by a recording device may not be retrieved by a person other than the owner of the motor vehicle in which the recording device is installed except:

(1) on court order;

(2) with the consent of the owner for any purpose, including for the purpose of diagnosing, servicing, or repairing the motor vehicle;

(3) for the purpose of improving motor vehicle safety, including for medical research on the human body's reaction to motor vehicle accidents, if the identity of the owner or driver of the vehicle is not disclosed in connection with the retrieved information; or

(4) for the purpose of determining the need for or facilitating emergency medical response in the event of a motor vehicle accident.

(d) For information recorded or transmitted by a recording device described by Subsection (a)(2)(B), a court order may be obtained only after a showing that:

(1) retrieval of the information is necessary to protect the public safety; or

(2) the information is evidence of an offense or constitutes evidence that a particular person committed an offense.

(e) For the purposes of Subsection (c)(3):

(1) disclosure of a motor vehicle's vehicle identification number with the last six digits deleted or redacted is not disclosure of the identity of the owner or driver; and

(2) retrieved information may be disclosed only:

(A) for the purposes of motor vehicle safety and medical research communities to advance the purposes described in Subsection (c)(3); or

(B) to a data processor solely for the purposes described in Subsection (c)(3).

(f) If a recording device is used as part of a subscription service, the subscription service agreement must disclose that the device may record or transmit information as described by Subsection (a)(2). Subsection (c) does not apply to a subscription service under this subsection.

Sec. 547.616. Radar Interference Devices; Offense.

(a) In this section, "radar interference device" means a device, a mechanism, an instrument, or equipment that is designed, manufactured, used, or intended to be used to interfere with, scramble, disrupt, or otherwise cause to malfunction a radar or laser device used to measure the speed of a motor vehicle by a law enforcement agency of this state or a political subdivision of this state, including a "radar jamming device," "jammer," "scrambler," or "diffuser." The term does not include a ham radio, band radio, or similar electronic device.

(b) A person, other than a law enforcement officer in the discharge of the officer's official duties, may not use, attempt to use, install, operate, or attempt to operate a radar interference device in a motor vehicle operated by the person.

(c) A person may not purchase, sell, or offer for sale a radar interference device to be used in a manner described by Subsection (b).

(d) A person who violates this section commits an offense. An offense under this subsection is a Class C misdemeanor.

Sec. 547.617. Motorcycle and Moped Footrests and Handholds Required.

(a) A motorcycle or moped that is designed to carry more than one person must be equipped with footrests and handholds for use by the passenger.

(b) This section does not apply to an autocycle as defined by Section 501.008 or a motorcycle as defined by Section 521.001(a)(6-a).

Transportation Code

Sec. 547.618. Equipment Required for Certain Automated Motor Vehicles.

(a) In this section, "automated motor vehicle" and "automated driving system" have the meanings assigned by Section 545.451.

(b) An automated motor vehicle that is designed to be operated exclusively by the automated driving system for all trips is not subject to motor vehicle equipment laws or regulations of this state that:

(1) relate to or support motor vehicle operation by a human driver; and

(2) are not relevant for an automated driving system.

(c) If a vehicle safety inspection is required under this code for the operation of a vehicle described by Subsection (b), the vehicle shall automatically be considered to pass the inspection with respect to any equipment:

(1) the requirements from which the vehicle is exempt under Subsection (b); or

(2) the inspection of which is not required under Section 548.051.

SUBCHAPTER L ADDITIONAL EQUIPMENT REQUIREMENTS FOR SCHOOL BUSES, AUTHORIZED EMERGENCY VEHICLES, AND SLOW-MOVING VEHICLES

Sec. 547.701. Additional Equipment Requirements for School Buses and Other Buses Used to Transport Schoolchildren.

(a) A school bus shall be equipped with:

(1) a convex mirror or other device that reflects to the school bus operator a clear view of the area immediately in front of the vehicle that would otherwise be hidden from view; and

(2) signal lamps that:

(A) are mounted as high and as widely spaced laterally as practicable;

(B) display four alternately flashing red lights, two located on the front at the same level and two located on the rear at the same level; and

(C) emit a light visible at a distance of 500 feet in normal sunlight.

(b) A school bus may be equipped with:

(1) rooftop warning lamps:

(A) that conform to and are placed on the bus in accordance with specifications adopted under Section 34.002, Education Code; and

(B) that are operated under rules adopted by the school district; and

(2) movable stop arms:

(A) that conform to regulations adopted under Section 34.002, Education Code; and

(B) that may be operated only when the bus is stopped to load or unload students.

(c) When a school bus is being stopped or is stopped on a highway to permit students to board or exit the bus, the operator of the bus shall activate all flashing warning signal lights and other equipment on the bus designed to warn other drivers that the bus is stopping to load or unload children.

(c-1) A person may not operate a light or other equipment described by Subsection (c) except when a school bus is being stopped or is stopped on a highway to:

(1) permit a student to board or exit the bus; or

(2) distribute to a student or the parent or guardian of a student:

(A) food; or

(B) technological equipment for use by the student for educational purposes.

(d) The exterior of a school bus may not bear advertising or another paid announcement directed at the public if the advertising or announcement distracts from the effectiveness of required safety warning equipment. The department shall adopt rules to implement this subsection. A school bus that violates this section or rules adopted under this section shall be placed out of service until it complies.

(e) In this subsection, "bus" includes a school bus, school activity bus, multifunction school activity bus, or school-chartered bus. A bus operated by or contracted for use by a school district for the transportation of schoolchildren shall be equipped with a three-point seat belt for each passenger, including the operator. This subsection does not apply to:

(1) a bus purchased by a school district that is a model year 2017 or earlier; or

(2) a bus purchased by a school district that is a model year 2018 or later if the board of trustees for the school district:

(A) determines that the district's budget does not permit the district to purchase a bus that is equipped with the seat belts required by this subsection; and

(B) votes to approve that determination in a public meeting.

(f) [Repealed by Acts 2017, 85th Leg., (S.B. 693), § 2, effective September 1, 2017.]

Sec. 547.7011. Additional Equipment Requirements for Other Buses.

(a) A bus, other than a school bus, that provides public transportation and that was acquired on or

Transportation Code

after September 1, 1997, shall be equipped with two or more hazard lamps that:

(1) are mounted at the same level on the rear of the bus;

(2) are visible at a distance of 500 feet in normal sunlight;

(3) flash; and

(4) emit amber light.

(b) An operator of a bus to which this section applies shall activate the hazard lamps if the bus stops to load or unload a person under 18 years of age.

(c) A bus to which this section applies must bear a sign on the rear of the bus stating: "Caution—children may be exiting".

Sec. 547.7012. Requirements for Multifunction School Activity Buses.

A multifunction school activity bus may not be painted National School Bus Glossy Yellow.

Sec. 547.7015. Rules Relating to School Buses.

(a) The department shall adopt and enforce rules governing the design, color, lighting and other equipment, construction, and operation of a school bus for the transportation of schoolchildren that is:

(1) owned and operated by a school district in this state; or

(2) privately owned and operated under a contract with a school district in this state.

(b) In adopting rules under this section, the department shall emphasize:

(1) safety features; and

(2) long-range, maintenance-free factors.

(c) Rules adopted under this section:

(1) apply to each school district, the officers and employees of a district, and each person employed under contract by a school district; and

(2) shall by reference be made a part of any contract that is entered into by a school district in this state for the transportation of schoolchildren on a privately owned school bus.

Sec. 547.702. Additional Equipment Requirements for Authorized Emergency Vehicles.

(a) An authorized emergency vehicle may be equipped with a siren, exhaust whistle, or bell:

(1) of a type approved by the department; and

(2) that emits a sound audible under normal conditions at a distance of at least 500 feet.

(b) The operator of an authorized emergency vehicle shall use the siren, whistle, or bell when necessary to warn other vehicle operators or pedestrians of the approach of the emergency vehicle.

(c) Except as provided by this section, an authorized emergency vehicle shall be equipped with signal lamps that:

(1) are mounted as high and as widely spaced laterally as practicable;

(2) display four alternately flashing red lights, two located on the front at the same level and two located on the rear at the same level; and

(3) emit a light visible at a distance of 500 feet in normal sunlight.

(d) A private vehicle operated by a volunteer firefighter responding to a fire alarm or a medical emergency may, but is not required to, be equipped with signal lamps that comply with the requirements of Subsection (c).

(e) A private vehicle operated by a volunteer firefighter responding to a fire alarm or a medical emergency may be equipped with a signal lamp that is temporarily attached to the vehicle roof and flashes a red light visible at a distance of at least 500 feet in normal sunlight.

(f) A police vehicle may, but is not required to, be equipped with signal lamps that comply with Subsection (c).

Sec. 547.703. Additional Equipment Requirements for Slow-Moving Vehicles.

(a) Except as provided by Subsection (b), a slow-moving vehicle shall display a slow-moving-vehicle emblem that:

(1) has a reflective surface designed to be clearly visible in daylight or at night from the light of standard automobile headlamps at a distance of at least 500 feet;

(2) is mounted base down on the rear of the vehicle and at a height that does not impair the visibility of the emblem; and

(3) is maintained in a clean, reflective condition.

(b) Subsection (a) does not apply to a vehicle that is used in construction or maintenance work and is traveling in a construction area that is marked as required by the Texas Transportation Commission.

(c) If a motor vehicle displaying a slow-moving-vehicle emblem tows machinery, including an implement of husbandry, and the visibility of the emblem is not obstructed, the towed unit is not required to display a slow-moving-vehicle emblem.

(d) A golf cart, neighborhood electric vehicle, or off-highway vehicle that is operated at a speed of not more than 25 miles per hour is required to display a slow-moving-vehicle emblem when it is operated on a highway.

(e) [Repealed by Acts 2009, 81st Leg., ch. 1136 (H.B. 2553), § 12(2), effective September 1, 2009.]

SUBCHAPTER M ADDITIONAL OR ALTERNATIVE EQUIPMENT REQUIREMENTS FOR MOTORCYCLES AND MOPEDS

Sec. 547.801. Lighting Equipment.

(a) A motorcycle or a moped shall be equipped with:

(1) not more than two headlamps mounted at a height from 24 to 54 inches;

(2) at least one taillamp mounted at a height from 20 to 72 inches;

(3) a taillamp or separate lamp to illuminate the rear license plate that complies with the requirements of Sections 547.322(f) and (g);

(4) at least one stoplamp that complies with the requirements of Section 547.323(d); and

(5) at least one rear red reflector that complies with the requirements of Section 547.325(b) and may be included as a part of the taillamp.

(b) A motorcycle, other than a motorcycle equipped with a motor that has an engine piston displacement of 250 cubic centimeters or less, shall be equipped with multiple-beam lighting equipment that produces:

(1) an uppermost distribution of light that reveals a person or vehicle at a distance of at least 300 feet ahead; and

(2) a lowermost distribution of light that:

(A) reveals a person or vehicle at a distance of at least 150 feet ahead; and

(B) is aimed so that no part of the high-intensity portion of the beam on the motorcycle that is on a straight and level road under any condition of loading projects into the eyes of an approaching vehicle operator.

(c) A moped or a motorcycle equipped with a motor that has an engine piston displacement of 250 cubic centimeters or less shall be equipped with:

(1) multiple-beam lighting equipment that complies with the requirements of Subsection (b); or

(2) single-beam lighting equipment that:

(A) emits light sufficient to reveal a person or vehicle:

(i) at a distance of at least 100 feet when the moped or motorcycle is operated at a speed less than 25 miles per hour;

(ii) at a distance of at least 200 feet when the moped or motorcycle is operated at a speed of 25 miles per hour or more; and

(iii) at a distance of at least 300 feet when the moped or motorcycle is operated at a speed of 35 miles per hour or more; and

(B) is aimed so that no part of the high-intensity portion of the beam from the lamp on a loaded moped or motorcycle projects a beam higher than the level center of the lamp for a distance of 25 feet ahead.

(d) A motorcycle may not be operated at any time unless at least one headlamp on the motorcycle is illuminated. This subsection does not apply to a motorcycle manufactured before the model year 1975.

Sec. 547.802. Brake Equipment.

(a) If a motorcycle or a moped complies with the performance requirements of Section 547.408, brakes are not required on the wheel of a sidecar attached to the motorcycle or moped.

(b) If a moped or a motorcycle equipped with a motor that has an engine piston displacement of 250 cubic centimeters or less complies with the performance standards of Section 547.408, brakes are not required on the front wheel of the moped or motorcycle.

(c) The director may require an inspection of the braking system of a moped or a motorcycle equipped with a motor that has an engine piston displacement of 250 cubic centimeters or less and may disapprove a system that:

(1) does not comply with the brake performance requirements in Section 547.408; or

(2) is not designed or constructed to ensure reasonable and reliable performance during actual use.

CHAPTER 548 COMPULSORY INSPECTION OF VEHICLES

SUBCHAPTER A GENERAL PROVISIONS

Sec. 548.001. Definitions.

In this chapter:

(1) "Commercial motor vehicle" means a self-propelled or towed vehicle, other than a farm

vehicle with a gross weight, registered weight, or gross weight rating of less than 48,000 pounds, that is used on a public highway to transport passengers or cargo if:

(A) the vehicle, including a school activity bus as defined in Section 541.201, or combination of vehicles has a gross weight, registered weight, or gross weight rating of more than 26,000 pounds;

(B) the vehicle, including a school activity bus as defined in Section 541.201, is designed or used to transport more than 15 passengers, including the driver; or

(C) the vehicle is used to transport hazardous materials in a quantity requiring placarding by a regulation issued under the Hazardous Materials Transportation Act (49 U.S.C. Section 5101 et seq.).

(2) "Commission" means the Public Safety Commission.

(3) "Conservation commission" means the Texas Commission on Environmental Quality.

(4) "Department" means the Department of Public Safety.

(5) "Farm vehicle" has the meaning assigned by the federal motor carrier safety regulations.

(6) "Federal motor carrier safety regulation" has the meaning assigned by Section 644.001.

(7) "Inspection station" means a facility certified to conduct inspections of vehicles under this chapter.

(8) "Inspector" means an individual certified to conduct inspections of vehicles under this chapter.

(9) "Nonattainment area" means an area so designated within the meaning of Section 107(d) of the Clean Air Act (42 U.S.C. Section 7407).

(10) "Vehicle inspection report" means a report issued by an inspector or an inspection station for a vehicle that indicates whether the vehicle has passed the safety and, if applicable, emissions inspections required by this chapter.

Sec. 548.002. Department Rules.

The department may adopt rules to administer and enforce this chapter.

Sec. 548.003. Department Certification and Supervision of Inspection Stations.

(a) The department may certify inspection stations to carry out this chapter and may instruct and supervise the inspection stations and mechanics for the inspection of vehicles and equipment subject to this chapter.

(b) The department shall certify at least one inspection station for each county.

Sec. 548.004. Department Certification of Inspection Stations for Political Subdivisions and State Agencies.

(a) The department may certify a vehicle maintenance facility owned and operated by a political subdivision or agency of this state as an inspection station.

(b) An inspection station certified under this section is subject to the requirements of this chapter applicable to another inspection station, except as otherwise provided by this chapter.

(c) The facility may inspect only a vehicle owned by the political subdivision or state agency.

Sec. 548.005. Inspection Only by Certain Inspection Stations.

A compulsory inspection under this chapter may be made only by an inspection station, except that the department may:

(1) permit inspection to be made by an inspector under terms and conditions the department prescribes;

(2) authorize the acceptance in this state of a certificate of inspection and approval issued in another state having a similar inspection law;

(3) authorize the acceptance in this state of a certificate of inspection and approval issued in compliance with 49 C.F.R. Part 396 to a motor bus, as defined by Section 502.001, that is registered in this state but is not domiciled in this state; and

(4) authorize the acceptance in this state of a certificate of inspection and approval issued:

(A) by an inspector qualified under 49 C.F.R. Part 396 acting as an employee or authorized agent of the owner of a commercial fleet, as defined in Section 502.001; and

(B) to a motor vehicle or trailer that is:

(i) part of the fleet; and

(ii) registered or in the process of being registered in this state.

Sec. 548.006. Advisory Committee.

(a) An advisory committee consisting of nine members shall:

(1) advise the conservation commission and the department on the conservation commission's and department's rules relating to the operation of the vehicle inspection program under this chapter;

(2) make recommendations to the conservation commission and the department relating to the content of rules involving the operation of the vehicle inspection program; and

Transportation Code

(3) perform any other advisory function requested by the conservation commission or the department in administering this chapter and Chapter 382, Health and Safety Code.

(b) The members of the commission shall appoint seven members of the committee as follows:

(1) four persons to represent inspection station owners and operators, with two of those persons from counties conducting vehicle emissions testing under Subchapter F and two of those persons from counties conducting safety only inspections;

(2) one person to represent manufacturers of motor vehicle emissions inspection devices;

(3) one person to represent independent vehicle equipment repair technicians; and

(4) one person to represent the public interest.

(c) The presiding officer of the conservation commission and the presiding officer of the commission shall each appoint one member of the committee who will alternate serving as the presiding officer of the committee.

(d) Committee members serve staggered three-year terms.

(e) A vacancy on the committee is filled in the same manner as other appointments to the committee.

(f) A member of the committee is not entitled to compensation, but is entitled to reimbursement of the member's travel expenses as provided in the General Appropriations Act for state employees.

(g) The committee may elect an assistant presiding officer and a secretary from among its members and may adopt rules for the conduct of its own activities.

(h) The committee is entitled to review and comment on rules to be considered for adoption by the conservation commission, the commission, or the department under this chapter or Chapter 382, Health and Safety Code, before the rules are adopted.

(i) The committee shall hold a meeting at least once each quarter.

(j) Chapter 2110, Government Code, does not apply to the committee.

Sec. 548.007. Contracts and Instruments to Implement Certain Inspection and Maintenance Programs.

The department may execute any contract or instrument that is necessary or convenient to exercise its powers or perform its duties in implementing a motor vehicle emissions inspection and maintenance program under Section 382.302, Health and Safety Code.

Sec. 548.008. Vehicle Inspection Program Director.

(a) The vehicle inspection program is managed by a program director. The program director may not be a commissioned officer.

(b) The office of the vehicle inspection program director must be located in Austin, Texas.

(c) The duties of the program director include:

(1) responsibility for the quality of the vehicle inspection program;

(2) coordination of the regional offices;

(3) compilation of regional and statewide performance data;

(4) the establishment of best practices and distribution of those practices to the regional offices;

(5) setting goals for the entire program, in consultation with the public safety director or the public safety director's designee, and setting goals for each regional office in consultation with the regional managers;

(6) monitoring the progress toward the goals set in Subdivision (5) and evaluating the program based on that progress; and

(7) coordination with the Texas Highway Patrol to enforce provisions related to vehicle inspection.

(d) The regional offices shall make reports as requested by the program director.

Sec. 548.009. Assembled Vehicles.

(a) In this section, "assembled vehicle" has the meaning assigned by Section 731.001.

(b) A provision of this chapter does not apply to an assembled vehicle if the provision:

(1) conflicts with Chapter 731 or a rule adopted under that chapter; or

(2) is a provision that an assembled vehicle, by its nature, cannot comply with or otherwise meet.

SUBCHAPTER B VEHICLES AND EQUIPMENT SUBJECT TO INSPECTION AND REINSPECTION

Sec. 548.051. Vehicles and Equipment Subject to Inspection.

(a) A motor vehicle, trailer, semitrailer, pole trailer, or mobile home, registered in this state, must have the following items inspected at an inspection station or by an inspector:

(1) tires;

(2) wheel assembly;

(3) safety guards or flaps, if required by Section 547.606;
(4) brake system, including power brake unit;
(5) steering system, including power steering;
(6) lighting equipment;
(7) horns and warning devices;
(8) mirrors;
(9) windshield wipers;
(10) sunscreening devices, unless the vehicle is exempt from sunscreen device restrictions under Section 547.613;
(11) front seat belts in vehicles on which seat belt anchorages were part of the manufacturer's original equipment;
(12) exhaust system;
(13) exhaust emission system;
(14) fuel tank cap, using pressurized testing equipment approved by department rule; and
(15) emissions control equipment as designated by department rule.

(b) A moped is subject to inspection in the same manner as a motorcycle, except that the only items of equipment required to be inspected are the brakes, headlamps, rear lamps, and reflectors, which must comply with the standards prescribed by Sections 547.408 and 547.801.

Sec. 548.052. Vehicles Not Subject to Inspection.

This chapter does not apply to:
(1) a trailer, semitrailer, pole trailer, or mobile home moving under or bearing a current factory-delivery license plate or current in-transit license plate;
(2) a vehicle moving under or bearing a paper dealer in-transit tag, machinery license, disaster license, parade license, prorate tab, one-trip permit, vehicle temporary transit permit, antique license, custom vehicle license, street rod license, temporary 24-hour permit, or permit license;
(3) a trailer, semitrailer, pole trailer, or mobile home having an actual gross weight or registered gross weight of 7,500 pounds or less;
(4) farm machinery, road-building equipment, a farm trailer, or a vehicle required to display a slow-moving-vehicle emblem under Section 547.703;
(5) a former military vehicle, as defined by Section 504.502;
(6) a vehicle qualified for a tax exemption under Section 152.092, Tax Code; or
(7) a vehicle for which a certificate of title has been issued but that is not required to be registered, including an off-highway vehicle registered under Section 502.140(c).

Sec. 548.053. Reinspection of Vehicle Requiring Adjustment, Correction, or Repair.

(a) If an inspection discloses the necessity for adjustment, correction, or repair, an inspection station or inspector may not issue a passing vehicle inspection report until the adjustment, correction, or repair is made. The owner of the vehicle may have the adjustment, correction, or repair made by a qualified person of the owner's choice, subject to reinspection. The vehicle shall be reinspected once free of charge within 15 days after the date of the original inspection, not including the date the original inspection is made, at the same inspection station after the adjustment, correction, or repair is made.

(b) A vehicle that is inspected and is subsequently involved in an accident affecting the safe operation of an item of inspection must be reinspected following repair. The reinspection must be at an inspection station and shall be treated and charged as an initial inspection.

(c) [Repealed by Acts 2013, 83rd Leg., ch. 1291 (H.B. 2305), § 50(1), effective March 1, 2015.]

SUBCHAPTER C
PERIODS OF INSPECTION; PREREQUISITES TO ISSUANCE OF PASSING VEHICLE INSPECTION REPORT

Sec. 548.101. General One-Year Inspection Period.

Except as provided by Section 548.102, the department shall require an annual inspection. The department shall set the periods of inspection and may make rules with respect to those periods. The rules must provide that:
(1) a vehicle owner may obtain an inspection not earlier than 90 days before the date of expiration of the vehicle's registration; and
(2) a used motor vehicle sold by a dealer, as defined by Section 503.001, must be inspected in the 180 days preceding the date the dealer sells the vehicle.

Sec. 548.102. Two-Year Initial Inspection Period for Passenger Car or Light Truck.

(a) The initial inspection period is two years for a passenger car or light truck that:
(1) is sold in this state or purchased by a commercial fleet buyer described by Section 501.0234(b)(4) for use in this state;

(2) has not been previously registered in this or another state; and

(3) on the date of sale is of the current or preceding model year.

(b) This section does not affect a requirement that a motor vehicle emission inspection be conducted during an initial inspection period in a county covered by an inspection and maintenance program approved by the United States Environmental Protection Agency under Section 548.301 and the Clean Air Act (42 U.S.C. Section 7401 et seq.).

Sec. 548.103. Extended Inspection Period for Certain Vehicles.

The department may extend the time within which the resident owner of a vehicle that is not in this state when an inspection is required must obtain a vehicle inspection report in this state.

Sec. 548.104. Equipment-Related Prerequisites to Issuance of Passing Vehicle Inspection Report.

(a) The commission shall adopt uniform standards of safety applicable to each item required to be inspected by Section 548.051. The standards and the list of items to be inspected shall be posted in each inspection station.

(b) An inspection station or inspector may issue a passing vehicle inspection report only if the vehicle is inspected and found to be in proper and safe condition and to comply with this chapter and the rules adopted under this chapter.

(c) An inspection station or inspector may inspect only the equipment required to be inspected by Section 548.051 and may not:

(1) falsely and fraudulently represent to an applicant that equipment required to be inspected must be repaired, adjusted, or replaced before the vehicle will pass inspection; or

(2) require an applicant to have another part of the vehicle or other equipment inspected as a prerequisite for issuance of a passing vehicle inspection report.

(d) An inspection station or inspector may not issue a passing vehicle inspection report for a vehicle equipped with:

(1) a sunscreening device prohibited by Section 547.613, except that the department by rule shall provide procedures for issuance of a passing vehicle inspection report for a vehicle exempt under Section 547.613(c); or

(2) a compressed natural gas container unless the owner demonstrates in accordance with department rules proof:

(A) that:

(i) the container has met the inspection requirements under 49 C.F.R. Section 571.304; and

(ii) the manufacturer's recommended service life for the container, as stated on the container label required by 49 C.F.R. Section 571.304, has not expired; or

(B) that the vehicle is a fleet vehicle for which the fleet operator employs a technician certified to inspect the container.

(e) The department shall adopt rules relating to inspection of and issuance of a vehicle inspection report for a moped.

Sec. 548.105. Evidence of Financial Responsibility As Prerequisite to Issuance of Passing Vehicle Inspection Report.

(a) An inspection station or inspector may not issue a passing vehicle inspection report for a vehicle unless the owner or operator furnishes evidence of financial responsibility at the time of inspection. Evidence of financial responsibility may be shown in the manner specified under Section 601.053(a). A personal automobile insurance policy used as evidence of financial responsibility must be written for a term of 30 days or more as required by Section 1952.054, Insurance Code.

(b) An inspection station is not liable to a person, including a third party, for issuing a passing vehicle inspection report in reliance on evidence of financial responsibility furnished to the station. An inspection station that is the seller of a motor vehicle may rely on an oral insurance binder.

SUBCHAPTER D INSPECTION OF COMMERCIAL MOTOR VEHICLES

Sec. 548.201. Commercial Motor Vehicle Inspection Program.

(a) The commission shall establish an inspection program for commercial motor vehicles that:

(1) meets the requirements of federal motor carrier safety regulations; and

(2) requires a commercial motor vehicle registered in this state to pass an annual inspection of all safety equipment required by the federal motor carrier safety regulations.

(b) A program under this section also applies to any:

(1) vehicle or combination of vehicles with a gross weight rating of more than 10,000 pounds that is

Transportation Code

operated in interstate commerce and registered in this state;

(2) school activity bus, as defined in Section 541.201, that has a gross weight, registered weight, or gross weight rating of more than 26,000 pounds, or is designed to transport more than 15 passengers, including the driver; and

(3) school bus that will operate at a speed authorized by Section 545.352(b)(5)(A).

Sec. 548.202. General Applicability of Chapter to Commercial Motor Vehicles.

This chapter applies to a commercial motor vehicle inspection program established under Section 548.201 except as otherwise provided.

Sec. 548.203. Exemptions.

(a) The commission by rule may exempt a type of commercial motor vehicle from the application of this subchapter if the vehicle:

(1) was manufactured before September 1, 1995;

(2) is operated only temporarily on a highway of this state and at a speed of less than 30 miles per hour; and

(3) complies with Section 548.051 and each applicable provision in Title 49, Code of Federal Regulations.

(b) Notwithstanding Subchapter B, a commercial motor vehicle is not subject to the inspection requirements of this chapter if the vehicle:

(1) is not domiciled in this state;

(2) is registered in this state or under the International Registration Plan as authorized by Section 502.091; and

(3) has been issued a certificate of inspection in compliance with federal motor carrier safety regulations.

(c) A commercial motor vehicle described by Subsection (b) is subject to any fees established by this code that would apply to the vehicle if the vehicle were subject to the inspection requirements of this chapter, including a fee under Section 548.504 or 548.5055.

SUBCHAPTER E ISSUANCE OF VEHICLE INSPECTION REPORTS; SUBMISSION OF INFORMATION TO DEPARTMENT DATABASE

Sec. 548.251. Department to Maintain Database.

The department shall maintain an electronic database to which inspection stations may electronically submit the information required by Section 548.253.

Sec. 548.252. Issuance of Vehicle Inspection Reports.

(a) The department by rule shall require an inspection station to:

(1) issue a vehicle inspection report to the owner or operator of each vehicle inspected by the station; and

(2) issue a passing vehicle inspection report to the owner or operator of each vehicle inspected by the station that passes the inspections required by this chapter.

(b) The department may adopt rules regarding the issuance of vehicle inspection reports, including rules providing for the format and safekeeping of the reports.

(c) The department may adopt rules providing for the inclusion on a vehicle inspection report for a vehicle inspected under this chapter notification regarding whether the vehicle is subject to a safety recall for which the vehicle has not been repaired or the repairs are incomplete. The department may accept gifts, grants, and donations from any source, including private and nonprofit organizations, for the purpose of providing the notification described by this subsection.

Sec. 548.253. Information to Be Submitted on Completion of Inspection.

An inspection station or inspector, on completion of an inspection, shall electronically submit to the department's inspection database:

(1) the vehicle identification number of the inspected vehicle and an indication of whether the vehicle passed the inspections required by this chapter; and

(2) any additional information required by rule by the department for the type of vehicle inspected.

Sec. 548.254. Validity of Vehicle Inspection Report.

A vehicle inspection report is invalid after the end of the 12th month following the month in which the report is issued.

Sec. 548.255. Attachment or Production of Inspection Certificate. [Repealed]

Sec. 548.256. Proof of Compliance with Inspection Requirements Required to Register Vehicle.

(a) Except as provided by Subsection (b) or (c), before a vehicle may be registered, the Texas Department of Motor Vehicles or the county assessor-collector registering the vehicle shall verify that the vehicle complies with the applicable inspection requirements under this chapter and Chapter 382, Health and Safety Code, as indicated in the department's inspection database. If the database information is not available, the owner of the vehicle may present a vehicle inspection report issued for the vehicle.

(b) The Texas Department of Motor Vehicles or a county assessor-collector may register a vehicle that is not in compliance with the applicable inspection requirements under this chapter or Chapter 382, Health and Safety Code, if the vehicle is located in another state at the time the applicant applies for registration or registration renewal under Chapter 502 and the applicant certifies that the vehicle is located in another state and the applicant will comply with the applicable inspection requirements under this chapter, Chapter 382, Health and Safety Code, and the department's administrative rules regarding inspection requirements once the vehicle is operated in this state. The Texas Department of Motor Vehicles or the county assessor-collector shall add a notation to the Texas Department of Motor Vehicles' registration database for law enforcement to verify the inspection status of the vehicle.

(c) Subsection (a) does not apply to:

(1) a vehicle that is being registered under the International Registration Plan as authorized by Section 502.091; or

(2) a token trailer that is being registered under Section 502.255, including a token trailer that is being registered for an extended period under Section 502.0023.

Sec. 548.257. Lost, Stolen, or Destroyed Certificate. [Repealed]

Sec. 548.258. Use of State Electronic Internet Portal.

(a) In this section, "state electronic Internet portal" has the meaning assigned by Section 2054.003, Government Code.

(b) The department may adopt rules to require an inspection station to use the state electronic Internet portal to send to the department a record, report, or other information required by the department.

SUBCHAPTER F MOTOR VEHICLE EMISSIONS INSPECTION AND MAINTENANCE

Sec. 548.301. Commission to Establish Program.

(a) The commission shall establish a motor vehicle emissions inspection and maintenance program for vehicles as required by any law of the United States or the state's air quality state implementation plan.

(b) The commission by rule may establish a motor vehicle emissions inspection and maintenance program for vehicles specified by the conservation commission in a county for which the conservation commission has adopted a resolution requesting the commission to establish such a program and for which the county and the municipality with the largest population in the county by resolution have formally requested a proactive air quality plan consisting of such a program.

(b-1) The commission by rule may establish a motor vehicle emissions inspection and maintenance program for vehicles subject to an early action compact as defined by Section 382.301, Health and Safety Code, that is consistent with the early action compact.

(c) A program established under this section must include registration and reregistration-based enforcement.

(d) A vehicle emissions inspection under this section may be performed by the same facility that performs a safety inspection if the facility is authorized and certified by the department to perform the vehicle emissions inspection and certified by the department to perform the safety inspection.

Sec. 548.3011. Emissions Test on Resale.

(a) This section applies only to a vehicle:

(1) the most recent certificate of title for which or registration of which was issued in a county without a motor vehicle emissions inspection and maintenance program; and

Transportation Code

(2) the ownership of which has changed and which has been the subject of a retail sale as defined by Section 2301.002, Occupations Code.

(b) Notwithstanding Subsection (a), this section does not apply to a vehicle that is a 1996 or newer model that has less than 50,000 miles.

(c) A vehicle subject to this section is not eligible for a title receipt under Section 501.024, a certificate of title under Section 501.027, or registration under Chapter 502 in a county with a motor vehicle emissions inspection and maintenance program unless proof is presented with the application for certificate of title or registration, as appropriate, that the vehicle, not earlier than the 90th day before the date on which the new owner's application for certificate of title or registration is filed with the county clerk or county assessor-collector, as appropriate, has passed an approved vehicle emissions test in the county in which it is to be titled or registered.

(d) The proof required by Subsection (c) may be in the form of a Vehicle Inspection Report (VIR) or other proof of program compliance as authorized by the department.

Transportation Code

Sec. 548.3012. Exemption: Vehicle Not Used Primarily in County of Registration.

(a) This section applies only to a vehicle that:

(1) is to be registered in a county with a motor vehicle emissions inspection and maintenance program; and

(2) will be used in that county for fewer than 60 days during the registration period for which registration is sought.

(b) The owner of a vehicle described by Subsection (a) may obtain for that vehicle an exemption from the vehicle emissions test requirements of this subchapter by submitting to the county assessor-collector an affidavit stating that the named vehicle will be used in the county of registration for fewer than 60 calendar days during the registration period for which registration is sought.

Sec. 548.302. Commission to Adopt Standards and Requirements.

The commission shall:

(1) adopt standards for emissions-related inspection criteria consistent with requirements of the United States and the conservation commission applicable to a county in which a program is established under this subchapter; and

(2) develop and impose requirements necessary to ensure that a passing vehicle inspection report is not issued to a vehicle subject to a program established under this subchapter and that information stating that a vehicle has passed an inspection is not submitted to the department's database unless the vehicle has passed a motor vehicle emissions inspection at a facility authorized and certified by the department.

Sec. 548.303. Program Administration.

The commission shall administer the motor vehicle emissions inspection and maintenance program under this subchapter.

Sec. 548.304. Stations Licensed to Conduct Emissions Inspections.

The department may authorize and certify inspection stations as necessary to implement the emissions-related inspection requirements of the motor vehicle emissions inspection and maintenance program established under this subchapter if the station meets the department's certification requirements.

Sec. 548.3045. Appointment of Decentralized Facility.

(a) The department may issue an inspection station certificate to a decentralized facility authorized and licensed by the department under Section 548.304 if the facility meets the certification requirements of that section and the department.

(b) A decentralized facility issued a certificate under Subsection (a) is authorized to perform an inspection under this subchapter or Subchapter B.

Sec. 548.305. Dealer Authority Regarding Emissions-Related Inspections [Repealed].

Repealed by Acts 1997, 75th Leg., ch. 1069 (S.B. 1856), § 19(2), effective June 19, 1997.

Sec. 548.306. Excessive Motor Vehicle Emissions.

(a) This section applies to a motor vehicle registered or operated for more than 60 days per calendar year in:

(1) a county or a portion of a county designated by department rule in accordance with Section 548.301; or

(2) a county adjacent to a county described in Subdivision (1).

(b) The registered owner of a motor vehicle commits an offense if the vehicle, in an area described by Subsection (a), emits:

(1) hydrocarbons, carbon monoxide, or nitrogen oxide in an amount that is excessive under United States Environmental Protection Agency standards or standards provided by department rule; or

(2) another vehicle-related pollutant that is listed by a department rule adopted to comply with Part A, National Emission Standards Act (42 U.S.C. Sections 7602-7619), or rules of the United States Environmental Protection Agency in an amount identified as excessive under that rule.

(c) The department shall provide a notice of violation to the registered owner of a vehicle that is detected violating Subsection (b). The notice of violation must be made by personal delivery to the registered owner or by mailing the notice to the registered owner at the last known address of the owner. The department shall include in the notice the date and location of the violation detected and instructions for the registered owner explaining how the owner must proceed to obtain and pass a verification emissions inspection and to make any repair to the vehicle necessary to pass the inspection and explaining any extension or assistance that may be available to the owner for making any necessary repair. Notice by mail is presumed delivered on the 10th day after the date the notice is deposited in the mail.

(d) A registered owner of a vehicle commits an offense if:

(1) notice is delivered to the owner under Subsection (c); and

(2) the owner fails to comply with any provision of the notice before the 31st day after the date the notice is delivered.

(e) An offense under this section is a misdemeanor punishable by a fine of not less than $1 and not more than $350. If a person has previously been convicted of an offense under this section, an offense under this section is a misdemeanor punishable by a fine of not less than $200 and not more than $1,000.

(f) It is an affirmative defense to an offense under this section that the registered owner of the vehicle, before the 31st day after the date the owner receives a notice of violation:

(1) after a verification emissions inspection indicated that the vehicle did not comply with applicable emissions standards, repaired the vehicle as necessary and passed another verification emissions inspection; and

(2) has complied with rules of the department concerning a violation under this section.

(g) The department may contract with a private person to implement this section. The person must comply with terms, policies, rules, and procedures the department adopts to administer this section.

(h) The Texas Department of Transportation may deny reregistration of a vehicle if the registered owner of the vehicle has received notification under Subsection (c) and the vehicle has not passed a verification emissions inspection.

(i) A hearing for a citation issued under this section shall be heard by a justice of the peace of any precinct in the county in which the vehicle is registered.

(j) Enforcement of the remote sensing component of the vehicle emissions inspection and maintenance program may not involve any method of screening in which the registered owner of a vehicle found to have allowable emissions by remote sensing technology is charged a fee.

(k) The department by rule may require that a vehicle determined by on-road testing to have excessive emissions be assessed an on-road emissions testing fee not to exceed the emissions testing fee charged by a certified emissions testing facility.

(*l*) The department by rule may establish procedures for reimbursing a fee for a verification test required by Subsection (c) if the owner demonstrates to the department's satisfaction that:

(1) the vehicle passed the verification emissions test not later than the 30th day after the date the vehicle owner received notice that the vehicle was detected as having excessive emissions; and

(2) the vehicle did not receive any repair, modification, alteration, or additive to the fuel, fuel tank, fuel delivery system, engine, exhaust system, or any attached emissions control components that would have, or could have, caused the vehicle to experience improved emissions performance between the date of detection and the date of the verification emissions test.

Sec. 548.3065. Administrative Penalty.

(a) In lieu of criminal proceedings for a violation of Section 548.306, the department may impose an administrative penalty against a person who knowingly violates this chapter or a rule adopted by the commission under this chapter.

(b) The amount of the administrative penalty may not exceed $1,000 for each violation. The aggregate penalty for multiple violations may not exceed $10,000. Each day a violation continues or occurs is a separate violation for purposes of imposing a penalty.

(c) For purposes of Subsection (a), the procedures for determining and administering an administrative penalty against a person charged with violating this chapter are the same as those prescribed by Section 643.251 for determining and administering an administrative penalty against a motor carrier under that section.

(c-1) The conservation commission may impose an administrative penalty on a person in the amount of not more than $500 for each violation of this subchapter or a rule adopted by the conservation commission under this subchapter.

(d) An administrative penalty collected under this section shall be deposited in a special account in the general revenue fund and may be used only by the department.

Sec. 548.307. Alternative Testing Methodology for Certain Counties.

The commission by rule may establish procedures for testing and enforcing vehicle emissions standards by use of alternative testing methodology that meets or exceeds United States Environmental Protection Agency requirements in a county participating in an early action compact under Subchapter H, Chapter 382, Health and Safety Code.

Sec. 548.3075. Limited Emissions Inspections.

(a) In this section, "limited emissions inspection" means an emissions inspection of a motor vehicle conducted only by using the onboard diagnostic system of the vehicle.

(b) A department rule that allows an inspection station to perform a limited emissions inspection of a motor vehicle may not restrict the number of limited emissions inspections conducted by the station.

SUBCHAPTER G CERTIFICATION OF INSPECTION STATION OR INSPECTOR

Sec. 548.401. Certification Generally.

A person may perform an inspection, issue a vehicle inspection report, or submit inspection information to the department's inspection database only if certified to do so by the department under rules adopted by the department.

Sec. 548.402. Application for Certification As Inspection Station.

(a) To operate as an inspection station, a person must apply to the department for certification. The application must:

(1) be filed with the department on a form prescribed and provided by the department; and

(2) state:

(A) the name of the applicant;

(B) if the applicant is an association, the names and addresses of the persons constituting the association;

(C) if the applicant is a corporation, the names and addresses of its principal officers;

(D) the name under which the applicant transacts or intends to transact business;

(E) the location of the applicant's place of business in the state; and

(F) other information required by the department, including information required by the department for identification.

(b) The application must be signed and sworn or affirmed by:

(1) if the applicant is an individual, the owner; or

(2) if the applicant is a corporation, an executive officer or person specifically authorized by the corporation to sign the application, to which shall be attached written evidence of the person's authority.

(c) An applicant who has or intends to have more than one place of business in this state must file a separate application for each place of business.

Sec. 548.403. Approval and Certification As Inspection Station.

(a) The department may approve an application for certification as an inspection station only if:

(1) the location complies with department requirements; and

(2) the applicant complies with department rules.

(b) On approval of an application, the department shall issue to the applicant an inspection station certificate. The certificate is valid for each person in whose name the certificate is issued and for the transaction of business at the location designated in the certificate. A certificate is not assignable.

(c) An inspection station certificate shall be conspicuously displayed at the station for which the certificate was issued.

Sec. 548.4035. Entry onto Premises.

(a) A member, employee, or agent of the department may enter an inspection station during normal business hours to conduct an investigation, inspection, or audit of the inspection station or an inspector to determine whether the inspection station or inspector is in compliance with:

(1) this chapter;

(2) department rules under this chapter; or

(3) Chapter 382, Health and Safety Code.

(b) A member, employee, or agent of the department who enters an inspection station for a purpose described by Subsection (a):

(1) shall notify the manager or person in charge of the inspection station of the presence of the member, employee, or agent;

(2) shall present the manager or person in charge of the inspection station with proper credentials identifying the member, employee, or agent as a member, employee, or agent of the department; and

(3) is entitled to have access to emissions testing equipment, inspection records, and any required inspection station certificate or inspector certificate.

(c) A member, employee, or agent of the department who enters an inspection station to conduct an investigation, inspection, or audit under Subsection (a) must observe the inspection station's rules relating to safety, security, and fire protection.

(d) Subsection (b) does not prohibit the department from conducting an undercover investigation or a covert audit of an inspection station.

Sec. 548.404. Application for Certification As Inspector.

An application for certification as an inspector shall:

(1) be made on a form prescribed and provided by the department; and

(2) state:

(A) the name of the applicant;

(B) the address of the applicant's residence and place of employment;

(C) the applicant's driver's license number; and

(D) other information required by the department.

Sec. 548.4045. Bond Required for Certain Inspection Stations.

(a) This section applies only to an inspection station that:

(1) is located in a county in which the conservation commission has established a motor vehicle emissions inspection and maintenance program under Subchapter F; and

(2) has been convicted of a violation of this chapter relating to an emissions inspection.

(b) An application for certification as an inspection station must be accompanied by a surety bond in the amount of $5,000, payable to this state and conditioned on the future compliance with this chapter and rules adopted by the department or the conservation commission under this chapter.

(c) The attorney general or the district or county attorney for the county in which the inspection station is located or in which the inspection station that employs the inspector is located may bring suit in the name of this state to recover on the bond.

Sec. 548.405. Denial, Revocation, or Suspension of Certificate.

(a) The commission may deny a person's application for a certificate, revoke or suspend the certificate of a person, inspection station, or inspector, place on probation a person who holds a suspended certificate, or reprimand a person who holds a certificate if:

(1) the station or inspector conducts an inspection, fails to conduct an inspection, or issues a certificate:

(A) in violation of this chapter or a rule adopted under this chapter; or

(B) without complying with the requirements of this chapter or a rule adopted under this chapter;

(2) the person, station, or inspector commits an offense under this chapter or violates this chapter or a rule adopted under this chapter;

(3) the applicant or certificate holder does not meet the standards for certification under this chapter or a rule adopted under this chapter;

(4) the station or inspector does not maintain the qualifications for certification or does not comply with a certification requirement under this subchapter;

(5) the certificate holder or the certificate holder's agent, employee, or representative commits an act or omission that would cause denial, revocation, or suspension of a certificate to an individual applicant or certificate holder; or

(6) the station or inspector does not pay a fee required by Subchapter H.

(b) [Repealed.]

(c) If the commission suspends a certificate because of a violation of Subchapter F, the suspension must be for a period of not less than six months.

(d) Until an inspector or inspection station whose certificate is suspended or revoked receives a new certificate, has the certificate reinstated, or has the suspension expire, the inspector or station may not be directly or indirectly involved in an inspection operation.

(e) An immediate family member of an inspector or owner of an inspection station whose certificate is suspended or revoked may not be granted a certificate under this subchapter if the location of the family member's place of business is the same as that of the inspector or owner whose certificate is suspended or revoked unless the family member proves that the inspector or owner whose certificate is suspended or revoked has no involvement with the family member's place of business.

(f) Subsection (a) applies to:

(1) each member of a partnership or association issued a certificate under this subchapter;

(2) each director or officer of a corporation issued a certificate under this subchapter; and

(3) a shareholder who receives compensation from the day-to-day operation of the corporation in the form of a salary.

(g) The commission may not suspend, revoke, or deny all certificates of a person who holds more than one inspection station certificate based on a suspension, revocation, or denial of one of that person's inspection station certificates without proof of culpability related to a prior action under this subsection.

(h) [Repealed.]

(i) [Repealed.]

Sec. 548.4055. Rules Regarding Criminal Convictions.

The commission shall adopt rules necessary to comply with Chapter 53, Occupations Code, with respect to the certification of persons under this subchapter. The commission's rules must list the specific offenses for each category of persons regulated under this subchapter for which a conviction would constitute grounds for the commission to take action under Section 53.021, Occupations Code.

Sec. 548.406. Certificate Holder on Probation May Be Required to Report. [Repealed]

Sec. 548.407. Hearing on Denial, Revocation, or Suspension of Certificate.

(a) Before an application for certification as an inspection station or inspector is denied, the director or a person the director designates shall give the person written notification of:

(1) the proposed denial;

(2) each reason for the proposed denial; and

(3) the person's right to an administrative hearing to determine whether the evidence warrants the denial.

(b) Before a certificate of appointment as an inspector or inspection station is revoked or suspended, the director or a person the director designates shall give written notification to the inspector or inspection station of the revocation or the period of suspension. The notice shall include:

(1) the effective date of the revocation or the period of the suspension, as applicable;

(2) each reason for the revocation or suspension; and

(3) a statement explaining the person's right to an administrative hearing to determine whether the evidence warrants the revocation or suspension.

(c) Notice under Subsection (a) or (b) must be made by personal delivery or by mail to the last address given to the department by the person.

(d) The commission may provide that a revocation or suspension takes effect on receipt of notice under Subsection (b) if the commission finds that the action is necessary to prevent or remedy a threat to public health, safety, or welfare. Violations that present a threat to public health, safety, or welfare include:

(1) issuing a passing vehicle inspection report or submitting inspection information to the department's database with knowledge that the issuance or submission is in violation of this chapter or rules adopted under this chapter;

(2) falsely or fraudulently representing to the owner or operator of a vehicle that equipment inspected or required to be inspected must be repaired, adjusted, or replaced for the vehicle to pass an inspection;

(3) issuing a vehicle inspection report or submitting inspection information to the department's database:

(A) without authorization to issue the report or submit the information; or

(B) without inspecting the vehicle;

(4) issuing a passing vehicle inspection report or submitting inspection information to the department's database for a vehicle with knowledge that the vehicle has not been repaired, adjusted, or corrected after an inspection has shown a repair, adjustment, or correction to be necessary;

(5) knowingly issuing a passing vehicle inspection report or submitting inspection information to the department's database:

(A) for a vehicle without conducting an inspection of each item required to be inspected; or

(B) for a vehicle that is missing an item required to be inspected or that has an item required to be inspected that is not in compliance with state law or department rules;

(6) refusing to allow a vehicle's owner to have a qualified person of the owner's choice make a required repair, adjustment, or correction;

(7) charging for an inspection an amount greater than the authorized fee;

(8) a violation of Subchapter F;

(9) a violation of Section 548.603; or

(10) a conviction of a felony or a Class A or B misdemeanor that directly relates to or affects

the duties or responsibilities of a vehicle inspection station or inspector or a conviction of a similar crime under the jurisdiction of another state or the federal government.

(e) The commission may adopt rules to implement this section.

(f) [Repealed.]

(g) [Repealed.]

(h) [Repealed.]

(i) [Repealed.]

(j) [Repealed.]

(k) [Repealed.]

(*l*) [Repealed.]

Sec. 548.408. Judicial Review of Administrative Action.

(a) A person dissatisfied with the final decision of the director may appeal the decision by filing a petition as provided by Subchapter G, Chapter 2001, Government Code.

(b) The district or county attorney or the attorney general shall represent the director in the appeal, except that an attorney who is a full-time employee of the department may represent the director in the appeal with the approval of the attorney general.

(c) The court in which the appeal is filed shall:

(1) set the matter for hearing after 10 days' written notice to the director and the attorney representing the director; and

(2) determine whether an enforcement action of the director shall be suspended pending hearing and enter an order for the suspension.

(d) The court order takes effect when served on the director.

(e) The director shall provide a copy of the petition and court order to the attorney representing the director.

(f) A stay under this section may not be effective for more than 90 days after the date the petition for appeal is filed. On the expiration of the stay, the director's enforcement action shall be reinstated or imposed. The department or court may not extend the stay or grant an additional stay.

(g) Judicial review of the final decision of the director is under the substantial evidence rule.

Sec. 548.409. Complaints. [Repealed]

Sec. 548.410. Expiration of Certificate.

A certificate issued to an inspector or an inspection station under this subchapter expires as determined by the department under Section 411.511, Government Code, but not later than the second anniversary of the date the certificate is issued.

SUBCHAPTER H INSPECTION AND CERTIFICATION FEES

Sec. 548.501. Inspection Fees Generally.

(a) Except as provided by Sections 548.503 and 548.504, the fee for inspection of a motor vehicle other than a moped is $12.50. The fee for inspection of a moped is $5.75.

(b) Out of each fee for an inspection, $5.50 shall be remitted to the state under Section 548.509.

Sec. 548.502. Inspection by Political Subdivision or State Agency.

A political subdivision or state agency for which the department certifies an inspection station under Section 548.004:

(1) shall pay to the state $5.50 for each inspection under Section 548.509; and

(2) may not be required to pay the remainder of the inspection fee.

Sec. 548.503. Initial Two-Year Inspection of Passenger Car or Light Truck.

(a) The fee for inspection of a passenger car or light truck under Section 548.102 shall be set by the department by rule on or before September 1 of each year. A fee set by the department under this subsection must be based on the costs of providing inspections and administering the program, but may not be less than $21.75.

(b) Out of each fee for an inspection under this section, $14.75 shall be remitted to the state under Section 548.509.

Sec. 548.504. Inspection of Commercial Motor Vehicle.

(a) The fee for inspection of a commercial motor vehicle under the program established under Section 548.201 is $50.

(b) Out of each fee for inspection of a commercial motor vehicle, $10 shall be remitted to the state under Section 548.509.

Sec. 548.505. Emissions-Related Inspection Fee.

(a) The department by rule may impose an inspection fee for a vehicle inspected under Section 548.301(a)

Transportation Code

in addition to the fee provided by Section 548.501, 548.502, 548.503, or 548.504. A fee imposed under this subsection must be based on the costs of:

(1) providing inspections; and

(2) administering the program.

(b) The department may provide a maximum fee for an inspection under this subchapter. The department may not set a minimum fee for an inspection under this subchapter.

Sec. 548.5055. Texas Emissions [Contingent Expiration – See editor's note] Reduction Plan Fee.

(a) In addition to other fees required by this subchapter, to fund the Texas emissions reduction plan established under Chapter 386, Health and Safety Code, the department shall collect for every commercial motor vehicle required to be inspected under Subchapter D, a fee of $10.

(b) The department shall remit fees collected under this section to the comptroller at the time and in the manner prescribed by the comptroller for deposit in the Texas emissions reduction plan fund.

(c) This section expires on the last day of the state fiscal biennium during which the conservation commission publishes in the Texas Register the notice required by Section 382.037, Health and Safety Code.

Sec. 548.506. Fee for Certification As Inspector.

(a) The commission by rule shall establish reasonable and necessary fees for certification as an inspector.

(b) The fees established under this section may not be less than an amount equal to:

(1) $25 for initial certification until August 31 of the even-numbered year following the date of certification; and

(2) $25 as a certificate fee for each subsequent two-year period.

Sec. 548.507. Fee for Certification As Inspection Station.

(a) The commission by rule shall establish reasonable and necessary fees for certification as an inspection station.

(b) The fees established under this section may not be less than:

(1) except as provided by Subdivision (2) or (3):

(A) $100 for certification until August 31 of the odd-numbered year after the date of appointment as an inspection station; and

(B) $100 for certification for each subsequent two-year period;

(2) if an applicant for certification as an inspection station has been convicted of a violation of this chapter relating to an emissions inspection under Subchapter F:

(A) $500 for certification until August 31 of the odd-numbered year after the date of appointment as an inspection station; and

(B) $100 for certification for each subsequent two-year period; and

(3) if an applicant for certification as an inspection station has been convicted of two or more violations of this chapter relating to an emissions inspection under Subchapter F:

(A) $1,500 for certification until August 31 of the odd-numbered year after the date of appointment as an inspection station; and

(B) $100 for certification for each subsequent two-year period.

Sec. 548.508. Disposition of Fees.

Except as provided by Sections 382.0622 and 382.202, Health and Safety Code, and Section 548.5055, each fee remitted to the comptroller under this subchapter shall be deposited to the credit of the Texas mobility fund.

Sec. 548.509. Collection of Fee During Registration.

The Texas Department of Motor Vehicles or a county assessor-collector that registers a motor vehicle that is subject to an inspection fee under this chapter shall collect at the time of registration of the motor vehicle the portion of the inspection fee that is required to be remitted to the state. The Texas Department of Motor Vehicles or the county assessor-collector shall remit the fee to the comptroller.

Sec. 548.510. Fee for Certain Vehicles Not Subject to Inspection; Collection of Fee During Registration.

(a) A vehicle described by Section 548.052(3) that has an actual gross weight or registered gross weight of more than 4,500 pounds is subject to a fee in the amount of $7.50.

(b) The Texas Department of Motor Vehicles or a county assessor-collector that registers a vehicle described by Subsection (a) shall collect at the time of registration of the vehicle the fee prescribed by Subsection (a). The Texas Department of Motor Vehicles or the county assessor-collector, as applicable, shall remit the fee to the comptroller. Each fee remitted to the comptroller under this section shall be deposited as follows:

(1) $3.50 to the credit of the Texas mobility fund;

(2) $2 to the credit of the general revenue fund; and

(3) $2 to the credit of the clean air account.

(c) The fee collected under Subsection (a) is not a motor vehicle registration fee and the revenue collected from the fee is not required to be used for a purpose specified by Section 7-a, Article VIII, Texas Constitution.

SUBCHAPTER I VIOLATIONS AND OFFENSES

Sec. 548.601. Offense Generally.

(a) A person, including an inspector or an inspection station, commits an offense if the person:

(1) submits information to the department's inspection database or issues a vehicle inspection report with knowledge that the submission or issuance is in violation of this chapter or rules adopted under this chapter;

(2) falsely or fraudulently represents to the owner or operator of a vehicle that equipment inspected or required to be inspected must be repaired, adjusted, or replaced for the vehicle to pass an inspection;

(3) misrepresents:

(A) material information in an application in violation of Section 548.402 or 548.403; or

(B) information filed with the department under this chapter or as required by department rule;

(4) submits information to the department's inspection database or issues a vehicle inspection report:

(A) without authorization to issue the report or submit the information; or

(B) without inspecting the vehicle;

(5) submits information to the department's inspection database indicating that a vehicle has passed the applicable inspections or issues a passing vehicle inspection report for a vehicle with knowledge that the vehicle has not been repaired, adjusted, or corrected after an inspection has shown a repair, adjustment, or correction to be necessary;

(6) knowingly submits information to the department's inspection database or issues a vehicle inspection report:

(A) for a vehicle without conducting an inspection of each item required to be inspected; or

(B) for a vehicle that is missing an item required to be inspected or that has an item required to be inspected that is not in compliance with state law or department rules;

(7) refuses to allow a vehicle's owner to have a qualified person of the owner's choice make a required repair, adjustment, or correction;

(8) charges for an inspection an amount greater than the authorized fee;

(9) discloses or sells information collected in relation to the vehicle inspection program under this chapter about a unique customer or a unique vehicle owner to a person other than the department or the person who is the subject of the information, including a customer or vehicle owner's name, address, or phone number; or

(10) performs an act prohibited by or fails to perform an act required by this chapter or a rule adopted under this chapter.

(b) Unless otherwise specified in this chapter, an offense under this section is a Class C misdemeanor.

(c) A designated representative of the department may issue a notice of an offense or a notice to appear to a person, including an inspector or inspection station, who violates this chapter or a rule adopted under this chapter.

Sec. 548.6015. Civil Penalties.

(a) An inspection station that violates a provision of this chapter relating to an emissions inspection under Subchapter F is liable for a civil penalty of not less than $250 or more than $500 for each violation. The district or county attorney for the county in which the inspection station is located or the attorney general may bring suit in the name of this state to collect the penalty.

(b) An inspector who violates a provision of this chapter relating to an emissions inspection under Subchapter F is liable for a civil penalty of not less than $50 or more than $150 for each violation. The district or county attorney for the county in which the inspection station that employs the inspector is located or the attorney general may bring suit in the name of this state to collect the penalty.

(c) A penalty imposed under this section is in lieu of a civil or administrative penalty imposed under another provision of this chapter for the same violation.

Sec. 548.602. Failure to Display Inspection Certificate. [Repealed]

Sec. 548.603. Fictitious or Counterfeit Inspection Certificate or Insurance Document.

(a) A person commits an offense if the person:

Transportation Code

(1) presents to an official of this state or a political subdivision of this state a vehicle inspection report or insurance document knowing that the report or document is counterfeit, tampered with, altered, fictitious, issued for another vehicle, issued for a vehicle failing to meet all emissions inspection requirements, or issued in violation of:

(A) this chapter, rules adopted under this chapter, or other law of this state; or

(B) a law of another state, the United States, the United Mexican States, a state of the United Mexican States, Canada, or a province of Canada;

(2) with intent to circumvent the emissions inspection requirements seeks an inspection of a vehicle at a station not certified to perform an emissions inspection if the person knows that the vehicle is required to be inspected under Section 548.301; or

(3) knowingly does not comply with an emissions inspection requirement for a vehicle.

(b) A person commits an offense if the person:

(1) makes or possesses, with the intent to sell, circulate, or pass, a counterfeit vehicle inspection report or insurance document; or

(2) possesses any part of a stamp, dye, plate, negative, machine, or other device that is used or designated for use in making a counterfeit vehicle inspection report or insurance document.

(c) The owner of a vehicle commits an offense if the owner knowingly allows the vehicle to be registered using a vehicle inspection report in violation of Subsection (a).

(d) An offense under Subsection (a) or (c) is a Class B misdemeanor. An offense under Subsection (b) is a third degree felony unless the person acts with the intent to defraud or harm another person, in which event the offense is a second degree felony.

(e) In this section:

(1) "Counterfeit" means an imitation of a document that is printed, engraved, copied, photographed, forged, or manufactured by a person not authorized to take that action under:

(A) this chapter, rules adopted under this chapter, or other law of this state; or

(B) a law of another state, the United States, the United Mexican States, a state of the United Mexican States, Canada, or a province of Canada.

(2) [Repealed by Acts 2013, 83rd Leg., ch. 1291 (H.B. 2305), §§ 44, 45, 50(5), (6), effective March 1, 2015.]

(3) "Insurance document" means a standard proof of motor vehicle insurance coverage that is:

(A) in a form prescribed by the Texas Department of Insurance or by a similarly authorized board, agency, or authority of another state; and

(B) issued by an insurer or insurer's agent who is authorized to write motor vehicle insurance coverage.

(4) "Person" includes an inspection station or inspector.

(f) Notwithstanding Subsection (c), an offense under Subsection (a)(1) that involves a fictitious vehicle inspection report is a Class B misdemeanor.

Sec. 548.6035. Fraudulent Emissions Inspection of Motor Vehicle.

(a) A person commits an offense if, in connection with a required emissions inspection of a motor vehicle, the person knowingly:

(1) submits information to the department's inspection database stating that a vehicle has passed the applicable inspections or issues a passing vehicle inspection report, if:

(A) the vehicle does not meet the emissions requirements established by the department; or

(B) the person has not inspected the vehicle;

(2) manipulates an emissions test result;

(3) uses or causes to be used emissions data from another motor vehicle as a substitute for the motor vehicle being inspected; or

(4) bypasses or circumvents a fuel cap test.

(b) A first offense under Subsections (a)(1)—(3) is a Class B misdemeanor.

(c) Except as provided by Subsection (d), a second or subsequent offense under Subsections (a)(1)—(3) is a Class A misdemeanor.

(d) If it is found on trial of an offense under Subsections (a)(1)—(3) that the person committing the offense acted with the intent to defraud or harm another person, the offense is a state jail felony.

(e) An offense under Subsection (a)(4) is a Class C misdemeanor.

(f) It is a defense to prosecution under Subsection (a)(4) that the analyzer used by the person developed a functional problem during the emissions inspection of the fuel cap that prevented the person from properly conducting the fuel cap test portion of the emissions inspection.

Sec. 548.6036. Actions of Employee.

(a) Except as provided by Subsection (b), an inspection station is not subject to an administrative or civil penalty or criminal prosecution under this subchapter for an act of an employee of the inspection station if the inspection station requires the employee to sign a written agreement to abide by the provisions of:

(1) this chapter;

(2) Chapter 382, Health and Safety Code; and

(3) all rules adopted under those chapters.

(b) An inspection station is subject to prosecution under this subchapter for an act of an employee of the inspection station if the inspection station:

(1) has received written notification from the department or another agency that the employee has committed an offense under this chapter; and

(2) continues to allow the employee to perform inspections under this chapter.

Sec. 548.604. Penalty for Certain Violations.

(a) A person commits an offense if the person operates or moves a motor vehicle, trailer, semitrailer, pole trailer, or mobile home, or a combination of those vehicles, that is:

(1) equipped in violation of this chapter or a rule adopted under this chapter; or

(2) in a mechanical condition that endangers a person, including the operator or an occupant, or property.

(b) An offense under this section is a misdemeanor punishable by a fine not to exceed $200.

Sec. 548.605. Operating a Vehicle Without Complying with Inspection Requirements As Certified; Offense; Dismissal of Charge.

(a) In this section, "working day" means any day other than a Saturday, a Sunday, or a holiday on which county offices are closed.

(b) A person commits an offense if:

(1) the person operates in this state a vehicle for which a certification was provided under Section 548.256(b); and

(2) the vehicle is not in compliance with the applicable inspection requirements under this chapter, Chapter 382, Health and Safety Code, or the department's administrative rules regarding inspection requirements.

(c) A peace officer may require the owner or operator to produce a vehicle inspection report issued for the vehicle if the Texas Department of Motor Vehicles' registration database includes a notation for law enforcement to verify the inspection status of the vehicle.

(d) It is a defense to prosecution under Subsection (b) that a passing vehicle inspection report issued for the vehicle is in effect at the time of the offense.

(e) A court shall:

(1) dismiss a charge under this section if the defendant remedies the defect:

(A) not later than the 20th working day after the date of the citation or before the defendant's first court appearance date, whichever is later; and

(B) not later than the 40th working day after the applicable deadline provided by this chapter, Chapter 382, Health and Safety Code, or the department's administrative rules regarding inspection requirements; and

(2) assess a reimbursement fee not to exceed $20 when the charge has been remedied under Subdivision (1).

(f) An offense under this section is a Class C misdemeanor.

CHAPTER 549
MOTOR CARRIER SAFETY STANDARDS [REPEALED]

SUBCHAPTER A GENERAL PROVISIONS

Sec. 549.001. Definitions [Repealed].

Repealed by Acts 1997, 75th Leg., ch. 165 (S.B. 898), § 30.124, effective September 1, 1997.

Sec. 549.002. Conflicts of Law [Repealed].

Repealed by Acts 1997, 75th Leg., ch. 165 (S.B. 898), § 30.124, effective September 1, 1997.

SUBCHAPTER B ADOPTION OF RULES

Sec. 549.101. Authority to Adopt Rules [Repealed].

Repealed by Acts 1997, 75th Leg., ch. 165 (S.B. 898), § 30.124, effective September 1, 1997.

Sec. 549.102. Purpose of Rules; Consistency with Federal Regulations [Repealed].

Repealed by Acts 1997, 75th Leg., ch. 165 (S.B. 898), § 30.124, effective September 1, 1997.

Sec. 549.103. Applicability of Rules [Repealed].

Repealed by Acts 1997, 75th Leg., ch. 165 (S.B. 898), § 30.124, effective September 1, 1997.

Sec. 549.104. Limitations of Rules [Repealed].

Repealed by Acts 1997, 75th Leg., ch. 165 (S.B. 898), § 30.124, effective September 1, 1997.

SUBCHAPTER C OTHER REQUIREMENTS

Sec. 549.201. Insurance [Repealed].

Repealed by Acts 1997, 75th Leg., ch. 165 (S.B. 898), § 30.124, effective September 1, 1997.

Sec. 549.202. Registration [Repealed].

Repealed by Acts 1997, 75th Leg., ch. 165 (S.B. 898), § 30.124, effective September 1, 1997.

SUBCHAPTER D ADMINISTRATIVE ENFORCEMENT

Sec. 549.301. Certification of Municipal Peace Officers [Repealed].

Repealed by Acts 1997, 75th Leg., ch. 165 (S.B. 898), § 30.124, effective September 1, 1997.

Sec. 549.302. Municipal Enforcement Requirements [Repealed].

Repealed by Acts 1997, 75th Leg., ch. 165 (S.B. 898), § 30.124, effective September 1, 1997.

Sec. 549.303. Detention of Vehicles [Repealed].

Repealed by Acts 1997, 75th Leg., ch. 165 (S.B. 898), § 30.124, effective September 1, 1997.

Sec. 549.304. Inspection of Premises [Repealed].

Repealed by Acts 1997, 75th Leg., ch. 165 (S.B. 898), § 30.124, effective September 1, 1997.

SUBCHAPTER E OFFENSES, PENALTIES, AND JUDICIAL ENFORCEMENT

Sec. 549.401. Offenses [Repealed].

Repealed by Acts 1997, 75th Leg., ch. 165 (S.B. 898), § 30.124, effective September 1, 1997.

Sec. 549.402. Civil Penalty [Repealed].

Repealed by Acts 1997, 75th Leg., ch. 165 (S.B. 898), § 30.124, effective September 1, 1997.

Sec. 549.403. Administrative Penalty [Repealed].

Repealed by Acts 1997, 75th Leg., ch. 165 (S.B. 898), § 30.124, effective September 1, 1997.

Sec. 549.404. Suit for Injunction [Repealed].

Repealed by Acts 1997, 75th Leg., ch. 165 (S.B. 898), § 30.124, effective September 1, 1997.

CHAPTER 550 ACCIDENTS AND ACCIDENT REPORTS

SUBCHAPTER A GENERAL PROVISIONS

Sec. 550.001. Applicability of Chapter.

This chapter applies only to:

(1) a road owned and controlled by a water control and improvement district;

(2) a private access way or parking area provided for a client or patron by a business, other than a private residential property, or the property of a garage or parking lot for which a charge is made for storing or parking a motor vehicle; and

(3) a highway or other public place.

SUBCHAPTER B DUTIES FOLLOWING ACCIDENT

Sec. 550.021. Accident Involving Personal Injury or Death.

(a) The operator of a vehicle involved in an accident that results or is reasonably likely to result in injury to or death of a person shall:

(1) immediately stop the vehicle at the scene of the accident or as close to the scene as possible;

(2) immediately return to the scene of the accident if the vehicle is not stopped at the scene of the accident;

(3) immediately determine whether a person is involved in the accident, and if a person is involved

in the accident, whether that person requires aid; and

(4) remain at the scene of the accident until the operator complies with the requirements of Section 550.023.

(b) An operator of a vehicle required to stop the vehicle by Subsection (a) shall do so without obstructing traffic more than is necessary.

(c) A person commits an offense if the person does not stop or does not comply with the requirements of this section. An offense under this section:

(1) involving an accident resulting in:

(A) death of a person is a felony of the second degree; or

(B) serious bodily injury, as defined by Section 1.07, Penal Code, to a person is a felony of the third degree; and

(2) involving an accident resulting in injury to which Subdivision (1) does not apply is punishable by:

(A) imprisonment in the Texas Department of Criminal Justice for not more than five years or confinement in the county jail for not more than one year;

(B) a fine not to exceed $5,000; or

(C) both the fine and the imprisonment or confinement.

Sec. 550.022. Accident Involving Damage to Vehicle.

(a) Except as provided by Subsection (b), the operator of a vehicle involved in an accident resulting only in damage to a vehicle that is driven or attended by a person shall:

(1) immediately stop the vehicle at the scene of the accident or as close as possible to the scene of the accident without obstructing traffic more than is necessary;

(2) immediately return to the scene of the accident if the vehicle is not stopped at the scene of the accident; and

(3) remain at the scene of the accident until the operator complies with the requirements of Section 550.023.

(b) If an accident occurs on a main lane, ramp, shoulder, median, or adjacent area of a freeway in a metropolitan area and each vehicle involved can be normally and safely driven, each operator shall move the operator's vehicle as soon as possible to a designated accident investigation site, if available, a location on the frontage road, the nearest suitable cross street, or other suitable location to complete the requirements of Section 550.023 and minimize interference with freeway traffic.

(c) A person commits an offense if the person does not stop or does not comply with the requirements of Subsection (a). An offense under this subsection is:

(1) a Class C misdemeanor, if the damage to all vehicles is less than $200; or

(2) a Class B misdemeanor, if the damage to all vehicles is $200 or more.

(c-1) A person commits an offense if the person does not comply with the requirements of Subsection (b). An offense under this subsection is a Class C misdemeanor.

(d) In this section, a vehicle can be normally and safely driven only if the vehicle:

(1) does not require towing; and

(2) can be operated under its own power and in its usual manner, without additional damage or hazard to the vehicle, other traffic, or the roadway.

Sec. 550.023. Duty to Give Information and Render Aid.

The operator of a vehicle involved in an accident resulting in the injury or death of a person or damage to a vehicle that is driven or attended by a person shall:

(1) give the operator's name and address, the registration number of the vehicle the operator was driving, and the name of the operator's motor vehicle liability insurer to any person injured or the operator or occupant of or person attending a vehicle involved in the collision;

(2) if requested and available, show the operator's driver's license to a person described by Subdivision (1); and

(3) provide any person injured in the accident reasonable assistance, including transporting or making arrangements for transporting the person to a physician or hospital for medical treatment if it is apparent that treatment is necessary, or if the injured person requests the transportation.

Sec. 550.024. Duty on Striking Unattended Vehicle.

(a) The operator of a vehicle that collides with and damages an unattended vehicle shall immediately stop and:

(1) locate the operator or owner of the unattended vehicle and give that person the name and address of the operator and the owner of the vehicle that struck the unattended vehicle; or

(2) leave in a conspicuous place in, or securely attach in a plainly visible way to, the unattended vehicle a written notice giving the name and address of the operator and the owner of the vehicle that

struck the unattended vehicle and a statement of the circumstances of the collision.

(b) A person commits an offense if the person violates Subsection (a). An offense under this section is:

(1) a Class C misdemeanor, if the damage to all vehicles involved is less than $200; or

(2) a Class B misdemeanor, if the damage to all vehicles involved is $200 or more.

Sec. 550.025. Duty on Striking Structure, Fixture, or Highway Landscaping.

(a) The operator of a vehicle involved in an accident resulting only in damage to a structure adjacent to a highway or a fixture or landscaping legally on or adjacent to a highway shall:

(1) take reasonable steps to locate and notify the owner or person in charge of the property of the accident and of the operator's name and address and the registration number of the vehicle the operator was driving; and

(2) if requested and available, show the operator's driver's license to the owner or person in charge of the property.

(b) A person commits an offense if the person violates Subsection (a). An offense under this section is:

(1) a Class C misdemeanor, if the damage to all fixtures and landscaping is less than $200; or

(2) a Class B misdemeanor, if the damage to all fixtures and landscaping is $200 or more.

Sec. 550.026. Immediate Report of Accident.

(a) The operator of a vehicle involved in an accident resulting in injury to or death of a person or damage to a vehicle to the extent that it cannot be normally and safely driven shall immediately by the quickest means of communication give notice of the accident to the:

(1) local police department if the accident occurred in a municipality;

(2) local police department or the sheriff's office if the accident occurred not more than 100 feet outside the limits of a municipality; or

(3) sheriff's office or the nearest office of the department if the accident is not required to be reported under Subdivision (1) or (2).

(b) If a section of road is within 100 feet of the limits of more than one municipality, the municipalities may agree regarding the maintenance of reports made under Subsection (a)(2). A county may agree with municipalities in the county regarding the maintenance of reports made under Subsection (a)(2). An agreement under this subsection does not affect the duty to report an accident under Subsection (a).

SUBCHAPTER C INVESTIGATION OF ACCIDENT

Sec. 550.041. Investigation by Peace Officer.

(a) A peace officer who is notified of a motor vehicle accident resulting in injury to or death of a person or property damage to an apparent extent of at least $1,000 may investigate the accident and file justifiable charges relating to the accident without regard to whether the accident occurred on property to which this chapter applies.

(b) This section does not apply to:

(1) a privately owned residential parking area; or

(2) a privately owned parking lot where a fee is charged for parking or storing a vehicle.

SUBCHAPTER D WRITTEN ACCIDENT REPORT

Sec. 550.0601. Definition.

In this subchapter, "department" means the Texas Department of Transportation.

Sec. 550.061. Operator's Accident Report. [Repealed]

Sec. 550.062. Officer's Accident Report.

(a) A law enforcement officer who in the regular course of duty investigates a motor vehicle accident shall make a written report of the accident if the accident resulted in injury to or the death of a person or damage to the property of any one person to the apparent extent of $1,000 or more.

(b) The report required by Subsection (a) must be filed electronically with the department not later than the 10th day after the date of the accident.

(b-1) If the motor vehicle accident involved a combination of vehicles operating under a permit issued under Section 623.402, the report required by Subsection (a) must include the weight and the number of axles of the vehicle combination.

(c) This section applies without regard to whether the officer investigates the accident at the location of the accident and immediately after the accident or afterwards by interviewing those involved in the accident or witnesses to the accident.

Sec. 550.063. Report on Appropriate Form.

The form of all written accident reports must be approved by the department and the Department of Public Safety. A person who is required to file a written accident report shall report on the appropriate form and shall disclose all information required by the form unless the information is not available.

Sec. 550.064. Accident Report Forms.

(a) The department shall prepare and when requested supply to police departments, coroners, sheriffs, garages, and other suitable agencies or individuals the accident report forms appropriate for the persons required to make a report and appropriate for the purposes to be served by those reports.

(b) An accident report form prepared by the department must:

(1) require sufficiently detailed information to disclose the cause and conditions of and the persons and vehicles involved in an accident if the form is for the report to be made by a person investigating the accident;

(2) include a way to designate and identify a peace officer, firefighter, or emergency medical services employee who is involved in an accident while driving a law enforcement vehicle, fire department vehicle, or emergency medical services vehicle while performing the person's duties;

(3) require a statement by a person described by Subdivision (2) as to the nature of the accident; and

(4) include a way to designate whether an individual involved in an accident wants to be contacted by a person seeking to obtain employment as a professional described by Section 38.01(12), Penal Code.

Sec. 550.065. Release of Certain Information Relating to Accidents.

(a) This section applies only to the following information that is held by the department or another governmental entity:

(1) a written report of an accident required under:

(A) Section 550.062; or

(B) former Section 550.061 or 601.004 before September 1, 2017; or

(2) accident report information compiled under Section 201.806.

(b) Except as provided by Subsection (c), (c-1), or (e), the information is privileged and for the confidential use of:

(1) the department; and

(2) an agency of the United States, this state, or a local government of this state that has use for the information for accident prevention purposes.

(c) On written request and payment of any required fee, the department or the governmental entity shall release the information to:

(1) an entity described by Subsection (b);

(2) the law enforcement agency that employs the peace officer who investigated the accident and sent the information to the department, including an agent of the law enforcement agency authorized by contract to obtain the information;

(3) the court in which a case involving a person involved in the accident is pending if the report is subpoenaed; or

(4) any person directly concerned in the accident or having a proper interest therein, including:

(A) any person involved in the accident;

(B) the authorized representative of any person involved in the accident;

(C) a driver involved in the accident;

(D) an employer, parent, or legal guardian of a driver involved in the accident;

(E) the owner of a vehicle or property damaged in the accident;

(F) a person who has established financial responsibility for a vehicle involved in the accident in a manner described by Section 601.051, including a policyholder of a motor vehicle liability insurance policy covering the vehicle;

(G) an insurance company that issued an insurance policy covering a vehicle involved in the accident;

(H) an insurance company that issued a policy covering any person involved in the accident;

(I) a person under contract to provide claims or underwriting information to a person described by Paragraph (F), (G), or (H);

(J) a radio or television station that holds a license issued by the Federal Communications Commission;

(K) a newspaper that is:

(i) a free newspaper of general circulation or qualified under Section 2051.044, Government Code, to publish legal notices;

(ii) published at least once a week; and

(iii) available and of interest to the general public in connection with the dissemination of news; or

(L) any person who may sue because of death resulting from the accident.

(c-1) On receiving information to which this section applies, the department or the governmental entity that receives the information shall create a redacted accident report that may be requested by any person. The redacted accident report may not

Transportation Code

include the items of information described by Subsection (f)(2). A report released under this subsection is not considered personal information under Section 730.003.

(d) The fee for a copy of the accident report is $6. The copy may be certified by the department or the governmental entity for an additional fee of $2. The department or the governmental entity may issue a certification that no report or information is on file for a fee of $6.

(e) In addition to the information required to be released under Subsection (c), the department may release:

(1) accident report information compiled under Section 201.806; or

(2) a vehicle identification number and specific accident information relating to that vehicle.

(f) The department when releasing information under Subsection (c-1) or (e):

(1) may not release personal information, as defined by Section 730.003; and

(2) shall withhold or redact the following items:

(A) the first, middle, and last name of any person listed in an accident report, including a vehicle driver, occupant, owner, or lessee, a bicyclist, a pedestrian, or a property owner;

(B) the number of any driver's license, commercial driver's license, or personal identification certificate issued to any person listed in an accident report;

(C) the date of birth, other than the year, of any person listed in an accident report;

(D) the address, other than zip code, and telephone number of any person listed in an accident report;

(E) the license plate number of any vehicle listed in an accident report;

(F) the name of any insurance company listed as a provider of financial responsibility for a vehicle listed in an accident report;

(G) the number of any insurance policy issued by an insurance company listed as a provider of financial responsibility;

(H) the date the peace officer who investigated the accident was notified of the accident;

(I) the date the investigating peace officer arrived at the accident site;

(J) the badge number or identification number of the investigating officer;

(K) the date on which any person who died as a result of the accident died;

(L) the date of any commercial motor vehicle report; and

(M) the place where any person injured or killed in an accident was taken and the person or entity that provided the transportation.

(g) The amount that may be charged for information provided under Subsection (e) shall be calculated in the manner specified by Chapter 552, Government Code, for public information provided by a governmental body under that chapter.

Sec. 550.066. Admissibility of Certain Accident Report Information.

An individual's response to the information requested on an accident report form as provided by Section 550.064(b)(4) is not admissible evidence in a civil trial.

Sec. 550.067. Municipal Authority to Require Accident Reports.

(a) A municipality by ordinance may require the operator of a vehicle involved in an accident to file with a designated municipal department:

(1) a report of the accident, if the accident results in injury to or the death of a person or the apparent total property damage is $25 or more; or

(2) a copy of a report required by this chapter to be filed with the department.

(b) A report filed under Subsection (a) is for the confidential use of the municipal department and subject to the provisions of Section 550.065.

(c) A municipality by ordinance may require the person in charge of a garage or repair shop where a motor vehicle is brought if the vehicle shows evidence of having been involved in an accident described by Section 550.062(a) or shows evidence of having been struck by a bullet to report to a department of the municipality within 24 hours after the garage or repair shop receives the motor vehicle, giving the engine number, registration number, and the name and address of the owner or operator of the vehicle.

Sec. 550.068. Changing Accident Report.

(a) Except as provided by Subsection (b), a change in or a modification of a written report of a motor vehicle accident prepared by a peace officer that alters a material fact in the report may be made only by the peace officer who prepared the report.

(b) A change in or a modification of the written report of the accident may be made by a person other than the peace officer if:

(1) the change is made by a written supplement to the report; and

(2) the written supplement clearly indicates the name of the person who originated the change.

SUBCHAPTER E
OTHER REPORTS

Sec. 550.081. Report of Medical Examiner or Justice of the Peace.

(a) In this section:

(1) "Department" means the Texas Department of Transportation.

(2) "Bridge collapse" means the abrupt failure of the basic structure of a bridge that impairs the ability of the bridge to serve its intended purpose and that damages a highway located on or under the structure.

(b) A medical examiner or justice of the peace acting as coroner in a county that does not have a medical examiner's office or that is not part of a medical examiner's district shall submit a report in writing to the department of the death of a person that was the result of a traffic accident or bridge collapse:

(1) to which this chapter applies; and

(2) that occurred within the jurisdiction of the medical examiner or justice of the peace in the preceding calendar quarter.

(c) The report must be submitted before the 11th day of each calendar month and include:

(1) the name of the deceased and a statement as to whether the deceased was:

(A) the operator of or a passenger in a vehicle involved in the accident; or

(B) a pedestrian or other nonoccupant of a vehicle;

(2) the date of the accident and the name of the county in which the accident occurred, and, if a bridge collapse, the location of the bridge in that county;

(3) the name of any laboratory, medical examiner's office, or other facility that conducted toxicological testing relative to the deceased; and

(4) the results of any toxicological testing that was conducted.

(d) A report required by this section shall be sent to:

(1) the crash records bureau of the department at its headquarters in Austin; or

(2) any other office or bureau of the department that the department designates.

(e) If toxicological test results are not available to the medical examiner or justice of the peace on the date a report must be submitted, the medical examiner or justice shall:

(1) submit a report that includes the statement "toxicological test results unavailable"; and

(2) submit a supplement to the report that contains the information required by Subsections (c)(3) and (4) as soon as practicable after the toxicological test results become available.

(f) The department shall prepare and when requested supply to medical examiners' offices and justices of the peace the forms necessary to make the reports required by this section.

CHAPTER 551
OPERATION OF BICYCLES AND MOPEDS, GOLF CARTS, AND OTHER LOW-POWERED VEHICLES

SUBCHAPTER A
APPLICATION OF CHAPTER

Sec. 551.001. Applicability.

Unless specifically provided otherwise, a provision of this chapter that applies to a person operating a bicycle applies only to a person operating a bicycle on:

(1) a highway; or

(2) a path set aside for the exclusive operation of bicycles.

Sec. 551.002. Moped and Electric Bicycle Included.

A provision of this subtitle applicable to a bicycle also applies to:

(1) a moped, other than a provision that by its nature cannot apply to a moped; and

(2) an electric bicycle, other than a provision that by its nature cannot apply to an electric bicycle.

SUBCHAPTER B
BICYCLES

Sec. 551.101. Rights and Duties.

(a) A person operating a bicycle has the rights and duties applicable to a driver operating a vehicle under this subtitle, unless:

(1) a provision of this chapter alters a right or duty; or

(2) a right or duty applicable to a driver operating a vehicle cannot by its nature apply to a person operating a bicycle.

(b) A parent of a child or a guardian of a ward may not knowingly permit the child or ward to violate this subtitle.

Sec. 551.102. General Operation.

(a) A person operating a bicycle shall ride only on or astride a permanent and regular seat attached to the bicycle.

(b) A person may not use a bicycle to carry more persons than the bicycle is designed or equipped to carry.

(c) A person operating a bicycle may not use the bicycle to carry an object that prevents the person from operating the bicycle with at least one hand on the handlebars of the bicycle.

(d) A person operating a bicycle, coaster, sled, or toy vehicle or using roller skates may not attach either the person or the bicycle, coaster, sled, toy vehicle, or roller skates to a streetcar or vehicle on a roadway.

Sec. 551.103. Operation on Roadway.

(a) Except as provided by Subsection (b), a person operating a bicycle on a roadway who is moving slower than the other traffic on the roadway shall ride as near as practicable to the right curb or edge of the roadway, unless:

(1) the person is passing another vehicle moving in the same direction;

(2) the person is preparing to turn left at an intersection or onto a private road or driveway;

(3) a condition on or of the roadway, including a fixed or moving object, parked or moving vehicle, pedestrian, animal, or surface hazard prevents the person from safely riding next to the right curb or edge of the roadway; or

(4) the person is operating a bicycle in an outside lane that is:

(A) less than 14 feet in width and does not have a designated bicycle lane adjacent to that lane; or

(B) too narrow for a bicycle and a motor vehicle to safely travel side by side.

(b) A person operating a bicycle on a one-way roadway with two or more marked traffic lanes may ride as near as practicable to the left curb or edge of the roadway.

(c) Persons operating bicycles on a roadway may ride two abreast. Persons riding two abreast on a laned roadway shall ride in a single lane. Persons riding two abreast may not impede the normal and reasonable flow of traffic on the roadway. Persons may not ride more than two abreast unless they are riding on a part of a roadway set aside for the exclusive operation of bicycles.

(d) [Repealed by Acts 2001, 77th Leg., ch. 1085 (H.B. 2204), § 13, effective September 1, 2001.]

Sec. 551.104. Safety Equipment.

(a) A person may not operate a bicycle unless the bicycle is equipped with a brake capable of making a braked wheel skid on dry, level, clean pavement.

(b) A person may not operate a bicycle at nighttime unless the bicycle is equipped with:

(1) a lamp on the front of the bicycle that emits a white light visible from a distance of at least 500 feet in front of the bicycle; and

(2) on the rear of the bicycle:

(A) a red reflector that is:

(i) of a type approved by the department; and

(ii) visible when directly in front of lawful upper beams of motor vehicle headlamps from all distances from 50 to 300 feet to the rear of the bicycle; or

(B) a lamp that emits a red light visible from a distance of 500 feet to the rear of the bicycle.

Sec. 551.105. Competitive Racing.

(a) In this section, "bicycle" means a nonmotorized vehicle propelled by human power.

(b) A sponsoring organization may hold a competitive bicycle race on a public road only with the approval of the appropriate local law enforcement agencies.

(c) The local law enforcement agencies and the sponsoring organization may agree on safety regulations governing the movement of bicycles during a competitive race or during training for a competitive race, including the permission for bicycle operators to ride abreast.

Sec. 551.106. Regulation of Bicycles by Department or Local Authority.

(a) The department or a local authority may not prohibit the operation of an electric bicycle:

(1) on a highway that is used primarily by motor vehicles; or

(2) in an area in which the operation of a nonelectric bicycle is permitted, unless the area is a path that:

(A) is not open to motor vehicles; and

(B) has a natural surface tread made by clearing and grading the native soil without adding surfacing materials.

(b) The department or a local authority may:

(1) prohibit the operation of a bicycle on a sidewalk; and

(2) establish speed limits for bicycles on paths set aside for the exclusive operation of bicycles and other paths on which bicycles may be operated.

(c) The department may establish rules for the administration of this section if necessary.

Sec. 551.107. Operation of Electric Bicycle.

(a) Subtitles A, B, and D and Chapter 551A do not apply to the operation of an electric bicycle.

(b) A person may not operate an electric bicycle unless the electric motor disengages or ceases to function either:

(1) when the operator stops pedaling; or

(2) when the brakes are applied.

(c) A person may not operate a Class 3 electric bicycle, as defined by Section 664.001, unless the person is at least 15 years of age. This subsection does not prohibit a person who is under 15 years of age from riding on a Class 3 bicycle as a passenger.

SUBCHAPTER C ELECTRIC PERSONAL ASSISTIVE MOBILITY DEVICES

Sec. 551.201. Definition.

In this subchapter, "electric personal assistive mobility device" means a two non-tandem wheeled device designed for transporting one person that is:

(1) self-balancing; and

(2) propelled by an electric propulsion system with an average power of 750 watts or one horsepower.

Sec. 551.202. Operation on Roadway.

(a) A person may operate an electric personal assistive mobility device on a residential street, roadway, or public highway with a speed limit of 30 miles per hour or less only:

(1) while making a direct crossing of a highway in a marked or unmarked crosswalk;

(2) where no sidewalk is available; or

(3) when so directed by a traffic control device or by a law enforcement officer.

(b) A person may operate an electric personal assistive mobility device on a path set aside for the exclusive operation of bicycles.

(c) Any person operating an electric personal assistive mobility device on a residential street, roadway, or public highway shall ride as close as practicable to the right-hand edge.

(d) Except as otherwise provided by this section, provisions of this title applicable to the operation of bicycles apply to the operation of electric personal assistive mobility devices.

Sec. 551.203. Sidewalks.

A person may operate an electric personal assistive mobility device on a sidewalk.

SUBCHAPTER D NEIGHBORHOOD ELECTRIC VEHICLES

Sec. 551.301. Definition.

In this subchapter, "neighborhood electric vehicle" means a vehicle that can attain a maximum speed of 35 miles per hour on a paved level surface and otherwise complies with Federal Motor Vehicle Safety Standard 500 (49 C.F.R. Section 571.500).

Sec. 551.302. Registration.

The Texas Department of Motor Vehicles may adopt rules relating to the registration and issuance of license plates to neighborhood electric vehicles.

Sec. 551.303. Operation on Roadways.

(a) A neighborhood electric vehicle may be operated only on a street or highway for which the posted speed limit is 45 miles per hour or less. A neighborhood electric vehicle may cross a road or street at an intersection where the road or street has a posted speed limit of more than 45 miles per hour. A neighborhood electric vehicle may not be operated on a street or highway at a speed that exceeds the lesser of:

(1) the posted speed limit; or

(2) 35 miles per hour.

(b) A county or municipality may prohibit the operation of a neighborhood electric vehicle on a street or highway if the governing body of the county or municipality determines that the prohibition is necessary in the interest of safety.

(c) The Texas Department of Transportation may prohibit the operation of a neighborhood electric vehicle on a highway if that department determines that the prohibition is necessary in the interest of safety.

Sec. 551.304. Limited Operation.

(a) An operator may operate a neighborhood electric vehicle:

(1) in a master planned community:

(A) that has in place a uniform set of restrictive covenants; and

(B) for which a county or municipality has approved a plat;

(2) on a public or private beach; or

(3) on a public highway for which the posted speed limit is not more than 35 miles per hour, if the neighborhood electric vehicle is operated:

(A) during the daytime; and

(B) not more than two miles from the location where the neighborhood electric vehicle is usually parked and for transportation to or from a golf course.

(b) A person is not required to register a neighborhood electric vehicle operated in compliance with this section.

SUBCHAPTER E MOTOR-ASSISTED SCOOTERS

Sec. 551.351. Definitions.

In this subchapter:

(1) "Motor-assisted scooter":

(A) means a self-propelled device with:

(i) at least two wheels in contact with the ground during operation;

(ii) a braking system capable of stopping the device under typical operating conditions;

(iii) a gas or electric motor not exceeding 40 cubic centimeters;

(iv) a deck designed to allow a person to stand or sit while operating the device; and

(v) the ability to be propelled by human power alone; and

(B) does not include a pocket bike or a minimotorbike.

(2) "Pocket bike or minimotorbike" means a self-propelled vehicle that is equipped with an electric motor or internal combustion engine having a piston displacement of less than 50 cubic centimeters, is designed to propel itself with not more than two wheels in contact with the ground, has a seat or saddle for the use of the operator, is not designed for use on a highway, and is ineligible for a certificate of title under Chapter 501. The term does not include:

(A) a moped or motorcycle;

(B) an electric bicycle;

(C) a motorized mobility device, as defined by Section 552A.0101;

(D) an electric personal assistive mobility device, as defined by Section 551.201; or

(E) a neighborhood electric vehicle, as defined by Section 551.301.

Sec. 551.352. Operation on Roadways or Sidewalks.

(a) A motor-assisted scooter may be operated only on a street or highway for which the posted speed limit is 35 miles per hour or less. The motor-assisted scooter may cross a road or street at an intersection where the road or street has a posted speed limit of more than 35 miles per hour.

(b) A county or municipality may prohibit the operation of a motor-assisted scooter on a street, highway, or sidewalk if the governing body of the county or municipality determines that the prohibition is necessary in the interest of safety.

(c) The department may prohibit the operation of a motor-assisted scooter on a highway if it determines that the prohibition is necessary in the interest of safety.

(d) A person may operate a motor-assisted scooter on a path set aside for the exclusive operation of bicycles or on a sidewalk. Except as otherwise provided by this section, a provision of this title applicable to the operation of a bicycle applies to the operation of a motor-assisted scooter.

(e) A provision of this title applicable to a motor vehicle does not apply to a motor-assisted scooter.

Sec. 551.353. Application of Subchapter to Pocket Bike or Minimotorbike.

This subchapter may not be construed to authorize the operation of a pocket bike or minimotorbike on any:

(1) highway, road, or street;

(2) path set aside for the exclusive operation of bicycles; or

(3) sidewalk.

SUBCHAPTER F GOLF CARTS

Sec. 551.401. Definition.

In this subchapter, "golf cart" means a motor vehicle designed by the manufacturer primarily for use on a golf course.

Sec. 551.402. Registration Not Authorized; License Plates.

(a) The Texas Department of Motor Vehicles may not register a golf cart for operation on a highway regardless of whether any alteration has been made to the golf cart.

(b) A person may operate a golf cart on a highway in a manner authorized by this subchapter only if the vehicle displays a license plate issued under this section.

(c) The Texas Department of Motor Vehicles:

(1) shall by rule establish a procedure to issue license plates for golf carts; and

(2) may charge a fee not to exceed $10 for the cost of the license plate, to be deposited to the credit of the Texas Department of Motor Vehicles fund.

(d) A golf cart license plate does not expire. A person who becomes the owner of a golf cart for which the previous owner obtained a license plate may not use the previous owner's license plate.

Sec. 551.403. Operation Authorized in Certain Areas.

(a) An operator may operate a golf cart:

(1) in a master planned community:

(A) that is a residential subdivision as defined by Section 209.002(9), Property Code, or has in place a uniform set of restrictive covenants; and

(B) for which a county or municipality has approved one or more plats;

(2) on a public or private beach that is open to vehicular traffic; or

(3) on a highway for which the posted speed limit is not more than 35 miles per hour, if the golf cart is operated:

(A) during the daytime; and

(B) not more than five miles from the location where the golf cart is usually parked and for transportation to or from a golf course.

(b) Notwithstanding Section 551.402(b), a person may operate a golf cart in a master planned community described by Subsection (a) without a golf cart license plate on a highway for which the posted speed limit is not more than 35 miles per hour, including through an intersection of a highway for which the posted speed limit is more than 35 miles per hour.

Sec. 551.4031. Prohibition of Operation on Highway by Municipality, County, or Department.

(a) A county or municipality may prohibit the operation of a golf cart on a highway under Section 551.403 if the governing body of the county or municipality determines that the prohibition is necessary in the interest of safety.

(b) The Texas Department of Transportation may prohibit the operation of a golf cart on a highway under Section 551.403 if the department determines that the prohibition is necessary in the interest of safety.

Sec. 551.404. Operation on Highway Authorized by Municipality or Certain Counties.

(a) In addition to the operation authorized by Section 551.403, the governing body of a municipality may allow an operator to operate a golf cart on all or part of a highway that:

(1) is in the corporate boundaries of the municipality; and

(2) has a posted speed limit of not more than 35 miles per hour.

(b) In addition to the operation authorized by Section 551.403, the commissioners court of a county described by Subsection (c) may allow an operator to operate a golf cart on all or part of a highway that:

(1) is located in the unincorporated area of the county; and

(2) has a speed limit of not more than 35 miles per hour.

(c) Subsection (b) applies only to a county that:

(1) borders or contains a portion of the Red River; or

(2) borders the Gulf of Mexico and has a population of less than 500,000.

Sec. 551.4041. Equipment.

A golf cart operated under Section 551.404 must have the following equipment:

(1) headlamps;

(2) taillamps;

(3) reflectors;

(4) parking brake; and

(5) mirrors.

Sec. 551.405. Crossing Intersections.

A golf cart may cross a highway at an intersection, including an intersection with a highway that has a posted speed limit of more than 35 miles per hour.

SUBCHAPTER G
PACKAGE DELIVERY VEHICLES

Sec. 551.451. Definitions.

In this subchapter:

(1) [Repealed.]

(2) "Golf cart" has the meaning assigned by Section 551.401.

(3) "Motor carrier" has the meaning assigned by Section 643.001.

(4) "Neighborhood electric vehicle" has the meaning assigned by Section 551.301.

(4-a) "Off-highway vehicle" has the meaning assigned by Section 551A.001.

(5) "Public highway" has the meaning assigned by Section 502.001.

(6) [Repealed.]

(7) [Repealed.]

Sec. 551.452. License Plates for Package Delivery Vehicles.

(a) The Texas Department of Motor Vehicles may issue distinguishing license plates for a vehicle operated by a motor carrier for the purpose of picking up and delivering mail, parcels, and packages if the vehicle:

(1) is a golf cart, a neighborhood electric vehicle, or an off-highway vehicle; and

(2) is equipped with headlamps, taillamps, reflectors, a parking brake, and mirrors, in addition to any other equipment required by law.

(b) The Texas Department of Motor Vehicles by rule shall establish a procedure to issue the license plates to be used only for operation in accordance with this subchapter.

(c) The license plates must include the words "Package Delivery."

(d) The Texas Department of Motor Vehicles may charge a license plate fee not to exceed $25 annually to be deposited to the credit of the Texas Department of Motor Vehicles fund.

Sec. 551.453. Limited Operation.

(a) A motor carrier may operate, for the purpose of picking up or delivering mail, parcels, or packages, a vehicle bearing license plates issued under Section 551.452 on a public highway that is not an interstate or a limited-access or controlled-access highway and that has a speed limit of not more than 35 miles per hour.

(b) The Department of Motor Vehicles may not require the registration of a vehicle operated under Subsection (a) unless the registration is required by other law.

Sec. 551.454. Operation on Property of Subdivision or Condominium.

(a) In this section:

(1) "Condominium" has the meaning assigned by Section 82.003, Property Code.

(2) "Declaration" has the meaning assigned by Section 82.003, Property Code.

(3) "Property owners' association" has the meaning assigned by Section 202.001, Property Code.

(4) "Restrictions" has the meaning assigned by Section 209.002, Property Code.

(5) "Subdivision" has the meaning assigned by Section 209.002, Property Code.

(b) A property owners' association may adopt reasonable safety and use rules for the operation, for the purpose of picking up or delivering mail, parcels, or packages, of a vehicle bearing license plates issued under Section 551.452 on the property of a subdivision or condominium managed or regulated by the association.

(c) A motor carrier may operate, for the purpose of picking up or delivering mail, parcels, or packages, a vehicle bearing license plates issued under Section 551.452 on the property of a subdivision subject to restrictions or a condominium that has in place a declaration, in a manner that complies with any applicable rules adopted by a property owners' association that manages or regulates the subdivision or condominium.

Sec. 551.455. Operation in Municipalities and Counties.

(a) In addition to the operation authorized by Sections 551.453 and 551.454, the governing body of a municipality may allow a motor carrier to operate, for the purpose of picking up or delivering mail, parcels, or packages, a vehicle bearing license plates issued under Section 551.452 on all or part of a public highway that:

(1) is in the corporate boundaries of the municipality; and

(2) has a speed limit of not more than 35 miles per hour.

(b) In addition to the operation authorized by Sections 551.453 and 551.454, a county commissioners court may allow a motor carrier to operate, for the purpose of picking up or delivering mail, parcels, or packages, a vehicle bearing license plates issued under Section 551.452 on all or part of a public highway that:

(1) is located in the unincorporated area of the county; and

(2) has a speed limit of not more than 35 miles per hour.

Sec. 551.456. Crossing Certain Roadways.

A vehicle bearing license plates issued under Section 551.452 may cross intersections, including on or through a road or street that has a speed limit of more than 35 miles per hour.

Sec. 551.457. Conflicts.

In the case of a conflict between this subchapter and other law, including Chapters 502 and 551A, this subchapter controls.

CHAPTER 551A. OFF-HIGHWAY VEHICLES

SUBCHAPTER A GENERAL PROVISIONS

Sec. 551A.001. Definitions.

In this chapter:

(1) "All-terrain vehicle" means a motor vehicle that is:

(A) equipped with a seat or seats for the use of:

(i) the rider; and

(ii) a passenger, if the motor vehicle is designed by the manufacturer to transport a passenger;

(B) designed to propel itself with three or more tires in contact with the ground;

(C) designed by the manufacturer for off-highway use;

(D) not designed by the manufacturer primarily for farming or lawn care; and

(E) not more than 50 inches wide.

(1-b) "Commission" means the Texas Commission of Licensing and Regulation.

(1-c) "Department" means the Texas Department of Licensing and Regulation.

(1-d) "Off-highway vehicle" means:

(A) an all-terrain vehicle or recreational off-highway vehicle;

(B) a sand rail; or

(C) a utility vehicle.

(2) "Beach" means a beach area, publicly or privately owned, that borders the seaward shore of the Gulf of Mexico.

(3) "Sand rail" means a vehicle, as defined by Section 502.001, that:

(A) is designed or built primarily for off-highway use in sandy terrains, including for use on sand dunes;

(B) has a tubular frame, an integrated roll cage, and an engine that is rear-mounted or placed midway between the front and rear axles of the vehicle; and

(C) has a gross vehicle weight, as defined by Section 541.401, of:

(i) not less than 700 pounds; and

(ii) not more than 2,000 pounds.

(4) "Public off-highway vehicle land" means land on which off-highway recreation is authorized under Chapter 29, Parks and Wildlife Code.

(5) "Recreational off-highway vehicle" means a motor vehicle that is:

(A) equipped with a seat or seats for the use of:

(i) the rider; and

(ii) a passenger or passengers, if the vehicle is designed by the manufacturer to transport a passenger or passengers;

(B) designed to propel itself with four or more tires in contact with the ground;

(C) designed by the manufacturer for off-highway use by the operator only; and

(D) not designed by the manufacturer primarily for farming or lawn care.

(6) "Utility vehicle" means a motor vehicle that is not a golf cart, as defined by Section 551.401, or lawn mower and is:

(A) equipped with side-by-side seating for the use of the operator and a passenger;

(B) designed to propel itself with at least four tires in contact with the ground;

(C) designed by the manufacturer for off-highway use only; and

(D) designed by the manufacturer primarily for utility work and not for recreational purposes.

Sec. 551A.002. Nonapplicability of Certain Other Laws.

(a) Chapter 521 does not apply to the operation or ownership of an off-highway vehicle on public off-highway vehicle land.

(b) Chapter 1001, Education Code, does not apply to instruction in the operation of an off-highway vehicle provided under the operator education and certification program established by this chapter.

SUBCHAPTER B. OFF-HIGHWAY VEHICLE OPERATOR EDUCATION AND CERTIFICATION FOR OPERATION ON PUBLIC LAND OR BEACH

Sec. 551A.011. Administration of Program.

The department shall administer an off-highway vehicle operator education and certification program and enforce the laws governing the program.

Sec. 551A.012. Purpose of Program.

The purpose of the off-highway vehicle operator education and certification program is to make available courses in basic training and safety skills relating to the operation of off-highway vehicles and to issue safety certificates to operators who successfully complete the educational program requirements or pass a test established under the program.

Sec. 551A.013. Program Standards.

(a) The department shall supervise the off-highway vehicle operator education and certification program and shall determine:

(1) locations at which courses will be offered;

(2) fees for the courses;

(3) qualifications of instructors;

(4) course curriculum; and

(5) standards for operator safety certification.

(b) In establishing standards for instructors, curriculum, and operator certification, the department shall consult and be guided by standards established by recognized off-highway vehicle safety organizations.

Sec. 551A.014. Contracts.

To administer the education program and certify off-highway vehicle operators, the department may contract with nonprofit safety organizations, nonprofit educational organizations, institutions of higher education or agencies of local governments.

Sec. 551A.015. Teaching and Testing Methods.

(a) If the department determines that vehicle operation is not feasible in a program component or at a particular program location, the operator education and certification program for persons who are at least 14 years of age may use teaching or testing methods that do not involve the actual operation of an off-highway vehicle.

(b) An operator safety certificate may not be issued to a person younger than 14 years of age unless the person has successfully completed a training course that involves the actual operation of an off-highway vehicle.

Sec. 551A.016. Fee for Course.

A person may charge, for a course under the off-highway vehicle operator education and certification program, a fee that is reasonably related to the costs of administering the course.

Sec. 551A.017. Denial, Suspension, or Cancellation of Approval.

(a) The executive director or commission may deny, suspend, or cancel its approval for a program sponsor to conduct or for an instructor to teach a course offered under this chapter if the applicant, sponsor, or instructor:

(1) does not satisfy the requirements established under this chapter to receive or retain approval;

(2) permits fraud or engages in fraudulent practices with reference to an application to the department;

(3) induces or countenances fraud or fraudulent practices by a person applying for a driver's license or permit;

(4) permits or engages in a fraudulent practice in an action between the applicant or license holder and the public; or

(5) fails to comply with rules of the department.

(b) Before the executive director or commission may deny, suspend, or cancel the approval of a program sponsor or an instructor, notice and opportunity for a hearing must be given as provided by:

(1) Chapter 2001, Government Code; and

(2) Chapter 53, Occupations Code.

Sec. 551A.018. Rules.

The commission may adopt rules to administer this chapter.

Sec. 551A.019. Exemptions.

The commission by rule may temporarily exempt the residents of any county from Section 551A.015 or from Section 551A.031(b)(1) until the appropriate education and certification program is established at a location that is reasonably accessible to the residents of that county.

SUBCHAPTER C
OFF-HIGHWAY OPERATION OF OFF-HIGHWAY VEHICLES

Sec. 551A.031. Operation on Public Land or Beach; Safety Certificate Required.

(a) A person may not operate an off-highway vehicle on land owned or leased by the state or a political subdivision of the state that is not open to vehicular traffic unless:

(1) the land is public off-highway vehicle land; and

(2) the operation is in compliance with:
(A) this chapter; and
(B) Chapter 29, Parks and Wildlife Code.
(b) A person may not operate an off-highway vehicle on public off-highway vehicle land or a beach unless the person:
(1) holds a safety certificate issued under this chapter or under the authority of another state;
(2) is taking a safety training course under the direct supervision of a certified off-highway vehicle safety instructor; or
(3) is under the direct supervision of an adult who holds a safety certificate issued under this chapter or under the authority of another state.
(c) A person to whom a safety certificate required by Subsection (b) has been issued shall:
(1) carry the certificate when the person operates an off-highway vehicle on public off-highway vehicle land or a beach; and
(2) display the certificate at the request of any law enforcement officer.

Sec. 551A.032. Operation on Public Off-Highway Vehicle Land by Person Younger Than 14.

A person younger than 14 years of age who is operating an off-highway vehicle on public off-highway vehicle land must be accompanied by and be under the direct supervision of:
(1) the person's parent or guardian; or
(2) an adult who is authorized by the person's parent or guardian.

Sec. 551A.033. Operation on Beach.

(a) A person may operate an off-highway vehicle on a beach only as provided by this section.
(b) A person operating an off-highway vehicle on a beach must hold and have in the person's possession a driver's license.
(c) Except as provided by Chapters 61 and 63, Natural Resources Code, an operator of an off-highway vehicle may drive the vehicle on a beach that is open to motor vehicle traffic.
(d) Except as provided by Chapters 61 and 63, Natural Resources Code, a person who is authorized to operate an off-highway vehicle that is owned by the state, a county, or a municipality may drive the vehicle on any beach if the vehicle is registered under Section 502.140(c).
(e) The Texas Department of Transportation or a county or municipality may prohibit the operation of an off-highway vehicle on a beach if the department or the governing body of the county or municipality determines that the prohibition is necessary in the interest of safety.

Sec. 551A.034. Crossing Highway at Point Other Than Intersection.

(a) The operator of an off-highway vehicle may drive the vehicle across a highway that is not an interstate or limited-access highway at a point other than an intersection if the operator:
(1) brings the vehicle to a complete stop before crossing the shoulder or main traveled way of the roadway;
(2) yields the right-of-way to oncoming traffic that is an immediate hazard; and
(3) makes the crossing:
(A) at an angle of approximately 90 degrees to the roadway;
(B) at a place where no obstruction prevents a quick and safe crossing; and
(C) with the vehicle's headlights and taillights lighted.
(b) Notwithstanding Subsection (a), the operator of an off-highway vehicle may drive the vehicle across a divided highway other than an interstate or limited access highway only at an intersection of the highway with another highway.

SUBCHAPTER D. OPERATION ON HIGHWAY

Sec. 551A.051. Applicability.

(a) A person may operate an off-highway vehicle on a highway only as provided by this chapter.
(b) This subchapter does not apply to the operation of an off-highway vehicle that is owned and registered as authorized by Section 502.140(c) by the state, a county, or a municipality by a person who is an authorized operator of the vehicle.

Sec. 551A.052. Registration; License Plates.

(a) Except as provided by Section 502.140(c), the Texas Department of Motor Vehicles may not register an off-highway vehicle for operation on a highway regardless of whether any alteration has been made to the vehicle.
(b) An operator may operate an unregistered off-highway vehicle on a highway in a manner authorized by this subchapter only if the vehicle displays a license plate issued under this section.
(c) The Texas Department of Motor Vehicles:

Transportation Code

(1) shall by rule establish a procedure to issue license plates for unregistered off-highway vehicles; and

(2) may charge a fee not to exceed $10 for the cost of the license plate, to be deposited to the credit of the Texas Department of Motor Vehicles fund.

(d) An off-highway vehicle license plate issued under Subsection (c) does not expire. A person who becomes the owner of an off-highway vehicle for which the previous owner obtained a license plate may not use the previous owner's license plate.

Sec. 551A.053. Operation on Highway Authorized by Municipality or Certain Counties.

(a) In addition to the operation authorized by Section 551A.055, the governing body of a municipality may allow an operator to operate an unregistered off-highway vehicle on all or part of a highway that:

(1) is in the corporate boundaries of the municipality; and

(2) has a posted speed limit of not more than 35 miles per hour.

(b) In addition to the operation authorized by Section 551A.055, the commissioners court of a county described by Subsection (c) may allow an operator to operate an unregistered off-highway vehicle on all or part of a highway that:

(1) is located in the unincorporated area of the county; and

(2) has a posted speed limit of not more than 35 miles per hour.

(c) Subsection (b) applies only to a county that:

(1) borders or contains a portion of the Red River;

(2) borders or contains a portion of the Guadalupe River and contains a part of a barrier island that borders the Gulf of Mexico; or

(3) is adjacent to a county described by Subdivision (2) and:

(A) has a population of less than 37,000; and

(B) contains a part of a barrier island or peninsula that borders the Gulf of Mexico.

Sec. 551A.054. Prohibition of Operation in Certain Areas by Municipality, County, or Department.

(a) A county or municipality may prohibit the operation of an unregistered off-highway vehicle on a highway under Section 551A.055 if the governing body of the county or municipality determines that the prohibition is necessary in the interest of safety.

(b) The Texas Department of Transportation may prohibit the operation of an unregistered off-highway vehicle on a highway under Section 551A.055 if that department determines that the prohibition is necessary in the interest of safety.

Sec. 551A.055. Operation Authorized in Certain Areas.

An operator may operate an unregistered off-highway vehicle:

(1) in a master planned community:

(A) that has in place a uniform set of restrictive covenants; and

(B) for which a county or municipality has approved a plat; or

(2) on a highway for which the posted speed limit is not more than 35 miles per hour, if the off-highway vehicle is operated:

(A) during the daytime; and

(B) not more than two miles from the location where the off-highway vehicle is usually parked and for transportation to or from a golf course.

Sec. 551A.056. Crossing Intersections.

An unregistered off-highway vehicle may cross a highway at an intersection, including an intersection with a highway that has a posted speed limit of more than 35 miles per hour.

Sec. 551A.057. Agricultural or Utility Operation on Highway.

(a) The operator of an unregistered off-highway vehicle may operate the vehicle on a highway that is not an interstate or limited-access highway if:

(1) the transportation is in connection with:

(A) the production, cultivation, care, harvesting, preserving, drying, processing, canning, storing, handling, shipping, marketing, selling, or use of agricultural products, as defined by Section 52.002, Agriculture Code; or

(B) utility work performed by a utility;

(2) the operator attaches to the back of the vehicle a triangular orange flag that is at least six feet above ground level;

(3) the vehicle's headlights and taillights are illuminated;

(4) the operation of the vehicle occurs in the daytime; and

(5) the operation of the vehicle does not exceed a distance of 25 miles from the point of origin to the destination.

(b) Notwithstanding Section 551A.052, an off-highway vehicle operated under this section is not required to display a license plate.

(c) Provisions of this code regarding helmet and eye protection use, safety certification, and other vehicular restrictions do not apply to the operation of an off-highway vehicle under this section.

Sec. 551A.058. Law Enforcement Operation.

(a) A peace officer or other person who provides law enforcement, firefighting, ambulance, medical, or other emergency services, including a volunteer firefighter, may operate an off-highway vehicle on a public street, road, or highway that is not an interstate or limited-access highway only if:

(1) the transportation is in connection with the performance of the operator's official duty

(2) the operator attaches to the back of the vehicle a triangular orange flag that is at least six feet above ground level;

(3) the vehicle's headlights and taillights are illuminated;

(4) the operator holds a driver's license, as defined by Section 521.001; and

(5) the operation of the vehicle does not exceed a distance of 10 miles from the point of origin to the destination.

(b) Notwithstanding Section 551A.052, an off-highway vehicle operated under this section is not required to display a license plate.

Sec. 551A.059. Flag Standards.

The commission shall adopt standards and specifications that apply to the color, size, and mounting position of flags required under Sections 551A.057 and 551A.058.

SUBCHAPTER E. EQUIPMENT AND SAFETY REQUIREMENTS

Sec. 551A.071. Required Equipment; Display of Lights.

(a) An off-highway vehicle that is operated on public off-highway vehicle land, a beach, or a highway must be equipped with:

(1) a brake system maintained in good operating condition;

(2) an adequate muffler system in good working condition; and

(3) a United States Forest Service qualified spark arrester.

(b) An off-highway vehicle that is operated on public off-highway vehicle land, a beach, or a highway must display a lighted headlight and taillight:

(1) during the period from one-half hour after sunset to one-half hour before sunrise; and

(2) at any time when visibility is reduced because of insufficient light or atmospheric conditions.

(c) A person may not operate an off-highway vehicle on public off-highway vehicle land, a beach, or a highway if:

(1) the vehicle has an exhaust system that has been modified with a cutout, bypass, or similar device; or

(2) the spark arrester has been removed or modified, unless the vehicle is being operated in a closed-course competition event.

(d) The department or executive director may exempt off-highway vehicles that are participating in certain competitive events from the requirements of this section.

Sec. 551A.072. Safety Apparel Required.

(a) A person may not operate, ride, or be carried on an off-highway vehicle on public off-highway vehicle land, a beach, or a highway unless the person wears:

(1) a safety helmet that complies with United States Department of Transportation standards;

(2) eye protection; and

(3) seat belts, if the vehicle is equipped with seat belts.

(b) Subsections (a)(1) and (2) do not apply to a motor vehicle that has four wheels, is equipped with bench or bucket seats and seat belts, and includes a roll bar or roll cage construction to reduce the risk of injury to an occupant of the vehicle in case of vehicle rollover.

(c) This section does not apply to a motor vehicle that is in the process of being loaded into or unloaded from a trailer or another vehicle used to transport the vehicle.

Sec. 551A.073. Reckless or Careless Operation Prohibited.

A person may not operate an off-highway vehicle on public off-highway vehicle land or a beach in a careless or reckless manner that endangers, injures, or damages any person or property.

Sec. 551A.074. Carrying Passengers.

A person may not carry a passenger on an off-highway vehicle operated on public off-highway vehicle land, a beach, or a highway unless the vehicle is designed by the manufacturer to transport a passenger.

SUBCHAPTER F
CERTAIN OFFENSES

Sec. 551A.091. Violation of Chapter on Public Off-Highway Vehicle Land or Beach.

Anoffense for a violation of this chapter committed on public off-highway vehicle land or a beach is a Class C misdemeanor.

CHAPTER 552
PEDESTRIANS

Sec. 552.001. Traffic Control Signals.

(a) A traffic control signal displaying green, red, and yellow lights or lighted arrows applies to a pedestrian as provided by this section unless the pedestrian is otherwise directed by a special pedestrian control signal.

(b) A pedestrian facing a green signal may proceed across a roadway within a marked or unmarked crosswalk unless the sole green signal is a turn arrow.

(c) A pedestrian facing a steady red signal alone or a steady yellow signal may not enter a roadway.

Sec. 552.002. Pedestrian Right-of-Way If Control Signal Present.

(a) A pedestrian control signal displaying "Walk," "Don't Walk," or "Wait" applies to a pedestrian as provided by this section.

(b) A pedestrian facing a "Walk" signal may proceed across a roadway in the direction of the signal, and the operator of a vehicle shall stop and yield the right-of-way to the pedestrian.

(c) A pedestrian may not start to cross a roadway in the direction of a "Don't Walk" signal or a "Wait" signal. A pedestrian who has partially crossed while the "Walk" signal is displayed shall proceed to a sidewalk or safety island while the "Don't Walk" signal or "Wait" signal is displayed.

Sec. 552.003. Pedestrian Right-of-Way at Crosswalk.

(a) The operator of a vehicle shall stop and yield the right-of-way to a pedestrian crossing a roadway in a crosswalk if:

(1) no traffic control signal is in place or in operation; and

(2) the pedestrian is:

(A) on the half of the roadway in which the vehicle is traveling; or

(B) approaching so closely from the opposite half of the roadway as to be in danger.

(b) Notwithstanding Subsection (a), a pedestrian may not suddenly leave a curb or other place of safety and proceed into a crosswalk in the path of a vehicle so close that it is impossible for the vehicle operator to stop and yield.

(c) The operator of a vehicle approaching from the rear of a vehicle that is stopped at a crosswalk to permit a pedestrian to cross a roadway may not pass the stopped vehicle.

(d) If it is shown on the trial of an offense under Subsection (a) that as a result of the commission of the offense a collision occurred causing serious bodily injury or death to a visually impaired or disabled person, the offense is a misdemeanor punishable by:

(1) a fine of not more than $500; and

(2) 30 hours of community service to an organization or agency that primarily serves visually impaired or disabled persons, to be completed in not less than six months and not more than one year.

(d-1) A portion of the community service required under Subsection (d)(2) shall include sensitivity training.

(e) For the purposes of this section:

(1) "Visually impaired" has the meaning assigned by Section 91.002, Human Resources Code.

(2) "Disabled" means a person who cannot walk without the use or assistance of:

(A) a device, including a brace, cane, crutch, prosthesis, or wheelchair; or

(B) another person.

(f) If conduct constituting an offense under this section also constitutes an offense under another section of this code or the Penal Code, the actor may be prosecuted under either section or both sections.

Sec. 552.004. Pedestrian to Keep to Right.

A pedestrian shall proceed on the right half of a crosswalk if possible.

Sec. 552.005. Crossing at Point Other Than Crosswalk.

(a) A pedestrian shall yield the right-of-way to a vehicle on the highway if crossing a roadway at a place:

(1) other than in a marked crosswalk or in an unmarked crosswalk at an intersection; or

Transportation Code

(2) where a pedestrian tunnel or overhead pedestrian crossing has been provided.

(b) Between adjacent intersections at which traffic control signals are in operation, a pedestrian may cross only in a marked crosswalk.

(c) A pedestrian may cross a roadway intersection diagonally only if and in the manner authorized by a traffic control device.

Sec. 552.006. Use of Sidewalk.

(a) A pedestrian may not walk along and on a roadway if an adjacent sidewalk is provided and is accessible to the pedestrian.

(b) If a sidewalk is not provided, a pedestrian walking along and on a highway shall if possible walk on:

(1) the left side of the roadway; or

(2) the shoulder of the highway facing oncoming traffic.

(c) The operator of a vehicle emerging from or entering an alley, building, or private road or driveway shall stop and yield the right-of-way to a pedestrian approaching on a sidewalk extending across the alley, building entrance or exit, road, or driveway.

Sec. 552.007. Solicitation by Pedestrians.

(a) A person may not stand in a roadway to solicit a ride, contribution, employment, or business from an occupant of a vehicle, except that a person may stand in a roadway to solicit a charitable contribution if authorized to do so by the local authority having jurisdiction over the roadway.

(b) A person may not stand on or near a highway to solicit the watching or guarding of a vehicle parked or to be parked on the highway.

(c) In this section, "charitable contribution" means a contribution to an organization defined as charitable by the standards of the United States Internal Revenue Service.

Sec. 552.0071. Local Authorization for Solicitation by Pedestrian.

(a) A local authority shall grant authorization for a person to stand in a roadway to solicit a charitable contribution as provided by Section 552.007(a) if the persons to be engaged in the solicitation are employees or agents of the local authority and the other requirements of this section are met.

(b) A person seeking authorization under this section shall file a written application with the local authority not later than the 11th day before the date the solicitation is to begin. The application must include:

(1) the date or dates and times when the solicitation is to occur;

(2) each location at which solicitation is to occur; and

(3) the number of solicitors to be involved in solicitation at each location.

(c) This section does not prohibit a local authority from requiring a permit or the payment of reasonable fees to the local authority.

(d) The applicant shall also furnish to the local authority advance proof of liability insurance in the amount of at least $1 million to cover damages that may arise from the solicitation. The insurance must provide coverage against claims against the applicant and claims against the local authority.

(e) A local authority, by acting under this section or Section 552.007, does not waive or limit any immunity from liability applicable under law to the local authority. The issuance of an authorization under this section and the conducting of the solicitation authorized is a governmental function of the local authority.

(f) Notwithstanding any provision of this section, the existing rights of individuals or organizations under Section 552.007 are not impaired.

(g) For purposes of a solicitation under Subsection (a), a roadway is defined to include the roadbed, shoulder, median, curbs, safety zones, sidewalks, and utility easements located adjacent to or near the roadway.

Sec. 552.008. Drivers to Exercise Due Care.

Notwithstanding another provision of this chapter, the operator of a vehicle shall:

(1) exercise due care to avoid colliding with a pedestrian on a roadway;

(2) give warning by sounding the horn when necessary; and

(3) exercise proper precaution on observing a child or an obviously confused or incapacitated person on a roadway.

Sec. 552.009. Ordinances Relating to Pedestrians.

A local authority may by ordinance:

(1) require pedestrians to comply strictly with the directions of an official traffic control signal; and

(2) prohibit pedestrians from crossing a roadway in a business district or a designated highway except in a crosswalk.

Sec. 552.010. Blind Pedestrians.

(a) No person may carry a white cane on a public street or highway unless the person is totally or partially blind.

(b) The driver of a vehicle approaching an intersection or crosswalk where a pedestrian guided by an assistance animal or carrying a white cane is crossing or attempting to cross shall take necessary precautions to avoid injuring or endangering the pedestrian. The driver shall bring the vehicle to a full stop if injury or danger can be avoided only by that action.

(c) If it is shown on the trial of an offense under this section that as a result of the commission of the offense a collision occurred causing serious bodily injury or death to a blind person, the offense is a misdemeanor punishable by:

(1) a fine of not more than $500; and

(2) 30 hours of community service to an organization or agency that primarily serves visually impaired or disabled persons, to be completed in not less than six months and not more than one year.

(c-1) A portion of the community service required under Subsection (c)(2) shall include sensitivity training.

(d) For the purposes of this section:

(1) "Assistance animal" has the meaning assigned by Section 121.002, Human Resources Code.

(2) "White cane" has the meaning assigned by Section 121.002, Human Resources Code.

(e) If conduct constituting an offense under this section also constitutes an offense under another section of this code or the Penal Code, the actor may be prosecuted under either section or both sections.

Sec. 552.011. Train Occupying Crossing.

A pedestrian may not move in front of, under, between, or through the cars of a moving or stationary train occupying any part of a railroad grade crossing.

CHAPTER 552A DEVICES SUBJECT TO PEDESTRIAN LAWS

SUBCHAPTER A PERSONAL DELIVERY AND MOBILE CARRYING DEVICES

Sec. 552A.0001. Definitions.

In this subchapter:

(1) "Agent" has the meaning assigned by Section 7.21, Penal Code.

(2) "Business entity" means a legal entity, including a corporation, partnership, or sole proprietorship, that is formed for the purpose of making a profit.

(3) "Mobile carrying device" means a device that:

(A) transports cargo while remaining within 25 feet of a human operator; and

(B) is equipped with technology that allows the operator to actively monitor the device.

(4) "Pedestrian area" includes a sidewalk, crosswalk, school crosswalk, school crossing zone, or safety zone.

(5) "Personal delivery device" means a device that:

(A) is manufactured primarily for transporting cargo in a pedestrian area or on the side or shoulder of a highway; and

(B) is equipped with automated driving technology, including software and hardware, that enables the operation of the device with the remote support and supervision of a human.

Sec. 552A.0002. Applicable Law.

(a) The operation of a personal delivery or mobile carrying device in a pedestrian area or on the side or shoulder of a highway is governed exclusively by:

(1) this subchapter; and

(2) any applicable regulations adopted by a local authority that are not inconsistent with this subchapter, as authorized under Section 552A.0009.

(b) For the purposes of this title, including Section 545.422, a personal delivery or mobile carrying device operated in compliance with this subchapter is not considered to be a vehicle.

Sec. 552A.0003. Operator of Personal Delivery Device.

(a) A person may operate a personal delivery device under this subchapter only if:

(1) the person is a business entity; and

(2) a human who is an agent of the business entity has the capability to monitor or exercise physical control over the navigation and operation of the device.

(b) Except as provided by Subsection (c), when a personal delivery device operated by a business entity is engaged, the business entity is considered to be the operator of the device solely for the purpose of assessing compliance with applicable traffic laws.

(c) When a personal delivery device operated by a business entity is engaged and an agent of the entity controls the device in a manner that is outside the scope of the agent's office or employment, the agent is considered to be the operator of the device.

(d) A person is not considered to be the operator of a personal delivery device solely because the person:

(1) requests a delivery or service provided by the device; or

(2) dispatches the device.

Sec. 552A.0004. Operator of Mobile Carrying Device.

A person operating a mobile carrying device is considered to be the operator of the device for the purpose of assessing compliance with applicable traffic laws.

Sec. 552A.0005. Device Operation.

(a) A personal delivery or mobile carrying device operated under this subchapter must:

(1) operate in a manner that complies with the provisions of this subtitle applicable to pedestrians, unless the provision cannot by its nature apply to the device;

(2) yield the right-of-way to all other traffic, including pedestrians;

(3) not unreasonably interfere with or obstruct other traffic, including pedestrians;

(4) if operated at nighttime, display the lights required by Section 552A.0007 or 552A.0008, as applicable;

(5) comply with any applicable regulations adopted by a local authority under Section 552A.0009;

(6) not transport hazardous materials in a quantity requiring placarding by a regulation issued under the Hazardous Materials Transportation Act (49 U.S.C. Section 5101 et seq.); and

(7) be monitored or controlled as provided by Section 552A.0003(a) for a personal delivery device or by the operator for a mobile carrying device.

(b) A mobile carrying device operated under this subchapter must remain within 25 feet of the operator while the device is in motion.

Sec. 552A.0006. Areas and Speeds of Operation.

(a) A personal delivery or mobile carrying device operated under this subchapter may be operated only:

(1) in a pedestrian area at a speed of not more than 10 miles per hour; or

(2) on the side of a roadway or the shoulder of a highway at a speed of not more than 20 miles per hour.

(b) Notwithstanding Subsection (a)(1), a local authority may establish a maximum speed of less than 10 miles per hour in a pedestrian area in the jurisdiction of the local authority if the local authority determines that a maximum speed of 10 miles per hour is unreasonable or unsafe for that area. A maximum speed established under this subsection may not be less than seven miles per hour.

Sec. 552A.0007. Personal Delivery Device Equipment.

(a) A personal delivery device operated under this subchapter must:

(1) be equipped with a marker that clearly states the name and contact information of the owner and a unique identification number; and

(2) be equipped with a braking system that enables the device to come to a controlled stop.

(b) A personal delivery device operated under this subchapter at nighttime must be equipped with lights on the front and rear of the device that are visible and recognizable under normal atmospheric conditions on all sides of the device from 1 to 500 feet from the device when the light is directly in front of lawful lower beams of headlamps.

Sec. 552A.0008. Mobile Carrying Device Equipment.

(a) A mobile carrying device operated under this subchapter must be equipped with a braking system that enables the device to come to a controlled stop.

(b) A mobile carrying device operated under this subchapter at nighttime must be equipped with lights that are visible and recognizable under normal atmospheric conditions from 1 to 50 feet from the device when the light is directly in front of lawful lower beams of headlamps.

Sec. 552A.0009. Local Authority Regulation.

(a) A local authority may regulate the operation of a personal delivery or mobile carrying device on a highway or in a pedestrian area in a manner not inconsistent with this subchapter.

(b) This section does not affect the authority of a local authority's peace officers to enforce the laws of this state relating to the operation of a personal delivery or mobile carrying device.

Sec. 552A.0010. Insurance.

A business entity that operates a personal delivery device operated under this subchapter must maintain an insurance policy that includes general liability coverage of not less than $100,000 for damages arising from the operation of the device.

SUBCHAPTER B MOBILITY DEVICES

Sec. 552A.0101. Operators of Certain Mobility Devices.

(a) In this section, "motorized mobility device" means a device designed for transportation of persons with physical disabilities that:

(1) has three or more wheels;

(2) is propelled by a battery-powered motor;

(3) has not more than one forward gear; and

(4) is not capable of speeds exceeding eight miles per hour.

(b) For the purposes of this subtitle, a person operating a nonmotorized wheelchair or motorized mobility device is considered to be a pedestrian.

CHAPTER 553 ENACTMENT AND ENFORCEMENT OF CERTAIN TRAFFIC LAWS IN CERTAIN MUNICIPALITIES

Sec. 553.001. Applicability.

This chapter applies only to a municipality with a population of less than 2,500 in a county with a population of 250,000 or more.

Sec. 553.002. Traffic Signals or Signs in Municipality.

(a) A municipality may not enact an ordinance governing the erection or operation of a traffic signal or sign in the municipality on a state highway funded in whole or in part by the state without prior approval by the Texas Department of Transportation.

(b) A municipality intending to erect or operate a traffic signal or sign described by Subsection (a) must apply in writing to the Texas Department of Transportation. After the application is filed, the Texas Department of Transportation shall designate an employee to investigate the application and shall grant or refuse the application not later than the 90th day after the date of the designation.

(c) In granting an application, the Texas Department of Transportation:

(1) may prescribe the conditions under which the municipality may erect and operate the signal or sign and all other aspects of the signal or sign; and

(2) shall consider the convenience of the traveling public in raising speed limits in noncongested areas and the control of traffic for the protection of schoolchildren and other inhabitants of small communities where there are areas of congestion and cross-traffic.

(d) This section does not apply to an ordinance enacted or a temporary speed limit sign erected or operated under Section 545.3561.

Sec. 553.003. Injunction Against Unauthorized Signal or Sign.

(a) If a municipality erects or maintains a traffic signal or sign without meeting the requirements of this chapter, the district or county attorney of the county where the signal or sign is located shall bring a suit to enjoin the erection and maintenance of the signal or sign.

(b) If the district or county attorney does not institute a suit under Subsection (a) within 15 days after the date a request to do so is received from a resident of the state, any state resident may institute and prosecute the suit.

CHAPTER 600 MISCELLANEOUS PROVISIONS

Sec. 600.001. Removing Material from Highway.

(a) A person who drops or permits to be dropped or thrown on a highway destructive or injurious material shall immediately remove the material or cause it to be removed.

(b) A person who removes a wrecked or damaged vehicle from a highway shall remove glass or another injurious substance dropped on the highway from the vehicle.

Sec. 600.002. Identification Required for Vehicle Near Mexican Border.

On demand of a peace officer within 250 feet of the Mexican border at a checkpoint authorized by Section 411.0095, Government Code, as added by Chapter 497, Acts of the 73rd Legislature, Regular Session, 1993, the driver of a vehicle shall produce a driver's license and proof of compliance with Chapter 601.

Sec. 600.003. Enforcement of Certain Traffic Laws by Private Institutions of Higher Education.

(a) In this section, "private or independent institution of higher education" has the meaning assigned by Section 61.003(15), Education Code.

(b) A private or independent institution of higher education may enforce a traffic law of this state under Chapter 545 restricting or prohibiting the operation or movement of vehicles on a road of the institution if:

(1) the road of the institution is open to the public at the time the traffic law is enforced;

(2) the governing body of the institution adopts a regulation to enforce the traffic law; and

(3) the restriction or prohibition on the operation and movement of vehicles adopted by the institution:

(A) is posted by means of a sign, marking, signal, or other device visible to and, if it contains writing, able to be read by an operator of a vehicle to whom the restriction or prohibition applies in the same manner as a similar restriction or prohibition on the operation and movement of vehicles would be posted by a municipality; and

(B) has been approved by:

(i) the commissioners court of the county in which the applicable road of the institution is located, if the road is located in the unincorporated area of a county; or

(ii) the governing body of the municipality in which the applicable road of the institution is located, if the road is located in a municipality.

(c) Campus security personnel of the institution commissioned under Section 51.212, Education Code, are authorized to enforce the provisions of this section and have the authority to issue and use traffic tickets and summons in a form prescribed by the Texas Department of Public Safety to enforce this chapter only on the property of the institution that commissioned the campus security personnel under Section 51.212, Education Code.

(d) The same procedures that apply to a traffic ticket or summons by a commissioned peace officer of an institution of higher education under Sections 51.206 and 51.210, Education Code, also apply to a ticket or summons issued under this section.

(e) The governing body of the municipality or the commissioners court of the county that approves the enforcement of traffic laws under Subsection (b) shall also determine the disposition of funds collected under this section from any fees or fines from the enforcement of a traffic law of this state.

Sec. 600.004. Training of School Crossing Guard.

(a) A local authority may authorize a school crossing guard to direct traffic in a school crossing zone if the guard successfully completes a training program in traffic direction as defined by the basic peace officer course curriculum established by the Commission on Law Enforcement Standards and Education.

(b) A school crossing guard trained under this section:

(1) is not a peace officer; and

(2) may not carry a weapon while directing traffic in a school crossing zone.

SUBTITLE D MOTOR VEHICLE SAFETY RESPONSIBILITY

CHAPTER 601 MOTOR VEHICLE SAFETY RESPONSIBILITY ACT

SUBCHAPTER A GENERAL PROVISIONS

Sec. 601.001. Short Title.

This chapter may be cited as the Texas Motor Vehicle Safety Responsibility Act.

Sec. 601.002. Definitions.

In this chapter:

(1) "Department" means the Department of Public Safety.

(2) "Driver's license" has the meaning assigned by Section 521.001.

(3) "Financial responsibility" means the ability to respond in damages for liability for an accident that:

(A) occurs after the effective date of the document evidencing the establishment of the financial responsibility; and

(B) arises out of the ownership, maintenance, or use of a motor vehicle.

(4) "Highway" means the entire width between property lines of a road, street, or way in this state that is not privately owned or controlled and:

(A) some part of which is open to the public for vehicular traffic; and

(B) over which the state has legislative jurisdiction under its police power.

(5) "Motor vehicle" means a self-propelled vehicle designed for use on a highway, a trailer or

semitrailer designed for use with a self-propelled vehicle, or a vehicle propelled by electric power from overhead wires and not operated on rails. The term does not include:

(A) a traction engine;

(B) a road roller or grader;

(C) a tractor crane;

(D) a power shovel;

(E) a well driller;

(F) an implement of husbandry; or

(G) an electric personal assistive mobility device, as defined by Section 551.201.

(6) "Nonresident" means a person who is not a resident of this state.

(7) "Nonresident's operating privilege" means the privilege conferred on a nonresident by the laws of this state relating to the operation of a motor vehicle in this state by the nonresident or the use in this state of a motor vehicle owned by the nonresident.

(8) "Operator" means the person in actual physical control of a motor vehicle.

(9) "Owner" means:

(A) the person who holds legal title to a motor vehicle;

(B) the purchaser or lessee of a motor vehicle subject to an agreement for the conditional sale or lease of the vehicle, if the person has:

(i) the right to purchase the vehicle on performing conditions stated in the agreement; and

(ii) an immediate right to possess the vehicle; or

(C) a mortgagor of a motor vehicle who is entitled to possession of the vehicle.

(10) "Person" means an individual, firm, partnership, association, or corporation.

(11) "State" means:

(A) a state, territory, or possession of the United States; or

(B) the District of Columbia.

(12) "Vehicle registration" means:

(A) a registration certificate, registration receipt, or number plate issued under Chapter 502; or

(B) a dealer's license plate or temporary tag issued under Chapter 503.

Sec. 601.003. Judgment; Satisfied Judgment.

(a) For purposes of this chapter, judgment refers only to a final judgment that is no longer appealable or has been finally affirmed on appeal and that was rendered by a court of any state, a province of Canada, or the United States on a cause of action:

(1) for damages for bodily injury, death, or damage to or destruction of property arising out of the ownership, maintenance, or use of a motor vehicle; or

(2) on an agreement of settlement for damages for bodily injury, death, or damage to or destruction of property arising out of the ownership, maintenance, or use of a motor vehicle.

(b) For purposes of this chapter, a judgment is considered to be satisfied as to the appropriate part of the judgment set out by this subsection if:

(1) the total amount credited on one or more judgments for bodily injury to or death of one person resulting from one accident equals or exceeds the amount required under Section 601.072(a)(1) to establish financial responsibility;

(2) the total amount credited on one or more judgments for bodily injury to or death of two or more persons resulting from one accident equals or exceeds the amount required under Section 601.072(a)(2) to establish financial responsibility; or

(3) the total amount credited on one or more judgments for damage to or destruction of property of another resulting from one accident equals or exceeds the amount required under Section 601.072(a)(3) to establish financial responsibility.

(c) In determining whether a judgment is satisfied under Subsection (b), a payment made in settlement of a claim for damages for bodily injury, death, or damage to or destruction of property is considered to be an amount credited on a judgment.

(d) For purposes of this section:

(1) damages for bodily injury or death include damages for care and loss of services; and

(2) damages for damage to or destruction of property include damages for loss of use.

Sec. 601.004. Accident Report. [Repealed]

Sec. 601.005. Evidence in Civil Suit.

A person at a trial for damages may not refer to or offer as evidence of the negligence or due care of a party:

(1) an action taken by the department under this chapter;

(2) the findings on which that action is based; or

(3) the security or evidence of financial responsibility filed under this chapter.

Sec. 601.006. Applicability to Certain Owners and Operators.

If an owner or operator of a motor vehicle involved in an accident in this state does not have a driver's license or vehicle registration or is a nonresident, the person may not be issued a driver's

Transportation Code

license or registration until the person has complied with this chapter to the same extent that would be necessary if, at the time of the accident, the person had a driver's license or registration.

Sec. 601.007. Applicability of Chapter to Government Vehicles.

(a) This chapter does not apply to a government vehicle.

(b) The provisions of this chapter do not apply to an officer, agent, or employee of the United States, this state, or a political subdivision of this state while operating a government vehicle in the course of that person's employment.

(c) The provisions of this chapter, other than Section 601.054, do not apply to a motor vehicle that is subject to Chapter 643.

(d) In this section, "government vehicle" means a motor vehicle owned by the United States, this state, or a political subdivision of this state.

Sec. 601.008. Violation of Chapter; Offense.

(a) A person commits an offense if the person violates a provision of this chapter for which a penalty is not otherwise provided.

(b) An offense under this section is a misdemeanor punishable by:

(1) a fine not to exceed $500;

(2) confinement in county jail for a term not to exceed 90 days; or

(3) both the fine and the confinement.

Sec. 601.009. Report from Other State or Canada.

(a) On receipt of a certification by the department that the operating privilege of a resident of this state has been suspended or revoked in another state or a province of Canada under a financial responsibility law, the department shall contact the official who issued the certification to request information relating to the specific nature of the resident's failure to comply.

(b) Except as provided by Subsection (c), the department shall suspend the resident's driver's license and vehicle registrations if the evidence shows that the resident's operating privilege was suspended in the other state or the province for violation of a financial responsibility law under circumstances that would require the department to suspend a nonresident's operating privilege had the accident occurred in this state.

(c) The department may not suspend the resident's driver's license and registration if the alleged failure to comply is based on the failure of the resident's insurance company or surety company to:

(1) obtain authorization to write motor vehicle liability insurance in the other state or the province; or

(2) execute a power of attorney directing the appropriate official in the other state or the province to accept on the company's behalf service of notice or process in an action under the policy arising out of an accident.

(d) Suspension of a driver's license and vehicle registrations under this section continues until the resident furnishes evidence of compliance with the financial responsibility law of the other state or the province.

(e) In this section, "financial responsibility law" means a law authorizing suspension or revocation of an operating privilege for failure to:

(1) deposit security for the payment of a judgment;

(2) satisfy a judgment; or

(3) file evidence of financial responsibility.

SUBCHAPTER B ADMINISTRATION BY DEPARTMENT

Sec. 601.021. Department Powers and Duties; Rules.

The department shall:

(1) administer and enforce this chapter; and

(2) provide for hearings on the request of a person aggrieved by an act of the department under this chapter.

Sec. 601.022. Department to Provide Operating Record [Repealed].

Repealed by Acts 2003, 78th Leg., ch. 991 (S.B. 1904), § 14(3), effective September 1, 2003.

Sec. 601.023. Payment of Statutory Fees.

The department may pay:

(1) a statutory fee required by the Texas Department of Motor Vehicles for a certified abstract or in connection with suspension of a vehicle registration; or

(2) a statutory fee payable to the comptroller for issuance of a certificate of deposit required by Section 601.122.

SUBCHAPTER C FINANCIAL RESPONSIBILITY; REQUIREMENTS

Sec. 601.051. Requirement of Financial Responsibility.

A person may not operate a motor vehicle in this state unless financial responsibility is established for that vehicle through:

(1) a motor vehicle liability insurance policy that complies with Subchapter D;

(2) a surety bond filed under Section 601.121;

(3) a deposit under Section 601.122;

(4) a deposit under Section 601.123; or

(5) self-insurance under Section 601.124.

Sec. 601.052. Exceptions to Financial Responsibility Requirement.

(a) Section 601.051 does not apply to:

(1) the operation of a motor vehicle that:

(A) is a former military vehicle or is at least 25 years old;

(B) is used only for exhibitions, club activities, parades, and other functions of public interest and not for regular transportation; and

(C) for which the owner files with the department an affidavit, signed by the owner, stating that the vehicle is a collector's item and used only as described by Paragraph (B);

(2) a neighborhood electric vehicle that is operated only as authorized by Section 551.304;

(2-a) a golf cart that is operated only as authorized by Section 551.403;

(2-b) an off-highway vehicle that is operated only as authorized by Subchapter C, Chapter 551A, or Section 551A.055 of this code or Chapter 29, Parks and Wildlife Code; or

(3) a volunteer fire department for the operation of a motor vehicle the title of which is held in the name of a volunteer fire department.

(b) Subsection (a)(3) does not exempt from the requirement of Section 601.051 a person who is operating a vehicle described by that subsection.

(c) In this section:

(1) "Former military vehicle" has the meaning assigned by Section 504.502(i).

(2) "Volunteer fire department" means a company, department, or association that is:

(A) organized in an unincorporated area to answer fire alarms and extinguish fires or to answer fire alarms, extinguish fires, and provide emergency medical services; and

(B) composed of members who:

(i) do not receive compensation; or

(ii) receive only nominal compensation.

Sec. 601.053. Evidence of Financial Responsibility.

(a) As a condition of operating in this state a motor vehicle to which Section 601.051 applies, the operator of the vehicle on request shall provide to a peace officer, as defined by Article 2.12, Code of Criminal Procedure, or a person involved in an accident with the operator evidence of financial responsibility by exhibiting:

(1) a motor vehicle liability insurance policy covering the vehicle that satisfies Subchapter D or a photocopy of the policy;

(2) a standard proof of motor vehicle liability insurance form prescribed by the Texas Department of Insurance under Section 601.081 and issued by a liability insurer for the motor vehicle;

(2-a) an image displayed on a wireless communication device that includes the information required by Section 601.081 as provided by a liability insurer;

(3) an insurance binder that confirms the operator is in compliance with this chapter;

(4) a surety bond certificate issued under Section 601.121;

(5) a certificate of a deposit with the comptroller covering the vehicle issued under Section 601.122;

(6) a copy of a certificate of a deposit with the appropriate county judge covering the vehicle issued under Section 601.123; or

(7) a certificate of self-insurance covering the vehicle issued under Section 601.124 or a photocopy of the certificate.

(b) Except as provided by Subsection (c), an operator who does not exhibit evidence of financial responsibility under Subsection (a) is presumed to have operated the vehicle in violation of Section 601.051.

(c) Subsection (b) does not apply if the peace officer determines through use of the verification program established under Subchapter N that financial responsibility has been established for the vehicle. A peace officer may not issue a citation for an offense under Section 601.191 unless the officer attempts to verify through the verification program that financial responsibility has been established for the vehicle and is unable to make that verification.

(d) The display of an image that includes financial responsibility information on a wireless communication device under Subsection (a)(2-a) does not constitute effective consent for a law enforcement officer, or any other person, to access the contents of the wireless communication device except to view the financial responsibility information.

(e) The authorization of the use of a wireless communication device to display financial responsibility information under Subsection (a)(2-a) does not prevent:

(1) a court of competent jurisdiction from requiring a person to provide a paper copy of the person's evidence of financial responsibility in a hearing or trial or in connection with discovery proceedings; or

(2) the commissioner of insurance from requiring a person to provide a paper copy of the person's evidence of financial responsibility in connection with any inquiry or transaction conducted by or on behalf of the commissioner.

(f) A telecommunications provider, as defined by Section 51.002, Utilities Code, may not be held liable to the operator of the motor vehicle for the failure of a wireless communication device to display financial responsibility information under Subsection (a)(2-a).

Sec. 601.054. Owner May Provide Evidence of Financial Responsibility for Others.

(a) The department shall accept evidence of financial responsibility from an owner for another person required to establish evidence of financial responsibility if the other person is:

(1) an operator employed by the owner; or

(2) a member of the owner's immediate family or household.

(b) The evidence of financial responsibility applies to a person who becomes subject to Subsection (a)(1) or (2) after the effective date of that evidence.

(c) Evidence of financial responsibility accepted by the department under Subsection (a) is a substitute for evidence by the other person and permits the other person to operate a motor vehicle for which the owner has provided evidence of financial responsibility.

(d) The department shall designate the restrictions imposed by this section on the face of the other person's driver's license.

Sec. 601.055. Substitution of Evidence of Financial Responsibility.

(a) If a person who has filed evidence of financial responsibility substitutes other evidence of financial responsibility that complies with this chapter, and the department accepts the other evidence, the department shall:

(1) consent to the cancellation of a bond or certificate of insurance filed as evidence of financial responsibility; or

(2) direct the comptroller to return money or securities deposited with the comptroller as evidence of financial responsibility to the person entitled to the return of the money or securities.

(b) The comptroller shall return money or securities deposited with the comptroller in accordance with the direction of the department under Subsection (a)(2).

Sec. 601.056. Cancellation, Return, or Waiver of Evidence of Financial Responsibility.

(a) As provided by this section, the department, on request, shall:

(1) consent to the cancellation of a bond or certificate of insurance filed as evidence of financial responsibility;

(2) direct the comptroller to return money or securities deposited with the comptroller as evidence of financial responsibility to the person entitled to the return of the money or securities; or

(3) waive the requirement of filing evidence of financial responsibility.

(b) Evidence of financial responsibility may be canceled, returned, or waived under Subsection (a) if:

(1) the department, during the two years preceding the request, has not received a record of a conviction or a forfeiture of bail that would require or permit the suspension or revocation of the driver's license, vehicle registration, or nonresident's operating privilege of the person by or for whom the evidence was provided;

(2) the person for whom the evidence of financial responsibility was provided dies or has a permanent incapacity to operate a motor vehicle; or

(3) the person for whom the evidence of financial responsibility was provided surrenders the person's license and vehicle registration to the department.

(c) A cancellation, return, or waiver under Subsection (b)(1) may be made only after the second anniversary of the date the evidence of financial responsibility was required.

(d) The comptroller shall return the money or securities as directed by the department under Subsection (a)(2).

(e) The department may not act under Subsection (a)(1) or (2) if:

(1) an action for damages on a liability covered by the evidence of financial responsibility is pending;

(2) a judgment for damages on a liability covered by the evidence of financial responsibility is not satisfied; or

Transportation Code

(3) the person for whom the bond has been filed or for whom money or securities have been deposited has, within the two years preceding the request for cancellation or return of the evidence of financial responsibility, been involved as an operator or owner in a motor vehicle accident resulting in bodily injury to, or property damage to the property of, another person.

(f) In the absence of evidence to the contrary in the records of the department, the department shall accept as sufficient an affidavit of the person requesting action under Subsection (a) stating that:

(1) the facts described by Subsection (e) do not exist; or

(2) the person has been released from the liability or has been finally adjudicated as not liable for bodily injury or property damage described by Subsection (e)(3).

(g) A person whose evidence of financial responsibility has been canceled or returned under Subsection (b)(3) may not be issued a new driver's license or vehicle registration unless the person establishes financial responsibility for the remainder of the two-year period beginning on the date the evidence of financial responsibility was required.

Sec. 601.057. Evidence That Does Not Fulfill Requirements; Suspension.

If evidence filed with the department does not continue to fulfill the purpose for which it was required, the department shall suspend the driver's license and all vehicle registrations or nonresident's operating privilege of the person who filed the evidence pending the filing of other evidence of financial responsibility.

SUBCHAPTER D ESTABLISHMENT OF FINANCIAL RESPONSIBILITY THROUGH MOTOR VEHICLE LIABILITY INSURANCE

Sec. 601.071. Motor Vehicle Liability Insurance; Requirements.

For purposes of this chapter, a motor vehicle liability insurance policy must be an owner's or operator's policy that:

(1) except as provided by Section 601.083, is issued by an insurance company authorized to write motor vehicle liability insurance in this state;

(2) is written to or for the benefit of the person named in the policy as the insured; and

(3) meets the requirements of this subchapter.

Sec. 601.072. Minimum Coverage Amounts; Exclusions.

(a) [Expired pursuant to Acts 2007, 80th Leg., ch. 1298 (S.B. 502), § 1, effective December 31, 2010.]

(a-1) Effective January 1, 2011, the minimum amounts of motor vehicle liability insurance coverage required to establish financial responsibility under this chapter are:

(1) $30,000 for bodily injury to or death of one person in one accident;

(2) $60,000 for bodily injury to or death of two or more persons in one accident, subject to the amount provided by Subdivision (1) for bodily injury to or death of one of the persons; and

(3) $25,000 for damage to or destruction of property of others in one accident.

(b) The coverage required under this section may exclude, with respect to one accident:

(1) the first $250 of liability for bodily injury to or death of one person;

(2) the first $500 of liability for bodily injury to or death of two or more persons, subject to the amount provided by Subdivision (1) for bodily injury to or death of one of the persons; and

(3) the first $250 of liability for property damage to or destruction of property of others.

(c) The Texas Department of Insurance shall establish an outreach program to inform persons of the requirements of this chapter and the ability to comply with the financial responsibility requirements of this chapter through motor vehicle liability insurance coverage. The commissioner, by rule, shall establish the requirements for the program. The program must be designed to encourage compliance with the financial responsibility requirements, and must be made available in English and Spanish.

(d) [Expired pursuant to Acts 2007, 80th Leg., ch. 1298 (S.B. 502), § 1, effective December 31, 2010.]

Sec. 601.073. Required Policy Terms.

(a) A motor vehicle liability insurance policy must state:

(1) the name and address of the named insured;

(2) the coverage provided under the policy;

(3) the premium charged for the policy;

(4) the policy period; and

(5) the limits of liability.

(b) The policy must contain an agreement or endorsement that the insurance coverage provided under the policy is:

(1) provided in accordance with the coverage required by this chapter for bodily injury, death, and property damage; and

(2) subject to this chapter.

(c) The liability of the insurance company for the insurance required by this chapter becomes absolute at the time bodily injury, death, or damage covered by the policy occurs. The policy may not be canceled as to this liability by an agreement between the insurance company and the insured that is entered into after the occurrence of the injury or damage. A statement made by or on behalf of the insured or a violation of the policy does not void the policy.

(d) The policy may not require the insured to satisfy a judgment for bodily injury, death, or property damage as a condition precedent under the policy to the right or duty of the insurance company to make payment for the injury, death, or damage.

(e) The insurance company may settle a claim covered by the policy. If the settlement is made in good faith, the amount of the settlement is deductible from the amounts specified in Section 601.072.

(f) The policy, any written application for the policy, and any rider or endorsement that does not conflict with this chapter constitute the entire contract between the parties.

(g) Subsections (c)—(f) apply to the policy without regard to whether those provisions are stated in the policy.

Sec. 601.074. Optional Terms.

(a) A motor vehicle liability insurance policy may provide that the insured shall reimburse the insurance company for a payment that, in the absence of this chapter, the insurance company would not have been obligated to make under the terms of the policy.

(b) A policy may allow prorating of the insurance provided under the policy with other collectible insurance.

Sec. 601.075. Prohibited Terms.

A motor vehicle liability insurance policy may not insure against liability:

(1) for which the insured or the insured's insurer may be held liable under a workers' compensation law;

(2) for bodily injury to or death of an employee of the insured while engaged in the employment, other than domestic, of the insured, or in domestic employment if benefits for the injury are payable or required to be provided under a workers' compensation law; or

(3) for injury to or destruction of property owned by, rented to, in the care of, or transported by the insured.

Sec. 601.076. Required Terms: Owner's Policy.

An owner's motor vehicle liability insurance policy must:

(1) cover each motor vehicle for which coverage is to be granted under the policy; and

(2) pay, on behalf of the named insured or another person who, as insured, uses a covered motor vehicle with the express or implied permission of the named insured, amounts the insured becomes obligated to pay as damages arising out of the ownership, maintenance, or use of the motor vehicle in the United States or Canada, subject to the amounts, excluding interest and costs, and exclusions of Section 601.072.

Sec. 601.077. Required Terms: Operator's Policy.

An operator's motor vehicle liability insurance policy must pay, on behalf of the named insured, amounts the insured becomes obligated to pay as damages arising out of the use by the insured of a motor vehicle the insured does not own, subject to the same territorial limits, payment limits, and exclusions as for an owner's policy under Section 601.076.

Sec. 601.078. Additional Coverage.

(a) An insurance policy that provides the coverage required for a motor vehicle liability insurance policy may also provide lawful coverage in excess of or in addition to the required coverage.

(b) The excess or additional coverage is not subject to this chapter.

(c) In the case of a policy that provides excess or additional coverage, the term "motor vehicle liability insurance policy" applies only to that part of the coverage that is required under this subchapter.

Sec. 601.079. Multiple Policies.

The requirements for a motor vehicle liability insurance policy may be satisfied by a combination of policies of one or more insurance companies if the policies in combination meet the requirements.

Sec. 601.080. Insurance Binder.

A binder issued pending the issuance of a motor vehicle liability insurance policy satisfies the requirements for such a policy.

Sec. 601.081. Standard Proof of Motor Vehicle Liability Insurance Form.

(a) [Repealed.]

(b) A standard proof of motor vehicle liability insurance form prescribed by the Texas Department of Insurance must include:

(1) the name of the insurer;

(2) the insurance policy number;

(3) the policy period;

(4) the name and address of each insured;

(5) the policy limits or a statement that the coverage of the policy complies with the minimum amounts of motor vehicle liability insurance required by this chapter; and

(6) the make and model of each covered vehicle.

Sec. 601.082. Motor Vehicle Liability Insurance; Certification.

If evidence of financial responsibility is required to be filed with the department under this chapter, a motor vehicle liability insurance policy that is to be used as evidence must be certified under Section 601.083 or 601.084.

Sec. 601.083. Certificate of Motor Vehicle Liability Insurance.

(a) A person may provide evidence of financial responsibility by filing with the department the certificate of an insurance company authorized to write motor vehicle liability insurance in this state certifying that a motor vehicle liability insurance policy for the benefit of the person required to provide evidence of financial responsibility is in effect.

(b) The certificate must state the effective date of the policy, which must be the same date as the effective date of the certificate.

(c) The certificate must cover each motor vehicle owned by the person required to provide the evidence of financial responsibility, unless the policy is issued to a person who does not own a motor vehicle.

(d) A motor vehicle may not be registered in the name of a person required to provide evidence of financial responsibility unless the vehicle is covered by a certificate.

(e) If a person files a certificate of insurance to establish financial responsibility under Section 601.153, the certificate must state that the requirements of Section 601.153(b) are satisfied.

Sec. 601.084. Nonresident Certificate.

(a) Subject to Subsection (c), a nonresident owner of a motor vehicle that is not registered in this state may provide evidence of financial responsibility by filing with the department the certificate of an insurance company authorized to transact business in the state in which the vehicle is registered certifying that a motor vehicle liability insurance policy for the benefit of the person required to provide evidence of financial responsibility is in effect.

(b) Subject to Subsection (c), a nonresident who does not own a motor vehicle may provide evidence of financial responsibility by filing with the department the certificate of an insurance company authorized to transact business in the state in which the nonresident resides.

(c) The department shall accept the certificate of an insurer not authorized to transact business in this state if the certificate otherwise complies with this chapter and the insurance company:

(1) executes a power of attorney authorizing the department to accept on its behalf service of notice or process in an action arising out of a motor vehicle accident in this state; and

(2) agrees in writing that its policies will be treated as conforming to the laws of this state relating to the terms of a motor vehicle liability insurance policy.

(d) The department may not accept a certificate of an insurance company not authorized to transact business in this state during the period that the company is in default in any undertaking or agreement under this section.

Sec. 601.085. Termination of Certified Policy.

(a) If an insurer has certified a policy under Section 601.083 or 601.084, the policy may not be terminated before the sixth day after the date a notice of the termination is received by the department except as provided by Subsection (b).

(b) A policy that is obtained and certified terminates a previously certified policy on the effective date of the certification of a subsequent policy.

Sec. 601.086. Response of Insurance Company If Policy Not in Effect.

An insurance company that is notified by the department of an accident in connection with which an owner or operator has reported a motor vehicle liability insurance policy with the company shall advise the department if a policy is not in effect as reported.

Sec. 601.087. Governmental Record: Unauthorized Certificate or Form [Repealed].

Repealed by Acts 1999, 76th Leg., ch. 659 (H.B. 319), § 4, effective September 1, 1999.

Transportation Code

Sec. 601.088. Effect on Certain Other Policies.

(a) This chapter does not apply to or affect a policy of motor vehicle liability insurance required by another law of this state. If that policy contains an agreement or is endorsed to conform to the requirements of this chapter, the policy may be certified as evidence of financial responsibility under this chapter.

(b) This chapter does not apply to or affect a policy that insures only the named insured against liability resulting from the maintenance or use of a motor vehicle that is not owned by the insured by persons who are:

(1) employed by the insured; or

(2) acting on the insured's behalf.

SUBCHAPTER E ALTERNATIVE METHODS OF ESTABLISHING FINANCIAL RESPONSIBILITY

Sec. 601.121. Surety Bond.

(a) A person may establish financial responsibility by filing with the department a bond:

(1) with at least two individual sureties, each of whom owns real property in this state that is not exempt from execution under the constitution or laws of this state;

(2) conditioned for payment in the amounts and under the same circumstances as required under a motor vehicle liability insurance policy;

(3) that is not cancelable before the sixth day after the date the department receives written notice of the cancellation;

(4) accompanied by the fee required by Subsection (e); and

(5) approved by the department.

(b) The real property required by Subsection (a)(1) must be described in the bond approved by a judge of a court of record. The assessor-collector of the county in which the property is located must certify the property as free of any tax lien. The sureties in combination must have equity in the property in an amount equal to at least twice the amount of the bond.

(c) The bond is a lien in favor of the state on the real property described in the bond. The lien exists in favor of a person who holds a final judgment against the person who filed the bond.

(d) On filing of a bond, the department shall issue to the person who filed the bond a certificate of compliance with this section.

(e) The department shall file notice of the bond in the office of the county clerk of the county in which the real property is located. The notice must include a description of the property described in the bond. The county clerk or the county clerk's deputy, on receipt of the notice, shall acknowledge the notice and record it in the lien records. The recording of the notice is notice in accordance with statutes governing the recordation of a lien on real property.

(f) If a judgment rendered against the person who files a bond under this section is not satisfied before the 61st day after the date the judgment becomes final, the judgment creditor, for the judgment creditor's own use and benefit and at the judgment creditor's expense, may bring an action in the name of the state against the sureties on the bond, including an action to foreclose a lien on the real property of a surety. The foreclosure action must be brought in the same manner as, and is subject to the law applicable to, an action to foreclose a mortgage on real property.

(g) Cancellation of a bond filed under this section does not prevent recovery for a right or cause of action arising before the date of the cancellation.

Sec. 601.122. Deposit of Cash or Securities with Comptroller.

(a) A person may establish financial responsibility by depositing $55,000 with the comptroller in:

(1) cash; or

(2) securities that:

(A) are of the type that may legally be purchased by savings banks or trust funds; and

(B) have a market value equal to the required amount.

(b) On receipt of the deposit, the comptroller shall issue to the person making the deposit a certificate stating that a deposit complying with this section has been made.

(c) The comptroller may not accept the deposit and the department may not accept the certificate unless the deposit or certificate is accompanied by evidence that an unsatisfied judgment of any character against the person making the deposit does not exist in the county in which the person making the deposit resides.

(d) The comptroller shall hold a deposit made under this section to satisfy, in accordance with this chapter, an execution on a judgment issued against the person making the deposit for damages that:

(1) result from the ownership, maintenance, use, or operation of a motor vehicle after the date the deposit was made; and

(2) are for:

Transportation Code

(A) bodily injury to or death of any person, including damages for care and loss of services; or

(B) damage to or destruction of property, including the loss of use of the property.

(e) Money or securities deposited under this section are not subject to attachment or execution unless the attachment or execution arises out of a suit for damages described by Subsection (d).

Sec. 601.123. Deposit of Cash or Cashier's Check with County Judge.

(a) A person may establish financial responsibility by making a deposit with the county judge of the county in which the motor vehicle is registered.

(b) The deposit must be made in cash or a cashier's check in the amount of at least $55,000.

(c) On receipt of the deposit, the county judge shall issue to the person making the deposit a certificate stating that a deposit complying with this section has been made. The certificate must be acknowledged by the sheriff of that county and filed with the department.

Sec. 601.124. Self-Insurance.

(a) A person in whose name more than 25 motor vehicles are registered may qualify as a self-insurer by obtaining a certificate of self-insurance issued by the department as provided by this section.

(b) The department may issue a certificate of self-insurance to a person if:

(1) the person applies for the certificate; and

(2) the department is satisfied that the person has and will continue to have the ability to pay judgments obtained against the person.

(c) The self-insurer must supplement the certificate with an agreement that, for accidents occurring while the certificate is in force, the self-insurer will pay the same judgments in the same amounts as an insurer would be obligated to pay under an owner's motor vehicle liability insurance policy issued to the self-insurer if such policy were issued.

(d) The department for cause may cancel a certificate of self-insurance after a hearing. Cause includes failure to pay a judgment before the 31st day after the date the judgment becomes final.

(e) A self-insurer must receive at least five days' notice of a hearing held under Subsection (d). The department shall send notice of the hearing to the self-insurer by:

(1) first class mail; or

(2) e-mail if the self-insurer has provided an e-mail address to the department and has elected to receive notice electronically.

SUBCHAPTER F SECURITY FOLLOWING ACCIDENT

Sec. 601.151. Applicability of Subchapter.

(a) This subchapter applies only to a motor vehicle accident in this state that results in bodily injury or death or in damage to the property of one person of at least $1,000.

(b) This subchapter does not apply to:

(1) an owner or operator who has in effect at the time of the accident a motor vehicle liability insurance policy that covers the motor vehicle involved in the accident;

(2) an operator who is not the owner of the motor vehicle, if a motor vehicle liability insurance policy or bond for the operation of a motor vehicle the person does not own is in effect at the time of the accident;

(3) an owner or operator whose liability for damages resulting from the accident, in the judgment of the department, is covered by another liability insurance policy or bond;

(4) an owner or operator, if there was not bodily injury to or damage of the property of a person other than the owner or operator;

(5) the owner or operator of a motor vehicle that at the time of the accident was legally parked or legally stopped at a traffic signal;

(6) the owner of a motor vehicle that at the time of the accident was being operated without the owner's express or implied permission or was parked by a person who had been operating the vehicle without that permission; or

(7) a person qualifying as a self-insurer under Section 601.124 or a person operating a motor vehicle for a self-insurer.

Sec. 601.152. Suspension of Driver's License and Vehicle Registration or Privilege.

(a) Subject to Section 601.153, the department shall suspend the driver's license and vehicle registrations of the owner and operator of a motor vehicle if:

(1) the vehicle is involved in any manner in an accident; and

(2) the department finds that there is a reasonable probability that a judgment will be rendered against the person as a result of the accident.

(b) If the owner or operator is a nonresident, the department shall suspend the person's nonresident operating privilege and the privilege of use of any motor vehicle owned by the nonresident.

Sec. 601.153. Deposit of Security; Evidence of Financial Responsibility.

(a) The department may not suspend a driver's license, vehicle registration, or nonresident's privilege under this subchapter if the owner or operator:

(1) deposits with the department security in an amount determined to be sufficient under Section 601.154 or 601.157 as appropriate; and

(2) files evidence of financial responsibility as required by this chapter.

(b) If the owner or operator chooses to establish financial responsibility under Subsection (a)(2) by filing evidence of motor vehicle liability insurance, the owner or operator must file a certificate of insurance for a policy that has a policy period of at least six months and for which the premium for the entire policy period is paid in full.

(c) Notwithstanding Section 601.085, coverage for a motor vehicle under a motor vehicle liability policy for which a person files with the department a certificate of insurance under Subsection (b) may not be canceled unless:

(1) the person no longer owns the motor vehicle;

(2) the person dies;

(3) the person has a permanent incapacity that renders the person unable to drive the motor vehicle; or

(4) the person surrenders to the department the person's driver's license and the vehicle registration for the motor vehicle.

Sec. 601.154. Department Determination of Probability of Liability.

(a) Subject to Subsection (d), if the department finds that there is a reasonable probability that a judgment will be rendered against an owner or operator as a result of an accident, the department shall determine the amount of security sufficient to satisfy any judgment for damages resulting from the accident that may be recovered from the owner or operator.

(b) The department may not require security in an amount:

(1) less than $1,000; or

(2) more than the limits prescribed by Section 601.072.

(c) In determining whether there is a reasonable probability that a judgment will be rendered against the person as a result of an accident and the amount of security that is sufficient under Subsection (a), the department may consider:

(1) a report of an investigating officer; and

(2) an affidavit of a person who has knowledge of the facts.

(d) The department shall make the determination required by Subsection (a) only if the department has not received, before the 21st day after the date the department receives a report of a motor vehicle accident, satisfactory evidence that the owner or operator has:

(1) been released from liability;

(2) been finally adjudicated not to be liable; or

(3) executed an acknowledged written agreement providing for the payment of an agreed amount in installments for all claims for injuries or damages resulting from the accident.

Sec. 601.155. Notice of Determination.

(a) The department shall notify the affected person of a determination made under Section 601.154 by:

(1) personal service;

(2) first class mail; or

(3) e-mail if the person has provided an e-mail address to the department and has elected to receive notice electronically.

(b) The notice must state that:

(1) the person's driver's license and vehicle registration or the person's nonresident's operating privilege will be suspended unless the person, not later than the 20th day after the date the notice was personally served or sent, establishes that:

(A) this subchapter does not apply to the person, and the person has previously provided this information to the department; or

(B) there is no reasonable probability that a judgment will be rendered against the person as a result of the accident; and

(2) the person is entitled to a hearing under this subchapter if a written request for a hearing is delivered or mailed to the department not later than the 20th day after the date the notice was personally served or sent.

(c) Notice under this section that is mailed by first class mail must be mailed to the person's last known address, as shown by the department's records.

(d) For purposes of this section, notice is presumed to be received if the notice was sent to the person's last known address or e-mail address, as shown by the department's records.

Sec. 601.156. Setting of Hearing.

(a) A hearing under this subchapter is subject to the notice and hearing procedures of Sections 521.295—521.303 and shall be heard by a judge of a municipal court or a justice of the peace of the county in which the person requesting the hearing resides. A party is not entitled to a jury.

Transportation Code

(b) The court shall set a date for the hearing. The hearing must be held at the earliest practical time after notice is given to the person requesting the hearing.

(c) The department shall summon the person requesting the hearing to appear at the hearing. Notice under this subsection:

(1) shall be:

(A) delivered through personal service;

(B) mailed by first class mail to the person's last known address, as shown by the department's records; or

(C) sent by e-mail if the person has provided an e-mail address to the department and has elected to receive notice electronically; and

(2) must include written charges issued by the department.

Sec. 601.157. Hearing Procedures.

(a) The judge may administer oaths and issue subpoenas for the attendance of witnesses and the production of relevant books and papers.

(b) The judge at the hearing shall determine:

(1) whether there is a reasonable probability that a judgment will be rendered against the person requesting the hearing as a result of the accident; and

(2) if there is a reasonable probability that a judgment will be rendered, the amount of security sufficient to satisfy any judgment for damages resulting from the accident.

(c) The amount of security under Subsection (b)(2) may not be less than the amount specified as a minimum by Section 601.154.

(d) The judge shall report the judge's determination to the department.

(e) The judge may receive a fee to be paid from the general revenue fund of the county for holding a hearing under this subchapter. The fee must be approved by the commissioners court of the county and may not be more than $5 for each hearing.

Sec. 601.158. Appeal.

(a) If, after a hearing under this subchapter, the judge determines that there is a reasonable probability that a judgment will be rendered against the person requesting the hearing as a result of the accident, the person may appeal the determination.

(b) To appeal a determination under Subsection (a), the person must file a petition not later than the 30th day after the date of the determination in the county court at law of the county in which the person resides, or, if there is no county court at law, in the county court of the county.

(c) A person who files an appeal under this section shall send a file-stamped copy of the petition by certified mail to the department at the department's headquarters in Austin. The copy must be certified by the clerk of the court in which the petition is filed.

(d) The filing of a petition of appeal as provided by this section stays an order of suspension until the earlier of the 91st day after the date the appeal petition is filed or the date the trial is completed and final judgment is rendered.

(e) On expiration of the stay, the department shall impose the suspension. The stay may not be extended, and an additional stay may not be granted.

(f) A trial on appeal is de novo.

Sec. 601.159. Procedures for Suspension of Driver's License and Vehicle Registration or Privilege.

The department shall suspend the driver's license and each vehicle registration of an owner or operator or the nonresident's operating privilege of an owner or operator unless:

(1) if a hearing is not requested, the person, not later than the 20th day after the date the notice under Section 601.155 was personally served or sent:

(A) delivers or mails to the department a written request for a hearing;

(B) shows that this subchapter does not apply to the person; or

(C) complies with Section 601.153; or

(2) the person complies with Section 601.153 not later than the 20th day after:

(A) the date of the expiration of the period in which an appeal may be brought, if the determination at a hearing is rendered against the owner or operator and the owner or operator does not appeal; or

(B) the date of a decision against the person following the appeal.

Sec. 601.160. Suspension Stayed Pending Hearing or Appeal.

The department may not suspend a driver's license, vehicle registration, or nonresident's operating privilege pending the outcome of a hearing and any appeal under this subchapter.

Sec. 601.161. Notice of Suspension.

Not later than the 11th day before the effective date of a suspension under Section 601.159, the department shall send notice of the suspension to each affected owner or operator. The department shall send the notice by first class mail or by e-mail to any owner or operator who has provided an e-mail address to the department and who has elected to receive notice electronically. The notice must state the amount required as security under Section 601.153 and the necessity for the owner or operator to file evidence of financial responsibility with the department.

Sec. 601.162. Duration of Suspension.

(a) The suspension of a driver's license, vehicle registration, or nonresident's operating privilege under this subchapter remains in effect, the license, registration, or privilege may not be renewed, and a license or vehicle registration may not be issued to the holder of the suspended license, registration, or privilege, until:

(1) the date the person, or a person acting on the person's behalf, deposits security and files evidence of financial responsibility under Section 601.153;

(2) the second anniversary of the date of the accident, if evidence satisfactory to the department is filed with the department that, during the two-year period, an action for damages arising out of the accident has not been instituted; or

(3) the date evidence satisfactory to the department is filed with the department of:

(A) a release from liability for claims arising out of the accident;

(B) a final adjudication that the person is not liable for claims arising out of the accident; or

(C) an installment agreement described by Section 601.154(d)(3).

(b) If a suspension is terminated under Subsection (a)(3)(C), on notice of a default in the payment of an installment under the agreement, the department shall promptly suspend the driver's license and vehicle registration or nonresident's operating privilege of the person defaulting. A suspension under this subsection continues until:

(1) the person deposits and maintains security in accordance with Section 601.153 in an amount determined by the department at the time of suspension under this subsection and files evidence of financial responsibility in accordance with Section 601.153; or

(2) the second anniversary of the date security was required under Subdivision (1) if, during that period, an action on the agreement has not been instituted in a court in this state.

Sec. 601.163. Form of Security.

(a) The security required under this subchapter shall be made:

(1) by cash deposit;

(2) through a bond that complies with Section 601.168; or

(3) in another form as required by the department.

(b) A person depositing security shall specify in writing the person on whose behalf the deposit is made. A single deposit of security is applicable only on behalf of persons required to provide security because of the same accident and the same motor vehicle.

(c) The person depositing the security may amend in writing the specification of the person on whose behalf the deposit is made to include an additional person. This amendment may be made at any time the deposit is in the custody of the department or the comptroller.

Sec. 601.164. Reduction in Security.

(a) The department may reduce the amount of security ordered in a case within six months after the date of the accident if, in the department's judgment, the amount is excessive.

(b) The amount of security originally deposited that exceeds the reduced amount shall be returned promptly to the depositor or the depositor's personal representative.

Sec. 601.165. Custody of Cash Security.

The department shall place cash deposited in compliance with this subchapter in the custody of the comptroller.

Sec. 601.166. Payment of Cash Security.

(a) Cash security may be applied only to the payment of:

(1) a judgment rendered against the person on whose behalf the deposit is made for damages arising out of the accident; or

(2) a settlement, agreed to by the depositor, of a claim arising out of the accident.

(b) For payment under Subsection (a), the action under which the judgment was rendered must have been instituted before the second anniversary of the later of:

(1) the date of the accident; or

(2) the date of the deposit, in the case of a deposit of security under Section 601.162(b).

Sec. 601.167. Return of Cash Security.

Cash security or any balance of the security shall be returned to the depositor or the depositor's personal representative when:

(1) evidence satisfactory to the department is filed with the department that there has been:

(A) a release of liability;

(B) a final adjudication that the person on whose behalf the deposit is made is not liable; or

(C) an agreement as described by Section 601.154(d)(3);

(2) reasonable evidence is provided to the department after the second anniversary of the date of the accident that no action arising out of the accident is pending and no judgment rendered in such an action is unpaid; or

(3) in the case of a deposit of security under Section 601.162(b), reasonable evidence is provided to the department after the second anniversary of the date of the deposit that no action arising out of the accident is pending and no unpaid judgment rendered in such an action is unpaid.

Sec. 601.168. Insurance Policy or Bond; Limits.

(a) A bond or motor vehicle liability insurance policy under this subchapter must:

(1) be issued by a surety company or insurance company:

(A) authorized to write motor vehicle liability insurance in this state; or

(B) that complies with Subsection (b); and

(2) cover the amounts, excluding interest and costs, required to establish financial responsibility under Section 601.072.

(b) A bond or motor vehicle liability insurance policy issued by a surety company or insurance company that is not authorized to do business in this state is effective under this subchapter only if:

(1) the bond or policy is issued for a motor vehicle that:

(A) is not registered in this state; or

(B) was not registered in this state on the effective date of the most recent renewal of the policy; and

(2) the surety company or insurance company executes a power of attorney authorizing the department to accept on the company's behalf service of notice or process in an action arising out of the accident on the bond or policy.

(c) The bond must be filed with and approved by the department.

Sec. 601.169. Reasonable Probability Not Admissible in Civil Suit.

A determination under Section 601.154 or 601.157 that there is a reasonable probability that a judgment will be rendered against a person as a result of an accident may not be introduced in evidence in a suit for damages arising from that accident.

Sec. 601.170. Department Acting on Erroneous Information.

If the department is given erroneous information relating to a matter covered by Section 601.151(b)(1) or (b)(2) or to a person's status as an employee of the United States acting within the scope of the person's employment, the department shall take appropriate action as provided by this subchapter not later than the 60th day after the date the department receives correct information.

SUBCHAPTER G FAILURE TO MAINTAIN MOTOR VEHICLE LIABILITY INSURANCE OR OTHERWISE ESTABLISH FINANCIAL RESPONSIBILITY; CRIMINAL PENALTIES

Sec. 601.191. Operation of Motor Vehicle in Violation of Motor Vehicle Liability Insurance Requirement; Offense.

(a) A person commits an offense if the person operates a motor vehicle in violation of Section 601.051.

(b) Except as provided by Subsections (c) and (d), an offense under this section is a misdemeanor punishable by a fine of not less than $175 or more than $350.

(c) If a person has been previously convicted of an offense under this section, an offense under this section is a misdemeanor punishable by a fine of not less than $350 or more than $1,000.

(d) If the court determines that a person who has not been previously convicted of an offense under this section is economically unable to pay the fine, the court may reduce the fine to less than $175.

(e) A citation issued for an offense under this section must include an affirmative indication that the peace officer was unable at the time of the alleged offense to verify financial responsibility for the vehicle through the verification program established under Subchapter N.

Sec. 601.192. Court Costs [Repealed].

Repealed by Acts 1997, 75th Leg., ch. 1100 (H.B. 2272), § 6(5), effective September 1, 1997.

Sec. 601.193. Defense: Financial Responsibility in Effect at Time of Alleged Offense.

(a) It is a defense to prosecution under Section 601.191 or 601.195 that the person charged produces to the court one of the documents listed in Section 601.053(a) that was valid at the time that the offense is alleged to have occurred.

(b) After the court verifies a document produced under Subsection (a), the court shall dismiss the charge.

Sec. 601.194. Defense: Possession of Motor Vehicle for Maintenance or Repair.

It is a defense to prosecution of an offense under Section 601.191 that the motor vehicle operated by the person charged:

(1) was in the possession of that person for the sole purpose of maintenance or repair; and

(2) was not owned in whole or in part by that person.

Sec. 601.195. Operation of Motor Vehicle in Violation of Requirement to Establish Financial Responsibility; Offense.

(a) A person commits an offense if the person:

(1) is required to establish financial responsibility under Subchapter F or K;

(2) does not maintain evidence of financial responsibility; and

(3) during the period evidence of financial responsibility must be maintained:

(A) operates on a highway a motor vehicle owned by the person; or

(B) knowingly permits another person, who is not otherwise permitted to operate a vehicle under this chapter, to operate on a highway a motor vehicle owned by the person.

(b) An offense under this section is a misdemeanor punishable by:

(1) a fine not to exceed $500;

(2) confinement in county jail for a term not to exceed six months; or

(3) both the fine and the confinement.

Sec. 601.196. Evidence Forged or Signed Without Authority; Offense [Repealed].

Repealed by Acts 1999, 76th Leg., ch. 659 (H.B. 319), § 4, effective September 1, 1999.

SUBCHAPTER H FAILURE TO MAINTAIN EVIDENCE OF FINANCIAL RESPONSIBILITY; SUSPENSION OF DRIVER'S LICENSE AND MOTOR VEHICLE REGISTRATION

Sec. 601.231. Suspension of Driver's License and Vehicle Registration.

(a) If a person is convicted of an offense under Section 601.191 and a prior conviction of that person under that section has been reported to the department by a magistrate or the judge or clerk of a court, the department shall suspend the driver's license and vehicle registrations of the person unless the person files and maintains evidence of financial responsibility with the department until the second anniversary of the date of the subsequent conviction.

(b) The department may waive the requirement of maintaining evidence of financial responsibility under Subsection (a) if satisfactory evidence is filed with the department showing that at the time of arrest the person was in compliance with the financial responsibility requirement of Section 601.051 or was exempt from that section under Section 601.007 or 601.052(a)(3).

Sec. 601.232. Notice of Suspension.

(a) The department shall send in a timely manner a notice to each person whose driver's license and vehicle registrations are suspended under Section 601.231.

(b) The notice must state that the person's driver's license and registration are suspended and that the person may apply for reinstatement of the license and vehicle registration or issuance of a new license and registration as provided by Sections 601.162 and 601.376.

Sec. 601.233. Notice of Potential Suspension.

(a) A citation for an offense under Section 601.191 issued as a result of Section 601.053 must include, in type larger than other type on the citation, the following statement: "A second or subsequent conviction of an offense under the Texas Motor Vehicle Safety Responsibility Act will result in the suspension of your driver's license and motor vehicle registration unless you file and maintain evidence

Transportation Code

of financial responsibility with the Department of Public Safety for two years from the date of conviction. The department may waive the requirement to file evidence of financial responsibility if you file satisfactory evidence with the department showing that at the time this citation was issued, the vehicle was covered by a motor vehicle liability insurance policy or that you were otherwise exempt from the requirements to provide evidence of financial responsibility."

(b) A judge presiding at a trial at which a person is convicted of an offense under Section 601.191 shall notify the person that the person's driver's license is subject to suspension if the person fails to provide to the department evidence of financial responsibility as required by Section 601.231.

Sec. 601.234. Issuance or Continuation of Vehicle Registration.

A motor vehicle may not be registered in the name of a person required to file evidence of financial responsibility unless evidence of financial responsibility is furnished for the vehicle.

SUBCHAPTER I FAILURE TO MAINTAIN EVIDENCE OF FINANCIAL RESPONSIBILITY; IMPOUNDMENT OF MOTOR VEHICLE

Sec. 601.261. Impoundment of Motor Vehicle.

On a second or subsequent conviction for an offense under Section 601.191, the court shall order the sheriff of the county in which the court has jurisdiction to impound the motor vehicle operated by the defendant at the time of the offense if the defendant:

(1) was an owner of the motor vehicle at the time of the offense; and

(2) is an owner on the date of that conviction.

Sec. 601.262. Duration of Impoundment.

(a) The duration of an impoundment under Section 601.261 is 180 days.

(b) The court may not order the release of the vehicle unless the defendant applies to the court for the vehicle's release and provides evidence of financial responsibility that complies with Section 601.053 and this section.

(c) The evidence of financial responsibility must cover the two-year period immediately following the date the defendant applies for release of the impounded vehicle. The court, by order, shall permit a defendant to provide evidence of insurability in increments of a period of not less than six months.

(d) If an insurance binder is offered as evidence of financial responsibility under this section, the binder must confirm to the court's satisfaction that the defendant is in compliance with this chapter for the period required by Subsection (c).

Sec. 601.263. Reimbursement Fee for Impoundment.

The court shall impose against the defendant a reimbursement fee of $15 a day for each day of impoundment of the defendant's vehicle.

Sec. 601.264. Penalties Cumulative.

Impoundment of a motor vehicle under this subchapter is in addition to any other punishment imposed under this chapter.

Sec. 601.265. Transfer of Title of Impounded Motor Vehicle.

(a) To transfer title to a motor vehicle impounded under Section 601.261, the owner must apply to the court for permission.

(b) If the court finds that the transfer is being made in good faith and is not being made to circumvent this chapter, the court shall approve the transfer.

Sec. 601.266. Release on Involuntary Transfer of Title of Impounded Motor Vehicle.

(a) Notwithstanding Section 601.262, the court shall order the release of a motor vehicle impounded under Section 601.261 if, while the vehicle is impounded, title to the vehicle is transferred by:

(1) foreclosure;

(2) sale on execution;

(3) cancellation of a conditional sales contract; or

(4) judicial order.

Sec. 601.267. Release of Impounded Motor Vehicle by Sheriff.

A sheriff who impounds a motor vehicle shall release the vehicle:

(1) on presentation of an order of release from the court and payment of the fee for the impoundment

by the defendant or a person authorized by the owner; or

(2) to a person who is shown as a lienholder on the vehicle's certificate of title on presentation of the certificate of title and an accompanying affidavit from an officer of the lienholder establishing that the debt secured by the vehicle is in default or has matured.

SUBCHAPTER J
IMPOUNDMENT OF MOTOR VEHICLE NOT REGISTERED IN THIS STATE

Sec. 601.291. Applicability of Subchapter.

This subchapter applies only to the owner or operator of a motor vehicle that:

(1) is not registered in this state; and

(2) is involved in a motor vehicle accident in this state that results in bodily injury, death, or damage to the property of one person to an apparent extent of at least $500.

Sec. 601.292. Duty to Provide Evidence of Financial Responsibility to Investigating Officer.

A person to whom this subchapter applies shall provide evidence of financial responsibility to a law enforcement officer of this state or a political subdivision of this state who is conducting an investigation of the accident.

Sec. 601.293. Failure to Provide Evidence of Financial Responsibility; Magistrate's Inquiry and Order.

(a) A person to whom this subchapter applies who fails to provide evidence under Section 601.292 shall be taken before a magistrate as soon as practicable.

(b) The magistrate shall conduct an inquiry on the issues of negligence and liability for bodily injury, death, or property damage sustained in the accident.

(c) If the magistrate determines that there is a reasonable possibility that a judgment will be rendered against the person for bodily injury, death, or property damage sustained in the accident, the magistrate shall order the person to provide:

(1) evidence of financial responsibility for the bodily injury, death, or property damage; or

(2) evidence that the person is exempt from the requirement of Section 601.051.

(d) A determination of negligence or liability under Subsection (c) does not act as collateral estoppel on an issue in a criminal or civil adjudication arising from the accident.

Sec. 601.294. Impoundment of Motor Vehicle.

If a person to whom this subchapter applies does not provide evidence required under Section 601.293(c), the magistrate shall enter an order directing the sheriff of the county or the chief of police of the municipality to impound the motor vehicle owned or operated by the person that was involved in the accident.

Sec. 601.295. Duration of Impoundment; Release.

(a) A motor vehicle impounded under Section 601.294 remains impounded until the owner, operator, or person authorized by the owner presents to the person authorized to release the vehicle:

(1) a certificate of release obtained from the department; and

(2) payment for the cost of impoundment.

(b) On presentation of the items described by Subsection (a), the person authorized to release an impounded motor vehicle shall release the vehicle.

Sec. 601.296. Certificate of Release.

(a) The department shall issue a certificate of release of an impounded motor vehicle to the owner, operator, or person authorized by the owner on submission to the department of:

(1) evidence of financial responsibility under Section 601.053 that shows that at the time of the accident the vehicle was in compliance with Section 601.051 or was exempt from the requirement of Section 601.051;

(2) a release executed by each person damaged in the accident other than the operator of the vehicle for which the certificate of release is requested; or

(3) security in a form and amount determined by the department to secure the payment of damages for which the operator may be liable.

(b) A person may satisfy the requirement of Subsection (a)(1) or (2) by submitting a photocopy of the item required.

(c) The department shall adopt the form, content, and procedures for issuance of a certificate of release.

(d) Security provided under this section is subject to Sections 601.163—601.167.

Transportation Code

Sec. 601.297. Liability for Cost of Impoundment.

The owner of an impounded vehicle is liable for the costs of the impoundment.

SUBCHAPTER K

EVIDENCE OF FINANCIAL RESPONSIBILITY FOLLOWING JUDGMENT, CONVICTION, PLEA, OR FORFEITURE OR FOLLOWING SUSPENSION OR REVOCATION

Sec. 601.331. Report of Unsatisfied Judgment or Conviction, Plea, or Forfeiture of Bail; Nonresident.

(a) If a person does not satisfy a judgment before the 61st day after the date of the judgment, the clerk of the court, on the written request of a judgment creditor or a judgment creditor's attorney, immediately shall send a certified copy of the judgment to the department.

(b) The clerk of the court immediately shall send to the department a certified copy of the action of the court in relation to:

(1) a conviction for a violation of a motor vehicle law; or

(2) a guilty plea or forfeiture of bail by a person charged with violation of a motor vehicle law.

(c) A certified copy sent to the department under Subsection (b) is prima facie evidence of the conviction, plea, forfeiture, or other action.

(d) If the court does not have a clerk, the judge of the court shall send the certified copy required by this section.

(e) If the defendant named in a judgment reported to the department is a nonresident, the department shall send a certified copy of the judgment to the official in charge of issuing driver's licenses and vehicle registrations of the state, province of Canada, or state of Mexico in which the defendant resides.

Sec. 601.332. Suspension of Driver's License and Vehicle Registration or Nonresident's Operating Privilege for Unsatisfied Judgment.

(a) Except as provided by Sections 601.333, 601.334, and 601.336, on receipt of a certified copy of a judgment under Section 601.331, the department shall suspend the judgment debtor's:

(1) driver's license and vehicle registrations; or

(2) nonresident's operating privilege.

(b) Subject to Sections 601.333, 601.334, and 601.336, the suspension continues, and the person's driver's license, vehicle registrations, or nonresident's operating privilege may not be renewed or the person issued a driver's license or registration in the person's name, until:

(1) the judgment is stayed or satisfied; and

(2) the person provides evidence of financial responsibility.

Sec. 601.333. Relief from Suspension: Motor Vehicle Liability Insurance.

(a) A person whose driver's license, vehicle registrations, or nonresident's operating privilege has been suspended or is subject to suspension under Section 601.332 may file with the department:

(1) evidence that there was a motor vehicle liability insurance policy covering the motor vehicle involved in the accident out of which the judgment arose in effect at the time of the accident;

(2) an affidavit stating that the person was insured at the time of the accident, that the insurance company is liable to pay the judgment, and the reason, if known, that the insurance company has not paid the judgment;

(3) the original policy of insurance or a certified copy of the policy, if available; and

(4) any other documents required by the department to show that the loss, injury, or damage for which the judgment was rendered was covered by the insurance.

(b) The department may not suspend the driver's license, vehicle registrations, or nonresident's operating privilege, and shall reinstate a license, registration, or privilege that has been suspended, if it is satisfied from the documents filed under Subsection (a) that:

(1) there was a motor vehicle liability insurance policy in effect for the vehicle at the time of the accident;

(2) the insurance company that issued the policy was authorized to issue the policy in this state at the time the policy was issued; and

(3) the insurance company is liable to pay the judgment to the extent and for the amounts required by this chapter.

Sec. 601.334. Relief from Suspension: Consent of Judgment Creditor.

(a) The department may allow a judgment debtor's driver's license and vehicle registrations or nonresident's operating privilege to continue, notwithstanding Section 601.332, if:

(1) the judgment creditor consents to the continuation in writing in the form prescribed by the department; and

(2) the judgment debtor provides evidence of financial responsibility to the department.

(b) Continuation of a judgment debtor's driver's license and vehicle registrations or nonresident's operating privilege expires on the later of:

(1) the date the consent of the judgment creditor is revoked in writing; or

(2) the expiration of six months after the effective date of the consent.

(c) Subsection (b) applies notwithstanding default in the payment of the judgment or any installments to be made under Section 601.335.

Sec. 601.335. Installment Payments Authorized.

(a) A judgment debtor, on notice to the judgment creditor, may apply to the court in which judgment was rendered to pay the judgment in installments.

(b) The court may order payment in installments and may establish the amounts and times of the payments.

(c) An order issued under this section is issued without prejudice to any other legal remedy that the judgment creditor has.

Sec. 601.336. Relief from Suspension: Installment Payments; Default.

(a) Subject to Subsection (c), the department may not suspend a judgment debtor's driver's license, vehicle registration, or nonresident's operating privilege under Section 601.332 if the judgment debtor:

(1) files evidence of financial responsibility with the department; and

(2) obtains an order under Section 601.335 permitting the payment of the judgment in installments.

(b) Subject to Subsection (c), the department shall restore a judgment debtor's driver's license, vehicle registrations, or nonresident's operating privilege that was suspended following nonpayment of a judgment if the judgment debtor complies with Subsections (a)(1) and (2).

(c) On notice that a judgment debtor has failed to pay an installment as specified in an order issued under Section 601.335, the department shall suspend the judgment debtor's driver's license, vehicle registrations, or nonresident's operating privilege. The suspensions continue until the judgment is satisfied as provided by this chapter.

Sec. 601.337. Effect of Bankruptcy.

A discharge in bankruptcy after a judgment is rendered relieves the judgment debtor from the requirements of this chapter, except for financial responsibility requirements arising after the date of the discharge.

Sec. 601.338. Evidence of Financial Responsibility or Suspension of Driver's License and Vehicle Registration of Owner of Motor Vehicle.

(a) The department shall suspend the driver's license and vehicle registrations of the owner of a motor vehicle that was used with the owner's consent by another person at the time of an offense resulting in conviction or a plea of guilty, if under state law the department:

(1) suspends or revokes the driver's license of the other person on receipt of a record of a conviction; or

(2) suspends the vehicle registration of the other person on receipt of a record of a plea of guilty.

(b) The department may not suspend the driver's license and vehicle registration of an owner under this section if the owner files and maintains evidence of financial responsibility with the department for each motor vehicle registered in the name of the owner.

Sec. 601.339. Evidence of Financial Responsibility Following Conviction, Plea, or Forfeiture.

(a) Except as provided by Subsection (c), the department may not issue a driver's license to a person who does not hold a driver's license and who:

(1) enters a plea of guilty to an offense or is convicted by a final order or a judgment that:

(A) requires the suspension or revocation of a driver's license;

(B) is imposed for operating a motor vehicle on a highway without a driver's license; or

(C) is imposed for operating an unregistered motor vehicle on a highway; or

(2) forfeits bail or collateral deposited to secure an appearance for trial for an offense described by Subdivision (1).

(b) Except as described by Subsection (c), a motor vehicle may not be registered in the name of a person described by Subsection (a).

(c) Notwithstanding Subsections (a) and (b), a driver's license may be issued or a motor vehicle may be registered if the person files and maintains evidence of financial responsibility with the department.

Transportation Code

Sec. 601.340. Evidence of Financial Responsibility or Suspension of Vehicle Registration Following Suspension or Revocation of Driver's License.

(a) Except as provided by Subsection (b) or (c), the department shall suspend the registration of each motor vehicle registered in the name of a person if the department:

(1) under any state law, other than Section 521.341(7), suspends or revokes the person's driver's license on receipt of a record of a conviction or a forfeiture of bail; or

(2) receives a record of a guilty plea of the person entered for an offense for which the department would be required to suspend the driver's license of a person convicted of the offense.

(b) The department, unless otherwise required by law, may not suspend a registration under Subsection (a) if the person files and maintains evidence of financial responsibility with the department for each motor vehicle registered in the name of the person.

(c) This section does not apply to a suspension of a driver's license for an offense under Chapter 106, Alcoholic Beverage Code, other than an offense that includes confinement as an authorized sanction.

Sec. 601.341. Evidence of Financial Responsibility; Termination of Penalty.

Unless a person whose driver's license or vehicle registration has been suspended or revoked under this subchapter files and maintains evidence of financial responsibility with the department:

(1) the suspension or revocation may not be terminated;

(2) the driver's license or registration may not be renewed;

(3) a new driver's license may not be issued to the person; or

(4) a motor vehicle may not be registered in the name of the person.

Sec. 601.342. Evidence of Financial Responsibility Following Suspension or Revocation of Nonresident's Operating Privilege.

The department may not terminate the suspension or revocation of a nonresident's operating privilege suspended or revoked under this subchapter because of a conviction, forfeiture of bail, or guilty plea unless the person files and maintains evidence of financial responsibility with the department.

SUBCHAPTER L EFFECT OF SUSPENSION

Sec. 601.371. Operation of Motor Vehicle in Violation of Suspension; Offense.

(a) A person commits an offense if the person, during a period that a suspension of the person's vehicle registration is in effect under this chapter, knowingly permits a motor vehicle owned by the person to be operated on a highway.

(b) It is an affirmative defense to prosecution under this section that the person had not received notice of a suspension order concerning the person's vehicle registration. For purposes of this subsection, notice is presumed to be received if the notice was sent in accordance with this chapter to the last known address or e-mail address of the person as shown by department records.

(c) Except as provided by Subsection (d), an offense under this section is a misdemeanor punishable by:

(1) a fine of not less than $100 or more than $500; and

(2) confinement in county jail for a term of not less than 72 hours or more than six months.

(d) If it is shown on the trial of an offense under this section that the person has previously been convicted of an offense under this section, the offense is punishable as a Class A misdemeanor.

(e) In this section, a conviction for an offense that involves operation of a motor vehicle after August 31, 1987, is a final conviction, whether the sentence for the conviction is imposed or probated.

Sec. 601.372. Return of Driver's License and Vehicle Registration to Department.

(a) The department shall give written notice of a suspension of a driver's license and vehicle registration to a person who is required to maintain a motor vehicle liability insurance policy or bond under this chapter and whose policy or bond is canceled or terminated or who does not provide other evidence of financial responsibility on the request of the department.

(b) The notice must be provided by:

(1) personal delivery to the person;

(2) deposit in the United States mail addressed to the person at the last address supplied to the department by the person; or

(3) e-mail if the person has provided an e-mail address to the department and has elected to receive notice electronically.

(b-1) Notice provided under Subsection (b) by mail or e-mail is presumed to be received on the 10th day after the date the notice is sent.

(c) The department by rule may require the person to send the person's driver's license and vehicle registrations not later than the 10th day after the date the person receives written notice from the department.

(d) Proof of the notice may be made by the certificate of a department employee stating that:

(1) the notice was prepared in the regular course of business and placed in the United States mail or sent by e-mail as part of the regular organized activity of the department; or

(2) the employee delivered the notice in person.

(e) A certificate under Subsection (d)(2) must specify the name of the person to whom the notice was given and the time, place, and manner of the delivery of the notice.

Sec. 601.373. Failure to Return Driver's License or Vehicle Registration; Offense.

(a) A person commits an offense if the person wilfully fails to send a driver's license or vehicle registration as required by Section 601.372. An offense under this subsection is a misdemeanor punishable by a fine not to exceed $200.

(b) The department may direct a department employee to obtain and send to the department the driver's license and vehicle registration of a person who fails to send the person's license or registration in accordance with Section 601.372. The director of the department or the person designated by the director may file a complaint against a person for an offense under Subsection (a).

Sec. 601.374. Transfer of Vehicle Registration Prohibited.

(a) An owner whose vehicle registration has been suspended under this chapter may not:

(1) transfer the registration unless the transfer is authorized under Subsection (b); or

(2) register in another name the motor vehicle to which the registration applies.

(b) The department may authorize the transfer of vehicle registration if the department is satisfied that the transfer is proposed in good faith and not to defeat the purposes of this chapter.

(c) This section does not affect the rights of a conditional vendor or lessor of, or person with a security interest in, a motor vehicle owned by a person who is subject to this section if the vendor, lessor, or secured party is not the registered owner of the vehicle.

Sec. 601.375. Cooperation with Other State or Canada.

(a) The department shall send a certified copy of the record of the department's action suspending a nonresident's operating privilege under Subchapter F or under Sections 601.332, 601.333, and 601.334 to the official in charge of issuing driver's licenses and vehicle registrations of the state or province of Canada in which the nonresident resides.

(b) Subsection (a) applies only if the law of the other state or the province provides for action similar to the action required by Section 601.009.

Sec. 601.376. Reinstatement Fee.

(a) A driver's license, vehicle registration, or nonresident's operating privilege that has been suspended under this chapter may not be reinstated and a new license or registration may not be issued to the holder of the suspended license, registration, or privilege until the person:

(1) pays to the department a fee of $100; and

(2) complies with the other requirements of this chapter.

(b) The fee imposed by this section is in addition to other fees imposed by law.

(c) A person is required to pay only one fee under this section, without regard to the number of driver's licenses and vehicle registrations to be reinstated for or issued to the person in connection with the payment.

SUBCHAPTER M APPEAL OF DEPARTMENT ACTION

Sec. 601.401. Department Actions Subject to Review.

(a) An action of the department under this chapter may be appealed, unless:

(1) an order of suspension by the department is based on an existing unsatisfied final judgment rendered against a person by a court in this state arising out of the use of a motor vehicle in this state; or

(2) the suspension is automatic under Section 601.231(a).

(b) To appeal an action of the department, the person must file a petition not later than the 30th day after the date of the action in the county court at law in the county in which the person resides or the county court of the county in which the person resides, if the county does not have a county court at law.

(c) A person who files an appeal under this section shall send a file-stamped copy of the petition by certified mail to the department at the department's headquarters in Austin. The copy must be certified by the clerk of the court in which the petition is filed.

(d) The filing of a petition of appeal as provided by this section stays an order of suspension until the earlier of the 91st day after the date the appeal petition is filed or the date the trial is completed and final judgment is rendered.

(e) On expiration of the stay, the department shall impose the suspension. The stay may not be extended, and an additional stay may not be granted.

(f) A trial on appeal is de novo.

Sec. 601.402. Time for Appeal [Repealed].

Repealed by Acts 1999, 76th Leg., ch. 1117 (H.B. 3641), § 9, effective September 1, 2000.

Sec. 601.403. Trial [Repealed].

Repealed by Acts 1999, 76th Leg., ch. 1117 (H.B. 3641), § 9, effective September 1, 2000.

Sec. 601.404. Stay of Act on Appeal [Repealed].

Repealed by Acts 1999, 76th Leg., ch. 1117 (H.B. 3641), § 9, effective September 1, 2000.

Sec. 601.405. Filing of Evidence of Financial Responsibility; Effect on Appeal [Repealed].

Repealed by Acts 1999, 76th Leg., ch. 1117 (H.B. 3641), § 9, effective September 1, 2000.

Sec. 601.406. Temporary Stay of Departments Order on Filing of Affidavit [Repealed].

Repealed by Acts 1999, 76th Leg., ch. 1117 (H.B. 3641), § 9, effective September 1, 2000.

Sec. 601.407. Stay After Plea or Conviction [Repealed].

Repealed by Acts 1999, 76th Leg., ch. 1117 (H.B. 3641), § 9, effective September 1, 2000.

Sec. 601.408. Stay After Acquittal or Dismissal [Repealed].

Repealed by Acts 1999, 76th Leg., ch. 1117 (H.B. 3641), § 9, effective September 1, 2000.

Sec. 601.409. Maintenance of Evidence of Financial Responsibility [Repealed].

Repealed by Acts 1999, 76th Leg., ch. 1117 (H.B. 3641), § 9, effective September 1, 2000.

Sec. 601.410. Limit on Courts [Repealed].

Repealed by Acts 1999, 76th Leg., ch. 1117 (H.B. 3641), § 9, effective September 1, 2000.

SUBCHAPTER N
FINANCIAL RESPONSIBILITY VERIFICATION PROGRAM

Sec. 601.450. Feasibility Study [Repealed].

Repealed by Acts 2009, 81st Leg., ch. 933 (H.B. 3097), § 2J.03, effective September 1, 2009 and by Acts 2009, 81st Leg., ch. 1146 (H.B. 2730), § 15A.02, effective September 1, 2009.

Sec. 601.451. Definition.

In this subchapter, "implementing agencies" means:

(1) the department;

(2) the Texas Department of Motor Vehicles;

(3) the Texas Department of Insurance; and

(4) the Department of Information Resources.

Sec. 601.452. Implementation of Program; Rules.

(a) The Texas Department of Insurance in consultation with the other implementing agencies shall establish a program for verification of whether owners of motor vehicles have established financial responsibility. The program established must be:

(1) the program most likely to:

(A) reduce the number of uninsured motorists in this state;

(B) operate reliably;

(C) be cost-effective;

(D) sufficiently protect the privacy of the motor vehicle owners;

(E) sufficiently safeguard the security and integrity of information provided by insurance companies;

(F) identify and employ a method of compliance that improves public convenience; and

(G) provide information that is accurate and current; and

Transportation Code

(2) capable of being audited by an independent auditor.

(b) The implementing agencies shall jointly adopt rules to administer this subchapter.

(c) The implementing agencies shall convene a working group to facilitate the implementation of the program, assist in the development of rules, and coordinate a testing phase and necessary changes identified in the testing phase. The working group must consist of representatives of the implementing agencies and the insurance industry and technical experts with the skills and knowledge, including knowledge of privacy laws, required to create and maintain the program.

Sec. 601.453. Agent.

(a) The Texas Department of Insurance in consultation with the other implementing agencies, under a competitive bidding procedure, shall select an agent to develop, implement, operate, and maintain the program.

(b) The implementing agencies shall jointly enter into a contract with the selected agent.

(c) A contract under this section may not have a term of more than five years.

Sec. 601.454. Information Provided by Insurance Company; Privacy.

(a) Each insurance company providing motor vehicle liability insurance policies in this state shall provide necessary information for those policies to allow the agent to carry out this subchapter, subject to the agent's contract with the implementing agencies and rules adopted under this subchapter.

(b) The agent is entitled only to information that is at that time available from the insurance company and that is determined by the implementing agencies to be necessary to carry out this subchapter.

(c) Information obtained under this subchapter is confidential. The agent:

(1) may use the information only for a purpose authorized under this subchapter;

(2) may not use the information for a commercial purpose; and

(3) on request, and subject to appropriate safeguards to protect the privacy of motor vehicle owners developed by the implementing agencies and the attorney general, may provide the information to the attorney general for the purpose of enforcing child support obligations.

(d) A person commits an offense if the person knowingly uses information obtained under this subchapter for any purpose not authorized under this subchapter. An offense under this subsection is a Class B misdemeanor.

Sec. 601.455. Access by Court.

(a) A justice or municipal court may access the verification program established under this subchapter to verify financial responsibility for the purpose of court proceedings.

(b) The costs associated with accessing the verification program under this section shall be paid out of the county treasury by order of the commissioners court or the municipal treasury by order of the governing body of the municipality, as applicable.

SUBTITLE E
VEHICLE SIZE AND WEIGHT

CHAPTER 621
GENERAL PROVISIONS RELATING TO VEHICLE SIZE AND WEIGHT

SUBCHAPTER A
GENERAL PROVISIONS

Sec. 621.001. Definitions.

In this chapter:

(1) "Commercial motor vehicle" means a motor vehicle, other than a motorcycle, designed or used for:

(A) the transportation of property; or

(B) delivery purposes.

(2) "Commission" means the Texas Transportation Commission.

(3) "Department" means the Texas Department of Motor Vehicles.

(4) "Director" means:

(A) the executive director of the department; or

(B) an employee of the department who is:

(i) a division or special office director or holds a rank higher than division or special office director; and

(ii) designated by the executive director.

(5) "Motor vehicle" means a vehicle that is self-propelled.

(6) "Semitrailer" means a vehicle without motive power that is designed, or used with a motor

vehicle, so that some of its weight and the weight of its load rests on or is carried by the motor vehicle.

(7) "Trailer" means a vehicle without motive power that is:

(A) designed or used to carry property or passengers on its own structure exclusively; and

(B) drawn by a motor vehicle.

(8) "Truck-tractor" means a motor vehicle designed or used primarily for drawing another vehicle:

(A) that is not constructed to carry a load other than a part of the weight of the vehicle and load being drawn; or

(B) that is engaged with a semitrailer in the transportation of automobiles or boats and that transports the automobiles or boats on part of the truck-tractor.

(9) "Vehicle" means a mechanical device, other than a device moved by human power or used exclusively upon stationary rails or tracks, in, on, or by which a person or property can be transported on a public highway. The term includes a motor vehicle, commercial motor vehicle, truck-tractor, trailer, or semitrailer but does not include manufactured housing as defined by Chapter 1201, Occupations Code.

(10) "Single axle weight" means the total weight transmitted to the road by all wheels whose centers may be included between two parallel transverse vertical planes 40 inches apart, extending across the full width of the vehicle.

(11) "Tandem axle weight" means the total weight transmitted to the road by two or more consecutive axles whose centers may be included between parallel transverse vertical planes spaced more than 40 inches and not more than 96 inches apart, extending across the full width of the vehicle.

(12) "Port of entry" means a place designated by executive order of the president of the United States, by order of the United States secretary of the treasury, or by act of the United States Congress at which a customs officer is authorized to accept entries of merchandise, collect duties, and enforce customs and navigation laws. The term includes a publicly owned or privately owned international port of entry between this state and the United Mexican States.

(13) "Board" means the board of the Texas Department of Motor Vehicles.

Sec. 621.002. Vehicle Registration Receipt for Certain Heavy Vehicles.

(a) A copy of the registration receipt issued under Section 502.057 for a commercial motor vehicle, truck-tractor, trailer, or semitrailer shall be:

(1) carried on the vehicle when the vehicle is on a public highway; and

(2) presented to an officer authorized to enforce this chapter on request of the officer.

(b) A copy of the registration receipt is:

(1) admissible in evidence in any cause in which the gross registered weight of the vehicle is an issue; and

(2) prima facie evidence of the gross weight for which the vehicle is registered.

Sec. 621.003. Reciprocal Agreement with Another State for Issuance of Permits.

(a) The board by rule may authorize the director to enter into with the proper authority of another state an agreement that authorizes:

(1) the authority of the other state to issue on behalf of the department to the owner or operator of a vehicle, or combination of vehicles, that exceeds the weight or size limits allowed by this state a permit that authorizes the operation or transportation on a highway in this state of the vehicle or combination of vehicles; and

(2) the department to issue on behalf of the authority of the other state to the owner or operator of a vehicle, or combination of vehicles, that exceeds the weight or size limits allowed by that state a permit that authorizes the operation or transportation on a highway of that state of the vehicle or combination of vehicles.

(b) A permit issued by the authority of another state under an agreement entered into under this section has the same validity in this state as a permit issued by the department.

(c) The holder of a permit issued by the authority of another state under an agreement entered into under this section is subject to all applicable laws of this state and rules of the department.

(d) The department may contract with a third party to act as the department's agent in the processing of a permit application and the distribution of a permit issued by the department under this section.

(e) An agreement entered into under this section may provide for a third party to act as the agent of each state in the processing of a permit application and the distribution of a permit issued by a state under this section.

Sec. 621.004. Admissibility of Certificate of Vertical Clearance.

In each civil or criminal proceeding in which a violation of this chapter may be an issue, a certificate of the vertical clearance of a structure, including a

Transportation Code

bridge or underpass, signed by the executive director of the Texas Department of Transportation is admissible in evidence for all purposes.

Sec. 621.005. Effect of Increased Limits by United States.

If the United States prescribes or adopts vehicle size or weight limits greater than those prescribed by 23 U.S.C. Section 127 on March 18, 1975, for the national system of interstate and defense highways, the increased limits apply to the national system of interstate and defense highways in this state.

Sec. 621.006. Restricted Operation on Certain Holidays.

The commission by rule may impose restrictions on the weight and size of vehicles to be operated on state highways on the following holidays only:

(1) New Year's Day;

(2) Memorial Day;

(3) Independence Day;

(4) Labor Day;

(5) Thanksgiving Day; and

(6) Christmas Day.

Sec. 621.007. Evidence of Violation.

(a) In a proceeding in which a violation of a weight restriction under this subtitle may be an issue, a document is admissible as relevant evidence of the violation if:

(1) the document is:

(A) a record kept under Section 621.410; or

(B) a bill of lading, freight bill, weight certification, or similar document that is issued by a person consigning cargo for shipment or engaged in the business of transporting or forwarding cargo; and

(2) the document states:

(A) a gross weight of the vehicle or combination of vehicles and cargo that exceeds a weight restriction under this subtitle; or

(B) a gross weight of the cargo that combined with the empty weight of the vehicle or combination of vehicles exceeds a weight restriction under this subtitle.

(b) This section does not limit the admissibility of any other evidence relating to the violation.

Sec. 621.008. Rulemaking Authority.

The board may adopt rules necessary to implement and enforce this chapter.

SUBCHAPTER B WEIGHT LIMITATIONS

Sec. 621.101. Maximum Weight of Vehicle or Combination.

(a) A vehicle or combination of vehicles may not be operated over or on a public highway or at a port-of-entry between Texas and the United Mexican States if the vehicle or combination has:

(1) a single axle weight heavier than 20,000 pounds, including all enforcement tolerances;

(2) a tandem axle weight heavier than 34,000 pounds, including all enforcement tolerances;

(3) an overall gross weight on a group of two or more consecutive axles heavier than the weight computed using the following formula and rounding the result to the nearest 500 pounds:

$$W = 500((LN/(N - 1)) + 12N + 36)$$

where:

"W" is maximum overall gross weight on the group;

"L" is distance in feet between the axles of the group that are the farthest apart; and

"N" is number of axles in the group; or

(4) tires that carry a weight heavier than the weight specified and marked on the sidewall of the tire, unless the vehicle is being operated under the terms of a special permit.

(b) Notwithstanding Subsection (a)(3), two consecutive sets of tandem axles may carry a gross load of not more than 34,000 pounds each if the overall distance between the first and last axles of the consecutive sets is 36 feet or more. The overall gross weight on a group of two or more consecutive axles may not be heavier than 80,000 pounds, including all enforcement tolerances, regardless of tire ratings, axle spacing (bridge), and number of axles.

(b-1) Notwithstanding any other provision of this section, a vehicle or combination of vehicles that is powered by an engine fueled primarily by natural gas may exceed any weight limitation under this section by an amount that is equal to the difference between the weight of the vehicle attributable to the natural gas tank and fueling system carried by that vehicle and the weight of a comparable diesel tank and fueling system, provided that the maximum gross weight of the vehicle or combination of vehicles may not exceed 82,000 pounds.

(c) This section does not:

(1) authorize size or weight limits on the national system of interstate and defense highways in this state greater than those permitted under 23 U.S.C. Section 127, as amended;

(2) prohibit the operation of a vehicle or combination of vehicles that could be lawfully operated on a highway or road of this state on December 16, 1974; or

(3) apply to a vehicle or combination of vehicles that operates exclusively:

(A) at a private port of entry;

(B) on private roads associated with the port of entry; and

(C) across a public highway between private roads associated with the port of entry under a contract under Section 623.052.

Sec. 621.102. Authority to Set Maximum Weights.

(a) The executive director of the Texas Department of Transportation may set the maximum single axle weight, tandem axle weight, or gross weight of a vehicle, or maximum single axle weight, tandem axle weight, or gross weight of a combination of vehicles and loads, that may be moved over a state highway or a farm or ranch road if the executive director finds that heavier maximum weight would rapidly deteriorate or destroy the road or a bridge or culvert along the road. A maximum weight set under this subsection may not exceed the maximum set by statute for that weight.

(b) The executive director of the Texas Department of Transportation must make the finding under this section on an engineering and traffic investigation and in making the finding shall consider the width, condition, and type of pavement structures and other circumstances on the road.

(c) A maximum weight or load set under this section becomes effective on a highway or road when appropriate signs giving notice of the maximum weight or load are erected on the highway or road by the Texas Department of Transportation.

(d) A vehicle operating under a permit issued under Section 623.011, 623.071, 623.094, 623.121, 623.142, 623.181, 623.192, 623.212, or 623.321, as added by Chapter 1135 (H.B. 2741), Acts of the 83rd Legislature, Regular Session, 2013, may operate under the conditions authorized by the permit over a road for which the executive director of the Texas Department of Transportation has set a maximum weight under this section.

(e) For the purpose of this section, a farm or ranch road is a state highway that is shown in the records of the commission to be a farm-to-market or ranch-to-market road.

(f) This section does not apply to a vehicle delivering groceries, farm products, or liquefied petroleum gas.

SUBCHAPTER C
SIZE LIMITATIONS

Sec. 621.201. Maximum Width.

(a) The total width of a vehicle operated on a public highway other than a vehicle to which Subsection (b) applies, including a load on the vehicle but excluding any safety device determined by the United States Department of Transportation or the Texas Department of Public Safety to be necessary for the safe and efficient operation of motor vehicles of that type, may not be greater than 102 inches.

(b) The total width of a passenger vehicle and its load may not be greater than eight feet. This subsection does not apply to a motor bus or trolley bus operated exclusively in the territory of a municipality, in suburbs contiguous to the municipality, or in the county in which the municipality is located.

(c) A passenger vehicle may not carry a load extending more than three inches beyond the left side line of its fenders or more than six inches beyond the right side line of its fenders.

Sec. 621.202. Commission's Authority to Set Maximum Width.

(a) To comply with safety and operational requirements of federal law, the commission by order may set the maximum width of a vehicle, including the load on the vehicle, at eight feet for a designated highway or segment of a highway if the results of an engineering and traffic study, conducted by the Texas Department of Transportation, that includes an analysis of structural capacity of bridges and pavements, traffic volume, unique climatic conditions, and width of traffic lanes support the change.

(b) An order under this section becomes effective on the designated highway or segment when appropriate signs giving notice of the limitations are erected by the Texas Department of Transportation.

(c) This section is intended to comply with the Surface Transportation Assistance Act of 1982 (23 U.S.C.A. Section 101 et seq.) and is conditioned on that Act and federal regulations implementing that Act.

Sec. 621.203. Maximum Length of Motor Vehicle.

(a) A motor vehicle, other than a truck-tractor, may not be longer than 45 feet.

(b) A motor bus as defined by Section 502.001 that is longer than 35 feet but not longer than 45 feet may be operated on a highway if the motor bus is equipped with air brakes and has either three or more axles or a minimum of four tires on the rear axle.

(c) The limitation prescribed by Subsection (a) does not apply to a house trailer or towable recreational vehicle or a combination of a house trailer or towable recreational vehicle and a motor vehicle. A house trailer or towable recreational vehicle and motor vehicle combination may not be longer than 65 feet.

(d) In this section, "house trailer" and "towable recreational vehicle" have the meanings assigned by Section 541.201.

Sec. 621.204. Maximum Length of Semitrailer or Trailer.

(a) A semitrailer that is operated in a truck-tractor and semitrailer combination may not be longer than 59 feet, excluding the length of the towing device.

(b) A semitrailer or trailer that is operated in a truck-tractor, semitrailer, and trailer combination may not be longer than 28-½ feet, excluding the length of the towing device.

(c) The limitations prescribed by this section do not include any safety device determined by regulation of the United States Department of Transportation or by rule of the Department of Public Safety to be necessary for the safe and efficient operation of motor vehicles.

(d) The limitations prescribed by this section do not apply to a semitrailer or trailer that has the dimensions of a semitrailer or trailer, as appropriate, that was being operated lawfully in this state on December 1, 1982.

Sec. 621.205. Maximum Length of Vehicle Combinations.

(a) Except as provided by this section, a combination of not more than three vehicles, including a truck and semitrailer, truck and trailer, truck-tractor and semitrailer and trailer, or a truck-tractor and two trailers, may be coupled together if the combination of vehicles, other than a truck-tractor combination, is not longer than 65 feet.

(b) A passenger car or another motor vehicle that has an unloaded weight of less than 2,500 pounds may not be coupled with more than one other vehicle or towing device at one time. This subsection does not apply to the towing of a disabled vehicle to the nearest intake place for repair.

(c) A motor vehicle, including a passenger car, that has an unloaded weight of 2,500 pounds or more may be coupled with a towing device and one other vehicle.

(d) In this section:

(1) "Passenger car" means a motor vehicle designed to transport 10 or fewer persons simultaneously.

(2) "Towing device" means a device used to tow a vehicle behind a motor vehicle by supporting one end of the towed vehicle above the surface of the road and permitting the wheels at the other end of the towed vehicle to remain in contact with the road.

Sec. 621.206. Maximum Extended Length of Load.

(a) A vehicle or combination of vehicles may not carry a load that extends more than three feet beyond its front or, except as permitted by other law, more than four feet beyond its rear.

(b) Subsection (a) does not apply to vehicles collecting garbage, rubbish, refuse, or recyclable materials which are equipped with front-end loading attachments and containers provided that the vehicle is actively engaged in the collection of garbage, rubbish, refuse, or recyclable materials.

Sec. 621.2061. Exception to Maximum Extended Length of Load: Certain Motor Vehicles.

Notwithstanding Section 621.206, a trailer may carry a load that extends more than four feet beyond the rear of the trailer if the load consists of a motor vehicle that:

(1) is designed and intended to be carried at the rear of the trailer;

(2) is used or intended to be used to load or unload a commodity on or off the trailer;

(3) does not extend more than seven feet beyond the rear of the trailer; and

(4) complies with each applicable federal motor carrier safety regulation.

Sec. 621.207. Maximum Height.

(a) A vehicle and its load may not be higher than 14 feet.

(b) The operator of a vehicle that is higher than 13 feet 6 inches shall ensure that the vehicle will pass through each vertical clearance of a structure in its path without touching the structure.

(c) The owner of a vehicle is strictly liable for any damage to a bridge, underpass, or similar structure that is caused by the height of the vehicle unless at the time the damage was caused:

(1) the vehicle was stolen;

(2) the vertical clearance of the structure was less than that posted on the structure;

(3) the vehicle was being operated under the immediate direction of a law enforcement agency; or

(4) the vehicle was being operated in compliance with a permit authorizing the movement of the vehicle issued by the department or a political subdivision of this state.

SUBCHAPTER D LOCAL REGULATIONS

Sec. 621.301. County's Authority to Set Maximum Weights.

(a) The commissioners court of a county may establish load limits for any county road or bridge only with the concurrence of the Texas Department of Transportation. A load limit shall be deemed concurred with by the Texas Department of Transportation 30 days after the county submits to the Texas Department of Transportation the load limit accompanied by supporting documentation and calculations reviewed and sealed by an engineer licensed in this state, though the Texas Department of Transportation may review the load limit and withdraw concurrence at any time after the 30-day period.

(b) The commissioners court may limit the maximum weights to be moved on or over a county road, bridge, or culvert by exercising its authority under this subsection in the same manner and under the same conditions provided by Section 621.102 for the Texas Department of Transportation to limit maximum weights on highways and roads to which that section applies.

(c) The commissioners court shall record an action under Subsection (b) in its minutes.

(d) A maximum weight set under this section becomes effective on a road when appropriate signs giving notice of the maximum weight are erected by the Texas Department of Transportation on the road under order of the commissioners court.

(e) A vehicle operating under a permit issued under Section 623.011, 623.071, 623.094, 623.121, 623.142, 623.181, 623.192, 623.212, or 623.321, as added by Chapter 1135 (H.B. 2741), Acts of the 83rd Legislature, Regular Session, 2013, may operate under the conditions authorized by the permit over a road for which the commissioners court has set a maximum weight under this section.

Sec. 621.302. Exception to County's Weight Limitations.

A maximum weight set under Section 621.301 does not apply to a vehicle delivering groceries or farm products to a destination requiring travel over a road for which the maximum is set.

Sec. 621.303. Municipal Regulation of Loads and Equipment.

(a) The governing body of any municipality may regulate the movement and operation on a public road, other than a state highway in the territory of the municipality, of:

(1) an overweight, oversize, or overlength commodity that cannot reasonably be dismantled; and

(2) superheavy or oversize equipment for the transportation of an overweight, oversize, or overlength commodity that cannot be reasonably dismantled.

(b) The governing body of a municipality may not, because of weight, regulate the movement and operation on a state highway or county or municipal road of a combination of vehicles operating under a permit issued under Section 623.402.

Sec. 621.304. Restriction on Local Government Authority to Regulate Overweight Vehicles and Loads on State Highway System.

Except as expressly authorized by this subtitle, a county or municipality may not require a permit, bond, fee, or license for the movement of a vehicle or combination of vehicles or any load carried by the vehicle or vehicles on the state highway system in the county or municipality that exceeds the weight or size limits on the state highway system.

SUBCHAPTER E FEES

Sec. 621.351. Escrow Account for Prepayment of Permit Fees.

(a) The department may establish one or more escrow accounts in the Texas Department of Motor Vehicles fund for the prepayment of a fee for a permit issued by the department that authorizes the operation of a vehicle and its load or a combination of vehicles and load exceeding size or weight limitations.

(b) The fees and any fees established by the department for the administration of this section shall be administered in accordance with an agreement containing terms and conditions agreeable to the department.

(c) The department shall deposit each fee established under this section to the credit of the Texas Department of Motor Vehicles fund. The fees may be appropriated only to the department for purposes of administering this section.

Sec. 621.352. Fees for Permits Issued Under Reciprocal Agreement.

(a) The board by rule may establish fees for the administration of Section 621.003 in an amount that, when added to the other fees collected by the department, does not exceed the amount sufficient to recover the actual cost to the department of administering that section. An administrative fee collected under this section shall be sent to the comptroller for deposit to the credit of the Texas Department of Motor Vehicles fund and may be appropriated only to the department for the administration of Section 621.003.

(b) A permit fee collected by the department under Section 621.003 for another state shall be sent to the comptroller for deposit to the credit of the permit distributive account in the general revenue fund. The comptroller shall distribute money in the permit distributive account only to the proper authorities of other states and only as directed by the department.

Sec. 621.353. Distribution of Fee for Permit for Excess Weight.

(a) The comptroller shall send $50 of each base fee collected under Section 623.011 for an excess weight permit to the counties of the state, with each county receiving an amount determined according to the ratio of the total number of miles of county roads maintained by the county to the total number of miles of county roads maintained by all of the counties of this state. The comptroller shall deposit $40 of each base fee, plus each fee collected under Section 623.0112, to the credit of the Texas Department of Motor Vehicles fund. Money deposited to the credit of that fund under this subsection may be appropriated only to the department to administer this section and Sections 623.011, 623.0111, and 623.0112.

(b) The comptroller shall send the amount due each county under Subsection (a) to the county treasurer or officer performing the function of that office at least twice each fiscal year.

(c) The comptroller shall send each fee collected under Section 623.0111 for an excess weight permit to the counties designated on the application for the permit, with each county shown on the application receiving an amount determined according to the ratio of the total number of miles of county roads maintained by the county to the total number of miles of county roads maintained by all of the counties designated on the application.

(d) The county treasurer or officer shall deposit amounts received under this section to the credit of the county road and bridge fund. Money deposited to the credit of that fund under this subsection may be used only for a purpose authorized by Section 256.001(a).

Sec. 621.354. Disposition of Fees for Permit for Movement of Cylindrical Hay Bales.

Of each fee collected under Section 623.017, the department shall deposit:

(1) 90 percent in the state treasury to the credit of the state highway fund; and

(2) 10 percent in the state treasury to the credit of the Texas Department of Motor Vehicles fund.

Sec. 621.355. Distribution of Fees for Registration of Additional Weight.

(a) If an operator or owner is required to pay for registration of additional weight under Section 621.406 in a county other than the county in which the owner resides, the assessor-collector of the county in which the payment is made shall send the amount collected to the department for deposit to the credit of the state highway fund.

(b) The department shall send the county's share of the amount collected under Section 621.406 to the county in which the owner resides.

Sec. 621.356. Form of Payment.

The board may adopt rules prescribing the method for payment of a fee for a permit issued by the department that authorizes the operation of a vehicle and its load or a combination of vehicles and load exceeding size or weight limitations. The rules may:

(1) authorize the use of electronic funds transfer or a credit card issued by:

(A) a financial institution chartered by a state or the federal government; or

(B) a nationally recognized credit organization approved by the board; and

(2) require the payment of a discount or service charge for a credit card payment in addition to the fee.

SUBCHAPTER F ENFORCEMENT

Sec. 621.401. Definition.

In this subchapter, "weight enforcement officer" means:

(1) a license and weight inspector of the Department of Public Safety;

(2) a highway patrol officer;

(3) a sheriff or sheriff's deputy;

(4) a municipal police officer in a municipality with a population of:

(A) 100,000 or more; or

(B) 74,000 or more in a county with a population of more than 1.5 million;

(5) a police officer certified under Section 644.101; or

(6) a constable or deputy constable designated under Section 621.4015.

Sec. 621.4015. Designation by Commissioners Court.

(a) A county commissioners court may designate a constable or deputy constable of the county as a weight enforcement officer in a county:

(1) that is a county with a population of 1.5 million or more and is within 200 miles of an international border; or

(2) that is adjacent to a county with a population of 3.3 million or more; and

(3) in which a planned community is located that has 20,000 or more acres of land, that was originally established under the Urban Growth and New Community Development Act of 1970 (42 U.S.C. Section 4501 et seq.), and that is subject to restrictive covenants containing ad valorem or annual variable budget based assessments on real property.

(b) A constable or deputy constable designated under this section shall be subject to the requirements of Subchapter C, Chapter 644, Transportation Code.

Sec. 621.402. Weighing Loaded Vehicle.

(a) A weight enforcement officer who has reason to believe that the single axle weight, tandem axle weight, or gross weight of a loaded motor vehicle is unlawful may:

(1) weigh the vehicle using portable or stationary scales furnished or approved by the Department of Public Safety; or

(2) require the vehicle to be weighed by a public weigher.

(b) The officer may require that the vehicle be driven to the nearest available scales.

(c) A noncommissioned employee of the Department of Public Safety who is certified for the purpose by the public safety director and who is supervised by an officer of the Department of Public Safety may, in a port of entry or at a commercial motor vehicle inspection site, weigh a vehicle, require the vehicle to be weighed, or require a vehicle to be driven to the nearest scale under Subsections (a) and (b).

(d) Prior to assessment of a penalty for weight which exceeds the maximum allowable axle weights, the owner or operator is authorized to shift the load to reduce or eliminate such excess axle weight penalties as long as no part of the shipment is removed.

(e) The Department of Public Safety:

(1) shall establish by rule uniform weighing procedures for weight enforcement officers to ensure an accurate weight is obtained for a motor vehicle; and

(2) may revoke or rescind the authority of:

(A) a weight enforcement officer who fails to comply with those rules; or

(B) weight enforcement officers of a municipal police department, sheriff's department, or constable's office that fails to comply with those rules.

Sec. 621.403. Unloading Vehicle If Gross Weight Exceeded.

(a) If the gross weight of a motor vehicle weighed under Section 621.402 is heavier than the weight equal to the maximum gross weight authorized by law for that vehicle plus a tolerance allowance equal to five percent of that maximum weight, the weight enforcement officer shall require the operator or owner of the vehicle to unload a part of the load necessary to decrease the gross weight of the vehicle to a gross weight that is not heavier than the weight equal to the vehicle's maximum gross weight plus the applicable tolerance allowance.

(b) The operator or owner of the vehicle immediately shall unload the vehicle to the extent necessary to reduce the gross weight as required by Subsection (a), and the vehicle may not be operated further over a public highway or road of this state until the gross weight has been reduced as required by Subsection (a).

Sec. 621.404. Unloading Vehicle If Axle Weight Exceeded.

(a) If the axle weight of a motor vehicle weighed under Section 621.402 is heavier than the maximum axle weight authorized by law for the vehicle plus a tolerance allowance equal to five percent of

Transportation Code

that maximum weight, the weight enforcement officer shall require the operator or owner of the vehicle to rearrange the vehicle's cargo, if possible, to bring the vehicle's axles within the maximum axle weight allowed by law for that vehicle. If the requirement cannot be satisfied by rearrangement of cargo, a part of the vehicle's load shall be unloaded to decrease the axle weight to a weight that is not heavier than the maximum axle weight allowed by law for the vehicle plus the applicable tolerance allowance.

(b) The vehicle may not be operated further over the public highways or roads of the state until the axle weight of the vehicle has been reduced as required by Subsection (a).

Sec. 621.405. Unloading Exceptions.

(a) The operator or owner of a vehicle is not required to unload any part of the vehicle's load under Section 621.403 or 621.404 if the vehicle is:

(1) a motor vehicle loaded with timber, pulp wood, or agricultural products in their natural state being transported from the place of production to the place of marketing or first processing; or

(2) a vehicle crossing a highway as provided by Subchapter C, Chapter 623.

(b) The operator of a motor vehicle may proceed to the vehicle's destination without unloading the vehicle as required by Section 621.403 or 621.404 if the vehicle is loaded with livestock.

Sec. 621.406. Additional Gross Weight Registration.

(a) If the gross weight of the motor vehicle is not heavier than the maximum gross weight allowed for the vehicle but is heavier than the registered gross weight for the vehicle, the weight enforcement officer shall require the operator or owner of the vehicle to apply to the nearest available county assessor-collector to increase the gross weight for which the vehicle is registered to a weight equal to or heavier than the gross weight of the vehicle before the operator or owner may proceed.

(b) The vehicle may not be operated further over the public highways or roads of the state until the registered gross weight of the vehicle has been increased as required by Subsection (a) unless the load consists of livestock or perishable merchandise, in which event the operator or owner may proceed with the vehicle in the direction of the vehicle's destination to the nearest practical location at which the vehicle's load can be protected from damage or destruction before increasing the registered weight.

(c) If an operator or owner is found to be carrying a load that is heavier than the load allowed for the registered gross weight of the vehicle, the operator or owner shall pay for the registration of the additional weight for the entire period for which the vehicle is registered without regard to whether the owner or operator has been carrying similar loads from the date of purchase of the vehicle's current license registration for that registration period.

Sec. 621.407. Forms; Accounting Procedures.

The department shall prescribe all forms and accounting procedures necessary to carry out Sections 621.401—621.406.

Sec. 621.408. Powers of Weight Enforcement Officers.

(a) Except for the authority granted to a port-of-entry supervisor or inspector by Section 621.409, weight enforcement officers have exclusive authority to enforce this subchapter in any area of this state, including all ports of entry between Texas and the United Mexican States.

(b) If a noncommissioned employee weighs a vehicle under Section 621.402 and determines that an enforcement action, such as the issuance of a citation, is warranted, the employee may take enforcement action only if the employee is under the supervision of an officer of the Department of Public Safety.

Sec. 621.409. Weighing of Loaded Vehicles by Port-of-Entry Supervisors, Inspectors, or Weight Enforcement Officers.

(a) A port-of-entry supervisor, an inspector employed by the Alcoholic Beverage Commission, or a weight enforcement officer who has reason to believe that the axle or gross weight of a loaded motor vehicle is unlawful may weigh the vehicle using portable or stationary scales furnished or approved by the Department of Public Safety.

(b) If the vehicle exceeds the maximum gross weight authorized by law, plus the tolerance allowance provided by Section 621.403, the supervisor, inspector, or weight enforcement officer may prohibit the vehicle from proceeding farther into the state.

Sec. 621.410. Weight Record.

(a) This section applies only to cargo other than timber or another agricultural product in its natural state transported by a commercial motor vehicle.

Transportation Code

(b) A person who weighs cargo before or after unloading shall keep a written record, in the form prescribed by the department, containing the information required by Subsection (c).

(c) A record under this section must state:

(1) the origin, weight, and composition of the cargo;

(2) the date of loading or unloading, as applicable;

(3) the name and address of the shipper;

(4) the total number of axles on the vehicle or combination of vehicles transporting the cargo;

(5) an identification number of the vehicle or other identification of the vehicle required by department rules; and

(6) any other information required by the department.

(d) A person required to keep a record under this section shall keep the record for not less than 180 days after the date it is created. The person shall make the record available to inspection and copying by a weight enforcement officer on demand.

(e) This section does not apply to a vehicle that:

(1) transports material regulated under Section 623.161;

(2) is weighed by a weight enforcement officer;

(3) is weighed on scales owned by the state or a political subdivision of the state; or

(4) is weighed on scales owned by an enterprise principally engaged in the retail sale of motor fuels to the general public.

Sec. 621.411. Joint Operation of Certain Fixed-Site Facilities.

A county and the Department of Public Safety may enter into an agreement for the joint operation of a fixed-site facility located within the boundaries of the county.

SUBCHAPTER G OFFENSES AND PENALTIES

Sec. 621.501. Failure to Carry or Present Vehicle License Receipt.

(a) A person commits an offense if the person fails in violation of Section 621.002 to carry or present a vehicle registration receipt.

(b) An offense under this section is a misdemeanor punishable by a fine not to exceed $200.

Sec. 621.502. Prohibitions on Size and Weight; Restrictions on Construction and Equipment.

(a) A person may not operate or move a vehicle on a highway if:

(1) the vehicle's size is larger than the applicable maximum size authorized for that vehicle by this subtitle;

(2) the vehicle's single axle weight, tandem axle weight, or gross weight is greater than the applicable weight authorized for that vehicle by this subtitle; or

(3) the vehicle is not constructed or equipped as required by this subtitle.

(b) The owner of a vehicle the size of which or the weight, axle load, or wheel load of which is greater than the applicable maximum size, weight, or load authorized for that vehicle by this subtitle or a vehicle that is not constructed or equipped as required by this chapter may not cause or allow the vehicle to be operated or moved on a highway.

(c) A person may not transport on a vehicle a load the size or weight of which is more than the applicable maximum size, weight, or load authorized for that vehicle by this subtitle.

(d) Intent to operate a vehicle at a weight that is heavier than the weight authorized by a permit issued under Section 623.011 is presumed if:

(1) the vehicle is operated at a weight that is heavier than the applicable weight plus the tolerance allowance provided by Section 623.011(a); and

(2) a permit to operate at that weight has not been issued for the vehicle.

Sec. 621.503. Prohibition of Loading More Than Size or Weight Limitation.

(a) A person may not load, or cause to be loaded, a vehicle for operation on a public highway of this state that exceeds the height, width, length, or weight limitations for operation of that vehicle provided by this subtitle.

(b) Intent to violate a weight limitation is presumed if the weight of the loaded vehicle is heavier than the applicable axle or gross weight limit by 15 percent or more.

(c) This section does not apply to the loading of an agricultural or a forestry commodity before the commodity is changed in processing from its natural state.

(d) A violation of this section is subject to administrative enforcement under Subchapter N, Chapter 623, except that administrative enforcement may not be imposed on a person described by Subsection (a) if the person is an entity or is owned by the same entity that operated the loaded vehicle and has been assessed a criminal penalty under this subtitle for a violation associated with the load.

Sec. 621.504. Bridge or Underpass Clearance; Offense.

(a) A person commits an offense if the person operates or attempts to operate a vehicle over or on a bridge or through an underpass or similar structure unless the height of the vehicle, including load, is less than the vertical clearance of the structure as shown by the records of the Texas Department of Transportation.

(b) Except as provided by Subsection (c), an offense under this section is a Class C misdemeanor.

(c) If it is shown on the trial of an offense under this section that the person was not in compliance with all applicable license and permit requirements for the operation of the vehicle, an offense under this section is a Class B misdemeanor punishable by:

(1) a fine not to exceed $500;

(2) confinement in county jail for a term not to exceed 30 days; or

(3) both the fine and the confinement.

(d) It is an affirmative defense to prosecution of an offense under this section that at the time of the offense:

(1) the vertical clearance of the structure was less than that posted on the structure;

(2) the vehicle was being operated under the immediate direction of a law enforcement agency; or

(3) the vehicle was being operated in compliance with a permit authorizing the movement of the vehicle issued by the department or a political subdivision of this state.

Sec. 621.505. Maximum Size and Weight of Containers [Repealed].

Repealed by Acts 2001, 77th Leg., ch. 941 (S.B. 886), § 44, effective September 1, 2001.

Sec. 621.506. Offense of Operating or Loading Overweight Vehicle; Penalty; Defense.

(a) A person commits an offense if the person:

(1) operates a vehicle or combination of vehicles in violation of Section 621.101, 622.012, 622.031, 622.041, 622.0435, 622.051, 622.061, 622.133, 622.953, or 623.162; or

(2) loads a vehicle or causes a vehicle to be loaded in violation of Section 621.503.

(b) Except as provided by Subsections (b-1), (b-2), and (b-3), an offense under this section is a misdemeanor punishable:

(1) by a fine of not less than $100 and not more than $250;

(2) on conviction of an offense involving a vehicle having a single axle weight or tandem axle weight that is heavier than the vehicle's allowable weight, by a fine according to the following schedule:

Pounds Overweight	Fine Range
less than 2,500	$100 to $500
2,500-5,000	$500 to $1,000
more than 5,000	$1,000 to $2,500; or

(3) on conviction of an offense involving a vehicle having a gross weight that is heavier than the vehicle's allowable weight, by a fine according to the following schedule:

Pounds Overweight	Fine Range
less than 2,500	$100 to $500
2,500-5,000	$500 to $1,000
5,001-10,000	$1,000 to $2,500
10,001-20,000	$2,500 to $5,000
20,001-40,000	$5,000 to $7,000
more than 40,000	$7,000 to $10,000.

(b-1) On conviction of a third offense punishable under Subsection (b)(2) or (3), before the first anniversary of the date of a previous conviction of an offense punishable under Subsection (b)(2) or (3), the defendant shall be punished by a fine in an amount not to exceed twice the maximum amount specified by Subsection (b)(2) or (3).

(b-2) A defendant operating a vehicle or combination of vehicles at a weight for which a permit issued under this subtitle would authorize the operation, but who does not hold the permit, shall be punished by a fine in addition to the fine imposed under Subsection (b) of not less than $500 or more than $1,000, except that for a second or subsequent conviction under this section, the offense is punishable by an additional fine of not less than $2,500 or more than $5,000.

(b-3) A defendant operating a vehicle or combination of vehicles at a weight in excess of 84,000 pounds with a load that can reasonably be dismantled shall be punished by a fine in addition to the fine imposed under Subsection (b) of not less than $500 or more than $1,000, except that for a second or subsequent conviction under this section, the offense is punishable by an additional fine of not less than $2,500 or more than $5,000.

(c) On conviction of a violation of an axle weight limitation, the court may assess a fine less than the applicable minimum amount prescribed by Subsection (b) if the court finds that when the violation occurred:

Transportation Code

(1) the vehicle was registered to carry the maximum gross weight authorized for that vehicle under Section 621.101; and

(2) the gross weight of the vehicle did not exceed that maximum gross weight.

(d) A judge or justice shall promptly report to the Department of Public Safety each conviction obtained in the judge's or the justice's court under this section. The Department of Public Safety shall keep a record of each conviction reported to it under this subsection.

(e) If a corporation fails to pay the fine assessed on conviction of an offense under this section, the district or county attorney in the county in which the conviction occurs may file suit against the corporation to collect the fine.

(f) A justice or municipal court has jurisdiction of an offense under this section.

(g) Except as provided by Subsection (h), a governmental entity that collects a fine under this section for an offense involving a vehicle having a single axle weight, tandem axle weight, or gross weight that is more than 5,000 pounds heavier than the vehicle's allowable weight shall send an amount equal to 50 percent of the fine to the comptroller in the manner provided by Subchapter B, Chapter 133, Local Government Code.

(h) If the offense described by Subsection (g) occurred within 20 miles of an international border, the entire amount of the fine shall be deposited for the purposes of road maintenance in:

(1) the municipal treasury, if the fine was imposed by a municipal court; or

(2) the county treasury, if the fine was imposed by a justice court.

(i) A fine may not be imposed under this section that exceeds the minimum dollar amount that may be imposed unless the vehicle's weight was determined by a portable or stationary scale furnished or approved by the Department of Public Safety.

Sec. 621.507. General Offense; Penalty.

(a) A person commits an offense if the person violates a provision of this subtitle for which an offense is not specified by another section of this subtitle.

(b) An offense under this section is a misdemeanor punishable:

(1) by a fine not to exceed $200;

(2) on conviction before the first anniversary of the date of a previous conviction under this section:

(A) by a fine not to exceed $500, by confinement in a county jail for not more than 60 days, or by both the fine and confinement; or

(B) if the convicted person is a corporation, by a fine not to exceed $1,000; or

(3) on a conviction before the first anniversary of the date of a previous conviction under this section that was punishable under Subdivision (2) or this subdivision:

(A) by a fine not to exceed $1,000, by confinement in the county jail for not more than six months, or by both the fine and confinement; or

(B) if the convicted person is a corporation, by a fine not to exceed $2,000.

Sec. 621.508. Affirmative Defense for Operating Vehicle Over Maximum Allowable Weight.

(a) Except as provided by Subsection (a-1), it is an affirmative defense to prosecution of, or an action under Subchapter F for, the offense of operating a vehicle with a single axle weight or tandem axle weight heavier than the axle weight authorized by law that at the time of the offense the vehicle:

(1) had a single axle weight or tandem axle weight that was not heavier than the axle weight authorized by law plus 12 percent;

(2) was loaded with timber, pulp wood, wood chips, or cotton, livestock, or other agricultural products that are:

(A) in their natural state; and

(B) being transported from the place of production to the place of first marketing or first processing; and

(3) was not being operated on a portion of the national system of interstate and defense highways.

(a-1) The affirmative defense provided by Subsection (a) does not apply to the excess weights authorized under Section 623.421(b).

(b) It is an affirmative defense to prosecution of, or an action under Subchapter F for, the offense of operating a vehicle with a single axle weight, tandem axle weight, or gross weight heavier than the weight authorized by law that at the time of the offense the weight enforcement officer failed to follow the weighing procedures established under Section 621.402(e) when determining the weight of the vehicle.

Sec. 621.509. Failure to Maintain Weight Record.

(a) A person commits an offense if the person fails to keep a weight record in violation of Section 621.410.

(b) An offense under this section is a Class C misdemeanor.

Sec. 621.510. Permit Void.

A permit issued under this chapter is void on the failure of the owner or the owner's representative to comply with a rule of the board or with a condition placed on the permit by the department.

Sec. 621.511. Name on Permit; Offense.

(a) A person commits an offense if:

(1) the person operates or moves on a public highway a vehicle that is issued a permit under this subtitle; and

(2) the person operating or moving the vehicle is not the person named on the permit for the vehicle or an employee of that person.

(b) An offense under this section is a Class C misdemeanor.

(c) It is an exception to the application of this section that:

(1) the vehicle being operated or moved is a combination of a tow truck and a disabled, abandoned, or accident-damaged vehicle or vehicle combination; and

(2) the tow truck is towing the other vehicle or vehicle combination directly to the nearest terminal, vehicle storage facility, or authorized place of repair.

CHAPTER 622 SPECIAL PROVISIONS AND EXCEPTIONS FOR OVERSIZE OR OVERWEIGHT VEHICLES

SUBCHAPTER A GENERAL PROVISIONS

Sec. 622.001. Definitions.

In this chapter:

(1) "Commission" means the Texas Transportation Commission.

(2) "Department" means the Texas Department of Motor Vehicles.

Sec. 622.002. Rulemaking Authority.

The board of the department may adopt rules necessary to implement and enforce this chapter.

SUBCHAPTER B VEHICLES TRANSPORTING READY-MIXED CONCRETE

Sec. 622.011. Definition; Designation As Perishable.

(a) In this subchapter, "ready-mixed concrete truck" means:

(1) a vehicle designed exclusively to transport or manufacture ready-mixed concrete and includes a vehicle designed exclusively to transport and manufacture ready-mixed concrete; or

(2) a concrete pump truck.

(b) Ready-mixed concrete is a perishable product.

Sec. 622.012. Axle Weight Restrictions.

(a) A ready-mixed concrete truck may be operated on a public highway of this state only if the tandem axle weight is not heavier than 46,000 pounds and the single axle weight is not heavier than 23,000 pounds.

(b) A truck may be operated at a weight that exceeds the maximum single axle or tandem axle weight limitation by not more than 10 percent if the gross weight is not heavier than 69,000 pounds and the department has issued a permit that authorizes the operation of the vehicle under Section 623.0171.

Sec. 622.013. Surety Bond [Repealed].

Repealed by Acts 2013, 83rd Leg., ch. 1135 (H.B. 2741), § 140(2), effective September 1, 2013.

Sec. 622.014. Local Regulation.

(a) The governing body of a county or municipality that determines a public highway under its jurisdiction is insufficient to carry a load authorized by Section 622.012 may prescribe, by order or ordinance, rules governing the operation of a ready-mixed concrete truck over a public highway maintained by the county or municipality.

(b) The rules may include weight limitations on a truck with:

(1) a tandem axle weight that is heavier than 36,000 pounds;

(2) a single axle weight that is heavier than 12,000 pounds; or

(3) a gross weight that is heavier than 48,000 pounds.

Sec. 622.015. Local Surety Bond.

The governing body of a county or municipality may require the owner of a ready-mixed concrete truck to file a surety bond in an amount not to exceed $15,000 and conditioned that the owner of the truck will pay to the county or municipality any damage to a highway caused by the operation of the truck with a tandem axle weight that is heavier than 34,000 pounds.

Transportation Code

Sec. 622.016. Interstate and Defense Highways.

(a) This subchapter does not authorize the operation on the national system of interstate and defense highways in this state of a vehicle of a size or weight greater than that authorized by 23 U.S.C. Section 127, as amended.

(b) If the United States authorizes the operation on the national system of interstate and defense highways of a vehicle of a size or weight greater than that authorized on January 1, 1977, the new limit automatically takes effect on the national system of interstate and defense highways in this state.

Sec. 622.017. Penalties [Repealed].

Repealed by Acts 2013, 83rd Leg., ch. 1135 (H.B. 2741), § 140(2), effective September 1, 2013.

Sec. 622.018. Defense to Prosecution: Bond in Effect [Repealed].

Repealed by Acts 2013, 83rd Leg., ch. 1135 (H.B. 2741), § 140(2), effective September 1, 2013.

SUBCHAPTER C VEHICLES TRANSPORTING MILK

Sec. 622.031. Length and Axle Weight Restrictions.

A vehicle used exclusively to transport milk may be operated on a public highway of this state only if:

(1) the distance between the front wheel of the forward tandem axle and the rear wheel of the rear tandem axle, measured longitudinally, is 28 feet or more; and

(2) the weight carried on any group of axles is not heavier than 68,000 pounds.

Sec. 622.032. Interstate and Defense Highways.

(a) This subchapter does not authorize the operation on the national system of interstate and defense highways in this state of a vehicle of a size or weight greater than that authorized by 23 U.S.C. Section 127, as amended.

(b) If the United States authorizes the operation on the national system of interstate and defense highways of a vehicle of a size or weight greater than that authorized by 23 U.S.C. Section 127 on August 29, 1977, the new limit takes effect on the national system of interstate and defense highways in this state.

Sec. 622.033. Penalties [Repealed].

Repealed by Acts 2001, 77th Leg., ch. 941 (S.B. 886), § 44, effective September 1, 2001.

SUBCHAPTER D VEHICLES TRANSPORTING TIMBER OR TIMBER PRODUCTS

Sec. 622.041. Length Limitation.

(a) A person may operate over a highway or road of this state a vehicle or combination of vehicles that is used exclusively for transporting poles, piling, or unrefined timber from the point of origin of the timber (the forest where the timber is felled) to a wood processing mill if:

(1) the vehicle, or combination of vehicles, is not longer than 90 feet, including the load; and

(2) the distance from the point of origin to the destination or delivery point does not exceed 125 miles.

(b) Subsection (a)(1) does not apply to a truck-tractor or truck-tractor combination transporting poles, piling, or unrefined timber.

Sec. 622.042. Time of Operation; Display of Flag, Cloth, or Strobe Light.

(a) A vehicle subject to this subchapter may be operated only during daytime.

(b) In this section, "daytime" has the meaning assigned by Section 541.401.

(c) A red flag or cloth not less than 12 inches square or a strobe light must be displayed at the rear of the load carried on the vehicle so that the light or the entire area of the flag or cloth is visible to the driver of a vehicle approaching from the rear.

Sec. 622.043. Conformity with General Provisions Relating to Vehicle Size and Weight.

The width, height, and gross weight of a vehicle or combination of vehicles subject to this subchapter shall conform to Chapter 621.

Sec. 622.0435. Vehicles Transporting Raw Wood Products.

(a) The width, height, and gross weight of a vehicle or combination of vehicles subject to this subchapter that is transporting raw wood products shall conform to Chapters 621 and 623, except that a vehicle or combination of vehicles transporting raw wood products that has an outer bridge of 39 feet or more may have a maximum gross weight of 80,000 pounds.

(b) Notwithstanding any other provision of law, Subsection (a) does not authorize the operation of a vehicle or combination of vehicles subject to this subchapter that is transporting raw wood products on a bridge with a load limitation at a weight that exceeds that limitation.

Sec. 622.044. Extension of Load Beyond Rear of Vehicle.

Section 621.206(a) does not apply to a vehicle to which this subchapter applies to the extent that section prescribes a limit on the extension of the load beyond the rear of the vehicle.

Sec. 622.045. Interstate and Defense Highways.

(a) This subchapter does not authorize the operation on the national system of interstate and defense highways in this state of a vehicle of a size or weight greater than those permitted under 23 U.S.C. Section 127, as amended.

(b) If the United States authorizes the operation on the national system of interstate and defense highways of a vehicle of a size or weight greater than those permitted under 23 U.S.C. Section 127 on August 29, 1997, the new limit automatically takes effect on the national system of interstate and defense highways in this state.

SUBCHAPTER E VEHICLES TRANSPORTING ELECTRIC POWER TRANSMISSION POLES

Sec. 622.051. Length Limitation; Fee.

(a) A person may operate over a highway or road of this state a vehicle or combination of vehicles that is used exclusively for transporting poles required for the maintenance of electric power transmission and distribution lines if:

(1) the vehicle, or combination of vehicles, is not longer than 75 feet, including the load; and

(2) the operator of the vehicle, or combination of vehicles, pays to the department $120 each calendar year.

(b) Subsection (a)(1) does not apply to a truck-tractor or truck-tractor combination transporting poles for the maintenance of electric power transmission or distribution lines.

Sec. 622.052. Time of Operation; Speed; Lighting Requirements.

(a) A vehicle to which this subchapter applies may be operated only:

(1) between sunrise and sunset as defined by law; and

(2) at a speed not to exceed 50 miles per hour.

(b) A vehicle to which this subchapter applies shall display on the extreme end of the load:

(1) two red lamps visible at a distance of at least 500 feet from the rear;

(2) two red reflectors that indicate the maximum width and are visible, when light is insufficient or atmospheric conditions are unfavorable, at all distances from 100 to 600 feet from the rear when directly in front of lawful lower beams of headlamps; and

(3) two red lamps, one on each side, that indicate the maximum overhang and are visible at a distance of at least 500 feet from the side.

(c) The limitation in Subsection (a)(1) does not apply to a vehicle being operated to prevent interruption or impairment of electric service or to restore electric service that has been interrupted.

Sec. 622.053. Conformity with General Provisions Relating to Vehicle Size and Weight.

The width, height, and gross weight of a vehicle or combination of vehicles to which this subchapter applies shall conform to Chapter 621.

SUBCHAPTER F VEHICLES TRANSPORTING POLES OR PIPE

Sec. 622.061. Length Limitation.

(a) A person may operate over a highway or road of this state a vehicle or combination of vehicles exclusively for the transportation of poles or pipe if

Transportation Code

the vehicle or combination of vehicles is not longer than 65 feet, including the load.

(b) Subsection (a) does not apply to a truck-tractor or truck-tractor combination transporting poles or pipe.

Sec. 622.062. Time of Operation; Lighting Requirements.

(a) A vehicle to which this subchapter applies may be operated only during daytime.

(b) A vehicle to which this subchapter applies shall display on the extreme end of the load:

(1) two red lamps visible at a distance of at least 500 feet from the rear;

(2) two red reflectors that indicate the maximum width and are visible, when light is insufficient or atmospheric conditions are unfavorable, at all distances from 100 to 600 feet from the rear when directly in front of lawful lower beams of headlamps; and

(3) two red lamps, one on each side, that indicate the maximum overhang and are visible at a distance of at least 500 feet from the side.

(c) In this section, "daytime" has the meaning assigned by Section 541.401.

Sec. 622.063. Conformity with General Provisions Relating to Vehicle Size and Weight.

A vehicle or combination of vehicles to which this subchapter applies shall conform to the length, width, height, and weight requirements of Chapter 621.

SUBCHAPTER G SPECIAL MOBILE EQUIPMENT

Sec. 622.071. Definition.

In this subchapter, "special mobile equipment" has the meaning assigned by Section 541.201.

Sec. 622.072. Identification Markings on Special Mobile Equipment; Offense.

(a) Before the 31st day after the date a person becomes the owner of a unit of special mobile equipment, the person shall mark in a conspicuous place on the main chassis the manufacturer's serial number, an operation identification number recognized by law enforcement agencies, or a company identification number in a manner that is visible from not less than 50 feet.

(b) A person commits an offense if the person:

(1) owns a unit of special mobile equipment; and

(2) fails to mark the unit as provided by this section.

(c) An offense under this section is a misdemeanor punishable by a fine of not less than $10 or more than $100 for each unit.

Sec. 622.073. Transportation of Special Mobile Equipment; Offense.

(a) A person commits an offense if the person transports on a public road or highway a unit of special mobile equipment that is not marked as required by Section 622.072.

(b) Except as provided by Subsection (c), an offense under this section is a misdemeanor punishable by a fine of not less than $25 or more than $200.

(c) An offense under this section is a misdemeanor punishable by a fine of not less than $200 or more than $500, confinement in the county jail for a term of not less than 60 days or more than 180 days, or both the fine and the confinement if:

(1) the person committing the offense fails or refuses to exhibit, on demand of a peace officer, a document that contains:

(A) the name, address, and telephone number of the owner of the unit of special mobile equipment;

(B) the place of origin of the unit, including the address of and telephone number at that point and the date the unit was picked up;

(C) the destination of the unit, including the address or telephone number;

(D) a description of the unit being transported, including the manufacturer's serial number and other identification numbers;

(E) a description of the motor vehicle transporting the unit; and

(F) the name, address, and telephone number of the person operating the motor vehicle transporting the unit;

(2) the person committing the offense exhibits a false or forged document purporting to contain the information described by Subdivision (1); or

(3) on inspection by the peace officer, the peace officer determines that the identification number of the unit of special mobile equipment has been removed, covered, or altered.

(d) For purposes of Subsection (c)(3), a peace officer has probable cause to inspect a unit of special mobile equipment to determine the identification numbers of the unit if:

(1) the person operating the motor vehicle transporting the unit fails or refuses to exhibit on demand a document described by Subsection (c)(1); or

(2) the unit is not marked as required by Section 622.072.

Sec. 622.074. Nonapplicability of Subchapter.

This subchapter does not apply to:

(1) farm equipment used for a purpose other than construction;

(2) special mobile equipment owned by a dealer or distributor;

(3) a vehicle used to propel special mobile equipment that is registered as a farm vehicle under Section 502.433; or

(4) equipment while being used by a commercial hauler to transport special mobile equipment under hire of a person who derives $500 in gross receipts annually from a farming or ranching enterprise.

SUBCHAPTER H VEHICLES TRANSPORTING LUMBER

Sec. 622.081. Weight of Lumber [Repealed].

Repealed by Acts 2001, 77th Leg., ch. 941 (S.B. 886), § 44, effective September 1, 2001.

SUBCHAPTER I VEHICLES TRANSPORTING CERTAIN AGRICULTURAL PRODUCTS OR EQUIPMENT

Sec. 622.101. Vehicles Transporting Certain Agricultural Products or Processing Equipment.

(a) A single motor vehicle used exclusively to transport chile pepper modules, seed cotton, cotton, cotton burrs, or equipment used to transport or process chile pepper modules or cotton, including a motor vehicle or burr spreader, may not be operated on a highway or road if the vehicle is:

(1) wider than 10 feet and the highway has not been designated by the commission under Section 621.202;

(2) longer than 48 feet; or

(3) higher than 14 feet 6 inches.

(b) A single motor vehicle that transports agricultural products under Subsection (a) must be registered under Section 504.505.

(c) A truck-tractor operated in combination with a semitrailer and used to transport seed cotton or cotton may not be operated on a highway or road if the vehicle is higher than 14 feet 6 inches.

SUBCHAPTER J CERTAIN VEHICLES TRANSPORTING RECYCLABLE MATERIALS

Sec. 622.131. Definition.

In this subchapter, "recyclable material" has the meaning assigned by Section 361.421, Health and Safety Code.

Sec. 622.132. Applicability of Subchapter.

This subchapter applies only to a vehicle other than a tractor-trailer combination, only if equipped with a container roll-off unit or a front-end loader.

Sec. 622.133. Axle Weight Restrictions.

A single motor vehicle used exclusively to transport recyclable materials may be operated on a public highway only if the tandem axle weight is not heavier than 44,000 pounds, a single axle load is not heavier than 21,000 pounds, and the gross load is not heavier than 64,000 pounds.

Sec. 622.134. Surety Bond.

(a) Except as provided by Subsection (c), the owner of a vehicle covered by this subchapter with a tandem axle weight heavier than 34,000 pounds shall before operating the vehicle on a public highway of this state file with the department a surety bond subject to the approval of the Texas Department of Transportation in the principal amount set by the Texas Department of Transportation not to exceed $15,000 for each vehicle.

(b) The bond must be conditioned that the owner of the vehicle will pay, within the limits of the bond, to the Texas Department of Transportation any damage to a highway, to a county any damage to a county road, and to a municipality any damage to a municipal street caused by the operation of the vehicle.

(c) Subsection (a) does not apply to a vehicle owned by a municipality or a county.

(d) A copy of the bond shall be:

(1) carried on the vehicle when the vehicle is on a public highway; and

(2) presented to an officer authorized to enforce this chapter on request of the officer.

Transportation Code

Sec. 622.135. Interstate and Defense Highways.

(a) This subchapter does not authorize the operation on the national system of interstate and defense highways in this state of a vehicle of a size or weight greater than authorized in 23 U.S.C. Section 127, as amended.

(b) If the United States government authorizes the operation on the national system of interstate and defense highways of vehicles of a size or weight greater than those authorized on January 1, 1983, the new limit automatically takes effect on the national system of interstate and defense highways in this state.

Sec. 622.136. Penalty.

A person commits an offense if the person fails in violation of Section 622.134(d) to carry or present the copy of the bond filed with the department. An offense under this section is a misdemeanor punishable by a fine not to exceed $200.

Sec. 622.137. Defense to Prosecution: Bond in Effect.

(a) It is a defense to prosecution under Section 622.136 that the person charged produces a surety bond that complies with Section 622.134 that was valid at the time the offense is alleged to have occurred.

(b) If the court verifies the bond produced by the person, the court shall dismiss the charge.

SUBCHAPTER K AUTOMOBILE TRANSPORTERS

Sec. 622.151. Definitions.

In this subchapter:

(1) "Automobile transporter" has the meaning assigned by 49 U.S.C. Section 31111.

(2) "Backhaul" means the return trip of a vehicle transporting cargo or general freight.

(3) "Stinger-steered" means a truck-tractor and semitrailer combination in which the fifth wheel is located on a drop frame located behind and below the rearmost axle of the truck-tractor.

Sec. 622.152. Automobile Transporter Backhauls.

(a) An automobile transporter that complies with the weight and size limitations for a truck-tractor and semitrailer combination under this subtitle may transport cargo or general freight on a backhaul.

(b) For purposes of Subsection (a), an automobile transporter is presumed to be on a backhaul if the automobile transporter is transporting cargo or general freight back over all or part of the same route.

Sec. 622.153. Maximum Extended Length of Load.

Notwithstanding Section 621.206, an automobile transporter that is stinger-steered may carry a load that extends not more than:

(1) four feet beyond its front; and

(2) six feet beyond its rear.

SUBCHAPTER Y MISCELLANEOUS SIZE EXCEPTIONS

Sec. 622.901. Width Exceptions.

(a) In this section, "farm tractor" and "implement of husbandry" have the meanings assigned by Section 541.201.

(b) The width limitation provided by Section 621.201 does not apply to:

(1) highway building or maintenance machinery that is traveling:

(A) during daylight on a public highway other than a highway that is part of the national system of interstate and defense highways; or

(B) for not more than 50 miles on a highway that is part of the national system of interstate and defense highways;

(2) a vehicle traveling during daylight on a public highway other than a highway that is part of the national system of interstate and defense highways or traveling for not more than 50 miles on a highway that is part of the national system of interstate and defense highways if the vehicle is:

(A) a farm tractor or implement of husbandry; or

(B) a vehicle on which a farm tractor, implement of husbandry, or equipment used in the harvesting and production of timber, other than a tractor, implement, or equipment being transported from one dealer to another, is being moved by the owner of the tractor, implement, or equipment or by an agent or employee of the owner:

(i) to deliver the tractor, implement, or equipment to a new owner;

Transportation Code

(ii) to transport the tractor, implement, or equipment to or from a mechanic for maintenance or repair; or

(iii) in the course of an agricultural or forestry operation;

(3) machinery that is used solely for drilling water wells, including machinery that is a unit or a unit mounted on a conventional vehicle or chassis, and that is traveling:

(A) during daylight on a public highway other than a highway that is part of the national system of interstate and defense highways; or

(B) for not more than 50 miles on a highway that is part of the national system of interstate and defense highways;

(4) a vehicle owned or operated by a public, private, or volunteer fire department;

(5) a vehicle registered under Section 502.431; or

(6) a recreational vehicle to which Section 622.903 applies.

Sec. 622.902. Length Exceptions.

The length limitations provided by Sections 621.203 to 621.205 do not apply to:

(1) machinery used exclusively for drilling water wells, including machinery that is itself a unit or that is a unit mounted on a conventional vehicle or chassis;

(2) a vehicle owned or operated by a public, private, or volunteer fire department;

(3) a vehicle or combination of vehicles operated exclusively in the territory of a municipality or to a combination of vehicles operated by a municipality in a suburb adjoining the municipality in which the municipality has been using the equipment or similar equipment in connection with an established service to the suburb;

(4) a truck-tractor, truck-tractor combination, or truck-trailer combination exclusively transporting machinery, materials, and equipment used in the construction, operation, and maintenance of facilities, including pipelines, that are used for the discovery, production, and processing of natural gas or petroleum;

(5) a drive-away saddlemount vehicle transporter combination or a drive-away saddlemount with fullmount vehicle transporter combination, as defined by 23 C.F.R. Part 658 or its successor, if:

(A) the overall length of the combination is not longer than 97 feet; and

(B) the combination does not have more than three saddlemounted vehicles if the combination does not include more than one fullmount vehicle;

(6) the combination of a tow truck and another vehicle or vehicle combination if:

(A) the other vehicle or vehicle combination cannot be normally or safely driven or was abandoned on a highway; and

(B) the tow truck is towing the other vehicle or vehicle combination directly to the nearest authorized place of repair, terminal, or destination of unloading;

(7) a vehicle or combination of vehicles used to transport a harvest machine that is used in farm custom harvesting operations on a farm if the overall length of the vehicle or combination is not longer than:

(A) 75 feet if the vehicle is traveling on a highway that is part of the national system of interstate and defense highways or the federal aid primary highway system; or

(B) 81-1/2 feet if the vehicle is not traveling on a highway that is part of the national system of interstate and defense highways or the federal aid primary highway system;

(8) a truck-tractor operated in combination with a semitrailer and trailer or semitrailer and semitrailer if:

(A) the combination is used to transport a harvest machine that is used in farm custom harvesting operations on a farm;

(B) the overall length of the combination, excluding the length of the truck-tractor, is not longer than 81-1/2 feet; and

(C) the combination is traveling on a highway that:

(i) is not part of the national system of interstate and defense highways or the federal aid primary highway system; and

(ii) is located in a county with a population of less than 300,000; or

(9) a towaway trailer transporter combination, as defined by 49 U.S.C. Section 31111, if the overall length of the combination is not longer than 82 feet.

Sec. 622.903. Width Limitation on Certain Recreational Vehicles.

(a) In this section:

(1) "Appurtenance" includes an awning, a grab handle, lighting equipment, or a vent. The term does not include a load-carrying device.

(2) "Recreational vehicle" has the meaning assigned by Section 522.004.

(b) A recreational vehicle may exceed a width limitation established by Section 621.201 or 621.202 if the excess width is attributable to an appurtenance that extends six inches or less beyond a fender on one or both sides of the vehicle.

SUBCHAPTER Z
MISCELLANEOUS WEIGHT EXCEPTIONS

Sec. 622.951. Oil Field Service Equipment [Repealed].

Repealed by Acts 2001, 77th Leg., ch. 941 (S.B. 886), § 44, effective September 1, 2001.

Sec. 622.952. Emergency Vehicle.

(a) The weight limitations of Section 621.101 do not apply to an emergency vehicle.

(b) The weight of an emergency vehicle may not exceed the greater of:

(1) the manufacturer's gross vehicle weight capacity or axle design rating; or

(2) including all enforcement tolerances, a:

(A) gross weight of 86,000 pounds;

(B) single steering axle weight of 24,000 pounds;

(C) single drive axle weight of 33,500 pounds;

(D) tandem axle weight of 62,000 pounds; or

(E) tandem rear drive steer axle weight of 52,000 pounds.

(c) In this section, "emergency vehicle" means a vehicle designed to be used under emergency conditions:

(1) to transport personnel and equipment; and

(2) to support the suppression of fires and mitigation of other hazardous situations.

Transportation Code

Sec. 622.953. Vehicle Transporting Seed Cotton or Chile Pepper Modules.

(a) The weight limitations of Section 621.101 do not apply to a single motor vehicle used exclusively to transport chile pepper modules, seed cotton, or equipment, including a motor vehicle, used to transport or process chile pepper modules or seed cotton.

(b) The overall gross weight of a single motor vehicle used to transport seed cotton or equipment used to transport or process seed cotton may not be heavier than 64,000 pounds.

(c) The overall gross weight of a single motor vehicle used to transport chile pepper modules or equipment used to transport or process chile pepper modules may not be heavier than 54,000 pounds.

(d) The owner of a single motor vehicle to which this section applies that has a gross weight above the gross weight authorized by this section that is applicable to the vehicle is liable to the state, county, or municipality for any damage to a highway, street, road, or bridge caused by the weight of the load.

(e) A vehicle to which this section applies may not be operated on the national system of interstate and defense highways if the vehicle exceeds the maximum weight authorized by 23 U.S.C. Section 127, as amended.

Sec. 622.954. Tow Trucks.

(a) A permit is not required to exceed the weight limitations of Section 621.101 by a combination of a tow truck and another vehicle or vehicle combination if:

(1) the nature of the service provided by the tow truck is needed to remove disabled, abandoned, or accident-damaged vehicles; and

(2) the tow truck is towing the other vehicle or vehicle combination directly to the nearest authorized place of repair, terminal, or vehicle storage facility.

(b) This section does not authorize the operation on the national system of interstate and defense highways in this state of vehicles with a weight greater than authorized by federal law.

Sec. 622.955. Increase of Maximum Weight for Vehicles with Idle Reduction Systems.

(a) For purposes of this section, "idle reduction system" means a system that provides heating, cooling, or electrical service to a commercial vehicle's sleeper berth for the purpose of reducing the idling of a motor vehicle.

(b) Notwithstanding any provision to the contrary, the maximum gross vehicle weight limit and axle weight limit for any vehicle or combination of vehicles equipped with an idle reduction system shall be increased by an amount necessary to compensate for the additional weight of the idle reduction system.

(c) The weight increase under Subsection (b) may not be greater than 550 pounds.

(d) On request by an appropriate law enforcement officer or an official of an appropriate regulatory agency, the vehicle operator shall provide proof that:

(1) the idle reduction technology is fully functional at all times; and

(2) the weight increase is not used for any purpose other than the use of an idle reduction system.

CHAPTER 623
PERMITS FOR OVERSIZE OR OVERWEIGHT VEHICLES

SUBCHAPTER A GENERAL PROVISIONS

Sec. 623.001. Definitions.

In this chapter:

(1) "Department" means the Texas Department of Motor Vehicles.

(2) "Shipper" means a person who consigns the movement of a shipment.

(3) "Shipper's certificate of weight" means a document described by Section 623.274.

(4) "Board" means the board of the Texas Department of Motor Vehicles.

(5) "Commission" means the Texas Transportation Commission.

Sec. 623.002. Rulemaking Authority.

The board may adopt rules necessary to implement and enforce this chapter.

Sec. 623.003. Route Determination.

(a) To the extent the department is required to determine a route under this chapter, the department shall base the department's routing decision on information provided by the Texas Department of Transportation.

(b) The Texas Department of Transportation shall provide the department with all routing information necessary to complete a permit issued under Section 623.071, 623.121, 623.142, 623.192, 623.402, or 623.421.

Sec. 623.004. Denial of Permit.

(a) The department may deny an application for a permit under this subtitle submitted by an applicant who:

(1) is the subject of an out-of-service order issued by the Federal Motor Carrier Safety Administration; or

(2) the Department of Public Safety has determined has:

(A) an unsatisfactory safety rating under 49 C.F.R. Part 385; or

(B) multiple violations of Chapter 644, a rule adopted under that chapter, or Subtitle C.

(b) A denial of an application for a permit under this section is not required to be preceded by notice and an opportunity for hearing.

(c) An applicant may appeal a denial under this section by filing an appeal with the department not later than the 26th day after the date the department issues notice of the denial to the applicant.

Sec. 623.005. Disposition of Permit Fee in Texas Department of Motor Vehicles Fund.

(a) This section applies only to a permit authorized by the legislature on or after September 1, 2019.

(b) Ten percent of the fee collected for a permit issued by the department under this subtitle shall be deposited to the credit of the Texas Department of Motor Vehicles fund with the remaining fee distribution to be adjusted proportionately, if needed.

(c) Subsection (b) does not apply if a provision of this subtitle expressly requires a different amount of a fee collected to be deposited to the credit of the Texas Department of Motor Vehicles fund.

Sec. 623.006. Disposition and Use of Permit Fees Due to County or Municipality.

Except as otherwise specified by this subtitle:

(1) at least once each fiscal year, the comptroller shall send from fees collected for a permit issued by the department under this chapter any amounts due to a county or municipality;

(2) amounts due to a county must be sent to the county treasurer or office performing the function of that office for deposit to the credit of the county road and bridge fund; and

(3) amounts due to a municipality must be sent to the office performing the function of treasurer for the municipality and may be used by the municipality only to fund commercial motor vehicle enforcement programs or road and bridge maintenance or infrastructure projects.

Sec. 623.007. Permit to Be Carried in Vehicle.

A permit issued by the department under this subtitle must be carried, in a manner prescribed by the department, in the vehicle that is being operated under the permit.

Sec. 623.008. Authority to Require Escort Flag Vehicles and Escort Flaggers.

(a) In this section:

(1) "Escort flag vehicle" means a vehicle that precedes or follows an oversize or overweight vehicle operating under a permit issued by the department for the purpose of facilitating the safe movement of the oversize or overweight vehicle over roads.

(2) "Escort flagger" means a person who:

(A) has successfully completed a training program in traffic direction as defined by the basic

Transportation Code

peace officer course curriculum established by the Texas Commission on Law Enforcement; and

(B) in accordance with a permit issued by the department under this subtitle, operates an escort flag vehicle or directs and controls the flow of traffic using a hand signaling device or an automated flagger assistance device.

(b) In addition to any other specific requirement under this subtitle, the department may require a person operating under a permit issued by the department under this subtitle to use one or more escort flag vehicles and escort flaggers if required:

(1) by the Texas Department of Transportation; or

(2) for the safe movement over roads of an oversize or overweight vehicle and its load.

SUBCHAPTER B
GENERAL PERMITS

Sec. 623.011. Permit for Excess Axle or Gross Weight.

(a) The department may issue a permit that authorizes the operation of a commercial motor vehicle, trailer, semitrailer, or combination of those vehicles, or a truck-tractor or combination of a truck-tractor and one or more other vehicles:

(1) at an axle weight that is not heavier than the weight equal to the maximum allowable axle weight for the vehicle or combination plus a tolerance allowance of 10 percent of that allowable weight; and

(2) at a gross weight that is not heavier than the weight equal to the maximum allowable gross weight for the vehicle or combination plus a tolerance allowance of five percent.

(b) To qualify for a permit under this section:

(1) the vehicle must be registered under Chapter 502 for the maximum gross weight applicable to the vehicle under Section 621.101, not to exceed 80,000 pounds;

(2) the security requirement of Section 623.012 must be satisfied; and

(3) a base permit fee of $90, any additional fee required by Section 623.0111, and any additional fee set by the board under Section 623.0112 must be paid.

(c) A permit issued under this section:

(1) is valid for one year; and

(2) must be carried in the vehicle for which it is issued.

(d) When the department issues a permit under this section, the department shall issue a sticker to be placed on the front windshield of the vehicle. The department shall design the form of the sticker to aid in the enforcement of weight limits for vehicles.

(e) The sticker must:

(1) indicate the expiration date of the permit; and

(2) be removed from the vehicle when:

(A) the permit for operation of the vehicle expires;

(B) a lease of the vehicle expires; or

(C) the vehicle is sold.

(f) A person commits an offense if the person fails to display the sticker in the manner required by Subsection (d). An offense under this subsection is a Class C misdemeanor. Section 623.019(g) applies to an offense under this subsection.

(g) A vehicle operating under a permit issued under this section may exceed the maximum allowable gross weight tolerance allowance by not more than five percent, regardless of the weight of any one axle or tandem axle, if no axle or tandem axle exceeds the tolerance permitted by Subsection (a).

Sec. 623.0111. Additional Fee for Operation of Vehicle Under Permit.

(a) When a person applies for a permit under Section 623.011, the person must:

(1) designate in the application each county in which the vehicle will be operated; and

(2) pay in addition to other fees an annual fee in an amount determined according to the following table:

Number of Counties Designated	Fee
1—5	$175
6—20	$250
21—40	$450
41—60	$625
61—80	$800
81—100	$900
101—254	$1,000

(b) A permit issued under Section 623.011 does not authorize the operation of the vehicle in a county that is not designated in the application.

(c) Of the fees collected under Subsection (a), the following amounts shall be deposited to the general revenue fund, 90 percent of the remainder shall be deposited to the credit of the state highway fund, and 10 percent of the remainder shall be deposited to the credit of the Texas Department of Motor Vehicles fund:

Number of Counties Designated	Amount Allocated to General Revenue Fund
1—5	$125
6—20	$125
21—40	$345
41—60	$565
61—80	$785
81—100	$900
101—254	$1,000

Sec. 623.0112. Additional Administrative Fee.

When a person applies for a permit under Section 623.011, the person must pay in addition to other fees an administrative fee adopted by board rule in an amount not to exceed the direct and indirect cost to the department of:

(1) issuing a sticker under Section 623.011(d);

(2) distributing fees under Section 621.353; and

(3) maintaining the list under Section 623.013.

Sec. 623.0113. Route Restrictions.

(a) Except as provided by Subsection (b), a permit issued under Section 623.011 does not authorize the operation of a vehicle on:

(1) the national system of interstate and defense highways in this state if the weight of the vehicle is greater than authorized by federal law; or

(2) a bridge for which a maximum weight and load limit has been established and posted by the Texas Transportation Commission under Section 621.102 or the commissioners court of a county under Section 621.301, if the gross weight of the vehicle and load or the axles and wheel loads are greater than the limits established and posted under those sections.

(b) The restrictions under Subsection (a)(2) do not apply if a bridge described by Subsection (a)(2) provides the only public vehicular access from an origin or to a destination by a holder of a permit issued under Section 623.011.

Sec. 623.012. Security for Permit.

(a) An applicant for a permit under Section 623.011, other than a permit under that section to operate a vehicle loaded with timber or pulp wood, wood chips, cotton, or agricultural products in their natural state, and an applicant for a permit under Section 623.321 shall file with the department:

(1) a blanket bond; or

(2) an irrevocable letter of credit issued by a financial institution the deposits of which are guaranteed by the Federal Deposit Insurance Corporation.

(b) The bond or letter of credit must:

(1) be in the amount of $15,000 payable to the counties of this state;

(2) be conditioned that the applicant will pay a county for any damage to a road or bridge of the county caused by the operation of the vehicle:

(A) for which the permit is issued at a heavier weight than the maximum weights authorized by Subchapter B of Chapter 621 or Section 621.301 or 623.321; or

(B) that is in violation of Section 623.323; and

(3) provide that the issuer is to notify the county and the applicant in writing promptly after a payment is made by the issuer on the bond or letter of credit.

(c) If an issuer of a bond or letter of credit pays under the bond or letter of credit, the permit holder shall file with the department before the 31st day after the date on which the payment is made:

(1) a replacement bond or letter of credit in the amount prescribed by Subsection (b) for the original bond or letter of credit; or

(2) a notification from the issuer of the existing bond or letter of credit that the bond or letter of credit has been restored to the amount prescribed by Subsection (b).

(d) If the filing is not made as required by Subsection (c), each permit held by the permit holder under Section 623.011 automatically expires on the 31st day after the date on which the payment is made on the bond or letter of credit.

Sec. 623.013. List of Permits Issued.

(a) The department shall make available on the department's Internet website a searchable and downloadable list by county of each permit issued under Section 623.011. The list must include the following information for each permit:

(1) the name and address of the person for whom the permit was issued;

(2) the vehicle identification number and license plate number of the vehicle;

(3) the permit number; and

(4) the effective date of the permit.

(b) On request of a county, the department shall send a copy of the permit and the bond or letter of credit required for the permit to the county.

Sec. 623.014. Transfer of Permit.

(a) A permit issued under Section 623.011 may not be transferred.

(b) If the vehicle for which a permit was issued is destroyed or permanently inoperable, a person may

Transportation Code

apply to the department for a credit for the remainder of the permit period.

(c) The department shall issue the prorated credit if the person:

(1) pays the fee adopted by the board; and

(2) provides the department with:

(A) the original permit; or

(B) if the original permit does not exist, written evidence in a form approved by the department that the vehicle has been destroyed or is permanently inoperable.

(d) The fee adopted by the board under Subsection (c)(1) may not exceed the cost of issuing the credit. A fee collected by the department under Subsection (c)(1) shall be deposited to the credit of the Texas Department of Motor Vehicles fund.

(e) A credit issued under Subsection (c) may be used only toward the payment of a permit fee under this subchapter.

Sec. 623.015. Liability for Damage.

(a) The liability of a holder of a permit issued under Section 623.011 for damage to a county road is not limited to the amount of the bond or letter of credit required for the issuance of the permit.

(b) The holder of a permit issued under Section 623.011 who has filed the bond or letter of credit required for the permit is liable to the county only for the actual damage to a county road, bridge, or culvert with a load limitation established under Subchapter B of Chapter 621 or Section 621.301 caused by the operation of the vehicle in excess of the limitation. If a county judge, county commissioner, county road supervisor, or county traffic officer requires the vehicle to travel over a designated route, it is presumed that the designated route, including a bridge or culvert on the route, is of sufficient strength and design to carry and withstand the weight of the vehicle traveling over the designated route.

Sec. 623.0155. Indemnification from Motor Carrier Prohibited.

(a) A person may not require indemnification from a motor carrier as a condition to:

(1) the transportation of property for compensation or hire by the carrier;

(2) entrance on property by the carrier for the purpose of loading, unloading, or transporting property for compensation or hire; or

(3) a service incidental to an activity described by Subdivision (1) or (2), including storage of property.

(b) Subsection (a) does not apply to:

(1) a claim arising from damage or loss from a wrongful or negligent act or omission of the carrier; or

(2) services or goods other than those described by Subsection (a).

(c) In this section, "motor carrier" means a common carrier, specialized carrier, or contract carrier that transports property for hire. The term does not include a person who transports property as an incidental activity of a nontransportation business activity regardless of whether the person imposes a separate charge for the transportation.

(d) A provision that is contrary to Subsection (a) is not enforceable.

Sec. 623.016. Recovery on Permit Security.

(a) A county may recover on the bond or letter of credit required for a permit issued under Section 623.011 only by a suit against the permit holder and the issuer of the bond or letter of credit.

(b) Venue for a suit under this section is in district court in:

(1) the county in which the defendant resides;

(2) the county in which the defendant has its principal place of business in this state; or

(3) the county in which the damage occurred.

Sec. 623.017. Permit for Movement of Cylindrical Hay Bales.

(a) The department may issue an annual permit to authorize the movement of a vehicle that is used to carry cylindrical bales of hay and that is wider than the maximum allowable vehicle width but not wider than 12 feet.

(b) A $10 permit fee must accompany an application for a permit under this section.

Sec. 623.0171. Permit for Ready-Mixed Concrete Trucks.

(a) In this section, "ready-mixed concrete truck" has the meaning assigned by Section 622.011.

(b) The department may issue a permit that authorizes the operation of a ready-mixed concrete truck with three axles.

(c) To qualify for a permit under this section, a base permit fee of $1,000 must be paid, except as provided by Subsection (g).

(d) A permit issued under this section:

(1) is valid for one year, except as provided by Subsection (g); and

(2) must be carried in the vehicle for which it is issued.

Transportation Code

(e) When the department issues a permit under this section, the department shall issue a sticker to be placed on the front windshield of the vehicle above the inspection certificate issued to the vehicle. The department shall design the form of the sticker to aid in the enforcement of weight limits for vehicles.

(f) The sticker must:

(1) indicate the expiration date of the permit; and

(2) be removed from the vehicle when:

(A) the permit for operation of the vehicle expires;

(B) a lease of the vehicle expires; or

(C) the vehicle is sold.

(g) The department may issue a permit under this section that is valid for a period of less than one year. The department shall prorate the applicable fee required by Subsection (c) for a permit issued under this subsection as necessary to reflect the term of the permit.

(h) Unless otherwise provided by state or federal law, a county or municipality may not require a permit, fee, or license for the operation of a ready-mixed concrete truck in addition to a permit, fee, or license required by state law.

(i) Section 622.015 does not apply to an owner of a ready-mixed concrete truck who holds a permit under this section for the truck.

(j) Unless otherwise provided by state or federal law, a ready-mixed concrete truck may operate on a state, county, or municipal road, including a load-zoned county road or a frontage road adjacent to a federal interstate highway, if the truck displays a sticker required by Subsection (e) and does not exceed the maximum gross weight authorized under Section 622.012.

(k) For the purposes of Subsection (*l*), the department by rule shall require an applicant to designate in the permit application the counties in which the applicant intends to operate.

(*l*) Of the fee collected under this section for a permit:

(1) 50 percent of the amount collected shall be deposited to the credit of the state highway fund; and

(2) the other 50 percent shall be divided among and distributed to the counties designated in permit applications under Subsection (k) according to department rule.

(m) [Repealed.]

Sec. 623.0172. Permit for Intermodal Shipping Container.

(a) In this section, "intermodal shipping container" means an enclosed, standardized, reusable container that:

(1) is used to pack, ship, move, or transport cargo;

(2) is designed to be carried on a semitrailer and loaded onto or unloaded from:

(A) a ship or vessel for international transportation; or

(B) a rail system for international transportation; and

(3) when combined with vehicles transporting the container, has a gross weight or axle weight that exceeds the limits allowed by law to be transported over a state highway or county or municipal road.

(b) The department shall issue an annual permit for the international transportation of an intermodal shipping container moving by a truck-tractor and semitrailer combination that has six total axles and is equipped with a roll stability support safety system and truck blind spot systems only if:

(1) the gross weight of the combination does not exceed 93,000 pounds;

(2) the distance between the front axle of the truck-tractor and the last axle of the semitrailer, measured longitudinally, is approximately 647 inches;

(3) the truck-tractor is configured as follows:

(A) one single axle that does not exceed 13,000 pounds;

(B) one two-axle group that does not exceed 37,000 pounds, in which no axle in the group exceeds 18,500 pounds; and

(C) the distance between the individual axles on the two-axle group of the truck-tractor, measured longitudinally, is not less than 51 inches and not more than 52 inches; and

(4) the semitrailer is configured as follows:

(A) one three-axle group that does not exceed 49,195 pounds, in which no axle in the group exceeds 16,400 pounds; and

(B) the distance between the individual axles in the three-axle group of the semitrailer, measured longitudinally, is 60 inches.

(c) The department shall restrict vehicles operating under a permit issued under this section to routes that are:

(1) located in a county with a population of more than 90,000;

(2) on highways in the state highway system; and

(3) not more than five miles from the border between this state and Arkansas.

(d) An intermodal shipping container being moved under a permit issued under this section must be continuously sealed from the point of origin to the point of destination with a seal that is required by:

(1) the United States Customs and Border Protection;

Transportation Code

(2) the United States Food and Drug Administration; or

(3) federal law or regulation.

(e) A permit issued under this section does not authorize the operation of a vehicle combination described by Subsection (b) on:

(1) load-restricted roads or bridges, including a road or bridge for which a maximum weight and load limit has been established and posted by the Texas Department of Transportation under Section 621.102; or

(2) routes for which the Texas Department of Transportation has not authorized the operation of a vehicle combination described by Subsection (b).

(f) A permit issued under this subchapter does not authorize the transportation of a material designated as of January 1, 2017, as a hazardous material by the United States secretary of transportation under 49 U.S.C. Section 5103(a).

(g) An applicant for a permit under this section must designate each Texas Department of Transportation district in which the permit will be used.

(h) The department shall initially set the fee for a permit issued under this section in an amount not to exceed $2,000. Beginning in 2022, on September 1 of each even-numbered year the department shall set the fee for a permit issued under this section in an amount based on a reasonable estimate of the costs associated with the operation of vehicles issued a permit under this section over routes described by Subsection (c), including any increase in the costs necessary to maintain or repair those highways. The estimate shall be based on the results of the study conducted under Subsection (l).

(i) Of the fee collected under this section for a permit:

(1) 90 percent shall be deposited to the credit of the state highway fund;

(2) 5 percent shall be deposited to the credit of the Texas Department of Motor Vehicles fund; and

(3) 5 percent shall be deposited to the appropriate county road and bridge fund.

(j) A fee deposited under Subsection (i)(1) may only be used for transportation projects in the Texas Department of Transportation district designated in the permit application for which the fee was assessed.

(k) The department may suspend a permit issued under this section if the department receives notice from the Federal Highway Administration that the operation of a vehicle under a permit authorized by this section would result in the loss of federal highway funding.

(l) Beginning in 2022, not later than September 1 of each even-numbered year, the Texas Department of Transportation shall conduct a study concerning vehicles operating under a permit issued under this section and publish the results of the study. In conducting the study, the Texas Department of Transportation shall collect and examine the following information:

(1) the weight and configuration of vehicles operating under a permit under this section that are involved in a motor vehicle accident;

(2) the types of vehicles operating under a permit issued under this section;

(3) traffic volumes and variations of vehicles operating under a permit issued under this section;

(4) weigh-in-motion data for highways located in and around the area described by Subsection (c);

(5) impacts to state and local bridges, including long-term bridge performance, for bridges located in and around the area described by Subsection (c); and

(6) impacts to state and local roads, including changes in pavement design standards, construction specification details, maintenance frequency and types, and properties of pavement and underlying soils resulting from or necessitated by vehicles operating under a permit issued under this section.

Sec. 623.018. County Permit.

(a) The commissioners court of a county, through the county judge, may issue a permit for:

(1) the transportation over highways of that county, other than state highways and public roads in the territory of a municipality, of an overweight, oversize, or overlength commodity that cannot be reasonably dismantled; or

(2) the operation over a highway of that county other than a state highway or public road in the territory of a municipality of:

(A) superheavy or oversize equipment for the transportation of an overweight, oversize, or overlength commodity that cannot be reasonably dismantled; or

(B) vehicles or combinations of vehicles that exceed the weights authorized under Subchapter B, Chapter 621, or Section 621.301.

(b) A permit under Subsection (a) may not be issued for longer than 90 days.

(c) The commissioners court of a county, through the county judge, may issue an annual permit to a dealer in implements of husbandry to allow the dealer to use vehicles that exceed the width limitations provided by this chapter to transport an implement on a highway. The county judge may exercise authority under this subsection independently of the commissioners court until the commissioners court takes action on the request.

(d) If a vehicle is being operated in compliance with a permit issued under Section 623.011 or 623.402, a commissioners court may not:

(1) issue a permit under this section or charge an additional fee for or otherwise regulate or restrict the operation of the vehicle because of weight; or

(2) require the owner or operator to:

(A) execute or comply with a road use agreement or indemnity agreement;

(B) make a filing or application; or

(C) provide a bond or letter of credit, other than the bond or letter of credit prescribed by Section 623.012 for a vehicle issued a permit under Section 623.011.

(e) The commissioners court may require a bond to be executed by an applicant in an amount sufficient to guarantee the payment of any damage to a road or bridge sustained as a consequence of the transportation authorized by the permit.

Sec. 623.0181. Permits for Auxiliary Power Units.

The department may issue a permit that authorizes the operation of a commercial motor vehicle, trailer, semitrailer, or combination of those vehicles, or a truck-tractor or combination of a truck-tractor and one or more other vehicles, that exceeds the maximum weight limit as set by the department due to the presence of an auxiliary power unit that allows the vehicle to operate on electricity or battery power if the department finds that such an exemption would reduce nitrogen oxide emissions.

Sec. 623.019. Violations of Subchapter; Offenses.

(a) A person who holds a permit issued under Section 623.011 commits an offense if:

(1) the person:

(A) operates or directs the operation of the vehicle for which the permit was issued on a public highway or road; and

(B) is criminally negligent with regard to the operation of the vehicle at a weight heavier than the weight limit authorized by Section 623.011; or

(2) the person operates or directs the operation of the vehicle for which the permit was issued:

(A) in a county not designated in the person's application under Section 623.0111; and

(B) at a weight heavier than a weight limit established under:

(i) Subchapter E, Chapter 251;

(ii) Chapter 621 or 622; or

(iii) this chapter.

(b) Except as provided by Subsections (c) and (d), an offense under Subsection (a) is a misdemeanor punishable by a fine of not less than $100 or more than $250.

(c) An offense under Subsection (a) is a misdemeanor and, except as provided by Subsection (d), is punishable by a fine according to the following schedules if the offense involves a vehicle:

(1) having a single axle weight or tandem axle weight that is heavier than the vehicle's allowable weight:

Pounds Overweight	Fine Range
less than 2,500	$100 to $500
2,500-5,000	$500 to $1,000
more than 5,000	$1,000 to $2,500; or

(2) having a gross weight that is heavier than the vehicle's allowable gross weight:

Pounds Overweight	Fine Range
less than 2,500	$100 to $500
2,500-5,000	$500 to $1,000
5,001-10,000	$1,000 to $2,500
10,001-20,000	$2,500 to $5,000
20,001-40,000	$5,000 to $7,000
more than 40,000	$7,000 to $10,000.

(d) On conviction of a third offense under Subsection (a), before the first anniversary of the date of a previous conviction under that subsection, the defendant shall be punished by a fine in an amount not to exceed twice the maximum amount specified by Subsection (c).

(e) A governmental entity collecting a fine under Subsection (c) shall send an amount equal to 50 percent of the fine to the comptroller.

(f) A justice or municipal court has jurisdiction of an offense under this section.

(g) A justice or judge who renders a conviction under this section shall report the conviction to the Department of Public Safety. The Department of Public Safety shall keep a record of each conviction reported under this subsection.

(h) A fine may not be imposed under this section that exceeds the minimum dollar amount that may be imposed unless the vehicle's weight was determined by a portable or stationary scale furnished or approved by the Department of Public Safety.

SUBCHAPTER C CONTRACTS FOR CROSSING ROADS

Transportation Code

Sec. 623.051. Contract Allowing Oversize or Overweight Vehicle to Cross Road; Surety Bond.

(a) A person may operate a vehicle that cannot comply with one or more of the restrictions of Subchapter C of Chapter 621 or Section 621.101 to cross the width of any road or highway under the jurisdiction of the Texas Department of Transportation, other than a controlled access highway as defined by Section 203.001, from private property to other private property if the person contracts with the commission to indemnify the Texas Department of Transportation for the cost of maintenance and repair of the part of the highway crossed by the vehicle.

(b) The commission shall adopt rules relating to the forms and procedures to be used under this section and other matters that the commission considers necessary to carry out this section.

(c) To protect the safety of the traveling public, minimize any delays and inconveniences to the operators of vehicles in regular operation, and assure payment for the added wear on the highways in proportion to the reduction of service life, the commission, in adopting rules under this section, shall consider:

(1) the safety and convenience of the general traveling public;

(2) the suitability of the roadway and subgrade on the road or highway to be crossed, variation in soil grade prevalent in the different regions of the state, and the seasonal effects on highway load capacity, the highway shoulder design, and other highway geometrics; and

(3) the state's investment in its highway system.

(d) Before exercising any right under a contract under this section, a person must execute with a corporate surety authorized to do business in this state a surety bond in an amount determined by the commission to compensate for the cost of maintenance and repairs as provided by this section. The bond must be approved by the comptroller and the attorney general and must be conditioned on the person fulfilling the obligations of the contract.

(e) [Repealed by Acts 1997, 75th Leg., ch. 165 (S.B. 898), § 30.140, effective September 1, 1997.]

Sec. 623.052. Contract Allowing Overweight Vehicle with Commodities or Products to Cross Highway; Surety Bond.

(a) A person may operate a vehicle that exceeds the overall gross weight limits provided by Section 621.101 to cross the width of a highway from private property to other private property if:

(1) the vehicle is transporting grain, sand, or another commodity or product and the vehicle's overall gross weight is not heavier than 110,000 pounds; or

(2) the vehicle is an unlicensed vehicle that is transporting sand, gravel, stones, rock, caliche, or a similar commodity.

(b) Before a person may operate a vehicle under this section, the person must:

(1) contract with the Texas Department of Transportation to indemnify the Texas Department of Transportation for the cost of the maintenance and repair for damage caused by a vehicle crossing that part of the highway; and

(2) execute an adequate surety bond to compensate for the cost of maintenance and repair, approved by the comptroller and the attorney general, with a corporate surety authorized to do business in this state, conditioned on the person fulfilling each obligation of the agreement.

Sec. 623.070. Nonapplicability of Subchapter.

This subchapter does not apply to the transportation of an intermodal shipping container as defined by Section 623.401, regardless of whether the container is sealed or unsealed.

SUBCHAPTER D HEAVY EQUIPMENT

Sec. 623.071. Permit to Move Certain Equipment.

(a) The department may issue a permit to allow the operation on a state highway of equipment that exceeds the weight and size limits provided by law for the movement of equipment or a commodity that cannot reasonably be dismantled

(b) The department may issue a permit to a person to operate over a farm-to-market or ranch-to-market road superheavy or oversize equipment that:

(1) is used to transport oilfield drill pipe or drill collars stored in a pipe box; and

(2) has a gross weight or size that exceeds the limits allowed by law to be transported over a state highway.

(c) The department may issue an annual permit to allow the operation on a state highway of equipment that exceeds weight and size limits provided by law for the movement of:

(1) an implement of husbandry by a dealer;

(2) water well drilling machinery and equipment or harvesting equipment being moved as part of an agricultural operation; or

(3) equipment or a commodity that:

Transportation Code

(A) cannot reasonably be dismantled; and

(B) does not exceed:

(i) 12 feet in width;

(ii) 14 feet in height;

(iii) 110 feet in length; or

(iv) 120,000 pounds gross weight.

(c-1) The department may issue an annual permit that allows a person to operate over a state highway or road a vehicle or combination of vehicles transporting a load that cannot reasonably be dismantled that exceeds the length and height limits provided by law, except that:

(1) the maximum length allowed may not exceed 110 feet; and

(2) the maximum height allowed may not exceed 14 feet.

(d) The department may issue an annual permit to a motor carrier, as defined by Section 643.001, that allows the motor carrier to operate on a state highway two or more vehicles for the movement of superheavy or oversize equipment described by Subsection (c)(3). An application under this subsection must be on the form prescribed by the department and include a description of each vehicle to be operated by the motor carrier under the permit. A permit issued under this subsection:

(1) may not authorize the operation of more than one vehicle at the same time; and

(2) must be carried in the vehicle that is being operated to move the superheavy or oversize equipment under the permit.

(e) The department may not issue a permit under this section unless the equipment may be operated without material damage to the highway.

(f) In this section, "pipe box" means a container specifically constructed to safely transport and handle oilfield drill pipe and drill collars.

(g) A single trip permit that increases the height or width limits established in Subsection (c)(3)(B)(i) or (ii) may be issued by the department and used in conjunction with an annual permit issued under Subsection (c).

(h) If on completion of a route and engineering study the department determines that the additional length can be transported safely, the department may issue to a person a single trip permit that allows the person to operate over a highway in this state superheavy or oversize equipment exceeding the length limitation established by Subsection (c) and that may be used in conjunction with an annual permit issued under that subsection.

Sec. 623.0711. Permits Authorized by Board.

(a) The board by rule may authorize the department to issue a permit to a motor carrier, as defined by Section 643.001, to transport multiple loads of the same commodity over a state highway if all of the loads are traveling between the same general locations.

(b) The board may not authorize the issuance of a permit that would allow a vehicle to:

(1) violate federal regulations on size and weight requirements; or

(2) transport equipment that could reasonably be dismantled for transportation as separate loads.

(c) The board rules must require that, before the department issues a permit under this section, the department:

(1) determine that the state will benefit from the consolidated permitting process; and

(2) complete a route and engineering study that considers:

(A) the estimated number of loads to be transported by the motor carrier under the permit;

(B) the size and weight of the commodity;

(C) available routes that can accommodate the size and weight of the vehicle and load to be transported;

(D) the potential roadway damage caused by repeated use of the road by the permitted vehicle;

(E) any disruption caused by the movement of the permitted vehicle; and

(F) the safety of the traveling public.

(d) The board rules may authorize the department to impose on the motor carrier any condition regarding routing, time of travel, axle weight, and escort vehicles necessary to ensure safe operation and minimal damage to the roadway.

(e) A permit issued under this section may provide multiple routes to minimize damage to the roadways.

(f) [Repealed.]

(g) **[2 Versions: As amended by Acts 2013, 83rd Leg., ch. 1135]** An application for a permit under this section must be accompanied by the permit fee established by the board for the permit, not to exceed $9,000. The department shall send each fee to the comptroller for deposit to the credit of the state highway fund.

(g) **[2 Versions: As amended by Acts 2013, 83rd Leg., ch. 1287]** An application for a permit under this section must be accompanied by the permit fee established by the department, in consultation with the commission, for the permit, not to exceed $9,000. The department shall send each fee to the comptroller, who shall deposit:

(1) 90 percent of the fee to the credit of the state highway fund; and

(2) 10 percent of the fee to the credit of the Texas Department of Motor Vehicles fund.

(h) In addition to the fee established under Subsection (g), the board rules must authorize the department to collect a consolidated permit payment for a permit under this section in an amount not to exceed 15 percent of the fee established under Subsection (g), of which:

(1) 90 percent shall be deposited to the credit of the state highway fund; and

(2) 10 percent shall be deposited to the credit of the Texas Department of Motor Vehicles fund.

(i) The executive director of the department or the executive director's designee may suspend a permit issued under this section or alter a designated route because of:

(1) a change in pavement conditions;

(2) a change in traffic conditions;

(3) a geometric change in roadway configuration;

(4) construction or maintenance activity; or

(5) emergency or incident management.

(j) A violation of a permit issued under this section is subject to the administrative sanctions of Subchapter N.

(k) [Repealed by Acts 2013, 83rd Leg., ch. 1135 (H.B 2741), § 140(2), effective September 1, 2013.]

Sec. 623.072. Designated Route in Municipality.

(a) A municipality having a state highway in its territory shall designate to the department the route in the municipality to be used by equipment described by Section 623.071 operating over the state highway. The department shall show the designated route on each map routing the equipment.

(b) If a municipality does not designate a route, the department shall determine the route of the equipment and the commodity on each state highway in the municipality.

(c) A municipality may not require a fee, permit, or license for movement of superheavy or oversize equipment on the route of a state highway designated by the municipality or department.

Sec. 623.073. Agent [Repealed].

Repealed by Acts 1997, 75th Leg., ch. 515 (S.B. 1631), § 3, effective September 1, 1997.

Sec. 623.074. Application.

(a) The department may issue a permit under this subchapter on the receipt of an application for the permit.

(b) The application must:

(1) be in writing;

(2) state the kind of equipment to be operated;

(3) describe the equipment;

(4) give the weight and dimensions of the equipment;

(5) give the width, height, and length of the equipment;

(6) state the kind of commodity to be transported and the weight of the total load; and

(7) be dated and signed by the applicant.

(c) An application for a permit under Section 623.071(a) or (b) must also also state:

(1) each highway over which the equipment is to be operated, if the permit is for a single trip; or

(2) the region or area, as required by rule, over which the equipment is to be operated, if the permit is for other than a single trip.

(d) The department may by rule authorize an applicant to submit an application electronically. An electronically submitted application shall be considered signed if a digital signature is transmitted with the application and intended by the applicant to authenticate the application. For purposes of this subsection, "digital signature" means an electronic identifier intended by the person using it to have the same force and effect as the use of a manual signature.

Sec. 623.075. Additional Requirements for Issuance of Permit.

(a) Except as provided by Subsection (b), the department may issue a permit under this subchapter only to an applicant registered under Chapter 643.

(b) Subsection (a) does not apply to a permit for:

(1) the driving or transporting of farm equipment that is being used for an agricultural purpose and is driven or transported by or under the authority of the owner of the equipment; or

(2) a vehicle or equipment that is not subject to Chapter 643.

(c) Before the department issues a permit under this subchapter for a vehicle or equipment described by Subsection (b)(2), the applicant shall file with the department a bond in an amount set by the Texas Department of Transportation, payable to the Texas Department of Transportation, and conditioned that the applicant will pay to the Texas Department of Transportation any damage that might be sustained to the highway because of the operation of the vehicle or equipment for which a permit is issued. Venue of a suit for recovery on the bond is in Travis County.

Sec. 623.076. Permit Fee.

(a) An application for a permit under this subchapter must be accompanied by a permit fee of:

(1) $60 for a single-trip permit;

(2) $120 for a permit that is valid for a period not exceeding 30 days;

(3) $180 for a permit that is valid for a period of 31 days or more but not exceeding 60 days;

(4) $240 for a permit that is valid for a period of 61 days or more but not exceeding 90 days;

(5) $270 for a permit issued under Section 623.071(c)(1) or (2); or

(6) $960 for a permit issued under Section 623.071(c-1).

(a-1) The following amounts collected under Subsection (a) shall be deposited to the general revenue fund, 90 percent of the remainder shall be deposited to the credit of the state highway fund, and 10 percent of the remainder shall be deposited to the credit of the Texas Department of Motor Vehicles fund:

Amount of Fee	Amount Allocated to General Revenue Fund
$60 (single-trip permit)	$30
$120 (30-day permit)	$60
$180	$90
$240	$120
$270	$135
$960	$480

(b) The board may adopt rules for the payment of a fee under Subsection (a). The rules may:

(1) authorize the use of electronic funds transfer;

(2) authorize the use of a credit card issued by:

(A) a financial institution chartered by a state or the United States; or

(B) a nationally recognized credit organization approved by the board; and

(3) require the payment of a discount or service charge for a credit card payment in addition to the fee prescribed by Subsection (a).

(b-1) The department shall deposit a fee collected under Subsection (b)(3) to the credit of the Texas Department of Motor Vehicles fund.

(c) An application for a permit under Section 623.071(c)(3) or (d) must be accompanied by the permit fee established by the board, in consultation with the commission, for the permit, not to exceed $7,000. Of each fee collected under this subsection, the department shall send:

(1) the first $1,000 to the comptroller for deposit to the credit of the general revenue fund; and

(2) any amount in excess of $1,000 to the comptroller, who shall deposit:

(A) 90 percent of the excess to the credit of the state highway fund; and

(B) 10 percent of the excess to the credit of the Texas Department of Motor Vehicles fund.

Sec. 623.077. Highway Maintenance Fee.

(a) An applicant for a permit under this subchapter, other than a permit under Section 623.071(c)(3), must also pay a highway maintenance fee in an amount determined according to the following table:

Vehicle Weight in Pounds	Fee
80,001 to 120,000	$150
120,001 to 160,000	$225
160,001 to 200,000	$300
200,001 and above	$375

(b) The department shall send each fee collected under Subsection (a) to the comptroller, who shall deposit:

(1) 90 percent of the fee to the credit of the state highway fund; and

(2) 10 percent of the fee to the credit of the Texas Department of Motor Vehicles fund.

Sec. 623.078. Vehicle Supervision Fee.

(a) Each applicant for a permit under this subchapter for a vehicle that is heavier than 200,000 pounds must also pay a vehicle supervision fee in an amount determined by the Texas Department of Transportation and designed to recover the direct cost of providing safe transportation of the vehicle over the state highway system, including the cost of:

(1) bridge structural analysis;

(2) the monitoring of the trip process; and

(3) moving traffic control devices.

(b) The department shall send each fee collected under Subsection (a) to the comptroller for deposit to the credit of the state highway fund.

Sec. 623.079. Registration of Equipment.

A permit under this subchapter may be issued only if the equipment to be operated under the permit is registered under Chapter 502 for maximum gross weight applicable to the vehicle under Section 621.101 that is not heavier than 80,000 pounds overall gross weight.

Sec. 623.080. Contents of Permit.

(a) Except as provided by Subsection (b), a permit under this subchapter must include:

(1) the name of the applicant;
(2) the date of issuance;
(3) the signature of the director of the department;
(4) a statement of the kind of equipment to be transported over the highway, the weight and dimensions of the equipment, and the kind and weight of each commodity to be transported; and
(5) a statement of any condition on which the permit is issued.

(b) A permit issued under Section 623.071(a) or (b) must also state:
(1) each highway over which the equipment is to be transported, if the permit is for a single trip; or
(2) the region or area, as required by rule, over which the equipment is to be operated, if the permit is for other than a single trip.

Sec. 623.081. Permit Issued by Telephone. [Repealed]

Sec. 623.082. Penalties.

(a) A person commits an offense if the person violates this subchapter.

(b) Except as provided by Subsection (c), an offense under this section is a misdemeanor punishable:
(1) by a fine of not more than $200;
(2) on conviction within one year after the date of a prior conviction under this section that was punishable under Subdivision (1), by a fine of not more than $500, by confinement in the county jail for not more than 60 days, or by both the fine and the confinement; or
(3) on conviction within one year after the date of a prior conviction under this section that was punishable under Subdivision (2) or this subdivision, by a fine of not more than $1,000, by confinement in the county jail for not more than six months, or by both the fine and the confinement.

(c) A corporation is not subject to confinement for an offense under this section, but two times the maximum fine provided for in the applicable subdivision of Subsection (b) may be imposed against the corporation.

(d) The judge shall report a conviction under this section to the Department of Public Safety. The Department of Public Safety shall keep a record of each conviction.

(e) If a corporation does not pay a fine assessed under this section, the district or county attorney for the county in which the conviction was obtained may file suit to collect the fine.

SUBCHAPTER E MANUFACTURED AND INDUSTRIALIZED HOUSING

Sec. 623.091. Definition.

In this subchapter, "manufactured house" means "industrialized building" as defined by Chapter 1202, Occupations Code, "industrialized housing" as defined by Chapter 1202, Occupations Code, or "manufactured home" as defined by Chapter 1201, Occupations Code. The term includes a temporary chassis system or returnable undercarriage used for the transportation of a manufactured house and a transportable section of a manufactured house that is transported on a chassis system or returnable undercarriage and that is constructed so that it cannot, without dismantling or destruction, be transported within the legal size limits for a motor vehicle.

Sec. 623.092. Permit Requirement.

(a) A manufactured house in excess of legal size limits for a motor vehicle may not be moved over a highway, road, or street in this state except in accordance with a permit issued by the department.

(b) A county or municipality may not require a permit, bond, fee, or license, in addition to that required by state law, for the movement of a manufactured house.

Sec. 623.093. Contents of Application and Permit.

(a) The application for a permit and the permit must be in the form prescribed by the department. The permit must show:
(1) the length, width, and height of the manufactured house and the towing vehicle in combination;
(2) the complete identification or serial number, the Department of Housing and Urban Development label number, or the state seal number of the house;
(3) the name of the owner of the house;
(4) the location from which the house is being transported;
(5) the location to which the house is being transported; and
(6) the route for the transportation of the house.

(b) The length of the manufactured house and the towing vehicle in combination includes the length of the hitch or towing device. The height is measured from the roadbed to the highest elevation of the manufactured house. The width of the house or section includes any roof or eave extension or overhang on either side.

(c) The route must be the shortest distance from the place where the transportation begins in this state to the place where the transportation ends in this state and include divided and interstate systems, except where construction is in progress or bridge or overpass width or height creates a safety hazard. A county or municipality may designate to the department the route to be used inside the territory of the county or municipality.

(d) [Repealed by Acts 2005, 79th Leg., ch. 1284 (H.B. 2438), § 34(3), effective June 18, 2005.]

(e) [Repealed.]

(f) [Repealed by Acts 2013, 83rd Leg., ch. 1135 (H.B. 2741), § 140(2), effective September 1, 2013.]

Sec. 623.094. Permit Issuance.

(a) Except as authorized by Section 623.095, the department may issue a permit only to:

(1) a person licensed by the Texas Department of Housing and Community Affairs as a manufacturer, retailer, or installer; or

(2) motor carriers registered with the department.

(b) The license or registration number of the person to whom the permit is issued shall be affixed to the rear of the manufactured house during transportation and have letters and numbers that are at least eight inches high.

Sec. 623.095. Permit Types.

(a) The department may issue a single-trip permit for the transportation of a manufactured house to:

(1) the owner of a manufactured house if:

(A) the title to the manufactured house and the title to the towing vehicle show that the owner of the manufactured house and the owner of the towing vehicle are the same person; or

(B) a lease shows that the owner of the manufactured house and the lessee of the towing vehicle are the same person;

(2) a person authorized to be issued permits by Section 623.094.

(b) A person or owner must have proof of the insurance coverage required by Section 623.103.

(c) In lieu of a single-trip permit, the department may issue an annual permit to any person authorized to be issued permits by Section 623.094 for the transportation of new manufactured homes from a manufacturing facility to a temporary storage location not to exceed 20 miles from the point of manufacture. A copy of the permit must be carried in the vehicle transporting a manufactured home from the manufacturer to temporary storage. The department may adopt rules concerning requirements for a permit issued under this subsection.

Sec. 623.096. Permit Fee.

(a) The department shall collect a fee of $40 for each permit issued under this subchapter. Of each fee, $19.70 shall be deposited to the credit of the general revenue fund and of the remainder:

(1) 90 percent shall be deposited to the credit of the state highway fund; and

(2) 10 percent shall be deposited to the credit of the Texas Department of Motor Vehicles fund.

(b) The board, in consultation with the Texas Department of Transportation, shall adopt rules concerning fees for each annual permit issued under Section 623.095(c) at a cost not to exceed $3,000.

(c) The department may establish an escrow account within the Texas Department of Motor Vehicles fund for the payment of permit fees.

Sec. 623.097. Duration of Permit.

A permit is valid for a five-day period.

Sec. 623.0975. List of Permits Issued.

The department shall make available on the department's Internet website a searchable and downloadable list by county of each permit issued under this subchapter. The list must include the following information for each permit:

(1) the permit number and issue date of the permit;

(2) the name of the person for whom the permit was issued;

(3) the length, width, and height of the manufactured house and the towing vehicle in combination;

(4) the name of the owner of the house;

(5) the model and year of manufacture of the house;

(6) the complete identification or serial number, the United States Department of Housing and Urban Development label number, or the state seal number of the house; and

(7) the origin county and address and destination county and address of the house.

Sec. 623.098. Caution Lights.

(a) A manufactured house that is wider than 12 feet must have one rotating amber beacon of not

Transportation Code

less than eight inches mounted at the rear of the manufactured house on the roof or one flashing amber light mounted at each rear corner of the manufactured house approximately six feet above ground level. In addition, the towing vehicle must have one rotating amber beacon of not less than eight inches mounted on top of the cab.

(b) Each beacon shall be operated during a move under a permit and while on a highway, road, or street in this state.

Sec. 623.099. Escort Flag Vehicle.

(a) A manufactured house that is wider than 16 feet, but is not wider than 18 feet, must have one escort flag vehicle that must:

(1) precede the house on a two-lane roadway; or

(2) follow the house on a roadway of four or more lanes.

(b) A manufactured house that is wider than 18 feet must be preceded and followed by escort flag vehicles while moving over a highway, road, or street in this state.

(c) An escort flag vehicle must have:

(1) on top of the vehicle and visible from the front and rear:

(A) two lights flashing simultaneously; or

(B) one rotating amber beacon of not less than eight inches;

(2) four red 16-inch square flags mounted on the four corners of the vehicle so that one flag is on each corner; and

(3) signs that:

(A) are mounted on the front and rear of the vehicle; and

(B) have a yellow background and black letters at least eight inches high stating "wide load."

(d) Two transportable sections of a multisection manufactured house or two single-section manufactured houses towed in convoy are considered one house for purposes of the escort flag vehicle requirements of this section if the distance between the two does not exceed 1,000 feet.

(e) The Texas Department of Transportation shall publish and annually revise a map or list of the bridges or overpasses that because of height or width require an escort flag vehicle to stop oncoming traffic while a manufactured house crosses the bridge or overpass.

(f) An escort flag vehicle may not be required under this subchapter except as expressly provided by this section.

(g) A county or municipality may not require the use of an escort flag vehicle or any other kind of escort for the movement of a manufactured house under a permit issued under this subchapter that is in addition to the escort flag vehicle requirements of this section.

Sec. 623.100. Times and Days of Movement.

(a) Movement authorized by a permit issued under this subchapter may be made on any day, except a national holiday, but shall be made only during daylight hours.

(b) The Texas Department of Transportation may limit the hours for travel on certain routes because of heavy traffic conditions.

(c) The Texas Department of Transportation shall publish the limitation on movements prescribed by this section and the limitations adopted under Subsection (b) and shall make the publications available to the public. Each limitation adopted by the Texas Department of Transportation must be made available to the public before it takes effect.

Sec. 623.101. Speed Limit.

(a) A manufactured house or house trailer may not be towed in excess of the posted speed limit or 55 miles per hour, whichever is less.

(b) In this section, "house trailer" has the meaning assigned by Section 541.201.

Sec. 623.102. Equipment.

(a) The brakes on a towing vehicle and a manufactured house must be capable of stopping the vehicle and house from an initial velocity of 20 miles per hour in not more than 40 feet.

(b) Each manufactured house must be equipped with a wiring harness during transportation over a roadway to provide on the rear of the house:

(1) right-turn and left-turn signal lights;

(2) braking or stopping lights; and

(3) parking lights.

Sec. 623.103. Liability Insurance.

A vehicle towing a manufactured house shall be covered by liability insurance of not less than $300,000 combined single limit.

Sec. 623.104. Civil and Criminal Penalties.

(a) A person commits an offense if the person violates this subchapter. An offense under this subsection is a Class C misdemeanor, except as provided by Subsection (d).

(b) A person convicted of an offense under Subsection (a) may also be assessed a civil penalty of not less than $200 or more than $500 for failure to:

(1) obtain a permit;

(2) have a required rotating amber beacon on the manufactured house or towing vehicle;

(3) provide a required escort flag vehicle; or

(4) have the required insurance.

(c) The civil penalty:

(1) may be awarded by a court having jurisdiction over a Class C misdemeanor; and

(2) shall be paid to the county in which the person was convicted.

(d) Except as provided by Subsection (e), if the offense involves the movement of a manufactured house over a highway, road, or street in this state without a permit issued by the department, the offense is a misdemeanor punishable by a fine of $1,000.

(e) If it is shown on the trial of an offense punishable under Subsection (d) that the defendant has previously been punished under Subsection (d):

(1) one time, the offense is punishable by a fine of $2,000; or

(2) two or more times, the offense is punishable by a fine of $4,000.

Sec. 623.105. Penalty for Compensating Certain Unlawful Actions.

(a) A person commits an offense if the person:

(1) provides compensation to another for the movement of a manufactured home over a highway, road, or street in this state; and

(2) knows the other person is not authorized by law to move the home.

(b) An offense under this section is a misdemeanor punishable by a fine of $1,000.

SUBCHAPTER F PORTABLE BUILDING UNITS

Sec. 623.121. Permit to Move Portable Building Unit.

(a) The department may issue a permit to a person to operate equipment to move over a state highway one or more portable building units that in combination with the towing vehicle are in excess of the length or width limitations provided by law but less than 80 feet in length.

(b) The length limitation in this section does not apply to a truck-tractor or truck-tractor combination towing or carrying the portable building units.

(c) In this section, "portable building unit" means the prefabricated structural and other components incorporated and delivered by the manufacturer as a complete inspected unit with a distinct serial number. The term includes a fully assembled configuration, a partially assembled configuration, or a kit or unassembled configuration, when loaded for transport.

Sec. 623.122. Designated Route in Municipality.

(a) A municipality having a state highway in its territory shall designate to the department the route in the municipality to be used by equipment described by Section 623.121 moving over the state highway. The department shall show the designated route on each map routing the equipment.

(b) If a municipality does not designate a route, the department shall determine the route to be used by the equipment on the state highway within the municipality.

(c) A municipality may not require a fee or license for movement of a portable building unit on the route of a state highway designated by the department or the municipality.

Sec. 623.123. Application.

The application for a permit under Section 623.121 must:

(1) be in writing;

(2) state the make and model of the portable building unit or units;

(3) state the length and width of the portable building unit or units;

(4) state the make and model of the towing vehicle;

(5) state the length and width of the towing vehicle;

(6) state the length and width of the combined portable building unit or units and towing vehicle;

(7) state each highway over which the portable building unit or units are to be moved;

(8) indicate the point of origin and destination; and

(9) be dated and signed by the applicant.

Sec. 623.124. Fee.

(a) An application for a permit must be accompanied by a fee of $15.

(b) The department shall send each fee collected under this section to the comptroller. Of each fee received from the department, the comptroller shall deposit:

(1) $7.50 to the credit of the general revenue fund; and

(2) of the remainder:

(A) 90 percent to the credit of the state highway fund; and

(B) 10 percent to the credit of the Texas Department of Motor Vehicles fund.

Sec. 623.125. Agent [Repealed].

Repealed by Acts 1997, 75th Leg., ch. 515 (S.B. 1631), § 8, effective September 1, 1997.

Sec. 623.126. Form of Permit.

(a) A permit issued under this subchapter must:

(1) contain the name of the applicant;

(2) be dated and signed by the director of the department or a designated agent;

(3) state the make and model of the portable building unit or units to be transported over the highways;

(4) state the make and model of the towing vehicle;

(5) state the combined length and width of the portable building unit or units and towing vehicle; and

(6) state each highway over which the portable building unit or units are to be moved.

(b) A permit is valid if it is substantially in the form provided by this section.

Sec. 623.127. Duration of Permit.

A permit issued under this subchapter is effective for a 10-day period and valid only for a single continuous movement.

Sec. 623.128. Time of Movement.

Movement authorized by a permit issued under this subchapter shall be made only during daylight hours.

Sec. 623.129. Escort Flag Vehicle.

The escort flag vehicle requirements provided by Section 623.099 apply to the movement of portable building units and compatible cargo under this subchapter as if such building units and cargo were a manufactured house.

Sec. 623.130. Compatible Cargo.

(a) A permit issued under this subchapter may authorize the movement of cargo, other than a portable building unit, manufactured, assembled, or distributed by a portable building unit manufacturer, as an authorized distributor if:

(1) the movement is conducted by employees of the manufacturer or by independent drivers and equipment under exclusive contract to the manufacturer during the movement;

(2) the movement is to or from a location where the manufacturer's building units may be legally stored, sold, or delivered; and

(3) the cargo is compatible with the movement of portable building units in that:

(A) the cargo does not cause the load to exceed applicable height or weight limits; and

(B) the cargo is loaded to properly distribute weight, width, and height to maximize safety and economy without exceeding size or weight limits authorized for movement of portable building units.

(b) If cargo moved under this section exceeds any width limit that would apply to the cargo if it were moved in a manner not governed by this section, the department shall collect an amount equal to any fee that would apply to movement of the cargo if the cargo were moved in a manner not governed by this section in addition to the fee required under this subchapter.

SUBCHAPTER G
OIL WELL SERVICING AND DRILLING MACHINERY

Sec. 623.141. Optional Procedure.

This subchapter provides an optional procedure for the issuance of a permit for the movement of oversize or overweight oil well servicing or oil well drilling machinery and equipment.

Sec. 623.142. Permit to Move Oil Well Servicing or Drilling Machinery.

(a) The department may, on application, issue a permit for the movement over a road or highway under the jurisdiction of the Texas Department of Transportation of a vehicle that:

(1) is a piece of fixed-load mobile machinery or equipment used to service, clean out, or drill an oil well; and

(2) cannot comply with the restrictions set out in Subchapter C of Chapter 621 and Section 621.101.

(b) The department may not issue a permit under this section unless the vehicle may be moved without material damage to the highway or serious inconvenience to highway traffic.

Sec. 623.143. Designated Route in Municipality.

(a) A municipality having a state highway in its territory may designate to the department the

Transportation Code

route in the municipality to be used by a vehicle described by Section 623.142 operating over the state highway. When the route is designated, the department shall show the route on each map routing the vehicles.

(b) If a municipality does not designate a route, the department shall determine the route to be used by a vehicle on a state highway in the municipality.

(c) A municipality may not require a fee, permit, or license for movement of vehicles on the route of a state highway designated by the municipality or department.

Sec. 623.144. Registration of Vehicle.

(a) A person may not operate a vehicle permitted under this subchapter on a public highway unless the vehicle is registered under Chapter 502 for the maximum gross weight applicable to the vehicle under Section 621.101 or has distinguishing license plates as provided by Section 502.146 if applicable to the vehicle.

(b) The department may not issue distinguishing license plates to a vehicle described by Section 502.146(b)(3) unless the applicant complies with the requirements of that subsection.

Sec. 623.145. Rules; Forms and Procedures; Fees.

(a) The board, in consultation with the commission, by rule shall provide for the issuance of permits under this subchapter. The rules must include each matter the board and commission determine necessary to implement this subchapter and:

(1) requirements for forms and procedures used in applying for a permit;

(2) conditions with regard to route and time of movement;

(3) requirements for flags, flaggers, and warning devices;

(4) the fee for a permit; and

(5) standards to determine whether a permit is to be issued for one trip only or for a period established by the commission.

(b) In adopting a rule or establishing a fee, the board and commission shall consider and be guided by:

(1) the state's investment in its highway system;

(2) the safety and convenience of the general traveling public;

(3) the registration or license fee paid on the vehicle for which the permit is requested;

(4) the fees paid by vehicles operating within legal limits;

(5) the suitability of roadways and subgrades on the various classes of highways of the system;

(6) the variation in soil grade prevalent in the different regions of the state;

(7) the seasonal effects on highway load capacity;

(8) the highway shoulder design and other highway geometrics;

(9) the load capacity of the highway bridges;

(10) administrative costs;

(11) added wear on highways; and

(12) compensation for inconvenience and necessary delays to highway users.

Sec. 623.146. Violation of Rule.

A permit under this subchapter is void on the failure of an owner or the owner's representative to comply with a rule of the board or with a condition placed on the permit, and immediately on the violation, further movement over the highway of an oversize or overweight vehicle violates the law regulating the size or weight of a vehicle on a public highway.

Sec. 623.147. Deposit of Fee in State Highway Fund and in Texas Department of Motor Vehicles Fund.

A fee collected under this subchapter shall be deposited as follows:

(1) 90 percent to the credit of the state highway fund; and

(2) 10 percent to the credit of the Texas Department of Motor Vehicles fund.

Sec. 623.148. Liability for Damage to Highways.

(a) By issuing a permit under this subchapter, the department does not guarantee that a highway can safely accommodate the movement.

(b) Except as provided by Section 621.207, the owner of a vehicle involved in the movement of an oversize or overweight vehicle, even if a permit has been issued for the movement, is strictly liable for any damage the movement causes the highway system or any of its structures or appurtenances.

Sec. 623.149. Determination Whether Vehicle Subject to Registration or Eligible for Distinguishing License Plate.

(a) The department may establish criteria to determine whether oil well servicing, oil well clean out, or oil well drilling machinery or equipment is subject to registration under Chapter 502 or eligible for the distinguishing license plate provided by Section 502.146.

(b) Notwithstanding Subsection (a), a vehicle authorized by the department before August 22, 1963, to operate without registration under Chapter 502 may not be required to register under that chapter.

(c) In this section, "oil well servicing, oil well clean out, or oil well drilling machinery or equipment" means a vehicle constructed as a machine used solely for servicing, cleaning out, or drilling an oil well and consisting in general of a mast, an engine for power, a draw works, and a chassis permanently constructed or assembled for one or more of those purposes.

Sec. 623.150. Nonapplicability of Subchapter.

This subchapter does not apply to a person issued a registration certificate under Chapter 643, even if not all the operations of the person are performed under that certificate.

SUBCHAPTER H VEHICLES TRANSPORTING SOLID WASTE

Sec. 623.161. Definition.

In this subchapter, "solid waste" has the meaning assigned by Chapter 361, Health and Safety Code, except that it does not include hazardous waste.

Sec. 623.162. Axle Weight Restrictions.

A single vehicle used exclusively to transport solid waste may be operated on a public highway of this state only if the tandem axle weight is not heavier than 44,000 pounds, the single axle weight is not heavier than 21,000 pounds, and the gross weight is not heavier than 64,000 pounds.

Sec. 623.163. Surety Bond.

(a) The owner of a vehicle used exclusively to transport solid waste with a tandem axle load heavier than 34,000 pounds shall before operating the vehicle on a public highway of this state file with the department a surety bond subject to the approval of the Texas Department of Transportation in the principal amount set by the Texas Department of Transportation not to exceed $15,000 for each vehicle.

(b) The bond must be conditioned that the owner of the vehicle will pay to the Texas Department of Transportation and to any municipality in which the vehicle is operated on a municipal street, within the limit of the bond, any damages to a highway or municipal street caused by the operation of the vehicle.

(c) This section does not apply to a vehicle owned by a municipality.

(d) A copy of the bond shall be:

(1) carried on the vehicle when the vehicle is on a public highway; and

(2) presented to an officer authorized to enforce this chapter on request of the officer.

Sec. 623.164. Interstate and Defense Highways.

(a) This subchapter does not authorize the operation on the national system of interstate and defense highways in this state of a vehicle of a size or weight greater than that authorized by 23 U.S.C. Section 127, as amended.

(b) If the United States authorizes the operation on the national system of interstate and defense highways of a vehicle of a size or weight greater than that authorized on January 1, 1983, the new limit automatically takes effect on the national system of interstate and defense highways in this state.

Sec. 623.165. Penalty.

A person commits an offense if the person fails in violation of Section 623.163(d) to carry or present the copy of the bond filed with the department. An offense under this section is a misdemeanor punishable by a fine not to exceed $200.

Sec. 623.166. Defense to Prosecution: Bond in Effect.

(a) It is a defense to prosecution under Section 623.165 that the person charged produces a surety bond that complies with Section 623.163 that was valid at the time the offense is alleged to have occurred.

(b) If the court verifies the bond produced by the person, the court shall dismiss the charge.

SUBCHAPTER I UNLADEN LIFT EQUIPMENT MOTOR VEHICLES; ANNUAL PERMIT

Sec. 623.181. Annual Permit.

(a) The department may issue an annual permit for the movement over a highway or road of this state of an unladen lift equipment motor vehicle that because of its design for use as lift equipment exceeds the maximum weight or width limitations prescribed by statute.

(b) The department may issue a permit on receipt of an application for the permit.

Sec. 623.182. Permit Fee.

(a) The fee for a permit under this subchapter is $100.

(b) The department shall send each fee collected under this subchapter to the comptroller. Of each fee received from the department, the comptroller shall deposit $50 to the credit of the general revenue fund and of the remainder the department shall deposit:

(1) 90 percent to the credit of the state highway fund; and

(2) 10 percent to the credit of the Texas Department of Motor Vehicles fund.

SUBCHAPTER J UNLADEN LIFT EQUIPMENT MOTOR VEHICLES; TRIP PERMITS

Sec. 623.191. Optional Procedure.

This subchapter provides an optional procedure for the issuance of a permit for the movement of an unladen lift equipment motor vehicle that because of its design for use as lift equipment exceeds the maximum weight and width limitations prescribed by statute.

Sec. 623.192. Permit to Move Unladen Lift Equipment Motor Vehicles.

(a) The department may, on application, issue a permit to a person to move over a road or highway under the jurisdiction of the Texas Department of Transportation an unladen lift equipment motor vehicle that cannot comply with the restrictions set out in Subchapter C of Chapter 621 and Section 621.101.

(b) The department may not issue a permit under this section unless the vehicle may be moved without material damage to the highway or serious inconvenience to highway traffic.

Sec. 623.193. Designated Route in Municipality.

(a) A municipality having a state highway in its territory may designate to the department the route in the municipality to be used by a vehicle described by Section 623.192 operating over the state highway. The department shall show the designated route on each map routing the vehicle.

(b) If a municipality does not designate a route, the department shall determine the route of the vehicle on each state highway in the municipality.

(c) A municipality may not require a fee, permit, or license for movement of the vehicles on the route of a state highway designated by the municipality or department.

Sec. 623.194. Registration of Vehicle.

A permit under this subchapter may be issued only if the vehicle to be moved is registered under Chapter 502 for the maximum gross weight applicable to the vehicle under Section 621.101 or has the distinguishing license plates as provided by Section 502.146 if applicable to the vehicle.

Sec. 623.195. Rules; Forms and Procedures; Fees.

(a) The board, in consultation with the commission, by rule shall provide for the issuance of a permit under this subchapter. The rules must include each matter the board and the commission determine necessary to implement this subchapter and:

(1) requirements for forms and procedures used in applying for a permit;

(2) conditions with regard to route and time of movement;

(3) requirements for flags, flaggers, and warning devices;

(4) the fee for a permit; and

(5) standards to determine whether a permit is to be issued for one trip only or for a period established by the commission.

(b) In adopting a rule or establishing a fee, the board and the commission shall consider and be guided by:

(1) the state's investment in its highway system;

(2) the safety and convenience of the general traveling public;

(3) the registration or license fee paid on the vehicle for which the permit is requested;

(4) the fees paid by vehicles operating within legal limits;

(5) the suitability of roadways and subgrades on the various classes of highways of the system;

(6) the variation in soil grade prevalent in the different regions of the state;

(7) the seasonal effects on highway load capacity;

(8) the highway shoulder design and other highway geometrics;

(9) the load capacity of highway bridges;

(10) administrative costs;

(11) added wear on highways; and

(12) compensation for inconvenience and necessary delays to highway users.

Sec. 623.196. Violation of Rule.

A permit under this subchapter is void on the failure of an owner or the owner's representative to comply with a rule of the board or with a condition placed on the permit, and immediately on the violation, further movement over a highway of an oversize or overweight vehicle violates the law regulating the size or weight of a vehicle on a public highway.

Sec. 623.197. Deposit of Fee in State Highway Fund and in Texas Department of Motor Vehicles Fund.

A fee collected under this subchapter shall be deposited as follows:

(1) 90 percent to the credit of the state highway fund; and

(2) 10 percent to the credit of the Texas Department of Motor Vehicles fund.

Sec. 623.198. Liability for Damage to Highways.

(a) By issuing a permit under this subchapter, the department does not guarantee that a highway can safely accommodate the movement.

(b) Except as provided by Section 621.207, the owner of a vehicle involved in the movement of an oversize or overweight vehicle, even if a permit has been issued for the movement, is strictly liable for any damage the movement causes the highway system or any of its structures or appurtenances.

Sec. 623.199. Determination Whether Vehicle Subject to Registration or Eligible for Distinguishing License Plate.

(a) The department may establish criteria to determine whether an unladen lift equipment motor vehicle that because of its design for use as lift equipment exceeds the maximum weight and width limitations prescribed by statute is subject to registration under Chapter 502 or eligible for the distinguishing license plate provided by Section 502.146.

(b) Notwithstanding Subsection (a), a vehicle authorized by the department before June 11, 1985, to operate without registration under Chapter 502 may not be required to register under that chapter.

Sec. 623.200. Nonapplicability of Subchapter.

This subchapter does not apply to a person issued a registration certificate under Chapter 643, even if not all the operations of the person are performed under that certificate.

SUBCHAPTER K
PORT AUTHORITY PERMITS

Sec. 623.210. Optional Procedure.

This subchapter provides an optional procedure for the issuance of a permit for the movement of oversize or overweight vehicles carrying cargo on state highways located in counties:

(1) contiguous to the Gulf of Mexico or a bay or inlet opening into the gulf and:

(A) adjacent to at least two counties with a population of 550,000 or more; or

(B) bordering the United Mexican States; or

(2) contiguous to the Gulf of Mexico or a bay or inlet opening into the gulf with a population of not more than 200,000 and adjacent to a county described by Subdivision (1)(A).

Sec. 623.211. Definition.

In this subchapter, "port authority" means a port authority or navigation district created or operating under Section 52, Article III, or Section 59, Article XVI, Texas Constitution.

Sec. 623.212. Permits by Port Authority.

The commission may authorize a port authority to issue permits for the movement of oversize or overweight vehicles carrying cargo on state highways located in counties:

(1) contiguous to the Gulf of Mexico or a bay or inlet opening into the gulf and:

(A) adjacent to at least two counties with a population of 550,000 or more; or

(B) bordering the United Mexican States; or

(2) contiguous to the Gulf of Mexico or a bay or inlet opening into the gulf with a population of not more than 200,000 and adjacent to a county described by Subdivision (1)(A).

Sec. 623.213. Maintenance Contracts [Repealed].

Repealed by Acts 2009, 81st Leg., ch. 61 (S.B. 1373), § 1.04, effective May 19, 2009.

Sec. 623.214. Permit Fees.

(a) A port authority may collect a fee for permits issued under this subchapter. Such fees shall not exceed $120 per trip.

(b) Fees collected under Subsection (a), less administrative costs, shall be used solely to provide funds for the maintenance and improvement of state highways subject to this subchapter. The administrative costs, which may not exceed 15 percent of the fees collected, may be retained by the port authority. The fees, less administrative costs, shall be deposited in the State Highway Fund.

Sec. 623.215. Permit Requirements.

(a) A permit issued under this subchapter must include:

(1) the name of the applicant;

(2) the date of issuance;

(3) the signature of the director of the port authority;

(4) a statement of the kind of cargo being transported under the permit, the maximum weight and dimensions of the equipment, and the kind and weight of each commodity to be transported provided the gross weight of such equipment and commodities shall not exceed 125,000 pounds;

(5) a statement of any condition on which the permit is issued;

(6) a statement of the route designated under Section 623.219;

(7) the name of the driver of the vehicle in which the cargo is to be transported; and

(8) the location where the cargo was loaded.

(b) A port authority shall report to the Texas Department of Transportation all permits issued under this subchapter.

Sec. 623.216. Time of Movement.

A permit issued under this subchapter shall specify the time in which movement authorized by the permit is allowed.

Sec. 623.217. Speed Limit.

Movement authorized by a permit issued under this subchapter shall not exceed the posted speed limit or 55 miles per hour, whichever is less. Violation of this provision shall constitute a moving violation.

Sec. 623.218. Enforcement.

The Department of Public Safety shall have authority to enforce the provisions of this subchapter.

Sec. 623.219. Route Designation.

(a) For a permit issued by a port authority located in a county that borders the United Mexican States, the commission shall, with the consent of the port authority, designate the most direct route from:

(1) the Gateway International Bridge or the Veterans International Bridge at Los Tomates to the entrance of the Port of Brownsville using State Highways 48 and 4 or United States Highways 77 and 83 or using United States Highway 77 and United States Highway 83, East Loop Corridor, and State Highway 4; and

(2) the Free Trade International Bridge to:

(A) the entrance of the Port of Brownsville using Farm-to-Market Road 509, United States Highways 77 and 83, Farm-to-Market Road 511, State Highway 550, and East Loop (State Highway 32);

(B) the eastern entrance of the Port of Harlingen using Farm-to-Market Road 509, United States Highway 77 Business, and Farm-to-Market Road 1846;

(C) the western entrance of the Port of Harlingen using Farm-to-Market Roads 509 and 106;

(D) the southern entrance of the Harlingen Industrial Park using Farm-to-Market Road 509; and

(E) the southern entrance of the Harlingen Aerotropolis at Valley International Airport using Farm-to-Market Road 509.

(b) For a permit issued by a port authority located in a county that is adjacent to at least two counties with a population of 550,000 or more, the commission shall, with the consent of the port authority, designate the most direct route from:

(1) the intersection of Farm-to-Market Road 523 and Moller Road to the entrance of Port Freeport using Farm-to-Market Roads 523 and 1495;

(2) the intersection of State Highway 288 and Chlorine Road to the entrance of Port Freeport using State Highway 288;

(3) the intersection of State Highway 288 and Chlorine Road to the entrance of Port Freeport using State Highways 288 and 332 and Farm-to-Market Roads 523 and 1495;

(4) the intersection of North Velasco Boulevard and South Avenue J in the city of Freeport to the entrance of Port Freeport using North Velasco Boulevard and Farm-to-Market Road 1495;

(5) 21441 Loop 419 in the city of Sweeny to the entrance of Port Freeport using Loop 419, State Highways 35 and 36, and Farm-to-Market Road 1495; and

(6) 5261 Seventh Street in Bay City to the entrance of Port Freeport using State Highway 35,

Loop 419, State Highway 36, and Farm-to-Market Road 1495.

(b-1) For a permit issued by a port authority contiguous to the Gulf of Mexico or a bay or inlet opening into the gulf with a population of not more than 200,000 that is adjacent to a county described in Subsection (b), the commission shall, with the consent of the port authority, designate the most direct route from:

(1) the Matagorda County line to the entrance of the Port of Palacios using State Highway 35;

(2) the Matagorda County line to the entrance of the Port of Palacios using State Highway 60;

(3) the Matagorda County line to the entrance of the Port of Palacios using FM 521; and

(4) the Matagorda County line to the entrance of the Port of Palacios using State Highway 71.

(c) If the commission designates a route or changes the route designated under this section, the commission shall notify the port authority of the route not later than the 60th day before the date that the designation takes effect.

Transportation Code

SUBCHAPTER L VICTORIA COUNTY NAVIGATION DISTRICT PERMITS

Sec. 623.230. Optional Procedure.

This subchapter provides an optional procedure for the issuance of a permit by the Victoria County Navigation District for the movement of oversize or overweight vehicles carrying cargo in Victoria County.

Sec. 623.231. Definition.

In this subchapter, "district" means the Victoria County Navigation District.

Sec. 623.232. Issuance of Permits.

The Texas Transportation Commission may authorize the district to issue permits for the movement of oversize or overweight vehicles carrying cargo only on the following highways and roads located in Victoria County:

(1) Farm-to-Market Road 1432 between the Port of Victoria and State Highway 185;

(2) State Highway 185 between U.S. Highway 59 and McCoy Road;

(3) U.S. Highway 59, including a frontage road of U.S. Highway 59, between State Highway 185 and Loop 463; and

(4) Loop 463 between U.S. Highway 59 and North Lone Tree Road.

Sec. 623.233. Maintenance Contracts.

The district shall make payments to the Texas Department of Transportation to provide funds for the maintenance of state highways subject to this subchapter.

Sec. 623.234. Permit Fees.

(a) The district may collect a fee for permits issued under this subchapter. The fees shall not exceed $100 per trip.

(b) Fees collected under Subsection (a) shall be used solely to provide funds for the payments provided for under Section 623.233 less administrative costs, which shall not exceed 15 percent of the fees collected. The fees shall be deposited in the state highway fund. Fees deposited in the state highway fund under this section are exempt from the application of Section 403.095, Government Code.

Sec. 623.235. Permit Requirements.

(a) A permit issued under this subchapter must include:

(1) the name of the applicant;

(2) the date of issuance;

(3) the signature of the director of the district or the director's designee;

(4) a statement of the kind of cargo being transported, the maximum weight and dimensions of the equipment, and the kind and weight of each commodity to be transported, provided that the gross weight of such equipment and commodities shall not exceed 140,000 pounds;

(5) a statement of any condition on which the permit is issued;

(6) a statement that the cargo shall only be transported on a road designated under Section 623.232;

(7) the name of the driver of the vehicle in which the cargo is to be transported; and

(8) the location where the cargo was loaded.

(b) The district shall report to the Texas Department of Transportation all permits issued under this subchapter.

Sec. 623.236. Time of Movement.

A permit issued under this subchapter shall specify the time in which movement authorized by the permit is allowed.

Sec. 623.237. Speed Limit.

Movement authorized by a permit issued under this subchapter shall not exceed the posted speed limit or 55 miles per hour, whichever is less. Violation of this provision shall constitute a moving violation.

Sec. 623.238. Enforcement.

The Department of Public Safety shall have authority to enforce the provisions of this subchapter.

Sec. 623.239. Rules.

The Texas Transportation Commission may adopt rules necessary to implement this subchapter.

SUBCHAPTER M CHAMBERS COUNTY PERMITS

Sec. 623.250. Optional Procedure.

This subchapter provides an optional procedure for the issuance of a permit by Chambers County for the movement of oversize or overweight vehicles carrying cargo on certain state highways located in Chambers County.

Sec. 623.251. Definition.

In this subchapter, "county" means Chambers County.

Sec. 623.252. Issuance of Permits.

(a) The Texas Transportation Commission may authorize the county to issue permits for the movement of oversize or overweight vehicles carrying cargo on state highways located in Chambers County.

(b) A permit issued under this subchapter may authorize:

(1) the transport of cargo only on the following roads in Chambers County:

(A) Farm-to-Market Road 1405 between its intersection with Farm-to-Market Road 2354 and its intersection with Farm-to-Market Road 565;

(B) State Highway 99, including the frontage road of State Highway 99 but excluding any portion of the highway for which payment of a toll is required, between its crossing with Cedar Bayou and its intersection with Interstate Highway 10;

(C) Farm-to-Market Road 565 from its intersection with Farm-to-Market Road 1405 to its intersection with State Highway 99; and

(D) Farm-to-Market Road 2354 from its intersection with Farm-to-Market Road 1405 northwest approximately 300 linear feet to the termination of the state-maintained portion of the road; and

(2) the movement of equipment and commodities weighing 100,000 pounds or less.

Sec. 623.253. Maintenance Contracts.

The county shall make payments to the Texas Department of Transportation to provide funds for the maintenance of state highways subject to this subchapter.

Sec. 623.254. Permit Fees.

(a) The county may collect a fee for permits issued under this subchapter. The fee may not exceed $80 per trip.

(b) Fees collected under Subsection (a) may be used only to provide funds for the payments under Section 623.253 and for the county's administrative costs, which may not exceed 15 percent of the fees collected. The fees shall be deposited in the state highway fund. Fees deposited in the state highway fund under this section are exempt from the application of Section 403.095, Government Code.

Sec. 623.255. Permit Requirements.

(a) A permit issued under this subchapter must include:

(1) the name of the applicant;

(2) the date of issuance;

(3) the signature of the designated agent for the county;

(4) a statement of the kind of cargo being transported, the maximum weight and dimensions of the equipment, and the kind and weight of each commodity to be transported;

(5) a statement of any condition on which the permit is issued;

(6) a statement that the cargo may be transported in Chambers County only over the roads described by Section 623.252(b)(1); and

(7) the location where the cargo was loaded.

(b) The county shall report to the department all permits issued under this subchapter.

Sec. 623.256. Time of Movement.

A permit issued under this subchapter must specify the time during which movement authorized by the permit is allowed.

Sec. 623.257. Speed Limit.

Movement authorized by a permit issued under this subchapter may not exceed the posted speed

Transportation Code

limit or 55 miles per hour, whichever is less. A violation of this provision constitutes a moving violation.

Sec. 623.258. Enforcement.

The Department of Public Safety has authority to enforce this subchapter.

Sec. 623.259. Rules.

The Texas Transportation Commission may adopt rules necessary to implement this subchapter.

SUBCHAPTER N ADMINISTRATIVE SANCTIONS

Sec. 623.271. Administrative Enforcement.

(a) The department may investigate and, except as provided by Subsection (f), may impose an administrative penalty or revoke an oversize or overweight permit issued under this chapter if the person or the holder of the permit, as applicable:

(1) provides false information on the permit application or another form required by the department for the issuance of an oversize or overweight permit;

(2) violates this chapter, Chapter 621, or Chapter 622;

(3) violates a rule or order adopted under this chapter, Chapter 621, or Chapter 622; or

(4) fails to obtain an oversize or overweight permit if a permit is required.

(b) The notice and hearing requirements of Section 643.2525 apply to the imposition of an administrative penalty or the revocation of a permit under this section as if the action were being taken under that section.

(c) It is an affirmative defense to administrative enforcement under this section that the person or holder of the permit relied on the shipper's certificate of weight.

(d) The amount of an administrative penalty imposed under this section is calculated in the same manner as the amount of an administrative penalty imposed under Section 643.251.

(e) A person who has been ordered to pay an administrative penalty under this section and the vehicle that is the subject of the enforcement order may not be issued a permit under this chapter until the amount of the penalty has been paid to the department.

(f) This subsection applies only to a vehicle or combination that is used to transport agricultural products or timber products from the place of production to the place of first marketing or first processing. In connection with a violation of a vehicle or combination weight restriction or limitation in this chapter, Chapter 621, or Chapter 622, the department may not impose an administrative penalty against a person or the holder of an overweight permit if the weight of the vehicle or combination involved in the violation did not exceed the allowable weight by more than three percent.

Sec. 623.272. Administrative Penalty for Failure to Provide Certificate or for False Information on Certificate.

(a) The department may investigate and impose an administrative penalty on a shipper who:

(1) does not provide a shipper's certificate of weight required under Section 623.274(b); or

(2) provides false information on a shipper's certificate of weight that the shipper delivers to a person transporting a shipment.

(b) The notice and hearing requirements of Section 643.2525 apply to the imposition of an administrative penalty under this section as if the action were being taken under that section.

(c) The amount of an administrative penalty imposed under this section is calculated in the same manner as the amount of an administrative penalty imposed under Section 643.251.

Sec. 623.273. Injunctive Relief.

(a) The attorney general, at the request of the department, may petition a district court for appropriate injunctive relief to prevent or abate a violation of this chapter or a rule or order adopted under this chapter.

(b) Venue in a suit for injunctive relief under this section is in Travis County.

(c) On application for injunctive relief and a finding that a person is violating or has violated this chapter or a rule or order adopted under this chapter, the court shall grant the appropriate relief without bond.

(d) The attorney general and the department may recover reasonable expenses incurred in obtaining injunctive relief under this section, including court costs, reasonable attorney's fees, investigative costs, witness fees, and deposition expenses.

(e) Money collected by the department under Subsection (d) shall be deposited to the credit of the Texas Department of Motor Vehicles fund.

Transportation Code

Sec. 623.274. Shipper's Certificate of Weight.

(a) The department shall prescribe a form to be used for a shipper's certificate of weight. The form must provide space for the maximum weight of the shipment being transported.

(b) On the written request of the person transporting the shipment, a shipper must:

(1) certify that the information contained on the certificate of weight is accurate; and

(2) deliver the certificate of weight to the person transporting the shipment.

(c) A person transporting a shipment must provide the department with a copy of the certificate of weight before the issuance of an overweight permit under this chapter if the combined weight of the vehicle or vehicles and load is more than 200,000 pounds.

SUBCHAPTER O PORT OF CORPUS CHRISTI AUTHORITY ROADWAY PERMITS

Sec. 623.280. Optional Procedure.

This subchapter provides an optional procedure for the issuance of a permit by the Port of Corpus Christi Authority for the movement of oversize or overweight vehicles carrying cargo on a roadway owned and maintained by the Port of Corpus Christi Authority that is located in San Patricio County or Nueces County.

Sec. 623.281. Definition.

In this subchapter, "port authority" means the Port of Corpus Christi Authority.

Sec. 623.282. Issuance of Permits.

The port authority may issue permits for the movement of oversize or overweight vehicles carrying cargo on a roadway owned and maintained by the port authority that is located in San Patricio County or Nueces County. A permit issued under this subchapter is in addition to other permits required by law.

Sec. 623.283. Permit Fees.

(a) The port authority may collect a fee for permits issued under this subchapter. The fees may not exceed $80 per trip.

(b) Fees collected under Subsection (a) shall be used solely for the construction and maintenance of port authority roadways.

Sec. 623.284. Permit Requirements.

A permit issued under this subchapter must include:

(1) the name of the applicant;

(2) the date of issuance;

(3) the signature of the manager of transportation of the port authority;

(4) a statement of the kind of cargo being transported, the maximum weight and dimensions of the equipment, and the kind and weight of each commodity to be transported;

(5) a statement of any condition on which the permit is issued;

(6) a statement that the cargo may only be transported on roadways that are owned and maintained by the port authority and located in San Patricio County or Nueces County; and

(7) the location where the cargo was loaded.

Sec. 623.285. Time of Movement.

A permit issued under this subchapter must specify the time in which movement authorized by the permit is allowed.

Sec. 623.286. Speed Limit.

Movement authorized by a permit issued under this subchapter may not exceed the posted speed limit or 55 miles per hour, whichever is less. Violation of this provision shall constitute a moving violation.

Sec. 623.287. Enforcement.

The Department of Public Safety shall have authority to enforce the provisions of this subchapter.

Sec. 623.288. Rules.

The Texas Transportation Commission may adopt rules necessary to implement this subchapter.

SUBCHAPTER P PORT OF CORPUS CHRISTI AUTHORITY PERMITS

Sec. 623.301. Optional Procedure.

This subchapter provides an optional procedure for the issuance of a permit by the Port of Corpus

Christi Authority for the movement of oversize or overweight vehicles carrying cargo on certain roads located in San Patricio and Nueces Counties.

Sec. 623.302. Definition.

In this subchapter, "portauthority" means the Port of Corpus Christi Authority.

Sec. 623.303. Issuance of Permits.

(a) The Texas Transportation Commission may authorize the port authority to issue permits for the movement of oversize or overweight vehicles carrying cargo in San Patricio and Nueces Counties on:

(1) the following roads:

(A) U.S. Highway 181 between its intersection with Burleson Street in the city of Corpus Christi and its intersection with County Road 3567 (Midway Road) in San Patricio County;

(B) State Highway 35 between its intersection with Burleson Street in the city of Corpus Christi and its intersection with Farm-to-Market Road 3512;

(C) State Highway 361 between its intersection with State Highway 35 and its intersection with Farm-to-Market Road 1069 (Main Street) in the city of Ingleside; and

(D) proposed State Highway 200 between its intersection with State Highway 361 and its intersection with Farm-to-Market Road 1069 (Main Street) in the city of Ingleside, if proposed State Highway 200 is constructed; or

(2) another route designated by the commission in consultation with the authority.

(b) The port authority may issue a permit under this subchapter only if the cargo being transported weighs 125,000 pounds or less.

Sec. 623.304. Maintenance Contracts.

The port authority shall make payments to the Texas Department of Transportation to provide funds for the maintenance of state highways subject to this subchapter.

Sec. 623.305. Permit Fees.

(a) The port authority may collect a fee for permits issued under this subchapter. The fees may not exceed $80 per trip.

(b) Fees collected under Subsection (a) shall be used solely to provide funds for the payments provided for under Section 623.304 and for the port authority's administrative costs, which may not exceed 15 percent of the fees collected. The fees shall be deposited in the state highway fund. Fees deposited in the state highway fund under this section are exempt from the application of Section 403.095, Government Code.

Sec. 623.306. Permit Requirements.

(a) A permit issued under this subchapter must include:

(1) the name of the applicant;

(2) the date of issuance;

(3) the signature of the manager of transportation of the port authority;

(4) a statement of the kind of cargo being transported, the maximum weight and dimensions of the equipment, and the kind and weight of each commodity to be transported;

(5) a statement of any condition on which the permit is issued;

(6) a statement that the cargo may be transported in San Patricio and Nueces Counties only over the roads described by or designated under Section 623.303; and

(7) the location where the cargo was loaded.

(b) The port authority shall report to the department all permits issued under this subchapter.

Sec. 623.307. Time of Movement.

A permit issued under this subchapter must specify the time in which movement authorized by the permit is allowed.

Sec. 623.308. Speed Limit.

Movement authorized by a permit issued under this subchapter may not exceed the posted speed limit or 55 miles per hour, whichever is less. Violation of this provision shall constitute a moving violation.

Sec. 623.309. Enforcement.

The Department of Public Safety may enforce the provisions of this subchapter.

Sec. 623.310. Rules.

The Texas Transportation Commission may adopt rules necessary to implement this subchapter.

SUBCHAPTER Q VEHICLES TRANSPORTING TIMBER

Sec. 623.321. Permit.

(a) The department may issue a permit under this subchapter, as an alternative to a permit issued under Section 623.011, authorizing a person to operate a vehicle or combination of vehicles that is being used to transport unrefined timber, wood chips, or woody biomass or equipment used to load timber on a vehicle in a county identified as a timber producing county in the most recent edition of the Texas A&M Forest Service's Harvest Trends Report as of May 15, 2013, at the weight limits prescribed by Subsection (b).

(b) A person may operate over a road or highway a vehicle or combination of vehicles issued a permit under this section at a gross weight that is not heavier than 84,000 pounds, if the gross load carried on any tandem axle of the vehicle or combination of vehicles does not exceed 44,000 pounds.

(c) Section 621.508 does not apply to a vehicle or combination of vehicles operated under this section.

(d) The department shall annually update the number of timber producing counties described by Subsection (a) based on the most recent edition of the Texas A&M Forest Service's Harvest Trends Report.

Sec. 623.322. Qualification; Requirements.

(a) To qualify for a permit under this subchapter for a vehicle or combination of vehicles, a person must:

(1) pay a permit fee of $900;

(2) designate in the permit application the timber producing counties described by Section 623.321(a) in which the vehicle or combination of vehicles will be operated; and

(3) satisfy the security requirement of Section 623.012.

(b) A permit issued under this subchapter:

(1) is valid for one year; and

(2) must be carried in the vehicle for which it is issued.

Sec. 623.323. Notification.

(a) For purposes of this section, "financially responsible party" means the owner of the vehicle or combination of vehicles, the party operating the vehicle or combination of vehicles, or a person that hires, leases, rents, or subcontracts the vehicle or combination of vehicles for use on a road maintained by a county or a state highway.

(b) Before a vehicle or combination of vehicles for which a permit is issued under this subchapter may be operated on a road maintained by a county or a state highway, the financially responsible party shall execute a notification document and agree to reimburse the county or the state, as applicable, for damage to a road or highway sustained as a consequence of the transportation authorized by the permit. At a minimum, the notification document must include:

(1) the name and address of the financially responsible party;

(2) a description of each permit issued for the vehicle or combination of vehicles;

(3) a description of the method of compliance by the financially responsible party with Section 601.051, 623.012, 643.101, or 643.102;

(4) the address or location of the geographic area in which the financially responsible party wishes to operate a vehicle or combination of vehicles and a designation of the specific route of travel anticipated by the financially responsible party, including the name or number of each road maintained by a county or state highway;

(5) a calendar or schedule of duration that includes the days and hours of operation during which the financially responsible party reasonably anticipates using the county road or state highway identified in Subdivision (4); and

(6) a list of each vehicle or combination of vehicles by license plate number or other registration information, and a description of the means by which financial responsibility is established for each vehicle or combination of vehicles if each vehicle or combination of vehicles is not covered by a single insurance policy, surety bond, deposit, or other means of financial assurance.

(c) A financially responsible party shall electronically file the notification document described by Subsection (b) with the department under rules adopted by the department not later than the second business day before the first business day listed by the financially responsible party under Subsection (b)(5). The department shall immediately send an electronic copy of the notification document to each county identified in the notification document and the Texas Department of Transportation and an electronic receipt for the notification document to the financially responsible party. Not later than the first business day listed by the financially responsible party under Subsection (b)(5), a county or the Texas Department of Transportation may

Transportation Code

inspect a road or highway identified in the notification document. If an inspection is conducted under this subsection, a county or the Texas Department of Transportation shall:

(1) document the condition of the roads or highways and take photographs of the roads or highways as necessary to establish a baseline for any subsequent assessment of damage sustained by the financially responsible party's use of the roads or highways; and

(2) provide a copy of the documentation to the financially responsible party.

(d) If an inspection has been conducted under Subsection (c), a county or the Texas Department of Transportation, as applicable, shall, not later than the fifth business day after the expiration of the calendar or schedule of duration described by Subsection (b)(5):

(1) conduct an inspection described by Subsection (c)(1) to determine any damage sustained by the financially responsible party's use of the roads or highways; and

(2) provide a copy of the inspection documentation to the financially responsible party.

(e) The state or a county required to be notified under this section may assert a claim against any security posted under Section 623.012 or insurance filed under Section 643.103 for damage to a road or highway sustained as a consequence of the transportation authorized by the permit.

(f) This section does not apply to a vehicle or combination of vehicles that are being used to transport unrefined timber, wood chips, or woody biomass or equipment used to load timber on a vehicle from:

(1) a storage yard to the place of first processing; or

(2) outside this state to a place of first processing in this state.

Sec. 623.324. Disposition of Fee.

(a) Of the fee collected under Section 623.322 for a permit:

(1) 50 percent of the amount collected shall be deposited to the credit of the state highway fund; and

(2) the other 50 percent shall be divided equally among all counties designated in the permit application under Section 623.322(a)(2).

(b) [Repealed.]

Sec. 623.325. Interstate and Defense Highways.

(a) This subchapter does not authorize the operation on the national system of interstate and defense highways in this state of a vehicle of a size or weight greater than those permitted under 23 U.S.C. Section 127.

(b) If the United States authorizes the operation on the national system of interstate and defense highways of a vehicle of a size or weight greater than those permitted under 23 U.S.C. Section 127 on September 1, 2013, the new limit automatically takes effect on the national system of interstate and defense highways in this state.

SUBCHAPTER R
PERMIT TO DELIVER RELIEF SUPPLIES DURING NATIONAL EMERGENCY

Sec. 623.341. Permit to Deliver Relief Supplies.

(a) Notwithstanding any other law, the department may issue a special permit during a major disaster as declared by the president of the United States under the Robert T. Stafford Disaster Relief and Emergency Assistance Act (42 U.S.C. Section 5121 et seq.) to an overweight or oversize vehicle or load that:

(1) can easily be dismantled or divided; and

(2) will be used only to deliver relief supplies.

(b) A permit issued under this section expires not later than the 120th day after the date of the major disaster declaration.

Sec. 623.342. Rules.

The board may adopt rules necessary to implement this subchapter, including rules that establish the requirements for obtaining a permit.

Sec. 623.343. Permit Conditions.

The department may impose conditions on a permit holder to ensure the safe operation of a permitted vehicle and minimize damage to roadways, including requirements related to vehicle routing, hours of operation, weight limits, and lighting and requirements for escort vehicles.

SUBCHAPTER S
REGIONAL MOBILITY AUTHORITY PERMITS

Sec. 623.361. Optional Procedure.

This subchapter provides an optional procedure for the issuance of a permit by a regional mobility authority for the movement of oversize or overweight vehicles carrying cargo on certain roads located in Hidalgo County.

Sec. 623.362. Definition.

In this subchapter, "authority" means the regional mobility authority authorized to issue permits under Section 623.363.

Sec. 623.363. Issuance of Permits.

(a) The commission may authorize a regional mobility authority to issue permits for the movement of oversize or overweight vehicles carrying cargo in Hidalgo County on:

(1) the following roads:

(A) U.S. Highway 281 between its intersection with the Pharr-Reynosa International Bridge and its intersection with State Highway 336;

(B) State Highway 336 between its intersection with U.S. Highway 281 and its intersection with Farm-to-Market Road 1016;

(C) Farm-to-Market Road 1016 between its intersection with State Highway 336 and its intersection with Trinity Road;

(D) Trinity Road between its intersection with Farm-to-Market Road 1016 and its intersection with Farm-to-Market Road 396;

(E) Farm-to-Market Road 396 between its intersection with Trinity Road and its intersection with the Anzalduas International Bridge;

(F) Farm-to-Market Road 2061 between its intersection with Farm-to-Market Road 3072 and its intersection with U.S. Highway 281;

(G) U.S. Highway 281 between its intersection with the Pharr-Reynosa International Bridge and its intersection with Spur 29;

(H) Spur 29 between its intersection with U.S. Highway 281 and its intersection with Doffin Canal Road;

(I) Doffin Canal Road between its intersection with the Pharr-Reynosa International Bridge and its intersection with Spur 29;

(J) Farm-to-Market Road 1015 between its intersection with U.S. Highway 281 and its intersection with U.S. Highway 83 Business;

(K) U.S. Highway 83 Business between its intersection with Farm-to-Market Road 1015 and its intersection with South Pleasantview Drive;

(L) Farm-to-Market Road 1015 between its intersection with U.S. Highway 83 Business and its intersection with Mile 9 Road North; and

(M) Mile 9 Road North between its intersection with Farm-to-Market Road 1015 and its intersection with Joe Stephens Avenue; or

(2) another route designated by the commission in consultation with the authority.

(b) The authority authorized under this section must serve the same geographic location as the roads over which the permit is valid.

Sec. 623.364. Permit Fees.

(a) The authority may collect a fee for permits issued under this subchapter. Beginning September 1, 2017, the maximum amount of the fee may not exceed $200 per trip. On September 1 of each subsequent year, the authority may adjust the maximum fee amount as necessary to reflect the percentage change during the preceding year in the Consumer Price Index for All Urban Consumers (CPI-U), U.S. City Average, published monthly by the United States Bureau of Labor Statistics or its successor in function.

(b) Fees collected under Subsection (a) shall be used only for the construction and maintenance of the roads described by or designated under Section 623.363 and for the authority's administrative costs, which may not exceed 15 percent of the fees collected. The authority shall make payments to the Texas Department of Transportation to provide funds for the maintenance of roads and highways subject to this subchapter.

Sec. 623.365. Permit Requirements.

(a) A permit issued under this subchapter must include:

(1) the name of the applicant;

(2) the date of issuance;

(3) the signature of the designated agent for the authority;

(4) a statement of the kind of cargo being transported, the maximum weight and dimensions of the equipment, and the kind and weight of each commodity to be transported;

(5) a statement:

(A) that the gross weight of the vehicle for which a permit is issued may not exceed 125,000 pounds; and

(B) of any other condition on which the permit is issued;

(6) a statement that the cargo may be transported in Hidalgo County only over the roads described by or designated under Section 623.363; and

(7) the location where the cargo was loaded.

(b) The authority shall report to the department all permits issued under this subchapter.

Sec. 623.366. Time of Movement.

A permit issued under this subchapter must specify the time during which movement authorized by the permit is allowed.

Transportation Code

Sec. 623.367. Speed Limit.

Movement authorized by a permit issued under this subchapter may not exceed the posted speed limit or 55 miles per hour, whichever is less. A violation of this provision constitutes a moving violation.

Sec. 623.368. Enforcement.

The Department of Public Safety has authority to enforce this subchapter.

Sec. 623.369. Rules.

The commission may adopt rules necessary to implement this subchapter.

Sec. 623.370. Bond.

(a) The authority shall file with the Texas Department of Transportation a bond in an amount set by the Texas Department of Transportation under Subsection (b), payable to the Texas Department of Transportation, and conditioned that the authority will pay to the Texas Department of Transportation the amount by which the annual cost to repair any damage to roads and highways subject to this subchapter from the movement of oversize and overweight vehicles for which permits are issued under this subchapter exceeds the annual amount paid to the Texas Department of Transportation under Section 623.364(b).

(b) The Texas Department of Transportation shall set the amount of the bond required under Subsection (a) in an amount equal to the estimated annual cost to repair any damage to roads and highways subject to this subchapter from the movement of oversize and overweight vehicles for which permits are issued under this subchapter.

SUBCHAPTER T. WEBB COUNTY PERMITS

Sec. 623.381. Optional Procedure.

This subchapter provides an optional procedure for the issuance of a permit by the City of Laredo for the movement of oversize or overweight vehicles carrying cargo on certain roadways located in Webb County.

Sec. 623.382. Issuance of Permits.

(a) The commission may authorize the City of Laredo to issue permits for the movement of oversize or overweight vehicles carrying cargo in Webb County on the following roadways:

(1) Farm-to-Market Road 1472 between its intersection with State Highway Loop 20 and the northernmost of its intersections with World Trade Center Loop;

(2) Farm-to-Market Road 1472 between the northernmost of its intersections with World Trade Center Loop and its intersection with Hachar Loop, if the Hachar Loop project in Webb County is constructed;

(3) Hachar Loop between its intersection with Farm-to-Market Road 1472 and its intersection with Interstate Highway 35, if the Hachar Loop project in Webb County is constructed; and

(4) Beltway Parkway between its intersection with Hachar Loop and its intersection with Interstate Highway 35, if the Hachar Loop project in Webb County is constructed.

(b) In addition to the roadways described by Subsection (a), the City of Laredo may designate and issue permits for the movement of oversize or overweight vehicles carrying cargo in Webb County on roadways under the city's jurisdiction and control.

Sec. 623.383. Surety Bond.

The commission may require the City of Laredo to execute, at its own expense, a surety bond payable to the Texas Department of Transportation in an amount of not less than $500,000 for costs of maintenance for the roadways described by Section 623.382(a).

Sec. 623.384. Permit Fees.

(a) The City of Laredo may collect a fee for permits issued under this subchapter. Except as otherwise provided by this subsection, the maximum amount of the fee may not exceed $200 per trip. On September 1 of each year, the city may adjust the maximum fee amount as necessary to reflect the percentage change during the preceding year in the Consumer Price Index for All Urban Consumers (CPI-U), U.S. City Average, published monthly by the United States Bureau of Labor Statistics or its successor in function.

(b) Fees collected under Subsection (a) may be used only for the operation and maintenance of the roadways described by or designated under Section 623.382 and for the City of Laredo's administrative costs, which may not exceed 15 percent of the fees collected.

(c) The distribution of the fees collected under Subsection (a) less the City of Laredo's administrative costs must be distributed between the state

Transportation Code

and the city based on lane mile calculations between on and off system roadways subject to this subchapter. Lane mile calculations must be adjusted on a biannual basis.

(d) The City of Laredo shall send the state's portion of the fees collected under Subsection (a) to the comptroller for deposit to the credit of the state highway fund. Fees deposited in the state highway fund under this section are exempt from the application of Section 403.095, Government Code.

Sec. 623.385. Permit Requirements.

(a) A permit issued under this subchapter must include:

(1) the name of the applicant;

(2) the date of issuance;

(3) the signature of the designated agent for the City of Laredo;

(4) a statement of the kind of cargo being transported, the maximum weight and dimensions of the equipment, and the kind and weight of each commodity to be transported;

(5) a statement:

(A) that the gross weight of the vehicle for which a permit is issued may not exceed 125,000 pounds; and

(B) of any other condition on which the permit is issued;

(6) a statement that the cargo may be transported in Webb County only over the roadways described by or designated under Section 623.382;

(7) a statement that the permit does not authorize the transportation of the cargo on an interstate highway; and

(8) the location where the cargo was loaded.

(b) The City of Laredo shall report to the department all permits issued under this subchapter.

Sec. 623.386. Time of Movement.

A permit issued under this subchapter must specify the time during which movement authorized by the permit is allowed.

Sec. 623.387. Speed Limit.

Movement authorized by a permit issued under this subchapter may not exceed the posted speed limit or 55 miles per hour, whichever is less. A violation of this provision constitutes a moving violation.

Sec. 623.388. Enforcement.

The Department of Public Safety has authority to enforce this subchapter.

Sec. 623.389. Pavement Management Plan.

The Texas Department of Transportation shall create a pavement management plan for the roadways described by Section 623.382(a).

Sec. 623.390. Rules.

The commission may adopt rules necessary to implement this subchapter.

SUBCHAPTER U INTERMODAL SHIPPING CONTAINERS

Sec. 623.401. [2 Versions: As added by Acts 2017, 85th Leg., ch. 108] Definition.

In this subchapter, "intermodal shipping container" means an enclosed, standardized, reusable container that:

(1) is used to pack, ship, move, or transport cargo;

(2) is designed to be carried on a semitrailer and loaded onto or unloaded from:

(A) a ship or vessel for international transportation; or

(B) a rail system for international transportation; and

(3) when combined with vehicles transporting the container, has a gross weight or axle weight that exceeds the limits allowed by law to be transported over a state highway or county or municipal road.

SUBCHAPTER U VEHICLES TRANSPORTING FLUID MILK

Sec. 623.401. [2 Versions: As added by Acts 2017, 85th Leg., ch. 750] Permit for Vehicles Transporting Fluid Milk. [Renumbered]

Sec. 623.402. [2 Versions: As added by Acts 2017, 85th Leg., ch. 108] Issuance of Permit.

(a) The department may issue an annual permit authorizing the movement of a sealed intermodal shipping container moving in international transportation by a truck-tractor and semitrailer combination that has six total axles and is equipped with a roll stability support safety system and truck blind spot systems only if:

Transportation Code

(1) the gross weight of the combination does not exceed 93,000 pounds;

(2) the distance between the front axle of the truck-tractor and the last axle of the semitrailer, measured longitudinally, is approximately 647 inches;

(3) the truck-tractor is configured as follows:

(A) one single axle that does not exceed 13,000 pounds;

(B) one two-axle group that does not exceed 37,000 pounds, in which no axle in the group exceeds 18,500 pounds; and

(C) the distance between the individual axles on the two-axle group of the truck-tractor, measured longitudinally, is not less than 51 inches and not more than 52 inches; and

(4) the semitrailer is configured as follows:

(A) one three-axle group that does not exceed 49,195 pounds, in which no axle in the group exceeds 16,400 pounds; and

(B) the distance between the individual axles in the three-axle group of the semitrailer, measured longitudinally, is 60 inches.

(b) The department may issue an annual permit authorizing the movement of a sealed intermodal shipping container moving in international transportation by a truck-tractor and semitrailer combination that has seven total axles and is equipped with a roll stability support safety system and truck blind spot systems only if:

(1) the gross weight of the combination does not exceed 100,000 pounds;

(2) the distance between the front axle of the truck-tractor and the last axle of the semitrailer, measured longitudinally, is approximately 612 inches;

(3) the truck-tractor is configured as follows:

(A) one single axle that does not exceed 15,000 pounds;

(B) one three-axle group that does not exceed 44,500 pounds, in which no axle in the group exceeds 14,900 pounds; and

(C) the distance between the individual axles on the three-axle group of the truck-tractor, measured longitudinally, is not less than 51 inches and not more than 52 inches; and

(4) the semitrailer is configured as follows:

(A) one three-axle group that does not exceed 46,200 pounds, in which no axle in the group exceeds 15,400 pounds; and

(B) the distance between the individual axles in the three-axle group of the semitrailer, measured longitudinally, is 60 inches.

(c) For purposes of Subsections (a) and (b), the gross weight, group weights, and axle weights listed in those subsections include all enforcement tolerances.

Sec. 623.402. [2 Versions: As added by Acts 2017, 85th Leg., ch. 750] Permit Sticker. [Renumbered]

Sec. 623.403. County Designation; Distribution of Fee. [Renumbered]

Sec. 623.403. [2 Versions: As added by Acts 2017, 85th Leg., ch. 108] County and Municipality Designation.

(a) An applicant for a permit under this subchapter must designate each county and municipality in which the permit will be used.

(b) A permit issued under this subchapter is not valid in a county or municipality that is not designated in the permit application.

Sec. 623.404. [2 Versions: As added by Acts 2017, 85th Leg., ch. 750] Permit Conditions. [Renumbered]

Sec. 623.405. [2 Versions: As added by Acts 2017, 85th Leg., ch. 750] Certain County or Municipal Actions Prohibited. [Renumbered]

Sec. 623.405. [2 Versions: As added by Acts 2017, 85th Leg., ch. 108] Route Restrictions.

(a) A permit issued under this subchapter does not authorize the operation of a truck-tractor and semitrailer combination on:

(1) the national system of interstate and defense highways; or

(2) load-restricted roads or bridges, including a road or bridge for which a maximum weight and load limit has been established and posted by the Texas Department of Transportation under Section 621.102 or the commissioners court of a county under Section 621.301.

(b) Subject to Section 623.406, a permit issued under this subchapter authorizes the operation of a truck-tractor and semitrailer combination only on highways and roads approved by the Texas Department of Transportation.

Sec. 623.406. [2 Versions: As added by Acts 2017, 85th Leg., ch. 108] Permit Conditions.

(a) In this section:

Transportation Code

(1) "Port authority" means a port authority or navigation district created or operating under Section 52, Article III, or Section 59, Article XVI, Texas Constitution.

(2) "Port of entry" has the meaning assigned by Section 621.001.

(b) The transportation of a sealed intermodal shipping container under a permit issued under this subchapter:

(1) must begin or end at a port authority or port of entry that is located in a county contiguous to the Gulf of Mexico or a bay or inlet opening into the gulf; and

(2) may not exceed 30 miles from the port authority or port of entry and must be on a highway or road described by Section 623.405(b).

(c) In addition to the requirements of Subsection (b), the intermodal shipping container must be continuously sealed from the point of origin to the point of destination with a seal that is required by:

(1) the United States Customs and Border Protection;

(2) the United States Food and Drug Administration; or

(3) federal law or regulation.

(d) A permit issued under this subchapter does not authorize the transportation of a material designated as of January 1, 2017, as a hazardous material by the United States secretary of transportation under 49 U.S.C. Section 5103(a).

(e) A permit issued under this subchapter does not authorize the transportation of a sealed intermodal shipping container in a county that borders New Mexico and the United Mexican States.

Sec. 623.406. [2 Versions: As added by Acts 2017, 85th Leg., ch. 750] Exclusive Permit. [Renumbered]

Sec. 623.407. [2 Versions: As added by Acts 2017, 85th Leg., ch. 750] Rules. [Renumbered]

Sec. 623.407. [2 Versions: As added by Acts 2017, 85th Leg., ch. 108] Permit Sticker.

(a) When the department issues a permit under this subchapter, the department shall issue a sticker to be placed on the front windshield of the truck-tractor. The department shall design the form of the sticker to aid in the enforcement of weight limits.

(b) The sticker must:

(1) indicate the expiration date of the permit; and

(2) be removed from the truck-tractor when:

(A) the permit for operation of the truck-tractor expires;

(B) a lease of the truck-tractor expires; or

(C) the truck-tractor is sold.

Sec. 623.408. Permit and Weight Record Documents.

(a) A permit issued under this subchapter must be carried in the truck-tractor for which the permit is issued.

(b) A copy of the weight record in the form prescribed by the department must contain the information required by Section 621.410(c) and must be:

(1) carried in the truck-tractor if the truck-tractor is:

(A) on a public highway or road; and

(B) transporting an intermodal shipping container that contains cargo; and

(2) presented, on request, to an officer authorized to enforce this subtitle, regardless of whether a weight record is required under Section 621.410.

Sec. 623.409. Offense.

(a) A person commits an offense if the person fails to:

(1) display the sticker described by Section 623.407(a) in the manner required by that section;

(2) carry a permit issued under this subchapter as required by Section 623.408(a); or

(3) carry or present a weight record as required by Section 623.408(b).

(b) An offense under this section is a Class C misdemeanor.

Sec. 623.410. Study.

Beginning in 2022, not later than September 1 of each even-numbered year, the Texas Department of Transportation shall conduct a study concerning vehicles operating under a permit issued under this subchapter and publish the results of the study. In conducting the study, the Texas Department of Transportation shall collect and examine the following information:

(1) the weight and configuration of vehicles operating under a permit issued under this subchapter that are involved in a motor vehicle accident;

(2) the types of vehicles operating under a permit issued under this subchapter;

(3) traffic volumes and variations of vehicles operating under a permit issued under this subchapter;

(4) weigh-in-motion data for highways and roads located in and around the area described by Section 623.405(b);

(5) impacts to state and local bridges, including long-term bridge performance, for bridges located in and around the area described by Section 623.405(b); and

(6) impacts to state and local roads, including changes in pavement design standards, construction specification details, maintenance frequency and types, and properties of pavement and underlying soils resulting from or necessitated by vehicles operating under a permit issued under this subchapter.

Sec. 623.425. Certain County or Municipal Actions Prohibited.

Unless otherwise provided by state or federal law, a county or municipality may not require a permit, fee, or license for the operation of a vehicle combination described by Section 623.421(a) or (b) in addition to a permit, fee, or license required by state law.

SUBCHAPTER V VEHICLES TRANSPORTING FLUID MILK

Sec. 623.421. Permit for Vehicles Transporting Fluid Milk.

(a) The department may issue a permit authorizing the movement of fluid milk by a truck-tractor and semitrailer combination that has six total axles and is equipped with a roll stability support safety system and truck blind spot systems:

(1) at a gross weight that is not heavier than 90,000 pounds; and

(2) with axle weights that comply with the requirements of Section 621.101(a), except as authorized by Subsection (b).

(b) A vehicle combination operating under a permit issued under Subsection (a) may exceed the axle weights listed in Section 621.101(a) for the following axle groups if the overall distance between the first axle of the truck-tractor and the first axle of the first consecutive set of tandem axles is 15 feet or more, the overall distance between the first and last axles of two consecutive sets of tandem axles is 36 feet or more, the distance between each individual axle in each axle group, measured from the center of the axle, is between 48 inches and 54 inches, and:

(1) a two-axle group does not exceed 36,500 pounds; and

(2) a three-axle group does not exceed 42,500 pounds.

(c) To qualify for a permit under this subchapter, a permit fee of $1,200 must be paid.

(d) A permit issued under this subchapter:

(1) is valid for one year; and

(2) must be carried in the truck-tractor for which it is issued.

Sec. 623.422. Permit Sticker.

(a) When the department issues a permit under this subchapter, the department shall issue a sticker to be placed on the front windshield of the truck-tractor. The department shall design the form of the sticker to aid in the enforcement of weight limits for vehicles.

(b) The sticker must:

(1) indicate the expiration date of the permit; and

(2) be removed from the truck-tractor when:

(A) the permit for operation of the vehicle combination expires;

(B) a lease of the truck-tractor expires; or

(C) the truck-tractor is sold.

Sec. 623.423. County Designation; Distribution of Fee.

(a) An applicant for a permit under this subchapter must designate in the permit application the counties in which the applicant intends to operate. A permit issued under this subchapter is not valid in a county that is not designated in the permit application.

(b) Of the fee collected under this subchapter for a permit:

(1) 75 percent of the amount collected shall be deposited to the credit of the state highway fund;

(2) 15 percent of the amount collected shall be divided equally among and distributed to the counties designated in the permit application; and

(3) 10 percent of the amount collected shall be deposited to the credit of the Texas Department of Motor Vehicles fund.

(c) [Repealed.]

Sec. 623.424. Permit Conditions.

(a) Except as provided by Subsections (b) and (c), a vehicle combination operating under a permit under this subchapter may operate on a federal interstate highway or a state, county, or municipal road, including a frontage road adjacent to a federal interstate highway, if the truck-tractor displays a sticker required by Section 623.422 and the vehicle combination does not exceed the maximum axle or gross weight applicable to the combination under the terms of the permit.

(b) A permit issued under this subchapter authorizes the operation of a truck-tractor and semitrailer combination only on highways and roads approved by the Texas Department of Transportation.

(c) A permit issued under this subchapter does not authorize the operation of a truck-tractor and semitrailer combination on a county road or bridge for which a maximum weight and load limit has been established and posted under Section 621.301.

Sec. 623.425. Certain County or Municipal Actions Prohibited.

Unless otherwise provided by state or federal law, a county or municipality may not require a permit, fee, or license for the operation of a vehicle combination described by Section 623.421(a) or (b) in addition to a permit, fee, or license required by state law.

Sec. 623.426. Exclusive Permit.

A permit issued under this subchapter is the only permit issued by the department under this chapter that may be used to transport fluid milk.

Sec. 623.427. Rules.

(a) The department shall adopt rules necessary to implement this subchapter, including rules governing the application for a permit under this subchapter.

(b) The Department of Public Safety shall adopt rules requiring additional safety and driver training for permits issued under this subchapter.

SUBTITLE F COMMERCIAL MOTOR VEHICLES

CHAPTER 641 OPERATION OF LEASED COMMERCIAL MOTOR VEHICLES AND TRUCK-TRACTORS [REPEALED]

SUBCHAPTER A GENERAL PROVISIONS

Sec. 641.001. Definitions [Repealed].

Repealed by Acts 1997, 75th Leg., ch. 165 (S.B. 898), § 30.148, effective September 1, 1997.

Sec. 641.002. Effect of Compliance with Chapter [Repealed].

Repealed by Acts 1997, 75th Leg., ch. 165 (S.B. 898), § 30.148, effective September 1, 1997.

SUBCHAPTER B VEHICLE OPERATED UNDER LEASE

Sec. 641.021. Filing of Lease Required [Repealed].

Repealed by Acts 1997, 75th Leg., ch. 165 (S.B. 898), § 30.148, effective September 1, 1997.

Sec. 641.022. Contents of Lease [Repealed].

Repealed by Acts 1997, 75th Leg., ch. 165 (S.B. 898), § 30.148, effective September 1, 1997.

Sec. 641.023. Manner of Filing; Fee [Repealed].

Repealed by Acts 1997, 75th Leg., ch. 165 (S.B. 898), § 30.148, effective September 1, 1997.

Sec. 641.024. Acknowledgment [Repealed].

Repealed by Acts 1997, 75th Leg., ch. 165 (S.B. 898), § 30.148, effective September 1, 1997.

Sec. 641.025. Maintenance and Display of Lease or Acknowledgment [Repealed].

Repealed by Acts 1997, 75th Leg., ch. 165 (S.B. 898), § 30.148, effective September 1, 1997.

Sec. 641.026. Subsequent Lease; Fee [Repealed].

Repealed by Acts 1997, 75th Leg., ch. 165 (S.B. 898), § 30.148, effective September 1, 1997.

Sec. 641.027. Lease Confidential [Repealed].

Repealed by Acts 1997, 75th Leg., ch. 165 (S.B. 898), § 30.148, effective September 1, 1997.

SUBCHAPTER C SIGNS

Sec. 641.041. Signs Required [Repealed].

Repealed by Acts 1997, 75th Leg., ch. 165 (S.B. 898), § 30.148, effective September 1, 1997.

Sec. 641.042. Placement and Content of Signs [Repealed].

Repealed by Acts 1997, 75th Leg., ch. 165 (S.B. 898), § 30.148, effective September 1, 1997.

SUBCHAPTER D EXCEPTIONS

Sec. 641.061. Operation by Agent [Repealed].

Repealed by Acts 1997, 75th Leg., ch. 165 (S.B. 898), § 30.148, effective September 1, 1997.

Sec. 641.062. Farm Vehicles [Repealed].

Repealed by Acts 1997, 75th Leg., ch. 165 (S.B. 898), § 30.148, effective September 1, 1997.

Sec. 641.063. Vehicles Used to Transport Earth and Road-Building Materials [Repealed].

Repealed by Acts 1997, 75th Leg., ch. 165 (S.B. 898), § 30.148, effective September 1, 1997.

Sec. 641.064. Passenger Car Used to Deliver Mail [Repealed].

Repealed by Acts 1997, 75th Leg., ch. 165 (S.B. 898), § 30.148, effective September 1, 1997.

Sec. 641.065. Vehicles Used to Transport Liquefied Petroleum Gas [Repealed].

Repealed by Acts 1997, 75th Leg., ch. 165 (S.B. 898), § 30.148, effective September 1, 1997.

Sec. 641.066. Vehicles Used to Transport Household and Office Goods [Repealed].

Repealed by Acts 1997, 75th Leg., ch. 165 (S.B. 898), § 30.148, effective September 1, 1997.

Sec. 641.067. Vehicles Leased from Certain Leasing Companies [Repealed].

Repealed by Acts 1997, 75th Leg., ch. 165 (S.B. 898), § 30.148, effective September 1, 1997.

SUBCHAPTER E VIOLATION; PENALTIES

Sec. 641.081. Offense [Repealed].

Repealed by Acts 1997, 75th Leg., ch. 165 (S.B. 898), § 30.148, effective September 1, 1997.

Sec. 641.082. Defense: Loan of Vehicle Without Compensation [Repealed].

Repealed by Acts 1997, 75th Leg., ch. 165 (S.B. 898), § 30.148, effective September 1, 1997.

CHAPTER 642 IDENTIFYING MARKINGS ON COMMERCIAL MOTOR VEHICLES

Sec. 642.001. Definitions.

In this chapter:

(1) "Motor vehicle" means a motor vehicle, other than a motorcycle, that is designed or used primarily for the transportation of persons or property.

(2) "Operator" means the person who is in actual physical control of a motor vehicle.

(3) "Owner" means a person who has:

(A) legal title to a motor vehicle; or

(B) the right to possess or control the vehicle.

(4) "Road-tractor" means a motor vehicle that is:

(A) used for towing manufactured housing; or

(B) designed and used for drawing other vehicles and not constructed so as to carry any load independently or as a part of the weight of a vehicle or load it is drawing.

(5) "Truck-tractor" means a motor vehicle that:

(A) transports passenger cars loaded on the vehicle while the vehicle is engaged with a semitrailer transporting passenger cars; or

(B) is designed or used primarily for pulling other vehicles and constructed to carry only a part of the weight of a vehicle it is pulling.

(6) "Tow truck" has the meaning assigned that term by Section 2308.002, Occupations Code.

Sec. 642.002. Identifying Markings on Certain Vehicles Required; Offense; Penalty.

(a) A person commits an offense if:

(1) the person operates on a public street, road, or highway:

(A) a commercial motor vehicle that has three or more axles;

(B) a truck-tractor;

(C) a road-tractor; or

(D) a tow truck; and

(2) the vehicle does not have on each side of the power unit identifying markings that comply with the identifying marking requirements specified by 49 C.F.R. Section 390.21 or that:

(A) show the name of the owner or operator of the vehicle;

(B) have clearly legible letters and numbers of a height of at least two inches; and

(C) show the motor carrier registration number in clearly legible letters and numbers, if the vehicle is required to be registered under this chapter or Chapter 643.

(b) A person commits an offense if the person operates on a public street, road, or highway a tow truck that does not show on each side of the power unit, in addition to the markings required by Subsection (a)(2), the city in which the owner or operator maintains its place of business and the telephone number, including area code, at that place of business in clearly legible letters and numbers.

(c) The owner of a vehicle commits an offense if the owner or operator permits another to operate a vehicle in violation of Subsection (a) or (b).

(d) The Texas Department of Motor Vehicles by rule may prescribe additional requirements regarding the form of the markings required by Subsection (a)(2) that are not inconsistent with that subsection.

(e) An offense under this section is a Class C misdemeanor.

Sec. 642.003. Nonapplicability.

Section 642.002 does not apply to a commercial motor vehicle, road-tractor, or truck-tractor that is:

(1) registered under Section 502.433;

(2) required to be registered under Section 113.131, Natural Resources Code;

(3) operated in private carriage that is subject to Title 49, Code of Federal Regulations, Part 390.21;

(4) operated under the direct control, supervision, or authority of a public utility, as recognized by the legislature, that is otherwise visibly marked; or

(5) transporting timber products in their natural state from first point of production or harvest to first point of processing.

CHAPTER 643 MOTOR CARRIER REGISTRATION

SUBCHAPTER A GENERAL PROVISIONS

Sec. 643.001. Definitions.

In this chapter:

(1) "Department" means the Texas Department of Motor Vehicles.

(2) "Director" means:

(A) the executive director of the department; or

(B) an employee of the department who:

(i) is a division or special office director or holds a higher rank; and

(ii) is designated by the director.

(3) "Hazardous material" has the meaning assigned by 49 U.S.C. Section 5102.

(4) "Household goods" has the meaning assigned by 49 U.S.C. Section 13102.

(5) "Insurer" means a person, including a surety, authorized in this state to write lines of insurance coverage required by this chapter.

(6) "Motor carrier" means an individual, association, corporation, or other legal entity that controls, operates, or directs the operation of one or more vehicles that transport persons or cargo over a road or highway in this state.

(7) [Repealed by Acts 2007, 80th Leg., ch. 1046 (H.B. 2094), § 5.01(a)(1), effective September 1, 2007.]

(7-a) [Repealed by Acts 2017, 85th Leg., (H.B. 3254), §17, effective January 1, 2018.]

(8) "Vehicle requiring registration" means a vehicle described by Section 643.051.

Sec. 643.002. Exemptions.

This chapter does not apply to:

(1) motor carrier operations exempt from registration by the Unified Carrier Registration Act of

Transportation Code

2005 (49 U.S.C. Section 14504a) or a motor vehicle registered under the single state registration system established under 49 U.S.C. Section 14504(c) when operating exclusively in interstate or international commerce;

(2) a motor vehicle registered as a cotton vehicle under Section 504.505;

(3) a motor vehicle the department by rule exempts because the vehicle is subject to comparable registration and a comparable safety program administered by another governmental entity;

(4) a motor vehicle used to transport passengers operated by an entity whose primary function is not the transportation of passengers, such as a vehicle operated by a hotel, day-care center, public or private school, nursing home, or similar organization;

(5) a vehicle operating under:

(A) Section 14.071, Alcoholic Beverage Code;

(B) Section 16.10, Alcoholic Beverage Code;

(C) Section 19.06, Alcoholic Beverage Code; or

(D) Section 20.04, Alcoholic Beverage Code;

(6) a vehicle operated by a governmental entity; or

(7) a tow truck, as defined by Section 2308.002, Occupations Code.

Transportation Code

Sec. 643.003. Rules.

The department may adopt rules to administer this chapter.

Sec. 643.004. Payment of Fees.

(a) The department may adopt rules on the method of payment of a fee under this chapter, including:

(1) authorizing the use of:

(A) escrow accounts described by Subsection (b); and

(B) electronic funds transfer or a credit card issued by a financial institution chartered by a state or the United States or by a nationally recognized credit organization approved by the department; and

(2) requiring the payment of a discount or service charge for a credit card payment in addition to the fee.

(b) The department may establish one or more escrow accounts in the Texas Department of Motor Vehicles fund for the prepayment of a fee under this chapter. Prepaid fees and any fees established by the department for the administration of this section shall be:

(1) administered under an agreement approved by the department; and

(2) deposited to the credit of the Texas Department of Motor Vehicles fund to be appropriated only to the department for the purposes of administering this chapter.

SUBCHAPTER B REGISTRATION

Sec. 643.051. Registration Required.

(a) A motor carrier may not operate a commercial motor vehicle, as defined by Section 548.001, on a road or highway of this state unless the carrier registers with the department under this subchapter.

(b) A motor carrier may not operate a vehicle, regardless of size of the vehicle, to transport household goods for compensation unless the carrier registers with the department under this subchapter.

Sec. 643.052. Application.

To register under this subchapter a motor carrier must submit to the department an application on a form prescribed by the department. The application must include:

(1) the name of the owner and the principal business address of the motor carrier;

(2) the name and address of the legal agent for service of process on the carrier in this state, if different;

(3) a description of each vehicle requiring registration the carrier proposes to operate, including the motor vehicle identification number, make, and unit number;

(4) a statement as to whether the carrier proposes to transport household goods or a hazardous material;

(5) a declaration that the applicant has knowledge of all laws and rules relating to motor carrier safety, including this chapter, Chapter 644, and Subtitle C;

(6) a certification that the carrier is in compliance with the drug testing requirements of 49 C.F.R. Part 382, and if the carrier belongs to a consortium, as defined by 49 C.F.R. Part 382, the names of the persons operating the consortium;

(7) a valid identification number issued to the motor carrier by or under the authority of the Federal Motor Carrier Safety Administration or its successor; and

(8) any other information the department by rule determines is necessary for the safe operation of a motor carrier under this chapter.

Sec. 643.053. Filing of Application.

An application under Section 643.052 must be filed with the department and accompanied by:

(1) an application fee of $100 plus a $10 fee for each vehicle requiring registration;

(2) evidence of insurance or financial responsibility as required by Section 643.103(a); and

(3) any insurance filing fee required under Section 643.103(c).

Sec. 643.054. Department Approval and Denial; Issuance of Certificate.

(a) The department shall register a motor carrier under this subchapter if the carrier complies with Sections 643.052 and 643.053.

(a-1) The department may deny a registration if the applicant has had a registration revoked under Section 643.252.

(a-2) The department may deny a registration if the applicant is owned, operated, managed, or otherwise controlled by or affiliated with a person, including a family member, corporate officer, entity, or shareholder, that the Department of Public Safety has determined has:

(1) an unsatisfactory safety rating under 49 C.F.R. Part 385; or

(2) multiple violations of Chapter 644, a rule adopted under that chapter, or Subtitle C.

(a-3) The department may deny a registration if the applicant is owned, operated, managed, or otherwise controlled by or affiliated with a person, including a family member, corporate officer, entity, or shareholder, that:

(1) owned, operated, managed, or otherwise controlled a motor carrier that the Federal Motor Carrier Safety Administration has placed out of service for unacceptable safety compliance; or

(2) has unpaid administrative penalties assessed under this chapter or Subtitle E.

(b) The department shall issue a certificate containing a single registration number to a motor carrier, regardless of the number of vehicles requiring registration the carrier operates.

(c) To avoid multiple registrations of a single motor carrier, the department shall adopt simplified procedures for the registration of motor carriers transporting household goods as agents for carriers required to register under this chapter.

Sec. 643.055. Conditional Acceptance.

(a) The department may conditionally accept an incomplete application for registration under this subchapter if the motor carrier complies with Section 643.053.

(b) The department shall notify a motor carrier that an application is incomplete and inform the carrier of the information required for completion. If the motor carrier fails to provide the information before the 46th day after the date the department provides the notice, the application is considered withdrawn, and the department shall retain each fee required by Section 643.053(1).

Sec. 643.056. Supplemental Registration.

(a) A motor carrier required to register under this subchapter shall supplement the carrier's application for registration before:

(1) the carrier transports a hazardous material or household goods if the carrier has not provided notice of the transportation to the department in the carrier's initial or a supplemental application for registration;

(2) the carrier operates a vehicle requiring registration that is not described on the carrier's initial or a supplemental application for registration; or

(3) the carrier changes the carrier's principal business address, legal agent, ownership, consortium, as defined by 49 C.F.R. Part 382, or name.

(b) The department shall prescribe the form of a supplemental application for registration under Subsection (a).

(c) The department may deny a supplement to a motor carrier's application for registration if the motor carrier is owned, operated, managed, or otherwise controlled by or affiliated with a person, including a family member, corporate officer, entity, or shareholder, that has unpaid administrative penalties assessed under this chapter or Subtitle E.

Sec. 643.057. Additional Vehicles and Fees.

(a) A motor carrier may not operate an additional vehicle requiring registration unless the carrier pays a registration fee of $10 for each additional vehicle and shows the department evidence of insurance or financial responsibility for the vehicle in an amount at least equal to the amount set by the department under Section 643.101.

(b) A motor carrier is not required to pay the applicable registration fee under Subsection (a) for a vehicle for which the same fee is required and that replaces a vehicle for which the fee has been paid.

(c) A registered motor carrier may not transport household goods or a hazardous material unless the carrier shows the department evidence of insurance or financial responsibility in an amount at least equal to the amount set by the department under Section 643.101 for a vehicle carrying household goods or a hazardous material.

(d) The department may not collect more than $10 in equipment registration fees for a vehicle registered under both this subchapter and Chapter 645.

Sec. 643.058. Renewal of Registration.

(a) Except as provided in Section 643.061, a registration issued under this subchapter is valid for one year. The department may adopt a system under which registrations expire at different times during the year.

(b) At least 30 days before the date on which a motor carrier's registration expires, the department shall notify the carrier of the impending expiration. The notice must be in writing and sent to the motor carrier's last known address according to the records of the department.

(c) A motor carrier may renew a registration under this subchapter by:

(1) supplementing the application with any new information required under Section 643.056;

(2) paying a $10 fee for each vehicle requiring registration; and

(3) providing the department evidence of continuing insurance or financial responsibility in an amount at least equal to the amount set by the department under Section 643.101.

(d) A motor carrier may not renew a registration that has been expired for more than 180 days. The motor carrier may obtain a new registration by complying with the requirements and procedures for obtaining an original registration under this chapter.

(e) The department may deny a motor carrier's application to renew a registration if the motor carrier is owned, operated, managed, or otherwise controlled by or affiliated with a person, including a family member, corporate officer, entity, or shareholder, that:

(1) the Department of Public Safety has determined has:

(A) an unsatisfactory safety rating under 49 C.F.R. Part 385; or

(B) multiple violations of Chapter 644, a rule adopted under that chapter, or Subtitle C;

(2) owned, operated, managed, or otherwise controlled a motor carrier that the Federal Motor Carrier Safety Administration has placed out of service for unacceptable safety compliance; or

(3) has unpaid administrative penalties assessed under this chapter or Subtitle E.

Sec. 643.0585. Reregistration.

(a) If a motor carrier's registration has been revoked, the motor carrier may apply to the department for reregistration not later than the 180th day after the date the registration was revoked.

(b) An application for reregistration must be submitted on a form prescribed by the department and accompanied by:

(1) a $10 fee for each vehicle requiring registration;

(2) evidence of insurance or financial responsibility as required by Section 643.103(a); and

(3) any insurance filing fee required under Section 643.103(c).

(c) The department may deny a motor carrier's application for reregistration if the motor carrier is owned, operated, managed, or otherwise controlled by or affiliated with a person, including a family member, corporate officer, entity, or shareholder, that:

(1) the Department of Public Safety has determined has:

(A) an unsatisfactory safety rating under 49 C.F.R. Part 385; or

(B) multiple violations of Chapter 644, a rule adopted under that chapter, or Subtitle C;

(2) owned, operated, managed, or otherwise controlled a motor carrier that the Federal Motor Carrier Safety Administration has placed out of service for unacceptable safety compliance; or

(3) has unpaid administrative penalties assessed under this chapter or Subtitle E.

Sec. 643.059. Cab Cards.

(a) The department shall issue a cab card for each vehicle requiring registration. A cab card must:

(1) show the registration number of the certificate issued under Section 643.054(b);

(2) show the vehicle unit number;

(3) show the vehicle identification number; and

(4) contain a statement that the vehicle is registered to operate under this subchapter.

(b) The department shall issue cab cards at the time a motor carrier pays a registration fee under this subchapter. The department may charge a fee of $1 for each cab card.

(c) A motor carrier required to register under this subchapter must keep the cab card in the cab of each vehicle requiring registration the carrier operates.

(d) The department may order a motor carrier to surrender a cab card if the carrier's registration is suspended or revoked under Section 643.252.

(e) If the department determines that the cab card system described by Subsections (a)—(c) is not an efficient means of enforcing this subchapter, the department by rule may adopt an alternative method that is accessible by law enforcement personnel in the field and provides for the enforcement of the registration requirements of this subchapter.

(f) A cab card or a vehicle registration issued under the alternative method described in Subsection (e) must be valid for the same duration of time as a motor carrier's certificate issued under Section 643.054(b) or Section 643.061(c)(1).

Sec. 643.060. Temporary Registration of International Motor Carrier.

The department by rule may provide for the temporary registration of an international motor carrier that provides evidence of insurance as required for a domestic motor carrier. The department may charge a fee for a temporary registration in an amount not to exceed the cost of administering this section.

Sec. 643.061. Optional Registration Periods.

(a) The department may vary the registration period under this subchapter by adopting rules that provide for:

(1) an optional two-year registration; and

(2) an optional temporary registration that is valid for less than one year.

(b) A motor carrier applying for registration under this section must pay:

(1) a $20 fee for each vehicle registered under Subsection (a)(1);

(2) a $10 fee for each vehicle registered under Subsection (a)(2); and

(3) application and insurance filing fees the department by rule adopts in an amount not to exceed $100 each.

(c) The department shall issue to a motor carrier registering under this section:

(1) a motor carrier's certificate, in the manner provided by Section 643.054; and

(2) a cab card or the equivalent of a cab card, in the manner provided by Section 643.059.

Sec. 643.062. Limitation on International Motor Carrier.

(a) A foreign-based international motor carrier required to register under this chapter or registered under Chapter 645 may not transport persons or cargo in intrastate commerce in this state.

(b) A person may not assist a foreign-based international motor carrier in violating Subsection (a).

Sec. 643.063. Vehicles Operated Under Short-Term Lease and Substitute Vehicles.

(a) In this section:

(1) "Leasing business" means a person that leases vehicles requiring registration.

(2) "Short-term lease" means a lease of 30 days or less.

(b) A vehicle requiring registration operated under a short-term lease is exempt from the registration requirements of Sections 643.052—643.059. The department shall adopt rules providing for the operation of these vehicles under flexible procedures. A vehicle requiring registration operated under a short-term lease is not required to carry a cab card or other proof of registration if a copy of the lease agreement is carried in the cab of the vehicle.

(c) A motor carrier may operate a substitute vehicle without notifying the department in advance if the substitute is a temporary replacement because of maintenance, repair, or other unavailability of the vehicle originally leased. A substitute vehicle is not required to carry a cab card or other proof of registration if a copy of the lease agreement for the vehicle originally leased is carried in the cab of the substitute.

(d) Instead of the registration procedures described by Sections 643.052—643.059, the department shall adopt rules that allow a leasing business to report annually to the department on the number of vehicles requiring registration that the leasing business actually operated in the previous 12 months. The rules may not require the vehicles operated to be described with particularity. The registration fee for each vehicle operated may be paid at the time the report is filed.

(e) A leasing business that registers its vehicles under Subsection (d) may comply with the liability insurance requirements of Subchapter C by filing evidence of a contingency liability policy satisfactory to the department.

(f) Rules adopted by the department under this section:

(1) must be designed to avoid requiring a vehicle to be registered more than once in a calendar year; and

(2) may allow a leasing business to register a vehicle on behalf of a lessee.

Sec. 643.064. United States Department of Transportation Numbers.

(a) [Repealed by Acts 2017, 85th Leg., (H.B. 3254), § 17, effective January 1, 2018.]

(b) A motor carrier required to register under this subchapter shall maintain an authorized

Transportation Code

identification number issued to the motor carrier by the Federal Motor Carrier Safety Administration, its successor, or another person authorized to issue the number.

SUBCHAPTER C INSURANCE

Sec. 643.101. Amount Required.

(a) A motor carrier required to register under Subchapter B shall maintain liability insurance in an amount set by the department for each vehicle requiring registration the carrier operates.

(b) Except as provided by Section 643.1015, the department by rule may set the amount of liability insurance required at an amount that does not exceed the amount required for a motor carrier under a federal regulation adopted under 49 U.S.C. Section 13906(a)(1). In setting the amount the department shall consider:

(1) the class and size of the vehicle; and

(2) the persons or cargo being transported.

(c) A motor carrier required to register under Subchapter B that transports household goods shall maintain cargo insurance in the amount required for a motor carrier transporting household goods under federal law.

(d) [Repealed by Acts 2007, 80th Leg., ch. 1046 (H.B. 2094), § 5.01(a)(2), effective September 1, 2007.]

(e) Unless state law permits a commercial motor vehicle to be self-insured, any insurance required for a commercial motor vehicle must be obtained from:

(1) an insurer authorized to do business in this state whose aggregate net risk, after reinsurance, under any one insurance policy is not in excess of 10 percent of the insurer's policyholders' surplus, and credit for such reinsurance is permitted by law; or

(2) an insurer that meets the eligibility requirements of a surplus lines insurer pursuant to Chapter 981, Insurance Code. Notwithstanding any other provision in law, an insurer in compliance with this subsection shall be deemed to be in compliance with any rating or financial criteria established for motor carriers by any political subdivision of the state.

Sec. 643.1015. Amount Required for Certain School Buses.

(a) This section applies only to a school bus that:

(1) is owned by a motor carrier required to be registered under Subchapter B;

(2) is in compliance with the requirements of Chapter 548; and

(3) is operated exclusively within the boundaries of a municipality by a person who:

(A) holds a driver's license or commercial driver's license of the appropriate class required for the operation of the school bus; and

(B) meets the requirements of Section 521.022.

(b) The owner of a school bus shall maintain liability insurance in the amount of at least $500,000 combined single limit.

(c) In this section, "school bus" means a motor vehicle that is operated by a motor carrier and used to transport preprimary, primary, or secondary school students on a route between the students' residences and a public, private, or parochial school or day-care facility.

Sec. 643.102. Self-Insurance.

A motor carrier may comply with Section 643.101 through self-insurance if the carrier demonstrates to the department that it can satisfy its obligations for liability for bodily injury or property damage. In the interest of public safety, the department by rule shall provide for a responsible system of self-insurance for a motor carrier.

Sec. 643.103. Filing; Evidence of Insurance; Fees.

(a) A motor carrier that is required to register under Subchapter B must file with the department evidence of insurance in the amounts required by Section 643.101 or 643.1015, or evidence of financial responsibility as described by Section 643.102, in a form prescribed by the department. The form must be filed:

(1) at the time of the initial registration;

(2) at the time of a subsequent registration if the motor carrier was required to be continuously registered under Subchapter B and the carrier failed to maintain continuous registration;

(3) at the time a motor carrier changes insurers; and

(4) at the time a motor carrier changes ownership, as determined by rules adopted by the department.

(b) A motor carrier shall keep evidence of insurance in a form approved by the department in the cab of each vehicle requiring registration the carrier operates.

(c) The department may charge a fee of $100 for a filing under Subsection (a).

Transportation Code

Sec. 643.104. Termination of Insurance Coverage.

(a) An insurer may not terminate coverage provided to a motor carrier registered under Subchapter B unless the insurer provides the department with notice at least 30 days before the date the termination takes effect.

(b) Notice under Subsection (a) must be in a form approved by the department and the Texas Department of Insurance. The department shall notify the Department of Public Safety and other law enforcement agencies of each motor carrier whose certificate of registration has been revoked for failing to maintain liability insurance coverage.

(c) The Department of Public Safety or a local law enforcement agency shall confirm that no operations are being performed by a motor carrier if notice has been received under Subsection (b) that the certificate of registration for that carrier has been revoked.

(d) A law enforcement officer may detain or impound any commercial vehicle operating without liability insurance until such coverage is properly filed with the department.

Sec. 643.105. Insolvency of Insurer.

If an insurer for a motor carrier becomes insolvent, is placed in receivership, or has its certificate of authority suspended or revoked and if the carrier no longer has insurance coverage as required by this subchapter, the carrier shall file with the department, not later than the 10th day after the date the coverage lapses:

(1) evidence of insurance as required by Section 643.103; and

(2) an affidavit that:

(A) indicates that an accident from which the carrier may incur liability did not occur while the coverage was not in effect; or

(B) contains a plan acceptable to the department indicating how the carrier will satisfy claims of liability against the carrier for an accident that occurred while the coverage was not in effect.

Sec. 643.106. Insurance for Employees.

(a) Notwithstanding any provision of any law or regulation, a motor carrier that is required to register under Subchapter B and whose primary business is transportation for compensation or hire between two or more municipalities shall protect its employees by obtaining:

(1) workers' compensation insurance coverage as defined under Subtitle A, Title 5, Labor Code; or

(2) accidental insurance coverage approved by the department from:

(A) a reliable insurance company authorized to write accidental insurance policies in this state; or

(B) a surplus lines insurer under Chapter 981, Insurance Code.

(b) The department shall determine the amount of insurance coverage under Subsection (a)(2). The amount may not be less than:

(1) $300,000 for medical expenses for at least 104 weeks;

(2) $100,000 for accidental death and dismemberment;

(3) 70 percent of an employee's pre-injury income for at least 104 weeks when compensating for loss of income; and

(4) $500 for the maximum weekly benefit.

SUBCHAPTER D ECONOMIC REGULATION

Sec. 643.151. Prohibition.

Except as provided by this subchapter, the department may not regulate the prices, routes, or services provided by a motor carrier.

Sec. 643.152. Voluntary Standards.

The department may establish voluntary standards for uniform cargo liability, uniform bills of lading or receipts for cargo being transported, and uniform cargo credit. A standard adopted under this section must be consistent with Subtitle IV, Title 49, United States Code, or a regulation adopted under that law.

Sec. 643.153. Motor Carrier Transporting Household Goods.

(a) The department shall adopt rules to protect a consumer using the service of a motor carrier who is transporting household goods for compensation.

(b) The department may adopt rules necessary to ensure that a customer of a motor carrier transporting household goods is protected from deceptive or unfair practices and unreasonably hazardous activities. The rules must:

(1) establish a formal process for resolving a dispute over a fee or damage;

(2) require a motor carrier to indicate clearly to a customer whether an estimate is binding or nonbinding and disclose the maximum price a customer could be required to pay;

Transportation Code

(3) create a centralized process for making complaints about a motor carrier that also allows a customer to inquire about a carrier's complaint record; and

(4) require a motor carrier transporting household goods to list a place of business with a street address in this state and the carrier's registration number issued under this article in any print advertising published in this state.

(c) [Repealed by Acts 2005, 79th Leg., ch. 281 (H.B. 2702), § 6.06, effective June 14, 2005.]

(d) A motor carrier that is required to register under Subchapter B and that transports household goods shall file a tariff with the department that establishes maximum charges for all transportation services. A motor carrier may comply with this requirement by filing, in a manner determined by the department, a copy of the carrier's tariff governing interstate transportation services. The department shall make tariffs filed under this subsection available for public inspection.

(e) The department may not adopt rules regulating the rates, except as provided by this section, or routes of a motor carrier transporting household goods.

(f) The unauthorized practice of the insurance business under Chapter 101, Insurance Code, does not include the offer of insurance by a household goods motor carrier, or its agent, that transports goods for up to the full value of a customer's property transported or stored, if the offer is authorized by a rule adopted under Subsection (b).

(g) A motor carrier may designate an association or an agent of an association as its collective maximum ratemaking association for the purpose of the filing of a tariff under Subsection (d).

Transportation Code

Sec. 643.154. Antitrust Exemption.

(a) Chapter 15, Business & Commerce Code, does not apply to a discussion or agreement between a motor carrier that is required to register under Subchapter B and that transports household goods and an agent of the carrier involving:

(1) the following matters if they occur under the authority of the principal carrier:

(A) a rate for the transportation of household goods;

(B) an access, terminal, storage, or other charge incidental to the transportation of household goods; or

(C) an allowance relating to the transportation of household goods; or

(2) ownership of the carrier by the agent or membership on the board of directors of the carrier by the agent.

(b) An agent under Subsection (a) may itself be a motor carrier required to register under Subchapter B.

(c) The department by rule may exempt a motor carrier required to register under Subchapter B from Chapter 15, Business & Commerce Code, for an activity relating to the establishment of a joint line rate, route, classification, or mileage guide.

(d) A motor carrier that is required to register under Subchapter B and that transports household goods, or an agent of the carrier, may enter into a collective ratemaking agreement with another motor carrier of household goods or an agent of that carrier concerning the establishment and filing of maximum rates, classifications, rules, or procedures. The agreement must be submitted to the department for approval.

(e) The department shall approve an agreement submitted under Subsection (d) if the agreement provides that each meeting of parties to the agreement is open to the public and that notice of each meeting must be given to customers who are multiple users of the services of a motor carrier that is a party to the agreement. The department may withhold approval of the agreement if it determines, after notice and hearing, that the agreement fails to comply with this subsection.

(f) Unless disapproved by the department, an agreement made under Subsection (d) is valid, and Chapter 15, Business & Commerce Code, does not apply to a motor carrier that is a party to the agreement.

Sec. 643.155. Rules Advisory Committee.

(a) The department shall appoint a rules advisory committee consisting of representatives of motor carriers transporting household goods using small, medium, and large equipment, the public, and the department.

(b) Members of the committee serve at the pleasure of the department and are not entitled to compensation or reimbursement of expenses for serving on the committee. The department may adopt rules to govern the operations of the advisory committee.

(c) The committee shall examine the rules adopted by the department under Sections 643.153(a) and (b) and make recommendations to the department on modernizing and streamlining the rules.

Sec. 643.156. Regulation of Advertising.

(a) The department may not by rule restrict competitive bidding or advertising by a motor carrier except to prohibit false, misleading, or deceptive practices.

(b) A rule to prohibit false, misleading, or deceptive practices may not:

(1) restrict the use of:

(A) any medium for an advertisement;

(B) a motor carrier's advertisement under a trade name; or

(C) a motor carrier's personal appearance or voice in an advertisement, if the motor carrier is an individual; or

(2) relate to the size or duration of an advertisement by a motor carrier.

SUBCHAPTER E TOW TRUCKS

Sec. 643.201. Tow Truck Regulation by Political Subdivisions [Renumbered].

Renumbered to Tex.Occ. Code § 2308.201 by Acts 2007, 80th Leg., ch. 1046 (H.B. 2094), § 2.01, effective September 1, 2007.

Sec. 643.202. Rules Advisory Committee [Repealed].

Repealed by Acts 2007, 80th Leg., ch. 1046 (H.B. 2094), § 5.01(a)(3), effective September 1, 2007.

Sec. 643.203. Regulation by Political Subdivisions of Fees for Nonconsent Tows [Renumbered].

Renumbered to Tex.Occ. Code § 2308.202 by Acts 2007, 80th Leg., ch. 1046 (H.B. 2094), § 2.01, effective September 1, 2007.

Sec. 643.204. Towing Fee Studies [Renumbered].

Renumbered to Tex.Occ. Code § 2308.203 by Acts 2007, 80th Leg., ch. 1046 (H.B. 2094), § 2.01, effective September 1, 2007.

Sec. 643.205. Fees for Nonconsent Tows in Other Areas [Renumbered].

Renumbered to Tex.Occ. Code § 2308.204 by Acts 2007, 80th Leg., ch. 1046 (H.B. 2094), § 2.01, effective September 1, 2007.

Sec. 643.206. Storage of Towed Vehicles [Renumbered].

Renumbered to Tex.Occ. Code § 2308.205 by Acts 2007, 80th Leg., ch. 1046 (H.B. 2094), § 2.01, effective September 1, 2007.

Sec. 643.207. Required Filing [Renumbered].

Renumbered to Tex.Occ. Code § 2308.206 by Acts 2007, 80th Leg., ch. 1046 (H.B. 2094), § 2.01, effective September 1, 2007.

Sec. 643.208. Required Posting [Renumbered].

Renumbered to Tex.Occ. Code § 2308.207 by Acts 2007, 80th Leg., ch. 1046 (H.B. 2094), § 2.01, effective September 1, 2007.

Sec. 643.209. Tow Rotation List in Certain Counties [Renumbered].

Renumbered to Tex.Occ. Code § 2308.209 by Acts 2009, 81st Leg., ch. 87 (S.B. 1969), § 27.001(109), effective September 1, 2009.

SUBCHAPTER F ENFORCEMENT

Sec. 643.251. Administrative Penalty.

(a) The department may impose an administrative penalty against a motor carrier required to register under Subchapter B that violates this chapter or a rule or order adopted under this chapter.

(b) Except as provided by this section, the amount of an administrative penalty may not exceed $5,000. If it is found that the motor carrier knowingly committed the violation, the penalty may not exceed $15,000. If it is found that the motor carrier knowingly committed multiple violations, the aggregate penalty for the multiple violations may not exceed $30,000. Each day a violation continues or occurs is a separate violation for purposes of imposing a penalty.

(c) The amount of the penalty shall be based on:

(1) the seriousness of the violation, including the nature, circumstances, extent, and gravity of any prohibited act, and the hazard or potential hazard created to the health, safety, or economic welfare of the public;

(2) the economic harm to property or the environment caused by the violation;

(3) the history of previous violations;

(4) the amount necessary to deter future violations;

(5) efforts to correct the violation; and

(6) any other matter that justice may require.

(d) to (r) [Repealed by Acts 2007, 80th Leg., ch. 1396 (H.B. 2093), § 26(1), effective September 1, 2007.]

Transportation Code

Sec. 643.252. Administrative Sanctions.

(a) The department may suspend, revoke, or deny a registration issued under this chapter or place on probation a motor carrier whose registration is suspended if a motor carrier:

(1) fails to maintain insurance or evidence of financial responsibility as required by Section 643.101(a), (b), or (c);

(2) fails to keep evidence of insurance in the cab of each vehicle as required by Section 643.103(b);

(3) fails to register a vehicle requiring registration;

(4) violates any other provision of this chapter or Chapter 621, 622, or 623;

(5) knowingly provides false information on any form filed with the department under this chapter or Chapter 621, 622, or 623;

(6) violates a rule or order adopted under this chapter or Chapter 621, 622, or 623; or

(7) is owned, operated, managed, or otherwise controlled by or affiliated with a person, including a family member, corporate officer, entity, or shareholder:

(A) whose registration has previously been revoked or denied; or

(B) that has unpaid administrative penalties assessed under this chapter or Subtitle E.

(b) The Department of Public Safety may request that the department suspend or revoke a registration issued under this chapter or place on probation a motor carrier whose registration is suspended if a motor carrier has:

(1) an unsatisfactory safety rating under 49 C.F.R. Part 385; or

(2) multiple violations of Chapter 644, a rule adopted under that chapter, or Subtitle C.

(c) The department shall revoke or deny a registration issued under this chapter to a for-hire motor carrier of passengers if the motor carrier is required to register with the Federal Motor Carrier Safety Administration and the federal registration is denied, revoked, suspended, or otherwise terminated.

(d), (e) [Repealed by Acts 2007, 80th Leg., ch. 1396 (H.B. 2093), § 26(2), effective September 1, 2007.]

Sec. 643.2525. Administrative Hearing Process.

(a) If the department determines that a violation has occurred for which an enforcement action is being taken under Section 643.251 or 643.252, the department shall give written notice to the motor carrier by first class mail to the carrier's address as shown in the records of the department.

(b) A notice required by Subsection (a) must include:

(1) a brief summary of the alleged violation;

(2) a statement of each administrative sanction being taken;

(3) the effective date of each sanction;

(4) a statement informing the carrier of the carrier's right to request a hearing; and

(5) a statement as to the procedure for requesting a hearing, including the period during which a request must be made.

(c) If not later than the 26th day after the date the notice is mailed the department receives a written request for a hearing, the department shall set a hearing and provide the carrier notice of the hearing and the opportunity to present evidence at the hearing. The hearing shall be conducted by an administrative law judge of the State Office of Administrative Hearings.

(d) If the motor carrier does not timely request a hearing under Subsection (c), the department's decision becomes final on the expiration of the period described by Subsection (c).

(e) If a hearing set under Subsection (c) is held and evidence is presented at the hearing, the administrative law judge shall make findings of fact and conclusions of law and promptly issue to the director a proposal for a decision as to the occurrence of the violation and the administrative penalties or sanctions.

(f) In addition to a penalty or sanction proposed under Subsection (e), the administrative law judge shall include in the proposal for a decision a finding setting out costs, fees, expenses, and reasonable and necessary attorney's fees incurred by the state in bringing the proceeding. The director may adopt the finding and make it a part of a final order entered in the proceeding.

(g) Based on the findings of fact, conclusions of law, and proposal for a decision, the director by order may find that a violation has occurred and impose the sanctions or may find that a violation has not occurred.

(h) The director shall provide written notice to the motor carrier of a finding made under Subsection (g) and shall include in the notice a statement of the right of the carrier to judicial review of the order.

(i) Before the 31st day after the date the director's order under Subsection (g) becomes final as provided by Section 2001.144, Government Code, the motor carrier may appeal the order by filing a petition for judicial review contesting the order. Judicial review is under the substantial evidence rule.

(j) A petition filed under Subsection (i) stays the enforcement of the administrative action until the earlier of the 550th day after the date the petition was filed or the date a final judgment is rendered by the court.

(k) If the motor carrier is required to pay a penalty or cost under Subsection (f), failure to pay the penalty or cost before the 61st day after the date the requirement becomes final is a violation of this chapter and may result in an additional penalty, revocation or suspension of a motor carrier registration, or denial of a motor carrier registration renewal or reregistration.

(*l*) A motor carrier that is required to pay a penalty, cost, fee, or expense under this section or Section 643.251 is not eligible for a registration, reregistration, or registration renewal under this chapter until all required amounts have been paid to the department.

(m) If the suspension of a motor carrier's registration is probated, the department may require the carrier to report regularly to the department on any matter that is the basis of the probation. Any violation of the probation may result in the imposition of an administrative penalty or the revocation of the registration.

(n) All proceedings under this section are subject to Chapter 2001, Government Code.

Sec. 643.2526. Appeal of Denial of Registration, Renewal, or Reregistration.

(a) Notwithstanding any other law, a denial of an application for registration, renewal of registration, or reregistration under this chapter is not required to be preceded by notice and an opportunity for hearing.

(b) An applicant may appeal a denial under this chapter by filing an appeal with the department not later than the 26th day after the date the department issues notice of the denial to the applicant.

(c) If the appeal of the denial is successful and the application is found to be compliant with this chapter, the application shall be considered to have been properly filed on the date the finding is entered.

Sec. 643.253. Offenses and Penalties.

(a) A person commits an offense if the person fails to:

(1) register as required by Subchapter B;

(2) maintain insurance or evidence of financial responsibility as required by Subchapter C; or

(3) keep a cab card in the cab of a vehicle as required by Section 643.059.

(b) A person commits an offense if the person engages in or solicits the transportation of household goods for compensation and is not registered as required by Subchapter B.

(c) Except as provided by Subsection (e), an offense under this section is a Class C misdemeanor.

(d) [Renumbered to Tex.Occ. Code § 2308.505 by Acts 2007, 80th Leg., ch. 1046 (H.B. 2094), § 2.10, effective September 1, 2007.]

(e) An offense under Subsection (b) is a Class C misdemeanor, except that the offense is:

(1) a Class B misdemeanor if the person has previously been convicted one time of an offense under Subsection (b); and

(2) a Class A misdemeanor if the person has previously been convicted two or more times of an offense under Subsection (b).

(f) A peace officer may issue a citation for a violation under this section.

(g) As soon as practicable after the date a person is convicted of an offense under Subsection (b), the convicting court shall notify the Department of Public Safety of the conviction. The notice must be in a form prescribed by the Department of Public Safety and must contain the person's driver's license number.

(h) A conviction under Subsection (b) shall be recorded in the person's driving record maintained by the Department of Public Safety.

Sec. 643.254. Inspection of Documents.

(a) To investigate an alleged violation of this chapter or a rule or order adopted under this chapter, an officer or employee of the department who has been certified for the purpose by the director may enter a motor carrier's premises to inspect, copy, or verify the correctness of a document, including an operation log or insurance certificate.

(b) The officer or employee may conduct the inspection:

(1) at a reasonable time;

(2) after stating the purpose of the inspection; and

(3) by presenting to the motor carrier:

(A) appropriate credentials; and

(B) a written statement from the department to the motor carrier indicating the officer's or employee's authority to inspect.

(c) A motor carrier domiciled outside this state must:

(1) designate a location in the state for inspection of records concerning the alleged violation; or

(2) request that an officer or employee of the department conduct the inspection at an office of the motor carrier located outside this state.

(d) A motor carrier requesting an out-of-state inspection will be responsible for payment of actual expenses incurred by the department in conducting the inspection.

Sec. 643.255. Injunctive Relief.

(a) The attorney general, at the request of the department, may petition a district court for appropriate injunctive relief to prevent or abate a violation of this chapter or a rule or order adopted under this chapter.

(b) Venue in a suit for injunctive relief under this section is in Travis County.

(c) On application for injunctive relief and a finding that a person is violating or has violated this chapter or a rule or order adopted under this chapter, the court shall grant the appropriate relief without bond.

(d) The attorney general and the department may recover reasonable expenses incurred in obtaining injunctive relief under this section, including court costs, reasonable attorney's fees, investigative costs, witness fees, and deposition expenses.

Sec. 643.256. Cease and Desist Order.

The department may issue a cease and desist order if the department determines that the action is necessary to:

(1) prevent a violation of this chapter; and

(2) protect the public health and safety.

Sec. 643.257. Refund by Motor Carriers Transporting Household Goods.

The department may order a motor carrier that violates this chapter or a rule or order adopted under this chapter to pay a refund to a consumer who paid the motor carrier to transport household goods.

CHAPTER 644
COMMERCIAL MOTOR VEHICLE SAFETY STANDARDS

SUBCHAPTER A
GENERAL PROVISIONS

Sec. 644.001. Definitions.

In this chapter:

(1) "Commercial motor vehicle" means:

(A) a commercial motor vehicle as defined by 49 C.F.R. Section 390.5, if operated interstate; or

(B) a commercial motor vehicle as defined by Section 548.001, if operated intrastate.

(2) "Department" means the Department of Public Safety.

(3) "Director" means the public safety director.

(4) "Federal hazardous material regulation" means a federal regulation in 49 C.F.R. Parts 101—199.

(5) "Federal motor carrier safety regulation" means a federal regulation in Subtitle A, Title 49, or Subchapter B, Chapter III, Subtitle B, Title 49, Code of Federal Regulations.

(6) "Federal safety regulation" means a federal hazardous material regulation or a federal motor carrier safety regulation.

(7) "Port of entry" has the meaning assigned by Section 621.001.

Sec. 644.002. Conflicts of Law.

(a) A federal motor carrier safety regulation prevails over a conflicting provision of this title applicable to a commercial vehicle operated in interstate commerce. A rule adopted by the director under this chapter prevails over a conflicting provision of a federal motor carrier safety regulation applicable to a commercial vehicle operated in intrastate commerce.

(b) A safety rule adopted under this chapter prevails over a conflicting rule adopted by a local government, authority, or state agency or officer, other than a conflicting rule adopted by the Railroad Commission of Texas under Chapter 113, Natural Resources Code.

Sec. 644.003. Rules.

The department may adopt rules to administer this chapter.

Sec. 644.004. Applicability to Foreign Commercial Motor Vehicles.

Except as otherwise provided by law, this chapter also applies to a foreign commercial motor vehicle, as defined by Section 648.001.

Sec. 644.005. Department Database.

The department shall develop and maintain a database on roadside vehicle inspection reports for defects on any intermodal equipment. The database shall include all citations involving intermodal equipment issued by officers certified under Section 644.101. The database shall be used to identify violations discovered on intermodal equipment during a roadside inspection.

SUBCHAPTER B ADOPTION OF RULES

Sec. 644.051. Authority to Adopt Rules.

(a) The director shall, after notice and a public hearing, adopt rules regulating:

(1) the safe transportation of hazardous materials; and

(2) the safe operation of commercial motor vehicles.

(b) A rule adopted under this chapter must be consistent with federal regulations, including federal safety regulations.

(c) The director may adopt all or part of the federal safety regulations by reference.

(d) Rules adopted under this chapter must ensure that:

(1) a commercial motor vehicle is safely maintained, equipped, loaded, and operated;

(2) the responsibilities imposed on a commercial motor vehicle's operator do not impair the operator's ability to operate the vehicle safely; and

(3) the physical condition of a commercial motor vehicle's operator enables the operator to operate the vehicle safely.

(e) A motor carrier safety rule adopted by a local government, authority, or state agency or officer must be consistent with corresponding federal regulations.

Sec. 644.052. Applicability of Rules.

(a) Notwithstanding an exemption provided in the federal safety regulations, other than an exemption relating to intracity or commercial zone operations provided in 49 C.F.R. Part 395, a rule adopted by the director under this chapter applies uniformly throughout this state.

(b) A rule adopted under this chapter applies to a vehicle that requires a hazardous material placard.

(c) A rule adopted under this chapter may not apply to a vehicle that is operated intrastate and that is:

(1) a machine generally consisting of a mast, engine, draw works, and chassis permanently constructed or assembled to be used and used in oil or water well servicing or drilling;

(2) a mobile crane that is an unladen, self-propelled vehicle constructed as a machine to raise, shift, or lower weight; or

(3) a vehicle transporting seed cotton.

Sec. 644.053. Limitations of Rules.

(a) A rule adopted under this chapter may not:

(1) prevent an intrastate operator from operating a vehicle up to 12 hours following eight consecutive hours off;

(2) require a person to meet the medical standards provided in the federal motor carrier safety regulations if the person:

(A) was regularly employed in this state as a commercial motor vehicle operator in intrastate commerce before August 28, 1989; and

(B) is not transporting property that requires a hazardous material placard;

(3) require a person who returns to the work-reporting location, is released from work within 12 consecutive hours, has at least eight consecutive hours off between each 12-hour period the person is on duty, and operates within a 150-air-mile radius of the normal work-reporting location to maintain a driver's record of duty status as described by 49 C.F.R. Section 395.8, provided that the person maintains time records in compliance with 49 C.F.R. Section 395.1(e)(5) and documents that verify the truth and accuracy of the time records such as:

(A) business records maintained by the owner that provide the date, time, and location of the delivery of a product or service; or

(B) documents required to be maintained by law, including delivery tickets or sales invoices, that provide the date of delivery and the quantity of merchandise delivered; or

(4) impose during a planting or harvesting season maximum driving and on-duty times on an operator of a vehicle transporting an agricultural commodity in intrastate commerce for agricultural purposes from the source of the commodity to the first place of processing or storage or the distribution point for the commodity, if the place is located within 150 air miles of the source.

(b) For purposes of Subsection (a)(3)(A), an owner's time records must at a minimum include:

(1) the time an operator reports for duty each day;

(2) the number of hours an operator is on duty each day;

(3) the time an operator is released from duty each day; and

(4) an operator's signed statement in compliance with 49 C.F.R. Section 395.8(j)(2).

(c) In this section, "agricultural commodity" means an agricultural, horticultural, viticultural, silvicultural, or vegetable product, bees or honey, planting seed, cottonseed, rice, livestock or a livestock product, or poultry or a poultry product that is produced in this state, either in its natural form or as processed by the producer, including woodchips.

(d) A rule adopted by the director under this chapter that relates to hours of service, an operator's record of duty status, or an operator's daily log, for operations outside a 150-mile radius of the normal work-reporting location, also applies to and must be complied with by a motor carrier of household goods not using a commercial motor vehicle. In this subsection:

(1) "commercial motor vehicle" has the meaning assigned by Section 548.001; and

(2) "motor carrier" has the meaning assigned by Section 643.001.

Sec. 644.054. Regulation of Contract Carriers of Certain Passengers.

(a) This section applies only to a contract carrier that transports an operating employee of a railroad on a road or highway of this state in a vehicle designed to carry 15 or fewer passengers.

(b) The department shall adopt rules regulating the operation of a contract carrier to which this section applies. The rules must:

(1) prohibit a person from operating a vehicle for more than 12 hours in a day;

(2) require a person who operates a vehicle for the number of consecutive hours or days the department determines is excessive to rest for a period determined by the department;

(3) require a contract carrier to keep a record of all hours a vehicle subject to regulation under this section is operated;

(4) require a contract carrier to perform alcohol and drug testing of vehicle operators on employment, on suspicion of alcohol or drug abuse, and periodically as determined by the department;

(5) require a contract carrier, at a minimum, to maintain liability insurance in the amount of $1.5 million for each vehicle; and

(6) be determined by the department to be necessary to protect the safety of a passenger being transported or the general public.

(c) The department shall inform contract carriers and railroad companies that employ contract carriers of the requirements of state statutes applicable to contract carriers.

SUBCHAPTER C ADMINISTRATIVE ENFORCEMENT

Sec. 644.101. Certification of Certain Peace Officers.

(a) The department shall establish procedures, including training, for the certification of municipal police officers, sheriffs, and deputy sheriffs to enforce this chapter.

(b) A police officer of any of the following municipalities is eligible to apply for certification under this section:

(1) a municipality with a population of 50,000 or more;

(2) a municipality with a population of 25,000 or more any part of which is located in a county with a population of 500,000 or more;

(3) a municipality with a population of less than 25,000:

(A) any part of which is located in a county with a population of 3.3 million; and

(B) that contains or is adjacent to an international port;

(4) a municipality with a population of at least 34,000 that is located in a county that borders two or more states;

(5) a municipality any part of which is located in a county bordering the United Mexican States;

(6) a municipality with a population of less than 5,000 that is located:

(A) adjacent to a bay connected to the Gulf of Mexico; and

(B) in a county adjacent to a county with a population greater than 3.3 million;

(7) a municipality that is located:

(A) within 25 miles of an international port; and

(B) in a county that does not contain a highway that is part of the national system of interstate and defense highways and is adjacent to a county with a population greater than 3.3 million;

(8) a municipality with a population of less than 8,500 that:

(A) is the county seat; and

(B) contains a highway that is part of the national system of interstate and defense highways;

(9) a municipality located in a county with a population between 60,000 and 66,000 adjacent to a bay connected to the Gulf of Mexico;

(10) a municipality with a population of more than 40,000 and less than 50,000 that is located in a county with a population of more than 285,000 and less than 300,000 that borders the Gulf of Mexico;

(11) a municipality with a population between 32,000 and 50,000 that is located entirely in a county that:

(A) has a population of less than 250,000;

(B) is adjacent to two counties that each have a population of more than 1.2 million; and

(C) contains two highways that are part of the national system of interstate and defense highways;

(12) a municipality with a population of more than 3,000 and less than 10,000 that:

(A) contains a highway that is part of the national system of interstate and defense highways; and

(B) is located in a county with a population between 150,000 and 155,000;

(13) a municipality with a population of less than 75,000 that is located in three counties, at least one of which has a population greater than 3.3 million;

(14) a municipality with a population between 14,000 and 17,000 that:

(A) contains three or more numbered United States highways; and

(B) is located in a county that is adjacent to a county with a population of more than 200,000; or

(15) a municipality with a population of less than 50,000 that is located in:

(A) a county that generated $20 million or more in tax revenue collected under Chapters 201 and 202, Tax Code, from oil and gas production during the preceding state fiscal year; or

(B) a county that is adjacent to two or more counties described by Paragraph (A).

(c) A sheriff or a deputy sheriff of any of the following counties is eligible to apply for certification under this section:

(1) a county bordering the United Mexican States;

(2) a county with a population of less than 1,000, part of which is located within 75 miles of an international border;

(3) a county with a population of 700,000 or more;

(4) a county with a population of 400,000 or more that borders the county in which the State Capitol is located;

(5) a county:

(A) any part of which is within 30 miles of New Mexico; and

(B) that is adjacent to two or more counties that generated $100 million or more in tax revenue collected under Chapters 201 and 202, Tax Code, from oil and gas production during the preceding state fiscal year; or

(6) a county with a population of more than 40,000 and less than 300,000 that is adjacent to a county described by Subdivision (4).

(d) A sheriff, a deputy sheriff, or any peace officer that does not attend continuing education courses on the enforcement of traffic and highway laws and on the use of radar equipment as prescribed by Subchapter F, Chapter 1701, Occupations Code, shall not enforce traffic and highway laws.

(e) The department by rule shall establish reasonable fees sufficient to recover from a municipality or a county the cost of certifying its peace officers under this section.

Sec. 644.102. Municipal and County Enforcement Requirements.

(a) The department by rule shall establish uniform standards for municipal or county enforcement of this chapter.

(b) A municipality or county that engages in enforcement under this chapter:

(1) shall pay all costs relating to the municipality's or county's enforcement;

(2) may not be considered, in the context of a federal grant related to this chapter:

(A) a party to a federal grant agreement, except as provided by Subsection (b-1); or

(B) a grantee under a federal grant to the department; and

(3) must comply with the standards established under Subsection (a).

(b-1) Subsection (b) does not prohibit a municipality or county from receiving High Priority Activity Funds provided under the federal Motor Carrier Safety Assistance Program.

(c) Municipal or county enforcement under Section 644.103(b) is not considered departmental enforcement for purposes of maintaining levels of effort required by a federal grant.

(d) In each fiscal year, a municipality may retain fines from the enforcement of this chapter in an amount not to exceed 110 percent of the municipality's actual expenses for enforcement of this chapter in the preceding fiscal year, as determined by the comptroller after reviewing the most recent municipal audit conducted under Section 103.001, Local Government Code. If there are no actual expenses for enforcement of this chapter in the most recent municipal audit, a municipality may retain fines in an amount not to exceed 110 percent of the amount the comptroller estimates would be the municipality's actual expenses for enforcement of this chapter during the year.

(e) In each fiscal year, a county may retain fines from the enforcement of this chapter in an amount not to exceed 110 percent of the county's actual expenses for enforcement of this chapter in the preceding fiscal year, as determined by the comptroller after reviewing the most recent county audit conducted under Chapter 115, Local Government Code. If there are no actual expenses for enforcement of this chapter in the most recent county audit, a county may retain fines in an amount not to exceed 110 percent of the amount the comptroller estimates would be the county's actual expenses for enforcement of this chapter during the year.

(f) A municipality or county shall send to the comptroller the proceeds of all fines that exceed the limit imposed by Subsection (d) or (e). The

Transportation Code

comptroller shall then deposit the remaining funds to the credit of the Texas Department of Transportation.

(f-1) A municipality or county that retains a fine from the enforcement of this chapter shall annually file with the comptroller a report that details the amount of fines retained from the enforcement of this chapter and the actual expenses claimed by the municipality or county for the enforcement of this chapter during the previous fiscal year. A municipality or county that fails to file a report as required by this subsection shall send to the comptroller for deposit to the credit of the Texas Department of Transportation an amount equal to the amount retained by the municipality or county in the fiscal year the report would cover.

(f-2) The comptroller shall adopt rules as necessary to implement and enforce Subsection (f-1).

(g) The department shall revoke or rescind the certification of any peace officer who fails to comply with any standard established under Subsection (a).

(h) The department may revoke or rescind the authority of a municipality or county to engage in enforcement under this chapter if the municipality or county fails to comply with this section or any standard established under Subsection (a).

Sec. 644.103. Detention of Vehicles.

(a) An officer of the department may stop, enter, or detain on a highway or at a port of entry a motor vehicle that is subject to this chapter.

(b) A municipal police officer who is certified under Section 644.101 may stop, enter, or detain on a highway or at a port of entry within the territory of the municipality a motor vehicle that is subject to this chapter. A sheriff or deputy sheriff who is certified under Section 644.101 may stop, enter, or detain on a highway or at a port of entry within the territory of the county a motor vehicle that is subject to this chapter.

(c) A person who detains a vehicle under this section may prohibit the further operation of the vehicle on a highway if the vehicle or operator of the vehicle is in violation of a federal safety regulation or a rule adopted under this chapter.

(d) A noncommissioned employee of the department who is certified for the purpose by the director and who is supervised by an officer of the department may, at a commercial motor vehicle inspection site, stop, enter, or detain a motor vehicle that is subject to this chapter. If the employee's inspection shows that an enforcement action, such as the issuance of a citation, is warranted for a violation of this title or a rule adopted under this title, including a federal safety regulation adopted under this chapter, the noncommissioned employee may take enforcement action only if the employee is under the supervision of an officer of the department.

(e) The department's training and other requirements for certification of a noncommissioned employee of the department under this section must be the same as the training and requirements, other than the training and requirements for becoming and remaining a peace officer, for officers who enforce this chapter.

Sec. 644.104. Inspection of Premises.

(a) An officer or employee of the department who has been certified for the purpose by the director may enter a motor carrier's premises to:

(1) inspect real property, including a building, or equipment; or

(2) copy or verify the correctness of documents, including records or reports, required to be kept or made by rules adopted under this chapter.

(b) The officer or employee may conduct the inspection:

(1) at a reasonable time;

(2) after stating the purpose of the inspection; and

(3) by presenting to the motor carrier:

(A) appropriate credentials; and

(B) a written statement from the department to the motor carrier indicating the officer's or employee's authority to inspect.

(c) The department may use an officer to conduct an inspection under this section if the inspection involves a situation that the department determines to reasonably require the use or presence of an officer to accomplish the inspection.

(d) The department's training and other requirements for certification of a noncommissioned employee of the department under this section must be the same as the training and requirements, other than the training and requirements for becoming and remaining a peace officer, for officers who enforce this chapter.

(e) A municipal police officer who is certified under Section 644.101 may enter a motor carrier's premises to inspect equipment on a per unit basis or in a manner agreeable between the motor carrier and the enforcement entity:

(1) at a reasonable time;

(2) after stating the purpose of the inspection; and

(3) by presenting to the motor carrier appropriate credentials.

SUBCHAPTER D OFFENSES, PENALTIES, AND JUDICIAL ENFORCEMENT

Sec. 644.151. Criminal Offense.

(a) A person commits an offense if the person:

(1) violates a rule adopted under this chapter;

(2) does not permit an inspection authorized under Section 644.104; or

(3) knowingly operates a commercial motor vehicle in violation of an out-of-service order issued under 49 C.F.R. Section 385.13(d)(1) or owns, leases, or assigns a person to drive a commercial motor vehicle that is knowingly operated in violation of an out-of-service order issued under 49 C.F.R. Section 385.13(d)(1).

(b) An offense under Subsection (a)(1) or (2) is a Class C misdemeanor.

(b-1) An offense under Subsection (a)(3) is a Class A misdemeanor, except that the offense is:

(1) a state jail felony if it is shown on the trial of the offense that at the time of the offense the commercial motor vehicle was involved in a motor vehicle accident that resulted in bodily injury; or

(2) a felony of the second degree if it is shown on the trial of the offense that at the time of the offense the commercial motor vehicle was involved in a motor vehicle accident that resulted in the death of a person.

(c) Each day a violation continues under Subsection (a)(1) or each day a person refuses to allow an inspection described under Subsection (a)(2) is a separate offense.

Sec. 644.152. Civil Penalty.

(a) A person who does not permit an inspection authorized by Section 644.104 is liable to the state for a civil penalty in an amount not to exceed $1,000.

(b) The attorney general may sue to collect the penalty in:

(1) the county in which the violation is alleged to have occurred; or

(2) Travis County.

(c) The penalty provided by this section is in addition to the penalty provided by Section 644.151.

(d) Each day a person refuses to permit an inspection described by Subsection (a) is a separate violation for purposes of imposing a penalty.

Sec. 644.153. Administrative Penalty.

(a) The department may impose an administrative penalty against a person who violates:

(1) a rule adopted under this chapter; or

(2) a provision of Subchapter C that the department by rule subjects to administrative penalties.

(b) To be designated as subject to an administrative penalty under Subsection (a)(2), a provision must relate to the safe operation of a commercial motor vehicle.

(c) The department shall:

(1) designate one or more employees to investigate violations and conduct audits of persons subject to this chapter; and

(2) impose an administrative penalty if the department discovers a violation that is covered by Subsection (a) or (b).

(d) A penalty under this section may not exceed the maximum penalty provided for a violation of a similar federal safety regulation.

(e) If the department determines to impose a penalty, the department shall issue a notice of claim. The department shall send the notice of claim by certified mail, registered mail, personal delivery, or another manner of delivery that records the receipt of the notice by the person responsible. The notice of claim must include a brief summary of the alleged violation and a statement of the amount of the recommended penalty and inform the person that the person is entitled to a hearing on the occurrence of the violation, the amount of the penalty, or both the occurrence of the violation and the amount of the penalty. A person who is subject to an administrative penalty imposed by the department under this section is required to pay the penalty or respond to the department within 20 days of receipt of the department's notice of claim.

(f) Before the 21st day after the date the person receives the notice of claim, the person may:

(1) accept the determination and pay the recommended penalty; or

(2) make a written request for an informal hearing or an administrative hearing on the occurrence of the violation, the amount of the penalty, or both the occurrence of the violation and the amount of the penalty.

(g) At the conclusion of an informal hearing requested under Subsection (f), the department may modify the recommendation for a penalty.

(h) If the person requests an administrative hearing, the department shall set a hearing and give notice of the hearing to the person. The hearing shall be held by an administrative law judge of the State Office of Administrative Hearings. The administrative law judge shall make findings of fact and conclusions of law and promptly issue to the director a proposal for a decision as to the occurrence of the violation and the amount of a proposed penalty.

(i) If a penalty is proposed under Subsection (h), the administrative law judge shall include in the proposal for a decision a finding setting out costs, fees, expenses, and reasonable and necessary attorney's fees incurred by the state in bringing the proceeding. The director may adopt the finding and make it a part of a final order entered in the proceeding.

(j) Based on the findings of fact, conclusions of law, and proposal for a decision, the director by order may find that a violation has occurred and impose a penalty or may find that no violation occurred. The director may, pursuant to Section 2001.058(e), Government Code, increase or decrease the amount of the penalty recommended by the administrative law judge within the limits prescribed by this chapter.

(k) Notice of the director's order shall be given to the affected person in the manner required by Chapter 2001, Government Code, and must include a statement that the person is entitled to seek a judicial review of the order.

(*l*) Before the 31st day after the date the director's order becomes final as provided by Section 2001.144, Government Code, the person must:

(1) pay the amount of the penalty;

(2) pay the amount of the penalty and file a petition for judicial review contesting:

(A) the occurrence of the violation;

(B) the amount of the penalty; or

(C) both the occurrence of the violation and the amount of the penalty; or

(3) without paying the amount of the penalty, file a petition for judicial review contesting:

(A) the occurrence of the violation;

(B) the amount of the penalty; or

(C) both the occurrence of the violation and the amount of the penalty.

(m) Within the 30-day period under Subsection (*l*), a person who acts under Subsection (*l*) may:

(1) stay enforcement of the penalty by:

(A) paying the amount of the penalty to the court for placement in an escrow account; or

(B) filing with the court a supersedeas bond approved by the court for the amount of the penalty that is effective until all judicial review of the director's order is final; or

(2) request the court to stay enforcement of the penalty by:

(A) filing with the court an affidavit of the person stating that the person is financially unable to pay the amount of the penalty and is financially unable to give the supersedeas bond; and

(B) sending a copy of the affidavit to the director by certified mail.

(n) Before the sixth day after the date the director receives a copy of an affidavit filed under Subsection (m)(2), the department may file with the court a contest to the affidavit. The court shall hold a hearing on the facts alleged in the affidavit as soon as practicable and shall stay the enforcement of the penalty if the court finds that the alleged facts are true. The person who files an affidavit under Subsection (m)(2) has the burden of proving that the person is financially unable to:

(1) pay the amount of the penalty; and

(2) file the supersedeas bond.

(o) If the person does not pay the amount of the penalty and the enforcement of the penalty is not stayed, the director may:

(1) refer the matter to the attorney general for collection of the amount of the penalty;

(2) initiate an impoundment proceeding under Subsection (q); or

(3) refer the matter to the attorney general and initiate the impoundment proceeding.

(p) A person who fails to pay, or becomes delinquent in the payment of an administrative penalty imposed by the department under this subchapter may not operate or direct the operation of a commercial motor vehicle on the highways of this state until the administrative penalty has been remitted to the department.

(q) The department shall impound any commercial motor vehicle owned or operated by a person in violation of Subsection (p) after the department has first served the person with a notice of claim. Service of the notice may be by certified mail, registered mail, personal delivery, or any other manner of delivery showing receipt of the notice.

(r) A commercial motor vehicle impounded by the department under Subsection (q) shall remain impounded until the administrative penalties imposed against the person are remitted to the department, except that an impounded commercial motor vehicle left at a vehicle storage facility controlled by the department or any other person shall be considered an abandoned motor vehicle on the 11th day after the date of impoundment if the delinquent administrative penalty is not remitted to the department before that day. Chapter 683 applies to the commercial motor vehicle, except that the department is entitled to receive from the proceeds of the sale the amount of the delinquent administrative penalty and costs.

(s) All costs associated with the towing and storage of the commercial motor vehicle and load shall be the responsibility of the person and not the department or the State of Texas.

(t) A proceeding under this section is subject to Chapter 2001, Government Code.

(u) Each penalty collected under this section shall be deposited to the credit of the Texas mobility fund.

Sec. 644.154. Suit for Injunction.

(a) The attorney general shall sue to enjoin a violation or a threatened violation of a rule adopted under this chapter on request of the director.

(b) The suit must be brought in the county in which the violation or threat is alleged to have occurred.

(c) The court may grant the director, without bond or other undertaking:

(1) a prohibitory or mandatory injunction, including a temporary restraining order; or

(2) after notice and hearing, a temporary or permanent injunction.

Sec. 644.155. Compliance Review and Safety Audit Program.

The department shall implement and enforce a compliance review and safety audit program similar to the federal program established under 49 C.F.R. Part 385 for any person who owns or operates a commercial motor vehicle that is domiciled in this state.

SUBCHAPTER E ROUTING OF HAZARDOUS MATERIALS

Sec. 644.201. Adoption of Rules.

(a) The Texas Transportation Commission shall adopt rules under this subchapter consistent with 49 C.F.R. Part 397 for the routing of nonradioactive hazardous materials.

(b) Rules concerning signage, public participation, and procedural requirements may impose more stringent requirements than provided by 49 C.F.R. Part 397.

(c) The rules must provide for consultation with a political subdivision when a route is being proposed within the jurisdiction of the political subdivision.

Sec. 644.202. Designation of Route.

(a) A political subdivision of this state or a state agency may designate a route for the transportation of nonradioactive hazardous materials over a public road or highway in this state only if the Texas Department of Transportation approves the route.

(b) A municipality with a population of more than 850,000 shall develop a route for commercial motor vehicles carrying hazardous materials on a road or highway in the municipality and submit the route to the Texas Department of Transportation for approval. If the Texas Department of Transportation determines that the route complies with all applicable federal and state regulations regarding the transportation of hazardous materials, the Texas Department of Transportation shall approve the route and notify the municipality of the approved route.

(c) The Texas Transportation Commission may designate a route for the transportation of nonradioactive hazardous materials over any public road or highway in this state. The designation may include a road or highway that is not a part of the state highway system only on the approval of the governing body of the political subdivision that maintains the road or highway.

Sec. 644.203. Signs.

(a) The Texas Department of Transportation shall provide signs for a designated route under Section 644.202(c) over a road or highway that is not part of the state highway system. Notwithstanding Section 222.001, the Texas Department of Transportation may use money in the state highway fund to pay for the signs.

(b) The political subdivision that maintains the road or highway shall bear the costs for installation and maintenance of the signs.

SUBCHAPTER F REPORT ON ALCOHOL AND DRUG TESTING

Sec. 644.251. Definitions.

In this subchapter:

(1) "Employee" has the meaning assigned by 49 C.F.R. Section 40.3.

(2) "Valid positive result" means:

(A) an alcohol concentration of 0.04 or greater on an alcohol confirmation test; or

(B) a result at or above the cutoff concentration levels listed in 49 C.F.R. Section 40.87 on a confirmation drug test.

Sec. 644.252. Report of Refusal and Certain Results.

(a) An employer required to conduct alcohol and drug testing of an employee who holds a commercial driver's license under Chapter 522 under federal safety regulations as part of the employer's drug testing program or consortium, as defined by 49 C.F.R. Part 382, shall report to the department:

(1) a valid positive result on an alcohol or drug test performed and whether the specimen producing the result was a dilute specimen, as defined by 49 C.F.R. Section 40.3;

(2) a refusal to provide a specimen for an alcohol or drug test; or

(3) an adulterated specimen or substituted specimen, as those terms are defined by 49 C.F.R. Section 40.3, on an alcohol or drug test performed.

(b) The department shall maintain the information provided under this section.

(c) Information maintained under this section is confidential and only subject to release as provided by Section 521.053.

CHAPTER 645
UNIFIED CARRIER REGISTRATION

Sec. 645.001. Federal Unified Carrier Registration; Definition.

(a) In this chapter, "unified carrier registration plan and agreement" means the federal unified carrier registration plan and agreement provided by 49 U.S.C. Section 14504a.

(b) The Texas Department of Motor Vehicles may, to the fullest extent practicable, participate in the unified carrier registration plan and agreement.

Sec. 645.002. Fees.

(a) [Repealed.]

(b) The department may adopt rules regarding the method of payment of a fee required under the unified carrier registration plan and agreement. The rules may:

(1) authorize the use of an escrow account described by Subsection (c), an electronic funds transfer, or a valid credit card issued by a financial institution chartered by a state or the United States or by a nationally recognized credit organization approved by the department; and

(2) require the payment of a discount or service charge for a credit card payment in addition to the fee.

(c) The department may establish one or more escrow accounts in the Texas Department of Motor Vehicles fund for the prepayment of a fee under this chapter. A prepaid fee or any fee established by the department for the administration of this section shall be:

(1) administered under an agreement approved by the department; and

(2) deposited to the credit of the Texas Department of Motor Vehicles fund to be appropriated only to the department for the purposes of administering this chapter.

Sec. 645.003. Enforcement Rules.

(a) The department may adopt rules providing for administrative penalties for a failure to register or submit information and documents under the unified carrier registration plan and agreement or for a violation of the unified carrier registration plan and agreement.

(b) The notice, hearing, and other procedural requirements of Section 643.2525 apply to the imposition of an administrative penalty under this section as if the action were being taken under that section.

(c) The amount of an administrative penalty imposed under this section is calculated in the same manner as the amount of an administrative penalty imposed under Section 643.251.

Sec. 645.004. Criminal Offense.

(a) A person commits an offense if the person fails to:

(1) register as required by the unified carrier registration plan and agreement; or

(2) submit information and documents as required by the unified carrier registration plan and agreement.

(b) An offense under this section is a Class C misdemeanor.

(c) Each day a violation occurs is a separate offense under this section.

CHAPTER 646
MOTOR TRANSPORTATION BROKERS

Sec. 646.001. Definitions.

In this chapter:

(1) "Department" means the Texas Department of Motor Vehicles.

(2) "Motor transportation broker" means a person who:

(A) sells, offers for sale, provides, or negotiates for the transportation of cargo by a motor carrier operated by another person; or

(B) aids or abets a person in performing an act described by Paragraph (A).

Sec. 646.002. Exception.

This chapter does not apply to a motor transportation broker who:

(1) is registered as a motor carrier under Chapter 643; or

(2) holds a permit issued under Subtitle IV, Title 49, United States Code.

Sec. 646.003. Bond Required.

(a) A person may not act as a motor transportation broker unless the person provides a bond to the department.

(b) The bond must be in an amount of at least $10,000 and must be:

(1) executed by a bonding company authorized to do business in this state;

(2) payable to this state or a person to whom the motor transportation broker provides services; and

(3) conditioned on the performance of the contract for transportation services between the broker and the person for whom services are provided.

(c) The department may charge the broker a bond review fee in an amount not to exceed the cost of reviewing the bond. The department shall deposit a fee collected under this subsection to the credit of the Texas Department of Motor Vehicles fund.

(d) The department may adopt rules regarding the method of payment of a fee under this chapter. The rules may:

(1) authorize the use of electronic funds transfer or a credit card issued by a financial institution chartered by a state or the United States or by a nationally recognized credit organization approved by the department; and

(2) require the payment of a discount or service charge for a credit card payment in addition to the fee.

Sec. 646.004. Criminal Offense.

(a) A person commits an offense if the person fails to provide the bond required by Section 646.003.

(b) An offense under this section is a Class C misdemeanor.

CHAPTER 647
MOTOR TRANSPORTATION OF MIGRANT AGRICULTURAL WORKERS

Sec. 647.001. Definitions.

In this chapter:

(1) "Bus" means a motor vehicle that is designed, constructed, and used to transport passengers. The term does not include a passenger automobile or a station wagon other than a taxicab.

(2) "Highway" has the meaning assigned by Section 541.302.

(3) "Migrant agricultural worker" means a person who:

(A) performs or seeks to perform farm labor of a seasonal nature, including labor necessary to process an agricultural food product; and

(B) occupies living quarters other than the individual's permanent home during the period of employment.

(4) "Motor vehicle" means any vehicle, machine, tractor, trailer, or semitrailer propelled or drawn by mechanical power and used on a highway to transport passengers or property or both. The term does not include:

(A) a vehicle, locomotive, or car that operates exclusively on one or more rails; or

(B) a trolley bus that operates on electricity generated from a fixed overhead wire and that provides local passenger transportation in street-railway service.

(5) "Operator" means a person who operates a motor vehicle.

(6) "Semitrailer" has the meaning assigned by Section 541.201.

(7) "Truck" has the meaning assigned by Section 541.201.

(8) "Truck tractor" has the meaning assigned by Section 541.201.

Sec. 647.002. Application of Chapter.

(a) This chapter applies to any carrier, including a carrier under contract, who at any time uses a motor vehicle to transport to or from a place of employment in this state at least five migrant agricultural workers for a total distance of more than 50 miles.

(b) This chapter does not apply if:

(1) the carrier is a common carrier;

(2) the motor vehicle used is a station wagon or passenger automobile; or

(3) the carrier is a migrant agricultural worker transporting the worker or a member of the worker's immediate family.

Sec. 647.003. Type of Vehicle Allowed.

(a) A carrier may transport migrant agricultural workers only in a:

Transportation Code

(1) bus;
(2) truck to which a trailer is not attached; or
(3) semitrailer attached to a truck tractor.

(b) A carrier may not:
(1) attach a trailer to a semitrailer described by Subsection (a)(3); or
(2) use a closed van that does not have windows or a method to ensure ventilation.

Sec. 647.004. Compliance with Requirements of Chapter.

(a) A carrier shall comply with the requirements and specifications of this chapter.

(b) An officer, agent, representative, or employee of a carrier who operates a motor vehicle used to transport migrant agricultural workers or who hires, supervises, trains, assigns, or dispatches operators of those motor vehicles shall comply with the requirements of Sections 647.006, 647.007, and 647.008.

(c) An officer, agent, representative, operator, or employee of a carrier who is directly involved in the management, maintenance, or operation of a motor vehicle used to transport migrant agricultural workers shall comply with the requirements of Sections 647.003, 647.005, 647.009, 647.010, 647.011, 647.012, 647.014, 647.016, and 647.017. The carrier shall instruct its officers, agents, representatives, and operators with the requirements of those sections and shall take necessary measures to ensure compliance with those requirements.

(d) An officer, agent, representative, operator, or employee of a carrier who is directly involved with the installation or maintenance of equipment and accessories of a motor vehicle used to transport migrant agricultural workers shall comply with the requirements and specifications of Sections 647.012, 647.013, 647.014, 647.015, and 647.016. A carrier may not operate a motor vehicle transporting migrant agricultural workers or cause or permit the vehicle to be operated unless the vehicle is equipped as required by those sections.

(e) A carrier shall systematically inspect and maintain each motor vehicle used to transport migrant agricultural workers and their accessories subject to its control to ensure that the vehicle and its accessories are in safe and proper operating condition.

Sec. 647.005. Operation in Accordance with Law.

If this chapter imposes a greater affirmative obligation or restraint on the operation of a motor vehicle transporting migrant agricultural workers than the laws, ordinances, and regulations of the jurisdiction in which the vehicle is operated, the operator shall comply with this chapter.

Sec. 647.006. Operator Age and Experience Requirements.

A person may not operate a motor vehicle transporting migrant agricultural workers and a carrier may not permit or require a person to operate the motor vehicle unless the person:
(1) is at least 18 years of age;
(2) has at least one year of experience in operating any type of motor vehicle, including a private automobile, during the different seasons;
(3) is familiar with the law relating to operating a motor vehicle; and
(4) is authorized by law to operate that type of motor vehicle.

Sec. 647.007. Operator Physical Requirements.

(a) A person may not operate a motor vehicle transporting migrant agricultural workers and a carrier may not permit or require a person to operate the motor vehicle if the person:
(1) is missing a foot, leg, hand, or arm;
(2) has a mental, nervous, organic, or functional disorder that is likely to interfere with the person's ability to safely operate the motor vehicle;
(3) is missing fingers, has impaired use of a foot, leg, finger, hand, or arm, or has another structural defect or limitation likely to interfere with the person's ability to safely operate the motor vehicle;
(4) has a visual acuity of less than 20/40 (Snellen) in each eye either without glasses or with corrective lenses;
(5) has a form field of vision in the horizontal median of less than a total of 140 degrees;
(6) cannot distinguish the colors red, green, and yellow;
(7) has hearing ability of less than 10/20 in the better ear for conversational tones without the use of a hearing aid; or
(8) is addicted to alcohol, narcotics, or habit-forming drugs.

(b) An operator who requires corrective lenses for vision shall use properly prescribed corrective lenses when operating the motor vehicle.

Sec. 647.008. Physical Examination Requirement.

(a) A person may not operate a motor vehicle transporting migrant agricultural workers and a carrier may not permit or require a person to operate the motor vehicle unless:

(1) the person has been physically examined by a licensed doctor of medicine or osteopathy during the preceding 36 months; and

(2) the doctor certifies that the person is physically qualified in accordance with Section 647.007.

(b) The doctor's certificate must state:

"Doctor's Certificate

(Operator of Migrant Agricultural Workers)

This is to certify that I have this day examined ______________ in accordance with the Texas law governing physical qualifications of operators of migrant agricultural workers and that I find ______________

Qualified under that law

Qualified only when wearing glasses or corrective lenses

I have kept on file in my office a completed examination.

(Date) (Place) (Signature of Examining Doctor)

(Address of Doctor)

Signature of Operator: ______________

Address of Operator: ______________"

(c) A carrier shall keep in its files at the carrier's principal place of business a legible doctor's certificate or a legible photographically reproduced copy of the doctor's certificate for each operator it employs or uses.

(d) An operator shall carry the operator's legible doctor's certificate or a legible photographically reproduced copy of the doctor's certificate when operating the motor vehicle.

Sec. 647.009. Limitation on Operation of Motor Vehicle.

(a) Except in an emergency, a person assigned to operate a motor vehicle transporting migrant workers may not allow another person to operate the motor vehicle without the carrier's authorization.

(b) A person may not operate a motor vehicle if the person's alertness or ability to operate the vehicle is impaired for any reason, including fatigue or illness, to the extent that it is not safe for the person to begin or to continue. This subsection does not apply if there is a grave emergency in which failure to operate a motor vehicle would result in a greater hazard to passengers. However, the person may operate the motor vehicle only to the nearest location at which the passengers' safety is ensured.

(c) A carrier may not permit or require a person to operate a motor vehicle from one location to another in a period that would necessitate the operation of the vehicle at a speed in excess of the applicable speed limit.

(d) An operator shall make a meal stop of not less than 30 minutes at least every six hours. The carrier shall provide for reasonable rest stops at least once between each meal stop.

(e) The operator of a truck transporting migrant agricultural workers for more than 500 miles shall stop for at least eight hours to provide rest for the operator and passengers either before or at the completion of each 500 miles.

(f) A person may not operate and a carrier may not permit or require the person to operate a motor vehicle for more than 10 hours in the aggregate, excluding meal and rest stops, during any 24-hour period unless the person rests for at least eight consecutive hours at the end of the 10-hour period. For purposes of this subsection, the 24-hour period begins at the time the operator reports for duty.

Sec. 647.010. Required Stop at Railroad Crossing.

(a) An operator transporting migrant agricultural workers who approaches a railroad grade crossing:

(1) shall stop the motor vehicle not less than 15 feet or more than 50 feet from the nearest rail of the crossing; and

(2) may proceed only after the operator determines that the course is clear.

(b) An operator is not required to stop at:

(1) a streetcar crossing that is in a municipal business or residential district;

(2) a railroad grade crossing at which a police officer or traffic-control signal other than a railroad flashing signal directs traffic to proceed; or

(3) a grade crossing that the proper state authority has clearly marked as being abandoned or exempted if the marking can be read from the operator's position.

(c) The motor vehicle must display a sign on the rear of the vehicle that states: "This Vehicle Stops at Railroad Crossings."

Sec. 647.011. Fuel Restrictions.

(a) An operator or carrier employee fueling a motor vehicle used to transport migrant agricultural workers may not:

(1) fuel the motor vehicle while the engine is running unless running the engine is required to fuel the vehicle;

(2) smoke or expose any open flame in the vicinity of the motor vehicle;

(3) fuel the motor vehicle when the nozzle of the fuel hose is not in continuous contact with the intake pipe of the fuel tank; or

(4) permit any other person to engage in an activity that would likely result in a fire or explosion.

(b) A person may carry fuel on the motor vehicle for use in the motor vehicle or an accessory only in a properly mounted fuel tank.

Sec. 647.012. Required Vehicle Equipment; Use of Required Equipment.

(a) A motor vehicle used to transport migrant agricultural workers must be equipped with:

(1) at least one properly mounted fire extinguisher;

(2) road warning devices, including at least one red-burning fusee and at least three red flares, red electric lanterns, or red emergency reflectors;

(3) coupling devices as prescribed by Subsection (c), if the vehicle is a truck tractor or dolly; and

(4) tires as prescribed by Subsection (d).

(b) A person may not operate a motor vehicle unless the person is satisfied that the equipment required under Subsection (a) and the following equipment is in good working order:

(1) the brakes, including service brakes, trailer brake connections, and hand parking brakes;

(2) lighting devices and reflectors;

(3) the steering mechanism;

(4) the horn;

(5) each windshield wiper; and

(6) each rearview mirror.

(c) Adequate means must be provided positively to prevent the shifting of the lower half of each fifth wheel attached to the frame of a truck tractor or dolly. The lower half of each fifth wheel must be securely fastened to the frame by U-bolts that are of adequate size and are securely tightened. Another method may be used if the method provides equivalent security. A U-bolt may not be of welded construction and must be installed so as not to crack, warp, or deform the frame. The upper half of each fifth wheel must be fastened with at least the security required for the lower half. A locking means must be provided in each fifth wheel mechanism, including adapters when used, so that the upper and lower half will not separate without the use of a positive manual release, such as a release mechanism that the operator uses from the cab. If the fifth wheel is designed and constructed to be readily separable, the requirement for a fifth wheel coupling device applies to a vehicle manufactured after December 31, 1952.

(d) Vehicle tires must be of adequate capacity to support the vehicle's gross weight. Each tire must have a tread configuration on the part of the tire that is in contact with the road and may not be so smooth as to expose any tread fabric. A tire may not have a defect likely to cause failure. A front tire may not be regrooved, recapped, or retreaded.

(e) An operator shall use required equipment as necessary.

Sec. 647.013. Passenger Safety Provisions on Motor Vehicle Other Than Bus.

(a) A motor vehicle other than a bus transporting migrant agricultural workers must have a passenger compartment in accordance with this section.

(b) The floor of the passenger compartment must be substantially smooth and without cracks or holes. Except as necessary to secure the seats or other devices attached to the floor, the floor may not have any object that protrudes more than two inches in height.

(c) The side walls and ends of the passenger compartment must extend at least 60 inches from the floor. If necessary, sideboards may be attached to the body of the motor vehicle. Stake body construction meets the requirements of this subsection only if the space six inches or larger between any two stakes is suitably closed to prevent the passengers from falling off the vehicle.

(d) The floor and interior of the sides and ends of the passenger compartment must be free of protruding nails, screws, splinters, or any other protruding object that is likely to injure a passenger or the passenger's clothes.

(e) The motor vehicle must have an adequate means of exiting and entering the passenger compartment from the rear or from the right side of the vehicle. Each exit and entrance must have a gate or door that has at least one latch or fastening device that will keep the gate or door securely closed during transportation. The latch or fastening device must be readily operative without the use of tools. An exit or entrance must:

(1) be at least 18 inches wide;

(2) have a top and clear opening of at least 60 inches or as high as the passenger compartment side wall if the side wall is less than 60 inches high; and

(3) have a bottom that is at the floor of the passenger compartment.

(f) If the motor vehicle has a permanently attached roof, the vehicle must have at least one emergency exit on a side or rear of the vehicle that does not have a regular exit or entrance. The exit must have a gate or door and a latch and hold as prescribed by Subsection (e).

(g) If necessary, a ladder or steps shall be used to enter and exit the passenger compartment. The maximum vertical spacing of footholds may not exceed 12 inches and the lowest step may not be more than 18 inches above the ground when the vehicle is empty.

(h) The motor vehicle must include handholds or other devices that will enable passengers to enter and exit the vehicle without hazard.

(i) The motor vehicle must have a way for passengers to communicate with the operator, including a telephone, speaker tube, buzzer, pull cord, or other mechanical or electrical device.

Sec. 647.014. Passenger Seating.

One seat must be provided for each passenger. Passengers shall remain seated while the vehicle is in motion.

Sec. 647.015. Passenger Seating Requirements for Certain Trips.

(a) A motor vehicle transporting migrant agricultural workers for a total distance of 100 miles or more must have a passenger compartment in accordance with this section.

(b) Each passenger seat must:

(1) be securely attached to the vehicle during use;

(2) be not less than 16 or more than 19 inches above the floor;

(3) be at least 13 inches deep;

(4) be equipped with backrests that extend at least 36 inches above the floor;

(5) have at least 24 inches of space between the backrests or the edges of the opposite seats when positioned face to face;

(6) provide at least 18 inches of seat area for each passenger;

(7) not have any cracks that are more than one-fourth inch wide;

(8) not have any cracks in the backrests, if slatted, that are more than two inches wide; and

(9) have any exposed wood surfaces planed or sanded smooth and free of splinters.

Sec. 647.016. Passenger Protection from Weather.

(a) If necessary to protect passengers from inclement weather, including rain, snow, or sleet, the passenger compartment must be equipped with a top that is at least 80 inches above the floor and with a means of closing the sides and ends. A tarpaulin or other removable protective device may be used if secured in place.

(b) The motor vehicle must have a safe method of protecting the passengers from cold or undue exposure. A motor vehicle may not have a heater that:

(1) conducts engine exhaust gases or engine compartment air into or through a space occupied by an individual;

(2) uses a flame that is not completely enclosed;

(3) might spill or leak fuel if the vehicle is tilted or overturned;

(4) uses heated or unheated air that comes from or through the engine compartment or from direct contact with any part of the exhaust system unless the heater ducts prevent contamination of the air from the exhaust or engine compartment gases; or

(5) is not securely fastened to the motor vehicle.

Sec. 647.017. Operational Requirements.

(a) A person may not operate a motor vehicle transporting migrant agricultural workers that is loaded or that has a load that is distributed or secured in a manner that prevents the vehicle's safe operation.

(b) A person may not operate a motor vehicle if:

(1) a tailgate, tailboard, tarpaulin, door, fastening device, or equipment or rigging is not securely in place;

(2) an object:

(A) obscures the operator's view in any direction;

(B) interferes with the free movement of the operator's arms or legs;

(C) obstructs the operator's access to emergency accessories; or

(D) obstructs a person's entrance or exit from the cab or operator's compartment; or

(3) property on the vehicle is stowed so that it:

Transportation Code

(A) restricts the operator's freedom of motion in properly operating the vehicle;

(B) obstructs a person's exit from the vehicle; or

(C) does not provide adequate protection to passengers and others from injury resulting from a falling or displaced article.

(c) An operator who leaves a motor vehicle unattended shall securely set the parking brake, chock the wheels, and take all reasonable precautions to prevent the vehicle from moving.

Sec. 647.018. Certificate of Compliance.

A carrier is considered to be in compliance with this chapter if the carrier holds a certificate of compliance with the United States Department of Transportation regulations governing transportation of migrant agricultural workers in interstate commerce.

Sec. 647.019. Penalty.

(a) A carrier who violates this chapter commits an offense.

(b) An offense under this section is a misdemeanor punishable by a fine of not less than $5 or more than $50.

CHAPTER 648 FOREIGN COMMERCIAL MOTOR TRANSPORTATION

SUBCHAPTER A GENERAL PROVISIONS

Sec. 648.001. Definitions.

In this chapter:

(1) "Border" means the border between this state and the United Mexican States.

(2) "Border commercial zone" means a commercial zone established under 49 C.F.R. Part 372, Subpart B, any portion of which is contiguous to the border in this state.

(3) "Commercial motor vehicle" includes a foreign commercial motor vehicle.

(4) "Foreign commercial motor vehicle" means a commercial motor vehicle, as defined by 49 C.F.R. Section 390.5, that is owned by a person or entity that is domiciled in or a citizen of a country other than the United States.

(5) "Motor carrier" includes a foreign motor carrier and a foreign motor private carrier, as defined in 49 U.S.C. Sections 13102(6) and (7).

Sec. 648.002. Rules.

In addition to rules required by this chapter, the Texas Department of Motor Vehicles, the Department of Public Safety, and the Texas Department of Insurance may adopt other rules to carry out this chapter.

Sec. 648.003. Reference to Federal Statute or Regulation.

A reference in this chapter to a federal statute or regulation includes any subsequent amendment or redesignation of the statute or regulation.

SUBCHAPTER B BORDER COMMERCIAL ZONE

Sec. 648.051. Border Commercial Zone Exclusive; Boundaries.

(a) A law or agreement of less than statewide application that is adopted by an agency or political subdivision of this state and that regulates motor carriers or commercial motor vehicles or the operation of those carriers or vehicles in the transportation of cargo across the border or within an area adjacent to the border by foreign commercial motor vehicles has no effect unless the law or agreement applies uniformly to an entire border commercial zone and only in a border commercial zone.

(b) This subchapter supersedes that portion of any paired city, paired state, or similar understanding governing foreign commercial motor vehicles or motor carriers entered into under Section 502.091 or any other law.

Sec. 648.052. Modification of Zone Boundaries.

The boundaries of a border commercial zone may be modified or established only as provided by federal law.

SUBCHAPTER C REGULATION OF OPERATION OF FOREIGN COMMERCIAL MOTOR VEHICLES

Sec. 648.101. Registration Exemption in Border Commercial Zone.

(a) A foreign commercial motor vehicle is exempt from Chapter 502 and any other law of this state requiring the vehicle to be registered in this state, including a law providing for a temporary registration permit, if:

(1) the vehicle is engaged solely in transportation of cargo across the border into or from a border commercial zone;

(2) for each load of cargo transported the vehicle remains in this state:

(A) not more than 24 hours; or

(B) not more than 48 hours, if:

(i) the vehicle is unable to leave this state within 24 hours because of circumstances beyond the control of the motor carrier operating the vehicle; and

(ii) all financial responsibility requirements applying to the vehicle are satisfied;

(3) the vehicle is registered and licensed as required by the country in which the person that owns the vehicle is domiciled or is a citizen as evidenced by a valid metal license plate attached to the front or rear of the exterior of the vehicle; and

(4) the country in which the person that owns the vehicle is domiciled or is a citizen provides a reciprocal exemption for commercial motor vehicles owned by residents of this state.

(b) A foreign commercial motor vehicle operating under the exemption provided by this section and the vehicle's driver may be considered unregistered if the vehicle is operated in this state outside a border commercial zone or in violation of United States law.

(c) A valid reciprocity agreement between this state and another state of the United States or a Canadian province that exempts currently registered vehicles owned by nonresidents is effective in a border commercial zone.

(d) A foreign commercial motor vehicle that engages primarily in transportation of cargo across the border into or from a border commercial zone must be:

(1) registered in this state; or

(2) operated under the exemption provided by this section.

(e) A vehicle located in a border commercial zone must display a valid Texas registration if the vehicle is owned by a person who:

(1) owns a leasing facility or a leasing terminal located in this state; and

(2) leases the vehicle to a foreign motor carrier.

Sec. 648.102. Financial Responsibility.

(a) The Texas Department of Motor Vehicles shall adopt rules that conform with 49 C.F.R. Part 387 requiring motor carriers operating foreign commercial motor vehicles in this state to maintain financial responsibility.

(b) This chapter prevails over any other requirement of state law relating to financial responsibility for operation of foreign commercial motor vehicles in this state.

Sec. 648.103. Domestic Transportation.

A foreign motor carrier or foreign motor private carrier may not transport persons or cargo in intrastate commerce in this state unless the carrier is authorized to conduct operations in interstate and foreign commerce domestically between points in the United States under federal law or international agreement.

SUBTITLE G
MOTORCYCLES, OFF-HIGHWAY VEHICLES, AND ELECTRIC BICYCLES

CHAPTER 661
PROTECTIVE HEADGEAR FOR MOTORCYCLE OPERATORS AND PASSENGERS

Sec. 661.001. Definitions.

In this chapter:

(1) "Motorcycle" means a motor vehicle designed to propel itself with not more than three wheels in contact with the ground, and having a saddle for the use of the rider. The term does not include a tractor or a three-wheeled vehicle equipped with a cab or occupant compartment, seat, and seat belt and designed to contain the operator in the cab or occupant compartment.

(2) "Department" means the Department of Public Safety.

Sec. 661.0015. Protective Headgear for Autocycle.

(a) In this section, "autocycle" means a motor vehicle, other than a tractor, that is:

(1) designed to have when propelled not more than three wheels on the ground;

(2) equipped with a steering wheel;

(3) equipped with seating that does not require the operator to straddle or sit astride the seat; and

(4) manufactured and certified to comply with federal safety requirements for a motorcycle.

(b) For purposes of this chapter, an autocycle is considered to be a motorcycle.

Sec. 661.002. Department to Prescribe Minimum Safety Standards for Protective Headgear.

(a) To provide for the safety and welfare of motorcycle operators and passengers, the department shall prescribe minimum safety standards for protective headgear used by motorcyclists in this state.

(b) The department may adopt any part or all of the American National Standards Institute's standards for protective headgear for vehicular users.

(c) On request of a manufacturer of protective headgear, the department shall make the safety standards prescribed by the department available to the manufacturer.

Sec. 661.003. Offenses Relating to Not Wearing Protective Headgear.

(a) A person commits an offense if the person:

(1) operates or rides as a passenger on a motorcycle on a public street or highway; and

(2) is not wearing protective headgear that meets safety standards adopted by the department.

(b) A person commits an offense if the person carries on a motorcycle on a public street or highway a passenger who is not wearing protective headgear that meets safety standards adopted by the department.

(c) It is an exception to the application of Subsection (a) or (b) that at the time the offense was committed, the person required to wear protective headgear was at least 21 years old and had successfully completed a motorcycle operator training and safety course under Chapter 662 or was covered by a health insurance plan providing the person with medical benefits for injuries incurred as a result of an accident while operating or riding on a motorcycle. A peace officer may not arrest a person or issue a citation to a person for a violation of Subsection (a) or (b) if the person required to wear protective headgear is at least 21 years of age and presents evidence sufficient to show that the person required to wear protective headgear has successfully completed a motorcycle operator training and safety course or is covered by a health insurance plan as described by this subsection.

(c-1) A peace officer may not stop or detain a person who is the operator of or a passenger on a motorcycle for the sole purpose of determining whether the person has successfully completed the motorcycle operator training and safety course or is covered by a health insurance plan.

(c-2) The Texas Department of Insurance shall prescribe a standard proof of health insurance for issuance to persons who are at least 21 years of age and covered by a health insurance plan described by Subsection (c).

(d) to (g) [Repealed by Acts 2009, 81st Leg., ch. 1391 (S.B. 1967), § 12, effective September 1, 2009.]

(h) An offense under this section is a misdemeanor punishable by a fine of not less than $10 or more than $50.

(i) In this section, "health insurance plan" means an individual, group, blanket, or franchise insurance policy, insurance agreement, evidence of coverage, group hospital services contract, health maintenance organization membership, or employee benefit plan that provides benefits for health care services or for medical or surgical expenses incurred as a result of an accident.

Sec. 661.004. Authority of Peace Officer to Inspect Protective Headgear.

Any peace officer may stop and detain a person who is a motorcycle operator or passenger to inspect the person's protective headgear for compliance with the safety standards prescribed by the department.

CHAPTER 662 MOTORCYCLE OPERATOR TRAINING AND SAFETY

Sec. 662.0005. Definitions.

In this chapter:

(1) "Commission" means the Texas Commission of Licensing and Regulation.

(2) "Department" means the Texas Department of Licensing and Regulation.

(3) "Institution of higher education" has the meaning assigned by Section 61.003, Education Code.

(4) "Instructor" means an individual who holds a license issued under this chapter that entitles the individual to provide instruction on motorcycle operation and safety as an employee of or under contract with a motorcycle school.

(5) "Motorcycle school" means a person who holds a license issued under this chapter that entitles the person to offer and conduct courses on motorcycle operation and safety for consideration as part of the motorcycle operator training and safety program.

Sec. 662.001. Administration of Program.

The department shall administer a motorcycle operator training and safety program and enforce the laws governing the program.

Sec. 662.002. Purpose of Program.

(a) The purpose of the motorcycle operator training and safety program is:

(1) to make available to motorcycle operators:

(A) information relating to the operation of motorcycles; and

(B) courses in knowledge, skills, and safety relating to the operation of motorcycles; and

(2) to provide information to the public on sharing roadways with motorcycles.

(b) [Repealed.]

Sec. 662.003. Program Director. [Repealed]

Sec. 662.0033. Minimum Curriculum Standards.

(a) The commission by rule shall establish minimum curriculum standards for courses provided under the motorcycle operator training and safety program.

(b) The department shall approve all courses that meet the curriculum standards established under Subsection (a).

(c) In establishing the minimum curriculum standards for entry-level courses, the commission shall consider the standards for motorcycle operator training and safety courses adopted by the National Highway Traffic Safety Administration.

Sec. 662.0035. Fees.

The commission may set fees in amounts reasonable and necessary to cover the costs of administering this chapter, including fees for:

(1) the issuance and renewal of a motorcycle school license and instructor license; and

(2) courses provided under the motorcycle operator training and safety program.

Sec. 662.0037. Motorcycle Safety Advisory Board.

(a) The commission shall establish an advisory board to advise the department on matters related to the motorcycle operator training and safety program established under this chapter.

(b) The advisory board must consist of nine members appointed by the presiding officer of the commission, on approval of the commission, as follows:

(1) three members:

(A) each of whom must be a licensed instructor or represent a licensed motorcycle school; and

(B) who must collectively represent the diversity in size and type of the motorcycle schools licensed under this chapter;

(2) one member who represents the motorcycle dealer retail industry;

(3) one representative of a law enforcement agency;

(4) one representative of the Texas A&M Transportation Institute;

(5) one representative of the Texas A&M Engineering Extension Service; and

(6) two public members who hold a valid Class M driver's license issued under Chapter 521.

(c) The advisory board members serve staggered six-year terms. The terms of three members expire September 1 of each odd-numbered year.

(d) If a vacancy occurs on the advisory board, the presiding officer of the commission, on approval of the commission, shall appoint a replacement who meets the qualifications for the vacant position to serve for the remainder of the term.

(e) The presiding officer of the commission, on approval of the commission, shall designate a member of the advisory board to serve as the presiding officer of the advisory board for a one-year term. The presiding officer of the advisory board may vote on any matter before the advisory board.

(f) The advisory board shall meet at the call of the executive director or the presiding officer of the commission.

(g) An advisory board member may not receive compensation for service on the advisory board but is entitled to reimbursement for actual and necessary expenses incurred in performing the functions as a member of the advisory board, subject to the General Appropriations Act.

(h) Chapter 2110, Government Code, does not apply to the advisory board.

(i) The department may call a joint meeting of the advisory board and the advisory committee established under Section 1001.058, Education Code, for the committees to collaborate on matters determined by the department.

Sec. 662.004. Motorcycle Safety Coordinator. [Repealed]

Transportation Code

Sec. 662.005. Contracts.

(a) The department may contract with qualified persons, including institutions of higher education, to:

(1) offer and conduct motorcycle operator training and safety courses under the program; or

(2) research motorcycle safety in this state.

(b) The department shall consult with the motorcycle safety advisory board regarding any proposal to contract under this section.

Sec. 662.006. Unauthorized Training Prohibited.

(a) A person may not offer or conduct training in motorcycle operation for consideration unless the person:

(1) is licensed as a motorcycle school under this chapter;

(2) offers and conducts training in accordance with a motorcycle operator training curriculum approved by the department; and

(3) employs or contracts with an instructor licensed under this chapter to conduct the training.

(b) A person who violates Subsection (a) commits an offense. An offense under this subsection is a Class B misdemeanor, except that the offense is a Class A misdemeanor if it is shown on the trial of the offense that the defendant has been previously convicted of an offense under this section.

Sec. 662.0062. Eligibility; Application.

(a) To be eligible for an instructor license, an applicant must:

(1) have completed a commission-approved training program on motorcycle operator training and safety instruction administered by the Texas A&M Engineering Extension Service;

(2) have held for the two years preceding the date of submitting the application a valid driver's license that entitles the applicant to operate a motorcycle on a public road; and

(3) have accumulated less than 10 points under the driver responsibility program established by Chapter 708.

(b) The commission by rule may adopt additional requirements for issuance of an instructor license.

(c) To be eligible for a motorcycle school license, an applicant must meet the minimum standards established by commission rule for:

(1) health and safety;

(2) the school's facility; and

(3) consumer protection.

(d) The department shall issue a license to an applicant who meets the eligibility requirements established under this chapter and department rule and who pays the required fee.

(e) The department may prescribe an application form for applicants to submit when applying for a license under this section.

Sec. 662.0064. Instructor Training; Administrator.

The Texas A&M Engineering Extension Service, in consultation with the department, shall administer the training program required by Section 662.0062(a)(1).

Sec. 662.0068. Program Certificates.

The department shall issue a certificate of completion to a person who completes a department-approved motorcycle operator training and safety course conducted by a motorcycle school on receipt of notice from the motorcycle school that conducted the course. The department may develop a process that allows a motorcycle school to issue a certificate of completion to the person.

Sec. 662.007. Fee for Course. [Repealed]

Sec. 662.008. Denial, Suspension, or Revocation of Instructor or Motorcycle School License.

(a) The executive director or commission may deny an application for, suspend, or revoke a license issued under this chapter if the applicant, instructor, or motorcycle school:

(1) does not satisfy the requirements established under this chapter to receive or retain the license;

(2) permits fraud or engages in a fraudulent practice with reference to an application for the license;

(3) induces or countenances fraud or a fraudulent practice by a person applying for a driver's license or permit;

(4) permits fraud or engages in a fraudulent practice in an action between the applicant or license holder and the public; or

(5) fails to comply with this chapter or rules adopted under this chapter.

(b) Following denial of an application for a license or the suspension or revocation of a license issued under this chapter, notice and opportunity for a hearing must be given as provided by:

(1) Chapter 2001, Government Code; and

(2) Chapter 53, Occupations Code.

Transportation Code

Sec. 662.009. Rules.

The commission may adopt rules to administer this chapter.

Sec. 662.010. Nonapplicability of Certain Other Law.

Chapter 1001, Education Code, does not apply to training offered or conducted under this chapter.

Sec. 662.011. Motorcycle Education Fund Account.

(a) Of each fee collected under Sections 521.421(b) and (g) and Sections 522.029(f) and (g), the Department of Public Safety shall send $5 to the comptroller for deposit to the credit of the motorcycle education fund account.

(b) Money deposited to the credit of the motorcycle education fund account may be used only to defray the cost of:

(1) administering the motorcycle operator training and safety program;

(2) conducting the motorcyclist safety and share the road campaign described by Section 201.621; and

(3) administering the grant program under Section 662.0115.

(c) The comptroller shall report to the governor and legislature not later than the first Monday in November of each even-numbered year on the condition of the account. The report must contain:

(1) a statement of the amount of money deposited to the credit of the account for the year;

(2) a statement of the amount of money disbursed by the comptroller from the account for the year;

(3) a statement of the balance of money in the account;

(4) a list of persons and entities that have received money from the account, including information for each person or entity that shows the amount of money received; and

(5) a statement of any significant problems encountered in administering the account, with recommendations for their solution.

(d) The department may apply for and accept gifts, grants, and donations from any organization to be deposited in the motorcycle education fund account for the purpose of improving motorcycle safety in this state.

Sec. 662.0115. Motorcycle Safety Grant Program.

(a) Using money from the motorcycle education fund account, the department may establish and administer a grant program to improve motorcycle safety in this state.

(b) The department may award a person a grant to:

(1) promote the motorcycle operator training and safety program or any other motorcycle safety program in this state;

(2) increase the number of individuals seeking motorcycle operator training or licensure as an instructor to conduct motorcycle operator training; or

(3) support any other goal reasonably likely to improve motorcycle safety in this state.

(c) To administer the grant program, the department shall prescribe:

(1) grant application procedures;

(2) guidelines relating to grant amounts; and

(3) criteria for evaluating grant applications.

(d) The department shall consult with the motorcycle safety advisory board regarding any proposal to award a grant under this section.

(e) An institution of higher education is eligible to receive a grant awarded under this section and, if applicable, may use the grant money awarded to perform a duty imposed under Section 662.0064 or 662.013.

Sec. 662.012. Reports.

(a) The department shall require each motorcycle school to report on the school's program in the form and manner prescribed by the department. The report must include:

(1) the number and types of courses provided in the reporting period;

(2) the number of persons who took each course in the reporting period;

(3) the number of instructors available to provide training under the school's program in the reporting period;

(4) information collected by surveying persons taking each course as to the length of any waiting period the person experienced before being able to enroll in the course;

(5) the number of persons on a waiting list for a course at the end of the reporting period; and

(6) any other information the department reasonably requires.

(b) The department shall maintain the reports submitted under Subsection (a) on a by-site basis.

(c) The department shall provide without charge a copy of the most recent reports submitted under Subsection (a) to any member of the legislature on request.

Sec. 662.013. Research, Advocacy, and Education.

The Texas A&M Transportation Institute, in consultation with the department, shall:

(1) research motorcycle safety in this state;
(2) provide advocacy on motorcycle safety issues in this state; and
(3) provide education to the public on motorcycle safety issues in this state.

CHAPTER 663 [HEADING REPEALED–SEE EDITOR'S NOTE]

SUBCHAPTER A GENERAL PROVISIONS [RENUMBERED]

Sec. 663.001. Definitions. [Renumbered]

Sec. 663.002. Nonapplicability of Certain Other Laws. [Renumbered]

Sec. 663.003. Recreational Off-Highway Vehicles. [Repealed]

SUBCHAPTER B OFF-HIGHWAY VEHICLE OPERATOR EDUCATION AND CERTIFICATION [RENUMBERED]

Sec. 663.011. Designated Division or State Agency. [Renumbered]

Sec. 663.012. Purpose of Program. [Renumbered]

Sec. 663.013. Off-Highway Vehicle Safety Coordinator. [Renumbered]

Sec. 663.014. Contracts. [Renumbered]

Sec. 663.015. Teaching and Testing Methods. [Renumbered]

Sec. 663.016. Fee for Course. [Renumbered]

Sec. 663.017. Denial, Suspension, or Cancellation of Approval. [Renumbered]

Sec. 663.018. Rules. [Renumbered]

Sec. 663.019. Exemptions. [Renumbered]

SUBCHAPTER C OPERATION OF OFF-HIGHWAY VEHICLES [RENUMBERED]

Sec. 663.031. Safety Certificate Required. [Renumbered]

Sec. 663.032. Operation by Person Younger Than 14. [Renumbered]

Sec. 663.033. Required Equipment; Display of Lights. [Renumbered]

Sec. 663.034. Safety Apparel Required. [Renumbered]

Sec. 663.035. Reckless or Careless Operation Prohibited. [Renumbered]

Sec. 663.036. Carrying Passengers. [Renumbered]

Sec. 663.037. [Heading Repealed-See Editor's Note]

(a) [Renumbered to Tex. Transp. Code § 551A.051]
(b) [Renumbered to Tex. Transp. Code § 551A.034]
(c) [Renumbered to Tex. Transp. Code § 551A.034]
(d) [Renumbered to Tex. Transp. Code § 551A.057]
(d-1) [Renumbered to Tex. Transp. Code § 551A.057]
(e) [Renumbered to Tex. Transp. Code § 551A.059]
(f) [Renumbered to Tex. Transp. Code § 551A.051]
(g) [Renumbered to Tex. Transp. Code § 551A.058]

Sec. 663.0371. Operation on Beach. [Renumbered]

Transportation Code

Sec. 663.038. Violation of Chapter; Offense. [Renumbered]

CHAPTER 664 STANDARDS FOR ELECTRIC BICYCLES

Sec. 664.001. Definitions.

In this chapter:

(1) "Class 1 electric bicycle" means an electric bicycle:

(A) equipped with a motor that assists the rider only when the rider is pedaling; and

(B) with a top assisted speed of 20 miles per hour or less.

(2) "Class 2 electric bicycle" means an electric bicycle:

(A) equipped with a motor that may be used to propel the bicycle without the pedaling of the rider; and

(B) with a top assisted speed of 20 miles per hour or less.

(3) "Class 3 electric bicycle" means an electric bicycle:

(A) equipped with a motor that assists the rider only when the rider is pedaling; and

(B) with a top assisted speed of more than 20 but less than 28 miles per hour.

(4) "Electric bicycle" means a bicycle:

(A) equipped with:

(i) fully operable pedals; and

(ii) an electric motor of fewer than 750 watts; and

(B) with a top assisted speed of 28 miles per hour or less.

(5) "Top assisted speed" means the speed at which the bicycle's motor ceases propelling the bicycle or assisting the rider.

Sec. 664.002. Labeling.

(a) A person who manufactures or sells an electric bicycle shall apply a permanent label to the electric bicycle in a prominent location that shows in Arial font in at least 9-point type:

(1) whether the electric bicycle is a Class 1, Class 2, or Class 3 electric bicycle;

(2) the top assisted speed of the electric bicycle; and

(3) the motor wattage of the electric bicycle.

(b) A person who changes the motor-powered speed capability or engagement of an electric bicycle shall replace the label required by Subsection (a) to show accurate information about the electric bicycle.

Sec. 664.003. Federal Standards.

A person who manufactures or sells an electric bicycle shall ensure that the bicycle complies with the equipment and manufacturing requirements for bicycles adopted by the United States Consumer Product Safety Commission under 16 C.F.R. Part 1512.

Sec. 664.004. Speedometer.

A person who manufactures or sells a Class 3 electric bicycle shall ensure that the bicycle is equipped with a speedometer.

CHAPTER 680 MISCELLANEOUS PROVISIONS

SUBCHAPTER A SALE OF MOTORCYCLE WITHOUT SERIAL NUMBERS

Sec. 680.001. Definitions.

In this subchapter:

(1) "Department" means the Department of Public Safety.

(2) "Motorcycle" has the meaning assigned that term by Section 661.001.

(3) "Person" means an individual, partnership, firm, corporation, association, or other private entity.

Sec. 680.002. Sale of Motorcycle Without Serial Numbers.

A person may not sell a motorcycle manufactured after January 1, 1976, unless:

(1) the serial number of the frame and the serial number of the engine are affixed so that they may not be removed without defacing the frame or engine; and

(2) the manufacturer has filed with the department a statement that:

(A) identifies the part to which each number is affixed;

(B) gives the exact dimensions of the part; and

(C) gives the location on the part to which the number is affixed.

Sec. 680.003. Offense; Penalty.

(a) An individual who violates Section 680.002 commits an offense.

(b) An offense under this section is a misdemeanor punishable by:

(1) a fine not to exceed $200;

(2) confinement in county jail for a term not to exceed 30 days; or

(3) both the fine and confinement.

(c) Each sale of a motorcycle in violation of this subchapter is a separate offense.

Sec. 680.004. Civil Penalty.

A partnership, firm, corporation, or association that violates Section 680.002 is liable to the state for a civil penalty of not more than $500 for each offense.

Sec. 680.005. Director to Adopt Rules and Develop Forms.

The director of the department shall adopt rules and develop forms to administer this subchapter.

SUBCHAPTER B
TOLLS FOR MOTORCYCLE; USE OF PREFERENTIAL LANE BY MOTORCYCLE

Sec. 680.011. Definitions.

In this subchapter:

(1) "Motorcycle" has the meaning assigned by Section 502.001 and includes a motorcycle equipped with a sidecar.

(2) "Preferential lane" means a traffic lane on a street or highway where motor vehicle usage is limited to:

(A) buses;

(B) vehicles occupied by a minimum number of persons; or

(C) car pool vehicles.

Sec. 680.012. Toll for Motorcycle.

A person who operates a toll road, toll bridge, or turnpike may not impose a toll for the operation of a motorcycle on the road, bridge, or turnpike that is greater than the toll imposed for the operation of a passenger car on the road, bridge, or turnpike.

Sec. 680.013. Use of Preferential Lane by Motorcycle.

A motorcycle, including a motorcycle described by Section 521.001(a)(6-a), may be operated in a preferential lane that is not closed to all vehicular traffic.

SUBTITLE H
PARKING, TOWING, AND STORAGE OF VEHICLES

CHAPTER 681
PRIVILEGED PARKING

Sec. 681.001. Definitions.

In this chapter:

(1) "Department" means the Texas Department of Motor Vehicles.

(2) "Disability" means a condition in which a person has:

(A) mobility problems that substantially impair the person's ability to ambulate;

(B) visual acuity of 20/200 or less in the better eye with correcting lenses; or

(C) visual acuity of more than 20/200 but with a limited field of vision in which the widest diameter of the visual field subtends an angle of 20 degrees or less.

(3) "Disabled parking placard" means a placard issued under Section 681.002.

(4) "International symbol of access" means the symbol adopted by Rehabilitation International in 1969 at its Eleventh World Congress on Rehabilitation of the Disabled.

(5) "Mobility problem that substantially impairs a person's ability to ambulate" means that the person:

(A) cannot walk 200 feet without stopping to rest;

(B) cannot walk without the use of or assistance from an assistance device, including a brace, a cane, a crutch, another person, or a prosthetic device;

(C) cannot ambulate without a wheelchair or similar device;

(D) is restricted by lung disease to the extent that the person's forced respiratory expiratory volume for one second, measured by spirometry, is less than one liter, or the arterial oxygen tension is less than 60 millimeters of mercury on room air at rest;

(E) uses portable oxygen;

(F) has a cardiac condition to the extent that the person's functional limitations are classified in severity as Class III or Class IV according to standards set by the American Heart Association;

(G) is severely limited in the ability to walk because of an arthritic, neurological, or orthopedic condition;

(H) has a disorder of the foot that, in the opinion of a person licensed to practice podiatry in this state or in a state adjacent to this state, limits or impairs the person's ability to walk; or

(I) has another debilitating condition that, in the opinion of a physician licensed to practice medicine in this state or a state adjacent to this state, or authorized by applicable law to practice medicine in a hospital or other health facility of the Veterans Administration, limits or impairs the person's ability to walk.

(6) "Podiatry" has the meaning assigned by Section 202.001, Occupations Code.

(7) "Stand" or "standing" means to halt an occupied or unoccupied vehicle, other than temporarily while receiving or discharging passengers.

Sec. 681.002. Disabled Parking Placard.

(a) The department shall provide for the issuance of a disabled parking placard to a person with a disability.

(b) A disabled parking placard must be two-sided and hooked and include on each side:

(1) the international symbol of access, which must be at least three inches in height, be centered on the placard, and be:

(A) white on a blue shield for a placard issued to a person with a permanent disability; or

(B) white on a red shield for a placard issued to a person with a temporary disability;

(2) an identification number;

(3) an expiration date at least three inches in height; and

(4) the seal or other identification of the department.

(c) The department shall furnish the disabled parking placards to each county assessor-collector.

(d) A disabled parking placard must bear a hologram designed to prevent the reproduction of the placard or the production of a counterfeit placard.

(e) In addition to the expiration date included on a disabled parking placard under Subsection (b), the expiration date must be indicated on the placard by a month and year hole-punch system.

Sec. 681.003. Parking Placard Application.

(a) An owner of a motor vehicle regularly operated by or for the transportation of a person with a disability may apply for a disabled parking placard.

(b) An application for a disabled parking placard must be:

(1) on a form furnished by the department;

(2) submitted to the county assessor-collector of the county in which the person with the disability:

(A) resides; or

(B) is seeking medical treatment; and

(3) accompanied by a fee of $5 if the application is for a temporary placard.

(c) Subject to Subsections (e) and (f), the first application must be accompanied by a notarized written statement or written prescription of a physician licensed to practice medicine in this state or a state adjacent to this state, or authorized by applicable law to practice medicine in a hospital or other health facility of the United States Department of Veterans Affairs, certifying and providing evidence acceptable to the department that the person making the application or on whose behalf the application is made is legally blind or has a mobility problem that substantially impairs the person's ability to ambulate. The statement or prescription must include a certification of whether the disability is temporary or permanent and information acceptable to the department to determine the type of disabled parking placard for which the applicant is eligible. The department shall determine a person's eligibility based on evidence provided by the applicant establishing legal blindness or mobility impairment.

(d) Information concerning the name or address of a person to whom a disabled parking placard is issued or in whose behalf a disabled parking placard is issued is confidential and not subject to disclosure under Chapter 552, Government Code.

(e) If a first application for a disabled parking placard under this section is made by or on behalf of a person with:

(1) a mobility problem caused by a disorder of the foot, the notarized written statement or written prescription required by Subsection (c) may be issued by a person licensed to practice podiatry in this state or a state adjacent to this state; or

(2) a disability caused by an impairment of vision as provided by Section 681.001(2), the notarized written statement or written prescription required by Subsection (c) may be issued by a person licensed to engage in the practice of optometry or the practice of therapeutic optometry in this state or a state adjacent to this state.

(f) This subsection applies only to the first application for a disabled parking placard submitted by a person. The notarized written statement or prescription may be issued by:

(1) a person acting under the delegation and supervision of a licensed physician in conformance

with Subchapter B, Chapter 157, Occupations Code; or

(2) a physician assistant licensed to practice in this state acting as the agent of a licensed physician under Section 204.202(e), Occupations Code.

(g) In this section, "practice of optometry" and "practice of therapeutic optometry" have the meanings assigned by Section 351.002, Occupations Code.

Sec. 681.0031. Applicant's Identification.

(a) The applicant shall include on the application the applicant's:

(1) driver's license number or the number of a personal identification card issued to the applicant under Chapter 521;

(2) military identification number; or

(3) driver's license number of a driver's license issued by another state or country if the applicant is not a resident of this state and is seeking medical treatment in this state.

(b) The county assessor-collector shall record on any disabled parking placard issued to the applicant the following information in the following order:

(1) the county number assigned by the comptroller to the county issuing the placard;

(2) the first four digits of the applicant's driver's license number, personal identification card number, or military identification number; and

(3) the applicant's initials.

Sec. 681.0032. Issuance of Disabled Parking Placards to Certain Institutions.

(a) The department shall provide for the issuance of disabled parking placards described by Section 681.002 for a van or bus operated by an institution, facility, or residential retirement community for the elderly in which a person described by Section 504.201(a) resides, including an institution licensed under Chapter 242, Health and Safety Code, and a facility licensed under Chapter 246 or 247 of that code.

(b) The application for a disabled parking placard must be made in the manner provided by Section 681.003(b) and be accompanied by a written statement signed by the administrator or manager of the institution, facility, or retirement community certifying to the department that the institution, facility, or retirement community regularly transports, as a part of the services that the institution, facility, or retirement community provides, one or more persons described by Section 504.201(a) who reside in the institution, facility, or retirement community. The department shall determine the eligibility of the institution, facility, or retirement community on the evidence the applicant provides.

Sec. 681.004. Issuance of Parking Placard; Expiration. [Effective until January 1, 2022]

(a) A person with a permanent disability may receive:

(1) two disabled parking placards, if the person does not receive a set of special license plates under Section 504.201;

(2) one disabled parking placard, if the person receives a set of special license plates under Section 504.201; or

(3) two disabled parking placards, if the person receives two sets of special license plates under Section 504.202.

(b) A person with a temporary disability may receive two disabled parking placards.

(c) A disabled parking placard issued to a person with a permanent disability:

(1) is valid for:

(A) four years for a resident of this state; and

(B) six months for a person who is not a resident of this state; and

(2) shall be replaced or renewed on request of the person to whom the initial card was issued without presentation of evidence of eligibility.

(d) A disabled parking placard issued to a person with a temporary disability expires after the period set by the department and may be renewed at the end of that period if the disability remains as evidenced by a physician's statement or prescription submitted as required for a first application under Section 681.003(c).

(e) The department shall include with each disabled parking placard a document that provides:

(1) information on laws governing parking for persons with disabilities; and

(2) instructions for reporting alleged violations of this chapter.

Sec. 681.004. Issuance of Parking Placard; Expiration. [Effective January 1, 2022]

(a) A person with a permanent disability may receive:

(1) two disabled parking placards, if the person does not receive a set of special license plates under Section 504.201;

(2) one disabled parking placard, if the person receives a set of special license plates under Section 504.201; or

Transportation Code

(3) two disabled parking placards, if the person receives two sets of special license plates under Section 504.202(b-1).

(b) A person with a temporary disability may receive two disabled parking placards.

(c) A disabled parking placard issued to a person with a permanent disability:

(1) is valid for:

(A) four years for a resident of this state; and

(B) six months for a person who is not a resident of this state; and

(2) shall be replaced or renewed on request of the person to whom the initial card was issued without presentation of evidence of eligibility.

(d) A disabled parking placard issued to a person with a temporary disability expires after the period set by the department and may be renewed at the end of that period if the disability remains as evidenced by a physician's statement or prescription submitted as required for a first application under Section 681.003(c).

(e) The department shall include with each disabled parking placard a document that provides:

(1) information on laws governing parking for persons with disabilities; and

(2) instructions for reporting alleged violations of this chapter.

Sec. 681.005. Duties of County Assessor-Collector.

Each county assessor-collector shall send to the department each fee collected under Section 681.003, to be deposited in the Texas Department of Motor Vehicles fund to defray the cost of providing the disabled parking placard.

Sec. 681.006. Parking Privileges: Persons with Disabilities.

(a) Subject to Section 681.009(e), a vehicle may be parked for an unlimited period in a parking space or area that is designated specifically for persons with physical disabilities if:

(1) the vehicle is being operated by or for the transportation of a person with a disability; and

(2) there are:

(A) displayed on the vehicle special license plates issued under Section 504.201; or

(B) placed on the rearview mirror of the vehicle's front windshield a disabled parking placard.

(b) The owner of a vehicle is exempt from the payment of a fee or penalty imposed by a governmental unit for parking at a meter if:

(1) the vehicle is being operated by or for the transportation of a person with a disability; and

(2) there are:

(A) displayed on the vehicle special license plates issued under Section 504.201; or

(B) placed on the rearview mirror of the vehicle's front windshield a disabled parking placard.

(c) The exemption provided by Subsection (b) or (e) does not apply to a fee or penalty:

(1) imposed by a branch of the United States government; or

(2) imposed by a governmental unit for parking at a meter, in a parking garage or lot, or in a space located within the boundaries of a municipal airport.

(d) This section does not permit a vehicle to be parked at a time when or a place where parking is prohibited.

(e) A governmental unit may provide by ordinance or order that the exemption provided by Subsection (b) also applies to payment of a fee or penalty imposed by the governmental unit for parking in a parking garage or lot or in a space with a limitation on the length of time for parking.

Sec. 681.007. Parking Privileges: Vehicles Displaying International Symbol of Access.

A vehicle may be parked and is exempt from the payment of a fee or penalty in the same manner as a vehicle that has displayed on the vehicle special license plates issued under Section 504.201 or a disabled parking placard as provided by Section 681.006 if there is displayed on the vehicle a license plate or placard that:

(1) bears the international symbol of access; and

(2) is issued by a state or by a state or province of a foreign country to the owner or operator of the vehicle for the transportation of a person with a disability.

Sec. 681.008. Parking Privileges: Certain Veterans and Military Award Recipients. [Effective until January 1, 2022]

(a) A vehicle may be parked for an unlimited period in a parking space or area that is designated specifically for persons with physical disabilities if the vehicle:

(1) is being operated by or for the transportation of:

(A) the person who registered the vehicle under Section 504.202(a) or a person described by Section 504.202(b) if the vehicle is registered under that subsection; and

(B) displays special license plates issued under Section 504.202; or

Transportation Code

(2) displays license plates issued by another state of the United States that indicate on the face of the license plates that the owner or operator of the vehicle is a disabled veteran of the United States armed forces.

(a-1) A vehicle described by Subsection (a) may be parked for an unlimited period in a parking space or area that is designated specifically for persons with physical disabilities on the property of an institution of higher education, as defined by Section 61.003, Education Code, regardless of whether a permit is generally required for the use of the space or area. An institution of higher education may require a vehicle described by Subsection (a) to display a parking permit issued by the institution specifically for the purpose of implementing this subsection, but may not charge a fee for the permit. This subsection does not entitle a person to park a vehicle described by Subsection (a) in a parking space or area that has not been designated specifically for persons with physical disabilities on the property of the institution if the vehicle has not been granted or assigned a parking permit required by the institution.

(a-2) Subsection (a-1) does not apply to a parking space or area located in:

(1) a controlled access parking facility if at least 50 percent of the number of parking spaces or areas designated specifically for persons with physical disabilities on the property of the institution of higher education are located outside a controlled access parking facility;

(2) an area temporarily designated for special event parking; or

(3) an area where parking is temporarily prohibited for health or safety concerns.

(b) A vehicle on which license plates described by Subsection (a)(2) or issued under Section 504.202, 504.308, 504.310, 504.315, 504.316, or 504.319 are displayed is exempt from the payment of a parking fee collected through a parking meter charged by a governmental authority other than a branch of the federal government, when being operated by or for the transportation of:

(1) the person who registered the vehicle under Section 504.202(a), 504.308, 504.310, 504.315, 504.316, or 504.319;

(2) a person described in Section 504.202(b) if the vehicle is registered under that subsection; or

(3) the owner or operator of a vehicle displaying license plates described by Subsection (a)(2).

(c) This section does not permit a vehicle to be parked at a time when or a place where parking is prohibited.

(d) A governmental unit may provide by ordinance or order that the exemption provided by Subsection (b) also applies to payment of a fee or penalty imposed by the governmental unit for parking in a parking garage or lot or in a space with a limitation on the length of time for parking.

Sec. 681.008. Parking Privileges: Certain Veterans and Military Award Recipients. [Effective January 1, 2022]

(a) A vehicle may be parked for an unlimited period in a parking space or area that is designated specifically for persons with physical disabilities if:

(1) the vehicle:

(A) displays special license plates issued under Section 504.202(b-1); and

(B) is being operated by or for the transportation of the person to whom the plates were issued; or

(2) the vehicle displays license plates issued by another state of the United States that indicate on the face of the license plates that the owner or operator of the vehicle is a disabled veteran of the United States armed forces.

(a-1) A vehicle described by Subsection (a) may be parked for an unlimited period in a parking space or area that is designated specifically for persons with physical disabilities on the property of an institution of higher education, as defined by Section 61.003, Education Code, regardless of whether a permit is generally required for the use of the space or area. An institution of higher education may require a vehicle described by Subsection (a) to display a parking permit issued by the institution specifically for the purpose of implementing this subsection, but may not charge a fee for the permit. This subsection does not entitle a person to park a vehicle described by Subsection (a) in a parking space or area that has not been designated specifically for persons with physical disabilities on the property of the institution if the vehicle has not been granted or assigned a parking permit required by the institution.

(a-2) Subsection (a-1) does not apply to a parking space or area located in:

(1) a controlled access parking facility if at least 50 percent of the number of parking spaces or areas designated specifically for persons with physical disabilities on the property of the institution of higher education are located outside a controlled access parking facility;

(2) an area temporarily designated for special event parking; or

(3) an area where parking is temporarily prohibited for health or safety concerns.

(b) A vehicle on which license plates described by Subsection (a)(2) or issued under Section 504.202, 504.308, 504.310, 504.315, 504.316, or 504.319 are displayed is exempt from the payment of a parking fee collected through a parking meter charged by a governmental authority other than a branch of the federal government, when being operated by or for the transportation of:

(1) the person who registered the vehicle under Section 504.202(a), 504.308, 504.310, 504.315, 504.316, or 504.319;

(2) a person described in Section 504.202(b) if the vehicle is registered under that subsection; or

(3) the owner or operator of a vehicle displaying license plates described by Subsection (a)(2).

(c) This section does not permit a vehicle to be parked at a time when or a place where parking is prohibited.

(d) A governmental unit may provide by ordinance or order that the exemption provided by Subsection (b) also applies to payment of a fee or penalty imposed by the governmental unit for parking in a parking garage or lot or in a space with a limitation on the length of time for parking.

Sec. 681.009. Designation of Parking Spaces by Political Subdivision or Private Property Owner. [Effective until January 1, 2022]

(a) A political subdivision or a person who owns or controls property used for parking may designate one or more parking spaces or a parking area for the exclusive use of vehicles transporting persons with disabilities.

(b) A political subdivision must designate a parking space or area by conforming to the standards and specifications adopted by the Texas Commission of Licensing and Regulation under Section 469.052, Government Code, relating to the identification and dimensions of parking spaces for persons with disabilities. A person who owns or controls private property used for parking may designate a parking space or area without conforming to those standards and specifications, unless required to conform by law.

(c) A political subdivision may require a private property owner or a person who controls property used for parking:

(1) to designate one or more parking spaces or a parking area for the exclusive use of vehicles transporting persons with disabilities; or

(2) to conform to the standards and specifications referred to in Subsection (b) when designating a parking space or area for persons with disabilities.

(d) The department shall provide at cost a design and stencil for use by a political subdivision or person who owns or controls property used for parking to designate spaces as provided by this section.

(e) Parking spaces or areas designated for the exclusive use of vehicles transporting persons with disabilities may be used by vehicles displaying a white on blue shield disabled parking placard, license plates issued under Section 504.201 or 504.202, or a white on red shield disabled parking placard.

Sec. 681.009. Designation of Parking Spaces by Political Subdivision or Private Property Owner. [Effective January 1, 2022]

(a) A political subdivision or a person who owns or controls property used for parking may designate one or more parking spaces or a parking area for the exclusive use of vehicles transporting persons with disabilities.

(b) A political subdivision must designate a parking space or area by conforming to the standards and specifications adopted by the Texas Commission of Licensing and Regulation under Section 469.052, Government Code, relating to the identification and dimensions of parking spaces for persons with disabilities. A person who owns or controls private property used for parking may designate a parking space or area without conforming to those standards and specifications, unless required to conform by law.

(c) A political subdivision may require a private property owner or a person who controls property used for parking:

(1) to designate one or more parking spaces or a parking area for the exclusive use of vehicles transporting persons with disabilities; or

(2) to conform to the standards and specifications referred to in Subsection (b) when designating a parking space or area for persons with disabilities.

(d) The department shall provide at cost a design and stencil for use by a political subdivision or person who owns or controls property used for parking to designate spaces as provided by this section.

(e) Parking spaces or areas designated for the exclusive use of vehicles transporting persons with disabilities may be used by vehicles displaying a white on blue shield disabled parking placard, license plates issued under Section 504.201 or 504.202(b-1), or a white on red shield disabled parking placard.

Sec. 681.010. Enforcement.

(a) A peace officer or a person designated by a political subdivision to enforce parking regulations may file a charge against a person who commits an offense under this chapter at a parking space or area designated as provided by Section 681.009.

(b) A security officer commissioned under Chapter 1702, Occupations Code, and employed by the owner of private property may file a charge against a person who commits an offense under this chapter at a parking space or area designated by the owner of the property as provided by Section 681.009.

Sec. 681.0101. Enforcement by Certain Appointed Persons.

(a) A political subdivision may appoint a person to have authority to file a charge against a person who commits an offense under this chapter.

(b) A person appointed under this section must:

(1) be a United States citizen of good moral character who has not been convicted of a felony;

(2) take and subscribe to an oath of office that the political subdivision prescribes; and

(3) successfully complete a training program of at least four hours in length developed by the political subdivision.

(c) A person appointed under this section:

(1) is not a peace officer;

(2) has no authority other than the authority applicable to a citizen to enforce a law other than this chapter; and

(3) may not carry a weapon while performing duties under this section.

(d) A person appointed under this section is not entitled to compensation for performing duties under this section or to indemnification from the political subdivision or the state for injury or property damage the person sustains or liability the person incurs in performing duties under this section.

(e) The political subdivision and the state are not liable for any damage arising from an act or omission of a person appointed under Subsection (a) in performing duties under this section.

Sec. 681.011. Offenses; Presumption. [Effective until January 1, 2022]

(a) A person commits an offense if:

(1) the person stands a vehicle on which are displayed license plates issued under Section 504.201 or 504.202 or a disabled parking placard in a parking space or area designated specifically for persons with disabilities by:

(A) a political subdivision; or

(B) a person who owns or controls private property used for parking as to which a political subdivision has provided for the application of this section under Subsection (f); and

(2) the standing of the vehicle in that parking space or area is not authorized by Section 681.006, 681.007, or 681.008.

(b) A person commits an offense if the person stands a vehicle on which license plates issued under Section 504.201 or 504.202 are not displayed and a disabled parking placard is not displayed in a parking space or area designated specifically for individuals with disabilities by:

(1) a political subdivision; or

(2) a person who owns or controls private property used for parking as to which a political subdivision has provided for the application of this section under Subsection (f).

(c) A person commits an offense if the person stands a vehicle so that the vehicle blocks an architectural improvement designed to aid persons with disabilities, including an access aisle or curb ramp.

(d) A person commits an offense if the person lends a disabled parking placard issued to the person to a person who uses the placard in violation of this section.

(e) In a prosecution under this section, it is presumed that the registered owner of the motor vehicle is the person who left the vehicle standing at the time and place the offense occurred.

(f) A political subdivision may provide that this section applies to a parking space or area for persons with disabilities on private property that is designated in compliance with the identification requirements referred to in Section 681.009(b).

(g) Except as provided by Subsections (h)—(k), an offense under this section is a misdemeanor punishable by a fine of not less than $500 or more than $750.

(h) If it is shown on the trial of an offense under this section that the person has been previously convicted one time of an offense under this section, the offense is punishable by:

(1) **[2 Versions: As added by Acts 2009, 81st Leg., ch. 1160]** a fine of not less than $550 or more than $800; and

(1) **[2 Versions: As added by Acts 2009, 81st Leg., ch. 1336]** a fine of not less than $500 or more than $800; and

(2) 10 hours of community service.

(i) If it is shown on the trial of an offense under this section that the person has been previously convicted two times of an offense under this section, the offense is punishable by:

(1) a fine of not less than $550 or more than $800; and

(2) **[2 Versions: As amended by Acts 2009, 81st Leg., ch. 1160]** not less than 20 or more than 30 hours of community service.

(2) **[2 Versions: As amended by Acts 2009, 81st Leg., ch. 1336]** 20 hours of community service.

Transportation Code

(j) If it is shown on the trial of an offense under this section that the person has been previously convicted three times of an offense under this section, the offense is punishable by:

(1) a fine of not less than $800 or more than $1,100; and

(2) **[2 Versions: As amended by Acts 2009, 81st Leg., ch. 1160]** 50 hours of community service.

(2) **[2 Versions: As amended by Acts 2009, 81st Leg., ch. 1336]** 30 hours of community service.

(k) If it is shown on the trial of an offense under this section that the person has been previously convicted four times of an offense under this section, the offense is punishable by a fine of $1,250 and 50 hours of community service.

(*l*) A person commits an offense if the person:

(1) stands a vehicle on which are displayed license plates issued under Section 504.201 or a disabled parking placard in a parking space or area for which this chapter creates an exemption from payment of a fee or penalty imposed by a governmental unit;

(2) does not have a disability;

(3) is not transporting a person with disability; and

(4) does not pay any applicable fee related to standing in the space or area imposed by a governmental unit or exceeds a limitation on the length of time for standing in the space or area.

Sec. 681.011. Offenses; Presumption. [Effective January 1, 2022]

(a) A person commits an offense if:

(1) the person stands a vehicle on which are displayed license plates issued under Section 504.201 or 504.202(b-1) or a disabled parking placard in a parking space or area designated specifically for persons with disabilities by:

(A) a political subdivision; or

(B) a person who owns or controls private property used for parking as to which a political subdivision has provided for the application of this section under Subsection (f); and

(2) the standing of the vehicle in that parking space or area is not authorized by Section 681.006, 681.007, or 681.008.

(b) A person commits an offense if the person stands a vehicle on which license plates issued under Section 504.201 or 504.202(b-1) are not displayed and a disabled parking placard is not displayed in a parking space or area designated specifically for individuals with disabilities by:

(1) a political subdivision; or

(2) a person who owns or controls private property used for parking as to which a political subdivision has provided for the application of this section under Subsection (f).

(c) A person commits an offense if the person stands a vehicle so that the vehicle blocks an architectural improvement designed to aid persons with disabilities, including an access aisle or curb ramp.

(d) A person commits an offense if the person lends a disabled parking placard issued to the person to a person who uses the placard in violation of this section.

(e) In a prosecution under this section, it is presumed that the registered owner of the motor vehicle is the person who left the vehicle standing at the time and place the offense occurred.

(f) A political subdivision may provide that this section applies to a parking space or area for persons with disabilities on private property that is designated in compliance with the identification requirements referred to in Section 681.009(b).

(g) Except as provided by Subsections (h)—(k), an offense under this section is a misdemeanor punishable by a fine of not less than $500 or more than $750.

(h) If it is shown on the trial of an offense under this section that the person has been previously convicted one time of an offense under this section, the offense is punishable by:

(1) **[2 Versions: As added by Acts 2009, 81st Leg., ch. 1160]** a fine of not less than $550 or more than $800; and

(1) **[2 Versions: As added by Acts 2009, 81st Leg., ch. 1336]** a fine of not less than $500 or more than $800; and

(2) 10 hours of community service.

(i) If it is shown on the trial of an offense under this section that the person has been previously convicted two times of an offense under this section, the offense is punishable by:

(1) a fine of not less than $550 or more than $800; and

(2) **[2 Versions: As amended by Acts 2009, 81st Leg., ch. 1160]** not less than 20 or more than 30 hours of community service.

(2) **[2 Versions: As amended by Acts 2009, 81st Leg., ch. 1336]** 20 hours of community service.

(j) If it is shown on the trial of an offense under this section that the person has been previously convicted three times of an offense under this section, the offense is punishable by:

(1) a fine of not less than $800 or more than $1,100; and

(2) **[2 Versions: As amended by Acts 2009, 81st Leg., ch. 1160]** 50 hours of community service.

(2) **[2 Versions: As amended by Acts 2009, 81st Leg., ch. 1336]** 30 hours of community service.

(k) If it is shown on the trial of an offense under this section that the person has been previously convicted four times of an offense under this section, the offense is punishable by a fine of $1,250 and 50 hours of community service.

(*l*) A person commits an offense if the person:

(1) stands a vehicle on which are displayed license plates issued under Section 504.201 or 504.202(b-1) or a disabled parking placard in a parking space or area for which this chapter creates an exemption from payment of a fee or penalty imposed by a governmental unit;

(2) does not have a disability;

(3) is not transporting a person with disability; and

(4) does not pay any applicable fee related to standing in the space or area imposed by a governmental unit or exceeds a limitation on the length of time for standing in the space or area.

Sec. 681.0111. Manufacture, Sale, Possession, or Use of Counterfeit or Altered Placard.

(a) A person commits an offense if, without the department's authorization, the person:

(1) manufactures, sells, or possesses a placard that is deceptively similar to a disabled parking placard; or

(2) alters a genuine disabled parking placard.

(b) A person commits an offense if the person knowingly parks a vehicle displaying a counterfeit or altered placard in a parking space or area designated specifically for persons with disabilities.

(c) An offense under Subsection (a) is a Class A misdemeanor. An offense under Subsection (b) is a Class C misdemeanor.

(d) For purposes of this section, a placard is deceptively similar to a disabled parking placard if the placard is not a genuine disabled parking placard but a reasonable person would presume that it is a genuine disabled parking placard.

Sec. 681.012. Seizure and Revocation of Placard.

(a) A law enforcement officer who believes that an offense under Section 681.011(a) or (d) has occurred in the officer's presence shall seize any disabled parking placard involved in the offense. Not later than 48 hours after the seizure, the officer shall determine whether probable cause existed to believe that the offense was committed. If the officer does not find that probable cause existed, the officer shall promptly return each placard to the person from whom it was seized. If the officer finds that probable cause existed, the officer, not later than the fifth day after the date of the seizure, shall destroy the placard and notify the department.

(a-1) A peace officer may seize a disabled parking placard from a person who operates a vehicle on which a disabled parking placard is displayed if the peace officer determines by inspecting the person's driver's license, personal identification certificate, or military identification that the disabled parking placard does not contain the first four digits of the driver's license number, personal identification certificate number, or military identification number and the initials of:

(1) the person operating the vehicle;

(2) the applicant on behalf of a person being transported by the vehicle; or

(3) a person being transported by the vehicle.

(a-2) A peace officer shall destroy a seized placard and notify the department.

(b) On seizure of a placard under Subsection (a) or (a-1), a placard is revoked. A person from whom the placard was seized may apply for a new placard by submitting an application under Section 681.003.

Sec. 681.013. Dismissal of Charge; Fine.

(a) In this section, "working day" means any day other than a Saturday, a Sunday, or a holiday on which county offices are closed.

(b) The court shall:

(1) dismiss a charge for an offense under Section 681.011(b)(1) if:

(A) the vehicle displayed a disabled parking placard that was not valid as expired;

(B) the defendant remedies the defect by renewing the expired disabled parking placard within 20 working days from the date of the offense or before the defendant's first court appearance date, whichever is later; and

(C) the disabled parking placard has not been expired for more than 60 days; and

(2) assess a reimbursement fee not to exceed $20 when the charge has been remedied.

(c) Notwithstanding Subsection (b)(1)(C), the court may dismiss a charge of unlawfully parking a vehicle in a space designated specifically for persons with disabilities, if at the time of the offense the defendant's vehicle displays a disabled parking placard that has been expired for more than 60 days.

CHAPTER 682 ADMINISTRATIVE ADJUDICATION OF VEHICLE PARKING AND STOPPING OFFENSES

Sec. 682.001. [2 Versions: As amended by Acts 1999, 76th Leg., ch. 156] Applicability.

This chapter applies only to:

(1) a municipality that:

(A) has a population greater than 30,000 and operates under a council-manager form of government; or

(B) has a population of 500,000 or more; and

(2) an airport operated by a joint board to which Section 22.074(d) applies.

Sec. 682.001. [2 Versions: As amended by Acts 1999, 76th Leg., ch. 310] Applicability.

This chapter applies only to a municipality that has a population greater than 30,000.

Sec. 682.002. Civil Offense.

(a) A municipality may declare the violation of a municipal ordinance relating to parking or stopping a vehicle to be a civil offense.

(b) A joint board to which Section 22.074(d) applies may declare the violation of a resolution, rule, or order of the joint board relating to parking or stopping a vehicle to be a civil offense.

Sec. 682.003. Adoption of Hearing Procedure.

A municipality may by ordinance or a joint board may by resolution, rule, or order establish an administrative adjudication hearing procedure under which a civil fine may be imposed.

Sec. 682.004. Content of Ordinance.

An ordinance, resolution, rule, or order adopted under this chapter must provide that a person charged with violating a parking or stopping ordinance, resolution, rule, or order is entitled to a hearing and provide for:

(1) the period during which a hearing must be held;

(2) the appointment of a hearing officer with authority to administer oaths and issue orders compelling the attendance of witnesses and the production of documents; and

(3) the amount and disposition of civil fines, costs, and fees.

Sec. 682.005. Enforcement of Order Concerning Witnesses and Documents.

A municipal court may enforce an order of the hearing officer compelling the attendance of a witness or the production of a document.

Sec. 682.006. Citation or Summons.

(a) A citation or summons issued for a vehicle parking or stopping civil offense under this chapter must:

(1) provide information as to the time and place of an administrative adjudication hearing; and

(2) contain a notification that the person charged with the civil offense has the right to an instanter hearing.

(b) The original or any copy of the summons or citation shall be kept as a record in the ordinary course of business of the municipality and is rebuttable proof of the facts it contains.

Sec. 682.007. Appearance at Hearing.

(a) A person charged with a civil offense who fails to appear at an administrative adjudication hearing authorized under this chapter is considered to admit liability for the offense charged.

(b) The person who issued the citation or summons is not required to attend an instanter hearing.

Sec. 682.008. Presumptions.

In an administrative adjudication hearing under this chapter:

(1) it is presumed that the registered owner of the motor vehicle is the person who parked or stopped the vehicle at the time and place of the offense charged; and

(2) the Texas Department of Motor Vehicles' computer-generated record of the registered vehicle owner is prima facie evidence of the contents of the record.

Sec. 682.009. Order.

(a) The hearing officer at an administrative adjudication hearing under this chapter shall issue an order stating:

(1) whether the person charged with the violation is liable for the violation; and

Transportation Code

(2) the amount of any fine, cost, or fee assessed against the person.

(b) The order issued under Subsection (a) may be filed with the clerk or secretary of the municipality or a person designated by the joint board. The clerk, secretary, or designated person shall keep the order in a separate index and file. The order may be recorded using microfilm, microfiche, or data processing techniques.

Sec. 682.010. Enforcement.

(a) An order filed under Section 682.009, or a fine, cost, or fee imposed under this chapter following a failure by the person charged to appear within the time specified by a municipality's ordinance, resolution, rule, or order, may be enforced by:

(1) impounding the vehicle if the offender has committed three or more vehicle parking or stopping offenses in a calendar year;

(2) placing a device on the vehicle that prohibits movement of the motor vehicle;

(3) imposing an additional fine if the original fine is not paid within a specified time;

(4) denying issuance of or revoking a parking or operating permit, as applicable; or

(5) filing an action to collect the fine, cost, or fee in a court of competent jurisdiction.

(b) An action to collect a fine, cost, or fee under Subsection (a)(5) must be brought:

(1) in the name of the municipality served by the hearing officer; and

(2) in a county in which all or part of that municipality is located.

Sec. 682.011. Appeal.

(a) A person whom the hearing officer determines to be in violation of a vehicle parking or stopping ordinance may appeal the determination by filing a petition with the clerk of a municipal court and paying the costs required by law for municipal court not later than the 30th day after the date on which the order is filed.

(b) The municipal court clerk shall schedule a hearing and notify each party of the date, time, and place of the hearing.

(c) An appeal does not stay enforcement and collection of the judgment unless the person, before appealing, posts bond with, as applicable:

(1) the agency of the municipality designated by ordinance to accept payment for a violation of a parking or stopping ordinance; or

(2) the agency of the joint board designated by the resolution, rule, or order to accept payment for a violation of a parking or stopping resolution, rule, or order.

CHAPTER 683 ABANDONED MOTOR VEHICLES

SUBCHAPTER A GENERAL PROVISIONS

Sec. 683.001. Definitions.

In this chapter:

(1) "Department" means the Texas Department of Motor Vehicles.

(2) "Garagekeeper" means an owner or operator of a storage facility.

(3) "Law enforcement agency" means:

(A) the Department of Public Safety;

(B) the police department of a municipality;

(C) the police department of an institution of higher education; or

(D) a sheriff or a constable.

(4) "Motor vehicle" means a vehicle that is subject to registration under Chapter 501.

(5) "Motor vehicle demolisher" means a person in the business of:

(A) converting motor vehicles into processed scrap or scrap metal; or

(B) wrecking or dismantling motor vehicles.

(6) "Outboard motor" means an outboard motor subject to registration under Chapter 31, Parks and Wildlife Code.

(7) "Storage facility" includes a garage, parking lot, or establishment for the servicing, repairing, or parking of motor vehicles.

(8) "Watercraft" means a vessel subject to registration under Chapter 31, Parks and Wildlife Code.

(9) "Abandoned nuisance vehicle" means a motor vehicle that is at least 10 years old and is of a condition only to be junked, crushed, or dismantled.

(10) "Vehicle storage facility" means a vehicle storage facility, as defined by Section 2303.002, Occupations Code, that is operated by a person who holds a license issued under Chapter 2303 of that code to operate that vehicle storage facility.

(11) "Aircraft" has the meaning assigned by Section 24.001.

Sec. 683.002. Abandoned Motor Vehicle.

(a) For the purposes of this chapter, a motor vehicle is abandoned if the motor vehicle:

(1) is inoperable, is more than five years old, and has been left unattended on public property for more than 48 hours;

Transportation Code

(2) has remained illegally on public property for more than 48 hours;

(3) has remained on private property without the consent of the owner or person in charge of the property for more than 48 hours;

(4) has been left unattended on the right-of-way of a designated county, state, or federal highway for more than 48 hours;

(5) has been left unattended for more than 24 hours on the right-of-way of a turnpike project constructed and maintained by the Texas Turnpike Authority division of the Texas Department of Transportation or a controlled access highway; or

(6) is considered an abandoned motor vehicle under Section 644.153(r).

(b) In this section, "controlled access highway" has the meaning assigned by Section 541.302.

Sec. 683.003. Conflict of Laws; Effect on Other Laws.

(a) Sections 683.051—683.055 may not be read as conflicting with Sections 683.074—683.078.

(b) This chapter does not affect a law authorizing the immediate removal of a vehicle left on public property that is an obstruction to traffic.

SUBCHAPTER B ABANDONED MOTOR VEHICLES: SEIZURE AND AUCTION

Sec. 683.011. Authority to Take Abandoned Motor Vehicle into Custody.

(a) A law enforcement agency may take into custody an abandoned motor vehicle, aircraft, watercraft, or outboard motor found on public or private property.

(b) A law enforcement agency may use agency personnel, equipment, and facilities or contract for other personnel, equipment, and facilities to remove, preserve, store, send notice regarding, and dispose of an abandoned motor vehicle, aircraft, watercraft, or outboard motor taken into custody by the agency under this subchapter.

Sec. 683.012. Taking Abandoned Motor Vehicle into Custody: Notice.

(a) A law enforcement agency shall send notice of abandonment to:

(1) the last known registered owner of each motor vehicle, aircraft, watercraft, or outboard motor taken into custody by the agency or for which a report is received under Section 683.031; and

(2) each lienholder recorded:

(A) under Chapter 501 for the motor vehicle;

(B) with the Federal Aviation Administration or the secretary of state for the aircraft; or

(C) under Chapter 31, Parks and Wildlife Code, for the watercraft or outboard motor.

(a-1) A law enforcement agency that takes into custody an aircraft shall contact the Federal Aviation Administration in the manner described by Section 22.901 to attempt to identify the owner of the aircraft before sending the notice required by Subsection (a).

(b) The notice under Subsection (a) must:

(1) be sent by certified mail not later than the 10th day after the date the agency:

(A) takes the abandoned motor vehicle, aircraft, watercraft, or outboard motor into custody; or

(B) receives the report under Section 683.031;

(2) specify the year, make, model, and identification number of the item;

(3) give the location of the facility where the item is being held;

(4) inform the owner and lienholder of the right to claim the item not later than the 20th day after the date of the notice on payment of:

(A) towing, preservation, and storage charges; or

(B) garagekeeper's charges and fees under Section 683.032 and, if the vehicle is a commercial motor vehicle impounded under Section 644.153(q), the delinquent administrative penalty and costs; and

(5) state that failure of the owner or lienholder to claim the item during the period specified by Subdivision (4) is:

(A) a waiver by that person of all right, title, and interest in the item; and

(B) consent to the sale of the item at a public auction.

(c) Notice by publication in one newspaper of general circulation in the area where the motor vehicle, aircraft, watercraft, or outboard motor was abandoned is sufficient notice under this section if:

(1) the identity of the last registered owner cannot be determined;

(2) the registration has no address for the owner; or

(3) the determination with reasonable certainty of the identity and address of all lienholders is impossible.

(d) Notice by publication:

(1) must be published in the same period that is required by Subsection (b) for notice by certified mail and contain all of the information required by that subsection; and

Transportation Code

(2) may contain a list of more than one abandoned motor vehicle, aircraft, watercraft, or outboard motor.

(e) A law enforcement agency is not required to send a notice, as otherwise required by Subsection (a), if the agency has received notice from a vehicle storage facility that an application has or will be submitted to the department for the disposal of the vehicle.

(f) In addition to the notice required under Subsection (a), if a law enforcement agency takes an abandoned motor vehicle into custody, the agency shall notify a person that files a theft report or similar report prepared by any law enforcement agency for the vehicle of that fact. The notice must be sent by regular mail on the next business day after the agency takes the vehicle into custody. The law enforcement agency shall also provide the name and address of the person that filed the theft report or similar report to the vehicle storage facility or governmental vehicle storage facility that is storing the vehicle.

Sec. 683.013. Storage Fees.

A law enforcement agency or the agent of a law enforcement agency that takes into custody an abandoned motor vehicle, aircraft, watercraft, or outboard motor is entitled to reasonable storage fees:

(1) for not more than 10 days, beginning on the day the item is taken into custody and ending on the day the required notice is mailed; and

(2) beginning on the day after the day the agency mails notice and ending on the day accrued charges are paid and the vehicle, aircraft, watercraft, or outboard motor is removed.

Sec. 683.014. Auction or Use of Abandoned Items; Waiver of Rights.

(a) If an abandoned motor vehicle, aircraft, watercraft, or outboard motor is not claimed under Section 683.012:

(1) the owner or lienholder:

(A) waives all rights and interests in the item; and

(B) consents to the sale of the item by public auction or the transfer of the item, if a watercraft, as provided by Subsection (d); and

(2) the law enforcement agency may sell the item at a public auction, transfer the item, if a watercraft, as provided by Subsection (d), or use the item as provided by Section 683.016.

(b) Proper notice of the auction shall be given. A garagekeeper who has a garagekeeper's lien shall be notified of the time and place of the auction.

(c) The purchaser of a motor vehicle, aircraft, watercraft, or outboard motor:

(1) takes title free and clear of all liens and claims of ownership;

(2) shall receive a sales receipt from the law enforcement agency; and

(3) is entitled to register the motor vehicle, aircraft, watercraft, or outboard motor with and receive a certificate of title from the appropriate authority.

(d) On consent of the Parks and Wildlife Department, the law enforcement agency may transfer a watercraft that is not claimed under Section 683.012 to the Parks and Wildlife Department for use as part of an artificial reef under Chapter 89, Parks and Wildlife Code, or for other use by the Parks and Wildlife Department permitted under the Parks and Wildlife Code. On transfer of the watercraft, the Parks and Wildlife Department:

(1) takes title free and clear of all liens and claims of ownership; and

(2) is entitled to register the watercraft and receive a certificate of title.

Sec. 683.015. Auction Proceeds.

(a) A law enforcement agency is entitled to reimbursement from the proceeds of the sale of an abandoned motor vehicle, aircraft, watercraft, or outboard motor for:

(1) the cost of the auction;

(2) towing, preservation, and storage fees resulting from the taking into custody;

(3) the cost of notice or publication as required by Section 683.012; and

(4) any compensation made by the agency under Subsection (f) to property owners whose property was damaged as a result of a pursuit involving the motor vehicle.

(b) After deducting the reimbursement allowed under Subsection (a), the proceeds of the sale shall be held for 90 days for the owner or lienholder of the vehicle.

(c) After the period provided by Subsection (b), proceeds unclaimed by the owner or lienholder shall be deposited in an account that may be used for the payment of auction, towing, preservation, storage, and notice and publication fees resulting from taking other vehicles, aircraft, watercraft, or outboard motors into custody if the proceeds from the sale of the other items are insufficient to meet those fees.

(d) A municipality or county may transfer funds in excess of $1,000 from the account to the municipality's or county's general revenue account to be used by the law enforcement agency or, if the vehicle, aircraft, watercraft, or outboard motor was located in a county with a population of less than 150,000, by the attorney representing the state.

(e) If the vehicle is a commercial motor vehicle impounded under Section 644.153(q), the Department of Public Safety is entitled from the proceeds of the sale to an amount equal to the amount of the delinquent administrative penalty and costs.

(f) A law enforcement agency or an attorney representing the state may use funds transferred under Subsection (d) to compensate property owners whose property was damaged as a result of a pursuit involving a law enforcement agency or a federal law enforcement agency, regardless of whether the agency would be liable under Chapter 101, Civil Practice and Remedies Code.

(g) Before a law enforcement agency or an attorney representing the state may compensate a property owner under Subsection (f) using funds transferred to a county under Subsection (d), the sheriff, constable, or attorney representing the state must submit the proposed payment for compensation for consideration, and the commissioners court shall consider the proposed payment for compensation, at the next regularly scheduled meeting of the commissioners court.

(h) In this section, "attorney representing the state" means a district attorney, criminal district attorney, or county attorney performing the duties of a district attorney.

Sec. 683.016. Law Enforcement Agency Use of Certain Abandoned Motor Vehicles.

(a) The law enforcement agency that takes an abandoned motor vehicle into custody that is not claimed under Section 683.012 may:

(1) use the vehicle for agency purposes; or

(2) transfer the vehicle to any other municipal or county agency, a groundwater conservation district governed by Chapter 36, Water Code, or a school district for the use of that agency or district.

(b) The law enforcement agency shall auction the vehicle as provided by this subchapter if the law enforcement agency or the municipal or county agency, groundwater conservation district, or school district to which the vehicle was transferred under Subsection (a) discontinues use of the vehicle.

(c) This section does not apply to an abandoned vehicle on which there is a garagekeeper's lien.

(d) This section does not apply to a vehicle that is:

(1) taken into custody by a law enforcement agency located in a county with a population of 3.3 million or more; and

(2) removed to a privately owned storage facility.

(e) A law enforcement agency must comply with the notice requirements of Section 683.012 before the law enforcement agency may transfer a vehicle under Subsection (a)(2).

SUBCHAPTER C
VEHICLE ABANDONED IN STORAGE FACILITY

Sec. 683.031. Garagekeeper's Duty: Abandoned Motor Vehicles.

(a) A motor vehicle is abandoned if the vehicle is left in a storage facility operated for commercial purposes after the 10th day after the date on which:

(1) the garagekeeper gives notice by registered or certified mail, return receipt requested, to the last known registered owner of the vehicle and to each lienholder of record of the vehicle under Chapter 501 to remove the vehicle;

(2) a contract for the vehicle to remain on the premises of the facility expires; or

(3) the vehicle was left in the facility, if the vehicle was left by a person other than the registered owner or a person authorized to have possession of the vehicle under a contract of use, service, storage, or repair.

(b) If notice sent under Subsection (a)(1) is returned unclaimed by the post office, substituted notice is sufficient if published in one newspaper of general circulation in the area where the vehicle was left.

(c) The garagekeeper shall report the abandonment of the motor vehicle to a law enforcement agency with jurisdiction where the vehicle is located and shall pay a $10 fee to be used by the law enforcement agency for the cost of the notice required by this subchapter or other cost incurred in disposing of the vehicle.

(d) The garagekeeper shall retain custody of an abandoned motor vehicle until the law enforcement agency takes the vehicle into custody under Section 683.034.

Sec. 683.032. Garagekeeper's Fees and Charges.

(a) A garagekeeper who acquires custody of a motor vehicle for a purpose other than repair is entitled to towing, preservation, and notification charges and reasonable storage fees, in addition to storage fees earned under a contract, for each day:

(1) not to exceed five days, until the notice described by Section 683.031(a) is mailed; and

Transportation Code

(2) after notice is mailed, until the vehicle is removed and all accrued charges are paid.

(b) A garagekeeper who fails to report an abandoned motor vehicle to a law enforcement agency within seven days after the date it is abandoned may not claim reimbursement for storage of the vehicle.

(c) This subchapter does not impair any lien that a garagekeeper has on a vehicle except for the termination or limitation of claim for storage for the failure to report the vehicle to the law enforcement agency.

Sec. 683.033. Unauthorized Storage Fee; Offense.

(a) A person commits an offense if the person charges a storage fee for a period for which the fee is not authorized by Section 683.032.

(b) An offense under this subsection is a misdemeanor punishable by a fine of not less than $200 or more than $1,000.

Sec. 683.034. Disposal of Vehicle Abandoned in Storage Facility.

(a) A law enforcement agency shall take into custody an abandoned vehicle left in a storage facility that has not been claimed in the period provided by the notice under Section 683.012. In this section, a law enforcement agency has custody if the agency:

(1) has physical custody of the vehicle;

(2) has given notice to the storage facility that the law enforcement agency intends to dispose of the vehicle under this section; or

(3) has received a report under Section 683.031(c) and the garagekeeper has met all of the requirements of that subsection.

(b) The law enforcement agency may use the vehicle as authorized by Section 683.016 or sell the vehicle at auction as provided by Section 683.014. If a vehicle is sold, the proceeds of the sale shall first be applied to a garagekeeper's charges for providing notice regarding the vehicle and for service, towing, impoundment, storage, and repair of the vehicle.

(c) As compensation for expenses incurred in taking the vehicle into custody and selling it, the law enforcement agency shall retain:

(1) two percent of the gross proceeds of the sale of the vehicle; or

(2) all the proceeds if the gross proceeds of the sale are less than $10.

(d) Surplus proceeds shall be distributed as provided by Section 683.015.

(e) If the law enforcement agency does not take the vehicle into custody before the 31st day after the date the vehicle was reported abandoned under Section 683.031:

(1) the law enforcement agency may not take the vehicle into custody; and

(2) the storage facility may dispose of the vehicle under:

(A) Chapter 70, Property Code, except that notice under Section 683.012 satisfies the notice requirements of that chapter; or

(B) Chapter 2303, Occupations Code, if the storage facility is a vehicle storage facility.

SUBCHAPTER D DEMOLITION OF MOTOR VEHICLES

Sec. 683.051. Application for Authorization to Dispose of Certain Motor Vehicles.

A person may apply to the department for authority:

(1) to sell, give away, or dispose of a motor vehicle to a motor vehicle demolisher for demolition, wrecking, or dismantling if:

(A) the person is the recorded owner or has been transferred ownership of the motor vehicle; or

(B) the vehicle is an abandoned motor vehicle and is:

(i) in the possession of the person; or

(ii) located on property owned by the person; or

(2) to dispose of a motor vehicle to a motor vehicle demolisher for demolition, wrecking, or dismantling if:

(A) the motor vehicle is in the possession of a lienholder under:

(i) Chapter 54, 59, or 70, Property Code; or

(ii) Chapter 2303, Occupations Code;

(B) the lienholder has complied with all notification requirements of the applicable chapter to foreclose on the lien; and

(C) the lienholder determines:

(i) the motor vehicle's only residual value is as a source of parts or scrap metal; or

(ii) it is not economical to dispose of the vehicle at a public sale.

Sec. 683.052. Contents of Application; Application Fee.

(a) An application under Section 683.051 must be made in a manner prescribed by the department and include:

(1) the name and address of the applicant;

(2) the year, make, model, body style, and vehicle identification number of the vehicle, if ascertainable;

(3) a certification by the applicant that the facts stated in the application are true and that the applicant:

(A) is the recorded owner or has been transferred ownership of the vehicle if the application is submitted under Section 683.051(1)(A); or

(B) is a lienholder listed in Section 683.051(2)(A) that has complied with all applicable notification requirements if the application is submitted under Section 683.051(2);

(4) any proof required by the department to verify compliance with notification requirements described by Section 683.051(2)(B); and

(5) the physical location of the motor vehicle.

(b) The department is not required to obtain an ownership document or any other verification of ownership in the name of an applicant under Section 683.051(1)(A) if the department is able to verify that the applicant is the recorded owner in the department's automated registration and titling system.

(c) The application must be accompanied by a fee of $2, unless the application is made by a unit of government. Fees collected under this subsection shall be deposited to the credit of the Texas Department of Motor Vehicles fund.

Sec. 683.053. Department to Provide Notice.

(a) If an application is submitted to sell, give away, or dispose of an abandoned motor vehicle under Section 683.051(1)(B), the department shall:

(1) send notice to any owners and lienholders of the abandoned motor vehicle identified in the department's automated registration and titling system; or

(2) if the department has no record of owners or lienholders for the abandoned motor vehicle, publish notice of abandonment on the department's website.

(b) The notice required by Subsection (a) must include:

(1) the year, make, model, body style, and vehicle identification number of the motor vehicle;

(2) the physical location of the motor vehicle;

(3) a statement:

(A) that an application has been submitted to the department for authorization to dispose of the motor vehicle to a motor vehicle demolisher;

(B) informing the motor vehicle's owners or lienholders of the right to claim the motor vehicle not later than the 20th day after the date the notice is sent or published; and

(C) that failure to claim the motor vehicle and notify the department that the vehicle has been claimed before the 21st day after the date the notice is sent or published:

(i) waives a person's rights, title, and interest in the motor vehicle; and

(ii) is considered consent for the department to issue to the applicant a certificate of authority under Section 683.054 to dispose of the motor vehicle to a motor vehicle demolisher; and

(4) the date the notice was sent or published.

(c) The department is not required to send or publish notice for an application submitted for a motor vehicle described by Section 683.051(1)(A) or (2).

(d) Notice sent under Subsection (a)(1) must be sent by first class mail.

Sec. 683.054. Certificate of Authority to Dispose of Vehicle.

(a) The department shall issue the applicant a certificate of authority to dispose of the vehicle to a motor vehicle demolisher for demolition, wrecking, or dismantling if the application submitted under Section 683.051:

(1) is properly executed;

(2) is accompanied by the required fee under Section 683.052; and

(3) contains any proof of notification or ownership required by the department to enforce this subchapter.

(b) A motor vehicle demolisher shall accept the certificate of authority in lieu of a certificate of title for the vehicle.

Sec. 683.055. Rules and Forms.

The department may adopt rules and prescribe forms to implement Sections 683.051—683.054.

Sec. 683.056. Demolisher's Duty.

(a) A motor vehicle demolisher who acquires a motor vehicle for dismantling or demolishing shall obtain from the person delivering the vehicle:

(1) the motor vehicle's certificate of title;

(2) a sales receipt for the motor vehicle;

(3) a transfer document for the vehicle as provided by Subchapter B or Subchapter E; or

(4) a certificate of authority for the disposal of the motor vehicle.

(b) A demolisher is not required to obtain a certificate of title for the vehicle in the demolisher's name.

(c) On the department's demand, the demolisher shall surrender for cancellation the certificate of title or certificate of authority.

(d) The department shall adopt rules and forms necessary to regulate the surrender of auction sales receipts and certificates of title.

Sec. 683.057. Demolisher's Records; Offense.

(a) A motor vehicle demolisher shall keep a record of a motor vehicle that is acquired in the course of business.

(b) The record must contain:

(1) the name and address of the person from whom the vehicle was acquired; and

(2) the date of acquisition of the vehicle.

(c) The demolisher shall keep the record until the first anniversary of the date of acquisition of the vehicle.

(d) The record shall be open to inspection by the department or any law enforcement agency at any time during normal business hours.

(e) A motor vehicle demolisher commits an offense if the demolisher fails to keep a record as provided by this section.

(f) An offense under Subsection (e) is a misdemeanor punishable by:

(1) a fine of not less than $100 or more than $1,000;

(2) confinement in the county jail for a term of not less than 10 days or more than six months; or

(3) both the fine and confinement.

Transportation Code

SUBCHAPTER E
JUNKED VEHICLES: PUBLIC NUISANCE; ABATEMENT

Sec. 683.071. Definition and Applicability.

(a) In this subchapter, "junked vehicle" means a vehicle that:

(1) is self-propelled; and

(2) is:

(A) wrecked, dismantled or partially dismantled, or discarded; or

(B) inoperable and has remained inoperable for more than:

(i) 72 consecutive hours, if the vehicle is on public property; or

(ii) 30 consecutive days, if the vehicle is on private property.

(b) For purposes of this subchapter, "junked vehicle" includes a motor vehicle, aircraft, or watercraft. This subchapter applies only to:

(1) a motor vehicle that displays an expired license plate or does not display a license plate;

(2) an aircraft that does not have lawfully printed on the aircraft an unexpired federal aircraft identification number registered under Federal Aviation Administration aircraft registration regulations in 14 C.F.R. Part 47; or

(3) a watercraft that:

(A) does not have lawfully on board an unexpired certificate of number; and

(B) is not a watercraft described by Section 31.055, Parks and Wildlife Code.

Sec. 683.0711. Municipal Requirements.

An ordinance adopted by a governing body of a municipality may provide for a more inclusive definition of a junked vehicle subject to regulation under this subchapter.

Sec. 683.072. Junked Vehicle Declared to Be Public Nuisance.

A junked vehicle, including a part of a junked vehicle, that is visible at any time of the year from a public place or public right-of-way:

(1) is detrimental to the safety and welfare of the public;

(2) tends to reduce the value of private property;

(3) invites vandalism;

(4) creates a fire hazard;

(5) is an attractive nuisance creating a hazard to the health and safety of minors;

(6) produces urban blight adverse to the maintenance and continuing development of municipalities; and

(7) is a public nuisance.

Sec. 683.073. Offense.

(a) A person commits an offense if the person maintains a public nuisance described by Section 683.072.

(b) An offense under this section is a misdemeanor punishable by a fine not to exceed $200.

(c) The court shall order abatement and removal of the nuisance on conviction.

Sec. 683.074. Authority to Abate Nuisance; Procedures.

(a) A municipality or county may adopt procedures that conform to this subchapter for the abatement and removal from private or public property or a public right-of-way of a junked vehicle or part of a junked vehicle as a public nuisance.

(b) The procedures must:

(1) prohibit a vehicle from being reconstructed or made operable after removal;

(2) require a public hearing on request of a person who receives notice as provided by Section 683.075 if the request is made not later than the date by which the nuisance must be abated and removed; and

(3) require that notice identifying the vehicle or part of the vehicle be given to the department not later than the fifth day after the date of removal.

(c) An appropriate court of the municipality or county may issue necessary orders to enforce the procedures.

(d) Procedures for abatement and removal of a public nuisance must be administered by regularly salaried, full-time employees of the municipality or county, except that any authorized person may remove the nuisance.

(e) A person authorized to administer the procedures may enter private property to examine a public nuisance, to obtain information to identify the nuisance, and to remove or direct the removal of the nuisance.

(f) On receipt of notice of removal of a motor vehicle under Subsection (b)(3), the department shall immediately cancel the certificate of title issued for the vehicle.

(g) The procedures may provide that the relocation of a junked vehicle that is a public nuisance to another location in the same municipality or county after a proceeding for the abatement and removal of the public nuisance has commenced has no effect on the proceeding if the junked vehicle constitutes a public nuisance at the new location.

(h) On receipt of notice of removal of a watercraft under Subsection (b)(3), the department shall notify the Parks and Wildlife Department of the removal. On receipt of the notice from the department, the Parks and Wildlife Department shall immediately cancel the certificate of title issued for the watercraft.

Sec. 683.075. Notice.

(a) The procedures for the abatement and removal of a public nuisance under this subchapter must provide not less than 10 days' notice of the nature of the nuisance. The notice must be personally delivered, sent by certified mail with a five-day return requested, or delivered by the United States Postal Service with signature confirmation service to:

(1) the last known registered owner of the nuisance;

(2) each lienholder of record of the nuisance; and

(3) the owner or occupant of:

(A) the property on which the nuisance is located; or

(B) if the nuisance is located on a public right-of-way, the property adjacent to the right-of-way.

(b) The notice must state that:

(1) the nuisance must be abated and removed not later than the 10th day after the date on which the notice was personally delivered or mailed; and

(2) any request for a hearing must be made before that 10-day period expires.

(c) If the post office address of the last known registered owner of the nuisance is unknown, notice may be placed on the nuisance or, if the owner is located, personally delivered.

(d) If notice is returned undelivered, action to abate the nuisance shall be continued to a date not earlier than the 11th day after the date of the return.

Sec. 683.076. Hearing.

(a) The governing body of the municipality or county or a board, commission, or official designated by the governing body shall conduct hearings under the procedures adopted under this subchapter.

(b) If a hearing is requested by a person for whom notice is required under Section 683.075(a)(3), the hearing shall be held not earlier than the 11th day after the date of the service of notice.

(c) At the hearing, the junked motor vehicle is presumed, unless demonstrated otherwise by the owner, to be inoperable.

(d) If the information is available at the location of the nuisance, a resolution or order requiring removal of the nuisance must include:

(1) for a motor vehicle, the vehicle's:

(A) description;

(B) vehicle identification number; and

(C) license plate number;

(2) for an aircraft, the aircraft's:

(A) description; and

(B) federal aircraft identification number as described by Federal Aviation Administration aircraft registration regulations in 14 C.F.R. Part 47; and

(3) for a watercraft, the watercraft's:

(A) description; and

(B) identification number as set forth in the watercraft's certificate of number.

Sec. 683.0765. Alternative Procedure for Administrative Hearing.

A municipality by ordinance may provide for an administrative adjudication process under which

Transportation Code

an administrative penalty may be imposed for the enforcement of an ordinance adopted under this subchapter. If a municipality provides for an administrative adjudication process under this section, the municipality shall use the procedure described by Section 54.044, Local Government Code.

Sec. 683.077. Inapplicability of Subchapter.

(a) Procedures adopted under Section 683.074 or 683.0765 may not apply to a vehicle or vehicle part:

(1) that is completely enclosed in a building in a lawful manner and is not visible from the street or other public or private property; or

(2) that is stored or parked in a lawful manner on private property in connection with the business of a licensed vehicle dealer or junkyard, or that is an antique or special interest vehicle stored by a motor vehicle collector on the collector's property, if the vehicle or part and the outdoor storage area, if any, are:

(A) maintained in an orderly manner;

(B) not a health hazard; and

(C) screened from ordinary public view by appropriate means, including a fence, rapidly growing trees, or shrubbery.

(b) In this section:

(1) "Antique vehicle" means a passenger car or truck that is at least 25 years old.

(2) "Motor vehicle collector" means a person who:

(A) owns one or more antique or special interest vehicles; and

(B) acquires, collects, or disposes of an antique or special interest vehicle or part of an antique or special interest vehicle for personal use to restore and preserve an antique or special interest vehicle for historic interest.

(3) "Special interest vehicle" means a motor vehicle of any age that has not been changed from original manufacturer's specifications and, because of its historic interest, is being preserved by a hobbyist.

Sec. 683.078. Junked Vehicle Disposal.

(a) A junked vehicle, including a part of a junked vehicle, may be removed to a scrapyard, a motor vehicle demolisher, or a suitable site operated by a municipality or county.

(b) A municipality or county may operate a disposal site if its governing body determines that commercial disposition of junked vehicles is not available or is inadequate. A municipality or county may:

(1) finally dispose of a junked vehicle or vehicle part; or

(2) transfer it to another disposal site if the disposal is scrap or salvage only.

CHAPTER 684
REMOVAL OF UNAUTHORIZED VEHICLES FROM PARKING FACILITY OR PUBLIC ROADWAY
[REPEALED AND RENUMBERED]

SUBCHAPTER A
GENERAL PROVISIONS [REPEALED.]

Sec. 684.001. Definitions [Repealed].

Repealed by Acts 2007, 80th Leg., ch. 1046 (H.B. 2094), § 5.01(a)(4), effective September 1, 2007.

SUBCHAPTER B
UNAUTHORIZED VEHICLES [REPEALED.]

Sec. 684.011. Prohibition Against Unattended Vehicles in Certain Areas [Renumbered].

Renumbered to Tex.Occ. Code § 2308.251 by Acts 2007, 80th Leg., ch. 1046 (H.B. 2094), § 2.03, effective September 1, 2007.

Sec. 684.012. Removal and Storage of Unauthorized Vehicle [Renumbered].

Renumbered to Tex.Occ. Code § 2308.252 by Acts 2007, 80th Leg., ch. 1046 (H.B. 2094), § 2.03, effective September 1, 2007.

Sec. 684.0125. Unattended Vehicles on Parking Facility of Apartment Complex; Removal and Storage of Vehicles [Renumbered].

Renumbered to Tex.Occ. Code § 2308.253 by Acts 2007, 80th Leg., ch. 1046 (H.B. 2094), § 2.03, effective September 1, 2007.

Sec. 684.013. Limitation on Parking Facility Owner's Authority to Remove Unauthorized Vehicle [Renumbered].

Renumbered to Tex.Occ. Code § 2308.254 by Acts 2007, 80th Leg., ch. 1046 (H.B. 2094), § 2.03, effective September 1, 2007.

Sec. 684.014. Towing Company's Authority to Remove and Store Unauthorized Vehicle [Renumbered].

Renumbered to Tex.Occ. Code § 2308.255 by Acts 2007, 80th Leg., ch. 1046 (H.B. 2094), § 2.03, effective September 1, 2007.

Sec. 684.015. Vehicle Storage Facility's Duty to Report After Accepting Unauthorized Vehicle [Renumbered].

Renumbered to Tex.Occ. Code § 2308.256 by Acts 2007, 80th Leg., ch. 1046 (H.B. 2094), § 2.03, effective September 1, 2007.

SUBCHAPTER C SIGNS PROHIBITING UNAUTHORIZED VEHICLES AND DESIGNATING RESTRICTED AREAS

Sec. 684.031. General Requirements for Sign Prohibiting Unauthorized Vehicles [Renumbered].

Renumbered to Tex.Occ. Code § 2308.301 by Acts 2007, 80th Leg., ch. 1046 (H.B. 2094), § 2.04, effective September 1, 2007.

Sec. 684.032. Color, Layout, and Lettering Height Requirements [Renumbered].

Renumbered to Tex.Occ. Code § 2308.302 by Acts 2007, 80th Leg., ch. 1046 (H.B. 2094), § 2.04, effective September 1, 2007.

Sec. 684.033. Telephone Number for Locating Towed Vehicle Required [Renumbered].

Renumbered to Tex.Occ. Code § 2308.303 by Acts 2007, 80th Leg., ch. 1046 (H.B. 2094), § 2.04, effective September 1, 2007.

Sec. 684.034. Designation of Restricted Parking Spaces on Otherwise Unrestricted Parking Facility [Renumbered].

Renumbered to Tex.Occ. Code § 2308.304 by Acts 2007, 80th Leg., ch. 1046 (H.B. 2094), § 2.04, effective September 1, 2007.

Sec. 684.035. Individual Parking Restrictions in Restricted Area [Renumbered].

Renumbered to Tex.Occ. Code § 2308.305 by Acts 2007, 80th Leg., ch. 1046 (H.B. 2094), § 2.04, effective September 1, 2007.

SUBCHAPTER D REGULATION OF PARKING ON CERTAIN PUBLIC ROADWAY AREAS

Sec. 684.051. Removal of Unauthorized Vehicle from Leased Right-of-Way [Renumbered].

Renumbered to Tex.Occ. Code § 2308.351 by Acts 2007, 80th Leg., ch. 1046 (H.B. 2094), § 2.05, effective September 1, 2007.

Sec. 684.052. Removal of Unauthorized Vehicle from Area Between Parking Facility and Public Roadway [Renumbered].

Renumbered to Tex.Occ. Code § 2308.352 by Acts 2007, 80th Leg., ch. 1046 (H.B. 2094), § 2.05, effective September 1, 2007.

Sec. 684.053. Removal Under Governmental Entity's Authority of Unauthorized Vehicle Parked in Right-of-Way [Renumbered].

Renumbered to Tex.Occ. Code § 2308.353 by Acts 2007, 80th Leg., ch. 1046 (H.B. 2094), § 2.05, effective September 1, 2007.

Sec. 684.054. Authority for Removal of Vehicle from Public Roadway [Renumbered].

Renumbered to Tex.Occ. Code § 2308.354 by Acts 2007, 80th Leg., ch. 1046 (H.B. 2094), § 2.05, effective September 1, 2007.

SUBCHAPTER E REGULATION OF TOWING COMPANIES AND PARKING FACILITY OWNERS

Transportation Code

Sec. 684.081. Parking Facility Owner Prohibited from Receiving Financial Gain from Towing Company [Renumbered].

Renumbered to Tex.Occ. Code § 2308.401 by Acts 2007, 80th Leg., ch. 1046 (H.B. 2094), § 2.06, effective September 1, 2007.

Sec. 684.082. Towing Company Prohibited from Financial Involvement with Parking Facility Owner [Renumbered].

Renumbered to Tex.Occ. Code § 2308.402 by Acts 2007, 80th Leg., ch. 1046 (H.B. 2094), § 2.06, effective September 1, 2007.

Sec. 684.083. Limitation on Liability of Parking Facility Owner for Removal or Storage of Unauthorized Vehicle [Renumbered].

Renumbered to Tex.Occ. Code § 2308.403 by Acts 2007, 80th Leg., ch. 1046 (H.B. 2094), § 2.06, effective September 1, 2007.

Sec. 684.084. Civil Liability of Towing Company or Parking Facility Owner for Violation of Chapter [Renumbered].

Renumbered to Tex.Occ. Code § 2308.404 by Acts 2007, 80th Leg., ch. 1046 (H.B. 2094), § 2.06, effective September 1, 2007.

Sec. 684.085. Violation of Chapter; Fine [Renumbered].

Renumbered to Tex.Occ. Code § 2308.405 by Acts 2007, 80th Leg., ch. 1046 (H.B. 2094), § 2.06, effective September 1, 2007.

Sec. 684.086. Violation of Chapter; Injunction [Renumbered].

Renumbered to Tex.Occ. Code § 2308.406 by Acts 2007, 80th Leg., ch. 1046 (H.B. 2094), § 2.06, effective September 1, 2007.

Sec. 684.087. Minor Sign or Lettering Height Variations [Renumbered].

Renumbered to Tex.Occ. Code § 2308.407 by Acts 2007, 80th Leg., ch. 1046 (H.B. 2094), § 2.06, effective September 1, 2007.

SUBCHAPTER F MISCELLANEOUS PROVISIONS [REPEALED.]

Sec. 684.101. Municipal Ordinance Regulating Unauthorized Vehicles [Renumbered].

Renumbered to Tex.Occ. Code § 2308.208 by Acts 2007, 80th Leg., ch. 1046 (H.B. 2094), § 2.02, effective September 1, 2007.

CHAPTER 685 RIGHTS OF OWNERS AND OPERATORS OF STORED VEHICLES

[REPEALED AND RENUMBERED]

Sec. 685.001. Definitions [Repealed].

Repealed by Acts 2007, 80th Leg., ch. 1046 (H.B. 2094), § 5.01(a)(5), effective September 1, 2007.

Sec. 685.002. Payment of Cost of Removal and Storage of Vehicle [Renumbered].

Renumbered to Tex.Occ. Code § 2308.451 by Acts 2007, 80th Leg., ch. 1046 (H.B. 2094), § 2.07, effective September 1, 2007.

Sec. 685.003. Right of Owner or Operator of Vehicle to Hearing [Renumbered].

Renumbered to Tex.Occ. Code § 2308.452 by Acts 2007, 80th Leg., ch. 1046 (H.B. 2094), § 2.07, effective September 1, 2007.

Sec. 685.004. Jurisdiction [Renumbered].

Renumbered to Tex.Occ. Code § 2308.453 by Acts 2007, 80th Leg., ch. 1046 (H.B. 2094), § 2.07, effective September 1, 2007.

Sec. 685.005. Notice to Vehicle Owner or Operator [Renumbered].

Renumbered to Tex.Occ. Code § 2308.454 by Acts 2007, 80th Leg., ch. 1046 (H.B. 2094), § 2.07, effective September 1, 2007.

Sec. 685.006. Contents of Notice [Renumbered].

Renumbered to Tex.Occ. Code § 2308.455 by Acts 2007, 80th Leg., ch. 1046 (H.B. 2094), § 2.07, effective September 1, 2007.

Sec. 685.007. Request for Hearing [Renumbered].

Renumbered to Tex.Occ. Code § 2308.456 by Acts 2007, 80th Leg., ch. 1046 (H.B. 2094), § 2.07, effective September 1, 2007.

Sec. 685.008. Filing Fee Authorized [Renumbered].

Renumbered to Tex.Occ. Code § 2308.457 by Acts 2007, 80th Leg., ch. 1046 (H.B. 2094), § 2.07, effective September 1, 2007.

Sec. 685.009. Hearing [Renumbered].

Renumbered to Tex.Occ. Code § 2308.458 by Acts 2007, 80th Leg., ch. 1046 (H.B. 2094), § 2.07, effective September 1, 2007.

Sec. 685.010. Appeal [Renumbered].

Renumbered to Tex.Occ. Code § 2308.459 by Acts 2007, 80th Leg., ch. 1046 (H.B. 2094), § 2.07, effective September 1, 2007.

CHAPTER 686
VALET PARKING SERVICES

Sec. 686.001. Definitions.

In this chapter:

(1) "Financial responsibility" means the ability to respond in damages for liability for an accident that:

(A) occurs after the effective date of the document evidencing the establishment of the financial responsibility; and

(B) arises out of the operation of a motor vehicle by an employee of a valet parking service.

(2) "Public accommodation" means any:

(A) inn, hotel, or motel;

(B) restaurant, cafeteria, or other facility principally engaged in selling food for consumption on the premises;

(C) bar, nightclub, or other facility engaged in selling alcoholic beverages for consumption on the premises;

(D) motion picture house, theater, concert hall, stadium, or other place of exhibition or entertainment; or

(E) other facility used by or open to members of the public.

(3) "Valet parking service" means a parking service through which the motor vehicles of patrons of a public accommodation are parked for a fee by a third party who is not an employee of the public accommodation.

Sec. 686.002. Requirement of Financial Responsibility for Valet Parking Services.

A person may not operate a valet parking service unless financial responsibility for each employee who operates a motor vehicle for the service is established through:

(1) a motor vehicle liability or comprehensive general liability and garage insurance policy in an amount established by Section 686.004;

(2) a surety bond filed under Section 601.121; or

(3) a deposit in the amount of $450,000 under Section 601.122, notwithstanding any other amount prescribed by that section.

Sec. 686.003. Evidence of Financial Responsibility.

(a) The owner or operator of a valet parking service shall provide evidence of financial responsibility in the same manner as required under Section 601.053.

(b) In addition to complying with Subsection (a), an owner or operator of a valet parking service shall exhibit, for public inspection, evidence of financial responsibility at a public accommodation whose patrons use the service.

Sec. 686.004. Minimum Coverage Amounts.

(a) The minimum amounts of motor vehicle liability insurance coverage required to establish financial responsibility under this chapter are:

(1) $100,000 for bodily injury to or death of one person in one accident;

(2) $300,000 for bodily injury to or death of two or more persons in one accident, subject to the amount provided by Subdivision (1) for bodily injury to or death of one of the persons; and

(3) $50,000 for damage to or destruction of property of others in one accident.

(b) The comprehensive general liability insurance must be on a broad form and provide limits of liability for bodily injury and property damage of not less than $300,000 combined single limit or the equivalent.

Transportation Code

(c) The garage insurance must provide limits of liability for bodily injury and property damage of not less than $300,000 combined single limit, or the equivalent, and must provide the following coverages:

(1) comprehensive and collision coverage for physical damage;

(2) coverage for vehicle storage; and

(3) coverage for a vehicle driven by or at the direction of the valet parking service.

Sec. 686.005. Common Law Defenses.

In an action against an owner or operator of a valet parking service that has not established financial responsibility as required by this chapter to recover damages for personal injuries, death, or property damage sustained in a motor vehicle accident arising out of the operation of a valet parking service, it is not a defense that the party who brings the action:

(1) was guilty of contributory negligence; or

(2) assumed the risk of injury, death, or property damage.

Sec. 686.006. Operation of Motor Vehicle in Violation of Financial Responsibility Requirement; Offense.

(a) A person commits an offense if the person, while in the course and scope of the person's employment with a valet parking service, operates a motor vehicle of a patron of the service without the financial responsibility required by this chapter.

(b) Except as provided by Subsections (c) and (d), an offense under this section is a misdemeanor punishable by a fine of not less than $175 or more than $350.

(c) If a person has been previously convicted of an offense under this section, an offense under this section is a misdemeanor punishable by a fine of not less than $350 or more than $1,000.

(d) If the court determines that a person who has not been previously convicted of an offense under this section is economically unable to pay the fine, the court may reduce the fine to not less than $175.

Sec. 686.007. Defense: Financial Responsibility in Effect at Time of Alleged Offense.

It is a defense to prosecution under Section 686.002 that the person charged produces one of the documents listed in Section 601.053 that was valid at the time the offense is alleged to have occurred.

SUBTITLE I ENFORCEMENT OF TRAFFIC LAWS

CHAPTER 701 COUNTY TRAFFIC OFFICERS

Sec. 701.001. Authorization.

(a) Except as provided by Subsection (c), acting in conjunction with the sheriff of the county, the commissioners court of a county may employ not more than five regular deputies as county traffic officers.

(b) Except as provided by Subsection (c), the commissioners court may employ not more than two additional deputies as county traffic officers to aid the regular officers in special emergencies.

(c) The limitation on the number of deputies that may be employed under Subsections (a) and (b) does not apply to a county with a population of more than two million.

Sec. 701.002. Power to Act; Guidance.

(a) A county traffic officer:

(1) must be deputized by the sheriff or a constable of the county in which the officer is employed;

(2) must give a bond and take an oath of office as other deputy sheriffs;

(3) must work under the direction of the sheriff; and

(4) has the same right and duty as a deputy sheriff to arrest a person who violates a law.

(b) [Repealed by Acts 2009, 81st Leg., ch. 471 (S.B. 376), § 2, effective June 19, 2009.]

Sec. 701.003. Duties.

(a) A county traffic officer shall:

(1) be a motorcycle rider when practicable;

(2) cooperate with the police department of each municipality in the county to enforce state traffic laws in that municipality and in the county;

(3) enforce state laws that regulate the operation of a motor vehicle on a highway, street, or alley; and

(4) remain on and patrol the highway at all times when performing the officer's duties.

(b) An officer may leave a highway only in pursuit of an offender the officer is unable to apprehend on the highway.

Transportation Code

Sec. 701.004. Compensation.

(a) The compensation to be paid a county traffic officer shall be set before the officer is employed.

(b) Salary paid to the officer is independent of a salary paid to the sheriff and sheriff's deputies who do not act as highway officers. Compensation for an officer may not be included in the sheriff's settlement in accounting for a fee of office or as salary paid to the sheriff or a sheriff's deputy.

(c) The commissioners court may provide necessary equipment for the officer at the county's expense. An officer's equipment may include a motorcycle and maintenance of that motorcycle.

Sec. 701.005. Fees.

A fee may not be charged for a service of a county traffic officer.

Sec. 701.006. Dismissal.

The commissioners court on its own initiative, or on recommendation of the sheriff, may dismiss a county traffic officer if the officer is no longer needed or if the officer's service is unsatisfactory.

CHAPTER 702 CONTRACTS FOR ENFORCEMENT OF CERTAIN ARREST WARRANTS

Sec. 702.001. Definitions.

In this chapter:

(1) "Department" means the Texas Department of Motor Vehicles.

(2) "Registration" of a motor vehicle includes a renewal of the registration of that vehicle.

(3) "Traffic law" means a statute or ordinance, a violation of which is a misdemeanor punishable by a fine not to exceed $200, that regulates, on a street, road, or highway of this state:

(A) the conduct or condition of a person while operating a motor vehicle; or

(B) the condition of a motor vehicle being operated.

Sec. 702.002. Application [Repealed].

Repealed by Acts 2011, 82nd Leg., ch. 871 (S.B. 86), § 1, effective June 17, 2011.

Sec. 702.003. Refusal to Register Vehicle.

(a) A county assessor-collector or the department may refuse to register a motor vehicle if the assessor-collector or the department receives under a contract information from a municipality that the owner of the vehicle has an outstanding warrant from that municipality for failure to appear or failure to pay a fine on a complaint that involves the violation of a traffic law.

(b) A municipality may contract with a county in which the municipality is located or the department to provide information to the county assessor-collector or department necessary to make a determination under Subsection (a).

(c) A municipality that has a contract under Subsection (b) shall notify the county assessor-collector or the department regarding a person for whom the county assessor-collector or the department has refused to register a motor vehicle on:

(1) entry of a judgment against the person and the person's payment to the court of the fine for the violation and of all court costs;

(2) perfection of an appeal of the case for which the arrest warrant was issued; or

(3) dismissal of the charge for which the arrest warrant was issued.

(d) After notice is received under Subsection (c), the county assessor-collector or the department may not refuse to register the motor vehicle under Subsection (a).

(e) A contract under Subsection (b) must be entered into in accordance with Chapter 791, Government Code, and is subject to the ability of the parties to provide or pay for the services required under the contract.

(e-1) A municipality that has a contract under Subsection (b) may impose an additional $20 reimbursement fee to a person who has an outstanding warrant from the municipality for failure to appear or failure to pay a fine on a complaint that involves the violation of a traffic law. The additional reimbursement fee may be used only to reimburse the department or the county assessor-collector for its expenses for providing services under the contract, or another county department for expenses related to services under the contract.

(f) This section does not apply to the registration of a motor vehicle under Section 501.0234.

Sec. 702.004. Warning; Citation.

(a) A peace officer authorized to issue citations in a municipality that has a contract under Section 702.003 shall issue a written warning to each person to whom the officer issues a citation for a violation of a traffic law in the municipality.

(b) The warning must state that if the person fails to appear in court as provided by law for the prosecution of the offense or fails to pay a fine for the violation, the person might not be permitted to register a motor vehicle in this state.

(c) The warning required by this section may be printed on the citation.

Sec. 702.005. Warning; Citation [Renumbered].

Renumbered to Tex. Transp. Code § 702.004 by Acts 1997, 75th Leg., ch. 165 (S.B. 898), § 30.160(d), effective September 1, 1997.

CHAPTER 703 NONRESIDENT VIOLATOR COMPACT OF 1977

Sec. 703.001. Definitions.

In this chapter:

(1) "Citation" and "motorist" have the meanings assigned by Article II, Section (b), Nonresident Violator Compact of 1977.

(2) "Department" and "licensing authority" mean the Department of Public Safety.

Sec. 703.002. Enactment; Terms of Compact.

The Nonresident Violator Compact of 1977 is enacted and entered into as follows:

NONRESIDENT VIOLATOR COMPACT OF 1977

Art. I. FINDINGS, DECLARATION OF POLICY, AND PURPOSE

(a) The party jurisdictions find that:

(1) In most instances, a motorist who is cited for a traffic violation in a jurisdiction other than his home jurisdiction:

(i) Must post collateral or bond to secure appearance for trial at a later date; or

(ii) If unable to post collateral or bond, is taken into custody until the collateral or bond is posted; or

(iii) Is taken directly to court for his trial to be held.

(2) In some instances, the motorist's driver's license may be deposited as collateral to be returned after he has complied with the terms of the citation.

(3) The purpose of the practices described in paragraphs (1) and (2) above is to ensure compliance with the terms of a traffic citation by the motorist who, if permitted to continue on his way after receiving the traffic citation, could return to his home jurisdiction and disregard his duty under the terms of the traffic citation.

(4) A motorist receiving a traffic citation in his home jurisdiction is permitted, except for certain violations, to accept the citation from the officer at the scene of the violation and to immediately continue on his way after promising or being instructed to comply with the terms of the citation.

(5) The practice described in paragraph (1) above causes unnecessary inconvenience and, at times, a hardship for the motorist who is unable at the time to post collateral, furnish a bond, stand trial, or pay the fine, and thus is compelled to remain in custody until some arrangement can be made.

(6) The deposit of a driver's license as a bail bond, as described in paragraph (2) above, is viewed with disfavor.

(7) The practices described herein consume an undue amount of law enforcement time.

(b) It is the policy of the party jurisdictions to:

(1) Seek compliance with the laws, ordinances, and administrative rules and regulations relating to the operation of motor vehicles in each of the jurisdictions.

(2) Allow motorists to accept a traffic citation for certain violations and proceed on their way without delay whether or not the motorist is a resident of the jurisdiction in which the citation was issued.

(3) Extend cooperation to its fullest extent among the jurisdictions for obtaining compliance with the terms of a traffic citation issued in one jurisdiction to a resident of another jurisdiction.

(4) Maximize effective utilization of law enforcement personnel and assist court systems in the efficient disposition of traffic violations.

(c) The purpose of this compact is to:

(1) Provide a means through which the party jurisdictions may participate in a reciprocal program to effectuate the policies enumerated in paragraph (b) above in a uniform and orderly manner.

(2) Provide for the fair and impartial treatment of traffic violators operating within party jurisdictions in recognition of the motorist's right of due process and the sovereign status of a party jurisdiction.

Art. II. DEFINITIONS

(a) In the Nonresident Violator Compact, the following words have the meaning indicated, unless the context requires otherwise.

(b) (1) "Citation" means any summons, ticket, or other official document issued by a police officer for a traffic violation containing an order which requires the motorist to respond.

(2) "Collateral" means any cash or other security deposited to secure an appearance for trial,

Transportation Code

following the issuance by a police officer of a citation for a traffic violation.

(3) "Court" means a court of law or traffic tribunal.

(4) "Driver's license" means any license or privilege to operate a motor vehicle issued under the laws of the home jurisdiction.

(5) "Home jurisdiction" means the jurisdiction that issued the driver's license of the traffic violator.

(6) "Issuing jurisdiction" means the jurisdiction in which the traffic citation was issued to the motorist.

(7) "Jurisdiction" means a state, territory, or possession of the United States, the District of Columbia, or the Commonwealth of Puerto Rico.

(8) "Motorist" means a driver of a motor vehicle operating in a party jurisdiction other than the home jurisdiction.

(9) "Personal recognizance" means an agreement by a motorist made at the time of issuance of the traffic citation that he will comply with the terms of that traffic citation.

(10) "Police officer" means any individual authorized by the party jurisdiction to issue a citation for a traffic violation.

(11) "Terms of the citation" means those options expressly stated upon the citation.

Art. III. PROCEDURE FOR ISSUING JURISDICTION

(a) When issuing a citation for a traffic violation, a police officer shall issue the citation to a motorist who possesses a driver's license issued by a party jurisdiction and shall not, subject to the exceptions noted in paragraph (b) of this article, require the motorist to post collateral to secure appearance, if the officer receives the motorist's personal recognizance that he or she will comply with the terms of the citation.

(b) Personal recognizance is acceptable only if not prohibited by law. If mandatory appearance is required, it must take place immediately following issuance of the citation.

(c) Upon failure of a motorist to comply with the terms of a traffic citation, the appropriate official shall report the failure to comply to the licensing authority of the jurisdiction in which the traffic citation was issued. The report shall be made in accordance with procedures specified by the issuing jurisdiction and shall contain information as specified in the Compact Manual as minimum requirements for effective processing by the home jurisdiction.

(d) Upon receipt of the report, the licensing authority of the issuing jurisdiction shall transmit to the licensing authority in the home jurisdiction of the motorist the information in a form and content as contained in the Compact Manual.

(e) The licensing authority of the issuing jurisdiction may not suspend the privilege of a motorist for whom a report has been transmitted.

(f) The licensing authority of the issuing jurisdiction shall not transmit a report on any violation if the date of transmission is more than six months after the date on which the traffic citation was issued.

(g) The licensing authority of the issuing jurisdiction shall not transmit a report on any violation where the date of issuance of the citation predates the most recent of the effective dates of entry for the two jurisdictions affected.

Art. IV. PROCEDURE FOR HOME JURISDICTION

(a) Upon receipt of a report of a failure to comply from the licensing authority of the issuing jurisdiction, the licensing authority of the home jurisdiction shall notify the motorist and initiate a suspension action, in accordance with the home jurisdiction's procedures, to suspend the motorist's driver's license until satisfactory evidence of compliance with the terms of the traffic citation has been furnished to the home jurisdiction licensing authority. Due process safeguards will be accorded.

(b) The licensing authority of the home jurisdiction shall maintain a record of actions taken and make reports to issuing jurisdictions as provided in the Compact Manual.

Art. V. APPLICABILITY OF OTHER LAWS

Except as expressly required by provisions of this compact, nothing contained herein shall be construed to affect the right of any party jurisdiction to apply any of its other laws relating to licenses to drive to any person or circumstance, or to invalidate or prevent any driver license agreement or other cooperative arrangement between a party jurisdiction and a nonparty jurisdiction.

Art. VI. COMPACT ADMINISTRATOR PROCEDURES

(a) For the purpose of administering the provisions of this compact and to serve as a governing body for the resolution of all matters relating to the operation of this compact, a Board of Compact Administrators is established. The board shall be composed of one representative from each party jurisdiction to be known as the compact administrator. The compact administrator shall be appointed by the jurisdiction executive and will serve and be subject to removal in accordance with the laws of

Transportation Code

the jurisdiction he represents. A compact administrator may provide for the discharge of his duties and the performance of his functions as a board member by an alternate. An alternate may not be entitled to serve unless written notification of his identity has been given to the board.

(b) Each member of the Board of Compact Administrators shall be entitled to one vote. No action of the board shall be binding unless taken at a meeting at which a majority of the total number of votes on the board are cast in favor. Action by the board shall be only at a meeting at which a majority of the party jurisdictions are represented.

(c) The board shall elect annually, from its membership, a chairman and a vice chairman.

(d) The board shall adopt bylaws, not inconsistent with the provisions of this compact or the laws of a party jurisdiction, for the conduct of its business and shall have the power to amend and rescind its bylaws.

(e) The board may accept for any of its purposes and functions under this compact any and all donations, and grants of money, equipment, supplies, materials, and services, conditional or otherwise, from any jurisdiction, the United States, or any other governmental agency, and may receive, utilize, and dispose of the same.

(f) The board may contract with, or accept services or personnel from, any governmental or intergovernmental agency, person, firm, or corporation, or any private nonprofit organization or institution.

(g) The board shall formulate all necessary procedures and develop uniform forms and documents for administering the provisions of this compact. All procedures and forms adopted pursuant to board action shall be contained in the Compact Manual.

Art. VII. ENTRY INTO COMPACT AND WITHDRAWAL

(a) This compact shall become effective when it has been adopted by at least two jurisdictions.

(b) (1) Entry into the compact shall be made by a Resolution of Ratification executed by the authorized officials of the applying jurisdiction and submitted to the chairman of the board.

(2) The resolution shall be in a form and content as provided in the Compact Manual and shall include statements that in substance are as follows:

(i) A citation of the authority by which the jurisdiction is empowered to become a party to this compact.

(ii) Agreement to comply with the terms and provisions of the compact.

(iii) That compact entry is with all jurisdictions then party to the compact and with any jurisdiction that legally becomes a party to the compact.

(3) The effective date of entry shall be specified by the applying jurisdiction, but it shall not be less than 60 days after notice has been given by the chairman of the Board of Compact Administrators or by the secretariat of the board to each party jurisdiction that the resolution from the applying jurisdiction has been received.

(c) A party jurisdiction may withdraw from this compact by official written notice to the other party jurisdictions, but a withdrawal shall not take effect until 90 days after notice of withdrawal is given. The notice shall be directed to the compact administrator of each member jurisdiction. No withdrawal shall affect the validity of this compact as to the remaining party jurisdictions.

Art. VIII. EXCEPTIONS

The provisions of this compact shall not apply to offenses which mandate personal appearance, moving traffic violations which alone carry a suspension, equipment violations, inspection violations, parking or standing violations, size and weight limit violations, violations of law governing the transportation of hazardous materials, motor carrier violations, lease law violations, and registration law violations.

Art. IX. AMENDMENTS TO THE COMPACT

(a) This compact may be amended from time to time. Amendments shall be presented in resolution form to the chairman of the Board of Compact Administrators and may be initiated by one or more party jurisdictions.

(b) Adoption of an amendment shall require endorsement of all party jurisdictions and shall become effective 30 days after the date of the last endorsement.

(c) Failure of a party jurisdiction to respond to the compact chairman within 120 days after receipt of the proposed amendment shall constitute endorsement.

Art. X. CONSTRUCTION AND SEVERABILITY

This compact shall be liberally construed so as to effectuate the purposes stated herein. The provisions of this compact shall be severable and if any phrase, clause, sentence, or provision of this compact is declared to be contrary to the constitution of any party jurisdiction or of the United States or the applicability thereof to any government, agency, person, or circumstance, the compact shall not be affected thereby. If this compact shall be held contrary to the constitution of any jurisdiction party thereto, the compact shall remain in full force and effect as to the remaining jurisdictions and in full force and effect as to the jurisdiction affected as to all severable matters.

Art. XI. TITLE

This compact shall be known as the Nonresident Violator Compact of 1977.

Sec. 703.003. Nonresident Violator Compact Administrator.

(a) The office of nonresident violator compact administrator is created.

(b) The governor shall appoint the compact administrator with the advice and consent of the senate to a two-year term that expires on February 1 of each odd-numbered year.

(c) The compact administrator is entitled to compensation and reimbursement for expenses as provided by legislative appropriation.

Sec. 703.004. Reports of Failure to Comply with Citation.

(a) The department shall report the failure of a motorist to comply with the terms of a citation.

(b) The department shall establish procedures for making the reports required by Subsection (a).

CHAPTER 704
FORFEITURE OF CERTAIN MOTOR VEHICLES [REPEALED]

Sec. 704.001. Grounds for Forfeiture; Notice [Repealed].

Repealed by Acts 2005, 79th Leg., ch. 617 (H.B. 2275), § 2, effective September 1, 2005.

Sec. 704.002. Temporary Restraining Order Prohibiting Disposition of Vehicle Pending Trial of Offense [Repealed].

Repealed by Acts 2005, 79th Leg., ch. 617 (H.B. 2275), § 2, effective September 1, 2005.

Sec. 704.003. Forfeiture of Vehicle Following Conviction [Repealed].

Repealed by Acts 2005, 79th Leg., ch. 617 (H.B. 2275), § 2, effective September 1, 2005.

Sec. 704.004. Sale of Forfeited Vehicle; Certificate of Title [Repealed].

Repealed by Acts 2005, 79th Leg., ch. 617 (H.B. 2275), § 2, effective September 1, 2005.

CHAPTER 705
ALLOWING DANGEROUS DRIVER TO BORROW MOTOR VEHICLE

Sec. 705.001. Allowing Dangerous Driver to Borrow Motor Vehicle; Offense.

(a) A person commits an offense if the person:

(1) knowingly permits another to operate a motor vehicle owned by the person; and

(2) knows that at the time permission is given the other person's license has been suspended as a result of a:

(A) conviction of an offense under:

(i) Section 49.04, Penal Code;

(ii) Section 49.07, Penal Code, if the offense involved operation of a motor vehicle; or

(iii) Article 6701*l*-1, Revised Statutes, as that law existed before September 1, 1994; or

(B) failure to give a specimen under:

(i) Chapter 724; or

(ii) Chapter 434, Acts of the 61st Legislature, Regular Session, 1969 (Article 6701*l*-5, Vernon's Texas Civil Statutes), as that law existed before September 1, 1995.

(b) An offense under this section is a Class C misdemeanor.

CHAPTER 706
DENIAL OF RENEWAL OF LICENSE FOR FAILURE TO APPEAR

Sec. 706.001. Definitions.

In this chapter:

(1) "Complaint" means a notice of an offense as described by Article 27.14(d) or 45.019, Code of Criminal Procedure.

(2) "Department" means the Department of Public Safety.

(3) "Driver's license" has the meaning assigned by Section 521.001.

(4) "Highway or street" has the meaning assigned by Section 541.302.

(5) "Motor vehicle" has the meaning assigned by Section 541.201.

(6) "Operator" has the meaning assigned by Section 541.001.

(7) "Political subdivision" means a municipality or county.

(8) "Public place" has the meaning assigned by Section 1.07, Penal Code.

(9) "Traffic law" means a statute or ordinance, a violation of which is a misdemeanor punishable by a fine in an amount not to exceed $1,000, that:

(A) regulates an operator's conduct or condition while operating a motor vehicle on a highway or street or in a public place;

(B) regulates the condition of a motor vehicle while it is being operated on a highway or street;

(C) relates to the driver's license status of an operator while operating a motor vehicle on a highway or street; or

(D) relates to the registration status of a motor vehicle while it is being operated on a highway or street.

Sec. 706.002. Contract with Department.

(a) A political subdivision may contract with the department to provide information necessary for the department to deny renewal of the driver's license of a person who fails to appear for a complaint or citation or fails to pay or satisfy a judgment ordering payment of a fine and cost in the manner ordered by the court in a matter involving any offense that a court has jurisdiction of under Chapter 4, Code of Criminal Procedure.

(b) A contract under this section:

(1) must be made in accordance with Chapter 791, Government Code; and

(2) is subject to the ability of the parties to provide or pay for the services required under the contract.

Sec. 706.003. Warning; Citation.

(a) If a political subdivision has contracted with the department, a peace officer authorized to issue a citation in the jurisdiction of the political subdivision shall issue a written warning to each person to whom the officer issues a citation for a violation of a traffic law in the jurisdiction of the political subdivision.

(b) The warning under Subsection (a):

(1) is in addition to any other warning required by law;

(2) must state in substance that if the person fails to appear in court as provided by law for the prosecution of the offense or if the person fails to pay or satisfy a judgment ordering the payment of a fine and cost in the manner ordered by the court, the person may be denied renewal of the person's driver's license; and

(3) may be printed on the same instrument as the citation.

Sec. 706.004. Denial of Renewal of Driver's License.

(a) If a political subdivision has contracted with the department, on receiving the necessary information from the political subdivision the department may deny renewal of the person's driver's license for failure to appear based on a complaint or citation or failure to pay or satisfy a judgment ordering the payment of a fine and cost in the manner ordered by the court in a matter involving an offense described by Section 706.002(a).

(b) The information must include:

(1) the name, date of birth, and driver's license number of the person;

(2) the nature and date of the alleged violation;

(3) a statement that the person failed to appear as required by law or failed to satisfy a judgment ordering the payment of a fine and cost in the manner ordered by the court in a matter involving an offense described by Section 706.002(a); and

(4) any other information required by the department.

Sec. 706.005. Clearance Notice to Department.

(a) A political subdivision shall immediately notify the department that there is no cause to continue to deny renewal of a person's driver's license based on the person's previous failure to appear or failure to pay or satisfy a judgment ordering the payment of a fine and cost in the manner ordered by the court in a matter involving an offense described by Section 706.002(a), on payment of a reimbursement fee as provided by Section 706.006 and:

(1) the perfection of an appeal of the case for which the warrant of arrest was issued or judgment arose;

(2) the dismissal of the charge for which the warrant of arrest was issued or judgment arose, other than a dismissal with prejudice by motion of the appropriate prosecuting attorney for lack of evidence;

(3) the posting of bond or the giving of other security to reinstate the charge for which the warrant was issued;

(4) the payment or discharge of the fine and cost owed on an outstanding judgment of the court; or

(5) other suitable arrangement to pay the fine and cost within the court's discretion.

(b) The department may not continue to deny the renewal of the person's driver's license under this chapter after the department receives notice:

(1) under Subsection (a);

(2) that the person was acquitted of the charge on which the person failed to appear;

(3) that the charge on which the person failed to appear was dismissed with prejudice by motion of the appropriate prosecuting attorney for lack of evidence; or

(4) from the political subdivision that the failure to appear report or court order to pay a fine or cost relating to the person:

(A) was sent to the department in error; or

(B) has been destroyed in accordance with the political subdivision's records retention policy.

Sec. 706.006. Payment of Reimbursement Fee.

(a) Except as provided by Subsection (d), a person who fails to appear for a complaint or citation for an offense described by Section 706.002(a) shall be required to pay a reimbursement fee of $10 for each complaint or citation reported to the department under this chapter, unless:

(1) the person is acquitted of the charges for which the person failed to appear;

(2) the charges on which the person failed to appear were dismissed with prejudice by motion of the appropriate prosecuting attorney for lack of evidence;

(3) the failure to appear report was sent to the department in error; or

(4) the case regarding the complaint or citation is closed and the failure to appear report has been destroyed in accordance with the applicable political subdivision's records retention policy.

(a-1) A person who is required to pay a reimbursement fee under Subsection (a) shall pay the fee when:

(1) the court enters judgment on the underlying offense reported to the department;

(2) the underlying offense is dismissed, other than a dismissal described by Subsection (a)(2); or

(3) bond or other security is posted to reinstate the charge for which the warrant was issued.

(b) Except as provided by Subsection (d), a person who fails to pay or satisfy a judgment ordering the payment of a fine and cost in the manner the court orders shall be required to pay a reimbursement fee of $10.

(c) The department may deny renewal of the driver's license of a person who does not pay a reimbursement fee due under this section until the fee is paid. The fee required by this section is in addition to any other fee required by law.

(d) If the court having jurisdiction over the underlying offense makes a finding that the person is indigent, the person may not be required to pay a reimbursement fee under this section. For purposes of this subsection, a person is presumed to be indigent if the person:

(1) is required to attend school full time under Section 25.085, Education Code;

(2) is a member of a household with a total annual income that is below 125 percent of the applicable income level established by the federal poverty guidelines; or

(3) receives assistance from:

(A) the financial assistance program established under Chapter 31, Human Resources Code;

(B) the medical assistance program under Chapter 32, Human Resources Code;

(C) the supplemental nutrition assistance program established under Chapter 33, Human Resources Code;

(D) the federal special supplemental nutrition program for women, infants, and children authorized by 42 U.S.C. Section 1786; or

(E) the child health plan program under Chapter 62, Health and Safety Code.

Sec. 706.007. Disposition of Fees.

(a) An officer collecting a reimbursement fee under Section 706.006 shall remit the money to the municipal or county treasurer, as applicable.

(b) [Repealed.]

(c) [Repealed.]

(d) The custodian of a municipal or county treasury shall deposit the money collected under Section 706.006 to the credit of the general fund of the municipality or county for the purposes of Section 706.008.

(e) [Repealed.]

Sec. 706.008. Contract with Private Vendor; Compensation.

(a) The department may contract with a private vendor to implement this chapter.

(b) The vendor performing the contract may be compensated by each political subdivision that has contracted with the department.

(c) Except for an action based on a citation issued by a peace officer employed by the department, the vendor may not be compensated with state money.

Sec. 706.009. Vendor to Provide Customer Support Services.

(a) A vendor must establish and maintain customer support services as directed by the department, including a toll-free telephone service line to answer and resolve questions from persons who are denied renewal of a driver's license under this chapter.

(b) The vendor shall comply with terms, policies, and rules adopted by the department to administer this chapter.

Sec. 706.010. Use of Information Collected by Vendor.

Information collected under this chapter by a vendor may not be used by a person other than the department, the political subdivision, or a vendor as provided by this chapter.

Sec. 706.011. Liability of State or Political Subdivision.

(a) An action for damages may not be brought against the state or a political subdivision based on an act or omission under this chapter, including the denial of renewal of a driver's license.

(b) The state or a political subdivision may not be held liable in damages based on an act or omission under this chapter, including the denial of renewal of a driver's license.

Transportation Code

Sec. 706.012. Rules.

The department may adopt rules to implement this chapter.

CHAPTER 707
PHOTOGRAPHIC TRAFFIC SIGNAL ENFORCEMENT SYSTEM PROHIBITED

Sec. 707.001. Definitions.

In this chapter:

(1) "Local authority" has the meaning assigned by Section 541.002.

(2) [Repealed.]

(3) "Photographic traffic signal enforcement system" means a system that:

(A) consists of a camera system and vehicle sensor installed to exclusively work in conjunction with an electrically operated traffic-control signal; and

(B) is capable of producing at least two recorded images that depict the license plate attached to the front or the rear of a motor vehicle that is not operated in compliance with the instructions of the traffic-control signal.

(4) "Recorded image" means a photographic or digital image that depicts the front or the rear of a motor vehicle.

(5) "Traffic-control signal" has the meaning assigned by Section 541.304.

Sec. 707.002. Authority to Provide for Civil Penalty. [Repealed]

Sec. 707.0021. Imposition of Civil Penalty on Owner of Authorized Emergency Vehicle. [Repealed]

Sec. 707.003. Installation and Operation of Photographic Traffic Signal Enforcement System. [Repealed]

Sec. 707.004. Report of Accidents. [Repealed]

Sec. 707.005. Minimum Change Interval. [Repealed]

Sec. 707.006. General Surveillance Prohibited; Offense. [Repealed]

Sec. 707.007. Amount of Civil Penalty; Late Payment Penalty. [Repealed]

Sec. 707.008. Deposit of Revenue from Certain Traffic Penalties. [Repealed]

Sec. 707.009. Required Ordinance Provisions. [Repealed]

Sec. 707.010. Effect on Other Enforcement. [Repealed]

Sec. 707.011. Notice of Violation; Contents. [Repealed]

Sec. 707.012. Admission of Liability. [Repealed]

Sec. 707.013. Presumption. [Repealed]

Sec. 707.014. Administrative Adjudication Hearing. [Repealed]

Sec. 707.015. Untimely Request for Administrative Adjudication Hearing. [Repealed]

Sec. 707.016. Appeal. [Repealed]

Sec. 707.017. Enforcement. [Repealed]

Sec. 707.018. Imposition of Civil Penalty Not a Conviction. [Repealed]

Sec. 707.019. Failure to Pay Civil Penalty. [Repealed]

Sec. 707.020. Photographic Traffic Signal Enforcement System Prohibited.

(a) Notwithstanding any other law, a local authority may not implement or operate a photographic traffic signal enforcement system with respect to a highway or street under the jurisdiction of the authority.

(b) The attorney general shall enforce this section.

Sec. 707.021. Use of Evidence From Photographic Traffic Signal Enforcement System Prohibited.

Notwithstanding any other law, a local authority may not issue a civil or criminal charge or citation for an offense or violation based on a recorded image produced by a photographic traffic signal enforcement system.

CHAPTER 708
DRIVER RESPONSIBILITY PROGRAM [REPEALED]

SUBCHAPTER A
GENERAL PROVISIONS [REPEALED]

Sec. 708.001. Definitions. [Repealed]

Sec. 708.002. Rules. [Repealed]

Sec. 708.003. Final Convictions. [Repealed]

SUBCHAPTER B
DRIVER'S LICENSE POINTS SURCHARGE [REPEALED]

Sec. 708.051. Nonapplicability. [Repealed]

Sec. 708.052. Assignment of Points for Certain Convictions. [Repealed]

Sec. 708.053. Annual Surcharge for Points. [Repealed]

Sec. 708.054. Amount of Points Surcharge. [Repealed]

Sec. 708.055. Notice of Assignment of Fifth Point. [Repealed]

Sec. 708.056. Deduction of Points. [Repealed]

SUBCHAPTER C
SURCHARGES FOR CERTAIN CONVICTIONS AND LICENSE SUSPENSIONS [REPEALED]

Sec. 708.101. Nonapplicability. [Repealed]

Sec. 708.102. Surcharge for Conviction of Certain Intoxicated Driver Offenses. [Repealed]

Sec. 708.103. Surcharge for Conviction of Driving While License Invalid or Without Financial Responsibility. [Repealed]

Sec. 708.104. Surcharge for Conviction of Driving Without Valid License. [Repealed]

Sec. 708.105. Notice of Potential Surcharge. [Repealed]

Sec. 708.106. Deferral of Surcharges for Deployed Military Personnel. [Repealed]

SUBCHAPTER D COLLECTION OF SURCHARGES [REPEALED]

Sec. 708.151. Notice of Surcharge. [Repealed]

Sec. 708.152. Failure to Pay Surcharge. [Repealed]

Sec. 708.153. Installment Payment of Surcharge. [Repealed]

Sec. 708.154. Credit Card Payment of Surcharge. [Repealed]

Sec. 708.155. Contracts for Collection of Surcharges. [Repealed]

Sec. 708.156. Remittance of Surcharges Collected to Comptroller. [Repealed]

Sec. 708.157. Amnesty and Incentives. [Repealed]

Sec. 708.158. Indigent Status and Reduction of Surcharges. [Repealed]

Sec. 708.159. Advance Payment of Surcharges. [Repealed]

CHAPTER 709. MISCELLANEOUS TRAFFIC FINES

Sec. 709.001. Traffic Fine for Conviction of Certain Intoxicated Driver Offenses.

(a) In this section, "offense relating to the operating of a motor vehicle while intoxicated" has the meaning assigned by Section 49.09, Penal Code.

(b) Except as provided by Subsection (c), in addition to the fine prescribed for the specific offense, a person who has been finally convicted of an offense relating to the operating of a motor vehicle while intoxicated shall pay a fine of:

(1) $3,000 for the first conviction within a 36-month period;

(2) $4,500 for a second or subsequent conviction within a 36-month period; and

(3) $6,000 for a first or subsequent conviction if it is shown on the trial of the offense that an analysis of a specimen of the person's blood, breath, or urine showed an alcohol concentration level of 0.15 or more at the time the analysis was performed.

(c) If the court having jurisdiction over an offense that is the basis for a fine imposed under this section makes a finding that the person is indigent, the court shall waive all fines and costs imposed on the person under this section.

(d) A person must provide information to the court in which the person is convicted of the offense that is the basis for the fine to establish that the person is indigent. The following documentation may be used as proof:

(1) a copy of the person's most recent federal income tax return that shows that the person's income or the person's household income does not exceed 125 percent of the applicable income level established by the federal poverty guidelines;

(2) a copy of the person's most recent statement of wages that shows that the person's income or the person's household income does not exceed 125 percent of the applicable income level established by the federal poverty guidelines; or

(3) documentation from a federal agency, state agency, or school district that indicates that the person or, if the person is a dependent as defined by Section 152, Internal Revenue Code of 1986, the taxpayer claiming the person as a dependent, receives assistance from:

(A) the food stamp program or the financial assistance program established under Chapter 31, Human Resources Code;

(B) the federal special supplemental nutrition program for women, infants, and children authorized by 42 U.S.C. Section 1786;

(C) the medical assistance program under Chapter 32, Human Resources Code;

(D) the child health plan program under Chapter 62, Health and Safety Code; or

(E) the national free or reduced-price lunch program established under 42 U.S.C. Section 1751 et seq.

Sec. 709.002. Remittance of Traffic Fines Collected to Comptroller.

(a) An officer collecting a traffic fine under Section 709.001 in a case in a justice, county, or district court shall keep separate records of the money collected and shall deposit the money in the county treasury.

(b) Each calendar quarter, an officer collecting a traffic fine under Section 709.001 shall submit a report to the comptroller. The report must comply with Articles 103.005(c) and (d), Code of Criminal Procedure.

(c) The custodian of money in a municipal or county treasury may deposit money collected under Section 709.001 in an interest-bearing account. The custodian shall:

(1) keep records of the amount of money collected under this section that is on deposit in the treasury; and

(2) not later than the last day of the month following each calendar quarter, remit to the comptroller money collected under this section during the preceding quarter, as required by the comptroller.

(d) A municipality or county may retain four percent of the money collected under Section 709.001 as a service fee for the collection if the county remits the funds to the comptroller within the period described by Subsection (c). The municipality or county may retain any interest accrued on the money if the custodian of the money deposited in the treasury keeps records of the amount of money collected under this section that is on deposit in the treasury and remits the funds to the comptroller within the period prescribed in Subsection (c).

(e) Of the money received by the comptroller under this section, the comptroller shall deposit:

(1) 80 percent to the credit of the undedicated portion of the general revenue fund, to be used only for criminal justice purposes; and

(2) 20 percent to the credit of the designated trauma facility and emergency medical services account under Section 780.003, Health and Safety Code, to be used only for the criminal justice purpose of funding designated trauma facilities, county and regional emergency medical services, and trauma care systems that provide trauma care and emergency medical services to victims of accidents resulting from traffic offenses.

(f) Money collected under this section is subject to audit by the comptroller. Money spent is subject to audit by the state auditor.

CHAPTER 720 MISCELLANEOUS PROVISIONS

Sec. 720.001. Badge of Sheriff, Constable, or Deputy.

(a) A sheriff, constable, or deputy sheriff or deputy constable may not arrest or accost a person for driving a motor vehicle on a highway in violation of a law relating to motor vehicles unless the sheriff, constable, or deputy displays a badge showing the sheriff's, constable's, or deputy's title.

(b) A person commits an offense if the person violates this section. An offense under this section is a misdemeanor punishable in the same manner as an offense under Section 86.011, Local Government Code.

(c) An officer charged by law to take or prosecute a complaint under this section shall be removed from office if the officer refuses to do so.

Sec. 720.002. Prohibition on Traffic-Offense Quotas.

(a) A political subdivision or an agency of this state may not establish or maintain, formally or informally, a plan to evaluate, promote, compensate, or discipline:

(1) a peace officer according to the officer's issuance of a predetermined or specified number of any type or combination of types of traffic citations; or

(2) a justice of the peace or a judge of a county court, statutory county court, municipal court, or municipal court of record according to the amount of money the justice or judge collects from persons convicted of a traffic offense.

(b) A political subdivision or an agency of this state may not require or suggest to a peace officer, a justice of the peace, or a judge of a county court, statutory county court, municipal court, or municipal court of record:

(1) that the peace officer is required or expected to issue a predetermined or specified number of any type or combination of types of traffic citations within a specified period; or

(2) that the justice or judge is required or expected to collect a predetermined amount of money from persons convicted of a traffic offense within a specified period.

(c) [Repealed by Acts 2009, 81st Leg., ch. 737 (S.B. 420), § 1, effective June 19, 2009.]

(d) This section does not prohibit a municipality from obtaining budgetary information from a municipal court or a municipal court of record,

Transportation Code

including an estimate of the amount of money the court anticipates will be collected in a budget year.

(e) A violation of this section by an elected official is misconduct and a ground for removal from office. A violation of this section by a person who is not an elected official is a ground for removal from the person's position.

(f) In this section:

(1) "Conviction" means the rendition of an order by a court imposing a punishment of incarceration or a fine.

(2) "Traffic offense" means an offense under:

(A) Chapter 521; or

(B) Subtitle C.

SUBTITLE J MISCELLANEOUS PROVISIONS

CHAPTER 721 INSCRIPTION REQUIRED ON STATE, MUNICIPAL, AND COUNTY MOTOR VEHICLES

Sec. 721.001. Definition.

In this chapter, "state agency" means a department, bureau, board, commission, or office of state government.

Sec. 721.002. Inscription Required on State-Owned Motor Vehicles.

(a) The official having control of a state-owned motor vehicle shall have printed on each side of the vehicle the word "Texas," followed by the title of the state agency having custody of the vehicle.

(b) The inscription must be in a color sufficiently different from the body of the motor vehicle so that the lettering is plainly legible at a distance of not less than 100 feet.

(c) The title of the state agency must be in letters not less than two inches high.

Sec. 721.003. Exemption from Inscription Requirement for Certain State-Owned Motor Vehicles.

(a) The governing bodies of the following state agencies or divisions by rule may exempt from the requirements of Section 721.002 a motor vehicle that is under the control and custody of the agency or division:

(1) Texas Commission on Fire Protection;

(2) Texas State Board of Pharmacy;

(3) Department of State Health Services and Department of Aging and Disability Services;

(4) Department of Public Safety of the State of Texas;

(5) Texas Department of Criminal Justice;

(6) Board of Pardons and Paroles;

(7) Parks and Wildlife Department;

(8) Railroad Commission of Texas;

(9) Texas Alcoholic Beverage Commission;

(10) Texas Department of Banking;

(11) Department of Savings and Mortgage Lending;

(12) Texas Juvenile Justice Department;

(13) Texas Commission on Environmental Quality;

(14) Texas Lottery Commission;

(15) the office of the attorney general;

(16) Texas Department of Insurance;

(17) Texas Military Department; and

(18) an agency that receives an appropriation under an article of the General Appropriations Act that appropriates money to the legislature.

(b) [Repealed by Acts 2001, 77th Leg., ch. 81 (S.B. 817), § 2, effective September 1, 2001.]

(c) A rule adopted under this section must specify:

(1) the purpose served by not printing on the motor vehicle the inscription required by Section 721.002; and

(2) the primary use of the motor vehicle.

(d) A rule adopted under this section is not effective until the rule is filed with the secretary of state.

(e) A rule adopted by the Texas Lottery Commission under Subsection (a) may exempt from the requirements of Section 721.002 only a motor vehicle used exclusively for surveillance purposes.

Sec. 721.004. Inscription Required on Municipal and County-Owned Motor Vehicles and Heavy Equipment.

(a) The office having control of a motor vehicle or piece of heavy equipment owned by a municipality or county shall have printed on each side of the vehicle or equipment the name of the municipality or county, followed by the title of the department or office having custody of the vehicle or equipment.

(b) The inscription must be in a color sufficiently different from the body of the vehicle or equipment so that the lettering is plainly legible.

(c) The title of the department or office must be in letters plainly legible at a distance of not less than 100 feet.

Sec. 721.005. Exemption from Inscription Requirement for Certain Municipal and County-Owned Motor Vehicles.

(a) The governing body of a municipality may exempt from the requirements of Section 721.004:

(1) an automobile when used to perform an official duty by a:

(A) police department;

(B) magistrate as defined by Article 2.09, Code of Criminal Procedure;

(C) medical examiner;

(D) municipal code enforcement officer designated to enforce environmental criminal laws; or

(E) municipal fire marshal or arson investigator; or

(2) an automobile used by a municipal employee only when conducting an investigation involving suspected fraud or other mismanagement within the municipality.

(b) The commissioners court of a county may exempt from the requirements of Section 721.004:

(1) an automobile when used to perform an official duty by a:

(A) police department;

(B) sheriff's office;

(C) constable's office;

(D) criminal district attorney's office;

(E) district attorney's office;

(F) county attorney's office;

(G) magistrate as defined by Article 2.09, Code of Criminal Procedure;

(H) county fire marshal's office; or

(I) medical examiner; or

(2) a juvenile probation department vehicle used to transport children, when used to perform an official duty.

(c) An exemption provided under this section does not apply to a contract deputy.

Sec. 721.006. Operation of Vehicle in Violation of Chapter; Offense.

(a) A person commits an offense if the person:

(1) operates on a municipal street or on a highway a motor vehicle or piece of equipment that does not have the inscription required by this chapter; or

(2) uses a motor vehicle that is exempt by rule under Section 721.003, and that use is not expressly specified by the rule.

(b) An offense under this section is a misdemeanor punishable by a fine of not less than $25 or more than $100.

CHAPTER 722 AUTOMOBILE CLUB SERVICES

Sec. 722.001. Short Title.

This chapter may be cited as the Automobile Club Services Act.

Sec. 722.002. Definitions.

In this chapter:

(1) "Agent" means a salesman or other individual appointed by an automobile club to sell memberships in the club to the public.

(2) "Automobile club" means a person who, for consideration, promises the membership assistance in matters relating to travel, and to the operation, use, or maintenance of a motor vehicle, by supplying services such as services related to:

(A) community traffic safety;

(B) travel and touring;

(C) theft prevention or rewards;

(D) maps;

(E) towing;

(F) emergency road assistance;

(G) bail bonds and legal fee reimbursement in the defense of traffic offenses; and

(H) purchase of accidental injury and death benefits insurance coverage from an authorized insurance company.

Sec. 722.003. Certificate of Authority Required.

(a) A person may not engage in business as an automobile club unless the person meets the requirements of this chapter and obtains an automobile club certificate of authority from the secretary of state.

(b) A person may not solicit or aid in the solicitation of another person to purchase a service contract or membership issued by an automobile club that does not hold an automobile club certificate of authority.

Sec. 722.004. Application.

(a) Each applicant for an automobile club certificate of authority must file an application with the secretary of state in the form and manner prescribed by the secretary. The secretary shall adopt the forms necessary for an applicant to comply with this chapter and shall furnish those forms on request to an applicant for a certificate of authority.

(b) An application must be executed under oath by the club president or other principal club officer and must be accompanied by:

(1) the first year's annual fee for the certificate of authority;

(2) a certificate by the secretary of state stating that the applicant has complied with the corporation laws of this state, if the applicant is a corporation;

(3) a list of each person who holds an ownership interest in the applicant and each officer of the applicant, if the applicant is not incorporated;

(4) a copy of any operating agreement or management agreement affecting the club and a list of each party to the agreement if the applicant is not incorporated; and

(5) proof of security in a manner that complies with Section 722.005.

(c) The secretary of state shall issue the automobile club certificate of authority or deny the application not later than the 15th day after the day the secretary receives the application, certificate, or security. Failure to issue the certificate of authority within the prescribed time entitles the applicant to a refund of all money and security deposited with the application.

Sec. 722.005. Security Requirements.

(a) An applicant for an automobile club certificate of authority may provide the security required for that certificate by depositing with the state or pledging in the form prescribed by the secretary of state:

(1) $25,000 in securities approved by the secretary;

(2) $25,000 in cash; or

(3) a $25,000 bond in the form prescribed by the secretary that is:

(A) payable to the state;

(B) executed by a corporate surety licensed to do business in this state; and

(C) conditioned on the faithful performance of the automobile club in selling or providing club services and the payment of any fines or penalties levied against the club for failure to comply with this chapter.

(b) The aggregate liability of the surety for all breaches of the bond conditions and for payment of all fines and penalties may not exceed the amount of the bond.

(c) The required security shall be maintained as long as the automobile club has any liability or obligation in this state. On showing to the satisfaction of the secretary of state that the club has ceased to do business and that all liabilities and obligations of the club have been satisfied, the secretary may return the security to the club or deliver the security in accordance with a court order.

Sec. 722.006. Renewal.

(a) An automobile club certificate of authority expires annually on August 31. The certificate may be renewed by filing a renewal application in the manner prescribed by the secretary of state and paying the annual fee.

(b) The secretary of state may adopt forms for the renewal application.

Sec. 722.007. Annual Fee.

The annual fee for an automobile club certificate of authority is $150.

Sec. 722.008. Certificate Revocation or Suspension.

(a) After a public hearing, the secretary of state shall revoke or suspend an automobile club's certificate of authority if the secretary determines, for good cause shown, that:

(1) the club:

(A) has violated this chapter;

(B) is not acting as an automobile club;

(C) is insolvent or has assets valued at less than its liabilities;

(D) has refused to submit to an examination by the secretary; or

(E) is transacting business in a fraudulent manner; or

(2) an owner, officer, or manager of the club is not of good moral character.

(b) The secretary of state shall give public notice of the suspension or revocation in the manner the secretary considers appropriate.

Sec. 722.009. Service Contract; Membership Information.

(a) Each automobile club operating under this chapter shall furnish to the membership a service contract or membership card that includes the following information:

(1) the club's name;

(2) the street address of the club's home office and of its usual place of business in this state; and

(3) a description of the services or benefits to which the members are entitled.

(b) For purposes of this chapter, the completed application for an automobile club certificate of authority and the description of services listed under Subsection (a) constitute the service contract.

Sec. 722.010. Filing of Information.

(a) Each automobile club shall file a certified copy of its service contract with the secretary of state.

(b) If an automobile club provides participation in a group accidental injury or death policy, the club shall file with the service contract a copy of the certificate of participation.

(c) An automobile club shall file with the secretary of state any change to the service contract.

Sec. 722.011. Agent Registration.

(a) An automobile club that operates in this state under an automobile club certificate of authority shall file with the secretary of state a notice of appointment of each agent not later than the 30th day after the date on which that agent is employed by the club.

(b) The notice of appointment must be in the form prescribed by the secretary of state and must contain:

(1) the name, address, age, sex, and social security number of the agent; and

(2) proof satisfactory to the secretary that the agent is of good moral character.

(c) Registration under this section is valid for one year from the date of the initial registration and may be renewed on each anniversary of that date. The annual registration fee is $10.

(d) Each automobile club shall notify the secretary of state of the termination of an agent's employment by the club not later than the 30th day after the date of the termination.

Sec. 722.012. Advertising Restrictions.

An automobile club operating under this chapter may not:

(1) refer to its certificate of authority or to approval by the secretary of state in any advertising, contract, or membership card; or

(2) advertise or describe its services in a manner that would lead the public to believe that the services include automobile insurance.

Sec. 722.013. Exemption from Certain Insurance Laws; Group Policy Requirements [Repealed].

Repealed by Acts 1999, 76th Leg., ch. 1530 (S.B. 957), § 5.02, effective September 1, 1999.

Sec. 722.014. Criminal Penalty.

(a) A person commits an offense if the person violates this chapter.

(b) An offense under this section is a misdemeanor punishable by:

(1) a fine not to exceed $500; and

(2) confinement in the county jail for a term not to exceed six months.

CHAPTER 723
TEXAS TRAFFIC SAFETY ACT

SUBCHAPTER A
GENERAL PROVISIONS

Sec. 723.001. Short Title.

This chapter may be cited as the Texas Traffic Safety Act.

Sec. 723.002. Governmental Purpose.

The establishment, development, and maintenance of a traffic safety program is a vital governmental purpose and function of the state and its legal and political subdivisions.

Sec. 723.003. Traffic Safety Fund Account.

(a) The traffic safety fund account is an account in the general revenue fund. Money received from any source to implement this chapter shall be:

(1) deposited to the credit of the traffic safety fund account; and

(2) spent with other state money spent to implement this chapter in the manner in which the other state money is spent.

(b) A payment from the traffic safety fund account shall be made in compliance with this chapter and rules adopted by the governor.

SUBCHAPTER B
PREPARATION AND ADMINISTRATION OF TRAFFIC SAFETY PROGRAM

Sec. 723.011. Governor's Responsibility for Program.

(a) The governor shall:

Transportation Code

(1) prepare and administer a statewide traffic safety program designed to reduce traffic accidents and the death, injury, and property damage that result from traffic accidents;

(2) adopt rules for the administration of this chapter, including rules, procedures, and policy statements governing grants-in-aid and contractual relations;

(3) receive on the state's behalf for the implementation of this chapter money made available by the United States under federal law; and

(4) allocate money appropriated by the legislature in the General Appropriations Act to implement this chapter.

(b) In preparing and administering the traffic safety program, the governor may:

(1) cooperate with the United States or a legal or political subdivision of the state in research designed to aid in traffic safety;

(2) accept federal money available for research relating to traffic safety; and

(3) employ personnel necessary to administer this chapter.

Sec. 723.012. Traffic Safety Program.

The statewide traffic safety program must include:

(1) a driver education and training program administered by the governor through appropriate agencies that complies with Section 723.013;

(2) plans for improving:

(A) driver licensing;

(B) accident records;

(C) vehicle inspection, registration, and titling;

(D) traffic engineering;

(E) personnel;

(F) police traffic supervision;

(G) traffic courts;

(H) highway design; and

(I) uniform traffic laws; and

(3) plans for local traffic safety programs by legal and political subdivisions of this state that may be implemented if the programs:

(A) are approved by the governor; and

(B) conform with uniform standards adopted under the Highway Safety Act of 1966 (23 U.S.C. Sec. 401 et seq.).

Sec. 723.013. Driver Education and Training Program.

(a) The statewide driver education and training program required by Section 723.012 shall provide for:

(1) rules that permit controlled innovation and experimentation and that set minimum standards for:

(A) classroom instruction;

(B) driving skills training;

(C) instructor qualifications;

(D) program content; and

(E) supplementary materials and equipment;

(2) a method for continuing evaluation of approved driver education and training programs to identify the practices most effective in preventing traffic accidents; and

(3) contracts between the governing bodies of centrally located independent school districts or other appropriate public or private agencies and the state to provide approved driver education and training programs.

(b) Instruction offered under a contract authorized by this section must be offered to any applicant who is over 15 years of age.

Sec. 723.014. Cooperation of State Agencies, Officers, and Employees.

On the governor's request, a state agency or institution, state officer, or state employee shall cooperate in an activity of the state that is consistent with:

(1) this chapter; and

(2) the agency's, institution's, officer's, or employee's official functions.

Sec. 723.015. Participation in Program by Legal or Political Subdivision.

A legal or political subdivision of this state may:

(1) cooperate and contract with the state, another legal or political subdivision of this state, or a private person in establishing, developing, and maintaining a statewide traffic safety program;

(2) spend money from any source for an activity related to performing a part of the traffic safety program; and

(3) contract and pay for a personal service or property to be used in the traffic safety program or for an activity related to the program.

SUBCHAPTER C
GIFTS, GRANTS, DONATIONS, GRANTS-IN-AID, AND PAYMENTS

Sec. 723.031. Gifts, Grants, and Donations.

To implement this chapter, the state may accept and spend a gift, grant, or donation of money or other property from a private source.

Sec. 723.032. Grants-in-Aid and Contractual Payments.

(a) A grant-in-aid for a governmental purpose or a contractual payment may be made to a legal or political subdivision of this state to carry out a duty or activity that is part of the statewide traffic safety program.

(b) To implement this chapter, a contractual payment may be made from money in the traffic safety fund account for a service rendered or property furnished by a private person or an agency that is not a legal or political subdivision of this state.

CHAPTER 724 IMPLIED CONSENT

SUBCHAPTER A GENERAL PROVISIONS

Sec. 724.001. Definitions.

In this chapter:

(1) "Alcohol concentration" has the meaning assigned by Section 49.01, Penal Code.

(2) "Arrest" includes the taking into custody of a child, as defined by Section 51.02, Family Code.

(3) "Controlled substance" has the meaning assigned by Section 481.002, Health and Safety Code.

(4) "Criminal charge" includes a charge that may result in a proceeding under Title 3, Family Code.

(5) "Criminal proceeding" includes a proceeding under Title 3, Family Code.

(6) "Dangerous drug" has the meaning assigned by Section 483.001, Health and Safety Code.

(7) "Department" means the Department of Public Safety.

(8) "Drug" has the meaning assigned by Section 481.002, Health and Safety Code.

(9) "Intoxicated" has the meaning assigned by Section 49.01, Penal Code.

(10) "License" has the meaning assigned by Section 521.001.

(11) "Operate" means to drive or be in actual control of a motor vehicle or watercraft.

(12) "Public place" has the meaning assigned by Section 1.07, Penal Code.

Sec. 724.002. Applicability.

The provisions of this chapter that apply to suspension of a license for refusal to submit to the taking of a specimen (Sections 724.013, 724.015, and 724.048 and Subchapters C and D) apply only to a person arrested for an offense involving the operation of a motor vehicle or watercraft powered with an engine having a manufacturer's rating of 50 horsepower or above.

Sec. 724.003. Rulemaking.

The department and the State Office of Administrative Hearings shall adopt rules to administer this chapter.

SUBCHAPTER B TAKING AND ANALYSIS OF SPECIMEN

Sec. 724.011. Consent to Taking of Specimen.

(a) If a person is arrested for an offense arising out of acts alleged to have been committed while the person was operating a motor vehicle in a public place, or a watercraft, while intoxicated, or an offense under Section 106.041, Alcoholic Beverage Code, the person is deemed to have consented, subject to this chapter, to submit to the taking of one or more specimens of the person's breath or blood for analysis to determine the alcohol concentration or the presence in the person's body of a controlled substance, drug, dangerous drug, or other substance.

(b) A person arrested for an offense described by Subsection (a) may consent to submit to the taking of any other type of specimen to determine the person's alcohol concentration.

Sec. 724.012. Taking of Specimen.

(a) One or more specimens of a person's breath or blood may be taken if the person is arrested and at the request of a peace officer having reasonable grounds to believe the person:

(1) while intoxicated was operating a motor vehicle in a public place, or a watercraft; or

(2) was in violation of Section 106.041, Alcoholic Beverage Code.

(a-1) A peace officer shall require the taking of a specimen of the person's blood if:

(1) the officer arrests the person for an offense under Chapter 49, Penal Code, involving the operation of a motor vehicle or a watercraft;

(2) the person refuses the officer's request to submit to the taking of a specimen voluntarily;

(3) the person was the operator of a motor vehicle or a watercraft involved in an accident that the officer reasonably believes occurred as a result of the offense; and

Transportation Code

(4) at the time of the arrest, the officer reasonably believes that as a direct result of the accident any individual has died, will die, or has suffered serious bodily injury.

(b) Subject to Subsection (a-1), a peace officer shall require the taking of a specimen of the person's breath or blood under any of the following circumstances if the officer arrests the person for an offense under Chapter 49, Penal Code, involving the operation of a motor vehicle or a watercraft and the person refuses the officer's request to submit to the taking of a specimen voluntarily:

(1) the person was the operator of a motor vehicle or a watercraft involved in an accident that the officer reasonably believes occurred as a result of the offense and, at the time of the arrest, the officer reasonably believes that as a direct result of the accident an individual other than the person has suffered bodily injury and been transported to a hospital or other medical facility for medical treatment;

(2) the offense for which the officer arrests the person is an offense under Section 49.045, Penal Code; or

(3) at the time of the arrest, the officer possesses or receives reliable information from a credible source that the person:

(A) has been previously convicted of or placed on community supervision for an offense under Section 49.045, 49.07, or 49.08, Penal Code, or an offense under the laws of another state containing elements substantially similar to the elements of an offense under those sections; or

(B) on two or more occasions, has been previously convicted of or placed on community supervision for an offense under Section 49.04, 49.05, 49.06, or 49.065, Penal Code, or an offense under the laws of another state containing elements substantially similar to the elements of an offense under those sections.

(c) Except as provided by Subsection (a-1), the peace officer shall designate the type of specimen to be taken.

(d) In this section, "bodily injury" and "serious bodily injury" have the meanings assigned by Section 1.07, Penal Code.

(e) A peace officer may not require the taking of a specimen under this section unless the officer:

(1) obtains a warrant directing that the specimen be taken; or

(2) has probable cause to believe that exigent circumstances exist.

Sec. 724.013. Prohibition on Taking Specimen If Person Refuses; Exception.

Except as provided by Section 724.012(a-1) or (b), a specimen may not be taken if a person refuses to submit to the taking of a specimen designated by a peace officer.

Sec. 724.014. Person Incapable of Refusal.

(a) A person who is dead, unconscious, or otherwise incapable of refusal is considered not to have withdrawn the consent provided by Section 724.011.

(b) If the person is dead, a specimen may be taken by:

(1) the county medical examiner or the examiner's designated agent; or

(2) a licensed mortician or a person authorized under Section 724.016 or 724.017 if there is not a county medical examiner for the county.

(c) If the person is alive but is incapable of refusal, a specimen may be taken by a person authorized under Section 724.016 or 724.017.

Sec. 724.015. Information Provided by Officer Before Requesting Specimen; Statement of Consent.

(a) Before requesting a person to submit to the taking of a specimen, the officer shall inform the person orally and in writing that:

(1) if the person refuses to submit to the taking of the specimen, that refusal may be admissible in a subsequent prosecution;

(2) if the person refuses to submit to the taking of the specimen, the person's license to operate a motor vehicle will be automatically suspended, whether or not the person is subsequently prosecuted as a result of the arrest, for not less than 180 days;

(3) if the person refuses to submit to the taking of a specimen, the officer may apply for a warrant authorizing a specimen to be taken from the person;

(4) if the person is 21 years of age or older and submits to the taking of a specimen designated by the officer and an analysis of the specimen shows the person had an alcohol concentration of a level specified by Chapter 49, Penal Code, the person's license to operate a motor vehicle will be automatically suspended for not less than 90 days, whether or not the person is subsequently prosecuted as a result of the arrest;

(5) if the person is younger than 21 years of age and has any detectable amount of alcohol in the person's system, the person's license to operate a motor vehicle will be automatically suspended for not less than 60 days even if the person submits to the taking of the specimen, but that if the person submits to the taking of the specimen and an analysis of the specimen shows that the person had an alcohol concentration less than the level specified

by Chapter 49, Penal Code, the person may be subject to criminal penalties less severe than those provided under that chapter;

(6) if the officer determines that the person is a resident without a license to operate a motor vehicle in this state, the department will deny to the person the issuance of a license, whether or not the person is subsequently prosecuted as a result of the arrest, under the same conditions and for the same periods that would have applied to a revocation of the person's driver's license if the person had held a driver's license issued by this state;

(7) the person has a right to a hearing on the suspension or denial if, not later than the 15th day after the date on which the person receives the notice of suspension or denial or on which the person is considered to have received the notice by mail as provided by law, the department receives, at its headquarters in Austin, a written demand, including a facsimile transmission, or a request in another form prescribed by the department for the hearing; and

(8) if the person submits to the taking of a blood specimen, the specimen will be retained and preserved in accordance with Article 38.50, Code of Criminal Procedure.

(b) If a person consents to the request of an officer to submit to the taking of a specimen, the officer shall request the person to sign a statement that:

(1) the officer requested that the person submit to the taking of a specimen;

(2) the person was informed of the consequences of not submitting to the taking of a specimen; and

(3) the person voluntarily consented to the taking of a specimen.

Sec. 724.016. Breath Specimen.

(a) A breath specimen taken at the request or order of a peace officer must be taken and analyzed under rules of the department by an individual possessing a certificate issued by the department certifying that the individual is qualified to perform the analysis.

(b) The department may:

(1) adopt rules approving satisfactory analytical methods; and

(2) ascertain the qualifications of an individual to perform the analysis.

(c) The department may revoke a certificate for cause.

Sec. 724.017. Taking of Blood Specimen.

(a) Only the following may take a blood specimen at the request or order of a peace officer under this chapter:

(1) a physician;

(2) a qualified technician;

(3) a registered professional nurse;

(4) a licensed vocational nurse; or

(5) a licensed or certified emergency medical technician-intermediate or emergency medical technician-paramedic authorized to take a blood specimen under Subsection (c).

(a-1) The blood specimen must be taken in a sanitary place.

(b) If the blood specimen was taken according to recognized medical procedures, the person who takes the blood specimen under this chapter, the facility that employs the person who takes the blood specimen, or the hospital where the blood specimen is taken is immune from civil liability for damages arising from the taking of the blood specimen at the request or order of the peace officer or pursuant to a search warrant as provided by this chapter and is not subject to discipline by any licensing or accrediting agency or body. This subsection does not relieve a person from liability for negligence in the taking of a blood specimen. The taking of a specimen from a person who objects to the taking of the specimen or who is resisting the taking of the specimen does not in itself constitute negligence and may not be considered evidence of negligence.

(c) A licensed or certified emergency medical technician-intermediate or emergency medical technician-paramedic may take a blood specimen only if authorized by the medical director for the entity that employs the technician-intermediate or technician-paramedic. The specimen must be taken according to a protocol developed by the medical director that provides direction to the technician-intermediate or technician-paramedic for the taking of a blood specimen at the request or order of a peace officer. In this subsection, "medical director" means a licensed physician who supervises the provision of emergency medical services by a public or private entity that:

(1) provides those services; and

(2) employs one or more licensed or certified emergency medical technician-intermediates or emergency medical technician-paramedics.

(c-1) A protocol developed under Subsection (c) may address whether an emergency medical technician-intermediate or emergency medical technician-paramedic engaged in the performance of official duties is entitled to refuse to:

(1) go to the location of a person from whom a peace officer requests or orders the taking of a blood specimen solely for the purpose of taking that blood specimen;

(2) take a blood specimen if the technician-intermediate or technician-paramedic reasonably

believes that complying with the peace officer's request or order to take the specimen would impair or interfere with the provision of patient care or the performance of other official duties; or

(3) provide the equipment or supplies necessary to take a blood specimen.

(c-2) If a licensed or certified emergency medical technician-intermediate or emergency medical technician-paramedic takes a blood specimen at the request or order of a peace officer, a peace officer must:

(1) observe the taking of the specimen; and

(2) immediately take possession of the specimen for purposes of establishing a chain of custody.

(d) A person whose blood specimen is taken under this chapter in a hospital is not considered to be present in the hospital for medical screening or treatment unless the appropriate hospital personnel determine that medical screening or treatment is required for proper medical care of the person.

Sec. 724.018. Furnishing Information Concerning Test Results.

On the request of a person who has given a specimen at the request of a peace officer, full information concerning the analysis of the specimen shall be made available to the person or the person's attorney.

Sec. 724.019. Additional Analysis by Request.

(a) A person who submits to the taking of a specimen of breath, blood, urine, or another bodily substance at the request or order of a peace officer may, on request and within a reasonable time not to exceed two hours after the arrest, have a physician, qualified technician, chemist, or registered professional nurse selected by the person take for analysis an additional specimen of the person's blood.

(b) The person shall be allowed a reasonable opportunity to contact a person specified by Subsection (a).

(c) A peace officer or law enforcement agency is not required to transport for testing a person who requests that a blood specimen be taken under this section.

(d) The failure or inability to obtain an additional specimen or analysis under this section does not preclude the admission of evidence relating to the analysis of the specimen taken at the request or order of the peace officer.

(e) A peace officer, another person acting for or on behalf of the state, or a law enforcement agency is not liable for damages arising from a person's request to have a blood specimen taken.

SUBCHAPTER C SUSPENSION OR DENIAL OF LICENSE ON REFUSAL OF SPECIMEN

Sec. 724.031. Statement Requested on Refusal.

If a person refuses the request of a peace officer to submit to the taking of a specimen, the peace officer shall request the person to sign a statement that:

(1) the officer requested that the person submit to the taking of a specimen;

(2) the person was informed of the consequences of not submitting to the taking of a specimen; and

(3) the person refused to submit to the taking of a specimen.

Sec. 724.032. Officer's Duties for License Suspension; Written Refusal Report.

(a) If a person refuses to submit to the taking of a specimen, whether expressly or because of an intentional failure of the person to give the specimen, the peace officer shall:

(1) serve notice of license suspension or denial on the person;

(2) take possession of any license issued by this state and held by the person arrested;

(3) issue a temporary driving permit to the person unless department records show or the officer otherwise determines that the person does not hold a license to operate a motor vehicle in this state; and

(4) make a written report of the refusal to the director of the department.

(b) The director must approve the form of the refusal report. The report must:

(1) show the grounds for the officer's belief that the person had been operating a motor vehicle or watercraft powered with an engine having a manufacturer's rating of 50 horsepower or above while intoxicated; and

(2) contain a copy of:

(A) the refusal statement requested under Section 724.031; or

(B) a statement signed by the officer that the person refused to:

(i) submit to the taking of the requested specimen; and

(ii) sign the requested statement under Section 724.031.

(c) The officer shall forward to the department not later than the fifth business day after the date of the arrest:

(1) a copy of the notice of suspension or denial;
(2) any license taken by the officer under Subsection (a);
(3) a copy of any temporary driving permit issued under Subsection (a); and
(4) a copy of the refusal report.

(d) The department shall develop forms for notices of suspension or denial and temporary driving permits to be used by all state and local law enforcement agencies.

(e) A temporary driving permit issued under this section expires on the 41st day after the date of issuance. If the person was driving a commercial motor vehicle, as defined by Section 522.003, a temporary driving permit that authorizes the person to drive a commercial motor vehicle is not effective until 24 hours after the time of arrest.

Sec. 724.033. Issuance by Department of Notice of Suspension or Denial of License.

(a) On receipt of a report of a peace officer under Section 724.032, if the officer did not serve notice of suspension or denial of a license at the time of refusal to submit to the taking of a specimen, the department shall mail notice of suspension or denial, by first class mail, to the address of the person shown by the records of the department or to the address given in the peace officer's report, if different.

(b) Notice is considered received on the fifth day after the date it is mailed.

Sec. 724.034. Contents of Notice of Suspension or Denial of License.

A notice of suspension or denial of a license must state:
(1) the reason and statutory grounds for the action;
(2) the effective date of the suspension or denial;
(3) the right of the person to a hearing;
(4) how to request a hearing; and
(5) the period in which a request for a hearing must be received by the department.

Sec. 724.035. Suspension or Denial of License.

(a) If a person refuses the request of a peace officer to submit to the taking of a specimen, the department shall:
(1) suspend the person's license to operate a motor vehicle on a public highway for 180 days; or
(2) if the person is a resident without a license, issue an order denying the issuance of a license to the person for 180 days.

(b) The period of suspension or denial is two years if the person's driving record shows one or more alcohol-related or drug-related enforcement contacts, as defined by Section 524.001(3), during the 10 years preceding the date of the person's arrest.

(c) A suspension or denial takes effect on the 40th day after the date on which the person:
(1) receives notice of suspension or denial under Section 724.032(a); or
(2) is considered to have received notice of suspension or denial under Section 724.033.

SUBCHAPTER D HEARING

Sec. 724.041. Hearing on Suspension or Denial.

(a) If, not later than the 15th day after the date on which the person receives notice of suspension or denial under Section 724.032(a) or is considered to have received notice under Section 724.033, the department receives at its headquarters in Austin, in writing, including a facsimile transmission, or by another manner prescribed by the department, a request that a hearing be held, the State Office of Administrative Hearings shall hold a hearing.

(b) A hearing shall be held not earlier than the 11th day after the date the person is notified, unless the parties agree to waive this requirement, but before the effective date of the notice of suspension or denial.

(c) A request for a hearing stays the suspension or denial until the date of the final decision of the administrative law judge. If the person's license was taken by a peace officer under Section 724.032(a), the department shall notify the person of the effect of the request on the suspension of the person's license before the expiration of any temporary driving permit issued to the person, if the person is otherwise eligible, in a manner that will permit the person to establish to a peace officer that the person's license is not suspended.

(d) A hearing shall be held by an administrative law judge employed by the State Office of Administrative Hearings.

(e) A hearing shall be held:
(1) at a location designated by the State Office of Administrative Hearings:
(A) in the county of arrest if the county has a population of 300,000 or more; or
(B) in the county in which the person was alleged to have committed the offense for which the person

Transportation Code

was arrested or not more than 75 miles from the county seat of the county of arrest if the population of the county of arrest is less than 300,000; or

(2) with the consent of the person requesting the hearing and the department, by telephone conference call.

(f) The State Office of Administrative Hearings shall provide for the stenographic or electronic recording of a hearing under this subchapter.

(g) An administrative hearing under this section is governed by Sections 524.032(b) and (c), 524.035(e), 524.037(a), and 524.040.

Sec. 724.042. Issues at Hearing.

The issues at a hearing under this subchapter are whether:

(1) reasonable suspicion or probable cause existed to stop or arrest the person;

(2) probable cause existed to believe that the person was:

(A) operating a motor vehicle in a public place while intoxicated; or

(B) operating a watercraft powered with an engine having a manufacturer's rating of 50 horsepower or above while intoxicated;

(3) the person was placed under arrest by the officer and was requested to submit to the taking of a specimen; and

(4) the person refused to submit to the taking of a specimen on request of the officer.

Sec. 724.043. Findings of Administrative Law Judge.

(a) If the administrative law judge finds in the affirmative on each issue under Section 724.042, the suspension order is sustained. If the person is a resident without a license, the department shall continue to deny to the person the issuance of a license for the applicable period provided by Section 724.035.

(b) If the administrative law judge does not find in the affirmative on each issue under Section 724.042, the department shall return the person's license to the person, if the license was taken by a peace officer under Section 724.032(a), and reinstate the person's license or rescind any order denying the issuance of a license because of the person's refusal to submit to the taking of a specimen under Section 724.032(a).

Sec. 724.044. Waiver of Right to Hearing.

A person waives the right to a hearing under this subchapter and the department's suspension or denial is final and may not be appealed if the person:

(1) fails to request a hearing under Section 724.041; or

(2) requests a hearing and fails to appear, without good cause.

Sec. 724.045. Prohibition on Probation of Suspension.

A suspension under this chapter may not be probated.

Sec. 724.046. Reinstatement of License or Issuance of New License.

(a) A license suspended under this chapter may not be reinstated or a new license issued until the person whose license has been suspended pays to the department a fee of $125 in addition to any other fee required by law. A person subject to a denial order issued under this chapter may not obtain a license after the period of denial has ended until the person pays to the department a fee of $125 in addition to any other fee required by law.

(b) If a suspension or denial under this chapter is rescinded by the department, an administrative law judge, or a court, payment of the fee under this section is not required for reinstatement or issuance of a license.

(c) Each fee collected under this section shall be deposited to the credit of the Texas mobility fund.

Sec. 724.047. Appeal.

Chapter 524 governs an appeal from an action of the department, following an administrative hearing under this chapter, in suspending or denying the issuance of a license.

Sec. 724.048. Relationship of Administrative Proceeding to Criminal Proceeding.

(a) The determination of the department or administrative law judge:

(1) is a civil matter;

(2) is independent of and is not an estoppel as to any matter in issue in an adjudication of a criminal charge arising from the occurrence that is the basis for the suspension or denial; and

(3) does not preclude litigation of the same or similar facts in a criminal prosecution.

(b) Except as provided by Subsection (c), the disposition of a criminal charge does not affect a license suspension or denial under this chapter and is not an estoppel as to any matter in issue in a suspension or denial proceeding under this chapter.

(c) If a criminal charge arising from the same arrest as a suspension under this chapter results in an acquittal, the suspension under this chapter may not be imposed. If a suspension under this chapter has already been imposed, the department shall rescind the suspension and remove references to the suspension from the computerized driving record of the individual.

SUBCHAPTER E ADMISSIBILITY OF EVIDENCE

Sec. 724.061. Admissibility of Refusal of Person to Submit to Taking of Specimen.

A person's refusal of a request by an officer to submit to the taking of a specimen of breath or blood, whether the refusal was express or the result of an intentional failure to give the specimen, may be introduced into evidence at the person's trial.

Sec. 724.062. Admissibility of Refusal of Request for Additional Test.

The fact that a person's request to have an additional analysis under Section 724.019 is refused by the officer or another person acting for or on behalf of the state, that the person was not provided a reasonable opportunity to contact a person specified by Section 724.019(a) to take the specimen, or that reasonable access was not allowed to the arrested person may be introduced into evidence at the person's trial.

Sec. 724.063. Admissibility of Alcohol Concentration or Presence of Substance.

Evidence of alcohol concentration or the presence of a controlled substance, drug, dangerous drug, or other substance obtained by an analysis authorized by Section 724.014 is admissible in a civil or criminal action.

Sec. 724.064. Admissibility in Criminal Proceeding of Specimen Analysis.

On the trial of a criminal proceeding arising out of an offense under Chapter 49, Penal Code, involving the operation of a motor vehicle or a watercraft, or an offense under Section 106.041, Alcoholic Beverage Code, evidence of the alcohol concentration or presence of a controlled substance, drug, dangerous drug, or other substance as shown by analysis of a specimen of the person's blood, breath, or urine or any other bodily substance taken at the request or order of a peace officer is admissible.

CHAPTER 725 TRANSPORTATION OF LOOSE MATERIALS

SUBCHAPTER A GENERAL PROVISIONS

Sec. 725.001. Definitions.

In this chapter:

(1) "Load" means a load of loose material.

(2) "Loose material" means material that can be blown or spilled from a vehicle because of movement or exposure to air, wind currents, or other weather. The term includes dirt, sand, gravel, refuse, and wood chips but excludes an agricultural product in its natural state.

(3) "Motor vehicle" has the meaning assigned by Section 621.001.

(4) "Public highway" includes a public road or street.

(4-a) "Refuse" means trash, rubbish, garbage, or any other discarded material.

(5) "Semitrailer" has the meaning assigned by Section 621.001.

(6) "Trailer" has the meaning assigned by Section 621.001.

(7) "Vehicle" has the meaning assigned by Section 621.001.

Sec. 725.002. Applicability.

This chapter applies to any motor vehicle, trailer, or semitrailer operated on a public highway except a vehicle or construction or mining equipment that is:

(1) moving between construction barricades on a public works project; or

(2) crossing a public highway.

Sec. 725.003. Offense; Penalty.

(a) A person or the person's agent or employee may not transport loose material in violation of this chapter.

(b) A person, excluding this state or a political subdivision of this state but including an agent or employee of this state or a political subdivision of this state, commits an offense if the person violates Subsection (a).

(c) An offense under this section is a misdemeanor punishable by a fine of not less than $25 or more than $500.

SUBCHAPTER B REQUIREMENTS FOR TRANSPORTING LOOSE MATERIALS

Sec. 725.021. Containing Loose Materials.

(a) A vehicle subject to this chapter shall be equipped and maintained as required by this section to prevent loose material from escaping by blowing or spilling.

(b) A vehicle bed carrying a load:

(1) may not have a hole, crack, or other opening through which loose material can escape; and

(2) shall be enclosed:

(A) on both sides by side panels;

(B) on the front by a panel or the vehicle cab; and

(C) on the rear by a tailgate or panel.

(c) Except as provided by Subsection (e), the load shall be covered and the covering firmly secured at the front and back, unless the load:

(1) is completely enclosed by the load-carrying compartment; or

(2) does not blow from or spill over the top of the load-carrying compartment.

(d) The tailgate of the vehicle shall be securely closed to prevent spillage during transportation.

(e) If the vehicle is a commercial motor vehicle transporting loose material, the load shall be covered and the covering firmly secured at the front and back or shall be completely enclosed by the load-carrying compartment. For purposes of this section, "commercial motor vehicle" means a motor vehicle, trailer, or semitrailer used primarily in the business of transporting property.

Sec. 725.022. Maintaining Non-Load-Carrying Vehicle Parts.

(a) Loose material that is spilled because of loading on a vehicle part that does not carry the load shall be removed before the vehicle is operated on a public highway.

(b) After the vehicle is unloaded and before the vehicle is operated on a public highway, residue of transported loose material on a vehicle part that does not carry the load shall be removed from the vehicle part.

CHAPTER 726 TESTING AND INSPECTION OF MOTOR VEHICLES BY CERTAIN MUNICIPALITIES

Sec. 726.001. Applicability.

(a) This chapter applies only to a municipality with a population of more than 290,000.

(b) This section or an ordinance adopted under this section does not apply to a motor vehicle, trailer, or semitrailer operated under a registration certificate issued under Chapter 643.

Sec. 726.002. Testing and Inspection of Motor Vehicles.

A municipality may adopt an ordinance:

(1) requiring each resident of the municipality, including a corporation having its principal office or place of business in the municipality, who owns a motor vehicle used for the transportation of persons or property and each person operating a motor vehicle on the public thoroughfares of the municipality to have each motor vehicle owned or operated, as appropriate, tested and inspected not more than four times in each calendar year;

(2) requiring each motor vehicle involved in an accident to be tested and inspected before it may be operated on the public thoroughfares of the municipality; or

(3) requiring that a motor vehicle operated on the public thoroughfares of the municipality be tested, inspected, and approved by the testing and inspecting authority.

Sec. 726.003. Motor Vehicle Testing Stations; Testing and Inspection Fee.

(a) A municipality may acquire, establish, improve, operate, and maintain motor vehicle testing stations and pay for the stations from fees charged for testing and inspecting motor vehicles.

(b) A municipality may impose a fee for the testing and inspecting of a motor vehicle. The fee may not exceed $1 a year. Fees collected under this subsection shall be placed in a separate fund from which may be paid the costs in connection with automotive and safety education programs and the acquisition, establishment, improvement, operation, and maintenance of the testing stations.

Sec. 726.004. Financing of Motor Vehicle Testing Stations.

(a) A municipality may borrow money to finance all or part of the cost of the acquisition, establishment, improvement, or repair of motor vehicle testing stations and may pledge all or part of the fees or other receipts derived from the operation of the stations for payment of principal and interest on the loan.

(b) A municipality may encumber a testing station, including things acquired pertaining to the station, to secure the payment of funds to construct all or part of the station or to improve, operate, or maintain the station. An encumbrance is not a debt of the municipality but is solely a charge on the property encumbered and may not be considered in determining the power of the municipality to issue bonds.

CHAPTER 727
MODIFICATION OF, TAMPERING WITH, AND EQUIPMENT OF MOTOR VEHICLES

Sec. 727.001. Minimum Road Clearance of Certain Vehicles; Offense.

(a) A person commits an offense if the person operates on a public roadway a passenger or commercial vehicle that has been modified from its original design or weighted so that the clearance between any part of the vehicle other than the wheels and the surface of the level roadway is less than the clearance between the roadway and the lowest part of the rim of any wheel in contact with the roadway.

(b) An offense under this section is a misdemeanor punishable by a fine not to exceed $50.

Sec. 727.002. Tampering with Odometer; Offense.

(a) A person commits an offense if the person, with intent to defraud, disconnects or resets an odometer to reduce the number of miles indicated on the odometer.

(b) Except as provided by Subsection (c), an offense under this section is punishable by:

(1) confinement in the county jail for not more than two years;

(2) a fine not to exceed $1,000; or

(3) both the confinement and fine.

(c) If it is shown on the trial of an offense under this section that the person has previously been convicted of an offense under this section, the offense is punishable by:

(1) confinement in the county jail for not less than 30 days or more than two years; and

(2) a fine not to exceed $2,000.

(d) In this section, "odometer" means an instrument for measuring and recording the distance a motor vehicle travels while in operation but does not include an auxiliary odometer designed to be reset by the operator to record mileage on trips.

Sec. 727.003. Tire Equipment of Motor Vehicle, Trailer, or Tractor; Offense.

(a) A person commits an offense if the person operates or permits to be operated on a public highway a motor vehicle, trailer, semitrailer, or tractor equipped with:

(1) solid rubber tires less than one inch in thickness at any point from the surface to the rim; or

(2) pneumatic tires, one or more of which has been removed.

(b) An offense under this section is a misdemeanor punishable by a fine not to exceed $200.

Sec. 727.004. Rim or Tire Width; Offense.

(a) A person commits an offense if the person sells or offers for sale a road vehicle, including a wagon, that has a rim or tire width less than:

(1) three inches, if the vehicle has an intended carrying capacity of more than 2,000 pounds and not more than 4,500 pounds; or

(2) four inches, if the vehicle has an intended carrying capacity of more than 4,500 pounds.

(b) This section does not apply to an individual who sells or offers for sale a road vehicle purchased for the individual's use.

(c) An offense under this section is punishable by a fine of not less than $100 or more than $1,000.

CHAPTER 728
SALE OR TRANSFER OF MOTOR VEHICLES AND MASTER KEYS

SUBCHAPTER A
SALE OF MOTOR VEHICLES ON CONSECUTIVE SATURDAY AND SUNDAY

Sec. 728.001. Definitions.

In this subchapter:

(1) "Employer" means a person who:

(A) owns a facility that sells or offers for sale motor vehicles; or

(B) has the authority to determine the hours of operation of the facility.

(2) "Motor vehicle" means a self-propelled vehicle of two or more wheels designed to transport a person or property.

Sec. 728.002. Sale of Motor Vehicles on Consecutive Saturday and Sunday Prohibited.

(a) A person may not, on consecutive days of Saturday and Sunday:

(1) sell or offer for sale a motor vehicle; or

(2) compel an employee to sell or offer for sale a motor vehicle.

(b) Each day a motor vehicle is offered for sale is a separate violation. Each sale of a motor vehicle is a separate violation.

(c) This section does not prohibit the occasional sale of a motor vehicle by a person not in a business that includes the sale of motor vehicles.

(d) This section does not prohibit the quoting of a price for a motor home or tow truck at a show or exhibition described by Section 2301.358, Occupations Code.

Sec. 728.003. Civil Penalty.

(a) A person who violates Section 728.002 is subject to a civil penalty of:

(1) not more than $500 for a first violation;

(2) not less than $500 or more than $1,000 for a second violation; or

(3) not less than $1,000 or more than $5,000 for a third or subsequent violation.

(b) On a finding by the trier of fact that a person wilfully or with conscious indifference violated Section 728.002, the court may triple the penalty due under Subsection (a).

Sec. 728.004. Enforcement; Injunction.

(a) The attorney general or a district, county, or municipal attorney may enforce this subchapter and may bring an action in the county in which a violation is alleged.

(b) The operation of a business in violation of this subchapter is a public nuisance. Any person, including a district, county, or municipal attorney, may obtain an injunction restraining a violation of this subchapter. A person who obtains an injunction under this subsection may recover the person's costs, including court costs and reasonable attorney's fees.

(c) An employer is a necessary party to an action brought against its employee under this section. An employer is strictly liable for all amounts, including civil penalties, damages, costs, and attorney's fees, resulting from a violation of Section 728.002 by its employee.

SUBCHAPTER B
SALE OF MASTER KEY FOR MOTOR VEHICLE IGNITIONS

Sec. 728.011. Sale of Master Key for Motor Vehicle Ignitions.

(a) A person commits an offense if the person sells or offers to sell a master key knowingly designed to fit the ignition switch on more than one motor vehicle.

(b) An offense under this section is a misdemeanor punishable by a fine of not less than $25 or more than $200.

SUBCHAPTER C
TRANSFER OF OWNERSHIP OF CERTAIN EMERGENCY VEHICLES

Sec. 728.021. Transfer of Ownership of Certain Emergency Vehicles; Offense.

(a) The owner of an authorized emergency vehicle that is used to transport sick or injured persons commits an offense if the owner transfers ownership of the vehicle without:

(1) removing from the vehicle any vehicle equipment, including a light, siren, or device, that under Subtitle C only an authorized emergency vehicle may be equipped with; and

(2) removing or obliterating any emblem or marking on the vehicle that identifies the vehicle as an authorized emergency vehicle.

(b) Subsection (a) does not apply if the owner of the vehicle transfers ownership of the vehicle to a person:

(1) who holds a license as an emergency medical services provider under Chapter 773, Health and Safety Code;

(2) who is in the business of buying and selling used vehicles in this state and who specializes in authorized emergency vehicles; or

(3) described by Section 541.201 or a similar person operating in a foreign country.

(c) An offense under this section is a Class C misdemeanor.

(d) In this section:

(1) "Authorized emergency vehicle" has the meaning assigned by Section 541.201.

(2) "Vehicle equipment" has the meaning assigned by Section 547.001.

Sec. 728.022. Sale or Transfer of Law Enforcement Vehicle.

(a) A person may not sell or transfer a marked patrol car or other law enforcement motor vehicle to the public unless the person first removes any equipment or insignia that could mislead a reasonable person to believe that the vehicle is a law enforcement motor vehicle, including any police light, siren, amber warning light, spotlight, grill light, antenna, emblem, outline of an emblem, or emergency vehicle equipment.

(b) A person may not sell or transfer a marked patrol car or other law enforcement motor vehicle to a security services contractor who is regulated by the Department of Public Safety and licensed under Chapter 1702, Occupations Code, unless each emblem or insignia that identifies the vehicle as a law enforcement motor vehicle is removed before the sale or transfer.

(c) A person who sells or transfers a marked patrol car or other law enforcement motor vehicle to the public in violation of this section is liable:

(1) for damages proximately caused by the use of that vehicle during the commission of a crime; and

(2) to this state for a civil penalty of $1,000.

(d) The attorney general may bring an action to recover the civil penalty imposed under Subsection (c)(2).

CHAPTER 729 OPERATION OF MOTOR VEHICLE BY MINOR

Sec. 729.001. Operation of Motor Vehicle by Minor in Violation of Traffic Laws; Offense.

(a) A person who is younger than 17 years of age commits an offense if the person operates a motor vehicle on a public road or highway, a street or alley in a municipality, or a public beach in violation of any traffic law of this state, including:

(1) Chapter 502, other than Section 502.282 or 502.412;

(2) Chapter 521, other than an offense under Section 521.457;

(3) Subtitle C, other than an offense punishable by imprisonment or by confinement in jail under Section 550.021, 550.022, 550.024, or 550.025;

(4) Chapter 601;

(5) Chapter 621;

(6) Chapter 661; and

(7) Chapter 681.

(b) In this section, "beach" means a beach bordering on the Gulf of Mexico that extends inland from the line of mean low tide to the natural line of vegetation bordering on the seaward shore of the Gulf of Mexico, or the larger contiguous area to which the public has acquired a right of use or easement to or over by prescription, dedication, or estoppel, or has retained a right by virtue of continuous right in the public since time immemorial as recognized by law or custom.

(c) An offense under this section is punishable by the fine or other sanction, other than confinement or imprisonment, authorized by statute for violation of the traffic law listed under Subsection (a) that is the basis of the prosecution under this section.

Sec. 729.002. Operation of Motor Vehicle by Minor Without License.

(a) A person who is younger than 17 years of age commits an offense if the person operates a motor vehicle without a driver's license authorizing the operation of a motor vehicle on a:

(1) public road or highway;

(2) street or alley in a municipality; or

(3) public beach as defined by Section 729.001.

(b) An offense under this section is punishable in the same manner as if the person was 17 years of age or older and operated a motor vehicle without a license as described by Subsection (a), except that an offense under this section is not punishable by confinement or imprisonment.

Sec. 729.003. Procedure in Cases Involving Minors [Repealed].

Repealed by Acts 2005, 79th Leg., ch. 949 (H.B. 1575), § 52(2), effective September 1, 2005.

Sec. 729.004. Fine for Offense in Construction or Maintenance Work Zone [Repealed].

Repealed by Acts 2003, 78th Leg., ch. 283 (H.B. 2319), § 61(2), effective September 1, 2003.

CHAPTER 730
MOTOR VEHICLE RECORDS DISCLOSURE ACT

Sec. 730.001. Short Title.

This chapter may be cited as the Motor Vehicle Records Disclosure Act.

Sec. 730.002. Purpose.

The purpose of this chapter is to implement 18 U.S.C. Chapter 123 and to protect the interest of an individual in the individual's personal privacy by prohibiting the disclosure and use of personal information contained in motor vehicle records, except as authorized by the individual or by law.

Sec. 730.003. Definitions.

In this chapter:

(1) "Agency" includes any agency or political subdivision of this state, or an authorized agent or contractor of an agency or political subdivision of this state, that compiles or maintains motor vehicle records.

(1-a) "Authorized recipient" means a person who is permitted to receive and use personal information from an agency in a manner authorized by this chapter.

(2) "Disclose" means to make available or make known personal information contained in a motor vehicle record about a person to another person, by any means of communication.

(3) "Individual record" means a motor vehicle record obtained by an agency containing personal information about an individual who is the subject of the record as identified in a request.

(4) "Motor vehicle record" means a record that pertains to a motor vehicle operator's or driver's license or permit, motor vehicle registration, motor vehicle title, or identification document issued by an agency of this state or a local agency authorized to issue an identification document. The term does not include:

(A) a record that pertains to a motor carrier; or

(B) an accident report prepared under:

(i) Chapter 550; or

(ii) former Section 601.004 before September 1, 2017.

(5) "Person" means an individual, organization, or entity but does not include this state or an agency of this state.

(6) "Personal information" means information that identifies a person, including an individual's photograph or computerized image, social security number, date of birth, driver identification number, name, address, but not the zip code, e-mail address, telephone number, and medical or disability information. The term does not include:

(A) information on vehicle accidents, driving or equipment-related violations, or driver's license or registration status; or

(B) information contained in an accident report prepared under:

(i) Chapter 550; or

(ii) former Section 601.004 before September 1, 2017.

(7) "Record" includes any book, paper, photograph, photostat, card, film, tape, recording, electronic data, printout, or other documentary material regardless of physical form or characteristics.

Sec. 730.004. Prohibition on Disclosure and Use of Personal Information from Motor Vehicle Records.

Notwithstanding any other provision of law to the contrary, including Chapter 552, Government Code, except as provided by Sections 730.005—730.007, an agency may not disclose personal information about any person obtained by the agency in connection with a motor vehicle record.

Sec. 730.005. Required Disclosure.

Personal information obtained by an agency in connection with a motor vehicle record shall be disclosed for use in connection with any matter of:

(1) motor vehicle or motor vehicle operator safety;

(2) motor vehicle theft;

(3) motor vehicle emissions;

(4) motor vehicle product alterations, recalls, or advisories;

(5) performance monitoring of motor vehicles or motor vehicle dealers by a motor vehicle manufacturer;

(6) removal of nonowner records from the original owner records of a motor vehicle manufacturer to carry out the purposes of:

(A) the Automobile Information Disclosure Act, 15 U.S.C. Section 1231 et seq.;

(B) 49 U.S.C. Chapters 301, 305, 323, 325, 327, 329, and 331;

(C) the Anti Car Theft Act of 1992, 18 U.S.C. Sections 553, 981, 982, 2119, 2312, 2313, and 2322, 19 U.S.C. Sections 1646b and 1646c, and 42 U.S.C. Section 3750a et seq., all as amended;

(D) the Clean Air Act, 42 U.S.C. Section 7401 et seq., as amended; and

(E) any other statute or regulation enacted or adopted under or in relation to a law included in Paragraphs (A)—(D);

(7) child support enforcement under Chapter 231, Family Code;

(8) enforcement by the Texas Workforce Commission under Title 4, Labor Code; or

(9) voter registration or the administration of elections by the secretary of state.

Sec. 730.006. Required Disclosure with Consent.

Personal information obtained by an agency in connection with a motor vehicle record shall be disclosed to a requestor who:

(1) is the subject of the information; or

(2) demonstrates, in such form and manner as the agency requires, that the requestor has obtained the written consent of the person who is the subject of the information.

Sec. 730.007. Permitted Disclosures of Certain Personal Information.

(a) Personal information obtained by an agency in connection with a motor vehicle record may be disclosed to any requestor by an agency if the requestor:

(1) provides the requestor's name and address and any proof of that information required by the agency; and

(2) represents that the use of the personal information will be strictly limited to:

(A) use by:

(i) a government agency, including any court or law enforcement agency, in carrying out its functions; or

(ii) a private person or entity acting on behalf of a government agency in carrying out the functions of the agency;

(B) use in connection with a matter of:

(i) motor vehicle or motor vehicle operator safety;

(ii) motor vehicle theft;

(iii) motor vehicle product alterations, recalls, or advisories;

(iv) performance monitoring of motor vehicles, motor vehicle parts, or motor vehicle dealers; or

(v) removal of nonowner records from the original owner records of motor vehicle manufacturers;

(C) use in the normal course of business by a legitimate business or an authorized agent of the business, but only:

(i) to verify the accuracy of personal information submitted by the individual to the business or the agent of the business; and

(ii) if the information is not correct, to obtain the correct information, for the sole purpose of preventing fraud by, pursuing a legal remedy against, or recovering on a debt or security interest against the individual;

(D) use in conjunction with a civil, criminal, administrative, or arbitral proceeding in any court or government agency or before any self-regulatory body, including service of process, investigation in anticipation of litigation, execution or enforcement of a judgment or order, or under an order of any court;

(E) use in research or in producing statistical reports, but only if the personal information is not published, redisclosed, or used to contact any individual;

(F) use by an insurer, insurance support organization, or self-insured entity, or an authorized agent of an insurer, insurance support organization, or self-insured entity, in connection with claims processing or investigation activities, antifraud activities, rating, or underwriting;

(G) use in providing notice to an owner of a vehicle that was towed or impounded and is in the possession of a vehicle storage facility;

(H) use by a licensed private investigator agency or licensed security service for a purpose permitted under this section;

(I) use by an employer or an agent or insurer of the employer to obtain or verify information relating to a holder of a commercial driver's license that is required under 49 U.S.C. Chapter 313;

(J) use in connection with the operation of a toll transportation facility or another type of transportation project described by Section 370.003;

(K) use by a consumer reporting agency, as defined by the Fair Credit Reporting Act (15 U.S.C. Section 1681 et seq.), for a purpose permitted under that Act;

(L) use by a motor vehicle manufacturer, dealership, or distributor, or an agent of or provider of services to a motor vehicle manufacturer, dealership, or distributor, for motor vehicle market research activities, including survey research;

(M) use in the ordinary course of business by a person or authorized agent of a person who:

(i) holds a salvage vehicle dealer license issued under Chapter 2302, Occupations Code;

(ii) holds an independent motor vehicle dealer or wholesale motor vehicle auction general distinguishing number issued under Chapter 503 of this code;

(iii) holds a used automotive parts recycler license issued under Chapter 2309, Occupations Code; or

(iv) is licensed by, registered with, or subject to regulatory oversight by the Texas Department of Motor Vehicles, the Texas Department of Banking, the Department of Savings and Mortgage Lending, the Credit Union Department, the Office of Consumer Credit Commissioner, the Texas Department of Insurance, the Board of Governors of the Federal Reserve System, the Office of the Comptroller of the Currency, the Federal Deposit Insurance Corporation, the Consumer Financial Protection Bureau, or the National Credit Union Administration; or

(N) use by an employer, principal, general contractor, nonprofit organization, charitable organization, or religious institution to obtain or verify information relating to a person who holds a driver's license or the driving history of a person who holds a driver's license if the person is employed by, works under a contract with, or volunteers for the employer, principal, contractor, organization, or institution.

(a-1) Personal information obtained by the Texas Department of Motor Vehicles in connection with a motor vehicle record may be disclosed:

(1) when referring potential violations to the Texas Office of Consumer Credit Commissioner, the Department of Public Safety, law enforcement agencies, or the comptroller, if the personal information is necessary for carrying out regulatory functions;

(2) to the attorney general as part of a response by the Texas Department of Motor Vehicles to a subpoena or a discovery request, if the personal information is necessary for litigation purposes; or

(3) to a county assessor-collector if the personal information is related to a finding from an audit or investigation conducted under Section 520.010.

(a-2) Subsection (a)(2)(C) does not authorize the disclosure of personal information to a natural person who is not a business licensed by, registered with, or subject to regulatory oversight by a government agency.

(b) The only personal information an agency may release under this section is the individual's:

(1) name and address;

(2) date of birth; and

(3) driver's license number.

(c) This section does not:

(1) prohibit the disclosure of a person's photographic image to:

(A) a law enforcement agency, the Texas Department of Motor Vehicles, a county tax assessor-collector, or a criminal justice agency for an official purpose;

(B) an agency of this state investigating an alleged violation of a state or federal law relating to the obtaining, selling, or purchasing of a benefit authorized by Chapter 31 or 33, Human Resources Code; or

(C) an agency of this state investigating an alleged violation of a state or federal law under authority provided by Title 4, Labor Code; or

(2) prevent a court from compelling by subpoena the production of a person's photographic image.

(d) Personal information obtained by an agency in connection with a motor vehicle record shall be disclosed to a requestor by an agency if the requestor:

(1) provides the requestor's name and address and any proof of that information required by the agency; and

(2) represents that the intent of the requestor is to use personal information in the motor vehicle record only for the purpose of preventing, detecting, or protecting against personal identity theft or other acts of fraud and provides any proof of the requestor's intent required by the agency.

(e) If the agency determines that the requestor intends to use personal information requested under Subsection (d) only for the represented purpose, the agency shall release to the requestor any requested personal information in the motor vehicle record.

(f) Personal information obtained by an agency under Section 411.0845, Government Code, in connection with a motor vehicle record may be disclosed as provided by that section.

(g) An agency may request that an authorized recipient or other person in possession of personal information disclosed for a use authorized by this section provide to the agency information sufficient for the agency to determine whether the authorized recipient or person has complied with this chapter, agency rules, or other law that applies to the disclosed personal information. The authorized recipient or person shall provide the requested information not later than the fifth business day after the date the agency submits the request unless the agency extends the deadline to provide a reasonable period to produce the requested information.

Sec. 730.008. Disclosure of Individual Record [Repealed].

Repealed by Acts 2001, 77th Leg., ch. 1032 (H.B. 1544), § 9(1), effective September 1, 2001.

Sec. 730.009. Requests to Prohibit Disclosure [Repealed].

Repealed by Acts 2001, 77th Leg., ch. 1032 (H.B. 1544), § 9(1), effective September 1, 2001.

Sec. 730.010. Disclosure of Thumb or Finger Images Prohibited.

Notwithstanding any other provision of this chapter, if an agency obtains an image of an individual's thumb or finger in connection with the issuance of a license, permit, or certificate to the individual, the agency may:

(1) use the image only:

(A) in connection with the issuance of the license, permit, or certificate; or

(B) to verify the identity of an individual as provided by Section 521.059; and

(2) disclose the image only if disclosure is expressly authorized by law.

Sec. 730.011. Fees.

Unless a fee is imposed by law, an agency that has obtained information in connection with a motor vehicle may adopt reasonable fees for disclosure of that personal information under this chapter.

Sec. 730.012. Additional Conditions.

(a) In addition to the payment of a fee adopted under Section 730.011, an agency may require a requestor to provide reasonable assurance:

(1) as to the identity of the requestor; and

(2) that use of the personal information will be only as authorized or that the consent of the person who is the subject of the information has been obtained.

(b) An agency may require the requestor to make or file a written application in the form and containing any certification requirement the agency may prescribe.

Sec. 730.0121. Deletion of Information Required If Not Authorized Recipient.

An agency by rule shall require a requestor to delete from the requestor's records personal information received from the agency under this chapter if the requestor becomes aware that the requestor is not an authorized recipient of that information.

Sec. 730.0122. Sale Prohibited.

(a) A person may not sell to a person who is not an authorized recipient personal information obtained by an agency in connection with a motor vehicle record.

(b) A person commits an offense if the person violates Subsection (a). An offense under this subsection is a misdemeanor punishable by a fine not to exceed $100,000.

Sec. 730.0123. Civil Suit.

(a) A person who sells to a person who is not an authorized recipient personal information obtained by an agency in connection with a motor vehicle record is liable to the person who is the subject of the information for:

(1) actual damages;

(2) if the actual damages to the person are less than $2,500, an additional amount so that the total amount of damages equals $2,500; and

(3) court costs incurred by the person who is the subject of the information in bringing the action.

(b) A person whose personal information has been disclosed for compensation to a person who is not an authorized recipient may sue for:

(1) the damages, costs, and fees authorized under Subsection (a);

(2) injunctive relief; and

(3) any other equitable remedy determined to be appropriate by the court.

(c) A district court has exclusive original jurisdiction over a cause of action brought under this section.

Sec. 730.013. Redisclosure; Offense.

(a) An authorized recipient of personal information may not redisclose the personal information in the identical or a substantially identical format the personal information was disclosed to the recipient by the applicable agency.

(b) An authorized recipient of personal information may redisclose the information, including redisclosure for compensation, only for a use permitted under Section 730.007.

(c) An authorized recipient who rediscloses personal information obtained from an agency shall be required by that agency to:

(1) maintain for a period of not less than five years records as to any person or entity receiving that information and the permitted use for which it was obtained; and

(2) provide copies of those records to the agency on request.

(c-1) A person who receives personal information under Subsection (b) may not redisclose the personal information, including redisclosure for compensation, to a person who is not an authorized recipient.

(c-2) An authorized recipient shall notify each person who receives personal information from the authorized recipient that the person may not redisclose the personal information to a person who is not an authorized recipient.

(d) A person commits an offense if the person violates this section. An offense under this subsection

Transportation Code

is a misdemeanor punishable by a fine not to exceed $100,000.

Sec. 730.014. Agency Rules, Records, and Contracts.

(a) Each agency may adopt rules to implement and administer this chapter.

(b) An agency that maintains motor vehicle records in relation to motor vehicles is not required to also maintain those records in relation to the individuals named in those records.

(c) An agency that provides a requestor access to personal information in motor vehicle records in bulk under a contract under Section 730.007 shall include in the contract:

(1) a requirement that the requestor post a performance bond in an amount of not more than $1 million;

(2) a prohibition on the sale or redisclosure of the personal information for the purpose of marketing extended vehicle warranties by telephone;

(3) a requirement that the requestor provide proof of general liability and cyber-threat insurance coverage in an amount specified by the contracting agency that is:

(A) at least $3 million; and

(B) reasonably related to the risks associated with unauthorized access and use of the records;

(4) a requirement that if a requestor experiences a breach of system security, as defined by Section 521.053, Business & Commerce Code, that includes data obtained under Section 730.007, the requestor must notify the agency of the breach not later than 48 hours after the discovery of the breach;

(5) a requirement that the requestor include in each contract with a third party that receives the personal information from the requestor that the third party must comply with federal and state laws regarding the records;

(6) a requirement that the requestor and any third party receiving the personal information from the requestor protect the personal information with appropriate and accepted industry standard security measures for the type of information and the known risks from unauthorized access and use of the information; and

(7) a requirement that the requestor annually provide to the agency a report of all third parties to which the personal information was disclosed under this section and the purpose of the disclosure.

(d) The bond and insurance requirements in Subsections (c)(1) and (3) do not apply to a contract under Section 730.007 between a government agency and another government agency, including a court or law enforcement agency.

(e) An agency that discloses any motor vehicle records in bulk under Section 730.007 shall include in the records at least two records that are created solely for the purpose of monitoring compliance with this chapter and detecting, by receipt of certain forms of communications or actions directed at the subjects of the created records, potential violations of this chapter or contract terms required by this section.

(f) An agency that discloses motor vehicle records shall designate an employee to be responsible for:

(1) monitoring compliance with this chapter and contract terms required by this section;

(2) referring potential violations of this chapter to law enforcement agencies; and

(3) making recommendations to the administrative head of the agency or the designee of the administrative head of the agency on the eligibility of a person under Section 730.016 to receive personal information.

(g) This subsection does not affect any rights or remedies available under a contract or any other law. If an agency determines that a person has violated a term of a contract with the agency for the disclosure under this chapter of personal information obtained by the agency in connection with a motor vehicle record, the agency may:

(1) cease disclosing personal information to that person; and

(2) allow the person to remedy the violation and resume receiving personal information.

Sec. 730.015. Penalty for False Representation.

(a) A person who requests the disclosure of personal information from an agency's records under this chapter and misrepresents the person's identity or who makes a false statement to the agency on an application required by the agency under this chapter commits an offense.

(b) An offense under Subsection (a) is a Class A misdemeanor.

Sec. 730.016. Ineligibility of Certain Persons to Receive, Retain, or Redisclose Personal Information; Offense.

(a) A person who is convicted of an offense under this chapter, or who violates a rule adopted by an agency relating to the terms or conditions for a release of personal information, including a rule adopted under Section 730.0121:

(1) is ineligible to receive personal information under Section 730.007;

Transportation Code

(2) not later than one year after the date of conviction or the court's final determination under this subsection, shall delete from the person's records all personal information received under this chapter; and

(3) may not redisclose personal information received under this chapter.

(b) For purposes of Subsection (a), a person is considered to have been convicted in a case if:

(1) a sentence is imposed;

(2) the defendant receives probation or deferred adjudication; or

(3) the court defers final disposition of the case.

(c) A person commits an offense if the person violates this section. An offense under this subsection is a misdemeanor punishable by a fine not to exceed $100,000.

CHAPTER 731
ASSEMBLED VEHICLES

SUBCHAPTER A
GENERAL PROVISIONS

Sec. 731.001. Definitions.

(a) In this chapter:

(1) "Assembled motorcycle" means a motorcycle, as defined by Section 541.201, that is built or assembled by a hobbyist.

(2) "Assembled motor vehicle" means a motor vehicle, as defined by Section 501.002(17)(A), that:

(A) has a motor, body, and frame; and

(B) is built or assembled by a hobbyist.

(3) "Assembled trailer" means a trailer, semitrailer, or travel trailer, as those terms are defined by Section 501.002, that is built or assembled by a hobbyist.

(4) "Assembled vehicle" means:

(A) an assembled motor vehicle;

(B) an assembled motorcycle;

(C) an assembled trailer;

(D) a custom vehicle;

(E) a street rod;

(F) a replica; or

(G) a glider kit.

(5) "Board" means the board of the department.

(6) "Custom vehicle" and "street rod" have the meanings assigned by Section 504.501.

(7) "Department" means the Texas Department of Motor Vehicles.

(8) "Glider kit" means a truck tractor, as defined by Section 541.201, that is built or assembled using:

(A) a kit that typically consists of a new cab, frame, and front axle and new accessories; and

(B) a used powertrain.

(9) "Hobbyist" means a person who:

(A) builds or assembles an assembled vehicle for personal use;

(B) does not engage in the continuous sale of vehicles, as defined by the department; and

(C) is not the maker of a kit or a manufacturer, as defined by Section 2301.002, Occupations Code.

(10) "Master technician" means a person who holds a master technician certification issued by the National Institute for Automotive Service Excellence.

(11) "Owner" has the meaning assigned by Section 541.001.

(12) "Replica" means a vehicle that uses a manufactured prefabricated body or a body constructed from materials not original to the vehicle and that resembles an established make of a previous year vehicle model. The term may include a custom vehicle or street rod.

(13) "Title" and "vehicle identification number" have the meanings assigned by Section 501.002.

(14) "Vehicle" has the meaning assigned by Section 502.001.

(b) For purposes of Subsection (a)(4), the term "assembled vehicle" does not include a golf cart, as defined by Section 551.401, or an off-highway vehicle, as defined by Section 551A.001, regardless of whether the vehicle is built or assembled by a hobbyist.

Sec. 731.002. Rules.

The board may adopt rules as necessary to implement and administer this chapter.

Sec. 731.003. Conflict of Law.

To the extent of a conflict between this chapter, including a rule adopted under this chapter, and another law, this chapter controls.

SUBCHAPTER B
TITLE AND REGISTRATION

Sec. 731.051. Eligibility for Title and Registration.

(a) Except as provided by Subsection (b), an owner of an assembled vehicle shall apply for a title for the vehicle and register the vehicle as provided by Chapters 501 and 502, as applicable, and in accordance with rules adopted under this chapter, regardless of whether the assembled vehicle was built or assembled using a vehicle that was previously titled in this state or another jurisdiction.

(b) An assembled vehicle may not be titled or registered in this state if the vehicle:

(1) is built or assembled from the merging of two or more vehicle classes, provided that component parts from the following vehicle classes may be interchanged:

(A) two-axle, four-tire passenger cars;

(B) two-axle, four-tire pickups, panels, and vans; and

(C) six-tire dually pickups, of which the rear tires are dual tires;

(2) uses the frame or body of a nonrepairable motor vehicle, as defined by Section 501.091;

(3) contains any electrical or mechanical components from a flood-damaged vehicle;

(4) is designed for off-highway use only;

(5) is designed by the manufacturer for on-track racing only;

(6) has been stripped to the extent that the vehicle loses its original identity; or

(7) uses any parts that do not meet federal motor vehicle safety standards, if standards have been developed for those parts.

Sec. 731.052. Procedures and Requirements for Title and Registration.

(a) The board by rule shall establish procedures and requirements for:

(1) issuance of a title for an assembled vehicle; and

(2) registration of an assembled vehicle.

(b) Rules adopted under Subsection (a):

(1) may not exclude a type of assembled vehicle, other than an assembled vehicle described by Section 731.051(b), from eligibility for title and registration;

(2) must establish the form of a title issued for an assembled vehicle; and

(3) must exempt an assembled vehicle or a type of assembled vehicle from any provision of Chapter 501 or 502 that an assembled vehicle or type of assembled vehicle, by its nature, cannot comply with or otherwise meet the requirements of.

Sec. 731.053. Certificate of Title Requirements.

(a) The title for an assembled vehicle that has never been titled in this state or any other jurisdiction must:

(1) list the owner of the assembled vehicle as the purchaser;

(2) contain the notation "NONE" in the space for the seller's name;

(3) list the municipality and state in which the vehicle was completed in the space for the seller's municipality and state; and

(4) contain the odometer reading and the notation "NOT ACTUAL MILEAGE".

(b) Except as provided by Subsection (a), a title issued for an assembled vehicle must contain all of the information required under Section 501.021.

Sec. 731.054. Assignment of Vehicle Identification Number.

The department shall assign a vehicle identification number under Section 501.033 to an assembled vehicle unless the vehicle has a discernible vehicle identification number assigned by:

(1) the manufacturer of the component part by which the vehicle may be identified; or

(2) the maker of the kit from which the vehicle is built or assembled.

SUBCHAPTER C INSPECTION BY MASTER TECHNICIAN

Sec. 731.101. Inspection Required for Issuance of Title.

(a) In addition to the inspection required under Chapter 548, an assembled vehicle must pass an inspection conducted by a master technician for the type of assembled vehicle being inspected. The inspection must be conducted before issuance of a title for the assembled vehicle.

(b) On application for title for an assembled vehicle, the owner of the assembled vehicle must provide:

(1) proof acceptable to the department that the vehicle passed an inspection conducted under this section; and

(2) a copy of the master technician's Automobile and Light Truck certification or a successor certification.

(c) The board by rule shall establish procedures and requirements for the inspection required by this section. Rules adopted under this subsection:

(1) must establish inspection criteria;

(2) may specify additional items of equipment that must be inspected by a master technician and may specify different items of equipment that must be inspected based on the type of assembled vehicle; and

(3) must require an owner of an assembled vehicle that is being inspected under this section to pay all fees required for the inspection, including any reinspection, in addition to all applicable fees

required under Chapter 548 for an inspection or reinspection conducted under that chapter.

Sec. 731.102. Equipment Subject to Inspection.

An inspection conducted under Section 731.101 must:

(1) as applicable, include the following items of an assembled vehicle:

(A) frame, chassis, and any structural components of the vehicle;

(B) wheel assembly;

(C) brake system, including each brake and power brake unit;

(D) steering system, including power steering; and

(E) front seat belts in vehicles that contain seat belt anchorages; and

(2) include an evaluation of the structural integrity of the assembled vehicle and, as applicable, the connection points of the:

(A) frame, chassis, or body;

(B) steering system;

(C) drive train; and

(D) suspension.

CHAPTER 731 DISCLOSURE OF PERSONAL INFORMATION FROM MOTOR VEHICLE RECORDS [REPEALED]

Sec. 731.001. Definitions [Repealed].

Repealed by Acts 2001, 77th Leg., ch. 1032 (H.B. 1544), § 9(2), effective September 1, 2001.

Sec. 731.002. Release of Personal Information by Agency [Repealed].

Repealed by Acts 2001, 77th Leg., ch. 1032 (H.B. 1544), § 9(2), effective September 1, 2001.

Sec. 731.003. Publication or Disclosure of Personal Information on Internet [Repealed].

Repealed by Acts 2001, 77th Leg., ch. 1032 (H.B. 1544), § 9(2), effective September 1, 2001.

Sec. 731.004. Civil Enforcement [Repealed].

Repealed by Acts 2001, 77th Leg., ch. 1032 (H.B. 1544), § 9(2), effective September 1, 2001.

Sec. 731.005. Civil Cause of Action [Repealed].

Repealed by Acts 2001, 77th Leg., ch. 1032 (H.B. 1544), § 9(2), effective September 1, 2001.

Sec. 731.006. False Statement to Agency; Penalty [Repealed].

Repealed by Acts 2001, 77th Leg., ch. 1032 (H.B. 1544), § 9(2), effective September 1, 2001.

Sec. 731.007. Dissemination or Publication of Personal Information on Internet Prohibited; Penalty [Repealed].

Repealed by Acts 2001, 77th Leg., ch. 1032 (H.B. 1544), § 9(2), effective September 1, 2001.

Sec. 731.008. Affirmative Defense to Civil Action or Prosecution [Repealed].

Repealed by Acts 2001, 77th Leg., ch. 1032 (H.B. 1544), § 9(2), effective September 1, 2001.

Sec. 731.009. Rules [Repealed].

Repealed by Acts 2001, 77th Leg., ch. 1032 (H.B. 1544), § 9(2), effective September 1, 2001.

CHAPTER 750 MISCELLANEOUS PROVISIONS

Sec. 750.001. Children Standing in School Bus [Repealed].

Repealed by Acts 1997, 75th Leg., ch. 165 (S.B. 898), § 30.169, effective September 1, 1997.

Sec. 750.002. Speed of Vehicle in Park in County Bordering Gulf of Mexico.

(a) A person commits an offense if the person drives a vehicle at a speed greater than 30 miles per hour within the boundaries of a county park located in a county that borders on the Gulf of Mexico, other than on a beach as that term is defined by Section 61.012, Natural Resources Code, in the park.

(b) An offense under this section is a misdemeanor punishable by a fine of not less than $1 or more than $200.

Sec. 750.003. Operation of Vehicle on Dune Seaward of Dune Protection Line Prohibited.

(a) In this section, "vehicle" means a device that is designed to transport persons or property and is self-propelled or propelled by external means.

(b) A person commits an offense if the person operates a vehicle on a sand dune seaward of the dune protection line as defined in Section 63.012, Natural Resources Code, except on a roadway designated by a subdivision of the state.

(c) An offense under this section is a Class C misdemeanor.

ALCOHOLIC BEVERAGE CODE

TITLE 1
GENERAL PROVISIONS

CHAPTER 1
GENERAL PROVISIONS

Sec. 1.03. Public Policy.

This code is an exercise of the police power of the state for the protection of the welfare, health, peace, temperance, and safety of the people of the state. It shall be liberally construed to accomplish this purpose.

Sec. 1.04. Definitions. [Effective until January 1, 2022]

In this code:

(1) "Alcoholic beverage" means alcohol, or any beverage containing more than one-half of one percent of alcohol by volume, which is capable of use for beverage purposes, either alone or when diluted.

(2) "Consignment sale" means:

(A) the delivery of alcoholic beverages under an agreement, arrangement, condition, or system by which the person receiving the beverages has the right at any time to relinquish possession to them or to return them to the shipper and in which title to the beverages remains in the shipper;

(B) the delivery of alcoholic beverages under an agreement, arrangement, condition, or system by which the person designated as the receiver merely acts as an intermediary for the shipper or seller and the actual receiver;

(C) the delivery of alcoholic beverages to a factor or broker;

(D) any method employed by a shipper or seller by which a person designated as the purchaser of alcoholic beverages does not in fact purchase the beverages;

(E) any method employed by a shipper or seller by which a person is placed in actual or constructive possession of an alcoholic beverage without acquiring title to the beverage; or

(F) any other type of transaction which may legally be construed as a consignment sale.

(3) "Distilled spirits" means alcohol, spirits of wine, whiskey, rum, brandy, gin, or any liquor produced in whole or in part by the process of distillation, including all dilutions or mixtures of them, and includes spirit coolers that may have an alcoholic content as low as four percent alcohol by volume and that contain plain, sparkling, or carbonated water and may also contain one or more natural or artificial blending or flavoring ingredients.

(4) "Illicit beverage" means an alcoholic beverage:

(A) manufactured, distributed, bought, sold, bottled, rectified, blended, treated, fortified, mixed, processed, warehoused, stored, possessed, imported, or transported in violation of this code;

(B) on which a tax imposed by the laws of this state has not been paid and to which the tax stamp, if required, has not been affixed; or

(C) possessed, kept, stored, owned, or imported with intent to manufacture, sell, distribute, bottle, rectify, blend, treat, fortify, mix, process, warehouse, store, or transport in violation of this code.

(5) "Liquor" means any alcoholic beverage, other than a malt beverage, containing alcohol in excess of five percent by volume, unless otherwise indicated. Proof that an alcoholic beverage is alcohol, spirits of wine, whiskey, liquor, wine, brandy, gin, rum, tequila, mescal, habanero, or barreteago, is prima facie evidence that it is liquor.

(6) "Person" means a natural person or association of natural persons, trustee, receiver, partnership, corporation, organization, or the manager, agent, servant, or employee of any of them.

(7) "Wine and vinous liquor" means the product obtained from the alcoholic fermentation of juice of sound ripe grapes, fruits, berries, or honey, and includes wine coolers and saké.

(8) "Hotel" means the premises of an establishment:

(A) where, in consideration of payment, travelers are furnished food and lodging;

(B) in which are located:

(i) at least 10 adequately furnished completely separate rooms with adequate facilities so comfortably disposed that persons usually apply for and receive overnight accommodations in the establishment, either in the course of usual and regular travel or as a residence; or

(ii) at least five rooms described by Subparagraph (i) if the building being used as a hotel is a historic structure as defined by Section 442.001, Government Code; and

(C) which operates a regular dining room constantly frequented by customers each day.

(9) "Applicant" means a person who submits or files an original or renewal application with the commission for a license or permit.

(10) "Commission" means the Texas Alcoholic Beverage Commission.

(11) "Permittee" means a person who is the holder of a permit provided for in this code, or an agent, servant, or employee of that person.

(12) [Repealed.]

(13) "Mixed beverage" means one or more servings of a beverage composed in whole or part of an alcoholic beverage in a sealed or unsealed container of any legal size for consumption on the premises where served or sold by the holder of a mixed beverage permit, the holder of certain nonprofit entity temporary event permits, the holder of a private club registration permit, or the holder of certain retailer late hours certificates.

(14) "Barrel" means, as a standard of measure, a quantity of malt beverages equal to 31 standard gallons.

(15) "Malt beverage" means a fermented beverage of any name or description containing one-half of one percent or more of alcohol by volume, brewed or produced from malt, in whole or in part, or from any malt substitute.

(16) "Licensee" means a person who is the holder of a license provided in this code, or any agent, servant, or employee of that person.

(17) "Brewer " means a person engaged in the brewing of malt beverages, whether located inside or outside the state.

(18) "Original package," as applied to malt beverages, means a container holding malt beverages in bulk, or any box, crate, carton, or other device used in packing malt beverages that is contained in bottles or other containers.

(19) "Premises" has the meaning given it in Section 11.49 of this code.

(20) "Citizen of Texas" and "citizen of this state" mean a person who is a citizen of both the United States and Texas.

(21) "Minibar" means a closed container in a hotel guestroom with access to the interior of the container restricted by a locking device which requires the use of a key, magnetic card, or similar device.

(22) "Minibar key" means the key, magnetic card, or similar device which permits access to the interior of a minibar.

(23) "Guestroom" means a sleeping room, including any adjacent private living area, in a hotel which is rented to guests for their use as an overnight accommodation.

(24) "Wine cooler" means an alcoholic beverage consisting of vinous liquor plus plain, sparkling, or carbonated water and which may also contain one or more natural or artificial blending or flavoring ingredients. A wine cooler may have an alcohol content as low as one-half of one percent by volume.

(25) "Executive management" includes the administrator, the assistant administrator, individuals who report directly to the administrator, and the head of each division of the commission.

(26) "Alternating brewery proprietorship" means an arrangement in which two or more parties take turns using the physical premises of a brewery as permitted under this code and federal law.

(27) "Contract brewing arrangement" means an arrangement in which two breweries, each of which has a separate facility, contract for one brewery to brew malt beverages on behalf of the other brewery due to the limited capacity or other reasonable business necessity of one party to the arrangement.

(28) "Criminal negligence" has the meaning assigned by Section 6.03, Penal Code.

Sec. 1.04. Definitions. [Effective January 1, 2022]

In this code:

(1) "Alcoholic beverage" means alcohol, or any beverage containing more than one-half of one percent of alcohol by volume, which is capable of use for beverage purposes, either alone or when diluted.

(2) "Consignment sale" means:

(A) the delivery of alcoholic beverages under an agreement, arrangement, condition, or system by which the person receiving the beverages has the right at any time to relinquish possession to them or to return them to the shipper and in which title to the beverages remains in the shipper;

(B) the delivery of alcoholic beverages under an agreement, arrangement, condition, or system by which the person designated as the receiver merely acts as an intermediary for the shipper or seller and the actual receiver;

(C) the delivery of alcoholic beverages to a factor or broker;

(D) any method employed by a shipper or seller by which a person designated as the purchaser of alcoholic beverages does not in fact purchase the beverages;

(E) any method employed by a shipper or seller by which a person is placed in actual or constructive possession of an alcoholic beverage without acquiring title to the beverage; or

(F) any other type of transaction which may legally be construed as a consignment sale.

Alcoholic Beverage Code

(3) "Distilled spirits" means alcohol, spirits of wine, whiskey, rum, brandy, gin, or any liquor produced in whole or in part by the process of distillation, including all dilutions or mixtures of them, and includes spirit coolers that may have an alcoholic content as low as four percent alcohol by volume and that contain plain, sparkling, or carbonated water and may also contain one or more natural or artificial blending or flavoring ingredients.

(4) "Illicit beverage" means an alcoholic beverage:

(A) manufactured, distributed, bought, sold, bottled, rectified, blended, treated, fortified, mixed, processed, warehoused, stored, possessed, imported, or transported in violation of this code;

(B) on which a tax imposed by the laws of this state has not been paid and to which the tax stamp, if required, has not been affixed; or

(C) possessed, kept, stored, owned, or imported with intent to manufacture, sell, distribute, bottle, rectify, blend, treat, fortify, mix, process, warehouse, store, or transport in violation of this code.

(5) "Liquor" means any alcoholic beverage, other than a malt beverage, containing alcohol in excess of five percent by volume, unless otherwise indicated. Proof that an alcoholic beverage is alcohol, spirits of wine, whiskey, liquor, wine, brandy, gin, rum, tequila, mescal, habanero, or barreteago, is prima facie evidence that it is liquor.

(6) "Person" means a natural person or association of natural persons, trustee, receiver, partnership, corporation, organization, or the manager, agent, servant, or employee of any of them.

(7) "Wine and vinous liquor" means the product obtained from the alcoholic fermentation of juice of sound ripe grapes, fruits, berries, or honey, and includes wine coolers and saké.

(8) "Hotel" means the premises of an establishment:

(A) where, in consideration of payment, travelers are furnished food and lodging;

(B) in which are located:

(i) at least 10 adequately furnished completely separate rooms with adequate facilities so comfortably disposed that persons usually apply for and receive overnight accommodations in the establishment, either in the course of usual and regular travel or as a residence; or

(ii) at least five rooms described by Subparagraph (i) if the building being used as a hotel is a historic structure as defined by Section 442.001, Government Code; and

(C) which operates a regular dining room constantly frequented by customers each day.

(9) "Applicant" means a person who submits or files an original or renewal application with the commission for a license or permit.

(10) "Commission" means the Texas Alcoholic Beverage Commission.

(11) "Permittee" means a person who is the holder of a permit provided for in this code, or an agent, servant, or employee of that person.

(12) [Repealed.]

(13) "Mixed beverage" means one or more servings of a beverage composed in whole or part of an alcoholic beverage in a sealed or unsealed container of any legal size for consumption on the premises where served or sold by the holder of a mixed beverage permit, the holder of certain nonprofit entity temporary event permits, the holder of a private club registration permit, or the holder of certain retailer late hours certificates.

(14) "Barrel" means, as a standard of measure, a quantity of malt beverages equal to 31 standard gallons.

(15) "Malt beverage" means a fermented beverage of any name or description containing one-half of one percent or more of alcohol by volume, brewed or produced from malt, in whole or in part, or from any malt substitute.

(16) "Licensee" means a person who is the holder of a license provided in this code, or any agent, servant, or employee of that person.

(17) "Brewer" means a person engaged in the brewing of malt beverages, whether located inside or outside the state.

(18) "Original package," as applied to malt beverages, means a container holding malt beverages in bulk, or any box, crate, carton, or other device used in packing malt beverages that is contained in bottles or other containers.

(19) "Premises" has the meaning given it in Section 11.49 of this code.

(20) "Citizen of Texas" and "citizen of this state" mean a person who is a citizen of both the United States and Texas.

(21) "Minibar" means a closed container in a hotel guestroom with access to the interior of the container restricted by a locking device which requires the use of a key, magnetic card, or similar device.

(22) "Minibar key" means the key, magnetic card, or similar device which permits access to the interior of a minibar.

(23) "Guestroom" means a sleeping room, including any adjacent private living area, in a hotel which is rented to guests for their use as an overnight accommodation.

(24) "Wine cooler" means an alcoholic beverage consisting of vinous liquor plus plain, sparkling, or carbonated water and which may also contain one or more natural or artificial blending or flavoring ingredients. A wine cooler may have an alcohol content as low as one-half of one percent by volume.

(25) "Executive management" includes the administrator, the assistant administrator, individuals who report directly to the administrator, and the head of each division of the commission.

(26) "Alternating brewery proprietorship" means an arrangement in which two or more parties take turns using the physical premises of a brewery as permitted under this code and federal law.

(27) "Contract brewing arrangement" means an arrangement in which two breweries, each of which has a separate facility, contract for one brewery to brew malt beverages on behalf of the other brewery due to the limited capacity or other reasonable business necessity of one party to the arrangement.

(28) "Criminal negligence" has the meaning assigned by Section 6.03, Penal Code.

(29) "Restaurant" means a business that:

(A) operates its own permanent food service facility with commercial cooking equipment on its premises; and

(B) prepares and offers to sell multiple entrees for consumption on or off the premises.

Sec. 1.05. General Penalty.

(a) A person who violates a provision of this code for which a specific penalty is not provided is guilty of a misdemeanor and on conviction is punishable by a fine of not less than $100 nor more than $1,000 or by confinement in the county jail for not more than one year or by both.

(b) The term "specific penalty," as used in this section, means a penalty which might be imposed as a result of a criminal prosecution.

Sec. 1.08. Criminal Negligence Defined [Repealed].

Repealed by Acts 2013, 83rd Leg., ch. 1190 (S.B. 1090), § 26(1), effective September 1, 2013.

Sec. 1.09. References to Certain Terms.

A reference in this code to:

(1) "Ale," "beer," or "malt liquor" means a malt beverage.

(2) "Brewer's permit" or "manufacturer's license" means a brewer's license.

(3) "Nonresident brewer's permit" or "nonresident manufacturer's license" means a nonresident brewer's license.

(4) "Wine and beer retailer's off-premise permit" means a wine and malt beverage retailer's off-premise permit.

(5) "Wine and beer retailer's permit" means a wine and malt beverage retailer's permit.

TITLE 2 ADMINISTRATION OF CODE

CHAPTER 5 ALCOHOLIC BEVERAGE COMMISSION

SUBCHAPTER B POWERS AND DUTIES

Sec. 5.361. Enforcement; Inspections.

(a) The commission shall develop a risk-based approach to conducting its enforcement activities that focuses on:

(1) detecting serious violations that impact public safety;

(2) monitoring entities that have a history of complaints and violations of this code; and

(3) any other factors the commission considers important.

(a-1) As part of the commission's enforcement activities under this section, the commission by rule shall develop a plan for inspecting permittees and licensees using a risk-based approach that prioritizes public safety. The inspection plan may provide for a virtual inspection of the permittee or licensee that may include a review of the permittee's or licensee's records or it may also require a physical inspection of the permittee's or licensee's premises.

(a-2) The inspection plan must:

(1) establish a timeline for the inspection of each permittee and licensee that ensures that high-risk permittees and licensees are prioritized; and

(2) require the commission to physically inspect the premises of each permittee and licensee within a reasonable time as set by rule.

(b) The commission shall develop benchmarks and goals to track key enforcement activities and the results of those activities. For each type of enforcement activity, the commission shall track the number of violations detected by the enforcement activity, the amount of time spent on the enforcement activity, and any other information the commission considers necessary. The commission shall use the information collected under this subsection and other information to compare the enforcement performance of each region and to determine the most effective enforcement activities.

(c) The commission shall track, on a statewide and regional basis, the type of violations detected, the disposition of the violations, and the entities that committed the most serious violations.

(d) The commission shall compile detailed statistics and analyze trends related to its enforcement activities. The commission shall:

(1) summarize the statistics and trends for executive management on a monthly basis and for the members of the commission on a quarterly basis; and

(2) make summary information available to the public, including by posting the information on the commission's Internet website.

Sec. 5.362. Schedule of Sanctions.

(a) The commission by rule shall adopt a schedule of sanctions that may be imposed on a license or permit holder for violations of this code or rules adopted under this code. In adopting the schedule of sanctions, the commission shall ensure that the severity of the sanction imposed is appropriate to the type of violation that is the basis for disciplinary action.

(b) For each violation for which a license or permit may be suspended, the schedule of sanctions must include the number of days a permit or license would be suspended and the corresponding civil penalty under Section 11.64.

(c) In determining the appropriate sanction for a violation under the schedule, the commission or administrator shall consider:

(1) the type of license or permit held by the person who committed the violation;

(2) the type of violation;

(3) any aggravating or ameliorating circumstances concerning the violation; and

(4) the license or permit holder's previous violations of this code.

(d) The schedule must:

(1) allow deviations from the schedule for clearly established mitigating circumstances, including circumstances listed in Section 11.64(c), or aggravating circumstances; and

(2) include a list of the most common violations by members of the manufacturing, wholesaling, and retailing tiers of the alcoholic beverage industry and the sanctions assessed for those violations.

(e) The commission shall develop policies to guide commission staff in determining the circumstances when it is appropriate to deviate from the schedule of sanctions. The policies must identify the circumstances when approval is required in order to deviate from the schedule.

(f) The commission shall make the schedule of sanctions available to the public, including by posting the schedule on the commission's Internet website.

Sec. 5.363. Disciplinary Authority of Administrator and Commission.

(a) The commission by rule may delegate to the administrator the authority to take disciplinary and enforcement actions against a person subject to the commission's regulation under this code, including the authority to enter into an agreed settlement of a disciplinary action. In the rules adopted under this subsection, the commission shall specify a threshold for the types of disciplinary and enforcement actions that are delegated to the administrator.

(b) The commission shall make the final decision in any disciplinary action in a contested case that has had an administrative hearing.

TITLE 3 LICENSES AND PERMITS

SUBTITLE A PERMITS

CHAPTER 26 WINE AND MALT BEVERAGE RETAILER'S OFF-PREMISE PERMIT

Sec. 26.05. Warning Sign Required.

(a) Each holder of a wine and malt beverage retailer's off-premise permit shall display in a prominent place on the permittee's premises a sign stating in letters at least two inches high: IT IS A CRIME (MISDEMEANOR) TO CONSUME LIQUOR OR MALT BEVERAGES ON THESE PREMISES. The commission or administrator may require the holder of the permit to also display the sign in a language other than English if it can be observed or determined that a substantial portion of the expected customers speak the other language as their familiar language.

(b) A permittee who fails to comply with this section commits a misdemeanor punishable by a fine of not more than $25.

CHAPTER 28
MIXED BEVERAGE PERMIT

Sec. 28.13. Issuance of Permit for Certain Boats. [Repealed]

CHAPTER 30
NONPROFIT ENTITY TEMPORARY MIXED BEVERAGE PERMIT

Sec. 30.01. Definition.

In this chapter, "nonprofit entity" means:

(1) a nonprofit corporation;

(2) a nonprofit charitable, civic, or religious organization;

(3) a political party or political association supporting a candidate for public office or a proposed amendment to the Texas Constitution or other ballot measure;

(4) a fraternal organization with a regular membership that has been in continuous existence for more than five years; or

(5) a person or group of persons who are subject to recordkeeping requirements under Chapter 254, Election Code.

Sec. 30.02. Authorized Activities.

The holder of a nonprofit entity temporary event permit may sell for consumption on the premises for which the permit is issued any alcoholic beverage that is authorized to be sold where the event is held.

CHAPTER 48A.
PASSENGER BUS BEVERAGE PERMIT [REPEALED]

Sec. 48A.01. Authorized Activities; Applicability of Chapter. [Repealed]

Sec. 48A.02. Fee. [Repealed]

Sec. 48A.03. Eligibility for Permit; Application and Payment of Fee. [Repealed]

Sec. 48A.04. Exemption From Taxes. [Repealed]

Sec. 48A.05. Sale of Liquor to Permittee. [Repealed]

Sec. 48A.06. Inapplicable Provision. [Repealed]

TITLE 4
REGULATORY AND PENAL PROVISIONS

CHAPTER 101
GENERAL CRIMINAL PROVISIONS

SUBCHAPTER A
PROCEDURAL PROVISIONS

Sec. 101.01. Restraining Orders and Injunctions.

(a) If a credible person by affidavit informs the attorney general or a county or district attorney that a person is violating or is about to violate a provision of this code, or that a permit or license was wrongfully issued, the attorney general or county or district attorney shall begin proceedings in district court to restrain the person from violating the code or operating under the permit or license.

(b) The court may issue a restraining order without a hearing, and on notice and hearing may grant an injunction, to prevent the threatened or further violation or operation. The court may require the complaining party to file a bond in an amount and with the conditions the court finds necessary.

(c) If the court finds that a person has violated a restraining order or injunction issued under this section, it shall enter a judgment to that effect. The judgment operates to cancel without further proceedings any license or permit held by the person. The district clerk shall notify the commission when a judgment is entered that operates to cancel a license or permit.

(d) A license or permit may not be issued to a person whose license or permit is cancelled under

Alcoholic Beverage Code

Subsection (c) until the first anniversary of the date the license or permit is cancelled.

Sec. 101.02. Arrest Without Warrant.

A peace officer may arrest without a warrant any person he observes violating any provision of this code or any rule or regulation of the commission. The officer shall take possession of all illicit beverages the person has in his possession or on his premises as provided in Chapter 103 of this code.

Sec. 101.03. Search and Seizure.

(a) A search warrant may issue under Chapter 18, Code of Criminal Procedure, 1965, as amended, to search for, seize, and destroy or otherwise dispose of in accordance with this code:

(1) an illicit beverage;

(2) any equipment or instrumentality used, or capable or designed to be used, to manufacture an illicit beverage;

(3) a vehicle or instrumentality used or to be used for the illegal transportation of an illicit beverage;

(4) unlawful equipment or materials used or to be used in the illegal manufacturing of an illicit beverage;

(5) a forged or counterfeit stamp, die, plate, official signature, certificate, evidence of tax payment, license, permit, or other instrument pertaining to this code; or

(6) any instrumentality or equipment, or parts of either of them, used or to be used, or designed or capable of use, to manufacture, print, etch, indite, or otherwise make a forged or counterfeit instrument covered by Subdivision (5) of this subsection.

(b) Any magistrate may issue a search warrant on the affidavit of a credible person, setting forth the name or description of the owner or person in charge of the premises (or stating that the name and description are unknown), the address or description of the premises, and showing that the described premises is a place where this code has been or is being violated. If the place to be searched is a private dwelling occupied as such and no part of it is used as a store, shop, hotel, boarding house, or for any other purpose except as a private residence, the affidavit must be made by two credible persons.

(c) All provisions of Chapter 18, Code of Criminal Procedure, 1965, as amended, apply to the application, issuance, and execution of the warrant except those that conflict with this section.

(d) The officer executing the warrant shall seize all items described in Subsection (a) of this section, and those items may not be taken from his custody by a writ of replevin or any other process. The officer shall retain the items pending final judgment in the proceedings.

(e) This section does not require a peace officer to obtain a search warrant to search premises covered by a license or permit.

Sec. 101.04. Consent to Inspection; Penalty.

(a) By accepting a license or permit, the holder consents to the commission, an authorized representative of the commission, or a peace officer entering the licensed premises at any time to conduct an investigation or inspect the premises for the purpose of performing any duty imposed by this code.

(b) A person commits an offense if the person refuses to allow the commission, an authorized representative of the commission, or a peace officer to enter a licensed or permitted premises as required by Subsection (a). An offense under this section is a Class A misdemeanor.

Sec. 101.07. Duty of Peace Officers.

All peace officers in the state, including those of cities, counties, and state, shall enforce the provisions of this code and cooperate with and assist the commission in detecting violations and apprehending offenders.

SUBCHAPTER B OFFENSES RELATING TO DRY AREAS

Sec. 101.31. Alcoholic Beverages in Dry Areas.

(a) Except as otherwise provided in this code, no person in a dry area may manufacture, distill, brew, sell, import into the state, export from the state, transport, distribute, warehouse, store, solicit or take orders for, or possess with intent to sell an alcoholic beverage.

(b) An offense under this section is a Class B misdemeanor.

(c) If it is shown on the trial of an offense under this section that the person has previously been convicted two or more times of an offense under this section, the offense is a state jail felony.

Sec. 101.32. Prima Facie Evidence of Intent to Sell. [Repealed]

SUBCHAPTER D MISCELLANEOUS OFFENSES

Sec. 101.61. Violation of Code or Rule.

A person who fails or refuses to comply with a requirement of this code or a valid rule of the commission violates this code.

Sec. 101.62. Offensive Noise on Premises. [Repealed]

Sec. 101.63. Sale or Delivery to Certain Persons.

(a) A person commits an offense if the person with criminal negligence sells an alcoholic beverage to an habitual drunkard or an intoxicated or insane person.

(a-1) A person commits an offense if the person with criminal negligence delivers for commercial purposes an alcoholic beverage to an intoxicated person.

(b) Except as provided in Subsection (c) of this section, a violation of this section is a misdemeanor punishable by a fine of not less than $100 nor more than $500, by confinement in jail for not more than one year, or by both.

(c) If a person has been previously convicted of a violation of this section or of Section 106.03 of this code, a violation is a misdemeanor punishable by a fine of not less than $500 nor more than $1,000, by confinement in jail for not more than one year, or by both.

Sec. 101.64. Indecent Graphic Material.

No holder of a license or permit may possess or display on the licensed premises a card, calendar, placard, picture, or handbill that is immoral, indecent, lewd, or profane.

Sec. 101.65. Beverages Made from Certain Materials Prohibited.

No person may manufacture, import, sell, or possess for the purpose of sale an alcoholic beverage made from:

(1) any compound made from synthetic materials;

(2) substandard wines;

(3) imitation wines; or

(4) must concentrated at any time to more than 80 degrees Balling.

Sec. 101.66. Beverages of Certain Alcohol Content Prohibited.

A person may not manufacture, sell, barter, or exchange a beverage that contains more than one-half of one percent alcohol by volume and not more than five percent alcohol by volume, except malt beverages, wine coolers, and spirit coolers.

Sec. 101.67. Prior Approval of Malt Beverages.

(a) Before an authorized licensee may ship or cause to be shipped into the state, import into the state, manufacture and offer for sale in the state, or distribute, sell, or store in the state any malt beverages, the licensee must register the malt beverages with the commission. The registration application must include a certificate of label approval issued by the United States Alcohol and Tobacco Tax and Trade Bureau for the product.

(b) Only a brewer's or nonresident brewer's licensee, or a brewpub licensee may apply to register malt beverages with the commission.

(c) This section does not apply to the importation of malt beverages for personal consumption and not for sale.

(d) On registration of a certificate of label approval issued by the United States Alcohol and Tobacco Tax and Trade Bureau, the commission shall approve the product under this section and issue a letter to that effect to the licensee unless the commission determines the product, despite having a valid federal certificate of label approval, would create a public safety concern, create a cross-tier violation, or otherwise violate this code.

(d-1) If the commission approves the product, the commission shall issue a certificate of approval upon receipt of a fee in an amount that is sufficient to cover the cost of administering this section. A copy of the certificate shall be kept on file in the office of the commission.

(e) Not later than the 30th day after the date the commission receives an application for registration of a product under this section, the commission shall either approve or deny the registration application. If the commission denies the application for a product with a valid federal certificate of label approval or fails to act on the application within the time required by this subsection, the licensee submitting the application is entitled to an administrative hearing before the State Office of Administrative Hearings.

(f) The commission by rule shall establish procedures for:

(1) accepting federal certificates of label approval for registration under this section;

(2) registering alcoholic beverage products that are not eligible to receive a certificate of label approval issued by the United States Alcohol and Tobacco Tax and Trade Bureau; and

(3) registering alcoholic beverage products during periods when the United States Alcohol and Tobacco Tax and Trade Bureau has ceased processing applications for a certificate of label approval.

(g) The commission shall consider the nutrition label requirements of the United States Food and Drug Administration and the alcohol label requirements of the United States Alcohol and Tobacco Tax and Trade Bureau in developing the label requirements to register products described by Subsection (f)(2).

(h) The rules adopted under this section may not require testing for alcohol content as part of the process for registering an alcoholic beverage with the commission.

Sec. 101.6701. Label Approval Not Required for Certain Malt Beverages.

(a) This section applies only to the holder of a brewer's license authorized under Section 62.122 to sell malt beverages produced on the brewer's premises under the license to ultimate consumers on the brewer's premises for responsible consumption on the brewer's premises and for off-premises consumption.

(b) Notwithstanding Sections 101.41 and 101.67 or any other law, a license holder to whom this section applies may sell malt beverages to ultimate consumers for consumption on the license holder's premises or for off-premises consumption without receiving label approval for the malt beverages.

(c) A license holder who sells malt beverages under Subsection (b) shall:

(1) post in a conspicuous place on the license holder's premises the alcohol content of the malt beverages in percentage of alcohol by volume; and

(2) provide in writing to an ultimate consumer who purchases a malt beverage for off-premises consumption:

(A) the product name of the malt beverage; and

(B) the alcohol content of the malt beverage in percentage of alcohol by volume.

(d) A license holder satisfies the requirements of Subsection (c)(2) if the license holder:

(1) writes the product name and alcohol content on the container of the malt beverage; or

(2) applies a label with the product name and alcohol content to the container of the malt beverage.

Sec. 101.671. Prior Approval of Distilled Spirits and Wine.

(a) Before an authorized permittee may ship distilled spirits or wine into the state or sell distilled spirits or wine within the state, the permittee must register the distilled spirits or wine with the commission and provide proof that the permittee is the primary American source of supply for purposes of Section 37.10. Except for rare or vintage wine that is acquired at auction and for which no certificate is available, the registration application must include a certificate of label approval issued by the United States Alcohol and Tobacco Tax and Trade Bureau for the product. Rare or vintage wine purchased at auction and registered by the commission under this subsection must comply with all other provisions of this code, including provisions regarding the sale, purchase, importation, and distribution of that wine.

(b) On registration of a certificate of label approval issued by the United States Alcohol and Tobacco Tax and Trade Bureau, the commission shall approve the product under this section and issue a letter to that effect to the permittee unless the commission determines the product, despite having a valid federal certificate of label approval, would create a public safety concern, create a cross-tier violation, or otherwise violate this code. The commission may not require additional approval for the product unless there is a change to the label or product that requires reissuance of the federal certificate of label approval. The commission shall accept the certificate of label approval as constituting full compliance only with any applicable standards adopted under Section 5.38 regarding quality, purity, and identity of distilled spirits or wine.

(c) The commission may not register a product unless the application is accompanied by a fee set by the commission in an amount that is sufficient to cover the cost of administering this section. A copy of the registration shall be kept on file in the office of the commission.

(c-1) Not later than the 30th day after the date the commission receives an application for registration of a product under this section, the commission shall either approve or deny the registration application. If the commission denies the application for a product with a valid federal certificate of label approval or fails to act on the application within the time required by this subsection, the permittee submitting the application is entitled to an administrative hearing before the State Office of Administrative Hearings.

(d) The commission by rule shall establish procedures for:

(1) accepting:

Alcoholic Beverage Code

(A) federal certificates of label approval for registration under this section; and

(B) proof, such as a letter of authorization, that a permittee is the primary American source of supply of the product or brand for purposes of Section 37.10; and

(2) registering alcoholic beverage products that are not eligible to receive a certificate of label approval issued by the United States Alcohol and Tobacco Tax and Trade Bureau.

(e) The commission shall consider the nutrition label requirements of the United States Food and Drug Administration and the alcohol label requirements of the United States Alcohol and Tobacco Tax and Trade Bureau in developing the label requirements to register products described by Subsection (d)(2).

(f) The rules adopted under this section may not require testing for alcohol content as part of the process for registering an alcoholic beverage with the commission.

Sec. 101.673. Use of American Viticultural Area, County, or Vineyard on Wine Label.

(a) In this section, "American viticultural area" has the meaning assigned by 27 C.F.R. Section 4.25.

(b) A wine that is otherwise entitled under federal law to an appellation of origin indicating the wine's origin is an American viticultural area or county located in this state may use that appellation only if the wine is 100 percent by volume fermented juice of grapes or other fruit grown in this state.

(c) A wine that is otherwise entitled under federal law to use the name of a specific vineyard in this state on the wine's label may use the name of the vineyard on the label only if the wine is 100 percent by volume fermented juice of grapes or other fruit grown in this state.

Sec. 101.68. Consignment Sale Prohibited.

A person commits an offense if he is a party to, or directly or indirectly interested in or connected with, a consignment sale of an alcoholic beverage.

Sec. 101.69. False Statement.

Except as provided in Section 103.05(d), a person who knowingly makes a false statement or false representation in an application for a permit or license or in a statement, report, or other instrument to be filed with the commission and required to be sworn commits an offense punishable by imprisonment in the Texas Department of Criminal Justice for not less than 2 nor more than 10 years.

Sec. 101.70. Common Nuisance.

(a) A room, building, boat, structure, or other place where alcoholic beverages are sold, bartered, manufactured, stored, possessed, or consumed in violation of this code or under circumstances contrary to the purposes of this code, the beverages themselves, and all property kept or used in the place, are a common nuisance. A person who maintains or assists in maintaining the nuisance commits an offense.

(b) The county or district attorney in the county where the nuisance exists or the attorney general may sue in the name of the state for an injunction to abate and temporarily and permanently enjoin it. Except as otherwise provided in this section, the proceeding is conducted as other similar proceedings.

(b-1) The city attorney in the city where the nuisance exists may sue in the name of the city for an injunction to abate and temporarily and permanently enjoin it. Except as otherwise provided in this section, the proceeding is conducted as other similar proceedings.

(c) The plaintiff is not required to give a bond. The final judgment is a judgment in rem against the property and a judgment against the defendant. If the court finds against the defendant, on final judgment it shall order that the place where the nuisance exists be closed for one year or less and until the owner, lessee, tenant, or occupant gives bond with sufficient surety as approved by the court in the penal sum of at least $1,000. The bond must be payable to the state and conditioned:

(1) that this code will not be violated;

(2) that no person will be permitted to resort to the place to drink alcoholic beverages in violation of this code; and

(3) that the defendant will pay all fines, costs, and damages assessed against him for any violation of this code.

(d) On appeal, the judgment may not be superseded except on filing an appeal bond in the penal sum of not more than $500, in addition to the bond for costs of the appeal. That bond must be approved by the trial court and must be posted before the judgment of the court may be superseded on appeal. The bond must be conditioned that if the judgment of the trial court is finally affirmed it may be forfeited in the same manner and for any cause for which a bond required on final judgment may be forfeited for an act committed during the pendency of an appeal.

Sec. 101.71. Inspection of Vehicle.

No holder of a permit issued under Title 3, Subtitle A, of this code, may refuse to allow the commission or its authorized representative or a peace

Alcoholic Beverage Code

officer, on request, to make a full inspection, investigation, or search of any vehicle.

Sec. 101.72. Consumption of Alcoholic Beverage on Premises Licensed for Off-Premises Consumption.

(a) A person commits an offense if the person knowingly consumes liquor or malt beverages on the premises of a holder of a wine and malt beverage retailer's off-premise permit or a retail dealer's off-premise license.

(b) A person is presumed to have knowingly violated Subsection (a) of this section if the warning sign required by either Section 26.05 or 71.10 of this code is displayed on the premises.

(c) Except as provided in Subsection (d) of this section, a violation of this section is a misdemeanor punishable by a fine of not less than $25 nor more than $200.

(d) If a person has been convicted of a violation of this section occurring within a year of a subsequent violation, the subsequent violation is a misdemeanor punishable by a fine of not less than $100 nor more than $200.

Sec. 101.73. Expungement of Conviction for Consumption on Premises Licensed for Off-Premises Consumption.

(a) A person convicted of not more than one violation of Section 101.72 of this code within 12 months, after the first anniversary of the conviction, may apply to the court in which he was convicted to have the conviction expunged.

(b) The application shall contain the applicant's sworn statement that he was not convicted of an additional violation of Section 101.72 of this code during the previous 12 months.

(c) If the court finds that the applicant was not convicted of another violation of Section 101.72 of this code during the preceding 12 months, the court shall order the conviction, together with all complaints, verdicts, fines, and other documents relating to the offense, to be expunged from the applicant's record. After entry of the order, the applicant is released from all disabilities resulting from the conviction, and the conviction may not be shown or made known for any purpose.

Sec. 101.74. Offenses Relating to Bingo.

(a) An organization licensed to conduct bingo under Chapter 2001, Occupations Code, may not offer an alcoholic beverage as a bingo prize or as a door prize at a bingo occasion.

(b) A person who holds a permit or license at the manufacturing or wholesale levels of the alcoholic beverage industry or a person who holds a package store permit may not participate in advertising any bingo game or pay or contribute toward payment of the printing of bingo cards or of the supplying of any novelties of any sort to be used during or in connection with the conduct of a bingo game.

Sec. 101.75. Consumption of Alcoholic Beverages Near Schools.

(a) A person commits an offense if the person possesses an open container or consumes an alcoholic beverage on a public street, public alley, or public sidewalk within 1,000 feet of the property line of a facility that is a public or private school, including a parochial school, that provides all or any part of prekindergarten through twelfth grade.

(b) This section does not apply to the possession of an open container or the consumption at an event duly authorized by appropriate authorities and held in compliance with all other applicable provisions of this code.

(c) An offense under this section is a Class C misdemeanor.

(d) In this section, "open container" has the meaning assigned in Section 109.35.

Sec. 101.76. Unlawful Display or Use of Permit or License.

(a) A person commits an offense if the person knowingly allows another person to display or use a permit or license issued by the commission in any manner not allowed by law.

(b) A person commits an offense if the person displays or uses a permit or license issued by the commission to another person in any manner not allowed by law.

(c) Except as provided by Subsection (d), an offense under this section is a Class B misdemeanor.

(d) If it is shown on the trial of an offense under this section that the person has previously been convicted of an offense under this section, the offense is a Class A misdemeanor.

CHAPTER 103
ILLICIT BEVERAGES

Sec. 103.01. Illicit Beverages Prohibited.

No person may possess, manufacture, transport, or sell an illicit beverage.

Sec. 103.02. Equipment or Material for Manufacture of Illicit Beverages.

No person may possess equipment or material designed for, capable of use for, or used in manufacturing an illicit beverage.

Sec. 103.03. Seizure of Illicit Beverages, Etc.

A peace officer may seize without a warrant:

(1) any illicit beverage, its container, and its packaging;

(2) any vehicle, including an aircraft or watercraft, used to transport an illicit beverage;

(3) any equipment designed for use in or used in manufacturing an illicit beverage; or

(4) any material to be used in manufacturing an illicit beverage.

Sec. 103.04. Arrest of Person in Possession.

A peace officer may arrest without a warrant any person found in possession of:

(1) an illicit beverage;

(2) any equipment designed for use in or used in manufacturing an illicit beverage; or

(3) any material to be used in manufacturing an illicit beverage.

Sec. 103.05. Report of Seizure.

(a) A peace officer who makes a seizure under Section 103.03 of this code shall make a report in triplicate which lists each item seized and the place and name of the owner, operator, or other person from whom it is seized. One copy of the report shall be verified by oath.

(b) The verified copy shall be retained in the permanent files of the commission or other agency making the seizure. The copy is subject to inspection by any member of the legislature or by any authorized law enforcement agency of the state.

(c) One copy of the report shall be delivered to the person from whom the seizure is made.

(d) A peace officer who makes a false report of the property seized commits a felony punishable by confinement in the Texas Department of Criminal Justice for not less than two years and not more than five years.

(e) A peace officer who fails to file the reports of a seizure as required by this section commits a misdemeanor punishable by a fine of not less than $50 nor more than $100 or by confinement in jail for not less than 10 nor more than 90 days or by both. The commission shall insure that the reports are made by peace officers.

Sec. 103.06. Beverage Seized by Peace Officer.

Any alcoholic beverage, its container, and its packaging which has been seized by a peace officer, as provided in Section 103.03:

(1) may not be replevied; and

(2) shall be:

(A) destroyed or disposed of by a peace officer; or

(B) delivered to the commission for immediate public or private sale in the manner the commission considers best.

Sec. 103.07. Beverage of Illicit Manufacture or Unfit for Consumption.

(a) The commission may not sell alcoholic beverages seized by a peace officer, as provided in Section 103.03, that are unfit for public consumption or are of illicit manufacture.

(b) Alcoholic beverages are unfit for public consumption if:

(1) the manufacturer or wholesaler of the beverages determines that the beverages are inappropriate for sale to a consumer;

(2) the beverages are damaged; or

(3) the code date affixed by the manufacturer to the beverages has expired.

(c) If the commission determines that seized alcoholic beverages are unfit for public consumption or are of illicit manufacture, the commission shall destroy the alcoholic beverages.

CHAPTER 105
HOURS OF SALE AND CONSUMPTION

Sec. 105.01. Hours of Sale: Liquor.

(a) Except as provided in Sections 105.02, 105.03, 105.04, 105.08, and 105.091, no person may sell, offer for sale, or deliver any liquor:

(1) on New Year's Day, Thanksgiving Day, or Christmas Day;

(2) on Sunday; or

(3) before 10 a.m. or after 9 p.m. on any other day.

(b) When Christmas Day or New Year's Day falls on a Sunday, Subsection (a) of this section applies to the following Monday.

Sec. 105.02. Hours of Sale: Wholesalers and Local Distributors to Retailers.

(a) A holder of a wholesaler's permit may sell, offer for sale, or deliver liquor to a retailer anytime except Sunday and Christmas Day.

Alcoholic Beverage Code

(b) A local distributor's permittee may sell, offer for sale, or deliver liquor to a retailer between 5 a.m. and 9 p.m. on any day except:

(1) Sunday;

(2) Christmas Day; or

(3) a day on which a package store permittee is prohibited from selling liquor.

Sec. 105.03. Hours of Sale: Mixed Beverages.

(a) No person may sell or offer for sale mixed beverages at any time not permitted by this section.

(b) A mixed beverage permittee may sell and offer for sale mixed beverages between 7 a.m. and midnight on any day except Sunday. On Sunday he may sell mixed beverages between midnight and 1:00 a.m. and between 10 a.m. and midnight, except that an alcoholic beverage served to a customer between 10 a.m. and 12 noon on Sunday must be provided during the service of food to the customer.

(c) In a city or county having a population of 800,000 or more, according to the last preceding federal census, or 500,000 or more, according to the 22nd Decennial Census of the United States, as released by the Bureau of the Census on March 12, 2001, a holder of a mixed beverage permit who holds a retailer late hours certificate may also sell and offer for sale mixed beverages between midnight and 2 a.m. on any day.

(d) In a city or county other than a city or county described by Subsection (c), the extended hours prescribed in Subsection (c) are effective for the sale of mixed beverages and the offer to sell them by a holder of a mixed beverage permit who holds a retailer late hours certificate:

(1) in the unincorporated areas of the county if the extended hours are adopted by an order of the commissioners court; and

(2) in an incorporated city or town if the extended hours are adopted by an ordinance of the governing body of the city or town.

(e) A violation of a city ordinance or order of a commissioners court adopted pursuant to Subsection (d) of this section is a violation of this code.

Sec. 105.04. Hours of Sale: Wine and Malt Beverage Retailer.

The hours of sale and delivery for alcoholic beverages sold under a wine and malt beverage retailer's permit or a wine and malt beverage retailer's off-premise permit are the same as those prescribed for the sale of malt beverages under Section 105.05.

Sec. 105.05. Hours of Sale: Malt Beverages.

(a) A person may sell, offer for sale, or deliver malt beverages only at a time permitted by this section.

(b) A person may sell, offer for sale, or deliver malt beverages between 7 a.m. and midnight on any day except Sunday. On Sunday a person may sell malt beverages between midnight and 1:00 a.m. and between noon and midnight, except that:

(1) permittees or licensees authorized to sell for on-premise consumption may sell malt beverages between 10:00 a.m. and noon if the malt beverages are served to a customer during the service of food to the customer; and

(2) holders of a retail dealer's on-premise license or a retail dealer's off-premise license may also sell malt beverages for off-premise consumption between 10:00 a.m. and noon.

(c) In a city or county having a population of 800,000 or more, according to the last preceding federal census, or 500,000 or more, according to the 22nd Decennial Census of the United States, as released by the Bureau of the Census on March 12, 2001, a holder of a retail dealer's on-premise license who holds a retailer late hours certificate may also sell, offer for sale, and deliver malt beverages between midnight and 2 a.m. on any day.

(d) In a city or county other than a city or county described by Subsection (c), the extended hours prescribed in Subsection (c) or any part of the extended hours prescribed in Subsection (c) are effective for the sale, offer to sell, and delivery of malt beverages by a holder of a retail dealer's on-premise license who holds a retailer late hours certificate:

(1) in the unincorporated areas of the county if the extended hours are adopted by an order of the commissioners court; and

(2) in an incorporated city or town if the extended hours are adopted by an ordinance of the governing body of the city or town.

(e) A violation of a city ordinance or order of a commissioners court adopted pursuant to Subsection (d) is a violation of this code.

Sec. 105.051. Sale of Malt Beverages by Distributor's Licensee.

The holder of a general or branch distributor's license may sell, offer for sale, or deliver malt beverages 24 hours a day Monday through Saturday and between midnight and 1 a.m. and between noon and midnight on Sunday.

Sec. 105.052. Sale of Beer by Distributor's Licensee in Certain Metropolitan Areas [Repealed].

Repealed by Acts 2009, 81st Leg., ch. 7 (H.B. 2594), § 3, effective May 5, 2009.

Sec. 105.06. Hours of Consumption.

(a) In this section:

(1) "Extended hours area" means an area subject to the extended hours of sale provided in Section 105.03 or 105.05 of this code.

(2) "Standard hours area" means an area which is not an extended hours area.

(a-1) For the purposes of this section, a licensed or permitted premises is a public place.

(b) Except as provided by Subsection (f), in a standard hours area, a person commits an offense if the person consumes or possesses with intent to consume an alcoholic beverage in a public place at any time on Sunday between 1:15 a.m. and 12 noon or on any other day between 12:15 a.m. and 7 a.m.

(c) Except as provided by Subsection (f), in an extended hours area, a person commits an offense if the person consumes or possesses with intent to consume an alcoholic beverage in a public place at any time on Sunday between 2:15 a.m. and 12 noon and on any other day between 2:15 a.m. and 7 a.m.

(d) Proof that an alcoholic beverage was possessed with intent to consume in violation of this section requires evidence that the person consumed an alcoholic beverage on that day in violation of this section.

(e) An offense under this section is a Class C misdemeanor.

(f) A person who is a registered guest of a hotel may consume or possess alcoholic beverages in the hotel bar, as defined by Section 105.091, at any time.

Sec. 105.07. Hours of Sale and Consumption: Sports Venue.

(a) In this section, "sports venue" means a public entertainment facility property, as defined by Section 108.73, that is primarily designed and used for live sporting events.

(b) Notwithstanding any other provision of this code, in addition to any other period during which the sale and consumption of alcohol is authorized under this code:

(1) a licensed or permitted premises located in a sports venue may sell alcoholic beverages between 10 a.m. and noon; and

(2) a person may consume alcoholic beverages at a sports venue between 10 a.m. and noon.

Sec. 105.08. Hours of Sale and Consumption: Winery.

The holder of a winery permit may sell, offer for sale, and deliver wine, and a person may consume wine on the premises of a winery:

(1) between 8 a.m. and midnight on any day except Sunday;

(2) between 10 a.m. and midnight on Sunday; and

(3) between midnight and 2 a.m. on New Year's Day.

Sec. 105.081. Hours of Sale and Consumption: Distillery.

(a) The holder of a distiller's and rectifier's permit may sell and offer for sale distilled spirits for on-premises consumption and a person may consume distilled spirits on the permitted premises during the same hours mixed beverages may be sold and offered for sale by a mixed beverage permit holder under Section 105.03(b).

(b) The holder of a distiller's and rectifier's permit may sell and offer for sale distilled spirits to ultimate consumers for off-premises consumption during the same hours as the holder of a package store permit may sell and offer for sale distilled spirits to ultimate consumers for off-premises consumption.

Sec. 105.082. Hours of Sale and Consumption: Brewer.

The holder of a brewer's license may sell, offer for sale, and deliver malt beverages and a person may consume malt beverages on the brewer's premises:

(1) between 8 a.m. and midnight on any day except Sunday; and

(2) between 10 a.m. and midnight on Sunday.

Sec. 105.09. Hours of Sale and Consumption: Certain Events.

Notwithstanding any other provision of this code, in addition to any other period during which the sale and consumption of alcohol is authorized under this code:

(1) a licensed or permitted premises located at a festival, fair, or concert may sell alcoholic beverages between 10 a.m. and noon; and

(2) a person may consume alcoholic beverages at a festival, fair, or concert between 10 a.m. and noon.

Sec. 105.091. Hours of Sale; Hotel Bar.

(a) In this section, "hotel bar" means an establishment that is located in a hotel and holds a permit

Alcoholic Beverage Code

or license providing for the on-premises consumption of alcoholic beverages.

(b) Notwithstanding any other law, a hotel bar may sell or offer for sale alcoholic beverages at any time to a registered guest of the hotel.

Sec. 105.10. Penalty.

(a) A person commits an offense if the person, in violation of this chapter or Section 32.17(a)(7):

(1) sells or offers for sale an alcoholic beverage during prohibited hours; or

(2) consumes or permits the consumption of an alcoholic beverage on the person's licensed or permitted premises during prohibited hours.

(b) An offense under this section is a Class A misdemeanor.

CHAPTER 106 PROVISIONS RELATING TO AGE

Sec. 106.01. Definition.

In this code, "minor" means a person under 21 years of age.

Sec. 106.02. Purchase of Alcohol by a Minor.

(a) A minor commits an offense if the minor purchases an alcoholic beverage. A minor does not commit an offense if the minor purchases an alcoholic beverage under the immediate supervision of a commissioned peace officer engaged in enforcing the provisions of this code.

(b) An offense under this section is punishable as provided by Section 106.071.

Sec. 106.025. Attempt to Purchase Alcohol by a Minor.

(a) A minor commits an offense if, with specific intent to commit an offense under Section 106.02 of this code, the minor does an act amounting to more than mere preparation that tends but fails to effect the commission of the offense intended.

(b) An offense under this section is punishable as provided by Section 106.071.

Sec. 106.03. Sale to Minors.

(a) A person commits an offense if with criminal negligence he sells an alcoholic beverage to a minor.

(b) A person who sells a minor an alcoholic beverage does not commit an offense if the minor falsely represents himself to be 21 years old or older by displaying an apparently valid proof of identification that contains a physical description and photograph consistent with the minor's appearance, purports to establish that the minor is 21 years of age or older, and was issued by a governmental agency. The proof of identification may include a driver's license or identification card issued by the Department of Public Safety, a passport, or a military identification card.

(c) An offense under this section is a Class A misdemeanor.

(d) Subsection (b) does not apply to a person who accesses electronically readable information under Section 109.61 that identifies a driver's license or identification certificate as invalid.

Sec. 106.04. Consumption of Alcohol by a Minor.

(a) A minor commits an offense if he consumes an alcoholic beverage.

(b) It is an affirmative defense to prosecution under this section that the alcoholic beverage was consumed in the visible presence of the minor's adult parent, guardian, or spouse.

(c) An offense under this section is punishable as provided by Section 106.071.

(d) A minor who commits an offense under this section and who has been previously convicted twice or more of offenses under this section is not eligible for deferred disposition. For the purposes of this subsection:

(1) an adjudication under Title 3, Family Code, that the minor engaged in conduct described by this section is considered a conviction of an offense under this section; and

(2) an order of deferred disposition for an offense alleged under this section is considered a conviction of an offense under this section.

(e) Subsection (a) does not apply to a minor who:

(1) requested emergency medical assistance in response to the possible alcohol overdose of the minor or another person;

(2) was the first person to make a request for medical assistance under Subdivision (1); and

(3) if the minor requested emergency medical assistance for the possible alcohol overdose of another person:

(A) remained on the scene until the medical assistance arrived; and

(B) cooperated with medical assistance and law enforcement personnel.

(f) Except as provided by Subsection (g), Subsection (a) does not apply to a minor who reports the sexual assault of the minor or another person, or is the victim of a sexual assault reported by another person, to:

(1) a health care provider treating the victim of the sexual assault;

(2) an employee of a law enforcement agency, including an employee of a campus police department of an institution of higher education; or

(3) the Title IX coordinator of an institution of higher education or another employee of the institution responsible for responding to reports of sexual assault.

(g) A minor is entitled to raise the defense provided by Subsection (f) in the prosecution of an offense under this section only if the minor is in violation of this section at the time of the commission of a sexual assault that is:

(1) reported by the minor under Subsection (f); or

(2) committed against the minor and reported by another person under Subsection (f).

(h) A minor who commits a sexual assault that is reported under Subsection (f) is not entitled to raise the defense provided by Subsection (f) in the prosecution of the minor for an offense under this section.

Sec. 106.041. Driving or Operating Watercraft Under the Influence of Alcohol by Minor.

(a) A minor commits an offense if the minor operates a motor vehicle in a public place, or a watercraft, while having any detectable amount of alcohol in the minor's system.

(b) Except as provided by Subsection (c), an offense under this section is a Class C misdemeanor.

(c) If it is shown at the trial of the defendant that the defendant is a minor who is not a child and who has been previously convicted at least twice of an offense under this section, the offense is punishable by:

(1) a fine of not less than $500 or more than $2,000;

(2) confinement in jail for a term not to exceed 180 days; or

(3) both the fine and confinement.

(d) In addition to any fine and any order issued under Section 106.115, the court shall order a minor convicted of an offense under this section to perform community service for:

(1) not less than 20 or more than 40 hours, if the minor has not been previously convicted of an offense under this section; or

(2) not less than 40 or more than 60 hours, if the minor has been previously convicted of an offense under this section.

(e) Community service ordered under this section must be related to education about or prevention of misuse of alcohol.

(f) A minor who commits an offense under this section and who has been previously convicted twice or more of offenses under this section is not eligible for deferred disposition or deferred adjudication.

(g) An offense under this section is not a lesser included offense under Section 49.04, 49.045, or 49.06, Penal Code.

(h) For the purpose of determining whether a minor has been previously convicted of an offense under this section:

(1) an adjudication under Title 3, Family Code, that the minor engaged in conduct described by this section is considered a conviction under this section; and

(2) an order of deferred disposition for an offense alleged under this section is considered a conviction of an offense under this section.

(i) A peace officer who is charging a minor with committing an offense under this section is not required to take the minor into custody but may issue a citation to the minor that contains written notice of the time and place the minor must appear before a magistrate, the name and address of the minor charged, and the offense charged.

(j) In this section:

(1) "Child" has the meaning assigned by Section 51.02, Family Code.

(2) "Motor vehicle" has the meaning assigned by Section 32.34(a), Penal Code.

(3) "Public place" has the meaning assigned by Section 1.07, Penal Code.

(4) "Watercraft" has the meaning assigned by Section 49.01, Penal Code.

Sec. 106.05. Possession of Alcohol by a Minor.

(a) Except as provided in Subsection (b) of this section, a minor commits an offense if he possesses an alcoholic beverage.

(b) A minor may possess an alcoholic beverage:

(1) while in the course and scope of the minor's employment if the minor is an employee of a licensee or permittee and the employment is not prohibited by this code;

(2) if the minor is in the visible presence of his adult parent, guardian, or spouse, or other adult to whom the minor has been committed by a court;

(3) if the minor is under the immediate supervision of a commissioned peace officer engaged in enforcing the provisions of this code; or

(4) if the beverage is lawfully provided to the minor under Section 106.16.

(c) An offense under this section is punishable as provided by Section 106.071.

(d) Subsection (a) does not apply to a minor who:

(1) requested emergency medical assistance in response to the possible alcohol overdose of the minor or another person;

(2) was the first person to make a request for medical assistance under Subdivision (1); and

(3) if the minor requested emergency medical assistance for the possible alcohol overdose of another person:

(A) remained on the scene until the medical assistance arrived; and

(B) cooperated with medical assistance and law enforcement personnel.

(e) Except as provided by Subsection (f), Subsection (a) does not apply to a minor who reports the sexual assault of the minor or another person, or is the victim of a sexual assault reported by another person, to:

(1) a health care provider treating the victim of the sexual assault;

(2) an employee of a law enforcement agency, including an employee of a campus police department of an institution of higher education; or

(3) the Title IX coordinator of an institution of higher education or another employee of the institution responsible for responding to reports of sexual assault.

(f) A minor is entitled to raise the defense provided by Subsection (e) in the prosecution of an offense under this section only if the minor is in violation of this section at the time of the commission of a sexual assault that is:

(1) reported by the minor under Subsection (e); or

(2) committed against the minor and reported by another person under Subsection (e).

(g) A minor who commits a sexual assault that is reported under Subsection (e) is not entitled to raise the defense provided by Subsection (e) in the prosecution of the minor for an offense under this section.

Sec. 106.06. Purchase of Alcohol for a Minor; Furnishing Alcohol to a Minor.

(a) **[2 versions: As amended by Acts 1993, 73rd Leg., ch. 437]** Except as provided in Subsection (b) of this section, a person commits an offense if he purchases an alcoholic beverage for or gives or makes available an alcoholic beverage to a minor with criminal negligence.

(a) **[2 versions: As amended by Acts 1993, 73rd Leg., ch. 934]** Except as provided in Subsection (b) of this section, a person commits an offense if he purchases an alcoholic beverage for or gives or with criminal negligence makes available an alcoholic beverage to a minor.

(b) A person may purchase an alcoholic beverage for or give an alcoholic beverage to a minor if the person is:

(1) the minor's adult parent, guardian, or spouse, or an adult in whose custody the minor has been committed by a court, and is visibly present when the minor possesses or consumes the alcoholic beverage; or

(2) a person lawfully providing an alcoholic beverage to a minor under Section 106.16.

(c) An offense under this section is a Class A misdemeanor.

(d) A judge, acting under Chapter 42A, Code of Criminal Procedure, who places a defendant charged with an offense under this section on community supervision under that chapter shall, if the defendant committed the offense at a gathering where participants were involved in the abuse of alcohol, including binge drinking or forcing or coercing individuals to consume alcohol, in addition to any other condition imposed by the judge:

(1) require the defendant to:

(A) perform community service for not less than 20 or more than 40 hours; and

(B) attend an alcohol awareness program approved under Section 106.115; and

(2) order the Department of Public Safety to suspend the driver's license or permit of the defendant or, if the defendant does not have a driver's license or permit, to deny the issuance of a driver's license or permit to the defendant for 180 days.

(e) Community service ordered under Subsection (d) is in addition to any community service ordered by the judge under Article 42A.304, Code of Criminal Procedure, and must be related to education about or prevention of misuse of alcohol if programs or services providing that education are available in the community in which the court is located. If programs or services providing that education are not available, the court may order community service that the court considers appropriate for rehabilitative purposes.

Sec. 106.07. Misrepresentation of Age by a Minor.

(a) A minor commits an offense if he falsely states that he is 21 years of age or older or presents any document that indicates he is 21 years of age or older to a person engaged in selling or serving alcoholic beverages.

(b) An offense under this section is punishable as provided by Section 106.071.

Sec. 106.071. Punishment for Alcohol-Related Offense by Minor.

(a) This section applies to an offense under Section 106.02, 106.025, 106.04, 106.05, or 106.07.

(b) Except as provided by Subsection (c), an offense to which this section applies is a Class C misdemeanor.

(c) If it is shown at the trial of the defendant that the defendant is a minor who is not a child and who has been previously convicted at least twice of an offense to which this section applies, the offense is punishable by:

(1) a fine of not less than $250 or more than $2,000;

(2) confinement in jail for a term not to exceed 180 days; or

(3) both the fine and confinement.

(d) In addition to any fine and any order issued under Section 106.115:

(1) the court shall order a minor placed on deferred disposition for or convicted of an offense to which this section applies to perform community service for:

(A) not less than eight or more than 12 hours, if the minor has not been previously convicted of an offense to which this section applies; or

(B) not less than 20 or more than 40 hours, if the minor has been previously convicted once of an offense to which this section applies; and

(2) the court shall order the Department of Public Safety to suspend the driver's license or permit of a minor convicted of an offense to which this section applies or, if the minor does not have a driver's license or permit, to deny the issuance of a driver's license or permit for:

(A) 30 days, if the minor has not been previously convicted of an offense to which this section applies;

(B) 60 days, if the minor has been previously convicted once of an offense to which this section applies; or

(C) 180 days, if the minor has been previously convicted twice or more of an offense to which this section applies.

(e) Community service ordered under this section must be related to education about or prevention of misuse of alcohol or drugs, as applicable, if programs or services providing that education are available in the community in which the court is located. If programs or services providing that education are not available, the court may order community service that it considers appropriate for rehabilitative purposes.

(f) In this section:

(1) a prior adjudication under Title 3, Family Code, that the minor engaged in conduct described by this section is considered a conviction; and

(2) a prior order of deferred disposition for an offense alleged under this section is considered a conviction.

(g) In this section, "child" has the meaning assigned by Section 51.02, Family Code.

(h) A driver's license suspension under this section takes effect on the 11th day after the date the minor is convicted.

(i) A defendant who is not a child and who has been previously convicted at least twice of an offense to which this section applies is not eligible to receive a deferred disposition or deferred adjudication.

Sec. 106.08. Importation by a Minor.

No minor may import into this state or possess with intent to import into this state any alcoholic beverage.

Sec. 106.09. Employment of Minors.

(a) Except as provided by Subsections (b), (c), (e), and (f), no person may employ a person under 18 years of age to sell, prepare, serve, or otherwise handle liquor, or to assist in doing so.

(b) A holder of a wine only package store permit may employ a person 16 years old or older to work in any capacity.

(c) A holder of a permit or license providing for the on-premises consumption of alcoholic beverages may employ a person under 18 years of age to work in any capacity other than the actual selling, preparing, or serving of alcoholic beverages.

(d) A person who is 18, 19, or 20 years of age is not prohibited from acting as an agent under Chapter 35, 36, or 73, provided the person may carry out the activities authorized by those chapters only while in the actual course and scope of the person's employment.

(e) The holder of a permit or license providing for the on-premises consumption of alcoholic beverages who also holds a food and beverage certificate may employ a person under 18 years of age to work as a cashier for transactions involving the sale of alcoholic beverages if the alcoholic beverages are served by a person 18 years of age or older.

(f) The holder of a permit or license providing for the on-premises consumption of alcoholic beverages that derives less than 50 percent of its gross receipts for the premises from the sale or service of alcoholic beverages may employ a person under

Alcoholic Beverage Code

18 years of age to work as a cashier for transactions involving the sale of alcoholic beverages if the alcoholic beverages are served by a person 18 years of age or older.

Sec. 106.10. Plea of Guilty by Minor.

No minor may plead guilty to an offense under this chapter except in open court before a judge.

Sec. 106.11. Parent or Guardian at Trial [Repealed].

Repealed by Acts 2005, 79th Leg., ch. 949 (H.B. 1575), § 52(1), effective September 1, 2005.

Sec. 106.115. Alcohol Awareness Program; License Suspension.

(a) **[As amended by Acts 2021, 87th Leg., ch. XXX (SB 1480)]** On the placement of a minor on deferred disposition for an offense under Section 49.02, Penal Code, or under Section 106.02, 106.025, 106.04, 106.041, 106.05, or 106.07, the court shall require the defendant to successfully complete one of the following programs:

(1) an alcohol awareness program under this section that is regulated under Chapter 171, Government Code;

(2) a drug education program under Section 521.374(a)(1), Transportation Code, that is regulated under Chapter 171, Government Code; or

(3) a drug and alcohol driving awareness program under Section 1001.103, Education Code.

(a) **[As amended by Acts 2021, 87th Leg., ch. XXX (HB 1560)]** On the placement of a minor on deferred disposition for an offense under Section 49.02, Penal Code, or under Section 106.02, 106.025, 106.04, 106.041, 106.05, or 106.07, the court shall require the defendant to attend an alcohol awareness program approved by the Texas Department of Licensing and Regulation under this section or a drug education program approved by the Department of State Health Services in accordance with Section 521.374, Transportation Code. On conviction of a minor of an offense under one or more of those sections, the court, in addition to assessing a fine as provided by those sections, shall require a defendant who has not been previously convicted of an offense under one of those sections to attend an alcohol awareness program or a drug education program described by this subsection. If the defendant has been previously convicted once or more of an offense under one or more of those sections, the court may require the defendant to attend an alcohol awareness program or a drug education program described by this subsection. If the defendant is younger than 18 years of age, the court may require the parent or guardian of the defendant to attend the program with the defendant. The Texas Department of Licensing and Regulation or Texas Commission of Licensing and Regulation, as appropriate:

(1) is responsible for the administration of the certification of approved alcohol awareness programs;

(2) may charge a nonrefundable application fee for:

(A) initial certification of the approval; or

(B) renewal of the certification;

(3) shall adopt rules regarding alcohol awareness programs approved under this section; and

(4) shall monitor, coordinate, and provide training to a person who provides an alcohol awareness program.

(a-1) On conviction of a minor of an offense under Section 49.02, Penal Code, or Section 106.02, 106.025, 106.04, 106.041, 106.05, or 106.07, the court, in addition to assessing a fine as provided by those sections, shall require a defendant who has not been previously convicted of an offense under one of those sections to successfully complete an alcohol awareness program, a drug education program, or a drug and alcohol driving awareness program described by Subsection (a). If the defendant has been previously convicted once or more of an offense under one or more of those sections, the court may require the defendant to successfully complete an alcohol awareness program, a drug education program, or a drug and alcohol driving awareness program described by Subsection (a).

(a-2) If the defendant is younger than 18 years of age, the court may require the parent or guardian of the defendant to attend the program described by Subsection (a) with the defendant.

(b) [Repealed.]

(b-1) If the defendant resides in a county with a population of 75,000 or less and access to an alcohol awareness program is not readily available in the county, the court may allow the defendant to take an online alcohol awareness program if the Texas Department of Licensing and Regulation approves online courses or require the defendant to perform not less than eight hours of community service related to alcohol abuse prevention or treatment and approved by the Texas Department of Licensing and Regulation under Subsection (b-3) instead of attending the alcohol awareness program. Community service ordered under this subsection is in addition to community service ordered under Section 106.071(d).

Alcoholic Beverage Code

(b-2) For purposes of Subsection (b-1), if the defendant is enrolled in an institution of higher education located in a county in which access to an alcohol awareness program is readily available, the court may consider the defendant to be a resident of that county. If the defendant is not enrolled in such an institution of higher education or if the court does not consider the defendant to be a resident of the county in which the institution is located, the defendant's residence is the residence listed on the defendant's driver's license or personal identification certificate issued by the Department of Public Safety. If the defendant does not have a driver's license or personal identification certificate issued by the Department of Public Safety, the defendant's residence is the residence on the defendant's voter registration certificate. If the defendant is not registered to vote, the defendant's residence is the residence on file with the public school district on which the defendant's enrollment is based. If the defendant is not enrolled in public school, the defendant's residence is determined by the court.

(b-3) The Texas Department of Licensing and Regulation shall create a list of community services related to alcohol abuse prevention or treatment in each county in the state to which a judge may sentence a defendant under Subsection (b-1).

(c) The court shall require the defendant to present to the court, within 90 days of the date of final conviction, evidence in the form prescribed by the court that the defendant, as ordered by the court, has satisfactorily completed an alcohol awareness program or performed the required hours of community service. For good cause the court may extend this period by not more than 90 days. If the defendant presents the required evidence within the prescribed period, the court may reduce the assessed fine to an amount equal to no less than one-half of the amount of the initial fine.

(d) If the defendant does not present the required evidence within the prescribed period, the court:

(1) shall order the Department of Public Safety to:

(A) suspend the defendant's driver's license or permit for a period not to exceed six months or, if the defendant does not have a license or permit, to deny the issuance of a license or permit to the defendant for that period; or

(B) if the defendant has been previously convicted of an offense under one or more of the sections listed in Subsection (a), suspend the defendant's driver's license or permit for a period not to exceed one year or, if the defendant does not have a license or permit, to deny the issuance of a license or permit to the defendant for that period; and

(2) may order the defendant or the parent, managing conservator, or guardian of the defendant to do any act or refrain from doing any act if the court determines that doing the act or refraining from doing the act will increase the likelihood that the defendant will present evidence to the court that the defendant has satisfactorily completed an alcohol awareness program or performed the required hours of community service.

(e) The Department of Public Safety shall send notice of the suspension or prohibition order issued under Subsection (d) by first class mail to the defendant. The notice must include the date of the suspension or prohibition order, the reason for the suspension or prohibition, and the period covered by the suspension or prohibition.

Sec. 106.116. Reports of Court to Commission.

Unless the clerk is otherwise required to include the information in a report submitted under Section 101.09, the clerk of a court, including a justice court, municipal court, or juvenile court, shall furnish to the commission on request a notice of a conviction of an offense under this chapter or an adjudication under Title 3, Family Code, for conduct that constitutes an offense under this chapter. The report must be in the form prescribed by the commission.

Sec. 106.117. Report of Court to Department of Public Safety.

(a) Each court, including a justice court, municipal court, or juvenile court, shall furnish to the Department of Public Safety a notice of each:

(1) adjudication under Title 3, Family Code, for conduct that constitutes an offense under this chapter;

(2) conviction of an offense under this chapter;

(3) order of deferred disposition for an offense alleged under this chapter; and

(4) acquittal of an offense under Section 106.041.

(b) The notice must be in a form prescribed by the Department of Public Safety and must contain the driver's license number of the defendant, if the defendant holds a driver's license.

(c) The Department of Public Safety shall maintain appropriate records of information in the notices and shall provide the information to law enforcement agencies and courts as necessary to enable those agencies and courts to carry out their official duties. The information is admissible in any action in which it is relevant. A person who holds a driver's license having the same number that is contained in a record maintained under this section is presumed to be the person to whom the record relates. The presumption may be rebutted only by evidence presented under oath.

(d) The information maintained under this section is confidential and may not be disclosed except as provided by this section. A provision of Chapter 58, Family Code, or other law limiting collection or reporting of information on a juvenile or other minor or requiring destruction of that information does not apply to information reported and maintained under this section.

Sec. 106.12. Expunction of Conviction or Arrest Records of a Minor.

(a) Any person convicted of not more than one violation of this code while a minor, on attaining the age of 21 years, may apply to the court in which he was convicted to have the conviction expunged.

(b) The application shall contain the applicant's sworn statement that he was not convicted of any violation of this code while a minor other than the one he seeks to have expunged.

(c) If the court finds that the applicant was not convicted of any other violation of this code while he was a minor, the court shall order the conviction, together with all complaints, verdicts, sentences, prosecutorial and law enforcement records, and other documents relating to the offense, to be expunged from the applicant's record. After entry of the order, the applicant shall be released from all disabilities resulting from the conviction, and the conviction may not be shown or made known for any purpose.

(d) Any person placed under a custodial or noncustodial arrest for not more than one violation of this code while a minor and who was not convicted of the violation may apply to the court in which the person was charged to have the records of the arrest expunged. The application must contain the applicant's sworn statement that the applicant was not arrested for a violation of this code other than the arrest the applicant seeks to expunge. If the court finds the applicant was not arrested for any other violation of this code while a minor, the court shall order all complaints, verdicts, prosecutorial and law enforcement records, and other documents relating to the violation to be expunged from the applicant's record.

(e) The court shall charge an applicant a reimbursement fee in the amount of $30 for each application for expunction filed under this section to defray the cost of notifying state agencies of orders of expunction under this section.

(f) The procedures for expunction provided under this section are separate and distinct from the expunction procedures under Chapter 55, Code of Criminal Procedure.

Sec. 106.13. Sanctions Against Retailer.

(a) Except as provided in Subsections (b) and (c) of this section, the commission or administrator may cancel or suspend for not more than 90 days a retail license or permit or a private club registration permit if it is found, on notice and hearing, that the licensee or permittee with criminal negligence sold, served, dispensed, or delivered an alcoholic beverage to a minor or with criminal negligence permitted a minor to violate Section 106.04 or 106.05 of this code on the licensed premises.

(b) For a second offense the commission or administrator may cancel the license or permit or suspend it for not more than six months. For a third offense within a period of 36 consecutive months the commission or administrator may cancel the permit or suspend it for not more than 12 months.

(c) The commission or administrator may relax the provisions of this section concerning suspension and cancellation and assess a sanction the commission or administrator finds just under the circumstances if, at a hearing, the licensee or permittee establishes to the satisfaction of the commission or administrator:

(1) that the violation could not reasonably have been prevented by the permittee or licensee by the exercise of due diligence;

(2) that the permittee or licensee was entrapped; or

(3) that an agent, servant, or employee of the permittee or licensee violated this code without the knowledge of the permittee or licensee.

Sec. 106.14. Actions of Employee.

(a) For purposes of this chapter and any other provision of this code relating to the sales, service, dispensing, or delivery of alcoholic beverages to a person who is not a member of a private club on the club premises, a minor, or an intoxicated person or the consumption of alcoholic beverages by a person who is not a member of a private club on the club premises, a minor, or an intoxicated person, the actions of an employee shall not be attributable to the employer if:

(1) the employer requires its employees to attend a commission-approved seller training program;

(2) the employee has actually attended such a training program; and

(3) the employer has not directly or indirectly encouraged the employee to violate such law.

(b) The commission shall adopt rules or policies establishing the minimum requirements for approved seller training programs. Upon application, the commission shall approve seller training programs meeting such requirements that are sponsored either privately, by public community colleges, or by public or private institutions of higher education that offer a four-year undergraduate program and a degree or certificate in hotel or motel management, restaurant management, or travel or tourism management. The commission may charge an application fee to be set by the commission in such amount as is necessary to defray the expense of processing the application.

(c) The commission may approve under this section a seller training program sponsored by a licensee or permittee for the purpose of training its employees whether or not such employees are located at the same premises. This subsection shall only apply to licensees or permittees who employ at least 150 persons at any one time during the license or permit year who sell, serve, or prepare alcoholic beverages.

(d) The commission may approve under this section a seller training program conducted by a hotel management company or a hotel operating company for the employees of five or more hotels operated or managed by the company if:

(1) the seller training program is administered through the corporate offices of the company; and

(2) the hotels employ a total of at least 200 persons at one time during the license or permit year who sell, serve, or prepare alcoholic beverages.

(e) After notice and hearing, the commission may cancel or suspend the commission's approval of a seller training program, the commission's certification of a trainer to teach a seller training program, or the commission's certification of a seller-server if the program, trainer, or seller-server violates this code or a commission rule. The commission may give a program, trainer, or seller-server the opportunity to pay a civil penalty rather than be subject to suspension under this subsection. Sections 11.62 through 11.67 apply to the program approval or certification as if the program approval or certification were a license or permit under this code.

Sec. 106.15. Prohibited Activities by Persons Younger Than 18.

(a) A permittee or licensee commits an offense if he employs, authorizes, permits, or induces a person younger than 18 years of age to dance with another person in exchange for a benefit, as defined by Section 1.07, Penal Code, on the premises covered by the permit or license.

(b) An offense under Subsection (a) is a Class A misdemeanor.

(c) In addition to a penalty imposed under Subsection (b), the commission or administrator shall:

(1) suspend for a period of five days the license or permit of a person convicted of a first offense under Subsection (a);

(2) suspend for a period of 60 days the license or permit of a person convicted of a second offense under Subsection (a); and

(3) cancel the license or permit of a person convicted of a third offense under Subsection (a).

(d) This section does not apply to a gift or benefit given for a dance at a wedding, anniversary, or similar event.

(e) A person does not commit an offense under Subsection (a) if the person younger than 18 years of age falsely represents the person's age to be at least 18 years of age by displaying an apparently valid Texas driver's license or an identification card issued by the Department of Public Safety containing a physical description consistent with the person's appearance.

Sec. 106.16. Exception for Certain Course Work.

(a) In this section:

(1) "Career school or college" has the meaning assigned by Section 132.001, Education Code.

(2) "Taste" means to draw a beverage into the mouth without swallowing or otherwise consuming the beverage.

(b) Notwithstanding any other law, a minor may taste an alcoholic beverage if:

(1) the minor:

(A) is at least 18 years old; and

(B) is enrolled:

(i) as a student at a public or private institution of higher education or a career school or college that offers a program in culinary arts, viticulture, enology or wine technology, brewing or malt beverage technology, or distilled spirits production or technology; and

(ii) in a course that is part of a program described by Subparagraph (i);

(2) the beverage is tasted for educational purposes as part of the curriculum for the course described by Subdivision (1)(B)(ii);

(3) the beverage is not purchased by the minor; and

(4) the service and tasting of the beverage is supervised by a faculty or staff member who is at least 21 years of age.

(c) A public or private institution of higher education or a career school or college is not required to hold a license or permit to engage in the activities authorized under this section.

Sec. 106.17. Presence or Employment of Certain Persons at Permitted or Licensed Premises Operating As Sexually Oriented Business.

(a) An individual younger than 18 years of age may not be on premises covered by a permit or license issued under this code if a sexually oriented business, as defined by Section 243.002, Local Government Code, operates on the premises.

(b) The holder of a permit or license covering a premises described by Subsection (a) may not:

(1) knowingly or recklessly allow an individual younger than 18 years of age to be on the premises; or

(2) enter into a contract, other than a contract described by Section 51.016(g), Labor Code, with an individual younger than 21 years of age for the performance of work or the provision of a service on the premises.

(c) Notwithstanding any other provision of this code, if it is found, after notice and hearing, that a permittee or licensee has violated Subsection (b) the commission or administrator shall:

(1) suspend the permit or license for 30 days for the first violation;

(2) suspend the permit or license for 60 days for the second violation; and

(3) cancel the permit or license for the third violation.

CHAPTER 107
TRANSPORTATION AND IMPORTATION

Sec. 107.01. Transportation of Liquor: Statement Required.

(a) No person may transport liquor into this state or on a public highway, street, or alley in this state unless the person accompanying or in charge of the shipment has with him, available for exhibition and inspection, a written statement furnished and signed by the shipper showing the name and address of the consignor and the consignee, the origin and destination of the shipment, and any other information required by rule or regulation of the commission.

(b) The person in charge of the shipment while it is being transported shall exhibit the statement to the commission, an authorized representative of the commission, or a peace officer on demand, and it is a violation of this code to fail or refuse to do so. The representative or officer shall accept the written statement as prima facie evidence of the legal right to transport the liquor.

Sec. 107.02. Transportation of Malt Beverages: Statement Required.

(a) It is lawful for a person to transport malt beverages from any place where its sale, manufacture, or distribution is authorized to another place in the state where its sale, manufacture, or distribution is authorized, or from the state boundary to a place where its sale, manufacture, or distribution is authorized, even though the route of transportation may cross a dry area.

(a-1) A person transporting malt beverages to the premises of a distributor, including to a location from which the distributor is temporarily conducting business under Section 109.62, shall provide to the consignee a shipping invoice that clearly states:

(1) the name and address of the consignor and consignee;

(2) the origin and destination of the shipment; and

(3) any other information required by this code or commission rule, including the brands, sizes of containers, and quantities of malt beverages contained in the shipment.

(b) A shipment of malt beverages must be accompanied by a written statement furnished and signed by the shipper showing:

(1) the name and address of the consignor and consignee;

(2) the origin and destination of the shipment; and

(3) any other information required by the commission or administrator.

(c) The person in charge of the shipment while it is being transported shall exhibit the written statement to any representative of the commission or peace officer who demands to see it. The statement shall be accepted by the representative or peace officer as prima facie evidence of the legal right to transport the malt beverages.

(d) A person who transports malt beverages not accompanied by the required statement, or who fails to exhibit the statement after a lawful demand, violates this code.

Sec. 107.08. Transportation of Beverages for Personal Consumption.

A person who purchases an alcoholic beverage for the person's own consumption may personally transport it from a place where its sale is legal to a place where its possession is legal without holding a license or permit.

CONSTITUTION OF THE STATE OF TEXAS 1876

ARTICLE I
BILL OF RIGHTS

Sec. 9. Searches and Seizures.

The people shall be secure in their persons, houses, papers and possessions, from all unreasonable seizures or searches, and no warrant to search any place, or to seize any person or thing, shall issue without describing them as near as may be, nor without probable cause, supported by oath or affirmation.

Sec. 10. Rights of Accused in Criminal Prosecutions.

In all criminal prosecutions the accused shall have a speedy public trial by an impartial jury. He shall have the right to demand the nature and cause of the accusation against him, and to have a copy thereof. He shall not be compelled to give evidence against himself, and shall have the right of being heard by himself or counsel, or both, shall be confronted by the witnesses against him and shall have compulsory process for obtaining witnesses in his favor, except that when the witness resides out of the State and the offense charged is a violation of any of the anti-trust laws of this State, the defendant and the State shall have the right to produce and have the evidence admitted by deposition, under such rules and laws as the Legislature may hereafter provide; and no person shall be held to answer for a criminal offense, unless on an indictment of a grand jury, except in cases in which the punishment is by fine or imprisonment, otherwise than in the penitentiary, in cases of impeachment, and in cases arising in the army or navy, or in the militia, when in actual service in time of war or public danger.

Sec. 11. Bail.

All prisoners shall be bailable by sufficient sureties, unless for capital offenses, when the proof is evident; but this provision shall not be so construed as to prevent bail after indictment found upon examination of the evidence, in such manner as may be prescribed by law.

Sec. 11a. Denial of Bail After Multiple Felonies.

(a) Any person (1) accused of a felony less than capital in this State, who has been theretofore twice convicted of a felony, the second conviction being subsequent to the first, both in point of time of commission of the offense and conviction therefor, (2) accused of a felony less than capital in this State, committed while on bail for a prior felony for which he has been indicted, (3) accused of a felony less than capital in this State involving the use of a deadly weapon after being convicted of a prior felony, or (4) accused of a violent or sexual offense committed while under the supervision of a criminal justice agency of the State or a political subdivision of the State for a prior felony, after a hearing, and upon evidence substantially showing the guilt of the accused of the offense in (1) or (3) above, of the offense committed while on bail in (2) above, or of the offense in (4) above committed while under the supervision of a criminal justice agency of the State or a political subdivision of the State for a prior felony, may be denied bail pending trial, by a district judge in this State, if said order denying bail pending trial is issued within seven calendar days subsequent to the time of incarceration of the accused; provided, however, that if the accused is not accorded a trial upon the accusation under (1) or (3) above, the accusation and indictment used under (2) above, or the accusation or indictment used under (4) above within sixty (60) days from the time of his incarceration upon the accusation, the order denying bail shall be automatically set aside, unless a continuance is obtained upon the motion or request of the accused; provided, further, that the right of appeal to the Court of Criminal Appeals of this State is expressly accorded the accused for a review of any judgment or order made hereunder, and said appeal shall be given preference by the Court of Criminal Appeals.

(b) In this section:

(1) "Violent offense" means:

(A) murder;

(B) aggravated assault, if the accused used or exhibited a deadly weapon during the commission of the assault;

(C) aggravated kidnapping; or

(D) aggravated robbery.

(2) "Sexual offense" means:

(A) aggravated sexual assault;

(B) sexual assault; or

(C) indecency with a child.

ARTICLE III
LEGISLATIVE DEPARTMENT

Sec. 14. Privilege from Arrest During Legislative Session.

Senators and Representatives shall, except in cases of treason, felony, or breach of the peace, be privileged from arrest during the session of the Legislature, and in going to and returning from the same.

ARTICLE VI
SUFFRAGE

Sec. 5. Voters Privileged from Arrest.

Voters shall, in all cases, except treason, felony or breach of the peace, be privileged from arrest during their attendance at elections, and in going to and returning therefrom.

ARTICLE XVII
MODE OF AMENDING THE CONSTITUTION OF THIS STATE

Sec. 1. Proposed Amendments; Publication; Submission to Voters; Adoption.

(a) The Legislature, at any regular session, or at any special session when the matter is included within the purposes for which the session is convened, may propose amendments revising the Constitution, to be voted upon by the qualified voters for statewide offices and propositions, as defined in the Constitution and statutes of this State. The date of the elections shall be specified by the Legislature. The proposal for submission must be approved by a vote of two-thirds of all the members elected to each House, entered by yeas and nays on the journals.

(b) A brief explanatory statement of the nature of a proposed amendment, together with the date of the election and the wording of the proposition as it is to appear on the ballot, shall be published twice in each newspaper in the State which meets requirements set by the Legislature for the publication of official notices of offices and departments of the state government. The explanatory statement shall be prepared by the Secretary of State and shall be approved by the Attorney General. The Secretary of State shall send a full and complete copy of the proposed amendment or amendments to each county clerk who shall post the same in a public place in the courthouse at least 30 days prior to the election on said amendment. The first notice shall be published not more than 60 days nor less than 50 days before the date of the election, and the second notice shall be published on the same day in the succeeding week. The Legislature shall fix the standards for the rate of charge for the publication, which may not be higher than the newspaper's published national rate for advertising per column inch.

(c) The election shall be held in accordance with procedures prescribed by the Legislature, and the returning officer in each county shall make returns to the Secretary of State of the number of legal votes cast at the election for and against each amendment. If it appears from the returns that a majority of the votes cast have been cast in favor of an amendment, it shall become a part of this Constitution, and proclamation thereof shall be made by the Governor.

AGRICULTURE CODE

TITLE 5
PRODUCTION, PROCESSING, AND SALE OF HORTICULTURAL PRODUCTS

SUBTITLE D
HANDLING AND MARKETING OF HORTICULTURAL PRODUCTS

CHAPTER 102
HANDLING AND MARKETING OF CITRUS FRUIT

SUBCHAPTER B
TRANSPORTATION OF CITRUS FRUIT

Sec. 102.101. Identification Signs.

(a) A motor vehicle, including a truck or tractor, that hauls citrus fruit in bulk or in open containers for commercial purposes on the highways of this state must be identified by signs showing:

(1) the name of the person who owns the vehicle; or

(2) the name of the person who leases or operates the vehicle.

(b) If a person licensed under Subchapter A of this chapter is the owner or operator of the vehicle, each identification sign must also show "Licensed Citrus Fruit Dealer" under the name of the person.

(c) The lettering on each identification sign must be at least three inches in height.

(d) An identification sign must appear on both sides of the vehicle or on both the front and the rear and must be affixed permanently or in another manner in which it may not easily be removed. If both a tractor and a trailer or two units are used in hauling the citrus fruit, both the tractor and the trailer or both units must be labeled with identification signs in the manner required by this subsection.

Sec. 102.102. Certificate.

A person who operates a motor vehicle, including a truck or tractor, or a motor vehicle and a trailer for hauling citrus fruit in bulk or in open containers for commercial purposes on the highways of this state shall, when operating the vehicle, have on his or her person a certificate or other document showing:

(1) the approximate amount of citrus fruit being hauled;

(2) the name of the owner of the citrus fruit; and

(3) the origin of the citrus fruit.

Sec. 102.103. Exception.

This subchapter does not apply to citrus fruit being hauled from the farm or grove to market or the place of first processing by the producer of the citrus fruit operating the producer's vehicle or by an employee of the producer operating a vehicle owned by the producer.

Sec. 102.104. Penalty.

(a) A person commits an offense if the person:

(1) operates a motor vehicle or a motor vehicle and trailer not identified in accordance with Section 102.101 of this code; or

(2) operates a motor vehicle or motor vehicle and trailer without a certificate or document required by Section 102.102 of this code.

(b) An offense under this section is a Class B misdemeanor.

SUBTITLE F
HEMP

CHAPTER 122.
CULTIVATION OF HEMP

SUBCHAPTER A
GENERAL PROVISIONS

Sec. 122.001. Definitions.

In this chapter:

(1) "Cultivate" means to plant, irrigate, cultivate, or harvest a hemp plant.

(2) "Governing person" has the meaning assigned by Section 1.002, Business Organizations Code.

(3) "Handle" means to possess or store a hemp plant:

(A) on premises owned, operated, or controlled by a license holder for any period of time; or

(B) in a vehicle for any period of time other than during the actual transport of the plant from a premises owned, operated, or controlled by a license holder to:

(i) a premises owned, operated, or controlled by another license holder; or

(ii) a person licensed under Chapter 443, Health and Safety Code.

(4) "Hemp" has the meaning assigned by Section 121.001.

(5) "Institution of higher education" has the meaning assigned by Section 61.003, Education Code.

(6) "License" means a hemp grower's license issued under Subchapter C.

(7) "License holder" means an individual or business entity holding a license.

(8) "Nonconsumable hemp product" means a product that contains hemp, other than a consumable hemp product as defined by Section 443.001, Health and Safety Code. The term includes cloth, cordage, fiber, fuel, paint, paper, particleboard, and plastics derived from hemp.

(9) "Plot" means a contiguous area in a field, greenhouse, or indoor growing structure containing the same variety or cultivar of hemp throughout the area.

Sec. 122.002. Local Regulation Prohibited.

A municipality, county, or other political subdivision of this state may not enact, adopt, or enforce a rule, ordinance, order, resolution, or other regulation that prohibits the cultivation, handling, transportation, or sale of hemp as authorized by this chapter.

Sec. 122.003. State Hemp Production Account.

(a) The state hemp production account is an account in the general revenue fund administered by the department.

(b) The account consists of:

(1) appropriations of money to the account by the legislature;

(2) public or private gifts, grants, or donations, including federal funds, received for the account;

(3) fees received under Section 122.052;

(4) interest and income earned on the investment of money in the account;

(5) penalties collected under this chapter other than a civil penalty collected under Subchapter H; and

(6) funds from any other source deposited in the account.

(c) The department may accept appropriations and gifts, grants, or donations from any source to administer and enforce this subtitle. Money received under this subsection shall be deposited in the account.

(d) Money in the account may be appropriated only to the department for the administration and enforcement of this subtitle.

Sec. 122.004. Severability.

(a) A provision of this chapter or its application to any person or circumstance is invalid if the secretary of the United States Department of Agriculture determines that the provision or application conflicts with 7 U.S.C. Chapter 38, Subchapter VII, and prevents the approval of the state plan submitted under Chapter 121.

(b) The invalidity of a provision or application under Subsection (a) does not affect the other provisions or applications of this chapter that can be given effect without the invalid provision or application, and to this end the provisions of this chapter are declared to be severable.

SUBCHAPTER B POWERS AND DUTIES OF DEPARTMENT

Sec. 122.051. Department Rules and Procedures.

(a) The department shall adopt rules and procedures necessary to implement, administer, and enforce this chapter.

(b) Rules adopted under Subsection (a) must:

(1) prescribe sampling, inspection, and testing procedures, including standards and procedures for the calibration of laboratory equipment, to ensure that the delta-9 tetrahydrocannabinol concentration of hemp plants cultivated in this state is not more than 0.3 percent on a dry weight basis; and

(2) provide due process consistent with Chapter 2001, Government Code, including an appeals

process, to protect license holders from the consequences of imperfect test results.

Sec. 122.052. Fees.

(a) The department shall set and collect:

(1) an application fee for an initial license in an amount not to exceed $100;

(2) a license renewal fee in an amount not to exceed $100;

(3) a participation fee for each location described by Section 122.103(a)(1) and each location added after the application is submitted in an amount not to exceed $100;

(4) a site modification fee for each change to a location described by Section 122.103(a)(1) in an amount not to exceed $500; and

(5) a collection and testing fee for each preharvest test or postharvest test if performed by the department in an amount not to exceed $300.

(b) A fee set by the department under this section may not exceed the amount necessary to administer this chapter. The comptroller may authorize the department to collect a fee described by Subsection (a) in an amount greater than the maximum amount provided by that subsection if necessary to cover the department's costs of administering this chapter.

(c) The department may not set or collect a fee associated with the cultivation of hemp that is not listed in Subsection (a), other than:

(1) a fee for the organic certification of hemp under Chapter 18 or for participation in another optional marketing program; or

(2) a fee for the certification of seed or plants under Chapter 62.

(d) Fees collected by the department under this chapter are not refundable and may be appropriated only to the department for the purpose of administering this chapter.

Sec. 122.053. Inspections.

(a) The department may randomly inspect land where hemp is grown to determine whether hemp is being cultivated in compliance with this chapter.

(b) The department may enter onto land described by Section 122.103(a)(1), conduct inspections, and collect and test plant samples.

(c) Using participation fees set and collected under Section 122.052(a)(3), the department shall pay the cost of inspections under this section.

(d) The Department of Public Safety may inspect, collect samples from, or test plants from any portion of a plot to ensure compliance with this chapter. A license holder shall allow the Department of Public Safety access to the plot and the property on which the plot is located for purposes of this subsection.

(e) If, after conducting an inspection or performing testing under this section, the department or the Department of Public Safety determines any portion of a plot is not compliant with this chapter, the department or the Department of Public Safety may report the license holder to the other department or to the attorney general.

Sec. 122.054. Sample Collection and Testing.

The department may collect samples and perform testing or contract with a laboratory for the performance of that collection and testing on behalf of the department. A test performed by a laboratory on behalf of the department is considered to be performed by the department for purposes of this chapter.

Sec. 122.055. Shipping Certificate or Cargo Manifest.

(a) The department shall develop a shipping certificate or cargo manifest which the department shall issue to a license holder in connection with the transportation of a shipment of hemp plant material originating in this state, other than sterilized seeds that are incapable of beginning germination.

(b) A certificate or manifest developed under Subsection (a) must include a unique identifying number for the shipment and the department's contact information to allow law enforcement during a roadside inspection of a motor vehicle transporting the shipment to verify that the shipment consists of hemp cultivated in compliance with this chapter.

(c) The department may coordinate with the Department of Public Safety to determine whether information included on a certificate or manifest issued under Subsection (a), including the unique identifying number, may be made available to law enforcement personnel through the Texas Law Enforcement Telecommunications System or a successor system of telecommunication used by law enforcement agencies and operated by the Department of Public Safety.

(d) A person commits an offense if the person, with intent to deceive law enforcement, forges, falsifies, or alters a shipping certificate or cargo manifest issued under this section. An offense under this subsection is a third degree felony.

SUBCHAPTER C
HEMP GROWER'S LICENSE

Sec. 122.101. License Required; Exceptions.

(a) Except as provided by Subsection (b), a person or the person's agent may not cultivate or handle hemp in this state or transport hemp outside of this state unless the person holds a license under this subchapter.

(b) A person is not required to hold a license under this subchapter to manufacture a consumable hemp product in accordance with Subtitle A, Title 6, Health and Safety Code.

Sec. 122.102. License Ineligibility.

(a) An individual who is or has been convicted of a felony relating to a controlled substance under federal law or the law of any state may not, before the 10th anniversary of the date of the conviction:

(1) hold a license under this subchapter; or

(2) be a governing person of a business entity that holds a license under this subchapter.

(b) The department may not issue a license under this subchapter to a person who materially falsifies any information contained in an application submitted to the department under Section 122.103.

Sec. 122.103. Application; Issuance.

(a) A person may apply for a license under this subchapter by submitting an application to the department on a form and in the manner prescribed by the department. The application must be accompanied by:

(1) a legal description of each location where the applicant intends to cultivate or handle hemp and the global positioning system coordinates for the perimeter of each location;

(2) written consent from the applicant or the property owner if the applicant is not the property owner allowing the department, the Department of Public Safety, and any other state or local law enforcement agency to enter onto all premises where hemp is cultivated or handled to conduct a physical inspection or to ensure compliance with this chapter and rules adopted under this chapter;

(3) the application fee; and

(4) any other information required by department rule.

(b) Except as provided by Subsection (c), the department shall issue a license to a qualified applicant not later than the 60th day after the date the department receives the completed application and the required application fees.

(c) A qualified applicant who along with the application submits proof to the department that the applicant holds a license under Chapter 487, Health and Safety Code, is not required to pay an application fee, and the department shall issue the license to the applicant within the time prescribed by Subsection (b).

Sec. 122.104. Term; Renewal.

(a) A license is valid for one year and may be renewed as provided by this section.

(b) The department shall renew a license if the license holder:

(1) is not ineligible to hold the license under Section 122.102;

(2) submits to the department the license renewal fee; and

(3) does not owe any outstanding fee described by Section 122.052.

Sec. 122.105. Revocation.

The department shall revoke a license if the license holder is convicted of a felony relating to a controlled substance under federal law or the law of any state.

SUBCHAPTER D
TESTING

Sec. 122.151. Testing Laboratories.

(a) Subject to Subsection (b), testing under this subchapter or Section 122.053 must be performed by:

(1) the department;

(2) an institution of higher education; or

(3) an independent testing laboratory registered under Section 122.152.

(b) To perform testing under this chapter, a laboratory described by Subsection (a) must be accredited by an independent accreditation body in accordance with International Organization for Standardization ISO/IEC 17025 or a comparable or successor standard.

(c) A license holder shall select a laboratory described by Subsection (a) to perform preharvest or postharvest testing of a sample taken from the license holder's plot. A license holder may not select an independent testing laboratory under Subsection (a)(3) unless the license holder has:

Agriculture Code

(1) no ownership interest in the laboratory; or

(2) less than a 10 percent ownership interest in the laboratory if the laboratory is a publicly traded company.

(d) A license holder must pay the costs of preharvest or postharvest sample collection and testing in the amount prescribed by the laboratory selected by the license holder.

(e) The department shall recognize and accept the results of a test performed by an institution of higher education or an independent testing laboratory described by Subsection (a). The department shall require that a copy of the test results be sent by the institution of higher education or independent testing laboratory directly to the department and the license holder.

(f) The department shall notify the license holder of the results of the test not later than the 14th day after the date the sample was collected under Section 122.154 or the date the department receives test results under Subsection (e).

Sec. 122.152. Registration of Independent Testing Laboratories.

(a) The department shall register independent testing laboratories authorized to conduct testing under Section 122.151(a)(3).

(b) A laboratory is eligible for registration if the laboratory submits to the department proof of accreditation by an independent accreditation body in accordance with International Organization for Standardization ISO/IEC 17025 or a comparable or successor standard and any required fee.

(c) The department shall annually prepare a registry of all independent testing laboratories registered by the department and make the registry available to license holders.

(d) The department may charge a registration fee to recover the costs of administering this section.

Sec. 122.153. Preharvest Testing Required.

(a) A license holder may not harvest a hemp plant or plant intended or believed to be hemp unless a representative sample of plants from the plot where the plant is grown is collected before harvest and subsequently tested using post-decarboxylation, high-performance liquid chromatography, or another similarly reliable method to determine the delta-9 tetrahydrocannabinol concentration of the sample in the manner required by this subchapter.

(b) For purposes of Subsection (a), a representative sample of plants from a plot consists of cuttings taken from at least five plants throughout the plot. The department by rule shall prescribe the minimum distance between plants from which cuttings may be taken based on the size of the plot.

(c) A laboratory performing preharvest testing under this section shall homogenize all the cuttings in the sample and test the delta-9 tetrahydrocannabinol concentration of a random sample of the homogenized material.

(d) This section does not prohibit a license holder from harvesting plants immediately after a preharvest sample is collected.

Sec. 122.154. Preharvest Sample Collection.

(a) A license holder shall notify the department at least 20 days before the date the license holder expects to harvest plants from a plot in the manner prescribed by department rule.

(b) A sample must be collected by the department or another entity described by Section 122.151(a) for purposes of preharvest testing under Section 122.153.

(c) The department by rule may prescribe reasonable procedures for submitting a preharvest sample collected under this section to a testing laboratory selected by the license holder.

Sec. 122.155. Optional Postharvest Testing.

(a) The department by rule shall allow a license holder to have a single postharvest test performed on a representative sample of plants from a plot if the results of the preharvest test representing the plot show a delta-9 tetrahydrocannabinol concentration of more than 0.3 percent on a dry weight basis.

(b) The department by rule shall prescribe the requirements for a representative sample and for sample collection under this section.

(c) If a license holder fails to request postharvest testing on or before the 15th day after the date the license holder is notified of the results of the preharvest test, the results of the preharvest test are final.

Sec. 122.156. Shipping Documentation for Test Samples.

The department shall issue documentation to an entity authorized to collect samples of plants for testing that authorizes the transportation of those samples from the place of collection to a testing laboratory described by Section 122.151(a).

Sec. 122.157. False Laboratory Report; Criminal Offense.

(a) A person commits an offense if the person, with the intent to deceive, forges, falsifies, or alters the results of a laboratory test required or authorized under this chapter.

(b) An offense under Subsection (a) is a third degree felony.

SUBCHAPTER E HARVEST AND USE OR DISPOSAL OF PLANTS

Sec. 122.201. Harvest.

(a) A license holder shall harvest the plants from a plot not later than the 30th day after the date a preharvest sample is collected under Section 122.154 unless field conditions delay harvesting or the department authorizes the license holder to delay harvesting. This subsection does not prohibit the license holder from harvesting the plants immediately after the preharvest sample is collected.

(b) A license holder may not sell or use harvested plants before the results of a preharvest and, if applicable, postharvest test performed on a sample representing the plants are received. If the test results are not received before the plants are harvested, the license holder shall dry and store the harvested plants until the results are received.

(c) A license holder may not commingle harvested plants represented by one sample with plants represented by another sample until the results of the tests are received.

Sec. 122.202. Use or Disposal of Harvested Plants.

(a) If the results of a preharvest or postharvest test performed on a sample show a delta-9 tetrahydrocannabinol concentration of not more than 0.3 percent on a dry weight basis, the license holder may sell or use the plants represented by the sample for any purpose allowed by law.

(b) If the results of a preharvest and, if applicable, postharvest test performed on a sample show a delta-9 tetrahydrocannabinol concentration of more than 0.3 percent on a dry weight basis:

(1) the license holder shall dispose of or destroy all plants represented by the sample:

(A) in the manner prescribed by federal law; or

(B) in a manner approved by the department that does not conflict with federal law; or

(2) if the department determines the plants represented by the sample reached that concentration solely as a result of negligence, the license holder is subject to Section 122.403(c) and may:

(A) trim the plants until the delta-9 tetrahydrocannabinol concentration of the plants is not more than 0.3 percent on a dry weight basis and dispose of the noncompliant parts of the plants in a manner approved by the department;

(B) process the plants into fiber with a delta-9 tetrahydrocannabinol concentration of not more than 0.3 percent on a dry weight basis and dispose of any remaining parts of the plants in a manner approved by the department; or

(C) take any other corrective action consistent with federal regulations adopted under 7 U.S.C. Chapter 38, Subchapter VII.

SUBCHAPTER F HEMP SEED

Sec. 122.251. Applicability of Subchapter.

This subchapter does not apply to sterilized seeds that are incapable of beginning germination.

Sec. 122.252. Certification or Approval.

(a) The department or an entity authorized to certify seed under Chapter 62 shall identify and certify or approve seed confirmed to produce hemp.

(b) The department or entity may not certify or approve a variety of hemp seed if the seed is tested and confirmed to produce a plant that has delta-9 tetrahydrocannabinol concentration of more than 0.3 percent on a dry weight basis. For purposes of this subsection, the department may partner with a private entity or an institution of higher education to test seed for the purpose of certification or approval under this section.

(c) The department may authorize the importation of hemp seed certified in accordance with the law of another state or jurisdiction that requires as a condition of certification that hemp be produced in compliance with:

(1) that state or jurisdiction's plan approved by the United States Department of Agriculture under 7 U.S.C. Section 1639p; or

(2) a plan established under 7 U.S.C. Section 1639q if that plan applies in the state or jurisdiction.

(d) The department shall maintain and make available to license holders a list of hemp seeds certified or approved under this section.

Sec. 122.253. Prohibited Use of Certain Hemp Seed.

A person may not sell, offer for sale, distribute, or use hemp seed in this state unless the seed is certified or approved under Section 122.252.

SUBCHAPTER G NONCONSUMABLE HEMP PRODUCTS

Sec. 122.301. Manufacture.

(a) Except as provided by Subsection (b), a state agency may not prohibit a person who manufactures a product regulated by the agency, other than an article regulated under Chapter 431, Health and Safety Code, from applying for or obtaining a permit or other authorization to manufacture the product solely on the basis that the person intends to manufacture the product as a nonconsumable hemp product.

(b) A state agency may not authorize a person to manufacture a product containing hemp for smoking, as defined by Section 443.001, Health and Safety Code.

Sec. 122.302. Possession, Transportation, and Sale.

(a) Notwithstanding any other law, a person may possess, transport, sell, and purchase legally produced nonconsumable hemp products in this state.

(b) The department by rule must provide to a retailer of nonconsumable hemp products fair notice of a potential violation concerning hemp products sold by the retailer and an opportunity to cure a violation made unintentionally or negligently.

Sec. 122.303. Retail Sale of Out-Of-State Products.

A nonconsumable hemp product manufactured outside of this state may be sold at retail in this state unless:

(1) the hemp used to manufacture the product was cultivated illegally; or

(2) the retail sale of the product in this state violates federal law.

Sec. 122.304. Transportation and Exportation Out of State.

Nonconsumable hemp products may be legally transported across state lines and exported to foreign jurisdictions in a manner that is consistent with federal law and the laws of respective foreign jurisdictions.

SUBCHAPTER H TRANSPORTATION REQUIREMENTS

Sec. 122.351. Definition.

In this subchapter, "peace officer" has the meaning assigned by Article 2.12, Code of Criminal Procedure.

Sec. 122.352. Policy.

It is the policy of this state to not interfere with the interstate commerce of hemp or the transshipment of hemp through this state.

Sec. 122.353. Interstate Transportation.

To the extent of a conflict between a provision of this chapter and a provision of federal law involving interstate transportation of hemp, including a United States Department of Agriculture regulation, federal law controls and conflicting provisions of this chapter do not apply.

Sec. 122.354. Department Rules.

The department, in consultation with the Department of Public Safety, shall adopt rules regulating the transportation of hemp in this state to ensure that illegal marihuana is not transported into or through this state disguised as legal hemp.

Sec. 122.355. Hemp Transportation Account.

(a) The hemp transportation account is a dedicated account in the general revenue fund administered by the department. The account consists of:

(1) civil penalties collected under this subchapter; and

(2) interest and income earned on the investment of money in the account.

(b) Money in the account may be appropriated only to the department for the administration and enforcement of this subchapter. The department may transfer money appropriated under this subsection to the Department of Public Safety for the administration and enforcement of that department's powers and duties under this subchapter, unless prohibited by other law.

Sec. 122.356. Documentation and Other Shipping Requirements.

(a) A person may not transport hemp plant material in this state unless the hemp:

(1) is produced in compliance with:

(A) a state or tribal plan approved by the United States Department of Agriculture under 7 U.S.C. Section 1639p; or

(B) a plan established under 7 U.S.C. Section 1639q if the hemp was cultivated in an area where that plan applies; and

(2) is accompanied by:

(A) a shipping certificate or cargo manifest issued under Section 122.055 if the hemp originated in this state; or

(B) documentation containing the name and address of the place where the hemp was cultivated and a statement that the hemp was produced in compliance with 7 U.S.C. Chapter 38, Subchapter VII, if the hemp originated outside this state.

(b) A person transporting hemp plant material in this state:

(1) may not concurrently transport any cargo that is not hemp plant material; and

(2) shall furnish the documentation required by this section to the department or any peace officer on request.

Sec. 122.357. Agricultural Pests and Diseases.

A person may not transport in this state hemp that contains an agricultural pest or disease as provided by department rule.

Sec. 122.358. Powers and Duties of Peace Officers.

(a) A peace officer may inspect and collect a reasonably sized sample of any material from the plant Cannabis sativa L. found in a vehicle to determine the delta-9 tetrahydrocannabinol concentration of the plant material. Unless a peace officer has probable cause to believe the plant material is marihuana, the peace officer may not:

(1) seize the plant material; or

(2) arrest the person transporting the plant material.

(b) A peace officer may detain any hemp being transported in this state until the person transporting the hemp provides the documentation required by Section 122.356. The peace officer shall immediately release the hemp to the person if the person produces documentation required by that section.

(c) If a peace officer has probable cause to believe that a person transporting hemp in this state is also transporting marihuana or a controlled substance, as defined by Section 481.002, Health and Safety Code, or any other illegal substance under state or federal law, the peace officer may seize and impound the hemp along with the controlled or illegal substance.

(d) This subchapter does not limit or restrict a peace officer from enforcing to the fullest extent the laws of this state regulating marihuana and controlled substances, as defined by Section 481.002, Health and Safety Code.

Sec. 122.359. Civil Penalty.

(a) A person who violates Section 122.356 is liable to this state for a civil penalty in an amount not to exceed $500 for each violation.

(b) The attorney general or any district or county attorney may bring an action to recover the civil penalty.

(c) A civil penalty collected under this section must be deposited in the hemp transportation account under Section 122.355.

Sec. 122.360. Criminal Offense.

(a) A person commits an offense if the person violates Section 122.356.

(b) An offense under this section is a misdemeanor punishable by a fine of not more than $1,000.

SUBCHAPTER I ENFORCEMENT; PENALTIES

Sec. 122.401. Penalty Schedule.

(a) The department by rule shall adopt a schedule of sanctions and penalties for violations of this chapter and rules adopted under this chapter that does not conflict with 7 U.S.C. Section 1639p(e).

(b) A penalty collected under this chapter other than a civil penalty collected under Subchapter H must be deposited in the state hemp production account under Section 122.003.

Sec. 122.402. Administrative Penalty.

Except as provided by Section 122.403 and to the extent permitted under 7 U.S.C. Section 1639p(e), the department may impose an administrative penalty or other administrative sanction for a violation of this chapter or a rule or order adopted under this chapter, including a penalty or sanction under Section 12.020 or 12.0201.

Sec. 122.403. Negligent Violations by License Holder.

(a) If the department determines that a license holder negligently violated this chapter or a rule adopted under this chapter, the department shall enforce the violation in the manner provided by 7 U.S.C. Section 1639p(e).

(b) A license holder described by Subsection (a) is not subject to a civil, criminal, or administrative enforcement action other than an enforcement action provided by this chapter.

(c) A license holder who violates this chapter by cultivating plants described by Section 122.202(b)(2):

(1) must comply with an enhanced testing protocol developed by the department;

(2) shall pay a fee in the amount of $500 for each violation to cover the department's costs of administering the enhanced testing protocol; and

(3) shall be included on a list maintained by the department of license holders with negligent violations, which is public information for purposes of Chapter 552, Government Code.

(d) A person who negligently violates this chapter three times in any five-year period may not cultivate, process, or otherwise produce hemp in this state before the fifth anniversary of the date of the third violation. The department shall include each person subject to this subsection on a list of banned producers, which is public information for purposes of Chapter 552, Government Code.

Sec. 122.404. Other Violations by License Holder.

If the department suspects or determines that a license holder violated this chapter or a rule adopted under this chapter with a culpable mental state greater than negligence, the department shall immediately report the license holder to:

(1) the United States attorney general; and

(2) the attorney general of this state, who may:

(A) investigate the violation;

(B) institute proceedings for injunctive or other appropriate relief on behalf of the department; or

(C) report the matter to the Department of Public Safety and any other appropriate law enforcement agency.

TITLE 6
PRODUCTION, PROCESSING, AND SALE OF ANIMAL PRODUCTS

SUBTITLE B
LIVESTOCK

CHAPTER 143
FENCES; RANGE RESTRICTIONS

SUBCHAPTER D
LOCAL OPTION TO PREVENT CATTLE OR DOMESTIC TURKEYS FROM RUNNING AT LARGE

Sec. 143.082. Penalty.

(a) A person commits an offense if the person knowingly permits a head of cattle or a domestic turkey to run at large in a county or area that has adopted this subchapter.

(b) An offense under this section is a Class C misdemeanor.

SUBCHAPTER E
ANIMALS RUNNING AT LARGE ON HIGHWAYS

Sec. 143.101. Definition.

In this subchapter, "highway" means a U.S. highway or a state highway in this state, but does not include a numbered farm-to-market road. The term includes the portion of Recreation Road Number 255 that is located in Newton County between State Highway Number 87 and the boundary line with Jasper County.

Sec. 143.102. Running at Large on Highway Prohibited.

A person who owns or has responsibility for the control of a horse, mule, donkey, cow, bull, steer, hog, sheep, or goat may not knowingly permit the animal to traverse or roam at large, unattended, on the right-of-way of a highway.

Sec. 143.103. Immunity from Liability.

A person whose vehicle strikes, kills, injures, or damages an unattended animal running at large on a highway is not liable for damages to the animal except on a finding of:

(1) gross negligence in the operation of the vehicle; or

(2) wilful intent to strike, kill, injure, or damage the animal.

Sec. 143.104. Herding of Livestock Along Highway.

This subchapter does not prevent the movement of livestock from one location to another by herding, leading, or driving the livestock on, along, or across a highway.

Sec. 143.105. Impounding of Livestock [Repealed].

Repealed by Acts 1987, 70th Leg., ch. 51 (S.B. 20), § 5(12), effective September 1, 1987.

Sec. 143.106. Enforcement.

Each state highway patrolman or county or local law enforcement officer shall enforce this subchapter and may enforce it without the use of a written warrant.

Sec. 143.107. Conflict with Other Law.

This subchapter prevails to the extent of any conflict with another provision of this chapter.

Sec. 143.108. Penalty.

(a) A person commits an offense if the person violates Section 143.102 of this code.

(b) An offense under this section is a Class C misdemeanor.

(c) A person commits a separate offense for each day that an animal is permitted to roam at large in violation of Section 143.102 of this code.

CHAPTER 146
SALE AND SHIPMENT OF LIVESTOCK

SUBCHAPTER A
GENERAL PROVISIONS

Sec. 146.005. Permits to Transport Animals.

(a) A person who drives a vehicle, including a truck or an automobile, containing livestock, domestic fowl, slaughtered livestock or domestic fowl, or butchered portions of livestock or domestic fowl on a highway, public street, or thoroughfare or on property owned or leased by a person other than the driver shall obtain a permit authorizing the movement.

(b) A permit must be signed by the owner or caretaker of the shipment or by the owner or person in control of the land from which the driver began movement. In addition, the permit must state the following information:

(1) the point of origin of the shipment, including the name of the ranch or other place;

(2) the point of destination of the shipment, including the name of the ranch, market center, packinghouse, or other place;

(3) the number of living animals, slaughtered animals, or butchered portions; and

(4) the description of the shipment, including the kind, breed, color, and marks and brands of living or slaughtered animals.

(c) On demand of a peace officer or any other person, the driver shall exhibit the permit required by this section or shall provide a signed, written statement containing all of the information required for a permit under this section.

(d) Failure or refusal of a driver to exhibit a permit or provide a statement in accordance with this section is probable cause for a search of the vehicle to determine if it contains stolen property and for detaining the shipment a reasonable length of time to make that determination.

Sec. 146.006. Penalty for Driving Stock to Market Without Bill of Sale or Sworn List.

(a) A person commits an offense if the person drives to market animals of a class listed in Section 146.001 of this code without possessing:

(1) a bill of sale or transfer for each animal that shows the marks and brands of the animal and is certified as recorded by the county clerk of the county from which the animals were driven; or

(2) if the person raised the animals, a list of the marks and brands that is certified as recorded by the county clerk of the county from which the animals were driven.

(b) An offense under this section is a misdemeanor punishable by a fine not to exceed $2,000.

Sec. 146.008. Penalty for Transporting Animals Without Permit or with Fraudulent Permit.

(a) A person commits an offense if, under Section 146.005 of this code, the person:

(1) transports living animals, slaughtered animals, or butchered portions of animals without possessing a permit;

(2) fails to exhibit a permit or provide a statement on demand;

(3) transports living animals, slaughtered animals, or butchered portions of animals that are not covered by a permit;

(4) possesses a false or forged permit; or

(5) provides a false written statement.

(b) An offense under Subsection (a)(1) or (a)(2) of this section is a misdemeanor punishable by a fine of not less than $25 nor more than $200 for each animal in the shipment.

(c) An offense under Subsection (a)(3) of this section is a misdemeanor punishable by a fine of not less than $25 nor more than $200 for each animal that is not covered by the permit.

(d) An offense under Subsection (a)(4) or (a)(5) of this section is a misdemeanor punishable by:

(1) a fine of not less than $200 nor more than $500;

(2) confinement in county jail for not less than 60 days nor more than 6 months; or

(3) both fine and confinement under this subsection.

BUSINESS AND COMMERCE CODE

TITLE 5 REGULATION OF BUSINESSES AND SERVICES

SUBTITLE C BUSINESS OPERATIONS

CHAPTER 102 SEXUALLY ORIENTED BUSINESSES

SUBCHAPTER C NOTICE REQUIREMENTS ON PREMISES OF SEXUALLY ORIENTED BUSINESSES

Sec. 102.101. Posting of Certain Sign Required.

(a) A sexually oriented business shall post by the sink area in each restroom on the premises one sign that directs a victim of human trafficking to contact the National Human Trafficking Resource Center. Except as provided by Subsection (c), the sign must be 11 inches by 17 inches in size.

(b) The attorney general by rule shall prescribe the design, content, and manner of display of the sign required by this section. The sign must:

(1) be in both English and Spanish;

(2) include the telephone number and Internet website of the National Human Trafficking Resource Center; and

(3) include the contact information for reporting suspicious activity to the Department of Public Safety.

(c) The attorney general by rule may require the sign to:

(1) be in an additional language other than English or Spanish;

(2) be larger than 11 inches by 17 inches in size if the attorney general determines that a larger sign is appropriate; and

(3) include other information the attorney general considers necessary and appropriate.

Sec. 102.102. Criminal Penalty.

(a) A person commits an offense if the person:

(1) is an owner or operator of a sexually oriented business; and

(2) fails to post the sign required by Section 102.101 in compliance with that section and rules adopted under that section.

(b) An offense under this section is a Class C misdemeanor.

CHAPTER 109 BUSINESS ENTITIES ENGAGED IN PUBLICATION OF CERTAIN CRIMINAL RECORD OR JUVENILE RECORD INFORMATION

Sec. 109.001. Definitions.

In this chapter:

(1) "Criminal justice agency" has the meaning assigned by Section 411.082, Government Code.

(2) "Criminal record information" means information about a person's involvement in the criminal justice system. The term includes:

(A) a description or notation of any arrests, any formal criminal charges, and the dispositions of those criminal charges;

(B) a photograph of the person taken pursuant to an arrest or other involvement in the criminal justice system; and

(C) personal identifying information of a person displayed in conjunction with any other record of the person's involvement in the criminal justice system.

(3) "Personal identifying information" means information that alone or in conjunction with other information identifies a person, including a person's name, address, date of birth, photograph, and social security number or other government-issued identification number.

Business and Commerce Code

(4) "Publish" means to communicate or make information available to another person in writing or by means of telecommunications and includes communicating information on a computer bulletin board or similar system.

(5) "Confidential criminal record information of a child" means information about a person's involvement in the criminal justice system resulting from conduct that occurred or was alleged to occur when the person was younger than 17 years of age that is confidential under Chapter 45, Code of Criminal Procedure, or other law. The term does not include:

(A) criminal record information of a person certified to stand trial as an adult for that conduct, as provided by Section 54.02, Family Code; or

(B) information relating to a traffic offense.

(6) "Confidential juvenile record information" means information about a person's involvement in the juvenile justice system that is confidential, sealed, under restricted access, or required to be destroyed under Chapter 58, Family Code, or other law, including:

(A) a description or notation of any referral to a juvenile probation department or court with jurisdiction under Title 3, Family Code, including any instances of being taken into custody, any informal disposition of a custodial or referral event, or any formal charges and the disposition of those charges;

(B) a photograph of the person taken pursuant to a custodial event or other involvement in the juvenile justice system under Title 3, Family Code; and

(C) personal identifying information of the person contained in any other records of the person's involvement in the juvenile justice system.

(7) "Information service" has the meaning assigned by 47 U.S.C. Section 153.

(8) "Interactive computer service" has the meaning assigned by 47 U.S.C. Section 230(f).

(9) "Telecommunications provider" has the meaning assigned by Section 51.002, Utilities Code.

Sec. 109.002. Applicability of Chapter.

(a) Except as provided by Subsection (b), this chapter applies to:

(1) a business entity that:

(A) publishes criminal record information, including information:

(i) originally obtained pursuant to a request for public information under Chapter 552, Government Code; or

(ii) purchased or otherwise obtained by the entity or an affiliated business entity from the Department of Public Safety under Subchapter F, Chapter 411, Government Code; and

(B) requires the payment:

(i) of a fee in an amount of $150 or more or other consideration of comparable value to remove criminal record information; or

(ii) of a fee or other consideration to correct or modify criminal record information; or

(2) a business entity that publishes confidential juvenile record information or confidential criminal record information of a child in a manner not permitted by Chapter 58, Family Code, Chapter 45, Code of Criminal Procedure, or other law, regardless of:

(A) the source of the information; or

(B) whether the business entity charges a fee for access to or removal or correction of the information.

(b) This chapter does not apply to:

(1) a statewide juvenile information and case management system authorized by Subchapter E, Chapter 58, Family Code;

(2) a publication of general circulation or an Internet website related to such a publication that contains news or other information, including a magazine, periodical newsletter, newspaper, pamphlet, or report;

(3) a radio or television station that holds a license issued by the Federal Communications Commission;

(4) an entity that provides an information service or that is an interactive computer service; or

(5) a telecommunications provider.

Sec. 109.003. Duty to Publish Complete and Accurate Criminal Record Information.

(a) A business entity must ensure that criminal record information the entity publishes is complete and accurate.

(b) For purposes of this chapter, criminal record information published by a business entity is considered:

(1) complete if the information reflects the notations of arrest and the filing and disposition of criminal charges, as applicable; and

(2) accurate if the information:

(A) reflects the most recent information received by the entity from the Department of Public Safety in accordance with Section 411.0851(b)(1)(B), Government Code; or

(B) was obtained by the entity from a law enforcement agency or criminal justice agency, including the Department of Public Safety, or any other governmental agency or entity within the 60-day period preceding the date of publication.

Sec. 109.004. Disputing Completeness or Accuracy of Information.

(a) A business entity shall clearly and conspicuously publish an e-mail address, fax number, or mailing address to enable a person who is the subject of criminal record information published by the entity to dispute the completeness or accuracy of the information.

(b) If a business entity receives a dispute regarding the completeness or accuracy of criminal record information from a person who is the subject of the information, the business entity shall:

(1) verify with the appropriate law enforcement agency or criminal justice agency, including the Department of Public Safety, or any other governmental agency or entity, free of charge the disputed information; and

(2) complete the investigation described by Subdivision (1) not later than the 45th business day after the date the entity receives notice of the dispute.

(c) If a business entity finds incomplete or inaccurate criminal record information after conducting an investigation prescribed by this section, the entity shall promptly remove the inaccurate information from the website or other publication or shall promptly correct the information, as applicable. The entity may not:

(1) charge a fee to remove, correct, or modify incomplete or inaccurate information; or

(2) continue to publish incomplete or inaccurate information.

(d) A business entity shall provide written notice to the person who disputed the completeness or accuracy of information of the results of an investigation conducted under this section not later than the fifth business day after the date on which the investigation is completed.

Sec. 109.0045. Publication of Confidential Juvenile Record Information or Confidential Criminal Record Information of a Child Prohibited.

(a) A business entity may not publish confidential juvenile record information or confidential criminal record information of a child.

(b) If a business entity receives a written notice by any person that the business entity is publishing information in violation of this section, the business entity must immediately remove the information from the website or publication.

(c) If the business entity confirms that the information is not confidential juvenile record information or confidential criminal record information of a child and is not otherwise prohibited from publication, the business entity may republish the information.

(d) This section does not entitle a business entity to access confidential juvenile record information or confidential criminal record information of a child.

(e) A business entity does not violate this chapter if the business entity published confidential juvenile record information or confidential criminal record information of a child and:

(1) the child who is the subject of the records gives written consent to the publication on or after the 18th birthday of the child;

(2) the publication of the information is authorized or required by other law; or

(3) the business entity is an interactive computer service, as defined by 47 U.S.C. Section 230, and published material provided by another person.

Sec. 109.005. Publication of Certain Criminal Record Information Prohibited; Civil Liability.

(a) A business entity may not publish any criminal record information in the business entity's possession with respect to which the business entity has knowledge or has received notice that:

(1) an order of expunction has been issued under Article 55.02, Code of Criminal Procedure; or

(2) an order of nondisclosure of criminal history record information has been issued under Subchapter E-1, Chapter 411, Government Code.

(a-1) Except as provided by Section 109.0045(e), a business entity may not publish any information with respect to which the business entity has knowledge or has received notice that the information is confidential juvenile record information or confidential criminal record information of a child.

(b) A business entity that publishes information in violation of this section is liable to the individual who is the subject of the information in an amount not to exceed $500 for each separate violation and, in the case of a continuing violation, an amount not to exceed $500 for each subsequent day on which the violation occurs.

(c) In an action brought under this section, the court may grant injunctive relief to prevent or restrain a violation of this section.

(d) An individual who prevails in an action brought under this section is also entitled to recover court costs and reasonable attorney's fees.

Sec. 109.006. Civil Penalty; Injunction.

(a) A business entity that publishes criminal record information, confidential juvenile record information, or confidential criminal record information of a child in violation of this chapter is liable to the state for a civil penalty in an amount not to exceed $500 for each separate violation and, in the case of a continuing violation, an amount not to exceed $500 for each subsequent day on which the violation occurs. For purposes of this subsection, each record published in violation of this chapter constitutes a separate violation.

(b) The attorney general or an appropriate prosecuting attorney may sue to collect a civil penalty under this section.

(c) A civil penalty collected under this section shall be deposited in the state treasury to the credit of the general revenue fund.

(d) The attorney general may bring an action in the name of the state to restrain or enjoin a violation or threatened violation of this chapter.

(e) The attorney general or an appropriate prosecuting attorney is entitled to recover reasonable expenses incurred in obtaining injunctive relief or a civil penalty, or both, under this chapter, including court costs and reasonable attorney's fees.

Sec. 109.007. Venue.

An action under this chapter must be brought in a district court:

(1) in Travis County if the action is brought by the attorney general;

(2) in the county in which the person who is the subject of the criminal record information, confidential juvenile record information, or confidential criminal record information of a child resides; or

(3) in the county in which the business entity is located.

Sec. 109.008. Cumulative Remedies.

The actions and remedies provided by this chapter are not exclusive and are in addition to any other action or remedy provided by law.

CHAPTER 110 COMPUTER TECHNICIANS REQUIRED TO REPORT CHILD PORNOGRAPHY

Sec. 110.001. Definitions.

In this chapter:

(1) "Child pornography" means an image of a child engaging in sexual conduct or sexual performance.

(2) "Commercial mobile service provider" has the meaning assigned by Section 64.201, Utilities Code.

(3) "Computer technician" means an individual who in the course and scope of employment or business installs, repairs, or otherwise services a computer for a fee.

(4) "Information service provider" includes an Internet service provider and hosting service provider.

(5) "Sexual conduct" and "sexual performance" have the meanings assigned by Section 43.25, Penal Code.

(6) "Telecommunications provider" has the meaning assigned by Section 51.002, Utilities Code.

Sec. 110.002. Reporting of Images of Child Pornography.

(a) A computer technician who, in the course and scope of employment or business, views an image on a computer that is or appears to be child pornography shall immediately report the discovery of the image to a local or state law enforcement agency or the Cyber Tipline at the National Center for Missing and Exploited Children. The report must include the name and address of the owner or person claiming a right to possession of the computer, if known, and as permitted by federal law.

(b) Except in a case of wilful or wanton misconduct, a computer technician may not be held liable in a civil action for reporting or failing to report the discovery of an image under Subsection (a).

(c) A telecommunications provider, commercial mobile service provider, or information service provider may not be held liable under this chapter for the failure to report child pornography that is transmitted or stored by a user of the service.

Sec. 110.003. Criminal Penalty.

(a) A person who intentionally fails to report an image in violation of this chapter commits an offense. An offense under this subsection is a Class B misdemeanor.

(b) It is a defense to prosecution under this section that the actor did not report the discovery of an image of child pornography because the child in the image appeared to be at least 18 years of age.

TITLE 6 SALE OR TRANSFER OF GOODS

CHAPTER 202 SALES OF MOTOR VEHICLES WITH STOPLAMP COVERINGS

Sec. 202.001. Sale of Motor Vehicle with Certain Stoplamp Covering Prohibited.

(a) In this section, "motor vehicle" has the meaning assigned by Section 541.201, Transportation Code.

(b) A person in the business of selling motor vehicles may not sell a motor vehicle with a transparent or semitransparent covering:

(1) placed over a stoplamp that is mounted on the rear center line of the vehicle either in or on the rear window or within six inches from the rear window of the vehicle for the purpose of emitting light when the vehicle's brakes are applied; and

(2) on which is impressed or imprinted a name, trade name, logotype, or other message that a person behind the vehicle can read when the stoplamp is illuminated.

(c) A person who violates this section commits an offense. An offense under this section is a Class C misdemeanor.

TITLE 10 USE OF TELECOMMUNICATIONS

SUBTITLE B ELECTRONIC COMMUNICATIONS

CHAPTER 326 AUTOMATED SALES SUPPRESSION DEVICES; PHANTOM-WARE

Sec. 326.001. Definitions.

In this chapter:

(1) "Automated sales suppression device" means a device or software program that falsifies an electronic record, including transaction data or a transaction report, of an electronic cash register or other point-of-sale system. The term includes a device that carries the software program or an Internet link to the software program.

(2) "Electronic cash register" means a device or point-of-sale system that maintains a register or documentation through an electronic device or computer system that is designed to record transaction data for the purpose of computing, compiling, or processing retail sales transaction data.

(3) "Phantom-ware" means a hidden programming option that is embedded in the operating system of an electronic cash register or hardwired into an electronic cash register and that may be used to create a second set of transaction reports or to eliminate or manipulate an original transaction report, which may or may not be preserved in a digital format, to represent the original or manipulated report of a transaction in the electronic cash register.

(4) "Transaction data" includes data identifying an item purchased by a customer, a price for an item, a taxability determination for an item, a segregated tax amount for an item, an amount of cash or credit tendered for an item, a net amount of cash returned to a customer who purchased an item, a date or time of a purchase, a receipt or invoice number for a transaction, and a vendor's name, address, or identification number.

(5) "Transaction report" means a report that:

(A) contains documentation of each sale, amount of tax or fee collected, media total, or discount void at an electronic cash register and that is printed on a cash register tape at the end of a day or a shift; or

(B) documents every action at an electronic cash register and is stored electronically.

Sec. 326.002. Automated Sales Suppression Devices and Phantom-Ware Prohibited; Criminal Offense.

(a) A person commits an offense if the person knowingly sells, purchases, installs, transfers, uses, or possesses an automated sales suppression device or phantom-ware.

(b) An offense under this section is a state jail felony.

TITLE 11 PERSONAL IDENTITY INFORMATION

SUBTITLE A IDENTIFYING INFORMATION

CHAPTER 504 PROHIBITED USE OF CRIME VICTIM OR MOTOR VEHICLE ACCIDENT INFORMATION

Business and Commerce Code

Sec. 504.001. Definitions.

In this chapter:

(1) "Crime victim information" means information that:

(A) is collected or prepared by a law enforcement agency; and

(B) identifies or serves to identify a person who, according to a record of the agency, may have been the victim of a crime in which:

(i) physical injury to the person occurred or was attempted; or

(ii) the offender entered or attempted to enter the dwelling of the person.

(2) "Motor vehicle accident information" means information that:

(A) is collected or prepared by a law enforcement agency; and

(B) identifies or serves to identify a person who, according to a record of the agency, may have been involved in a motor vehicle accident.

Sec. 504.002. Prohibition on Use for Solicitation or Sale of Information.

(a) A person who possesses crime victim or motor vehicle accident information that the person obtained or knows was obtained from a law enforcement agency may not:

(1) use the information to contact directly any of the following persons for the purpose of soliciting business from the person:

(A) a crime victim;

(B) a person who was involved in a motor vehicle accident; or

(C) a member of the family of a person described by Paragraph (A) or (B); or

(2) sell the information to another person for financial gain.

(b) The attorney general may bring an action against a person who violates Subsection (a) pursuant to Section 17.47.

(c) A person commits an offense if the person violates Subsection (a). An offense under this subsection is a Class C misdemeanor unless the defendant has been previously convicted under this section three or more times, in which event the offense is a felony of the third degree.

CHAPTER 506
REIDENTIFICATION OF DEIDENTIFIED INFORMATION

Sec. 506.001. Definitions.

In this chapter:

(1) "Covered information" means deidentified information released by a board, commission, department, or other agency of this state, including an institution of higher education as defined by Section 61.003, Education Code, or a hospital that is maintained or operated by the state.

(2) "Deidentified information" means information with respect to which the holder of the information has made a good faith effort to remove all personal identifying information or other information that may be used by itself or in combination with other information to identify the subject of the information. The term includes aggregate statistics, redacted information, information for which random or fictitious alternatives have been substituted for personal identifying information, and information for which personal identifying information has been encrypted and for which the encryption key is maintained by a person otherwise authorized to have access to the information in an identifiable format.

(3) "Personal identifying information" has the meaning assigned by Section 521.002(a)(1).

CHAPTER 507
CONCEALED HANDGUN LICENSES AS VALID FORMS OF PERSONAL IDENTIFICATION

Sec. 507.001. Concealed Handgun License As Valid Proof of Identification.

(a) A person may not deny the holder of a concealed handgun license issued under Subchapter H, Chapter 411, Government Code, access to goods, services, or facilities, except as provided by Section 521.460, Transportation Code, or in regard to the operation of a motor vehicle, because the holder has or presents a concealed handgun license rather than a driver's license or other acceptable form of personal identification.

(b) This section does not affect:

(1) the requirement under Section 411.205, Government Code, that a person subject to that section present a driver's license or identification certificate in addition to a concealed handgun license; or

(2) the types of identification required under federal law to access airport premises or pass through airport security.

Business and Commerce Code

CIVIL PRACTICE AND REMEDIES CODE

TITLE 2
TRIAL, JUDGMENT, AND APPEAL

SUBTITLE A
GENERAL PROVISIONS

CHAPTER 7
LIABILITY OF COURT OFFICERS

SUBCHAPTER A
LIABILITY OF OFFICER

Sec. 7.003. Liability Regarding Execution of Writs.

(a) Except as provided by Section 34.061, an officer is not liable for damages resulting from the execution of a writ issued by a court of this state if the officer in good faith executes or attempts to execute the writ as provided by law and by the Texas Rules of Civil Procedure.

(b) An officer shall execute a writ issued by a court of this state without requiring that bond be posted for the indemnification of the officer.

(c) An officer shows that the officer acted in good faith when the officer shows that a reasonably prudent officer, under the same or similar circumstances, could have believed that the officer's conduct was justified based on the information the officer possessed when the conduct occurred.

SUBTITLE B
TRIAL MATTERS

CHAPTER 22
WITNESSES

SUBCHAPTER B
PRIVILEGES

Sec. 22.011. Privilege from Arrest.

(a) A witness is privileged from arrest while attending, going to, and returning from court.

(b) The privilege provided by this section extends for a period computed by allowing one day of travel for each 150 miles of the distance from the courthouse to the witness's residence.

(c) This section does not apply to an arrest for a felony, treason, or breach of the peace.

SUBTITLE C
JUDGMENTS

CHAPTER 34
EXECUTION ON JUDGMENTS

SUBCHAPTER B
RECOVERY OF SEIZED PROPERTY

Sec. 34.021. Recovery of Property Before Sale.

A person is entitled to recover his property that has been seized through execution of a writ issued by a court if the judgment on which execution is issued is reversed or set aside and the property has not been sold at execution.

Sec. 34.022. Recovery of Property Value After Sale.

(a) A person is entitled to recover from the judgment creditor the market value of the person's property that has been seized through execution of a writ issued by a court if the judgment on which execution is issued is reversed or set aside but the property has been sold at execution.

(b) The amount of recovery is determined by the market value at the time of sale of the property sold.

TITLE 4
LIABILITY IN TORT

CHAPTER 78A
LIABILITY OF FIRST RESPONDERS FOR ROADSIDE ASSISTANCE

Sec. 78A.001. Definitions.

In this chapter:

(1) "First responder" means a law enforcement, fire protection, or emergency medical services employee or volunteer, including:

(A) a peace officer as defined by Article 2.12, Code of Criminal Procedure;

(B) fire protection personnel as defined by Section 419.021, Government Code;

(C) a volunteer firefighter who is:

(i) certified by the Texas Commission on Fire Protection or by the State Firefighters' and Fire Marshals' Association of Texas; or

(ii) a member of an organized volunteer firefighting unit that renders fire-fighting services without remuneration and conducts a minimum of two drills each month, each two hours long; and

(D) an individual certified as emergency medical services personnel by the Department of State Health Services.

(2) "Roadside assistance" means assistance to the owner, operator, or passenger of a motor vehicle with an incident related to the operation of the motor vehicle, including jump-starting or replacing a motor vehicle battery, lockout assistance, replacing a flat tire, and roadside vehicle breakdown assistance.

Sec. 78A.002. Liability of First Responder.

A first responder who in good faith provides roadside assistance is not liable in civil damages for damage to the motor vehicle affected by the incident for which the roadside assistance is provided that is caused by an act or omission that occurs during the performance of the act of roadside assistance unless the act or omission constitutes gross negligence, recklessness, or intentional misconduct.

CHAPTER 83
USE OF FORCE OR DEADLY FORCE

Sec. 83.001. Civil Immunity.

A defendant who uses force or deadly force that is justified under Chapter 9, Penal Code, is immune from civil liability for personal injury or death that results from the defendant's use of force or deadly force, as applicable.

Sec. 83.002. Liability [Renumbered].

Renumbered to Tex. Civ. Prac. & Rem. Code § 85.002 by Acts 1997, 75th Leg., ch. 165 (S.B. 898), § 31.01(7), effective September 1, 1997.

Sec. 83.003. Proof [Renumbered].

Renumbered to Tex. Civ. Prac. & Rem. Code § 85.003 by Acts 1997, 75th Leg., ch. 165 (S.B. 898), § 31.01(7), effective September 1, 1997.

Sec. 83.004. Damages [Renumbered].

Renumbered to Tex. Civ. Prac. & Rem. Code § 85.004 by Acts 1997, 75th Leg., ch. 165 (S.B. 898), § 31.01(7), effective September 1, 1997.

Sec. 83.005. Defense [Renumbered].

Renumbered to Tex. Civ. Prac. & Rem. Code § 85.005 by Acts 1997, 75th Leg., ch. 165 (S.B. 898), § 31.01(7), effective September 1, 1997.

Sec. 83.006. Cause of Action Cumulative [Renumbered].

Renumbered to Tex. Civ. Prac. & Rem. Code § 85.006 by Acts 1997, 75th Leg., ch. 165 (S.B. 898), § 31.01(7), effective September 1, 1997.

CHAPTER 85
LIABILITY FOR STALKING

Sec. 85.001. Definitions.

In this chapter:

(1) "Claimant" means a party seeking to recover damages under this chapter, including a plaintiff, counterclaimant, cross-claimant, or third-party plaintiff. In an action in which a party seeks recovery of damages under this chapter on behalf of another person, "claimant" includes both that other person and the party seeking recovery of damages.

(2) "Defendant" includes any party from whom a claimant seeks recovery of damages under this chapter.

(3) "Family" has the meaning assigned by Section 71.003, Family Code.

(4) "Harassing behavior" means conduct by the defendant directed specifically toward the claimant, including following the claimant, that is reasonably likely to harass, annoy, alarm, abuse, torment, or embarrass the claimant.

Sec. 85.002. Liability.

A defendant is liable, as provided by this chapter, to a claimant for damages arising from stalking of the claimant by the defendant.

Sec. 85.003. Proof.

(a) A claimant proves stalking against a defendant by showing:

(1) on more than one occasion the defendant engaged in harassing behavior;

(2) as a result of the harassing behavior, the claimant reasonably feared for the claimant's safety or the safety of a member of the claimant's family; and

(3) the defendant violated a restraining order prohibiting harassing behavior or:

(A) the defendant, while engaged in harassing behavior, by acts or words threatened to inflict bodily injury on the claimant or to commit an offense against the claimant, a member of the claimant's family, or the claimant's property;

(B) the defendant had the apparent ability to carry out the threat;

(C) the defendant's apparent ability to carry out the threat caused the claimant to reasonably fear for the claimant's safety or the safety of a family member;

(D) the claimant at least once clearly demanded that the defendant stop the defendant's harassing behavior;

(E) after the demand to stop by the claimant, the defendant continued the harassing behavior; and

(F) the harassing behavior has been reported to the police as a stalking offense.

(b) The claimant must, as part of the proof of the behavior described by Subsection (a)(1), submit evidence other than evidence based on the claimant's own perceptions and beliefs.

Sec. 85.004. Damages.

A claimant who prevails in a suit under this chapter may recover actual damages and, subject to Chapter 41, exemplary damages.

Sec. 85.005. Defense.

It is a defense to an action brought under this chapter that the defendant was engaged in conduct that consisted of activity in support of constitutionally or statutorily protected rights.

Sec. 85.006. Cause of Action Cumulative.

The cause of action created by this chapter is cumulative of any other remedy provided by common law or statute.

CHAPTER 92A. LIMITATION OF LIABILITY FOR REMOVING CERTAIN INDIVIDUALS FROM MOTOR VEHICLE

Sec. 92A.001. Definitions.

In this chapter:

(1) "Motor vehicle" means a vehicle that is self-propelled or a trailer or semitrailer designed for use with a self-propelled vehicle.

(2) "Vulnerable individual" means:

(A) a child younger than seven years of age; or

(B) an individual who by reason of age or physical or mental disease, defect, or injury is substantially unable to protect the individual's self from harm.

Sec. 92A.002. Limitation of Liability.

A person who, by force or otherwise, enters a motor vehicle for the purpose of removing a vulnerable individual from the vehicle is immune from civil liability for damages resulting from that entry or removal if the person:

(1) determines that:

(A) the motor vehicle is locked; or

(B) there is no reasonable method for the individual to exit the motor vehicle without assistance;

(2) has a good faith and reasonable belief, based on known circumstances, that entry into the motor vehicle is necessary to avoid imminent harm to the individual;

(3) before entering the motor vehicle, ensures that law enforcement is notified or 911 is called if the person is not a law enforcement officer or other first responder;

(4) uses no more force to enter the motor vehicle and remove the individual than is necessary; and

(5) remains with the individual in a safe location that is in reasonable proximity to the motor

vehicle until a law enforcement officer or other first responder arrives.

Sec. 92A.003. Effect on Other Laws.

This chapter does not affect limitation under Section 74.151 or 74.152 of a person's liability for good faith administration of emergency care.

TITLE 6
MISCELLANEOUS PROVISIONS

CHAPTER 124
PRIVILEGE TO INVESTIGATE THEFT

Sec. 124.001. Detention.

A person who reasonably believes that another has stolen or is attempting to steal property is privileged to detain that person in a reasonable manner and for a reasonable time to investigate ownership of the property.

CHAPTER 125
COMMON AND PUBLIC NUISANCES

SUBCHAPTER A
SUIT TO ABATE CERTAIN COMMON NUISANCES

Sec. 125.001. Definitions.

In this chapter:

(1) "Common nuisance" is a nuisance described by Section 125.0015.

(1-a) "Computer network" means the interconnection of two or more computers or computer systems by satellite, microwave, line, or other communication medium with the capability to transmit information between the computers.

(2) "Public nuisance" is a nuisance described by Section 125.062 or 125.063.

(3) "Multiunit residential property" means improved real property with at least three dwelling units, including an apartment building, condominium, hotel, or motel. The term does not include a single-family home or duplex.

(4) "Web address" means a website operating on the Internet.

Sec. 125.0015. Common Nuisance.

(a) A person who maintains a place to which persons habitually go for the following purposes and who knowingly tolerates the activity and furthermore fails to make reasonable attempts to abate the activity maintains a common nuisance:

(1) discharge of a firearm in a public place as prohibited by the Penal Code;

(2) reckless discharge of a firearm as prohibited by the Penal Code;

(3) engaging in organized criminal activity as a member of a combination as prohibited by the Penal Code;

(4) delivery, possession, manufacture, or use of a substance or other item in violation of Chapter 481, Health and Safety Code;

(5) gambling, gambling promotion, or communicating gambling information as prohibited by the Penal Code;

(6) prostitution as described by Section 43.02, Penal Code, solicitation of prostitution as described by Section 43.021, Penal Code, promotion of prostitution as described by Section 43.03, Penal Code, or aggravated promotion of prostitution as described by Section 43.04, Penal Code;

(7) compelling prostitution as prohibited by the Penal Code;

(8) commercial manufacture, commercial distribution, or commercial exhibition of obscene material as prohibited by the Penal Code;

(9) aggravated assault as described by Section 22.02, Penal Code;

(10) sexual assault as described by Section 22.011, Penal Code;

(11) aggravated sexual assault as described by Section 22.021, Penal Code;

(12) robbery as described by Section 29.02, Penal Code;

(13) aggravated robbery as described by Section 29.03, Penal Code;

(14) unlawfully carrying a weapon as described by Section 46.02, Penal Code;

(15) murder as described by Section 19.02, Penal Code;

(16) capital murder as described by Section 19.03, Penal Code;

(17) continuous sexual abuse of young child or disabled individual as described by Section 21.02, Penal Code;

(18) massage therapy or other massage services in violation of Chapter 455, Occupations Code;

(19) employing or entering into a contract for the performance of work or the provision of a service with an individual younger than 21 years of age for work or services performed at a sexually oriented business as defined by Section 243.002, Local Government Code;

(20) trafficking of persons as described by Section 20A.02, Penal Code;

(21) sexual conduct or performance by a child as described by Section 43.25, Penal Code;

(22) employment harmful to a child as described by Section 43.251, Penal Code;

(23) criminal trespass as described by Section 30.05, Penal Code;

(24) disorderly conduct as described by Section 42.01, Penal Code;

(25) arson as described by Section 28.02, Penal Code;

(26) criminal mischief as described by Section 28.03, Penal Code, that causes a pecuniary loss of $500 or more;

(27) a graffiti offense in violation of Section 28.08, Penal Code; or

(28) permitting an individual younger than 18 years of age to enter the premises of a sexually oriented business as defined by Section 243.002, Local Government Code.

(b) A person maintains a common nuisance if the person maintains a multiunit residential property to which persons habitually go to commit acts listed in Subsection (a) and knowingly tolerates the acts and furthermore fails to make reasonable attempts to abate the acts.

(c) A person operating a web address or computer network in connection with an activity described by Subsection (a)(3), (6), (7), (10), (11), (17), (18), (19), (20), (21), or (22) maintains a common nuisance.

(d) Subsection (c) does not apply to:

(1) a provider of remote computing services or electronic communication services to the public;

(2) a provider of an interactive computer service as defined by 47 U.S.C. Section 230;

(3) an Internet service provider;

(4) a search engine operator;

(5) a browsing or hosting company;

(6) an operating system provider; or

(7) a device manufacturer.

(e) This section does not apply to an activity exempted, authorized, or otherwise lawful activity regulated by federal law.

Sec. 125.0017. [2 Versions: As added by Acts 2017, 85th Leg., ch. 1135] Notice of Arrest for Certain Activities. [Repealed]

SUBCHAPTER D MEMBERSHIP IN CRIMINAL STREET GANG

Sec. 125.061. Definitions.

In this subchapter:

(1) "Combination" and "criminal street gang" have the meanings assigned by Section 71.01, Penal Code.

(2) "Continuously or regularly" means at least five times in a period of not more than 12 months.

(3) "Gang activity" means the following types of conduct:

(A) organized criminal activity as described by Section 71.02, Penal Code;

(B) terroristic threat as described by Section 22.07, Penal Code;

(C) coercing, soliciting, or inducing gang membership as described by Section 71.022(a) or (a-1), Penal Code;

(D) criminal trespass as described by Section 30.05, Penal Code;

(E) disorderly conduct as described by Section 42.01, Penal Code;

(F) criminal mischief as described by Section 28.03, Penal Code, that causes a pecuniary loss of $500 or more;

(G) a graffiti offense in violation of Section 28.08, Penal Code;

(H) a weapons offense in violation of Chapter 46, Penal Code; or

(I) unlawful possession of a substance or other item in violation of Chapter 481, Health and Safety Code.

Sec. 125.062. Public Nuisance; Combination.

A combination or criminal street gang that continuously or regularly associates in gang activities is a public nuisance.

Sec. 125.063. Public Nuisance; Use of Place.

The habitual use of a place by a combination or criminal street gang for engaging in gang activity is a public nuisance.

Sec. 125.070. Civil Action for Violation of Injunction.

(a) In this section, "governmental entity" means a political subdivision of this state, including any city, county, school district, junior college district,

Civil Practice and Remedies Code

levee improvement district, drainage district, irrigation district, water improvement district, water control and improvement district, water control and preservation district, freshwater supply district, navigation district, conservation and reclamation district, soil conservation district, communication district, public health district, and river authority.

(b) A criminal street gang or a member of a criminal street gang is liable to the state or a governmental entity injured by the violation of a temporary or permanent injunctive order under this subchapter.

(c) In an action brought against a member of a criminal street gang, the plaintiff must show that the member violated the temporary or permanent injunctive order.

(d) A district, county, or city attorney or the attorney general may sue for money damages on behalf of the state or a governmental entity. If the state or a governmental entity prevails in a suit under this section, the state or governmental entity may recover:

(1) actual damages;

(2) a civil penalty in an amount not to exceed $20,000 for each violation; and

(3) court costs and attorney's fees in accordance with Section 125.005.

(e) The property of the criminal street gang or a member of the criminal street gang may be seized in execution on a judgment under this section. Property may not be seized under this subsection if the owner or interest holder of the property proves by a preponderance of the evidence that the owner or interest holder was not a member of the criminal street gang and did not violate the temporary or permanent injunctive order. The owner or interest holder of property that is in the possession of a criminal street gang or a member of the criminal street gang and that is subject to execution under this subsection must show that the property:

(1) was stolen from the owner or interest holder; or

(2) was used or intended to be used without the effective consent of the owner or interest holder by the criminal street gang or a member of the criminal street gang.

(f) The attorney general shall deposit money received under this section for damages or as a civil penalty in the neighborhood and community recovery fund held by the attorney general outside the state treasury. Money in the fund is held by the attorney general in trust for the benefit of the community or neighborhood harmed by the violation of a temporary or permanent injunctive order. Money in the fund may be used only for the benefit of the community or neighborhood harmed by the violation of the injunctive order. Interest earned on money in the fund shall be credited to the fund. The attorney general shall account for money in the fund so that money held for the benefit of a community or neighborhood, and interest earned on that money, are not commingled with money in the fund held for the benefit of a different community or neighborhood.

(g) A district, county, or city attorney who brings suit on behalf of a governmental entity shall deposit money received for damages or as a civil penalty in an account to be held in trust for the benefit of the community or neighborhood harmed by the violation of a temporary or permanent injunctive order. Money in the account may be used only for the benefit of the community or neighborhood harmed by the violation of the injunctive order. Interest earned on money in the account shall be credited to the account. The district, county, or city attorney shall account for money in the account so that money held for the benefit of a community or neighborhood, and interest earned on that money, are not commingled with money in the account held for the benefit of a different community or neighborhood.

(h) An action under this section brought by the state or a governmental entity does not waive sovereign or governmental immunity for any purpose.

EDUCATION CODE

TITLE 2
PUBLIC EDUCATION

SUBTITLE F
CURRICULUM, PROGRAMS, AND SERVICES

CHAPTER 33
SERVICE PROGRAMS AND EXTRACURRICULAR ACTIVITIES

SUBCHAPTER C
MISSING CHILD PREVENTION AND IDENTIFICATION PROGRAMS

Sec. 33.051. Definitions.

In this subchapter:

(1) "Child" and "minor" have the meanings assigned by Section 101.003, Family Code.

(2) "Missing child" means a child whose whereabouts are unknown to the legal custodian of the child and:

(A) the circumstances of whose absence indicate that the child did not voluntarily leave the care and control of the custodian and that the taking of the child was not authorized by law; or

(B) the child has engaged in conduct indicating a need for supervision under Section 51.03(b)(2), Family Code.

Sec. 33.052. Missing Child Prevention and Identification Programs.

(a) The board of trustees of a school district or of a private school may participate in missing child prevention and identification programs, including fingerprinting and photographing as provided by this subchapter.

(b) The board of trustees of a school district may delegate responsibility for implementation of the program to the district's school administration or to the district's community education services administration.

(c) The chief administrative officer of each private primary or secondary school may participate in the programs and may contract with the regional education service center in which the school is located for operation of all or any part of the program through a shared services arrangement.

Sec. 33.053. Fingerprints of Children.

(a) A missing child prevention and identification program may include a procedure for taking the fingerprints of each student registered in the school whose parent or legal custodian has consented in writing to the fingerprinting. Fingerprints obtained under this section may be used only for the identification and location of a missing child.

(b) The board of trustees of a school district or the chief administrative officer of a private school may establish a reasonable fee to cover the costs of fingerprinting not provided by volunteer assistance. The fee may not exceed $3 for each child fingerprinted. If the school charges a fee, the school may waive all or a portion of the costs of fingerprinting for educationally disadvantaged children.

(c) A representative of a law enforcement agency of the county or the municipality in which the school district is located or of the Department of Public Safety, or a person trained in fingerprinting technique by a law enforcement agency or the Department of Public Safety, shall make one complete set of fingerprints on a fingerprint card for each child participating in the program. If the school requests, the Department of Public Safety may provide fingerprint training to persons designated by the school.

(d) A fingerprint card shall include a description of the child, including the name, address, date and place of birth, color of eyes and hair, weight, and sex of the child.

(e) Except as provided by Section 33.054(b), the fingerprint card and other materials developed under this subchapter shall be made part of the school's permanent student records.

(f) A state agency, law enforcement agency, or other person may not retain a copy of a child's fingerprints taken under this program.

Sec. 33.0531. Child Identification Program.

(a) The agency shall provide to all school districts and open-enrollment charter schools inkless, in-home fingerprint and DNA identification kits to be distributed through the district or school on request to the parent or legal custodian of any kindergarten, elementary, or middle school student.

(b) A parent or legal custodian who receives a fingerprint and DNA identification kit may submit the kit to federal, state, tribal, or local law enforcement to help locate and return a missing or trafficked child.

Sec. 33.054. Photographs of Children.

(a) A participating school shall retain a current photograph of each child registered in the school whose parent or legal custodian has consented in writing. Photographs retained under this section may be used only for the identification and location of a missing child.

(b) The photograph shall be retained by the participating school until the photograph is replaced by a subsequently made photograph under this section or until the expiration of three years, whichever is earlier.

(c) On the request of a parent or legal custodian of a missing child, or of a peace officer who is engaged in the investigation of a missing child, a participating school may give to the parent, legal custodian, or peace officer a copy of that child's photograph held by the school under this section. Except as provided by this subsection, a photograph held under this section may not be given to any person.

(d) A participating school may charge a fee for making and keeping records of photographs under this section. If the school charges a fee, the school may waive this fee for educationally disadvantaged children.

Sec. 33.055. Fingerprints and Photographs Not Used As Evidence.

(a) A child's fingerprint card made under Section 33.053 or a photograph of a child made or kept under Section 33.054 may not be used as evidence in any criminal proceeding in which the child is a defendant or in any case under Title 3, Family Code, in which the child is alleged to have engaged in delinquent conduct or in conduct indicating a need for supervision.

(b) This subchapter does not apply to the use by a law enforcement agency for an official purpose of a photograph published in a school annual.

(c) This subchapter does not prevent the use of a videotape or photograph taken to monitor the activity of students for disciplinary reasons or in connection with a criminal prosecution or an action under Title 3, Family Code.

Sec. 33.056. Liability for Nonperformance.

A person is not liable in any suit for damages for negligent performance or nonperformance of any requirement of this subchapter.

Sec. 33.057. Destruction of Fingerprints and Photographs.

The agency shall adopt rules relating to the destruction of fingerprints and photographs made or kept under Section 33.053 or 33.054.

CHAPTER 34
TRANSPORTATION

Sec. 34.002. Safety Standards.

(a) The Department of Public Safety, with the advice of the Texas Education Agency, shall establish safety standards for school buses used to transport students in accordance with Section 34.003.

(b) Each school district shall meet or exceed the safety standards for school buses established under Subsection (a).

(c) A school district that fails or refuses to meet the safety standards for school buses established under this section is ineligible to share in the transportation allotment under Section 48.151 until the first anniversary of the date the district begins complying with the safety standards.

Sec. 34.003. Operation of School Buses.

(a) School buses or mass transit authority motor buses shall be used for the transportation of students to and from schools on routes having 10 or more students. On those routes having fewer than 10 students, passenger cars may be used for the transportation of students to and from school.

(b) To transport students in connection with school activities other than on routes to and from school:

(1) only school buses or motor buses may be used to transport 15 or more students in any one vehicle; and

(2) passenger cars or passenger vans may be used to transport fewer than 15 students.

(c) In all circumstances in which passenger cars or passenger vans are used to transport students, the operator of the vehicle shall ensure that the number of passengers in the vehicle does not exceed the designed capacity of the vehicle and that each passenger is secured by a safety belt.

(d) In this section, "passenger van" means a motor vehicle other than a motorcycle or passenger car, used to transport persons and designed to transport 15 or fewer passengers, including the driver.

(e) "Motor bus" means a vehicle designed to transport more than 15 passengers, including the driver.

Sec. 34.004. Standing Children.

A school district may not require or allow a child to stand on a school bus or passenger van that is in motion.

Sec. 34.008. Contract with Transit Authority, Commercial Transportation Company, or Juvenile Board.

(a) A board of county school trustees or school district board of trustees may contract with a mass transit authority, commercial transportation company, or juvenile board for all or any part of a district's public school transportation if the authority, company, or board:

(1) requires its school bus drivers to have the qualifications required by and to be certified in accordance with standards established by the Department of Public Safety; and

(2) uses only those school buses or mass transit authority buses in transporting 15 or more public school students that meet or exceed safety standards for school buses established under Section 34.002.

(b) This section does not prohibit the county or school district board from supplementing the state transportation cost allotment with local funds necessary to provide complete transportation services.

(c) A mass transit authority contracting under this section for daily transportation of pre-primary, primary, or secondary students to or from school shall conduct, in a manner and on a schedule approved by the county or district school board, the following education programs:

(1) a program to inform the public that public school students will be riding on the authority's or company's buses;

(2) a program to educate the drivers of the buses to be used under the contract of the special needs and problems of public school students riding on the buses; and

(3) a program to educate public school students on bus riding safety and any special considerations arising from the use of the authority's or company's buses.

Sec. 34.009. Contracts for Use, Acquisition, or Lease of School Bus.

(a) As an alternative to purchasing a school bus, a board of county school trustees or school district board of trustees may contract with any person for use, acquisition, or lease with option to purchase of a school bus if the county or school district board determines the contract to be economically advantageous to the county or district. A contract in the form of an installment purchase or any form other than a lease or lease with option to purchase is subject to Section 34.001.

(b) A school bus that is leased or leased with an option to purchase under this section must meet or exceed the safety standards for school buses established under Section 34.002, Education Code.

(c) Each contract that reserves to the county or school district board the continuing right to terminate the contract at the expiration of each budget period of the board during the term of the contract is considered to be a commitment of current revenues only.

(d) Termination penalties may not be included in any contract under this section. The net effective interest rate on any contract must comply with Chapter 1204, Government Code.

(e) The competitive bidding requirements of Subchapter B, Chapter 44, apply to a contract under this section.

(f) The commissioner shall adopt a recommended contract form for the use, acquisition, or lease with option to purchase of school buses. A district is not required to use the contract.

(g) After a contract providing for payment aggregating $100,000 or more by a school district is authorized by the board of trustees, the board may submit the contract and the record relating to the contract to the attorney general for the attorney general's examination as to the validity of the contract. The approval is not required as a term of the contract. If the contract has been made in accordance with the constitution and laws of the state, the attorney general shall approve the contract, and the comptroller shall register the contract. After the contract has been approved by the attorney general and registered by the comptroller, the validity of the contract is incontestable for any cause. The legal obligations of the lessor, vendor, or supplier of the property to the board are not diminished in any respect by the approval and registration of a contract.

(h) The decision of a board of county school trustees or school district board of trustees to use an alternative form of use, acquisition, or purchase of a school bus does not affect a district's eligibility for participation in the transportation funding provisions of the Foundation School Program or any other state funding program.

(i) A contract entered into under this section is a legal and authorized investment for banks, savings banks, trust companies, building and loan associations, savings and loan associations, insurance companies, fiduciaries, and trustees and for the sinking funds of school districts.

(j) A contract under this section may have any lawful term of not less than two or more than 10 years.

(k) A school district may use the provisions of any other law not in conflict with this section to the extent convenient or necessary to carry out any power or authority, express or implied, granted by this section.

SUBTITLE G
SAFE SCHOOLS

CHAPTER 37
DISCIPLINE; LAW AND ORDER

SUBCHAPTER A
ALTERNATIVE SETTINGS FOR BEHAVIOR MANAGEMENT

Sec. 37.0151. Report to Local Law Enforcement Regarding Certain Conduct Constituting Assault or Harassment; Liability.

(a) The principal of a public primary or secondary school, or a person designated by the principal under Subsection (c), may make a report to any school district police department, if applicable, or the police department of the municipality in which the school is located or, if the school is not in a municipality, the sheriff of the county in which the school is located if, after an investigation is completed, the principal has reasonable grounds to believe that a student engaged in conduct that constitutes an offense under Section 22.01 or 42.07(a)(7), Penal Code.

(b) A person who makes a report under this section may include the name and address of each student the person believes may have participated in the conduct.

(c) The principal of a public primary or secondary school may designate a school employee, other than a school counselor, who is under the supervision of the principal to make the report under this section.

(d) A person who is not a school employee but is employed by an entity that contracts with a district or school to use school property is not required to make a report under this section and may not be designated by the principal of a public primary or secondary school to make a report. A person who voluntarily makes a report under this section is immune from civil or criminal liability.

(e) A person who takes any action under this section is immune from civil or criminal liability or disciplinary action resulting from that action.

(f) Notwithstanding any other law, this section does not create a civil, criminal, or administrative cause of action or liability or create a standard of care, obligation, or duty that provides a basis for a cause of action for an act under this section.

(g) A school district and school personnel and school volunteers are immune from suit resulting from an act under this section, including an act under related policies and procedures.

(h) An act by school personnel or a school volunteer under this section, including an act under related policies and procedures, is the exercise of judgment or discretion on the part of the school personnel or school volunteer and is not considered to be a ministerial act for purposes of liability of the school district or the district's employees.

SUBCHAPTER C
LAW AND ORDER

Sec. 37.0813. School Marshals: Private Schools.

(a) The governing body of a private school may appoint one or more school marshals.

(b) The governing body of a private school may select for appointment as a school marshal under this section an applicant who is an employee of the school and certified as eligible for appointment under Section 1701.260, Occupations Code.

(c) A school marshal appointed by the governing body of a private school may carry a concealed handgun or possess a handgun on the physical premises of a school, but only in the manner provided by written regulations adopted by the governing body.

(d) Any written regulations adopted for purposes of Subsection (c) must provide that a school marshal may carry a concealed handgun on the school marshal's person or possess the handgun on the physical premises of a school in a locked and secured safe or other locked and secured location. The written regulations must also require that a handgun carried or possessed by a school marshal may be loaded only with frangible duty ammunition approved for that purpose by the Texas Commission on Law Enforcement.

(e) A school marshal may use a handgun the school marshal is authorized to carry or possess under this section only under circumstances that would justify the use of deadly force under Section 9.32 or 9.33, Penal Code.

(f) A private school employee's status as a school marshal becomes inactive on:

(1) expiration of the employee's school marshal license under Section 1701.260, Occupations Code;

(2) suspension or revocation of the employee's license to carry a handgun issued under Subchapter H, Chapter 411, Government Code;

(3) termination of the employee's employment with the private school; or

(4) notice from the governing body that the employee's services as school marshal are no longer required.

(g) The identity of a school marshal appointed under this section is confidential, except as provided by Section 1701.260(j), Occupations Code, and is not subject to a request under Chapter 552, Government Code.

(h) If a parent or guardian of a student enrolled at a private school inquires in writing, the school shall provide the parent or guardian written notice indicating whether any employee of the school is currently appointed a school marshal. The notice may not disclose information that is confidential under Subsection (g).

(i) This section does not apply to a school whose students meet the definition provided by Section 29.916(a)(1).

Sec. 37.0815. Transportation or Storage of Firearm and Ammunition by License Holder in School Parking Area.

(a) A school district or open-enrollment charter school may not prohibit a person, including a school employee, who holds a license to carry a handgun under Subchapter H, Chapter 411, Government Code, from transporting or storing a handgun or other firearm or ammunition in a locked, privately owned or leased motor vehicle in a parking lot, parking garage, or other parking area provided by the district or charter school and may not regulate the manner in which the handgun, firearm, or ammunition is stored in the vehicle, provided that the handgun, firearm, or ammunition is not in plain view.

(b) This section does not authorize a person to possess, transport, or store a handgun, a firearm, or ammunition in violation of Section 37.125 of this code, Section 46.03, Penal Code, or other law.

Sec. 37.085. Arrests Prohibited for Certain Class C Misdemeanors.

Notwithstanding any other provision of law, a warrant may not be issued for the arrest of a person for a Class C misdemeanor under this code committed when the person was younger than 17 years of age.

SUBCHAPTER D PROTECTION OF BUILDINGS AND GROUNDS

Sec. 37.107. Trespass on School Grounds.

An unauthorized person who trespasses on the grounds of any school district of this state commits an offense. An offense under this section is a Class C misdemeanor.

Sec. 37.1081. Public Hearing on Multihazard Emergency Operations Plan Noncompliance.

(a) If the board of trustees of a school district receives notice of noncompliance under Section 37.207(e) or 37.2071(g), the board shall hold a public hearing to notify the public of:

(1) the district's failure to:

(A) submit or correct deficiencies in a multihazard emergency operations plan; or

(B) report the results of a safety and security audit to the Texas School Safety Center as required by law;

(2) the dates during which the district has not been in compliance; and

(3) the names of each member of the board of trustees and the superintendent serving in that capacity during the dates the district was not in compliance.

(b) The school district shall provide the information required under Subsection (a)(3) in writing to each person in attendance at the hearing.

(c) The board shall give members of the public a reasonable opportunity to appear before the board and to speak on the issue of the district's failure to submit or correct deficiencies in a multihazard emergency operations plan or report the results of a safety and security audit during a hearing held under this section.

(d) A school district required to hold a public hearing under Subsection (a) shall provide written confirmation to the Texas School Safety Center that the district held the hearing.

Sec. 37.1081. [Expired September 1, 2017] School Safety Certification Program.

Sec. 37.1082. [Expired September 1, 2017] School Safety Task Force.

Sec. 37.1082. Multihazard Emergency Operations Plan Noncompliance; Appointment of Conservator or Board of Managers.

(a) If the agency receives notice from the Texas School Safety Center of a school district's failure to submit a multihazard emergency operations plan, the commissioner may appoint a conservator for the district under Chapter 39A. The conservator may order the district to adopt, implement, and submit a multihazard emergency operations plan.

(b) If a district fails to comply with a conservator's order to adopt, implement, and submit a multihazard emergency operations plan within the time frame imposed by the commissioner, the commissioner may appoint a board of managers under Chapter 39A to oversee the operations of the district.

(c) The commissioner may adopt rules as necessary to administer this section.

Sec. 37.110. Information Regarding Gang-Free Zones.

The superintendent of each public school district and the administrator of each private elementary or secondary school located in the public school district shall ensure that the student handbook for each campus in the public school district includes information on gang-free zones and the consequences of engaging in organized criminal activity within those zones.

SUBCHAPTER E PENAL PROVISIONS

Sec. 37.121. Fraternities, Sororities, Secret Societies, and Gangs.

(a) A person commits an offense if the person:

(1) is a member of, pledges to become a member of, joins, or solicits another person to join or pledge to become a member of a public school fraternity, sorority, secret society, or gang; or

(2) is not enrolled in a public school and solicits another person to attend a meeting of a public school fraternity, sorority, secret society, or gang or a meeting at which membership in one of those groups is encouraged.

(b) A school district board of trustees or an educator shall recommend placing in a disciplinary alternative education program any student under the person's control who violates Subsection (a).

(c) An offense under this section is a Class C misdemeanor.

(d) In this section, "public school fraternity, sorority, secret society, or gang" means an organization composed wholly or in part of students of public primary or secondary schools that seeks to perpetuate itself by taking in additional members from the students enrolled in school on the basis of the decision of its membership rather than on the free choice of a student in the school who is qualified by the rules of the school to fill the special aims of the organization. The term does not include an agency for public welfare, including Boy Scouts, Hi-Y, Girl Reserves, DeMolay, Rainbow Girls, Pan-American Clubs, scholarship societies, or other similar educational organizations sponsored by state or national education authorities.

Sec. 37.122. Possession of Intoxicants on Public School Grounds.

(a) A person commits an offense if the person possesses an intoxicating beverage for consumption, sale, or distribution while:

(1) on the grounds or in a building of a public school; or

(2) entering or inside any enclosure, field, or stadium where an athletic event sponsored or participated in by a public school of this state is being held.

(a-1) It is a defense to prosecution under this section that the person possessed the intoxicating beverage:

(1) at a performing arts facility; and

Education Code

(2) during an event held outside of regular school hours and not sponsored or sanctioned by a school district.

(b) An officer of this state who sees a person violating this section shall immediately seize the intoxicating beverage and, within a reasonable time, deliver it to the county or district attorney to be held as evidence until the trial of the accused possessor.

(c) An offense under this section is a Class C misdemeanor.

Sec. 37.123. Disruptive Activities.

(a) A person commits an offense if the person, alone or in concert with others, intentionally engages in disruptive activity on the campus or property of any private or public school.

(b) For purposes of this section, disruptive activity is:

(1) obstructing or restraining the passage of persons in an exit, entrance, or hallway of a building without the authorization of the administration of the school;

(2) seizing control of a building or portion of a building to interfere with an administrative, educational, research, or other authorized activity;

(3) preventing or attempting to prevent by force or violence or the threat of force or violence a lawful assembly authorized by the school administration so that a person attempting to participate in the assembly is unable to participate due to the use of force or violence or due to a reasonable fear that force or violence is likely to occur;

(4) disrupting by force or violence or the threat of force or violence a lawful assembly in progress; or

(5) obstructing or restraining the passage of a person at an exit or entrance to the campus or property or preventing or attempting to prevent by force or violence or by threats of force or violence the ingress or egress of a person to or from the property or campus without the authorization of the administration of the school.

(c) An offense under this section is a Class B misdemeanor.

(d) Any person who is convicted the third time of violating this section is ineligible to attend any institution of higher education receiving funds from this state before the second anniversary of the third conviction.

(e) This section may not be construed to infringe on any right of free speech or expression guaranteed by the constitution of the United States or of this state.

Sec. 37.124. Disruption of Classes.

(a) A person other than a primary or secondary grade student enrolled in the school commits an offense if the person, on school property or on public property within 500 feet of school property, alone or in concert with others, intentionally disrupts the conduct of classes or other school activities.

(b) An offense under this section is a Class C misdemeanor.

(c) In this section:

(1) "Disrupting the conduct of classes or other school activities" includes:

(A) emitting noise of an intensity that prevents or hinders classroom instruction;

(B) enticing or attempting to entice a student away from a class or other school activity that the student is required to attend;

(C) preventing or attempting to prevent a student from attending a class or other school activity that the student is required to attend; and

(D) entering a classroom without the consent of either the principal or the teacher and, through either acts of misconduct or the use of loud or profane language, disrupting class activities.

(2) "Public property" includes a street, highway, alley, public park, or sidewalk.

(3) "School property" includes a public school campus or school grounds on which a public school is located and any grounds or buildings used by a school for an assembly or other school-sponsored activity.

(d) It is an exception to the application of Subsection (a) that, at the time the person engaged in conduct prohibited under that subsection, the person was younger than 12 years of age.

Sec. 37.125. Exhibition, Use, or Threat of Exhibition or Use of Firearms.

(a) A person commits an offense if, in a manner intended to cause alarm or personal injury to another person or to damage school property, the person intentionally:

(1) exhibits or uses a firearm:

(A) in or on any property, including a parking lot, parking garage, or other parking area, that is owned by a private or public school; or

(B) on a school bus being used to transport children to or from school-sponsored activities of a private or public school;

(2) threatens to exhibit or use a firearm in or on property described by Subdivision (1)(A) or on a bus described by Subdivision (1)(B) and was in possession of or had immediate access to the firearm; or

(3) threatens to exhibit or use a firearm in or on property described by Subdivision (1)(A) or on a bus described by Subdivision (1)(B).

(b) An offense under Subsection (a)(1) or (2) is a third degree felony.

(c) An offense under Subsection (a)(3) is a Class A misdemeanor.

Sec. 37.126. Disruption of Transportation.

(a) Except as provided by Section 37.125, a person other than a primary or secondary grade student commits an offense if the person intentionally disrupts, prevents, or interferes with the lawful transportation of children:

(1) to or from school on a vehicle owned or operated by a county or independent school district; or

(2) to or from an activity sponsored by a school on a vehicle owned or operated by a county or independent school district.

(b) An offense under this section is a Class C misdemeanor.

(c) It is an exception to the application of Subsection (a)(1) that, at the time the person engaged in conduct prohibited under that subdivision, the person was younger than 12 years of age.

SUBCHAPTER E-1 CRIMINAL PROCEDURE

Sec. 37.141. Definitions.

In this subchapter:

(1) "Child" means a person who is:

(A) a student; and

(B) at least 10 years of age and younger than 18 years of age.

(2) "School offense" means an offense committed by a child enrolled in a public school that is a Class C misdemeanor other than a traffic offense and that is committed on property under the control and jurisdiction of a school district.

Sec. 37.142. Conflict of Law.

To the extent of any conflict, this subchapter controls over any other law applied to a school offense alleged to have been committed by a child.

Sec. 37.143. Citation Prohibited; Custody of Child.

(a) A peace officer, law enforcement officer, or school resource officer may not issue a citation to a child who is alleged to have committed a school offense.

(b) This subchapter does not prohibit a child from being taken into custody under Section 52.01, Family Code.

Sec. 37.144. Graduated Sanctions for Certain School Offenses.

(a) A school district that commissions peace officers under Section 37.081 may develop a system of graduated sanctions that the school district may require to be imposed on a child before a complaint is filed under Section 37.145 against the child for a school offense that is an offense under Section 37.124 or 37.126 or under Section 42.01(a)(1), (2), (3), (4), or (5), Penal Code. A system adopted under this section must include multiple graduated sanctions. The system may require:

(1) a warning letter to be issued to the child and the child's parent or guardian that specifically states the child's alleged school offense and explains the consequences if the child engages in additional misconduct;

(2) a behavior contract with the child that must be signed by the child, the child's parent or guardian, and an employee of the school and that includes a specific description of the behavior that is required or prohibited for the child and the penalties for additional alleged school offenses, including additional disciplinary action or the filing of a complaint in a criminal court;

(3) the performance of school-based community service by the child; and

(4) the referral of the child to counseling, community-based services, or other in-school or out-of-school services aimed at addressing the child's behavioral problems.

(b) A referral made under Subsection (a)(4) may include participation by the child's parent or guardian if necessary.

Sec. 37.145. Complaint.

If a child fails to comply with or complete graduated sanctions under Section 37.144, or if the school district has not elected to adopt a system of graduated sanctions under that section, the school may file a complaint against the child with a criminal court in accordance with Section 37.146.

Sec. 37.146. Requisites of Complaint.

(a) A complaint alleging the commission of a school offense must, in addition to the requirements imposed by Article 45.019, Code of Criminal Procedure:

Education Code

(1) be sworn to by a person who has personal knowledge of the underlying facts giving rise to probable cause to believe that an offense has been committed; and

(2) be accompanied by a statement from a school employee stating:

(A) whether the child is eligible for or receives special services under Subchapter A, Chapter 29; and

(B) the graduated sanctions, if required under Section 37.144, that were imposed on the child before the complaint was filed.

(b) After a complaint has been filed under this subchapter, a summons may be issued under Articles 23.04 and 45.057(e), Code of Criminal Procedure.

(c) A complaint under this subchapter may include a recommendation by a school employee that the child attend a teen court program under Article 45.052, Code of Criminal Procedure, if the school employee believes attending a teen court program is in the best interest of the child.

Sec. 37.147. Prosecuting Attorneys.

An attorney representing the state in a court with jurisdiction may adopt rules pertaining to the filing of a complaint under this subchapter that the state considers necessary in order to:

(1) determine whether there is probable cause to believe that the child committed the alleged offense;

(2) review the circumstances and allegations in the complaint for legal sufficiency; and

(3) see that justice is done.

Sec. 37.148. Right to Report Crime.

(a) An employee of a school district or open-enrollment charter school may report a crime witnessed at the school to any peace officer with authority to investigate the crime.

(b) A school district or open-enrollment charter school may not adopt a policy requiring a school employee to:

(1) refrain from reporting a crime witnessed at the school; or

(2) report a crime witnessed at the school only to certain persons or peace officers.

SUBCHAPTER F HAZING

Sec. 37.151. Definitions.

In this subchapter:

(1) "Educational institution" includes a public or private high school.

(2) "Pledge" means any person who has been accepted by, is considering an offer of membership from, or is in the process of qualifying for membership in an organization.

(3) "Pledging" means any action or activity related to becoming a member of an organization.

(4) "Student" means any person who:

(A) is registered in or in attendance at an educational institution;

(B) has been accepted for admission at the educational institution where the hazing incident occurs; or

(C) intends to attend an educational institution during any of its regular sessions after a period of scheduled vacation.

(5) "Organization" means a fraternity, sorority, association, corporation, order, society, corps, club, or student government, a band or musical group or an academic, athletic, cheerleading, or dance team, including any group or team that participates in National Collegiate Athletic Association competition, or a service, social, or similar group, whose members are primarily students.

(6) "Hazing" means any intentional, knowing, or reckless act, occurring on or off the campus of an educational institution, by one person alone or acting with others, directed against a student for the purpose of pledging, being initiated into, affiliating with, holding office in, or maintaining membership in an organization if the act:

(A) is any type of physical brutality, such as whipping, beating, striking, branding, electronic shocking, placing of a harmful substance on the body, or similar activity;

(B) involves sleep deprivation, exposure to the elements, confinement in a small space, calisthenics, or other similar activity that subjects the student to an unreasonable risk of harm or that adversely affects the mental or physical health or safety of the student;

(C) involves consumption of a food, liquid, alcoholic beverage, liquor, drug, or other substance, other than as described by Paragraph (E), that subjects the student to an unreasonable risk of harm or that adversely affects the mental or physical health or safety of the student;

(D) is any activity that induces, causes, or requires the student to perform a duty or task that involves a violation of the Penal Code; or

(E) involves coercing, as defined by Section 1.07, Penal Code, the student to consume:

(i) a drug; or

(ii) an alcoholic beverage or liquor in an amount that would lead a reasonable person to believe

Education Code

that the student is intoxicated, as defined by Section 49.01, Penal Code.

Sec. 37.152. Personal Hazing Offense.

(a) A person commits an offense if the person:

(1) engages in hazing;

(2) solicits, encourages, directs, aids, or attempts to aid another in engaging in hazing;

(3) recklessly permits hazing to occur; or

(4) has firsthand knowledge of the planning of a specific hazing incident involving a student in an educational institution, or has firsthand knowledge that a specific hazing incident has occurred, and knowingly fails to report that knowledge in writing to the dean of students or other appropriate official of the institution.

(b) The offense of failing to report is a Class B misdemeanor.

(c) Any other offense under this section that does not cause serious bodily injury to another is a Class B misdemeanor.

(d) Any other offense under this section that causes serious bodily injury to another is a Class A misdemeanor.

(e) Any other offense under this section that causes the death of another is a state jail felony.

(f) Except if an offense causes the death of a student, in sentencing a person convicted of an offense under this section, the court may require the person to perform community service, subject to the same conditions imposed on a person placed on community supervision under Chapter 42A, Code of Criminal Procedure, for an appropriate period of time in lieu of confinement in county jail or in lieu of a part of the time the person is sentenced to confinement in county jail.

Sec. 37.153. Organization Hazing Offense.

(a) An organization commits an offense if the organization condones or encourages hazing or if an officer or any combination of members, pledges, or alumni of the organization commits or assists in the commission of hazing.

(b) An offense under this section is a misdemeanor punishable by:

(1) a fine of not less than $5,000 nor more than $10,000; or

(2) if the court finds that the offense caused personal injury, property damage, or other loss, a fine of not less than $5,000 nor more than double the amount lost or expenses incurred because of the injury, damage, or loss.

Sec. 37.154. Consent Not a Defense.

It is not a defense to prosecution of an offense under this subchapter that the person against whom the hazing was directed consented to or acquiesced in the hazing activity.

Sec. 37.155. Immunity From Prosecution or Civil Liability Available.

(a) In the prosecution of an offense under this subchapter, the court may grant immunity from prosecution for the offense to each person who is subpoenaed to testify for the prosecution and who does testify for the prosecution.

(b) Any person who voluntarily reports a specific hazing incident involving a student in an educational institution to the dean of students or other appropriate official of the institution is immune from civil or criminal liability that might otherwise be incurred or imposed as a result of the reported hazing incident if the person:

(1) reports the incident before being contacted by the institution concerning the incident or otherwise being included in the institution's investigation of the incident; and

(2) as determined by the dean of students or other appropriate official of the institution designated by the institution, cooperates in good faith throughout any institutional process regarding the incident.

(c) Immunity under Subsection (b) extends to participation in any judicial proceeding resulting from the report.

(d) A person is not immune under Subsection (b) if the person:

(1) reports the person's own act of hazing; or

(2) reports an incident of hazing in bad faith or with malice.

Sec. 37.156. Offenses in Addition to Other Penal Provisions.

This subchapter does not affect or repeal any penal law of this state. This subchapter does not limit or affect the right of an educational institution to enforce its own penalties against hazing.

Sec. 37.157. Reporting by Medical Authorities.

A doctor or other medical practitioner who treats a student who may have been subjected to hazing activities:

(1) may report the suspected hazing activities to police or other law enforcement officials; and

(2) is immune from civil or other liability that might otherwise be imposed or incurred as a result of the report, unless the report is made in bad faith or with malice.

Sec. 37.158. Venue.

(a) In this section, "prosecuting attorney" means a county attorney, district attorney, or criminal district attorney.

(b) An offense under this subchapter may be prosecuted:

(1) in any county in which the offense may be prosecuted under other law; or

(2) if the consent required by Subsection (c) is provided, in a county, other than a county described by Subdivision (1), in which is located the educational institution campus at which a victim of the offense is enrolled.

(c) An offense under this subchapter may be prosecuted in a county described by Subsection (b)(2) only with the written consent of a prosecuting attorney of a county described by Subsection (b)(1) who has authority to prosecute an offense under this subchapter.

ELECTION CODE

TITLE 2
VOTER QUALIFICATIONS AND REGISTRATION

CHAPTER 20
VOTER REGISTRATION AGENCIES

SUBCHAPTER C
DEPARTMENT OF PUBLIC SAFETY

Sec. 20.061. Applicability of Other Provisions.

The other provisions of this chapter apply to the Department of Public Safety except provisions that conflict with this subchapter.

Sec. 20.062. Department Forms and Procedure.

(a) The Department of Public Safety shall prescribe and use a form and procedure that combines the department's application form for a license or card with an officially prescribed voter registration application form.

(b) The department shall prescribe and use a change of address form and procedure that combines department and voter registration functions. The form must allow a licensee or cardholder to indicate whether the change of address is also to be used for voter registration purposes.

(c) The design, content, and physical characteristics of the department forms must be approved by the secretary of state.

Sec. 20.063. Registration Procedures.

(a) The Department of Public Safety shall provide to each person who applies in person at the department's offices for an original or renewal of a driver's license, a personal identification card, or a duplicate or corrected license or card an opportunity to complete a voter registration application form.

(b) When the department processes a license or card for renewal by mail, the department shall deliver to the applicant by mail a voter registration application form.

(c) A change of address that relates to a license or card and that is submitted to the department in person or by mail serves as a change of address for voter registration unless the licensee or cardholder indicates that the change is not for voter registration purposes. The date of submission of a change of address to a department employee is considered to be the date of submission to the voter registrar for the purpose of determining the effective date of registration only.

(d) If a completed voter registration application submitted to a department employee does not include the applicant's correct driver's license number or personal identification card number, a department employee shall enter the appropriate information on the application. If a completed application does not include the applicant's correct residence address or mailing address, a department employee shall obtain the appropriate information from the applicant and enter the information on the application.

Sec. 20.064. Declination Form Not Required.

The Department of Public Safety is not required to comply with the procedures prescribed by this chapter relating to the form for a declination of voter registration.

Sec. 20.065. Delivery of Applications and Changes of Address.

(a) At the end of each day a Department of Public Safety office is regularly open for business, the manager of the office shall deliver by mail or in person to the voter registrar of the county in which the office is located each completed voter registration application and applicable change of address submitted to a department employee.

(b) Each weekday the department is regularly open for business, the department shall electronically transfer to the secretary of state the name of each person who completes a voter registration application submitted to the department. The secretary shall prescribe procedures necessary to implement this subsection.

(c) On the weekday the secretary of state is regularly open for business following the date the secretary receives information under Subsection (b), the secretary shall inform the appropriate voter registrar of the name of each person who completes a voter registration application submitted to the department. The registrar may verify that the registrar has received each application as indicated by the information provided by the secretary under this subsection.

Sec. 20.066. Registration Procedures.

(a) If a person completes a voter registration application as provided by Section 20.063, the Department of Public Safety shall:

(1) input the information provided on the application into the department's electronic data system; and

(2) inform the applicant that the applicant's electronic signature provided to the department will be used for submitting the applicant's voter registration application.

(b) Not later than the fifth day after the date a person completes a voter registration application and provides an electronic signature to the department, the department shall electronically transfer the applicant's voter registration data, including the applicant's signature, to the secretary of state.

(c) The secretary of state shall prescribe additional procedures as necessary to implement this section.

(d), (e) [Expired pursuant to Acts 2005, 79th Leg., ch. 1105 (H.B. 2280), § 9, effective January 2, 2008.]

TITLE 16 MISCELLANEOUS PROVISIONS

CHAPTER 276 MISCELLANEOUS OFFENSES AND OTHER PROVISIONS

Sec. 276.005. Voter's Privilege from Arrest.

A voter may not be arrested during the voter's attendance at an election and while going to and returning from a polling place except for treason, a felony, or a breach of peace.

TEXAS FAMILY CODE

TITLE 2
CHILD IN RELATION TO THE FAMILY

SUBTITLE A
LIMITATIONS OF MINORITY

CHAPTER 32
CONSENT TO TREATMENT OF CHILD BY NON-PARENT OR CHILD

SUBCHAPTER A
CONSENT TO MEDICAL, DENTAL, PSYCHOLOGICAL, AND SURGICAL TREATMENT

Sec. 32.001. Consent by Non-Parent.

(a) The following persons may consent to medical, dental, psychological, and surgical treatment of a child when the person having the right to consent as otherwise provided by law cannot be contacted and that person has not given actual notice to the contrary:

(1) a grandparent of the child;

(2) an adult brother or sister of the child;

(3) an adult aunt or uncle of the child;

(4) an educational institution in which the child is enrolled that has received written authorization to consent from a person having the right to consent;

(5) an adult who has actual care, control, and possession of the child and has written authorization to consent from a person having the right to consent;

(6) a court having jurisdiction over a suit affecting the parent-child relationship of which the child is the subject;

(7) an adult responsible for the actual care, control, and possession of a child under the jurisdiction of a juvenile court or committed by a juvenile court to the care of an agency of the state or county; or

(8) a peace officer who has lawfully taken custody of a minor, if the peace officer has reasonable grounds to believe the minor is in need of immediate medical treatment.

(b) Except as otherwise provided by this subsection, the Texas Juvenile Justice Department may consent to the medical, dental, psychological, and surgical treatment of a child committed to the department under Title 3 when the person having the right to consent has been contacted and that person has not given actual notice to the contrary. Consent for medical, dental, psychological, and surgical treatment of a child for whom the Department of Family and Protective Services has been appointed managing conservator and who is committed to the Texas Juvenile Justice Department is governed by Sections 266.004, 266.009, and 266.010.

(c) This section does not apply to consent for the immunization of a child.

(d) A person who consents to the medical treatment of a minor under Subsection (a)(7) or (8) is immune from liability for damages resulting from the examination or treatment of the minor, except to the extent of the person's own acts of negligence. A physician or dentist licensed to practice in this state, or a hospital or medical facility at which a minor is treated is immune from liability for damages resulting from the examination or treatment of a minor under this section, except to the extent of the person's own acts of negligence.

Sec. 32.002. Consent Form.

(a) Consent to medical treatment under this subchapter must be in writing, signed by the person giving consent, and given to the doctor, hospital, or other medical facility that administers the treatment.

(b) The consent must include:

(1) the name of the child;

(2) the name of one or both parents, if known, and the name of any managing conservator or guardian of the child;

(3) the name of the person giving consent and the person's relationship to the child;

(4) a statement of the nature of the medical treatment to be given; and

(5) the date the treatment is to begin.

Sec. 32.003. Consent to Treatment by Child.

Texas Family Code

(a) A child may consent to medical, dental, psychological, and surgical treatment for the child by a licensed physician or dentist if the child:

(1) is on active duty with the armed services of the United States of America;

(2) is:

(A) 16 years of age or older and resides separate and apart from the child's parents, managing conservator, or guardian, with or without the consent of the parents, managing conservator, or guardian and regardless of the duration of the residence; and

(B) managing the child's own financial affairs, regardless of the source of the income;

(3) consents to the diagnosis and treatment of an infectious, contagious, or communicable disease that is required by law or a rule to be reported by the licensed physician or dentist to a local health officer or the Texas Department of Health, including all diseases within the scope of Section 81.041, Health and Safety Code;

(4) is unmarried and pregnant and consents to hospital, medical, or surgical treatment, other than abortion, related to the pregnancy;

(5) consents to examination and treatment for drug or chemical addiction, drug or chemical dependency, or any other condition directly related to drug or chemical use;

(6) is unmarried, is the parent of a child, and has actual custody of his or her child and consents to medical, dental, psychological, or surgical treatment for the child; or

(7) is serving a term of confinement in a facility operated by or under contract with the Texas Department of Criminal Justice, unless the treatment would constitute a prohibited practice under Section 164.052(a)(19), Occupations Code.

(b) Consent by a child to medical, dental, psychological, and surgical treatment under this section is not subject to disaffirmance because of minority.

(c) Consent of the parents, managing conservator, or guardian of a child is not necessary in order to authorize hospital, medical, surgical, or dental care under this section.

(d) A licensed physician, dentist, or psychologist may, with or without the consent of a child who is a patient, advise the parents, managing conservator, or guardian of the child of the treatment given to or needed by the child.

(e) A physician, dentist, psychologist, hospital, or medical facility is not liable for the examination and treatment of a child under this section except for the provider's or the facility's own acts of negligence.

(f) A physician, dentist, psychologist, hospital, or medical facility may rely on the written statement of the child containing the grounds on which the child has capacity to consent to the child's medical treatment.

Sec. 32.004. Consent to Counseling.

(a) A child may consent to counseling for:

(1) suicide prevention;

(2) chemical addiction or dependency; or

(3) sexual, physical, or emotional abuse.

(b) A licensed or certified physician, psychologist, counselor, or social worker having reasonable grounds to believe that a child has been sexually, physically, or emotionally abused, is contemplating suicide, or is suffering from a chemical or drug addiction or dependency may:

(1) counsel the child without the consent of the child's parents or, if applicable, managing conservator or guardian;

(2) with or without the consent of the child who is a client, advise the child's parents or, if applicable, managing conservator or guardian of the treatment given to or needed by the child; and

(3) rely on the written statement of the child containing the grounds on which the child has capacity to consent to the child's own treatment under this section.

(c) Unless consent is obtained as otherwise allowed by law, a physician, psychologist, counselor, or social worker may not counsel a child if consent is prohibited by a court order.

(d) A physician, psychologist, counselor, or social worker counseling a child under this section is not liable for damages except for damages resulting from the person's negligence or wilful misconduct.

(e) A parent, or, if applicable, managing conservator or guardian, who has not consented to counseling treatment of the child is not obligated to compensate a physician, psychologist, counselor, or social worker for counseling services rendered under this section.

Sec. 32.005. Examination Without Consent of Abuse or Neglect of Child.

(a) Except as provided by Subsection (c), a physician, dentist, or psychologist having reasonable grounds to believe that a child's physical or mental condition has been adversely affected by abuse or neglect may examine the child without the consent of the child, the child's parents, or other person authorized to consent to treatment under this subchapter.

(b) An examination under this section may include X-rays, blood tests, photographs, and penetration of tissue necessary to accomplish those tests.

(c) Unless consent is obtained as otherwise allowed by law, a physician, dentist, or psychologist may not examine a child:

(1) 16 years of age or older who refuses to consent; or

(2) for whom consent is prohibited by a court order.

(d) A physician, dentist, or psychologist examining a child under this section is not liable for damages except for damages resulting from the physician's or dentist's negligence.

CHAPTER 34 AUTHORIZATION AGREEMENT FOR NONPARENT ADULT CAREGIVER

Sec. 34.001. Applicability. [Repealed]

Sec. 34.0015. Definitions.

In this chapter:

(1) "Adult caregiver" means an adult person whom a parent has authorized to provide temporary care for a child under this chapter.

(2) "Parent" has the meaning assigned by Section 101.024.

Sec. 34.002. Authorization Agreement.

(a) A parent or both parents of a child may enter into an authorization agreement with an adult caregiver to authorize the adult caregiver to perform the following acts in regard to the child:

(1) to authorize medical, dental, psychological, or surgical treatment and immunization of the child, including executing any consents or authorizations for the release of information as required by law relating to the treatment or immunization;

(2) to obtain and maintain health insurance coverage for the child and automobile insurance coverage for the child, if appropriate;

(3) to enroll the child in a day-care program or preschool or in a public or private elementary or secondary school;

(4) to authorize the child to participate in age-appropriate extracurricular, civic, social, or recreational activities, including athletic activities;

(5) to authorize the child to obtain a learner's permit, driver's license, or state-issued identification card;

(6) to authorize employment of the child;

(7) to apply for and receive public benefits on behalf of the child; and

(8) to obtain:

(A) copies or originals of state-issued personal identification documents for the child, including the child's birth certificate; and

(B) to the extent authorized under federal law, copies or originals of federally issued personal identification documents for the child, including the child's social security card.

(b) To the extent of any conflict or inconsistency between this chapter and any other law relating to the eligibility requirements other than parental consent to obtain a service under Subsection (a), the other law controls.

(c) An authorization agreement under this chapter does not confer on an adult caregiver the right to authorize the performance of an abortion on the child or the administration of emergency contraception to the child.

(d) Only one authorization agreement may be in effect for a child at any time. An authorization agreement is void if it is executed while a prior authorization agreement remains in effect.

Sec. 34.0021. Authorization Agreement by Parent in Child Protective Services Case.

A parent may enter into an authorization agreement with an adult caregiver with whom a child is placed under a parental child safety placement agreement approved by the Department of Family and Protective Services to allow the person to perform the acts described by Section 34.002(a) with regard to the child:

(1) during an investigation of abuse or neglect; or

(2) while the department is providing services to the parent.

Sec. 34.0022. Inapplicability of Certain Laws.

(a) An authorization agreement executed under this chapter between a child's parent and an adult caregiver does not subject the adult caregiver to any law or rule governing the licensing or regulation of a residential child-care facility under Chapter 42, Human Resources Code.

(b) A child who is the subject of an authorization agreement executed under this chapter is not considered to be placed in foster care and the parties to the authorization agreement are not subject to any law or rule governing foster care providers.

Sec. 34.003. Contents of Authorization Agreement.

(a) The authorization agreement must contain:

(1) the following information from the adult caregiver:

(A) the name and signature of the adult caregiver;

(B) the adult caregiver's relationship to the child; and

(C) the adult caregiver's current physical address and telephone number or the best way to contact the adult caregiver;

(2) the following information from the parent:

(A) the name and signature of the parent; and

(B) the parent's current address and telephone number or the best way to contact the parent;

(3) the information in Subdivision (2) with respect to the other parent, if applicable;

(4) a statement that the adult caregiver has been given authorization to perform the functions listed in Section 34.002(a) as a result of a voluntary action of the parent and that the adult caregiver has voluntarily assumed the responsibility of performing those functions;

(5) statements that neither the parent nor the adult caregiver has knowledge that a parent, guardian, custodian, licensed child-placing agency, or other authorized agency asserts any claim or authority inconsistent with the authorization agreement under this chapter with regard to actual physical possession or care, custody, or control of the child;

(6) statements that:

(A) to the best of the parent's and adult caregiver's knowledge:

(i) there is no court order or pending suit affecting the parent-child relationship concerning the child;

(ii) there is no pending litigation in any court concerning:

(a) custody, possession, or placement of the child; or

(b) access to or visitation with the child; and

(iii) a court does not have continuing jurisdiction concerning the child; or

(B) the court with continuing jurisdiction concerning the child has given written approval for the execution of the authorization agreement accompanied by the following information:

(i) the county in which the court is located;

(ii) the number of the court; and

(iii) the cause number in which the order was issued or the litigation is pending;

(7) a statement that to the best of the parent's and adult caregiver's knowledge there is no current, valid authorization agreement regarding the child;

(8) a statement that the authorization is made in conformance with this chapter;

(9) a statement that the parent and the adult caregiver understand that each party to the authorization agreement is required by law to immediately provide to each other party information regarding any change in the party's address or contact information;

(10) a statement by the parent that:

(A) indicates the authorization agreement is for a term of:

(i) six months from the date the parties enter into the agreement, which renews automatically for six-month terms unless the agreement is terminated as provided by Section 34.008; or

(ii) the time provided in the agreement with a specific expiration date earlier than six months after the date the parties enter into the agreement; and

(B) identifies the circumstances under which the authorization agreement may be:

(i) terminated as provided by Section 34.008 before the term of the agreement expires; or

(ii) continued beyond the term of the agreement by a court as provided by Section 34.008(b); and

(11) space for the signature and seal of a notary public.

(b) The authorization agreement must contain the following warnings and disclosures:

(1) that the authorization agreement is an important legal document;

(2) that the parent and the adult caregiver must read all of the warnings and disclosures before signing the authorization agreement;

(3) that the persons signing the authorization agreement are not required to consult an attorney but are advised to do so;

(4) that the parent's rights as a parent may be adversely affected by placing or leaving the parent's child with another person;

(5) that the authorization agreement does not confer on the adult caregiver the rights of a managing or possessory conservator or legal guardian;

(6) that a parent who is a party to the authorization agreement may terminate the authorization agreement and resume custody, possession, care, and control of the child on demand and that at any time the parent may request the return of the child;

(7) that failure by the adult caregiver to return the child to the parent immediately on request may have criminal and civil consequences;

(8) that, under other applicable law, the adult caregiver may be liable for certain expenses relating to the child in the adult caregiver's care but that the parent still retains the parental obligation to support the child;

(9) that, in certain circumstances, the authorization agreement may not be entered into without written permission of the court;

(10) that the authorization agreement may be terminated by certain court orders affecting the child;

(11) that the authorization agreement does not supersede, invalidate, or terminate any prior authorization agreement regarding the child;

(12) that the authorization agreement is void if a prior authorization agreement regarding the child is in effect and has not expired or been terminated;

(13) that, except as provided by Section 34.005(a-2), the authorization agreement is void unless not later than the 10th day after the date the authorization agreement is signed, the parties mail to a parent who was not a party to the authorization agreement at the parent's last known address, if the parent is living and the parent's parental rights have not been terminated:

(A) one copy of the authorization agreement by certified mail, return receipt requested, or international registered mail, return receipt requested, as applicable; and

(B) one copy of the authorization agreement by first class mail or international first class mail, as applicable; and

(14) that the authorization agreement does not confer on an adult caregiver the right to authorize the performance of an abortion on the child or the administration of emergency contraception to the child.

Sec. 34.004. Execution of Authorization Agreement.

(a) The authorization agreement must be signed and sworn to before a notary public by the parent and the adult caregiver.

(b) A parent may not execute an authorization agreement without a written order by the appropriate court if:

(1) there is a court order or pending suit affecting the parent-child relationship concerning the child;

(2) there is pending litigation in any court concerning:

(A) custody, possession, or placement of the child; or

(B) access to or visitation with the child; or

(3) a court has continuing, exclusive jurisdiction over the child.

(c) An authorization agreement obtained in violation of Subsection (b) is void.

Sec. 34.005. Duties of Parties to Authorization Agreement.

(a) If both parents did not sign the authorization agreement, not later than the 10th day after the date the authorization agreement is executed the parties shall mail to the parent who was not a party to the authorization agreement at the parent's last known address, if that parent is living and that parent's parental rights have not been terminated:

(1) one copy of the executed authorization agreement by certified mail, return receipt requested, or international registered mail, return receipt requested, as applicable; and

(2) one copy of the executed authorization agreement by first class mail or international first class mail, as applicable.

(a-1) Except as otherwise provided by Subsection (a-2), an authorization agreement is void if the parties fail to comply with Subsection (a).

(a-2) Subsection (a) does not apply to an authorization agreement if the parent who was not a party to the authorization agreement:

(1) does not have court-ordered possession of or access to the child who is the subject of the authorization agreement; and

(2) has previously committed an act of family violence, as defined by Section 71.004, or assault against the parent who is a party to the authorization agreement, the child who is the subject of the authorization agreement, or another child of the parent who is a party to the authorization agreement, as documented by one or more of the following:

(A) the issuance of a protective order against the parent who was not a party to the authorization agreement as provided under Chapter 85 or under a similar law of another state; or

(B) the conviction of the parent who was not a party to the authorization agreement of an offense under Title 5, Penal Code, or of another criminal offense in this state or in another state an element of which involves a violent act or prohibited sexual conduct.

(b) A party to the authorization agreement shall immediately inform each other party of any change in the party's address or contact information. If a party fails to comply with this subsection, the authorization agreement is voidable by the other party.

Sec. 34.006. Authorization Voidable.

An authorization agreement is voidable by a party if the other party knowingly:

(1) obtained the authorization agreement by fraud, duress, or misrepresentation; or

(2) made a false statement on the authorization agreement.

Sec. 34.007. Effect of Authorization Agreement.

(a) A person who is not a party to the authorization agreement who relies in good faith on an authorization agreement under this chapter, without actual knowledge that the authorization agreement is void, revoked, or invalid, is not subject to civil or criminal liability to any person, and is not subject to professional disciplinary action, for that reliance if the agreement is completed as required by this chapter.

(b) The authorization agreement does not affect the rights of the child's parent or legal guardian regarding the care, custody, and control of the child, and does not mean that the adult caregiver has legal custody of the child.

(c) An authorization agreement executed under this chapter does not confer or affect standing or a right of intervention in any proceeding under Title 5.

Sec. 34.0075. Term of Authorization Agreement.

An authorization agreement executed under this chapter is for a term of six months from the date the parties enter into the agreement and renews automatically for six-month terms unless:

(1) an earlier expiration date is stated in the authorization agreement;

(2) the authorization agreement is terminated as provided by Section 34.008; or

(3) a court authorizes the continuation of the agreement as provided by Section 34.008(b).

Sec. 34.008. Termination of Authorization Agreement.

(a) Except as provided by Subsection (b), an authorization agreement under this chapter terminates if, after the execution of the authorization agreement, a court enters an order:

(1) affecting the parent-child relationship;

(2) concerning custody, possession, or placement of the child;

(3) concerning access to or visitation with the child; or

(4) regarding the appointment of a guardian for the child under Subchapter B, Chapter 1104, Estates Code.

(b) An authorization agreement may continue after a court order described by Subsection (a) is entered if the court entering the order gives written permission.

(c) An authorization agreement under this chapter terminates on written revocation by a party to the authorization agreement if the party:

(1) gives each party written notice of the revocation;

(2) files the written revocation with the clerk of the county in which:

(A) the child resides;

(B) the child resided at the time the authorization agreement was executed; or

(C) the adult caregiver resides; and

(3) files the written revocation with the clerk of each court:

(A) that has continuing, exclusive jurisdiction over the child;

(B) in which there is a court order or pending suit affecting the parent-child relationship concerning the child;

(C) in which there is pending litigation concerning:

(i) custody, possession, or placement of the child; or

(ii) access to or visitation with the child; or

(D) that has entered an order regarding the appointment of a guardian for the child under Subchapter B, Chapter 1104, Estates Code.

(d) [Repealed.]

(e) If both parents have signed the authorization agreement, either parent may revoke the authorization agreement without the other parent's consent.

(f) Execution of a subsequent authorization agreement does not by itself supersede, invalidate, or terminate a prior authorization agreement.

Sec. 34.009. Penalty.

(a) A person commits an offense if the person knowingly:

(1) presents a document that is not a valid authorization agreement as a valid authorization agreement under this chapter;

(2) makes a false statement on an authorization agreement; or

(3) obtains an authorization agreement by fraud, duress, or misrepresentation.

(b) An offense under this section is a Class B misdemeanor.

SUBTITLE B PARENTAL LIABILITY

CHAPTER 41 LIABILITY OF PARENTS FOR CONDUCT OF CHILD

Sec. 41.001. Liability.

A parent or other person who has the duty of control and reasonable discipline of a child is liable for any property damage proximately caused by:

(1) the negligent conduct of the child if the conduct is reasonably attributable to the negligent failure of the parent or other person to exercise that duty; or

(2) the wilful and malicious conduct of a child who is at least 10 years of age but under 18 years of age.

SUBTITLE C
CHANGE OF NAME

CHAPTER 45
CHANGE OF NAME

SUBCHAPTER B
CHANGE OF NAME OF ADULT

Sec. 45.101. Who May File; Venue.

An adult may file a petition requesting a change of name in the county of the adult's place of residence.

Sec. 45.102. Requirements of Petition.

(a) A petition to change the name of an adult must be verified and include:

(1) the present name and place of residence of the petitioner;

(2) the full name requested for the petitioner;

(3) the reason the change in name is requested;

(4) whether the petitioner has been the subject of a final felony conviction;

(5) whether the petitioner is subject to the registration requirements of Chapter 62, Code of Criminal Procedure; and

(6) a legible and complete set of the petitioner's fingerprints on a fingerprint card format acceptable to the Department of Public Safety and the Federal Bureau of Investigation.

(b) The petition must include each of the following or a reasonable explanation why the required information is not included:

(1) the petitioner's:

(A) full name;

(B) sex;

(C) race;

(D) date of birth;

(E) driver's license number for any driver's license issued in the 10 years preceding the date of the petition;

(F) social security number; and

(G) assigned FBI number, state identification number, if known, or any other reference number in a criminal history record system that identifies the petitioner;

(2) any offense above the grade of Class C misdemeanor for which the petitioner has been charged; and

(3) the case number and the court if a warrant was issued or a charging instrument was filed or presented for an offense listed in Subsection (b)(2).

(c) A petitioner is not required to provide the street address of the petitioner's place of residence or the petitioner's reason for the requested change of name as otherwise required by Subsection (a) if the petitioner provides a copy of an authorization card certifying in accordance with Article 58.059, Code of Criminal Procedure, that the petitioner is a participant in the address confidentiality program administered by the attorney general under Subchapter B, Chapter 58, Code of Criminal Procedure.

Sec. 45.103. Order.

(a) The court shall order a change of name under this subchapter for a person other than a person with a final felony conviction or a person subject to the registration requirements of Chapter 62, Code of Criminal Procedure, if the change is in the interest or to the benefit of the petitioner and in the interest of the public.

(a-1) For purposes of Subsection (a), it is presumed that a change of name is in the interest or to the benefit of the petitioner and in the interest of the public if the petitioner provides a copy of an authorization card certifying in accordance with Article 58.059, Code of Criminal Procedure, that the petitioner is a participant in the address confidentiality program administered by the attorney general under Subchapter B, Chapter 58, Code of Criminal Procedure.

(b) A court may order a change of name under this subchapter for a person with a final felony conviction if:

(1) in addition to the requirements of Subsection (a), the person has:

(A) received a certificate of discharge by the Texas Department of Criminal Justice or completed a period of community supervision or juvenile probation ordered by a court and not less than two years have passed from the date of the receipt of discharge or completion of community supervision or juvenile probation; or

(B) been pardoned; or

(2) the person is requesting to change the person's name to the primary name used in the person's criminal history record information.

(c) A court may order a change of name under this subchapter for a person subject to the registration requirements of Chapter 62, Code of Criminal Procedure, if the person:

(1) meets the requirements of Subsection (a) or is requesting to change the person's name to the primary name used in the person's criminal history record information; and

(2) provides the court with proof that the person has notified the appropriate local law enforcement authority of the proposed name change.

(c-1) An order issued under this section to change the name of a petitioner described by Subsection (a-1) is confidential and may not be released by the court to any person, regardless of whether the petitioner continues to participate in the address confidentiality program following the change of name under this subchapter.

(d) In this section:

(1) "Criminal history record information" has the meaning assigned by Section 411.082, Government Code.

(2) "Local law enforcement authority" has the meaning assigned by Article 62.001, Code of Criminal Procedure.

Sec. 45.104. Liabilities and Rights Unaffected.

A change of name under this subchapter does not release a person from liability incurred in that person's previous name or defeat any right the person had in the person's previous name.

Sec. 45.107. Waiver of Citation.

(a) A party to a suit under this subchapter may waive the issuance or service of citation after the suit is filed by filing with the clerk of the court in which the suit is filed the waiver of the party acknowledging receipt of a copy of the filed petition.

(b) The party executing the waiver may not sign the waiver using a digitized signature.

(c) The waiver must contain the mailing address of the party executing the waiver.

(d) The waiver must be sworn before a notary public who is not an attorney in the suit or conform to the requirements for an unsworn declaration under Section 132.001, Civil Practice and Remedies Code. This subsection does not apply if the party executing the waiver is incarcerated.

(e) The Texas Rules of Civil Procedure do not apply to a waiver executed under this section.

(f) For purposes of this section, "digitized signature" has the meaning assigned by Section 101.0096.

TITLE 3
JUVENILE JUSTICE CODE

CHAPTER 51
GENERAL PROVISIONS

Sec. 51.01. Purpose and Interpretation.

This title shall be construed to effectuate the following public purposes:

(1) to provide for the protection of the public and public safety;

(2) consistent with the protection of the public and public safety:

(A) to promote the concept of punishment for criminal acts;

(B) to remove, where appropriate, the taint of criminality from children committing certain unlawful acts; and

(C) to provide treatment, training, and rehabilitation that emphasizes the accountability and responsibility of both the parent and the child for the child's conduct;

(3) to provide for the care, the protection, and the wholesome moral, mental, and physical development of children coming within its provisions;

(4) to protect the welfare of the community and to control the commission of unlawful acts by children;

(5) to achieve the foregoing purposes in a family environment whenever possible, separating the child from the child's parents only when necessary for the child's welfare or in the interest of public safety and when a child is removed from the child's family, to give the child the care that should be provided by parents; and

(6) to provide a simple judicial procedure through which the provisions of this title are executed and enforced and in which the parties are assured a fair hearing and their constitutional and other legal rights recognized and enforced.

Sec. 51.02. Definitions.

In this title:

(1) "Aggravated controlled substance felony" means an offense under Subchapter D, Chapter 481, Health and Safety Code, that is punishable by:

(A) a minimum term of confinement that is longer than the minimum term of confinement for a felony of the first degree; or

(B) a maximum fine that is greater than the maximum fine for a felony of the first degree.

(2) "Child" means a person who is:

(A) ten years of age or older and under 17 years of age; or

(B) seventeen years of age or older and under 18 years of age who is alleged or found to have engaged in delinquent conduct or conduct indicating a need for supervision as a result of acts committed before becoming 17 years of age.

(3) "Custodian" means the adult with whom the child resides.

(3-a) "Dual status child" means a child who has been referred to the juvenile justice system and is:

(A) in the temporary or permanent managing conservatorship of the Department of Family and Protective Services;

(B) the subject of a case for which family-based safety services have been offered or provided by the department;

(C) an alleged victim of abuse or neglect in an open child protective investigation; or

(D) a victim in a case in which, after an investigation, the department concluded there was reason to believe the child was abused or neglected.

(4) "Guardian" means the person who, under court order, is the guardian of the person of the child or the public or private agency with whom the child has been placed by a court.

(5) "Judge" or "juvenile court judge" means the judge of a juvenile court.

(6) "Juvenile court" means a court designated under Section 51.04 of this code to exercise jurisdiction over proceedings under this title.

(7) "Law-enforcement officer" means a peace officer as defined by Article 2.12, Code of Criminal Procedure.

(8) "Nonoffender" means a child who:

(A) is subject to jurisdiction of a court under abuse, dependency, or neglect statutes under Title 5 for reasons other than legally prohibited conduct of the child; or

(B) has been taken into custody and is being held solely for deportation out of the United States.

(8-a) "Nonsecure correctional facility" means a facility described by Section 51.126.

(9) "Parent" means the mother or the father of a child, but does not include a parent whose parental rights have been terminated.

(10) "Party" means the state, a child who is the subject of proceedings under this subtitle, or the child's parent, spouse, guardian, or guardian ad litem.

(11) "Prosecuting attorney" means the county attorney, district attorney, or other attorney who regularly serves in a prosecutory capacity in a juvenile court.

(12) "Referral to juvenile court" means the referral of a child or a child's case to the office or official, including an intake officer or probation officer, designated by the juvenile board to process children within the juvenile justice system.

(13) "Secure correctional facility" means any public or private residential facility, including an alcohol or other drug treatment facility, that:

(A) includes construction fixtures designed to physically restrict the movements and activities of juveniles or other individuals held in lawful custody in the facility; and

(B) is used for the placement of any juvenile who has been adjudicated as having committed an offense, any nonoffender, or any other individual convicted of a criminal offense.

(14) "Secure detention facility" means any public or private residential facility that:

(A) includes construction fixtures designed to physically restrict the movements and activities of juveniles or other individuals held in lawful custody in the facility; and

(B) is used for the temporary placement of any juvenile who is accused of having committed an offense, any nonoffender, or any other individual accused of having committed a criminal offense.

(15) "Status offender" means a child who is accused, adjudicated, or convicted for conduct that would not, under state law, be a crime if committed by an adult, including:

(A) running away from home under Section 51.03(b)(2);

(B) a fineable only offense under Section 51.03(b)(1) transferred to the juvenile court under Section 51.08(b), but only if the conduct constituting the offense would not have been criminal if engaged in by an adult;

(C) a violation of standards of student conduct as described by Section 51.03(b)(4);

(D) a violation of a juvenile curfew ordinance or order;

(E) a violation of a provision of the Alcoholic Beverage Code applicable to minors only; or

(F) a violation of any other fineable only offense under Section 8.07(a)(4) or (5), Penal Code, but only if the conduct constituting the offense would not have been criminal if engaged in by an adult.

(16) "Traffic offense" means:

(A) a violation of a penal statute cognizable under Chapter 729, Transportation Code, except for conduct for which the person convicted may be sentenced to imprisonment or confinement in jail; or

(B) a violation of a motor vehicle traffic ordinance of an incorporated city or town in this state.

(17) "Valid court order" means a court order entered under Section 54.04 concerning a child adjudicated to have engaged in conduct indicating a need for supervision as a status offender.

Sec. 51.03. Delinquent Conduct; Conduct Indicating a Need for Supervision.

(a) Delinquent conduct is:

(1) conduct, other than a traffic offense, that violates a penal law of this state or of the United States punishable by imprisonment or by confinement in jail;

(2) conduct that violates a lawful order of a court under circumstances that would constitute contempt of that court in:

(A) a justice or municipal court;

(B) a county court for conduct punishable only by a fine; or

(C) a truancy court;

(3) conduct that violates Section 49.04, 49.05, 49.06, 49.07, or 49.08, Penal Code; or

(4) conduct that violates Section 106.041, Alcoholic Beverage Code, relating to driving under the influence of alcohol by a minor (third or subsequent offense).

(b) Conduct indicating a need for supervision is:

(1) subject to Subsection (f), conduct, other than a traffic offense, that violates:

(A) the penal laws of this state of the grade of misdemeanor that are punishable by fine only; or

(B) the penal ordinances of any political subdivision of this state;

(2) the voluntary absence of a child from the child's home without the consent of the child's parent or guardian for a substantial length of time or without intent to return;

(3) conduct prohibited by city ordinance or by state law involving the inhalation of the fumes or vapors of paint and other protective coatings or glue and other adhesives and the volatile chemicals itemized in Section 485.001, Health and Safety Code;

(4) an act that violates a school district's previously communicated written standards of student conduct for which the child has been expelled under Section 37.007(c), Education Code;

(5) notwithstanding Subsection (a)(1), conduct described by Section 43.02 or 43.021, Penal Code;

(6) notwithstanding Subsection (a)(1), conduct that violates Section 43.261, Penal Code; or

(7) notwithstanding Subsection (a)(1), conduct that violates Section 42.0601, Penal Code, if the child has not previously been adjudicated as having engaged in conduct violating that section.

(c) Nothing in this title prevents criminal proceedings against a child for perjury.

(d) [Repealed by Acts 2015, 84th Leg., ch. 935 (H.B. 2398), § 41(3), effective September 1, 2015.]

(e) For the purposes of Subsection (b)(2) , "child" does not include a person who is married, divorced, or widowed.

(e-1) [Repealed by Acts 2015, 84th Leg., ch. 935 (H.B. 2398), § 41(3), effective September 1, 2015.]

(f) Conduct described under Subsection (b)(1) does not constitute conduct indicating a need for supervision unless the child has been referred to the juvenile court under Section 51.08(b).

(g) [Repealed by Acts 2015, 84th Leg., ch. 935 (H.B. 2398), § 41(3), effective September 1, 2015.]

Sec. 51.031. Habitual Felony Conduct.

(a) Habitual felony conduct is conduct violating a penal law of the grade of felony, other than a state jail felony, if:

(1) the child who engaged in the conduct has at least two previous final adjudications as having engaged in delinquent conduct violating a penal law of the grade of felony;

(2) the second previous final adjudication is for conduct that occurred after the date the first previous adjudication became final; and

(3) all appeals relating to the previous adjudications considered under Subdivisions (1) and (2) have been exhausted.

(b) For purposes of this section, an adjudication is final if the child is placed on probation or committed to the Texas Juvenile Justice Department.

(c) An adjudication based on conduct that occurred before January 1, 1996, may not be considered in a disposition made under this section.

Sec. 51.04. Jurisdiction.

(a) This title covers the proceedings in all cases involving the delinquent conduct or conduct indicating a need for supervision engaged in by a person who was a child within the meaning of this title at the time the person engaged in the conduct, and, except as provided by Subsection (h) or Section 51.0414, the juvenile court has exclusive original jurisdiction over proceedings under this title.

(b) In each county, the county's juvenile board shall designate one or more district, criminal district, domestic relations, juvenile, or county courts or county courts at law as the juvenile court, subject to Subsections (c), (d), and (i).

(c) If the county court is designated as a juvenile court, at least one other court shall be designated as the juvenile court. A county court does not have jurisdiction of a proceeding involving a petition approved by a grand jury under Section 53.045 of this code.

(d) If the judge of a court designated in Subsection (b) or (c) of this section is not an attorney licensed in this state, there shall also be designated an alternate court, the judge of which is an attorney licensed in this state.

(e) A designation made under Subsection (b), (c), or (i) may be changed from time to time by the authorized boards or judges for the convenience of the people and the welfare of children. However, there must be at all times a juvenile court designated for each county. It is the intent of the legislature that in selecting a court to be the juvenile court of each county, the selection shall be made as far as practicable so that the court designated as the juvenile court will be one which is presided over by a judge who has a sympathetic understanding of the problems of child welfare and that changes in the designation of juvenile courts be made only when the best interest of the public requires it.

(f) If the judge of the juvenile court or any alternate judge named under Subsection (b) or (c) is not in the county or is otherwise unavailable, any magistrate may make a determination under Section 53.02(f) or may conduct the detention hearing provided for in Section 54.01.

(g) The juvenile board may appoint a referee to make determinations under Section 53.02(f) or to conduct hearings under this title. The referee shall be an attorney licensed to practice law in this state and shall comply with Section 54.10. Payment of any referee services shall be provided from county funds.

(h) A judge exercising jurisdiction over a child in a suit instituted under Subtitle E, Title 5, may refer any aspect of a suit involving a dual status child that is instituted under this title to the appropriate associate judge appointed under Subchapter C, Chapter 201, serving in the county and exercising jurisdiction over the child under Subtitle E, Title 5, if the associate judge consents to the referral. The scope of an associate judge's authority over a suit referred under this subsection is subject to any limitations placed by the court judge in the order of referral.

(i) If the court designated as the juvenile court under Subsection (b) does not have jurisdiction over proceedings under Subtitle E, Title 5, the county's juvenile board may designate at least one other court that does have jurisdiction over proceedings under Subtitle E, Title 5, as a juvenile court or alternative juvenile court.

Sec. 51.041. Jurisdiction After Appeal.

(a) The court retains jurisdiction over a person, without regard to the age of the person, for conduct engaged in by the person before becoming 17 years of age if, as a result of an appeal by the person or the state under Chapter 56 of an order of the court, the order is reversed or modified and the case remanded to the court by the appellate court.

(b) If the respondent is at least 18 years of age when the order of remand from the appellate court is received by the juvenile court, the juvenile court shall proceed as provided by Sections 54.02(o)-(r) for the detention of a person at least 18 years of age in discretionary transfer proceedings. Pending retrial of the adjudication or transfer proceeding, the juvenile court may:

(1) order the respondent released from custody;

(2) order the respondent detained in a juvenile detention facility; or

(3) set bond and order the respondent detained in a county adult facility if bond is not made.

Sec. 51.0411. Jurisdiction for Transfer or Release Hearing.

The court retains jurisdiction over a person, without regard to the age of the person, who is referred to the court under Section 54.11 for transfer to the Texas Department of Criminal Justice or release under supervision.

Sec. 51.0412. Jurisdiction over Incomplete Proceedings.

The court retains jurisdiction over a person, without regard to the age of the person, who is a respondent in an adjudication proceeding, a disposition proceeding, a proceeding to modify disposition, a proceeding for waiver of jurisdiction and transfer to criminal court under Section 54.02(a), or a motion for transfer of determinate sentence probation to an appropriate district court if:

(1) the petition or motion was filed while the respondent was younger than 18 or 19 years of age, as applicable;

(2) the proceeding is not complete before the respondent becomes 18 or 19 years of age, as applicable; and

(3) the court enters a finding in the proceeding that the prosecuting attorney exercised due diligence in an attempt to complete the proceeding

before the respondent became 18 or 19 years of age, as applicable.

Sec. 51.0413. Jurisdiction over and Transfer of Combination of Proceedings.

(a) A juvenile court designated under Section 51.04(b) or, if that court does not have jurisdiction over proceedings under Subtitle E, Title 5, the juvenile court designated under Section 51.04(i) may simultaneously exercise jurisdiction over proceedings under this title and proceedings under Subtitle E, Title 5, if there is probable cause to believe that the child who is the subject of those proceedings engaged in delinquent conduct or conduct indicating a need for supervision and cause to believe that the child may be the victim of conduct that constitutes an offense under Section 20A.02, Penal Code.

(b) If a proceeding is instituted under this title in a juvenile court designated under Section 51.04(b) that does not have jurisdiction over proceedings under Subtitle E, Title 5, the court shall assess the case and may transfer the proceedings to a court designated as a juvenile court or alternative juvenile court under Section 51.04(i) if the receiving court agrees and if, in the course of the proceedings, evidence is presented that constitutes cause to believe that the child who is the subject of those proceedings is a child described by Subsection (a).

Sec. 51.0414. Discretionary Transfer to Combine Proceedings.

(a) The juvenile court may transfer a dual status child's case, including transcripts of records and documents for the case, to a district or statutory county court located in another county that is exercising jurisdiction over the child in a suit instituted under Subtitle E, Title 5. A case may only be transferred under this section with the consent of the judge of the court to which the case is being transferred.

(b) Notwithstanding Section 51.04, a district or statutory county court to which a case is transferred under this section has jurisdiction over the transferred case regardless of whether the court is a designated juvenile court or alternative juvenile court in the county.

(c) If the court exercising jurisdiction over the child under Subtitle E, Title 5, consents to a transfer under this section, the juvenile court shall file the transfer order with the clerk of the transferring court. On receipt and without a hearing or further order from the juvenile court, the clerk of the transferring court shall transfer the files, including transcripts of records and documents for the case as soon as practicable but not later than the 10th day after the date an order of transfer is filed.

(d) On receipt of the pleadings, documents, and orders from the transferring court, the clerk of the receiving court shall notify the judge of the receiving court, all parties, and the clerk of the transferring court.

Sec. 51.042. Objection to Jurisdiction Because of Age of the Child.

(a) A child who objects to the jurisdiction of the court over the child because of the age of the child must raise the objection at the adjudication hearing or discretionary transfer hearing, if any.

(b) A child who does not object as provided by Subsection (a) waives any right to object to the jurisdiction of the court because of the age of the child at a later hearing or on appeal.

Sec. 51.045. Juries in County Courts at Law.

If a provision of this title requires a jury of 12 persons, that provision prevails over any other law that limits the number of members of a jury in a particular county court at law. The state and the defense are entitled to the same number of peremptory challenges allowed in a district court.

Sec. 51.05. Court Sessions and Facilities.

(a) The juvenile court shall be deemed in session at all times. Suitable quarters shall be provided by the commissioners court of each county for the hearing of cases and for the use of the judge, the probation officer, and other employees of the court.

(b) The juvenile court and the juvenile board shall report annually to the commissioners court on the suitability of the quarters and facilities of the juvenile court and may make recommendations for their improvement.

Sec. 51.06. Venue.

(a) A proceeding under this title shall be commenced in

(1) the county in which the alleged delinquent conduct or conduct indicating a need for supervision occurred; or

(2) the county in which the child resides at the time the petition is filed, but only if:

(A) the child was under probation supervision in that county at the time of the commission of the delinquent conduct or conduct indicating a need for supervision;

(B) it cannot be determined in which county the delinquent conduct or conduct indicating a need for supervision occurred; or

(C) the county in which the child resides agrees to accept the case for prosecution, in writing, prior to the case being sent to the county of residence for prosecution.

(b) An application for a writ of habeas corpus brought by or on behalf of a person who has been committed to an institution under the jurisdiction of the Texas Juvenile Justice Department and which attacks the validity of the judgment of commitment shall be brought in the county in which the court that entered the judgment of commitment is located.

Sec. 51.07. Transfer to Another County for Disposition.

(a) When a child has been found to have engaged in delinquent conduct or conduct indicating a need for supervision under Section 54.03, the juvenile court may transfer the case and transcripts of records and documents to the juvenile court of the county where the child resides for disposition of the case under Section 54.04. Consent by the court of the county where the child resides is not required.

(b) For purposes of Subsection (a), while a child is the subject of a suit under Title 5, the child is considered to reside in the county in which the court of continuing exclusive jurisdiction over the child is located.

Sec. 51.071. Transfer of Probation Supervision Between Counties: Courtesy Supervision Prohibited.

Except as provided by Section 51.075, a juvenile court or juvenile probation department may not engage in the practice of courtesy supervision of a child on probation.

Sec. 51.072. Transfer of Probation Supervision Between Counties: Interim Supervision.

(a) In this section:

(1) "Receiving county" means the county to which a child on probation has moved or intends to move.

(2) "Sending county" means the county that:

(A) originally placed the child on probation; or

(B) assumed permanent supervision of the child under an inter-county transfer of probation supervision.

(b) When a child on probation moves or intends to move from one county to another and intends to remain in the receiving county for at least 60 days, the juvenile probation department of the sending county shall request that the juvenile probation department of the receiving county provide interim supervision of the child. If the receiving county and the sending county are member counties within a judicial district served by one juvenile probation department, then a transfer of probation supervision is not required.

(c) The juvenile probation department of the receiving county may refuse the request to provide interim supervision only if:

(1) the residence of the child in the receiving county is in a residential placement facility arranged by the sending county; or

(2) the residence of the child in the receiving county is in a foster care placement arranged by the Department of Family and Protective Services.

(d) The juvenile probation department of the sending county shall initiate the request for interim supervision by electronic communication to the probation officer designated as the inter-county transfer officer for the juvenile probation department of the receiving county or, in the absence of this designation, to the chief juvenile probation officer.

(e) The juvenile probation department of the sending county shall provide the juvenile probation department of the receiving county with the following information in the request for interim supervision initiated under Subsection (d):

(1) the child's name, sex, age, race, and date of birth;

(2) the name, address, date of birth, and social security or driver's license number, and telephone number, if available, of the person with whom the child proposes to reside or is residing in the receiving county;

(3) the offense for which the child is on probation;

(4) the length of the child's probation term;

(5) a brief summary of the child's history of referrals;

(6) a brief statement of any special needs of the child;

(7) the name and telephone number of the child's school in the receiving county, if available; and

(8) the reason for the child moving or intending to move to the receiving county.

(f) Not later than 10 business days after a receiving county has agreed to provide interim supervision of a child, the juvenile probation department of the sending county shall provide the juvenile probation department of the receiving county with a copy of the following documents:

(1) the petition and the adjudication and disposition orders for the child, including the child's thumbprint;

(2) the child's conditions of probation;

(3) the social history report for the child;

(4) any psychological or psychiatric reports concerning the child;

(5) the Department of Public Safety CR 43J form or tracking incident number concerning the child;

(6) any law enforcement incident reports concerning the offense for which the child is on probation;

(7) any sex offender registration information concerning the child;

(8) any juvenile probation department progress reports concerning the child and any other pertinent documentation for the child's probation officer;

(9) case plans concerning the child;

(10) the Texas Juvenile Justice Department standard assessment tool results for the child;

(11) the computerized referral and case history for the child, including case disposition;

(12) the child's birth certificate;

(13) the child's social security number or social security card, if available;

(14) the name, address, and telephone number of the contact person in the sending county's juvenile probation department;

(15) Title IV-E eligibility screening information for the child, if available;

(16) the address in the sending county for forwarding funds collected to which the sending county is entitled;

(17) any of the child's school or immunization records that the juvenile probation department of the sending county possesses;

(18) any victim information concerning the case for which the child is on probation; and

(19) if applicable, documentation that the sending county has required the child to provide a DNA sample to the Department of Public Safety under Section 54.0405 or 54.0409 or under Subchapter G, Chapter 411, Government Code.

(f-1) The inter-county transfer officers in the sending and receiving counties shall agree on the official start date for the period of interim supervision, which must begin no later than three business days after the date the documents required under Subsection (f) have been received and accepted by the receiving county.

(f-2) On initiating a transfer of probation supervision under this section, for a child ordered to submit a DNA sample as a condition of probation, the sending county shall provide to the receiving county documentation of compliance with the requirements of Section 54.0405 or 54.0409 or of Subchapter G, Chapter 411, Government Code, as applicable. If the sending county has not provided the documentation required under this section within the time provided by Subsection (f), the receiving county may refuse to accept interim supervision until the sending county has provided the documentation.

(g) The juvenile probation department of the receiving county shall supervise the child under the probation conditions imposed by the sending county and provide services similar to those provided to a child placed on probation under the same conditions in the receiving county. On request of the juvenile probation department of the receiving county, the juvenile court of the receiving county may modify the original probation conditions and impose new conditions using the procedures in Section 54.05. The juvenile court of the receiving county may not modify a financial probation condition imposed by the juvenile court of the sending county or the length of the child's probation term. The juvenile court of the receiving county shall designate a cause number for identifying the modification proceedings.

(h) The juvenile court of the sending county may revoke probation for a violation of a condition imposed by the juvenile court of the sending county only if the condition has not been specifically modified or replaced by the juvenile court of the receiving county. The juvenile court of the receiving county may revoke probation for a violation of a condition of probation that the juvenile court of the receiving county has modified or imposed.

(i) If a child is reasonably believed to have violated a condition of probation imposed by the juvenile court of the sending county, the juvenile court of the sending or receiving county may issue a directive to apprehend or detain the child in a certified detention facility, as in other cases of probation violation. In order to respond to a probation violation under this subsection, the juvenile court of the receiving county may:

(1) modify the conditions of probation or extend the probation term; or

(2) require that the juvenile probation department of the sending county resume direct supervision for the child.

(j) On receiving a directive from the juvenile court of the receiving county under Subsection (i)(2), the juvenile probation department of the sending county shall arrange for the prompt transportation of the child back to the sending county at the expense of the sending county. The juvenile probation department in the receiving county shall provide the sending county with supporting written documentation of the incidents of violation of probation on which the request to resume direct supervision is based.

(j-1) Notwithstanding Subsection (j), the sending county may request interim supervision from the receiving county that issued a directive under Subsection (i)(2). Following the conclusion of any judicial proceedings in the sending county or on the completion of any residential placement ordered by the juvenile court of the sending county, the sending and receiving counties may mutually agree to return the child to the receiving county. The sending and receiving counties may take into consideration whether:

(1) the person having legal custody of the child resides in the receiving county;

(2) the child has been ordered by the juvenile court of the sending county to reside with a parent, guardian, or other person who resides in the sending county or any other county; and

(3) the case meets the statutory requirements for collaborative supervision.

(j-2) The period of interim supervision under Subsection (j-1) may not exceed the period under Subsection (m).

(k) The juvenile probation department of the receiving county is entitled to any probation supervision fees collected from the child or the child's parent while providing interim supervision for the child. During the period of interim supervision, the receiving county shall collect and distribute to the victim monetary restitution payments in the manner specified by the sending county. At the expiration of the period of interim supervision, the receiving county shall collect and distribute directly to the victim any remaining payments.

(*l*) The sending county is financially responsible for any special treatment program or placement that the juvenile court of the sending county requires as a condition of probation if the child's family is financially unable to pay for the program or placement.

(m) Except as provided by Subsection (n), a period of interim supervision may not exceed 180 days. Permanent supervision automatically transfers to the juvenile probation department of the receiving county after the expiration of the period of interim supervision. The juvenile probation department of the receiving county may request permanent supervision from the juvenile probation department of the sending county at any time before the 180-day interim supervision period expires. After signing and entry of an order of transfer of permanent supervision by the sending county juvenile court, the juvenile probation department shall, in accordance with Section 51.073(b), promptly send the permanent supervision order and related documents to the receiving county.

(m-1) If a child on interim supervision moves to another county of residence or is otherwise no longer in the receiving county before the expiration of 180 days, the receiving county shall direct the sending county to resume supervision of the child.

(n) Notwithstanding Subsection (m), the period of interim supervision of a child who is placed on probation under Section 54.04(q) does not expire until the child has satisfactorily completed the greater of either 180 days or one-third of the term of probation, including one-third of the term of any extension of the probation term ordered under Section 54.05. Permanent supervision automatically transfers to the probation department of the receiving county after the expiration of the period of interim supervision under this subsection. If the state elects to initiate transfer proceedings under Section 54.051, the juvenile court of the sending county may order transfer of the permanent supervision before the expiration of the period of interim supervision under this subsection.

(o) At least once every 90 days during the period of interim supervision, the juvenile probation department of the receiving county shall provide the juvenile probation department of the sending county with a progress report of supervision concerning the child.

Sec. 51.073. Transfer of Probation Supervision Between Counties: Permanent Supervision.

(a) In this section:

(1) "Receiving county" means the county to which a child on probation has moved or intends to move.

(2) "Sending county" means the county that:

(A) originally placed the child on probation; or

(B) assumed permanent supervision of the child under an inter-county transfer of probation supervision.

(b) On transfer of permanent supervision of a child under Section 51.072(m) or (n), the juvenile court of the sending county shall order the juvenile probation department of the sending county to provide the juvenile probation department of the receiving county with the order of transfer. On receipt of the order of transfer, the juvenile probation department of the receiving county shall ensure that the order of transfer, the petition, the order of adjudication, the order of disposition, and the conditions of probation are filed with the clerk of the juvenile court of the receiving county.

(c) The juvenile court of the receiving county shall require that the child be brought before the court in order to impose new or different conditions of probation than those originally ordered by the sending county or ordered by the receiving county during the period of interim supervision. The child shall be represented by counsel as provided by Section 51.10.

(d) Once permanent supervision is transferred to the juvenile probation department of the receiving county, the receiving county is fully responsible for selecting and imposing conditions of probation, providing supervision, modifying conditions of probation, and revoking probation. The sending county has no further jurisdiction over the child's case.

(d-1) On the final transfer of a case involving a child who has been adjudicated as having committed an offense for which registration is required under Chapter 62, Code of Criminal Procedure, the receiving county shall have jurisdiction to conduct a hearing under that chapter. This subsection does not prohibit the receiving county juvenile court from considering the written recommendations of the sending county juvenile court.

(e) This section does not affect the sending county's jurisdiction over any new offense committed by the child in the sending county.

Sec. 51.074. Transfer of Probation Supervision Between Counties: Deferred Prosecution.

(a) A juvenile court may transfer interim supervision, but not permanent supervision, to the county where a child on deferred prosecution resides.

(b) On an extension of a previous order of deferred prosecution authorized under Section 53.03(j), the child shall remain on interim supervision for an additional period not to exceed 180 days.

(c) On a violation of the conditions of the original deferred prosecution agreement, the receiving county shall forward the case to the sending county for prosecution or other action in the manner provided by Sections 51.072(i) and (j), except that the original conditions of deferred prosecution may not be modified by the receiving county.

Sec. 51.075. Collaborative Supervision Between Adjoining Counties.

(a) If a child who is on probation in one county spends substantial time in an adjoining county, including residing, attending school, or working in the adjoining county, the juvenile probation departments of the two counties may enter into a collaborative supervision arrangement regarding the child.

(b) Under a collaborative supervision arrangement, the juvenile probation department of the adjoining county may authorize a probation officer for the county to provide supervision and other services for the child as an agent of the juvenile probation department of the county in which the child was placed on probation. The probation officer providing supervision and other services for the child in the adjoining county shall provide the probation officer supervising the child in the county in which the child was placed on probation with periodic oral, electronic, or written reports concerning the child.

(c) The juvenile court of the county in which the child was placed on probation retains sole authority to modify, amend, extend, or revoke the child's probation.

Sec. 51.08. Transfer from Criminal Court.

(a) If the defendant in a criminal proceeding is a child who is charged with an offense other than perjury, a traffic offense, a misdemeanor punishable by fine only, or a violation of a penal ordinance of a political subdivision, unless the child has been transferred to criminal court under Section 54.02, the court exercising criminal jurisdiction shall transfer the case to the juvenile court, together with a copy of the accusatory pleading and other papers, documents, and transcripts of testimony relating to the case, and shall order that the child be taken to the place of detention designated by the juvenile court, or shall release the child to the custody of the child's parent, guardian, or custodian, to be brought before the juvenile court at a time designated by that court.

(b) A court in which there is pending a complaint against a child alleging a violation of a misdemeanor offense punishable by fine only other than a traffic offense or a violation of a penal ordinance of a political subdivision other than a traffic offense:

(1) except as provided by Subsection (d), shall waive its original jurisdiction and refer the child to juvenile court if:

(A) the complaint pending against the child alleges a violation of a misdemeanor offense under Section 43.261, Penal Code, that is punishable by fine only; or

(B) the child has previously been convicted of:

(i) two or more misdemeanors punishable by fine only other than a traffic offense;

(ii) two or more violations of a penal ordinance of a political subdivision other than a traffic offense; or

(iii) one or more of each of the types of misdemeanors described in Subparagraph (i) or (ii); and

(2) may waive its original jurisdiction and refer the child to juvenile court if the child:

(A) has not previously been convicted of a misdemeanor punishable by fine only other than a traffic

Texas Family Code

offense or a violation of a penal ordinance of a political subdivision other than a traffic offense; or

(B) has previously been convicted of fewer than two misdemeanors punishable by fine only other than a traffic offense or two violations of a penal ordinance of a political subdivision other than a traffic offense.

(c) A court in which there is pending a complaint against a child alleging a violation of a misdemeanor offense punishable by fine only other than a traffic offense or a violation of a penal ordinance of a political subdivision other than a traffic offense shall notify the juvenile court of the county in which the court is located of the pending complaint and shall furnish to the juvenile court a copy of the final disposition of any matter for which the court does not waive its original jurisdiction under Subsection (b).

(d) A court that has implemented a juvenile case manager program under Article 45.056, Code of Criminal Procedure, may, but is not required to, waive its original jurisdiction under Subsection (b)(1)(B).

(e) [Repealed by Acts 2015, 84th Leg., ch. 935 (H.B. 2398), § 41(3), effective September 1, 2015.]

(f) A court shall waive original jurisdiction for a complaint against a child alleging a violation of a misdemeanor offense punishable by fine only, other than a traffic offense, and refer the child to juvenile court if the court or another court has previously dismissed a complaint against the child under Section 8.08, Penal Code.

Sec. 51.09. Waiver of Rights.

Unless a contrary intent clearly appears elsewhere in this title, any right granted to a child by this title or by the constitution or laws of this state or the United States may be waived in proceedings under this title if:

(1) the waiver is made by the child and the attorney for the child;

(2) the child and the attorney waiving the right are informed of and understand the right and the possible consequences of waiving it;

(3) the waiver is voluntary; and

(4) the waiver is made in writing or in court proceedings that are recorded.

Sec. 51.095. Admissibility of a Statement of a Child.

(a) Notwithstanding Section 51.09, the statement of a child is admissible in evidence in any future proceeding concerning the matter about which the statement was given if:

(1) the statement is made in writing under a circumstance described by Subsection (d) and:

(A) the statement shows that the child has at some time before the making of the statement received from a magistrate a warning that:

(i) the child may remain silent and not make any statement at all and that any statement that the child makes may be used in evidence against the child;

(ii) the child has the right to have an attorney present to advise the child either prior to any questioning or during the questioning;

(iii) if the child is unable to employ an attorney, the child has the right to have an attorney appointed to counsel with the child before or during any interviews with peace officers or attorneys representing the state; and

(iv) the child has the right to terminate the interview at any time;

(B) and:

(i) the statement must be signed in the presence of a magistrate by the child with no law enforcement officer or prosecuting attorney present, except that a magistrate may require a bailiff or a law enforcement officer if a bailiff is not available to be present if the magistrate determines that the presence of the bailiff or law enforcement officer is necessary for the personal safety of the magistrate or other court personnel, provided that the bailiff or law enforcement officer may not carry a weapon in the presence of the child; and

(ii) the magistrate must be fully convinced that the child understands the nature and contents of the statement and that the child is signing the same voluntarily, and if a statement is taken, the magistrate must sign a written statement verifying the foregoing requisites have been met;

(C) the child knowingly, intelligently, and voluntarily waives these rights before and during the making of the statement and signs the statement in the presence of a magistrate; and

(D) the magistrate certifies that the magistrate has examined the child independent of any law enforcement officer or prosecuting attorney, except as required to ensure the personal safety of the magistrate or other court personnel, and has determined that the child understands the nature and contents of the statement and has knowingly, intelligently, and voluntarily waived these rights;

(2) the statement is made orally and the child makes a statement of facts or circumstances that are found to be true and tend to establish the child's guilt, such as the finding of secreted or stolen property, or the instrument with which the child states the offense was committed;

(3) the statement was res gestae of the delinquent conduct or the conduct indicating a need for supervision or of the arrest;

(4) the statement is made:

(A) in open court at the child's adjudication hearing;

(B) before a grand jury considering a petition, under Section 53.045, that the child engaged in delinquent conduct; or

(C) at a preliminary hearing concerning the child held in compliance with this code, other than at a detention hearing under Section 54.01; or

(5) subject to Subsection (f), the statement is made orally under a circumstance described by Subsection (d) and the statement is recorded by an electronic recording device, including a device that records images, and:

(A) before making the statement, the child is given the warning described by Subdivision (1)(A) by a magistrate, the warning is a part of the recording, and the child knowingly, intelligently, and voluntarily waives each right stated in the warning;

(B) the recording device is capable of making an accurate recording, the operator of the device is competent to use the device, the recording is accurate, and the recording has not been altered;

(C) each voice on the recording is identified; and

(D) not later than the 20th day before the date of the proceeding, the attorney representing the child is given a complete and accurate copy of each recording of the child made under this subdivision.

(b) This section and Section 51.09 do not preclude the admission of a statement made by the child if:

(1) the statement does not stem from interrogation of the child under a circumstance described by Subsection (d); or

(2) without regard to whether the statement stems from interrogation of the child under a circumstance described by Subsection (d), the statement is:

(A) voluntary and has a bearing on the credibility of the child as a witness; or

(B) recorded by an electronic recording device, including a device that records images, and is obtained:

(i) in another state in compliance with the laws of that state or this state; or

(ii) by a federal law enforcement officer in this state or another state in compliance with the laws of the United States.

(c) An electronic recording of a child's statement made under Subsection (a)(5) or (b)(2)(B) shall be preserved until all juvenile or criminal matters relating to any conduct referred to in the statement are final, including the exhaustion of all appeals, or barred from prosecution.

(d) Subsections (a)(1) and (a)(5) apply to the statement of a child made:

(1) while the child is in a detention facility or other place of confinement;

(2) while the child is in the custody of an officer; or

(3) during or after the interrogation of the child by an officer if the child is in the possession of the Department of Family and Protective Services and is suspected to have engaged in conduct that violates a penal law of this state.

(e) A juvenile law referee or master may perform the duties imposed on a magistrate under this section without the approval of the juvenile court if the juvenile board of the county in which the statement of the child is made has authorized a referee or master to perform the duties of a magistrate under this section.

(f) A magistrate who provides the warnings required by Subsection (a)(5) for a recorded statement may at the time the warnings are provided request by speaking on the recording that the officer return the child and the recording to the magistrate at the conclusion of the process of questioning. The magistrate may then view the recording with the child or have the child view the recording to enable the magistrate to determine whether the child's statements were given voluntarily. The magistrate's determination of voluntariness shall be reduced to writing and signed and dated by the magistrate. If a magistrate uses the procedure described by this subsection, a child's statement is not admissible unless the magistrate determines that the statement was given voluntarily.

Sec. 51.10. Right to Assistance of Attorney; Compensation.

(a) A child may be represented by an attorney at every stage of proceedings under this title, including:

(1) the detention hearing required by Section 54.01 of this code;

(2) the hearing to consider transfer to criminal court required by Section 54.02 of this code;

(3) the adjudication hearing required by Section 54.03 of this code;

(4) the disposition hearing required by Section 54.04 of this code;

(5) the hearing to modify disposition required by Section 54.05 of this code;

(6) hearings required by Chapter 55 of this code;

(7) habeas corpus proceedings challenging the legality of detention resulting from action under this title; and

(8) proceedings in a court of civil appeals or the Texas Supreme Court reviewing proceedings under this title.

(b) The child's right to representation by an attorney shall not be waived in:

(1) a hearing to consider transfer to criminal court as required by Section 54.02;

(2) an adjudication hearing as required by Section 54.03;

(3) a disposition hearing as required by Section 54.04;

(4) a hearing prior to commitment to the Texas Juvenile Justice Department as a modified disposition in accordance with Section 54.05(f); or

(5) hearings required by Chapter 55.

(c) If the child was not represented by an attorney at the detention hearing required by Section 54.01 of this code and a determination was made to detain the child, the child shall immediately be entitled to representation by an attorney. The court shall order the retention of an attorney according to Subsection (d) or appoint an attorney according to Subsection (f).

(d) The court shall order a child's parent or other person responsible for support of the child to employ an attorney to represent the child, if:

(1) the child is not represented by an attorney;

(2) after giving the appropriate parties an opportunity to be heard, the court determines that the parent or other person responsible for support of the child is financially able to employ an attorney to represent the child; and

(3) the child's right to representation by an attorney:

(A) has not been waived under Section 51.09 of this code; or

(B) may not be waived under Subsection (b) of this section.

(e) The court may enforce orders under Subsection (d) by proceedings under Section 54.07 or by appointing counsel and ordering the parent or other person responsible for support of the child to pay a reasonable attorney's fee set by the court. The order may be enforced under Section 54.07.

(f) The court shall appoint an attorney to represent the interest of a child entitled to representation by an attorney, if:

(1) the child is not represented by an attorney;

(2) the court determines that the child's parent or other person responsible for support of the child is financially unable to employ an attorney to represent the child; and

(3) the child's right to representation by an attorney:

(A) has not been waived under Section 51.09 of this code; or

(B) may not be waived under Subsection (b) of this section.

(g) The juvenile court may appoint an attorney in any case in which it deems representation necessary to protect the interests of the child.

(h) Any attorney representing a child in proceedings under this title is entitled to 10 days to prepare for any adjudication or transfer hearing under this title.

(i) Except as provided in Subsection (d) of this section, an attorney appointed under this section to represent the interests of a child shall be paid from the general fund of the county in which the proceedings were instituted according to the schedule in Article 26.05 of the Texas Code of Criminal Procedure, 1965. For this purpose, a bona fide appeal to a court of civil appeals or proceedings on the merits in the Texas Supreme Court are considered the equivalent of a bona fide appeal to the Texas Court of Criminal Appeals.

(j) The juvenile board of a county may make available to the public the list of attorneys eligible for appointment to represent children in proceedings under this title as provided in the plan adopted under Section 51.102. The list of attorneys must indicate the level of case for which each attorney is eligible for appointment under Section 51.102(b)(2).

(k) Subject to Chapter 61, the juvenile court may order the parent or other person responsible for support of the child to reimburse the county for payments the county made to counsel appointed to represent the child under Subsection (f) or (g). The court may:

(1) order payment for each attorney who has represented the child at any hearing, including a detention hearing, discretionary transfer hearing, adjudication hearing, disposition hearing, or modification of disposition hearing;

(2) include amounts paid to or on behalf of the attorney by the county for preparation time and investigative and expert witness costs; and

(3) require full or partial reimbursement to the county.

(*l*) The court may not order payments under Subsection (k) that exceed the financial ability of the parent or other person responsible for support of the child to meet the payment schedule ordered by the court.

Sec. 51.101. Appointment of Attorney and Continuation of Representation.

(a) If an attorney is appointed under Section 54.01(b-1) or (d) to represent a child at the initial detention hearing and the child is detained, the attorney shall continue to represent the child until the case is terminated, the family retains an attorney, or a new attorney is appointed by the juvenile court. Release of the child from detention does not terminate the attorney's representation.

(b) If there is an initial detention hearing without an attorney and the child is detained, the attorney appointed under Section 51.10(c) shall continue to represent the child until the case is terminated, the family retains an attorney, or a new attorney is appointed by the juvenile court. Release of the child from detention does not terminate the attorney's representation.

(c) The juvenile court shall determine, on the filing of a petition, whether the child's family is indigent if:

(1) the child is released by intake;

(2) the child is released at the initial detention hearing; or

(3) the case was referred to the court without the child in custody.

(d) A juvenile court that makes a finding of indigence under Subsection (c) shall appoint an attorney to represent the child on or before the fifth working day after the date the petition for adjudication or discretionary transfer hearing was served on the child. An attorney appointed under this subsection shall continue to represent the child until the case is terminated, the family retains an attorney, or a new attorney is appointed by the juvenile court.

(e) The juvenile court shall determine whether the child's family is indigent if a motion or petition is filed under Section 54.05 seeking to modify disposition by committing the child to the Texas Juvenile Justice Department or placing the child in a secure correctional facility. A court that makes a finding of indigence shall appoint an attorney to represent the child on or before the fifth working day after the date the petition or motion has been filed. An attorney appointed under this subsection shall continue to represent the child until the court rules on the motion or petition, the family retains an attorney, or a new attorney is appointed.

Sec. 51.102. Appointment of Counsel Plan.

(a) The juvenile board in each county shall adopt a plan that:

(1) specifies the qualifications necessary for an attorney to be included on an appointment list from which attorneys are appointed to represent children in proceedings under this title; and

(2) establishes the procedures for:

(A) including attorneys on the appointment list and removing attorneys from the list; and

(B) appointing attorneys from the appointment list to individual cases.

(b) A plan adopted under Subsection (a) must:

(1) to the extent practicable, comply with the requirements of Article 26.04, Code of Criminal Procedure, except that:

(A) the income and assets of the child's parent or other person responsible for the child's support must be used in determining whether the child is indigent; and

(B) any alternative plan for appointing counsel is established by the juvenile board in the county; and

(2) recognize the differences in qualifications and experience necessary for appointments to cases in which:

(A) the allegation is:

(i) conduct indicating a need for supervision or delinquent conduct, and commitment to the Texas Juvenile Justice Department is not an authorized disposition; or

(ii) delinquent conduct, and commitment to the department without a determinate sentence is an authorized disposition; or

(B) determinate sentence proceedings have been initiated or proceedings for discretionary transfer to criminal court have been initiated.

Sec. 51.11. Guardian Ad Litem.

(a) In this section:

(1) "Dual-system child" means a child who, at any time before the child's 18th birthday, was referred to the juvenile justice system and was involved in the child welfare system by being:

(A) placed in the temporary or permanent managing conservatorship of the Department of Family and Protective Services;

(B) the subject of a family-based safety services case with the Department of Family and Protective Services;

(C) an alleged victim of abuse or neglect in an active case being investigated by the Department of Family and Protective Services child protective investigations division; or

(D) a victim in a case in which the Department of Family and Protective Services investigation concluded that there was a reason to believe that abuse or neglect occurred.

(2) "Dual-status child" means a dual-system child who is involved with both the child welfare and juvenile justice systems at the same time.

(a-1) If a child appears before the juvenile court without a parent or guardian, the court shall appoint a guardian ad litem to protect the interests of the child. The juvenile court need not appoint a guardian ad litem if a parent or guardian appears with the child.

(b) In any case in which it appears to the juvenile court that the child's parent or guardian is incapable or unwilling to make decisions in the best interest of the child with respect to proceedings under this title, the court may appoint a guardian ad litem to protect the interests of the child in the proceedings.

(c) An attorney for a child may also be his guardian ad litem. A law-enforcement officer, probation officer, or other employee of the juvenile court may not be appointed guardian ad litem.

(d) The juvenile court may appoint the guardian ad litem appointed under Chapter 107 for a child in a suit affecting the parent-child relationship filed by the Department of Family and Protective Services to serve as the guardian ad litem for the child in a proceeding held under this title.

(e) A non-attorney guardian ad litem in a case involving a dual-system child may not:

(1) investigate any charges involving a dual-status child that are pending with the juvenile court; or

(2) offer testimony concerning the guilt or innocence of a dual-status child.

Sec. 51.115. Attendance at Hearing: Parent or Other Guardian.

(a) Each parent of a child, each managing and possessory conservator of a child, each court-appointed custodian of a child, and a guardian of the person of the child shall attend each hearing affecting the child held under:

(1) Section 54.02 (waiver of jurisdiction and discretionary transfer to criminal court);

(2) Section 54.03 (adjudication hearing);

(3) Section 54.04 (disposition hearing);

(4) Section 54.05 (hearing to modify disposition); and

(5) Section 54.11 (release or transfer hearing).

(b) Subsection (a) does not apply to:

(1) a person for whom, for good cause shown, the court waives attendance;

(2) a person who is not a resident of this state; or

(3) a parent of a child for whom a managing conservator has been appointed and the parent is not a conservator of the child.

(c) A person required under this section to attend a hearing is entitled to reasonable written or oral notice that includes a statement of the place, date, and time of the hearing and that the attendance of the person is required. The notice may be included with or attached to any other notice required by this chapter to be given the person. Separate notice is not required for a disposition hearing that convenes on the adjournment of an adjudication hearing. If a person required under this section fails to attend a hearing, the juvenile court may proceed with the hearing.

(d) A person who is required by Subsection (a) to attend a hearing, who receives the notice of the hearing, and who fails to attend the hearing may be punished by the court for contempt by a fine of not less than $100 and not more than $1,000. In addition to or in lieu of contempt, the court may order the person to receive counseling or to attend an educational course on the duties and responsibilities of parents and skills and techniques in raising children.

Sec. 51.116. Right to Reemployment.

(a) An employer may not terminate the employment of a permanent employee because the employee is required under Section 51.115 to attend a hearing.

(b) An employee whose employment is terminated in violation of this section is entitled to return to the same employment that the employee held when notified of the hearing if the employee, as soon as practical after the hearing, gives the employer actual notice that the employee intends to return.

(c) A person who is injured because of a violation of this section is entitled to reinstatement to the person's former position and to damages, but the damages may not exceed an amount equal to six months' compensation at the rate at which the person was compensated when required to attend the hearing.

(d) The injured person is also entitled to reasonable attorney's fees in an amount approved by the court.

(e) It is a defense to an action brought under this section that the employer's circumstances changed while the employee attended the hearing so that reemployment was impossible or unreasonable. To establish a defense under this subsection, an employer must prove that the termination of employment was because of circumstances other than the employee's attendance at the hearing.

Sec. 51.12. Place and Conditions of Detention.

(a) Except as provided by Subsection (h), a child may be detained only in a:

(1) juvenile processing office in compliance with Section 52.025;

(2) place of nonsecure custody in compliance with Article 45.058, Code of Criminal Procedure;

(3) certified juvenile detention facility that complies with the requirements of Subsection (f);

(4) secure detention facility as provided by Subsection (j);

(5) county jail or other facility as provided by Subsection (*l*); or

(6) nonsecure correctional facility as provided by Subsection (j-1).

(b) The proper authorities in each county shall provide a suitable place of detention for children who are parties to proceedings under this title, but the juvenile board shall control the conditions and terms of detention and detention supervision and shall permit visitation with the child at all reasonable times.

(b-1) A pre-adjudication secure detention facility may be operated only by:

(1) a governmental unit in this state as defined by Section 101.001, Civil Practice and Remedies Code; or

(2) a private entity under a contract with a governmental unit in this state.

(c) In each county, each judge of the juvenile court and a majority of the members of the juvenile board shall personally inspect all public or private juvenile pre-adjudication secure detention facilities that are located in the county at least annually and shall certify in writing to the authorities responsible for operating and giving financial support to the facilities and to the Texas Juvenile Justice Department that the facilities are suitable or unsuitable for the detention of children. In determining whether a facility is suitable or unsuitable for the detention of children, the juvenile court judges and juvenile board members shall consider:

(1) current monitoring and inspection reports and any noncompliance citation reports issued by the department, including the report provided under Subsection (c-1), and the status of any required corrective actions;

(2) current governmental inspector certification regarding the facility's compliance with local fire codes;

(3) current building inspector certification regarding the facility's compliance with local building codes;

(4) for the 12-month period preceding the inspection, the total number of allegations of abuse, neglect, or exploitation reported by the facility and a summary of the findings of any investigations of abuse, neglect, or exploitation conducted by the facility, a local law enforcement agency, and the department;

(5) the availability of health and mental health services provided to facility residents;

(6) the availability of educational services provided to facility residents; and

(7) the overall physical appearance of the facility, including the facility's security, maintenance, cleanliness, and environment.

(c-1) The Texas Juvenile Justice Department shall annually inspect each public or private juvenile pre-adjudication secure detention facility. The department shall provide a report to each juvenile court judge presiding in the same county as an inspected facility indicating whether the facility is suitable or unsuitable for the detention of children in accordance with:

(1) the requirements of Subsections (a), (f), and (g); and

(2) minimum professional standards for the detention of children in pre-adjudication secure confinement promulgated by the department or, at the election of the juvenile board of the county in which the facility is located, the current standards promulgated by the American Correctional Association.

(d) Except as provided by Subsections (j) and (*l*), a child may not be placed in a facility that has not been certified under Subsection (c) as suitable for the detention of children and registered under Subsection (i). Except as provided by Subsections (j) and (*l*), a child detained in a facility that has not been certified under Subsection (c) as suitable for the detention of children or that has not been registered under Subsection (i) shall be entitled to immediate release from custody in that facility.

(e) If there is no certified place of detention in the county in which the petition is filed, the designated place of detention may be in another county.

(f) A child detained in a building that contains a jail, lockup, or other place of secure confinement, including an alcohol or other drug treatment facility, shall be separated by sight and sound from adults detained in the same building. Children and adults are separated by sight and sound only if they are unable to see each other and conversation between them is not possible. The separation must extend to all areas of the facility, including sally ports and passageways, and those areas used for admission, counseling, sleeping, toileting, showering, dining, recreational, educational, or vocational activities, and health care. The separation may be accomplished through architectural design. A person who has been transferred for prosecution in criminal court under Section 54.02 and is under 17 years of age is considered a child for the purposes of this subsection.

(g) Except for a child detained in a juvenile processing office, a place of nonsecure custody, a secure detention facility as provided by Subsection (j), or a facility as provided by Subsection (*l*), a child detained in a building that contains a jail or lockup may not have any contact with:

(1) part-time or full-time security staff, including management, who have contact with adults detained in the same building; or

(2) direct-care staff who have contact with adults detained in the same building.

(h) This section does not apply to a person:

(1) who has been transferred to criminal court for prosecution under Section 54.02 and is at least 17 years of age; or

(2) who is at least 17 years of age and who has been taken into custody after having:

(A) escaped from a juvenile facility operated by or under contract with the Texas Juvenile Justice Department; or

(B) violated a condition of release under supervision of the department.

(i) Except for a facility as provided by Subsection (l), a governmental unit or private entity that operates or contracts for the operation of a juvenile pre-adjudication secure detention facility under Subsection (b-1) in this state shall:

(1) register the facility annually with the Texas Juvenile Justice Department; and

(2) adhere to all applicable minimum standards for the facility.

(j) After being taken into custody, a child may be detained in a secure detention facility until the child is released under Section 53.01, 53.012, or 53.02 or until a detention hearing is held under Section 54.01(a), regardless of whether the facility has been certified under Subsection (c), if:

(1) a certified juvenile detention facility is not available in the county in which the child is taken into custody;

(2) the detention facility complies with:

(A) the short-term detention standards adopted by the Texas Juvenile Justice Department; and

(B) the requirements of Subsection (f); and

(3) the detention facility has been designated by the county juvenile board for the county in which the facility is located.

(j-1) After being taken into custody, a child may be detained in a nonsecure correctional facility until the child is released under Section 53.01, 53.012, or 53.02 or until a detention hearing is held under Section 54.01(a), if:

(1) the nonsecure correctional facility has been appropriately registered and certified;

(2) a certified secure detention facility is not available in the county in which the child is taken into custody;

(3) the nonsecure correctional facility complies with the short-term detention standards adopted by the Texas Juvenile Justice Department; and

(4) the nonsecure correctional facility has been designated by the county juvenile board for the county in which the facility is located.

(k) If a child who is detained under Subsection (j) or (*l*) is not released from detention at the conclusion of the detention hearing for a reason stated in Section 54.01(e), the child may be detained after the hearing only in a certified juvenile detention facility.

(*l*) A child who is taken into custody and required to be detained under Section 53.02(f) may be detained in a county jail or other facility until the child is released under Section 53.02(f) or until a detention hearing is held as required by Section 54.01(p), regardless of whether the facility complies with the requirements of this section, if:

(1) a certified juvenile detention facility or a secure detention facility described by Subsection (j) is not available in the county in which the child is taken into custody or in an adjacent county;

(2) the facility has been designated by the county juvenile board for the county in which the facility is located;

(3) the child is separated by sight and sound from adults detained in the same facility through architectural design or time-phasing;

(4) the child does not have any contact with management or direct-care staff that has contact with adults detained in the same facility on the same work shift;

(5) the county in which the child is taken into custody is not located in a metropolitan statistical area as designated by the United States Bureau of the Census; and

(6) each judge of the juvenile court and a majority of the members of the juvenile board of the county in which the child is taken into custody have personally inspected the facility at least annually and have certified in writing to the Texas Juvenile Justice Department that the facility complies with the requirements of Subdivisions (3) and (4).

(m) The Texas Juvenile Justice Department may deny, suspend, or revoke the registration of any facility required to register under Subsection (i) if the facility fails to:

(1) adhere to all applicable minimum standards for the facility; or

(2) timely correct any notice of noncompliance with minimum standards.

Sec. 51.125. Post-Adjudication Correctional Facilities.

(a) A post-adjudication secure correctional facility for juvenile offenders may be operated only by:

Texas Family Code

(1) a governmental unit in this state as defined by Section 101.001, Civil Practice and Remedies Code; or

(2) a private entity under a contract with a governmental unit in this state.

(b) In each county, each judge of the juvenile court and a majority of the members of the juvenile board shall personally inspect all public or private juvenile post-adjudication secure correctional facilities that are not operated by the Texas Juvenile Justice Department and that are located in the county at least annually and shall certify in writing to the authorities responsible for operating and giving financial support to the facilities and to the department that the facility or facilities are suitable or unsuitable for the confinement of children. In determining whether a facility is suitable or unsuitable for the confinement of children, the juvenile court judges and juvenile board members shall consider:

(1) current monitoring and inspection reports and any noncompliance citation reports issued by the department, including the report provided under Subsection (c), and the status of any required corrective actions; and

(2) the other factors described under Sections 51.12(c)(2)-(7).

(c) The Texas Juvenile Justice Department shall annually inspect each public or private juvenile post-adjudication secure correctional facility that is not operated by the department. The department shall provide a report to each juvenile court judge presiding in the same county as an inspected facility indicating whether the facility is suitable or unsuitable for the confinement of children in accordance with minimum professional standards for the confinement of children in post-adjudication secure confinement promulgated by the department or, at the election of the juvenile board of the county in which the facility is located, the current standards promulgated by the American Correctional Association.

(d) A governmental unit or private entity that operates or contracts for the operation of a juvenile post-adjudication secure correctional facility in this state under Subsection (a), except for a facility operated by or under contract with the Texas Juvenile Justice Department, shall:

(1) register the facility annually with the department; and

(2) adhere to all applicable minimum standards for the facility.

(e) The Texas Juvenile Justice Department may deny, suspend, or revoke the registration of any facility required to register under Subsection (d) if the facility fails to:

(1) adhere to all applicable minimum standards for the facility; or

(2) timely correct any notice of noncompliance with minimum standards.

Sec. 51.126. Nonsecure Correctional Facilities.

(a) A nonsecure correctional facility for juvenile offenders may be operated only by:

(1) a governmental unit, as defined by Section 101.001, Civil Practice and Remedies Code; or

(2) a private entity under a contract with a governmental unit in this state.

(b) In each county, each judge of the juvenile court and a majority of the members of the juvenile board shall personally inspect, at least annually, all nonsecure correctional facilities that are located in the county and shall certify in writing to the authorities responsible for operating and giving financial support to the facilities and to the Texas Juvenile Justice Department that the facility or facilities are suitable or unsuitable for the confinement of children. In determining whether a facility is suitable or unsuitable for the confinement of children, the juvenile court judges and juvenile board members shall consider:

(1) current monitoring and inspection reports and any noncompliance citation reports issued by the Texas Juvenile Justice Department, including the report provided under Subsection (c), and the status of any required corrective actions; and

(2) the other factors described under Sections 51.12(c)(2)-(7).

(c) The Texas Juvenile Justice Department shall annually inspect each nonsecure correctional facility. The Texas Juvenile Justice Department shall provide a report to each juvenile court judge presiding in the same county as an inspected facility indicating whether the facility is suitable or unsuitable for the confinement of children in accordance with minimum professional standards for the confinement of children in nonsecure confinement promulgated by the Texas Juvenile Justice Department or, at the election of the juvenile board of the county in which the facility is located, the current standards promulgated by the American Correctional Association.

(d) A governmental unit or private entity that operates or contracts for the operation of a juvenile nonsecure correctional facility in this state under Subsection (a), except for a facility operated by or under contract with the Texas Juvenile Justice Department, shall:

(1) register the facility annually with the Texas Juvenile Justice Department; and

(2) adhere to all applicable minimum standards for the facility.

(e) The Texas Juvenile Justice Department may deny, suspend, or revoke the registration of any facility required to register under Subsection (d) if the facility fails to:

(1) adhere to all applicable minimum standards for the facility; or

(2) timely correct any notice of noncompliance with minimum standards.

(f) [Expired pursuant to Acts 2011, 82nd Leg., ch. 85 (S.B. 653), § 2.001, effective December 1, 2011.]

Sec. 51.13. Effect of Adjudication or Disposition.

(a) Except as provided by Subsections (d) and (e), an order of adjudication or disposition in a proceeding under this title is not a conviction of crime. Except as provided by Chapter 841, Health and Safety Code, an order of adjudication or disposition does not impose any civil disability ordinarily resulting from a conviction or operate to disqualify the child in any civil service application or appointment.

(b) The adjudication or disposition of a child or evidence adduced in a hearing under this title may be used only in subsequent:

(1) proceedings under this title in which the child is a party;

(2) sentencing proceedings in criminal court against the child to the extent permitted by the Texas Code of Criminal Procedure, 1965; or

(3) civil commitment proceedings under Chapter 841, Health and Safety Code.

(c) A child may not be committed or transferred to a penal institution or other facility used primarily for the execution of sentences of persons convicted of crime, except:

(1) for temporary detention in a jail or lockup pending juvenile court hearing or disposition under conditions meeting the requirements of Section 51.12;

(2) after transfer for prosecution in criminal court under Section 54.02, unless the juvenile court orders the detention of the child in a certified juvenile detention facility under Section 54.02(h);

(3) after transfer from the Texas Juvenile Justice Department under Section 245.151(c), Human Resources Code; or

(4) after transfer from a post-adjudication secure correctional facility, as that term is defined by Section 54.04011.

(d) An adjudication under Section 54.03 that a child engaged in conduct that occurred on or after January 1, 1996, and that constitutes a felony offense resulting in commitment to the Texas Juvenile Justice Department under Section 54.04(d)(2), (d)(3), or (m) or 54.05(f) or commitment to a post-adjudication secure correctional facility under Section 54.04011 for conduct that occurred on or after December 1, 2013, is a final felony conviction only for the purposes of Sections 12.42(a), (b), and (c)(1) or Section 12.425, Penal Code.

(e) A finding that a child engaged in conduct indicating a need for supervision as described by Section 51.03(b)(6) is a conviction only for the purposes of Sections 43.261(c) and (d), Penal Code.

Sec. 51.14. Files and Records [Repealed].

Repealed by Acts 1995, 74th Leg., ch. 262 (H.B. 327), § 100(a), effective January 1, 1996.

Sec. 51.15. Fingerprints and Photographs [Repealed].

Repealed by Acts 1995, 74th Leg., ch. 262 (H.B. 327), § 100(a), effective January 1, 1996.

Sec. 51.151. Polygraph Examination.

If a child is taken into custody under Section 52.01 of this code, a person may not administer a polygraph examination to the child without the consent of the child's attorney or the juvenile court unless the child is transferred to criminal court for prosecution under Section 54.02 of this code.

Sec. 51.16. Sealing of Files and Records [Repealed].

Repealed by Acts 1995, 74th Leg., ch. 262 (H.B. 327), § 100(a), effective January 1, 1996 and by Acts 1997 75th Leg., ch. 165 (S.B. 898), § 10.05(b), effective September 1, 1997.

Sec. 51.17. Procedure and Evidence.

(a) Except as provided by Section 56.01(b-1) and except for the burden of proof to be borne by the state in adjudicating a child to be delinquent or in need of supervision under Section 54.03(f) or otherwise when in conflict with a provision of this title, the Texas Rules of Civil Procedure govern proceedings under this title.

(b) Discovery in a proceeding under this title is governed by the Code of Criminal Procedure and by case decisions in criminal cases.

(c) Except as otherwise provided by this title, the Texas Rules of Evidence applicable to criminal cases and Articles 33.03 and 37.07 and Chapter 38,

Code of Criminal Procedure, apply in a judicial proceeding under this title.

(d) When on the motion for appointment of an interpreter by a party or on the motion of the juvenile court, in any proceeding under this title, the court determines that the child, the child's parent or guardian, or a witness does not understand and speak English, an interpreter must be sworn to interpret for the person as provided by Article 38.30, Code of Criminal Procedure.

(e) In any proceeding under this title, if a party notifies the court that the child, the child's parent or guardian, or a witness is deaf, the court shall appoint a qualified interpreter to interpret the proceedings in any language, including sign language, that the deaf person can understand, as provided by Article 38.31, Code of Criminal Procedure.

(f) Any requirement under this title that a document contain a person's signature, including the signature of a judge or a clerk of the court, is satisfied if the document contains the signature of the person as captured on an electronic device or as a digital signature. Article 2.26, Code of Criminal Procedure, applies in a proceeding held under this title.

(g) Articles 21.07, 26.07, 26.08, 26.09, and 26.10, Code of Criminal Procedure, relating to the name of an adult defendant in a criminal case, apply to a child in a proceeding held under this title.

(h) Articles 58.001, 58.101, 58.102, 58.103, 58.104, 58.105, and 58.106, Code of Criminal Procedure, relating to the use of a pseudonym by a victim in a criminal case, apply in a proceeding held under this title.

(i) Except as provided by Section 56.03(f), the state is not required to pay any cost or fee otherwise imposed for court proceedings in either the trial or appellate courts.

Sec. 51.18. Election Between Juvenile Court and Alternate Juvenile Court.

(a) This section applies only to a child who has a right to a trial before a juvenile court the judge of which is not an attorney licensed in this state.

(b) On any matter that may lead to an order appealable under Section 56.01 of this code, a child may be tried before either the juvenile court or the alternate juvenile court.

(c) The child may elect to be tried before the alternate juvenile court only if the child files a written notice with that court not later than 10 days before the date of the trial. After the notice is filed, the child may be tried only in the alternate juvenile court. If the child does not file a notice as provided by this subsection, the child may be tried only in the juvenile court.

(d) If the child is tried before the juvenile court, the child is not entitled to a trial de novo before the alternate juvenile court.

(e) The child may appeal any order of the juvenile court or alternate juvenile court only as provided by Section 56.01 of this code.

Sec. 51.19. Limitation Periods.

(a) The limitation periods and the procedures for applying the limitation periods under Chapter 12, Code of Criminal Procedure, and other statutory law apply to proceedings under this title.

(b) For purposes of computing a limitation period, a petition filed in juvenile court for a transfer or an adjudication hearing is equivalent to an indictment or information and is treated as presented when the petition is filed in the proper court.

(c) The limitation period is two years for an offense or conduct that is not given a specific limitation period under Chapter 12, Code of Criminal Procedure, or other statutory law.

Sec. 51.20. Physical or Mental Examination.

(a) At any stage of the proceedings under this title, including when a child is initially detained in a pre-adjudication secure detention facility or a post-adjudication secure correctional facility, the juvenile court may, at its discretion or at the request of the child's parent or guardian, order a child who is referred to the juvenile court or who is alleged by a petition or found to have engaged in delinquent conduct or conduct indicating a need for supervision to be examined by a disinterested expert, including a physician, psychiatrist, or psychologist, qualified by education and clinical training in mental health or mental retardation and experienced in forensic evaluation, to determine whether the child has a mental illness as defined by Section 571.003, Health and Safety Code, is a person with mental retardation as defined by Section 591.003, Health and Safety Code, or suffers from chemical dependency as defined by Section 464.001, Health and Safety Code. If the examination is to include a determination of the child's fitness to proceed, an expert may be appointed to conduct the examination only if the expert is qualified under Subchapter B, Chapter 46B, Code of Criminal Procedure, to examine a defendant in a criminal case, and the examination and the report resulting from an examination under this subsection must comply with the requirements under Subchapter B, Chapter 46B, Code of Criminal Procedure, for the examination and resulting report of a defendant in a criminal case.

(b) If, after conducting an examination of a child ordered under Subsection (a) and reviewing any other relevant information, there is reason to believe that the child has a mental illness or mental retardation or suffers from chemical dependency, the probation department shall refer the child to the local mental health or mental retardation authority or to another appropriate and legally authorized agency or provider for evaluation and services, unless the prosecuting attorney has filed a petition under Section 53.04.

(c) If, while a child is under deferred prosecution supervision or court-ordered probation, a qualified professional determines that the child has a mental illness or mental retardation or suffers from chemical dependency and the child is not currently receiving treatment services for the mental illness, mental retardation, or chemical dependency, the probation department shall refer the child to the local mental health or mental retardation authority or to another appropriate and legally authorized agency or provider for evaluation and services.

(d) A probation department shall report each referral of a child to a local mental health or mental retardation authority or another agency or provider made under Subsection (b) or (c) to the Texas Juvenile Justice Department in a format specified by the department.

(e) At any stage of the proceedings under this title, the juvenile court may order a child who has been referred to the juvenile court or who is alleged by the petition or found to have engaged in delinquent conduct or conduct indicating a need for supervision to be subjected to a physical examination by a licensed physician.

Sec. 51.21. Mental Health Screening and Referral.

(a) A probation department that administers the mental health screening instrument or clinical assessment required by Section 221.003, Human Resources Code, shall refer the child to the local mental health authority for assessment and evaluation if:

(1) the child's scores on the screening instrument or clinical assessment indicate a need for further mental health assessment and evaluation; and

(2) the department and child do not have access to an internal, contract, or private mental health professional.

(b) A probation department shall report each referral of a child to a local mental health authority made under Subsection (a) to the Texas Juvenile Justice Department in a format specified by the Texas Juvenile Justice Department.

CHAPTER 52 PROCEEDINGS BEFORE AND INCLUDING REFERRAL TO COURT

Sec. 52.01. Taking into Custody; Issuance of Warning Notice.

(a) A child may be taken into custody:

(1) pursuant to an order of the juvenile court under the provisions of this subtitle;

(2) pursuant to the laws of arrest;

(3) by a law-enforcement officer, including a school district peace officer commissioned under Section 37.081, Education Code, if there is probable cause to believe that the child has engaged in:

(A) conduct that violates a penal law of this state or a penal ordinance of any political subdivision of this state;

(B) delinquent conduct or conduct indicating a need for supervision; or

(C) conduct that violates a condition of probation imposed by the juvenile court;

(4) by a probation officer if there is probable cause to believe that the child has violated a condition of probation imposed by the juvenile court;

(5) pursuant to a directive to apprehend issued as provided by Section 52.015; or

(6) by a probation officer if there is probable cause to believe that the child has violated a condition of release imposed by the juvenile court or referee under Section 54.01.

(b) The taking of a child into custody is not an arrest except for the purpose of determining the validity of taking him into custody or the validity of a search under the laws and constitution of this state or of the United States.

(c) A law-enforcement officer authorized to take a child into custody under Subdivisions (2) and (3) of Subsection (a) of this section may issue a warning notice to the child in lieu of taking the child into custody if:

(1) guidelines for warning disposition have been issued by the law-enforcement agency in which the officer works;

(2) the guidelines have been approved by the juvenile board of the county in which the disposition is made;

(3) the disposition is authorized by the guidelines;

(4) the warning notice identifies the child and describes the child's alleged conduct;

(5) a copy of the warning notice is sent to the child's parent, guardian, or custodian as soon as practicable after disposition; and

Texas Family Code

(6) a copy of the warning notice is filed with the law-enforcement agency and the office or official designated by the juvenile board.

(d) A warning notice filed with the office or official designated by the juvenile board may be used as the basis of further action if necessary.

(e) A law-enforcement officer who has probable cause to believe that a child is in violation of the compulsory school attendance law under Section 25.085, Education Code, may take the child into custody for the purpose of returning the child to the school campus of the child to ensure the child's compliance with compulsory school attendance requirements.

Sec. 52.011. Duty of Law Enforcement Officer to Notify Probate Court.

(a) In this section, "ward" has the meaning assigned by Section 22.033, Estates Code.

(b) As soon as practicable, but not later than the first working day after the date a law enforcement officer takes a child who is a ward into custody under Section 52.01(a)(2) or (3), the law enforcement officer or other person having custody of the child shall notify the court with jurisdiction over the child's guardianship of the child's detention or arrest.

Sec. 52.015. Directive to Apprehend.

(a) On the request of a law-enforcement or probation officer, a juvenile court may issue a directive to apprehend a child if the court finds there is probable cause to take the child into custody under the provisions of this title.

(b) On the issuance of a directive to apprehend, any law-enforcement or probation officer shall take the child into custody.

(c) An order under this section is not subject to appeal.

Sec. 52.0151. Bench Warrant; Attachment of Witness in Custody.

(a) If a witness is in a placement in the custody of the Texas Juvenile Justice Department, a juvenile secure detention facility, or a juvenile secure correctional facility, the court may issue a bench warrant or direct that an attachment issue to require a peace officer or probation officer to secure custody of the person at the placement and produce the person in court. Once the person is no longer needed as a witness or the period prescribed by Subsection (c) has expired without extension, the court shall order the peace officer or probation officer to return the person to the placement from which the person was released.

(b) The court may order that the person who is the witness be detained in a certified juvenile detention facility if the person is younger than 17 years of age. If the person is at least 17 years of age, the court may order that the person be detained without bond in an appropriate county facility for the detention of adults accused of criminal offenses.

(c) A witness held in custody under this section may be placed in a certified juvenile detention facility for a period not to exceed 30 days. The length of placement may be extended in 30-day increments by the court that issued the original bench warrant. If the placement is not extended, the period under this section expires and the witness may be returned as provided by Subsection (a).

Sec. 52.02. Release or Delivery to Court.

(a) Except as provided by Subsection (c), a person taking a child into custody, without unnecessary delay and without first taking the child to any place other than a juvenile processing office designated under Section 52.025, shall do one of the following:

(1) release the child to a parent, guardian, custodian of the child, or other responsible adult upon that person's promise to bring the child before the juvenile court as requested by the court;

(2) bring the child before the office or official designated by the juvenile board if there is probable cause to believe that the child engaged in delinquent conduct, conduct indicating a need for supervision, or conduct that violates a condition of probation imposed by the juvenile court;

(3) bring the child to a detention facility designated by the juvenile board;

(4) bring the child to a secure detention facility as provided by Section 51.12(j);

(5) bring the child to a medical facility if the child is believed to suffer from a serious physical condition or illness that requires prompt treatment;

(6) dispose of the case under Section 52.03; or

(7) if school is in session and the child is a student, bring the child to the school campus to which the child is assigned if the principal, the principal's designee, or a peace officer assigned to the campus agrees to assume responsibility for the child for the remainder of the school day.

(b) A person taking a child into custody shall promptly give notice of the person's action and a statement of the reason for taking the child into custody, to:

(1) the child's parent, guardian, or custodian; and

Texas Family Code

(2) the office or official designated by the juvenile board.

(c) A person who takes a child into custody and who has reasonable grounds to believe that the child has been operating a motor vehicle in a public place while having any detectable amount of alcohol in the child's system may, before complying with Subsection (a):

(1) take the child to a place to obtain a specimen of the child's breath or blood as provided by Chapter 724, Transportation Code; and

(2) perform intoxilyzer processing and videotaping of the child in an adult processing office of a law enforcement agency.

(d) Notwithstanding Section 51.09(a), a child taken into custody as provided by Subsection (c) may submit to the taking of a breath specimen or refuse to submit to the taking of a breath specimen without the concurrence of an attorney, but only if the request made of the child to give the specimen and the child's response to that request is videotaped. A videotape made under this subsection must be maintained until the disposition of any proceeding against the child relating to the arrest is final and be made available to an attorney representing the child during that period.

Sec. 52.025. Designation of Juvenile Processing Office.

(a) The juvenile board may designate an office or a room, which may be located in a police facility or sheriff's offices, as the juvenile processing office for the temporary detention of a child taken into custody under Section 52.01. The office may not be a cell or holding facility used for detentions other than detentions under this section. The juvenile board by written order may prescribe the conditions of the designation and limit the activities that may occur in the office during the temporary detention.

(b) A child may be detained in a juvenile processing office only for:

(1) the return of the child to the custody of a person under Section 52.02(a)(1);

(2) the completion of essential forms and records required by the juvenile court or this title;

(3) the photographing and fingerprinting of the child if otherwise authorized at the time of temporary detention by this title;

(4) the issuance of warnings to the child as required or permitted by this title; or

(5) the receipt of a statement by the child under Section 51.095(a)(1), (2), (3), or (5).

(c) A child may not be left unattended in a juvenile processing office and is entitled to be accompanied by the child's parent, guardian, or other custodian or by the child's attorney.

(d) A child may not be detained in a juvenile processing office for longer than six hours.

Sec. 52.026. Responsibility for Transporting Juvenile Offenders.

(a) It shall be the duty of the law enforcement officer who has taken a child into custody to transport the child to the appropriate detention facility or to the school campus to which the child is assigned as provided by Section 52.02(a)(7) if the child is not released to the parent, guardian, or custodian of the child.

(b) If the juvenile detention facility is located outside the county in which the child is taken into custody, it shall be the duty of the law enforcement officer who has taken the child into custody or, if authorized by the commissioners court of the county, the sheriff of that county to transport the child to the appropriate juvenile detention facility unless the child is:

(1) detained in a secure detention facility under Section 51.12(j); or

(2) released to the parent, guardian, or custodian of the child.

(c) On adoption of an order by the juvenile board and approval of the juvenile board's order by record vote of the commissioners court, it shall be the duty of the sheriff of the county in which the child is taken into custody to transport the child to and from all scheduled juvenile court proceedings and appearances and other activities ordered by the juvenile court.

Sec. 52.027. Children Taken into Custody for Traffic Offenses, Other Fineable Only Offenses, or As a Status Offender [Repealed].

Repealed by Acts 2003, 78th Leg., ch. 283 (H.B. 2319), § 61(1), effective September 1, 2003 and by Acts 2003, 78th Leg., ch. 1276 (H.B. 3507), § 7.001(a), effective September 1, 2003.

Sec. 52.028. Children Taken into Custody for Violation of Juvenile Curfew Ordinance or Order [Repealed].

Repealed by Acts 2001, 77th Leg., ch. 1514 (S.B. 1432), § 19(b), effective September 1, 2001.

Sec. 52.03. Disposition Without Referral to Court.

(a) A law-enforcement officer authorized by this title to take a child into custody may dispose of the case of a child taken into custody or accused of a Class C misdemeanor, other than a traffic offense, without referral to juvenile court or charging a child in a court of competent criminal jurisdiction, if:

(1) guidelines for such disposition have been adopted by the juvenile board of the county in which the disposition is made as required by Section 52.032;

(2) the disposition is authorized by the guidelines; and

(3) the officer makes a written report of the officer's disposition to the law-enforcement agency, identifying the child and specifying the grounds for believing that the taking into custody or accusation of criminal conduct was authorized.

(b) No disposition authorized by this section may involve:

(1) keeping the child in law-enforcement custody; or

(2) requiring periodic reporting of the child to a law-enforcement officer, law-enforcement agency, or other agency.

(c) A disposition authorized by this section may involve:

(1) referral of the child to an agency other than the juvenile court;

(2) a brief conference with the child and his parent, guardian, or custodian; or

(3) referral of the child and the child's parent, guardian, or custodian for services under Section 264.302.

(d) Statistics indicating the number and kind of dispositions made by a law-enforcement agency under the authority of this section shall be reported at least annually to the office or official designated by the juvenile board, as ordered by the board.

Sec. 52.031. First Offender Program.

(a) A juvenile board may establish a first offender program under this section for the referral and disposition of children taken into custody, or accused prior to the filing of a criminal charge, of:

(1) conduct indicating a need for supervision;

(2) a Class C misdemeanor, other than a traffic offense; or

(3) delinquent conduct other than conduct that constitutes:

(A) a felony of the first, second, or third degree, an aggravated controlled substance felony, or a capital felony; or

(B) a state jail felony or misdemeanor involving violence to a person or the use or possession of a firearm, location-restricted knife, or club, as those terms are defined by Section 46.01, Penal Code, or a prohibited weapon, as described by Section 46.05, Penal Code.

(a-1) A child accused of a Class C misdemeanor, other than a traffic offense, may be referred to a first offender program established under this section prior to the filing of a complaint with a criminal court.

(b) Each juvenile board in the county in which a first offender program is established shall designate one or more law enforcement officers and agencies, which may be law enforcement agencies, to process a child under the first offender program.

(c) The disposition of a child under the first offender program may not take place until guidelines for the disposition have been adopted by the juvenile board of the county in which the disposition is made as required by Section 52.032.

(d) **[2 Versions: As amended by Acts 2013, 83rd Leg., ch. 1407]** A law enforcement officer taking a child into custody or accusing a child of an offense described in Subsection (a)(2) may refer the child to the law enforcement officer or agency designated under Subsection (b) for disposition under the first offender program and not refer the child to juvenile court or a court of competent criminal jurisdiction only if:

(1) the child has not previously been adjudicated as having engaged in delinquent conduct;

(2) the referral complies with guidelines for disposition under Subsection (c); and

(3) the officer reports in writing the referral to the agency, identifying the child and specifying the grounds for taking the child into custody or accusing a child of an offense described in Subsection (a)(2).

(d) **[2 Versions: As amended by Acts 2013, 83rd Leg., ch. 1409]** A law enforcement officer taking a child into custody for conduct described by Subsection (a) or before issuing a citation to a child for an offense described by Subsection (a-1) may refer the child to the law enforcement officer or agency designated under Subsection (b) for disposition under the first offender program and not refer the child to juvenile court for the conduct or file a complaint with a criminal court for the offense only if:

(1) the child has not previously been adjudicated as having engaged in delinquent conduct;

(2) the referral complies with guidelines for disposition under Subsection (c); and

(3) the officer reports in writing the referral to the agency, identifying the child and specifying the grounds for taking the child into custody or for accusing the child of an offense.

(e) A child referred for disposition under the first offender program may not be detained in law enforcement custody.

(f) **[2 Versions: As amended by Acts 2013, 83rd Leg., ch. 1407]** The parent, guardian, or other custodian of the child must receive notice that the child has been referred for disposition under the first offender program. The notice must:

(1) state the grounds for taking the child into custody or accusing a child of an offense described in Subsection (a)(2);

(2) identify the law enforcement officer or agency to which the child was referred;

(3) briefly describe the nature of the program; and

(4) state that the child's failure to complete the program will result in the child being referred to the juvenile court or a court of competent criminal jurisdiction.

(f) **[2 Versions: As amended by Acts 2013, 83rd Leg., ch. 1409]** The parent, guardian, or other custodian of the child must receive notice that the child has been referred for disposition under the first offender program. The notice must:

(1) state the grounds for taking the child into custody for conduct described by Subsection (a), or for accusing the child of an offense described by Subsection (a-1);

(2) identify the law enforcement officer or agency to which the child was referred;

(3) briefly describe the nature of the program; and

(4) state that the child's failure to complete the program will result in the child being referred to the juvenile court for the conduct or a complaint being filed with a criminal court for the offense.

(g) The child and the parent, guardian, or other custodian of the child must consent to participation by the child in the first offender program.

(h) Disposition under a first offender program may include:

(1) voluntary restitution by the child or the parent, guardian, or other custodian of the child to the victim of the conduct of the child;

(2) voluntary community service restitution by the child;

(3) educational, vocational training, counseling, or other rehabilitative services; and

(4) periodic reporting by the child to the law enforcement officer or agency to which the child has been referred.

(i) **[2 Versions: As amended by Acts 2013, 83rd Leg., ch. 1407]** The case of a child who successfully completes the first offender program is closed and may not be referred to juvenile court or a court of competent criminal jurisdiction, unless the child is taken into custody under circumstances described by Subsection (j)(3).

(i) **[2 Versions: As amended by Acts 2013, 83rd Leg., ch. 1409]** The case of a child who successfully completes the first offender program is closed and may not be referred to juvenile court or filed with a criminal court, unless the child is taken into custody under circumstances described by Subsection (j)(3).

(j) **[2 Versions: As amended by Acts 2013, 83rd Leg., ch. 1407]** The case of a child referred for disposition under the first offender program shall be referred to juvenile court or a court of competent criminal jurisdiction if:

(1) the child fails to complete the program;

(2) the child or the parent, guardian, or other custodian of the child terminates the child's participation in the program before the child completes it; or

(3) the child completes the program but is taken into custody under Section 52.01 before the 90th day after the date the child completes the program for conduct other than the conduct for which the child was referred to the first offender program.

(j) **[2 Versions: As amended by Acts 2013, 83rd Leg., ch. 1409]** The case of a child referred for disposition under the first offender program shall be referred to juvenile court or, if the child is accused of an offense described by Subsection (a-1), filed with a criminal court if:

(1) the child fails to complete the program;

(2) the child or the parent, guardian, or other custodian of the child terminates the child's participation in the program before the child completes it; or

(3) the child completes the program but is taken into custody under Section 52.01 before the 90th day after the date the child completes the program for conduct other than the conduct for which the child was referred to the first offender program.

(k) A statement made by a child to a person giving advice or supervision or participating in the first offender program may not be used against the child in any proceeding under this title or any criminal proceeding.

(*l*) The law enforcement agency must report to the juvenile board in December of each year the following:

(1) the last known address of the child, including the census tract;

(2) the gender and ethnicity of the child referred to the program; and

(3) the offense committed by the child.

Sec. 52.032. Informal Disposition Guidelines.

(a) The juvenile board of each county, in cooperation with each law enforcement agency in the county, shall adopt guidelines for the disposition of a child under Section 52.03 or 52.031. The guidelines adopted under this section shall not be considered mandatory.

(b) The guidelines adopted under Subsection (a) may not allow for the case of a child to be disposed of under Section 52.03 or 52.031 if there is probable cause to believe that the child engaged in delinquent conduct or conduct indicating a need for supervision and cause to believe that the child may be the victim of conduct that constitutes an offense under Section 20A.02, Penal Code.

Sec. 52.04. Referral to Juvenile Court; Notice to Parents.

(a) The following shall accompany referral of a child or a child's case to the office or official designated by the juvenile board or be provided as quickly as possible after referral:

(1) all information in the possession of the person or agency making the referral pertaining to the identity of the child and the child's address, the name and address of the child's parent, guardian, or custodian, the names and addresses of any witnesses, and the child's present whereabouts;

(2) a complete statement of the circumstances of the alleged delinquent conduct or conduct indicating a need for supervision;

(3) when applicable, a complete statement of the circumstances of taking the child into custody; and

(4) when referral is by an officer of a law-enforcement agency, a complete statement of all prior contacts with the child by officers of that law-enforcement agency.

(b) The office or official designated by the juvenile board may refer the case to a law-enforcement agency for the purpose of conducting an investigation to obtain necessary information.

(c) If the office of the prosecuting attorney is designated by the juvenile court to conduct the preliminary investigation under Section 53.01, the referring entity shall first transfer the child's case to the juvenile probation department for statistical reporting purposes only. On the creation of a statistical record or file for the case, the probation department shall within three business days forward the case to the prosecuting attorney for review under Section 53.01.

(d) On referral of the case of a child who has not been taken into custody to the office or official designated by the juvenile board, the office or official designated by the juvenile board shall promptly give notice of the referral and a statement of the reason for the referral to the child's parent, guardian, or custodian.

Sec. 52.041. Referral of Child to Juvenile Court After Expulsion.

(a) A school district that expels a child shall refer the child to juvenile court in the county in which the child resides.

(b) The board of the school district or a person designated by the board shall deliver a copy of the order expelling the student and any other information required by Section 52.04 on or before the second working day after the date of the expulsion hearing to the authorized officer of the juvenile court.

(c) Within five working days of receipt of an expulsion notice under this section by the office or official designated by the juvenile board, a preliminary investigation and determination shall be conducted as required by Section 53.01.

(d) The office or official designated by the juvenile board shall within two working days notify the school district that expelled the child if:

(1) a determination was made under Section 53.01 that the person referred to juvenile court was not a child within the meaning of this title;

(2) a determination was made that no probable cause existed to believe the child engaged in delinquent conduct or conduct indicating a need for supervision;

(3) no deferred prosecution or formal court proceedings have been or will be initiated involving the child;

(4) the court or jury finds that the child did not engage in delinquent conduct or conduct indicating a need for supervision and the case has been dismissed with prejudice; or

(5) the child was adjudicated but no disposition was or will be ordered by the court.

(e) In any county where a juvenile justice alternative education program is operated, no student shall be expelled without written notification by the board of the school district or its designated agent to the juvenile board's designated representative. The notification shall be made not later than two business days following the board's determination that the student is to be expelled. Failure to timely notify the designated representative of the juvenile board shall result in the child's duty to continue attending the school district's educational program, which shall be provided to that child until such time as the notification to the juvenile board's designated representative is properly made.

CHAPTER 53
PROCEEDINGS PRIOR TO JUDICIAL PROCEEDINGS

Sec. 53.01. Preliminary Investigation and Determinations; Notice to Parents.

(a) On referral of a person believed to be a child or on referral of the person's case to the office or official designated by the juvenile board, the intake officer, probation officer, or other person authorized by the board shall conduct a preliminary investigation to determine whether:

(1) the person referred to juvenile court is a child within the meaning of this title; and

(2) there is probable cause to believe the person:

(A) engaged in delinquent conduct or conduct indicating a need for supervision; or

(B) is a nonoffender who has been taken into custody and is being held solely for deportation out of the United States.

(b) If it is determined that the person is not a child or there is no probable cause, the person shall immediately be released.

(b-1) The person who is conducting the preliminary investigation shall, as appropriate, refer the child's case to a community resource coordination group, a local-level interagency staffing group, or other community juvenile service provider for services under Section 53.011, if the person determines that:

(1) the child is younger than 12 years of age;

(2) there is probable cause to believe the child engaged in delinquent conduct or conduct indicating a need for supervision;

(3) the child's case does not require referral to the prosecuting attorney under Subsection (d) or (f);

(4) the child is eligible for deferred prosecution under Section 53.03; and

(5) the child and the child's family are not currently receiving services under Section 53.011 and would benefit from receiving the services.

(c) When custody of a child is given to the office or official designated by the juvenile board, the intake officer, probation officer, or other person authorized by the board shall promptly give notice of the whereabouts of the child and a statement of the reason the child was taken into custody to the child's parent, guardian, or custodian unless the notice given under Section 52.02(b) provided fair notice of the child's present whereabouts.

(d) Unless the juvenile board approves a written procedure proposed by the office of prosecuting attorney and chief juvenile probation officer which provides otherwise, if it is determined that the person is a child and, regardless of a finding of probable cause, or a lack thereof, there is an allegation that the child engaged in delinquent conduct of the grade of felony, or conduct constituting a misdemeanor offense involving violence to a person or the use or possession of a firearm, location-restricted knife, or club, as those terms are defined by Section 46.01, Penal Code, or prohibited weapon, as described by Section 46.05, Penal Code, the case shall be promptly forwarded to the office of the prosecuting attorney, accompanied by:

(1) all documents that accompanied the current referral; and

(2) a summary of all prior referrals of the child to the juvenile court, juvenile probation department, or a detention facility.

(e) If a juvenile board adopts an alternative referral plan under Subsection (d), the board shall register the plan with the Texas Juvenile Justice Department.

(f) A juvenile board may not adopt an alternate referral plan that does not require the forwarding of a child's case to the prosecuting attorney as provided by Subsection (d) if probable cause exists to believe that the child engaged in delinquent conduct that violates Section 19.03, Penal Code (capital murder), or Section 19.02, Penal Code (murder).

Sec. 53.011. Services Provided to Certain Children and Families.

(a) In this section:

(1) "Community resource coordination group" has the meaning assigned by Section 531.421, Government Code.

(2) "Local-level interagency staffing group" means a group established under the memorandum of understanding described by Section 531.055, Government Code.

(b) On receipt of a referral under Section 53.01(b-1), a community resource coordination group, a local-level interagency staffing group, or another community juvenile services provider shall evaluate the child's case and make recommendations to the juvenile probation department for appropriate services for the child and the child's family.

(c) The probation officer shall create and coordinate a service plan or system of care for the child or the child's family that incorporates the service recommendations for the child or the child's family provided to the juvenile probation department under Subsection (b). The child and the child's parent, guardian, or custodian must consent to the services with knowledge that consent is voluntary.

(d) For a child who receives a service plan or system of care under this section, the probation officer may hold the child's case open for not more than three months to monitor adherence to the service plan or system of care. The probation officer may adjust the service plan or system of care as necessary during the monitoring period. The probation officer may refer the child to the prosecuting attorney if the child fails to successfully participate in required services during that period.

Sec. 53.012. Review by Prosecutor.

(a) The prosecuting attorney shall promptly review the circumstances and allegations of a referral made under Section 53.01 for legal sufficiency and the desirability of prosecution and may file a petition without regard to whether probable cause was found under Section 53.01.

(b) If the prosecuting attorney does not file a petition requesting the adjudication of the child referred to the prosecuting attorney, the prosecuting attorney shall:

(1) terminate all proceedings, if the reason is for lack of probable cause; or

(2) return the referral to the juvenile probation department for further proceedings.

(c) The juvenile probation department shall promptly refer a child who has been returned to the department under Subsection (b)(2) and who fails or refuses to participate in a program of the department to the prosecuting attorney for review of the child's case and determination of whether to file a petition.

Sec. 53.013. Progressive Sanctions Program.

Each juvenile board may adopt a progressive sanctions program using the model for progressive sanctions in Chapter 59.

Sec. 53.02. Release from Detention.

(a) If a child is brought before the court or delivered to a detention facility as authorized by Sections 51.12(a)(3) and (4), the intake or other authorized officer of the court shall immediately make an investigation and shall release the child unless it appears that his detention is warranted under Subsection (b). The release may be conditioned upon requirements reasonably necessary to insure the child's appearance at later proceedings, but the conditions of the release must be in writing and filed with the office or official designated by the court and a copy furnished to the child.

(b) A child taken into custody may be detained prior to hearing on the petition only if:

(1) the child is likely to abscond or be removed from the jurisdiction of the court;

(2) suitable supervision, care, or protection for the child is not being provided by a parent, guardian, custodian, or other person;

(3) the child has no parent, guardian, custodian, or other person able to return the child to the court when required;

(4) the child may be dangerous to himself or herself or the child may threaten the safety of the public if released;

(5) the child has previously been found to be a delinquent child or has previously been convicted of a penal offense punishable by a term in jail or prison and is likely to commit an offense if released; or

(6) the child's detention is required under Subsection (f).

(c) If the child is not released, a request for detention hearing shall be made and promptly presented to the court, and an informal detention hearing as provided in Section 54.01 of this code shall be held promptly, but not later than the time required by Section 54.01 of this code.

(d) A release of a child to an adult under Subsection (a) must be conditioned on the agreement of the adult to be subject to the jurisdiction of the juvenile court and to an order of contempt by the court if the adult, after notification, is unable to produce the child at later proceedings.

(e) Unless otherwise agreed in the memorandum of understanding under Section 37.011, Education Code, in a county with a population greater than 125,000, if a child being released under this section is expelled under Section 37.007, Education Code, the release shall be conditioned on the child's attending a juvenile justice alternative education program pending a deferred prosecution or formal court disposition of the child's case.

(f) A child who is alleged to have engaged in delinquent conduct and to have used, possessed, or exhibited a firearm, as defined by Section 46.01, Penal Code, in the commission of the offense shall be detained until the child is released at the direction of the judge of the juvenile court, a substitute judge authorized by Section 51.04(f), or a referee appointed under Section 51.04(g), including an oral direction by telephone, or until a detention hearing is held as required by Section 54.01.

Sec. 53.03. Deferred Prosecution.

(a) Subject to Subsections (e) and (g), if the preliminary investigation required by Section 53.01 of this code results in a determination that further proceedings in the case are authorized, the probation officer or other designated officer of the court, subject to the direction of the juvenile court, may advise the parties for a reasonable period of time not to exceed six months concerning deferred prosecution and rehabilitation of a child if:

(1) deferred prosecution would be in the interest of the public and the child;

(2) the child and his parent, guardian, or custodian consent with knowledge that consent is not obligatory; and

(3) the child and his parent, guardian, or custodian are informed that they may terminate the

deferred prosecution at any point and petition the court for a court hearing in the case.

(b) Except as otherwise permitted by this title, the child may not be detained during or as a result of the deferred prosecution process.

(c) An incriminating statement made by a participant to the person giving advice and in the discussions or conferences incident thereto may not be used against the declarant in any court hearing.

(d) The juvenile board may adopt a fee schedule for deferred prosecution services and rules for the waiver of a fee for financial hardship in accordance with guidelines that the Texas Juvenile Justice Department shall provide. The maximum fee is $15 a month. If the board adopts a schedule and rules for waiver, the probation officer or other designated officer of the court shall collect the fee authorized by the schedule from the parent, guardian, or custodian of a child for whom a deferred prosecution is authorized under this section or waive the fee in accordance with the rules adopted by the board. The officer shall deposit the fees received under this section in the county treasury to the credit of a special fund that may be used only for juvenile probation or community-based juvenile corrections services or facilities in which a juvenile may be required to live while under court supervision. If the board does not adopt a schedule and rules for waiver, a fee for deferred prosecution services may not be imposed.

(e) A prosecuting attorney may defer prosecution for any child. A probation officer or other designated officer of the court:

(1) may not defer prosecution for a child for a case that is required to be forwarded to the prosecuting attorney under Section 53.01(d); and

(2) may defer prosecution for a child who has previously been adjudicated for conduct that constitutes a felony only if the prosecuting attorney consents in writing.

(f) The probation officer or other officer designated by the court supervising a program of deferred prosecution for a child under this section shall report to the juvenile court any violation by the child of the program.

(g) Prosecution may not be deferred for a child alleged to have engaged in conduct that:

(1) is an offense under Section 49.04, 49.05, 49.06, 49.07, or 49.08, Penal Code; or

(2) is a third or subsequent offense under Section 106.04 or 106.041, Alcoholic Beverage Code.

(h) If the child is alleged to have engaged in delinquent conduct or conduct indicating a need for supervision that violates Section 28.08, Penal Code, deferred prosecution under this section may include:

(1) voluntary attendance in a class with instruction in self-responsibility and empathy for a victim of an offense conducted by a local juvenile probation department, if the class is available; and

(2) voluntary restoration of the property damaged by the child by removing or painting over any markings made by the child, if the owner of the property consents to the restoration.

(h-1) If the child is alleged to have engaged in delinquent conduct or conduct indicating a need for supervision that violates Section 481.115, 481.1151, 481.116, 481.1161, 481.117, 481.118, or 481.121, Health and Safety Code, deferred prosecution under this section may include a condition that the child successfully complete a drug education program that is designed to educate persons on the dangers of drug abuse in accordance with Section 521.374(a)(1), Transportation Code, and that is regulated by the Texas Department of Licensing and Regulation under Chapter 171, Government Code.

(h-2) If the child is alleged to have engaged in delinquent conduct or conduct indicating a need for supervision that violates Section 106.02, 106.025, 106.04, 106.041, 106.05, or 106.07, Alcoholic Beverage Code, or Section 49.02, Penal Code, deferred prosecution under this section may include a condition that the child successfully complete an alcohol awareness program described by Section 106.115, Alcoholic Beverage Code, that is regulated by the Texas Department of Licensing and Regulation under Chapter 171, Government Code.

(i) The court may defer prosecution for a child at any time:

(1) for an adjudication that is to be decided by a jury trial, before the jury is sworn;

(2) for an adjudication before the court, before the first witness is sworn; or

(3) for an uncontested adjudication, before the child pleads to the petition or agrees to a stipulation of evidence.

(j) The court may add the period of deferred prosecution under Subsection (i) to a previous order of deferred prosecution, except that the court may not place the child on deferred prosecution for a combined period longer than one year.

(k) In deciding whether to grant deferred prosecution under Subsection (i), the court may consider professional representations by the parties concerning the nature of the case and the background of the respondent. The representations made under this subsection by the child or counsel for the child are not admissible against the child at trial should the court reject the application for deferred prosecution.

Sec. 53.035. Grand Jury Referral.

(a) The prosecuting attorney may, before filing a petition under Section 53.04, refer an offense to a grand jury in the county in which the offense is alleged to have been committed.

(b) The grand jury has the same jurisdiction and powers to investigate the facts and circumstances concerning an offense referred to the grand jury under this section as it has to investigate other criminal activity.

(c) If the grand jury votes to take no action on an offense referred to the grand jury under this section, the prosecuting attorney may not file a petition under Section 53.04 concerning the offense unless the same or a successor grand jury approves the filing of the petition.

(d) If the grand jury votes for approval of the prosecution of an offense referred to the grand jury under this section, the prosecuting attorney may file a petition under Section 53.04.

(e) The approval of the prosecution of an offense by a grand jury under this section does not constitute approval of a petition by a grand jury for purposes of Section 53.045.

Sec. 53.04. Court Petition; Answer.

(a) If the preliminary investigation, required by Section 53.01 of this code[,] results in a determination that further proceedings are authorized and warranted, a petition for an adjudication or transfer hearing of a child alleged to have engaged in delinquent conduct or conduct indicating a need for supervision may be made as promptly as practicable by a prosecuting attorney who has knowledge of the facts alleged or is informed and believes that they are true.

(b) The proceedings shall be styled "In the matter of ______."

(c) The petition may be on information and belief.

(d) The petition must state:

(1) with reasonable particularity the time, place, and manner of the acts alleged and the penal law or standard of conduct allegedly violated by the acts;

(2) the name, age, and residence address, if known, of the child who is the subject of the petition;

(3) the names and residence addresses, if known, of the parent, guardian, or custodian of the child and of the child's spouse, if any;

(4) if the child's parent, guardian, or custodian does not reside or cannot be found in the state, or if their places of residence are unknown, the name and residence address of any known adult relative residing in the county or, if there is none, the name and residence address of the known adult relative residing nearest to the location of the court; and

(5) if the child is alleged to have engaged in habitual felony conduct, the previous adjudications in which the child was found to have engaged in conduct violating penal laws of the grade of felony.

(e) An oral or written answer to the petition may be made at or before the commencement of the hearing. If there is no answer, a general denial of the alleged conduct is assumed.

Sec. 53.045. Offenses Eligible for Determinate Sentence.

(a) Except as provided by Subsection (e), the prosecuting attorney may refer the petition to the grand jury of the county in which the court in which the petition is filed presides if the petition alleges that the child engaged in delinquent conduct that constitutes habitual felony conduct as described by Section 51.031 or that included the violation of any of the following provisions:

(1) Section 19.02, Penal Code (murder);

(2) Section 19.03, Penal Code (capital murder);

(3) Section 19.04, Penal Code (manslaughter);

(4) Section 20.04, Penal Code (aggravated kidnapping);

(5) Section 22.011, Penal Code (sexual assault) or Section 22.021, Penal Code (aggravated sexual assault);

(6) Section 22.02, Penal Code (aggravated assault);

(7) Section 29.03, Penal Code (aggravated robbery);

(8) Section 22.04, Penal Code (injury to a child, elderly individual, or disabled individual), if the offense is punishable as a felony, other than a state jail felony;

(9) Section 22.05(b), Penal Code (felony deadly conduct involving discharging a firearm);

(10) Subchapter D, Chapter 481, Health and Safety Code, if the conduct constitutes a felony of the first degree or an aggravated controlled substance felony (certain offenses involving controlled substances);

(11) Section 15.03, Penal Code (criminal solicitation);

(12) Section 21.11(a)(1), Penal Code (indecency with a child);

(13) Section 15.031, Penal Code (criminal solicitation of a minor);

(14) Section 15.01, Penal Code (criminal attempt), if the offense attempted was an offense under Section 19.02, Penal Code (murder), or Section 19.03,

Texas Family Code

Penal Code (capital murder), or an offense listed by Article 42A.054(a), Code of Criminal Procedure;

(15) Section 28.02, Penal Code (arson), if bodily injury or death is suffered by any person by reason of the commission of the conduct;

(16) Section 49.08, Penal Code (intoxication manslaughter); or

(17) Section 15.02, Penal Code (criminal conspiracy), if the offense made the subject of the criminal conspiracy includes a violation of any of the provisions referenced in Subdivisions (1) through (16).

(b) A grand jury may approve a petition submitted to it under this section by a vote of nine members of the grand jury in the same manner that the grand jury votes on the presentment of an indictment.

(c) The grand jury has all the powers to investigate the facts and circumstances relating to a petition submitted under this section as it has to investigate other criminal activity but may not issue an indictment unless the child is transferred to a criminal court as provided by Section 54.02 of this code.

(d) If the grand jury approves of the petition, the fact of approval shall be certified to the juvenile court, and the certification shall be entered in the record of the case. For the purpose of the transfer of a child to the Texas Department of Criminal Justice as provided by Section 152.00161(c) or 245.151(c), Human Resources Code, as applicable, a juvenile court petition approved by a grand jury under this section is an indictment presented by the grand jury.

(e) The prosecuting attorney may not refer a petition that alleges the child engaged in conduct that violated Section 22.011(a)(2), Penal Code, or Sections 22.021(a)(1)(B) and (2)(B), Penal Code, unless the child is more than three years older than the victim of the conduct.

Sec. 53.05. Time Set for Hearing.

(a) After the petition has been filed, the juvenile court shall set a time for the hearing.

(b) The time set for the hearing shall not be later than 10 working days after the day the petition was filed if:

(1) the child is in detention; or

(2) the child will be taken into custody under Section 53.06(d) of this code.

Sec. 53.06. Summons.

(a) The juvenile court shall direct issuance of a summons to:

(1) the child named in the petition;

(2) the child's parent, guardian, or custodian;

(3) the child's guardian ad litem; and

(4) any other person who appears to the court to be a proper or necessary party to the proceeding.

(b) The summons must require the persons served to appear before the court at the time set to answer the allegations of the petition. A copy of the petition must accompany the summons.

(c) The court may endorse on the summons an order directing the person having the physical custody or control of the child to bring the child to the hearing. A person who violates an order entered under this subsection may be proceeded against under Section 53.08 or 54.07 of this code.

(d) If it appears from an affidavit filed or from sworn testimony before the court that immediate detention of the child is warranted under Section 53.02(b) of this code, the court may endorse on the summons an order that a law-enforcement officer shall serve the summons and shall immediately take the child into custody and bring him before the court.

(e) A party, other than the child, may waive service of summons by written stipulation or by voluntary appearance at the hearing.

Sec. 53.07. Service of Summons.

(a) If a person to be served with a summons is in this state and can be found, the summons shall be served upon him personally at least two days before the day of the adjudication hearing. If he is in this state and cannot be found, but his address is known or can with reasonable diligence be ascertained, the summons may be served on him by mailing a copy by registered or certified mail, return receipt requested, at least five days before the day of the hearing. If he is outside this state but he can be found or his address is known, or his whereabouts or address can with reasonable diligence be ascertained, service of the summons may be made either by delivering a copy to him personally or mailing a copy to him by registered or certified mail, return receipt requested, at least five days before the day of the hearing.

(b) The juvenile court has jurisdiction of the case if after reasonable effort a person other than the child cannot be found nor his post-office address ascertained, whether he is in or outside this state.

(c) Service of the summons may be made by any suitable person under the direction of the court.

(d) The court may authorize payment from the general funds of the county of the costs of service and of necessary travel expenses incurred by persons summoned or otherwise required to appear at the hearing.

(e) Witnesses may be subpoenaed in accordance with the Texas Code of Criminal Procedure, 1965.

Sec. 53.08. Writ of Attachment.

(a) The juvenile court may issue a writ of attachment for a person who violates an order entered under Section 53.06(c).

(b) A writ of attachment issued under this section is executed in the same manner as in a criminal proceeding as provided by Chapter 24, Code of Criminal Procedure.

CHAPTER 54
JUDICIAL PROCEEDINGS

Sec. 54.01. Detention Hearing.

(a) Except as provided by Subsection (p), if the child is not released under Section 53.02, a detention hearing without a jury shall be held promptly, but not later than the second working day after the child is taken into custody; provided, however, that when a child is detained on a Friday or Saturday, then such detention hearing shall be held on the first working day after the child is taken into custody.

(b) Reasonable notice of the detention hearing, either oral or written, shall be given, stating the time, place, and purpose of the hearing. Notice shall be given to the child and, if they can be found, to his parents, guardian, or custodian. Prior to the commencement of the hearing, the court shall inform the parties of the child's right to counsel and to appointed counsel if they are indigent and of the child's right to remain silent with respect to any allegations of delinquent conduct, conduct indicating a need for supervision, or conduct that violates an order of probation imposed by a juvenile court.

(b-1) Unless the court finds that the appointment of counsel is not feasible due to exigent circumstances, the court shall appoint counsel within a reasonable time before the first detention hearing is held to represent the child at that hearing.

(c) At the detention hearing, the court may consider written reports from probation officers, professional court employees, guardians ad litem appointed under Section 51.11(d), or professional consultants in addition to the testimony of witnesses. Prior to the detention hearing, the court shall provide the attorney for the child with access to all written matter to be considered by the court in making the detention decision. The court may order counsel not to reveal items to the child or the child's parent, guardian, or guardian ad litem if such disclosure would materially harm the treatment and rehabilitation of the child or would substantially decrease the likelihood of receiving information from the same or similar sources in the future.

(d) A detention hearing may be held without the presence of the child's parents if the court has been unable to locate them. If no parent or guardian is present, the court shall appoint counsel or a guardian ad litem for the child, subject to the requirements of Subsection (b-1).

(e) At the conclusion of the hearing, the court shall order the child released from detention unless it finds that:

(1) he is likely to abscond or be removed from the jurisdiction of the court;

(2) suitable supervision, care, or protection for him is not being provided by a parent, guardian, custodian, or other person;

(3) he has no parent, guardian, custodian, or other person able to return him to the court when required;

(4) he may be dangerous to himself or may threaten the safety of the public if released; or

(5) he has previously been found to be a delinquent child or has previously been convicted of a penal offense punishable by a term in jail or prison and is likely to commit an offense if released.

(f) Unless otherwise agreed in the memorandum of understanding under Section 37.011, Education Code, a release may be conditioned on requirements reasonably necessary to insure the child's appearance at later proceedings, but the conditions of the release must be in writing and a copy furnished to the child. In a county with a population greater than 125,000, if a child being released under this section is expelled under Section 37.007, Education Code, the release shall be conditioned on the child's attending a juvenile justice alternative education program pending a deferred prosecution or formal court disposition of the child's case.

(g) No statement made by the child at the detention hearing shall be admissible against the child at any other hearing.

(h) A detention order extends to the conclusion of the disposition hearing, if there is one, but in no event for more than 10 working days. Further detention orders may be made following subsequent detention hearings. The initial detention hearing may not be waived but subsequent detention hearings may be waived in accordance with the requirements of Section 51.09. Each subsequent detention order shall extend for no more than 10 working days, except that in a county that does not have a certified juvenile detention facility, as described by

Section 51.12(a)(3), each subsequent detention order shall extend for no more than 15 working days.

(i) A child in custody may be detained for as long as 10 days without the hearing described in Subsection (a) of this section if:

(1) a written request for shelter in detention facilities pending arrangement of transportation to his place of residence in another state or country or another county of this state is voluntarily executed by the child not later than the next working day after he was taken into custody;

(2) the request for shelter contains:

(A) a statement by the child that he voluntarily agrees to submit himself to custody and detention for a period of not longer than 10 days without a detention hearing;

(B) an allegation by the person detaining the child that the child has left his place of residence in another state or country or another county of this state, that he is in need of shelter, and that an effort is being made to arrange transportation to his place of residence; and

(C) a statement by the person detaining the child that he has advised the child of his right to demand a detention hearing under Subsection (a) of this section; and

(3) the request is signed by the juvenile court judge to evidence his knowledge of the fact that the child is being held in detention.

(j) The request for shelter may be revoked by the child at any time, and on such revocation, if further detention is necessary, a detention hearing shall be held not later than the next working day in accordance with Subsections (a) through (g) of this section.

(k) Notwithstanding anything in this title to the contrary, the child may sign a request for shelter without the concurrence of an adult specified in Section 51.09 of this code.

(*l*) The juvenile board may appoint a referee to conduct the detention hearing. The referee shall be an attorney licensed to practice law in this state. Such payment or additional payment as may be warranted for referee services shall be provided from county funds. Before commencing the detention hearing, the referee shall inform the parties who have appeared that they are entitled to have the hearing before the juvenile court judge or a substitute judge authorized by Section 51.04(f). If a party objects to the referee conducting the detention hearing, an authorized judge shall conduct the hearing within 24 hours. At the conclusion of the hearing, the referee shall transmit written findings and recommendations to the juvenile court judge or substitute judge. The juvenile court judge or substitute judge shall adopt, modify, or reject the referee's recommendations not later than the next working day after the day that the judge receives the recommendations. Failure to act within that time results in release of the child by operation of law. A recommendation that the child be released operates to secure the child's immediate release, subject to the power of the juvenile court judge or substitute judge to reject or modify that recommendation. The effect of an order detaining a child shall be computed from the time of the hearing before the referee.

(m) The detention hearing required in this section may be held in the county of the designated place of detention where the child is being held even though the designated place of detention is outside the county of residence of the child or the county in which the alleged delinquent conduct, conduct indicating a need for supervision, or probation violation occurred.

(n) An attorney appointed by the court under Section 51.10(c) because a determination was made under this section to detain a child who was not represented by an attorney may request on behalf of the child and is entitled to a de novo detention hearing under this section. The attorney must make the request not later than the 10th working day after the date the attorney is appointed. The hearing must take place not later than the second working day after the date the attorney filed a formal request with the court for a hearing.

(o) The court or referee shall find whether there is probable cause to believe that a child taken into custody without an arrest warrant or a directive to apprehend has engaged in delinquent conduct, conduct indicating a need for supervision, or conduct that violates an order of probation imposed by a juvenile court. The court or referee must make the finding within 48 hours, including weekends and holidays, of the time the child was taken into custody. The court or referee may make the finding on any reasonably reliable information without regard to admissibility of that information under the Texas Rules of Evidence. A finding of probable cause is required to detain a child after the 48th hour after the time the child was taken into custody. If a court or referee finds probable cause, additional findings of probable cause are not required in the same cause to authorize further detention.

(p) If a child is detained in a county jail or other facility as provided by Section 51.12(*l*) and the child is not released under Section 53.02(f), a detention hearing without a jury shall be held promptly, but not later than the 24th hour, excluding weekends and holidays, after the time the child is taken into custody.

Texas Family Code

(q) If a child has not been released under Section 53.02 or this section and a petition has not been filed under Section 53.04 or 54.05 concerning the child, the court shall order the child released from detention not later than:

(1) the 30th working day after the date the initial detention hearing is held, if the child is alleged to have engaged in conduct constituting a capital felony, an aggravated controlled substance felony, or a felony of the first degree; or

(2) the 15th working day after the date the initial detention hearing is held, if the child is alleged to have engaged in conduct constituting an offense other than an offense listed in Subdivision (1) or conduct that violates an order of probation imposed by a juvenile court.

(q-1) The juvenile board may impose an earlier deadline than the specified deadlines for filing petitions under Subsection (q) and may specify the consequences of not filing a petition by the deadline the juvenile board has established. The juvenile board may authorize but not require the juvenile court to release a respondent from detention for failure of the prosecutor to file a petition by the juvenile board's deadline.

(r) On the conditional release of a child from detention by judicial order under Subsection (f), the court, referee, or detention magistrate may order that the child's parent, guardian, or custodian present in court at the detention hearing engage in acts or omissions specified by the court, referee, or detention magistrate that will assist the child in complying with the conditions of release. The order must be in writing and a copy furnished to the parent, guardian, or custodian. An order entered under this subsection may be enforced as provided by Chapter 61.

Sec. 54.011. Detention Hearings for Status Offenders and Nonoffenders; Penalty.

(a) The detention hearing for a status offender or nonoffender who has not been released administratively under Section 53.02 shall be held before the 24th hour after the time the child arrived at a detention facility, excluding hours of a weekend or a holiday. Except as otherwise provided by this section, the judge or referee conducting the detention hearing shall release the status offender or nonoffender from secure detention.

(b) The judge or referee may order a child in detention accused of the violation of a valid court order as defined by Section 51.02 detained not longer than 72 hours after the time the detention order was entered, excluding weekends and holidays, if:

(1) the judge or referee finds at the detention hearing that there is probable cause to believe the child violated the valid court order; and

(2) the detention of the child is justified under Section 54.01(e)(1), (2), or (3).

(c) Except as provided by Subsection (d), a detention order entered under Subsection (b) may be extended for one additional 72-hour period, excluding weekends and holidays, only on a finding of good cause by the juvenile court.

(d) A detention order for a child under this section may be extended on the demand of the child's attorney only to allow the time that is necessary to comply with the requirements of Section 51.10(h), entitling the attorney to 10 days to prepare for an adjudication hearing.

(e) A status offender may be detained for a necessary period, not to exceed the period allowed under the Interstate Compact for Juveniles, to enable the child's return to the child's home in another state under Chapter 60.

(f) Except as provided by Subsection (a), a nonoffender, including a person who has been taken into custody and is being held solely for deportation out of the United States, may not be detained for any period of time in a secure detention facility or secure correctional facility, regardless of whether the facility is publicly or privately operated. A nonoffender who is detained in violation of this subsection is entitled to immediate release from the facility and may bring a civil action for compensation for the illegal detention against any person responsible for the detention. A person commits an offense if the person knowingly detains or assists in detaining a nonoffender in a secure detention facility or secure correctional facility in violation of this subsection. An offense under this subsection is a Class B misdemeanor.

Sec. 54.012. Interactive Video Recording of Detention Hearing.

(a) A detention hearing under Section 54.01 may be held using interactive video equipment if:

(1) the child and the child's attorney agree to the video hearing; and

(2) the parties to the proceeding have the opportunity to cross-examine witnesses.

(b) A detention hearing may not be held using video equipment unless the video equipment for the hearing provides for a two-way communication of image and sound among the child, the court, and other parties at the hearing.

(c) A recording of the communications shall be made. The recording shall be preserved until the earlier of:

(1) the 91st day after the date on which the recording is made if the child is alleged to have engaged in conduct constituting a misdemeanor;

(2) the 120th day after the date on which the recording is made if the child is alleged to have engaged in conduct constituting a felony; or

(3) the date on which the adjudication hearing ends.

(d) An attorney for the child may obtain a copy of the recording on payment of the reasonable costs of reproducing the copy.

Sec. 54.02. Waiver of Jurisdiction and Discretionary Transfer to Criminal Court.

(a) The juvenile court may waive its exclusive original jurisdiction and transfer a child to the appropriate district court or criminal district court for criminal proceedings if:

(1) the child is alleged to have violated a penal law of the grade of felony;

(2) the child was:

(A) 14 years of age or older at the time he is alleged to have committed the offense, if the offense is a capital felony, an aggravated controlled substance felony, or a felony of the first degree, and no adjudication hearing has been conducted concerning that offense; or

(B) 15 years of age or older at the time the child is alleged to have committed the offense, if the offense is a felony of the second or third degree or a state jail felony, and no adjudication hearing has been conducted concerning that offense; and

(3) after a full investigation and a hearing, the juvenile court determines that there is probable cause to believe that the child before the court committed the offense alleged and that because of the seriousness of the offense alleged or the background of the child the welfare of the community requires criminal proceedings.

(b) The petition and notice requirements of Sections 53.04, 53.05, 53.06, and 53.07 of this code must be satisfied, and the summons must state that the hearing is for the purpose of considering discretionary transfer to criminal court.

(c) The juvenile court shall conduct a hearing without a jury to consider transfer of the child for criminal proceedings.

(d) Prior to the hearing, the juvenile court shall order and obtain a complete diagnostic study, social evaluation, and full investigation of the child, his circumstances, and the circumstances of the alleged offense.

(e) At the transfer hearing the court may consider written reports from probation officers, professional court employees, guardians ad litem appointed under Section 51.11(d), or professional consultants in addition to the testimony of witnesses. At least five days prior to the transfer hearing, the court shall provide the attorney for the child and the prosecuting attorney with access to all written matter to be considered by the court in making the transfer decision. The court may order counsel not to reveal items to the child or the child's parent, guardian, or guardian ad litem if such disclosure would materially harm the treatment and rehabilitation of the child or would substantially decrease the likelihood of receiving information from the same or similar sources in the future.

(f) In making the determination required by Subsection (a) of this section, the court shall consider, among other matters:

(1) whether the alleged offense was against person or property, with greater weight in favor of transfer given to offenses against the person;

(2) the sophistication and maturity of the child;

(3) the record and previous history of the child; and

(4) the prospects of adequate protection of the public and the likelihood of the rehabilitation of the child by use of procedures, services, and facilities currently available to the juvenile court.

(g) If the petition alleges multiple offenses that constitute more than one criminal transaction, the juvenile court shall either retain or transfer all offenses relating to a single transaction. Except as provided by Subsection (g-1), a child is not subject to criminal prosecution at any time for any offense arising out of a criminal transaction for which the juvenile court retains jurisdiction.

(g-1) A child may be subject to criminal prosecution for an offense committed under Chapter 19 or Section 49.08, Penal Code, if:

(1) the offense arises out of a criminal transaction for which the juvenile court retained jurisdiction over other offenses relating to the criminal transaction; and

(2) on or before the date the juvenile court retained jurisdiction, one or more of the elements of the offense under Chapter 19 or Section 49.08, Penal Code, had not occurred.

(h) If the juvenile court waives jurisdiction, it shall state specifically in the order its reasons for waiver and certify its action, including the written order and findings of the court, and shall transfer the person to the appropriate court for criminal proceedings and cause the results of the diagnostic study of the person ordered under Subsection (d), including psychological information, to be transferred to the appropriate criminal prosecutor. On transfer of the person for criminal proceedings, the person shall be dealt with as an adult and in accordance with the Code of Criminal Procedure, except that if detention in a certified juvenile detention facility is authorized under Section 152.0015, Human Resources Code, the juvenile court may order the person to be detained in the facility pending trial or until the criminal court enters an order under Article 4.19, Code of Criminal Procedure. A transfer of custody made under this subsection is an arrest.

(h-1) If the juvenile court orders a person detained in a certified juvenile detention facility under Subsection (h), the juvenile court shall set or deny bond for the person as required by the Code of Criminal Procedure and other law applicable to the pretrial detention of adults accused of criminal offenses.

(i) A waiver under this section is a waiver of jurisdiction over the child and the criminal court may not remand the child to the jurisdiction of the juvenile court.

(j) The juvenile court may waive its exclusive original jurisdiction and transfer a person to the appropriate district court or criminal district court for criminal proceedings if:

(1) the person is 18 years of age or older;

(2) the person was:

(A) 10 years of age or older and under 17 years of age at the time the person is alleged to have committed a capital felony or an offense under Section 19.02, Penal Code;

(B) 14 years of age or older and under 17 years of age at the time the person is alleged to have committed an aggravated controlled substance felony or a felony of the first degree other than an offense under Section 19.02, Penal Code; or

(C) 15 years of age or older and under 17 years of age at the time the person is alleged to have committed a felony of the second or third degree or a state jail felony;

(3) no adjudication concerning the alleged offense has been made or no adjudication hearing concerning the offense has been conducted;

(4) the juvenile court finds from a preponderance of the evidence that:

(A) for a reason beyond the control of the state it was not practicable to proceed in juvenile court before the 18th birthday of the person; or

(B) after due diligence of the state it was not practicable to proceed in juvenile court before the 18th birthday of the person because:

(i) the state did not have probable cause to proceed in juvenile court and new evidence has been found since the 18th birthday of the person;

(ii) the person could not be found; or

(iii) a previous transfer order was reversed by an appellate court or set aside by a district court; and

(5) the juvenile court determines that there is probable cause to believe that the child before the court committed the offense alleged.

(k) The petition and notice requirements of Sections 53.04, 53.05, 53.06, and 53.07 of this code must be satisfied, and the summons must state that the hearing is for the purpose of considering waiver of jurisdiction under Subsection (j). The person's parent, custodian, guardian, or guardian ad litem is not considered a party to a proceeding under Subsection (j) and it is not necessary to provide the parent, custodian, guardian, or guardian ad litem with notice.

(*l*) The juvenile court shall conduct a hearing without a jury to consider waiver of jurisdiction under Subsection (j). Except as otherwise provided by this subsection, a waiver of jurisdiction under Subsection (j) may be made without the necessity of conducting the diagnostic study or complying with the requirements of discretionary transfer proceedings under Subsection (d). If requested by the attorney for the person at least 10 days before the transfer hearing, the court shall order that the person be examined pursuant to Section 51.20(a) and that the results of the examination be provided to the attorney for the person and the attorney for the state at least five days before the transfer hearing.

(m) Notwithstanding any other provision of this section, the juvenile court shall waive its exclusive original jurisdiction and transfer a child to the appropriate district court or criminal court for criminal proceedings if:

(1) the child has previously been transferred to a district court or criminal district court for criminal proceedings under this section, unless:

(A) the child was not indicted in the matter transferred by the grand jury;

(B) the child was found not guilty in the matter transferred;

(C) the matter transferred was dismissed with prejudice; or

(D) the child was convicted in the matter transferred, the conviction was reversed on appeal, and the appeal is final; and

(2) the child is alleged to have violated a penal law of the grade of felony.

(n) A mandatory transfer under Subsection (m) may be made without conducting the study required in discretionary transfer proceedings by Subsection (d). The requirements of Subsection (b) that the summons state that the purpose of the hearing is to consider discretionary transfer to criminal court does not apply to a transfer proceeding under Subsection (m). In a proceeding under Subsection (m), it is sufficient that the summons

Texas Family Code

provide fair notice that the purpose of the hearing is to consider mandatory transfer to criminal court.

(o) If a respondent is taken into custody for possible discretionary transfer proceedings under Subsection (j), the juvenile court shall hold a detention hearing in the same manner as provided by Section 54.01, except that the court shall order the respondent released unless it finds that the respondent:

(1) is likely to abscond or be removed from the jurisdiction of the court;

(2) may be dangerous to himself or herself or may threaten the safety of the public if released; or

(3) has previously been found to be a delinquent child or has previously been convicted of a penal offense punishable by a term of jail or prison and is likely to commit an offense if released.

(p) If the juvenile court does not order a respondent released under Subsection (o), the court shall, pending the conclusion of the discretionary transfer hearing, order that the respondent be detained in:

(1) a certified juvenile detention facility as provided by Subsection (q); or

(2) an appropriate county facility for the detention of adults accused of criminal offenses.

(q) The detention of a respondent in a certified juvenile detention facility must comply with the detention requirements under this title, except that, to the extent practicable, the person shall be kept separate from children detained in the same facility.

(r) If the juvenile court orders a respondent detained in a county facility under Subsection (p), the county sheriff shall take custody of the respondent under the juvenile court's order. The juvenile court shall set or deny bond for the respondent as required by the Code of Criminal Procedure and other law applicable to the pretrial detention of adults accused of criminal offenses.

(s) If a child is transferred to criminal court under this section, only the petition for discretionary transfer, the order of transfer, and the order of commitment, if any, are a part of the district clerk's public record.

Sec. 54.021. County, Justice, or Municipal Court: Truancy. [Repealed]

Sec. 54.022. Justice or Municipal Court: Certain Misdemeanors [Repealed].

Repealed by Acts 2001, 77th Leg., ch. 1297 (H.B. 1118), § 71(2), effective September 1, 2001 and by Acts 2001, 77th Leg., ch. 1514 (S.B. 1432), § 19(b), effective September 1, 2001.

Sec. 54.023. Justice or Municipal Court: Enforcement [Repealed].

Repealed by Acts 2003, 78th Leg., ch. 283 (H.B. 2319), § 61(1), effective September 1, 2003.

Sec. 54.03. Adjudication Hearing.

(a) A child may be found to have engaged in delinquent conduct or conduct indicating a need for supervision only after an adjudication hearing conducted in accordance with the provisions of this section.

(b) At the beginning of the adjudication hearing, the juvenile court judge shall explain to the child and his parent, guardian, or guardian ad litem:

(1) the allegations made against the child;

(2) the nature and possible consequences of the proceedings, including the law relating to the admissibility of the record of a juvenile court adjudication in a criminal proceeding;

(3) the child's privilege against self-incrimination;

(4) the child's right to trial and to confrontation of witnesses;

(5) the child's right to representation by an attorney if he is not already represented; and

(6) the child's right to trial by jury.

(c) Trial shall be by jury unless jury is waived in accordance with Section 51.09. If the hearing is on a petition that has been approved by the grand jury under Section 53.045, the jury must consist of 12 persons and be selected in accordance with the requirements in criminal cases. If the hearing is on a petition that alleges conduct that violates a penal law of this state of the grade of misdemeanor, the jury must consist of the number of persons required by Article 33.01(b), Code of Criminal Procedure. Jury verdicts under this title must be unanimous.

(d) Except as provided by Section 54.031, only material, relevant, and competent evidence in accordance with the Texas Rules of Evidence applicable to criminal cases and Chapter 38, Code of Criminal Procedure, may be considered in the adjudication hearing. Except in a detention or discretionary transfer hearing, a social history report or social service file shall not be viewed by the court before the adjudication decision and shall not be viewed by the jury at any time.

(e) A child alleged to have engaged in delinquent conduct or conduct indicating a need for supervision need not be a witness against nor otherwise incriminate himself. An extrajudicial statement which was obtained without fulfilling the requirements of this title or of the constitution of this state or the United States, may not be used in an adjudication hearing. A statement made by the child

Texas Family Code

out of court is insufficient to support a finding of delinquent conduct or conduct indicating a need for supervision unless it is corroborated in whole or in part by other evidence. An adjudication of delinquent conduct or conduct indicating a need for supervision cannot be had upon the testimony of an accomplice unless corroborated by other evidence tending to connect the child with the alleged delinquent conduct or conduct indicating a need for supervision; and the corroboration is not sufficient if it merely shows the commission of the alleged conduct. Evidence illegally seized or obtained is inadmissible in an adjudication hearing.

(f) At the conclusion of the adjudication hearing, the court or jury shall find whether or not the child has engaged in delinquent conduct or conduct indicating a need for supervision. The finding must be based on competent evidence admitted at the hearing. The child shall be presumed to be innocent of the charges against the child and no finding that a child has engaged in delinquent conduct or conduct indicating a need for supervision may be returned unless the state has proved such beyond a reasonable doubt. In all jury cases the jury will be instructed that the burden is on the state to prove that a child has engaged in delinquent conduct or is in need of supervision beyond a reasonable doubt. A child may be adjudicated as having engaged in conduct constituting a lesser included offense as provided by Articles 37.08 and 37.09, Code of Criminal Procedure.

(g) If the court or jury finds that the child did not engage in delinquent conduct or conduct indicating a need for supervision, the court shall dismiss the case with prejudice.

(h) If the finding is that the child did engage in delinquent conduct or conduct indicating a need for supervision, the court or jury shall state which of the allegations in the petition were found to be established by the evidence. The court shall also set a date and time for the disposition hearing.

(i) In order to preserve for appellate or collateral review the failure of the court to provide the child the explanation required by Subsection (b), the attorney for the child must comply with Rule 33.1, Texas Rules of Appellate Procedure, before testimony begins or, if the adjudication is uncontested, before the child pleads to the petition or agrees to a stipulation of evidence.

(j) When the state and the child agree to the disposition of the case, in whole or in part, the prosecuting attorney shall inform the court of the agreement between the state and the child. The court shall inform the child that the court is not required to accept the agreement. The court may delay a decision on whether to accept the agreement until after reviewing a report filed under Section 54.04(b). If the court decides not to accept the agreement, the court shall inform the child of the court's decision and give the child an opportunity to withdraw the plea or stipulation of evidence. If the court rejects the agreement, no document, testimony, or other evidence placed before the court that relates to the rejected agreement may be considered by the court in a subsequent hearing in the case. A statement made by the child before the court's rejection of the agreement to a person writing a report to be filed under Section 54.04(b) may not be admitted into evidence in a subsequent hearing in the case. If the court accepts the agreement, the court shall make a disposition in accordance with the terms of the agreement between the state and the child.

Sec. 54.031. Hearsay Statement of Certain Abuse Victims.

(a) This section applies to a hearing under this title in which a child is alleged to be a delinquent child on the basis of a violation of any of the following provisions of the Penal Code, if a child 12 years of age or younger or a person with a disability is the alleged victim of the violation:

(1) Chapter 21 (Sexual Offenses) or 22 (Assaultive Offenses);

(2) Section 25.02 (Prohibited Sexual Conduct);

(3) Section 43.25 (Sexual Performance by a Child);

(4) Section 20A.02(a)(7) or (8) (Trafficking of Persons); or

(5) Section 43.05(a)(2) (Compelling Prostitution).

(b) This section applies only to statements that describe the alleged violation that:

(1) were made by the child or person with a disability who is the alleged victim of the violation; and

(2) were made to the first person, 18 years of age or older, to whom the child or person with a disability made a statement about the violation.

(c) A statement that meets the requirements of Subsection (b) is not inadmissible because of the hearsay rule if:

(1) on or before the 14th day before the date the hearing begins, the party intending to offer the statement:

(A) notifies each other party of its intention to do so;

(B) provides each other party with the name of the witness through whom it intends to offer the statement; and

(C) provides each other party with a written summary of the statement;

(2) the juvenile court finds, in a hearing conducted outside the presence of the jury, that the

Texas Family Code

statement is reliable based on the time, content, and circumstances of the statement; and

(3) the child or person with a disability who is the alleged victim testifies or is available to testify at the hearing in court or in any other manner provided by law.

(d) In this section, "person with a disability" means a person 13 years of age or older who because of age or physical or mental disease, disability, or injury is substantially unable to protect the person's self from harm or to provide food, shelter, or medical care for the person's self.

Sec. 54.032. Deferral of Adjudication and Dismissal of Certain Cases on Completion of Teen Court Program. [Effective until January 1, 2022]

(a) A juvenile court may defer adjudication proceedings under Section 54.03 for not more than 180 days if the child:

(1) is alleged to have engaged in conduct indicating a need for supervision that violated a penal law of this state of the grade of misdemeanor that is punishable by fine only or a penal ordinance of a political subdivision of this state;

(2) waives, under Section 51.09, the privilege against self-incrimination and testifies under oath that the allegations are true;

(3) presents to the court an oral or written request to attend a teen court program; and

(4) has not successfully completed a teen court program in the two years preceding the date that the alleged conduct occurred.

(b) The teen court program must be approved by the court.

(c) A child for whom adjudication proceedings are deferred under Subsection (a) shall complete the teen court program not later than the 90th day after the date the teen court hearing to determine punishment is held or the last day of the deferral period, whichever date is earlier. The court shall dismiss the case with prejudice at the time the child presents satisfactory evidence that the child has successfully completed the teen court program.

(d) A case dismissed under this section may not be part of the child's records for any purpose.

(e) The court may require a child who requests a teen court program to pay a reimbursement fee not to exceed $10 that is set by the court to cover the costs of administering this section. The court shall deposit the fee in the county treasury of the county in which the court is located. A child who requests a teen court program and does not complete the program is not entitled to a refund of the fee.

(f) A court may transfer a case in which proceedings have been deferred as provided by this section to a court in another county if the court to which the case is transferred consents. A case may not be transferred unless it is within the jurisdiction of the court to which it is transferred.

(g) In addition to the reimbursement fee authorized by Subsection (e), the court may require a child who requests a teen court program to pay a $10 reimbursement fee to cover the cost to the teen court for performing its duties under this section. The court shall pay the fee to the teen court program, and the teen court program must account to the court for the receipt and disbursal of the fee. A child who pays a fee under this subsection is not entitled to a refund of the fee, regardless of whether the child successfully completes the teen court program.

(h) Notwithstanding Subsection (e) or (g), a juvenile court that is located in the Texas-Louisiana border region, as defined by Section 2056.002, Government Code, may charge a reimbursement fee of $20 under those subsections.

Sec. 54.032. Deferral of Adjudication and Dismissal of Certain Cases on Completion of Teen Court Program. [Effective January 1, 2022]

(a) A juvenile court may defer adjudication proceedings under Section 54.03 for not more than 180 days if the child:

(1) is alleged to have engaged in conduct indicating a need for supervision that violated a penal law of this state of the grade of misdemeanor that is punishable by fine only or a penal ordinance of a political subdivision of this state;

(2) waives, under Section 51.09, the privilege against self-incrimination and testifies under oath that the allegations are true;

(3) presents to the court an oral or written request to attend a teen court program; and

(4) has not successfully completed a teen court program in the two years preceding the date that the alleged conduct occurred.

(b) The teen court program must be approved by the court.

(c) A child for whom adjudication proceedings are deferred under Subsection (a) shall complete the teen court program not later than the 90th day after the date the teen court hearing to determine punishment is held or the last day of the deferral period, whichever date is earlier. The court shall dismiss the case with prejudice at the time the child presents satisfactory evidence that the child has successfully completed the teen court program.

(d) A case dismissed under this section may not be part of the child's records for any purpose.

(e) [Repealed.]

(f) A court may transfer a case in which proceedings have been deferred as provided by this section to a court in another county if the court to which the case is transferred consents. A case may not be transferred unless it is within the jurisdiction of the court to which it is transferred.

(g) [Repealed.]

(h) [Repealed.]

Sec. 54.0325. Deferral of Adjudication and Dismissal of Certain Cases on Completion of Teen Dating Violence Court Program. [Effective until January 1, 2022]

(a) In this section:

(1) "Dating violence" has the meaning assigned by Section 71.0021.

(2) "Family violence" has the meaning assigned by Section 71.004.

(3) "Teen dating violence court program" means a program that includes:

(A) a 12-week program designed to educate children who engage in dating violence and encourage them to refrain from engaging in that conduct;

(B) a dedicated teen victim advocate who assists teen victims by offering referrals to additional services, providing counseling and safety planning, and explaining the juvenile justice system;

(C) a court-employed resource coordinator to monitor children's compliance with the 12-week program;

(D) one judge who presides over all of the cases in the jurisdiction that qualify for the program; and

(E) an attorney in the district attorney's office or the county attorney's office who is assigned to the program.

(b) On the recommendation of the prosecuting attorney, the juvenile court may defer adjudication proceedings under Section 54.03 for not more than 180 days if the child is a first offender who is alleged to have engaged in conduct:

(1) that violated a penal law of this state of the grade of misdemeanor; and

(2) involving dating violence.

(c) For the purposes of Subsection (b), a first offender is a child who has not previously been referred to juvenile court for allegedly engaging in conduct constituting dating violence, family violence, or an assault.

(d) Before implementation, the teen dating violence court program must be approved by:

(1) the court; and

(2) the commissioners court of the county.

(e) A child for whom adjudication proceedings are deferred under Subsection (b) shall:

(1) complete the teen dating violence court program not later than the last day of the deferral period; and

(2) appear in court once a month for monitoring purposes.

(f) The court shall dismiss the case with prejudice at the time the child presents satisfactory evidence that the child has successfully completed the teen dating violence court program.

(g) The court may require a child who participates in a teen dating violence court program to pay a fee not to exceed $10 that is set by the court to cover the costs of administering this section. The court shall deposit the fee in the county treasury of the county in which the court is located.

(h) In addition to the fee authorized by Subsection (g), the court may require a child who participates in a teen dating violence court program to pay a fee of $10 to cover the cost to the teen dating violence court program for performing its duties under this section. The court shall pay the fee to the teen dating violence court program, and the teen dating violence court program must account to the court for the receipt and disbursal of the fee.

(i) The court shall track the number of children ordered to participate in the teen dating violence court program, the percentage of victims meeting with the teen victim advocate, and the compliance rate of the children ordered to participate in the program.

Sec. 54.0325. Deferral of Adjudication and Dismissal of Certain Cases on Completion of Teen Dating Violence Court Program. [Effective January 1, 2022]

(a) In this section:

(1) "Dating violence" has the meaning assigned by Section 71.0021.

(2) "Family violence" has the meaning assigned by Section 71.004.

(3) "Teen dating violence court program" means a program that includes:

(A) a 12-week program designed to educate children who engage in dating violence and encourage them to refrain from engaging in that conduct;

(B) a dedicated teen victim advocate who assists teen victims by offering referrals to additional services, providing counseling and safety planning, and explaining the juvenile justice system;

(C) a court-employed resource coordinator to monitor children's compliance with the 12-week program;

(D) one judge who presides over all of the cases in the jurisdiction that qualify for the program; and

(E) an attorney in the district attorney's office or the county attorney's office who is assigned to the program.

(b) On the recommendation of the prosecuting attorney, the juvenile court may defer adjudication proceedings under Section 54.03 for not more than 180 days if the child is a first offender who is alleged to have engaged in conduct:

(1) that violated a penal law of this state of the grade of misdemeanor; and

(2) involving dating violence.

(c) For the purposes of Subsection (b), a first offender is a child who has not previously been referred to juvenile court for allegedly engaging in conduct constituting dating violence, family violence, or an assault.

(d) Before implementation, the teen dating violence court program must be approved by:

(1) the court; and

(2) the commissioners court of the county.

(e) A child for whom adjudication proceedings are deferred under Subsection (b) shall:

(1) complete the teen dating violence court program not later than the last day of the deferral period; and

(2) appear in court once a month for monitoring purposes.

(f) The court shall dismiss the case with prejudice at the time the child presents satisfactory evidence that the child has successfully completed the teen dating violence court program.

(g) [Repealed.]

(h) [Repealed.]

(i) The court shall track the number of children ordered to participate in the teen dating violence court program, the percentage of victims meeting with the teen victim advocate, and the compliance rate of the children ordered to participate in the program.

Sec. 54.0326. Deferral of Adjudication and Dismissal of Certain Cases on Completion of Trafficked Persons Program.

(a) This section applies to a juvenile court or to an alternative juvenile court exercising simultaneous jurisdiction over proceedings under this title and Subtitle E, Title 5, in the manner authorized by Section 51.0413.

(b) A juvenile court may defer adjudication proceedings under Section 54.03 until the child's 18th birthday and require a child to participate in a program established under Section 152.0017, Human Resources Code, if the child:

(1) is alleged to have engaged in delinquent conduct or conduct indicating a need for supervision and may be a victim of conduct that constitutes an offense under Section 20A.02, Penal Code; and

(2) presents to the court an oral or written request to participate in the program.

(c) Following a child's completion of the program, the court shall dismiss the case with prejudice at the time the child presents satisfactory evidence that the child successfully completed the program.

Sec. 54.033. Sexually Transmitted Disease, AIDS, and HIV Testing.

(a) A child found at the conclusion of an adjudication hearing under Section 54.03 of this code to have engaged in delinquent conduct that included a violation of Sections 21.11(a)(1), 22.011, or 22.021, Penal Code, shall undergo a medical procedure or test at the direction of the juvenile court designed to show or help show whether the child has a sexually transmitted disease, acquired immune deficiency syndrome (AIDS), human immunodeficiency virus (HIV) infection, antibodies to HIV, or infection with any other probable causative agent of AIDS. The court may direct the child to undergo the procedure or test on the court's own motion or on the request of the victim of the delinquent conduct.

(b) If the child or another person who has the power to consent to medical treatment for the child refuses to submit voluntarily or consent to the procedure or test, the court shall require the child to submit to the procedure or test.

(c) The person performing the procedure or test shall make the test results available to the local health authority. The local health authority shall be required to notify the victim of the delinquent conduct and the person found to have engaged in the delinquent conduct of the test result.

(d) The state may not use the fact that a medical procedure or test was performed on a child under this section or use the results of the procedure or test in any proceeding arising out of the delinquent conduct.

(e) Testing under this section shall be conducted in accordance with written infectious disease control protocols adopted by the Texas Board of Health that clearly establish procedural guidelines that provide criteria for testing and that respect the rights of the child and the victim of the delinquent conduct.

(f) Nothing in this section allows a court to release a test result to anyone other than a person specifically authorized under this section. Section 81.103(d), Health and Safety Code, may not be construed to allow the disclosure of test results under this section except as provided by this section.

Sec. 54.034. Limited Right to Appeal: Warning.

Before the court may accept a child's plea or stipulation of evidence in a proceeding held under this title, the court shall inform the child that if the court accepts the plea or stipulation and the court makes a disposition in accordance with the agreement between the state and the child regarding the disposition of the case, the child may not appeal an order of the court entered under Section 54.03, 54.04, or 54.05, unless:

(1) the court gives the child permission to appeal; or

(2) the appeal is based on a matter raised by written motion filed before the proceeding in which the child entered the plea or agreed to the stipulation of evidence.

Sec. 54.04. Disposition Hearing.

(a) The disposition hearing shall be separate, distinct, and subsequent to the adjudication hearing. There is no right to a jury at the disposition hearing unless the child is in jeopardy of a determinate sentence under Subsection (d)(3) or (m), in which case, the child is entitled to a jury of 12 persons to determine the sentence, but only if the child so elects in writing before the commencement of the voir dire examination of the jury panel. If a finding of delinquent conduct is returned, the child may, with the consent of the attorney for the state, change the child's election of one who assesses the disposition.

(b) At the disposition hearing, the juvenile court, notwithstanding the Texas Rules of Evidence or Chapter 37, Code of Criminal Procedure, may consider written reports from probation officers, professional court employees, guardians ad litem appointed under Section 51.11(d), or professional consultants in addition to the testimony of witnesses. On or before the second day before the date of the disposition hearing, the court shall provide the attorney for the child and the prosecuting attorney with access to all written matter to be considered by the court in disposition. The court may order counsel not to reveal items to the child or the child's parent, guardian, or guardian ad litem if such disclosure would materially harm the treatment and rehabilitation of the child or would substantially decrease the likelihood of receiving information from the same or similar sources in the future.

(c) No disposition may be made under this section unless the child is in need of rehabilitation or the protection of the public or the child requires that disposition be made. If the court or jury does not so find, the court shall dismiss the child and enter a final judgment without any disposition. No disposition placing the child on probation outside the child's home may be made under this section unless the court or jury finds that the child, in the child's home, cannot be provided the quality of care and level of support and supervision that the child needs to meet the conditions of the probation.

(d) If the court or jury makes the finding specified in Subsection (c) allowing the court to make a disposition in the case:

(1) the court or jury may, in addition to any order required or authorized under Section 54.041 or 54.042, place the child on probation on such reasonable and lawful terms as the court may determine:

(A) in the child's own home or in the custody of a relative or other fit person; or

(B) subject to the finding under Subsection (c) on the placement of the child outside the child's home, in:

(i) a suitable foster home;

(ii) a suitable public or private residential treatment facility licensed by a state governmental entity or exempted from licensure by state law, except a facility operated by the Texas Juvenile Justice Department; or

(iii) a suitable public or private post-adjudication secure correctional facility that meets the requirements of Section 51.125, except a facility operated by the Texas Juvenile Justice Department;

(2) if the court or jury found at the conclusion of the adjudication hearing that the child engaged in delinquent conduct that violates a penal law of this state or the United States of the grade of felony, the court or jury made a special commitment finding under Section 54.04013, and the petition was not approved by the grand jury under Section 53.045, the court may commit the child to the Texas Juvenile Justice Department under Section 54.04013, or a post-adjudication secure correctional facility under Section 54.04011(c)(1), as applicable, without a determinate sentence;

(3) if the court or jury found at the conclusion of the adjudication hearing that the child engaged in delinquent conduct that included a violation of a penal law listed in Section 53.045(a) and if the petition was approved by the grand jury under Section 53.045, the court or jury may sentence the child to commitment in the Texas Juvenile Justice Department or a post-adjudication secure correctional facility under Section 54.04011(c)(2) with a possible transfer to the Texas Department of Criminal Justice for a term of:

(A) not more than 40 years if the conduct constitutes:

(i) a capital felony;
(ii) a felony of the first degree; or
(iii) an aggravated controlled substance felony;
(B) not more than 20 years if the conduct constitutes a felony of the second degree; or
(C) not more than 10 years if the conduct constitutes a felony of the third degree;
(4) the court may assign the child an appropriate sanction level and sanctions as provided by the assignment guidelines in Section 59.003;
(5) the court may place the child in a suitable nonsecure correctional facility that is registered and meets the applicable standards for the facility as provided by Section 51.126; or
(6) if applicable, the court or jury may make a disposition under Subsection (m) or Section 54.04011(c)(2)(A).
(e) The Texas Juvenile Justice Department shall accept a person properly committed to it by a juvenile court even though the person may be 17 years of age or older at the time of commitment.
(f) The court shall state specifically in the order its reasons for the disposition and shall furnish a copy of the order to the child. If the child is placed on probation, the terms of probation shall be written in the order.
(g) If the court orders a disposition under Subsection (d)(3) or (m) and there is an affirmative finding that the defendant used or exhibited a deadly weapon during the commission of the conduct or during immediate flight from commission of the conduct, the court shall enter the finding in the order. If there is an affirmative finding that the deadly weapon was a firearm, the court shall enter that finding in the order.
(h) At the conclusion of the dispositional hearing, the court shall inform the child of:
(1) the child's right to appeal, as required by Section 56.01; and
(2) the procedures for the sealing of the child's records under Subchapter C-1, Chapter 58.
(i) If the court places the child on probation outside the child's home or commits the child to the Texas Juvenile Justice Department, the court:
(1) shall include in its order its determination that:
(A) it is in the child's best interests to be placed outside the child's home;
(B) reasonable efforts were made to prevent or eliminate the need for the child's removal from the home and to make it possible for the child to return to the child's home; and
(C) the child, in the child's home, cannot be provided the quality of care and level of support and supervision that the child needs to meet the conditions of probation; and
(2) may approve an administrative body to conduct permanency hearings pursuant to 42 U.S.C. Section 675 if required during the placement or commitment of the child.
(j) If the court or jury found that the child engaged in delinquent conduct that included a violation of a penal law of the grade of felony or jailable misdemeanor, the court:
(1) shall require that the child's thumbprint be affixed or attached to the order; and
(2) may require that a photograph of the child be attached to the order.
(k) Except as provided by Subsection (m), the period to which a court or jury may sentence a person to commitment to the Texas Juvenile Justice Department with a transfer to the Texas Department of Criminal Justice under Subsection (d)(3) applies without regard to whether the person has previously been adjudicated as having engaged in delinquent conduct.
(*l*) Except as provided by Subsection (q), a court or jury may place a child on probation under Subsection (d)(1) for any period, except that probation may not continue on or after the child's 18th birthday. Except as provided by Subsection (q), the court may, before the period of probation ends, extend the probation for any period, except that the probation may not extend to or after the child's 18th birthday.
(m) The court or jury may sentence a child adjudicated for habitual felony conduct as described by Section 51.031 to a term prescribed by Subsection (d)(3) and applicable to the conduct adjudicated in the pending case if:
(1) a petition was filed and approved by a grand jury under Section 53.045 alleging that the child engaged in habitual felony conduct; and
(2) the court or jury finds beyond a reasonable doubt that the allegation described by Subdivision (1) in the grand jury petition is true.
(n) A court may order a disposition of secure confinement of a status offender adjudicated for violating a valid court order only if:
(1) before the order is issued, the child received the full due process rights guaranteed by the Constitution of the United States or the Texas Constitution; and
(2) the juvenile probation department in a report authorized by Subsection (b):
(A) reviewed the behavior of the child and the circumstances under which the child was brought before the court;
(B) determined the reasons for the behavior that caused the child to be brought before the court; and
(C) determined that all dispositions, including treatment, other than placement in a secure

detention facility or secure correctional facility, have been exhausted or are clearly inappropriate.

(o) In a disposition under this title:

(1) a status offender may not, under any circumstances, be committed to the Texas Juvenile Justice Department for engaging in conduct that would not, under state or local law, be a crime if committed by an adult;

(2) a status offender may not, under any circumstances other than as provided under Subsection (n), be placed in a post-adjudication secure correctional facility; and

(3) a child adjudicated for contempt of a county, justice, or municipal court order may not, under any circumstances, be placed in a post-adjudication secure correctional facility or committed to the Texas Juvenile Justice Department for that conduct.

(p) Except as provided by Subsection (*l*), a court that places a child on probation under Subsection (d)(1) for conduct described by Section 54.0405(b) and punishable as a felony shall specify a minimum probation period of two years.

(q) If a court or jury sentences a child to commitment in the Texas Juvenile Justice Department or a post-adjudication secure correctional facility under Subsection (d)(3) for a term of not more than 10 years, the court or jury may place the child on probation under Subsection (d)(1) as an alternative to making the disposition under Subsection (d)(3). The court shall prescribe the period of probation ordered under this subsection for a term of not more than 10 years. The court may, before the sentence of probation expires, extend the probationary period under Section 54.05, except that the sentence of probation and any extension may not exceed 10 years. The court may, before the child's 19th birthday, discharge the child from the sentence of probation. If a sentence of probation ordered under this subsection and any extension of probation ordered under Section 54.05 will continue after the child's 19th birthday, the court shall discharge the child from the sentence of probation on the child's 19th birthday unless the court transfers the child to an appropriate district court under Section 54.051.

(r) If the judge orders a disposition under this section and there is an affirmative finding that the victim or intended victim was younger than 17 years of age at the time of the conduct, the judge shall enter the finding in the order.

(s), (t) [Repealed by Acts 2007, 80th Leg., ch. 263 (S.B. 103), § 64(1), effective June 8, 2007.]

(u) For the purposes of disposition under Subsection (d)(2), delinquent conduct that violates a penal law of this state of the grade of felony does not include conduct that violates a lawful order of a county, municipal, justice, or juvenile court under circumstances that would constitute contempt of that court.

(v) If the judge orders a disposition under this section for delinquent conduct based on a violation of an offense, on the motion of the attorney representing the state the judge shall make an affirmative finding of fact and enter the affirmative finding in the papers in the case if the judge determines that, regardless of whether the conduct at issue is the subject of the prosecution or part of the same criminal episode as the conduct that is the subject of the prosecution, a victim in the trial:

(1) is or has been a victim of a severe form of trafficking in persons, as defined by 22 U.S.C. Section 7102(8); or

(2) has suffered substantial physical or mental abuse as a result of having been a victim of criminal activity described by 8 U.S.C. Section 1101(a)(15)(U)(iii).

(w) That part of the papers in the case containing an affirmative finding under Subsection (v):

(1) must include specific information identifying the victim, as available;

(2) may not include information identifying the victim's location; and

(3) is confidential, unless written consent for the release of the affirmative finding is obtained from the victim or, if the victim is younger than 18 years of age, the victim's parent or guardian.

(x) A child may be detained in an appropriate detention facility following disposition of the child's case under Subsection (d) or (m) pending:

(1) transportation of the child to the ordered placement; and

(2) the provision of medical or other health care services for the child that may be advisable before transportation, including health care services for children in the late term of pregnancy.

(y) A juvenile court conducting a hearing under this section involving a child for whom the Department of Family and Protective Services has been appointed managing conservator may communicate with the court having continuing jurisdiction over the child before the disposition hearing. The juvenile court may allow the parties to the suit affecting the parent-child relationship in which the Department of Family and Protective Services is a party to participate in the communication under this subsection.

(z) Nothing in this section may be construed to prohibit a juvenile court or jury in a county to which Section 54.04011 applies from committing a child to a post-adjudication secure correctional facility in accordance with that section after a disposition hearing held in accordance with this section.

Sec. 54.0401. Community-Based Programs.

(a) This section applies only to a county that has a population of at least 335,000.

(b) A juvenile court of a county to which this section applies may require a child who is found to have engaged in delinquent conduct that violates a penal law of the grade of misdemeanor and for whom the requirements of Subsection (c) are met to participate in a community-based program administered by the county's juvenile board.

(c) A juvenile court of a county to which this section applies may make a disposition under Subsection (b) for delinquent conduct that violates a penal law of the grade of misdemeanor:

(1) if:

(A) the child has been adjudicated as having engaged in delinquent conduct violating a penal law of the grade of misdemeanor on at least two previous occasions;

(B) of the previous adjudications, the conduct that was the basis for one of the adjudications occurred after the date of another previous adjudication; and

(C) the conduct that is the basis of the current adjudication occurred after the date of at least two previous adjudications; or

(2) if:

(A) the child has been adjudicated as having engaged in delinquent conduct violating a penal law of the grade of felony on at least one previous occasion; and

(B) the conduct that is the basis of the current adjudication occurred after the date of that previous adjudication.

(d) The Texas Juvenile Justice Department shall establish guidelines for the implementation of community-based programs described by this section. The juvenile board of each county to which this section applies shall implement a community-based program that complies with those guidelines.

(e) The Texas Juvenile Justice Department shall provide grants to selected juvenile boards to assist with the implementation of a system of community-based programs under this section.

(f) [Expired pursuant to Acts 2007, 80th Leg., ch. 263 (S.B. 103), § 8, effective February 1, 2009].

Sec. 54.04011. Commitment to Post-Adjudication Secure Correctional Facility. [Expired]

Sec. 54.04012. Trafficked Persons Program.

(a) This section applies to a juvenile court or to an alternative juvenile court exercising simultaneous jurisdiction over proceedings under this title and Subtitle E, Title 5, in the manner authorized by Section 51.0413.

(b) A juvenile court may require a child adjudicated to have engaged in delinquent conduct or conduct indicating a need for supervision and who is believed to be a victim of an offense of trafficking of persons as defined by Article 56B.003, Code of Criminal Procedure, to participate in a program established under Section 152.0017, Human Resources Code.

(c) The court may require a child participating in the program to periodically appear in court for monitoring and compliance purposes.

(d) Following a child's successful completion of the program, the court may order the sealing of the records of the case in the manner provided by Subchapter C-1, Chapter 58.

Sec. 54.04013. Special Commitment to Texas Juvenile Justice Department.

Notwithstanding any other provision of this code, after a disposition hearing held in accordance with Section 54.04, the juvenile court may commit a child who is found to have engaged in delinquent conduct that constitutes a felony offense to the Texas Juvenile Justice Department without a determinate sentence if the court makes a special commitment finding that the child has behavioral health or other special needs that cannot be met with the resources available in the community. The court should consider the findings of a validated risk and needs assessment and the findings of any other appropriate professional assessment available to the court.

Sec. 54.0402. Dispositional Order for Failure to Attend School. [Repealed]

Sec. 54.0404. Electronic Transmission of Certain Visual Material Depicting Minor: Educational Programs.

(a) If a child is found to have engaged in conduct indicating a need for supervision described by Section 51.03(b)(6), the juvenile court may enter an order requiring the child to attend and successfully complete an educational program described by Section 37.218, Education Code, or another equivalent educational program.

(b) A juvenile court that enters an order under Subsection (a) shall require the child or the child's parent or other person responsible for the child's support to pay the cost of attending an educational

Texas Family Code

program under Subsection (a) if the court determines that the child, parent, or other person is financially able to make payment.

Sec. 54.0405. Child Placed on Probation for Conduct Constituting Sexual Offense.

(a) If a court or jury makes a disposition under Section 54.04 in which a child described by Subsection (b) is placed on probation, the court:

(1) may require as a condition of probation that the child:

(A) attend psychological counseling sessions for sex offenders as provided by Subsection (e); and

(B) submit to a polygraph examination as provided by Subsection (f) for purposes of evaluating the child's treatment progress; and

(2) shall require as a condition of probation that the child:

(A) register under Chapter 62, Code of Criminal Procedure; and

(B) submit a blood sample or other specimen to the Department of Public Safety under Subchapter G, Chapter 411, Government Code, for the purpose of creating a DNA record of the child, unless the child has already submitted the required specimen under other state law.

(b) This section applies to a child placed on probation for conduct constituting an offense for which the child is required to register as a sex offender under Chapter 62, Code of Criminal Procedure.

(c) Psychological counseling required as a condition of probation under Subsection (a) must be with an individual or organization that:

(1) provides sex offender treatment or counseling;

(2) is specified by the local juvenile probation department supervising the child; and

(3) meets minimum standards of counseling established by the local juvenile probation department.

(d) A polygraph examination required as a condition of probation under Subsection (a) must be administered by an individual who is specified by the local juvenile probation department supervising the child.

(e) A local juvenile probation department that specifies a sex offender treatment provider under Subsection (c) to provide counseling to a child shall:

(1) establish with the cooperation of the treatment provider the date, time, and place of the first counseling session between the child and the treatment provider;

(2) notify the child and the treatment provider, not later than the 21st day after the date the order making the disposition placing the child on probation under Section 54.04 becomes final, of the date, time, and place of the first counseling session between the child and the treatment provider; and

(3) require the treatment provider to notify the department immediately if the child fails to attend any scheduled counseling session.

(f) A local juvenile probation department that specifies a polygraph examiner under Subsection (d) to administer a polygraph examination to a child shall arrange for a polygraph examination to be administered to the child:

(1) not later than the 60th day after the date the child attends the first counseling session established under Subsection (e); and

(2) after the initial polygraph examination, as required by Subdivision (1), on the request of the treatment provider specified under Subsection (c).

(g) A court that requires as a condition of probation that a child attend psychological counseling under Subsection (a) may order the parent or guardian of the child to:

(1) attend four sessions of instruction with an individual or organization specified by the court relating to:

(A) sexual offenses;

(B) family communication skills;

(C) sex offender treatment;

(D) victims' rights;

(E) parental supervision; and

(F) appropriate sexual behavior; and

(2) during the period the child attends psychological counseling, participate in monthly treatment groups conducted by the child's treatment provider relating to the child's psychological counseling.

(h) A court that orders a parent or guardian of a child to attend instructional sessions and participate in treatment groups under Subsection (g) shall require:

(1) the individual or organization specified by the court under Subsection (g) to notify the court immediately if the parent or guardian fails to attend any scheduled instructional session; and

(2) the child's treatment provider specified under Subsection (c) to notify the court immediately if the parent or guardian fails to attend a session in which the parent or guardian is required to participate in a scheduled treatment group.

(i) A court that requires as a condition of probation that a child attend psychological counseling under Subsection (a) may, before the date the probation period ends, extend the probation for any additional period necessary to complete the required counseling as determined by the treatment provider, except that the probation may not be extended to a date after the date of the child's 18th birthday, or 19th birthday if the child is placed on determinate sentence probation under Section 54.04(q).

Sec. 54.0406. Child Placed on Probation for Conduct Involving a Handgun.

(a) If a court or jury places a child on probation under Section 54.04(d) for conduct that violates a penal law that includes as an element of the offense the possession, carrying, using, or exhibiting of a handgun, as defined by Section 46.01, Penal Code, and if at the adjudication hearing the court or jury affirmatively finds that the child personally possessed, carried, used, or exhibited the handgun, the court shall require as a condition of probation that the child, not later than the 30th day after the date the court places the child on probation, notify the juvenile probation officer who is supervising the child of the manner in which the child acquired the handgun, including the date and place of and any person involved in the acquisition.

(b) On receipt of information described by Subsection (a), a juvenile probation officer shall promptly notify the appropriate local law enforcement agency of the information.

(c) Information provided by a child to a juvenile probation officer as required by Subsection (a) and any other information derived from that information may not be used as evidence against the child in any juvenile or criminal proceeding.

Sec. 54.0407. Cruelty to Animals: Counseling Required.

If a child is found to have engaged in delinquent conduct constituting an offense under Section 42.09 or 42.092, Penal Code, the juvenile court shall order the child to participate in psychological counseling for a period to be determined by the court.

Sec. 54.0408. Referral of Child Exiting Probation to Mental Health or Mental Retardation Authority.

A juvenile probation officer shall refer a child who has been determined to have a mental illness or mental retardation to an appropriate local mental health or mental retardation authority at least three months before the child is to complete the child's juvenile probation term unless the child is currently receiving treatment from the local mental health or mental retardation authority of the county in which the child resides.

Sec. 54.0409. DNA Sample Required on Certain Felony Adjudications.

(a) This section applies only to conduct constituting the commission of a felony:

(1) that is listed in Article 42A.054(a), Code of Criminal Procedure; or

(2) for which it is shown that a deadly weapon, as defined by Section 1.07, Penal Code, was used or exhibited during the commission of the conduct or during immediate flight from the commission of the conduct.

(b) If a court or jury makes a disposition under Section 54.04 in which a child is adjudicated as having engaged in conduct constituting the commission of a felony to which this section applies and the child is placed on probation, the court shall require as a condition of probation that the child provide a DNA sample under Subchapter G, Chapter 411, Government Code, for the purpose of creating a DNA record of the child, unless the child has already submitted the required sample under other state law.

Sec. 54.041. Orders Affecting Parents and Others. [Effective until January 1, 2022]

(a) When a child has been found to have engaged in delinquent conduct or conduct indicating a need for supervision and the juvenile court has made a finding that the child is in need of rehabilitation or that the protection of the public or the child requires that disposition be made, the juvenile court, on notice by any reasonable method to all persons affected, may:

(1) order any person found by the juvenile court to have, by a wilful act or omission, contributed to, caused, or encouraged the child's delinquent conduct or conduct indicating a need for supervision to do any act that the juvenile court determines to be reasonable and necessary for the welfare of the child or to refrain from doing any act that the juvenile court determines to be injurious to the welfare of the child;

(2) enjoin all contact between the child and a person who is found to be a contributing cause of the child's delinquent conduct or conduct indicating a need for supervision;

(3) after notice and a hearing of all persons affected order any person living in the same household with the child to participate in social or psychological counseling to assist in the rehabilitation of the child and to strengthen the child's family environment; or

(4) after notice and a hearing of all persons affected order the child's parent or other person responsible for the child's support to pay all or part of the reasonable costs of treatment programs in which the child is required to participate during the period of probation if the court finds the child's parent or person responsible for the child's support is able to pay the costs.

Texas Family Code

(b) If a child is found to have engaged in delinquent conduct or conduct indicating a need for supervision arising from the commission of an offense in which property damage or loss or personal injury occurred, the juvenile court, on notice to all persons affected and on hearing, may order the child or a parent to make full or partial restitution to the victim of the offense. The program of restitution must promote the rehabilitation of the child, be appropriate to the age and physical, emotional, and mental abilities of the child, and not conflict with the child's schooling. When practicable and subject to court supervision, the court may approve a restitution program based on a settlement between the child and the victim of the offense. An order under this subsection may provide for periodic payments by the child or a parent of the child for the period specified in the order but except as provided by Subsection (h), that period may not extend past the date of the 18th birthday of the child or past the date the child is no longer enrolled in an accredited secondary school in a program leading toward a high school diploma, whichever date is later.

(c) Restitution under this section is cumulative of any other remedy allowed by law and may be used in addition to other remedies; except that a victim of an offense is not entitled to receive more than actual damages under a juvenile court order.

(d) A person subject to an order proposed under Subsection (a) of this section is entitled to a hearing on the order before the order is entered by the court.

(e) An order made under this section may be enforced as provided by Section 54.07 of this code.

(f), (g) [Repealed by Acts 2015, 84th Leg., ch. 935 (H.B. 2398), § 41(3), effective September 1, 2015.]

(h) If the juvenile court places the child on probation in a determinate sentence proceeding initiated under Section 53.045 and transfers supervision on the child's 19th birthday to a district court for placement on community supervision, the district court shall require the payment of any unpaid restitution as a condition of the community supervision. The liability of the child's parent for restitution may not be extended by transfer to a district court for supervision.

Sec. 54.041. Orders Affecting Parents and Others. [Effective January 1, 2022]

(a) When a child has been found to have engaged in delinquent conduct or conduct indicating a need for supervision and the juvenile court has made a finding that the child is in need of rehabilitation or that the protection of the public or the child requires that disposition be made, the juvenile court, on notice by any reasonable method to all persons affected, may:

(1) order any person found by the juvenile court to have, by a wilful act or omission, contributed to, caused, or encouraged the child's delinquent conduct or conduct indicating a need for supervision to do any act that the juvenile court determines to be reasonable and necessary for the welfare of the child or to refrain from doing any act that the juvenile court determines to be injurious to the welfare of the child;

(2) enjoin all contact between the child and a person who is found to be a contributing cause of the child's delinquent conduct or conduct indicating a need for supervision; or

(3) after notice and a hearing of all persons affected order any person living in the same household with the child to participate in social or psychological counseling to assist in the rehabilitation of the child and to strengthen the child's family environment.

(b) If a child is found to have engaged in delinquent conduct or conduct indicating a need for supervision arising from the commission of an offense in which property damage or loss or personal injury occurred, the juvenile court, on notice to all persons affected and on hearing, may order the child or a parent to make full or partial restitution to the victim of the offense. The program of restitution must promote the rehabilitation of the child, be appropriate to the age and physical, emotional, and mental abilities of the child, and not conflict with the child's schooling. When practicable and subject to court supervision, the court may approve a restitution program based on a settlement between the child and the victim of the offense. An order under this subsection may provide for periodic payments by the child or a parent of the child for the period specified in the order but except as provided by Subsection (h), that period may not extend past the date of the 18th birthday of the child or past the date the child is no longer enrolled in an accredited secondary school in a program leading toward a high school diploma, whichever date is later.

(c) Restitution under this section is cumulative of any other remedy allowed by law and may be used in addition to other remedies; except that a victim of an offense is not entitled to receive more than actual damages under a juvenile court order.

(d) A person subject to an order proposed under Subsection (a) of this section is entitled to a hearing on the order before the order is entered by the court.

(e) An order made under this section may be enforced as provided by Section 54.07 of this code.

(f), (g) [Repealed by Acts 2015, 84th Leg., ch. 935 (H.B. 2398), § 41(3), effective September 1, 2015.]

(h) If the juvenile court places the child on probation in a determinate sentence proceeding initiated under Section 53.045 and transfers supervision on the child's 19th birthday to a district court for placement on community supervision, the district court shall require the payment of any unpaid restitution as a condition of the community supervision. The liability of the child's parent for restitution may not be extended by transfer to a district court for supervision.

Sec. 54.0411. Juvenile Probation Diversion Fund. [Repealed effective January 1, 2022]

(a) If a disposition hearing is held under Section 54.04 of this code, the juvenile court, after giving the child, parent, or other person responsible for the child's support a reasonable opportunity to be heard, shall order the child, parent, or other person, if financially able to do so, to pay a fee as costs of court of $20.

(b) Orders for the payment of fees under this section may be enforced as provided by Section 54.07 of this code.

(c) An officer collecting costs under this section shall keep separate records of the funds collected as costs under this section and shall deposit the funds in the county treasury.

(d) Each officer collecting court costs under this section shall file the reports required under Article 103.005, Code of Criminal Procedure. If no funds due as costs under this section have been collected in any quarter, the report required for each quarter shall be filed in the regular manner, and the report must state that no funds due under this section were collected.

(e) The custodian of the county treasury may deposit the funds collected under this section in interest-bearing accounts. The custodian shall keep records of the amount of funds on deposit collected under this section and not later than the last day of the month following each calendar quarter shall send to the comptroller of public accounts the funds collected under this section during the preceding quarter. A county may retain 10 percent of the funds as a service fee and may retain the interest accrued on the funds if the custodian of a county treasury keeps records of the amount of funds on deposit collected under this section and remits the funds to the comptroller within the period prescribed under this subsection.

(f) Funds collected are subject to audit by the comptroller and funds expended are subject to audit by the State Auditor.

(g) The comptroller shall deposit the funds in a special fund to be known as the juvenile probation diversion fund.

(h) The legislature shall determine and appropriate the necessary amount from the juvenile probation diversion fund to the Texas Juvenile Justice Department for the purchase of services the department considers necessary for the diversion of any juvenile who is at risk of commitment to the department. The department shall develop guidelines for the use of the fund. The department may not purchase the services if a person responsible for the child's support or a local juvenile probation department is financially able to provide the services.

Sec. 54.0411. Juvenile Probation Diversion Fund. [Repealed effective January 1, 2022]

Sec. 54.042. License Suspension.

(a) A juvenile court, in a disposition hearing under Section 54.04, shall:

(1) order the Department of Public Safety to suspend a child's driver's license or permit, or if the child does not have a license or permit, to deny the issuance of a license or permit to the child if the court finds that the child has engaged in conduct that:

(A) violates a law of this state enumerated in Section 521.342(a), Transportation Code; or

(B) violates a penal law of this state or the United States, an element or elements of which involve a severe form of trafficking in persons, as defined by 22 U.S.C. Section 7102; or

(2) notify the Department of Public Safety of the adjudication, if the court finds that the child has engaged in conduct that violates a law of this state enumerated in Section 521.372(a), Transportation Code.

(b) A juvenile court, in a disposition hearing under Section 54.04, may order the Department of Public Safety to suspend a child's driver's license or permit or, if the child does not have a license or permit, to deny the issuance of a license or permit to the child, if the court finds that the child has engaged in conduct that violates Section 28.08, Penal Code.

(c) The order under Subsection (a)(1) shall specify a period of suspension or denial of 365 days.

(d) The order under Subsection (b) shall specify a period of suspension or denial:

(1) not to exceed 365 days; or

(2) of 365 days if the court finds the child has been previously adjudicated as having engaged in conduct violating Section 28.08, Penal Code.

(e) A child whose driver's license or permit has been suspended or denied pursuant to this section may, if the child is otherwise eligible for, and fulfils [fulfills] the requirements for issuance of, a provisional driver's license or permit under Chapter 521, Transportation Code, apply for and receive an occupational license in accordance with the provisions of Subchapter L of that chapter.

(f) A juvenile court, in a disposition hearing under Section 54.04, may order the Department of Public Safety to suspend a child's driver's license or permit or, if the child does not have a license or permit, to deny the issuance of a license or permit to the child for a period not to exceed 12 months if the court finds that the child has engaged in conduct in need of supervision or delinquent conduct other than the conduct described by Subsection (a).

(g) A juvenile court that places a child on probation under Section 54.04 may require as a reasonable condition of the probation that if the child violates the probation, the court may order the Department of Public Safety to suspend the child's driver's license or permit or, if the child does not have a license or permit, to deny the issuance of a license or permit to the child for a period not to exceed 12 months. The court may make this order if a child that is on probation under this condition violates the probation. A suspension under this subsection is cumulative of any other suspension under this section.

(h) If a child is adjudicated for conduct that violates Section 49.04, 49.07, or 49.08, Penal Code, and if any conduct on which that adjudication is based is a ground for a driver's license suspension under Chapter 524 or 724, Transportation Code, each of the suspensions shall be imposed. The court imposing a driver's license suspension under this section shall credit a period of suspension imposed under Chapter 524 or 724, Transportation Code, toward the period of suspension required under this section, except that if the child was previously adjudicated for conduct that violates Section 49.04, 49.07, or 49.08, Penal Code, credit may not be given.

Sec. 54.043. Monitoring School Attendance.

If the court places a child on probation under Section 54.04(d) and requires as a condition of probation that the child attend school, the probation officer charged with supervising the child shall monitor the child's school attendance and report to the court if the child is voluntarily absent from school.

Sec. 54.044. Community Service.

(a) If the court places a child on probation under Section 54.04(d), the court shall require as a condition of probation that the child work a specified number of hours at a community service project approved by the court and designated by the juvenile probation department as provided by Subsection (e), unless the court determines and enters a finding on the order placing the child on probation that:

(1) the child is physically or mentally incapable of participating in the project;

(2) participating in the project will be a hardship on the child or the family of the child; or

(3) the child has shown good cause that community service should not be required.

(b) The court may also order under this section that the child's parent perform community service with the child.

(c) The court shall order that the child and the child's parent perform a total of not more than 500 hours of community service under this section.

(d) A municipality or county that establishes a program to assist children and their parents in rendering community service under this section may purchase insurance policies protecting the municipality or county against claims brought by a person other than the child or the child's parent for a cause of action that arises from an act of the child or parent while rendering community service. The municipality or county is not liable under this section to the extent that damages are recoverable under a contract of insurance or under a plan of self-insurance authorized by statute. The liability of the municipality or county for a cause of action that arises from an action of the child or the child's parent while rendering community service may not exceed $100,000 to a single person and $300,000 for a single occurrence in the case of personal injury or death, and $10,000 for a single occurrence of property damage. Liability may not extend to punitive or exemplary damages. This subsection does not waive a defense, immunity, or jurisdictional bar available to the municipality or county or its officers or employees, nor shall this section be construed to waive, repeal, or modify any provision of Chapter 101, Civil Practice and Remedies Code.

(e) For the purposes of this section, a court may submit to the juvenile probation department a list of organizations or projects approved by the court for community service. The juvenile probation department may:

(1) designate an organization or project for community service only from the list submitted by the court; and

(2) reassign or transfer a child to a different organization or project on the list submitted by the court under this subsection without court approval.

(f) A person subject to an order proposed under Subsection (a) or (b) is entitled to a hearing on the order before the order is entered by the court.

(g) On a finding by the court that a child's parents or guardians have made a reasonable good faith effort to prevent the child from engaging in delinquent conduct or engaging in conduct indicating a need for supervision and that, despite the parents' or guardians' efforts, the child continues to engage in such conduct, the court shall waive any requirement for community service that may be imposed on a parent under this section.

(h) An order made under this section may be enforced as provided by Section 54.07.

(i) In a disposition hearing under Section 54.04 in which the court finds that a child engaged in conduct violating Section 521.453, Transportation Code, the court, in addition to any other order authorized under this title and if the court is located in a municipality or county that has established a community service program, may order the child to perform eight hours of community service as a condition of probation under Section 54.04(d) unless the child is shown to have previously engaged in conduct violating Section 521.453, Transportation Code, in which case the court may order the child to perform 12 hours of community service.

Sec. 54.045. Admission of Unadjudicated Conduct.

(a) During a disposition hearing under Section 54.04, a child may:

(1) admit having engaged in delinquent conduct or conduct indicating a need for supervision for which the child has not been adjudicated; and

(2) request the court to take the admitted conduct into account in the disposition of the child.

(b) If the prosecuting attorney agrees in writing, the court may take the admitted conduct into account in the disposition of the child.

(c) A court may take into account admitted conduct over which exclusive venue lies in another county only if the court obtains the written permission of the prosecuting attorney for that county.

(d) A child may not be adjudicated by any court for having engaged in conduct taken into account under this section, except that, if the conduct taken into account included conduct over which exclusive venue lies in another county and the written permission of the prosecuting attorney of that county was not obtained, the child may be adjudicated for that conduct, but the child's admission under this section may not be used against the child in the adjudication.

Sec. 54.046. Conditions of Probation for Damaging Property with Graffiti.

(a) If a juvenile court places on probation under Section 54.04(d) a child adjudicated as having engaged in conduct in violation of Section 28.08, Penal Code, in addition to other conditions of probation, the court:

(1) shall order the child to:

(A) reimburse the owner of the property for the cost of restoring the property; or

(B) with consent of the owner of the property, restore the property by removing or painting over any markings made by the child on the property; and

(2) if the child made markings on public property, a street sign, or an official traffic-control device in violation of Section 28.08, Penal Code, shall order the child to:

(A) make to the political subdivision that owns the public property or erected the street sign or official traffic-control device restitution in an amount equal to the lesser of the cost to the political subdivision of replacing or restoring the public property, street sign, or official traffic-control device; or

(B) with the consent of the political subdivision, restore the public property, street sign, or official traffic-control device by removing or painting over any markings made by the child on the property, sign, or device.

(a-1) For purposes of Subsection (a), "official traffic-control device" has the meaning assigned by Section 541.304, Transportation Code.

(b) In addition to a condition imposed under Subsection (a), the court may require the child as a condition of probation to attend a class with instruction in self-responsibility and empathy for a victim of an offense conducted by a local juvenile probation department.

(c) If a juvenile court orders a child to make restitution under Subsection (a) and the child, child's parent, or other person responsible for the child's support is financially unable to make the restitution, the court may order the child to perform a specific number of hours of community service, in addition to the hours required under Subsection (d), to satisfy the restitution.

(d) If a juvenile court places on probation under Section 54.04(d) a child adjudicated as having engaged in conduct in violation of Section 28.08, Penal Code, in addition to other conditions of probation, the court shall order the child to perform:

(1) at least 15 hours of community service if the amount of pecuniary loss resulting from the conduct is $50 or more but less than $500; or

(2) at least 30 hours of community service if the amount of pecuniary loss resulting from the conduct is $500 or more.

(e) The juvenile court shall direct a child ordered to make restitution under this section to deliver the amount or property due as restitution to a juvenile probation department for transfer to the owner. The juvenile probation department shall notify the juvenile court when the child has delivered the full amount of restitution ordered.

Sec. 54.0461. Payment of Juvenile Delinquency Prevention Fees. [Repealed effective January 1, 2022]

(a) If a child is adjudicated as having engaged in delinquent conduct that violates Section 28.08, Penal Code, the juvenile court shall order the child, parent, or other person responsible for the child's support to pay to the court a $50 juvenile delinquency prevention fee as a cost of court.

(b) The court shall deposit fees received under this section to the credit of the county juvenile delinquency prevention fund provided for under Article 102.0171, Code of Criminal Procedure.

(c) If the court finds that a child, parent, or other person responsible for the child's support is unable to pay the juvenile delinquency prevention fee required under Subsection (a), the court shall enter into the child's case records a statement of that finding. The court may waive a fee under this section only if the court makes the finding under this subsection.

Sec. 54.0461. Payment of Juvenile Delinquency Prevention Fees. [Repealed effective January 1, 2022]

Sec. 54.0462. Payment of Fees for Offenses Requiring DNA Testing. [Repealed effective January 1, 2022]

(a) If a child is adjudicated as having engaged in delinquent conduct that constitutes the commission of a felony and the provision of a DNA sample is required under Section 54.0409 or other law, the juvenile court shall order the child, parent, or other person responsible for the child's support to pay to the court as a cost of court:

(1) a $50 fee if the disposition of the case includes a commitment to a facility operated by or under contract with the Texas Juvenile Justice Department; and

(2) a $34 fee if the disposition of the case does not include a commitment described by Subdivision (1) and the child is required to submit a DNA sample under Section 54.0409 or other law.

(b) The clerk of the court shall transfer to the comptroller any funds received under this section. The comptroller shall credit the funds to the Department of Public Safety to help defray the cost of any analyses performed on DNA samples provided by children with respect to whom a court cost is collected under this section.

(c) If the court finds that a child, parent, or other person responsible for the child's support is unable to pay the fee required under Subsection (a), the court shall enter into the child's case records a statement of that finding. The court may waive a fee under this section only if the court makes the finding under this subsection.

Sec. 54.0462. Payment of Fees for Offenses Requiring DNA Testing. [Repealed effective January 1, 2022]

Sec. 54.047. Alcohol or Drug Related Offense. [Effective until January 1, 2022]

(a) If the court or jury finds at an adjudication hearing for a child that the child engaged in delinquent conduct or conduct indicating a need for supervision that constitutes a violation of Section 481.115, 481.1151, 481.116, 481.1161, 481.117, 481.118, or 481.121, Health and Safety Code, the court may order that the child successfully complete a drug education program that is designed to educate persons on the dangers of drug abuse in accordance with Section 521.374(a)(1), Transportation Code, and that is regulated by the Texas Department of Licensing and Regulation under Chapter 171, Government Code.

(b) If the court or jury finds at an adjudication hearing for a child that the child engaged in delinquent conduct or conduct indicating a need for supervision that violates the alcohol-related offenses in Section 106.02, 106.025, 106.04, 106.041, 106.05, or 106.07, Alcoholic Beverage Code, or Section 49.02, Penal Code, the court may order that the child successfully complete an alcohol awareness program described by Section 106.115, Alcoholic Beverage Code, that is regulated by the Texas Department of Licensing and Regulation under Chapter 171, Government Code.

(c) The court shall, in addition to any order described by Subsection (a) or (b), order that, in the manner provided by Section 106.071(d), Alcoholic Beverage Code:

(1) the child perform community service; and

(2) the child's driver's license or permit be suspended or that the child be denied issuance of a driver's license or permit.

(d) An order under this section:

(1) is subject to a finding under Section 54.04(c); and

(2) may be issued in addition to any other order authorized by this title.

(e) [Repealed.]

(f) If the court orders a child under Subsection (a) or (b) to successfully complete a drug education program or alcohol awareness program, unless the court determines that the parent or guardian of the child is indigent and unable to pay the cost, the court shall require the child's parent or a guardian of the child to pay the cost of the program. The court shall allow the child's parent or guardian to pay the cost of the program in installments.

Sec. 54.047. Alcohol or Drug Related Offense. [Effective January 1, 2022]

(a) If the court or jury finds at an adjudication hearing for a child that the child engaged in delinquent conduct or conduct indicating a need for supervision that constitutes a violation of Section 481.115, 481.1151, 481.116, 481.1161, 481.117, 481.118, or 481.121, Health and Safety Code, the court may order that the child successfully complete a drug education program that is designed to educate persons on the dangers of drug abuse in accordance with Section 521.374(a)(1), Transportation Code, and that is regulated by the Texas Department of Licensing and Regulation under Chapter 171, Government Code.

(b) If the court or jury finds at an adjudication hearing for a child that the child engaged in delinquent conduct or conduct indicating a need for supervision that violates the alcohol-related offenses in Section 106.02, 106.025, 106.04, 106.041, 106.05, or 106.07, Alcoholic Beverage Code, or Section 49.02, Penal Code, the court may order that the child successfully complete an alcohol awareness program described by Section 106.115, Alcoholic Beverage Code, that is regulated by the Texas Department of Licensing and Regulation under Chapter 171, Government Code.

(c) The court shall, in addition to any order described by Subsection (a) or (b), order that, in the manner provided by Section 106.071(d), Alcoholic Beverage Code:

(1) the child perform community service; and

(2) the child's driver's license or permit be suspended or that the child be denied issuance of a driver's license or permit.

(d) An order under this section:

(1) is subject to a finding under Section 54.04(c); and

(2) may be issued in addition to any other order authorized by this title.

(e) [Repealed.]

(f) [Repealed.]

Sec. 54.048. Restitution.

(a) A juvenile court, in a disposition hearing under Section 54.04, may order restitution to be made by the child and the child's parents.

(b) This section applies without regard to whether the petition in the case contains a plea for restitution.

Sec. 54.0481. Restitution for Damaging Property with Graffiti.

(a) A juvenile court, in a disposition hearing under Section 54.04 regarding a child who has been adjudicated to have engaged in delinquent conduct that violates Section 28.08, Penal Code:

(1) may order the child or a parent or other person responsible for the child's support to make restitution by:

(A) reimbursing the owner of the property for the cost of restoring the property; or

(B) with the consent of the owner of the property, personally restoring the property by removing or painting over any markings the child made; and

(2) if the child made markings on public property, a street sign, or an official traffic-control device in violation of Section 28.08, Penal Code, may order the child or a parent or other person responsible for the child's support to:

(A) make to the political subdivision that owns the public property or erected the street sign or official traffic-control device restitution in an amount equal to the lesser of the cost to the political subdivision of replacing or restoring the public property, street sign, or official traffic-control device; or

(B) with the consent of the political subdivision, restore the public property, street sign, or official traffic-control device by removing or painting over any markings made by the child on the property, sign, or device.

(b) If a juvenile court orders a child to make restitution under Subsection (a) and the child, child's parent, or other person responsible for the child's support is financially unable to make the restitution, the court may order the child to perform a specific number of hours of community service to satisfy the restitution.

(c) For purposes of Subsection (a), "official traffic-control device" has the meaning assigned by Section 541.304, Transportation Code.

Sec. 54.0482. Treatment of Restitution Payments.

(a) A juvenile probation department that receives a payment to a victim as the result of a juvenile court order for restitution shall immediately:

(1) deposit the payment in an interest-bearing account in the county treasury; and

(2) notify the victim that a payment has been received.

(b) The juvenile probation department shall promptly remit the payment to a victim who has been notified under Subsection (a) and makes a claim for payment.

(b-1) If the victim does not make a claim for payment on or before the 30th day after the date of being notified under Subsection (a), the juvenile probation department shall notify the victim by certified mail, sent to the last known address of the victim, that a payment has been received.

(c) On or before the fifth anniversary of the date the juvenile probation department receives a payment for a victim that is not claimed by the victim, the department shall make and document a good faith effort to locate and notify the victim that an unclaimed payment exists, including:

(1) confirming, if possible, the victim's most recent address with the Department of Public Safety; and

(2) making at least one additional certified mailing to the victim.

(d) A juvenile probation department satisfies the good faith requirement under Subsection (c) by sending by certified mail to the victim, during the period the child is required by the juvenile court order to make payments to the victim, a notice that the victim is entitled to an unclaimed payment.

(e) If a victim claims a payment on or before the fifth anniversary of the date on which the juvenile probation department mailed a notice to the victim under Subsection (b-1), the juvenile probation department shall pay the victim the amount of the original payment, less any interest earned while holding the payment.

(f) If a victim does not claim a payment on or before the fifth anniversary of the date on which the juvenile probation department mailed a notice to the victim under Subsection (b-1), the department:

(1) has no liability to the victim or anyone else in relation to the payment; and

(2) shall transfer the payment from the interest-bearing account to a special fund of the county treasury, the unclaimed juvenile restitution fund.

(g) The county may spend money in the unclaimed juvenile restitution fund only for the same purposes for which the county may spend juvenile state aid.

Sec. 54.049. Conditions of Probation for Desecrating a Cemetery or Abusing a Corpse.

(a) If a juvenile court places on probation under Section 54.04(d) a child adjudicated to have engaged in conduct in violation of Section 28.03(f), Penal Code, involving damage or destruction inflicted on a place of human burial or under Section 42.08, Penal Code, in addition to other conditions of probation, the court shall order the child to make restitution to a cemetery organization operating a cemetery affected by the conduct in an amount equal to the cost to the cemetery of repairing any damage caused by the conduct.

(b) If a juvenile court orders a child to make restitution under Subsection (a) and the child is financially unable to make the restitution, the court may order:

(1) the child to perform a specific number of hours of community service to satisfy the restitution; or

(2) a parent or other person responsible for the child's support to make the restitution in the amount described by Subsection (a).

(c) In this section, "cemetery" and "cemetery organization" have the meanings assigned by Section 711.001, Health and Safety Code.

Sec. 54.0491. Gang-Related Conduct.

(a) In this section:

(1) "Criminal street gang" has the meaning assigned by Section 71.01, Penal Code.

(2) "Gang-related conduct" means conduct that violates a penal law of the grade of Class B misdemeanor or higher and in which a child engages with the intent to:

(A) further the criminal activities of a criminal street gang of which the child is a member;

(B) gain membership in a criminal street gang; or

(C) avoid detection as a member of a criminal street gang.

(b) A juvenile court, in a disposition hearing under Section 54.04 regarding a child who has been adjudicated to have engaged in delinquent conduct that is also gang-related conduct, shall order the child to participate in a criminal street gang intervention program that is appropriate for the child based on the child's level of involvement in the criminal activities of a criminal street gang. The intervention program:

(1) must include at least 12 hours of instruction; and

(2) may include voluntary tattoo removal.

(c) If a child required to attend a criminal street gang intervention program is committed to the

Texas Juvenile Justice Department as a result of the gang-related conduct, the child must complete the intervention program before being discharged from the custody of or released under supervision by the department.

Sec. 54.05. Hearing to Modify Disposition.

(a) Except as provided by Subsection (a-1), any disposition, except a commitment to the Texas Juvenile Justice Department, may be modified by the juvenile court as provided in this section until:

(1) the child reaches:

(A) the child's 18th birthday; or

(B) the child's 19th birthday, if the child was placed on determinate sentence probation under Section 54.04(q); or

(2) the child is earlier discharged by the court or operation of law.

(a-1) [Repealed by Acts 2015, 84th Leg., ch. 935 (H.B. 2398), § 41(3), effective September 1, 2015.]

(b) Except for a commitment to the Texas Juvenile Justice Department or to a post-adjudication secure correctional facility under Section 54.04011 or a placement on determinate sentence probation under Section 54.04(q), all dispositions automatically terminate when the child reaches the child's 18th birthday.

(c) There is no right to a jury at a hearing to modify disposition.

(d) A hearing to modify disposition shall be held on the petition of the child and his parent, guardian, guardian ad litem, or attorney, or on the petition of the state, a probation officer, or the court itself. Reasonable notice of a hearing to modify disposition shall be given to all parties.

(e) After the hearing on the merits or facts, the court may consider written reports from probation officers, professional court employees, guardians ad litem appointed under Section 51.11(d), or professional consultants in addition to the testimony of other witnesses. On or before the second day before the date of the hearing to modify disposition, the court shall provide the attorney for the child and the prosecuting attorney with access to all written matter to be considered by the court in deciding whether to modify disposition. The court may order counsel not to reveal items to the child or the child's parent, guardian, or guardian ad litem if such disclosure would materially harm the treatment and rehabilitation of the child or would substantially decrease the likelihood of receiving information from the same or similar sources in the future.

(f) Except as provided by Subsection (j), a disposition based on a finding that the child engaged in delinquent conduct that violates a penal law of this state or the United States of the grade of felony may be modified so as to commit the child to the Texas Juvenile Justice Department or, if applicable, a post-adjudication secure correctional facility operated under Section 152.0016, Human Resources Code, if the court after a hearing to modify disposition finds by a preponderance of the evidence that the child violated a reasonable and lawful order of the court. A disposition based on a finding that the child engaged in habitual felony conduct as described by Section 51.031 or in delinquent conduct that included a violation of a penal law listed in Section 53.045(a) may be modified to commit the child to the Texas Juvenile Justice Department or, if applicable, a post-adjudication secure correctional facility operated under Section 152.0016, Human Resources Code, with a possible transfer to the Texas Department of Criminal Justice for a definite term prescribed by, as applicable, Section 54.04(d)(3) or Section 152.0016(g), Human Resources Code, if the original petition was approved by the grand jury under Section 53.045 and if after a hearing to modify the disposition the court finds that the child violated a reasonable and lawful order of the court.

(g) Except as provided by Subsection (j), a disposition based solely on a finding that the child engaged in conduct indicating a need for supervision may not be modified to commit the child to the Texas Juvenile Justice Department. A new finding in compliance with Section 54.03 must be made that the child engaged in delinquent conduct that meets the requirements for commitment under Section 54.04.

(h) A hearing shall be held prior to placement in a post-adjudication secure correctional facility for a period longer than 30 days or commitment to the Texas Juvenile Justice Department as a modified disposition. In other disposition modifications, the child and the child's parent, guardian, guardian ad litem, or attorney may waive hearing in accordance with Section 51.09.

(i) The court shall specifically state in the order its reasons for modifying the disposition and shall furnish a copy of the order to the child.

(j) If, after conducting a hearing to modify disposition without a jury, the court finds by a preponderance of the evidence that a child violated a reasonable and lawful condition of probation ordered under Section 54.04(q), the court may modify the disposition to commit the child to the Texas Juvenile Justice Department under Section 54.04(d)(3) or, if applicable, a post-adjudication secure correctional facility operated under Section 152.0016, Human Resources Code, for a term that does not exceed the original sentence assessed by the court or jury.

(k) [Repealed by Acts 2007, 80th Leg., ch. 263 (S.B. 103), § 64(2), effective June 8, 2007.]

(*l*) The court may extend a period of probation under this section at any time during the period of probation or, if a motion for revocation or modification of probation is filed before the period of supervision ends, before the first anniversary of the date on which the period of probation expires.

(m) If the court places the child on probation outside the child's home or commits the child to the Texas Juvenile Justice Department or to a post-adjudication secure correctional facility operated under Section 152.0016, Human Resources Code, the court:

(1) shall include in the court's order a determination that:

(A) it is in the child's best interests to be placed outside the child's home;

(B) reasonable efforts were made to prevent or eliminate the need for the child's removal from the child's home and to make it possible for the child to return home; and

(C) the child, in the child's home, cannot be provided the quality of care and level of support and supervision that the child needs to meet the conditions of probation; and

(2) may approve an administrative body to conduct a permanency hearing pursuant to 42 U.S.C. Section 675 if required during the placement or commitment of the child.

Sec. 54.051. Transfer of Determinate Sentence Probation to Appropriate District Court.

(a) On motion of the state concerning a child who is placed on probation under Section 54.04(q) for a period, including any extension ordered under Section 54.05, that will continue after the child's 19th birthday, the juvenile court shall hold a hearing to determine whether to transfer the child to an appropriate district court or discharge the child from the sentence of probation.

(b) The hearing must be conducted before the person's 19th birthday, or before the person's 18th birthday if the offense for which the person was placed on probation occurred before September 1, 2011, and must be conducted in the same manner as a hearing to modify disposition under Section 54.05.

(c) If, after a hearing, the court determines to discharge the child, the court shall specify a date on or before the child's 19th birthday to discharge the child from the sentence of probation.

(d) If, after a hearing, the court determines to transfer the child, the court shall transfer the child to an appropriate district court on the child's 19th birthday.

(d-1) After a transfer to district court under Subsection (d), only the petition, the grand jury approval, the judgment concerning the conduct for which the person was placed on determinate sentence probation, and the transfer order are a part of the district clerk's public record.

(e) A district court that exercises jurisdiction over a person transferred under Subsection (d) shall place the person on community supervision under Chapter 42A, Code of Criminal Procedure, for the remainder of the person's probationary period and under conditions consistent with those ordered by the juvenile court.

(e-1) The restrictions on a judge placing a defendant on community supervision imposed by Article 42A.054, Code of Criminal Procedure, do not apply to a case transferred from the juvenile court. The minimum period of community supervision imposed by Article 42A.053(d), Code of Criminal Procedure, does not apply to a case transferred from the juvenile court.

(e-2) If a person who is placed on community supervision under this section violates a condition of that supervision or if the person violated a condition of probation ordered under Section 54.04(q) and that probation violation was not discovered by the state before the person's 19th birthday, the district court shall dispose of the violation of community supervision or probation, as appropriate, in the same manner as if the court had originally exercised jurisdiction over the case. If the judge revokes community supervision, the judge may reduce the prison sentence to any length without regard to the minimum term imposed by Article 42A.755(a), Code of Criminal Procedure.

(e-3) The time that a person serves on probation ordered under Section 54.04(q) is the same as time served on community supervision ordered under this section for purposes of determining the person's eligibility for early discharge from community supervision under Article 42A.701, Code of Criminal Procedure.

(f) The juvenile court may transfer a child to an appropriate district court as provided by this section without a showing that the child violated a condition of probation ordered under Section 54.04(q).

(g) If the juvenile court places the child on probation for an offense for which registration as a sex offender is required by Chapter 62, Code of Criminal Procedure, and defers the registration requirement until completion of treatment for the sex offense under Subchapter H, Chapter 62, Code of Criminal Procedure, the authority under that article to reexamine the need for registration on completion of treatment is transferred to the court to which probation is transferred.

(h) If the juvenile court places the child on probation for an offense for which registration as a sex offender is required by Chapter 62, Code of Criminal Procedure, and the child registers, the authority of the court to excuse further compliance with the registration requirement under Subchapter H, Chapter 62, Code of Criminal Procedure, is transferred to the court to which probation is transferred.

(i) If the juvenile court exercises jurisdiction over a person who is 18 or 19 years of age or older, as applicable, under Section 51.041 or 51.0412, the court or jury may, if the person is otherwise eligible, place the person on probation under Section 54.04(q). The juvenile court shall set the conditions of probation and immediately transfer supervision of the person to the appropriate court exercising criminal jurisdiction under Subsection (e).

Sec. 54.052. Credit for Time Spent in Detention Facility for Child with Determinate Sentence.

(a) This section applies only to a child who is committed to:

(1) the Texas Juvenile Justice Department under a determinate sentence under Section 54.04(d)(3) or (m) or Section 54.05(f); or

(2) a post-adjudication secure correctional facility under a determinate sentence under Section 54.04011(c)(2).

(b) The judge of the court in which a child is adjudicated shall give the child credit on the child's sentence for the time spent by the child, in connection with the conduct for which the child was adjudicated, in a secure detention facility before the child's transfer to a Texas Juvenile Justice Department facility or a post-adjudication secure correctional facility, as applicable.

(c) If a child appeals the child's adjudication and is retained in a secure detention facility pending the appeal, the judge of the court in which the child was adjudicated shall give the child credit on the child's sentence for the time spent by the child in a secure detention facility pending disposition of the child's appeal. The court shall endorse on both the commitment and the mandate from the appellate court all credit given the child under this subsection.

(d) The Texas Juvenile Justice Department or the juvenile board or local juvenile probation department operating or contracting for the operation of the post-adjudication secure correctional facility under Section 152.0016, Human Resources Code, as applicable, shall grant any credit under this section in computing the child's eligibility for parole and discharge.

Sec. 54.06. Judgments for Support. [Effective until January 1, 2022]

(a) At any stage of the proceeding, when a child has been placed outside the child's home, the juvenile court, after giving the parent or other person responsible for the child's support a reasonable opportunity to be heard, shall order the parent or other person to pay in a manner directed by the court a reasonable sum for the support in whole or in part of the child or the court shall waive the payment by order. The court shall order that the payment for support be made to the local juvenile probation department to be used only for residential care and other support for the child unless the child has been committed to the Texas Juvenile Justice Department, in which case the court shall order that the payment be made to the Texas Juvenile Justice Department for deposit in a special account in the general revenue fund that may be appropriated only for the care of children committed to the Texas Juvenile Justice Department.

(b) At any stage of the proceeding, when a child has been placed outside the child's home and the parent of the child is obligated to pay support for the child under a court order under Title 5, the juvenile court shall order that the person entitled to receive the support assign the person's right to support for the child placed outside the child's home to the local juvenile probation department to be used for residential care and other support for the child unless the child has been committed to the Texas Juvenile Justice Department, in which event the court shall order that the assignment be made to the Texas Juvenile Justice Department.

(c) A court may enforce an order for support under this section by ordering garnishment of the wages of the person ordered to pay support or by any other means available to enforce a child support order under Title 5.

(d) [Repealed by Acts 2003, 78th Leg., ch. 283 (H.B. 2319), § 61(1), effective September 1, 2003.]

(e) The court shall apply the child support guidelines under Subchapter C, Chapter 154, in an order requiring the payment of child support under this section. The court shall also require in an order to pay child support under this section that health insurance and dental insurance be provided for the child. Subchapter D, Chapter 154, applies to an order requiring health insurance and dental insurance for a child under this section.

(f) An order under this section prevails over any previous child support order issued with regard to the child to the extent of any conflict between the orders.

Sec. 54.06. Judgments for Support. [Effective January 1, 2022]

(a) [Repealed.]

(b) At any stage of the proceeding, when a child has been placed outside the child's home and the parent of the child is obligated to pay support for the child under a court order under Title 5, the juvenile court shall order that the person entitled to receive the support assign the person's right to support for the child placed outside the child's home to the local juvenile probation department to be used for residential care and other support for the child unless the child has been committed to the Texas Juvenile Justice Department, in which event the court shall order that the assignment be made to the Texas Juvenile Justice Department.

(c) A court may enforce an order for support under this section by ordering garnishment of the wages of the person ordered to pay support or by any other means available to enforce a child support order under Title 5.

(d) [Repealed by Acts 2003, 78th Leg., ch. 283 (H.B. 2319), § 61(1), effective September 1, 2003.]

(e) The court shall apply the child support guidelines under Subchapter C, Chapter 154, in an order requiring the payment of child support under this section. The court shall also require in an order to pay child support under this section that health insurance and dental insurance be provided for the child. Subchapter D, Chapter 154, applies to an order requiring health insurance and dental insurance for a child under this section.

(f) An order under this section prevails over any previous child support order issued with regard to the child to the extent of any conflict between the orders.

Texas Family Code

Sec. 54.061. Payment of Probation Fees.

(a) If a child is placed on probation under Section 54.04(d)(1) of this code, the juvenile court, after giving the child, parent, or other person responsible for the child's support a reasonable opportunity to be heard, shall order the child, parent, or other person, if financially able to do so, to pay to the court a fee of not more than $15 a month during the period that the child continues on probation.

(b) Orders for the payment of fees under this section may be enforced as provided by Section 54.07 of this code.

(c) The court shall deposit the fees received under this section in the county treasury to the credit of a special fund that may be used only for juvenile probation or community-based juvenile corrections services or facilities in which a juvenile may be required to live while under court supervision.

(d) If the court finds that a child, parent, or other person responsible for the child's support is financially unable to pay the probation fee required under Subsection (a), the court shall enter into the records of the child's case a statement of that finding. The court may waive a fee under this section only if the court makes the finding under this subsection.

Sec. 54.07. Enforcement of Order.

(a) Except as provided by Subsection (b) or a juvenile court child support order, any order of the juvenile court may be enforced as provided by Chapter 61.

(b) A violation of any of the following orders of the juvenile court may not be enforced by contempt of court proceedings against the child:

(1) an order setting conditions of probation;

(2) an order setting conditions of deferred prosecution; and

(3) an order setting conditions of release from detention.

(c) This section and Chapter 61 do not preclude a juvenile court from summarily finding a child or other person in direct contempt of the juvenile court for conduct occurring in the presence of the judge of the court. Direct contempt of the juvenile court by a child is punishable by a maximum of 10 days' confinement in a secure juvenile detention facility or by a maximum of 40 hours of community service, or both. The juvenile court may not impose a fine on a child for direct contempt.

(d) This section and Chapter 61 do not preclude a juvenile court in an appropriate case from using a civil or coercive contempt proceeding to enforce an order.

Sec. 54.08. Public Access to Court Hearings.

(a) Except as provided by this section, the court shall open hearings under this title to the public unless the court, for good cause shown, determines that the public should be excluded.

(b) The court may not prohibit a person who is a victim of the conduct of a child, or the person's family, from personally attending a hearing under this title relating to the conduct by the child unless the victim or member of the victim's family is to testify in the hearing or any subsequent hearing relating to the conduct and the court determines that the victim's or family member's testimony would be materially affected if the victim or member of the victim's family hears other testimony at trial.

(c) If a child is under the age of 14 at the time of the hearing, the court shall close the hearing to the public unless the court finds that the interests of the child or the interests of the public would be better served by opening the hearing to the public.

(d) In this section, "family" has the meaning assigned by Section 71.003.

Sec. 54.09. Recording of Proceedings.

All judicial proceedings under this chapter except detention hearings shall be recorded by stenographic notes or by electronic, mechanical, or other appropriate means. Upon request of any party, a detention hearing shall be recorded.

Sec. 54.10. Hearings Before Referee.

(a) Except as provided by Subsection (e), a hearing under Section 54.03, 54.04, or 54.05, including a jury trial, a hearing under Chapter 55, including a jury trial, or a hearing under the Interstate Compact for Juveniles (Chapter 60) may be held by a referee appointed in accordance with Section 51.04(g) or an associate judge appointed under Chapter 54A, Government Code, provided:

(1) the parties have been informed by the referee or associate judge that they are entitled to have the hearing before the juvenile court judge; and

(2) after each party is given an opportunity to object, no party objects to holding the hearing before the referee or associate judge.

(b) The determination under Section 53.02(f) whether to release a child may be made by a referee appointed in accordance with Section 51.04(g) if:

(1) the child has been informed by the referee that the child is entitled to have the determination made by the juvenile court judge or a substitute judge authorized by Section 51.04(f); or

(2) the child and the attorney for the child have in accordance with Section 51.09 waived the right to have the determination made by the juvenile court judge or a substitute judge.

(c) If a child objects to a referee making the determination under Section 53.02(f), the juvenile court judge or a substitute judge authorized by Section 51.04(f) shall make the determination.

(d) At the conclusion of the hearing or immediately after making the determination, the referee shall transmit written findings and recommendations to the juvenile court judge. The juvenile court judge shall adopt, modify, or reject the referee's recommendations not later than the next working day after the day that the judge receives the recommendations. Failure to act within that time results in release of the child by operation of law and a recommendation that the child be released operates to secure the child's immediate release subject to the power of the juvenile court judge to modify or reject that recommendation.

(e) Except as provided by Subsection (f), the hearings provided by Sections 54.03, 54.04, and 54.05 may not be held before a referee if the grand jury has approved of the petition and the child is subject to a determinate sentence.

(f) When the state and a child who is subject to a determinate sentence agree to the disposition of the case, wholly or partly, a referee or associate judge may hold a hearing for the purpose of allowing the child to enter a plea or stipulation of evidence. After the hearing under this subsection, the referee or associate judge shall transmit the referee's or associate judge's written findings and recommendations regarding the plea or stipulation of evidence to the juvenile court judge for consideration. The juvenile court judge may accept or reject the plea or stipulation of evidence in accordance with Section 54.03(j).

Sec. 54.11. Release or Transfer Hearing.

(a) On receipt of a referral under Section 244.014(a), Human Resources Code, for the transfer to the Texas Department of Criminal Justice of a person committed to the Texas Juvenile Justice Department under Section 54.04(d)(3), 54.04(m), or 54.05(f), on receipt of a request by the Texas Juvenile Justice Department under Section 245.051(d), Human Resources Code, for approval of the release under supervision of a person committed to the Texas Juvenile Justice Department under Section 54.04(d)(3), 54.04(m), or 54.05(f), or on receipt of a referral under Section 152.0016(g) or (j), Human Resources Code, the court shall set a time and place for a hearing on the possible transfer or release of the person, as applicable.

(b) The court shall notify the following of the time and place of the hearing:

(1) the person to be transferred or released under supervision;

(2) the parents of the person;

(3) any legal custodian of the person, including the Texas Juvenile Justice Department or a juvenile board or local juvenile probation department if the child is committed to a post-adjudication secure correctional facility;

(4) the office of the prosecuting attorney that represented the state in the juvenile delinquency proceedings;

(5) the victim of the offense that was included in the delinquent conduct that was a ground for the disposition, or a member of the victim's family; and

(6) any other person who has filed a written request with the court to be notified of a release hearing with respect to the person to be transferred or released under supervision.

(c) Except for the person to be transferred or released under supervision and the prosecuting attorney, the failure to notify a person listed in Subsection (b) of this section does not affect the validity of a hearing conducted or determination made under this section if the record in the case reflects that the whereabouts of the persons who did not receive notice were unknown to the court and a reasonable effort was made by the court to locate those persons.

(d) At a hearing under this section the court may consider written reports and supporting documents from probation officers, professional court employees, guardians ad litem appointed under Section 51.11(d), professional consultants, employees of the Texas Juvenile Justice Department, or employees of a post-adjudication secure correctional facility in addition to the testimony of witnesses. On or before the fifth day before the date of the hearing, the court shall provide the attorney for the person to be transferred or released under supervision with access to all written matter to be considered by the court. All written matter is admissible in evidence at the hearing.

(e) At the hearing, the person to be transferred or released under supervision is entitled to an attorney, to examine all witnesses against him, to present evidence and oral argument, and to previous examination of all reports on and evaluations and examinations of or relating to him that may be used in the hearing.

(f) A hearing under this section is open to the public unless the person to be transferred or released under supervision waives a public hearing with the consent of his attorney and the court.

(g) A hearing under this section must be recorded by a court reporter or by audio or video tape recording, and the record of the hearing must be retained by the court for at least two years after the date of the final determination on the transfer or release of the person by the court.

(h) The hearing on a person who is referred for transfer under Section 152.0016(j) or 244.014(a), Human Resources Code, shall be held not later than the 60th day after the date the court receives the referral.

(i) On conclusion of the hearing on a person who is referred for transfer under Section 152.0016(j) or 244.014(a), Human Resources Code, the court may, as applicable, order:

(1) the return of the person to the Texas Juvenile Justice Department or post-adjudication secure correctional facility; or

(2) the transfer of the person to the custody of the Texas Department of Criminal Justice for the completion of the person's sentence.

(j) On conclusion of the hearing on a person who is referred for release under supervision under Section 152.0016(g) or 245.051(c), Human Resources Code, the court may, as applicable, order the return of the person to the Texas Juvenile Justice Department or post-adjudication secure correctional facility:

(1) with approval for the release of the person under supervision; or

(2) without approval for the release of the person under supervision.

(k) In making a determination under this section, the court may consider the experiences and character of the person before and after commitment to the Texas Juvenile Justice Department or post-adjudication secure correctional facility, the nature of the penal offense that the person was found to have committed and the manner in which the offense was committed, the abilities of the person to contribute to society, the protection of the victim of the offense or any member of the victim's family, the recommendations of the Texas Juvenile Justice Department, county juvenile board, local juvenile probation department, and prosecuting attorney, the best interests of the person, and any other factor relevant to the issue to be decided.

(*l*) Pending the conclusion of a transfer hearing, the juvenile court shall order that the person who is referred for transfer be detained in a certified juvenile detention facility as provided by Subsection (m). If the person is at least 17 years of age, the juvenile court may order that the person be detained without bond in an appropriate county facility for the detention of adults accused of criminal offenses.

(m) The detention of a person in a certified juvenile detention facility must comply with the detention requirements under this title, except that, to the extent practicable, the person must be kept separate from children detained in the same facility.

(n) If the juvenile court orders that a person who is referred for transfer be detained in a county facility under Subsection (*l*), the county sheriff shall take custody of the person under the juvenile court's order.

(o) In this section, "post-adjudication secure correctional facility" has the meaning assigned by Section 54.04011.

CHAPTER 55
PROCEEDINGS CONCERNING CHILDREN WITH MENTAL ILLNESS OR INTELLECTUAL DISABILITY

SUBCHAPTER A
GENERAL PROVISIONS

Sec. 55.01. Meaning of "Having a Mental Illness".

For purposes of this chapter, a child who is described as having a mental illness means a child with a mental illness as defined by Section 571.003, Health and Safety Code.

Sec. 55.02. Mental Health and Intellectual Disability Jurisdiction.

For the purpose of initiating proceedings to order mental health or intellectual disability services for a child or for commitment of a child as provided by this chapter, the juvenile court has jurisdiction of proceedings under Subtitle C or D, Title 7, Health and Safety Code.

Sec. 55.03. Standards of Care.

(a) Except as provided by this chapter, a child for whom inpatient mental health services is ordered by a court under this chapter shall be cared for as provided by Subtitle C, Title 7, Health and Safety Code.

(b) Except as provided by this chapter, a child who is committed by a court to a residential care facility due to an intellectual disability shall be cared for as provided by Subtitle D, Title 7, Health and Safety Code.

CHAPTER 56
APPEAL

Sec. 56.01. Right to Appeal.

(a) Except as provided by Subsection (b-1), an appeal from an order of a juvenile court is to a court of appeals and the case may be carried to the Texas Supreme Court by writ of error or upon certificate, as in civil cases generally.

(b) The requirements governing an appeal are as in civil cases generally. When an appeal is sought by filing a notice of appeal, security for costs of appeal, or an affidavit of inability to pay the costs of appeal, and the filing is made in a timely fashion after the date the disposition order is signed, the appeal must include the juvenile court adjudication and all rulings contributing to that adjudication. An appeal of the adjudication may be sought notwithstanding that the adjudication order was signed more than 30 days before the date the notice of appeal, security for costs of appeal, or affidavit of inability to pay the costs of appeal was filed.

(b-1) A motion for new trial seeking to vacate an adjudication is:

(1) timely if the motion is filed not later than the 30th day after the date on which the disposition order is signed; and

(2) governed by Rule 21, Texas Rules of Appellate Procedure.

(c) An appeal may be taken:

(1) except as provided by Subsection (n), by or on behalf of a child from an order entered under:

(A) Section 54.02 respecting transfer of the child for prosecution as an adult;

(B) Section 54.03 with regard to delinquent conduct or conduct indicating a need for supervision;

(C) Section 54.04 disposing of the case;

(D) Section 54.05 respecting modification of a previous juvenile court disposition; or

(E) Chapter 55 by a juvenile court committing a child to a facility for the mentally ill or intellectually disabled; or

(2) by a person from an order entered under Section 54.11(i)(2) transferring the person to the custody of the Texas Department of Criminal Justice.

(d) A child has the right to:

(1) appeal, as provided by this subchapter;

(2) representation by counsel on appeal; and

(3) appointment of an attorney for the appeal if an attorney cannot be obtained because of indigency.

(e) On entering an order that is appealable under this section, the court shall advise the child and the child's parent, guardian, or guardian ad litem of the child's rights listed under Subsection (d) of this section.

(f) If the child and his parent, guardian, or guardian ad litem express a desire to appeal, the attorney who represented the child before the juvenile court shall file a notice of appeal with the juvenile court and inform the court whether that attorney will handle the appeal. Counsel shall be appointed under the standards provided in Section 51.10 of this code unless the right to appeal is waived in accordance with Section 51.09 of this code.

(g) An appeal does not suspend the order of the juvenile court, nor does it release the child from the custody of that court or of the person, institution, or agency to whose care the child is committed, unless the juvenile court so orders. However, the appellate court may provide for a personal bond.

(g-1) An appeal from an order entered under Section 54.02 respecting transfer of the child for prosecution as an adult does not stay the criminal proceedings pending the disposition of that appeal.

(h) If the order appealed from takes custody of the child from the child's parent, guardian, or custodian or waives jurisdiction under Section 54.02 and transfers the child to criminal court for prosecution, the appeal has precedence over all other cases.

(h-1) The supreme court shall adopt rules accelerating the disposition by the appellate court and the supreme court of an appeal of an order waiving jurisdiction under Section 54.02 and transferring a child to criminal court for prosecution.

(i) The appellate court may affirm, reverse, or modify the judgment or order, including an order of disposition or modified disposition, from which appeal was taken. It may reverse or modify an order of disposition or modified order of disposition while affirming the juvenile court adjudication that the child engaged in delinquent conduct or conduct indicating a need for supervision. It may remand an order that it reverses or modifies for further proceedings by the juvenile court.

(j) Neither the child nor his family shall be identified in an appellate opinion rendered in an appeal or habeas corpus proceedings related to juvenile court proceedings under this title. The appellate opinion shall be styled, "In the matter of __," identifying the child by his initials only.

(k) The appellate court shall dismiss an appeal on the state's motion, supported by affidavit showing that the appellant has escaped from custody pending the appeal and, to the affiant's knowledge, has not voluntarily returned to the state's custody on or before the 10th day after the date of the escape. The court may not dismiss an appeal, or if the appeal has been dismissed, shall reinstate the appeal, on the filing of an affidavit of an officer or other credible person showing that the appellant voluntarily returned to custody on or before the 10th day after the date of the escape.

(*l*) The court may order the child, the child's parent, or other person responsible for support of the child to pay the child's costs of appeal, including the costs of representation by an attorney, unless the court determines the person to be ordered to pay the costs is indigent.

(m) For purposes of determining indigency of the child under this section, the court shall consider the assets and income of the child, the child's parent, and any other person responsible for the support of the child.

(n) A child who enters a plea or agrees to a stipulation of evidence in a proceeding held under this title may not appeal an order of the juvenile court entered under Section 54.03, 54.04, or 54.05 if the court makes a disposition in accordance with the agreement between the state and the child regarding the disposition of the case, unless:

(1) the court gives the child permission to appeal; or

(2) the appeal is based on a matter raised by written motion filed before the proceeding in which the child entered the plea or agreed to the stipulation of evidence.

(o) This section does not limit a child's right to obtain a writ of habeas corpus.

Sec. 56.02. Transcript on Appeal.

(a) An attorney retained to represent a child on appeal who desires to have included in the record on appeal a transcription of notes of the reporter has the responsibility of obtaining and paying for the transcription and furnishing it to the clerk in duplicate in time for inclusion in the record.

(b) The juvenile court shall order the reporter to furnish a transcription without charge to the attorney if the court finds, after hearing or on an affidavit filed by the child's parent or other person responsible for support of the child that the parent or other responsible person is unable to pay or to give security therefor.

(c) On certificate of the court that a transcription has been provided without charge, payment therefor shall be made from the general funds of the county in which the proceedings appealed from occurred.

(d) The court reporter shall report any portion of the proceedings requested by either party or directed by the court and shall report the proceedings in question and answer form unless a narrative transcript is requested.

Sec. 56.03. Appeal by State in Cases of Offenses Eligible for Determinate Sentence.

(a) In this section, "prosecuting attorney" means the county attorney, district attorney, or criminal district attorney who has the primary responsibility of presenting cases in the juvenile court. The term does not include an assistant prosecuting attorney.

(b) The state is entitled to appeal an order of a court in a juvenile case in which the grand jury has approved of the petition under Section 53.045 if the order:

(1) dismisses a petition or any portion of a petition;

(2) arrests or modifies a judgment;

(3) grants a new trial;

(4) sustains a claim of former jeopardy; or

(5) grants a motion to suppress evidence, a confession, or an admission and if:

(A) jeopardy has not attached in the case;

(B) the prosecuting attorney certifies to the trial court that the appeal is not taken for the purpose of delay; and

(C) the evidence, confession, or admission is of substantial importance in the case.

(c) The prosecuting attorney may not bring an appeal under Subsection (b) later than the 15th day after the date on which the order or ruling to be appealed is entered by the court.

(d) The state is entitled to a stay in the proceedings pending the disposition of an appeal under Subsection (b).

(e) The court of appeals shall give preference in its docket to an appeal filed under Subsection (b).

(f) The state shall pay all costs of appeal under Subsection (b), other than the cost of attorney's fees for the respondent.

(g) If the respondent is represented by appointed counsel, the counsel shall continue to represent the respondent as appointed counsel on the appeal. If the respondent is not represented by appointed counsel, the respondent may seek the appointment of counsel to represent the respondent on appeal. The juvenile court shall determine whether the parent or other person responsible for support of the child is financially able to obtain an attorney to represent the respondent on appeal. If the court determines that the parent or other person is financially unable to obtain counsel for the appeal, the court shall appoint counsel to represent the respondent on appeal.

(h) If the state appeals under this section and the respondent is not detained, the court shall permit the respondent to remain at large subject only to the condition that the respondent appear in court for further proceedings when required by the court. If the respondent is detained, on the state's filing of notice of appeal under this section, the respondent is entitled to immediate release from detention on the allegation that is the subject of the appeal. The court shall permit the respondent to remain at large regarding that allegation subject only to the condition that the respondent appear in court for further proceedings when required by the court.

(i) The Texas Rules of Appellate Procedure apply to a petition by the state to the supreme court for review of a decision of a court of appeals in a juvenile case.

CHAPTER 57
RIGHTS OF VICTIMS

Sec. 57.001. Definitions.

In this chapter:

(1) "Close relative of a deceased victim" means a person who was the spouse of a deceased victim at the time of the victim's death or who is a parent or adult brother, sister, or child of the deceased victim.

(2) "Guardian of a victim" means a person who is the legal guardian of the victim, whether or not the legal relationship between the guardian and victim exists because of the age of the victim or the physical or mental incompetency of the victim.

(3) "Victim" means a person who as the result of the delinquent conduct of a child suffers a pecuniary loss or personal injury or harm.

Sec. 57.002. Victim's Rights.

(a) A victim, guardian of a victim, or close relative of a deceased victim is entitled to the following rights within the juvenile justice system:

(1) the right to receive from law enforcement agencies adequate protection from harm and threats of harm arising from cooperation with prosecution efforts;

(2) the right to have the court or person appointed by the court take the safety of the victim or the victim's family into consideration as an element in determining whether the child should be detained before the child's conduct is adjudicated;

(3) the right, if requested, to be informed of relevant court proceedings, including appellate proceedings, and to be informed in a timely manner if those court proceedings have been canceled or rescheduled;

(4) the right to be informed, when requested, by the court or a person appointed by the court concerning the procedures in the juvenile justice system, including general procedures relating to:

(A) the preliminary investigation and deferred prosecution of a case; and

(B) the appeal of the case;

(5) the right to provide pertinent information to a juvenile court conducting a disposition hearing concerning the impact of the offense on the victim and the victim's family by testimony, written statement, or any other manner before the court renders its disposition;

(6) the right to receive information regarding compensation to victims as provided by Chapter 56B, Code of Criminal Procedure, including information related to the costs that may be compensated under that chapter and the amount of compensation, eligibility for compensation, and procedures for application for compensation under that chapter, the payment of medical expenses under Subchapter F, Chapter 56A, Code of Criminal Procedure, for a victim of a sexual assault, and when requested, to referral to available social service agencies that may offer additional assistance;

(7) the right to be informed, upon request, of procedures for release under supervision or transfer of the person to the custody of the Texas Department of Criminal Justice for parole, to participate in the release or transfer for parole process, to be notified, if requested, of the person's release, escape, or transfer for parole proceedings concerning the person, to provide to the Texas Juvenile Justice Department for inclusion in the person's file information to be considered by the department before the release under supervision or transfer for parole of the person, and to be notified, if requested, of the person's release or transfer for parole;

(8) the right to be provided with a waiting area, separate or secure from other witnesses, including the child alleged to have committed the conduct and relatives of the child, before testifying in any proceeding concerning the child, or, if a separate waiting area is not available, other safeguards should be taken to minimize the victim's contact with the child and the child's relatives and witnesses, before and during court proceedings;

(9) the right to prompt return of any property of the victim that is held by a law enforcement agency or the attorney for the state as evidence when the property is no longer required for that purpose;

(10) the right to have the attorney for the state notify the employer of the victim, if requested, of the necessity of the victim's cooperation and testimony in a proceeding that may necessitate the absence of the victim from work for good cause;

(11) the right to be present at all public court proceedings related to the conduct of the child as provided by Section 54.08, subject to that section; and

(12) any other right appropriate to the victim that a victim of criminal conduct has under Subchapter B, Chapter 56A, Code of Criminal Procedure.

(b) In notifying a victim of the release or escape of a person, the Texas Juvenile Justice Department shall use the same procedure established for the notification of the release or escape of an adult offender under Subchapter K, Chapter 56A, Code of Criminal Procedure.

Sec. 57.003. Duties of Juvenile Board and Victim Assistance Coordinator.

(a) The juvenile board shall ensure to the extent practicable that a victim, guardian of a victim, or close relative of a deceased victim is afforded the rights granted by Section 57.002 and, on request, an explanation of those rights.

(b) The juvenile board may designate a person to serve as victim assistance coordinator in the juvenile board's jurisdiction for victims of juvenile offenders.

(c) The victim assistance coordinator shall ensure that a victim, or close relative of a deceased victim, is afforded the rights granted victims, guardians, and relatives by Section 57.002 and, on request, an explanation of those rights. The victim assistance coordinator shall work closely with appropriate law enforcement agencies, prosecuting attorneys, and the Texas Juvenile Justice Department in carrying out that duty.

(d) The victim assistance coordinator shall ensure that at a minimum, a victim, guardian of a victim, or close relative of a deceased victim receives:

(1) a written notice of the rights outlined in Section 57.002;

(2) an application for compensation under the Crime Victims' Compensation Act (Chapter 56B, Code of Criminal Procedure); and

(3) a victim impact statement with information explaining the possible use and consideration of the victim impact statement at detention, adjudication, and release proceedings involving the juvenile.

(e) The victim assistance coordinator shall, on request, offer to assist a person receiving a form under Subsection (d) to complete the form.

(f) The victim assistance coordinator shall send a copy of the victim impact statement to the court conducting a disposition hearing involving the juvenile.

(g) The juvenile board, with the approval of the commissioners court of the county, may approve a program in which the victim assistance coordinator may offer not more than 10 hours of posttrial psychological counseling for a person who serves as a juror or an alternate juror in an adjudication hearing involving graphic evidence or testimony and who requests the posttrial psychological counseling not later than the 180th day after the date on which the jury in the adjudication hearing is dismissed. The victim assistance coordinator may provide the counseling using a provider that assists local juvenile justice agencies in providing similar services to victims.

Sec. 57.0031. Notification of Rights of Victims of Juveniles.

Texas Family Code

At the initial contact or at the earliest possible time after the initial contact between the victim of a reported crime and the juvenile probation office having the responsibility for the disposition of the juvenile, the office shall provide the victim a written notice:

(1) containing information about the availability of emergency and medical services, if applicable;

(2) stating that the victim has the right to receive information regarding compensation to victims of crime as provided by the Crime Victims' Compensation Act (Chapter 56B, Code of Criminal Procedure), including information about:

(A) the costs that may be compensated and the amount of compensation, eligibility for compensation, and procedures for application for compensation;

(B) the payment for a medical examination for a victim of a sexual assault; and

(C) referral to available social service agencies that may offer additional assistance;

(3) stating the name, address, and phone number of the victim assistance coordinator for victims of juveniles;

(4) containing the following statement: "You may call the crime victim assistance coordinator for the status of the case and information about victims' rights.";

(5) stating the rights of victims of crime under Section 57.002;

(6) summarizing each procedural stage in the processing of a juvenile case, including preliminary investigation, detention, informal adjustment of a case, disposition hearings, release proceedings, restitution, and appeals;

(7) suggesting steps the victim may take if the victim is subjected to threats or intimidation;

(8) stating the case number and assigned court for the case; and

(9) stating that the victim has the right to file a victim impact statement and to have it considered in juvenile proceedings.

Sec. 57.004. Notification.

A court, a person appointed by the court, or the Texas Juvenile Justice Department is responsible for notifying a victim, guardian of a victim, or close relative of a deceased victim of a proceeding under this chapter only if the victim, guardian of a victim, or close relative of a deceased victim requests the notification in writing and provides a current address to which the notification is to be sent.

Sec. 57.005. Liability.

The Texas Juvenile Justice Department, a juvenile board, a court, a person appointed by a court, an attorney for the state, a peace officer, or a law enforcement agency is not liable for a failure or inability to provide a right listed under Section 57.002.

Sec. 57.006. Appeal.

The failure or inability of any person to provide a right or service listed under Section 57.002 of this code may not be used by a child as a ground for appeal or for a post conviction writ of habeas corpus.

Sec. 57.007. Standing.

A victim, guardian of a victim, or close relative of a victim does not have standing to participate as a party in a juvenile proceeding or to contest the disposition of any case.

Sec. 57.008. Court Order for Protection from Juveniles.

(a) A court may issue an order for protection from juveniles directed against a child to protect a victim of the child's conduct who, because of the victim's participation in the juvenile justice system, risks further harm by the child.

(b) In the order, the court may prohibit the child from doing specified acts or require the child to do specified acts necessary or appropriate to prevent or reduce the likelihood of further harm to the victim by the child.

CHAPTER 58
RECORDS; JUVENILE JUSTICE INFORMATION SYSTEM

SUBCHAPTER A
CREATION AND CONFIDENTIALITY OF JUVENILE RECORDS

Sec. 58.001. Law Enforcement Collection and Transmittal of Records of Children.

(a) Law enforcement officers and other juvenile justice personnel shall collect information described by Section 58.104 as a part of the juvenile justice information system created under Subchapter B.

(b) [Repealed.]

(c) A law enforcement agency shall forward information, including fingerprints, relating to a child who has been taken into custody under Section 52.01 by the agency to the Department of Public Safety for inclusion in the juvenile justice information system created under Subchapter B, but only if the child is referred to juvenile court on or before the 10th day after the date the child is taken into custody under Section 52.01. If the child is not referred to juvenile court within that time, the law enforcement agency shall destroy all information, including photographs and fingerprints, relating to the child unless the child is placed in a first offender program under Section 52.031 or on informal disposition under Section 52.03. The law enforcement agency may not forward any information to the Department of Public Safety relating to the child while the child is in a first offender program under Section 52.031, or during the 90 days following successful completion of the program or while the child is on informal disposition under Section 52.03. Except as provided by Subsection (f), after the date the child completes an informal disposition under Section 52.03 or after the 90th day after the date the child successfully completes a first offender program under Section 52.031, the law enforcement agency shall destroy all information, including photographs and fingerprints, relating to the child.

(d) If information relating to a child is contained in a document that also contains information relating to an adult and a law enforcement agency is required to destroy all information relating to the child under this section, the agency shall alter the document so that the information relating to the child is destroyed and the information relating to the adult is preserved.

(e) The deletion of a computer entry constitutes destruction of the information contained in the entry.

(f) A law enforcement agency may maintain information relating to a child after the 90th day after the date the child successfully completes a first offender program under Section 52.031 only to determine the child's eligibility to participate in a first offender program.

Sec. 58.002. Photographs and Fingerprints of Children.

(a) Except as provided by Chapter 63, Code of Criminal Procedure, a child may not be photographed or fingerprinted without the consent of the juvenile court unless the child is:

(1) taken into custody; or

(2) referred to the juvenile court for conduct that constitutes a felony or a misdemeanor punishable by confinement in jail, regardless of whether the child has been taken into custody.

(b) On or before December 31 of each year, the head of each municipal or county law enforcement agency located in a county shall certify to the juvenile board for that county that the photographs and fingerprints required to be destroyed under Section 58.001 have been destroyed. The juvenile board may conduct or cause to be conducted an audit of the records of the law enforcement agency to verify the destruction of the photographs and fingerprints and the law enforcement agency shall make its records available for this purpose. If the audit shows that the certification provided by the head of the law enforcement agency is false, that person is subject to prosecution for perjury under Chapter 37, Penal Code.

(c) This section does not prohibit a law enforcement officer from photographing or fingerprinting a child who is not in custody or who has not been referred to the juvenile court for conduct that constitutes a felony or misdemeanor punishable by confinement in jail if the child's parent or guardian voluntarily consents in writing to the photographing or fingerprinting of the child. Consent of the child's parent or guardian is not required to photograph or fingerprint a child described by Subsection (a)(1) or (2).

(d) This section does not apply to fingerprints that are required or authorized to be submitted or obtained for an application for a driver's license or personal identification card.

(e) This section does not prohibit a law enforcement officer from fingerprinting or photographing a child as provided by Section 58.0021.

Sec. 58.0021. Fingerprints or Photographs for Comparison in Investigation.

(a) A law enforcement officer may take temporary custody of a child to take the child's fingerprints if:

(1) the officer has probable cause to believe that the child has engaged in delinquent conduct;

(2) the officer has investigated that conduct and has found other fingerprints during the investigation; and

(3) the officer has probable cause to believe that the child's fingerprints will match the other fingerprints.

(b) A law enforcement officer may take temporary custody of a child to take the child's photograph, or may obtain a photograph of a child from a juvenile probation department in possession of a photograph of the child, if:

(1) the officer has probable cause to believe that the child has engaged in delinquent conduct; and

(2) the officer has probable cause to believe that the child's photograph will be of material assistance in the investigation of that conduct.

(c) Temporary custody for the purpose described by Subsection (a) or (b):

(1) is not a taking into custody under Section 52.01; and

(2) may not be reported to the juvenile justice information system under Subchapter B.

(d) If a law enforcement officer does not take the child into custody under Section 52.01, the child shall be released from temporary custody authorized under this section as soon as the fingerprints or photographs are obtained.

(e) A law enforcement officer who under this section obtains fingerprints or photographs from a child shall:

(1) immediately destroy them if they do not lead to a positive comparison or identification; and

(2) make a reasonable effort to notify the child's parent, guardian, or custodian of the action taken.

(f) A law enforcement officer may under this section obtain fingerprints or photographs from a child at:

(1) a juvenile processing office; or

(2) a location that affords reasonable privacy to the child.

Sec. 58.0022. Fingerprints or Photographs to Identify Runaways.

A law enforcement officer who takes a child into custody with probable cause to believe that the child has engaged in conduct indicating a need for supervision as described by Section 51.03(b)(2) and who after reasonable effort is unable to determine the identity of the child, may fingerprint or photograph the child to establish the child's identity. On determination of the child's identity or that the child cannot be identified by the fingerprints or photographs, the law enforcement officer shall immediately destroy all copies of the fingerprint records or photographs of the child.

Sec. 58.003. Sealing of Records.

(a)-(c-2) [Repealed.] [See Editor's Notes]

(c-3) [Repealed.]

(c-4)-(p) [Repealed.] [See Editor's Notes]

Sec. 58.004. Redaction of Victim's Personally Identifiable Information.

(a) Notwithstanding any other law, before disclosing any juvenile court record of a child as authorized by this chapter or other law, the custodian of the record must redact any personally identifiable information about a victim of the child's delinquent conduct or conduct indicating a need for supervision who was under 18 years of age on the date the conduct occurred.

(b) This section does not apply to information that is:

(1) necessary for an agency to provide services to the victim;

(2) necessary for law enforcement purposes;

(3) shared within the statewide juvenile information and case management system established under Subchapter E;

(4) shared with an attorney representing the child in a proceeding under this title; or

(5) shared with an attorney representing any other person in a juvenile or criminal court proceeding arising from the same act or conduct for which the child was referred to juvenile court.

Sec. 58.005. Confidentiality of Facility Records.

(a) This section applies only to the inspection, copying, and maintenance of a record concerning a child and to the storage of information from which a record could be generated, including personally identifiable information, information obtained for the purpose of diagnosis, examination, evaluation, or treatment of the child or for making a referral for treatment of the child, and other records or information, created by or in the possession of:

(1) the Texas Juvenile Justice Department;

(2) an entity having custody of the child under a contract with the Texas Juvenile Justice Department; or

(3) another public or private agency or institution having custody of the child under order of the juvenile court, including a facility operated by or under contract with a juvenile board or juvenile probation department.

(a-1) Except as provided by Article 15.27, Code of Criminal Procedure, the records and information to which this section applies may be disclosed only to:

(1) the professional staff or consultants of the agency or institution;

(2) the judge, probation officers, and professional staff or consultants of the juvenile court;

(3) an attorney for the child;

(4) a governmental agency if the disclosure is required or authorized by law;

(5) an individual or entity to whom the child is referred for treatment or services, including assistance in transitioning the child to the community after the child's release or discharge from a juvenile facility;

(6) the Texas Department of Criminal Justice and the Texas Juvenile Justice Department for the

purpose of maintaining statistical records of recidivism and for diagnosis and classification;

(7) a prosecuting attorney;

(8) a parent, guardian, or custodian with whom a child will reside after the child's release or discharge from a juvenile facility;

(9) a governmental agency or court if the record is necessary for an administrative or legal proceeding and the personally identifiable information about the child is redacted before the record is disclosed; or

(10) with permission from the juvenile court, any other individual, agency, or institution having a legitimate interest in the proceeding or in the work of the court.

(b) This section does not affect the collection, dissemination, or maintenance of information as provided by Subchapter B or D-1.

(c) An individual or entity that receives confidential information under this section may not disclose the information unless otherwise authorized by law.

Sec. 58.0051. Interagency Sharing of Educational Records.

(a) In this section:

(1) "Educational records" means records in the possession of a primary or secondary educational institution that contain information relating to a student, including information relating to the student's:

(A) identity;

(B) special needs;

(C) educational accommodations;

(D) assessment or diagnostic test results;

(E) attendance records;

(F) disciplinary records;

(G) medical records; and

(H) psychological diagnoses.

(2) "Juvenile service provider" means a governmental entity that provides juvenile justice or prevention, medical, educational, or other support services to a juvenile. The term includes:

(A) a state or local juvenile justice agency as defined by Section 58.101;

(B) health and human services agencies, as defined by Section 531.001, Government Code, and the Health and Human Services Commission;

(C) the Department of Family and Protective Services;

(D) the Department of Public Safety;

(E) the Texas Education Agency;

(F) an independent school district;

(G) a juvenile justice alternative education program;

(H) a charter school;

(I) a local mental health or mental retardation authority;

(J) a court with jurisdiction over juveniles;

(K) a district attorney's office;

(L) a county attorney's office; and

(M) a children's advocacy center established under Section 264.402.

(3) "Student" means a person who:

(A) is registered or in attendance at a primary or secondary educational institution; and

(B) is younger than 18 years of age.

(b) At the request of a juvenile service provider, an independent school district or a charter school shall disclose to the juvenile service provider confidential information contained in the student's educational records if the student has been:

(1) taken into custody under Section 52.01; or

(2) referred to a juvenile court for allegedly engaging in delinquent conduct or conduct indicating a need for supervision.

(c) An independent school district or charter school that discloses confidential information to a juvenile service provider under Subsection (b) may not destroy a record of the disclosed information before the seventh anniversary of the date the information is disclosed.

(d) An independent school district or charter school shall comply with a request under Subsection (b) regardless of whether other state law makes that information confidential.

(e) A juvenile service provider that receives confidential information under this section shall:

(1) certify in writing that the juvenile service provider receiving the confidential information has agreed not to disclose it to a third party, other than another juvenile service provider; and

(2) use the confidential information only to:

(A) verify the identity of a student involved in the juvenile justice system; and

(B) provide delinquency prevention or treatment services to the student.

(f) A juvenile service provider may establish an internal protocol for sharing information with other juvenile service providers as necessary to efficiently and promptly disclose and accept the information. The protocol may specify the types of information that may be shared under this section without violating federal law, including any federal funding requirements. A juvenile service provider may enter into a memorandum of understanding with another juvenile service provider to share information according to the juvenile service provider's protocols. A juvenile service provider shall comply with this section regardless of whether the juvenile service provider establishes an internal protocol or enters into a memorandum of understanding under this subsection unless compliance with this section violates federal law.

(g) This section does not affect the confidential status of the information being shared. The information may be released to a third party only as directed by a court order or as otherwise authorized by law. Personally identifiable information disclosed to a juvenile service provider under this section is not subject to disclosure to a third party under Chapter 552, Government Code.

(h) A juvenile service provider that requests information under this section shall pay a fee to the disclosing juvenile service provider in the same amounts charged for the provision of public information under Subchapter F, Chapter 552, Government Code, unless:

(1) a memorandum of understanding between the requesting provider and the disclosing provider:

(A) prohibits the payment of a fee;

(B) provides for the waiver of a fee; or

(C) provides an alternate method of assessing a fee;

(2) the disclosing provider waives the payment of the fee; or

(3) disclosure of the information is required by law other than this subchapter.

Sec. 58.0052. Interagency Sharing of Certain Noneducational Records.

(a) In this section:

(1) "Juvenile justice agency" has the meaning assigned by Section 58.101.

(2) "Juvenile service provider" has the meaning assigned by Section 58.0051.

(3) "Multi-system youth" means a person who:

(A) is younger than 19 years of age; and

(B) has received services from two or more juvenile service providers.

(4) "Personal health information" means personally identifiable information regarding a multi-system youth's physical or mental health or the provision of or payment for health care services, including case management services, to a multi-system youth. The term does not include clinical psychological notes or substance abuse treatment information.

(b) Subject to Subsection (c), at the request of a juvenile service provider, another juvenile service provider shall disclose to that provider a multi-system youth's personal health information or a history of governmental services provided to the multi-system youth, including:

(1) identity records;

(2) medical and dental records;

(3) assessment or diagnostic test results;

(4) special needs;

(5) program placements;

(6) psychological diagnoses; and

(7) other related records or information.

(b-1) In addition to the information provided under Subsection (b), the Department of Family and Protective Services and the Texas Juvenile Justice Department shall coordinate and develop protocols for sharing with each other, on request, any other information relating to a multi-system youth necessary to:

(1) identify and coordinate the provision of services to the youth and prevent duplication of services;

(2) enhance rehabilitation of the youth; and

(3) improve and maintain community safety.

(b-2) At the request of the Department of Family and Protective Services or a single source continuum contractor who contracts with the department to provide foster care services, a state or local juvenile justice agency shall share with the department or contractor information in the possession of the juvenile justice agency that is necessary to improve and maintain community safety or that assists the department or contractor in the continuation of services for or providing services to a multi-system youth who is or has been in the custody or control of the juvenile justice agency.

(b-3) At the request of a state or local juvenile justice agency, the Department of Family and Protective Services or a single source continuum contractor who contracts with the department to provide foster care services shall, not later than the 14th business day after the date of the request, share with the juvenile justice agency information in the possession of the department or contractor that is necessary to improve and maintain community safety or that assists the agency in the continuation of services for or providing services to a multi-system youth who:

(1) is or has been in the temporary or permanent managing conservatorship of the department;

(2) is or was the subject of a family-based safety services case with the department;

(3) has been reported as an alleged victim of abuse or neglect to the department;

(4) is the perpetrator in a case in which the department investigation concluded that there was a reason to believe that abuse or neglect occurred; or

(5) is a victim in a case in which the department investigation concluded that there was a reason to believe that abuse or neglect occurred.

(c) A juvenile service provider may disclose personally identifiable information under this section only for the purposes of:

(1) identifying a multi-system youth;

(2) coordinating and monitoring care for a multi-system youth; and

(3) improving the quality of juvenile services provided to a multi-system youth.

(d) To the extent that this section conflicts with another law of this state with respect to confidential information held by a governmental agency, this section controls.

(e) A juvenile service provider may establish an internal protocol for sharing information with other juvenile service providers as necessary to efficiently and promptly disclose and accept the information. The protocol may specify the types of information that may be shared under this section without violating federal law, including any federal funding requirements. A juvenile service provider may enter into a memorandum of understanding with another juvenile service provider to share information according to the juvenile service provider's protocols. A juvenile service provider shall comply with this section regardless of whether the juvenile service provider establishes an internal protocol or enters into a memorandum of understanding under this subsection unless compliance with this section violates federal law.

(f) This section does not affect the confidential status of the information being shared. The information may be released to a third party only as directed by a court order or as otherwise authorized by law. Personally identifiable information disclosed to a juvenile service provider under this section is not subject to disclosure to a third party under Chapter 552, Government Code.

(g) This section does not affect the authority of a governmental agency to disclose to a third party for research purposes information that is not personally identifiable as provided by the governmental agency's protocol.

(h) A juvenile service provider that requests information under this section shall pay a fee to the disclosing juvenile service provider in the same amounts charged for the provision of public information under Subchapter F, Chapter 552, Government Code, unless:

(1) a memorandum of understanding between the requesting provider and the disclosing provider:

(A) prohibits the payment of a fee;

(B) provides for the waiver of a fee; or

(C) provides an alternate method of assessing a fee;

(2) the disclosing provider waives the payment of the fee; or

(3) disclosure of the information is required by law other than this subchapter.

Sec. 58.0053. Interagency Sharing of Juvenile Probation Records. [Repealed]

Sec. 58.006. Destruction of Certain Records. [Repealed]

Sec. 58.007. Confidentiality of Probation Department, Prosecutor, and Court Records.

(a) This section applies only to the inspection, copying, and maintenance of a record concerning a child and the storage of information, by electronic means or otherwise, concerning the child from which a record could be generated and does not affect the collection, dissemination, or maintenance of information as provided by Subchapter B or D-1. This section does not apply to a record relating to a child that is:

(1) required or authorized to be maintained under the laws regulating the operation of motor vehicles in this state;

(2) maintained by a municipal or justice court; or

(3) subject to disclosure under Chapter 62, Code of Criminal Procedure.

(b) Except as provided by Section 54.051(d-1) and by Article 15.27, Code of Criminal Procedure, the records, whether physical or electronic, of a juvenile court, a clerk of court, a juvenile probation department, or a prosecuting attorney relating to a child who is a party to a proceeding under this title may be inspected or copied only by:

(1) the judge, probation officers, and professional staff or consultants of the juvenile court;

(2) a juvenile justice agency as that term is defined by Section 58.101;

(3) an attorney representing the child's parent in a proceeding under this title;

(4) an attorney representing the child;

(5) a prosecuting attorney;

(6) an individual or entity to whom the child is referred for treatment or services, including assistance in transitioning the child to the community after the child's release or discharge from a juvenile facility;

(7) a public or private agency or institution providing supervision of the child by arrangement of the juvenile court, or having custody of the child under juvenile court order; or

(8) with permission from the juvenile court, any other individual, agency, or institution having a legitimate interest in the proceeding or in the work of the court.

(b-1) A person who is the subject of the records is entitled to access the records for the purpose of

Texas Family Code

preparing and presenting a motion or application to seal the records.

(c) An individual or entity that receives confidential information under this section may not disclose the information unless otherwise authorized by law.

(d) to (f) [Repealed.]

(g) For the purpose of offering a record as evidence in the punishment phase of a criminal proceeding, a prosecuting attorney may obtain the record of a defendant's adjudication that is admissible under Section 3(a), Article 37.07, Code of Criminal Procedure, by submitting a request for the record to the juvenile court that made the adjudication. If a court receives a request from a prosecuting attorney under this subsection, the court shall, if the court possesses the requested record of adjudication, certify and provide the prosecuting attorney with a copy of the record. If a record has been sealed under this chapter, the juvenile court may not provide a copy of the record to a prosecuting attorney under this subsection.

(h) The juvenile court may disseminate to the public the following information relating to a child who is the subject of a directive to apprehend or a warrant of arrest and who cannot be located for the purpose of apprehension:

(1) the child's name, including other names by which the child is known;

(2) the child's physical description, including sex, weight, height, race, ethnicity, eye color, hair color, scars, marks, and tattoos;

(3) a photograph of the child; and

(4) a description of the conduct the child is alleged to have committed, including the level and degree of the alleged offense.

(i) In addition to the authority to release information under Subsection (b)(6), a juvenile probation department may release information contained in its records without leave of the juvenile court pursuant to guidelines adopted by the juvenile board.

(j) [Repealed.]

Sec. 58.0071. Destruction of Certain Physical Records and Files. [Repealed]

Sec. 58.00711. Records Relating to Children Charged with, Convicted of, or Receiving Deferred Disposition for Fine-Only Misdemeanors. [Repealed]

Sec. 58.0072. Dissemination of Juvenile Justice Information. [Renumbered]

Sec. 58.008. Confidentiality of Law Enforcement Records.

(a) This section applies only to the inspection, copying, and maintenance of a record concerning a child and to the storage of information, by electronic means or otherwise, concerning the child from which a record could be generated and does not affect the collection, dissemination, or maintenance of information as provided by Subchapter B. This section does not apply to a record relating to a child that is:

(1) required or authorized to be maintained under the laws regulating the operation of motor vehicles in this state;

(2) maintained by a municipal or justice court; or

(3) subject to disclosure under Chapter 62, Code of Criminal Procedure.

(b) Except as provided by Subsection (c), law enforcement records concerning a child and information concerning a child that are stored by electronic means or otherwise and from which a record could be generated may not be disclosed to the public and shall be:

(1) if maintained on paper or microfilm, kept separate from adult records;

(2) if maintained electronically in the same computer system as adult records, accessible only under controls that are separate and distinct from the controls to access electronic data concerning adults; and

(3) maintained on a local basis only and not sent to a central state or federal depository, except as provided by Subsection (c) or Subchapter B, D, or E.

(c) The law enforcement records of a person with a determinate sentence who is transferred to the Texas Department of Criminal Justice may be transferred to a central state or federal depository for adult records after the date of transfer and may be shared in accordance with the laws governing the adult records in the depository.

(d) Law enforcement records concerning a child may be inspected or copied by:

(1) a juvenile justice agency, as defined by Section 58.101;

(2) a criminal justice agency, as defined by Section 411.082, Government Code;

(3) the child;

(4) the child's parent or guardian; or

(5) the chief executive officer or the officer's designee of a primary or secondary school where the child is enrolled only for the purpose of conducting a threat assessment or preparing a safety plan related to the child.

(d-1) For purposes of Subsection (d), "chief executive officer" includes:

Texas Family Code

(1) the superintendent of a public school;

(2) the director of an open-enrollment charter school; and

(3) the chief executive officer of a private school.

(e) Before a child or a child's parent or guardian may inspect or copy a record concerning the child under Subsection (d), the custodian of the record shall redact:

(1) any personally identifiable information about a juvenile suspect, offender, victim, or witness who is not the child; and

(2) any information that is excepted from required disclosure under Chapter 552, Government Code, or any other law.

(f) If a child has been reported missing by a parent, guardian, or conservator of that child, information about the child may be forwarded to and disseminated by the Texas Crime Information Center and the National Crime Information Center.

Sec. 58.009. Dissemination of Juvenile Justice Information by the Texas Juvenile Justice Department.

(a) Except as provided by this section, juvenile justice information collected and maintained by the Texas Juvenile Justice Department for statistical and research purposes is confidential information for the use of the department and may not be disseminated by the department.

(b) Juvenile justice information consists of information of the type described by Section 58.104, including statistical data in any form or medium collected, maintained, or submitted to the Texas Juvenile Justice Department under Section 221.007, Human Resources Code.

(c) The Texas Juvenile Justice Department may grant the following entities access to juvenile justice information for research and statistical purposes or for any other purpose approved by the department:

(1) criminal justice agencies as defined by Section 411.082, Government Code;

(2) the Texas Education Agency, as authorized under Section 37.084, Education Code;

(3) any agency under the authority of the Health and Human Services Commission;

(4) the Department of Family and Protective Services; or

(5) a public or private university.

(d) The Texas Juvenile Justice Department may grant the following individuals or entities access to juvenile justice information only for a purpose beneficial to and approved by the department to:

(1) an individual or entity working on a research or statistical project that:

(A) is funded in whole or in part by state or federal funds; and

(B) meets the requirements of and is approved by the department; or

(2) an individual or entity that:

(A) is working on a research or statistical project that meets the requirements of and is approved by the department; and

(B) has a specific agreement with the department that:

(i) specifically authorizes access to information;

(ii) limits the use of information to the purposes for which the information is given;

(iii) ensures the security and confidentiality of the information; and

(iv) provides for sanctions if a requirement imposed under Subparagraph (i), (ii), or (iii) is violated.

(e) The Texas Juvenile Justice Department shall grant access to juvenile justice information for legislative purposes under Section 552.008, Government Code.

(f) The Texas Juvenile Justice Department may not release juvenile justice information in identifiable form, except for information released under Subsection (c)(1), (2), (3), or (4) or under the terms of an agreement entered into under Subsection (d)(2). For purposes of this subsection, identifiable information means information that contains a juvenile offender's name or other personal identifiers or that can, by virtue of sample size or other factors, be reasonably interpreted as referring to a particular juvenile offender.

(g) Except as provided by Subsection (e), the Texas Juvenile Justice Department is permitted but not required to release or disclose juvenile justice information to any person identified under this section.

SUBCHAPTER B JUVENILE JUSTICE INFORMATION SYSTEM

Sec. 58.101. Definitions.

In this subchapter:

(1) "Criminal justice agency" has the meaning assigned by Section 411.082, Government Code.

(2) "Department" means the Department of Public Safety of the State of Texas.

(3) "Disposition" means an action that results in the termination, transfer of jurisdiction, or indeterminate suspension of the prosecution of a juvenile offender.

(4) "Incident number" means a unique number assigned to a child during a specific custodial or detention period or for a specific referral to the office or official designated by the juvenile board, if the juvenile offender was not taken into custody before the referral.

(5) "Juvenile justice agency" means an agency that has custody or control over juvenile offenders.

(6) "Juvenile offender" means a child who has been assigned an incident number.

(7) "State identification number" means a unique number assigned by the department to a child in the juvenile justice information system.

(8) "Uniform incident fingerprint card" means a multiple-part form containing a unique incident number with space for information relating to the conduct for which a child has been taken into custody, detained, or referred, the child's fingerprints, and other relevant information.

Sec. 58.102. Juvenile Justice Information System.

(a) The department is responsible for recording data and maintaining a database for a computerized juvenile justice information system that serves:

(1) as the record creation point for the juvenile justice information system maintained by the state; and

(2) as the control terminal for entry of records, in accordance with federal law, rule, and policy, into the federal records system maintained by the Federal Bureau of Investigation.

(b) The department shall develop and maintain the system with the cooperation and advice of the:

(1) Texas Juvenile Justice Department; and

(2) juvenile courts and clerks of juvenile courts.

(c) The department may not collect, retain, or share information relating to a juvenile except as provided by this chapter.

(d) The database must contain the information required by this subchapter.

(e) The department shall designate the offense codes and has the sole responsibility for designating the state identification number for each juvenile whose name appears in the juvenile justice system.

Sec. 58.103. Purpose of System.

The purpose of the juvenile justice information system is to:

(1) provide agencies and personnel within the juvenile justice system accurate information relating to children who come into contact with the juvenile justice system of this state;

(2) provide, where allowed by law, adult criminal justice agencies accurate and easily accessible information relating to children who come into contact with the juvenile justice system;

(3) provide an efficient conversion, where appropriate, of juvenile records to adult criminal records;

(4) improve the quality of data used to conduct impact analyses of proposed legislative changes in the juvenile justice system; and

(5) improve the ability of interested parties to analyze the functioning of the juvenile justice system.

Sec. 58.104. Types of Information Collected.

(a) Subject to Subsection (f), the juvenile justice information system shall consist of information relating to delinquent conduct committed or alleged to have been committed by a juvenile offender that, if the conduct had been committed by an adult, would constitute a criminal offense other than an offense punishable by a fine only, including information relating to:

(1) the juvenile offender;

(2) the intake or referral of the juvenile offender into the juvenile justice system;

(3) the detention of the juvenile offender;

(4) the prosecution of the juvenile offender;

(5) the disposition of the juvenile offender's case, including the name and description of any program to which the juvenile offender is referred;

(6) the probation or commitment of the juvenile offender; and

(7) the termination of probation supervision or discharge from commitment of the juvenile offender.

(b) To the extent possible and subject to Subsection (a), the department shall include in the juvenile justice information system the following information for each juvenile offender taken into custody, detained, or referred under this title for delinquent conduct:

(1) the juvenile offender's name, including other names by which the juvenile offender is known;

(2) the juvenile offender's date and place of birth;

(3) the juvenile offender's physical description, including sex, weight, height, race, ethnicity, eye color, hair color, scars, marks, and tattoos;

(4) the juvenile offender's state identification number, and other identifying information, as determined by the department;

(5) the juvenile offender's fingerprints;

(6) the juvenile offender's last known residential address, including the census tract number designation for the address;

Texas Family Code

(7) the name and identifying number of the agency that took into custody or detained the juvenile offender;

(8) the date of detention or custody;

(9) the conduct for which the juvenile offender was taken into custody, detained, or referred, including level and degree of the alleged offense;

(10) the name and identifying number of the juvenile intake agency or juvenile probation office;

(11) each disposition by the juvenile intake agency or juvenile probation office;

(12) the date of disposition by the juvenile intake agency or juvenile probation office;

(13) the name and identifying number of the prosecutor's office;

(14) each disposition by the prosecutor;

(15) the date of disposition by the prosecutor;

(16) the name and identifying number of the court;

(17) each disposition by the court, including information concerning probation or custody of a juvenile offender by a juvenile justice agency;

(18) the date of disposition by the court;

(19) the date any probation supervision, including deferred prosecution supervision, was terminated;

(20) any commitment or release under supervision by the Texas Juvenile Justice Department;

(21) the date of any commitment or release under supervision by the Texas Juvenile Justice Department; and

(22) a description of each appellate proceeding.

(c) The department may designate codes relating to the information described by Subsection (b).

(d) The department shall designate a state identification number for each juvenile offender.

(e) This subchapter does not apply to a disposition that represents an administrative status notice of an agency described by Section 58.102(b).

(f) Records maintained by the department in the depository are subject to being sealed under Subchapter C-1.

Sec. 58.105. Duties of Juvenile Board.

Each juvenile board shall provide for:

(1) the compilation and maintenance of records and information needed for reporting information to the department under this subchapter;

(2) the transmittal to the department, in the manner provided by the department, of all records and information required by the department under this subchapter; and

(3) access by the department to inspect records and information to determine the completeness and accuracy of information reported.

Sec. 58.106. Dissemination of Confidential Information in Juvenile Justice Information System.

(a) Except as otherwise provided by this section, information contained in the juvenile justice information system is confidential information for the use of the department and may not be disseminated by the department except:

(1) with the permission of the juvenile offender, to military personnel of this state or the United States;

(2) to a criminal justice agency as defined by Section 411.082, Government Code;

(3) to a noncriminal justice agency authorized by federal statute or federal executive order to receive juvenile justice record information;

(4) to a juvenile justice agency;

(5) to the Texas Juvenile Justice Department;

(6) to the office of independent ombudsman of the Texas Juvenile Justice Department;

(7) to a district, county, justice, or municipal court exercising jurisdiction over a juvenile; and

(8) to the Department of Family and Protective Services or the Health and Human Services Commission as provided by Section 411.114, Government Code.

(a-1) [Repealed.]

(a-2) Information disseminated under Subsection (a) remains confidential after dissemination and may be disclosed by the recipient only as provided by this title.

(b) Subsection (a) does not apply to a document maintained by a juvenile justice or law enforcement agency that is the source of information collected by the department.

(c) The department may, if necessary to protect the welfare of the community, disseminate to the public the following information relating to a juvenile who has escaped from the custody of the Texas Juvenile Justice Department or from another secure detention or correctional facility:

(1) the juvenile's name, including other names by which the juvenile is known;

(2) the juvenile's physical description, including sex, weight, height, race, ethnicity, eye color, hair color, scars, marks, and tattoos;

(3) a photograph of the juvenile; and

(4) a description of the conduct for which the juvenile was committed to the Texas Juvenile Justice Department or detained in the secure detention or correctional facility, including the level and degree of the alleged offense.

(d) The department may, if necessary to protect the welfare of the community, disseminate to the public the information listed under Subsection (c) relating to a juvenile offender when notified by a law enforcement agency of this state that the law enforcement agency has been issued a directive to apprehend the offender or an arrest warrant for the offender or that the law enforcement agency is otherwise authorized to arrest the offender and that the offender is suspected of having:

(1) committed a felony offense under the following provisions of the Penal Code:

(A) Title 5;

(B) Section 29.02; or

(C) Section 29.03; and

(2) fled from arrest or apprehension for commission of the offense.

Sec. 58.107. Compatibility of Data.

Data supplied to the juvenile justice information system must be compatible with the system and must contain both incident numbers and state identification numbers.

Sec. 58.108. Duties of Agencies and Courts.

(a) A juvenile justice agency and a clerk of a juvenile court shall:

(1) compile and maintain records needed for reporting data required by the department;

(2) transmit to the department in the manner provided by the department data required by the department;

(3) give the department or its accredited agents access to the agency or court for the purpose of inspection to determine the completeness and accuracy of data reported; and

(4) cooperate with the department to enable the department to perform its duties under this chapter.

(b) A juvenile justice agency and clerk of a court shall retain documents described by this section.

Sec. 58.109. Uniform Incident Fingerprint Card.

(a) The department may provide for the use of a uniform incident fingerprint card in the maintenance of the juvenile justice information system.

(b) The department shall design, print, and distribute to each law enforcement agency and juvenile intake agency uniform incident fingerprint cards.

(c) The incident cards must:

(1) be serially numbered with an incident number in a manner that allows each incident of referral of a juvenile offender who is the subject of the incident fingerprint card to be readily ascertained; and

(2) be multiple-part forms that can be transmitted with the juvenile offender through the juvenile justice process and that allow each agency to report required data to the department.

(d) Subject to available telecommunications capacity, the department shall develop the capability to receive by electronic means from a law enforcement agency the information on the uniform incident fingerprint card. The information must be in a form that is compatible to the form required of data supplied to the juvenile justice information system.

Sec. 58.110. Reporting.

(a) The department by rule shall develop reporting procedures that ensure that the juvenile offender processing data is reported from the time a juvenile offender is initially taken into custody, detained, or referred until the time a juvenile offender is released from the jurisdiction of the juvenile justice system.

(b) The law enforcement agency or the juvenile intake agency that initiates the entry of the juvenile offender into the juvenile justice information system for a specific incident shall prepare a uniform incident fingerprint card and initiate the reporting process for each incident reportable under this subchapter.

(c) The clerk of the court exercising jurisdiction over a juvenile offender's case shall report the disposition of the case to the department.

(d) In each county, the reporting agencies may make alternative arrangements for reporting the required information, including combined reporting or electronic reporting, if the alternative reporting is approved by the juvenile board and the department.

(e) Except as otherwise required by applicable state laws or regulations, information required by this chapter to be reported to the department shall be reported promptly. The information shall be reported not later than the 30th day after the date the information is received by the agency responsible for reporting the information, except that a juvenile offender's custody or detention without previous custody shall be reported to the department not later than the seventh day after the date of the custody or detention.

(f) Subject to available telecommunications capacity, the department shall develop the capability to receive by electronic means the information required under this section to be reported to the department. The information must be in a form that is compatible to the form required of data to be reported under this section.

Sec. 58.111. Local Data Advisory Boards.

The commissioners court of each county may create a local data advisory board to perform the same duties relating to the juvenile justice information system as the duties performed by a local data advisory board in relation to the criminal history record system under Article 66.354, Code of Criminal Procedure.

Sec. 58.112. Report to Legislature. [Renumbered]

Sec. 58.113. Warrants.

The department shall maintain in a computerized database that is accessible by the same entities that may access the juvenile justice information system information relating to a warrant of arrest, as that term is defined by Article 15.01, Code of Criminal Procedure, or a directive to apprehend under Section 52.015 for any child, without regard to whether the child has been taken into custody.

SUBCHAPTER C AUTOMATIC RESTRICTION OF ACCESS TO RECORDS [REPEALED]

Sec. 58.201. Definition. [Repealed]

Sec. 58.202. Exempted Records. [Repealed]

Sec. 58.203. Certification. [Repealed]

Sec. 58.204. Restricted Access on Certification. [Repealed]

Sec. 58.205. Request to the Federal Bureau of Investigation on Certification. [Repealed]

Sec. 58.206. Effect of Certification in Relation to the Protected Person. [Repealed]

Sec. 58.207. Juvenile Court Orders on Certification. [Repealed]

Sec. 58.208. Information to Child on Discharge. [Repealed]

Sec. 58.209. Information to Child by Probation Officer or Texas Juvenile Justice Department. [Repealed]

Sec. 58.210. Sealing or Destruction of Records Not Affected. [Repealed]

Sec. 58.211. Rescinding Restricted Access. [Repealed]

SUBCHAPTER C-1 SEALING AND DESTRUCTION OF JUVENILE RECORDS

Sec. 58.251. Definitions.

In this subchapter:

(1) "Electronic record" means an entry in a computer file or information on microfilm, microfiche, or any other electronic storage media.

(2) "Juvenile matter" means a referral to a juvenile court or juvenile probation department and all related court proceedings and outcomes, if any.

(3) "Physical record" means a paper copy of a record.

(4) "Record" means any documentation related to a juvenile matter, including information contained in that documentation.

Sec. 58.252. Exempted Records.

The following records are exempt from this subchapter:

(1) records relating to a criminal combination or criminal street gang maintained by the Department of Public Safety or a local law enforcement agency under Chapter 67, Code of Criminal Procedure;

(2) sex offender registration records maintained by the Department of Public Safety or a local law enforcement agency under Chapter 62, Code of Criminal Procedure; and

(3) records collected or maintained by the Texas Juvenile Justice Department for statistical and research purposes, including data submitted under Section 221.007, Human Resources Code, and personally identifiable information.

Texas Family Code

Sec. 58.253. Sealing Records Without Application: Delinquent Conduct.

(a) This section does not apply to the records of a child referred to a juvenile court or juvenile probation department solely for conduct indicating a need for supervision.

(b) A person who was referred to a juvenile probation department for delinquent conduct is entitled to have all records related to the person's juvenile matters, including records relating to any matters involving conduct indicating a need for supervision, sealed without applying to the juvenile court if the person:

(1) is at least 19 years of age;

(2) has not been adjudicated as having engaged in delinquent conduct or, if adjudicated for delinquent conduct, was not adjudicated for delinquent conduct violating a penal law of the grade of felony;

(3) does not have any pending delinquent conduct matters;

(4) has not been transferred by a juvenile court to a criminal court for prosecution under Section 54.02;

(5) has not as an adult been convicted of a felony or a misdemeanor punishable by confinement in jail; and

(6) does not have any pending charges as an adult for a felony or a misdemeanor punishable by confinement in jail.

Sec. 58.254. Certification of Eligibility for Sealing Records Without Application for Delinquent Conduct.

(a) The Department of Public Safety shall certify to a juvenile probation department that has submitted records to the juvenile justice information system that the records relating to a person referred to the juvenile probation department appear to be eligible for sealing under Section 58.253.

(b) The Department of Public Safety may issue the certification described by Subsection (a) by electronic means, including by electronic mail.

(c) Except as provided by Subsection (d), not later than the 60th day after the date the juvenile probation department receives a certification under Subsection (a), the juvenile probation department shall:

(1) give notice of the receipt of the certification to the juvenile court; and

(2) provide the court with a list of all referrals received by the department relating to that person and the outcome of each referral.

(d) If a juvenile probation department has reason to believe the records of the person for whom the department received a certification under Subsection (a) are not eligible to be sealed, the juvenile probation department shall notify the Department of Public Safety not later than the 15th day after the date the juvenile probation department received the certification. If the juvenile probation department later determines that the person's records are eligible to be sealed, the juvenile probation department shall notify the juvenile court and provide the court the information described by Subsection (c) not later than the 30th day after the date of the determination.

(e) If, after receiving a certification under Subsection (a), the juvenile probation department determines that the person's records are not eligible to be sealed, the juvenile probation department and the Department of Public Safety shall update the juvenile justice information system to reflect that determination and no further action related to the records is required.

(f) Not later than the 60th day after the date a juvenile court receives notice from a juvenile probation department under Subsection (c), the juvenile court shall issue an order sealing all records relating to the person named in the certification.

Sec. 58.255. Sealing Records Without Application: Conduct Indicating Need for Supervision.

(a) A person who was referred to a juvenile court for conduct indicating a need for supervision is entitled to have all records related to all conduct indicating a need for supervision matters sealed without applying to the juvenile court if the person:

(1) has records relating to the conduct filed with the court clerk;

(2) is at least 18 years of age;

(3) has not been referred to the juvenile probation department for delinquent conduct;

(4) has not as an adult been convicted of a felony; and

(5) does not have any pending charges as an adult for a felony or a misdemeanor punishable by confinement in jail.

(b) The juvenile probation department shall:

(1) give the juvenile court notice that a person's records are eligible for sealing under Subsection (a); and

(2) provide the juvenile court with a list of all referrals relating to that person received by the department and the outcome of each referral.

(c) Not later than the 60th day after the date the juvenile court receives notice from the juvenile probation department under Subsection (b), the

Texas Family Code

juvenile court shall issue an order sealing all records relating to the person named in the notice.

Sec. 58.2551. Sealing Records Without Application: Finding of Not True.

A juvenile court, on the court's own motion and without a hearing, shall immediately order the sealing of all records related to the alleged conduct if the court enters a finding that the allegations are not true.

Sec. 58.256. Application for Sealing Records.

(a) Notwithstanding Sections 58.253 and 58.255, a person may file an application for the sealing of records related to the person in the juvenile court served by the juvenile probation department to which the person was referred. The court may not charge a fee for filing the application, regardless of the form of the application.

(a-1) An application filed under this section may be sent to the juvenile court by any reasonable method authorized under Rule 21, Texas Rules of Civil Procedure, including secure electronic means.

(b) An application filed under this section must include either the following information or the reason that one or more of the following is not included in the application:

(1) the person's:

(A) full name;

(B) sex;

(C) race or ethnicity;

(D) date of birth;

(E) driver's license or identification card number; and

(F) social security number;

(2) the conduct for which the person was referred to the juvenile probation department, including the date on which the conduct was alleged or found to have been committed;

(3) the cause number assigned to each petition relating to the person filed in juvenile court, if any, and the court in which the petition was filed; and

(4) a list of all entities the person believes have possession of records related to the person, including the applicable entities listed under Section 58.258(b).

(c) Except as provided by Subsection (d), the juvenile court may order the sealing of records related to all matters for which the person was referred to the juvenile probation department if the person:

(1) is at least 17 years of age, or is younger than 17 years of age and at least one year has elapsed after the date of final discharge in each matter for which the person was referred to the juvenile probation department;

(2) does not have any delinquent conduct matters pending with any juvenile probation department or juvenile court;

(3) was not transferred by a juvenile court to a criminal court for prosecution under Section 54.02;

(4) has not as an adult been convicted of a felony; and

(5) does not have any pending charges as an adult for a felony or a misdemeanor punishable by confinement in jail.

(d) A court may not order the sealing of the records of a person who:

(1) received a determinate sentence for engaging in:

(A) delinquent conduct that violated a penal law listed under Section 53.045; or

(B) habitual felony conduct as described by Section 51.031;

(2) is currently required to register as a sex offender under Chapter 62, Code of Criminal Procedure; or

(3) was committed to the Texas Juvenile Justice Department or to a post-adjudication secure correctional facility under Section 54.04011, unless the person has been discharged from the agency to which the person was committed.

(e) On receipt of an application under this section, the court may:

(1) order the sealing of the person's records immediately, without a hearing; or

(2) hold a hearing under Section 58.257 at the court's discretion to determine whether to order the sealing of the person's records.

Sec. 58.257. Hearing Regarding Sealing of Records.

(a) A hearing regarding the sealing of a person's records must be held not later than the 60th day after the date the court receives the person's application under Section 58.256.

(b) The court shall give reasonable notice of a hearing under this section to:

(1) the person who is the subject of the records;

(2) the person's attorney who made the application for sealing on behalf of the person, if any;

(3) the prosecuting attorney for the juvenile court;

(4) all entities named in the application that the person believes possess eligible records related to the person; and

(5) any individual or entity whose presence at the hearing is requested by the person or prosecutor.

Texas Family Code

Sec. 58.258. Order Sealing Records.

(a) An order sealing the records of a person under this subchapter must include either the following information or the reason one or more of the following is not included in the order:

(1) the person's:

(A) full name;

(B) sex;

(C) race or ethnicity;

(D) date of birth;

(E) driver's license or identification card number; and

(F) social security number;

(2) each instance of conduct indicating a need for supervision or delinquent conduct alleged against the person or for which the person was referred to the juvenile justice system;

(3) the date on which and the county in which each instance of conduct was alleged to have occurred;

(4) if any petitions relating to the person were filed in juvenile court, the cause number assigned to each petition and the court and county in which each petition was filed; and

(5) a list of the entities believed to be in possession of the records that have been ordered sealed, including the entities listed under Subsection (b).

(b) Not later than the 60th day after the date of the entry of the order, the court shall provide a copy of the order to:

(1) the Department of Public Safety;

(2) the Texas Juvenile Justice Department, if the person was committed to the department;

(3) the clerk of court;

(4) the juvenile probation department serving the court;

(5) the prosecutor's office;

(6) each law enforcement agency that had contact with the person in relation to the conduct that is the subject of the sealing order;

(7) each public or private agency that had custody of or that provided supervision or services to the person in relation to the conduct that is the subject of the sealing order; and

(8) each official, agency, or other entity that the court has reason to believe has any record containing information that is related to the conduct that is the subject of the sealing order.

(c) On entry of the order, all adjudications relating to the person are vacated and the proceedings are dismissed and treated for all purposes as though the proceedings had never occurred. The clerk of court shall:

(1) seal all court records relating to the proceedings, including any records created in the clerk's case management system; and

(2) send copies of the order to all entities listed in the order by any reasonable method, including certified mail or secure electronic means.

Sec. 58.259. Actions Taken on Receipt of Order to Seal Records.

(a) An entity receiving an order to seal the records of a person issued under this subchapter shall, not later than the 61st day after the date of receiving the order, take the following actions, as applicable:

(1) the Department of Public Safety shall:

(A) limit access to the records relating to the person in the juvenile justice information system to only the Texas Juvenile Justice Department for the purpose of conducting research and statistical studies;

(B) destroy any other records relating to the person in the department's possession, including DNA records as provided by Section 411.151, Government Code; and

(C) send written verification of the limitation and destruction of the records to the issuing court;

(2) the Texas Juvenile Justice Department shall:

(A) seal all records relating to the person, other than those exempted from sealing under Section 58.252; and

(B) send written verification of the sealing of the records to the issuing court;

(3) a public or private agency or institution that had custody of or provided supervision or services to the person who is the subject of the records, the juvenile probation department, a law enforcement entity, or a prosecuting attorney shall:

(A) seal all records relating to the person; and

(B) send written verification of the sealing of the records to the issuing court; and

(4) any other entity that receives an order to seal a person's records shall:

(A) send any records relating to the person to the issuing court;

(B) delete all index references to the person's records; and

(C) send written verification of the deletion of the index references to the issuing court.

(b) Physical or electronic records are considered sealed if the records are not destroyed but are stored in a manner that allows access to the records only by the custodian of records for the entity possessing the records.

(c) If an entity that received an order to seal records relating to a person later receives an inquiry about a person or the matter contained in the records, the entity must respond that no records relating to the person or the matter exist.

(d) If an entity receiving an order to seal records under this subchapter is unable to comply with the order because the information in the order is incorrect or insufficient to allow the entity to identify the records that are subject to the order, the entity shall notify the issuing court not later than the 30th day after the date of receipt of the order. The court shall take any actions necessary and possible to provide the needed information to the entity, including contacting the person who is the subject of the order or the person's attorney.

(e) If an entity receiving a sealing order under this subchapter has no records related to the person who is the subject of the order, the entity shall provide written verification of that fact to the issuing court not later than the 30th day after the date of receipt of the order.

Sec. 58.260. Inspection and Release of Sealed Records.

(a) A juvenile court may allow, by order, the inspection of records sealed under this subchapter or under Section 58.003, as that law existed before September 1, 2017, only by:

(1) a person named in the order, on the petition of the person who is the subject of the records;

(2) a prosecutor, on the petition of the prosecutor, for the purpose of reviewing the records for possible use:

(A) in a capital prosecution; or

(B) for the enhancement of punishment under Section 12.42, Penal Code; or

(3) a court, the Texas Department of Criminal Justice, or the Texas Juvenile Justice Department for the purposes of Article 62.007(e), Code of Criminal Procedure.

(b) After a petitioner inspects records under this section, the court may order the release of any or all of the records to the petitioner on the motion of the petitioner.

Sec. 58.261. Effect of Sealing Records.

(a) A person whose records have been sealed under this subchapter or under Section 58.003, as that law existed before September 1, 2017, is not required to state in any proceeding or in any application for employment, licensing, admission, housing, or other public or private benefit that the person has been the subject of a juvenile matter.

(b) If a person's records have been sealed, the information in the records, the fact that the records once existed, or the person's denial of the existence of the records or of the person's involvement in a juvenile matter may not be used against the person in any manner, including in:

(1) a perjury prosecution or other criminal proceeding;

(2) a civil proceeding, including an administrative proceeding involving a governmental entity;

(3) an application process for licensing or certification; or

(4) an admission, employment, or housing decision.

(c) A person who is the subject of the sealed records may not waive the protected status of the records or the consequences of the protected status.

Sec. 58.262. Information Given to Child Regarding Sealing of Records.

(a) When a child is referred to the juvenile probation department, an employee of the juvenile probation department shall give the child and the child's parent, guardian, or custodian a written explanation describing the process of sealing records under this subchapter and a copy of this subchapter.

(b) On the final discharge of a child, or on the last official action in the matter if there is no adjudication, a probation officer or official at the Texas Juvenile Justice Department, as appropriate, shall give the child and the child's parent, guardian, or custodian a written explanation regarding the eligibility of the child's records for sealing under this subchapter and a copy of this subchapter.

(c) The written explanation provided to a child under Subsections (a) and (b) must include the requirements for a record to be eligible for sealing, including an explanation of the records that are exempt from sealing under Section 58.252, and the following information:

(1) that, regardless of whether the child's conduct was adjudicated, the child has a juvenile record with the Department of Public Safety and the Federal Bureau of Investigation;

(2) the child's juvenile record is a permanent record unless the record is sealed under this subchapter;

(3) except as provided by Section 58.260, the child's juvenile record, other than treatment records made confidential by law, may be accessed by a police officer, sheriff, prosecutor, probation officer, correctional officer, or other criminal or juvenile justice official unless the record is sealed as provided by this subchapter;

(4) sealing of the child's records under Section 58.253 or Section 58.255, as applicable, does not require any action by the child or the child's family, including the filing of an application or

hiring of a lawyer, but occurs automatically at age 18 or 19 as applicable based on the child's referral and adjudication history;

(5) the child's juvenile record may be eligible for an earlier sealing date under Section 58.256, but an earlier sealing requires the child or an attorney for the child to file an application with the court;

(6) the impact of sealing records on the child; and

(7) the circumstances under which a sealed record may be reopened.

(d) The Texas Juvenile Justice Department shall adopt rules to implement this section and to facilitate the effective explanation of the information required to be communicated by this section.

Sec. 58.263. Destruction of Records: No Probable Cause.

The court shall order the destruction of the records relating to the conduct for which a child is taken into custody or referred to juvenile court without being taken into custody, including records contained in the juvenile justice information system, if:

(1) a determination is made under Section 53.01 that no probable cause exists to believe the child engaged in the conduct and the case is not referred to a prosecutor for review under Section 53.012; or

(2) a determination that no probable cause exists to believe the child engaged in the conduct is made by a prosecutor under Section 53.012.

Sec. 58.264. Permissible Destruction of Records.

(a) Subject to Subsections (b) and (c) of this section, Section 202.001, Local Government Code, and any other restrictions imposed by an entity's records retention guidelines, the following persons may authorize the destruction of records in a closed juvenile matter, regardless of the date the records were created:

(1) a juvenile board, in relation to the records in the possession of the juvenile probation department;

(2) the head of a law enforcement agency, in relation to the records in the possession of the agency; and

(3) a prosecuting attorney, in relation to the records in the possession of the prosecuting attorney's office.

(b) The records related to a person referred to a juvenile probation department may be destroyed if the person:

(1) is at least 18 years of age, and:

(A) the most serious conduct for which the person was referred was conduct indicating a need for supervision, whether or not the person was adjudicated; or

(B) the referral or information did not relate to conduct indicating a need for supervision or delinquent conduct and the juvenile probation department, prosecutor, or juvenile court did not take action on the referral or information for that reason;

(2) is at least 21 years of age, and:

(A) the most serious conduct for which the person was adjudicated was delinquent conduct that violated a penal law of the grade of misdemeanor; or

(B) the most serious conduct for which the person was referred was delinquent conduct and the person was not adjudicated as having engaged in the conduct; or

(3) is at least 31 years of age and the most serious conduct for which the person was adjudicated was delinquent conduct that violated a penal law of the grade of felony.

(c) If a record contains information relating to more than one person referred to a juvenile probation department, the record may only be destroyed if:

(1) the destruction of the record is authorized under this section; and

(2) information in the record that may be destroyed under this section can be separated from information that is not authorized to be destroyed.

(d) Electronic records are considered to be destroyed if the electronic records, including the index to the records, are deleted.

(e) Converting physical records to electronic records and subsequently destroying the physical records while maintaining the electronic records is not considered destruction of a record under this subchapter.

(f) This section does not authorize the destruction of the records of the juvenile court or clerk of court.

(g) This section does not authorize the destruction of records maintained for statistical and research purposes by the Texas Juvenile Justice Department in a juvenile information and case management system authorized under Section 58.403.

(h) This section does not affect the destruction of physical records and files authorized by the Texas State Library Records Retention Schedule.

Sec. 58.265. Juvenile Records Not Subject to Expunction.

Records to which this chapter applies are not subject to an order of expunction issued by any court.

SUBCHAPTER D LOCAL JUVENILE JUSTICE INFORMATION SYSTEM

Sec. 58.301. Definitions.

In this subchapter:

(1) "County juvenile board" means a juvenile board created under Chapter 152, Human Resources Code.

(2) "Juvenile facility" means a facility that:

(A) serves juveniles under a juvenile court's jurisdiction; and

(B) is operated as a holdover facility, a preadjudication detention facility, a nonsecure facility, or a post-adjudication secure correctional facility.

(2-a) "Governmental juvenile facility" means a juvenile facility operated by a unit of government.

(3) "Governmental service provider" means a juvenile justice service provider operated by a unit of government.

(4) "Local juvenile justice information system" means a county or multicounty computerized database of information concerning children, with data entry and access by the partner agencies that are members of the system.

(5) "Partner agency" means a service provider or juvenile facility that is authorized by this subchapter to be a member of a local juvenile justice information system or that has applied to be a member of a local juvenile justice information system and has been approved by the county juvenile board or regional juvenile board committee as a member of the system.

(6) "Regional juvenile board committee" means a committee that is composed of two members from each county juvenile board in a region that comprises a multicounty local juvenile information system.

Sec. 58.302. Purposes of System.

The purposes of a local juvenile justice information system are to:

(1) provide accurate information at the county or regional level relating to children who come into contact with the juvenile justice system;

(2) assist in the development and delivery of services to children in the juvenile justice system;

(3) assist in the development and delivery of services to children:

(A) who school officials have reasonable cause to believe have committed an offense for which a report is required under Section 37.015, Education Code; or

(B) who have been expelled, the expulsion of which school officials are required to report under Section 52.041;

(4) provide for an efficient transmission of juvenile records from justice and municipal courts to county juvenile probation departments and the juvenile court and from county juvenile probation departments and juvenile court to the state juvenile justice information system created by Subchapter B;

(5) provide efficient computerized case management resources to juvenile courts, prosecutors, court clerks, county juvenile probation departments, and partner agencies authorized by this subchapter;

(6) provide a directory of services available to children to the partner agencies to facilitate the delivery of services to children;

(7) provide an efficient means for municipal and justice courts to report filing of charges, adjudications, and dispositions of juveniles to the juvenile court as required by Section 51.08; and

(8) provide a method for agencies to fulfill their duties under Section 58.108, including the electronic transmission of information required to be sent to the Department of Public Safety by Section 58.110(f).

Sec. 58.303. Local Juvenile Justice Information System.

(a) Juvenile justice agencies in a county or region of this state may jointly create and maintain a local juvenile justice information system to aid in processing the cases of children under this code, to facilitate the delivery of services to children in the juvenile justice system, and to aid in the early identification of at-risk and delinquent children.

(b) A local juvenile justice information system may contain the following components:

(1) case management resources for juvenile courts, court clerks, prosecuting attorneys, and county juvenile probation departments;

(2) reporting systems to fulfill statutory requirements for reporting in the juvenile justice system;

(3) service provider directories and indexes of agencies providing services to children;

(4) victim-witness notices required under Chapter 57;

(5) electronic filing of complaints or petitions, court orders, and other documents filed with the court, including documents containing electronic signatures;

(6) electronic offense and intake processing;

(7) case docket management and calendaring;

(8) communications by email or other electronic communications between partner agencies;

Texas Family Code

(9) reporting of charges filed, adjudications and dispositions of juveniles by municipal and justice courts and the juvenile court, and transfers of cases to the juvenile court as authorized or required by Section 51.08;

(10) reporting to schools under Article 15.27, Code of Criminal Procedure, by law enforcement agencies, prosecuting attorneys, and juvenile courts;

(11) records of adjudications and dispositions, including probation conditions ordered by the juvenile court;

(12) warrant management and confirmation capabilities; and

(13) case management for juveniles in juvenile facilities.

(c) [Redesignated as a portion of Tex.Fam. Code § 58.303(b) by Acts 2005, 79th Leg., ch. 949 (H.B. 1575), § 24, effective September 1, 2005.]

(d) [Repealed.]

Sec. 58.304. Types of Information Contained in a Local Juvenile Information System.

(a) A local juvenile justice information system must consist of:

(1) information relating to all referrals to the juvenile court of any type, including referrals for conduct indicating a need for supervision and delinquent conduct; and

(2) information relating to:

(A) the juvenile;

(B) the intake or referral of the juvenile into the juvenile justice system for any offense or conduct;

(C) the detention of the juvenile;

(D) the prosecution of the juvenile;

(E) the disposition of the juvenile's case, including the name and description of any program to which the juvenile is referred; and

(F) the probation, placement, or commitment of the juvenile.

(b) To the extent possible and subject to Subsection (a), the local juvenile justice information system may include the following information for each juvenile taken into custody, detained, or referred under this title:

(1) the juvenile's name, including other names by which the juvenile is known;

(2) the juvenile's date and place of birth;

(3) the juvenile's physical description, including sex, weight, height, race, ethnicity, eye color, hair color, scars, marks, and tattoos;

(4) the juvenile's state identification number and other identifying information;

(5) the juvenile's fingerprints and photograph;

(6) the juvenile's last known residential address, including the census tract number designation for the address;

(7) the name, address, and phone number of the juvenile's parent, guardian, or custodian;

(8) the name and identifying number of the agency that took into custody or detained the juvenile;

(9) each date of custody or detention;

(10) a detailed description of the conduct for which the juvenile was taken into custody, detained, or referred, including the level and degree of the alleged offense;

(11) the name and identifying number of the juvenile intake agency or juvenile probation office;

(12) each disposition by the juvenile intake agency or juvenile probation office;

(13) the date of disposition by the juvenile intake agency or juvenile probation office;

(14) the name and identifying number of the prosecutor's office;

(15) each disposition by the prosecutor;

(16) the date of disposition by the prosecutor;

(17) the name and identifying number of the court;

(18) each disposition by the court, including information concerning custody of a juvenile by a juvenile justice agency or county juvenile probation department;

(19) the date of disposition by the court;

(20) any commitment or release under supervision by the Texas Juvenile Justice Department, including the date of the commitment or release;

(21) information concerning each appellate proceeding;

(22) electronic copies of all documents filed with the court; and

(23) information obtained for the purpose of diagnosis, examination, evaluation, treatment, or referral for treatment of a child by a public or private agency or institution providing supervision of a child by arrangement of the juvenile court or having custody of the child under order of the juvenile court.

(c) If the Department of Public Safety assigns a state identification number for the juvenile, the identification number shall be entered in the local juvenile information system.

(d) [Repealed.]

Sec. 58.305. Partner Agencies.

(a) A local juvenile justice information system shall to the extent possible include the following partner agencies within that county:

(1) the juvenile court and court clerk;

(2) justice of the peace and municipal courts;
(3) the county juvenile probation department;
(4) the prosecuting attorneys who prosecute juvenile cases in juvenile court, municipal court, or justice court;
(5) law enforcement agencies;
(6) each public school district in the county;
(7) service providers approved by the county juvenile board; and
(8) juvenile facilities approved by the county juvenile board.

(b) A local juvenile justice information system for a multicounty region shall to the extent possible include the partner agencies listed in Subsections (a)(1)-(6) for each county in the region and the following partner agencies from within the multicounty region that have applied for membership in the system and have been approved by the regional juvenile board committee:
(1) service providers; and
(2) juvenile facilities.

Sec. 58.306. Access to Information; Levels.

(a) This section describes the level of access to information to which each partner agency in a local juvenile justice information system is entitled.

(b) Information is at Access Level 1 if the information relates to a child:
(1) who:
(A) a school official has reasonable grounds to believe has committed an offense for which a report is required under Section 37.015, Education Code; or
(B) has been expelled, the expulsion of which is required to be reported under Section 52.041; and
(2) who has not been charged with a fineable only offense, a status offense, or delinquent conduct.

(c) Information is at Access Level 2 if the information relates to a child who:
(1) is alleged in a justice or municipal court to have committed a fineable only offense, municipal ordinance violation, or status offense; and
(2) has not been charged with delinquent conduct or conduct indicating a need for supervision.

(d) Information is at Access Level 3 if the information relates to a child who is alleged to have engaged in delinquent conduct or conduct indicating a need for supervision.

(e) Except as provided by Subsection (i), Level 1 Access is by public school districts in the county or region served by the local juvenile justice information system.

(f) Except as provided by Subsection (i), Level 2 Access is by:
(1) justice of the peace courts that process juvenile cases; and
(2) municipal courts that process juvenile cases.

(g) Except as provided by Subsection (i), Level 3 Access is by:
(1) the juvenile court and court clerk;
(2) the prosecuting attorney;
(3) the county juvenile probation department;
(4) law enforcement agencies;
(5) governmental service providers that are partner agencies;
(6) governmental juvenile facilities that are partner agencies; and
(7) a private juvenile facility that is a partner agency, except the access is limited to information that relates to a child detained or placed in the custody of the facility.

(h) Access for Level 1 agencies is only to information at Level 1. Access for Level 2 agencies is only to information at Levels 1 and 2. Access for Level 3 agencies is to information at Levels 1, 2, and 3.

(i) Information described by Section 58.304(b)(23) may be accessed only by:
(1) the juvenile court and court clerk;
(2) the county juvenile probation department;
(3) a governmental juvenile facility that is a partner agency; and
(4) a private juvenile facility that is a partner agency, except the access is limited to information that relates to a child detained or placed in the custody of the facility.

Sec. 58.307. Confidentiality of Information.

(a) Information that is part of a local juvenile justice information system is not public information and may not be released to the public, except as authorized by law.

(b) Information that is part of a local juvenile justice information system is for the professional use of the partner agencies that are members of the system and may be used only by authorized employees of those agencies to discharge duties of those agencies.

(c) Information from a local juvenile justice information system may not be disclosed to persons, agencies, or organizations that are not members of the system except to the extent disclosure is authorized or mandated by this title.

(d) Information in a local juvenile justice information system is subject to destruction, sealing, or restricted access as provided by this title.

(e) Information in a local juvenile justice information system, including electronic signature systems, shall be protected from unauthorized access by a system of access security and any access to information in a local juvenile information system performed by browser software shall be at the level of at least

2048-bit encryption. A juvenile board or a regional juvenile board committee shall require all partner agencies to maintain security and restrict access in accordance with the requirements of this title.

SUBCHAPTER D-1 REPORTS ON COUNTY INTERNET WEBSITES

Sec. 58.351. Applicability.

This subchapter applies only to a county with a population of 600,000 or more.

Sec. 58.352. Information Posted on County Website.

(a) A juvenile court judge in a county to which this subchapter applies shall post a report on the Internet website of the county in which the court is located. The report must include:

(1) the total number of children committed by the judge to:

(A) a correctional facility operated by the Texas Juvenile Justice Department; or

(B) a post-adjudication secure correctional facility as that term is defined by Section 54.04011; and

(2) for each child committed to a facility described by Subdivision (1):

(A) a general description of the offense committed by the child or the conduct of the child that led to the child's commitment to the facility;

(B) the year the child was committed to the facility; and

(C) the age range, race, and gender of the child.

(b) Not later than the 10th day following the first day of each quarter, a juvenile court judge shall update the information posted on a county Internet website under Subsection (a).

Sec. 58.353. Confidentiality.

A record posted on a county Internet website under this subchapter may not include any information that personally identifies a child.

SUBCHAPTER E STATEWIDE JUVENILE INFORMATION AND CASE MANAGEMENT SYSTEM

Sec. 58.401. Definitions.

In this subchapter:

(1) "Department" means the Texas Juvenile Justice Department.

(2) "Criminal justice agency" has the meaning assigned by Section 411.082, Government Code.

(3) "Juvenile justice agency" means an agency that has custody or control over juvenile offenders.

(4) "Partner agencies" means those agencies described in Section 58.305 as well as private service providers to the juvenile justice system.

(5) "System" means an automated statewide juvenile information and case management system.

Sec. 58.402. Purposes of System.

The purposes of the system are to:

(1) provide accurate information at the statewide level relating to children who come into contact with the juvenile justice system;

(2) facilitate communication and information sharing between authorized entities in criminal and juvenile justice agencies and partner agencies regarding effective and efficient identification of and service delivery to juvenile offenders; and

(3) provide comprehensive juvenile justice information and case management abilities that will meet the common data collection, reporting, and management needs of juvenile probation departments in this state and provide the flexibility to accommodate individualized requirements.

Sec. 58.403. Juvenile Information System.

(a) Through the adoption of an interlocal contract under Chapter 791, Government Code, with one or more counties, the department may participate in and assist counties in the creation, operation, and maintenance of a system that is intended for statewide use to:

(1) aid in processing the cases of children under this title;

(2) facilitate the delivery of services to children in the juvenile justice system;

(3) aid in the early identification of at-risk and delinquent children; and

(4) facilitate cross-jurisdictional sharing of information related to juvenile offenders between authorized criminal and juvenile justice agencies and partner agencies.

(b) The department may use funds appropriated for the implementation of this section to pay costs incurred under an interlocal contract described by Subsection (a), including license fees, maintenance and operations costs, administrative costs, and any other costs specified in the interlocal contract.

(c) The department may provide training services to counties on the use and operation of a system created, operated, or maintained by one or more counties under Subsection (a).

(d) Subchapter L, Chapter 2054, Government Code, does not apply to the statewide juvenile information and case management system created under this subchapter.

Sec. 58.404. Information Collected by Department.

The department may collect and maintain all information related to juvenile offenders and all offenses committed by a juvenile offender, including all information collected and maintained under Subchapters B and D.

Sec. 58.405. Authority Cumulative.

The authority granted by this subchapter is cumulative of all other authority granted by this chapter to a county, the department, or a juvenile justice agency and nothing in this subchapter limits the authority of a county, the department, or a juvenile justice agency under this chapter to create an information system or to share information related to a juvenile.

CHAPTER 59
PROGRESSIVE SANCTIONS MODEL

Sec. 59.001. Purposes.

The purposes of the progressive sanctions model are to:

(1) ensure that juvenile offenders face uniform and consistent consequences and punishments that correspond to the seriousness of each offender's current offense, prior delinquent history, special treatment or training needs, and effectiveness of prior interventions;

(2) balance public protection and rehabilitation while holding juvenile offenders accountable;

(3) permit flexibility in the decisions made in relation to the juvenile offender to the extent allowed by law;

(4) consider the juvenile offender's circumstances;

(5) recognize that departure of a disposition from this model is not necessarily undesirable and in some cases is highly desirable; and

(6) improve juvenile justice planning and resource allocation by ensuring uniform and consistent reporting of disposition decisions at all levels.

Sec. 59.002. Sanction Level Assignment by Probation Department.

(a) The probation department may assign a sanction level of one to a child referred to the probation department under Section 53.012.

(b) The probation department may assign a sanction level of two to a child for whom deferred prosecution is authorized under Section 53.03.

Sec. 59.003. Sanction Level Assignment Model.

(a) Subject to Subsection (e), after a child's first commission of delinquent conduct or conduct indicating a need for supervision, the probation department or prosecuting attorney may, or the juvenile court may, in a disposition hearing under Section 54.04 or a modification hearing under Section 54.05, assign a child one of the following sanction levels according to the child's conduct:

(1) for conduct indicating a need for supervision, other than conduct described in Section 51.03(b)(3) or (4) or a Class A or B misdemeanor, the sanction level is one;

(2) for conduct indicating a need for supervision under Section 51.03(b)(3) or (4) or a Class A or B misdemeanor, other than a misdemeanor involving the use or possession of a firearm, or for delinquent conduct under Section 51.03(a)(2), the sanction level is two;

(3) for a misdemeanor involving the use or possession of a firearm or for a state jail felony or a felony of the third degree, the sanction level is three;

(4) for a felony of the second degree, the sanction level is four;

(5) for a felony of the first degree, other than a felony involving the use of a deadly weapon or causing serious bodily injury, the sanction level is five;

(6) for a felony of the first degree involving the use of a deadly weapon or causing serious bodily injury, for an aggravated controlled substance felony, or for a capital felony, the sanction level is six; or

(7) for a felony of the first degree involving the use of a deadly weapon or causing serious bodily injury, for an aggravated controlled substance felony, or for a capital felony, if the petition has been approved by a grand jury under Section 53.045, or if a petition to transfer the child to criminal court has been filed under Section 54.02, the sanction level is seven.

Texas Family Code

(b) Subject to Subsection (e), if the child subsequently is found to have engaged in delinquent conduct in an adjudication hearing under Section 54.03 or a hearing to modify a disposition under Section 54.05 on two separate occasions and each involves a violation of a penal law of a classification that is less than the classification of the child's previous conduct, the juvenile court may assign the child a sanction level that is one level higher than the previously assigned sanction level, unless the child's previously assigned sanction level is six.

(c) Subject to Subsection (e), if the child's subsequent commission of delinquent conduct or conduct indicating a need for supervision involves a violation of a penal law of a classification that is the same as or greater than the classification of the child's previous conduct, the juvenile court may assign the child a sanction level authorized by law that is one level higher than the previously assigned sanction level.

(d) Subject to Subsection (e), if the child's previously assigned sanction level is four or five and the child's subsequent commission of delinquent conduct is of the grade of felony, the juvenile court may assign the child a sanction level that is one level higher than the previously assigned sanction level.

(e) The probation department may, in accordance with Section 54.05, request the extension of a period of probation specified under sanction levels one through five if the circumstances of the child warrant the extension.

(f) Before the court assigns the child a sanction level that involves the revocation of the child's probation and the commitment of the child to the Texas Juvenile Justice Department, the court shall hold a hearing to modify the disposition as required by Section 54.05.

Sec. 59.004. Sanction Level One.

(a) For a child at sanction level one, the juvenile court or probation department may:

(1) require counseling for the child regarding the child's conduct;

(2) inform the child of the progressive sanctions that may be imposed on the child if the child continues to engage in delinquent conduct or conduct indicating a need for supervision;

(3) inform the child's parents or guardians of the parents' or guardians' responsibility to impose reasonable restrictions on the child to prevent the conduct from recurring;

(4) provide information or other assistance to the child or the child's parents or guardians in securing needed social services;

(5) require the child or the child's parents or guardians to participate in a program for services under Section 264.302, if a program under Section 264.302 is available to the child or the child's parents or guardians;

(6) refer the child to a community-based citizen intervention program approved by the juvenile court;

(7) release the child to the child's parents or guardians; and

(8) require the child to attend and successfully complete an educational program described by Section 37.218, Education Code, or another equivalent educational program.

(b) The probation department shall discharge the child from the custody of the probation department after the provisions of this section are met.

Sec. 59.005. Sanction Level Two.

(a) For a child at sanction level two, the juvenile court, the prosecuting attorney, or the probation department may, as provided by Section 53.03:

(1) place the child on deferred prosecution for not less than three months or more than six months;

(2) require the child to make restitution to the victim of the child's conduct or perform community service restitution appropriate to the nature and degree of harm caused and according to the child's ability;

(3) require the child's parents or guardians to identify restrictions the parents or guardians will impose on the child's activities and requirements the parents or guardians will set for the child's behavior;

(4) provide the information required under Sections 59.004(a)(2) and (4);

(5) require the child or the child's parents or guardians to participate in a program for services under Section 264.302, if a program under Section 264.302 is available to the child or the child's parents or guardians;

(6) refer the child to a community-based citizen intervention program approved by the juvenile court; and

(7) if appropriate, impose additional conditions of probation.

(b) The juvenile court or the probation department shall discharge the child from the custody of the probation department on the date the provisions of this section are met or on the child's 18th birthday, whichever is earlier.

Sec. 59.006. Sanction Level Three.

(a) For a child at sanction level three, the juvenile court may:

Texas Family Code

(1) place the child on probation for not less than six months;

(2) require the child to make restitution to the victim of the child's conduct or perform community service restitution appropriate to the nature and degree of harm caused and according to the child's ability;

(3) impose specific restrictions on the child's activities and requirements for the child's behavior as conditions of probation;

(4) require a probation officer to closely monitor the child's activities and behavior;

(5) require the child or the child's parents or guardians to participate in programs or services designated by the court or probation officer; and

(6) if appropriate, impose additional conditions of probation.

(b) The juvenile court shall discharge the child from the custody of the probation department on the date the provisions of this section are met or on the child's 18th birthday, whichever is earlier.

Sec. 59.007. Sanction Level Four.

(a) For a child at sanction level four, the juvenile court may:

(1) require the child to participate as a condition of probation for not less than three months or more than 12 months in an intensive services probation program that emphasizes frequent contact and reporting with a probation officer, discipline, intensive supervision services, social responsibility, and productive work;

(2) after release from the program described by Subdivision (1), continue the child on probation supervision;

(3) require the child to make restitution to the victim of the child's conduct or perform community service restitution appropriate to the nature and degree of harm caused and according to the child's ability;

(4) impose highly structured restrictions on the child's activities and requirements for behavior of the child as conditions of probation;

(5) require a probation officer to closely monitor the child;

(6) require the child or the child's parents or guardians to participate in programs or services designed to address their particular needs and circumstances; and

(7) if appropriate, impose additional sanctions.

(b) The juvenile court shall discharge the child from the custody of the probation department on the date the provisions of this section are met or on the child's 18th birthday, whichever is earlier.

Sec. 59.008. Sanction Level Five.

(a) For a child at sanction level five, the juvenile court may:

(1) as a condition of probation, place the child for not less than six months or more than 12 months in a post-adjudication secure correctional facility;

(2) after release from the program described by Subdivision (1), continue the child on probation supervision;

(3) require the child to make restitution to the victim of the child's conduct or perform community service restitution appropriate to the nature and degree of harm caused and according to the child's ability;

(4) impose highly structured restrictions on the child's activities and requirements for behavior of the child as conditions of probation;

(5) require a probation officer to closely monitor the child;

(6) require the child or the child's parents or guardians to participate in programs or services designed to address their particular needs and circumstances; and

(7) if appropriate, impose additional sanctions.

(b) The juvenile court shall discharge the child from the custody of the probation department on the date the provisions of this section are met or on the child's 18th birthday, whichever is earlier.

Sec. 59.009. Sanction Level Six.

(a) For a child at sanction level six, the juvenile court may commit the child to the custody of the Texas Juvenile Justice Department or a post-adjudication secure correctional facility under Section 54.04011(c)(1). The department, juvenile board, or local juvenile probation department, as applicable, may:

(1) require the child to participate in a highly structured residential program that emphasizes discipline, accountability, fitness, training, and productive work for not less than nine months or more than 24 months unless the department, board, or probation department extends the period and the reason for an extension is documented;

(2) require the child to make restitution to the victim of the child's conduct or perform community service restitution appropriate to the nature and degree of the harm caused and according to the child's ability, if there is a victim of the child's conduct;

(3) require the child and the child's parents or guardians to participate in programs and services for their particular needs and circumstances; and

(4) if appropriate, impose additional sanctions.

(b) On release of the child under supervision, the Texas Juvenile Justice Department parole programs or the juvenile board or local juvenile probation department operating parole programs under Section 152.0016(c)(2), Human Resources Code, may:

(1) impose highly structured restrictions on the child's activities and requirements for behavior of the child as conditions of release under supervision;

(2) require a parole officer to closely monitor the child for not less than six months; and

(3) if appropriate, impose any other conditions of supervision.

(c) The Texas Juvenile Justice Department, juvenile board, or local juvenile probation department may discharge the child from the custody of the department, board, or probation department, as applicable, on the date the provisions of this section are met or on the child's 19th birthday, whichever is earlier.

Sec. 59.010. Sanction Level Seven.

(a) For a child at sanction level seven, the juvenile court may certify and transfer the child under Section 54.02 or sentence the child to commitment to the Texas Juvenile Justice Department under Section 54.04(d)(3), 54.04(m), or 54.05(f) or to a post-adjudication secure correctional facility under Section 54.04011(c)(2). The department, juvenile board, or local juvenile probation department, as applicable, may:

(1) require the child to participate in a highly structured residential program that emphasizes discipline, accountability, fitness, training, and productive work for not less than 12 months or more than 10 years unless the department, board, or probation department extends the period and the reason for the extension is documented;

(2) require the child to make restitution to the victim of the child's conduct or perform community service restitution appropriate to the nature and degree of harm caused and according to the child's ability, if there is a victim of the child's conduct;

(3) require the child and the child's parents or guardians to participate in programs and services for their particular needs and circumstances; and

(4) impose any other appropriate sanction.

(b) On release of the child under supervision, the Texas Juvenile Justice Department parole programs or the juvenile board or local juvenile probation department parole programs under Section 152.0016(c)(2), Human Resources Code, may:

(1) impose highly structured restrictions on the child's activities and requirements for behavior of the child as conditions of release under supervision;

(2) require a parole officer to monitor the child closely for not less than 12 months; and

(3) impose any other appropriate condition of supervision.

Sec. 59.011. Duty of Juvenile Board.

A juvenile board shall require the juvenile probation department to report progressive sanction data electronically to the Texas Juvenile Justice Department in the format and time frames specified by the Texas Juvenile Justice Department.

Sec. 59.012. Reports by Criminal Justice Policy Council [Repealed].

Repealed by Acts 2013, 83rd Leg., ch. 1312 (S.B. 59), § 99(9), effective September 1, 2013.

Sec. 59.013. Liability.

The Texas Juvenile Justice Department, a juvenile board, a court, a person appointed by a court, an attorney for the state, a peace officer, or a law enforcement agency is not liable for a failure or inability to provide a service listed under Sections 59.004-59.010.

Sec. 59.014. Appeal.

A child may not bring an appeal or a postconviction writ of habeas corpus based on:

(1) the failure or inability of any person to provide a service listed under Sections 59.004–59.010;

(2) the failure of a court or of any person to make a sanction level assignment as provided in Section 59.002 or 59.003;

(3) a departure from the sanction level assignment model provided by this chapter; or

(4) the failure of a juvenile court or probation department to report a departure from the model.

Sec. 59.015. Waiver of Sanctions on Parents or Guardians.

On a finding by the juvenile court or probation department that a child's parents or guardians have made a reasonable good faith effort to prevent the child from engaging in delinquent conduct or engaging in conduct indicating a need for supervision and that, despite the parents' or guardians' efforts, the child continues to engage in such conduct, the court or probation department shall waive any sanction that may be imposed on the parents or guardians at any sanction level.

CHAPTER 60
UNIFORM INTERSTATE COMPACT ON JUVENILES

Sec. 60.001. Definitions.

In this chapter:

(1) "Commission" means the Interstate Commission for Juveniles.

(2) "Compact" means the Interstate Compact for Juveniles.

(3) "Compact administrator" has the meaning assigned by Article II of the compact.

Sec. 60.002. Execution of Interstate Compact [Repealed].

Repealed by Acts 2005, 79th Leg., ch. 1007 (H.B. 706), § 3.02, effective August 26, 2008.

Sec. 60.003. Execution of Additional Article [Repealed].

Repealed by Acts 2005, 79th Leg., ch. 1007 (H.B. 706), § 3.02, effective August 26, 2008.

Sec. 60.004. Execution of Amendment [Repealed].

Repealed by Acts 2005, 79th Leg., ch. 1007 (H.B. 706), § 3.02, effective August 26, 2008.

Sec. 60.005. Juvenile Compact Administrator.

Under the compact, the governor may designate an officer as the compact administrator. The administrator, acting jointly with like officers of other party states, shall adopt regulations to carry out more effectively the terms of the compact. The compact administrator serves at the pleasure of the governor. The compact administrator shall cooperate with all departments, agencies, and officers of and in the government of this state and its subdivisions in facilitating the proper administration of the compact or of a supplementary agreement entered into by this state.

Sec. 60.006. Supplementary Agreements.

A compact administrator may make supplementary agreements with appropriate officials of other states pursuant to the compact. If a supplementary agreement requires or contemplates the use of an institution or facility of this state or requires or contemplates the provision of a service of this state, the supplementary agreement has no force or effect until approved by the head of the department or agency under whose jurisdiction the institution is operated, or whose department or agency is charged with performing the service.

Sec. 60.007. Financial Arrangements.

The compact administrator may make or arrange for the payments necessary to discharge the financial obligations imposed upon this state by the compact or by a supplementary agreement made under the compact, subject to legislative appropriations.

Sec. 60.008. Enforcement.

The courts, departments, agencies, and officers of this state and its subdivisions shall enforce this compact and shall do all things appropriate to effectuate its purposes and intent which are within their respective jurisdictions.

Sec. 60.009. Additional Procedures Not Precluded.

In addition to any procedures developed under the compact for the return of a runaway juvenile, the particular states, the juvenile, or his parents, the courts, or other legal custodian involved may agree upon and adopt any plan or procedure legally authorized under the laws of this state and the other respective party states for the return of the runaway juvenile.

Sec. 60.010. Interstate Compact for Juveniles.

ARTICLE I
PURPOSE

The compacting states to this Interstate Compact recognize that each state is responsible for the proper supervision or return of juveniles, delinquents, and status offenders who are on probation or parole and who have absconded, escaped, or run away from supervision and control and in so doing have endangered their own safety and the safety of others. The compacting states also recognize that each state is responsible for the safe return of juveniles who have run away from home and in doing so have left their state of residence. The compacting states also recognize that congress, by enacting the Crime Control Act, 4 U.S.C. Section 112 (1965), has authorized and encouraged compacts for cooperative efforts and mutual assistance in the prevention of crime.

It is the purpose of this compact, through means of joint and cooperative action among the compacting states to: (A) ensure that the juveniles who are moved under this compact to another state for probation or parole supervision and services are governed in the receiving state by the same standards that apply to juveniles receiving such supervision and services in the receiving state; (B) ensure that the public safety interests of the citizens, including the victims of juvenile offenders, in both the sending and receiving states are adequately protected and balanced with the juvenile's and the juvenile's family's best interests and welfare when an interstate movement is under consideration; (C) return juveniles who have run away, absconded, or escaped from supervision or control or have been accused of an offense to the state requesting their return through a fair and prompt judicial review process that ensures that the requisition is in order and that the transport is properly supervised; (D) make provisions for contracts between member states for the cooperative institutionalization in public facilities in member states for delinquent youth needing special services; (E) provide for the effective tracking of juveniles who move interstate under the compact's provisions; (F) equitably allocate the costs, benefits, and obligations of the compacting states; (G) establish procedures to manage the movement between states of juvenile offenders released to the community under the jurisdiction of courts, juvenile departments, or any other criminal or juvenile justice agency which has jurisdiction over juvenile offenders, ensuring that a receiving state accepts supervision of a juvenile when the juvenile's parent or other person having legal custody resides or is undertaking residence there; (H) ensure immediate notice to jurisdictions where defined offenders are authorized to travel or to relocate across state lines; (I) establish a system of uniform data collection on information pertaining to juveniles who move interstate under this compact that prevents public disclosure of identity and individual treatment information but allows access by authorized juvenile justice and criminal justice officials and regular reporting of compact activities to heads of state executive, judicial, and legislative branches and juvenile and criminal justice administrators; (J) monitor compliance with rules governing interstate movement of juveniles and initiate interventions to address and correct noncompliance; (K) coordinate training and education regarding the regulation of interstate movement of juveniles for officials involved in such activity; and (L) coordinate the implementation and operation of the compact with the Interstate Compact for the Placement of Children, the Interstate Compact for Adult Offender Supervision and other compacts affecting juveniles particularly in those cases where concurrent or overlapping supervision issues arise. It is the policy of the compacting states that the activities conducted by the Interstate Commission created herein are the formation of public policies and therefore are public business. Furthermore, the compacting states shall cooperate and observe their individual and collective duties and responsibilities for the prompt return and acceptance of juveniles subject to the provisions of this compact. The provisions of this compact shall be reasonably and liberally construed to accomplish the purposes and policies of the compact.

ARTICLE II
DEFINITIONS

As used in this compact, unless the context clearly requires a different construction:

A. "Bylaws" means those bylaws established by the Interstate Commission for its governance or for directing or controlling the Interstate Commission's actions or conduct.

B. "Compact administrator" means the individual in each compacting state appointed pursuant to the terms of this compact responsible for the administration and management of the state's supervision and transfer of juveniles subject to the terms of this compact and to the rules adopted by the Interstate Commission under this compact.

C. "Compacting state" means any state which has enacted the enabling legislation for this compact.

D. "Commissioner" means the voting representative of each compacting state appointed pursuant to Article III of this compact.

E. "Court" means any court having jurisdiction over delinquent, neglected, or dependent children.

F. "Deputy compact administrator" means the individual, if any, in each compacting state appointed to act on behalf of a compact administrator pursuant to the terms of this compact, responsible for the administration and management of the state's supervision and transfer of juveniles subject to the terms of this compact and to the rules adopted by the Interstate Commission under this compact.

G. "Interstate Commission" means the Interstate Commission for Juveniles created by Article III of this compact.

H. "Juvenile" means any person defined as a juvenile in any member state or by the rules of the Interstate Commission, including:

(1) Accused Delinquent — a person charged with an offense that, if committed by an adult, would be a criminal offense;

(2) Adjudicated Delinquent — a person found to have committed an offense that, if committed by an adult, would be a criminal offense;

(3) Accused Status Offender — a person charged with an offense that would not be a criminal offense if committed by an adult;

(4) Adjudicated Status Offender — a person found to have committed an offense that would not be a criminal offense if committed by an adult; and

(5) Nonoffender — a person in need of supervision who has not been accused or adjudicated a status offender or delinquent.

I. "Noncompacting state" means any state which has not enacted the enabling legislation for this compact.

J. "Probation or parole" means any kind of supervision or conditional release of juveniles authorized under the laws of the compacting states.

K. "Rule" means a written statement by the Interstate Commission promulgated pursuant to Article VI of this compact that is of general applicability, implements, interprets, or prescribes a policy or provision of the compact, or an organizational, procedural, or practice requirement of the Interstate Commission, and has the force and effect of statutory law in a compacting state, and includes the amendment, repeal, or suspension of an existing rule.

L. "State" means a state of the United States, the District of Columbia (or its designee), the Commonwealth of Puerto Rico, the U.S.Virgin Islands, Guam, American Samoa, and the Northern Marianas Islands.

ARTICLE III
INTERSTATE COMMISSION FOR JUVENILES

A. The compacting states hereby create the Interstate Commission for Juveniles. The Interstate Commission shall be a body corporate and joint agency of the compacting states. The commission shall have all the responsibilities, powers, and duties set forth herein, and such additional powers as may be conferred upon it by subsequent action of the respective legislatures of the compacting states in accordance with the terms of this compact.

B. The Interstate Commission shall consist of commissioners appointed by the appropriate appointing authority in each state pursuant to the rules and requirements of each compacting state. The commissioner shall be the compact administrator, deputy compact administrator, or designee from that state who shall serve on the Interstate Commission in such capacity under or pursuant to the applicable law of the compacting state.

C. In addition to the commissioners who are the voting representatives of each state, the Interstate Commission shall include individuals who are not commissioners, but who are members of interested organizations. Such noncommissioner members must include a member of the national organizations of governors, legislators, state chief justices, attorneys general, Interstate Compact for Adult Offender Supervision, Interstate Compact for the Placement of Children, juvenile justice and juvenile corrections officials, and crime victims. All noncommissioner members of the Interstate Commission shall be ex officio (nonvoting) members. The Interstate Commission may provide in its bylaws for such additional ex officio (nonvoting) members, including members of other national organizations, in such numbers as shall be determined by the commission.

D. Each compacting state represented at any meeting of the Interstate Commission is entitled to one vote. A majority of the compacting states shall constitute a quorum for the transaction of business, unless a larger quorum is required by the bylaws of the Interstate Commission.

E. The Interstate Commission shall meet at least once each calendar year. The chairperson may call additional meetings and, upon the request of a simple majority of the compacting states, shall call additional meetings. Public notice shall be given of all meetings and meetings shall be open to the public.

F. The Interstate Commission shall establish an executive committee, which shall include commission officers, members, and others as determined by the bylaws. The executive committee shall have the power to act on behalf of the Interstate Commission during periods when the Interstate Commission is not in session, with the exception of rulemaking or amendment to the compact. The executive committee shall oversee the day-to-day activities of the administration of the compact managed by an executive director and Interstate Commission staff; administers enforcement and compliance with the provisions of the compact, its bylaws and rules, and performs such other duties as directed by the Interstate Commission or set forth in the bylaws.

G. Each member of the Interstate Commission shall have the right and power to cast a vote to which that compacting state is entitled and to participate in the business and affairs of the Interstate Commission. A member shall vote in person and shall not delegate a vote to another compacting state. However, a commissioner shall appoint another authorized representative, in the absence of the commissioner from that state, to cast a vote on behalf of the compacting state at a specified meeting. The bylaws may provide for members' participation in meetings by telephone or other means of telecommunication or electronic communication.

H. The Interstate Commission's bylaws shall establish conditions and procedures under which the Interstate Commission shall make its information and official records available to the public for inspection or copying. The Interstate Commission may exempt from disclosure any information or official records to the extent they would adversely affect personal privacy rights or proprietary interests.

I. Public notice shall be given of all meetings and all meetings shall be open to the public, except as set forth in the rules or as otherwise provided in the compact. The Interstate Commission and any of its committees may close a meeting to the public when it determines by two-thirds vote that an open meeting would be likely to:

1. Relate solely to the Interstate Commission's internal personnel practices and procedures;

2. Disclose matters specifically exempted from disclosure by statute;

3. Disclose trade secrets or commercial or financial information which is privileged or confidential;

4. Involve accusing any person of a crime or formally censuring any person;

5. Disclose information of a personal nature where disclosure would constitute a clearly unwarranted invasion of personal privacy;

6. Disclose investigative records compiled for law enforcement purposes;

7. Disclose information contained in or related to examination, operating or condition reports prepared by, or on behalf of or for the use of, the Interstate Commission with respect to a regulated person or entity for the purpose of regulation or supervision of such person or entity;

8. Disclose information, the premature disclosure of which would significantly endanger the stability of a regulated person or entity; or

9. Specifically relate to the Interstate Commission's issuance of a subpoena, or its participation in a civil action or other legal proceeding.

J. For every meeting closed pursuant to this provision, the Interstate Commission's legal counsel shall publicly certify that, in the legal counsel's opinion, the meeting may be closed to the public, and shall reference each relevant exemptive provision. The Interstate Commission shall keep minutes which shall fully and clearly describe all matters discussed in any meeting and shall provide a full and accurate summary of any actions taken, and the reasons therefore, including a description of each of the views expressed on any item and the record of any roll call vote (reflected in the vote of each member on the question). All documents considered in connection with any action shall be identified in such minutes.

K. The Interstate Commission shall collect standardized data concerning the interstate movement of juveniles as directed through its rules which shall specify the data to be collected, the means of collection and data exchange, and reporting requirements. Such methods of data collection, exchange, and reporting shall insofar as is reasonably possible conform to up-to-date technology and coordinate the Interstate Commission's information functions with the appropriate repository of records.

ARTICLE IV
POWERS AND DUTIES OF THE INTERSTATE COMMISSION

The commission shall have the following powers and duties:

1. To provide for dispute resolution among compacting states.

2. To promulgate rules to effect the purposes and obligations as enumerated in this compact, which shall have the force and effect of statutory law and shall be binding in the compacting states to the extent and in the manner provided in this compact.

3. To oversee, supervise, and coordinate the interstate movement of juveniles subject to the terms of this compact and any bylaws adopted and rules promulgated by the Interstate Commission.

4. To enforce compliance with the compact provisions, the rules promulgated by the Interstate Commission, and the bylaws, using all necessary and proper means, including but not limited to the use of judicial process.

5. To establish and maintain offices which shall be located within one or more of the compacting states.

6. To purchase and maintain insurance and bonds.

7. To borrow, accept, hire, or contract for services of personnel.

8. To establish and appoint committees and hire staff which it deems necessary for the carrying out of its functions including, but not limited to, an executive committee as required by Article III of this compact, which shall have the power to act on behalf of the Interstate Commission in carrying out its powers and duties hereunder.

9. To elect or appoint officers, attorneys, employees, agents, or consultants, and to fix their compensation, define their duties, and determine their qualifications, and to establish the Interstate Commission's personnel policies and programs relating to, inter alia, conflicts of interest, rates of compensation, and qualifications of personnel.

10. To accept any and all donations and grants of money, equipment, supplies, materials, and services, and to receive, utilize, and dispose of same.

11. To lease, purchase, accept contributions or donations of, or otherwise to own, hold, improve, or use any property, whether real, personal, or mixed.

12. To sell, convey, mortgage, pledge, lease, exchange, abandon, or otherwise dispose of any property, whether real, personal, or mixed.

13. To establish a budget and make expenditures and levy dues as provided in Article VIII of this compact.

14. To sue and be sued.

15. To adopt a seal and bylaws governing the management and operation of the Interstate Commission.

16. To perform such functions as may be necessary or appropriate to achieve the purposes of this compact.

17. To report annually to the legislatures, governors, and judiciary of the compacting states concerning the activities of the Interstate Commission during the preceding year. Such reports shall also include any recommendations that may have been adopted by the Interstate Commission.

18. To coordinate education, training, and public awareness regarding the interstate movement of juveniles for officials involved in such activity.

19. To establish uniform standards of the reporting, collecting, and exchanging of data.

20. The Interstate Commission shall maintain its corporate books and records in accordance with the bylaws.

ARTICLE V
ORGANIZATION AND OPERATION OF THE INTERSTATE COMMISSION

Sec. A. Bylaws

1. The Interstate Commission shall, by a majority of the members present and voting, within 12 months of the first Interstate Commission meeting, adopt bylaws to govern its conduct as may be necessary or appropriate to carry out the purposes of the compact, including, but not limited to:

a. Establishing the fiscal year of the Interstate Commission;

b. Establishing an executive committee and such other committees as may be necessary;

c. Providing for the establishment of committees governing any general or specific delegation of any authority or function of the Interstate Commission;

d. Providing reasonable procedures for calling and conducting meetings of the Interstate Commission and ensuring reasonable notice of each such meeting;

e. Establishing the titles and responsibilities of the officers of the Interstate Commission;

f. Providing a mechanism for concluding the operations of the Interstate Commission and the return of any surplus funds that may exist upon the termination of the compact after the payment or reserving of all of its debts and obligations;

g. Providing start-up rules for initial administration of the compact; and

h. Establishing standards and procedures for compliance and technical assistance in carrying out the compact.

Sec. B. Officers and Staff

1. The Interstate Commission shall, by a majority of the members, elect annually from among its members a chairperson and a vice chairperson, each of whom shall have such authority and duties as may be specified in the bylaws. The chairperson or, in the chairperson's absence or disability, the vice chairperson shall preside at all meetings of the Interstate Commission. The officers so elected shall serve without compensation or remuneration from the Interstate Commission, provided that, subject to the availability of budgeted funds, the officers shall be reimbursed for any ordinary and necessary costs and expenses incurred by them in the performance of their duties and responsibilities as officers of the Interstate Commission.

2. The Interstate Commission shall, through its executive committee, appoint or retain an executive director for such period, upon such terms and conditions, and for such compensation as the Interstate Commission may deem appropriate. The executive director shall serve as secretary to the Interstate Commission, but shall not be a member and shall hire and supervise such other staff as may be authorized by the Interstate Commission.

Sec. C. Qualified Immunity, Defense, and Indemnification

1. The Interstate Commission's executive director and employees shall be immune from suit and liability, either personally or in their official capacity, for any claim for damage to or loss of property or personal injury or other civil liability caused or arising out of or relating to any actual or alleged act, error, or omission that occurred, or that such person had a reasonable basis for believing occurred, within the scope of Interstate Commission employment, duties, or responsibilities, provided that any such person shall not be protected from suit or liability for any damage, loss, injury, or liability caused by the intentional or wilful and wanton misconduct of any such person.

2. The liability of any commissioner, or the employee or agent of a commissioner, acting within the scope of such person's employment or duties for acts, errors, or omissions occurring within such person's state may not exceed the limits of liability set forth under the constitution and laws of that state for state officials, employees, and agents. Nothing in this subsection shall be construed to protect any

such person from suit or liability for any damage, loss, injury, or liability caused by the intentional or wilful and wanton misconduct of any such person.

3. The Interstate Commission shall defend the executive director or the employees or representatives of the Interstate Commission and, subject to the approval of the attorney general of the state represented by any commissioner of a compacting state, shall defend such commissioner or the commissioner's representatives or employees in any civil action seeking to impose liability arising out of any actual or alleged act, error, or omission that occurred within the scope of Interstate Commission employment, duties, or responsibilities, or that the defendant had a reasonable basis for believing occurred within the scope of Interstate Commission employment, duties, or responsibilities, provided that the actual or alleged act, error, or omission did not result from intentional or wilful and wanton misconduct on the part of such person.

4. The Interstate Commission shall indemnify and hold the commissioner of a compacting state, or the commissioner's representatives or employees, or the Interstate Commission's representatives or employees, harmless in the amount of any settlement or judgment obtained against such persons arising out of any actual or alleged act, error, or omission that occurred within the scope of Interstate Commission employment, duties, or responsibilities, or that such persons had a reasonable basis for believing occurred within the scope of Interstate Commission employment, duties, or responsibilities, provided that the actual or alleged act, error, or omission did not result from intentional or wilful and wanton misconduct on the part of such persons.

ARTICLE VI
RULEMAKING FUNCTIONS OF THE INTERSTATE COMMISSION

A. The Interstate Commission shall promulgate and publish rules in order to effectively and efficiently achieve the purposes of the compact.

B. Rulemaking shall occur pursuant to the criteria set forth in this article and the bylaws and rules adopted pursuant thereto. Such rulemaking shall substantially conform to the principles of the "Model State Administrative Procedures Act," 1981 Act, Uniform Laws Annotated, Vol. 15, p.1 (2000), or such other administrative procedures act, as the Interstate Commission deems appropriate consistent with due process requirements under the United States Constitution as now or hereafter interpreted by the United States Supreme Court. All rules and amendments shall become binding as of the date specified, as published with the final version of the rule as approved by the Interstate Commission.

C. When promulgating a rule, the Interstate Commission shall, at a minimum:

1. Publish the proposed rule's entire text stating the reason or reasons for that proposed rule;

2. Allow and invite persons to submit written data, facts, opinions, and arguments, which information shall be added to the record and be made publicly available;

3. Provide an opportunity for an informal hearing, if petitioned by 10 or more persons; and

4. Promulgate a final rule and its effective date, if appropriate, based on input from state or local officials, or interested parties.

D. Allow, not later than 60 days after a rule is promulgated, any interested person to file a petition in the United States District Court for the District of Columbia or in the federal district court where the Interstate Commission's principal office is located for judicial review of the rule. If the court finds that the Interstate Commission's action is not supported by substantial evidence in the rulemaking record, the court shall hold the rule unlawful and set it aside. For purposes of this subsection, evidence is substantial if it would be considered substantial evidence under the Model State Administrative Procedures Act.

E. If a majority of the legislatures of the compacting states rejects a rule, those states may, by enactment of a statute or resolution in the same manner used to adopt the compact, cause that such rule shall have no further force and effect in any compacting state.

F. The existing rules governing the operation of the Interstate Compact on Juveniles superceded by this Act shall be null and void 12 months after the first meeting of the Interstate Commission created under this compact.

G. Upon determination by the Interstate Commission that an emergency exists, the Interstate Commission may promulgate an emergency rule which shall become effective immediately upon adoption, provided that the usual rulemaking procedures provided hereunder shall be retroactively applied to said rule as soon as reasonably possible, but no later than 90 days after the effective date of the emergency rule.

ARTICLE VII
OVERSIGHT, ENFORCEMENT, AND DISPUTE RESOLUTION BY THE INTERSTATE COMMISSION

Sec. A. Oversight

1. The Interstate Commission shall oversee the administration and operations of the interstate

movement of juveniles subject to this compact in the compacting states and shall monitor such activities being administered in noncompacting states which may significantly affect compacting states.

2. The courts and executive agencies in each compacting state shall enforce this compact and shall take all actions necessary and appropriate to effectuate the compact's purposes and intent. The provisions of this compact and the rules promulgated hereunder shall be received by all the judges, public officers, commissions, and departments of the state government as evidence of the authorized statute and administrative rules. All courts shall take judicial notice of the compact and the rules. In any judicial or administrative proceeding in a compacting state pertaining to the subject matter of this compact which may affect the powers, responsibilities, or actions of the Interstate Commission, the Interstate Commission shall be entitled to receive all service of process in any such proceeding, and shall have standing to intervene in the proceeding for all purposes.

Sec. B. Dispute Resolution

1. The compacting states shall report to the Interstate Commission on all issues and activities necessary for the administration of the compact as well as issues and activities pertaining to compliance with the provisions of the compact and its bylaws and rules.

2. The Interstate Commission shall attempt, upon the request of a compacting state, to resolve any disputes or other issues which are subject to the compact and which may arise among compacting states and between compacting and noncompacting states. The Interstate Commission shall promulgate a rule providing for both mediation and binding dispute resolution for disputes among the compacting states.

3. The Interstate Commission, in the reasonable exercise of its discretion, shall enforce the provisions and rules of this compact using any or all means set forth in Article X of this compact.

ARTICLE VIII
FINANCE

A. The Interstate Commission shall pay or provide for the payment of the reasonable expenses of its establishment, organization, and ongoing activities.

B. The Interstate Commission shall levy on and collect an annual assessment from each compacting state to cover the cost of the internal operations and activities of the Interstate Commission and its staff which must be in a total amount sufficient to cover the Interstate Commission's annual budget as approved each year. The aggregate annual assessment amount shall be allocated based upon a formula to be determined by the Interstate Commission, taking into consideration the population of each compacting state and the volume of interstate movement of juveniles in each compacting state. The Interstate Commission shall promulgate a rule binding upon all compacting states that governs said assessment.

C. The Interstate Commission shall not incur any obligations of any kind prior to securing the funds adequate to meet the same, nor shall the Interstate Commission pledge the credit of any of the compacting states, except by and with the authority of the compacting state.

D. The Interstate Commission shall keep accurate accounts of all receipts and disbursements. The receipts and disbursements of the Interstate Commission shall be subject to the audit and accounting procedures established under its bylaws. However, all receipts and disbursements of funds handled by the Interstate Commission shall be audited yearly by a certified or licensed public accountant and the report of the audit shall be included in and become part of the annual report of the Interstate Commission.

ARTICLE IX
COMPACTING STATES, EFFECTIVE DATE, AND AMENDMENT

A. Any state, as defined in Article II of this compact, is eligible to become a compacting state.

B. The compact shall become effective and binding upon legislative enactment of the compact into law by no less than 35 of the states. The initial effective date shall be the later of July 1, 2004, or upon enactment into law by the 35th jurisdiction. Thereafter, the compact shall become effective and binding, as to any other compacting state, upon enactment of the compact into law by that state. The governors of noncompacting states or their designees shall be invited to participate in Interstate Commission activities on a nonvoting basis prior to adoption of the compact by all states.

C. The Interstate Commission may propose amendments to the compact for enactment by the compacting states. No amendment shall become effective and binding upon the Interstate Commission and the compacting states unless and until it is enacted into law by unanimous consent of the compacting states.

ARTICLE X
WITHDRAWAL, DEFAULT, TERMINATION, AND JUDICIAL ENFORCEMENT

Sec. A. Withdrawal

1. Once effective, the compact shall continue in force and remain binding upon each and every compacting

state, provided that a compacting state may withdraw from the compact by specifically repealing the statute which enacted the compact into law.

2. The effective date of withdrawal is the effective date of the repeal.

3. The withdrawing state shall immediately notify the chairperson of the Interstate Commission in writing upon the introduction of legislation repealing this compact in the withdrawing state. The Interstate Commission shall notify the other compacting states of the withdrawing state's intent to withdraw within 60 days of its receipt thereof.

4. The withdrawing state is responsible for all assessments, obligations, and liabilities incurred through the effective date of withdrawal, including any obligations, the performance of which extend beyond the effective date of withdrawal.

5. Reinstatement following withdrawal of any compacting state shall occur upon the withdrawing state reenacting the compact or upon such later date as determined by the Interstate Commission.

Sec. B. Technical Assistance, Fines, Suspension, Termination, and Default

1. If the Interstate Commission determines that any compacting state has at any time defaulted in the performance of any of its obligations or responsibilities under this compact, or the bylaws or duly promulgated rules, the Interstate Commission may impose any or all of the following penalties:

a. Remedial training and technical assistance as directed by the Interstate Commission;

b. Alternative dispute resolution;

c. Fines, fees, and costs in such amounts as are deemed to be reasonable as fixed by the Interstate Commission; and

d. Suspension or termination of membership in the compact, which shall be imposed only after all other reasonable means of securing compliance under the bylaws and rules have been exhausted and the Interstate Commission has determined that the offending state is in default. Immediate notice of suspension shall be given by the Interstate Commission to the governor, the chief justice or the chief judicial officer of the state, and the majority and minority leaders of the defaulting state's legislature. The grounds for default include, but are not limited to, failure of a compacting state to perform such obligations or responsibilities imposed upon it by this compact, the bylaws or duly promulgated rules, and any other grounds designated in commission bylaws and rules. The Interstate Commission shall immediately notify the defaulting state in writing of the penalty imposed by the Interstate Commission and of the default pending a cure of the default. The Interstate Commission shall stipulate the conditions and the time period within which the defaulting state must cure its default. If the defaulting state fails to cure the default within the time period specified by the Interstate Commission, the defaulting state shall be terminated from the compact upon an affirmative vote of a majority of the compacting states and all rights, privileges, and benefits conferred by this compact shall be terminated from the effective date of termination.

2. Within 60 days of the effective date of termination of a defaulting state, the Interstate Commission shall notify the governor, the chief justice or chief judicial officer of the state, and the majority and minority leaders of the defaulting state's legislature of such termination.

3. The defaulting state is responsible for all assessments, obligations, and liabilities incurred through the effective date of termination including any obligations, the performance of which extends beyond the effective date of termination.

4. The Interstate Commission shall not bear any costs relating to the defaulting state unless otherwise mutually agreed upon in writing between the Interstate Commission and the defaulting state.

5. Reinstatement following termination of any compacting state requires both a reenactment of the compact by the defaulting state and the approval of the Interstate Commission pursuant to the rules.

Sec. C. Judicial Enforcement

The Interstate Commission may, by majority vote of the members, initiate legal action in the United States District Court for the District of Columbia or, at the discretion of the Interstate Commission, in the federal district where the Interstate Commission has its offices, to enforce compliance with the provisions of the compact, its duly promulgated rules and bylaws, against any compacting state in default. In the event judicial enforcement is necessary the prevailing party shall be awarded all costs of such litigation including reasonable attorney's fees.

Sec. D. Dissolution of Compact

1. The compact dissolves effective upon the date of the withdrawal or default of the compacting state, which reduces membership in the compact to one compacting state.

2. Upon the dissolution of this compact, the compact becomes null and void and shall be of no further force or effect, and the business and affairs of the Interstate Commission shall be concluded and any surplus funds shall be distributed in accordance with the bylaws.

ARTICLE XI
SEVERABILITY AND CONSTRUCTION

A. The provisions of this compact shall be severable, and if any phrase, clause, sentence, or provision is deemed unenforceable, the remaining provisions of the compact shall be enforceable.

B. The provisions of this compact shall be liberally construed to effectuate its purposes.

ARTICLE XII BINDING EFFECT OF COMPACT AND OTHER LAWS

Sec. A. Other Laws

1. Nothing herein prevents the enforcement of any other law of a compacting state that is not inconsistent with this compact.

2. All compacting states' laws other than state constitutions and other interstate compacts conflicting with this compact are superseded to the extent of the conflict.

Sec. B. Binding Effect of the Compact

1. All lawful actions of the Interstate Commission, including all rules and bylaws promulgated by the Interstate Commission, are binding upon the compacting states.

2. All agreements between the Interstate Commission and the compacting states are binding in accordance with their terms.

3. Upon the request of a party to a conflict over meaning or interpretation of Interstate Commission actions, and upon a majority vote of the compacting states, the Interstate Commission may issue advisory opinions regarding such meaning or interpretation.

4. In the event any provision of this compact exceeds the constitutional limits imposed on the legislature of any compacting state, the obligations, duties, powers, or jurisdiction sought to be conferred by such provision upon the Interstate Commission shall be ineffective and such obligations, duties, powers, or jurisdiction shall remain in the compacting state and shall be exercised by the agency thereof to which such obligations, duties, powers, or jurisdiction are delegated by law in effect at the time this compact becomes effective.

Sec. 60.011. Effect of Texas Laws.

If the laws of this state conflict with the compact, the compact controls, except that in the event of a conflict between the compact and the Texas Constitution, as determined by the courts of this state, the Texas Constitution controls.

Sec. 60.012. Liabilities for Certain Commission Agents.

The compact administrator and each member, officer, executive director, employee, or agent of the commission acting within the scope of the person's employment or duties is, for the purpose of acts or omissions occurring within this state, entitled to the same protections under Chapter 104, Civil Practice and Remedies Code, as an employee, a member of the governing board, or any other officer of a state agency, institution, or department.

CHAPTER 61 RIGHTS AND RESPONSIBILITIES OF PARENTS AND OTHER ELIGIBLE PERSONS

SUBCHAPTER A ENTRY OF ORDERS AGAINST PARENTS AND OTHER ELIGIBLE PERSONS

Sec. 61.001. Definitions.

In this chapter:

(1) "Juvenile court order" means an order by a juvenile court in a proceeding to which this chapter applies requiring a parent or other eligible person to act or refrain from acting.

(2) "Other eligible person" means the respondent's guardian, the respondent's custodian, or any other person described in a provision under this title authorizing the court order.

Sec. 61.002. Applicability. [Effective until January 1, 2022]

(a) Except as provided by Subsection (b), this chapter applies to a proceeding to enter a juvenile court order:

(1) for payment of probation fees under Section 54.061;

(2) for restitution under Sections 54.041(b) and 54.048;

(3) for payment of graffiti eradication fees under Section 54.0461;

(4) for community service under Section 54.044(b);

(5) for payment of costs of court under Section 54.0411 or other provisions of law;

(6) requiring the person to refrain from doing any act injurious to the welfare of the child under Section 54.041(a)(1);

Texas Family Code

(7) enjoining contact between the person and the child who is the subject of a proceeding under Section 54.041(a)(2);

(8) ordering a person living in the same household with the child to participate in counseling under Section 54.041(a)(3);

(9) requiring a parent or other eligible person to pay reasonable attorney's fees for representing the child under Section 51.10(e);

(10) requiring the parent or other eligible person to reimburse the county for payments the county has made to an attorney appointed to represent the child under Section 51.10(j);

(11) requiring payment of deferred prosecution supervision fees under Section 53.03(d);

(12) requiring a parent or other eligible person to attend a court hearing under Section 51.115;

(13) requiring a parent or other eligible person to act or refrain from acting to aid the child in complying with conditions of release from detention under Section 54.01(r);

(14) requiring a parent or other eligible person to act or refrain from acting under any law imposing an obligation of action or omission on a parent or other eligible person because of the parent's or person's relation to the child who is the subject of a proceeding under this title;

(15) for payment of fees under Section 54.0462; or

(16) for payment of the cost of attending an educational program under Section 54.0404.

(b) This subchapter does not apply to the entry and enforcement of a child support order under Section 54.06.

Sec. 61.002. Applicability. [Effective January 1, 2022]

(a) Except as provided by Subsection (b), this chapter applies to a proceeding to enter a juvenile court order:

(1) for payment of probation fees under Section 54.061;

(2) for restitution under Sections 54.041(b) and 54.048;

(3) for community service under Section 54.044(b);

(4) requiring the person to refrain from doing any act injurious to the welfare of the child under Section 54.041(a)(1);

(5) enjoining contact between the person and the child who is the subject of a proceeding under Section 54.041(a)(2);

(6) ordering a person living in the same household with the child to participate in counseling under Section 54.041(a)(3);

(7) requiring a parent or other eligible person to pay reasonable attorney's fees for representing the child under Section 51.10(e);

(8) requiring the parent or other eligible person to reimburse the county for payments the county has made to an attorney appointed to represent the child under Section 51.10(j);

(9) requiring payment of deferred prosecution supervision fees under Section 53.03(d);

(10) requiring a parent or other eligible person to attend a court hearing under Section 51.115;

(11) requiring a parent or other eligible person to act or refrain from acting to aid the child in complying with conditions of release from detention under Section 54.01(r);

(12) requiring a parent or other eligible person to act or refrain from acting under any law imposing an obligation of action or omission on a parent or other eligible person because of the parent's or person's relation to the child who is the subject of a proceeding under this title; or

(13) for payment of the cost of attending an educational program under Section 54.0404.

(b) This subchapter does not apply to the entry and enforcement of a child support order under Section 54.06.

Sec. 61.003. Entry of Juvenile Court Order Against Parent or Other Eligible Person.

(a) To comply with the requirements of due process of law, the juvenile court shall:

(1) provide sufficient notice in writing or orally in a recorded court hearing of a proposed juvenile court order; and

(2) provide a sufficient opportunity for the parent or other eligible person to be heard regarding the proposed order.

(b) A juvenile court order must be in writing and a copy promptly furnished to the parent or other eligible person.

(c) The juvenile court may require the parent or other eligible person to provide suitable identification to be included in the court's file. Suitable identification includes fingerprints, a driver's license number, a social security number, or similar indicia of identity.

Sec. 61.0031. Transfer of Order Affecting Parent or Other Eligible Person to County of Child's Residence.

(a) This section applies only when:

(1) a juvenile court has placed a parent or other eligible person under a court order under this chapter;

(2) the child who was the subject of the juvenile court proceedings in which the order was entered:

(A) resides in a county other than the county in which the order was entered;

(B) has moved to a county other than the county in which the order was entered and intends to remain in that county for at least 60 days; or

(C) intends to move to a county other than the county in which the order was entered and to remain in that county for at least 60 days; and

(3) the parent or other eligible person resides or will reside in the same county as the county in which the child now resides or to which the child has moved or intends to move.

(b) A juvenile court that enters an order described by Subsection (a)(1) may transfer the order to the juvenile court of the county in which the parent now resides or to which the parent has moved or intends to move.

(c) The juvenile court shall provide the parent or other eligible person written notice of the transfer. The notification must identify the court to which the order has been transferred.

(d) The juvenile court to which the order has been transferred shall require the parent or other eligible person to appear before the court to notify the person of the existence and terms of the order, unless the permanent supervision hearing under Section 51.073(c) has been waived. Failure to do so renders the order unenforceable.

(e) If the notice required by Subsection (d) is provided, the juvenile court to which the order has been transferred may modify, extend, or enforce the order as though the court originally entered the order.

Sec. 61.004. Appeal.

(a) The parent or other eligible person against whom a final juvenile court order has been entered may appeal as provided by law from judgments entered in civil cases.

(b) The movant may appeal from a judgment denying requested relief regarding a juvenile court order as provided by law from judgments entered in civil cases.

(c) The pendency of an appeal initiated under this section does not abate or otherwise affect the proceedings in juvenile court involving the child.

SUBCHAPTER B
ENFORCEMENT OF ORDER AGAINST PARENT OR OTHER ELIGIBLE PERSON

Sec. 61.051. Motion for Enforcement.

(a) A party initiates enforcement of a juvenile court order by filing a written motion. In ordinary and concise language, the motion must:

(1) identify the provision of the order allegedly violated and sought to be enforced;

(2) state specifically and factually the manner of the person's alleged noncompliance;

(3) state the relief requested; and

(4) contain the signature of the party filing the motion.

(b) The movant must allege in the same motion for enforcement each violation by the person of the juvenile court orders described by Section 61.002(a) that the movant had a reasonable basis for believing the person was violating when the motion was filed.

(c) The juvenile court retains jurisdiction to enter a contempt order if the motion for enforcement is filed not later than six months after the child's 18th birthday.

Sec. 61.052. Notice and Appearance.

(a) On the filing of a motion for enforcement, the court shall by written notice set the date, time, and place of the hearing and order the person against whom enforcement is sought to appear and respond to the motion.

(b) The notice must be given by personal service or by certified mail, return receipt requested, on or before the 10th day before the date of the hearing on the motion. The notice must include a copy of the motion for enforcement. Personal service must comply with the Code of Criminal Procedure.

(c) If a person moves to strike or specially excepts to the motion for enforcement, the court shall rule on the exception or motion to strike before the court hears evidence on the motion for enforcement. If an exception is sustained, the court shall give the movant an opportunity to replead and continue the hearing to a designated date and time without the requirement of additional service.

(d) If a person who has been personally served with notice to appear at the hearing does not appear, the juvenile court may not hold the person in contempt, but may issue a capias for the arrest of the person. The court shall set and enforce bond as provided by Subchapter C, Chapter 157. If a person served by certified mail, return receipt requested, with notice to appear at the hearing does not appear, the juvenile court may require immediate personal service of notice.

Sec. 61.053. Attorney for the Person.

(a) In a proceeding on a motion for enforcement where incarceration is a possible punishment against a person who is not represented by an attorney, the court shall inform the person of the right to be represented by an attorney and, if the person is indigent, of the right to the appointment of an attorney.

(b) If the person claims indigency and requests the appointment of an attorney, the juvenile court may require the person to file an affidavit of indigency. The court may hear evidence to determine the issue of indigency.

(c) The court shall appoint an attorney to represent the person if the court determines that the person is indigent.

(d) The court shall allow an appointed or retained attorney at least 10 days after the date of the attorney's appointment or retention to respond to the movant's pleadings and to prepare for the hearing. The attorney may waive the preparation time or agree to a shorter period for preparation.

Sec. 61.054. Compensation of Appointed Attorney.

(a) An attorney appointed to represent an indigent person is entitled to a reasonable fee for services to be paid from the general fund of the county according to the schedule for compensation adopted by the county juvenile board. The attorney must meet the qualifications required of attorneys for appointment to Class B misdemeanor cases in juvenile court.

(b) For purposes of compensation, a proceeding in the supreme court is the equivalent of a proceeding in the court of criminal appeals.

(c) The juvenile court may order the parent or other eligible person for whom it has appointed counsel to reimburse the county for the fees the county pays to appointed counsel.

Sec. 61.055. Conduct of Enforcement Hearing.

(a) The juvenile court shall require that the enforcement hearing be recorded as provided by Section 54.09.

(b) The movant must prove beyond a reasonable doubt that the person against whom enforcement is sought engaged in conduct constituting contempt of a reasonable and lawful court order as alleged in the motion for enforcement.

(c) The person against whom enforcement is sought has a privilege not to be called as a witness or otherwise to incriminate himself or herself.

(d) The juvenile court shall conduct the enforcement hearing without a jury.

(e) The juvenile court shall include in its judgment findings as to each violation alleged in the motion for enforcement and the punishment, if any, to be imposed.

(f) If the person against whom enforcement is sought was not represented by counsel during any previous court proceeding involving a motion for enforcement, the person may through counsel raise any defense or affirmative defense to the proceeding that could have been lodged in the previous court proceeding but was not because the person was not represented by counsel.

(g) It is an affirmative defense to enforcement of a juvenile court order that the juvenile court did not provide the parent or other eligible person with due process of law in the proceeding in which the court entered the order.

Sec. 61.056. Affirmative Defense of Inability to Pay.

(a) In an enforcement hearing in which the motion for enforcement alleges that the person against whom enforcement is sought failed to pay restitution, court costs, supervision fees, or any other payment ordered by the court, it is an affirmative defense that the person was financially unable to pay.

(b) The burden of proof to establish the affirmative defense of inability to pay is on the person asserting it.

(c) In order to prevail on the affirmative defense of inability to pay, the person asserting it must show that the person could not have reasonably paid the court-ordered obligation after the person discharged the person's other important financial obligations, including payments for housing, food, utilities, necessary clothing, education, and preexisting debts.

Sec. 61.057. Punishment for Contempt.

(a) On a finding of contempt, the juvenile court may commit the person to the county jail for a term not to exceed six months or may impose a fine in an amount not to exceed $500, or both.

(b) The court may impose only a single jail sentence not to exceed six months or a single fine not to exceed $500, or both, during an enforcement proceeding, without regard to whether the court has entered multiple findings of contempt.

(c) On a finding of contempt in an enforcement proceeding, the juvenile court may, instead of issuing a commitment to jail, enter an order requiring the person's future conduct to comply with the court's previous orders.

(d) Violation of an order entered under Subsection (c) may be the basis of a new enforcement proceeding.

(e) The juvenile court may assign a juvenile probation officer to assist a person in complying with a court order issued under Subsection (c).

(f) A juvenile court may reduce a term of incarceration or reduce payment of all or part of a fine at any time before the sentence is fully served or the fine fully paid.

(g) A juvenile court may reduce the burden of complying with a court order issued under Subsection (c) at any time before the order is fully satisfied, but may not increase the burden except following a new finding of contempt in a new enforcement proceeding.

SUBCHAPTER C RIGHTS OF PARENTS

Sec. 61.101. Definition.

In this subchapter, "parent" includes the guardian or custodian of a child.

Sec. 61.102. Right to Be Informed of Proceeding.

(a) The parent of a child referred to a juvenile court is entitled as soon as practicable after the referral to be informed by staff designated by the juvenile board, based on the information accompanying the referral to the juvenile court, of:

(1) the date and time of the offense;

(2) the date and time the child was taken into custody;

(3) the name of the offense and its penal category;

(4) the type of weapon, if any, that was used;

(5) the type of property taken or damaged and the extent of damage, if any;

(6) the physical injuries, if any, to the victim of the offense;

(7) whether there is reason to believe that the offense was gang-related;

(8) whether there is reason to believe that the offense was related to consumption of alcohol or use of an illegal controlled substance;

(9) if the child was taken into custody with adults or other juveniles, the names of those persons;

(10) the aspects of the juvenile court process that apply to the child;

(11) if the child is in detention, the visitation policy of the detention facility that applies to the child;

(12) the child's right to be represented by an attorney and the local standards and procedures for determining whether the parent qualifies for appointment of counsel to represent the child; and

(13) the methods by which the parent can assist the child with the legal process.

(b) If the child was released on field release citation, or from the law enforcement station by the police, by intake, or by the judge or associate judge at the initial detention hearing, the information required by Subsection (a) may be communicated to the parent in person, by telephone, or in writing.

(c) If the child is not released before or at the initial detention hearing, the information required by Subsection (a) shall be communicated in person to the parent unless that is not feasible, in which event it may be communicated by telephone or in writing.

(d) Information disclosed to a parent under Subsection (a) is not admissible in a judicial proceeding under this title as substantive evidence or as evidence to impeach the testimony of a witness for the state.

Sec. 61.103. Right of Access to Child.

(a) The parent of a child taken into custody for delinquent conduct, conduct indicating a need for supervision, or conduct that violates a condition of probation imposed by the juvenile court has the right to communicate in person privately with the child for reasonable periods of time while the child is in:

(1) a juvenile processing office;

(2) a secure detention facility;

(3) a secure correctional facility;

(4) a court-ordered placement facility; or

(5) the custody of the Texas Juvenile Justice Department.

(b) The time, place, and conditions of the private, in-person communication may be regulated to prevent disruption of scheduled activities and to maintain the safety and security of the facility.

Sec. 61.104. Parental Written Statement.

(a) When a petition for adjudication, a motion or petition to modify disposition, or a motion or petition for discretionary transfer to criminal court is served on a parent of the child, the parent must be provided with a form prescribed by the Texas Juvenile Justice Department on which the parent can make a written statement about the needs of the child or family or any other matter relevant to disposition of the case.

(b) The parent shall return the statement to the juvenile probation department, which shall transmit the statement to the court along with the

Texas Family Code

discretionary transfer report authorized by Section 54.02(e), the disposition report authorized by Section 54.04(b), or the modification of disposition report authorized by Section 54.05(e), as applicable. The statement shall be disclosed to the parties as appropriate and may be considered by the court at the disposition, modification, or discretionary transfer hearing.

Sec. 61.105. Parental Oral Statement.

(a) After all the evidence has been received but before the arguments of counsel at a hearing for discretionary transfer to criminal court, a disposition hearing without a jury, or a modification of disposition hearing, the court shall give a parent who is present in court a reasonable opportunity to address the court about the needs or strengths of the child or family or any other matter relevant to disposition of the case.

(b) The parent may not be required to make the statement under oath and may not be subject to cross-examination, but the court may seek clarification or expansion of the statement from the person giving the statement.

(c) The court may consider and act on the statement as the court considers appropriate.

Sec. 61.106. Appeal or Collateral Challenge.

The failure or inability of a person to perform an act or to provide a right or service listed under this subchapter may not be used by the child or any party as a ground for:

(1) appeal;

(2) an application for a post-adjudication writ of habeas corpus; or

(3) exclusion of evidence against the child in any proceeding or forum.

Sec. 61.107. Liability.

The Texas Juvenile Justice Department, a juvenile board, a court, a person appointed by the court, an employee of a juvenile probation department, an attorney for the state, a peace officer, or a law enforcement agency is not liable for a failure or inability to provide a right listed in this chapter.

TITLE 3A TRUANCY COURT PROCEEDINGS

CHAPTER 65 TRUANCY COURT PROCEEDINGS

SUBCHAPTER A GENERAL PROVISIONS

Sec. 65.001. Scope and Purpose.

(a) This chapter details the procedures and proceedings in cases involving allegations of truant conduct.

(b) The purpose of this chapter is to encourage school attendance by creating simple civil judicial procedures through which children are held accountable for excessive school absences.

(c) The best interest of the child is the primary consideration in adjudicating truant conduct of the child.

Sec. 65.002. Definitions.

In this chapter:

(1) "Child" means a person who is 12 years of age or older and younger than 19 years of age.

(2) "Juvenile court" means a court designated under Section 51.04 to exercise jurisdiction over proceedings under Title 3.

(3) "Qualified telephone interpreter" means a telephone service that employs licensed court interpreters, as defined by Section 157.001, Government Code.

(4) "Truancy court" means a court designated under Section 65.004 to exercise jurisdiction over cases involving allegations of truant conduct.

Sec. 65.003. Truant Conduct.

(a) A child engages in truant conduct if the child is required to attend school under Section 25.085, Education Code, and fails to attend school on 10 or more days or parts of days within a six-month period in the same school year.

(b) Truant conduct may be prosecuted only as a civil case in a truancy court.

(c) It is an affirmative defense to an allegation of truant conduct that one or more of the absences required to be proven:

(1) have been excused by a school official or by the court;

(2) were involuntary; or

Texas Family Code

(3) were due to the child's voluntary absence from the child's home because of abuse, as defined by Section 261.001.

(d) The affirmative defense provided by Subsection (c) is not available if, after deducting the absences described by that subsection, there remains a sufficient number of absences to constitute truant conduct.

(e) In asserting an affirmative defense described by Subsection (c), the burden is on the child to show by a preponderance of the evidence that the absence:

(1) has been or should be excused;

(2) was involuntary; or

(3) was due to the child's voluntary absence from the child's home because of abuse, as defined by Section 261.001.

(f) A decision by the court to excuse an absence for purposes of an affirmative defense under Subsection (c) does not affect the ability of the school district to determine whether to excuse the absence for another purpose.

Sec. 65.004. Truancy Courts; Jurisdiction.

(a) The following are designated as truancy courts:

(1) in a county with a population of 1.75 million or more, the constitutional county court;

(2) justice courts; and

(3) municipal courts.

(b) A truancy court has exclusive original jurisdiction over cases involving allegations of truant conduct.

(c) A municipality may enter into an agreement with a contiguous municipality or a municipality with boundaries that are within one-half mile of the municipality seeking to enter into the agreement to establish concurrent jurisdiction of the municipal courts in the municipalities and provide original jurisdiction to a municipal court in which a truancy case is brought as if the municipal court were located in the municipality in which the case arose.

(d) A truancy court retains jurisdiction over a person, without regard to the age of the person, who was referred to the court under Section 65.051 for engaging in truant conduct before the person's 19th birthday, until final disposition of the case.

Sec. 65.005. Court Sessions.

A truancy court is considered to be in session at all times.

Sec. 65.006. Venue.

Venue for a proceeding under this chapter is the county in which the school in which the child is enrolled is located or the county in which the child resides.

Sec. 65.007. Right to Jury Trial.

(a) A child alleged to have engaged in truant conduct is entitled to a jury trial.

(b) The number of jurors in a case involving an allegation of truant conduct is six. The state and the child are each entitled to three peremptory challenges.

(c) There is no jury fee for a trial under this chapter.

Sec. 65.008. Waiver of Rights.

A right granted to a child by this chapter or by the constitution or laws of this state or the United States is waived in proceedings under this chapter if:

(1) the right is one that may be waived;

(2) the child and the child's parent or guardian are informed of the right, understand the right, understand the possible consequences of waiving the right, and understand that waiver of the right is not required;

(3) the child signs the waiver;

(4) the child's parent or guardian signs the waiver; and

(5) the child's attorney signs the waiver, if the child is represented by counsel.

Sec. 65.009. Effect of Adjudication.

(a) An adjudication of a child as having engaged in truant conduct is not a conviction of crime. An order of adjudication does not impose any civil disability ordinarily resulting from a conviction or operate to disqualify the child in any civil service application or appointment.

(b) The adjudication of a child as having engaged in truant conduct may not be used in any subsequent court proceedings, other than for the purposes of determining an appropriate remedial action under this chapter or in an appeal under this chapter.

Sec. 65.010. Burden of Proof.

A court or jury may not return a finding that a child has engaged in truant conduct unless the state has proved the conduct beyond a reasonable doubt.

Sec. 65.011. Applicable Statutes Regarding Discovery.

Discovery in a proceeding under this chapter is governed by Chapter 39, Code of Criminal Procedure, other than Articles 39.14(i) and (j).

Sec. 65.012. Procedural Rules.

The supreme court may promulgate rules of procedure applicable to proceedings under this chapter, including guidelines applicable to the informal disposition of truancy cases.

Sec. 65.013. Interpreters.

(a) When on the motion for appointment of an interpreter by a party or on the motion of the court, in any proceeding under this chapter, the court determines that the child, the child's parent or guardian, or a witness does not understand and speak English, an interpreter must be sworn to interpret for the person. Articles 38.30(a), (b), and (c), Code of Criminal Procedure, apply in a proceeding under this chapter. A qualified telephone interpreter may be sworn to provide interpretation services if an interpreter is not available to appear in person before the court.

(b) In any proceeding under this chapter, if a party notifies the court that the child, the child's parent or guardian, or a witness is deaf, the court shall appoint a qualified interpreter to interpret the proceedings in any language, including sign language, that the deaf person can understand. Articles 38.31(d), (e), (f), and (g), Code of Criminal Procedure, apply in a proceeding under this chapter.

Sec. 65.014. Signatures.

Any requirement under this chapter that a document be signed or that a document contain a person's signature, including the signature of a judge or a clerk of the court, is satisfied if the document contains the signature of the person as captured on an electronic device or as a digital signature.

Sec. 65.015. Public Access to Court Hearings.

(a) Except as provided by Subsection (b), a truancy court shall open a hearing under this chapter to the public unless the court, for good cause shown, determines that the public should be excluded.

(b) The court may prohibit a person from personally attending a hearing if the person is expected to testify at the hearing and the court determines that the person's testimony would be materially affected if the person hears other testimony at the hearing.

Sec. 65.016. Recording of Proceedings.

(a) The proceedings in a truancy court that is not a court of record may not be recorded.

(b) The proceedings in a truancy court that is a court of record must be recorded by stenographic notes or by electronic, mechanical, or other appropriate means.

Sec. 65.017. Juvenile Case Managers.

A truancy court may employ a juvenile case manager in accordance with Article 45.056, Code of Criminal Procedure, to provide services to children who have been referred to the truancy court or who are in jeopardy of being referred to the truancy court.

SUBCHAPTER B
INITIAL PROCEDURES

Sec. 65.051. Initial Referral to Truancy Court.

When a truancy court receives a referral under Section 25.0915, Education Code, and the court is not required to dismiss the referral under that section, the court shall forward the referral to a truant conduct prosecutor who serves the court.

Sec. 65.052. Truant Conduct Prosecutor.

In a justice or municipal court or a constitutional county court that is designated as a truancy court, the attorney who represents the state in criminal matters in that court shall serve as the truant conduct prosecutor.

Sec. 65.053. Review by Prosecutor.

(a) The truant conduct prosecutor shall promptly review the facts described in a referral received under Section 65.051.

(b) The prosecutor may, in the prosecutor's discretion, determine whether to file a petition with the truancy court requesting an adjudication of the child for truant conduct. If the prosecutor decides not to file a petition requesting an adjudication, the prosecutor shall inform the truancy court and the school district of the decision.

(c) The prosecutor may not file a petition for an adjudication of a child for truant conduct if the referral was not made in compliance with Section 25.0915, Education Code.

Sec. 65.054. State's Petition.

(a) A petition for an adjudication of a child for truant conduct initiates an action of the state against a child who has allegedly engaged in truant conduct.

(b) The proceedings shall be styled "In the matter of ______________, Child," identifying the child by the child's initials only.

(c) The petition may be on information and belief.

(d) The petition must state:

(1) with reasonable particularity the time, place, and manner of the acts alleged to constitute truant conduct;

(2) the name, age, and residence address, if known, of the child who is the subject of the petition;

(3) the names and residence addresses, if known, of at least one parent, guardian, or custodian of the child and of the child's spouse, if any; and

(4) if the child's parent, guardian, or custodian does not reside or cannot be found in the state, or if their places of residence are unknown, the name and residence address of any known adult relative residing in the county or, if there is none, the name and residence address of the known adult relative residing nearest to the location of the court.

(e) Filing fees may not be charged for the filing of the state's petition.

Sec. 65.055. Limitations Period.

A petition may not be filed after the 45th day after the date of the last absence giving rise to the act of truant conduct.

Sec. 65.056. Hearing Date.

(a) After the petition has been filed, the truancy court shall set a date and time for an adjudication hearing.

(b) The hearing may not be held on or before the 10th day after the date the petition is filed.

Sec. 65.057. Summons.

(a) After setting the date and time of an adjudication hearing, the truancy court shall direct the issuance of a summons to:

(1) the child named in the petition;

(2) the child's parent, guardian, or custodian;

(3) the child's guardian ad litem, if any; and

(4) any other person who appears to the court to be a proper or necessary party to the proceeding.

(b) The summons must require the persons served to appear before the court at the place, date, and time of the adjudication hearing to answer the allegations of the petition. A copy of the petition must accompany the summons. If a person, other than the child, required to appear under this section fails to attend a hearing, the truancy court may proceed with the hearing.

(c) The truancy court may endorse on the summons an order directing the person having the physical custody or control of the child to bring the child to the hearing.

(d) A party, other than the child, may waive service of summons by written stipulation or by voluntary appearance at the hearing.

Sec. 65.058. Service of Summons.

(a) If a person to be served with a summons is in this state and can be found, the summons shall be served on the person personally or by registered or certified mail, return receipt requested, at least five days before the date of the adjudication hearing.

(b) Service of the summons may be made by any suitable person under the direction of the court.

Sec. 65.059. Representation by Attorney.

(a) A child may be represented by an attorney in a case under this chapter. Representation by an attorney is not required.

(b) A child is not entitled to have an attorney appointed to represent the child, but the court may appoint an attorney if the court determines it is in the best interest of the child.

(c) The court may order a child's parent or other responsible person to pay for the cost of an attorney appointed under this section if the court determines that the person has sufficient financial resources.

Sec. 65.060. Child's Answer.

After the petition has been filed, the child may answer, orally or in writing, the petition at or before the commencement of the hearing. If the child does not answer, a general denial of the alleged truant conduct is assumed.

Sec. 65.061. Guardian Ad Litem.

(a) If a child appears before the truancy court without a parent or guardian, or it appears to the court that the child's parent or guardian is incapable or unwilling to make decisions in the best interest of the child with respect to proceedings under this chapter, the court may appoint a guardian ad litem to protect the interests of the child in the proceedings.

(b) An attorney for a child may also be the child's guardian ad litem. A law enforcement officer, probation officer, or other employee of the truancy court may not be appointed as a guardian ad litem.

(c) The court may order a child's parent or other person responsible to support the child to reimburse the county or municipality for the cost of the guardian ad litem. The court may issue the order only after determining that the parent or other responsible person has sufficient financial resources to offset the cost of the child's guardian ad litem wholly or partly.

Sec. 65.062. Attendance at Hearing.

(a) The child must be personally present at the adjudication hearing. The truancy court may not proceed with the adjudication hearing in the absence of the child.

(b) A parent or guardian of a child and any court-appointed guardian ad litem of a child is required to attend the adjudication hearing.

(c) Subsection (b) does not apply to:

(1) a person for whom, for good cause shown, the court excuses attendance;

(2) a person who is not a resident of this state; or

(3) a parent of a child for whom a managing conservator has been appointed and the parent is not a conservator of the child.

Sec. 65.063. Right to Reemployment.

(a) An employer may not terminate the employment of a permanent employee because the employee is required under Section 65.062(b) to attend a hearing.

(b) Notwithstanding any other law, an employee whose employment is terminated in violation of this section is entitled to return to the same employment that the employee held when notified of the hearing if the employee, as soon as practical after the hearing, gives the employer actual notice that the employee intends to return.

(c) A person who is injured because of a violation of this section is entitled to:

(1) reinstatement to the person's former position;

(2) damages not to exceed an amount equal to six times the amount of monthly compensation received by the person on the date of the hearing; and

(3) reasonable attorney's fees in an amount approved by the court.

(d) It is a defense to an action brought under this section that the employer's circumstances changed while the employee attended the hearing and caused reemployment to be impossible or unreasonable. To establish a defense under this subsection, an employer must prove that the termination of employment was because of circumstances other than the employee's attendance at the hearing.

Sec. 65.064. Subpoena of Witness.

A witness may be subpoenaed in accordance with the procedures for the subpoena of a witness under the Code of Criminal Procedure.

Sec. 65.065. Child Alleged to Be Mentally Ill.

(a) A party may make a motion requesting that a petition alleging a child to have engaged in truant conduct be dismissed because the child has a mental illness, as defined by Section 571.003, Health and Safety Code. In response to the motion, the truancy court shall temporarily stay the proceedings to determine whether probable cause exists to believe the child has a mental illness. In making a determination, the court may:

(1) consider the motion, supporting documents, professional statements of counsel, and witness testimony; and

(2) observe the child.

(b) If the court determines that probable cause exists to believe that the child has a mental illness, the court shall dismiss the petition. If the court determines that evidence does not exist to support a finding that the child has a mental illness, the court shall dissolve the stay and continue with the truancy court proceedings.

SUBCHAPTER C ADJUDICATION HEARING AND REMEDIES

Sec. 65.101. Adjudication Hearing; Judgment.

(a) A child may be found to have engaged in truant conduct only after an adjudication hearing conducted in accordance with the provisions of this chapter.

(b) At the beginning of the adjudication hearing, the judge of the truancy court shall explain to the child and the child's parent, guardian, or guardian ad litem:

(1) the allegations made against the child;

(2) the nature and possible consequences of the proceedings;

(3) the child's privilege against self-incrimination;

(4) the child's right to trial and to confrontation of witnesses;

(5) the child's right to representation by an attorney if the child is not already represented; and

(6) the child's right to a jury trial.

(c) Trial is by jury unless jury is waived in accordance with Section 65.008. Jury verdicts under this chapter must be unanimous.

(d) The Texas Rules of Evidence do not apply in a truancy proceeding under this chapter except:

(1) when the judge hearing the case determines that a particular rule of evidence applicable to criminal cases must be followed to ensure that the proceedings are fair to all parties; or

(2) as otherwise provided by this chapter.

(e) A child alleged to have engaged in truant conduct need not be a witness against nor otherwise incriminate himself or herself. An extrajudicial statement of the child that was obtained in violation of the constitution of this state or the United States may not be used in an adjudication hearing. A statement made by the child out of court is insufficient to support a finding of truant conduct unless it is corroborated wholly or partly by other evidence.

(f) At the conclusion of the adjudication hearing, the court or jury shall find whether the child has engaged in truant conduct. The finding must be based on competent evidence admitted at the hearing. The child shall be presumed to have not engaged in truant conduct and no finding that a child has engaged in truant conduct may be returned unless the state has proved the conduct beyond a reasonable doubt. In all jury cases the jury will be instructed that the burden is on the state to prove that a child has engaged in truant conduct beyond a reasonable doubt.

(g) If the court or jury finds that the child did not engage in truant conduct, the court shall dismiss the case with prejudice.

(h) If the court or jury finds that the child did engage in truant conduct, the court shall proceed to issue a judgment finding the child has engaged in truant conduct and order the remedies the court finds appropriate under Section 65.103. The jury is not involved in ordering remedies for a child who has been adjudicated as having engaged in truant conduct.

Sec. 65.102. Remedial Actions.

(a) The truancy court shall determine and order appropriate remedial actions in regard to a child who has been found to have engaged in truant conduct.

(b) The truancy court shall orally pronounce the court's remedial actions in the child's presence and enter those actions in a written order.

(c) After pronouncing the court's remedial actions, the court shall advise the child and the child's parent, guardian, or guardian ad litem of:

(1) the child's right to appeal, as detailed in Subchapter D; and

(2) the procedures for the sealing of the child's records under Section 65.201.

Sec. 65.103. Remedial Order.

(a) A truancy court may enter a remedial order requiring a child who has been found to have engaged in truant conduct to:

(1) attend school without unexcused absences;

(2) attend a preparatory class for the high school equivalency examination administered under Section 7.111, Education Code, if the court determines that the individual is unlikely to do well in a formal classroom environment due to the individual's age;

(3) if the child is at least 16 years of age, take the high school equivalency examination administered under Section 7.111, Education Code, if that is in the best interest of the child;

(4) attend a nonprofit, community-based special program that the court determines to be in the best interest of the child, including:

(A) an alcohol and drug abuse program;

(B) a rehabilitation program;

(C) a counseling program, including a self-improvement program;

(D) a program that provides training in self-esteem and leadership;

(E) a work and job skills training program;

(F) a program that provides training in parenting, including parental responsibility;

(G) a program that provides training in manners;

(H) a program that provides training in violence avoidance;

(I) a program that provides sensitivity training; and

(J) a program that provides training in advocacy and mentoring;

(5) complete not more than 50 hours of community service on a project acceptable to the court; and

(6) participate for a specified number of hours in a tutorial program covering the academic subjects in which the child is enrolled that are provided by the school the child attends.

(b) A truancy court may not order a child who has been found to have engaged in truant conduct to:

Texas Family Code

(1) attend a juvenile justice alternative education program, a boot camp, or a for-profit truancy class; or

(2) perform more than 16 hours of community service per week under this section.

(c) In addition to any other order authorized by this section, a truancy court may order the Department of Public Safety to suspend the driver's license or permit of a child who has been found to have engaged in truant conduct. If the child does not have a driver's license or permit, the court may order the Department of Public Safety to deny the issuance of a license or permit to the child. The period of the license or permit suspension or the order that the issuance of a license or permit be denied may not extend beyond the maximum time period that a remedial order is effective as provided by Section 65.104.

Sec. 65.104. Maximum Time Remedial Order Is Effective.

A truancy court's remedial order under Section 65.103 is effective until the later of:

(1) the date specified by the court in the order, which may not be later than the 180th day after the date the order is entered; or

(2) the last day of the school year in which the order was entered.

Sec. 65.105. Orders Affecting Parents and Others.

(a) If a child has been found to have engaged in truant conduct, the truancy court may:

(1) order the child and the child's parent to attend a class for students at risk of dropping out of school that is designed for both the child and the child's parent;

(2) order any person found by the court to have, by a wilful act or omission, contributed to, caused, or encouraged the child's truant conduct to do any act that the court determines to be reasonable and necessary for the welfare of the child or to refrain from doing any act that the court determines to be injurious to the child's welfare;

(3) enjoin all contact between the child and a person who is found to be a contributing cause of the child's truant conduct, unless that person is related to the child within the third degree by consanguinity or affinity, in which case the court may contact the Department of Family and Protective Services, if necessary;

(4) after notice to, and a hearing with, all persons affected, order any person living in the same household with the child to participate in social or psychological counseling to assist in the child's rehabilitation;

(5) order the child's parent or other person responsible for the child's support to pay all or part of the reasonable costs of treatment programs in which the child is ordered to participate if the court finds the child's parent or person responsible for the child's support is able to pay the costs;

(6) order the child's parent to attend a program for parents of students with unexcused absences that provides instruction designed to assist those parents in identifying problems that contribute to the child's unexcused absences and in developing strategies for resolving those problems; and

(7) order the child's parent to perform not more than 50 hours of community service with the child.

(b) A person subject to an order proposed under Subsection (a) is entitled to a hearing before the order is entered by the court.

(c) On a finding by the court that a child's parents have made a reasonable good faith effort to prevent the child from engaging in truant conduct and that, despite the parents' efforts, the child continues to engage in truant conduct, the court shall waive any requirement for community service that may be imposed on a parent under this section.

Sec. 65.106. Liability for Claims Arising from Community Service.

(a) A municipality or county that establishes a program to assist children and their parents in rendering community service under this subchapter may purchase an insurance policy protecting the municipality or county against a claim brought by a person other than the child or the child's parent for a cause of action that arises from an act of the child or parent while rendering the community service. The municipality or county is not liable for the claim to the extent that damages are recoverable under a contract of insurance or under a plan of self-insurance authorized by statute.

(b) The liability of the municipality or county for a claim that arises from an action of the child or the child's parent while rendering community service may not exceed $100,000 to a single person and $300,000 for a single occurrence in the case of personal injury or death, and $10,000 for a single occurrence of property damage. Liability may not extend to punitive or exemplary damages.

(c) This section does not waive a defense, immunity, or jurisdictional bar available to the municipality or county or its officers or employees, nor shall this section be construed to waive, repeal, or modify any provision of Chapter 101, Civil Practice and Remedies Code.

Sec. 65.107. Court Cost.

(a) If a child is found to have engaged in truant conduct, the truancy court, after giving the child, parent, or other person responsible for the child's support a reasonable opportunity to be heard, shall order the child, parent, or other person, if financially able to do so, to pay a court cost of $50 to the clerk of the court.

(b) The court's order to pay the $50 court cost is not effective unless the order is reduced to writing and signed by the judge. The written order to pay the court cost may be part of the court's order detailing the remedial actions in the case.

(c) The clerk of the court shall keep a record of the court costs collected under this section and shall forward the funds to the county treasurer, municipal treasurer, or person fulfilling the role of a county treasurer or municipal treasurer, as appropriate.

(d) The court costs collected under this section shall be deposited in a special account that can be used only to offset the cost of the operations of the truancy court.

Sec. 65.108. Hearing to Modify Remedy.

(a) A truancy court may hold a hearing to modify any remedy imposed by the court. A remedy may only be modified during the period the order is effective under Section 65.104.

(b) There is no right to a jury at a hearing under this section.

(c) A hearing to modify a remedy imposed by the court shall be held on the petition of the state, the court, or the child and the child's parent, guardian, guardian ad litem, or attorney. Reasonable notice of a hearing to modify disposition shall be given to all parties.

(d) Notwithstanding any other law, in considering a motion to modify a remedy imposed by the court, the truancy court may consider a written report from a school district official or employee, juvenile case manager, or professional consultant in addition to the testimony of witnesses. The court shall provide the attorney for the child and the prosecuting attorney with access to all written matters to be considered by the court. The court may order counsel not to reveal items to the child or to the child's parent, guardian, or guardian ad litem if the disclosure would materially harm the treatment and rehabilitation of the child or would substantially decrease the likelihood of receiving information from the same or similar sources in the future.

(e) The truancy court shall pronounce in court, in the presence of the child, the court's changes to the remedy, if any. The court shall specifically state the new remedy and the court's reasons for modifying the remedy in a written order. The court shall furnish a copy of the order to the child.

Sec. 65.109. Motion for New Trial.

The order of a truancy court may be challenged by filing a motion for new trial. Rules 505.3(c) and (e), Texas Rules of Civil Procedure, apply to a motion for new trial.

SUBCHAPTER D
APPEAL

Sec. 65.151. Right to Appeal.

(a) The child, the child's parent or guardian, or the state may appeal any order of a truancy court. A person subject to an order entered under Section 65.105 may appeal that order.

(b) An appeal from a truancy court shall be to a juvenile court. The case must be tried de novo in the juvenile court. This chapter applies to the de novo trial in the juvenile court. On appeal, the judgment of the truancy court is vacated.

(c) A judgment of a juvenile court in a trial conducted under Subsection (b) may be appealed in the same manner as an appeal under Chapter 56.

Sec. 65.152. Governing Law.

Rule 506, Texas Rules of Civil Procedure, applies to the appeal of an order of a truancy court to a juvenile court in the same manner as the rule applies to an appeal of a judgment of a justice court to a county court, except an appeal bond is not required.

Sec. 65.153. Counsel on Appeal.

(a) A child may be represented by counsel on appeal.

(b) If the child and the child's parent, guardian, or guardian ad litem request an appeal, the attorney who represented the child before the truancy court, if any, shall file a notice of appeal with the court that will hear the appeal and inform that court whether that attorney will handle the appeal.

(c) An appeal serves to vacate the order of the truancy court.

SUBCHAPTER E
RECORDS

Sec. 65.201. Sealing of Records.

(a) A child who has been found to have engaged in truant conduct may apply, on or after the child's 18th birthday, to the truancy court that made the finding to seal the records relating to the allegation and finding of truant conduct held by:

(1) the court;

(2) the truant conduct prosecutor; and

(3) the school district.

(b) The application must include the following information or an explanation of why one or more of the following is not included:

(1) the child's:

(A) full name;

(B) sex;

(C) race or ethnicity;

(D) date of birth;

(E) driver's license or identification card number; and

(F) social security number;

(2) the dates on which the truant conduct was alleged to have occurred; and

(3) if known, the cause number assigned to the petition and the court and county in which the petition was filed.

(c) The truancy court shall order that the records be sealed after determining the child complied with the remedies ordered by the court in the case.

(d) All index references to the records of the truancy court that are ordered sealed shall be deleted not later than the 30th day after the date of the sealing order.

(e) A truancy court, clerk of the court, truant conduct prosecutor, or school district shall reply to a request for information concerning a child's sealed truant conduct case that no record exists with respect to the child.

(f) Inspection of the sealed records may be permitted by an order of the truancy court on the petition of the person who is the subject of the records and only by those persons named in the order.

(g) A person whose records have been sealed under this section is not required in any proceeding or in any application for employment, information, or licensing to state that the person has been the subject of a proceeding under this chapter. Any statement that the person has never been found to have engaged in truant conduct may not be held against the person in any criminal or civil proceeding.

(h) On or after the fifth anniversary of a child's 16th birthday, on the motion of the child or on the truancy court's own motion, the truancy court may order the destruction of the child's records that have been sealed under this section if the child has not been convicted of a felony.

Sec. 65.202. Confidentiality of Records.

Records and files created under this chapter may be disclosed only to:

(1) the judge of the truancy court, the truant conduct prosecutor, and the staff of the judge and prosecutor;

(2) the child or an attorney for the child;

(3) a governmental agency if the disclosure is required or authorized by law;

(4) a person or entity to whom the child is referred for treatment or services if the agency or institution disclosing the information has entered into a written confidentiality agreement with the person or entity regarding the protection of the disclosed information;

(5) the Texas Department of Criminal Justice and the Texas Juvenile Justice Department for the purpose of maintaining statistical records of recidivism and for diagnosis and classification;

(6) the agency; or

(7) with leave of the truancy court, any other person, agency, or institution having a legitimate interest in the proceeding or in the work of the court.

Sec. 65.203. Destruction of Certain Records.

A truancy court shall order the destruction of records relating to allegations of truant conduct that are held by the court or by the prosecutor if a prosecutor decides not to file a petition for an adjudication of truant conduct after a review of the referral under Section 65.053.

SUBCHAPTER F
ENFORCEMENT OF ORDERS

Sec. 65.251. Failure to Obey Truancy Court Order; Child in Contempt of Court.

(a) If a child fails to obey an order issued by a truancy court under Section 65.103(a) or a child is in direct contempt of court, the truancy court, after providing notice and an opportunity for a hearing, may hold the child in contempt of court and order either or both of the following:

(1) that the child pay a fine not to exceed $100; or

(2) that the Department of Public Safety suspend the child's driver's license or permit or, if the child does not have a license or permit, order that the Department of Public Safety deny the issuance of a license or permit to the child until the child fully complies with the court's orders.

(b) If a child fails to obey an order issued by a truancy court under Section 65.103(a) or a child is in direct contempt of court and the child has failed to obey an order or has been found in direct contempt of court on two or more previous occasions, the truancy court, after providing notice and an opportunity for a hearing, may refer the child to the juvenile probation department as a request for truancy intervention, unless the child failed to obey the truancy court order or was in direct contempt of court while 17 years of age or older.

(c) On referral of the child to the juvenile probation department, the truancy court shall provide to the juvenile probation department:

(1) documentation of all truancy prevention measures taken by the originating school district;

(2) documentation of all truancy orders for each of the child's previous truancy referrals, including:

(A) court remedies and documentation of the child's failure to comply with the truancy court's orders, if applicable, demonstrating all interventions that were exhausted by the truancy court; and

(B) documentation describing the child's direct contempt of court, if applicable;

(3) the name, birth date, and last known address of the child and the school in which the child is enrolled; and

(4) the name and last known address of the child's parent or guardian.

(d) The juvenile probation department may, on review of information provided under Subsection (c):

(1) offer further remedies related to the local plan for truancy intervention strategies adopted under Section 25.0916, Education Code; or

(2) refer the child to a juvenile court for a hearing to be conducted under Section 65.252.

(e) A truancy court may not order the confinement of a child for the child's failure to obey an order of the court issued under Section 65.103(a).

Sec. 65.252. Proceedings in Juvenile Court.

(a) After a referral by the local juvenile probation department, the juvenile court prosecutor shall determine if probable cause exists to believe that the child engaged in direct contempt of court or failed to obey an order of the truancy court under circumstances that would constitute contempt of court. On a finding that probable cause exists, the prosecutor shall determine whether to request an adjudication. Not later than the 20th day after the date the juvenile court receives a request for adjudication from the prosecutor, the juvenile court shall conduct a hearing to determine if the child engaged in conduct that constitutes contempt of the order issued by the truancy court or engaged in direct contempt of court.

(b) If the juvenile court finds that the child engaged in conduct that constitutes contempt of the order issued by the truancy court or direct contempt of court, the juvenile court shall:

(1) enter an order requiring the child to comply with the truancy court's order;

(2) forward a copy of the order to the truancy court within five days; and

(3) admonish the child, orally and in writing, of the consequences of subsequent referrals to the juvenile court, including:

(A) a possible charge of delinquent conduct for contempt of the truancy court's order or direct contempt of court; and

(B) a possible detention hearing.

(c) If the juvenile court prosecutor finds that probable cause does not exist to believe that the child engaged in direct contempt or in conduct that constitutes contempt of the order issued by the truancy court, or if the juvenile probation department finds that extenuating circumstances caused the original truancy referral, the juvenile court shall enter an order requiring the child's continued compliance with the truancy court's order and notify the truancy court not later than the fifth day after the date the order is entered.

(d) This section does not limit the discretion of a juvenile prosecutor or juvenile court to prosecute a child for conduct under Section 51.03.

Sec. 65.253. Parent or Other Person in Contempt of Court.

(a) A truancy court may enforce the following orders by contempt:

(1) an order that a parent of a child, guardian of a child, or any court-appointed guardian ad litem of a child attend an adjudication hearing under Section 65.062(b);

(2) an order requiring a person other than a child to take a particular action under Section 65.105(a);

(3) an order that a child's parent, or other person responsible to support the child, reimburse the municipality or county for the cost of the guardian ad litem appointed for the child under Section 65.061(c); and

(4) an order that a parent, or person other than the child, pay the $50 court cost under Section 65.107.

(b) A truancy court may find a parent or person other than the child in direct contempt of the court.

(c) The penalty for a finding of contempt under Subsection (a) or (b) is a fine in an amount not to exceed $100.

(d) In addition to the assessment of a fine under Subsection (c), direct contempt of the truancy court by a parent or person other than the child is punishable by:

(1) confinement in jail for a maximum of three days;

(2) a maximum of 40 hours of community service; or

(3) both confinement and community service.

Sec. 65.254. Writ of Attachment.

A truancy court may issue a writ of attachment for a person who violates an order entered under Section 65.057(c). The writ of attachment is executed in the same manner as in a criminal proceeding as provided by Chapter 24, Code of Criminal Procedure.

Sec. 65.255. Entry of Truancy Court Order Against Parent or Other Eligible Person.

(a) The truancy court shall:

(1) provide notice to a person who is the subject of a proposed truancy court order under Section 65.253; and

(2) provide a sufficient opportunity for the person to be heard regarding the proposed order.

(b) A truancy court order under Section 65.253 must be in writing and a copy promptly furnished to the parent or other eligible person.

(c) The truancy court may require the parent or other eligible person to provide suitable identification to be included in the court's file. Suitable identification includes fingerprints, a driver's license number, a social security number, or similar indicia of identity.

Sec. 65.256. Appeal.

(a) The parent or other eligible person against whom a final truancy court order has been entered under Section 65.253 may appeal as provided by law from judgments entered by a justice court in civil cases.

(b) Rule 506, Texas Rules of Civil Procedure, applies to an appeal under this section, except an appeal bond is not required.

(c) The pendency of an appeal initiated under this section does not abate or otherwise affect the proceedings in the truancy court involving the child.

Sec. 65.257. Motion for Enforcement.

(a) The state may initiate enforcement of a truancy court order under Section 65.253 against a parent or person other than the child by filing a written motion. In ordinary and concise language, the motion must:

(1) identify the provision of the order allegedly violated and sought to be enforced;

(2) state specifically and factually the manner of the person's alleged noncompliance;

(3) state the relief requested; and

(4) contain the signature of the party filing the motion.

(b) The state must allege the particular violation by the person of the truancy court order that the state had a reasonable basis for believing the person was violating when the motion was filed.

(c) The truancy court may also initiate enforcement of an order under this section on its own motion.

Sec. 65.258. Notice and Appearance.

(a) On the filing of a motion for enforcement, the truancy court shall by written notice set the date, time, and place of the hearing and order the person against whom enforcement is sought to appear and respond to the motion.

(b) The notice must be given by personal service or by certified mail, return receipt requested, on or before the 10th day before the date of the hearing on the motion. The notice must include a copy of the motion for enforcement. Personal service must comply with the Code of Criminal Procedure.

(c) If a person moves to strike or specially excepts to the motion for enforcement, the truancy court shall rule on the exception or motion to strike before the court hears evidence on the motion for enforcement. If an exception is sustained, the court shall give the movant an opportunity to replead and continue the hearing to a designated date and time without the requirement of additional service.

(d) If a person who has been personally served with notice to appear at the hearing does not appear, the truancy court may not hold the person in contempt, but may issue a warrant for the arrest of the person.

Sec. 65.259. Conduct of Enforcement Hearing.

(a) The movant must prove beyond a reasonable doubt that the person against whom enforcement is sought engaged in conduct constituting contempt of a reasonable and lawful court order as alleged in the motion for enforcement.

(b) The person against whom enforcement is sought has a privilege not to be called as a witness or otherwise to incriminate himself or herself.

(c) The truancy court shall conduct the enforcement hearing without a jury.

(d) The truancy court shall include in the court's judgment:

(1) findings for each violation alleged in the motion for enforcement; and

(2) the punishment, if any, to be imposed.

(e) If the person against whom enforcement is sought was not represented by counsel during any previous court proceeding involving a motion for enforcement, the person may, through counsel, raise any defense or affirmative defense to the proceeding that could have been asserted in the previous court proceeding that was not asserted because the person was not represented by counsel.

(f) It is an affirmative defense to enforcement of a truancy court order under Section 65.253 that the court did not provide the parent or other eligible person with due process of law in the proceeding in which the court entered the order.

TITLE 4
PROTECTIVE ORDERS AND FAMILY VIOLENCE

SUBTITLE A
GENERAL PROVISIONS

CHAPTER 71
DEFINITIONS

Sec. 71.001. Applicability of Definitions.

(a) Definitions in this chapter apply to this title.

(b) If, in another part of this title, a term defined by this chapter has a meaning different from the meaning provided by this chapter, the meaning of that other provision prevails.

(c) Except as provided by this chapter, the definitions in Chapter 101 apply to terms used in this title.

Sec. 71.002. Court.

"Court" means the district court, court of domestic relations, juvenile court having the jurisdiction of a district court, statutory county court, constitutional county court, or other court expressly given jurisdiction under this title.

Sec. 71.0021. Dating Violence.

(a) "Dating violence" means an act, other than a defensive measure to protect oneself, by an actor that:

(1) is committed against a victim or applicant for a protective order:

(A) with whom the actor has or has had a dating relationship; or

(B) because of the victim's or applicant's marriage to or dating relationship with an individual with whom the actor is or has been in a dating relationship or marriage; and

(2) is intended to result in physical harm, bodily injury, assault, or sexual assault or that is a threat that reasonably places the victim or applicant in fear of imminent physical harm, bodily injury, assault, or sexual assault.

(b) For purposes of this title, "dating relationship" means a relationship between individuals who have or have had a continuing relationship of a romantic or intimate nature. The existence of such a relationship shall be determined based on consideration of:

(1) the length of the relationship;

(2) the nature of the relationship; and

(3) the frequency and type of interaction between the persons involved in the relationship.

(c) A casual acquaintanceship or ordinary fraternization in a business or social context does not constitute a "dating relationship" under Subsection (b).

Sec. 71.003. Family.

"Family" includes individuals related by consanguinity or affinity, as determined under Sections 573.022 and 573.024, Government Code, individuals who are former spouses of each other, individuals who are the parents of the same child, without regard to marriage, and a foster child and foster parent, without regard to whether those individuals reside together.

Sec. 71.004. Family Violence.

"Family violence" means:

(1) an act by a member of a family or household against another member of the family or household that is intended to result in physical harm, bodily injury, assault, or sexual assault or that is a threat that reasonably places the member in fear of imminent physical harm, bodily injury, assault, or sexual assault, but does not include defensive measures to protect oneself;

(2) abuse, as that term is defined by Sections 261.001(1)(C), (E), (G), (H), (I), (J), (K), and

(M), by a member of a family or household toward a child of the family or household; or

(3) dating violence, as that term is defined by Section 71.0021.

Sec. 71.005. Household.

"Household" means a unit composed of persons living together in the same dwelling, without regard to whether they are related to each other.

Sec. 71.006. Member of a Household.

"Member of a household" includes a person who previously lived in a household.

Sec. 71.007. Prosecuting Attorney.

"Prosecuting attorney" means the attorney, determined as provided in this title, who represents the state in a district or statutory county court in the county in which venue of the application for a protective order is proper.

Sec. 71.008. Protective Order from Another Jurisdiction [Repealed].

Repealed by Acts 2001, 77th Leg., ch. 48 (H.B. 919), § 3, effective September 1, 2001.

SUBTITLE B
PROTECTIVE ORDERS

CHAPTER 82
APPLYING FOR PROTECTIVE ORDER

SUBCHAPTER A
APPLICATION FOR PROTECTIVE ORDER

Sec. 82.001. Application.

A proceeding under this subtitle is begun by filing "An Application for a Protective Order" with the clerk of the court.

Sec. 82.002. Who May File Application.

(a) With regard to family violence under Section 71.004(1) or (2), an adult member of the family or household may file an application for a protective order to protect the applicant or any other member of the applicant's family or household.

(b) **[2 Versions: As amended by Acts 2011, 82nd Leg., ch. 632 (S.B. 819)]** With regard to family violence under Section 71.004(3), an application for a protective order to protect the applicant may be filed by a member of the dating relationship, regardless of whether the member is an adult or a child.

(b) **[2 Versions: As amended by Acts 2011, 82nd Leg., ch. 872 (S.B. 116)]** With regard to family violence under Section 71.004(3), an application for a protective order to protect the applicant may be filed by:

(1) an adult member of the dating relationship; or

(2) an adult member of the marriage, if the victim is or was married as described by Section 71.0021(a)(1)(B).

(c) Any adult may apply for a protective order to protect a child from family violence.

(d) In addition, an application may be filed for the protection of any person alleged to be a victim of family violence by:

(1) a prosecuting attorney; or

(2) the Department of Family and Protective Services.

(e) The person alleged to be the victim of family violence in an application filed under Subsection (c) or (d) is considered to be the applicant for a protective order under this subtitle.

Sec. 82.003. Venue.

An application may be filed in:

(1) the county in which the applicant resides;

(2) the county in which the respondent resides; or

(3) any county in which the family violence is alleged to have occurred.

Sec. 82.004. Contents of Application.

An application must state:

(1) the name and county of residence of each applicant;

(2) the name and county of residence of each individual alleged to have committed family violence;

(3) the relationships between the applicants and the individual alleged to have committed family violence;

(4) a request for one or more protective orders; and

(5) whether an applicant is receiving services from the Title IV-D agency in connection with a child support case and, if known, the agency case number for each open case.

Sec. 82.005. Application Filed During Suit for Dissolution of Marriage or Suit Affecting Parent-Child Relationship.

A person who wishes to apply for a protective order with respect to the person's spouse and who is a party to a suit for the dissolution of a marriage or a suit affecting the parent-child relationship that is pending in a court must file the application as required by Subchapter D, Chapter 85.

Sec. 82.006. Application Filed After Dissolution of Marriage.

If an applicant for a protective order is a former spouse of the individual alleged to have committed family violence, the application must include:

(1) a copy of the decree dissolving the marriage; or

(2) a statement that the decree is unavailable to the applicant and that a copy of the decree will be filed with the court before the hearing on the application.

Sec. 82.007. Application Filed for Child Subject to Continuing Jurisdiction.

An application that requests a protective order for a child who is subject to the continuing exclusive jurisdiction of a court under Title 5 or alleges that a child who is subject to the continuing exclusive jurisdiction of a court under Title 5 has committed family violence must include:

(1) a copy of each court order affecting the conservatorship, support, and possession of or access to the child; or

(2) a statement that the orders affecting the child are unavailable to the applicant and that a copy of the orders will be filed with the court before the hearing on the application.

Sec. 82.008. Application Filed After Expiration of Former Protective Order.

(a) An application for a protective order that is filed after a previously rendered protective order has expired must include:

(1) a copy of the expired protective order attached to the application or, if a copy of the expired protective order is unavailable, a statement that the order is unavailable to the applicant and that a copy of the order will be filed with the court before the hearing on the application;

(2) a description of either:

(A) the violation of the expired protective order, if the application alleges that the respondent violated the expired protective order by committing an act prohibited by that order before the order expired; or

(B) the threatened harm that reasonably places the applicant in fear of imminent physical harm, bodily injury, assault, or sexual assault; and

(3) if a violation of the expired order is alleged, a statement that the violation of the expired order has not been grounds for any other order protecting the applicant that has been issued or requested under this subtitle.

(b) The procedural requirements for an original application for a protective order apply to a protective order requested under this section.

Sec. 82.0085. Application Filed Before Expiration of Previously Rendered Protective Order.

(a) If an application for a protective order alleges that an unexpired protective order applicable to the respondent is due to expire not later than the 30th day after the date the application was filed, the application for the subsequent protective order must include:

(1) a copy of the previously rendered protective order attached to the application or, if a copy of the previously rendered protective order is unavailable, a statement that the order is unavailable to the applicant and that a copy of the order will be filed with the court before the hearing on the application; and

(2) a description of the threatened harm that reasonably places the applicant in fear of imminent physical harm, bodily injury, assault, or sexual assault.

(b) The procedural requirements for an original application for a protective order apply to a protective order requested under this section.

Sec. 82.009. Application for Temporary Ex Parte Order.

(a) An application that requests the issuance of a temporary ex parte order under Chapter 83 must:

(1) contain a detailed description of the facts and circumstances concerning the alleged family violence and the need for the immediate protective order; and

(2) be signed by each applicant under an oath that the facts and circumstances contained in the application are true to the best knowledge and belief of each applicant.

(b) For purposes of this section, a statement signed under oath by a child is valid if the statement otherwise complies with this chapter.

Sec. 82.010. Confidentiality of Application.

(a) This section applies only in a county with a population of 3.4 million or more.

(b) Except as otherwise provided by law, an application for a protective order is confidential, is excepted from required public disclosure under Chapter 552, Government Code, and may not be released to a person who is not a respondent to the application until after the date of service of notice of the application or the date of the hearing on the application, whichever date is sooner.

(c) Except as otherwise provided by law, an application requesting the issuance of a temporary ex parte order under Chapter 83 is confidential, is excepted from required public disclosure under Chapter 552, Government Code, and may not be released to a person who is not a respondent to the application until after the date that the court or law enforcement informs the respondent of the court's order.

Sec. 82.011. Confidentiality of Certain Information.

On request by an applicant, the court may protect the applicant's mailing address by rendering an order:

(1) requiring the applicant to:

(A) disclose the applicant's mailing address to the court;

(B) designate a person to receive on behalf of the applicant any notice or documents filed with the court related to the application; and

(C) disclose the designated person's mailing address to the court;

(2) requiring the court clerk to:

(A) strike the applicant's mailing address from the public records of the court, if applicable; and

(B) maintain a confidential record of the applicant's mailing address for use only by the court; and

(3) prohibiting the release of the information to the respondent.

SUBCHAPTER B PLEADINGS BY RESPONDENT

Sec. 82.021. Answer.

A respondent to an application for a protective order who is served with notice of an application for a protective order may file an answer at any time before the hearing. A respondent is not required to file an answer to the application.

Sec. 82.022. Request by Respondent for Protective Order.

To apply for a protective order, a respondent to an application for a protective order must file a separate application.

SUBCHAPTER C NOTICE OF APPLICATION FOR PROTECTIVE ORDER

Sec. 82.041. Contents of Notice of Application.

(a) A notice of an application for a protective order must:

(1) be styled "The State of Texas";

(2) be signed by the clerk of the court under the court's seal;

(3) contain the name and location of the court;

(4) show the date the application was filed;

(5) show the date notice of the application for a protective order was issued;

(6) show the date, time, and place of the hearing;

(7) show the file number;

(8) show the name of each applicant and each person alleged to have committed family violence;

(9) be directed to each person alleged to have committed family violence;

(10) show:

(A) the name and address of the attorney for the applicant; or

(B) if the applicant is not represented by an attorney:

(i) the mailing address of the applicant; or

(ii) if applicable, the name and mailing address of the person designated under Section 82.011; and

(11) contain the address of the clerk of the court.

(b) The notice of an application for a protective order must state: "An application for a protective order has been filed in the court stated in this notice alleging that you have committed family violence. You may employ an attorney to defend you against this allegation. You or your attorney may, but are not required to, file a written answer to the application. Any answer must be filed before the hearing on the application. If you receive this notice within 48 hours before the time set for the hearing, you may request the court to reschedule the hearing not later than 14 days after the date set for the hearing. If you do not attend the hearing, a default judgment may be taken and a protective order may be issued against you."

Sec. 82.042. Issuance of Notice of Application.

(a) On the filing of an application, the clerk of the court shall issue a notice of an application for a protective order and deliver the notice as directed by the applicant.

(b) On request by the applicant, the clerk of the court shall issue a separate or additional notice of an application for a protective order.

Sec. 82.043. Service of Notice of Application.

(a) Each respondent to an application for a protective order is entitled to service of notice of an application for a protective order.

(b) An applicant for a protective order shall furnish the clerk with a sufficient number of copies of the application for service on each respondent.

(c) Notice of an application for a protective order must be served in the same manner as citation under the Texas Rules of Civil Procedure, except that service by publication is not authorized.

(d) Service of notice of an application for a protective order is not required before the issuance of a temporary ex parte order under Chapter 83.

(e) The requirements of service of notice under this subchapter do not apply if the application is filed as a motion in a suit for dissolution of a marriage. Notice for the motion is given in the same manner as any other motion in a suit for dissolution of a marriage.

CHAPTER 83
TEMPORARY EX PARTE ORDERS

Sec. 83.001. Requirements for Temporary Ex Parte Order.

(a) If the court finds from the information contained in an application for a protective order that there is a clear and present danger of family violence, the court, without further notice to the individual alleged to have committed family violence and without a hearing, may enter a temporary ex parte order for the protection of the applicant or any other member of the family or household of the applicant.

(b) In a temporary ex parte order, the court may direct a respondent to do or refrain from doing specified acts.

Sec. 83.002. Duration of Order; Extension.

(a) A temporary ex parte order is valid for the period specified in the order, not to exceed 20 days.

(b) On the request of an applicant or on the court's own motion, a temporary ex parte order may be extended for additional 20-day periods.

Sec. 83.003. Bond Not Required.

The court, at the court's discretion, may dispense with the necessity of a bond for a temporary ex parte order.

Sec. 83.004. Motion to Vacate.

Any individual affected by a temporary ex parte order may file a motion at any time to vacate the order. On the filing of the motion to vacate, the court shall set a date for hearing the motion as soon as possible.

Sec. 83.005. Conflicting Orders.

During the time the order is valid, a temporary ex parte order prevails over any other court order made under Title 5 to the extent of any conflict between the orders.

Sec. 83.006. Exclusion of Party from Residence.

(a) Subject to the limitations of Section 85.021(2), a person may only be excluded from the occupancy of the person's residence by a temporary ex parte order under this chapter if the applicant:

(1) files a sworn affidavit that provides a detailed description of the facts and circumstances requiring the exclusion of the person from the residence; and

(2) appears in person to testify at a temporary ex parte hearing to justify the issuance of the order without notice.

(b) Before the court may render a temporary ex parte order excluding a person from the person's residence, the court must find from the required affidavit and testimony that:

(1) the applicant requesting the excluding order either resides on the premises or has resided there within 30 days before the date the application was filed;

(2) the person to be excluded has within the 30 days before the date the application was filed committed family violence against a member of the household; and

(3) there is a clear and present danger that the person to be excluded is likely to commit family violence against a member of the household.

(c) The court may recess the hearing on a temporary ex parte order to contact the respondent by telephone and provide the respondent the opportunity to be present when the court resumes the hearing. Without regard to whether the respondent is able to be present at the hearing, the court shall resume the hearing before the end of the working day.

Sec. 83.007. Recess of Hearing to Contact Respondent [Repealed].

Repealed by Acts 2011, 82nd Leg., ch. 632 (S.B. 819), § 6(1), effective September 1, 2011.

CHAPTER 84
HEARING

Sec. 84.001. Time Set for Hearing.

(a) On the filing of an application for a protective order, the court shall set a date and time for the hearing unless a later date is requested by the applicant. Except as provided by Section 84.002, the court may not set a date later than the 14th day after the date the application is filed.

(b) The court may not delay a hearing on an application in order to consolidate it with a hearing on a subsequently filed application.

Sec. 84.002. Extended Time for Hearing in District Court in Certain Counties.

(a) On the request of the prosecuting attorney in a county with a population of more than two million or in a county in a judicial district that is composed of more than one county, the district court shall set the hearing on a date and time not later than 20 days after the date the application is filed or 20 days after the date a request is made to reschedule a hearing under Section 84.003.

(b) The district court shall grant the request of the prosecuting attorney for an extended time in which to hold a hearing on a protective order either on a case-by-case basis or for all cases filed under this subtitle.

Sec. 84.003. Hearing Rescheduled for Failure of Service.

(a) If a hearing set under this chapter is not held because of the failure of a respondent to receive service of notice of an application for a protective order, the applicant may request the court to reschedule the hearing.

(b) Except as provided by Section 84.002, the date for a rescheduled hearing shall be not later than 14 days after the date the request is made.

Sec. 84.004. Hearing Rescheduled for Insufficient Notice.

(a) If a respondent receives service of notice of an application for a protective order within 48 hours before the time set for the hearing, on request by the respondent, the court shall reschedule the hearing for a date not later than 14 days after the date set for the hearing.

(b) The respondent is not entitled to additional service for a hearing rescheduled under this section.

Sec. 84.005. Legislative Continuance.

If a proceeding for which a legislative continuance is sought under Section 30.003, Civil Practice and Remedies Code, includes an application for a protective order, the continuance is discretionary with the court.

Sec. 84.006. Hearsay Statement of Child Victim of Family Violence.

In a hearing on an application for a protective order, a statement made by a child 12 years of age or younger that describes alleged family violence against the child is admissible as evidence in the same manner that a child's statement regarding alleged abuse against the child is admissible under Section 104.006 in a suit affecting the parent-child relationship.

CHAPTER 85
ISSUANCE OF PROTECTIVE ORDER

SUBCHAPTER A
FINDINGS AND ORDERS

Sec. 85.001. Required Findings and Orders.

(a) At the close of a hearing on an application for a protective order, the court shall find whether:

(1) family violence has occurred; and

(2) family violence is likely to occur in the future.

(b) If the court finds that family violence has occurred and that family violence is likely to occur in the future, the court:

(1) shall render a protective order as provided by Section 85.022 applying only to a person found to have committed family violence; and

(2) may render a protective order as provided by Section 85.021 applying to both parties that is in the best interest of the person protected by the order or member of the family or household of the person protected by the order.

(c) A protective order that requires the first applicant to do or refrain from doing an act under Section 85.022 shall include a finding that the first applicant has committed family violence and is likely to commit family violence in the future.

(d) If the court renders a protective order for a period of more than two years, the court must include in the order a finding described by Section 85.025(a-1).

Sec. 85.002. Exception for Violation of Expired Protective Order.

If the court finds that a respondent violated a protective order by committing an act prohibited by the order as provided by Section 85.022, that the order was in effect at the time of the violation, and that the order has expired after the date that the violation occurred, the court, without the necessity of making the findings described by Section 85.001(a), shall render a protective order as provided by Section 85.022 applying only to the respondent and may render a protective order as provided by Section 85.021.

Sec. 85.003. Separate Protective Orders Required.

(a) A court that renders separate protective orders that apply to both parties and require both parties to do or refrain from doing acts under Section 85.022 shall render two distinct and separate protective orders in two separate documents that reflect the appropriate conditions for each party.

(b) A court that renders protective orders that apply to both parties and require both parties to do or refrain from doing acts under Section 85.022 shall render the protective orders in two separate documents. The court shall provide one of the documents to the applicant and the other document to the respondent.

(c) A court may not render one protective order under Section 85.022 that applies to both parties.

Sec. 85.004. Protective Order in Suit for Dissolution of Marriage.

A protective order in a suit for dissolution of a marriage must be in a separate document entitled "PROTECTIVE ORDER."

Sec. 85.005. Agreed Order.

(a) To facilitate settlement, the parties to a proceeding may agree in writing to a protective order as provided by Sections 85.021 and 85.022. An agreement under this subsection is subject to the approval of the court. The court may not approve an agreement that requires the applicant for the protective order to do or refrain from doing an act under Section 85.022.

(b) An agreed protective order is enforceable civilly or criminally, regardless of whether the court makes the findings required by Section 85.001.

(c) If the court approves an agreement between the parties, the court shall render an agreed protective order that is in the best interest of the applicant, the family or household, or a member of the family or household.

(d) An agreed protective order is not enforceable as a contract.

(e) An agreed protective order expires on the date the court order expires.

Sec. 85.006. Default Order.

(a) Notwithstanding Rule 107, Texas Rules of Civil Procedure, a court may render a protective order that is binding on a respondent who does not attend a hearing if:

(1) the respondent received service of the application and notice of the hearing; and

(2) proof of service was filed with the court before the hearing.

(b) If the court reschedules the hearing under Chapter 84, a protective order may be rendered if the respondent does not attend the rescheduled hearing.

Sec. 85.007. Confidentiality of Certain Information.

(a) On request by a person protected by an order or member of the family or household of a person protected by an order, the court may exclude from a protective order the address and telephone number of:

(1) a person protected by the order, in which case the order shall state the county in which the person resides;

(2) the place of employment or business of a person protected by the order; or

Texas Family Code

(3) the child-care facility or school a child protected by the order attends or in which the child resides.

(b) On granting a request for confidentiality under this section, the court shall order the clerk to:

(1) strike the information described by Subsection (a) from the public records of the court; and

(2) maintain a confidential record of the information for use only by:

(A) the court; or

(B) a law enforcement agency for purposes of entering the information required by Section 411.042(b)(6), Government Code, into the statewide law enforcement information system maintained by the Department of Public Safety.

Sec. 85.008. Dismissal of Application Prohibited If Divorce Filed; Exception [Repealed].

Repealed by Acts 1997, 75th Leg., ch. 1193 (S.B. 1253), § 24, effective September 1, 1997.

Sec. 85.009. Order Valid Until Superseded.

A protective order rendered under this chapter is valid and enforceable pending further action by the court that rendered the order until the order is properly superseded by another court with jurisdiction over the order.

SUBCHAPTER B CONTENTS OF PROTECTIVE ORDER

Sec. 85.021. Requirements of Order Applying to Any Party.

In a protective order, the court may:

(1) prohibit a party from:

(A) removing a child who is a member of the family or household from:

(i) the possession of a person named in the order; or

(ii) the jurisdiction of the court;

(B) transferring, encumbering, or otherwise disposing of property, other than in the ordinary course of business, that is mutually owned or leased by the parties; or

(C) removing a pet, companion animal, or assistance animal, as defined by Section 121.002, Human Resources Code, from the possession or actual or constructive care of a person named in the order;

(2) grant exclusive possession of a residence to a party and, if appropriate, direct one or more parties to vacate the residence if the residence:

(A) is jointly owned or leased by the party receiving exclusive possession and a party being denied possession;

(B) is owned or leased by the party retaining possession; or

(C) is owned or leased by the party being denied possession and that party has an obligation to support the party or a child of the party granted possession of the residence;

(3) provide for the possession of and access to a child of a party if the person receiving possession of or access to the child is a parent of the child;

(4) require the payment of support for a party or for a child of a party if the person required to make the payment has an obligation to support the other party or the child; or

(5) award to a party the use and possession of specified property that is community property or jointly owned or leased property.

Sec. 85.022. Requirements of Order Applying to Person Who Committed Family Violence.

(a) In a protective order, the court may order the person found to have committed family violence to perform acts specified by the court that the court determines are necessary or appropriate to prevent or reduce the likelihood of family violence and may order that person to:

(1) complete a battering intervention and prevention program accredited under Article 42.141, Code of Criminal Procedure;

(2) beginning on September 1, 2008, if the referral option under Subdivision (1) is not available, complete a program or counsel with a provider that has begun the accreditation process described by Subsection (a-1); or

(3) if the referral option under Subdivision (1) or, beginning on September 1, 2008, the referral option under Subdivision (2) is not available, counsel with a social worker, family service agency, physician, psychologist, licensed therapist, or licensed professional counselor who has completed family violence intervention training that the community justice assistance division of the Texas Department of Criminal Justice has approved, after consultation with the licensing authorities described by Chapters 152, 501, 502, 503, and 505, Occupations Code, and experts in the field of family violence.

(a-1) Beginning on September 1, 2009, a program or provider serving as a referral option for the courts under Subsection (a)(1) or (2) must be accredited under Section 4A, Article 42.141, Code of Criminal Procedure, as conforming to program guidelines under that article.

(b) In a protective order, the court may prohibit the person found to have committed family violence from:

(1) committing family violence;

(2) communicating:

(A) directly with a person protected by an order or a member of the family or household of a person protected by an order, in a threatening or harassing manner;

(B) a threat through any person to a person protected by an order or a member of the family or household of a person protected by an order; and

(C) if the court finds good cause, in any manner with a person protected by an order or a member of the family or household of a person protected by an order, except through the party's attorney or a person appointed by the court;

(3) going to or near the residence or place of employment or business of a person protected by an order or a member of the family or household of a person protected by an order;

(4) going to or near the residence, child-care facility, or school a child protected under the order normally attends or in which the child normally resides;

(5) engaging in conduct directed specifically toward a person who is a person protected by an order or a member of the family or household of a person protected by an order, including following the person, that is reasonably likely to harass, annoy, alarm, abuse, torment, or embarrass the person;

(6) possessing a firearm, unless the person is a peace officer, as defined by Section 1.07, Penal Code, actively engaged in employment as a sworn, full-time paid employee of a state agency or political subdivision; and

(7) harming, threatening, or interfering with the care, custody, or control of a pet, companion animal, or assistance animal, as defined by Section 121.002, Human Resources Code, that is possessed by or is in the actual or constructive care of a person protected by an order or by a member of the family or household of a person protected by an order.

(c) In an order under Subsection (b)(3) or (4), the court shall specifically describe each prohibited location and the minimum distances from the location, if any, that the party must maintain. This subsection does not apply to an order in which Section 85.007 applies.

(d) In a protective order, the court shall suspend a license to carry a handgun issued under Subchapter H, Chapter 411, Government Code, that is held by a person found to have committed family violence.

(e) In this section, "firearm" has the meaning assigned by Section 46.01, Penal Code.

Sec. 85.0225. Separation of Wireless Telephone Service Account.

(a) A petitioner who is the primary user of a wireless telephone number associated with the respondent's wireless telephone service account may submit to the court that renders a protective order for the petitioner under this chapter a request for the court to order:

(1) the separation of that wireless telephone number from the respondent's wireless telephone service account; and

(2) if applicable, the separation of each wireless telephone number primarily used by a child in the petitioner's care or custody.

(b) The request must include each wireless telephone number for which the petitioner requests separation.

(c) If the petitioner shows by a preponderance of the evidence that for each wireless telephone number listed in the request the petitioner or, if applicable, a child in the petitioner's care or custody is the primary user, the court shall render a separate order directing the wireless telephone service provider to transfer the billing responsibilities and rights to each listed wireless telephone number to the petitioner.

(d) An order rendered under Subsection (c) must include:

(1) the name and billing wireless telephone number of the wireless telephone service account holder;

(2) each wireless telephone number to be transferred; and

(3) a statement requiring the wireless telephone service provider to transfer to the petitioner all financial responsibility for and the right to use each wireless telephone number transferred.

(e) For purposes of Subsection (d)(3), financial responsibility includes the monthly service costs associated with any mobile device associated with the wireless telephone number.

(f) The court shall serve a copy of the order described by Subsection (c) on the registered agent for the wireless telephone service provider designated under Chapter 5, Business Organizations Code.

(g) The court shall ensure that the contact information of the petitioner is not provided to the respondent as the wireless telephone service account holder in a proceeding under this section.

Texas Family Code

Sec. 85.023. Effect on Property Rights.

A protective order or an agreement approved by the court under this subtitle does not affect the title to real property.

Sec. 85.024. Enforcement of Counseling Requirement.

(a) A person found to have engaged in family violence who is ordered to attend a program or counseling under Section 85.022(a)(1), (2), or (3) shall file with the court an affidavit before the 60th day after the date the order was rendered stating either that the person has begun the program or counseling or that a program or counseling is not available within a reasonable distance from the person's residence. A person who files an affidavit that the person has begun the program or counseling shall file with the court before the date the protective order expires a statement that the person completed the program or counseling not later than the 30th day before the expiration date of the protective order or the 30th day before the first anniversary of the date the protective order was issued, whichever date is earlier. An affidavit under this subsection must be accompanied by a letter, notice, or certificate from the program or counselor that verifies the person's completion of the program or counseling. A person who fails to comply with this subsection may be punished for contempt of court under Section 21.002, Government Code.

(b) A protective order under Section 85.022 must specifically advise the person subject to the order of the requirement of this section and the possible punishment if the person fails to comply with the requirement.

Sec. 85.025. Duration of Protective Order.

(a) Except as otherwise provided by this section, an order under this subtitle is effective:

(1) for the period stated in the order, not to exceed two years; or

(2) if a period is not stated in the order, until the second anniversary of the date the order was issued.

(a-1) The court may render a protective order sufficient to protect the applicant and members of the applicant's family or household that is effective for a period that exceeds two years if the court finds that the person who is the subject of the protective order:

(1) committed an act constituting a felony offense involving family violence against the applicant or a member of the applicant's family or household, regardless of whether the person has been charged with or convicted of the offense;

(2) caused serious bodily injury to the applicant or a member of the applicant's family or household; or

(3) was the subject of two or more previous protective orders rendered:

(A) to protect the person on whose behalf the current protective order is sought; and

(B) after a finding by the court that the subject of the protective order:

(i) has committed family violence; and

(ii) is likely to commit family violence in the future.

(b) A person who is the subject of a protective order may file a motion not earlier than the first anniversary of the date on which the order was rendered requesting that the court review the protective order and determine whether there is a continuing need for the order.

(b-1) Following the filing of a motion under Subsection (b), a person who is the subject of a protective order issued under Subsection (a-1) that is effective for a period that exceeds two years may file not more than one subsequent motion requesting that the court review the protective order and determine whether there is a continuing need for the order. The subsequent motion may not be filed earlier than the first anniversary of the date on which the court rendered an order on the previous motion by the person.

(b-2) After a hearing on a motion under Subsection (b) or (b-1), if the court does not make a finding that there is no continuing need for the protective order, the protective order remains in effect until the date the order expires under this section. Evidence of the movant's compliance with the protective order does not by itself support a finding by the court that there is no continuing need for the protective order. If the court finds there is no continuing need for the protective order, the court shall order that the protective order expires on a date set by the court.

(b-3) Subsection (b) does not apply to a protective order issued under Subchapter A, Chapter 7B, Code of Criminal Procedure.

(c) If a person who is the subject of a protective order is confined or imprisoned on the date the protective order would expire under Subsection (a) or (a-1), or if the protective order would expire not later than the first anniversary of the date the person is released from confinement or imprisonment, the period for which the order is effective is extended, and the order expires on:

(1) the first anniversary of the date the person is released from confinement or imprisonment, if the

person was sentenced to confinement or imprisonment for more than five years; or

(2) the second anniversary of the date the person is released from confinement or imprisonment, if the person was sentenced to confinement or imprisonment for five years or less.

Sec. 85.026. Warning on Protective Order.

(a) Each protective order issued under this subtitle, including a temporary ex parte order, must contain the following prominently displayed statements in boldfaced type, capital letters, or underlined:

"A PERSON WHO VIOLATES THIS ORDER MAY BE PUNISHED FOR CONTEMPT OF COURT BY A FINE OF AS MUCH AS $500 OR BY CONFINEMENT IN JAIL FOR AS LONG AS SIX MONTHS, OR BOTH."

"NO PERSON, INCLUDING A PERSON WHO IS PROTECTED BY THIS ORDER, MAY GIVE PERMISSION TO ANYONE TO IGNORE OR VIOLATE ANY PROVISION OF THIS ORDER. DURING THE TIME IN WHICH THIS ORDER IS VALID, EVERY PROVISION OF THIS ORDER IS IN FULL FORCE AND EFFECT UNLESS A COURT CHANGES THE ORDER."

"IT IS UNLAWFUL FOR ANY PERSON, OTHER THAN A PEACE OFFICER, AS DEFINED BY SECTION 1.07, PENAL CODE, ACTIVELY ENGAGED IN EMPLOYMENT AS A SWORN, FULL-TIME PAID EMPLOYEE OF A STATE AGENCY OR POLITICAL SUBDIVISION, WHO IS SUBJECT TO A PROTECTIVE ORDER TO POSSESS A FIREARM OR AMMUNITION."

IF A PERSON SUBJECT TO A PROTECTIVE ORDER IS RELEASED FROM CONFINEMENT OR IMPRISONMENT FOLLOWING THE DATE THE ORDER WOULD HAVE EXPIRED, OR IF THE ORDER WOULD HAVE EXPIRED NOT LATER THAN THE FIRST ANNIVERSARY OF THE DATE THE PERSON IS RELEASED FROM CONFINEMENT OR IMPRISONMENT, THE ORDER IS AUTOMATICALLY EXTENDED TO EXPIRE ON:

(1) THE FIRST ANNIVERSARY OF THE DATE THE PERSON IS RELEASED, IF THE PERSON WAS SENTENCED TO CONFINEMENT OR IMPRISONMENT FOR A TERM OF MORE THAN FIVE YEARS; OR

"(2) THE SECOND ANNIVERSARY OF THE DATE THE PERSON IS RELEASED, IF THE PERSON WAS SENTENCED TO CONFINEMENT OR IMPRISONMENT FOR A TERM OF FIVE YEARS OR LESS."

"A VIOLATION OF THIS ORDER BY COMMISSION OF AN ACT PROHIBITED BY THE ORDER MAY BE PUNISHABLE BY A FINE OF AS MUCH AS $4,000 OR BY CONFINEMENT IN JAIL FOR AS LONG AS ONE YEAR, OR BOTH. AN ACT THAT RESULTS IN FAMILY VIOLENCE MAY BE PROSECUTED AS A SEPARATE MISDEMEANOR OR FELONY OFFENSE. IF THE ACT IS PROSECUTED AS A SEPARATE FELONY OFFENSE, IT IS PUNISHABLE BY CONFINEMENT IN PRISON FOR AT LEAST TWO YEARS."

(b) [Repealed by Acts 2011, 82nd Leg., ch. 632 (S.B. 819), § 6(2), effective September 1, 2011.]

(c) Each protective order issued under this subtitle, including a temporary ex parte order, must contain the following prominently displayed statement in boldfaced type, capital letters, or underlined:

"NO PERSON, INCLUDING A PERSON WHO IS PROTECTED BY THIS ORDER, MAY GIVE PERMISSION TO ANYONE TO IGNORE OR VIOLATE ANY PROVISION OF THIS ORDER. DURING THE TIME IN WHICH THIS ORDER IS VALID, EVERY PROVISION OF THIS ORDER IS IN FULL FORCE AND EFFECT UNLESS A COURT CHANGES THE ORDER."

SUBCHAPTER C DELIVERY OF PROTECTIVE ORDER

Sec. 85.041. Delivery to Respondent.

(a) A protective order rendered under this subtitle shall be:

(1) delivered to the respondent as provided by Rule 21a, Texas Rules of Civil Procedure;

(2) served in the same manner as a writ of injunction; or

(3) served in open court at the close of the hearing as provided by this section.

(b) The court shall serve an order in open court to a respondent who is present at the hearing by giving to the respondent a copy of the order, reduced to writing and signed by the judge or master. A certified copy of the signed order shall be given to the applicant at the time the order is given to the respondent. If the applicant is not in court at the conclusion of the hearing, the clerk of the court shall mail a certified copy of the order to the applicant not later than the third business day after the date the hearing is concluded.

(c) If the order has not been reduced to writing, the court shall give notice orally to a respondent who is present at the hearing of the part of the order that contains prohibitions under Section 85.022

or any other part of the order that contains provisions necessary to prevent further family violence. The clerk of the court shall mail a copy of the order to the respondent and a certified copy of the order to the applicant not later than the third business day after the date the hearing is concluded.

(d) If the respondent is not present at the hearing and the order has been reduced to writing at the conclusion of the hearing, the clerk of the court shall immediately provide a certified copy of the order to the applicant and mail a copy of the order to the respondent not later than the third business day after the date the hearing is concluded.

Sec. 85.042. Delivery of Order to Other Persons.

(a) Not later than the next business day after the date the court issues an original or modified protective order under this subtitle, the clerk of the court shall send a copy of the order, along with the information provided by the applicant or the applicant's attorney that is required under Section 411.042(b)(6), Government Code, to:

(1) the chief of police of the municipality in which the person protected by the order resides, if the person resides in a municipality;

(2) the appropriate constable and the sheriff of the county in which the person resides, if the person does not reside in a municipality; and

(3) the Title IV-D agency, if the application for the protective order indicates that the applicant is receiving services from the Title IV-D agency.

(a-1) This subsection applies only if the respondent, at the time of issuance of an original or modified protective order under this subtitle, is a member of the state military forces or is serving in the armed forces of the United States in an active-duty status and the applicant or the applicant's attorney provides to the clerk of the court the mailing address of the staff judge advocate or provost marshal, as applicable. In addition to complying with Subsection (a), the clerk of the court shall also provide a copy of the protective order and the information described by that subsection to the staff judge advocate at Joint Force Headquarters or the provost marshal of the military installation to which the respondent is assigned with the intent that the commanding officer will be notified, as applicable.

(b) If a protective order made under this chapter prohibits a respondent from going to or near a child-care facility or school, the clerk of the court shall send a copy of the order to the child-care facility or school.

(c) The clerk of a court that vacates an original or modified protective order under this subtitle shall notify each individual or entity who received a copy of the original or modified order from the clerk under this section that the order is vacated.

(d) The applicant or the applicant's attorney shall provide to the clerk of the court:

(1) the name and address of each law enforcement agency, child-care facility, school, and other individual or entity to which the clerk is required to send a copy of the order under this section; and

(2) any other information required under Section 411.042(b)(6), Government Code.

(e) The clerk of the court issuing an original or modified protective order under Section 85.022 that suspends a license to carry a handgun shall send a copy of the order to the appropriate division of the Department of Public Safety at its Austin headquarters. On receipt of the order suspending the license, the department shall:

(1) record the suspension of the license in the records of the department;

(2) report the suspension to local law enforcement agencies, as appropriate; and

(3) demand surrender of the suspended license from the license holder.

(f) A clerk of the court may transmit the order and any related information electronically or in another manner that can be accessed by the recipient.

(g) A clerk of the court may delay sending a copy of the order under Subsection (a) only if the clerk lacks information necessary to ensure service and enforcement.

(h) In this section, "business day" means a day other than a Saturday, Sunday, or state or national holiday.

SUBCHAPTER D RELATIONSHIP BETWEEN PROTECTIVE ORDER AND SUIT FOR DISSOLUTION OF MARRIAGE AND SUIT AFFECTING PARENT-CHILD RELATIONSHIP

Sec. 85.061. Dismissal of Application Prohibited; Subsequently Filed Suit for Dissolution of Marriage or Suit Affecting Parent-Child Relationship.

If an application for a protective order is pending, a court may not dismiss the application or delay a hearing on the application on the grounds that a suit for dissolution of marriage or suit affecting the parent-child relationship is filed after the date the application was filed.

Sec. 85.062. Application Filed While Suit for Dissolution of Marriage or Suit Affecting Parent-Child Relationship Pending.

(a) If a suit for dissolution of a marriage or suit affecting the parent-child relationship is pending, a party to the suit may apply for a protective order against another party to the suit by filing an application:

(1) in the court in which the suit is pending; or

(2) in a court in the county in which the applicant resides if the applicant resides outside the jurisdiction of the court in which the suit is pending.

(b) An applicant subject to this section shall inform the clerk of the court that renders a protective order that a suit for dissolution of a marriage or a suit affecting the parent-child relationship is pending in which the applicant is party.

(c) If a final protective order is rendered by a court other than the court in which a suit for dissolution of a marriage or a suit affecting the parent-child relationship is pending, the clerk of the court that rendered the protective order shall:

(1) inform the clerk of the court in which the suit is pending that a final protective order has been rendered; and

(2) forward a copy of the final protective order to the court in which the suit is pending.

(d) A protective order rendered by a court in which an application is filed under Subsection (a)(2) is subject to transfer under Section 85.064.

Sec. 85.063. Application Filed After Final Order Rendered in Suit for Dissolution of Marriage or Suit Affecting Parent-Child Relationship.

(a) If a final order has been rendered in a suit for dissolution of marriage or suit affecting the parent-child relationship, an application for a protective order by a party to the suit against another party to the suit filed after the date the final order was rendered, and that is:

(1) filed in the county in which the final order was rendered, shall be filed in the court that rendered the final order; and

(2) filed in another county, shall be filed in a court having jurisdiction to render a protective order under this subtitle.

(b) A protective order rendered by a court in which an application is filed under Subsection (a)(2) is subject to transfer under Section 85.064.

Sec. 85.064. Transfer of Protective Order.

(a) If a protective order was rendered before the filing of a suit for dissolution of marriage or suit affecting the parent-child relationship or while the suit is pending as provided by Section 85.062, the court that rendered the order may, on the motion of a party or on the court's own motion, transfer the protective order to the court having jurisdiction of the suit if the court makes the finding prescribed by Subsection (c).

(b) If a protective order that affects a party's right to possession of or access to a child is rendered after the date a final order was rendered in a suit affecting the parent-child relationship, on the motion of a party or on the court's own motion, the court may transfer the protective order to the court of continuing, exclusive jurisdiction if the court makes the finding prescribed by Subsection (c).

(c) A court may transfer a protective order under this section if the court finds that the transfer is:

(1) in the interest of justice; or

(2) for the safety or convenience of a party or a witness.

(d) The transfer of a protective order under this section shall be conducted according to the procedures provided by Section 155.207.

(e) Except as provided by Section 81.002, the fees or costs associated with the transfer of a protective order shall be paid by the movant.

Sec. 85.065. Effect of Transfer.

(a), (b) [Repealed by Acts 2011, 82nd Leg., ch. 632 (S.B. 819), § 6(3), effective September 1, 2011.]

(c) A protective order that is transferred is subject to modification by the court that receives the order to the same extent modification is permitted under Chapter 87 by a court that rendered the order.

CHAPTER 86
LAW ENFORCEMENT DUTIES RELATING TO PROTECTIVE ORDERS

Sec. 86.001. Adoption of Procedures by Law Enforcement Agency.

(a) To ensure that law enforcement officers responding to calls are aware of the existence and terms of protective orders issued under this subtitle, each law enforcement agency shall establish procedures in the agency to provide adequate information or access to information for law enforcement officers of the names of each person protected by an order issued under this subtitle and of each person against whom protective orders are directed.

(b) A law enforcement agency may enter a protective order in the agency's computer records of outstanding warrants as notice that the order has been issued and is currently in effect. On receipt of notification by a clerk of court that the court has vacated or dismissed an order, the law enforcement agency shall remove the order from the agency's computer record of outstanding warrants.

Sec. 86.0011. Duty to Enter Information Into Statewide Law Enforcement Information System.

(a) On receipt of an original or modified protective order from the clerk of the issuing court, or on receipt of information pertaining to the date of confinement or imprisonment or date of release of a person subject to the protective order, a law enforcement agency shall immediately, but not later than the third business day after the date the order or information is received, enter the information required by Section 411.042(b)(6), Government Code, into the statewide law enforcement information system maintained by the Department of Public Safety.

(b) In this section, "business day" means a day other than a Saturday, Sunday, or state or national holiday.

Sec. 86.002. Duty to Provide Information to Firearms Dealers.

(a) On receipt of a request for a law enforcement information system record check of a prospective transferee by a licensed firearms dealer under the Brady Handgun Violence Prevention Act, 18 U.S.C. Section 922, the chief law enforcement officer shall determine whether the Department of Public Safety has in the department's law enforcement information system a record indicating the existence of an active protective order directed to the prospective transferee.

(b) If the department's law enforcement information system indicates the existence of an active protective order directed to the prospective transferee, the chief law enforcement officer shall immediately advise the dealer that the transfer is prohibited.

Sec. 86.003. Court Order for Law Enforcement Assistance Under Temporary Order.

On request by an applicant obtaining a temporary ex parte protective order that excludes the respondent from the respondent's residence, the court granting the temporary order shall render a written order to the sheriff, constable, or chief of police to provide a law enforcement officer from the department of the chief of police, constable, or sheriff to:

(1) accompany the applicant to the residence covered by the order;

(2) inform the respondent that the court has ordered that the respondent be excluded from the residence;

(3) protect the applicant while the applicant takes possession of the residence; and

(4) protect the applicant if the respondent refuses to vacate the residence while the applicant takes possession of the applicant's necessary personal property.

Sec. 86.004. Court Order for Law Enforcement Assistance Under Final Order.

On request by an applicant obtaining a final protective order that excludes the respondent from the respondent's residence, the court granting the final order shall render a written order to the sheriff, constable, or chief of police to provide a law enforcement officer from the department of the chief of police, constable, or sheriff to:

(1) accompany the applicant to the residence covered by the order;

(2) inform the respondent that the court has ordered that the respondent be excluded from the residence;

(3) protect the applicant while the applicant takes possession of the residence and the respondent takes possession of the respondent's necessary personal property; and

(4) if the respondent refuses to vacate the residence:

(A) remove the respondent from the residence; and

(B) arrest the respondent for violating the court order.

Sec. 86.005. Protective Order from Another Jurisdiction.

To ensure that law enforcement officers responding to calls are aware of the existence and terms of a protective order from another jurisdiction, each law enforcement agency shall establish procedures in the agency to provide adequate information or access to information for law enforcement officers regarding the name of each person protected by an order rendered in another jurisdiction and of each person against whom the protective order is directed.

CHAPTER 87
MODIFICATION OF PROTECTIVE ORDERS

Sec. 87.001. Modification of Protective Order.

On the motion of any party, the court, after notice and hearing, may modify an existing protective order to:

(1) exclude any item included in the order; or

(2) include any item that could have been included in the order.

Sec. 87.002. Modification May Not Extend Duration of Order.

A protective order may not be modified to extend the period of the order's validity beyond the second anniversary of the date the original order was rendered or beyond the date the order expires under Section 85.025(a-1) or (c), whichever date occurs later.

Sec. 87.003. Notification of Motion to Modify.

Notice of a motion to modify a protective order is sufficient if delivery of the motion is attempted on the respondent at the respondent's last known address by registered or certified mail as provided by Rule 21a, Texas Rules of Civil Procedure.

Sec. 87.004. Change of Address or Telephone Number.

(a) If a protective order contains the address or telephone number of a person protected by the order, of the place of employment or business of the person, or of the child-care facility or school of a child protected by the order and that information is not confidential under Section 85.007, the person protected by the order may file a notification of change of address or telephone number with the court that rendered the order to modify the information contained in the order.

(b) The clerk of the court shall attach the notification of change to the protective order and shall deliver a copy of the notification to the respondent by registered or certified mail as provided by Rule 21a, Texas Rules of Civil Procedure.

(c) The filing of a notification of change of address or telephone number and the attachment of the notification to a protective order does not affect the validity of the order.

CHAPTER 88
UNIFORM INTERSTATE ENFORCEMENT OF DOMESTIC-VIOLENCE PROTECTION ORDERS ACT

Sec. 88.001. Short Title.

This chapter may be cited as the Uniform Interstate Enforcement of Domestic Violence Protection Orders Act.

Sec. 88.002. Definitions.

In this chapter:

(1) "Foreign protective order" means a protective order issued by a tribunal of another state.

(2) "Issuing state" means the state in which a tribunal issues a protective order.

(3) "Mutual foreign protective order" means a foreign protective order that includes provisions issued in favor of both the protected individual seeking enforcement of the order and the respondent.

(4) "Protected individual" means an individual protected by a protective order.

(5) "Protective order" means an injunction or other order, issued by a tribunal under the domestic violence or family violence laws or another law of the issuing state, to prevent an individual from engaging in violent or threatening acts against, harassing, contacting or communicating with, or being in physical proximity to another individual.

(6) "Respondent" means the individual against whom enforcement of a protective order is sought.

(7) "State" means a state of the United States, the District of Columbia, the Commonwealth of Puerto Rico, the United States Virgin Islands, or a territory or insular possession subject to the jurisdiction of the United States. The term includes a military tribunal of the United States, an Indian tribe or band, and an Alaskan native village that has jurisdiction to issue protective orders.

(8) "Tribunal" means a court, agency, or other entity authorized by law to issue or modify a protective order.

Sec. 88.003. Judicial Enforcement of Order.

(a) A tribunal of this state shall enforce the terms of a foreign protective order, including a term that provides relief that a tribunal of this state would not have power to provide but for this section. The tribunal shall enforce the order regardless of whether the order was obtained by independent action or in another proceeding, if the order is an order issued in response to a complaint, petition, or motion filed by or on behalf of an individual seeking protection. In a proceeding to enforce a foreign protective order, the tribunal shall follow the procedures of this state for the enforcement of protective orders.

(b) A tribunal of this state shall enforce the provisions of the foreign protective order that govern the possession of and access to a child if the provisions were issued in accordance with the jurisdictional requirements governing the issuance of possession and access orders in the issuing state.

(c) A tribunal of this state may enforce a provision of the foreign protective order relating to child support if the order was issued in accordance with the jurisdictional requirements of Chapter 159 and the federal Full Faith and Credit for Child Support Orders Act, 28 U.S.C. Section 1738B, as amended.

(d) A foreign protective order is valid if the order:

(1) names the protected individual and the respondent;

(2) is currently in effect;

(3) was rendered by a tribunal that had jurisdiction over the parties and the subject matter under the law of the issuing state; and

(4) was rendered after the respondent was given reasonable notice and an opportunity to be heard consistent with the right to due process, either:

(A) before the tribunal issued the order; or

(B) in the case of an ex parte order, within a reasonable time after the order was rendered.

(e) A protected individual seeking enforcement of a foreign protective order establishes a prima facie case for its validity by presenting an order that is valid on its face.

(f) It is an affirmative defense in an action seeking enforcement of a foreign protective order that the order does not meet the requirements for a valid order under Subsection (d).

(g) A tribunal of this state may enforce the provisions of a mutual foreign protective order that favor a respondent only if:

(1) the respondent filed a written pleading seeking a protective order from the tribunal of the issuing state; and

(2) the tribunal of the issuing state made specific findings in favor of the respondent.

Sec. 88.004. Nonjudicial Enforcement of Order.

(a) A law enforcement officer of this state, on determining that there is probable cause to believe that a valid foreign protective order exists and that the order has been violated, shall enforce the foreign protective order as if it were an order of a tribunal of this state. A law enforcement officer has probable cause to believe that a foreign protective order exists if the protected individual presents a foreign protective order that identifies both the protected individual and the respondent and on its face, is currently in effect.

(b) For the purposes of this section, a foreign protective order may be inscribed on a tangible medium or may be stored in an electronic or other medium if it is retrievable in a perceivable form. Presentation of a certified copy of a protective order is not required for enforcement.

(c) If a protected individual does not present a foreign protective order, a law enforcement officer may determine that there is probable cause to believe that a valid foreign protective order exists by relying on any relevant information.

(d) A law enforcement officer of this state who determines that an otherwise valid foreign protective order cannot be enforced because the respondent has not been notified or served with the order shall inform the respondent of the order and make a reasonable effort to serve the order on the respondent. After informing the respondent and attempting to serve the order, the officer shall allow the respondent a reasonable opportunity to comply with the order before enforcing the order.

(e) The registration or filing of an order in this state is not required for the enforcement of a valid foreign protective order under this chapter.

Sec. 88.005. Registration of Order.

(a) An individual may register a foreign protective order in this state. To register a foreign protective order, an individual shall:

(1) present a certified copy of the order to a sheriff, constable, or chief of police responsible for the registration of orders in the local computer records and in the statewide law enforcement system maintained by the Texas Department of Public Safety; or

(2) present a certified copy of the order to the Department of Public Safety and request that the order be registered in the statewide law enforcement system maintained by the Department of Public Safety.

(b) On receipt of a foreign protective order, the agency responsible for the registration of protective orders shall register the order in accordance with this section and furnish to the individual registering the order a certified copy of the registered order.

(c) The agency responsible for the registration of protective orders shall register a foreign protective order on presentation of a copy of a protective order that has been certified by the issuing state. A registered foreign protective order that is inaccurate or not currently in effect shall be corrected or removed from the registry in accordance with the law of this state.

(d) An individual registering a foreign protective order shall file an affidavit made by the protected individual that, to the best of the protected individual's knowledge, the order is in effect.

(e) A foreign protective order registered under this section may be entered in any existing state or federal registry of protective orders, in accordance with state or federal law.

(f) A fee may not be charged for the registration of a foreign protective order.

Sec. 88.006. Immunity.

A state or local governmental agency, law enforcement officer, prosecuting attorney, clerk of court, or any state or local governmental official acting in an official capacity is immune from civil and criminal liability for an act or omission arising from the registration or enforcement of a foreign protective order or the detention or arrest of a person alleged to have violated a foreign protective order if the act or omission was done in good faith in an effort to comply with this chapter.

Sec. 88.007. Other Remedies.

A protected individual who pursues a remedy under this chapter is not precluded from pursuing other legal or equitable remedies against the respondent.

Sec. 88.008. Uniformity of Application and Construction.

In applying and construing this chapter, consideration shall be given to the need to promote uniformity of the law with respect to its subject matter among the states that enact the Uniform Interstate Enforcement of Domestic Violence Protection Orders Act.

SUBTITLE C FAMILY VIOLENCE REPORTING AND SERVICES

CHAPTER 91 REPORTING FAMILY VIOLENCE

Sec. 91.001. Definitions.

In this subtitle:

(1) "Family violence" has the meaning assigned by Section 71.004.

(2) "Medical professional" means a licensed doctor, nurse, physician assistant, or emergency medical technician.

Sec. 91.002. Reporting by Witnesses Encouraged.

A person who witnesses family violence is encouraged to report the family violence to a local law enforcement agency.

Sec. 91.003. Information Provided by Medical Professionals.

A medical professional who treats a person for injuries that the medical professional has reason to believe were caused by family violence shall:

(1) immediately provide the person with information regarding the nearest family violence shelter center;

(2) document in the person's medical file:

(A) the fact that the person has received the information provided under Subdivision (1); and

(B) the reasons for the medical professional's belief that the person's injuries were caused by family violence; and

(3) give the person a written notice in substantially the following form, completed with the required information, in both English and Spanish:

"NOTICE TO ADULT VICTIMS OF FAMILY VIOLENCE

"It is a crime for any person to cause you any physical injury or harm even if that person is a member or former member of your family or household.

"You may report family violence to a law enforcement officer by calling the following telephone numbers: ________________

"If you, your child, or any other household resident has been injured or if you feel you are going to be in danger after a law enforcement officer investigating family violence leaves your residence or at a later time, you have the right to:

"Ask the local prosecutor to file a criminal complaint against the person committing family violence; and

"Apply to a court for an order to protect you. You may want to consult with a legal aid office, a prosecuting attorney, or a private attorney. A court can enter an order that:

"(1) prohibits the abuser from committing further acts of violence;

"(2) prohibits the abuser from threatening, harassing, or contacting you at home;

"(3) directs the abuser to leave your household; and

"(4) establishes temporary custody of the children or any property.

"A VIOLATION OF CERTAIN PROVISIONS OF COURT-ORDERED PROTECTION MAY BE A FELONY.

"CALL THE FOLLOWING VIOLENCE SHELTERS OR SOCIAL ORGANIZATIONS IF YOU NEED PROTECTION: ____________________"

Sec. 91.004. Application of Subtitle.

This subtitle does not affect a duty to report child abuse under Chapter 261.

CHAPTER 92 IMMUNITY

Sec. 92.001. Immunity.

(a) Except as provided by Subsection (b), a person who reports family violence under Section 91.002 or provides information under Section 91.003 is immune from civil liability that might otherwise be incurred or imposed.

(b) A person who reports the person's own conduct or who otherwise reports family violence in bad faith is not protected from liability under this section.

CHAPTER 93 CONFIDENTIAL AND PRIVILEGED COMMUNICATIONS

Sec. 93.001. Definitions.

In this chapter:

(1) "Advocate" means a person who has at least 20 hours of training in assisting victims of family violence and is an employee or volunteer of a family violence center.

(2) "Family violence center" means a public or private nonprofit organization that provides, as its primary purpose, services to victims of family violence, including the services described by Section 51.005(b)(3), Human Resources Code.

(3) "Victim" has the meaning assigned to "victim of family violence" by Section 51.002, Human Resources Code.

Sec. 93.002. Confidential Communications.

A written or oral communication between an advocate and a victim made in the course of advising, advocating for, counseling, or assisting the victim is confidential and may not be disclosed.

Sec. 93.003. Privileged Communications.

(a) A victim has a privilege to refuse to disclose and to prevent another from disclosing a confidential communication described by Section 93.002.

(b) The privilege may be claimed by:

(1) a victim or a victim's attorney on a victim's behalf;

(2) a parent, guardian, or conservator of a victim under 18 years of age; or

(3) an advocate or a family violence center on a victim's behalf.

Sec. 93.004. Exceptions.

(a) A communication that is confidential under this chapter may be disclosed only:

(1) to another individual employed by or volunteering for a family violence center for the purpose of furthering the advocacy process;

(2) for the purpose of seeking evidence that is admissible under Article 38.49, Code of Criminal Procedure, following an in camera review and a determination that the communication is admissible under that article;

(3) to other persons in the context of a support group or group counseling in which a victim is a participant; or

(4) for the purposes of making a report under Chapter 261 of this code or Section 48.051, Human Resources Code.

(b) Notwithstanding Subsection (a), the Texas Rules of Evidence govern the disclosure of a communication that is confidential under this chapter in a criminal or civil proceeding by an expert witness who relies on facts or data from the communication to form the basis of the expert's opinion.

(c) If the family violence center, at the request of the victim, discloses a communication privileged under this chapter for the purpose of a criminal or civil proceeding, the family violence center shall disclose the communication to all parties to that criminal or civil proceeding.

TITLE 5 THE PARENT-CHILD RELATIONSHIP AND THE SUIT AFFECTING THE PARENT-CHILD RELATIONSHIP

SUBTITLE A GENERAL PROVISIONS

CHAPTER 105 SETTINGS, HEARINGS, AND ORDERS

Sec. 105.0011. Information Regarding Protective Orders.

At any time while a suit is pending, if the court believes, on the basis of any information received by the court, that a party to the suit or a member of the party's family or household may be a victim of family violence, the court shall inform that party of the party's right to apply for a protective order under Title 4.

SUBTITLE B SUITS AFFECTING THE PARENT-CHILD RELATIONSHIP

CHAPTER 151 RIGHTS AND DUTIES IN PARENT-CHILD RELATIONSHIP

Sec. 151.001. Rights and Duties of Parent.

(a) A parent of a child has the following rights and duties:

(1) the right to have physical possession, to direct the moral and religious training, and to designate the residence of the child;

(2) the duty of care, control, protection, and reasonable discipline of the child;

(3) the duty to support the child, including providing the child with clothing, food, shelter, medical and dental care, and education;

(4) the duty, except when a guardian of the child's estate has been appointed, to manage the estate of the child, including the right as an agent of the child to act in relation to the child's estate if the child's action is required by a state, the United States, or a foreign government;

(5) except as provided by Section 264.0111, the right to the services and earnings of the child;

(6) the right to consent to the child's marriage, enlistment in the armed forces of the United States, medical and dental care, and psychiatric, psychological, and surgical treatment;

(7) the right to represent the child in legal action and to make other decisions of substantial legal significance concerning the child;

(8) the right to receive and give receipt for payments for the support of the child and to hold or disburse funds for the benefit of the child;

(9) the right to inherit from and through the child;

(10) the right to make decisions concerning the child's education; and

(11) any other right or duty existing between a parent and child by virtue of law.

(b) The duty of a parent to support his or her child exists while the child is an unemancipated minor and continues as long as the child is fully enrolled in a secondary school in a program leading toward a high school diploma and complies with attendance requirements described by Section 154.002(a)(2).

(c) A parent who fails to discharge the duty of support is liable to a person who provides necessaries to those to whom support is owed.

(d) The rights and duties of a parent are subject to:

(1) a court order affecting the rights and duties;

(2) an affidavit of relinquishment of parental rights; and

(3) an affidavit by the parent designating another person or agency to act as managing conservator.

(e) Only the following persons may use corporal punishment for the reasonable discipline of a child:

(1) a parent or grandparent of the child;

(2) a stepparent of the child who has the duty of control and reasonable discipline of the child; and

(3) an individual who is a guardian of the child and who has the duty of control and reasonable discipline of the child.

Sec. 151.003. Limitation on State Agency Action.

A state agency may not adopt rules or policies or take any other action that violates the fundamental right and duty of a parent to direct the upbringing of the parent's child.

CHAPTER 153 CONSERVATORSHIP, POSSESSION, AND ACCESS

SUBCHAPTER A GENERAL PROVISIONS

Sec. 153.013. False Report of Child Abuse.

(a) If a party to a pending suit affecting the parent-child relationship makes a report alleging child abuse by another party to the suit that the reporting party knows lacks a factual foundation, the court shall deem the report to be a knowingly false report.

(b) Evidence of a false report of child abuse is admissible in a suit between the involved parties regarding the terms of conservatorship of a child.

(c) If the court makes a finding under Subsection (a), the court shall impose a civil penalty not to exceed $500.

SUBCHAPTER B PARENT APPOINTED AS CONSERVATOR: IN GENERAL

Sec. 153.074. Rights and Duties During Period of Possession.

Unless limited by court order, a parent appointed as a conservator of a child has the following rights and duties during the period that the parent has possession of the child:

(1) the duty of care, control, protection, and reasonable discipline of the child;

(2) the duty to support the child, including providing the child with clothing, food, shelter, and medical and dental care not involving an invasive procedure;

(3) the right to consent for the child to medical and dental care not involving an invasive procedure; and

(4) the right to direct the moral and religious training of the child.

CHAPTER 157 ENFORCEMENT

SUBCHAPTER B PROCEDURE

Sec. 157.066. Failure to Appear.

If a respondent who has been personally served with notice to appear at a hearing does not appear at the designated time, place, and date to respond to a motion for enforcement of an existing court order, regardless of whether the motion is joined with other claims or remedies, the court may not hold the respondent in contempt but may, on proper proof, grant a default judgment for the relief sought and issue a capias for the arrest of the respondent.

SUBCHAPTER C
FAILURE TO APPEAR; BOND OR SECURITY

Sec. 157.102. Capias or Warrant; Duty of Law Enforcement Officials.

Law enforcement officials shall treat a capias or arrest warrant ordered under this chapter in the same manner as an arrest warrant for a criminal offense and shall enter the capias or warrant in the computer records for outstanding warrants maintained by the local police, sheriff, and Department of Public Safety. The capias or warrant shall be forwarded to and disseminated by the Texas Crime Information Center and the National Crime Information Center.

Sec. 157.114. Failure to Appear.

The court may order a capias to be issued for the arrest of the respondent if:

(1) the motion for enforcement requests contempt;

(2) the respondent was personally served; and

(3) the respondent fails to appear.

CHAPTER 160
UNIFORM PARENTAGE ACT

SUBCHAPTER F
GENETIC TESTING

Sec. 160.512. Offense: Falsification of Specimen.

(a) A person commits an offense if the person alters, destroys, conceals, fabricates, or falsifies genetic evidence in a proceeding to adjudicate parentage, including inducing another person to provide a specimen with the intent to affect the outcome of the proceeding.

(b) An offense under this section is a felony of the third degree.

(c) An order excluding a man as the biological father of a child based on genetic evidence shown to be altered, fabricated, or falsified is void and unenforceable.

SUBTITLE C
JUDICIAL RESOURCES AND SERVICES

CHAPTER 203
DOMESTIC RELATIONS OFFICES

Sec. 203.007. Access to Records; Offense.

(a) A domestic relations office may obtain the records described by Subsections (b), (c), (d), and (e) that relate to a person who has:

(1) been ordered to pay child support;

(2) been designated as a conservator of a child;

(3) been designated to be the father of a child;

(4) executed an acknowledgment of paternity;

(5) court-ordered possession of a child; or

(6) filed suit to adopt a child.

(b) A domestic relations office is entitled to obtain from the Department of Public Safety records that relate to:

(1) a person's date of birth;

(2) a person's most recent address;

(3) a person's current driver's license status;

(4) motor vehicle accidents involving a person;

(5) reported traffic-law violations of which a person has been convicted; and

(6) a person's criminal history record information.

(c) A domestic relations office is entitled to obtain from the Texas Workforce Commission records that relate to:

(1) a person's address;

(2) a person's employment status and earnings;

(3) the name and address of a person's current or former employer; and

(4) unemployment compensation benefits received by a person.

(d) To the extent permitted by federal law, a domestic relations office is entitled to obtain from the national directory of new hires established under 42 U.S.C. Section 653(i), as amended, records that relate to a person described by Subsection (a), including records that relate to:

(1) the name, telephone number, and address of the person's employer;

(2) information provided by the person on a W-4 form; and

(3) information provided by the person's employer on a Title IV-D form.

(e) To the extent permitted by federal law, a domestic relations office is entitled to obtain from the state case registry records that relate to a person described by Subsection (a), including records that relate to:

(1) the street and mailing address and the social security number of the person;

(2) the name, telephone number, and address of the person's employer;

(3) the location and value of real and personal property owned by the person; and

(4) the name and address of each financial institution in which the person maintains an account and the account number for each account.

(f) An agency required to provide records under this section may charge a domestic relations office a fee for providing the records in an amount that does not exceed the amount paid for those records by the agency responsible for Title IV-D cases.

(g) The Department of Public Safety, the Texas Workforce Commission, or the office of the secretary of state may charge a domestic relations office a fee not to exceed the charge paid by the Title IV-D agency for furnishing records under this section.

(h) Information obtained by a domestic relations office under this section that is confidential under a constitution, statute, judicial decision, or rule is privileged and may be used only by that office.

(i) A person commits an offense if the person releases or discloses confidential information obtained under this section without the consent of the person to whom the information relates. An offense under this subsection is a Class C misdemeanor.

(j) A domestic relations office is entitled to obtain from the office of the secretary of state the following information about a registered voter to the extent that the information is available:

(1) complete name;

(2) current and former street and mailing address;

(3) sex;

(4) date of birth;

(5) social security number; and

(6) telephone number.

SUBTITLE D ADMINISTRATIVE SERVICES

CHAPTER 232 SUSPENSION OF LICENSE

Sec. 232.001. Definitions.

In this chapter:

(1) "License" means a license, certificate, registration, permit, or other authorization that:

(A) is issued by a licensing authority;

(B) is subject before expiration to renewal, suspension, revocation, forfeiture, or termination by a licensing authority; and

(C) a person must obtain to:

(i) practice or engage in a particular business, occupation, or profession;

(ii) operate a motor vehicle on a public highway in this state; or

(iii) engage in any other regulated activity, including hunting, fishing, or other recreational activity for which a license or permit is required.

(2) "Licensing authority" means a department, commission, board, office, or other agency of the state or a political subdivision of the state that issues or renews a license or that otherwise has authority to suspend or refuse to renew a license.

(3) "Order suspending license" means an order issued by the Title IV-D agency or a court directing a licensing authority to suspend or refuse to renew a license.

(3-a) "Renewal" means any instance when a licensing authority:

(A) renews, extends, recertifies, or reissues a license; or

(B) periodically certifies a licensee to be in good standing with the licensing authority based on the required payment of fees or dues or the performance of some other mandated action or activity.

(4) "Subpoena" means a judicial or administrative subpoena issued in a parentage determination or child support proceeding under this title.

Sec. 232.002. Licensing Authorities Subject to Chapter.

Unless otherwise restricted or exempted, all licensing authorities are subject to this chapter.

Sec. 232.0021. Application of Chapter to Texas Lottery Commission.

With respect to the Texas Lottery Commission, this chapter applies only to a lottery ticket sales agent license issued under Chapter 466, Government Code.

Sec. 232.0022. Suspension or Nonrenewal of Motor Vehicle Registration.

(a) The Texas Department of Motor Vehicles is the appropriate licensing authority for suspension or nonrenewal of a motor vehicle registration under this chapter.

(b) The suspension or nonrenewal of a motor vehicle registration under this chapter does not:

(1) encumber the title to the motor vehicle or otherwise affect the transfer of the title to the vehicle; or

(2) affect the sale, purchase, or registration of the motor vehicle by a person who holds a general

Texas Family Code

distinguishing number issued under Chapter 503, Transportation Code.

Sec. 232.003. Suspension of License.

(a) A court or the Title IV-D agency may issue an order suspending a license as provided by this chapter if an individual who is an obligor:

(1) owes overdue child support in an amount equal to or greater than the total support due for three months under a support order;

(2) has been provided an opportunity to make payments toward the overdue child support under a court-ordered or agreed repayment schedule; and

(3) has failed to comply with the repayment schedule.

(b) A court or the Title IV-D agency may issue an order suspending a license as provided by this chapter if a parent or alleged parent has failed, after receiving appropriate notice, to comply with a subpoena.

(c) A court may issue an order suspending license as provided by this chapter for an individual for whom a court has rendered an enforcement order under Chapter 157 finding that the individual has failed to comply with the terms of a court order providing for the possession of or access to a child.

Sec. 232.004. Petition for Suspension of License.

(a) A child support agency or obligee may file a petition to suspend, as provided by this chapter, a license of an obligor who has an arrearage equal to or greater than the total support due for three months under a support order.

(b) In a Title IV-D case, the petition shall be filed with the Title IV-D agency, the court of continuing jurisdiction, or the tribunal in which a child support order has been registered under Chapter 159. The tribunal in which the petition is filed obtains jurisdiction over the matter.

(c) In a case other than a Title IV-D case, the petition shall be filed in the court of continuing jurisdiction or the court in which a child support order has been registered under Chapter 159.

(d) A proceeding in a case filed with the Title IV-D agency under this chapter is governed by the contested case provisions of Chapter 2001, Government Code, except that Section 2001.054 does not apply to the proceeding. The director of the Title IV-D agency or the director's designee may render a final decision in a contested case proceeding under this chapter.

Sec. 232.005. Contents of Petition.

(a) A petition under this chapter must state that license suspension is required under Section 232.003 and allege:

(1) the name and, if known, social security number of the individual;

(2) the name of the licensing authority that issued a license the individual is believed to hold; and

(3) the amount of arrearages owed under the child support order or the facts associated with the individual's failure to comply with:

(A) a subpoena; or

(B) the terms of a court order providing for the possession of or access to a child.

(b) A petition under this chapter may include as an attachment a copy of:

(1) the record of child support payments maintained by the Title IV-D registry or local registry;

(2) the subpoena with which the individual has failed to comply, together with proof of service of the subpoena; or

(3) with respect to a petition for suspension under Section 232.003(c):

(A) the enforcement order rendered under Chapter 157 describing the manner in which the individual was found to have not complied with the terms of a court order providing for the possession of or access to a child; and

(B) the court order containing the provisions that the individual was found to have violated.

Sec. 232.006. Notice.

(a) On the filing of a petition under Section 232.004, the clerk of the court or the Title IV-D agency shall deliver to the individual:

(1) notice of the individual's right to a hearing before the court or agency;

(2) notice of the deadline for requesting a hearing; and

(3) a hearing request form if the proceeding is in a Title IV-D case.

(b) Notice under this section may be served:

(1) if the party has been ordered under Chapter 105 to provide the court and registry with the party's current mailing address, by mailing a copy of the notice to the respondent, together with a copy of the petition, by first class mail to the last mailing address of the respondent on file with the court and the state case registry; or

(2) as in civil cases generally.

(c) The notice must contain the following prominently displayed statement in boldfaced type, capital letters, or underlined:

Texas Family Code

"AN ACTION TO SUSPEND ONE OR MORE LICENSES ISSUED TO YOU HAS BEEN FILED AS PROVIDED BY CHAPTER 232, TEXAS FAMILY CODE. YOU MAY EMPLOY AN ATTORNEY TO REPRESENT YOU IN THIS ACTION. IF YOU OR YOUR ATTORNEY DO NOT REQUEST A HEARING BEFORE THE 21ST DAY AFTER THE DATE OF SERVICE OF THIS NOTICE, AN ORDER SUSPENDING YOUR LICENSE MAY BE RENDERED."

Sec. 232.007. Hearing on Petition to Suspend License.

(a) A request for a hearing and motion to stay suspension must be filed with the court or Title IV-D agency by the individual not later than the 20th day after the date of service of the notice under Section 232.006.

(b) If a request for a hearing is filed, the court or Title IV-D agency shall:

(1) promptly schedule a hearing;

(2) notify each party of the date, time, and location of the hearing; and

(3) stay suspension pending the hearing.

(c) In a case involving support arrearages, a record of child support payments made by the Title IV-D agency or a local registry is evidence of whether the payments were made. A copy of the record appearing regular on its face shall be admitted as evidence at a hearing under this chapter, including a hearing on a motion to revoke a stay. Either party may offer controverting evidence.

(d) In a case in which an individual has failed to comply with a subpoena, proof of service is evidence of delivery of the subpoena.

Sec. 232.008. Order Suspending License for Failure to Pay Child Support.

(a) On making the findings required by Section 232.003, the court or Title IV-D agency shall render an order suspending the license unless the individual:

(1) proves that all arrearages and the current month's support have been paid;

(2) shows good cause for failure to comply with the subpoena or the terms of the court order providing for the possession of or access to a child; or

(3) establishes an affirmative defense as provided by Section 157.008(c).

(b) Subject to Subsection (b-1), the court or Title IV-D agency may stay an order suspending a license conditioned on the individual's compliance with:

(1) a reasonable repayment schedule that is incorporated in the order;

(2) the requirements of a reissued and delivered subpoena; or

(3) the requirements of any court order pertaining to the possession of or access to a child.

(b-1) The court or Title IV-D agency may not stay an order under Subsection (b)(1) unless the individual makes an immediate partial payment in an amount specified by the court or Title IV-D agency. The amount specified may not be less than $200.

(c) An order suspending a license with a stay of the suspension may not be served on the licensing authority unless the stay is revoked as provided by this chapter.

(d) A final order suspending license rendered by a court or the Title IV-D agency shall be forwarded to the appropriate licensing authority by the clerk of the court or Title IV-D agency. The clerk shall collect from an obligor a fee of $5 for each order mailed.

(e) If the court or Title IV-D agency renders an order suspending license, the individual may also be ordered not to engage in the licensed activity.

(f) If the court or Title IV-D agency finds that the petition for suspension should be denied, the petition shall be dismissed without prejudice, and an order suspending license may not be rendered.

Sec. 232.009. Default Order.

The court or Title IV-D agency shall consider the allegations of the petition for suspension to be admitted and shall render an order suspending the license of an obligor without the requirement of a hearing if the court or Title IV-D agency determines that the individual failed to respond to a notice issued under Section 232.006 by:

(1) requesting a hearing; or

(2) appearing at a scheduled hearing.

Sec. 232.010. Review of Final Administrative Order.

An order issued by a Title IV-D agency under this chapter is a final agency decision and is subject to review under the substantial evidence rule as provided by Chapter 2001, Government Code.

Sec. 232.011. Action by Licensing Authority.

(a) On receipt of a final order suspending license, the licensing authority shall immediately determine if the authority has issued a license to the individual named on the order and, if a license has been issued:

(1) record the suspension of the license in the licensing authority's records;

(2) report the suspension as appropriate; and

(3) demand surrender of the suspended license if required by law for other cases in which a license is suspended.

(b) A licensing authority shall implement the terms of a final order suspending license without additional review or hearing. The authority may provide notice as appropriate to the license holder or to others concerned with the license.

(c) A licensing authority may not modify, remand, reverse, vacate, or stay an order suspending license issued under this chapter and may not review, vacate, or reconsider the terms of a final order suspending license.

(d) An individual who is the subject of a final order suspending license is not entitled to a refund for any fee or deposit paid to the licensing authority.

(e) An individual who continues to engage in the business, occupation, profession, or other licensed activity after the implementation of the order suspending license by the licensing authority is liable for the same civil and criminal penalties provided for engaging in the licensed activity without a license or while a license is suspended that apply to any other license holder of that licensing authority.

(f) A licensing authority is exempt from liability to a license holder for any act authorized under this chapter performed by the authority.

(g) Except as provided by this chapter, an order suspending license or dismissing a petition for the suspension of a license does not affect the power of a licensing authority to grant, deny, suspend, revoke, terminate, or renew a license.

(h) The denial or suspension of a driver's license under this chapter is governed by this chapter and not by the general licensing provisions of Chapter 521, Transportation Code.

(i) An order issued under this chapter to suspend a license applies to each license issued by the licensing authority subject to the order for which the obligor is eligible. The licensing authority may not issue or renew any other license for the obligor until the court or the Title IV-D agency renders an order vacating or staying an order suspending license.

Sec. 232.012. Motion to Revoke Stay.

(a) The obligee, support enforcement agency, court, or Title IV-D agency may file a motion to revoke the stay of an order suspending license if the individual who is subject of an order suspending license does not comply with:

(1) the terms of a reasonable repayment plan entered into by the individual;

(2) the requirements of a reissued subpoena; or

(3) the terms of any court order pertaining to the possession of or access to a child.

(b) Notice to the individual of a motion to revoke stay under this section may be given by personal service or by mail to the address provided by the individual, if any, in the order suspending license. The notice must include a notice of hearing. The notice must be provided to the individual not less than 10 days before the date of the hearing.

(c) A motion to revoke stay must allege the manner in which the individual failed to comply with the repayment plan, the reissued subpoena, or the court order pertaining to possession of or access to a child.

(d) If the court or Title IV-D agency finds that the individual is not in compliance with the terms of the repayment plan, reissued subpoena, or court order pertaining to possession of or access to a child, the court or agency shall revoke the stay of the order suspending license and render a final order suspending license.

Sec. 232.013. Vacating or Staying Order Suspending License.

(a) The court or Title IV-D agency may render an order vacating or staying an order suspending an individual's license if:

(1) the individual has:

(A) paid all delinquent child support or has established a satisfactory payment record;

(B) complied with the requirements of a reissued subpoena; or

(C) complied with the terms of any court order providing for the possession of or access to a child; or

(2) the court or Title IV-D agency determines that good cause exists for vacating or staying the order.

(b) The clerk of the court or Title IV-D agency shall promptly deliver an order vacating or staying an order suspending license to the appropriate licensing authority. The clerk shall collect from an obligor a fee of $5 for each order mailed.

(c) On receipt of an order vacating or staying an order suspending license, the licensing authority shall promptly issue the affected license to the individual if the individual is otherwise qualified for the license.

(d) An order rendered under this section does not affect the right of the child support agency or obligee to any other remedy provided by law, including the right to seek relief under this chapter. An order rendered under this section does not affect the power of a licensing authority to grant, deny, suspend, revoke, terminate, or renew a license as otherwise provided by law.

Sec. 232.0135. Denial of License Issuance or Renewal.

(a) A child support agency, as defined by Section 101.004, may provide notice to a licensing authority concerning an obligor who has failed to pay child support under a support order for six months or more that requests the authority to refuse to approve an application for issuance of a license to the obligor or renewal of an existing license of the obligor.

(b) A licensing authority that receives the information described by Subsection (a) shall refuse to approve an application for issuance of a license to the obligor or renewal of an existing license of the obligor until the authority is notified by the child support agency that the obligor has:

(1) paid all child support arrearages;

(2) made an immediate payment of not less than $200 toward child support arrearages owed and established with the agency a satisfactory repayment schedule for the remainder or is in compliance with a court order for payment of the arrearages;

(3) been granted an exemption from this subsection as part of a court-supervised plan to improve the obligor's earnings and child support payments; or

(4) successfully contested the denial of issuance or renewal of license under Subsection (d).

(c) On providing a licensing authority with the notice described by Subsection (a), the child support agency shall send a copy to the obligor by first class mail and inform the obligor of the steps the obligor must take to permit the authority to approve the obligor's application for license issuance or renewal.

(d) An obligor receiving notice under Subsection (c) may request a review by the child support agency to resolve any issue in dispute regarding the identity of the obligor or the existence or amount of child support arrearages. The agency shall promptly provide an opportunity for a review, either by telephone or in person, as appropriate to the circumstances. After the review, if appropriate, the agency may notify the licensing authority that it may approve the obligor's application for issuance or renewal of license. If the agency and the obligor fail to resolve any issue in dispute, the obligor, not later than the 30th day after the date of receiving notice of the agency's determination from the review, may file a motion with the court to direct the agency to withdraw the notice under Subsection (a) and request a hearing on the motion. The obligor's application for license issuance or renewal may not be approved by the licensing authority until the court rules on the motion. If, after a review by the agency or a hearing by the court, the agency withdraws the notice under Subsection (a), the agency shall reimburse the obligor the amount of any fee charged the obligor under Section 232.014.

(e) If an obligor enters into a repayment agreement with the child support agency under this section, the agency may incorporate the agreement in an order to be filed with and confirmed by the court in the manner provided for agreed orders under Chapter 233.

(f) In this section, "licensing authority" does not include the State Securities Board.

Sec. 232.014. Fee by Licensing Authority.

(a) A licensing authority may charge a fee to an individual who is the subject of an order suspending license or of an action of a child support agency under Section 232.0135 to deny issuance or renewal of license in an amount sufficient to recover the administrative costs incurred by the authority under this chapter.

(b) A fee collected by the Texas Department of Motor Vehicles shall be deposited to the credit of the Texas Department of Motor Vehicles fund. A fee collected by the Department of Public Safety shall be deposited to the credit of the state highway fund.

Sec. 232.015. Cooperation Between Licensing Authorities and Title IV-D Agency.

(a) The Title IV-D agency may request from each licensing authority the name, address, social security number, license renewal date, and other identifying information for each individual who holds, applies for, or renews a license issued by the authority.

(b) A licensing authority shall provide the requested information in the form and manner identified by the Title IV-D agency.

(c) The Title IV-D agency may enter into a cooperative agreement with a licensing authority to administer this chapter in a cost-effective manner.

(d) The Title IV-D agency may adopt a reasonable implementation schedule for the requirements of this section.

(e) The Title IV-D agency, the comptroller, and the Texas Alcoholic Beverage Commission shall by rule specify additional prerequisites for the suspension of licenses relating to state taxes collected under Title 2, Tax Code. The joint rules must be adopted not later than March 1, 1996.

Sec. 232.016. Rules, Forms, and Procedures.

The Title IV-D agency by rule shall prescribe forms and procedures for the implementation of this chapter.

SUBTITLE E PROTECTION OF THE CHILD

CHAPTER 261 INVESTIGATION OF REPORT OF CHILD ABUSE OR NEGLECT

SUBCHAPTER A GENERAL PROVISIONS

Sec. 261.001. Definitions.

In this chapter:

(1) "Abuse" includes the following acts or omissions by a person:

(A) mental or emotional injury to a child that results in an observable and material impairment in the child's growth, development, or psychological functioning;

(B) causing or permitting the child to be in a situation in which the child sustains a mental or emotional injury that results in an observable and material impairment in the child's growth, development, or psychological functioning;

(C) physical injury that results in substantial harm to the child, or the genuine threat of substantial harm from physical injury to the child, including an injury that is at variance with the history or explanation given and excluding an accident or reasonable discipline by a parent, guardian, or managing or possessory conservator that does not expose the child to a substantial risk of harm;

(D) failure to make a reasonable effort to prevent an action by another person that results in physical injury that results in substantial harm to the child;

(E) sexual conduct harmful to a child's mental, emotional, or physical welfare, including conduct that constitutes the offense of continuous sexual abuse of young child or disabled individual under Section 21.02, Penal Code, indecency with a child under Section 21.11, Penal Code, sexual assault under Section 22.011, Penal Code, or aggravated sexual assault under Section 22.021, Penal Code;

(F) failure to make a reasonable effort to prevent sexual conduct harmful to a child;

(G) compelling or encouraging the child to engage in sexual conduct as defined by Section 43.01, Penal Code, including compelling or encouraging the child in a manner that constitutes an offense of trafficking of persons under Section 20A.02(a)(7) or (8), Penal Code, solicitation of prostitution under Section 43.021, Penal Code, or compelling prostitution under Section 43.05(a)(2), Penal Code;

(H) causing, permitting, encouraging, engaging in, or allowing the photographing, filming, or depicting of the child if the person knew or should have known that the resulting photograph, film, or depiction of the child is obscene as defined by Section 43.21, Penal Code, or pornographic;

(I) the current use by a person of a controlled substance as defined by Chapter 481, Health and Safety Code, in a manner or to the extent that the use results in physical, mental, or emotional injury to a child;

(J) causing, expressly permitting, or encouraging a child to use a controlled substance as defined by Chapter 481, Health and Safety Code;

(K) causing, permitting, encouraging, engaging in, or allowing a sexual performance by a child as defined by Section 43.25, Penal Code;

(L) knowingly causing, permitting, encouraging, engaging in, or allowing a child to be trafficked in a manner punishable as an offense under Section 20A.02(a)(5), (6), (7), or (8), Penal Code, or the failure to make a reasonable effort to prevent a child from being trafficked in a manner punishable as an offense under any of those sections; or

(M) forcing or coercing a child to enter into a marriage.

(2) "Department" means the Department of Family and Protective Services.

(3) "Exploitation" means the illegal or improper use of a child or of the resources of a child for monetary or personal benefit, profit, or gain by an employee, volunteer, or other individual working under the auspices of a facility or program as further described by rule or policy.

(4) **[As amended by Acts 2021, 87th Leg., ch. 29 (HB 2536)]** "Neglect":

(A) includes:

(i) the leaving of a child in a situation where the child would be exposed to a substantial risk of physical or mental harm, without arranging for necessary care for the child, and the demonstration of an intent not to return by a parent, guardian, or managing or possessory conservator of the child;

(ii) the following acts or omissions by a person:

(a) placing a child in or failing to remove a child from a situation that a reasonable person would realize requires judgment or actions beyond the child's level of maturity, physical condition, or mental abilities and that results in bodily injury or a substantial risk of immediate harm to the child;

(b) failing to seek, obtain, or follow through with medical care for a child, with the failure resulting in or presenting a substantial risk of death, disfigurement, or bodily injury or with the failure resulting in an observable and material impairment to the growth, development, or functioning of the child;

(c) the failure to provide a child with food, clothing, or shelter necessary to sustain the life or health of the child, excluding failure caused primarily by financial inability unless relief services had been offered and refused;

(d) placing a child in or failing to remove the child from a situation in which the child would be exposed to a substantial risk of sexual conduct harmful to the child; or

(e) placing a child in or failing to remove the child from a situation in which the child would be exposed to acts or omissions that constitute abuse under Subdivision (1)(E), (F), (G), (H), or (K) committed against another child;

(iii) the failure by the person responsible for a child's care, custody, or welfare to permit the child to return to the child's home without arranging for the necessary care for the child after the child has been absent from the home for any reason, including having been in residential placement or having run away; or

(iv) a negligent act or omission by an employee, volunteer, or other individual working under the auspices of a facility or program, including failure to comply with an individual treatment plan, plan of care, or individualized service plan, that causes or may cause substantial emotional harm or physical injury to, or the death of, a child served by the facility or program as further described by rule or policy; and

(B) does not include:

(i) the refusal by a person responsible for a child's care, custody, or welfare to permit the child to remain in or return to the child's home resulting in the placement of the child in the conservatorship of the department if:

(a) the child has a severe emotional disturbance;

(b) the person's refusal is based solely on the person's inability to obtain mental health services necessary to protect the safety and well-being of the child; and

(c) the person has exhausted all reasonable means available to the person to obtain the mental health services described by Sub-subparagraph (b); or

(ii) a decision by a person responsible for a child's care, custody, or welfare to:

(a) obtain an opinion from more than one medical provider relating to the child's medical care;

(b) transfer the child's medical care to a new medical provider; or

(c) transfer the child to another health care facility.

(4) **[As amended by Acts 2021, 87th Leg., ch. 8 (HB 567)]** "Neglect" means an act or failure to act by a person responsible for a child's care, custody, or welfare evidencing the person's blatant disregard for the consequences of the act or failure to act that results in harm to the child or that creates an immediate danger to the child's physical health or safety and:

(A) includes:

(i) the leaving of a child in a situation where the child would be exposed to an immediate danger of physical or mental harm, without arranging for necessary care for the child, and the demonstration of an intent not to return by a parent, guardian, or managing or possessory conservator of the child;

(ii) the following acts or omissions by a person:

(a) placing a child in or failing to remove a child from a situation that a reasonable person would realize requires judgment or actions beyond the child's level of maturity, physical condition, or mental abilities and that results in bodily injury or an immediate danger of harm to the child;

(b) failing to seek, obtain, or follow through with medical care for a child, with the failure resulting in or presenting an immediate danger of death, disfigurement, or bodily injury or with the failure resulting in an observable and material impairment to the growth, development, or functioning of the child;

(c) the failure to provide a child with food, clothing, or shelter necessary to sustain the life or health of the child, excluding failure caused primarily by financial inability unless relief services had been offered and refused;

(d) placing a child in or failing to remove the child from a situation in which the child would be exposed to an immediate danger of sexual conduct harmful to the child; or

(e) placing a child in or failing to remove the child from a situation in which the child would be exposed to acts or omissions that constitute abuse under Subdivision (1)(E), (F), (G), (H), or (K) committed against another child;

(iii) the failure by the person responsible for a child's care, custody, or welfare to permit the child to return to the child's home without arranging for the necessary care for the child after the child has been absent from the home for any reason, including having been in residential placement or having run away; or

(iv) a negligent act or omission by an employee, volunteer, or other individual working under the auspices of a facility or program, including failure to comply with an individual treatment plan, plan of care, or individualized service plan, that causes or may cause substantial emotional harm or physical injury to, or the death of, a child served by the facility or program as further described by rule or policy; and

(B) does not include:

(i) the refusal by a person responsible for a child's care, custody, or welfare to permit the child to remain in or return to the child's home resulting in the placement of the child in the conservatorship of the department if:

(a) the child has a severe emotional disturbance;

(b) the person's refusal is based solely on the person's inability to obtain mental health services necessary to protect the safety and well-being of the child; and

(c) the person has exhausted all reasonable means available to the person to obtain the mental health services described by Sub-subparagraph (b); or

(ii) allowing the child to engage in independent activities that are appropriate and typical for the child's level of maturity, physical condition, developmental abilities, or culture.

(5) "Person responsible for a child's care, custody, or welfare" means a person who traditionally is responsible for a child's care, custody, or welfare, including:

(A) a parent, guardian, managing or possessory conservator, or foster parent of the child;

(B) a member of the child's family or household as defined by Chapter 71;

(C) a person with whom the child's parent cohabits;

(D) school personnel or a volunteer at the child's school;

(E) personnel or a volunteer at a public or private child-care facility that provides services for the child or at a public or private residential institution or facility where the child resides; or

(F) an employee, volunteer, or other person working under the supervision of a licensed or unlicensed child-care facility, including a family home, residential child-care facility, employer-based day-care facility, or shelter day-care facility, as those terms are defined in Chapter 42, Human Resources Code.

(6) "Report" means a report that alleged or suspected abuse or neglect of a child has occurred or may occur.

(7) [Repealed.]

(8) [Repealed by Acts 2015, 84th Leg., ch. 1 (S.B. 219), § 1.203(4), effective April 2, 2015.]

(9) "Severe emotional disturbance" means a mental, behavioral, or emotional disorder of sufficient duration to result in functional impairment that substantially interferes with or limits a person's role or ability to function in family, school, or community activities.

Sec. 261.002. Central Registry.

(a) The department shall establish and maintain a central registry of the names of individuals found by the department to have abused or neglected a child.

(b) The executive commissioner shall adopt rules necessary to carry out this section. The rules shall:

(1) prohibit the department from making a finding of abuse or neglect against a person in a case in which the department is named managing conservator of a child who has a severe emotional disturbance only because the child's family is unable to obtain mental health services for the child;

(2) establish guidelines for reviewing the records in the registry and removing those records in which the department was named managing conservator of a child who has a severe emotional disturbance only because the child's family was unable to obtain mental health services for the child;

(3) require the department to remove a person's name from the central registry maintained under this section not later than the 10th business day after the date the department receives notice that a finding of abuse and neglect against the person is overturned in:

(A) an administrative review or an appeal of the review conducted under Section 261.309(c);

(B) a review or an appeal of the review conducted by the office of consumer affairs of the department; or

(C) a hearing or an appeal conducted by the State Office of Administrative Hearings; and

(4) require the department to update any relevant department files to reflect an overturned finding of abuse or neglect against a person not later than the 10th business day after the date the finding is overturned in a review, hearing, or appeal described by Subdivision (3).

(c) The department may enter into agreements with other states to allow for the exchange of reports of child abuse and neglect in other states' central registry systems. The department shall use information obtained under this subsection in performing the background checks required under Section 42.056, Human Resources Code. The department shall cooperate with federal agencies and shall provide information and reports of child abuse and neglect to the appropriate federal agency that maintains the national registry for child abuse and neglect, if a national registry exists.

Sec. 261.003. Application to Students in School for Deaf or School for Blind and Visually Impaired.

This chapter applies to the investigation of a report of abuse or neglect of a student, without regard to the age of the student, in the Texas School for the Deaf or the Texas School for the Blind and Visually Impaired.

Sec. 261.004. Tracking of Recurrence of Child Abuse or Neglect Reports.

(a) The department shall collect and monitor data regarding repeated reports of abuse or neglect:

(1) involving the same child, including reports of abuse or neglect of the child made while the child resided in other households and reports of abuse or neglect of the child by different alleged perpetrators made while the child resided in the same household; or

(2) by the same alleged perpetrator.

(b) In monitoring reports of abuse or neglect under Subsection (a), the department shall group together separate reports involving different children residing in the same household.

(c) The department shall consider any report collected under Subsection (a) involving any child or adult who is a part of a child's household when making case priority determinations or when conducting service or safety planning for the child or the child's family.

Sec. 261.004. Reference to Executive Commissioner or Commission. [Renumbered]

Sec. 261.005. Reference to Executive Commissioner or Commission.

In this chapter:

(1) a reference to the executive commissioner or the executive commissioner of the Health and Human Services Commission means the commissioner of the department; and

(2) a reference to the Health and Human Services Commission means the department.

SUBCHAPTER B
REPORT OF ABUSE OR NEGLECT; IMMUNITIES

Sec. 261.101. Persons Required to Report; Time to Report.

(a) A person having reasonable cause to believe that a child's physical or mental health or welfare has been adversely affected by abuse or neglect by any person shall immediately make a report as provided by this subchapter.

(b) If a professional has reasonable cause to believe that a child has been abused or neglected or may be abused or neglected, or that a child is a victim of an offense under Section 21.11, Penal Code, and the professional has reasonable cause to believe that the child has been abused as defined by Section 261.001, the professional shall make a report not later than the 48th hour after the hour the professional first has reasonable cause to believe that the child has been or may be abused or neglected or is a victim of an offense under Section 21.11, Penal Code. A professional may not delegate to or rely on another person to make the report. In this subsection, "professional" means an individual who is licensed or certified by the state or who is an employee of a facility licensed, certified, or operated by the state and who, in the normal course of official duties or duties for which a license or certification is required, has direct contact with children. The term includes teachers, nurses, doctors, day-care employees, employees of a clinic or health care facility that provides reproductive services, juvenile probation officers, and juvenile detention or correctional officers.

(b-1) In addition to the duty to make a report under Subsection (a) or (b), a person or professional shall make a report in the manner required by Subsection (a) or (b), as applicable, if the person or professional has reasonable cause to believe that an adult was a victim of abuse or neglect as a child and the person or professional determines in good faith that disclosure of the information is necessary to protect the health and safety of:

(1) another child; or

(2) an elderly person or person with a disability as defined by Section 48.002, Human Resources Code.

(c) The requirement to report under this section applies without exception to an individual whose personal communications may otherwise be privileged, including an attorney, a member of the clergy, a medical practitioner, a social worker, a mental health professional, an employee or member of a board that licenses or certifies a professional, and an employee of a clinic or health care facility that provides reproductive services.

(d) Unless waived in writing by the person making the report, the identity of an individual making a report under this chapter is confidential and may be disclosed only:

(1) as provided by Section 261.201; or

(2) to a law enforcement officer for the purposes of conducting a criminal investigation of the report.

Sec. 261.102. Matters to Be Reported.

A report should reflect the reporter's belief that a child has been or may be abused or neglected or has died of abuse or neglect.

Sec. 261.103. Report Made to Appropriate Agency.

(a) Except as provided by Subsections (b) and (c) and Section 261.405, a report shall be made to:

(1) any local or state law enforcement agency;

(2) the department; or

(3) the state agency that operates, licenses, certifies, or registers the facility in which the alleged abuse or neglect occurred.

(b) A report may be made to the Texas Juvenile Justice Department instead of the entities listed under Subsection (a) if the report is based on information provided by a child while under the supervision of the Texas Juvenile Justice Department concerning the child's alleged abuse of another child.

(c) Notwithstanding Subsection (a), a report, other than a report under Subsection (a)(3) or Section 261.405, must be made to the department if the alleged or suspected abuse or neglect involves a person responsible for the care, custody, or welfare of the child.

Sec. 261.104. Contents of Report.

The person making a report shall identify, if known:

(1) the name and address of the child;

(2) the name and address of the person responsible for the care, custody, or welfare of the child; and

(3) any other pertinent information concerning the alleged or suspected abuse or neglect.

Sec. 261.105. Referral of Report by Department or Law Enforcement.

(a) All reports received by a local or state law enforcement agency that allege abuse or neglect by a person responsible for a child's care, custody, or welfare shall be referred immediately to the department.

(b) The department shall immediately notify the appropriate state or local law enforcement agency of any report it receives, other than a report from a law enforcement agency, that concerns the suspected abuse or neglect of a child or death of a child from abuse or neglect.

(c) In addition to notifying a law enforcement agency, if the report relates to a child in a facility operated, licensed, certified, or registered by a state agency, the department shall refer the report to the agency for investigation.

(c-1) Notwithstanding Subsections (b) and (c), if a report under this section relates to a child with an intellectual disability receiving services in a state supported living center as defined by Section 531.002, Health and Safety Code, or the ICF-IID component of the Rio Grande State Center, the department shall proceed with the investigation of the report as provided by Section 261.404.

(d) If the department initiates an investigation and determines that the abuse or neglect does not involve a person responsible for the child's care, custody, or welfare, the department shall refer the report to a law enforcement agency for further investigation. If the department determines that the abuse or neglect involves an employee of a public or private elementary or secondary school, and that the child is a student at the school, the department shall orally notify the superintendent of the school district, the director of the open-enrollment charter school, or the chief executive officer of the private school in which the employee is employed about the investigation.

(e) In cooperation with the department, the Texas Juvenile Justice Department by rule shall adopt guidelines for identifying a report made to the Texas Juvenile Justice Department under Section 261.103(b) that is appropriate to refer to the department or a law enforcement agency for investigation. Guidelines adopted under this subsection must require the Texas Juvenile Justice Department to consider the severity and immediacy of the alleged abuse or neglect of the child victim.

Sec. 261.1055. Notification of District Attorneys.

(a) A district attorney may inform the department that the district attorney wishes to receive notification of some or all reports of suspected abuse or neglect of children who were in the county at the time the report was made or who were in the county at the time of the alleged abuse or neglect.

(b) If the district attorney makes the notification under this section, the department shall, on receipt of a report of suspected abuse or neglect, immediately notify the district attorney as requested and the department shall forward a copy of the reports to the district attorney on request.

Sec. 261.106. Immunities.

(a) A person acting in good faith who reports or assists in the investigation of a report of alleged child abuse or neglect or who testifies or otherwise participates in a judicial proceeding arising from a report, petition, or investigation of alleged child abuse or neglect is immune from civil or criminal liability that might otherwise be incurred or imposed.

(b) Immunity from civil and criminal liability extends to an authorized volunteer of the department or a law enforcement officer who participates at the request of the department in an investigation of alleged or suspected abuse or neglect or in an action arising from an investigation if the person was acting in good faith and in the scope of the person's responsibilities.

(c) A person who reports the person's own abuse or neglect of a child or who acts in bad faith or with malicious purpose in reporting alleged child abuse or neglect is not immune from civil or criminal liability.

Sec. 261.107. False Report; Criminal Penalty; Civil Penalty.

(a) A person commits an offense if, with the intent to deceive, the person knowingly makes a report as provided in this chapter that is false. An offense under this subsection is a state jail felony unless it is shown on the trial of the offense that the person has previously been convicted under this section, in which case the offense is a felony of the third degree.

(b) A finding by a court in a suit affecting the parent-child relationship that a report made under this chapter before or during the suit was false or lacking factual foundation may be grounds for the court to modify an order providing for possession of or access to the child who was the subject of the report by restricting further access to the child by the person who made the report.

(c) The appropriate county prosecuting attorney shall be responsible for the prosecution of an offense under this section.

(d) The court shall order a person who is convicted of an offense under Subsection (a) to pay any reasonable attorney's fees incurred by the person who was falsely accused of abuse or neglect in any proceeding relating to the false report.

(e) A person who engages in conduct described by Subsection (a) is liable to the state for a civil penalty of $1,000. The attorney general shall bring an action to recover a civil penalty authorized by this subsection.

Sec. 261.108. Frivolous Claims Against Person Reporting.

(a) In this section:

(1) "Claim" means an action or claim by a party, including a plaintiff, counterclaimant, cross-claimant, or third-party plaintiff, requesting recovery of damages.

(2) "Defendant" means a party against whom a claim is made.

(b) A court shall award a defendant reasonable attorney's fees and other expenses related to the defense of a claim filed against the defendant for damages or other relief arising from reporting or assisting in the investigation of a report under this chapter or participating in a judicial proceeding resulting from the report if:

(1) the court finds that the claim is frivolous, unreasonable, or without foundation because the defendant is immune from liability under Section 261.106; and

(2) the claim is dismissed or judgment is rendered for the defendant.

(c) To recover under this section, the defendant must, at any time after the filing of a claim, file a written motion stating that:

(1) the claim is frivolous, unreasonable, or without foundation because the defendant is immune from liability under Section 261.106; and

(2) the defendant requests the court to award reasonable attorney's fees and other expenses related to the defense of the claim.

Sec. 261.109. Failure to Report; Penalty.

(a) A person commits an offense if the person is required to make a report under Section 261.101(a) and knowingly fails to make a report as provided in this chapter.

(a-1) A person who is a professional as defined by Section 261.101(b) commits an offense if the person is required to make a report under Section 261.101(b) and knowingly fails to make a report as provided in this chapter.

(b) An offense under Subsection (a) is a Class A misdemeanor, except that the offense is a state jail felony if it is shown on the trial of the offense that the child was a person with an intellectual disability who resided in a state supported living center, the ICF-IID component of the Rio Grande State Center, or a facility licensed under Chapter 252, Health and Safety Code, and the actor knew that the child had suffered serious bodily injury as a result of the abuse or neglect.

(c) An offense under Subsection (a-1) is a Class A misdemeanor, except that the offense is a state jail felony if it is shown on the trial of the offense that the actor intended to conceal the abuse or neglect.

Sec. 261.110. Employer Retaliation Prohibited.

(a) In this section:

(1) "Adverse employment action" means an action that affects an employee's compensation, promotion, transfer, work assignment, or performance evaluation, or any other employment action that would dissuade a reasonable employee from making or supporting a report of abuse or neglect under Section 261.101.

(2) "Professional" has the meaning assigned by Section 261.101(b).

(b) An employer may not suspend or terminate the employment of, discriminate against, or take any other adverse employment action against a person who is a professional and who in good faith:

(1) reports child abuse or neglect to:

(A) the person's supervisor;

(B) an administrator of the facility where the person is employed;

(C) a state regulatory agency; or

(D) a law enforcement agency; or

(2) initiates or cooperates with an investigation or proceeding by a governmental entity relating to an allegation of child abuse or neglect.

(c) A person may sue for injunctive relief, damages, or both if, in violation of this section, the person:

(1) is suspended or terminated from the person's employment;

(2) is discriminated against; or

(3) suffers any other adverse employment action.

(d) A plaintiff who prevails in a suit under this section may recover:

(1) actual damages, including damages for mental anguish even if an injury other than mental anguish is not shown;

(2) exemplary damages under Chapter 41, Civil Practice and Remedies Code, if the employer is a private employer;

(3) court costs; and

(4) reasonable attorney's fees.

(e) In addition to amounts recovered under Subsection (d), a plaintiff who prevails in a suit under this section is entitled to:

(1) reinstatement to the person's former position or a position that is comparable in terms of compensation, benefits, and other conditions of employment;

(2) reinstatement of any fringe benefits and seniority rights lost because of the suspension, termination, or discrimination; and

(3) compensation for wages lost during the period of suspension or termination.

(f) A public employee who alleges a violation of this section may sue the employing state or local governmental entity for the relief provided for by this section. Sovereign immunity is waived and abolished to the extent of liability created by this section. A person having a claim under this section may sue a governmental unit for damages allowed by this section.

(g) In a suit under this section against an employing state or local governmental entity, a plaintiff may not recover compensatory damages for future pecuniary losses, emotional pain, suffering, inconvenience, mental anguish, loss of enjoyment of life, and other nonpecuniary losses in an amount that exceeds:

(1) $50,000, if the employing state or local governmental entity has fewer than 101 employees in each of 20 or more calendar weeks in the calendar year in which the suit is filed or in the preceding year;

(2) $100,000, if the employing state or local governmental entity has more than 100 and fewer than 201 employees in each of 20 or more calendar weeks in the calendar year in which the suit is filed or in the preceding year;

(3) $200,000, if the employing state or local governmental entity has more than 200 and fewer than 501 employees in each of 20 or more calendar weeks in the calendar year in which the suit is filed or in the preceding year; and

(4) $250,000, if the employing state or local governmental entity has more than 500 employees in each of 20 or more calendar weeks in the calendar year in which the suit is filed or in the preceding year.

(h) If more than one subdivision of Subsection (g) applies to an employing state or local governmental entity, the amount of monetary damages that may be recovered from the entity in a suit brought under this section is governed by the applicable provision that provides the highest damage award.

(i) A plaintiff suing under this section has the burden of proof, except that there is a rebuttable presumption that the plaintiff's employment was suspended or terminated or that the plaintiff was otherwise discriminated against for reporting abuse or neglect if the suspension, termination, or discrimination occurs before the 61st day after the date on which the person made a report in good faith.

(j) A suit under this section may be brought in a district or county court of the county in which:

(1) the plaintiff was employed by the defendant; or

(2) the defendant conducts business.

(k) It is an affirmative defense to a suit under Subsection (b) that an employer would have taken the action against the employee that forms the basis of the suit based solely on information, observation, or evidence that is not related to the fact that the employee reported child abuse or neglect or initiated or cooperated with an investigation or proceeding relating to an allegation of child abuse or neglect.

(*l*) A public employee who has a cause of action under Chapter 554, Government Code, based on conduct described by Subsection (b) may not bring an action based on that conduct under this section.

(m) This section does not apply to a person who reports the person's own abuse or neglect of a child or who initiates or cooperates with an investigation or proceeding by a governmental entity relating to an allegation of the person's own abuse or neglect of a child.

Sec. 261.111. Refusal of Psychiatric or Psychological Treatment of Child.

(a) In this section, "psychotropic medication" has the meaning assigned by Section 266.001.

(b) The refusal of a parent, guardian, or managing or possessory conservator of a child to administer or consent to the administration of a psychotropic medication to the child, or to consent to any other psychiatric or psychological treatment of the child, does not by itself constitute neglect of the child unless the refusal to consent:

(1) presents a substantial risk of death, disfigurement, or bodily injury to the child; or

(2) has resulted in an observable and material impairment to the growth, development, or functioning of the child.

SUBCHAPTER C CONFIDENTIALITY AND PRIVILEGED COMMUNICATION

Sec. 261.201. Confidentiality and Disclosure of Information.

(a) Except as provided by Section 261.203, the following information is confidential, is not subject to public release under Chapter 552, Government Code, and may be disclosed only for purposes consistent with this code and applicable federal or state law or under rules adopted by an investigating agency:

(1) a report of alleged or suspected abuse or neglect made under this chapter and the identity of the person making the report; and

(2) except as otherwise provided in this section, the files, reports, records, communications, audiotapes, videotapes, and working papers used or developed in an investigation under this chapter or in providing services as a result of an investigation.

(b) A court may order the disclosure of information that is confidential under this section if:

(1) a motion has been filed with the court requesting the release of the information;

(2) a notice of hearing has been served on the investigating agency and all other interested parties; and

(3) after hearing and an in camera review of the requested information, the court determines that the disclosure of the requested information is:

(A) essential to the administration of justice; and

(B) not likely to endanger the life or safety of:

(i) a child who is the subject of the report of alleged or suspected abuse or neglect;

(ii) a person who makes a report of alleged or suspected abuse or neglect; or

(iii) any other person who participates in an investigation of reported abuse or neglect or who provides care for the child.

(b-1) On a motion of one of the parties in a contested case before an administrative law judge relating to the license or certification of a professional, as defined by Section 261.101(b), or an educator, as defined by Section 5.001, Education Code, the administrative law judge may order the disclosure of information that is confidential under this section that relates to the matter before the administrative law judge after a hearing for which notice is provided as required by Subsection (b)(2) and making the review and determination required by Subsection (b)(3). Before the department may release information under this subsection, the department must edit the information to protect the confidentiality of the identity of any person who makes a report of abuse or neglect.

(c) In addition to Subsection (b), a court, on its own motion, may order disclosure of information that is confidential under this section if:

(1) the order is rendered at a hearing for which all parties have been given notice;

(2) the court finds that disclosure of the information is:

(A) essential to the administration of justice; and

(B) not likely to endanger the life or safety of:

(i) a child who is the subject of the report of alleged or suspected abuse or neglect;

(ii) a person who makes a report of alleged or suspected abuse or neglect; or

(iii) any other person who participates in an investigation of reported abuse or neglect or who provides care for the child; and

(3) the order is reduced to writing or made on the record in open court.

(d) The adoptive parents of a child who was the subject of an investigation and an adult who was the subject of an investigation as a child are entitled to examine and make copies of any report, record, working paper, or other information in the possession, custody, or control of the state that pertains to the history of the child. The department may edit the documents to protect the identity of the biological parents and any other person whose identity is confidential, unless this information is already known to the adoptive parents or is readily available through other sources, including the court records of a suit to terminate the parent-child relationship under Chapter 161.

(e) Before placing a child who was the subject of an investigation, the department shall notify the prospective adoptive parents of their right to examine any report, record, working paper, or other information in the possession, custody, or control of the department that pertains to the history of the child.

(f) The department shall provide prospective adoptive parents an opportunity to examine information under this section as early as practicable before placing a child.

(f-1) The department shall provide to a relative or other individual with whom a child is placed any information the department considers necessary to ensure that the relative or other individual is prepared to meet the needs of the child. The information required by this subsection may include information related to any abuse or neglect suffered by the child.

(g) Notwithstanding Subsection (b), the department, on request and subject to department rule, shall provide to the parent, managing conservator, or other legal representative of a child who is the subject of reported abuse or neglect information concerning the reported abuse or neglect that would otherwise be confidential under this section if the department has edited the information to protect the confidentiality of the identity of the person who made the report and any other person whose life or safety may be endangered by the disclosure.

(h) This section does not apply to an investigation of child abuse or neglect in a home or facility regulated under Chapter 42, Human Resources Code.

(i) Notwithstanding Subsection (a), the Texas Juvenile Justice Department shall release a report of alleged or suspected abuse or neglect made under this chapter if:

(1) the report relates to a report of abuse or neglect involving a child committed to the Texas Juvenile Justice Department during the period that the child is committed to that department; and

(2) the Texas Juvenile Justice Department is not prohibited by Chapter 552, Government Code, or other law from disclosing the report.

(j) The Texas Juvenile Justice Department shall edit any report disclosed under Subsection (i) to protect the identity of:

(1) a child who is the subject of the report of alleged or suspected abuse or neglect;

(2) the person who made the report; and

(3) any other person whose life or safety may be endangered by the disclosure.

(k) Notwithstanding Subsection (a), an investigating agency, other than the department or the Texas Juvenile Justice Department, on request, shall provide to the parent, managing conservator, or other legal representative of a child who is the subject of reported abuse or neglect, or to the child if the child is at least 18 years of age, information concerning the reported abuse or neglect that would otherwise be confidential under this section. The investigating agency shall withhold information under this subsection if the parent, managing conservator, or other legal representative of the child requesting the information is alleged to have committed the abuse or neglect.

(*l*) Before a child or a parent, managing conservator, or other legal representative of a child may inspect or copy a record or file concerning the child under Subsection (k), the custodian of the record or file must redact:

(1) any personally identifiable information about a victim or witness under 18 years of age unless that victim or witness is:

(A) the child who is the subject of the report; or

(B) another child of the parent, managing conservator, or other legal representative requesting the information;

(2) any information that is excepted from required disclosure under Chapter 552, Government Code, or other law; and

(3) the identity of the person who made the report.

Sec. 261.202. Privileged Communication.

In a proceeding regarding the abuse or neglect of a child, evidence may not be excluded on the ground of privileged communication except in the case of communications between an attorney and client.

Sec. 261.203. Information Relating to Child Fatality.

(a) Not later than the fifth day after the date the department receives a request for information about a child fatality with respect to which the department is conducting an investigation of alleged abuse or neglect, the department shall release:

(1) the age and sex of the child;

(2) the date of death;

(3) whether the state was the managing conservator of the child at the time of the child's death; and

(4) whether the child resided with the child's parent, managing conservator, guardian, or other person entitled to possession of the child at the time of the child's death.

(b) If, after a child abuse or neglect investigation described by Subsection (a) is completed, the department determines a child's death or a child's near fatality was caused by abuse or neglect, the department on request shall promptly release investigation information not prohibited from release under federal law, including the following information:

(1) the information described by Subsection (a), if not previously released to the person requesting the information;

(2) information on whether a child's death or near fatality:

(A) was determined by the department to be attributable to abuse or neglect; or

(B) resulted in a criminal investigation or the filing of criminal charges if known at the time the investigation is completed;

(3) for cases in which the child's death or near fatality occurred while the child was living with the child's parent, managing conservator, guardian, or other person entitled to possession of the child:

(A) a summary of any previous reports of abuse or neglect of the child or another child made while the child was living with that parent, managing conservator, guardian, or other person entitled to possession of the child;

(B) the disposition of any report under Paragraph (A);

(C) a description of any services, including family-based safety services, that were provided or offered by the department to the child or the child's family as a result of any report under Paragraph (A) and whether the services were accepted or declined; and

(D) the results of any risk or safety assessment completed by the department relating to the child; and

(4) for a case in which the child's death or near fatality occurred while the child was in substitute care with the department or with a residential child-care provider regulated under Chapter 42, Human Resources Code, the following information:

(A) the date the substitute care provider with whom the child was residing at the time of death or near fatality was licensed or verified;

(B) a summary of any previous reports of abuse or neglect investigated by the department relating to the substitute care provider, including the disposition of any investigation resulting from a report;

(C) any reported licensing violations, including notice of any action taken by the department regarding a violation; and

(D) records of any training completed by the substitute care provider while the child was placed with the provider.

(c) If the department is unable to release the information required by Subsection (b) before the 11th day after the date the department receives a request for the information or the date the investigation of the child fatality is completed, whichever is later, the department shall inform the person requesting the information of the date the department will release the information.

(d) [Repealed by Acts 2015, 84th Leg., ch. 944 (S.B. 206), § 86(7), effective September 1, 2015.]

(e) Before the department releases any information under Subsection (b), the department shall redact from the records any information the release of which would:

(1) identify:

(A) the individual who reported the abuse or neglect; or

(B) any other individual other than the deceased child or an alleged perpetrator of the abuse or neglect;

(2) jeopardize an ongoing criminal investigation or prosecution;

(3) endanger the life or safety of any individual; or

(4) violate other state or federal law.

(f) The executive commissioner of the Health and Human Services Commission shall adopt rules to implement this section.

Sec. 261.204. Annual Child Fatality Report.

(a) Not later than March 1 of each year, the department shall publish an aggregated report using information compiled from each child fatality investigation for which the department made a finding regarding abuse or neglect, including cases in which the department determined the fatality was not the result of abuse or neglect. The report must protect the identity of individuals involved and contain the following information:

(1) the age and sex of the child and the county in which the fatality occurred;

(2) whether the state was the managing conservator of the child or whether the child resided with the child's parent, managing conservator, guardian, or other person entitled to the possession of the child at the time of the fatality;

(3) the relationship to the child of the individual alleged to have abused or neglected the child, if any;

(4) the number of any department abuse or neglect investigations involving the child or the individual alleged to have abused or neglected the child during the two years preceding the date of the fatality and the results of the investigations;

(5) whether the department offered family-based safety services or conservatorship services to the child or family;

(6) the types of abuse and neglect alleged in the reported investigations, if any; and

(7) any trends identified in the investigations contained in the report.

(b) The report published under Subsection (a) must:

(1) accurately represent all abuse-related and neglect-related child fatalities in this state, including child fatalities investigated under Subchapter F, Chapter 264, and other child fatalities investigated by the department; and

(2) aggregate the fatalities by investigative findings and case disposition, including the following dispositions:

(A) abuse and neglect ruled out;

(B) unable to determine cause of death;

(C) reason to believe abuse or neglect occurred;

(D) reason to believe abuse or neglect contributed to child's death;

(E) unable to complete review; and

(F) administrative closure.

(c) The department may release additional information in the annual report if the release of the information is not prohibited by state or federal law.

(d) The department shall post the annual report on the department's Internet website and otherwise make the report available to the public.

(e) The executive commissioner of the Health and Human Services Commission may adopt rules to implement this section.

(f) At least once every 10 years, the department shall use the information reported under this section to provide guidance for possible department policy changes.

SUBCHAPTER D INVESTIGATIONS

Sec. 261.301. Investigation of Report.

(a) With assistance from the appropriate state or local law enforcement agency as provided by this section, the department shall make a prompt and thorough investigation of a report of child abuse or neglect allegedly committed by a person responsible for a child's care, custody, or welfare. The investigation shall be conducted without regard to any pending suit affecting the parent-child relationship.

(b) A state agency shall investigate a report that alleges abuse, neglect, or exploitation occurred in a facility operated, licensed, certified, or registered by that agency as provided by Subchapter E. In conducting an investigation for a facility operated, licensed, certified, registered, or listed by the department, the department shall perform the investigation as provided by:

(1) Subchapter E; and

(2) the Human Resources Code.

(c) The department is not required to investigate a report that alleges child abuse, neglect, or exploitation by a person other than a person responsible for a child's care, custody, or welfare. The appropriate state or local law enforcement agency shall investigate that report if the agency determines an investigation should be conducted.

(d) The executive commissioner shall by rule assign priorities and prescribe investigative procedures for investigations based on the severity and immediacy of the alleged harm to the child. The primary purpose of the investigation shall be the protection of the child. The rules must require the department, subject to the availability of funds, to:

(1) immediately respond to a report of abuse and neglect that involves circumstances in which the death of the child or substantial bodily harm to the child would result unless the department immediately intervenes;

(2) respond within 24 hours to a report of abuse and neglect that is assigned the highest priority, other than a report described by Subdivision (1); and

(3) respond within 72 hours to a report of abuse and neglect that is assigned the second highest priority.

(e) As necessary to provide for the protection of the child, the department shall determine:

(1) the nature, extent, and cause of the abuse or neglect;

(2) the identity of the person responsible for the abuse or neglect;

(3) the names and conditions of the other children in the home;

(4) an evaluation of the parents or persons responsible for the care of the child;

(5) the adequacy of the home environment;

(6) the relationship of the child to the persons responsible for the care, custody, or welfare of the child; and

(7) all other pertinent data.

(f) An investigation of a report to the department that alleges that a child has been or may be the victim of conduct that constitutes a criminal offense that poses an immediate risk of physical or sexual abuse of a child that could result in the death of or serious harm to the child shall be conducted jointly by a peace officer, as defined by Article 2.12, Code of Criminal Procedure, from the appropriate local law enforcement agency and the department or the agency responsible for conducting an investigation under Subchapter E.

(g) The inability or unwillingness of a local law enforcement agency to conduct a joint investigation under this section does not constitute grounds to prevent or prohibit the department from performing its duties under this subtitle. The department shall document any instance in which a law enforcement agency is unable or unwilling to conduct a joint investigation under this section.

(h) The department and the appropriate local law enforcement agency shall conduct an investigation, other than an investigation under Subchapter E, as provided by this section and Article 2.27, Code of Criminal Procedure, if the investigation is of a report that alleges that a child has been or may be the victim of conduct that constitutes a criminal offense that poses an immediate risk of physical or sexual abuse of a child that could result in the death of or serious harm to the child. Immediately on receipt of a report described by this subsection, the department shall notify the appropriate local law enforcement agency of the report.

(i) If at any time during an investigation of a report of child abuse or neglect to which the department has assigned the highest priority the department is unable to locate the child who is the subject of the report of abuse or neglect or the child's family, the department shall notify the Department of Public Safety that the location of the child and the child's family is unknown. If the Department of Public Safety locates the child and the child's family, the Department of Public Safety shall notify the department of the location of the child and the child's family.

(j) In geographic areas with demonstrated need, the department shall designate employees to serve specifically as investigators and responders for after-hours reports of child abuse or neglect.

(k) In an investigation of a report of abuse or neglect allegedly committed by a person responsible for a child's care, custody, or welfare, the department shall determine whether the person is an active duty member of the United States armed forces or the spouse of a member on active duty. If the department determines the person is an active duty member of the United States armed forces or the spouse of a member on active duty, the department shall notify the United States Department of Defense Family Advocacy Program at the closest active duty military installation of the investigation.

Sec. 261.3011. Joint Investigation Guidelines and Training.

(a) The department shall, in consultation with the appropriate law enforcement agencies, develop guidelines and protocols for joint investigations by the department and the law enforcement agency under Section 261.301. The guidelines and protocols must:

(1) clarify the respective roles of the department and law enforcement agency in conducting the investigation;

(2) require that mutual child protective services and law enforcement training and agreements be implemented by both entities to ensure the integrity and best outcomes of joint investigations; and

(3) incorporate the use of forensic methods in determining the occurrence of child abuse and neglect.

(b) The department shall collaborate with law enforcement agencies to provide to department investigators and law enforcement officers responsible for investigating reports of abuse and neglect joint training relating to methods to effectively conduct joint investigations under Section 261.301. The training must include information on interviewing techniques, evidence gathering, and testifying in court for criminal investigations, as well as instruction on rights provided by the Fourth Amendment to the United States Constitution.

Sec. 261.3012. Completion of Paperwork. [Repealed]

Sec. 261.3013. Case Closure Agreements Prohibited.

(a) Except as provided by Subsection (b), on closing a case, the department may not enter into a written agreement with a child's parent or another adult with whom the child resides that requires the parent or other adult to take certain actions after the case is closed to ensure the child's safety.

(b) This section does not apply to an agreement that is entered into by a parent or other adult:

(1) following the removal of a child and that is subject to the approval of a court with continuing jurisdiction over the child;

(2) as a result of the person's participation in family group conferencing; or

(3) as part of a formal case closure plan agreed to by the person who will continue to care for a child as a result of a parental child safety placement.

(c) The department shall develop policies to guide caseworkers in the development of case closure agreements authorized under Subsections (b)(2) and (3).

Sec. 261.3015. Alternative Response System.

(a) In assigning priorities and prescribing investigative procedures based on the severity and immediacy of the alleged harm to a child under Section 261.301(d), the department shall establish an alternative response system to allow the department to make the most effective use of resources to investigate and respond to reported cases of abuse and neglect.

(b) Notwithstanding Section 261.301, the department may, in accordance with this section and department rules, conduct an alternative response to a report of abuse or neglect if the report does not:

(1) allege sexual abuse of a child;

(2) allege abuse or neglect that caused the death of a child; or

(3) indicate a risk of serious physical injury or immediate serious harm to a child.

(c) The department may administratively close a reported case of abuse or neglect without completing the investigation or alternative response and without providing services or making a referral to another entity for assistance if the department determines, after contacting a professional or other credible source, that the child's safety can be assured without further investigation, response, services, or assistance.

(d) In determining how to classify a reported case of abuse or neglect under the alternative response system, the child's safety is the primary concern. The classification of a case may be changed as warranted by the circumstances.

(e) An alternative response to a report of abuse or neglect must include:

(1) a safety assessment of the child who is the subject of the report;

(2) an assessment of the child's family; and

(3) in collaboration with the child's family, identification of any necessary and appropriate service or support to reduce the risk of future harm to the child.

(f) An alternative response to a report of abuse or neglect may not include a formal determination of whether the alleged abuse or neglect occurred.

(g) The department may implement the alternative response in one or more of the department's administrative regions before implementing the system statewide. The department shall study the results of the system in the regions where the system has been implemented in determining the method by which to implement the system statewide.

Sec. 261.3016. Training of Personnel Receiving Reports of Abuse and Neglect.

The department shall develop, in cooperation with local law enforcement officials and the Commission on State Emergency Communications, a training program for department personnel who receive reports of abuse and neglect. The training program must include information on:

(1) the proper methods of screening reports of abuse and neglect; and

(2) ways to determine the seriousness of a report, including determining whether a report alleges circumstances that could result in the death of or serious harm to a child or whether the report is less serious in nature.

Sec. 261.3017. Consultation with Physician Networks and Systems Regarding Certain Medical Conditions.

(a) In this section:

(1) "Network" means the Forensic Assessment Center Network.

(2) "System" means the entities that receive grants under the Texas Medical Child Abuse Resources and Education System (MEDCARES) authorized by Chapter 1001, Health and Safety Code.

(b) Any agreement between the department and the network or between the Department of State Health Services and the system to provide assistance in connection with abuse and neglect investigations conducted by the department must require the network and the system to have the ability to obtain consultations with physicians licensed to practice medicine in this state and board certified in the relevant field or specialty, including radiologists, geneticists, orthopedists, and endocrinologists, to diagnose and treat certain unique health conditions, including:

(1) rickets;

(2) Ehlers-Danlos Syndrome;

(3) osteogenesis imperfecta;

(4) vitamin D deficiency; and

(5) other medical conditions that mimic child maltreatment or increase the risk of misdiagnosis of child maltreatment.

(c) During an abuse or neglect investigation authorized by this subchapter or an assessment provided under Subsection (b), the department shall refer the child's case for a specialty consultation if:

(1) the department determines the child requires a specialty consultation with a physician;

(2) the child's primary care physician or other primary health care provider who provided health care or treatment or otherwise evaluated the child recommends a specialty consultation; or

(3) the child's parent or legal guardian or, if represented by an attorney, the attorney of the parent or legal guardian requests a specialty consultation.

(c-1) For a case in which a specialty consultation is required by Subsection (c), the department shall refer the case to a physician who:

(1) is licensed to practice medicine in this state under Subtitle B, Title 3, Occupations Code;

(2) is board certified in a field or specialty relevant to diagnosing and treating the conditions described by Subsection (b); and

(3) was not involved with the report of suspected abuse or neglect.

(c-2) Before referring a child's case under Subsection (c), the department shall provide to the child's parent or legal guardian or, if represented by an attorney, the attorney of the parent or legal guardian written notice of the name, contact information, and credentials of the specialist. The parent, legal guardian, or attorney, as applicable, may object to the proposed referral and request referral to another specialist. The department and the parent, legal guardian, or attorney, as applicable, shall collaborate in good faith to select an acceptable specialist from the proposed specialists; however the department may refer the child's case to a specialist over the objection of the parent, legal guardian, or attorney.

(d) In providing assessments to the department as provided by Subsection (b), the network and the system must use a blind peer review process to resolve cases where physicians in the network or system disagree in the assessment of the causes of a child's injuries or in the presence of a condition listed under Subsection (b).

(e) This section may not be construed to prohibit a child's parent or legal guardian or, if represented by an attorney, the attorney of the parent or legal guardian from otherwise obtaining an alternative opinion at the parent's, legal guardian's, or attorney's, as applicable, own initiative and expense. The department shall accept and consider an alternative opinion obtained and provided under this section and shall document its analysis and determinations regarding the opinion.

Sec. 261.30171. Forensic Assessment Center Network Evaluation. [Effective until September 2, 2023; Expires September 1, 2023]

(a) In this section, "network" means the Forensic Assessment Center Network.

(b) The department, with the assistance of the Supreme Court of Texas Children's Commission, shall:

(1) evaluate the department's use of the network; and

(2) develop joint recommendations to improve:

(A) the evaluation of agreements between the department and the network; and

(B) the best practices for using assessments provided by the network in connection with abuse and neglect investigations conducted by the department.

(c) Not later than September 1, 2022, the department shall prepare and submit to the legislature a written report containing the department's findings and recommendations under Subsection (b) and any recommendations for legislative or other action.

(d) This section expires September 1, 2023.

Sec. 261.30175. Mitigation of Provider Conflicts in Abuse or Neglect Investigation Consultations.

(a) In this section:

(1) "Forensic assessment" means a medical examination, psychosocial evaluation, medical case review, specialty evaluation, or other forensic evaluation service conducted by a physician under Section 261.3017 in connection with any investigation of a suspected case of abuse or neglect for the primary purpose of providing the department, law enforcement, or the court with expert advice, recommendations, or testimony on the case.

(2) "Health care practitioner" means an individual licensed, certified, or otherwise authorized to administer health care services in the ordinary course of business or professional practice. The term includes a physician, medical student, resident physician, child abuse fellow, advanced practice registered nurse, nurse, and physician assistant.

(3) "Network" has the meaning assigned by Section 261.3017.

(4) "System" has the meaning assigned by Section 261.3017.

(b) A health care practitioner who reports suspected abuse or neglect of a child may not provide forensic assessment services in connection with an investigation resulting from the report. This subsection applies regardless of whether the practitioner is a member of the network or system.

(c) When referring a case for forensic assessment, the department shall refer the case to a physician authorized to practice medicine in this state under Subtitle B, Title 3, Occupations Code, who was not involved with the report of suspected abuse or neglect.

(d) This section may not be construed to:

(1) prohibit the department from interviewing the health care practitioner in the practitioner's capacity as a principal or collateral source; or

(2) otherwise restrict the department's ability to conduct an investigation as provided by this subchapter.

Sec. 261.3018. Abbreviated Investigation and Administrative Closure of Certain Cases.

(a) A department caseworker may refer a reported case of child abuse or neglect to a department supervisor for abbreviated investigation or administrative closure at any time before the 60th day after the date the report is received if:

(1) there is no prior report of abuse or neglect of the child who is the subject of the report;

(2) the department has not received an additional report of abuse or neglect of the child following the initial report;

(3) after contacting a professional or other credible source, the caseworker determines that the child's safety can be assured without further investigation, response, services, or assistance; and

(4) the caseworker determines that no abuse or neglect occurred.

(b) A department supervisor shall review each reported case of child abuse or neglect that has remained open for more than 60 days and administratively close the case if:

(1) the supervisor determines that:

(A) the circumstances described by Subsections (a)(1)-(4) exist; and

(B) closing the case would not expose the child to an undue risk of harm; and

(2) the department director grants approval for the administrative closure of the case.

(c) A department supervisor may reassign a reported case of child abuse or neglect that does not qualify for abbreviated investigation or administrative closure under Subsection (a) or (b) to a different department caseworker if the supervisor determines that reassignment would allow the department to make the most effective use of resources to investigate and respond to reported cases of abuse or neglect.

(d) The executive commissioner shall adopt rules necessary to implement this section.

(e) In this section, "professional" means an individual who is licensed or certified by the state or who is an employee of a facility licensed, certified, or operated by the state and who, in the normal course of official duties or duties for which a license or certification is required, has direct contact with children. The term includes teachers, nurses, doctors, day-care employees, employees of a clinic or health care facility that provides reproductive services, juvenile probation officers, and juvenile detention or correctional officers.

Sec. 261.3019. Pilot Programs for Investigations of Child Abuse [Expired].

Expired pursuant to Acts 1997, 75th Leg., ch. 1022 (S.B. 359), § 72, effective September 1, 2001.

Sec. 261.302. Conduct of Investigation.

(a) The investigation may include:

(1) a visit to the child's home, unless the alleged abuse or neglect can be confirmed or clearly ruled out without a home visit; and

(2) an interview with and examination of the subject child, which may include a medical, psychological, or psychiatric examination.

(b) The interview with and examination of the child may:

(1) be conducted at any reasonable time and place, including the child's home or the child's school;

(2) include the presence of persons the department determines are necessary; and

(3) include transporting the child for purposes relating to the interview or investigation.

(b-1) Before the department may transport a child as provided by Subsection (b)(3), the department shall attempt to notify the parent or other person having custody of the child of the transport.

(c) The investigation may include an interview with the child's parents and an interview with and medical, psychological, or psychiatric examination of any child in the home.

(d) If, before an investigation is completed, the investigating agency believes that the immediate removal of a child from the child's home is necessary to protect the child from further abuse or neglect, the investigating agency shall file a petition or take other action under Chapter 262 to provide for the temporary care and protection of the child.

(e) An interview with a child in which the allegations of the current investigation are discussed and that is conducted by the department during the investigation stage shall be audiotaped or videotaped unless:

Texas Family Code

(1) the recording equipment malfunctions and the malfunction is not the result of a failure to maintain the equipment or bring adequate supplies for the equipment;

(2) the child is unwilling to allow the interview to be recorded after the department makes a reasonable effort consistent with the child's age and development and the circumstances of the case to convince the child to allow the recording; or

(3) due to circumstances that could not have been reasonably foreseen or prevented by the department, the department does not have the necessary recording equipment because the department employee conducting the interview does not ordinarily conduct interviews.

(e-1) An interview with a child alleged to be a victim of physical abuse or sexual abuse conducted by an investigating agency other than the department shall be audiotaped or videotaped unless the investigating agency determines that good cause exists for not audiotaping or videotaping the interview in accordance with rules of the agency. Good cause may include, but is not limited to, such considerations as the age of the child and the nature and seriousness of the allegations under investigation. Nothing in this subsection shall be construed as prohibiting the investigating agency from audiotaping or videotaping an interview of a child on any case for which such audiotaping or videotaping is not required under this subsection. The fact that the investigating agency failed to audiotape or videotape an interview is admissible at the trial of the offense that is the subject of the interview.

(f) A person commits an offense if the person is notified of the time of the transport of a child by the department and the location from which the transport is initiated and the person is present at the location when the transport is initiated and attempts to interfere with the department's investigation. An offense under this subsection is a Class B misdemeanor. It is an exception to the application of this subsection that the department requested the person to be present at the site of the transport.

Sec. 261.3021. Casework Documentation and Management.

Subject to the appropriation of money, the department shall identify critical investigation actions that impact child safety and require department caseworkers to document those actions in a child's case file not later than the day after the action occurs.

Sec. 261.3022. Child Safety Check Alert List.

(a) The Department of Public Safety of the State of Texas shall maintain a child safety check alert list as part of the Texas Crime Information Center to help locate a child or the child's family for purposes of:

(1) investigating a report of child abuse or neglect;

(2) providing protective services to a family receiving family-based support services; or

(3) providing protective services to the family of a child in the managing conservatorship of the department.

(b) If the department is unable to locate a child or the child's family for a purpose described by Subsection (a) after the department has attempted to locate the child for not more than 20 days, the department shall notify the Texas Department of Public Safety that the department is unable to locate the child or the child's family. The notice must include the information required by Subsections (c)(1)-(10).

(c) On receipt of the notice from the department, the Texas Department of Public Safety shall notify the Texas Crime Information Center to place the child and the child's family on a child safety check alert list. The alert list must include the following information if known or readily available:

(1) the name, sex, race, date of birth, any known identifying numbers, including social security number and driver's license number, and personal descriptions of the family member alleged to have abused or neglected a child according to the report the department is attempting to investigate;

(2) the name, sex, race, date of birth, any known identifying numbers, including social security number and driver's license number, and personal descriptions of any parent, managing conservator, or guardian of the child who cannot be located for the purposes described by Subsection (a);

(3) the name, sex, race, date of birth, any known identifying numbers, including social security number and driver's license number, and personal descriptions of the child who is the subject of the report or is receiving services described by Subsection (a)(2) or (3);

(4) if applicable, a code identifying the type of child abuse or neglect alleged or determined to have been committed against the child;

(5) the family's last known address;

(6) any known description of the motor vehicle, including the vehicle's make, color, style of body, model year, and vehicle identification number, in which the child is suspected to be transported;

(7) the case number assigned by the department;

(8) the department's dedicated law-enforcement telephone number for statewide intake;

(9) the date and time when and the location where the child was last seen; and

(10) any other information required for an entry as established by the center.

Sec. 261.3023. Law Enforcement Response to Child Safety Check Alert.

If a law enforcement officer encounters a child or other person listed on the Texas Crime Information Center's child safety check alert list, the law enforcement officer shall follow the procedures described by Article 2.272, Code of Criminal Procedure.

Sec. 261.3024. Removal from Child Safety Check Alert List.

(a) A law enforcement officer who locates a child listed on the Texas Crime Information Center's child safety check alert list shall report that the child has been located in the manner prescribed by Article 2.272, Code of Criminal Procedure.

(b) If the department locates a child who has been placed on the child safety check alert list established under Section 261.3022 through a means other than information reported to the department by a law enforcement officer under Article 2.272, Code of Criminal Procedure, the department shall report to the Texas Crime Information Center that the child has been located.

(c) On receipt of notice that a child has been located, the Texas Crime Information Center shall remove the child and the child's family from the child safety check alert list.

Sec. 261.3025. [Expires February 2, 2021] Child Safety Check Alert List Progress Report.

(a) Not later than February 1 of each year, the Department of Public Safety, with the assistance of the department, shall prepare and submit a report on the use of the Texas Crime Information Center's child safety check alert list to the standing committees of the senate and the house of representatives with primary jurisdiction over child protective services.

(b) The report must include the following information for the preceding calendar year:

(1) the number of law enforcement officers who completed the training program established under Section 1701.266, Occupations Code;

(2) the number of children who have been placed on the child safety check alert list and the number of those children who have been located; and

(3) the number of families who have been placed on the child safety check alert list and the number of those families who have been located.

(c) This section expires February 2, 2021.

Sec. 261.3027. Notice of Right to Record Interview.

(a) Before conducting an interview with an alleged perpetrator, the department shall inform the person orally and in writing that:

(1) the person may create an audio or video recording of the interview but may not record the interview in any other manner;

(2) any audio or video recording made by the person may be subject to subpoena under a court order; and

(3) the person may request and receive a copy of the department's current recording policy.

(b) The department shall document in the case file that the department provided the notice required by Subsection (a).

(c) The department shall provide two copies of the written notice to be signed by the person. The department shall provide one signed notice to the person and retain the other signed notice in the case file.

(d) An audio or video recording of the department's interview with an alleged perpetrator may not be posted on an Internet website in a manner that could identify a party involved in the interview.

Sec. 261.303. Interference with Investigation; Court Order.

(a) A person may not interfere with an investigation of a report of child abuse or neglect conducted by the department.

(b) If admission to the home, school, or any place where the child may be cannot be obtained, then for good cause shown the court having family law jurisdiction shall order the parent, the person responsible for the care of the children, or the person in charge of any place where the child may be to allow entrance for the interview, examination, and investigation.

(c) If a parent or person responsible for the child's care does not consent to release of the child's prior medical, psychological, or psychiatric records or to a medical, psychological, or psychiatric examination of the child that is requested by the department, the court having family law jurisdiction shall, for good cause shown, order the records to be released or the examination to be made at the times and places designated by the court.

(d) A person, including a medical facility, that makes a report under Subchapter B shall release to the department, as part of the required report under Section 261.103, records that directly relate to the suspected abuse or neglect without requiring parental consent or a court order. If a child is transferred from a reporting medical facility to another medical facility to treat the injury or condition that formed the basis for the original report, the transferee medical facility shall, at the department's request, release to the department records relating to the injury or condition without requiring parental consent or a court order.

(e) A person, including a utility company, that has confidential locating or identifying information regarding a family that is the subject of an investigation under this chapter shall release that information to the department on request. The release of information to the department as required by this subsection by a person, including a utility company, is not subject to Section 552.352, Government Code, or any other law providing liability for the release of confidential information.

Sec. 261.3031. Failure to Cooperate with Investigation; Department Response.

(a) If a parent or other person refuses to cooperate with the department's investigation of the alleged abuse or neglect of a child and the refusal poses a risk to the child's safety, the department shall seek assistance from the appropriate attorney with responsibility for representing the department as provided by Section 264.009 to obtain a court order as described by Section 261.303.

(b) A person's failure to report to an agency authorized to investigate abuse or neglect of a child within a reasonable time after receiving proper notice constitutes a refusal by the person to cooperate with the department's investigation. A summons may be issued to locate the person.

Sec. 261.3032. Interference with Investigation; Criminal Penalty.

(a) A person commits an offense if, with the intent to interfere with the department's investigation of a report of abuse or neglect of a child, the person relocates the person's residence, either temporarily or permanently, without notifying the department of the address of the person's new residence or conceals the child and the person's relocation or concealment interferes with the department's investigation.

(b) An offense under this section is a Class B misdemeanor.

(c) If conduct that constitutes an offense under this section also constitutes an offense under any other law, the actor may be prosecuted under this section or the other law.

Sec. 261.304. Investigation of Anonymous Report.

(a) If the department receives an anonymous report of child abuse or neglect by a person responsible for a child's care, custody, or welfare, the department shall conduct a preliminary investigation to determine whether there is any evidence to corroborate the report.

(b) An investigation under this section may include a visit to the child's home, unless the alleged abuse or neglect can be confirmed or clearly ruled out without a home visit, an interview with and examination of the child, and an interview with the child's parents. In addition, the department may interview any other person the department believes may have relevant information.

(c) Unless the department determines that there is some evidence to corroborate the report of abuse, the department may not conduct the thorough investigation required by this chapter or take any action against the person accused of abuse.

Sec. 261.305. Access to Mental Health Records.

(a) An investigation may include an inquiry into the possibility that a parent or a person responsible for the care of a child who is the subject of a report under Subchapter B has a history of medical or mental illness.

(b) If the parent or person does not consent to an examination or allow the department to have access to medical or mental health records requested by the department, the court having family law jurisdiction, for good cause shown, shall order the examination to be made or that the department be permitted to have access to the records under terms and conditions prescribed by the court.

(c) If the court determines that the parent or person is indigent, the court shall appoint an attorney to represent the parent or person at the hearing. The fees for the appointed attorney shall be paid as provided by Chapter 107.

(d) A parent or person responsible for the child's care is entitled to notice and a hearing when the department seeks a court order to allow a medical, psychological, or psychiatric examination or access to medical or mental health records.

(e) This access does not constitute a waiver of confidentiality.

Sec. 261.306. Removal of Child from State.

(a) If the department has reason to believe that a person responsible for the care, custody, or welfare of the child may remove the child from the state before the investigation is completed, the department may file an application for a temporary restraining order in a district court without regard to continuing jurisdiction of the child as provided in Chapter 155.

(b) The court may render a temporary restraining order prohibiting the person from removing the child from the state pending completion of the investigation if the court:

(1) finds that the department has probable cause to conduct the investigation; and

(2) has reason to believe that the person may remove the child from the state.

Sec. 261.307. Information Relating to Investigation Procedure and Child Placement Resources.

(a) As soon as possible after initiating an investigation of a parent or other person having legal custody of a child, the department shall provide to the person:

(1) a summary that:

(A) is brief and easily understood;

(B) is written in a language that the person understands, or if the person is illiterate, is read to the person in a language that the person understands; and

(C) contains the following information:

(i) the department's procedures for conducting an investigation of alleged child abuse or neglect, including:

(a) a description of the circumstances under which the department would request to remove the child from the home through the judicial system; and

(b) an explanation that the law requires the department to refer all reports of alleged child abuse or neglect to a law enforcement agency for a separate determination of whether a criminal violation occurred;

(ii) the person's right to file a complaint with the department or to request a review of the findings made by the department in the investigation;

(iii) the person's right to review all records of the investigation unless the review would jeopardize an ongoing criminal investigation or the child's safety;

(iv) the person's right to seek legal counsel;

(v) references to the statutory and regulatory provisions governing child abuse and neglect and how the person may obtain copies of those provisions; and

(vi) the process the person may use to acquire access to the child if the child is removed from the home;

(2) if the department determines that removal of the child may be warranted, a proposed child placement resources form that:

(A) instructs the parent or other person having legal custody of the child to:

(i) complete and return the form to the department or agency;

(ii) identify in the form at least three individuals who could be relative caregivers or designated caregivers, as those terms are defined by Section 264.751;

(iii) ask the child in a developmentally appropriate manner to identify any adult, particularly an adult residing in the child's community, who could be a relative caregiver or designated caregiver for the child; and

(iv) list on the form the name of each individual identified by the child as a potential relative caregiver or designated caregiver; and

(B) informs the parent or other person of a location that is available to the parent or other person to submit the information in the form 24 hours a day either in person or by facsimile machine or e-mail; and

(3) an informational manual required by Section 261.3071.

(b) The child placement resources form described by Subsection (a)(2) must include information on the periods of time by which the department must complete a background check.

Sec. 261.3071. Informational Manuals.

(a) In this section:

(1) "Designated caregiver" and "relative caregiver" have the meanings assigned those terms by Section 264.751.

(2) "Voluntary caregiver" means a person who voluntarily agrees to provide temporary care for a child:

(A) who is the subject of an investigation by the department or whose parent, managing conservator, possessory conservator, guardian, caretaker, or custodian is receiving family-based safety services from the department;

(B) who is not in the conservatorship of the department; and

(C) who is placed in the care of the person by the parent or other person having legal custody of the child.

(b) The department shall develop and publish informational manuals that provide information for:

(1) a parent or other person having custody of a child who is the subject of an investigation under this chapter;

(2) a person who is selected by the department to be the child's relative or designated caregiver; and

(3) a voluntary caregiver.

(c) Information provided in the manuals must be in both English and Spanish and must include, as appropriate:

(1) useful indexes of information such as telephone numbers;

(2) the information required to be provided under Section 261.307(a)(1);

(3) information describing the rights and duties of a relative or designated caregiver;

(4) information regarding:

(A) the relative and other designated caregiver program under Subchapter I, Chapter 264, and the option for the relative or other designated caregiver to become verified by a licensed child-placing agency to operate an agency foster home, if applicable; and

(B) the permanency care assistance program under Subchapter K, Chapter 264; and

(5) information regarding the role of a voluntary caregiver, including information on how to obtain any documentation necessary to provide for a child's needs.

Sec. 261.308. Submission of Investigation Report.

(a) The department shall make a complete written report of the investigation.

(b), (c) [Repealed by Acts 2015, 84th Leg., ch. 944 (S.B. 206), § 86(9) effective September 1, 2015.]

(d) The department shall release information regarding a person alleged to have committed abuse or neglect to persons who have control over the person's access to children, including, as appropriate, the Texas Education Agency, the State Board for Educator Certification, the local school board or the school's governing body, the superintendent of the school district, the public school principal or director, the director of the open-enrollment charter school, or the chief executive officer of the private school if the department determines that:

(1) the person alleged to have committed abuse or neglect poses a substantial and immediate risk of harm to one or more children outside the family of a child who is the subject of the investigation; and

(2) the release of the information is necessary to assist in protecting one or more children from the person alleged to have committed abuse or neglect.

(e) On request, the department shall release information about a person alleged to have committed abuse or neglect to the State Board for Educator Certification if the board has a reasonable basis for believing that the information is necessary to assist the board in protecting children from the person alleged to have committed abuse or neglect.

Sec. 261.309. Review of Department Investigations.

(a) The executive commissioner shall by rule establish policies and procedures to resolve complaints relating to and conduct reviews of child abuse or neglect investigations conducted by the department.

(b) If a person under investigation for allegedly abusing or neglecting a child requests clarification of the status of the person's case or files a complaint relating to the conduct of the department's staff or to department policy, the department shall conduct an informal review to clarify the person's status or resolve the complaint. The division of the department responsible for investigating complaints shall conduct the informal review as soon as possible but not later than the 14th day after the date the request or complaint is received.

(c) If, after the department's investigation, the person who is alleged to have abused or neglected a child disputes the department's determination of whether child abuse or neglect occurred, the person may request an administrative review of the findings. A department employee in administration who was not involved in or did not directly supervise the investigation shall conduct the review. The review must sustain, alter, or reverse the department's original findings in the investigation.

(d) The department employee shall conduct the review prescribed by Subsection (c) as soon as possible but not later than the 45th day after the date the department receives the request, unless the department has good cause for extending the deadline. If a civil or criminal court proceeding or an ongoing criminal investigation relating to the alleged abuse or neglect investigated by the department is pending, the department may postpone the review until the court proceeding is completed.

(e) A person is not required to exhaust the remedies provided by this section before pursuing a judicial remedy provided by law.

(f) This section does not provide for a review of an order rendered by a court.

Sec. 261.3091. Notice of Right to Request Administrative Review.

(a) Before conducting an interview with an alleged perpetrator, the department shall notify the person in writing that the person may request an administrative review of the department's findings under Section 261.309. The person shall sign the written notice to acknowledge receipt of the notice.

(b) The department shall document in the case file that the department provided the notice required by Subsection (a).

Sec. 261.310. Investigation Standards.

(a) The executive commissioner shall by rule develop and adopt standards for persons who investigate suspected child abuse or neglect at the state or local level. The standards shall encourage professionalism and consistency in the investigation of suspected child abuse or neglect.

(b) The standards must provide for a minimum number of hours of annual professional training for interviewers and investigators of suspected child abuse or neglect.

(c) [Repealed by Acts 2015, 84th Leg., ch. 944 (S.B. 206), § 86(10), effective September 1, 2015.]

(d) The standards shall:

(1) recommend that videotaped and audiotaped interviews be uninterrupted;

(2) recommend a maximum number of interviews with and examinations of a suspected victim;

(3) provide procedures to preserve evidence, including the original recordings of the intake telephone calls, original notes, videotapes, and audiotapes, for one year; and

(4) provide that an investigator of suspected child abuse or neglect make a reasonable effort to locate and inform each parent of a child of any report of abuse or neglect relating to the child.

(e) The department, in conjunction with the Department of Public Safety, shall provide to the department's residential child-care facility licensing investigators advanced training in investigative protocols and techniques.

Sec. 261.3101. Forensic Investigation Support. [Repealed]

Sec. 261.311. Notice of Report.

(a) When during an investigation of a report of suspected child abuse or neglect a representative of the department conducts an interview with or an examination of a child, the department shall make a reasonable effort before 24 hours after the time of the interview or examination to notify each parent of the child and the child's legal guardian, if one has been appointed, of the nature of the allegation and of the fact that the interview or examination was conducted.

(b) If a report of suspected child abuse or neglect is administratively closed by the department as a result of a preliminary investigation that did not include an interview or examination of the child, the department shall make a reasonable effort before the expiration of 24 hours after the time the investigation is closed to notify each parent and legal guardian of the child of the disposition of the investigation.

(c) The notice required by Subsection (a) or (b) is not required if the department or agency determines that the notice is likely to endanger the safety of the child who is the subject of the report, the person who made the report, or any other person who participates in the investigation of the report.

(d) The notice required by Subsection (a) or (b) may be delayed at the request of a law enforcement agency if notification during the required time would interfere with an ongoing criminal investigation.

Sec. 261.312. Review Teams; Offense.

(a) The department shall establish review teams to evaluate department casework and decision-making related to investigations by the department of child abuse or neglect. The department may create one or more review teams for each region of the department for child protective services. A review team is a citizen review panel or a similar entity for the purposes of federal law relating to a state's child protection standards.

(b) A review team consists of at least five members who serve staggered two-year terms. Review team members are appointed by the commissioner of the department and consist of volunteers who live in and are broadly representative of the region in which the review team is established and have expertise in the prevention and treatment of child abuse and neglect. At least two members of a review team must be parents who have not been convicted of or indicted for an offense involving child abuse or neglect, have not been determined by the department to have engaged in child abuse or neglect, and are not under investigation by the department for child abuse or neglect. A member of a review team is a department volunteer for the purposes of Section 411.114, Government Code.

(c) A review team conducting a review of an investigation may conduct the review by examining the facts of the case as outlined by the department caseworker and law enforcement personnel. A review team member acting in the member's official capacity may receive information made confidential under Section 40.005, Human Resources Code, or Section 261.201.

(d) A review team shall report to the department the results of the team's review of an investigation. The review team's report may not include confidential information. The findings contained in a review team's report are subject to disclosure under Chapter 552, Government Code. This section does not require a law enforcement agency to divulge information to a review team that the agency believes would compromise an ongoing criminal case, investigation, or proceeding.

(e) A member of a review team commits an offense if the member discloses confidential information. An offense under this subsection is a Class C misdemeanor.

Sec. 261.3125. Child Safety Specialists.

(a) The department shall employ in each of the department's administrative regions at least one child safety specialist. The job responsibilities of the child safety specialist must focus on child abuse and neglect investigation issues, including reports of child abuse required by Section 261.101, to achieve a greater compliance with that section, and on assessing and improving the effectiveness of the department in providing for the protection of children in the region.

(b) The duties of a child safety specialist must include the duty to:

(1) conduct staff reviews and evaluations of cases determined to involve a high risk to the health or safety of a child, including cases of abuse reported under Section 261.101, to ensure that risk assessment tools are fully and correctly used;

(2) review and evaluate cases in which there have been multiple referrals to the department of child abuse or neglect involving the same family, child, or person alleged to have committed the abuse or neglect; and

(3) approve decisions and assessments related to investigations of cases of child abuse or neglect that involve a high risk to the health or safety of a child.

Sec. 261.3126. Colocation of Investigators.

(a) In each county, to the extent possible, the department and the local law enforcement agencies that investigate child abuse in the county shall colocate in the same offices investigators from the department and the law enforcement agencies to improve the efficiency of child abuse investigations. With approval of the local children's advocacy center and its partner agencies, in each county in which a children's advocacy center established under Section 264.402 is located, the department shall attempt to locate investigators from the department and county and municipal law enforcement agencies at the center.

(b) A law enforcement agency is not required to comply with the colocation requirements of this section if the law enforcement agency does not have a full-time peace officer solely assigned to investigate reports of child abuse and neglect.

(c) If a county does not have a children's advocacy center, the department shall work with the local community to encourage one as provided by Section 264.402.

Sec. 261.314. Testing.

(a) The department shall provide testing as necessary for the welfare of a child who the department believes, after an investigation under this chapter, has been sexually abused, including human immunodeficiency virus (HIV) testing of a child who was abused in a manner by which HIV may be transmitted.

(b) Except as provided by Subsection (c), the results of a test under this section are confidential.

(c) If requested, the department shall report the results of a test under this section to:

(1) a court having jurisdiction of a proceeding involving the child or a proceeding involving a person suspected of abusing the child;

(2) a person responsible for the care and custody of the child as a foster parent; and

(3) a person seeking to adopt the child.

Sec. 261.315. Removal of Certain Investigation Information from Records.

(a) At the conclusion of an investigation in which the department determines that the person alleged to have abused or neglected a child did not commit abuse or neglect, the department shall notify the person of the person's right to request the department to remove information about the person's alleged role in the abuse or neglect report from the department's records.

(b) On request under Subsection (a) by a person whom the department has determined did not commit abuse or neglect, the department shall remove information from the department's records concerning the person's alleged role in the abuse or neglect report.

(c) The executive commissioner shall adopt rules necessary to administer this section.

Sec. 261.316. Exemption from Fees for Medical Records.

The department is exempt from the payment of a fee otherwise required or authorized by law to obtain a medical record from a hospital or health care provider if the request for a record is made in the course of an investigation by the department.

SUBCHAPTER E INVESTIGATIONS OF ABUSE, NEGLECT, OR EXPLOITATION IN CERTAIN FACILITIES

Sec. 261.401. Agency Investigation.

(a) [Repealed.]

(b) Except as provided by Section 261.404 of this code and Section 531.02013(1)(D), Government Code, a state agency that operates, licenses, certifies, registers, or lists a facility in which children are located or provides oversight of a program that serves children shall make a prompt, thorough investigation of a report that a child has been or may be abused, neglected, or exploited in the facility or program. The primary purpose of the investigation shall be the protection of the child.

(c) A state agency shall adopt rules relating to the investigation and resolution of reports received as provided by this subchapter. The executive commissioner shall review and approve the rules of agencies other than the Texas Department of Criminal Justice or the Texas Juvenile Justice Department to ensure that those agencies implement appropriate standards for the conduct of investigations and that uniformity exists among agencies in the investigation and resolution of reports.

(d) The Texas School for the Blind and Visually Impaired and the Texas School for the Deaf shall adopt policies relating to the investigation and resolution of reports received as provided by this subchapter. The executive commissioner shall review and approve the policies to ensure that the Texas School for the Blind and Visually Impaired and the Texas School for the Deaf adopt those policies in a manner consistent with the minimum standards adopted by the executive commissioner under Section 261.407.

Sec. 261.402. Investigative Reports.

(a) A state agency shall prepare and keep on file a complete written report of each investigation conducted by the agency under this subchapter.

(b) A state agency shall immediately notify the appropriate state or local law enforcement agency of any report the agency receives, other than a report from a law enforcement agency, that concerns the suspected abuse, neglect, or exploitation of a child or the death of a child from abuse or neglect. If the state agency finds evidence indicating that a child may have been abused, neglected, or exploited, the agency shall report the evidence to the appropriate law enforcement agency.

(c) A state agency that licenses, certifies, or registers a facility in which children are located shall compile, maintain, and make available statistics on the incidence in the facility of child abuse, neglect, and exploitation that is investigated by the agency.

(d) A state agency shall compile, maintain, and make available statistics on the incidence of child abuse, neglect, and exploitation in a facility operated by the state agency.

Sec. 261.403. Complaints.

(a) If a state agency receives a complaint relating to an investigation conducted by the agency concerning a facility operated by that agency in which children are located, the agency shall refer the complaint to the agency's governing body.

(b) The governing body of a state agency that operates a facility in which children are located shall ensure that the procedure for investigating abuse, neglect, and exploitation allegations and inquiries in the agency's facility is periodically reviewed under the agency's internal audit program required by Chapter 2102, Government Code.

Sec. 261.404. Investigations Regarding Certain Children Receiving Services from Certain Providers.

(a) The department shall investigate a report of abuse, neglect, or exploitation of a child receiving services from a provider, as those terms are defined by Section 48.251, Human Resources Code, or as otherwise defined by rule. The department shall also investigate, under Subchapter F, Chapter 48, Human Resources Code, a report of abuse, neglect, or exploitation of a child receiving services from an officer, employee, agent, contractor, or subcontractor of a home and community support services agency licensed under Chapter 142, Health and Safety Code, if the officer, employee, agent, contractor, or subcontractor is or may be the person alleged to have committed the abuse, neglect, or exploitation.

(a-1) For an investigation of a child living in a residence owned, operated, or controlled

Texas Family Code

by a provider of services under the home and community-based services waiver program described by Section 534.001(11)(B), Government Code, the department, in accordance with Subchapter E, Chapter 48, Human Resources Code, may provide emergency protective services necessary to immediately protect the child from serious physical harm or death and, if necessary, obtain an emergency order for protective services under Section 48.208, Human Resources Code.

(a-2) For an investigation of a child living in a residence owned, operated, or controlled by a provider of services under the home and community-based services waiver program described by Section 534.001(11)(B), Government Code, regardless of whether the child is receiving services under that waiver program from the provider, the department shall provide protective services to the child in accordance with Subchapter E, Chapter 48, Human Resources Code.

(a-3) For purposes of this section, Subchapters E and F, Chapter 48, Human Resources Code, apply to an investigation of a child and to the provision of protective services to that child in the same manner those subchapters apply to an investigation of an elderly person or person with a disability and the provision of protective services to that person.

(b) The department shall investigate the report under rules developed by the executive commissioner.

(c) If a report under this section relates to a child with an intellectual disability receiving services in a state supported living center or the ICF-IID component of the Rio Grande State Center, the department shall, within one hour of receiving the report, notify the facility in which the child is receiving services of the allegations in the report.

(d) If during the course of the department's investigation of reported abuse, neglect, or exploitation a caseworker of the department or the caseworker's supervisor has cause to believe that a child with an intellectual disability described by Subsection (c) has been abused, neglected, or exploited by another person in a manner that constitutes a criminal offense under any law, including Section 22.04, Penal Code, the caseworker shall immediately notify the Health and Human Services Commission's office of inspector general and promptly provide the commission's office of inspector general with a copy of the department's investigation report.

(e) The definitions of "abuse" and "neglect" prescribed by Section 261.001 do not apply to an investigation under this section.

(f) [Repealed by Acts 2015, 84th Leg., ch. 860 (S.B. 1880), § 15(1), effective September 1, 2015 and by Acts 2015, 84th Leg., ch. 1272 (S.B. 760), § 19(1), effective September 1, 2015.]

Sec. 261.405. Investigations in Juvenile Justice Programs and Facilities.

(a) Notwithstanding Section 261.001, in this section:

(1) "Abuse" means an intentional, knowing, or reckless act or omission by an employee, volunteer, or other individual working under the auspices of a facility or program that causes or may cause emotional harm or physical injury to, or the death of, a child served by the facility or program as further described by rule or policy.

(2) "Exploitation" means the illegal or improper use of a child or of the resources of a child for monetary or personal benefit, profit, or gain by an employee, volunteer, or other individual working under the auspices of a facility or program as further described by rule or policy.

(3) "Juvenile justice facility" means a facility operated wholly or partly by the juvenile board, by another governmental unit, or by a private vendor under a contract with the juvenile board, county, or other governmental unit that serves juveniles under juvenile court jurisdiction. The term includes:

(A) a public or private juvenile pre-adjudication secure detention facility, including a holdover facility;

(B) a public or private juvenile post-adjudication secure correctional facility except for a facility operated solely for children committed to the Texas Juvenile Justice Department; and

(C) a public or private non-secure juvenile post-adjudication residential treatment facility that is not licensed by the Department of Family and Protective Services or the Department of State Health Services.

(4) "Juvenile justice program" means a program or department operated wholly or partly by the juvenile board or by a private vendor under a contract with a juvenile board that serves juveniles under juvenile court jurisdiction. The term includes:

(A) a juvenile justice alternative education program;

(B) a non-residential program that serves juvenile offenders under the jurisdiction of the juvenile court; and

(C) a juvenile probation department.

(5) "Neglect" means a negligent act or omission by an employee, volunteer, or other individual working under the auspices of a facility or program, including failure to comply with an individual treatment plan, plan of care, or individualized service plan, that causes or may cause substantial emotional harm or physical injury to, or the death of, a child served by the facility or program as further described by rule or policy.

(b) A report of alleged abuse, neglect, or exploitation in any juvenile justice program or facility shall be made to the Texas Juvenile Justice Department and a local law enforcement agency for investigation.

(c) The Texas Juvenile Justice Department shall make a prompt, thorough investigation as provided by this chapter if that department receives a report of alleged abuse, neglect, or exploitation in any juvenile justice program or facility. The primary purpose of the investigation shall be the protection of the child.

(d) In an investigation required under this section, the investigating agency shall have access to medical and mental health records as provided by Subchapter D.

(e) As soon as practicable after a child is taken into custody or placed in a juvenile justice facility or juvenile justice program, the facility or program shall provide the child's parents with:

(1) information regarding the reporting of suspected abuse, neglect, or exploitation of a child in a juvenile justice facility or juvenile justice program to the Texas Juvenile Justice Department; and

(2) the Texas Juvenile Justice Department's toll-free number for this reporting.

Sec. 261.406. Investigations in Schools.

(a) On receipt of a report of alleged or suspected abuse or neglect of a child in a public or private school, the department shall perform an investigation as provided by this chapter.

(b) The department shall send a copy of the completed report of the department's investigation to the Texas Education Agency or, in the case of a private school, the school's chief executive officer. On request, the department shall provide a copy of the completed report of the department's investigation to the State Board for Educator Certification, the local school board or the school's governing body, the superintendent of the school district, the public school principal or director, or the chief executive officer of the private school, unless the principal, director, or chief executive officer is alleged to have committed the abuse or neglect, for appropriate action. On request, the department shall provide a copy of the report of investigation to the parent, managing conservator, or legal guardian of a child who is the subject of the investigation and to the person alleged to have committed the abuse or neglect. The report of investigation shall be edited to protect the identity of the persons who made the report of abuse or neglect. Except as otherwise provided by this subsection, Section 261.201(b) applies to the release of the report relating to the investigation of abuse or neglect under this section and to the identity of the person who made the report of abuse or neglect.

(c) Nothing in this section may prevent a law enforcement agency from conducting an investigation of a report made under this section.

(d) The executive commissioner shall adopt rules necessary to implement this section.

Sec. 261.407. Minimum Standards.

(a) The executive commissioner by rule shall adopt minimum standards for the investigation under Section 261.401 of suspected child abuse, neglect, or exploitation in a facility.

(b) A rule or policy adopted by a state agency or institution under Section 261.401 must be consistent with the minimum standards adopted by the executive commissioner.

(c) This section does not apply to a facility under the jurisdiction of the Texas Department of Criminal Justice or the Texas Juvenile Justice Department.

Sec. 261.408. Information Collection.

(a) The executive commissioner by rule shall adopt uniform procedures for collecting information under Section 261.401, including procedures for collecting information on deaths that occur in facilities.

(b) The department shall receive and compile information on investigations in facilities. An agency submitting information to the department is responsible for ensuring the timeliness, accuracy, completeness, and retention of the agency's reports.

(c) This section does not apply to a facility under the jurisdiction of the Texas Department of Criminal Justice or the Texas Juvenile Justice Department.

Sec. 261.409. Investigations in Facilities Under Texas Juvenile Justice Department Jurisdiction.

The board of the Texas Juvenile Justice Department by rule shall adopt standards for:

(1) the investigation under Section 261.401 of suspected child abuse, neglect, or exploitation in a facility under the jurisdiction of the Texas Juvenile Justice Department; and

(2) compiling information on those investigations.

Sec. 261.410. Report of Abuse by Other Children.

Texas Family Code

(a) In this section:

(1) "Physical abuse" means:

(A) physical injury that results in substantial harm to the child requiring emergency medical treatment and excluding an accident or reasonable discipline by a parent, guardian, or managing or possessory conservator that does not expose the child to a substantial risk of harm; or

(B) failure to make a reasonable effort to prevent an action by another person that results in physical injury that results in substantial harm to the child.

(2) "Sexual abuse" means:

(A) sexual conduct harmful to a child's mental, emotional, or physical welfare; or

(B) failure to make a reasonable effort to prevent sexual conduct harmful to a child.

(b) An agency that operates, licenses, certifies, or registers a facility shall require a residential child-care facility to report each incident of physical or sexual abuse committed by a child against another child.

(c) Using information received under Subsection (b), the agency that operates, licenses, certifies, or registers a facility shall, subject to the availability of funds, compile a report that includes information:

(1) regarding the number of cases of physical and sexual abuse committed by a child against another child;

(2) identifying the residential child-care facility;

(3) regarding the date each allegation of abuse was made;

(4) regarding the date each investigation was started and concluded;

(5) regarding the findings and results of each investigation; and

(6) regarding the number of children involved in each incident investigated.

SUBCHAPTER F PROTECTIVE ORDER IN CERTAIN CASES OF ABUSE OR NEGLECT. [CONTINGENTLY ENACTED] [SEE EDITOR'S NOTES]

Sec. 261.501. Filing Application for Protective Order in Certain Cases of Abuse or Neglect. [Contingently enacted] [See Editor's Notes]

The department may file an application for a protective order for a child's protection under this subchapter on the department's own initiative or jointly with a parent, relative, or caregiver of the child who requests the filing of the application if the department:

(1) has temporary managing conservatorship of the child;

(2) determines that:

(A) the child:

(i) is a victim of abuse or neglect; or

(ii) has a history of being abused or neglected; and

(B) there is a threat of:

(i) immediate or continued abuse or neglect to the child;

(ii) someone illegally taking the child from the home in which the child is placed;

(iii) behavior that poses a threat to the caregiver with whom the child is placed; or

(iv) someone committing an act of violence against the child or the child's caregiver; and

(3) is not otherwise authorized to apply for a protective order for the child's protection under Chapter 82.

Sec. 261.502. Certification of Findings. [Contingently enacted] [See Editor's Notes]

(a) In making the application under this subchapter, the department must certify that:

(1) the department has diligently searched for and:

(A) was unable to locate the child's parent, legal guardian, or custodian, other than the respondent to the application; or

(B) located and provided notice of the proposed application to the child's parent, legal guardian, or custodian, other than the respondent to the application; and

(2) if applicable, the relative or caregiver who is jointly filing the petition, or with whom the child would reside following an entry of the protective order, has not abused or neglected the child and does not have a history of abuse or neglect.

(b) An application for a temporary ex parte order under Section 261.503 may be filed without making the findings required by Subsection (a) if the department certifies that the department believes there is an immediate danger of abuse or neglect to the child.

Sec. 261.503. Temporary Ex Parte Order. [Contingently enacted] [See Editor's Notes]

If the court finds from the information contained in an application for a protective order that there is an immediate danger of abuse or neglect to the child, the court, without further notice to the respondent and without a hearing, may enter a temporary ex parte order for the protection of the child.

Sec. 261.504. Required Findings; Issuance of Protective Order.

(a) At the close of a hearing on an application for a protective order under this subchapter, the court shall find whether there are reasonable grounds to believe that:

(1) the child:

(A) is a victim of abuse or neglect; or

(B) has a history of being abused or neglected; and

(2) there is a threat of:

(A) immediate or continued abuse or neglect to the child;

(B) someone illegally taking the child from the home in which the child is placed;

(C) behavior that poses a threat to the caregiver with whom the child is placed; or

(D) someone committing an act of violence against the child or the child's caregiver.

(a-1) In making a determination whether the child is or has been a victim of abuse or neglect, the court shall consider the opinion of a medical professional obtained by an individual against whom a protective order is sought.

(b) If the court makes an affirmative finding under Subsection (a), the court shall issue a protective order that includes a statement of that finding.

Sec. 261.505. Application of Other Law. [Contingently enacted] [See Editor's Notes]

To the extent applicable, except as otherwise provided by this subchapter, Title 4 applies to a protective order issued under this subchapter.

Texas Family Code

CHAPTER 262
PROCEDURES IN SUIT BY GOVERNMENTAL ENTITY TO PROTECT HEALTH AND SAFETY OF CHILD

SUBCHAPTER A
GENERAL PROVISIONS

Sec. 262.001. Authorized Actions by Governmental Entity.

(a) A governmental entity with an interest in the child may file a suit affecting the parent-child relationship requesting an order or take possession of a child without a court order as provided by this chapter.

(b) In determining the reasonable efforts that are required to be made with respect to preventing or eliminating the need to remove a child from the child's home or to make it possible to return a child to the child's home, the child's health and safety is the paramount concern.

Sec. 262.002. Jurisdiction.

A suit brought by a governmental entity requesting an order under this chapter may be filed in a court with jurisdiction to hear the suit in the county in which the child is found.

Sec. 262.0022. Review of Placement; Findings.

At each hearing under this chapter, the court shall review the placement of each child in the temporary or permanent managing conservatorship of the Department of Family and Protective Services who is not placed with a relative caregiver or designated caregiver as defined by Section 264.751. The court shall include in its findings a statement on whether the department:

(1) asked the child in a developmentally appropriate manner to identify any adult, particularly an adult residing in the child's community, who could be a relative caregiver or designated caregiver for the child; and

(2) has the option of placing the child with a relative caregiver or designated caregiver.

Sec. 262.003. Civil Liability.

A person who takes possession of a child without a court order is immune from civil liability if, at the time possession is taken, there is reasonable cause to believe there is an immediate danger to the physical health or safety of the child.

Sec. 262.004. Accepting Voluntary Delivery of Possession of Child.

A law enforcement officer or a juvenile probation officer may take possession of a child without a court order on the voluntary delivery of the child by the parent, managing conservator, possessory conservator, guardian, caretaker, or custodian who is presently entitled to possession of the child.

Sec. 262.005. Filing Petition After Accepting Voluntary Delivery of Possession of Child.

When possession of the child has been acquired through voluntary delivery of the child to a law enforcement officer or juvenile probation officer, the law enforcement officer or juvenile probation officer taking the child into possession shall cause a suit to be filed not later than the 60th day after the date the child is taken into possession.

Sec. 262.006. Living Child After Abortion.

(a) An authorized representative of the Department of Family and Protective Services may assume the care, control, and custody of a child born alive as the result of an abortion as defined by Chapter 161.

(b) The department shall file a suit and request an emergency order under this chapter.

(c) A child for whom possession is assumed under this section need not be delivered to the court except on the order of the court.

Sec. 262.007. Possession and Delivery of Missing Child.

(a) A law enforcement officer who, during a criminal investigation relating to a child's custody, discovers that a child is a missing child and believes that a person may flee with or conceal the child shall take possession of the child and provide for the delivery of the child as provided by Subsection (b).

(b) An officer who takes possession of a child under Subsection (a) shall deliver or arrange for the delivery of the child to a person entitled to possession of the child.

(c) If a person entitled to possession of the child is not immediately available to take possession of the child, the law enforcement officer shall deliver the child to the Department of Family and Protective Services. Until a person entitled to possession of the child takes possession of the child, the department may, without a court order, retain possession of the child not longer than five days after the date the child is delivered to the department. While the department retains possession of a child under this subsection, the department may place the child in foster care. If a parent or other person entitled to possession of the child does not take possession of the child before the sixth day after the date the child is delivered to the department, the department shall proceed under this chapter as if the law enforcement officer took possession of the child under Section 262.104.

Sec. 262.008. Abandoned Children.

(a) An authorized representative of the Department of Family and Protective Services may assume the care, control, and custody of a child:

(1) who is abandoned without identification or a means for identifying the child; and

(2) whose identity cannot be ascertained by the exercise of reasonable diligence.

(b) The department shall immediately file a suit to terminate the parent-child relationship of a child under Subsection (a).

(c) [Repealed by Acts 2015, 84th Leg., ch. 1 (S.B. 219), § 1.203(5), effective April 2, 2015.]

Sec. 262.009. Temporary Care of Child Taken into Possession.

An employee of or volunteer with a law enforcement agency who successfully completes a background and criminal history check approved by the law enforcement agency may assist a law enforcement officer or juvenile probation officer with the temporary care of a child who is taken into possession by a governmental entity without a court order under this chapter until further arrangements regarding the custody of the child can be made.

Sec. 262.010. Child with Sexually Transmitted Disease.

(a) If during an investigation by the Department of Family and Protective Services the department discovers that a child younger than 11 years of age has a sexually transmitted disease, the department shall:

(1) appoint a special investigator to assist in the investigation of the case; and

(2) file an original suit requesting an emergency order under this chapter for possession of the child unless the department determines, after taking the following actions, that emergency removal is not necessary for the protection of the child:

(A) reviewing the medical evidence to determine whether the medical evidence supports a finding that abuse likely occurred;

(B) interviewing the child and other persons residing in the child's home;

(C) conferring with law enforcement;

(D) determining whether any other child in the home has a sexually transmitted disease and, if so, referring the child for a sexual abuse examination;

(E) if the department determines a forensic interview is appropriate based on the child's age and development, ensuring that each child alleged to have been abused undergoes a forensic interview by a children's advocacy center established under Section 264.402 or another professional with specialized training in conducting forensic interviews if a children's advocacy center is not available in the county in which the child resides;

(F) consulting with a department staff nurse or other medical expert to obtain additional information regarding the nature of the sexually transmitted disease and the ways the disease is transmitted and an opinion as to whether abuse occurred based on the facts of the case;

(G) contacting any additional witness who may have information relevant to the investigation, including other individuals who had access to the child; and

(H) if the department determines after taking the actions described by Paragraphs (A)—(G) that a finding of sexual abuse is not supported, obtaining an opinion from the Forensic Assessment Center Network as to whether the evidence in the case supports a finding that abuse likely occurred.

(b) If the department determines that abuse likely occurred, the department shall work with law enforcement to obtain a search warrant to require an individual the department reasonably believes may have sexually abused the child to undergo medically appropriate diagnostic testing for sexually transmitted diseases.

Sec. 262.011. Placement in Secure Agency Foster Home.

A court in an emergency, initial, or full adversary hearing conducted under this chapter may order that the child who is the subject of the hearing be placed in a secure agency foster home verified in accordance with Section 42.0531, Human Resources Code, if the court finds that:

(1) the placement is in the best interest of the child; and

(2) the child's physical health or safety is in danger because the child has been recruited, harbored, transported, provided, or obtained for forced labor or commercial sexual activity, including any child subjected to an act specified in Section 20A.02 or 20A.03, Penal Code.

Sec. 262.012. Sealing of Court Records Filed Electronically.

For purposes of determining whether to seal documents in accordance with Rule 76a, Texas Rules of Civil Procedure, in a suit under this subtitle, the court shall consider documents filed through an electronic filing system in the same manner as any other document filed with the court.

Sec. 262.013. Voluntary Temporary Managing Conservatorship.

In a suit affecting the parent-child relationship filed by the Department of Family and Protective Services, the existence of a parent's voluntary agreement to temporarily place the parent's child in the managing conservatorship of the department is not an admission by the parent that the parent engaged in conduct that endangered the child.

Sec. 262.014. Disclosure of Certain Evidence.

On the request of the attorney for a parent who is a party in a suit affecting the parent-child relationship filed under this chapter, or the attorney ad litem for the parent's child, the Department of Family and Protective Services shall, before the full adversary hearing, provide:

(1) the name of any person, excluding a department employee, whom the department will call as a witness to any of the allegations contained in the petition filed by the department;

(2) a copy of any offense report relating to the allegations contained in the petition filed by the department that will be used in court to refresh a witness's memory; and

(3) a copy of any photograph, video, or recording that will be presented as evidence.

Sec. 262.015. Filing Requirement for Petition Regarding More Than One Child.

Each suit under this chapter based on allegations of abuse or neglect arising from the same incident or occurrence and involving children that live in the same home must be filed in the same court.

SUBCHAPTER B TAKING POSSESSION OF CHILD

Sec. 262.101. Filing Petition Before Taking Possession of Child.

An original suit filed by a governmental entity that requests permission to take possession of a child without prior notice and a hearing must be supported by an affidavit sworn to by a person with personal knowledge and stating facts sufficient to satisfy a person of ordinary prudence and caution that:

(1) there is an immediate danger to the physical health or safety of the child or the child has been a victim of neglect or sexual abuse;

(2) continuation in the home would be contrary to the child's welfare;

(3) there is no time, consistent with the physical health or safety of the child, for a full adversary hearing under Subchapter C; and

(4) reasonable efforts, consistent with the circumstances and providing for the safety of the child, were made to prevent or eliminate the need for the removal of the child.

Sec. 262.1015. Removal of Alleged Perpetrator; Offense.

(a) If the Department of Family and Protective Services determines after an investigation that child abuse has occurred and that the child would be protected in the child's home by the removal of the alleged perpetrator of the abuse, the department shall file a petition for the removal of the alleged perpetrator from the residence of the child rather than attempt to remove the child from the residence.

(a-1) Notwithstanding Subsection (a), if the Department of Family and Protective Services determines that a protective order issued under Title 4 provides a reasonable alternative to obtaining an order under that subsection, the department may:

(1) file an application for a protective order on behalf of the child instead of or in addition to obtaining a temporary restraining order under this section; or

(2) assist a parent or other adult with whom a child resides in obtaining a protective order.

(b) A court may issue a temporary restraining order in a suit by the department for the removal of an alleged perpetrator under Subsection (a) if the department's petition states facts sufficient to satisfy the court that:

(1) there is an immediate danger to the physical health or safety of the child or the child has been a victim of sexual abuse;

(2) there is no time, consistent with the physical health or safety of the child, for an adversary hearing;

(3) the child is not in danger of abuse from a parent or other adult with whom the child will continue to reside in the residence of the child;

(4) the parent or other adult with whom the child will continue to reside in the child's home is likely to:

(A) make a reasonable effort to monitor the residence; and

(B) report to the department and the appropriate law enforcement agency any attempt by the alleged perpetrator to return to the residence; and

(5) the issuance of the order is in the best interest of the child.

(c) The order shall be served on the alleged perpetrator and on the parent or other adult with whom the child will continue to reside.

(d) A temporary restraining order under this section expires not later than the 14th day after the date the order was rendered, unless the court grants an extension under Section 262.201(e).

(e) A temporary restraining order under this section and any other order requiring the removal of an alleged perpetrator from the residence of a child shall require that the parent or other adult with whom the child will continue to reside in the child's home make a reasonable effort to monitor the residence and report to the department and the appropriate law enforcement agency any attempt by the alleged perpetrator to return to the residence.

(f) The court shall order the removal of an alleged perpetrator if the court finds that the child is not in danger of abuse from a parent or other adult with whom the child will continue to reside in the child's residence and that:

(1) the presence of the alleged perpetrator in the child's residence constitutes a continuing danger to the physical health or safety of the child; or

(2) the child has been the victim of sexual abuse and there is a substantial risk that the child will be the victim of sexual abuse in the future if the alleged perpetrator remains in the residence.

(g) A person commits an offense if the person is a parent or other person with whom a child resides, the person is served with an order containing the requirement specified by Subsection (e), and the person fails to make a reasonable effort to monitor the residence of the child or to report to the department and the appropriate law enforcement agency an attempt by the alleged perpetrator to return to the residence. An offense under this section is a Class A misdemeanor.

(h) A person commits an offense if, in violation of a court order under this section, the person returns to the residence of the child the person is alleged to have abused. An offense under this subsection is a Class A misdemeanor, except that the offense is a felony of the third degree if the person has previously been convicted under this subsection.

Sec. 262.102. Emergency Order Authorizing Possession of Child.

(a) Before a court may, without prior notice and a hearing, issue a temporary order for the conservatorship of a child under Section 105.001(a)(1) or a temporary restraining order or attachment of a child authorizing a governmental entity to take possession of a child in a suit brought by a governmental entity, the court must find that:

(1) there is an immediate danger to the physical health or safety of the child or the child has been a victim of neglect or sexual abuse;

(2) continuation in the home would be contrary to the child's welfare;

(3) there is no time, consistent with the physical health or safety of the child and the nature of the emergency, for a full adversary hearing under Subchapter C; and

(4) reasonable efforts, consistent with the circumstances and providing for the safety of the child, were made to prevent or eliminate the need for removal of the child.

(b) In determining whether there is an immediate danger to the physical health or safety of a child, the court may consider whether the child's household includes a person who has:

(1) abused or neglected another child in a manner that caused serious injury to or the death of the other child; or

(2) sexually abused another child.

(b-1) A determination under this section that there is an immediate danger to the physical health or safety of a child or that the child has been a victim of neglect or sexual abuse may not be based solely on the opinion of a medical professional under contract with the Department of Family and Protective Services who did not conduct a physical examination of the child.

(c) If, based on the recommendation of or a request by the Department of Family and Protective Services, the court finds that child abuse or neglect has occurred and that the child requires protection from family violence by a member of the child's family or household, the court shall render a temporary order under Title 4 for the protection of the child. In this subsection, "family violence" has the meaning assigned by Section 71.004.

(d) The temporary order, temporary restraining order, or attachment of a child rendered by the court under Subsection (a) must contain the following statement prominently displayed in boldface type, capital letters, or underlined:

"YOU HAVE THE RIGHT TO BE REPRESENTED BY AN ATTORNEY. IF YOU ARE INDIGENT AND UNABLE TO AFFORD AN ATTORNEY, YOU HAVE THE RIGHT TO REQUEST THE APPOINTMENT OF AN ATTORNEY BY CONTACTING THE COURT AT [ADDRESS], [TELEPHONE NUMBER]. IF YOU APPEAR IN OPPOSITION TO THE SUIT, CLAIM INDIGENCE, AND REQUEST THE APPOINTMENT OF AN ATTORNEY, THE COURT WILL REQUIRE YOU TO SIGN AN AFFIDAVIT OF INDIGENCE AND THE COURT MAY HEAR EVIDENCE TO DETERMINE IF YOU ARE INDIGENT. IF THE COURT DETERMINES YOU ARE INDIGENT AND ELIGIBLE FOR APPOINTMENT OF AN ATTORNEY, THE COURT WILL APPOINT AN ATTORNEY TO REPRESENT YOU."

Sec. 262.103. Duration of Temporary Order, Temporary Restraining Order, and Attachment.

A temporary order, temporary restraining order, or attachment of the child issued under Section 262.102(a) expires not later than 14 days after the date it is issued unless it is extended as provided by the Texas Rules of Civil Procedure or Section 262.201(e).

Sec. 262.104. Taking Possession of a Child in Emergency Without a Court Order.

(a) If there is no time to obtain a temporary order, temporary restraining order, or attachment under Section 262.102(a) before taking possession of a child consistent with the health and safety of that child, an authorized representative of the Department of Family and Protective Services, a law enforcement officer, or a juvenile probation officer may take possession of a child without a court order under the following conditions, only:

(1) on personal knowledge of facts that would lead a person of ordinary prudence and caution to believe that there is an immediate danger to the physical health or safety of the child;

(2) on information furnished by another that has been corroborated by personal knowledge of facts and all of which taken together would lead a person of ordinary prudence and caution to believe that there is an immediate danger to the physical health or safety of the child;

(3) on personal knowledge of facts that would lead a person of ordinary prudence and caution to believe that the child has been the victim of sexual abuse or of trafficking under Section 20A.02 or 20A.03, Penal Code;

(4) on information furnished by another that has been corroborated by personal knowledge of facts and all of which taken together would lead a person of ordinary prudence and caution to believe that the child has been the victim of sexual abuse or of trafficking under Section 20A.02 or 20A.03, Penal Code; or

(5) on information furnished by another that has been corroborated by personal knowledge of facts and all of which taken together would lead a person of ordinary prudence and caution to believe that the parent or person who has possession of the child is currently using a controlled substance as

defined by Chapter 481, Health and Safety Code, and the use constitutes an immediate danger to the physical health or safety of the child.

(b) An authorized representative of the Department of Family and Protective Services, a law enforcement officer, or a juvenile probation officer may take possession of a child under Subsection (a) on personal knowledge or information furnished by another, that has been corroborated by personal knowledge, that would lead a person of ordinary prudence and caution to believe that the parent or person who has possession of the child has permitted the child to remain on premises used for the manufacture of methamphetamine.

(c) An authorized representative of the Department of Family and Protective Services, a law enforcement officer, or a juvenile probation officer may not take possession of a child under Subsection (a) based solely on the opinion of a medical professional under contract with the Department of Family and Protective Services who did not conduct a physical examination of the child.

Sec. 262.1041. Release of Child by Law Enforcement or Juvenile Probation Officer. [Repealed]

Sec. 262.105. Filing Petition After Taking Possession of Child in Emergency.

(a) When a child is taken into possession without a court order, the person taking the child into possession, without unnecessary delay, shall:

(1) file a suit affecting the parent-child relationship;

(2) request the court to appoint an attorney ad litem for the child; and

(3) request an initial hearing to be held by no later than the first business day after the date the child is taken into possession.

(b) An original suit filed by a governmental entity after taking possession of a child under Section 262.104 must be supported by an affidavit stating facts sufficient to satisfy a person of ordinary prudence and caution that:

(1) based on the affiant's personal knowledge or on information furnished by another person corroborated by the affiant's personal knowledge, one of the following circumstances existed at the time the child was taken into possession:

(A) there was an immediate danger to the physical health or safety of the child;

(B) the child was the victim of sexual abuse or of trafficking under Section 20A.02 or 20A.03, Penal Code;

(C) the parent or person who had possession of the child was using a controlled substance as defined by Chapter 481, Health and Safety Code, and the use constituted an immediate danger to the physical health or safety of the child; or

(D) the parent or person who had possession of the child permitted the child to remain on premises used for the manufacture of methamphetamine; and

(2) based on the affiant's personal knowledge:

(A) continuation of the child in the home would have been contrary to the child's welfare;

(B) there was no time, consistent with the physical health or safety of the child, for a full adversary hearing under Subchapter C; and

(C) reasonable efforts, consistent with the circumstances and providing for the safety of the child, were made to prevent or eliminate the need for the removal of the child.

Sec. 262.106. Initial Hearing After Taking Possession of Child in Emergency Without Court Order.

(a) The court in which a suit has been filed after a child has been taken into possession without a court order by a governmental entity shall hold an initial hearing on or before the first business day after the date the child is taken into possession. The court shall render orders that are necessary to protect the physical health and safety of the child. If the court is unavailable for a hearing on the first business day, then, and only in that event, the hearing shall be held no later than the first business day after the court becomes available, provided that the hearing is held no later than the third business day after the child is taken into possession.

(b) The initial hearing may be ex parte and proof may be by sworn petition or affidavit if a full adversary hearing is not practicable.

(c) If the initial hearing is not held within the time required, the child shall be returned to the parent, managing conservator, possessory conservator, guardian, caretaker, or custodian who is presently entitled to possession of the child.

(d) For the purpose of determining under Subsection (a) the first business day after the date the child is taken into possession, the child is considered to have been taken into possession by the Department of Family and Protective Services on the expiration of the five-day period permitted under Section 262.007(c) or 262.110(b), as appropriate.

Sec. 262.107. Standard for Decision at Initial Hearing After Taking Possession of Child Without a Court Order in Emergency.

(a) The court shall order the return of the child at the initial hearing regarding a child taken in possession without a court order by a governmental entity unless the court is satisfied that:

(1) the evidence shows that one of the following circumstances exists:

(A) there is a continuing danger to the physical health or safety of the child if the child is returned to the parent, managing conservator, possessory conservator, guardian, caretaker, or custodian who is presently entitled to possession of the child;

(B) the child has been the victim of sexual abuse or of trafficking under Section 20A.02 or 20A.03, Penal Code, on one or more occasions and that there is a substantial risk that the child will be the victim of sexual abuse or of trafficking in the future;

(C) the parent or person who has possession of the child is currently using a controlled substance as defined by Chapter 481, Health and Safety Code, and the use constitutes an immediate danger to the physical health or safety of the child; or

(D) the parent or person who has possession of the child has permitted the child to remain on premises used for the manufacture of methamphetamine;

(2) continuation of the child in the home would be contrary to the child's welfare; and

(3) reasonable efforts, consistent with the circumstances and providing for the safety of the child, were made to prevent or eliminate the need for removal of the child.

(b) In determining whether there is a continuing danger to the physical health or safety of a child, the court may consider whether the household to which the child would be returned includes a person who has:

(1) abused or neglected another child in a manner that caused serious injury to or the death of the other child; or

(2) sexually abused another child.

Sec. 262.108. Unacceptable Facilities for Housing Child.

When a child is taken into possession under this chapter, that child may not be held in isolation or in a jail, juvenile detention facility, or other secure detention facility.

Sec. 262.109. Notice to Parent, Conservator, or Guardian.

(a) The Department of Family and Protective Services or other agency must give written notice as prescribed by this section to each parent of the child or to the child's conservator or legal guardian when a representative of the department or other agency takes possession of a child under this chapter.

(b) The written notice must be given as soon as practicable, but in any event not later than the first business day after the date the child is taken into possession.

(c) The written notice must include:

(1) the reasons why the department or agency is taking possession of the child and the facts that led the department to believe that the child should be taken into custody;

(2) the name of the person at the department or agency that the parent, conservator, or other custodian may contact for information relating to the child or a legal proceeding relating to the child;

(3) a summary of legal rights of a parent, conservator, guardian, or other custodian under this chapter and an explanation of the probable legal procedures relating to the child; and

(4) a statement that the parent, conservator, or other custodian has the right to hire an attorney.

(d) The written notice may be waived by the court at the initial hearing:

(1) on a showing that:

(A) the parents, conservators, or other custodians of the child could not be located; or

(B) the department took possession of the child under Subchapter D; or

(2) for other good cause.

Sec. 262.1095. Information Provided to Relatives and Certain Individuals; Investigation.

(a) When the Department of Family and Protective Services or another agency takes possession of a child under this chapter, the department:

(1) shall provide information as prescribed by this section in writing to each adult the department is able to identify and locate who is:

(A) related to the child within the fourth degree by consanguinity as determined under Chapter 573, Government Code;

(B) an adult relative of the alleged father of the child if the department has a reasonable basis to believe the alleged father is the child's biological father; or

(C) identified as a potential relative or designated caregiver, as defined by Section 264.751, on the proposed child placement resources form provided under Section 261.307; and

(2) may provide information as prescribed by this section to each adult the department is able to identify and locate who has a long-standing and significant relationship with the child.

(b) The information provided under Subsection (a) must:

(1) state that the child has been removed from the child's home and is in the temporary managing conservatorship of the department;

(2) explain the options available to the individual to participate in the care and placement of the child and the support of the child's family, the methods by which the individual may exercise those options, and any requirements the individual must satisfy to exercise those options, including:

(A) the requirement that the individual be evaluated by the Department of Family and Protective Services under Section 262.114 before the individual may serve as a substitute caregiver; and

(B) the deadlines before which the individual must respond to exercise those options;

(3) identify the options available to the individual that may be lost if the individual fails to respond in a timely manner;

(4) include, if applicable, the date, time, and location of the hearing under Subchapter C, Chapter 263; and

(5) include information regarding the procedures and timeline for a suit affecting the parent-child relationship under this chapter.

(c) The department is not required to provide information to an individual if the individual has received service of citation under Section 102.009 or if the department determines providing information is inappropriate because the individual has a criminal history or a history of family violence.

(d) The department shall use due diligence to identify and locate all individuals described by Subsection (a) not later than the 30th day after the date the department files a suit affecting the parent-child relationship. In order to identify and locate the individuals described by Subsection (a), the department shall seek information from:

(1) each parent, relative, and alleged father of the child; and

(2) the child in an age-appropriate manner.

(d-1) Immediately after the Department of Family and Protective Services identifies and locates an individual described by Subsection (a)(1), the department shall provide the information required by this section.

(e) The failure of a parent or alleged father of the child to complete the proposed child placement resources form does not relieve the department of its duty to seek information about the person under Subsection (d).

Sec. 262.110. Taking Possession of Child in Emergency with Intent to Return Home.

(a) An authorized representative of the Department of Family and Protective Services, a law enforcement officer, or a juvenile probation officer may take temporary possession of a child without a court order on discovery of a child in a situation of danger to the child's physical health or safety when the sole purpose is to deliver the child without unnecessary delay to the parent, managing conservator, possessory conservator, guardian, caretaker, or custodian who is presently entitled to possession of the child.

(b) Until a parent or other person entitled to possession of the child takes possession of the child, the department may retain possession of the child without a court order for not more than five days. On the expiration of the fifth day, if a parent or other person entitled to possession does not take possession of the child, the department shall take action under this chapter as if the department took possession of the child under Section 262.104.

Sec. 262.111. Finding That Child Cannot Remain in or Be Returned to Home [Repealed].

Repealed by Acts 2001, 77th Leg., ch. 849 (H.B. 1566), § 10, effective September 1, 2001.

Sec. 262.112. Expedited Hearing and Appeal.

(a) The Department of Family and Protective Services is entitled to an expedited hearing under this chapter in any proceeding in which a hearing is required if the department determines that a child should be removed from the child's home because of an immediate danger to the physical health or safety of the child.

(b) In any proceeding in which an expedited hearing is held under Subsection (a), the department, parent, guardian, or other party to the proceeding is entitled to an expedited appeal on a ruling by a court that the child may not be removed from the child's home.

(c) If a child is returned to the child's home after a removal in which the department was entitled to an expedited hearing under this section and the child is the subject of a subsequent allegation of abuse or neglect, the department or any other interested party is entitled to an expedited hearing on the removal of the child from the child's home in the manner provided by Subsection (a) and to an expedited appeal in the manner provided by Subsection (b).

Sec. 262.113. Filing Suit Without Taking Possession of Child. [Repealed]

Sec. 262.1131. Temporary Restraining Order Before Full Adversary Hearing. [Repealed]

Sec. 262.114. Evaluation of Identified Relatives and Other Designated Individuals; Placement.

(a) Before a full adversary hearing under Subchapter C, the Department of Family and Protective Services must perform a background and criminal history check of the relatives or other designated individuals identified as a potential relative or designated caregiver, as defined by Section 264.751, on the proposed child placement resources form provided under Section 261.307, including any adult identified by the child. The department shall evaluate each person listed on the form to determine the relative or other designated individual who would be the most appropriate substitute caregiver for the child and must complete a home study of the most appropriate substitute caregiver, if any, before the full adversary hearing. Until the department identifies a relative or other designated individual qualified to be a substitute caregiver, the department must continue to explore substitute caregiver options, including asking the child in a developmentally appropriate manner to identify any adult, particularly an adult residing in the child's community, who could be a relative or designated caregiver for the child. The time frames in this subsection do not apply to a relative or other designated individual located in another state.

(a-1) At the full adversary hearing under Section 262.201, the department shall, after redacting any social security numbers, file with the court:

(1) a copy of each proposed child placement resources form completed by the parent or other person having legal custody of the child;

(2) a copy of any completed home study performed under Subsection (a); and

(3) the name of the relative or other designated caregiver, if any, with whom the child has been placed.

(a-2) If the child has not been placed with a relative or other designated caregiver by the time of the full adversary hearing under Section 262.201, the department shall file with the court a statement that explains:

(1) the reasons why the department has not placed the child with a relative or other designated caregiver listed on the proposed child placement resources form, including any adult identified by the child; and

(2) the actions the department is taking, if any, to place the child with a relative or other designated caregiver.

(b) The department may place a child with a relative or other designated caregiver identified on the proposed child placement resources form, including any adult identified by the child, if the department determines that the placement is in the best interest of the child. The department must complete the background and criminal history check and conduct a preliminary evaluation of the relative or other designated caregiver's home before the child is placed with the relative or other designated caregiver. The department may place the child with the relative or designated caregiver before conducting the home study required under Subsection (a). Not later than 48 hours after the time that the child is placed with the relative or other designated caregiver, the department shall begin the home study of the relative or other designated caregiver. The department shall complete the home study as soon as possible unless otherwise ordered by a court. The department shall provide a copy of an informational manual required under Section 261.3071 to the relative or other designated caregiver at the time of the child's placement.

(c) The department shall consider placing a child who has previously been in the managing conservatorship of the department with a foster parent with whom the child previously resided if:

(1) the department determines that placement of the child with a relative or designated caregiver is not in the child's best interest; and

(2) the placement is available and in the child's best interest.

(d) In making a placement decision for a child, the department shall give preference to persons in the following order:

(1) a person related to the child by blood, marriage, or adoption;

(2) a person with whom the child has a longstanding and significant relationship;

(3) a foster home; and

(4) a general residential operation.

Sec. 262.115. Visitation with Certain Children; Temporary Visitation Schedule.

(a) In this section, "department" means the Department of Family and Protective Services.

(b) This section applies only to a child:

(1) who is in the temporary managing conservatorship of the department; and

(2) for whom the department's goal is reunification of the child with the child's parent.

(c) The department shall ensure that a parent who is otherwise entitled to possession of the child has an opportunity to visit the child not later than the fifth day after the date the department

Texas Family Code

is named temporary managing conservator of the child unless:

(1) the department determines that visitation is not in the child's best interest; or

(2) visitation with the parent would conflict with a court order relating to possession of or access to the child.

(d) Before a hearing conducted under Subchapter C, the department in collaboration with each parent of the child must develop a temporary visitation schedule for the child's visits with each parent. The visitation schedule may conform to the department's minimum visitation policies. The department shall consider the factors listed in Section 263.107(c) in developing the temporary visitation schedule. Unless modified by court order, the schedule remains in effect until a visitation plan is developed under Section 263.107.

(e) The department may include the temporary visitation schedule in any report the department submits to the court before or during a hearing under Subchapter C. The court may render any necessary order regarding the temporary visitation schedule.

Sec. 262.116. Limits on Removal

(a) **[As amended by Acts 2021, 87th Leg., ch. 29 (HB 2536)]** The Department of Family and Protective Services may not take possession of a child under this subchapter based on evidence that the parent:

(1) homeschooled the child;

(2) is economically disadvantaged;

(3) has been charged with a nonviolent misdemeanor offense other than:

(A) an offense under Title 5, Penal Code;

(B) an offense under Title 6, Penal Code; or

(C) an offense that involves family violence, as defined by Section 71.004 of this code;

(4) provided or administered low-THC cannabis to a child for whom the low-THC cannabis was prescribed under Chapter 169, Occupations Code;

(5) declined immunization for the child for reasons of conscience, including a religious belief; or

(6) sought an opinion from more than one medical provider relating to the child's medical care, transferred the child's medical care to a new medical provider, or transferred the child to another health care facility.

(a) **[As amended by Acts 2021, 87th Leg., ch. 8 (HB 567)]**The Department of Family and Protective Services may not take possession of a child under this subchapter based on evidence that the parent:

(1) homeschooled the child;

(2) is economically disadvantaged;

(3) has been charged with a nonviolent misdemeanor offense other than:

(A) an offense under Title 5, Penal Code;

(B) an offense under Title 6, Penal Code; or

(C) an offense that involves family violence, as defined by Section 71.004 of this code;

(4) provided or administered low-THC cannabis to a child for whom the low-THC cannabis was prescribed under Chapter 169, Occupations Code;

(5) declined immunization for the child for reasons of conscience, including a religious belief;

(6) allowed the child to engage in independent activities that are appropriate and typical for the child's level of maturity, physical condition, developmental abilities, or culture; or

(7) tested positive for marihuana, unless the department has evidence that the parent's use of marihuana has caused significant impairment to the child's physical or mental health or emotional development.

(b) The department shall train child protective services caseworkers regarding the prohibitions on removal provided under Subsection (a).

(c) The executive commissioner of the Health and Human Services Commission may adopt rules to implement this section.

(d) This section does not prohibit the department from gathering or offering evidence described by Subsection (a) as part of an action to take possession of a child under this subchapter.

SUBCHAPTER C ADVERSARY HEARING

Sec. 262.201. Full Adversary Hearing; Findings of the Court.

(a) In a suit filed under Section 262.101 or 262.105, unless the child has already been returned to the parent, managing conservator, possessory conservator, guardian, caretaker, or custodian entitled to possession and the temporary order, if any, has been dissolved, a full adversary hearing shall be held not later than the 14th day after the date the child was taken into possession by the governmental entity, unless the court grants an extension under Subsection (e) or (e-1).

(a-1) [Expired.]

(a-2) [Expired.]

(a-3) [Expired.]

(a-4) [Expired.]

(a-5) [Repealed.]

(b) [Repealed.]

(c) Before commencement of the full adversary hearing, the court must inform each parent not represented by an attorney of:

(1) the right to be represented by an attorney; and

(2) if a parent is indigent and appears in opposition to the suit, the right to a court-appointed attorney.

(d) If a parent claims indigence and requests the appointment of an attorney before the full adversary hearing, the court shall require the parent to complete and file with the court an affidavit of indigence. The court may consider additional evidence to determine whether the parent is indigent, including evidence relating to the parent's income, source of income, assets, property ownership, benefits paid in accordance with a federal, state, or local public assistance program, outstanding obligations, and necessary expenses and the number and ages of the parent's dependents. If the appointment of an attorney for the parent is requested, the court shall make a determination of indigence before commencement of the full adversary hearing. If the court determines the parent is indigent, the court shall appoint an attorney to represent the parent.

(e) The court may, for good cause shown, postpone the full adversary hearing for not more than seven days from the date of the attorney's appointment to provide the attorney time to respond to the petition and prepare for the hearing. The court may shorten or lengthen the extension granted under this subsection if the parent and the appointed attorney agree in writing. If the court postpones the full adversary hearing, the court shall extend a temporary order, temporary restraining order, or attachment issued by the court under Section 262.102(a) for the protection of the child until the date of the rescheduled full adversary hearing.

(e-1) If a parent who is not indigent appears in opposition to the suit, the court may, for good cause shown, postpone the full adversary hearing for not more than seven days from the date of the parent's appearance to allow the parent to hire an attorney or to provide the parent's attorney time to respond to the petition and prepare for the hearing. A postponement under this subsection is subject to the limits and requirements prescribed by Subsection (e) and Section 155.207.

(f) The court shall ask all parties present at the full adversary hearing whether the child or the child's family has a Native American heritage and identify any Native American tribe with which the child may be associated.

(g) In a suit filed under Section 262.101 or 262.105, at the conclusion of the full adversary hearing, the court shall order the return of the child to the parent, managing conservator, possessory conservator, guardian, caretaker, or custodian entitled to possession from whom the child is removed unless the court finds sufficient evidence to satisfy a person of ordinary prudence and caution that:

(1) there was a danger to the physical health or safety of the child, including a danger that the child would be a victim of trafficking under Section 20A.02 or 20A.03, Penal Code, which was caused by an act or failure to act of the person entitled to possession and for the child to remain in the home is contrary to the welfare of the child;

(2) the urgent need for protection required the immediate removal of the child and reasonable efforts, consistent with the circumstances and providing for the safety of the child, were made to eliminate or prevent the child's removal; and

(3) reasonable efforts have been made to enable the child to return home, but there is a substantial risk of a continuing danger if the child is returned home.

(g-1) In a suit filed under Section 262.101 or 262.105, if the court does not order the return of the child under Subsection (g) and finds that another parent, managing conservator, possessory conservator, guardian, caretaker, or custodian entitled to possession did not cause the immediate danger to the physical health or safety of the child or was not the perpetrator of the neglect or abuse alleged in the suit, the court shall order possession of the child by that person unless the court finds sufficient evidence to satisfy a person of ordinary prudence and caution that, specific to each person entitled to possession:

(1) the person cannot be located after the exercise of due diligence by the Department of Family and Protective Services, or the person is unable or unwilling to take possession of the child; or

(2) reasonable efforts have been made to enable the person's possession of the child, but possession by that person presents a continuing danger to the physical health or safety of the child caused by an act or failure to act of the person, including a danger that the child would be a victim of trafficking under Section 20A.02 or 20A.03, Penal Code.

(h) In a suit filed under Section 262.101 or 262.105, if the court finds sufficient evidence to make the applicable finding under Subsection (g) or (g-1), the court shall issue an appropriate temporary order under Chapter 105.

(i) In determining whether there is a continuing danger to the physical health or safety of the child under Subsection (g), the court may consider whether the household to which the child would be returned includes a person who:

(1) has abused or neglected another child in a manner that caused serious injury to or the death of the other child; or

(2) has sexually abused another child.

(i-1) In making a determination whether there is an immediate danger to the physical health or safety of a child, the court shall consider the opinion of a medical professional obtained by the child's parent, managing conservator, possessory conservator, guardian, caretaker, or custodian.

(j) [Repealed.]

(k) If the court finds that the child requires protection from family violence, as that term is defined by Section 71.004, by a member of the child's family or household, the court shall render a protective order for the child under Title 4.

(l) The court shall require each parent, alleged father, or relative of the child before the court to complete the proposed child placement resources form provided under Section 261.307 and file the form with the court, if the form has not been previously filed with the court, and provide the Department of Family and Protective Services with information necessary to locate any other absent parent, alleged father, or relative of the child. The court shall inform each parent, alleged father, or relative of the child before the court that the person's failure to submit the proposed child placement resources form will not delay any court proceedings relating to the child.

(l-1) The court shall ask all parties present at the full adversary hearing whether:

(1) the child has had the opportunity, in a developmentally appropriate manner, to identify any adult, particularly an adult residing in the child's community, who could be a relative or designated caregiver for the child; and

(2) each individual identified by the child as a potential relative or designated caregiver is listed on the proposed child placement resources form.

(m) The court shall inform each parent in open court that parental and custodial rights and duties may be subject to restriction or to termination unless the parent or parents are willing and able to provide the child with a safe environment.

(n) If the court does not order possession of a child by a parent, managing conservator, possessory conservator, guardian, caretaker, or custodian entitled to possession under Subsection (g) or (g-1), the court shall place the child with a relative of the child unless the court finds that the placement with a relative is not in the best interest of the child.

(n-1) For a child placed with a relative of the child, the court shall inform the relative of:

(1) the option to become verified by a licensed child-placing agency to operate an agency foster home, if applicable; and

(2) the permanency care assistance program under Subchapter K, Chapter 264.

(o) When citation by publication is needed for a parent or alleged or probable father in an action brought under this chapter because the location of the parent, alleged father, or probable father is unknown, the court may render a temporary order without delay at any time after the filing of the action without regard to whether notice of the citation by publication has been published.

(p) For the purpose of determining under Subsection (a) the 14th day after the date the child is taken into possession, a child is considered to have been taken into possession by the Department of Family and Protective Services on the expiration of the five-day period permitted under Section 262.007(c) or 262.110(b), as appropriate.

(q) On receipt of a written request for possession of the child from a parent, managing conservator, possessory conservator, guardian, caretaker, or custodian entitled to possession of the child who was not located before the adversary hearing, the Department of Family and Protective Services shall notify the court and request a hearing to determine whether the parent, managing conservator, possessory conservator, guardian, caretaker, or custodian is entitled to possession of the child under Subsection (g-1).

Sec. 262.2015. Aggravated Circumstances.

(a) The court may waive the requirement of a service plan and the requirement to make reasonable efforts to return the child to a parent and may accelerate the trial schedule to result in a final order for a child under the care of the Department of Family and Protective Services at an earlier date than provided by Subchapter D, Chapter 263, if the court finds that the parent has subjected the child to aggravated circumstances.

(b) The court may find under Subsection (a) that a parent has subjected the child to aggravated circumstances if:

(1) the parent abandoned the child without identification or a means for identifying the child;

(2) the child or another child of the parent is a victim of serious bodily injury or sexual abuse inflicted by the parent or by another person with the parent's consent;

(3) the parent has engaged in conduct against the child or another child of the parent that would constitute an offense under the following provisions of the Penal Code:

(A) Section 19.02 (murder);

(B) Section 19.03 (capital murder);

(C) Section 19.04 (manslaughter);

(D) Section 21.11 (indecency with a child);
(E) Section 22.011 (sexual assault);
(F) Section 22.02 (aggravated assault);
(G) Section 22.021 (aggravated sexual assault);
(H) Section 22.04 (injury to a child, elderly individual, or disabled individual);
(I) Section 22.041 (abandoning or endangering child);
(J) Section 25.02 (prohibited sexual conduct);
(K) Section 43.25 (sexual performance by a child);
(L) Section 43.26 (possession or promotion of child pornography);
(M) Section 21.02 (continuous sexual abuse of young child or disabled individual);
(N) Section 43.05(a)(2) (compelling prostitution); or
(O) Section 20A.02(a)(7) or (8) (trafficking of persons);
(4) the parent voluntarily left the child alone or in the possession of another person not the parent of the child for at least six months without expressing an intent to return and without providing adequate support for the child;
(5) the parent has been convicted for:
(A) the murder of another child of the parent and the offense would have been an offense under 18 U.S.C. Section 1111(a) if the offense had occurred in the special maritime or territorial jurisdiction of the United States;
(B) the voluntary manslaughter of another child of the parent and the offense would have been an offense under 18 U.S.C. Section 1112(a) if the offense had occurred in the special maritime or territorial jurisdiction of the United States;
(C) aiding or abetting, attempting, conspiring, or soliciting an offense under Paragraph (A) or (B); or
(D) the felony assault of the child or another child of the parent that resulted in serious bodily injury to the child or another child of the parent; or
(6) the parent is required under any state or federal law to register with a sex offender registry.
(c) On finding that reasonable efforts to make it possible for the child to safely return to the child's home are not required, the court shall at any time before the 30th day after the date of the finding, conduct an initial permanency hearing under Subchapter D, Chapter 263. Separate notice of the permanency plan is not required but may be given with a notice of a hearing under this section.
(d) The Department of Family and Protective Services shall make reasonable efforts to finalize the permanent placement of a child for whom the court has made the finding described by Subsection (c). The court shall set the suit for trial on the merits as required by Subchapter D, Chapter 263, in order to facilitate final placement of the child.

Sec. 262.202. Identification of Court of Continuing, Exclusive Jurisdiction.

If at the conclusion of the full adversary hearing the court renders a temporary order, the governmental entity shall request identification of a court of continuing, exclusive jurisdiction as provided by Chapter 155.

Sec. 262.203. Transfer of Suit.

(a) On the motion of a party or the court's own motion, if applicable, the court that rendered the temporary order shall in accordance with procedures provided by Chapter 155:
(1) transfer the suit to the court of continuing, exclusive jurisdiction, if any, within the time required by Section 155.207(a), if the court finds that the transfer is:
(A) necessary for the convenience of the parties; and
(B) in the best interest of the child;
(2) order transfer of the suit from the court of continuing, exclusive jurisdiction; or
(3) if grounds exist for transfer based on improper venue, order transfer of the suit to the court having venue of the suit under Chapter 103.
(b) Notwithstanding Section 155.204, a motion to transfer relating to a suit filed under this chapter may be filed separately from the petition and is timely if filed while the case is pending.
(c) Notwithstanding Sections 6.407 and 103.002, a court exercising jurisdiction under this chapter is not required to transfer the suit to a court in which a parent has filed a suit for dissolution of marriage before a final order for the protection of the child has been rendered under Subchapter E, Chapter 263.
(d) An order of transfer must include:
(1) the date of any future hearings in the case that have been scheduled by the transferring court;
(2) any date scheduled by the transferring court for the dismissal of the suit under Section 263.401; and
(3) the name and contact information of each attorney ad litem or guardian ad litem appointed in the suit.
(e) The court to which a suit is transferred may retain an attorney ad litem or guardian ad litem appointed by the transferring court. If the court finds that the appointment of a new attorney ad litem or guardian ad litem is appropriate, the court shall appoint that attorney ad litem or guardian ad litem before the earlier of:
(1) the 10th day after the date of receiving the order of transfer; or

(2) the date of the first scheduled hearing after the transfer.

Sec. 262.204. Temporary Order in Effect Until Superseded.

(a) A temporary order rendered under this chapter is valid and enforceable until properly superseded by a court with jurisdiction to do so.

(b) A court to which the suit has been transferred may enforce by contempt or otherwise a temporary order properly issued under this chapter.

Sec. 262.205. Hearing When Child Not in Possession of Governmental Entity. [Repealed]

Sec. 262.206. Ex Parte Hearings Prohibited.

Unless otherwise authorized by this chapter or other law, a hearing held by a court in a suit under this chapter may not be ex parte.

SUBCHAPTER D EMERGENCY POSSESSION OF CERTAIN ABANDONED CHILDREN

Sec. 262.301. Definitions.

In this chapter:

(1) "Designated emergency infant care provider" means:

(A) an emergency medical services provider;

(B) a hospital;

(C) a freestanding emergency medical care facility licensed under Chapter 254, Health and Safety Code; or

(D) a child-placing agency licensed by the Department of Family and Protective Services under Chapter 42, Human Resources Code, that:

(i) agrees to act as a designated emergency infant care provider under this subchapter; and

(ii) has on staff a person who is licensed as a registered nurse under Chapter 301, Occupations Code, or who provides emergency medical services under Chapter 773, Health and Safety Code, and who will examine and provide emergency medical services to a child taken into possession by the agency under this subchapter.

(2) "Emergency medical services provider" has the meaning assigned that term by Section 773.003, Health and Safety Code.

Sec. 262.302. Accepting Possession of Certain Abandoned Children.

(a) A designated emergency infant care provider shall, without a court order, take possession of a child who appears to be 60 days old or younger if the child is voluntarily delivered to the provider by the child's parent and the parent did not express an intent to return for the child.

(b) A designated emergency infant care provider who takes possession of a child under this section has no legal duty to detain or pursue the parent and may not do so unless the child appears to have been abused or neglected. The designated emergency infant care provider has no legal duty to ascertain the parent's identity and the parent may remain anonymous. However, the parent may be given a form for voluntary disclosure of the child's medical facts and history.

(c) A designated emergency infant care provider who takes possession of a child under this section shall perform any act necessary to protect the physical health or safety of the child. The designated emergency infant care provider is not liable for damages related to the provider's taking possession of, examining, or treating the child, except for damages related to the provider's negligence.

Sec. 262.303. Notification of Possession of Abandoned Child.

(a) Not later than the close of the first business day after the date on which a designated emergency infant care provider takes possession of a child under Section 262.302, the provider shall notify the Department of Family and Protective Services that the provider has taken possession of the child.

(b) The department shall assume the care, control, and custody of the child immediately on receipt of notice under Subsection (a).

Sec. 262.304. Filing Petition After Accepting Possession of Abandoned Child.

A child for whom the Department of Family and Protective Services assumes care, control, and custody under Section 262.303 shall be treated as a child taken into possession without a court order, and the department shall take action as required by Section 262.105 with regard to the child.

Sec. 262.305. Report to Law Enforcement Agency; Investigation.

(a) Immediately after assuming care, control, and custody of a child under Section 262.303, the

Texas Family Code

Department of Family and Protective Services shall report the child to appropriate state and local law enforcement agencies as a potential missing child.

(b) A law enforcement agency that receives a report under Subsection (a) shall investigate whether the child is reported as missing.

Sec. 262.306. Notice.

Each designated emergency infant care provider shall post in a conspicuous location a notice stating that the provider is a designated emergency infant care provider location and will accept possession of a child in accordance with this subchapter.

Sec. 262.307. Reimbursement for Care of Abandoned Child.

The Department of Family and Protective Services shall reimburse a designated emergency infant care provider that takes possession of a child under Section 262.302 for the cost to the provider of assuming the care, control, and custody of the child.

Sec. 262.308. Confidentiality.

(a) All identifying information, documentation, or other records regarding a person who voluntarily delivers a child to a designated emergency infant care provider under this subchapter is confidential and not subject to release to any individual or entity except as provided by Subsection (b).

(b) Any pleading or other document filed with a court under this subchapter is confidential, is not public information for purposes of Chapter 552, Government Code, and may not be released to a person other than to a party in a suit regarding the child, the party's attorney, or an attorney ad litem or guardian ad litem appointed in the suit.

(c) In a suit concerning a child for whom the Department of Family and Protective Services assumes care, control, and custody under this subchapter, the court shall close the hearing to the public unless the court finds that the interests of the child or the public would be better served by opening the hearing to the public.

(d) Unless the disclosure, receipt, or use is permitted by this section, a person commits an offense if the person knowingly discloses, receives, uses, or permits the use of information derived from records or files described by this section or knowingly discloses identifying information concerning a person who voluntarily delivers a child to a designated emergency infant care provider. An offense under this subsection is a Class B misdemeanor.

Sec. 262.309. Search for Relatives Not Required.

The Department of Family and Protective Services is not required to conduct a search for the relatives of a child for whom the department assumes care, control, and custody under this subchapter.

SUBCHAPTER E
RELINQUISHING CHILD TO OBTAIN CERTAIN SERVICES

Sec. 262.351. Definitions.

In this subchapter:

(1) "Commission" means the Health and Human Services Commission.

(1-a) "Department" means the Department of Family and Protective Services.

(1-b) "Relinquishment avoidance program" means the Health and Human Services Commission's program that provides mental health services to a child with a severe emotional disturbance without the child entering the managing conservatorship of the department.

(2) "Severe emotional disturbance" has the meaning assigned by Section 261.001.

Sec. 262.352. Joint Managing Conservatorship of Child.

(a) Before the department files a suit affecting the parent-child relationship requesting managing conservatorship of a child who suffers from a severe emotional disturbance in order to obtain mental health services for the child, the department must, unless it is not in the best interest of the child, discuss with the child's parent or legal guardian the option of seeking a court order for joint managing conservatorship of the child with the department.

(b) **[Expires September 1, 2019]** Not later than November 1 of each even-numbered year, the department shall report the following information to the legislature:

(1) with respect to children described by Subsection (a):

(A) the number of children for whom the department has been appointed managing conservator;

(B) the number of children for whom the department has been appointed joint managing conservator; and

(C) the number of children who were diverted to community or residential mental health services through another agency; and

Texas Family Code

(2) the number of persons whose names were entered into the central registry of cases of child abuse and neglect only because the department was named managing conservator of a child who has a severe emotional disturbance because the child's family was unable to obtain mental health services for the child.

(c) **[Expires September 1, 2019]** Subsection (b) and this subsection expire September 1, 2019.

Sec. 262.353. Procedure for Relinquishing Child to Obtain Services.

(a) The commission may not require the department to conduct a child abuse or neglect investigation before allowing a child to participate in the relinquishment avoidance program unless there is an allegation of abuse or neglect of the child.

(b) A local mental or behavioral health authority may refer a child directly to the relinquishment avoidance program without first contacting the department.

(c) The department and the commission shall:

(1) jointly adopt comprehensive guidance for providers and families that describes:

(A) how to access services under the relinquishment avoidance program; and

(B) the child's and family's rights when the child's parent or legal guardian:

(i) relinquishes the child in order to obtain mental health services for the child; or

(ii) accesses services under the relinquishment avoidance program;

(2) publish the information described by Subdivision (1) on the agency's Internet website; and

(3) make the information described by Subdivision (1) available to caseworkers and families with a child who has a severe emotional disturbance.

(d) The department and the commission shall jointly adopt clear and concise protocols for families at risk of relinquishing a child for the sole purpose of accessing mental health services for the child. The protocols must:

(1) include procedures for determining eligibility for the relinquishment avoidance program, including emergency eligibility procedures for children who are at immediate risk of relinquishment;

(2) include procedures for applying for the relinquishment avoidance program;

(3) identify who will manage the case of a family eligible for the relinquishment avoidance program;

(4) identify the funding and resources for the relinquishment avoidance program; and

(5) identify the role of each party involved in the relinquishment avoidance program, including the department, the commission, contracted residential treatment centers, and local mental and behavioral health authorities.

(e) The department and local mental and behavioral health authorities shall follow the protocols adopted under Subsection (d).

SUBCHAPTER F
FAMILY PRESERVATION SERVICES PILOT PROGRAM

Sec. 262.401. Definitions.

In this subchapter:

(1) "Child who is a candidate for foster care" means a child who is at imminent risk of being removed from the child's home and placed into the conservatorship of the department because of a continuing danger to the child's physical health or safety caused by an act or failure to act of a person entitled to possession of the child but for whom a court of competent jurisdiction has issued an order allowing the child to remain safely in the child's home or in a kinship placement with the provision of family preservation services.

(2) "Department" means the Department of Family and Protective Services.

(3) "Family preservation service" means a time-limited, family-focused service, including a service subject to the Family First Prevention Services Act (Title VII, Div. E, Pub. L. No. 115-123), provided to the family of a child who is:

(A) a candidate for foster care to prevent or eliminate the need to remove the child and to allow the child to remain safely with the child's family; or

(B) a pregnant or parenting foster youth.

(4) "Family preservation services plan" means a written plan, based on a professional assessment, listing the family preservation services, including services subject to the Family First Prevention Services Act (Title VII, Div. E, Pub. L. No. 115-123), to be provided to the family of a child who is:

(A) a candidate for foster care; or

(B) a pregnant or parenting foster youth.

(5) "Foster care" means substitute care as defined by Section 263.001.

Sec. 262.402. Pilot Program for Family Preservation Services.

(a) The department shall establish a pilot program that allows the department to dispose of an investigation by referring the family of a child who is a candidate for foster care for family preservation services and allowing the child to return home instead of entering foster care or by providing services to a pregnant or parenting foster youth. The department shall implement the pilot program in two child protective services regions in this state, one urban and one rural.

(b) The pilot program must be implemented in at least one child protective services region in this state in which community-based care has been implemented under Subchapter B-1, Chapter 264.

(c) In authorizing family preservation services for a child who is a candidate for foster care, the child's safety is the primary concern. The services may be modified as necessary to accommodate the child's circumstances.

(d) In implementing the pilot program, the department shall use:

(1) Title IV-E funds to:

(A) pay for legal representation for parents in the manner provided by Section 107.015; or

(B) provide to counties a matching reimbursement for the cost of the legal representation; and

(2) funds received under the Temporary Assistance for Needy Families (TANF) program or other department funds to provide enhanced in-home support services to families qualifying for prevention services under this subchapter to achieve the objectives in the family preservation services plan.

Sec. 262.403. Court Order Required.

(a) Subject to Subsection (b), the department must obtain a court order from a court of competent jurisdiction to compel the family of a child who is a candidate for foster care to obtain family preservation services and complete the family preservation services plan.

(b) The department is not required to obtain a court order to provide family preservation services to a pregnant or parenting foster youth.

Sec. 262.404. Filing Suit; Petition Requirements.

(a) The department may file a suit requesting the court to render an order requiring the parent, managing conservator, guardian, or other member of the child's household to:

(1) participate in the family preservation services for which the department makes a referral or services the department provides or purchases to:

(A) alleviate the effects of the abuse or neglect that has occurred;

(B) reduce a continuing danger to the physical health or safety of the child caused by an act or failure to act of the parent, managing conservator, guardian, or other member of the child's household; or

(C) reduce a substantial risk of abuse or neglect caused by an act or failure to act of the parent, managing conservator, guardian, or other member of the child's household;

(2) permit the child and any siblings of the child to receive the services; and

(3) complete all actions and services required under the family preservation services plan.

(b) A suit requesting an order under this section may be filed in a court with jurisdiction to hear the suit in the county in which the child is located.

(c) Except as otherwise provided by this subchapter, the suit is governed by the Texas Rules of Civil Procedure applicable to the filing of an original lawsuit.

(d) The petition for suit must be supported by:

(1) a sworn affidavit based on personal knowledge and stating facts sufficient to support a finding that:

(A) the child has been a victim of abuse or neglect or is at substantial risk of abuse or neglect; and

(B) there is a continuing danger to the child's physical health or safety caused by an act or failure to act of the parent, managing conservator, guardian, or other member of the child's household unless that person participates in family preservation services requested by the department; and

(2) a safety risk assessment for the child that documents:

(A) the process for the child to remain at home with appropriate family preservation services instead of foster care;

(B) the specific reasons the department should provide family preservation services to the family; and

(C) the manner in which family preservation services will mitigate the risk of the child entering foster care.

(e) In a suit filed under this section, the court may render a temporary restraining order as provided by Section 105.001.

(f) The court shall hold a hearing on the petition not later than the 14th day after the date the petition is filed unless the court finds good cause for extending that date for not more than 14 days.

Sec. 262.405. Ad Litem Appointments.

(a) The court shall appoint an attorney ad litem to represent the interests of the child immediately after a suit is filed under Section 262.404 but before the hearing to ensure adequate representation of the child. The attorney ad litem for the child has the powers and duties of an attorney ad litem for a child under Chapter 107.

Texas Family Code

(b) The court shall appoint an attorney ad litem to represent the interests of a parent for whom participation in family preservation services is being requested immediately after the suit is filed but before the hearing to ensure adequate representation of the parent. The attorney ad litem for the parent has the powers and duties of an attorney ad litem for a parent under Section 107.0131.

(c) Before the hearing commences, the court shall inform each parent of:

(1) the parent's right to be represented by an attorney; and

(2) for a parent who is indigent and appears in opposition to the motion, the parent's right to a court-appointed attorney.

(d) If a parent claims indigence, the court shall require the parent to complete and file with the court an affidavit of indigence. The court may consider additional evidence to determine whether the parent is indigent, including evidence relating to the parent's income, source of income, assets, property ownership, benefits paid in accordance with a federal, state, or local public assistance program, outstanding obligations, and necessary expenses and the number and ages of the parent's dependents. If the court finds the parent is indigent, the attorney ad litem appointed to represent the interests of the parent may continue the representation. If the court finds the parent is not indigent, the court shall discharge the attorney ad litem from the appointment after the hearing and order the parent to pay the cost of the attorney ad litem's representation.

(e) The court may, for good cause shown, postpone any subsequent proceedings for not more than seven days after the date of the attorney ad litem's discharge to allow the parent to hire an attorney or to provide the parent's attorney time to prepare for the subsequent proceeding.

Sec. 262.406. Court Order.

(a) Except as provided by Subsection (d), at the conclusion of the hearing in a suit filed under Section 262.404, the court shall order the department to provide family preservation services and to execute a family preservation services plan developed in collaboration with the family of the child who is a candidate for foster care if the court finds sufficient evidence to satisfy a person of ordinary prudence and caution that:

(1) abuse or neglect occurred or there is a substantial risk of abuse or neglect or continuing danger to the child's physical health or safety caused by an act or failure to act of the parent, managing conservator, guardian, or other member of the child's household;

(2) family preservation services are necessary to ensure the child's physical health or safety; and

(3) family preservation services are appropriate based on the child's safety risk assessment and the child's family assessment.

(b) The court's order for family preservation services must:

(1) identify and require specific services narrowly tailored to address the factors that make the child a candidate for foster care; and

(2) include a statement on whether the services to be provided to the family are appropriate to address the factors that place the child at risk of removal.

(c) The court may, in its discretion, order family preservation services for a parent whose parental rights to another child were previously terminated.

(d) If the court finds, by clear and convincing evidence, that the parent has subjected the child to aggravated circumstances described by Section 262.2015, the court may order that family preservation services not be provided.

Sec. 262.407. Family Preservation Services Plan; Contents.

(a) On order of the court under Section 262.406, the department in consultation with the child's family shall develop a family preservation services plan. The department and the family shall discuss each term and condition of the plan.

(b) The family preservation services plan must be written in a manner that is clear and understandable to the parent, managing conservator, guardian, or other member of the child's household and in a language the person understands.

(c) The family preservation services plan must:

(1) include a safety risk assessment of the child who is the subject of the investigation and an assessment of the child's family;

(2) state the reasons the department is involved with the family;

(3) be narrowly tailored to address the specific reasons the department is involved with the family and the factors that make the child a candidate for foster care;

(4) list the specific family preservation services the family will receive under the plan and identify the manner in which those services will mitigate the child's specific risk factors and allow the child to remain safely at home;

(5) specify the tasks the family must complete during the effective period of the plan and include a schedule with appropriate completion dates for those tasks; and

(6) include the name of the department or single source continuum contractor representative who

will serve as a contact for the family in obtaining information related to the plan.

(d) The family preservation services plan must include the following statement:

"TO THE PARENT OF THE CHILD SERVED BY THIS PLAN: THIS DOCUMENT IS VERY IMPORTANT. ITS PURPOSE IS TO HELP YOU PROVIDE YOUR CHILD WITH A SAFE ENVIRONMENT WITHIN THE REASONABLE PERIOD SPECIFIED IN THIS PLAN. IF YOU ARE UNWILLING OR UNABLE TO PROVIDE YOUR CHILD WITH A SAFE ENVIRONMENT, YOUR CHILD MAY BE REMOVED FROM YOU, AND YOUR PARENTAL AND CUSTODIAL DUTIES AND RIGHTS MAY BE RESTRICTED OR TERMINATED. A COURT HEARING WILL BE HELD AT WHICH A JUDGE WILL REVIEW THIS FAMILY PRESERVATION SERVICES PLAN."

Sec. 262.408. Family Preservation Services Plan: Signing and Effect.

(a) The family of a child who is a candidate for foster care and the department shall sign the family preservation services plan, and the department shall submit a copy of the signed plan to the court for review.

(b) If the family is unwilling to participate in the development of the family preservation services plan, the department may submit the plan to the court without the parents' signatures.

(c) The family preservation services plan takes effect on the date the court certifies that the plan complies with the court's order for family preservation services and is narrowly tailored to address the factors that make the child a candidate for foster care. The court may hold a hearing to review the plan for compliance.

(d) The family preservation services plan remains in effect until:

(1) the 180th day after the date the court's order for family preservation services is signed, unless renewed by an order of the court; or

(2) the date the plan is amended or revoked by the court.

(e) A person subject to the family preservation services plan may file a motion with the court at any time to request a modification or revocation of the original or any amended plan.

Sec. 262.409. Amended Family Preservation Services Plan.

(a) A family preservation services plan may be amended at any time. The department or single source continuum contractor and the parents of a child who is a candidate for foster care shall jointly develop any amendment to the plan. The department or contractor must inform the parents of their rights related to the amended family preservation services plan process.

(b) The parents and the person preparing the amended family preservation services plan shall sign the amended plan, and the department or single source continuum contractor shall submit the amended plan to the court for review.

(c) If the parents are unwilling to participate in the development of the amended family preservation services plan, the department or single source continuum contractor may submit the amended plan to the court without the parents' signatures.

(d) The amended family preservation services plan takes effect on the date the court certifies that the amended plan complies with the court's order for family preservation services and is narrowly tailored to address the factors that make the child a candidate for foster care. The court may hold a hearing to review the amended plan for compliance.

(e) The amended family preservation services plan is in effect until:

(1) the 180th day after the date the court's order for family preservation services is signed, unless renewed by an order of the court; or

(2) the date the amended plan is modified or revoked by the court.

Sec. 262.410. Court Implementation of Family Preservation Services Plan.

(a) After reviewing and certifying an original or any amended family preservation services plan, the court shall incorporate the original and any amended plan into the court's order and may render additional appropriate orders to implement or require compliance with an original or amended plan.

(b) In rendering an order, a court may omit any service prescribed under the family preservation services plan that the court finds is not appropriate or is not narrowly tailored to address the factors that make the child a candidate for foster care and place the child at risk of removal.

Sec. 262.411. Selection of Service Provider.

(a) A parent, managing conservator, guardian, or other member of a household ordered to participate in family preservation services under this subchapter may obtain those services from a qualified or licensed provider selected by the person.

(b) Services provided by a provider selected under Subsection (a) must be similar in scope and duration to services described by the family preservation services plan adopted under Section 262.407 and achieve the stated goals of the service plan. The service provider must certify in writing that the parent, managing conservator, guardian, or other member of a household completed the services.

(c) A parent, managing conservator, guardian, or other member of a household who obtains family preservation services from a provider selected by the person is responsible for the cost of those services.

(d) A parent, managing conservator, guardian, or other member of a household who successfully completes the required family preservation services must obtain verification from the service provider of that completion. The department shall accept the service provider's verification provided under this subsection as proof that the person successfully completed the court-ordered family preservation services.

Sec. 262.412. Status Hearing.

Not later than the 90th day after the date the court renders an order for family preservation services under this subchapter, the court shall hold a hearing to review the status of each person required to participate in the services and of the child and to review the services provided, purchased, or referred. The court shall set subsequent review hearings every 90 days to review the continued need for the order.

Sec. 262.413. Extension of Order.

(a) The court may extend an order for family preservation services rendered under this subchapter on a showing by the department of a continuing need for the order, after notice and hearing. Except as provided by Subsection (b), the court may extend the order only one time for not more than 180 days.

(b) The court may extend an order rendered under this subchapter for not more than an additional 180 days only if:

(1) the court finds that:

(A) the extension is necessary to allow the person required to participate in family preservation services under the family preservation services plan time to complete those services;

(B) the department made a good faith effort to timely provide the services to the person;

(C) the person made a good faith effort to complete the services; and

(D) the completion of the services is necessary to ensure the physical health and safety of the child; and

(2) the extension is requested by the person required to participate in family preservation services under the family preservation services plan or the person's attorney.

Sec. 262.414. Expiration of Order.

On expiration of a court order for family preservation services under this subchapter, the court shall dismiss the case.

Sec. 262.415. Contract for Services.

(a) The department may contract with one or more persons to provide family preservation services under the pilot program. In a child protective services region in this state in which community-based care under Subchapter B-1, Chapter 264, has been implemented and in which the pilot program is implemented, the department may contract with the single source continuum contractor to provide family preservation services under the pilot program.

(b) The contract with the person selected to provide family preservation services must include performance-based measures that require the person to show that as a result of the services:

(1) fewer children enter foster care in the pilot program region in comparison to other regions of this state;

(2) fewer children are removed from their families after receiving the services in the pilot program region in comparison to other regions of this state; and

(3) fewer children enter foster care in the five years following completion of the services in the pilot program region in comparison to other regions of this state.

(c) The department shall collaborate with a person selected to provide family preservation services to identify children who are candidates for foster care or who are pregnant or parenting foster youth and to ensure that the services are appropriate for children referred by the department.

Sec. 262.416. Limit on Finance of Services.

If a court order for services under this subchapter includes services that are not subject to the Family First Prevention Services Act (Title VII, Div. E., Pub. L. No. 115-123), the order must identify a method of financing for the services and the local jurisdiction that will pay for the services.

Sec. 262.417. Report to Legislature.

(a) Not later than the first anniversary of the date the department commences a pilot program under this subchapter and every two years after that date, the department shall contract with an entity based in this state that is independent of the department and has demonstrated expertise in statistical, financial, logistical, and operational analysis to evaluate the implementation of the pilot program under this subchapter, assess its progress, and report its findings to the appropriate standing committees of the legislature having jurisdiction over child protective services and foster care matters. The report must include:

(1) a detailed description of the actions taken by the department to ensure the successful implementation of the pilot program;

(2) a detailed analysis of the role each of the following entities has in the pilot program:

(A) the courts;

(B) legal representatives;

(C) the investigations division of the department; and

(D) the department or other entity implementing the pilot program;

(3) an analysis of any barrier to the successful implementation of the pilot program and recommendations for overcoming those barriers;

(4) data on the performance-based outcomes described by Subsection (b) and achieved in the child protective services region in which the pilot program is implemented;

(5) a detailed comparison of outcomes achieved in the child protective services region in which the pilot program is implemented with outcomes achieved in other child protective services regions;

(6) a detailed description of the costs of the pilot program and services provided; and

(7) recommendations on whether to expand services described in this subchapter to other child protective services regions in this state based on the outcomes and performance of the pilot program.

(b) Performance-based outcomes for evaluating the pilot program must include:

(1) the number of children served;

(2) the number of families served;

(3) the percentage of children who do not have a reported finding of abuse, neglect, or exploitation;

(4) the percentage of children served who did not enter foster care at case closure;

(5) the percentage of children served who did not enter foster care within six months and one year of the date the case was closed;

(6) the number of families who received family preservation services under the pilot program for whom the department opens an investigation of abuse or neglect involving the family before the second anniversary of the date the case was closed; and

(7) the average length of time services are provided from the entry of an order for family preservation services to case dismissal.

CHAPTER 264
CHILD WELFARE SERVICES

SUBCHAPTER F
CHILD FATALITY REVIEW AND INVESTIGATION

Sec. 264.513. Report of Death of Child.

(a) A person who knows of the death of a child younger than six years of age shall immediately report the death to the medical examiner of the county in which the death occurs or, if the death occurs in a county that does not have a medical examiner's office or that is not part of a medical examiner's district, to a justice of the peace in that county.

(b) The requirement of this section is in addition to any other reporting requirement imposed by law, including any requirement that a person report child abuse or neglect under this code.

(c) A person is not required to report a death under this section that is the result of a motor vehicle accident. This subsection does not affect a duty imposed by another law to report a death that is the result of a motor vehicle accident.

SUBCHAPTER I
RELATIVE AND OTHER DESIGNATED CAREGIVER PLACEMENT PROGRAM

Sec. 264.7551. Fraudulent Agreement; Criminal Offense; Civil Penalty.

(a) A person commits an offense if, with intent to defraud or deceive the department, the person knowingly makes or causes to be made a false statement or misrepresentation of a material fact that allows a person to enter into a caregiver assistance agreement.

(b) An offense under this section is:

(1) a Class C misdemeanor if the person entered into a fraudulent caregiver assistance agreement and received no monetary assistance under the agreement or received monetary assistance under the agreement for less than 7 days;

(2) a Class B misdemeanor if the person entered into a fraudulent caregiver assistance agreement and received monetary assistance under the agreement for 7 days or more but less than 31 days;

(3) a Class A misdemeanor if the person entered into a fraudulent caregiver assistance agreement and received monetary assistance under the agreement for 31 days or more but less than 91 days; or

(4) a state jail felony if the person entered into a fraudulent caregiver assistance agreement and received monetary assistance under the agreement for 91 days or more.

(c) If conduct that constitutes an offense under this section also constitutes an offense under any other law, the actor may be prosecuted under this section, the other law, or both.

(d) The appropriate county prosecuting attorney shall be responsible for the prosecution of an offense under this section.

(e) A person who engaged in conduct described by Subsection (a) is liable to the state for a civil penalty of $1,000. The attorney general shall bring an action to recover a civil penalty as authorized by this subsection.

(f) The commissioner of the department may adopt rules necessary to determine whether fraudulent activity that violates Subsection (a) has occurred.

FINANCE CODE

TITLE 3 FINANCIAL INSTITUTIONS AND BUSINESSES

SUBTITLE E OTHER FINANCIAL BUSINESSES

CHAPTER 151 REGULATION OF MONEY SERVICES BUSINESSES

SUBCHAPTER A GENERAL PROVISIONS

Sec. 151.001. Short Title.

This chapter may be cited as the Money Services Act.

Sec. 151.002. Definitions.

(a) This section defines general terms that apply to an applicant for or holder of a money services license issued under this chapter, regardless of whether the license is a money transmission license or a currency exchange license. Additional terms that apply specifically to money transmission are defined in Section 151.301. Additional terms that apply specifically to currency exchange are defined in Section 151.501.

(b) In this chapter:

(1) "Applicant" means a person that files an application for a license under this chapter.

(2) "Authorized delegate" means a person a license holder appoints under Section 151.402 to conduct money transmission on behalf of the license holder.

(3) "Bank Secrecy Act" means the Bank Secrecy Act (31 U.S.C. Section 5311 et seq.), and its implementing regulations.

(4) "Commission" means the Finance Commission of Texas.

(5) "Commissioner" means the Banking Commissioner of Texas or a person designated by the banking commissioner and acting under the banking commissioner's direction and authority.

(6) "Control" means ownership of, or the power to directly or indirectly vote, 25 percent or more of the outstanding voting interests of a license holder or applicant, and includes an individual whose ownership is through one or more legal entities.

(7) "Currency exchange" has the meaning assigned by Section 151.501.

(8) "Currency exchange license" means a license issued under Subchapter F.

(9) "Department" means the Texas Department of Banking.

(9-a) [Repealed.]

(9-b) [Repealed.]

(9-c) [Repealed.]

(10) "Executive officer" means a president, a presiding officer of the executive committee, a treasurer or chief financial officer, or any other individual who performs similar functions.

(11) "License holder" means a person that holds a money transmission license or a currency exchange license.

(12) "Location" means a place at which activity regulated by this chapter occurs.

(13) "Material litigation" means any litigation that, according to generally accepted accounting principles, is considered significant to an applicant's or license holder's financial health and would be required to be referenced in that entity's audited financial statements, report to shareholders, or similar documents.

(14) "Money services" means money transmission or currency exchange services.

(15) "Money transmission" has the meaning assigned by Section 151.301.

(16) "Money transmission license" means a license issued under Subchapter D.

(17) "Person" means an individual or legal entity.

(18) "Principal" means:

(A) with respect to a sole proprietorship, an owner; or

(B) with respect to a legal entity other than a sole proprietorship, an executive officer, director, general partner, trustee, or manager, as applicable.

(19) "Record" means information that is:

(A) inscribed on a tangible medium; or

(B) stored in an electronic or other medium and retrievable in perceivable form.

(20) "Responsible individual" means an individual who has direct control over or significant management policy and decision-making authority with respect to a license holder's ongoing, daily money services operations in this state.

(20-a) "Tangible net worth" means the total value of all assets, minus any liabilities and intangible assets.

(21) "USA PATRIOT ACT" means the Uniting and Strengthening America by Providing Appropriate Tools Required to Intercept and Obstruct Terrorism (USA PATRIOT ACT) Act of 2001 (Pub. L. No. 107-56, 115 Stat. 272).

Sec. 151.003. Exclusions.

The following persons are not required to be licensed under this chapter:

(1) the United States or an instrumentality of the United States, including the United States Post Office or a contractor acting on behalf of the United States Post Office;

(2) a state or an agency, political subdivision, or other instrumentality of a state;

(3) a federally insured financial institution, as that term is defined by Section 201.101, that is organized under the laws of this state, another state, or the United States;

(4) a foreign bank branch or agency in the United States established under the federal International Banking Act of 1978 (12 U.S.C. Section 3101 et seq.);

(5) a person acting as an agent for an entity excluded under Subdivision (3) or (4), to the extent of the person's actions in that capacity, provided that:

(A) the entity is liable for satisfying the money services obligation owed to the purchaser on the person's receipt of the purchaser's money; and

(B) the entity and person enter into a written contract that appoints the person as the entity's agent and the person acts only within the scope of authority conferred by the contract;

(6) a person that, on behalf of the United States or a department, agency, or instrumentality of the United States, or a state or county, city, or any other governmental agency or political subdivision of a state, provides electronic funds transfer services of governmental benefits for a federal, state, county, or local governmental agency;

(7) a person that acts as an intermediary on behalf of and at the direction of a license holder in the process by which the license holder, after receiving money or monetary value from a purchaser, either directly or through an authorized delegate, transmits the money or monetary value to the purchaser's designated recipient, provided that the license holder is liable for satisfying the obligation owed to the purchaser;

(8) an attorney or title company that in connection with a real property transaction receives and disburses domestic currency or issues an escrow or trust fund check only on behalf of a party to the transaction;

(9) a person engaged in the business of currency transportation who is both a registered motor carrier under Chapter 643, Transportation Code, and a licensed armored car company or courier company under Chapter 1702, Occupations Code, provided that the person:

(A) only transports currency:

(i) from a person to the same person at another location;

(ii) from a person to a financial institution to be deposited in an account belonging to the same person; or

(iii) to a person from a financial institution after being withdrawn from an account belonging to the same person; and

(B) does not otherwise engage in the money transmission or currency exchange business without a license issued under this chapter;

(9-a) a trust company, as defined by Section 187.001(a), that is organized under the laws of this state; and

(10) any other person, transaction, or class of persons or transactions exempted by commission rule or any other person or transaction exempted by the commissioner's order on a finding that the licensing of the person is not necessary to achieve the purposes of this chapter.

Sec. 151.051. Incorporation Requirement [Repealed].

Repealed by Acts 1999, 76th leg., ch. 62 (S.B. 1368), § 7.17(b), effective September 1, 1999.

Sec. 151.052. Purposes of Incorporation [Repealed].

Repealed by Acts 1999, 76th leg., ch. 62 (S.B. 1368), § 7.17(b), effective September 1, 1999.

Sec. 151.053. Paid-In Capital [Repealed].

Repealed by Acts 1999, 76th leg., ch. 62 (S.B. 1368), § 7.17(b), effective September 1, 1999.

Sec. 151.054. Determination of Application for Charter; Appeal [Repealed].

Repealed by Acts 1999, 76th leg., ch. 62 (S.B. 1368), § 7.17(b), effective September 1, 1999.

SUBCHAPTER B ADMINISTRATIVE PROVISIONS

Sec. 151.101. Administration.

The department shall administer this chapter.

Sec. 151.102. Rules.

(a) The commission may adopt rules to administer and enforce this chapter, including rules necessary or appropriate to:

(1) implement and clarify this chapter;

(2) preserve and protect the safety and soundness of money services businesses;

(3) protect the interests of purchasers of money services and the public;

(4) protect against drug trafficking, terrorist funding, and money laundering, structuring, or a related financial crime; and

(5) recover the cost of maintaining and operating the department and the cost of administering and enforcing this chapter and other applicable law by imposing and collecting proportionate and equitable fees and costs for notices, applications, examinations, investigations, and other actions required to achieve the purposes of this chapter.

(b) The presence or absence of a specific reference in this chapter to a rule regarding a particular subject is not intended to and does not limit the general rulemaking authority granted to the commission by this section.

Sec. 151.103. Commissioner's General Authority.

(a) Each power granted to the commissioner under this chapter is in addition to, and not in limitation of, each other power granted under this chapter. The fact that the commissioner possesses, or has exercised, a power under a provision of this chapter does not preclude the commissioner from exercising a power under any other provision of this chapter.

(b) Each power granted to the commissioner under this chapter is in addition to, and not in limitation of, powers granted to the commissioner under other law. The fact that the commissioner possesses, or has exercised, a power under any other provision of law does not preclude the commissioner from exercising any power under this chapter. The fact that the commissioner possesses, or has exercised, a power under a provision of this chapter does not preclude the commissioner from exercising a power under any other law.

(c) The commissioner may impose on any authority, approval, exemption, license, or order issued or granted under this chapter any condition the commissioner considers reasonably necessary or appropriate to carry out and achieve the purposes of this chapter.

Sec. 151.104. Investigations.

(a) The commissioner may conduct investigations in or outside this state and the United States as the commissioner considers necessary or appropriate to administer and enforce this chapter, including investigations to:

(1) determine whether to approve an application for a license or a request for approval or exemption filed under this chapter or a rule adopted or order issued under this chapter;

(2) determine whether a person has violated or is likely to violate this chapter or a rule adopted or order issued under this chapter;

(3) determine whether a license or authorized delegate designation should be revoked or suspended;

(4) otherwise aid in the enforcement of this chapter or a rule adopted or order issued under this chapter; and

(5) aid in the adoption of rules or issuance of orders under this chapter.

(b) For purposes of an investigation, examination, or other proceeding under this chapter, the commissioner may administer or cause to be administered oaths, subpoena witnesses, compel the attendance of witnesses, take evidence, and require the production of any document that the commissioner determines to be relevant to the inquiry.

(c) If a person refuses to obey a subpoena, a district court of Travis County, on application by the commissioner, may issue an order requiring the person to appear before the commissioner and produce documents or give evidence regarding the matter under investigation.

(d) The commissioner may employ a person or request the attorney general, the Department of Public Safety, or any other state, federal, or local law enforcement agency to assist in enforcing this chapter.

(e) The commissioner may recover the reasonable costs incurred in connection with an investigation conducted under this chapter from the person that is the subject of the investigation.

Sec. 151.105. Regulatory Cooperation.

(a) To efficiently and effectively administer and enforce this chapter and to minimize regulatory burden, the commissioner may cooperate, coordinate, and share information with another state, federal, or foreign governmental agency that:

(1) regulates or supervises persons engaged in money services businesses or activities subject to this chapter; or

(2) is authorized to investigate or prosecute violations of a state, federal, or foreign law related to persons engaged in money services businesses or activities subject to this chapter, including a state attorney general's office.

(b) The commissioner, with respect to an agency described by and for the purposes set forth in Subsection (a), may:

(1) enter into a written cooperation, coordination, or information-sharing contract or agreement with the agency;

(2) share information with the agency, subject to the confidentiality provisions of Section 151.606(b)(3);

(3) conduct a joint or concurrent on-site examination or other investigation or enforcement action with the agency;

(4) accept a report of examination or investigation by, or a report submitted to, the agency, in which event the accepted report is an official report of the commissioner for all purposes;

(5) engage the services of the agency to assist the commissioner in performing or discharging a duty or responsibility imposed by this chapter or other law and pay a reasonable fee for the services;

(6) share with the agency any supervisory or examination fees assessed against a license holder or authorized delegate under this chapter and receive a portion of supervisory or examination fees assessed by the agency against a license holder or authorized delegate; and

(7) take other action as the commissioner considers reasonably necessary or appropriate to carry out and achieve the purposes of this chapter.

(b-1) To efficiently and effectively administer and enforce this chapter and to minimize regulatory burden, the commissioner may cooperate, coordinate, and share information with an organization the membership of which is made up of state or federal governmental agencies described by Subsection (a). The commissioner may:

(1) enter into a written cooperation, coordination, or information-sharing contract or agreement with the organization; and

(2) share information, provided that the organization agrees in writing to maintain the confidentiality and security of the shared information.

(c) The commissioner may not waive, and nothing in this section constitutes a waiver of, the commissioner's authority to conduct an examination or investigation or otherwise take independent action authorized by this chapter or a rule adopted or order issued under this chapter to enforce compliance with applicable state or federal law.

(d) A joint examination or investigation, or acceptance of an examination or investigation report, does not waive an examination assessment provided for in this chapter.

(e) Chapter 2254, Government Code, does not apply to a contract or agreement entered into under this section.

Sec. 151.106. Consent to Service of Process.

A license holder, an authorized delegate, or a person who knowingly engages in activities that are regulated and require a license under this chapter, with or without filing an application for a license or holding a license under this chapter, is considered to have consented to the jurisdiction of the courts of this state for all actions arising under this chapter.

Sec. 151.107. Compliance with the Securities Act [Repealed].

Repealed by Acts 1999, 76th Leg., ch. 62 (S.B. 1368), § 7.17(b), effective September 1, 1999.

Sec. 151.151. Restrictions on Foreign Trust Companies and Corporations [Repealed].

Repealed by Acts 1999, 76th Leg., ch. 62 (S.B. 1368), § 7.17(b), effective September 1, 1999.

Sec. 151.152. Examination [Repealed].

Repealed by Acts 1999, 76th Leg., ch. 62 (S.B. 1368), § 7.17(b), effective September 1, 1999.

Sec. 151.153. Applicability of Provisions to Certain Foreign Corporations [Repealed].

Repealed by Acts 1999, 76th Leg., ch. 62 (S.B. 1368), § 7.17(b), effective September 1, 1999.

Sec. 151.154. Acquisition or Control of Trust Company by Foreign Trust Company or Corporation [Repealed].

Repealed by Acts 1999, 76th Leg., ch. 62 (S.B. 1368), § 7.17(b), effective September 1, 1999.

Sec. 151.155. Establishment of Trust Relationship Regardless of Domicile [Repealed].

Repealed by Acts 1999, 76th Leg., ch. 62 (S.B. 1368), § 7.17(b), effective September 1, 1999.

SUBCHAPTER C
GENERAL QUALIFICATIONS AND PROVISIONS APPLICABLE TO MONEY SERVICES LICENSES

Sec. 151.201. Scope.

This subchapter sets out the general qualifications and provisions that apply to a money services license, regardless of whether the license is a money transmission license or a currency exchange license. Subchapters D and E set forth the additional qualifications and provisions that apply specifically to a money transmission license. Subchapter F sets forth the additional qualifications and provisions that apply specifically to a currency exchange license.

Sec. 151.202. Qualifications for License.

(a) Subject to Subsections (b) and (c), to qualify for a license under this chapter, an applicant must demonstrate to the satisfaction of the commissioner that:

(1) the financial responsibility and condition, financial and business experience, competence, character, and general fitness of the applicant justify the confidence of the public and warrant the belief that the applicant will conduct business in compliance with this chapter and the rules adopted under this chapter and other applicable state and federal law;

(2) the issuance of the license is in the public interest;

(3) the applicant, a principal of the applicant, or a person in control of the applicant does not owe the department a delinquent fee, assessment, administrative penalty, or other amount imposed under this chapter or a rule adopted or order issued under this chapter;

(4) the applicant, if a partnership, and any partner that would generally be liable for the obligations of the partnership, does not owe a delinquent federal tax;

(5) the applicant, if a corporation:

(A) is in good standing and statutory compliance in the state or country of incorporation;

(B) is authorized to engage in business in this state; and

(C) does not owe any delinquent franchise or other taxes to this state;

(6) the applicant, if not a corporation, is properly registered under the laws of this state or another state or country and, if required, is authorized to engage in business in this state; and

(7) the applicant, a principal of the applicant, or a principal of a person in control of the applicant is not listed on the specifically designated nationals and blocked persons list prepared by the United States Department of the Treasury, or designated successor agency, as a potential threat to commit or fund terrorist acts.

(b) In determining whether an applicant has demonstrated satisfaction of the qualifications identified in Subsection (a)(1), the commissioner shall consider the financial responsibility and condition, financial and business experience, competence, character, and general fitness of each principal of, person in control of, principal of a person in control of, and proposed responsible individual of the applicant and may deny approval of the application on the basis that the applicant has failed to demonstrate satisfaction of the requisite qualifications with respect to one or more of those persons.

(c) The commissioner may not issue a license to an applicant if the applicant or one of the following persons has been convicted within the preceding 10 years of a criminal offense specified in Subsection (e):

(1) if the applicant is an individual, the spouse or proposed responsible individual or individuals of the applicant;

(2) if the applicant is an entity that is wholly owned, directly or indirectly, by a single individual, the spouse of the individual; or

(3) if the applicant is a person other than an individual, a principal of, person in control of, principal of a person in control of, or proposed responsible individual or individuals of the applicant.

(d) The commissioner, on a finding that the conviction does not reflect adversely on the present likelihood that the applicant will conduct business in compliance with this chapter, rules adopted under this chapter, and other applicable state and federal law, may waive a disqualification under Subsection (c) based on the conviction of a spouse or a corporate applicant or corporate person in control of an applicant.

(e) For purposes of Subsection (c), a disqualifying conviction is a conviction for a felony criminal offense:

(1) under state or federal law that involves or relates to:

Finance Code

(A) deception, dishonesty, or defalcation;

(B) money transmission or other money services, including a reporting, recordkeeping or registration requirement of the Bank Secrecy Act, the USA PATRIOT ACT, or Chapter 271;

(C) money laundering, structuring, or a related financial crime;

(D) drug trafficking; or

(E) terrorist funding; and

(2) under a similar law of a foreign country unless the applicant demonstrates to the satisfaction of the commissioner that the conviction was based on extenuating circumstances unrelated to the person's reputation for honesty and obedience to law.

(f) For purposes of Subsection (c), a person is considered to have been convicted of an offense if the person has been found guilty or pleaded guilty or nolo contendere to the charge or has been placed on probation or deferred adjudication without regard to whether a judgment of conviction has been entered by the court.

Sec. 151.203. Application for License.

(a) An application for a license under this chapter must be made under oath and in the form and medium required by the commissioner. The application must contain:

(1) the legal name and residential and business address of the applicant and each principal of the applicant;

(2) the taxpayer identification number, social security number, driver's license number, or other identifying information the commissioner requires of the applicant and each principal of the applicant; and

(3) any other information or documentation the commissioner reasonably requires to determine whether the applicant qualifies for and should be issued the license for which application is made.

(b) The commissioner, at the time the application is submitted or in connection with an investigation of the application under Section 151.204, may require the applicant, the spouse of the applicant, a principal of, individual who is a person in control of, or proposed responsible individual of the applicant, or any other individual associated with the applicant and the proposed licensed activities, to provide the department a complete set of fingerprints for purposes of a criminal background investigation.

(c) An applicant must certify in writing on the application that the applicant and each principal of, person in control of, and proposed responsible individual of the applicant:

(1) is familiar with and agrees to fully comply with all applicable state and federal laws and regulations pertaining to the applicant's proposed money services business, including this chapter, relevant provisions of the Bank Secrecy Act, the USA PATRIOT ACT, and Chapter 271;

(2) has not within the preceding three years knowingly failed to file or evaded the obligation to file a report, including a currency transaction or suspicious activity report required by the Bank Secrecy Act, the USA PATRIOT ACT, or Chapter 271; and

(3) has not knowingly accepted money for transmission or exchange in which a portion of the money was derived from an illegal transaction or activity.

(d) The commissioner may waive an application requirement or permit the submission of substituted information in lieu of the information generally required in an application, either with respect to a specific applicant or a category of applicants, if the commissioner determines that the waiver or substitution of information is consistent with achievement of the purposes of this chapter.

Sec. 151.2031. Use of Nationwide Multistate Licensing System and Registry.

(a) In this section, "Nationwide Multistate Licensing System and Registry" or "nationwide registry" means a licensing system developed and maintained by the Conference of State Bank Supervisors or an affiliated organization to manage mortgage licenses and other financial services licenses, or a successor registry.

(b) The commissioner may require that a person submit through the Nationwide Multistate Licensing System and Registry in the form and manner prescribed by the commissioner and acceptable to the registry any information or document or payment of a fee required to be submitted under this chapter or rules adopted under this chapter.

(c) The commissioner may use the nationwide registry as a channeling agent for obtaining information required for licensing purposes under this chapter or rules adopted under this chapter, including:

(1) criminal history record information from the Federal Bureau of Investigation, the United States Department of Justice, or any other agency or entity at the commissioner's discretion;

(2) information related to any administrative, civil, or criminal findings by a governmental jurisdiction; and

(3) information requested by the commissioner under Section 151.203(a)(3).

Sec. 151.204. Processing and Investigation of Application.

(a) An application for a license under this chapter shall be processed and acted on according to the time periods established by commission rule.

(b) On receipt of an application that meets the requirements of Section 151.203 and Section 151.304 or 151.504, as applicable, the commissioner shall investigate the applicant to determine whether the prescribed qualifications have been met. The commissioner may:

(1) conduct an on-site investigation of the applicant;

(2) employ a screening service to assist with the investigation;

(3) to the extent the commissioner considers reasonably necessary to evaluate the application and the applicant's qualifications, investigate the financial responsibility and condition, financial and business experience, character and general fitness of each principal of, person in control of, principal of a person in control of, or proposed responsible individual of the applicant or any other person that is or will be associated with the applicant's licensed activities in this state; or

(4) require additional information and take other action the commissioner considers reasonably necessary.

(c) The commissioner may collect from the applicant the reasonable expenses of an on-site examination or third-party investigation. Additionally, depending on the nature and extent of the investigation required in connection with a particular application, the commissioner may require an applicant to pay a nonrefundable investigation fee in an amount established by commission rule.

(d) The commissioner may suspend consideration of an application for a license if the applicant or a principal of, person in control of, or proposed responsible individual of the applicant is the subject of a pending state or federal criminal prosecution, state or federal government enforcement action, or state or federal asset forfeiture proceeding until the conclusion of the prosecution, action, or proceeding.

Sec. 151.205. Issuance of License.

(a) The commissioner shall issue a license if the commissioner, with respect to the license for which application has been made, finds that:

(1) the applicant meets the prescribed qualifications and it is reasonable to believe that the applicant's business will be conducted fairly and lawfully, according to applicable state and federal law, and in a manner commanding the public's trust and confidence;

(2) the issuance of the license is in the public interest;

(3) the documentation and forms required to be submitted by the applicant are acceptable; and

(4) the applicant has satisfied all requirements for licensure.

(b) If the commissioner finds that the applicant for any reason fails to possess the qualifications or satisfy the requirements for the license for which application is made, the commissioner shall inform the applicant in writing that the application is denied and state the reasons for the denial. The applicant may appeal the denial by filing a written request for a hearing with the commissioner not later than the 30th day after the date the notice is mailed. A hearing on the denial must be held not later than the 45th day after the date the commissioner receives the written request unless the administrative law judge extends the period for good cause or the parties agree to a later hearing date. The hearing is considered a contested case hearing and is subject to Section 151.801.

Sec. 151.206. Transfer or Assignment of License.

A license issued under this chapter may not be transferred or assigned.

Sec. 151.207. Continuation of License; Annual Report and Fee.

(a) If a license holder does not continue to meet the qualifications or satisfy the requirements that apply to an applicant for a new money transmission license or currency exchange license, as applicable, the commissioner may suspend or revoke the license holder's license.

(b) In addition to complying with Subsection (a), a license holder must annually:

(1) pay a license fee in an amount established by commission rule; and

(2) submit a report that is under oath, is in the form and medium required by the commissioner, and contains:

(A) if the license is a money transmission license, an audited unconsolidated financial statement dated as of the last day of the license holder's fiscal year that ended in the immediately preceding calendar year;

(B) if the license is a currency exchange license, a financial statement, audited or unaudited, dated as of the last day of the license holder's fiscal year that ended in the immediately preceding calendar year; and

(C) documentation and certification, or any other information the commissioner reasonably requires to determine the security, net worth, permissible

Finance Code

investments, and other requirements the license holder must satisfy and whether the license holder continues to meet the qualifications and requirements for licensure.

(c) If the department does not receive a license holder's annual license fee and complete annual report on or before the due date prescribed by the commissioner under this section, the commissioner shall notify the license holder in writing that:

(1) the license holder shall submit the report and pay the license fee not later than the 45th day after the due date prescribed by the commissioner; and

(2) the license holder must pay a late fee, in an amount that is established by commission rule and not subject to appeal, for each business day after the report due date specified by the commissioner that the commissioner does not receive the completed report and license fee.

(d) If the license holder fails to submit the completed annual report and pay the annual license fee and any late fee due within the time prescribed by Subsection (c)(1), the license expires, and the license holder must cease and desist from engaging in the business of money transmission or currency exchange, as applicable, as of that date. The expiration of a license is not subject to appeal.

(e) On timely receipt of a license holder's complete annual report, annual license fee, and any late fee due, the department shall review the report and, if necessary, investigate the business and records of the license holder. On completion of the review and investigation, if any, the commissioner may:

(1) impose conditions on the license the commissioner considers reasonably necessary or appropriate; or

(2) suspend or revoke the license on the basis of a ground specified in Section 151.703.

(f) On written application and for good cause shown, the commissioner may extend the due date for filing the annual license fee and annual report required under this section.

(g) The holder or principal of or the person in control of the holder of an expired license, or the holder or principal of or person in control of the holder of a license surrendered under Section 151.208, that wishes to conduct activities for which a license is required under this chapter must file a new license application and satisfy all requirements for licensure that apply at the time the new application is filed.

Sec. 151.208. Surrender of License.

(a) A license holder may surrender the license holder's license by delivering the original license to the commissioner along with a written notice of surrender that includes the location at which the license holder's records will be stored and the name, address, telephone number, and other contact information for an individual who is authorized to provide access to the records.

(b) A license holder shall surrender the license holder's license if the license holder becomes ineligible for a license under Section 151.202(c).

(c) The surrender of a license does not reduce or eliminate a license holder's civil or criminal liability arising from any acts or omissions before the surrender of the license, including any administrative action undertaken by the commissioner to revoke or suspend a license, to assess an administrative penalty, to order the payment of restitution, or to exercise any other authority under this chapter. Further, the surrender of a license does not release the security required of the license holder under Section 151.308 or 151.506.

Sec. 151.209. Refunds.

A fee or cost paid under this chapter is not refundable.

Sec. 151.251. Administrative Penalty [Repealed].

Repealed by Acts 1999, 76th Leg., ch. 62 (S.B. 1368), § 7.17(b), effective September 1, 1999.

Sec. 151.252. Revocation of Certificate of Foreign Corporation [Repealed].

Repealed by Acts 1999, 76th Leg., ch. 62 (S.B. 1368), § 7.17(b), effective September 1, 1999.

Sec. 151.253. Forfeiture of Charter of Trust Company [Repealed].

Repealed by Acts 1999, 76th Leg., ch. 62 (S.B. 1368), § 7.17(b), effective September 1, 1999.

Sec. 151.254. Enforcement Order [Repealed].

Repealed by Acts 1999, 76th Leg., ch. 62 (S.B. 1368), § 7.17(b), effective September 1, 1999.

Sec. 151.255. Supervision or Conservatorship [Repealed].

Repealed by Acts 1999, 76th Leg., ch. 62 (S.B. 1368), § 7.17(b), effective September 1, 1999.

Sec. 151.256. Priority of Claims on Liquidation [Repealed].

Repealed by Acts 1999, 76th Leg., ch. 62 (S.B. 1368), § 7.17(b), effective September 1, 1999.

Sec. 151.257. Venue for Liquidation Action [Repealed].

Repealed by Acts 1999, 76th Leg., ch. 62 (S.B. 1368), § 7.17(b), effective September 1, 1999.

SUBCHAPTER D MONEY TRANSMISSION LICENSE

Sec. 151.301. Definitions.

(a) This section defines terms that apply to an applicant for or holder of a money transmission license issued under this subchapter.

(b) In this subchapter:

(1) "Currency" means the coin and paper money of the United States or another country that is designated as legal tender and circulates and is customarily used and accepted as a medium of exchange in the country of issuance.

(2) "Electronic instrument" means a card or other tangible object for the transmission, transfer, or payment of money or monetary value, that contains an electronic chip or strip for the storage of information or that provides access to information.

(3) "Money" or "monetary value" means currency or a claim that can be converted into currency through a financial institution, electronic payments network, or other formal or informal payment system.

(4) "Money transmission" means the receipt of money or monetary value by any means in exchange for a promise to make the money or monetary value available at a later time or different location. The term:

(A) includes:

(i) selling or issuing stored value or payment instruments, including checks, money orders, and traveler's checks;

(ii) receiving money or monetary value for transmission, including by payment instrument, wire, facsimile, electronic transfer, or ACH debit;

(iii) providing third-party bill paying services; or

(iv) receiving currency or an instrument payable in currency to physically transport the currency or its equivalent from one location to another by motor vehicle or other means of transportation or through the use of the mail or a shipping, courier, or other delivery service; and

(B) does not include the provision solely of online or telecommunication services or connection services to the Internet.

(5) "Outstanding" means:

(A) with respect to a payment instrument or stored value, a payment instrument or stored value that has been issued and sold in the United States directly by the license holder, or sold by an authorized delegate of the license holder in the United States and reported to the license holder, that has not yet been paid by or for the license holder; or

(B) with respect to transmission, a money transmission for which the license holder, directly or through an authorized delegate of the license holder, has received money or monetary value from the customer for transmission, but has not yet completed the money transmission by delivering the money or monetary value to the person designated by the customer or refunded the money or monetary value to the customer.

(6) "Payment instrument" means a written or electronic equivalent of a check, draft, money order, traveler's check, or other written or electronic instrument, service, or device for the transmission or payment of money or monetary value, sold or issued to one or more persons, regardless of whether negotiable. The term does not include an instrument, service, or device that:

(A) transfers money directly from a purchaser to a creditor of the purchaser or to an agent of the creditor;

(B) is redeemed by the issuer in goods or services or a cash or credit refund under circumstances not designed to evade the obligations and responsibilities imposed by this chapter; or

(C) is a credit card voucher or letter of credit.

(7) [Repealed by Acts 2015, 84th Leg., ch. 75 (S.B. 899), § 7, effective September 1, 2015.]

(8) "Stored value" means monetary value evidenced by an electronic record that is prefunded and for which value is reduced on each use. The term includes prepaid access as defined by 31 C.F.R. Section 1010.100(ww). The term does not include an electronic record that is:

(A) loaded with points, miles, or other nonmonetary value;

(B) not sold to the public but distributed as a reward or charitable donation; or

(C) redeemable only for goods or services from a specified merchant or set of affiliated merchants, such as:

(i) a specified retailer or retail chain;

(ii) a set of affiliated companies under common ownership;

(iii) a college campus; or

(iv) a mass transportation system.

(9) "Unsafe or unsound act or practice" means a practice of or conduct by a license holder or an authorized delegate of the license holder that creates the likelihood of material loss, insolvency, or dissipation of the license holder's assets, or that otherwise materially prejudices the interests of the license holder or the license holder's customers.

Sec. 151.302. License Required.

(a) A person may not engage in the business of money transmission in this state or advertise, solicit, or represent that the person engages in the business of money transmission in this state unless the person:

(1) is licensed under this subchapter;

(2) is an authorized delegate of a person licensed under this subchapter, appointed by the license holder in accordance with Section 151.402;

(3) is excluded from licensure under Section 151.003; or

(4) has been granted an exemption under Subsection (c).

(b) For purposes of this chapter, a person engages in the business of money transmission if the person receives compensation or expects to receive compensation, directly or indirectly, for conducting money transmission.

(c) On application and a finding that the exemption is in the public interest, the commissioner may exempt a person that:

(1) incidentally engages in the money transmission business only to the extent reasonable and necessary to accomplish a primary business objective unrelated to the money transmission business;

(2) does not advertise or offer money transmission services to the public except to the extent reasonable and necessary to fairly advertise or offer the person's primary business services; and

(3) transmits money without a fee as an inducement for customer participation in the person's primary business.

(d) A license holder may engage in the money transmission business at one or more locations in this state owned, directly or indirectly by the license holder, or through one or more authorized delegates, or both, under a single license granted to the license holder.

Sec. 151.303. Additional Qualifications.

In addition to the general qualifications for licensure set forth in Section 151.202, an applicant for a money transmission license must demonstrate to the satisfaction of the commissioner that:

(1) the applicant has and will maintain the minimum net worth required under Section 151.307;

(2) the applicant's financial condition will enable the applicant to safely and soundly engage in the business of money transmission; and

(3) the applicant does not engage in any activity or practice that adversely affects the applicant's safety and soundness.

Sec. 151.304. Application and Accompanying Fee, Statements, and Security.

(a) An applicant for a money transmission license must submit an application in accordance with Section 151.203.

(b) At the time an application for a money transmission license is submitted, an applicant must file with the department:

(1) an application fee in the amount established by commission rule;

(2) audited financial statements that are satisfactory to the commissioner for purposes of determining whether the applicant has the minimum net worth required under Section 151.307 and is likely to maintain the required minimum net worth if a license is issued; and

(3) security that meets the requirements of Section 151.308, and an undertaking or agreement that the applicant will increase or supplement the security to equal the aggregate security required by the commissioner under that section before the issuance of the license and the start of operations.

Sec. 151.305. Investigation and Action on Application.

The commissioner shall investigate the applicant and act on the application in accordance with Sections 151.204 and 151.205.

Sec. 151.306. Temporary License.

(a) The commissioner may issue a temporary license to a person that is engaging in money transmission, but has not obtained a license under this subchapter, if the person:

(1) certifies in writing that the person qualifies for the license and will submit a completed license application not later than the 60th day after the date the temporary license is issued;

(2) submits a recent financial statement acceptable to the commissioner that reflects the minimum net worth required under Section 151.307;

Finance Code

(3) provides security that meets the requirements of Section 151.308 in an amount specified by the commissioner, but not less than $300,000;

(4) agrees in writing that, until a permanent license is issued, the person will engage only in activities being conducted at existing locations; and

(5) pays the application fee and a nonrefundable temporary license fee in the amount established by commission rule.

(b) The effective period for a temporary license may not exceed 90 days from the date the license is issued, provided that the commissioner may extend the period for not more than an additional 90 days if necessary to complete the processing of a timely filed application for which approval is likely.

Sec. 151.307. Net Worth.

(a) An applicant for a money transmission license must possess, and a money transmission license holder must maintain at all times, a minimum net worth computed in accordance with generally accepted accounting principles of:

(1) $100,000, if business is proposed to be or is conducted, directly or through an authorized delegate, at four or fewer locations; or

(2) $500,000, if business is proposed to be or is conducted, directly or through an authorized delegate, at five or more locations or over the Internet.

(b) The commissioner may increase the amount of net worth required of an applicant or license holder, up to a maximum of $1 million, if the commissioner determines, with respect to the applicant or license holder, that a higher net worth is necessary to achieve the purposes of this chapter based on:

(1) the nature and volume of the projected or established business;

(2) the number of locations at or through which money transmission is or will be conducted;

(3) the amount, nature, quality, and liquidity of its assets;

(4) the amount and nature of its liabilities;

(5) the history of its operations and prospects for earning and retaining income;

(6) the quality of its operations;

(7) the quality of its management;

(8) the nature and quality of its principals and persons in control;

(9) the history of its compliance with applicable state and federal law; and

(10) any other factor the commissioner considers relevant.

(c) At least 50 percent of the applicant's or license holder's total net worth under this section must be tangible net worth.

Sec. 151.308. Security.

(a) An applicant for a money transmission license must provide, and a money transmission license holder must maintain at all times, security consisting of a surety bond, an irrevocable letter of credit, or a deposit instead of a bond in accordance with this section.

(b) The amount of the required security is the greater of $300,000 or an amount equal to one percent of the license holder's total yearly dollar volume of money transmission business in this state or the applicant's projected total volume of business in this state for the first year of licensure, up to a maximum of $2 million.

(b-1) The commissioner may increase the amount of security required of an applicant who intends to provide, or a license holder who is providing, third-party bill payments in conjunction with loan acceleration services, up to a total amount of $2 million, by multiplying the amount of security required under this section by a factor of up to two, if the commissioner determines, with respect to the applicant or license holder, that a higher amount of the required security is necessary to achieve the purposes of this chapter based on the factors listed under Section 151.307(b).

(b-2) When the amount of the required security exceeds $1 million, the applicant or license holder may, in the alternative, provide security in the amount of $1 million, plus a dollar for dollar increase in the net worth of the applicant or license holder over the amount required under Section 151.307, up to a total amount of $2 million.

(c) The security must:

(1) be in a form satisfactory to the commissioner;

(2) be payable to any claimant or to the commissioner, on behalf of a claimant or this state, for any liability arising out of the license holder's money transmission business in this state, incurred under, subject to, or by virtue of this chapter; and

(3) if the security is a bond, be issued by a qualified surety company authorized to engage in business in this state and acceptable to the commissioner or, if the security is an irrevocable letter of credit, be issued by a financial institution acceptable to the commissioner.

(d) A claimant may bring suit directly on the security, or the commissioner may bring suit on behalf of the claimant or the state, either in one action or in successive actions.

(e) The commissioner may collect from the security or proceeds of the security any delinquent fee, assessment, cost, penalty, or other amount imposed on and owed by a license holder. If the security is a surety bond, the commissioner shall give the surety

Finance Code

reasonable prior notice of a hearing to impose an administrative penalty against the license holder, provided that a surety may not be considered an interested, aggrieved, or affected person for purposes of an administrative proceeding under Section 151.801 or Chapter 2001, Government Code.

(f) The security remains in effect until canceled, which may occur only after providing 30 days' written notice to the commissioner. Cancellation does not affect any liability incurred or accrued during the period covered by the security.

(g) The security shall cover claims for at least five years after the license holder surrenders its license or otherwise ceases to engage in activities for which a license is required under this subchapter. However, the commissioner may permit the amount of the security to be reduced or eliminated before that time to the extent that the amount of the license holder's obligations to the department and to purchasers in this state is reduced. The commissioner may permit a license holder to substitute another form of security when the license holder ceases to provide money transmission in this state.

(h) If the commissioner at any time reasonably determines that the required security is insecure, deficient in amount, or exhausted in whole or in part, the commissioner by written order shall require the license holder to file or make new or additional security to comply with this section.

(i) Instead of providing all or part of the amount of the security required by this section, an applicant or license holder may deposit, with a financial institution possessing trust powers that is authorized to conduct a trust business in this state and is acceptable to the commissioner, an aggregate amount of United States currency, certificates of deposit, or other cash equivalents that equals the total amount of the required security or the remaining part of the security. The deposit:

(1) must be held in trust in the name of and be pledged to the commissioner;

(2) must secure the same obligations as the security; and

(3) is subject to other conditions and terms the commissioner may reasonably require.

(j) The security is considered by operation of law to be held in trust for the benefit of this state and any individual to whom an obligation arising under this chapter is owed, and may not be considered an asset or property of the license holder in the event of bankruptcy, receivership, or a claim against the license holder unrelated to the license holder's obligations under this chapter.

Sec. 151.309. Permissible Investments.

(a) A money transmission license holder must maintain at all times permissible investments that have an aggregate market value computed in accordance with generally accepted accounting principles in an amount not less than:

(1) if the license holder has a net worth of less than $5 million, the aggregate face amount of the license holder's average outstanding money transmission obligations in the United States, computed in the manner prescribed by commission rule; or

(2) if the license holder has a net worth of $5 million or more, 50 percent of the amount required by Subdivision (1).

(b) Except to the extent limited by Subsection (d), the following constitute a permissible investment for purposes of this section:

(1) 40 percent of the receivables due a license holder from authorized delegates resulting from money transmission under this chapter that is not past due or doubtful of collection;

(2) cash in demand or interest-bearing accounts with a federally insured depository institution, including certificates of deposit;

(3) certificates of deposit or senior debt obligations of a domestic federally insured depository institution that are readily marketable and insured by an agency of the federal government;

(4) investment grade bonds and other legally created general obligations of a state, an agency or political subdivision of a state, the United States, or an instrumentality of the United States;

(5) obligations that a state, an agency or political subdivision of a state, the United States, or an instrumentality of the United States has unconditionally agreed to purchase, insure, or guarantee and that bear a rating of one of the three highest grades as defined by a nationally recognized organization that rates securities;

(6) shares in a money market mutual fund if the mutual fund, under the terms of the mutual fund's governing documents, is authorized to invest only in securities of the type described by Subdivisions (4) and (5) or permitted by commission rule; and

(7) other assets and investments permitted by rule of the commission or approved by the commissioner in writing, based on a determination that the assets or investments have a safety substantially equivalent to other permissible investments.

(c) In addition to investments listed in Subsection (b), a permissible investment for purposes of Subsection (a) includes:

(1) the security provided under Section 151.308;

(2) a surety bond or letter of credit in addition to the security provided under Section 151.308, if the additional surety bond or letter of credit satisfies the requirements of Section 151.308; and

(3) that portion of a surety bond maintained for the benefit of the purchasers of the license holder's outstanding money transmission obligations in another state that is not in excess of the amount of the outstanding obligations in that state, provided:

(A) the license holder maintains a surety bond or letter of credit or has on hand other permissible investments, or a combination of investments, in an amount sufficient to satisfy the requirements of Subsection (a) with respect to the outstanding money transmission obligations in this state; and

(B) the surety bond is issued by a surety rated within the top two rating categories of a nationally recognized United States rating service.

(d) The commissioner, with respect to a license holder, may limit or disallow for purposes of determining compliance with Subsection (a) an investment, surety bond, or letter of credit otherwise permitted by this section if the commissioner determines it to be unsatisfactory for investment purposes or to pose a significant supervisory concern.

(e) A permissible investment subject to this section, even if commingled with other assets of the license holder, is considered by operation of law to be held in trust for the benefit of any individual to whom an obligation arising under this chapter is owed, and may not be considered an asset or property of the license holder in the event of bankruptcy, receivership, or a claim against the license holder unrelated to any of the license holder's obligations under this chapter.

SUBCHAPTER E
CONDUCT OF MONEY TRANSMISSION BUSINESS

Sec. 151.401. Liability of License Holder.

A money transmission license holder is liable for the payment of all money or monetary value received for transmission directly or by an authorized delegate appointed in accordance with Section 151.402.

Sec. 151.402. Conduct of Business Through Authorized Delegate.

(a) A money transmission license holder may conduct business regulated under this chapter through an authorized delegate appointed by the license holder in accordance with this section. A license holder is responsible for the acts of the authorized delegate, of which the license holder has or reasonably should have knowledge, that are conducted pursuant to the authority granted by the license holder and that relate to the license holder's money transmission business.

(b) Before a license holder is authorized to conduct business through an authorized delegate or allows a person to act as the license holder's authorized delegate, the license holder must:

(1) adopt, and update as necessary, written policies and procedures designed to ensure that the license holder's authorized delegate complies with applicable state and federal law;

(2) enter into a written contract that complies with Subsection (c); and

(3) conduct a reasonable risk-based background investigation sufficient for the license holder to determine whether the authorized delegate has complied with applicable state and federal law.

(c) The written contract required by Subsection (b)(2) must be signed by the license holder and the authorized delegate and, at a minimum, must:

(1) appoint the person signing the contract as the license holder's authorized delegate with the authority to conduct money transmission on behalf of the license holder;

(2) set forth the nature and scope of the relationship between the license holder and the authorized delegate and the respective rights and responsibilities of the parties;

(3) require the authorized delegate to certify that the delegate is familiar with and agrees to fully comply with all applicable state and federal laws, rules, and regulations pertaining to money transmission, including this chapter and rules adopted under this chapter, relevant provisions of the Bank Secrecy Act and the USA PATRIOT ACT, and Chapter 271;

(4) require the authorized delegate to remit and handle money and monetary value in accordance with Sections 151.403(b) and (c);

(5) impose a trust on money and monetary value received in accordance with Section 151.404;

(6) require the authorized delegate to prepare and maintain records as required by this chapter or a rule adopted under this chapter or as reasonably requested by the commissioner;

(7) acknowledge that the authorized delegate consents to examination or investigation by the commissioner;

(8) state that the license holder is subject to regulation by the commissioner and that, as part of that regulation, the commissioner may suspend or revoke an authorized delegate designation or require the license holder to terminate an authorized delegate designation;

(9) acknowledge receipt of the written policies and procedures required under Subsection (b)(1); and

Finance Code

(10) acknowledge that the authorized delegate has been provided regulatory website addresses through which the authorized delegate can access this chapter and rules adopted under this chapter and the Bank Secrecy Act, the USA PATRIOT ACT, and Chapter 271.

(d) A license holder must report to the commissioner the theft or loss of payment instruments or stored value from the license holder or an authorized delegate in this state if the total value of the instruments or stored value exceeds $10,000. The license holder must make the report as soon as the license holder has knowledge of the theft or loss.

(e) A license holder must notify the license holder's authorized delegates and require the delegates to take any action required by the commissioner if:

(1) the license holder's license expired or is surrendered or revoked; or

(2) the license holder is subject to an emergency or final order that affects the conduct of the license holder's business through an authorized delegate.

(f) A license holder must maintain a current list of authorized delegates located in this state or doing business with persons located in this state that includes the name and business address of each delegate and must provide the list to the commissioner on request. A license holder that engages in business through 11 or more authorized delegates located in this state must include on the license holder's website a list of the names and addresses of the authorized delegates of the license holder located in this state and the delegates' business addresses. The license holder must update the list quarterly.

(g) The commission by rule may exempt from one or more of the requirements of this chapter an authorized delegate that is a federally insured financial institution excluded under Section 151.003(3) or a foreign bank branch or agency excluded under Section 151.003(4).

Sec. 151.403. Authorized Delegate Conduct.

(a) An authorized delegate of a license holder:

(1) is under a duty to and must act only as authorized under the contract with the license holder and in strict compliance with the license holder's written policies and procedures;

(2) must not commit fraud or misrepresentation or make any fraudulent or false statement or misrepresentation to a license holder or the commissioner;

(3) must cooperate with an investigation or examination conducted by the commissioner and is considered to have consented to the commissioner's examination of the delegate's books and records;

(4) must not commit an unsafe or unsound act or practice or conduct business in an unsafe and unsound manner;

(5) must, on discovery, immediately report to the license holder the theft or loss of payment instruments or stored value;

(6) must prominently display on the form prescribed by the commissioner a notice that indicates that the person is an authorized delegate of the license holder under this subchapter; and

(7) must cease to provide money services as an authorized delegate of a license holder or take other required action immediately on receipt of notice from the commissioner or the license holder as provided by Section 151.402(e).

(b) An authorized delegate shall remit all money owed to the license holder:

(1) not later than the 10th business day after the date the authorized delegate receives the money;

(2) in accordance with the contract between the license holder and the authorized delegate; or

(3) as directed by the commissioner.

(c) Notwithstanding Subsection (b)(1), an authorized delegate may remit the money at a later date if the authorized delegate maintains on deposit with an office of a federally insured financial institution located in the United States an amount that:

(1) is in an account solely in the name of the license holder; and

(2) for each day by which the period before the remittance exceeds 10 business days, is not less than the outstanding obligations of the license holder routinely incurred by the authorized delegate on a daily basis.

(d) Any business for which a license is required under this subchapter that is conducted by an authorized delegate outside the scope of authority conferred in the contract between the authorized delegate and the license holder is unlicensed activity.

Sec. 151.404. Trust Imposed.

(a) A license holder shall hold in trust all money received for transmission directly or from an authorized delegate from the time of receipt until the time the transmission obligation is discharged. A trust resulting from the license holder's actions is in favor of the persons to whom the related money transmission obligations are owed.

(b) A license holder's authorized delegate shall hold in trust all money received for transmission by or for the license holder from the time of receipt until the time the money is remitted by the authorized delegate to the license holder. A trust resulting from the authorized delegate's actions is in favor of the license holder.

(c) A license holder's authorized delegate may not commingle the money received for transmission by or for the license holder with the authorized delegate's own money or other property, except to use in the ordinary course of the delegate's business for the purpose of making change, if the money is accounted for at the end of each business day.

(d) If a license holder or the license holder's authorized delegate commingles any money received for transmission with money or other property owned or controlled by the license holder or delegate, all commingled money and other property are impressed with a trust as provided by this section in an amount equal to the amount of money received for transmission, less the amount of fees paid for the transmission.

(e) If the commissioner revokes a license holder's license under Section 151.703, all money held in trust by the license holder and the license holder's authorized delegates is assigned to the commissioner for the benefit of the persons to whom the related money transmission obligations are owed.

(f) Money of a license holder or authorized delegate impressed with a trust under this section may not be considered an asset or property of the license holder or authorized delegate in the event of bankruptcy, receivership, or a claim against the license holder or authorized delegate unrelated to the license holder's or delegate's obligations under this chapter.

Sec. 151.405. Disclosure Requirements.

(a) A license holder's name and mailing address or telephone number must be provided to the purchaser in connection with each money transmission transaction conducted by the license holder directly or through an authorized delegate.

(b) A license holder receiving currency or an instrument payable in currency for transmission must comply with Chapter 278.

SUBCHAPTER F CURRENCY EXCHANGE LICENSE

Sec. 151.501. Definitions.

(a) This section defines terms that apply specifically to an applicant for or holder of a currency exchange license issued under this subchapter.

(b) In this subchapter:

(1) "Currency" means the coin and paper money of the United States or any country that is designated as legal tender and circulates and is customarily used and accepted as a medium of exchange in the country of issuance.

(2) "Currency exchange" means:

(A) receiving the currency of one government and exchanging it for the currency of another government; or

(B) receiving a negotiable instrument and exchanging it for the currency of another government.

(3) "Negotiable instrument" has the meaning assigned by Section 3.104, Business & Commerce Code.

Sec. 151.502. License Required.

(a) A person may not engage in the business of currency exchange or advertise, solicit, or hold itself out as providing currency exchange unless the person:

(1) is licensed under this subchapter;

(2) is licensed for money transmission under Subchapter D;

(3) is an authorized delegate of a person licensed for money transmission under Subchapter D;

(4) is excluded under Section 151.003; or

(5) has been granted an exemption under Subsection (d).

(b) For purposes of this chapter, a person engages in the business of currency exchange if the person exchanges currency and receives compensation or expects to receive compensation, directly or indirectly, for the currency exchange.

(c) A license holder may engage in the currency exchange business at one or more locations in this state owned, directly or indirectly by the license holder, under a single license.

(d) On application and a finding that the exemption is in the public interest, the commissioner may exempt a retailer, wholesaler, or service provider that in the ordinary course of business accepts currency of a foreign country or government as payment for goods or services, provided that a person is not eligible for the exemption if:

(1) the value of the goods or services purchased in a single transaction exceeds $10,000;

(2) the change given or made as a result of the transaction exceeds $100;

(3) an attempt is made to structure a transaction in a manner that evades the licensing requirements of this subchapter or avoids using a business licensed under this chapter;

(4) the person is engaged in the business of cashing checks, drafts, or other payment instruments for consideration and is not otherwise exempt from licensing under this chapter; or

(5) the person would not be eligible for a license under this chapter.

(e) In accordance with the investigation provisions of this chapter, the commissioner may examine a person to verify the person's exempt status under Subsection (d).

Sec. 151.503. Qualifications.

An applicant for a currency exchange license must have the qualifications set forth in Section 151.202.

Sec. 151.504. Application and Accompanying Fee and Security.

(a) An applicant for a currency exchange license must submit an application in accordance with Section 151.203.

(b) At the time an application for a currency exchange license is submitted, an applicant must file with the department:

(1) an application fee in the amount established by commission rule; and

(2) security in the amount required under Section 151.506.

Sec. 151.505. Investigation and Action on Application.

The commissioner shall investigate the applicant and act on the application in accordance with Sections 151.204 and 151.205.

Sec. 151.506. Security.

(a) An applicant for a currency exchange license must provide and a currency exchange license holder must maintain at all times security in the amount applicable to the applicant or license holder under this section. The security must satisfy the requirements of and is subject to Sections 151.308(c)-(j).

(b) An applicant must provide and a license holder must maintain security in the amount of $2,500 if the applicant will conduct or the license holder conducts business with persons located in this state exclusively at one or more physical locations through in-person, contemporaneous transactions.

(c) Except as provided by Subsection (d), if Subsection (b) does not apply to:

(1) the applicant, the applicant must provide security in the amount that is the greater of:

(A) $2,500; or

(B) an amount equal to one percent of the applicant's projected total dollar volume of currency exchange business in this state for the first year of licensure; or

(2) the license holder, the license holder must maintain security in the amount that is the greater of:

(A) $2,500; or

(B) an amount equal to one percent of the license holder's total dollar volume of currency exchange business in this state for the preceding year.

(d) The maximum amount of security that may be required under Subsection (c) is $1 million.

SUBCHAPTER G EXAMINATIONS, REPORTS, AND RECORDS

Sec. 151.601. Examinations.

(a) The commissioner may examine a license holder or authorized delegate of a license holder as reasonably necessary or appropriate to administer and enforce this chapter and rules adopted and orders issued under this chapter and other applicable law, including the Bank Secrecy Act, the USA PATRIOT ACT, and Chapter 271.

(b) The commissioner may:

(1) conduct an examination annually or at other times as the commissioner may reasonably require;

(2) conduct an on-site examination or an off-site review of records;

(3) conduct an examination in conjunction with an examination conducted by representatives of other state agencies or agencies of another state or of the federal government;

(4) accept the examination report of another state agency or an agency of another state or of the federal government, or a report prepared by an independent accounting firm, which on being accepted is considered for all purposes as an official report of the commissioner; and

(5) summon and examine under oath a principal, responsible individual, or employee of a license holder or authorized delegate of a license holder and require the person to produce records regarding any matter related to the condition and business of the license holder or authorized delegate.

(c) A license holder or authorized delegate of a license holder shall provide, and the commissioner shall have full and complete access to, all records the commissioner may reasonably require to conduct a complete examination. The records must be provided at the location and in the format specified by the commissioner.

(d) Unless otherwise directed by the commissioner, a license holder shall pay all costs reasonably incurred in connection with an examination of

Finance Code

the license holder or the license holder's authorized delegate.

(e) Disclosure of information to the commissioner under an examination request does not waive or otherwise affect or diminish confidentiality or a privilege to which the information is otherwise subject. Information disclosed to the commissioner in connection with an examination is confidential under Section 151.606.

Sec. 151.602. Records.

(a) A license holder must prepare, maintain, and preserve the following books, accounts, and other records for at least five years or another period as may be prescribed by rule of the commission:

(1) a record of each money transmission transaction or currency exchange transaction, as applicable;

(2) a general ledger posted in accordance with generally accepted accounting principles containing all asset, liability, capital, income, and expense accounts, unless directed otherwise by the commissioner;

(3) bank statements and bank reconciliation records;

(4) all records and reports required by applicable state and federal law, including the reporting and recordkeeping requirements imposed by the Bank Secrecy Act, the USA PATRIOT ACT, and Chapter 271, and other federal and state laws pertaining to money laundering, drug trafficking, or terrorist funding; and

(5) any other records required by commission rule or reasonably requested by the commissioner to determine compliance with this chapter.

(b) The records required under this section may be:

(1) maintained in a photographic, electronic, or other similar form; and

(2) maintained at the license holder's principal place of business or another location as may be reasonably requested by the commissioner.

(c) An authorized delegate must prepare, maintain, and preserve the records required by commission rule or reasonably requested by the commissioner.

(d) The records required under this section are subject to inspection by the commissioner under Section 151.601.

(e) The records required under this section and the reports required under Section 151.603 must be in English and the financial information contained in the records and reports must be denominated in United States dollars.

Sec. 151.603. Reports.

(a) An applicant or license holder shall file a written report with the commissioner not later than the 15th day after the date the applicant or license holder knows or has reason to know of a material change in the information reported in an application or annual report required under Section 151.207(b)(2). The report must describe the change and the anticipated impact of the change on the activities of the applicant or license holder in this state.

(b) A money transmission license holder shall prepare written reports and statements as follows:

(1) the annual report required by Section 151.207(b)(2), including an audited unconsolidated financial statement that is dated as of the last day of the license holder's fiscal year that ended in the immediately preceding calendar year;

(2) a quarterly interim financial statement and report regarding the permissible investments required to be maintained under Section 151.309 that reflect the license holder's financial condition and permissible investments as of the last day of the calendar quarter to which the statement and report relate and that are prepared not later than the 45th day after the last day of the calendar quarter; and

(3) any other report required by rule of the commission or reasonably requested by the commissioner to determine compliance with this chapter.

(c) A currency exchange license holder shall prepare a written report or statement as follows:

(1) the annual report required by Section 151.207(b)(2), including a financial statement that may be audited or unaudited and that is dated as of the last day of the license holder's fiscal year that ended in the immediately preceding calendar year;

(2) a quarterly interim financial statement and transaction report that reflects the license holder's financial condition and currency exchange business as of the last day of the calendar quarter to which the statement and report relate and that are prepared not later than the 45th day after the last day of the calendar quarter; and

(3) any other report required by rule of the commission or reasonably requested by the commissioner to determine compliance with this chapter.

(c-1) [Repealed.]

(d) A license holder shall file the statements and reports required under this section with the commissioner as required by this chapter, by commission rule, or as requested by the commissioner.

(e) On written application and for good cause shown, the commissioner may extend the time for preparing or filing a statement or report required under this section.

Sec. 151.604. Extraordinary Reporting Requirements.

(a) A license holder shall file a written report with the commissioner not later than the 15th day after the date the license holder knows or has reason to know of a material change in the information reported in an application or annual report required under Section 151.207(b)(2). The report must describe the change and the anticipated impact of the change on the license holder's activities in this state.

(b) A license holder must file a written report with the commissioner not later than 24 hours after the license holder knows or has reason to know of:

(1) the filing of a petition by or against the license holder for bankruptcy or reorganization;

(2) the filing of a petition by or against the license holder for receivership, the commencement of any other judicial or administrative proceeding for its dissolution or reorganization, or the making of a general assignment for the benefit of the license holder's creditors;

(3) the institution of a proceeding to revoke or suspend the license holder's license, or to enjoin or otherwise require the license holder to cease and desist from engaging in an activity related to a business activity that, if conducted in this state, would be subject to this chapter, by a state or country in which the license holder engages in business or is licensed;

(4) the felony indictment or conviction of the license holder or a principal of, person in control of, responsible individual of, or authorized delegate of the license holder for an offense identified in Section 151.202(e);

(5) the cancellation or other impairment of the license holder's security; or

(6) the inability to meet the license holder's transmission obligations under this chapter for a period of 24 hours or longer.

Sec. 151.605. Change of Control.

(a) This section applies to a proposed change of control of a license holder that results in a person or group of persons acting in concert, a "proposed person in control," after consummation of the acquisition transaction, controlling the license holder or a person in control of a license holder.

(b) A person may not directly or indirectly acquire control of a license holder or a person in control of a license holder without the prior written approval of the commissioner, except as provided by this section.

(c) A license holder or proposed person in control shall:

(1) give the commissioner written notice of a proposed change of control at least 45 days before the date the proposed transaction is to be consummated;

(2) request approval of the proposed change of control; and

(3) submit a nonrefundable fee in an amount established by commission rule.

(d) A proposed person in control is subject to the same standards and qualifications that apply to a principal of an applicant for a new license under this chapter. The commissioner may require the license holder or proposed person in control to provide the same type of information, documentation, and certifications and may conduct the same type of investigation the commissioner requires and conducts in connection with a new license application.

(e) The commissioner shall approve a proposed change of control if the commissioner determines that the proposed person in control has the financial responsibility, financial condition, business experience, competence, character, and general fitness to warrant the belief that the business of the license holder will be conducted in compliance with this chapter, rules adopted under this chapter, and other applicable state and federal law and that the change of control will not jeopardize the public interest.

(f) If the commissioner determines that the proposed person in control fails to meet the qualifications, standards, and requirements of this chapter, the commissioner shall inform the license holder and the proposed person in control in writing that the application is denied and state the reasons for the denial. The license holder or the proposed person in control may appeal the denial by filing a written request for a hearing with the commissioner not later than the 30th day after the date the notice is mailed. A hearing on the denial must be held not later than the 45th day after the date the commissioner receives the written request unless the administrative law judge extends the period for good cause or the parties agree to a later hearing date. The hearing is considered a contested case hearing and is subject to Section 151.801.

(g) The following persons are exempt from the requirements of Subsection (a), but the license holder must notify the commissioner not later than the 15th day after the date the change of control becomes effective:

Finance Code

(1) a person that acts as proxy for the sole purpose of voting at a designated meeting of the security holders or holders of voting interests of a license holder or controlling person;

(2) a person that acquires control of a license holder by devise or descent;

(3) a person exempted in the public interest by rule of the commission or by order of the commissioner; and

(4) a person that has previously complied with and received approval under this chapter or that was identified as a person in control in a prior application filed with and approved by the commissioner.

(h) Subsection (b) does not apply to a public offering of securities.

(i) Before filing an application for approval of a proposed change of control, a license holder may submit a written request asking the commissioner to determine whether a person would be considered a proposed person in control of the license holder and whether the requirements of this section apply to the proposed transaction. The request must be accompanied by a fee in an amount established by commission rule and must correctly and fully represent the facts relevant to the person and the proposed transaction. If the commissioner determines that the person would not be a person in control of the license holder for purposes of this section, the commissioner shall advise the license holder in writing that this section does not apply to the proposed person and transaction.

Sec. 151.606. Confidentiality.

(a) Except as otherwise provided by Subsection (b) or by rule of the commission, all financial information and all other personal information obtained by the commissioner under this chapter through application, examination, investigation, or otherwise, and any related file or record of the department, is confidential and not subject to disclosure.

(b) The commissioner may disclose confidential information if:

(1) the applicant, license holder, or authorized delegate consents to the release of the information or has published the information contained in the release;

(2) the commissioner finds that release of the information is necessary to protect the public or purchasers or potential purchasers of money services from the license holder or authorized delegate from immediate and irreparable harm;

(3) the information is disclosed to an agency identified in Section 151.105(a), in which event the information remains confidential and the agency must take appropriate measures to maintain that confidentiality;

(4) the commissioner finds that release of the information is required for an administrative hearing; or

(5) the commissioner discloses the information to a person acting on behalf of or for the commissioner for regulatory or enforcement purposes, subject to an agreement that maintains the confidentiality of the information.

(c) This section does not prohibit the commissioner from disclosing to the public:

(1) a list of license holders or authorized delegates, including addresses and the names of contact individuals;

(2) the identity of a license holder or authorized delegate subject to an emergency or final order of the commissioner and the basis for the commissioner's action; or

(3) information regarding or included in a consumer complaint against a license holder or authorized delegate.

SUBCHAPTER H ENFORCEMENT

Sec. 151.701. Injunctive Relief.

(a) Whenever it appears that a person has violated, or that reasonable cause exists to believe that a person is likely to violate, this chapter or a rule adopted under this chapter, the following persons may bring an action for injunctive relief to enjoin the violation or enforce compliance with the provision:

(1) the commissioner, through the attorney general;

(2) the attorney general;

(3) the district attorney of Travis County; or

(4) the prosecuting attorney of the county in which the violation is alleged to have occurred.

(b) In addition to the authority granted to the commissioner under Subsection (a), the commissioner, through the attorney general, may bring an action for injunctive relief if the commissioner has reason to believe that a person has violated or is likely to violate an order of the commissioner issued under this chapter.

(c) An action for injunctive relief brought by the commissioner, the attorney general, or the district attorney of Travis County under Subsection (a), or brought by the commissioner under Subsection (b), must be brought in a district court in Travis County. An action brought by a prosecuting attorney under Subsection (a)(4) must be brought in a district court in the county in which all or part of the violation is alleged to have occurred.

(d) On a proper showing, the court may issue a restraining order, an order freezing assets, a preliminary or permanent injunction, or a writ of mandate, or may appoint a receiver for the defendant or the defendant's assets.

(e) A receiver appointed by the court under Subsection (d) may, with approval of the court, exercise all of the powers of the defendant's directors, officers, partners, trustees, or persons who exercise similar powers and perform similar duties.

(f) An action brought under this section may include a claim for ancillary relief, including a claim by the commissioner for costs or civil penalties authorized under this chapter, or for restitution or damages on behalf of the persons injured by the act constituting the subject matter of the action, and the court has jurisdiction to award that relief.

Sec. 151.702. Cease and Desist Orders for Unlicensed Persons.

(a) If the commissioner has reason to believe that an unlicensed person has engaged or is likely to engage in an activity for which a license is required under this chapter, the commissioner may order the person to cease and desist from the violation until the person is issued a license under this chapter. The commissioner's order is subject to Section 151.709, unless the order is issued as an emergency order. The commissioner may issue an emergency cease and desist order in accordance with Section 151.710 if the commissioner finds that the person's violation or likely violation threatens immediate and irreparable harm to the public.

(b) A cease and desist order under this section may require the unlicensed person to take affirmative action to correct any condition resulting from or contributing to the activity or violation, including the payment of restitution to each resident of this state damaged by the violation.

Sec. 151.703. Suspension and Revocation of License.

(a) The commissioner must revoke a license if the commissioner finds that:

(1) the net worth of the license holder is less than the amount required under this chapter; or

(2) the license holder does not provide the security required under this chapter.

(b) The commissioner may suspend or revoke a license or order a license holder to revoke the designation of an authorized delegate if the commissioner has reason to believe that:

(1) the license holder has violated this chapter, a rule adopted or order issued under this chapter, a written agreement entered into with the department or commissioner, or any other state or federal law applicable to the license holder's money services business;

(2) the license holder has refused to permit or has not cooperated with an examination or investigation authorized by this chapter;

(3) the license holder has engaged in fraud, knowing misrepresentation, deceit, or gross negligence in connection with the operation of the license holder's money services business or any transaction subject to this chapter;

(4) an authorized delegate of the license holder has knowingly violated this chapter, a rule adopted or order issued under this chapter, or a state or federal anti-money-laundering or terrorist funding law, and the license holder knows or should have known of the violation and has failed to make a reasonable effort to prevent or correct the violation;

(5) the competence, experience, character, or general fitness of the license holder or an authorized delegate of the license holder, or a principal of, person in control of, or responsible person of a license holder or authorized delegate, indicates that it is not in the public interest to permit the license holder or authorized delegate to provide money services;

(6) the license holder has engaged in an unsafe or unsound act or practice or has conducted business in an unsafe or unsound manner;

(7) the license holder has suspended payment of the license holder's obligations, made a general assignment for the benefit of the license holder's creditors, or admitted in writing the license holder's inability to pay debts of the license holder as they become due;

(8) the license holder has failed to terminate the authority of an authorized delegate after the commissioner has issued and served on the license holder a final order finding that the authorized delegate has violated this chapter;

(9) a fact or condition exists that, if it had been known at the time the license holder applied for the license, would have been grounds for denying the application;

(10) the license holder has engaged in false, misleading, or deceptive advertising;

(11) the license holder has failed to pay a judgment entered in favor of a claimant or creditor in an action arising out of the license holder's activities under this chapter not later than the 30th day after the date the judgment becomes final or not

later than the 30th day after the date the stay of execution expires or is terminated, as applicable;

(12) the license holder has knowingly made a material misstatement or has suppressed or withheld material information on an application, request for approval, report, or other document required to be filed with the department under this chapter; or

(13) the license holder has committed a breach of trust or of a fiduciary duty.

(c) In determining whether a license holder has engaged in an unsafe or unsound act or practice or has conducted business in an unsafe or unsound manner, the commissioner may consider factors that include:

(1) the size and condition of the license holder's provision of money services;

(2) the magnitude of the loss or potential loss;

(3) the gravity of the violation of this chapter or rule adopted or order issued under this chapter;

(4) any action taken against the license holder by this state, another state, or the federal government; and

(5) the previous conduct of the license holder.

(d) The commissioner's order suspending or revoking a license or directing a license holder to revoke the designation of an authorized delegate is subject to Section 151.709, unless the order is issued as an emergency order. The commissioner may issue an emergency order suspending a license or directing a license holder to revoke the designation of an authorized delegate in accordance with Section 151.710 if the commissioner finds that the factors identified in Section 151.710(b) exist.

Sec. 151.704. Suspension and Revocation of Authorized Delegate Designation.

(a) The commissioner may suspend or revoke the designation of an authorized delegate if the commissioner has reason to believe that:

(1) the authorized delegate has violated this chapter, a rule adopted or order issued under this chapter, a written agreement entered into with the commissioner or the department, or any other state or federal law applicable to a money services business;

(2) the authorized delegate has refused to permit or has not cooperated with an examination or investigation under this chapter;

(3) the authorized delegate has engaged in fraud, knowing misrepresentation, deceit, gross negligence, or an unfair or deceptive act or practice in connection with the operation of the delegate's business on behalf of the license holder or any transaction subject to this chapter;

(4) the competence, experience, character, or general fitness of the authorized delegate, or a principal of, person in control of, or responsible person of the authorized delegate, indicates that it is not in the public interest to permit the authorized delegate to provide money services;

(5) the authorized delegate has engaged in an unsafe or unsound act or practice or conducted business in an unsafe and unsound manner;

(6) the authorized delegate, or a principal or responsible person of the authorized delegate, is listed on the specifically designated nationals and blocked persons list prepared by the United States Department of the Treasury as a potential threat to commit terrorist acts or to fund terrorist acts; or

(7) the authorized delegate, or a principal or responsible person of the authorized delegate, has been convicted of a state or federal anti-money-laundering or terrorist funding law.

(b) In determining whether an authorized delegate has engaged in an unsafe or unsound act or practice or conducted business in an unsafe or unsound manner, the commissioner may consider factors that include:

(1) the size and condition of the authorized delegate's provision of money services;

(2) the magnitude of the loss or potential loss;

(3) the gravity of the violation of this chapter or rule adopted or order issued under this chapter;

(4) any action taken against the authorized delegate by this state, another state, or the federal government; and

(5) the previous conduct of the authorized delegate.

(c) The commissioner's order suspending or revoking the designation of an authorized delegate is subject to Section 151.709, unless the order is issued as an emergency order. The commissioner may issue an emergency order suspending the designation of an authorized delegate in accordance with Section 151.710 if the commissioner finds that the factors identified in Section 151.710(b) exist.

Sec. 151.705. Cease and Desist Orders for License Holders or Authorized Delegates.

(a) The commissioner may issue an order to cease and desist if the commissioner finds that:

(1) an action, violation, or condition listed in Section 151.703 or 151.704 exists with respect to a license holder or authorized delegate; and

(2) a cease and desist order is necessary to protect the interests of the license holder, the purchasers of the license holder's money services, or the public.

(b) A cease and desist order may require a license holder or authorized delegate to cease and desist from the action or violation or to take affirmative

Finance Code

action to correct any condition resulting from or contributing to the action or violation, and the requirements of the order may apply to a principal or responsible person of the license holder or authorized delegate.

(c) The cease and desist order is subject to Section 151.709, unless the order is issued as an emergency order. The commissioner may issue an emergency cease and desist order in accordance with Section 151.710 if the commissioner finds that the factors identified in Section 151.710(b) exist.

Sec. 151.706. Consent Orders.

(a) The commissioner may enter into a consent order at any time with a person to resolve a matter arising under this chapter or a rule adopted or order issued under this chapter.

(b) A consent order must be signed by the person to whom the order is issued or by the person's authorized representative and must indicate agreement with the terms contained in the order. However, a consent order may provide that the order does not constitute an admission by a person that this chapter or a rule adopted or order issued under this chapter has been violated.

(c) A consent order is a final order and may not be appealed.

Sec. 151.707. Administrative Penalty.

(a) After notice and hearing, the commissioner may assess an administrative penalty against a person that:

(1) has violated this chapter or a rule adopted or order issued under this chapter and has failed to correct the violation not later than the 30th day after the date the department sends written notice of the violation to the person;

(2) if the person is a license holder, has engaged in conduct specified in Section 151.703;

(3) has engaged in a pattern of violations; or

(4) has demonstrated wilful disregard for the requirements of this chapter, the rules adopted under this chapter, or an order issued under this chapter.

(b) A violation corrected after a person receives written notice from the department of the violation may be considered for purposes of determining whether a person has engaged in a pattern of violations under Subsection (a)(3) or demonstrated wilful disregard under Subsection (a)(4).

(c) The amount of the penalty may not exceed $5,000 for each violation or, in the case of a continuing violation, $5,000 for each day that the violation continues. Each transaction in violation of this chapter and each day that a violation continues is a separate violation.

(d) In determining the amount of the penalty, the commissioner shall consider factors that include the seriousness of the violation, the person's compliance history, and the person's good faith in attempting to comply with this chapter, provided that if the person is found to have demonstrated wilful disregard under Subsection (a)(4), the trier of fact may recommend that the commissioner impose the maximum administrative penalty permitted under Subsection (c).

(e) A hearing to assess an administrative penalty is considered a contested case hearing and is subject to Section 151.801.

(f) An order imposing an administrative penalty after notice and hearing becomes effective and is final for purposes of collection and appeal immediately on issuance.

(g) The commissioner may collect an administrative penalty assessed under this section:

(1) in the same manner that a money judgment is enforced in court; or

(2) if the penalty is imposed against a license holder or a license holder's authorized delegate, from the proceeds of the license holder's security in accordance with Section 151.308(e).

Sec. 151.708. Criminal Penalty.

(a) A person commits an offense if the person:

(1) intentionally makes a false statement, misrepresentation, or certification in a record or application filed with the department or required to be maintained under this chapter or a rule adopted or order issued under this chapter, or intentionally makes a false entry or omits a material entry in the record or application; or

(2) knowingly engages in an activity for which a license is required under Subchapter D or F without being licensed under this chapter.

(b) An offense under this section is a felony of the third degree.

(c) An offense under this section may be prosecuted in Travis County or in the county in which the offense is alleged to have been committed.

(d) Nothing in this section limits the power of the state to punish a person for an act that constitutes an offense under this or any other law.

Sec. 151.709. Notice, Hearing, and Other Procedures for Nonemergency Orders.

(a) This section applies to an order issued by the commissioner under this subchapter that is not an emergency order.

(b) An order to which this section applies becomes effective only after notice and an opportunity for hearing. The order must:

(1) state the grounds on which the order is based;

(2) to the extent applicable, state the action or violation from which the person subject to the order must cease and desist or the affirmative action the person must take to correct a condition resulting from the violation or that is otherwise appropriate;

(3) be delivered by personal delivery or sent by certified mail, return receipt requested, to the person against whom the order is directed at the person's last known address;

(4) state the effective date of the order, which may not be before the 21st day after the date the order is delivered or mailed; and

(5) include a notice that a person may file a written request for a hearing on the order with the commissioner not later than the 20th day after the date the order is delivered or mailed.

(c) Unless the commissioner receives a written request for hearing from the person against whom the order is directed not later than the 20th day after the date the order is delivered or mailed, the order takes effect as stated in the order and is final against and nonappealable by that person from that date.

(d) A hearing on the order must be held not later than the 45th day after the date the commissioner receives the written request for the hearing unless the administrative law judge extends the period for good cause or the parties agree to a later hearing date.

(e) An order that has been affirmed or modified after a hearing becomes effective and is final for purposes of enforcement and appeal immediately on issuance. The order may be appealed to the district court of Travis County as provided by Section 151.801(b).

Sec. 151.710. Requirements and Notice and Hearing Procedures for Emergency Orders.

(a) This section applies to an emergency order issued by the commissioner under this subchapter.

(b) The commissioner may issue an emergency order, without prior notice and an opportunity for hearing, if the commissioner finds that:

(1) the action, violation, or condition that is the basis for the order:

(A) has caused or is likely to cause the insolvency of the license holder;

(B) has caused or is likely to cause the substantial dissipation of the license holder's assets or earnings;

(C) has seriously weakened or is likely to seriously weaken the condition of the license holder; or

(D) has seriously prejudiced or is likely to seriously prejudice the interests of the license holder, a purchaser of the license holder's money services, or the public; and

(2) immediate action is necessary to protect the interests of the license holder, a purchaser of the license holder's money services, or the public.

(c) In connection with and as directed by an emergency order, the commissioner may seize the records and assets of a license holder or authorized delegate that relate to the license holder's money services business.

(d) An emergency order must:

(1) state the grounds on which the order is based;

(2) advise the person against whom the order is directed that the order takes effect immediately, and, to the extent applicable, require the person to immediately cease and desist from the conduct or violation that is the subject of the order or to take the affirmative action stated in the order as necessary to correct a condition resulting from the conduct or violation or as otherwise appropriate;

(3) be delivered by personal delivery or sent by certified mail, return receipt requested, to the person against whom the order is directed at the person's last known address; and

(4) include a notice that a person may request a hearing on the order by filing a written request for hearing with the commissioner not later than the 15th day after the date the order is delivered or mailed.

(e) An emergency order takes effect as soon as the person against whom the order is directed has actual or constructive knowledge of the issuance of the order.

(f) A license holder or authorized delegate against whom an emergency order is directed must submit a written certification to the commissioner, signed by the license holder or authorized delegate, and their principals and responsible individuals, as applicable, and each person named in the order, stating that each person has received a copy of and has read and understands the order.

(g) Unless the commissioner receives a written request for a hearing from a person against whom an emergency order is directed not later than the 15th day after the date the order is delivered or mailed, the order is final and nonappealable as to that person on the 16th day after the date the order is delivered or mailed.

(h) A request for a hearing does not stay an emergency order.

(i) A hearing on an emergency order takes precedence over any other matter pending before the commissioner, and must be held not later than the 10th day after the date the commissioner receives the written request for hearing unless the administrative law judge extends the period for good cause or the parties agree to a later hearing date.

(j) An emergency order that has been affirmed or modified after a hearing is final for purposes of enforcement and appeal. The order may be appealed to the district court of Travis County as provided in Section 151.801(b).

SUBCHAPTER I ADMINISTRATIVE PROCEDURES AND JUDICIAL REVIEW

Sec. 151.801. Administrative Procedures.

(a) All administrative proceedings under this chapter must be conducted in accordance with Chapter 2001, Government Code, and Title 7, Chapter 9, Texas Administrative Code.

(b) A person affected by a final order of the commissioner issued under this chapter after a hearing may appeal the order by filing a petition for judicial review in a district court of Travis County. A petition for judicial review filed in the district court under this subsection does not stay or vacate the appealed order unless the court, after notice and hearing, specifically stays or vacates the order.

SUBCHAPTER J. DEPOSITORY AGENT LICENSE [REPEALED]

Sec. 151.851. Definitions. [Repealed]

Sec. 151.852. Applicability to Depository Agent Services. [Repealed]

Sec. 151.853. License Required. [Repealed]

Sec. 151.854. Additional Qualifications. [Repealed]

Sec. 151.855. Application and Accompanying Fee, Statements, and Security. [Repealed]

Sec. 151.856. Investigation and Action on Application. [Repealed]

Sec. 151.857. Temporary License. [Repealed]

Sec. 151.858. Liability of License Holder. [Repealed]

Sec. 151.859. Trust Imposed. [Repealed]

Sec. 151.860. Disclosure Requirements. [Repealed]

CHAPTER 158 RESIDENTIAL MORTGAGE LOAN SERVICERS

SUBCHAPTER C INVESTIGATIONS, COMPLAINTS, AND ACTIONS AGAINST REGISTRANT

Sec. 158.1045. Issuance and Enforcement of Subpoena.

(a) During an investigation, the commissioner may issue a subpoena that is addressed to a peace officer of this state or other person authorized by law to serve citation or perfect service. The subpoena may require a person to give a deposition, produce documents, or both.

(b) If a person disobeys a subpoena or if a person appearing in a deposition in connection with the investigation refuses to testify, the commissioner may petition a district court in Travis County to issue an order requiring the person to obey the subpoena, testify, or produce documents relating to the matter. The court shall promptly set an application to enforce a subpoena issued under Subsection (a) for hearing and shall cause notice of the application and the hearing to be served on the person to whom the subpoena is directed.

SUBTITLE Z MISCELLANEOUS PROVISIONS RELATING TO FINANCIAL INSTITUTIONS AND BUSINESSES

CHAPTER 271
FINANCIAL TRANSACTION REPORTING REQUIREMENTS

Sec. 271.001. Reporting Requirement for Crimes and Suspected Crimes and Currency and Foreign Transactions.

(a) A financial institution that is required to file a report with respect to a transaction in this state under the Currency and Foreign Transactions Reporting Act (31 U.S.C. Section 5311 et seq.), 31 C.F.R. Part 103, or 12 C.F.R. Section 21.11, and their subsequent amendments, shall file a copy of the report with the attorney general.

(b) A financial institution that timely files the report described by Subsection (a) with the appropriate federal agency as required by federal law complies with that subsection unless the attorney general:

(1) notifies the financial institution that the report is not of a type that is regularly and comprehensively transmitted by the federal agency to the attorney general following the attorney general's request to that agency;

(2) requests that the financial institution provide the attorney general with a copy of the report; and

(3) reimburses the financial institution for the actual cost of duplicating and delivering the report or 25 cents for each page, whichever is less.

(c) In this section, "financial institution" has the meaning assigned by 31 U.S.C. Section 5312 and its subsequent amendments.

Sec. 271.002. Reporting Requirement for Cash Receipts of More Than $10,000.

(a) A person engaged in a trade or business who, in the course of the trade or business, receives more than $10,000 in one transaction or in two or more related transactions in this state and who is required to file a return under Section 6050I, Internal Revenue Code of 1986 (26 U.S.C. Section 6050I), or 26 C.F.R. Section 1.6050I-1, and their subsequent amendments, shall file a copy of the return with the attorney general.

(b) A person who timely files the return described by Subsection (a) with the appropriate federal agency as required by federal law complies with that subsection unless the attorney general:

(1) notifies the person that the return is not of a type that is regularly and comprehensively transmitted by the federal agency to the attorney general; and

(2) requests that the person provide the attorney general with a copy of the return.

Sec. 271.003. Use of Reported Information.

The attorney general may report a possible violation indicated by analysis of a report or return described by this chapter or information obtained under this chapter to an appropriate law enforcement agency for use in the proper discharge of the agency's official duties.

Sec. 271.004. Failure to Comply with Reporting Requirements; Criminal Penalty.

(a) A person commits an offense if the person:

(1) is requested by the attorney general to submit information required by Section 271.001 or 271.002 to the attorney general; and

(2) knowingly fails to provide the requested information to the attorney general before the 30th day after the date of the request.

(b) An offense under this section is a Class A misdemeanor.

Sec. 271.005. Suppression of Physical Evidence; Criminal Penalty.

(a) A person commits an offense if the person knowingly suppresses physical evidence connected with information contained in a report or return required by this chapter through concealment, alteration, or destruction.

(b) An offense under this section is a Class A misdemeanor.

Sec. 271.006. Notification to Target of Criminal Investigation; Criminal Penalty.

(a) A person commits an offense if the person:

(1) is required to submit a report or return under this chapter; and

(2) knowingly notifies an individual who is the target of a criminal investigation involving an offense under Chapter 34, Penal Code, that:

(A) the attorney general has requested the person to provide information required by this chapter related to the targeted individual; or

(B) the individual may be subject to impending criminal prosecution.

(b) An offense under this section is a Class A misdemeanor.

TITLE 5
PROTECTION OF CONSUMERS OF FINANCIAL SERVICES

CHAPTER 391
FURNISHING FALSE CREDIT INFORMATION

Sec. 391.001. Definition.

In this chapter, "credit reporting bureau" means a person who engages in the practice of assembling or reporting credit information about individuals for the purpose of furnishing the information to a third party.

Sec. 391.002. Furnishing False Information; Penalty.

(a) A person commits an offense if the person knowingly furnishes false information about another person's creditworthiness, credit standing, or credit capacity to a credit reporting bureau.

(b) A credit reporting bureau commits an offense if the credit reporting bureau knowingly furnishes false information about a person's creditworthiness, credit standing, or credit capacity to a third party.

(c) An offense under this section is a misdemeanor punishable by a fine of not more than $200.

Finance Code

GOVERNMENT CODE

TITLE 2
JUDICIAL BRANCH

SUBTITLE I
COURT FEES AND COSTS [REPEALE]

CHAPTER 102
COURT COSTS IN CRIMINAL PROCEEDINGS [REPEALED]

SUBCHAPTER B
COURT COSTS ON CONVICTION [REPEALED]

Sec. 102.021. Court Costs on Conviction: Code of Criminal Procedure. [Repealed]

Sec. 102.0211. Court Costs on Conviction: Government Code. [Repealed; Effective until January 1, 2022]

Sec. 102.0211. Court Costs on Conviction: Government Code. [Repealed effective January 1, 2022]

Sec. 102.0212. Court Costs on Conviction: Local Government Code. [Repealed]

Sec. 102.0213. Court Costs on Conviction: Transportation Code. [Repealed]

Sec. 102.0213. Court Costs on Conviction: Transportation Code. [Repealed effective January 1, 2022]

Sec. 102.0214. Court Costs on Conviction: Parks and Wildlife Code. [Repealed]

SUBTITLE I
COURT FEES AND COSTS

CHAPTER 102
COURT COSTS IN CRIMINAL PROCEEDINGS

SUBCHAPTER B
COURT COSTS ON CONVICTION

Sec. 102.0215. Additional Court Costs on Conviction: Code of Criminal Procedure [Repealed].

Repealed by Acts 2009, 81st Leg., ch. 87 (S.B. 1969), § 11.111(b), effective September 1, 2009; Acts 2009, 81st Leg., ch. 902 (H.B. 666), § 2(b), effective September 1, 2009; and Acts 2009 81st Leg., ch. 1209 (S.B. 727), § 7(b), effective September 1, 2009.

SUBCHAPTER F
CRIMINAL COURT COSTS IN JUSTICE COURT [REPEALED]

Sec. 102.102. Additional Court Costs on Conviction in Justice Court: Business & Commerce Code. [Repealed]

SUBTITLE K
SPECIALTY COURTS

CHAPTER 126
COMMERCIALLY SEXUALLY EXPLOITED PERSONS COURT PROGRAM

Sec. 126.001. Commercially Sexually Exploited Persons Court Program; Procedures for Certain Defendants.

(a) In this chapter, "commercially sexually exploited persons court program" means a program that has the following essential characteristics:

(1) the integration of services in the processing of cases in the judicial system;

(2) the use of a nonadversarial approach involving prosecutors and defense attorneys to promote public safety, to reduce the demand for the commercial sex trade and trafficking of persons by educating offenders, and to protect the due process rights of program participants;

(3) early identification and prompt placement of eligible participants in the program;

(4) access to information, counseling, and services relating to sex addiction, sexually transmitted diseases, mental health, and substance abuse;

(5) a coordinated strategy to govern program responses to participant compliance;

(6) monitoring and evaluation of program goals and effectiveness;

(7) continuing interdisciplinary education to promote effective program planning, implementation, and operations; and

(8) development of partnerships with public agencies and community organizations.

(b) If a defendant successfully completes a commercially sexually exploited persons court program, regardless of whether the defendant was convicted of the offense for which the defendant entered the program or whether the court deferred further proceedings without entering an adjudication of guilt, after notice to the state and a hearing on whether the defendant is otherwise entitled to the petition, including whether the required time has elapsed, and whether issuance of the order is in the best interest of justice, the court shall enter an order of nondisclosure of criminal history record information under Subchapter E-1, Chapter 411, as if the defendant had received a discharge and dismissal under Article 42A.111, Code of Criminal Procedure, with respect to all records and files related to the defendant's arrest for the offense for which the defendant entered the program.

Sec. 126.002. Authority to Establish Program; Eligibility.

(a) The commissioners court of a county or governing body of a municipality may establish a commercially sexually exploited persons court program for defendants charged with an offense under Section 43.02(a), Penal Code.

(b) A defendant is eligible to participate in a commercially sexually exploited persons court program established under this chapter only if the attorney representing the state consents to the defendant's participation in the program.

(c) The court in which the criminal case is pending shall allow an eligible defendant to choose whether to participate in the commercially sexually exploited persons court program or otherwise proceed through the criminal justice system.

Sec. 126.003. Establishment of Regional Program.

The commissioners courts of two or more counties, or the governing bodies of two or more municipalities, may elect to establish a regional commercially sexually exploited persons court program under this chapter for the participating counties or municipalities.

Sec. 126.004. Program Powers and Duties.

(a) A commercially sexually exploited persons court program established under this chapter must:

(1) ensure that a person eligible for the program is provided legal counsel before volunteering to proceed through the program and while participating in the program;

(2) allow any participant to withdraw from the program at any time before a trial on the merits has been initiated;

(3) provide each participant with information, counseling, and services relating to sex addiction, sexually transmitted diseases, mental health, and substance abuse; and

(4) provide each participant with instruction related to the prevention of prostitution.

(b) To provide each program participant with information, counseling, and services described by Subsection (a)(3), a program established under this chapter may employ a person or solicit a volunteer who is:

(1) a health care professional;

(2) a psychologist;

(3) a licensed social worker or counselor;

(4) a former prostitute;

(5) a family member of a person arrested for soliciting prostitution;

(6) a member of a neighborhood association or community that is adversely affected by the commercial sex trade or trafficking of persons; or

(7) an employee of a nongovernmental organization specializing in advocacy or laws related to sex trafficking or human trafficking or in providing services to victims of those offenses.

(c) A program established under this chapter shall establish and publish local procedures to promote maximum participation of eligible defendants in programs established in the county or municipality in which the defendants reside.

(d) A program established under this chapter shall provide each program participant with information related to the right to petition for an order of nondisclosure of criminal history record information under Section 411.0728.

Sec. 126.005. Documentation Regarding Insufficient Funding.

A legislative committee may require a county that does not establish a commercially sexually exploited persons court program under this chapter due to a lack of sufficient funding, as provided by Section 126.007(c), to provide the committee with any documentation in the county's possession that concerns federal or state funding received by the county.

Sec. 126.006. Reimbursement Fees.

(a) A commercially sexually exploited persons court program established under this chapter may collect from a participant in the program a nonrefundable reimbursement fee for the program in a reasonable amount not to exceed $1,000, from which the following must be paid:

(1) a counseling and services reimbursement fee in an amount necessary to cover the costs of the counseling and services provided by the program; and

(2) a law enforcement training reimbursement fee, in an amount equal to five percent of the total amount paid under Subdivision (1), to be deposited to the credit of the treasury of the county or municipality that established the program to cover costs associated with the provision of training to law enforcement personnel on domestic violence, prostitution, and the trafficking of persons.

(b) Reimbursement fees collected under this section may be paid on a periodic basis or on a deferred payment schedule at the discretion of the judge, magistrate, or coordinator. The fees must be based on the participant's ability to pay.

Sec. 126.007. Program in Certain Counties Mandatory.

(a) If a municipality in the county has not established a commercially sexually exploited persons court program, the commissioners court of a county with a population of more than 200,000 shall:

(1) establish a commercially sexually exploited persons court program under this chapter; and

(2) direct the judge, magistrate, or coordinator to comply with Section 121.002(c)(1).

(b) A county required under this section to establish a commercially sexually exploited persons court program shall apply for federal and state funds available to pay the costs of the program. The criminal justice division of the governor's office may assist a county in applying for federal funds as required by this subsection.

(b-1) A county may apply to the criminal justice division of the governor's office for a grant for the establishment or operation of a commercially sexually exploited persons court program.

(c) Notwithstanding Subsection (a), a county is required to establish a commercially sexually exploited persons court program under this section only if:

(1) the county receives sufficient federal or state funding specifically for that purpose; and

(2) the judge, magistrate, or coordinator receives the verification described by Section 121.002(c)(2).

(d) A county that does not establish a commercially sexually exploited persons court program as required by this section and maintain the program is ineligible to receive funds for a community supervision and corrections department from the state.

Sec. 126.008. Suspension or Dismissal of Community Service Requirement.

(a) To encourage participation in a commercially sexually exploited persons court program established under this chapter, the judge or magistrate administering the program may suspend any requirement that, as a condition of community supervision, a participant in the program work a specified number of hours at a community service project..

(b) On a participant's successful completion of a commercially sexually exploited persons court program, a judge or magistrate may excuse the participant from any condition of community supervision previously suspended under Subsection (a).

SUBTITLE L COURT PROFESSIONS REGULATION

CHAPTER 158 COURT SECURITY OFFICERS

Sec. 158.001. Definition.

In this chapter, "court security officer" means a constable, sheriff, sheriff's deputy, municipal peace officer, or any other person assigned to provide security for an appellate, district, statutory county, county, municipal, or justice court in this state.

Sec. 158.002. Court Security Certification.

(a) Except as provided by Subsection (b), a person may not serve as a court security officer for an appellate, district, statutory county, county, municipal, or justice court in this state unless the person holds a court security certification issued by a training program approved by the Texas Commission on Law Enforcement..

(b) A court security officer is not required to hold a court security certification to provide security to a court described by Subsection (a) before the first anniversary of the date the officer begins providing security for the court.

Sec. 158.003. Verification.

The sheriff, constable, law enforcement agency, or other entity that provides security for a court shall verify that each court security officer holds the court security certification as required by this chapter.

TITLE 4 EXECUTIVE BRANCH

SUBTITLE B LAW ENFORCEMENT AND PUBLIC PROTECTION

CHAPTER 411 DEPARTMENT OF PUBLIC SAFETY OF THE STATE OF TEXAS

SUBCHAPTER A GENERAL PROVISIONS AND ADMINISTRATION

Sec. 411.001. Definitions.

In this chapter:

(1) "Commission" means the Public Safety Commission.

(2) "Department" means the Department of Public Safety of the State of Texas.

(3) "Director" means the public safety director.

(4) "Internet" means the largest nonproprietary nonprofit cooperative public computer network, popularly known as the Internet.

Sec. 411.0011. Certain Local Government Corporations Engaged in Criminal Identification Activities.

For purposes of this chapter, a reference to "criminal justice agency" includes a local government corporation created under Subchapter D, Chapter 431, Transportation Code, for governmental purposes relating to criminal identification activities, including forensic analysis, that allocates a substantial part of its annual budget to those criminal identification activities.

Sec. 411.002. Department of Public Safety of the State of Texas.

(a) The Department of Public Safety of the State of Texas is an agency of the state to enforce the laws protecting the public safety and provide for the prevention and detection of crime. The department is composed of the Texas Rangers, the Texas Highway Patrol, the administrative division, and other divisions that the commission considers necessary.

(b) The department shall have its principal office and headquarters in Austin.

(c) The Department of Public Safety of the State of Texas is subject to Chapter 325 (Texas Sunset Act). Unless continued in existence as provided by that chapter, the department is abolished and Subsections (a) and (b) expire September 1, 2031.

(d), (e) [Expired pursuant to Acts 2009, 81st Leg., ch. 1146 (H.B. 2730), § 5.01, effective August 31, 2011.]

Sec. 411.003. Public Safety Commission.

(a) The Public Safety Commission controls the department.

(b) The commission is composed of five citizens of this state appointed by the governor with the advice and consent of the senate. Members must be selected because of their peculiar qualifications for the position and must reflect the diverse geographic regions and population groups of this

Government Code

state. Members must have and maintain a secret security clearance granted by the United States government. A member may serve on the commission upon the granting of an interim secret security clearance, but may not be given access to classified information, participate in a briefing involving classified information, or vote on an issue involving classified information until a secret security clearance has been finally approved by the United States government. Appointments to the commission shall be made without regard to race, color, disability, sex, religion, age, or national origin. In making an appointment the governor shall consider, among other things, the person's knowledge of laws, experience in the enforcement of law, honesty, integrity, education, training, and executive ability.

(c) Members serve staggered six-year terms with the terms of either one or two members expiring January 1 of each even-numbered year.

(d) The governor shall designate one member of the commission as chairman of the commission to serve in that capacity at the pleasure of the governor. The commission shall meet at the times and places specified by commission rule or at the call of the chairman. The chairman shall oversee the preparation of an agenda for each meeting and ensure that a copy is provided to each member at least seven days before the meeting.

(e) A member serves without compensation for service on the commission but is entitled to per diem for expenses as provided by the General Appropriations Act.

(f) The commission shall develop and implement policies that provide the public with a reasonable opportunity to appear before the commission and to speak on any issue under the jurisdiction of the commission.

Sec. 411.0031. Training for Commission Members.

(a) A person who is appointed to and qualifies for office as a member of the commission may not vote, deliberate, or be counted as a member in attendance at a meeting of the commission until the person completes a training program that complies with this section.

(b) The training program must provide the person with information regarding:

(1) the law governing the department's operations;

(2) the programs, functions, rules, and budget of the department;

(3) the scope of and limitations on the rulemaking authority of the commission;

(4) the results of the most recent formal audit of the department;

(5) the requirements of:

(A) laws relating to open meetings, public information, administrative procedure, and disclosing conflicts of interest; and

(B) other laws applicable to members of the commission in performing their duties; and

(6) any applicable ethics policies adopted by the department or the Texas Ethics Commission.

(c) A person appointed to the commission is entitled to reimbursement, as provided by the General Appropriations Act, for the travel expenses incurred in attending the training program regardless of whether the attendance at the program occurs before or after the person qualifies for office.

(d) The director shall create a training manual that includes the information required by Subsection (b). The director shall distribute a copy of the training manual annually to each member of the commission. Each member of the commission shall sign and submit to the director a statement acknowledging that the member received and has reviewed the training manual.

Sec. 411.0035. Member and General Counsel Restriction.

(a) In this section, "Texas trade association" means a cooperative and voluntarily joined statewide association of business or professional competitors in this state designed to assist its members and its industry or profession in dealing with mutual business or professional problems and in promoting their common interest.

(b) A person may not be a member of the commission and may not be a department employee employed in a "bona fide executive, administrative, or professional capacity," as that phrase is used for purposes of establishing an exemption to the overtime provisions of the federal Fair Labor Standards Act of 1938 (29 U.S.C. Section 201 et seq.), if:

(1) the person is an officer, employee, or paid consultant of a Texas trade association in the field of law enforcement or private security; or

(2) the person's spouse is an officer, manager, or paid consultant of a Texas trade association in the field of law enforcement or private security.

(c) A person may not be a member of the commission or act as the general counsel to the commission if the person is required to register as a lobbyist under Chapter 305 because of the person's activities for compensation on behalf of a profession related to the operation of the commission.

Sec. 411.0036. Removal of Commission Member.

(a) It is a ground for removal from the commission if a member:

(1) does not have at the time of appointment the qualifications required by Section 411.003;

(2) does not maintain during service on the commission the qualifications required by Section 411.003;

(3) violates a prohibition established by Section 411.0035;

(4) cannot discharge the member's duties for a substantial part of the term for which the member is appointed because of illness or disability; or

(5) is absent from more than half of the regularly scheduled commission meetings that the member is eligible to attend during a calendar year unless the absence is excused by majority vote of the commission.

(b) The validity of an action of the commission is not affected by the fact that it is taken when a ground for removal of a commission member exists.

(c) If the director has knowledge that a potential ground for removal exists, the director shall notify the chairman of the commission of the potential ground. The chairman shall then notify the governor and the attorney general that a potential ground for removal exists. If the potential ground for removal involves the chairman, the director shall notify the member with the longest tenure on the commission, other than the chairman, who shall then notify the governor and the attorney general that a potential ground for removal exists.

Sec. 411.004. Duties and Powers of Commission.

The commission shall:

(1) formulate plans and policies for:

(A) enforcement of state criminal, traffic, and safety laws;

(B) prevention of crime;

(C) detection and apprehension of persons who violate laws; and

(D) education of citizens of this state in the promotion of public safety and the observance of law;

(2) organize the department and supervise its operation;

(3) adopt rules considered necessary for carrying out the department's work;

(4) maintain records of all proceedings and official orders; and

(5) biennially submit a report of its work to the governor and legislature, including the commission's and director's recommendations.

Sec. 411.0041. Open Meetings Exception: Criminal Investigations.

A discussion or deliberation of the commission regarding an ongoing criminal investigation, including a vote to issue a directive or take other action regarding the investigation, is not subject to the open meetings law, Chapter 551.

Sec. 411.0042. Division of Responsibilities.

The commission shall develop and implement policies that clearly separate the policymaking responsibilities of the commission and the management responsibilities of the director and the staff of the department.

Sec. 411.0043. Technology Policy; Review.

(a) The commission shall implement a policy requiring the department to use appropriate technological solutions to improve the department's ability to perform its functions. The policy must ensure that the public is able to interact with the department on the Internet.

(b) The department shall periodically:

(1) review the department's existing information technology system to determine whether:

(A) the system's security should be upgraded; and

(B) the system provides the department with the best ability to monitor and investigate criminal activity on the Internet; and

(2) make any necessary improvements to the department's information technology system.

Sec. 411.0044. Negotiated Rulemaking and Alternative Dispute Resolution.

(a) The commission shall develop and implement a policy to encourage the use of:

(1) negotiated rulemaking procedures under Chapter 2008 for the adoption of department rules; and

(2) appropriate alternative dispute resolution procedures under Chapter 2009 to assist in the resolution of internal and external disputes under the department's jurisdiction.

(b) The department's procedures relating to alternative dispute resolution must conform, to the extent possible, to any model guidelines issued by the State Office of Administrative Hearings for the use of alternative dispute resolution by state agencies.

(c) The commission shall designate a trained person to:

(1) coordinate the implementation of the policy adopted under Subsection (a);

(2) serve as a resource for any training needed to implement the procedures for negotiated rulemaking or alternative dispute resolution; and

(3) collect data concerning the effectiveness of those procedures, as implemented by the department.

Sec. 411.0045. Physical Fitness Programs.

The commission shall adopt:

(1) physical fitness programs in accordance with Section 614.172; and

(2) a resolution certifying that the programs adopted under Subdivision (1) are consistent with generally accepted scientific standards and meet all applicable requirements of state and federal labor and employment law.

Sec. 411.005. Director, Deputy Directors, and Assistant Directors.

(a) The commission shall appoint a citizen of the United States as public safety director. The director serves until removed by the commission.

(b) The director may appoint, with the advice and consent of the commission, deputy directors and assistant directors who shall perform the duties that the director designates. Deputy directors and assistant directors serve until removed by the director.

(c) The commission shall select the director, and the director shall select deputy directors and assistant directors, on the basis of the person's training, experience, and qualifications for the position. The director, deputy directors, and assistant directors are entitled to annual salaries as provided by the legislature.

Sec. 411.006. Duties of Director.

(a) The director shall:

(1) be directly responsible to the commission for the conduct of the department's affairs;

(2) act as executive director of the department;

(3) act with the commission in an advisory capacity, without vote;

(4) adopt rules, subject to commission approval, considered necessary for the control of the department;

(5) issue commissions as law enforcement officers, under the commission's direction, to all members of the Texas Rangers and the Texas Highway Patrol and to other officers of the department;

(6) appoint, with the advice and consent of the commission, the head of a division or bureau provided for by this chapter;

(7) quarterly, annually, and biennially submit to the commission detailed reports of the operation of the department, including statements of its expenditures; and

(8) prepare, swear to, submit to the governor, and file in the department's records a quarterly statement containing an itemized list of all money received and its source and all money spent and the purposes for which it was spent.

(b) The director or the director's designee shall provide to members of the commission and to department employees, as often as necessary, information regarding the requirements for office or employment under this chapter, including information regarding a person's responsibilities under applicable laws relating to standards of conduct for state officers or employees.

Sec. 411.0061. Commercial Carrier Inspections: Implementation Schedule for Noncommissioned Personnel [Expired].

Expired pursuant to Acts 1999, 76th Leg., ch. 1189 (S.B. 370), § 5, effective January 1, 2005.

Sec. 411.007. Officers and Employees.

(a) Subject to the provisions of this chapter, the director may appoint, promote, reduce, suspend, or discharge any officer or employee of the department.

(b) Appointment or promotion of an officer or employee must be based on merit determined under commission rules that take into consideration the applicant's age and physical condition, if appropriate and to the extent allowed under federal law, and that take into consideration the applicant's experience and education. For promotions of commissioned officers, other than those positions covered under Section 411.0071, the department, with the advice and consent of the commission, shall establish processes to be consistently applied and based on merit. Each person who has an application on file for a position in the department for which an applicant must take an examination shall be given reasonable written notice of the time and place of those examinations.

(c) An applicant for a position in the department must be a United States citizen. An applicant may not be questioned regarding the applicant's political affiliation or religious faith or beliefs. The department may not prohibit an officer or employee of the department, while off duty and out of

Government Code

uniform, from placing a bumper sticker endorsing political activities or a candidate for political office on a personal vehicle, placing a campaign sign in the person's private yard, making a political contribution, or wearing a badge endorsing political activities or a candidate. An officer commissioned by the department may not be suspended, terminated, or subjected to any form of discrimination by the department because of the refusal of the officer to take a polygraph examination. Section 411.0074 does not authorize the department to require an officer commissioned by the department to take a polygraph examination.

(d) At least annually the heads of the divisions and bureaus, after due investigation, shall make a report to the director of the efficiency of each employee within the division or bureau. These reports shall be kept in the department's permanent files and shall be given proper consideration in all matters of promotion and discharge.

(e) An officer or employee of the department may not be discharged without just cause. The director shall determine whether an officer or employee is to be discharged. A commissioned officer ordered discharged may appeal to the commission, and during the appeal the officer shall be suspended without pay.

(e-1) Except as provided by Subsection (g), the department may not discharge, suspend, or demote a commissioned officer except for the violation of a specific commission rule. If the department discharges, suspends, or demotes the officer, the department shall deliver to the officer a written statement giving the reasons for the action taken. The written statement must point out each commission rule alleged to have been violated by the officer and must describe the alleged acts of the officer that the department contends are in violation of the commission rules.

(e-2) The commission shall establish necessary policies and procedures for the appointment, promotion, reduction, suspension, and discharge of all employees.

(f) A discharged commissioned officer is entitled, on application to the commission, to a public hearing before the commission, who shall affirm or set aside the discharge. The commission shall affirm or set aside a discharge on the basis of the evidence presented. If the commission affirms the discharge, the discharged officer may seek judicial review, not later than the 90th day after the date the commission affirms the discharge, in a district court under the substantial evidence standard of review, and the officer remains suspended without pay while the case is under judicial review.

(g) A noncommissioned employee inducted into the service of the department is on probation for the first one year of service, and an officer is on probation from the date the officer is inducted into the service of the department until the anniversary of the date the officer is commissioned. At any time during the probationary period, an officer or employee may be discharged if the director, with the advice and consent of the commission, finds the officer or employee to be unsuitable for the work.

Sec. 411.0071. Direct Appointment to Management Team Positions by Director.

(a) The director may designate a head of a division or a position that involves working directly with the director as a management team position.

(b) The director may directly appoint a person to a position designated as a management team position under Subsection (a) under criteria determined by the director and approved by the commission. The director's appointment of a person to a management team position or transfer of a person from a management team position to another position for which the person is qualified, as determined by the director, is not subject to Section 411.007.

(c) A person appointed to a management team position under this section, on removal from that position, shall be returned to the position the person held immediately before appointment to the management team position or to a position of equivalent rank. If a person is removed from a management team position as a result of the filing of a formal charge of misconduct, this subsection applies only if the person is exonerated for the misconduct charged.

Sec. 411.0072. Employment-Related Grievances and Appeals of Disciplinary Actions Within the Department.

(a) In this section:

(1) "Disciplinary action" means discharge, suspension, or demotion.

(2) "Employment-related grievance" means an employment-related issue, other than a disciplinary action, in regard to which an employee wishes to express dissatisfaction, including promotions, leave requests, performance evaluations, transfers, benefits, working environment, shift or duty assignments, harassment, retaliation, and relationships with supervisors or other employees or any other issue the commission determines by rule.

(b) The commission shall establish procedures and practices governing the appeal of a disciplinary action within the department.

(c) The commission shall establish procedures and practices through which the department will address an employment-related grievance that include:

(1) a form on which an employee may state an employment-related grievance and request a specific corrective action;

(2) time limits for submitting a grievance and for management to respond to a grievance;

(3) a multilevel process in which an employee's grievance is submitted to the lowest appropriate level of management, with each subsequent appeal submitted to a higher level in the chain of command;

(4) an assurance that confidentiality of all parties involved will be maintained, except to the extent that information is subject to disclosure under Section 411.00755 and Chapter 552, and that retaliation against an employee who files a grievance is prohibited; and

(5) a program to advertise and explain the grievance procedure to all employees.

(d) The department shall submit annually to the commission, and as part of its biennial report to the legislature required under Section 411.004, a report on the department's use of the employment-related grievance process under Subsection (c). The report must include:

(1) the number of grievances filed;

(2) a brief description of the subject of each grievance filed; and

(3) the final disposition of each grievance.

Sec. 411.0073. Mediation of Personnel Disputes.

(a) The commission shall establish procedures for an employee to resolve an employment-related grievance covered by Section 411.0072 through mediation if the employee chooses. The procedures must include mediation procedures and establish the circumstances under which mediation is appropriate for an employment-related grievance.

(b) Except for Section 2008.054, Chapter 2008, as added by Chapter 934, Acts of the 75th Legislature, Regular Session, 1997, does not apply to the mediation. The mediator must be trained in mediation techniques.

Sec. 411.0074. Polygraph Examinations for Certain Applicants.

(a) This section does not apply to:

(1) an applicant who is currently a peace officer of the department commissioned by the department; or

(2) an applicant for a police communications operator position who is currently employed by the department in another police communications operator position.

(b) Before commissioning an applicant as a peace officer or employing an applicant for a police communications operator position, the department shall require the applicant to submit to the administration of a polygraph examination in accordance with rules adopted under Subsection (e).

(c) The polygraph examination required by this section may only be administered by a polygraph examiner who:

(1) is a peace officer commissioned by the department; or

(2) has a minimum of two years of experience conducting preemployment polygraph examinations for a law enforcement agency.

(d) The department and the polygraph examiner shall maintain the confidentiality of the results of a polygraph examination administered under this section, except that the department may disclose any admission of criminal conduct made during the course of an examination to another appropriate governmental entity.

(e) The department shall adopt reasonable rules to specify the point in the hiring process at which the department shall require a polygraph examination to be administered under this section and the manner in which the examination shall be administered. Rules relating to the administration of a polygraph examination shall be adopted in accordance with the guidelines published by the American Polygraph Association or the American Association of Police Polygraphists.

(f) The department shall use the results of a polygraph examination under this section as a factor in determining whether to commission a peace officer or employ an applicant for the position of police communications operator.

Sec. 411.00741. Polygraph Examinations for Certain Officers and Employees.

(a) The department may require a commissioned or noncommissioned officer or employee of the department to submit to the administration of a polygraph examination administered by a polygraph examiner if:

(1) the officer or employee is assigned to a position that requires the officer or employee to work with a federal agency on national security issues; and

(2) the federal agency requires that the officer or employee submit to a polygraph examination.

(b) If an officer or employee does not submit to the administration of a polygraph examination required under Subsection (a), the department may, as applicable:

(1) remove the officer or employee from an assignment to a position described by Subsection (a)(1); or

(2) refuse to assign the officer or employee to that position.

Sec. 411.0075. Personnel Policies.

(a) The director or the director's designee shall develop an intraagency career ladder program. The program shall require intraagency postings of all non-entry-level positions concurrently with any public posting.

(b) The director or the director's designee shall prepare and maintain a written policy statement to assure implementation of a program of equal employment opportunity under which all personnel transactions are made without regard to race, color, disability, sex, religion, age, or national origin. The policy statement must include:

(1) personnel policies, including policies related to recruitment, evaluation, selection, appointment, training, and promotion of personnel;

(2) a comprehensive analysis of the department work force that meets federal and state guidelines;

(3) procedures by which a determination can be made of significant underuse in the department work force of all persons for whom federal or state guidelines encourage a more equitable balance; and

(4) reasonable methods to appropriately address those areas of significant underuse.

(c) A policy statement prepared under Subsection (b) of this section must cover an annual period, be updated at least annually, and be filed with the governor's office.

(d) [Repealed by Acts 2011, 82nd Leg., ch. 1083 (S.B. 1179), § 25(30), effective June 17, 2011.]

Sec. 411.00755. Personnel Records of Commissioned Officers.

(a) In this section:

(1) "Personnel record" includes any letter, memorandum, or document maintained by the department that relates to a commissioned officer of the department, including background investigations, employment applications, employment contracts, service and training records, requests for off-duty employment, birth records, reference letters, letters of recommendation, performance evaluations and counseling records, results of physical tests, polygraph questionnaires and results, proficiency tests, the results of health examinations and other medical records, workers' compensation files, the results of psychological examinations, leave requests, requests for transfers of shift or duty assignments, commendations, promotional processes, demotions, complaints and complaint investigations, employment-related grievances, and school transcripts.

(2) "Disciplinary action" has the meaning assigned by Section 411.0072(a)(1).

(b) The personnel records of a commissioned officer of the department may not be disclosed or otherwise made available to the public, except the department shall release in accordance with Chapter 552:

(1) any letter, memorandum, or document relating to:

(A) a commendation, congratulation, or honor bestowed on the officer for an action, duty, or activity that relates to the officer's official duties; and

(B) misconduct by the officer, if the letter, memorandum, or document resulted in disciplinary action;

(2) the state application for employment submitted by the officer, but not including any attachments to the application;

(3) any reference letter submitted by the officer;

(4) any letter of recommendation for the officer;

(5) any employment contract with the officer;

(6) any periodic evaluation of the officer by a supervisor;

(7) any document recording a promotion or demotion of the officer;

(8) any request for leave by the officer;

(9) any request by the officer for transfers of shift or duty assignments;

(10) any documents presented to the commission in connection with a public hearing under Section 411.007(f);

(11) the officer's:

(A) name;

(B) age;

(C) dates of employment;

(D) positions held; and

(E) gross salary; and

(12) information about the location of the officer's department duty assignments.

(c) The department may release any personnel record of a commissioned officer:

(1) pursuant to a subpoena or court order, including a discovery order;

(2) for use by the department in an administrative hearing; or

(3) with the written authorization of the officer who is the subject of the record.

(d) A release of information under Subsection (c) does not waive the right to assert in the future that the information is excepted from required disclosure under this section or other law.

Sec. 411.0076. Minority Recruiting.

(a) The department shall continue to place emphasis on minority recruiting and hiring efforts for noncommissioned positions.

(b) The department's minority recruiter and equal employment opportunity positions created for personnel and equal employment opportunity matters shall continue to pertain to both commissioned and noncommissioned employees.

(c) The department by September, 1994, shall study job requirements for all noncommissioned positions and thereafter shall limit promotion-from-within only to positions where department experience is essential for reasonable job performance.

Sec. 411.0077. Limitation on Restrictions on Certain Off-Duty Activities.

(a) During the period that the officer is off duty, a commissioned officer of the department is entitled to attend educational programs or courses or to engage in any outside employment that does not adversely affect the operations or the reputation of the department. The rights of a commissioned officer under this section are subject to any reasonable department requirements that the officer be accessible to the department during off-duty periods for the possible performance of official duties.

(b) The department shall adopt reasonable guidelines relating to acceptable off-duty employment. The guidelines shall be uniformly applied to all supervisory and nonsupervisory commissioned officers.

(b-1) If the department denies approval of a commissioned officer's secondary employment or proposed secondary employment, the director or the director's designee must promptly notify the officer in writing of the specific guideline adopted under Subsection (b) on which the department's decision is based. The notice must explain why the secondary employment or proposed secondary employment is prohibited by the referenced guideline.

(c) If a commissioned officer is engaged in off-duty employment that the officer believes, in good faith, is not prohibited by a specific guideline adopted under Subsection (b), the officer is authorized to engage in the off-duty employment until the director or the director's designee informs the officer in writing that the employment is not acceptable.

Sec. 411.0078. Use of Uniform While Performing Certain Off-Duty Activities.

(a) An officer commissioned by the department may purchase from the department at fair market value a uniform to be used by the officer while providing law enforcement services for a person or entity other than the department. If an officer who purchased a uniform under this subsection leaves the service of the department for any reason, the officer shall return the uniform to the department. The department shall pay the officer the fair market value of the uniform at the time it is returned. For purposes of this subsection:

(1) a uniform does not include a handgun or other weapon; and

(2) the fair market value of a uniform is determined by the department.

(b) An officer wearing a uniform purchased under Subsection (a) may not act in a manner that adversely affects the operations or reputation of the department.

(c) The department shall adopt reasonable guidelines regarding:

(1) the types of law enforcement services for which an officer may purchase and wear a uniform under Subsection (a) and the circumstances under which the officer may perform those services; and

(2) the standards of behavior to be maintained by an officer who wears a uniform purchased under Subsection (a).

Sec. 411.0079. Working Conditions for Certain Pregnant Officers.

(a) The director shall make reasonable efforts to accommodate the request of a commissioned officer of the department who is determined by a physician to be partially physically restricted by a pregnancy if the request is related to the officer's working conditions.

(b) If the physician of an officer certifies that, because of the officer's pregnancy, the officer is unable to perform the duties of the officer's permanent work assignment and a temporary work assignment that the officer may perform is available, the director shall, on request of the officer, assign the officer to the temporary work assignment.

Sec. 411.008. District Headquarters.

The commission may establish district headquarters and stations at various places in the state and provide personnel and equipment necessary for their functioning and operation.

Sec. 411.0085. Driver's License Facilities: Personnel.

The department may not assign more than 123 commissioned officers plus supervising personnel to driver's license facilities.

Sec. 411.0086. Driver's License Facilities Personnel Reduction Schedule [Expired].

Expired pursuant to Acts 1995, 74th Leg., ch. 165 (S.B. 971), § 4, September 1, 1996.

Sec. 411.009. Local Cooperation.

(a) The sheriff and constables of each county and chief of police of each municipality are associate members of the department and are entitled to the rights and privileges granted to them by the department.

(b) The director may require a sheriff or other police officer in a county or municipality, within the limits of the officer's jurisdiction, to aid or assist in the performance of a duty imposed by this chapter. The officer shall comply with the order to the extent requested.

(c) The director with the advice and consent of the commission shall formulate and put into effect plans and means of cooperating with sheriffs, local police, and other peace officers throughout the state to prevent and discover crime, apprehend criminals, and promote public safety. Each local police and peace officer shall cooperate with the director in the plans.

(d) Each telegraph and telephone company and radio station operating in the state shall grant priority of service to a police agency and the department when notified that the service is urgent in the interests of the public welfare.

(e) The commissioners court of each county may furnish to the department necessary building space for establishing a branch crime detection laboratory to serve the general area of the state in which the county is located. If the county offers to furnish necessary space, the department may equip and operate the laboratory within the limits of its general authority and available appropriations. Unless the legislature has specifically directed the establishment and operation of a branch laboratory, the commission has discretion to decide whether a branch laboratory should be established or maintained.

(f) If the Commissioners Court of El Paso County furnishes without cost to the state the necessary building space, the department shall establish and operate a branch crime detection laboratory in El Paso County to serve the West Texas area, if the department determines that efficient enforcement of law requires establishment of the laboratory and sufficient funds are available in the department.

Sec. 411.0091. Sex Offender Compliance Unit.

(a) The director shall create a sex offender compliance unit to be operated by the department.

(b) The sex offender compliance unit shall investigate and arrest individuals determined to have committed a sexually violent offense, as defined by Article 62.001, Code of Criminal Procedure.

(c) The legislature may appropriate funds to the department from the fugitive apprehension account for the purpose of paying the costs to the department of implementing this section.

(d) The department may adopt rules as necessary to implement this section.

Sec. 411.0095. Vehicle Theft Checkpoints at Border Crossing.

(a) The department may establish a program for the purpose of establishing border crossing checkpoints to prevent stolen vehicles, farm tractors or implements, construction equipment, aircraft, or watercraft from entering Mexico.

(b) A checkpoint may be established under Subsection (a) if the checkpoint is:

(1) located within 250 yards of a federally designated crossing facility located at or near the actual boundary between this state and Mexico;

(2) located on a public highway or street leading directly to an international border crossing;

(3) designed to stop only traffic bound for Mexico; and

(4) operated in such a manner as to stop only vehicles, tractors or implements, equipment, aircraft, or watercraft for which law enforcement authorities have probable cause to believe is stolen and bound for Mexico.

(c) The department may establish the border crossing checkpoint program in conjunction with local law enforcement authorities. The department and local law enforcement authorities may share the cost of staffing the checkpoints.

(d) The department shall establish procedures governing the encounter between the driver and the peace officers operating the checkpoint that ensure that any intrusion on the driver is minimized and that the inquiries made are reasonably related to the purpose of the checkpoint. A peace officer at the checkpoint may not direct a driver or a passenger in a motor vehicle to leave the vehicle or move the vehicle off the roadway unless the officer has reasonable suspicion or probable cause to believe that the person committed or is committing an offense. However, a peace officer may require that each motor vehicle passing through the checkpoint be diverted to a location immediately adjacent to the roadway, if desirable, to ensure safety.

(e) In this section:

(1) "Motor vehicle" and "vehicle" have the meanings assigned to those terms by Section 541.201, Transportation Code.

(2) "Watercraft" has the meaning assigned by Section 49.01, Penal Code.

Sec. 411.0096. Memorandum of Understanding with Criminal Justice Division of the Office of the Governor.

(a) The department and the office of the governor, criminal justice division, by rule shall adopt a joint memorandum of understanding on coordinating the drug law enforcement efforts of the department and the criminal justice division.

(b) The memorandum of understanding shall:

(1) provide that the department shall advise the criminal justice division about the statewide drug policy planning efforts of the division;

(2) provide for representation by the department on any advisory board advising the governor about drug policy;

(3) require the criminal justice division and the department to define their respective roles relating to drug task forces;

(4) require the criminal justice division and the department to jointly determine the areas of law enforcement focus for drug task force efforts; and

(5) require the criminal justice division and the department to jointly develop guidelines and procedures to govern drug task force operations that are funded by the state.

(c) The criminal justice division and the department shall update and revise the memorandum of understanding as necessary and by rule adopt all revisions to the memorandum.

(d) [Expired pursuant to Acts 1993, 73rd Leg., ch. 790 (S.B. 510), § 8, effective January 2, 1994.]

Sec. 411.0097. [2 Versions: As added by Acts 2005, 79th Leg., ch. 556] Multicounty Drug Task Forces.

(a) The department shall establish policies and procedures for multicounty drug task forces, as defined by Section 362.001, Local Government Code, and may exercise the authority necessary to ensure compliance with those policies and procedures.

(b) The department shall evaluate each multicounty drug task force with respect to whether the task force:

(1) complies with state and federal requirements, including policies and procedures established by department rule; and

(2) demonstrates effective performance outcomes.

(c) [Repealed by Acts 2013, 83rd Leg., ch. 1312 (S.B. 59), § 99(13), effective September 1, 2013.]

Sec. 411.0097. [2 Versions: As added by Acts 2005, 79th Leg., ch. 693] Transportation and Inspections Meeting with Representatives of Mexican States.

(a) The department shall initiate efforts to meet at least quarterly with the department's counterparts in the Mexican states bordering this state to discuss issues relating to truck inspections and transportation and infrastructure involved in truck inspections and transportation.

(b) To assist the department in carrying out this section, the department shall contact the border commerce coordinator designated under Section 772.010 and the mayors of each municipality in this state in which a port of entry for land traffic is located.

(c) At least one department representative participating in a meeting under Subsection (a) must be proficient in Spanish.

(d) The department, in conjunction with the border commerce coordinator, shall develop short-range and long-range plans, including recommendations to increase bilateral relations with Mexico and expedite trade by mitigating delays in border crossing inspections for northbound truck traffic. In developing the plans, the department and coordinator shall consider information obtained from any meetings under Subsection (a). The department shall update the plan biennially.

Sec. 411.0098. Coordination with Department of Transportation.

(a) The department and the Texas Department of Transportation shall establish procedures to ensure effective coordination of the development of transportation infrastructure projects that affect both agencies.

(b) Procedures established under this section shall:

(1) allow each agency to provide comments and advice to the other agency on an ongoing basis regarding statewide transportation planning efforts that affect traffic law enforcement;

(2) define the role of each agency in transportation infrastructure efforts; and

(3) require the department and the Texas Department of Transportation to develop a plan for

applying for and using federal funds to address infrastructure needs that affect enforcement efforts.

(c) The department and the Texas Department of Transportation shall update and revise the procedures established under this section as necessary.

Sec. 411.0099. Needs Assessment for Enforcement of Commercial Motor Vehicle Rules.

(a) The department shall conduct a long-term needs assessment for the enforcement of commercial motor vehicle rules that considers at a minimum:

(1) the inventory of current facilities and equipment used for enforcement, including types of scales, structures, space, and other equipment;

(2) enforcement activity, including trend information, at fixed-site facilities;

(3) staffing levels and operating hours for each facility; and

(4) needed infrastructure improvements and the associated costs and projected increase in activity that would result from the improvements.

(b) The department shall submit a biennial report to the legislative committees with primary jurisdiction over state budgetary matters and the Texas Transportation Commission that reflects the results of the needs assessment conducted under Subsection (a). The report shall be submitted to the legislature in conjunction with the department's legislative appropriations request.

Sec. 411.010. Assistance of State Agencies.

The attorney general, the Texas Department of Transportation, the Texas Department of Health, and all other departments of state government shall cooperate with the department in the execution of this chapter and the enforcement of state laws concerning public safety and crime prevention and detection.

Sec. 411.0105. Public Safety Radio Communications Council [Repealed].

Repealed by Acts 2005, 79th Leg., ch. 1337 (S.B. 9), § 22(a), effective June 18, 2005.

Sec. 411.011. Assistance of State Educational Institutions.

(a) The University of Texas and all other state-supported educational institutions shall:

(1) cooperate with the department in carrying out this chapter;

(2) assist in the giving of instruction in the training schools conducted by the bureau of education; and

(3) assist the bureau of identification and records in making necessary chemical tests and analyses and in making statistical analyses, charts, and reports of law enforcement and violations of law.

(b) The commission and the president of the educational institution called on for assistance shall agree on and arrange the nature and extent of the assistance.

Sec. 411.0111. Provision of Certain Information to Comptroller.

(a) Not later than June 1 of every fifth year, the department shall provide to the comptroller, for the purpose of assisting the comptroller in the identification of persons entitled to unclaimed property reported to the comptroller, the name, address, social security number, date of birth, and driver's license or state identification number of each person about whom the department has such information in its records.

(b) Information provided to the comptroller under this section is confidential and may not be disclosed to the public.

(c) The department shall provide the information in the format prescribed by rule of the comptroller.

Sec. 411.012. Command by Governor.

The governor may assume command and direct the activities of the commission and department during a public disaster, riot, insurrection, or formation of a dangerous resistance to enforcement of law, or to perform the governor's constitutional duty to enforce law. The governor shall use the personnel of the Texas Highway Patrol only if the other personnel of the department are unable to cope with the emergency.

Sec. 411.013. Expenditures, Donations, and Appropriations.

(a) [Repealed by Acts 1997, 75th Leg., ch. 1206 (S.B. 1752), § 28, effective September 1, 1997.]

(b) The department may accept donations of money and other real or personal property from any individual, group, association, corporation, or governmental agency and may use those donations for any purpose designated by the donor that furthers the exercise of duties imposed by law on the department.

(c) Appropriations for the Texas Highway Patrol must be made from the state highway fund.

Government Code

(d) [Repealed by Acts 2011, 82nd Leg., ch. 1083 (S.B. 1179), § 25(31), effective June 17, 2011.]

Sec. 411.0131. Use of Seized and Forfeited Assets.

(a) The commission by rule shall establish a process under which the commission approves all of the department's dispositions of assets seized or forfeited under state or federal law and received by or appropriated to the department. The commission shall adopt rules under this section in accordance with Chapter 2001. Before approving a disposition, the commission shall consider how the disposition supports priorities established in the department's strategic plan and whether the disposition complies with applicable federal guidelines.

(b) The department shall file annually with the governor and the presiding officer of each house of the legislature a report on seized and forfeited assets. The report must include:

(1) a summary of receipts, dispositions, and fund balances for the fiscal year derived from both federal and state sources;

(2) regarding receipts, the court in which each case involving seized or forfeited assets was adjudicated, the nature and value of the assets, and the specific intended use of the assets;

(3) regarding dispositions, the departmental control number and category, the division making the request, the specific item and amount requested, the amount the commission approved, and the actual amount expended per item; and

(4) regarding planned dispositions, a description of the broad categories of anticipated dispositions and how they relate to the department's strategic plan.

(c) The department shall, within 30 days after the end of each quarter, report and justify any dispositions of seized or forfeited assets during the quarter that:

(1) differ from the planned dispositions reported under Subsection (b); and

(2) were used for a purpose not considered a priority in the department's strategic plan or not required by law or applicable federal guidelines.

Sec. 411.0132. Use of Funds to Support Certain Persons.

The department may use appropriated funds to purchase food and beverages for:

(1) training functions required of peace officers of the department subject to director approval; and

(2) a person who is:

(A) activated to provide services in response to an emergency situation, incident, or disaster; and

(B) unable to leave or required to remain at the person's assignment area due to the emergency situation, incident, or disaster.

Sec. 411.0133. Missing or Exploited Children Prevention Grants. [Renumbered]

Sec. 411.0135. Method of Payment of Fees and Charges.

(a) The department may adopt rules regarding the method of payment of any fee or charge that is imposed or collected by the department.

(b) Rules adopted under Subsection (a) may authorize payment, under circumstances prescribed by the department:

(1) in person, by mail, by telephone, or over the Internet;

(2) by means of electronic funds transfer; or

(3) by means of a valid credit card issued by a financial institution chartered by a state or the federal government or by a nationally recognized credit organization approved by the department.

(c) The department by rule may require, in addition to the amount of the fee or charge, the payment of:

(1) a discount, convenience, or service charge for a payment transaction; or

(2) a service charge in connection with the payment of a payment transaction that is dishonored or refused for lack of funds or insufficient funds.

Sec. 411.014. Buildings and Equipment.

(a) The state shall provide the necessary buildings, offices, and quarters for the department and its officers and employees in Austin and other places in the state where district headquarters are located. The state shall provide furniture, fixtures, automobiles, motorcycles, horses, firearms, ammunition, uniforms, appliances, and other materials necessary to the proper functioning and operation of the department.

(b) The department's physical plant in Austin is under the department's control and management for the use and benefit of the state in the discharge of the official duties of the department.

Sec. 411.0141. Multiuse Training and Operations Center Facility.

(a) The Texas Facilities Commission shall construct a multiuse training and operations center facility to be used by the department, the Texas military forces, county and municipal law enforcement agencies, and any other military or law enforcement agency, including agencies of the federal government:

(1) for training purposes;

(2) to house law enforcement assets and equipment; and

(3) to support and initiate tactical operations and law enforcement missions.

(b) The Texas Facilities Commission, with the assistance of the department, shall locate and acquire real property for the purpose of constructing the training and operations center facility. The governing body of a county, municipality, or navigation district, on behalf of the county, municipality, or navigation district, may donate real property to the department for the facility. The donation may be in fee simple or otherwise.

(c) The department shall, with the assistance of the Texas Facilities Commission, design the training and operations center facility.

(d) On completion of the construction of the training and operations center facility, the Texas Facilities Commission shall transfer ownership of the facility, including the real property and buildings, to the department.

(e) The department shall manage the training and operations center facility and may adopt rules necessary to implement this section. The department shall make the facility available for use by the department, the Texas military forces, county and municipal law enforcement agencies, and any other military or law enforcement agency, including agencies of the federal government. The department may set and collect fees for the use of the facility.

Sec. 411.015. Organization.

(a) Except as provided by Subsection (b), the designation by this chapter of certain divisions and division chiefs is not mandatory and this chapter does not prevent the commission from reorganization or consolidation within the department in the interest of more efficient and economical management and direction of the department. The director, with the commission's approval, may organize and maintain within the department divisions of service considered necessary for the efficient conduct of the department's work.

(b) The division relating to the Texas Rangers may not be abolished.

Sec. 411.016. Compensatory Time; Overtime Pay.

(a) This section applies to an officer commissioned by the department who is not employed in a position that the director has declared to be administrative, executive, or professional.

(b) If, during a 24-hour period, the total number of hours worked by a commissioned officer equals more than eight hours, the excess is overtime.

(b-1) If, during a work week, the total number of hours worked by a commissioned officer equals more than 40 hours, the excess is overtime.

(c) This section applies only to the computation of overtime entitlements and does not apply to the method of compensating a commissioned officer for working on regularly scheduled state holidays.

(d) A commissioned officer may receive a supplement paid by the federal government earned while working on a project funded by the federal government, and that supplement may not be considered in determining a commissioned officer's entitlement under this section.

(e) The department may compensate an officer commissioned by the department for the overtime earned by the officer by:

(1) allowing or requiring the officer to take compensatory leave at the rate of 1-1/2 hours of leave for each hour of overtime earned; or

(2) paying the officer for the overtime hours earned at the rate equal to 1-1/2 times the officer's regular hourly pay rate.

(f) If a conflict exists between this section and Section 659.015, this section controls.

Sec. 411.0161. Donation of Accrued Compensatory Time or Accrued Annual Leave for Legislative Purposes.

(a) The director shall allow a department employee to voluntarily transfer to a legislative leave pool up to eight hours of compensatory time or annual leave per year earned by the employee.

(b) The director or designee shall administer the legislative leave pool.

(c) The Public Safety Commission shall adopt rules and prescribe procedures relating to the operation of the legislative leave pool.

(d) The director or designee shall credit the legislative leave pool with the amount of time contributed by an employee and deduct a corresponding amount of time from the employee's earned compensatory time or annual leave as if the employee had used the time for personal purposes.

(e) An employee is entitled to use time contributed to the legislative leave pool if the employee uses the time for legislative leave on behalf of a law enforcement association of at least 1,000 active or retired members governed by a board of directors.

(f) The director of the pool administrator shall transfer time from the pool to the employee and credit the time to the employee.

(g) An employee may only withdraw time from the legislative leave pool in coordination and with the consent of the president or designee of the law enforcement association described in Subsection (e), and may not draw more than 80 hours of time from the pool in a 160-hours work cycle with the maximum time taken not to exceed 480 hours per fiscal year.

(h) In addition to Subsection (g), the use of any time from the legislative leave pool must also be in accordance with rules adopted by the Public Safety Commission.

Sec. 411.0162. Salaries for Certain Troopers.

(a) Notwithstanding any other provision of law and subject to the availability of money appropriated for that purpose, the department may pay its employees classified as Trooper Trainee, Probationary Trooper, and Trooper I at rates that exceed the maximum rates designated in Salary Schedule C of the position classification schedule prescribed by the General Appropriations Act for the state fiscal biennium ending August 31, 2013, for that position by up to 10 percent.

(b) [Expired pursuant to Acts 2013, 83rd Leg., ch. 680 (H.B. 2100), § 1, effective September 1, 2014]

Sec. 411.0163. Hiring Officers with Previous Law Enforcement Experience.

Notwithstanding any other provision of law, the department may, at the time a commissioned officer is hired, elect to credit up to four years of experience as a peace officer in the state as years of service for the purpose of calculating the officer's salary under Schedule C. All officers are subject to the one-year probationary period under Section 411.007(g) notwithstanding the officer's rank or salary classification.

Sec. 411.0164. 50-Hour Workweek for Commissioned Officers.

Notwithstanding any other law, the department may implement a 10-hour workday and 50-hour workweek for commissioned officers of the department.

Sec. 411.0165. Veteran Applicants for Trooper Training.

The department may accept a person applying to the department's trooper trainee academy if the person:

(1) has served four or more years in the United States armed forces as a member of the military police or other security force and received an honorable discharge; and

(2) meets all other department requirements for a commissioned officer.

Sec. 411.017. Unauthorized Acts Involving Department Name, Insignia, or Division Name.

(a) A person commits an offense if, without the director's authorization, the person:

(1) manufactures, sells, or possesses a badge, identification card, or other item bearing a department insignia or an insignia deceptively similar to the department's;

(2) makes a copy or likeness of a badge, identification card, or department insignia, with intent to use or allow another to use the copy or likeness to produce an item bearing the department insignia or an insignia deceptively similar to the department's; or

(3) uses the term "Texas Department of Public Safety," "Department of Public Safety," "Texas Ranger," or "Texas Highway Patrol" in connection with an object, with the intent to create the appearance that the object belongs to or is being used by the department.

(b) In this section, "department insignia" means an insignia or design prescribed by the director for use by officers and employees of the department in connection with their official activities. An insignia is deceptively similar to the department's if it is not prescribed by the department but a reasonable person would presume that it was prescribed by the department.

(c) A district or county court, on application of the attorney general or of the district attorney or prosecuting attorney performing the duties of district attorney for the district in which the court is located, may enjoin a violation or threatened violation of this section on a showing that a violation has occurred or is likely to occur.

(d) It is an affirmative defense to a prosecution under this section that the object is used exclusively:

(1) for decorative purposes, maintained or preserved in a decorative state, and not offered for sale; or

(2) in an artistic or dramatic presentation, and before the use of the object the producer of the presentation notifies the director in writing of the

intended use, the location where the use will occur, and the period during which the use will occur.

(e) An offense under this section is a Class A misdemeanor, unless the object is shipped by United States mail or by any type of commercial carrier from a point outside the State of Texas to a point inside the state if the shipper or his agent has been sent notification by registered United States mail of this section prior to the shipment, in which event the offense is a felony of the third degree.

Sec. 411.0175. Accident Reports [Repealed].

Repealed by Acts 2007, 80th Leg., ch. 1407 (S.B. 766), § 6, effective September 1, 2007.

Sec. 411.018. Hazardous Materials.

(a) The director shall adopt rules relating to the reporting of all transportation incidents involving releases of reportable quantities of hazardous materials occurring on public roads or railroads that are not on a private industrial site. The rules must be consistent with federal rules relating to hazardous materials adopted under federal law. The director may adopt all or part of the federal hazardous materials rules by reference.

(b) The department by rule shall require that all carriers of hazardous materials report all incidents involving a release of reportable quantities of hazardous materials to the department.

(c) The department shall serve as the central repository of statistical information relating to incidents involving release of hazardous materials.

(d) The department is responsible for the on-site coordination of all hazardous materials transportation emergencies. The director shall adopt necessary rules to implement this subsection.

Sec. 411.019. Toll-Free Number.

(a) The department shall provide a 24-hour toll-free telephone number for use by the public in reporting traffic offenses, including driving while intoxicated, suspected criminal activity, and traffic accidents and other emergencies.

(b) On receiving a report of an offense, the department shall contact the law enforcement agency of the jurisdiction where the reported suspected driver or incident was observed or shall dispatch department officers.

Sec. 411.0195. Public Complaints.

(a) The department shall maintain a system to promptly and efficiently act on complaints filed with the department. The department shall maintain information about parties to the complaint, the subject matter of the complaint, a summary of the results of the review or investigation of the complaint, and its disposition.

(b) The department shall make information available describing its procedures for complaint investigation and resolution.

(c) The department shall periodically notify the complaint parties of the status of the complaint until final disposition.

(d), (e) [Repealed by Acts 2009, 81st Leg., ch. 1146 (H.B. 2730), § 5.15, effective September 1, 2009.]

Sec. 411.0196. Access to Programs.

The department shall prepare and maintain a written plan that describes how a person who does not speak English or who has a physical, mental, or developmental disability can be provided reasonable access to the department's programs.

Sec. 411.0197. Advisory Oversight Community Outreach Committee. [Repealed]

Sec. 411.020. Purchase of Firearm from Department by Officer.

(a) A commissioned officer of the department may purchase for an amount set by the department, not to exceed fair market value, a firearm issued to the officer by the department if the firearm is not listed as a prohibited weapon under Section 46.05, Penal Code, and if the firearm is retired by the department for replacement purposes.

(b) The department may adopt rules for the sale of a retired firearm to an officer of the department.

Sec. 411.0201. Reproduction of Records.

(a) Except as provided by Subsection (b), the department may photograph, microphotograph, or film any record in connection with the issuance of a driver's license or commercial driver's license and any record of any division of the department.

(b) None of the following may be photographed or filmed to dispose of the original record:

(1) an original fingerprint card;

(2) any evidence submitted in connection with a criminal case; or

(3) a confession or statement made by the defendant in a criminal case.

(c) The department may create original records in micrographic form on media, such as computer output microfilm.

(d) A photograph, microphotograph, or film of a record reproduced under Subsection (a) is equivalent to the original record for all purposes, including introduction as evidence in all courts and administrative agency proceedings. A certified or authenticated copy of such a photograph, microphotograph, or film is admissible as evidence equally with the original photograph, microphotograph, or film.

(e) The director or an authorized representative may certify the authenticity of a photograph, microphotograph, or film of a record reproduced under this section and shall charge a fee for the certified photograph, microphotograph, or film as provided by law.

(f) Certified records shall be furnished to any person who is authorized by law to receive them.

Sec. 411.0202. Disposal of Records.

(a) Unless otherwise required by law and subject to Chapter 441, the department may dispose of or destroy records that the department determines are not required for the performance of the department's duties and functions.

(b) The department may dispose of or destroy a defendant's original fingerprint card if:

(1) the department has on file and retains another original fingerprint card for the defendant; or

(2) the defendant has attained the age of 80.

Sec. 411.0205. Crime Laboratory Accreditation Process. [Renumbered]

Sec. 411.0206. Abatement or Deferral for Victims of Identity Theft.

(a) In this section:

(1) "License" means a license, certificate, permit, or other authorization issued by the department.

(2) "Victim of identity theft" means an individual who has filed a criminal complaint alleging the commission of an offense under Section 32.51, Penal Code, other than a person who is convicted of an offense under Section 37.08, Penal Code, with respect to that complaint.

(b) The department may abate or defer a mandatory suspension or revocation of a license if the license holder presents evidence acceptable to the department that:

(1) the license holder is the victim of identity theft; and

(2) the person against whom a criminal complaint alleging the commission of an offense under Section 32.51, Penal Code, has been filed, and not the license holder, engaged in the act or omission that mandates the suspension or revocation.

Sec. 411.0207. Public Corruption Unit.

(a) In this section, "organized criminal activity" means conduct that constitutes an offense under Section 71.02, Penal Code.

(b) A public corruption unit is created within the department to investigate and assist in the management of allegations of participation in organized criminal activity by:

(1) an individual elected, appointed, or employed to serve as a peace officer for a governmental entity of this state under Article 2.12, Code of Criminal Procedure; or

(2) a federal law enforcement officer while performing duties in this state.

(c) The unit shall:

(1) assist district attorneys and county attorneys in the investigation and prosecution of allegations described by Subsection (b);

(2) if requested by the agency, assist a state or local law enforcement agency with the investigation of such allegations against law enforcement officers in the agency;

(3) assist the United States Department of Justice or any other appropriate federal department or agency in the investigation and prosecution of allegations described by Subsection (b);

(4) if requested by the agency, assist a federal law enforcement agency with the investigation of such allegations against law enforcement officers in the agency;

(5) serve as a clearinghouse for information relating to the investigation and prosecution of allegations described by Subsection (b); and

(6) report to the highest-ranking officer of the Texas Rangers division of the department.

(d) On written approval of the director or of the chair of the commission, the highest-ranking officer of the Texas Rangers division of the department may initiate an investigation of an allegation of participation in organized criminal activity by a law enforcement officer described by Subsection (b)(1). Written approval under this subsection must be based on cause.

(e) To the extent allowed by law, a state or local law enforcement agency shall cooperate with the public corruption unit by providing information requested by the unit as necessary to carry out the purposes of this section. Information described by this subsection is excepted from required disclosure under Chapter 552 in the manner provided by Section 552.108.

Sec. 411.0208. Reserve Officer Corps.

(a) The commission may provide for the establishment of a reserve officer corps consisting of retired or previously commissioned peace officers, as defined by Article 2.12, Code of Criminal Procedure, who retired or resigned in good standing.

(b) The commission shall establish qualifications and standards of training for members of the reserve officer corps.

(c) The commission may limit the size of the reserve officer corps.

(d) The director shall appoint the members of the reserve officer corps. Members serve at the director's discretion.

(e) The director may call the reserve officer corps into service at any time the director considers it necessary to have additional officers to assist the department in conducting background investigations, sex offender compliance checks, and other duties as determined necessary by the director.

Sec. 411.0209. Department Assistance at International Border Checkpoints.

(a) To prevent the unlawful transfer of contraband from this state to the United Mexican States and other unlawful activity, the department shall implement a strategy for providing to federal authorities and to local law enforcement authorities working with those federal authorities at international border checkpoints assistance in the interdiction of weapons, bulk currency, stolen vehicles, and other contraband, and of fugitives, being smuggled into the United Mexican States.

(b) The department may share with the federal government the cost of staffing any international border checkpoints for the purposes described by this section.

(c) The director and applicable local law enforcement authorities shall adopt procedures as necessary to administer this section.

Sec. 411.02095. Statewide Program for the Prevention and Detection of Certain Criminal Offenses.

(a) The department may establish a program throughout this state for preventing and detecting:

(1) the unlawful possession or the unlawful and imminent movement or transfer between this state and an adjacent state or the United Mexican States of:

(A) firearms, in violation of Section 46.14, Penal Code;

(B) controlled substances, in violation of Chapter 481, Health and Safety Code; or

(C) currency, in violation of Section 34.02, Penal Code; and

(2) the commission or imminent commission of the offenses of smuggling of persons under Section 20.05, Penal Code, and trafficking of persons under Section 20A.02, Penal Code, occurring in this state or involving travel between this state and an adjacent state or the United Mexican States.

(b) A peace officer participating in a program established under this section must have reasonable suspicion or probable cause to believe that firearms, controlled substances, or currency are unlawfully possessed or being unlawfully and imminently moved or transferred between this state and an adjacent state or the United Mexican States or that an offense described by Subsection (a)(2) has been committed or imminently will be committed, as applicable, before exercising the officer's authority under the program, including stopping a person or vehicle or coming into contact with a person.

(c) In developing the program, the department shall establish:

(1) clear guidelines and procedures to mitigate any unnecessary negative impact on the flow of trade, commerce, or daily business activities in locations where the program is implemented; and

(2) protocols, standards, and guidelines to minimize any intrusion on a person in an encounter with a peace officer exercising the officer's authority under the program.

(d) The department shall implement the program established under this section in conjunction with federal and local law enforcement agencies.

(e) The director shall adopt rules as necessary to implement and administer a program established under this section.

Sec. 411.02096. Report Regarding Certain Firearm Statistics. [Effective until September 2, 2028; Expires September 1, 2028]

(a) Not later than January 31 of each year, the department shall collect information for the preceding calendar year related to the carrying of firearms by persons in this state, including:

(1) the number of persons who applied for a license to carry a handgun under Subchapter H compared to the yearly average number of people who applied for a license from 2010 through 2020; and

(2) any other relevant information related to the carrying of firearms by persons in this state.

(b) The department shall identify the entities that possess information required by Subsection (a) and require each entity to report the information to the department in the manner prescribed by the department.

(c) Not later than February 1 of each year, the department shall prepare and submit to the governor, the lieutenant governor, and each member of the legislature a report that includes the information described by Subsection (a).

(d) This section expires September 1, 2028.

Sec. 411.02097. Firearm Safety.

The department shall develop and post on the department's Internet website a course on firearm safety and handling. The course must be accessible to the public free of charge.

SUBCHAPTER B TEXAS RANGERS

Sec. 411.021. Composition.

The Texas Rangers are a major division of the department consisting of the number of rangers authorized by the legislature. The highest ranking officer of the Texas Rangers is responsible to and reports directly to the director. Officers are entitled to compensation as provided by the legislature.

Sec. 411.022. Authority of Officers.

(a) An officer of the Texas Rangers is governed by the law regulating and defining the powers and duties of sheriffs performing similar duties, except that the officer may make arrests, execute process in a criminal case in any county and, if specially directed by the judge of a court of record, execute process in a civil case.

(b) An officer of the Texas Rangers who arrests a person charged with a criminal offense shall immediately convey the person to the proper officer of the county where the person is charged and shall obtain a receipt. The state shall pay all necessary expenses incurred under this subsection.

(c) An officer of the Texas Rangers has the authority to investigate offenses against public administration prosecuted under Subchapter B-1.

Sec. 411.0221. Qualifications.

(a) To be commissioned as an officer of the Texas Rangers, a person must:

(1) have at least eight years of experience as a full-time, paid peace officer, including at least four years of experience in the department; and

(2) be a commissioned member of the department.

(b) The Texas Rangers is an equal employment opportunity employer; all personnel decisions shall be made without regard to race, color, sex, national origin, or religion.

Sec. 411.0222. Eligibility for Promotion.

Except as provided by Section 411.0223, an officer of the Texas Rangers is eligible for promotion only if the officer has served in the next lower position for at least two years before the date of promotion.

Sec. 411.0223. Appointment of Highest-Ranking Officers.

(a) Except as provided by Subsection (c), an officer is eligible for appointment by the director to chief of the Texas Rangers only if the officer has at least five years of supervisory experience as a commissioned member of the Texas Rangers.

(b) Except as provided by Subsection (c), an officer is eligible for appointment by the director to assistant chief of the Texas Rangers only if the officer has at least four years of supervisory experience as a commissioned member of the Texas Rangers.

(c) If there are fewer than two qualified officers for appointment to chief or assistant chief of the Texas Rangers, the director may appoint an officer to the position of chief or assistant chief of the Texas Rangers only if the officer has at least two years of supervisory experience as a commissioned member of the Texas Rangers.

(d) Except as provided by Subsection (e), an officer is eligible for appointment by the director to the rank of major of the Texas Rangers only if the officer has at least one year of supervisory experience as a captain of the Texas Rangers.

(e) If there are fewer than two qualified captains for appointment to the rank of major of the Texas Rangers, the director may appoint a lieutenant to the position of major of the Texas Rangers only if the lieutenant has at least two years of supervisory experience as a commissioned member of the Texas Rangers.

Sec. 411.023. Special Rangers.

(a) The commission may appoint as special rangers honorably retired commissioned officers of the department and not more than 300 other persons.

(b) A special ranger is subject to the orders of the commission and the governor for special duty to the same extent as other law enforcement officers provided for by this chapter, except that a special ranger may not enforce a law except one designed to protect life and property and may not enforce a law regulating the use of a state highway by a motor vehicle. A special ranger is not connected with a ranger company or uniformed unit of the department.

(c) Before issuance of a commission to a special ranger the person shall enter into a good and sufficient bond executed by a surety company authorized to do business in the state in the amount of $2,500, approved by the director, and indemnifying all persons against damages resulting from an unlawful act of the special ranger.

(d) A special ranger is not entitled to compensation from the state for service as a special ranger.

(e) A special ranger commission expires January 1 of the first odd-numbered year after appointment. The director may revoke a special ranger commission at any time for cause.

(f) The commission shall authorize a badge for persons appointed as special rangers under this section that is distinct in appearance from the badge authorized for special Texas Rangers under Section 411.024 and from any badge issued to a Texas Ranger.

Sec. 411.024. Special Texas Rangers.

(a) The commission may appoint as a special Texas Ranger an honorably retired or retiring commissioned officer of the department whose position immediately preceding retirement is an officer of the Texas Rangers.

(b) A special Texas Ranger is subject to the orders of the commission and the governor for special duty to the same extent as other law enforcement officers provided for by this chapter, except that a special Texas Ranger may not enforce a law except one designed to protect life and property and may not enforce a law regulating the use of a state highway by a motor vehicle. A special Texas Ranger is not connected with a ranger company or uniformed unit of the department.

(c) Before issuance of a commission to a special Texas Ranger the person shall enter into a good and sufficient bond executed by a surety company authorized to do business in the state in the amount of $2,500, approved by the director, and indemnifying all persons against damages resulting from an unlawful act of the special Texas Ranger.

(d) A special Texas Ranger is not entitled to compensation from the state for service as a special Texas Ranger.

(e) A special Texas Ranger commission expires January 1 of the first odd-numbered year after appointment. The commission may revoke the commission of a special Texas Ranger who commits a violation of a rule of the department for which an active officer of the Texas Rangers would be discharged.

(f) The commission shall authorize a badge for persons appointed as special Texas Rangers under this section that is distinct in appearance from the badge authorized for special rangers under Section 411.023.

SUBCHAPTER B-1 PUBLIC INTEGRITY UNIT

Sec. 411.0251. Definitions.

In this subchapter:

(1) "Offense" means a prohibited act for which state law imposes a criminal or civil penalty.

(2) "Prosecuting attorney" means a district attorney, criminal district attorney, or county attorney.

(3) "State agency" means a department, commission, board, office, council, authority, or other agency in the executive branch of state government that is created by the constitution or a statute of this state, including a university system or institution of higher education as defined by Section 61.003, Education Code.

(4) "State employee" means an individual, other than a state officer, who is employed by:

(A) a state agency;

(B) the Supreme Court of Texas, the Court of Criminal Appeals of Texas, a court of appeals, or the Texas Judicial Council; or

(C) either house of the legislature or a legislative agency, council, or committee, including the Legislative Budget Board, the Texas Legislative Council, the State Auditor's Office, and the Legislative Reference Library.

(5) "State officer" means an elected officer, an appointed officer, a salaried appointed officer, an appointed officer of a major state agency, or the executive head of a state agency.

Sec. 411.0252. Offenses Against Public Administration.

For purposes of this subchapter, the following are offenses against public administration:

(1) an offense under Title 8, Penal Code, committed by a state officer or a state employee in

connection with the powers and duties of the state office or state employment;

(2) an offense under Chapter 301, 302, 571, 572, or 2004 committed by a state officer or a state employee in connection with the powers and duties of the state office or state employment or by a candidate for state office;

(3) an offense under Chapter 573 committed by a state officer in connection with the powers and duties of the state office; and

(4) an offense under Title 15, Election Code, committed in connection with:

(A) a campaign for or the holding of state office; or

(B) an election on a proposed constitutional amendment.

Sec. 411.0253. Public Integrity Unit.

(a) The Texas Rangers division of the department shall establish and support a public integrity unit.

(b) On receiving a formal or informal complaint regarding an offense against public administration or on request of a prosecuting attorney or law enforcement agency, the public integrity unit may perform an initial investigation into whether a person has committed an offense against public administration.

(c) The Texas Rangers have authority to investigate an offense against public administration, any lesser included offense, and any other offense arising from conduct that constitutes an offense against public administration.

(d) If an initial investigation by the public integrity unit demonstrates a reasonable suspicion that an offense against public administration occurred, the matter shall be referred to the prosecuting attorney of the county in which venue is proper under Section 411.0256 or Chapter 13, Code of Criminal Procedure, as applicable.

(e) The public integrity unit shall, on request of the prosecuting attorney described by Subsection (d), assist the attorney in the investigation of an offense against public administration.

Sec. 411.0254. Notification Regarding Disposition of Case.

The prosecuting attorney shall notify the public integrity unit of:

(1) the termination of a case investigated by the public integrity unit; or

(2) the results of the final disposition of a case investigated by the public integrity unit, including the final adjudication or entry of a plea.

Sec. 411.0255. Disqualification of Prosecuting Attorney or Judge; Selection of Prosecuting Attorney by Presiding Judge of Administrative Judicial Region.

(a) In this section, "presiding judges" means the presiding judges of the administrative judicial regions.

(b) A prosecuting attorney may request that the court with jurisdiction over the complaint permit the attorney to recuse himself or herself for good cause in a case investigated under this subchapter, and on submitting the notice of recusal, the attorney is disqualified.

(b-1) The judge of a court with jurisdiction over a complaint may request that the presiding judges permit the judge to recuse himself or herself for good cause in a case investigated under this subchapter, and on submitting the notice of recusal, the judge is disqualified.

(b-2) The public integrity unit shall inform the judge of the court with jurisdiction over a complaint if the prosecuting attorney is disqualified for purposes of Article 2.07, Code of Criminal Procedure, because the prosecuting attorney is the subject of a criminal investigation under this subchapter based on credible evidence of criminal misconduct. On showing that the prosecuting attorney is the subject of the investigation, the judge shall order the prosecuting attorney disqualified under Article 2.08, Code of Criminal Procedure.

(b-3) If the judge of the court with jurisdiction over a complaint described by Subsection (b-2) is also disqualified, the public integrity unit shall inform the presiding judges of the prosecuting attorney's disqualification under that subsection.

(b-4) The public integrity unit shall inform the presiding judges if a judge of a court with jurisdiction over a complaint is disqualified because the judge is the subject of a criminal investigation under this subchapter based on credible evidence of criminal misconduct. On showing that the judge is the subject of the investigation, the presiding judges shall order the judge disqualified. Disqualification under this subsection applies only to the judge's access to the criminal investigation pending against the judge and to any prosecution of a criminal charge resulting from that investigation.

(c) Following the disqualification or recusal of a prosecuting attorney under this section, the presiding judges shall appoint a prosecuting attorney from another county in that administrative judicial region by majority vote. A prosecuting attorney selected under this subsection has the authority to represent the state in the prosecution of the offense.

(c-1) Following the disqualification of a judge of a court with jurisdiction over a complaint under this section, the presiding judges by majority vote shall appoint a judge from a county within the administrative judicial region. A judge selected under this subsection has jurisdiction over the complaint.

(d) The prosecutor selected under this section may pursue a waiver to extend the statute of limitations by no more than two years. If the waiver adds less than two years to limitations, the prosecutor may pursue a successive waiver for good cause shown to the court, providing that the total time of all waivers does not exceed two years.

Sec. 411.0256. Venue.

Notwithstanding Chapter 13, Code of Criminal Procedure, or other law, if the defendant is a natural person, venue for prosecution of an offense against public administration and lesser included offenses arising from the same transaction is the county in which the defendant resided at the time the offense was committed.

Sec. 411.0257. Residence.

For the purposes of this subchapter, a person resides in the county where that person:

(1) claims a residence homestead under Chapter 41, Property Code, if that person is a member of the legislature;

(2) claimed to be a resident before being subject to residency requirements under Article IV, Texas Constitution, if that person is a member of the executive branch of this state;

(3) claims a residence homestead under Chapter 41, Property Code, if that person is a justice on the supreme court or judge on the court of criminal appeals; or

(4) otherwise claims residence if no other provision of this section applies.

Sec. 411.0258. Cooperation of State Agencies and Local Law Enforcement Agencies.

(a) To the extent allowed by law, a state agency or local law enforcement agency shall cooperate with the public integrity unit and prosecuting attorney by providing resources and information requested by the unit as necessary to carry out the purposes of this subchapter.

(b) Information disclosed under this section is confidential and not subject to disclosure under Chapter 552.

Sec. 411.0259. Subpoenas.

(a) In connection with an investigation of an alleged offense against public administration, the public integrity unit may issue a subpoena to compel the production, for inspection or copying, of relevant evidence that is in this state.

(b) A subpoena may be served personally or by certified mail.

(c) If a person fails to comply with a subpoena, the public integrity unit, acting through the general counsel of the department, may file suit to enforce the subpoena in a district court in this state. On finding that good cause exists for issuing the subpoena, the court shall order the person to comply with the subpoena. The court may punish a person who fails to obey the court order.

SUBCHAPTER C TEXAS HIGHWAY PATROL

Sec. 411.031. Composition.

The Texas Highway Patrol is a division of the department consisting of the chief patrol officer, the number of captains, sergeants, and privates authorized by the legislature, and administrative and clerical help as the commission determines. A person's literary attainment does not preclude the person's appointment as a private if the person is otherwise qualified. The chief patrol officer is the executive officer of the patrol. Officers are entitled to compensation as provided by the legislature.

Sec. 411.032. Powers and Duties of Officers.

In addition to the powers and duties provided by law for the officers, noncommissioned officers, and enlisted persons of the Texas Highway Patrol, they have the powers and authority provided by law for members of the Texas Rangers force.

Sec. 411.033. Certain Equipment for Vehicles.

The department shall equip all motor vehicles used by officers of the Texas Highway Patrol in discharging the officers' official duties with bullet-resistant windshields.

SUBCHAPTER D ADMINISTRATIVE DIVISION

Sec. 411.041. Composition.

The administrative division of the department consists of the bureaus of identification and records, communications, intelligence, and training. The director, with the advice and consent of the commission, shall employ chiefs, experts, operators, instructors, and assistants as necessary for the operation of this division and its bureaus.

Sec. 411.042. Bureau of Identification and Records.

(a) The director shall appoint, with the advice and consent of the commission, a chief of the bureau of identification and records to be the executive officer of the bureau. The chief and at least one assistant must be recognized identification experts with at least three years' actual experience.

(b) The bureau of identification and records shall:

(1) procure and file for record photographs, pictures, descriptions, fingerprints, measurements, and other pertinent information of all persons arrested for or charged with a criminal offense or convicted of a criminal offense, regardless of whether the conviction is probated;

(2) collect information concerning the number and nature of offenses reported or known to have been committed in the state and the legal steps taken in connection with the offenses, and other information useful in the study of crime and the administration of justice, including information that enables the bureau to create a statistical breakdown of:

(A) offenses in which family violence was involved;

(B) offenses under Sections 22.011 and 22.021, Penal Code; and

(C) offenses under Sections 20A.02, 43.02, 43.021, 43.03, 43.031, 43.04, 43.041, and 43.05, Penal Code;

(3) make ballistic tests of bullets and firearms and chemical analyses of bloodstains, cloth, materials, and other substances for law enforcement officers of the state;

(4) cooperate with identification and crime records bureaus in other states and the United States Department of Justice;

(5) maintain a list of all previous background checks for applicants for any position regulated under Chapter 1702, Occupations Code, who have undergone a criminal history background check as required by that chapter, if the check indicates a Class B misdemeanor or equivalent offense or a greater offense;

(6) collect information concerning the number and nature of protective orders and magistrate's orders of emergency protection and all other pertinent information about all persons subject to active orders, including pertinent information about persons subject to conditions of bond imposed for the protection of the victim in any family violence, sexual assault or abuse, indecent assault, stalking, or trafficking case. Information in the law enforcement information system relating to an active order shall include:

(A) the name, sex, race, date of birth, personal descriptors, address, and county of residence of the person to whom the order is directed;

(B) any known identifying number of the person to whom the order is directed, including the person's social security number or driver's license number;

(C) the name and county of residence of the person protected by the order;

(D) the residence address and place of employment or business of the person protected by the order;

(E) the child-care facility or school where a child protected by the order normally resides or which the child normally attends;

(F) the relationship or former relationship between the person who is protected by the order and the person to whom the order is directed;

(G) the conditions of bond imposed on the person to whom the order is directed, if any, for the protection of a victim in any family violence, sexual assault or abuse, indecent assault, stalking, or trafficking case;

(H) any minimum distance the person subject to the order is required to maintain from the protected places or persons; and

(I) the date the order expires;

(7) grant access to criminal history record information in the manner authorized under Subchapter F;

(8) collect and disseminate information regarding offenders with mental impairments in compliance with Chapter 614, Health and Safety Code; and

(9) record data and maintain a state database for a computerized criminal history record system and computerized juvenile justice information system that serves:

(A) as the record creation point for criminal history record information and juvenile justice information maintained by the state; and

(B) as the control terminal for the entry of records, in accordance with federal law and regulations, federal executive orders, and federal policy, into the federal database maintained by the Federal Bureau of Investigation.

(c) The bureau chief shall offer assistance and, if practicable, instruction to sheriffs, chiefs of police, and other peace officers in establishing efficient local bureaus of identification in their districts.

(d) The department may charge each person and charge each entity or agency that is not primarily a criminal justice agency a fee for processing inquiries for information that is not criminal history record information regarding a person. A person, entity, or agency that receives information must be entitled to receive the information under state or federal statutes, rules, regulations, or case law. The department may charge actual costs for processing all inquiries under this section.

(e) The department shall deposit all fees collected under this section in the operators and chauffeurs license fund.

(f) The department may keep any record or other information submitted to the department under this section, unless otherwise prohibited by law.

(g) The department may adopt reasonable rules under this section relating to:

(1) law enforcement information systems maintained by the department;

(2) the collection, maintenance, and correction of records;

(3) reports of criminal history information submitted to the department;

(4) active protective orders and reporting procedures that ensure that information relating to the issuance and dismissal of an active protective order is reported to the local law enforcement agency at the time of the order's issuance or dismissal and entered by the local law enforcement agency in the state's law enforcement information system;

(5) the collection of information described by Subsection (h);

(6) a system for providing criminal history record information through the criminal history clearinghouse under Section 411.0845; and

(7) active conditions of bond imposed on a defendant for the protection of a victim in any family violence, sexual assault or abuse, indecent assault, stalking, or trafficking case, and reporting procedures that ensure that information relating to the issuance, modification, or removal of the conditions of bond is reported, at the time of the issuance, modification, or removal, to:

(A) the victim or, if the victim is deceased, a close relative of the victim; and

(B) the local law enforcement agency for entry by the local law enforcement agency in the state's law enforcement information system.

(h) Information collected to perform a statistical breakdown of offenses under Sections 22.011 and 22.021, Penal Code, as required by Subsection (b)(2) must include information indicating the specific offense committed and information regarding:

(1) the victim;

(2) the offender and the offender's relationship to the victim;

(3) any weapons used or exhibited in the commission of the offense; and

(4) any injuries sustained by the victim.

(i) A law enforcement agency shall report offenses under Section 22.011 or 22.021, Penal Code, to the department in the form and manner and at regular intervals as prescribed by rules adopted by the department. The report must include the information described by Subsection (h).

(j) The department may contract with private vendors as necessary in implementing this section.

Sec. 411.0421. Information Regarding Fraudulent Use of Identification.

(a) The department shall create a record of each individual who:

(1) in conjunction with the attorney representing the state in the prosecution of felonies in the county in which the individual resides and the sheriff of that county or, if the individual is not a resident of a county in this state, the attorney and sheriff in a county that the individual frequents, signs a declaration that the individual's identity has been used by another person to frustrate proper law enforcement without the individual's consent; and

(2) files that declaration with the department.

(b) A declaration filed under this section must include:

(1) the individual's name, social security number, driver's license number, date of birth, and other identifying data requested by the department;

(2) a statement that the individual's name, social security number, driver's license number, date of birth, or other data has been used by another person to frustrate proper law enforcement; and

(3) a name, word, number, letter, or combination of 30 or fewer characters designated by the individual as a unique password to verify the individual's identity.

(c) On receipt of a declaration under this section, the department shall create a record of the individual's identity, including a record of the individual's unique password, in the criminal history record information maintained by the department under Subchapter F. The department shall ensure that this record, including the unique password, is available online to any entity authorized to receive information from the department under Subchapter F.

Sec. 411.043. Bureau of Communications.

(a) The director, with the advice and consent of the commission, shall appoint the chief of the bureau of communications.

(b) The bureau of communications shall:

(1) provide for the rapid exchange between law enforcement agencies of the state, counties, municipalities, other states, and the federal government of information concerning the commission of crimes and the detection of violators of the law; and

(2) establish and operate, in coordination with state, county, and municipal law enforcement agencies, a state roads blockade system.

(c) If funds are provided, the bureau of communications may install and operate a police radio broadcasting system for broadcasting information concerning the activities of violators of the law and for directing the activities and functions of the law enforcement agencies of the state, counties, and municipalities. The bureau shall cooperate with county and municipal police authorities and police radio stations in this state and other states.

Sec. 411.044. Bureau of Intelligence.

(a) The director, with the advice and consent of the commission, shall appoint the chief of the bureau of intelligence.

(b) The bureau of intelligence shall:

(1) accumulate and analyze, with the aid of the other department divisions and bureaus, information of crime activities in the state and make the information available for use of the department and county and municipal law enforcement agencies; and

(2) aid in the detection and apprehension of violators of the law.

Sec. 411.045. Bureau of Training.

(a) The director, with the advice and consent of the commission, shall appoint the chief of the bureau of training. The chief must have substantial experience in law enforcement and in instruction of law enforcement officers.

(b) The bureau of training shall:

(1) establish and operate schools for training department personnel in their duties and functions;

(2) establish and operate schools for training county and municipal police officers who are selected to attend the schools by the authorities of the law enforcement agencies that employ them; and

(3) establish and carry out a comprehensive plan for the education of citizens of this state in matters of public safety and crime prevention and detection.

(c) The chief of the bureau of training shall organize schools for department members and other peace officers and give instruction in the schools.

(d) The adjutant general shall provide, for use of the bureau of training in conducting its training schools, suitable buildings, land, and state-owned equipment at Camp Mabry in Austin.

Sec. 411.046. Hate Crime Reporting.

(a) The bureau of identification and records shall establish and maintain a central repository for the collection and analysis of information relating to crimes that are motivated by prejudice, hatred, or advocacy of violence, including, but not limited to, incidents for which statistics are or were kept under Public Law No. 101-275, as that law existed on July 3, 1996. On establishing the repository, the department shall develop a procedure to monitor, record, classify, and analyze information relating to incidents directed against persons and property that are apparently motivated by the factors listed in this subsection.

(b) Local law enforcement agencies shall report offenses described by Subsection (a) in the form and manner and at regular intervals as prescribed by rules adopted by the department. The department shall summarize and analyze information received under this subsection and file an annual report with the governor and legislature containing the summary and analysis.

(c) The department shall make information, records, and statistics collected under this section available to any local enforcement agency, political subdivision, or state agency to the extent the information is reasonably necessary or useful to the agency or subdivision in carrying out duties imposed by law on the agency or subdivision. This subsection may not be construed to limit access to information, records, or statistics which access if permitted by other law. Dissemination of the names of defendants and victims is subject to all confidentiality requirements otherwise imposed by law.

Sec. 411.047. Reporting Related to Certain Handgun Incidents Involving License Holders.

(a) The department may maintain statistics on its website related to responses by law enforcement agencies to incidents in which a person licensed to carry a handgun under Subchapter H is convicted of an offense only if the offense is prohibited under Subchapter H or under Title 5, Chapter 29, Chapter 46, or Section 30.02, Penal Code.

(b) Such statistics shall be drawn and reported annually from the Department of Public Safety computerized criminal history file on persons

Government Code

21 years of age and older and shall be compared in numerical and graphical format to all like offenses committed in the state for the reporting period as a percentage of the total of such reported offenses.

(c) The department by rule shall adopt procedures for local law enforcement to make reports to the department described by Subsection (a).

Sec. 411.048. Threats Against Peace Officers and Detention Officers.

(a) In this section:

(1) "Criminal justice agency" has the meaning assigned by Article 66.001, Code of Criminal Procedure.

(2) "Peace officer" has the meaning assigned by Section 1.07, Penal Code.

(3) "Detention officer" means a person who is employed to ensure the safekeeping of prisoners and the security of a municipal or county jail.

(b) The bureau of identification and records shall establish and maintain a central index in the law enforcement information system maintained by the department to:

(1) collect and disseminate information relating to an individual's expression of intent to inflict serious bodily injury or death on a peace officer or detention officer; and

(2) alert a peace officer or detention officer of an expression of intent to inflict serious bodily injury or death on the officer.

(c) A criminal justice agency, after making each determination required under Subsection (d), shall immediately enter into the information system an electronic report of an individual who expresses an intent to inflict serious bodily injury or death on a peace officer or detention officer. The agency shall enter the information in the form and manner provided by rules adopted by the director.

(d) Before entering information collected under this section into the information system, a criminal justice agency must determine that the report described by Subsection (c):

(1) is not from an anonymous source; and

(2) consists of an expression of intent to inflict serious bodily injury or death on a peace officer or detention officer.

(e) On proper inquiry into the information system, the department shall disseminate information collected under this section to a criminal justice agency as reasonably necessary to protect the safety of a peace officer or detention officer. The criminal justice agency may use information disseminated under this subsection in the manner provided by rules adopted by the director.

(f) The department shall promptly respond to a request to disclose information collected under this section by an individual who is the subject of the information.

(g) An individual who is the subject of information collected under this section may request that the director, the director's designee, or a court review the information to determine whether the information complies with rules adopted by the director. The review shall be conducted using the same procedure for reviewing criminal information collected under Chapter 67, Code of Criminal Procedure.

(h) A peace officer, detention officer, or criminal justice agency is not liable for an act or omission relating to the collection, use, or dissemination of information collected under this section in accordance with rules adopted by the director.

(i) The director may adopt rules to implement and enforce this section. Any rule adopted by the director under this section must comply with the provisions of the Code of Federal Regulations, Title 28, Part 23, as it applies to criminal intelligence systems.

Sec. 411.0485. Protection for Judges.

Any commissioned peace officer in this state, including a commissioned officer of the department, may provide personal security to a state judge at any location in this state, regardless of the location of the law enforcement agency or department that employs or commissions the peace officer.

Sec. 411.049. Report Related to Certain Intoxication Offenses.

(a) In this section, "offense relating to the operating of a motor vehicle while intoxicated" has the meaning assigned by Section 49.09, Penal Code.

(b) The department shall compile and maintain statistical information on the prosecution of offenses relating to the operating of a motor vehicle while intoxicated, including:

(1) the number of arrests;

(2) the number of arrests resulting in release with no charges;

(3) the number of charges resulting in a plea of not guilty and a trial;

(4) the number of charges resulting in a plea of guilty or nolo contendere;

(5) the number of charges resulting in a conviction of the offense charged in the original information, indictment, complaint, or other charging instrument;

(6) the number of charges resulting in a conviction of an offense other than the offense charged in the original information, indictment, complaint, or other charging instrument; and

(7) the number of charges resulting in a dismissal.

(c) Each law enforcement agency that enforces Chapter 49, Penal Code, and each appropriate prosecuting attorney's office and court in this state shall report in the manner and on a form prescribed by the department the information necessary for the department to compile the information required by Subsection (b).

(d) The department shall identify law enforcement agencies, prosecuting attorney's offices, and courts required to report under Subsection (c) that fail to timely report or that report incomplete information to the department.

(e) The department shall submit to the legislature not later than February 15 of each year a report of the statistical information described in Subsection (b) compiled for the preceding calendar year. The report must include a list of the law enforcement agencies, prosecuting attorney's offices, and courts identified by the department under Subsection (d).

(f) The department may adopt rules to implement this section.

Sec. 411.050. Crime Statistic Mapping.

The department, in conjunction with Texas State University, may annually produce maps of the state that include information regarding crime statistics correlated with the various regions of the state.

Sec. 411.051. Analysis of Information Identifying Persons Committing or Suspected of Committing Certain Property Offenses Against Elderly Individuals.

(a) This section applies to an offense under Chapter 31 or 32, Penal Code, or any other offense under that code involving an intent to steal or defraud if the offense was committed against an elderly individual as defined by Section 22.04(c), Penal Code.

(b) For purposes of this section, the victim's status as an elderly individual is determined according to the victim's age at the time of the offense.

(c) A law enforcement agency that investigates an offense described by Subsection (a) shall report the investigation to the department in the form and manner and at regular intervals as prescribed by rules adopted by the department. The rules must require submission of the original investigative report and any supplemental investigative report containing new, significant information.

(d) To identify a person committing or suspected of committing an offense described by Subsection (a) or a victim of an offense described by that subsection, the department shall analyze information received under this section and any other corresponding information possessed by the department.

(e) The department shall make the analysis required by this section available to any local law enforcement agency, political subdivision, or state agency to the extent the analysis is reasonably necessary or useful to the agency or subdivision in carrying out duties imposed by law on the agency or subdivision. This subsection may not be construed to enable direct access by a person to information analyzed by the department under this section if the person does not otherwise have direct access to that information. Dissemination of the analysis required by this section is subject to all confidentiality requirements imposed by other law.

Sec. 411.052. Federal Firearm Reporting.

(a) In this section, "federal prohibited person information" means information that identifies an individual as:

(1) a person ordered by a court to receive inpatient mental health services under Chapter 574, Health and Safety Code;

(2) a person acquitted in a criminal case by reason of insanity or lack of mental responsibility, regardless of whether the person is ordered by a court to receive inpatient treatment or residential care under Chapter 46C, Code of Criminal Procedure;

(3) a person determined to have mental retardation and committed by a court for long-term placement in a residential care facility under Chapter 593, Health and Safety Code;

(4) an incapacitated adult individual for whom a court has appointed a guardian of the individual under Title 3, Estates Code, based on the determination that the person lacks the mental capacity to manage the person's affairs; or

(5) a person determined to be incompetent to stand trial under Chapter 46B, Code of Criminal Procedure.

(b) The department by rule shall establish a procedure to provide federal prohibited person information to the Federal Bureau of Investigation for use with the National Instant Criminal Background Check System. Except as otherwise provided by state law, the department may disseminate federal prohibited person information under this subsection only to the extent necessary to allow the Federal Bureau of Investigation to collect and maintain a list of persons who are prohibited under federal law from engaging in certain activities with respect to a firearm.

(c) The department shall grant access to federal prohibited person information to the person who is the subject of the information.

(d) Federal prohibited person information maintained by the department is confidential information for the use of the department and, except as otherwise provided by this section and other state law, may not be disseminated by the department.

(e) The department by rule shall establish a procedure to correct department records and transmit those corrected records to the Federal Bureau of Investigation when a person provides:

(1) a copy of a judicial order or finding that a person is no longer an incapacitated adult or is entitled to relief from disabilities under Section 574.088, Health and Safety Code; or

(2) proof that the person has obtained notice of relief from disabilities under 18 U.S.C. Section 925.

Sec. 411.0521. Report to Department Concerning Certain Persons' Access to Firearms.

(a) The clerk of the court shall prepare and forward to the department the information described by Subsection (b) not later than the 30th day after the date the court:

(1) orders a person to receive inpatient mental health services under Chapter 574, Health and Safety Code;

(2) acquits a person in a criminal case by reason of insanity or lack of mental responsibility, regardless of whether the person is ordered to receive inpatient treatment or residential care under Chapter 46C, Code of Criminal Procedure;

(3) commits a person determined to have mental retardation for long-term placement in a residential care facility under Chapter 593, Health and Safety Code;

(4) appoints a guardian of the incapacitated adult individual under Title 3, Estates Code, based on the determination that the person lacks the mental capacity to manage the person's affairs;

(5) determines a person is incompetent to stand trial under Chapter 46B, Code of Criminal Procedure; or

(6) finds a person is entitled to relief from disabilities under Section 574.088, Health and Safety Code.

(b) The clerk of the court shall prepare and forward the following information under Subsection (a):

(1) the complete name, race, and sex of the person;

(2) any known identifying number of the person, including social security number, driver's license number, or state identification number;

(3) the person's date of birth; and

(4) the federal prohibited person information that is the basis of the report required by this section.

(c) If practicable, the clerk of the court shall forward to the department the information described by Subsection (b) in an electronic format prescribed by the department.

(d) If an order previously reported to the department under Subsection (a) is reversed by order of any court, the clerk shall notify the department of the reversal not later than 30 days after the clerk receives the mandate from the appellate court.

(e) The duty of a clerk to prepare and forward information under this section is not affected by:

(1) any subsequent appeal of the court order;

(2) any subsequent modification of the court order; or

(3) the expiration of the court order.

Sec. 411.053. Preservation of Evidence Containing Biological Material.

(a) The department:

(1) shall maintain a storage space for the preservation of evidence containing biological material that is delivered to the department under Article 38.43(f), Code of Criminal Procedure; and

(2) may maintain a storage space for the preservation of evidence of a sexual assault or other sex offense.

(b) The department shall adopt rules relating to the delivery, cataloging, and preservation of evidence stored under this section.

Sec. 411.054. Incident-Based Crime Statistics Reporting Goal.

(a) The department shall establish a goal that, not later than September 1, 2019, all local law enforcement agencies:

(1) will have implemented an incident-based reporting system that meets the reporting requirements of the National Incident-Based Reporting System of the Uniform Crime Reporting Program of the Federal Bureau of Investigation; and

(2) will use the system described by Subdivision (1) to submit to the department information and statistics concerning criminal offenses committed in the jurisdiction of the local law enforcement agency.

(b) Not later than January 1, 2017, the department shall submit a report to the legislature that identifies the number of local law enforcement agencies that have implemented the system described by Subsection (a).

Government Code

Sec. 411.055. Annual Report on Border Crime and Other Criminal Activity.

(a) Not later than May 30 of each year, the department shall submit to the legislature a report on border crime and other criminal activity. The report must include:

(1) statistics for each month of the preceding calendar year and yearly totals of all border crime, as defined by Section 772.0071, and other criminal activity, including transnational criminal activity, the department determines relates to border security that occurred in each county included in a department region that is adjacent to the Texas-Mexico border; and

(2) statewide crime statistics for the crimes reported under Subdivision (1).

(b) In compiling the information for the report, the department shall use information available in the National Incident-Based Reporting System of the Uniform Crime Reporting Program of the Federal Bureau of Investigation and the Texas Incident-Based Reporting System of the department.

SUBCHAPTER D-1 CENTRAL INDEX OF CERTAIN ADDITIONAL OFFENSES SUSPECTED TO HAVE BEEN COMMITTED BY CRIMINAL DEFENDANTS

Sec. 411.0601. Definition.

In this subchapter, "criminal justice agency" has the meaning assigned by Article 66.001, Code of Criminal Procedure.

Sec. 411.0602. Establishment of Central Index; Entry of Information.

(a) In the law enforcement information system maintained by the department, the bureau of identification and records shall establish and maintain a central index to collect and disseminate information regarding additional offenses that forensic DNA test results indicate may have been committed by a defendant who has been arrested for or charged with any felony or misdemeanor offense, other than a misdemeanor offense punishable by fine only.

(b) Information relating to a defendant described by Subsection (a) may be entered in the central index only if the information is based on forensic DNA test results indicating that the DNA profile of the defendant cannot be excluded as a donor to the DNA profile of a person suspected to have committed an offense, regardless of whether the defendant has been or will be arrested for or charged with that offense. The information must be:

(1) submitted in the form of an affidavit signed by a representative of an investigating criminal justice agency and approved by a district judge; and

(2) accompanied by a set of the defendant's fingerprints.

Sec. 411.0603. Confidentiality and Dissemination of Information in Central Index.

(a) Information maintained by the department in the central index established under this subchapter is confidential. The department may not disseminate the information except as otherwise provided by this section.

(b) On proper inquiry, the department shall disseminate to a criminal justice agency the information collected under Section 411.0602. The criminal justice agency may disseminate the information to any other criminal justice agency if the dissemination of that information is for a criminal justice purpose.

(c) A criminal justice agency or an employee of a criminal justice agency is not liable for an act or omission relating to the collection, use, or dissemination of information collected under Section 411.0602 if that collection, use, or dissemination is performed in accordance with rules adopted by the director.

Sec. 411.0604. Rules.

The director shall adopt rules to implement and enforce this subchapter.

Sec. 411.0605. Right to Request Notice of Entry in Central Index.

(a) A defendant described by Section 411.0602(a) may submit to the bureau of identification and records a request to determine whether the bureau has entered information relating to the defendant in the central index established under Section 411.0602. The bureau shall respond to the request not later than the 10th business day after the date the bureau receives the request.

(b) Before responding to a request under Subsection (a), the bureau may require reasonable written

Government Code

verification of the identity of the defendant submitting the request, including written verification of an address, date of birth, driver's license number, state identification card number, or social security number.

Sec. 411.0606. Right to Request Review of Entry in Central Index.

(a) On receipt by the bureau of identification and records of a written request that is submitted by a defendant described by Section 411.0602(a), that is accompanied by a set of the defendant's fingerprints, and that alleges that the bureau may have entered inaccurate information relating to the defendant in the central index established under Section 411.0602, the head of the bureau or that person's designee and the head of the department's crime laboratory in Austin each shall review the information to determine whether there is a high likelihood that the information is accurate.

(b) If after review the head of the bureau or that person's designee or the head of the department's crime laboratory in Austin determines there is not a high likelihood that the information relating to the defendant is accurate, the bureau shall:

(1) promptly remove that information from the central index; and

(2) notify other appropriate divisions of the department, the investigating criminal justice agency, and the defendant of the bureau's determination and the removal of the information.

(c) If after review the head of the bureau or that person's designee and the head of the department's crime laboratory in Austin jointly determine there is a high likelihood that the information relating to the defendant is accurate, the bureau shall notify the defendant of that determination.

SUBCHAPTER E CAPITOL COMPLEX

Sec. 411.061. Definition.

(a) In this subchapter, "Capitol Complex" means the following property that is located in Austin, Texas, to the extent the property is owned by or under the control of the state:

(1) the area bounded on the north by the inside curb of Martin Luther King, Jr., Boulevard, on the east by the outside curb of Trinity Street, on the south by the outside curb of 10th Street, and on the west by the outside curb of Lavaca Street;

(2) the William P. Clements State Office Building located at 300 West 15th Street; and

(3) other locations under the jurisdiction of the capitol police district as may be approved by the director.

(b) The provisions of this subchapter do not apply to the property or parking facility under the management and control of the Texas Employment Commission and located within the bounds set forth in Subsection (a).

Sec. 411.062. Law Enforcement and Security Authority.

(a) The department has primary responsibility for law enforcement and security services on the Capitol Complex.

(b) Subsection (a) does not prohibit the department from requesting or receiving assistance from another law enforcement agency.

(c) This section does not prohibit a peace officer who is not a member of the department from exercising the officer's authority on the Capitol Complex in an emergency or in a situation where the officer reasonably believes that immediate action is necessary.

(d) The department shall adopt rules relating to security of persons and access to and protection of the grounds, public buildings, and property of the state within the Capitol Complex, except that public use of the capitol, the capitol extension, the capitol grounds, and the General Land Office building shall be governed by the State Preservation Board.

(d-1) The director shall adopt rules governing the use of unmanned aircraft in the Capitol Complex. The rules adopted under this subsection may:

(1) prohibit the use of unmanned aircraft in the Capitol Complex; or

(2) authorize limited use of unmanned aircraft in the Capitol Complex.

(e) The department may enforce the rules of the State Preservation Board, adopted under Section 443.018.

(f) The department and the City of Austin shall execute an interlocal cooperation agreement that defines the respective responsibilities of the department and the city for traffic and parking enforcement and general security in the Capitol Complex, including private property within the boundaries of the complex.

(g) The commission may authorize the director to impose within the Capitol Complex measures the director determines to be necessary to protect the safety and security of persons and property within the complex.

Sec. 411.0625. Pass for Expedited Access to Capitol.

(a) The department shall allow a person to enter the Capitol and the Capitol Extension, including any public space in the Capitol or Capitol Extension, in the same manner as the department allows entry to a person who presents a license to carry a handgun under Subchapter H if the person:

(1) obtains from the department a Capitol access pass; and

(2) presents the pass to the appropriate law enforcement official when entering the building or a space within the building.

(b) To be eligible for a Capitol access pass, a person must meet the eligibility requirements applicable to a license to carry a handgun under Subchapter H, other than requirements regarding evidence of handgun proficiency.

(c) The department shall adopt rules to establish a procedure by which a resident of the state may apply for and be issued a Capitol access pass. Rules adopted under this section must include provisions for eligibility, application, approval, issuance, and renewal that:

(1) require the department to conduct the same background check on an applicant for a Capitol access pass that is conducted on an applicant for a license to carry a handgun under Subchapter H;

(2) enable the department to conduct the background check described by Subdivision (1); and

(3) establish application and renewal fees in amounts sufficient to cover the cost of administering this section, not to exceed the amounts of similar fees required under Section 411.174 for a license to carry a handgun.

Sec. 411.063. Rules Relating to Parking and Vehicles.

(a) The State Preservation Board shall adopt rules for the safe movement and the parking of vehicles in the Capitol Complex. The department shall administer and enforce the rules adopted by the preservation board and shall administer and enforce this subchapter. This subsection does not affect the authority of the department to adopt rules under Section 411.067.

(b) Rules adopted under this section may:

(1) regulate the type, flow, and direction of vehicular traffic;

(2) designate, mark, and assign areas and spaces for parking for elected state officials, chief executives and employees of state agencies located in the Capitol Complex, state-owned vehicles, business vehicles, and visitors to the Capitol Complex;

(3) establish a system of registration for vehicle identification;

(4) prohibit or restrict the use of areas and spaces for parking;

(5) establish a reasonable fee for parking in a parking space on a parking lot or in a parking garage that is located in the Capitol Complex, other than a space in the capitol driveway or capitol extension garage; and

(6) provide for the towing and storing, at the expense of the owner, of a vehicle parked in violation of a rule.

(c) Rules that govern parking in the parking spaces in the capitol driveways and the parking lots and parking garages near the capitol, to the extent that parking in such places is not otherwise regulated by the State Preservation Board, shall provide for:

(1) assigning and marking reserved parking spaces for the unrestricted use of the governor, lieutenant governor, speaker of the house of representatives, and secretary of state;

(2) when the legislature is in session, assigning and marking reserved parking spaces requested by each house of the legislature for the unrestricted use of members and administrative staff of the legislature; and

(3) when the legislature is not in session, assigning and marking parking spaces requested by each house of the legislature for the use of members and administrative staff of the legislature.

(d) Except as provided by Section 443.015, the department shall remit to the comptroller for deposit to the credit of State Parking Fund No. 125 any fee collected for the parking of a vehicle in the Capitol Complex. Money in the fund may be appropriated only to the department for the operation, maintenance, and improvement of state parking facilities on, and for security in, the Capitol Complex.

(e) To the extent that the City of Austin on January 1, 1997, operated and maintained parking meters along either side of the streets forming the perimeter of the Capitol Complex, the city is entitled to continue to operate, maintain, and receive the revenue from those meters, except that the city may not operate or maintain along those streets meters that accept only quarters.

Sec. 411.064. Assistance of Texas Department of Transportation or Texas Facilities Commission.

(a) On request of the department, the Texas Department of Transportation and the Texas Facilities Commission shall:

(1) assist the department in the marking and designation of parking lots, parking garages, and parking spaces;

Government Code

(2) maintain the painting of lines and curb markings; and

(3) furnish and erect direction and information signs.

(b) The department may recover the cost of providing the services described in Subsection (a) from the agency or agencies for which the service was provided. To the extent that either the Texas Facilities Commission or the Texas Department of Transportation provides or assists in providing the services described in Subsection (a), that agency shall be reimbursed by the department from its funds or the funds received from another agency under this subsection.

Sec. 411.0645. Transportation Planning Committee.

(a) The department, the City of Austin, the Capital Metropolitan Transportation Authority, the Texas Facilities Commission, the State Preservation Board, and The University of Texas at Austin shall each designate a representative to a committee established for the purpose of coordinating transportation in and adjacent to the Capitol Complex. The representative of the department shall convene the initial meeting of the committee, and the committee shall elect officers and meet as decided by the committee.

(b) The committee may develop and recommend to the agencies represented agreements and memoranda of understanding relating to transportation in and adjacent to the Capitol Complex, including agreements or understandings relating to parking, vehicle traffic, and the location of light rail or other mass transit terminals and facilities in that area.

Sec. 411.065. Offenses.

(a) A person commits an offense if the person violates a rule of the department adopted under Section 411.062 or a rule of the State Preservation Board adopted under Section 411.063.

(b) An offense under this section is a Class C misdemeanor, except that an offense is a Class B misdemeanor if the person violates a rule adopted under Section 411.062(d-1).

Sec. 411.066. Jurisdiction.

The municipal court of a municipality and the justice courts of a county in which an offense under Section 411.065 was committed have concurrent original jurisdiction over such an offense.

Sec. 411.067. Administrative Parking Violations.

(a) The department may adopt rules for the assessment of an administrative fine of $25 for violations of the parking rules adopted under Section 411.063. Notwithstanding the provisions of Sections 411.065 and 411.066, the department may issue an administrative citation for a parking violation.

(b) Rules adopted under this section shall:

(1) establish a system for enforcement of administrative citations, including assessment of a late fee not to exceed $5 and towing, impoundment, or immobilization of vehicles; and

(2) provide a procedure of administrative review within the highway patrol district that includes the Capitol Complex and, on request of the person assessed an administrative fine, further judicial review by the department filing the appropriate citation or complaint in a court, as provided in Section 411.066.

(c) The administrative review provided for in Subsection (b) shall not be considered a contested case under Chapter 2001 or Chapter 2003.

(d) The department shall remit to the comptroller for deposit in the general revenue fund each administrative fine and late fee collected under this section. The money deposited may be appropriated only to the department for security and parking in the highway patrol district that includes the Capitol Complex.

SUBCHAPTER E-1 ORDER OF NONDISCLOSURE OF CRIMINAL HISTORY RECORD INFORMATION

Sec. 411.071. Definitions.

In this subchapter, "criminal history record information," "criminal justice agency," and "criminal justice purpose" have the meanings assigned by Section 411.082.

Sec. 411.0715. Definition of Deferred Adjudication Community Supervision for Purpose of Receiving Order of Nondisclosure.

For purposes of an order of nondisclosure of criminal history record information under this subchapter, a person is considered to have been placed on deferred adjudication community supervision if, regardless of the statutory authorization:

(1) the person entered a plea of guilty or nolo contendere;

(2) the judge deferred further proceedings without entering an adjudication of guilt and placed the person under the supervision of the court or an officer under the supervision of the court; and

(3) at the end of the period of supervision the judge dismissed the proceedings and discharged the person.

Sec. 411.0716. Applicability of Subchapter.

(a) Except as provided by Subsection (b), this subchapter applies to the issuance of an order of nondisclosure of criminal history record information for an offense committed before, on, or after September 1, 2017.

(b) Section 411.072 applies only to a person described by Subsection (a) of that section who receives a discharge and dismissal under Article 42A.111, Code of Criminal Procedure, on or after September 1, 2017.

Sec. 411.072. Procedure for Deferred Adjudication Community Supervision; Certain Nonviolent Misdemeanors.

(a) This section applies only to a person who:

(1) was placed on deferred adjudication community supervision under Subchapter C, Chapter 42A, Code of Criminal Procedure, for a misdemeanor other than a misdemeanor:

(A) under:

(i) Section 49.04 or 49.06, Penal Code; or

(ii) Chapter 20, 21, 22, 25, 42, 43, 46, or 71, Penal Code; or

(B) with respect to which an affirmative finding under Article 42A.105(f), Code of Criminal Procedure, or former Section 5(k), Article 42.12, Code of Criminal Procedure, was filed in the papers of the case; and

(2) has never been previously convicted of or placed on deferred adjudication community supervision for another offense other than a traffic offense that is punishable by fine only.

(b) Notwithstanding any other provision of this subchapter or Subchapter F, if a person described by Subsection (a) receives a discharge and dismissal under Article 42A.111, Code of Criminal Procedure, and satisfies the requirements of Section 411.074, the court that placed the person on deferred adjudication community supervision shall issue an order of nondisclosure of criminal history record information under this subchapter prohibiting criminal justice agencies from disclosing to the public criminal history record information related to the offense giving rise to the deferred adjudication community supervision. The court shall determine whether the person satisfies the requirements of Section 411.074, and if the court makes a finding that the requirements of that section are satisfied, the court shall issue the order of nondisclosure of criminal history record information:

(1) at the time the court discharges and dismisses the proceedings against the person, if the discharge and dismissal occurs on or after the 180th day after the date the court placed the person on deferred adjudication community supervision; or

(2) as soon as practicable on or after the 180th day after the date the court placed the person on deferred adjudication community supervision, if the discharge and dismissal occurred before that date.

(c) The person shall present to the court any evidence necessary to establish that the person is eligible to receive an order of nondisclosure of criminal history record information under this section. The person must pay a $28 fee to the clerk of the court before the court issues the order.

(d) A person who is not eligible to receive an order of nondisclosure of criminal history record information under this section solely because an affirmative finding under Article 42A.105(f), Code of Criminal Procedure, or former Section 5(k), Article 42.12, Code of Criminal Procedure, was filed in the papers of the case may file a petition for an order of nondisclosure of criminal history record information under Section 411.0725 if the person otherwise satisfies the requirements of that section.

Sec. 411.0725. Procedure for Deferred Adjudication Community Supervision; Felonies and Certain Misdemeanors.

(a) This section applies only to a person placed on deferred adjudication community supervision under Subchapter C, Chapter 42A, Code of Criminal Procedure, who:

(1) is not eligible to receive an order of nondisclosure of criminal history record information under Section 411.072; and

(2) was placed on deferred adjudication community supervision for an offense other than an offense under Section 49.04 or 49.06, Penal Code.

(b) Notwithstanding any other provision of this subchapter or Subchapter F, if a person described by Subsection (a) receives a discharge and dismissal under Article 42A.111, Code of Criminal Procedure, and satisfies the requirements of Section 411.074, the person may petition the court that placed the person on deferred adjudication community supervision for an order of nondisclosure of criminal history record information under this section.

(c) Except as provided by Section 411.074, a person may petition the court for an order of nondisclosure under this section regardless of whether the person has been previously convicted of or placed on deferred adjudication community supervision for another offense.

(d) After notice to the state, an opportunity for a hearing, and a determination that the person is entitled to file the petition and issuance of the order is in the best interest of justice, the court shall issue an order prohibiting criminal justice agencies from disclosing to the public criminal history record information related to the offense giving rise to the deferred adjudication community supervision.

(e) A person may petition the court that placed the person on deferred adjudication community supervision for an order of nondisclosure of criminal history record information under this section only on or after:

(1) the discharge and dismissal, if the offense for which the person was placed on deferred adjudication was a misdemeanor other than a misdemeanor described by Subdivision (2);

(2) the second anniversary of the discharge and dismissal, if the offense for which the person was placed on deferred adjudication was a misdemeanor under Chapter 20, 21, 22, 25, 42, 43, or 46, Penal Code; or

(3) the fifth anniversary of the discharge and dismissal, if the offense for which the person was placed on deferred adjudication was a felony.

Sec. 411.0726. Procedure for Deferred Adjudication Community Supervision; Certain Driving While Intoxicated and Boating While Intoxicated Misdemeanors.

(a) This section applies only to a person who was placed on deferred adjudication community supervision under Subchapter C, Chapter 42A, Code of Criminal Procedure, for a misdemeanor:

(1) under Section 49.04 or 49.06, Penal Code; and

(2) with respect to which no affirmative finding under Article 42A.105(f), Code of Criminal Procedure, was filed in the papers of the case.

(b) Notwithstanding any other provision of this subchapter or Subchapter F, a person may petition the court that placed the person on deferred adjudication community supervision for an order of nondisclosure if the person:

(1) receives a discharge and dismissal under Article 42A.111, Code of Criminal Procedure;

(2) satisfies the requirements of Section 411.074; and

(3) has never been previously convicted of or placed on deferred adjudication community supervision for another offense, other than a traffic offense that is punishable by fine only.

(c) A petition for an order of nondisclosure of criminal history record information filed under this section must include evidence that the person is entitled to file the petition.

(d) Except as provided by Subsection (e), after notice to the state, an opportunity for a hearing, and a determination that the person is entitled to file the petition and issuance of an order of nondisclosure of criminal history record information is in the best interest of justice, the court shall issue an order prohibiting criminal justice agencies from disclosing to the public criminal history record information related to the offense giving rise to the deferred adjudication community supervision.

(e) A court may not issue an order of nondisclosure of criminal history record information under this section if the attorney representing the state presents evidence sufficient to the court demonstrating that the commission of the offense for which the order is sought resulted in a motor vehicle accident involving another person, including a passenger in a motor vehicle operated by the person seeking the order of nondisclosure.

(f) A person may petition the court that placed the person on deferred adjudication community supervision for an order of nondisclosure of criminal history record information under this section only on or after the second anniversary of the date of completion of the deferred adjudication community supervision and the discharge and dismissal of the case.

Sec. 411.0727. Procedure Following Successful Completion of Veterans Treatment Court Program.

(a) This section applies only to a person who successfully completes a veterans treatment court program under Chapter 124 or former law.

(b) Notwithstanding any other provision of this subchapter or Subchapter F, a person described by Subsection (a) is entitled to file with the court that placed the person in the veterans treatment court program a petition for an order of nondisclosure of criminal history record information under this section if the person:

(1) satisfies the requirements of this section and Section 411.074;

(2) has never been previously convicted of an offense listed in Article 42A.054(a), Code of Criminal Procedure, or a sexually violent offense, as defined by Article 62.001, Code of Criminal Procedure; and

(3) is not convicted of any felony offense between the date on which the person successfully completed the program and the second anniversary of that date.

(c) Regardless of whether the person was convicted of or placed on deferred adjudication community supervision for the offense for which the person entered the veterans treatment court program or whether the case against the person was dismissed under Section 124.001(b), after notice to the state, an opportunity for a hearing, and a determination that the person is entitled to file the petition and issuance of the order is in the best interest of justice, the court shall issue an order prohibiting criminal justice agencies from disclosing to the public criminal history record information related to the offense for which the person entered the veterans treatment court program.

(d) A person may file with the court that placed the person in the veterans treatment court program a petition for an order of nondisclosure of criminal history record information under this section only on or after the second anniversary of the date the person successfully completed the program.

(e) A person is not entitled to petition the court for an order of nondisclosure of criminal history record information under this section if the person's entry into the veterans treatment court program arose as the result of a conviction of an offense involving the operation of a motor vehicle while intoxicated.

Sec. 411.0728. Procedure for Certain Victims of Trafficking of Persons or Compelling Prostitution.

(a) This section applies only to a person:

(1) who is convicted of or placed on deferred adjudication community supervision for an offense under:

(A) Section 481.120, Health and Safety Code, if the offense is punishable under Subsection (b)(1);

(B) Section 481.121, Health and Safety Code, if the offense is punishable under Subsection (b)(1);

(C) Section 31.03, Penal Code, if the offense is punishable under Subsection (e)(1) or (2); or

(D) Section 43.02, Penal Code; and

(2) who, if requested by the applicable law enforcement agency or prosecuting attorney to provide assistance in the investigation or prosecution of an offense under Section 20A.02, 20A.03, or 43.05, Penal Code, or a federal offense containing elements that are substantially similar to the elements of an offense under any of those sections:

(A) provided assistance in the investigation or prosecution of the offense; or

(B) did not provide assistance in the investigation or prosecution of the offense due to the person's age or a physical or mental disability resulting from being a victim of an offense described by this subdivision.

(b) Notwithstanding any other provision of this subchapter or Subchapter F, a person described by Subsection (a) who satisfies the requirements of Section 411.074(b) may petition the court that convicted the person or placed the person on deferred adjudication community supervision for an order of nondisclosure of criminal history record information under this section on the grounds that the person committed the offense solely as a victim of an offense under Section 20A.02, 20A.03, or 43.05, Penal Code.

(b-1) A petition under Subsection (b) must:

(1) be in writing;

(2) allege specific facts that, if proved, would establish that the petitioner committed the offense described by Subsection (a)(1) solely as a victim of an offense under Section 20A.02, 20A.03, or 43.05, Penal Code; and

(3) assert that if the person has previously submitted a petition for an order of nondisclosure under this section, the person has not committed an offense described by Subsection (a)(1) on or after the date on which the person's first petition under this section was submitted.

(b-2) On the filing of the petition under Subsection (b), the clerk of the court shall promptly serve a copy of the petition and any supporting document on the appropriate office of the attorney representing the state. Any response to the petition by the attorney representing the state must be filed not later than the 20th business day after the date of service under this subsection.

(b-3) A person convicted of or placed on deferred adjudication community supervision for more than one offense described by Subsection (a)(1) that the person committed solely as a victim of an offense under Section 20A.02, 20A.03, or 43.05, Penal Code, may file a petition for an order of nondisclosure of criminal history record information under this section with respect to each offense, and may request consolidation of those petitions, in a district court in the county where the person was most recently convicted or placed on deferred adjudication community supervision as described by this subsection. On receipt of a request for consolidation, the court shall consolidate the petitions and exercise jurisdiction over the petitions, regardless of the county in which the offenses described by Subsection (a)(1) occurred. For each offense that is the subject of a consolidated petition and that occurred in a county other than the county in which the court consolidating the petitions is located, the clerk of the court, in addition to the clerk's duties under Subsection (b-2), shall promptly serve a copy of the consolidated petition and any supporting document related to the applicable offense on the appropriate office of the attorney representing the state on behalf of the other county. Each attorney representing the state who receives a copy of a consolidated petition under this subsection may file a response to the petition in accordance with Subsection (b-2).

(b-4) A district court that consolidates petitions under Subsection (b-3) shall allow an attorney representing the state who receives a petition involving an offense that was committed outside the county in which the court is located to appear at any hearing regarding the consolidated petition by telephone or video conference call.

(c) After notice to the state and an opportunity for a hearing, the court having jurisdiction over the petition shall issue an order prohibiting criminal justice agencies from disclosing to the public criminal history record information related to the offense if the court determines that:

(1) the person committed the offense described by Subsection (a)(1) solely as a victim of an offense under Section 20A.02, 20A.03, or 43.05, Penal Code;

(2) if applicable, the person did not commit another offense described by Subsection (a)(1) on or after the date on which the person's first petition for an order of nondisclosure under this section was submitted; and

(3) issuance of the order is in the best interest of justice.

(c-1) In determining whether a person committed an offense described by Subsection (a)(1) solely as a victim of an offense under Section 20A.02, 20A.03, or 43.05, Penal Code, the court may consider any order of nondisclosure previously granted to the person under this section.

(d) A person may petition the applicable court for an order of nondisclosure of criminal history record information under this section only on or after the first anniversary of the date the person:

(1) completed the sentence, including any term of confinement imposed and payment of all fines, costs, and restitution imposed; or

(2) received a dismissal and discharge under Article 42A.111, Code of Criminal Procedure, if the person was placed on deferred adjudication community supervision.

Sec. 411.0729. Procedure for Certain Veterans Placed on Community Supervision.

(a) On successful completion of the veterans reemployment program under Subchapter H-1, Chapter 42A, Code of Criminal Procedure, and all other conditions of the defendant's community supervision, including deferred adjudication community supervision, after notice to the state and a hearing on whether issuance of an order of nondisclosure is in the best interest of justice, the court shall enter an order of nondisclosure with respect to all records of the offense for which the defendant was placed on community supervision.

(b) Subsection (a) applies regardless of whether the defendant meets the other eligibility criteria under this subchapter.

Sec. 411.073. Procedure for Community Supervision Following Conviction; Certain Misdemeanors.

(a) This section applies only to a person placed on community supervision under Chapter 42A, Code of Criminal Procedure:

(1) following a conviction of a misdemeanor other than a misdemeanor under Section 106.041, Alcoholic Beverage Code, Section 49.04, 49.05, 49.06, or 49.065, Penal Code, or Chapter 71, Penal Code; and

(2) under a provision of Chapter 42A, Code of Criminal Procedure, other than Subchapter C, including:

(A) a provision that requires the person to serve a term of confinement as a condition of community supervision; or

(B) another provision that authorizes placing a person on community supervision after the person has served part of a term of confinement imposed for the offense.

(b) Notwithstanding any other provision of this subchapter or Subchapter F, a person described by Subsection (a) whose community supervision is not revoked and who completes the period of community supervision, including any term of confinement imposed and payment of all fines, costs, and restitution imposed, may petition the court that placed the person on community supervision for an order of nondisclosure of criminal history record information under this section if the person:

(1) satisfies the requirements of this section and Section 411.074; and

(2) has never been previously convicted of or placed on deferred adjudication community supervision for another offense other than a traffic offense that is punishable by fine only.

(c) After notice to the state, an opportunity for a hearing, and a determination that the person is entitled to file the petition and issuance of the order is in the best interest of justice, the court shall issue an order prohibiting criminal justice agencies from disclosing to the public criminal history record information related to the offense giving rise to the community supervision.

(d) A person may petition the court that placed the person on community supervision for an order of nondisclosure of criminal history record information under this section only on or after:

(1) the completion of the community supervision, if the offense for which the person was placed on community supervision was a misdemeanor other than a misdemeanor described by Subdivision (2); or

(2) the second anniversary of the date of completion of the community supervision, if the offense for which the person was placed on community supervision was a misdemeanor under Chapter 20, 21, 22, 25, 42, 43, or 46, Penal Code.

Sec. 411.0731. Procedure for Community Supervision following Conviction; Certain Driving while Intoxicated Convictions.

(a) This section applies only to a person placed on community supervision under Chapter 42A, Code of Criminal Procedure:

(1) following a conviction of an offense under Section 49.04, Penal Code, other than an offense punishable under Subsection (d) of that section; and

(2) under a provision of Chapter 42A, Code of Criminal Procedure, other than Subchapter C, including:

(A) a provision that requires the person to serve a term of confinement as a condition of community supervision; or

(B) another provision that authorizes placing a person on community supervision after the person has served part of a term of confinement imposed for the offense.

(b) Notwithstanding any other provision of this subchapter or Subchapter F, a person described by Subsection (a) whose community supervision is not revoked and who completes the period of community supervision, including any term of confinement imposed and payment of all fines, costs, and restitution imposed, may petition the court that placed the person on community supervision for an order of nondisclosure of criminal history record information under this section if the person:

(1) satisfies the requirements of this section and Section 411.074; and

(2) has never been previously convicted of or placed on deferred adjudication community supervision for another offense other than a traffic offense that is punishable by fine only.

(c) A petition for an order of nondisclosure of criminal history record information filed under this section must include evidence that the person is entitled to file the petition.

(d) Except as provided by Subsection (e), after notice to the state, an opportunity for a hearing, and a determination that the person is entitled to file the petition and issuance of an order of nondisclosure of criminal history record information is in the best interest of justice, the court shall issue an order prohibiting criminal justice agencies from disclosing to the public criminal history record information related to the offense giving rise to the community supervision.

(e) A court may not issue an order of nondisclosure of criminal history record information under this section if the attorney representing the state presents evidence sufficient to the court demonstrating that the commission of the offense for which the order is sought resulted in a motor vehicle accident involving another person, including a passenger in a motor vehicle operated by the person seeking the order of nondisclosure.

(f) A person may petition the court that placed the person on community supervision for an order of nondisclosure of criminal history record information under this section only on or after:

(1) the second anniversary of the date of completion of the community supervision, if the person successfully complied with a condition of community supervision that, for a period of not less than six months, restricted the person's operation of a motor vehicle to a motor vehicle equipped with an ignition interlock device; or

(2) the fifth anniversary of the date of completion of the community supervision, if the court that placed the person on community supervision did not order the person to comply with a condition of community supervision described by Subdivision (1) for the period described by that subdivision.

Sec. 411.0735. Procedure for Conviction; Certain Misdemeanors.

(a) This section applies only to a person who:

(1) is convicted of a misdemeanor other than a misdemeanor under Section 106.041, Alcoholic Beverage Code, Section 49.04, 49.05, 49.06, or 49.065, Penal Code, or Chapter 71, Penal Code; and

(2) is not eligible for an order of nondisclosure of criminal history record information under Section 411.073.

(b) Notwithstanding any other provision of this subchapter or Subchapter F, a person described by Subsection (a) who completes the person's sentence, including any term of confinement imposed and payment of all fines, costs, and restitution imposed, may petition the court that imposed the sentence for an order of nondisclosure of criminal history record information under this section if the person:

(1) satisfies the requirements of this section and Section 411.074; and

(2) has never been previously convicted of or placed on deferred adjudication community supervision for another offense other than a traffic offense that is punishable by fine only.

(c) Except as provided by Subsection (c-1), after notice to the state, an opportunity for a hearing, and a determination that the person is entitled to file the petition and issuance of the order is in the best interest of justice, the court shall issue an order prohibiting criminal justice agencies from disclosing to the public criminal history record information related to the offense for which the person was convicted.

(c-1) A court may not issue an order of nondisclosure of criminal history record information under this section if the court determines that the offense for which the order is sought, other than an offense under Section 22.01, Penal Code, was violent or sexual in nature.

(d) A person may petition the court that imposed the sentence for an order of nondisclosure of criminal history record information under this section only on or after:

(1) the date of completion of the person's sentence, if the offense of which the person was convicted was a misdemeanor punishable by fine only; or

(2) the second anniversary of the date of completion of the person's sentence, if the offense of which the person was convicted was a misdemeanor other than a misdemeanor described by Subdivision (1).

Sec. 411.0736. Procedure for Conviction; Certain Driving While Intoxicated Convictions.

(a) This section applies only to a person who:

(1) is convicted of an offense under Section 49.04, Penal Code, other than an offense punishable under Subsection (d) of that section; and

(2) is not eligible for an order of nondisclosure of criminal history record information under Section 411.0731.

(b) Notwithstanding any other provision of this subchapter or Subchapter F, a person described by Subsection (a) who completes the person's sentence, including any term of confinement imposed and payment of all fines, costs, and restitution imposed, may petition the court that imposed the sentence for an order of nondisclosure of criminal history record information under this section if the person:

(1) satisfies the requirements of this section and Section 411.074; and

(2) has never been previously convicted of or placed on deferred adjudication community supervision for another offense other than a traffic offense that is punishable by fine only.

(c) A petition for an order of nondisclosure of criminal history record information filed under this section must include evidence that the person is entitled to file the petition.

(d) Except as provided by Subsection (e), after notice to the state, an opportunity for a hearing, and a determination that the person is entitled to file the petition and issuance of an order of nondisclosure of criminal history record information is in the best interest of justice, the court shall issue an order prohibiting criminal justice agencies from disclosing to the public criminal history record information related to the offense for which the person was convicted.

(e) A court may not issue an order of nondisclosure of criminal history record information under this section if the attorney representing the state presents evidence sufficient to the court demonstrating that the commission of the offense for which the order is sought resulted in a motor vehicle accident involving another person, including a passenger in a motor vehicle operated by the person seeking the order of nondisclosure.

(f) A person may petition the court that imposed the sentence for an order of nondisclosure of criminal history record information under this section on or after:

(1) the third anniversary of the date of completion of the person's sentence, if the person successfully complied with a condition of the sentence that, for a period of not less than six months, restricted the person's operation of a motor vehicle to a motor vehicle equipped with an ignition interlock device; or

(2) the fifth anniversary of the date of completion of the person's sentence, if the court that imposed the sentence did not order the person to comply with a condition described by Subdivision (1) for the period described by that subdivision.

Sec. 411.074. Required Conditions for Receiving an Order of Nondisclosure.

(a) A person may be granted an order of nondisclosure of criminal history record information under this subchapter and, when applicable, is entitled to petition the court to receive an order under this subchapter only if, during the period after the court pronounced the sentence or placed the person on community supervision, including deferred adjudication community supervision, for the offense for which the order of nondisclosure is requested, and during any applicable waiting period for the person under this subchapter following completion of the person's sentence or community supervision, including deferred adjudication community supervision, the person is not convicted of or placed on deferred adjudication community supervision for any offense other than a traffic offense that is punishable by fine only.

(b) A person may not be granted an order of nondisclosure of criminal history record information under this subchapter and is not entitled to petition the court for an order of nondisclosure under this subchapter if:

(1) the person requests the order of nondisclosure for, or the person has been previously convicted of or placed on deferred adjudication community supervision for:

(A) an offense requiring registration as a sex offender under Chapter 62, Code of Criminal Procedure;

(B) an offense under Section 20.04, Penal Code, regardless of whether the offense is a reportable conviction or adjudication for purposes of Chapter 62, Code of Criminal Procedure;

(C) an offense under Section 19.02, 19.03, 20A.02, 20A.03, 22.04, 22.041, 25.07, 25.072, or 42.072, Penal Code; or

(D) any other offense involving family violence, as defined by Section 71.004, Family Code; or

(2) the court makes an affirmative finding that the offense for which the order of nondisclosure is requested involved family violence, as defined by Section 71.004, Family Code.

Sec. 411.0745. Petition and Order. [Effective until January 1, 2022]

(a) A person who petitions the court for an order of nondisclosure of criminal history record information under this subchapter, when a petition is required, may file the petition in person, electronically, or by mail.

(b) The petition must be accompanied by payment of a $28 fee to the clerk of the court in addition to any other fee that generally applies to the filing of a civil petition.

(c) The Office of Court Administration of the Texas Judicial System shall prescribe a form for the filing of a petition electronically or by mail. The form must provide for the petition to be accompanied by the required fees and any other supporting material determined necessary by the office of court administration, including evidence that the person is entitled to file the petition.

(d) The office of court administration shall make available on its Internet website the electronic application and printable application form. Each county or district clerk's office that maintains an Internet website shall include on that website a link to the electronic application and printable application form available on the office of court administration's Internet website.

(e) On receipt of a petition under this section, the court shall provide notice to the state and an opportunity for a hearing on whether the person is entitled to file the petition and issuance of the order is in the best interest of justice. The court shall hold a hearing before determining whether to issue an order of nondisclosure of criminal history record information, except that a hearing is not required if:

(1) the state does not request a hearing on the issue before the 45th day after the date on which the state receives notice under this subsection; and

(2) the court determines that:

(A) the person is entitled to file the petition; and

(B) the order is in the best interest of justice.

Sec. 411.0745. Petition and Order. [Effective January 1, 2022]

(a) A person who petitions the court for an order of nondisclosure of criminal history record information under this subchapter, when a petition is required, may file the petition in person, electronically, or by mail.

(b) The petition must be accompanied by payment of a fee that generally applies to the filing of a civil case.

(c) The Office of Court Administration of the Texas Judicial System shall prescribe a form for the filing of a petition electronically or by mail. The form must provide for the petition to be accompanied by the required fees and any other supporting material determined necessary by the office of court administration, including evidence that the person is entitled to file the petition.

(d) The office of court administration shall make available on its Internet website the electronic application and printable application form. Each county or district clerk's office that maintains an Internet website shall include on that website a link to the electronic application and printable application form available on the office of court administration's Internet website.

(e) On receipt of a petition under this section, the court shall provide notice to the state and an opportunity for a hearing on whether the person is entitled to file the petition and issuance of the order is in the best interest of justice. The court shall hold a hearing before determining whether to issue an order of nondisclosure of criminal history record information, except that a hearing is not required if:

(1) the state does not request a hearing on the issue before the 45th day after the date on which the state receives notice under this subsection; and

(2) the court determines that:

(A) the person is entitled to file the petition; and

(B) the order is in the best interest of justice.

Sec. 411.075. Procedure After Order.

(a) Not later than the 15th business day after the date an order of nondisclosure of criminal history record information is issued under this subchapter, the clerk of the court shall send all relevant criminal history record information contained in the order or a copy of the order by certified mail, return receipt requested, or secure electronic mail, electronic transmission, or facsimile transmission to the Crime Records Service of the department.

(b) Not later than 10 business days after receipt of relevant criminal history record information contained in an order or a copy of an order under Subsection (a), the department shall seal any criminal history record information maintained by the department that is the subject of the order. The department shall also send all relevant criminal history record information contained in the order or a copy of the order by certified mail, return receipt requested, or secure electronic mail, electronic transmission, or facsimile transmission to all:

(1) law enforcement agencies, jails or other detention facilities, magistrates, courts, prosecuting attorneys, correctional facilities, central state depositories of criminal records, and other officials or agencies or other entities of this state or of any political subdivision of this state;

(2) central federal depositories of criminal records that there is reason to believe have criminal history record information that is the subject of the order; and

(3) private entities that purchase criminal history record information from the department or that otherwise are likely to have criminal history record information that is subject to the order.

(c) The director shall adopt rules regarding minimum standards for the security of secure electronic mail, electronic transmissions, and facsimile transmissions under Subsections (a) and (b). In adopting rules under this subsection, the director shall consult with the Office of Court Administration of the Texas Judicial System.

(d) Not later than 30 business days after receipt of relevant criminal history record information contained in an order or a copy of an order from the department under Subsection (b), an individual or entity described by Subsection (b)(1) shall seal any criminal history record information maintained by the individual or entity that is the subject of the order.

(e) The department may charge to a private entity that purchases criminal history record information from the department a fee in an amount sufficient to recover costs incurred by the department in providing relevant criminal history record information contained in an order or a copy of an order under Subsection (b)(3) to the entity.

Sec. 411.0755. Statement in Application for Employment, Information, or Licensing.

A person whose criminal history record information is the subject of an order of nondisclosure of criminal history record information issued under this subchapter is not required in any application for employment, information, or licensing to state that the person has been the subject of any criminal proceeding related to the information that is the subject of the order.

Sec. 411.076. Disclosure by Court.

(a) A court may not disclose to the public any information contained in the court records that is the subject of an order of nondisclosure of criminal history record information issued under this subchapter. The court may disclose information contained in the court records that is the subject of an order of nondisclosure of criminal history record information only to:

(1) criminal justice agencies for criminal justice or regulatory licensing purposes;

(2) an agency or entity listed in Section 411.0765; or

(3) the person who is the subject of the order.

(b) The clerk of the court issuing an order of nondisclosure of criminal history record information under this subchapter shall seal any court records containing information that is the subject of the order as soon as practicable after the date the clerk of the court sends all relevant criminal history record information contained in the order or a copy of the order to the department under Section 411.075(a).

Sec. 411.0765. Disclosure by Criminal Justice Agency.

(a) A criminal justice agency may disclose criminal history record information that is the subject of an order of nondisclosure of criminal history record information under this subchapter only:

(1) to other criminal justice agencies;

(2) for criminal justice or regulatory licensing purposes;

(3) to an agency or entity listed in Subsection (b);

(4) to the person who is the subject of the order; or

(5) for the purpose of complying with a requirement under federal law or if federal law requires the disclosure as a condition of receiving federal highway funds.

(b) A criminal justice agency may disclose criminal history record information that is the subject of an order of nondisclosure of criminal history record information under this subchapter to the following noncriminal justice agencies or entities only:

(1) the State Board for Educator Certification;

(2) a school district, charter school, private school, regional education service center, commercial transportation company, or education shared services arrangement;

(3) the Texas Medical Board;

(4) the Texas School for the Blind and Visually Impaired;

(5) the Board of Law Examiners;

(6) the State Bar of Texas;

(7) a district court regarding a petition for name change under Subchapter B, Chapter 45, Family Code;

(8) the Texas School for the Deaf;

(9) the Department of Family and Protective Services;

(10) the Texas Juvenile Justice Department;

(11) the Department of Assistive and Rehabilitative Services;

(12) the Department of State Health Services, a local mental health service, a local intellectual and developmental disability authority, or a community center providing services to persons with mental illness or intellectual or developmental disabilities;

(13) the Texas Private Security Board;

(14) a municipal or volunteer fire department;

(15) the Texas Board of Nursing;

(16) a safe house providing shelter to children in harmful situations;

(17) a public or nonprofit hospital or hospital district, or a facility as defined by Section 250.001, Health and Safety Code;

(18) the securities commissioner, the banking commissioner, the savings and mortgage lending commissioner, the consumer credit commissioner, or the credit union commissioner;

(19) the Texas State Board of Public Accountancy;

(20) the Texas Department of Licensing and Regulation;

(21) the Health and Human Services Commission;

(22) the Department of Aging and Disability Services;

(23) the Texas Education Agency;

(24) the Judicial Branch Certification Commission;

(25) a county clerk's office in relation to a proceeding for the appointment of a guardian under Title 3, Estates Code;

(26) the Department of Information Resources but only regarding an employee, applicant for employment, contractor, subcontractor, intern, or volunteer who provides network security services under Chapter 2059 to:

(A) the Department of Information Resources; or

(B) a contractor or subcontractor of the Department of Information Resources;

(27) the Texas Department of Insurance;

(28) the Teacher Retirement System of Texas;

(29) the Texas State Board of Pharmacy;

(30) the Texas Civil Commitment Office;

(31) a bank, savings bank, savings and loan association, credit union, or mortgage banker, a subsidiary or affiliate of those entities, or another financial institution regulated by a state regulatory entity listed in Subdivision (18) or by a corresponding federal regulatory entity, but only regarding an employee, contractor, subcontractor, intern, or volunteer of or an applicant for employment by that bank, savings bank, savings and loan association, credit union, mortgage banker, subsidiary or affiliate, or financial institution; and

(32) an employer that has a facility that handles or has the capability of handling, transporting, storing, processing, manufacturing, or controlling hazardous, explosive, combustible, or flammable materials, if:

(A) the facility is critical infrastructure, as defined by 42 U.S.C. Section 5195c(e), or the employer is required to submit to a risk management plan under Section 112(r) of the federal Clean Air Act (42 U.S.C. Section 7412) for the facility; and

(B) the information concerns an employee, applicant for employment, contractor, or subcontractor whose duties involve or will involve the handling, transporting, storing, processing, manufacturing, or controlling hazardous, explosive, combustible, or flammable materials and whose background is required to be screened under a federal provision described by Paragraph (A).

Sec. 411.077. Disposition of Fee; Department of Public Safety Report. [Effective until January 1, 2022]

(a) The clerk of a court that collects a fee in connection with a petition or order for nondisclosure of criminal history record information under this subchapter shall remit the fee to the comptroller not later than the last day of the month following the end of the calendar quarter in which the fee is collected, and the comptroller shall deposit the fee in the general revenue fund.

(b) The department shall submit a report to the legislature not later than December 1 of each even-numbered year that includes information on:

(1) the number of petitions for nondisclosure of criminal history record information and orders of nondisclosure of criminal history record information received by the department in each of the previous two years;

(2) the actions taken by the department with respect to the petitions and orders received;

(3) the costs incurred by the department in taking those actions; and

(4) the number of persons who are the subject of an order of nondisclosure of criminal history record information and who became the subject of criminal charges for an offense committed after the order was issued.

Sec. 411.077. Department of Public Safety Report. [Effective January 1, 2022]

(a) [Repealed.]

(b) The department shall submit a report to the legislature not later than December 1 of each even-numbered year that includes information on:

(1) the number of petitions for nondisclosure of criminal history record information and orders of nondisclosure of criminal history record information received by the department in each of the previous two years;

(2) the actions taken by the department with respect to the petitions and orders received;

(3) the costs incurred by the department in taking those actions; and

(4) the number of persons who are the subject of an order of nondisclosure of criminal history record information and who became the subject of criminal charges for an offense committed after the order was issued.

Sec. 411.0775. Admissibility and Use of Certain Criminal History Record Information in Subsequent Criminal Proceeding.

Notwithstanding any other law, criminal history record information that is related to a conviction and is the subject of an order of nondisclosure of criminal history record information under this subchapter may be:

(1) admitted into evidence during the trial of any subsequent offense if the information is admissible under the Texas Rules of Evidence or another law; or

(2) disclosed to a prosecuting attorney for a criminal justice purpose.

SUBCHAPTER F CRIMINAL HISTORY RECORD INFORMATION

Sec. 411.0971. Access to Criminal History Record Information: Teacher Retirement System of Texas.

(a) The Teacher Retirement System of Texas is entitled to obtain from the department, the Federal Bureau of Investigation Criminal Justice Information Services Division, or another law enforcement agency criminal history record information maintained by the department, division, or agency that relates to a person who:

(1) is an employee or an applicant for employment with the retirement system;

(2) is a consultant, contract employee, independent contractor, intern, or volunteer for the retirement system or an applicant to serve in one of those positions;

(3) proposes to enter into a contract with or has a contract with the retirement system to perform services for or supply goods to the retirement system; or

(4) is an employee or subcontractor, or an applicant to be an employee or subcontractor, of a contractor that provides services to the retirement system.

(b) Criminal history record information obtained by the Teacher Retirement System of Texas under Subsection (a) may not be released or disclosed to any person except:

(1) on court order;

(2) with the consent of the person who is the subject of the criminal history record information; or

(3) to a federal agency as required by federal law or executive order.

(c) The Teacher Retirement System of Texas shall destroy criminal history record information obtained under this section after the information is used for the purposes authorized by this section.

(d) The Teacher Retirement System of Texas may provide a copy of the criminal history record information obtained from the department, the Federal Bureau of Investigation Criminal Justice Information Services Division, or other law enforcement agency to the individual who is the subject of the information.

(e) The failure or refusal of an employee or applicant to provide the following on request constitutes good cause for dismissal or refusal to hire:

(1) a complete set of fingerprints;

(2) a true and complete name; or

(3) other information necessary for a law enforcement entity to obtain criminal history record information.

Sec. 411.135. Access to Certain Information by Public.

(a) Any person is entitled to obtain from the department:

(1) any information described as public information under Chapter 62, Code of Criminal Procedure, including, to the extent available, a recent photograph of each person subject to registration under that chapter; and

(2) criminal history record information maintained by the department that relates to the conviction of or a grant of deferred adjudication to a person for any criminal offense, including arrest information that relates to the conviction or grant of deferred adjudication.

(b) The department by rule shall design and implement a system to respond to electronic inquiries and other inquiries for information described by Subsection (a).

(c) A person who obtains information from the department under Subsection (a) may:

(1) use the information for any purpose; or

(2) release the information to any other person.

SUBCHAPTER G
DNA DATABASE SYSTEM

Sec. 411.141. Definitions.

In this subchapter:

(1) "CODIS" means the FBI's Combined DNA Index System. The term includes the national DNA index system sponsored by the FBI.

(2) "Conviction" includes conviction by a jury or a court, a guilty plea, a plea of nolo contendere, or a finding of not guilty by reason of insanity.

(3) "Criminal justice agency" means:

(A) a federal or state agency that is engaged in the administration of criminal justice under a statute or executive order and that allocates a substantial part of its annual budget to the administration of criminal justice;

(B) a secure correctional facility as defined by Section 1.07, Penal Code; or

(C) a community supervision and corrections department, a parole office, or a local juvenile probation department or parole office.

(4) "DNA" means deoxyribonucleic acid.

(5) "DNA database" means one or more databases that contain forensic DNA records maintained by the director.

(6) "DNA laboratory" means a laboratory that performs forensic DNA analysis on samples or specimens derived from a human body, physical evidence, or a crime scene. The term includes a department crime laboratory facility that conducts forensic DNA analysis.

(7) "DNA record" means the results of a forensic DNA analysis performed by a DNA laboratory. The term includes a DNA profile and related records, which may include a code or other identifying number referenced to a separate database to locate:

(A) the originating entity; and

(B) if known, the name and other personally identifying information concerning the individual who is the subject of the analysis.

(8) "DNA sample" means a blood sample or other biological sample or specimen provided by an individual under this subchapter or submitted to the director under this subchapter for DNA analysis or storage.

(9) "FBI" means the Federal Bureau of Investigation.

(10) "Forensic analysis" has the meaning assigned by Article 38.35, Code of Criminal Procedure.

(11) "Institution of higher education" has the meaning assigned by Section 61.003, Education Code.

(12) "Penal institution" has the meaning assigned by Section 1.07, Penal Code.

Sec. 411.142. DNA Database.

(a) The director shall record DNA data and establish and maintain a computerized database that serves as the central depository in the state for DNA records.

(b) The director may maintain the DNA database in the department's crime laboratory in Austin or another suitable location.

(c) The director may receive, analyze, store, and destroy a DNA record or DNA sample for the purposes described by Section 411.143. If a DNA sample was collected solely for the purpose of creating a DNA record, the director may destroy the sample after any test results associated with the sample are entered into the DNA database and the CODIS database.

(d) The DNA database must be capable of classifying, matching, and storing the results of analyses of DNA.

(e) The director, with advice from the Department of Information Resources, shall develop biennial plans to:

(1) improve the reporting and accuracy of the DNA database; and

(2) develop and maintain a monitoring system capable of identifying inaccurate or incomplete information.

(f) The DNA database must be compatible with the national DNA identification index system (CODIS) used by the FBI to the extent required by the FBI to permit the useful exchange and storage of DNA records or information derived from those records.

(g) The DNA database may contain DNA records for the following:

(1) an individual described by this subchapter, including Section 411.1471, 411.148, or 411.154;

(2) a biological specimen of a deceased victim of a crime;

(3) a biological specimen that is legally obtained in the investigation of a crime, regardless of origin;

(4) results of testing ordered by a court under this subchapter, Article 64.03, Code of Criminal Procedure, or other law permitting or requiring the creation of a DNA record;

(5) an unidentified missing person, or unidentified skeletal remains or body parts;

(6) a close biological relative of a person who has been reported missing to a law enforcement agency;

(7) a person at risk of becoming lost, such as a child or a person declared by a court to be mentally incapacitated, if the record is required by court order or a parent, conservator, or guardian of the person consents to the record; or

(8) an unidentified person, if the record does not contain personal identifying information.

(h) The director shall establish standards for DNA analysis by the DNA laboratory that meet or exceed the current standards for quality assurance and proficiency testing for forensic DNA analysis issued by the FBI. The DNA database may contain only DNA records of DNA analyses performed according to the standards adopted by the director.

Sec. 411.1425. Grant Funds.

The director shall apply for any available federal grant funds applicable to the creation and storage of DNA records of persons arrested for certain offenses.

Sec. 411.143. Purposes.

(a) The principal purpose of the DNA database is to assist a federal, state, or local criminal justice agency in the investigation or prosecution of sex-related offenses or other offenses in which biological evidence is recovered.

(b) In criminal cases, the purposes of the DNA database are only for use in the investigation of an offense, the exclusion or identification of suspects or offenders, and the prosecution or defense of the case.

(c) Other purposes of the database include:

(1) assisting in the recovery or identification of human remains from a disaster or for humanitarian purposes;

(2) assisting in the identification of living or deceased missing persons;

(3) if personal identifying information is removed:

(A) establishing a population statistics database; and

(B) assisting in identification research, forensic validation studies, or forensic protocol development; and

(4) retesting to validate or update the original analysis or assisting in database or DNA laboratory quality control.

(d) The information contained in the DNA database may not be collected, analyzed, or stored to obtain information about human physical traits or predisposition for disease unless the purpose for obtaining the information is related to a purpose described by this section.

(e) The director may not store a name or other personal identifying information in the CODIS database. A file or reference number to another information system may be included in the CODIS database only if the director determines the information is necessary to:

(1) generate an investigative lead or exclusion;

(2) support the statistical interpretation of a test result; or

(3) allow for the successful implementation of the DNA database.

(f) Except as provided by this subchapter, the DNA database may not include criminal history record information.

(g) A party contracting to carry out a function of another entity under this subchapter shall comply with:

(1) a requirement imposed by this subchapter on the other entity, unless the party or other entity is exempted by the director; and

(2) any additional requirement imposed by the director on the party.

Sec. 411.144. Regulation of DNA Laboratories; Penalties.

(a) The director by rule shall establish procedures for a DNA laboratory or criminal justice agency in the collection, preservation, shipment, analysis, and use of a DNA sample for forensic DNA analysis in a manner that permits the exchange of DNA evidence between DNA laboratories and the use of the evidence in a criminal case.

(b) A DNA laboratory or criminal justice agency shall follow the procedures:

(1) established by the director under this section; and

(2) specified by the FBI, including use of comparable test procedures, laboratory equipment, supplies, and computer software.

(c) The director may at any reasonable time enter and inspect the premises or audit the records, reports, procedures, or other quality assurance matters of any DNA laboratory that:

(1) provides DNA records to the director under this subchapter; or

(2) conducts forensic analysis.

(d) A DNA laboratory conducting a forensic DNA analysis under this subchapter shall:

(1) forward the DNA record of the analysis to the director at the department's crime laboratory or another location as required by the director; and

(2) comply with this subchapter and rules adopted under this subchapter.

(e) The director is the Texas liaison for DNA data, records, evidence, and other related matters between:

(1) the FBI; and

(2) a DNA laboratory or a criminal justice agency.

(f) The director may:

(1) conduct DNA analyses; or

(2) contract with a laboratory, state agency, private entity, or institution of higher education for services to perform DNA analyses for the director.

Sec. 411.145. Fees.

(a) The director may collect a reasonable fee under this subchapter for:

(1) the DNA analysis of a DNA sample submitted voluntarily to the director; or

(2) providing population statistics data or other appropriate research data.

(b) If the director provides a copy of an audit or other report made under this subchapter, the director may charge $6 for the copy, in addition to any other cost permitted under Chapter 552 or a rule adopted under that chapter.

(c) A fee collected under this section shall be deposited in the state treasury to the credit of the state highway fund, and money deposited to the state highway fund under this section and under Chapter 42A, Code of Criminal Procedure, may be used only to defray the cost of administering this subchapter.

Sec. 411.146. DNA Samples.

(a) The director may not accept a DNA record or DNA sample collected from an individual who at the time of collection is alive, unless the director reasonably believes the sample was submitted voluntarily or as required by this subchapter and is:

(1) a blood sample collected in a medically approved manner by:

(A) a physician, registered nurse, licensed vocational nurse, licensed clinical laboratory technologist; or

(B) an individual who is trained to properly collect blood samples under this subchapter; or

(2) a specimen other than a blood sample collected:

(A) in a manner approved by the director by rule adopted under this section; and

(B) by an individual who is trained to properly collect the specimen under this subchapter.

(b) The director shall provide at no cost to a person collecting a DNA sample as described by Subsection (a) the collection kits, labels, report forms, instructions, and training for collection of DNA samples under this section.

(c) (1) The director shall adopt rules regarding the collection, preservation, shipment, and analysis of a DNA database sample under this subchapter, including the type of sample or specimen taken.

(2) A criminal justice agency permitted or required to collect a DNA sample for forensic DNA analysis under this subchapter:

(A) may collect the sample or contract with a phlebotomist, laboratory, state agency, private entity, or institution of higher education for services to collect the sample at the time determined by the agency; and

(B) shall:

(i) preserve each sample collected until it is forwarded to the director under Subsection (d); and

(ii) maintain a record of the collection of the sample.

(d) A criminal justice agency that collects a DNA sample under this section shall send the sample to:

(1) the director at the department's crime laboratory; or

(2) another location as required by the director by rule.

(e) A DNA laboratory may analyze a DNA sample collected under this section only:

(1) to type the genetic markers contained in the sample;

(2) for criminal justice or law enforcement purposes; or

(3) for other purposes described by this subchapter.

(f) If possible, a second DNA sample must be collected from an individual in a criminal investigation if forensic DNA evidence is necessary for use as substantive evidence in the investigation, prosecution, or defense of a case.

Sec. 411.147. Access to DNA Database Information.

(a) The director by rule shall establish procedures:

(1) to prevent unauthorized access to the DNA database; and

(2) to release from the DNA database a DNA sample, analysis, record, or other information maintained under this subchapter.

(b) The director may adopt rules relating to the internal disclosure, access, or use of a sample or DNA record in a DNA laboratory.

(c) The director may release a DNA sample, analysis, or record only:

(1) to a criminal justice agency for criminal justice or law enforcement identification purposes;

(2) for a judicial proceeding, if otherwise admissible under law;

(3) for criminal defense purposes to a defendant, if related to the case in which the defendant is charged or released from custody under Article 17.47, Code of Criminal Procedure, or other court order; or

(4) for another purpose:

(A) described in Section 411.143; or

(B) required under federal law as a condition for obtaining federal funding.

(d) The director may release a record of the number of requests made for a defendant's individual DNA record and the name of the requesting person.

(e) A criminal justice agency may have access to a DNA sample for a law enforcement purpose through:

(1) the agency's laboratory; or

(2) a laboratory used by the agency.

(f) The director shall maintain a record of requests made under this section.

Sec. 411.1471. DNA Records of Persons Arrested for or Convicted of Certain Offenses.

(a) This section applies to a defendant who is:

(1) arrested for a felony prohibited under any of the following Penal Code sections:

(A) Section 19.02;
(B) Section 19.03;
(C) Section 20.03;
(D) Section 20.04;
(E) Section 20.05;
(F) Section 20.06;
(G) Section 20A.02;
(H) Section 20A.03;
(I) Section 21.02;
(J) Section 21.11;
(K) Section 22.01;
(L) Section 22.011;
(M) Section 22.02;
(N) Section 22.021;
(O) Section 25.02;
(P) Section 29.02;
(Q) Section 29.03;
(R) Section 30.02;
(S) Section 31.03;
(T) Section 43.03;
(U) Section 43.04;
(V) Section 43.05;
(W) Section 43.25; or
(X) Section 43.26; or

(2) convicted of an offense:

(A) under Title 5, Penal Code, other than an offense described by Subdivision (1), that is punishable as a Class A misdemeanor or any higher category of offense, except for an offense punishable as a Class A misdemeanor under Section 22.05, Penal Code; or

(B) under Section 21.08, 25.04, 43.021, or 43.24, Penal Code.

(b) A law enforcement agency arresting a defendant described by Subsection (a)(1), immediately after fingerprinting the defendant and at the same location as the fingerprinting occurs, shall require the defendant to provide one or more specimens for the purpose of creating a DNA record.

(b-1) After a defendant described by Subsection (a)(3) is convicted, the court shall require the defendant to provide to a law enforcement agency one or more specimens for the purpose of creating a DNA record.

(c) [Repealed]

(d) The director by rule shall require law enforcement agencies taking a specimen under this section to preserve the specimen and maintain a record of the collection of the specimen. A law enforcement agency taking a specimen under this section may use any method to take the specimen approved by the director in the rule adopted under this subsection. The rule adopted by the director must prohibit a law enforcement agency from taking a blood sample for the purpose of creating a DNA record under this section. The agency may either send the

Government Code

specimen to the director or send to the director an analysis of the sample performed at a laboratory chosen by the agency and approved by the director.

(e) Notwithstanding Subsection (d), on acquittal of a defendant described by Subsection (a)(1) or dismissal of the case against the defendant, or after an individual has been granted relief in accordance with a writ of habeas corpus that is based on a court finding or determination that the person is actually innocent of a crime for which the person was sentenced, the law enforcement agency taking the specimen shall immediately destroy the record of the collection of the specimen, and the department shall destroy the specimen and the record of its receipt. As soon as practicable after the acquittal of the defendant or the dismissal of the case, the court shall provide notice of the acquittal or dismissal to the applicable law enforcement agency and the department.

(f) A defendant who provides a DNA sample under this section is not required to provide a DNA sample under Section 411.148 of this code or under Article 42A.352, Code of Criminal Procedure, unless the attorney representing the state in the prosecution of the felony offense that makes Section 411.148 or Article 42A.352 applicable to the defendant establishes to the satisfaction of the director that the interests of justice or public safety require that the defendant provide additional samples.

Sec. 411.1472. DNA Records of Persons Placed on Community Supervision for Certain Offenses [Repealed].

Repealed by Acts 2005, 79th Leg., ch. 1224 (H.B. 1068), § 19(1), effective September 1, 2005.

Sec. 411.1473. DNA Records of Certain Registered Sex Offenders.

(a) This section applies only to a person who is required to register under Chapter 62, Code of Criminal Procedure.

(b) The department by rule shall require a law enforcement agency serving as a person's primary registration authority under Chapter 62, Code of Criminal Procedure, to:

(1) take one or more specimens from a person described by Subsection (a) for the purpose of creating a DNA record; and

(2) preserve the specimen and maintain a record of the collection of the specimen.

(c) A law enforcement agency taking a specimen under this section may either send the specimen to the director or send to the director an analysis of the specimen performed by a laboratory chosen by the agency and approved by the director.

(d) A law enforcement agency is not required to take and a person is not required to provide a specimen under this section if the person is required to and has provided a specimen under this chapter or other law.

Sec. 411.148. Mandatory DNA Record.

(a) This section applies to:

(1) an individual, other than a juvenile, who is:

(A) ordered by a magistrate or court to provide a DNA sample under Section 411.154 or other law, including as part of an order granting community supervision to the individual; or

(B) confined in a penal institution operated by or under contract with the Texas Department of Criminal Justice; or

(2) a juvenile who, following an adjudication for conduct constituting a felony, is:

(A) confined in a facility operated by or under contract with the Texas Juvenile Justice Department; or

(B) placed on probation, if the conduct constitutes a felony described by Section 54.0409, Family Code.

(b) An individual described by Subsection (a) shall provide one or more DNA samples for the purpose of creating a DNA record.

(c) A criminal justice agency shall collect a sample ordered by a magistrate or court in compliance with the order.

(d) If an individual described by Subsection (a)(1)(B) is received into custody by the Texas Department of Criminal Justice, that department shall collect the sample from the individual during the diagnostic process or at another time determined by the Texas Department of Criminal Justice. If an individual described by Subsection (a)(2)(A) is received into custody by the Texas Juvenile Justice Department, that department shall collect the sample from the individual during the initial examination or at another time it determines. If an individual who is required under this section or other law to provide a DNA sample is in the custody or under the supervision of another criminal justice agency, such as a community supervision and corrections department, a parole office, or a local juvenile probation department or parole office, that agency shall collect the sample from the individual at a time determined by the agency.

(e) [Repealed by Acts 2009, 81st Leg., ch. 1209 (S.B. 727), § 11, effective September 1, 2009.]

(f) The Texas Department of Criminal Justice shall notify the director that an individual described by Subsection (a)(1)(B) is to be released from custody not earlier than the 120th day before the individual's statutory release date and not later than the 90th day before the individual's statutory release date. An individual described by Subsection (a)(1)(B) may not be held past the individual's statutory release date if the individual fails or refuses to provide a DNA sample under this section. The Texas Department of Criminal Justice may take lawful administrative action, including disciplinary action resulting in the loss of good conduct time, against an individual described by Subsection (a)(1)(B) who refuses to provide a sample under this section. In this subsection, "statutory release date" means the date on which an individual is discharged from the individual's controlling sentence.

(f-1) The Texas Juvenile Justice Department shall notify the director that an individual described by Subsection (a)(2)(A) is to be released from custody not earlier than the 120th day before the individual's release date.

(f-2) The Texas Department of Criminal Justice and the Texas Juvenile Justice Department, in consultation with the director, shall determine the form of the notification described by Subsections (f) and (f-1).

(g) A medical staff employee of a criminal justice agency may collect a voluntary sample from an individual at any time.

(h) An employee of a criminal justice agency may use force against an individual required to provide a DNA sample under this section when and to the degree the employee reasonably believes the force is immediately necessary to collect the sample.

(i) (1) The Texas Department of Criminal Justice as soon as practicable shall cause a sample to be collected from an individual described by Subsection (a)(1)(B) if:

(A) the individual is confined in another penal institution after sentencing and before admission to the department; and

(B) the department determines that the individual is likely to be released before being admitted to the department.

(2) The administrator of the other penal institution shall cooperate with the Texas Department of Criminal Justice as necessary to allow the Texas Department of Criminal Justice to perform its duties under this subsection.

(j) (1) The Texas Juvenile Justice Department as soon as practicable shall cause a sample to be collected from an individual described by Subsection (a)(2)(A) if:

(A) the individual is detained in another juvenile detention facility after adjudication and before admission to the Texas Juvenile Justice Department; and

(B) the Texas Juvenile Justice Department determines the individual is likely to be released before being admitted to that department.

(2) The administrator of the other juvenile detention facility shall cooperate with the Texas Juvenile Justice Department as necessary to allow that department to perform its duties under this subsection.

(k) When a criminal justice agency of this state agrees to accept custody or supervision of an individual from another state or jurisdiction under an interstate compact or a reciprocal agreement with a local, county, state, or federal agency, the criminal justice agency that agrees to accept custody or supervision of the individual shall collect a DNA sample under this subchapter if the individual was convicted of or adjudicated as having engaged in conduct constituting a felony and is otherwise required to provide a DNA sample under this section.

(*l*) If, in consultation with the director, it is determined that an acceptable sample has already been received from an individual, additional samples are not required unless requested by the director.

Sec. 411.1481. DNA Records: Capital Murder [Repealed].

Repealed by Acts 2005, 79th Leg., ch. 1224 (H.B. 1068), § 19(1), effective September 1, 2005.

Sec. 411.149. Voluntary DNA Record.

An individual, including an individual required to provide a DNA sample under this subchapter, may at any time voluntarily provide or cause to be provided to a criminal justice agency a sample to be forwarded to the director for the purpose of creating a DNA record under this subchapter.

Sec. 411.150. DNA Records of Certain Juveniles [Repealed].

Repealed by Acts 2007, 80th Leg., ch. 760 (H.B. 3295), § 5, effective June 15, 2007.

Sec. 411.151. Expunction or Removal of DNA Records.

(a) The director shall expunge a DNA record of an individual from a DNA database if the person:

(1) notifies the director in writing that the DNA record has been ordered to be expunged under this section or Chapter 55, Code of Criminal Procedure, and provides the director with a certified copy of the court order that expunges the DNA record; or

(2) provides the director with a certified copy of a court order issued under Subchapter C-1, Chapter 58, Family Code, that seals the juvenile record of the adjudication that resulted in the DNA record.

(b) A person may petition for the expunction of a DNA record under the procedures established under Article 55.02, Code of Criminal Procedure, if the person is entitled to the expunction of records relating to the offense to which the DNA record is related under Article 55.01, Code of Criminal Procedure.

(c) This section does not require the director to expunge a record or destroy a sample if the director determines that the individual is otherwise required to submit a DNA sample under this subchapter.

(d) The director by rule may permit administrative removal of a record, sample, or other information erroneously included in a database.

(e) The department's failure to expunge a DNA record as required by this section may not serve as the sole grounds for a court in a criminal proceeding to exclude evidence based on or derived from the contents of that record.

Sec. 411.152. Rules.

(a) The director may adopt rules permitted by this subchapter that are necessary to administer or enforce this subchapter but shall adopt a rule expressly required by this subchapter.

(b) The director by rule may release or permit access to information to confirm or deny whether an individual has a preexisting record under this subchapter. After receiving a request regarding an individual whose DNA record has been expunged or removed under Section 411.151, the director shall deny the preexisting record.

(c) The director by rule may exempt:

(1) a laboratory conducting non-human forensic DNA analysis from a rule adopted under this subchapter; and

(2) certain categories of individuals from a requirement to provide an additional sample after an acceptable DNA record exists for the individual.

(d) The director by rule may determine whether a DNA sample complies with a collection provision of this subchapter.

Sec. 411.153. Confidentiality of DNA Records.

(a) A DNA record stored in the DNA database is confidential and is not subject to disclosure under the public information law, Chapter 552.

(b) A person commits an offense if the person knowingly discloses to an unauthorized recipient information in a DNA record or information related to a DNA analysis of a sample collected under this subchapter.

(c) An offense under this section is a state jail felony.

(d) A violation under this section constitutes official misconduct.

Sec. 411.1531. Segregation of Records [Repealed].

Repealed by Acts 2005, 79th Leg., ch. 1224 (H.B. 1068), § 19(1), effective September 1, 2005.

Sec. 411.1532. Confidentiality of Preconfinement DNA Records [Repealed].

Repealed by Acts 2005, 79th Leg., ch. 1224 (H.B. 1068), § 19(1), effective September 1, 2005.

Sec. 411.154. Enforcement by Court Order.

(a) On the request of the director, a district or county attorney or the attorney general may petition a district court for an order requiring a person to:

(1) comply with this subchapter or a rule adopted under this subchapter; or

(2) refrain from acting in violation of this subchapter or a rule adopted under this subchapter.

(b) The court may issue an order requiring a person:

(1) to act in compliance with this subchapter or a rule adopted under this subchapter;

(2) to refrain from acting in violation of this subchapter or a rule adopted under this subchapter;

(3) to provide a DNA sample; or

(4) if the person has already provided a DNA sample, to provide another sample if good cause is shown.

(c) An order issued under this section is appealable as a criminal matter and if appealed is to be reviewed under an abuse of discretion standard.

SUBCHAPTER H LICENSE TO CARRY A HANDGUN

Sec. 411.171. Definitions.

In this subchapter:

(1) "Approved online course provider" means a person who is certified by the department to offer in an online format the classroom instruction part

of the handgun proficiency course and to administer the associated written exam.

(2) "Chemically dependent person" means a person who frequently or repeatedly becomes intoxicated by excessive indulgence in alcohol or uses controlled substances or dangerous drugs so as to acquire a fixed habit and an involuntary tendency to become intoxicated or use those substances as often as the opportunity is presented.

(3) [Repealed by Acts 2015, 84th Leg., ch. 437 (H.B. 910), § 50, effective January 1, 2016.]

(4) "Convicted" means an adjudication of guilt or, except as provided in Section 411.1711, an order of deferred adjudication entered against a person by a court of competent jurisdiction whether or not the imposition of the sentence is subsequently probated and the person is discharged from community supervision. The term does not include an adjudication of guilt or an order of deferred adjudication that has been subsequently:

(A) expunged;

(B) pardoned under the authority of a state or federal official; or

(C) otherwise vacated, set aside, annulled, invalidated, voided, or sealed under any state or federal law.

(4-a) "Federal judge" means:

(A) a judge of a United States court of appeals;

(B) a judge of a United States district court;

(C) a judge of a United States bankruptcy court; or

(D) a magistrate judge of a United States district court.

(4-b) "State judge" means:

(A) the judge of an appellate court, a district court, or a county court at law of this state;

(B) an associate judge appointed under Chapter 201, Family Code; or

(C) a justice of the peace.

(5) "Handgun" has the meaning assigned by Section 46.01, Penal Code.

(6) "Intoxicated" has the meaning assigned by Section 49.01, Penal Code.

(7) "Qualified handgun instructor" means a person who is certified to instruct in the use of handguns by the department.

(8) [Repealed by Acts 1999, 76th Leg., ch. 62 (S.B. 1368), § 9.02(a), effective September 1, 1999.]

Sec. 411.1711. Certain Exemptions from Convictions.

A person is not convicted, as that term is defined by Section 411.171, if an order of deferred adjudication was entered against the person on a date not less than 10 years preceding the date of the person's application for a license under this subchapter unless the order of deferred adjudication was entered against the person for:

(1) a felony offense under:

(A) Title 5, Penal Code;

(B) Chapter 29, Penal Code;

(C) Section 25.07 or 25.072, Penal Code; or

(D) Section 30.02, Penal Code, if the offense is punishable under Subsection (c)(2) or (d) of that section; or

(2) an offense under the laws of another state if the offense contains elements that are substantially similar to the elements of an offense listed in Subdivision (1).

Sec. 411.172. Eligibility.

(a) A person is eligible for a license to carry a handgun if the person:

(1) is a legal resident of this state for the six-month period preceding the date of application under this subchapter or is otherwise eligible for a license under Section 411.173(a);

(2) is at least 21 years of age;

(3) has not been convicted of a felony;

(4) is not charged with the commission of a Class A or Class B misdemeanor or equivalent offense, or of an offense under Section 42.01, Penal Code, or equivalent offense, or of a felony under an information or indictment;

(5) is not a fugitive from justice for a felony or a Class A or Class B misdemeanor or equivalent offense;

(6) is not a chemically dependent person;

(7) is not incapable of exercising sound judgment with respect to the proper use and storage of a handgun;

(8) has not, in the five years preceding the date of application, been convicted of a Class A or Class B misdemeanor or equivalent offense or of an offense under Section 42.01, Penal Code, or equivalent offense;

(9) is fully qualified under applicable federal and state law to purchase a handgun;

(10) has not been finally determined to be delinquent in making a child support payment administered or collected by the attorney general;

(11) has not been finally determined to be delinquent in the payment of a tax or other money collected by the comptroller, the tax collector of a political subdivision of the state, or any agency or subdivision of the state;

(12) is not currently restricted under a court protective order or subject to a restraining order affecting the spousal relationship, other than a restraining order solely affecting property interests;

Government Code

(13) has not, in the 10 years preceding the date of application, been adjudicated as having engaged in delinquent conduct violating a penal law of the grade of felony; and

(14) has not made any material misrepresentation, or failed to disclose any material fact, in an application submitted pursuant to Section 411.174.

(b) For the purposes of this section, an offense under the laws of this state, another state, or the United States is:

(1) except as provided by Subsection (b-1), a felony if the offense, at the time the offense is committed:

(A) is designated by a law of this state as a felony;

(B) contains all the elements of an offense designated by a law of this state as a felony; or

(C) is punishable by confinement for one year or more in a penitentiary; and

(2) a Class A misdemeanor if the offense is not a felony and confinement in a jail other than a state jail felony facility is affixed as a possible punishment.

(b-1) An offense is not considered a felony for purposes of Subsection (b) if, at the time of a person's application for a license to carry a handgun, the offense:

(1) is not designated by a law of this state as a felony; and

(2) does not contain all the elements of any offense designated by a law of this state as a felony.

(c) An individual who has been convicted two times within the 10-year period preceding the date on which the person applies for a license of an offense of the grade of Class B misdemeanor or greater that involves the use of alcohol or a controlled substance as a statutory element of the offense is a chemically dependent person for purposes of this section and is not qualified to receive a license under this subchapter. This subsection does not preclude the disqualification of an individual for being a chemically dependent person if other evidence exists to show that the person is a chemically dependent person.

(d) For purposes of Subsection (a)(7), a person is incapable of exercising sound judgment with respect to the proper use and storage of a handgun if the person:

(1) has been diagnosed by a licensed physician as suffering from a psychiatric disorder or condition that causes or is likely to cause substantial impairment in judgment, mood, perception, impulse control, or intellectual ability;

(2) suffers from a psychiatric disorder or condition described by Subdivision (1) that:

(A) is in remission but is reasonably likely to redevelop at a future time; or

(B) requires continuous medical treatment to avoid redevelopment;

(3) has been diagnosed by a licensed physician, determined by a review board or similar authority, or declared by a court to be incompetent to manage the person's own affairs; or

(4) has entered in a criminal proceeding a plea of not guilty by reason of insanity.

(e) The following constitutes evidence that a person has a psychiatric disorder or condition described by Subsection (d)(1):

(1) involuntary psychiatric hospitalization;

(2) psychiatric hospitalization;

(3) inpatient or residential substance abuse treatment in the preceding five-year period;

(4) diagnosis in the preceding five-year period by a licensed physician that the person is dependent on alcohol, a controlled substance, or a similar substance; or

(5) diagnosis at any time by a licensed physician that the person suffers or has suffered from a psychiatric disorder or condition consisting of or relating to:

(A) schizophrenia or delusional disorder;

(B) bipolar disorder;

(C) chronic dementia, whether caused by illness, brain defect, or brain injury;

(D) dissociative identity disorder;

(E) intermittent explosive disorder; or

(F) antisocial personality disorder.

(f) Notwithstanding Subsection (d), a person who has previously been diagnosed as suffering from a psychiatric disorder or condition described by Subsection (d) or listed in Subsection (e) is not because of that disorder or condition incapable of exercising sound judgment with respect to the proper use and storage of a handgun if the person provides the department with a certificate from a licensed physician whose primary practice is in the field of psychiatry stating that the psychiatric disorder or condition is in remission and is not reasonably likely to develop at a future time.

(g) Notwithstanding Subsection (a)(2), a person who is at least 18 years of age but not yet 21 years of age is eligible for a license to carry a handgun if the person:

(1) is a member or veteran of the United States armed forces, including a member or veteran of the reserves or national guard;

(2) was discharged under honorable conditions, if discharged from the United States armed forces, reserves, or national guard; and

(3) meets the other eligibility requirements of Subsection (a) except for the minimum age required by federal law to purchase a handgun.

(h) The issuance of a license to carry a handgun to a person eligible under Subsection (g) does not affect the person's ability to purchase a handgun or ammunition under federal law.

(i) Notwithstanding Subsection (a)(2), a person who is at least 18 years of age but not yet 21 years of age is eligible for a license to carry a handgun if the person:

(1) is protected under:

(A) an active protective order issued under:

(i) Title 4, Family Code; or

(ii) Subchapter A, Chapter 7B, Code of Criminal Procedure; or

(B) an active magistrate's order for emergency protection under Article 17.292, Code of Criminal Procedure; and

(2) meets the other eligibility requirements of Subsection (a) except for the minimum age required by federal law to purchase a handgun.

Sec. 411.173. Nonresident License.

(a) The department by rule shall establish a procedure for a person who meets the eligibility requirements of this subchapter other than the residency requirement established by Section 411.172(a)(1) to obtain a license under this subchapter if the person is a legal resident of another state or if the person relocates to this state with the intent to establish residency in this state. The procedure must include payment of a fee in an amount sufficient to recover the average cost to the department of obtaining a criminal history record check and investigation on a nonresident applicant. A license issued in accordance with the procedure established under this subsection:

(1) remains in effect until the license expires under Section 411.183; and

(2) may be renewed under Section 411.185.

(a-1) [Repealed by Acts 2005, 79th Leg., ch. 915 (H.B. 225), § 4, effective September 1, 2005.]

(b) The governor shall negotiate an agreement with any other state that provides for the issuance of a license to carry a handgun under which a license issued by the other state is recognized in this state or shall issue a proclamation that a license issued by the other state is recognized in this state if the attorney general of the State of Texas determines that a background check of each applicant for a license issued by that state is initiated by state or local authorities or an agent of the state or local authorities before the license is issued. For purposes of this subsection, "background check" means a search of the National Crime Information Center database and the Interstate Identification Index maintained by the Federal Bureau of Investigation.

(c) The attorney general of the State of Texas shall annually:

(1) submit a report to the governor, lieutenant governor, and speaker of the house of representatives listing the states the attorney general has determined qualify for recognition under Subsection (b); and

(2) review the statutes of states that the attorney general has determined do not qualify for recognition under Subsection (b) to determine the changes to their statutes that are necessary to qualify for recognition under that subsection.

(d) The attorney general of the State of Texas shall submit the report required by Subsection (c)(1) not later than January 1 of each calendar year.

Sec. 411.1735. Protective Order Designation.

(a) Notwithstanding any other provision of this subchapter, a person who establishes eligibility for a license to carry a handgun under Section 411.172(i) may only hold a license under this subchapter that bears a protective order designation on the face of the license.

(b) A person described by this section must submit a copy of the applicable court order described by Section 411.172(i)(1) with the application materials described by Section 411.174. The person's application is not considered complete for purposes of this subchapter unless the application includes the documentation and materials required by this section.

(c) Notwithstanding Section 411.183, a license that bears a protective order designation under this section expires on the earlier of:

(1) the date on which the applicable court order described by Section 411.172(i)(1) is rescinded or expires; or

(2) the 22nd birthday of the license holder.

(d) A holder of a license with a protective order designation under this section who becomes 21 years of age may apply for a license under this subchapter that does not bear the designation by using the renewal procedure under Section 411.185, regardless of whether the license that bears the designation has expired or is about to expire.

(e) The director shall adopt rules establishing a process by which the department periodically verifies a license holder's eligibility for a license to carry a handgun under Section 411.172(i) if the license holder's license bears a protective order designation under this section. The rules may specify different intervals at which the department must verify the license holder's eligibility based on the court order used to satisfy the eligibility requirement described by Section 411.172(i)(1).

Sec. 411.174. Application.

(a) An applicant for a license to carry a handgun must submit to the director's designee described by Section 411.176:

(1) a completed application on a form provided by the department that requires only the information listed in Subsection (b);

(2) one or more photographs of the applicant that meet the requirements of the department;

(3) a certified copy of the applicant's birth certificate or certified proof of age;

(4) proof of residency in this state;

(5) two complete sets of legible and classifiable fingerprints of the applicant taken by a person appropriately trained in recording fingerprints who is employed by a law enforcement agency or by a private entity designated by a law enforcement agency as an entity qualified to take fingerprints of an applicant for a license under this subchapter;

(6) a nonrefundable application and license fee of $40 paid to the department;

(7) evidence of handgun proficiency, in the form and manner required by the department;

(8) an affidavit signed by the applicant stating that the applicant:

(A) has read and understands each provision of this subchapter that creates an offense under the laws of this state and each provision of the laws of this state related to use of deadly force; and

(B) fulfills all the eligibility requirements listed under Section 411.172; and

(9) a form executed by the applicant that authorizes the director to make an inquiry into any noncriminal history records that are necessary to determine the applicant's eligibility for a license under Section 411.172(a).

(b) An applicant must provide on the application a statement of the applicant's:

(1) full name and place and date of birth;

(2) race and sex;

(3) residence and business addresses for the preceding five years;

(4) hair and eye color;

(5) height and weight;

(6) driver's license number or identification certificate number issued by the department;

(7) criminal history record information of the type maintained by the department under this chapter, including a list of offenses for which the applicant was arrested, charged, or under an information or indictment and the disposition of the offenses; and

(8) history, if any, of treatment received by, commitment to, or residence in:

(A) a drug or alcohol treatment center licensed to provide drug or alcohol treatment under the laws of this state or another state, but only if the treatment, commitment, or residence occurred during the preceding five years; or

(B) a psychiatric hospital.

(b-1) The application must provide space for the applicant to:

(1) list any military service that may qualify the applicant to receive a license with a veteran's designation under Section 411.179(e); and

(2) include proof required by the department to determine the applicant's eligibility to receive that designation.

(c) The department shall distribute on request a copy of this subchapter and application materials.

(d) The department may not request or require an applicant to provide the applicant's social security number as part of an application under this section.

Sec. 411.1741. Voluntary Contribution to Fund for Veterans' Assistance.

(a) When a person applies for an original or renewal license to carry a handgun under this subchapter, the person may make a voluntary contribution in any amount to the fund for veterans' assistance established by Section 434.017.

(b) The department shall:

(1) include space on the first page of each application for an original or renewal license to carry a handgun that allows a person applying for an original or renewal license to carry a handgun to indicate the amount that the person is voluntarily contributing to the fund; and

(2) provide an opportunity for the person to contribute to the fund during the application process for an original or renewal license to carry a handgun on the department's Internet website.

(c) The department shall send any contribution made under this section to the comptroller for deposit in the state treasury to the credit of the fund for veterans' assistance not later than the 14th day of each month. Before sending the money to the fund, the department may deduct money equal to the amount of reasonable expenses for administering this section.

Sec. 411.175. Procedures for Submitting Fingerprints.

The department shall establish procedures for the submission of legible and classifiable fingerprints by an applicant for a license under this subchapter who:

(1) is required to submit those fingerprints to the department, including an applicant under Section 411.199, 411.1991, or 411.201; and

(2) resides in a county having a population of 46,000 or less and does not reside within a 25-mile radius of a facility with the capability to process digital or electronic fingerprints.

Sec. 411.176. Review of Application Materials.

(a) On receipt of application materials by the department at its Austin headquarters, the department shall conduct the appropriate criminal history record check of the applicant through its computerized criminal history system. Not later than the 30th day after the date the department receives the application materials, the department shall forward the materials to the director's designee in the geographical area of the applicant's residence so that the designee may conduct the investigation described by Subsection (b). For purposes of this section, the director's designee may be a noncommissioned employee of the department.

(b) The director's designee as needed shall conduct an additional criminal history record check of the applicant and an investigation of the applicant's local official records to verify the accuracy of the application materials. The director's designee may access any records necessary for purposes of this subsection. The scope of the record check and the investigation are at the sole discretion of the department, except that the director's designee shall complete the record check and investigation not later than the 60th day after the date the department receives the application materials. The department shall send a fingerprint card to the Federal Bureau of Investigation for a national criminal history check of the applicant. On completion of the investigation, the director's designee shall return all materials and the result of the investigation to the appropriate division of the department at its Austin headquarters.

(c) The director's designee may submit to the appropriate division of the department, at the department's Austin headquarters, along with the application materials a written recommendation for disapproval of the application, accompanied by an affidavit stating personal knowledge or naming persons with personal knowledge of a ground for denial under Section 411.172. The director's designee may also submit the application and the recommendation that the license be issued.

(d) On receipt at the department's Austin headquarters of the application materials and the result of the investigation by the director's designee, the department shall conduct any further record check or investigation the department determines is necessary if a question exists with respect to the accuracy of the application materials or the eligibility of the applicant, except that the department shall complete the record check and investigation not later than the 180th day after the date the department receives the application materials from the applicant.

Sec. 411.177. Issuance or Denial of License.

(a) The department shall issue a license to carry a handgun to an applicant if the applicant meets all the eligibility requirements and submits all the application materials. The department shall administer the licensing procedures in good faith so that any applicant who meets all the eligibility requirements and submits all the application materials shall receive a license. The department may not deny an application on the basis of a capricious or arbitrary decision by the department.

(b) Except as otherwise provided by Subsection (b-1), the department shall, not later than the 60th day after the date of the receipt by the director's designee of the completed application materials:

(1) issue the license;

(2) notify the applicant in writing that the application was denied:

(A) on the grounds that the applicant failed to qualify under the criteria listed in Section 411.172;

(B) based on the affidavit of the director's designee submitted to the department under Section 411.176(c); or

(C) based on the affidavit of the qualified handgun instructor submitted to the department under Section 411.188(k); or

(3) notify the applicant in writing that the department is unable to make a determination regarding the issuance or denial of a license to the applicant within the 60-day period prescribed by this subsection and include in that notification an explanation of the reason for the inability and an estimation of the additional period the department will need to make the determination.

(b-1) If the applicant submits with the completed application materials an application for a designation under Section 411.184, the department shall, without charging an additional fee, expedite the application. Not later than the 10th day after the receipt of the materials under this subsection, the department shall:

(1) issue the license with the designation; or

(2) notify the applicant in writing that the applicant is not eligible for the designation under Section 411.184 and the application for the license will be processed in the regular course of business.

(b-2) Notwithstanding Subsection (b-1), if the department determines that the applicant is eligible for the designation under Section 411.184 but is unable to quickly make a determination regarding the issuance or denial of a license to the applicant, the department shall provide written notice of that fact to the applicant and shall include in that notice an explanation of the reason for the inability and an estimation of the additional period the department will need to make the determination.

(b-3) The director shall adopt policies for expedited processing under Subsection (b-1).

(c) Failure of the department to issue or deny a license for a period of more than 30 days after the department is required to act under Subsection (b) constitutes denial, regardless of whether the applicant was eligible for expedited processing of the application under Subsection (b-1).

(d) A license issued under this subchapter is effective from the date of issuance.

Sec. 411.178. Notice to Local Law Enforcement.

On request of a local law enforcement agency, the department shall notify the agency of the licenses that have been issued to license holders who reside in the county in which the agency is located.

Sec. 411.179. Form of License.

(a) **[As amended by Acts 2021, 87th Leg., chs. XXX (HB 918) and XXX (SB 1134)]** The department by rule shall adopt the form of the license. A license must include:

(1) a number assigned to the license holder by the department;

(2) a statement of the period for which the license is effective;

(3) a photograph of the license holder;

(4) the license holder's full name, date of birth, hair and eye color, height, weight, and signature;

(5) the license holder's residence address or, as provided by Subsection (d), the street address of the courthouse in which the license holder or license holder's spouse or parent serves as a federal judge or the license holder serves as a state judge;

(6) the number of a driver's license or an identification certificate issued to the license holder by the department;

(7) the designation "VETERAN" if required under Subsection (e); and

(8) if applicable, a protective order designation under Section 411.1735.

(a) **[As amended by Acts 2021, 87th Leg., chs. XXX (HB 2675) and XXX (SB 1134)]** The department by rule shall adopt the form of the license. A license must include:

(1) a number assigned to the license holder by the department;

(2) a statement of the period for which the license is effective;

(3) a photograph of the license holder;

(4) the license holder's full name, date of birth, hair and eye color, height, weight, and signature;

(5) the license holder's residence address or, as provided by Subsection (d), the street address of the courthouse in which the license holder or license holder's spouse or parent serves as a federal judge or the license holder serves as a state judge;

(6) the number of a driver's license or an identification certificate issued to the license holder by the department;

(7) the designation "VETERAN" if required under Subsection (e); and

(8) any at-risk designation for which the license holder has established eligibility under Section 411.184.

(b) [Repealed by Acts 2013, 83rd Leg., ch. 1302 (H.B. 3142), § 14(2), effective June 14, 2013.]

(c) In adopting the form of the license under Subsection (a), the department shall establish a procedure for the license of a qualified handgun instructor or of the attorney general or a judge, justice, United States attorney, assistant United States attorney, assistant attorney general, prosecuting attorney, or assistant prosecuting attorney, as described by Section 46.15(a)(4), (6), or (7), Penal Code, to indicate on the license the license holder's status as a qualified handgun instructor or as the attorney general or a judge, justice, United States attorney, assistant United States attorney, assistant attorney general, district attorney, criminal district attorney, or county attorney. In establishing the procedure, the department shall require sufficient documentary evidence to establish the license holder's status under this subsection.

(d) In adopting the form of the license under Subsection (a), the department shall establish a procedure for the license of a federal judge, including a federal bankruptcy judge, a marshal of the United States Marshals Service, a United States attorney, a state judge, or a family member of a federal judge, including a federal bankruptcy judge, a marshal of the United States Marshals Service, a United States attorney, or a state judge to omit the license holder's residence address and to include, in lieu of that address, the street address of the courthouse in which the license holder or license holder's spouse or parent serves as a federal judge, including a federal bankruptcy judge, a marshal of the United States Marshals Service, a United States attorney, or a state judge. In establishing the procedure, the department shall require sufficient documentary evidence to establish the license holder's status as a federal judge, including a federal bankruptcy judge, a marshal of the United States Marshals Service, a United States attorney, or a state judge, or a family member of a federal judge, including a federal bankruptcy judge, a marshal of the United States Marshals Service, a United States attorney, or a state judge.

(e) In this subsection, "veteran" has the meaning assigned by Section 411.1951. The department shall include the designation "VETERAN" on the face of any original, duplicate, modified, or renewed license under this subchapter or on the reverse side of the license, as determined by the department, if the license is issued to a veteran who:

(1) requests the designation; and

(2) provides proof sufficient to the department of the veteran's military service and honorable discharge.

(f) In this section, "family member" has the meaning assigned by Section 31.006, Finance Code.

Sec. 411.180. Notification of Denial, Revocation, or Suspension of License; Review.

(a) The department shall give written notice to each applicant for a handgun license of any denial, revocation, or suspension of that license. Not later than the 30th day after the notice is received by the applicant, according to the records of the department, the applicant or license holder may request a hearing on the denial, revocation, or suspension. The applicant must make a written request for a hearing addressed to the department at its Austin address. The request for hearing must reach the department in Austin prior to the 30th day after the date of receipt of the written notice. On receipt of a request for hearing from a license holder or applicant, the department shall promptly schedule a hearing in the appropriate justice court in the county of residence of the applicant or license holder. The justice court shall conduct a hearing to review the denial, revocation, or suspension of the license. In a proceeding under this section, a justice of the peace shall act as an administrative hearing officer. A hearing under this section is not subject to Chapter 2001 (Administrative Procedure Act). A district attorney or county attorney, the attorney general, or a designated member of the department may represent the department.

(b) The department, on receipt of a request for hearing, shall file the appropriate petition in the justice court selected for the hearing and send a copy of that petition to the applicant or license holder at the address contained in departmental records. A hearing under this section must be scheduled within 30 days of receipt of the request for a hearing. The hearing shall be held expeditiously but in no event more than 60 days after the date that the applicant or license holder requested the hearing. The date of the hearing may be reset on the motion of either party, by agreement of the parties, or by the court as necessary to accommodate the court's docket.

(c) The justice court shall determine if the denial, revocation, or suspension is supported by a preponderance of the evidence. Both the applicant or license holder and the department may present evidence. The court shall affirm the denial, revocation, or suspension if the court determines that denial, revocation, or suspension is supported by a preponderance of the evidence. If the court determines that the denial, revocation, or suspension is not supported by a preponderance of the evidence, the court shall order the department to immediately issue or return the license to the applicant or license holder.

(d) A proceeding under this section is subject to Chapter 105, Civil Practice and Remedies Code, relating to fees, expenses, and attorney's fees.

(e) A party adversely affected by the court's ruling following a hearing under this section may appeal the ruling by filing within 30 days after the ruling a petition in a county court at law in the county in which the applicant or license holder resides or, if there is no county court at law in the county, in the county court of the county. A person who appeals under this section must send by certified mail a copy of the person's petition, certified by the clerk of the court in which the petition is filed, to the appropriate division of the department at its Austin headquarters. The trial on appeal shall be a trial de novo without a jury. A district or county attorney or the attorney general may represent the department.

(f) A suspension of a license may not be probated.

(g) If an applicant or a license holder does not petition the justice court, a denial becomes final and a revocation or suspension takes effect on the 30th day after receipt of written notice.

(h) The department may use and introduce into evidence certified copies of governmental records to establish the existence of certain events that could result in the denial, revocation, or suspension of a license under this subchapter, including records regarding convictions, judicial findings regarding mental competency, judicial findings regarding chemical dependency, or other matters that may be established by governmental records that have been properly authenticated.

(i) This section does not apply to a suspension of a license under Section 85.022, Family Code, or Article 17.292, Code of Criminal Procedure.

Sec. 411.181. Notice of Change of Information; Duplicate License.

(a) If a person who is a current license holder moves from any residence address stated on the license, if the name of the person is changed by marriage or otherwise, or if the person's status becomes inapplicable for purposes of the information required to be displayed on the license under Section 411.179, the person shall, not later than the 30th day after the date of the address, name, or status change, notify the department and provide the department with the number of the person's license and, as applicable, the person's:

(1) former and new addresses;

(2) former and new names; or

(3) former and new status.

(a-1) If a license holder whose license will expire under Section 411.183(a)(1)(B) or (b)(1)(B) is granted an extension for the license holder's lawful presence in the United States as determined by the United States agency responsible for citizenship and immigration in compliance with federal law, the license holder may apply to the department for a duplicate license with an updated expiration date by providing to the department the person's license number and evidence of the extension. The duplicate license must provide for an expiration date, calculated in accordance with Section 411.183(a) or (b), as applicable, that takes into account the extension of the period for which the license holder may be lawfully present in the United States.

(b) If the name of the license holder is changed by marriage or otherwise, or if the person's status becomes inapplicable as described by Subsection (a), the person shall apply for a duplicate license. The duplicate license must reflect the person's current name, residence address, and status.

(c) If a license holder moves from the address stated on the license, the person shall apply for a duplicate license.

(d) The department shall charge a license holder a fee of $25 for a duplicate license.

(e) The department shall make the forms available on request.

(f) On request of a local law enforcement agency, the department shall notify the agency of changes made under Subsection (a) by license holders who reside in the county in which the agency is located.

(g) If a license is lost, stolen, or destroyed, the license holder shall apply for a duplicate license not later than the 30th day after the date of the loss, theft, or destruction of the license.

(h) If a license holder is required under this section to apply for a duplicate license and the license expires not later than the 60th day after the date of the loss, theft, or destruction of the license, the applicant may renew the license with the modified information included on the new license. The applicant must pay only the nonrefundable renewal fee.

(i) A license holder whose application fee for a duplicate license under this section is dishonored or reversed may reapply for a duplicate license at any time, provided the application fee and a dishonored payment charge of $25 is paid by cashier's check or money order made payable to the "Texas Department of Public Safety."

Sec. 411.182. Notice.

(a) For the purpose of a notice required by this subchapter, the department may assume that the address currently reported to the department by the applicant or license holder is the correct address.

(b) A written notice meets the requirements under this subchapter if the notice is sent by certified mail to the current address reported by the applicant or license holder to the department.

(c) If a notice is returned to the department because the notice is not deliverable, the department may give notice by publication once in a newspaper of general interest in the county of the applicant's or license holder's last reported address. On the 31st day after the date the notice is published, the department may take the action proposed in the notice.

Sec. 411.183. Expiration.

(a) A license issued under this subchapter expires on:

(1) the earlier of:

(A) the first birthday of the license holder occurring after the fourth anniversary of the date of issuance; or

(B) the expiration of the license holder's lawful presence in the United States as determined by the United States agency responsible for citizenship and immigration in compliance with federal law; or

(2) the first anniversary of the date of issuance, if there is no definite expiration date for the applicant's lawful presence in the United States.

(b) A renewed license expires on:

(1) the earlier of:

(A) the license holder's birthdate, five years after the date of the expiration of the previous license; or

(B) the expiration of the license holder's lawful presence in the United States as determined by the United States agency responsible for citizenship and immigration in compliance with federal law; or

(2) the first anniversary of the date of renewal, if there is no definite expiration date for the applicant's lawful presence in the United States.

(c) Except as otherwise provided by Section 411.181(a-1), a duplicate license expires on the date the license that was duplicated would have expired.

(d) A modified license expires on the date the license that was modified would have expired.

(e) [Expired pursuant to Acts 1997, 75th Leg., ch. 165 (S.B. 898), § 10.01, effective January 1, 2005.]

Sec. 411.184. At-Risk Designation.

(a) The department shall develop a procedure for persons who are at increased risk of becoming a victim of violence to:

(1) obtain a handgun license on an expedited basis, if the person is not already a license holder; and

(2) qualify for an at-risk designation on the license.

(b) A person is eligible for an at-risk designation under this section if:

(1) the person is protected under, or a member of the person's household or family is protected under:

(A) a temporary restraining order or temporary injunction issued under Subchapter F, Chapter 6, Family Code;

(B) a temporary ex parte order issued under Chapter 83, Family Code;

(C) a protective order issued under Chapter 85, Family Code;

(D) a protective order issued under Chapter 7B, Code of Criminal Procedure; or

(E) a magistrate's order for emergency protection issued under Article 17.292, Code of Criminal Procedure; or

(2) the person participates in the address confidentiality program under Subchapter B, Chapter 58, Code of Criminal Procedure.

(c) The director may adopt rules to accept alternative documentation not described by Subsection (b) that shows that the person is at increased risk of becoming a victim of violence.

(d) A person may receive an at-risk designation under this section if the person submits to the department, in the form and manner provided by the department:

(1) an application for the designation;

(2) evidence of the increased risk of becoming a victim of violence, as provided by Subsection (b) or rules adopted under Subsection (c); and

(3) any other information that the department may require.

(e) A license holder may apply for the designation under this section by making an application for a duplicate license. A person who is not a license holder may apply for the designation with the person's application for an original license to carry a handgun.

(f) A person with a designation granted under this section shall annually certify that the person continues to qualify for the designation and shall submit to the department any information the department requires to verify the person's continuing eligibility. A person who no longer qualifies for the designation under this section shall immediately notify the department.

(g) If based on the information received under Subsection (f) the department determines that the person is no longer eligible for a designation under this section, the department shall notify the person and issue to the person a duplicate license without a designation.

(h) On receipt of a duplicate license without a designation under Subsection (g), the license holder shall return the license with the designation to the department.

(i) The department may not charge a fee for issuing a duplicate license with a designation under this section or for issuing a duplicate license without a designation if the person no longer qualifies for the designation. If a person applies for a designation at the same time the person applies for an original license under this subchapter, the department may charge only the licensing fee.

Sec. 411.185. License Renewal Procedure.

(a) To renew a license, a license holder must, on or before the date the license expires, submit to the department by mail or, in accordance with the procedure adopted under Subsection (f), on the Internet:

(1) a renewal application on a form provided by the department;

(2) payment of a nonrefundable renewal fee of $40; and

(3) the informational form described by Subsection (c) signed or electronically acknowledged by the applicant.

(b) The director by rule shall adopt a renewal application form requiring an update of the information on the original completed application.

(c) The director by rule shall adopt an informational form that describes state law regarding the use of deadly force and the places where it is unlawful for the holder of a license issued under this subchapter to carry a handgun. An applicant for a renewed license must sign and return the informational form to the department by mail or acknowledge the form electronically on the Internet according to the procedure adopted under Subsection (f).

(d) Not later than the 60th day before the expiration date of the license, the department shall mail to each license holder a written notice of the expiration of the license, a renewal application form, and the informational form described by Subsection (c).

(e) The department shall renew the license of a license holder who meets all the eligibility requirements to continue to hold a license and submits all the renewal materials described by Subsection (a). Not later than the 45th day after receipt of the renewal materials, the department shall issue the renewed license or notify the license holder in writing that the department denied the license holder's renewal application.

(f) The director by rule shall adopt a procedure by which a license holder who satisfies the eligibility requirements to continue to hold a license may submit the renewal materials described by Subsection (a) by mail or on the Internet.

(g) The department may not request or require a license holder to provide the license holder's social security number to renew a license under this section.

Sec. 411.186. Revocation.

(a) The department shall revoke a license under this section if the license holder:

(1) was not entitled to the license at the time it was issued;

(2) made a material misrepresentation or failed to disclose a material fact in an application submitted under this subchapter;

(3) subsequently becomes ineligible for a license under Section 411.172, unless the sole basis for the ineligibility is that the license holder is charged with the commission of a Class A or Class B misdemeanor or equivalent offense, or of an offense under Section 42.01, Penal Code, or equivalent offense, or of a felony under an information or indictment;

(4) is determined by the department to have engaged in conduct constituting a reason to suspend a license listed in Section 411.187(a) after the person's license has been previously suspended twice for the same reason; or

(5) submits an application fee that is dishonored or reversed if the applicant fails to submit a cashier's check or money order made payable to the "Department of Public Safety of the State of Texas" in the amount of the dishonored or reversed fee, plus $25, within 30 days of being notified by the department that the fee was dishonored or reversed.

(b) If a peace officer believes a reason listed in Subsection (a) to revoke a license exists, the officer shall prepare an affidavit on a form provided by the department stating the reason for the revocation of the license and giving the department all of the information available to the officer at the time of the preparation of the form. The officer shall attach the officer's reports relating to the license holder to the form and send the form and attachments to the appropriate division of the department at its Austin headquarters not later than the fifth working day after the date the form is prepared. The officer shall send a copy of the form and the attachments to the license holder. If the license holder has not surrendered the license or the license was not seized as evidence, the license holder shall surrender the license to the appropriate division of the department not later than the 10th day after the date the license holder receives the notice of revocation from the department, unless the license holder requests a hearing from the department. The license holder may request that the justice court in the justice court precinct in which the license holder resides review the revocation as provided by Section 411.180. If a request is made for the justice court to review the revocation and hold a hearing, the license holder shall surrender the license on the date an order of revocation is entered by the justice court.

(c) A license holder whose license is revoked for a reason listed in Subsections (a)(1)-(4) may reapply as a new applicant for the issuance of a license under this subchapter after the second anniversary of the date of the revocation if the cause for revocation does not exist on the date of the second anniversary. If the cause for revocation exists on the date of the second anniversary after the date of revocation, the license holder may not apply for a new license until the cause for revocation no longer exists and has not existed for a period of two years.

(d) A license holder whose license is revoked under Subsection (a)(5) may reapply for an original or renewed license at any time, provided the application fee and a dishonored payment charge of $25 is paid by cashier's check or money order made payable to the "Texas Department of Public Safety."

Sec. 411.187. Suspension of License.

(a) The department shall suspend a license under this section if the license holder:

(1) is charged with the commission of a Class A or Class B misdemeanor or equivalent offense, or of an offense under Section 42.01, Penal Code, or

equivalent offense, or of a felony under an information or indictment;

(2) fails to notify the department of a change of address, name, or status as required by Section 411.181;

(3) commits an act of family violence and is the subject of an active protective order rendered under Title 4, Family Code; or

(4) is arrested for an offense involving family violence or an offense under Section 42.072, Penal Code, and is the subject of an order for emergency protection issued under Article 17.292, Code of Criminal Procedure.

(b) If a peace officer believes a reason listed in Subsection (a) to suspend a license exists, the officer shall prepare an affidavit on a form provided by the department stating the reason for the suspension of the license and giving the department all of the information available to the officer at the time of the preparation of the form. The officer shall attach the officer's reports relating to the license holder to the form and send the form and the attachments to the appropriate division of the department at its Austin headquarters not later than the fifth working day after the date the form is prepared. The officer shall send a copy of the form and the attachments to the license holder. If the license holder has not surrendered the license or the license was not seized as evidence, the license holder shall surrender the license to the appropriate division of the department not later than the 10th day after the date the license holder receives the notice of suspension from the department unless the license holder requests a hearing from the department. The license holder may request that the justice court in the justice court precinct in which the license holder resides review the suspension as provided by Section 411.180. If a request is made for the justice court to review the suspension and hold a hearing, the license holder shall surrender the license on the date an order of suspension is entered by the justice court.

(c) The department shall suspend a license under this section:

(1) for 30 days, if the person's license is subject to suspension for a reason listed in Subsection (a) (2), (3), or (4), except as provided by Subdivision (2);

(2) for not less than one year and not more than three years, if the person's license:

(A) is subject to suspension for a reason listed in Subsection (a), other than the reason listed in Subsection (a)(1); and

(B) has been previously suspended for the same reason;

(3) until dismissal of the charges, if the person's license is subject to suspension for the reason listed in Subsection (a)(1); or

(4) for the duration of or the period specified by:

(A) the protective order issued under Title 4, Family Code, if the person's license is subject to suspension for the reason listed in Subsection (a) (5); or

(B) the order for emergency protection issued under Article 17.292, Code of Criminal Procedure, if the person's license is subject to suspension for the reason listed in Subsection (a)(6).

Sec. 411.1871. Notice of Suspension or Revocation of Certain Licenses.

The department shall notify the Texas Commission on Law Enforcement Officer Standards and Education if the department takes any action against the license of a person identified by the commission as a person certified under Section 1701.260, Occupations Code, including suspension or revocation.

Sec. 411.188. Handgun Proficiency Requirement.

(a) The director by rule shall establish minimum standards for handgun proficiency and shall develop a course to teach handgun proficiency and examinations to measure handgun proficiency. The course to teach handgun proficiency is required for each person who seeks to obtain a license and must contain training sessions divided into two parts. One part of the course must be classroom instruction and the other part must be range instruction and an actual demonstration by the applicant of the applicant's ability to safely and proficiently use a handgun. An applicant must be able to demonstrate, at a minimum, the degree of proficiency that is required to effectively operate a handgun. The department shall distribute the standards, course requirements, and examinations on request to any qualified handgun instructor or approved online course provider seeking to administer the course or a part of the course as described by Subsection (b).

(b) Only qualified handgun instructors may administer the range instruction part of the handgun proficiency course. A qualified handgun instructor or approved online course provider may administer the classroom instruction part of the handgun proficiency course. The classroom instruction part of the course must include not less than four hours and not more than six hours of instruction on:

(1) the laws that relate to weapons and to the use of deadly force;

(2) handgun use and safety, including use of restraint holsters and methods to ensure the secure carrying of openly carried handguns;

(3) nonviolent dispute resolution; and

(4) proper storage practices for handguns with an emphasis on storage practices that eliminate the possibility of accidental injury to a child.

(c) An approved online course provider shall administer the classroom instruction part of the handgun proficiency course in an online format. A course administered online must include not less than four hours and not more than six hours of instruction.

(d) Except as provided by Subsection (e), only a qualified handgun instructor may administer the proficiency examination to obtain a license. The proficiency examination must include:

(1) a written section on the subjects listed in Subsection (b); and

(2) a physical demonstration of proficiency in the use of one or more handguns and in handgun safety procedures.

(d-1) A qualified handgun instructor shall require an applicant who successfully completed an online version of the classroom instruction part of the handgun proficiency course to complete not less than one hour but not more than two hours of the range instruction part of the handgun proficiency course before allowing a physical demonstration of handgun proficiency as described by Subsection (d)(2).

(e) An approved online course provider may administer online through a secure portal the written portion of the proficiency examination described by Subsection (d)(1).

(f) The department shall develop and distribute directions and materials for course instruction, test administration, and recordkeeping. All test results shall be sent to the department, and the department shall maintain a record of the results.

(g) A person who wishes to obtain a license to carry a handgun must apply in person to a qualified handgun instructor to take the range instruction part of the handgun proficiency course and to demonstrate handgun proficiency as required by the department. A person must apply in person to a qualified handgun instructor or online to an approved online course provider, as applicable, to take the classroom instruction part of the handgun proficiency course.

(h) [Repealed by Acts 2013, 83rd Leg., ch. 1302 (H.B. 3142), § 14(4), effective June 14, 2013.]

(i) A certified firearms instructor of the department may monitor any class or training presented by a qualified handgun instructor. A qualified handgun instructor shall cooperate with the department in the department's efforts to monitor the presentation of training by the qualified handgun instructor.

(j) A qualified handgun instructor or approved online course provider shall make available for inspection to the department any and all records maintained by the instructor or course provider under this subchapter. The qualified handgun instructor or approved online course provider shall keep a record of all information required by department rule.

(k) A qualified handgun instructor may submit to the department a written recommendation for disapproval of the application for a license or modification of a license, accompanied by an affidavit stating personal knowledge or naming persons with personal knowledge of facts that lead the instructor to believe that an applicant does not possess the required handgun proficiency. The department may use a written recommendation submitted under this subsection as the basis for denial of a license only if the department determines that the recommendation is made in good faith and is supported by a preponderance of the evidence. The department shall make a determination under this subsection not later than the 45th day after the date the department receives the written recommendation. The 60-day period in which the department must take action under Section 411.177(b) is extended one day for each day a determination is pending under this subsection.

Sec. 411.1881. Exemption from Instruction for Certain Persons.

(a) Notwithstanding any other provision of this subchapter, a person may not be required to complete the range instruction portion of a handgun proficiency course to obtain a license issued under this subchapter if the person:

(1) is currently serving in or is honorably discharged from:

(A) the army, navy, air force, coast guard, or marine corps of the United States or an auxiliary service or reserve unit of one of those branches of the armed forces; or

(B) the Texas military forces, as defined by Section 437.001; and

(2) has, within the 10 years preceding the date of the person's application for the license, completed as part of the person's service with the armed forces or Texas military forces:

(A) a course of training in firearm proficiency or familiarization; or

(B) a range qualification process for firearm usage.

(b) The director by rule shall adopt a procedure by which a license holder who is exempt under Subsection (a) from the range instruction portion of the handgun proficiency requirement may submit a form demonstrating the license holder's qualification for an exemption under that subsection. The form must provide sufficient information to allow the department to verify whether the license holder qualifies for the exemption.

Sec. 411.1882. Evidence of Handgun Proficiency for Certain Persons.

(a) A person who is serving in this state as the attorney general or as a judge or justice of a federal court, as an active judicial officer as defined by Section 411.201, as a United States attorney, assistant United States attorney, assistant attorney general, district attorney, assistant district attorney, criminal district attorney, assistant criminal district attorney, county attorney, or assistant county attorney, as a supervision officer as defined by Article 42A.001, Code of Criminal Procedure, or as a juvenile probation officer may establish handgun proficiency for the purposes of this subchapter by obtaining from a handgun proficiency instructor approved by the Texas Commission on Law Enforcement for purposes of Section 1702.1675, Occupations Code, a sworn statement that indicates that the person, during the 12-month period preceding the date of the person's application to the department, demonstrated to the instructor proficiency in the use of handguns.

(b) The director by rule shall adopt a procedure by which a person described under Subsection (a) may submit a form demonstrating the person's qualification for an exemption under that subsection. The form must provide sufficient information to allow the department to verify whether the person qualifies for the exemption.

(c) A license issued under this section automatically expires on the six-month anniversary of the date the person's status under Subsection (a) becomes inapplicable. A license that expires under this subsection may be renewed under Section 411.185.

Sec. 411.189. Handgun Proficiency Certificate [Repealed].

Repealed by Acts 2009, 81st Leg., ch. 1146 (H.B. 2730), § 11.25, effective September 1, 2009.

Sec. 411.190. Qualified Handgun Instructors and Approved Online Course Providers.

(a) The director may certify as a qualified handgun instructor a person who:

(1) is certified by the Texas Commission on Law Enforcement or under Chapter 1702, Occupations Code, to instruct others in the use of handguns;

(2) regularly instructs others in the use of handguns and has graduated from a handgun instructor school that uses a nationally accepted course designed to train persons as handgun instructors; or

(3) is certified by the National Rifle Association of America as a handgun instructor.

(a-1) The director may certify as an approved online course provider a person who has:

(1) at least three years of experience in providing online instruction;

(2) experience working with governmental entities; and

(3) direct knowledge of handgun training.

(b) In addition to the qualifications described by Subsection (a) or (a-1), as appropriate, a qualified handgun instructor or approved online course provider must be qualified to instruct persons in:

(1) the laws that relate to weapons and to the use of deadly force;

(2) handgun use, proficiency, and safety, including use of restraint holsters and methods to ensure the secure carrying of openly carried handguns;

(3) nonviolent dispute resolution; and

(4) proper storage practices for handguns, including storage practices that eliminate the possibility of accidental injury to a child.

(c) In the manner applicable to a person who applies for a license to carry a handgun, the department shall conduct a background check of a person who applies for certification as a qualified handgun instructor or approved online course provider. If the background check indicates that the applicant for certification would not qualify to receive a handgun license, the department may not certify the applicant as a qualified handgun instructor or approved online course provider. If the background check indicates that the applicant for certification would qualify to receive a handgun license, the department shall provide handgun instructor or online course provider training to the applicant. The applicant shall pay a fee of $100 to the department for the training. The applicant must take and successfully complete the training offered by the department and pay the training fee before the department may certify the applicant as a qualified handgun instructor or approved online course provider. The department shall issue a license to carry a handgun under the authority of this subchapter to any person who is certified as a qualified handgun instructor or approved online course provider and who pays to the department a fee of

$40 in addition to the training fee. The department by rule may prorate or waive the training fee for an employee of another governmental entity.

(d) The certification of a qualified handgun instructor or approved online course provider expires on the second anniversary after the date of certification. To renew a certification, the qualified handgun instructor or approved online course provider must pay a fee of $100 and take and successfully complete the retraining courses required by department rule.

(d-1) The department shall ensure that an applicant may renew certification under Subsection (d) from any county in this state by using an online format to complete the required retraining courses if:

(1) the applicant is renewing certification for the first time; or

(2) the applicant completed the required retraining courses in person the previous time the applicant renewed certification.

(e) After certification, a qualified handgun instructor or approved online course provider may conduct training for applicants for a license under this subchapter.

(f) If the department determines that a reason exists to revoke, suspend, or deny a license to carry a handgun with respect to a person who is a qualified handgun instructor or approved online course provider or an applicant for certification as a qualified handgun instructor or approved online course provider, the department shall take that action against the person's:

(1) license to carry a handgun if the person is an applicant for or the holder of a license issued under this subchapter; and

(2) certification as a qualified handgun instructor or approved online course provider.

Sec. 411.1901. School Safety Certification for Qualified Handgun Instructors.

(a) The department shall establish a process to enable qualified handgun instructors certified under Section 411.190 to obtain an additional certification in school safety. The process must include a school safety certification course that provides training in the following:

(1) the protection of students;

(2) interaction of license holders with first responders;

(3) tactics for denying an intruder entry into a classroom or school facility; and

(4) methods for increasing a license holder's accuracy with a handgun while under duress.

(b) The school safety certification course under Subsection (a) must include not less than 15 hours and not more than 20 hours of instruction.

(c) A qualified handgun instructor certified in school safety under this section may provide school safety training, including instruction in the subjects listed under Subsection (a), to employees of a school district or an open-enrollment charter school who hold a license to carry a handgun issued under this subchapter.

(d) The department shall establish a fee in an amount that is sufficient to cover the costs of the school safety certification under this section.

(e) The department may adopt rules to administer this section.

Sec. 411.191. Review of Denial, Revocation, or Suspension of Certification As Qualified Handgun Instructor or Approved Online Course Provider.

The procedures for the review of a denial, revocation, or suspension of a license under Section 411.180 apply to the review of a denial, revocation, or suspension of certification as a qualified handgun instructor or approved online course provider. The notice provisions of this subchapter relating to denial, revocation, or suspension of handgun licenses apply to the proposed denial, revocation, or suspension of a certification of a qualified handgun instructor or approved online course provider or an applicant for certification as a qualified handgun instructor or approved online course provider.

Sec. 411.192. Confidentiality of Records.

(a) The department shall disclose to a criminal justice agency information contained in its files and records regarding whether a named individual or any individual named in a specified list is licensed under this subchapter. Information on an individual subject to disclosure under this section includes the individual's name, date of birth, gender, race, zip code, telephone number, e-mail address, and Internet website address. Except as otherwise provided by this section and by Section 411.193, all other records maintained under this subchapter are confidential and are not subject to mandatory disclosure under the open records law, Chapter 552.

(b) An applicant or license holder may be furnished a copy of disclosable records regarding the applicant or license holder on request and the payment of a reasonable fee.

(c) The department shall notify a license holder of any request that is made for information relating to the license holder under this section and provide the name of the agency making the request.

(d) The department shall make public and distribute to the public at no cost lists of individuals who are certified as qualified handgun instructors by the department and who request to be included as provided by Subsection (e) and lists of approved online course providers. The department shall include on the lists each individual's name, telephone number, e-mail address, and Internet website address. The department shall make the lists available on the department's Internet website.

(e) An individual who is certified as a qualified handgun instructor may request in writing that the department disclose all or part of the information described by Subsection (d) regarding the individual. The department shall include all or part of the individual's information on the list as requested.

Sec. 411.193. Statistical Report.

The department shall make available, on request and payment of a reasonable fee to cover costs of copying, a statistical report that includes the number of licenses issued, denied, revoked, or suspended by the department during the preceding month, listed by age, gender, race, and zip code of the applicant or license holder.

Sec. 411.194. Reduction of Certain Fees Due to Indigency.

(a) Notwithstanding any other provision of this subchapter, if the department determines that an applicant is indigent, the department shall reduce by:

(1) 50 percent any fee required for the issuance of a duplicate or modified license under this subchapter; and

(2) $5 any fee required for the issuance of a renewed license under this subchapter.

(b) The department shall require an applicant requesting a reduction of a fee to submit proof of indigency with the application materials.

(c) For purposes of this section, an applicant is indigent if the applicant's income is not more than 100 percent of the applicable income level established by the federal poverty guidelines.

Sec. 411.195. Reduction of Certain Fees for Senior Citizens.

Notwithstanding any other provision of this subchapter, if an applicant for the license is 60 years of age or older, the department shall reduce by:

(1) 50 percent any fee required for the issuance of a duplicate or modified license under this subchapter; and

(2) $5 any fee required for the issuance of a renewed license under this subchapter.

Sec. 411.1951. Waiver or Reduction of Fees for Members or Veterans of United States Armed Forces.

(a) In this section, "veteran" means a person who:

(1) has served in:

(A) the army, navy, air force, coast guard, or marine corps of the United States;

(B) the Texas military forces as defined by Section 437.001; or

(C) an auxiliary service of one of those branches of the armed forces; and

(2) has been honorably discharged from the branch of the service in which the person served.

(b) Notwithstanding any other provision of this subchapter, the department shall waive any fee required for the issuance of an original, duplicate, modified, or renewed license under this subchapter if the applicant for the license is:

(1) a member of the United States armed forces, including a member of the reserves, national guard, or state guard; or

(2) a veteran who, within 365 days preceding the date of the application, was honorably discharged from the branch of service in which the person served.

(c) Notwithstanding any other provision of this subchapter, if the applicant is a veteran who, more than 365 days preceding the date of the application, was honorably discharged from the branch of the service in which the applicant served:

(1) the applicant must pay a fee of $25 for the issuance of an original or renewed license under this subchapter; and

(2) the department shall reduce by 50 percent any fee required of the applicant for a duplicate or modified license under this subchapter.

Sec. 411.1952. Reduction of Fees for Employees of Texas Department of Criminal Justice. [Repealed]

Sec. 411.1953. Reduction of Fees for Community Supervision and Corrections Department Officers and Juvenile Probation Officers.

Notwithstanding any other provision of this subchapter, an applicant who is serving in this state as

Government Code

a supervision officer, as defined by Article 42A.001, Code of Criminal Procedure, or as a juvenile probation officer shall pay a fee of $25 for the issuance of an original or renewed license under this subchapter.

Sec. 411.1954. Waiver of Certain Fees for Certain Applicants Who Hold Cardiopulmonary Resuscitation Certification.

(a) Notwithstanding any other provision of this subchapter, the department shall waive any fee required for the issuance of an original or renewed license under this subchapter if at the time of the application the applicant for the license submits to the department satisfactory evidence that the applicant:

(1) holds a current certification in cardiopulmonary resuscitation issued by the American Heart Association, the American Red Cross, or another nationally recognized association; and

(2) is not required to hold the certification described by Subdivision (1) as a condition of obtaining or maintaining employment or an occupational license.

(b) For purposes of Subsection (a)(2), "occupational license" means a license, certificate, registration, permit, or other form of authorization that a person must obtain to practice or engage in a particular business, occupation, or profession.

Sec. 411.196. Method of Payment.

A person may pay a fee required by this subchapter by cash, credit card, personal check, cashier's check, or money order. A person who pays a fee required by this subchapter by cash must pay the fee in person. Checks or money orders must be made payable to the "Texas Department of Public Safety." A person whose payment for a fee required by this subchapter is dishonored or reversed must pay any future fees required by this subchapter by cashier's check or money order made payable to the "Texas Department of Public Safety." A fee received by the department under this subchapter is nonrefundable.

Sec. 411.197. Rules.

The director shall adopt rules to administer this subchapter.

Sec. 411.198. Law Enforcement Officer Alias Handgun License.

(a) On written approval of the director, the department may issue to a law enforcement officer an alias license to carry a handgun to be used in supervised activities involving criminal investigations.

(b) [Repealed.]

Sec. 411.199. Honorably Retired Peace Officers.

(a) The following peace officers may apply for a license issued under this subchapter at any time after retirement:

(1) a person who is licensed as a peace officer under Chapter 1701, Occupations Code, and who has been employed full-time as a peace officer by a law enforcement agency;

(2) a railroad peace officer appointed by the director under Article 2.121, Code of Criminal Procedure, who holds a certificate of authority issued by the director under that article and a peace officer license issued by the Texas Commission on Law Enforcement; or

(3) a special ranger of the Texas and Southwestern Cattle Raisers Association appointed by the director under Article 2.125, Code of Criminal Procedure, who holds a certificate of authority issued by the director under that article and a peace officer license issued by the Texas Commission on Law Enforcement.

(b) The person shall submit two complete sets of legible and classifiable fingerprints and a sworn statement from the head of the law enforcement agency that employed the applicant or other former employer of the applicant, as applicable. A head of a law enforcement agency or other former employer may not refuse to issue a statement under this subsection. If the applicant alleges that the statement is untrue, the department shall investigate the validity of the statement. The statement must include:

(1) the name and rank of the applicant;

(2) the status of the applicant before retirement;

(3) whether the applicant was accused of misconduct at the time of the retirement;

(4) the physical and mental condition of the applicant;

(5) the type of weapons the applicant had demonstrated proficiency with during the last year of employment;

(6) whether the applicant would be eligible for reemployment with the agency or employer, and if not, the reasons the applicant is not eligible;

(7) a recommendation from the agency head or the employer regarding the issuance of a license under this subchapter; and

Government Code

(8) whether the applicant holds a current certificate of proficiency under Section 1701.357, Occupations Code.

(c) The department may issue a license issued under this subchapter to an applicant under this section if the applicant is honorably retired and physically and emotionally fit to possess a handgun. In this subsection, "honorably retired" means the applicant:

(1) did not retire in lieu of any disciplinary action;

(2) was eligible to retire from the law enforcement agency or other former employer or was ineligible to retire only as a result of an injury received in the course of the applicant's employment; and

(3) for a peace officer described by Subsection (a)(1), is entitled to receive a pension or annuity for service as a law enforcement officer or is not entitled to receive a pension or annuity only because the law enforcement agency that employed the applicant does not offer a pension or annuity to its employees.

(d) The department shall waive any fee required for a license issued under this subchapter to an applicant under this section.

(e) An applicant under this section who complies with Subsections (b) and (c) or Subsection (g), as applicable, and with the other requirements of this subchapter is not required to complete the classroom instruction portion of the handgun proficiency course described by Section 411.188 to obtain a license under this subchapter.

(e-1) An applicant described by Subsection (e) who holds a current certificate of proficiency under Section 1701.357, Occupations Code, is not required to complete the range instruction portion of the handgun proficiency course described by Section 411.188 to obtain a license under this subchapter.

(f) A license issued under this subchapter to an applicant under this section expires as provided by Section 411.183.

(g) A retired officer of the United States who was eligible to carry a firearm in the discharge of the officer's official duties is eligible to apply under this section for a license issued under this subchapter. An applicant described by this subsection may submit the application at any time after retirement. The applicant shall submit with the application proper proof of retired status by presenting the following documents prepared by the agency from which the applicant retired:

(1) retirement credentials; and

(2) a letter from the agency head stating the applicant retired in good standing.

Sec. 411.1991. Peace Officers.

(a) A person may apply for a license issued under this subchapter if the person is:

(1) licensed as a peace officer under Chapter 1701, Occupations Code, and employed as a peace officer by a law enforcement agency;

(2) a railroad peace officer appointed by the director under Article 2.121, Code of Criminal Procedure, who holds a certificate of authority issued by the director under that article and a peace officer license issued by the Texas Commission on Law Enforcement;

(3) a special ranger of the Texas and Southwestern Cattle Raisers Association appointed by the director under Article 2.125, Code of Criminal Procedure, who holds a certificate of authority issued by the director under that article and a peace officer license issued by the Texas Commission on Law Enforcement; or

(4) a member of the Texas military forces, excluding Texas State Guard members who are serving in the Texas Legislature.

(a-1) An applicant who is a peace officer described by Subsection (a)(1), (2), or (3) shall submit to the department:

(1) the name and rank of the applicant; and

(2) a current copy of the applicant's license issued by the Texas Commission on Law Enforcement and evidence of employment as a peace officer, railroad peace officer, or special ranger, as applicable.

(a-2) The department shall adopt rules regarding the information required to be included in an application submitted by a member of the Texas military forces under this section.

(b) The department may issue a license under this subchapter to an applicant under this section if the applicant complies with Subsection (a-1) or rules adopted under Subsection (a-2), as applicable.

(b-1) An applicant under this section who is a peace officer described by Subsection (a)(1), (2), or (3) and who complies with Subsection (a-1) and the other requirements of this subchapter is not required to complete the handgun proficiency course described by Section 411.188 to obtain a license under this subchapter.

(c) The department shall waive any fee required for a license issued under this subchapter to an applicant under this section.

(d) A license issued under this section expires as provided by Section 411.183.

Sec. 411.1992. Former Reserve Law Enforcement Officers.

(a) A person who served as a reserve law enforcement officer, as defined by Section 1701.001,

Occupations Code, not less than a total of 10 years of cumulative service with one or more state or local law enforcement agencies may apply for a license under this subchapter at any time.

(b) The applicant shall submit to the department two complete sets of legible and classifiable fingerprints and a sworn statement from the head of the law enforcement agency at which the applicant last served as a reserve law enforcement officer. A head of a law enforcement agency may not refuse to issue a statement under this subsection. If the applicant alleges that the statement is untrue, the department shall investigate the validity of the statement. The statement must include:

(1) the name and rank of the applicant;

(2) the status of the applicant;

(3) whether the applicant was accused of misconduct at any time during the applicant's term of service and the disposition of that accusation;

(4) a description of the physical and mental condition of the applicant;

(5) a list of the types of weapons the applicant demonstrated proficiency with during the applicant's term of service; and

(6) a recommendation from the agency head regarding the issuance of a license under this subchapter.

(c) The department may issue a license under this subchapter to an applicant under this section if the applicant was a reserve law enforcement officer for not less than a total of 10 years of cumulative service with one or more state or local law enforcement agencies and is physically and emotionally fit to possess a handgun.

(d) An applicant under this section must pay a fee of $25 for a license issued under this subchapter.

(e) [Repealed.]

(f) A license issued under this section expires as provided by Section 411.183.

Sec. 411.1993. County Jailers.

(a) In this section, "county jailer" has the meaning assigned by Section 1701.001, Occupations Code.

(b) A county jailer who holds a county jailer license issued under Chapter 1701, Occupations Code, may apply for a license under this subchapter.

(c) An applicant under this section who is a county jailer shall submit to the department:

(1) the name and job title of the applicant;

(2) a current copy of the applicant's county jailer license and evidence of employment as a county jailer; and

(3) evidence that the applicant has satisfactorily completed the preparatory training program required under Section 1701.310, Occupations Code, including the demonstration of weapons proficiency required as part of the training program under Section 1701.307 of that code.

(d) The department may issue a license under this subchapter to an applicant under this section if the applicant complies with Subsection (c) and meets all other requirements of this subchapter, except that the applicant is not required to complete the range instruction part of the handgun proficiency course described by Section 411.188 if the department is satisfied, on the basis of the evidence provided under Subsection (c)(3), that the applicant is proficient in the use of handguns.

(e) The department shall waive any fee required for a license issued under this subchapter to an applicant under this section.

(f) A license issued to an applicant under this section expires as provided by Section 411.183.

Sec. 411.1994. State Correctional Officers.

(a) A correctional officer of the Texas Department of Criminal Justice may apply for a license under this subchapter.

(b) An applicant under this section shall submit to the department:

(1) the name and job title of the applicant;

(2) evidence of employment as a correctional officer of the Texas Department of Criminal Justice; and

(3) evidence that the applicant has satisfactorily completed the correctional officer training program offered by the Texas Department of Criminal Justice, including a demonstration of weapons proficiency.

(c) The department may issue a license under this subchapter to an applicant under this section if the applicant complies with Subsection (b) and meets all other requirements of this subchapter, except that the applicant is not required to complete the range instruction part of the handgun proficiency course described by Section 411.188 if the department is satisfied, on the basis of the evidence provided under Subsection (b)(3), that the applicant is proficient in the use of handguns.

(d) The department shall waive any fee required for a license issued under this subchapter to an applicant under this section.

(e) A license issued to an applicant under this section expires as provided by Section 411.183.

Sec. 411.200. Application to Licensed Security Officers.

This subchapter does not exempt a license holder who is also employed as a security officer and licensed under Chapter 1702, Occupations Code, from the duty to comply with Chapter 1702, Occupations Code, or Section 46.02, Penal Code.

Sec. 411.201. Active and Retired Judicial Officers.

(a) In this section:

(1) "Active judicial officer" means:

(A) a person serving as a judge or justice of the supreme court, the court of criminal appeals, a court of appeals, a district court, a criminal district court, a constitutional county court, a statutory county court, a justice court, or a municipal court;

(B) a federal judge who is a resident of this state; or

(C) a person appointed and serving as an associate judge under Chapter 201, Family Code.

(2) "Federal judge" means:

(A) a judge of a United States court of appeals;

(B) a judge of a United States district court;

(C) a judge of a United States bankruptcy court; or

(D) a magistrate judge of a United States district court.

(3) "Retired judicial officer" means:

(A) a visiting judge appointed under Section 26.023 or 26.024;

(B) a senior judge designated under Section 75.001 or a judicial officer as designated or defined by Section 75.001, 831.001, or 836.001; or

(C) a retired federal judge who is a resident of this state.

(b) Notwithstanding any other provision of this subchapter, the department shall issue a license under this subchapter to an active or retired judicial officer who meets the requirements of this section.

(c) An active judicial officer is eligible for a license to carry a handgun under the authority of this subchapter. A retired judicial officer is eligible for a license to carry a handgun under the authority of this subchapter if the officer:

(1) has not been convicted of a felony;

(2) has not, in the five years preceding the date of application, been convicted of a Class A or Class B misdemeanor or equivalent offense;

(3) is not charged with the commission of a Class A or Class B misdemeanor or equivalent offense or of a felony under an information or indictment;

(4) is not a chemically dependent person; and

(5) is not a person of unsound mind.

(d) An applicant for a license who is an active or retired judicial officer must submit to the department:

(1) a completed application, including all required affidavits, on a form prescribed by the department;

(2) one or more photographs of the applicant that meet the requirements of the department;

(3) two complete sets of legible and classifiable fingerprints of the applicant, including one set taken by a person employed by a law enforcement agency who is appropriately trained in recording fingerprints;

(4) evidence of handgun proficiency, in the form and manner required by the department for an applicant under this section;

(5) a nonrefundable application and license fee of $25; and

(6) if the applicant is a retired judicial officer, a form executed by the applicant that authorizes the department to make an inquiry into any noncriminal history records that are necessary to determine the applicant's eligibility for a license under this subchapter.

(e) On receipt of all the application materials required by this section, the department shall:

(1) if the applicant is an active judicial officer, issue a license to carry a handgun under the authority of this subchapter; or

(2) if the applicant is a retired judicial officer, conduct an appropriate background investigation to determine the applicant's eligibility for the license and, if the applicant is eligible, issue a license to carry a handgun under the authority of this subchapter.

(f) Except as otherwise provided by this subsection, an applicant for a license under this section must satisfy the handgun proficiency requirements of Section 411.188. The classroom instruction part of the proficiency course for an active judicial officer is not subject to a minimum hour requirement. The instruction must include instruction only on:

(1) handgun use, proficiency, and safety; and

(2) proper storage practices for handguns with an emphasis on storage practices that eliminate the possibility of accidental injury to a child.

(g) A license issued under this section expires as provided by Section 411.183 and may be renewed in accordance with Section 411.185.

(h) The department shall issue a license to carry a handgun under the authority of this subchapter to a United States attorney or an assistant United States attorney, or to an attorney elected or employed to represent the state in the prosecution of felony cases, who meets the requirements of this section for an active judicial officer. The department shall waive any fee required for the issuance of an original, duplicate, or renewed license under this subchapter for an applicant who is a United

States attorney or an assistant United States attorney or who is an attorney elected or employed to represent the state in the prosecution of felony cases.

Sec. 411.202. License a Benefit.

The issuance of a license under this subchapter is a benefit to the license holder for purposes of those sections of the Penal Code to which the definition of "benefit" under Section 1.07, Penal Code, applies.

Sec. 411.203. Rights of Employers.

This subchapter does not prevent or otherwise limit the right of a public or private employer to prohibit persons who are licensed under this subchapter from carrying a handgun on the premises of the business. In this section, "premises" has the meaning assigned by Section 46.03, Penal Code.

Sec. 411.2031. Carrying of Handguns by License Holders on Certain Campuses.

(a) For purposes of this section:

(1) "Campus" means all land and buildings owned or leased by an institution of higher education or private or independent institution of higher education.

(2) "Institution of higher education" and "private or independent institution of higher education" have the meanings assigned by Section 61.003, Education Code.

(3) "Premises" has the meaning assigned by Section 46.03, Penal Code.

(b) A license holder may carry a concealed handgun on or about the license holder's person while the license holder is on the campus of an institution of higher education or private or independent institution of higher education in this state.

(c) Except as provided by Subsection (d), (d-1), or (e), an institution of higher education or private or independent institution of higher education in this state may not adopt any rule, regulation, or other provision prohibiting license holders from carrying handguns on the campus of the institution.

(d) An institution of higher education or private or independent institution of higher education in this state may establish rules, regulations, or other provisions concerning the storage of handguns in dormitories or other residential facilities that are owned or leased and operated by the institution and located on the campus of the institution.

(d-1) After consulting with students, staff, and faculty of the institution regarding the nature of the student population, specific safety considerations, and the uniqueness of the campus environment, the president or other chief executive officer of an institution of higher education in this state shall establish reasonable rules, regulations, or other provisions regarding the carrying of concealed handguns by license holders on the campus of the institution or on premises located on the campus of the institution. The president or officer may not establish provisions that generally prohibit or have the effect of generally prohibiting license holders from carrying concealed handguns on the campus of the institution. The president or officer may amend the provisions as necessary for campus safety. The provisions take effect as determined by the president or officer unless subsequently amended by the board of regents or other governing board under Subsection (d-2). The institution must give effective notice under Section 30.06, Penal Code, with respect to any portion of a premises on which license holders may not carry.

(d-2) Not later than the 90th day after the date that the rules, regulations, or other provisions are established as described by Subsection (d-1), the board of regents or other governing board of the institution of higher education shall review the provisions. The board of regents or other governing board may, by a vote of not less than two-thirds of the board, amend wholly or partly the provisions established under Subsection (d-1). If amended under this subsection, the provisions are considered to be those of the institution as established under Subsection (d-1).

(d-3) An institution of higher education shall widely distribute the rules, regulations, or other provisions described by Subsection (d-1) to the institution's students, staff, and faculty, including by prominently publishing the provisions on the institution's Internet website.

(d-4) Not later than September 1 of each even-numbered year, each institution of higher education in this state shall submit a report to the legislature and to the standing committees of the legislature with jurisdiction over the implementation and continuation of this section that:

(1) describes its rules, regulations, or other provisions regarding the carrying of concealed handguns on the campus of the institution; and

(2) explains the reasons the institution has established those provisions.

(e) A private or independent institution of higher education in this state, after consulting with students, staff, and faculty of the institution, may establish rules, regulations, or other provisions prohibiting license holders from carrying handguns on the campus of the institution, any grounds or building on which an activity sponsored by the institution is being conducted, or a passenger transportation vehicle owned by the institution.

Sec. 411.2032. Transportation and Storage of Firearms and Ammunition by License Holders in Private Vehicles on Certain Campuses.

(a) For purposes of this section:

(1) "Campus" means all land and buildings owned or leased by an institution of higher education or private or independent institution of higher education.

(2) "Institution of higher education" and "private or independent institution of higher education" have the meanings assigned by Section 61.003, Education Code.

(b) An institution of higher education or private or independent institution of higher education in this state may not adopt or enforce any rule, regulation, or other provision or take any other action, including posting notice under Section 30.06 or 30.07, Penal Code, prohibiting or placing restrictions on the storage or transportation of a firearm or ammunition in a locked, privately owned or leased motor vehicle by a person, including a student enrolled at that institution, who holds a license to carry a handgun under this subchapter and lawfully possesses the firearm or ammunition:

(1) on a street or driveway located on the campus of the institution; or

(2) in a parking lot, parking garage, or other parking area located on the campus of the institution.

Sec. 411.204. Notice Required on Certain Premises.

(a) A business that has a permit or license issued under Chapter 25, 28, 32, 69, or 74, Alcoholic Beverage Code, and that derives 51 percent or more of its income from the sale of alcoholic beverages for on-premises consumption as determined by the Texas Alcoholic Beverage Commission under Section 104.06, Alcoholic Beverage Code, shall prominently display at each entrance to the business premises a sign that complies with the requirements of Subsection (c).

(b) A hospital licensed under Chapter 241, Health and Safety Code, or a nursing home licensed under Chapter 242, Health and Safety Code, shall prominently display at each entrance to the hospital or nursing home, as appropriate, a sign that complies with the requirements of Subsection (c) other than the requirement that the sign include on its face the number "51".

(c) The sign required under Subsections (a) and (b) must give notice in both English and Spanish that it is unlawful for a person licensed under this subchapter to carry a handgun on the premises. The sign must appear in contrasting colors with block letters at least one inch in height and must include on its face the number "51" printed in solid red at least five inches in height. The sign shall be displayed in a conspicuous manner clearly visible to the public.

(d) [Repealed.]

(e) This section does not apply to a business that has a food and beverage certificate issued under the Alcoholic Beverage Code.

Sec. 411.205. Requirement to Display License.

If a license holder is carrying a handgun on or about the license holder's person when a magistrate or a peace officer demands that the license holder display identification, the license holder shall display:

(1) both the license holder's driver's license or identification certificate issued by the department and the license holder's handgun license; and

(2) if the license holder's handgun license bears a protective order designation, a copy of the applicable court order under which the license holder is protected.

Sec. 411.206. Seizure of Handgun and License.

(a) If a peace officer arrests and takes into custody a license holder who is carrying a handgun under the authority of this subchapter, the officer shall seize the license holder's handgun and license as evidence.

(b) The provisions of Article 18.19, Code of Criminal Procedure, relating to the disposition of weapons seized in connection with criminal offenses, apply to a handgun seized under this subsection.

(c) [Repealed.]

Sec. 411.207. Authority of Peace Officer to Disarm.

(a) A peace officer who is acting in the lawful discharge of the officer's official duties may disarm a license holder at any time the officer reasonably believes it is necessary for the protection of the license holder, officer, or another individual. The peace officer shall return the handgun to the license holder before discharging the license holder from the scene if the officer determines that the license holder is not a threat to the officer, license holder, or another individual and if the license holder has not violated any provision of this subchapter or committed any other violation that results in the arrest of the license holder.

(b) A peace officer who is acting in the lawful discharge of the officer's official duties may temporarily disarm a license holder when a license holder enters a nonpublic, secure portion of a law enforcement facility, if the law enforcement agency provides a gun locker where the peace officer can secure the license holder's handgun. The peace officer shall secure the handgun in the locker and shall return the handgun to the license holder immediately after the license holder leaves the nonpublic, secure portion of the law enforcement facility.

(c) A law enforcement facility shall prominently display at each entrance to a nonpublic, secure portion of the facility a sign that gives notice in both English and Spanish that, under this section, a peace officer may temporarily disarm a license holder when the license holder enters the nonpublic, secure portion of the facility. The sign must appear in contrasting colors with block letters at least one inch in height. The sign shall be displayed in a clearly visible and conspicuous manner.

(d) In this section:

(1) "Law enforcement facility" means a building or a portion of a building used exclusively by a law enforcement agency that employs peace officers as described by Articles 2.12(1) and (3), Code of Criminal Procedure, and support personnel to conduct the official business of the agency. The term does not include:

(A) any portion of a building not actively used exclusively to conduct the official business of the agency; or

(B) any public or private driveway, street, sidewalk, walkway, parking lot, parking garage, or other parking area.

(2) "Nonpublic, secure portion of a law enforcement facility" means that portion of a law enforcement facility to which the general public is denied access without express permission and to which access is granted solely to conduct the official business of the law enforcement agency.

Sec. 411.208. Limitation of Liability.

(a) A court may not hold the state, an agency or subdivision of the state, an officer or employee of the state, an institution of higher education, an officer or employee of an institution of higher education, a private or independent institution of higher education that has not adopted rules under Section 411.2031(e), an officer or employee of a private or independent institution of higher education that has not adopted rules under Section 411.2031(e), a peace officer, a qualified handgun instructor, or an approved online course provider liable for damages caused by:

(1) an action authorized under this subchapter or a failure to perform a duty imposed by this subchapter; or

(2) the actions of an applicant or license holder that occur after the applicant has received a license or been denied a license under this subchapter.

(b) A cause of action in damages may not be brought against the state, an agency or subdivision of the state, an officer or employee of the state, an institution of higher education, an officer or employee of an institution of higher education, a private or independent institution of higher education that has not adopted rules under Section 411.2031(e), an officer or employee of a private or independent institution of higher education that has not adopted rules under Section 411.2031(e), a peace officer, a qualified handgun instructor, or an approved online course provider for any damage caused by the actions of an applicant or license holder under this subchapter.

(c) The department is not responsible for any injury or damage inflicted on any person by an applicant or license holder arising or alleged to have arisen from an action taken by the department under this subchapter.

(d) The immunities granted under Subsections (a), (b), and (c) do not apply to:

(1) an act or a failure to act by the state, an agency or subdivision of the state, an officer of the state, an institution of higher education, an officer or employee of an institution of higher education, a private or independent institution of higher education that has not adopted rules under Section 411.2031(e), an officer or employee of a private or independent institution of higher education that has not adopted rules under Section 411.2031(e), or a peace officer if the act or failure to act was capricious or arbitrary; or

(2) any officer or employee of an institution of higher education or private or independent institution of higher education described by Subdivision (1) who possesses a handgun on the campus of that institution and whose conduct with regard to the handgun is made the basis of a claim for personal injury or property damage.

(e) The immunities granted under Subsection (a) to a qualified handgun instructor or approved online course provider do not apply to a cause of action for fraud or a deceptive trade practice.

(f) For purposes of this section:

(1) "Campus" has the meaning assigned by Section 411.2031.

(2) "Institution of higher education" and "private or independent institution of higher education" have the meanings assigned by Section 61.003, Education Code.

Sec. 411.209. Wrongful Exclusion of Handgun License Holder.

(a) Except as provided by Subsection (i), a state agency or a political subdivision of the state may not take any action, including an action consisting of the provision of notice by a communication described by Section 30.06 or 30.07, Penal Code, that states or implies that a license holder who is carrying a handgun under the authority of this subchapter is prohibited from entering or remaining on a premises or other place owned or leased by the governmental entity unless license holders are prohibited from carrying a handgun on the premises or other place by Section 46.03, Penal Code, or other law.

(b) A state agency or a political subdivision of the state that violates Subsection (a) is liable for a civil penalty of:

(1) not less than $1,000 and not more than $1,500 for the first violation; and

(2) not less than $10,000 and not more than $10,500 for the second or a subsequent violation.

(c) Each day of a continuing violation of Subsection (a) constitutes a separate violation.

(d) A resident of this state or a person licensed to carry a handgun under this subchapter may file a complaint with the attorney general that a state agency or political subdivision is in violation of Subsection (a) if the resident or license holder provides the agency or subdivision a written notice that describes the location and general facts of the violation and the agency or subdivision does not cure the violation before the end of the third business day after the date of receiving the written notice. A complaint filed with the attorney general under this subsection must include evidence of the violation and a copy of the written notice provided to the agency or subdivision.

(e) A civil penalty collected by the attorney general under this section shall be deposited to the credit of the compensation to victims of crime fund established under Subchapter J, Chapter 56B, Code of Criminal Procedure.

(f) Before a suit may be brought against a state agency or a political subdivision of the state for a violation of Subsection (a), the attorney general must investigate the complaint to determine whether legal action is warranted. If legal action is warranted, the attorney general must give the chief administrative officer of the agency or political subdivision charged with the violation a written notice that:

(1) describes the violation;

(2) states the amount of the proposed penalty for the violation; and

(3) gives the agency or political subdivision 15 days from receipt of the notice to cure the violation to avoid the penalty, unless the agency or political subdivision was found liable by a court for previously violating Subsection (a).

(g) If the attorney general determines that legal action is warranted and that the state agency or political subdivision has not cured the violation within the 15-day period provided by Subsection (f)(3), the attorney general or the appropriate county or district attorney may sue to collect the civil penalty provided by Subsection (b). The attorney general may also file a petition for a writ of mandamus or apply for other appropriate equitable relief. A suit or petition under this subsection may be filed in a district court in Travis County or in a county in which the principal office of the state agency or political subdivision is located. The attorney general may recover reasonable expenses incurred in obtaining relief under this subsection, including court costs, reasonable attorney's fees, investigative costs, witness fees, and deposition costs.

(h) Sovereign immunity to suit is waived and abolished to the extent of liability created by this section.

(i) Subsection (a) does not apply to a written notice provided by a state hospital under Section 552.002, Health and Safety Code.

(j) In this section, "premises" has the meaning assigned by Section 46.03, Penal Code.

SUBCHAPTER I
INTERNAL OVERSIGHT

Sec. 411.241. Office of Audit and Review.

The commission shall establish the office of audit and review. The office shall coordinate activities designed to promote effectiveness in departmental operations and to keep the commission and the legislature fully informed about deficiencies within the department. The office shall:

(1) inspect and audit departmental programs and operations for efficiency, uniformity, and compliance with established procedures and develop recommendations for improvement;

(2) coordinate and be responsible for promoting accountability, integrity, and efficiency in the department; and

(3) provide the commission with information relevant to its oversight of the department.

Sec. 411.242. Director of Audit and Review.

(a) The commission shall appoint the director of the office of audit and review. The director of audit and review serves until removed by the commission.

(b) The director of audit and review must satisfy the requirements to be the agency's internal auditor under Section 2102.006(b) and is considered to be the agency's internal auditor for purposes of Chapter 2102.

(c) The department shall provide the director of audit and review with access to any records, data, or other information necessary to fulfill the purposes of this section and Section 411.243.

(d) The director of audit and review shall, with the advice and consent of the commission, determine which audits and inspections to perform and may publish the findings and recommendations of the office of audit and review.

(e) The director of audit and review shall:

(1) report to the commission regarding audits and inspections planned and the status and findings of those audits and inspections; and

(2) report to the director for administrative purposes and keep the director informed of the office's findings.

Sec. 411.243. Powers and Duties.

(a) The office of audit and review shall:

(1) independently and objectively inspect all divisions of the department to:

(A) ensure that operations are conducted efficiently, uniformly, and in compliance with established procedures; and

(B) make recommendations for improvements in operational performance;

(2) independently and objectively audit all divisions of the department to:

(A) promote economy, effectiveness, and efficiency within the department;

(B) prevent and detect fraud, waste, and abuse in department programs and operations; and

(C) make recommendations about the adequacy and effectiveness of the department's system of internal control policies and procedures;

(3) advise in the development and evaluation of the department's performance measures;

(4) review actions taken by the department to improve program performance and make recommendations for improvement;

(5) review and make recommendations to the commission and the legislature regarding rules, laws, and guidelines relating to department programs and operations;

(6) keep the commission, director, and legislature fully informed of problems in department programs and operations; and

(7) ensure effective coordination and cooperation among the state auditor's office, legislative oversight committees, and other governmental bodies while attempting to avoid duplication.

(b) Chapter 2102 applies to the office of audit and review.

Sec. 411.244. Office of Inspector General [Renumbered].

Renumbered to Sec. 411.251 to 411.256 by Acts 2011, 82nd Leg., ch. 1308 (H.B. 3099), § 2, effective September 1, 2011.

SUBCHAPTER I-1 OFFICE OF INSPECTOR GENERAL

Sec. 411.251. Establishment and Purpose.

(a) The commission shall establish the office of inspector general.

(b) The office of inspector general is responsible for:

(1) acting to prevent and detect serious breaches of departmental policy, fraud, and abuse of office, including any acts of criminal conduct within the department; and

(2) independently and objectively reviewing, investigating, delegating, and overseeing the investigation of:

(A) conduct described in Subdivision (1);

(B) criminal activity occurring in all divisions of the department;

(C) allegations of wrongdoing by department employees;

(D) crimes committed on department property; and

(E) serious breaches of department policy.

Sec. 411.252. Oversight of Investigations.

(a) The office of inspector general has departmental jurisdiction for oversight and coordination over all investigations occurring on department property or involving department employees.

(b) The office shall coordinate and provide oversight, but is not required to conduct all investigations under this subchapter.

(c) The inspector general shall delegate any investigation considered potentially appropriate for criminal prosecution to the Texas Ranger division or the criminal investigations division of the department for investigation or referral back to the inspector general for further action.

(d) The inspector general shall continually monitor an investigation referred to another division of the department under Subsection (c), and the inspector general and the division shall report to the commission on the status of the investigation while pending.

Sec. 411.253. Initiation of Investigations.

The office of inspector general may only initiate an investigation based on:

(1) authorization from the commission;

(2) approval of the inspector general or deputy inspector general;

(3) approval of the director, a deputy director, an assistant director of the Texas Rangers, or an assistant director of the criminal investigations division for criminal investigations; or

(4) commission rules or approved commission policies.

Sec. 411.254. Commission Appointment and Oversight.

(a) The commission shall appoint the inspector general and may appoint a deputy inspector general. The inspector general serves until removed by the commission.

(b) The inspector general is not required to be a peace officer as that term is defined by Article 2.12, Code of Criminal Procedure. The commission or director may commission the inspector general as a commissioned peace officer of the department if the inspector general holds a permanent peace officer license issued under Chapter 1701, Occupations Code.

(c) The commission has direct oversight over the office of inspector general, including decisions regarding budget and staffing. The inspector general shall coordinate with the director for administrative support as provided by the commission.

(d) The commission shall establish policies to ensure that the commission continues to oversee the office of inspector general as required by this section and to ensure that the office of inspector general retains and exercises its original jurisdiction under Section 411.252.

Sec. 411.255. Reports.

(a) The inspector general shall report directly to the commission regarding performance of and activities related to investigations and provide the director with information regarding investigations as appropriate.

(b) The inspector general shall present at each regularly scheduled commission meeting and at other appropriate times:

(1) reports of investigations; and

(2) a summary of information relating to investigations conducted under this subchapter that includes analysis of the number, type, and outcome of investigations, trends in the investigations, and recommendations to avoid future complaints.

Sec. 411.256. Authority of State Auditor.

This chapter or other law related to the operation of the department's office of inspector general does not preempt the authority of the state auditor to conduct an audit or investigation under Chapter 321 or other law.

SUBCHAPTER J UNSOLVED CRIMES INVESTIGATION PROGRAM

Sec. 411.261. Definitions.

In this subchapter:

(1) "Attorney representing the state" means a district attorney, criminal district attorney, or county attorney performing the duties of a district attorney.

(2) "Unsolved crime" means a criminal offense:

(A) that is an unsolved homicide or an unsolved felony that is one offense arising out of the same criminal episode as other unsolved felonies; and

(B) the investigation of which requires a level of expertise that is not readily available to local law enforcement agencies.

Sec. 411.262. Unsolved Crimes Investigation Program.

(a) The unsolved crimes investigation program is an investigative program within the department.

(b) The program is a function of the Texas Rangers and will be commanded by the chief of the Texas Rangers.

(c) The director may employ commissioned peace officers and noncommissioned employees to perform duties required of the program.

(d) To be eligible for employment under this section, a peace officer must be a sergeant or higher-ranked officer of the Texas Rangers and must have two or more years of experience in the investigation of homicides or other major felonies.

(e) To be eligible for employment under this section, a noncommissioned employee must meet the experience, training, and educational qualifications set by the director as requirements for investigating or assisting in the investigation of an unsolved crime.

Sec. 411.263. Assistance on Request.

On the request of an attorney representing the state and with the approval of the director, employees of the unsolved crimes investigation program of the department may assist local law enforcement in the investigation of crime.

SUBCHAPTER K DEPARTMENT OF PUBLIC SAFETY HISTORICAL MUSEUM AND RESEARCH CENTER

Sec. 411.281. Definition.

In this subchapter, "museum" means the nonprofit organization, known as the Department of Public Safety Historical Museum and Research Center, established by employees and former employees of the department for the purposes of creating and operating a museum and research facility to:

(1) inform the public about the personnel and history of the department; and

(2) educate young people about law enforcement procedures through an interactive facility.

Sec. 411.282. General Provisions.

The commission may:

(1) establish a support staff in the department to assist the museum;

(2) use department property to fulfill the purposes of this subchapter; and

(3) enter into a contract with the museum.

Sec. 411.283. Personnel.

(a) The director may appoint and assign duties to department personnel to serve as paid support staff for the museum.

(b) The support staff may consist of a historian, a librarian, and other personnel as needed to administer the museum.

(c) The department may spend funds to hire support staff.

Sec. 411.284. Funding.

(a) The Department of Public Safety Historical Museum and Research Center account is created as a special account outside the state treasury to be held at the Department of Public Safety Credit Union and to be administered by the commission. The money in the account may be used only to administer this subchapter.

(b) The account is composed of gifts, grants, and donations collected by the department from any public or private source for the purposes of this subchapter.

Sec. 411.301. Definitions [Renumbered].

Renumbered to Tex. Gov't Code § 411.281 by Acts 2003, 78th Leg., ch. 1275 (H.B. 3506), § 2(59), effective September 1, 2003.

Sec. 411.302. General Provisions [Renumbered].

Renumbered to Tex. Gov't Code § 411.282 by Acts 2003, 78th Leg., ch. 1275 (H.B. 3506), § 2(59), effective September 1, 2003.

Sec. 411.303. Personnel [Renumbered].

Renumbered to Tex. Gov't Code § 411.283 by Acts 2003, 78th Leg., ch. 1275 (H.B. 3506), § 2(59), effective September 1, 2003.

Sec. 411.304. Funding [Renumbered].

Renumbered to Tex. Gov't Code § 411.284 by Acts 2003, 78th Leg., ch. 1275 (H.B. 3506), § 2(59), effective September 1, 2003.

SUBCHAPTER K-1 POWER OUTAGE ALERT

Sec. 411.301. Power Outage Alert.

(a) With the cooperation of the Texas Department of Transportation, the Texas Division of Emergency Management, the office of the governor, and the Public Utility Commission of Texas, the department shall develop and implement an alert to be activated when the power supply in this state may be inadequate to meet demand.

(b) The Public Utility Commission of Texas by rule shall adopt criteria for the content, activation, and termination of the alert described by Subsection (a). The criteria must provide for an alert to be regional or statewide.

Sec. 411.302. Administration.

(a) The director is the statewide coordinator of the power outage alert.

(b) The director shall adopt rules and issue directives as necessary to ensure proper implementation of the power outage alert. The rules and directives must include the procedures to be used by the Public Utility Commission of Texas and the independent organization certified under Section 39.151, Utilities Code, to communicate with the director about the power outage alert.

Sec. 411.303. Department to Recruit Participants.

The department shall recruit public and commercial television and radio broadcasters, private commercial entities, state or local governmental entities, the public, and other appropriate persons to assist in developing and implementing the power outage alert system.

Sec. 411.304. State Agencies.

(a) A state agency participating in the power outage alert system shall:

(1) cooperate with the department and assist in developing and implementing the alert system; and

(2) establish a plan for providing relevant information to its officers, investigators, or employees, as appropriate, once the power outage alert system has been activated.

(b) In addition to its duties as a state agency under Subsection (a), the Texas Department of Transportation shall establish a plan for providing relevant information to the public through an existing system of dynamic message signs located across the state.

Sec. 411.305. Activation of Power Outage Alert.

(a) When the Public Utility Commission of Texas or an independent organization certified under Section 39.151, Utilities Code, notifies the department that the criteria adopted under Section 411.301(b) for the activation of the alert has been met, the department shall confirm the accuracy of the information and, if confirmed, immediately issue a power outage alert under this subchapter in accordance with department rules.

(b) In issuing the power outage alert, the department shall send the alert to designated media outlets in this state. Following receipt of the alert, participating radio stations and television stations and other participating media outlets may issue the alert at designated intervals.

Sec. 411.306. Content of Power Outage Alert.

The power outage alert must include a statement that electricity customers may experience a power outage.

Sec. 411.307. Termination of Power Outage Alert.

The director shall terminate any activation of the power outage alert as soon as practicable after the Public Utility Commission of Texas or the Electric Reliability Council of Texas notifies the department that the criteria adopted under Section 411.301(b) for the termination of the alert has been met.

Sec. 411.308. Limitation on Participation by Texas Department of Transportation.

Notwithstanding Section 411.304(b), the Texas Department of Transportation is not required to use any existing system of dynamic message signs in a statewide alert system created under this subchapter if that department receives notice from the United States Department of Transportation Federal Highway Administration that the use of the signs would result in the loss of federal highway funding or other punitive actions taken against this state due to noncompliance with federal laws, regulations, or policies.

SUBCHAPTER L STATEWIDE AMERICA'S MISSING: BROADCAST EMERGENCY RESPONSE (AMBER) ALERT SYSTEM FOR ABDUCTED CHILDREN AND MISSING PERSONS WITH INTELLECTUAL DISABILITIES

Sec. 411.351. Definitions.

In this subchapter:

(1) "Abducted child" means a child 17 years of age or younger whose whereabouts are unknown and whose disappearance poses a credible threat to the safety and health of the child, as determined by a local law enforcement agency.

(2) "Alert system" means the statewide America's Missing: Broadcast Emergency Response (AMBER) alert system for abducted children and missing persons with intellectual disabilities.

(2-a) "Intellectual disability" means significantly subaverage general intellectual functioning that is concurrent with deficits in adaptive behavior and originates during the developmental period. The term includes a pervasive developmental disorder.

(3) "Local law enforcement agency" means a local law enforcement agency with jurisdiction over the investigation of:

(A) the abduction of a child; or

(B) a missing person with an intellectual disability.

(3-a) "Pervasive developmental disorder" means a disorder that meets the criteria for a pervasive developmental disorder established in the most recent Diagnostic and Statistical Manual of Mental Disorders published by the American Psychiatric Association.

(4) "Serious bodily injury" has the meaning assigned by Section 1.07, Penal Code.

Sec. 411.352. Statewide America's Missing: Broadcast Emergency Response (AMBER) Alert System for Abducted Children and Missing Persons with Intellectual Disabilities.

With the cooperation of the Texas Department of Transportation, the office of the governor, and other appropriate law enforcement agencies in this state, the department shall develop and implement a statewide alert system to be activated on behalf of an abducted child or a missing person with an intellectual disability.

Sec. 411.353. Administration.

(a) The director is the statewide coordinator of the alert system.

(b) The director shall adopt rules and issue directives as necessary to ensure proper implementation of the alert system. The rules and directives must include instructions on the procedures for activating and deactivating the alert system.

(c) The director shall prescribe forms for use by local law enforcement agencies in requesting activation of the alert system.

Sec. 411.354. Department to Recruit Participants.

(a) The department shall recruit public and commercial television and radio broadcasters, private commercial entities, state or local governmental entities, the public, and other appropriate persons to assist in developing and implementing the alert system.

(b) The department may enter into agreements with participants in the alert system to provide necessary support for the alert system.

Sec. 411.355. Activation.

(a) On the request of a local law enforcement agency regarding an abducted child, the department shall activate the alert system and notify appropriate participants in the alert system, as established by rule, if:

(1) the local law enforcement agency believes that a child has been abducted, including a child who:

(A) is younger than 14 years of age; and

(B) regardless of whether the child departed willingly with the other person, has been taken from the care and custody of the child's parent or legal guardian without the permission of the parent or legal guardian by another person who is:

(i) more than three years older than the child; and

(ii) not related to the child by any degree of consanguinity or affinity as defined under Subchapter B, Chapter 573, Government Code;

(2) the local law enforcement agency believes that the abducted child is in immediate danger of serious bodily injury or death or of becoming the victim of a sexual assault;

(3) the local law enforcement agency confirms that a preliminary investigation has taken place that verifies the abduction and eliminates alternative explanations for the child's disappearance; and

(4) sufficient information is available to disseminate to the public that could assist in locating the child, a person suspected of abducting the child, or a vehicle suspected of being used in the abduction.

(b) On the request of a local law enforcement agency regarding a missing person with an intellectual disability, the department shall activate the alert system and notify appropriate participants in the alert system, as established by rule, if:

(1) the local law enforcement agency receives notice of a missing person with an intellectual disability;

(2) the local law enforcement agency verifies that at the time the person is reported missing:

(A) the person has an intellectual disability, as determined according to the procedure provided by Section 593.005, Health and Safety Code; and

(B) the person's location is unknown;

(3) the local law enforcement agency determines that the person's disappearance poses a credible threat to the person's health and safety; and

(4) sufficient information is available to disseminate to the public that could assist in locating the person.

(c) The department may modify the criteria described by Subsection (a) or (b) as necessary for the proper implementation of the alert system.

Sec. 411.356. Local Law Enforcement Agencies.

Before requesting activation of the alert system, a local law enforcement agency must verify that the criteria described by Section 411.355(a) or (b), as applicable, have been satisfied. On verification of the applicable criteria, the local law enforcement agency shall immediately contact the department to request activation and shall supply the necessary information on the forms prescribed by the director.

Sec. 411.357. State Agencies.

(a) A state agency participating in the alert system shall:

(1) cooperate with the department and assist in developing and implementing the alert system; and

(2) establish a plan for providing relevant information to its officers, investigators, or employees, as appropriate, once the alert system has been activated.

(b) In addition to its duties as a state agency under Subsection (a), the Texas Department of Transportation shall establish a plan for providing relevant information to the public through an existing system of dynamic message signs located across the state.

Sec. 411.358. Termination.

The director shall terminate any activation of the alert system with respect to a particular abducted child or a particular missing person with an intellectual disability if:

(1) the abducted child or missing person is recovered or the situation is otherwise resolved; or

(2) the director determines that the alert system is no longer an effective tool for locating and recovering the abducted child or missing person.

Sec. 411.359. System Name.

The director by rule may assign a name other than America's Missing: Broadcast Emergency Response (AMBER) to the alert system when the system is activated regarding a missing person with an intellectual disability.

SUBCHAPTER L-1
TEXAS ACTIVE SHOOTER ALERT SYSTEM

Sec. 411.371. Definition.

In this subchapter, "alert system" means the Texas Active Shooter Alert System established under this subchapter.

Sec. 411.372. Development and Implementation of Alert System.

With the cooperation of the Texas Department of Transportation, the office of the governor, and other appropriate law enforcement agencies in this state, the department shall develop and implement an alert system to be activated on report of an active shooter.

Sec. 411.373. Administration.

(a) The director is the statewide coordinator of the alert system.

(b) The director shall adopt rules and issue directives as necessary to ensure proper implementation of the alert system. The rules and directives must include instructions on the procedures for activating and deactivating the alert system.

(c) The director shall prescribe forms for local law enforcement agencies to use in requesting activation of the alert system.

Sec. 411.374. Department to Recruit Participants.

(a) The department shall recruit public and commercial television and radio broadcasters, mobile telephone service providers by use of the federal Wireless Emergency Alert system, private commercial entities, state or local governmental entities, the public, and other appropriate persons to assist in developing and implementing the alert system.

(b) The department may enter into agreements with participants in the alert system to provide necessary support for the alert system.

Sec. 411.375. Activation.

(a) On the request of a local law enforcement agency or as the department determines appropriate to assist a local law enforcement agency regarding an active shooter, the department shall activate the alert system and notify appropriate participants in the alert system as established by rule if the local law enforcement agency or department:

(1) believes an active shooter is in the agency's jurisdiction;

(2) determines an active shooter alert would assist individuals near the active shooter's location;

(3) verifies the active shooter situation through a preliminary investigation; and

(4) provides the active shooter's last known location and any identifiable information for the active shooter.

(b) The department may modify the criteria described by Subsection (a) as necessary for the proper implementation of the alert system.

Sec. 411.376. Local Law Enforcement Agencies.

Before requesting activation of the alert system, a local law enforcement agency must verify that the criteria described by Section 411.375(a) have been satisfied. On verification of the applicable criteria, the local law enforcement agency may immediately contact the department to request activation and supply the necessary information on forms prescribed by the director.

Sec. 411.377. State Agencies.

(a) A state agency participating in the alert system shall:

(1) cooperate with the department and assist in developing and implementing the alert system; and

(2) establish a plan for providing relevant information to its officers, investigators, or employees, as appropriate, on activation of the alert system.

(b) In addition to its duties as a state agency under Subsection (a), the Texas Department of Transportation shall establish a plan for providing relevant information to the public within 50 miles of an active shooter for which an alert has been issued through an existing system of dynamic message signs located across the state.

Sec. 411.378. Limitation on Participation by Texas Department of Transportation.

Notwithstanding Section 411.377(b), the Texas Department of Transportation is not required to use any existing system of dynamic message signs in a statewide alert system created under this subchapter if the Texas Department of Transportation receives notice from the United States Department of Transportation Federal Highway Administration that the use of the signs would result in the loss of federal highway funding or other punitive actions taken against this state due to noncompliance with federal laws, regulations, or policies.

Sec. 411.379. Termination.

The director shall terminate any activation of the alert system for a particular active shooter if:

(1) the active shooter situation is resolved; or

(2) the director or a local law enforcement agency determines the alert system is no longer an effective tool for providing relevant information to the public about the active shooter.

Sec. 411.380. Limitation of Liability.

The department or a local law enforcement agency is not liable for failure to activate the alert system.

SUBCHAPTER M
SILVER ALERT FOR MISSING SENIOR CITIZENS AND PERSONS WITH ALZHEIMER'S DISEASE

Sec. 411.381. Definitions.

In this subchapter:

(1) "Alert" means the statewide silver alert for missing senior citizens and persons with Alzheimer's disease, as developed and implemented under this subchapter.

(2) "Local law enforcement agency" means a local law enforcement agency with jurisdiction over the investigation of a missing senior citizen or person with Alzheimer's disease.

(3) "Senior citizen" means a person who is 65 years of age or older.

Government Code

Sec. 411.382. Silver Alert for Missing Senior Citizens and Persons with Alzheimer's Disease.

With the cooperation of the Texas Department of Transportation, the office of the governor, and other appropriate law enforcement agencies in this state, the department shall develop and implement a statewide silver alert to be activated on behalf of a missing senior citizen or person with Alzheimer's disease.

Sec. 411.383. Administration.

(a) The director is the statewide coordinator of the alert.

(b) The director shall adopt rules and issue directives as necessary to ensure proper implementation of the alert. The rules and directives must include:

(1) the procedures to be used by a local law enforcement agency to verify whether a person reported missing is a senior citizen with

an impaired mental condition or a person with Alzheimer's disease and whether the person's location is unknown;

(2) a description of the circumstances under which a local law enforcement agency is required to report a missing senior citizen or person with Alzheimer's disease to the department; and

(3) the procedures to be used by an individual or entity to report information about a missing senior citizen or person with Alzheimer's disease to designated media outlets in Texas.

Sec. 411.384. Department to Recruit Participants.

The department shall recruit public and commercial television and radio broadcasters, private commercial entities, state or local governmental entities, the public, and other appropriate persons to assist in developing and implementing the alert.

Sec. 411.385. Duties of Texas Department of Transportation.

The Texas Department of Transportation shall:

(1) cooperate with the department and assist in developing and implementing the alert; and

(2) establish a plan for providing relevant information to the public through an existing system of dynamic message signs located across the state.

Sec. 411.386. Notification to Department of Missing Senior Citizen or Person with Alzheimer's Disease.

(a) A local law enforcement agency may notify the department if the agency:

(1) receives notice of a missing senior citizen or person with Alzheimer's disease;

(2) verifies that at the time the senior citizen or person with Alzheimer's disease is reported missing:

(A) the person reported missing:

(i) is 65 years of age or older and has an impaired mental condition; or

(ii) is a person with Alzheimer's disease; and

(B) the person's location is unknown; and

(3) determines that the person's disappearance poses a credible threat to the person's health and safety.

(b) The local law enforcement agency shall:

(1) require the family or legal guardian of the missing senior citizen or person with Alzheimer's disease to provide documentation of the person's age and condition to verify the person's status as described by Subsection (a)(2)(A); and

(2) as soon as practicable, determine whether the person's disappearance poses a credible threat to the person's health and safety for purposes of Subsection (a)(3).

Sec. 411.387. Activation of Silver Alert.

(a) When a local law enforcement agency notifies the department under Section 411.386, the department shall confirm the accuracy of the information and, if confirmed, immediately issue an alert under this subchapter in accordance with department rules.

(b) In issuing the alert, the department shall send the alert to designated media outlets in Texas. Following receipt of the alert, participating radio stations and television stations and other participating media outlets may issue the alert at designated intervals to assist in locating the missing senior citizen or person with Alzheimer's disease.

Sec. 411.388. Content of Silver Alert.

The alert must include:

(1) all appropriate information that is provided by the local law enforcement agency and that may lead to the safe recovery of the missing senior citizen or person with Alzheimer's disease; and

(2) a statement instructing any person with information related to the missing senior citizen or person with Alzheimer's disease to contact a local law enforcement agency.

Sec. 411.389. Termination of Silver Alert.

(a) The director shall terminate any activation of the alert with respect to a particular missing senior citizen or person with Alzheimer's disease not later than the earlier of the date on which:

(1) the missing person is located or the situation is otherwise resolved; or

(2) the notification period ends, as determined by department rule.

(b) A local law enforcement agency that locates a missing senior citizen or person with Alzheimer's disease who is the subject of an alert under this subchapter shall notify the department as soon as possible that the missing person has been located.

SUBCHAPTER N INTEROPERABLE STATEWIDE EMERGENCY RADIO INFRASTRUCTURE

Sec. 411.401. Definition.

In this subchapter, "emergency radio infrastructure" means radio frequency hardware, software, or auxiliary equipment that:

(1) provides dispatch communications for this state and local governments to public safety agencies; and

(2) allows interoperable communication between public safety agencies, including communication between different types of public safety agencies.

Sec. 411.4015. Grants to Finance Interoperable Statewide Emergency Radio Infrastructure.

(a) The office of the governor shall establish a program to provide grants as provided by Section 411.402.

(b) The office of the governor shall establish procedures to administer the grant program, including a procedure for the submission of a proposal and a procedure to be used by the office to evaluate a proposal.

(c) The office of the governor shall enter into a contract that includes performance requirements with each grant recipient. The office shall monitor and enforce the terms of the contract.

(d) The office of the governor shall adopt rules to administer this section.

Sec. 411.402. Use of Grants.

(a) A grant provided under Section 411.4015 may only:

(1) be used for the planning, development, provision, enhancement, or ongoing maintenance of an interoperable statewide emergency radio infrastructure;

(2) be used in accordance with the statewide integrated public safety radio communications plan developed under Subchapter F, Chapter 421;

(3) be used for the development of a regional or state interoperable radio communication system;

(4) be made to:

(A) regional councils of government that have entered into interlocal agreements authorized under state law; and

(B) state agencies requiring emergency radio infrastructure; or

(5) be used for other public safety purposes.

(b) A grant provided under Section 411.4015 may not be used to purchase or maintain radio subscriber equipment.

Sec. 411.403. Emergency Radio Infrastructure Account.

(a) The emergency radio infrastructure account is an account in the general revenue fund.

(b) The account consists of fees deposited in the account as provided by Section 133.102(e)(9), Local Government Code.

(c) Money in the account may be used only for grants made under this subchapter.

(d) Section 403.095 does not apply to the account.

SUBCHAPTER O PREVENTION OF SCRAP METAL THEFT GRANT PROGRAM

Sec. 411.421. Definition.

In this subchapter, "regulated material" has the meaning assigned by Section 1956.001, Occupations Code.

Sec. 411.422. Grants to Fund Scrap Metal Theft Prevention.

(a) From fines collected and distributed to the department under Sections 1956.040(a-2) and (a-4), Occupations Code, the commission by rule shall establish and implement a grant program to provide funding to assist local law enforcement agencies in preventing the theft of regulated material.

(b) To be eligible for a grant, a recipient must be a local law enforcement agency that has established a program designed to prevent the theft of regulated material.

(c) Rules adopted under this section must:

(1) include accountability measures for grant recipients and provisions for loss of eligibility for grant recipients that fail to comply with the measures; and

(2) require grant recipients to provide to the department information on program outcomes.

SUBCHAPTER P BLUE ALERT SYSTEM

Sec. 411.441. Definitions.

In this subchapter:

(1) "Alert system" means the statewide blue alert system that is developed and implemented under this subchapter.

(2) "Law enforcement agency" means a law enforcement agency with jurisdiction over the investigation of an alleged offense that resulted in the death or serious bodily injury of a law enforcement officer.

(3) "Law enforcement officer" means a person who is a peace officer under Article 2.12, Code of Criminal Procedure, or a person who is a federal law enforcement officer, as defined by 5 U.S.C. Section 8331(20).

(4) "Serious bodily injury" has the meaning assigned by Section 1.07, Penal Code.

Sec. 411.442. Blue Alert System.

With the cooperation of the Texas Department of Transportation, the office of the governor, and other appropriate law enforcement agencies in this state, the department shall develop and implement a statewide blue alert system to be activated to aid in the apprehension of an individual suspected of killing or causing serious bodily injury to a law enforcement officer.

Sec. 411.443. Administration.

(a) The director is the statewide coordinator of the alert system.

(b) The director shall adopt rules and issue directives as necessary to ensure proper implementation of the alert system. The rules and directives must include:

(1) the procedures to be used by a law enforcement agency to verify whether:

(A) an individual is suspected of killing or causing serious bodily injury to a law enforcement officer and is not yet apprehended; and

(B) the activation of the alert system would aid in the apprehension of that individual;

(2) a description of the circumstances under which a law enforcement agency is required to report a missing suspect to the department; and

(3) the procedures to be used by an individual or entity to report information about a missing suspect to designated media outlets in Texas.

(c) The director shall prescribe forms for use by law enforcement agencies in requesting activation of the alert system.

Sec. 411.444. Department to Recruit Participants.

The department shall recruit public and commercial television and radio broadcasters, private commercial entities, state or local governmental entities, the public, and other appropriate persons to assist in developing and implementing the alert system.

Sec. 411.445. State Agencies.

(a) A state agency participating in the alert system shall:

(1) cooperate with the department and assist in developing and implementing the alert system; and

(2) establish a plan for providing relevant information to its officers, investigators, or employees, as appropriate, once the alert system has been activated.

(b) In addition to its duties as a state agency under Subsection (a), the Texas Department of Transportation shall establish a plan for providing relevant information to the public through an existing system of dynamic message signs located across the state.

Sec. 411.446. Notification to Department.

(a) A law enforcement agency that receives notice of an individual who is suspected of killing or causing serious bodily injury to a law enforcement officer and who has not yet been apprehended shall:

(1) confirm the accuracy of the information; and

(2) if the agency believes the missing suspect poses a threat to other law enforcement officers and to the public, provide notice to the department.

(b) A law enforcement agency providing notice to the department under Subsection (a) shall include with that notice a detailed description of the missing suspect and, if applicable, any available portion of the license plate number of a motor vehicle being used by the suspect.

Sec. 411.447. Activation of Blue Alert System.

(a) When a law enforcement agency notifies the department under Section 411.446, the department shall confirm the accuracy of the information and, if confirmed, immediately issue an alert through the alert system in accordance with department rules.

(b) In issuing the alert, the department shall send the alert to designated media outlets in Texas. Following receipt of the alert, participating radio stations and television stations and other participating media outlets may issue the alert at designated intervals to assist in locating the missing suspect.

(c) The department shall also send the alert to:

(1) any appropriate law enforcement agency;

(2) the Texas Department of Transportation; and

(3) a state agency described by Section 411.445.

Sec. 411.448. Content of Alert.

The alert must include:

(1) all appropriate information that is provided by the law enforcement agency under Section 411.446 and that may lead to the apprehension of the missing suspect; and

(2) a statement instructing any person with information related to the missing suspect to contact a law enforcement agency.

Sec. 411.449. Termination of Alert System.

(a) The director shall terminate any activation of the alert system with respect to a particular missing suspect not later than the earlier of the date on which:

(1) the missing suspect is apprehended;

(2) the department receives evidence that the missing suspect has left this state; or

(3) the department determines that the alert system will no longer aid in the apprehension of the missing suspect.

(b) A law enforcement agency that apprehends a missing suspect who is the subject of an alert under this subchapter shall notify the department as soon as possible that the missing suspect has been apprehended.

SUBCHAPTER Z MISCELLANEOUS PROVISIONS

Sec. 411.951. Study on Digital Identification and Proof of Licensure. [Expired.]

CHAPTER 420A TEXAS CIVIL COMMITMENT OFFICE [EXPIRES SEPTEMBER 1, 2027]

Sec. 420A.001. Definitions. [Expires September 1, 2027]

In this chapter:

(1) "Board" means the governing board of the Texas Civil Commitment Office.

(2) "Office" means the Texas Civil Commitment Office.

Sec. 420A.002. Office; Governing Board. [Expires September 1, 2027]

(a) The Texas Civil Commitment Office is a state agency.

(b) The office is governed by a board composed of five members appointed by the governor, including:

(1) one member experienced in the management of sex offenders;

(2) one member experienced in the investigation or prosecution of sex offenses; and

(3) one member experienced in counseling or advocating on behalf of victims of sexual assault.

(c) Members of the board serve staggered six-year terms, with the terms of one or two members expiring on February 1 of each odd-numbered year.

(d) A member of the board is entitled to travel expenses incurred in performing official duties and to a per diem equal to the maximum amount allowed on January 1 of that year for federal employees per diem for federal income tax purposes, subject to the same limitations provided for members of state boards and commissions in the General Appropriations Act.

Sec. 420A.003. Presiding Officer; Meetings. [Expires September 1, 2027]

(a) The governor shall designate a member of the board as presiding officer. The presiding officer serves at the discretion of the governor.

(a-1) The presiding officer shall select a member of the board as an assistant presiding officer and may create board committees.

(b) The board shall meet at least quarterly and at other times at the call of the presiding officer.

Sec. 420A.004. Sunset Provision. [Expires September 1, 2027]

The Texas Civil Commitment Office is subject to Chapter 325 (Texas Sunset Act). Unless continued in existence as provided by that chapter, the office is abolished and this chapter expires September 1, 2027.

Sec. 420A.005. Grants and Donations. [Expires September 1, 2027]

On behalf of the state, the office may apply for and accept grants and donations from any source to be used by the office in the performance of the duties of the office.

Sec. 420A.006. Public Interest Information. [Expires September 1, 2027]

The office shall prepare information of public interest describing the functions of the office and the procedures by which complaints are filed with and resolved by the office. The office shall make the information available to the public and appropriate state agencies.

Sec. 420A.007. Biennial Report. [Expires September 1, 2027]

Not later than December 1 of each even-numbered year, the office shall submit to the governor, the lieutenant governor, and the speaker of the house of representatives a report concerning the operation of the office. The office may include in the report any recommendations that the office considers appropriate.

Sec. 420A.008. Staff. [Expires September 1, 2027]

The office may select and employ a general counsel, staff attorneys, and other staff necessary to perform the office's functions.

Sec. 420A.009. Salary Career Ladder for Case Managers. [Expires September 1, 2027]

(a) The board shall adopt a salary career ladder for case managers. The salary career ladder must base a case manager's salary on the manager's classification and years of service with the office.

(b) [Repealed by Acts 2017, 85th Leg., ch. 34 (S.B. 1576), § 40, effective September 1, 2017.]

(c) [Repealed by Acts 2017, 85th Leg., ch. 34 (S.B. 1576), § 40, effective September 1, 2017.]

Sec. 420A.010. Powers and Duties. [Expires September 1, 2027]

The office shall perform appropriate functions related to the sex offender civil commitment program provided under Chapter 841, Health and Safety Code, including functions related to the provision of treatment and supervision to civilly committed sex offenders.

Sec. 420A.011. Administrative Attachment; Support. [Expires September 1, 2027]

(a) The office is administratively attached to the Health and Human Services Commission.

(b) The Health and Human Services Commission shall provide administrative support services, including human resources, budgetary, accounting, purchasing, payroll, information technology, and legal support services, to the office as necessary to carry out the purposes of this chapter.

(c) The office, in accordance with the rules and procedures of the Legislative Budget Board, shall prepare, approve, and submit a legislative appropriations request that is separate from the legislative appropriations request for the Health and Human Services Commission and is used to develop the office's budget structure. The office shall maintain the office's legislative appropriations request and budget structure separately from those of the commission.

CHAPTER 423
USE OF UNMANNED AIRCRAFT

Sec. 423.001. Definition.

In this chapter, "image" means any capturing of sound waves, thermal, infrared, ultraviolet, visible light, or other electromagnetic waves, odor, or other conditions existing on or about real property in this state or an individual located on that property.

Sec. 423.002. Nonapplicability.

(a) It is lawful to capture an image using an unmanned aircraft in this state:

(1) for the purpose of professional or scholarly research and development or for another academic purpose by a person acting on behalf of an institution of higher education or a private or independent institution of higher education, as those terms are defined by Section 61.003, Education Code, including a person who:

(A) is a professor, employee, or student of the institution; or

(B) is under contract with or otherwise acting under the direction or on behalf of the institution;

(2) in airspace designated as a test site or range authorized by the Federal Aviation Administration for the purpose of integrating unmanned aircraft systems into the national airspace;

(3) as part of an operation, exercise, or mission of any branch of the United States military;

(4) if the image is captured by a satellite for the purposes of mapping;

(5) if the image is captured by or for an electric or natural gas utility or a telecommunications provider:

(A) for operations and maintenance of utility or telecommunications facilities for the purpose of maintaining utility or telecommunications system reliability and integrity;

(B) for inspecting utility or telecommunications facilities to determine repair, maintenance, or replacement needs during and after construction of such facilities;

(C) for assessing vegetation growth for the purpose of maintaining clearances on utility or telecommunications easements; and

(D) for utility or telecommunications facility routing and siting for the purpose of providing utility or telecommunications service;

(6) with the consent of the individual who owns or lawfully occupies the real property captured in the image;

(7) pursuant to a valid search or arrest warrant;

(8) if the image is captured by a law enforcement authority or a person who is under contract with or otherwise acting under the direction or on behalf of a law enforcement authority:

(A) in immediate pursuit of a person law enforcement officers have reasonable suspicion or probable cause to suspect has committed an offense, not including misdemeanors or offenses punishable by a fine only;

(B) for the purpose of documenting a crime scene where an offense, not including misdemeanors or offenses punishable by a fine only, has been committed;

(C) for the purpose of investigating the scene of:

(i) a human fatality;

(ii) a motor vehicle accident causing death or serious bodily injury to a person; or

(iii) any motor vehicle accident on a state highway or federal interstate or highway;

(D) in connection with the search for a missing person;

(E) for the purpose of conducting a high-risk tactical operation that poses a threat to human life;

(F) of private property that is generally open to the public where the property owner consents to law enforcement public safety responsibilities; or

(G) of real property or a person on real property that is within 25 miles of the United States border for the sole purpose of ensuring border security;

(9) if the image is captured by state or local law enforcement authorities, or a person who is under contract with or otherwise acting under the direction or on behalf of state authorities, for the purpose of:

(A) surveying the scene of a catastrophe or other damage to determine whether a state of emergency should be declared;

(B) preserving public safety, protecting property, or surveying damage or contamination during a lawfully declared state of emergency; or

(C) conducting routine air quality sampling and monitoring, as provided by state or local law;

(10) at the scene of a spill, or a suspected spill, of hazardous materials;

(11) for the purpose of fire suppression;

(12) for the purpose of rescuing a person whose life or well-being is in imminent danger;

(13) if the image is captured by a Texas licensed real estate broker in connection with the marketing, sale, or financing of real property, provided that no individual is identifiable in the image;

(14) from a height no more than eight feet above ground level in a public place, if the image was captured without using any electronic, mechanical, or other means to amplify the image beyond normal human perception;

(15) of public real property or a person on that property;

(16) if the image is captured by the owner or operator of an oil, gas, water, or other pipeline for the purpose of inspecting, maintaining, or repairing pipelines or other related facilities, and is captured without the intent to conduct surveillance on an individual or real property located in this state;

(17) in connection with oil pipeline safety and rig protection;

(18) in connection with port authority surveillance and security;

(19) if the image is captured by a registered professional land surveyor in connection with the practice of professional surveying, as those terms are defined by Section 1071.002, Occupations Code, provided that no individual is identifiable in the image;

(20) if the image is captured by a professional engineer licensed under Subchapter G, Chapter 1001, Occupations Code, in connection with the practice of engineering, as defined by Section 1001.003, Occupations Code, provided that no individual is identifiable in the image; or

(21) if:

(A) the image is captured by an employee of an insurance company or of an affiliate of the company in connection with the underwriting of an insurance policy, or the rating or adjusting of an insurance claim, regarding real property or a structure on real property; and

(B) the operator of the unmanned aircraft is authorized by the Federal Aviation Administration to conduct operations within the airspace from which the image is captured.

(b) This chapter does not apply to the manufacture, assembly, distribution, or sale of an unmanned aircraft.

Sec. 423.003. Offense: Illegal Use of Unmanned Aircraft to Capture Image.

(a) A person commits an offense if the person uses an unmanned aircraft to capture an image of an individual or privately owned real property in this state with the intent to conduct surveillance on the individual or property captured in the image.

(b) An offense under this section is a Class C misdemeanor.

(c) It is a defense to prosecution under this section that the person destroyed the image:

(1) as soon as the person had knowledge that the image was captured in violation of this section; and

(2) without disclosing, displaying, or distributing the image to a third party.

(d) In this section, "intent" has the meaning assigned by Section 6.03, Penal Code.

Sec. 423.004. Offense: Possession, Disclosure, Display, Distribution, or Use of Image.

(a) A person commits an offense if the person:

(1) captures an image in violation of Section 423.003; and

(2) possesses, discloses, displays, distributes, or otherwise uses that image.

(b) An offense under this section for the possession of an image is a Class C misdemeanor. An offense under this section for the disclosure, display, distribution, or other use of an image is a Class B misdemeanor.

(c) Each image a person possesses, discloses, displays, distributes, or otherwise uses in violation of this section is a separate offense.

(d) It is a defense to prosecution under this section for the possession of an image that the person destroyed the image as soon as the person had knowledge that the image was captured in violation of Section 423.003.

(e) It is a defense to prosecution under this section for the disclosure, display, distribution, or other use of an image that the person stopped disclosing, displaying, distributing, or otherwise using the image as soon as the person had knowledge that the image was captured in violation of Section 423.003.

Sec. 423.0045. Offense: Operation of Unmanned Aircraft Over Correctional Facility, Detention Facility, or Critical Infrastructure Facility.

(a) In this section:

(1) "Correctional facility" means:

(A) a confinement facility operated by or under contract with any division of the Texas Department of Criminal Justice;

(B) a municipal or county jail;

(C) a confinement facility operated by or under contract with the Federal Bureau of Prisons; or

(D) a secure correctional facility or secure detention facility, as defined by Section 51.02, Family Code.

(1-a) "Critical infrastructure facility" means:

(A) one of the following, if completely enclosed by a fence or other physical barrier that is obviously designed to exclude intruders, or if clearly marked with a sign or signs that are posted on the property, are reasonably likely to come to the attention of intruders, and indicate that entry is forbidden:

(i) a petroleum or alumina refinery;

(ii) an electrical power generating facility, substation, switching station, or electrical control center;

(iii) a chemical, polymer, or rubber manufacturing facility;

(iv) a water intake structure, water treatment facility, wastewater treatment plant, or pump station;

(v) a natural gas compressor station;

(vi) a liquid natural gas terminal or storage facility;

(vii) a telecommunications central switching office or any structure used as part of a system to provide wired or wireless telecommunications services;

(viii) a port, a public or private airport depicted in any current aeronautical chart published by the Federal Aviation Administration, a railroad switching yard, a trucking terminal, or any other freight transportation facility;

(ix) a gas processing plant, including a plant used in the processing, treatment, or fractionation of natural gas;

(x) a transmission facility used by a federally licensed radio or television station;

(xi) a steelmaking facility that uses an electric arc furnace to make steel;

(xii) a dam that is classified as a high hazard by the Texas Commission on Environmental Quality;

(xiii) a concentrated animal feeding operation, as defined by Section 26.048, Water Code; or

(xiv) a military installation owned or operated by or for the federal government, the state, or another governmental entity; or

(B) if enclosed by a fence or other physical barrier obviously designed to exclude intruders:

(i) any portion of an aboveground oil, gas, or chemical pipeline;

(ii) an oil or gas drilling site;

(iii) a group of tanks used to store crude oil, such as a tank battery;

(iv) an oil, gas, or chemical production facility;

(v) an oil or gas wellhead; or

(vi) any oil and gas facility that has an active flare.

(2) "Dam" means any barrier, including any appurtenant structures, that is constructed for the purpose of permanently or temporarily impounding water.

(3) "Detention facility" means a facility operated by or under contract with United States Immigration and Customs Enforcement for the purpose of detaining aliens and placing them in removal proceedings.

(b) A person commits an offense if the person intentionally or knowingly:

(1) operates an unmanned aircraft over a correctional facility, detention facility, or critical infrastructure facility and the unmanned aircraft is not higher than 400 feet above ground level;

(2) allows an unmanned aircraft to make contact with a correctional facility, detention facility, or critical infrastructure facility, including any person or object on the premises of or within the facility; or

(3) allows an unmanned aircraft to come within a distance of a correctional facility, detention facility, or critical infrastructure facility that is close enough to interfere with the operations of or cause a disturbance to the facility.

(c) This section does not apply to:

(1) conduct described by Subsection (b) that involves a correctional facility, detention facility, or critical infrastructure facility and is committed by:

(A) the federal government, the state, or a governmental entity;

(B) a person under contract with or otherwise acting under the direction or on behalf of the federal government, the state, or a governmental entity;

(C) a law enforcement agency;

(D) a person under contract with or otherwise acting under the direction or on behalf of a law enforcement agency; or

(E) an operator of an unmanned aircraft that is being used for a commercial purpose, if the operation is conducted in compliance with:

(i) each applicable Federal Aviation Administration rule, restriction, or exemption; and

(ii) all required Federal Aviation Administration authorizations; or

(2) conduct described by Subsection (b) that involves a critical infrastructure facility and is committed by:

(A) an owner or operator of the critical infrastructure facility;

(B) a person under contract with or otherwise acting under the direction or on behalf of an owner or operator of the critical infrastructure facility;

(C) a person who has the prior written consent of the owner or operator of the critical infrastructure facility; or

(D) the owner or occupant of the property on which the critical infrastructure facility is located or a person who has the prior written consent of the owner or occupant of that property.

(d) An offense under this section is a Class B misdemeanor, except that the offense is a Class A misdemeanor if the actor has previously been convicted under this section or Section 423.0046.

Sec. 423.0046. Offense: Operation of Unmanned Aircraft Over Sports Venue.

(a) In this section, "sports venue" means an arena, automobile racetrack, coliseum, stadium, or other type of area or facility that:

(1) has a seating capacity of 30,000 or more people; and

(2) is primarily used for one or more professional or amateur sports or athletics events.

(b) A person commits an offense if the person intentionally or knowingly operates an unmanned aircraft over a sports venue and the unmanned aircraft is not higher than 400 feet above ground level.

(c) This section does not apply to conduct described by Subsection (b) that is committed by:

(1) the federal government, the state, or a governmental entity;

(2) a person under contract with or otherwise acting under the direction or on behalf of the federal government, the state, or a governmental entity;

(3) a law enforcement agency;

(4) a person under contract with or otherwise acting under the direction or on behalf of a law enforcement agency;

(5) an operator of an unmanned aircraft that is being used for a commercial purpose, if the operation is conducted in compliance with:

(A) each applicable Federal Aviation Administration rule, restriction, or exemption; and

(B) all required Federal Aviation Administration authorizations;

(6) an owner or operator of the sports venue;

(7) a person under contract with or otherwise acting under the direction or on behalf of an owner or operator of the sports venue; or

(8) a person who has the prior written consent of the owner or operator of the sports venue.

(d) An offense under this section is a Class B misdemeanor, except that the offense is a Class A misdemeanor if the actor has previously been convicted under this section or Section 423.0045.

Sec. 423.005. Illegally or Incidentally Captured Images Not Subject to Disclosure.

(a) Except as otherwise provided by Subsection (b), an image captured in violation of Section 423.003, or an image captured by an unmanned aircraft that was incidental to the lawful capturing of an image:

(1) may not be used as evidence in any criminal or juvenile proceeding, civil action, or administrative proceeding;

(2) is not subject to disclosure, inspection, or copying under Chapter 552; and

(3) is not subject to discovery, subpoena, or other means of legal compulsion for its release.

(b) An image described by Subsection (a) may be disclosed and used as evidence to prove a violation of this chapter and is subject to discovery, subpoena, or other means of legal compulsion for that purpose.

Sec. 423.006. Civil Action.

(a) An owner or tenant of privately owned real property located in this state may bring against a person who, in violation of Section 423.003, captured an image of the property or the owner or tenant while on the property an action to:

(1) enjoin a violation or imminent violation of Section 423.003 or 423.004;

(2) recover a civil penalty of:

(A) $5,000 for all images captured in a single episode in violation of Section 423.003; or

(B) $10,000 for disclosure, display, distribution, or other use of any images captured in a single episode in violation of Section 423.004; or

(3) recover actual damages if the person who captured the image in violation of Section 423.003 discloses, displays, or distributes the image with malice.

(b) For purposes of recovering the civil penalty or actual damages under Subsection (a), all owners of a parcel of real property are considered to be a single owner and all tenants of a parcel of real property are considered to be a single tenant.

(c) In this section, "malice" has the meaning assigned by Section 41.001, Civil Practice and Remedies Code.

(d) In addition to any civil penalties authorized under this section, the court shall award court costs and reasonable attorney's fees to the prevailing party.

(e) Venue for an action under this section is governed by Chapter 15, Civil Practice and Remedies Code.

(f) An action brought under this section must be commenced within two years from the date the image was:

(1) captured in violation of Section 423.003; or

(2) initially disclosed, displayed, distributed, or otherwise used in violation of Section 423.004.

Sec. 423.007. Rules for Use by Law Enforcement.

The Department of Public Safety shall adopt rules and guidelines for use of an unmanned aircraft by a law enforcement authority in this state.

Sec. 423.008. Reporting by Law Enforcement Agency.

(a) Not earlier than January 1 and not later than January 15 of each odd-numbered year, each state law enforcement agency and each county or municipal law enforcement agency located in a county or municipality, as applicable, with a population greater than 150,000, that used or operated an unmanned aircraft during the preceding 24 months shall issue a written report to the governor, the lieutenant governor, and each member of the legislature and shall:

(1) retain the report for public viewing; and

(2) post the report on the law enforcement agency's publicly accessible website, if one exists.

(b) The report must include:

(1) the number of times an unmanned aircraft was used, organized by date, time, location, and the types of incidents and types of justification for the use;

(2) the number of criminal investigations aided by the use of an unmanned aircraft and a description of how the unmanned aircraft aided each investigation;

(3) the number of times an unmanned aircraft was used for a law enforcement operation other than a criminal investigation, the dates and locations of those operations, and a description of how the unmanned aircraft aided each operation;

(4) the type of information collected on an individual, residence, property, or area that was not the subject of a law enforcement operation and the frequency of the collection of this information; and

(5) the total cost of acquiring, maintaining, repairing, and operating or otherwise using each unmanned aircraft for the preceding 24 months.

Sec. 423.009. Regulation of Unmanned Aircraft by Political Subdivision.

(a) In this section:

(1) "Political subdivision" includes a county, a joint board created under Section 22.074, Transportation Code, and a municipality.

(2) "Special event" means a festival, celebration, or other gathering that:

(A) involves:

(i) the reservation and temporary use of all or a portion of a public park, road, or other property of a political subdivision; and

(ii) entertainment, the sale of merchandise, food, or beverages, or mass participation in a sports event; and

(B) requires a significant use or coordination of a political subdivision's services.

(b) Except as provided by Subsection (c), a political subdivision may not adopt or enforce any ordinance, order, or other similar measure regarding the operation of an unmanned aircraft.

(c) A political subdivision may adopt and enforce an ordinance, order, or other similar measure regarding:

(1) the use of an unmanned aircraft during a special event;

(2) the political subdivision's use of an unmanned aircraft; or

(3) the use of an unmanned aircraft near a facility or infrastructure owned by the political subdivision, if the political subdivision:

(A) applies for and receives authorization from the Federal Aviation Administration to adopt the regulation; and

(B) after providing reasonable notice, holds a public hearing on the political subdivision's intent to apply for the authorization.

(d) An ordinance, order, or other similar measure that violates Subsection (b) is void and unenforceable.

SUBTITLE C
STATE MILITARY FORCES AND VETERANS

CHAPTER 431
STATE MILITIA

SUBCHAPTER F
SERVICE AND DUTIES [REPEALED]

Sec. 431.086. Exemption from Arrest [Repealed].

Repealed by Acts 2013, 83rd Leg., ch. 1217 (S.B. 1536), § 4.01(2), effective September 1, 2013.

SUBTITLE G
CORRECTIONS

CHAPTER 508
PAROLE AND MANDATORY SUPERVISION

SUBCHAPTER F
MANDATORY CONDITIONS OF PAROLE OR MANDATORY SUPERVISION

Sec. 508.181. Residence During Release.

(a) Except as provided by Subsections (b) and (c), a parole panel shall require as a condition of parole or mandatory supervision that the releasee reside in the county in which:

(1) the releasee resided at the time of committing the offense for which the releasee was sentenced to the institutional division; or

(2) the releasee committed the offense for which the releasee was sentenced to the institutional division, if the releasee was not a resident of this state at the time of committing the offense.

(b) A parole panel may require a releasee to reside in a county other than the county required under Subsection (a) to:

(1) protect the life or safety of:

(A) a victim of the releasee's offense;

(B) the releasee;

(C) a witness in the case; or

(D) any other person; or

(2) increase the likelihood of the releasee's successful completion of parole or mandatory supervision, because of:

(A) written expressions of significant public concern in the county in which the releasee would otherwise be required to reside;

(B) the presence of family members or friends in the other county who have expressed a willingness to assist the releasee in successfully completing the conditions of the releasee's parole or mandatory supervision;

Government Code

(C) the verified existence of a job offer in the other county; or

(D) the availability of a treatment program, educational program, or other social service program in the other county that is not available in the county in which the releasee is otherwise required to reside under Subsection (a).

(c) At any time after a releasee is released on parole or to mandatory supervision, a parole panel may modify the conditions of parole or mandatory supervision to require the releasee to reside in a county other than the county required by the original conditions. In making a decision under this subsection, a parole panel must consider the factors listed under Subsection (b).

(d) If a parole panel initially requires the releasee to reside in a county other than the county required under Subsection (a), the parole panel shall subsequently require the releasee to reside in the county described under Subsection (a) if the requirement that the releasee reside in the other county was based on:

(1) the verified existence of a job offer under Subsection (b)(2)(C) and the releasee is no longer employed or actively seeking employment; or

(2) the availability of a treatment program, educational program, or other social service program under Subsection (b)(2)(D) and the releasee:

(A) no longer regularly participates in the program as required by a condition of parole or mandatory supervision; or

(B) has successfully completed the program but has violated another condition of the releasee's parole or mandatory supervision.

(e) If a parole panel requires the releasee to reside in a county other than the county required under Subsection (a), the panel shall:

(1) state in writing the reason for the panel's decision; and

(2) place the statement in the releasee's permanent record.

(f) This section does not apply to a decision by a parole panel to require a releasee to serve the period of parole or mandatory supervision in another state.

(g) The division shall, on the first working day of each month, notify the sheriff of any county in which the total number of sex offenders under the supervision and control of the division residing in the county exceeds 10 percent of the total number of sex offenders in the state under the supervision and control of the division. The notice must be provided by e-mail or other electronic communication. If the total number of sex offenders under the supervision and control of the division residing in a county exceeds 22 percent of the total number of sex offenders in the state under the supervision and control of the division, a parole panel may require a sex offender to reside in that county only as required by Subsection (a) or for the reason stated in Subsection (b)(2)(B). In this subsection, "sex offender" means a person who is released on parole or to mandatory supervision after serving a sentence for an offense described by Section 508.187(a).

(h) If a parole panel requires a releasee to reside in a county other than the county required under Subsection (a), the division shall include the reason for residency exemption in the required notification to the sheriff of the county in which the defendant is to reside, the chief of police of the municipality in which the halfway house is located, and the attorney who represents the state in the prosecution of felonies in that county.

Sec. 508.182. Parole Supervision Fee; Administrative Fee.

(a) A parole panel shall require as a condition of parole or mandatory supervision that a releasee pay to the division for each month during which the releasee is under parole supervision:

(1) a parole supervision fee of $10; and

(2) an administrative fee of $8.

(b) A fee under this section applies to an inmate released in another state who is required as a condition of the inmate's release to report to a parole officer or supervisor in this state for parole supervision.

(c) On the request of the releasee, a parole panel may allow the releasee to defer one or more payments under this section. The releasee remains responsible for payment of the fee and shall pay the amount of the deferred payment not later than the second anniversary of the date the payment becomes due.

(d) The Texas Board of Criminal Justice shall adopt rules relating to the method of payment required of the releasee.

(e) The division shall remit fees collected under this section to the comptroller. The comptroller shall deposit the fees collected under:

(1) Subsection (a)(1) in the general revenue fund; and

(2) Subsection (a)(2) in the compensation to victims of crime fund.

(f) In a parole or mandatory supervision revocation hearing under Section 508.281 at which it is alleged only that the releasee failed to make a payment under this section, it is an affirmative defense to revocation that the releasee is unable to pay the amount as ordered by a parole panel. The releasee must prove the affirmative defense by a preponderance of the evidence.

Sec. 508.183. Educational Skill Level.

(a) A parole panel shall require as a condition of release on parole or release to mandatory supervision that an inmate demonstrate to the parole panel whether the inmate has an educational skill level that is equal to or greater than the average skill level of students who have completed the sixth grade in a public school in this state.

(b) If the parole panel determines that the inmate has not attained that skill level, the parole panel shall require as a condition of parole or mandatory supervision that the inmate as a releasee attain that level of educational skill, unless the parole panel determines that the inmate lacks the intellectual capacity or the learning ability to ever achieve that level of skill.

Sec. 508.184. Controlled Substance Testing.

(a) A parole panel shall require as a condition of parole or mandatory supervision that a releasee submit to testing for controlled substances on evidence that:

(1) a controlled substance is present in the releasee's body;

(2) the releasee has used a controlled substance; or

(3) the use of a controlled substance is related to the offense for which the releasee was convicted.

(b) The Texas Board of Criminal Justice by rule shall adopt procedures for the administration of a test required under this section.

Sec. 508.185. Substance Abuse Treatment.

(a) A parole panel shall require as a condition of release on parole or release to mandatory supervision that an inmate who immediately before release is a participant in the program established under Section 501.0931 participate as a releasee in a drug or alcohol abuse continuum of care treatment program.

(b) The Texas Commission on Alcohol and Drug Abuse shall develop the continuum of care treatment program.

Sec. 508.186. Sex Offender Registration.

A parole panel shall require as a condition of parole or mandatory supervision that a releasee required to register as a sex offender under Chapter 62, Code of Criminal Procedure:

(1) register under that chapter; and

(2) submit a blood sample or other specimen to the Department of Public Safety under Subchapter G, Chapter 411, for the purpose of creating a DNA record of the releasee, unless the releasee has already submitted the required specimen under other state law.

Sec. 508.1861. Prohibitions on Internet Access for Certain Sex Offenders.

(a) This section applies only to a person who, on release, will be required to register as a sex offender under Chapter 62, Code of Criminal Procedure, by court order or otherwise, and:

(1) is serving a sentence for an offense under Section 21.11, 22.011(a)(2), 22.021(a)(1)(B), 33.021, or 43.25, Penal Code;

(2) used the Internet or any other type of electronic device used for Internet access to commit the offense or engage in the conduct for which the person is required to register under Chapter 62, Code of Criminal Procedure; or

(3) is assigned a numeric risk level of two or three based on an assessment conducted under Article 62.007, Code of Criminal Procedure.

(b) If the parole panel releases on parole or to mandatory supervision a person described by Subsection (a), the parole panel as a condition of parole or mandatory supervision shall:

(1) prohibit the releasee from using the Internet to:

(A) access material that is obscene as defined by Section 43.21, Penal Code;

(B) access a commercial social networking site, as defined by Article 62.0061(f), Code of Criminal Procedure;

(C) communicate with any individual concerning sexual relations with an individual who is younger than 17 years of age; or

(D) communicate with another individual the releasee knows is younger than 17 years of age; and

(2) to ensure the releasee's compliance with Subdivision (1), require the releasee to submit to regular inspection or monitoring of each electronic device used by the releasee to access the Internet.

(c) The parole panel may modify at any time the condition described by Subsection (b)(1)(D) if:

(1) the condition interferes with the releasee's ability to attend school or become or remain employed and consequently constitutes an undue hardship for the releasee; or

(2) the releasee is the parent or guardian of an individual who is younger than 17 years of age and the releasee is not otherwise prohibited from communicating with that individual.

Sec. 508.1862. Sex Offender Treatment.

A parole panel shall require as a condition of release on parole or to mandatory supervision that a releasee participate in a sex offender treatment program developed by the department if:

(1) the releasee:

(A) was serving a sentence for an offense under Chapter 21, Penal Code; or

(B) is required to register as a sex offender under Chapter 62, Code of Criminal Procedure; and

(2) immediately before release, the releasee is participating in a sex offender treatment program established under Section 499.054.

Sec. 508.1864. Notification to Department of Public Safety and Licensing Authority.

(a) In this section, "health care professional," "license," and "licensing authority" have the meanings assigned by Section 108.051, Occupations Code.

(b) A parole panel that knows an inmate holds or has submitted an application for a license as a health care professional shall immediately notify the Department of Public Safety and the applicable licensing authority if the parole panel requires the inmate as a condition of release on parole or to mandatory supervision to register as a sex offender under Chapter 62, Code of Criminal Procedure.

Sec. 508.187. Child Safety Zone.

(a) This section applies only to a releasee serving a sentence for an offense under:

(1) Section 43.25 or 43.26, Penal Code;

(2) Section 21.02, 21.11, 22.011, 22.021, or 25.02, Penal Code;

(3) Section 20.04(a)(4), Penal Code, if the releasee committed the offense with the intent to violate or abuse the victim sexually;

(4) Section 30.02, Penal Code, punishable under Subsection (d) of that section, if the releasee committed the offense with the intent to commit a felony listed in Subdivision (2) or (3);

(5) Section 43.05(a)(2), Penal Code; or

(6) Section 20A.02, Penal Code, if the defendant:

(A) trafficked the victim with the intent or knowledge that the victim would engage in sexual conduct, as defined by Section 43.25, Penal Code; or

(B) benefited from participating in a venture that involved a trafficked victim engaging in sexual conduct, as defined by Section 43.25, Penal Code.

(b) A parole panel shall establish a child safety zone applicable to a releasee if the panel determines that a child as defined by Section 22.011(c), Penal Code, was the victim of the offense, by requiring as a condition of parole or mandatory supervision that the releasee:

(1) not:

(A) supervise or participate in any program that includes as participants or recipients persons who are 17 years of age or younger and that regularly provides athletic, civic, or cultural activities; or

(B) go in, on, or within a distance specified by the panel of premises where children commonly gather, including a school, day-care facility, playground, public or private youth center, public swimming pool, or video arcade facility; and

(2) attend for a period of time determined necessary by the panel psychological counseling sessions for sex offenders with an individual or organization that provides sex offender treatment or counseling as specified by the parole officer supervising the releasee after release.

(b-1) Notwithstanding Subsection (b)(1)(B), a requirement that a releasee not go in, on, or within a distance specified by a parole panel of certain premises does not apply to a releasee while the releasee is in or going immediately to or from:

(1) a parole office;

(2) premises at which the releasee is participating in a program or activity required as a condition of release;

(3) a residential facility in which the releasee is required to reside as a condition of release;

(4) a private residence in which the releasee is required to reside as a condition of release; or

(5) any other premises, facility, or location that is:

(A) designed to rehabilitate or reform the releasee; or

(B) authorized by the division as a premises, facility, or location where it is reasonable and necessary for the releasee to be present and at which the releasee has legitimate business, including a church, synagogue, or other established place of religious worship, a workplace, a health care facility, or a location of a funeral.

(c) A parole officer who under Subsection (b)(2) specifies a sex offender treatment provider to provide counseling to a releasee shall:

(1) contact the provider before the releasee is released;

(2) establish the date, time, and place of the first session between the releasee and the provider; and

(3) request the provider to immediately notify the officer if the releasee fails to attend the first session or any subsequent scheduled session.

(d) At any time after the imposition of a condition under Subsection (b)(1), the releasee may request the parole panel to modify the child safety zone applicable to the releasee because the zone as created by the panel:

Government Code

(1) interferes with the releasee's ability to attend school or hold a job and consequently constitutes an undue hardship for the releasee; or

(2) is broader than necessary to protect the public, given the nature and circumstances of the offense.

(e) A parole officer supervising a releasee may permit the releasee to enter on an event-by-event basis into the child safety zone that the releasee is otherwise prohibited from entering if:

(1) the releasee has served at least two years of the period of supervision imposed on release;

(2) the releasee enters the zone as part of a program to reunite with the releasee's family;

(3) the releasee presents to the parole officer a written proposal specifying:

(A) where the releasee intends to go within the zone;

(B) why and with whom the releasee is going; and

(C) how the releasee intends to cope with any stressful situations that occur;

(4) the sex offender treatment provider treating the releasee agrees with the officer that the releasee should be allowed to attend the event; and

(5) the officer and the treatment provider agree on a chaperon to accompany the releasee, and the chaperon agrees to perform that duty.

(f) In this section, "playground," "premises," "school," "video arcade facility," and "youth center" have the meanings assigned by Section 481.134, Health and Safety Code.

Sec. 508.188. Community Service for Certain Releasees.

A parole panel shall require as a condition of parole or mandatory supervision that a releasee for whom the court has made an affirmative finding under Article 42.014, Code of Criminal Procedure, perform not less than 300 hours of community service at a project designated by the parole panel that primarily serves the person or group that was the target of the releasee.

Sec. 508.189. Parole Fee for Certain Releasees.

(a) A parole panel shall require as a condition of parole or mandatory supervision that a releasee convicted of an offense under Section 21.02, 21.08, 21.11, 22.011, 22.021, 25.02, 43.25, or 43.26, Penal Code, pay to the division a parole supervision fee of $5 each month during the period of parole supervision.

(b) The division shall send fees collected under this section to the comptroller. The comptroller shall deposit the fees in the general revenue fund to the credit of the sexual assault program fund established under Section 44.0061, Health and Safety Code.

Sec. 508.190. Avoiding Victim of Stalking Offense.

(a) A parole panel shall require as a condition of parole or mandatory supervision that a releasee serving a sentence for an offense under Section 42.072, Penal Code, not:

(1) communicate directly or indirectly with the victim;

(2) go to or near the residence, place of employment, or business of the victim; or

(3) go to or near a school, day-care facility, or similar facility where a dependent child of the victim is in attendance.

(b) If a parole panel requires the prohibition contained in Subsection (a)(2) or (3) as a condition of parole or mandatory supervision, the parole panel shall specifically describe the prohibited locations and the minimum distances, if any, that the releasee must maintain from the locations.

Sec. 508.191. No Contact with Victim.

(a) If a parole panel releases a defendant on parole or to mandatory supervision, the panel shall require as a condition of parole or mandatory supervision that the defendant not intentionally or knowingly communicate directly or indirectly with a victim of the offense or intentionally or knowingly go near a residence, school, place of employment, or business of a victim. At any time after the defendant is released on parole or to mandatory supervision, a victim of the offense may petition the panel for a modification of the conditions of the defendant's parole or mandatory supervision allowing the defendant contact with the victim subject to reasonable restrictions.

(b) Notwithstanding Subsection (a), a defendant may participate in victim-offender mediation authorized by Section 508.324 on the request of the victim or a guardian of the victim or a close relative of a deceased victim.

(c) In this section, "victim" has the meaning assigned by Article 56A.001, Code of Criminal Procedure.

Sec. 508.192. Reentry into the United States Prohibited.

(a) In this section, "illegal criminal alien" has the meaning assigned by Section 493.015.

(b) A parole panel shall require as a condition of parole or mandatory supervision that an illegal criminal alien released to the custody of United States Immigration and Customs Enforcement:

(1) regardless of whether a final order of deportation is issued with reference to the illegal criminal alien, leave the United States as soon as possible after release; and

(2) not unlawfully return to or unlawfully reenter the United States in violation of the Immigration Reform and Control Act of 1986 (8 U.S.C. Section 1101 et seq.).

SUBCHAPTER G DISCRETIONARY CONDITIONS OF PAROLE OR MANDATORY SUPERVISION

Sec. 508.221. Conditions Permitted Generally.

A parole panel may impose as a condition of parole or mandatory supervision any condition that a court may impose on a defendant placed on community supervision under Chapter 42A, Code of Criminal Procedure, including the condition that a releasee submit to testing for controlled substances or submit to electronic monitoring if the parole panel determines that without testing for controlled substances or participation in an electronic monitoring program the inmate would not be released on parole.

Sec. 508.222. Payment of Certain Damages.

A parole panel may require as a condition of parole or mandatory supervision that a releasee make payments in satisfaction of damages for which the releasee is liable under Section 500.002.

Sec. 508.223. Psychological Counseling.

A parole panel may require as a condition of parole or mandatory supervision that a releasee serving a sentence for an offense under Section 42.072, Penal Code, attend psychological counseling sessions of a type and for a duration as specified by the parole panel, if the parole panel determines in consultation with a local mental health services provider that appropriate mental health services are available through the Texas Department of Mental Health and Mental Retardation in accordance with Section 534.053, Health and Safety Code, or through another mental health services provider.

Sec. 508.224. Substance Abuse Counseling.

A parole panel may require as a condition of parole or mandatory supervision that the releasee attend counseling sessions for substance abusers or participate in substance abuse treatment services in a program or facility approved or licensed by the Texas Commission on Alcohol and Drug Abuse if:

(1) the releasee was sentenced for an offense involving a controlled substance; or

(2) the panel determines that the releasee's substance abuse was related to the commission of the offense.

Sec. 508.225. Child Safety Zone.

(a) If the nature of the offense for which an inmate is serving a sentence warrants the establishment of a child safety zone, a parole panel may establish a child safety zone applicable to an inmate serving a sentence for an offense listed in Article 42A.054(a), Code of Criminal Procedure, or for which the judgment contains an affirmative finding under Article 42A.054(c) or (d), Code of Criminal Procedure, by requiring as a condition of parole or release to mandatory supervision that the inmate not:

(1) supervise or participate in any program that includes as participants or recipients persons who are 17 years of age or younger and that regularly provides athletic, civic, or cultural activities; or

(2) go in or on, or within a distance specified by the panel of, a premises where children commonly gather, including a school, day-care facility, playground, public or private youth center, public swimming pool, or video arcade facility.

(a-1) Notwithstanding Subsection (a)(2), a requirement that an inmate not go in, on, or within a distance specified by a parole panel of certain premises does not apply to an inmate while the inmate is in or going immediately to or from:

(1) a parole office;

(2) premises at which the inmate is participating in a program or activity required as a condition of release;

(3) a residential facility in which the inmate is required to reside as a condition of release;

(4) a private residence in which the inmate is required to reside as a condition of release; or

(5) any other premises, facility, or location that is:

(A) designed to rehabilitate or reform the inmate; or

(B) authorized by the division as a premises, facility, or location where it is reasonable and necessary for the inmate to be present and at which the inmate has legitimate business, including a church,

Government Code

synagogue, or other established place of religious worship, a workplace, a health care facility, or a location of a funeral.

(b) At any time after the imposition of a condition under Subsection (a), the inmate may request the parole panel to modify the child safety zone applicable to the inmate because the zone as created by the panel:

(1) interferes with the ability of the inmate to attend school or hold a job and consequently constitutes an undue hardship for the inmate; or

(2) is broader than is necessary to protect the public, given the nature and circumstances of the offense.

(c) This section does not apply to an inmate described by Section 508.187.

(d) In this section, "playground," "premises," "school," "video arcade facility," and "youth center" have the meanings assigned by Section 481.134, Health and Safety Code.

Sec. 508.226. Orchiectomy As Condition Prohibited.

A parole panel may not require an inmate to undergo an orchiectomy as a condition of release on parole or to mandatory supervision.

Sec. 508.227. Electronic Monitoring of Certain Members of Criminal Street Gang.

(a) This section applies only to a releasee who:

(1) is identified as a member of a criminal street gang in an intelligence database established under Chapter 67, Code of Criminal Procedure; and

(2) has three or more times been convicted of, or received a grant of deferred adjudication community supervision or another functionally equivalent form of community supervision or probation for, a felony offense under the laws of this state, another state, or the United States.

(b) A parole panel may require as a condition of release on parole or to mandatory supervision that a releasee described by Subsection (a) submit to tracking under an electronic monitoring service or other appropriate technological service designed to track a person's location.

Sec. 508.228. Sex Offender Treatment.

A parole panel may require as a condition of release on parole or to mandatory supervision that a releasee participate in a sex offender treatment program as specified by the parole panel if:

(1) the releasee:

(A) was serving a sentence for an offense under Chapter 21, Penal Code; or

(B) is required to register as a sex offender under Chapter 62, Code of Criminal Procedure; or

(2) a designated agent of the board after conducting a hearing that allows the releasee to contest the evidence, on evidence that a sex offense occurred during the commission of the offense for which the releasee was serving a sentence, makes an affirmative finding that, regardless of the offense for which the releasee was serving a sentence, the releasee constitutes a threat to society because of the releasee's lack of sexual control.

SUBCHAPTER H WARRANTS

Sec. 508.251. Issuance of Warrant or Summons.

(a) In a case of parole or mandatory supervision, the director or a designated agent of the director or, in another case, the board on order by the governor, may issue a warrant as provided by Section 508.252 for the return of:

(1) a releasee;

(2) an inmate released although not eligible for release;

(3) a resident released to a preparole or work program;

(4) an inmate released on emergency reprieve or on emergency absence under escort; or

(5) a person released on a conditional pardon.

(b) A warrant issued under Subsection (a) must require the return of the person to the institution from which the person was paroled or released.

(c) Instead of the issuance of a warrant under this section, the division:

(1) may issue to the person a summons requiring the person to appear for a hearing under Section 508.281 if the person:

(A) is not a releasee who is:

(i) on intensive supervision or superintensive supervision;

(ii) an absconder; or

(iii) determined by the division to be a threat to public safety; or

(B) is charged only with committing a new offense that is alleged to have been committed after the first anniversary of the date the person was released on parole or to mandatory supervision if:

(i) the new offense is a Class C misdemeanor under the Penal Code, other than an offense committed against a child younger than 17 years of age or an offense involving family violence, as defined by Section 71.004, Family Code;

Government Code

(ii) the person has maintained steady employment for at least one year;

(iii) the person has maintained a stable residence for at least one year; and

(iv) the person has not previously been charged with an offense after the person was released on parole or to mandatory supervision; and

(2) shall issue to the person a summons requiring the person to appear for a hearing under Section 508.281 if the person:

(A) is charged only with committing an administrative violation of release that is alleged to have been committed after the first anniversary of the date the person was released on parole or to mandatory supervision;

(B) is not serving a sentence for, and has not been previously convicted of, an offense listed in or described by Article 62.001(5), Code of Criminal Procedure; and

(C) is not a releasee with respect to whom a summons may not be issued under Subdivision (1).

(c-1) A summons issued under Subsection (c) must state the time, date, place, and purpose of the hearing.

(d) A designated agent of the director acts independently from a parole officer and must receive specialized training as determined by the director.

Sec. 508.252. Grounds for Issuance of Warrant or Summons.

A warrant or summons may be issued under Section 508.251 if:

(1) there is reason to believe that the person has been released although not eligible for release;

(2) the person has been arrested for an offense;

(3) there is a document that is self-authenticating as provided by Rule 902, Texas Rules of Evidence, stating that the person violated a rule or condition of release; or

(4) there is reliable evidence that the person has exhibited behavior during the person's release that indicates to a reasonable person that the person poses a danger to society that warrants the person's immediate return to custody.

Sec. 508.253. Effect on Sentence After Issuance of Warrant.

If it appears a releasee has violated a condition or provision of the releasee's parole or mandatory supervision, the date of the issuance of the warrant to the date of the releasee's arrest is not counted as a part of the time served under the releasee's sentence.

Sec. 508.254. Detention Under Warrant.

(a) A person who is the subject of a warrant may be held in custody pending a determination of all facts surrounding the alleged offense, violation of a rule or condition of release, or dangerous behavior.

(b) A warrant authorizes any officer named by the warrant to take custody of the person and detain the person until a parole panel orders the return of the person to the institution from which the person was released.

(c) Except as provided by Subsection (d), pending a hearing on a charge of parole violation, ineligible release, or violation of a condition of mandatory supervision, a person returned to custody shall remain confined.

(d) A magistrate of the county in which the person is held in custody may release the person on bond pending the hearing if:

(1) the person is arrested or held in custody only on a charge that the person committed an administrative violation of release;

(2) the division, in accordance with Subsection (e), included notice on the warrant for the person's arrest that the person is eligible for release on bond; and

(3) the magistrate determines that the person is not a threat to public safety.

(e) The division shall include a notice on the warrant for the person's arrest indicating that the person is eligible for release on bond under Subsection (d) if the division determines that the person:

(1) has not been previously convicted of:

(A) an offense under Chapter 29, Penal Code;

(B) an offense under Title 5, Penal Code, punishable as a felony; or

(C) an offense involving family violence, as defined by Section 71.004, Family Code;

(2) is not on intensive supervision or super-intensive supervision;

(3) is not an absconder; and

(4) is not a threat to public safety.

(f) The provisions of Chapters 17 and 22, Code of Criminal Procedure, apply to a person released under Subsection (d) in the same manner as those provisions apply to a person released pending an appearance before a court or magistrate, except that the release under that subsection is conditioned on the person's appearance at a hearing under this subchapter.

Sec. 508.255. Status As Fugitive from Justice.

(a) After the issuance of a warrant, a person for whose return a warrant was issued is a fugitive from justice.

(b) The law relating to the right of the state to extradite a person and return a fugitive from justice and Article 42.11, Code of Criminal Procedure, relating to the waiver of all legal requirements to obtain extradition of a fugitive from justice from another state to this state, are not impaired by this chapter and remain in full force and effect.

Sec. 508.256. Withdrawal of Warrant.

At any time before setting a revocation hearing date under Section 508.282, the division may withdraw a warrant and continue supervision of a releasee.

SUBCHAPTER I HEARINGS AND SANCTIONS

Sec. 508.281. Hearing.

(a) A releasee, a person released although ineligible for release, or a person granted a conditional pardon is entitled to a hearing before a parole panel or a designated agent of the board under the rules adopted by the board and within a period that permits a parole panel, a designee of the board, or the department to dispose of the charges within the periods established by Sections 508.282(a) and (b) if the releasee or person:

(1) is accused of a violation of the releasee's parole or mandatory supervision or the person's conditional pardon, on information and complaint by a peace officer or parole officer; or

(2) is arrested after an ineligible release.

(b) If a parole panel or designated agent of the board determines that a releasee or person granted a conditional pardon has been convicted of a felony offense committed while an administrative releasee and has been sentenced to a term of confinement in a penal institution, the determination is considered to be a sufficient hearing to revoke the parole or mandatory supervision or recommend to the governor revocation of a conditional pardon without further hearing, except that the parole panel or designated agent shall conduct a hearing to consider mitigating circumstances if requested by the releasee or person granted a conditional pardon.

(c) **[2 Versions: As amended by Acts 2015, 84th Leg., ch. 472]** If a designated agent of the board determines that a releasee who appears in compliance with a summons has violated a condition of release, the agent shall notify the board. After the board or a parole panel makes a final determination regarding the violation, the division may issue a warrant requiring the releasee to be held in a county jail pending the return of the releasee to the institution from which the releasee was released.

(c) **[2 Versions: As amended by Acts 2015, 84th Leg., ch. 693]** If a hearing before a designated agent of the board is held under this section for a releasee who appears in compliance with a summons, the sheriff of the county in which the releasee is required to appear shall provide the designated agent with a place at the county jail to hold the hearing. After the board or a parole panel makes a final determination that a releasee has violated a condition of release, a warrant may be issued requiring the releasee to be held in the county jail pending:

(1) transfer to an intermediate sanction facility; or

(2) the return of the releasee to the institution from which the releasee was released.

(d) If a parole panel or designated agent of the board determines that a releasee has violated a condition of release required under Section 508.192 and confirms the violation with a peace officer or other law enforcement officer of this state who is authorized under federal law to verify a person's immigration status or, in accordance with 8 U.S.C. Section 1373(c), with a federal law enforcement officer, the determination is considered to be a sufficient hearing to revoke the parole or mandatory supervision without further hearing or determination, except that the parole panel or designated agent shall conduct a hearing to consider mitigating circumstances, if requested by the releasee.

(e) A parole panel or designated agent of the board may not revoke the parole or mandatory supervision of a releasee if the parole panel or designated agent finds that the only evidence supporting the alleged violation of a condition of release is the uncorroborated results of a polygraph examination.

(f) Any hearing required to be conducted by a parole panel under this chapter may be conducted by a designated agent of the board. The designated agent may make recommendations to a parole panel that has responsibility for making a final determination.

Sec. 508.2811. Preliminary Hearing.

A parole panel or a designee of the board shall provide within a reasonable time to an inmate or person described by Section 508.281(a) a preliminary hearing to determine whether probable cause or reasonable grounds exist to believe that the inmate or person has committed an act that would constitute a violation of a condition of release, unless the inmate or person:

(1) waives the preliminary hearing; or

(2) after release:

(A) has been charged only with an administrative violation of a condition of release; or

(B) has been adjudicated guilty of or has pleaded guilty or nolo contendere to an offense committed after release, other than an offense punishable by fine only involving the operation of a motor vehicle, regardless of whether the court has deferred disposition of the case, imposed a sentence in the case, or placed the inmate or person on community supervision.

Sec. 508.282. Deadlines.

(a) Except as provided by Subsection (b), a parole panel, a designee of the board, or the department shall dispose of the charges against an inmate or person described by Section 508.281(a):

(1) before the 41st day after the date on which:

(A) a warrant issued as provided by Section 508.251 is executed, if the inmate or person is arrested only on a charge that the inmate or person has committed an administrative violation of a condition of release, and the inmate or person is not charged before the 41st day with the commission of an offense described by Section 508.2811(2)(B); or

(B) the sheriff having custody of an inmate or person alleged to have committed an offense after release notifies the department that:

(i) the inmate or person has discharged the sentence for the offense; or

(ii) the prosecution of the alleged offense has been dismissed by the attorney representing the state in the manner provided by Article 32.02, Code of Criminal Procedure; or

(2) within a reasonable time after the date on which the inmate or person is returned to the custody of the department, if:

(A) immediately before the return the inmate or person was in custody in another state or in a federal correctional system; or

(B) the inmate or person is transferred to the custody of the department under Section 508.284.

(b) A parole panel, a designee of the board, or the department is not required to dispose of the charges against an inmate or person within the period required by Subsection (a) if:

(1) the inmate or person is in custody in another state or a federal correctional institution;

(2) the parole panel or a designee of the board is not provided a place by the sheriff to hold the hearing, in which event the department, parole panel, or designee is not required to dispose of the charges against the inmate or person until the 30th day after the date on which the sheriff provides a place to hold the hearing; or

(3) the inmate or person is granted a continuance by a parole panel or a designee of the board in the inmate's or person's hearing under Section 508.281(a), but in no event may a parole panel, a designee of the board, or the department dispose of the charges against the person later than the 15th day after the date on which the parole panel, designee, or department would otherwise be required to dispose of the charges under this section, unless the inmate or person is released from custody and a summons is issued under Section 508.251 requiring the inmate or person to appear for a hearing under Section 508.281.

(c) In Subsections (a), (b), and (f), charges against an inmate or person are disposed of when:

(1) the inmate's or person's conditional pardon, parole, or release to mandatory supervision is:

(A) revoked; or

(B) continued or modified and the inmate or person is released from the county jail;

(2) the warrant for the inmate or person issued under Section 508.251 is withdrawn; or

(3) the inmate or person is transferred to a facility described by Section 508.284 for further proceedings.

(d) A sheriff, not later than the 10th day before the date on which the sheriff intends to release from custody an inmate or person described by Section 508.281(a) or transfer the inmate or person to the custody of an entity other than the department, shall notify the department of the intended release or transfer.

(e) If a warrant for an inmate or person issued under Section 508.251 is withdrawn, a summons may be issued requiring the inmate or person to appear for a hearing under Section 508.281.

(f) A parole panel, a designee of the board, or the department shall dispose of the charges against a releasee for whom a warrant is issued under Section 508.281(c) not later than the 31st day after the date on which the warrant is issued.

Sec. 508.283. Sanctions.

(a) After a parole panel or designated agent of the board has held a hearing under Section 508.281, in any manner warranted by the evidence:

(1) the board may recommend to the governor to continue, revoke, or modify the conditional pardon; and

(2) a parole panel may continue, revoke, or modify the parole or mandatory supervision.

(b) If the parole, mandatory supervision, or conditional pardon of a person described by Section 508.149(a) is revoked, the person may be required to serve the remaining portion of the sentence on which the person was released. The remaining portion is computed without credit for the time from the date of the person's release to the date of revocation.

(c) If the parole, mandatory supervision, or conditional pardon of a person other than a person described by Section 508.149(a) is revoked, the person may be required to serve the remaining portion of the sentence on which the person was released. For a person who on the date of issuance of a warrant or summons initiating the revocation process is subject to a sentence the remaining portion of which is greater than the amount of time from the date of the person's release to the date of issuance of the warrant or summons, the remaining portion is to be served without credit for the time from the date of the person's release to the date of revocation. For a person who on the date of issuance of the warrant or summons is subject to a sentence the remaining portion of which is less than the amount of time from the date of the person's release to the date of issuance of the warrant or summons, the remaining portion is to be served without credit for an amount of time equal to the remaining portion of the sentence on the date of issuance of the warrant or citation.

(d) If a warrant is issued charging a violation of a release condition or a summons is issued for a hearing under Section 508.281, the sentence time credit may be suspended until a determination is made in the case. The suspended time credit may be reinstated if the parole, mandatory supervision, or conditional pardon is continued.

(e) If a person's parole or mandatory supervision is modified after it is established that the person violated conditions of release, the board may require the releasee to remain under custodial supervision in a county jail for a period of not less than 60 days or more than 180 days. A sheriff is required to accept an inmate sanctioned under this subsection only if the commissioners court of the county in which the sheriff serves and the Texas Department of Criminal Justice have entered into a contract providing for the housing of persons sanctioned under this subsection.

Sec. 508.284. Transfer Pending Revocation Hearing.

The department, as provided by Section 508.282(c), may authorize a facility that is otherwise required to detain and house an inmate or person to transfer the inmate or person to a correctional facility operated by the department or under contract with the department if:

(1) the department determines that adequate space is available in the facility to which the inmate or person is to be transferred; and

(2) the facility to which the inmate or person is to be transferred is located not more than 150 miles from the facility from which the inmate or person is to be transferred.

SUBCHAPTER J MISCELLANEOUS

Sec. 508.311. Duty to Provide Information.

On request of a member of the board or employee of the board or department, a public official of the state, including a judge, district attorney, county attorney, or police officer, who has information relating to an inmate eligible for parole shall send to the department in writing the information in the official's possession or under the official's control.

Sec. 508.312. Information on Recidivism of Releasees.

The Texas Board of Criminal Justice shall collect information on recidivism of releasees under the supervision of the division and shall use the information to evaluate operations.

Sec. 508.313. Confidential Information.

(a) All information obtained and maintained, including a victim protest letter or other correspondence, a victim impact statement, a list of inmates eligible for release on parole, and an arrest record of an inmate, is confidential and privileged if the information relates to:

(1) an inmate of the institutional division subject to release on parole, release to mandatory supervision, or executive clemency;

(2) a releasee; or

(3) a person directly identified in any proposed plan of release for an inmate.

(b) Statistical and general information relating to the parole and mandatory supervision system, including the names of releasees and data recorded relating to parole and mandatory supervision services, is not confidential or privileged and must be made available for public inspection at any reasonable time.

Government Code

(c) The department, on request or in the normal course of official business, shall provide information that is confidential and privileged under Subsection (a) to:

(1) the governor;

(2) a member of the board or a parole commissioner;

(3) the Criminal Justice Policy Council in performing duties of the council under Section 413.017; or

(4) an eligible entity requesting information for a law enforcement, prosecutorial, correctional, clemency, or treatment purpose.

(d) In this section, "eligible entity" means:

(1) a government agency, including the office of a prosecuting attorney;

(2) an organization with which the department contracts or an organization to which the department provides a grant; or

(3) an organization to which inmates are referred for services by the department.

(e) This section does not apply to information relating to a sex offender that is authorized for release under Chapter 62, Code of Criminal Procedure.

(f) This section does not apply to information that is subject to required public disclosure under Section 552.029.

Sec. 508.314. Access to Inmates.

The department shall:

(1) grant to a member or employee of the board access at all reasonable times to any inmate;

(2) provide for the member or employee or a representative of the member or employee facilities for communicating with or observing an inmate; and

(3) furnish to the member or employee:

(A) any report the member or employee requires relating to the conduct or character of an inmate; or

(B) other facts a parole panel considers pertinent in determining whether an inmate will be released on parole.

Sec. 508.315. Electronic Monitoring Programs.

(a) To establish and maintain an electronic monitoring program under this chapter, the department may:

(1) fund an electronic monitoring program in a parole office;

(2) develop standards for the operation of an electronic monitoring program in a parole office; and

(3) fund the purchase, lease, or maintenance of electronic monitoring equipment.

(b) In determining whether electronic monitoring equipment should be leased or purchased, the department shall consider the rate at which technological change makes electronic monitoring equipment obsolete.

Sec. 508.316. Special Programs.

(a) The department may contract for services for releasees if funds are appropriated to the department for the services, including services for releasees who have a history of:

(1) mental impairment or mental retardation;

(2) substance abuse; or

(3) sexual offenses.

(b) The department shall seek funding for a contract under this section as a priority item.

Sec. 508.317. Intensive Supervision Program; Super-Intensive Supervision Program.

(a) The department shall establish a program to provide intensive supervision to inmates released under Subchapter B, Chapter 499, and other inmates determined by a parole panel or the department to require intensive supervision.

(b) The Texas Board of Criminal Justice shall adopt rules that establish standards for determining which inmates require intensive supervision.

(c) The program must provide the level of supervision the department provides that is higher than any level of supervision other than the level of supervision described by Subsection (d).

(d) The department shall establish a program to provide super-intensive supervision to inmates released on parole or mandatory supervision and determined by parole panels to require super-intensive supervision. The program must provide the highest level of supervision provided by the department.

Sec. 508.318. Continuing Education Program.

(a) The Texas Board of Criminal Justice and the Texas Education Agency shall adopt a memorandum of understanding that establishes the respective responsibilities of the board and the agency in implementing a continuing education program to increase the literacy of releasees.

(b) The Texas Board of Criminal Justice and the agency shall coordinate the development of the memorandum of understanding and each by rule shall adopt the memorandum.

Sec. 508.319. Program to Assess and Enhance Educational and Vocational Skills.

(a) The department, with the assistance of public school districts, community and public junior colleges, public and private institutions of higher education, and other appropriate public and private entities, may establish a developmental program based on information obtained under Section 508.183 for an inmate to be released to the supervision of the division.

(b) The developmental program may provide the inmate with the educational and vocational training necessary to:

(1) meet the average skill level required under Section 508.183; and

(2) acquire employment while in the custody of the division to lessen the likelihood that the inmate will return to the institutional division.

(c) To decrease state expense for a program established under this section, the Texas Workforce Commission shall provide to the department and the other entities described by Subsection (a) information relating to obtaining financial assistance under applicable programs of public or private entities.

(d) The department may establish a developmental program similar to the program described by Subsection (a) for inmates released from the institutional division who will not be supervised by the department.

Sec. 508.320. Contracts for Lease of Federal Facilities.

(a) The department may contract with the federal government for the lease of a military base or other federal facility that is not being used by the federal government.

(b) The department may use a facility leased under this section to house releasees in the custody of the division.

(c) The department may not enter into a contract under this section unless funds have been appropriated specifically to make payments on a contract under this section.

(d) The department shall attempt to enter into contracts that will provide the department with facilities located in various parts of the state.

Sec. 508.321. Reporting, Management, and Collection Services.

The department, with the approval of the Texas Board of Criminal Justice, may contract with a public or private vendor to provide telephone reporting, automated caseload management, or collection services for:

(1) fines, fees, restitution, or other costs ordered to be paid by a court; or

(2) fees collected by the division.

Sec. 508.322. Releasee Restitution Fund.

(a) The releasee restitution fund is a fund outside the treasury and consists of restitution payments made by releasees. Money in the fund may be used only to pay restitution as required by a condition of parole or mandatory supervision to victims of criminal offenses.

(b) The comptroller is the trustee of the releasee restitution fund as provided by Section 404.073.

(c) When a parole panel orders the payment of restitution from a releasee as provided by Article 42.037(h), Code of Criminal Procedure, the department shall:

(1) collect the payment for disbursement to the victim;

(2) deposit the payment in the releasee restitution fund; and

(3) transmit the payment to the victim as soon as practicable.

(d) If a victim who is entitled to restitution cannot be located, immediately after receiving a final payment in satisfaction of an order of restitution for the victim, the department shall attempt to notify the victim of that fact by certified mail, mailed to the last known address of the victim. If a victim then makes a claim for payment, the department promptly shall remit the payment to the victim.

(e) If a victim who is entitled to restitution does not make a claim for payment before the fifth anniversary of the date the department receives the initial restitution payment or if, after the victim makes a claim for payment, the department is unable to locate the victim for a period of five years after the date the department last made a payment to the victim, any unclaimed restitution payments being held by the department for payment to the victim are presumed abandoned. The department shall report and deliver to the comptroller all unclaimed restitution payments presumed abandoned under this section in the manner provided by Chapter 77, Property Code.

(f) If on March 1 a department is not holding unclaimed restitution payments that are presumed abandoned under this section, the department shall file a property report under Section 77.051, Property Code, that certifies that the department is not holding any unclaimed restitution payments that are presumed abandoned under this section.

Sec. 508.323. Audit.

The financial transactions of the division and the board are subject to audit by the state auditor in accordance with Chapter 321.

Sec. 508.324. Victim-Offender Mediation.

If the pardons and paroles division receives notice from the victim services office of the department that a victim of the defendant, or the victim's guardian or close relative, wishes to participate in victim-offender mediation with a person released on parole or to mandatory supervision, the division shall cooperate and assist the person if the person chooses to participate in the mediation program provided by the office. The pardons and paroles division may not require the defendant to participate and may not reward the person for participation by modifying conditions of release or the person's level of supervision or by granting any other benefit to the person.

TITLE 5
OPEN GOVERNMENT; ETHICS

SUBTITLE A
OPEN GOVERNMENT

CHAPTER 552
PUBLIC INFORMATION

SUBCHAPTER I
CRIMINAL VIOLATIONS

Sec. 552.351. Destruction, Removal, or Alteration of Public Information.

(a) A person commits an offense if the person wilfully destroys, mutilates, removes without permission as provided by this chapter, or alters public information.

(b) An offense under this section is a misdemeanor punishable by:

(1) a fine of not less than $25 or more than $4,000;

(2) confinement in the county jail for not less than three days or more than three months; or

(3) both the fine and confinement.

(c) It is an exception to the application of Subsection (a) that the public information was transferred under Section 441.204.

Sec. 552.352. Distribution or Misuse of Confidential Information.

(a) A person commits an offense if the person distributes information considered confidential under the terms of this chapter.

(a-1) An officer or employee of a governmental body who obtains access to confidential information under Section 552.008 commits an offense if the officer or employee knowingly:

(1) uses the confidential information for a purpose other than the purpose for which the information was received or for a purpose unrelated to the law that permitted the officer or employee to obtain access to the information, including solicitation of political contributions or solicitation of clients;

(2) permits inspection of the confidential information by a person who is not authorized to inspect the information; or

(3) discloses the confidential information to a person who is not authorized to receive the information.

(a-2) For purposes of Subsection (a-1), a member of an advisory committee to a governmental body who obtains access to confidential information in that capacity is considered to be an officer or employee of the governmental body.

(b) An offense under this section is a misdemeanor punishable by:

(1) a fine of not more than $1,000;

(2) confinement in the county jail for not more than six months; or

(3) both the fine and confinement.

(c) A violation under this section constitutes official misconduct.

Sec. 552.353. Failure or Refusal of Officer for Public Information to Provide Access to or Copying of Public Information.

(a) An officer for public information, or the officer's agent, commits an offense if, with criminal negligence, the officer or the officer's agent fails or refuses to give access to, or to permit or provide copying of, public information to a requestor as provided by this chapter.

(b) It is an affirmative defense to prosecution under Subsection (a) that the officer for public information reasonably believed that public access to the requested information was not required and that:

(1) the officer acted in reasonable reliance on a court order or a written interpretation of this chapter contained in an opinion of a court of record or of the attorney general issued under Subchapter G;

(2) the officer requested a decision from the attorney general in accordance with Subchapter G, and the decision is pending; or

(3) not later than the 10th calendar day after the date of receipt of a decision by the attorney general

that the information is public, the officer or the governmental body for whom the defendant is the officer for public information filed a petition for a declaratory judgment against the attorney general in a Travis County district court seeking relief from compliance with the decision of the attorney general, as provided by Section 552.324, and the cause is pending.

(c) It is an affirmative defense to prosecution under Subsection (a) that a person or entity has, not later than the 10th calendar day after the date of receipt by a governmental body of a decision by the attorney general that the information is public, filed a cause of action seeking relief from compliance with the decision of the attorney general, as provided by Section 552.325, and the cause is pending.

(d) It is an affirmative defense to prosecution under Subsection (a) that the defendant is the agent of an officer for public information and that the agent reasonably relied on the written instruction of the officer for public information not to disclose the public information requested.

(e) An offense under this section is a misdemeanor punishable by:

(1) a fine of not more than $1,000;

(2) confinement in the county jail for not more than six months; or

(3) both the fine and confinement.

(f) A violation under this section constitutes official misconduct.

CHAPTER 557
SEDITION, SABOTAGE, AND COMMUNISM

SUBCHAPTER A
SEDITION

Sec. 557.001. Sedition.

(a) A person commits an offense if the person knowingly:

(1) commits, attempts to commit, or conspires with one or more persons to commit an act intended to overthrow, destroy, or alter the constitutional form of government of this state or of any political subdivision of this state by force or violence;

(2) under circumstances that constitute a clear and present danger to the security of this state or a political subdivision of this state, advocates, advises, or teaches or conspires with one or more persons to advocate, advise, or teach a person to commit or attempt to commit an act described in Subdivision (1); or

(3) participates, with knowledge of the nature of the organization, in the management of an organization that engages in or attempts to engage in an act intended to overthrow, destroy, or alter the constitutional form of government of this state or of any political subdivision of this state by force or violence.

(b) An offense under this section is a felony punishable by:

(1) a fine not to exceed $20,000;

(2) confinement in the Texas Department of Criminal Justice for a term of not less than one year or more than 20 years; or

(3) both fine and imprisonment.

(c) A person convicted of an offense under this section may not receive community supervision under Chapter 42A, Code of Criminal Procedure.

Sec. 557.002. Disqualification.

A person who is finally convicted of an offense under Section 557.001 may not hold office or a position of profit, trust, or employment with the state or any political subdivision of the state.

Sec. 557.003. Seditious Organizations.

(a) An organization, either incorporated or unincorporated, may not engage in or have as a purpose activities intended to overthrow, destroy, or alter the constitutional form of government of this state or a political subdivision of this state by force or violence.

(b) An organization that violates Subsection (a):

(1) may not lawfully exist, function, or operate in this state; and

(2) is not entitled to the rights, privileges, and immunities granted to organizations under the law of this state.

(c) A district attorney, criminal district attorney, or county attorney may bring an action against an organization in a court of competent jurisdiction. If the court finds that the organization has violated Subsection (a), the court shall order:

(1) the organization dissolved;

(2) if the organization is incorporated in the state or has a permit to do business in the state, the organization's charter or permit revoked;

(3) all funds, records, and property of the organization forfeited to the state; and

(4) all books, records, and files of the organization turned over to the attorney general.

(d) It is prima facie evidence that an organization engages in or has as a purpose engaging in activities intended to overthrow, destroy, or alter the constitutional form of the government of this state or a political subdivision of this state by force or violence if it is shown that the organization has a parent or superior organization that engages in or has as a purpose engaging in activities intended to overthrow, destroy, or alter the constitutional form of the government of this state or a political subdivision of this state by force or violence.

Sec. 557.004. Enforcement.

(a) A district court may, on application by a district attorney, criminal district attorney, or county attorney, order injunctive or other equitable relief appropriate to enforce this subchapter.

(b) The procedure for relief sought under Subsection (a) of this section is the same as that for other similar relief in the district court except that the proceeding may not be instituted unless the director of the Department of Public Safety of the State of Texas or the director's assistant in charge is notified by telephone, telegraph, or in person that injunctive or other equitable relief will be sought.

(c) An affidavit that states that the notice described in Subsection (b) was given and that accompanies the application for relief is sufficient to permit filing of the application.

(d) Injunctive or other equitable relief sought to enforce this subchapter may not be granted in a labor dispute.

(e) The internal security section of the Department of Public Safety of the State of Texas shall assist in the enforcement of this subchapter.

Sec. 557.005. Judicial Powers in Labor Disputes.

This subchapter does not affect the powers of the courts of this state or of the United States under the law of this state in a labor dispute.

SUBCHAPTER B SABOTAGE

Sec. 557.011. Sabotage.

(a) A person commits an offense if the person, with the intent to injure the United States, this state, or any facility or property used for national defense sabotages or attempts to sabotage any property or facility used or to be used for national defense.

(b) An offense under this section is a felony punishable by confinement in the Texas Department of Criminal Justice for a term of not less than two years or more than 20 years.

(c) If conduct constituting an offense under this section also constitutes an offense under another provision of law, the actor may be prosecuted under both sections.

(d) In this section, "sabotage" means to wilfully and maliciously damage or destroy property.

Sec. 557.012. Capital Sabotage.

(a) A person commits an offense if the person commits an offense under Section 557.011(a) and the sabotage or attempted sabotage causes the death of an individual.

(b) An offense under this section is punishable by:

(1) death; or

(2) confinement in the Texas Department of Criminal Justice for:

(A) life; or

(B) a term of not less than two years.

(c) If conduct constituting an offense under this section also constitutes an offense under other law, the actor may be prosecuted under both sections.

Sec. 557.013. Enforcement.

The attorney general, a district or county attorney, the department, and any law enforcement officer of this state shall enforce this subchapter.

SUBCHAPTER C COMMUNISM

Sec. 557.021. Definitions.

In this subchapter:

(1) "Communist" means a person who commits an act reasonably calculated to further the overthrow of the government:

(A) by force or violence; or

(B) by unlawful or unconstitutional means and replace it with a communist government.

(2) "Department" means the Department of Public Safety of the State of Texas.

(3) "Government" means the government of this state or any of its political subdivisions.

Sec. 557.022. Restrictions.

(a) The name of a communist may not be printed on the ballot for any primary or general election in this state or a political subdivision of this state.

(b) A person may not hold a nonelected office or position with the state or any political subdivision of the state if:

(1) any of the compensation for the office or position comes from public funds of this state or a political subdivision of this state; and

(2) the employer or superior of the person has reasonable grounds to believe that the person is a communist.

Sec. 557.023. Enforcement.

The attorney general, a district or county attorney, the department, and any law enforcement officer of this state shall enforce this subchapter.

TITLE 7 INTERGOVERNMENTAL RELATIONS

CHAPTER 772 GOVERNMENTAL PLANNING

SUBCHAPTER A PLANNING ENTITIES

Sec. 772.0072. Missing or Exploited Children Prevention Grants.

(a) In this section, "nonprofit organization" means an organization exempt from federal income taxation under Section 501(a), Internal Revenue Code of 1986, as an organization described by Section 501(c)(3) of that code.

(b) This section applies to a nonprofit organization that is formed to offer programs and provide information to parents or other legal custodians, children, schools, public officials, organizations serving youths, nonprofit organizations, and the general public concerning child safety and Internet safety and the prevention of child abductions and child sexual exploitation.

(c) The criminal justice division established under Section 772.006 may award a grant to a nonprofit organization described by Subsection (b) that is operating in this state to provide programs and information described by that subsection to assist the Department of Public Safety in the performance of its duties related to missing or exploited children, including any duty related to the missing children and missing persons information clearinghouse under Chapter 63, Code of Criminal Procedure.

HEALTH AND SAFETY CODE

TITLE 2 HEALTH

SUBTITLE A DEPARTMENT OF STATE HEALTH SERVICES

CHAPTER 12 POWERS AND DUTIES OF DEPARTMENT OF STATE HEALTH SERVICES

SUBCHAPTER H MEDICAL ADVISORY BOARD

Sec. 12.091. Definition.

In this subchapter, "panel"means a panel of the medical advisory board.

Sec. 12.092. Medical Advisory Board; Board Members.

(a) The commissioner shall appoint the medical advisory board members from:

(1) persons licensed to practice medicine in this state, including physicians who are board certified in internal medicine, psychiatry, neurology, physical medicine, or ophthalmology and who are jointly recommended by the department and the Texas Medical Association; and

(2) persons licensed to practice optometry in this state who are jointly recommended by the department and the Texas Optometric Association.

(b) The medical advisory board shall assist the Department of Public Safety of the State of Texas in determining whether:

(1) an applicant for a driver's license or a license holder is capable of safely operating a motor vehicle; or

(2) an applicant for or holder of a license to carry a handgun under the authority of Subchapter H, Chapter 411, Government Code, or an applicant for or holder of a commission as a security officer under Chapter 1702, Occupations Code, is capable of exercising sound judgment with respect to the proper use and storage of a handgun.

Sec. 12.093. Administration.

(a) The medical advisory board is administratively attached to the department.

(b) The department:

(1) shall provide administrative support for the medical advisory board and panels of the medical advisory board; and

(2) may collect and maintain the individual medical records necessary for use by the medical advisory board and the panels under this section from a physician, hospital, or other health care provider.

Sec. 12.094. Rules Relating to Medical Advisory Board Members.

(a) The executive commissioner:

(1) may adopt rules to govern the activities of the medical advisory board;

(2) by rule may establish a reasonable fee to pay a member of the medical advisory board for the member's professional consultation services; and

(3) if appropriate, may authorize reimbursement for travel expenses as provided by Section 2110.004, Government Code, for each meeting a member attends.

(b) The fee under Subsection (a)(2) may not be less than $75 or more than $150 for each meeting that the member attends.

Sec. 12.095. Board Panels; Powers and Duties.

(a) If the Department of Public Safety of the State of Texas requests an opinion or recommendation from the medical advisory board as to the ability of an applicant or license holder to operate a motor vehicle safely or to exercise sound judgment with respect to the proper use and storage of a handgun, the commissioner or a person designated by the commissioner shall convene a panel to consider the case or question submitted by that department.

(b) To take action as a panel, at least three members of the medical advisory board must be present.

Health and Safety Code

(c) Each panel member shall prepare an individual independent written report for the Department of Public Safety of the State of Texas that states the member's opinion as to the ability of the applicant or license holder to operate a motor vehicle safely or to exercise sound judgment with respect to the proper use and storage of a handgun, as appropriate. In the report the panel member may also make recommendations relating to that department's subsequent action.

(d) In its deliberations, a panel may examine any medical record or report that contains material that may be relevant to the ability of the applicant or license holder.

(e) The panel may require the applicant or license holder to undergo a medical or other examination at the applicant's or holder's expense. A person who conducts an examination under this subsection may be compelled to testify before the panel and in any subsequent proceedings under Subchapter H, Chapter 411, Government Code, or Subchapter N, Chapter 521, Transportation Code, as applicable, concerning the person's observations and findings.

Sec. 12.096. Physician Report.

(a) A physician licensed to practice medicine in this state may inform the Department of Public Safety of the State of Texas or the medical advisory board, orally or in writing, of the name, date of birth, and address of a patient older than 15 years of age whom the physician has diagnosed as having a disorder or disability specified in a rule of the Department of Public Safety of the State of Texas.

(b) The release of information under this section is an exception to the patient-physician privilege requirements imposed under Section 159.002, Occupations Code.

Sec. 12.097. Confidentiality Requirements.

(a) All records, reports, and testimony relating to the medical condition of an applicant or license holder:

(1) are for the confidential use of the medical advisory board, a panel, or the Department of Public Safety of the State of Texas;

(2) are privileged information; and

(3) may not be disclosed to any person or used as evidence in a trial except as provided by Subsection (b).

(b) In a subsequent proceeding under Subchapter H, Chapter 411, Government Code, or Subchapter N, Chapter 521, Transportation Code, the department may provide a copy of the report of the medical advisory board or panel and a medical record or report relating to an applicant or license holder to:

(1) the Department of Public Safety of the State of Texas;

(2) the applicant or license holder; and

(3) the officer who presides at the hearing.

Sec. 12.098. Liability.

A member of the medical advisory board, a member of a panel, a person who makes an examination for or on the recommendation of the medical advisory board, or a physician who reports to the medical advisory board or a panel under Section 12.096 is not liable for a professional opinion, recommendation, or report made under this subchapter.

SUBTITLE G
LICENSES AND OTHER REGULATION

CHAPTER 142
HOME AND COMMUNITY SUPPORT SERVICES

SUBCHAPTER A
HOME AND COMMUNITY SUPPORT SERVICES LICENSE

Sec. 142.0061. Possession of Sterile Water or Saline.

A home and community support services agency or its employees who are registered nurses or licensed vocational nurses may purchase, store, or transport for the purpose of administering to their home health or hospice patients under physician's orders:

(1) sterile water for injection and irrigation; and

(2) sterile saline for injection and irrigation.

Sec. 142.0062. Possession of Certain Vaccines or Tuberculin.

(a) A home and community support services agency or its employees who are registered nurses or licensed vocational nurses may purchase, store, or transport for the purpose of administering to the agency's employees, home health or hospice

Health and Safety Code

patients, or patient family members under physician's standing orders the following dangerous drugs:

(1) hepatitis B vaccine;

(2) influenza vaccine;

(3) tuberculin purified protein derivative for tuberculosis testing;

(4) pneumococcal polysaccharide vaccine; and

(5) any other vaccine approved, authorized for emergency use, or otherwise permitted for use by the United States Food and Drug Administration to treat or mitigate the spread of a communicable disease, as defined by Section 81.003.

(b) A home and community support services agency that purchases, stores, or transports a vaccine or tuberculin under this section shall ensure that any standing order for the vaccine or tuberculin:

(1) is signed and dated by the physician;

(2) identifies the vaccine or tuberculin covered by the order;

(3) indicates that the recipient of the vaccine or tuberculin has been assessed as an appropriate candidate to receive the vaccine or tuberculin and has been assessed for the absence of any contraindication;

(4) indicates that appropriate procedures are established for responding to any negative reaction to the vaccine or tuberculin; and

(5) orders that a specific medication or category of medication be administered if the recipient has a negative reaction to the vaccine or tuberculin.

Sec. 142.0063. Possession of Certain Dangerous Drugs.

(a) A home and community support services agency in compliance with this section or its employees who are registered nurses or licensed vocational nurses may purchase, store, or transport for the purpose of administering to their home health or hospice patients in accordance with Subsection (c) the following dangerous drugs:

(1) any of the following items in a sealed portable container of a size determined by the dispensing pharmacist:

(A) 1,000 milliliters of 0.9 percent sodium chloride intravenous infusion;

(B) 1,000 milliliters of five percent dextrose in water injection; or

(C) sterile saline; or

(2) not more than five dosage units of any of the following items in an individually sealed, unused portable container:

(A) heparin sodium lock flush in a concentration of 10 units per milliliter or 100 units per milliliter;

(B) epinephrine HCl solution in a concentration of 1 to 1,000;

(C) diphenhydramine HCl solution in a concentration of 50 milligrams per milliliter;

(D) methylprednisolone in a concentration of 125 milligrams per two milliliters;

(E) naloxone in a concentration of one milligram per milliliter in a two-milliliter vial;

(F) promethazine in a concentration of 25 milligrams per milliliter;

(G) glucagon in a concentration of one milligram per milliliter;

(H) furosemide in a concentration of 10 milligrams per milliliter;

(I) lidocaine 2.5 percent and prilocaine 2.5 percent cream in a five-gram tube; or

(J) lidocaine HCl solution in a concentration of one percent in a two-milliliter vial.

(b) A home and community support services agency or the agency's authorized employees may purchase, store, or transport dangerous drugs in a sealed portable container under this section only if the agency has established policies and procedures to ensure that:

(1) the container is handled properly with respect to storage, transportation, and temperature stability;

(2) a drug is removed from the container only on a physician's written or oral order;

(3) the administration of any drug in the container is performed in accordance with a specific treatment protocol; and

(4) the agency maintains a written record of the dates and times the container is in the possession of a registered nurse or licensed vocational nurse.

(c) A home and community support services agency or the agency's authorized employee who administers a drug listed in Subsection (a) may administer the drug only in the patient's residence under physician's orders in connection with the provision of emergency treatment or the adjustment of:

(1) parenteral drug therapy; or

(2) vaccine or tuberculin administration.

(d) If a home and community support services agency or the agency's authorized employee administers a drug listed in Subsection (a) pursuant to a physician's oral order, the physician shall promptly send a signed copy of the order to the agency, and the agency shall:

(1) not later than 24 hours after receipt of the order, reduce the order to written form and send a copy of the form to the dispensing pharmacy by mail or facsimile transmission; and

(2) not later than 20 days after receipt of the order, send a copy of the order as signed by and

received from the physician to the dispensing pharmacy.

(e) A pharmacist that dispenses a sealed portable container under this section shall ensure that the container:

(1) is designed to allow access to the contents of the container only if a tamper-proof seal is broken;

(2) bears a label that lists the drugs in the container and provides notice of the container's expiration date, which is the earlier of:

(A) the date that is six months after the date on which the container is dispensed; or

(B) the earliest expiration date of any drug in the container; and

(3) remains in the pharmacy or under the control of a pharmacist, registered nurse, or licensed vocational nurse.

(f) If a home and community support services agency or the agency's authorized employee purchases, stores, or transports a sealed portable container under this section, the agency shall deliver the container to the dispensing pharmacy for verification of drug quality, quantity, integrity, and expiration dates not later than the earlier of:

(1) the seventh day after the date on which the seal on the container is broken; or

(2) the date for which notice is provided on the container label.

(g) A pharmacy that dispenses a sealed portable container under this section shall take reasonable precautionary measures to ensure that the home and community support services agency receiving the container complies with Subsection (f). On receipt of a container under Subsection (f), the pharmacy shall perform an inventory of the drugs used from the container and shall restock and reseal the container before delivering the container to the agency for reuse.

SUBCHAPTER B PERMITS TO ADMINISTER MEDICATION

Sec. 142.021. Administration of Medication.

A person may not administer medication to a client of a home and community support services agency unless the person:

(1) holds a license under state law that authorizes the person to administer medication;

(2) holds a permit issued under Section 142.025 and acts under the delegated authority of a person who holds a license under state law that authorizes the person to administer medication;

(3) administers a medication to a client of a home and community support service agency in accordance with rules of the Texas Board of Nursing that permit delegation of the administration of medication to a person not holding a permit under Section 142.025; or

(4) administers noninjectable medication under circumstances authorized by the memorandum of understanding executed by the department and the Texas Board of Nursing.

Sec. 142.022. Exemptions for Nursing Students and Medication Aide Trainees.

(a) Sections 142.021 and 142.029 do not apply to:

(1) a graduate nurse holding a temporary permit issued by the Texas Board of Nursing;

(2) a student enrolled in an accredited school of nursing or program for the education of registered nurses who is administering medications as part of the student's clinical experience;

(3) a graduate vocational nurse holding a temporary permit issued by the Texas Board of Nursing;

(4) a student enrolled in an accredited school of vocational nursing or program for the education of vocational nurses who is administering medications as part of the student's clinical experience; or

(5) a trainee in a medication aide training program approved by the department under Section 142.024 who is administering medications as part of the trainee's clinical experience.

(b) The administration of medications by persons exempted under Subdivisions (1) through (4) of Subsection (a) is governed by the terms of the memorandum of understanding executed by the department and the Texas Board of Nursing.

Sec. 142.029. Administration of Medication; Criminal Penalty.

(a) A person commits an offense if the person knowingly administers medication to a client of a home and community support services agency and the person is not authorized to administer the medication under Section 142.021 or 142.022.

(b) An offense under this section is a Class B misdemeanor.

Sec. 142.030. Dispensing Dangerous Drugs or Controlled Substances; Criminal Penalty.

(a) A person authorized by this subchapter to administer medication to a client of a home and community support services agency may not dispense dangerous drugs or controlled substances without complying with Subtitle J, Title 3, Occupations Code.

Health and Safety Code

(b) An offense under this section is a Class A misdemeanor.

SUBTITLE H PUBLIC HEALTH PROVISIONS

CHAPTER 161 PUBLIC HEALTH PROVISIONS

SUBCHAPTER H DISTRIBUTION OF CIGARETTES, E-CIGARETTES, OR TOBACCO PRODUCTS

Sec. 161.081. Definitions.

In this subchapter:

(1) "Cigarette" has the meaning assigned by Section 154.001, Tax Code.

(1-a) (A) "E-cigarette" means:

(i) an electronic cigarette or any other device that simulates smoking by using a mechanical heating element, battery, or electronic circuit to deliver nicotine or other substances to the individual inhaling from the device; or

(ii) a consumable liquid solution or other material aerosolized or vaporized during the use of an electronic cigarette or other device described by this subdivision.

(B) The term "e-cigarette" does not include a prescription medical device unrelated to the cessation of smoking.

(C) The term "e-cigarette" includes:

(i) a device described by this subdivision regardless of whether the device is manufactured, distributed, or sold as an e-cigarette, e-cigar, or e-pipe or under another product name or description; and

(ii) a component, part, or accessory for the device, regardless of whether the component, part, or accessory is sold separately from the device.

(1-b) "Minor" means a person under 21 years of age.

(2) "Permit holder" has the meaning assigned by Section 147.0001 of this code or Section 154.001 or 155.001, Tax Code, as applicable.

(3) "Retail sale" means a transfer of possession from a retailer to a consumer in connection with a purchase, sale, or exchange for value of cigarettes, e-cigarettes, or tobacco products.

(4) "Retailer" means a person who engages in the practice of selling cigarettes, e-cigarettes, or tobacco products to consumers and includes the owner of a coin-operated cigarette, e-cigarette, or tobacco product vending machine. The term includes a retailer as defined by Section 154.001 or 155.001, Tax Code, and an e-cigarette retailer as defined by Section 147.0001 of this code, as applicable.

(5) "Tobacco product" has the meaning assigned by Section 155.001, Tax Code.

(6) "Wholesaler" has the meaning assigned by Section 154.001 or 155.001, Tax Code, as applicable.

Sec. 161.0815. Nonapplicability.

This subchapter does not apply to a product that is:

(1) approved by the United States Food and Drug Administration for use in the treatment of nicotine or smoking addiction; and

(2) labeled with a "Drug Facts" panel in accordance with regulations of the United States Food and Drug Administration.

Sec. 161.082. Sale of Cigarettes, E-Cigarettes, or Tobacco Products to Persons Younger Than 21 Years of Age Prohibited; Proof of Age Required.

(a) A person commits an offense if the person, with criminal negligence:

(1) sells, gives, or causes to be sold or given a cigarette, e-cigarette, or tobacco product to someone who is younger than 21 years of age; or

(2) sells, gives, or causes to be sold or given a cigarette, e-cigarette, or tobacco product to another person who intends to deliver it to someone who is younger than 21 years of age.

(b) If an offense under this section occurs in connection with a sale by an employee of the owner of a store in which cigarettes, e-cigarettes, or tobacco products are sold at retail, the employee is criminally responsible for the offense and is subject to prosecution.

(c) An offense under this section is a Class C misdemeanor.

(d) It is a defense to prosecution under Subsection (a)(1) that the person to whom the cigarette, e-cigarette, or tobacco product was sold or given presented to the defendant apparently valid proof of identification.

(e) A proof of identification satisfies the requirements of Subsection (d) if it contains a physical description and photograph consistent with the person's appearance, purports to establish that the person is 21 years of age or older, and was issued by a governmental agency. The proof of identification may include a driver's license issued by this state or another state, a passport, or an identification card issued by a state or the federal government.

(f) It is an exception to the application of Subsection (a)(1) that the person to whom the cigarette, e-cigarette, or tobacco product was sold:

(1) is at least 18 years of age; and

(2) presented at the time of purchase a valid military identification card of the United States military forces or the state military forces.

Sec. 161.0825. Use of Certain Electronically Readable Information.

(a) In this section, "transaction scan device" means a device capable of deciphering electronically readable information on a driver's license, commercial driver's license, or identification certificate.

(b) A person may access electronically readable information on a driver's license, commercial driver's license, or identification certificate for the purpose of complying with Section 161.082.

(c) Information accessed under this section may not be sold or otherwise disseminated to a third party for any purpose, including any marketing, advertising, or promotional activities. The information may be obtained by court order or on proper request by the comptroller, a law enforcement officer, or a law enforcement agency.

(d) A person who violates this section commits an offense. An offense under this section is a Class A misdemeanor.

(e) It is an affirmative defense to prosecution under Section 161.082 that:

(1) a transaction scan device identified a license or certificate as valid and the defendant accessed the information and relied on the results in good faith; or

(2) if the defendant is the owner of a store in which cigarettes, e-cigarettes, or tobacco products are sold at retail, the offense under Section 161.082 occurs in connection with a sale by an employee of the owner, and the owner had provided the employee with:

(A) a transaction scan device in working condition; and

(B) adequate training in the use of the transaction scan device.

Sec. 161.083. Sale of Cigarettes, E-Cigarettes, or Tobacco Products to Persons Younger Than 30 Years of Age.

(a) A person may not sell, give, or cause to be sold or given a cigarette, e-cigarette, or tobacco product to someone who is younger than 30 years of age unless the person to whom the cigarette, e-cigarette, or tobacco product was sold or given presents an apparently valid proof of identification.

(a-1) [Repealed.]

(b) A retailer shall adequately supervise and train the retailer's agents and employees to prevent a violation of Subsection (a).

(c) A proof of identification described by Section 161.082(e) satisfies the requirements of Subsection (a).

(d) Notwithstanding any other provision of law, a violation of this section is not a violation of this subchapter for purposes of Section 161.0901.

Sec. 161.084. Warning Notice.

(a) Each person who sells cigarettes, e-cigarettes, or tobacco products at retail or by vending machine shall post a sign in a location that is conspicuous to all employees and customers and that is close to the place at which the cigarettes, e-cigarettes, or tobacco products may be purchased.

(b) The sign must include the statement:

PURCHASING OR ATTEMPTING TO PURCHASE CIGARETTES, E-CIGARETTES, OR TOBACCO PRODUCTS BY A PERSON UNDER 21 YEARS OF AGE IS PROHIBITED BY LAW. SALE OR PROVISION OF CIGARETTES, E-CIGARETTES, OR TOBACCO PRODUCTS TO A PERSON UNDER 21 YEARS OF AGE IS PROHIBITED BY LAW. UPON CONVICTION, A CLASS C MISDEMEANOR, INCLUDING A FINE OF UP TO $500, MAY BE IMPOSED. VIOLATIONS MAY BE REPORTED TO THE TEXAS COMPTROLLER'S OFFICE BY CALLING (insert toll-free telephone number). PREGNANT WOMEN SHOULD NOT SMOKE. SMOKERS ARE MORE LIKELY TO HAVE BABIES WHO ARE BORN PREMATURE OR WITH LOW BIRTH WEIGHT. THE PROHIBITIONS ON THE PURCHASE OR ATTEMPT TO PURCHASE DESCRIBED ABOVE DO NOT APPLY TO A PERSON WHO IS IN THE UNITED STATES MILITARY FORCES OR STATE MILITARY FORCES.

(b-1) [Expires September 1, 2022] Immediately following the statement described by Subsection (b), the sign described by that subsection must include the statement:

THE PROHIBITIONS ON THE PURCHASE OR ATTEMPT TO PURCHASE DESCRIBED ABOVE DO NOT APPLY TO A PERSON WHO WAS BORN ON OR BEFORE AUGUST 31, 2001.

(b-2) [Expires September 1, 2022] This subsection and Subsection (b-1) expire September 1, 2022.

(c) The comptroller by rule shall determine the design and size of the sign.

(d) The comptroller on request shall provide the sign without charge to any person who sells cigarettes, e-cigarettes, or tobacco products. The comptroller may provide the sign without charge to distributors of cigarettes, e-cigarettes, or tobacco products or wholesale dealers of cigarettes, e-cigarettes, or tobacco products in this state for distribution to persons who sell cigarettes, e-cigarettes, or tobacco products. A distributor or wholesale dealer may not charge for distributing a sign under this subsection.

(e) A person commits an offense if the person fails to display a sign as prescribed by this section. An offense under this subsection is a Class C misdemeanor.

(f) The comptroller may accept gifts or grants from any public or private source to perform the comptroller's duties under this section.

Sec. 161.085. Notification of Employees and Agents.

(a) Each retailer shall notify each individual employed by that retailer who is to be engaged in retail sales of cigarettes, e-cigarettes, or tobacco products that state law:

(1) prohibits the sale or distribution of cigarettes, e-cigarettes, or tobacco products to any person who is younger than 21 years of age as provided by Section 161.082 and that a violation of that section is a Class C misdemeanor; and

(2) requires each person who sells cigarettes, e-cigarettes, or tobacco products at retail or by vending machine to post a warning notice as provided by Section 161.084, requires each employee to ensure that the appropriate sign is always properly displayed while that employee is exercising the employee's duties, and provides that a violation of Section 161.084 is a Class C misdemeanor.

(b) The notice required by this section must be provided within 72 hours of the date an individual begins to engage in retail sales of cigarettes, e-cigarettes, or tobacco products. The individual shall signify that the individual has received the notice required by this section by signing a form stating that the law has been fully explained, that the individual understands the law, and that the individual, as a condition of employment, agrees to comply with the law.

(c) Each form signed by an individual under this section shall indicate the date of the signature and the current address and social security number of the individual. The retailer shall retain the form signed by each individual employed as a retail sales clerk until the 60th day after the date the individual has left the employer's employ.

(d) A retailer required by this section to notify employees commits an offense if the retailer fails, on demand of a peace officer or an agent of the comptroller, to provide the forms prescribed by this section. An offense under this section is a Class C misdemeanor.

(e) It is a defense to prosecution under Subsection (d) to show proof that the employee did complete, sign, and date the forms required by Subsections (b) and (c). Proof must be shown to the comptroller or an agent of the comptroller not later than the seventh day after the date of a demand under Subsection (d).

Sec. 161.086. Vendor Assisted Sales Required; Vending Machines.

(a) Except as provided by Subsection (b), a retailer or other person may not:

(1) offer cigarettes, e-cigarettes, or tobacco products for sale in a manner that permits a customer direct access to the cigarettes, e-cigarettes, or tobacco products; or

(2) install or maintain a vending machine containing cigarettes, e-cigarettes, or tobacco products.

(b) Subsection (a) does not apply to:

(1) a facility or business that is not open to persons younger than 21 years of age at any time;

(2) that part of a facility or business that is a humidor or other enclosure designed to store cigars in a climate-controlled environment and that is not open to persons younger than 21 years of age at any time; or

(3) a premises for which a person holds a package store permit issued under the Alcoholic Beverage Code and that is not open to persons younger than 21 years of age at any time.

(c) The comptroller or a peace officer may, with or without a warrant, seize, seal, or disable a vending machine installed or maintained in violation of this section. Property seized under this subsection must be seized in accordance with, and is subject to forfeiture to the state in accordance with, Subchapter H, Chapter 154, Tax Code, and Subchapter E, Chapter 155, Tax Code.

(d) A person commits an offense if the person violates Subsection (a). An offense under this subsection is a Class C misdemeanor.

Sec. 161.087. Distribution of Cigarettes, E-Cigarettes, or Tobacco Products.

(a) A person may not distribute:

(1) a free sample of a cigarette, e-cigarette, or tobacco product; or

(2) a coupon or other item that the recipient may use to receive a free cigarette, e-cigarette, or tobacco product or a sample cigarette, e-cigarette, or tobacco product.

(a-1) A person may not distribute to persons younger than 21 years of age a coupon or other item that the recipient may use to receive a discounted cigarette, e-cigarette, or tobacco product.

(b) Except as provided by Subsection (c), a person, including a permit holder, may not accept or redeem, offer to accept or redeem, or hire a person to accept or redeem:

(1) a coupon or other item that the recipient may use to receive a free cigarette, e-cigarette, or tobacco product or a sample cigarette, e-cigarette, or tobacco product; or

(2) a coupon or other item that the recipient may use to receive a discounted cigarette, e-cigarette, or tobacco product if the recipient is younger than 21 years of age.

(b-1) A coupon or other item that a recipient described by Subsection (b) may use to receive a discounted cigarette, e-cigarette, or tobacco product may not be redeemable through mail or courier delivery.

(c) Subsections (a)(2), (a-1), (b), and (b-1) do not apply to a transaction between permit holders unless the transaction is a retail sale.

(d) A person commits an offense if the person violates this section. An offense under this subsection is a Class C misdemeanor.

Sec. 161.0875. Sale of E-Cigarette Nicotine Containers.

(a) A person may not sell or cause to be sold a container that contains liquid with nicotine and that is an accessory for an e-cigarette unless:

(1) the container satisfies the child-resistant effectiveness standards under 16 C.F.R. Section 1700.15(b)(1) when tested in accordance with the method described by 16 C.F.R. Section 1700.20; or

(2) the container is a cartridge that is prefilled and sealed by the manufacturer and is not intended to be opened by a consumer.

(b) If the federal government adopts standards for the packaging of a container described by Subsection (a), a person who complies with those standards is considered to be in compliance with this section.

Sec. 161.088. Enforcement; Unannounced Inspections.

(a) The comptroller shall enforce this subchapter in partnership with local law enforcement agencies and with their cooperation and shall ensure the state's compliance with Section 1926 of the federal Public Health Service Act (42 U.S.C. Section 300x-26) and any implementing regulations adopted by the United States Department of Health and Human Services. Except as expressly authorized by law, the comptroller may not adopt any rules governing the subject matter of this subchapter or Subchapter K, N, or O.

(b) The comptroller may make block grants to counties and municipalities to be used by local law enforcement agencies to enforce this subchapter and Subchapter R in a manner that can reasonably be expected to reduce the extent to which cigarettes, e-cigarettes, and tobacco products are sold or distributed, including by delivery sale, to persons who are younger than 21 years of age. At least annually, random unannounced inspections shall be conducted at various locations where cigarettes, e-cigarettes, and tobacco products are sold or distributed, including by delivery sale, to ensure compliance with this subchapter and Subchapter R. The comptroller shall rely, to the fullest extent possible, on local law enforcement agencies to enforce this subchapter and Subchapter R.

(c) To facilitate the effective administration and enforcement of this subchapter, the comptroller may enter into interagency contracts with other state agencies, and those agencies may assist the comptroller in the administration and enforcement of this subchapter.

(d) The use of a person younger than 21 years of age to act as a minor decoy to test compliance with this subchapter and Subchapter R shall be conducted in a fashion that promotes fairness. A person may be enlisted by the comptroller or a local law enforcement agency to act as a minor decoy only if the following requirements are met:

(1) written parental consent is obtained for the use of a person younger than 18 years of age to act as a minor decoy to test compliance with this subchapter and Subchapter R;

(2) at the time of the inspection, order, or delivery, the minor decoy is younger than 21 years of age;

(3) the minor decoy has an appearance that would cause a reasonably prudent seller of cigarettes, e-cigarettes, or tobacco products to request identification and proof of age;

(4) the minor decoy carries either the minor's own identification showing the minor's correct date of birth or carries no identification, and a minor decoy who carries identification presents it on request to any seller of or any person who delivers cigarettes, e-cigarettes, or tobacco products; and

(5) the minor decoy answers truthfully any questions about the minor's age at the time of the inspection, order, or delivery.

(e) The comptroller shall annually prepare for submission by the governor to the secretary of the United States Department of Health and Human Services the report required by Section 1926 of the federal Public Health Service Act (42 U.S.C. Section 300x-26).

Sec. 161.089. Preemption of Local Law.

(a) Except as provided by Subsection (b), this subchapter does not preempt a local regulation of the sale, distribution, or use of cigarettes or tobacco products or affect the authority of a political subdivision to adopt or enforce an ordinance or requirement relating to the sale, distribution, or use of cigarettes or tobacco products if the regulation, ordinance, or requirement:

(1) is compatible with and equal to or more stringent than a requirement prescribed by this subchapter; or

(2) relates to an issue that is not specifically addressed by this subchapter or Chapter 154 or 155, Tax Code.

(b) A political subdivision may not adopt or enforce an ordinance or requirement relating to the lawful age to sell, distribute, or use cigarettes, e-cigarettes, or tobacco products that is more stringent than a requirement prescribed by this subchapter.

Sec. 161.090. Reports of Violation.

A local or state law enforcement agency or other governmental unit shall notify the comptroller, on the 10th day of each month, or the first working day after that date, of any violation of this subchapter that occurred in the preceding month that the agency or unit detects, investigates, or prosecutes.

Sec. 161.0901. Disciplinary Action Against Cigarette, E-Cigarette, and Tobacco Product Retailers.

(a) A retailer is subject to disciplinary action as provided by this section if an agent or employee of the retailer commits an offense under this subchapter.

(b) If the comptroller finds, after notice and an opportunity for a hearing as provided by Chapter 2001, Government Code, that a permit holder has violated this subchapter at a place of business for which a permit is issued, the comptroller may suspend the permit for that place of business and administratively assess a fine as follows:

(1) for the first violation of this subchapter during the 24-month period preceding the violation at that place of business, the comptroller may require the permit holder to pay a fine in an amount not to exceed $1,000;

(2) for the second violation of this subchapter during the 24-month period preceding the most recent violation at that place of business, the comptroller may require the permit holder to pay a fine in an amount not to exceed $2,000; and

(3) for the third violation of this subchapter during the 24-month period preceding the most recent violation at that place of business, the comptroller may:

(A) require the permit holder to pay a fine in an amount not to exceed $3,000; and

(B) suspend the permit for that place of business for not more than five days.

(c) Except as provided by Subsection (e), for the fourth or a subsequent violation of this subchapter during the 24-month period preceding the most recent violation at that place of business, the comptroller shall revoke the permit issued under Chapter 147 of this code or Chapter 154 or 155, Tax Code, as applicable. If the permit holder does not hold a permit under Chapter 147 of this code or Chapter 154 or 155, Tax Code, the comptroller shall revoke the permit issued under Section 151.201, Tax Code.

(d) A permit holder whose permit has been revoked under this section may not apply for a permit for the same place of business before the expiration of six months after the effective date of the revocation.

(e) For purposes of this section, the comptroller may suspend a permit for a place of business but may not revoke the permit under Subsection (c) if the comptroller finds that:

(1) the permit holder has not violated this subchapter more than seven times at the place of business in the 48-month period preceding the violation in question;

(2) the permit holder requires its employees to attend a comptroller-approved seller training program;

(3) the employees have actually attended a comptroller-approved seller training program; and

(4) the permit holder has not directly or indirectly encouraged the employees to violate the law.

(f) The comptroller may adopt rules to implement this section.

Sec. 161.0902. E-Cigarette Report.

(a) Not later than January 5th of each odd-numbered year, the department shall report to the governor, lieutenant governor, and speaker of the house of representatives on the status of the use of e-cigarettes in this state.

(b) The report must include, at a minimum:

(1) a baseline of statistics and analysis regarding retail compliance with this subchapter and Subchapter R;

(2) a baseline of statistics and analysis regarding illegal e-cigarette sales, including:

(A) sales to minors;

(B) enforcement actions concerning minors; and

(C) sources of citations;

(3) e-cigarette controls and initiatives by the department, or any other state agency, including an evaluation of the effectiveness of the controls and initiatives;

(4) the future goals and plans of the department to decrease the use of e-cigarettes;

(5) the educational programs of the department and the effectiveness of those programs; and

(6) the incidence of use of e-cigarettes by regions in this state, including use of e-cigarettes by ethnicity.

(c) The department may include the report required by this section with a similar report for cigarettes or tobacco products required by law.

Sec. 161.0903. Use of Certain Revenue.

Revenue from fees collected under Section 161.123 and from the sale of permits under Chapter 147 of this code, retailer permits under Chapter 154, Tax Code, and retailer permits under Chapter 155, Tax Code, shall be deposited in the general revenue fund and may be appropriated only as provided by this section. The revenue shall be appropriated, in order of priority, to:

(1) the comptroller for the purpose of administering retailer permitting under Chapter 147 of this code and Chapters 154 and 155, Tax Code; and

(2) the comptroller for the purpose of administering and enforcing this subchapter and Subchapters K and N.

SUBCHAPTER N
E-CIGARETTE AND TOBACCO USE BY MINORS

Sec. 161.251. Definitions.

In this subchapter:

(1) "Cigarette" has the meaning assigned by Section 154.001, Tax Code.

(1-a) "E-cigarette" has the meaning assigned by Section 161.081.

(1-b) "Minor" means a person under 21 years of age.

(2) "Tobacco product" has the meaning assigned by Section 155.001, Tax Code.

Sec. 161.252. Possession, Purchase, Consumption, or Receipt of Cigarettes, E-Cigarettes, or Tobacco Products by Minors Prohibited.

(a) An individual who is younger than 21 years of age commits an offense if the individual:

(1) possesses, purchases, consumes, or accepts a cigarette, e-cigarette, or tobacco product; or

(2) falsely represents himself or herself to be 21 years of age or older by displaying proof of age that is false, fraudulent, or not actually proof of the individual's own age in order to obtain possession of, purchase, or receive a cigarette, e-cigarette, or tobacco product.

(b) It is an exception to the application of this section that the individual younger than 21 years of age possessed the cigarette, e-cigarette, or tobacco product in the presence of an employer of the individual, if possession or receipt of the cigarette, e-cigarette, or tobacco product is required in the performance of the employee's duties as an employee.

(c) It is an exception to the application of this section that the individual younger than 21 years of age is participating in an inspection or test of compliance in accordance with Section 161.088.

(c-1) It is an exception to the application of this section that the individual younger than 21 years of age:

(1) is at least 18 years of age; and

(2) presents at the time of purchase a valid military identification card of the United States military forces or the state military forces.

(d) An offense under this section is punishable by a fine not to exceed $100.

(e) On conviction of an individual under this section, the court shall give notice to the individual that the individual may apply to the court to have the individual's conviction expunged as provided by Section 161.255 on or after the individual's 21st birthday.

Sec. 161.253. E-Cigarette and Tobacco Awareness Program; Community Service.

(a) On conviction of an individual for an offense under Section 161.252, the court shall suspend execution of sentence and shall require the defendant to attend an e-cigarette and tobacco awareness program approved by the commissioner. The court may require the parent or guardian of the defendant to attend the e-cigarette and tobacco awareness program with the defendant.

(b) On request, an e-cigarette and tobacco awareness program may be taught in languages other than English.

(c) If the defendant resides in a rural area of this state or another area of this state in which access to an e-cigarette and tobacco awareness program is not readily available, the court shall require the defendant to perform eight to 12 hours of e-cigarette- and tobacco-related community service instead of attending the e-cigarette and tobacco awareness program.

(d) The e-cigarette and tobacco awareness program and the e-cigarette- and tobacco-related community service are remedial and are not punishment.

(e) Not later than the 90th day after the date of a conviction under Section 161.252, the defendant shall present to the court, in the manner required by the court, evidence of satisfactory completion of the e-cigarette and tobacco awareness program or the e-cigarette- and tobacco-related community service.

(f) On receipt of the evidence required under Subsection (e), the court shall:

(1) if the defendant has been previously convicted of an offense under Section 161.252, execute the sentence, and at the discretion of the court, reduce the fine imposed to not less than half the fine previously imposed by the court; or

(2) if the defendant has not been previously convicted of an offense under Section 161.252, discharge the defendant and dismiss the complaint or information against the defendant.

(g) If the court discharges the defendant under Subsection (f)(2), the defendant is released from all penalties and disabilities resulting from the offense except that the defendant is considered to have been convicted of the offense if the defendant is subsequently convicted of an offense under Section 161.252 committed after the dismissal under Subsection (f)(2).

Sec. 161.254. Driver's License Suspension or Denial. [Repealed]

Sec. 161.255. Expungement of Conviction.

(a) An individual convicted of an offense under Section 161.252 may apply to the court to have the conviction expunged on or after the individual's 21st birthday. The court shall order the conviction and any complaint, verdict, sentence, or other document relating to the offense to be expunged from the individual's record and the conviction may not be shown or made known for any purpose.

(b) The court shall charge an applicant a reimbursement fee in the amount of $30 for each application for expungement filed under this section to defray the cost of notifying state agencies of orders of expungement under this section.

Sec. 161.256. Jurisdiction of Courts.

A justice court or municipal court may exercise jurisdiction over any matter in which a court under this subchapter may impose a requirement that a defendant attend an e-cigarette and tobacco awareness program or perform e-cigarette- and tobacco-related community service.

Sec. 161.257. Application of Other Law.

Title 3, Family Code, does not apply to a proceeding under this subchapter.

CHAPTER 166 ADVANCE DIRECTIVES

SUBCHAPTER B DIRECTIVE TO PHYSICIANS

Sec. 166.048. Criminal Penalty; Prosecution.

(a) A person commits an offense if the person intentionally conceals, cancels, defaces, obliterates, or damages another person's directive without that person's consent. An offense under this subsection is a Class A misdemeanor.

(b) A person is subject to prosecution for criminal homicide under Chapter 19, Penal Code, if the person, with the intent to cause life-sustaining treatment to be withheld or withdrawn from another person contrary to the other person's desires, falsifies or forges a directive or intentionally conceals or withholds personal knowledge of a revocation and thereby directly causes life-sustaining treatment to be withheld or withdrawn from the other person with the result that the other person's death is hastened.

CHAPTER 167 FEMALE GENITAL MUTILATION

Sec. 167.001. Female Genital Mutilation Prohibited.

(a) A person commits an offense if the person:

(1) knowingly circumcises, excises, or infibulates any part of the labia majora or labia minora or clitoris of another person who is younger than 18 years of age;

(2) is a parent or legal guardian of another person who is younger than 18 years of age and knowingly consents to or permits an act described by Subdivision (1) to be performed on that person; or

(3) knowingly transports or facilitates the transportation of another person who is younger than 18 years of age within this state or from this state for the purpose of having an act described by Subdivision (1) performed on that person.

(b) An offense under this section is a state jail felony.

(c) It is a defense to prosecution under Subsection (a) that:

(1) the person performing the act is a physician or other licensed health care professional and the act is within the scope of the person's license; and

(2) the act is performed for medical purposes.

(d) It is not a defense to prosecution under this section that:

(1) the person on whom the circumcision, excision, or infibulation was performed or was to be performed, or another person authorized to consent to medical treatment of that person, including that person's parent or legal guardian, consented to the circumcision, excision, or infibulation;

(2) the circumcision, excision, or infibulation is required by a custom or practice of a particular group; or

(3) the circumcision, excision, or infibulation was performed or was to be performed as part of or in connection with a religious or other ritual.

CHAPTER 169 FIRST OFFENDER PROSTITUTION PREVENTION PROGRAM

Sec. 169.001. First Offender Solicitation of Prostitution Prevention Program; Procedures for Certain Defendants.

(a) In this chapter, "first offender solicitation of prostitution prevention program" means a program that has the following essential characteristics:

(1) the integration of services in the processing of cases in the judicial system;

(2) the use of a nonadversarial approach involving prosecutors and defense attorneys to promote public safety, to reduce the demand for the commercial sex trade and trafficking of persons by educating offenders, and to protect the due process rights of program participants;

(3) early identification and prompt placement of eligible participants in the program;

(4) access to information, counseling, and services relating to sex addiction, sexually transmitted diseases, mental health, and substance abuse;

(5) a coordinated strategy to govern program responses to participant compliance;

(6) monitoring and evaluation of program goals and effectiveness;

(7) continuing interdisciplinary education to promote effective program planning, implementation, and operations; and

(8) development of partnerships with public agencies and community organizations.

(b) If a defendant successfully completes a first offender solicitation of prostitution prevention program, regardless of whether the defendant was convicted of the offense for which the defendant entered the program or whether the court deferred further proceedings without entering an adjudication of guilt, after notice to the state and a hearing on whether the defendant is otherwise entitled to the petition, including whether the required time period has elapsed, and whether issuance of the order is in the best interest of justice, the court shall enter an order of nondisclosure of criminal history record information under Subchapter E-1, Chapter 411, Government Code, as if the defendant had received a discharge and dismissal under Article 42A.111, Code of Criminal Procedure, with respect to all records and files related to the defendant's arrest for the offense for which the defendant entered the program if the defendant:

(1) has not been previously convicted of a felony offense; and

(2) is not convicted of any other felony offense before the second anniversary of the defendant's successful completion of the program.

Sec. 169.002. Authority to Establish Program; Eligibility.

(a) The commissioners court of a county or governing body of a municipality may establish a first offender solicitation of prostitution prevention program for defendants charged with an offense under Section 43.021, Penal Code.

(b) A defendant is eligible to participate in a first offender solicitation of prostitution prevention program established under this chapter only if:

(1) the attorney representing the state consents to the defendant's participation in the program; and

Health and Safety Code

(2) the court in which the criminal case is pending finds that the defendant has not been previously convicted of:

(A) an offense under Section 20A.02, 43.02(b), as that law existed before September 1, 2021, 43.021, 43.03, 43.031, 43.04, 43.041, or 43.05, Penal Code;

(B) an offense listed in Article 42A.054(a), Code of Criminal Procedure; or

(C) an offense punishable as a felony under Chapter 481.

(c) For purposes of Subsection (b), a defendant has been previously convicted of an offense listed in that subsection if:

(1) the defendant was adjudged guilty of the offense or entered a plea of guilty or nolo contendere in return for a grant of deferred adjudication, regardless of whether the sentence for the offense was ever imposed or whether the sentence was probated and the defendant was subsequently discharged from community supervision; or

(2) the defendant was convicted under the laws of another state for an offense containing elements that are substantially similar to the elements of an offense listed in Subsection (b).

(d) A defendant is not eligible to participate in the first offender solicitation of prostitution prevention program if the defendant offered or agreed to hire a person to engage in sexual conduct and the person was younger than 18 years of age at the time of the offense.

(e) The court in which the criminal case is pending shall allow an eligible defendant to choose whether to participate in the first offender solicitation of prostitution prevention program or otherwise proceed through the criminal justice system.

(f) If a defendant who chooses to participate in the first offender solicitation of prostitution prevention program fails to attend any portion of the program, the court in which the defendant's criminal case is pending shall issue a warrant for the defendant's arrest and proceed on the criminal case as if the defendant had chosen not to participate in the program.

Sec. 169.003. Program Powers and Duties.

(a) A first offender solicitation of prostitution prevention program established under this chapter must:

(1) ensure that a person eligible for the program is provided legal counsel before volunteering to proceed through the program and while participating in the program;

(2) allow any participant to withdraw from the program at any time before a trial on the merits has been initiated;

(3) provide each participant with information, counseling, and services relating to sex addiction, sexually transmitted diseases, mental health, and substance abuse; and

(4) provide each participant with classroom instruction related to the prevention of the solicitation of prostitution.

(b) To provide each program participant with information, counseling, and services described by Subsection (a)(3), a program established under this chapter may employ a person or solicit a volunteer who is:

(1) a health care professional;

(2) a psychologist;

(3) a licensed social worker or counselor;

(4) a former prostitute;

(5) a family member of a person arrested for soliciting prostitution;

(6) a member of a neighborhood association or community that is adversely affected by the commercial sex trade or trafficking of persons; or

(7) an employee of a nongovernmental organization specializing in advocacy or laws related to sex trafficking or human trafficking or in providing services to victims of those offenses.

(c) A program established under this chapter shall establish and publish local procedures to promote maximum participation of eligible defendants in programs established in the county or municipality in which the defendants reside.

Sec. 169.004. Oversight.

(a) The lieutenant governor and the speaker of the house of representatives may assign to appropriate legislative committees duties relating to the oversight of first offender solicitation of prostitution prevention programs established under this chapter.

(b) A legislative committee or the governor may request the state auditor to perform a management, operations, or financial or accounting audit of a first offender solicitation of prostitution prevention program established under this chapter.

(c) A first offender solicitation of prostitution prevention program established under this chapter shall:

(1) notify the criminal justice division of the governor's office before or on implementation of the program; and

(2) provide information regarding the performance of the program to the division on request.

Sec. 169.005. Reimbursement Fees.

(a) A first offender solicitation of prostitution prevention program established under this chapter may collect from a participant in the program a nonrefundable reimbursement fee for the program in a reasonable amount not to exceed $1,000, from which the following must be paid:

(1) a counseling and services reimbursement fee in an amount necessary to cover the costs of the counseling and services provided by the program; and

(2) a law enforcement training reimbursement fee, in an amount equal to five percent of the total amount paid under Subdivision (1), to be deposited to the credit of the treasury of the county or municipality that established the program to cover costs associated with the provision of training to law enforcement personnel on domestic violence, prostitution, and the trafficking of persons.

(b) Reimbursement fees collected under this section may be paid on a periodic basis or on a deferred payment schedule at the discretion of the judge, magistrate, or program director administering the first offender solicitation of prostitution prevention program. The fees must be based on the participant's ability to pay.

Sec. 169.006. Suspension or Dismissal of Community Service Requirement.

(a) To encourage participation in a first offender solicitation of prostitution prevention program established under this chapter, the judge or magistrate administering the program may suspend any requirement that, as a condition of community supervision, a participant in the program work a specified number of hours at a community service project.

(b) On a participant's successful completion of a first offender solicitation of prostitution prevention program, a judge or magistrate may excuse the participant from any condition of community supervision previously suspended under Subsection (a).

CHAPTER 169A PROSTITUTION PREVENTION PROGRAM [RENUMBERED]

Sec. 169A.001. Prostitution Prevention Program; Procedures for Certain Defendants. [Renumbered]

(a) In this chapter, "prostitution prevention program" means a program that has the following essential characteristics:

(1) the integration of services in the processing of cases in the judicial system;

(2) the use of a nonadversarial approach involving prosecutors and defense attorneys to promote public safety, to reduce the demand for the commercial sex trade and trafficking of persons by educating offenders, and to protect the due process rights of program participants;

(3) early identification and prompt placement of eligible participants in the program;

(4) access to information, counseling, and services relating to sex addiction, sexually transmitted diseases, mental health, and substance abuse;

(5) a coordinated strategy to govern program responses to participant compliance;

(6) monitoring and evaluation of program goals and effectiveness;

(7) continuing interdisciplinary education to promote effective program planning, implementation, and operations; and

(8) development of partnerships with public agencies and community organizations.

(b) If a defendant successfully completes a prostitution prevention program, regardless of whether the defendant was convicted of the offense for which the defendant entered the program or whether the court deferred further proceedings without entering an adjudication of guilt, after notice to the state and a hearing on whether the defendant is otherwise entitled to the petition, including whether the required time has elapsed, and whether issuance of the order is in the best interest of justice, the court shall enter an order of nondisclosure under Section 411.081, Government Code, as if the defendant had received a discharge and dismissal under Article 42A.111, Code of Criminal Procedure, with respect to all records and files related to the defendant's arrest for the offense for which the defendant entered the program.

Sec. 169A.002. Authority to Establish Program; Eligibility. [Renumbered]

Sec. 169A.0025. Establishment of Regional Program. [Renumbered]

Sec. 169A.003. Program Powers and Duties. [Renumbered]

Sec. 169A.004. Oversight. [Renumbered]

Sec. 169A.005. Fees. [Renumbered]

Health and Safety Code

Sec. 169A.0055. Program in Certain Counties Mandatory. [Renumbered]

Sec. 169A.006. Suspension or Dismissal of Community Service Requirement. [Renumbered]

CHAPTER 170A PERFORMANCE OF ABORTION

Sec. 170A.001. Definitions.

In this chapter:

(1) "Abortion" has the meaning assigned by Section 245.002.

(2) "Fertilization" means the point in time when a male human sperm penetrates the zona pellucida of a female human ovum.

(3) "Pregnant" means the female human reproductive condition of having a living unborn child within the female's body during the entire embryonic and fetal stages of the unborn child's development from fertilization until birth.

(4) "Reasonable medical judgment" means a medical judgment made by a reasonably prudent physician, knowledgeable about a case and the treatment possibilities for the medical conditions involved.

(5) "Unborn child" means an individual living member of the homo sapiens species from fertilization until birth, including the entire embryonic and fetal stages of development.

Sec. 170A.002. Prohibited Abortion; Exceptions.

(a) A person may not knowingly perform, induce, or attempt an abortion.

(b) The prohibition under Subsection (a) does not apply if:

(1) the person performing, inducing, or attempting the abortion is a licensed physician;

(2) in the exercise of reasonable medical judgment, the pregnant female on whom the abortion is performed, induced, or attempted has a life-threatening physical condition aggravated by, caused by, or arising from a pregnancy that places the female at risk of death or poses a serious risk of substantial impairment of a major bodily function unless the abortion is performed or induced; and

(3) the person performs, induces, or attempts the abortion in a manner that, in the exercise of reasonable medical judgment, provides the best opportunity for the unborn child to survive unless, in the reasonable medical judgment, that manner would create:

(A) a greater risk of the pregnant female's death; or

(B) a serious risk of substantial impairment of a major bodily function of the pregnant female.

(c) A physician may not take an action authorized under Subsection (b) if, at the time the abortion was performed, induced, or attempted, the person knew the risk of death or a substantial impairment of a major bodily function described by Subsection (b)(2) arose from a claim or diagnosis that the female would engage in conduct that might result in the female's death or in substantial impairment of a major bodily function.

(d) Medical treatment provided to the pregnant female by a licensed physician that results in the accidental or unintentional injury or death of the unborn child does not constitute a violation of this section.

Sec. 170A.003. Construction of Chapter.

This chapter may not be construed to authorize the imposition of criminal, civil, or administrative liability or penalties on a pregnant female on whom an abortion is performed, induced, or attempted.

Sec. 170A.004. Criminal Offense.

(a) A person who violates Section 170A.002 commits an offense.

(b) An offense under this section is a felony of the second degree, except that the offense is a felony of the first degree if an unborn child dies as a result of the offense.

Sec. 170A.005. Civil Penalty.

A person who violates Section 170A.002 is subject to a civil penalty of not less than $100,000 for each violation. The attorney general shall file an action to recover a civil penalty assessed under this section and may recover attorney's fees and costs incurred in bringing the action.

Sec. 170A.006. Civil Remedies Unaffected.

The fact that conduct is subject to a civil or criminal penalty under this chapter does not abolish or impair any remedy for the conduct that is available in a civil suit.

Sec. 170A.007. Disciplinary Action.

In addition to any other penalty that may be imposed under this chapter, the appropriate licensing authority shall revoke the license, permit, registration, certificate, or other authority of a physician or other health care professional who performs, induces, or attempts an abortion in violation of Section 170A.002.

CHAPTER 171
ABORTION

SUBCHAPTER F. PARTIAL-BIRTH ABORTIONS

Sec. 171.101. Definitions.

In this subchapter:

(1) "Partial-birth abortion" means an abortion in which the person performing the abortion:

(A) for the purpose of performing an overt act that the person knows will kill the partially delivered living fetus, deliberately and intentionally vaginally delivers a living fetus until:

(i) for a head-first presentation, the entire fetal head is outside the body of the mother; or

(ii) for a breech presentation, any part of the fetal trunk past the navel is outside the body of the mother; and

(B) performs the overt act described in Paragraph (A), other than completion of delivery, that kills the partially delivered living fetus.

(2) "Physician" means an individual who is licensed to practice medicine in this state, including a medical doctor and a doctor of osteopathic medicine.

Sec. 171.102. Partial-Birth Abortions Prohibited.

(a) A physician or other person may not knowingly perform a partial-birth abortion.

(b) Subsection (a) does not apply to a physician who performs a partial-birth abortion that is necessary to save the life of a mother whose life is endangered by a physical disorder, physical illness, or physical injury, including a life-endangering physical condition caused by or arising from the pregnancy.

Sec. 171.103. Criminal Penalty.

A person who violates Section 171.102 commits an offense. An offense under this section is a state jail felony.

Sec. 171.104. Civil Liability.

(a) Except as provided by Subsection (b), the father of the fetus or a parent of the mother of the fetus, if the mother is younger than 18 years of age at the time of the partial-birth abortion, may bring a civil action to obtain appropriate relief, including:

(1) money damages for physical injury, mental anguish, and emotional distress; and

(2) exemplary damages equal to three times the cost of the partial-birth abortion.

(b) A person may not bring or maintain an action under this section if:

(1) the person consented to the partial-birth abortion; or

(2) the person's criminally injurious conduct resulted in the pregnancy.

Sec. 171.105. Hearing.

(a) A physician who is the subject of a criminal or civil action for a violation of Section 171.102 may request a hearing before the Texas Medical Board on whether the physician's conduct was necessary to save the life of a mother whose life was endangered by a physical disorder, physical illness, or physical injury, including a life-endangering physical condition caused by or arising from the pregnancy.

(b) The board's findings under Subsection (a) are admissible in any court proceeding against the physician arising from that conduct. On the physician's motion, the court shall delay the beginning of a criminal or civil trial for not more than 60 days for the hearing to be held under Subsection (a).

Sec. 171.106. Applicability.

A woman on whom a partial-birth abortion is performed or attempted in violation of this subchapter may not be prosecuted under this subchapter or for conspiracy to commit a violation of this subchapter.

SUBCHAPTER G. DISMEMBERMENT ABORTIONS

Sec. 171.151. Definition.

In this subchapter, "dismemberment abortion" means an abortion in which a person, with the purpose of causing the death of an unborn child, dismembers the living unborn child and extracts the unborn child one piece at a time from the uterus through the use of clamps, grasping forceps, tongs, scissors, or a similar instrument that, through the convergence of two rigid levers, slices, crushes, or grasps, or performs any combination of those actions on, a piece of the unborn child's body to cut or rip the piece from the body. The term does not include an abortion that uses suction to dismember the body of an unborn child by sucking pieces of the unborn child into a collection container. The term includes a dismemberment abortion that is used to cause the death of an unborn child and in which suction is subsequently used to extract pieces of the unborn child after the unborn child's death.

Sec. 171.152. Dismemberment Abortions Prohibited.

(a) A person may not intentionally perform a dismemberment abortion unless the dismemberment abortion is necessary in a medical emergency.

(b) A woman on whom a dismemberment abortion is performed, an employee or agent acting under the direction of a physician who performs a dismemberment abortion, or a person who fills a prescription or provides equipment used in a dismemberment abortion does not violate Subsection (a).

Sec. 171.153. Criminal Penalty.

(a) A person who violates Section 171.152 commits an offense.

(b) An offense under this section is a state jail felony.

Sec. 171.154. Construction of Subchapter.

(a) This subchapter shall be construed, as a matter of state law, to be enforceable to the maximum possible extent consistent with but not further than federal constitutional requirements, even if that construction is not readily apparent, as such constructions are authorized only to the extent necessary to save the subchapter from judicial invalidation. Judicial reformation of statutory language is explicitly authorized only to the extent necessary to save the statutory provision from invalidity.

(b) If any court determines that a provision of this subchapter is unconstitutionally vague, the court shall interpret the provision, as a matter of state law, to avoid the vagueness problem and shall enforce the provision to the maximum possible extent. If a federal court finds any provision of this subchapter or its application to any person, group of persons, or circumstances to be unconstitutionally vague and declines to impose the saving construction described by this subsection, the Supreme Court of Texas shall provide an authoritative construction of the objectionable statutory provisions that avoids the constitutional problems while enforcing the statute's restrictions to the maximum possible extent and shall agree to answer any question certified from a federal appellate court regarding the statute.

(c) A state executive or administrative official may not decline to enforce this subchapter, or adopt a construction of this subchapter in a way that narrows its applicability, based on the official's own beliefs concerning the requirements of the state or federal constitution, unless the official is enjoined by a state or federal court from enforcing this subchapter.

(d) This subchapter may not be construed to:

(1) authorize the prosecution of or a cause of action to be brought against a woman on whom an abortion is performed or induced in violation of this subchapter; or

(2) create or recognize a right to abortion or a right to a particular method of abortion.

TITLE 3
VITAL STATISTICS

CHAPTER 192
BIRTH RECORDS

SUBCHAPTER A
GENERAL REGISTRATION PROVISIONS

Sec. 192.0021. Heirloom Birth Certificate.

(a) The department shall promote and sell copies of an heirloom birth certificate. The department shall solicit donated designs for the certificate from Texas artists and select the best donated designs for the form of the certificate. An heirloom birth certificate must contain the same information as, and have the same effect of, a certified copy of another birth record. The executive commissioner by rule shall prescribe a fee for the issuance of an heirloom birth certificate in an amount that does not exceed $50. The heirloom birth certificate must be printed on high-quality paper with the appearance of parchment not smaller than 11 inches by 14 inches.

(b) The department shall deposit 50 percent of the proceeds from the sale of heirloom birth certificates to the credit of the childhood immunization account and the other 50 percent to the credit of the undedicated portion of the general revenue fund. The childhood immunization account is an account in the general revenue fund. Money in the account may be used only by the department for:

(1) making grants to fund childhood immunizations and related education programs; and

(2) administering this section.

(c) The department may sell an heirloom birth certificate only for an individual born in this state.

TITLE 5 SANITATION AND ENVIRONMENTAL QUALITY

SUBTITLE B SOLID WASTE, TOXIC CHEMICALS, SEWAGE, LITTER, AND WATER

CHAPTER 365 LITTER

SUBCHAPTER A GENERAL PROVISIONS

Sec. 365.001. Short Title.

This chapter may be cited as the Texas Litter Abatement Act.

Sec. 365.002. Water Pollution Controlled by Water Code.

The pollution of water in the state is controlled by Chapter 26, Water Code, and other applicable law.

Sec. 365.003. Litter on Beaches Controlled by Natural Resources Code.

The regulation of litter on public beaches is controlled by Subchapters C and D, Chapter 61, Natural Resources Code.

Sec. 365.004. Disposal of Garbage, Refuse, and Sewage in Certain Areas Under Control of Parks and Wildlife Department.

The Parks and Wildlife Commission may adopt rules to govern the disposal of garbage, refuse, and sewage in state parks, public water in state parks, historic sites, scientific areas, and forts under the control of the Parks and Wildlife Department.

Sec. 365.005. Venue and Recovery of Costs.

(a) Venue for the prosecution of a criminal offense under Subchapter B or Section 365.032 or 365.033 or for a suit for injunctive relief under any of those provisions is in the county in which the defendant resides, in the county in which the offense or the violation occurs, or in Travis County.

(b) If the attorney general or a local government brings a suit for injunctive relief under Subchapter B or Section 365.032 or 365.033, a prevailing party may recover its reasonable attorney fees, court costs, and reasonable investigative costs incurred in relation to the proceeding.

SUBCHAPTER B CERTAIN ACTIONS PROHIBITED

Sec. 365.011. Definitions.

In this subchapter:

(1) "Approved solid waste site" means:

(A) a solid waste site permitted or registered by the Texas Natural Resource Conservation Commission;

(B) a solid waste site licensed by a county under Chapter 361; or

(C) a designated collection area for ultimate disposal at a permitted or licensed municipal solid waste site.

(2) "Boat" means a vehicle, including a barge, airboat, motorboat, or sailboat, used for transportation on water.

(3) "Commercial purpose" means the purpose of economic gain.

(4) "Commercial vehicle" means a vehicle that is operated by a person for a commercial purpose or that is owned by a business or commercial enterprise.

(5) "Dispose" and "dump" mean to discharge, deposit, inject, spill, leak, or place litter on or into land or water.

(6) "Litter" means:

Health and Safety Code

(A) decayable waste from a public or private establishment, residence, or restaurant, including animal and vegetable waste material from a market or storage facility handling or storing produce or other food products, or the handling, preparation, cooking, or consumption of food, but not including sewage, body wastes, or industrial by-products; or

(B) nondecayable solid waste, except ashes, that consists of:

(i) combustible waste material, including paper, rags, cartons, wood, excelsior, furniture, rubber, plastics, yard trimmings, leaves, or similar materials;

(ii) noncombustible waste material, including glass, crockery, tin or aluminum cans, metal furniture, and similar materials that do not burn at ordinary incinerator temperatures of 1800 degrees Fahrenheit or less; and

(iii) discarded or worn-out manufactured materials and machinery, including motor vehicles and parts of motor vehicles, tires, aircraft, farm implements, building or construction materials, appliances, and scrap metal.

(7) "Motor vehicle" has the meaning assigned by Section 541.201, Transportation Code.

(8) "Public highway" means the entire width between property lines of a road, street, way, thoroughfare, bridge, public beach, or park in this state, not privately owned or controlled, if any part of the road, street, way, thoroughfare, bridge, public beach, or park:

(A) is opened to the public for vehicular traffic;

(B) is used as a public recreational area; or

(C) is under the state's legislative jurisdiction through its police power.

(9) "Solid waste" has the meaning assigned by Section 361.003.

Sec. 365.012. Illegal Dumping; Discarding Lighted Materials; Criminal Penalties.

(a) A person commits an offense if the person disposes or allows or permits the disposal of litter or other solid waste at a place that is not an approved solid waste site, including a place on or within 300 feet of a public highway, on a right-of-way, on other public or private property, or into inland or coastal water of the state.

(a-1) A person commits an offense if:

(1) the person discards lighted litter, including a match, cigarette, or cigar, onto open-space land, a private road or the right-of-way of a private road, a public highway or other public road or the right-of-way of a public highway or other public road, or a railroad right-of-way; and

(2) a fire is ignited as a result of the conduct described by Subdivision (1).

(b) A person commits an offense if the person receives litter or other solid waste for disposal at a place that is not an approved solid waste site, regardless of whether the litter or other solid waste or the land on which the litter or other solid waste is disposed is owned or controlled by the person.

(c) A person commits an offense if the person transports litter or other solid waste to a place that is not an approved solid waste site for disposal at the site.

(d) An offense under Subsection (a), (b), or (c) is a Class C misdemeanor if the litter or other solid waste to which the offense applies weighs five pounds or less or has a volume of five gallons or less.

(d-1) An offense under Subsection (a-1) is a misdemeanor under this subsection if the litter or other solid waste to which the offense applies weighs less than 500 pounds or has a volume of less than 100 cubic feet and is punishable by:

(1) a fine not to exceed $500;

(2) confinement in jail for a term not to exceed 30 days; or

(3) both such fine and confinement.

(e) An offense under Subsection (a), (b), or (c) is a Class B misdemeanor if the litter or other solid waste to which the offense applies weighs more than five pounds but less than 500 pounds or has a volume of more than five gallons but less than 100 cubic feet.

(f) An offense under this section is a Class A misdemeanor if:

(1) the litter or other solid waste to which the offense applies weighs 500 pounds or more but less than 1,000 pounds or has a volume of 100 cubic feet or more but less than 200 cubic feet; or

(2) the litter or other solid waste is disposed for a commercial purpose and weighs more than five pounds but less than 200 pounds or has a volume of more than five gallons but less than 200 cubic feet.

(g) An offense under this section is a state jail felony if the litter or solid waste to which the offense applies:

(1) weighs 1,000 pounds or more or has a volume of 200 cubic feet or more;

(2) is disposed of for a commercial purpose and weighs 200 pounds or more or has a volume of 200 cubic feet or more; or

(3) is contained in a closed barrel or drum.

(h) If it is shown on the trial of the defendant for an offense under this section that the defendant has previously been convicted of an offense under this section, the punishment for the offense is increased to the punishment for the next highest category.

Health and Safety Code

(i) On conviction for an offense under this section, the court shall provide to the defendant written notice that a subsequent conviction for an offense under this section may result in the forfeiture under Chapter 59, Code of Criminal Procedure, of the vehicle used by the defendant in committing the offense.

(j) The offenses prescribed by this section include the unauthorized disposal of litter or other solid waste in a dumpster or similar receptacle.

(k) This section does not apply to the temporary storage for future disposal of litter or other solid waste by a person on land owned by that person, or by that person's agent. The commission by rule shall regulate temporary storage for future disposal of litter or other solid waste by a person on land owned by the person or the person's agent.

(*l*) This section does not apply to an individual's disposal of litter or other solid waste if:

(1) the litter or waste is generated on land the individual owns;

(2) the litter or waste is not generated as a result of an activity related to a commercial purpose;

(3) the disposal occurs on land the individual owns; and

(4) the disposal is not for a commercial purpose.

(m) A municipality or county may offer a reward of $50 for reporting a violation of this section that results in a prosecution under this section.

(n) An offense under this section may be prosecuted without alleging or proving any culpable mental state, unless the offense is a state jail felony.

(o) For purposes of a prosecution under Subsection (g), a generator creates a rebuttable presumption of lack of culpable mental state if the generator of the solid waste to be disposed of secures, prior to the hauler's receipt of the solid waste, a signed statement from the hauler that the solid waste will be disposed of legally. The statement shall include the hauler's valid Texas driver's license number.

(p) It is an affirmative defense to prosecution under Subsection (a-1) that the person discarded the lighted litter in connection with controlled burning the person was conducting in the area into which the lighted litter was discarded.

(q) The operator of a public conveyance in which smoking tobacco is allowed shall post a sign stating the substance of Subsections (a-1) and (d-1) in a conspicuous place within any portion of the public conveyance in which smoking is allowed.

(r) If conduct that constitutes an offense under Subsection (a-1) also constitutes an offense under Subsection (a), the actor may be prosecuted only under Subsection (a-1). If conduct that constitutes an offense under Subsection (a-1) also constitutes an offense under Chapter 28, Penal Code, the actor may be prosecuted under Subsection (a-1) or Chapter 28, Penal Code, but not both.

(s) On conviction of an offense under this section, the court shall require the defendant, in addition to any fine or other penalty, to perform community service as provided by Article 42A.304(e), Code of Criminal Procedure.

Sec. 365.013. Rules and Standards; Criminal Penalty.

(a) The Texas Natural Resource Conservation Commission shall adopt rules and standards regarding processing and treating litter disposed in violation of this subchapter.

(b) A person commits an offense if the person violates a rule adopted under this section.

(c) An offense under this section is a Class A misdemeanor.

(d) On conviction of an offense under this section, the court shall require the defendant, in addition to any fine or other penalty, to perform community service as provided by Article 42A.304(e), Code of Criminal Procedure.

Sec. 365.014. Application of Subchapter; Defenses; Presumptions.

(a) This subchapter does not apply to farmers:

(1) in handling anything necessary to grow, handle, and care for livestock; or

(2) in erecting, operating, and maintaining improvements necessary to handle, thresh, and prepare agricultural products or for conservation projects.

(b) A person who dumps more than five pounds or 13 gallons of litter or other solid waste from a commercial vehicle in violation of this subchapter is presumed to be dumping the litter or other solid waste for a commercial purpose.

(c) It is an affirmative defense to prosecution under Section 365.012 that:

(1) the storage, processing, or disposal took place on land owned or leased by the defendant;

(2) the defendant received the litter or other solid waste from another person;

(3) the defendant, after exercising due diligence, did not know and reasonably could not have known that litter or other solid waste was involved; and

(4) the defendant did not receive, directly or indirectly, compensation for the receipt, storage, processing, or treatment.

Sec. 365.015. Injunction; Venue; Recovery of Costs.

(a) A district attorney, a county attorney, or the attorney general may bring a civil suit for an injunction to prevent or restrain a violation of this subchapter. A person affected or to be affected by a violation is entitled to seek injunctive relief to enjoin the violation.

(b) Venue for a prosecution of a criminal offense under this subchapter or for a civil suit for injunctive relief under this subchapter is in the county in which the defendant resides, the county in which the offense or violation occurred, or in Travis County.

(c) In a suit for relief under this section, the prevailing party may recover its reasonable attorney fees, court costs, and reasonable investigative costs incurred in relation to the proceeding.

Sec. 365.016. Disposal of Litter in a Cave; Criminal Penalty.

(a) A person commits an offense if the person disposes litter, a dead animal, sewage, or any chemical in a cave.

(b) An offense under this section is a Class C misdemeanor unless:

(1) it is shown on the trial of the defendant that the defendant previously has been convicted once of an offense under this section, in which event the offense is a Class A misdemeanor; or

(2) it is shown on the trial of the defendant that the defendant previously has been convicted two or more times of an offense under this section, in which event the offense is a felony of the third degree.

(c) On conviction of an offense under this section, the court shall require the defendant, in addition to any fine or other penalty, to perform community service as provided by Article 42A.304(e), Code of Criminal Procedure.

Sec. 365.017. Regulation of Litter in Certain Counties.

(a) The commissioners court of a county may adopt regulations to control the disposal of litter and the removal of illegally dumped litter from private property in unincorporated areas of that county. The commissioners court may not adopt regulations under this section concerning the disposal of recyclable materials as defined in Chapter 361 of the Health and Safety Code.

(b) Prior to the adoption of regulations the commissioners court of a county must find that the proposed regulations are necessary to promote the public health, safety, and welfare of the residents of that county.

(c) The definitions of Section 365.011 apply in this Act. "Illegally dumped litter" means litter dumped anywhere other than in an approved solid waste site. "Litter" has the meaning assigned by Section 365.011, except that the term does not include equipment used for agricultural purposes.

(d) The regulations adopted by the commissioners court may require the record property owners to pay for the cost of removal after the commissioners court has given the record property owner 30 days written notice to remove the illegally dumped litter.

(e) Regulations adopted under this section are in addition to any other law regarding this issue and the stricter law shall apply.

(f) In addition to any other remedy provided by law, a district attorney, a county attorney, or the attorney general may bring a civil suit to enjoin violation of regulations adopted under this section and to recover the costs of removal of illegally dumped litter. In such a suit the prevailing party may recover its reasonable attorney fees, court fees, and reasonable investigative costs incurred in relation to that proceeding.

SUBCHAPTER C SPECIAL PROVISIONS

Sec. 365.031. Litter, Garbage, Refuse, and Rubbish in Lake Sabine.

The governing body of Port Arthur by ordinance may prohibit the depositing or placing of litter, garbage, refuse, or rubbish into or on the waters of Lake Sabine within the municipal limits.

Sec. 365.032. Throwing Certain Substances in or Near Lake Lavon; Criminal Penalty.

(a) The definitions provided by Section 365.011 apply to this section.

(b) A person commits an offense if the person throws, leaves, or causes to be thrown or left wastepaper, glass, metal, a tin can, refuse, garbage, waste, discarded or soiled personal property, or any other noxious or poisonous substance in the water of or near Lake Lavon in Collin County if the substance is detrimental to fish or to a person fishing in Lake Lavon.

(c) An offense under this section is a Class C misdemeanor unless it is shown on the trial of the defendant that the defendant has previously been convicted of an offense under this section, in which event the offense is a Class A misdemeanor.

Sec. 365.033. Discarding Refuse in Certain County Parks; Criminal Penalty.

(a) The definitions provided by Section 365.011 apply to this section.

(b) In this section, "beach" means an area in which the public has acquired a right of use or an easement and that borders on the seaward shore of the Gulf of Mexico or extends from the line of mean low tide to the line of vegetation bordering on the Gulf of Mexico.

(c) This section applies only to a county park located in a county that has the Gulf of Mexico as one boundary, but does not apply to a beach located in that park.

(d) A person commits an offense if the person discards in a county park any junk, garbage, rubbish, or other refuse in a place that is not an officially designated refuse container or disposal unit.

(e) An offense under this section is a Class C misdemeanor unless it is shown on the trial of the defendant that the defendant has previously been convicted of an offense under this section, in which event the offense is a Class A misdemeanor.

Sec. 365.034. County Regulation of Litter Near Public Highway; Criminal Penalty.

(a) The commissioners court of a county may:

(1) by order prohibit the accumulation of litter for more than 30 days on a person's property within 50 feet of a public highway in the county;

(2) provide for the removal and disposition of litter accumulated near a public highway in violation of an order adopted under this section; and

(3) provide for the assessment against a person who owns the property from which litter is removed under Subdivision (2) of the costs incurred by the county in removing and disposing of the litter.

(b) Before the commissioners court takes any action to remove or dispose of litter under this section, the court shall send a notice by certified mail to the record owners of the property on which the litter is accumulated in violation of an order adopted under this section. The court may not remove or dispose of the litter or assess the costs of the removal or disposition against a property owner before the 30th day after the date the notice is sent under this subsection.

(c) If a person assessed costs under this section does not pay the costs within 60 days after the date of assessment:

(1) a lien in favor of the county attaches to the property from which the litter was removed to secure the payment of the costs and interest accruing at an annual rate of 10 percent on any unpaid part of the costs; and

(2) the commissioners court shall file a record of the lien in the office of the county clerk.

(d) The violation of an order adopted under this section is a Class C misdemeanor.

(e) In this section:

(1) "Litter" has the meaning assigned by Section 365.011 except that the term does not include equipment used for agricultural purposes.

(2) "Public highway" has the meaning assigned by Section 365.011.

Sec. 365.035. Prohibition on Possessing Glass Containers Within Boundary of State-Owned Riverbed; Penalties.

(a) In this section, "glass container" means a glass container designed to contain a beverage, including a bottle or jar.

(b) A person commits an offense if the person knowingly possesses a glass container within the boundaries of a state-owned riverbed in a county:

(1) that is located within 85 miles of an international border; and

(2) in which at least four rivers are located.

(c) An offense under this section is a Class C misdemeanor.

(d) It is a defense to prosecution under Subsection (b) that the person who possessed the glass container:

(1) did not transport the glass container into the boundaries of the riverbed;

(2) possessed the glass container only for the purpose of lawfully disposing of the glass container in a designated waste receptacle; or

(3) is the owner of property adjacent to the section of the riverbed in which the person possessed the glass container.

(e) It is an exception to the application of Subsection (b) that the person possessed the glass container only for the purpose of water sampling or conducting scientific research as authorized by:

(1) a governmental entity;

(2) a utility as defined by Section 11.004, Utilities Code;

(3) a retail public utility as defined by Section 13.002, Water Code;

(4) a power generation company as defined by Section 31.002, Utilities Code;

(5) a surface coal mining and reclamation operation, as defined by Section 134.004, Natural Resources Code; or

(6) a school-sponsored or university-sponsored educational activity.

SUBTITLE C
AIR QUALITY

CHAPTER 382
CLEAN AIR ACT

SUBCHAPTER G
VEHICLE EMISSIONS

Sec. 382.201. Definitions.

In this subchapter:

(1) "Affected county" means a county with a motor vehicle emissions inspection and maintenance program established under Section 548.301, Transportation Code.

(2) "Commercial vehicle" means a vehicle that is owned or leased in the regular course of business of a commercial or business entity.

(3) "Fleet vehicle" means a motor vehicle operated as one of a group that consists of more than 10 motor vehicles and that is owned and operated by a public or commercial entity or by a private entity other than a single household.

(4) "Participating county" means an affected county in which the commissioners court by resolution has chosen to implement a low-income vehicle repair assistance, retrofit, and accelerated vehicle retirement program authorized by Section 382.209.

(5) "Retrofit" means to equip, or the equipping of, an engine or an exhaust or fuel system with new, emissions-reducing parts or equipment designed to reduce air emissions and improve air quality, after the manufacture of the original engine or exhaust or fuel system, so long as the parts or equipment allow the vehicle to meet or exceed state and federal air emissions reduction standards.

(6) "Retrofit equipment" means emissions-reducing equipment designed to reduce air emissions and improve air quality that is installed after the manufacture of the original engine or exhaust or fuel system.

(7) "Vehicle" includes a fleet vehicle.

Sec. 382.202. Vehicle Emissions Inspection and Maintenance Program.

(a) The commission by resolution may request the Public Safety Commission to establish a vehicle emissions inspection and maintenance program under Subchapter F, Chapter 548, Transportation Code, in accordance with this section and rules adopted under this section. The commission by rule may establish, implement, and administer a program requiring emissions-related inspections of motor vehicles to be performed at inspection facilities consistent with the requirements of the federal Clean Air Act (42 U.S.C. Section 7401 et seq.) and its subsequent amendments.

(b) The commission by rule may require emissions-related inspection and maintenance of land vehicles, including testing exhaust emissions, examining emission control devices and systems, verifying compliance with applicable standards, and other requirements as provided by federal law or regulation.

(c) If the program is established under this section, the commission:

(1) shall adopt vehicle emissions inspection and maintenance requirements for certain areas as required by federal law or regulation; and

(2) shall adopt vehicle emissions inspection and maintenance requirements for counties not subject to a specific federal requirement in response to a formal request by resolutions adopted by the county and the most populous municipality within the county according to the most recent federal decennial census.

(d) On adoption of a resolution by the commission and after proper notice, the Department of Public Safety of the State of Texas shall implement a system that requires, as a condition of obtaining a passing vehicle inspection report issued under Subchapter C, Chapter 548, Transportation Code, in a county that is included in a vehicle emissions inspection and maintenance program under Subchapter F of that chapter, that the vehicle, unless the vehicle is not covered by the system, be annually or biennially inspected under the vehicle emissions inspection and maintenance program as required by the state's air quality state implementation plan. The Department of Public Safety shall implement such a system when it is required by any provision of federal or state law, including any provision of the state's air quality state implementation plan.

(d-1) The commission may adopt rules providing for the inclusion on a vehicle inspection report for a vehicle inspected in a county that is included in a vehicle emissions inspection and maintenance program under Subchapter F, Chapter 548, Transportation Code, of notification regarding whether the vehicle is subject to a safety recall for which the vehicle has not been repaired or the repairs are incomplete. The commission may accept gifts, grants, and donations from any source, including private and nonprofit organizations, for the purpose of providing the notification described by this subsection.

(e) The commission may assess fees for vehicle emissions-related inspections performed at inspection or reinspection facilities authorized and licensed by the commission in amounts reasonably necessary to recover the costs of developing, administering, evaluating, and enforcing the vehicle emissions inspection and maintenance program. If the program relies on privately operated or contractor-operated inspection or reinspection stations, an appropriate portion of the fee as determined by commission rule may be retained by the station owner, contractor, or operator to recover the cost of performing the inspections and provide for a reasonable margin of profit. Any portion of the fee collected by the commission is a Clean Air Act fee under Section 382.0622.

(f) The commission:

(1) shall, no less frequently than biennially, review the fee established under Subsection (e); and

(2) may use part of the fee collected under Subsection (e) to provide incentives, including financial incentives, for participation in the testing network to ensure availability of an adequate number of testing stations.

(g) The commission shall:

(1) use part of the fee collected under Subsection (e) to fund low-income vehicle repair assistance, retrofit, and accelerated vehicle retirement programs created under Section 382.209; and

(2) to the extent practicable, distribute available funding created under Subsection (e) to participating counties in reasonable proportion to the amount of fees collected under Subsection (e) in those counties or in the regions in which those counties are located.

(h) Regardless of whether different tests are used for different vehicles as determined under Section 382.205, the commission may:

(1) set fees assessed under Subsection (e) at the same rate for each vehicle in a county or region; and

(2) set different fees for different counties or regions.

(i) The commission shall examine the efficacy of annually inspecting diesel vehicles for compliance with applicable federal emission standards, compliance with an opacity or other emissions-related standard established by commission rule, or both and shall implement that inspection program if the commission determines the program would minimize emissions. For purposes of this subsection, a diesel engine not used in a vehicle registered for use on public highways is not a diesel vehicle.

(j) The commission may not establish, before January 1, 2004, vehicle fuel content standards to provide for vehicle fuel content for clean motor vehicle fuels for any area of the state that are more stringent or restrictive than those standards promulgated by the United States Environmental Protection Agency applicable to that area except as provided in Subsection (o) unless the fuel is specifically authorized by the legislature.

(k) The commission by rule may establish classes of vehicles that are exempt from vehicle emissions inspections and by rule may establish procedures to allow and review petitions for the exemption of individual vehicles, according to criteria established by commission rule. Rules adopted by the commission under this subsection must be consistent with federal law. The commission by rule may establish fees to recover the costs of administering this subsection. Fees collected under this subsection shall be deposited to the credit of the clean air account, an account in the general revenue fund, and may be used only for the purposes of this section.

(*l*) Except as provided by this subsection, a person who sells or transfers ownership of a motor vehicle for which a passing vehicle inspection report has been issued is not liable for the cost of emission control system repairs that are required for the vehicle subsequently to receive a passing report. This subsection does not apply to repairs that are required because emission control equipment or devices on the vehicle were removed or tampered with before the sale or transfer of the vehicle.

(m) The commission may conduct audits to determine compliance with this section.

(n) The commission may suspend the emissions inspection program as it applies to pre-1996 vehicles in an affected county if:

(1) the department certifies that the number of pre-1996 vehicles in the county subject to the program is 20 percent or less of the number of those vehicles that were in the county on September 1, 2001; and

(2) an alternative testing methodology that meets or exceeds United States Environmental Protection Agency requirements is available.

(o) The commission may not require the distribution of Texas low-emission diesel as described in revisions to the State Implementation Plan for the control of ozone air pollution prior to February 1, 2005.

(p) The commission may consider, as an alternative method of compliance with Subsection (o), fuels to achieve equivalent emissions reductions.

(q), (r) [Repealed by Acts 2007, 80th Leg., ch. 262 (S.B. 12), § 1.10(2), effective June 8, 2007.]

Sec. 382.203. Vehicles Subject to Program; Exemptions.

(a) The inspection and maintenance program applies to any gasoline-powered vehicle that is:

(1) required to be registered in and is primarily operated in an affected county; and

(2) at least two and less than 25 years old; or

(3) subject to test-on-resale requirements under Section 548.3011, Transportation Code.

(b) In addition to a vehicle described by Subsection (a), the program applies to:

(1) a vehicle with United States governmental plates primarily operated in an affected county;

(2) a vehicle operated on a federal facility in an affected county; and

(3) a vehicle primarily operated in an affected county that is exempt from motor vehicle registration requirements or eligible under Chapter 502, Transportation Code, to display an "exempt" license plate.

(c) The Department of Public Safety of the State of Texas by rule may waive program requirements, in accordance with standards adopted by the commission, for certain vehicles and vehicle owners, including:

(1) the registered owner of a vehicle who cannot afford to comply with the program, based on reasonable income standards;

(2) a vehicle that cannot be brought into compliance with emissions standards by performing repairs;

(3) a vehicle:

(A) on which at least $100 has been spent to bring the vehicle into compliance; and

(B) that the department:

(i) can verify was driven fewer than 5,000 miles since the last safety inspection; and

(ii) reasonably determines will be driven fewer than 5,000 miles during the period before the next safety inspection is required; and

(4) a vehicle for which parts are not readily available.

(d) The program does not apply to a:

(1) motorcycle;

(2) slow-moving vehicle as defined by Section 547.001, Transportation Code; or

(3) vehicle that is registered but not operated primarily in a county or group of counties subject to a motor vehicle emissions inspection program established under Subchapter F, Chapter 548, Transportation Code.

Sec. 382.204. Remote Sensing Program Component.

(a) The commission and the Department of Public Safety of the State of Texas jointly shall develop a program component for enforcing vehicle emissions testing and standards by use of remote or automatic emissions detection and analysis equipment.

(b) The program component may be employed in any county designated as a nonattainment area within the meaning of Section 107(d) of the Clean Air Act (42 U.S.C. Section 7407) and its subsequent amendments, in any affected county, or in any county adjacent to an affected county.

(c) If a vehicle registered in a county adjacent to an affected county is detected under the program component authorized by this section as operating and exceeding acceptable emissions limitations in an affected county, the department shall provide notice of the violation under Section 548.306, Transportation Code.

Sec. 382.205. Inspection Equipment and Procedures.

(a) The commission by rule may adopt:

(1) standards and specifications for motor vehicle emissions testing equipment;

(2) recordkeeping and reporting procedures; and

(3) measurable emissions standards a vehicle must meet to pass the inspection.

(b) In adopting standards and specifications under Subsection (a), the commission may require different types of tests for different vehicle models.

(c) In consultation with the Department of Public Safety of the State of Texas, the commission may contract with one or more private entities to provide testing equipment, training, and related services to inspection stations in exchange for part of the testing fee. A contract under this subsection may apply to one specified area of the state or to the entire state. The commission at least once during each year shall review each contract entered into under this subsection to determine whether the contracting entity is performing satisfactorily under the terms of the contract. Immediately after completing the review, the commission shall prepare a report summarizing the review and send a copy of the report to the speaker of the house of representatives, the lieutenant governor, and the governor.

(d) The Department of Public Safety of the State of Texas by rule shall adopt:

(1) testing procedures in accordance with motor vehicle emissions testing equipment specifications; and

(2) procedures for issuing a vehicle inspection report following an emissions inspection and submitting information to the inspection database described by Section 548.251, Transportation Code, following an emissions inspection.

(e) The commission and the Department of Public Safety of the State of Texas by joint rule may adopt

Health and Safety Code

procedures to encourage a stable private market for providing emissions testing to the public in all areas of an affected county, including:

(1) allowing facilities to perform one or more types of emissions tests; and

(2) any other measure the commission and the Department of Public Safety consider appropriate.

(f) Rules and procedures under this section must ensure that approved repair facilities participating in a low-income vehicle repair assistance, retrofit, and accelerated vehicle retirement program established under Section 382.209 have access to adequate testing equipment.

(g) Subject to Subsection (h), the commission and the Department of Public Safety of the State of Texas by rule may allow alternative vehicle emissions testing if:

(1) the technology provides accurate and reliable results;

(2) the technology is widely and readily available to persons interested in performing alternative vehicle emissions testing; and

(3) the use of alternative testing is not likely to substantially affect federal approval of the state's air quality state implementation plan.

(h) A rule adopted under Subsection (g) may not be more restrictive than federal regulations governing vehicle emissions testing.

Sec. 382.206. Collection of Data; Report.

(a) The commission and the Department of Public Safety of the State of Texas may collect inspection and maintenance information derived from the emissions inspection and maintenance program, including:

(1) inspection results;

(2) inspection station information;

(3) information regarding vehicles operated on federal facilities;

(4) vehicle registration information; and

(5) other data the United States Environmental Protection Agency requires.

(b) The commission shall:

(1) report the information to the United States Environmental Protection Agency; and

(2) compare the information on inspection results with registration information for enforcement purposes.

Sec. 382.207. Inspection Stations; Quality Control Audits.

(a) The Department of Public Safety of the State of Texas by rule shall adopt standards and procedures for establishing vehicle emissions inspection stations authorized and licensed by the state.

(b) A vehicle emissions inspection may be performed at a decentralized independent inspection station or at a centralized inspection facility operated or licensed by the state. In developing the program for vehicle emissions inspections, the Department of Public Safety shall make all reasonable efforts to preserve the present decentralized system.

(c) After consultation with the Texas Department of Transportation, the commission shall require state and local transportation planning entities designated by the commission to prepare long-term projections of the combined impact of significant planned transportation system changes on emissions and air quality. The projections shall be prepared using air pollution estimation methodologies established jointly by the commission and the Texas Department of Transportation. This subsection does not restrict the Texas Department of Transportation's function as the transportation planning body for the state or its role in identifying and initiating specific transportation-related projects in the state.

(d) The Department of Public Safety may authorize enforcement personnel or other individuals to remove, disconnect, adjust, or make inoperable vehicle emissions control equipment, devices, or systems and to operate a vehicle in the tampered condition in order to perform a quality control audit of an inspection station or other quality control activities as necessary to assess and ensure the effectiveness of the vehicle emissions inspection and maintenance program.

(e) The Department of Public Safety shall develop a challenge station program to provide for the reinspection of a motor vehicle at the option of the owner of the vehicle to ensure quality control of a vehicle emissions inspection and maintenance system.

(f) The commission may contract with one or more private entities to operate a program established under this section.

(g) In addition to other procedures established by the commission, the commission shall establish procedures by which a private entity with whom the commission has entered into a contract to operate a program established under this section may agree to perform:

(1) testing at a fleet facility or dealership using mobile test equipment;

(2) testing at a fleet facility or dealership using test equipment owned by the fleet or dealership but calibrated and operated by the private entity's personnel; or

Health and Safety Code

(3) testing at a fleet facility or dealership using test equipment owned and operated by the private entity and installed at the fleet or dealership facility.

(h) The fee for a test conducted as provided by Subsection (g) shall be set by the commission in an amount not to exceed twice the fee otherwise provided by law or by rule of the commission. An appropriate portion of the fee, as determined by the commission, may be remitted by the private entity to the fleet facility or dealership.

Sec. 382.208. Attainment Program.

(a) Except as provided by Section 382.202(j) or another provision of this chapter, the commission shall coordinate with federal, state, and local transportation planning agencies to develop and implement transportation programs and other measures necessary to demonstrate and maintain attainment of national ambient air quality standards and to protect the public from exposure to hazardous air contaminants from motor vehicles.

(b) Participating agencies include the Texas Department of Transportation and metropolitan planning organizations designated by the governor.

Sec. 382.209. Low-Income Vehicle Repair Assistance, Retrofit, and Accelerated Vehicle Retirement Program.

(a) The commission and the Public Safety Commission by joint rule shall establish and authorize the commissioners court of a participating county to implement a low-income vehicle repair assistance, retrofit, and accelerated vehicle retirement program subject to agency oversight that may include reasonable periodic commission audits.

(b) The commission shall provide funding for local low-income vehicle repair assistance, retrofit, and accelerated vehicle retirement programs with available funds collected under Section 382.202, 382.302, or other designated and available funds. The programs shall be administered in accordance with Chapter 783, Government Code. Program costs may include call center management, application oversight, invoice analysis, education, outreach, and advertising. Not more than 10 percent of the money provided to a local low-income vehicle repair assistance, retrofit, and accelerated vehicle retirement program under this section may be used for the administration of the programs, including program costs.

(c) The rules adopted under Subsection (a) must provide procedures for ensuring that a program implemented under authority of that subsection does not apply to a vehicle that is:

(1) registered under Section 504.501 or 504.502, Transportation Code; and

(2) not regularly used for transportation during the normal course of daily activities.

(d) Subject to the availability of funds, a low-income vehicle repair assistance, retrofit, and accelerated vehicle retirement program established under this section shall provide monetary or other compensatory assistance for:

(1) repairs directly related to bringing certain vehicles that have failed a required emissions test into compliance with emissions requirements;

(2) a replacement vehicle or replacement assistance for a vehicle that has failed a required emissions test and for which the cost of repairs needed to bring the vehicle into compliance is uneconomical; and

(3) installing retrofit equipment on vehicles that have failed a required emissions test, if practically and economically feasible, in lieu of or in combination with repairs performed under Subdivision (1). The commission and the Department of Public Safety of the State of Texas shall establish standards and specifications for retrofit equipment that may be used under this section.

(e) A vehicle is not eligible to participate in a low-income vehicle repair assistance, retrofit, and accelerated vehicle retirement program established under this section unless:

(1) the vehicle is capable of being operated;

(2) the registration of the vehicle:

(A) is current; and

(B) reflects that the vehicle has been registered in the county implementing the program for at least 12 of the 15 months preceding the application for participation in the program;

(3) the commissioners court of the county administering the program determines that the vehicle meets the eligibility criteria adopted by the commission, the Texas Department of Motor Vehicles, and the Public Safety Commission;

(4) if the vehicle is to be repaired, the repair is done by a repair facility recognized by the Department of Public Safety, which may be an independent or private entity licensed by the state; and

(5) if the vehicle is to be retired under this subsection and Section 382.213, the replacement vehicle is a qualifying motor vehicle.

(f) A fleet vehicle, a vehicle owned or leased by a governmental entity, or a commercial vehicle is not eligible to participate in a low-income vehicle repair assistance, retrofit, and accelerated vehicle retirement program established and implemented under this section.

(g) A participating county may contract with any appropriate entity, including the regional council of governments or the metropolitan planning organization in the appropriate region, or with another county for services necessary to implement the participating county's low-income vehicle repair assistance, retrofit, and accelerated vehicle retirement program. The participating counties in a nonattainment region or counties participating in an early action compact under Subchapter H may agree to have the money collected in any one county be used in any other participating county in the same region.

(h) Participation by an affected county in a low-income vehicle repair assistance, retrofit, and accelerated vehicle retirement program is not mandatory. To the extent allowed by federal law, any emissions reductions attributable to a low-income vehicle repair assistance, retrofit, and accelerated vehicle retirement program in a county that are attained during a period before the county is designated as a nonattainment county shall be considered emissions reductions credit if the county is later determined to be a nonattainment county.

(i) Notwithstanding the vehicle replacement requirements provided by Subsection (d)(2), the commission by rule may provide monetary or other compensatory assistance under the low-income vehicle repair assistance, retrofit, and accelerated vehicle retirement program, subject to the availability of funds, for the replacement of a vehicle that meets the following criteria:

(1) the vehicle is gasoline-powered and is at least 10 years old;

(2) the vehicle owner meets applicable financial eligibility criteria;

(3) the vehicle meets the requirements provided by Subsections (e)(1) and (2); and

(4) the vehicle has passed a Department of Public Safety motor vehicle safety inspection or safety and emissions inspection within the 15-month period before the application is submitted.

(j) The commission may provide monetary or other compensatory assistance under the low-income vehicle repair assistance, retrofit, and accelerated vehicle retirement program for a replacement vehicle or replacement assistance for a pre-1996 model year replacement vehicle that passes the required United States Environmental Protection Agency Start-Up Acceleration Simulation Mode Standards emissions test but that would have failed the United States Environmental Protection Agency Final Acceleration Simulation Mode Standards emissions test or failed to meet some other criterion determined by the commission; provided, however, that a replacement vehicle under this subsection must be a qualifying motor vehicle.

Sec. 382.210. Implementation Guidelines and Requirements.

(a) The commission by rule shall adopt guidelines to assist a participating county in implementing a low-income vehicle repair assistance, retrofit, and accelerated vehicle retirement program authorized under Section 382.209. The guidelines at a minimum shall recommend:

(1) a minimum and maximum amount for repair assistance;

(2) a minimum and maximum amount toward the purchase price of a replacement vehicle qualified for the accelerated retirement program, based on vehicle type and model year, with the maximum amount not to exceed:

(A) $3,000 for a replacement car of the current model year or the previous three model years, except as provided by Paragraph (C);

(B) $3,000 for a replacement truck of the current model year or the previous two model years, except as provided by Paragraph (C); and

(C) $3,500 for a replacement vehicle of the current model year or the previous three model years that:

(i) is a hybrid vehicle, electric vehicle, or natural gas vehicle; or

(ii) has been certified to meet federal Tier 2, Bin 3 or a cleaner Bin certification under 40 C.F.R. Section 86.1811-04, as published in the February 10, 2000, Federal Register;

(3) criteria for determining eligibility, taking into account:

(A) the vehicle owner's income, which may not exceed 300 percent of the federal poverty level;

(B) the fair market value of the vehicle; and

(C) any other relevant considerations;

(4) safeguards for preventing fraud in the repair, purchase, or sale of a vehicle in the program; and

(5) procedures for determining the degree and amount of repair assistance a vehicle is allowed, based on:

(A) the amount of money the vehicle owner has spent on repairs;

(B) the vehicle owner's income; and

(C) any other relevant factors.

(b) A replacement vehicle described by Subsection (a)(2) must:

(1) except as provided by Subsection (c), be a vehicle in a class or category of vehicles that has been certified to meet federal Tier 2, Bin 5 or a cleaner Bin certification under 40 C.F.R. Section 86.1811-04, as published in the February 10, 2000, Federal Register;

(2) have a gross vehicle weight rating of less than 10,000 pounds;

Health and Safety Code

(3) have an odometer reading of not more than 70,000 miles; and

(4) be a vehicle the total cost of which does not exceed:

(A) for a vehicle described by Subsection (a)(2)(A) or (B), $35,000; or

(B) for a vehicle described by Subsection (a)(2)(C), $45,000.

(c) The commission may adopt any revisions made by the federal government to the emissions standards described by Subsection (b)(1).

(d) A participating county shall provide an electronic means for distributing vehicle repair or replacement funds once all program criteria have been met with regard to the repair or replacement. The county shall ensure that funds are transferred to a participating dealer under this section not later than the 10th business day after the date the county receives proof of the sale and any required administrative documents from the participating dealer.

(e) In rules adopted under this section, the commission shall require a mandatory procedure that:

(1) produces a document confirming that a person is eligible to purchase a replacement vehicle in the manner provided by this chapter, and the amount of money available to the participating purchaser;

(2) provides that a person who seeks to purchase a replacement vehicle in the manner provided by this chapter is required to have the document required by Subdivision (1) before the person enters into negotiation for a replacement vehicle in the manner provided by this chapter; and

(3) provides that a participating dealer who relies on a document issued as required by Subdivision (1) has no duty to otherwise confirm the eligibility of a person to purchase a replacement vehicle in the manner provided by this chapter.

(f) In this section, "total cost" means the total amount of money paid or to be paid for the purchase of a motor vehicle as set forth as "sales price" in the form entitled "Application for Texas Certificate of Title" promulgated by the Texas Department of Motor Vehicles. In a transaction that does not involve the use of that form, the term means an amount of money that is equivalent, or substantially equivalent, to the amount that would appear as "sales price" on the Application for Texas Certificate of Title if that form were involved.

Sec. 382.211. Local Advisory Panel.

(a) The commissioners court of a participating county may appoint one or more local advisory panels consisting of representatives of automobile dealerships, the automotive repair industry, safety inspection facilities, the public, antique and vintage car clubs, local nonprofit organizations, and locally affected governments to advise the county regarding the operation of the county's low-income vehicle repair assistance, retrofit, and accelerated vehicle retirement program, including the identification of a vehicle make or model with intrinsic value as an existing or future collectible.

(b) The commissioners court may delegate all or part of the administrative and financial matters to one or more local advisory panels established under Subsection (a).

Sec. 382.212. Emissions Reduction Credit.

(a) In this section, "emissions reduction credit" means an emissions reduction certified by the commission that is:

(1) created by eliminating future emissions, quantified during or before the period in which emissions reductions are made;

(2) expressed in tons or partial tons per year; and

(3) banked by the commission in accordance with commission rules relating to emissions banking.

(b) To the extent allowable under federal law, the commission by rule shall authorize:

(1) the assignment of a percentage of emissions reduction credit to a private, commercial, or business entity that purchases, for accelerated retirement, a qualified vehicle under a low-income vehicle repair assistance, retrofit, and accelerated vehicle retirement program;

(2) the transferability of an assigned emissions reduction credit;

(3) the use of emissions reduction credit by the holder of the credit against any state or federal emissions requirements applicable to a facility owned or operated by the holder of the credit;

(4) the assignment of a percentage of emissions reduction credit, on the retirement of a fleet vehicle, a vehicle owned or leased by a governmental entity, or a commercial vehicle, to the owner or lessor of the vehicle; and

(5) other actions relating to the disposition or use of emissions reduction credit that the commission determines will benefit the implementation of low-income vehicle repair assistance, retrofit, and accelerated vehicle retirement programs established under Section 382.209.

Sec. 382.213. Disposition of Retired Vehicle.

(a) Except as provided by Subsection (c) and Subdivision (5) of this subsection, a vehicle retired under an accelerated vehicle retirement program authorized by Section 382.209 may not be resold or reused in its entirety in this or another state. Subject to the provisions of Subsection (i), the automobile dealer who takes possession of the vehicle must submit to the program administrator proof, in a manner adopted by the commission, that the vehicle has been retired. The vehicle must be:

(1) destroyed;

(2) recycled;

(3) dismantled and its parts sold as used parts or used in the program;

(4) placed in a storage facility of a program established under Section 382.209 and subsequently destroyed, recycled, or dismantled and its parts sold or used in the program; or

(5) repaired, brought into compliance, and used as a replacement vehicle under Section 382.209(d)(2).

(a-1) The commission shall establish a partnership with representatives of the steel industry, automobile dismantlers, and the scrap metal recycling industry to ensure that:

(1) vehicles retired under Section 382.209 are scrapped or recycled; and

(2) proof of scrapping or recycling is provided to the commission.

(b) Not more than 10 percent of all vehicles eligible for retirement under this section may be used as replacement vehicles under Subsection (a)(5).

(c) A vehicle identified by a local advisory panel as an existing or future collectible vehicle under Section 382.211 may be sold to an individual if the vehicle:

(1) is repaired and brought into compliance;

(2) is removed from the state;

(3) is removed from an affected county; or

(4) is stored for future restoration and cannot be registered in an affected county except under Section 504.501 or 504.502, Transportation Code.

(d) Notwithstanding Subsection (a)(3), the dismantler of a vehicle shall scrap the emissions control equipment and engine. The dismantler shall certify that the equipment and engine have been scrapped and not resold into the marketplace. A person who causes, suffers, allows, or permits a violation of this subsection or of a rule adopted under this section is subject to a civil penalty under Subchapter D, Chapter 7, Water Code, for each violation. For purposes of this subsection, a separate violation occurs with each fraudulent certification or prohibited resale.

(e) Notwithstanding Subsection (d), vehicle parts not related to emissions control equipment or the engine may be resold in any state. The only cost to be paid by a recycler for the residual scrap metal of a vehicle retired under this section shall be the cost of transportation of the residual scrap metal to the recycling facility.

(f) Any dismantling of vehicles or salvaging of steel under this section must be performed at a facility located in this state.

(g) In dismantling a vehicle under this section, the dismantler shall remove any mercury switches in accordance with state and federal law.

(h) The commission shall adopt rules:

(1) defining "emissions control equipment" and "engine" for the purposes of this section; and

(2) providing a procedure for certifying that emissions control equipment and vehicle engines have been scrapped or recycled.

(i) Notwithstanding any other provision of this section, and except as provided by this subsection, a dealer is in compliance with this section and incurs no civil or criminal liability as a result of the disposal of a replaced vehicle if the dealer produces proof of transfer of the replaced vehicle by the dealer to a dismantler. The defense provided by this subsection is not available to a dealer who knowingly and intentionally conspires with another person to violate this section.

Sec. 382.214. Sale of Vehicle with Intent to Defraud.

(a) A person who with intent to defraud sells a vehicle in an accelerated vehicle retirement program established under Section 382.209 commits an offense that is a third degree felony.

(b) Sale of a vehicle in an accelerated vehicle retirement program includes:

(1) sale of the vehicle to retire the vehicle under the program; and

(2) sale of a vehicle purchased for retirement under the program.

Sec. 382.215. Sale of Vehicle Not Required.

Nothing in this subchapter may be construed to require a vehicle that has failed a required emissions test to be sold or destroyed by the owner.

Sec. 382.216. Incentives for Voluntary Participation in Vehicle Emissions Inspection and Maintenance Program.

The commission, the Texas Department of Transportation, and the Public Safety Commission may, subject to federal limitations:

(1) encourage counties likely to exceed federal clean air standards to implement voluntary:

(A) motor vehicle emissions inspection and maintenance programs; and

(B) low-income vehicle repair assistance, retrofit, and accelerated vehicle retirement programs;

Health and Safety Code

(2) establish incentives for counties to voluntarily implement motor vehicle emissions inspection and maintenance programs and low-income vehicle repair assistance, retrofit, and accelerated vehicle retirement programs; and

(3) designate a county that voluntarily implements a motor vehicle emissions inspection and maintenance program or a low-income vehicle repair assistance, retrofit, and accelerated vehicle retirement program as a "Clean Air County" and give preference to a county designated as a Clean Air County in any federal or state clean air grant program.

Sec. 382.217. Use of Unexpended Vehicle Repair Assistance, Retrofit, and Retirement Money [Repealed].

Repealed by Acts 2007, 80th Leg., ch. 262 (S.B. 12), § 1.10(3), effective June 8, 2007.

Sec. 382.218. Required Participation by Certain Counties.

(a) This section applies only to a county with a population of 800,000 or more that borders the United Mexican States.

(b) A county that was at any time required, because of the county's designation as a nonattainment area under Section 107(d) of the federal Clean Air Act (42 U.S.C. Section 7407), to participate in the vehicle emissions inspection and maintenance program under this subchapter and Subchapter F, Chapter 548, Transportation Code, shall continue to participate in the program even if the county is designated as an attainment area under the federal Clean Air Act.

Sec. 382.219. Purchase of Replacement Vehicle; Automobile Dealerships.

(a) An amount described by Section 382.210(a)(2) may be used as a down payment toward the purchase of a replacement vehicle.

(b) An automobile dealer that participates in the procedures and programs offered by this chapter must be located in the state. No dealer is required to participate in the procedures and programs provided by this chapter.

Sec. 382.220. Use of Funding for Local Initiative Projects.

(a) Money that is made available to participating counties under Section 382.202(g) or 382.302 may be appropriated only for programs administered in accordance with Chapter 783, Government Code, to improve air quality. A participating county may agree to contract with any appropriate entity, including a metropolitan planning organization or a council of governments to implement a program under Section 382.202, 382.209, or this section.

(b) A program under this section must be implemented in consultation with the commission and may include a program to:

(1) expand and enhance the AirCheck Texas Repair and Replacement Assistance Program;

(2) develop and implement programs or systems that remotely determine vehicle emissions and notify the vehicle's operator;

(3) develop and implement projects to implement the commission's smoking vehicle program;

(4) develop and implement projects in consultation with the director of the Department of Public Safety for coordinating with local law enforcement officials to reduce the use of counterfeit registration insignia and vehicle inspection reports by providing local law enforcement officials with funds to identify vehicles with counterfeit registration insignia and vehicle inspection reports and to carry out appropriate actions;

(5) develop and implement programs to enhance transportation system improvements; or

(6) develop and implement new air control strategies designed to assist local areas in complying with state and federal air quality rules and regulations.

(c) Money that is made available for the implementation of a program under Subsection (b) may not be expended for local government fleet or vehicle acquisition or replacement, call center management, application oversight, invoice analysis, education, outreach, or advertising purposes.

(d) Fees collected under Sections 382.202 and 382.302 may be used in an amount not to exceed $7 million per fiscal year for projects described by Subsection (b), of which $2 million may be used only for projects described by Subsection (b)(4). The remaining $5 million may be used for any project described by Subsection (b). The fees shall be made available only to counties participating in the low-income vehicle repair assistance, retrofit, and accelerated vehicle retirement programs created under Section 382.209 and only on a matching basis, whereby the commission provides money to a county in the same amount that the county dedicates to a project authorized by Subsection (b). The commission may reduce the match requirement for a county that proposes to develop and implement independent test facility fraud detection programs, including the use of remote sensing technology for coordinating with law enforcement officials to detect, prevent, and prosecute the use of counterfeit registration insignia and vehicle inspection reports.

SUBCHAPTER H
VEHICLE EMISSIONS PROGRAMS IN CERTAIN COUNTIES

Sec. 382.301. Definitions.

In this subchapter:

(1) "Early action compact" means an agreement entered into before January 1, 2003, by the United States Environmental Protection Agency, the commission, the governing body of a county that is in attainment of the one-hour national ambient air quality standard for ozone but that has incidents approaching, or monitors incidents that exceed, the eight-hour national ambient air quality standard for ozone, and the governing body of the most populous municipality in that county that results in the submission of:

(A) an early action plan to the commission that the commission finds to be adequate; and

(B) a state implementation plan revision to the United States Environmental Protection Agency on or before December 31, 2004, that provides for attainment of the eight-hour national ambient air quality standard for ozone on or before December 31, 2007.

(2) "Participating county" means a county that is a party to an early action compact.

Sec. 382.302. Inspection and Maintenance Program.

(a) A participating county whose early action plan contains provisions for a motor vehicle emissions inspection and maintenance program and has been found adequate by the commission may formally request the commission to adopt motor vehicle emissions inspection and maintenance program requirements for the county. The request must be made by a resolution adopted by the governing body of the participating county and the governing body of the most populous municipality in the county.

(b) After approving a request made under Subsection (a), the commission by resolution may request the Public Safety Commission to establish motor vehicle emissions inspection and maintenance program requirements for the participating county under Subchapter F, Chapter 548, Transportation Code, in accordance with this section and rules adopted under this section. The motor vehicle emissions inspection and maintenance program requirements for the participating county may include exhaust emissions testing, emissions control devices and systems inspections, or other testing methods that meet or exceed United States Environmental Protection Agency requirements, and a remote sensing component as provided by Section 382.204. The motor vehicle emissions inspection and maintenance program requirements adopted for the participating county may apply to all or to a defined subset of vehicles described by Section 382.203.

(c) The commission may assess a fee for a vehicle inspection performed in accordance with a program established under this section. The fee must be in an amount reasonably necessary to recover the costs of developing, administering, evaluating, and enforcing the participating county's motor vehicle emissions inspection and maintenance program. An appropriate part of the fee as determined by commission rule may be retained by the station owner, contractor, or operator to recover the cost of performing the inspection and provide for a reasonable margin of profit.

(d) The incentives for voluntary participation established under Section 382.216 shall be made available to a participating county.

(e) A participating county may participate in the program established under Section 382.209.

TITLE 6
FOOD, DRUGS, ALCOHOL, AND HAZARDOUS SUBSTANCES

SUBTITLE A
FOOD AND DRUG HEALTH REGULATIONS

CHAPTER 431
TEXAS FOOD, DRUG, AND COSMETIC ACT

SUBCHAPTER A
GENERAL PROVISIONS

Sec. 431.001. Short Title.

This chapter may be cited as the Texas Food, Drug, and Cosmetic Act.

Sec. 431.002. Definitions.

In this chapter:

(1) "Advertising" means all representations disseminated in any manner or by any means, other than by labeling, for the purpose of inducing, or that are likely to induce, directly or indirectly, the purchase of food, drugs, devices, or cosmetics.

(2) "Animal feed," as used in Subdivision (23), in Section 512 of the federal Act, and in provisions of this chapter referring to those paragraphs or sections, means an article intended for use as food for animals other than man as a substantial source of nutrients in the diet of the animals. The term is not limited to a mixture intended to be the sole ration of the animals.

(3), (4) [Repealed by Acts 2015, 84th Leg., ch. 1 (S.B. 219), § 3.1639(75), effective April 2, 2015.]

(5) "Butter" means the food product usually known as butter that is made exclusively from milk or cream, or both, with or without common salt or additional coloring matter, and containing not less than 80 percent by weight of milk fat, after allowing for all tolerances.

(6) (A) "Color additive" means a material that:

(i) is a dye, pigment, or other substance made by a process of synthesis or similar artifice, or extracted, isolated, or otherwise derived, with or without intermediate or final change of identity from a vegetable, animal, mineral, or other source; and

(ii) when added or applied to a food, drug, or cosmetic, or to the human body or any part of the human body, is capable, alone or through reaction with other substance, of imparting color. The term does not include any material exempted under the federal Act.

(B) "Color" includes black, white, and intermediate grays.

(C) Paragraph (A) does not apply to any pesticide chemical, soil or plant nutrient, or other agricultural chemical solely because of its effect in aiding, retarding, or otherwise affecting, directly or indirectly, the growth or other natural physiological processes of produce of the soil and thereby affecting its color, whether before or after harvest.

(7) [Repealed by Acts 2015, 84th Leg., ch. 1 (S.B. 219), § 3.1639(75), effective April 2, 2015.]

(8) "Consumer commodity," except as otherwise provided by this subdivision, means any food, drug, device, or cosmetic, as those terms are defined by this chapter or by the federal Act, and any other article, product, or commodity of any kind or class that is customarily produced or distributed for sale through retail sales agencies or instrumentalities for consumption by individuals, or for use by individuals for purposes of personal care or in the performance of services ordinarily rendered within the household, and that usually is consumed or expended in the course of the consumption or use. The term does not include:

(A) a meat or meat product, poultry or poultry product, or tobacco or tobacco product;

(B) a commodity subject to packaging or labeling requirements imposed under the Federal Insecticide, Fungicide, and Rodenticide Act (7 U.S.C. 136), or The Virus-Serum-Toxin Act (21 U.S.C. 151 et seq.);

(C) a drug subject to the provisions of Section 431.113(c)(1) or Section 503(b)(1) of the federal Act;

(D) a beverage subject to or complying with packaging or labeling requirements imposed under the Federal Alcohol Administration Act (27 U.S.C. 205(e)); or

(E) a commodity subject to the provisions of Chapter 61, Agriculture Code, relating to the inspection, labeling, and sale of agricultural and vegetable seed.

(9) "Contaminated with filth" applies to any food, drug, device, or cosmetic not securely protected from dust, dirt, and as far as may be necessary by all reasonable means, from all foreign or injurious contaminations.

(10) "Cosmetic" means articles intended to be rubbed, poured, sprinkled, or sprayed on, introduced into, or otherwise applied to the human body or any part of the human body for cleaning, beautifying, promoting attractiveness, or altering the appearance, and articles intended for use as a component of those articles. The term does not include soap.

(11) "Counterfeit drug" means a drug, or the container or labeling of a drug, that, without authorization, bears the trademark, trade name or other identifying mark, imprint, or device of a drug manufacturer, processor, packer, or distributor other than the person who in fact manufactured, processed, packed, or distributed the drug, and that falsely purports or is represented to be the product of, or to have been packed or distributed by, the other drug manufacturer, processor, packer, or distributor.

(12) [Repealed by Acts 2015, 84th Leg., ch. 1 (S.B. 219), § 3.1639(75), effective April 2, 2015.]

(13) "Device," except when used in Sections 431.003, 431.021(*l*), 431.082(g), 431.112(c) and 431.142(c), means an instrument, apparatus,

implement, machine, contrivance, implant, in vitro reagent, or other similar or related article, including any component, part, or accessory, that is:

(A) recognized in the official United States Pharmacopoeia National Formulary or any supplement to it;

(B) intended for use in the diagnosis of disease or other conditions, or in the cure, mitigation, treatment, or prevention of disease in man or other animals; or

(C) intended to affect the structure or any function of the body of man or other animals and that does not achieve any of its principal intended purposes through chemical action within or on the body of man or other animals and is not dependent on metabolization for the achievement of any of its principal intended purposes.

(14) "Drug" means articles recognized in the official United States Pharmacopoeia National Formulary, or any supplement to it, articles designed or intended for use in the diagnosis, cure, mitigation, treatment, or prevention of disease in man or other animals, articles, other than food, intended to affect the structure or any function of the body of man or other animals, and articles intended for use as a component of any article specified in this subdivision. The term does not include devices or their components, parts, or accessories. A food for which a claim is made in accordance with Section 403(r) of the federal Act, and for which the claim is approved by the secretary, is not a drug solely because the label or labeling contains such a claim.

(15) "Federal Act" means the Federal Food, Drug and Cosmetic Act (Title 21 U.S.C. 301 et seq.).

(16) "Food" means:

(A) articles used for food or drink for man;

(B) chewing gum; and

(C) articles used for components of any such article.

(17) "Food additive" means any substance the intended use of which results or may reasonably be expected to result, directly or indirectly, in its becoming a component or otherwise affecting the characteristics of any food (including any substance intended for use in producing, manufacturing, packing, processing, preparing, treating, packaging, transporting, or holding food; and including any source of radiation intended for any use), if such substance is not generally recognized, among experts qualified by scientific training and experience to evaluate its safety, as having been adequately shown through scientific procedures (or, in the case of a substance used in food prior to January 1, 1958, through either scientific procedures or experience based on common use in food) to be safe under the conditions of its intended use; except that such term does not include:

(A) a pesticide chemical in or on a raw agricultural commodity;

(B) a pesticide chemical to the extent that it is intended for use or is used in the production, storage, or transportation of any raw agricultural commodity;

(C) a color additive;

(D) any substance used in accordance with a sanction or approval granted prior to the enactment of the Food Additives Amendment of 1958, Pub. L. No. 85-929, 52 Stat. 1041 (codified as amended in various sections of 21 U.S.C.), pursuant to the federal Act, the Poultry Products Inspection Act (21 U.S.C. 451 et seq.) or the Meat Inspection Act of 1906 (21 U.S.C. 601 et seq.); or

(E) a new animal drug.

(18) "Health authority" means a physician designated to administer state and local laws relating to public health.

(19) "Immediate container" does not include package liners.

(20) "Infant formula" means a food that is represented for special dietary use solely as a food for infants by reason of its simulation of human milk or its suitability as a complete or partial substitute for human milk.

(21) "Label" means a display of written, printed, or graphic matter upon the immediate container of any article; and a requirement made by or under authority of this chapter that any word, statement, or other information that appears on the label shall not be considered to be complied with unless the word, statement, or other information also appears on the outside container or wrapper, if any, of the retail package of the article, or is easily legible through the outside container or wrapper.

(22) "Labeling" means all labels and other written, printed, or graphic matter (1) upon any article or any of its containers or wrappers, or (2) accompanying such article.

(23) "Manufacture" means:

(A) the process of combining or purifying food or packaging food for sale to a person at wholesale or retail, and includes repackaging, labeling, or relabeling of any food;

(B) the process of preparing, propagating, compounding, processing, packaging, repackaging, labeling, testing, or quality control of a drug or drug product, but does not include compounding that is done within the practice of pharmacy and pursuant to a prescription drug order or initiative from a practitioner for a patient or prepackaging that is done in accordance with Section 562.154, Occupations Code;

(C) the process of preparing, fabricating, assembling, processing, packing, repacking, labeling, or relabeling a device; or

(D) the making of any cosmetic product by chemical, physical, biological, or other procedures, including manipulation, sampling, testing, or control procedures applied to the product.

(24) "New animal drug" means any drug intended for use for animals other than man, including any drug intended for use in animal feed:

(A) the composition of which is such that the drug is not generally recognized among experts qualified by scientific training and experience to evaluate the safety and effectiveness of animal drugs as safe and effective for use under the conditions prescribed, recommended, or suggested in the labeling of the drug (except that such an unrecognized drug is not deemed to be a "new animal drug" if at any time before June 25, 1938, it was subject to the Food and Drug Act of June 30, 1906, and if at that time its labeling contained the same representations concerning the conditions of its use);

(B) the composition of which is such that the drug, as a result of investigations to determine its safety and effectiveness for use under those conditions, has become recognized but that has not, otherwise than in the investigations, been used to a material extent or for a material time under those conditions; or

(C) is composed wholly or partly of penicillin, streptomycin, chloratetracycline, chloramphenicol, or bacitracin, or any derivative of those substances, unless:

(i) a published order of the secretary is in effect that declares the drug not to be a new animal drug on the grounds that the requirement of certification of batches of the drug, as provided by Section 512(n) of the federal Act, is not necessary to ensure that the objectives specified in Section 512(n)(3) of that Act are achieved; and

(ii) Paragraph (A) or (B) of this subdivision does not apply to the drug.

(25) "New drug" means:

(A) any drug, except a new animal drug, the composition of which is such that such drug is not generally recognized among experts qualified by scientific training and experience to evaluate the safety and effectiveness of drugs, as safe and effective for use under the conditions prescribed, recommended, or suggested in the labeling thereof (except that such an unrecognized drug is not a "new drug" if at any time before May 26, 1985, it was subject to the Food and Drug Act of June 30, 1906, and if at that time its labeling contained the same representations concerning the conditions of its use); or

(B) any drug, except a new animal drug, the composition of which is such that such drug, as a result of investigations to determine its safety and effectiveness for use under such conditions, has become so recognized, but which has not, otherwise than in such investigations, been used to a material extent or for a material time under such conditions.

(26) "Official compendium" means the official United States Pharmacopoeia National Formulary, or any supplement to it.

(27) "Package" means any container or wrapping in which a consumer commodity is enclosed for use in the delivery or display of that consumer commodity to retail purchasers. The term includes wrapped meats enclosed in papers or other materials as prepared by the manufacturers thereof for sale. The term does not include:

(A) shipping containers or wrappings used solely for the transportation of a consumer commodity in bulk or in quantity to manufacturers, packers, or processors, or to wholesale or retail distributors;

(B) shipping containers or outer wrappings used by retailers to ship or deliver a commodity to retail customers if the containers and wrappings do not bear printed matter relating to any particular commodity; or

(C) containers subject to the provisions of the Standard Barrel Act (Apple Barrels) (15 U.S.C. 231, 21 U.S.C. 20) or the Standard Barrel Act (Fruits and Vegetables) (15 U.S.C. 234—236).

(28) "Person" includes individual, partnership, corporation, and association.

(29) "Pesticide chemical" means any substance which, alone, in chemical combination or in formulation with one or more other substances, is a "pesticide" within the meaning of the Federal Insecticide, Fungicide, and Rodenticide Act (7 U.S.C. 136(u)), as now in force or as amended, and that is used in the production, storage, or transportation of raw agricultural commodities.

(30) "Principal display panel" means that part of a label that is most likely to be displayed, presented, shown, or examined under normal and customary conditions of display for retail sale.

(31) "Raw agricultural commodity" means any food in its raw or natural state, including all fruits that are washed, colored, or otherwise treated in their unpeeled natural form prior to marketing.

(32) "Saccharin" includes calcium saccharin, sodium saccharin, and ammonium saccharin.

(33) "Safe" refers to the health of humans or animals.

(34) "Secretary" means the secretary of the United States Department of Health and Human Services.

Sec. 431.003. Article Misbranded Because of Misleading Labeling or Advertising.

If an article is alleged to be misbranded because the labeling or advertising is misleading, then in determining whether the labeling or advertising is misleading, there shall be taken into account, among other things, not only representations made or suggested by statement, word, design, device, sound, or any combination of these, but also the extent to which the labeling or advertising fails to reveal facts material in the light of such representations or material with respect to consequences which may result from the use of the article to which the labeling or advertising relates under the conditions of use prescribed in the labeling or advertising thereof, or under such conditions of use as are customary or usual.

Sec. 431.004. Representation of Drug As Antiseptic.

The representation of a drug, in its labeling, as an antiseptic shall be considered to be a representation that the drug is a germicide, except in the case of a drug purporting to be, or represented as, an antiseptic for inhibitory use as a wet dressing, ointment, dusting powder, or such other use as involves prolonged contact with the body.

Sec. 431.005. Provisions Regarding Sale of Food, Drugs, Devices, or Cosmetics.

The provisions of this chapter regarding the selling of food, drugs, devices, or cosmetics, shall be considered to include the manufacture, production, processing, packaging, exposure, offer, possession, and holding of any such article for sale; and the sale, dispensing, and giving of any such article, and the supplying or applying of any such articles in the conduct of any food, drug, or cosmetic establishment.

Sec. 431.006. Certain Combination Products.

If the United States Food and Drug Administration determines, with respect to a product that is a combination of a drug and a device, that:

(1) the primary mode of action of the product is as a drug, a person who engages in wholesale distribution of the product is subject to licensure under Subchapter I; and

(2) the primary mode of action of the product is as a device, a distributor or manufacturer of the product is subject to licensure under Subchapter L.

Sec. 431.007. Compliance with Other Law; Molluscan Shellfish.

A person who is subject to this chapter and who handles molluscan shellfish, as that term is defined by Section 436.002, shall comply with Section 436.105.

Sec. 431.008. Applicability of Chapter to Distressed or Reconditioned Merchandise and Certain Licensed Entities.

(a) This chapter applies to a food, drug, device, or cosmetic that is distressed merchandise for purposes of Chapter 432 or that has been subject to reconditioning in accordance with Chapter 432.

(b) Except as provided by Subsection (c), this chapter applies to the conduct of a person licensed under Chapter 432.

(c) A person who holds a license under Chapter 432 and is engaging in conduct within the scope of that license is not required to hold a license as a wholesale drug distributor under Subchapter I, a food wholesaler under Subchapter J, or a device distributor under Subchapter L.

Sec. 431.009. Applicability of Chapter to Frozen Desserts.

(a) This chapter applies to a frozen dessert, an imitation frozen dessert, a product sold in semblance of a frozen dessert, or a mix for one of those products subject to Chapter 440. A frozen dessert, an imitation frozen dessert, a product sold in semblance of a frozen dessert, or a mix for one of those products is food for purposes of this chapter.

(b) Except as provided by Subsection (c), this chapter applies to the conduct of a person licensed under Chapter 440.

(c) A person who holds a license under Chapter 440 related to the manufacturing of a product regulated under that chapter and is engaging in conduct within the scope of that license is not required to hold a license as a food manufacturer or food wholesaler under Subchapter J.

Sec. 431.010. Applicability of Chapter to Milk and Milk Products.

(a) This chapter applies to milk or a milk product subject to Chapter 435. Milk or a milk product is a food for purposes of this chapter.

(b) Except as provided by Subsection (c), this chapter applies to the conduct of a person who holds a permit under Chapter 435.

(c) A person who holds a permit under Chapter 435 related to the processing, producing, bottling, receiving, transferring, or transporting of Grade A milk or milk products and who is engaging in conduct within the scope of that permit is not required to hold a license as a food manufacturer or food wholesaler under Subchapter J.

Sec. 431.011. Applicability of Chapter to Consumable Hemp Products and Manufacturers.

(a) This chapter applies to a consumable hemp product subject to Chapter 443. An article regulated under this chapter may not be deemed to be adulterated solely on the basis that the article is a consumable hemp product.

(b) Except as provided by Subsection (c), this chapter applies to the conduct of a person who holds a license under Chapter 443.

(c) A person who holds a license under Chapter 443 related to the processing of hemp or the manufacturing of a consumable hemp product regulated under that chapter and is engaging in conduct within the scope of that license is not required to hold a license as a food manufacturer or food wholesaler under Subchapter J.

SUBCHAPTER B PROHIBITED ACTS

Sec. 431.021. Prohibited Acts.

The following acts and the causing of the following acts within this state are unlawful and prohibited:

(a) the introduction or delivery for introduction into commerce of any food, drug, device, or cosmetic that is adulterated or misbranded;

(b) the adulteration or misbranding of any food, drug, device, or cosmetic in commerce;

(c) the receipt in commerce of any food, drug, device, or cosmetic that is adulterated or misbranded, and the delivery or proffered delivery thereof for pay or otherwise;

(d) the distribution in commerce of a consumer commodity, if such commodity is contained in a package, or if there is affixed to that commodity a label that does not conform to the provisions of this chapter and of rules adopted under the authority of this chapter; provided, however, that this prohibition shall not apply to persons engaged in business as wholesale or retail distributors of consumer commodities except to the extent that such persons:

(1) are engaged in the packaging or labeling of such commodities; or

(2) prescribe or specify by any means the manner in which such commodities are packaged or labeled;

(e) the introduction or delivery for introduction into commerce of any article in violation of Section 431.084, 431.114, or 431.115;

(f) the dissemination of any false advertisement;

(g) the refusal to permit entry or inspection, or to permit the taking of a sample or to permit access to or copying of any record as authorized by Sections 431.042-431.044; or the failure to establish or maintain any record or make any report required under Section 512(j), (l), or (m) of the federal Act, or the refusal to permit access to or verification or copying of any such required record;

(h) the manufacture within this state of any food, drug, device, or cosmetic that is adulterated or misbranded;

(i) the giving of a guaranty or undertaking referred to in Section 431.059, which guaranty or undertaking is false, except by a person who relied on a guaranty or undertaking to the same effect signed by, and containing the name and address of the person residing in this state from whom the person received in good faith the food, drug, device, or cosmetic; or the giving of a guaranty or undertaking referred to in Section 431.059, which guaranty or undertaking is false;

(j) the use, removal, or disposal of a detained or embargoed article in violation of Section 431.048;

(k) the alteration, mutilation, destruction, obliteration, or removal of the whole or any part of the labeling of, or the doing of any other act with respect to a food, drug, device, or cosmetic, if such act is done while such article is held for sale after shipment in commerce and results in such article being adulterated or misbranded;

(*l*) (1) forging, counterfeiting, simulating, or falsely representing, or without proper authority using any mark, stamp, tag, label, or other identification device authorized or required by rules adopted under this chapter or the regulations promulgated under the provisions of the federal Act;

(2) making, selling, disposing of, or keeping in possession, control, or custody, or concealing any punch, die, plate, stone, or other thing designed to print, imprint, or reproduce the trademark, trade name, or other identifying mark, imprint, or device of another or any likeness of any of the foregoing on any drug or container or labeling thereof so as to render such drug a counterfeit drug;

(3) the doing of any act that causes a drug to be a counterfeit drug, or the sale or dispensing, or the holding for sale or dispensing, of a counterfeit drug;

(m) the using by any person to the person's own advantage, or revealing, other than to the department , to a health authority, or to the courts when relevant in any judicial proceeding under this chapter, of any information acquired under the authority of this chapter concerning any method or process that as a trade secret is entitled to protection;

(n) the using, on the labeling of any drug or device or in any advertising relating to such drug or device, of any representation or suggestion that approval of an application with respect to such drug or device is in effect under Section 431.114 or Section 505, 515, or 520(g) of the federal Act, as the case may be, or that such drug or device complies with the provisions of such sections;

(o) the using, in labeling, advertising or other sales promotion of any reference to any report or analysis furnished in compliance with Sections 431.042-431.044 or Section 704 of the federal Act;

(p) in the case of a prescription drug distributed or offered for sale in this state, the failure of the manufacturer, packer, or distributor of the drug to maintain for transmittal, or to transmit, to any practitioner licensed by applicable law to administer such drug who makes written request for information as to such drug, true and correct copies of all printed matter that is required to be included in any package in which that drug is distributed or sold, or such other printed matter as is approved under the federal Act. Nothing in this subsection shall be construed to exempt any person from any labeling requirement imposed by or under other provisions of this chapter;

(q) (1) placing or causing to be placed on any drug or device or container of any drug or device, with intent to defraud, the trade name or other identifying mark, or imprint of another or any likeness of any of the foregoing;

(2) selling, dispensing, disposing of or causing to be sold, dispensed, or disposed of, or concealing or keeping in possession, control, or custody, with intent to sell, dispense, or dispose of, any drug, device, or any container of any drug or device, with knowledge that the trade name or other identifying mark or imprint of another or any likeness of any of the foregoing has been placed thereon in a manner prohibited by Subdivision (1); or

(3) making, selling, disposing of, causing to be made, sold, or disposed of, keeping in possession, control, or custody, or concealing with intent to defraud any punch, die, plate, stone, or other thing designed to print, imprint, or reproduce the trademark, trade name, or other identifying mark, imprint, or device of another or any likeness of any of the foregoing on any drug or container or labeling of any drug or container so as to render such drug a counterfeit drug;

(r) dispensing or causing to be dispensed a different drug in place of the drug ordered or prescribed without the express permission in each case of the person ordering or prescribing;

(s) the failure to register in accordance with Section 510 of the federal Act, the failure to provide any information required by Section 510(j) or (k) of the federal Act, or the failure to provide a notice required by Section 510(j)(2) of the federal Act;

(t) (1) the failure or refusal to:

(A) comply with any requirement prescribed under Section 518 or 520(g) of the federal Act; or

(B) furnish any notification or other material or information required by or under Section 519 or 520(g) of the federal Act;

(2) with respect to any device, the submission of any report that is required by or under this chapter that is false or misleading in any material respect;

(u) the movement of a device in violation of an order under Section 304(g) of the federal Act or the removal or alteration of any mark or label required by the order to identify the device as detained;

(v) the failure to provide the notice required by Section 412(b) or 412(c), the failure to make the reports required by Section 412(d)(1)(B), or the failure to meet the requirements prescribed under Section 412(d)(2) of the federal Act;

(w) except as provided under Subchapter M of this chapter and Section 562.1085, Occupations Code, the acceptance by a person of an unused prescription or drug, in whole or in part, for the purpose of resale, after the prescription or drug has been originally dispensed, or sold;

(x) engaging in the wholesale distribution of drugs or operating as a distributor or manufacturer of devices in this state without obtaining a license issued by the department under Subchapter I, L, or N, as applicable;

(y) engaging in the manufacture of food in this state or operating as a warehouse operator in this state without having a license as required by Section 431.222 or operating as a food wholesaler in this state without having a license under Section 431.222 or being registered under Section 431.2211, as appropriate;

(z) unless approved by the United States Food and Drug Administration pursuant to the federal Act, the sale, delivery, holding, or offering for sale of a self-testing kit designed to indicate whether a person has a human immunodeficiency virus infection, acquired immune deficiency syndrome, or a related disorder or condition;

(aa) making a false statement or false representation in an application for a license or in a

Health and Safety Code

statement, report, or other instrument to be filed with or requested by the department under this chapter;

(bb) failing to comply with a requirement or request to provide information or failing to submit an application, statement, report, or other instrument required by the department;

(cc) performing, causing the performance of, or aiding and abetting the performance of an act described by Subsection (x);

(dd) purchasing or otherwise receiving a prescription drug from a pharmacy in violation of Section 431.411(a);

(ee) selling, distributing, or transferring a prescription drug to a person who is not authorized under state or federal law to receive the prescription drug in violation of Section 431.411(b);

(ff) failing to deliver prescription drugs to specified premises as required by Section 431.411(c);

(gg) failing to maintain or provide pedigrees as required by Section 431.412 or 431.413;

(hh) failing to obtain, pass, or authenticate a pedigree as required by Section 431.412 or 431.413;

(ii) the introduction or delivery for introduction into commerce of a drug or prescription device at a flea market;

(jj) the receipt of a prescription drug that is adulterated, misbranded, stolen, obtained by fraud or deceit, counterfeit, or suspected of being counterfeit, and the delivery or proffered delivery of such a drug for payment or otherwise; or

(kk) the alteration, mutilation, destruction, obliteration, or removal of all or any part of the labeling of a prescription drug or the commission of any other act with respect to a prescription drug that results in the prescription drug being misbranded.

Sec. 431.0211. Exception.

Any provision of Section 431.021 that relates to a prescription drug does not apply to a prescription drug manufacturer, or an agent of a prescription drug manufacturer, who is obtaining or attempting to obtain a prescription drug for the sole purpose of testing the prescription drug for authenticity.

Sec. 431.022. Offense: Transfer of Product Containing Ephedrine.

(a) A person commits an offense if the person knowingly sells, transfers, or otherwise furnishes a product containing ephedrine to a person 17 years of age or younger, unless:

(1) the actor is:

(A) a practitioner or other health care provider licensed by this state who has obtained, as required by law, consent to the treatment of the person to whom the product is furnished; or

(B) the parent, guardian, or managing conservator of the person to whom the product is furnished;

(2) the person to whom the product is furnished has had the disabilities of minority removed for general purposes under Chapter 31, Family Code; or

(3) the product is a drug.

(b) An offense under this section is a Class C misdemeanor unless it is shown on the trial of the offense that the defendant has been previously convicted of an offense under this section, in which event the offense is a Class B misdemeanor.

(c) A product containing ephedrine that is not described in Subsection (a)(3) must be labeled in accordance with department rules to indicate that sale to persons 17 years of age or younger is prohibited.

Sec. 431.023. Limited Exemption for Distressed Food, Drugs, Devices, or Cosmetics.

In relation to a food, drug, device, or cosmetic that is distressed merchandise for purposes of Chapter 432, Sections 431.021(a), (c), and (d) do not prohibit:

(1) the introduction or delivery for introduction into commerce of the merchandise for the purpose of reconditioning in accordance with Chapter 432 and not for sale to the ultimate consumer;

(2) the receipt in commerce of the merchandise for the purpose of reconditioning in accordance with Chapter 432 and not for sale to the ultimate consumer;

(3) the holding of merchandise for the purpose of reconditioning in accordance with Chapter 432 and not for resale to the ultimate consumer; or

(4) the reconditioning of the merchandise in accordance with Chapter 432.

SUBCHAPTER C ENFORCEMENT

Sec. 431.041. Definition.

In this subchapter, "detained or embargoed article" means a food, drug, device, cosmetic, or consumer commodity that has been detained or embargoed under Section 431.048.

Sec. 431.042. Inspection.

(a) To enforce this chapter, the department or a health authority may, on presenting appropriate credentials to the owner, operator, or agent in charge:

(1) enter at reasonable times an establishment, including a factory or warehouse, in which a food, drug, device, or cosmetic is manufactured, processed, packed, or held for introduction into commerce or held after the introduction;

(2) enter a vehicle being used to transport or hold the food, drug, device, or cosmetic in commerce; or

(3) inspect at reasonable times, within reasonable limits, and in a reasonable manner, the establishment or vehicle and all equipment, finished and unfinished materials, containers, and labeling of any item and obtain samples necessary for the enforcement of this chapter.

(b) The inspection of an establishment, including a factory, warehouse, or consulting laboratory, in which a prescription drug or restricted device is manufactured, processed, packed, or held for introduction into commerce extends to any place or thing, including a record, file, paper, process, control, or facility, in order to determine whether the drug or device:

(1) is adulterated or misbranded;

(2) may not be manufactured, introduced into commerce, sold, or offered for sale under this chapter; or

(3) is otherwise in violation of this chapter.

(c) An inspection under Subsection (b) may not extend to:

(1) financial data;

(2) sales data other than shipment data;

(3) pricing data;

(4) personnel data other than data relating to the qualifications of technical and professional personnel performing functions under this chapter;

(5) research data other than data:

(A) relating to new drugs, antibiotic drugs, and devices; and

(B) subject to reporting and inspection under regulations issued under Section 505(i) or (j), 519, or 520(g) of the federal Act; or

(6) data relating to other drugs or devices that, in the case of a new drug, would be subject to reporting or inspection under regulations issued under Section 505(j) of the federal Act.

(d) An inspection under Subsection (b) shall be started and completed with reasonable promptness.

(e) This section does not apply to:

(1) a pharmacy that:

(A) complies with Subtitle J, Title 3, Occupations Code;

(B) regularly engages in dispensing prescription drugs or devices on prescriptions of practitioners licensed to administer the drugs or devices to their patients in the course of their professional practice; and

(C) does not, through a subsidiary or otherwise, manufacture, prepare, propagate, compound, or process a drug or device for sale other than in the regular course of its business of dispensing or selling drugs or devices at retail;

(2) a practitioner licensed to prescribe or administer a drug who manufactures, prepares, propagates, compounds, or processes the drug solely for use in the course of the practitioner's professional practice;

(3) a practitioner licensed to prescribe or use a device who manufactures or processes the device solely for use in the course of the practitioner's professional practice; or

(4) a person who manufactures, prepares, propagates, compounds, or processes a drug or manufactures or processes a device solely for use in research, teaching, or chemical analysis and not for sale.

(f) The executive commissioner may exempt a class of persons from inspection under this section if the executive commissioner finds that inspection as applied to the class is not necessary for the protection of the public health.

(g) The department or a health authority who makes an inspection under this section to enforce the provisions of this chapter applicable to infant formula shall be permitted, at all reasonable times, to have access to and to copy and verify records:

(1) in order to determine whether the infant formula manufactured or held in the inspected facility meets the requirements of this chapter; or

(2) that are required by this chapter.

(h) If the department or a health authority while inspecting an establishment, including a factory or warehouse, obtains a sample, the department or health authority before leaving the establishment shall give to the owner, operator, or the owner's or operator's agent a receipt describing the sample.

Sec. 431.043. Access to Records.

A person who is required to maintain records under this chapter or Section 519 or 520(g) of the federal Act or a person who is in charge or custody of those records shall, at the request of the department or a health authority, permit the department or health authority at all reasonable times access to and to copy and verify the records, including records that verify that the hemp in a consumable hemp product was produced in accordance with Chapter 122, Agriculture Code, or 7 U.S.C. Chapter 38, Subchapter VII.

Health and Safety Code

Sec. 431.044. Access to Records Showing Movement in Commerce.

(a) To enforce this chapter, a carrier engaged in commerce or other person receiving a food, drug, device, or cosmetic in commerce or holding a food, drug, device, or cosmetic received in commerce shall, at the request of the department or a health authority, permit the department or health authority at all reasonable times to have access to and to copy all records showing:

(1) the movement in commerce of the food, drug, device, or cosmetic;

(2) the holding of the food, drug, device, or cosmetic after movement in commerce; and

(3) the quantity, shipper, and consignee of the food, drug, device, or cosmetic.

(b) The carrier or other person may not refuse access to and copying of the requested record if the request is accompanied by a written statement that specifies the nature or kind of food, drug, device, or cosmetic to which the request relates.

(c) Evidence obtained under this section or evidence that is directly or indirectly derived from the evidence obtained under this section may not be used in a criminal prosecution of the person from whom the evidence is obtained.

(d) A carrier is not subject to other provisions of this chapter because of the carrier's receipt, carriage, holding, or delivery of a food, drug, device, or cosmetic in the usual course of business as a carrier.

Sec. 431.045. Emergency Order.

(a) The commissioner or a person designated by the commissioner may issue an emergency order, either mandatory or prohibitory in nature, in relation to the manufacture or distribution of a food, drug, device, or cosmetic in the department's jurisdiction if the commissioner or the person designated by the commissioner determines that:

(1) the manufacture or distribution of the food, drug, device, or cosmetic creates or poses an immediate and serious threat to human life or health; and

(2) other procedures available to the department to remedy or prevent the occurrence of the situation will result in unreasonable delay.

(b) The commissioner or a person designated by the commissioner may issue the emergency order without notice and hearing if the commissioner or a person designated by the commissioner determines this is practicable under the circumstances.

(c) If an emergency order is issued without a hearing, the department shall propose a time and place for a hearing and refer the matter to the State Office of Administrative Hearings. An administrative law judge of that office shall set the time and place for the hearing at which the emergency order is affirmed, modified, or set aside. The hearing shall be held under the contested case provisions of Chapter 2001, Government Code, and the department's formal hearing rules.

(d) [Repealed by Acts 2015, 84th Leg., ch. 1 (S.B. 219), § 3.1639(75), effective April 2, 2015.]

Sec. 431.046. Violation of Rules.

A violation of a rule adopted under this chapter is a violation of this chapter.

Sec. 431.047. Violation; Injunction.

(a) The department or a health authority may petition the district court for a temporary restraining order to restrain a continuing violation of Subchapter B or a threat of a continuing violation of Subchapter B if the department or health authority finds that:

(1) a person has violated, is violating, or is threatening to violate Subchapter B; and

(2) the violation or threatened violation creates an immediate threat to the health and safety of the public.

(b) A district court, on petition of the department or a health authority, and on a finding by the court that a person is violating or threatening to violate Subchapter B shall grant any injunctive relief warranted by the facts.

(c) Venue for a suit brought under this section is in the county in which the violation or threat of violation is alleged to have occurred or in Travis County.

(d) The department and the attorney general may each recover reasonable expenses incurred in obtaining injunctive relief under this section, including investigative costs, court costs, reasonable attorney fees, witness fees, and deposition expenses. The expenses recovered by the department may be used by the department for the administration and enforcement of this chapter. The expenses recovered by the attorney general may be used by the attorney general.

Sec. 431.048. Detained or Embargoed Article.

(a) The department shall affix to an article that is a food, drug, device, cosmetic, or consumer commodity a tag or other appropriate marking that gives notice that the article is, or is suspected of being, adulterated or misbranded and that the article has been detained or embargoed if the department finds or has probable cause to believe that the article:

(1) is adulterated;

(2) is misbranded so that the article is dangerous or fraudulent under this chapter; or

(3) violates Section 431.084, 431.114, or 431.115.

(b) The tag or marking on a detained or embargoed article must warn all persons not to use the article, remove the article from the premises, or dispose of the article by sale or otherwise until permission for use, removal, or disposal is given by the department or a court.

(c) A person may not use a detained or embargoed article, remove a detained or embargoed article from the premises, or dispose of a detained or embargoed article by sale or otherwise without permission of the department or a court. The department may permit perishable goods to be moved to a place suitable for proper storage.

(d) The department shall remove the tag or other marking from an embargoed or detained article if the department finds that the article is not adulterated or misbranded.

(e) The department may not detain or embargo an article, including an article that is distressed merchandise, that is in the possession of a person licensed under Chapter 432 and that is being held for the purpose of reconditioning in accordance with Chapter 432, unless the department finds or has probable cause to believe that the article cannot be adequately reconditioned in accordance with that chapter and applicable rules.

Sec. 431.049. Removal Order for Detained or Embargoed Article.

(a) If the claimant of the detained or embargoed articles or the claimant's agent fails or refuses to transfer the articles to a secure place after the tag or other appropriate marking has been affixed as provided by Section 431.048, the department may order the transfer of the articles to one or more secure storage areas to prevent their unauthorized use, removal, or disposal.

(b) The department may provide for the transfer of the article if the claimant of the article or the claimant's agent does not carry out the transfer order in a timely manner. The costs of the transfer shall be assessed against the claimant of the article or the claimant's agent.

(c) The claimant of the article or the claimant's agent shall pay the costs of the transfer.

(d) The department may request the attorney general to bring an action in the district court in Travis County to recover the costs of the transfer. In a judgment in favor of the state, the court may award costs, attorney fees, court costs, and interest from the time the expense was incurred through the date the department is reimbursed.

Sec. 431.0495. Recall Orders.

(a) In conjunction with the issuance of an emergency order under Section 431.045 or the detention or embargo of an article under Section 431.048, the commissioner may order a food, drug, device, cosmetic, or consumer commodity to be recalled from commerce.

(b) The commissioner's recall order may require the articles to be removed to one or more secure areas approved by the department.

(c) The recall order must be in writing and signed by the commissioner.

(d) The recall order may be issued before or in conjunction with the affixing of the tag or other appropriate marking as provided by Section 431.048(a) or in conjunction with the commissioner's issuance of an emergency order under Section 431.045.

(e) The recall order is effective until the order:

(1) expires on its own terms;

(2) is withdrawn by the commissioner;

(3) is reversed by a court in an order denying condemnation under Section 431.050; or

(4) is set aside at the hearing provided to affirm, modify, or set aside an emergency order under Section 431.045.

(f) The claimant of the articles or the claimant's agent shall pay the costs of the removal and storage of the articles removed.

(g) If the claimant or the claimant's agent fails or refuses to carry out the recall order in a timely manner, the commissioner may provide for the recall of the articles. The costs of the recall shall be assessed against the claimant of the articles or the claimant's agent.

(h) The commissioner may request the attorney general to bring an action in the district court of Travis County to recover the costs of the recall. In a judgment in favor of the state, the court may award costs, attorney fees, court costs, and interest from the time the expense was incurred through the date the department is reimbursed.

Sec. 431.050. Condemnation.

An action for the condemnation of an article may be brought before a court in whose jurisdiction the article is located, detained, or embargoed if the article is adulterated, misbranded, or in violation of Section 431.084, 431.114, or 431.115.

Health and Safety Code

Sec. 431.051. Destruction of Article.

(a) A court shall order the destruction of a sampled article or a detained or embargoed article if the court finds that the article is adulterated or misbranded.

(b) After entry of the court's order, an authorized agent shall supervise the destruction of the article.

(c) The claimant of the article shall pay the cost of the destruction of the article.

(d) The court shall tax against the claimant of the article or the claimant's agent all court costs and fees, and storage and other proper expenses.

Sec. 431.052. Correction by Proper Labeling or Processing.

(a) A court may order the delivery of a sampled article or a detained or embargoed article that is adulterated or misbranded to the claimant of the article for labeling or processing under the supervision of the department if:

(1) the decree has been entered in the suit;

(2) the costs, fees, and expenses of the suit have been paid;

(3) the adulteration or misbranding can be corrected by proper labeling or processing; and

(4) a good and sufficient bond, conditioned on the correction of the adulteration or misbranding by proper labeling or processing, has been executed.

(b) The claimant shall pay the costs of the supervision.

(c) The court shall order that the article be returned to the claimant and the bond discharged on the representation to the court by the department that the article no longer violates this chapter and that the expenses of the supervision are paid.

Sec. 431.053. Condemnation of Perishable Articles.

(a) The department shall immediately condemn or render by any means unsalable as human food an article that is a nuisance under Subsection (b) and that the department finds in any room, building, or other structure or in a vehicle.

(b) Any meat, seafood, poultry, vegetable, fruit, or other perishable article is a nuisance if it:

(1) is unsound;

(2) contains a filthy, decomposed, or putrid substance; or

(3) may be poisonous or deleterious to health or otherwise unsafe.

Sec. 431.054. Administrative Penalty.

(a) The department may assess an administrative penalty against a person who violates Subchapter B or an order adopted or registration issued under this chapter.

(b) In determining the amount of the penalty, the department shall consider:

(1) the person's previous violations;

(2) the seriousness of the violation;

(3) any hazard to the health and safety of the public;

(4) the person's demonstrated good faith; and

(5) such other matters as justice may require.

(c) The penalty may not exceed $25,000 a day for each violation.

(d) Each day a violation continues may be considered a separate violation.

Sec. 431.055. Administrative Penalty Assessment Procedure.

(a) An administrative penalty may be assessed only after a person charged with a violation is given an opportunity for a hearing.

(b) If a hearing is held, an administrative law judge of the State Office of Administrative Hearings shall make findings of fact and shall issue to the department a written proposal for decision regarding the occurrence of the violation and the amount of the penalty that may be warranted.

(c) If the person charged with the violation does not request a hearing, the department may assess a penalty after determining that a violation has occurred and the amount of the penalty that may be warranted.

(d) After making a determination under this section that a penalty is to be assessed against a person, the department shall issue an order requiring that the person pay the penalty.

(e) [Repealed by Acts 2015, 84th Leg., ch. 1 (S.B. 219), § 3.1639(75), effective April 2, 2015.]

Sec. 431.056. Payment of Administrative Penalty.

(a) Not later than the 30th day after the date an order finding that a violation has occurred is issued, the department shall inform the person against whom the order is issued of the amount of the penalty for the violation.

(b) Not later than the 30th day after the date on which a decision or order charging a person with a penalty is final, the person shall:

(1) pay the penalty in full; or

(2) file a petition for judicial review of the department's order contesting the amount of the penalty, the fact of the violation, or both.

(b-1) If the person seeks judicial review within the period prescribed by Subsection (b), the person may:

(1) stay enforcement of the penalty by:

(A) paying the amount of the penalty to the court for placement in an escrow account; or

(B) posting with the court a supersedeas bond for the amount of the penalty; or

(2) request that the department stay enforcement of the penalty by:

(A) filing with the court a sworn affidavit of the person stating that the person is financially unable to pay the penalty and is financially unable to give the supersedeas bond; and

(B) sending a copy of the affidavit to the department.

(b-2) If the department receives a copy of an affidavit under Subsection (b-1)(2), the department may file with the court, within five days after the date the copy is received, a contest to the affidavit. The court shall hold a hearing on the facts alleged in the affidavit as soon as practicable and shall stay the enforcement of the penalty on finding that the alleged facts are true. The person who files an affidavit has the burden of proving that the person is financially unable to pay the penalty or to give a supersedeas bond.

(c) A bond posted under this section must be in a form approved by the court and be effective until all judicial review of the order or decision is final.

(d) A person who does not send money to, post the bond with, or file the affidavit with the court within the period prescribed by Subsection (b) waives all rights to contest the violation or the amount of the penalty.

Sec. 431.057. Refund of Administrative Penalty.

On the date the court's judgment that an administrative penalty against a person should be reduced or not assessed becomes final, the court shall order that:

(1) the appropriate amount of any penalty payment plus accrued interest be remitted to the person not later than the 30th day after that date; or

(2) the bond be released, if the person has posted a bond.

Sec. 431.058. Recovery of Administrative Penalty by Attorney General.

The attorney general at the request of the department may bring a civil action to recover an administrative penalty under this subchapter.

Sec. 431.0585. Civil Penalty.

(a) At the request of the department , the attorney general or a district, county, or city attorney shall institute an action in district court to collect a civil penalty from a person who has violated Section 431.021.

(b) The civil penalty may not exceed $25,000 a day for each violation. Each day of violation constitutes a separate violation for purposes of the penalty assessment.

(c) The court shall consider the following in determining the amount of the penalty:

(1) the person's history of any previous violations of Section 431.021;

(2) the seriousness of the violation;

(3) any hazard posed to the public health and safety by the violation; and

(4) demonstrations of good faith by the person charged.

(d) Venue for a suit brought under this section is in the city or county in which the violation occurred or in Travis County.

(e) A civil penalty recovered in a suit instituted by a local government under this section shall be paid to that local government.

Sec. 431.059. Criminal Penalty; Defenses.

(a) A person commits an offense if the person violates any of the provisions of Section 431.021 relating to unlawful or prohibited acts. A first offense under this subsection is a Class A misdemeanor unless it is shown on the trial of an offense under this subsection that the defendant was previously convicted of an offense under this subsection, in which event the offense is a state jail felony. In a criminal proceeding under this section, it is not necessary to prove intent, knowledge, recklessness, or criminal negligence of the defendant beyond the degree of culpability, if any, stated in Section 431.021 to establish criminal responsibility for the violation.

(a-1), (a-2) [Repealed by Acts 2007, 80th Leg., ch. 980 (S.B. 943), § 14, effective September 1, 2007.]

(b) A person is not subject to the penalties of Subsection (a):

(1) for having received an article in commerce and having delivered or offered delivery of the article, if the delivery or offer was made in good faith, unless the person refuses to furnish, on request of the department or a health authority, the name and address of the person from whom the article was received and copies of any documents relating to the receipt of the article;

(2) for having violated Section 431.021(a) or (e) if the person establishes a guaranty or undertaking

Health and Safety Code

signed by, and containing the name and address of, the person residing in this state from whom the person received in good faith the article, to the effect that:

(A) in the case of an alleged violation of Section 431.021(a), the article is not adulterated or misbranded within the meaning of this chapter; and

(B) in the case of an alleged violation of Section 431.021(e), the article is not an article that may not, under the provisions of Section 404 or 405 of the federal Act or Section 431.084 or 431.114, be introduced into commerce;

(3) for having violated Section 431.021, if the violation exists because the article is adulterated by reason of containing a color additive not from a batch certified in accordance with regulations promulgated under the federal Act, if the person establishes a guaranty or undertaking signed by, and containing the name and address of, the manufacturer of the color additive, to the effect that the color additive was from a batch certified in accordance with the applicable regulations promulgated under the federal Act;

(4) for having violated Section 431.021(b), (c), or (k) by failure to comply with Section 431.112(i) with respect to an article received in commerce to which neither Section 503(a) nor Section 503(b)(1) of the federal Act applies if the delivery or offered delivery was made in good faith and the labeling at the time of the delivery or offer contained the same directions for use and warning statements as were contained in the labeling at the same time of the receipt of the article; or

(5) for having violated Section 431.021(l)(2) if the person acted in good faith and had no reason to believe that use of the punch, die, plate, stone, or other thing would result in a drug being a counterfeit drug, or for having violated Section 431.021(l)(3) if the person doing the act or causing it to be done acted in good faith and had no reason to believe that the drug was a counterfeit drug.

(c) A publisher, radio-broadcast licensee, or agency or medium for the dissemination of an advertisement, except the manufacturer, packer, distributor, or seller of the article to which a false advertisement relates, is not liable under this section for the dissemination of the false advertisement, unless the person has refused, on the request of the department, to furnish the department the name and post-office address of the manufacturer, packer, distributor, seller, or advertising agency, residing in this state who caused the person to disseminate the advertisement.

(d) A person is not subject to the penalties of Subsection (a) for a violation of Section 431.021 involving misbranded food if the violation exists solely because the food is misbranded under Section 431.082 because of its advertising, and a person is not subject to the penalties of Subsection (a) for such a violation unless the violation is committed with the intent to defraud or mislead.

(e) It is an affirmative defense to prosecution under Subsection (a) that the conduct charged is exempt, in accordance with Section 431.023, from the application of Section 431.021.

Sec. 431.060. Initiation of Proceedings.

(a) The attorney general, or a district, county, or municipal attorney to whom the department or a health authority reports a violation of this chapter, shall initiate and prosecute appropriate proceedings without delay.

(b) The department or attorney general may, as authorized by Section 307 of the federal Act, bring in the name of this state a suit for civil penalties or to restrain a violation of Section 401 or Section 403(b) through (i), (k), (q), or (r) of the federal Act if the food that is the subject of the proceedings is located in this state.

(c) The department or attorney general may not bring a proceeding under Subsection (b):

(1) before the 31st day after the date on which the state has given notice to the secretary of its intent to bring a suit;

(2) before the 91st day after the date on which the state has given notice to the secretary of its intent to bring a suit if the secretary has, not later than the 30th day after receiving notice from the state, commenced an informal or formal enforcement action pertaining to the food that would be the subject of the suit brought by the state; or

(3) if the secretary is diligently prosecuting a suit in court pertaining to that food, has settled a suit pertaining to that food, or has settled the informal or formal enforcement action pertaining to that food.

Sec. 431.061. Minor Violation.

This chapter does not require the department or a health authority to report for prosecution or the institution of proceedings under this chapter a minor violation of this chapter if the department or health authority believes that the public interest is adequately served by a suitable written notice or warning.

SUBCHAPTER E DRUGS AND DEVICES

Sec. 431.111. Adulterated Drug or Device.

A drug or device shall be deemed to be adulterated:

(a) (1) if it consists in whole or in part of any filthy, putrid, or decomposed substance; or

(2) (A) if it has been prepared, packed, or held under insanitary conditions whereby it may have been contaminated with filth, or whereby it may have been rendered injurious to health; or

(B) if it is a drug and the methods used in, or the facilities or controls used for, its manufacture, processing, packing, or holding do not conform to or are not operated or administered in conformity with current good manufacturing practice to assure that such drug meets the requirements of this chapter as to safety and has the identity and strength, and meets the quality and purity characteristics, which it purports or is represented to possess; or

(3) if its container is composed, in whole or in part, of any poisonous or deleterious substance which may render the contents injurious to health; or

(4) if it:

(A) bears or contains, for purposes of coloring only, a color additive that is unsafe under Section 431.161(a); or

(B) is a color additive, the intended use of which in or on drugs or devices is for purposes of coloring only, and is unsafe under Section 431.161(a); or

(5) if it is a new animal drug that is unsafe under Section 512 of the federal Act;

(b) if it purports to be or is represented as a drug, the name of which is recognized in an official compendium, and its strength differs from, or its quality or purity falls below, the standards set forth in such compendium. Such determination as to strength, quality or purity shall be made in accordance with the tests or methods of assay set forth in such compendium, or in the absence of or inadequacy of such tests or methods of assay, those prescribed under the authority of the federal Act. No drug defined in an official compendium shall be deemed to be adulterated under this subsection because it differs from the standards of strength, quality, or purity therefor set forth in such compendium, if its difference in strength, quality, or purity from such standards is plainly stated on its label. Whenever a drug is recognized in The United States Pharmacopeia and The National Formulary (USP-NF), it shall be subject to the requirements of the USP-NF;

(c) if it is not subject to Subsection (b) and its strength differs from, or its purity or quality falls below, that which it purports or is represented to possess;

(d) if it is a drug and any substance has been:

(1) mixed or packed therewith so as to reduce its quality or strength; or

(2) substituted wholly or in part therefor;

(e) if it is, or purports to be or is represented as, a device that is subject to a performance standard established under Section 514 of the federal Act, unless the device is in all respects in conformity with the standard;

(f) (1) if it is a class III device:

(A) (i) that is required by a regulation adopted under Section 515(b) of the federal Act to have an approval under that section of an application for premarket approval and that is not exempt from Section 515 as provided by Section 520(g) of the federal Act; and

(ii) (I) for which an application for premarket approval or a notice of completion of a product development protocol was not filed with the United States Food and Drug Administration by the 90th day after the date of adoption of the regulation; or

(II) for which that application was filed and approval was denied or withdrawn, for which that notice was filed and was declared incomplete, or for which approval of the device under the protocol was withdrawn;

(B) that was classified under Section 513(f) of the federal Act into class III, which under Section 515(a) of the federal Act is required to have in effect an approved application for premarket approval, that is not exempt from Section 515 as provided by Section 520(g) of the federal Act, and that does not have the application in effect; or

(C) that was classified under Section 520(l) of the federal Act into class III, which under that section is required to have in effect an approved application under Section 515 of the federal Act, and that does not have the application in effect, except that:

(2) (A) in the case of a device classified under Section 513(f) of the federal Act into class III and intended solely for investigational use, Subdivision (1)(B) does not apply to the device during the period ending on the 90th day after the date of adoption of the regulations prescribing the procedures and conditions required by Section 520(g)(2) of the federal Act; and

(B) in the case of a device subject to a regulation adopted under Section 515(b) of the federal Act, Subdivision (1) does not apply to the device during the period ending on whichever of the following dates occurs later:

(i) the last day of the 30-day calendar month beginning after the month in which the classification of the device into class III became effective under Section 513 of the federal Act; or

Health and Safety Code

(ii) the 90th day after the date of adoption of the regulation;

(g) if it is a banned device;

(h) if it is a device and the methods used in, or the facilities or controls used for its manufacture, packing, storage, or installations are not in conformity with applicable requirements under Section 520(f)(1) of the federal Act or an applicable condition as prescribed by an order under Section 520(f)(2) of the federal Act; or

(i) if it is a device for which an exemption has been granted under Section 520(g) of the federal Act for investigational use and the person who was granted the exemption or any investigator who uses the device under the exemption fails to comply with a requirement prescribed by or under that section.

Sec. 431.112. Misbranded Drug or Device.

A drug or device shall be deemed to be misbranded:

(a) (1) if its labeling is false or misleading in any particular; or

(2) if its labeling or packaging fails to conform with the requirements of Section 431.181.

(b) if in a package form unless it bears a label containing (1) the name and place of business of the manufacturer, packer, or distributor; and (2) an accurate statement of the quantity of the contents in terms of weight, measure, or numerical count; provided, that under Subdivision (2) reasonable variations shall be permitted, and exemptions as to small packages shall be allowed in accordance with regulations prescribed by the secretary under the federal Act;

(c) if any word, statement, or other information required by or under authority of this chapter to appear on the label or labeling is not prominently placed thereon with such conspicuousness (as compared with other words, statements, designs, or devices, in the labeling) and in such terms as to render it likely to be read and understood by the ordinary individual under customary conditions of purchase and use;

(d) (1) if it is a drug, unless:

(A) its label bears, to the exclusion of any other nonproprietary name (except the applicable systematic chemical name or the chemical formula):

(i) the established name (as defined in Subdivision (3)) of the drug, if any; and

(ii) in case it is fabricated from two or more ingredients, the established name and quantity of each active ingredient, including the quantity, kind, and proportion of any alcohol, and also including, whether active or not, the established name and quantity or proportion of any bromides, ether, chloroform, acetanilid, acetphenetidin, amidopyrine, antipyrine, atropine, hyoscine, hyoscyamine, arsenic, digitalis, digitalis glucosides, mercury, ouabain, strophanthin, strychnine, thyroid, or any derivative or preparation of any such substances, contained therein; provided, that the requirement for stating the quantity of the active ingredients, other than the quantity of those specifically named in this subparagraph shall apply only to prescription drugs; and

(B) for any prescription drug the established name of the drug or ingredient, as the case may be, on the label (and on any labeling on which a name for such drug or ingredient is used) is printed prominently and in type at least half as large as that used thereon for any proprietary name or designation for such drug or ingredient; and provided, that to the extent that compliance with the requirements of Paragraph (A)(ii) or this paragraph is impracticable, exemptions shall be allowed under regulations promulgated by the secretary under the federal Act;

(2) if it is a device and it has an established name, unless its label bears, to the exclusion of any other nonproprietary name, its established name (as defined in Subdivision (4)) prominently printed in type at least half as large as that used thereon for any proprietary name or designation for such device, except that to the extent compliance with this subdivision is impracticable, exemptions shall be allowed under regulations promulgated by the secretary under the federal Act;

(3) as used in Subdivision (1), the term "established name," with respect to a drug or ingredient thereof, means:

(A) the applicable official name designated pursuant to Section 508 of the federal Act; or

(B) if there is no such name and such drug, or such ingredient, is an article recognized in an official compendium, then the official title thereof in such compendium; or

(C) if neither Paragraph (A) nor Paragraph (B) applies, then the common or usual name, if any, of such drug or of such ingredient; provided further, that where Paragraph (B) applies to an article recognized in the United States Pharmacopoeia National Formulary, the official title used in the United States Pharmacopoeia National Formulary shall apply;

(4) as used in Subdivision (2), the term "established name" with respect to a device means:

(A) the applicable official name of the device designated pursuant to Section 508 of the federal Act;

(B) if there is no such name and such device is an article recognized in an official compendium, then the official title thereof in such compendium; or

Health and Safety Code

(C) if neither Paragraph (A) nor Paragraph (B) applies, then any common or usual name of such device;

(e) unless its labeling bears:

(1) adequate directions for use; and

(2) such adequate warnings against use in those pathological conditions or by children where its use may be dangerous to health, or against unsafe dosage or methods or durations of administration or application, in such manner and form, as are necessary for the protection of users unless the drug or device has been exempted from those requirements by the regulations adopted by the secretary;

(f) if it purports to be a drug the name of which is recognized in an official compendium, unless it is packaged and labeled as prescribed therein unless the method of packing has been modified with the consent of the secretary. Whenever a drug is recognized in the United States Pharmacopoeia National Formulary, it shall be subject to the requirements of the United States Pharmacopoeia National Formulary with respect to packaging and labeling. If there is an inconsistency between the requirements of this subsection and those of Subsection (d) as to the name by which the drug or its ingredients shall be designated, the requirements of Subsection (d) prevail;

(g) if it has been found by the secretary to be a drug liable to deterioration, unless it is packaged in such form and manner, and its label bears a statement of such precautions, as the secretary shall by regulations require as necessary for the protection of public health;

(h) if:

(1) it is a drug and its container is so made, formed, or filled as to be misleading; or

(2) it is an imitation of another drug; or

(3) it is offered for sale under the name of another drug;

(i) if it is dangerous to health when used in the dosage, or manner or with the frequency or duration prescribed, recommended, or suggested in the labeling thereof;

(j) if it is a color additive, the intended use of which is for the purpose of coloring only, unless its packaging and labeling are in conformity with such packaging and labeling requirements applicable to such color additive, as may be contained in rules issued under Section 431.161(b);

(k) in the case of any prescription drug distributed or offered for sale in this state, unless the manufacturer, packer, or distributor thereof includes in all advertisements and other descriptive printed matter issued or caused to be issued by the manufacturer, packer, or distributor with respect to that drug a true statement of:

(1) the established name as defined in Subsection (d), printed prominently and in type at least half as large as that used for any trade or brand name;

(2) the formula showing quantitatively each ingredient of the drug to the extent required for labels under Subsection (d); and

(3) other information in brief summary relating to side effects, contraindications, and effectiveness as required in regulations issued under Section 701(e) of the federal Act;

(*l*) if it was manufactured, prepared, propagated, compounded, or processed in an establishment in this state not registered under Section 510 of the federal Act, if it was not included in a list required by Section 510(j) of the federal Act, if a notice or other information respecting it was not provided as required by that section or Section 510(k) of the federal Act, or if it does not bear symbols from the uniform system for identification of devices prescribed under Section 510(e) of the federal Act as required by regulation;

(m) if it is a drug and its packaging or labeling is in violation of an applicable regulation issued under Section 3 or 4 of the federal Poison Prevention Packaging Act of 1970 (15 U.S.C. 1472 or 1473);

(n) if a trademark, trade name, or other identifying mark, imprint or device of another, or any likeness of the foregoing has been placed thereon or on its container with intent to defraud;

(o) in the case of any restricted device distributed or offered for sale in this state, if:

(1) its advertising is false or misleading in any particular; or

(2) it is sold, distributed, or used in violation of regulations prescribed under Section 520(e) of the federal Act;

(p) in the case of any restricted device distributed or offered for sale in this state, unless the manufacturer, packer, or distributor thereof includes in all advertisements and other descriptive printed matter issued by the manufacturer, packer, or distributor with respect to that device:

(1) a true statement of the device's established name as defined in Section 502(e) of the federal Act, printed prominently and in type at least half as large as that used for any trade or brand name thereof; and

(2) a brief statement of the intended uses of the device and relevant warnings, precautions, side effects, and contraindications and in the case of specific devices made subject to regulations issued under the federal Act, a full description of the components of such device or the formula showing quantitatively each ingredient of such device to the extent required in regulations under the federal Act;

(q) if it is a device subject to a performance standard established under Section 514 of the federal Act, unless it bears such labeling as may be prescribed in such performance standard; or

(r) if it is a device and there was a failure or refusal:

(1) to comply with any requirement prescribed under Section 518 of the federal Act respecting the device; or

(2) to furnish material required by or under Section 519 of the federal Act respecting the device.

Sec. 431.113. Exemption for Certain Drugs and Devices.

(a) The executive commissioner shall adopt rules exempting from any labeling or packaging requirement of this chapter drugs and devices that are, in accordance with the practice of the trade, to be processed, labeled, or repacked in substantial quantities at establishments other than those where originally processed or packaged on condition that such drugs and devices are not adulterated or misbranded under the provisions of this chapter on removal from such processing, labeling, or repacking establishment.

(b) Drugs and device labeling or packaging exemptions adopted under the federal Act shall apply to drugs and devices in this state except insofar as modified or rejected by department rules.

(c) (1) A drug intended for use by man that:

(A) because of its toxicity or other potentiality for harmful effect, or the method of its use, or the collateral measures necessary to its use, is not safe for use except under the supervision of a practitioner licensed by law to administer such drug; or

(B) is limited by an approved application under Section 505 of the federal Act to use under the professional supervision of a practitioner licensed by law to administer such drug shall be dispensed only:

(i) on a written prescription of a practitioner licensed by law to administer such drug; or

(ii) on an oral prescription of such practitioner that is reduced promptly to writing and filed by the pharmacist; or

(iii) by refilling any such written or oral prescription if such refilling is authorized by the prescriber either in the original prescription or by oral order that is reduced promptly to writing and filed by the pharmacist. The act of dispensing a drug contrary to the provisions of this paragraph shall be deemed to be an act that results in a drug being misbranded while held for sale.

(2) Any drug dispensed by filling or refilling a written or oral prescription of a practitioner licensed by law to administer such drug shall be exempt from the requirements of Section 431.112, except Sections 431.112(a)(1), (h)(2), and (h)(3), and the packaging requirements of Sections 431.112(f), (g), and (m), if the drug bears a label containing the name and address of the dispenser, the serial number and date of the prescription or of its filling, the name of the prescriber, and, if stated in the prescription, the name of the patient, and the directions for use and cautionary statements, if any, contained in such prescription. This exemption shall not apply to any drugs dispensed in the course of the conduct of business of dispensing drugs pursuant to diagnosis by mail, or to a drug dispensed in violation of Subdivision (1).

(3) A drug that is subject to Subdivision (1) shall be deemed to be misbranded if at any time prior to dispensing its label fails to bear at a minimum, the symbol "RX Only." A drug to which Subdivision (1) does not apply shall be deemed to be misbranded if at any time prior to dispensing its label bears the caution statement quoted in the preceding sentence.

Sec. 431.114. New Drugs.

(a) A person shall not sell, deliver, offer for sale, hold for sale or give away any new drug unless:

(1) an application with respect thereto has been approved and the approval has not been withdrawn under Section 505 of the federal Act; and

(2) a copy of the letter of approval or approvability issued by the United States Food and Drug Administration is on file with the department if the product is manufactured in this state.

(b) A person shall not use in or on human beings or animals a new drug or new animal drug limited to investigational use unless the person has filed with the United States Food and Drug Administration a completed and signed investigational new drug (IND) application in accordance with 21 C.F.R. 312.20-312.38 and the exemption has not been terminated. The drug shall be plainly labeled in compliance with Section 505(i) of the federal Act.

(c) This section shall not apply:

(1) to any drug that is not a new drug as defined in the federal Act;

(2) to any drug that is licensed under the Public Health Service Act (42 U.S.C. 201 et seq.); or

(3) to any drug approved by the department by the authority of any prior law.

Sec. 431.115. New Animal Drugs.

(a) A new animal drug shall, with respect to any particular use or intended use of the drug, be deemed unsafe for the purposes of this chapter unless:

(1) there is in effect an approval of an application filed pursuant to Section 512(b) of the federal Act with respect to the use or intended use of the drug; and

(2) the drug, its labeling, and the use conforms to the approved application.

(b) A new animal drug shall not be deemed unsafe for the purposes of this chapter if the article is for investigational use and conforms to the terms of an exemption in effect with respect thereto under Section 512(j) of the federal Act.

(c) This section does not apply to any drug:

(1) licensed under the virus-serum-toxin law of March 4, 1913 (21 U.S.C. 151-159);

(2) approved by the United States Department of Agriculture; or

(3) approved by the department by the authority of any prior law.

Sec. 431.116. Average Manufacturer Price.

(a) In this section, "average manufacturer price" has the meaning assigned by 42 U.S.C. Section 1396r-8(k), as amended.

(b) A person who manufactures a drug, including a person who manufactures a generic drug, that is sold in this state shall file with the department:

(1) the average manufacturer price for the drug; and

(2) the price that each wholesaler in this state pays the manufacturer to purchase the drug.

(c) The information required under Subsection (b) must be filed annually or more frequently as determined by the department.

(d) The department and the attorney general may investigate the manufacturer to determine the accuracy of the information provided under Subsection (b). The attorney general may take action to enforce this section.

(e) [Repealed by Acts 2005, 79th Leg., ch. 349 (S.B. 1188), § 29, effective September 1, 2007.]

(f) Notwithstanding any other state law, pricing information disclosed by manufacturers or labelers under this section may be provided by the department only to the Medicaid vendor drug program for its sole use. The Medicaid vendor drug program may use the information only as necessary to administer its drug programs, including Medicaid drug programs.

(g) Notwithstanding any other state law, pricing information disclosed by manufacturers or labelers under this section is confidential and, except as necessary to permit the attorney general to enforce state and federal laws, may not be disclosed by the Health and Human Services Commission or any other state agency in a form that discloses the identity of a specific manufacturer or labeler or the prices charged by a specific manufacturer or labeler for a specific drug.

(h) The attorney general shall treat information obtained under this section in the same manner as information obtained by the attorney general through a civil investigative demand under Section 36.054, Human Resources Code.

(i) Notwithstanding any other state law, the penalties for unauthorized disclosure of confidential information under Chapter 552, Government Code, apply to unauthorized disclosure of confidential information under this section.

Sec. 431.117. Priority for Health Care Providers in Distribution of Influenza Vaccine.

The executive commissioner shall study the wholesale distribution of influenza vaccine in this state to determine the feasibility of implementing a system that requires giving a priority in filling orders for influenza vaccine to physicians and other licensed health care providers authorized to administer influenza vaccine over retail establishments. The executive commissioner may implement such a system if it is determined to be feasible.

SUBCHAPTER H FAIR PACKAGING AND LABELING; FALSE ADVERTISING

Sec. 431.181. Fair Packaging and Labeling.

(a) All labels of consumer commodities, as defined by this chapter, shall conform with the requirements for the declaration of net quantity of contents of Section 4 of the Fair Packaging and Labeling Act (15 U.S.C. 1451 et seq.) and the regulations promulgated pursuant thereto; provided, that consumer commodities exempted from the requirements of Section 4 of the Fair Packaging and Labeling Act shall also be exempt from this subsection.

(b) The label of any package of a consumer commodity that bears a representation as to the number of servings of the commodity contained in the package shall bear a statement of the net quantity (in terms of weight, measure, or numerical count) of each serving.

(c) No person shall distribute or cause to be distributed in commerce any packaged consumer commodity if any qualifying words or phrases appear in conjunction with the separate statement of the net quantity of contents required by Subsection (a), but nothing in this subsection shall prohibit supplemental statements at other places on the package describing in nondeceptive terms the net quantity of contents; provided, that the supplemental statements of net quantity of contents shall not include any term qualifying a unit of weight, measure, or count that tends to exaggerate the amount of the commodity contained in the package.

(d) Whenever the executive commissioner determines that rules containing prohibitions or requirements other than those prescribed by Subsection (a) are necessary to prevent the deception of consumers or to facilitate value comparisons as to any consumer commodity, the executive commissioner shall adopt with respect to that commodity rules effective to:

(1) establish and define standards for the characterization of the size of a package enclosing any consumer commodity, which may be used to supplement the label statement of net quantity of contents of packages containing such commodity, but this subdivision shall not be construed as authorizing any limitation on the size, shape, weight, dimensions, or number of packages that may be used to enclose any commodity;

(2) regulate the placement on any package containing any commodity, or on any label affixed to the commodity, of any printed matter stating or representing by implication that such commodity is offered for retail sale at a price lower than the ordinary and customary retail sale price or that a retail sale price advantage is accorded to purchasers thereof by reason of the size of that package or the quantity of its contents;

(3) require that the label on each package of a consumer commodity (other than one which is a food within the meaning of Section 431.002) bear:

(A) the common or usual name of the consumer commodity, if any; and

(B) in case the consumer commodity consists of two or more ingredients, the common or usual name of each ingredient listed in order of decreasing predominance, but nothing in this paragraph shall be deemed to require that any trade secret be divulged; or

(4) prevent the nonfunctional slack-fill of packages containing consumer commodities. For the purpose of this subdivision, a package shall be deemed to be nonfunctionally slack-filled if it is filled of substantially less than its capacity for reasons other than:

(A) protection of the contents of the package; or

(B) the requirements of the machine used for enclosing the contents in the package.

Sec. 431.182. False Advertisement.

(a) An advertisement of a food, drug, device, or cosmetic shall be deemed to be false if it is false or misleading in any particular.

(b) The advertising of a food that incorporates a health claim not in conformance with or defined by Section 403(r) of the federal Act is deemed to be false or misleading for the purposes of this chapter.

Sec. 431.183. False Advertisement of Drug or Device.

(a) An advertisement of a drug or device is false if the advertisement represents that the drug or device affects:

(1) infectious and parasitic diseases;

(2) neoplasms;

(3) endocrine, nutritional, and metabolic diseases and immunity disorders;

(4) diseases of blood and blood-forming organs;

(5) mental disorders;

(6) diseases of the nervous system and sense organs;

(7) diseases of the circulatory system;

(8) diseases of the respiratory system;

(9) diseases of the digestive system;

(10) diseases of the genitourinary system;

(11) complications of pregnancy, childbirth, and the puerperium;

(12) diseases of the skin and subcutaneous tissue;

(13) diseases of the musculoskeletal system and connective tissue;

(14) congenital anomalies;

(15) certain conditions originating in the perinatal period;

(16) symptoms, signs, and ill-defined conditions; or

(17) injury and poisoning.

(b) Subsection (a) does not apply to an advertisement of a drug or device if the advertisement does not violate Section 431.182 and is disseminated:

(1) to the public for self-medication and is consistent with the labeling claims permitted by the federal Food and Drug Administration;

(2) only to members of the medical, dental, and veterinary professions and appears only in the scientific periodicals of those professions; or

(3) only for the purpose of public health education by a person not commercially interested, directly or indirectly, in the sale of the drug or device.

(c) The executive commissioner by rule shall authorize the advertisement of a drug having a curative or therapeutic effect for a disease listed under Subsection (a) if the executive commissioner determines that an advance in medical science has made any type of self-medication safe for the disease. The executive commissioner may impose conditions and restrictions on the advertisement of the drug necessary in the interest of public health.

(d) This section does not indicate that self-medication for a disease other than a disease listed under Subsection (a) is safe or effective.

SUBCHAPTER I
WHOLESALE DISTRIBUTORS OF NONPRESCRIPTION DRUGS

Sec. 431.201. Definitions.

In this subchapter:

(1) "Nonprescription drug" means any drug that is not a prescription drug as defined by Section 431.401.

(2) "Place of business" means each location at which a drug for wholesale distribution is located.

(3) "Wholesale distribution" means distribution to a person other than a consumer or patient, and includes distribution by a manufacturer, repackager, own label distributor, broker, jobber, warehouse, or wholesaler.

Sec. 431.2011. Applicability of Subchapter.

This subchapter applies only to the wholesale distribution of nonprescription drugs.

Sec. 431.202. License Required.

(a) A person may not engage in wholesale distribution of nonprescription drugs in this state unless the person holds a wholesale drug distribution license issued by the department under this subchapter or Subchapter N.

(b) An applicant for a license under this subchapter must submit an application to the department on the form prescribed by the department or electronically on the state electronic Internet portal.

(c) A license issued under this subchapter expires on the second anniversary of the date of issuance.

Sec. 431.2021. Exemption from Licensing. [Repealed]

Sec. 431.203. Contents of License Statement.

The license statement must contain:

(1) the name under which the business is conducted;

(2) the address of each place of business that is licensed;

(3) the name and residence address of:

(A) the proprietor, if the business is a proprietorship;

(B) all partners, if the business is a partnership; or

(C) all principals, if the business is an association;

(4) the date and place of incorporation, if the business is a corporation;

(5) the names and residence addresses of the individuals in an administrative capacity showing:

(A) the managing proprietor, if the business is a proprietorship;

(B) the managing partner, if the business is a partnership;

(C) the officers and directors, if the business is a corporation; or

(D) the persons in a managerial capacity, if the business is an association; and

(6) the residence address of an individual in charge of each place of business.

Sec. 431.2031. Effect of Operation in Other Jurisdictions; Reports.

(a) A person who engages in the wholesale distribution of drugs outside this state may engage in the wholesale distribution of drugs in this state if the person holds a license issued by the department.

(b) The department may accept reports from authorities in other jurisdictions to determine the extent of compliance with this chapter and the minimum standards adopted under this chapter.

(c) The department may issue a license to a person who engages in the wholesale distribution of drugs outside this state to engage in the wholesale distribution of drugs in this state, if after an examination of the reports of the person's compliance history and current compliance record, the department determines that the person is in compliance with this subchapter and department rules.

(d) The department shall consider each licensing statement filed by a person who wishes to engage in wholesale distribution of drugs in this state on an individual basis.

Sec. 431.204. Fees.

(a) The department shall collect fees for:

(1) a license that is filed or renewed;

Health and Safety Code

(2) a license that is amended, including a notification of a change in the location of a licensed place of business required under Section 431.206; and

(3) an inspection performed in enforcing this subchapter and rules adopted under this subchapter.

(b) The executive commissioner by rule shall set the fees in amounts that allow the department to recover the biennial expenditures of state funds by the department in:

(1) reviewing and acting on a license;

(2) amending and renewing a license;

(3) inspecting a licensed facility; and

(4) implementing and enforcing this subchapter, including a rule or order adopted or a license issued under this subchapter.

(c) Fees collected under this section shall be deposited to the credit of the food and drug registration fee account of the general revenue fund and appropriated to the department to carry out the administration and enforcement of this chapter.

Sec. 431.205. Expiration Date [Repealed].

Repealed by Acts 2005, 79th Leg., ch. 282 (H.B. 164), § 3(k), effective September 1, 2005.

Sec. 431.206. Change of Location of Place of Business.

(a) Not fewer than 30 days in advance of the change, the licensee shall notify the department in writing of the licensee's intent to change the location of a licensed place of business.

(b) The notice shall include the address of the new location, and the name and residence address of the individual in charge of the business at the new location.

(c) Not more than 10 days after the completion of the change of location, the licensee shall notify the department in writing to confirm the completion of the change of location and provide verification of the information previously provided or correct and confirm any information that has changed since providing the notice of intent.

(d) The notice and confirmation required by this section are deemed adequate if the licensee sends the notices by certified mail, return receipt requested, to the central office of the department or submits them electronically through the state electronic Internet portal.

Sec. 431.207. Refusal to License; Suspension or Revocation of License.

(a) The department may refuse an application for a license or may suspend or revoke a license if the applicant or licensee:

(1) has been convicted of a felony or misdemeanor that involves moral turpitude;

(2) is an association, partnership, or corporation and the managing officer has been convicted of a felony or misdemeanor that involves moral turpitude;

(3) has been convicted in a state or federal court of the illegal use, sale, or transportation of intoxicating liquors, narcotic drugs, barbiturates, amphetamines, desoxyephedrine, their compounds or derivatives, or any other dangerous or habit-forming drugs;

(4) is an association, partnership, or corporation and the managing officer has been convicted in a state or federal court of the illegal use, sale, or transportation of intoxicating liquors, narcotic drugs, barbiturates, amphetamines, desoxyephedrine, their compounds or derivatives, or any other dangerous or habit-forming drugs;

(5) has not complied with this chapter or the rules implementing this chapter;

(6) has violated Section 431.021(l)(3), relating to the counterfeiting of a drug or the sale or holding for sale of a counterfeit drug;

(7) has violated Chapter 481 or 483;

(8) has violated the rules of the public safety director of the Department of Public Safety, including being responsible for a significant discrepancy in the records that state law requires the applicant or licensee to maintain; or

(9) fails to complete a license application or submits an application that contains false, misleading, or incorrect information or contains information that cannot be verified by the department.

(b) The executive commissioner by rule shall establish minimum standards required for the issuance or renewal of a license under this subchapter.

(c) The refusal to license an applicant or the suspension or revocation of a license by the department and the appeal from that action are governed by the procedures for a contested case hearing under Chapter 2001, Government Code.

Sec. 431.208. Reporting of Purchase Price.

(a) On the department's request, a person who engages in the wholesale distribution of drugs in this state shall file with the department information showing the actual price at which the wholesale distributor sells a particular drug to a retail pharmacy.

(b) The executive commissioner shall adopt rules to implement this section.

(c) The department and the attorney general may investigate the distributor to determine the accuracy of the information provided under Subsection (a). The attorney general may take action to enforce this section.

(d) [Repealed by Acts 2005, 79th Leg., ch. 349 (S.B. 1188), § 29, effective September 1, 2007.]

SUBCHAPTER K GENERAL ADMINISTRATIVE PROVISIONS AND RULEMAKING AUTHORITY

Sec. 431.241. Rulemaking Authority.

(a) The executive commissioner may adopt rules for the efficient enforcement of this chapter.

(b) The executive commissioner may conform rules adopted under this chapter, if practicable, with regulations adopted under the federal Act.

(c) The enumeration of specific federal laws and regulations in Sections 431.244 and 431.245 does not limit the general authority granted to the executive commissioner in Subsection (b) to conform rules adopted under this chapter to those adopted under the federal Act.

(d) The executive commissioner may adopt the federal regulations issued by the secretary pursuant to the Prescription Drug Marketing Act of 1987 (21 U.S.C. Sections 331, 333, 353, and 381), as necessary or desirable so that the state wholesale drug distributor licensing program in Subchapter N may achieve compliance with that Act.

(e) The executive commissioner shall not establish a drug formulary that restricts by any prior or retroactive approval process a physician's ability to treat a patient with a prescription drug that has been approved and designated as safe and effective by the United States Food and Drug Administration, in compliance with federal law and subject to review by the executive commissioner.

(f) Nothing in this section shall effect a prior approval program in operation on the effective date of this section nor shall any portion of this chapter prohibit a prior approval process on any federally exempted products.

(g) The department may assess a fee for the issuance of a certificate of free sale and another certification issued under this chapter. The executive commissioner by rule shall set each fee in an amount sufficient to recover the cost to the department of issuing the particular certificate.

Sec. 431.242. Contested Case Hearings and Appeals.

A hearing under this chapter or an appeal from a final administrative decision shall be conducted under Chapter 2001, Government Code.

Sec. 431.243. Persons to Conduct Hearings. [Repealed]

Sec. 431.244. Federal Regulations Adopted As State Rules.

(a) A regulation adopted by the secretary under the federal Act concerning pesticide chemicals, food additives, color additives, special dietary use, processed low acid food, acidified food, infant formula, bottled water, or vended bottled water is a rule for the purposes of this chapter, unless the executive commissioner modifies or rejects the rule.

(b) A regulation adopted under the Fair Packaging and Labeling Act (15 U.S.C. 1451 et seq.) is a rule for the purposes of this chapter, unless the executive commissioner modifies or rejects the rule. The executive commissioner may not adopt a rule that conflicts with the labeling requirements for the net quantity of contents required under Section 4 of the Fair Packaging and Labeling Act (15 U.S.C. 1453) and the regulations adopted under that Act.

(c) A regulation adopted by the secretary under Sections 403(b) through (i) of the federal Act is a rule for the purposes of this chapter unless the executive commissioner modifies or rejects the rule. The executive commissioner may not adopt a rule that conflicts with the limitations provided by Sections 403(q) and (r) of the federal Act.

(d) A federal regulation that this section provides as a rule for the purposes of this chapter is effective:

(1) on the date that the regulation becomes effective as a federal regulation; and

(2) whether or not the executive commissioner or department has fulfilled the rulemaking provisions of Chapter 2001, Government Code.

(e) If the executive commissioner modifies or rejects a federal regulation, the executive commissioner shall comply with the rulemaking provisions of Chapter 2001, Government Code.

(f) For any federal regulation adopted as a state rule under this chapter, including a regulation considered to be a rule for purposes of this chapter under Subsection (a), (b), or (c), the department shall provide on its Internet website:

(1) a link to the text of the federal regulation;

(2) a clear explanation of the substance of and purpose for the regulation; and

(3) information on providing comments in response to any proposed or pending federal regulation, including an address to which and the manner in which comments may be submitted.

Sec. 431.245. Definition or Standard of Identity, Quality, or Fill of Container.

(a) A definition or standard of identity, quality, or fill of container of the federal Act is a definition or standard of identity, quality, or fill of container in this chapter, except as modified by department rules.

(b) The executive commissioner by rule may establish definitions and standards of identity, quality, and fill of container for a food if:

(1) a federal regulation does not apply to the food; and

(2) the executive commissioner determines that adopting the rules will promote honest and fair dealing in the interest of consumers.

(c) A temporary permit granted for interstate shipment of an experimental pack of food that varies from the requirements of federal definitions and standards of identity is automatically effective in this state under the conditions of the permit.

(d) The department may issue additional permits if the department determines that:

(1) it is necessary for the completion of an otherwise adequate investigation; and

(2) the interests of consumers are safeguarded.

(e) A permit issued under Subsection (d) is subject to the terms and conditions of department rules.

Sec. 431.246. Removal of Adulterated Item From Stores.

The executive commissioner shall adopt rules that provide a system for removing adulterated items from the shelves of a grocery store or other retail establishment selling those items.

Sec. 431.247. Delegation of Powers or Duties.

(a) [Repealed by Acts 2015, 84th Leg., ch. xxx (S.B. 219), § 3.1639(75), effective April 2, 2015.]

(b) A health authority may, unless otherwise restricted by law, delegate a power or duty imposed on the health authority by this chapter to an employee of the local health department, the local health unit, or the public health district in which the health authority serves.

Sec. 431.2471. Texas Department of Health Peace Officers. [Repealed]

Sec. 431.248. Memorandum of Understanding with Department of Agriculture.

(a) The department and the Department of Agriculture shall execute a memorandum of understanding that:

(1) requires each agency to disclose to the other agency any positive results of testing conducted by the agency for pesticides in food; and

(2) specifies how each agency will assist the other in performing its duties regarding pesticides in food.

(b) The executive commissioner and the Department of Agriculture shall adopt the memorandum of understanding as a rule.

(c) The department and the Department of Agriculture shall request the federal Food and Drug Administration to join in execution of the memorandum of understanding.

Sec. 431.249. Dissemination of Information.

(a) The department may publish reports summarizing the judgments, decrees, and court orders rendered under this chapter, including the nature and disposition of the charge.

(b) The department may disseminate information regarding a food, drug, device, or cosmetic in a situation that the department determines to involve imminent danger to health or gross deception of consumers.

(c) This section does not prohibit the department from collecting, reporting, and illustrating the results of an investigation by the department.

Sec. 431.250. Public Comments for Federal Grants and Contracts.

(a) The department shall annually solicit comments from interested persons regarding the grants and contracts the department has requested from or entered into with the United States Food and Drug Administration for implementing the federal Act and its amendments, including the Food Safety Modernization Act (21 U.S.C. Section 2201 et seq.).

(b) The department shall solicit comments by posting on the department's Internet website a detailed description of and providing notice to interested persons of each grant and contract described by Subsection (a) requested or entered into during the previous year. The description and notice must include the benefits to this state, the department, the regulated community, and the public.

(c) The department shall respond to questions and comments about a grant or contract described by Subsection (a) to the best of the department's knowledge. If an interested person requests that the department decline to receive future federal funding from the grant or contract, the department shall consider the request and determine whether the benefits of the grant or contract outweigh the person's concerns.

SUBTITLE B ALCOHOL AND SUBSTANCE ABUSE PROGRAMS

CHAPTER 462 TREATMENT OF PERSONS WITH CHEMICAL DEPENDENCIES

SUBCHAPTER C EMERGENCY DETENTION

Sec. 462.041. Apprehension by Peace Officer Without Warrant.

(a) A peace officer, without a warrant, may take a person into custody if the officer:

(1) has reason to believe and does believe that:

(A) the person is chemically dependent; and

(B) because of that chemical dependency there is a substantial risk of harm to the person or to others unless the person is immediately restrained; and

(2) believes that there is not sufficient time to obtain a warrant before taking the person into custody.

(b) A substantial risk of serious harm to the person or others under Subsection (a)(1)(B) may be demonstrated by:

(1) the person's behavior; or

(2) evidence of severe emotional distress and deterioration in the person's mental or physical condition to the extent that the person cannot remain at liberty.

(c) The peace officer may form the belief that the person meets the criteria for apprehension:

(1) from a representation of a credible person; or

(2) on the basis of the conduct of the apprehended person or the circumstances under which the apprehended person is found.

(d) A peace officer who takes a person into custody under Subsection (a) shall immediately transport the apprehended person to:

(1) the nearest appropriate inpatient treatment facility; or

(2) if an appropriate inpatient treatment facility is not available, a facility considered suitable by the county's health authority.

(e) A person may not be detained in a jail or similar detention facility except in an extreme emergency. A person detained in a jail or a nonmedical facility shall be kept separate from any person who is charged with or convicted of a crime.

(f) A peace officer shall immediately file an application for detention after transporting a person to a facility under this section. The application for detention must contain:

(1) a statement that the officer has reason to believe and does believe that the person evidences chemical dependency;

(2) a statement that the officer has reason to believe and does believe that the person evidences a substantial risk of serious harm to himself or others;

(3) a specific description of the risk of harm;

(4) a statement that the officer has reason to believe and does believe that the risk of harm is imminent unless the person is immediately restrained;

(5) a statement that the officer's beliefs are derived from specific recent behavior, overt acts, attempts, or threats that were observed by or reliably reported to the officer;

(6) a detailed description of the specific behavior, acts, attempts, or threats; and

(7) the name and relationship to the apprehended person of any person who reported or observed the behavior, acts, attempts, or threats.

(g) The person shall be released on completion of a preliminary examination conducted under Section 462.044 unless the examining physician determines that emergency detention is necessary and provides the statement prescribed by Section 462.044(b). If a person is not admitted to a facility, is not arrested, and does not object, arrangements shall be made to immediately return the person to:

(1) the location of the person's apprehension;

(2) the person's residence in this state; or

(3) another suitable location.

(h) The county in which the person was apprehended shall pay the costs of the person's return.

(i) A treatment facility may provide to a person medical assistance regardless of whether the facility admits the person or refers the person to another facility.

CHAPTER 463 CONTRIBUTING TO DELINQUENCY OF HABITUAL DRUNKARD OR NARCOTIC ADDICT [REPEALED]

SUBCHAPTER A CONTRIBUTING TO DELINQUENCY OF HABITUAL DRUNKARD [REPEALED]

Sec. 463.001. Contributing to Delinquency of Habitual Drunkard; Criminal Penalty. [Repealed]

Sec. 463.002. Conflicting Offenses. [Repealed]

SUBCHAPTER B CONTRIBUTING TO NARCOTIC ADDICTION [REPEALED]

Sec. 463.011. Contributing to Delinquency of Narcotic Addict; Criminal Penalty. [Repealed]

Sec. 463.012. Conflicting Offenses. [Repealed]

Sec. 463.013. Exception. [Repealed]

Sec. 463.014. Mental Health Facility Requirements [Repealed].

Repealed by Acts 1991, 72nd Leg., ch. 14 (S.B. 404), § 178, effective September 1, 1991.

Sec. 463.015. Appointment of Attorney Ad Litem; Notice of Hearing [Repealed].

Repealed by Acts 1991, 72nd Leg., ch. 14 (S.B. 404), § 178, effective September 1, 1991.

Sec. 463.016. Time for Probable Cause Hearing [Repealed].

Repealed by Acts 1991, 72nd Leg., ch. 14 (S.B. 404), § 178, effective September 1, 1991.

Sec. 463.017. Probable Cause Hearing [Repealed].

Repealed by Acts 1991, 72nd Leg., ch. 14 (S.B. 404), § 178, effective September 1, 1991.

Sec. 463.018. Order for Release or Detention After Probable Cause Hearing [Repealed].

Repealed by Acts 1991, 72nd Leg., ch. 14 (S.B. 404), § 178, effective September 1, 1991.

Sec. 463.019. Notification of Probable Cause Hearing [Repealed].

Repealed by Acts 1991, 72nd Leg., ch. 14 (S.B. 404), § 178, effective September 1, 1991.

Sec. 463.020. Detention Pending Commitment Hearing [Repealed].

Repealed by Acts 1991, 72nd Leg., ch. 14 (S.B. 404), § 178, effective September 1, 1991.

Sec. 463.021. Appropriate Detention Facilities [Repealed].

Repealed by Acts 1991, 72nd Leg., ch. 14 (S.B. 404), § 178, effective September 1, 1991.

SUBCHAPTER C COMMITMENT OF DRUG-DEPENDENT PERSON TO MENTAL HEALTH FACILITY [REPEALED]

Sec. 463.041. Definition [Repealed].

Repealed by Acts 1991, 72nd Leg., ch. 14 (S.B. 404), § 178, effective September 1, 1991.

Sec. 463.042. Application for Extended Commitment [Repealed].

Repealed by Acts 1991, 72nd Leg., ch. 14 (S.B. 404), § 178, effective September 1, 1991.

Sec. 463.043. Physician's Certificate Filed with Application [Repealed].

Repealed by Acts 1991, 72nd Leg., ch. 14 (S.B. 404), § 178, effective September 1, 1991.

Sec. 463.044. Certificates Required [Repealed].

Repealed by Acts 1991, 72nd Leg., ch. 14 (S.B. 404), § 178, effective September 1, 1991.

Sec. 463.045. Time for Commitment Hearing; Continuance [Repealed].

Repealed by Acts 1991, 72nd Leg., ch. 14 (S.B. 404), § 178, effective September 1, 1991.

Sec. 463.046. Attorney Ad Litem; Attorney Access to Patient's Files [Repealed].

Repealed by Acts 1991, 72nd Leg., ch. 14 (S.B. 404), § 178, effective September 1, 1991.

Sec. 463.047. Jury [Repealed].

Repealed by Acts 1991, 72nd Leg., ch. 14 (S.B. 404), § 178, effective September 1, 1991.

Sec. 463.048. Burden of Proof; Hearing Evidence [Repealed].

Repealed by Acts 1991, 72nd Leg., ch. 14 (S.B. 404), § 178, effective September 1, 1991.

Sec. 463.049. Transfer [Repealed].

Repealed by Acts 1991, 72nd Leg., ch. 14 (S.B. 404), § 178, effective September 1, 1991.

Sec. 463.050. Findings [Repealed].

Repealed by Acts 1991, 72nd Leg., ch. 14 (S.B. 404), § 178, effective September 1, 1991.

Sec. 463.051. Order for Release or Commitment [Repealed].

Repealed by Acts 1991, 72nd Leg., ch. 14 (S.B. 404), § 178, effective September 1, 1991.

Sec. 463.052. Order for Outpatient Care or Services [Repealed].

Repealed by Acts 1991, 72nd Leg., ch. 14 (S.B. 404), § 178, effective September 1, 1991.

Sec. 463.053. New Trial [Repealed].

Repealed by Acts 1991, 72nd Leg., ch. 14 (S.B. 404), § 178, effective September 1, 1991.

Sec. 463.054. Appeal [Repealed].

Repealed by Acts 1991, 72nd Leg., ch. 14 (S.B. 404), § 178, effective September 1, 1991.

Sec. 463.055. Place of Commitment [Repealed].

Repealed by Acts 1991, 72nd Leg., ch. 14 (S.B. 404), § 178, effective September 1, 1991.

Sec. 463.056. Commitment to Private Mental Health Facility [Repealed].

Repealed by Acts 1991, 72nd Leg., ch. 14 (S.B. 404), § 178, effective September 1, 1991.

Sec. 463.057. Commitment to Federal Agency [Repealed].

Repealed by Acts 1991, 72nd Leg., ch. 14 (S.B. 404), § 178, effective September 1, 1991.

Sec. 463.058. Patient Transport [Repealed].

Repealed by Acts 1991, 72nd Leg., ch. 14 (S.B. 404), § 178, effective September 1, 1991.

Sec. 463.059. Duties of Clerk Concerning Patient Transport [Repealed].

Repealed by Acts 1991, 72nd Leg., ch. 14 (S.B. 404), § 178, effective September 1, 1991.

Sec. 463.060. Receipt of Patient [Repealed].

Repealed by Acts 1991, 72nd Leg., ch. 14 (S.B. 404), § 178, effective September 1, 1991.

SUBCHAPTER D COSTS, LIABILITY, AND VIOLATIONS: EXTENDED COMMITMENTS AND PROTECTIVE CUSTODY [REPEALED]

Sec. 463.071. Costs Relating to Detention or Commitment [Repealed].

Repealed by Acts 1991, 72nd Leg., ch. 14 (S.B. 404), § 178, effective September 1, 1991.

Sec. 463.072. Immunity from Liability [Repealed].

Repealed by Acts 1991, 72nd Leg., ch. 14 (S.B. 404), § 178, effective September 1, 1991.

Sec. 463.073. Unwarranted Commitment; Criminal Penalty [Repealed].

Repealed by Acts 1991, 72nd Leg., ch. 14 (S.B. 404), § 178, effective September 1, 1991.

Sec. 463.074. Criminal Penalty [Repealed].

Repealed by Acts 1991, 72nd Leg., ch. 14 (S.B. 404), § 178, effective September 1, 1991.

Sec. 463.075. Prosecution of Violation [Repealed].

Repealed by Acts 1991, 72nd Leg., ch. 14 (S.B. 404), § 178, effective September 1, 1991.

SUBCHAPTER E VOLUNTARY ADMISSION TO STATE HOSPITAL [REPEALED]

Sec. 463.081. Eligibility for Voluntary Admission to State Hospital [Repealed].

Repealed by Acts 1991, 72nd Leg., ch. 14 (S.B. 404), § 178, effective September 1, 1991.

Sec. 463.082. Admission to State Hospital; Certification [Repealed].

Repealed by Acts 1991, 72nd Leg., ch. 14 (S.B. 404), § 178, effective September 1, 1991.

Sec. 463.083. Denial of Admission [Repealed].

Repealed by Acts 1991, 72nd Leg., ch. 14 (S.B. 404), § 178, effective September 1, 1991.

Sec. 463.084. Costs of Treatment [Repealed].

Repealed by Acts 1991, 72nd Leg., ch. 14 (S.B. 404), § 178, effective September 1, 1991.

Sec. 463.085. Treatment and Release [Repealed].

Repealed by Acts 1991, 72nd Leg., ch. 14 (S.B. 404), § 178, effective September 1, 1991.

Sec. 463.086. Commitment of Child to State Hospital [Repealed].

Repealed by Acts 1991, 72nd Leg., ch. 14 (S.B. 404), § 178, effective September 1, 1991.

SUBCHAPTER F TREATMENT OF CHILDREN FOR DRUG ABUSE [REPEALED]

Sec. 463.101. Consent to Medical Treatment for Drug Use [Repealed].

Repealed by Acts 1991, 72nd Leg., ch. 14 (S.B. 404), § 178, effective September 1, 1991.

Sec. 463.102. Commitment of Child to Approved Treatment Program [Repealed].

Repealed by Acts 1991, 72nd Leg., ch. 14 (S.B. 404), § 178, effective September 1, 1991.

SUBCHAPTER G CONTRIBUTING TO NARCOTIC ADDICTION [RENUMBERED]

Sec. 463.121. Contributing to Delinquency of Narcotic Addict; Criminal Penalty [Renumbered].

Renumbered to Tex.Health & Safety Code § 463.011 by Acts 1991, 72nd Leg., ch. 14 (S.B. 404), § 179, effective September 1, 1991.

Sec. 463.122. Conflicting Offenses [Renumbered].

Renumbered to Tex.Health & Safety Code § 463.012 by Acts 1991, 72nd Leg., ch. 14 (S.B. 404), § 179, effective September 1, 1991.

CHAPTER 465 LOCAL DRUG AND ALCOHOL EDUCATION PROGRAMS

Sec. 465.001. Commission.

A municipality or county may create and support with public funds a commission to:

(1) educate the public on drug and alcohol abuse;

(2) promote drug and alcohol education at all levels of the schools;

(3) study the effectiveness of efforts, including the commission's efforts, in reducing drug and alcohol abuse; and

(4) create and administer a program to counsel or treat drug and alcohol abusers or to provide both counseling and treatment.

Sec. 465.002. Individual or Joint Action.

The municipality or county may create the commission by its own action or jointly by agreement with another municipality or county or a private foundation, nonprofit organization, church, or other entity. If the commission is created by agreement, all matters regarding the creation and operation of the commission are governed as provided by the agreement.

Sec. 465.003. Report.

The commission shall report annually to each entity that participates in the creation of the commission regarding the commission's activities.

CHAPTER 466
REGULATION OF NARCOTIC DRUG TREATMENT PROGRAMS

SUBCHAPTER A
GENERAL PROVISIONS

Sec. 466.001. Legislative Intent.

(a) It is the intent of the legislature that the department exercise its administrative powers and regulatory authority to ensure the proper use of approved narcotic drugs in the treatment of persons with a narcotic dependency.

(b) Treatment of narcotic addiction by permitted treatment programs is recognized as a specialty chemical dependency treatment area using the medical model.

(c) Short-term goals should have an emphasis of personal and public health, crime prevention, reintegration of persons with a narcotic addiction into the public work force, and social and medical stabilization. Narcotic treatment programs are an important component of the state's effort to prevent the further proliferation of the AIDS virus. Total drug abstinence is recognized as a long-term goal of treatment, subject to medical determination of the medical appropriateness and prognosis of the person with a narcotic addiction.

Sec. 466.002. Definitions.

In this chapter:

(1) "Approved narcotic drug" means a drug approved by the United States Food and Drug Administration for maintenance or detoxification of a person physiologically addicted to the opiate class of drugs.

(2), (3) [Repealed by Acts 2015, 84th Leg., ch. 1 (S.B. 219), § 3.1639(91), effective April 2, 2015.]

(4) "Commissioner" means the commissioner of state health services.

(5) "Department" means the Department of State Health Services.

(5-a) "Executive commissioner" means the executive commissioner of the Health and Human Services Commission.

(6) "Facility" includes a medical office, an outpatient clinic, a general or special hospital, a community mental health center, and any other location in which a structured narcotic dependency program is conducted.

(7) "Narcotic drug" has the meaning assigned by Chapter 481 (Texas Controlled Substances Act).

Sec. 466.003. Exclusion of Cocaine.

Cocaine is excluded for the purpose of this chapter.

Sec. 466.004. Powers and Duties of Executive Commissioner and Department.

(a) The executive commissioner shall adopt and the department shall administer and enforce rules to ensure the proper use of approved narcotic drugs in the treatment of persons with a narcotic drug dependency, including rules that:

(1) require an applicant or a permit holder to make annual, periodic, and special reports that the department determines are necessary;

(2) require an applicant or permit holder to keep records that the department determines are necessary;

(3) provide for investigations that the department determines are necessary; and

(4) provide for the coordination of the approval of narcotic drug treatment programs by the United States Food and Drug Administration and the United States Drug Enforcement Administration.

(b) The executive commissioner shall adopt rules for the issuance of permits to operate narcotic drug treatment programs including rules:

(1) governing the submission and review of applications;

(2) establishing the criteria for the issuance and renewal of permits; and

(3) establishing the criteria for the suspension and revocation of permits.

Sec. 466.005. Administration by Commission and Department [Repealed].

Repealed by Acts 1999, 76th Leg., ch. 1411 (H.B. 2085), § 1.18, effective September 1, 1999.

SUBCHAPTER B PERMIT

Sec. 466.021. Permit Required.

A person may not operate a narcotic drug treatment program unless the person has a permit issued under this chapter.

Sec. 466.022. Limitation on Prescription, Order, or Administration of Narcotic Drug.

A physician may not prescribe, order, or administer a narcotic drug for the purpose of treating drug dependency unless the physician prescribes, orders, or administers an approved narcotic drug for the maintenance or detoxification of persons with a drug dependency as part of a program permitted by the department.

Sec. 466.023. Application for Permit; Fees.

(a) The department shall issue a permit to an applicant who qualifies under rules and standards adopted by the executive commissioner.

(b) A permit issued under this section is valid until suspended or revoked by the department or surrendered by the permit holder in accordance with department rules.

(c) A person must obtain a permit for each facility that the person operates.

(d) A permit issued by the department is not transferable from one facility to another facility and must be returned to the department if the permit holder sells or otherwise conveys the facility to another person.

(e) The executive commissioner by rule shall establish and the department shall collect a nonrefundable application fee to defray the cost to the department of processing each application for a permit. The application fee must be submitted with the application. An application may not be considered unless the application is accompanied by the application fee.

(f) The executive commissioner shall adopt rules that set permit fees in amounts sufficient for the department to recover not less than half of the actual annual expenditures of state funds by the department to:

(1) amend permits;

(2) inspect facilities operated by permit holders; and

(3) implement and enforce this chapter.

(g) [Repealed by Acts 2015, 84th Leg., ch. 1 (S.B. 219), § 3.1639(92), effective April 2, 2015.]

Sec. 466.024. Permit Limitations.

(a) The department may issue a permit to:

(1) a person constituting a legal entity organized and operating under the laws of this state; or

(2) a physician.

(b) The department may issue a permit to a person other than a physician only if the person provides health care services under the supervision of one or more physicians licensed by the Texas Medical Board.

Sec. 466.025. Inspection.

(a) The department may enter the facility of a person who is an applicant for a permit or who is a permit holder during any hours in which the facility is in operation for the purpose of inspecting the facility to determine:

(1) if the person meets the standards set in department rules for the issuance of a permit; or

(2) if a person who holds a permit is in compliance with this chapter, the standards set in department rules for the operation of a facility, any special provisions contained in the permit, or an order of the commissioner or the department.

(b) The inspection may be conducted without prior notice to the applicant or the permit holder.

(c) The department shall provide the applicant or permit holder with a copy of the inspection report. An inspection report shall be made a part of the applicant's submission file or the permit holder's compliance record.

Sec. 466.026. Multiple Enrollment Prevention.

The department shall work with representatives from permitted narcotic treatment programs in this state to develop recommendations for a plan to prevent the simultaneous multiple enrollment of

Health and Safety Code

persons in narcotic treatment programs. The executive commissioner may adopt rules to implement these recommendations.

Sec. 466.027. Denial, Suspension, or Revocation of Permit.

(a) After notice to an applicant or a permit holder and after the opportunity for a hearing, the department may:

(1) deny an application of the person if the person fails to comply with this chapter or the rules establishing minimum standards for the issuance of a permit adopted under this chapter; or

(2) suspend or revoke the permit of a person who has violated this chapter, an order issued under this chapter, or a minimum standard required for the issuance of a permit.

(b) The executive commissioner may adopt rules that establish the criteria for the denial, suspension, or revocation of a permit.

(c) Hearings, appeals from, and judicial review of final administrative decisions under this section shall be conducted according to the contested case provisions of Chapter 2001, Government Code, and the department's formal hearing rules.

(d) This section does not prevent the informal reconsideration of a case before the setting of a hearing or before the issuance of the final administrative decision under this section. The program rules must contain provisions establishing the procedures for the initiation and conduct of the informal reconsideration by the department.

SUBCHAPTER C ENFORCEMENT

Sec. 466.041. Emergency Orders.

(a) The department may issue an emergency order, either mandatory or prohibitory in nature, in relation to the operation of a permitted facility or the treatment of patients by the facility staff, in the department's jurisdiction. The order may be issued if the department determines that the treatment of patients by the staff of the permit holder creates or poses an immediate and serious threat to human life or health and other procedures available to the department to remedy or prevent the occurrence of the situation will result in an unreasonable delay.

(b) The department may issue the emergency order, including an emergency order suspending or revoking a permit issued by the department, without notice and hearing, if the department determines that action to be practicable under the circumstances.

(c) If an emergency order is issued without a hearing, the department shall determine a time and place for a hearing at which the emergency order is affirmed, modified, or set aside. The hearing shall be held under the contested case provisions of Chapter 2001, Government Code, and the department's formal hearing rules.

(d) If an emergency order is issued to suspend or revoke the permit, the department shall ensure that treatment services for the patients are maintained at the same location until appropriate referrals to an alternate treatment program are made.

Sec. 466.042. Injunction.

(a) The department may request the attorney general or a district, county, or municipal attorney to petition the district court for a temporary restraining order to restrain:

(1) a continuing violation of this chapter, a rule adopted under this chapter, or an order or permit issued under this chapter; or

(2) a threat of a continuing violation of this chapter, a rule, or an order or permit.

(b) To request a temporary restraining order, the department must find that a person has violated, is violating, or is threatening to violate this chapter, a rule adopted under this chapter, or an order or permit issued under this chapter and:

(1) the violation or threatened violation creates an immediate threat to the health and safety of the public; or

(2) there is reasonable cause to believe that the permit holder or the staff of the permit holder is party to the diversion of a narcotic drug or drugs in violation of Chapter 481 (Texas Controlled Substances Act).

(c) On finding by the court that a person is violating or threatening to violate this chapter, a rule adopted under this chapter, or an order or permit issued under this chapter, the court shall grant the injunctive relief warranted by the facts.

(d) Venue for a suit brought under this section is in the county in which the violation or threat of violation is alleged to have occurred or in Travis County.

Sec. 466.043. Administrative Penalty.

If a person violates this chapter, a rule adopted under this chapter, or an order or permit issued under this chapter, the department may assess an administrative penalty against the person as provided by Chapter 431 (Texas Food, Drug, and Cosmetic Act).

Health and Safety Code

Sec. 466.044. Criminal Penalty.

(a) A person commits an offense if the person operates a narcotic drug treatment program without a permit issued by the department.

(b) An offense under this section is a Class A misdemeanor.

Sec. 466.045. Civil Penalty.

(a) If it appears that a person has violated this chapter, a rule adopted under this chapter, or an order or permit issued under this chapter, the department may request the attorney general or the district, county, or municipal attorney of the municipality or county in which the violation occurred to institute a civil suit for the assessment and recovery of a civil penalty.

(b) The penalty may be in an amount not to exceed $10,000 for each violation.

(c) In determining the amount of the penalty, the court shall consider:

(1) the person's history of previous violations;

(2) the seriousness of the violation;

(3) any hazard to the health and safety of the public; and

(4) the demonstrated good faith of the person charged.

(d) A civil penalty recovered in a suit instituted by the attorney general under this chapter shall be deposited in the state treasury to the credit of the General Revenue Fund. A civil penalty recovered in a suit instituted by a local government under this chapter shall be paid to the local government.

SUBTITLE C SUBSTANCE ABUSE REGULATION AND CRIMES

CHAPTER 481 TEXAS CONTROLLED SUBSTANCES ACT

SUBCHAPTER A GENERAL PROVISIONS

Sec. 481.001. Short Title.

This chapter may be cited as the Texas Controlled Substances Act.

Sec. 481.002. Definitions.

In this chapter:

(1) "Administer" means to directly apply a controlled substance by injection, inhalation, ingestion, or other means to the body of a patient or research subject by:

(A) a practitioner or an agent of the practitioner in the presence of the practitioner; or

(B) the patient or research subject at the direction and in the presence of a practitioner.

(2) "Agent" means an authorized person who acts on behalf of or at the direction of a manufacturer, distributor, or dispenser. The term does not include a common or contract carrier, public warehouseman, or employee of a carrier or warehouseman acting in the usual and lawful course of employment.

(3) "Commissioner" means the commissioner of state health services or the commissioner's designee.

(4) "Controlled premises" means:

(A) a place where original or other records or documents required under this chapter are kept or are required to be kept; or

(B) a place, including a factory, warehouse, other establishment, or conveyance, where a person registered under this chapter may lawfully hold, manufacture, distribute, dispense, administer, possess, or otherwise dispose of a controlled substance or other item governed by the federal Controlled Substances Act (21 U.S.C. Section 801 et seq.) or this chapter, including a chemical precursor and a chemical laboratory apparatus.

(5) "Controlled substance" means a substance, including a drug, an adulterant, and a dilutant, listed in Schedules I through V or Penalty Group 1, 1-A, 1-B, 2, 2-A, 3, or 4. The term includes the aggregate weight of any mixture, solution, or other substance containing a controlled substance. The term does not include hemp, as defined by Section 121.001, Agriculture Code, or the tetrahydrocannabinols in hemp.

(6) "Controlled substance analogue" means:

(A) a substance with a chemical structure substantially similar to the chemical structure of a controlled substance in Schedule I or II or Penalty Group 1, 1-A, 1-B, 2, or 2-A; or

(B) a substance specifically designed to produce an effect substantially similar to, or greater than, the effect of a controlled substance in Schedule I or II or Penalty Group 1, 1-A, 1-B, 2, or 2-A.

(7) "Counterfeit substance" means a controlled substance that, without authorization, bears or is in a container or has a label that bears an actual or simulated trademark, trade name, or other

identifying mark, imprint, number, or device of a manufacturer, distributor, or dispenser other than the person who in fact manufactured, distributed, or dispensed the substance.

(8) "Deliver" means to transfer, actually or constructively, to another a controlled substance, counterfeit substance, or drug paraphernalia, regardless of whether there is an agency relationship. The term includes offering to sell a controlled substance, counterfeit substance, or drug paraphernalia.

(9) "Delivery" or "drug transaction" means the act of delivering.

(10) "Designated agent" means an individual designated under Section 481.074(b-2) to communicate a practitioner's instructions to a pharmacist in an emergency.

(11) "Director" means the director of the Department of Public Safety or an employee of the department designated by the director.

(12) "Dispense" means the delivery of a controlled substance in the course of professional practice or research, by a practitioner or person acting under the lawful order of a practitioner, to an ultimate user or research subject. The term includes the prescribing, administering, packaging, labeling, or compounding necessary to prepare the substance for delivery.

(13) "Dispenser" means a practitioner, institutional practitioner, pharmacist, or pharmacy that dispenses a controlled substance.

(14) "Distribute" means to deliver a controlled substance other than by administering or dispensing the substance.

(15) "Distributor" means a person who distributes.

(16) "Drug" means a substance, other than a device or a component, part, or accessory of a device, that is:

(A) recognized as a drug in the official United States Pharmacopoeia, official Homeopathic Pharmacopoeia of the United States, official National Formulary, or a supplement to either pharmacopoeia or the formulary;

(B) intended for use in the diagnosis, cure, mitigation, treatment, or prevention of disease in man or animals;

(C) intended to affect the structure or function of the body of man or animals but is not food; or

(D) intended for use as a component of a substance described by Paragraph (A), (B), or (C).

(17) "Drug paraphernalia" means equipment, a product, or material that is used or intended for use in planting, propagating, cultivating, growing, harvesting, manufacturing, compounding, converting, producing, processing, preparing, testing, analyzing, packaging, repackaging, storing, containing, or concealing a controlled substance in violation of this chapter or in injecting, ingesting, inhaling, or otherwise introducing into the human body a controlled substance in violation of this chapter. The term includes:

(A) a kit used or intended for use in planting, propagating, cultivating, growing, or harvesting a species of plant that is a controlled substance or from which a controlled substance may be derived;

(B) a material, compound, mixture, preparation, or kit used or intended for use in manufacturing, compounding, converting, producing, processing, or preparing a controlled substance;

(C) an isomerization device used or intended for use in increasing the potency of a species of plant that is a controlled substance;

(D) testing equipment used or intended for use in identifying or in analyzing the strength, effectiveness, or purity of a controlled substance;

(E) a scale or balance used or intended for use in weighing or measuring a controlled substance;

(F) a dilutant or adulterant, such as quinine hydrochloride, mannitol, inositol, nicotinamide, dextrose, lactose, or absorbent, blotter-type material, that is used or intended to be used to increase the amount or weight of or to transfer a controlled substance regardless of whether the dilutant or adulterant diminishes the efficacy of the controlled substance;

(G) a separation gin or sifter used or intended for use in removing twigs and seeds from or in otherwise cleaning or refining marihuana;

(H) a blender, bowl, container, spoon, or mixing device used or intended for use in compounding a controlled substance;

(I) a capsule, balloon, envelope, or other container used or intended for use in packaging small quantities of a controlled substance;

(J) a container or other object used or intended for use in storing or concealing a controlled substance;

(K) a hypodermic syringe, needle, or other object used or intended for use in parenterally injecting a controlled substance into the human body; and

(L) an object used or intended for use in ingesting, inhaling, or otherwise introducing marihuana, cocaine, hashish, or hashish oil into the human body, including:

(i) a metal, wooden, acrylic, glass, stone, plastic, or ceramic pipe with or without a screen, permanent screen, hashish head, or punctured metal bowl;

(ii) a water pipe;

(iii) a carburetion tube or device;

(iv) a smoking or carburetion mask;

(v) a chamber pipe;
(vi) a carburetor pipe;
(vii) an electric pipe;
(viii) an air-driven pipe;
(ix) a chillum;
(x) a bong; or
(xi) an ice pipe or chiller.

(18) "Federal Controlled Substances Act" means the Federal Comprehensive Drug Abuse Prevention and Control Act of 1970 (21 U.S.C. Section 801 et seq.) or its successor statute.

(19) "Federal Drug Enforcement Administration" means the Drug Enforcement Administration of the United States Department of Justice or its successor agency.

(20) "Hospital" means:

(A) a general or special hospital as defined by Section 241.003;

(B) an ambulatory surgical center licensed under Chapter 243 and approved by the federal government to perform surgery paid by Medicaid on patients admitted for a period of not more than 24 hours; or

(C) a freestanding emergency medical care facility licensed under Chapter 254.

(21) "Human consumption" means the injection, inhalation, ingestion, or application of a substance to or into a human body.

(22) "Immediate precursor" means a substance the director finds to be and by rule designates as being:

(A) a principal compound commonly used or produced primarily for use in the manufacture of a controlled substance;

(B) a substance that is an immediate chemical intermediary used or likely to be used in the manufacture of a controlled substance; and

(C) a substance the control of which is necessary to prevent, curtail, or limit the manufacture of a controlled substance.

(23) "Institutional practitioner" means an intern, resident physician, fellow, or person in an equivalent professional position who:

(A) is not licensed by the appropriate state professional licensing board;

(B) is enrolled in a bona fide professional training program in a base hospital or institutional training facility registered by the Federal Drug Enforcement Administration; and

(C) is authorized by the base hospital or institutional training facility to administer, dispense, or prescribe controlled substances.

(24) "Lawful possession" means the possession of a controlled substance that has been obtained in accordance with state or federal law.

(25) "Manufacture" means the production, preparation, propagation, compounding, conversion, or processing of a controlled substance other than marihuana, directly or indirectly by extraction from substances of natural origin, independently by means of chemical synthesis, or by a combination of extraction and chemical synthesis, and includes the packaging or repackaging of the substance or labeling or relabeling of its container. However, the term does not include the preparation, compounding, packaging, or labeling of a controlled substance:

(A) by a practitioner as an incident to the practitioner's administering or dispensing a controlled substance in the course of professional practice; or

(B) by a practitioner, or by an authorized agent under the supervision of the practitioner, for or as an incident to research, teaching, or chemical analysis and not for delivery.

(26) "Marihuana" means the plant Cannabis sativa L., whether growing or not, the seeds of that plant, and every compound, manufacture, salt, derivative, mixture, or preparation of that plant or its seeds. The term does not include:

(A) the resin extracted from a part of the plant or a compound, manufacture, salt, derivative, mixture, or preparation of the resin;

(B) the mature stalks of the plant or fiber produced from the stalks;

(C) oil or cake made from the seeds of the plant;

(D) a compound, manufacture, salt, derivative, mixture, or preparation of the mature stalks, fiber, oil, or cake;

(E) the sterilized seeds of the plant that are incapable of beginning germination; or

(F) hemp, as that term is defined by Section 121.001, Agriculture Code.

(27) "Medical purpose" means the use of a controlled substance for relieving or curing a mental or physical disease or infirmity.

(28) "Medication order" means an order from a practitioner to dispense a drug to a patient in a hospital for immediate administration while the patient is in the hospital or for emergency use on the patient's release from the hospital.

(29) "Narcotic drug" means any of the following, produced directly or indirectly by extraction from substances of vegetable origin, independently by means of chemical synthesis, or by a combination of extraction and chemical synthesis:

(A) opium and opiates, and a salt, compound, derivative, or preparation of opium or opiates;

(B) a salt, compound, isomer, derivative, or preparation of a salt, compound, isomer, or derivative that is chemically equivalent or identical to a substance listed in Paragraph (A) other than the isoquinoline alkaloids of opium;

(C) opium poppy and poppy straw; or

(D) cocaine, including:

(i) its salts, its optical, position, or geometric isomers, and the salts of those isomers;

(ii) coca leaves and a salt, compound, derivative, or preparation of coca leaves; and

(iii) a salt, compound, derivative, or preparation of a salt, compound, or derivative that is chemically equivalent or identical to a substance described by Subparagraph (i) or (ii), other than decocainized coca leaves or extractions of coca leaves that do not contain cocaine or ecgonine.

(30) "Opiate" means a substance that has an addiction-forming or addiction-sustaining liability similar to morphine or is capable of conversion into a drug having addiction-forming or addiction-sustaining liability. The term includes its racemic and levorotatory forms. The term does not include, unless specifically designated as controlled under Subchapter B, the dextrorotatory isomer of 3-methoxy-n-methylmorphinan and its salts (dextromethorphan).

(31) "Opium poppy" means the plant of the species Papaver somniferum L., other than its seeds.

(32) "Patient" means a human for whom or an animal for which a drug:

(A) is administered, dispensed, delivered, or prescribed by a practitioner; or

(B) is intended to be administered, dispensed, delivered, or prescribed by a practitioner.

(33) "Person" means an individual, corporation, government, business trust, estate, trust, partnership, association, or any other legal entity.

(34) "Pharmacist" means a person licensed by the Texas State Board of Pharmacy to practice pharmacy and who acts as an agent for a pharmacy.

(35) "Pharmacist-in-charge" means the pharmacist designated on a pharmacy license as the pharmacist who has the authority or responsibility for the pharmacy's compliance with this chapter and other laws relating to pharmacy.

(36) "Pharmacy" means a facility licensed by the Texas State Board of Pharmacy where a prescription for a controlled substance is received or processed in accordance with state or federal law.

(37) "Poppy straw" means all parts, other than the seeds, of the opium poppy, after mowing.

(38) "Possession" means actual care, custody, control, or management.

(39) "Practitioner" means:

(A) a physician, dentist, veterinarian, podiatrist, scientific investigator, or other person licensed, registered, or otherwise permitted to distribute, dispense, analyze, conduct research with respect to, or administer a controlled substance in the course of professional practice or research in this state;

(B) a pharmacy, hospital, or other institution licensed, registered, or otherwise permitted to distribute, dispense, conduct research with respect to, or administer a controlled substance in the course of professional practice or research in this state;

(C) a person practicing in and licensed by another state as a physician, dentist, veterinarian, or podiatrist, having a current Federal Drug Enforcement Administration registration number, who may legally prescribe Schedule II, III, IV, or V controlled substances in that state; or

(D) an advanced practice registered nurse or physician assistant to whom a physician has delegated the authority to prescribe or order a drug or device under Section 157.0511, 157.0512, or 157.054, Occupations Code.

(40) "Prescribe" means the act of a practitioner to authorize a controlled substance to be dispensed to an ultimate user.

(41) "Prescription" means an order by a practitioner to a pharmacist for a controlled substance for a particular patient that specifies:

(A) the date of issue;

(B) the name and address of the patient or, if the controlled substance is prescribed for an animal, the species of the animal and the name and address of its owner;

(C) the name and quantity of the controlled substance prescribed with the quantity shown numerically followed by the number written as a word if the order is written or, if the order is communicated orally or telephonically, with the quantity given by the practitioner and transcribed by the pharmacist numerically;

(D) directions for the use of the drug;

(E) the intended use of the drug unless the practitioner determines the furnishing of this information is not in the best interest of the patient; and

(F) the legibly printed or stamped name, address, Federal Drug Enforcement Administration registration number, and telephone number of the practitioner at the practitioner's usual place of business.

(42) "Principal place of business" means a location where a person manufactures, distributes, dispenses, analyzes, or possesses a controlled substance. The term does not include a location where a practitioner dispenses a controlled substance on an outpatient basis unless the controlled substance is stored at that location.

(43) "Production" includes the manufacturing, planting, cultivating, growing, or harvesting of a controlled substance.

(44) "Raw material" means a compound, material, substance, or equipment used or intended for use, alone or in any combination, in manufacturing a controlled substance.

(45) "Registrant" means a person who has a current Federal Drug Enforcement Administration registration number.

(46) "Substitution" means the dispensing of a drug or a brand of drug other than that which is ordered or prescribed.

(47) "Official prescription form" means a prescription form that is used for a Schedule II controlled substance under Section 481.0755 and contains the prescription information required by Section 481.0755(e).

(48) "Ultimate user" means a person who has lawfully obtained and possesses a controlled substance for the person's own use, for the use of a member of the person's household, or for administering to an animal owned by the person or by a member of the person's household.

(49) "Adulterant or dilutant" means any material that increases the bulk or quantity of a controlled substance, regardless of its effect on the chemical activity of the controlled substance.

(50) "Abuse unit" means:

(A) except as provided by Paragraph (B):

(i) a single unit on or in any adulterant, dilutant, or similar carrier medium, including marked or perforated blotter paper, a tablet, gelatin wafer, sugar cube, or stamp, or other medium that contains any amount of a controlled substance listed in Penalty Group 1-A, if the unit is commonly used in abuse of that substance; or

(ii) each quarter-inch square section of paper, if the adulterant, dilutant, or carrier medium is paper not marked or perforated into individual abuse units; or

(B) if the controlled substance is in liquid or solid form, 40 micrograms of the controlled substance including any adulterant or dilutant.

(51) "Chemical precursor" means:

(A) Methylamine;

(B) Ethylamine;

(C) D-lysergic acid;

(D) Ergotamine tartrate;

(E) Diethyl malonate;

(F) Malonic acid;

(G) Ethyl malonate;

(H) Barbituric acid;

(I) Piperidine;

(J) N-acetylanthranilic acid;

(K) Pyrrolidine;

(L) Phenylacetic acid;

(M) Anthranilic acid;

(N) Ephedrine;

(O) Pseudoephedrine;

(P) Norpseudoephedrine; or

(Q) Phenylpropanolamine.

(52) "Department" means the Department of Public Safety.

(53) "Chemical laboratory apparatus" means any item of equipment designed, made, or adapted to manufacture a controlled substance or a controlled substance analogue, including:

(A) a condenser;

(B) a distilling apparatus;

(C) a vacuum drier;

(D) a three-neck or distilling flask;

(E) a tableting machine;

(F) an encapsulating machine;

(G) a filter, Buchner, or separatory funnel;

(H) an Erlenmeyer, two-neck, or single-neck flask;

(I) a round-bottom, Florence, thermometer, or filtering flask;

(J) a Soxhlet extractor;

(K) a transformer;

(L) a flask heater;

(M) a heating mantel; or

(N) an adaptor tube.

(54) "Health information exchange" means an organization that:

(A) assists in the transmission or receipt of health-related information among organizations transmitting or receiving the information according to nationally recognized standards and under an express written agreement;

(B) as a primary business function, compiles or organizes health-related information that is designed to be securely transmitted by the organization among physicians, health care providers, or entities within a region, state, community, or hospital system; or

(C) assists in the transmission or receipt of electronic health-related information among physicians, health care providers, or entities within:

(i) a hospital system;

(ii) a physician organization;

(iii) a health care collaborative, as defined by Section 848.001, Insurance Code;

(iv) an accountable care organization participating in the Pioneer Model under the initiative by the Innovation Center of the Centers for Medicare and Medicaid Services; or

(v) an accountable care organization participating in the Medicare shared savings program under 42 U.S.C. Section 1395jjj.

(55) **[2 Versions: As added by Acts 2015, 84th Leg., ch. 1]** "Executive commissioner" means the executive commissioner of the Health and Human Services Commission.

(55) **[2 Versions: As added by Acts 2015, 84th Leg., ch. 1268]** "Board" means the Texas State Board of Pharmacy.

Sec. 481.003. Rules.

(a) **[As amended by Acts 2019, 86th Leg., ch. 1105 (H.B. 2174)]** The director may adopt rules to administer and enforce this chapter, other than Sections 481.074, 481.075, 481.0755, 481.0756, 481.076, 481.0761, 481.0762, 481.0763, 481.07635, 481.07636, 481.0764, 481.0765, and 481.0766. The board may adopt rules to administer Sections 481.074, 481.075, 481.0755, 481.0756, 481.076, 481.0761, 481.0762, 481.0763, 481.07635, 481.07636, 481.0764, 481.0765, and 481.0766.

(a) **[As amended by Acts 2019, 86th Leg., ch. 1166 (H.B. 3284)]** The director may adopt rules to administer and enforce this chapter, other than Sections 481.073, 481.074, 481.075, 481.076, 481.0761, 481.0762, 481.0763, 481.0764, 481.0765, 481.0766, 481.0767, 481.0768, and 481.0769. The board may adopt rules to administer Sections 481.073, 481.074, 481.075, 481.076, 481.0761, 481.0762, 481.0763, 481.0764, 481.0765, 481.0766, 481.0767, 481.0768, and 481.0769.

(b) The director by rule shall prohibit a person in this state, including a person regulated by the Texas Department of Insurance under the Insurance Code or the other insurance laws of this state, from using a practitioner's Federal Drug Enforcement Administration number for a purpose other than a purpose described by federal law or by this chapter. A person who violates a rule adopted under this subsection commits a Class C misdemeanor.

SUBCHAPTER B SCHEDULES

Sec. 481.031. Nomenclature.

Controlled substances listed in Schedules I through V and Penalty Groups 1 through 4 are included by whatever official, common, usual, chemical, or trade name they may be designated.

Sec. 481.032. Schedules.

(a) The commissioner shall establish and modify the following schedules of controlled substances under this subchapter: Schedule I, Schedule II, Schedule III, Schedule IV, and Schedule V.

(b) A reference to a schedule in this chapter means the most current version of the schedule established or altered by the commissioner under this subchapter and published in the Texas Register on or after January 1, 1998.

Sec. 481.033. Exclusion from Schedules and Application of Act.

(a) A nonnarcotic substance is excluded from Schedules I through V if the substance may lawfully be sold over the counter without a prescription, under the Federal Food, Drug, and Cosmetic Act (21 U.S.C. Section 301 et seq.).

(b) The commissioner may not include in the schedules:

(1) a substance described by Subsection (a); or

(2) distilled spirits, wine, malt beverages, or tobacco.

(c) A compound, mixture, or preparation containing a stimulant substance listed in Schedule II and having a potential for abuse associated with a stimulant effect on the central nervous system is excepted from the application of this chapter if the compound, mixture, or preparation contains one or more active medicinal ingredients not having a stimulant effect on the central nervous system and if the admixtures are included in combinations, quantity, proportions, or concentrations that vitiate the potential for abuse of the substance having a stimulant effect on the central nervous system.

(d) A compound, mixture, or preparation containing a depressant substance listed in Schedule III or IV and having a potential for abuse associated with a depressant effect on the central nervous system is excepted from the application of this chapter if the compound, mixture, or preparation contains one or more active medicinal ingredients not having a depressant effect on the central nervous system and if the admixtures are included in combinations, quantity, proportions, or concentrations that vitiate the potential for abuse of the substance having a depressant effect on the central nervous system.

(e) A nonnarcotic prescription substance is exempted from Schedules I through V and the application of this chapter to the same extent that the substance has been exempted from the application of the Federal Controlled Substances Act, if the substance is listed as an exempt prescription product under 21 C.F.R. Section 1308.32 and its subsequent amendments.

(f) A chemical substance that is intended for laboratory, industrial, educational, or special research purposes and not for general administration to a human being or other animal is exempted from Schedules I through V and the application of this chapter to the same extent that the substance has been exempted from the application of the Federal Controlled Substances Act, if the substance is listed as an exempt chemical preparation under 21 C.F.R. Section 1308.24 and its subsequent amendments.

(g) An anabolic steroid product, which has no significant potential for abuse due to concentration, preparation, mixture, or delivery system, is exempted from Schedules I through V and the application of this chapter to the same extent that the

Health and Safety Code

substance has been exempted from the application of the Federal Controlled Substances Act, if the substance is listed as an exempt anabolic steroid product under 21 C.F.R. Section 1308.34 and its subsequent amendments.

Sec. 481.034. Establishment and Modification of Schedules by Commissioner.

(a) The commissioner shall annually establish the schedules of controlled substances. These annual schedules shall include the complete list of all controlled substances from the previous schedules and modifications in the federal schedules of controlled substances as required by Subsection (g). Any further additions to and deletions from these schedules, any rescheduling of substances and any other modifications made by the commissioner to these schedules of controlled substances shall be made:

(1) in accordance with Section 481.035;

(2) in a manner consistent with this subchapter; and

(3) with approval of the executive commissioner.

(b) Except for alterations in schedules required by Subsection (g), the commissioner may not make an alteration in a schedule unless the commissioner holds a public hearing on the matter in Austin and obtains approval from the executive commissioner.

(c) The commissioner may not:

(1) add a substance to the schedules if the substance has been deleted from the schedules by the legislature;

(2) delete a substance from the schedules if the substance has been added to the schedules by the legislature; or

(3) reschedule a substance if the substance has been placed in a schedule by the legislature.

(d) In making a determination regarding a substance, the commissioner shall consider:

(1) the actual or relative potential for its abuse;

(2) the scientific evidence of its pharmacological effect, if known;

(3) the state of current scientific knowledge regarding the substance;

(4) the history and current pattern of its abuse;

(5) the scope, duration, and significance of its abuse;

(6) the risk to the public health;

(7) the potential of the substance to produce psychological or physiological dependence liability; and

(8) whether the substance is a controlled substance analogue, chemical precursor, or an immediate precursor of a substance controlled under this chapter.

(e) After considering the factors listed in Subsection (d), the commissioner shall make findings with respect to those factors. If the commissioner finds the substance has a potential for abuse, the executive commissioner shall adopt a rule controlling the substance.

(f) [Repealed by Acts 2003, 78th Leg., ch. 1099 (H.B. 2192), § 17, effective September 1, 2003.]

(g) Except as otherwise provided by this subsection, if a substance is designated, rescheduled, or deleted as a controlled substance under federal law and notice of that fact is given to the commissioner, the commissioner similarly shall control the substance under this chapter. After the expiration of a 30-day period beginning on the day after the date of publication in the Federal Register of a final order designating a substance as a controlled substance or rescheduling or deleting a substance, the commissioner similarly shall designate, reschedule, or delete the substance, unless the commissioner objects during the period. If the commissioner objects, the commissioner shall publish the reasons for the objection and give all interested parties an opportunity to be heard. At the conclusion of the hearing, the commissioner shall publish a decision, which is final unless altered by statute. On publication of an objection by the commissioner, control as to that particular substance under this chapter is stayed until the commissioner publishes the commissioner's decision.

(h) Not later than the 10th day after the date on which the commissioner designates, deletes, or reschedules a substance under Subsection (a), the commissioner shall give written notice of that action to the director and to each state licensing agency having jurisdiction over practitioners.

Sec. 481.035. Findings.

(a) The commissioner shall place a substance in Schedule I if the commissioner finds that the substance:

(1) has a high potential for abuse; and

(2) has no accepted medical use in treatment in the United States or lacks accepted safety for use in treatment under medical supervision.

(b) The commissioner shall place a substance in Schedule II if the commissioner finds that:

(1) the substance has a high potential for abuse;

(2) the substance has currently accepted medical use in treatment in the United States; and

(3) abuse of the substance may lead to severe psychological or physical dependence.

(c) The commissioner shall place a substance in Schedule III if the commissioner finds that:

(1) the substance has a potential for abuse less than that of the substances listed in Schedules I and II;

(2) the substance has currently accepted medical use in treatment in the United States; and

(3) abuse of the substance may lead to moderate or low physical dependence or high psychological dependence.

(d) The commissioner shall place a substance in Schedule IV if the commissioner finds that:

(1) the substance has a lower potential for abuse than that of the substances listed in Schedule III;

(2) the substance has currently accepted medical use in treatment in the United States; and

(3) abuse of the substance may lead to a more limited physical or psychological dependence than that of the substances listed in Schedule III.

(e) The commissioner shall place a substance in Schedule V if the commissioner finds that the substance:

(1) has a lower potential for abuse than that of the substances listed in Schedule IV;

(2) has currently accepted medical use in treatment in the United States; and

(3) may lead to a more limited physical or psychological dependence liability than that of the substances listed in Schedule IV.

Sec. 481.0355. Emergency Scheduling; Legislative Report.

(a) Except as otherwise provided by Subsection (b) and subject to Subsection (c), the commissioner may emergency schedule a substance as a controlled substance if the commissioner determines the action is necessary to avoid an imminent hazard to the public safety.

(b) The commissioner may not emergency schedule a substance as a controlled substance under this section if:

(1) the substance is already scheduled;

(2) an exemption or approval is in effect for the substance under Section 505, Federal Food, Drug, and Cosmetic Act (21 U.S.C. Section 355); or

(3) the substance is an over-the-counter drug that qualifies for recognition as safe and effective under conditions established by federal regulations of the United States Food and Drug Administration governing over-the-counter drugs.

(c) Before emergency scheduling a substance as a controlled substance under this section, the commissioner shall consult with the Department of Public Safety and may emergency schedule the substance only in accordance with any recommendations provided by the department.

(d) In determining whether a substance poses an imminent hazard to the public safety, the commissioner shall consider:

(1) the scope, duration, symptoms, or significance of abuse;

(2) the degree of detriment that abuse of the substance may cause;

(3) whether the substance has been temporarily scheduled under federal law; and

(4) whether the substance has been temporarily or permanently scheduled under the law of another state.

(e) If the commissioner emergency schedules a substance as a controlled substance under this section, an emergency exists for purposes of Section 481.036(c) and the action takes effect on the date the schedule is published in the Texas Register.

(f) Except as otherwise provided by Subsection (f-1), an emergency scheduling under this section expires on September 1 of each odd-numbered year for any scheduling that occurs before January 1 of that year.

(f-1) The commissioner may extend the emergency scheduling of a substance under this section not more than once and for a period not to exceed one year by publishing the extension in the Texas Register. If the commissioner extends the emergency scheduling of a substance, an emergency exists for purposes of Section 481.036(c) and the action takes effect on the date the extension is published in the Texas Register.

(g) The commissioner shall post notice about each emergency scheduling of a substance or each extension of an emergency scheduling of a substance under this section on the Internet website of the Department of State Health Services.

(h) Not later than December 1 of each even-numbered year, the commissioner shall submit a report about each emergency scheduling action taken under this section during the preceding two-year period to the governor, the lieutenant governor, the speaker of the house of representatives, and each legislative standing committee with primary jurisdiction over the department and each legislative standing committee with primary jurisdiction over criminal justice matters.

Sec. 481.036. Publication of Schedules.

(a) The commissioner shall publish the schedules by filing a certified copy of the schedules with the secretary of state for publication in the Texas Register not later than the fifth working day after the date the commissioner takes action under this subchapter.

(b) Each published schedule must show changes, if any, made in the schedule since its latest publication.

Health and Safety Code

(c) An action by the commissioner that establishes or modifies a schedule under this subchapter may take effect not earlier than the 21st day after the date on which the schedule or modification is published in the Texas Register unless an emergency exists that necessitates earlier action to avoid an imminent hazard to the public safety.

Sec. 481.037. Carisoprodol.

Schedule IV includes carisoprodol.

Sec. 481.038. Alteration of Schedules by Commission [Renumbered].

Renumbered to Tex.Health & Safety Code § 481.034 by Acts 1997, 75th Leg., ch. 745 (H.B. 1070), § 4, effective January 1, 1998.

Sec. 481.039. Findings [Renumbered].

Renumbered to Tex.Health & Safety Code § 481.035 by Acts 1997, 75th Leg., ch. 745 (H.B. 1070), § 4, effective January 1, 1998.

Sec. 481.040. Publication of Schedules [Renumbered].

Renumbered to Tex.Health & Safety Code § 481.036 by Acts 1997, 75th Leg., ch. 745 (H.B. 1070), § 4, effective January 1, 1998.

SUBCHAPTER C

REGULATION OF MANUFACTURE, DISTRIBUTION, AND DISPENSATION OF CONTROLLED SUBSTANCES, CHEMICAL PRECURSORS, AND CHEMICAL LABORATORY APPARATUS

Sec. 481.061. Federal Registration Required.

(a) Except as otherwise provided by this chapter, a person who is not registered with or exempt from registration with the Federal Drug Enforcement Administration may not manufacture, distribute, prescribe, possess, analyze, or dispense a controlled substance in this state.

(b) A person who is registered with the Federal Drug Enforcement Administration to manufacture, distribute, analyze, dispense, or conduct research with a controlled substance may possess, manufacture, distribute, analyze, dispense, or conduct research with that substance to the extent authorized by the person's registration and in conformity with this chapter.

(c), (d) [Repealed by Acts 2015, 84th Leg., ch. 1268 (S.B. 195), § 25(1), effective September 1, 2016.]

Sec. 481.062. Exemptions.

(a) The following persons may possess a controlled substance under this chapter without registering with the Federal Drug Enforcement Administration:

(1) an agent or employee of a manufacturer, distributor, analyzer, or dispenser of the controlled substance who is registered with the Federal Drug Enforcement Administration and acting in the usual course of business or employment;

(2) a common or contract carrier, a warehouseman, or an employee of a carrier or warehouseman whose possession of the controlled substance is in the usual course of business or employment;

(3) an ultimate user or a person in possession of the controlled substance under a lawful order of a practitioner or in lawful possession of the controlled substance if it is listed in Schedule V;

(4) an officer or employee of this state, another state, a political subdivision of this state or another state, or the United States who is lawfully engaged in the enforcement of a law relating to a controlled substance or drug or to a customs law and authorized to possess the controlled substance in the discharge of the person's official duties;

(5) if the substance is tetrahydrocannabinol or one of its derivatives:

(A) a Department of State Health Services official, a medical school researcher, or a research program participant possessing the substance as authorized under Subchapter G; or

(B) a practitioner or an ultimate user possessing the substance as a participant in a federally approved therapeutic research program that the commissioner has reviewed and found, in writing, to contain a medically responsible research protocol; or

(6) a dispensing organization licensed under Chapter 487 that possesses low-THC cannabis.

(b) [Repealed by Acts 2015, 84th Leg., ch. 1268 (S.B. 195), § 25(1), effective September 1, 2016.]

Sec. 481.0621. Exceptions.

(a) This subchapter does not apply to an educational or research program of a school district or a public or private institution of higher education.

This subchapter does not apply to a manufacturer, wholesaler, retailer, or other person who sells, transfers, or furnishes materials covered by this subchapter to those educational or research programs.

(b) The department and the Texas Higher Education Coordinating Board shall adopt a memorandum of understanding that establishes the responsibilities of the board, the department, and the public or private institutions of higher education in implementing and maintaining a program for reporting information concerning controlled substances, controlled substance analogues, chemical precursors, and chemical laboratory apparatus used in educational or research activities of institutions of higher education.

(c) The department and the Texas Education Agency shall adopt a memorandum of understanding that establishes the responsibilities of the agency, the department, and school districts in implementing and maintaining a program for reporting information concerning controlled substances, controlled substance analogues, chemical precursors, and chemical laboratory apparatus used in educational or research activities of those schools and school districts.

Sec. 481.063. Registration Application; Issuance or Denial. [Repealed]

Sec. 481.064. Registration Fees. [Repealed]

Sec. 481.0645. Registration, Renewal, and Fees for Physicians. [Repealed]

Sec. 481.065. Authorization for Certain Activities.

(a) The director may authorize the possession, distribution, planting, and cultivation of controlled substances by a person engaged in research, training animals to detect controlled substances, or designing or calibrating devices to detect controlled substances. A person who obtains an authorization under this subsection does not commit an offense involving the possession or distribution of controlled substances to the extent that the possession or distribution is authorized.

(b) A person may conduct research with or analyze substances listed in Schedule I in this state only if the person is a practitioner registered under federal law to conduct research with or analyze those substances and the person provides the director with evidence of federal registration.

Sec. 481.066. Voluntary Surrender, Cancellation, Suspension, Probation, or Revocation of Registration. [Repealed]

Sec. 481.067. Records.

(a) A person who is registered with the Federal Drug Enforcement Administration to manufacture, distribute, analyze, or dispense a controlled substance shall keep records and maintain inventories in compliance with recordkeeping and inventory requirements of federal law and with additional rules the board or director adopts.

(b) The pharmacist-in-charge of a pharmacy shall maintain the records and inventories required by this section.

(c) A record required by this section must be made at the time of the transaction that is the basis of the record. A record or inventory required by this section must be kept or maintained for at least two years after the date the record or inventory is made.

Sec. 481.068. Confidentiality.

(a) The director may authorize a person engaged in research on the use and effects of a controlled substance to withhold the names and other identifying characteristics of individuals who are the subjects of the research. A person who obtains the authorization may not be compelled in a civil, criminal, administrative, legislative, or other proceeding to identify the individuals who are the subjects of the research for which the authorization is obtained.

(b) Except as provided by Sections 481.074 and 481.075, a practitioner engaged in authorized medical practice or research may not be required to furnish the name or identity of a patient or research subject to the department, the Department of State Health Services, or any other agency, public official, or law enforcement officer. A practitioner may not be compelled in a state or local civil, criminal, administrative, legislative, or other proceeding to furnish the name or identity of an individual that the practitioner is obligated to keep confidential.

(c) The director may not provide to a federal, state, or local law enforcement agency the name or identity of a patient or research subject whose identity could not be obtained under Subsection (b).

Sec. 481.069. Order Forms. [Repealed]

Sec. 481.070. Administering or Dispensing Schedule I Controlled Substance.

Except as permitted by this chapter, a person may not administer or dispense a controlled substance listed in Schedule I.

Sec. 481.071. Medical Purpose Required Before Prescribing, Dispensing, Delivering, or Administering Controlled Substance.

(a) A practitioner defined by Section 481.002(39)(A) may not prescribe, dispense, deliver, or administer a controlled substance or cause a controlled substance to be administered under the practitioner's direction and supervision except for a valid medical purpose and in the course of medical practice.

(b) An anabolic steroid or human growth hormone listed in Schedule III may only be:

(1) dispensed, prescribed, delivered, or administered by a practitioner, as defined by Section 481.002(39)(A), for a valid medical purpose and in the course of professional practice; or

(2) dispensed or delivered by a pharmacist according to a prescription issued by a practitioner, as defined by Section 481.002(39)(A) or (C), for a valid medical purpose and in the course of professional practice.

(c) For the purposes of Subsection (b), bodybuilding, muscle enhancement, or increasing muscle bulk or strength through the use of an anabolic steroid or human growth hormone listed in Schedule III by a person who is in good health is not a valid medical purpose.

Sec. 481.072. Medical Purpose Required Before Distributing or Dispensing Schedule V Controlled Substance.

A person may not distribute or dispense a controlled substance listed in Schedule V except for a valid medical purpose.

Sec. 481.073. Communication of Prescriptions by Agent. [Repealed]

Sec. 481.074. Prescriptions.

(a) A pharmacist may not:

(1) dispense or deliver a controlled substance or cause a controlled substance to be dispensed or delivered under the pharmacist's direction or supervision except under a valid prescription and in the course of professional practice;

(2) dispense a controlled substance if the pharmacist knows or should have known that the prescription was issued without a valid patient-practitioner relationship;

(3) fill a prescription that is not prepared or issued as prescribed by this chapter;

(4) permit or allow a person who is not a licensed pharmacist or pharmacist intern to dispense, distribute, or in any other manner deliver a controlled substance even if under the supervision of a pharmacist, except that after the pharmacist or pharmacist intern has fulfilled his professional and legal responsibilities, a nonpharmacist may complete the actual cash or credit transaction and delivery; or

(5) permit the delivery of a controlled substance to any person not known to the pharmacist, the pharmacist intern, or the person authorized by the pharmacist to deliver the controlled substance without first requiring identification of the person taking possession of the controlled substance, except as provided by Subsection (n).

(b) Except in an emergency as defined by board rule under Subsection (b-1) or as otherwise provided by Section 481.075(j) or (m) or 481.0755, a person may not dispense or administer a controlled substance without an electronic prescription that meets the requirements of and is completed by the practitioner in accordance with Section 481.075.

(b-1) In an emergency as defined by board rule, a person may dispense or administer a controlled substance on the oral or telephonically communicated prescription of a practitioner. The person who administers or dispenses the substance shall:

(1) if the person is a prescribing practitioner or a pharmacist, promptly comply with Subsection (c); or

(2) if the person is not a prescribing practitioner or a pharmacist, promptly write the oral or telephonically communicated prescription and include in the written record of the prescription the name, address, and Federal Drug Enforcement Administration number issued for prescribing a controlled substance in this state of the prescribing practitioner, all information required to be provided by a practitioner under Section 481.075(e)(1), and all information required to be provided by a dispensing pharmacist under Section 481.075(e)(2).

(b-2) In an emergency described by Subsection (b-1), an agent designated in writing by a practitioner defined by Section 481.002(39)(A) may communicate a prescription by telephone. A practitioner who designates a different agent shall designate that agent in writing and maintain the designation in the same manner in which the practitioner initially designated an agent under this subsection. On the request of a pharmacist, a practitioner shall furnish a copy of the written designation. This subsection does not relieve a practitioner or the practitioner's designated agent from the requirement

Health and Safety Code

of Subchapter A, Chapter 562, Occupations Code. A practitioner is personally responsible for the actions of the designated agent in communicating a prescription to a pharmacist.

(c) Not later than the seventh day after the date a prescribing practitioner authorizes an emergency oral or telephonically communicated prescription, the prescribing practitioner shall cause an electronic prescription, completed in the manner required by Section 481.075, to be delivered to the dispensing pharmacist at the pharmacy where the prescription was dispensed. On receipt of the electronic prescription, the pharmacist shall annotate the electronic prescription record with the original authorization and date of the emergency oral or telephonically communicated prescription.

(d) Except as specified in Subsections (e) and (f), the board, by rule and in consultation with the Texas Medical Board, shall establish the period after the date on which the prescription is issued that a person may fill a prescription for a controlled substance listed in Schedule II. A person may not refill a prescription for a substance listed in Schedule II.

(d-1) Notwithstanding Subsection (d), a prescribing practitioner may issue multiple prescriptions authorizing the patient to receive a total of up to a 90-day supply of a Schedule II controlled substance if:

(1) each separate prescription is issued for a legitimate medical purpose by a prescribing practitioner acting in the usual course of professional practice;

(2) the prescribing practitioner provides instructions on each prescription to be filled at a later date indicating the earliest date on which a pharmacy may fill each prescription;

(3) the prescribing practitioner concludes that providing the patient with multiple prescriptions in this manner does not create an undue risk of diversion or abuse; and

(4) the issuance of multiple prescriptions complies with other applicable state and federal laws.

(e) The partial filling of a prescription for a controlled substance listed in Schedule II is permissible in accordance with applicable federal law.

(f) A prescription for a Schedule II controlled substance for a patient in a long-term care facility (LTCF) or for a hospice patient with a medical diagnosis documenting a terminal illness may be filled in partial quantities to include individual dosage units. If there is any question about whether a hospice patient may be classified as having a terminal illness, the pharmacist must contact the practitioner before partially filling the prescription. Both the pharmacist and the practitioner have a corresponding responsibility to assure that the controlled substance is for a terminally ill hospice patient. The pharmacist must record the prescription in the electronic prescription record and must indicate in the electronic prescription record whether the patient is a "terminally ill hospice patient" or an "LTCF patient." A prescription that is partially filled and does not contain the notation "terminally ill hospice patient" or "LTCF patient" is considered to have been filled in violation of this chapter. For each partial filling, the dispensing pharmacist shall record in the electronic prescription record the date of the partial filling, the quantity dispensed, the remaining quantity authorized to be dispensed, and the identification of the dispensing pharmacist. Before any subsequent partial filling, the pharmacist must determine that the additional partial filling is necessary. The total quantity of Schedule II controlled substances dispensed in all partial fillings may not exceed the total quantity prescribed. Schedule II prescriptions for patients in a long-term care facility or hospice patients with a medical diagnosis documenting a terminal illness are valid for a period not to exceed 60 days following the issue date unless sooner terminated by discontinuance of the medication.

(g) A person may not dispense a controlled substance in Schedule III or IV that is a prescription drug under the Federal Food, Drug, and Cosmetic Act (21 U.S.C. Section 301 et seq.) without a prescription of a practitioner defined by Section 481.002(39)(A) or (D), except that the practitioner may dispense the substance directly to an ultimate user. A prescription for a controlled substance listed in Schedule III or IV may not be filled or refilled later than six months after the date on which the prescription is issued and may not be refilled more than five times, unless the prescription is renewed by the practitioner. A prescription under this subsection must comply with other applicable state and federal laws.

(h) A pharmacist may dispense a controlled substance listed in Schedule III, IV, or V under a prescription issued by a practitioner defined by Section 481.002(39)(C) only if the pharmacist determines that the prescription was issued for a valid medical purpose and in the course of professional practice. A prescription described by this subsection may not be filled or refilled later than six months after the date the prescription is issued and may not be refilled more than five times, unless the prescription is renewed by the practitioner.

(i) A person may not dispense a controlled substance listed in Schedule V and containing 200 milligrams or less of codeine, or any of its salts, per 100 milliliters or per 100 grams, or containing 100 milligrams or less of dihydrocodeine, or any of its salts, per 100 milliliters or per 100 grams, without the prescription of a practitioner defined by Section 481.002(39)(A), except that a practitioner may dispense the substance directly to an ultimate user. A prescription issued under this subsection may not be filled or refilled later than six months after the date the prescription is issued and may not be refilled more than five times, unless the prescription is renewed by the practitioner.

(j) A practitioner or institutional practitioner may not allow a patient, on the patient's release from the hospital, to possess a controlled substance prescribed by the practitioner unless:

(1) the substance was dispensed under a medication order while the patient was admitted to the hospital;

(2) the substance is in a properly labeled container; and

(3) the patient possesses not more than a seven-day supply of the substance.

(k) A prescription for a controlled substance must show:

(1) the quantity of the substance prescribed:

(A) numerically, if the prescription is electronic; or

(B) if the prescription is communicated orally or telephonically, as transcribed by the receiving pharmacist;

(2) the date of issue;

(2-a) if the prescription is issued for a Schedule II controlled substance to be filled at a later date under Subsection (d-1), the earliest date on which a pharmacy may fill the prescription;

(3) the name, address, and date of birth or age of the patient or, if the controlled substance is prescribed for an animal, the species of the animal and the name and address of its owner;

(4) the name and strength of the controlled substance prescribed;

(5) the directions for use of the controlled substance;

(6) the intended use of the substance prescribed unless the practitioner determines the furnishing of this information is not in the best interest of the patient; and

(7) the name, address, Federal Drug Enforcement Administration number, and telephone number of the practitioner at the practitioner's usual place of business.

(*l*) A pharmacist may exercise his professional judgment in refilling a prescription for a controlled substance in Schedule III, IV, or V without the authorization of the prescribing practitioner provided:

(1) failure to refill the prescription might result in an interruption of a therapeutic regimen or create patient suffering;

(2) either:

(A) a natural or manmade disaster has occurred which prohibits the pharmacist from being able to contact the practitioner; or

(B) the pharmacist is unable to contact the practitioner after reasonable effort;

(3) the quantity of prescription drug dispensed does not exceed a 72-hour supply;

(4) the pharmacist informs the patient or the patient's agent at the time of dispensing that the refill is being provided without such authorization and that authorization of the practitioner is required for future refills; and

(5) the pharmacist informs the practitioner of the emergency refill at the earliest reasonable time.

(*l*-1) Notwithstanding Subsection (*l*), in the event of a natural or manmade disaster, a pharmacist may dispense not more than a 30-day supply of a prescription drug, other than a controlled substance listed in Schedule II, without the authorization of the prescribing practitioner if:

(1) failure to refill the prescription might result in an interruption of a therapeutic regimen or create patient suffering;

(2) the natural or manmade disaster prohibits the pharmacist from being able to contact the practitioner;

(3) the governor has declared a state of disaster under Chapter 418, Government Code; and

(4) the Texas State Board of Pharmacy, through its executive director, has notified pharmacies in this state that pharmacists may dispense up to a 30-day supply of a prescription drug.

(*l*-2) The prescribing practitioner is not liable for an act or omission by a pharmacist in dispensing a prescription drug under Subsection (*l*-1).

(m) A pharmacist may permit the delivery of a controlled substance by an authorized delivery person, by a person known to the pharmacist, a pharmacist intern, or the authorized delivery person, or by mail to the person or address of the person authorized by the prescription to receive the controlled substance. If a pharmacist permits delivery of a controlled substance under this subsection, the pharmacist shall retain in the records of the pharmacy for a period of not less than two years:

(1) the name of the authorized delivery person, if delivery is made by that person;

(2) the name of the person known to the pharmacist, a pharmacist intern, or the authorized delivery person if delivery is made by that person; or

(3) the mailing address to which delivery is made, if delivery is made by mail.

(n) A pharmacist may permit the delivery of a controlled substance to a person not known to the pharmacist, a pharmacist intern, or the authorized delivery person without first requiring the identification of the person to whom the controlled substance is delivered if the pharmacist determines that an emergency exists and that the controlled substance is needed for the immediate well-being of the patient for whom the controlled substance is prescribed. If a pharmacist permits delivery of a controlled substance under this subsection, the pharmacist shall retain in the records of the pharmacy for a period of not less than two years all information relevant to the delivery known to the pharmacist, including the name, address, and date of birth or age of the person to whom the controlled substance is delivered.

(o) [Repealed.]

(p) [Repealed.]

(q) Each dispensing pharmacist shall send all required information to the board by electronic transfer or another form approved by the board not later than the next business day after the date the prescription is completely filled.

Sec. 481.075. Schedule II Prescriptions.

(a) A practitioner who prescribes a controlled substance listed in Schedule II shall, except as provided by Section 481.074(b-1) or 481.0755 or a rule adopted under Section 481.0761, record the prescription in an electronic prescription that includes the information required by this section.

(b) [Repealed.]

(c) [Repealed.]

(d) [Repealed.]

(e) Each prescription used to prescribe a Schedule II controlled substance must contain:

(1) information provided by the prescribing practitioner, including:

(A) the date the prescription is issued;

(B) the controlled substance prescribed;

(C) the quantity of controlled substance prescribed, shown numerically;

(D) the intended use of the controlled substance, or the diagnosis for which the controlled substance is prescribed, and the instructions for use of the substance;

(E) the practitioner's name, address, and Federal Drug Enforcement Administration number issued for prescribing a controlled substance in this state;

(F) the name, address, and date of birth or age of the person for whom the controlled substance is prescribed; and

(G) if the prescription is issued to be filled at a later date under Section 481.074(d-1), the earliest date on which a pharmacy may fill the prescription;

(2) information provided by the dispensing pharmacist, including the date the prescription is filled; and

(3) the prescribing practitioner's electronic signature or other secure method of validation authorized by federal law.

(f) [Repealed.]

(g) Except for an emergency oral or telephonically communicated prescription described by Section 481.074(b-1), the prescribing practitioner shall:

(1) record or direct a designated agent to record in the electronic prescription each item of information required to be provided by the prescribing practitioner under Subsection (e)(1), unless the practitioner determines that:

(A) under rule adopted by the board for this purpose, it is unnecessary for the practitioner or the practitioner's agent to provide the patient identification number; or

(B) it is not in the best interest of the patient for the practitioner or practitioner's agent to provide information regarding the intended use of the controlled substance or the diagnosis for which it is prescribed; and

(2) electronically sign or validate the electronic prescription as authorized by federal law and transmit the prescription to the dispensing pharmacy.

(h) In the case of an emergency oral or telephonically communicated prescription described by Section 481.074(b-1), the prescribing practitioner shall give the dispensing pharmacy the information needed to complete the electronic prescription record.

(i) [**As amended by Acts 2019, 86th Leg., chs. 1144 and 965 (H.B. 2847 and SB 683)**] Each dispensing pharmacist shall:

(1) fill in on the official prescription form or note in the electronic prescription record each item of information given orally to the dispensing pharmacy under Subsection (h) and the date the prescription is filled, and:

(A) for a written prescription, fill in the dispensing pharmacist's signature; or

(B) for an electronic prescription, appropriately record the identity of the dispensing pharmacist in the electronic prescription record;

(2) retain with the records of the pharmacy for at least two years:

(A) the official prescription form or the electronic prescription record, as applicable; and

(B) the name or other patient identification required by Section 481.074(m) or (n);

(3) send all required information, including any information required to complete an official prescription form or electronic prescription record, to the board by electronic transfer or another form approved by the board not later than the next

business day after the date the prescription is completely filled; and

(4) if the pharmacy does not dispense any controlled substance prescriptions during a period of seven consecutive days, send a report to the board indicating that the pharmacy did not dispense any controlled substance prescriptions during that period, unless the pharmacy has obtained a waiver or permission to delay reporting to the board.

(i) [**As amended by Acts 2019, 86th Leg., ch. 1105 (H.B. 2174)**]Each dispensing pharmacist shall:

(1) note in the electronic prescription record each item of information given orally to the dispensing pharmacy under Subsection (h) and the date the prescription is filled and appropriately record the identity of the dispensing pharmacist in the electronic prescription record;

(2) retain with the records of the pharmacy for at least two years:

(A) the electronic prescription record; and

(B) the name or other patient identification required by Section 481.074(m) or (n); and

(3) send all required information, including any information required to complete an electronic prescription record, to the board by electronic transfer or another form approved by the board not later than the next business day after the date the prescription is completely filled.

(j) A medication order written for a patient who is admitted to a hospital at the time the medication order is written and filled is not required to be recorded in an electronic prescription record that meets the requirements of this section.

(k) [Repealed.]

(*l*) [Repealed.]

(m) A pharmacy in this state may fill a prescription for a controlled substance listed in Schedule II issued by a practitioner in another state if:

(1) a share of the pharmacy's business involves the dispensing and delivery or mailing of controlled substances;

(2) the prescription is issued by a prescribing practitioner in the other state in the ordinary course of practice; and

(3) the prescription is filled in compliance with a written plan providing the manner in which the pharmacy may fill a Schedule II prescription issued by a practitioner in another state that:

(A) is submitted by the pharmacy to the board; and

(B) is approved by the board.

(n) A person dispensing a Schedule II controlled substance under a prescription shall provide written notice, as defined by board rule adopted under Subsection (o), on the safe disposal of controlled substance prescription drugs, unless:

(1) the Schedule II controlled substance prescription drug is dispensed at a pharmacy or other location that:

(A) is authorized to take back those drugs for safe disposal; and

(B) regularly accepts those drugs for safe disposal; or

(2) the dispenser provides to the person to whom the Schedule II controlled substance prescription drug is dispensed, at the time of dispensation and at no cost to the person:

(A) a mail-in pouch for surrendering unused controlled substance prescription drugs; or

(B) chemicals to render any unused drugs unusable or non-retrievable.

(o) The board shall adopt rules to prescribe the form of the written notice on the safe disposal of controlled substance prescription drugs required under Subsection (n). The notice must include information on locations at which Schedule II controlled substance prescription drugs are accepted for safe disposal. The notice, in lieu of listing those locations, may provide the address of an Internet website specified by the board that provides a searchable database of locations at which Schedule II controlled substance prescription drugs are accepted for safe disposal.

(p) The board may take disciplinary action against a person who fails to comply with Subsection (n).

Sec. 481.0755. Written, Oral, and Telephonically Communicated Prescriptions.

(a) Notwithstanding Sections 481.074 and 481.075, a prescription for a controlled substance is not required to be issued electronically and may be issued in writing if the prescription is issued:

(1) by a veterinarian;

(2) in circumstances in which electronic prescribing is not available due to temporary technological or electronic failure, as prescribed by board rule;

(3) by a practitioner to be dispensed by a pharmacy located outside this state, as prescribed by board rule;

(4) when the prescriber and dispenser are in the same location or under the same license;

(5) in circumstances in which necessary elements are not supported by the most recently implemented national data standard that facilitates electronic prescribing;

(6) for a drug for which the United States Food and Drug Administration requires additional information in the prescription that is not possible with electronic prescribing;

(7) for a non-patient-specific prescription pursuant to a standing order, approved protocol for drug therapy, collaborative drug management, or comprehensive medication management, in response to a public health emergency or in other circumstances in which the practitioner may issue a non-patient-specific prescription;

(8) for a drug under a research protocol;

(9) by a practitioner who has received a waiver under Section 481.0756 from the requirement to use electronic prescribing;

(10) under circumstances in which the practitioner has the present ability to submit an electronic prescription but reasonably determines that it would be impractical for the patient to obtain the drugs prescribed under the electronic prescription in a timely manner and that a delay would adversely impact the patient's medical condition; or

(11) before January 1, 2021.

(b) A dispensing pharmacist who receives a controlled substance prescription in a manner other than electronically is not required to verify that the prescription is exempt from the requirement that it be submitted electronically. The pharmacist may dispense a controlled substance pursuant to an otherwise valid written, oral, or telephonically communicated prescription consistent with the requirements of this subchapter.

(c) Except in an emergency, a practitioner must use a written prescription to submit a prescription described by Subsection (a). In an emergency, the practitioner may submit an oral or telephonically communicated prescription as authorized under Section 481.074(b-1).

(d) A written prescription for a controlled substance other than a Schedule II controlled substance must include the information required under Section 481.074(k) and the signature of the prescribing practitioner.

(e) A written prescription for a Schedule II controlled substance must be on an official prescription form and include the information required for an electronic prescription under Section 481.075(e), the signature of the practitioner, and the signature of the dispensing pharmacist after the prescription is filled.

(f) The board by rule shall authorize a practitioner to determine whether it is necessary to obtain a particular patient identification number and to provide that number on the official prescription form.

(g) On request of a practitioner, the board shall issue official prescription forms to the practitioner for a fee covering the actual cost of printing, processing, and mailing the forms. Before mailing or otherwise delivering prescription forms to a practitioner, the board shall print on each form the number of the form and any other information the board determines is necessary.

(h) Each official prescription form must be sequentially numbered.

(i) A person may not obtain an official prescription form unless the person is a practitioner as defined by Section 481.002(39)(A) or an institutional practitioner.

(j) Not more than one Schedule II prescription may be recorded on an official prescription form.

(k) Not later than the 30th day after the date a practitioner's Federal Drug Enforcement Administration number or license to practice has been denied, suspended, canceled, surrendered, or revoked, the practitioner shall return to the board all official prescription forms in the practitioner's possession that have not been used for prescriptions.

(l) Each prescribing practitioner:

(1) may use an official prescription form only to submit a prescription described by Subsection (a);

(2) shall date or sign an official prescription form only on the date the prescription is issued; and

(3) shall take reasonable precautionary measures to ensure that an official prescription form issued to the practitioner is not used by another person to violate this subchapter or a rule adopted under this subchapter.

(m) In the case of an emergency oral or telephonically communicated prescription described by Section 481.074(b-1), the prescribing practitioner shall give the dispensing pharmacy the information needed to complete the official prescription form if the pharmacy is not required to use the electronic prescription record.

(n) Each dispensing pharmacist receiving an oral or telephonically communicated prescription under Subsection (m) shall:

(1) fill in on the official prescription form each item of information given orally to the dispensing pharmacy under Subsection (m) and the date the prescription is filled and fill in the dispensing pharmacist's signature;

(2) retain with the records of the pharmacy for at least two years:

(A) the official prescription form; and

(B) the name or other patient identification required by Section 481.074(m) or (n); and

(3) send all required information, including any information required to complete an official prescription form, to the board by electronic transfer or another form approved by the board not later than the next business day after the date the prescription is completely filled.

Health and Safety Code

Sec. 481.0756. Waivers From Electronic Prescribing.

(a) The appropriate regulatory agency that issued the license, certification, or registration to a prescriber is authorized to grant a prescriber a waiver from the electronic prescribing requirement under the provisions of this section.

(b) The board shall convene an interagency workgroup that includes representatives of each regulatory agency that issues a license, certification, or registration to a prescriber.

(c) The work group described by Subsection (b) shall establish recommendations and standards for circumstances in which a waiver from the electronic prescribing requirement is appropriate and a process under which a prescriber may request and receive a waiver.

(d) The board shall adopt rules establishing the eligibility for a waiver, including:

(1) economic hardship;

(2) technological limitations not reasonably within the control of the prescriber; or

(3) other exceptional circumstances demonstrated by the prescriber.

(e) Each regulatory agency that issues a license, certification, or registration to a prescriber shall adopt rules for the granting of waivers consistent with the board rules adopted under Subsection (d).

(f) A waiver may be issued to a prescriber for a period of one year. A prescriber may reapply for a subsequent waiver not earlier than the 30th day before the date the waiver expires if the circumstances that necessitated the waiver continue.

Sec. 481.076. Official Prescription Information; Duties of Texas State Board of Pharmacy.

(a) The board may not permit any person to have access to information submitted to the board under Section 481.074(q) or 481.075 except:

(1) the board, the Texas Medical Board, the Texas Department of Licensing and Regulation, with respect to the regulation of podiatrists, the State Board of Dental Examiners, the State Board of Veterinary Medical Examiners, the Texas Board of Nursing, or the Texas Optometry Board for the purpose of:

(A) investigating a specific license holder; or

(B) monitoring for potentially harmful prescribing or dispensing patterns or practices under Section 481.0762;

(2) an authorized employee of the board engaged in the administration, investigation, or enforcement of this chapter or another law governing illicit drugs in this state or another state;

(3) the department or other law enforcement or prosecutorial official engaged in the administration, investigation, or enforcement of this chapter or another law governing illicit drugs in this state or another state, if the board is provided a warrant, subpoena, or other court order compelling the disclosure;

(4) a medical examiner conducting an investigation;

(5) provided that accessing the information is authorized under the Health Insurance Portability and Accountability Act of 1996 (Pub. L. No. 104-191) and regulations adopted under that Act:

(A) a pharmacist or a pharmacist-intern, pharmacy technician, or pharmacy technician trainee, as defined by Section 551.003, Occupations Code, acting at the direction of a pharmacist, who is inquiring about a recent Schedule II, III, IV, or V prescription history of a particular patient of the pharmacist; or

(B) a practitioner who:

(i) is a physician, dentist, veterinarian, podiatrist, optometrist, or advanced practice nurse or is a physician assistant described by Section 481.002(39)(D) or an employee or other agent of a practitioner acting at the direction of a practitioner; and

(ii) is inquiring about a recent Schedule II, III, IV, or V prescription history of a particular patient of the practitioner;

(6) a pharmacist or practitioner who is inquiring about the person's own dispensing or prescribing activity or a practitioner who is inquiring about the prescribing activity of an individual to whom the practitioner has delegated prescribing authority;

(7) one or more states or an association of states with which the board has an interoperability agreement, as provided by Subsection (j);

(8) a health care facility certified by the federal Centers for Medicare and Medicaid Services; or

(9) the patient, the patient's parent or legal guardian, if the patient is a minor, or the patient's legal guardian, if the patient is an incapacitated person, as defined by Section 1002.017(2), Estates Code, inquiring about the patient's prescription record, including persons who have accessed that record.

(a-1) A person authorized to receive information under Subsection (a)(4), (5), or (6) may access that information through a health information exchange, subject to proper security measures to ensure against disclosure to unauthorized persons.

(a-2) A person authorized to receive information under Subsection (a)(5) may include that information in any form in the medical or pharmacy record of the patient who is the subject of the information. Any information included in a patient's medical or

Health and Safety Code

pharmacy record under this subsection is subject to any applicable state or federal confidentiality or privacy laws.

(a-3) [Repealed.]

(a-4) [Repealed.]

(a-5) [Repealed.]

(a-6) A patient, the patient's parent or legal guardian, if the patient is a minor, or the patient's legal guardian, if the patient is an incapacitated person, as defined by Section 1002.017(2), Estates Code, is entitled to a copy of the patient's prescription record as provided by Subsection (a)(9), including a list of persons who have accessed that record, if a completed patient data request form and any supporting documentation required by the board is submitted to the board. The board may charge a reasonable fee for providing the copy. The board shall adopt rules to implement this subsection, including rules prescribing the patient data request form, listing the documentation required for receiving a copy of the prescription record, and setting the fee.

(b) This section does not prohibit the board from creating, using, or disclosing statistical data about information submitted to the board under this section if the board removes any information reasonably likely to reveal the identity of each patient, practitioner, or other person who is a subject of the information.

(c) The board by rule shall design and implement a system for submission of information to the board by electronic or other means and for retrieval of information submitted to the board under this section and Sections 481.074 and 481.075. The board shall use automated information security techniques and devices to preclude improper access to the information. The board shall submit the system design to the director and the Texas Medical Board for review and comment a reasonable time before implementation of the system and shall comply with the comments of those agencies unless it is unreasonable to do so.

(d) Information submitted to the board under this section may be used only for:

(1) the administration, investigation, or enforcement of this chapter or another law governing illicit drugs in this state or another state;

(2) investigatory, evidentiary, or monitoring purposes in connection with the functions of an agency listed in Subsection (a)(1);

(3) the prescribing and dispensing of controlled substances by a person listed in Subsection (a)(5); or

(4) dissemination by the board to the public in the form of a statistical tabulation or report if all information reasonably likely to reveal the identity of each patient, practitioner, or other person who is a subject of the information has been removed.

(e) The board shall remove from the information retrieval system, destroy, and make irretrievable the record of the identity of a patient submitted under this section to the board not later than the end of the 36th calendar month after the month in which the identity is entered into the system. However, the board may retain a patient identity that is necessary for use in a specific ongoing investigation conducted in accordance with this section until the 30th day after the end of the month in which the necessity for retention of the identity ends.

(f) If the board accesses information under Subsection (a)(2) relating to a person licensed or regulated by an agency listed in Subsection (a)(1), the board shall notify and cooperate with that agency regarding the disposition of the matter before taking action against the person, unless the board determines that notification is reasonably likely to interfere with an administrative or criminal investigation or prosecution.

(g) If the board provides access to information under Subsection (a)(3) relating to a person licensed or regulated by an agency listed in Subsection (a)(1), the board shall notify that agency of the disclosure of the information not later than the 10th working day after the date the information is disclosed.

(h) If the board withholds notification to an agency under Subsection (f), the board shall notify the agency of the disclosure of the information and the reason for withholding notification when the board determines that notification is no longer likely to interfere with an administrative or criminal investigation or prosecution.

(i) Information submitted to the board under Section 481.074(q) or 481.075 is confidential and remains confidential regardless of whether the board permits access to the information under this section.

(j) The board may enter into an interoperability agreement with one or more states or an association of states authorizing the board to access prescription monitoring information maintained or collected by the other state or states or the association, including information maintained on a central database such as the National Association of Boards of Pharmacy Prescription Monitoring Program InterConnect. Pursuant to an interoperability agreement, the board may authorize the prescription monitoring program of one or more states or an association of states to access information submitted to the board under Sections 481.074(q) and 481.075, including by submitting or sharing information through a central database such as the

National Association of Boards of Pharmacy Prescription Monitoring Program InterConnect.

(k) A person authorized to access information under Subsection (a)(4) or (5) who is registered with the board for electronic access to the information is entitled to directly access the information available from other states pursuant to an interoperability agreement described by Subsection (j).

Sec. 481.0761. Rules; Authority to Contract.

(a) The board shall by rule establish and revise as necessary a standardized database format that may be used by a pharmacy to transmit the information required by Sections 481.074(q) and 481.075(i) to the board electronically or to deliver the information on storage media, including disks, tapes, and cassettes.

(b) The director shall consult with the Department of State Health Services, the Texas State Board of Pharmacy, and the Texas Medical Board and by rule may:

(1) remove a controlled substance listed in Schedules II through V from the official prescription program, if the director determines that the burden imposed by the program substantially outweighs the risk of diversion of the particular controlled substance; or

(2) return a substance previously removed from Schedules II through V to the official prescription program, if the director determines that the risk of diversion substantially outweighs the burden imposed by the program on the particular controlled substance.

(c) The board by rule may:

(1) establish a procedure for the issuance of multiple prescriptions of a Schedule II controlled substance under Section 481.074(d-1);

(2) remove from or return to the official prescription program any aspect of a practitioner's or pharmacist's hospital practice, including administering or dispensing;

(3) waive or delay any requirement relating to the time or manner of reporting;

(4) establish compatibility protocols for electronic data transfer hardware, software, or format, including any necessary modifications for participation in a database described by Section 481.076(j);

(5) establish a procedure to control the release of information under Sections 481.074, 481.075, and 481.076; and

(6) establish a minimum level of prescription activity below which a reporting activity may be modified or deleted.

(d) The board by rule shall authorize a practitioner to determine whether it is necessary to obtain a particular patient identification number and to provide that number in the electronic prescription record.

(e) In adopting a rule relating to the electronic transfer of information under this subchapter, the board shall consider the economic impact of the rule on practitioners and pharmacists and, to the extent permitted by law, act to minimize any negative economic impact, including the imposition of costs related to computer hardware or software or to the transfer of information.

(f) The board may authorize a contract between the board and another agency of this state or a private vendor as necessary to ensure the effective operation of the official prescription program.

(g) The board may adopt rules providing for a person authorized to access information under Section 481.076(a)(5) to be enrolled in electronic access to the information described by Section 481.076(a) at the time the person obtains or renews the person's applicable professional or occupational license or registration.

(h) The board, in consultation with the department and the regulatory agencies listed in Section 481.076(a)(1), shall identify prescribing practices that may be potentially harmful and patient prescription patterns that may suggest drug diversion or drug abuse. The board shall determine the conduct that constitutes a potentially harmful prescribing pattern or practice and develop indicators for levels of prescriber or patient activity that suggest a potentially harmful prescribing pattern or practice may be occurring or drug diversion or drug abuse may be occurring.

(i) The board, based on the indicators developed under Subsection (h), may send an electronic notification to a dispenser or prescriber if the information submitted under Section 481.074(q) or 481.075 indicates a potentially harmful prescribing pattern or practice may be occurring or drug diversion or drug abuse may be occurring.

(j) The board by rule may develop guidelines identifying behavior suggesting a patient is obtaining controlled substances that indicate drug diversion or drug abuse is occurring. A pharmacist who observes behavior described by this subsection by a person who is to receive a controlled substance shall access the information under Section 481.076(a)(5) regarding the patient for whom the substance is to be dispensed.

(k) The board by rule may develop guidelines identifying patterns that may indicate that a particular patient to whom a controlled substance is prescribed or dispensed is engaging in drug abuse or drug diversion. These guidelines may be based on the frequency of prescriptions issued to and filled by the patient, the types of controlled substances prescribed, and the number of prescribers who prescribe controlled substances to the patient. The board may, based on the guidelines developed under this subsection, send a prescriber or dispenser an electronic notification if there is reason to believe that a particular patient is engaging in drug abuse or drug diversion.

Sec. 481.0762. Monitoring by Regulatory Agency.

(a) Each regulatory agency that issues a license, certification, or registration to a prescriber shall promulgate specific guidelines for prescribers regulated by that agency for the responsible prescribing of opioids, benzodiazepines, barbiturates, or carisoprodol.

(b) A regulatory agency that issues a license, certification, or registration to a prescriber shall periodically access the information submitted to the board under Sections 481.074(q) and 481.075 to determine whether a prescriber is engaging in potentially harmful prescribing patterns or practices.

(c) If the board sends a prescriber an electronic notification authorized under Section 481.0761(i), the board shall immediately send an electronic notification to the appropriate regulatory agency.

(d) In determining whether a potentially harmful prescribing pattern or practice is occurring, the appropriate regulatory agency, at a minimum, shall consider:

(1) the number of times a prescriber prescribes opioids, benzodiazepines, barbiturates, or carisoprodol; and

(2) for prescriptions described by Subdivision (1), patterns of prescribing combinations of those drugs and other dangerous combinations of drugs identified by the board.

(e) If, during a periodic check under this section, the regulatory agency finds evidence that a prescriber may be engaging in potentially harmful prescribing patterns or practices, the regulatory agency may notify that prescriber.

(f) A regulatory agency may open a complaint against a prescriber if the agency finds evidence during a periodic check under this section that the prescriber is engaging in conduct that violates this subchapter or any other statute or rule.

Sec. 481.0763. Registration by Regulatory Agency.

A regulatory agency that issues a license, certification, or registration to a prescriber or dispenser shall provide the board with any necessary information for each prescriber or dispenser, including contact information for the notifications described by Sections 481.0761(i) and (k), to register the prescriber or dispenser with the system by which the prescriber or dispenser receives information as authorized under Section 481.076(a)(5).

Sec. 481.07635. Continuing Education.

(a) A person authorized to receive information under Section 481.076(a)(5) shall, not later than the first anniversary after the person is issued a license, certification, or registration to prescribe or dispense controlled substances under this chapter, complete two hours of professional education related to approved procedures of prescribing and monitoring controlled substances.

(b) A person authorized to receive information may annually take the professional education course under this section to fulfil hours toward the ethics education requirement of the person's license, certification, or registration.

(c) The regulatory agency that issued the license, certification, or registration to a person authorized to receive information under Section 481.076(a)(5) shall approve professional education to satisfy the requirements of this section.

Sec. 481.07636. Opioid Prescription Limits.

(a) In this section, "acute pain" means the normal, predicted, physiological response to a stimulus such as trauma, disease, and operative procedures. Acute pain is time limited. The term does not include:

(1) chronic pain;

(2) pain being treated as part of cancer care;

(3) pain being treated as part of hospice or other end-of-life care; or

(4) pain being treated as part of palliative care.

(b) For the treatment of acute pain, a practitioner may not:

(1) issue a prescription for an opioid in an amount that exceeds a 10-day supply; or

(2) provide for a refill of an opioid.

(c) Subsection (b) does not apply to a prescription for an opioid approved by the United States Food and Drug Administration for the treatment of substance addiction that is issued by a practitioner for the treatment of substance addiction.

(d) A dispenser is not subject to criminal, civil, or administrative penalties for dispensing or refusing to dispense a controlled substance under a prescription that exceeds the limits provided by Subsection (b).

Sec. 481.0764. Duties of Prescribers, Pharmacists, and Related Health Care Practitioners.

(a) A person authorized to receive information under Section 481.076(a)(5), other than a veterinarian, shall access that information with respect to the patient before prescribing or dispensing opioids, benzodiazepines, barbiturates, or carisoprodol.

(b) A person authorized to receive information under Section 481.076(a)(5) may access that information with respect to the patient before prescribing or dispensing any controlled substance.

(c) A veterinarian authorized to access information under Subsection (b) regarding a controlled substance may access the information for prescriptions dispensed only for the animals of an owner and may not consider the personal prescription history of the owner.

(d) A violation of Subsection (a) is grounds for disciplinary action by the regulatory agency that issued a license, certification, or registration to the person who committed the violation.

(e) This section does not grant a person the authority to issue prescriptions for or dispense controlled substances.

(f) **[Expires August 31, 2023]** A prescriber or dispenser whose practice includes the prescription or dispensation of opioids shall annually attend at least one hour of continuing education covering best practices, alternative treatment options, and multi-modal approaches to pain management that may include physical therapy, psychotherapy, and other treatments. The board shall adopt rules to establish the content of continuing education described by this subsection. The board may collaborate with private and public institutions of higher education and hospitals in establishing the content of the continuing education. This subsection expires August 31, 2023.

Sec. 481.0765. Exceptions.

(a) A prescriber is not subject to the requirements of Section 481.0764(a) if:

(1) the patient has been diagnosed with cancer or sickle cell disease or the patient is receiving hospice care; and

(2) the prescriber clearly notes in the prescription record that the patient was diagnosed with cancer or sickle cell disease or is receiving hospice care, as applicable.

(b) A dispenser is not subject to the requirements of Section 481.0764(a) if it is clearly noted in the prescription record that the patient has been diagnosed with cancer or sickle cell disease or is receiving hospice care.

(c) A prescriber or dispenser is not subject to the requirements of Section 481.0764(a) and a dispenser is not subject to a rule adopted under Section 481.0761(j) if the prescriber or dispenser makes a good faith attempt to comply but is unable to access the information under Section 481.076(a)(5) because of circumstances outside the control of the prescriber or dispenser.

Sec. 481.0766. Reports of Wholesale Distributors.

(a) A wholesale distributor shall report to the board the distribution of all Schedules II, III, IV, and V controlled substances by the distributor to a person in this state. The distributor shall report the information to the board in the same format and with the same frequency as the information is reported to the Federal Drug Enforcement Administration.

(b) Information reported to the board under Subsection (a) is confidential and not subject to disclosure under Chapter 552, Government Code.

(c) The board shall make the information reported under Subsection (a) available to the State Board of Veterinary Medical Examiners for the purpose of routine inspections and investigations.

Sec. 481.0767. Advisory Committee.

(a) The board shall establish an advisory committee to make recommendations regarding information submitted to the board and access to that information under Sections 481.074, 481.075, 481.076, and 481.0761, including recommendations for:

(1) operational improvements to the electronic system that stores the information, including implementing best practices and improvements that address system weaknesses and workflow challenges;

(2) resolutions to identified data concerns;

(3) methods to improve data accuracy, integrity, and security and to reduce technical difficulties; and

(4) the addition of any new data set or service to the information submitted to the board or the access to that information.

(b) The board shall appoint the following members to the advisory committee:

(1) a physician licensed in this state who practices in pain management;

(2) a physician licensed in this state who practices in family medicine;

Health and Safety Code

(3) a physician licensed in this state who performs surgery;

(4) a physician licensed in this state who practices in emergency medicine at a hospital;

(5) a physician licensed in this state who practices in psychiatry;

(6) an oral and maxillofacial surgeon;

(7) a physician assistant or advanced practice registered nurse to whom a physician has delegated the authority to prescribe or order a drug;

(8) a pharmacist working at a chain pharmacy;

(9) a pharmacist working at an independent pharmacy;

(10) an academic pharmacist; and

(11) two representatives of the health information technology industry, at least one of whom is a representative of a company whose primary line of business is electronic medical records.

(c) Members of the advisory committee serve three-year terms. Each member shall serve until the member's replacement has been appointed.

(d) The advisory committee shall annually elect a presiding officer from its members.

(e) The advisory committee shall meet at least two times a year and at the call of the presiding officer or the board.

(f) A member of the advisory committee serves without compensation but may be reimbursed by the board for actual expenses incurred in performing the duties of the advisory committee.

Sec. 481.0768. Administrative Penalty: Disclosure or Use of Information.

(a) A person authorized to receive information under Section 481.076(a) may not disclose or use the information in a manner not authorized by this subchapter or other law.

(b) A regulatory agency that issues a license, certification, or registration to a prescriber or dispenser shall periodically update the administrative penalties, or any applicable disciplinary guidelines concerning the penalties, assessed by that agency for conduct that violates Subsection (a).

(c) The agency shall set the penalties in an amount sufficient to deter the conduct.

Sec. 481.0769. Criminal Offenses Related to Prescription Information.

(a) A person authorized to receive information under Section 481.076(a) commits an offense if the person discloses or uses the information in a manner not authorized by this subchapter or other law.

(b) A person requesting information under Section 481.076(a-6) commits an offense if the person makes a material misrepresentation or fails to disclose a material fact in the request for information under that subsection.

(c) An offense under Subsection (a) is a Class A misdemeanor.

(d) An offense under Subsection (b) is a Class C misdemeanor.

Sec. 481.077. Chemical Precursor Records and Reports.

(a) Except as provided by Subsection (*l*), a person who sells, transfers, or otherwise furnishes a chemical precursor to another person shall make an accurate and legible record of the transaction and maintain the record for at least two years after the date of the transaction.

(b) The director by rule may:

(1) name an additional chemical substance as a chemical precursor for purposes of Subsection (a) if the director determines that public health and welfare are jeopardized by evidenced proliferation or use of the chemical substance in the illicit manufacture of a controlled substance or controlled substance analogue; or

(2) exempt a chemical precursor from the requirements of Subsection (a) if the director determines that the chemical precursor does not jeopardize public health and welfare or is not used in the illicit manufacture of a controlled substance or a controlled substance analogue.

(b-1) If the director names a chemical substance as a chemical precursor for purposes of Subsection (a) or designates a substance as an immediate precursor, a substance that is a precursor of the chemical precursor or the immediate precursor is not subject to control solely because it is a precursor of the chemical precursor or the immediate precursor.

(c) This section does not apply to a person to whom a registration has been issued by the Federal Drug Enforcement Agency or who is exempt from such registration.

(d) Before selling, transferring, or otherwise furnishing to a person in this state a chemical precursor subject to Subsection (a), a manufacturer, wholesaler, retailer, or other person shall:

(1) if the recipient does not represent a business, obtain from the recipient:

(A) the recipient's driver's license number or other personal identification certificate number, date of birth, and residential or mailing address, other than a post office box number, from a driver's license or personal identification certificate issued by the department that contains a photograph of the recipient;

Health and Safety Code

(B) the year, state, and number of the motor vehicle license of the motor vehicle owned or operated by the recipient;

(C) a complete description of how the chemical precursor is to be used; and

(D) the recipient's signature; or

(2) if the recipient represents a business, obtain from the recipient:

(A) a letter of authorization from the business that includes the business license or comptroller tax identification number, address, area code, and telephone number and a complete description of how the chemical precursor is to be used; and

(B) the recipient's signature; and

(3) for any recipient, sign as a witness to the signature and identification of the recipient.

(e) [Repealed.]

(f) [Repealed.]

(g) [Repealed.]

(h) [Repealed.]

(i) A manufacturer, wholesaler, retailer, or other person who discovers a loss or theft of a chemical precursor subject to Subsection (a) shall:

(1) submit a report of the transaction to the director in accordance with department rule; and

(2) include in the report:

(A) any difference between the amount of the chemical precursor actually received and the amount of the chemical precursor shipped according to the shipping statement or invoice; or

(B) the amount of the loss or theft.

(j) A report under Subsection (i) must:

(1) be made not later than the third day after the date that the manufacturer, wholesaler, retailer, or other person learns of the discrepancy, loss, or theft; and

(2) if the discrepancy, loss, or theft occurred during a shipment of the chemical precursor, include the name of the common carrier or person who transported the chemical precursor and the date that the chemical precursor was shipped.

(k) A manufacturer, wholesaler, retailer, or other person who sells, transfers, or otherwise furnishes any chemical precursor subject to Subsection (a), or a commercial purchaser or other person who receives a chemical precursor subject to Subsection (a):

(1) shall maintain records and inventories in accordance with rules established by the director;

(2) shall allow a member of the department or a peace officer to conduct audits and inspect records of purchases and sales and all other records made in accordance with this section at any reasonable time; and

(3) may not interfere with the audit or with the full and complete inspection or copying of those records.

(*l*) This section does not apply to the sale or transfer of any compound, mixture, or preparation containing ephedrine, pseudoephedrine, or norpseudoephedrine that is in liquid, liquid capsule, or liquid gel capsule form.

Sec. 481.0771. Records and Reports on Pseudoephedrine.

(a) A wholesaler who sells, transfers, or otherwise furnishes a product containing ephedrine, pseudoephedrine, or norpseudoephedrine to a retailer shall:

(1) before delivering the product, obtain from the retailer the retailer's address, area code, and telephone number; and

(2) make an accurate and legible record of the transaction and maintain the record for at least two years after the date of the transaction.

(b) The wholesaler shall make all records available to the director in accordance with department rule, including:

(1) the information required by Subsection (a)(1);

(2) the amount of the product containing ephedrine, pseudoephedrine, or norpseudoephedrine delivered; and

(3) any other information required by the director.

(c) Not later than 10 business days after receipt of an order for a product containing ephedrine, pseudoephedrine, or norpseudoephedrine that requests delivery of a suspicious quantity of the product as determined by department rule, a wholesaler shall submit to the director a report of the order in accordance with department rule.

(d) A wholesaler who, with reckless disregard for the duty to report, fails to report as required by Subsection (c) may be subject to disciplinary action in accordance with department rule.

Sec. 481.078. Chemical Precursor Transfer Permit. [Repealed]

Sec. 481.079. Offense: Unlawful Transfer or Receipt of Chemical Precursor [Repealed].

Repealed by Acts 1997, 75th Leg., ch. 745 (H.B. 1070), § 37, effective January 1, 1998.

Sec. 481.080. Chemical Laboratory Apparatus Record-Keeping Requirements.

(a) A manufacturer, wholesaler, retailer, or other person who sells, transfers, or otherwise furnishes a chemical laboratory apparatus shall make an accurate and legible record of the transaction and maintain the record for at least two years after the date of the transaction.

(b) The director may adopt rules to implement this section.

(c) The director by rule may:

(1) name an additional item of equipment as a chemical laboratory apparatus for purposes of Subsection (a) if the director determines that public health and welfare are jeopardized by evidenced proliferation or use of the item of equipment in the illicit manufacture of a controlled substance or controlled substance analogue; or

(2) exempt a chemical laboratory apparatus from the requirement of Subsection (a) if the director determines that the apparatus does not jeopardize public health and welfare or is not used in the illicit manufacture of a controlled substance or a controlled substance analogue.

(d) This section does not apply to a person to whom a registration has been issued by the Federal Drug Enforcement Agency or who is exempt from such registration.

(d-1) This section does not apply to a chemical manufacturer engaged in commercial research and development:

(1) whose primary business is the manufacture, use, storage, or transportation of hazardous, combustible, or explosive materials;

(2) that operates a secure, restricted location that contains a physical plant not open to the public, the ingress into which is constantly monitored by security personnel; and

(3) that holds:

(A) a Voluntary Protection Program Certification under Section (2)(b)(1), Occupational Safety and Health Act of 1970 (29 U.S.C. Section 651 et seq.); or

(B) a Facility Operations Area authorization under the Texas Risk Reduction Program (30 T.A.C. Chapter 350).

(e) Before selling, transferring, or otherwise furnishing to a person in this state a chemical laboratory apparatus subject to Subsection (a), a manufacturer, wholesaler, retailer, or other person shall:

(1) if the recipient does not represent a business, obtain from the recipient:

(A) the recipient's driver's license number or other personal identification certificate number, date of birth, and residential or mailing address, other than a post office box number, from a driver's license or personal identification certificate issued by the department that contains a photograph of the recipient;

(B) the year, state, and number of the motor vehicle license of the motor vehicle owned or operated by the recipient;

(C) a complete description of how the apparatus is to be used; and

(D) the recipient's signature; or

(2) if the recipient represents a business, obtain from the recipient:

(A) a letter of authorization from the business that includes the business license or comptroller tax identification number, address, area code, and telephone number and a complete description of how the apparatus is to be used; and

(B) the recipient's signature; and

(3) for any recipient, sign as a witness to the signature and identification of the recipient.

(f) [Repealed.]

(g) [Repealed.]

(h) [Repealed.]

(i) [Repealed.]

(j) A manufacturer, wholesaler, retailer, or other person who discovers a loss or theft of such an apparatus shall:

(1) submit a report of the transaction to the director in accordance with department rule; and

(2) include in the report:

(A) any difference between the number of the apparatus actually received and the number of the apparatus shipped according to the shipping statement or invoice; or

(B) the number of the loss or theft.

(k) A report under Subsection (j) must:

(1) be made not later than the third day after the date that the manufacturer, wholesaler, retailer, or other person learns of the discrepancy, loss, or theft; and

(2) if the discrepancy, loss, or theft occurred during a shipment of the apparatus, include the name of the common carrier or person who transported the apparatus and the date that the apparatus was shipped.

(*l*) This subsection applies to a manufacturer, wholesaler, retailer, or other person who sells, transfers, or otherwise furnishes any chemical laboratory apparatus subject to Subsection (a) and to a commercial purchaser or other person who receives such an apparatus. A person covered by this subsection:

(1) shall maintain records and inventories in accordance with rules established by the director;

(2) shall allow a member of the department or a peace officer to conduct audits and inspect records of purchases and sales and all other records made in accordance with this section at any reasonable time; and

(3) may not interfere with the audit or with the full and complete inspection or copying of those records.

Sec. 481.081. Chemical Laboratory Apparatus Transfer Permit. [Repealed]

Sec. 481.082. Unlawful Transfer or Receipt of Chemical Laboratory Apparatus [Repealed].

Repealed by Acts 1997, 75th Leg., ch. 745 (H.B. 1070), § 37, effective January 1, 1998.

SUBCHAPTER D OFFENSES AND PENALTIES

Sec. 481.101. Criminal Classification.

For the purpose of establishing criminal penalties for violations of this chapter, controlled substances, including a material, compound, mixture, or preparation containing the controlled substance, are divided into Penalty Groups 1 through 4.

Sec. 481.102. Penalty Group 1.

Penalty Group 1 consists of:

(1) the following opiates, including their isomers, esters, ethers, salts, and salts of isomers, esters, and ethers, unless specifically excepted, if the existence of these isomers, esters, ethers, and salts is possible within the specific chemical designation:

Alfentanil;
Allylprodine;
Alphacetylmethadol;
Benzethidine;
Betaprodine;
Clonitazene;
Diampromide;
Diethylthiambutene;
Difenoxin not listed in Penalty Group 3 or 4;
Dimenoxadol;
Dimethylthiambutene;
Dioxaphetyl butyrate;
Dipipanone;
Ethylmethylthiambutene;
Etonitazene;
Etoxeridine;
Furethidine;
Hydroxypethidine;
Ketobemidone;
Levophenacylmorphan;
Meprodine;
Methadol;
Moramide;
Morpheridine;
Noracymethadol;
Norlevorphanol;
Normethadone;
Norpipanone;
Phenadoxone;
Phenampromide;
Phenomorphan;
Phenoperidine;
Piritramide;
Proheptazine;
Properidine;
Propiram;
Sufentanil;
Tilidine; and
Trimeperidine;

(2) the following opium derivatives, their salts, isomers, and salts of isomers, unless specifically excepted, if the existence of these salts, isomers, and salts of isomers is possible within the specific chemical designation:

Acetorphine;
Acetyldihydrocodeine;
Benzylmorphine;
Codeine methylbromide;
Codeine-N-Oxide;
Cyprenorphine;
Desomorphine;
Dihydromorphine;
Drotebanol;
Etorphine, except hydrochloride salt;
Heroin;
Hydromorphinol;
Methyldesorphine;
Methyldihydromorphine;
Monoacetylmorphine;
Morphine methylbromide;
Morphine methylsulfonate;
Morphine-N-Oxide;
Myrophine;
Nicocodeine;
Nicomorphine;
Normorphine;
Pholcodine; and
Thebacon;

(3) the following substances, however produced, except those narcotic drugs listed in another group:

(A) Opium and opiate not listed in Penalty Group 3 or 4, and a salt, compound, derivative, or preparation of opium or opiate, other than thebaine derived butorphanol, nalmefene and its salts, naloxone and its salts, and naltrexone and its salts, but including:

Codeine not listed in Penalty Group 3 or 4;
Dihydroetorphine;
Ethylmorphine not listed in Penalty Group 3 or 4;
Granulated opium;
Hydrocodone not listed in Penalty Group 3;
Hydromorphone;
Metopon;
Morphine not listed in Penalty Group 3;
Opium extracts;

Opium fluid extracts;
Oripavine;
Oxycodone;
Oxymorphone;
Powdered opium;
Raw opium;
Thebaine; and
Tincture of opium;

(B) a salt, compound, isomer, derivative, or preparation of a substance that is chemically equivalent or identical to a substance described by Paragraph (A), other than the isoquinoline alkaloids of opium;

(C) Opium poppy and poppy straw;

(D) Cocaine, including:

(i) its salts, its optical, position, and geometric isomers, and the salts of those isomers;

(ii) coca leaves and a salt, compound, derivative, or preparation of coca leaves; and

(iii) a salt, compound, derivative, or preparation of a salt, compound, or derivative that is chemically equivalent or identical to a substance described by Subparagraph (i) or (ii), other than decocainized coca leaves or extractions of coca leaves that do not contain cocaine or ecgonine; and

(E) concentrate of poppy straw, meaning the crude extract of poppy straw in liquid, solid, or powder form that contains the phenanthrine alkaloids of the opium poppy;

(4) the following opiates, including their isomers, esters, ethers, salts, and salts of isomers, if the existence of these isomers, esters, ethers, and salts is possible within the specific chemical designation:

Acetyl-alpha-methylfentanyl (N-[1-(1-methyl-2-phenethyl)-4-piperidinyl]-N-phenylacetamide);
Alpha-methylthiofentanyl (N-[1-methyl-2-(2- thienyl)ethyl-4-piperidinyl]-N-phenylpropanamide);
Alphaprodine;
Anileridine;
Beta-hydroxyfentanyl (N-[1-(2-hydroxy-2- phenethyl)-4-piperidinyl] -N-phenylpropanamide);
Beta-hydroxy-3-methylfentanyl;
Bezitramide;
Carfentanil;
Dihydrocodeine not listed in Penalty Group 3 or 4;
Diphenoxylate not listed in Penalty Group 3 or 4;
Isomethadone;
Levomethorphan;
Levorphanol;
Metazocine;
Methadone;
Methadone-Intermediate, 4-cyano-2-dimethylamino- 4, 4-diphenyl butane;
3-methylfentanyl(N-[3-methyl-1-(2-phenylethyl)- 4-piperidyl]-N-phenylpropanamide);
3-methylthiofentanyl(N-[3-methyl-1-(2-thienyl) ethyl-4-piperidinyl]-N-phenylpropanamide);
Moramide-Intermediate, 2-methyl-3-morpholino-1, 1-diphenyl-propane-carboxylic acid;
Para-fluorofentanyl(N-(4-fluorophenyl)-N-1-(2-phenylethyl)-4-piperidinylpropanamide);
PEPAP (1-(2-phenethyl)-4-phenyl-4- acetoxypiperidine);
Pethidine (Meperidine);
Pethidine-Intermediate-A, 4-cyano-1-methyl-4-phenylpiperidine;
Pethidine-Intermediate-B, ethyl-4- phenylpiperidine-4 carboxylate;
Pethidine-Intermediate-C, 1-methyl-4-phenylpiperidine-4-carboxylic acid;
Phenazocine;
Piminodine;
Racemethorphan;
Racemorphan;
Remifentanil; and
Thiofentanyl(N-phenyl-N-[1-(2-thienyl)ethyl-4-piperidinyl]-propanamide);

(5) Flunitrazepam (trade or other name: Rohypnol);

(6) Methamphetamine, including its salts, optical isomers, and salts of optical isomers;

(7) Phenylacetone and methylamine, if possessed together with intent to manufacture methamphetamine;

(8) Phencyclidine, including its salts;

(9) Gamma hydroxybutyric acid (some trade or other names: gamma hydroxybutyrate, GHB), including its salts;

(10) Ketamine;

(11) Phenazepam;

(12) U-47700;

(13) AH-7921;

(14) ADB-FUBINACA;

(15) AMB-FUBINACA; and

(16) MDMB-CHMICA.

Sec. 481.1021. Penalty Group 1-A.

(a) Penalty Group 1-A consists of:

(1) lysergic acid diethylamide (LSD), including its salts, isomers, and salts of isomers; and

(2) compounds structurally derived from 2,5-dimethoxyphenethylamine by substitution at the 1-amino nitrogen atom with a benzyl substituent, including:

(A) compounds further modified by:

(i) substitution in the phenethylamine ring at the 4-position to any extent (including alkyl, alkoxy, alkylenedioxy, haloalkyl, or halide substituents); or

(ii) substitution in the benzyl ring to any extent (including alkyl, alkoxy, alkylenedioxy, haloalkyl, or halide substituents); and

(B) by example, compounds such as:

4-Bromo-2,5-dimethoxy-N-(2-methoxybenzyl) phenethylamine (trade or other names: 25B-NBOMe, 2C-B-NBOMe);

4-Chloro-2,5-dimethoxy-N-(2-methoxybenzyl) phenethylamine (trade or other names: 25C-NBOMe, 2C-C-NBOMe);

2,5-Dimethoxy-4-methyl-N-(2-methoxybenzyl) phenethylamine (trade or other names: 25D-NBOMe, 2C-D-NBOMe);

4-Ethyl-2,5-dimethoxy-N-(2-methoxybenzyl) phenethylamine (trade or other names: 25E-NBOMe, 2C-E-NBOMe);

2,5-Dimethoxy-N-(2- methoxybenzyl)phenethylamine (some trade and other names: 25H-NBOMe, 2C-H-NBOMe);

4-Iodo-2,5-dimethoxy-N-(2-methoxybenzyl) phenethylamine (some trade and other names: 25I-NBOMe, 2C-I-NBOMe);

4-Iodo-2,5-dimethoxy-N- benzylphenethylamine (trade or other name: 25I-NB);

4-Iodo-2,5-dimethoxy-N-(2,3- methylenedioxybenzyl)phenethylamine (trade or other name: 25I-NBMD);

4-Iodo-2,5-dimethoxy-N-(2- fluorobenzyl) phenethylamine (trade or other name: 25I-NBF);

4-Iodo-2,5-dimethoxy-N-(2-hydroxybenzyl) phenethylamine (trade or other name: 25I-NBOH);

2,5-Dimethoxy-4-nitro-N-(2-methoxybenzyl) phenethylamine (trade or other names: 25N-NBOMe, 2C-N-NBOMe); and

2,5-Dimethoxy-4-(n)-propyl-N-(2- methoxybenzyl)phenethylamine (some trade and other names: 25P-NBOMe, 2C-P-NBOMe).

(b) To the extent Subsection (a)(2) conflicts with another provision of this subtitle or another law, the other provision or the other law prevails.

Sec. 481.1022. Penalty Group 1-B.

Penalty Group 1-B consists of fentanyl, alphamethylfentanyl, and any other derivative of fentanyl.

Sec. 481.103. Penalty Group 2.

(a) Penalty Group 2 consists of:

(1) any quantity of the following hallucinogenic substances, their salts, isomers, and salts of isomers, unless specifically excepted, if the existence of these salts, isomers, and salts of isomers is possible within the specific chemical designation:

5-(2-aminopropyl)benzofuran (5-APB);

6-(2-aminopropyl)benzofuran (6-APB);

5-(2-aminopropyl)-2,3-dihydrobenzofuran (5-APDB);

6-(2-aminopropyl)-2,3-dihydrobenzofuran (6-APDB);

5-(2-aminopropyl)indole (5-IT,5-API);

6-(2-aminopropyl)indole (6-IT,6-API);

1-(benzofuran-5-yl)-N-methylpropan-2-amine (5-MAPB);

1-(benzofuran-6-yl)-N-methylpropan-2-amine (6-MAPB);

Benzothiophenylcyclohexylpiperidine (BTCP);

8-bromo-alpha-methyl-benzo[1,2-b:4,5-b']difuran- 4-ethanamine (trade or other name: Bromo-DragonFLY);

Desoxypipradrol (2-benzhydrylpiperidine);

2, 5-dimethoxyamphetamine (some trade or other names: 2, 5-dimethoxy-alpha-methylpheneth ylamine; 2, 5-DMA);

Diphenylprolinol (diphenyl(pyrrolidin-2-yl) methanol, D2PM);

Dronabinol (synthetic) in sesame oil and encapsulated in a soft gelatin capsule in a U.S. Food and Drug Administration approved drug product (some trade or other names for Dronabinol: (a6aR-trans)-6a,7,8,10a-tetrahydro- 6,6, 9- trimethyl-3-pentyl-6H- dibenzo [b,d]pyran-1-ol or (-)-delta-9- (trans)-tetrahydrocannabinol);

Ethylamine Analog of Phencyclidine (some trade or other names: N-ethyl-1-phenylcyclohexylamine, (1- phenylcyclohexyl) ethylamine, N-(1-phenylcyclohexyl) ethylamine, cyclohexamine, PCE);

2-ethylamino-2-(3-methoxyphenyl)cyclohexanone (trade or other name: methoxetamine);

Ibogaine (some trade or other names: 7-Ethyl-6, 6, beta 7, 8, 9, 10, 12, 13-octahydro-2-methoxy-6, 9-methano-5H- pyrido [1', 2':1, 2] azepino [5, 4-b] indole; tabernanthe iboga.);

5-iodo-2-aminoindane (5-IAI);

Mescaline;

5-methoxy-3, 4-methylenedioxy amphetamine;

4-methoxyamphetamine (some trade or other names: 4-methoxy-alpha-methylphenethylamine; paramethoxyamphetamine; PMA);

4-methoxymethamphetamine (PMMA);

2-(2-methoxyphenyl)-2-(methylamino)cyclo hexanone (some trade and other names: 2-MeO-ketamine; methoxyketamine);

1-methyl- 4-phenyl-4-propionoxypiperidine (MPPP, PPMP);

4-methyl-2, 5-dimethoxyamphetamine (some trade and other names: 4-methyl-2, 5-dimethoxy-alpha- methylphenethylamine; "DOM"; "STP");

3,4-methylenedioxy methamphetamine (MDMA, MDM);

Health and Safety Code

3,4-methylenedioxy amphetamine;

3,4-methylenedioxy N-ethylamphetamine (Also known as N-ethyl MDA);

5,6-methylenedioxy-2-aminoindane (MDAI);

Nabilone (Another name for nabilone: (+)-trans-3-(1,1-dimethylheptyl)- 6,6a, 7,8,10,10a-hexahydro-1-hydroxy- 6, 6-dimethyl-9H-dibenzo[b,d] pyran-9-one;

N-benzylpiperazine (some trade or other names: BZP; 1-benzylpiperazine);

N-ethyl-3-piperidyl benzilate;

N-hydroxy-3,4-methylenedioxyamphetamine (Also known as N-hydroxy MDA);

4-methylaminorex;

N-methyl-3-piperidyl benzilate;

Parahexyl (some trade or other names: 3-Hexyl-1- hydroxy-7, 8, 9, 10-tetrahydro-6, 6, 9-trimethyl-6H-dibenzo [b, d] pyran; Synhexyl);

1-Phenylcyclohexylamine;

1-Piperidinocyclohexanecarbonitrile (PCC);

Pyrrolidine Analog of Phencyclidine (some trade or other names: 1-(1-phenylcyclohexyl)-pyrrolidine, PCPy, PHP);

Tetrahydrocannabinols, other than marihuana, and synthetic equivalents of the substances contained in the plant, or in the resinous extractives of Cannabis, or synthetic substances, derivatives, and their isomers with similar chemical structure and pharmacological activity such as:

delta-1 cis or trans tetrahydrocannabinol, and their optical isomers;

delta-6 cis or trans tetrahydrocannabinol, and their optical isomers;

delta-3, 4 cis or trans tetrahydrocannabinol, and its optical isomers; or

compounds of these structures, regardless of numerical designation of atomic positions, since nomenclature of these substances is not internationally standardized;

Thiophene Analog of Phencyclidine (some trade or other names: 1-[1-(2-thienyl) cyclohexyl] piperidine; 2-Thienyl Analog of Phencyclidine; TPCP, TCP);

1-pyrrolidine (some trade or other name: TCPy);

1-(3-trifluoromethylphenyl)piperazine (trade or other name: TFMPP); and

3,4,5-trimethoxy amphetamine;

(2) Phenylacetone (some trade or other names: Phenyl-2-propanone; P2P, Benzymethyl ketone, methyl benzyl ketone);

(3) unless specifically excepted or unless listed in another Penalty Group, a material, compound, mixture, or preparation that contains any quantity of the following substances having a potential for abuse associated with a depressant or stimulant effect on the central nervous system:

Aminorex (some trade or other names: aminoxaphen; 2-amino-5-phenyl-2-oxazoline; 4,5-dihydro-5-phenyl-2-oxazolamine);

Amphetamine, its salts, optical isomers, and salts of optical isomers;

Cathinone (some trade or other names: 2-amino-1-phenyl-1-propanone, alpha-aminopropiophenone, 2- aminopropiophenone);

Etaqualone and its salts;

Etorphine Hydrochloride;

Fenethylline and its salts;

Lisdexamfetamine, including its salts, isomers, and salts of isomers;

Mecloqualone and its salts;

Methaqualone and its salts;

Methcathinone (some trade or other names: 2-methylamino-propiophenone; alpha-(methylamino) propriophenone; 2-(methylamino)-1-phenylpropan-1-one; alpha-N- methylaminopropriophenone; monomethylpropion; ephedrone, N- methylcathinone; methylcathinone; AL-464; AL-422; AL-463; and UR 1431);

N-Ethylamphetamine, its salts, optical isomers, and salts of optical isomers; and

N,N-dimethylamphetamine (some trade or other names: N,N,alpha-trimethylbenzeneethanamine;

N,N,alpha-trimethylphenethylamine), its salts, optical isomers, and salts of optical isomers;

(4) any compound structurally derived from 2-aminopropanal by substitution at the 1-position with any monocyclic or fused-polycyclic ring system, including:

(A) compounds further modified by:

(i) substitution in the ring system to any extent (including alkyl, alkoxy, alkylenedioxy, haloalkyl, or halide substituents), whether or not further substituted in the ring system by other substituents;

(ii) substitution at the 3-position with an alkyl substituent; or

(iii) substitution at the 2-amino nitrogen atom with alkyl, benzyl, dialkyl, or methoxybenzyl groups, or inclusion of the 2-amino nitrogen atom in a cyclic structure; and

(B) by example, compounds such as:

4-Methylmethcathinone (Also known as Mephedrone);

3,4-Dimethylmethcathinone (Also known as 3,4-DMMC);

3-Fluoromethcathinone (Also known as 3-FMC);

4-Fluoromethcathinone (Also known as Flephedrone);

3,4-Methylenedioxy-N-methylcathinone (Also known as Methylone);

3,4-Methylenedioxypyrovalerone (Also known as MDPV);

Health and Safety Code

alpha-Pyrrolidinopentiophenone (Also known as alpha-PVP);

Naphthylpyrovalerone (Also known as Naphyrone);

alpha-Methylamino-valerophenone (Also known as Pentedrone);

beta-Keto-N-methylbenzodioxolylpropylamine (Also known as Butylone);

beta-Keto-N-methylbenzodioxolylpentanamine (Also known as Pentylone);

beta-Keto-Ethylbenzodioxolylbutanamine (Also known as Eutylone); and

3,4-methylenedioxy-N-ethylcathinone (Also known as Ethylone);

(5) any compound structurally derived from tryptamine (3-(2-aminoethyl)indole) or a ring-hydroxy tryptamine:

(A) by modification in any of the following ways:

(i) by substitution at the amine nitrogen atom of the sidechain to any extent with alkyl or alkenyl groups or by inclusion of the amine nitrogen atom of the side chain (and no other atoms of the side chain) in a cyclic structure;

(ii) by substitution at the carbon atom adjacent to the nitrogen atom of the side chain (alpha-position) with an alkyl or alkenyl group;

(iii) by substitution in the 6-membered ring to any extent with alkyl, alkoxy, haloalkyl, thioaklyl, alkylenedioxy, or halide substituents; or

(iv) by substitution at the 2-position of the tryptamine ring system with an alkyl substituent; and

(B) including:

(i) ethers and esters of the controlled substances listed in this subdivision; and

(ii) by example, compounds such as:

alpha-ethyltryptamine;

alpha-methyltryptamine;

Bufotenine (some trade and other names: 3-(beta-Dimethylaminoethyl)-5-hydroxyindole; 3-(2-dimethylaminoethyl)- 5- indolol; N, N-dimethylserotonin; 5-hydroxy-N, N- dimethyltryptamine; mappine);

Diethyltryptamine (some trade and other names: N, N-Diethyltryptamine, DET);

Dimethyltryptamine (trade or other name: DMT);

5-methoxy-N, N-diisopropyltryptamine (5-MeO-DiPT);

O-Acetylpsilocin (Trade or other name: 4-Aco-DMT);

Psilocin; and

Psilocybin;

(6) 2,5-Dimethoxyphenethylamine and any compound structurally derived from 2,5-Dimethoxyphenethylamine by substitution at the 4-position of the phenyl ring to any extent (including alkyl, alkoxy, alkylenedioxy, haloalkyl, or halide substituents), including, by example, compounds such as:

4-Bromo-2,5-dimethoxyphenethylamine (trade or other name: 2C-B);

4-Chloro-2,5-dimethoxyphenethylamine (trade or other name: 2C-C);

2,5-Dimethoxy-4-methylphenethylamine (trade or other name: 2C-D);

4-Ethyl-2,5-dimethoxyphenethylamine (trade or other name: 2C-E);

4-Iodo-2,5-dimethoxyphenethylamine (trade or other name: 2C-I);

2,5-Dimethoxy-4-nitrophenethylamine (trade or other name: 2C-N);

2,5-Dimethoxy-4-(n)-propylphenethylamine (trade or other name: 2C-P);

4-Ethylthio-2,5-dimethoxyphenethylamine (trade or other name: 2C-T-2);

4-Isopropylthio-2,5-dimethoxyphenethylamine (trade or other name: 2C-T-4); and

2,5-Dimethoxy-4-(n)-propylthiophenethylamine (trade or other name: 2C-T-7); and

(7) 2,5-Dimethoxyamphetamine and any compound structurally derived from 2,5-Dimethoxyamphetamine by substitution at the 4-position of the phenyl ring to any extent (including alkyl, alkoxy, alkylenedioxy, haloalkyl, or halide substituents), including, by example, compounds such as:

4-Ethylthio-2,5-dimethoxyamphetamine (trade or other name: Aleph-2);

4-Isopropylthio-2,5-dimethoxyamphetamine (trade or other name: Aleph-4);

4-Bromo-2,5-dimethoxyamphetamine (trade or other name: DOB);

4-Chloro-2,5-dimethoxyamphetamine (trade or other name: DOC);

2,5-Dimethoxy-4-ethylamphetamine (trade or other name: DOET);

4-Iodo-2,5-dimethoxyamphetamine (trade or other name: DOI);

2,5-Dimethoxy-4-methylamphetamine (trade or other name: DOM);

2,5-Dimethoxy-4-nitroamphetamine (trade or other name: DON);

4-Isopropyl-2,5-dimethoxyamphetamine (trade or other name: DOIP); and

2,5-Dimethoxy-4-(n)-propylamphetamine (trade or other name: DOPR).

(b) For the purposes of Subsection (a)(1) only, the term "isomer" includes an optical, position, or geometric isomer.

(c) To the extent Subsection (a)(4), (5), (6), or (7) conflicts with another provision or this subtitle or another law, the other provision or the other law prevails. If a substance listed in this section is also listed in another penalty group, the listing in the other penalty group controls.

(d) [Repealed.]

Sec. 481.1031. Penalty Group 2-A.

(a) In this section:

(1) "Core component" is one of the following: azaindole, benzimidazole, benzothiazole, carbazole, imidazole, indane, indazole, indene, indole, pyrazole, pyrazolopyridine, pyridine, or pyrrole.

(2) "Group A component" is one of the following: adamantane, benzene, cycloalkylmethyl, isoquinoline, methylpiperazine, naphthalene, phenyl, quinoline, tetrahydronaphthalene, tetramethylcyclopropane, amino oxobutane, amino dimethyl oxobutane, amino phenyl oxopropane, methyl methoxy oxobutane, methoxy dimethyl oxobutane, methoxy phenyl oxopropane, or an amino acid.

(3) "Link component" is one of the following functional groups: carboxamide, carboxylate, hydrazide, methanone (ketone), ethanone, methanediyl (methylene bridge), or methine.

(b) Penalty Group 2-A consists of any material, compound, mixture, or preparation that contains any quantity of a natural or synthetic chemical substance, including its salts, isomers, and salts of isomers, listed by name in this subsection or contained within one of the structural classes defined in this subsection:

(1) WIN-55,212-2;

(2) Cyclohexylphenol: any compound structurally derived from 2-(3-hydroxycyclohexyl)phenol by substitution at the 5-position of the phenolic ring, (N-methylpiperidin-2-yl)alkyl, (4-tetrahydropyran) alkyl, or 2-(4-morpholinyl)alkyl, whether or not substituted in the cyclohexyl ring to any extent, including:

JWH-337;

JWH-344;

CP-55,940;

CP-47,497; and

analogues of CP-47,497;

(3) Cannabinol derivatives, except where contained in marihuana, including tetrahydro derivatives of cannabinol and 3-alkyl homologues of cannabinol or of its tetrahydro derivatives, such as:

Nabilone;

HU-210; and

HU-211;

(4) Tetramethylcyclopropyl thiazole: any compound structurally derived from 2,2,3,3-tetramethyl-N-(thiazol- 2-ylidene)cyclopropanecarboxamide by substitution at the nitrogen atom of the thiazole ring, whether or not further substituted in the thiazole ring to any extent, whether or not substituted in the tetramethylcyclopropyl ring to any extent, including:

A-836,339;

(5) any compound containing a core component substituted at the 1-position to any extent, and substituted at the 3-position with a link component attached to a group A component, whether or not the core component or group A component are further substituted to any extent, including:

Naphthoylindane;

Naphthoylindazole (THJ-018);

Naphthyl methyl indene (JWH-171);

Naphthoylindole (JWH-018);

Quinolinoyl pyrazole carboxylate (Quinolinyl fluoropentyl fluorophenyl pyrazole carboxylate);

Naphthoyl pyrazolopyridine; and

Naphthoylpyrrole (JWH-030);

(6) any compound containing a core component substituted at the 1-position to any extent, and substituted at the 2-position with a link component attached to a group A component, whether or not the core component or group A component are further substituted to any extent, including:

Naphthoylbenzimidazole (JWH-018 Benzimidazole); and

Naphthoylimidazole;

(7) any compound containing a core component substituted at the 3-position to any extent, and substituted at the 2-position with a link component attached to a group A component, whether or not the core component or group A component are further substituted to any extent, including:

Naphthoyl benzothiazole; and

(8) any compound containing a core component substituted at the 9-position to any extent, and substituted at the 3-position with a link component attached to a group A component, whether or not the core component or group A component are further substituted to any extent, including:

Naphthoylcarbazole (EG-018).

Sec. 481.104. Penalty Group 3.

(a) Penalty Group 3 consists of:

(1) a material, compound, mixture, or preparation that contains any quantity of the following substances having a potential for abuse associated with a stimulant effect on the central nervous system:

Methylphenidate and its salts; and

Phenmetrazine and its salts;

(2) a material, compound, mixture, or preparation that contains any quantity of the following substances having a potential for abuse associated with a depressant effect on the central nervous system:

a substance that contains any quantity of a derivative of barbituric acid, or any salt of a derivative of barbituric acid not otherwise described by this subsection;

a compound, mixture, or preparation containing amobarbital, secobarbital, pentobarbital, or any salt of any of these, and one or more active medicinal ingredients that are not listed in any penalty group;

a suppository dosage form containing amobarbital, secobarbital, pentobarbital, or any salt of any of these drugs, and approved by the United States Food and Drug Administration for marketing only as a suppository;

Alprazolam;
Amobarbital;
Bromazepam;
Camazepam;
Carisoprodol;
Chlordiazepoxide;
Chlorhexadol;
Clobazam;
Clonazepam;
Clorazepate;
Clotiazepam;
Cloxazolam;
Delorazepam;
Diazepam;
Estazolam;
Ethyl loflazepate;
Etizolam;
Fludiazepam;
Flurazepam;
Glutethimide;
Halazepam;
Haloxzolam;
Ketazolam;
Loprazolam;
Lorazepam;
Lormetazepam;
Lysergic acid, including its salts, isomers, and salts of isomers;
Lysergic acid amide, including its salts, isomers, and salts of isomers;
Mebutamate;
Medazepam;
Methyprylon;
Midazolam;
Nimetazepam;
Nitrazepam;
Nordiazepam;
Oxazepam;
Oxazolam;
Pentazocine, its salts, derivatives, or compounds or mixtures thereof;
Pentobarbital;
Pinazepam;
Prazepam;
Quazepam;
Secobarbital;
Sulfondiethylmethane;
Sulfonethylmethane;
Sulfonmethane;
Temazepam;
Tetrazepam;
Tiletamine and zolazepam in combination, and its salts. (some trade or other names for a tiletamine-zolazepam combination product: Telazol, for tiletamine: 2-(ethylamino)- 2-(2-thienyl)-cyclohexanone, and for zolazepam: 4-(2- fluorophenyl)-6, 8-dihydro -1,3,8,-trimethylpyrazolo-[3,4- e](1,4)-d diazepin-7(1H)-one, flupyrazapon);
Tramadol;
Triazolam;
Zaleplon;
Zolpidem; and
Zopiclone;

(3) Nalorphine;

(4) a material, compound, mixture, or preparation containing limited quantities of the following narcotic drugs, or any of their salts:

not more than 1.8 grams of codeine, or any of its salts, per 100 milliliters or not more than 90 milligrams per dosage unit, with an equal or greater quantity of an isoquinoline alkaloid of opium;

not more than 1.8 grams of codeine, or any of its salts, per 100 milliliters or not more than 90 milligrams per dosage unit, with one or more active, nonnarcotic ingredients in recognized therapeutic amounts;

not more than 300 milligrams of dihydrocodeinone (hydrocodone), or any of its salts, per 100 milliliters or not more than 15 milligrams per dosage unit, with a fourfold or greater quantity of an isoquinoline alkaloid of opium;

not more than 300 milligrams of dihydrocodeinone (hydrocodone), or any of its salts, per 100 milliliters or not more than 15 milligrams per dosage unit, with one or more active, nonnarcotic ingredients in recognized therapeutic amounts;

not more than 1.8 grams of dihydrocodeine, or any of its salts, per 100 milliliters or not more than 90 milligrams per dosage unit, with one or more active, nonnarcotic ingredients in recognized therapeutic amounts;

not more than 300 milligrams of ethylmorphine, or any of its salts, per 100 milliliters or not more than 15 milligrams per dosage unit, with one or more active, nonnarcotic ingredients in recognized therapeutic amounts;

not more than 500 milligrams of opium per 100 milliliters or per 100 grams, or not more than 25 milligrams per dosage unit, with one or more active, nonnarcotic ingredients in recognized therapeutic amounts;

not more than 50 milligrams of morphine, or any of its salts, per 100 milliliters or per 100 grams with one or more active, nonnarcotic ingredients in recognized therapeutic amounts; and

not more than 1 milligram of difenoxin and not less than 25 micrograms of atropine sulfate per dosage unit;

(5) a material, compound, mixture, or preparation that contains any quantity of the following substances:

Barbital;
Chloral betaine;
Chloral hydrate;
Ethchlorvynol;
Ethinamate;
Meprobamate;
Methohexital;
Methylphenobarbital (Mephobarbital);
Paraldehyde;
Petrichloral; and
Phenobarbital;

(6) Peyote, unless unharvested and growing in its natural state, meaning all parts of the plant classified botanically as Lophophora, whether growing or not, the seeds of the plant, an extract from a part of the plant, and every compound, manufacture, salt, derivative, mixture, or preparation of the plant, its seeds, or extracts;

(7) unless listed in another penalty group, a material, compound, mixture, or preparation that contains any quantity of the following substances having a stimulant effect on the central nervous system, including the substance's salts, optical, position, or geometric isomers, and salts of the substance's isomers, if the existence of the salts, isomers, and salts of isomers is possible within the specific chemical designation:

Benzphetamine;
Cathine [(+)-norpseudoephedrine];
Chlorphentermine;
Clortermine;
Diethylpropion;
Fencamfamin;
Fenfluramine;
Fenproporex;
Mazindol;
Mefenorex;
Modafinil;
Pemoline (including organometallic complexes and their chelates);
Phendimetrazine;
Phentermine;
Pipradrol;
Sibutramine; and
SPA [(-)-1-dimethylamino-1,2-diphenylethane];

(8) unless specifically excepted or unless listed in another penalty group, a material, compound, mixture, or preparation that contains any quantity of the following substance, including its salts:

Dextropropoxyphene (Alpha-(+)-4-dimethyl amino- 1,2-diphenyl-3-methyl-2-propionoxybutane);

(9) an anabolic steroid, including any drug or hormonal substance, or any substance that is chemically or pharmacologically related to testosterone, other than an estrogen, progestin, dehydroepiandrosterone, or corticosteroid, and promotes muscle growth, including the following drugs and substances and any salt, ester, or ether of the following drugs and substances:

Androstanediol;
Androstanedione;
Androstenediol;
Androstenedione;
Bolasterone;
Boldenone;
Calusterone;
Clostebol;
Dehydrochlormethyltestosterone;
Delta-1-dihydrotestosterone;
Dihydrotestosterone (4-dihydrotestosterone);
Drostanolone;
Ethylestrenol;
Fluoxymesterone;
Formebulone;
Furazabol;
13beta-ethyl-17beta-hydroxygon-4-en-3-one;
4-hydroxytestosterone;
4-hydroxy-19-nortestosterone;
Mestanolone;
Mesterolone;
Methandienone;
Methandriol;
Methenolone;
17alpha-methyl-3beta, 17 beta-dihydroxy-5alpha- androstane;
17alpha-methyl-3alpha, 17 beta-dihydroxy-5alpha- androstane;
17alpha-methyl-3beta, 17beta-dihydroxyandrost-4- ene;
17alpha-methyl-4-hydroxynandrolone;
Methyldienolone;
Methyltestosterone;
Methyltrienolone;
17alpha-methyl-delta-1-dihydrotestosterone;
Mibolerone;
Nandrolone;
Norandrostenediol;
Norandrostenedione;
Norbolethone;

Norclostebol;
Norethandrolone;
Normethandrolone;
Oxandrolone;
Oxymesterone;
Oxymetholone;
Stanozolol;
Stenbolone;
Testolactone;
Testosterone;
Tetrahydrogestrinone; and
Trenbolone; and

(10) Salvia divinorum, unless unharvested and growing in its natural state, meaning all parts of that plant, whether growing or not, the seeds of that plant, an extract from a part of that plant, and every compound, manufacture, salt, derivative, mixture, or preparation of that plant, its seeds, or extracts, including Salvinorin A.

(b) Penalty Group 3 does not include a compound, mixture, or preparation containing a stimulant substance listed in Subsection (a)(1) if the compound, mixture, or preparation contains one or more active medicinal ingredients not having a stimulant effect on the central nervous system and if the admixtures are included in combinations, quantity, proportion, or concentration that vitiate the potential for abuse of the substances that have a stimulant effect on the central nervous system.

(c) Penalty Group 3 does not include a compound, mixture, or preparation containing a depressant substance listed in Subsection (a)(2) or (a)(5) if the compound, mixture, or preparation contains one or more active medicinal ingredients not having a depressant effect on the central nervous system and if the admixtures are included in combinations, quantity, proportion, or concentration that vitiate the potential for abuse of the substances that have a depressant effect on the central nervous system.

Sec. 481.105. Penalty Group 4.

Penalty Group 4 consists of:

(1) a compound, mixture, or preparation containing limited quantities of any of the following narcotic drugs that includes one or more nonnarcotic active medicinal ingredients in sufficient proportion to confer on the compound, mixture, or preparation valuable medicinal qualities other than those possessed by the narcotic drug alone:

not more than 200 milligrams of codeine per 100 milliliters or per 100 grams;

not more than 100 milligrams of dihydrocodeine per 100 milliliters or per 100 grams;

not more than 100 milligrams of ethylmorphine per 100 milliliters or per 100 grams;

not more than 2.5 milligrams of diphenoxylate and not less than 25 micrograms of atropine sulfate per dosage unit;

not more than 15 milligrams of opium per 29.5729 milliliters or per 28.35 grams; and

not more than 0.5 milligram of difenoxin and not less than 25 micrograms of atropine sulfate per dosage unit;

(2) unless specifically excepted or unless listed in another penalty group, a material, compound, mixture, or preparation containing any quantity of the narcotic drug Buprenorphine or Butorphanol or a salt of either; and

(3) unless specifically exempted or excluded or unless listed in another penalty group, any material, compound, mixture, or preparation that contains any quantity of pyrovalerone, a substance having a stimulant effect on the central nervous system, including its salts, isomers, and salts of isomers.

Sec. 481.106. Classification of Controlled Substance Analogue.

For the purposes of the prosecution of an offense under this subchapter involving the manufacture, delivery, or possession of a controlled substance, Penalty Groups 1, 1-A, 1-B, 2, and 2-A include a controlled substance analogue that:

(1) has a chemical structure substantially similar to the chemical structure of a controlled substance listed in the applicable penalty group; or

(2) is specifically designed to produce an effect substantially similar to, or greater than, a controlled substance listed in the applicable penalty group.

Sec. 481.107. Repeat Offenders [Repealed].

Repealed by Acts 1993, 73rd Leg., ch. 900 (S.B. 1067), § 2.07, effective September 1, 1994.

Sec. 481.108. Preparatory Offenses.

Title 4, Penal Code, applies to an offense under this chapter.

Sec. 481.109. Conditional Discharge [Repealed].

Repealed by Acts 1991, 72nd Leg., ch. 141 (S.B. 11), § 6, effective September 1, 1991.

Sec. 481.110. Resentencing [Repealed].

Repealed by Acts 1991, 72nd Leg., ch. 141 (S.B. 11), § 6, effective September 1, 1991.

Sec. 481.111. Exemptions.

(a) The provisions of this chapter relating to the possession and distribution of peyote do not apply to the use of peyote by a member of the Native American Church in bona fide religious ceremonies of the church or to a person who supplies the substance to the church. An exemption granted to a member of the Native American Church under this section does not apply to a member with less than 25 percent Indian blood.

(b) The provisions of this chapter relating to the possession of denatured sodium pentobarbital do not apply to possession by personnel of a humane society or an animal control agency for the purpose of destroying injured, sick, homeless, or unwanted animals if the humane society or animal control agency is registered with the Federal Drug Enforcement Administration. The provisions of this chapter relating to the distribution of denatured sodium pentobarbital do not apply to a person registered as required by Subchapter C, who is distributing the substance for that purpose to a humane society or an animal control agency registered with the Federal Drug Enforcement Administration.

(c) A person does not violate Section 481.113, 481.116, 481.1161, 481.121, or 481.125 if the person possesses or delivers tetrahydrocannabinols or their derivatives, or drug paraphernalia to be used to introduce tetrahydrocannabinols or their derivatives into the human body, for use in a federally approved therapeutic research program.

(d) The provisions of this chapter relating to the possession and distribution of anabolic steroids do not apply to the use of anabolic steroids that are administered to livestock or poultry.

(e) Sections 481.120, 481.121, 481.122, and 481.125 do not apply to a person who engages in the acquisition, possession, production, cultivation, delivery, or disposal of a raw material used in or by-product created by the production or cultivation of low-THC cannabis if the person:

(1) for an offense involving possession only of marihuana or drug paraphernalia, is a patient for whom low-THC cannabis is prescribed under Chapter 169, Occupations Code, or the patient's legal guardian, and the person possesses low-THC cannabis obtained under a valid prescription from a dispensing organization; or

(2) is a director, manager, or employee of a dispensing organization and the person, solely in performing the person's regular duties at the organization, acquires, possesses, produces, cultivates, dispenses, or disposes of:

(A) in reasonable quantities, any low-THC cannabis or raw materials used in or by-products created by the production or cultivation of low-THC cannabis; or

(B) any drug paraphernalia used in the acquisition, possession, production, cultivation, delivery, or disposal of low-THC cannabis.

(f) For purposes of Subsection (e):

(1) "Dispensing organization" has the meaning assigned by Section 487.001.

(2) "Low-THC cannabis" has the meaning assigned by Section 169.001, Occupations Code.

Sec. 481.112. Offense: Manufacture or Delivery of Substance in Penalty Group 1.

(a) Except as authorized by this chapter, a person commits an offense if the person knowingly manufactures, delivers, or possesses with intent to deliver a controlled substance listed in Penalty Group 1.

(b) An offense under Subsection (a) is a state jail felony if the amount of the controlled substance to which the offense applies is, by aggregate weight, including adulterants or dilutants, less than one gram.

(c) An offense under Subsection (a) is a felony of the second degree if the amount of the controlled substance to which the offense applies is, by aggregate weight, including adulterants or dilutants, one gram or more but less than four grams.

(d) An offense under Subsection (a) is a felony of the first degree if the amount of the controlled substance to which the offense applies is, by aggregate weight, including adulterants or dilutants, four grams or more but less than 200 grams.

(e) An offense under Subsection (a) is punishable by imprisonment in the Texas Department of Criminal Justice for life or for a term of not more than 99 years or less than 10 years, and a fine not to exceed $100,000, if the amount of the controlled substance to which the offense applies is, by aggregate weight, including adulterants or dilutants, 200 grams or more but less than 400 grams.

(f) An offense under Subsection (a) is punishable by imprisonment in the Texas Department of Criminal Justice for life or for a term of not more than 99 years or less than 15 years, and a fine not to exceed $250,000, if the amount of the controlled substance to which the offense applies is, by aggregate weight, including adulterants or dilutants, 400 grams or more.

Sec. 481.1121. Offense: Manufacture or Delivery of Substance in Penalty Group 1-A.

(a) Except as provided by this chapter, a person commits an offense if the person knowingly manufactures, delivers, or possesses with intent to deliver a controlled substance listed in Penalty Group 1-A.

(b) An offense under this section is:

(1) a state jail felony if the number of abuse units of the controlled substance is fewer than 20;

(2) a felony of the second degree if the number of abuse units of the controlled substance is 20 or more but fewer than 80;

(3) a felony of the first degree if the number of abuse units of the controlled substance is 80 or more but fewer than 4,000; and

(4) punishable by imprisonment in the Texas Department of Criminal Justice for life or for a term of not more than 99 years or less than 15 years and a fine not to exceed $250,000, if the number of abuse units of the controlled substance is 4,000 or more.

Sec. 481.1122. Manufacture of Substance in Penalty Group 1: Presence of Child.

If it is shown at the punishment phase of a trial for the manufacture of a controlled substance listed in Penalty Group 1 that when the offense was committed a child younger than 18 years of age was present on the premises where the offense was committed:

(1) the punishments specified by Sections 481.112(b) and (c) are increased by one degree;

(2) the minimum term of imprisonment specified by Section 481.112(e) is increased to 15 years and the maximum fine specified by that section is increased to $150,000; and

(3) the minimum term of imprisonment specified by Section 481.112(f) is increased to 20 years and the maximum fine specified by that section is increased to $300,000.

Sec. 481.1123. Offense: Manufacture or Delivery of Substance in Penalty Group 1-B.

(a) Except as authorized by this chapter, a person commits an offense if the person knowingly manufactures, delivers, or possesses with intent to deliver a controlled substance listed in Penalty Group 1-B.

(b) An offense under Subsection (a) is a state jail felony if the amount of the controlled substance to which the offense applies is, by aggregate weight, including adulterants or dilutants, less than one gram.

(c) An offense under Subsection (a) is a felony of the second degree if the amount of the controlled substance to which the offense applies is, by aggregate weight, including adulterants or dilutants, one gram or more but less than four grams.

(d) An offense under Subsection (a) is punishable by imprisonment in the Texas Department of Criminal Justice for life or for a term of not more than 99 years or less than 10 years, and a fine not to exceed $20,000, if the amount of the controlled substance to which the offense applies is, by aggregate weight, including adulterants or dilutants, four grams or more but less than 200 grams.

(e) An offense under Subsection (a) is punishable by imprisonment in the Texas Department of Criminal Justice for life or for a term of not more than 99 years or less than 15 years, and a fine not to exceed $200,000, if the amount of the controlled substance to which the offense applies is, by aggregate weight, including adulterants or dilutants, 200 grams or more but less than 400 grams.

(f) An offense under Subsection (a) is punishable by imprisonment in the Texas Department of Criminal Justice for life or for a term of not more than 99 years or less than 20 years, and a fine not to exceed $500,000, if the amount of the controlled substance to which the offense applies is, by aggregate weight, including adulterants or dilutants, 400 grams or more.

Sec. 481.113. Offense: Manufacture or Delivery of Substance in Penalty Group 2 or 2-A.

(a) Except as authorized by this chapter, a person commits an offense if the person knowingly manufactures, delivers, or possesses with intent to deliver a controlled substance listed in Penalty Group 2 or 2-A.

(b) An offense under Subsection (a) is a state jail felony if the amount of the controlled substance to which the offense applies is, by aggregate weight, including adulterants or dilutants, less than one gram.

(c) An offense under Subsection (a) is a felony of the second degree if the amount of the controlled substance to which the offense applies is, by aggregate weight, including adulterants or dilutants, one gram or more but less than four grams.

(d) An offense under Subsection (a) is a felony of the first degree if the amount of the controlled substance to which the offense applies is, by aggregate weight, including adulterants or dilutants, four grams or more but less than 400 grams.

(e) An offense under Subsection (a) is punishable by imprisonment in the Texas Department of Criminal Justice for life or for a term of not more than 99 years or less than 10 years, and a fine not to exceed $100,000, if the amount of the controlled substance to which the offense applies is, by aggregate weight, including adulterants or dilutants, 400 grams or more.

Sec. 481.1131. Cause of Action for Sale or Provision of Synthetic Cannabinoid.

(a) In this section, "synthetic cannabinoid" means a substance included in Penalty Group 2-A under Section 481.1031.

(b) This section does not affect the right of a person to bring a common law cause of action against an individual whose consumption or ingestion of a synthetic cannabinoid resulted in causing the person bringing the suit to suffer personal injury or property damage.

(c) Providing, selling, or serving a synthetic cannabinoid may be made the basis of a statutory cause of action under this section on proof that the intoxication of the recipient of the synthetic cannabinoid was a proximate cause of the damages suffered.

(d) The liability provided under this section for the actions of a retail establishment's employees, customers, members, or guests who are or become intoxicated by the consumption or ingestion of a synthetic cannabinoid is in lieu of common law or other statutory law warranties and duties of retail establishments.

(e) This chapter does not impose obligations on a retail establishment other than those expressly stated in this section.

Sec. 481.114. Offense: Manufacture or Delivery of Substance in Penalty Group 3 or 4.

(a) Except as authorized by this chapter, a person commits an offense if the person knowingly manufactures, delivers, or possesses with intent to deliver a controlled substance listed in Penalty Group 3 or 4.

(b) An offense under Subsection (a) is a state jail felony if the amount of the controlled substance to which the offense applies is, by aggregate weight, including adulterants or dilutants, less than 28 grams.

(c) An offense under Subsection (a) is a felony of the second degree if the amount of the controlled substance to which the offense applies is, by aggregate weight, including adulterants or dilutants, 28 grams or more but less than 200 grams.

(d) An offense under Subsection (a) is a felony of the first degree, if the amount of the controlled substance to which the offense applies is, by aggregate weight, including adulterants or dilutants, 200 grams or more but less than 400 grams.

(e) An offense under Subsection (a) is punishable by imprisonment in the Texas Department of Criminal Justice for life or for a term of not more than 99 years or less than 10 years, and a fine not to exceed $100,000, if the amount of the controlled substance to which the offense applies is, by aggregate weight, including any adulterants or dilutants, 400 grams or more.

Sec. 481.115. Offense: Possession of Substance in Penalty Group 1 or 1-B.

(a) Except as authorized by this chapter, a person commits an offense if the person knowingly or intentionally possesses a controlled substance listed in Penalty Group 1 or 1-B, unless the person obtained the substance directly from or under a valid prescription or order of a practitioner acting in the course of professional practice.

(b) An offense under Subsection (a) is a state jail felony if the amount of the controlled substance possessed is, by aggregate weight, including adulterants or dilutants, less than one gram.

(c) An offense under Subsection (a) is a felony of the third degree if the amount of the controlled substance possessed is, by aggregate weight, including adulterants or dilutants, one gram or more but less than four grams.

(d) An offense under Subsection (a) is a felony of the second degree if the amount of the controlled substance possessed is, by aggregate weight, including adulterants or dilutants, four grams or more but less than 200 grams.

(e) An offense under Subsection (a) is a felony of the first degree if the amount of the controlled substance possessed is, by aggregate weight, including adulterants or dilutants, 200 grams or more but less than 400 grams.

(f) An offense under Subsection (a) is punishable by imprisonment in the Texas Department of Criminal Justice for life or for a term of not more than 99 years or less than 10 years, and a fine not to exceed $100,000, if the amount of the controlled substance possessed is, by aggregate weight, including adulterants or dilutants, 400 grams or more.

(g) It is a defense to prosecution for an offense punishable under Subsection (b) that the actor:

(1) was the first person to request emergency medical assistance in response to the possible overdose of another person and:

(A) made the request for medical assistance during an ongoing medical emergency;

(B) remained on the scene until the medical assistance arrived; and

(C) cooperated with medical assistance and law enforcement personnel; or

(2) was the victim of a possible overdose for which emergency medical assistance was requested, by the actor or by another person, during an ongoing medical emergency.

(h) The defense to prosecution provided by Subsection (g) is not available if:

(1) at the time the request for emergency medical assistance was made:

(A) a peace officer was in the process of arresting the actor or executing a search warrant describing the actor or the place from which the request for medical assistance was made; or

(B) the actor is committing another offense, other than an offense punishable under Section 481.1151(b)(1), 481.116(b), 481.1161(b)(1) or (2), 481.117(b), 481.118(b), or 481.121(b)(1) or (2), or an offense under Section 481.119(b), 481.125(a), 483.041(a), or 485.031(a);

(2) the actor has been previously convicted of or placed on deferred adjudication community supervision for an offense under this chapter or Chapter 483 or 485;

(3) the actor was acquitted in a previous proceeding in which the actor successfully established the defense under that subsection or Section 481.1151(c), 481.116(f), 481.1161(c), 481.117(f), 481.118(f), 481.119(c), 481.121(c), 481.125(g), 483.041(e), or 485.031(c); or

(4) at any time during the 18-month period preceding the date of the commission of the instant offense, the actor requested emergency medical assistance in response to the possible overdose of the actor or another person.

(i) The defense to prosecution provided by Subsection (g) does not preclude the admission of evidence obtained by law enforcement resulting from the request for emergency medical assistance if that evidence pertains to an offense for which the defense described by Subsection (g) is not available.

Sec. 481.1151. Offense: Possession of Substance in Penalty Group 1-A.

(a) Except as provided by this chapter, a person commits an offense if the person knowingly possesses a controlled substance listed in Penalty Group 1-A.

(b) An offense under this section is:

(1) a state jail felony if the number of abuse units of the controlled substance is fewer than 20;

(2) a felony of the third degree if the number of abuse units of the controlled substance is 20 or more but fewer than 80;

(3) a felony of the second degree if the number of abuse units of the controlled substance is 80 or more but fewer than 4,000;

(4) a felony of the first degree if the number of abuse units of the controlled substance is 4,000 or more but fewer than 8,000; and

(5) punishable by imprisonment in the Texas Department of Criminal Justice for life or for a term of not more than 99 years or less than 15 years and a fine not to exceed $250,000, if the number of abuse units of the controlled substance is 8,000 or more.

(c) It is a defense to prosecution for an offense punishable under Subsection (b)(1) that the actor:

(1) was the first person to request emergency medical assistance in response to the possible overdose of another person and:

(A) made the request for medical assistance during an ongoing medical emergency;

(B) remained on the scene until the medical assistance arrived; and

(C) cooperated with medical assistance and law enforcement personnel; or

(2) was the victim of a possible overdose for which emergency medical assistance was requested, by the actor or by another person, during an ongoing medical emergency.

(d) The defense to prosecution provided by Subsection (c) is not available if:

(1) at the time the request for emergency medical assistance was made:

(A) a peace officer was in the process of arresting the actor or executing a search warrant describing the actor or the place from which the request for medical assistance was made; or

(B) the actor is committing another offense, other than an offense punishable under Section 481.115(b), 481.116(b), 481.1161(b)(1) or (2), 481.117(b), 481.118(b), or 481.121(b)(1) or (2), or an offense under Section 481.119(b), 481.125(a), 483.041(a), or 485.031(a);

(2) the actor has been previously convicted of or placed on deferred adjudication community supervision for an offense under this chapter or Chapter 483 or 485;

(3) the actor was acquitted in a previous proceeding in which the actor successfully established the defense under that subsection or Section 481.115(g), 481.116(f), 481.1161(c), 481.117(f), 481.118(f), 481.119(c), 481.121(c), 481.125(g), 483.041(e), or 485.031(c); or

(4) at any time during the 18-month period preceding the date of the commission of the instant offense, the actor requested emergency medical assistance in response to the possible overdose of the actor or another person.

(e) The defense to prosecution provided by Subsection (c) does not preclude the admission of evidence obtained by law enforcement resulting from the request for emergency medical assistance if that evidence pertains to an offense for which the defense described by Subsection (c) is not available.

Sec. 481.116. Offense: Possession of Substance in Penalty Group 2.

(a) Except as authorized by this chapter, a person commits an offense if the person knowingly or intentionally possesses a controlled substance listed in Penalty Group 2, unless the person obtained the substance directly from or under a valid prescription or order of a practitioner acting in the course of professional practice.

(b) An offense under Subsection (a) is a state jail felony if the amount of the controlled substance possessed is, by aggregate weight, including adulterants or dilutants, less than one gram.

(c) An offense under Subsection (a) is a felony of the third degree if the amount of the controlled substance possessed is, by aggregate weight, including adulterants or dilutants, one gram or more but less than four grams.

(d) An offense under Subsection (a) is a felony of the second degree if the amount of the controlled substance possessed is, by aggregate weight, including adulterants or dilutants, four grams or more but less than 400 grams.

(e) An offense under Subsection (a) is punishable by imprisonment in the Texas Department of Criminal Justice for life or for a term of not more than 99 years or less than five years, and a fine not to exceed $50,000, if the amount of the controlled substance possessed is, by aggregate weight, including adulterants or dilutants, 400 grams or more.

(f) It is a defense to prosecution for an offense punishable under Subsection (b) that the actor:

(1) was the first person to request emergency medical assistance in response to the possible overdose of another person and:

(A) made the request for medical assistance during an ongoing medical emergency;

(B) remained on the scene until the medical assistance arrived; and

(C) cooperated with medical assistance and law enforcement personnel; or

(2) was the victim of a possible overdose for which emergency medical assistance was requested, by the actor or by another person, during an ongoing medical emergency.

(g) The defense to prosecution provided by Subsection (f) is not available if:

(1) at the time the request for emergency medical assistance was made:

(A) a peace officer was in the process of arresting the actor or executing a search warrant describing the actor or the place from which the request for medical assistance was made; or

(B) the actor is committing another offense, other than an offense punishable under Section 481.115(b), 481.1151(b)(1), 481.1161(b)(1) or (2), 481.117(b), 481.118(b), or 481.121(b)(1) or (2), or an offense under Section 481.119(b), 481.125(a), 483.041(a), or 485.031(a);

(2) the actor has been previously convicted of or placed on deferred adjudication community supervision for an offense under this chapter or Chapter 483 or 485;

(3) the actor was acquitted in a previous proceeding in which the actor successfully established the defense under that subsection or Section 481.115(g), 481.1151(c), 481.1161(c), 481.117(f), 481.118(f), 481.119(c), 481.121(c), 481.125(g), 483.041(e), or 485.031(c); or

(4) at any time during the 18-month period preceding the date of the commission of the instant offense, the actor requested emergency medical assistance in response to the possible overdose of the actor or another person.

(h) The defense to prosecution provided by Subsection (f) does not preclude the admission of evidence obtained by law enforcement resulting from the request for emergency medical assistance if that evidence pertains to an offense for which the defense described by Subsection (f) is not available.

Sec. 481.1161. Offense: Possession of Substance in Penalty Group 2-A.

(a) Except as authorized by this chapter, a person commits an offense if the person knowingly possesses a controlled substance listed in Penalty Group 2-A, unless the person obtained the substance directly from or under a valid prescription or order of a practitioner acting in the course of professional practice.

(b) An offense under this section is:

(1) a Class B misdemeanor if the amount of the controlled substance possessed is, by aggregate weight, including adulterants or dilutants, two ounces or less;

(2) a Class A misdemeanor if the amount of the controlled substance possessed is, by aggregate weight, including adulterants or dilutants, four ounces or less but more than two ounces;

(3) a state jail felony if the amount of the controlled substance possessed is, by aggregate weight,

including adulterants or dilutants, five pounds or less but more than four ounces;

(4) a felony of the third degree if the amount of the controlled substance possessed is, by aggregate weight, including adulterants or dilutants, 50 pounds or less but more than 5 pounds;

(5) a felony of the second degree if the amount of the controlled substance possessed is, by aggregate weight, including adulterants or dilutants, 2,000 pounds or less but more than 50 pounds; and

(6) punishable by imprisonment in the Texas Department of Criminal Justice for life or for a term of not more than 99 years or less than 5 years, and a fine not to exceed $50,000, if the amount of the controlled substance possessed is, by aggregate weight, including adulterants or dilutants, more than 2,000 pounds.

(c) It is a defense to prosecution for an offense punishable under Subsection (b)(1) or (2) that the actor:

(1) was the first person to request emergency medical assistance in response to the possible overdose of another person and:

(A) made the request for medical assistance during an ongoing medical emergency;

(B) remained on the scene until the medical assistance arrived; and

(C) cooperated with medical assistance and law enforcement personnel; or

(2) was the victim of a possible overdose for which emergency medical assistance was requested, by the actor or by another person, during an ongoing medical emergency.

(d) The defense to prosecution provided by Subsection (c) is not available if:

(1) at the time the request for emergency medical assistance was made:

(A) a peace officer was in the process of arresting the actor or executing a search warrant describing the actor or the place from which the request for medical assistance was made; or

(B) the actor is committing another offense, other than an offense punishable under Section 481.115(b), 481.1151(b)(1), 481.116(b), 481.117(b), 481.118(b), or 481.121(b)(1) or (2), or an offense under Section 481.119(b), 481.125(a), 483.041(a), or 485.031(a);

(2) the actor has been previously convicted of or placed on deferred adjudication community supervision for an offense under this chapter or Chapter 483 or 485;

(3) the actor was acquitted in a previous proceeding in which the actor successfully established the defense under that subsection or Section 481.115(g), 481.1151(c), 481.116(f), 481.117(f), 481.118(f), 481.119(c), 481.121(c), 481.125(g), 483.041(e), or 485.031(c); or

(4) at any time during the 18-month period preceding the date of the commission of the instant offense, the actor requested emergency medical assistance in response to the possible overdose of the actor or another person.

(e) The defense to prosecution provided by Subsection (c) does not preclude the admission of evidence obtained by law enforcement resulting from the request for emergency medical assistance if that evidence pertains to an offense for which the defense described by Subsection (c) is not available.

Sec. 481.117. Offense: Possession of Substance in Penalty Group 3.

(a) Except as authorized by this chapter, a person commits an offense if the person knowingly or intentionally possesses a controlled substance listed in Penalty Group 3, unless the person obtains the substance directly from or under a valid prescription or order of a practitioner acting in the course of professional practice.

(b) An offense under Subsection (a) is a Class A misdemeanor if the amount of the controlled substance possessed is, by aggregate weight, including adulterants or dilutants, less than 28 grams.

(c) An offense under Subsection (a) is a felony of the third degree if the amount of the controlled substance possessed is, by aggregate weight, including adulterants or dilutants, 28 grams or more but less than 200 grams.

(d) An offense under Subsection (a) is a felony of the second degree, if the amount of the controlled substance possessed is, by aggregate weight, including adulterants or dilutants, 200 grams or more but less than 400 grams.

(e) An offense under Subsection (a) is punishable by imprisonment in the Texas Department of Criminal Justice for life or for a term of not more than 99 years or less than five years, and a fine not to exceed $50,000, if the amount of the controlled substance possessed is, by aggregate weight, including adulterants or dilutants, 400 grams or more.

(f) It is a defense to prosecution for an offense punishable under Subsection (b) that the actor:

(1) was the first person to request emergency medical assistance in response to the possible overdose of another person and:

(A) made the request for medical assistance during an ongoing medical emergency;

(B) remained on the scene until the medical assistance arrived; and

(C) cooperated with medical assistance and law enforcement personnel; or

(2) was the victim of a possible overdose for which emergency medical assistance was requested, by

the actor or by another person, during an ongoing medical emergency.

(g) The defense to prosecution provided by Subsection (f) is not available if:

(1) at the time the request for emergency medical assistance was made:

(A) a peace officer was in the process of arresting the actor or executing a search warrant describing the actor or the place from which the request for medical assistance was made; or

(B) the actor is committing another offense, other than an offense punishable under Section 481.115(b), 481.1151(b)(1), 481.116(b), 481.1161(b)(1) or (2), 481.118(b), or 481.121(b)(1) or (2), or an offense under Section 481.119(b), 481.125(a), 483.041(a), or 485.031(a);

(2) the actor has been previously convicted of or placed on deferred adjudication community supervision for an offense under this chapter or Chapter 483 or 485;

(3) the actor was acquitted in a previous proceeding in which the actor successfully established the defense under that subsection or Section 481.115(g), 481.1151(c), 481.116(f), 481.1161(c), 481.118(f), 481.119(c), 481.121(c), 481.125(g), 483.041(e), or 485.031(c); or

(4) at any time during the 18-month period preceding the date of the commission of the instant offense, the actor requested emergency medical assistance in response to the possible overdose of the actor or another person.

(h) The defense to prosecution provided by Subsection (f) does not preclude the admission of evidence obtained by law enforcement resulting from the request for emergency medical assistance if that evidence pertains to an offense for which the defense described by Subsection (f) is not available.

Sec. 481.118. Offense: Possession of Substance in Penalty Group 4.

(a) Except as authorized by this chapter, a person commits an offense if the person knowingly or intentionally possesses a controlled substance listed in Penalty Group 4, unless the person obtained the substance directly from or under a valid prescription or order of a practitioner acting in the course of practice.

(b) An offense under Subsection (a) is a Class B misdemeanor if the amount of the controlled substance possessed is, by aggregate weight, including adulterants or dilutants, less than 28 grams.

(c) An offense under Subsection (a) is a felony of the third degree if the amount of the controlled substance possessed is, by aggregate weight, including adulterants or dilutants, 28 grams or more but less than 200 grams.

(d) An offense under Subsection (a) is a felony of the second degree, if the amount of the controlled substance possessed is, by aggregate weight, including adulterants or dilutants, 200 grams or more but less than 400 grams.

(e) An offense under Subsection (a) is punishable by imprisonment in the Texas Department of Criminal Justice for life or for a term of not more than 99 years or less than five years, and a fine not to exceed $50,000, if the amount of the controlled substance possessed is, by aggregate weight, including adulterants or dilutants, 400 grams or more.

(f) It is a defense to prosecution for an offense punishable under Subsection (b) that the actor:

(1) was the first person to request emergency medical assistance in response to the possible overdose of another person and:

(A) made the request for medical assistance during an ongoing medical emergency;

(B) remained on the scene until the medical assistance arrived; and

(C) cooperated with medical assistance and law enforcement personnel; or

(2) was the victim of a possible overdose for which emergency medical assistance was requested, by the actor or by another person, during an ongoing medical emergency.

(g) The defense to prosecution provided by Subsection (f) is not available if:

(1) at the time the request for emergency medical assistance was made:

(A) a peace officer was in the process of arresting the actor or executing a search warrant describing the actor or the place from which the request for medical assistance was made; or

(B) the actor is committing another offense, other than an offense punishable under Section 481.115(b), 481.1151(b)(1), 481.116(b), 481.1161(b)(1) or (2), 481.117(b), or 481.121(b)(1) or (2), or an offense under Section 481.119(b), 481.125(a), 483.041(a), or 485.031(a);

(2) the actor has been previously convicted of or placed on deferred adjudication community supervision for an offense under this chapter or Chapter 483 or 485;

(3) the actor was acquitted in a previous proceeding in which the actor successfully established the defense under that subsection or Section 481.115(g), 481.1151(c), 481.116(f), 481.1161(c), 481.117(f), 481.119(c), 481.121(c), 481.125(g), 483.041(e), or 485.031(c); or

(4) at any time during the 18-month period preceding the date of the commission of the instant offense, the actor requested emergency medical

assistance in response to the possible overdose of the actor or another person.

(h) The defense to prosecution provided by Subsection (f) does not preclude the admission of evidence obtained by law enforcement resulting from the request for emergency medical assistance if that evidence pertains to an offense for which the defense described by Subsection (f) is not available.

Sec. 481.119. Offense: Manufacture, Delivery, or Possession of Miscellaneous Substances.

(a) A person commits an offense if the person knowingly manufactures, delivers, or possesses with intent to deliver a controlled substance listed in a schedule by an action of the commissioner under this chapter but not listed in a penalty group. An offense under this subsection is a Class A misdemeanor, except that the offense is:

(1) a state jail felony, if the person has been previously convicted of an offense under this subsection; or

(2) a felony of the third degree, if the person has been previously convicted two or more times of an offense under this subsection.

(b) A person commits an offense if the person knowingly or intentionally possesses a controlled substance listed in a schedule by an action of the commissioner under this chapter but not listed in a penalty group. An offense under this subsection is a Class B misdemeanor.

(c) It is a defense to prosecution for an offense under Subsection (b) that the actor:

(1) was the first person to request emergency medical assistance in response to the possible overdose of another person and:

(A) made the request for medical assistance during an ongoing medical emergency;

(B) remained on the scene until the medical assistance arrived; and

(C) cooperated with medical assistance and law enforcement personnel; or

(2) was the victim of a possible overdose for which emergency medical assistance was requested, by the actor or by another person, during an ongoing medical emergency.

(d) The defense to prosecution provided by Subsection (c) is not available if:

(1) at the time the request for emergency medical assistance was made:

(A) a peace officer was in the process of arresting the actor or executing a search warrant describing the actor or the place from which the request for medical assistance was made; or

(B) the actor is committing another offense, other than an offense punishable under Section 481.115(b), 481.1151(b)(1), 481.116(b), 481.1161(b)(1) or (2), 481.117(b), 481.118(b), or 481.121(b)(1) or (2), or an offense under Section 481.125(a), 483.041(a), or 485.031(a);

(2) the actor has been previously convicted of or placed on deferred adjudication community supervision for an offense under this chapter or Chapter 483 or 485;

(3) the actor was acquitted in a previous proceeding in which the actor successfully established the defense under that subsection or Section 481.115(g), 481.1151(c), 481.116(f), 481.1161(c), 481.117(f), 481.118(f), 481.121(c), 481.125(g), 483.041(e), or 485.031(c); or

(4) at any time during the 18-month period preceding the date of the commission of the instant offense, the actor requested emergency medical assistance in response to the possible overdose of the actor or another person.

(e) The defense to prosecution provided by Subsection (c) does not preclude the admission of evidence obtained by law enforcement resulting from the request for emergency medical assistance if that evidence pertains to an offense for which the defense described by Subsection (c) is not available.

Sec. 481.1191. Civil Liability for Engaging in or Aiding in Production, Distribution, Sale, or Provision of Synthetic Substances.

(a) In this section:

(1) "Minor" means a person younger than 18 years of age.

(2) "Synthetic substance" means an artificial substance that produces and is intended by the manufacturer to produce when consumed or ingested an effect similar to or in excess of the effect produced by the consumption or ingestion of a controlled substance or controlled substance analogue, as those terms are defined by Section 481.002.

(b) A person is liable for damages proximately caused by the consumption or ingestion of a synthetic substance by another person if the actor:

(1) produced, distributed, sold, or provided the synthetic substance to the other person; or

(2) aided in the production, distribution, sale, or provision of the synthetic substance to the other person.

(c) A person is strictly liable for all damages caused by the consumption or ingestion of a synthetic substance by a minor if the actor:

(1) produced, distributed, sold, or provided the synthetic substance to the minor; or

(2) aided in the production, distribution, sale, or provision of the synthetic substance to the minor.

(d) A person who is found liable under this section or other law for any amount of damages arising from the consumption or ingestion by another of a synthetic substance is jointly and severally liable with any other person for the entire amount of damages awarded.

(e) Chapter 33, Civil Practice and Remedies Code, does not apply to an action brought under this section or an action brought under Section 17.50, Business & Commerce Code, based on conduct made actionable under Subsection (f) of this section.

(f) Conduct for which Subsection (b) or (c) creates liability is a false, misleading, or deceptive act or practice or an unconscionable action or course of action for purposes of Section 17.50, Business & Commerce Code, and that conduct is:

(1) actionable under Subchapter E, Chapter 17, Business & Commerce Code; and

(2) subject to any remedy prescribed by that subchapter.

(g) An action brought under this section may include a claim for exemplary damages, which may be awarded in accordance with Section 41.003, Civil Practice and Remedies Code.

(h) Section 41.008, Civil Practice and Remedies Code, does not apply to the award of exemplary damages in an action brought under this section.

(i) Section 41.005, Civil Practice and Remedies Code, does not apply to a claim for exemplary damages in an action brought under this section.

(j) It is an affirmative defense to liability under this section that the synthetic substance produced, distributed, sold, or provided was approved for use, sale, or distribution by the United States Food and Drug Administration or other state or federal regulatory agency with authority to approve a substance for use, sale, or distribution.

(k) It is not a defense to liability under this section that a synthetic substance was in packaging labeled with "Not for Human Consumption" or other wording indicating the substance is not intended to be ingested.

Sec. 481.120. Offense: Delivery of Marihuana.

(a) Except as authorized by this chapter, a person commits an offense if the person knowingly or intentionally delivers marihuana.

(b) An offense under Subsection (a) is:

(1) a Class B misdemeanor if the amount of marihuana delivered is one-fourth ounce or less and the person committing the offense does not receive remuneration for the marihuana;

(2) a Class A misdemeanor if the amount of marihuana delivered is one-fourth ounce or less and the person committing the offense receives remuneration for the marihuana;

(3) a state jail felony if the amount of marihuana delivered is five pounds or less but more than one-fourth ounce;

(4) a felony of the second degree if the amount of marihuana delivered is 50 pounds or less but more than five pounds;

(5) a felony of the first degree if the amount of marihuana delivered is 2,000 pounds or less but more than 50 pounds; and

(6) punishable by imprisonment in the Texas Department of Criminal Justice for life or for a term of not more than 99 years or less than 10 years, and a fine not to exceed $100,000, if the amount of marihuana delivered is more than 2,000 pounds.

Sec. 481.121. Offense: Possession of Marihuana.

(a) Except as authorized by this chapter, a person commits an offense if the person knowingly or intentionally possesses a usable quantity of marihuana.

(b) An offense under Subsection (a) is:

(1) a Class B misdemeanor if the amount of marihuana possessed is two ounces or less;

(2) a Class A misdemeanor if the amount of marihuana possessed is four ounces or less but more than two ounces;

(3) a state jail felony if the amount of marihuana possessed is five pounds or less but more than four ounces;

(4) a felony of the third degree if the amount of marihuana possessed is 50 pounds or less but more than 5 pounds;

(5) a felony of the second degree if the amount of marihuana possessed is 2,000 pounds or less but more than 50 pounds; and

(6) punishable by imprisonment in the Texas Department of Criminal Justice for life or for a term of not more than 99 years or less than 5 years, and a fine not to exceed $50,000, if the amount of marihuana possessed is more than 2,000 pounds.

(c) It is a defense to prosecution for an offense punishable under Subsection (b)(1) or (2) that the actor:

(1) was the first person to request emergency medical assistance in response to the possible overdose of another person and:

(A) made the request for medical assistance during an ongoing medical emergency;

(B) remained on the scene until the medical assistance arrived; and

(C) cooperated with medical assistance and law enforcement personnel; or

(2) was the victim of a possible overdose for which emergency medical assistance was requested, by the actor or by another person, during an ongoing medical emergency.

(d) The defense to prosecution provided by Subsection (c) is not available if:

(1) at the time the request for emergency medical assistance was made:

(A) a peace officer was in the process of arresting the actor or executing a search warrant describing the actor or the place from which the request for medical assistance was made; or

(B) the actor is committing another offense, other than an offense punishable under Section 481.115(b), 481.1151(b)(1), 481.116(b), 481.1161(b)(1) or (2), 481.117(b), or 481.118(b), or an offense under Section 481.119(b), 481.125(a), 483.041(a), or 485.031(a);

(2) the actor has been previously convicted of or placed on deferred adjudication community supervision for an offense under this chapter or Chapter 483 or 485;

(3) the actor was acquitted in a previous proceeding in which the actor successfully established the defense under that subsection or Section 481.115(g), 481.1151(c), 481.116(f), 481.1161(c), 481.117(f), 481.118(f), 481.119(c), 481.125(g), 483.041(e), or 485.031(c); or

(4) at any time during the 18-month period preceding the date of the commission of the instant offense, the actor requested emergency medical assistance in response to the possible overdose of the actor or another person.

(e) The defense to prosecution provided by Subsection (c) does not preclude the admission of evidence obtained by law enforcement resulting from the request for emergency medical assistance if that evidence pertains to an offense for which the defense described by Subsection (c) is not available.

Sec. 481.122. Offense: Delivery of Controlled Substance or Marihuana to Child.

(a) A person commits an offense if the person knowingly delivers a controlled substance listed in Penalty Group 1, 1-A, 1-B, 2, or 3 or knowingly delivers marihuana and the person delivers the controlled substance or marihuana to a person:

(1) who is a child;

(2) who is enrolled in a public or private primary or secondary school; or

(3) who the actor knows or believes intends to deliver the controlled substance or marihuana to a person described by Subdivision (1) or (2).

(b) It is an affirmative defense to prosecution under this section that:

(1) the actor was a child when the offense was committed; or

(2) the actor:

(A) was younger than 21 years of age when the offense was committed;

(B) delivered only marihuana in an amount equal to or less than one-fourth ounce; and

(C) did not receive remuneration for the delivery.

(c) An offense under this section is a felony of the second degree.

(d) In this section, "child" means a person younger than 18 years of age.

(e) If conduct that is an offense under this section is also an offense under another section of this chapter, the actor may be prosecuted under either section or both.

Sec. 481.123. Defense to Prosecution for Offense Involving Controlled Substance Analogue.

(a) It is an affirmative defense to the prosecution of an offense under this subchapter involving the manufacture, delivery, or possession of a controlled substance analogue that the analogue:

(1) was a substance for which there is an approved new drug application under Section 505 of the Federal Food, Drug, and Cosmetic Act (21 U.S.C. Section 355); or

(2) was a substance for which an exemption for investigational use has been granted under Section 505 of the Federal Food, Drug, and Cosmetic Act (21 U.S.C. Section 355), if the actor's conduct with respect to the substance is in accord with the exemption.

(b) For the purposes of this section, Section 505 of the Federal Food, Drug, and Cosmetic Act (21 U.S.C. Section 355) applies to the introduction or delivery for introduction of any new drug into intrastate, interstate, or foreign commerce.

Sec. 481.124. Offense: Possession or Transport of Certain Chemicals with Intent to Manufacture Controlled Substance.

(a) A person commits an offense if, with intent to unlawfully manufacture a controlled substance, the person possesses or transports:

(1) anhydrous ammonia;

(2) an immediate precursor; or

(3) a chemical precursor or an additional chemical substance named as a precursor by the director under Section 481.077(b)(1).

(b) For purposes of this section, an intent to unlawfully manufacture the controlled substance

Health and Safety Code

methamphetamine is presumed if the actor possesses or transports:

(1) anhydrous ammonia in a container or receptacle that is not designed and manufactured to lawfully hold or transport anhydrous ammonia;

(2) lithium metal removed from a battery and immersed in kerosene, mineral spirits, or similar liquid that prevents or retards hydration; or

(3) in one container, vehicle, or building, phenylacetic acid, or more than nine grams, three containers packaged for retail sale, or 300 tablets or capsules of a product containing ephedrine or pseudoephedrine, and:

(A) anhydrous ammonia;

(B) at least three of the following categories of substances commonly used in the manufacture of methamphetamine:

(i) lithium or sodium metal or red phosphorus, iodine, or iodine crystals;

(ii) lye, sulfuric acid, hydrochloric acid, or muriatic acid;

(iii) an organic solvent, including ethyl ether, alcohol, or acetone;

(iv) a petroleum distillate, including naphtha, paint thinner, or charcoal lighter fluid; or

(v) aquarium, rock, or table salt; or

(C) at least three of the following items:

(i) an item of equipment subject to regulation under Section 481.080, if the person is not a registrant; or

(ii) glassware, a plastic or metal container, tubing, a hose, or other item specially designed, assembled, or adapted for use in the manufacture, processing, analyzing, storing, or concealing of methamphetamine.

(c) For purposes of this section, a substance is presumed to be anhydrous ammonia if the substance is in a container or receptacle that is:

(1) designed and manufactured to lawfully hold or transport anhydrous ammonia; or

(2) not designed and manufactured to lawfully hold or transport anhydrous ammonia, if:

(A) a properly administered field test of the substance using a testing device or instrument designed and manufactured for that purpose produces a positive result for anhydrous ammonia; or

(B) a laboratory test of a water solution of the substance produces a positive result for ammonia.

(d) An offense under this section is:

(1) a felony of the second degree if the controlled substance is listed in Penalty Group 1, 1-A, or 1-B;

(2) a felony of the third degree if the controlled substance is listed in Penalty Group 2;

(3) a state jail felony if the controlled substance is listed in Penalty Group 3 or 4; or

(4) a Class A misdemeanor if the controlled substance is listed in a schedule by an action of the commissioner under this chapter but not listed in a penalty group.

(e) If conduct constituting an offense under this section also constitutes an offense under another section of this code, the actor may be prosecuted under either section or under both sections.

(f) This section does not apply to a chemical precursor exempted by the director under Section 481.077(b)(2) from the requirements of that section.

Sec. 481.1245. Offense: Possession or Transport of Anhydrous Ammonia; Use of or Tampering with Equipment.

(a) A person commits an offense if the person:

(1) possesses or transports anhydrous ammonia in a container or receptacle that is not designed or manufactured to hold or transport anhydrous ammonia;

(2) uses, transfers, or sells a container or receptacle that is designed or manufactured to hold anhydrous ammonia without the express consent of the owner of the container or receptacle; or

(3) tampers with equipment that is manufactured or used to hold, apply, or transport anhydrous ammonia without the express consent of the owner of the equipment.

(b) An offense under this section is a felony of the third degree.

Sec. 481.125. Offense: Possession or Delivery of Drug Paraphernalia.

(a) A person commits an offense if the person knowingly or intentionally uses or possesses with intent to use drug paraphernalia to plant, propagate, cultivate, grow, harvest, manufacture, compound, convert, produce, process, prepare, test, analyze, pack, repack, store, contain, or conceal a controlled substance in violation of this chapter or to inject, ingest, inhale, or otherwise introduce into the human body a controlled substance in violation of this chapter.

(b) A person commits an offense if the person knowingly or intentionally delivers, possesses with intent to deliver, or manufactures with intent to deliver drug paraphernalia knowing that the person who receives or who is intended to receive the drug paraphernalia intends that it be used to plant, propagate, cultivate, grow, harvest, manufacture, compound, convert, produce, process, prepare, test, analyze, pack, repack, store, contain, or conceal a controlled substance in violation of this chapter or to inject, ingest, inhale, or otherwise introduce into the human body a controlled substance in violation of this chapter.

(c) A person commits an offense if the person commits an offense under Subsection (b), is 18 years of age or older, and the person who receives or who is intended to receive the drug paraphernalia is younger than 18 years of age and at least three years younger than the actor.

(d) An offense under Subsection (a) is a Class C misdemeanor.

(e) An offense under Subsection (b) is a Class A misdemeanor, unless it is shown on the trial of a defendant that the defendant has previously been convicted under Subsection (b) or (c), in which event the offense is punishable by confinement in jail for a term of not more than one year or less than 90 days.

(f) An offense under Subsection (c) is a state jail felony.

(g) It is a defense to prosecution for an offense under Subsection (a) that the actor:

(1) was the first person to request emergency medical assistance in response to the possible overdose of another person and:

(A) made the request for medical assistance during an ongoing medical emergency;

(B) remained on the scene until the medical assistance arrived; and

(C) cooperated with medical assistance and law enforcement personnel; or

(2) was the victim of a possible overdose for which emergency medical assistance was requested, by the actor or by another person, during an ongoing medical emergency.

(h) The defense to prosecution provided by Subsection (g) is not available if:

(1) at the time the request for emergency medical assistance was made:

(A) a peace officer was in the process of arresting the actor or executing a search warrant describing the actor or the place from which the request for medical assistance was made; or

(B) the actor is committing another offense, other than an offense punishable under Section 481.115(b), 481.1151(b)(1), 481.116(b), 481.1161(b)(1) or (2), 481.117(b), 481.118(b), or 481.121(b)(1) or (2), or an offense under Section 481.119(b), 483.041(a), or 485.031(a);

(2) the actor has been previously convicted of or placed on deferred adjudication community supervision for an offense under this chapter or Chapter 483 or 485;

(3) the actor was acquitted in a previous proceeding in which the actor successfully established the defense under that subsection or Section 481.115(g), 481.1151(c), 481.116(f), 481.1161(c), 481.117(f), 481.118(f), 481.119(c), 481.121(c), 483.041(e), or 485.031(c); or

(4) at any time during the 18-month period preceding the date of the commission of the instant offense, the actor requested emergency medical assistance in response to the possible overdose of the actor or another person.

(i) The defense to prosecution provided by Subsection (g) does not preclude the admission of evidence obtained by law enforcement resulting from the request for emergency medical assistance if that evidence pertains to an offense for which the defense described by Subsection (g) is not available.

Sec. 481.126. Offense: Illegal Barter, Expenditure, or Investment.

(a) A person commits an offense if the person:

(1) barters property or expends funds the person knows are derived from the commission of an offense under this chapter punishable by imprisonment in the Texas Department of Criminal Justice for life;

(2) barters property or expends funds the person knows are derived from the commission of an offense under Section 481.121(a) that is punishable under Section 481.121(b)(5);

(3) barters property or finances or invests funds the person knows or believes are intended to further the commission of an offense for which the punishment is described by Subdivision (1); or

(4) barters property or finances or invests funds the person knows or believes are intended to further the commission of an offense under Section 481.121(a) that is punishable under Section 481.121(b)(5).

(b) An offense under Subsection (a)(1) or (3) is a felony of the first degree. An offense under Subsection (a)(2) or (4) is a felony of the second degree.

Sec. 481.127. Offense: Unauthorized Disclosure of Information.

(a) A person commits an offense if the person knowingly gives, permits, or obtains unauthorized access to information submitted to the board under Section 481.074(q) or 481.075.

(b) An offense under this section is a state jail felony.

Sec. 481.128. Offense and Civil Penalty: Commercial Matters.

(a) A registrant or dispenser commits an offense if the registrant or dispenser knowingly:

(1) distributes, delivers, administers, or dispenses a controlled substance in violation of Subchapter C;

(2) manufactures a controlled substance not authorized by the person's Federal Drug Enforcement Administration registration or distributes or dispenses a controlled substance not authorized by the person's registration to another registrant or other person;

(3) refuses or fails to make, keep, or furnish a record, report, notification, order form, statement, invoice, or information required by this chapter;

(4) prints, manufactures, possesses, or produces an official prescription form without the approval of the board;

(5) delivers or possesses a counterfeit official prescription form;

(6) refuses an entry into a premise for an inspection authorized by this chapter;

(7) refuses or fails to return an official prescription form as required by Section 481.0755(k);

(8) refuses or fails to make, keep, or furnish a record, report, notification, order form, statement, invoice, or information required by a rule adopted by the director or the board; or

(9) refuses or fails to maintain security required by this chapter or a rule adopted under this chapter.

(b) If the registrant or dispenser knowingly refuses or fails to make, keep, or furnish a record, report, notification, order form, statement, invoice, or information or maintain security required by a rule adopted by the director or the board, the registrant or dispenser is liable to the state for a civil penalty of not more than $5,000 for each act.

(c) An offense under Subsection (a) is a state jail felony.

(d) If a person commits an act that would otherwise be an offense under Subsection (a) except that it was committed without the requisite culpable mental state, the person is liable to the state for a civil penalty of not more than $1,000 for each act.

(e) A district attorney of the county where the act occurred may file suit in district court in that county to collect a civil penalty under this section, or the district attorney of Travis County or the attorney general may file suit in district court in Travis County to collect the penalty.

Sec. 481.1285. Offense: Diversion of Controlled Substance by Registrants, Dispensers, and Certain Other Persons.

(a) This section applies only to a registrant, a dispenser, or a person who, pursuant to Section 481.062(a)(1) or (2), is not required to register under this subchapter.

(b) A person commits an offense if the person knowingly:

(1) converts to the person's own use or benefit a controlled substance to which the person has access by virtue of the person's profession or employment; or

(2) diverts to the unlawful use or benefit of another person a controlled substance to which the person has access by virtue of the person's profession or employment.

(c) An offense under Subsection (b)(1) is a state jail felony. An offense under Subsection (b)(2) is a felony of the third degree.

(d) If conduct that constitutes an offense under this section also constitutes an offense under any other law, the actor may be prosecuted under this section, the other law, or both.

Sec. 481.129. Offense: Fraud.

(a) A person commits an offense if the person knowingly:

(1) distributes as a registrant or dispenser a controlled substance listed in Schedule I or II, unless the person distributes the controlled substance as authorized under the federal Controlled Substances Act (21 U.S.C. Section 801 et seq.);

(2) uses in the course of manufacturing, prescribing, or distributing a controlled substance a Federal Drug Enforcement Administration registration number that is fictitious, revoked, suspended, or issued to another person;

(3) issues a prescription bearing a forged or fictitious signature;

(4) uses a prescription issued to another person to prescribe a Schedule II controlled substance;

(5) possesses, obtains, or attempts to possess or obtain a controlled substance or an increased quantity of a controlled substance:

(A) by misrepresentation, fraud, forgery, deception, or subterfuge;

(B) through use of a fraudulent prescription form;

(C) through use of a fraudulent oral or telephonically communicated prescription; or

(D) through the use of a fraudulent electronic prescription; or

(6) furnishes false or fraudulent material information in or omits material information from an application, report, record, or other document required to be kept or filed under this chapter.

(a-1) A person commits an offense if the person, with intent to obtain a controlled substance or combination of controlled substances that is not medically necessary for the person or an amount of a controlled substance or substances that is not

Health and Safety Code

medically necessary for the person, obtains or attempts to obtain from a practitioner a controlled substance or a prescription for a controlled substance by misrepresentation, fraud, forgery, deception, subterfuge, or concealment of a material fact. For purposes of this subsection, a material fact includes whether the person has an existing prescription for a controlled substance issued for the same period of time by another practitioner.

(b) A person commits an offense if the person knowingly or intentionally:

(1) makes, distributes, or possesses a punch, die, plate, stone, or other thing designed to print, imprint, or reproduce an actual or simulated trademark, trade name, or other identifying mark, imprint, or device of another on a controlled substance or the container or label of a container for a controlled substance, so as to make the controlled substance a counterfeit substance; or

(2) manufactures, delivers, or possesses with intent to deliver a counterfeit substance.

(c) A person commits an offense if the person knowingly or intentionally:

(1) delivers a prescription or a prescription form for other than a valid medical purpose in the course of professional practice; or

(2) possesses a prescription for a controlled substance or a prescription form unless the prescription or prescription form is possessed:

(A) during the manufacturing or distribution process;

(B) by a practitioner, practitioner's agent, or an institutional practitioner for a valid medical purpose during the course of professional practice;

(C) by a pharmacist or agent of a pharmacy during the professional practice of pharmacy;

(D) under a practitioner's order made by the practitioner for a valid medical purpose in the course of professional practice; or

(E) by an officer or investigator authorized to enforce this chapter within the scope of the officer's or investigator's official duties.

(d) An offense under Subsection (a) is:

(1) a felony of the second degree if the controlled substance that is the subject of the offense is listed in Schedule I or II;

(2) a felony of the third degree if the controlled substance that is the subject of the offense is listed in Schedule III or IV; and

(3) a Class A misdemeanor if the controlled substance that is the subject of the offense is listed in Schedule V.

(d-1) An offense under Subsection (a-1) is:

(1) a felony of the second degree if any controlled substance that is the subject of the offense is listed in Schedule I or II;

(2) a felony of the third degree if any controlled substance that is the subject of the offense is listed in Schedule III or IV; and

(3) a Class A misdemeanor if any controlled substance that is the subject of the offense is listed in Schedule V.

(e) An offense under Subsection (b) is a Class A misdemeanor.

(f) An offense under Subsection (c)(1) is:

(1) a felony of the second degree if the defendant delivers:

(A) a prescription form; or

(B) a prescription for a controlled substance listed in Schedule II; and

(2) a felony of the third degree if the defendant delivers a prescription for a controlled substance listed in Schedule III, IV, or V.

(g) An offense under Subsection (c)(2) is:

(1) a state jail felony if the defendant possesses:

(A) a prescription form; or

(B) a prescription for a controlled substance listed in Schedule II or III; and

(2) a Class B misdemeanor if the defendant possesses a prescription for a controlled substance listed in Schedule IV or V.

Sec. 481.130. Penalties Under Other Law.

A penalty imposed for an offense under this chapter is in addition to any civil or administrative penalty or other sanction imposed by law.

Sec. 481.131. Offense: Diversion of Controlled Substance Property or Plant.

(a) A person commits an offense if the person intentionally or knowingly:

(1) converts to the person's own use or benefit a controlled substance property or plant seized under Section 481.152 or 481.153; or

(2) diverts to the unlawful use or benefit of another person a controlled substance property or plant seized under Section 481.152 or 481.153.

(b) An offense under this section is a state jail felony.

Sec. 481.132. Multiple Prosecutions.

(a) In this section, "criminal episode" means the commission of two or more offenses under this chapter under the following circumstances:

(1) the offenses are committed pursuant to the same transaction or pursuant to two or more transactions that are connected or constitute a common scheme, plan, or continuing course of conduct; or

(2) the offenses are the repeated commission of the same or similar offenses.

(b) A defendant may be prosecuted in a single criminal action for all offenses arising out of the same criminal episode. If a single criminal action is based on more than one charging instrument within the jurisdiction of the trial court, not later than the 30th day before the date of the trial, the state shall file written notice of the action.

(c) If a judgment of guilt is reversed, set aside, or vacated and a new trial is ordered, the state may not prosecute in a single criminal action in the new trial any offense not joined in the former prosecution unless evidence to establish probable guilt for that offense was not known to the appropriate prosecution official at the time the first prosecution began.

(d) If the accused is found guilty of more than one offense arising out of the same criminal episode prosecuted in a single criminal action, sentence for each offense for which the accused has been found guilty shall be pronounced, and those sentences run concurrently.

(e) If it appears that a defendant or the state is prejudiced by a joinder of offenses, the court may order separate trials of the offenses or provide other relief as justice requires.

(f) This section provides the exclusive method for consolidation and joinder of prosecutions for offenses under this chapter. This section is not a limitation of Article 36.09 or 36.10, Code of Criminal Procedure.

Sec. 481.133. Offense: Falsification of Drug Test Results.

(a) A person commits an offense if the person knowingly or intentionally uses or possesses with intent to use any substance or device designed to falsify drug test results.

(b) A person commits an offense if the person knowingly or intentionally delivers, possesses with intent to deliver, or manufactures with intent to deliver a substance or device designed to falsify drug test results.

(c) In this section, "drug test" means a lawfully administered test designed to detect the presence of a controlled substance or marihuana.

(d) An offense under Subsection (a) is a Class B misdemeanor.

(e) An offense under Subsection (b) is a Class A misdemeanor.

Sec. 481.134. Drug-Free Zones.

(a) In this section:

(1) "Minor" means a person who is younger than 18 years of age.

(2) "Institution of higher education" means any public or private technical institute, junior college, senior college or university, medical or dental unit, or other agency of higher education as defined by Section 61.003, Education Code.

(3) "Playground" means any outdoor facility that is not on the premises of a school and that:

(A) is intended for recreation;

(B) is open to the public; and

(C) contains three or more play stations intended for the recreation of children, such as slides, swing sets, and teeterboards.

(4) "Premises" means real property and all buildings and appurtenances pertaining to the real property.

(5) "School" means a private or public elementary or secondary school or a day-care center, as defined by Section 42.002, Human Resources Code.

(6) "Video arcade facility" means any facility that:

(A) is open to the public, including persons who are 17 years of age or younger;

(B) is intended primarily for the use of pinball or video machines; and

(C) contains at least three pinball or video machines.

(7) "Youth center" means any recreational facility or gymnasium that:

(A) is intended primarily for use by persons who are 17 years of age or younger; and

(B) regularly provides athletic, civic, or cultural activities.

(8) "General residential operation" has the meaning assigned by Section 42.002, Human Resources Code.

(b) An offense otherwise punishable as a state jail felony under Section 481.112, 481.1121, 481.1123, 481.113, 481.114, or 481.120 is punishable as a felony of the third degree, an offense otherwise punishable as a felony of the third degree under any of those sections is punishable as a felony of the second degree, and an offense otherwise punishable as a felony of the second degree under any of those sections is punishable as a felony of the first degree, if it is shown at the punishment phase of the trial of the offense that the offense was committed:

(1) in, on, or within 1,000 feet of premises owned, rented, or leased by an institution of higher learning, the premises of a public or private youth center, or a playground;

(2) in, on, or within 300 feet of the premises of a public swimming pool or video arcade facility; or

(3) by any unauthorized person 18 years of age or older, in, on, or within 1,000 feet of premises owned,

rented, or leased by a general residential operation operating as a residential treatment center.

(c) The minimum term of confinement or imprisonment for an offense otherwise punishable under Section 481.112(c), (d), (e), or (f), 481.1121(b)(2), (3), or (4), 481.1123(c), (d), (e), or (f), 481.113(c), (d), or (e), 481.114(c), (d), or (e), 481.115(c)-(f), 481.1151(b)(2), (3), (4), or (5), 481.116(c), (d), or (e), 481.1161(b)(4), (5), or (6), 481.117(c), (d), or (e), 481.118(c), (d), or (e), 481.120(b)(4), (5), or (6), or 481.121(b)(4), (5), or (6) is increased by five years and the maximum fine for the offense is doubled if it is shown on the trial of the offense that the offense was committed:

(1) in, on, or within 1,000 feet of the premises of a school, the premises of a public or private youth center, or a playground;

(2) on a school bus; or

(3) by any unauthorized person 18 years of age or older, in, on, or within 1,000 feet of premises owned, rented, or leased by a general residential operation operating as a residential treatment center.

(d) An offense otherwise punishable under Section 481.112(b), 481.1121(b)(1), 481.113(b), 481.114(b), 481.115(b), 481.1151(b)(1), 481.116(b), 481.1161(b)(3), 481.120(b)(3), or 481.121(b)(3) is a felony of the third degree if it is shown on the trial of the offense that the offense was committed:

(1) in, on, or within 1,000 feet of any real property that is owned, rented, or leased to a school or school board, the premises of a public or private youth center, or a playground;

(2) on a school bus; or

(3) by any unauthorized person 18 years of age or older, in, on, or within 1,000 feet of premises owned, rented, or leased by a general residential operation operating as a residential treatment center.

(e) An offense otherwise punishable under Section 481.117(b), 481.119(a), 481.120(b)(2), or 481.121(b)(2) is a state jail felony if it is shown on the trial of the offense that the offense was committed:

(1) in, on, or within 1,000 feet of any real property that is owned, rented, or leased to a school or school board, the premises of a public or private youth center, or a playground;

(2) on a school bus; or

(3) by any unauthorized person 18 years of age or older, in, on, or within 1,000 feet of premises owned, rented, or leased by a general residential operation operating as a residential treatment center.

(f) An offense otherwise punishable under Section 481.118(b), 481.119(b), 481.120(b)(1), or 481.121(b)(1) is a Class A misdemeanor if it is shown on the trial of the offense that the offense was committed:

(1) in, on, or within 1,000 feet of any real property that is owned, rented, or leased to a school or school board, the premises of a public or private youth center, or a playground;

(2) on a school bus; or

(3) by any unauthorized person 18 years of age or older, in, on, or within 1,000 feet of premises owned, rented, or leased by a general residential operation operating as a residential treatment center.

(g) Subsection (f) does not apply to an offense if:

(1) the offense was committed inside a private residence; and

(2) no minor was present in the private residence at the time the offense was committed.

(h) Punishment that is increased for a conviction for an offense listed under this section may not run concurrently with punishment for a conviction under any other criminal statute.

Sec. 481.135. Maps As Evidence of Location or Area.

(a) In a prosecution under Section 481.134, a map produced or reproduced by a municipal or county engineer for the purpose of showing the location and boundaries of drug-free zones is admissible in evidence and is prima facie evidence of the location or boundaries of those areas if the governing body of the municipality or county adopts a resolution or ordinance approving the map as an official finding and record of the location or boundaries of those areas.

(b) A municipal or county engineer may, on request of the governing body of the municipality or county, revise a map that has been approved by the governing body of the municipality or county as provided by Subsection (a).

(c) A municipal or county engineer shall file the original or a copy of every approved or revised map approved as provided by Subsection (a) with the county clerk of each county in which the area is located.

(d) This section does not prevent the prosecution from:

(1) introducing or relying on any other evidence or testimony to establish any element of an offense for which punishment is increased under Section 481.134; or

(2) using or introducing any other map or diagram otherwise admissible under the Texas Rules of Evidence.

Sec. 481.136. Offense: Unlawful Transfer or Receipt of Chemical Precursor.

(a) A person commits an offense if the person sells, transfers, furnishes, or receives a chemical precursor subject to Section 481.077(a) and the person:

(1) does not comply with Section 481.077 or 481.0771;

(2) knowingly makes a false statement in a report or record required by Section 481.077 or 481.0771; or

(3) knowingly violates a rule adopted under Section 481.077 or 481.0771.

(b) An offense under this section is a state jail felony, unless it is shown on the trial of the offense that the defendant has been previously convicted of an offense under this section or Section 481.137, in which event the offense is a felony of the third degree.

Sec. 481.137. Offense: Transfer of Precursor Substance for Unlawful Manufacture.

(a) A person commits an offense if the person sells, transfers, or otherwise furnishes a chemical precursor subject to Section 481.077(a) with the knowledge or intent that the recipient will use the chemical precursor to unlawfully manufacture a controlled substance or controlled substance analogue.

(b) An offense under this section is a felony of the third degree.

Sec. 481.138. Offense: Unlawful Transfer or Receipt of Chemical Laboratory Apparatus.

(a) A person commits an offense if the person sells, transfers, furnishes, or receives a chemical laboratory apparatus subject to Section 481.080(a) and the person:

(1) does not comply with Section 481.080;

(2) knowingly makes a false statement in a report or record required by Section 481.080; or

(3) knowingly violates a rule adopted under Section 481.080.

(b) An offense under this section is a state jail felony, unless it is shown on the trial of the offense that the defendant has been previously convicted of an offense under this section, in which event the offense is a felony of the third degree.

Sec. 481.139. Offense: Transfer of Chemical Laboratory Apparatus for Unlawful Manufacture.

(a) A person commits an offense if the person sells, transfers, or otherwise furnishes a chemical laboratory apparatus with the knowledge or intent that the recipient will use the apparatus to unlawfully manufacture a controlled substance or controlled substance analogue.

(b) An offense under Subsection (a) is a felony of the third degree.

Sec. 481.140. Use of Child in Commission of Offense.

(a) If it is shown at the punishment phase of the trial of an offense otherwise punishable as a state jail felony, felony of the third degree, or felony of the second degree under Section 481.112, 481.1121, 481.1123, 481.113, 481.114, 481.120, or 481.122 that the defendant used or attempted to use a child younger than 18 years of age to commit or assist in the commission of the offense, the punishment is increased by one degree, unless the defendant used or threatened to use force against the child or another to gain the child's assistance, in which event the punishment for the offense is a felony of the first degree.

(b) Notwithstanding Article 42.08, Code of Criminal Procedure, if punishment for a defendant is increased under this section, the court may not order the sentence for the offense to run concurrently with any other sentence the court imposes on the defendant.

Sec. 481.141. Manufacture or Delivery of Controlled Substance Causing Death or Serious Bodily Injury.

(a) If at the guilt or innocence phase of the trial of an offense described by Subsection (b), the judge or jury, whichever is the trier of fact, determines beyond a reasonable doubt that a person died or suffered serious bodily injury as a result of injecting, ingesting, inhaling, or introducing into the person's body any amount of the controlled substance manufactured or delivered by the defendant, regardless of whether the controlled substance was used by itself or with another substance, including a drug, adulterant, or dilutant, the punishment for the offense is increased by one degree.

(b) This section applies to an offense otherwise punishable as a state jail felony, felony of the third degree, or felony of the second degree under Section 481.112, 481.1121, 481.1123, 481.113, 481.114, or 481.122.

(c) Notwithstanding Article 42.08, Code of Criminal Procedure, if punishment for a defendant is increased under this section, the court may not order the sentence for the offense to run concurrently with any other sentence the court imposes on the defendant.

SUBCHAPTER E
FORFEITURE

Sec. 481.151. Definitions.

In this subchapter:

(1) "Controlled substance property" means a controlled substance, mixture containing a controlled substance, controlled substance analogue, counterfeit controlled substance, drug paraphernalia, chemical precursor, chemical laboratory apparatus, or raw material.

(2) "Controlled substance plant" means a species of plant from which a controlled substance listed in Schedule I or II may be derived.

(2-a) "Crime laboratory" has the meaning assigned by Article 38.35, Code of Criminal Procedure.

(2-b) "Criminal justice agency" has the meaning assigned by Section 411.082, Government Code, and includes a local government corporation described by Section 411.0011 of that code.

(3) "Summary destruction" or "summarily destroy" means destruction without the necessity of any court action, a court order, or further proceedings.

(4) "Summary forfeiture" or "summarily forfeit" means forfeiture without the necessity of any court action, a court order, or further proceedings.

Sec. 481.152. Seizure, Summary Forfeiture, and Summary Destruction or Other Disposition of Controlled Substance Plants.

(a) Controlled substance plants are subject to seizure and summary forfeiture to the state if:

(1) the plants have been planted, cultivated, or harvested in violation of this chapter;

(2) the plants are wild growths; or

(3) the owners or cultivators of the plants are unknown.

(b) Subsection (a) does not apply to unharvested peyote growing in its natural state.

(c) If a person who occupies or controls land or premises on which the plants are growing fails on the demand of a peace officer to produce an appropriate registration or proof that the person is the holder of the registration, the officer may seize and summarily forfeit the plants.

(d) If a controlled substance plant is seized and forfeited under this section, a court may order the disposition of the plant under Section 481.159, or the department, a criminal justice agency, or a peace officer may summarily destroy the property under the rules of the department or dispose of the property in lieu of destruction as provided by Section 481.161.

Sec. 481.153. Seizure, Summary Forfeiture, and Summary Destruction or Other Disposition of Controlled Substance Property.

(a) Controlled substance property that is manufactured, delivered, or possessed in violation of this chapter is subject to seizure and summary forfeiture to the state.

(b) If an item of controlled substance property is seized and forfeited under this section, a court may order the disposition of the property under Section 481.159, or the department, a criminal justice agency, or a peace officer may summarily destroy the property under the rules of the department or dispose of the property in lieu of destruction as provided by Section 481.161.

Sec. 481.154. Rules.

(a) The director may adopt reasonable rules and procedures, not inconsistent with the provisions of this chapter, concerning:

(1) summary forfeiture and summary destruction of controlled substance property or plants;

(2) establishment and operation of a secure storage area;

(3) delegation by a law enforcement agency head of the authority to access a secure storage area; and

(4) minimum tolerance for and the circumstances of loss or destruction during an investigation.

(b) The rules for the destruction of controlled substance property or plants must require:

(1) more than one person to witness the destruction of the property or plants;

(2) the preparation of an inventory of the property or plants destroyed; and

(3) the preparation of a statement that contains the names of the persons who witness the destruction and the details of the destruction.

(c) A document prepared under a rule adopted under this section must be completed, retained, and made available for inspection by the director.

Sec. 481.155. Replevy [Repealed].

Repealed by Acts 1989, 71st Leg., 1st C.S., ch. 12 (H.B. 65), § 6, effective October 18, 1989.

Sec. 481.156. Deposit of Money Pending Disposition [Repealed].

Repealed by Acts 1989, 71st Leg., 1st C.S., ch. 12 (H.B. 65), § 6, effective October 18, 1989.

Sec. 481.157. Forfeiture Hearing [Repealed].

Repealed by Acts 1989, 71st Leg., 1st C.S., ch. 12 (H.B. 65), § 6, effective October 18, 1989; Acts 1991, 72nd Leg., ch. 14 (S.B. 404), § 198, effective September 1, 1991.

Sec. 481.158. Disposition of Money or Other Things of Value [Repealed].

Repealed by Acts 1989, 71st Leg., 1st C.S., ch. 12 (H.B. 65), § 6, effective October 18, 1989.

Sec. 481.159. Disposition of Controlled Substance Property or Plant.

(a) If a district court orders the forfeiture of a controlled substance property or plant under Chapter 59, Code of Criminal Procedure, or under this code, the court shall also order a law enforcement agency or a criminal justice agency to which the law enforcement agency transferred the property or plant for analysis and storage to:

(1) retain the property or plant for official law enforcement purposes, including use in the investigation of offenses under this code;

(2) deliver the property or plant to a government agency for official purposes;

(3) deliver the property or plant to a person authorized by the court to receive it;

(4) deliver the property or plant to a person authorized by the director to receive it; or

(5) destroy the property or plant that is not otherwise disposed of in the manner prescribed by this subchapter.

(b) The district court may not require the department to receive, analyze, or retain a controlled substance property or plant forfeited to a law enforcement agency other than the department.

(c) In order to ensure that a controlled substance property or plant is not diluted, substituted, diverted, or tampered with while being used in the investigation of offenses under this code, law enforcement agencies using the property or plant for this purpose shall:

(1) employ a qualified individual to conduct qualitative and quantitative analyses of the property or plant before and after their use in an investigation;

(2) maintain the property or plant in a secure storage area accessible only to the law enforcement agency head and the individual responsible for analyzing, preserving, and maintaining security over the property or plant; and

(3) maintain a log documenting:

(A) the date of issue, date of return, type, amount, and concentration of property or plant used in an investigation; and

(B) the signature and the printed or typed name of the peace officer to whom the property or plant was issued and the signature and the printed or typed name of the individual issuing the property or plant.

(d) A law enforcement agency may contract with another law enforcement agency to provide security that complies with Subsection (c) for controlled substance property or plants.

(e) A law enforcement agency may adopt a written policy with more stringent requirements than those required by Subsection (c). The director may enter and inspect, in accordance with Section 481.181, a location at which an agency maintains records or controlled substance property or plants as required by this section.

(f) If a law enforcement agency uses a controlled substance property or plant in the investigation of an offense under this code and the property or plant has been transported across state lines before the forfeiture, the agency shall cooperate with a federal agency in the investigation if requested to do so by the federal agency.

(g) Under the rules of the department, a law enforcement agency head may grant to another person access to a secure storage facility under Subsection (c)(2).

(h) A county, justice, or municipal court may order forfeiture of a controlled substance property or plant, unless the lawful possession of and title to the property or plant can be ascertained. If the court determines that a person had lawful possession of and title to the controlled substance property or plant before it was seized, the court shall order the controlled substance property or plant returned to the person, if the person so desires. The court may only order the destruction of a controlled substance property or plant that is not otherwise disposed of in the manner prescribed by Section 481.160.

(i) If a controlled substance property or plant seized under this chapter was forfeited to an agency for the purpose of destruction or disposition under Section 481.161 in lieu of destruction or for any purpose other than investigation, the property or plant may not be used in an investigation unless a district court orders disposition under this section and permits the use of the property or plant in the investigation.

Sec. 481.160. Disposition of Excess Quantities.

Health and Safety Code

(a) If a controlled substance property or plant is forfeited under this code or under Chapter 59, Code of Criminal Procedure, the law enforcement agency that seized the property or plant or to which the property or plant is forfeited or a criminal justice agency to which the law enforcement agency transferred the property or plant for analysis and storage may summarily destroy the property or plant without a court order, or otherwise dispose of the property or plant in lieu of destruction in accordance with Section 481.161, before the disposition of a case arising out of the forfeiture if the agency ensures that:

(1) at least five random and representative samples are taken from the total amount of the property or plant and a sufficient quantity is preserved to provide for discovery by parties entitled to discovery;

(2) photographs are taken that reasonably depict the total amount of the property or plant; and

(3) the gross weight or liquid measure of the property or plant is determined, either by actually weighing or measuring the property or plant or by estimating its weight or measurement after making dimensional measurements of the total amount seized.

(b) If the property consists of a single container of liquid, taking and preserving one representative sample complies with Subsection (a)(1).

(c) A representative sample, photograph, or record made under this section is admissible in civil or criminal proceedings in the same manner and to the same extent as if the total quantity of the suspected controlled substance property or plant was offered in evidence, regardless of whether the remainder of the property or plant has been destroyed or otherwise disposed of. An inference or presumption of spoliation does not apply to a property or plant destroyed or otherwise disposed of under this section.

(d) If hazardous waste, residuals, contaminated glassware, associated equipment, or by-products from illicit chemical laboratories or similar operations that create a health or environmental hazard or are not capable of being safely stored are forfeited, those items may be disposed of under Subsection (a) or may be seized by and summarily forfeited to a law enforcement agency and destroyed by the law enforcement agency or by a criminal justice agency to which the law enforcement agency transferred the items for analysis and storage without a court order before the disposition of a case arising out of the forfeiture if current environmental protection standards are followed.

(e) A law enforcement agency seizing and destroying or disposing of materials described in Subsection (d) shall ensure that photographs are taken that reasonably depict the total amount of the materials seized and the manner in which the materials were physically arranged or positioned before seizure.

(f) [Repealed by Acts 2005, 79th Leg., ch. 1224 (H.B. 1068), § 19(2), effective September 1, 2005.]

Sec. 481.161. Disposition of Controlled Substance Property or Plant in Lieu of Destruction.

(a) Controlled substance property or plants subject to summary destruction or ordered destroyed by a court may be disposed of in accordance with this section.

(b) A law enforcement agency or criminal justice agency may transfer the controlled substance property or plants to a crime laboratory to be used for the purposes of laboratory research, testing results validation, and training of analysts.

(c) The crime laboratory to which the controlled substance property or plants are transferred under Subsection (b) shall destroy or otherwise properly dispose of any unused quantities of the controlled substance property or plants.

(d) This section does not apply to evidence described by Section 481.160(d).

(e) The director may adopt rules to implement this section.

SUBCHAPTER F
INSPECTIONS, EVIDENCE, AND MISCELLANEOUS LAW ENFORCEMENT PROVISIONS

Sec. 481.181. Inspections.

(a) The director may enter controlled premises at any reasonable time and inspect the premises and items described by Subsection (b) in order to inspect, copy, and verify the correctness of a record, report, or other document required to be made or kept under this chapter and to perform other functions under this chapter. For purposes of this subsection, "reasonable time" means any time during the normal business hours of the person or activity regulated under this chapter or any time an activity regulated under this chapter is occurring on the premises. The director shall:

(1) state the purpose of the entry;

(2) display to the owner, operator, or agent in charge of the premises appropriate credentials; and

Health and Safety Code

(3) deliver to the owner, operator, or agent in charge of the premises a written notice of inspection authority.

(b) The director may:

(1) inspect and copy a record, report, or other document required to be made or kept under this chapter;

(2) inspect, within reasonable limits and in a reasonable manner, the controlled premises and all pertinent equipment, finished and unfinished drugs, other substances, and materials, containers, labels, records, files, papers, processes, controls, and facilities as appropriate to verify a record, report, or document required to be kept under this chapter or to administer this chapter;

(3) examine and inventory stock of a controlled substance and obtain samples of the controlled substance;

(4) examine a hypodermic syringe, needle, pipe, or other instrument, device, contrivance, equipment, control, container, label, or facility relating to a possible violation of this chapter; and

(5) examine a material used, intended to be used, or capable of being used to dilute or adulterate a controlled substance.

(c) Unless the owner, operator, or agent in charge of the controlled premises consents in writing, the director may not inspect:

(1) financial data;

(2) sales data other than shipment data; or

(3) pricing data.

Sec. 481.182. Evidentiary Rules Relating to Offer of Delivery.

For the purpose of establishing a delivery under this chapter, proof of an offer to sell must be corroborated by:

(1) a person other than the person to whom the offer is made; or

(2) evidence other than a statement of the person to whom the offer is made.

Sec. 481.183. Evidentiary Rules Relating to Drug Paraphernalia.

(a) In considering whether an item is drug paraphernalia under this chapter, a court or other authority shall consider, in addition to all other logically relevant factors, and subject to rules of evidence:

(1) statements by an owner or person in control of the object concerning its use;

(2) the existence of any residue of a controlled substance on the object;

(3) direct or circumstantial evidence of the intent of an owner or other person in control of the object to deliver it to a person whom the person knows or should reasonably know intends to use the object to facilitate a violation of this chapter;

(4) oral or written instructions provided with the object concerning its use;

(5) descriptive material accompanying the object that explains or depicts its use;

(6) the manner in which the object is displayed for sale;

(7) whether the owner or person in control of the object is a supplier of similar or related items to the community, such as a licensed distributor or dealer of tobacco products;

(8) direct or circumstantial evidence of the ratio of sales of the object to the total sales of the business enterprise;

(9) the existence and scope of uses for the object in the community;

(10) the physical design characteristics of the item; and

(11) expert testimony concerning the item's use.

(b) The innocence of an owner or other person in charge of an object as to a direct violation of this chapter does not prevent a finding that the object is intended or designed for use as drug paraphernalia.

Sec. 481.184. Burden of Proof; Liabilities.

(a) The state is not required to negate an exemption or exception provided by this chapter in a complaint, information, indictment, or other pleading or in any trial, hearing, or other proceeding under this chapter. A person claiming the benefit of an exemption or exception has the burden of going forward with the evidence with respect to the exemption or exception.

(b) In the absence of proof that a person is the duly authorized holder of an appropriate registration or order form issued under this chapter, the person is presumed not to be the holder of the registration or form. The presumption is subject to rebuttal by a person charged with an offense under this chapter.

(c) This chapter does not impose a liability on an authorized state, county, or municipal officer engaged in the lawful performance of official duties.

Sec. 481.185. Arrest Reports.

(a) Each law enforcement agency in this state shall file monthly with the director a report of all arrests made for drug offenses and quantities of controlled substances seized during the preceding month. The agency shall make the report on a form provided by the director and shall provide the information required by the form.

(b) The director shall publish an annual summary of all drug arrests and controlled substances seized in the state.

Sec. 481.186. Cooperative Arrangements.

(a) The director shall cooperate with federal and state agencies in discharging the director's responsibilities concerning traffic in controlled substances and in suppressing the abuse of controlled substances. The director may:

(1) arrange for the exchange of information among government officials concerning the use and abuse of controlled substances;

(2) cooperate in and coordinate training programs concerning controlled substances law enforcement at local and state levels;

(3) cooperate with the Federal Drug Enforcement Administration and state agencies by establishing a centralized unit to accept, catalog, file, and collect statistics, including records on drug-dependent persons and other controlled substance law offenders in this state and, except as provided by Section 481.068, make the information available for federal, state, and local law enforcement purposes; and

(4) conduct programs of eradication aimed at destroying wild or illegal growth of plant species from which controlled substances may be extracted.

(b) In the exercise of regulatory functions under this chapter, the director may rely on results, information, and evidence relating to the regulatory functions of this chapter received from the Federal Drug Enforcement Administration or a state agency.

SUBCHAPTER G THERAPEUTIC RESEARCH PROGRAM

Sec. 481.201. Research Program; Review Board.

(a) The executive commissioner may establish a controlled substance therapeutic research program for the supervised use of tetrahydrocannabinols for medical and research purposes to be conducted in accordance with this chapter.

(b) If the executive commissioner establishes the program, the executive commissioner shall create a research program review board. The review board members are appointed by the executive commissioner and serve at the will of the executive commissioner.

(c) The review board shall be composed of:

(1) a licensed physician certified by the American Board of Ophthalmology;

(2) a licensed physician certified by the American Board of Internal Medicine and certified in the subspecialty of medical oncology;

(3) a licensed physician certified by the American Board of Psychiatry;

(4) a licensed physician certified by the American Board of Surgery;

(5) a licensed physician certified by the American Board of Radiology; and

(6) a licensed attorney with experience in law pertaining to the practice of medicine.

(d) Members serve without compensation but are entitled to reimbursement for actual and necessary expenses incurred in performing official duties.

Sec. 481.202. Review Board Powers and Duties.

(a) The review board shall review research proposals submitted and medical case histories of persons recommended for participation in a research program and determine which research programs and persons are most suitable for the therapy and research purposes of the program. The review board shall approve the research programs, certify program participants, and conduct periodic reviews of the research and participants.

(b) The review board, after approval of the executive commissioner, may seek authorization to expand the research program to include diseases not covered by this subchapter.

(c) The review board shall maintain a record of all persons in charge of approved research programs and of all persons who participate in the program as researchers or as patients.

(d) The executive commissioner may terminate the distribution of tetrahydrocannabinols and their derivatives to a research program as the executive commissioner determines necessary.

Sec. 481.203. Patient Participation.

(a) A person may not be considered for participation as a recipient of tetrahydrocannabinols and their derivatives through a research program unless the person is recommended to a person in charge of an approved research program and the review board by a physician who is licensed by the Texas Medical Board and is attending the person.

(b) A physician may not recommend a person for the research program unless the person:

(1) has glaucoma or cancer;

Health and Safety Code

(2) is not responding to conventional treatment for glaucoma or cancer or is experiencing severe side effects from treatment; and

(3) has symptoms or side effects from treatment that may be alleviated by medical use of tetrahydrocannabinols or their derivatives.

Sec. 481.204. Acquisition and Distribution of Controlled Substances.

(a) The executive commissioner shall acquire the tetrahydrocannabinols and their derivatives for use in the research program by contracting with the National Institute on Drug Abuse to receive tetrahydrocannabinols and their derivatives that are safe for human consumption according to the regulations adopted by the institute, the United States Food and Drug Administration, and the Federal Drug Enforcement Administration.

(b) The executive commissioner shall supervise the distribution of the tetrahydrocannabinols and their derivatives to program participants. The tetrahydrocannabinols and derivatives of tetrahydrocannabinols may be distributed only by the person in charge of the research program to physicians caring for program participant patients, under rules adopted by the executive commissioner in such a manner as to prevent unauthorized diversion of the substances and in compliance with all requirements of the Federal Drug Enforcement Administration. The physician is responsible for dispensing the substances to patients.

Sec. 481.205. Rules; Reports.

(a) The executive commissioner shall adopt rules necessary for implementing the research program.

(b) If the executive commissioner establishes a program under this subchapter, the commissioner shall publish a report not later than January 1 of each odd-numbered year on the medical effectiveness of the use of tetrahydrocannabinols and their derivatives and any other medical findings of the research program.

SUBCHAPTER H ADMINISTRATIVE PENALTY

Sec. 481.301. Imposition of Penalty.

The department may impose an administrative penalty on a person who violates Section 481.067, 481.077, 481.0771, or 481.080 or a rule or order adopted under any of those sections.

Sec. 481.302. Amount of Penalty.

(a) The amount of the penalty may not exceed $1,000 for each violation, and each day a violation continues or occurs is a separate violation for purposes of imposing a penalty. The total amount of the penalty assessed for a violation continuing or occurring on separate days under this subsection may not exceed $20,000.

(b) The amount shall be based on:

(1) the seriousness of the violation, including the nature, circumstances, extent, and gravity of the violation;

(2) the threat to health or safety caused by the violation;

(3) the history of previous violations;

(4) the amount necessary to deter a future violation;

(5) whether the violator demonstrated good faith, including when applicable whether the violator made good faith efforts to correct the violation; and

(6) any other matter that justice may require.

Sec. 481.303. Report and Notice of Violation and Penalty.

(a) If the department initially determines that a violation occurred, the department shall give written notice of the report to the person by certified mail, registered mail, personal delivery, or another manner of delivery that records the person's receipt of the notice.

(b) The notice must:

(1) include a brief summary of the alleged violation;

(2) state the amount of the recommended penalty; and

(3) inform the person of the person's right to a hearing on the occurrence of the violation, the amount of the penalty, or both.

Sec. 481.304. Penalty to Be Paid or Informal Hearing Requested.

(a) Before the 21st day after the date the person receives notice under Section 481.303, the person in writing may:

(1) accept the determination and recommended penalty; or

(2) make a request for an informal hearing held by the department on the occurrence of the violation, the amount of the penalty, or both.

(b) At the conclusion of an informal hearing requested under Subsection (a), the department may modify the amount of the recommended penalty.

(c) If the person accepts the determination and recommended penalty, including any modification of the amount, or if the person fails to timely respond to the notice, the director by order shall approve the determination and impose the recommended penalty.

Sec. 481.305. Formal Hearing.

(a) The person may request a formal hearing only after participating in an informal hearing.

(b) The request must be submitted in writing and received by the department before the 21st day after the date the person is notified of the decision from the informal hearing.

(c) If a timely request for a formal hearing is not received, the director by order shall approve the determination from the informal hearing and impose the recommended penalty.

(d) If the person timely requests a formal hearing, the director shall refer the matter to the State Office of Administrative Hearings, which shall promptly set a hearing date and give written notice of the time and place of the hearing to the director and to the person. An administrative law judge of the State Office of Administrative Hearings shall conduct the hearing.

(e) The administrative law judge shall make findings of fact and conclusions of law and promptly issue to the director a proposal for a decision about the occurrence of the violation and the amount of any proposed penalty.

(f) If a penalty is proposed under Subsection (e), the administrative law judge shall include in the proposal for a decision a finding setting out costs, fees, expenses, and reasonable and necessary attorney's fees incurred by the state in bringing the proceeding. The director may adopt the finding and impose the costs, fees, and expenses on the person as part of the final order entered in the proceeding.

Sec. 481.306. Decision.

(a) Based on the findings of fact, conclusions of law, and proposal for a decision, the director by order may:

(1) find that a violation occurred and impose a penalty; or

(2) find that a violation did not occur.

(b) The notice of the director's order under Subsection (a) that is sent to the person in the manner provided by Chapter 2001, Government Code, must include a statement of the right of the person to judicial review of the order.

Sec. 481.307. Options Following Decision: Pay or Appeal.

Before the 31st day after the date the order under Section 481.306 that imposes an administrative penalty becomes final, the person shall:

(1) pay the penalty; or

(2) file a petition for judicial review of the order contesting the occurrence of the violation, the amount of the penalty, or both.

Sec. 481.308. Stay of Enforcement of Penalty.

(a) Within the period prescribed by Section 481.307, a person who files a petition for judicial review may:

(1) stay enforcement of the penalty by:

(A) paying the penalty to the court for placement in an escrow account; or

(B) giving the court a supersedeas bond approved by the court that:

(i) is for the amount of the penalty; and

(ii) is effective until all judicial review of the order is final; or

(2) request the court to stay enforcement of the penalty by:

(A) filing with the court a sworn affidavit of the person stating that the person is financially unable to pay the penalty and is financially unable to give the supersedeas bond; and

(B) sending a copy of the affidavit to the director by certified mail.

(b) Following receipt of a copy of an affidavit under Subsection (a)(2), the director may file with the court, before the sixth day after the date of receipt, a contest to the affidavit. The court shall hold a hearing on the facts alleged in the affidavit as soon as practicable and shall stay the enforcement of the penalty on finding that the alleged facts are true. The person who files an affidavit has the burden of proving that the person is financially unable to pay the penalty or to give a supersedeas bond.

Sec. 481.309. Collection of Penalty.

(a) If the person does not pay the penalty and the enforcement of the penalty is not stayed, the penalty may be collected.

(b) The attorney general may sue to collect the penalty.

Sec. 481.310. Decision by Court.

(a) If the court sustains the finding that a violation occurred, the court may uphold or reduce the amount of the penalty and order the person to pay the full or reduced amount of the penalty.

(b) If the court does not sustain the finding that a violation occurred, the court shall order that a penalty is not owed.

Sec. 481.311. Remittance of Penalty and Interest.

(a) If the person paid the penalty and if the amount of the penalty is reduced or the penalty is not upheld by the court, the court shall order, when the court's judgment becomes final, that the appropriate amount plus accrued interest be remitted to the person before the 31st day after the date that the judgment of the court becomes final.

(b) The interest accrues at the rate charged on loans to depository institutions by the New York Federal Reserve Bank.

(c) The interest shall be paid for the period beginning on the date the penalty is paid and ending on the date the penalty is remitted.

Sec. 481.312. Release of Bond.

(a) If the person gave a supersedeas bond and the penalty is not upheld by the court, the court shall order, when the court's judgment becomes final, the release of the bond.

(b) If the person gave a supersedeas bond and the amount of the penalty is reduced, the court shall order the release of the bond after the person pays the reduced amount.

Sec. 481.313. Administrative Procedure.

A proceeding to impose the penalty is considered to be a contested case under Chapter 2001, Government Code.

Sec. 481.314. Disposition of Penalty.

The department shall send any amount collected as a penalty under this subchapter to the comptroller for deposit to the credit of the general revenue fund.

SUBCHAPTER I INTERAGENCY PRESCRIPTION MONITORING WORK GROUP

Sec. 481.351. Interagency Prescription Monitoring Work Group.

The interagency prescription monitoring work group is created to evaluate the effectiveness of prescription monitoring under this chapter and offer recommendations to improve the effectiveness and efficiency of recordkeeping and other functions related to the regulation of dispensing controlled substances by prescription.

Sec. 481.352. Members.

The work group is composed of:

(1) the executive director of the board or the executive director's designee, who serves as chair of the work group;

(2) the commissioner of state health services or the commissioner's designee;

(3) the executive director of the Texas Medical Board or the executive director's designee;

(4) the executive director of the Texas Board of Nursing or the executive director's designee;

(5) the executive director of the Texas Physician Assistant Board or the executive director's designee;

(6) the executive director of the State Board of Dental Examiners or the executive director's designee;

(7) the executive director of the Texas Optometry Board or the executive director's designee;

(8) the executive director of the Texas Department of Licensing and Regulation or the executive director's designee;

(9) the executive director of the State Board of Veterinary Medical Examiners or the executive director's designee; and

(10) a medical examiner appointed by the board.

Sec. 481.353. Meetings.

(a) The work group shall meet when necessary as determined by the board.

(b) The work group is subject to Chapter 551, Government Code.

(c) The work group shall proactively engage stakeholders and solicit and take into account input from the public.

Sec. 481.354. Report.

Not later than December 1 of each even-numbered year, the work group shall submit to the legislature its recommendations relating to prescription monitoring.

CHAPTER 482 SIMULATED CONTROLLED SUBSTANCES

Sec. 482.001. Definitions.

In this chapter:

(1) "Controlled substance" has the meaning assigned by Section 481.002 (Texas Controlled Substances Act).

(2) "Deliver" means to transfer, actually or constructively, from one person to another a simulated controlled substance, regardless of whether there is an agency relationship. The term includes offering to sell a simulated controlled substance.

(3) "Manufacture" means to make a simulated controlled substance and includes the preparation of the substance in dosage form by mixing, compounding, encapsulating, tableting, or any other process.

(4) "Simulated controlled substance" means a substance that is purported to be a controlled substance, but is chemically different from the controlled substance it is purported to be.

Sec. 482.002. Unlawful Delivery or Manufacture with Intent to Deliver; Criminal Penalty.

(a) A person commits an offense if the person knowingly or intentionally manufactures with the intent to deliver or delivers a simulated controlled substance and the person:

(1) expressly represents the substance to be a controlled substance;

(2) represents the substance to be a controlled substance in a manner that would lead a reasonable person to believe that the substance is a controlled substance; or

(3) states to the person receiving or intended to receive the simulated controlled substance that the person may successfully represent the substance to be a controlled substance to a third party.

(b) It is a defense to prosecution under this section that the person manufacturing with the intent to deliver or delivering the simulated controlled substance was:

(1) acting in the discharge of the person's official duties as a peace officer;

(2) manufacturing the substance for or delivering the substance to a licensed medical practitioner for use as a placebo in the course of the practitioner's research or practice; or

(3) a licensed medical practitioner, pharmacist, or other person authorized to dispense or administer a controlled substance, and the person was acting in the legitimate performance of the person's professional duties.

(c) It is not a defense to prosecution under this section that the person manufacturing with the intent to deliver or delivering the simulated controlled substance believed the substance to be a controlled substance.

(d) An offense under this section is a state jail felony.

Sec. 482.003. Evidentiary Rules.

(a) In determining whether a person has represented a simulated controlled substance to be a controlled substance in a manner that would lead a reasonable person to believe the substance was a controlled substance, a court may consider, in addition to all other logically relevant factors, whether:

(1) the simulated controlled substance was packaged in a manner normally used for the delivery of a controlled substance;

(2) the delivery or intended delivery included an exchange of or demand for property as consideration for delivery of the substance and the amount of the consideration was substantially in excess of the reasonable value of the simulated controlled substance; and

(3) the physical appearance of the finished product containing the substance was substantially identical to a controlled substance.

(b) Proof of an offer to sell a simulated controlled substance must be corroborated by a person other than the offeree or by evidence other than a statement of the offeree.

Sec. 482.004. Summary Forfeiture.

A simulated controlled substance seized as a result of an offense under this chapter is subject to summary forfeiture and to destruction or disposition in the same manner as is a controlled substance property under Subchapter E, Chapter 481.

Sec. 482.005. Preparatory Offenses.

Title 4, Penal Code, applies to an offense under this chapter.

CHAPTER 483
DANGEROUS DRUGS

SUBCHAPTER A
GENERAL PROVISIONS

Sec. 483.0001. Short Title.

This Act may be cited as the Texas Dangerous Drug Act.

Sec. 483.001. Definitions.

In this chapter:

(1) "Board" means the Texas State Board of Pharmacy.

(2) "Dangerous drug" means a device or a drug that is unsafe for self-medication and that is not included in Schedules I through V or Penalty Groups 1 through 4 of Chapter 481 (Texas Controlled Substances Act). The term includes a device or a drug that bears or is required to bear the legend:

(A) "Caution: federal law prohibits dispensing without prescription" or "Rx only" or another legend that complies with federal law; or

(B) "Caution: federal law restricts this drug to use by or on the order of a licensed veterinarian."

(3) "Deliver" means to sell, dispense, give away, or supply in any other manner.

(4) "Designated agent" means:

(A) a licensed nurse, physician assistant, pharmacist, or other individual designated by a practitioner to communicate prescription drug orders to a pharmacist;

(B) a licensed nurse, physician assistant, or pharmacist employed in a health care facility to whom the practitioner communicates a prescription drug order; or

(C) a registered nurse or physician assistant authorized by a practitioner to carry out a prescription drug order for dangerous drugs under Subchapter B, Chapter 157, Occupations Code.

(5) "Dispense" means to prepare, package, compound, or label a dangerous drug in the course of professional practice for delivery under the lawful order of a practitioner to an ultimate user or the user's agent.

(6) "Manufacturer" means a person, other than a pharmacist, who manufactures dangerous drugs. The term includes a person who prepares dangerous drugs in dosage form by mixing, compounding, encapsulating, entableting, or any other process.

(7) "Patient" means:

(A) an individual for whom a dangerous drug is prescribed or to whom a dangerous drug is administered; or

(B) an owner or the agent of an owner of an animal for which a dangerous drug is prescribed or to which a dangerous drug is administered.

(8) "Person" includes an individual, corporation, partnership, and association.

(9) "Pharmacist" means a person licensed by the Texas State Board of Pharmacy to practice pharmacy.

(10) "Pharmacy" means a facility where prescription drug or medication orders are received, processed, dispensed, or distributed under this chapter, Chapter 481 of this code, and Subtitle J, Title 3, Occupations Code. The term does not include a narcotic drug treatment program that is regulated by Chapter 466, Health and Safety Code.

(11) "Practice of pharmacy" means:

(A) provision of those acts or services necessary to provide pharmaceutical care;

(B) interpretation and evaluation of prescription drug orders or medication orders;

(C) participation in drug and device selection as authorized by law, drug administration, drug regimen review, or drug or drug-related research;

(D) provision of patient counseling;

(E) responsibility for:

(i) dispensing of prescription drug orders or distribution of medication orders in the patient's best interest;

(ii) compounding and labeling of drugs and devices, except labeling by a manufacturer, repackager, or distributor of nonprescription drugs and commercially packaged prescription drugs and devices;

(iii) proper and safe storage of drugs and devices; or

(iv) maintenance of proper records for drugs and devices. In this subdivision, "device" has the meaning assigned by Subtitle J, Title 3, Occupations Code; or

(F) performance of a specific act of drug therapy management for a patient delegated to a pharmacist by a written protocol from a physician licensed by the state under Subtitle B, Title 3, Occupations Code.

(12) "Practitioner" means:

(A) a person licensed by:

(i) the Texas Medical Board, State Board of Dental Examiners, Texas Optometry Board, or State Board of Veterinary Medical Examiners to prescribe and administer dangerous drugs; or

(ii) the Texas Department of Licensing and Regulation, with respect to podiatry, to prescribe and administer dangerous drugs;

(B) a person licensed by another state in a health field in which, under the laws of this state, a licensee may legally prescribe dangerous drugs;

(C) a person licensed in Canada or Mexico in a health field in which, under the laws of this state, a licensee may legally prescribe dangerous drugs; or

(D) an advanced practice registered nurse or physician assistant to whom a physician has delegated the authority to prescribe or order a drug or device under Section 157.0511, 157.0512, or 157.054, Occupations Code.

(13) "Prescription" means an order from a practitioner, or an agent of the practitioner designated in writing as authorized to communicate

Health and Safety Code

prescriptions, or an order made in accordance with Subchapter B, Chapter 157, Occupations Code, or Section 203.353, Occupations Code, to a pharmacist for a dangerous drug to be dispensed that states:

(A) the date of the order's issue;

(B) the name and address of the patient;

(C) if the drug is prescribed for an animal, the species of the animal;

(D) the name and quantity of the drug prescribed;

(E) the directions for the use of the drug;

(F) the intended use of the drug unless the practitioner determines the furnishing of this information is not in the best interest of the patient;

(G) the name, address, and telephone number of the practitioner at the practitioner's usual place of business, legibly printed or stamped; and

(H) the name, address, and telephone number of the licensed midwife, registered nurse, or physician assistant, legibly printed or stamped, if signed by a licensed midwife, registered nurse, or physician assistant.

(14) "Warehouseman" means a person who stores dangerous drugs for others and who has no control over the disposition of the drugs except for the purpose of storage.

(15) "Wholesaler" means a person engaged in the business of distributing dangerous drugs to a person listed in Sections 483.041(c)(1)-(6).

Sec. 483.002. Rules.

The board may adopt rules for the proper administration and enforcement of this chapter.

Sec. 483.003. Department of State Health Services Hearings Regarding Certain Dangerous Drugs.

(a) The Department of State Health Services may hold public hearings in accordance with Chapter 2001, Government Code, to determine whether there is compelling evidence that a dangerous drug has been abused, either by being prescribed for nontherapeutic purposes or by the ultimate user.

(b) On finding that a dangerous drug has been abused, the Department of State Health Services may limit the availability of the abused drug by permitting its dispensing only on the prescription of a practitioner described by Section 483.001(12)(A), (B), or (D).

Sec. 483.004. Commissioner of State Health Services Emergency Authority Relating to Dangerous Drugs.

If the commissioner of state health services has compelling evidence that an immediate danger to the public health exists as a result of the prescription of a dangerous drug by practitioners described by Section 483.001(12)(C), the commissioner may use the commissioner's existing emergency authority to limit the availability of the drug by permitting its prescription only by practitioners described by Section 483.001(12)(A), (B), or (D).

SUBCHAPTER B DUTIES OF PHARMACISTS, PRACTITIONERS, AND OTHER PERSONS

Sec. 483.021. Determination by Pharmacist on Request to Dispense Drug.

(a) A pharmacist who is requested to dispense a dangerous drug under a prescription issued by a practitioner shall determine, in the exercise of the pharmacist's professional judgment, that the prescription is a valid prescription. A pharmacist may not dispense a dangerous drug if the pharmacist knows or should have known that the prescription was issued without a valid patient-practitioner relationship.

(b) A pharmacist who is requested to dispense a dangerous drug under a prescription issued by a therapeutic optometrist shall determine, in the exercise of the pharmacist's professional judgment, whether the prescription is for a dangerous drug that a therapeutic optometrist is authorized to prescribe under Section 351.358, Occupations Code.

Sec. 483.022. Practitioner's Designated Agent; Practitioner's Responsibilities.

(a) A practitioner shall provide in writing the name of each designated agent as defined by Section 483.001(4)(A) and (C), and the name of each healthcare facility which employs persons defined by Section 483.001(4)(B).

(b) The practitioner shall maintain at the practitioner's usual place of business a list of the designated agents or healthcare facilities as defined by Section 483.001(4).

(c) The practitioner shall provide a pharmacist with a copy of the practitioner's written authorization for a designated agent as defined by Section 483.001(4) on the pharmacist's request.

(d) This section does not relieve a practitioner or the practitioner's designated agent from the requirements of Subchapter A, Chapter 562, Occupations Code.

(e) A practitioner remains personally responsible for the actions of a designated agent who communicates a prescription to a pharmacist.

(f) A practitioner may designate a person who is a licensed vocational nurse or has an education equivalent to or greater than that required for a licensed vocational nurse to communicate prescriptions of an advanced practice nurse or physician assistant authorized by the practitioner to sign prescription drug orders under Subchapter B, Chapter 157, Occupations Code.

Sec. 483.023. Retention of Prescriptions.

A pharmacy shall retain a prescription for a dangerous drug dispensed by the pharmacy for two years after the date of the initial dispensing or the last refilling of the prescription, whichever date is later.

Sec. 483.024. Records of Acquisition or Disposal.

The following persons shall maintain a record of each acquisition and each disposal of a dangerous drug for two years after the date of the acquisition or disposal:

(1) a pharmacy;

(2) a practitioner;

(3) a person who obtains a dangerous drug for lawful research, teaching, or testing purposes, but not for resale;

(4) a hospital that obtains a dangerous drug for lawful administration by a practitioner; and

(5) a manufacturer or wholesaler licensed by the Department of State Health Services under Chapter 431 (Texas Food, Drug, and Cosmetic Act).

Sec. 483.025. Inspections; Inventories.

A person required to keep records relating to dangerous drugs shall:

(1) make the records available for inspection and copying at all reasonable hours by any public official or employee engaged in enforcing this chapter; and

(2) allow the official or employee to inventory all stocks of dangerous drugs on hand.

Sec. 483.026. Requirements Relating to Anabolic Steroids and Human Growth Hormones [Repealed].

Repealed by Acts 1989, 71st Leg., ch. 1100 (S.B. 1046), § 5.03(h), effective September 1, 1989.

SUBCHAPTER C CRIMINAL PENALTIES

Sec. 483.041. Possession of Dangerous Drug.

(a) A person commits an offense if the person possesses a dangerous drug unless the person obtains the drug from a pharmacist acting in the manner described by Section 483.042(a)(1) or a practitioner acting in the manner described by Section 483.042(a)(2).

(b) Except as permitted by this chapter, a person commits an offense if the person possesses a dangerous drug for the purpose of selling the drug.

(c) Subsection (a) does not apply to the possession of a dangerous drug in the usual course of business or practice or in the performance of official duties by the following persons or an agent or employee of the person:

(1) a pharmacy licensed by the board;

(2) a practitioner;

(3) a person who obtains a dangerous drug for lawful research, teaching, or testing, but not for resale;

(4) a hospital that obtains a dangerous drug for lawful administration by a practitioner;

(5) an officer or employee of the federal, state, or local government;

(6) a manufacturer or wholesaler licensed by the Department of State Health Services under Chapter 431 (Texas Food, Drug, and Cosmetic Act);

(7) a carrier or warehouseman;

(8) a home and community support services agency licensed under and acting in accordance with Chapter 142;

(9) a licensed midwife who obtains oxygen for administration to a mother or newborn or who obtains a dangerous drug for the administration of prophylaxis to a newborn for the prevention of ophthalmia neonatorum in accordance with Section 203.353, Occupations Code;

(10) a salvage broker or salvage operator licensed under Chapter 432; or

(11) a certified laser hair removal professional under Subchapter M, Chapter 401, who possesses and uses a laser or pulsed light device approved by and registered with the Department of State Health Services and in compliance with department rules for the sole purpose of cosmetic nonablative hair removal.

(d) An offense under this section is a Class A misdemeanor.

(e) It is a defense to prosecution for an offense under Subsection (a) that the actor:

(1) was the first person to request emergency medical assistance in response to the possible overdose of another person and:

(A) made the request for medical assistance during an ongoing medical emergency;

(B) remained on the scene until the medical assistance arrived; and

(C) cooperated with medical assistance and law enforcement personnel; or

(2) was the victim of a possible overdose for which emergency medical assistance was requested, by the actor or by another person, during an ongoing medical emergency.

(f) The defense to prosecution provided by Subsection (e) is not available if:

(1) at the time the request for emergency medical assistance was made:

(A) a peace officer was in the process of arresting the actor or executing a search warrant describing the actor or the place from which the request for medical assistance was made; or

(B) the actor is committing another offense, other than an offense punishable under Section 481.115(b), 481.1151(b)(1), 481.116(b), 481.1161(b)(1) or (2), 481.117(b), 481.118(b), or 481.121(b)(1) or (2), or an offense under Section 481.119(b), 481.125(a), or 485.031(a);

(2) the actor has been previously convicted of or placed on deferred adjudication community supervision for an offense under this chapter or Chapter 481 or 485;

(3) the actor was acquitted in a previous proceeding in which the actor successfully established the defense under that subsection or Section 481.115(g), 481.1151(c), 481.116(f), 481.1161(c), 481.117(f), 481.118(f), 481.119(c), 481.121(c), 481.125(g), or 485.031(c); or

(4) at any time during the 18-month period preceding the date of the commission of the instant offense, the actor requested emergency medical assistance in response to the possible overdose of the actor or another person.

(g) The defense to prosecution provided by Subsection (e) does not preclude the admission of evidence obtained by law enforcement resulting from the request for emergency medical assistance if that evidence pertains to an offense for which the defense described by Subsection (e) is not available.

Sec. 483.042. Delivery or Offer of Delivery of Dangerous Drug.

(a) A person commits an offense if the person delivers or offers to deliver a dangerous drug:

(1) unless:

(A) the dangerous drug is delivered or offered for delivery by a pharmacist under:

(i) a prescription issued by a practitioner described by Section 483.001(12)(A) or (B);

(ii) a prescription signed by a registered nurse or physician assistant in accordance with Subchapter B, Chapter 157, Occupations Code; or

(iii) an original written prescription issued by a practitioner described by Section 483.001(12)(C); and

(B) a label is attached to the immediate container in which the drug is delivered or offered to be delivered and the label contains the following information:

(i) the name and address of the pharmacy from which the drug is delivered or offered for delivery;

(ii) the date the prescription for the drug is dispensed;

(iii) the number of the prescription as filed in the prescription files of the pharmacy from which the prescription is dispensed;

(iv) the name of the practitioner who prescribed the drug and, if applicable, the name of the registered nurse or physician assistant who signed the prescription;

(v) the name of the patient and, if the drug is prescribed for an animal, a statement of the species of the animal; and

(vi) directions for the use of the drug as contained in the prescription; or

(2) unless:

(A) the dangerous drug is delivered or offered for delivery by:

(i) a practitioner in the course of practice; or

(ii) a registered nurse or physician assistant in the course of practice in accordance with Subchapter B, Chapter 157, Occupations Code; and

(B) a label is attached to the immediate container in which the drug is delivered or offered to be delivered and the label contains the following information:

(i) the name and address of the practitioner who prescribed the drug, and if applicable, the name and address of the registered nurse or physician assistant;

(ii) the date the drug is delivered;

(iii) the name of the patient and, if the drug is prescribed for an animal, a statement of the species of the animal; and

(iv) the name of the drug, the strength of the drug, and directions for the use of the drug.

(b) Subsection (a) does not apply to the delivery or offer for delivery of a dangerous drug to a person listed in Section 483.041(c) for use in the usual course of business or practice or in the performance of official duties by the person.

(c) Proof of an offer to sell a dangerous drug must be corroborated by a person other than the offeree or by evidence other than a statement by the offeree.

(d) An offense under this section is a state jail felony.

(e) The labeling provisions of Subsection (a) do not apply to a dangerous drug prescribed or dispensed for administration to a patient who is institutionalized. The board shall adopt rules for the labeling of such a drug.

(f) Provided all federal requirements are met, the labeling provisions of Subsection (a) do not apply to a dangerous drug prescribed or dispensed for administration to food production animals in an agricultural operation under a written medical directive or treatment guideline from a veterinarian licensed under Chapter 801, Occupations Code.

Sec. 483.043. Manufacture of Dangerous Drug.

(a) A person commits an offense if the person manufactures a dangerous drug and the person is not authorized by law to manufacture the drug.

(b) An offense under this section is a state jail felony.

Sec. 483.044. Prescribing, Delivering, and Administering Steroids and Growth Hormones [Repealed].

Repealed by Acts 1989, 71st Leg., ch. 1100 (S.B. 1046), § 5.03(h), effective September 1, 1989.

Sec. 483.045. Forging or Altering Prescription.

(a) A person commits an offense if the person:

(1) forges a prescription or increases the prescribed quantity of a dangerous drug in a prescription;

(2) issues a prescription bearing a forged or fictitious signature;

(3) obtains or attempts to obtain a dangerous drug by using a forged, fictitious, or altered prescription;

(4) obtains or attempts to obtain a dangerous drug by means of a fictitious or fraudulent telephone call; or

(5) possesses a dangerous drug obtained by a forged, fictitious, or altered prescription or by means of a fictitious or fraudulent telephone call.

(b) An offense under this section is a Class B misdemeanor unless it is shown on the trial of the defendant that the defendant has previously been convicted of an offense under this chapter, in which event the offense is a Class A misdemeanor.

Sec. 483.046. Failure to Retain Prescription.

(a) A pharmacist commits an offense if the pharmacist:

(1) delivers a dangerous drug under a prescription; and

(2) fails to retain the prescription as required by Section 483.023.

(b) An offense under this section is a Class B misdemeanor unless it is shown on the trial of the defendant that the defendant has previously been convicted of an offense under this chapter, in which event the offense is a Class A misdemeanor.

Sec. 483.047. Refilling Prescription Without Authorization.

(a) Except as authorized by Subsections (b) and (b-1), a pharmacist commits an offense if the pharmacist refills a prescription unless:

(1) the prescription contains an authorization by the practitioner for the refilling of the prescription, and the pharmacist refills the prescription in the manner provided by the authorization; or

(2) at the time of refilling the prescription, the pharmacist is authorized to do so by the practitioner who issued the prescription.

(b) A pharmacist may exercise his professional judgment in refilling a prescription for a dangerous drug without the authorization of the prescribing practitioner provided:

(1) failure to refill the prescription might result in an interruption of a therapeutic regimen or create patient suffering;

(2) either:

(A) a natural or manmade disaster has occurred which prohibits the pharmacist from being able to contact the practitioner; or

(B) the pharmacist is unable to contact the practitioner after reasonable effort;

(3) the quantity of drug dispensed does not exceed a 72-hour supply;

(4) the pharmacist informs the patient or the patient's agent at the time of dispensing that the refill is being provided without such authorization and that authorization of the practitioner is required for future refills; and

(5) the pharmacist informs the practitioner of the emergency refill at the earliest reasonable time.

(b-1) Notwithstanding Subsection (b), in the event of a natural or manmade disaster, a pharmacist may dispense not more than a 30-day supply of

Health and Safety Code

a dangerous drug without the authorization of the prescribing practitioner if:

(1) failure to refill the prescription might result in an interruption of a therapeutic regimen or create patient suffering;

(2) the natural or manmade disaster prohibits the pharmacist from being able to contact the practitioner;

(3) the governor has declared a state of disaster under Chapter 418, Government Code; and

(4) the board, through the executive director, has notified pharmacies in this state that pharmacists may dispense up to a 30-day supply of a dangerous drug.

(b-2) The prescribing practitioner is not liable for an act or omission by a pharmacist in dispensing a dangerous drug under Subsection (b-1).

(c) An offense under this section is a Class B misdemeanor unless it is shown on the trial of the defendant that the defendant has previously been convicted under this chapter, in which event the offense is a Class A misdemeanor.

Sec. 483.048. Unauthorized Communication of Prescription.

(a) An agent of a practitioner commits an offense if the agent communicates by telephone a prescription unless the agent is designated in writing under Section 483.022 as authorized by the practitioner to communicate prescriptions by telephone.

(b) An offense under this section is a Class B misdemeanor unless it is shown on the trial of the defendant that the defendant has previously been convicted of an offense under this chapter, in which event the offense is a Class A misdemeanor.

Sec. 483.049. Failure to Maintain Records.

(a) A person commits an offense if the person is required to maintain a record under Section 483.023 or 483.024 and the person fails to maintain the record in the manner required by those sections.

(b) An offense under this section is a Class B misdemeanor unless it is shown on the trial of the defendant that the defendant has previously been convicted of an offense under this chapter, in which event the offense is a Class A misdemeanor.

Sec. 483.050. Refusal to Permit Inspection.

(a) A person commits an offense if the person is required to permit an inspection authorized by Section 483.025 and fails to permit the inspection in the manner required by that section.

(b) An offense under this section is a Class B misdemeanor unless it is shown on the trial of the defendant that the defendant has previously been convicted of an offense under this chapter, in which event the offense is a Class A misdemeanor.

Sec. 483.051. Using or Revealing Trade Secret.

(a) A person commits an offense if the person uses for the person's advantage or reveals to another person, other than to an officer or employee of the board or to a court in a judicial proceeding relevant to this chapter, information relating to dangerous drugs required to be kept under this chapter, if that information concerns a method or process subject to protection as a trade secret.

(b) An offense under this section is a Class B misdemeanor unless it is shown on the trial of the defendant that the defendant has previously been convicted of an offense under this chapter, in which event the offense is a Class A misdemeanor.

Sec. 483.052. Violation of Other Provision.

(a) A person commits an offense if the person violates a provision of this chapter other than a provision for which a specific offense is otherwise described by this chapter.

(b) An offense under this section is a Class B misdemeanor, unless it is shown on the trial of the defendant that the defendant has previously been convicted of an offense under this chapter, in which event the offense is a Class A misdemeanor.

Sec. 483.053. Preparatory Offenses.

Title 4, Penal Code, applies to an offense under this subchapter.

SUBCHAPTER D CRIMINAL AND CIVIL PROCEDURE

Sec. 483.071. Exceptions; Burden of Proof.

(a) In a complaint, information, indictment, or other action or proceeding brought for the enforcement of this chapter, the state is not required to negate an exception, excuse, proviso, or exemption contained in this chapter.

(b) The defendant has the burden of proving the exception, excuse, proviso, or exemption.

Sec. 483.072. Uncorroborated Testimony.

A conviction under this chapter may be obtained on the uncorroborated testimony of a party to the offense.

Sec. 483.073. Search Warrant.

A peace officer may apply for a search warrant to search for dangerous drugs possessed in violation of this chapter. The peace officer must apply for and execute the search warrant in the manner prescribed by the Code of Criminal Procedure.

Sec. 483.074. Seizure and Destruction.

(a) A dangerous drug that is manufactured, sold, or possessed in violation of this chapter is contraband and may be seized by an employee of the board or by a peace officer authorized to enforce this chapter and charged with that duty.

(b) If a dangerous drug is seized under Subsection (a), the board may direct an employee of the board or an authorized peace officer to destroy the drug. The employee or authorized peace officer directed to destroy the drug must act in the presence of another employee of the board or authorized peace officer and shall destroy the drug in any manner designated as appropriate by the board.

(c) Before the dangerous drug is destroyed, an inventory of the drug must be prepared. The inventory must be accompanied by a statement that the dangerous drug is being destroyed at the direction of the board, by an employee of the board or an authorized peace officer, and in the presence of another employee of the board or authorized peace officer. The statement must also contain the names of the persons in attendance at the time of destruction, state the capacity in which each of those persons acts, be signed by those persons, and be sworn to by those persons that the statement is correct. The statement shall be filed with the board.

Sec. 483.075. Injunction.

The board may institute an action in its own name to enjoin a violation of this chapter.

Sec. 483.076. Legal Representation of Board.

(a) If the board institutes a legal proceeding under this chapter, the board may be represented only by a county attorney, a district attorney, or the attorney general.

(b) The board may not employ private counsel in any legal proceeding instituted by or against the board under this chapter.

SUBCHAPTER E OPIOID ANTAGONISTS

Sec. 483.101. Definitions.

In this subchapter:

(1) "Emergency services personnel" includes firefighters, emergency medical services personnel as defined by Section 773.003, emergency room personnel, and other individuals who, in the course and scope of employment or as a volunteer, provide services for the benefit of the general public during emergency situations.

(2) "Opioid antagonist" means any drug that binds to opioid receptors and blocks or otherwise inhibits the effects of opioids acting on those receptors.

(3) "Opioid-related drug overdose" means a condition, evidenced by symptoms such as extreme physical illness, decreased level of consciousness, constriction of the pupils, respiratory depression, or coma, that a layperson would reasonably believe to be the result of the consumption or use of an opioid.

(4) "Prescriber" means a person authorized by law to prescribe an opioid antagonist.

Sec. 483.102. Prescription of Opioid Antagonist; Standing Order.

(a) A prescriber may, directly or by standing order, prescribe an opioid antagonist to:

(1) a person at risk of experiencing an opioid-related drug overdose; or

(2) a family member, friend, or other person in a position to assist a person described by Subdivision (1).

(b) A prescription issued under this section is considered as issued for a legitimate medical purpose in the usual course of professional practice.

(c) A prescriber who, acting in good faith with reasonable care, prescribes or does not prescribe an opioid antagonist is not subject to any criminal or civil liability or any professional disciplinary action for:

(1) prescribing or failing to prescribe the opioid antagonist; or

(2) if the prescriber chooses to prescribe an opioid antagonist, any outcome resulting from the eventual administration of the opioid antagonist.

Sec. 483.103. Dispensing of Opioid Antagonist.

(a) A pharmacist may dispense an opioid antagonist under a valid prescription to:

(1) a person at risk of experiencing an opioid-related drug overdose; or

(2) a family member, friend, or other person in a position to assist a person described by Subdivision (1).

(b) A prescription filled under this section is considered as filled for a legitimate medical purpose in the usual course of professional practice.

(c) A pharmacist who, acting in good faith and with reasonable care, dispenses or does not dispense an opioid antagonist under a valid prescription is not subject to any criminal or civil liability or any professional disciplinary action for:

(1) dispensing or failing to dispense the opioid antagonist; or

(2) if the pharmacist chooses to dispense an opioid antagonist, any outcome resulting from the eventual administration of the opioid antagonist.

Sec. 483.104. Distribution of Opioid Antagonist; Standing Order.

A person or organization acting under a standing order issued by a prescriber may store an opioid antagonist and may distribute an opioid antagonist, provided the person or organization does not request or receive compensation for storage or distribution.

Sec. 483.105. Possession of Opioid Antagonist.

Any person may possess an opioid antagonist, regardless of whether the person holds a prescription for the opioid antagonist.

Sec. 483.106. Administration of Opioid Antagonist.

(a) A person who, acting in good faith and with reasonable care, administers or does not administer an opioid antagonist to another person whom the person believes is suffering an opioid-related drug overdose is not subject to criminal prosecution, sanction under any professional licensing statute, or civil liability, for an act or omission resulting from the administration of or failure to administer the opioid antagonist.

(b) Emergency services personnel are authorized to administer an opioid antagonist to a person who appears to be suffering an opioid-related drug overdose, as clinically indicated.

Sec. 483.107. Conflict of Law.

To the extent of a conflict between this subchapter and another law, this subchapter controls.

CHAPTER 484
ABUSABLE SYNTHETIC SUBSTANCES

Sec. 484.001. Definitions.

In this chapter:

(1) "Abusable synthetic substance" means a substance that:

(A) is not otherwise regulated under this title or under federal law;

(B) is intended to mimic a controlled substance or controlled substance analogue; and

(C) when inhaled, ingested, or otherwise introduced into a person's body:

(i) produces an effect on the central nervous system similar to the effect produced by a controlled substance or controlled substance analogue;

(ii) creates a condition of intoxication, hallucination, or elation similar to a condition produced by a controlled substance or controlled substance analogue; or

(iii) changes, distorts, or disturbs the person's eyesight, thinking process, balance, or coordination in a manner similar to a controlled substance or controlled substance analogue.

(2) "Business" includes trade and commerce and advertising, selling, and buying service or property.

(3) "Mislabeled" means varying from the standard of truth or disclosure in labeling prescribed by law or set by established commercial usage.

(4) "Sell" and "sale" include offer for sale, advertise for sale, expose for sale, keep for the purpose of sale, deliver for or after sale, solicit and offer to buy, and every disposition for value.

Sec. 484.002. Prohibited Acts.

(a) A person commits an offense if in the course of business the person knowingly produces, distributes, sells, or offers for sale a mislabeled abusable synthetic substance.

(b) An offense under this section is a Class C misdemeanor, except that the offense is a Class A misdemeanor if it is shown on the trial of the offense that the actor has previously been convicted of an offense under this section or of an offense under Section 32.42(b)(4), Penal Code, and the adulterated or mislabeled commodity was an abusable synthetic substance.

(c) If conduct constituting an offense under this section also constitutes an offense under another provision of law, the person may be prosecuted under either this section or the other provision.

Sec. 484.003. Civil Penalty.

(a) The attorney general or a district, county, or city attorney may institute an action in district court to collect a civil penalty from a person who in the course of business produces, distributes, sells, or offers for sale a mislabeled abusable synthetic substance.

(b) The civil penalty may not exceed $25,000 a day for each offense. Each day an offense is committed constitutes a separate violation for purposes of the penalty assessment.

(c) The court shall consider the following in determining the amount of the penalty:

(1) the person's history of any previous offenses under Section 484.002 or under Section 32.42(b)(4), Penal Code, relating to the sale of a mislabeled abusable synthetic substance;

(2) the seriousness of the offense;

(3) any hazard posed to the public health and safety by the offense; and

(4) demonstrations of good faith by the person charged.

(d) Venue for a suit brought under this section is in the city or county in which the offense occurred or in Travis County.

(e) A civil penalty recovered in a suit instituted by a local government under this section shall be paid to that local government.

Sec. 484.004. Affirmative Defense.

It is an affirmative defense to prosecution or liability under this chapter that:

(1) the abusable synthetic substance was approved for use, sale, or distribution by the United States Food and Drug Administration or other state or federal regulatory agency with authority to approve the substance's use, sale, or distribution; and

(2) the abusable synthetic substance was lawfully produced, distributed, sold, or offered for sale by the person who is the subject of the criminal or civil action.

Sec. 484.005. No Defense.

In a prosecution or civil action under this chapter, the fact that the abusable synthetic substance was in packaging labeled with "Not for Human Consumption," or other wording indicating the substance is not intended to be ingested, is not a defense.

CHAPTER 484
VOLATILE CHEMICALS [REPEALED]

Sec. 484.006. Proof of Offer to Sell or Deliver [Repealed].

Repealed by Acts 2001, 77th Leg., ch. 1463 (H.B. 2950), § 4, effective September 1, 2001.

Sec. 484.007. Summary Forfeiture [Repealed].

Repealed by Acts 2001, 77th Leg., ch. 1463 (H.B. 2950), § 4, effective September 1, 2001.

Sec. 484.008. Preparatory Offenses [Repealed].

Repealed by Acts 2001, 77th Leg., ch. 1463 (H.B. 2950), § 4, effective September 1, 2001.

CHAPTER 485
ABUSABLE VOLATILE CHEMICALS

SUBCHAPTER A
GENERAL PROVISIONS

Sec. 485.001. Definitions.

In this chapter:

(1) "Abusable volatile chemical" means:

(A) a chemical, including aerosol paint, that:

(i) is packaged in a container subject to the labeling requirements concerning precautions against inhalation established under the Federal Hazardous Substances Act (15 U.S.C. Section 1261 et seq.), as amended, and regulations adopted under that Act and is labeled with the statement of principal hazard on the principal display panel "VAPOR HARMFUL" or other labeling requirement subsequently established under that Act or those regulations;

(ii) when inhaled, ingested, or otherwise introduced into a person's body, may:

(a) affect the person's central nervous system;

(b) create or induce in the person a condition of intoxication, hallucination, or elation; or

(c) change, distort, or disturb the person's eyesight, thinking process, balance, or coordination; and

(iii) is not:

(a) a pesticide subject to Chapter 76, Agriculture Code, or to the Federal Environmental Pesticide Control Act of 1972 (7 U.S.C. Section 136 et seq.), as amended;

Health and Safety Code

(b) a food, drug, or cosmetic subject to Chapter 431 or to the Federal Food, Drug, and Cosmetic Act (21 U.S.C. Section 301 et seq.), as amended; or

(c) a beverage subject to the Federal Alcohol Administration Act (27 U.S.C. Section 201 et seq.), as amended; or

(B) nitrous oxide that is not:

(i) a pesticide subject to Chapter 76, Agriculture Code, or to the Federal Environmental Pesticide Control Act of 1972 (7 U.S.C. Section 136 et seq.), as amended;

(ii) a food, drug, or cosmetic subject to Chapter 431 or to the Federal Food, Drug, and Cosmetic Act (21 U.S.C. Section 301 et seq.), as amended; or

(iii) a beverage subject to the Federal Alcohol Administration Act (27 U.S.C. Section 201 et seq.), as amended.

(2) "Aerosol paint" means an aerosolized paint product, including a clear or pigmented lacquer or finish.

(3) [Repealed by Acts 2015, 84th Leg., ch. 1 (S.B. 219), § 3.1639(94), effective April 2, 2015.]

(4) "Commissioner" means the commissioner of state health services.

(5) "Deliver" means to make the actual or constructive transfer from one person to another of an abusable volatile chemical, regardless of whether there is an agency relationship. The term includes an offer to sell an abusable volatile chemical.

(6) "Delivery" means the act of delivering.

(7) "Department" means the Department of State Health Services.

(7-a) "Executive commissioner" means the executive commissioner of the Health and Human Services Commission.

(8) "Inhalant paraphernalia" means equipment or materials of any kind that are intended for use in inhaling, ingesting, or otherwise introducing into the human body an abusable volatile chemical. The term includes a tube, balloon, bag, fabric, bottle, or other container used to concentrate or hold in suspension an abusable volatile chemical or vapors of the chemical.

(9) "Sell" includes a conveyance, exchange, barter, or trade.

Sec. 485.002. Rules.

The executive commissioner may adopt rules necessary to comply with any labeling requirements concerning precautions against inhalation of an abusable volatile chemical established under the Federal Hazardous Substances Act (15 U.S.C. Section 1261 et seq.), as amended, or under regulations adopted under that Act.

SUBCHAPTER B
SALES PERMITS AND SIGNS

Sec. 485.011. Permit Required.

A person may not sell an abusable volatile chemical at retail unless the person or the person's employer holds, at the time of the sale, a volatile chemical sales permit for the location of the sale.

Sec. 485.012. Issuance and Renewal of Permit.

(a) To be eligible for the issuance or renewal of a volatile chemical sales permit, a person must:

(1) hold a sales tax permit that has been issued to the person;

(2) complete and return to the department an application as required by the department; and

(3) pay to the department the application fee established under Section 485.013 for each location at which an abusable volatile chemical may be sold by the person holding a volatile chemical sales permit.

(b) The executive commissioner shall adopt rules as necessary to administer this chapter, including application procedures and procedures by which the department shall give each permit holder reasonable notice of permit expiration and renewal requirements.

(c) The department shall issue or deny a permit and notify the applicant of the department's action not later than the 60th day after the date on which the department receives the complete application and appropriate fee. If the department denies an application, the department shall include in the notice the reasons for the denial.

(d) A permit issued or renewed under this chapter is valid for two years from the date of issuance or renewal.

(e) A permit is not valid if the permit holder has been convicted more than once in the preceding year of an offense committed:

(1) at a location for which the permit is issued; and

(2) under Section 485.031, 485.032, or 485.033.

(f) A permit issued by the department is the property of the department and must be surrendered on demand by the department.

(g) The department shall prepare an annual roster of permit holders.

(h) The department shall monitor and enforce compliance with this chapter.

Sec. 485.013. Fee.

The executive commissioner by rule may establish fees in amounts as prescribed by Section 12.0111.

Sec. 485.014. Permit Available for Inspection.

A permit holder must have the volatile chemical sales permit or a copy of the permit available for inspection by the public at each location where the permit holder sells an abusable volatile chemical.

Sec. 485.015. Refusal to Issue or Renew Permit.

A proceeding for the failure to issue or renew a volatile chemical sales permit under Section 485.012 or for an appeal from that proceeding is governed by the contested case provisions of Chapter 2001, Government Code.

Sec. 485.016. Disposition of Funds; Education and Prevention Programs.

(a) The department shall account for all amounts received under Section 485.013 and send those amounts to the comptroller.

(b) The comptroller shall deposit the amounts received under Subsection (a) in the state treasury to the credit of the general revenue fund to be used only by the department to:

(1) administer, monitor, and enforce this chapter; and

(2) finance statewide education projects concerning the hazards of abusable volatile chemicals and the prevention of inhalant abuse.

Sec. 485.017. Signs.

A business establishment that sells an abusable volatile chemical at retail shall display a conspicuous sign, in English and Spanish, that states the following:

It is unlawful for a person to sell or deliver an abusable volatile chemical to a person under 18 years of age. Except in limited situations, such an offense is a state jail felony.

It is also unlawful for a person to abuse a volatile chemical by inhaling, ingesting, applying, using, or possessing with intent to inhale, ingest, apply, or use a volatile chemical in a manner designed to affect the central nervous system. Such an offense is a Class B misdemeanor.

Sec. 485.018. Prohibited Ordinance and Rule.

(a) A political subdivision or an agency of this state may not enact an ordinance or rule that requires a business establishment to display an abusable volatile chemical, other than aerosol paint, in a manner that makes the chemical accessible to patrons of the business only with the assistance of personnel of the business.

(b) This section does not apply to an ordinance or rule that was enacted before September 1, 1989.

Sec. 485.019. Restriction of Access to Aerosol Paint.

(a) A business establishment that holds a permit under Section 485.012 and that displays aerosol paint shall display the paint:

(1) in a place that is in the line of sight of a cashier or in the line of sight from a workstation normally continuously occupied during business hours;

(2) in a manner that makes the paint accessible to a patron of the business establishment only with the assistance of an employee of the establishment; or

(3) in an area electronically protected, or viewed by surveillance equipment that is monitored, during business hours.

(b) This section does not apply to a business establishment that has in place a computerized checkout system at the point of sale for merchandise that alerts the cashier that a person purchasing aerosol paint must be over 18 years of age.

(c) A court may issue a warning to a business establishment or impose a civil penalty of $50 on the business establishment for a first violation of this section. After receiving a warning or penalty for the first violation, the business establishment is liable to the state for a civil penalty of $100 for each subsequent violation.

(d) For the third violation of this section in a calendar year, a court may issue an injunction prohibiting the business establishment from selling aerosol paint for a period of not more than two years. A business establishment that violates the injunction is liable to the state for a civil penalty of $100, in addition to any other penalty authorized by law, for each day the violation continues.

(e) If a business establishment fails to pay a civil penalty under this section, the court may issue an injunction prohibiting the establishment from selling aerosol paint until the establishment pays the penalty, attorney's fees, and court costs.

(f) The district or county attorney for the county in which a violation of this section is alleged to have

Health and Safety Code

occurred, or the attorney general, if requested by the district or county attorney for that county, may file suit for the issuance of a warning, the collection of a penalty, or the issuance of an injunction.

(g) A penalty collected under this section shall be sent to the comptroller for deposit in the state treasury to the credit of the general revenue fund.

(h) This section applies only to a business establishment that is located in a county with a population of 75,000 or more.

SUBCHAPTER C CRIMINAL PENALTIES

Sec. 485.031. Possession and Use.

(a) A person commits an offense if the person inhales, ingests, applies, uses, or possesses an abusable volatile chemical with intent to inhale, ingest, apply, or use the chemical in a manner:

(1) contrary to directions for use, cautions, or warnings appearing on a label of a container of the chemical; and

(2) designed to:

(A) affect the person's central nervous system;

(B) create or induce a condition of intoxication, hallucination, or elation; or

(C) change, distort, or disturb the person's eyesight, thinking process, balance, or coordination.

(b) An offense under this section is a Class B misdemeanor.

(c) It is a defense to prosecution for an offense under Subsection (a) that the actor:

(1) was the first person to request emergency medical assistance in response to the possible overdose of another person and:

(A) made the request for medical assistance during an ongoing medical emergency;

(B) remained on the scene until the medical assistance arrived; and

(C) cooperated with medical assistance and law enforcement personnel; or

(2) was the victim of a possible overdose for which emergency medical assistance was requested, by the actor or by another person, during an ongoing medical emergency.

(d) The defense to prosecution provided by Subsection (c) is not available if:

(1) at the time the request for emergency medical assistance was made:

(A) a peace officer was in the process of arresting the actor or executing a search warrant describing the actor or the place from which the request for medical assistance was made; or

(B) the actor is committing another offense, other than an offense punishable under Section 481.115(b), 481.1151(b)(1), 481.116(b), 481.1161(b)(1) or (2), 481.117(b), 481.118(b), or 481.121(b)(1) or (2), or an offense under Section 481.119(b), 481.125(a), or 483.041(a);

(2) the actor has been previously convicted of or placed on deferred adjudication community supervision for an offense under this chapter or Chapter 481 or 483;

(3) the actor was acquitted in a previous proceeding in which the actor successfully established the defense under that subsection or Section 481.115(g), 481.1151(c), 481.116(f), 481.1161(c), 481.117(f), 481.118(f), 481.119(c), 481.121(c), 481.125(g), or 483.041(e); or

(4) at any time during the 18-month period preceding the date of the commission of the instant offense, the actor requested emergency medical assistance in response to the possible overdose of the actor or another person.

(e) The defense to prosecution provided by Subsection (c) does not preclude the admission of evidence obtained by law enforcement resulting from the request for emergency medical assistance if that evidence pertains to an offense for which the defense described by Subsection (c) is not available.

Sec. 485.032. Delivery to a Minor.

(a) A person commits an offense if the person knowingly delivers an abusable volatile chemical to a person who is younger than 18 years of age.

(b) It is a defense to prosecution under this section that:

(1) the abusable volatile chemical that was delivered contains additive material that effectively discourages intentional abuse by inhalation; or

(2) the person making the delivery is not the manufacturer of the chemical and the manufacturer of the chemical failed to label the chemical with the statement of principal hazard on the principal display panel "VAPOR HARMFUL" or other labeling requirement subsequently established under the Federal Hazardous Substances Act (15 U.S.C. Section 1261 et seq.), as amended, or regulations subsequently adopted under that Act.

(c) It is an affirmative defense to prosecution under this section that:

(1) the person making the delivery is an adult having supervisory responsibility over the person younger than 18 years of age and:

(A) the adult permits the use of the abusable volatile chemical only under the adult's direct

Health and Safety Code

supervision and in the adult's presence and only for its intended purpose; and

(B) the adult removes the chemical from the person younger than 18 years of age on completion of that use; or

(2) the person to whom the abusable volatile chemical was delivered presented to the defendant an apparently valid Texas driver's license or an identification certificate, issued by the Department of Public Safety of the State of Texas and containing a physical description consistent with the person's appearance, that purported to establish that the person was 18 years of age or older.

(d) Except as provided by Subsections (e) and (f), an offense under this section is a state jail felony.

(e) An offense under this section is a Class B misdemeanor if it is shown on the trial of the defendant that at the time of the delivery the defendant or the defendant's employer held a volatile chemical sales permit for the location of the sale.

(f) An offense under this section is a Class A misdemeanor if it is shown on the trial of the defendant that at the time of the delivery the defendant or the defendant's employer:

(1) did not hold a volatile chemical sales permit but did hold a sales tax permit for the location of the sale; and

(2) had not been convicted previously under this section for an offense committed after January 1, 1988.

Sec. 485.033. Inhalant Paraphernalia.

(a) A person commits an offense if the person knowingly uses or possesses with intent to use inhalant paraphernalia to inhale, ingest, or otherwise introduce into the human body an abusable volatile chemical in violation of Section 485.031.

(b) A person commits an offense if the person:

(1) knowingly:

(A) delivers or sells inhalant paraphernalia;

(B) possesses, with intent to deliver or sell, inhalant paraphernalia; or

(C) manufactures, with intent to deliver or sell, inhalant paraphernalia; and

(2) at the time of the act described by Subdivision (1), knows that the person who receives or is intended to receive the paraphernalia intends that it be used to inhale, ingest, apply, use, or otherwise introduce into the human body a volatile chemical in violation of Section 485.031.

(c) An offense under Subsection (a) is a Class B misdemeanor, and an offense under Subsection (b) is a Class A misdemeanor.

Sec. 485.034. Failure to Post Sign.

(a) A person commits an offense if the person sells an abusable volatile chemical in a business establishment and the person does not display the sign required by Section 485.017.

(b) An offense under this section is a Class C misdemeanor.

Sec. 485.035. Sale Without Permit.

(a) A person commits an offense if the person sells an abusable volatile chemical in violation of Section 485.011 and the purchaser is 18 years of age or older.

(b) An offense under this section is a Class B misdemeanor.

Sec. 485.036. Proof of Offer to Sell.

Proof of an offer to sell an abusable volatile chemical must be corroborated by a person other than the offeree or by evidence other than a statement of the offeree.

Sec. 485.037. Summary Forfeiture.

An abusable volatile chemical or inhalant paraphernalia seized as a result of an offense under this chapter is subject to summary forfeiture and to destruction or disposition in the same manner as controlled substance property under Subchapter E, Chapter 481.

Sec. 485.038. Preparatory Offenses.

Title 4, Penal Code, applies to an offense under this subchapter.

Sec. 485.039. Preparatory Offense [Renumbered].

Renumbered to Tex.Health & Safety Code § 485.038 by Acts 2001, 77th Leg., ch. 1463 (H.B. 2950), § 2, effective September 1, 2001.

SUBCHAPTER D ADMINISTRATIVE PENALTY

Sec. 485.101. Imposition of Penalty.

(a) The department may impose an administrative penalty on a person who sells abusable glue or aerosol paint at retail who violates this chapter or a rule or order adopted under this chapter.

Health and Safety Code

(b) A penalty collected under this subchapter shall be deposited in the state treasury in the general revenue fund.

Sec. 485.102. Amount of Penalty.

(a) The amount of the penalty may not exceed $1,000 for each violation, and each day a violation continues or occurs is a separate violation for purposes of imposing a penalty. The total amount of the penalty assessed for a violation continuing or occurring on separate days under this subsection may not exceed $5,000.

(b) The amount shall be based on:

(1) the seriousness of the violation, including the nature, circumstances, extent, and gravity of the violation;

(2) the threat to health or safety caused by the violation;

(3) the history of previous violations;

(4) the amount necessary to deter a future violation;

(5) whether the violator demonstrated good faith, including when applicable whether the violator made good faith efforts to correct the violation; and

(6) any other matter that justice may require.

Sec. 485.103. Report and Notice of Violation and Penalty.

(a) If the department initially determines that a violation occurred, the department shall give written notice of the report by certified mail to the person.

(b) The notice must:

(1) include a brief summary of the alleged violation;

(2) state the amount of the recommended penalty; and

(3) inform the person of the person's right to a hearing on the occurrence of the violation, the amount of the penalty, or both.

Sec. 485.104. Penalty to Be Paid or Hearing Requested.

(a) Within 20 days after the date the person receives the notice sent under Section 485.103, the person in writing may:

(1) accept the determination and recommended penalty of the department; or

(2) make a request for a hearing on the occurrence of the violation, the amount of the penalty, or both.

(b) If the person accepts the determination and recommended penalty or if the person fails to respond to the notice, the department by order shall impose the recommended penalty.

Sec. 485.105. Hearing.

(a) If the person requests a hearing, the department shall refer the matter to the State Office of Administrative Hearings, which shall promptly set a hearing date. The department shall give written notice of the time and place of the hearing to the person. An administrative law judge of the State Office of Administrative Hearings shall conduct the hearing.

(b) The administrative law judge shall make findings of fact and conclusions of law and promptly issue to the department a written proposal for a decision about the occurrence of the violation and the amount of a proposed penalty.

Sec. 485.106. Decision by Department.

(a) Based on the findings of fact, conclusions of law, and proposal for a decision, the department by order may:

(1) find that a violation occurred and impose a penalty; or

(2) find that a violation did not occur.

(b) The notice of the department's order under Subsection (a) that is sent to the person in accordance with Chapter 2001, Government Code, must include a statement of the right of the person to judicial review of the order.

Sec. 485.107. Options Following Decision: Pay or Appeal.

Within 30 days after the date the order of the department under Section 485.106 that imposes an administrative penalty becomes final, the person shall:

(1) pay the penalty; or

(2) file a petition for judicial review of the department's order contesting the occurrence of the violation, the amount of the penalty, or both.

Sec. 485.108. Stay of Enforcement of Penalty.

(a) Within the 30-day period prescribed by Section 485.107, a person who files a petition for judicial review may:

(1) stay enforcement of the penalty by:

(A) paying the penalty to the court for placement in an escrow account; or

(B) giving the court a supersedeas bond approved by the court that:

(i) is for the amount of the penalty; and

(ii) is effective until all judicial review of the department's order is final; or

(2) request the court to stay enforcement of the penalty by:

(A) filing with the court a sworn affidavit of the person stating that the person is financially unable to pay the penalty and is financially unable to give the supersedeas bond; and

(B) sending a copy of the affidavit to the department by certified mail.

(b) If the department receives a copy of an affidavit under Subsection (a)(2), the department may file with the court, within five days after the date the copy is received, a contest to the affidavit. The court shall hold a hearing on the facts alleged in the affidavit as soon as practicable and shall stay the enforcement of the penalty on finding that the alleged facts are true. The person who files an affidavit has the burden of proving that the person is financially unable to pay the penalty or to give a supersedeas bond.

Sec. 485.109. Collection of Penalty.

(a) If the person does not pay the penalty and the enforcement of the penalty is not stayed, the penalty may be collected.

(b) The attorney general may sue to collect the penalty.

Sec. 485.110. Decision by Court.

(a) If the court sustains the finding that a violation occurred, the court may uphold or reduce the amount of the penalty and order the person to pay the full or reduced amount of the penalty.

(b) If the court does not sustain the finding that a violation occurred, the court shall order that a penalty is not owed.

Sec. 485.111. Remittance of Penalty and Interest.

(a) If the person paid the penalty and if the amount of the penalty is reduced or the penalty is not upheld by the court, the court shall order, when the court's judgment becomes final, that the appropriate amount plus accrued interest be remitted to the person within 30 days after the date that the judgment of the court becomes final.

(b) The interest accrues at the rate charged on loans to depository institutions by the New York Federal Reserve Bank.

(c) The interest shall be paid for the period beginning on the date the penalty is paid and ending on the date the penalty is remitted.

Sec. 485.112. Release of Bond.

(a) If the person gave a supersedeas bond and the penalty is not upheld by the court, the court shall order, when the court's judgment becomes final, the release of the bond.

(b) If the person gave a supersedeas bond and the amount of the penalty is reduced, the court shall order the release of the bond after the person pays the reduced amount.

Sec. 485.113. Administrative Procedure.

A proceeding to impose the penalty is considered to be a contested case under Chapter 2001, Government Code.

CHAPTER 486
OVER-THE-COUNTER SALES OF EPHEDRINE, PSEUDOEPHEDRINE, AND NORPSEUDOEPHEDRINE

SUBCHAPTER A
GENERAL PROVISIONS

Sec. 486.001. Definitions.

(a) In this chapter:

(1) "Commissioner" means the commissioner of state health services.

(2) [Repealed by Acts 2015, 84th Leg., ch. 1 (S.B. 219), § 3.1639(95), effective April 2, 2015.]

(3) "Department" means the Department of State Health Services.

(4) "Ephedrine," "pseudoephedrine," and "norpseudoephedrine" mean any compound, mixture, or preparation containing any detectable amount of that substance, including its salts, optical isomers, and salts of optical isomers. The term does not include any compound, mixture, or preparation that is in liquid, liquid capsule, or liquid gel capsule form.

(4-a) "Executive commissioner" means the executive commissioner of the Health and Human Services Commission.

(5) "Sale" includes a conveyance, exchange, barter, or trade.

(6) "Real-time electronic logging system" means a system intended to be used by law enforcement agencies and pharmacies or other business establishments that:

(A) is installed, operated, and maintained free of any one-time or recurring charge to the business establishment or to the state;

(B) is able to communicate in real time with similar systems operated in other states and similar systems containing information submitted by more than one state;

(C) complies with the security policy of the Criminal Justice Information Services division of the Federal Bureau of Investigation;

(D) complies with information exchange standards adopted by the National Information Exchange Model;

(E) uses a mechanism to prevent the completion of a sale of a product containing ephedrine, pseudoephedrine, or norpseudoephedrine that would violate state or federal law regarding the purchase of a product containing those substances; and

(F) is equipped with an override of the mechanism described in Paragraph (E) that:

(i) may be activated by an employee of a business establishment; and

(ii) creates a record of each activation of the override.

(b) A term that is used in this chapter but is not defined by Subsection (a) has the meaning assigned by Section 481.002.

Sec. 486.002. Applicability.

This chapter does not apply to the sale of any product dispensed or delivered by a pharmacist according to a prescription issued by a practitioner for a valid medical purpose and in the course of professional practice.

Sec. 486.003. Rules.

The executive commissioner shall adopt rules necessary to implement and enforce this chapter.

Sec. 486.004. Fees.

(a) The department shall collect fees for an inspection performed in enforcing this chapter and rules adopted under this chapter.

(b) The executive commissioner by rule shall set the fees in amounts that allow the department to recover the biennial expenditures of state funds by the department in implementing and enforcing this chapter.

(c) Fees collected under this section shall be deposited to the credit of a special account in the general revenue fund and appropriated to the department to implement and enforce this chapter.

Sec. 486.005. Statewide Application and Uniformity.

(a) To ensure uniform and equitable implementation and enforcement throughout this state, this chapter constitutes the whole field of regulation regarding over-the-counter sales of products that contain ephedrine, pseudoephedrine, or norpseudoephedrine.

(b) This chapter preempts and supersedes a local ordinance, rule, or regulation adopted by a political subdivision of this state pertaining to over-the-counter sales of products that contain ephedrine, pseudoephedrine, or norpseudoephedrine.

(c) This section does not preclude a political subdivision from imposing administrative sanctions on the holder of a business or professional license or permit issued by the political subdivision who engages in conduct that violates this chapter.

SUBCHAPTER B
OVER-THE-COUNTER SALES

Sec. 486.011. Sales by Pharmacies.

A business establishment that operates a pharmacy licensed by the Texas State Board of Pharmacy may engage in over-the-counter sales of ephedrine, pseudoephedrine, and norpseudoephedrine.

Sec. 486.012. Sales by Establishments Other Than Pharmacies; Certificate of Authority. [Repealed]

Sec. 486.013. Restriction of Access to Ephedrine, Pseudoephedrine, and Norpseudoephedrine.

A business establishment that engages in over-the-counter sales of products containing ephedrine, pseudoephedrine, or norpseudoephedrine shall:

(1) if the establishment operates a pharmacy licensed by the Texas State Board of Pharmacy, maintain those products:

(A) behind the pharmacy counter; or

(B) in a locked case within 30 feet and in a direct line of sight from a pharmacy counter staffed by an employee of the establishment; or

(2) if the establishment does not operate a pharmacy licensed by the Texas State Board of Pharmacy, maintain those products:

(A) behind a sales counter; or

(B) in a locked case within 30 feet and in a direct line of sight from a sales counter continuously staffed by an employee of the establishment.

Sec. 486.014. Prerequisites to and Restrictions on Sale.

(a) Before completing an over-the-counter sale of a product containing ephedrine, pseudoephedrine, or norpseudoephedrine, a business establishment that engages in those sales shall:

(1) require the person making the purchase to:

(A) display a driver's license or other form of government-issued identification containing the person's photograph and indicating that the person is 16 years of age or older; and

(B) sign for the purchase;

(2) make a record of the sale, including the name and date of birth of the person making the purchase, the address of the purchaser, the date and time of the purchase, the type of identification displayed by the person and the identification number, and the item and number of grams purchased; and

(3) transmit the record of sale as required by Section 486.0141.

(b) A business establishment may not sell to a person who makes over-the-counter purchases of one or more products containing ephedrine, pseudoephedrine, or norpseudoephedrine:

(1) within any calendar day, more than 3.6 grams of ephedrine, pseudoephedrine, norpseudoephedrine, or a combination of those substances; and

(2) within any 30-day period, more than nine grams of ephedrine, pseudoephedrine, norpseudoephedrine, or a combination of those substances.

Sec. 486.0141. Transmission of Sales Information to Real-Time Electronic Logging System.

(a) Before completing an over-the-counter sale of a product containing ephedrine, pseudoephedrine, or norpseudoephedrine, a business establishment that engages in those sales shall transmit the information in the record made under Section 486.014(a)(2) to a real-time electronic logging system.

(b) Except as provided by Subsection (c), a business establishment may not complete an over-the-counter sale of a product containing ephedrine, pseudoephedrine, or norpseudoephedrine if the real-time electronic logging system returns a report that the completion of the sale would result in the person obtaining an amount of ephedrine, pseudoephedrine, norpseudoephedrine, or a combination of those substances greater than the amount described by Section 486.014(b), regardless of whether all or some of the products previously obtained by the buyer were sold at the establishment or another business establishment.

(c) An employee of a business establishment may complete a sale prohibited by Subsection (b) by using the override mechanism described by Section 486.001(a)(6)(F) only if the employee has a reasonable fear of imminent bodily injury or death from the person attempting to obtain ephedrine, pseudoephedrine, or norpseudoephedrine.

(d) On request of the Department of Public Safety, the administrators of a real-time electronic logging system shall make available to the department a copy of each record of an over-the-counter sale of a product containing ephedrine, pseudoephedrine, or norpseudoephedrine that is submitted by a business establishment located in this state.

Sec. 486.0142. Temporary Exemption.

(a) On application by a business establishment that operates a pharmacy and engages in over-the-counter sales of products containing ephedrine, pseudoephedrine, or norpseudoephedrine as authorized by Section 486.011, the Texas State Board of Pharmacy may grant that business establishment a temporary exemption, not to exceed 180 days, from the requirement of using a real-time electronic logging system under this chapter.

(b) On application by a business establishment that engages in over-the-counter sales of products containing ephedrine, pseudoephedrine, or norpseudoephedrine, the department may grant that business establishment a temporary exemption, not to exceed 180 days, from the requirement of using a real-time electronic logging system under this chapter.

(c) A business establishment granted a temporary exemption under this section must keep records of sales in the same manner required under Section 486.0143 for a business establishment that experiences a mechanical or electronic failure of the real-time electronic logging system.

(d) An exemption granted under this section does not relieve a business establishment of any duty under this chapter other than the duty to use a real-time electronic logging system.

Sec. 486.0143. Written Log or Other Electronic Recordkeeping.

If a business establishment that engages in over-the-counter sales of a product containing ephedrine, pseudoephedrine, or norpseudoephedrine experiences a mechanical or electronic failure of the real-time electronic logging system, the business shall:

(1) maintain a written record or an electronic record made by any means that satisfies the requirements of Section 486.014(a)(2); and

(2) enter the information in the real-time electronic logging system as soon as practicable after the system becomes operational.

Sec. 486.0144. Online Portal.

The administrators of a real-time electronic logging system shall provide real-time access to the information in the system to the Department of Public Safety if the department executes a memorandum of understanding with the administrators.

Sec. 486.0145. Limitation on Civil Liability.

A person is not liable for an act done or omission made in compliance with the requirements of Section 486.014 or 486.0141.

Sec. 486.0146. Privacy Protections.

(a) The privacy protections provided an individual under 21 C.F.R. Section 1314.45 apply to information entered or stored in a real-time electronic logging system.

(b) A business establishment that engages in over-the-counter sales of a product containing ephedrine, pseudoephedrine, or norpseudoephedrine may disclose information entered or stored in a real-time electronic logging system only to the United States Drug Enforcement Administration and other federal, state, and local law enforcement agencies.

(c) A business establishment that engages in over-the-counter sales of a product containing ephedrine, pseudoephedrine, or norpseudoephedrine may not use information entered or stored in a real-time electronic logging system for any purpose other than for a disclosure authorized by Subsection (b) or to comply with the requirements of this chapter.

(d) Notwithstanding Subsection (c), a business establishment that engages in over-the-counter sales of a product containing ephedrine, pseudoephedrine, or norpseudoephedrine or an employee or agent of the business establishment is not civilly liable for the release of information entered or stored in a real-time electronic logging system unless the release constitutes negligence, recklessness, or wilful misconduct.

Sec. 486.015. Maintenance of Records.

(a) Except as provided by Subsection (b), a business establishment shall maintain each record made under Section 486.014(a)(2) until at least the second anniversary of the date the record is made and shall make each record available on request by the department or any local, state, or federal law enforcement agency, including the United States Drug Enforcement Administration.

(b) Subsection (a) does not apply to a business establishment that has used a real-time electronic logging system for longer than two years.

(c) A business establishment that has used a real-time electronic logging system for longer than two years shall destroy all paper records maintained under this section unless the destruction is otherwise prohibited by law.

SUBCHAPTER C ADMINISTRATIVE PENALTY

Sec. 486.021. Imposition of Penalty.

The department may impose an administrative penalty on a person who violates this chapter.

Sec. 486.022. Amount of Penalty.

(a) The amount of the penalty may not exceed $1,000 for each violation, and each day a violation continues or occurs is a separate violation for purposes of imposing a penalty. The total amount of the penalty assessed for a violation continuing or occurring on separate days under this subsection may not exceed $20,000.

(b) The amount shall be based on:

(1) the seriousness of the violation, including the nature, circumstances, extent, and gravity of the violation;

(2) the threat to health or safety caused by the violation;

(3) the history of previous violations;

(4) the amount necessary to deter a future violation;

(5) whether the violator demonstrated good faith, including when applicable whether the violator made good faith efforts to correct the violation; and

(6) any other matter that justice may require.

Sec. 486.023. Report and Notice of Violation and Penalty.

(a) If the department initially determines that a violation occurred, the department shall give

Health and Safety Code

written notice of the report by certified mail to the person.

(b) The notice must:

(1) include a brief summary of the alleged violation;

(2) state the amount of the recommended penalty; and

(3) inform the person of the person's right to a hearing on the occurrence of the violation, the amount of the penalty, or both.

Sec. 486.024. Penalty to Be Paid or Hearing Requested.

(a) Before the 21st day after the date the person receives notice under Section 486.023, the person in writing may:

(1) accept the determination and recommended penalty; or

(2) make a request for a hearing on the occurrence of the violation, the amount of the penalty, or both.

(b) If the person accepts the determination and recommended penalty or if the person fails to respond to the notice, the department by order shall impose the penalty.

Sec. 486.025. Hearing.

(a) If the person requests a hearing, the department shall refer the matter to the State Office of Administrative Hearings, which shall promptly set a hearing date, and the department shall give written notice of the time and place of the hearing to the person. An administrative law judge of the State Office of Administrative Hearings shall conduct the hearing.

(b) The administrative law judge shall make findings of fact and conclusions of law and promptly issue to the department a written proposal for a decision about the occurrence of the violation and the amount of a proposed penalty.

Sec. 486.026. Decision.

(a) Based on the findings of fact, conclusions of law, and proposal for a decision, the department by order may:

(1) find that a violation occurred and impose a penalty; or

(2) find that a violation did not occur.

(b) The notice of the department's order under Subsection (a) that is sent to the person in the manner provided by Chapter 2001, Government Code, must include a statement of the right of the person to judicial review of the order.

Sec. 486.027. Options Following Decision: Pay or Appeal.

Before the 31st day after the date the order under Section 486.026 that imposes an administrative penalty becomes final, the person shall:

(1) pay the penalty; or

(2) file a petition for judicial review of the order contesting the occurrence of the violation, the amount of the penalty, or both.

Sec. 486.028. Stay of Enforcement of Penalty.

(a) Within the period prescribed by Section 486.027, a person who files a petition for judicial review may:

(1) stay enforcement of the penalty by:

(A) paying the amount of the penalty to the court for placement in an escrow account; or

(B) giving the court a supersedeas bond approved by the court that:

(i) is for the amount of the penalty; and

(ii) is effective until all judicial review of the order is final; or

(2) request the court to stay enforcement of the penalty by:

(A) filing with the court an affidavit of the person stating that the person is financially unable to pay the penalty and is financially unable to give the supersedeas bond; and

(B) sending a copy of the affidavit to the department by certified mail.

(b) Following receipt of a copy of an affidavit under Subsection (a)(2), the department may file with the court, before the sixth day after the date of receipt, a contest to the affidavit. The court shall hold a hearing on the facts alleged in the affidavit as soon as practicable and shall stay the enforcement of the penalty on finding that the alleged facts are true. The person who files an affidavit has the burden of proving that the person is financially unable to pay the penalty or to give a supersedeas bond.

Sec. 486.029. Collection of Penalty.

(a) If the person does not pay the penalty and the enforcement of the penalty is not stayed, the penalty may be collected.

(b) The attorney general may sue to collect the penalty.

Sec. 486.030. Decision by Court.

(a) If the court sustains the finding that a violation occurred, the court may uphold or reduce the amount of the penalty and order the person to pay the full or reduced amount of the penalty.

(b) If the court does not sustain the finding that a violation occurred, the court shall order that a penalty is not owed.

Sec. 486.031. Remittance of Penalty and Interest.

(a) If the person paid the penalty and if the amount of the penalty is reduced or the penalty is not upheld by the court, the court shall order, when the court's judgment becomes final, that the appropriate amount plus accrued interest be remitted to the person before the 31st day after the date that the judgment of the court becomes final.

(b) The interest accrues at the rate charged on loans to depository institutions by the New York Federal Reserve Bank.

(c) The interest shall be paid for the period beginning on the date the penalty is paid and ending on the date the penalty is remitted.

Sec. 486.032. Release of Bond.

(a) If the person gave a supersedeas bond and the penalty is not upheld by the court, the court shall order, when the court's judgment becomes final, the release of the bond.

(b) If the person gave a supersedeas bond and the amount of the penalty is reduced, the court shall order the release of the bond after the person pays the reduced amount.

Sec. 486.033. Administrative Procedure.

A proceeding to impose the penalty under this subchapter is considered to be a contested case under Chapter 2001, Government Code.

TITLE 7 MENTAL HEALTH AND INTELLECTUAL DISABILITY

SUBTITLE B STATE FACILITIES

CHAPTER 552 STATE HOSPITALS

SUBCHAPTER A GENERAL PROVISIONS

Sec. 552.002. Carrying of Handgun by License Holder in State Hospital.

(a) In this section:

(1) "License holder" has the meaning assigned by Section 46.03, Penal Code.

(2) "State hospital" means the following facilities:

(A) the Austin State Hospital;

(B) the Big Spring State Hospital;

(C) the El Paso Psychiatric Center;

(D) the Kerrville State Hospital;

(E) the North Texas State Hospital;

(F) the Rio Grande State Center;

(G) the Rusk State Hospital;

(H) the San Antonio State Hospital;

(I) the Terrell State Hospital; and

(J) the Waco Center for Youth.

(3) "Written notice" means a sign that is posted on property and that:

(A) includes in both English and Spanish written language identical to the following: "Pursuant to Section 552.002, Health and Safety Code (carrying of handgun by license holder in state hospital), a person licensed under Subchapter H, Chapter 411, Government Code (handgun licensing law), may not enter this property with a handgun";

(B) appears in contrasting colors with block letters at least one inch in height; and

(C) is displayed in a conspicuous manner clearly visible to the public at each entrance to the property.

(b) A state hospital may prohibit a license holder from carrying a handgun under the authority of Subchapter H, Chapter 411, Government Code, on the property of the hospital by providing written notice.

(c) A license holder who carries a handgun under the authority of Subchapter H, Chapter 411, Government Code, on the property of a state hospital at which written notice is provided is liable for a civil penalty in the amount of:

(1) $100 for the first violation; or

(2) $500 for the second or subsequent violation.

(d) The attorney general or an appropriate prosecuting attorney may sue to collect a civil penalty under this section.

SUBTITLE C TEXAS MENTAL HEALTH CODE

CHAPTER 573
EMERGENCY DETENTION

SUBCHAPTER A
APPREHENSION BY PEACE OFFICER OR TRANSPORTATION FOR EMERGENCY DETENTION BY GUARDIAN

Sec. 573.0001. Definitions.

In this chapter:

(1) "Emergency medical services personnel" and "emergency medical services provider" have the meanings assigned by Section 773.003.

(2) "Law enforcement agency" has the meaning assigned by Article 59.01, Code of Criminal Procedure.

Sec. 573.001. Apprehension by Peace Officer Without Warrant.

(a) A peace officer, without a warrant, may take a person into custody, regardless of the age of the person, if the officer:

(1) has reason to believe and does believe that:

(A) the person is a person with mental illness; and

(B) because of that mental illness there is a substantial risk of serious harm to the person or to others unless the person is immediately restrained; and

(2) believes that there is not sufficient time to obtain a warrant before taking the person into custody.

(b) A substantial risk of serious harm to the person or others under Subsection (a)(1)(B) may be demonstrated by:

(1) the person's behavior; or

(2) evidence of severe emotional distress and deterioration in the person's mental condition to the extent that the person cannot remain at liberty.

(c) The peace officer may form the belief that the person meets the criteria for apprehension:

(1) from a representation of a credible person; or

(2) on the basis of the conduct of the apprehended person or the circumstances under which the apprehended person is found.

(d) A peace officer who takes a person into custody under Subsection (a) shall immediately:

(1) transport the apprehended person to:

(A) the nearest appropriate inpatient mental health facility; or

(B) a mental health facility deemed suitable by the local mental health authority, if an appropriate inpatient mental health facility is not available; or

(2) transfer the apprehended person to emergency medical services personnel of an emergency medical services provider in accordance with a memorandum of understanding executed under Section 573.005 for transport to a facility described by Subdivision (1)(A) or (B).

(e) A jail or similar detention facility may not be deemed suitable except in an extreme emergency.

(f) A person detained in a jail or a nonmedical facility shall be kept separate from any person who is charged with or convicted of a crime.

(g) A peace officer who takes a person into custody under Subsection (a) shall immediately inform the person orally in simple, nontechnical terms:

(1) of the reason for the detention; and

(2) that a staff member of the facility will inform the person of the person's rights within 24 hours after the time the person is admitted to a facility, as provided by Section 573.025(b).

(h) A peace officer who takes a person into custody under Subsection (a) may immediately seize any firearm found in possession of the person. After seizing a firearm under this subsection, the peace officer shall comply with the requirements of Article 18.191, Code of Criminal Procedure.

Sec. 573.002. Peace Officer's Notification of Detention.

(a) A peace officer shall immediately file with a facility a notification of detention after transporting a person to that facility in accordance with Section 573.001. Emergency medical services personnel of an emergency medical services provider who transport a person to a facility at the request of a peace officer made in accordance with a memorandum of understanding executed under Section 573.005 shall immediately file with the facility the notification of detention completed by the peace officer who made the request.

(b) The notification of detention must contain:

(1) a statement that the officer has reason to believe and does believe that the person evidences mental illness;

(2) a statement that the officer has reason to believe and does believe that the person evidences a substantial risk of serious harm to the person or others;

(3) a specific description of the risk of harm;

(4) a statement that the officer has reason to believe and does believe that the risk of harm is imminent unless the person is immediately restrained;

(5) a statement that the officer's beliefs are derived from specific recent behavior, overt acts,

attempts, or threats that were observed by or reliably reported to the officer;

(6) a detailed description of the specific behavior, acts, attempts, or threats; and

(7) the name and relationship to the apprehended person of any person who reported or observed the behavior, acts, attempts, or threats.

(c) The facility where the person is detained shall include in the detained person's clinical file the notification of detention described by this section.

(d) The peace officer shall provide the notification of detention on the following form:

Notification—Emergency Detention NO. ________

DATE:__________ TIME:__________

THE STATE OF TEXAS

FOR THE BEST INTEREST AND PROTECTION OF:

____

NOTIFICATION OF EMERGENCY DETENTION

Now comes ______________, a peace officer with (name of agency) ______________, of the State of Texas, and states as follows:

1. I have reason to believe and do believe that (name of person to be detained) ______________ evidences mental illness.

2. I have reason to believe and do believe that the above-named person evidences a substantial risk of serious harm to himself/herself or others based upon the following:

____

____

____

____

____

3. I have reason to believe and do believe that the above risk of harm is imminent unless the above-named person is immediately restrained.

4. My beliefs are based upon the following recent behavior, overt acts, attempts, statements, or threats observed by me or reliably reported to me:

____

____

____

____

____

5. The names, addresses, and relationship to the above-named person of those persons who reported or observed recent behavior, acts, attempts, statements, or threats of the above-named person are (if applicable):

____

____

____

____

For the above reasons, I present this notification to seek temporary admission to the (name of facility) ______________ inpatient mental health facility or hospital facility for the detention of (name of person to be detained) ______________ on an emergency basis.

Health and Safety Code

6. Was the person restrained in any way? Yes ☐ No ☐

BADGE NO.____________

PEACE OFFICER'S SIGNATURE

Address:______________________ Zip Code:____________________

Telephone:____________

____

SIGNATURE OF EMERGENCY MEDICAL SERVICES PERSONNEL

(if applicable)

Address:______________________ Zip Code: ____________________

Telephone:____________

A mental health facility or hospital emergency department may not require a peace officer or emergency medical services personnel to execute any form other than this form as a predicate to accepting for temporary admission a person detained by a peace officer under Section 573.001, Health and Safety Code, and transported by the officer under that section or by emergency medical services personnel of an emergency medical services provider at the request of the officer made in accordance with a memorandum of understanding executed under Section 573.005, Health and Safety Code.

(e) A mental health facility or hospital emergency department may not require a peace officer or emergency medical services personnel to execute any form other than the form provided by Subsection (d) as a predicate to accepting for temporary admission a person detained by a peace officer under Section 573.001 and transported by the officer under that section or by emergency medical services personnel of an emergency medical services provider at the request of the officer made in accordance with a memorandum of understanding executed under Section 573.005.

Sec. 573.0021. Duty of Peace Officer to Notify Probate Courts.

As soon as practicable, but not later than the first working day after the date a peace officer takes a person who is a ward into custody, the peace officer shall notify the court having jurisdiction over the ward's guardianship of the ward's detention or transportation to a facility in accordance with Section 573.001.

Sec. 573.005. Transportation for Emergency Detention by Emergency Medical Services Provider; Memorandum of Understanding.

(a) A law enforcement agency and an emergency medical services provider may execute a memorandum of understanding under which emergency medical services personnel employed by the provider may transport a person taken into custody under Section 573.001 by a peace officer employed by the law enforcement agency.

(b) A memorandum of understanding must:

(1) address responsibility for the cost of transporting the person taken into custody; and

(2) be approved by the county in which the law enforcement agency is located and the local mental health authority that provides services in that county with respect to provisions of the memorandum that address the responsibility for the cost of transporting the person.

(c) A peace officer may request that emergency medical services personnel transport a person taken into custody by the officer under Section 573.001 only if:

(1) the law enforcement agency that employs the officer and the emergency medical services provider that employs the personnel have executed a memorandum of understanding under this section; and

(2) the officer determines that transferring the person for transport is safe for both the person and the personnel.

(d) Emergency medical services personnel may, at the request of a peace officer, transport a person taken into custody by the officer under Section 573.001 to the appropriate facility, as provided by that section, if the law enforcement agency that employs the officer and the emergency medical services provider that employs the personnel have executed a memorandum of understanding under this section.

(e) A peace officer who transfers a person to emergency medical services personnel under a memorandum of understanding executed under this section for transport to the appropriate facility must provide:

(1) to the person the notice described by Section 573.001(g); and

(2) to the personnel a completed notification of detention about the person on the form provided by Section 573.002(d).

TITLE 9
SAFETY

SUBTITLE A
PUBLIC SAFETY

CHAPTER 751
MASS GATHERINGS

Sec. 751.001. Short Title.

This chapter may be cited as the Texas Mass Gatherings Act.

Sec. 751.002. Definitions.

In this chapter:

(1) "Mass gathering" means a gathering:

(A) that is held outside the limits of a municipality;

(B) that attracts or is expected to attract:

(i) more than 2,500 persons; or

(ii) more than 500 persons, if 51 percent or more of those persons may reasonably be expected to be younger than 21 years of age and it is planned or may reasonably be expected that alcoholic beverages will be sold, served, or consumed at or around the gathering; and

(C) at which the persons will remain:

(i) for more than five continuous hours; or

(ii) for any amount of time during the period beginning at 10 p.m. and ending at 4 a.m.

(2) "Person" means an individual, group of individuals, firm, corporation, partnership, or association.

(3) "Promote" includes organize, manage, finance, or hold.

(4) "Promoter" means a person who promotes a mass gathering.

Sec. 751.0021. Applicability to Certain Horse and Greyhound Races.

(a) This chapter applies to a horse or greyhound race that attracts or is expected to attract at least 100 persons, except that this chapter does not apply if the race is held at a location at which pari-mutuel wagering is authorized under Subtitle A-1, Title 13, Occupations Code (Texas Racing Act).

(b) This section does not legalize any activity prohibited under the Penal Code or other state law.

Sec. 751.003. Permit Requirement.

A person may not promote a mass gathering without a permit issued under this chapter.

Sec. 751.004. Application Procedure.

(a) At least 45 days before the date on which a mass gathering will be held, the promoter shall file a permit application with the county judge of the county in which the mass gathering will be held.

(b) The application must include:

(1) the promoter's name and address;

(2) a financial statement that reflects the funds being supplied to finance the mass gathering and each person supplying the funds;

(3) the name and address of the owner of the property on which the mass gathering will be held;

(4) a certified copy of the agreement between the promoter and the property owner;

(5) the location and a description of the property on which the mass gathering will be held;

(6) the dates and times that the mass gathering will be held;

(7) the maximum number of persons the promoter will allow to attend the mass gathering and the plan the promoter intends to use to limit attendance to that number;

(8) the name and address of each performer who has agreed to appear at the mass gathering and the name and address of each performer's agent;

(9) a description of each agreement between the promoter and a performer;

(10) a description of each step the promoter has taken to ensure that minimum standards of sanitation and health will be maintained during the mass gathering;

(11) a description of all preparations being made to provide traffic control, to ensure that the mass gathering will be conducted in an orderly manner, and to protect the physical safety of the persons who attend the mass gathering;

(12) a description of the preparations made to provide adequate medical and nursing care; and

(13) a description of the preparations made to supervise minors who may attend the mass gathering.

Health and Safety Code

Sec. 751.005. Investigation.

(a) After a permit application is filed with the county judge, the county judge shall send a copy of the application to the county health authority, the county fire marshal or the person designated under Subsection (c), and the sheriff.

(b) The county health authority shall inquire into preparations for the mass gathering. At least five days before the date on which the hearing prescribed by Section 751.006 is held, the county health authority shall submit to the county judge a report stating whether the health authority believes that the minimum standards of health and sanitation prescribed by state and local laws, rules, and orders will be maintained.

(c) The county fire marshal shall investigate preparations for the mass gathering. If there is no county fire marshal in that county, the commissioners court shall designate a person to act under this section. At least five days before the date on which the hearing prescribed by Section 751.006 is held, the county fire marshal or the commissioners court designee shall submit to the county judge a report stating whether the fire marshal or designee believes that the minimum standards for ensuring public fire safety and order as prescribed by state and local laws, rules, and orders will be maintained.

(d) The sheriff shall investigate preparations for the mass gathering. At least five days before the date on which the hearing prescribed by Section 751.006 is held, the sheriff shall submit to the county judge a report stating whether the sheriff believes that the minimum standards for ensuring public safety and order that are prescribed by state and local laws, rules, and orders will be maintained.

(e) The county judge may conduct any additional investigation that the judge considers necessary.

(f) The county health authority, county fire marshal or commissioners court designee, and sheriff shall be available at the hearing prescribed by Section 751.006 to give testimony relating to their reports.

Sec. 751.0055. Delegation of Duties of County Judge.

(a) The county judge of a county may file an order with the commissioners court of the county delegating to another county officer the duty to hear applications for a permit under this chapter. The order may provide for allowing the county officer to revoke a permit under Section 751.008.

(b) An order of a county officer acting under the delegated authority of the county judge in regard to a permit has the same effect as an order of the county judge.

(c) During the period in which the order is in effect, the county judge may withdraw the authority delegated in relation to an application and the county judge may hear the application.

(d) The county judge may at any time revoke an order delegating duties under this section.

Sec. 751.006. Hearing.

(a) Not later than the 10th day before the date on which a mass gathering will begin, the county judge shall hold a hearing on the application. The county judge shall set the date and time of the hearing.

(b) Notice of the time and place of the hearing shall be given to the promoter and to each person who has an interest in whether the permit is granted or denied.

(c) At the hearing, any person may appear and testify for or against granting the permit.

Sec. 751.007. Findings and Decision of County Judge.

(a) After the completion of the hearing prescribed by Section 751.006, the county judge shall enter his findings in the record and shall either grant or deny the permit.

(b) The county judge may deny the permit if he finds that:

(1) the application contains false or misleading information or omits required information;

(2) the promoter's financial backing is insufficient to ensure that the mass gathering will be conducted in the manner stated in the application;

(3) the location selected for the mass gathering is inadequate for the purpose for which it will be used;

(4) the promoter has not made adequate preparations to limit the number of persons attending the mass gathering or to provide adequate supervision for minors attending the mass gathering;

(5) the promoter does not have assurance that scheduled performers will appear;

(6) the preparations for the mass gathering do not ensure that minimum standards of sanitation and health will be maintained;

(7) the preparations for the mass gathering do not ensure that the mass gathering will be conducted in an orderly manner and that the physical safety of persons attending will be protected;

(8) adequate arrangements for traffic control have not been provided; or

(9) adequate medical and nursing care will not be available.

Health and Safety Code

Sec. 751.008. Permit Revocation.

(a) The county judge may revoke a permit issued under this chapter if the county judge finds that preparations for the mass gathering will not be completed by the time the mass gathering will begin or that the permit was obtained by fraud or misrepresentation.

(b) The county judge must give notice to the promoter that the permit will be revoked at least 24 hours before the revocation. If requested by the promoter, the county judge shall hold a hearing on the revocation.

Sec. 751.009. Appeal.

A promoter or a person affected by the granting, denying, or revoking of a permit may appeal that action to a district court having jurisdiction in the county in which the mass gathering will be held.

Sec. 751.010. Rules.

(a) After notice and a public hearing, the executive commissioner of the Health and Human Services Commission shall adopt rules relating to minimum standards of health and sanitation to be maintained at mass gatherings.

(b) After notice and a public hearing, the Department of Public Safety shall adopt rules relating to minimum standards that must be maintained at a mass gathering to protect public safety and maintain order.

Sec. 751.011. Criminal Penalty.

(a) A person commits an offense if the person violates Section 751.003.

(b) An offense under this section is a misdemeanor punishable by a fine of not more than $1,000, confinement in the county jail for not more than 90 days, or both.

Sec. 751.012. Inspections.

(a) The county health authority may inspect a mass gathering during the mass gathering to ensure that the minimum standards of health and sanitation prescribed by state and local laws, rules, and orders are being maintained. If the county health authority determines a violation of the minimum standards is occurring, the health authority may order the promoter of the mass gathering to correct the violation.

(b) The county fire marshal or the person designated under Section 751.005(c) may inspect a mass gathering during the mass gathering to ensure that the minimum standards for ensuring public fire safety and order as prescribed by state and local laws, rules, and orders are being maintained. If the marshal or commissioners court designee determines a violation of the minimum standards is occurring, the marshal or designee may order the promoter of the mass gathering to correct the violation.

(c) The sheriff may inspect a mass gathering during the mass gathering to ensure that the minimum standards for ensuring public safety and order prescribed by state and local laws, rules, and orders are being maintained. If the sheriff determines a violation of the minimum standards is occurring, the sheriff may order the promoter of the mass gathering to correct the violation.

(d) A promoter who fails to comply with an order issued under this section commits an offense. An offense under this section is a Class C misdemeanor.

Sec. 751.013. Inspection Fees.

(a) A commissioners court may establish and collect a fee for an inspection performed under Section 751.012. The fee may not exceed the amount necessary to defray the costs of performing the inspections. The fee shall be deposited into the general fund of the county.

(b) A commissioners court may use money collected under this section to reimburse the county department or, if a state agency performs the inspection on behalf of the county, the state agency, the cost of performing the inspection.

SUBTITLE B
EMERGENCIES

CHAPTER 784
CRITICAL INCIDENT STRESS MANAGEMENT AND CRISIS RESPONSE SERVICES

Sec. 784.001. Definitions.

In this chapter:

(1) "Crisis response service" means consultation, risk assessment, referral, and on-site crisis intervention services provided by an emergency response team member to an emergency service provider affected by a crisis or disaster.

(2) "Critical incident stress" means the acute or cumulative psychological stress or trauma that an

emergency service provider may experience in providing emergency services in response to a critical incident, including a crisis, disaster, or emergency. The stress or trauma is an unusually strong emotional, cognitive, or physical reaction that has the potential to interfere with normal functioning, including:

(A) physical and emotional illness;

(B) failure of usual coping mechanisms;

(C) loss of interest in the job;

(D) personality changes; and

(E) loss of ability to function.

(3) "Critical incident stress management service" means a service providing a process of crisis intervention designed to assist an emergency service provider in coping with critical incident stress. The term includes consultation, counseling, debriefing, defusing, intervention services, case management services, prevention, and referral.

(4) "Emergency response team member" means an individual providing critical incident stress management services or crisis response services, or both, who is designated by an appropriate state or local governmental unit to provide those services as a member of an organized team or in association with the governmental unit.

(5) "Emergency service provider" means an individual who provides emergency response services, including a law enforcement officer, firefighter, emergency medical services provider, dispatcher, or rescue service provider.

Sec. 784.002. Closed Meetings.

(a) Except as provided by Subsection (b) and notwithstanding Chapter 551, Government Code, or any other law, a meeting in which critical incident stress management services or crisis response services are provided to an emergency service provider:

(1) is closed to the general public; and

(2) may be closed to any individual who was not directly involved in the critical incident or crisis.

(b) Subsection (a) does not apply if:

(1) the emergency service provider or the legal representative of the provider expressly agrees that the meeting may be open to the general public or to certain individuals; or

(2) the emergency service provider is deceased.

Sec. 784.003. Confidentiality.

(a) Except as otherwise provided by this section:

(1) a communication made by an emergency service provider to an emergency response team member while the provider receives critical incident stress management services or crisis response services is confidential and may not be disclosed in a civil, criminal, or administrative proceeding; and

(2) a record kept by an emergency response team member relating to the provision of critical incident stress management services or crisis response services to an emergency service provider by the team is confidential and is not subject to subpoena, discovery, or introduction into evidence in a civil, criminal, or administrative proceeding.

(b) A court in a civil or criminal case or the decision-making entity in an administrative proceeding may allow disclosure of a communication or record described by Subsection (a) if the court or entity finds that the benefit of allowing disclosure of the communication or record is more important than protecting the privacy of the individual.

(c) A communication or record described by Subsection (a) is not confidential if:

(1) the emergency response team member reasonably needs to make an appropriate referral of the emergency service provider to or consult about the provider with another member of the team or an appropriate professional associated with the team;

(2) the communication conveys information that the emergency service provider is or appears to be an imminent threat to the provider or anyone else;

(3) the communication conveys information relating to a past, present, or future criminal act that does not directly relate to the critical incident or crisis;

(4) the emergency service provider or the legal representative of the provider expressly agrees that the communication or record is not confidential; or

(5) the emergency service provider is deceased.

(d) A communication or record described by Subsection (a) is not confidential to the extent that it conveys information concerning the services and care provided to or withheld by the emergency service provider to an individual injured in the critical incident or during the crisis.

Sec. 784.004. Limitation on Liability.

(a) Except as provided by Subsection (b), an emergency response team or an emergency response team member providing critical incident stress management services or crisis response services is not liable for damages, including personal injury, wrongful death, property damage, or other loss related to the team's or member's act, error, or omission in the performance of the services, unless the act, error, or omission constitutes wanton, wilful, or intentional misconduct.

Health and Safety Code

(b) Subsection (a) limits liability for damages in any civil action, other than an action under Chapter 74, Civil Practice and Remedies Code.

CHAPTER 785
SEARCH AND RESCUE DOGS

Sec. 785.001. Definitions.

In this chapter:

(1) "Handler" means a person who handles a search and rescue dog and who is certified by the National Association for Search and Rescue or another state or nationally recognized search and rescue agency.

(2) "Housing accommodations" has the meaning assigned by Section 121.002(3), Human Resources Code.

(3) "Public facility" means a facility described by Section 121.002(5), Human Resources Code.

(4) "Search and rescue dog" means a canine that is trained or being trained to assist a nationally recognized search and rescue agency in search and rescue activities.

Sec. 785.002. Discrimination Prohibited.

(a) The owner, manager, or operator of a public facility, or an employee or other agent of the owner, manager, or operator, may not deny a search and rescue dog admittance to the facility.

(b) The owner, manager, or operator of a public facility, or an employee or other agent of the owner, manager, or operator, may not deny a search and rescue dog's handler admittance to the facility because of the presence of the handler's search and rescue dog.

(c) The owner, manager, or operator of a common carrier, airplane, railroad train, motor bus, streetcar, boat, or other public conveyance or mode of transportation operating within this state, or an employee or other agent of the owner, manager, or operator, may not:

(1) refuse to accept as a passenger a search and rescue dog or the dog's handler; or

(2) require the dog's handler to pay an additional fare because of the search and rescue dog.

(d) The discrimination prohibited by this section includes:

(1) refusing to allow a search and rescue dog or the dog's handler to use or be admitted to a public facility;

(2) a ruse or subterfuge calculated to prevent or discourage a search and rescue dog or the dog's handler from using or being admitted to a public facility; and

(3) failing to make a reasonable accommodation in a policy, practice, or procedure to allow a search and rescue dog or the dog's handler to be admitted to a public facility.

(e) A policy relating to the use of a public facility by a designated class of persons from the general public may not prohibit the use of the particular public facility by a search and rescue dog or the dog's handler.

(f) A search and rescue dog's handler is entitled to full and equal access, in the same manner as other members of the general public, to all housing accommodations offered for rent, lease, or compensation in this state, subject to any condition or limitation established by law that applies to all persons, except that the handler may not be required to pay an extra fee or charge or security deposit for the search and rescue dog.

Sec. 785.003. Penalty for Discrimination.

(a) A person who violates Section 785.002 commits an offense. An offense under this subsection is a misdemeanor punishable by a fine of not less than $300 or more than $1,000.

(b) It is a defense to prosecution under Subsection (a) that the actor requested the search and rescue dog handler's credentials under Section 785.005 and the handler failed to provide the actor with the credentials.

Sec. 785.004. Responsibilities of Handlers; Civil Liability.

(a) A handler who accompanies a search and rescue dog shall keep the dog properly harnessed or leashed. A person may maintain a cause of action against a dog's handler for personal injury, property damage, or death resulting from the failure of the dog's handler to properly harness or leash the dog under the same law applicable to other causes brought for the redress of injuries caused by animals.

(b) The handler of a search and rescue dog is liable for any property damage caused by the search and rescue dog to a public facility or to housing accommodations.

(c) A governmental unit, as defined by Section 101.001, Civil Practice and Remedies Code, is subject to liability under this section only as provided by Chapter 101, Civil Practice and Remedies Code. A public servant, as defined by Section 108.001, Civil Practice and Remedies Code, is subject to liability under this section only as provided by Chapter 108, Civil Practice and Remedies Code.

Sec. 785.005. Canine Handler Credentials.

A person may ask a search and rescue dog handler to display proof that the handler is a person with a certification issued by the National Association for Search and Rescue or another state or nationally recognized search and rescue agency.

TITLE 10
HEALTH AND SAFETY OF ANIMALS

CHAPTER 821
TREATMENT AND DISPOSITION OF ANIMALS

SUBCHAPTER B
DISPOSITION OF CRUELLY TREATED ANIMALS

Sec. 821.022. Seizure of Cruelly Treated Animal.

(a) If a peace officer or an officer who has responsibility for animal control in a county or municipality has reason to believe that an animal has been or is being cruelly treated, the officer may apply to a justice court or magistrate in the county or to a municipal court in the municipality in which the animal is located for a warrant to seize the animal.

(b) On a showing of probable cause to believe that the animal has been or is being cruelly treated, the court or magistrate shall issue the warrant and set a time within 10 calendar days of the date of issuance for a hearing in the appropriate justice court or municipal court to determine whether the animal has been cruelly treated.

(c) The officer executing the warrant shall cause the animal to be impounded and shall give written notice to the owner of the animal of the time and place of the hearing.

CHAPTER 822
REGULATION OF ANIMALS

SUBCHAPTER A
GENERAL PROVISIONS; DOGS THAT ATTACK PERSONS OR ARE A DANGER TO PERSONS

Sec. 822.001. Definitions.

In this subchapter:

(1) "Animal control authority" means a municipal or county animal control office with authority over the area in which the dog is kept or the county sheriff in an area that does not have an animal control office.

(2) "Serious bodily injury" means an injury characterized by severe bite wounds or severe ripping and tearing of muscle that would cause a reasonably prudent person to seek treatment from a medical professional and would require hospitalization without regard to whether the person actually sought medical treatment.

(3) "Dangerous dog," "dog," "owner," and "secure enclosure" have the meanings assigned by Section 822.041.

(4) "Secure" means to take steps that a reasonable person would take to ensure a dog remains on the owner's property, including confining the dog in an enclosure that is capable of preventing the escape or release of the dog.

Sec. 822.0011. Application to Certain Property.

For purposes of this subchapter, a person's property includes property the person is entitled to possess or occupy under a lease or other agreement.

Sec. 822.0012. Animal Control Authority in Certain Municipalities.

(a) This section applies only to an incorporated municipality that has a population of more than 1,000 and that is the county seat of a county with a population of less than 1,600.

(b) Notwithstanding the definition in Section 822.001(1), for purposes of this subchapter the police department of a municipality described by Subsection (a) is the animal control authority for the municipality in all areas in which a dog is kept and that are subject to the authority of the police department.

Sec. 822.002. Seizure of a Dog Causing Death of or Serious Bodily Injury to a Person.

(a) A justice court, county court, or municipal court shall order the animal control authority to seize a dog and shall issue a warrant authorizing the seizure:

(1) on the sworn complaint of any person, including the county attorney, the city attorney, or a peace officer, that the dog has caused the death of or serious bodily injury to a person by attacking, biting, or mauling the person; and

(2) on a showing of probable cause to believe that the dog caused the death of or serious bodily injury to the person as stated in the complaint.

(b) The animal control authority shall seize the dog or order its seizure and shall provide for the impoundment of the dog in secure and humane conditions until the court orders the disposition of the dog.

Sec. 822.003. Hearing.

(a) The court shall set a time for a hearing to determine whether the dog caused the death of or serious bodily injury to a person by attacking, biting, or mauling the person. The hearing must be held not later than the 10th day after the date on which the warrant is issued.

(b) The court shall give written notice of the time and place of the hearing to:

(1) the owner of the dog or the person from whom the dog was seized; and

(2) the person who made the complaint.

(c) Any interested party, including the county attorney or city attorney, is entitled to present evidence at the hearing.

(d) The court shall order the dog destroyed if the court finds that the dog caused the death of a person by attacking, biting, or mauling the person. If that finding is not made, the court shall order the dog released to:

(1) its owner;

(2) the person from whom the dog was seized; or

(3) any other person authorized to take possession of the dog.

(e) The court may order the dog destroyed if the court finds that the dog caused serious bodily injury to a person by attacking, biting, or mauling the person. If that finding is not made, the court shall order the dog released to:

(1) its owner;

(2) the person from whom the dog was seized; or

(3) any other person authorized to take possession of the dog.

(f) The court may not order the dog destroyed if the court finds that the dog caused the serious bodily injury to a person by attacking, biting, or mauling the person and:

(1) the dog was being used for the protection of a person or person's property, the attack, bite, or mauling occurred in an enclosure in which the dog was being kept, and:

(A) the enclosure was reasonably certain to prevent the dog from leaving the enclosure on its own and provided notice of the presence of a dog; and

(B) the injured person was at least eight years of age, and was trespassing in the enclosure when the attack, bite, or mauling occurred;

(2) the dog was not being used for the protection of a person or person's property, the attack, bite, or mauling occurred in an enclosure in which the dog was being kept, and the injured person was at least eight years of age and was trespassing in the enclosure when the attack, bite, or mauling occurred;

(3) the attack, bite, or mauling occurred during an arrest or other action of a peace officer while the peace officer was using the dog for law enforcement purposes;

(4) the dog was defending a person from an assault or person's property from damage or theft by the injured person; or

(5) the injured person was younger than eight years of age, the attack, bite, or mauling occurred in an enclosure in which the dog was being kept, and the enclosure was reasonably certain to keep a person younger than eight years of age from entering.

Sec. 822.004. Destruction of Dog.

The destruction of a dog under this subchapter must be performed by:

(1) a licensed veterinarian;

(2) personnel of a recognized animal shelter or humane society who are trained in the humane destruction of animals; or

(3) personnel of a governmental agency responsible for animal control who are trained in the humane destruction of animals.

Sec. 822.005. Attack by Dog.

(a) A person commits an offense if the person is the owner of a dog and the person:

(1) with criminal negligence, as defined by Section 6.03, Penal Code, fails to secure the dog and the dog makes an unprovoked attack on another person that occurs at a location other than the owner's real property or in or on the owner's motor vehicle or boat and that causes serious bodily injury, as defined by Section 1.07, Penal Code, or death to the other person; or

(2) knows the dog is a dangerous dog by learning in a manner described by Section 822.042(g) that

the person is the owner of a dangerous dog, and the dangerous dog makes an unprovoked attack on another person that occurs at a location other than a secure enclosure in which the dog is restrained in accordance with Subchapter D and that causes serious bodily injury, as defined by Section 822.001, or death to the other person.

(b) An offense under this section is a felony of the third degree unless the attack causes death, in which event the offense is a felony of the second degree.

(c) If a person is found guilty of an offense under this section, the court may order the dog destroyed by a person listed in Section 822.004.

(d) A person who is subject to prosecution under this section and under any other law may be prosecuted under this section, the other law, or both.

Sec. 822.006. Defenses.

(a) It is a defense to prosecution under Section 822.005(a) that the person is a veterinarian, a veterinary clinic employee, a peace officer, a person employed by a recognized animal shelter, or a person employed by this state or a political subdivision of this state to deal with stray animals and has temporary ownership, custody, or control of the dog in connection with that position.

(b) It is a defense to prosecution under Section 822.005(a) that the person is an employee of the Texas Department of Criminal Justice or a law enforcement agency and trains or uses dogs for law enforcement or corrections purposes and is training or using the dog in connection with the person's official capacity.

(c) It is a defense to prosecution under Section 822.005(a) that the person is a dog trainer or an employee of a guard dog company under Chapter 1702, Occupations Code, and has temporary ownership, custody, or control of the dog in connection with that position.

(d) It is a defense to prosecution under Section 822.005(a) that the person is a person with a disability and uses the dog to provide assistance, the dog is trained to provide assistance to a person with a disability, and the person is using the dog to provide assistance in connection with the person's disability.

(e) It is a defense to prosecution under Section 822.005(a) that the person attacked by the dog was at the time of the attack engaged in conduct prohibited by Chapters 19, 20, 21, 22, 28, 29, and 30, Penal Code.

(f) It is an affirmative defense to prosecution under Section 822.005(a) that, at the time of the conduct charged, the person and the dog are participating in an organized search and rescue effort at the request of law enforcement.

(g) It is an affirmative defense to prosecution under Section 822.005(a) that, at the time of the conduct charged, the person and the dog are participating in an organized dog show or event sponsored by a nationally recognized or state-recognized kennel club.

(h) It is an affirmative defense to prosecution under Section 822.005(a) that, at the time of the conduct charged, the person and the dog are engaged in:

(1) a lawful hunting activity; or

(2) a farming or ranching activity, including herding livestock, typically performed by a working dog on a farm or ranch.

(i) It is a defense to prosecution under Section 822.005(a) that, at the time of the conduct charged, the person's dog was on a leash and the person:

(1) was in immediate control of the dog; or

(2) if the person was not in control of the dog, the person was making immediate and reasonable attempts to regain control of the dog.

Sec. 822.007. Local Regulation of Dogs.

This subchapter does not prohibit a municipality or county from adopting leash or registration requirements applicable to dogs.

SUBCHAPTER B DOGS AND COYOTES THAT ARE A DANGER TO ANIMALS

Sec. 822.011. Definitions.

In this subchapter:

(1) "Dog or coyote" includes a crossbreed between a dog and a coyote.

(2) "Livestock" includes exotic livestock as defined by Section 161.001, Agriculture Code.

Sec. 822.012. Certain Dogs and Coyotes Prohibited from Running at Large; Criminal Penalty.

(a) The owner, keeper, or person in control of a dog or coyote that the owner, keeper, or person knows is accustomed to run, worry, or kill livestock, domestic animals, or fowls may not permit the dog or coyote to run at large.

(b) A person who violates this section commits an offense. An offense under this subsection is punishable by a fine of not more than $100.

Health and Safety Code

(c) Each time a dog or coyote runs at large in violation of this section constitutes a separate offense.

Sec. 822.013. Dogs or Coyotes That Attack Animals.

(a) A dog or coyote that is attacking, is about to attack, or has recently attacked livestock, domestic animals, or fowls may be killed by:

(1) any person witnessing the attack; or

(2) the attacked animal's owner or a person acting on behalf of the owner if the owner or person has knowledge of the attack.

(b) A person who kills a dog or coyote as provided by this section is not liable for damages to the owner, keeper, or person in control of the dog or coyote.

(c) A person who discovers on the person's property a dog or coyote known or suspected of having killed livestock, domestic animals, or fowls may detain or impound the dog or coyote and return it to its owner or deliver the dog or coyote to the local animal control authority. The owner of the dog or coyote is liable for all costs incurred in the capture and care of the dog or coyote and all damage done by the dog or coyote.

(d) The owner, keeper, or person in control of a dog or coyote that is known to have attacked livestock, domestic animals, or fowls shall control the dog or coyote in a manner approved by the local animal control authority.

(e) A person is not required to acquire a hunting license under Section 42.002, Parks and Wildlife Code, to kill a dog or coyote under this section.

SUBCHAPTER C COUNTY REGISTRATION AND REGULATION OF DOGS

Sec. 822.021. Application to Counties That Adopt Subchapter.

This subchapter applies only to a county that adopts this subchapter by a majority vote of the qualified voters of the county voting at an election held under this subchapter. This subchapter shall not apply to any county or municipality that enacts or has enacted registration or restraint laws pursuant to Chapter 826 (Rabies Control Act of 1981).

Sec. 822.022. Petition for Election.

(a) On receiving a petition signed by at least 100 qualified property taxpaying voters of the county or a majority of the qualified property taxpaying voters of the county, whichever is less, the commissioners court of a county shall order an election to determine whether the registration of and registration fee for dogs will be required in the county.

(b) The election shall be held on the first authorized uniform election date prescribed by the Election Code that allows sufficient time to comply with other requirements of law.

Sec. 822.023. Notice.

In addition to the notice required by Section 4.003, Election Code, notice of an election under this subchapter shall be published at least once in an English language newspaper of general circulation in the county. If there is no English language newspaper of general circulation in the county, the notice shall be posted at the courthouse door for at least one week before the election.

Sec. 822.024. Ballot Proposition.

The ballot for an election under this subchapter shall be printed to provide for voting for or against the proposition: "Registration of and registration fee for dogs."

Sec. 822.025. Election Result.

(a) If a majority of those voting at the election vote in favor of the measure, the requirement that dogs be registered takes effect in the county on the 10th day after the date on which the result of the election is declared.

(b) The county judge shall issue a proclamation declaring the result of the election if the vote is in favor of the measure. The proclamation shall be published at least once in an English language newspaper of general circulation in the county or, if there is no English language newspaper of general circulation in the county, the proclamation shall be posted at the courthouse door.

Sec. 822.026. Interval Between Elections.

(a) If the result of an election is against the registration of and registration fee for dogs, another election on that subject may not be held for six months after the date of the election.

(b) If the result of an election is for the registration of and registration fee for dogs, an election to repeal the registration and fee may not be held for two years from the date of the election.

Sec. 822.027. Registration Tags and Certificate.

(a) The commissioners court of a county shall furnish the county treasurer the necessary dog identification tags.

(b) The tags must be numbered consecutively and must be printed or impressed with the name of the county issuing the tags.

(c) The county treasurer shall assign a registration number to each dog registered with the county and shall give the owner or person having control of the dog the identification tag and a registration certificate.

(d) The county treasurer shall record the registration of a dog, including the age, breed, color, sex, and registration date of the dog. If the registration information is not recorded on microfilm, as may be permitted under other law, it shall be recorded in a book kept for that purpose.

(e) If the ownership of a dog is transferred, the dog's registration certificate shall be transferred to the new owner.

Sec. 822.028. Registration Fee.

(a) An owner of a dog registered under this subchapter must pay a registration fee of $1. However, the commissioners court of the county may set the fee in an amount of more than $1 but not more than $5, and if the court sets the amount of the fee the owner must pay that amount.

(b) Registration is valid for one year from the date of registration.

(c) If a dog is moved to another county, the owner may present the registration certificate to the county treasurer of the county to which the dog is moved and receive without additional cost a registration certificate. The new registration certificate is valid for one year from the date of registration in the county from which the dog was moved.

Sec. 822.029. Disposition of Fee.

(a) The fee collected for the registration of a dog shall be deposited to the credit of a special fund of the county and used only to:

(1) defray the cost of administering this subchapter in the county, including the costs of registration and the identification tags; and

(2) reimburse the owner of any sheep, goats, calves, or other domestic animals or fowls killed in the county by a dog not owned by the person seeking reimbursement.

(b) Reimbursement under Subsection (a)(2) shall be made on the order of the commissioners court only on satisfactory proof of the killing.

(c) The commissioners court shall determine the amount and time of reimbursement. If there is insufficient money in the fund to reimburse all injured persons in full, reimbursement shall be made on a pro rata basis.

(d) The county treasurer shall keep an accurate record showing all amounts received into and paid from the fund.

Sec. 822.030. Registration Required; Exception for Temporary Visits.

(a) The owner or person having control of a dog six months of age or older in a county that has adopted this subchapter must register the dog not later than the 30th day after the date on which the proclamation is published or adopted.

(b) A dog brought into a county for not more than 10 days for breeding purposes, trial, or show is not required to be registered.

Sec. 822.031. Unregistered Dogs Prohibited from Running at Large.

The owner or person having control of a dog at least six months of age in a county adopting this subchapter may not allow the dog to run at large unless the dog:

(1) is registered under this subchapter with the county in which the dog runs at large; and

(2) has fastened about its neck a dog identification tag issued by the county.

Sec. 822.032. Unmuzzled Dogs Prohibited from Running at Large [Repealed].

Repealed by Acts 2003, 78th Leg., ch. 1002 (H.B. 151), § 2, effective September 1, 2003.

Sec. 822.033. Dogs That Attack Domestic Animals [Renumbered].

Renumbered to Tex.Health & Safety Code § 822.013 by Acts 2003, 78th Leg., ch. 1002 (H.B. 151), § 1, effective September 1, 2003.

Sec. 822.034. Protection of Domestic Animals [Repealed].

Repealed by Acts 2003, 78th Leg., ch. 1002 (H.B. 151), § 2, effective September 1, 2003.

Sec. 822.035. Criminal Penalty.

(a) A person commits an offense if the person intentionally:

(1) fails or refuses to register a dog required to be registered under this subchapter;

(2) fails or refuses to allow a dog to be killed when ordered by the proper authorities to do so; or

(3) violates this subchapter.

(b) An offense under this section is a misdemeanor punishable by a fine of not more than $100, confinement in the county jail for not more than 30 days, or both.

SUBCHAPTER D DANGEROUS DOGS

Sec. 822.041. Definitions.

In this subchapter:

(1) "Animal control authority" means a municipal or county animal control office with authority over the area where the dog is kept or a county sheriff in an area with no animal control office.

(2) "Dangerous dog" means a dog that:

(A) makes an unprovoked attack on a person that causes bodily injury and occurs in a place other than an enclosure in which the dog was being kept and that was reasonably certain to prevent the dog from leaving the enclosure on its own; or

(B) commits unprovoked acts in a place other than an enclosure in which the dog was being kept and that was reasonably certain to prevent the dog from leaving the enclosure on its own and those acts cause a person to reasonably believe that the dog will attack and cause bodily injury to that person.

(3) "Dog" means a domesticated animal that is a member of the canine family.

(4) "Secure enclosure" means a fenced area or structure that is:

(A) locked;

(B) capable of preventing the entry of the general public, including children;

(C) capable of preventing the escape or release of a dog;

(D) clearly marked as containing a dangerous dog; and

(E) in conformance with the requirements for enclosures established by the local animal control authority.

(5) "Owner" means a person who owns or has custody or control of the dog.

Sec. 822.0411. Animal Control Authority in Certain Municipalities.

(a) This section applies only to an incorporated municipality that has a population of more than 1,000 and that is the county seat of a county with a population of less than 1,600.

(b) Notwithstanding the definition in Section 822.041(1), for purposes of this subchapter the police department of a municipality described by Subsection (a) is the animal control authority for the municipality in all areas in which a dog is kept and that are subject to the authority of the police department.

Sec. 822.042. Requirements for Owner of Dangerous Dog.

(a) Not later than the 30th day after a person learns that the person is the owner of a dangerous dog, the person shall:

(1) register the dangerous dog with the animal control authority for the area in which the dog is kept;

(2) restrain the dangerous dog at all times on a leash in the immediate control of a person or in a secure enclosure;

(3) obtain liability insurance coverage or show financial responsibility in an amount of at least $100,000 to cover damages resulting from an attack by the dangerous dog causing bodily injury to a person and provide proof of the required liability insurance coverage or financial responsibility to the animal control authority for the area in which the dog is kept; and

(4) comply with an applicable municipal or county regulation, requirement, or restriction on dangerous dogs.

(b) The owner of a dangerous dog who does not comply with Subsection (a) shall deliver the dog to the animal control authority not later than the 30th day after the owner learns that the dog is a dangerous dog.

(c) If, on application of any person, a justice court, county court, or municipal court finds, after notice and hearing as provided by Section 822.0423, that the owner of a dangerous dog has failed to comply with Subsection (a) or (b), the court shall order the animal control authority to seize the dog and shall issue a warrant authorizing the seizure. The authority shall seize the dog or order its seizure and shall provide for the impoundment of the dog in secure and humane conditions.

(d) The owner shall pay any cost or fee assessed by the municipality or county related to the seizure, acceptance, impoundment, or destruction of the dog. The governing body of the municipality or county may prescribe the amount of the fees.

(e) Subject to Subsection (e-1), the court shall order the animal control authority to humanely destroy the dog if the owner has not complied with

Subsection (a) before the 11th day after the date on which the dog is seized or delivered to the authority. The court shall order the authority to return the dog to the owner if the owner complies with Subsection (a) before the 11th day after the date on which the dog is seized or delivered to the authority.

(e-1) Notwithstanding any other law or local regulation:

(1) any order to destroy a dog is stayed for a period of 10 calendar days from the date the order is issued, during which period the dog's owner may file a notice of appeal; and

(2) a court, including a justice court, may not order the destruction of a dog during the pendency of an appeal under Section 822.0424.

(f) The court may order the humane destruction of a dog if the owner of the dog has not been located before the 15th day after the seizure and impoundment of the dog.

(g) For purposes of this section, a person learns that the person is the owner of a dangerous dog when:

(1) the owner knows of an attack described in Section 822.041(2)(A) or (B);

(2) the owner receives notice that a justice court, county court, or municipal court has found that the dog is a dangerous dog under Section 822.0423; or

(3) the owner is informed by the animal control authority that the dog is a dangerous dog under Section 822.0421.

Sec. 822.0421. Determination That Dog Is Dangerous.

(a) If a person reports an incident described by Section 822.041(2), the animal control authority may investigate the incident. If, after receiving the sworn statements of any witnesses, the animal control authority determines the dog is a dangerous dog, the animal control authority shall notify the owner in writing of the determination.

(b) Notwithstanding any other law, including a municipal ordinance, an owner, not later than the 15th day after the date the owner is notified that a dog owned by the owner is a dangerous dog, may appeal the determination of the animal control authority to a justice, county, or municipal court of competent jurisdiction.

(c) To file an appeal under Subsection (b), the owner must:

(1) file a notice of appeal of the animal control authority's dangerous dog determination with the court;

(2) attach a copy of the determination from the animal control authority; and

(3) serve a copy of the notice of appeal on the animal control authority by mailing the notice through the United States Postal Service.

(d) An owner may appeal the decision of the justice or municipal court under Subsection (b) in the manner described by Section 822.0424.

Sec. 822.0422. Reporting of Incident in Certain Counties and Municipalities.

(a) This section applies only to a county with a population of more than 2,800,000, to a county in which the commissioners court has entered an order electing to be governed by this section, and to a municipality in which the governing body has adopted an ordinance electing to be governed by this section.

(b) A person may report an incident described by Section 822.041(2) to a municipal court, a justice court, or a county court. The owner of the dog shall deliver the dog to the animal control authority not later than the fifth day after the date on which the owner receives notice that the report has been filed. The authority may provide for the impoundment of the dog in secure and humane conditions until the court orders the disposition of the dog.

(c) If the owner fails to deliver the dog as required by Subsection (b), the court shall order the animal control authority to seize the dog and shall issue a warrant authorizing the seizure. The authority shall seize the dog or order its seizure and shall provide for the impoundment of the dog in secure and humane conditions until the court orders the disposition of the dog. The owner shall pay any cost incurred in seizing the dog.

(d) The court shall determine, after notice and hearing as provided in Section 822.0423, whether the dog is a dangerous dog.

(e) The court, after determining that the dog is a dangerous dog, may order the animal control authority to continue to impound the dangerous dog in secure and humane conditions until the court orders disposition of the dog under Section 822.042 and the dog is returned to the owner or destroyed.

(f) The owner shall pay a cost or fee assessed under Section 822.042(d).

Sec. 822.0423. Hearing.

(a) The court, on receiving a report of an incident under Section 822.0422 or on application under Section 822.042(c), shall set a time for a hearing to determine whether the dog is a dangerous dog or whether the owner of the dog has complied with Section 822.042. The hearing must be held not later than the 10th day after the date on which the dog is seized or delivered.

Health and Safety Code

(b) The court shall give written notice of the time and place of the hearing to:

(1) the owner of the dog or the person from whom the dog was seized; and

(2) the person who made the complaint.

(c) Any interested party, including the county or city attorney, is entitled to present evidence at the hearing.

(c-1) The court shall determine the estimated costs to house and care for the impounded dog during the appeal process and shall set the amount of bond for an appeal adequate to cover those estimated costs.

(d) An owner or person filing the action may appeal the decision of the municipal or justice court in the manner described by Section 822.0424.

Sec. 822.0424. Appeal.

(a) A party to an appeal under Section 822.0421(d) or a hearing under Section 822.0423 may appeal the decision to a county court or county court at law in the county in which the justice or municipal court is located and is entitled to a jury trial on request.

(b) As a condition of perfecting an appeal, not later than the 10th calendar day after the date the decision is issued, the appellant must file a notice of appeal and, if applicable, an appeal bond in the amount determined by the court from which the appeal is taken.

(c) Notwithstanding Section 30.00014, Government Code, or any other law, a person filing an appeal from a municipal court under Subsection (a) is not required to file a motion for a new trial to perfect an appeal.

(d) A decision of a county court or county court at law under this section may be appealed in the same manner as an appeal for any other case in a county court or county court at law.

(e) Notwithstanding any other law, a county court or a county court at law has jurisdiction to hear an appeal filed under this section.

Sec. 822.043. Registration.

(a) An animal control authority for the area in which the dog is kept shall annually register a dangerous dog if the owner:

(1) presents proof of:

(A) liability insurance or financial responsibility, as required by Section 822.042;

(B) current rabies vaccination of the dangerous dog; and

(C) the secure enclosure in which the dangerous dog will be kept; and

(2) pays an annual registration fee of $50.

(b) The animal control authority shall provide to the owner registering a dangerous dog a registration tag. The owner must place the tag on the dog's collar.

(c) If an owner of a registered dangerous dog sells or moves the dog to a new address, the owner, not later than the 14th day after the date of the sale or move, shall notify the animal control authority for the area in which the new address is located. On presentation by the current owner of the dangerous dog's prior registration tag and payment of a fee of $25, the animal control authority shall issue a new registration tag to be placed on the dangerous dog's collar.

(d) An owner of a registered dangerous dog shall notify the office in which the dangerous dog was registered of any attacks the dangerous dog makes on people.

Sec. 822.044. Attack by Dangerous Dog.

(a) A person commits an offense if the person is the owner of a dangerous dog and the dog makes an unprovoked attack on another person outside the dog's enclosure and causes bodily injury to the other person.

(b) An offense under this section is a Class C misdemeanor.

(c) If a person is found guilty of an offense under this section, the court may order the dangerous dog destroyed by a person listed in Section 822.004.

(d) [Repealed by Acts 2007, 80th Leg., ch. 669 (H.B. 1355), § 8, effective September 1, 2007.]

Sec. 822.045. Violations.

(a) A person who owns or keeps custody or control of a dangerous dog commits an offense if the person fails to comply with Section 822.042 or Section 822.0422(b) or an applicable municipal or county regulation relating to dangerous dogs.

(b) Except as provided by Subsection (c), an offense under this section is a Class C misdemeanor.

(c) An offense under this section is a Class B misdemeanor if it is shown on the trial of the offense that the defendant has previously been convicted under this section.

Sec. 822.046. Defense.

(a) It is a defense to prosecution under Section 822.044 or Section 822.045 that the person is a veterinarian, a peace officer, a person employed by a recognized animal shelter, or a person employed by the state or a political subdivision of the state to deal with stray animals and has temporary ownership, custody, or control of the dog in connection with that position.

(b) It is a defense to prosecution under Section 822.044 or Section 822.045 that the person is an employee of the institutional division of the Texas Department of Criminal Justice or a law enforcement agency and trains or uses dogs for law enforcement or corrections purposes.

(c) It is a defense to prosecution under Section 822.044 or Section 822.045 that the person is a dog trainer or an employee of a guard dog company under Chapter 1702, Occupations Code.

Sec. 822.047. Local Regulation of Dangerous Dogs.

A county or municipality may place additional requirements or restrictions on dangerous dogs if the requirements or restrictions:

(1) are not specific to one breed or several breeds of dogs; and

(2) are more stringent than restrictions provided by this subchapter.

SUBCHAPTER E DANGEROUS WILD ANIMALS

Sec. 822.101. Definitions.

In this subchapter:

(1) "Animal registration agency" means the municipal or county animal control office with authority over the area where a dangerous wild animal is kept or a county sheriff in an area that does not have an animal control office.

(2) [Repealed by Acts 2015, 84th Leg., ch. 1 (S.B. 219), § 3.1639(119), effective April 2, 2015.]

(3) "Commercial activity" means:

(A) an activity involving a dangerous wild animal conducted for profit that is not inherent to the animal's nature;

(B) an activity for which a fee is charged and that is entertainment using or an exhibition of the animal; or

(C) the selling, trading, bartering, or auctioning of a dangerous wild animal or a dangerous wild animal's body parts.

(4) "Dangerous wild animal" means:

(A) a lion;

(B) a tiger;

(C) an ocelot;

(D) a cougar;

(E) a leopard;

(F) a cheetah;

(G) a jaguar;

(H) a bobcat;

(I) a lynx;

(J) a serval;

(K) a caracal;

(L) a hyena;

(M) a bear;

(N) a coyote;

(O) a jackal;

(P) a baboon;

(Q) a chimpanzee;

(R) an orangutan;

(S) a gorilla; or

(T) any hybrid of an animal listed in this subdivision.

(4-a) "Executive commissioner" means the executive commissioner of the Health and Human Services Commission.

(5) "Owner" means any person who owns, harbors, or has custody or control of a dangerous wild animal.

(6) "Person" means an individual, partnership, corporation, trust, estate, joint stock company, foundation, or association of individuals.

(7) "Primary enclosure" means any structure used to immediately restrict an animal to a limited amount of space, including a cage, pen, run, room, compartment, or hutch.

Sec. 822.102. Applicability of Subchapter.

(a) This subchapter does not apply to:

(1) a county, municipality, or agency of the state or an agency of the United States or an agent or official of a county, municipality, or agency acting in an official capacity;

(2) a research facility, as that term is defined by Section 2(e), Animal Welfare Act (7 U.S.C. Section 2132), and its subsequent amendments, that is licensed by the secretary of agriculture of the United States under that Act;

(3) an organization that is an accredited member of the Association of Zoos and Aquariums;

(4) an injured, infirm, orphaned, or abandoned dangerous wild animal while being transported for care or treatment;

(5) an injured, infirm, orphaned, or abandoned dangerous wild animal while being rehabilitated, treated, or cared for by a licensed veterinarian, an incorporated humane society or animal shelter, or a person who holds a rehabilitation permit issued under Subchapter C, Chapter 43, Parks and Wildlife Code;

(6) a dangerous wild animal owned by and in the custody and control of a transient circus company that is not based in this state if:

(A) the animal is used as an integral part of the circus performances; and

(B) the animal is kept within this state only during the time the circus is performing in this state or for a period not to exceed 30 days while the circus is performing outside the United States;

(7) a dangerous wild animal while in the temporary custody or control of a television or motion picture production company during the filming of a television or motion picture production in this state;

(8) a dangerous wild animal owned by and in the possession, custody, or control of a college or university solely as a mascot for the college or university;

(9) a dangerous wild animal while being transported in interstate commerce through the state in compliance with the Animal Welfare Act (7 U.S.C. Section 2131 et seq.) and its subsequent amendments and the regulations adopted under that Act;

(10) a nonhuman primate owned by and in the control and custody of a person whose only business is supplying nonhuman primates directly and exclusively to biomedical research facilities and who holds a Class "A" or Class "B" dealer's license issued by the secretary of agriculture of the United States under the Animal Welfare Act (7 U.S.C. Section 2131 et seq.) and its subsequent amendments;

(11) a dangerous wild animal that is:

(A) owned by or in the possession, control, or custody of a person who is a participant in a species survival plan of the Association of Zoos and Aquariums for that species; and

(B) an integral part of that species survival plan; and

(12) in a county west of the Pecos River that has a population of less than 25,000, a cougar, bobcat, or coyote in the possession, custody, or control of a person that has trapped the cougar, bobcat, or coyote as part of a predator or depredation control activity.

(b) This subchapter does not require a municipality that does not have an animal control office to create that office.

Sec. 822.103. Certificate of Registration; Fees.

(a) A person may not own, harbor, or have custody or control of a dangerous wild animal for any purpose unless the person holds a certificate of registration for that animal issued by an animal registration agency.

(b) A certificate of registration issued under this subchapter is not transferrable and is valid for one year after its date of issuance or renewal unless revoked.

(c) The animal registration agency may establish and charge reasonable fees for application, issuance, and renewal of a certificate of registration in order to recover the costs associated with the administration and enforcement of this subchapter. The fee charged to an applicant may not exceed $50 for each animal registered and may not exceed $500 for each person registering animals, regardless of the number of animals owned by the person. The fees collected under this section may be used only to administer and enforce this subchapter.

Sec. 822.104. Certificate of Registration Application.

(a) An applicant for an original or renewal certificate of registration for a dangerous wild animal must file an application with an animal registration agency on a form provided by the animal registration agency.

(b) The application must include:

(1) the name, address, and telephone number of the applicant;

(2) a complete identification of each animal, including species, sex, age, if known, and any distinguishing marks or coloration that would aid in the identification of the animal;

(3) the exact location where each animal is to be kept;

(4) a sworn statement that:

(A) all information in the application is complete and accurate; and

(B) the applicant has read this subchapter and that all facilities used by the applicant to confine or enclose the animal comply with the requirements of this subchapter; and

(5) any other information the animal registration agency may require.

(c) An applicant shall include with each application:

(1) the nonrefundable fee;

(2) proof, in a form acceptable by the animal registration agency, that the applicant has liability insurance, as required by Section 822.107;

(3) a color photograph of each animal being registered taken not earlier than the 30th day before the date the application is filed;

(4) a photograph and a statement of the dimensions of the primary enclosure in which each animal is to be kept and a scale diagram of the premises where each animal will be kept, including the location of any perimeter fencing and any residence on the premises; and

(5) if an applicant holds a Class "A" or Class "B" dealer's license or Class "C" exhibitor's license issued by the secretary of agriculture of the United

Health and Safety Code

States under the Animal Welfare Act (7 U.S.C. Section 2131 et seq.) and its subsequent amendments, a clear and legible photocopy of the license.

(d) In addition to the items required under Subsection (c), an application for renewal must include a statement signed by a veterinarian licensed to practice in this state stating that the veterinarian:

(1) inspected each animal being registered not earlier than the 30th day before the date of the filing of the renewal application; and

(2) finds that the care and treatment of each animal by the owner meets or exceeds the standards prescribed under this subchapter.

Sec. 822.105. Denial or Revocation of Certificate of Registration; Appeal.

(a) If the animal registration agency finds that an application for an original or renewal certificate of registration under this subchapter does not meet the requirements of Section 822.104 or, after inspection, that an applicant has not complied with this subchapter, the animal registration agency shall deny the applicant a certificate of registration and give the applicant written notice of the denial and the reasons for the denial.

(b) If the animal registration agency finds, after inspection, that a registered owner provided false information in or in connection with the application or has not complied with this subchapter, the animal registration agency shall revoke the certificate of registration and give the owner written notice of the revocation and the reasons for the revocation.

(c) A person may appeal the denial of an original or renewal certificate of registration or the revocation of a certificate of registration to the justice court for the precinct in which the animal is located or the municipal court in the municipality in which the animal is located not later than the 15th day after the date the certificate of registration is denied or revoked. Either party may appeal the decision of the justice or municipal court to a county court or county court at law in the county in which the justice or municipal court is located. The decision of the county court or county court at law may not be appealed.

(d) The filing of an appeal of the denial or revocation of a certificate of registration under Subsection (c) stays the denial or revocation until the court rules on the appeal.

Sec. 822.106. Display of Certificate of Registration.

(a) A holder of a certificate of registration shall prominently display the certificate at the premises where each animal that is the subject of the certificate of registration is kept.

(b) Not later than the 10th day after the date a person receives a certificate of registration, the person shall file a clear and legible copy of the certificate of registration with the Department of State Health Services. The executive commissioner shall establish a procedure for filing a certificate of registration and by rule shall establish a reasonable fee to be collected by the department in an amount sufficient to recover the cost associated with filing a certificate of registration under this subsection.

Sec. 822.107. Liability Insurance.

An owner of a dangerous wild animal shall maintain liability insurance coverage in an amount of not less than $100,000 for each occurrence for liability for damages for destruction of or damage to property and death or bodily injury to a person caused by the dangerous wild animal.

Sec. 822.108. Inspection.

An owner of a dangerous wild animal, at all reasonable times, shall allow the animal registration agency, its staff, its agents, or a designated licensed veterinarian to enter the premises where the animal is kept and to inspect the animal, the primary enclosure for the animal, and the owner's records relating to the animal to ensure compliance with this subchapter.

Sec. 822.109. Relocation or Disposition of Animal.

(a) An owner of a dangerous wild animal may not permanently relocate the animal unless the owner first notifies the animal registration agency in writing of the exact location to which the animal will be relocated and provides the animal registration agency, with respect to the new location, the information required by Section 822.104.

(b) Within 10 days after the death, sale, or other disposition of the animal, the owner of the animal shall notify the animal registration agency in writing of the death, sale, or other disposition.

Sec. 822.110. Attack by Animal; Escape of Animal; Liability.

(a) An owner of a dangerous wild animal shall notify the animal registration agency of any attack of a human by the animal within 48 hours of the attack.

(b) An owner of a dangerous wild animal shall immediately notify the animal registration agency

Health and Safety Code

and the local law enforcement agency of any escape of the animal.

(c) An owner of a dangerous wild animal that escapes is liable for all costs incurred in apprehending and confining the animal.

(d) An animal registration agency, a law enforcement agency, or an employee of an animal registration agency or law enforcement agency is not liable to an owner of a dangerous wild animal for damages arising in connection with the escape of a dangerous wild animal, including liability for damage, injury, or death caused by the animal during or after the animal's escape, or for injury to or death of the animal as a result of apprehension or confinement of the animal after escape.

Sec. 822.111. Powers and Duties of Executive Commissioner; Caging Requirements and Standards.

(a) The executive commissioner by rule shall establish caging requirements and standards for the keeping and confinement of a dangerous wild animal to ensure that the animal is kept in a manner and confined in a primary enclosure that:

(1) protects and enhances the public's health and safety;

(2) prevents escape by the animal; and

(3) provides a safe, healthy, and humane environment for the animal.

(b) An owner of a dangerous wild animal shall keep and confine the animal in accordance with the caging requirements and standards established by the executive commissioner.

(c) An animal registration agency may approve a deviation from the caging requirements and standards established by the executive commissioner, only if:

(1) the animal registration agency has good cause for the deviation; and

(2) the deviation:

(A) does not compromise the public's health and safety;

(B) does not reduce the total area of the primary enclosure below that established by the executive commissioner; and

(C) does not otherwise adversely affect the overall welfare of the animal involved.

Sec. 822.112. Care, Treatment, and Transportation of Animal.

(a) For each dangerous wild animal, the owner shall comply with all applicable standards of the Animal Welfare Act (7 U.S.C. Section 2131 et seq.) and its subsequent amendments and the regulations adopted under that Act relating to:

(1) facilities and operations;

(2) animal health and husbandry; and

(3) veterinary care.

(b) An owner of a dangerous wild animal shall maintain a separate written log for each dangerous wild animal documenting the animal's veterinary care and shall make the log available to the animal registration agency or its agent on request. The log must:

(1) identify the animal treated;

(2) provide the date of treatment;

(3) describe the type or nature of treatment; and

(4) provide the name of the attending veterinarian, if applicable.

(c) When transporting a dangerous wild animal, the owner of the animal, or a designated carrier or intermediate handler of the animal, shall comply with all transportation standards that apply to that animal under the Animal Welfare Act (7 U.S.C. Section 2131 et seq.) and its subsequent amendments or the regulations adopted under that Act.

(d) A person is exempt from the requirements of this section if the person is caring for, treating, or transporting an animal for which the person holds a Class "A" or Class "B" dealer's license or a Class "C" exhibitor's license issued by the secretary of agriculture of the United States under the Animal Welfare Act (7 U.S.C. Section 2131 et seq.) and its subsequent amendments.

Sec. 822.113. Offense and Penalty.

(a) A person commits an offense if the person violates Section 822.103(a), Section 822.106, or Section 822.110(a) or (b). Each animal with respect to which there is a violation and each day that a violation continues is a separate offense.

(b) A person commits an offense if the person knowingly sells or otherwise transfers ownership of a dangerous wild animal to a person who does not have a certificate of registration for that animal as required by this subchapter.

(c) An offense under this section is a Class C misdemeanor.

Sec. 822.114. Civil Penalty.

(a) A person who violates Section 822.103(a) is liable for a civil penalty of not less than $200 and not more than $2,000 for each animal with respect to which there is a violation and for each day the violation continues.

(b) The county or municipality in which the violation occurs may sue to collect a civil penalty. A

Health and Safety Code

civil penalty collected under this subsection may be retained by the county or municipality.

(c) The county or municipality in which the violation occurs may also recover the reasonable costs of investigation, reasonable attorney's fees, and reasonable expert witness fees incurred by the animal registration agency in the civil action. Costs or fees recovered under this subsection shall be credited to the operating account from which payment for the animal registration agency's expenditures was made.

Sec. 822.115. Injunction.

Any person who is directly harmed or threatened with harm by a violation of this subchapter or a failure to enforce this subchapter may sue an owner of a dangerous wild animal to enjoin a violation of this subchapter or to enforce this subchapter.

Sec. 822.116. Effect of Subchapter on Other Law.

(a) This subchapter does not affect the applicability of any other law, rule, order, ordinance, or other legal requirement of this state or a political subdivision of this state.

(b) This subchapter does not prevent a municipality or county from prohibiting or regulating by ordinance or order the ownership, possession, confinement, or care of a dangerous wild animal.

CHAPTER 825
PREDATORY ANIMALS AND ANIMAL PESTS

SUBCHAPTER A
COOPERATION BETWEEN STATE AND FEDERAL AGENCIES IN CONTROLLING PREDATORY ANIMALS AND RODENTS

Sec. 825.008. Tampering with Traps; Criminal Penalty.

(a) A person commits an offense if the person maliciously or wilfully tampers with all or any part of a trap set under this subchapter or removes a trap from the position in which it is placed by a hunter or trapper acting under this subchapter.

(b) An offense under this section is punishable by a fine of not less than $50 or more than $200.

Sec. 825.009. Stealing Traps; Criminal Penalty.

(a) A person commits an offense if the person steals or fraudulently takes a trap belonging to the state or the United States Department of the Interior.

(b) An offense under this section is a misdemeanor punishable by a fine of not less than $100 or more than $200.

Sec. 825.010. Stealing Animals from Traps; Criminal Penalty.

(a) A person commits an offense if the person steals an animal listed in Section 825.001 from a trap set under this subchapter or takes the animal from the trap without authority.

(b) An offense under this section is a misdemeanor punishable by a fine of not less than $100 or more than $200.

(c) An animal stolen or taken in violation of this section is the property of the state. A complaint alleging a violation of this section must allege that the animal is owned by the state, and the only proof necessary to establish ownership shall consist of proving that the animal was taken from a trap that had been set by a hunter or trapper acting under this subchapter.

CHAPTER 826
RABIES

SUBCHAPTER C
RABIES VACCINATIONS

Sec. 826.021. Vaccination of Dogs and Cats Required.

(a) Except as otherwise provided by department rule, the owner of a dog or cat shall have the animal vaccinated against rabies by the time the animal is four months of age and at regular intervals thereafter as prescribed by department rule.

(b) A veterinarian who vaccinates a dog or cat against rabies shall issue to the animal's owner a vaccination certificate in a form that meets the minimum standards approved by the executive commissioner.

(c) A county or municipality may not register or license an animal that has not been vaccinated in accordance with this section.

Health and Safety Code

Sec. 826.022. Vaccination; Criminal Penalty.

(a) A person commits an offense if the person fails or refuses to have each dog or cat owned by the person vaccinated against rabies and the animal is required to be vaccinated under:

(1) Section 826.021 and department rules; or

(2) ordinances or rules adopted under this chapter by a county or municipality within whose jurisdiction the act occurs.

(b) An offense under this section is a Class C misdemeanor.

(c) If on the trial of an offense under this section the court finds that the person has been previously convicted of an offense under this section, the offense is a Class B misdemeanor.

SUBCHAPTER D REGISTRATION AND RESTRAINT OF DOGS AND CATS

Sec. 826.034. Restraint; Criminal Penalty.

(a) A person commits an offense if:

(1) the person fails or refuses to restrain a dog or cat owned by the person; and

(2) the animal is required to be restrained under the ordinances or rules adopted under this chapter by a county or municipality within whose jurisdiction the act occurs.

(b) An offense under this section is a Class C misdemeanor.

SUBCHAPTER E REPORTS AND QUARANTINE

Sec. 826.042. Quarantine of Animals.

(a) The executive commissioner shall adopt rules governing the testing of quarantined animals and the procedure for and method of quarantine.

(b) The local rabies control authority or a veterinarian shall quarantine or test in accordance with department rules any animal that the local rabies control authority or veterinarian has probable cause to believe is rabid, may have been exposed to rabies, or may have exposed a person to rabies.

(c) An owner shall submit for quarantine an animal that:

(1) is reported to be rabid or to have exposed an individual to rabies; or

(2) the owner knows or suspects is rabid or has exposed an individual to rabies.

(d) The owner shall submit the animal to the local rabies control authority of the county or municipality in which the exposure occurs.

(e) A veterinarian shall quarantine an animal that:

(1) is in the possession of the veterinarian; and

(2) the veterinarian knows or suspects is rabid or has exposed an individual to rabies.

(f) At the time an owner submits for quarantine an animal described by Subsection (b), the veterinarian or local rabies control authority, as applicable, shall:

(1) provide written notification to the animal's owner of the date the animal enters quarantine and the date the animal will be released from quarantine;

(2) obtain and retain with the animal's records a written statement signed by the animal's owner and a supervisor employed by the veterinarian or local rabies control authority acknowledging that the information required by Subdivision (1) has been provided to the animal's owner; and

(3) provide the animal's owner a copy of the signed written statement obtained under Subdivision (2).

(g) A veterinarian or local rabies control authority, as applicable, shall identify each animal quarantined under this section with a placard or other marking on the animal's kennel that indicates the animal is quarantined under this section.

Sec. 826.044. Quarantine; Criminal Penalty.

(a) A person commits an offense if the person fails or refuses to quarantine or present for quarantine or testing an animal that:

(1) is required to be placed in quarantine or presented for testing under Section 826.042 and department rules; or

(2) is required to be placed in quarantine under ordinances or rules adopted under this chapter by a county or municipality within whose jurisdiction the act occurs.

(b) An offense under this section is a Class C misdemeanor.

TITLE 11 CIVIL COMMITMENT OF SEXUALLY VIOLENT PREDATORS

CHAPTER 841 CIVIL COMMITMENT OF SEXUALLY VIOLENT PREDATORS

SUBCHAPTER A
GENERAL PROVISIONS

Sec. 841.001. Legislative Findings.

The legislature finds that a small but extremely dangerous group of sexually violent predators exists and that those predators have a behavioral abnormality that is not amenable to traditional mental illness treatment modalities and that makes the predators likely to engage in repeated predatory acts of sexual violence. The legislature finds that the existing involuntary commitment provisions of Subtitle C, Title 7, are inadequate to address the risk of repeated predatory behavior that sexually violent predators pose to society. The legislature further finds that treatment modalities for sexually violent predators are different from the traditional treatment modalities for persons appropriate for involuntary commitment under Subtitle C, Title 7. Thus, the legislature finds that a civil commitment procedure for the long-term supervision and treatment of sexually violent predators is necessary and in the interest of the state.

Sec. 841.002. Definitions.

In this chapter:

(1) "Attorney representing the state" means a district attorney, criminal district attorney, or county attorney with felony criminal jurisdiction who represents the state in a civil commitment proceeding under this chapter.

(2) "Behavioral abnormality" means a congenital or acquired condition that, by affecting a person's emotional or volitional capacity, predisposes the person to commit a sexually violent offense, to the extent that the person becomes a menace to the health and safety of another person.

(3) "Case manager" means a person employed by or under contract with the office to perform duties related to the treatment and supervision of a person committed under this chapter.

(3-a) "Civil commitment proceeding" means a trial or hearing conducted under Subchapter D, F, or G.

(4) "Office" means the Texas Civil Commitment Office.

(5) "Predatory act" means an act directed toward individuals, including family members, for the primary purpose of victimization.

(6) "Repeat sexually violent offender" has the meaning assigned by Section 841.003.

(7) "Secure correctional facility" means a county jail or a confinement facility operated by or under contract with any division of the Texas Department of Criminal Justice.

(7-a) "Sexually motivated conduct" means any conduct involving the intent to arouse or gratify the sexual desire of any person immediately before, during, or immediately after the commission of an offense.

(8) "Sexually violent offense" means:

(A) an offense under Section 21.02, 21.11(a)(1), 22.011, or 22.021, Penal Code;

(B) an offense under Section 20.04(a)(4), Penal Code, if the person committed the offense with the intent to violate or abuse the victim sexually;

(C) an offense under Section 30.02, Penal Code, if the offense is punishable under Subsection (d) of that section and the person committed the offense with the intent to commit an offense listed in Paragraph (A) or (B);

(D) an offense under Section 19.02 or 19.03, Penal Code, that, during the guilt or innocence phase or the punishment phase for the offense, during the adjudication or disposition of delinquent conduct constituting the offense, or subsequently during a civil commitment proceeding under Subchapter D, is determined beyond a reasonable doubt to have been based on sexually motivated conduct;

(E) an attempt, conspiracy, or solicitation, as defined by Chapter 15, Penal Code, to commit an offense listed in Paragraph (A), (B), (C), or (D);

(F) an offense under prior state law that contains elements substantially similar to the elements of an offense listed in Paragraph (A), (B), (C), (D), or (E); or

(G) an offense under the law of another state, federal law, or the Uniform Code of Military Justice that contains elements substantially similar to the elements of an offense listed in Paragraph (A), (B), (C), (D), or (E).

(9) "Sexually violent predator" has the meaning assigned by Section 841.003.

(10) "Tracking service" means an electronic monitoring service, global positioning satellite service, or other appropriate technological service that is designed to track a person's location.

Sec. 841.003. Sexually Violent Predator.

(a) A person is a sexually violent predator for the purposes of this chapter if the person:

(1) is a repeat sexually violent offender; and

(2) suffers from a behavioral abnormality that makes the person likely to engage in a predatory act of sexual violence.

(b) A person is a repeat sexually violent offender for the purposes of this chapter if the person is convicted of more than one sexually violent offense and a sentence is imposed for at least one of the offenses or if:

(1) the person:

(A) is convicted of a sexually violent offense, regardless of whether the sentence for the offense was ever imposed or whether the sentence was probated and the person was subsequently discharged from community supervision;

(B) enters a plea of guilty or nolo contendere for a sexually violent offense in return for a grant of deferred adjudication; or

(C) is adjudicated by a juvenile court as having engaged in delinquent conduct constituting a sexually violent offense and is committed to the Texas Juvenile Justice Department under Section 54.04(d)(3) or (m), Family Code; and

(2) after the date on which under Subdivision (1) the person is convicted, receives a grant of deferred adjudication, or is adjudicated by a juvenile court as having engaged in delinquent conduct, the person commits a sexually violent offense for which the person is convicted, but only if the sentence for the offense is imposed.

Sec. 841.004. Special Prosecution Unit. [Repealed]

Sec. 841.005. Office of State Counsel for Offenders.

(a) Except as provided by Subsection (b), the Office of State Counsel for Offenders shall represent an indigent person subject to a civil commitment proceeding under this chapter.

(b) If for any reason the Office of State Counsel for Offenders is unable to represent an indigent person described by Subsection (a) at a civil commitment proceeding under this chapter, the court shall appoint other counsel to represent the indigent person.

Sec. 841.006. Application of Chapter.

This chapter does not:

(1) prohibit a person committed under this chapter from filing at any time a petition for release under this chapter; or

(2) create for the committed person a cause of action against another person for failure to give notice within a period required by Subchapter B, C, or D.

Sec. 841.007. Duties of Texas Civil Commitment Office.

The Texas Civil Commitment Office is responsible for:

(1) providing appropriate and necessary treatment and supervision for committed persons through the case management system; and

(2) developing and implementing a sex offender treatment program for persons committed under this chapter.

SUBCHAPTER B NOTICE OF POTENTIAL PREDATOR; INITIAL DETERMINATIONS

Sec. 841.021. Notice of Potential Predator.

(a) Subject to Subsection (a-1) and except as provided by Subsection (d), before the person's anticipated release date, the Texas Department of Criminal Justice shall give to the multidisciplinary team established under Section 841.022 written notice of the anticipated release of a person who:

(1) is serving a sentence for:

(A) a sexually violent offense described by Section 841.002(8)(A), (B), or (C); or

(B) what is, or as described by this chapter what the department reasonably believes may be determined to be, a sexually violent offense described by Section 841.002(8)(D); and

(2) may be a repeat sexually violent offender.

(a-1) Regardless of whether any exigent circumstances are present, the Texas Department of Criminal Justice may give notice under this section with respect to a person who is scheduled to be released on parole or to mandatory supervision only if the person's anticipated release date is not later than 24 months after the date on which the notice will be given. The department may not give notice with respect to a person who is currently released on parole or to mandatory supervision, but the multidisciplinary team may perform the functions described by Section 841.022(c) within the applicable period required by that subsection if the written notice required by this section was received by the team before the date of the person's release.

(b) [Repealed by Acts 2015, 84th Leg., ch. 845 (S.B. 746), § 39(2), effective June 17, 2015.]

(c) The Texas Department of Criminal Justice shall give the notice described by Subsection (a) not later than the first day of the 24th month before the person's anticipated release date, but under exigent circumstances may give the notice at any time before that date, except as provided by Subsection (a-1). The notice must contain the following information:

(1) the person's name, identifying factors, anticipated residence after release, and criminal history;

(2) documentation of the person's institutional adjustment and actual treatment; and

(3) an assessment of the likelihood that the person will commit a sexually violent offense after release.

(d) The Texas Department of Criminal Justice may not provide notice under Subsection (a) of the anticipated release of a person for whom the department has previously provided notice under this section and who has been previously recommended for an assessment under Section 841.022 unless, after the recommendation for assessment was made:

(1) the person is convicted of a new sexually violent offense; or

(2) the person's parole or mandatory supervision is revoked based on:

(A) the commission of a new sexually violent offense;

(B) failure to adhere to the requirements of sex offender treatment and supervision; or

(C) failure to register as a sex offender.

Sec. 841.022. Multidisciplinary Team.

(a) The executive director of the Texas Department of Criminal Justice shall establish a multidisciplinary team to review available records of a person referred to the team under Section 841.021. The team must include:

(1) a mental health professional from the Department of State Health Services;

(2) two persons from the Texas Department of Criminal Justice as follows:

(A) one person from the victim services division; and

(B) one person from the sex offender rehabilitation program in the rehabilitation programs division;

(3) a licensed peace officer who is employed by the Department of Public Safety and who has at least five years' experience working for that department or the officer's designee;

(4) two persons from the office; and

(5) a licensed sex offender treatment provider from the Council on Sex Offender Treatment.

(a-1) The Texas Department of Criminal Justice, in consultation with the office, shall provide training to the members of the multidisciplinary team regarding the civil commitment program under this chapter, including training regarding:

(1) eligibility criteria for commitment;

(2) the process for evaluating persons for commitment; and

(3) the sex offender treatment program for persons committed under this chapter.

(b) The multidisciplinary team may request the assistance of other persons in making an assessment under this section.

(c) Not later than the 60th day after the date the multidisciplinary team receives notice under Section 841.021(a), the team shall:

(1) assess whether the person is a repeat sexually violent offender and whether the person is likely to commit a sexually violent offense after release;

(2) give notice of that assessment to the Texas Department of Criminal Justice; and

(3) recommend the assessment of the person for a behavioral abnormality, as appropriate.

Sec. 841.023. Assessment for Behavioral Abnormality.

(a) Not later than the 60th day after the date of a recommendation under Section 841.022(c), the Texas Department of Criminal Justice shall assess whether the person suffers from a behavioral abnormality that makes the person likely to engage in a predatory act of sexual violence. To aid in the assessment, the department shall use an expert to examine the person. The department may contract for the expert services required by this subsection. The expert shall make a clinical assessment based on testing for psychopathy, a clinical interview, and other appropriate assessments and techniques to aid the department in its assessment.

(b) If as a result of the assessment the Texas Department of Criminal Justice believes that the person suffers from a behavioral abnormality, not later than the 60th day after the date of a recommendation under Section 841.022(c) the department shall give notice of that assessment and provide corresponding documentation to the attorney representing the state for the county in which the person was most recently convicted of a sexually violent offense.

SUBCHAPTER C PETITION ALLEGING PREDATOR STATUS

Sec. 841.041. Petition Alleging Predator Status.

(a) If a person is referred to the attorney representing the state under Section 841.023, the attorney may file a petition alleging that the person is a sexually violent predator and stating facts sufficient to support the allegation.

(b) A petition described by Subsection (a) must be:

(1) filed in a district court in the county of the person's most recent conviction for a sexually violent offense;

(2) filed not later than the 90th day after the date the person is referred to the attorney representing the state; and

(3) served on the person as soon as practicable after the date the petition is filed.

(c) To the extent feasible, in filing the petition in a district court described by Subsection (b)(1), the attorney representing the state shall give preference to filing the petition in the applicable court of conviction.

Sec. 841.042. Assistance from Special Prosecution Unit.

On request of the attorney representing the state, the special prosecution unit shall provide legal, financial, and technical assistance to the attorney for a civil commitment proceeding conducted under this chapter.

SUBCHAPTER D TRIAL

Sec. 841.061. Trial.

(a) The judge shall commence a trial to determine whether the person is a sexually violent predator:

(1) except as provided by Section 841.063, not later than the 270th day after the date a petition is served on the person under Section 841.041; and

(2) not later than the person's sentence discharge date unless the judge determines that a delay is necessary in the due administration of justice.

(b) The person or the state is entitled to a jury trial on demand. A demand for a jury trial must be filed in writing not later than the 10th day before the date the trial is scheduled to begin.

(c) The person and the state are each entitled to an immediate clinical interview of the person by an expert. All components of the clinical interview must be completed not later than the 90th day before the date the trial begins.

(d) Additional rights of the person at the trial include the following:

(1) the right to appear at the trial;

(2) the right to waive the right to appear at the trial and appear through the person's attorney;

(3) except as provided by Subsection (f), the right to present evidence on the person's behalf;

(4) the right to cross-examine a witness who testifies against the person; and

(5) the right to view and copy all petitions and reports in the court file.

(e) The attorney representing the state may rely on the petition filed under Section 841.041 and supplement the petition with documentary evidence or live testimony.

(f) A person who is on trial to determine the person's status as a sexually violent predator is required to submit to all expert clinical interviews that are required or permitted of the state to prepare for the person's trial. A person who fails to submit to a clinical interview on the state's behalf as required by this subsection is subject to the following consequences:

(1) the person's failure to participate may be used as evidence against the person at trial;

(2) the person may be prohibited from offering into evidence the results of a clinical interview performed on the person's behalf; and

(3) the person may be subject to contempt proceedings if the person violates a court order by failing to submit to a clinical interview on the state's behalf.

(g) A judge assigned to preside over a trial under this subchapter is not subject to an objection under Section 74.053, Government Code, other than an objection made under Section 74.053(d), Government Code.

(h) Notwithstanding any other provision in this subchapter, the person may appear at the trial through the use of remote technology, including teleconference and videoconference technology.

Sec. 841.062. Determination of Predator Status.

(a) The judge or jury shall determine whether, beyond a reasonable doubt, the person is a sexually violent predator. Either the state or the person is entitled to appeal the determination and to a retrial if an appellate court remands the case to the trial court for a new trial.

(b) A jury determination in a civil commitment proceeding must be by unanimous verdict. If one or two of the 12 jurors have been discharged and there are no alternate jurors to be seated, the remaining jurors may render a verdict. If fewer than 12 jurors render a verdict, the verdict must be signed by each juror rendering the verdict.

Sec. 841.063. Continuance.

(a) Except as provided by Subsection (b), the judge may continue a trial or hearing conducted under this chapter if the person is not substantially prejudiced by the continuance and:

(1) on the request of either party and a showing of good cause; or

(2) on the judge's own motion in the due administration of justice.

(b) The judge may not continue a trial conducted under this chapter to a date occurring later than the person's sentence discharge date unless the judge determines that a continuance is necessary in the due administration of justice.

Sec. 841.064. Retrial.

(a) A trial following a mistrial must commence not later than the 90th day after the date a mistrial was declared in the previous trial, unless the later trial is continued as provided by Section 841.063.

(b) If an appellate court remands the case to the trial court for a new trial, the judge shall commence the retrial not later than the 90th day after the date the appellate court remanded the case. The retrial may be continued as provided by Section 841.063.

Sec. 841.065. Agreed Order.

An agreed order of civil commitment must require the person to submit to the treatment and supervision administered by the office.

SUBCHAPTER E CIVIL COMMITMENT

Sec. 841.081. Civil Commitment of Predator.

(a) If at a trial conducted under Subchapter D the judge or jury determines that the person is a sexually violent predator, the judge shall commit the person for treatment and supervision to be coordinated by the office. The commitment order is effective immediately on entry of the order, except that the treatment and supervision begins on the person's release from a secure correctional facility and continues until the person's behavioral abnormality has changed to the extent that the person is no longer likely to engage in a predatory act of sexual violence.

(b) At any time after entry of a commitment order under Subsection (a), the office may provide to the person instruction regarding the requirements associated with the order, regardless of whether the person is incarcerated at the time of the instruction.

Sec. 841.082. Commitment Requirements.

(a) Before entering an order directing a person's civil commitment, the judge shall impose on the person requirements necessary to ensure the person's compliance with treatment and supervision and to protect the community. The requirements shall include:

(1) requiring the person to reside where instructed by the office;

(2) prohibiting the person's contact with a victim of the person;

(3) requiring the person's participation in and compliance with the sex offender treatment program provided by the office and compliance with all written requirements imposed by the office;

(4) requiring the person to submit to appropriate supervision and:

(A) submit to tracking under a particular type of tracking service, if the person:

(i) while residing at a civil commitment center, leaves the center for any reason;

(ii) is in one of the two most restrictive tiers of treatment, as determined by the office;

(iii) is on disciplinary status, as determined by the office; or

(iv) resides in the community; and

(B) if required to submit to tracking under Paragraph (A), refrain from tampering with, altering, modifying, obstructing, removing, or manipulating the tracking equipment; and

(5) prohibiting the person from leaving the state without prior authorization from the office.

(b) A tracking service to which a person is required to submit under Subsection (a)(4) must:

(1) track the person's location in real time;

(2) be able to provide a real-time report of the person's location to the office on request; and

(3) periodically provide a cumulative report of the person's location to the office.

(c) The judge shall provide a copy of the requirements imposed under Subsection (a) to the person and to the office. The office shall provide a copy of those requirements to the case manager and to the service providers.

(d) The committing court retains jurisdiction of the case with respect to a proceeding conducted under this subchapter, other than a criminal proceeding involving an offense under Section 841.085, or to a civil commitment proceeding conducted under Subchapters F and G.

(e) The requirements imposed under Subsection (a) may be modified by the committing court at any time after notice to each affected party to the proceedings and a hearing.

Sec. 841.0821. Sex Offender Treatment Before Release From Secure Correctional Facility.

(a) The Texas Department of Criminal Justice shall prioritize enrolling in a sex offender treatment program established by the department any committed person who has not yet been released by the department.

(b) The Texas Department of Criminal Justice and the office shall adopt a memorandum of understanding that establishes their respective responsibilities to institute a continuity of care for committed persons enrolled in a sex offender treatment program established by the department.

Sec. 841.0822. Required Procedures Before Release From Secure Correctional Facility.

Before a committed person is released from a secure correctional facility, the Texas Department of Criminal Justice shall ensure that:

(1) the Department of Public Safety issues a personal identification card to the person; and

(2) the person completes an application for the following federal benefits, as appropriate, for which the person may be eligible:

(A) social security benefits, including disability benefits, administered by the United States Social Security Administration; and

(B) veterans benefits administered by the United States Department of Veterans Affairs.

Sec. 841.083. Treatment; Supervision.

(a) The office shall determine the conditions of supervision and treatment of a committed person.

(b) The office shall provide supervision to the person. The provision of supervision must include a tracking service and, if determined necessary by the office, supervised housing.

(c) The office shall enter into appropriate memoranda of understanding with the Texas Department of Criminal Justice for the provision of a tracking service and with the Department of Public Safety and local law enforcement authorities for assistance in the preparation of criminal complaints, warrants, and related documents and in the apprehension and arrest of a person.

(d) The office shall enter into appropriate contracts for the provision of any necessary supervised housing and other related services and may enter into appropriate contracts for medical and mental health services and sex offender treatment.

(e) The case manager shall:

(1) coordinate the treatment and supervision required by this chapter, including performing a periodic assessment of the success of that treatment and supervision; and

(2) provide a report to the office, semiannually or more frequently as necessary, which must includeany known change in the person's status that affects proper treatment and supervision.

Sec. 841.0831. Tiered Program.

(a) The office shall develop a tiered program for the supervision and treatment of a committed person.

(b) The tiered program must provide for the seamless transition of a committed person from a total confinement facility to less restrictive housing and supervision and eventually to release from civil commitment, based on the person's behavior and progress in treatment.

Sec. 841.0832. Housing Facilities.

(a) The office shall operate, or contract with a vendor to operate, one or more facilities provided for the purpose of housing committed persons.

(b) The office shall designate all or part of a facility under Subsection (a) to serve as an intake and orientation facility for committed persons on release from a secure correctional facility.

Sec. 841.0833. Security and Monitoring; Confidentiality.

(a) The office shall develop procedures for the security and monitoring of committed persons in each programming tier.

(b) Information regarding the security and monitoring procedures developed under Subsection (a) is confidential and not subject to disclosure under Chapter 552, Government Code.

Sec. 841.0834. Movement Between Programming Tiers.

(a) The office shall transfer a committed person to less restrictive housing and supervision if the transfer is in the best interests of the person and conditions can be imposed that adequately protect the community.

(b) Without the office's approval, a committed person may file a petition with the court for transfer to less restrictive housing and supervision. The court shall grant the transfer if the court determines that the transfer is in the best interests of the person and conditions can be imposed that adequately protect the community. A committed person who files a petition under this subsection shall serve a copy of the petition on the office.

(c) The office shall return a committed person who has been transferred to less restrictive housing and supervision to a more restrictive setting if the office considers the transfer necessary to further treatment and to protect the community. The decision to transfer the person must be based on the person's behavior or progress in treatment.

(d) Not later than the 90th day after the date a committed person is returned to a more restrictive setting under Subsection (c), the committing court shall hold a hearing via videoconference to review the office's determination. The court shall order the office to transfer the person to less restrictive housing and supervision only if the court determines by clear and convincing evidence that the office's determination was not made in accordance with Subsection (c). The committed person may waive the right to a hearing under this subsection.

(e) [Repealed.]

Sec. 841.0835. Committed Persons with Special Needs.

(a) The Health and Human Services Commission, after coordination with the office, shall provide psychiatric services, disability services, and housing for a committed person with an intellectual or developmental disability, a mental illness, or a physical disability that prevents the person from effectively participating in the sex offender treatment program administered by the office.

(b) For a committed person who the office has determined is unable to effectively participate in the sex offender treatment program because the person's mental illness prevents the person from understanding and internalizing the concepts presented by the program's treatment material, the Health and Human Services Commission shall provide inpatient mental health services until the person is able to participate effectively in the sex offender treatment program.

(c) A person who is adjudicated as a sexually violent predator under this chapter and who has a mental illness that prevents the person from effectively participating in a sex offender treatment program presents a substantial risk of serious harm to the person or others for purposes of Chapter 574.

Sec. 841.0836. Release From Housing.

(a) A committed person released from housing operated by or under contract with the office shall be released to:

(1) the county in which the person was most recently convicted of a sexually violent offense; or

(2) if the county described by Subdivision (1) does not provide adequate opportunities for the person's treatment and for the person's housing or other supervision, as determined by the office, a county designated by the office.

(b) The office may require a committed person released to a county under Subsection (a)(2) to change the person's residence to the county described by Subsection (a)(1) if the office determines that adequate opportunities for the person's treatment and for the person's housing or other supervision become available in that county.

Sec. 841.0837. Emergency Detention Order.

The office may issue an emergency detention order for a committed person's immediate apprehension and transportation to an office-designated location for the purpose of:

(1) returning the person to a more restrictive setting following:

(A) a transfer to less restrictive housing and supervision under Section 841.0834; or

(B) a release under Section 841.0836; or

(2) for a recently committed person who is not in the custody of the Texas Department of Criminal Justice at the time the commitment order is entered, bringing the person under the supervision of the office.

Sec. 841.0838. Use of Restraints.

(a) An employee of the office, or a person who contracts with the office or an employee of that person, may use mechanical or chemical restraints on a committed person residing in a civil commitment center or while transporting a committed person who resides at the center only if:

(1) the employee or person completes a training program approved by the office on the use of restraints that:

(A) includes instruction on the office's approved restraint techniques and devices and the office's verbal de-escalation policies, procedures, and practices; and

(B) requires the employee or person to demonstrate competency in the use of the restraint techniques and devices; and

(2) the restraint is:

(A) used as a last resort;

(B) necessary to stop or prevent:

(i) imminent physical injury to the committed person or another;

(ii) threatening behavior by the committed person while the person is using or exhibiting a weapon;

(iii) a disturbance by a group of committed persons; or

Health and Safety Code

(iv) an absconsion from the center; and

(C) the least restrictive restraint necessary, used for the minimum duration necessary, to prevent the injury, property damage, or absconsion.

(b) The office shall develop procedures governing the use of mechanical or chemical restraints on committed persons.

Sec. 841.084. Payment of Costs by Committed Person.

(a) Notwithstanding Section 841.146(c), a civilly committed person who is not indigent:

(1) is responsible for the cost of:

(A) housing and treatment provided under this chapter;

(B) the tracking service required by Section 841.082; and

(C) repairs to or replacement of the tracking equipment required by Section 841.082, if the person intentionally caused the damage to or loss of the equipment, as determined by the office; and

(2) shall pay to the office:

(A) a monthly amount that the office determines will be necessary to defray the cost of providing the housing, treatment, and service with respect to the person; and

(B) as directed by the office, any amount for which the person is responsible under Subdivision (1)(C).

(b) Money collected under this section shall be deposited to the credit of the account from which the costs were originally paid.

(c) A committed person, on request, shall provide to the office any financial records or other information regarding the person's income, assets, and expenses to assist the office in determining whether the person is indigent for purposes of this section.

Sec. 841.0845. Notice of Intent Regarding New Residence or Facility.

(a) The office shall provide advance notice of any intent to house one or more committed persons at a new residence or facility that has not previously served as housing for committed persons under this chapter.

(b) A vendor shall provide advance notice of any intent to submit a proposal to the office for the construction or renovation of a residence or facility that will serve as a new location for housing committed persons under this chapter.

(c) Notice must be provided in writing to each member of the legislature who represents a district containing territory in the affected county as follows:

(1) by a vendor, not later than the 30th day before the date that the vendor will submit a proposal described by Subsection (b) to the office; and

(2) by the office:

(A) as soon as practicable after awarding a contract for the construction or renovation of a residence or facility that will serve as a new location for housing committed persons under this chapter; or

(B) if a construction or renovation contract is unnecessary for the purpose, not later than the 30th day before the date that the residence or facility will first be used as housing for committed persons under this chapter, except as provided by Subsection (d).

(d) The office may provide notice required by Subsection (c)(2)(B) not later than 72 hours before transferring a committed person to the residence or facility if the transfer is necessary due to:

(1) a medical emergency;

(2) a serious behavioral or health and safety issue; or

(3) release from a secure correctional facility.

Sec. 841.085. Criminal Penalty; Prosecution of Offense.

(a) A person commits an offense if, after having been adjudicated and civilly committed as a sexually violent predator under this chapter, the person violates a civil commitment requirement imposed under Section 841.082(a)(1), (2), (4), or (5).

(b) An offense under this section is a felony of the third degree.

(c) On request of the local prosecuting attorney, the special prosecution unit may assist in the trial of an offense under this section.

SUBCHAPTER F COMMITMENT REVIEW

Sec. 841.101. Biennial Examination.

(a) A person committed under Section 841.081 shall receive a biennial examination. The office shall contract for an expert to perform the examination.

(b) In preparation for a judicial review conducted under Section 841.102, the office shall provide a report of the biennial examination to the judge and to the person. The report must include consideration of whether to modify a requirement imposed on the person under this chapter and whether to release the person from all requirements imposed on the person under this chapter.

Sec. 841.102. Biennial Review.

(a) Not later than the 60th day after the date of receipt of the report submitted under Section 841.101, the judge shall conduct a biennial review of the status of the committed person and issue an order concluding the review or setting a hearing under Subsection (c).

(b) The person is entitled to be represented by counsel at the biennial review, but the person is not entitled to be present at that review.

(c) The judge shall set a hearing if the judge determines at the biennial review that:

(1) a requirement imposed on the person under this chapter should be modified; or

(2) probable cause exists to believe that the person's behavioral abnormality has changed to the extent that the person is no longer likely to engage in a predatory act of sexual violence.

Sec. 841.103. Hearing.

(a) At a hearing set by the judge under Section 841.102, the person and the state are entitled to an immediate examination of the person by an expert.

(b) If the hearing is set under Section 841.102(c)(1), hearsay evidence is admissible if it is considered otherwise reliable by the judge.

(c) If the hearing is set under Section 841.102(c)(2), the committed person is entitled to be present and to have the benefit of all constitutional protections provided to the person at the initial civil commitment proceeding. On the request of the person or the attorney representing the state, the court shall conduct the hearing before a jury. The burden of proof at that hearing is on the state to prove beyond a reasonable doubt that the person's behavioral abnormality has not changed to the extent that the person is no longer likely to engage in a predatory act of sexual violence.

SUBCHAPTER G PETITION FOR RELEASE

Sec. 841.121. Authorized Petition for Release.

(a) If the office determines that the committed person's behavioral abnormality has changed to the extent that the person is no longer likely to engage in a predatory act of sexual violence, the office shall authorize the person to petition the court for release.

(b) The petitioner shall serve a petition under this section on the court and the attorney representing the state.

(c) The judge shall set a hearing on a petition under this section not later than the 30th day after the date the judge receives the petition. The petitioner and the state are entitled to an immediate examination of the petitioner by an expert.

(d) On request of the petitioner or the attorney representing the state, the court shall conduct the hearing before a jury.

(e) The burden of proof at the hearing is on the state to prove beyond a reasonable doubt that the petitioner's behavioral abnormality has not changed to the extent that the petitioner is no longer likely to engage in a predatory act of sexual violence.

Sec. 841.122. Right to File Unauthorized Petition for Release.

On a person's commitment and annually after that commitment, the office shall provide the person with written notice of the person's right to file with the court and without the office's authorization a petition for release.

Sec. 841.123. Review of Unauthorized Petition for Release.

(a) If the committed person files a petition for release without the office's authorization, the person shall serve the petition on the court and the attorney representing the state.

(b) The judge shall review and issue a ruling on a petition for release filed by the committed person without the office's authorization not later than the 60th day after the date of filing of the petition.

(c) Except as provided by Subsection (d), the judge shall deny without a hearing a petition for release filed without the office's authorization if the petition is frivolous or if:

(1) the petitioner previously filed without the office's authorization another petition for release; and

(2) the judge determined on review of the previous petition or following a hearing that:

(A) the petition was frivolous; or

(B) the petitioner's behavioral abnormality had not changed to the extent that the petitioner was no longer likely to engage in a predatory act of sexual violence.

(d) The judge is not required to deny a petition under Subsection (c) if probable cause exists to believe that the petitioner's behavioral abnormality has changed to the extent that the petitioner is no longer likely to engage in a predatory act of sexual violence.

Sec. 841.124. Hearing on Unauthorized Petition for Release.

(a) If as authorized by Section 841.123 the judge does not deny a petition for release filed by the committed person without the office's authorization, the judge shall conduct a hearing on the petition not later than the 60th day after the date of filing of the petition.

(b) The petitioner and the state are entitled to an immediate examination of the person by an expert.

(c) On request of the petitioner or the attorney representing the state, the court shall conduct the hearing before a jury.

(d) The burden of proof at the hearing is on the state to prove beyond a reasonable doubt that the petitioner's behavioral abnormality has not changed to the extent that the petitioner is no longer likely to engage in a predatory act of sexual violence.

SUBCHAPTER H MISCELLANEOUS PROVISIONS

Sec. 841.141. Rulemaking Authority.

(a) The office by rule shall administer this chapter. Rules adopted by the office under this section must be consistent with the purposes of this chapter.

(b) [Repealed].

Sec. 841.142. Release or Exchange of Information.

(a) To protect the public and to enable an assessment or determination relating to whether a person is a sexually violent predator, any entity that possesses relevant information relating to the person shall release the information to an entity charged with making an assessment or determination under this chapter.

(b) To protect the public and to enable the provision of supervision and treatment to a person who is a sexually violent predator, any entity that possesses relevant information relating to the person shall release the information to the office.

(c) On the written request of any attorney for another state or for a political subdivision in another state, the Texas Department of Criminal Justice, the office, a service provider contracting with one of those agencies, the multidisciplinary team, and the applicable attorney representing the state shall release to the attorney any available information relating to a person that is sought in connection with an attempt to civilly commit the person as a sexually violent predator in another state.

(d) To protect the public and to enable an assessment or determination relating to whether a person is a sexually violent predator or to enable the provision of supervision and treatment to a person who is a sexually violent predator, the Texas Department of Criminal Justice, the office, a service provider contracting with one of those agencies, the multidisciplinary team, and the applicable attorney representing the state may exchange any available information relating to the person.

(e) Information subject to release or exchange under this section includes information relating to the supervision, treatment, criminal history, or physical or mental health of the person, as appropriate, regardless of whether the information is otherwise confidential and regardless of when the information was created or collected. The person's consent is not required for release or exchange of information under this section.

Sec. 841.143. Report, Record, or Statement Submitted to Court.

(a) A psychological report, drug and alcohol report, treatment record, diagnostic report, medical record, or victim impact statement submitted to the court under this chapter is part of the record of the court.

(b) Notwithstanding Subsection (a), the report, record, or statement must be sealed and may be opened only:

(1) on order of the judge;

(2) as provided by this chapter; or

(3) in connection with a criminal proceeding as otherwise provided by law.

Sec. 841.144. Counsel.

(a) Immediately after the filing of a petition under Section 841.041, a person subject to a civil commitment proceeding under this chapter is entitled to the assistance of counsel at all stages of the proceeding.

(b) If the person is indigent, the court shall appoint counsel as appropriate under Section 841.005 to assist the person.

Sec. 841.145. Expert.

(a) At the person's own expense, a person who is examined under this chapter may retain an expert to perform an examination or participate in a civil commitment proceeding on the person's behalf, including a biennial examination or other civil

Health and Safety Code

commitment proceeding to assess the person's status as a sexually violent predator.

(b) On the request of an indigent person examined under this chapter, the judge shall determine whether expert services for the person are necessary. If the judge determines that the services are necessary, the judge shall appoint an expert to perform an examination or participate in a civil commitment proceeding on the person's behalf and shall approve compensation for the expert as appropriate under Subsection (c).

(c) The court shall approve reasonable compensation for expert services rendered on behalf of an indigent person on the filing of a certified compensation claim supported by a written statement specifying:

(1) time expended on behalf of the person;

(2) services rendered on behalf of the person;

(3) expenses incurred on behalf of the person; and

(4) compensation received in the same case or for the same services from any other source.

(d) The court shall ensure that an expert retained or appointed under this section has for purposes of examination reasonable access to a person examined under this chapter, as well as to all relevant medical and psychological records and reports.

Sec. 841.146. Civil Commitment Proceeding; Procedure and Costs.

(a) On request, a person subject to a civil commitment proceeding under this chapter and the attorney representing the state are entitled to a jury trial or a hearing before a jury for that proceeding, except for a proceeding set by the judge under Section 841.102(c)(1). The jury shall consist of 12 qualified jurors. The judge may direct that not more than four jurors in addition to the regular jury be called and impaneled to sit as alternate jurors. Each party is entitled to 10 peremptory challenges to the 12 qualified jurors and one peremptory challenge to the qualified alternate jurors.

(b) Except as otherwise provided by this subsection, a civil commitment proceeding is subject to the rules of procedure and appeal for civil cases. To the extent of any conflict between this chapter and the rules of procedure and appeal for civil cases, this chapter controls.

(c) In an amount not to exceed $2,500, the State of Texas shall pay all costs associated with a civil commitment proceeding conducted under Subchapter D. The State of Texas shall pay the reasonable costs of state or appointed counsel or experts for any other civil commitment proceeding conducted under this chapter and shall pay the reasonable costs of the person's treatment and supervision.

Sec. 841.1461. Certain Expert Testimony Not Required for Civil Commitment of Sexually Violent Predator.

A person who suffers from a behavioral abnormality as determined under this chapter is not because of that abnormality a person of unsound mind for purposes of Section 15-a, Article I, Texas Constitution.

Sec. 841.1462. Privilege for Personal Information That Identifies Victim.

Personal information, including a home address, home telephone number, and social security account number, that identifies the victim of a person subject to a civil commitment proceeding under this chapter is privileged from discovery by that person.

Sec. 841.1463. Failure to Give Notice Within Relevant Period Not Jurisdictional Error.

The periods within which notice must be given under this chapter are binding on all appropriate persons as provided by this chapter, but a failure to give notice within the relevant period is not a jurisdictional error.

Sec. 841.147. Immunity.

The following persons are immune from liability for good faith conduct under this chapter:

(1) an employee or officer of the Texas Department of Criminal Justice or the office;

(2) a member of the multidisciplinary team established under Section 841.022;

(3) the applicable attorney representing the state and an employee of the attorney; and

(4) a person providing, or contracting, appointed, or volunteering to perform, a tracking service or another service under this chapter.

Sec. 841.150. Effect of Subsequent Detention, Confinement, or Commitment on Order of Civil Commitment.

(a) The duties imposed on the office and the judge by this chapter are suspended for the duration of a detention or confinement of a committed person in a correctional facility, secure correctional facility, or secure detention facility, or if applicable any other commitment of the person to a community center, mental health facility, or state supported living center, by governmental action.

(b) In this section:

(1) "Community center" means a center established under Subchapter A, Chapter 534.

(2) "Correctional facility" has the meaning assigned by Section 1.07, Penal Code.

(3) "Mental health facility" has the meaning assigned by Section 571.003.

(4) "Secure correctional facility" and "secure detention facility" have the meanings assigned by Section 51.02, Family Code.

(5) "State supported living center" has the meaning assigned by Section 531.002.

Sec. 841.151. Notice of Release of Sexually Violent Predator.

(a) In this section:

(1) "Correctional facility" has the meaning assigned by Section 1.07, Penal Code.

(2) "Secure correctional facility" and "secure detention facility" have the meanings assigned by Section 51.02, Family Code.

(b) This section applies to a person who has been civilly committed under this chapter and who is detained or confined in a correctional facility, secure correctional facility, or secure detention facility as a result of violating:

(1) a civil commitment requirement imposed under Section 841.082(a)(1), (2), (4), or (5); or

(2) a law of this state.

(c) Except as provided by Subsection (c-1), as soon as practicable before, but not later than the third business day preceding, the date a correctional facility, secure correctional facility, or secure detention facility releases a person who, at the time of the person's detention or confinement, was civilly committed under this chapter as a sexually violent predator, the facility shall notify the office and the person's case manager in writing of the anticipated date and time of the person's release.

(c-1) Subsection (c) does not apply with respect to a person whom a court orders to be immediately released from a correctional facility, secure correctional facility, or secure detention facility.

(d) A case manager, on request, shall provide a correctional facility, a secure correctional facility, or a secure detention facility with the case manager's appropriate contact information for notification under Subsection (c).

Sec. 841.152. Certain Hearings by Closed-Circuit Video Teleconferencing Permitted.

(a) Notwithstanding Section 841.103(c), on motion by the attorney representing the state, the court shall require a committed person to appear via closed-circuit video teleconferencing at a hearing on the modification of civil commitment requirements under Section 841.082 or a hearing under Subchapter F or G.

(b) A recording of a hearing conducted as provided by Subsection (a) shall be made and preserved with the court's record of the hearing.

Sec. 841.153. State-Issued Identification; Necessary Documentation.

(a) On the release of a committed person from a correctional facility, secure correctional facility, or secure detention facility, as those terms are defined by Section 841.151, the office shall:

(1) determine whether the person has:

(A) a valid license issued under Chapter 521 or 522, Transportation Code; or

(B) a valid personal identification certificate issued under Chapter 521, Transportation Code; and

(2) if the person does not have a valid license or certificate described by Subdivision (1), submit to the Department of Public Safety on behalf of the person a request for the issuance of a personal identification certificate under Chapter 521, Transportation Code.

(b) The office shall submit a request under Subsection (a)(2) as soon as practicable.

(c) The office, the Department of Public Safety, and the vital statistics unit of the Department of State Health Services by rule shall adopt a memorandum of understanding that establishes their respective responsibilities with respect to the issuance of a personal identification certificate to a committed person, including responsibilities related to verification of the person's identity. The memorandum of understanding must require the Department of State Health Services to electronically verify the birth record of a committed person whose name and any other personal information is provided by the office and to electronically report the recorded filing information to the Department of Public Safety to validate the identity of a committed person under this section.

(d) The office shall reimburse the Department of Public Safety or the Department of State Health Services, as applicable, for the actual costs incurred by those agencies in performing responsibilities established under this section. The office may charge a committed person for the actual costs incurred under this section or for the fees required by Section 521.421, Transportation Code.

LABOR CODE

TITLE 2
PROTECTION OF LABORERS

SUBTITLE B
RESTRICTIONS ON LABOR

CHAPTER 52
MISCELLANEOUS RESTRICTIONS

SUBCHAPTER G
RESTRICTIONS ON PROHIBITING EMPLOYEE TRANSPORTATION OR STORAGE OF CERTAIN FIREARMS OR AMMUNITION

Sec. 52.061. Restriction on Prohibiting Employee Access to or Storage of Firearm or Ammunition.

A public or private employer may not prohibit an employee who holds a license to carry a handgun under Subchapter H, Chapter 411, Government Code, who otherwise lawfully possesses a firearm, or who lawfully possesses ammunition from transporting or storing a firearm or ammunition the employee is authorized by law to possess in a locked, privately owned motor vehicle in a parking lot, parking garage, or other parking area the employer provides for employees.

Sec. 52.062. Exceptions.

(a) Section 52.061 does not:

(1) authorize a person who holds a license to carry a handgun under Subchapter H, Chapter 411, Government Code, who otherwise lawfully possesses a firearm, or who lawfully possesses ammunition to possess a firearm or ammunition on any property where the possession of a firearm or ammunition is prohibited by state or federal law; or

(2) apply to:

(A) a vehicle owned or leased by a public or private employer and used by an employee in the course and scope of the employee's employment, unless the employee is required to transport or store a firearm in the official discharge of the employee's duties;

(B) a school district;

(C) an open-enrollment charter school, as defined by Section 5.001, Education Code;

(D) a private school, as defined by Section 22.081, Education Code;

(E) property owned or controlled by a person, other than the employer, that is subject to a valid, unexpired oil, gas, or other mineral lease that contains a provision prohibiting the possession of firearms on the property; or

(F) property owned or leased by a chemical manufacturer or oil and gas refiner with an air authorization under Chapter 382, Health and Safety Code, and on which the primary business conducted is the manufacture, use, storage, or transportation of hazardous, combustible, or explosive materials, except in regard to an employee who holds a license to carry a handgun under Subchapter H, Chapter 411, Government Code, and who stores a firearm or ammunition the employee is authorized by law to possess in a locked, privately owned motor vehicle in a parking lot, parking garage, or other parking area the employer provides for employees that is outside of a secured and restricted area:

(i) that contains the physical plant;

(ii) that is not open to the public; and

(iii) the ingress into which is constantly monitored by security personnel.

(b) Section 52.061 does not prohibit an employer from prohibiting an employee who holds a license to carry a handgun under Subchapter H, Chapter 411, Government Code, or who otherwise lawfully possesses a firearm, from possessing a firearm the employee is otherwise authorized by law to possess on the premises of the employer's business. In this subsection, "premises" has the meaning assigned by Section 46.03, Penal Code.

LOCAL GOVERNMENT CODE

TITLE 4 FINANCES

SUBTITLE C FINANCIAL PROVISIONS APPLYING TO MORE THAN ONE TYPE OF LOCAL GOVERNMENT

CHAPTER 133 CRIMINAL AND CIVIL FEES PAYABLE TO THE COMPTROLLER

SUBCHAPTER C CRIMINAL FEES

Sec. 133.105. Fee for Support of Court-Related Purposes. [Repealed]

Sec. 133.107. Fee for Support of Indigent Defense Representation. [Repealed]

TITLE 11 PUBLIC SAFETY

SUBTITLE A MUNICIPAL PUBLIC SAFETY

CHAPTER 341 MUNICIPAL LAW ENFORCEMENT

SUBCHAPTER Z MISCELLANEOUS PROVISIONS

Sec. 341.906. Limitations on Registered Sex Offenders in General-Law Municipalities.

(a) In this section:

(1) "Child safety zone" means premises where children commonly gather. The term includes a school, day-care facility, playground, public or private youth center, public swimming pool, video arcade facility, or other facility that regularly holds events primarily for children. The term does not include a church, as defined by Section 544.251, Insurance Code.

(2) "Playground," "premises," "school," "video arcade facility," and "youth center" have the meanings assigned by Section 481.134, Health and Safety Code.

(3) "Registered sex offender" means an individual who is required to register as a sex offender under Chapter 62, Code of Criminal Procedure.

(b) To provide for the public safety, the governing body of a general-law municipality by ordinance may restrict a registered sex offender from going in, on, or within a specified distance of a child safety zone in the municipality.

(c) It is an affirmative defense to prosecution of an offense under the ordinance that the registered sex offender was in, on, or within a specified distance of a child safety zone for a legitimate purpose, including transportation of a child that the registered sex offender is legally permitted to be with, transportation to and from work, and other work-related purposes.

(d) The ordinance may establish a distance requirement described by Subsection (b) at any distance of not more than 1,000 feet.

(e) The ordinance shall establish procedures for a registered sex offender to apply for an exemption from the ordinance.

(f) The ordinance must exempt a registered sex offender who established residency in a residence located within the specified distance of a child safety zone before the date the ordinance is adopted. The exemption must apply only to:

(1) areas necessary for the registered sex offender to have access to and to live in the residence; and

(2) the period the registered sex offender maintains residency in the residence.

SUBTITLE B
COUNTY PUBLIC SAFETY

CHAPTER 351
COUNTY JAILS AND LAW ENFORCEMENT

SUBCHAPTER Z
MISCELLANEOUS LAW ENFORCEMENT PROVISIONS

Sec. 351.904. Electronic Monitoring Program.

(a) A commissioners court of a county may establish and operate an electronic monitoring program for the purpose of monitoring defendants required by a court of the county to participate in an electronic monitoring program under:

(1) Article 43.09, Code of Criminal Procedure, to discharge a fine or costs; or

(2) Article 42.035, Code of Criminal Procedure, as an alternative to serving all or part of a sentence of confinement in county jail.

(b) The commissioners court shall provide for the sheriff or the community supervision and corrections department serving the county, under an agreement with the commissioners court, to oversee and operate, or, if the program is operated by a private vendor under Subsection (c), oversee the operation of, an electronic monitoring program established under this section.

(c) A commissioners court may contract with a private vendor to operate an electronic monitoring program under this section, including by enrolling and tracking participants in the program and performing periodic reviews with participants regarding compliance with the program.

(d) A commissioners court may use money that a defendant is ordered to pay to a county under Article 42.035(c), Code of Criminal Procedure, to pay for the services of a private vendor that operates an electronic monitoring program under Subsection (c).

(e) A commissioners court may subsidize all or part of the cost of a defendant's participation in an electronic monitoring program under this section if the defendant is indigent.

(f) A commissioners court may contract for any available electronic monitoring technology, including a technology that provides continuous positional tracking of the participant, that meets the approval of the commissioners court and either the sheriff or the community supervision and corrections department, as appropriate.

SUBTITLE C
PUBLIC SAFETY PROVISIONS APPLYING TO MORE THAN ONE TYPE OF LOCAL GOVERNMENT

CHAPTER 370
MISCELLANEOUS PROVISIONS RELATING TO MUNICIPAL AND COUNTY HEALTH AND PUBLIC SAFETY

Sec. 370.004. Notice of Damaged Fence.

(a) A peace officer employed by a political subdivision of this state who investigates or responds to an incident in which a motor vehicle damages a fence shall, if the peace officer reasonably believes that the fence is intended to contain livestock or other animals:

(1) immediately determine the owner of the land on which the damaged fence is located; and

(2) notify the owner of the type and extent of the damage, if the owner has registered with the political subdivision in accordance with Subsection (c).

(b) A peace officer is not liable to an owner of land or any other person for damage resulting from the peace officer's failure to notify the owner under Subsection (a).

(c) A landowner must provide an agency or department of a political subdivision that employs peace officers with the following information if the landowner would like a peace officer of that agency or department to notify the landowner of damage under Subsection (a):

(1) the landowner's name, address, and telephone number; and

(2) the location and a description of the landowner's property.

NATURAL RESOURCES CODE

TITLE 3
OIL AND GAS

SUBTITLE B
CONSERVATION AND REGULATION OF OIL AND GAS

CHAPTER 85
CONSERVATION OF OIL AND GAS

SUBCHAPTER K
PENALTIES, IMPRISONMENT, AND CONFINEMENT

Sec. 85.389. Criminal Penalty.

(a) A person who is not the owner or operator of an oil well, gas well, or oil and gas well, a purchaser under contract of oil, gas, or oil and gas from a well, a gatherer with written authorization from the owner, operator, or purchaser, or an authorized representative of the commission who knowingly destroys, breaks, removes, or otherwise tampers with or attempts to destroy, break, remove, or otherwise tamper with any cap, seal, or other device placed on an oil well, gas well, oil and gas well, or associated oil or gas gathering equipment by the owner or operator for the purpose of controlling or limiting the operation of the well or associated equipment commits an offense.

(b) An offense under this section is a felony of the third degree.

SUBTITLE D
REGULATION OF SPECIFIC BUSINESSES AND OCCUPATIONS

CHAPTER 112
USED OIL FIELD EQUIPMENT DEALERS

SUBCHAPTER A
GENERAL PROVISIONS

Sec. 112.001. Definitions.

In this chapter:

(1) "Pipeline equipment" means all pipe, fittings, pumps, telephone and telegraph lines, and all other material and equipment used as part of or incident to the construction, maintenance, and operation of a pipeline for the transportation of oil, gas, water, or other liquid or gaseous substance.

(2) "Oil and gas equipment" means equipment and materials that are part of or incident to the exploration, development, maintenance, and operation of oil and gas properties and includes equipment and materials that are part of or incident to the construction, maintenance, and operation of oil and gas wells, oil and gas leases, gasoline plants, and refineries.

(3) "Used materials" means pipeline equipment or oil and gas equipment after the equipment has once been placed in the use for which it first was manufactured and intended.

(4) "Dealer" means every person whose primary business is buying, selling, or otherwise dealing in used materials and who has a fixed, designated place or places of business within the state.

(5) "Broker" means every person whose primary business is buying, selling, or otherwise dealing in used materials as agent for the seller of the used materials, or as agent for the buyer of the used materials, or as agent for both.

(6) "Peddler" means every person who is not a dealer or broker and whose primary business is buying, selling, or otherwise dealing in used materials.

Sec. 112.002. Applicability.

The provisions of this chapter shall not apply if the reasonable market value of the purchase made is less than $25.

SUBCHAPTER B
SALE OF USED EQUIPMENT

Sec. 112.011. Bill of Sale.

Before purchasing or acquiring by exchange used materials, a dealer, broker, or peddler shall require that a bill of sale for the used materials be executed by the seller or the person who exchanges the materials. The dealer, broker, or peddler shall keep a copy of each bill of sale at his place of business.

Sec. 112.012. Required Information.

(a) The bill of sale shall include:

(1) the name and address of the dealer, broker, or peddler;

(2) the serial number, if any;

(3) the kind, make, size, weight, length, and quantity of the used materials purchased or acquired by exchange;

(4) the date of the purchase or acquisition by exchange, if different from the date of the bill of sale;

(5) the name and address of the seller or person who exchanged the materials;

(6) the place of location of the property at the time purchased or acquired by exchange;

(7) the license number of each motor vehicle used in transporting a purchased or exchanged item to the dealer's, broker's, or peddler's place of business; and

(8) the driver's license number of the seller or person who exchanged the materials.

(b) A dealer, broker, or peddler under this chapter shall keep at his regular place of business all records required to be kept by this chapter for two years after the date of the purchase or acquisition by exchange of the materials.

SUBCHAPTER C
ENFORCEMENT; PENALTY

Sec. 112.031. Injunctive Relief.

In the name and on behalf of the State of Texas, the attorney general or any district attorney or county attorney in this state may enjoin a dealer, peddler, or broker from continuing in business in this state as a dealer, peddler, or broker on violation of any of the provisions of this chapter.

Sec. 112.032. Criminal Penalty.

A person, dealer, peddler, or broker who violates any of the provisions of this chapter is guilty of a misdemeanor and on conviction is subject to a fine of not less than $500 for each violation.

Sec. 112.033. Inspection.

(a) Any Texas Ranger or other officer commissioned by the Department of Public Safety, any sheriff or deputy sheriff, or any municipal police officer may enter the business premises of a dealer, broker, or peddler under this chapter during normal business hours to inspect the premises and the records of the dealer, broker, or peddler to determine whether the dealer, broker, or peddler is in compliance with this chapter.

(b) A dealer, broker, or peddler under this chapter must allow and shall not interfere with inspections conducted pursuant to this chapter.

(c) Each inspection conducted under this chapter shall be commenced and completed with reasonable promptness and shall be conducted in a reasonable manner.

CHAPTER 115
REGULATION OF CERTAIN TRANSPORTERS OF OIL OR PETROLEUM PRODUCTS

SUBCHAPTER A
GENERAL PROVISIONS

Sec. 115.001. Definitions.

In this chapter:

(1) "Commission" means the Railroad Commission of Texas.

(2) "Commission order" includes a rule or order adopted by the commission under the oil and gas conservation statutes of this state, including this title and Subtitle B, Title 3, Utilities Code.

(3) "Gas" includes natural gas, bradenhead gas, casinghead gas, or gas produced from an oil or gas well.

(4) "Manifest" includes a document issued by a shipper that covers oil or a petroleum product transported by motor vehicle.

(5) "Oil" includes crude petroleum oil:
(A) in its natural state as produced; or
(B) from which only the basic sediment and water have been removed.
(6) "Person" includes an individual, corporation, association, partnership, receiver, trustee, guardian, executor, administrator, or representative.
(7) "Petroleum product" includes:
(A) refined crude oil;
(B) crude tops;
(C) topped crude;
(D) processed crude petroleum;
(E) residue from crude petroleum;
(F) cracking stock;
(G) uncracked fuel oil;
(H) fuel oil;
(I) treated crude oil;
(J) residuum;
(K) gas oil;
(L) casinghead gasoline;
(M) natural gas gasoline;
(N) naphtha;
(O) distillate;
(P) gasoline;
(Q) kerosene;
(R) benzine;
(S) wash oil;
(T) waste oil;
(U) blended gasoline;
(V) lubricating oil;
(W) blends or mixtures of petroleum; or
(X) any other liquid petroleum product or by-product derived from crude petroleum oil or gas.
(8) "Shipping papers" includes:
(A) a bill of lading that covers oil or a petroleum product transported by railway;
(B) a manifest; or
(C) a document that covers oil or a petroleum product transported by pipeline, boat, or barge.
(9) "Tender" means a permit or certificate of clearance for the transportation of oil or a petroleum product that is approved and issued or registered under the authority of the commission.
(10) "Unlawful gas" includes gas produced or transported in violation of a law of this state or commission order.
(11) "Unlawful petroleum product" includes a petroleum product:
(A) any part of which was processed or derived in whole or in part from:
(i) unlawful oil;
(ii) a product of unlawful oil; or
(iii) unlawful gas; or
(B) transported in violation of a law of this state or commission order.

Sec. 115.002. Exception.

This chapter does not apply to the retail purchase of a petroleum product if that product is:
(1) contained in the ordinary equipment of a motor vehicle; and
(2) used only to operate the motor vehicle in which it is contained.

Sec. 115.003. Definition of Unlawful Oil; Presumption.

(a) For purposes of this chapter, oil is unlawful if the oil is:
(1) produced in this state from a well in excess of the amount allowed by a commission order or otherwise in violation of a law of this state or commission order; or
(2) transported in violation of a law of this state or commission order.
(b) It is presumed that oil is "unlawful oil" for purposes of this chapter if the oil is retained in storage for more than six years without being used, consumed, or moved into regular commercial channels.
(c) The presumption under Subsection (b) may be rebutted by proof that the oil:
(1) was produced from a well within the production allowable then applying to that well;
(2) was not produced in violation of a law of this state or commission order; and
(3) if transported from the lease from which it was produced, was not transported in violation of a law of this state or commission order.

SUBCHAPTER B
TENDERS AND MANIFESTS

Sec. 115.011. Tender Requirements.

The commission by order may require that a tender be obtained before oil or a petroleum product may be transported or received for transportation by pipeline, railway, boat, or barge.

Sec. 115.012. Tender; Application Requirements.

(a) The commission by order shall prescribe the form of a tender and a tender application.
(b) The form must show:
(1) the name and address of the shipper or other person who tenders oil or a petroleum product for transportation;

Natural Resources Code

(2) the name and address of the transporter if the commission order requires the transporter to be designated;

(3) the quantity and classification of each commodity authorized to be transported;

(4) each location at which delivery is to be made to the transporter; and

(5) other related information as prescribed by commission order.

(c) Each tender must:

(1) bear a date and serial number;

(2) state the expiration date of the tender; and

(3) be executed by an agent authorized by the commission to deny, approve, or register tenders.

(d) An agent may not approve or register a tender for the transportation of unlawful oil or an unlawful petroleum product.

Sec. 115.013. Action on Tender Application.

(a) If an agent of the commission rejects an application for a tender, the agent shall return a copy of the application to the applicant with the reasons for the rejection indicated on the copy.

(b) A person whose tender application is not acted on before the 21st day after the date on which the application is filed is entitled to judicial review in the manner provided by Section 115.014 for the appeal of a rejection of a tender application.

Sec. 115.014. Judicial Review.

(a) A person whose tender application is rejected may appeal that action by filing a petition against the commission in a district court of Travis County for review of the agent's decision.

(b) The clerk of the court shall issue to the commission a notice setting forth briefly the cause of action stated in the petition. The court may not enter an order on the petition until the court conducts a hearing. The court must conduct the hearing not later than the fifth day after the date of issuance of the notice.

(c) The court may sustain, modify, or overrule the agent's decision and may issue a restraining order or injunction as warranted by the facts.

(d) A person dissatisfied with the decision of the district court may appeal to the court of appeals.

Sec. 115.015. Transfer Under Tender.

(a) A person who obtains a tender may not transport or deliver, or cause or permit to be transported or delivered, any more or any different commodity than that authorized by the tender.

(b) A connecting carrier or consignee who receives oil or a petroleum product from another transporter by pipeline, railway, boat, or barge under authority of shipping papers executed by the initial transporter that bear the date and serial number of a tender issued to that initial transporter is considered to receive the oil or petroleum product by authority of that tender if the commission order provides that a connecting carrier or consignee may rely on the shipping papers.

Sec. 115.016. Issuance of Manifest.

(a) A person who obtains a tender required under this subchapter shall sign and issue a manifest to the operator of each motor vehicle used to transport the oil or petroleum product that is covered by the tender.

(b) The person shall issue a separate manifest for each load carried by the motor vehicle.

Sec. 115.017. Form of Manifest.

(a) The commission by order may prescribe the form of a manifest.

(b) A manifest must:

(1) bear a certificate signed by the shipper that states the amount of oil or petroleum products to be transported and specifies each petroleum product to be transported; and

(2) include, if required by commission order:

(A) the date and serial number of the tender that authorizes the transportation or a seal, number, or other evidence of the tender, if a tender is required;

(B) the amount and classification of each petroleum product to be transported;

(C) the name and address of the transporter, the name and address of the shipper, and the name and address of the consignee, if known;

(D) the name and address of the operator of the motor vehicle;

(E) the license plate number of the motor vehicle;

(F) the date, time, and place at which the motor vehicle was loaded and the destination, if known, of the load; and

(G) other related information as required by commission order.

(c) If the form of the manifest is not prescribed by commission order, each shipper required to issue a manifest to a transporter shall use a form of manifest that is:

(1) commonly used in commercial transactions; or

(2) required by another state agency to accompany the movement of gasoline.

Sec. 115.018. Transfer Under Manifest; Restrictions.

(a) A person authorized to transport oil or a petroleum product on a manifest issued by a shipper may not receive:

(1) a commodity for transportation that is different from the commodity described in the manifest; or

(2) oil or a petroleum product in an amount exceeding the amount authorized by the manifest.

(b) A person authorized to transport oil or a petroleum product by a shipper-issued manifest that bears on its face the date and serial number of the tender may rely on the manifest delivered to that person and each consignee or person to whom the transporter delivers oil or a petroleum product covered by that manifest may rely on the manifest as authority to receive the commodity delivered if the manifest:

(1) appears to be valid on its face;

(2) is signed by the shipper; and

(3) bears the certificate of the shipper that the transportation of the oil or petroleum product is authorized by the tender.

(c) If the commission by order prohibits the transportation of oil or a petroleum product by motor vehicle without a manifest that shows the date and serial number of a tender authorizing the transportation, a person may not ship or transport or cause to be shipped or transported by motor vehicle oil or a petroleum product unless the person furnishes the manifest to the operator of the motor vehicle. The person transporting the oil or petroleum product shall maintain the manifest in the vehicle at all times during the shipment. If the person to whom the tender is issued is the operator of the motor vehicle and the tender identifies the motor vehicle by license number and covers one load, the person may carry the tender in the vehicle in lieu of a manifest.

Sec. 115.019. Receipt Required.

A person who transports oil or a petroleum product by motor vehicle under conditions that require a tender or manifest shall obtain a receipt from each person to whom any part of the oil or petroleum product is delivered. The receipt must be on the reverse side of the tender or manifest and must indicate:

(1) the number of gallons of oil or of each petroleum product delivered;

(2) the date of delivery; and

(3) the signature and address of the purchaser or consignee of the oil or petroleum product.

Sec. 115.020. Records; Inspection.

(a) A person who transports by motor vehicle and delivers oil or a petroleum product shall keep in this state for two years each tender or manifest issued to the person, together with the receipts and endorsements on the tender or manifest.

(b) A tender or manifest is at all times subject to inspection by the commission or an agent or inspector of the commission.

SUBCHAPTER C
FORFEITURE OF UNLAWFUL OIL OR PETROLEUM PRODUCT

Sec. 115.031. Forfeiture Authorized.

Unlawful oil and unlawful petroleum products, regardless of the date of production or manufacture, are declared to be a nuisance and shall be forfeited to this state as provided by this subchapter.

Sec. 115.032. Report to Attorney General.

On the discovery of unlawful oil or an unlawful petroleum product, a member of the commission, an agent or employee of the commission, or a peace officer shall immediately file with the attorney general a report that describes the unlawful oil or unlawful petroleum product. The report must state the ownership, party in possession, amount, location, and classification of the oil or petroleum product.

Sec. 115.033. Action in Rem.

(a) If the attorney general is advised of the presence of unlawful oil or an unlawful petroleum product, the attorney general shall bring an action in rem in the name of the state in Travis County or in the county in which the oil or petroleum product is located against the unlawful oil or petroleum product and against each person who owns, claims, or is in possession of the oil or petroleum product.

(b) If it appears to the court from an examination of the petition or after hearing evidence on the petition at a preliminary hearing that the unlawful oil or petroleum product mentioned in the petition is in danger of being removed, wasted, lost, or destroyed, the court shall:

(1) issue restraining orders or injunctive relief, either mandatory or prohibitive;

(2) appoint a receiver to take charge of the oil or petroleum product; or

(3) direct the sheriff of the county in which the unlawful oil or petroleum product is located to seize and impound the oil or petroleum product pending further orders of the court.

(c) A party to the action may demand a trial by jury on any issue of fact raised by the pleadings, and the case shall proceed to trial in the manner provided for other civil cases.

Sec. 115.034. Forfeiture Sale.

(a) If, on the trial of the action, the oil or petroleum product in controversy is found to be unlawful, the court shall render judgment forfeiting the oil or petroleum product to this state. The court shall issue an order of sale directing the sheriff or a constable of the county in which the oil or petroleum product is located to seize and sell the oil or petroleum product in the same manner as personal property is sold under execution. The court may order the oil or petroleum product sold in whole or in part.

(b) The sale shall be conducted at the courthouse door of the county in which the oil or petroleum product is located.

(c) The court shall apply the money realized from the sale first to the payment of the costs of the action and expenses incident to the sale of the oil or petroleum product. The court may then use not more than one-half of the money to compensate a person for expenses incurred in storing the unlawful oil or petroleum product. Any balance remaining shall be remitted to the comptroller.

(d) The officers of the court shall receive the same fees provided by law for other civil actions. The sheriff who executes the sale shall issue a bill of sale or certificate to the purchaser of the oil or petroleum product, and the commission, on presentation of that certificate of clearance, shall issue a tender, if a tender is required, permitting the purchaser of the oil or petroleum product to move the oil or petroleum product into commerce.

SUBCHAPTER D ENFORCEMENT AND PENALTIES

Sec. 115.041. Enforcement; Arrests.

(a) To enforce this chapter, an agent of the commission or a peace officer of this state who has probable cause and reasonable grounds to believe that a motor vehicle is transporting unlawful oil or an unlawful petroleum product may stop the vehicle to take samples of the cargo and to inspect the shipping papers.

(b) If, on examination of the motor vehicle, the agent or officer finds that the vehicle is transporting unlawful oil or an unlawful petroleum product or is transporting oil or a petroleum product without a required tender, the agent or officer, with or without a warrant, shall arrest the operator of the vehicle and file a complaint against the operator under this chapter.

(c) In a criminal action under this chapter, the agent or officer is not entitled to a fee for executing a warrant of arrest or capias or for making an arrest with or without a warrant.

Sec. 115.042. Publication of Commission Order Prior to Enforcement.

A criminal action may not be maintained against a person involving the violation of a rule or order that the commission adopts, modifies, or amends until the commission publishes a complete copy of the rule or order.

Sec. 115.043. Certificate As Evidence.

(a) A certificate that sets forth the terms of a commission order and states that the order has been adopted and published and was in effect on a specified date or during a specified period is prima facie evidence of those facts if the certificate is:

(1) made under the seal of the commission; and

(2) executed by a member or the secretary of the commission.

(b) The certificate is admissible in evidence in any civil or criminal action that involves the order without further proof of the adoption, publication, or contents of the order.

Sec. 115.044. Service of Process.

(a) In an action or proceeding that involves the enforcement of this chapter or a commission order, a Texas Ranger or agent of the commission may serve any judicial process, warrant, subpoena, or writ as directed by the court issuing the process and shall serve the process in the same manner as a peace officer.

(b) The ranger or agent may serve the process, warrant, or subpoena anywhere in this state although it may be directed to the sheriff or a constable of a particular county.

(c) The ranger or agent shall make the same return as any other officer, sign the return, and add under the name the title "State Ranger" or "Agent, Railroad Commission of Texas," as appropriate, which is sufficient to make the writ valid if the writ is otherwise properly prepared.

(d) A Texas Ranger or agent of the commission is not entitled to a fee in addition to that person's regular compensation for a service provided under this section.

Sec. 115.045. Pleading; Proof.

(a) In a complaint, information, or indictment that alleges a violation of a commission order, it is unnecessary to set forth fully the terms of the order and sufficient to allege the substance of the order or the pertinent terms of the order that are alleged to have been violated.

(b) In a criminal action filed under this chapter, a certificate executed by a member or the secretary of the commission that shows the amount of allowable oil that may be produced per day or during a stated period from an oil well, proof of production from which is involved in the criminal action, is admissible and is prima facie evidence of the facts stated in the certificate.

(c) This section does not limit the power of the commission to adopt rules or orders under the oil and gas conservation statutes of this state, including this title and Subtitle B, Title 3, Utilities Code.

Sec. 115.046. Venue.

A criminal action maintained under this chapter must be brought in:

(1) the county in which the oil or petroleum product involved in the criminal action is received or delivered; or

(2) any county in or through which that oil or petroleum product is transported.

Sec. 115.047. Penalties.

(a) A person commits an offense if the person is the operator of a motor vehicle that transports oil or a petroleum product and the person:

(1) intentionally fails to stop the vehicle on the command of an agent of the commission or peace officer; or

(2) intentionally fails to permit inspection by the agent or officer of the contents of or the shipping papers accompanying the vehicle.

(b) A person commits an offense if the person:

(1) knowingly violates Section 115.011, 115.015(a), 115.016, 115.018, 115.019, or 115.020;

(2) knowingly ships or transports or causes to be shipped or transported unlawful oil or an unlawful petroleum product by motor vehicle over a public highway in this state;

(3) knowingly ships or transports or causes to be shipped or transported by motor vehicle oil or a petroleum product without the authority of a tender if a tender is required by a commission order; or

(4) if a tender is required by a commission order, knowingly receives from a motor vehicle or knowingly delivers to a motor vehicle oil or a petroleum product that is not covered by a tender authorizing the transportation of the oil or petroleum product.

(c) A person commits an offense if the person:

(1) knowingly ships or transports or causes or permits to be shipped or transported by pipeline, railway, boat, or barge unlawful oil or an unlawful petroleum product;

(2) knowingly receives or delivers for transportation by pipeline, railway, boat, or barge unlawful oil or an unlawful petroleum product;

(3) knowingly ships or transports or causes or permits to be shipped or transported by pipeline, railway, boat, or barge oil or a petroleum product without authority of a tender if a tender is required by a commission order; or

(4) knowingly receives or delivers by pipeline, railway, boat, or barge oil or a petroleum product without authority of a tender if a tender is required by a commission order.

(d) An offense under this section is punishable by a fine of not less than $50 or more than $200.

TITLE 6
TIMBER

CHAPTER 151
PROVISIONS GENERALLY APPLICABLE

SUBCHAPTER B
UNAUTHORIZED HARVESTING OF TIMBER

Sec. 151.052. Criminal Offense.

(a) A person commits an offense if the person:

(1) harvests standing timber with knowledge that the harvesting is without the permission of the owner of the standing timber; or

(2) causes another person to harvest standing timber without the permission of the owner of the standing timber.

(b) An offense under this section is:

(1) a state jail felony if it is shown on the trial of the offense that the value of the timber harvested is at least $500 but less than $20,000;

(2) a felony of the third degree if it is shown on the trial of the offense that the value of the timber harvested is at least $20,000 but less than $100,000;

(3) a felony of the second degree if it is shown on the trial of the offense that the value of the timber harvested is at least $100,000 but less than $200,000; or

(4) a felony of the first degree if it is shown on the trial of the offense that the value of the timber harvested is at least $200,000.

OCCUPATIONS CODE

TITLE 3
HEALTH PROFESSIONS

SUBTITLE A
PROVISIONS APPLYING TO HEALTH PROFESSIONS GENERALLY

CHAPTER 107
INTRACTABLE PAIN TREATMENT

SUBCHAPTER A
GENERAL PROVISIONS

Sec. 107.001. Short Title.

This chapter may be cited as the Intractable Pain Treatment Act.

Sec. 107.002. Definitions.

In this chapter:

(1) "Board" means the Texas State Board of Medical Examiners.

(2) "Intractable pain" means a state of pain for which:

(A) the cause of the pain cannot be removed or otherwise treated; and

(B) in the generally accepted course of medical practice, relief or cure of the cause of the pain:

(i) is not possible; or

(ii) has not been found after reasonable efforts.

(3) "Physician" means a physician licensed by the board.

Sec. 107.003. Nonapplicability of Chapter to Certain Chemically Dependent Persons.

Except as provided by Subchapter C, this chapter does not apply to a person being treated by a physician for chemical dependency because of the person's use of a dangerous drug or controlled substance.

Sec. 107.004. Rules [Renumbered].

Renumbered to Tex.Occ. Code § 111.004 by Acts 2005, 79th Leg., ch. 728 (H.B. 2018), § 23.001(69), effective September 1, 2005.

SUBCHAPTER B
PRESCRIPTION AND ADMINISTRATION OF DANGEROUS DRUGS AND CONTROLLED SUBSTANCES

Sec. 107.051. Authority to Prescribe or Administer Dangerous Drug or Controlled Substance.

Notwithstanding any other law, a physician may prescribe or administer a dangerous drug or controlled substance to a person in the course of the physician's treatment of the person for intractable pain.

Sec. 107.052. Limitations on Prescription or Administration of Dangerous Drug or Controlled Substance.

This chapter does not authorize a physician to prescribe or administer to a person a dangerous drug or controlled substance:

(1) for a purpose that is not a legitimate medical purpose as defined by the board; and

(2) if the physician knows or should know the person is using drugs for a nontherapeutic purpose.

Sec. 107.053. Limitation on Authority of Hospital or Other Health Care Facility Regarding Use of Dangerous Drug or Controlled Substance.

A hospital or other health care facility may not prohibit or restrict the use of a dangerous drug or controlled substance prescribed or administered by a physician who holds staff privileges at the hospital or facility for a person diagnosed and treated by a physician for intractable pain.

SUBCHAPTER C TREATMENT OF CERTAIN PATIENTS

Sec. 107.101. Patient.

In this subchapter, "patient" includes a person who:

(1) is currently abusing a dangerous drug or controlled substance;

(2) is not currently abusing such a drug or substance but has a history of such abuse; or

(3) lives in an environment that poses a risk for misuse or diversion to illegitimate use of such a drug or substance.

Sec. 107.102. Authority to Treat.

This chapter authorizes a physician to treat a patient with an acute or chronic painful medical condition with a dangerous drug or controlled substance to relieve the patient's pain using appropriate doses, for an appropriate length of time, and for as long as the pain persists.

Sec. 107.103. Duty to Monitor Patient.

A physician who treats a patient under this subchapter shall monitor the patient to ensure that a prescribed dangerous drug or controlled substance is used only for the treatment of the patient's painful medical condition.

Sec. 107.104. Documentation and Consultation Required.

To ensure that a prescribed dangerous drug or controlled substance is not diverted to another use and to ensure the appropriateness of the treatment of the patient's targeted symptoms, the physician shall:

(1) specifically document:

(A) the understanding between the physician and patient about the patient's prescribed treatment;

(B) the name of the drug or substance prescribed;

(C) the dosage and method of taking the prescribed drug or substance;

(D) the number of dose units prescribed; and

(E) the frequency of prescribing and dispensing the drug or substance; and

(2) consult with a psychologist, psychiatrist, expert in the treatment of addictions, or other health care professional, as appropriate.

SUBCHAPTER D DISCIPLINARY ACTION

Sec. 107.151. Disciplinary Action Prohibited.

A physician is not subject to disciplinary action by the board for prescribing or administering a dangerous drug or controlled substance in the course of treatment of a person for intractable pain.

Sec. 107.152. Authority of Board to Revoke or Suspend License.

(a) This chapter does not affect the authority of the board to revoke or suspend the license of a physician who:

(1) prescribes, administers, or dispenses a drug or treatment:

(A) for a purpose that is not a legitimate medical purpose as defined by the board; and

(B) that is nontherapeutic in nature or nontherapeutic in the manner the drug or treatment is administered or prescribed;

(2) fails to keep a complete and accurate record of the purchase and disposal of:

(A) a drug listed in Chapter 481, Health and Safety Code; or

(B) a controlled substance scheduled in the Comprehensive Drug Abuse Prevention and Control Act of 1970 (21 U.S.C. Section 801 et seq.);

(3) writes a false or fictitious prescription for:

(A) a dangerous drug as defined by Chapter 483, Health and Safety Code;

(B) a controlled substance listed in a schedule under Chapter 481, Health and Safety Code; or

(C) a controlled substance scheduled in the Comprehensive Drug Abuse Prevention and Control Act of 1970 (21 U.S.C. Section 801 et seq.); or

(4) prescribes, administers, or dispenses in a manner inconsistent with public health and welfare:

(A) a dangerous drug as defined by Chapter 483, Health and Safety Code;

(B) a controlled substance listed in a schedule under Chapter 481, Health and Safety Code; or

(C) a controlled substance scheduled in the Comprehensive Drug Abuse Prevention and Control Act of 1970 (21 U.S.C. Section 801 et seq.).

(b) For purposes of Subsection (a)(2), the physician's records must include a record of:

(1) the date of purchase;

(2) the sale or disposal of the drug or substance by the physician;

(3) the name and address of the person receiving the drug or substance; and

(4) the reason for the disposal or dispensing of the drug or substance to the person.

SUBCHAPTER E PAIN TREATMENT REVIEW COMMITTEE

Sec. 107.201. Pain Treatment Review Committee [Expired].

Expired pursuant to Acts 2007, 80th Leg., ch. 1391 (S.B. 1879), § 6, effective July 1, 2009.

SUBTITLE B PHYSICIANS [EXPIRES SEPTEMBER 1, 2031]

CHAPTER 158 AUTHORITY OF PHYSICIAN TO PROVIDE CERTAIN DRUGS AND SUPPLIES [EXPIRES SEPTEMBER 1, 2031]

Sec. 158.001. Provision of Drugs and Other Supplies. [Expires September 1, 2031]

(a) A physician licensed under this subtitle may supply a patient with any drug, remedy, or clinical supply necessary to meet the patient's immediate needs.

(b) This section does not permit a physician to operate a retail pharmacy without complying with Chapter 558.

(c) This chapter does not prohibit a physician from supplying to a patient, free of charge, a drug provided to the physician by a drug manufacturer for an indigent pharmaceutical program if, in the physician's opinion, it is advantageous to the patient, in adhering to a course of treatment prescribed by the physician, to receive the drug.

Sec. 158.002. Provision of Free Samples. [Expires September 1, 2031]

(a) This chapter does not prohibit a physician from supplying a pharmaceutical sample to a patient free of charge if, in the physician's opinion, it is advantageous to the patient, in adhering to a course of treatment prescribed by the physician, to receive the sample.

(b) A pharmaceutical sample provided under this section must be:

(1) provided to the physician from the manufacturer free of charge and delivered to a patient free of any direct or indirect charge;

(2) prepackaged by the original manufacturer and not repackaged; and

(3) marked on the immediate container to indicate that it is a sample or recorded in records that indicate it is a sample.

(c) Each state and federal labeling and recordkeeping requirement must be followed and documented. A record maintained under Subsection (b)(3) must be accessible as provided under state and federal law.

Sec. 158.003. Dispensing of Dangerous Drugs in Certain Rural Areas. [Expires September 1, 2031]

(a) In this section, "reimbursement for cost" means an additional charge, separate from that imposed for the physician's professional services, that includes the cost of the drug product and all other actual costs to the physician incidental to providing the dispensing service. The term does not include a separate fee imposed for the act of dispensing the drug itself.

(b) This section applies to an area located in a county with a population of 5,000 or less, or in a municipality or an unincorporated town with a population of less than 2,500, that is within a 15-mile radius of the physician's office and in which a pharmacy is not located. This section does not apply to a municipality or an unincorporated town that is adjacent to a municipality with a population of 2,500 or more.

(c) A physician who practices medicine in an area described by Subsection (b) may:

(1) maintain a supply of dangerous drugs in the physician's office to be dispensed in the course of treating the physician's patients; and

(2) be reimbursed for the cost of supplying those drugs without obtaining a license under Chapter 558.

(d) A physician who dispenses dangerous drugs under Subsection (c) shall:

(1) comply with each labeling provision under Subtitle J applicable to that class of drugs; and

(2) oversee compliance with packaging and recordkeeping provisions applicable to that class of drugs.

(e) A physician who desires to dispense dangerous drugs under this section shall notify both the

Texas State Board of Pharmacy and the board that the physician practices in an area described by Subsection (b). The physician may continue to dispense dangerous drugs in the area until the Texas State Board of Pharmacy determines, after notice and hearing, that the physician no longer practices in an area described by Subsection (b).

CHAPTER 169
AUTHORITY TO PRESCRIBE LOW-THC CANNABIS TO CERTAIN PATIENTS FOR COMPASSIONATE USE [EXPIRES SEPTEMBER 1, 2031]

Sec. 169.001. Definitions. [Expires September 1, 2031]

In this chapter:

(1) "Department" means the Department of Public Safety.

(1–a) "Incurable neurodegenerative disease" means a disease designated as an incurable neurodegenerative disease by rule of the executive commissioner of the Health and Human Services Commission, adopted in consultation with the National Institutes of Health.

(2) [Repealed.]

(3) "Low-THC cannabis" means the plant Cannabis sativa L., and any part of that plant or any compound, manufacture, salt, derivative, mixture, preparation, resin, or oil of that plant that contains not more than one percent by weight of tetrahydrocannabinols.

(4) "Medical use" means the ingestion by a means of administration other than by smoking of a prescribed amount of low-THC cannabis by a person for whom low-THC cannabis is prescribed under this chapter.

(5) "Smoking" means burning or igniting a substance and inhaling the smoke.

(6) [Repealed.]

Sec. 169.0011. Prescription for Medical Use. [Expires September 1, 2031]

A reference in this chapter, Chapter 487, Health and Safety Code, or other law to a prescription for medical use or a prescription for low-THC cannabis means an entry in the compassionate-use registry established under Section 487.054, Health and Safety Code.

Sec. 169.002. Physician Qualified to Prescribe Low-THC Cannabis to Patients with Certain Medical Conditions. [Expires September 1, 2031]

(a) Only a physician qualified with respect to a patient's particular medical condition as provided by this section may prescribe low-THC cannabis in accordance with this chapter to treat the applicable medical condition.

(b) A physician is qualified to prescribe low-THC cannabis with respect to a patient's particular medical condition if the physician:

(1) is licensed under this subtitle;

(2) is board certified in a medical specialty relevant to the treatment of the patient's particular medical condition by a specialty board approved by the American Board of Medical Specialties or the Bureau of Osteopathic Specialists; and

(3) dedicates a significant portion of clinical practice to the evaluation and treatment of the patient's particular medical condition.

(c) A physician is qualified to prescribe low-THC cannabis for the treatment of a patient with a medical condition approved by rule of the executive commissioner of the Health and Human Services Commission for treatment in an approved research program conducted under Subchapter F, Chapter 487, Health and Safety Code, if the physician is:

(1) licensed under this subtitle; and

(2) certified by a compassionate-use institutional review board created under Section 487.253, Health and Safety Code, that oversees patient treatment undertaken as part of that approved research program.

Sec. 169.003. Prescription of Low-THC Cannabis. [Expires September 1, 2031]

A physician described by Section 169.002 may prescribe low-THC cannabis to a patient if:

(1) the patient is a permanent resident of the state;

(2) the physician complies with the registration requirements of Section 169.004; and

(3) the physician certifies to the department that:

(A) the patient is diagnosed with:

(i) epilepsy;

(ii) a seizure disorder;

(iii) multiple sclerosis;

(iv) spasticity;

(v) amyotrophic lateral sclerosis;

(vi) autism;

(vii) cancer;

(viii) an incurable neurodegenerative disease;

(ix) post-traumatic stress disorder; or

Occupations Code

(x) a medical condition that is approved for a research program under Subchapter F, Chapter 487, Health and Safety Code, and for which the patient is receiving treatment under that program; and

(B) the physician determines the risk of the medical use of low-THC cannabis by the patient is reasonable in light of the potential benefit for the patient.

Sec. 169.004. Low-THC Cannabis Prescriber Registration. [Expires September 1, 2031]

(a) Before a physician qualified to prescribe low-THC cannabis under Section 169.002 may prescribe or renew a prescription for low-THC cannabis for a patient under this chapter, the physician must register as the prescriber for that patient in the compassionate-use registry maintained by the department under Section 487.054, Health and Safety Code. The physician's registration must indicate:

(1) the physician's name;

(2) the patient's name and date of birth;

(3) the dosage prescribed to the patient;

(4) the means of administration ordered for the patient; and

(5) the total amount of low-THC cannabis required to fill the patient's prescription.

(b) The department may not publish the name of a physician registered under this section unless permission is expressly granted by the physician.

Sec. 169.005. Patient Treatment Plan. [Expires September 1, 2031]

A physician described by Section 169.002 who prescribes low-THC cannabis for a patient's medical use under this chapter must maintain a patient treatment plan that indicates:

(1) the dosage, means of administration, and planned duration of treatment for the low-THC cannabis;

(2) a plan for monitoring the patient's symptoms; and

(3) a plan for monitoring indicators of tolerance or reaction to low-THC cannabis.

SUBTITLE J PHARMACY AND PHARMACISTS [EXPIRES SEPTEMBER 1, 2029]

CHAPTER 551 GENERAL PROVISIONS [EXPIRES SEPTEMBER 1, 2029]

Sec. 551.001. [Expires September 1, 2029] Short Title.

This subtitle may be cited as the Texas Pharmacy Act.

Sec. 551.002. [Expires September 1, 2029] Legislative Declaration; Purpose.

(a) This subtitle shall be liberally construed to regulate in the public interest the practice of pharmacy in this state as a professional practice that affects the public health, safety, and welfare.

(b) It is a matter of public interest and concern that the practice of pharmacy merits and receives the confidence of the public and that only qualified persons be permitted to engage in the practice of pharmacy in this state.

(c) The purpose of this subtitle is to promote, preserve, and protect the public health, safety, and welfare through:

(1) effectively controlling and regulating the practice of pharmacy; and

(2) licensing pharmacies engaged in the sale, delivery, or distribution of prescription drugs and devices used in diagnosing and treating injury, illness, and disease.

Sec. 551.003. Definitions. [Expires September 1, 2029]

In Chapters 551-566:

(1) "Administer" means to directly apply a prescription drug to the body of a patient by any means, including injection, inhalation, or ingestion, by:

(A) a person authorized by law to administer the drug, including a practitioner or an authorized agent under a practitioner's supervision; or

(B) the patient at the direction of a practitioner.

(2) "Board" means the Texas State Board of Pharmacy.

(3) "Class A pharmacy license" or "community pharmacy license" means a license described by Section 560.051.

(4) "Class B pharmacy license" or "nuclear pharmacy license" means a license described by Section 560.051.

(5) "Class C pharmacy license" or "institutional pharmacy license" means a license described by Section 560.051.

(6) "Class D pharmacy license" or "clinic pharmacy license" means a license described by Section 560.051.

(7) "Class E pharmacy license" or "nonresident pharmacy license" means a license described by Section 560.051.

(8) "College of pharmacy" means a school, university, or college of pharmacy that:

(A) satisfies the accreditation standards of the American Council on Pharmaceutical Education as adopted by the board; or

(B) has degree requirements that meet the standards of accreditation set by the board.

(9) "Compounding" means the preparation, mixing, assembling, packaging, or labeling of a drug or device:

(A) as the result of a practitioner's prescription drug order based on the practitioner-patient-pharmacist relationship in the course of professional practice;

(B) for administration to a patient by a practitioner as the result of a practitioner's initiative based on the practitioner-patient-pharmacist relationship in the course of professional practice;

(C) in anticipation of a prescription drug order based on a routine, regularly observed prescribing pattern; or

(D) for or as an incident to research, teaching, or chemical analysis and not for selling or dispensing, except as allowed under Section 562.154 or Chapter 563.

(10) "Confidential record" means a health-related record, including a patient medication record, prescription drug order, or medication order, that:

(A) contains information that identifies an individual; and

(B) is maintained by a pharmacy or pharmacist.

(11) "Controlled substance" means a substance, including a drug:

(A) listed in Schedule I, II, III, IV, or V, as established by the commissioner of public health under Chapter 481, Health and Safety Code, or in Penalty Group 1, 1-A, 1-B, 2, 3, or 4, Chapter 481; or

(B) included in Schedule I, II, III, IV, or V of the Comprehensive Drug Abuse Prevention and Control Act of 1970 (21 U.S.C. Section 801 et seq.).

(12) "Dangerous drug" means a drug or device that:

(A) is not included in Penalty Group 1, 1-B, 2, 3, or 4, Chapter 481, Health and Safety Code, and is unsafe for self-medication; or

(B) bears or is required to bear the legend:

(i) "Caution: federal law prohibits dispensing without prescription" or "Rx only" or another legend that complies with federal law; or

(ii) "Caution: federal law restricts this drug to use by or on the order of a licensed veterinarian."

(13) "Deliver" or "delivery" means the actual, constructive, or attempted transfer of a prescription drug or device or controlled substance from one person to another, with or without consideration.

(14) "Designated agent" means:

(A) an individual, including a licensed nurse, physician assistant, or pharmacist:

(i) who is designated by a practitioner and authorized to communicate a prescription drug order to a pharmacist; and

(ii) for whom the practitioner assumes legal responsibility;

(B) a licensed nurse, physician assistant, or pharmacist employed in a health care facility to whom a practitioner communicates a prescription drug order; or

(C) a registered nurse or physician assistant authorized by a practitioner to administer a prescription drug order for a dangerous drug under Subchapter B, Chapter 157.

(15) "Device" means an instrument, apparatus, implement, machine, contrivance, implant, in vitro reagent, or other similar or related article, including a component part or accessory, that is required under federal or state law to be ordered or prescribed by a practitioner.

(15-a) "Direct supervision" means supervision by a pharmacist who directs the activities of a pharmacist-intern, pharmacy technician, or pharmacy technician trainee to a sufficient degree to ensure the activities are performed accurately, safely, and without risk of harm to patients, as specified by board rule.

(16) "Dispense" means to prepare, package, compound, or label, in the course of professional practice, a prescription drug or device for delivery to an ultimate user or the user's agent under a practitioner's lawful order.

(17) "Distribute" means to deliver a prescription drug or device other than by administering or dispensing.

(18) "Drug" means:

(A) a substance recognized as a drug in a drug compendium, including the current official United States Pharmacopoeia, official National Formulary, or official Homeopathic Pharmacopoeia, or in a supplement to a drug compendium;

(B) a substance intended for use in the diagnosis, cure, mitigation, treatment, or prevention of disease in a human or another animal;

(C) a substance, other than food, intended to affect the structure or a function of the body of a human or another animal;

(D) a substance intended for use as a component of a substance specified in Paragraph (A), (B), or (C);

(E) a dangerous drug; or
(F) a controlled substance.
(19) "Drug regimen review" includes evaluation of prescription drug or medication orders and a patient medication record for:
(A) a known allergy;
(B) a rational therapy-contraindication;
(C) a reasonable dose and route of administration;
(D) reasonable directions for use;
(E) duplication of therapy;
(F) a drug-drug interaction;
(G) drug-food interaction;
(H) drug-disease interaction;
(I) adverse drug reaction; and
(J) proper use, including overuse or underuse.
(20) "Internship" means a practical experience program that is approved by the board.
(21) "Label" means written, printed, or graphic matter on the immediate container of a drug or device.
(22) "Labeling" means the process of affixing a label, including all information required by federal and state statute or regulation, to a drug or device container. The term does not include:
(A) the labeling by a manufacturer, packer, or distributor of a nonprescription drug or commercially packaged prescription drug or device; or
(B) unit dose packaging.
(23) "Manufacturing" means the production, preparation, propagation, conversion, or processing of a drug or device, either directly or indirectly, by extraction from a substance of natural origin or independently by a chemical or biological synthesis. The term includes packaging or repackaging a substance or labeling or relabeling a container and promoting and marketing the drug or device and preparing and promoting a commercially available product from a bulk compound for resale by a person, including a pharmacy or practitioner. The term does not include compounding.
(24) "Medication order" means an order from a practitioner or a practitioner's designated agent for administration of a drug or device.
(25) "Nonprescription drug" means a nonnarcotic drug or device that may be sold without a prescription and that is labeled and packaged in compliance with state or federal law.
(26) "Patient counseling" means communication by a pharmacist of information, as specified by board rule, to a patient or caregiver to improve therapy by ensuring proper use of a drug or device.
(27) "Pharmaceutical care" means providing drug therapy and other pharmaceutical services defined by board rule and intended to assist in curing or preventing a disease, eliminating or reducing a patient's symptom, or arresting or slowing a disease process.
(28) "Pharmacist" means a person licensed by the board to practice pharmacy.
(29) "Pharmacist-in-charge" means the pharmacist designated on a pharmacy license as the pharmacist who has the authority or responsibility for the pharmacy's compliance with statutes and rules relating to the practice of pharmacy.
(30) "Pharmacist-intern" means:
(A) an undergraduate student who is enrolled in the professional sequence of a college of pharmacy approved by the board and who is participating in a board-approved internship program; or
(B) a graduate of a college of pharmacy who is participating in a board-approved internship.
(31) "Pharmacy" means a facility at which a prescription drug or medication order is received, processed, or dispensed under this subtitle, Chapter 481 or 483, Health and Safety Code, or the Comprehensive Drug Abuse Prevention and Control Act of 1970 (21 U.S.C. Section 801 et seq.). The term does not include a narcotic drug treatment program that is regulated under Chapter 466, Health and Safety Code.
(32) "Pharmacy technician" means an individual employed by a pharmacy whose responsibility is to provide technical services that do not require professional judgment regarding preparing and distributing drugs and who works under the direct supervision of and is responsible to a pharmacist. The term does not include a pharmacy technician trainee.
(32-a) "Pharmacy technician trainee" means an individual who is registered with the board as a pharmacy technician trainee and is authorized to participate in a pharmacy technician training program.
(33) "Practice of pharmacy" means:
(A) providing an act or service necessary to provide pharmaceutical care;
(B) interpreting or evaluating a prescription drug order or medication order;
(C) participating in drug or device selection as authorized by law, and participating in drug administration, drug regimen review, or drug or drug-related research;
(D) providing patient counseling;
(E) being responsible for:
(i) dispensing a prescription drug order or distributing a medication order;
(ii) compounding or labeling a drug or device, other than labeling by a manufacturer, repackager, or distributor of a nonprescription drug or commercially packaged prescription drug or device;
(iii) properly and safely storing a drug or device; or

(iv) maintaining proper records for a drug or device;

(F) performing for a patient a specific act of drug therapy management delegated to a pharmacist by a written protocol from a physician licensed in this state in compliance with Subtitle B; or

(G) administering an immunization or vaccination under a physician's written protocol.

(34) "Practitioner" means:

(A) a person licensed or registered to prescribe, distribute, administer, or dispense a prescription drug or device in the course of professional practice in this state, including a physician, dentist, podiatrist, or veterinarian but excluding a person licensed under this subtitle;

(B) a person licensed by another state, Canada, or the United Mexican States in a health field in which, under the law of this state, a license holder in this state may legally prescribe a dangerous drug;

(C) a person practicing in another state and licensed by another state as a physician, dentist, veterinarian, or podiatrist, who has a current federal Drug Enforcement Administration registration number and who may legally prescribe a Schedule II, III, IV, or V controlled substance, as specified under Chapter 481, Health and Safety Code, in that other state; or

(D) an advanced practice registered nurse or physician assistant to whom a physician has delegated the authority to prescribe or order a drug or device under Section 157.0511, 157.0512, or 157.054.

(35) "Preceptor" has the meaning assigned by Section 558.057.

(36) "Prescription drug" means:

(A) a substance for which federal or state law requires a prescription before the substance may be legally dispensed to the public;

(B) a drug or device that under federal law is required, before being dispensed or delivered, to be labeled with the statement:

(i) "Caution: federal law prohibits dispensing without prescription" or "Rx only" or another legend that complies with federal law; or

(ii) "Caution: federal law restricts this drug to use by or on the order of a licensed veterinarian"; or

(C) a drug or device that is required by federal or state statute or regulation to be dispensed on prescription or that is restricted to use by a practitioner only.

(37) "Prescription drug order" means:

(A) an order from a practitioner or a practitioner's designated agent to a pharmacist for a drug or device to be dispensed; or

(B) an order under Subchapter B, Chapter 157.

(38) "Prospective drug use review" means the review of a patient's drug therapy and prescription drug order or medication order, as defined by board rule, before dispensing or distributing a drug to the patient.

(39) "Provide" means to supply one or more unit doses of a nonprescription drug or dangerous drug to a patient.

(40) "Radioactive drug" means a drug that exhibits spontaneous disintegration of unstable nuclei with the emission of nuclear particles or photons, including a nonradioactive reagent kit or nuclide generator that is intended to be used in the preparation of the substance.

(41) "Substitution" means the dispensing of a drug or a brand of drug other than the drug or brand of drug ordered or prescribed.

(42) "Texas trade association" means a cooperative and voluntarily joined statewide association of business or professional competitors in this state designed to assist its members and its industry or profession in dealing with mutual business or professional problems and in promoting their common interest.

(42-a) "Therapeutic contact lens" means a contact lens that contains one or more drugs and that delivers the drugs into the wearer's eye.

(43) "Ultimate user" means a person who obtains or possesses a prescription drug or device for the person's own use or for the use of a member of the person's household or for administering to an animal owned by the person or by a member of the person's household.

(44) "Unit dose packaging" means the ordered amount of drug in a dosage form ready for administration to a particular patient, by the prescribed route at the prescribed time, and properly labeled with the name, strength, and expiration date of the drug.

(45) "Written protocol" means a physician's order, standing medical order, standing delegation order, or other order or protocol as defined by rule of the Texas Medical Board under Subtitle B.

Sec. 551.004. [Expires September 1, 2029] Applicability of Subtitle.

(a) This subtitle does not apply to:

(1) a practitioner licensed by the appropriate state board who supplies a patient of the practitioner with a drug in a manner authorized by state or federal law and who does not operate a pharmacy for the retailing of prescription drugs;

(2) a member of the faculty of a college of pharmacy recognized by the board who is a pharmacist

and who performs the pharmacist's services only for the benefit of the college;

(3) a person who procures prescription drugs for lawful research, teaching, or testing and not for resale;

(4) a home and community support services agency that possesses a dangerous drug as authorized by Section 142.0061, 142.0062, or 142.0063, Health and Safety Code; or

(5) a dispensing organization, as defined by Section 487.001, Health and Safety Code, that cultivates, processes, and dispenses low-THC cannabis, as authorized by Chapter 487, Health and Safety Code, to a patient listed in the compassionate-use registry established under that chapter.

(b) This subtitle does not prevent a practitioner from administering a drug to a patient of the practitioner.

(c) This subtitle does not prevent the sale by a person, other than a pharmacist, firm, joint stock company, partnership, or corporation, of:

(1) a nonprescription drug that is harmless if used according to instructions on a printed label on the drug's container and that does not contain a narcotic;

(2) an insecticide, a fungicide, or a chemical used in the arts if the insecticide, fungicide, or chemical is properly labeled; or

(3) an insecticide or fungicide that is mixed or compounded only for an agricultural purpose.

(d) A wholesaler or manufacturer may distribute a prescription drug as provided by state or federal law.

(e) This subtitle does not prevent a physician or therapeutic optometrist from dispensing and charging for therapeutic contact lenses. This subsection does not authorize a therapeutic optometrist to prescribe, administer, or dispense a drug that is otherwise outside the therapeutic optometrist's scope of practice.

Sec. 551.005. Application of Sunset Act. [Expires September 1, 2029]

The Texas State Board of Pharmacy is subject to Chapter 325, Government Code (Texas Sunset Act). Unless continued in existence as provided by that chapter, the board is abolished and this subtitle expires September 1, 2029.

Sec. 551.006. [Expires September 1, 2029] Exclusive Authority.

Notwithstanding any other law, a pharmacist has the exclusive authority to determine whether or not to dispense a drug.

Sec. 551.008. [Expires September 1, 2029] Prohibition on Rule Violating Sincerely Held Religious Belief.

(a) All rules, regulations, or policies adopted by the board may not violate Chapter 110, Civil Practice and Remedies Code.

(b) A person may assert a violation of Subsection (a) as an affirmative defense in an administrative hearing or as a claim or defense in a judicial proceeding under Chapter 37, Civil Practice and Remedies Code.

CHAPTER 563 PRESCRIPTION REQUIREMENTS; DELEGATION OF ADMINISTRATION AND PROVISION OF DANGEROUS DRUGS [EXPIRES SEPTEMBER 1, 2029]

SUBCHAPTER A PRESCRIPTION REQUIREMENTS FOR PRACTITIONERS [REPEALED]

Sec. 563.001. Prescription Issued by Practitioner [Repealed].

Repealed by Acts 2001, 77th Leg., ch. 1254 (S.B. 768), § 13(a)(2), effective June 1, 2002.

Sec. 563.002. Requirements Related to Prescription Forms [Repealed].

Repealed by Acts 2001, 77th Leg., ch. 1254 (S.B. 768), § 13(a)(2), effective June 1, 2002.

SUBCHAPTER B DELEGATION OF ADMINISTRATION AND PROVISION OF DANGEROUS DRUGS [EXPIRES SEPTEMBER 1, 2029]

Sec. 563.051. [Expires September 1, 2029] General Delegation of Administration and Provision of Dangerous Drugs.

(a) A physician may delegate to any qualified and properly trained person acting under the physician's supervision the act of administering or providing dangerous drugs in the physician's office, as ordered by the physician, that are used or required to meet the immediate needs of the physician's patients. The administration or provision of the dangerous drugs must be performed in compliance with laws relating to the practice of medicine and state and federal laws relating to those dangerous drugs.

(b) A physician may also delegate to any qualified and properly trained person acting under the physician's supervision the act of administering or providing dangerous drugs through a facility licensed by the board, as ordered by the physician, that are used or required to meet the needs of the physician's patients. The administration of those dangerous drugs must be in compliance with laws relating to the practice of medicine, professional nursing, and pharmacy and state and federal drug laws. The provision of those dangerous drugs must be in compliance with:

(1) laws relating to the practice of medicine, professional nursing, and pharmacy;

(2) state and federal drug laws; and

(3) rules adopted by the board.

(c) The administration or provision of the drugs may be delegated through a physician's order, a standing medical order, a standing delegation order, or another order defined by the Texas State Board of Medical Examiners.

(d) This section does not authorize a physician or a person acting under the supervision of a physician to keep a pharmacy, advertised or otherwise, for the retail sale of dangerous drugs, other than as authorized under Section 158.003, without complying with the applicable laws relating to the dangerous drugs.

(e) A practitioner may designate a licensed vocational nurse or a person having education equivalent to or greater than that required for a licensed vocational nurse to communicate the prescriptions of an advanced practice nurse or physician assistant authorized by the practitioner to sign prescription drug orders under Subchapter B, Chapter 157.

Sec. 563.052. [Expires September 1, 2029] Suitable Container Required.

A drug or medicine provided under this subchapter must be supplied in a suitable container labeled in compliance with applicable drug laws. A qualified and trained person, acting under the supervision of a physician, may specify at the time of the provision of the drug the inclusion on the container of the date of the provision and the patient's name and address.

Sec. 563.053. [Expires September 1, 2029] Dispensing of Dangerous Drugs in Certain Rural Areas.

(a) In this section, "reimbursement for cost" means an additional charge, separate from that imposed for the physician's professional services, that includes the cost of the drug product and all other actual costs to the physician incidental to providing the dispensing service. The term does not include a separate fee imposed for the act of dispensing the drug itself.

(b) This section applies to an area located in a county with a population of 5,000 or less, or in a municipality or an unincorporated town with a population of less than 2,500, that is within a 15-mile radius of the physician's office and in which a pharmacy is not located. This section does not apply to a municipality or an unincorporated town that is adjacent to a municipality with a population of 2,500 or more.

(c) A physician who practices medicine in an area described by Subsection (b) may:

(1) maintain a supply of dangerous drugs in the physician's office to be dispensed in the course of treating the physician's patients; and

(2) be reimbursed for the cost of supplying those drugs without obtaining a license under Chapter 558.

(d) A physician who dispenses dangerous drugs under Subsection (c) shall:

(1) comply with each labeling provision under this subtitle applicable to that class of drugs; and

(2) oversee compliance with packaging and recordkeeping provisions applicable to that class of drugs.

(e) A physician who desires to dispense dangerous drugs under this section shall notify both the board and the Texas State Board of Medical Examiners that the physician practices in an area described by Subsection (b). The physician may continue to dispense dangerous drugs in the area until the board determines, after notice and hearing, that the physician no longer practices in an area described by Subsection (b).

Sec. 563.054. [Expires September 1, 2029] Administration of Dangerous Drugs.

(a) A veterinarian may:

(1) administer or provide dangerous drugs to a patient in the veterinarian's office, or on the patient's premises, if the drugs are used or required to meet the needs of the veterinarian's patients;

(2) delegate the administration or provision of dangerous drugs to a person who:

(A) is qualified and properly trained; and

(B) acts under the veterinarian's supervision; and

(3) itemize and receive compensation for the administration or provision of the dangerous drugs under Subdivision (1).

(b) This section does not permit a veterinarian to maintain a pharmacy for the retailing of drugs without complying with applicable laws.

(c) The administration or provision of dangerous drugs must comply with:

(1) laws relating to the practice of veterinary medicine; and

(2) state and federal laws relating to dangerous drugs.

TITLE 10
OCCUPATIONS RELATED TO LAW ENFORCEMENT AND SECURITY

CHAPTER 1701
LAW ENFORCEMENT OFFICERS [EXPIRES SEPTEMBER 1, 2023]

SUBCHAPTER G
LICENSE REQUIREMENTS; DISQUALIFICATIONS AND EXEMPTIONS [EXPIRES SEPTEMBER 1, 2023]

Sec. 1701.301. License Required. [Expires September 1, 2023]

Except as provided by Sections 1701.310, 1701.311, and 1701.405, a person may not appoint or employ a person to serve as an officer, county jailer, school marshal, public security officer, or telecommunicator unless the person holds an appropriate license issued by the commission.

Sec. 1701.302. Certain Elected Law Enforcement Officers; License Required. [Expires September 1, 2023]

(a) An officer, including a sheriff, elected under the Texas Constitution or a statute or appointed to fill a vacancy in an elective office must obtain a license from the commission not later than the second anniversary of the date the officer takes office.

(b) The commission shall establish requirements for issuing the license and for revocation, suspension, or denial of the license.

(c) An officer to whom this section applies who does not obtain the license by the required date or does not remain licensed is incompetent and is subject to removal from office under Section 665.052, Government Code, or another removal statute.

Sec. 1701.303. License Application; Duties of Appointing Entity. [Expires September 1, 2023]

(a) A law enforcement agency or governmental entity that hires a person for whom a license is sought must file an application with the commission as provided by commission rule.

(b) A person who appoints an officer or county jailer licensed by the commission shall notify the commission not later than the 30th day after the date of the appointment. If the person appoints an individual who previously served as an officer or county jailer and the appointment occurs after the 180th day after the last date of service as an officer or county jailer, the person must have on file for the officer or county jailer in a form readily accessible to the commission:

(1) new criminal history record information;

(2) a new declaration of psychological and emotional health and lack of drug dependency or illegal drug use; and

(3) two completed fingerprint cards.

(c) A person who appoints or employs a telecommunicator licensed by the commission shall notify the commission not later than the 30th day after the date of the appointment or employment. If the person appoints or employs an individual who previously served as a telecommunicator and the appointment or employment occurs after the 180th day after the last date of service as a telecommunicator, the person must have on file in a form readily accessible to the commission:

(1) new criminal history record information; and

(2) two completed fingerprint cards.

Sec. 1701.304. Examination. [Expires September 1, 2023]

(a) The commission shall conduct an examination for each type of license issued by the commission at least four times each year at times and places designated by the commission. The commission shall:

(1) prescribe the content of an examination for each type of license;

(2) include in each examination a written examination that tests the applicant's knowledge of the appropriate occupation; and

(3) prescribe standards for acceptable performance on each examination.

(b) The commission by rule shall establish minimum qualifications for a person to be examined under this section. A person who is disqualified by law to be an officer or county jailer may not take an examination under this section.

(c) A law enforcement agency may request the commission to conduct examinations required by this chapter in the jurisdiction served by the agency. The commission may conduct the examinations in the jurisdiction if:

(1) the commission determines that doing so will not place a significant hardship on the commission's resources; and

(2) the requesting law enforcement agency reimburses the commission for additional costs incurred in conducting the examination in the agency's jurisdiction.

Sec. 1701.305. Examination Results. [Expires September 1, 2023]

(a) The commission shall notify each examinee of the examination results not later than the 30th day after the date the examination is administered. If an examination is graded or reviewed by a national testing service, the commission shall notify each examinee of the examination results not later than the 14th day after the date the commission receives the results from the testing service.

(b) If notice of the results of an examination graded or reviewed by a national testing service will be delayed for longer than 90 days after the examination date, the commission shall notify each examinee of the reason for the delay before the 90th day.

(c) If requested in writing by a person who fails an examination, the commission shall provide to the person an analysis of the person's performance on the examination.

Sec. 1701.306. Psychological and Physical Examination. [Expires September 1, 2023]

(a) The commission may not issue a license to a person unless the person is examined by:

(1) a licensed psychologist or by a psychiatrist who declares in writing that the person is in satisfactory psychological and emotional health to serve as the type of officer for which a license is sought; and

(2) a licensed physician who declares in writing that the person does not show any trace of drug dependency or illegal drug use after a blood test or other medical test.

(b) An agency hiring a person for whom a license is sought shall select the examining physician and the examining psychologist or psychiatrist. The agency shall prepare a report of each declaration required by Subsection (a) and shall maintain a copy of the report on file in a format readily accessible to the commission. A declaration is not public information.

(c) The commission shall adopt rules that:

(1) relate to appropriate standards and measures to be used by a law enforcement agency in reporting the declarations made under Subsection (a); and

(2) provide for exceptional circumstances in the administration of the examination of the applicant's psychological and emotional health, including permitting the examination to be made by a qualified licensed physician instead of a psychologist or psychiatrist.

(d) The commission may order an applicant to submit to an examination described by Subsection (a) by a psychologist, psychiatrist, or physician appointed by the commission if the commission:

(1) has cause to believe that a law enforcement agency failed to follow commission rules relating to an examination; or

(2) discovers that the applicant has submitted a false declaration.

Sec. 1701.307. Issuance of Officer or County Jailer License. [Expires September 1, 2023]

(a) The commission shall issue an appropriate officer or county jailer license to a person who, as required by this chapter:

(1) submits an application;

(2) completes the required training;

(3) passes the required examination;

(4) is declared to be in satisfactory psychological and emotional health and free from drug dependency or illegal drug use; and

(5) demonstrates weapons proficiency.

(b) The commission may issue a permanent license to a person who meets the requirements of this chapter and the rules prescribed by the commission to serve as an officer.

(c) The commission may issue a temporary or permanent license to a person to serve as a county jailer.

Sec. 1701.3071. Issuance of Telecommunicator License. [Expires September 1, 2023]

(a) The commission shall issue a telecommunicator license to a person who:

(1) submits an application;

(2) completes the required training;

(3) passes the required examination; and

(4) meets any other requirement of this chapter and the rules prescribed by the commission to qualify as a telecommunicator.

(a-1) The training required by Subsection (a)(2) must include telecommunicator cardiopulmonary resuscitation training that:

(1) uses the most current nationally recognized emergency cardiovascular care guidelines;

(2) incorporates recognition protocols for out-of-hospital cardiac arrest; and

(3) provides information on best practices for relaying compression-only cardiopulmonary resuscitation instructions to callers.

(b) The commission may issue a temporary or permanent license to a person to act as a telecommunicator.

Sec. 1701.3075. Qualified Applicant Awaiting Appointment. [Expires September 1, 2023]

(a) A person who meets the requirements set forth in Section 1701.307(a) has the same reporting responsibilities toward the commission under rules adopted by the commission as a license holder who has already been appointed as a peace officer.

(b) The commission may determine that a person who meets the requirements under Section 1701.307(a) is ineligible for appointment as a peace officer based on events that occur after the person meets the requirements in Section 1701.307(a) but before the person is appointed.

Sec. 1701.308. Weapons Proficiency. [Expires September 1, 2023]

The commission shall require a person applying for a peace officer license to demonstrate weapons proficiency.

Sec. 1701.309. Age Requirement. [Expires September 1, 2023]

The commission by rule shall set 21 years of age as the minimum age for obtaining a license as an officer. The rules must provide that a person at least 18 years of age may be issued a license as an officer if the person has:

(1) completed and received credit for at least 60 hours of study at an accredited college or university or received an associate degree from an accredited college or university; or

(2) received an honorable discharge from the United States armed forces after at least two years of service.

Sec. 1701.310. Appointment of County Jailer; Training Required. [Expires September 1, 2023]

(a) Except as provided by Subsection (e), a person may not be appointed as a county jailer, except on a temporary basis, unless the person has satisfactorily completed a preparatory training program, as required by the commission, in the operation of a county jail at a school operated or licensed by the commission. The training program must consist of at least eight hours of mental health training approved by the commission and the Commission on Jail Standards.

(b) A county jailer appointed on a temporary basis who does not satisfactorily complete the preparatory training program before the first anniversary of the date that the person is appointed shall be removed from the position. A county jailer appointed on a temporary basis shall be enrolled in the preparatory training program on or before the 90th day after their temporary appointment. A temporary appointment may not be renewed.

(c) A county jailer serving under permanent appointment before September 1, 1979, regardless of whether the person's employment was terminated before that date because of failure to satisfy standards adopted under Chapter 511, Government Code, is not required to meet a requirement of this section as a condition of continued employment or promotion unless:

(1) in an attempt to meet the standards the person took an examination and failed or was not allowed to finish the examination because the person acted dishonestly in regard to the examination;

(2) the person forged a document purporting to show that the person meets the standards; or

(3) the person seeks a new appointment as a county jailer on or after September 1, 1984.

(d) A county jailer serving under permanent appointment before September 1, 1979, is eligible to attend training courses in the operation of a county jail, subject to commission rules.

(e) A person trained and certified by the Texas Department of Criminal Justice to serve as a corrections officer in that agency's correctional institutions division is not required to complete the training requirements of this section to be appointed a part-time county jailer. Examinations under Section 1701.304 and psychological examinations under Section 1701.306 apply.

(f) A county jailer appointed on a temporary basis may not be promoted to a supervisory position in a county jail.

Sec. 1701.311. Provisional License for Workforce Shortage. [Expires September 1, 2023]

(a) The commission shall adopt rules to allow a law enforcement agency to petition for issuance of a provisional license for an officer if the agency proves that it has a workforce shortage.

(b) Except in an emergency, a peace officer holding a provisional license may not be required to work at the peace officer's employing agency and attend a commission-approved basic preparatory school for more than a total of 40 hours a week.

(c) An agency employing a peace officer who holds a provisional license may contract with the peace officer for reimbursement of the cost of a basic preparatory training course if the peace officer voluntarily resigns from the agency before a date specified in the contract that is not later than the first anniversary of the date the officer is appointed. The contract must state the cost of the course.

Sec. 1701.312. Disqualification: Felony Conviction or Placement on Community Supervision. [Expires September 1, 2023]

(a) A person who has been convicted of a felony is disqualified to be an officer, public security officer, telecommunicator, or county jailer, and the commission may not issue a license to, and a law enforcement agency may not appoint or employ, the person.

(b) For purposes of this section and Section 1701.502, a person is convicted of a felony if a court enters an adjudication of guilt against the person on a felony offense under the laws of this or another state or the United States, regardless of whether:

(1) the sentence is subsequently probated and the person is discharged from community supervision;

(2) the accusation, complaint, information, or indictment against the person is dismissed and the person is released from all penalties and disabilities resulting from the offense; or

(3) the person is pardoned for the offense, unless the pardon is granted expressly for subsequent proof of innocence.

(c) The commission, on receipt of a certified copy of a court's judgment under Article 42.011, Code of Criminal Procedure, shall note on the person's licensing records the conviction or community supervision indicated by the judgment.

Sec. 1701.313. Disqualification: Conviction of Barratry. [Expires September 1, 2023]

(a) A person who has been convicted of barratry under Section 38.12, Penal Code, is disqualified to be an officer, telecommunicator, or county jailer, and the commission may not issue a license to the person.

(b) For purposes of this section and Section 1701.503, a person is convicted of barratry if a court enters an adjudication of guilt against the person regardless of whether:

(1) the sentence is subsequently probated and the person is discharged from community supervision;

(2) the accusation, complaint, information, or indictment against the person is dismissed following community supervision; or

(3) the person is pardoned for the offense, unless the pardon is granted expressly for subsequent proof of innocence.

Sec. 1701.314. Exemption: Officer Appointed Before September 1, 1970. [Expires September 1, 2023]

A peace officer serving under a permanent appointment before September 1, 1970, is not required to obtain a license as a condition of tenure, continued employment, or promotion unless the officer seeks a new appointment. The officer is eligible to attend peace officer training courses subject to commission rules.

Sec. 1701.315. License Requirements for Persons with Military Special Forces Training. [Expires September 1, 2023]

(a) In this section, "special forces" means a special forces component of the United States armed forces, including:

(1) the United States Army Special Forces;

(2) the United States Navy SEALs;

(3) the United States Air Force Pararescue;

(4) the United States Marine Corps Force Reconnaissance; and

(5) any other component of the United States Special Operations Command approved by the commission.

(b) The commission shall adopt rules to allow an applicant to qualify to take an examination described by Section 1701.304 if the applicant:

(1) has served in the special forces;

(2) has successfully completed a special forces training course and provides to the commission documentation verifying completion of the course;

(3) completes a supplemental peace officer training course; and

(4) completes any other training required by the commission after the commission has reviewed the applicant's military training.

(c) Commission rules adopted under Subsection (b) shall include rules:

(1) to determine acceptable forms of documentation that satisfy the requirements of Subsection (b);

(2) under which the commission may waive any other license requirement for an applicant described by Subsection (b) based on other relevant military training the applicant has received, as determined by the commission, including intelligence or medical training; and

(3) to establish an expedited application process for an applicant described by Subsection (b).

(d) The commission shall review the content of the training course for each special forces component described by Subsection (a) and in adopting rules under Subsection (b) specify the training requirements an applicant who has completed that training course must complete and the training requirements from which an applicant who has completed that training course is exempt.

Sec. 1701.316. Reactivation of Peace Officer License. [Expires September 1, 2023]

(a) The commission shall adopt rules establishing requirements for reactivation of a peace officer's license after a break in employment.

(b) The commission may consider employment as a peace officer in another state in determining whether the person is required to obtain additional training or testing.

(c) The commission shall reactivate a peace officer's license after a break in employment if the former license holder:

(1) completed at least 10 years of full-time service as a peace officer in good standing before the break in employment;

(2) meets current licensing standards;

(3) successfully completes:

(A) an online or in-person supplemental peace officer course of not more than 120 hours; and

(B) other in-person training requirements of not more than 40 hours;

(4) passes a peace officer reactivation examination;

(5) files an application; and

(6) pays any required fees.

Sec. 1701.3161. Reactivation of Peace Officer License: Retired Peace Officers. [Expires September 1, 2023]

(a) In this section, "retired peace officer" means a person who served as a peace officer in this state who:

(1) is not currently serving as an elected, appointed, or employed peace officer under Article 2.12, Code of Criminal Procedure, or other law;

(2) was eligible to retire from a law enforcement agency in this state or was ineligible to retire only as a result of an injury received in the course of the officer's employment with the law enforcement agency; and

(3) is eligible to receive a pension or annuity for service as a law enforcement officer in this state or is ineligible to receive a pension or annuity only because the law enforcement agency that employed the officer does not offer a pension or annuity to its employees.

(b) The commission shall adopt rules for the reactivation of a retired peace officer's license after a break in employment. The rules must allow a retired peace officer to reactivate the officer's license by completing the continuing education requirements prescribed by Section 1701.351 and completing any other continuing education requirement imposed by law in lieu of successfully completing any examination required by the commission for reactivation.

(c) The commission may waive the reinstatement fee established for the reactivation of a peace officer's license for a retired peace officer who is eligible for reactivation as provided by Subsection (b).

Sec. 1701.317. Limitation on Information Required for License Renewal. [Expires September 1, 2023]

The requirements and procedures adopted by the commission for the renewal of a license issued under this chapter:

(1) may not require an applicant to provide unchanged criminal history information already included in one or more of the applicant's previous applications for licensure or for license renewal filed with the commission; and

(2) may require the applicant to provide only information relevant to the period occurring since the date of the applicant's last application for licensure or for license renewal, as applicable, including information relevant to any new requirement applicable to the license held by the applicant.

SUBCHAPTER H CONTINUING EDUCATION AND YEARLY WEAPONS PROFICIENCY [EXPIRES SEPTEMBER 1, 2023]

Sec. 1701.351. Continuing Education Required for Peace Officers. [Expires September 1, 2023]

(a) Each peace officer shall complete at least 40 hours of continuing education programs once every 24 months. The commission may suspend the license of a peace officer who fails to comply with this requirement.

(a-1) As part of the continuing education programs under Subsection (a), a peace officer must complete a training and education program that covers recent changes to the laws of this state and of the United States pertaining to peace officers.

(a-2) Before the first day of each 24-month training unit during which peace officers are required to complete 40 hours of continuing education programs under Subsection (a), the commission shall specify the mandated topics to be covered in up to 16 of the required hours.

(b) The commission by rule shall provide for waiver of the requirements of this section when mitigating circumstances exist.

(c) The commission shall credit a peace officer with meeting the continuing education requirements of this section if during the relevant 24-month period the peace officer serves on active duty as a member of the United States military for at least 12 months or serves as an elected member of the legislature. Credit for continuing education under this subsection does not affect any requirement to demonstrate continuing weapons proficiency under Section 1701.355.

(d) A peace officer who is second in command to a police chief of a law enforcement agency and who attends a continuing education program for command staff provided by the Bill Blackwood Law Enforcement Management Institute of Texas under Section 96.641, Education Code, is exempt from the continuing education requirements of this subchapter.

Sec. 1701.352. Continuing Education Programs. [Expires September 1, 2023]

(a) The commission shall recognize, prepare, or administer continuing education programs for officers and county jailers.

(b) The commission shall require a state, county, special district, or municipal agency that appoints or employs peace officers to provide each peace officer with a training program at least once every 48 months that is approved by the commission and consists of:

(1) topics selected by the agency; and

(2) for an officer holding only a basic proficiency certificate, not more than 20 hours of education and training that contain curricula incorporating the learning objectives developed by the commission regarding:

(A) civil rights, racial sensitivity, and cultural diversity;

(B) de-escalation and crisis intervention techniques to facilitate interaction with persons with mental impairments;

(C) de-escalation techniques to facilitate interaction with members of the public, including techniques for limiting the use of force resulting in bodily injury; and

(D) unless determined by the agency head to be inconsistent with the officer's assigned duties:

(i) the recognition, documentation, and investigation of cases that involve child abuse or neglect, family violence, and sexual assault, including the use of best practices and trauma-informed techniques to effectively recognize, document, and investigate those cases; and

(ii) issues concerning sex offender characteristics.

(c) A course provided under Subsection (b) may use instructional materials developed by the agency or its trainers or by entities having training agreements with the commission in addition to materials included in curricula developed by the commission.

(d) A peace officer who is appointed or will be appointed to the officer's first supervisory position must receive in-service training on supervision as part of the course provided for the officer under Subsection (b) not earlier than the 12th month before the date of that appointment or later than the first anniversary of the date of that appointment.

(e) The commission may require a state, county, special district, or municipal agency that appoints or employs a reserve law enforcement officer, county jailer, or public security officer to provide each of those persons with education and training in civil rights, racial sensitivity, and cultural diversity at least once every 48 months.

(f) Training in documentation of cases required by Subsection (b) shall include instruction in:

(1) making a written account of the extent of injuries sustained by the victim of an alleged offense;

(2) recording by photograph or videotape the area in which an alleged offense occurred and the victim's injuries;

(3) recognizing and recording a victim's statement that may be admissible as evidence in a proceeding concerning the matter about which the statement was made; and

(4) recognizing and recording circumstances indicating that a victim may have been assaulted in the manner described by Section 22.01(b)(2)(B), Penal Code.

(g) The training and education program on de-escalation and crisis intervention techniques to facilitate interaction with persons with mental impairments under Subsection (b)(2)(B) may not be provided as an online course. The commission shall:

(1) determine best practices for interacting with persons with mental impairments, in consultation with the Bill Blackwood Law Enforcement Management Institute of Texas; and

(2) review the education and training program under Subsection (b)(2)(B) at least once every 24 months.

(h) The commission shall require a state, county, special district, or municipal agency that employs telecommunicators to provide each telecommunicator with 24 hours of crisis communications instruction approved by the commission. The instruction must be provided on or before the first anniversary of the telecommunicator's first day of employment.

(i) A state agency, county, special district, or municipality that appoints or employs a telecommunicator shall provide training to the telecommunicator of not less than 20 hours during each 24-month period of employment that includes:

(1) telecommunicator cardiopulmonary resuscitation as described by Section 1701.3071(a-1); and

(2) other topics selected by the commission and the employing entity.

Sec. 1701.353. Continuing Education Procedures. [Expires September 1, 2023]

(a) The commission by rule shall adopt procedures to:

(1) ensure the timely and accurate reporting by agencies and persons licensed under this chapter of information related to training programs offered under this subchapter, including procedures for creating training records for license holders; and

(2) provide adequate notice to agencies and license holders of impending noncompliance with the training requirements of this subchapter so that the agencies and license holders may comply within the 24-month period or 48-month period, as appropriate.

(b) The commission shall require agencies to report to the commission in a timely manner the reasons that a license holder is in noncompliance after the agency receives notice by the commission of the license holder's noncompliance. The commission shall, following receipt of an agency's report or on a determination that the agency has failed to report in a timely manner, notify the license holder by certified mail of the reasons the license holder is in noncompliance and that the commission at the request of the license holder will hold a hearing as provided by this subsection if the license holder fails to obtain the required training within 60 days after the date the license holder receives notice under this subsection. The commission shall conduct a hearing consistent with Section 1701.504 if the license holder claims that:

(1) mitigating circumstances exist; or

(2) the license holder failed to complete the required training because the license holder's employing agency did not provide an adequate opportunity for the license holder to attend the required training course.

Sec. 1701.354. Continuing Education for Deputy Constables. [Expires September 1, 2023]

(a) If the commission requires a state, county, special district, or municipal agency that employs a deputy constable to provide the deputy constable with a training program under Section 1701.352, the commission shall require the deputy constable to attend at least 20 hours of instruction in civil process.

(b) The commission shall adopt rules and procedures concerning a civil process course, including rules providing for:

(1) approval of course content and standards; and

(2) issuance of course credit.

(c) The commission may waive the instruction requirements for a deputy constable under this section:

(1) if a constable requests a waiver for the deputy constable based on a representation that the deputy constable's duty assignment does not involve civil process responsibilities; or

(2) if the deputy constable requests a waiver because of hardship and the commission determines that a hardship exists.

Sec. 1701.3545. Initial Training and Continuing Education for Constables. [Expires September 1, 2023]

(a) A public institution of higher education selected by the commission shall establish and offer a program of initial training and a program of continuing education for constables. The curriculum for each program must relate to law enforcement management. The institution selected under this subsection shall develop the curriculum for the programs. The curriculum must be approved by the commission.

(b) Each constable must complete at least 40 hours of continuing education provided by the selected institution under Subsection (a) each 48-month period. The commission by rule shall establish a uniform 48-month continuing education training period.

(b-1) In addition to the requirements of Subsection (b), during each 48-month continuing education training period each constable must complete at least 20 hours of continuing education instruction on civil process to be provided by a public institution of higher education selected by the commission under this subsection. The commission shall establish minimum curriculum requirements for the continuing education course on civil process required by this subsection. The commission may waive the continuing education requirements of this subsection if:

(1) a constable requests a waiver because of hardship; and

(2) the commission determines that a hardship exists.

(c) An individual appointed or elected to that individual's first position as constable must complete at least 40 hours of initial training for new constables in accordance with Subsections (d) and (e).

(d) A newly appointed or elected constable shall complete the initial training program for new constables not later than the second anniversary of that individual's appointment or election as constable. The initial training program for new constables is in addition to the initial training required by this chapter. The commission by rule shall establish that the first continuing education training period for an individual under Subsection (b) begins on the first day of the first uniform continuing education training period that follows the date the individual completed the initial training program.

(e) The institution selected under Subsection (a) by rule may provide for the waiver of:

(1) all or part of the required 40 hours of initial training for new constables to the extent the new constable has satisfactorily completed equivalent training during the 24 months preceding the individual's appointment or election; or

(2) the continuing education requirements of Subsection (b) for an individual who has satisfactorily completed equivalent continuing education during the preceding 24 months.

(f) An individual who is subject to the continuing education requirements of Subsections (b) and (b-1) is exempt from other continuing education requirements under this subchapter.

(g) The commission shall establish procedures to annually determine the status of the peace officer license of each elected constable and to ensure that constables comply with this section. The commission shall forward to the attorney general's office documentation for each constable who does not comply with this section. A constable who does not comply with this section forfeits the office and the attorney general shall institute a quo warranto proceeding under Chapter 66, Civil Practice and Remedies Code, to remove the constable from office.

(h) To the extent of a conflict between this section and any other law, this section controls.

Sec. 1701.355. Continuing Demonstration of Weapons Proficiency. [Expires September 1, 2023]

(a) An agency that employs one or more peace officers shall designate a firearms proficiency officer and require each peace officer the agency employs to demonstrate weapons proficiency to the firearms proficiency officer at least annually. The agency shall maintain records of the weapons proficiency of the agency's peace officers.

(a-1) An agency that employs one or more county jailers who have been issued a certificate of firearms proficiency under Section 1701.2561 shall designate a firearms proficiency officer and require the jailers to demonstrate weapons proficiency to the firearms proficiency officer at least annually. The agency shall maintain records of the weapons proficiency of the agency's jailers. A county jailer's failure to demonstrate weapons proficiency does not affect the county jailer's license under this chapter.

(b) On request, the commission may waive the requirement that a peace officer or county jailer demonstrate weapons proficiency on a determination by the commission that the requirement causes a hardship.

(c) The commission by rule shall define weapons proficiency for purposes of this section.

Sec. 1701.356. Certain Officers: Reactivation and Continuing Education Not Required. [Expires September 1, 2023]

(a) An officer is not subject to Section 1701.351 or 1701.352 if the officer is:

(1) an honorably retired commissioned officer of the Department of Public Safety who is:

Occupations Code

(A) a special ranger under Section 411.023, Government Code; or

(B) a special Texas Ranger under Section 411.024, Government Code;

(2) an honorably retired commissioned officer of the Parks and Wildlife Department who is a special game warden under Section 11.0201, Parks and Wildlife Code; or

(3) an honorably retired commissioned officer of the Texas Alcoholic Beverage Commission who is a special inspector or representative under Section 5.142, Alcoholic Beverage Code.

(b) A person who is an honorably retired commissioned officer described by Subsection (a) or a retired state employee and who holds a permanent license issued before January 1981 and that was current on January 1, 1995:

(1) has the same rights and privileges as any other peace officer of this state;

(2) holds, notwithstanding Section 1701.316, an active license unless the license is revoked, suspended, or probated by the commission for a violation of this chapter; and

(3) is not subject to Section 1701.351.

(c) An honorably retired commissioned officer described by Subsection (a) may not be required to undergo training under Section 1701.253.

Sec. 1701.357. Weapons Proficiency for Qualified Retired Law Enforcement Officers. [Expires September 1, 2023]

(a) In this section:

(1) "Qualified handgun instructor" means a person certified as a qualified handgun instructor under Section 411.190, Government Code.

(2) "Qualified retired law enforcement officer" has the meaning assigned by 18 U.S.C. Section 926C.

(a-1) This section applies only to a qualified retired law enforcement officer who is entitled to carry a concealed firearm under 18 U.S.C. Section 926C.

(b) The head of a state or local law enforcement agency may allow a qualified retired law enforcement officer who is a retired commissioned peace officer an opportunity to demonstrate weapons proficiency if the officer provides to the agency a sworn affidavit stating that:

(1) the officer:

(A) honorably retired after not less than a total of 10 years of cumulative service as a commissioned officer with one or more state or local law enforcement agencies; or

(B) before completing 10 years of cumulative service as a commissioned officer with one or more state or local law enforcement agencies, separated from employment with the agency or agencies and is a qualified retired law enforcement officer;

(2) the officer's license as a commissioned officer was not revoked or suspended for any period during the officer's term of service as a commissioned officer; and

(3) the officer has no psychological or physical disability that would interfere with the officer's proper handling of a handgun.

(b-1) The commission shall issue a certificate of proficiency to a qualified retired law enforcement officer who:

(1) satisfactorily demonstrates weapons proficiency to a qualified handgun instructor under Subsection (b-2);

(2) provides to the commission a sworn affidavit stating that:

(A) the officer meets the requirements for a qualified retired law enforcement officer under 18 U.S.C. Section 926C;

(B) the officer's license as a qualified law enforcement officer was not revoked or suspended for any period during the officer's term of service; and

(C) the officer has no psychological or physical disability that would interfere with the officer's proper handling of a handgun; and

(3) otherwise satisfies the applicable procedures established by the commission under Subsection (c-1).

(b-2) A qualified handgun instructor may allow any qualified retired law enforcement officer an opportunity to demonstrate weapons proficiency if the officer provides to the instructor a copy of the sworn affidavit described by Subsection (b-1)(2).

(c) The state or local law enforcement agency shall establish written procedures for the issuance or denial of a certificate of proficiency under this subsection. The agency shall issue the certificate to a retired commissioned peace officer who satisfactorily demonstrates weapons proficiency under Subsection (b) and satisfies the written procedures established by the agency. The agency shall maintain records of any person who holds a certificate issued under this subsection.

(c-1) The commission shall establish written procedures and forms for qualified handgun instructors regarding the manner in which demonstrations are conducted and the communication of demonstration results to the commission and for the issuance or denial of certificates of proficiency to qualified retired law enforcement officers. The commission shall maintain records of any person who holds a certificate issued under Subsection (b-1).

(c-2) For purposes of this section, proof that an individual is a qualified retired law enforcement officer may include a retired peace officer identification

Occupations Code

card issued under Subchapter H, Chapter 614, Government Code, or other form of identification as described by 18 U.S.C. Section 926C(d).

(d) A certificate issued under this section expires on the first anniversary of the date the certificate was issued.

(e) The head of a state or local law enforcement agency may set and collect fees to recover the expenses the agency incurs in performing duties under this section.

(f) The amount of a fee set by a county law enforcement agency under Subsection (e) is subject to the approval of the commissioners court of the county. A county law enforcement agency that collects a fee under Subsection (e) shall deposit the amounts collected to the credit of the general fund of the county.

(f-1) A qualified handgun instructor may collect a reasonable fee for the purpose of evaluating a demonstration of weapons proficiency under this section.

(g) A county law enforcement agency must obtain approval of the program authorized by this section from the commissioners court of the county before issuing a certificate of proficiency under this section.

(h) The head of a state law enforcement agency may allow a qualified retired law enforcement officer, other than a retired commissioned peace officer, an opportunity to demonstrate weapons proficiency in the same manner as, and subject to the same requirements applicable to, a retired commissioned peace officer as described by Subsection (b). The agency shall establish written procedures for the issuance or denial of a certificate of proficiency under this subsection. The agency shall issue a certificate of proficiency to a qualified retired law enforcement officer who satisfactorily demonstrates weapons proficiency under this subsection and satisfies the written procedures established by the agency. The agency shall maintain records regarding the issuance of that certificate.

(i) On request of a qualified retired law enforcement officer who holds a certificate of proficiency under this section, the head of the state or local law enforcement agency from which the officer retired or most recently separated shall issue to the officer identification that indicates that the officer honorably retired or separated from the agency. An identification under this subsection must include a photograph of the officer.

(j) [Repealed.]

Sec. 1701.358. Initial Training and Continuing Education for Police Chiefs. [Expires September 1, 2023]

A police chief shall complete the initial training and continuing education required under Section 96.641, Education Code.

SUBCHAPTER I PROFESSIONAL TRAINING AND RECOGNITION [EXPIRES SEPTEMBER 1, 2023]

Sec. 1701.401. Professional Achievement. [Expires September 1, 2023]

(a) In this section:

(1) "Professional achievement" includes an instance in which an individual through personal initiative, fixity of purpose, persistence, or endeavor creates a program or system that has a significant positive impact on the law enforcement profession that exceeds the normal expectations of job performance.

(2) "Public service" includes an instance in which an individual through initiative creates or participates in a program or system that has a significant positive impact on the general population of a community that exceeds the normal expectations of job performance.

(3) "Valor" includes an act of personal heroism or bravery that exceeds the normal expectations of job performance, including placing one's own life in jeopardy to save another person's life, to prevent serious bodily injury to another, or to prevent the consequences of a criminal act.

(b) The commission shall issue certificates that recognize professional achievement. For this purpose the commission shall use the employment records of the employing agency.

(c) The commission shall adopt rules for issuing achievement awards to peace officers, reserve peace officers, jailers, custodial officers, or telecommunicators who are licensed by the commission. The commission's rules shall require recommendations from an elected official of this state or a political subdivision, an administrator of a law enforcement agency, or a person holding a license issued by the commission.

(d) The awards shall be given in the name of this state and presented at the State Capitol during May of each year. At a minimum the award shall consist of a document, an appropriate medal, and a ribbon suitable for wearing on a uniform.

(e) The awards shall be issued in three areas: valor, public service, and professional achievement.

(f) The commission may present awards relating to not more than a total of 20 incidents and accomplishments each year.

Sec. 1701.402. Proficiency Certificates. [Expires September 1, 2023]

(a) The commission shall issue certificates that recognize proficiency based on law enforcement

Occupations Code

training, education, and experience. For this purpose the commission shall use the employment records of the employing agency.

(b) As a requirement for a basic proficiency certificate, the commission shall require completion of local courses or programs of instruction on federal and state statutes that relate to employment issues affecting peace officers, telecommunicators, and county jailers, including:

(1) civil service;

(2) compensation, including overtime compensation, and vacation time;

(3) personnel files and other employee records;

(4) management-employee relations in law enforcement organizations;

(5) work-related injuries;

(6) complaints and investigations of employee misconduct; and

(7) disciplinary actions and the appeal of disciplinary actions.

(c) An employing agency is responsible for providing the training required by this section.

(d) As a requirement for an intermediate proficiency certificate, an officer must complete an education and training program on asset forfeiture established by the commission under Section 1701.253(g).

(e) As a requirement for an intermediate proficiency certificate, an officer must complete an education and training program on racial profiling established by the commission under Section 1701.253(h).

(f) As a requirement for an intermediate proficiency certificate, an officer must complete an education and training program on identity theft established by the commission under Section 1701.253(i).

(g) As a requirement for an intermediate proficiency certificate or an advanced proficiency certificate, an officer must complete the education and training program described by Section 1701.253 regarding de-escalation and crisis intervention techniques to facilitate interaction with persons with mental impairments.

(h) As a requirement for an intermediate proficiency certificate, an officer must complete an education and training program on investigative topics established by the commission under Section 1701.253(b).

(i) As a requirement for an intermediate proficiency certificate, an officer must complete an education and training program on civil rights, racial sensitivity, and cultural diversity established by the commission under Section 1701.253(c).

(j) As a requirement for an intermediate or advanced proficiency certificate issued by the commission on or after January 1, 2011, an officer must complete the basic education and training program on the trafficking of persons described by Section 1701.258(a).

(k) As a requirement for an intermediate or advanced proficiency certificate issued by the commission on or after January 1, 2015, an officer must complete an education and training program on missing and exploited children. The commission by rule shall establish the program. The program must:

(1) consist of at least four hours of training;

(2) include instruction on reporting an attempted child abduction to the missing children and missing persons information clearinghouse under Chapter 63, Code of Criminal Procedure;

(3) include instruction on responding to and investigating situations in which the Internet is used to commit crimes against children; and

(4) include a review of the substance of Chapters 20 and 43, Penal Code.

(*l*) As a requirement for an intermediate or advanced proficiency certificate issued by the commission on or after January 1, 2016, an officer must complete the canine encounter training program established by the commission under Section 1701.261.

(m) As a requirement for an intermediate or advanced proficiency certificate issued by the commission on or after January 1, 2016, an officer must complete an education and training program on the Texas Crime Information Center's child safety check alert list established by the commission under Section 1701.266.

(n) As a requirement for an intermediate proficiency certificate or an advanced proficiency certificate, an officer must complete the education and training program regarding de-escalation techniques to facilitate interaction with members of the public established by the commission under Section 1701.253(n).

(o) The commission shall adopt rules to allow an officer who has served in the military to receive credit toward meeting any training hours required for an intermediate, advanced, or master proficiency certificate based on that military service.

Sec. 1701.403. Investigative Hypnosis. [Expires September 1, 2023]

(a) The commission may establish minimum requirements for the training, testing, and certification of peace officers who use investigative hypnosis.

(b) A peace officer may not use a hypnotic interview technique unless the officer:

(1) completes a training course approved by the commission; and

(2) passes an examination administered by the commission that is designed to test the officer's knowledge of investigative hypnosis.

(c) The commission may issue a professional achievement or proficiency certificate to an officer who meets the requirements of Subsection (b).

Sec. 1701.404. Certification of Officers for Mental Health Assignments. [Expires September 1, 2023]

(a) The commission by rule may establish minimum requirements for the training, testing, and certification of special officers for offenders with mental impairments.

(b) The commission may certify a sheriff, sheriff's deputy, constable, other peace officer, county jailer, or justice of the peace as a special officer for offenders with mental impairments if the person:

(1) completes a training course in emergency first aid and lifesaving techniques approved by the commission;

(2) completes a training course administered by the commission on mental health issues and offenders with mental impairments; and

(3) passes an examination administered by the commission that is designed to test the person's:

(A) knowledge and recognition of the characteristics and symptoms of mental illness, mental retardation, and mental disabilities; and

(B) knowledge of mental health crisis intervention strategies for people with mental impairments.

(c) The commission may issue a professional achievement or proficiency certificate to an officer, county jailer, or justice of the peace who meets the requirements of Subsection (b).

Sec. 1701.4045. Certification of Officers for Family Violence and Sexual Assault Assignments. [Expires September 1, 2023]

(a) The commission by rule shall establish minimum requirements for the training, testing, and certification of special officers for responding to allegations of family violence or sexual assault.

(b) The commission may certify a peace officer as a special officer for responding to allegations of family violence or sexual assault if the person:

(1) completes an advanced training course administered by the commission on recognizing, documenting, and investigating family violence and sexual assault using best practices and trauma-informed techniques; and

(2) passes an examination administered by the commission that is designed to test the person's:

(A) knowledge and recognition of the signs of family violence and sexual assault; and

(B) skill at documenting and investigating family violence and sexual assault using best practices and trauma-informed techniques.

(c) The commission may issue a professional achievement or proficiency certificate to a peace officer who meets the requirements of Subsection (b).

Sec. 1701.405. Telecommunicators. [Expires September 1, 2023]

(a) In this section:

(1) [Repealed by Acts 2011, 82nd Leg., ch. 855 (H.B. 3823), § 12, effective September 1, 2011.]

(2) "Emergency" means the occurrence or imminent threat of damage, injury, or loss of life or property resulting from an extraordinary natural or man-made cause.

(3) [Repealed by Acts 2011, 82nd Leg., ch. 855 (H.B. 3823), § 12, effective September 1, 2011.]

(b) This state or a political subdivision of this state may not employ a person to act as a telecommunicator unless the person:

(1) has had at least 40 hours of telecommunicator training as determined by the commission;

(2) is at least 18 years of age;

(3) holds a high school diploma or high school equivalency certificate; and

(4) holds a license to act as a telecommunicator or agrees to obtain the license not later than the first anniversary of the date of employment.

(b-1) A person employed to act as a telecommunicator who has not obtained a license to act as a telecommunicator under this chapter may not continue to act as a telecommunicator after the first anniversary of the date of employment unless the person obtains the license.

(b-2) Notwithstanding this section, an officer is not required to obtain a telecommunicator license to act as a telecommunicator.

(c) The commission shall accredit telecommunicator training programs that fulfill the minimum requirements for a telecommunicator. The commission shall adopt rules providing for the accreditation of telecommunicator training programs developed and taught by the Department of Public Safety, an institution of higher education, including a junior college, community college, or technical school, or any other entity approved by the commission.

(d) A person who completes an accredited training program under this section may, by letter to the commission, request a written acknowledgment from the commission that the person has met the minimum requirements for a telecommunicator as determined by the commission. The request must be accompanied, in accordance with commission rules, by evidence of satisfactory completion of an accredited telecommunicator training program. On a determination by the commission that the person meets the minimum requirements for a telecommunicator, the commission shall issue the written acknowledgment to the person.

(e) [Repealed by Acts 2011, 82nd Leg., ch. 855 (H.B. 3823), § 12, effective September 1, 2011.]

(f) A person performing the duties of a telecommunicator and serving under permanent appointment on and before September 1, 1987, is not required to meet the requirements of this section as a condition of continued employment.

(g) Notwithstanding this section, a person may be appointed or serve as a telecommunicator on a temporary or probationary basis or may perform the duties of a telecommunicator in an emergency.

(h) A person appointed on a temporary or probationary basis after September 1, 1987, who does not satisfactorily complete an accredited telecommunicator training program before the first anniversary of the date the person is originally appointed shall be removed from the position. The person's temporary or probationary appointment may not be extended for more than one year except that not earlier than the first anniversary of the date the person is removed under this subsection, the employing agency may petition the commission for reinstatement of the person to temporary or probationary employment.

Sec. 1701.406. County Jail Personnel [Repealed].

Repealed by Acts 2009, 81st Leg., ch. 1172 (H.B. 3389), § 35, effective September 1, 2009.

SUBCHAPTER J
EMPLOYMENT RECORDS AND PREEMPLOYMENT PROCEDURE

Sec. 1701.451. Preemployment Procedure. [Expires September 1, 2023]

(a) Before a law enforcement agency may hire a person licensed under this chapter, the agency must, on a form and in the manner prescribed by the commission:

(1) obtain the person's written consent for the agency to review the information required to be reviewed under this section;

(2) request from the commission and any other applicable person information required to be reviewed under this section; and

(3) submit to the commission confirmation that the agency, to the best of the agency's ability before hiring the person:

(A) contacted each entity or individual necessary to obtain the information required to be reviewed under this section; and

(B) except as provided by Subsection (b), obtained and reviewed as related to the person, as applicable:

(i) personnel files and other employee records from each previous law enforcement agency employer, including the employment application submitted to the previous employer;

(ii) employment termination reports maintained by the commission under this subchapter;

(iii) service records maintained by the commission;

(iv) proof that the person meets the minimum qualifications for enrollment in a training program under Section 1701.251(a);

(v) a military veteran's United States Department of Defense Form DD-214 or other military discharge record;

(vi) criminal history record information;

(vii) information on pending warrants as available through the Texas Crime Information Center and National Crime Information Center;

(viii) evidence of financial responsibility as required by Section 601.051, Transportation Code;

(ix) a driving record from the Department of Public Safety;

(x) proof of United States citizenship; and

(xi) information on the person's background from at least three personal references and at least two professional references.

(a-1) [Repealed.]

(b) If an entity or individual contacted for information required to be reviewed under this section refused to provide the information or did not respond to the request for information, the confirmation submitted to the commission must document the manner of the request and the refusal or lack of response.

(c) If the commission or a law enforcement agency receives from a law enforcement agency a request for information under this section and the person's consent on the forms and in the manner prescribed by the commission, the commission or agency shall provide the information to the requesting agency.

(d) The confirmation form submitted to the commission under this section is not confidential and is subject to disclosure under Chapter 552, Government Code.

(e) The commission shall:

(1) by rule establish the forms and procedures required by this section, including:

(A) the process by which a law enforcement agency shall make a person's employment records electronically available to a law enforcement agency hiring a person licensed under this chapter;

(B) appropriate privacy and security protections for the process described by Paragraph (A); and

(C) a rule prohibiting a confirmation form submitted to the commission under this section from containing confidential information described by Section 552.1175(b), Government Code, regarding the person who is the subject of the confirmation form;

(2) post the forms and procedures on the commission's Internet website; and

(3) retain a record of each confirmation form submitted under this section.

(f) The head of a law enforcement agency or the agency head's designee shall review and sign each confirmation form required under this section before submission to the commission. The failure of an agency head or the agency head's designee to comply with this subsection constitutes grounds for suspension of the agency head's license under Section 1701.501.

Sec. 1701.452. Employment Termination Report. [Expires September 1, 2023]

(a) The head of a law enforcement agency or the head's designee shall submit a report to the commission on a form prescribed by the commission regarding a person licensed under this chapter who resigns or retires from employment with the law enforcement agency, whose appointment with the law enforcement agency is terminated, or who separates from the law enforcement agency for any other reason. The report must be submitted by the head or the designee not later than the seventh business day after the date the license holder:

(1) resigns, retires, is terminated, or separates from the agency; and

(2) exhausts all administrative appeals available to the license holder, if applicable.

(b) The head of a law enforcement agency or the head's designee shall include in the report required under Subsection (a) a statement on whether the license holder was honorably discharged, generally discharged, or dishonorably discharged and, as required by the commission, an explanation of the circumstances under which the person resigned, retired, or was terminated. For purposes of this subsection:

(1) "Honorably discharged" means a license holder who, while in good standing and not because of pending or final disciplinary actions or a documented performance problem, retired, resigned, or separated from employment with or died while employed by a law enforcement agency.

(2) "Generally discharged" means a license holder who:

(A) was terminated by, retired or resigned from, or died while in the employ of a law enforcement agency and the separation was related to a disciplinary investigation of conduct that is not included in the definition of dishonorably discharged; or

(B) was terminated by or retired or resigned from a law enforcement agency and the separation was for a documented performance problem and was not because of a reduction in workforce or an at-will employment decision.

(3) "Dishonorably discharged" means a license holder who:

(A) was terminated by a law enforcement agency or retired or resigned in lieu of termination by the agency in relation to allegations of criminal misconduct; or

(B) was terminated by a law enforcement agency or retired or resigned in lieu of termination by the agency for insubordination or untruthfulness.

(c) The commission by rule may further specify the circumstances that constitute honorably discharged, dishonorably discharged, and generally discharged within the definitions provided by Subsection (b).

(d) The head of the law enforcement agency from which a license holder resigns, retires, is terminated, or separates for reasons other than death, or the head's designee, shall provide to the license holder a copy of the report. The report must be provided to the license holder not later than the seventh business day after the date the license holder:

(1) resigns, retires, is terminated, or separates from the agency; and

(2) exhausts all administrative appeals available to the license holder, if applicable.

(e) If the person who is the subject of the employment termination report is deceased, the head of the law enforcement agency or the head's designee on request shall provide a copy of the report to the person's next of kin not later than the seventh business day after the date of the request.

(f) The head of a law enforcement agency or the head's designee satisfies the obligation to provide the report required under Subsection (d) or (e) by sending by certified mail:

(1) the report required under Subsection (d) to the last known address of the license holder if the license holder is not otherwise available; or

(2) the report required under Subsection (e) to the last known address of the next of kin if the next of kin who requested the report is not otherwise available.

(g) The head of a law enforcement agency or the head's designee must submit a report under this section each time a person licensed under this chapter resigns, retires, is terminated, or separates for any other reason from the agency. The report is an official government document.

Sec. 1701.4521. License Suspension for Officer Dishonorably Discharged. [Expires September 1, 2023]

(a) The commission shall suspend the license of an officer licensed under this chapter on notification that the officer has been dishonorably discharged if the officer has previously been dishonorably discharged from another law enforcement agency.

(b) An officer whose license is suspended under this section may appeal the suspension in writing to the commission not later than the 30th day after the date the officer is suspended.

(c) After a commission determination, the commission may revoke or reinstate the officer's license in accordance with rules or procedures adopted by the commission under this chapter related to revocation or reinstatement of a license. The commission shall revoke the officer's license if the officer does not appeal the suspension before the 30th day after the date the officer is suspended.

(d) The commission's decision does not affect:

(1) the employment relationship between an officer licensed under this chapter and a law enforcement agency; or

(2) any disciplinary action taken against an officer licensed under this chapter by a law enforcement agency.

Sec. 1701.4525. Petition for Correction of Report; Hearing. [Expires September 1, 2023]

(a) A person who is the subject of an employment termination report maintained by the commission under this subchapter may contest information contained in the report by submitting to the law enforcement agency and to the commission a written petition on a form prescribed by the commission for a correction of the report not later than the 30th day after the date the person receives a copy of the report. On receipt of the petition, the commission shall refer the petition to the State Office of Administrative Hearings.

(b), (c) [Repealed by Acts 2011, 82nd Leg., ch. 399 (S.B. 545), § 6, effective September 1, 2011.]

(d) A proceeding to contest information in an employment termination report is a contested case under Chapter 2001, Government Code.

(e) In a proceeding to contest information in an employment termination report for a report based on alleged misconduct, an administrative law judge shall determine if the alleged misconduct occurred by a preponderance of the evidence regardless of whether the person who is the subject of the report was terminated or the person resigned, retired, or separated in lieu of termination. If the alleged misconduct is not supported by a preponderance of the evidence, the administrative law judge shall order the commission to change the report. The commission shall send the changed report to the law enforcement agency that prepared the original employment termination report. The law enforcement agency shall replace the original employment termination report with the changed report.

(e-1) [Repealed by Acts 2013, 83rd Leg., ch. 109 (S.B. 965), § 3, effective September 1, 2013.]

(f) The commission shall adopt rules for the administration of this section.

(g) The commission is not considered a party in a proceeding conducted by the State Office of Administrative Hearings under this section.

Sec. 1701.453. Maintenance of Reports and Statements. [Expires September 1, 2023]

The commission shall maintain a copy of each report and statement submitted to the commission under this subchapter until at least the 10th anniversary of the date on which the report or statement is submitted.

Sec. 1701.454. Confidentiality. [Expires September 1, 2023]

(a) All information submitted to the commission under this subchapter is confidential and is not subject to disclosure under Chapter 552, Government Code, unless the person resigned or was terminated due to substantiated incidents of excessive force or violations of the law other than traffic offenses.

(b) Except as provided by this subchapter, a commission member or other person may not release information submitted under this subchapter.

Sec. 1701.455. Subpoena. [Expires September 1, 2023]

Information submitted to the commission under this subchapter is subject to subpoena only in a judicial proceeding.

Sec. 1701.456. Immunity from Liability. [Expires September 1, 2023]

(a) The commission is not liable for civil damages for providing information contained in a report or statement maintained by the commission under this subchapter if the commission released the information as provided by this subchapter.

(b) A law enforcement agency, agency head, or other law enforcement official is not liable for civil damages for:

(1) a report made by that agency or person if the report is made in good faith; or

(2) making a person's information available to a hiring law enforcement agency under Section 1701.451.

Sec. 1701.457. Limitation on Commission Authority. [Expires September 1, 2023]

This subchapter does not authorize the commission to review disciplinary action taken by a law enforcement agency against a person licensed under this chapter or to issue a subpoena to compel the production of a document prepared or maintained by the agency in connection with a disciplinary matter.

Sec. 1701.458. Venue. [Expires September 1, 2023]

Venue for the prosecution of an offense under Section 37.10, Penal Code, that arises from a report required under this subchapter lies in the county where the offense occurred or in Travis County.

SUBCHAPTER K DISCIPLINARY PROCEDURES [EXPIRES SEPTEMBER 1, 2023]

Sec. 1701.501. Disciplinary Action. [Expires September 1, 2023]

(a) Except as provided by Subsection (d), the commission shall revoke or suspend a license, place on probation a person whose license has been suspended, or reprimand a license holder for a violation of:

(1) this chapter;

(2) the reporting requirements provided by Articles 2.132 and 2.134, Code of Criminal Procedure; or

(3) a commission rule.

(b) The commission may establish procedures for the revocation of a license issued under this chapter.

(c) The commission by rule may adopt other necessary enforcement procedures.

(d) The commission may revoke a license issued under this chapter to an officer elected under the Texas Constitution only if the officer is convicted of:

(1) a felony; or

(2) a criminal offense directly involving the person's duties as an officer.

Sec. 1701.502. Felony Conviction or Placement on Community Supervision. [Expires September 1, 2023]

(a) The commission shall immediately revoke the license of a person licensed under this chapter who is convicted of a felony.

(b) The commission shall immediately suspend the license of a person licensed under this chapter who is charged with a felony and is placed on community supervision regardless of whether the court defers further proceedings without entering an adjudication of guilt.

(c) The commission may reinstate, as provided by commission rules, a license that is suspended under Subsection (b) when the license holder is released from community supervision.

Sec. 1701.503. Barratry Conviction. [Expires September 1, 2023]

The commission shall immediately revoke the license of a person licensed under this chapter who is convicted of barratry under Section 38.12, Penal Code.

Sec. 1701.504. Hearing. [Expires September 1, 2023]

(a) Except as provided by Sections 1701.502 and 1701.503, if the commission proposes to suspend or revoke a person's license, the person is entitled to a hearing conducted by the State Office of Administrative Hearings.

(b) If the commission proposes to refuse to renew a person's license, the person is entitled to a hearing conducted by the State Office of Administrative Hearings.

Sec. 1701.505. Administrative Procedure. [Expires September 1, 2023]

(a) Proceedings for a disciplinary action are governed by Chapter 2001, Government Code.

(b) Rules of practice adopted by the commission under Section 2001.004, Government Code, applicable to the proceedings for a disciplinary action may not conflict with rules adopted by the State Office of Administrative Hearings.

Sec. 1701.506. Appeal. [Expires September 1, 2023]

(a) A person dissatisfied with an action of the commission may appeal the action under Chapter 2001, Government Code. The court shall set the matter for hearing not earlier than 10 days after written notice of the appeal is given to the commission and the commission's attorney.

(b) The court may suspend an action of the commission pending a hearing. The order suspending the action takes effect when served on the commission. The commission shall provide its attorney a copy of the petition and order.

(c) The attorney general or the district or county attorney shall represent the commission in the appeal.

Sec. 1701.507. Administrative Penalties. [Expires September 1, 2023]

(a) In addition to other penalties imposed by law, a law enforcement agency or governmental entity that violates this chapter or a rule adopted under this chapter is subject to an administrative penalty in an amount set by the commission not to exceed $1,000 per day per violation. The administrative penalty shall be assessed in a proceeding conducted in accordance with Chapter 2001, Government Code.

(b) The amount of the penalty shall be based on:

(1) the seriousness of the violation;

(2) the respondent's history of violations;

(3) the amount necessary to deter future violations;

(4) efforts made by the respondent to correct the violation; and

(5) any other matter that justice may require.

(c) The commission by rule shall establish a written enforcement plan that provides notice of the specific ranges of penalties that apply to specific alleged violations and the criteria by which the commission determines the amount of a proposed administrative penalty.

SUBCHAPTER L CRIMINAL PENALTY [EXPIRES SEPTEMBER 1, 2023]

Sec. 1701.551. Criminal Penalty for Appointment or Retention of Certain Persons. [Expires September 1, 2023]

(a) A person commits an offense if the person appoints or retains another person as an officer, county jailer, or telecommunicator in violation of Section 1701.301, 1701.303, 1701.306, or 1701.405.

(b) An offense under Subsection (a) is a misdemeanor punishable by a fine of not less than $100 and not more than $1,000.

Sec. 1701.552. Criminal Penalty for Appointment of Person Not Certified for Investigative Hypnosis. [Expires September 1, 2023]

(a) A person commits an offense if the person appoints or retains another person in violation of Section 1701.403.

(b) An offense under Subsection (a) is a misdemeanor punishable by a fine of not less than $100 and not more than $1,000.

Sec. 1701.553. Criminal Penalty for Appointment or Retention of Persons with Certain Convictions. [Expires September 1, 2023]

(a) A person commits an offense if the person appoints, employs, or retains an individual as an officer, public security officer, telecommunicator, or county jailer in violation of Section 1701.312 or 1701.313.

(b) An offense under Subsection (a) is a state jail felony.

Sec. 1701.554. Venue. [Expires September 1, 2023]

Venue for the prosecution of an offense that arises from a violation of this chapter or in connection with the administration of this chapter lies in the county where the offense occurred or in Travis County.

SUBCHAPTER M VISITING RESOURCE OFFICER IN PUBLIC SCHOOL [EXPIRES SEPTEMBER 1, 2023]

Sec. 1701.601. Definition. [Expires September 1, 2023]

In this subchapter, "school resource officer" means a peace officer who is assigned by the officer's employing political subdivision to provide a police presence at a public school, safety or drug education to students of a public school, or other similar services. The term does not include a peace officer who provides law enforcement at:

(1) a public school only for extracurricular activities; or

(2) a public school event only for extracurricular activities.

Sec. 1701.602. License Required. [Expires September 1, 2023]

A peace officer who is a visiting school resource officer in a public school must be licensed as provided by this chapter.

Sec. 1701.603. Firearms Accident Prevention Program. [Expires September 1, 2023]

(a) A peace officer who is a visiting school resource officer in a public elementary school shall at least once each school year offer to provide instruction to students in a firearms accident prevention program, as determined by the school district.

(b) A firearms accident prevention program must include the safety message, "Stop! Don't Touch. Leave the Area. Tell an Adult.", and may include instructional materials from the National Rifle Association Eddie Eagle GunSafe Program, including animated videos and activity books.

SUBCHAPTER M-1
PEER SUPPORT NETWORK FOR LAW ENFORCEMENT OFFICERS

Sec. 1701.621. Definitions.

In this subchapter:

(1) "Law enforcement officer" means a person identified as a peace officer under Article 2.12(1), (2), (3), or (4), Code of Criminal Procedure.

(2) "Peer" means a person who is a law enforcement officer or retired law enforcement officer.

Sec. 1701.622. General Powers and Duties.

(a) The commission shall develop a peer support network for law enforcement officers. The network must include:

(1) peer-to-peer support;

(2) training for peer service coordinators and peers that includes suicide prevention training;

(3) technical assistance for program development, peer service coordinators, licensed mental health professionals, and peers; and

(4) identification, retention, and screening of licensed mental health professionals.

(b) As part of the peer support network for law enforcement officers, the commission shall ensure law enforcement officers have support in both urban and rural jurisdictions.

(c) The commission shall solicit and ensure that specialized training is provided to persons who are peers and who want to provide peer-to-peer support and other peer-to-peer services under the network.

(d) The commission may adopt rules necessary to implement this subchapter.

Sec. 1701.623. Contract with Institution of Higher Education.

The commission may contract with an institution of higher education that has appropriate expertise in mental health or law enforcement to develop the peer support network under this subchapter.

Sec. 1701.624. Confidentiality of Participant Information.

Information relating to a law enforcement officer's participation in peer-to-peer support and other peer-to-peer services under the network is confidential and may not be disclosed under Chapter 552, Government Code, by:

(1) the commission;

(2) a law enforcement agency that employs a law enforcement officer participant; or

(3) any other state agency or political subdivision in this state that employs a law enforcement officer participant.

Sec. 1701.625. Protections Related to Licensure.

A law enforcement officer's participation in peer-to-peer support and other peer-to-peer services under the network may not:

(1) serve as the basis for a revocation, suspension, or denial of a license issued under this chapter; or

(2) be considered in any proceeding related to the officer's licensure under this chapter.

Sec. 1701.626. Annual Report.

Not later than December 1 of each year, the commission shall submit a report to the governor and the legislature that includes:

(1) the number of law enforcement officers who received peer support through the peer support network for law enforcement officers;

(2) the number of peers and peer service coordinators trained;

(3) an evaluation of the services provided under this subchapter; and

(4) recommendations for program improvements.

SUBCHAPTER N BODY WORN CAMERA PROGRAM [EXPIRES SEPTEMBER 1, 2023]

Sec. 1701.651. Definitions. [Expires September 1, 2023]

In this subchapter:

(1) "Body worn camera" means a recording device that is:

(A) capable of recording, or transmitting to be recorded remotely, video or audio; and

(B) worn on the person of a peace officer, which includes being attached to the officer's clothing or worn as glasses.

(2) "Department" means the Department of Public Safety of the State of Texas.

(3) "Private space" means a location in which a person has a reasonable expectation of privacy, including a person's home.

Sec. 1701.652. Grants for Body Worn Cameras. [Expires September 1, 2023]

(a) A police department of a municipality in this state, a sheriff of a county in this state who has received the approval of the commissioners court for the purpose, or the department may apply to the office of the governor for a grant to defray the cost of implementing this subchapter and to equip peace officers with body worn cameras if that law enforcement agency employs officers who:

(1) are engaged in traffic or highway patrol or otherwise regularly detain or stop motor vehicles; or

(2) are primary responders who respond directly to calls for assistance from the public.

(b) The office of the governor shall set deadlines for applications for grants under this chapter.

(c) Except as provided by Subsection (d), the office of the governor shall create and implement a matching grant program under which matching funds from federal, state, local, and other funding sources may be required as a condition of the grant. A law enforcement agency that receives a grant under this section is required to match 25 percent of the grant money.

(d) The department is eligible for grants under this subchapter but may not be made subject to any requirement for matching funds.

(e) The governor's office may conditionally award a grant to a law enforcement agency that has not adopted and implemented the policy under Section 1701.655 or implemented the training required under Section 1701.656, but money may not be disbursed to a law enforcement agency until the agency fully complies with those sections.

Sec. 1701.6521. Grants for Body Worn Camera Data Storage. [Expires September 1, 2023]

(a) A law enforcement agency in this state that provides body worn cameras to its peace officers may apply to the office of the governor for a grant to defray the cost of data storage for recordings created with the body worn cameras.

(b) The grant program established by this section may be funded by federal funds or by gifts, grants, and donations.

Sec. 1701.653. Reporting. [Expires September 1, 2023]

(a) As a condition of receiving a grant under this subchapter, a law enforcement agency annually shall report to the commission regarding the costs of implementing a body worn camera program, including all known equipment costs and costs for data storage.

(b) The commission shall compile the information submitted under Subsection (a) into a report and submit the report to the office of the governor and the legislature not later than December 1 of each year.

Sec. 1701.654. Interagency or Interlocal Contracts. [Expires September 1, 2023]

A law enforcement agency in this state may enter into an interagency or interlocal contract to receive body worn camera services and have the identified operations performed through a program established by the Department of Information Resources.

Sec. 1701.655. Body Worn Camera Policy. [Expires September 1, 2023]

(a) A law enforcement agency that receives a grant to provide body worn cameras to its peace officers or that otherwise operates a body worn camera program shall adopt a policy for the use of body worn cameras.

(b) A policy described by Subsection (a) must ensure that a body worn camera is activated only for a law enforcement purpose and must include:

(1) guidelines for when a peace officer should activate a camera or discontinue a recording currently in progress, considering the need for privacy in certain situations and at certain locations;

(2) provisions relating to data retention, including a provision requiring the retention of video for a minimum period of 90 days;

(3) provisions relating to storage of video and audio, creation of backup copies of the video and audio, and maintenance of data security;

(4) provisions relating to the collection of a body worn camera, including the applicable video and audio recorded by the camera, as evidence;

(5) guidelines for public access, through open records requests, to recordings that are public information;

(6) provisions entitling an officer to access any recording of an incident involving the officer before the officer is required to make a statement about the incident;

(7) procedures for supervisory or internal review; and

(8) the handling and documenting of equipment and malfunctions of equipment.

(c) A policy described by Subsection (a) may not require a peace officer to keep a body worn camera activated for the entire period of the officer's shift.

(c-1) A policy described by Subsection (a) must require a peace officer who is equipped with a body worn camera and actively participating in an investigation to keep the camera activated for the entirety of the officer's active participation in the investigation unless the camera has been deactivated in compliance with that policy.

(d) A policy adopted under this section must be consistent with the Federal Rules of Evidence and Texas Rules of Evidence.

Sec. 1701.656. Training. [Expires September 1, 2023]

(a) Before a law enforcement agency may operate a body worn camera program, the agency must provide training to:

(1) peace officers who will wear the body worn cameras; and

(2) any other personnel who will come into contact with video and audio data obtained from the use of body worn cameras.

(b) The commission, in consultation with the department, the Bill Blackwood Law Enforcement Management Institute of Texas, the W. W. Caruth Jr. Police Institute at Dallas, and the Texas Police Chiefs Association, shall develop or approve a curriculum for a training program under this section.

Sec. 1701.657. Recording Interactions with the Public. [Expires September 1, 2023]

(a) A peace officer equipped with a body worn camera shall act in a manner that is consistent with the policy of the law enforcement agency that employs the officer with respect to when and under what circumstances a body worn camera must be activated.

(b) A peace officer equipped with a body worn camera may choose not to activate a camera or may choose to discontinue a recording currently in progress for any encounter with a person that is not related to an investigation.

(c) A peace officer who does not activate a body worn camera in response to a call for assistance must include in the officer's incident report or otherwise note in the case file or record the reason for not activating the camera.

(d) Any justification for failing to activate the body worn camera because it is unsafe, unrealistic, or impracticable is based on whether a reasonable officer under the same or similar circumstances would have made the same decision.

Sec. 1701.658. Use of Personal Equipment. [Expires September 1, 2023]

(a) If a law enforcement agency receives a grant under Section 1701.652, a peace officer who is employed by the agency and who is on duty may only use a body worn camera that is issued and maintained by that agency.

(b) Notwithstanding any previous policies, an agency may not allow its peace officers to use privately owned body worn cameras after receiving a grant described by this section.

(c) A peace officer who is employed by a law enforcement agency that has not received a grant described by this section or who has not otherwise been provided with a body worn camera by the agency that employs the officer may operate a body worn camera that is privately owned only if permitted by the employing agency.

(d) An agency that authorizes the use of privately owned body worn cameras under Subsection (c) must make provisions for the security and compatibility of the recordings made by those cameras.

Occupations Code

Sec. 1701.659. Offense. [Expires September 1, 2023]

(a) A peace officer or other employee of a law enforcement agency commits an offense if the officer or employee releases a recording created with a body worn camera under this subchapter without permission of the applicable law enforcement agency.

(b) An offense under this section is a Class A misdemeanor.

Sec. 1701.660. Recordings As Evidence. [Expires September 1, 2023]

(a) Except as provided by Subsections (a-1) and (b), a recording created with a body worn camera and documenting an incident that involves the use of deadly force by a peace officer or that is otherwise related to an administrative or criminal investigation of an officer may not be deleted, destroyed, or released to the public until all criminal matters have been finally adjudicated and all related administrative investigations have concluded.

(a-1) A law enforcement agency may permit a person who is depicted in a recording of an incident described by Subsection (a) or, if the person is deceased, the person's authorized representative, to view the recording, provided that the law enforcement agency determines that the viewing furthers a law enforcement purpose and provided that any authorized representative who is permitted to view the recording was not a witness to the incident. A person viewing a recording may not duplicate the recording or capture video or audio from the recording. A permitted viewing of a recording under this subsection is not considered to be a release of public information for purposes of Chapter 552, Government Code.

(b) A law enforcement agency may release to the public a recording described by Subsection (a) if the law enforcement agency determines that the release furthers a law enforcement purpose.

(c) This section does not affect the authority of a law enforcement agency to withhold under Section 552.108, Government Code, information related to a closed criminal investigation that did not result in a conviction or a grant of deferred adjudication community supervision.

Sec. 1701.661. Release of Information Recorded by Body Worn Camera. [Expires September 1, 2023]

(a) A member of the public is required to provide the following information when submitting a written request to a law enforcement agency for information recorded by a body worn camera:

(1) the date and approximate time of the recording;

(2) the specific location where the recording occurred; and

(3) the name of one or more persons known to be a subject of the recording.

(b) A failure to provide all of the information required by Subsection (a) to be part of a request for recorded information does not preclude the requestor from making a future request for the same recorded information.

(c) Except as provided by Subsection (d), information recorded by a body worn camera and held by a law enforcement agency under this subchapter is not subject to the requirements of Section 552.021, Government Code.

(d) Information that is or could be used as evidence in a criminal prosecution is subject to the requirements of Section 552.021, Government Code.

(e) A law enforcement agency may:

(1) seek to withhold information subject to Subsection (d) in accordance with procedures provided by Section 552.301, Government Code;

(2) assert any exceptions to disclosure in Chapter 552, Government Code, or other law; or

(3) release information requested in accordance with Subsection (a) after the agency redacts any information made confidential under Chapter 552, Government Code, or other law.

(f) A law enforcement agency may not release any portion of a recording made in a private space, or of a recording involving the investigation of conduct that constitutes a misdemeanor punishable by fine only and does not result in arrest, without written authorization from the person who is the subject of that portion of the recording or, if the person is deceased, from the person's authorized representative.

(g) The attorney general shall set a proposed fee to be charged to members of the public who seek to obtain a copy of a recording under this section. The fee amount must be sufficient to cover the cost of reviewing and making the recording. A law enforcement agency may provide a copy without charge or at a reduced charge if the agency determines that waiver or reduction of the charge is in the public interest.

(h) A recording is confidential and excepted from the requirements of Chapter 552, Government Code, if the recording:

(1) was not required to be made under this subchapter or another law or under a policy adopted by the appropriate law enforcement agency; and

(2) does not relate to a law enforcement purpose.

Sec. 1701.662. Body Worn Camera Recordings; Request for Attorney General Decision. [Expires September 1, 2023]

(a) Notwithstanding Section 552.301(b), Government Code, a governmental body's request for a decision from the attorney general about whether a requested body worn camera recording falls within an exception to public disclosure is considered timely if made not later than the 20th business day after the date of receipt of the written request.

(b) Notwithstanding Section 552.301(d), Government Code, a governmental body's response to a requestor regarding a requested body worn camera recording is considered timely if made not later than the 20th business day after the date of receipt of the written request.

(c) Notwithstanding Section 552.301(e), Government Code, a governmental body's submission to the attorney general of the information required by that subsection regarding a requested body worn camera recording is considered timely if made not later than the 25th business day after the date of receipt of the written request.

(d) Notwithstanding Section 552.301(e-1), Government Code, a governmental body's submission to a requestor of the information required by that subsection regarding a requested body worn camera recording is considered timely if made not later than the 25th business day after the date of receipt of the written request.

Sec. 1701.663. Production of Body Worn Camera Recording in Response to Voluminous Public Information Requests. [Expires September 1, 2023]

(a) Notwithstanding Section 552.221(d), Government Code, an officer for public information who is employed by a governmental body and who receives a voluminous request in accordance with Section 1701.661(a) is considered to have promptly produced the information for purposes of Section 552.221, Government Code, if the officer takes the actions required under Section 552.221 before the 21st business day after the date of receipt of the written request.

(b) For purposes of this section, "voluminous request" includes:

(1) a request for body worn camera recordings from more than five separate incidents;

(2) more than five separate requests for body worn camera recordings from the same person in a 24-hour period, regardless of the number of incidents included in each request; or

(3) a request or multiple requests from the same person in a 24-hour period for body worn camera recordings that, taken together, constitute more than five total hours of video footage.

SUBCHAPTER O EMERGENCY ADMINISTRATION OF EPINEPHRINE [EXPIRES SEPTEMBER 1, 2023]

Sec. 1701.701. Definitions. [Expires September 1, 2023]

In this subchapter:

(1) "Anaphylaxis" means a sudden, severe, and potentially life-threatening allergic reaction that occurs when a person is exposed to an allergen.

(2) "Epinephrine auto-injector" means a disposable medical drug delivery device that contains a premeasured single dose of epinephrine intended for use to treat anaphylaxis.

(3) "Physician" means a person who holds a license to practice medicine in this state.

Sec. 1701.702. Administration of Epinephrine. [Expires September 1, 2023]

(a) A law enforcement agency may acquire and possess epinephrine auto-injectors and a peace officer may possess and administer an epinephrine auto-injector in accordance with this subchapter.

(b) A peace officer may possess and administer an epinephrine auto-injector only if the peace officer has successfully completed training in the use of the device in a course approved by the commission.

(c) The commission, in consultation with the Department of State Health Services, shall approve a training course on the administration of an epinephrine auto-injector.

Sec. 1701.703. Prescription of Epinephrine. [Expires September 1, 2023]

(a) A physician, or a person who has been delegated prescriptive authority under Chapter 157, Occupations Code, may prescribe epinephrine auto-injectors in the name of a law enforcement agency.

(b) A physician or other person who prescribes epinephrine auto-injectors under Subsection (a) shall provide the law enforcement agency with a standing order for the administration of an epinephrine auto-injector to a person reasonably believed to be experiencing anaphylaxis.

(c) A standing order under Subsection (b) is not required to be patient-specific. An epinephrine auto-injector may be administered under this subchapter to a person without a previously established physician-patient relationship.

(d) Notwithstanding any other law, supervision or delegation by a physician is considered adequate if the physician:

(1) periodically reviews the order; and

(2) is available through direct telecommunication as needed for consultation, assistance, and direction.

(e) An order issued under this section must contain:

(1) the name and signature of the prescribing physician or other person;

(2) the name of the law enforcement agency to which the order is issued;

(3) the quantity of epinephrine auto-injectors to be obtained and maintained under the order; and

(4) the date the order was issued.

(f) A pharmacist may dispense an epinephrine auto-injector to a law enforcement agency without requiring the name of or any other identifying information relating to the user.

Sec. 1701.704. Maintenance and Administration of Epinephrine Auto-Injectors. [Expires September 1, 2023]

A law enforcement agency that acquires and possesses epinephrine auto-injectors under this subchapter shall adopt and implement a policy regarding the maintenance, administration, and disposal of the epinephrine auto-injectors. The policy must:

(1) establish a process for the agency to check the inventory of epinephrine auto-injectors at regular intervals for expiration and replacement; and

(2) require that the epinephrine auto-injectors be stored in a secure location.

Sec. 1701.705. Notification of Administration of Epinephrine Auto-Injector. [Expires September 1, 2023]

After an officer administers an epinephrine auto-injector under this subchapter, the law enforcement agency shall notify the physician or other person who prescribed the epinephrine auto-injector of:

(1) the age of the person to whom the epinephrine auto-injector was administered; and

(2) the number of epinephrine auto-injector doses administered to the person.

Sec. 1701.706. Gifts, Grants, and Donations. [Expires September 1, 2023]

A law enforcement agency may accept gifts, grants, donations, and federal and local money to implement this subchapter.

Sec. 1701.707. Not Practice of Health Care. [Expires September 1, 2023]

The administration by a peace officer of an epinephrine auto-injector to a person in accordance with the requirements of this subchapter or commission rules does not constitute the unlawful practice of any health care profession.

Sec. 1701.708. Immunity From Liability. [Expires September 1, 2023]

(a) A person who in good faith takes, or fails to take, action relating to the prescription of an epinephrine auto-injector to a law enforcement agency or the administration of an epinephrine auto-injector by a peace officer is immune from civil or criminal liability or disciplinary action resulting from that action or failure to act, including:

(1) issuing an order for epinephrine auto-injectors;

(2) supervising or delegating the administration of an epinephrine auto-injector;

(3) possessing, maintaining, storing, or disposing of an epinephrine auto-injector;

(4) prescribing an epinephrine auto-injector;

(5) dispensing an epinephrine auto-injector;

(6) administering, or assisting in administering, an epinephrine auto-injector;

(7) providing, or assisting in providing, training, consultation, or advice in the development, adoption, or implementation of policies, guidelines, rules, or plans; or

(8) undertaking any other act permitted or required under this subchapter.

(b) The immunities and protections provided by this subchapter are in addition to other immunities or limitations of liability provided by law.

(c) Notwithstanding any other law, this subchapter does not create a civil, criminal, or administrative cause of action or liability or create a standard of care, obligation, or duty that provides a basis for a cause of action for an act or omission under this subchapter.

(d) An act or omission described by this subchapter does not create a cause of action.

Sec. 1701.709. Governmental Immunity Not Waived. [Expires September 1, 2023]

This subchapter does not waive governmental immunity from suit or liability.

CHAPTER 1702
PRIVATE SECURITY

SUBCHAPTER I
PERSONAL PROTECTION OFFICER LICENSE REQUIREMENTS

Sec. 1702.206. Limited Authority to Carry Firearms.

(a) An individual acting as a personal protection officer may not carry a firearm unless the officer:

(1) is either:

(A) engaged in the exclusive performance of the officer's duties as a personal protection officer for the employer under whom the officer's personal protection officer license is issued; or

(B) traveling to or from the officer's place of assignment; and

(2) carries the officer's security officer commission and personal protection officer license on the officer's person while performing the officer's duties or traveling as described by Subdivision (1) and presents the commission and license on request.

(b) An individual who is acting as a personal protection officer and is wearing the uniform of a security officer, including any uniform or apparel described by Section 1702.323(d), may not conceal any firearm the individual is carrying and shall carry the firearm in plain view. An individual who is acting as a personal protection officer and is not wearing the uniform of a security officer shall conceal the firearm, regardless of whether the individual is authorized to openly carry the firearm under any other law.

TITLE 12
PRACTICES AND TRADES RELATED TO WATER, HEALTH, AND SAFETY

SUBTITLE B
PRACTICES RELATED TO HEALTH AND SAFETY

CHAPTER 1956
METAL RECYCLING ENTITIES

SUBCHAPTER A
GENERAL PROVISIONS

Sec. 1956.001. Definitions.

In this chapter:

(1) "Aluminum material" means a product made from aluminum, an aluminum alloy, or an aluminum by-product. The term includes aluminum wiring and an aluminum malt beverage keg but does not include another type of aluminum can used to contain a food or beverage.

(2) "Bronze material" means:

(A) a cemetery vase, receptacle, or memorial made from bronze;

(B) bronze statuary; or

(C) material readily identifiable as bronze, including bronze wiring.

(2-a) "Catalytic converter" includes any material removed from a catalytic converter.

(3) "Commission" means the Public Safety Commission.

(4) "Copper or brass material" means:

(A) a power inverter or insulated or noninsulated copper wire or cable that contains copper or an alloy of copper or zinc and is of the type used by:

(i) a public utility or common carrier;

(ii) a telecommunications provider as defined by Section 51.002, Utilities Code;

(iii) a cable service provider as defined by Section 66.002, Utilities Code; or

(iv) a video service provider as defined by Section 66.002, Utilities Code;

(B) a copper or brass item of a type commonly used in construction or by:

(i) a public utility;

(ii) a telecommunications provider as defined by Section 51.002, Utilities Code;

(iii) a cable service provider as defined by Section 66.002, Utilities Code; or

(iv) a video service provider as defined by Section 66.002, Utilities Code; or

(C) copper pipe or copper tubing.

(5) "Department" means the Texas Department of Public Safety.

(6) "Director" means the public safety director.

(6-a) "Explosive device" means a device or material that contains explosive powder, primer, fluid, or gas or a detonator. The term does not include:

Occupations Code

(A) a device that is designed, made, or adapted for delivering or shooting ammunition of .50 caliber or less and that is purchased for personal or security reasons recognized under state or federal law;

(B) a component of a motor vehicle or mechanical equipment, including equipment that is used in the exploration or production of minerals;

(C) any type of compressed cylinder that is commonly used in a residence or commercial business; or

(D) any type of scrap metal that is routinely purchased in the metal recycling industry and that is not associated with military weaponry.

(6-b) "Lead material" means:

(A) a commercial grade lead battery, lead-acid battery, or spiral cell battery; or

(B) a material or an item readily identifiable as being made of or containing lead.

(7) "Metal recycling entity" means a business that is operated from a fixed location and is predominantly engaged in:

(A) performing the manufacturing process by which scrap, used, or obsolete ferrous or nonferrous metal is converted into raw material products consisting of prepared grades and having an existing or potential economic value, by a method that in part requires the use of powered tools and equipment, including processes that involve processing, sorting, cutting, classifying, cleaning, baling, wrapping, shredding, shearing, or changing the physical form of that metal;

(B) the use of raw material products described under Paragraph (A) in the manufacture of producer or consumer goods; or

(C) purchasing or otherwise acquiring scrap, used, or obsolete ferrous or nonferrous metals for the eventual use of the metal for the purposes described by Paragraph (A) or (B).

(8) "Personal identification document" means:

(A) a valid driver's license issued by a state in the United States;

(B) a United States military identification card; or

(C) a personal identification certificate issued by the department under Section 521.101, Transportation Code, or a corresponding card or certificate issued by another state.

(9) "Regulated material" means:

(A) aluminum material;

(B) bronze material;

(C) copper or brass material;

(D) lead material; or

(E) regulated metal.

(10) "Regulated metal" means:

(A) manhole covers;

(B) guardrails;

(C) metal cylinders designed to contain compressed air, oxygen, gases, or liquids;

(D) malt beverage kegs made from metal other than aluminum;

(E) historical markers or cemetery vases, receptacles, or memorials made from metal other than aluminum;

(F) unused rebar;

(G) street signs;

(H) drain gates;

(I) safes;

(J) communication, transmission, and service wire or cable;

(K) condensing or evaporator coils for central heating or air conditioning units;

(L) utility structures, including the fixtures and hardware;

(M) aluminum or stainless steel containers designed to hold propane for fueling forklifts;

(N) metal railroad equipment, including tie plates, signal houses, control boxes, signs, signals, traffic devices, traffic control devices, traffic control signals, switch plates, e-clips, and rail tie functions;

(O) catalytic converters not attached to a vehicle;

(P) fire hydrants;

(Q) metal bleachers or other seating facilities used in recreational areas or sporting arenas;

(R) any metal item clearly and conspicuously marked with any form of the name, initials, or logo of a governmental entity, utility, cemetery, or railroad;

(S) insulated utility, communications, or electrical wire that has been burned in whole or in part to remove the insulation;

(T) backflow valves;

(U) metal in the form of commonly recognized products of the industrial metals recycling process, including bales, briquettes, billets, sows, ingots, pucks, and chopped or shredded metals; and

(V) commercial grade lead batteries or lead-acid batteries.

Sec. 1956.002. Exception.

This chapter does not apply to:

(1) a purchase of regulated material from a public utility, a telecommunications provider as defined by Section 51.002, Utilities Code, a cable service provider as defined by Section 66.002, Utilities Code, a video service provider as defined by Section 66.002, Utilities Code, or a manufacturing, industrial, commercial, retail, or other seller that sells regulated material in the ordinary course of the seller's business;

(2) a purchase of regulated material by a manufacturer whose primary business is the

manufacture of iron and steel products made from melting scrap iron and scrap steel; or

(3) the transport or hauling of recyclable materials to or from the metal recycling entity.

Sec. 1956.003. Local Law; Criminal Penalty.

(a) A county, municipality, or political subdivision of this state may adopt a rule, charter, or ordinance or issue an order or impose standards that are more stringent than but do not conflict with this chapter or rules adopted under this chapter.

(a-1) A county, municipality, or other political subdivision may require the record of purchase described under Section 1956.033 to contain a clear and legible thumbprint of a seller of regulated material.

(a-2) A county, municipality, or other political subdivision that, as authorized under Subsection (a), requires a metal recycling entity to report to the county, municipality, or political subdivision information relating to a sale of regulated material shall:

(1) include in any contract entered into by the county, municipality, or political subdivision relating to the reporting of the information a provision that:

(A) requires any contractor, subcontractor, or third party that has access to, comes into possession of, or otherwise obtains information relating to a sale of regulated material to maintain the confidentiality of all information received, including the name of the seller, the price paid for a purchase of regulated material, and the quantity of regulated material purchased; and

(B) allows the county, municipality, or political subdivision to terminate the contract of any contractor, subcontractor, or third party that violates the confidentiality provision required by Paragraph (A); and

(2) investigate a complaint alleging that a contractor, subcontractor, or third party has failed to maintain the confidentiality of information relating to a sale of regulated material.

(b) A county, municipality, or political subdivision of this state may issue a license or permit to a business to allow the business to act as a metal recycling entity in that county or municipality and may impose a fee not to exceed $250 for the issuance or renewal of the license or permit.

(b-1) [Expired pursuant to Acts 2007, 80th Leg., ch. 1316 (S.B. 1154), § 2, effective January 1, 2010.]

(c) A county, municipality, or political subdivision of this state that issues a license or permit to a business as authorized under Subsection (b) shall submit to the department in the manner required by the department information on each business that is issued a license or permit, including inspection reports for the business, information regarding violations of this chapter by the business, and information regarding disciplinary actions initiated against the business.

(d) A municipality or political subdivision of this state, other than a county, may not increase the local license or permit fee imposed on a metal recycling facility unless the increase is approved by the local governing body. A request for an increase in the local license or permit fee must be based on the costs associated with law enforcement and administration of the licensing or permitting program. The municipality or political subdivision must submit a report to the department on the law enforcement and administrative costs associated with the fee increase.

(e) A county may increase the local license or permit fee imposed on a metal recycling facility one additional time before the second anniversary of the date of the initial fee increase. The fee increase must be based on the average cost charged by municipalities statewide.

(f) A person commits an offense if the person owns or operates a metal recycling entity and does not hold a license or permit required by a county, municipality, or other political subdivision as authorized under Subsection (b). An offense under this subsection is a Class B misdemeanor unless it is shown on the trial of the offense that the person has been previously convicted under this subsection, in which event the offense is a Class A misdemeanor.

(f-1), (f-2) [Expired pursuant to Acts 2011, 82nd Leg., ch. 1234 (S.B. 694), § 3, effective March 1, 2013.]

(g) Notwithstanding any other law, a county, municipality, or other political subdivision must provide a minimum 30-day notice followed by a public hearing prior to enacting a prohibition on the sale or use of a recyclable product.

Sec. 1956.004. Civil Penalty.

(a) A person who owns or operates a metal recycling entity and does not hold a license or permit required by a county, municipality, or other political subdivision as authorized under Section 1956.003(b) is subject to a civil penalty of not more than $1,000 for each violation. In determining the amount of the civil penalty, the court shall consider:

(1) any other violations by the person; and

(2) the amount necessary to deter future violations.

Occupations Code

(b) A district attorney, county attorney, or municipal attorney may institute an action to collect the civil penalty provided by this section.

(c) Each day a violation occurs or continues to occur is a separate violation.

(d) The district attorney, county attorney, or municipal attorney may recover reasonable expenses incurred in obtaining a civil penalty under this section, including court costs, reasonable attorney's fees, investigative costs, witness fees, and deposition expenses.

(e), (f) [Expired pursuant to Acts 2011, 82nd Leg., ch. 1234 (S.B. 694), § 4, effective March 1, 2013.]

Sec. 1956.005. Record of Purchase [Renumbered].

Renumbered to Tex.Occ. Code § 1956.033 by Acts 2007, 80th Leg., ch. 1316 (S.B. 1154), § 2, effective September 1, 2007.

Sec. 1956.006. Preservation of Records [Renumbered].

Renumbered to Tex.Occ. Code § 1956.034 by Acts 2007, 80th Leg., ch. 1316 (S.B. 1154), § 2, effective September 1, 2007.

Sec. 1956.007. Inspection of Records by Peace Officer [Renumbered].

Renumbered to Tex.Occ. Code § 1956.035 by Acts 2007, 80th Leg., ch. 1316 (S.B. 1154), § 2, effective September 1, 2007.

Sec. 1956.008. Furnishing of Report to Department [Renumbered].

Renumbered to Tex.Occ. Code § 1956.036 by Acts 2007, 80th Leg., ch. 1316 (S.B. 1154), § 2, effective September 1, 2007.

Sec. 1956.009. Placement of Items on Hold [Renumbered].

Renumbered to Tex.Occ. Code § 1956.037 by Acts 2007, 80th Leg., ch. 1316 (S.B. 1154), § 2, effective September 1, 2007.

Sec. 1956.010. Prohibited Acts [Renumbered].

Renumbered to Tex.Occ. Code § 1956.038 by Acts 2007, 80th Leg., ch. 1316 (S.B. 1154), § 2, effective September 1, 2007.

SUBCHAPTER A-1 POWERS AND DUTIES

Sec. 1956.011. Administration of Chapter.

The department shall administer this chapter.

Sec. 1956.012. Department Staff.

The department may employ administrative and clerical staff as necessary to carry out this chapter.

Sec. 1956.013. Rules.

The commission may adopt rules to administer this chapter, including rules:

(1) establishing minimum requirements for registration under this chapter; and

(2) adopting forms required by this chapter.

Sec. 1956.014. Fees; Reports.

(a) The commission by rule shall prescribe fees in reasonable amounts sufficient to cover the costs of administering this chapter, including fees for:

(1) an initial application for a certificate of registration;

(2) issuance of a certificate of registration;

(3) issuance of a renewal certificate of registration; and

(4) issuance of a duplicate certificate of registration or duplicate renewal certificate of registration.

(b) [Repealed.]

(c) [Repealed.]

(d) [Expired pursuant to Acts 2007, 80th Leg., ch. 1316 (S.B. 1154), § 2, effective January 1, 2009.]

Sec. 1956.015. Statewide Electronic Reporting System.

(a) The department shall establish a statewide electronic reporting system to track the sales of regulated metal reported to the department under Section 1956.036.

(b) The department shall post a summary of the reports provided to the department under Section 1956.036 on the department's Internet website. The summary must include by county or region the frequency with which a person presents regulated materials for sale to a metal recycling entity. The summary may not identify any person to which the metal recycling entity sells the regulated materials.

(c) Subsection (b) does not apply to regulated material sold by a utility company, municipality, manufacturer, railroad, cemetery, cable or satellite entity, or other business entity that routinely has access to regulated metal.

(d) Information provided under this section is not subject to disclosure under Chapter 552, Government Code. The department may use information provided under this section for law enforcement purposes. Except as provided by this subsection, the department shall maintain the confidentiality of all information provided under this section, including the name of the seller, the price paid for a purchase of regulated material, and the quantity of regulated material purchased.

(e) The department may enter into contracts relating to the operation of the statewide electronic reporting system established by this section. A contract under this subsection must:

(1) require that any contractor, subcontractor, or third party that has access to, comes into possession of, or otherwise obtains information provided under this section maintain the confidentiality of all information provided under this section, including the name of the seller, the price paid for a purchase of regulated material, and the quantity of regulated material purchased; and

(2) provide that the department may terminate the contract of any contractor, subcontractor, or third party that violates the confidentiality provision required by Subdivision (1).

(f) The department shall investigate a complaint alleging that a contractor, subcontractor, or third party has failed to maintain the confidentiality of information relating to a sale of regulated material.

Sec. 1956.016. Registration Database.

The department shall make available on its Internet website a publicly accessible list of all registered metal recycling entities. The list must contain the following for each registered metal recycling entity:

(1) the entity's name;

(2) the entity's physical address; and

(3) the name of and contact information for a representative of the entity.

Sec. 1956.017. Advisory Committee.

(a) The department shall establish an advisory committee to advise the department on matters related to the department's regulation of metal recycling entities under this chapter.

(b) The advisory committee consists of 15 members appointed by the director as follows:

(1) one representative of the department;

(2) two representatives of local law enforcement agencies located in different municipalities, each with a population of 500,000 or more;

(3) two representatives of local law enforcement agencies located in different municipalities, each with a population of 200,000 or more but less than 500,000;

(4) one representative of a local law enforcement agency located in a municipality with a population of less than 200,000;

(5) five representatives of metal recycling entities;

(6) two members who represent industries that are impacted by theft of regulated material;

(7) one sheriff of a county with a population of 500,000 or more; and

(8) one sheriff of a county with a population of less than 500,000.

(c) The director shall ensure that the members of the advisory committee reflect the diverse geographic regions of this state.

(d) The advisory committee shall elect a presiding officer from among its members to serve a two-year term. A member may serve more than one term as presiding officer.

(e) The advisory committee shall meet annually and at the call of the presiding officer or the director.

(f) An advisory committee member is not entitled to compensation or reimbursement of expenses.

(g) Chapter 2110, Government Code, does not apply to the size, composition, or duration of the advisory committee or to the appointment of the committee's presiding officer.

SUBCHAPTER A-2 CERTIFICATE OF REGISTRATION

Sec. 1956.021. Registration Required.

A person may not act as a metal recycling entity or represent to the public that the person is a metal recycling entity unless the person is registered under this chapter.

Sec. 1956.022. Issuance of Certificate; Qualifications.

(a) The department shall issue a certificate of registration to an applicant who:

(1) applies and pays a registration fee; and

(2) presents any relevant evidence relating to the applicant's qualifications as required by commission rule.

(b) The commission by rule may establish qualifications for the holder of a certificate of registration under this chapter, which may include accepting copies of a license or permit issued by a county or municipality authorizing a metal recycling entity to conduct business in that county or municipality.

Sec. 1956.023. Term of Certificate.

(a) A certificate of registration is valid for two years after the date of issuance.

(b) The department shall adopt a system under which certificates of registration expire and are renewed on various dates.

(c) Not later than the 45th day before the date a person's certificate of registration is scheduled to expire, the department shall send written notice of the impending expiration to the person at the person's last known address according to the records of the department.

(d) A person whose certificate of registration has expired may not make a representation for which a certificate of registration is required under Section 1956.021 or perform collections services until the certificate has been renewed.

Sec. 1956.024. Renewal of Certificate.

(a) To renew a certificate of registration, a person must submit an application for renewal in the manner prescribed by the department.

(b) A person who is otherwise eligible to renew a certificate of registration may renew an unexpired certificate by paying the required renewal fee to the department before the expiration date of the certificate.

(c) A person whose certificate of registration has been expired for 90 days or less may renew the certificate by paying to the department a renewal fee that is equal to 1-½ times the normally required renewal fee.

(d) A person whose certificate of registration has been expired for more than 90 days but less than one year may renew the certificate by paying to the department a renewal fee that is equal to two times the normally required renewal fee.

(e) A person whose certificate of registration has been expired for one year or more may not renew the certificate. The person may obtain a new certificate of registration by complying with the requirements and procedures, including the examination requirements, for an original certificate.

SUBCHAPTER A-3 PRACTICE BY CERTIFICATE HOLDERS

Sec. 1956.031. Notice to Sellers.

(a) A metal recycling entity shall at all times maintain in a prominent place in the entity's place of business, in open view to a seller of regulated material, a notice in two-inch lettering that:

(1) includes the following language:

"A PERSON ATTEMPTING TO SELL ANY REGULATED MATERIAL MUST PRESENT SUFFICIENT IDENTIFICATION AND WRITTEN PROOF OF OWNERSHIP REQUIRED BY STATE LAW."

"WARNING: STATE LAW PROVIDES A CRIMINAL PENALTY FOR A PERSON WHO INTENTIONALLY PROVIDES A FALSE DOCUMENT OF IDENTIFICATION OR OTHER FALSE INFORMATION TO A METAL RECYCLING ENTITY WHILE ATTEMPTING TO SELL ANY REGULATED MATERIAL."; and

(2) states the metal recycling entity's usual business hours.

(b) The notice required by this section may be contained on a sign that contains another notice if the metal recycling entity is required to display another notice under applicable law.

Sec. 1956.032. Information Regarding Seller.

(a) Except as provided by Subsection (f), a person attempting to sell regulated material to a metal recycling entity shall:

(1) display to the metal recycling entity the person's personal identification document;

(2) provide to the metal recycling entity the make, model, color, and license plate number of the motor vehicle used to transport the regulated material and the name of the state issuing the license plate;

(3) either:

(A) present written documentation evidencing that the person is the legal owner or is lawfully entitled to sell the regulated material; or

(B) sign a written statement provided by the metal recycling entity that the person is the legal owner of or is lawfully entitled to sell the regulated material offered for sale;

(4) if the regulated material includes condensing or evaporator coils for central heating or air conditioning units, display to the metal recycling entity:

Occupations Code

(A) the person's air conditioning and refrigeration contractor license issued under Subchapter F or G, Chapter 1302;

(B) the person's air conditioning and refrigeration technician registration issued under Subchapter K, Chapter 1302;

(C) a receipt, bill of sale, or other documentation showing that the seller purchased the coils the seller is attempting to sell; or

(D) a receipt, bill of sale, or other documentation showing that the seller has purchased a replacement central heating or air conditioning unit; and

(5) if the regulated material includes insulated communications wire that has been burned wholly or partly to remove the insulation, display to the metal recycling entity documentation acceptable under the rules adopted under Subsection (h) that states that the material was salvaged from a fire.

(b) A person required by a municipality to prepare a signed statement consisting of the information required by Subsection (a)(3) may use the statement required by the municipality to comply with Subsection (a)(3).

(c) The metal recycling entity or the entity's agent shall visually verify the accuracy of the identification presented by the seller at the time of the purchase of regulated material and make a copy of the identification to be maintained by the entity in the entity's records, except as otherwise provided by Subsection (f).

(d) The metal recycling entity or the entity's agent for recordkeeping purposes may photograph the seller's entire face, not including any hat, and obtain the name of the seller's employer.

(e) The metal recycling entity or the entity's agent for recordkeeping purposes may take a photograph of the motor vehicle of the seller in which the make, model, and license plate number of the motor vehicle are identifiable in lieu of the information required under Subsection (a)(3).

(f) The metal recycling entity is not required to make a copy of the identification as required under Subsection (c) or collect the information required under Subsection (a)(3) if:

(1) the seller signs the written statement as required under Subsection (a)(3);

(2) the seller has previously provided the information required under Subsection (a); and

(3) the previously provided information has not changed.

(g) Notwithstanding Section 1956.002, the metal recycling entity shall verify the registration of a person attempting to sell regulated material who represents that the person is a metal recycling entity as follows:

(1) by using the database described by Section 1956.016; or

(2) by obtaining from the person a copy of the person's certificate of registration issued under Section 1956.022 in addition to the information required under Subsection (a).

(h) The commission shall adopt rules establishing the type of documentation that a seller of insulated communications wire described by Subsection (a)(5) must provide to a metal recycling entity to establish that the wire was salvaged from a fire.

Sec. 1956.0321. Additional Requirements Regarding Purchase of Catalytic Converter.

(a) In addition to the requirements of Section 1956.032, a person attempting to sell a catalytic converter to a metal recycling entity shall provide to the metal recycling entity:

(1) the year, make, model, and vehicle identification number for the vehicle from which the catalytic converter was removed; and

(2) a copy of the certificate of title or other documentation indicating that the person has an ownership interest in the vehicle described by Subdivision (1).

(b) A metal recycling entity may not purchase a catalytic converter from a seller who does not comply with the requirements of Subsection (a).

(c) A metal recycling entity may not purchase a catalytic converter unless the entity determines that the catalytic converter is consistent with the manufacturer's specifications for a catalytic converter from the vehicle for which the seller provided information under Subsection (a)(1).

(d) A metal recycling entity shall mark, in the manner prescribed by the commission by rule, each catalytic converter purchased by the entity with a unique number.

(e) A metal recycling entity shall keep an accurate electronic record or an accurate and legible written record of each purchase of a catalytic converter made in the course of the entity's business. The record must be in English and include:

(1) the information required by Section 1956.033;

(2) the vehicle information provided under Subsection (a)(1);

(3) a copy of the documentation described by Subsection (a)(2); and

(4) the unique number marked on the catalytic converter under Subsection (d).

Sec. 1956.033. Record of Purchase.

(a) Each metal recycling entity in this state shall keep an accurate electronic record or an accurate and legible written record of each purchase of regulated material made in the course of the entity's business from an individual.

(b) The record must be in English and include:

(1) the place, date, and amount of the purchase;

(2) the name and address of the seller in possession of the regulated material purchased;

(3) the identifying number of the seller's personal identification document;

(4) a description made in accordance with the custom of the trade of the commodity type and quantity of regulated material purchased;

(5) the information required by Sections 1956.032(a)(2) and (3);

(6) as applicable:

(A) the identifying number of the seller's air conditioning and refrigeration contractor license displayed under Section 1956.032(a)(4)(A);

(B) a copy of the seller's air conditioning and refrigeration technician registration displayed under Section 1956.032(a)(4)(B);

(C) a copy of the documentation described by Section 1956.032(a)(4)(C); or

(D) a copy of the documentation described by Section 1956.032(a)(4)(D);

(7) if applicable, a copy of the documentation described by Section 1956.032(a)(5);

(8) a copy of the documentation described by Section 1956.032(g);

(9) a copy of the documentation described by Section 1956.0381(b); and

(10) if the regulated material purchased is a catalytic converter, a clear and legible thumbprint of the seller unless the seller presents to the metal recycling entity a valid cash transaction card issued under Section 1956.0382.

Sec. 1956.0331. Photograph or Recording Requirement for Regulated Metal Transaction.

(a) In addition to the requirements of Sections 1956.032 and 1956.033, for each purchase by a metal recycling entity of an item of regulated metal, the entity shall obtain a digital photograph or video recording that accurately depicts the seller's entire face and each type of regulated metal purchased.

(b) A metal recycling entity shall preserve a photograph or recording required under Subsection (a) as follows:

(1) for a video recording, until the 91st day after the date of the transaction; and

(2) for a digital photograph, until the 181st day after the date of the transaction.

(c) The photograph or recording must be made available for inspection as provided by Section 1956.035 not later than 72 hours after the time of purchase.

Sec. 1956.034. Preservation of Records.

A metal recycling entity shall preserve each record required by Sections 1956.032, 1956.0321, and 1956.033 until the second anniversary of the date the record was made. The records must be kept in an easily retrievable format and must be available for inspection as provided by Section 1956.035 not later than 72 hours after the time of purchase.

Sec. 1956.035. Inspection of Records.

(a) On request, a metal recycling entity shall permit a peace officer of this state, a representative of the department, or a representative of a county, municipality, or other political subdivision that issues a license or permit under Section 1956.003(b) to inspect, during the entity's usual business hours:

(1) a record required by Section 1956.0321 or 1956.033;

(2) a digital photograph or video recording required by Section 1956.0331;

(3) regulated material in the entity's possession; or

(4) an application for a cash transaction card submitted to the entity.

(b) The person seeking to inspect a record or material shall:

(1) inform the entity of the officer's status as a peace officer; or

(2) if the person is a representative of the department or a representative of a county, municipality, or other political subdivision, inform the entity of the person's status and display to the entity an identification document or other appropriate documentation establishing the person's status as a representative of the department or of the appropriate county, municipality, or political subdivision.

Sec. 1956.036. Furnishing of Report to Department.

(a) Except as provided by Subsections (b) and (d), not later than the close of business on a metal recycling entity's second working day after the date of the purchase or other acquisition of material for which a record is required under Section 1956.0321 or 1956.033, the entity shall send an electronic transaction report to the department via the department's Internet website. Except as provided by Subsection (d-1), the report must contain the information required to be recorded under Sections 1956.0321 and 1956.033.

Occupations Code

(b) If a metal recycling entity purchases bronze material that is a cemetery vase, receptacle, memorial, or statuary or a pipe that can reasonably be identified as aluminum irrigation pipe, the entity shall:

(1) not later than the close of business on the entity's first working day after the purchase date, notify the department by telephone, by e-mail, or via the department's Internet website; and

(2) not later than the close of business on the entity's second working day after the purchase date, submit to the department electronically via the department's Internet website or file with the department a report containing the information required to be recorded under Section 1956.033.

(c) Subsection (b) does not apply to a purchase from:

(1) the manufacturer or fabricator of the material or pipe;

(2) a seller bearing a bill of sale for the material or pipe; or

(3) the owner of the material or pipe.

(d) A metal recycling entity may submit the transaction report required under Subsection (a) by facsimile if:

(1) the entity submits to the department annually:

(A) an application requesting an exception to the electronic reporting requirement; and

(B) an affidavit stating that the entity does not have an available and reliable means of submitting the transaction report electronically; and

(2) the department approves the entity's application under this subsection.

(d-1) A metal recycling entity is not required to include in a transaction report required by this section:

(1) the amount of the purchase; or

(2) a copy of the documentation described by Section 1956.0381(b).

(e) The department, after notice and an opportunity for a hearing, may prohibit a metal recycling entity from paying cash for a purchase of regulated material for a period determined by the department if the department finds that the entity has failed to comply with this section.

(f) A metal recycling entity shall report to the department by telephone, by e-mail, or through the department's Internet website the entity's possession of an explosive device unknowingly purchased or otherwise obtained by the entity not later than the close of business on the entity's first working day after the date the possession of the device is discovered. A metal recycling entity may also report to an appropriate law enforcement authority or the nearest military installation the possession of an explosive device that the entity unknowingly purchased or otherwise obtained so that the explosive device may be removed from the entity or disposed of as soon as possible.

Sec. 1956.037. Placement of Items on Hold.

(a) A metal recycling entity may not dispose of, process, sell, or remove from the premises an item of regulated metal unless:

(1) the entity acquired the item more than:

(A) eight days, excluding weekends and holidays, before the disposal, processing, sale, or removal, if the item is a cemetery vase, receptacle, or memorial made from a regulated material other than aluminum material;

(B) five days, excluding weekends and holidays, before the disposal, processing, sale, or removal, if the item is a catalytic converter; or

(C) 72 hours, excluding weekends and holidays, before the disposal, processing, sale, or removal, if the item is not an item described by Paragraph (A) or (B); or

(2) the entity purchased the item from a manufacturing, industrial, commercial, retail, or other seller that sells regulated material in the ordinary course of its business.

(b) A peace officer who has reasonable suspicion to believe that an item of regulated material in the possession of a metal recycling entity is stolen may place the item on hold by issuing to the entity a written notice that:

(1) specifically identifies the item alleged to be stolen and subject to the hold; and

(2) informs the entity of the requirements of Subsection (c).

(c) On receiving the notice, the entity may not, except as provided by Subsection (e), process or remove from the entity's premises the identified item before the 60th day after the date the notice is issued unless the hold is released at an earlier time in writing by a peace officer of this state or a court order.

(d) After the holding period expires, the entity may dispose of the item unless disposition violates a court order.

(e) If a hold is placed on a purchase of regulated material, a metal recycling entity may not dispose of, process, sell, or remove from the premises any item from the purchased material unless the hold on the material is released.

Sec. 1956.038. Prohibited Acts.

(a) A person may not, with the intent to deceive:

(1) display to a metal recycling entity a false or invalid personal identification document in

Occupations Code

connection with the person's attempted sale of regulated material;

(2) make a false, material statement or representation to a metal recycling entity in connection with:

(A) that person's execution of a written statement required by Section 1956.032(a)(3); or

(B) the entity's efforts to obtain the information required under Section 1956.033(b);

(3) display or provide to a metal recycling entity any information required under Section 1956.032 that the person knows is false or invalid; or

(4) display another individual's personal identification document in connection with the sale of regulated material.

(a-1) A metal recycling entity may only pay for a purchase of regulated material in the manner provided by Section 1956.0381.

(b) A metal recycling entity may not pay for a purchase of regulated material in cash if:

(1) the entity does not hold a certificate of registration under Subchapter A-2 and, if applicable, a license or permit required by a county, municipality, or other political subdivision as authorized under Section 1956.003(b); or

(2) the entity has been prohibited by the department from paying cash under Section 1956.036(e).

(c) Notwithstanding Section 1956.003(a) or any other law, a county, municipality, or other political subdivision may not adopt or enforce a rule, charter, or ordinance or issue an order or impose standards that limit the use of cash by a metal recycling entity in a manner more restrictive than that provided by Subsection (b).

(d) Subsection (c) does not apply to a rule, charter, ordinance, or order of a county, municipality, or other political subdivision in effect on January 1, 2011.

(d1), (d2) [Expired pursuant to Acts 2011, 82nd Leg., ch. 1234 (S.B. 694), § 15, effective March 1, 2012.]

(e) The department or a county, municipality, or other political subdivision may bring an action in the county in which a metal recycling entity is located to enjoin the business operations of the owner or operator of the metal recycling entity for a period of not less than 30 days and not more than 90 days if the owner or operator has not submitted an application for a certificate of registration or the appropriate license or permit required by a county, municipality, or other political subdivision.

(f) An action under Subsection (e) must be brought in the name of the state. If judgment is in favor of the state, the court shall:

(1) enjoin the owner or operator from maintaining or participating in the business of a metal recycling entity for a definite period of not less than 30 days and not more than 90 days, as determined by the court; and

(2) order that the place of business of the owner or operator be closed for the same period.

Sec. 1956.0381. Payment by Metal Recycling Entity.

(a) A metal recycling entity may pay for a purchase of regulated material only by:

(1) cash if the seller has been issued a cash transaction card under Section 1956.0382, unless the metal recycling entity is prohibited from paying in cash under Section 1956.038(b);

(2) debit card if the seller has been issued a cash transaction card under Section 1956.0382;

(3) check;

(4) money order; or

(5) direct deposit by electronic funds transfer.

(b) A metal recycling entity shall include in the record of purchase required by Section 1956.033, as applicable, a copy of:

(1) the seller's cash transaction card or approved application for a cash transaction card if the entity paid for a purchase of regulated material by cash;

(2) the debit card receipt and the seller's cash transaction card or approved application for a cash transaction card if the entity paid for a purchase of regulated material by debit card; or

(3) the check if the entity paid for a purchase of regulated material by check.

Sec. 1956.0382. Cash Transaction Card.

(a) A metal recycling entity may pay a seller for a purchase of regulated material by cash or debit card only if, before the entity issues payment:

(1) the seller presents to the entity a valid cash transaction card issued by the entity or by another metal recycling entity located in this state; or

(2) the entity obtains a copy of the seller's cash transaction card from the records of the entity.

(b) An application for the issuance or renewal of a cash transaction card must include:

(1) the name, address, sex, and birth date of the applicant;

(2) the identification number from the applicant's personal identification document;

(3) a digital photograph that accurately depicts the applicant's entire face taken at the time the applicant completes the application;

(4) a clear and legible thumbprint of the applicant; and

(5) the signature of the applicant.

(c) On receipt of an application that contains the information required by Subsection (b), a metal recycling entity may approve the application and issue a cash transaction card to the applicant. The individual approving the application on behalf of the metal recycling entity must sign the application.

(d) A cash transaction card must include:

(1) the name and address of the seller;

(2) a digital photograph of the seller that accurately depicts the seller's entire face;

(3) an identifying number that is unique to the individual card; and

(4) the expiration date of the card, which may not be later than two years from the date the card was issued or renewed.

(e) A metal recycling entity must mail the issued cash transaction card to the address provided on the application for the card.

(f) A cash transaction card issued under this section is not transferable.

(g) A metal recycling entity shall preserve:

(1) each application for a cash transaction card the entity receives until the second anniversary of the date the application was received; and

(2) a copy of each cash transaction card the entity issues or renews until the second anniversary of the date the card was issued or renewed.

Sec. 1956.039. Hours for Purchasing Material.

(a) Subject to Subsection (b), a county, municipality, or political subdivision may establish the hours during which a metal recycling entity may purchase regulated material.

(b) A metal recycling entity may not purchase from the general public regulated material:

(1) more than 15 consecutive hours in one day; or

(2) later than 9 p.m.

Sec. 1956.040. Criminal Penalty.

(a) A person commits an offense if the person knowingly violates Section 1956.038. Except as otherwise provided by this subsection, an offense under this subsection is a Class A misdemeanor unless it is shown on trial of the offense that the person has previously been convicted of a violation of this subchapter, in which event the offense is a state jail felony. An offense under this subsection involving a catalytic converter is a state jail felony unless it is shown on trial of the offense that the person has previously been convicted of a violation of this subchapter involving a catalytic converter, in which event the offense is a felony of the third degree.

(a-1) A person commits an offense if the person knowingly violates Section 1956.021, 1956.023(d), 1956.036(a), or 1956.039.

(a-2) An offense under Subsection (a-1) is a Class A misdemeanor, except that any fine imposed may not exceed $10,000. If it is shown on trial of an offense under Subsection (a-1) that the person has previously been convicted of a violation of that subsection, the offense is a state jail felony.

(a-3) It is an affirmative defense to prosecution of a violation of Section 1956.021 or 1956.023(d) that the person made a diligent effort to obtain or renew a certificate of registration at the time of the violation.

(a-4) A municipality or county may retain 10 percent of the money collected from a fine for a conviction of an offense under Subsection (a-1) as a service fee for that collection and the clerk of the court shall remit the remainder of the fine collected for conviction of an offense under Subsection (a-1) to the comptroller in the manner provided for the remission of fees to the comptroller under Subchapter B, Chapter 133, Local Government Code. The comptroller shall deposit proceeds received under this subsection to the credit of an account in the general revenue fund, and those proceeds may be appropriated only to the department and used to:

(1) finance the department's administration of Subchapters A, A-1, A-2, and A-3; and

(2) fund grants distributed under the prevention of scrap metal theft grant program established under Subchapter O, Chapter 411, Government Code.

(b) A person commits an offense if the person knowingly buys:

(1) stolen regulated material; or

(2) insulated communications wire that has been burned wholly or partly to remove the insulation, unless the wire is accompanied by documentation acceptable under the rules adopted under Section 1956.032(h) that states that the material was salvaged from a fire.

(b-1) Except as otherwise provided by Subsection (b-2), an offense under Subsection (b) is a Class A misdemeanor unless it is shown on trial of the offense that the person has previously been convicted under Subsection (b), in which event the offense is a state jail felony.

(b-2) An offense under Subsection (b)(1) in which the regulated material purchased was a catalytic converter is a state jail felony unless it is shown on trial of the offense that the person has previously been convicted of an offense under Subsection (b)(1) in which the regulated material purchased was a catalytic converter, in which event the offense is a felony of the third degree.

(c) A person commits an offense if the person knowingly sells stolen regulated material. An offense under this subsection is a state jail felony unless it is shown on trial of the offense that the person has previously been convicted under this subsection, in which event the offense is a third degree felony.

(c-1) A person commits an offense if the person knowingly sells an explosive device to a metal recycling entity.

(c-2) A metal recycling entity commits an offense if the entity knowingly buys an explosive device.

(c-3) Except as provided by Subsection (c-5), an offense under Subsection (c-1) or (c-2) is a Class A misdemeanor.

(c-4) A metal recycling entity commits an offense if the entity knowingly stores or allows to be stored on the entity's premises an explosive device. Except as provided by Subsection (c-5), an offense under this subsection is a Class A misdemeanor. For purposes of this subsection, a metal recycling entity is considered to store an explosive device on the entity's premises beginning not earlier than 72 hours after the time a person presents the explosive device to the entity for sale or an attempted sale and ending at the time the entity reports the presence of the explosive device on the entity's premises to the department. A metal recycling entity is not liable under this section for the time it takes for the department, a law enforcement agency, or a military installation to respond to the entity's report that the entity possesses an explosive device.

(c-5) An offense under Subsection (c-1), (c-2), or (c-4) is a felony of the second degree if it is shown at the trial of the offense that a person suffered death or serious bodily injury, as defined by Section 1.07, Penal Code, as a result of the detonation of an explosive device.

(d) On the conviction of a metal recycling entity for an offense punishable under Subsection (b), a court, in addition to imposing any other applicable penalty, may order that the entity cease doing business as a metal recycling entity for a period not to exceed:

(1) 30 days from the date of the order for each violation that forms the basis of the conviction for a first offense; and

(2) 180 days from the date of the order for each violation that forms the basis of the conviction if it is shown on trial of the offense that the person has previously been convicted under this section.

(d-1) On conviction of an offense under Subsection (c-1), (c-2), or (c-4), the court may order the defendant to make restitution to:

(1) the state or a political subdivision of the state for the costs incurred by the state or subdivision for responding to the offense and any removal, cleaning, sanitizing, demolition, reconstruction, or other treatment required as a result of the offense; and

(2) the owner of any property damaged as a result of the offense.

(e) If conduct that constitutes an offense under this section also constitutes an offense under any other law, the actor may be prosecuted under this section or the other law.

Sec. 1956.041. Administrative Penalty.

(a) The commission, after notice and an opportunity for a hearing, may impose an administrative penalty on a person who:

(1) violates this subchapter or Subchapter A-2 or a rule or order of the commission under this chapter; or

(2) engages in conduct that would constitute an offense under Section 1956.040(c-2) or (c-4).

(b) Except as provided by Subsection (b-1), the amount of the administrative penalty may not exceed $1,000. Each day a violation occurs or continues to occur is a separate violation for the purpose of imposing a penalty under this section. In determining the amount of the administrative penalty under this section, the commission shall consider:

(1) the seriousness of the violation, including the nature, circumstances, extent, and gravity of the violation;

(2) the economic harm caused by the violation;

(3) the history of previous violations;

(4) the amount necessary to deter a future violation;

(5) efforts to correct the violation; and

(6) any other matter that justice may require.

(b-1) The amount of an administrative penalty for engaging in conduct described by Subsection (a)(2) or for a violation of Section 1956.036(f) may not exceed $1,000 for each violation. The aggregate penalty under this subsection for multiple violations may not exceed $10,000.

(b-2) [Repealed.]

(c) [Repealed.]

(d) [Repealed.]

(e) [Repealed.]

(f) [Repealed.]

SUBCHAPTER B SALE OF CRAFTED PRECIOUS METAL TO DEALERS

Sec. 1956.051. Definitions.

In this subchapter:

(1) "Commission" means the Finance Commission of Texas.

(2) "Commissioner" means the consumer credit commissioner.

(3) "Crafted precious metal" means jewelry, silverware, an art object, or another object, made wholly or partly from precious metal and used primarily for personal, family, or household purchases. The term does not include:

(A) a coin;

(B) a bar;

(C) a commemorative medallion;

(D) an item selling at 105 percent or more of the scrap value of the item;

(E) an item made wholly or partly from precious metal and used for a dental, pharmaceutical, or medical application; or

(F) an item made wholly or partly from precious metal extracted, recovered, or salvaged from an industrial by-product or industrial waste product.

(4) "Dealer" means a person registered to engage in the business of purchasing and selling crafted precious metal, including purchases or sales made through the mail.

(5) "Department" means the Texas Department of Public Safety.

(5-a) "Jewelry store" means a retail establishment that derives 75 percent or more of its annual revenue from the sale to consumers of crafted precious metal or other items of personal adornment, including watches, bracelets, necklaces, brooches, rings, and earrings.

(6) "Precious metal" means gold, silver, platinum, palladium, iridium, rhodium, osmium, ruthenium, or an alloy of those metals.

Sec. 1956.0511. Administration by Commission.

(a) Notwithstanding any other provision of this chapter, the commission shall administer and enforce this subchapter, unless the context clearly requires another state agency to perform a specific duty.

(b) To the extent of any conflict between this subchapter and other provisions of this chapter, this subchapter prevails.

Sec. 1956.052. Applicability of Subchapter. [Repealed]

Sec. 1956.053. Exception: Precious Metal Extracted, Recovered, or Salvaged from Industrial By-Products or Industrial Waste Products. [Repealed]

Sec. 1956.054. Exception: Dental, Pharmaceutical, or Medical Application of Crafted Precious Metal. [Repealed]

Sec. 1956.055. Exception: Crafted Precious Metal Acquired from Another Dealer Who Previously Made Required Reports.

This subchapter does not apply to crafted precious metal acquired in good faith in a transaction involving the stock-in-trade of another dealer who previously made the reports concerning that metal as required by this subchapter if:

(1) the selling dealer delivers to the acquiring dealer a written document stating that the reports have been made;

(2) the acquiring dealer submits a copy of the statement to the chief of police of the municipality or the sheriff of the county in which the selling dealer is located; and

(3) each dealer involved in the transaction retains a copy of the statement until the third anniversary of the date of the transaction.

Sec. 1956.056. Exception: Crafted Precious Metal Acquired in Dissolution or Liquidation Sale.

This subchapter does not apply to crafted precious metal acquired in a nonjudicial sale, transfer, assignment, assignment for the benefit of creditors, or consignment of the assets or stock-in-trade, in bulk, or a substantial part of those assets, of an industrial or commercial enterprise, other than a dealer, for the voluntary dissolution or liquidation of the seller's business, or for disposing of an excessive quantity of personal property, or property that has been acquired in a nonjudicial sale or transfer from an owner other than a dealer, the seller's entire household of personal property, or a substantial part of that property, if the dealer:

(1) gives written notice to the chief of police of the municipality or the sheriff of the county in which the dealer's business is located that a reporting exemption is being claimed under this section;

(2) retains in the dealer's place of business, until the third anniversary of the date of the transaction, a copy of the bill of sale, receipt, inventory list, or other transfer document; and

(3) makes the record retained available for inspection by a peace officer.

Sec. 1956.057. Exception: Crafted Precious Metal Acquired in Judicial Sale.

This subchapter does not apply to crafted precious metal acquired in a sale made:

(1) by any public officer in the officer's official capacity as a trustee in bankruptcy, executor, administrator, receiver, or public official acting under judicial process or authority; or

(2) on the execution of, or by virtue of, any process issued by a court.

Sec. 1956.058. Exception: Crafted Precious Metal Acquired As Payment for Other Crafted Precious Metal by Person in Business of Selling to Consumers.

This subchapter does not apply to crafted precious metal acquired in good faith as part or complete payment for other crafted precious metal by a person whose principal business is primarily that of selling directly to the consumer crafted precious metal that has not been subject to a prior sale.

Sec. 1956.059. Exception: Crafted Precious Metal Acquired from or Reported to Governmental Agency.

This subchapter does not apply to crafted precious metal:

(1) acquired as surplus property from the United States, a state, a subdivision of a state, or a municipal corporation; or

(2) reported by a dealer as an acquisition or a purchase, or reported as destroyed or otherwise disposed of, to:

(A) a state agency under another law of this state; or

(B) a municipal or county office or agency under another law of this state or a municipal ordinance.

Sec. 1956.060. Exception: Crafted Precious Metal Acquired by Person Licensed Under Texas Pawnshop Act.

This subchapter does not apply to crafted precious metal acquired by:

(1) a person licensed under Chapter 371, Finance Code; or

(2) an entity affiliated with a person licensed under Chapter 371, Finance Code, if the entity's recordkeeping practices satisfy the requirements of that chapter.

Sec. 1956.061. Effect on Other Laws and Ordinances.

This subchapter does not:

(1) excuse noncompliance with another state law or municipal ordinance covering the reporting, holding, or releasing of crafted precious metal;

(2) prohibit a municipality from enacting, amending, or enforcing an ordinance relating to a dealer; or

(3) supersede a municipal ordinance except to the extent the ordinance does not require reporting for transactions involving crafted precious metal.

Sec. 1956.0611. Rulemaking.

The commission may adopt rules necessary to implement and enforce this subchapter.

Sec. 1956.0612. Registration As Dealer.

(a) A person may not engage in the business of purchasing and selling crafted precious metal unless the person is registered with the commissioner as a dealer under this section.

(b) To register as a dealer, a person must provide to the commissioner:

(1) a list of each location in this state at which the person will conduct business as a dealer; and

(2) a processing fee for each location included on the list furnished under Subdivision (1).

(b-1) A registration issued under this section is valid for the period prescribed by commission rule adopted under Section 14.112, Finance Code.

(c) The commissioner shall prescribe the processing fee in an amount necessary to cover the costs of administering this subchapter.

(d) The commission by rule shall establish a deadline for the submission of the information and fee required by Subsection (b) for initial issuance and renewal of registrations under this section.

(d-1) After the applicable deadline for initial or renewal registrations, a dealer may amend the registration required under Subsection (a) to reflect any change in the information provided by the registration.

(e) The commissioner shall make available to the public a list of dealers registered under this section.

(f) The commissioner may prescribe the registration form.

(g) A reference to a registration in another subchapter of this chapter does not apply to a person to the extent the person is registered under this subchapter.

(h) The commissioner may refuse to renew the registration of a person who fails to comply with an order issued by the commissioner to enforce this chapter.

Sec. 1956.0613. Investigation by Commissioner.

The commissioner shall:

(1) monitor the operations of a dealer to ensure compliance with this subchapter; and

(2) receive and investigate complaints against a dealer or a person acting as a dealer.

Sec. 1956.06131. Examination by Commissioner. [Effective January 1, 2022]

(a) At the times the commissioner considers necessary, the commissioner or the commissioner's representative may:

(1) examine each place of business of each dealer; and

(2) investigate the dealer's transactions and records, including books, accounts, papers, and correspondence, to the extent the transactions and records pertain to the business regulated under this subchapter.

(b) A dealer shall:

(1) give the commissioner or the commissioner's representative free access to the dealer's office, place of business, files, safes, and vaults; and

(2) allow the commissioner or the representative to make a copy of an item that may be investigated under Subsection (a)(2).

(c) The commissioner or the commissioner's representative shall examine under Subsection (a) at least 10 dealers each calendar year.

(d) This section does not apply with respect to a jewelry store.

Sec. 1956.0614. Revocation of Registration.

(a) The commissioner may revoke the registration of a dealer if the commissioner concludes that the dealer has violated this chapter or an order issued by the commissioner to enforce this chapter. The commissioner shall recite the basis of the decision in an order revoking the registration.

(b) If the commissioner proposes to revoke a registration, the dealer is entitled to a hearing before the commissioner or a hearings officer, who shall propose a decision to the commissioner. The commissioner or hearings officer shall prescribe the time and place of the hearing. The hearing is governed by Chapter 2001, Government Code.

(c) A dealer aggrieved by a ruling, order, or decision of the commissioner is entitled to appeal to a district court in the county in which the hearing was held. An appeal under this subsection is governed by Chapter 2001, Government Code.

Sec. 1956.0615. Administrative Penalty.

The commissioner may assess an administrative penalty not to exceed $500 against a person for each knowing and wilful violation of this chapter.

Sec. 1956.0616. Notice of Enforcement Order.

(a) As soon as practicable after an enforcement order against a dealer for a violation of this subchapter becomes final, including an order assessing an administrative penalty or an order to pay restitution under Section 14.251(b)(3), Finance Code, the commissioner shall provide notice of the order to:

(1) the chief of police of the municipality in which the violation occurred; or

(2) the sheriff of the county in which the violation occurred, if the violation did not occur in a municipality.

(b) The notice must include:

(1) a copy of the enforcement order;

(2) the information on complaint procedures described by Section 14.062(b), Finance Code; and

(3) any other information the commissioner considers necessary or proper to the enforcement of this subchapter.

Sec. 1956.062. Report of Purchase Required.

(a) A dealer shall, as required by Section 1956.063, report all identifiable crafted precious metal that the dealer purchases, takes in trade, accepts for sale on consignment, or accepts for auction.

(b) Before crafted precious metal is offered for sale or exchange, a dealer must notify each person intending to sell or exchange the metal that, before the dealer may accept any of the person's property, the person must file with the dealer a list describing all of the person's crafted precious metal to be accepted by the dealer. The list must contain:

(1) the proposed seller's name and address;

(2) a complete and accurate description of the crafted precious metal; and

(3) the proposed seller's certification that the information is true and complete.

(c) The dealer shall record the proposed seller's driver's license number or department personal identification certificate number on physical presentation of the license or personal identification certificate by the seller. The record must accompany the list.

(d) The dealer shall:

(1) provide to a peace officer, on demand, the list required by Subsection (b); and

Occupations Code

(2) mail or deliver a complete copy of the list to the chief of police or the sheriff as provided by Section 1956.063 not later than 48 hours after the list is filed with the dealer.

Sec. 1956.063. Form of Report; Filing.

(a) A report required by this subchapter must comply with this section unless a similar report is required by another state law or a municipal ordinance, in which event the required report must comply with the applicable law or ordinance.

(b) If a transaction regulated by this subchapter occurs in a municipality that maintains a police department, the original and a copy of the report required by this subchapter shall be submitted to the municipality's chief of police. If the transaction does not occur in such a municipality, the original and a copy of the report shall be submitted to the sheriff of the county in which the transaction occurs.

(c) For each transaction regulated by this subchapter, the dealer shall submit a report on a preprinted and prenumbered form prescribed by the commissioner or in the manner described by Subsection (c-1). The form must include the following:

(1) the date of the transaction;

(2) a description of the crafted precious metal purchased by the dealer;

(3) the name and physical address of the dealer; and

(4) the name, physical description, and physical address of the seller or transferor.

(c-1) A dealer may submit a list required by Section 1956.062(b) to satisfy the reporting requirement under this section if the list contains the information described by Subsection (c).

(d) The dealer shall retain a copy of the report until the third anniversary of the date the report is filed.

Sec. 1956.064. Required Retention of Crafted Precious Metal.

(a) A dealer may not melt, deface, alter, or dispose of crafted precious metal that is the subject of a report required by this subchapter before the 11th day after the date the report is filed unless:

(1) the peace officer to whom the report is submitted, for good cause, authorizes disposition of the metal;

(2) the dealer obtains the name, address, and description of the buyer and retains a record of that information; or

(3) the dealer is a pawnbroker and the disposition is the redemption of pledged property by the pledgor.

(b) A peace officer who has reasonable suspicion to believe that an item of crafted precious metal in the possession of a dealer is stolen may place the item on hold for a period not to exceed 60 days by issuing to the dealer a written notice that:

(1) specifically identifies the item alleged to be stolen and subject to the hold; and

(2) informs the dealer of the requirements of Subsection (c).

(c) On receiving the notice, the dealer may not melt, deface, alter, or dispose of the identified crafted precious metal until the hold is released in writing by a peace officer of this state or a court order.

Sec. 1956.065. Inspection of Crafted Precious Metal by Peace Officer.

(a) A dealer shall make crafted precious metal purchased by the dealer available for inspection by a peace officer during regular business hours while in the dealer's possession.

(b) Information obtained under this section is confidential except for use in a criminal investigation or prosecution or a civil court proceeding.

Sec. 1956.066. Purchase from Minor.

(a) A dealer may not purchase crafted precious metal from a person younger than 18 years of age unless the seller delivers to the dealer before the purchase a written statement from the seller's parent or legal guardian consenting to the transaction.

(b) The dealer shall retain the statement with the records required to be kept under this subchapter. The dealer may destroy the statement after the later of:

(1) the date the item is sold; or

(2) the first anniversary of the date the dealer purchased the item.

Sec. 1956.067. Purchase at Temporary Location of Dealer.

(a) A dealer who conducts business at a temporary location for a period of less than one year may not engage in the business of buying precious metal or used items made of precious metal unless, within a 12-month period at least 30 days before the date on which each purchase is made, the dealer has filed:

(1) a registration statement with the department;

(2) a copy of the registration statement and a copy of the dealer's certificate of registration issued under this subchapter with the local law enforcement agency of:

(A) the municipality in which the temporary location is located; or

(B) if the temporary location is not located in a municipality, the county in which the temporary location is located; and

(3) a copy of the dealer's certificate of registration issued under this subchapter with the county and, if applicable, the municipality in which the temporary location is located.

(b) The registration statement must contain:

(1) the name and address of the dealer;

(2) the location where business is to be conducted;

(3) if the dealer is an association, the name and address of each member of the association;

(4) if the dealer is a corporation, the name and address of each officer and director of the corporation; and

(5) other relevant information required by the department.

Sec. 1956.068. Purchase of Melted Items.

A dealer, in the course of business, may not purchase from a person other than a manufacturer of or a regular dealer in crafted precious metal an object formed as the result of the melting of crafted precious metal.

Sec. 1956.069. Criminal Penalty.

(a) A person commits an offense if the person:

(1) fails to make or permit inspection of a report as required by Section 1956.062 or 1956.063;

(2) violates Section 1956.0612 or 1956.064;

(3) fails to obtain or retain a statement as required by Section 1956.066;

(4) fails to file a registration statement as required by Section 1956.067; or

(5) purchases an object in violation of Section 1956.068.

(b) An offense under this section is a Class B misdemeanor.

SUBCHAPTER C RESTRICTIONS ON SALE OF CERTAIN ITEMS TO METAL RECYCLING ENTITIES

Sec. 1956.101. Definitions.

In this subchapter:

(1) [Repealed by Acts 2007, 80th Leg., ch. 1316 (S.B. 1154), § 5, effective September 1, 2007.]

(2) "Motor vehicle" has the meaning assigned by Section 541.201, Transportation Code.

(3) "PCB-containing capacitor" means a capacitor that contains polychlorinated biphenyls and is regulated under the federal Toxic Substances Control Act (15 U.S.C. Section 2601 et seq.).

(4) "Person" means an individual, corporation, partnership, sole proprietorship, or other business entity.

Sec. 1956.102. Exception.

This subchapter does not apply to a sale or transfer by or on behalf of a metal recycling entity.

Sec. 1956.103. Restrictions on Transfer of Certain Property.

(a) A person may not sell or otherwise transfer to a metal recycling entity:

(1) a lead-acid battery, fuel tank, or PCB-containing capacitor that is included with another type of scrap, used, or obsolete metal without first obtaining from the metal recycling entity a written and signed acknowledgment that the scrap, used, or obsolete metal includes one or more lead-acid batteries, fuel tanks, or PCB-containing capacitors;

(2) any of the following items that contain or enclose a lead-acid battery, fuel tank, or PCB-containing capacitor or of which a lead-acid battery, fuel tank, or PCB-containing capacitor is a part:

(A) a motor vehicle;

(B) a motor vehicle that has been junked, flattened, dismantled, or changed so that it has lost its character as a motor vehicle;

(C) an appliance; or

(D) any other item of scrap, used, or obsolete metal;

(3) a motor vehicle or a motor vehicle that has been junked, flattened, dismantled, or changed so that it has lost its character as a motor vehicle if the motor vehicle includes, contains, or encloses a tire or scrap tire; or

(4) a metal alcoholic beverage keg, regardless of condition, unless the seller is the manufacturer of the keg, the brewer or distiller of the beverage that was contained in the keg, or an authorized representative of the manufacturer, brewer, or distiller.

(b) Subsection (a)(3) does not apply to the sale or other transfer of a motor vehicle or a junked, flattened, dismantled, or changed motor vehicle from another state.

(c) Subsection (a) does not apply to a fuel tank that has been completely drained and rendered unusable in accordance with Texas Commission on Environmental Quality rules regardless of whether the fuel tank is attached to a motor vehicle.

Sec. 1956.104. Notice of Restrictions.

A metal recycling entity shall post in a conspicuous location a notice that:

(1) is readily visible to a person selling material to the metal recycling entity;

(2) is at least 24 inches horizontally by 18 inches vertically; and

(3) contains the following language:

TEXAS LAW PROHIBTS:

1. THE SALE OF A WHOLE, FLATTENED OR JUNKED MOTOR VEHICLE, AN APPLIANCE, OR ANY OTHER SCRAP METAL ITEM CONTAINING A LEAD-ACID BATTERY, FUEL TANK THAT HAS NOT BEEN COMPLETELY DRAINED AND RENDERED UNUSABLE, OR PCB-CONTAINING CAPACITOR; AND

2. THE SALE OF LEAD-ACID BATTERIES, FUEL TANKS THAT HAVE NOT BEEN COMPLETELY DRAINED AND RENDERED UNUSABLE, OR PCB-CONTAINING CAPACITORS INCLUDED WITH OTHER SCRAP METALS WITHOUT PRIOR WRITTEN ACKNOWLEDGMENT.

VIOLATION OF THIS LAW IS A MISDEMEANOR

Sec. 1956.105. Criminal Penalty.

(a) A person commits an offense if the person violates this subchapter.

(b) An offense under this section is a misdemeanor punishable by:

(1) a fine of not more than $1,000;

(2) confinement in the county jail for not more than 60 days; or

(3) both the fine and the confinement.

SUBCHAPTER D DISCIPLINARY PROCEDURES

Sec. 1956.151. Denial of Certificate; Disciplinary Action.

The commission shall deny an application for a certificate of registration, suspend or revoke a certificate of registration, or reprimand a person who is registered under this chapter if the person:

(1) obtains a certificate of registration by means of fraud, misrepresentation, or concealment of a material fact;

(2) sells, barters, or offers to sell or barter a certificate of registration;

(3) violates a provision of this chapter or a rule adopted under this chapter; or

(4) violates Section 1956.021.

Sec. 1956.152. Investigation. [Repealed]

Sec. 1956.153. Hearing.

(a) A person whose application for a certificate of registration is denied, whose certificate of registration is suspended or revoked, or who is reprimanded is entitled to a hearing before the department if the person submits to the department a written request for the hearing.

(b) A hearing is governed by department rules for a contested hearing and by Chapter 2001, Government Code.

SUBCHAPTER E OTHER PENALTIES AND ENFORCEMENT PROVISIONS

Sec. 1956.201. Enforcement Proceedings; Injunction.

(a) The department, the attorney general, or the district, county, or city attorney for the county or municipality in which an alleged violation of this chapter occurs may, on receipt of a verified complaint, bring an appropriate administrative or judicial proceeding to enforce this chapter or a rule adopted under this chapter.

(b) The attorney general or an attorney representing the state may initiate an action for an injunction to prohibit a person from violating this chapter or a rule adopted under this chapter.

Sec. 1956.202. Civil Penalty.

(a) Except as provided by Subsection (d), a person who violates this chapter or a rule adopted under this chapter is liable to this state for a civil penalty of not more than $1,000 for each violation.

(b) The amount of the penalty shall be based on:

(1) the seriousness of the violation;
(2) the history of previous violations;
(3) the amount necessary to deter a future violation; and
(4) any other matter that justice may require.

(c) The attorney general may sue to collect a civil penalty under this section. In the suit the attorney general may recover, on behalf of the state, the reasonable expenses incurred in obtaining the penalty, including investigation and court costs, reasonable attorney's fees, witness fees, and other expenses.

(d) A civil penalty may not be assessed under this section for conduct described by Section 1956.021, 1956.023(d), 1956.036(a), 1956.038, or 1956.039.

Sec. 1956.203. Criminal Penalty for Certain Solicitation.

(a) A person commits an offense if the person solicits the purchase of regulated material at a location other than a business location at which the material is produced as a by-product in the ordinary course of that business.

(b) An offense under this section is a Class B misdemeanor.

Sec. 1956.204. General Criminal Penalty.

(a) A person commits an offense if the person violates this chapter or a rule adopted under this chapter, including a rule, charter, or ordinance adopted, an order issued, or a standard imposed by a county, municipality, or political subdivision under Section 1956.003.

(b) An offense under this section is a Class C misdemeanor.

(c) If conduct that constitutes an offense under this section also constitutes an offense under another section in this chapter, the person may be prosecuted only under that other section.

TITLE 13
SPORTS, AMUSEMENTS, ENTERTAINMENT

SUBTITLE A
GAMING

CHAPTER 2002
CHARITABLE RAFFLES

SUBCHAPTER A
GENERAL PROVISIONS

Sec. 2002.001. Short Title.

This chapter may be cited as the Charitable Raffle Enabling Act.

Sec. 2002.002. Definitions.

In this chapter:

(1) "Charitable purposes" means:
(A) benefitting needy or deserving persons in this state, indefinite in number, by:
(i) enhancing their opportunities for religious or educational advancement;
(ii) relieving them from disease, suffering, or distress;
(iii) contributing to their physical well-being;
(iv) assisting them in establishing themselves in life as worthy and useful citizens; or
(v) increasing their comprehension of and devotion to the principles on which this nation was founded and enhancing their loyalty to their government;
(B) initiating, performing, or fostering worthy public works in this state; or
(C) enabling or furthering the erection or maintenance of public structures in this state.

(1-a) "Money" means coins, paper currency, or a negotiable instrument that represents and is readily convertible to coins or paper currency.

(2) "Qualified organization" means a qualified religious society, qualified volunteer fire department, qualified volunteer emergency medical service, or qualified nonprofit organization.

(3) "Qualified religious society" means a church, synagogue, or other organization or association organized primarily for religious purposes that:
(A) has been in existence in this state for at least 10 years; and
(B) does not distribute any of its income to its members, officers, or governing body, other than as reasonable compensation for services or for reimbursement of expenses.

(4) "Qualified volunteer emergency medical service" means an association that:
(A) is organized primarily to provide and actively provides emergency medical, rescue, or ambulance services;
(B) does not pay its members compensation other than nominal compensation; and
(C) does not distribute any of its income to its members, officers, or governing body other than for reimbursement of expenses.

Occupations Code

(5) "Qualified volunteer fire department" means an association that:

(A) operates fire-fighting equipment;

(B) is organized primarily to provide and actively provides fire-fighting services;

(C) does not pay its members compensation other than nominal compensation; and

(D) does not distribute any of its income to its members, officers, or governing body, other than for reimbursement of expenses.

(6) "Raffle" means the award of one or more prizes by chance at a single occasion among a single pool or group of persons who have paid or promised a thing of value for a ticket that represents a chance to win a prize.

(7) "Reverse raffle" means a raffle in which the last ticket or tickets drawn are considered the winning tickets.

Sec. 2002.003. Qualified Nonprofit Organization.

(a) An organization incorporated or holding a certificate of authority under the Texas Non-Profit Corporation Act (Article 1396-1.01 et seq., Vernon's Texas Civil Statutes) is a qualified nonprofit organization for the purposes of this chapter if the organization:

(1) does not distribute any of its income to its members, officers, or governing body, other than as reasonable compensation for services;

(2) has existed for the three preceding years;

(3) does not devote a substantial part of its activities to attempting to influence legislation and does not participate or intervene in any political campaign on behalf of any candidate for public office in any manner, including by publishing or distributing statements or making campaign contributions;

(4) qualifies for and has obtained an exemption from federal income tax from the Internal Revenue Service under Section 501(c), Internal Revenue Code of 1986; and

(5) does not have or recognize any local chapter, affiliate, unit, or subsidiary organization in this state.

(b) An organization that is formally recognized as and that operates as a local chapter, affiliate, unit, or subsidiary organization of a parent organization incorporated or holding a certificate of authority under the Texas Non-Profit Corporation Act (Article 1396-1.01 et seq., Vernon's Texas Civil Statutes) is a qualified nonprofit organization if:

(1) neither the local organization nor the parent organization distributes any of its income to its members, officers, or governing body, other than as reasonable compensation for services;

(2) the local organization has existed for the three preceding years and during those years has been formally recognized as a local chapter, affiliate, unit, or subsidiary organization of the parent organization;

(3) neither the local organization nor the parent organization:

(A) devotes a substantial part of its activities to attempting to influence legislation; or

(B) participates or intervenes in any political campaign on behalf of any candidate for public office in any manner, including by publishing or distributing statements or making campaign contributions; and

(4) either the local organization or the parent organization qualifies for and has obtained an exemption from federal income tax from the Internal Revenue Service under Section 501(c), Internal Revenue Code of 1986.

(b-1) An organization that is formally recognized as and that operates as a local chapter, affiliate, unit, or subordinate lodge of a grand lodge or other institution or order incorporated under Title 32, Revised Statutes, as authorized by Article 1399, Revised Statutes, is a qualified nonprofit organization if:

(1) neither the local organization nor the incorporated grand lodge or other institution or order distributes any of its income to its members, officers, or governing body, other than as reasonable compensation for services;

(2) the local organization has existed for the three preceding years and during those years:

(A) has had a governing body or officers elected by a vote of its members or by a vote of delegates elected by its members; or

(B) has been formally recognized as a local chapter, affiliate, unit, or subordinate lodge of the grand lodge or other institution or order;

(3) neither the local organization nor the incorporated grand lodge or other institution or order:

(A) devotes a substantial part of its activities to attempting to influence legislation; or

(B) participates or intervenes in any political campaign on behalf of any candidate for public office in any manner, including by publishing or distributing statements or making campaign contributions; and

(4) either the local organization or the incorporated grand lodge or other institution or order qualifies for and has obtained an exemption from federal income tax from the Internal Revenue Service under Section 501(c), Internal Revenue Code of 1986, or other applicable provision.

(c) An unincorporated organization, association, or society is a qualified nonprofit organization if it:

(1) does not distribute any of its income to its members, officers, or governing body, other than as reasonable compensation for services;

(2) for the three preceding years has been affiliated with a state or national organization organized to perform the same purposes as the unincorporated organization, association, or society;

(3) does not devote a substantial part of its activities to attempting to influence legislation and does not participate or intervene in any political campaign on behalf of any candidate for public office in any manner, including by publishing or distributing statements or making campaign contributions; and

(4) qualifies for and has obtained an exemption from federal income tax from the Internal Revenue Service under Section 501(c), Internal Revenue Code of 1986.

(d) An organization, association, or society is considered to devote a substantial part of its activities to attempting to influence legislation for purposes of this section if, in any 12-month period in the preceding three years, more than 10 percent of the organization's expenditures were made to influence legislation.

(e) A nonprofit wildlife conservation association and its local chapters, affiliates, wildlife cooperatives, or units are qualified nonprofit organizations under this chapter if the parent association meets the eligibility criteria under this section other than the requirement prescribed by Subsection (a)(3), (b)(3), (b-1)(3), or (c)(3), as applicable. An association or a local chapter, affiliate, wildlife cooperative, or unit that is eligible under this subsection may not use any proceeds from a raffle conducted under this chapter to attempt to influence legislation or participate or intervene in a political campaign on behalf of a candidate for public office in any manner, including by publishing or distributing a statement or making a campaign contribution. For purposes of this section, a nonprofit wildlife conservation association includes an association that supports wildlife, fish, or fowl.

Sec. 2002.004. Imputed Actions of Organization.

For purposes of this chapter, an organization performs an act if a member, officer, or agent of the organization performs the act with the consent or authorization of the organization.

Sec. 2002.005. Applicability.

This chapter does not apply to a savings promotion raffle authorized under Chapter 280, Finance Code.

SUBCHAPTER B OPERATION OF RAFFLE

Sec. 2002.051. Raffle Authorized.

A qualified organization may conduct a raffle subject to the conditions imposed by this subchapter.

Sec. 2002.052. Time and Frequency Restrictions.

(a) In this section, "calendar year" means a period beginning January 1 and ending on the succeeding December 31.

(b) A raffle is not authorized by this chapter if the organization awards prizes in the raffle in a calendar year in which the organization has previously awarded prizes in four other raffles. For purposes of this subsection, a raffle conducted in a preceding calendar year for which a prize or prizes are awarded on a later date set in accordance with Subsection (e) that occurs in a subsequent calendar year is not included in the number of raffles for which prizes are awarded by the organization in that subsequent calendar year.

(c) [Repealed.]

(d) Before selling or offering to sell tickets for a raffle, a qualified organization shall set a date on which the organization will award the prize or prizes in a raffle. The organization must award the prize or prizes on that date unless the organization becomes unable to award the prize or prizes on that date.

(e) A qualified organization that is unable to award a prize or prizes on the date set under Subsection (d) may set another date not later than 30 days from the date originally set on which the organization will award the prize or prizes.

(f) If the prize or prizes are not awarded within the 30 days as required by Subsection (e), the organization must refund or offer to refund the amount paid by each person who purchased a ticket for the raffle.

Sec. 2002.053. Use of Raffle Proceeds.

All proceeds from the sale of tickets for a raffle must be spent for the charitable purposes of the qualified organization.

Sec. 2002.054. Restrictions on Raffle Promotion and Ticket Sales.

(a) The organization may not:

(1) directly or indirectly, by the use of paid advertising, promote a raffle through a medium of mass communication, including television, radio, or newspaper;

(2) promote or advertise a raffle statewide, other than on the organization's Internet website or through a publication or solicitation, including a newsletter, social media, or electronic mail, provided only to previously identified supporters of the organization; or

(3) sell or offer to sell tickets for a raffle statewide.

(b) Except as provided by this subsection, the organization may not compensate a person directly or indirectly for organizing or conducting a raffle or for selling or offering to sell tickets to a raffle. A member of the organization who is employed by the organization may organize and conduct a raffle, but the member's work organizing or conducting a raffle may not be more than a de minimis portion of the member's employment with the organization.

(c) Except as provided by Section 2002.0541, the organization may not permit a person who is not authorized by the organization to sell or offer to sell raffle tickets.

Sec. 2002.0541. Reverse Raffle.

(a) A qualified organization may conduct a reverse raffle as provided by this section.

(b) Notwithstanding Section 2002.056(a), a refund of the purchase price of a ticket may be awarded as a raffle prize in a reverse raffle.

(c) Notwithstanding Section 2002.055(3), after the drawing of tickets in a reverse raffle has begun, the qualified organization conducting the raffle may auction off additional tickets to persons who are present at the drawing for a price other than the price printed on the ticket.

(d) After the drawing of tickets in a reverse raffle has begun, the qualified organization may permit a ticket holder present at the drawing to resell the ticket to another person present at the drawing for an amount greater than the original purchase price of the ticket. The sale must be made through a designated representative of the organization, and not less than 10 percent of the sale proceeds must be retained by the organization.

(e) Notwithstanding Section 2002.055(3), after the drawing of tickets in a reverse raffle has begun, the qualified organization may permit the holder of a previously drawn ticket:

(1) to purchase additional chances for the ticket to be selected to win a prize; or

(2) to purchase additional tickets for the raffle.

(f) Only the portion of the proceeds from the resale of a ticket under Subsection (d) retained by the organization are subject to Section 2002.053. All proceeds from the sale of additional chances for a ticket under Subsection (e) are considered to be proceeds from the sale of the ticket for purposes of Section 2002.053.

Sec. 2002.055. Ticket Disclosures.

The following information must be printed on each raffle ticket sold or offered for sale:

(1) the name of the organization conducting the raffle;

(2) the address of the organization or of a named officer of the organization;

(3) the ticket price;

(4) a general description of each prize having a value of more than $10 to be awarded in the raffle; and

(5) the date on which the raffle prize or prizes will be awarded.

Sec. 2002.056. Restrictions on Prizes.

(a) A prize offered or awarded at a raffle may not be money.

(b) Except as provided by Subsections (b-1) and (c), the value of a prize offered or awarded at a raffle that is purchased by the organization or for which the organization provides any consideration may not exceed $75,000.

(b-1) The value of a residential dwelling offered or awarded as a prize at a raffle that is purchased by the organization or for which the organization provides any consideration may not exceed $250,000.

(c) A raffle prize may consist of one or more tickets in the state lottery authorized by Chapter 466, Government Code, with a face value of $75,000 or less, without regard to whether a prize in the lottery game to which the ticket or tickets relate exceeds $75,000.

(d) A raffle is not authorized by this chapter unless the organization:

(1) has the prize to be offered in the raffle in its possession or ownership; or

(2) posts bond with the county clerk of the county in which the raffle is to be held for the full amount of the money value of the prize.

Sec. 2002.057. Ticket Sale on University Property.

An institution of higher education, as defined by Section 61.003, Education Code, shall allow a qualified organization that is a student organization recognized by the institution to sell raffle tickets at any facility of the institution, subject to reasonable restrictions on the time, place, and manner of the sale.

Sec. 2002.058. Injunctive Action Against Unauthorized Raffle.

(a) A county attorney, district attorney, criminal district attorney, or the attorney general may bring an action in county or district court for a permanent or temporary injunction or a temporary restraining order prohibiting conduct involving a raffle or similar procedure that:

(1) violates or threatens to violate state law relating to gambling; and

(2) is not authorized by this chapter or other law.

(b) Venue for an action under this section is in the county in which the conduct occurs or in which a defendant in the action resides.

CHAPTER 2003 INSPECTION AND REGULATION OF GAMBLING VESSELS

SUBCHAPTER A GENERAL PROVISIONS

Sec. 2003.001. Definition.

In this chapter, "department" means the Department of Public Safety of the State of Texas.

Sec. 2003.002. Application of Chapter.

This chapter applies only to a vessel on which activity described by Section 47.02(a), Penal Code, is regularly conducted, whether or not the activity occurs in this state.

SUBCHAPTER B STATE INSPECTION AND REGULATION

Sec. 2003.051. Criminal History Record Information.

(a) The department may request criminal history record information from the Federal Bureau of Investigation or any other law enforcement agency relating to a person who owns, has a financial interest in, operates, or is employed by a person who operates a vessel in this state, including the territorial waters of this state, whether or not the operation of the vessel is in violation of law.

(b) The department may maintain records of information obtained under Subsection (a).

Sec. 2003.052. Inspection.

The department may inspect a vessel located in this state, including the territorial waters of this state, to ensure that the vessel is operated in compliance with state or other law.

SUBCHAPTER C MUNICIPAL INSPECTION AND REGULATION

Sec. 2003.101. Regulation.

(a) A municipality, by ordinance, may impose regulations for the protection of the health and safety of the passengers or crew of a vessel that:

(1) regularly boards passengers in the municipality; or

(2) is regularly loaded, fueled, repaired, stored, or docked in the municipality.

(b) A municipal ordinance may not prohibit an activity relating to a vessel that is expressly permitted under Chapter 47, Penal Code, or other state law.

Sec. 2003.102. Inspection.

A municipality may inspect a vessel docked in the municipality to determine if the vessel is operated in compliance with Chapter 47, Penal Code, a municipal ordinance, or other law.

SUBTITLE D OTHER AMUSEMENTS AND ENTERTAINMENT

CHAPTER 2154 REGULATION OF FIREWORKS AND FIREWORKS DISPLAYS

SUBCHAPTER F PROHIBITED ACTS

Sec. 2154.254. Employment of Minors.

(a) Except as provided by Subsection (c), a person may not employ or allow a person younger than 16 years of age to manufacture, distribute, sell, or purchase fireworks in the course of the person's business.

(b) Except as provided by Subsection (c), a person may not employ a person 16 years of age or older but younger than 18 years of age to sell fireworks at a retail sales location unless the person selling fireworks at that location is accompanied by another person who is at least 18 years of age.

(c) An owner of a retail sales location may employ a person who is otherwise prohibited from engaging in that activity by Subsection (a) or (b) to sell fireworks at the owner's retail sales location if the person employed is:

(1) a member of the owner's immediate family;

(2) 12 years of age or older; and

(3) accompanied by another person who is at least 18 years of age while the person is engaged in selling fireworks at that location.

TITLE 14 REGULATION OF MOTOR VEHICLES AND TRANSPORTATION

SUBTITLE A REGULATIONS RELATED TO MOTOR VEHICLES

CHAPTER 2302 SALVAGE VEHICLE DEALERS

SUBCHAPTER A GENERAL PROVISIONS

Sec. 2302.001. Definitions.

In this chapter:

(1) "Casual sale," "damage," "insurance company," "major component part," "metal recycler," "motor vehicle," "nonrepairable motor vehicle," "nonrepairable vehicle title," "out-of-state buyer," "salvage motor vehicle," "salvage vehicle title," "salvage vehicle dealer," and "used part" have the meanings assigned by Section 501.091, Transportation Code.

(2) "Board" means the board of the Texas Department of Motor Vehicles.

(3) "Department" means the Texas Department of Motor Vehicles.

(4) "Federal safety certificate" means the label or tag required under 49 U.S.C. Section 30115 that certifies that a motor vehicle or equipment complies with applicable federal motor vehicle safety standards.

(5) "Salvage pool operator" means a person who engages in the business of selling nonrepairable motor vehicles or salvage motor vehicles at auction, including wholesale auction, or otherwise.

(6) [Repealed.]

Sec. 2302.0015. Consent to Entry and Inspection.

(a) A person consents to an entry or inspection described by Subsection (b) by:

(1) accepting a license under this chapter; or

(2) engaging in a business or activity regulated under this chapter.

(b) For the purpose of enforcing or administering this chapter or Chapter 501 or 502, Transportation Code, a member of the board, an employee or agent of the board or department, a member of the Public Safety Commission, an officer of the Department of Public Safety, or a peace officer may at a reasonable time:

(1) enter the premises of a business regulated under one of those chapters; and

(2) inspect or copy any document, record, vehicle, part, or other item regulated under one of those chapters.

(c) A person described by Subsection (a):

(1) may not refuse or interfere with an entry or inspection under this section; and

(2) shall cooperate fully with a person conducting an inspection under this section to assist in the recovery of stolen motor vehicles and parts and to prevent the sale or transfer of stolen motor vehicles and parts.

(d) An entry or inspection occurs at a reasonable time for purposes of Subsection (b) if the entry or inspection occurs:

(1) during normal business hours of the person or activity regulated under this chapter; or

(2) while an activity regulated under this chapter is occurring on the premises.

Sec. 2302.002. Classification of Vehicles [Repealed].

Repealed by Acts 2003, 78th Leg., ch. 1325 (H.B. 3588), § 17.09(2), effective September 1, 2003.

Sec. 2302.003. Classification As Metal Recycler [Repealed].

Repealed by Acts 2003, 78th Leg., ch. 1325 (H.B. 3588), § 17.09(2), effective September 1, 2003.

Sec. 2302.004. Sale of Certain Water-Damaged Vehicles [Repealed].

Repealed by Acts 2003, 78th Leg., ch. 1325 (H.B. 3588), § 17.09(2), effective September 1, 2003.

Sec. 2302.005. Applicability of Certain Municipal Ordinances, Licenses, and Permits.

This chapter:

(1) is in addition to any municipal ordinance relating to the regulation of a person who deals in nonrepairable or salvage motor vehicles or used parts; and

(2) does not prohibit the enforcement of a requirement of a municipal license or permit that is related to an activity regulated under this chapter.

Sec. 2302.006. Application of Chapter to Metal Recyclers.

(a) Except as provided by Subsections (b) and (c), this chapter does not apply to a transaction in which a metal recycler is a party.

(b) This chapter applies to a transaction in which a motor vehicle:

(1) is sold, transferred, released, or delivered to a metal recycler for the purpose of reuse or resale as a motor vehicle; and

(2) is used for that purpose.

(c) Sections 2302.0015 and 2302.205 apply to a metal recycler.

Sec. 2302.007. Application of Chapter to Insurance Companies.

This chapter does not apply to an insurance company.

Sec. 2302.008. Applicability of Chapter to Used Automotive Parts Recyclers.

This chapter does not apply to a used automotive parts recycler licensed under Chapter 2309.

Sec. 2302.009. Rebuilding of Assembled Vehicle Prohibited. [Renumbered to Tex. Occ. Code § 2302.010]

Sec. 2302.010. Rebuilding of Assembled Vehicle Prohibited. [Renumbered from Tex. Occ. Code § 2302.009]

A salvage vehicle dealer may not, as part of engaging in a business or activity regulated under this chapter, rebuild an assembled vehicle, as defined by Section 731.001, Transportation Code.

SUBCHAPTER B BOARD POWERS AND DUTIES

Sec. 2302.051. Rules and Enforcement Powers.

The board shall adopt rules as necessary to administer this chapter and may take other action as necessary to enforce this chapter.

Sec. 2302.052. Duty to Set Fees.

The board shall set application fees, license fees, renewal fees, and other fees as required to implement this chapter. The board shall set the fees in amounts reasonable and necessary to implement and enforce this chapter.

Sec. 2302.053. Rules Restricting Advertising or Competitive Bidding.

(a) The board may not adopt a rule under Section 2302.051 restricting advertising or competitive bidding by a person who holds a license issued under this chapter except to prohibit false, misleading, or deceptive practices by the person.

(b) The board may not include in its rules to prohibit false, misleading, or deceptive practices a rule that:

(1) restricts the use of any advertising medium;

(2) restricts the person's personal appearance or use of the person's voice in an advertisement;

(3) relates to the size or duration of an advertisement by the person; or

(4) restricts the use of a trade name in advertising by the person.

SUBCHAPTER C LICENSE REQUIREMENTS

Sec. 2302.101. [As amended by Acts 2019, 86th Leg., ch. XXX (S.B. 604)] Salvage Vehicle Dealer License.

(a) Unless a person holds a salvage vehicle dealer license issued under this chapter, the person may not:

(1) act as a salvage vehicle dealer or rebuilder; or

(2) store or display a motor vehicle as an agent or escrow agent of an insurance company.

(b) A person who holds a salvage vehicle dealer license issued under this chapter may perform any of the activities of a salvage vehicle dealer, including:

(1) buying salvage motor vehicles and nonrepairable motor vehicles or selling salvage motor vehicles and nonrepairable motor vehicles that have been issued a salvage vehicle title or nonrepairable vehicle title, as appropriate;

(2) engaging in the business of selling nonrepairable motor vehicles or salvage motor vehicles at auction, including wholesale auction;

(3) offering or negotiating to sell or buy salvage motor vehicles or nonrepairable motor vehicles owned by a license holder and to be purchased or sold by another license holder;

(4) acting as the agent or representative of a license holder in performing an act described by Subdivision (3); and

(5) acquiring and repairing, rebuilding, or reconstructing for operation on a public highway more than five salvage motor vehicles in a calendar year.

Sec. 2302.102. Salvage Vehicle Dealer License Classification. [Repealed]

Sec. 2302.103. Application for Salvage Vehicle Dealer License.

To apply for a salvage vehicle dealer license, a person must submit to the department an application on a form prescribed by the department and the application fee.

Sec. 2302.104. Contents of Application.

(a) An application for a salvage vehicle dealer license must include:

(1) the name, business address, and business telephone number of the applicant;

(2) the name under which the applicant proposes to conduct business;

(3) the location, by number, street, and municipality, of each office at which the applicant proposes to conduct business;

(4) a statement indicating whether the applicant previously applied for a license under this chapter and, if so, a statement indicating the result of the previous application and indicating whether the applicant has ever been the holder of a license issued under this chapter that was revoked or suspended;

(5) a statement of the previous history, record, and associations of the applicant to the extent sufficient to establish, to the satisfaction of the department, the business reputation and character of the applicant;

(6) the applicant's federal tax identification number, if any;

(7) the applicant's state sales tax number; and

(8) any other information required by rules adopted under this chapter.

(b) In addition to the information required by Subsection (a), the application of a corporation must include:

(1) the state of its incorporation;

(2) the name, address, date of birth, and social security number of each principal officer or director of the corporation;

(3) a statement of the previous history, record, and associations of each officer and each director to the extent sufficient to establish, to the satisfaction of the department, the business reputation and character of the applicant; and

(4) a statement showing whether an officer, director, or employee of the applicant has been refused a license as a salvage vehicle dealer or has been the holder of a license issued under this chapter that was revoked or suspended.

(c) In addition to the information required by Subsection (a), the application of a partnership must include:

(1) the name, address, date of birth, and social security number of each owner or partner;

(2) a statement of the previous history, record, and associations of each owner and each partner to the extent sufficient to establish, to the satisfaction of the department, the business reputation and character of the applicant; and

(3) a statement showing whether an owner, partner, or employee of the applicant has been refused a license as a salvage vehicle dealer or has been the holder of a license issued under this chapter that was revoked or suspended.

Sec. 2302.105. Department Investigation.

(a) The department may not issue a license under this chapter until the department completes an investigation of the applicant's qualifications.

(b) The department shall conduct the investigation not later than the 15th day after the date the department receives the application. The department shall report to the applicant the results of the investigation.

Sec. 2302.106. License Issuance.

(a) The department shall issue a license to an applicant who meets the license qualifications adopted under this chapter and pays the required fees.

(b) A license may not be issued in a fictitious name that may be confused with or is similar to that of a governmental entity or that is otherwise deceptive or misleading to the public.

Sec. 2302.107. Salvage Vehicle Agent License. [Repealed]

Sec. 2302.108. Disciplinary Action.

(a) The department may deny, suspend, revoke, or reinstate a license issued under this chapter.

(b) The board by rule shall establish the grounds for denial, suspension, revocation, or reinstatement of a license issued under this chapter and the procedures for disciplinary action. A rule adopted under this subsection may not conflict with a rule adopted by the State Office of Administrative Hearings.

(c) A proceeding under this section is subject to Chapter 2001, Government Code.

(d) A person whose license is revoked may not apply for a new license before the first anniversary of the date of the revocation.

SUBCHAPTER D LICENSE EXPIRATION AND RENEWAL

Sec. 2302.151. License Expiration.

(a) A license issued under this chapter is valid for the period prescribed by the board.

(b) A person whose license has expired may not engage in the activities that require a license until the license has been renewed under this subchapter.

(c) If the board prescribes the term of a license under this chapter for a period other than one year, the board shall prorate the applicable fee required under this chapter as necessary to reflect the term of the license.

Sec. 2302.152. Notice of Expiration.

Not later than the 31st day before the expiration date of a person's license, the department shall send written notice of the impending expiration to the person at the person's last known address according to department records.

Sec. 2302.153. Procedures for Renewal.

(a) A person who is otherwise eligible to renew a license issued under this chapter may renew an unexpired license by paying the required renewal fee to the department on or before the expiration date of the license.

(b) A person whose license has been expired for 90 days or less may renew the license by paying to the department a renewal fee that is equal to 1-½ times the normally required renewal fee.

(c) A person whose license has been expired for more than 90 days but less than one year may renew the license by paying to the department a renewal fee that is equal to two times the normally required renewal fee.

(d) A person whose license has been expired for one year or longer may not renew the license. The person may obtain a new license by complying with the requirements and procedures for obtaining an original license.

(e) A person who was licensed in this state, moved to another state, and has been doing business in the other state for the two years preceding the date of application may renew an expired license. The person must pay to the department a renewal fee that is equal to two times the normally required renewal fee.

SUBCHAPTER E CONDUCTING BUSINESS

Sec. 2302.201. Duties on Acquisition of Salvage Motor Vehicle.

(a) Except as provided by Section 501.0935, Transportation Code, a salvage vehicle dealer who acquires ownership of a salvage motor vehicle from an owner must receive from the owner a properly assigned title.

(b) The dealer shall comply with Subchapter E, Chapter 501, Transportation Code.

Sec. 2302.202. Records of Purchases.

A salvage vehicle dealer shall maintain a record of each salvage motor vehicle purchased or sold by the dealer.

Sec. 2302.203. Registration of New Business Location.

Occupations Code

Before moving a place of business or opening an additional place of business, a salvage vehicle dealer must register the new location with the department.

Sec. 2302.204. Casual Sales.

This chapter does not apply to a person who purchases fewer than five nonrepairable motor vehicles or salvage motor vehicles from a salvage vehicle dealer, an insurance company or salvage pool operator in a casual sale at auction, except that:

(1) the board shall adopt rules as necessary to regulate casual sales by salvage vehicle dealers, insurance companies, or salvage pool operators and to enforce this section; and

(2) a salvage vehicle dealer, insurance company, or salvage pool operator who sells a motor vehicle in a casual sale shall comply with those rules and Subchapter E, Chapter 501, Transportation Code.

Sec. 2302.205. Duty of Metal Recycler.

A metal recycler who purchases a motor vehicle shall submit a regular certificate of title or a nonrepairable or salvage vehicle title or comparable out-of-state ownership document to the department and comply with Subchapter E, Chapter 501, Transportation Code.

SUBCHAPTER F ADDITIONAL DUTIES OF SALVAGE VEHICLE DEALER IN CONNECTION WITH MOTOR VEHICLE COMPONENT PARTS

Sec. 2302.251. Definitions.

In this subchapter:

(1) "Component part" means a major component part as defined in Section 501.091, Transportation Code, or a minor component part.

(2) "Interior component part" means a seat or radio of a motor vehicle.

(3) "Minor component part" means an interior component part, a special accessory part, or a motor vehicle part that displays or should display one or more of the following:

(A) a federal safety certificate;

(B) a motor number;

(C) a serial number or a derivative; or

(D) a manufacturer's permanent vehicle identification number or a derivative.

(4) "Special accessory part" means a tire, wheel, tailgate, or removable glass top of a motor vehicle.

Sec. 2302.252. Removal of License Plates; Inventory.

(a) Immediately on receipt of a motor vehicle, a salvage vehicle dealer shall remove any unexpired license plates from the vehicle and place the license plates in a secure, locked place.

(b) A salvage vehicle dealer shall maintain on a form provided by the department an inventory of unexpired license plates removed under Subsection (a). The inventory must include:

(1) each license plate number;

(2) the make of the motor vehicle from which the license plate was removed;

(3) the motor number of that vehicle; and

(4) the vehicle identification number of that vehicle.

Sec. 2302.253. Receipt of Motor Vehicle by Holder of Endorsement As Used Vehicle Parts Dealer [Repealed].

Repealed by Acts 2009, 81st Leg., ch. 783 (S.B. 1095), § 12, effective September 1, 2009 and by Acts 2009, 81st Leg., ch. 933 (H.B. 3097), § 4.12, effective September 1, 2009.

Sec. 2302.254. Record of Purchase; Inventory of Parts.

(a) A salvage vehicle dealer shall keep an accurate and legible inventory of each used component part purchased by or delivered to the dealer. The inventory must contain a record of each part that includes:

(1) the date of purchase or delivery;

(2) the name, age, address, sex, and driver's license number of the seller and a legible photocopy of the seller's driver's license;

(3) the license plate number of the motor vehicle in which the part was delivered;

(4) a complete description of the part, including the type of material and, if applicable, the make, model, color, and size of the part; and

(5) the vehicle identification number of the motor vehicle from which the part was removed.

(b) Instead of the information required by Subsection (a), a salvage vehicle dealer may record:

(1) the name of the person who sold the part or the motor vehicle from which the part was obtained; and

(2) the Texas certificate of inventory number or the federal taxpayer identification number of that person.

(c) The department shall prescribe the form of the record required under Subsection (a) and shall make the form available to salvage vehicle dealers.

(d) This section does not apply to:

(1) an interior component part or special accessory part that is from a motor vehicle more than 10 years of age; or

(2) a part delivered to a salvage vehicle dealer by a commercial freight line or commercial carrier.

Sec. 2302.255. Assignment of Inventory Number.

(a) A salvage vehicle dealer shall:

(1) assign a unique inventory number to each transaction in which the dealer purchases or takes delivery of a component part;

(2) attach the unique inventory number to each component part the dealer obtains in the transaction; and

(3) retain each component part in its original condition on the business premises of the dealer for at least three calendar days, excluding Sundays, after the date the dealer obtains the part.

(b) An inventory number attached to a component part under Subsection (a) may not be removed while the part remains in the inventory of the salvage vehicle dealer.

(c) A salvage vehicle dealer shall record a component part on an affidavit bill of sale if:

(1) the component part does not have a vehicle identification number or the vehicle identification number has been removed; or

(2) the vehicle identification number of the vehicle from which the component part was removed is not available.

(d) The department shall prescribe and make available the form for the affidavit bill of sale.

(e) This section does not apply to the purchase by a salvage vehicle dealer of a nonoperational engine, transmission, or rear axle assembly from another salvage vehicle dealer or an automotive-related business.

Sec. 2302.256. Maintenance of Records.

A salvage vehicle dealer shall keep a record required under this subchapter on a form prescribed by the department. The dealer shall maintain two copies of each record required under this subchapter until the first anniversary of the date the dealer sells or disposes of the item for which the record is maintained.

Sec. 2302.257. Surrender of Certain Documents or License Plates.

(a) On demand, a salvage vehicle dealer shall surrender to the department for cancellation a certificate of title or authority, sales receipt or transfer document, license plate, or inventory list that the dealer is required to possess or maintain.

(b) The department shall provide a signed receipt for a surrendered certificate of title or license plate.

Sec. 2302.258. Inspection of Records.

(a) A peace officer at any reasonable time may inspect a record required to be maintained under this subchapter, including an inventory record and affidavit bill of sale.

(b) On demand of a peace officer, a salvage vehicle dealer shall give to the officer a copy of a record required to be maintained under this subchapter.

(c) A peace officer may inspect the inventory on the premises of a salvage vehicle dealer at any reasonable time in order to verify, check, or audit the records required to be maintained under this subchapter.

(d) A salvage vehicle dealer or an employee of the dealer shall allow and may not interfere with a peace officer's inspection of the dealer's inventory, premises, or required inventory records or affidavit bills of sale.

SUBCHAPTER G MOTOR VEHICLE SALVAGE YARDS IN CERTAIN COUNTIES

Sec. 2302.301. Application of Subchapter.

This subchapter applies only to a motor vehicle salvage yard located in a county with a population of 2.8 million or more.

Sec. 2302.302. Limits on Operation of Heavy Machinery.

(a) A salvage vehicle dealer may not operate heavy machinery in a motor vehicle salvage yard between the hours of 7 p.m. of one day and 7 a.m. of the following day.

(b) This section does not apply to conduct necessary to a sale or purchase by the dealer.

SUBCHAPTER H PENALTIES AND ENFORCEMENT

Sec. 2302.351. Injunctions.

(a) The prosecutor in the county where a motor vehicle salvage yard is located or the city attorney in the municipality where the salvage yard is located may bring suit to enjoin for a period of less than one year a violation of this chapter.

(b) If a salvage vehicle dealer or an employee of the dealer acting in the course of employment is convicted of more than one offense under Section 2302.353(a), the district attorney for a county in which the dealer's salvage business is located may bring an action in that county to enjoin the dealer's business operations for a period of at least one year.

(c) An action under Subsection (b) must be brought in the name of the state. If judgment is in favor of the state, the court shall:

(1) enjoin the dealer from maintaining or participating in the business of a salvage vehicle dealer for a definite period of at least one year or indefinitely, as determined by the court; and

(2) order that the dealer's place of business be closed for the same period.

Sec. 2302.352. Seizure of Vehicle or Part [Repealed].

Repealed by Acts 2003, 78th Leg., ch. 1325 (H.B. 3588), § 17.09(2), effective September 1, 2003.

Sec. 2302.353. Offenses.

(a) A person commits an offense if the person knowingly violates:

(1) a provision of this chapter other than Subchapter G; or

(2) a rule adopted under a provision of this chapter other than Subchapter G.

(b) A person commits an offense if the person knowingly violates Subchapter G.

(c) An offense under Subsection (a) is a Class A misdemeanor unless it is shown on the trial of the offense that the defendant has been previously convicted of an offense under that subsection, in which event the offense is punishable as a state jail felony.

(d) An offense under Subsection (b) is a Class C misdemeanor.

Sec. 2302.354. Administrative Penalty.

(a) The department may impose an administrative penalty against a person licensed under this chapter who violates this chapter or a rule or order adopted under this chapter.

(b) The penalty may not be less than $50 or more than $1,000, and each day a violation continues or occurs is a separate violation for the purpose of imposing a penalty. The amount of the penalty shall be based on:

(1) the seriousness of the violation, including the nature, circumstances, extent, and gravity of the violation;

(2) the economic harm caused by the violation;

(3) the history of previous violations;

(4) the amount necessary to deter a future violation;

(5) efforts to correct the violation; and

(6) any other matter that justice requires.

(c) The person may stay enforcement during the time the order is under judicial review if the person pays the penalty to the court clerk or files a supersedeas bond with the court in the amount of the penalty. A person who cannot afford to pay the penalty or file the bond may stay enforcement by filing an affidavit in the manner required by the Texas Rules of Civil Procedure for a party who cannot afford to file security for costs, subject to the right of the department to contest the affidavit as provided by those rules.

(d) A proceeding to impose an administrative penalty is subject to Chapter 2001, Government Code.

Sec. 2302.355. Cease and Desist Order.

If it appears to the board that a person who is not licensed under this chapter is violating this chapter or a rule or order adopted under this chapter, the board, after notice and opportunity for a hearing, may issue a cease and desist order prohibiting the person from engaging in the activity.

CHAPTER 2303 VEHICLE STORAGE FACILITIES

SUBCHAPTER A GENERAL PROVISIONS

Sec. 2303.001. Short Title.

This chapter may be cited as the Vehicle Storage Facility Act.

Sec. 2303.002. Definitions.

In this chapter:

(1) "Abandoned nuisance vehicle" means a motor vehicle that is:

(A) at least 10 years old; and

(B) of a condition only to be demolished, wrecked, or dismantled.

(2) "Commission" means the Texas Commission of Licensing and Regulation.

(3) "Department" means the Texas Department of Licensing and Regulation.

(4) "Executive director" means the executive director of the department.

(5) "Owner of a vehicle" means a person:

(A) named as the purchaser or transferee in the certificate of title issued for the vehicle under Chapter 501, Transportation Code;

(B) in whose name the vehicle is registered under Chapter 502, Transportation Code, or a member of the person's immediate family;

(C) who holds the vehicle through a lease agreement;

(D) who is an unrecorded lienholder entitled to possess the vehicle under the terms of a chattel mortgage; or

(E) who is a lienholder, holds an affidavit of repossession, and is entitled to repossess the vehicle.

(6) "Principal" means an individual who:

(A) personally or constructively holds, including as the beneficiary of a trust:

(i) at least 10 percent of a corporation's outstanding stock; or

(ii) more than $25,000 of the fair market value of a business entity;

(B) has the controlling interest in a business entity;

(C) has a direct or indirect participating interest through shares, stock, or otherwise, regardless of whether voting rights are included, of more than 10 percent of the profits, proceeds, or capital gains of a business entity;

(D) is a member of the board of directors or other governing body of a business entity; or

(E) serves as an elected officer of a business entity.

(7) "Vehicle" means:

(A) a motor vehicle for which the issuance of a certificate of title is required under Chapter 501, Transportation Code; or

(B) any other device designed to be self-propelled or transported on a public highway.

(8) "Vehicle storage facility" means a garage, parking lot, or other facility that is:

(A) owned by a person other than a governmental entity; and

(B) used to store or park at least 10 vehicles each year.

Sec. 2303.003. Exemptions.

(a) This chapter does not apply to a vehicle stored or parked at a vehicle storage facility with the consent of the owner of the vehicle.

(b) This chapter does not apply to a vehicle storage facility operated by a person licensed under Chapter 2301.

SUBCHAPTER B POWERS AND DUTIES OF COMMISSION AND DEPARTMENT

Sec. 2303.051. Rulemaking: License Requirements.

The commission shall adopt rules that:

(1) establish the requirements for a person to be licensed to operate a vehicle storage facility to ensure that the facility maintains adequate standards for the care of stored vehicles;

(2) relate to the administrative sanctions that may be imposed on a person licensed under this chapter;

(3) govern the administration of this chapter.

Sec. 2303.052. Issuance of License; Fees.

(a) The department may issue licenses to operate vehicle storage facilities.

(b) The department may impose and collect a fee for a license in an amount sufficient to cover the costs incurred by the department in administering this chapter.

Sec. 2303.053. Rules Regarding Payment of Fee.

(a) The commission may adopt rules regarding the method of payment of a fee under this chapter.

(b) The rules may authorize the use of:

(1) electronic funds transfer; or

(2) a credit card issued by a financial institution chartered by:

(A) a state or the federal government; or

(B) a nationally recognized credit organization approved by the department.

(c) The rules may require the payment of a discount or a service charge for a credit card payment in addition to the fee.

Sec. 2303.054. Rules Restricting Advertising or Competitive Bidding.

(a) The commission may not adopt a rule restricting advertising or competitive bidding by a person licensed under this chapter except to prohibit a false, misleading, or deceptive practice.

(b) In its rules to prohibit a false, misleading, or deceptive practice, the commission may not include a rule that:

(1) restricts the person's use of any advertising medium;

(2) restricts the person's personal appearance or the use of the person's voice in an advertisement;

(3) relates to the size or duration of an advertisement by the person; or

(4) restricts the person's advertisement under a trade name.

Sec. 2303.055. Examination of Criminal Conviction.

The department may conduct an examination of any criminal conviction of an applicant, including by obtaining any criminal history record information permitted by law.

Sec. 2303.056. Periodic Inspections.

(a) The department may enter and inspect at any time during business hours:

(1) the place of business of any person regulated under this chapter; or

(2) any place in which the department has reasonable cause to believe that a license holder is in violation of this chapter or in violation of a rule or order of the commission or executive director.

(b) [Repealed.]

(c) [Repealed.]

(d) [Repealed.]

Sec. 2303.057. Personnel.

The department may employ personnel necessary to administer and enforce this chapter.

Sec. 2303.058. Advisory Board.

The Towing and Storage Advisory Board under Chapter 2308 shall advise the commission in adopting vehicle storage rules under this chapter.

SUBCHAPTER C LICENSE REQUIREMENTS, ISSUANCE, AND RENEWAL

Sec. 2303.101. Facility License Required.

(a) A person may not operate a vehicle storage facility unless the person holds a license issued under this chapter.

(b) A license issued under this chapter:

(1) is valid only for the person who applied for the license; and

(2) applies only to a single vehicle storage facility named on the license.

Sec. 2303.1015. Employee License Required.

(a) A person may not work at a vehicle storage facility unless the person holds:

(1) a license issued under this chapter;

(2) an incident management towing operator's license under Section 2308.153;

(3) a private property towing operator's license under Section 2308.154; or

(4) a consent towing operator's license under Section 2308.155.

(b) The commission shall adopt rules governing the application for and issuance of a license under this section.

Sec. 2303.1016. Vehicle Storage Facility Employee and Towing Operator; Dual License. [Repealed]

Sec. 2303.102. License Application.

(a) The commission by rule shall determine the types of information to be included in an application for a license under this chapter on a form prescribed by the executive director.

(b) The rules adopted under this section must require an application for a facility license to list:

(1) the name and address of each partner, if the applicant is a partnership; and

(2) the name and address of the president, secretary, and treasurer of the corporation, if the applicant is a corporation.

(c) A corporation's application must be signed and sworn to by the president and secretary of the corporation.

Sec. 2303.103. Eligibility.

The department shall approve an application submitted as provided by Section 2303.102 unless the department determines that:

(1) the applicant knowingly supplied false or incomplete information on the application;

(2) in the three years preceding the date of application, the applicant, a partner, principal, or officer of the applicant, or the general manager of the applicant, was convicted of:

(A) a felony; or

(B) a misdemeanor punishable by confinement in jail or by a fine exceeding $500; or

(3) the vehicle storage facility for which the license is sought does not meet the standards for storage facilities established by commission rules.

Sec. 2303.104. Notice of Denial; Opportunity to Comply.

(a) If the department denies an application for a license under this chapter, the department shall send written notice of the decision to the applicant at the address shown on the application by certified mail, return receipt requested.

(b) The notice must state the reason for the department's decision and that the applicant is entitled to a hearing before the department under Subchapter E.

(c) The notice may state that the decision is temporary pending compliance by the applicant. If the decision is temporary and the applicant complies with this chapter and commission rules not later than the 14th day after the date the applicant receives the notice, the department shall approve the application.

Sec. 2303.105. Term of License; Notice of Expiration.

(a) A license issued under this chapter is valid for the period set by the department.

(b) Not later than the 30th day before the expiration date of a person's license, the department shall send written notice of the impending license expiration to the person at the person's last known address according to the department's records.

Sec. 2303.106. Procedure for Renewal.

(a) A person may apply to the department to renew the person's license. The application for renewal must be:

(1) made on a form approved by the department;

(2) submitted to the department before the expiration date of the license; and

(3) accompanied by a nonrefundable fee.

(b) A person whose license expires and is not renewed under this section may apply for a new license under Section 2303.102.

SUBCHAPTER D PRACTICE BY LICENSE HOLDER

Sec. 2303.151. Notice to Vehicle Owner or Lienholder.

(a) The operator of a vehicle storage facility who receives a vehicle that is registered in this state and that is towed to the facility for storage shall send a written notice to the registered owner and the primary lienholder of the vehicle not later than the fifth day after the date but not earlier than 24 hours after the date the operator receives the vehicle.

(b) Except as provided by Section 2303.152, the operator of a vehicle storage facility who receives a vehicle that is registered outside this state shall send a written notice to the registered owner and each recorded lienholder of the vehicle not later than the 14th day after the date but not earlier than 24 hours after the date the operator receives the vehicle.

(b-1) The operator of a vehicle storage facility shall send a written notice required under Subsection (b) to an address obtained, by mail or electronically, either:

(1) directly from the governmental entity responsible for maintaining the motor vehicle title and registration database for the state in which the vehicle is registered; or

(2) from a private entity authorized by that governmental entity to obtain title, registration, and lienholder information using a single vehicle identification number inquiry submitted through a secure access portal to the governmental entity's motor vehicle records.

(b-2) An address obtained electronically from a governmental entity under Subsection (b-1)(1) must be obtained through the governmental entity's secure access portal.

(c) It is a defense to an action initiated by the department for a violation of this section that the operator of the facility unsuccessfully attempted in writing or electronically to obtain information from the governmental entity with which the vehicle is registered.

(d) A notice under this section must:

(1) be correctly addressed;

(2) carry sufficient postage; and

(3) be sent by certified mail, return receipt requested or electronic certified mail.

(e) A notice under this section is considered to have been given on the date indicated on the postmark and to be timely filed if:

(1) the postmark indicates that the notice was mailed within the period described by Subsection (a) or (b), as applicable; or

(2) the notice was published as provided by Section 2303.152.

(f) If the operator of a vehicle storage facility sends a notice required under this section after the time prescribed by Subsection (a) or (b):

(1) the deadline for sending any subsequent notice is determined based on the date notice required by this section is actually sent;

(2) the operator may not begin to charge the daily storage fee authorized under Section 2303.155(b)(3) for the vehicle that is the subject of the notice until 24 hours after the operator sends the notice required under this section; and

(3) the ability of the operator to seek foreclosure of a lien for storage charges on the vehicle that is the subject of the notice is not affected.

(g) Notwithstanding any other law, a state agency or county office may not require proof of delivery of a notice sent under this section in order to issue a title for the vehicle that is the subject of the notice if proof is provided that the notice was mailed in accordance with this section.

Sec. 2303.1511. Vehicle Storage Facility's Duty to Report After Accepting Unauthorized Vehicle.

(a) A vehicle storage facility accepting a vehicle that is towed under this chapter shall, within two hours after receiving the vehicle, report to the local law enforcement agency with jurisdiction over the area from which the vehicle was towed:

(1) a general description of the vehicle;

(2) the state and number of the vehicle's license plate, if any;

(3) the vehicle identification number of the vehicle, if it can be ascertained;

(4) the location from which the vehicle was towed; and

(5) the name and location of the vehicle storage facility where the vehicle is being stored.

(b) The report required by this section must be made by telephone or electronically or delivered personally or by facsimile.

(c) This section does not apply to a vehicle received as a result of an incident management tow requested by a law enforcement agency unless the law enforcement agency requests a report of incident management tows within the jurisdiction of the agency. In this subsection, "incident management tow" has the meaning assigned by Section 2308.002.

Sec. 2303.152. Notice by Publication.

(a) Notice to the registered owner and the primary lienholder of a vehicle towed to a vehicle storage facility may be provided by publication in a newspaper of general circulation in the county in which the vehicle is stored if:

(1) the vehicle is registered in another state;

(2) the operator of the storage facility submits to the governmental entity responsible for maintaining the motor vehicle title and registration database for the state in which the vehicle is registered a request for information relating to the identity of the registered owner and any lienholder of record that is either:

(A) written; or

(B) electronic, through the governmental entity's secure access portal;

(3) the identity of the registered owner cannot be determined;

(4) the registration does not contain an address for the registered owner; or

(5) the operator of the storage facility cannot reasonably determine the identity and address of each lienholder.

(b) A written request under Subsection (a)(2)(A) must:

(1) be correctly addressed;

(2) carry sufficient postage; and

(3) be sent by certified mail, return receipt requested, or electronic certified mail.

(b-1) An electronic request under Subsection (a)(2)(B) must be submitted either:

(1) directly to the governmental entity through the governmental entity's secure access portal; or

(2) to a private entity authorized by the governmental entity to obtain title, registration, and lienholder information using a single vehicle identification number inquiry submitted through a secure access portal to the governmental entity's motor vehicle records.

(c) Notice by publication is not required if each notice sent as provided by Section 2303.151 is returned because:

(1) the notice was unclaimed or refused; or

(2) the person to whom the notice was sent moved without leaving a forwarding address.

(d) Only one notice is required to be published for an abandoned nuisance vehicle.

(e) Notice to the registered owner and the primary lienholder of a vehicle towed to a vehicle storage facility may be provided by publication in a newspaper of general circulation in the county in which the vehicle is stored if:

(1) the vehicle does not display a license plate or a vehicle inspection certificate indicating the state of registration;

(2) the identity of the registered owner cannot reasonably be determined by the operator of the storage facility; or

(3) the operator of the storage facility cannot reasonably determine the identity and address of each lienholder.

Sec. 2303.1521. Certain Vehicles with State of Registration Unknown.

(a) An operator of a vehicle storage facility who receives a motor vehicle as defined by Section 501.002(17)(A), Transportation Code, and does not know the state in which the vehicle is registered may give notice by publication under Section 2303.152 only if the operator:

(1) obtains, using the motor vehicle's vehicle identification number, by mail or electronically, a report from the National Motor Vehicle Title Information System operated by the United States Department of Justice, or a successor system, showing the state in which the motor vehicle is titled; and

(2) either:

(A) is unable to determine from the report the governmental entity that is responsible for maintaining the registration information for the motor vehicle; or

(B) attempts to and is unable to obtain, from the governmental entity indicated in the report, the identity and address of any registered owner and any lienholder.

(b) An operator who attempts to obtain owner and lienholder information under Subsection (a)(2) must attempt to obtain the information, by mail or electronically, either:

(1) directly from the governmental entity; or

(2) from a private entity authorized by the governmental entity to obtain title, registration, and lienholder information using a single vehicle identification number inquiry submitted through a secure access portal to the governmental entity's motor vehicle records.

(c) An address obtained electronically from a governmental entity under Subsection (b)(1) must be obtained through the governmental entity's secure access portal.

Sec. 2303.153. Contents of Notice.

(a) A notice by mail provided under Section 2303.151 must include:

(1) the date the vehicle was accepted for storage;

(2) the first day for which a storage fee is assessed;

(3) the daily storage rate;

(4) the type and amount of any other charge to be paid when the vehicle is claimed;

(5) the full name, street address, and telephone number of the vehicle storage facility;

(6) the hours during which the owner may claim the vehicle; and

(7) the facility license number preceded by "Texas Department of Licensing and Regulation Vehicle Storage Facility License Number" or "TDLR VSF Lic. No."

(b) A notice by publication provided under Section 2303.152 must include:

(1) the vehicle description;

(2) the total charges;

(3) the full name, street address, and telephone number of the facility; and

(4) the department registration number.

(c) Notice by publication is not required to include any information other than that listed in Subsection (b).

(d) Notice by publication may include a list of more than one vehicle, watercraft, or outboard motor.

Sec. 2303.154. Second Notice; Consent to Sale.

(a) If a vehicle is not claimed by a person permitted to claim the vehicle before the 10th day after the date notice is mailed or published under Section 2303.151 or 2303.152, the operator of the vehicle storage facility shall consider the vehicle to be abandoned and, if required by the law enforcement agency with jurisdiction where the vehicle is located, report the abandonment to the law enforcement agency. If the law enforcement agency notifies the vehicle storage facility that the agency will send notices and dispose of the abandoned vehicle under Subchapter B, Chapter 683, Transportation Code, the vehicle storage facility shall pay the fee required under Section 683.031, Transportation Code.

(b) Notice under this section must include:

(1) the information listed in Section 2303.153(a);

(2) a statement of the right of the facility to dispose of the vehicle under Section 2303.157; and

(3) a statement that the failure of the owner or lienholder to claim the vehicle before the 30th day after the date the notice is provided is:

(A) a waiver by that person of all right, title, or interest in the vehicle; and

(B) a consent to the sale of the vehicle at a public sale.

(c) Notwithstanding Subsection (b), if publication is required for notice under this section, the notice must include:

(1) the information listed in Section 2303.153(b); and

(2) a statement that the failure of the owner or lienholder to claim the vehicle before the date of sale is:

(A) a waiver of all right, title, and interest in the vehicle; and

(B) a consent to the sale of the vehicle at a public sale.

(d) Not earlier than the 15th day and before the 21st day after the date notice is mailed or published under Section 2303.151 or 2303.152, the operator of a vehicle storage facility shall send a second notice to the registered owner and each recorded lienholder of the vehicle if the facility:

(1) was not required to make a report under Subsection (a); or

(2) has made a required report under Subsection (a) and the law enforcement agency:

(A) has notified the facility that the law enforcement agency will not take custody of the vehicle;

(B) has not taken custody of the vehicle; or

(C) has not responded to the report.

(e) If the operator of a vehicle storage facility sends a notice required under this section outside of the time described by Subsection (d):

(1) the deadline for sending any subsequent notice is determined based on the date notice under this section is actually sent;

(2) the operator may not charge the daily storage fee authorized under Section 2303.155(b)(3) for the vehicle that is the subject of the notice during the period beginning on the 21st day after the date that notice under Section 2303.151 is sent and ending 24 hours after notice under this section is sent; and

(3) the ability of the operator to seek foreclosure of a lien for storage charges on the vehicle that is the subject of the notice is not affected.

(f) Notwithstanding any other law, a state agency or county office may not require proof of delivery of a notice sent under this section in order to issue a title for the vehicle that is the subject of the notice if proof is provided that the notice was mailed in accordance with this section.

(g) A report sent under Subsection (a) may, at the discretion of the law enforcement agency, contain a list of more than one vehicle, watercraft, or outboard motor.

(h) A vehicle sold in compliance with this chapter shall be titled and registered without the imposition by a county office of additional requirements not otherwise permitted by law.

Sec. 2303.1545. Disposition of Abandoned Nuisance Vehicle.

(a) A vehicle storage facility that holds an abandoned nuisance vehicle is not required to send or publish a second notice and is entitled to dispose of the vehicle on the 30th day after the date the notice is mailed or published under Section 2303.151 or 2303.152.

(b) The facility may:

(1) notify the department that notices under Chapter 683, Transportation Code, have been provided and shall pay a fee of $10 to the department; or

(2) in the alternative, notify the appropriate law enforcement agency and pay a fee of $10 to that agency.

(c) A law enforcement agency described by Subsection (b)(2) may sign a document issued by the department.

Sec. 2303.155. Charges Related to Storage.

(a) For the purposes of this section, "governmental vehicle storage facility" means a garage, parking lot, or other facility that is:

(1) owned by a governmental entity; and

(2) used to store or park at least 10 vehicles each year.

(b) The operator of a vehicle storage facility or governmental vehicle storage facility may charge the owner of a vehicle stored or parked at the facility:

(1) a notification fee set in a reasonable amount for providing notice under this subchapter, including notice under Section 2303.154(c);

(2) an impoundment fee of $20, subject to Section 2303.1552, for any action that:

(A) is taken by or at the direction of the owner or operator of the facility; and

(B) is necessary to preserve, protect, or service a vehicle stored or parked at the facility;

(3) a daily storage fee, subject to Section 2303.1552, of:

(A) $20 for each day or part of a day the vehicle is stored at the facility if the vehicle is not longer than 25 feet; or

(B) $35 for each day or part of a day the vehicle is stored at the facility if the vehicle is longer than 25 feet; and

(4) any fee that is required to be submitted to a law enforcement agency, the agency's authorized agent, or a governmental entity.

(c) A notification fee under Subsection (b) may not exceed $50, except that if notice by publication is required by this chapter and the cost of publication exceeds 50 percent of the notification fee, the vehicle storage facility may recover the additional amount of the cost of publication from the vehicle owner or agent.

(d) For purposes of imposing a daily storage fee, a day is considered to begin at midnight and to end at the next following midnight. A daily storage fee may be charged regardless of whether the vehicle is stored for 24 hours of the day, except that a daily storage fee may not be charged for more than one day if the vehicle remains at the facility for less than 12 hours.

(e) The operator of a vehicle storage facility or governmental vehicle storage facility may charge a daily storage fee under Subsection (b):

(1) for not more than five days before the date notice is mailed or published under this subchapter, if the vehicle is registered in this state;

(2) for not more than five days before the date the request for owner information is sent to the appropriate governmental entity as required by this subchapter, if the vehicle is registered in another state; and

(3) for each day the vehicle is in storage after the date the notice is mailed or published until the vehicle is removed and all accrued charges are paid.

(f) The operator of a vehicle storage facility or governmental vehicle storage facility may not charge an additional fee related to the storage of a vehicle other than a fee authorized by this section or a towing fee authorized by Chapter 2308.

(g) This section controls over any conflicting municipal ordinance or charter provision.

Sec. 2303.1551. Required Posting.

(a) All storage fees shall be posted at the licensed vehicle storage facility to which the motor vehicle has been delivered and shall be posted in view of the person who claims the vehicle.

(b) A vehicle storage facility accepting a nonconsent towed vehicle shall post a sign that complies with commission rules and states "Nonconsent tow fees schedules available on request." The vehicle storage facility shall provide a copy of a nonconsent towing fees schedule on request. The commission shall adopt rules for signs required under this subsection.

Sec. 2303.1552. Biennial Adjustment of Certain Fees.

(a) In this section, "consumer price index" means the Consumer Price Index for All Urban Consumers (CPI-U) published by the Bureau of Labor Statistics of the United States Department of Labor.

(b) Each odd-numbered year, the commission, not later than November 1:

(1) by rule may adjust the impoundment fee under Section 2303.155(b)(2) and the storage fees under Section 2303.155(b)(3) by an amount equal to the amount of the applicable fee in effect on December 31 of the preceding year multiplied by the percentage increase or decrease in the consumer price index during the preceding state fiscal biennium; and

(2) if the fees are adjusted under Subdivision (1), shall publish the adjusted fees on the department's Internet website.

(c) A fee adjusted under Subsection (b) is effective beginning the January 1 following the adoption of a rule under that subsection.

(d) If a fee is decreased under this section, the operator of a vehicle storage facility or governmental vehicle storage facility, as defined by Section 2303.155, shall begin charging the adjusted fee on the effective date of the decrease. If a fee is increased under this section, the operator may begin charging the adjusted fee at any time on or after the effective date of the increase.

Sec. 2303.156. Payment by Lienholder or Insurance Company.

(a) A lienholder who repossesses a vehicle delivered to a vehicle storage facility is liable to the operator of the facility for any money owed to the operator in relation to delivery of the vehicle to or storage of the vehicle in the facility regardless of whether an amount accrued before the lienholder repossessed the vehicle.

(b) An insurance company that pays a claim of total loss on a vehicle in a vehicle storage facility is liable to the operator of the facility for any money owed to the operator in relation to delivery of the vehicle to or storage of the vehicle in the facility regardless of whether an amount accrued before the insurance company paid the claim.

Sec. 2303.157. Disposal of Certain Abandoned Vehicles.

(a) The operator of a vehicle storage facility may dispose of a vehicle for which notice is given under Section 2303.154 if, before the 30th day after the date notice is mailed, the vehicle is not:

(1) claimed by a person entitled to claim the vehicle; or

(2) taken into custody by a law enforcement agency under Chapter 683, Transportation Code.

(b) An operator entitled to dispose of a vehicle under this section may sell the vehicle at a public sale without obtaining a release or discharge of any lien on the vehicle, regardless of whether notice was provided by mail or by publication under this chapter. The proceeds from the sale of the vehicle shall be applied to the charges incurred for the vehicle under Section 2303.155. The operator shall pay any excess proceeds to the person entitled to those proceeds.

(c) Notwithstanding Subsection (a), the operator of a vehicle storage facility may dispose of a vehicle

(2) employs an individual who does not hold an appropriate license required by this chapter.

(b) An offense under this section is a Class C misdemeanor.

Sec. 2303.303. Authority to Arrest.

A peace officer or license and weight inspector for the Department of Public Safety may make an arrest for a violation of a rule adopted under this chapter.

Sec. 2303.304. Administrative Penalty.

(a) The commission may impose an administrative penalty on a person under Subchapter F, Chapter 51, regardless of whether the person holds a registration, permit, or license under this chapter, if the person violates:

(1) this chapter or a rule adopted under this chapter; or

(2) a rule or order of the executive director or commission.

(b) An administrative penalty may not be imposed unless the person charged with a violation is provided the opportunity for a hearing.

Sec. 2303.305. Cease and Desist Order; Injunction; Civil Penalty.

(a) The executive director may issue a cease and desist order as necessary to enforce this chapter if the executive director determines that the action is necessary to prevent a violation of this chapter and to protect public health and safety.

(b) The attorney general or executive director may institute an action for an injunction or a civil penalty under this chapter as provided by Section 51.352.

CHAPTER 2304 NONMECHANICAL REPAIRS TO MOTOR VEHICLES

SUBCHAPTER A GENERAL PROVISIONS

Sec. 2304.001. Definitions.

In this chapter:

(1) "Commission" means the Texas Natural Resource Conservation Commission.

(2) "Executive director" means the executive director of the Texas Natural Resource Conservation Commission.

(3) "Motor vehicle" means a vehicle with at least four wheels that is self-propelled and that can transport a person or property on a public street or highway. The term does not include a vehicle that is used exclusively on stationary tracks.

(4) "Repair facility" means a person that engages in the business of repairing or replacing the nonmechanical exterior or interior body parts of a damaged motor vehicle.

Sec. 2304.002. Application of Chapter.

This chapter does not apply to a repair facility located in a county with a population of 50,000 or less.

SUBCHAPTER B CERTIFICATE OF REGISTRATION

Sec. 2304.051. Registration Required.

A repair facility shall register with the commission as provided by this chapter and the rules adopted by the commission.

Sec. 2304.052. Application.

(a) The commission by rule shall:

(1) prescribe an application form for the issuance or renewal of a certificate of registration; and

(2) determine the information to be disclosed on the application.

(b) The application must include:

(1) the name, street address, and mailing address of each location at which the applicant operates a repair facility;

(2) the name and address of:

(A) each owner, partner, officer, or director of the applicant; and

(B) if the applicant is a corporation, each shareholder holding 10 percent or more of the outstanding shares;

(3) the identification number assigned by, or a statement of other evidence of compliance with any applicable requirements of:

(A) the United States Environmental Protection Agency;

(B) the United States Occupational Safety and Health Administration;

(C) the commission;

(D) the Texas Department of Health;

Occupations Code

(E) the comptroller; and
(F) a municipality or county; and
(4) a statement of each conviction obtained against the applicant or a partner or officer of the applicant during the three years preceding the date of the application of:
(A) a felony; or
(B) a misdemeanor punishable by confinement in jail or by a fine exceeding $200.

Sec. 2304.053. Issuance and Renewal of Certificate.

(a) An applicant for the issuance or renewal of a certificate of registration shall submit to the executive director a sworn application on the form prescribed by the commission accompanied by a $50 fee.
(b) On receipt of the application and required fee, the executive director shall issue a certificate of registration to the applicant.
(c) A certificate of registration expires on the first anniversary of the date of issuance and may be renewed annually in the manner prescribed by the commission. An application for renewal must be submitted to the executive director within 30 days before the expiration date of the certificate.

Sec. 2304.054. Form of Certificate; Transferability.

A certificate of registration:
(1) must contain a unique number;
(2) applies only to the person whose name appears on the certificate or an employee of that person; and
(3) is not transferable.

Sec. 2304.055. Replacement Certificate.

(a) If a certificate of registration is lost or destroyed, the certificate holder may apply to the executive director for a replacement certificate of registration.
(b) The certificate holder must submit:
(1) an affidavit verifying that the certificate of registration was lost or destroyed; and
(2) a $25 replacement fee.
(c) The executive director shall issue a replacement certificate of registration on receipt of the affidavit and replacement fee.
(d) A replacement certificate of registration must be clearly identified as a replacement certificate on the certificate and in the records of the commission.

Sec. 2304.056. Voluntary Surrender of Certificate.

A certificate holder may terminate a certificate of registration at any time by voluntarily surrendering the certificate.

Sec. 2304.057. Cancellation of Certificate.

(a) On the expiration, termination, or surrender of a certificate of registration, the certificate holder shall deliver the certificate to the executive director.
(b) The executive director shall:
(1) cancel the certificate; or
(2) endorse on the certificate the date of expiration, termination, or surrender.

Sec. 2304.058. Maintenance of Registration Information.

(a) The executive director shall maintain each application for a certificate of registration and a copy of each certificate of registration in a convenient form that is available to the public.
(b) The executive director shall annually publish a list of:
(1) the name and address of each person registered under this chapter; and
(2) the name of each person whose registration has been revoked, suspended, or surrendered during the period and the specific date of the suspension, revocation, or surrender.

SUBCHAPTER C
PRACTICE BY CERTIFICATE HOLDER

Sec. 2304.101. Display of Certificate.

A certificate holder shall publicly display the current certificate of registration at the certificate holder's place of business in a location readily visible to a customer paying for repairs.

Sec. 2304.102. Registration Number.

A certificate holder shall include the certificate holder's registration number:
(1) on each repair estimate, repair order, or correspondence; and
(2) in each advertisement for motor vehicle repairs by the repair facility.

Sec. 2304.103. False Statements.

A certificate holder may not make a false or fraudulent statement in connection with:

(1) a repair; or

(2) an attempt to collect compensation for a repair.

Sec. 2304.104. Record of Vehicle Repairs.

(a) A certificate holder shall maintain in a convenient place a record of each motor vehicle that enters the certificate holder's premises for a repair. Except as provided by Subsection (b), the certificate holder shall include in the record:

(1) a description of the vehicle;

(2) the vehicle identification number;

(3) the date the vehicle entered the certificate holder's premises;

(4) the odometer reading at the time the vehicle is received;

(5) the name and address of the person from whom the vehicle is received; and

(6) a signed authorization for the work to be performed on the vehicle.

(b) If a motor vehicle is towed to the certificate holder's repair facility without the consent of the owner of the vehicle, the information in the record is the information provided by the law enforcement agency that initiated the towing process.

SUBCHAPTER D ENFORCEMENT PROVISIONS

Sec. 2304.151. Inspection of Premises and Record.

The executive director or an employee of the commission may, at any time, inspect:

(1) a record maintained under Section 2304.104; and

(2) the premises of a certificate holder's place of business.

Sec. 2304.152. Administrative Disciplinary Action and Procedures.

(a) The commission shall adopt rules establishing:

(1) grounds for suspension, revocation, or reinstatement of a certificate of registration; and

(2) procedures for taking disciplinary action.

(b) The executive director may suspend or revoke a certificate of registration based on a ground established under this section.

(c) Procedures for the suspension or revocation of a certificate of registration are governed by Chapter 2001, Government Code.

Sec. 2304.153. Failure to Register; Civil Penalty.

(a) A repair facility that fails to register under this chapter is liable to the state for a civil penalty of $250.

(b) The executive director shall waive the penalty if the repair facility applies for registration not later than the 10th day after the date of notice of the violation.

Sec. 2304.154. Violation of Chapter; Civil Penalty.

Except as provided by Section 2304.153, a person that violates this chapter is liable to the state for a civil penalty in an amount not to exceed $100.

CHAPTER 2305 RECORDS OF CERTAIN VEHICLE REPAIRS, SALES, AND PURCHASES

SUBCHAPTER A RECORDS MAINTAINED BY CERTAIN ENTITIES

Sec. 2305.001. Definitions.

In this subchapter:

(1) "Person" means an individual, corporation, or firm.

(2) "Repair" includes the rebuilding of a motor vehicle, the installation of a new or used part or accessory on a motor vehicle, and the performance of electrical work in connection with the repair of a motor vehicle. The term does not include a repair covered by Chapter 2304.

(3) "Used motor vehicle" includes a secondhand motor vehicle.

(4) "Motor vehicle" has the meaning assigned by Section 501.002, Transportation Code.

(5) "Board" means the board of the Texas Department of Motor Vehicles.

(6) "Department" means the Texas Department of Motor Vehicles.

Sec. 2305.002. Application of Subchapter.

This subchapter applies to any person who:

(1) operates a shop or garage that is engaged in the business of repairing motor vehicles; or

(2) engages in the business of purchasing or selling used motor vehicles in this state.

Sec. 2305.003. Register of Repairs.

(a) A person subject to this subchapter shall maintain a register of each repair the person makes to a motor vehicle. The register must contain a substantially complete and accurate description of each motor vehicle that is repaired.

(b) This section does not apply to a repair having a value of $1 or less.

Sec. 2305.004. Register of Used Motor Vehicle Sales and Purchases.

(a) A person subject to this subchapter shall maintain a register of each sale or purchase the person makes of a used motor vehicle.

(b) If the person buys a used motor vehicle, the register must contain:

(1) the make and model, the number of cylinders, the motor number, the vehicle identification number, and the passenger capacity of the motor vehicle, if applicable;

(2) the name, date of birth, usual place of address, and official identification number of each person claiming to be the owner of the motor vehicle; and

(3) the state registration number of the motor vehicle, if applicable.

(c) If the person sells a used motor vehicle, in addition to the requirements of Subsection (b), the register must contain the name and address of the purchaser of the motor vehicle.

Sec. 2305.005. Record of Replaced Cylinder Block.

The owner of the garage or repair shop that installs a replacement cylinder block and stamps the original engine number on the block as required by Section 2305.051 shall record in a substantially bound book:

(1) the name and address of the vehicle's owner; and

(2) the engine number and registration number of the vehicle.

Sec. 2305.0051. Records Related to Catalytic Converters.

(a) The owner of a garage or repair shop that sells to a metal recycling entity registered under Chapter 1956 a catalytic converter that the person removed in connection with a motor vehicle repair shall maintain a record of all repairs for the vehicle that includes:

(1) the name and address of the vehicle's owner; and

(2) copies of all related invoices.

(b) Notwithstanding Section 2305.006(a), a record required by this section shall be kept until at least the second anniversary of the date of the repair.

Sec. 2305.006. Maintenance of Records.

(a) All records required to be maintained under this subchapter shall be kept until at least the first anniversary of the date the record is made.

(b) The registers required by Sections 2305.003 and 2305.004 shall be maintained in a clear and intelligent manner in a well-bound book or an electronic recordkeeping system and kept in a secure place in the office or place of business where the work is performed or the business is conducted.

Sec. 2305.007. Entry and Inspection.

(a) Except as provided by Subsection (b), for the purpose of enforcing or administering this chapter, Chapter 2302 of this code, or Chapter 501 or 502, Transportation Code, a member of the board, an employee of the department, a member of the Public Safety Commission, an officer of the Department of Public Safety, or another peace officer who is interested in tracing or locating a stolen motor vehicle may at a reasonable time:

(1) enter the premises of a business regulated under one of those chapters; and

(2) inspect or copy any document, record, vehicle, part, or other item regulated under one of those chapters.

(b) For the purposes of tracing or locating a stolen motor vehicle on the premises of a person engaging in a business or activity regulated under this chapter who is also licensed under Chapter 348 or 353, Finance Code, only an officer of the Department of Public Safety may at a reasonable time:

(1) enter the premises of the person's business; and

(2) inspect or copy any document, record, vehicle, part, or other item regulated under:

(A) this chapter; or

(B) Chapter 348 or 353, Finance Code.

(c) A person engaging in a business or activity regulated under this chapter shall cooperate with a person conducting an inspection under this section to assist in the recovery of stolen motor vehicles and parts and to prevent the sale or transfer of stolen motor vehicles and parts.

(d) An entry or inspection occurs at a reasonable time for purposes of Subsection (a) or (b) if the entry or inspection occurs:

(1) during normal business hours of the person or activity regulated under a chapter listed in Subsection (a) or (b); or

(2) while an activity regulated under a chapter listed in Subsection (a) or (b) is occurring on the premises.

SUBCHAPTER B REQUIREMENT APPLICABLE TO OWNERS OF CERTAIN MOTOR VEHICLES

Sec. 2305.051. Replacement of Cylinder Block.

The owner of a motor vehicle registered under Chapter 502, Transportation Code, that has a damaged cylinder block replaced shall have the original engine number of the motor vehicle stamped with a steel die on the replacement cylinder block.

SUBCHAPTER C ENFORCEMENT

Sec. 2305.101. Criminal Penalty.

(a) A person commits an offense if the person violates this chapter or a rule adopted under this chapter.

(b) Except as provided by Subsection (c), an offense under this section is punishable by a fine of not less than $10 and not more than $100.

(c) An offense under this chapter that consists of the violation of Section 2305.007 is a Class A misdemeanor.

CHAPTER 2308 VEHICLE TOWING AND BOOTING

SUBCHAPTER A GENERAL PROVISIONS

Sec. 2308.001. Short Title.

This chapter may be cited as the Texas Towing and Booting Act.

Sec. 2308.002. Definitions.

In this chapter:

(1) "Advisory board" means the Towing and Storage Advisory Board.

(1-a) "Boot" means a lockable road wheel clamp or similar vehicle immobilization device that is designed to immobilize a parked vehicle and prevent its movement until the device is unlocked or removed.

(1-b) "Booting company" means a person that controls, installs, or directs the installation and removal of one or more boots.

(1-c) "Boot operator" means an individual who installs or removes a boot on or from a vehicle.

(2) "Commission" means the Texas Commission of Licensing and Regulation.

(3) "Consent tow" means any tow of a motor vehicle in which the tow truck is summoned by the owner or operator of the vehicle or by a person who has possession, custody, or control of the vehicle. The term does not include an incident management tow or a private property tow.

(4) "Department" means the Texas Department of Licensing and Regulation.

(5) "Driver's license" has the meaning assigned by Section 521.001, Transportation Code.

(5-a) "Incident management tow" means any tow of a vehicle in which the tow truck is summoned to the scene of a traffic accident or to an incident, including the removal of a vehicle, commercial cargo, and commercial debris from an accident or incident scene.

(5-b) "Local authority" means a state or local governmental entity authorized to regulate traffic or parking and includes:

(A) an institution of higher education; and

(B) a political subdivision, including a county, municipality, special district, junior college district, housing authority, or other political subdivision of this state.

(6) "Nonconsent tow" means any tow of a motor vehicle that is not a consent tow, including:

(A) an incident management tow; and

(B) a private property tow.

(7) "Parking facility" means public or private property used, wholly or partly, for restricted or paid vehicle parking. The term includes:

(A) a restricted space on a portion of an otherwise unrestricted parking facility; and

(B) a commercial parking lot, a parking garage, and a parking area serving or adjacent to a business, church, school, home that charges a fee for parking, apartment complex, property governed by a property owners' association, or government-owned property leased to a private person, including:

(i) a portion of the right-of-way of a public roadway that is leased by a governmental entity to the parking facility owner; and

(ii) the area between the facility's property line abutting a county or municipal public roadway and the center line of the roadway's drainage way or the curb of the roadway, whichever is farther from the facility's property line.

(7-a) "Parking facility authorized agent" means an employee or agent of a parking facility owner with the authority to:

(A) authorize the removal of a vehicle from the parking facility on behalf of the parking facility owner; and

(B) accept service on behalf of the parking facility owner of a notice of hearing requested under this chapter.

(8) "Parking facility owner" means:

(A) an individual, corporation, partnership, limited partnership, limited liability company, association, trust, or other legal entity owning or operating a parking facility;

(B) a property owners' association having control under a dedicatory instrument, as that term is defined in Section 202.001, Property Code, over assigned or unassigned parking areas; or

(C) a property owner having an exclusive right under a dedicatory instrument, as that term is defined in Section 202.001, Property Code, to use a parking space.

(8-a) "Peace officer" means a person who is a peace officer under Article 2.12, Code of Criminal Procedure.

(8-b) "Private property tow" means any tow of a vehicle authorized by a parking facility owner without the consent of the owner or operator of the vehicle.

(9) [Repealed.]

(10) "Public roadway" means a public street, alley, road, right-of-way, or other public way, including paved and unpaved portions of the right-of-way.

(11) "Tow truck" means a motor vehicle, including a wrecker, equipped with a mechanical device used to tow, winch, or otherwise move another motor vehicle. The term does not include:

(A) a motor vehicle owned and operated by a governmental entity, including a public school district;

(B) a motor vehicle towing:

(i) a race car;

(ii) a motor vehicle for exhibition; or

(iii) an antique motor vehicle;

(C) a recreational vehicle towing another vehicle;

(D) a motor vehicle used in combination with a tow bar, tow dolly, or other mechanical device if the vehicle is not operated in the furtherance of a commercial enterprise;

(E) a motor vehicle that is controlled or operated by a farmer or rancher and used for towing a farm vehicle;

(F) a motor vehicle that:

(i) is owned or operated by an entity the primary business of which is the rental of motor vehicles; and

(ii) only tows vehicles rented by the entity;

(G) a truck-trailer combination that is owned or operated by a dealer licensed under Chapter 2301 and used to transport new vehicles during the normal course of a documented transaction in which the dealer is a party and ownership or the right of possession of the transported vehicle is conveyed or transferred; or

(H) a car hauler that is used solely to transport, other than in a consent or nonconsent tow, motor vehicles as cargo:

(i) in the course of:

(a) a prearranged shipping transaction; or

(b) a commercial transaction for transport of a damaged vehicle arranged or authorized by an insurance company and delivered to a salvage pool operator as defined by Section 2302.001; or

(ii) for use in mining, drilling, or construction operations.

(12) "Towing company" means an individual, association, corporation, or other legal entity that controls, operates, or directs the operation of one or more tow trucks over a public roadway in this state but does not include a political subdivision of the state.

(13) "Unauthorized vehicle" means a vehicle parked, stored, or located on a parking facility without the consent of the parking facility owner.

(14) "Vehicle" means a device in, on, or by which a person or property may be transported on a public roadway. The term includes an operable or inoperable automobile, truck, motorcycle, recreational vehicle, or trailer but does not include a device moved by human power or used exclusively on a stationary rail or track.

(15) "Vehicle owner" means a person:

(A) named as the purchaser or transferee in the certificate of title issued for the vehicle under Chapter 501, Transportation Code;

(B) in whose name the vehicle is registered under Chapter 502, Transportation Code, or a member of the person's immediate family;

(C) who holds the vehicle through a lease agreement;

(D) who is an unrecorded lienholder entitled to possess the vehicle under the terms of a chattel mortgage; or

(E) who is a lienholder holding an affidavit of repossession and entitled to repossess the vehicle.

(16) "Vehicle storage facility" means a vehicle storage facility, as defined by Section 2303.002, that is operated by a person who holds a license issued under Chapter 2303 to operate the facility.

Sec. 2308.003. Study of Nonconsent Towing Fees [Expired].

Expired pursuant to Acts 2007, 80th Leg., ch. 1046 (H.B. 2094), § 1.12, effective September 1, 2009.

Sec. 2308.004. Exemption.

Sections 2308.151(b), 2308.2085, 2308.257, and 2308.258 do not apply to:

(1) a person who, while exercising a statutory or contractual lien right with regard to a vehicle:

(A) installs or removes a boot; or

(B) controls, installs, or directs the installation and removal of one or more boots; or

(2) a commercial office building owner or manager who installs or removes a boot in the building's parking facility.

SUBCHAPTER B ADVISORY BOARD

Sec. 2308.051. Towing, Storage, and Booting Advisory Board.

(a) The advisory board consists of the following members appointed by the presiding officer of the commission with the approval of the commission:

(1) one representative of a towing company operating in a county with a population of less than one million;

(2) one representative of a towing company operating in a county with a population of one million or more;

(3) one representative of a vehicle storage facility located in a county with a population of less than one million;

(4) one representative of a vehicle storage facility located in a county with a population of one million or more;

(5) one parking facility representative;

(6) one peace officer from a county with a population of less than one million;

(7) one peace officer from a county with a population of one million or more;

(8) one representative of a member insurer, as defined by Section 462.004, Insurance Code, of the Texas Property and Casualty Insurance Guaranty Association who writes automobile insurance in this state; and

(9) one person who operates both a towing company and a vehicle storage facility.

(b) The advisory board must include representation for each classification of towing.

(c) An appointment to the advisory board shall be made without regard to the race, color, disability, sex, religion, age, or national origin of the appointee.

Sec. 2308.052. Terms; Vacancies.

(a) Advisory board members serve terms of six years, with the terms of two or three members, as appropriate, expiring on February 1 of each odd-numbered year.

(b) A member may not serve more than two full consecutive terms.

(c) If a vacancy occurs during a term, the presiding officer of the commission shall appoint a replacement who meets the qualifications of the vacated position to serve for the remainder of the term.

Sec. 2308.053. Presiding Officer.

The presiding officer of the commission shall appoint one of the advisory board members to serve as presiding officer of the advisory board for a term of one year. The presiding officer of the advisory board may vote on any matter before the advisory board.

Sec. 2308.054. Compensation; Reimbursement of Expenses.

Advisory board members may not receive compensation but are entitled to reimbursement for actual and necessary expenses incurred in performing the functions of the advisory board, subject to the General Appropriations Act.

Sec. 2308.055. Meetings. [Repealed]

Sec. 2308.056. General Powers and Duties.

The executive director or commission, as appropriate, may take action as necessary to administer and enforce this chapter.

Sec. 2308.057. Rules.

(a) The commission shall adopt rules for permitting tow trucks and licensing towing operators, towing companies, booting companies, and boot operators. The commission may adopt different rules applicable to each type of permit or license.

(a-1) The commission shall adopt rules for denial of applications and permits if the applicant, a partner, principal, officer, or general manager of the applicant, or other license or permit holder has:

(1) a criminal conviction, or has pleaded guilty or nolo contendere to an offense, before the date of the application, for:

(A) a felony; or

(B) a misdemeanor punishable by confinement in jail or by a fine in an amount that exceeds $500;

(2) violated an order of the commission or executive director, including an order for sanctions or administrative penalties;

(3) failed to submit a license or permit bond in an amount established by the commission;

(4) knowingly submitted false or incomplete information on the application; or

(5) filed an application to permit a tow truck previously permitted by a license or permit holder.

(b) The commission by rule shall adopt:

(1) standards of conduct for license and permit holders under this chapter; and

(2) requirements for a consent tow, private property tow, and incident management tow.

Sec. 2308.0575. Rules on Fees; Contract for Study; Confidential Information.

(a) To protect the public health and safety, the commission by rule shall establish:

(1) the fees that may be charged in connection with a private property tow;

(2) the maximum amount that may be charged for fees, other than tow fees, that may be assessed by a towing company in connection with a private property tow; and

(3) a maximum amount that may be charged for the following private property tows:

(A) standard light-duty tows of motor vehicles with a gross weight rating of 10,000 pounds or less;

(B) medium-duty tows of motor vehicles with a gross weight rating of more than 10,000 pounds, but less than 25,000 pounds; and

(C) heavy-duty tows of motor vehicles with a gross weight rating that exceeds 25,000 pounds.

(b) In adopting rules under Subsection (a), the commission shall contract for a study that:

(1) examines towing fee studies conducted by municipalities in this state; and

(2) analyzes the cost of towing services by company, the consumer price index, the geographic area, and individual cost components.

(c) The commission may structure the maximum amounts that may be charged for private property tows based on hourly or flat fees or by geographic location.

(d) The commission shall maintain the confidentiality of information contained in a study conducted under this section that is claimed to be confidential for competitive purposes and may not release information that identifies a person or company. The confidential information is exempt from disclosure under Chapter 552, Government Code.

(e) To protect the confidentiality of the information, the commission shall aggregate the information to the maximum extent possible considering the purpose of the study.

(f) The department shall contract to conduct a study on private property towing fees under this section at least once every two years.

Sec. 2308.058. Fees.

The commission shall establish and collect reasonable and necessary fees in amounts sufficient to cover the costs of administering this chapter.

Sec. 2308.059. Periodic Inspections.

(a) The department may enter and inspect at any time during business hours:

(1) the place of business of any person regulated under this chapter; or

(2) any place in which the department has reasonable cause to believe that a license or permit holder is in violation of this chapter or in violation of a rule or order of the commission or executive director.

(b) [Repealed.]

(c) [Repealed.]

(d) In conducting an inspection under this section, the department may inspect a vehicle, a facility, business records, or any other place or thing reasonably required to enforce this chapter or a rule or order adopted under this chapter.

Sec. 2308.060. Powers and Duties of Advisory Board.

The advisory board shall provide advice and recommendations to the department on technical matters relevant to the administration and enforcement of this chapter, including examination content, licensing standards, continuing education requirements, and maximum amounts that may be charged for fees related to private property tows.

Sec. 2308.061. Personnel.

The department may employ personnel necessary to administer and enforce this chapter.

SUBCHAPTER C
TOW TRUCK PERMIT REQUIREMENTS

Sec. 2308.101. Permit Required.

A tow truck may not be used for consent towing or nonconsent towing on a public roadway in this state unless an appropriate permit has been issued for the tow truck under this subchapter. Each tow truck requires a separate permit.

Sec. 2308.102. Application Requirements.

(a) An applicant for a permit under this subchapter must submit to the department:

(1) a completed application on a form prescribed by the executive director;

(2) evidence of insurance or financial responsibility required under this subchapter;

(3) the required fees; and

(4) any other information required by the executive director.

(b) The department may conduct an examination of any criminal conviction of an applicant, including by obtaining any criminal history record information permitted by law.

Sec. 2308.103. Requirements for Incident Management Towing Permit.

(a) An incident management towing permit is required for a tow truck used to perform any nonconsent tow initiated by a peace officer, including a tow authorized under Section 545.3051, Transportation Code.

(b) To be eligible for an incident management towing permit, an applicant must submit evidence that:

(1) the tow truck is equipped to tow light-duty or heavy-duty vehicles according to the manufacturer's towing guidelines;

(2) the applicant has at least $500,000 of liability insurance for the tow truck; and

(3) the applicant has at least $50,000 of cargo insurance for the tow truck.

(c) A tow truck permitted under this section may also be used for private property towing and consent towing.

(d) [Repealed.]

Sec. 2308.104. Requirements for Private Property Towing Permit.

(a) A private property towing permit is required for a tow truck used to perform a nonconsent tow authorized by a parking facility owner under this chapter.

(b) To be eligible for a private property towing permit, an applicant must submit evidence that:

(1) the tow truck is equipped to tow light-duty or heavy-duty vehicles according to the manufacturer's towing guidelines;

(2) the applicant has at least $300,000 of liability insurance for the tow truck; and

(3) the applicant has at least $50,000 of cargo insurance for the tow truck.

(c) A tow truck permitted under this section may also be used for consent towing but not for incident management towing.

Sec. 2308.105. Requirements for Consent Towing Permit.

(a) A consent towing permit is required for a tow truck used to perform a consent tow authorized by the vehicle owner.

(b) To be eligible for a consent towing permit, an applicant must submit evidence that:

(1) the tow truck is equipped to tow light-duty or heavy-duty vehicles according to the manufacturer's towing guidelines; and

(2) the applicant has at least $300,000 of liability insurance for the tow truck.

(c) A tow truck permitted under this section may not be used for nonconsent towing, including incident management towing and private property towing.

Sec. 2308.106. Department Approval; Issuance of Permit.

(a) The department shall issue a permit under this subchapter to an applicant who meets the requirements for a permit. The department may deny an application if the applicant has had a permit revoked under this chapter.

(b) The department shall issue a certificate containing a single unique permit number for each tow truck, regardless of whether the permit holder holds more than one permit.

Sec. 2308.107. Permit Renewal.

(a) A permit issued under this chapter is valid for one year. The department may adopt a system under which permits expire at different times during the year.

(b) The department shall notify the permit holder at least 30 days before the date a permit expires. The notice must be in writing and sent to the permit holder's last known address according to the records of the department.

(c) A permit holder may renew a permit under this chapter by:

(1) paying a fee for each tow truck; and

(2) providing to the department evidence of continuing insurance or financial responsibility in an amount required by this chapter.

Sec. 2308.108. Cab Cards.

(a) The department shall issue a cab card for each tow truck issued a permit. The cab card must:

(1) show the permit number of the certificate issued under Section 2308.106(b);

(2) show the type of permit issued;

(3) show the vehicle unit number;

(4) show the vehicle identification number; and

(5) contain a statement that the vehicle has been issued a permit under this subchapter.

(b) The department shall issue a cab card when the department issues or renews a permit under this subchapter.

(c) A permit holder must keep the cab card in the cab of each permitted tow truck.

(d) The department may order a permit holder to surrender a cab card if the permit is suspended or revoked under this chapter.

(e) If the department determines that the cab card system described by Subsections (a) through (c) is not an efficient means of enforcing this subchapter, the executive director by rule may adopt an alternative method that is accessible by law enforcement personnel in the field and provides for the enforcement of the permit requirements of this subchapter.

(f) A cab card or a permit issued under the alternative method described in Subsection (e) must be valid for the same duration as a certificate issued under Section 2308.106.

Sec. 2308.109. Display of Information on Tow Truck.

(a) A permit holder shall display on each permitted tow truck:

(1) the permit holder's name;

(2) the permit holder's telephone number;

(3) the city and state where the permit holder is located; and

(4) the permit number for the tow truck.

(b) The information required to be displayed must be:

(1) printed in letters and numbers that are at least two inches high and in a color that contrasts with the color of the background surface; and

(2) permanently affixed in conspicuous places on both sides of the tow truck.

Sec. 2308.110. Financial Responsibility.

(a) A permit holder shall maintain liability insurance for each tow truck according to the requirements under this subchapter.

(b) Unless state law permits a tow truck to be self-insured, any insurance required for a tow truck must be obtained from an insurer authorized to do business in this state.

(c) An applicant or permit holder must file with the department evidence of insurance as required by this subchapter.

(d) A permit holder shall keep evidence of insurance in a form approved by the department in the cab of each permitted tow truck.

SUBCHAPTER D LICENSE REQUIREMENTS

Sec. 2308.151. License or Local Authorization Required.

(a) Unless the person holds an appropriate license under this subchapter, a person may not:

(1) perform towing operations; or

(2) operate a towing company.

(b) Unless prohibited by a local authority under Section 2308.2085, a person may:

(1) perform booting operations; and

(2) operate a booting company.

Sec. 2308.152. General License Application Requirements.

An applicant for a license under this subchapter must submit to the department:

(1) a completed application on a form prescribed by the executive director;

(2) the required fees; and

(3) any other information required by commission rule.

Sec. 2308.1521. Vehicle Storage Facility Employee and Towing Operator; Dual License. [Repealed]

Sec. 2308.153. Incident Management Towing Operator's License.

(a) An incident management towing operator's license is required to operate a tow truck permitted under Section 2308.103.

(b) An applicant for an incident management towing operator's license must:

(1) hold a valid driver's license issued by a state in the United States; and

(2) be certified by a program approved by the department.

(c) A person holding a license described by this section may work at a vehicle storage facility regulated under Chapter 2303.

Sec. 2308.154. Private Property Towing Operator's License.

(a) A private property towing operator's license is required to operate a tow truck permitted under Section 2308.104.

(b) An applicant for a private property towing operator's license must:

(1) hold a valid driver's license issued by a state in the United States; and

(2) be certified by a program approved by the department.

(c) A person holding a license described by this section may work at a vehicle storage facility regulated under Chapter 2303.

Sec. 2308.155. Consent Towing Operator's License.

(a) A consent towing operator's license is required to operate a tow truck permitted under Section 2308.105.

(b) An applicant for a consent towing operator's license must hold a valid driver's license issued by a state in the United States.

(c) A person holding a license described by this section may work at a vehicle storage facility regulated under Chapter 2303.

Sec. 2308.1551. Training License. [Repealed]

Sec. 2308.1555. Boot Operator's License. [Repealed]

Sec. 2308.1556. Booting Company License. [Repealed]

Sec. 2308.156. Nontransferability of License.

A license issued by the executive director is valid throughout this state and is not transferable.

Sec. 2308.157. Requirement for Initial Renewal of Incident Management Towing Operator's License.

To renew an incident management towing operator's license the first time, a license holder must complete a professional development course relating to incident management towing that is approved and administered by the department.

Sec. 2308.158. Alcohol and Drug Testing of Towing Operators.

(a) A towing company shall establish an alcohol and drug testing policy for towing operators. A towing company that establishes an alcohol and drug testing policy under this subsection may adopt the model alcohol and drug testing policy adopted by the commission or may use another alcohol and drug testing policy that the department determines is at least as stringent as the policy adopted by the commission.

(b) The commission by rule shall adopt a model alcohol and drug testing policy for use by a towing company. The model alcohol and drug testing policy must be designed to ensure the safety of the public through appropriate alcohol and drug testing and to protect the rights of employees. The model alcohol and drug testing policy must:

(1) require at least one scheduled drug test each year for each towing operator; and

(2) authorize random, unannounced alcohol and drug testing for towing operators.

Sec. 2308.159. License Renewal.

(a) A license issued under this subchapter is valid for one year. The department may adopt a system under which licenses expire at different times during the year.

(b) The department shall notify the license holder at least 30 days before the date a license expires. The notice must be in writing and sent to the license holder's last known address according to the records of the department.

(c) A license holder may renew a license issued under this chapter by:

(1) submitting an application on a form prescribed by the executive director;

(2) submitting evidence demonstrating compliance with the requirements for the license type as required by this chapter or commission rule;

(3) paying a renewal fee; and

(4) completing any applicable continuing education requirements.

SUBCHAPTER E
LOCAL REGULATION OF TOWING AND BOOTING

Sec. 2308.201. Tow Truck Regulation by Political Subdivisions.

(a) A political subdivision of this state may regulate the operation of a tow truck to the extent allowed by federal law, except that a political subdivision may not issue a more restrictive regulation for the use of lighting equipment on a tow truck than is imposed by Title 7, Transportation Code.

(b) A political subdivision may not require the registration of a tow truck that performs consent tows in the political subdivision unless the owner of the tow truck has a place of business in the territory of the political subdivision.

(c) A political subdivision may require the registration of a tow truck that performs a nonconsent tow in the political subdivision, regardless of whether the owner of the tow truck has a place of business in the territory of the political subdivision.

(d) A political subdivision may not require a person who holds a driver's license or commercial driver's license to obtain a license or permit for operating a tow truck unless the person performs nonconsent tows in the territory of the political subdivision. A fee charged for a license or permit may not exceed $15.

Sec. 2308.202. Regulation by Political Subdivisions of Fees for Nonconsent Tows.

The governing body of a political subdivision may regulate the fees that may be charged or collected in connection with a nonconsent tow originating in the territory of the political subdivision if the private property tow fees:

(1) are authorized by commission rule; and

(2) do not exceed the maximum amount authorized by commission rule.

Sec. 2308.203. Towing Fee Studies.

(a) The governing body of a political subdivision that regulates nonconsent tow fees shall establish procedures by which a towing company may request that a towing fee study be performed.

(b) The governing body of the political subdivision shall establish or amend the allowable fees for nonconsent tows at amounts that represent the fair value of the services of a towing company and are reasonably related to any financial or accounting information provided to the governing body.

Sec. 2308.204. Fees for Private Property Tows in Other Areas [Repealed].

Repealed by Acts 2011, 82nd Leg., ch. 353 (H.B. 3510), § 19(a)(1), effective September 1, 2011.

Sec. 2308.205. Towing of Vehicles to Licensed Vehicle Storage Facilities or Other Locations on Parking Facilities.

(a) A towing company that makes a nonconsent tow shall tow the vehicle to a vehicle storage facility that is operated by a person who holds a license to operate the facility under Chapter 2303, unless:

(1) the towing company agrees to take the vehicle to a location designated by the vehicle's owner; or

(2) the vehicle is towed under:

(A) rules adopted under Subsection (a-1); or

(B) Section 2308.259(b).

(a-1) The commission shall adopt rules authorizing a towing company that makes a nonconsent tow from a parking facility to tow the vehicle to another location on the same parking facility under the direction of:

(1) the parking facility owner;

(2) a parking facility authorized agent; or

(3) a peace officer.

(b) A storage or notification fee imposed in connection with a motor vehicle towed to a vehicle storage facility is governed by Chapter 2303.

(c) Except as provided by this chapter, Article 18.23, Code of Criminal Procedure, or Chapter 2303, a fee may not be charged or collected without the prior written consent of the vehicle owner or operator.

Sec. 2308.206. Required Filing [Repealed].

Repealed by Acts 2011, 82nd Leg., ch. 353 (H.B. 3510), § 19(a)(2), effective September 1, 2011.

Sec. 2308.2065. Fees for Nonconsent Tows; Refunds.

(a) A license or permit holder may not charge a fee for a nonconsent tow that is greater than:

(1) the fee for a nonconsent tow established under Section 2308.0575; or

(2) a fee for a nonconsent tow authorized by a political subdivision.

(b) A license or permit holder may not charge a fee for a service related to a nonconsent tow that is not included in the list of fees established:

(1) under Section 2308.0575; or

(2) by a political subdivision.

(c) The department may require a license or permit holder to refund to a vehicle owner or operator the:

(1) amount charged to the owner or operator in excess of the amounts established by commission rule or by a political subdivision; or

(2) total amount of the charges for a service not listed in the amounts established by commission rule or by a political subdivision.

Sec. 2308.207. Required Posting [Repealed].

Repealed by Acts 2009, 81st Leg., ch. 757 (S.B. 702), § 13, effective September 1, 2009.

Sec. 2308.208. Municipal or County Ordinance Regulating Unauthorized Vehicles and Towing of Motor Vehicles.

The governing body of a municipality or the commissioners court of a county may adopt an ordinance that is identical to this chapter or that imposes additional requirements that exceed the minimum standards of this chapter but may not adopt an ordinance conflicting with this chapter.

Sec. 2308.2085. Local Authority Regulation of Booting Activities.

(a) A local authority may regulate, in areas in which the entity regulates parking or traffic, booting activities, including:

(1) operation of booting companies and operators that operate on a parking facility;

(2) any permit and sign requirements in connection with the booting of a vehicle; and

(3) fees that may be charged in connection with the booting of a vehicle.

(b) Regulations adopted under this section must:

(1) incorporate the requirements of Sections 2308.257 and 2308.258;

(2) include procedures for vehicle owners and operators to file a complaint with the local authority regarding a booting company or operator; and

(3) provide for the imposition of a penalty on a booting company or operator for a violation of Section 2308.258.

Sec. 2308.209. Tow Rotation List in Certain Counties.

(a) [Repealed by Acts 2009, 81st Leg., ch. 87 (S.B. 1969), § 27.002(37), effective September 1, 2009.]

(b) This section applies only to the unincorporated area of a county:

(1) with a population of 450,000 or more that is adjacent to a county with a population of 3.3 million or more;

(2) with a population of less than 10,000 that is located in a national forest; or

(3) adjacent to a county described by Subdivision (2) that has a population of less than 75,000.

(c) The sheriff's office may maintain a list of towing companies to perform nonconsent tows of motor vehicles initiated by a peace officer investigating a traffic accident or a traffic incident. The towing companies must operate in a county to which this section applies.

(d) A peace officer initiating a nonconsent tow of a motor vehicle involved in a traffic accident or traffic incident that the officer is investigating shall notify the sheriff's office that the tow is being initiated. The sheriff's office shall contact successive towing companies on the tow rotation list until a company agrees to carry out the tow.

(e) The sheriff's office may assess a towing company an administrative fee to be included on the tow rotation list in an amount not to exceed the amount necessary to implement this section.

(f) The commissioners court of a county in which a list is maintained under Subsection (c) shall adopt policies to implement this section in a manner that ensures:

(1) equal distribution of nonconsent tows among the towing companies that perform nonconsent tows in the county; and

(2) consumer protection, including fair pricing, for owners or operators of motor vehicles towed by towing companies on the tow rotation list.

(g) The sheriff's office shall make a list maintained under this section available for public inspection.

(h) In a county in which a list is maintained under Subsection (c), a person commits an offense if:

(1) the person arrives at the scene of a traffic accident or traffic incident to perform a nonconsent tow of a motor vehicle without first being contacted by the sheriff's office;

(2) the person directly or indirectly solicits, on streets located in the county, towing services, including towing, removing, repairing, wrecking, storing, trading, selling, or purchasing related to a vehicle that has been damaged in an accident to the extent that it cannot be normally and safely driven; or

(3) the person enters the scene of a traffic accident, traffic incident, or other area under the control of a peace officer without the permission of the peace officer.

(i) An offense under Subsection (h) is a misdemeanor punishable by a fine of not less than $1 or more than $200.

Sec. 2308.210. Roadway Clearance Program in Certain Counties; Offense.

(a) In this section, "freeway" has the meaning assigned by Section 541.302, Transportation Code.

(b) The commissioners court of a county adjacent to a county with a population of more than 3.3 million by order may establish a program:

(1) for maintaining the safe movement of traffic on county freeways; and

(2) under which a peace officer designated by the sheriff's office or the commissioners court is authorized to direct, at the scene of an incident or remotely, a towing company, only for the purpose of the program, to:

(A) remove from a freeway, including the shoulder of a freeway, a vehicle that is impeding the safe movement of traffic; and

(B) relocate the vehicle to the closest safe location for the vehicle to be stored.

(c) An order under Subsection (b) must ensure the protection of the public and the safe and efficient operation of towing and storage services in the county.

(d) The commissioners court of a county operating a program under this section:

(1) may enter into an agreement with a federal agency, state agency, municipality, adjacent county, metropolitan rapid transit authority, or regional planning organization or any other governmental entity for the purpose of carrying out the program; and

(2) may apply for grants and other funding to carry out the program.

(e) A towing company or towing operator commits an offense if the company or operator violates a provision of an order establishing a program under this section relating to:

(1) the presence of a tow truck at the scene of an incident on a freeway or other area under the jurisdiction of the program; or

(2) the offering of towing or related services on a freeway or other area under the jurisdiction of the program.

(f) An offense under Subsection (e) is a misdemeanor punishable by a fine of not less than $1 or more than $200.

SUBCHAPTER F UNAUTHORIZED VEHICLES

Sec. 2308.251. Prohibition Against Unattended Vehicles in Certain Areas.

(a) The owner or operator of a vehicle may not leave unattended on a parking facility a vehicle that:

(1) is in or obstructs a vehicular traffic aisle, entry, or exit of the parking facility;

(2) prevents a vehicle from exiting a parking space in the facility;

(3) is in or obstructs a fire lane marked according to Subsection (c);

(4) does not display the special license plates issued under Section 504.201, Transportation Code, or the disabled parking placard issued under Chapter 681, Transportation Code, for a vehicle transporting a disabled person and is in a parking space that is designated for the exclusive use of a vehicle transporting a disabled person; or

(5) is leaking a fluid that presents a hazard or threat to persons or property.

(b) Subsection (a) does not apply to an emergency vehicle that is owned by, or the operation of which is authorized by, a governmental entity.

(c) If a government regulation governing the marking of a fire lane applies to a parking facility, a fire lane in the facility must be marked as provided by the regulation. If a government regulation on the marking of a fire lane does not apply to the parking facility, all curbs of fire lanes must be painted red and be conspicuously and legibly marked with the warning "FIRE LANE—TOW AWAY ZONE" in white letters at least three inches tall, at intervals not exceeding 50 feet.

Sec. 2308.252. Removal and Storage of Unauthorized Vehicle.

(a) A parking facility owner may, without the consent of the owner or operator of an unauthorized vehicle, cause the vehicle and any property on or in the vehicle to be removed and stored at a vehicle storage facility at the vehicle owner's or operator's expense if:

(1) signs that comply with Subchapter G prohibiting unauthorized vehicles are located on the parking facility at the time of towing and for the preceding 24 hours and remain installed at the time of towing;

(2) the owner or operator of the vehicle has received actual notice from the parking facility owner

that the vehicle will be towed at the vehicle owner's or operator's expense if it is in or not removed from an unauthorized space;

(3) the parking facility owner gives notice to the owner or operator of the vehicle under Subsection (b); or

(4) on request the parking facility owner provides to the owner or operator of the vehicle information on the name of the towing company and vehicle storage facility that will be used to remove and store the vehicle and the vehicle is:

(A) left in violation of Section 2308.251 or 2308.253; or

(B) in or obstructing a portion of a paved driveway or abutting public roadway used for entering or exiting the facility.

(b) A parking facility owner is considered to have given notice under Subsection (a)(3) if:

(1) a conspicuous notice has been attached to the vehicle's front windshield or, if the vehicle has no front windshield, to a conspicuous part of the vehicle stating:

(A) that the vehicle is in a parking space in which the vehicle is not authorized to be parked;

(B) a description of all other unauthorized areas in the parking facility;

(C) that the vehicle will be towed at the expense of the owner or operator of the vehicle if it remains in an unauthorized area of the parking facility; and

(D) a telephone number that is answered 24 hours a day to enable the owner or operator of the vehicle to locate the vehicle; and

(2) a notice is mailed after the notice is attached to the vehicle as provided by Subdivision (1) to the owner of the vehicle by certified mail, return receipt requested, to the last address shown for the owner according to the vehicle registration records of the Texas Department of Motor Vehicles, or if the vehicle is registered in another state, the appropriate agency of that state.

(c) The notice under Subsection (b)(2) must:

(1) state that the vehicle is in a space in which the vehicle is not authorized to park;

(2) describe all other unauthorized areas in the parking facility;

(3) contain a warning that the unauthorized vehicle will be towed at the expense of the owner or operator of the vehicle if it is not removed from the parking facility before the 15th day after the postmark date of the notice; and

(4) state a telephone number that is answered 24 hours a day to enable the owner or operator to locate the vehicle.

(d) The mailing of a notice under Subsection (b)(2) is not required if after the notice is attached under Subsection (b)(1) the owner or operator of the vehicle leaves the vehicle in another location where parking is unauthorized for the vehicle according to the notice.

Sec. 2308.253. Unattended Vehicles on Parking Facility of Apartment Complex; Removal and Storage of Vehicles.

(a) This section applies only to a parking facility serving or adjacent to an apartment complex consisting of one or more residential apartment units and any adjacent real property serving the apartment complex.

(b) The owner or operator of a vehicle may not leave unattended on a parking facility a vehicle that:

(1) obstructs a gate that is designed or intended for the use of pedestrians or vehicles;

(2) obstructs pedestrian or vehicular access to an area that is used for the placement of a garbage or refuse receptacle used in common by residents of the apartment complex;

(3) is in or obstructs a restricted parking area or parking space designated under Subchapter G, including a space designated for the use of employees or maintenance personnel of the parking facility or apartment complex;

(4) is in a tow away zone, other than a fire lane covered by Section 2308.251(c), that is brightly painted and is conspicuously and legibly marked with the warning "TOW AWAY ZONE" in contrasting letters at least three inches tall;

(5) is a semitrailer, trailer, or truck-tractor, as defined by Chapter 502, Transportation Code, unless the owner or operator of the vehicle is permitted under the terms of a rental or lease agreement with the apartment complex to leave the unattended vehicle on the parking facility; or

(6) is leaking a fluid that presents a hazard or threat to persons or property.

(c) A parking facility owner may not have an emergency vehicle described by Section 2308.251(b) towed from the parking facility.

(d) Except as provided by a contract described by Subsection (e), a parking facility owner may not have a vehicle towed from the parking facility merely because the vehicle does not display an unexpired license plate or registration insignia issued for the vehicle under Chapter 502, Transportation Code, or the vehicle registration law of another state or country.

(e) A contract provision providing for the towing from a parking facility of a vehicle that does not display an unexpired license plate or registration insignia is valid only if the provision requires the owner or operator of the vehicle to be given at least 10 days' written notice that the vehicle will be towed from the parking facility at the vehicle owner's or operator's expense if it is not removed from the parking facility. The notice must:

(1) state:

(A) that the vehicle does not display an unexpired license plate or registration insignia;

(B) that the vehicle will be towed at the expense of the owner or operator of the vehicle if the vehicle does not display an unexpired license plate or registration insignia; and

(C) a telephone number that is answered 24 hours a day to enable the owner or operator of the vehicle to locate the vehicle; and

(2) be:

(A) delivered in person to the owner or operator of the vehicle;

(B) sent by certified mail, return receipt requested, to that owner or operator; or

(C) attached:

(i) to the vehicle's front windshield;

(ii) to the vehicle's driver's side window; or

(iii) if the vehicle has no front windshield or driver's side window, to a conspicuous part of the vehicle.

(f) This section may not be construed:

(1) to authorize the owner or operator of a vehicle to leave an unattended vehicle on property that is not designed or intended for the parking of vehicles; or

(2) to limit or restrict the enforcement of Chapter 683, Transportation Code, the abandoned motor vehicle law.

(g) A provision of an apartment lease or rental agreement entered into or renewed on or after January 1, 2004, that is in conflict or inconsistent with this section is void and may not be enforced.

Sec. 2308.254. Limitation on Parking Facility Owner's Authority to Remove Unauthorized Vehicle.

A parking facility owner may not have an unauthorized vehicle removed from the facility except:

(1) as provided by this chapter or a municipal ordinance that complies with Section 2308.208; or

(2) under the direction of a peace officer or the owner or operator of the vehicle.

Sec. 2308.255. Towing Company's Authority to Tow and Store Unauthorized Vehicle.

(a) A towing company may, without the consent of an owner or operator of an unauthorized vehicle, tow the vehicle to and store the vehicle at a vehicle storage facility at the expense of the owner or operator of the vehicle if:

(1) the towing company has received written verification from the parking facility owner that:

(A) the signs required by Section 2308.252(a)(1) are posted; or

(B) the owner or operator received notice under Section 2308.252(a)(2) or the parking facility owner gave notice complying with Section 2308.252(a)(3); or

(2) on request the parking facility owner provides to the owner or operator of the vehicle information on the name of the towing company and vehicle storage facility that will be used to tow and store the vehicle and the vehicle is:

(A) left in violation of Section 2308.251;

(B) in or obstructing a portion of a paved driveway; or

(C) on a public roadway used for entering or exiting the facility and the tow is approved by a peace officer.

(b) A towing company may not tow an unauthorized vehicle except under:

(1) this chapter;

(2) a municipal ordinance that complies with Section 2308.208; or

(3) the direction of:

(A) a peace officer; or

(B) the owner or operator of the vehicle.

(c) Only a towing company that is insured against liability for property damage incurred in towing a vehicle may tow and store an unauthorized vehicle under this section.

(d) A towing company may tow and store a vehicle under Subsection (a) only if the parking facility owner:

(1) requests that the towing company tow and store the specific vehicle; or

(2) has a standing written agreement with the towing company to enforce parking restrictions in the parking facility.

(e) When a tow truck is used for a nonconsent tow authorized by a peace officer under Section 545.3051, Transportation Code, the operator of the tow truck and the towing company are agents of the law enforcement agency and are subject to Section 545.3051(e), Transportation Code.

Sec. 2308.2555. Removal of Certain Unauthorized Vehicles in Rural Areas.

(a) This section applies only to an abandoned vehicle that has damaged a fence on private property in a rural area.

(b) A law enforcement agency directing a towing company or tow operator to remove an abandoned vehicle that is located on private property shall provide the towing company or tow operator with the name and telephone number of the property owner or the owner's agent if the owner or agent has provided the information to the law enforcement agency.

(c) A towing company or tow operator provided with information under Subsection (b) shall contact the property owner or the owner's agent before entering private property to tow a vehicle described by Subsection (a).

Sec. 2308.256. Vehicle Storage Facility's Duty to Report After Accepting Unauthorized Vehicle [Repealed].

Repealed by Acts 2009, 81st Leg., ch. 757 (S.B. 702), § 13, effective September 1, 2009; Acts 2011, 82nd Leg., ch. 91 (S.B. 1303), § 18.005, effective September 1, 2011 and by Acts 2011, 82nd Leg., ch. 353 (H.B. 3510), § 19(b), effective September 1, 2011.

Sec. 2308.2565. Vehicle Storage Facility Duty to Report After Accepting Unauthorized Vehicle.

(a) Except for an incident management tow requested by a law enforcement agency, a vehicle storage facility accepting a vehicle that is towed under this chapter shall within two hours after receiving the vehicle report to the police department of the municipality from which the vehicle was towed or, if the vehicle was towed from a location that is not in a municipality with a police department, to the sheriff of the county from which the vehicle was towed:

(1) a general description of the vehicle;

(2) the state and number of the vehicle's license plate, if any;

(3) the vehicle identification number of the vehicle, if it can be ascertained;

(4) the location from which the vehicle was towed; and

(5) the name and location of the vehicle storage facility in which the vehicle is being stored.

(b) A law enforcement agency may request a vehicle storage facility to provide a report, in a manner prescribed by the law enforcement agency, of incident management tows within the jurisdiction of the agency. A vehicle storage facility must provide the report not later than 48 hours after the time the facility receives the request.

Sec. 2308.257. Booting of Unauthorized Vehicle.

(a) A parking facility owner may, without the consent of the owner or operator of an unauthorized vehicle, cause a boot to be installed on the vehicle in the parking facility if signs that comply with Subchapter G prohibiting unauthorized vehicles are located on the parking facility at the time of the booting and for the preceding 24 hours and remain installed at the time of the booting.

(b) A boot operator that installs a boot on a vehicle must affix a conspicuous notice to the vehicle's front windshield or driver's side window stating:

(1) that the vehicle has been booted and damage may occur if the vehicle is moved;

(2) the date and time the boot was installed;

(3) the name, address, and telephone number of the booting company;

(4) a telephone number that is answered 24 hours a day to enable the owner or operator of the vehicle to arrange for removal of the boot;

(5) the amount of the fee for removal of the boot and any associated parking fees;

(6) notice of the right of a vehicle owner or vehicle operator to a hearing under Subchapter J; and

(7) in the manner prescribed by the local authority, notice of the procedure to file a complaint with the local authority for violation of this chapter by a boot operator.

(c) On removal of a boot, the boot operator shall provide a receipt to the vehicle owner or operator stating:

(1) the name of the person who removed the boot;

(2) the date and time the boot was removed;

(3) the name of the person to whom the vehicle was released;

(4) the amount of fees paid for removal of the boot and any associated parking fees; and

(5) the right of the vehicle owner or operator to a hearing under Subchapter J.

(d) The booting company shall maintain a copy of the receipt at its place of business for a period of three years. A peace officer has the right, on request, to inspect and copy the records to determine compliance with the requirements of this section.

(e) A booting company shall accept payment by an electronic check, debit card, or credit card for any fee or charge associated with the removal of a boot. A booting company may not collect a fee for any charge associated with the removal of a boot from a person who offers to pay the charge with an electronic check, debit card, or credit card form of payment that the booting company is not equipped to accept.

Sec. 2308.258. Boot Removal.

(a) A booting company responsible for the installation of a boot on a vehicle shall remove the boot not later than one hour after the time the owner or operator of the vehicle contacts the company to request removal of the boot.

(b) A booting company shall waive the amount of the fee for removal of a boot, excluding any associated parking fees, if the company fails to have the boot removed within the time prescribed by Subsection (a).

(c) A booting company responsible for the installation of more than one boot on a vehicle may not charge a total amount for the removal of the boots that is greater than the amount of the fee for the removal of a single boot.

Sec. 2308.259. Towing Company's Authority to Tow Vehicle from University Parking Facility.

(a) In this section:

(1) "Special event" means a university-sanctioned, on-campus activity, including parking lot maintenance.

(2) "University" means:

(A) a public senior college or university, as defined by Section 61.003, Education Code; or

(B) a private or independent institution of higher education, as defined by Section 61.003, Education Code.

(b) Subject to Subsection (c), an individual designated by a university may, to facilitate a special event, request that a vehicle parked at a university parking facility be towed to another location on the university campus.

(c) A vehicle may not be towed under Subsection (b) unless signs complying with this section are installed on the parking facility for the 72 hours preceding towing enforcement for the special event and for 48 hours after the conclusion of the special event.

(d) Each sign required under Subsection (c) must:

(1) contain:

(A) a statement of:

(i) the nature of the special event; and

(ii) the dates and hours of towing enforcement; and

(B) the number, including the area code, of a telephone that is answered 24 hours a day to identify the location of a towed vehicle;

(2) face and be conspicuously visible to the driver of a vehicle that enters the facility;

(3) be located:

(A) on the right or left side of each driveway or curb-cut through which a vehicle can enter the facility, including an entry from an alley abutting the facility; or

(B) at intervals along the entrance so that no entrance is farther than 25 feet from a sign if:

(i) curbs, access barriers, landscaping, or driveways do not establish definite vehicle entrances onto a parking facility from a public roadway other than an alley; and

(ii) the width of an entrance exceeds 35 feet;

(4) be made of weather-resistant material;

(5) be at least 18 inches wide and 24 inches tall;

(6) be mounted on a pole, post, wall, or free-standing board; and

(7) be installed so that the bottom edge of the sign is no lower than two feet and no higher than six feet above ground level.

(e) If a vehicle is towed under Subsection (b), personnel must be available to:

(1) release the vehicle within two hours after a request for release of the vehicle; and

(2) accept any payment required for the release of the vehicle.

(f) A university may not charge a fee for a tow under Subsection (b) that exceeds 75 percent of the private property tow fee established under Section 2308.0575.

(g) A vehicle towed under Subsection (b) that is not claimed by the vehicle owner or operator within 48 hours after the conclusion of the special event may only be towed:

(1) without further expense to the vehicle owner or operator; and

(2) to another location on the university campus.

(h) The university must notify the owner or operator of a vehicle towed under Subsection (b) of the right of the vehicle owner or operator to a hearing under Subchapter J.

SUBCHAPTER G SIGNS PROHIBITING UNAUTHORIZED VEHICLES AND DESIGNATING RESTRICTED AREAS

Sec. 2308.301. General Requirements for Sign Prohibiting Unauthorized Vehicles.

(a) Except as provided by Subsection (a)(2)(B) and Section 2308.304 or 2308.305, an unauthorized vehicle may not be towed under Section 2308.252(a)(1) or booted under Section 2308.257 unless a sign prohibiting unauthorized vehicles on a parking facility is:

(1) facing and conspicuously visible to the driver of a vehicle that enters the facility;

(2) located:

(A) on the right or left side of each driveway or curb-cut through which a vehicle can enter the facility, including an entry from an alley abutting the facility; or

(B) at intervals along the entrance so that no entrance is farther than 25 feet from a sign if:

(i) curbs, access barriers, landscaping, or driveways do not establish definite vehicle entrances onto a parking facility from a public roadway other than an alley; and

(ii) the width of an entrance exceeds 35 feet;

(3) permanently mounted on a pole, post, permanent wall, or permanent barrier;

(4) installed on the parking facility; and

(5) installed so that the bottom edge of the sign is no lower than five feet and no higher than eight feet above ground level.

(b) Except as provided by Section 2308.305, an unauthorized vehicle may be towed under Section 2308.252(a)(1) or booted under Section 2308.257 only if each sign prohibiting unauthorized vehicles:

(1) is made of weather-resistant material;

(2) is at least 18 inches wide and 24 inches tall;

(3) contains the international symbol for towing vehicles;

(4) contains a statement describing who may park in the parking facility and prohibiting all others;

(5) bears the words, as applicable:

(A) "Unauthorized Vehicles Will Be Towed or Booted at Owner's or Operator's Expense";

(B) "Unauthorized Vehicles Will Be Towed at Owner's or Operator's Expense"; or

(C) "Unauthorized Vehicles Will Be Booted at Owner's or Operator's Expense";

(6) contains a statement of the days and hours of towing and booting enforcement; and

(7) contains a number, including the area code, of a telephone that is answered 24 hours a day to enable an owner or operator of a vehicle to locate a towed vehicle or to arrange for removal of a boot from a vehicle.

Sec. 2308.302. Color, Layout, and Lettering Height Requirements.

(a) Except as provided by Section 2308.305, each sign required by this chapter must comply with the color, layout, and lettering height requirements of this section.

(b) A bright red international towing symbol, which is a solid silhouette of a tow truck towing a vehicle on a generally rectangular white background, at least four inches in height, must be on the uppermost portion of a sign or on a separate sign placed immediately above the sign.

(c) The portion of the sign immediately below the international towing symbol must:

(1) in lettering at least two inches in height, contain the words, as applicable:

(A) "Towing and Booting Enforced";

(B) "Towing Enforced"; or

(C) "Booting Enforced"; and

(2) consist of white letters on a bright red background.

(d) Except as provided by Subsection (e), the next lower portion of the sign must contain the remaining information required by Section 2308.301(b) displayed in bright red letters at least one inch in height on a white background.

(e) The bottommost portion of the sign must contain the telephone numbers required by Section 2308.301(b), in lettering at least one inch in height and may, if the facility owner chooses or if an applicable municipal ordinance requires, include the name and address of the storage facility to which an unauthorized vehicle will be removed. The lettering on this portion of the sign must consist of white letters on a bright red background.

Sec. 2308.303. Telephone Number for Locating Towed Vehicle Required.

If a parking facility owner posts a sign described by Sections 2308.301 and 2308.302, the owner of a vehicle that is towed from the facility under this chapter must be able to locate the vehicle by calling the telephone number on the sign.

Sec. 2308.304. Designation of Restricted Parking Spaces on Otherwise Unrestricted Parking Facility.

A parking facility owner may designate one or more spaces as restricted parking spaces on a portion of an otherwise unrestricted parking facility. Instead of installing a sign at each entrance to the parking facility as provided by Section 2308.301(a)(2), an owner may place a sign that prohibits unauthorized vehicles from parking in designated spaces and that otherwise complies with Sections 2308.301 and 2308.302:

(1) at the right or left side of each entrance to a designated area or group of parking spaces located on the restricted portion of the parking facility; or

(2) at the end of a restricted parking space so that the sign, the top of which must not be higher than seven feet above the ground, is in front of a vehicle that is parked in the space and the rear of which is at the entrance of the space.

Sec. 2308.305. Individual Parking Restrictions in Restricted Area.

Occupations Code

(a) A parking facility owner who complies with Sections 2308.301 and 2308.302 may impose further specific parking restrictions in an area to which the signs apply for individual spaces by installing or painting a weather-resistant sign or notice on a curb, pole, post, permanent wall, or permanent barrier so that the sign is in front of a vehicle that is parked in the space and the rear of which is at the entrance of the space.

(b) The top of the sign or notice may not be higher than seven feet above the ground.

(c) The sign or notice must include an indication that the space is reserved for a particular unit number, person, or type of person.

(d) The letters on the sign or notice must be at least two inches in height and must contrast to the color of the curb, wall, or barrier so they can be read during the day and at night. The letters are not required to be illuminated or made of reflective material.

SUBCHAPTER H
REGULATION OF PARKING ON CERTAIN PUBLIC ROADWAY AREAS

Sec. 2308.351. Removal of Unauthorized Vehicle from Leased Right-of-Way.

Unless prohibited by the lease, a parking facility owner or towing company may remove an unauthorized vehicle parked in a leased area described by Section 2308.002(7)(B)(i) if the owner or towing company gives notice under Section 2308.252(a)(1), (2), or (3) and otherwise complies with this chapter.

Sec. 2308.352. Removal of Unauthorized Vehicle from Area Between Parking Facility and Public Roadway.

Unless prohibited by a municipal ordinance, a parking facility owner or towing company may remove an unauthorized vehicle any part of which is in an area described by Section 2308.002(7)(B)(ii) if notice provided by Section 2308.252(a)(2) or (3) is given and the owner or towing company has otherwise complied with this chapter.

Sec. 2308.353. Removal Under Governmental Entity's Authority of Unauthorized Vehicle Parked in Right-of-Way.

(a) A governmental entity that has jurisdiction over a public roadway and that has posted one or more signs in the right-of-way stating that parking is prohibited in the right-of-way may:

(1) remove or contract with a towing company to remove an unauthorized vehicle parked in the right-of-way of the public roadway; or

(2) grant written permission to an abutting parking facility owner to:

(A) post one or more "No parking in R.O.W." signs along a common property line of the facility and the roadway; and

(B) remove vehicles from the right-of-way of the public roadway under this chapter.

(b) A sign under Subsection (a)(2) must:

(1) state that a vehicle parked in the right-of-way may be towed at the expense of the owner or operator of the vehicle;

(2) be placed facing the public roadway:

(A) on the parking facility owner's property not more than two feet from the common boundary line; and

(B) at intervals so that no point in the boundary line is less than 25 feet from a sign posted under this subsection; and

(3) in all other respects comply with Subchapter G.

(c) After signs have been posted under Subsection (b), the parking facility owner or a towing company may remove an unauthorized vehicle from the right-of-way subject to the governmental entity's written permission given under Subsection (a)(2).

Sec. 2308.354. Authority for Removal of Vehicle From Public Roadway.

(a) Under an ordinance of a municipality regulating the parking of vehicles in the municipality, to aid in the enforcement of the ordinance, an employee designated by the municipality may be authorized to:

(1) immobilize a vehicle parked in the municipality;

(2) remove an immobilized vehicle from a public roadway in the municipality; and

(3) request the removal and storage of a vehicle that is located in an area where on-street parking is regulated by the ordinance and that:

(A) is parked illegally; or

(B) is parked legally and:

(i) has been unattended for more than 48 hours; and

(ii) the employee has reasonable grounds to believe is abandoned.

(b) A parking facility owner or towing company may not remove a vehicle from a public roadway except under:

(1) this chapter or a municipal ordinance that complies with Section 2308.208; or

(2) the direction of a peace officer, a municipal employee under Subsection (a)(3), or the owner or operator of the vehicle.

(c) Subsection (a) does not apply to a vehicle owned by an electric, gas, water, or telecommunications utility while the vehicle is parked for the purpose of conducting work on a facility of the utility that is located below, above, or adjacent to the street.

SUBCHAPTER I REGULATION OF TOWING COMPANIES AND PARKING FACILITY OWNERS

Sec. 2308.401. Parking Facility Owner Prohibited from Receiving Financial Gain from Towing Company or Booting Company.

(a) A parking facility owner may not directly or indirectly accept anything of value from:

(1) a towing company in connection with the removal of a vehicle from a parking facility; or

(2) a booting company in connection with booting a vehicle in a parking facility.

(b) A parking facility owner may not have a direct or indirect monetary interest in:

(1) a towing company that for compensation removes unauthorized vehicles from a parking facility in which the parking facility owner has an interest; or

(2) a booting company that for compensation boots vehicles in a parking facility in which the parking facility owner has an interest.

(c) This section does not apply to a sign required under Section 2308.301 provided by a towing or booting company to a parking facility owner.

Sec. 2308.402. Towing Company and Booting Company Prohibited from Financial Involvement with Parking Facility Owner.

(a) A towing company or booting company may not directly or indirectly give anything of value to a parking facility owner in connection with:

(1) the removal of a vehicle from a parking facility; or

(2) the booting of a vehicle in a parking facility.

(b) A towing company or booting company may not have a direct or indirect monetary interest in a parking facility:

(1) from which the towing company for compensation removes unauthorized vehicles; or

(2) in which the booting company for compensation installs boots on unauthorized vehicles.

(c) This section does not apply to a sign required under Section 2308.301 provided by a towing or booting company to a parking facility owner.

Sec. 2308.403. Limitation on Liability of Parking Facility Owner for Removal or Storage of Unauthorized Vehicle.

A parking facility owner who causes the removal of an unauthorized vehicle is not liable for damages arising from the removal or storage of the vehicle if the vehicle:

(1) was removed in compliance with this chapter; and

(2) is:

(A) removed by a towing company insured against liability for property damage incurred in towing a vehicle; and

(B) stored by a vehicle storage facility insured against liability for property damage incurred in storing a vehicle.

Sec. 2308.404. Civil Liability of Towing Company, Booting Company, or Parking Facility Owner for Violation of Chapter.

(a) A towing company, booting company, or parking facility owner who violates this chapter is liable to the owner or operator of the vehicle that is the subject of the violation for:

(1) damages arising from the removal, storage, or booting of the vehicle; and

(2) towing, storage, or booting fees assessed in connection with the vehicle's removal, storage, or booting.

(b) A vehicle's owner or operator is not required to prove negligence of a parking facility owner, towing company, or booting company to recover under Subsection (a).

(c) A towing company, booting company, or parking facility owner who intentionally, knowingly, or recklessly violates this chapter is liable to the owner or operator of the vehicle that is the subject of the violation for $1,000 plus three times the amount of fees assessed in the vehicle's removal, towing, storage, or booting.

(d) [Repealed by Acts 2011, 82nd Leg., ch. 353 (H.B. 3510), § 19(a)(3), effective September 1, 2011.]

Sec. 2308.405. Criminal Penalty.

A person commits an offense if the person violates this chapter. An offense under this section is a misdemeanor punishable by a fine of not less than $500 or more than $1,500 unless it is shown on trial of the offense that the person knowingly or intentionally violated this chapter, in which event the offense is a Class B misdemeanor.

Sec. 2308.406. Violation of Chapter; Injunction.

A violation of this chapter may be enjoined under Subchapter E, Chapter 17, Business & Commerce Code.

Sec. 2308.407. Minor Sign or Lettering Height Variations.

A minor variation of a required or minimum height of a sign or lettering is not a violation of this chapter.

SUBCHAPTER J RIGHTS OF OWNERS AND OPERATORS OF STORED OR BOOTED VEHICLES

Sec. 2308.451. Payment of Cost of Removal, Storage, and Booting of Vehicle.

(a) If in a hearing held under this chapter the court finds that a person or law enforcement agency authorized, with probable cause, the removal and storage in a vehicle storage facility of a vehicle, the person who requested the hearing shall pay the costs of the removal and storage.

(b) If in a hearing held under this chapter the court does not find that a person or law enforcement agency authorized, with probable cause, the removal and storage in a vehicle storage facility of a vehicle, the towing company, vehicle storage facility, or parking facility owner or law enforcement agency that authorized the removal shall:

(1) pay the costs of the removal and storage; or

(2) reimburse the owner or operator for the cost of the removal and storage paid by the owner or operator.

(c) If in a hearing held under this chapter the court finds that a person authorized, with probable cause, the booting of a vehicle in a parking facility, the person who requested the hearing shall pay the costs of the booting.

(c-1) If, in a hearing held under this chapter, regardless of whether the court finds that there was probable cause for the removal and storage of a vehicle, the court finds that the towing charge collected exceeded fees regulated by a political subdivision or authorized by this chapter or Chapter 2303, the towing company shall reimburse the owner or operator of the vehicle an amount equal to the overcharge.

(d) If in a hearing held under this chapter the court does not find that a person authorized, with probable cause, the booting of a vehicle, the person that authorized the booting shall:

(1) pay the costs of the booting and any related parking fees; or

(2) reimburse the owner or operator for the cost of the booting and any related parking fees paid by the owner or operator.

Sec. 2308.452. Right of Owner or Operator of Vehicle to Hearing.

The owner or operator of a vehicle that has been removed and placed in a vehicle storage facility or booted without the consent of the owner or operator of the vehicle is entitled to a hearing on whether probable cause existed for the removal and placement or booting.

Sec. 2308.453. Jurisdiction.

A hearing under this chapter shall be in any justice court in:

(1) the county from which the motor vehicle was towed; or

(2) for booted vehicles, the county in which the parking facility is located.

Sec. 2308.454. Notice to Vehicle Owner or Operator.

(a) If before a hearing held under this chapter the owner or operator of a vehicle pays the costs of the vehicle's removal or storage, the towing company or vehicle storage facility that received the payment shall at the time of payment give the owner or operator written notice of the person's rights under this chapter.

(b) The operator of a vehicle storage facility that sends a notice under Subchapter D, Chapter 2303, shall include with that notice a notice of the person's rights under this chapter.

(c) If before a hearing held under this chapter the owner or operator of a vehicle pays the costs for removal of a boot, the booting company shall at the time of payment give the owner or operator written notice of the person's rights under this chapter.

(d) The booting operator that places a notice on a booted vehicle under Section 2308.257 shall include with that notice a notice of the person's rights under this chapter.

(e) If the towing company or vehicle storage facility that received the payment fails to furnish to the owner or operator of the vehicle the name, address, and telephone number of the parking facility owner or law enforcement agency that authorized the removal of the vehicle, the towing company or vehicle storage facility that received the payment is liable if the court, after a hearing, does not find probable cause for the removal and storage of the vehicle.

Sec. 2308.455. Contents of Notice.

The notice under Section 2308.454 must include:

(1) a statement of:

(A) the person's right to submit a request within 14 days for a court hearing to determine whether probable cause existed to remove, or install a boot on, the vehicle;

(B) the information that a request for a hearing must contain;

(C) any filing fee for the hearing; and

(D) the person's right to request a hearing in any justice court in:

(i) the county from which the vehicle was towed; or

(ii) for booted vehicles, the county in which the parking facility is located;

(2) the name, address, and telephone number of the towing company that removed the vehicle or the booting company that booted the vehicle;

(3) the name, address, telephone number, and county of the vehicle storage facility in which the vehicle was placed;

(4) the name, street address including city, state, and zip code, and telephone number of the person, parking facility owner, or law enforcement agency that authorized the removal of the vehicle; and

(5) the name, address, and telephone number of each justice court in the county from which the vehicle was towed or, for booted vehicles, the county in which the parking facility is located, or the address of an Internet website maintained by the Office of Court Administration of the Texas Judicial System that contains the name, address, and telephone number of each justice court in that county.

Sec. 2308.456. Request for Hearing.

(a) Except as provided by Subsections (c) and (c-1), a person entitled to a hearing under this chapter must deliver a written request for the hearing to the court before the 14th day after the date the vehicle was removed and placed in the vehicle storage facility or booted, excluding Saturdays, Sundays, and legal holidays.

(b) A request for a hearing must contain:

(1) the name, address, and telephone number of the owner or operator of the vehicle;

(2) the location from which the vehicle was removed or in which the vehicle was booted;

(3) the date when the vehicle was removed or booted;

(4) the name, address, and telephone number of the person or law enforcement agency that authorized the removal or booting;

(5) the name, address, and telephone number of the vehicle storage facility in which the vehicle was placed;

(6) the name, address, and telephone number of the towing company that removed the vehicle or of the booting company that installed a boot on the vehicle;

(7) a copy of any receipt or notification that the owner or operator received from the towing company, the booting company, or the vehicle storage facility; and

(8) if the vehicle was removed from or booted in a parking facility:

(A) one or more photographs that show the location and text of any sign posted at the facility restricting parking of vehicles; or

(B) a statement that no sign restricting parking was posted at the parking facility.

(c) If notice was not given under Section 2308.454, the 14-day deadline for requesting a hearing under Subsection (a) does not apply, and the owner or operator of the vehicle may deliver a written request for a hearing at any time.

(c-1) The 14-day period for requesting a hearing under Subsection (a) does not begin until the date on which the towing company or vehicle storage facility provides to the vehicle owner or operator the information necessary for the vehicle owner or operator to complete the material for the request for hearing required under Subsections (b)(2) through (6).

(d) A person who fails to deliver a request in accordance with Subsection (a) waives the right to a hearing.

Sec. 2308.457. Filing Fee Authorized. [Repealed effective January 1, 2022]

The court may charge a filing fee of $20 for a hearing under this chapter.

Sec. 2308.457. Filing Fee Authorized. [Repealed effective January 1, 2022]

Sec. 2308.458. Hearing.

Occupations Code

(a) A hearing under this chapter shall be held before the 21st calendar day after the date the court receives the request for the hearing.

(b) The court shall notify the person who requested the hearing for a towed vehicle, the parking facility owner or law enforcement agency that authorized the removal of the vehicle, the towing company, and the vehicle storage facility in which the vehicle was placed of the date, time, and place of the hearing in a manner provided by Rule 21a, Texas Rules of Civil Procedure. The notice of the hearing to the towing company and the parking facility owner or law enforcement agency that authorized the removal of the vehicle must include a copy of the request for hearing. Notice to the law enforcement agency that authorized the removal of the vehicle is sufficient as notice to the political subdivision in which the law enforcement agency is located.

(b-1) At a hearing under this section:

(1) the burden of proof is on the person who requested the hearing; and

(2) hearsay evidence is admissible if it is considered otherwise reliable by the justice of the peace.

(b-2) The court shall notify the person who requested the hearing for a booted vehicle, the parking facility in which the vehicle was booted, and the booting company of the date, time, and place of the hearing in a manner provided by Rule 21a, Texas Rules of Civil Procedure. The notice of hearing to the person that authorized the booting of the vehicle must include a copy of the request for hearing.

(c) The issues in a hearing regarding a towed vehicle under this chapter are:

(1) whether probable cause existed for the removal and placement of the vehicle;

(2) whether a towing charge imposed or collected in connection with the removal or placement of the vehicle was greater than the amount authorized by the political subdivision under Section 2308.201 or 2308.202;

(3) whether a towing charge imposed or collected in connection with the removal or placement of the vehicle was greater than the amount authorized under Section 2308.203; or

(4) whether a towing charge imposed or collected in connection with the removal or placement of the vehicle was greater than the amount authorized under Section 2308.0575.

(c-1) The issues in a hearing regarding a booted vehicle under this chapter are:

(1) whether probable cause existed for the booting of the vehicle; and

(2) whether a boot removal charge imposed or collected in connection with the removal of the boot from the vehicle was greater than the amount authorized by the political subdivision under Section 2308.2085.

(d) The court shall make written findings of fact and a conclusion of law.

(e) The court may award:

(1) court costs and attorney's fees to the prevailing party;

(2) the reasonable cost of photographs submitted under Section 2308.456(b)(8) to a vehicle owner or operator who is the prevailing party;

(3) an amount equal to the amount that the towing charge or booting removal charge and associated parking fees exceeded fees regulated by a political subdivision or authorized by this code or by Chapter 2303; and

(4) reimbursement of fees paid for vehicle towing, storage, or removal of a boot.

Sec. 2308.459. Appeal.

An appeal from a hearing under this chapter is governed by the rules of procedure applicable to civil cases in justice court, except that no appeal bond may be required by the court.

Sec. 2308.460. Enforcement of Award.

(a) An award under this chapter may be enforced by any means available for the enforcement of a judgment for a debt.

(b) The department shall suspend a license holder's license on the license holder's failure to pay a final judgment awarded to an owner or operator of a vehicle before the 60th day after the date of the final judgment. The department must provide notice of the suspension to the license holder at least 30 days before the date the license is to be suspended.

(c) The owner or operator of the vehicle shall submit a certified copy of the final judgment to the department.

(d) On receipt of the certified copy of the unpaid final judgment, the department shall disqualify a person from renewing a license or permit or deny the person the opportunity of taking a licensing examination on the grounds that the person, towing company, or vehicle storage facility has not paid a final judgment awarded to an owner or operator of a vehicle.

(e) The department shall reinstate the license on submission of evidence satisfactory to the department of payment of the final judgment by the person, towing company, or vehicle storage facility.

SUBCHAPTER K ENFORCEMENT

Sec. 2308.501. Administrative Penalty.

(a) The commission may impose an administrative penalty on a person under Subchapter F, Chapter 51, regardless of whether the person holds a registration, permit, or license under this chapter, if the person violates:

(1) this chapter or a rule adopted under this chapter; or

(2) a rule or order of the executive director or commission.

(b) An administrative penalty may not be imposed unless the person charged with a violation is provided the opportunity for a hearing.

Sec. 2308.502. Cease and Desist Order; Injunction; Civil Penalty.

(a) The executive director may issue a cease and desist order as necessary to enforce this chapter if the executive director determines that the action is necessary to prevent a violation of this chapter and to protect public health and safety.

(b) The attorney general or executive director may institute an action for an injunction or a civil penalty under this chapter as provided by Section 51.352.

Sec. 2308.503. Sanctions.

The department may impose sanctions as provided by Section 51.353.

Sec. 2308.504. Criminal Penalty; Licensing.

(a) A person commits an offense if the person:

(1) violates the permitting or licensing requirements of this chapter;

(2) performs towing without a license to perform towing in this state;

(3) employs an individual who does not hold the appropriate license required by this chapter; or

(4) falsifies a certification or training.

(b) An offense under this section is a Class C misdemeanor. An offense under this section is enforceable by law enforcement.

Sec. 2308.505. Criminal Penalty; Towing.

(a) A person commits an offense if the person:

(1) violates an ordinance, resolution, order, rule, or regulation of a political subdivision adopted under Section 2308.201, 2308.202, or 2308.2085 for which the political subdivision does not prescribe the penalty;

(2) charges or collects a fee in a political subdivision that regulates the operation of tow trucks under Section 2308.201 or 2308.202 or booting under Section 2308.2085 that is not authorized or is greater than the authorized amount of the fee;

(3) charges or collects a fee greater than the amount authorized under Section 2308.204;

(4) charges or collects a fee in excess of the amount filed with the department under Section 2308.206;

(5) violates Section 2308.205; or

(6) violates a rule of the department applicable to a tow truck, towing company, or booting company.

(b) An offense under this section is a misdemeanor punishable by a fine of not less than $200 or more than $1,000 per violation. An offense under this section is enforceable by law enforcement.

CHAPTER 2309 USED AUTOMOTIVE PARTS RECYCLERS

SUBCHAPTER A GENERAL PROVISIONS

Sec. 2309.001. Short Title.

This chapter may be cited as the Texas Used Automotive Parts Recycling Act.

Sec. 2309.002. Definitions.

In this chapter:

(1) "Insurance company," "metal recycler," "motor vehicle," "nonrepairable motor vehicle," "nonrepairable vehicle title," "salvage motor vehicle," "salvage vehicle title," and "salvage vehicle dealer" have the meanings assigned by Section 501.091, Transportation Code.

(2) "Commission" means the Texas Commission of Licensing and Regulation.

(3) "Department" means the Texas Department of Licensing and Regulation.

(4) "Executive director" means the executive director of the department.

(5) "Used automotive part" has the meaning assigned to "used part" by Section 501.091, Transportation Code.

(6) "Used automotive parts recycler" means a person licensed under this chapter to operate a used automotive parts recycling business.

(7) "Used automotive parts recycling" means the dismantling and reuse or resale of used automotive parts and the safe disposal of salvage motor vehicles or nonrepairable motor vehicles, including the resale of those vehicles.

Sec. 2309.003. Applicability of Chapter to Metal Recyclers.

(a) Except as provided by Subsection (b), this chapter does not apply to a transaction to which a metal recycler is a party.

(b) This chapter applies to a transaction in which a motor vehicle:

(1) is sold, transferred, released, or delivered to a metal recycler as a source of used automotive parts; and

(2) is used as a source of used automotive parts.

Sec. 2309.004. Applicability of Chapter to Salvage Vehicle Dealers.

(a) Except as provided by Subsection (b), this chapter does not apply to a transaction in which a salvage vehicle dealer is a party.

(b) This chapter applies to a salvage vehicle dealer who deals in used automotive parts as more than an incidental part of the salvage vehicle dealer's primary business.

Sec. 2309.005. Applicability of Chapter to Insurance Companies.

This chapter does not apply to an insurance company.

SUBCHAPTER B ADVISORY BOARD

Sec. 2309.051. Used Automotive Parts Recycling Advisory Board.

(a) The advisory board consists of five members representing the used automotive parts industry in this state appointed by the presiding officer of the commission with the approval of the commission.

(b) The advisory board shall include members who represent used automotive parts businesses owned by domestic entities, as defined by Section 1.002, Business Organizations Code.

(c) The advisory board shall include one member who represents a used automotive parts business owned by a foreign entity, as defined by Section 1.002, Business Organizations Code.

(d) The advisory board may not include more than one member from any one used automotive parts business entity.

(e) Appointments to the advisory board shall be made without regard to the race, color, disability, sex, religion, age, or national origin of the appointee.

Sec. 2309.052. Terms; Vacancies.

(a) Advisory board members serve terms of six years, with the terms of one or two members expiring on February 1 of each odd-numbered year.

(b) A member may not serve more than two full consecutive terms.

(c) If a vacancy occurs during a term, the presiding officer of the commission shall appoint a replacement who meets the qualifications of the vacated position to serve for the remainder of the term.

Sec. 2309.053. Presiding Officer.

The presiding officer of the commission shall appoint one of the advisory board members to serve as presiding officer of the advisory board for a term of one year. The presiding officer of the advisory board may vote on any matter before the advisory board.

Sec. 2309.054. Powers and Duties of Advisory Board.

The advisory board shall provide advice and recommendations to the department on technical matters relevant to the administration and enforcement of this chapter, including licensing standards.

Sec. 2309.055. Compensation; Reimbursement of Expenses.

Advisory board members may not receive compensation but are entitled to reimbursement for actual and necessary expenses incurred in performing the functions of the advisory board, subject to the General Appropriations Act.

Sec. 2309.056. Meetings. [Repeale]

SUBCHAPTER C POWERS AND DUTIES OF COMMISSION AND DEPARTMENT

Sec. 2309.101. General Powers and Duties.

The executive director or commission, as appropriate, may take action as necessary to administer and enforce this chapter.

Sec. 2309.102. Rules.

(a) The commission shall adopt rules for licensing used automotive parts recyclers.

(b) The commission by rule shall adopt standards of conduct for license holders under this chapter.

Sec. 2309.103. Rules Regarding Licensing and Standards of Conduct.

(a) The commission shall adopt rules for licensing applicants, including rules for denial of an application if the applicant, a partner, principal, officer, or general manager of the applicant, or another license or permit holder with a connection to the applicant, has:

(1) before the application date, been convicted of, pleaded guilty or nolo contendere to, or been placed on deferred adjudication for:

(A) a felony; or

(B) a misdemeanor punishable by confinement in jail or by a fine exceeding $500;

(2) violated an order of the commission or executive director, including an order for sanctions or administrative penalties; or

(3) knowingly submitted false information on the application.

(b) The commission by rule shall adopt standards of conduct for license holders under this chapter.

Sec. 2309.104. Fees.

The commission shall establish and collect reasonable and necessary fees in amounts sufficient to cover the costs of administering this chapter.

Sec. 2309.105. Rules Restricting Advertising or Competitive Bidding.

(a) The commission may not adopt a rule restricting advertising or competitive bidding by a person who holds a license issued under this chapter except to prohibit false, misleading, or deceptive practices by the person.

(b) The commission may not include in its rules to prohibit false, misleading, or deceptive practices a rule that:

(1) restricts the use of any advertising medium;

(2) restricts the person's personal appearance or use of the person's voice in an advertisement;

(3) relates to the size or duration of an advertisement by the person; or

(4) restricts the use of a trade name in advertising by the person.

Sec. 2309.106. Periodic Inspections.

(a) [Repealed.]

(b) The department may enter and inspect at any time during business hours:

(1) the place of business of any person regulated under this chapter; or

(2) any place in which the department has reasonable cause to believe that a license holder is in violation of this chapter or in violation of a rule or order of the commission or executive director.

(c) [Repealed.]

(d) [Repealed.]

(e) In conducting an inspection under this section, the department may inspect a facility, a used automotive part, a business record, or any other place or thing reasonably required to enforce this chapter or a rule or order adopted under this chapter.

Sec. 2309.107. Personnel.

The department may employ personnel necessary to administer and enforce this chapter.

SUBCHAPTER D
LICENSE REQUIREMENTS

Sec. 2309.151. Used Automotive Parts Recycler License Required.

(a) Unless the person holds a used automotive parts recycler license issued under this chapter, a person may not own or operate a used automotive parts recycling business or sell used automotive parts.

(b) A used automotive parts recycler license:

(1) is valid only with respect to the person who applied for the license; and

(2) authorizes the license holder to operate a used automotive parts recycling business only at the one facility listed on the license.

Sec. 2309.152. General License Application Requirements.

An applicant for a used automotive parts recycler license under this chapter must submit to the department:

(1) a completed application on a form prescribed by the executive director;

(2) the required fees; and
(3) any other information required by commission rule.

Sec. 2309.153. License Requirements.

An applicant for a used automotive parts recycler license under this chapter must provide in a manner prescribed by the executive director:
(1) a federal tax identification number;
(2) proof of general liability insurance in an amount not less than $250,000; and
(3) proof of a storm water permit if the applicant is required by the Texas Commission on Environmental Quality to obtain a permit.

Sec. 2309.154. Used Automotive Parts Employee License Required. [Repealed]

Sec. 2309.155. Nontransferability of License.

A license issued by the executive director is valid throughout this state and is not transferable.

Sec. 2309.156. License Renewal.

(a) A license issued under this chapter is valid for one year. The department may adopt a system under which licenses expire at different times during the year.
(b) The department shall notify the license holder at least 30 days before the date a license expires. The notice must be in writing and sent to the license holder's last known address according to the records of the department.
(c) The commission by rule shall adopt requirements to renew a license issued under this chapter.

SUBCHAPTER E LOCAL REGULATION

Sec. 2309.201. Applicability of Certain Municipal Ordinances, Licenses, and Permits.

(a) The requirements of this chapter apply in addition to the requirements of any applicable municipal ordinance relating to the regulation of a person who deals in used automotive parts.
(b) This chapter does not prohibit the enforcement of an applicable municipal license or permit requirement that is related to an activity regulated under this chapter.

SUBCHAPTER F ENFORCEMENT

Sec. 2309.251. Administrative Penalty.

(a) The commission may impose an administrative penalty on a person under Subchapter F, Chapter 51, regardless of whether the person holds a license under this chapter, if the person violates:
(1) this chapter or a rule adopted under this chapter; or
(2) a rule or order of the executive director or commission.
(b) An administrative penalty may not be imposed unless the person charged with a violation is provided the opportunity for a hearing.

Sec. 2309.252. Cease and Desist Order; Injunction; Civil Penalty.

(a) The executive director may issue a cease and desist order as necessary to enforce this chapter if the executive director determines that the action is necessary to prevent a violation of this chapter and to protect public health and safety.
(b) The attorney general or executive director may institute an action for an injunction or a civil penalty under this chapter as provided by Section 51.352.

Sec. 2309.253. Sanctions.

The department may impose sanctions as provided by Section 51.353.

Sec. 2309.254. Criminal Penalty; Licensing.

(a) A person commits an offense if the person:
(1) violates the licensing requirements of this chapter;
(2) deals in used parts without a license required by this chapter; or
(3) employs an individual who does not hold the appropriate license required by this chapter.
(b) An offense under this section is a Class C misdemeanor.

SUBCHAPTER G CONDUCTING BUSINESS

Sec. 2309.301. Duties on Acquisition of Salvage Motor Vehicle.

(a) A used automotive parts recycler who acquires ownership of a salvage motor vehicle shall obtain a properly assigned title from the previous owner of the vehicle.

(b) A used automotive parts recycler who acquires ownership of a motor vehicle, nonrepairable motor vehicle, or salvage motor vehicle for the purpose of dismantling, scrapping, or destroying the motor vehicle, shall, before the 31st day after the date of acquiring the motor vehicle, submit to the Texas Department of Transportation a properly assigned manufacturer's certificate of origin, regular certificate of title, nonrepairable vehicle title, salvage vehicle title, other ownership document, or comparable out-of-state ownership document for the motor vehicle.

(c) After receiving the title or document, the Texas Department of Transportation shall issue the used automotive parts recycler a receipt for the manufacturer's certificate of origin, regular certificate of title, nonrepairable vehicle title, salvage vehicle title, other ownership document, or comparable out-of-state ownership document.

(d) The recycler shall comply with Subchapter E, Chapter 501, Transportation Code.

Sec. 2309.302. Records of Purchases.

A used automotive parts recycler shall maintain a record of or sales receipt for each motor vehicle, salvage motor vehicle, nonrepairable motor vehicle, and used automotive part purchased.

Sec. 2309.303. Registration of New Business Location.

Before moving a place of business, a used automotive parts recycler must notify the department of the new location. The used automotive parts recycler shall provide a storm water permit for the location if a permit is required by the Texas Commission on Environmental Quality.

SUBCHAPTER H
ADDITIONAL DUTIES OF USED AUTOMOTIVE PARTS RECYCLER IN CONNECTION WITH MOTOR VEHICLE COMPONENT PARTS

Sec. 2309.351. Definitions.

In this subchapter:

(1) "Component part" means a major component part as defined by Section 501.091, Transportation Code, or a minor component part.

(2) "Interior component part" means a motor vehicle's seat or radio.

(3) "Minor component part" means an interior component part, a special accessory part, or a motor vehicle part that displays or should display at least one of the following:

(A) a federal safety certificate;

(B) a motor number;

(C) a serial number or a derivative; or

(D) a manufacturer's permanent vehicle identification number or a derivative.

(4) "Special accessory part" means a motor vehicle's tire, wheel, tailgate, or removable glass top.

Sec. 2309.352. Removal of License Plates.

Immediately on receipt of a motor vehicle, a used automotive parts recycler shall:

(1) remove any unexpired license plates from the vehicle; and

(2) place the license plates in a secure place until destroyed by the used automotive parts recycler.

Sec. 2309.353. Dismantlement or Disposition of Motor Vehicle.

A used automotive parts recycler may not dismantle or dispose of a motor vehicle unless the recycler first obtains:

(1) a certificate of authority to dispose of the vehicle, a sales receipt, or a transfer document for the vehicle issued under Chapter 683, Transportation Code; or

(2) a certificate of title showing that there are no liens on the vehicle or that all recorded liens have been released.

Sec. 2309.354. Record of Purchase; Inventory of Parts.

(a) A used automotive parts recycler shall keep an accurate and legible record of each used component part purchased by or delivered to the recycler. The record must include:

(1) the date of purchase or delivery;

(2) the driver's license number of the seller and a legible photocopy of the seller's driver's license; and

(3) a description of the part and, if applicable, the make and model of the part.

(b) As an alternative to the information required by Subsection (a), a used automotive parts recycler may record:

(1) the name of the person who sold the part or the motor vehicle from which the part was obtained; and

(2) the Texas certificate of inventory number or the federal taxpayer identification number of the person.

(c) The department shall prescribe the form of the record required by Subsection (a) and shall make the form available to used automotive parts recyclers.

(d) This section does not apply to:

(1) an interior component part or special accessory part from a motor vehicle more than 10 years old; or

(2) a part delivered to a used automotive parts recycler by a commercial freight line, commercial carrier, or licensed used automotive parts recycler.

Sec. 2309.355. Retention of Component Parts.

(a) A used automotive parts recycler shall retain each component part in its original condition on the business premises of the recycler for at least three calendar days, excluding Sundays, after the date the recycler obtains the part.

(b) This section does not apply to the purchase by a used automotive parts recycler of a nonoperational engine, transmission, or rear axle assembly from another used automotive parts recycler or an automotive-related business.

Sec. 2309.356. Maintenance of Records.

A used automotive parts recycler shall maintain copies of each record required under this subchapter until the first anniversary of the purchase date of the item for which the record is maintained.

Sec. 2309.357. Surrender of Certain Documents or License Plates.

(a) A used automotive parts recycler shall surrender to the Texas Department of Transportation for cancellation a certificate of title or authority, sales receipt, or transfer document, as required by the department.

(b) The Texas Department of Transportation shall provide a signed receipt for a surrendered certificate of title.

Sec. 2309.358. Inspection of Records.

(a) A peace officer at any reasonable time may inspect a record required to be maintained under this subchapter, including an inventory record.

(b) On demand by a peace officer, a used automotive parts recycler shall provide to the officer a copy of a record required to be maintained under this subchapter.

(c) A peace officer may inspect the inventory on the premises of a used automotive parts recycler at any reasonable time to verify, check, or audit the records required to be maintained under this subchapter.

(d) A used automotive parts recycler or an employee of the recycler shall allow and may not interfere with a peace officer's inspection of the recycler's inventory, premises, or required inventory records.

SUBCHAPTER I
MOTOR VEHICLE SALVAGE YARDS IN CERTAIN COUNTIES

Sec. 2309.401. Applicability of Subchapter.

This subchapter applies only to a used automotive parts facility located in a county with a population of 2.8 million or more.

Sec. 2309.402. Limits on Operation of Heavy Machinery.

(a) A used automotive parts recycler may not operate heavy machinery in a used automotive parts recycling facility between the hours of 7 p.m. of one day and 7 a.m. of the following day.

(b) This section does not apply to conduct necessary to a sale or purchase by the recycler.

PARKS AND WILDLIFE

TITLE 5
WILDLIFE AND PLANT CONSERVATION

SUBTITLE I
PROTECTED FRESHWATER AREAS

CHAPTER 90
ACCESS TO PROTECTED FRESHWATER AREAS

Sec. 90.001. Definitions.

In this chapter:

(1) "Emergency" means a condition or circumstance in which a person reasonably believes that an individual has sustained serious bodily injury or is in imminent danger of serious bodily injury or that property has sustained significant damage or destruction or is in imminent danger of significant damage or destruction.

(2) "Motor vehicle" means any wheeled or tracked vehicle, machine, tractor, trailer, or semitrailer propelled or drawn by mechanical power and used to transport a person or thing.

(3) "Navigable river or stream" means a river or stream that retains an average width of 30 or more feet from the mouth or confluence up.

(4) "Protected freshwater area" means that portion of the bed, bottom, or bank of any navigable river or stream that lies at or below the gradient boundary of the river or stream. The term does not include that portion of a bed, bottom, or bank that lies below tidewater limits.

Sec. 90.002. Operation of Motor Vehicle in Protected Freshwater Area Prohibited.

Except as provided by Section 90.003 or 90.004, a person may not operate a motor vehicle in or on a protected freshwater area on or after January 1, 2004.

Sec. 90.003. Exemptions.

(a) Section 90.002 does not apply to:

(1) a state, county, or municipal road right-of-way;

(2) a private road crossing established on or before December 31, 2003; or

(3) operation of a motor vehicle by:

(A) a federal, state, or local government employee if operation of a motor vehicle is necessary for conducting official business;

(B) a person if operation of a motor vehicle is necessary for reasonable purposes related to usual and customary agricultural activities;

(C) a person if operation of a motor vehicle is necessary to and is authorized by a mineral lease;

(D) a person if operation of a motor vehicle is necessary to and authorized by a crossing easement granted by the General Land Office under the Natural Resources Code;

(E) a person if operation of a motor vehicle is necessary to an activity authorized by Chapter 86;

(F) a person in response to an emergency;

(G) a person if operation of a motor vehicle is necessary for the lawful construction, operation, or maintenance of equipment, facilities, or structures used for:

(i) the production, transportation, transmission, or distribution of electric power;

(ii) the provision of telecommunications services or other services delivered through a cable system;

(iii) the transportation of aggregates, oil, natural gas, coal, or any product of oil, natural gas, or coal;

(iv) the production, treatment, or transportation of water or wastewater; or

(v) dredge material disposal placement;

(H) an owner of the uplands adjacent to a protected freshwater area, the owner's agent, lessee, sublessee, or the lessee or sublessee's agent, representative, licensee, invitee, or guest for reasonable purposes related to usual and customary operation of:

(i) a camp regulated under Chapter 141, Health and Safety Code; or

(ii) a retreat facility owned and operated by a nonprofit corporation chartered under the laws of this state before January 1, 1970; or

(I) an owner of the adjacent uplands on both sides of a protected freshwater area and the owner's agents, employees, representatives, and lessees only for the purpose of accessing the owner's property on the opposite side of the protected freshwater area when no reasonable alternate access is available.

(b) This chapter does not apply to any river with headwaters in a state other than Texas and a mouth or confluence in a state other than Texas.

(c) A person exempt under this section who operates a motor vehicle in or on a protected freshwater area shall do so in a manner that avoids, to the extent reasonably possible, harming or disturbing vegetation, wildlife, or wildlife habitat within the protected freshwater area. A person exempt under this section who is crossing a protected freshwater area shall cross by the most direct feasible route.

Sec. 90.0035. Operation of Aircraft in or on Protected Freshwater Area.

(a) In this section, "aircraft" means a device that can be used for flight in the air, including an airplane, ultralight airplane, or helicopter.

(b) Notwithstanding any other provision of this chapter, a person may operate an aircraft in or on a protected freshwater area.

(c) A person who operates an aircraft in or on a protected freshwater area shall do so in a manner that avoids, to the extent reasonably possible, harming or disturbing vegetation, wildlife, or wildlife habitat within the protected freshwater area.

Sec. 90.004. Local River Access Plan.

(a) A county, municipality, or river authority may adopt a written local plan to provide access to a protected freshwater area located within the county's geographical boundaries or the river authority's or municipality's jurisdiction.

(b) A local plan adopted under Subsection (a) may:

(1) notwithstanding Section 90.002, allow limited motor vehicle use in a protected freshwater area;

(2) provide for the county, municipality, or river authority to collect a fee from a person accessing a protected freshwater area, the amount of which may not exceed the estimated cost that the county, municipality, or river authority incurs by allowing the limited use of motorized vehicles in protected freshwater areas within its jurisdiction; or

(3) establish other measures consistent with the policy and purposes of this chapter.

(c) Before a local plan adopted under Subsection (a) may take effect, a county, municipality, or river authority must file the plan with the department. A local plan does not take effect until the plan is approved in writing by the department.

(d) The department may approve, disapprove, or modify a local plan filed under Subsection (c). In determining whether to approve, disapprove, or modify a local plan, the department shall consider whether the plan:

(1) protects fish, wildlife, water quality, and other natural resources;

(2) protects public safety;

(3) provides for adequate enforcement;

(4) coordinates with adjacent and overlapping jurisdictions;

(5) provides for and publicizes adequate public access to a protected freshwater area;

(6) provides for adequate public services relating to access to a protected freshwater area; and

(7) protects private property rights.

(e) The department by rule may adopt additional criteria or procedures to govern approval of local plans. Lack of rules adopted under this section alone is not a sufficient basis for rejecting a local plan.

(f) The department may conduct periodic reviews of a local plan filed under Subsection (c) to monitor the effectiveness of the plan.

(g) A person who has reason to believe that a local plan filed under Subsection (c) does not comply with this section may file a petition for revocation of the plan with the department.

(h) The department shall revoke approval of a local plan if the department finds, as a result of a periodic review conducted under Subsection (f) or a petition for revocation filed under Subsection (g), that the plan as implemented fails to meet any of the criteria for approval established by Subsection (d).

(i) The department may adopt rules necessary to implement this section and Section 90.002, including rules relating to locations from which a person may launch or retrieve a vessel by trailer from the banks of a protected freshwater area. For purposes of this subsection, "vessel" has the meaning assigned by Section 12.101.

Sec. 90.0085. Camping and Building Fires Prohibited in Certain Areas.

(a) This section applies to a section of the Blanco River that is not located in a county adjacent to a county with a municipality with a population greater than 1.5 million.

(b) Notwithstanding Section 90.008(a), a person may not camp or build a fire in a dry riverbed.

Sec. 90.010. Enforcement.

All peace officers of this state shall enforce the provisions of this chapter.

Sec. 90.011. Penalty.

(a) A person commits an offense if the person violates Section 90.002, 90.008, or 90.0085.

(b) Except as provided by Subsection (c), an offense under Subsection (a) is a Class C misdemeanor.

(c) If it is shown on the trial of an offense under this section that the defendant was previously convicted two or more times under Section 90.002 or 90.008, on conviction the defendant shall be punished for a Class B misdemeanor.

(d) Each violation under this section is a separate offense.

(e) Notwithstanding Section 12.403 of this code, Subchapter B, Chapter 12, Penal Code, applies to punishments under this section.

TITLE 7
LOCAL AND SPECIAL LAWS

CHAPTER 284
DIMMIT, EDWARDS, FRIO, KENEDY, LLANO, MAVERICK, REAL, UVALDE, AND ZAVALA COUNTIES

Sec. 284.001. Discharge of Firearm Prohibited.

(a) In this section:

(1) "Archery equipment" means a longbow, recurved bow, compound bow, or crossbow.

(2) "Firearm" has the meaning assigned by Section 62.014.

(3) "Navigable river or stream" has the meaning assigned by Section 90.001.

(b) This section applies only to a navigable river or stream located wholly or partly in Dimmit, Edwards, Frio, Hall, Kenedy, Llano, Maverick, Real, Uvalde, or Zavala County.

(c) Except as provided by Subsection (d), a person may not discharge a firearm or shoot an arrow from any kind of bow if:

(1) the person is located in or on the bed or bank of a navigable river or stream at the time the firearm is discharged or the arrow is shot from the bow; or

(2) any portion of the ammunition discharged or arrow shot could physically contact the bed or bank of a navigable river or stream.

(d) This section does not apply to:

(1) an individual acting in the scope of the individual's duties as a peace officer or department employee;

(2) the discharge of a shotgun loaded with ammunition that releases only shot when discharged; or

(3) an individual engaging in fishing using archery equipment, if the individual is in compliance with Subsection (f).

(e) This section does not limit the ability of a license holder to carry a handgun under the authority of Subchapter H, Chapter 411, Government Code.

(f) An individual engaging in fishing using archery equipment may not possess while fishing:

(1) an arrow equipped with fletching of any kind;

(2) an unbarbed arrow; or

(3) a bow that is not equipped with a reel and line.

CHAPTER 287
POLK COUNTY
[REPEALED]

SUBCHAPTER A
APPLICABILITY OF UNIFORM WILDLIFE REGULATORY ACT [REPEALED.]

Sec. 287.001. Conservation Act: Applicability [Repealed].

Repealed by Acts 1997, 75th Leg., ch. 1256 (H.B. 2542), § 130, effective September 1, 1997.

CHAPTER 287.
POTTER COUNTY

Sec. 287.001. Discharge of Firearm Prohibited.

(a) In this section, "firearm" has the meaning assigned by Section 62.014.

(b) This section applies only to the segment of the Canadian River extending from the intersection of United States Highways 287 and 87 and the Canadian River to:

(1) a point 1.2 miles west of the intersection, marked by a structure serving as a railroad trestle; and

(2) a point 1.5 miles east of the intersection, where the Canadian River enters the Lake Meredith National Recreational Area.

(c) Except as provided by Subsection (d), a person may not discharge a firearm or shoot an arrow from any kind of bow if the person is located in or on the bed or bank of the portion of the Canadian River to which this chapter applies at the time the firearm is discharged or the arrow is shot from the bow.

(d) This section does not apply to:

(1) an individual acting in the scope of the individual's duties as a peace officer or department employee; or

(2) the discharge of a shotgun loaded with ammunition that releases only shot when discharged.

(e) This section does not limit the ability of a license holder to carry a concealed handgun under the authority of Subchapter H, Chapter 411, Government Code.

(e) A peace officer who provides assistance under this section in good faith and with reasonable diligence is not:

(1) civilly liable for an act or omission of the officer that arises in connection with providing the assistance; or

(2) civilly or criminally liable for the wrongful appropriation of any personal property by the person the officer is assisting.

Sec. 24A.004. Immunity From Liability.

A landlord or a landlord's agent who permits or facilitates entry into a residence in accordance with a writ issued under this chapter is not civilly or criminally liable for an act or omission that arises in connection with permitting or facilitating the entry.

Sec. 24A.005. Offense.

(a) A person commits an offense if the person interferes with a person or peace officer entering a residence and retrieving personal property under the authority of a writ issued under Section 24A.002 or 24A.0021.

(b) An offense under this section is a Class B misdemeanor.

(c) It is a defense to prosecution under this section that the actor did not receive a copy of the writ or other notice that the entry or property retrieval was authorized.

Sec. 24A.006. Hearing; Review.

(a) The occupant of a residence that is the subject of a writ issued under Section 24A.002 or 24A.0021, not later than the 10th day after the date of the authorized entry, may file a complaint in the court that issued the writ alleging that the applicant has appropriated property belonging to the occupant or the occupant's dependent.

(b) The court shall promptly hold a hearing on a complaint submitted under this section and rule on the disposition of the disputed property.

(c) This section does not limit the occupant's remedies under any other law for recovery of the property of the occupant or the occupant's dependent.

TAX CODE

TITLE 2
STATE TAXATION

SUBTITLE B
ENFORCEMENT AND COLLECTION

CHAPTER 111
COLLECTION PROCEDURES

SUBCHAPTER A
COLLECTION DUTIES AND POWERS

Sec. 111.021. Notice to Holders of and Levy upon Assets Belonging to Delinquent.

(a) If a person is delinquent in the payment of an amount required to be paid or has not paid an amount claimed in a determination made against the person, the comptroller may notify personally, by mail, or by means of facsimile or electronic transmission any other person who:

(1) possesses or controls a credit, bank or savings account, deposit, or other intangible or personal property belonging to the delinquent or the person against whom the unpaid determination is made, hereafter referred to as "assets"; or

(2) owes a debt to the delinquent or person against whom the unpaid determination is made.

(b) A notice under this section to a state officer, department, or agency must be given before the officer, department, or agency presents to the comptroller the claim of the delinquent or person to whom the unpaid determination applies.

(c) A notice under this section may be given at any time within three years after the payment becomes delinquent or within three years after the last recording of a lien filed under this title, but not thereafter. The notice must state the amount of taxes, penalties and interest due and owing, and an additional amount of penalties and interest that will accrue by operation of law in a period not to exceed 30 days and, in the case of a credit, bank or savings account or deposit, is effective only up to that amount.

(d) On receipt of a notice given under this section, the person receiving the notice:

(1) within 20 days after receiving the notice shall advise the comptroller of each such asset belonging to the delinquent or person to whom an unpaid determination applies that is possessed or controlled by the person receiving the notice and of each debt owed by the person receiving the notice to the delinquent person or person to whom an unpaid determination applies;

(2) may not transfer or dispose of the asset or debt possessed, controlled, or owed by the person at the time the person received the notice for a period of 60 days after receipt of the notice, unless the comptroller consents to an earlier disposal; and

(3) may not avoid or attempt to avoid compliance with this section by filing an interpleader action in court and depositing the delinquent's or person's funds or other assets into the registry of the court.

(e) A notice under this section that attempts to prohibit the transfer or disposal of an asset possessed or controlled by a bank or other financial institution is governed by Section 59.008, Finance Code, and also is effective if it is delivered or mailed to the principal or any branch office of the bank or other financial institution including any office of the bank or other financial institution at which the deposit is carried or the credit or property is held.

(f) A person who has received a notice under this section and who violates Subdivision (2) of Subsection (d) of this section is liable to the state for the amount of indebtedness of the person with respect to whose obligation the notice was given to the extent of the value of the asset or debt transferred or disposed of.

(f-1) A person who fails or refuses to comply with this section after receiving a notice of freeze or levy is liable for a penalty in an amount equal to 50 percent of the amount sought to be frozen or levied. This penalty is in addition to the liability imposed under Subsection (f). The penalty may be assessed and collected by the comptroller using any remedy available to collect other amounts under this title.

(g) At any time during the 60-day period as stated in Subdivision (2) of Subsection (d) of this section, the comptroller may levy upon the asset or debt. The levy shall be accomplished by delivery of a notice of levy, upon receipt of which the person possessing the asset or debt shall transfer the asset to the comptroller or pay to the comptroller the amount owed to the delinquent or to the person against whom the unpaid determination is made.

(h) A notice delivered under this section is effective:

(1) at the time of delivery against all property, rights to property, credits, and/or debts involving the delinquent taxpayer which are not at the time of the notice subject to an attachment, garnishment, or execution issued through a judicial process; and

(2) against all property, rights to property, credits and/or debts involving the delinquent taxpayer that come into the possession or control of the person served with the notice within the 60-day period provided by Subdivision (2) of Subsection (d) of this section.

(i) Any person acting in accordance with the terms of the notice of freeze or levy issued by the comptroller is discharged from any obligation or liability to the delinquent taxpayer with respect to such property or rights to property, credits, and/or debts of the taxpayer affected by compliance with the notice of freeze or levy.

(j) [Repealed by Acts 2015, 84th Leg., ch. 1255 (H.B. 1905), effective September 1, 2015.]

SUBTITLE E
SALES, EXCISE, AND USE TAXES

CHAPTER 159
CONTROLLED SUBSTANCES TAX [REPEALED]

SUBCHAPTER A
GENERAL PROVISIONS [REPEALED]

Sec. 159.001. Definitions. [Repealed]

Sec. 159.002. Measurements. [Repealed]

Sec. 159.003. Tax Payment Certificates. [Repealed]

Sec. 159.004. No Defense or Immunity. [Repealed]

Sec. 159.005. Confidential Information. [Repealed]

SUBCHAPTER B
IMPOSITION, RATE, AND PAYMENT OF TAX [REPEALED]

Sec. 159.101. Tax Imposed; Rate of Tax. [Repealed]

Sec. 159.102. Tax Payment Certificate Required. [Repealed]

Sec. 159.103. Exemption. [Repealed]

SUBCHAPTER C
CRIMINAL PROVISIONS [REPEALED]

Sec. 159.201. Possession of Item If Tax Unpaid. [Repealed]

Sec. 159.202. Counterfeit Tax Payment Certificates. [Repealed]

Sec. 159.203. Previously Used Certificates. [Repealed]

Sec. 159.204. Property Subject to Seizure [Repealed].

Repealed by Acts 1995, 74th Leg., ch. 1000 (S.B. 640), § 73, effective October 1, 1995.

Sec. 159.205. Right to Collect Subordinate to Other Laws. [Repealed]

Sec. 159.206. Settlement or Compromise of Tax. [Repealed]

SUBCHAPTER D
DISPOSITION OF PROCEEDS [REPEALED]

Sec. 159.301. Disposition of Proceeds. [Repealed]

UTILITIES CODE

TITLE 2 PUBLIC UTILITY REGULATORY ACT [EXPIRES SEPTEMBER 1, 2023]

SUBTITLE C TELECOMMUNICATIONS UTILITIES

CHAPTER 55 REGULATION OF TELECOMMUNICATIONS SERVICES [EXPIRES SEPTEMBER 1, 2025]

SUBCHAPTER E CALLER IDENTIFICATION SERVICE [EXPIRES SEPTEMBER 1, 2023]

Sec. 55.101. Definitions. [Expires September 1, 2023]

In this subchapter:

(1) "Caller identification information" means any information that may be used to identify the specific originating number or originating location of a wire or electronic communication transmitted by a telephone, including the telephone listing number or the name of the customer from whose telephone a telephone number is dialed.

(2) "Caller identification service" means a service that provides caller identification information to a device that can display the information.

(3) "Per-call blocking" means a telecommunications service that prevents caller identification information from being transmitted to a called party on an individual call when the calling party affirmatively acts to prevent the transmission.

(4) "Per-line blocking" means a telecommunications service that prevents caller identification information from being transmitted to a called party on each call unless the calling party affirmatively acts to permit the transmission.

Sec. 55.102. Applicability. [Expires September 1, 2023]

(a) This subchapter applies only to the provision of caller identification service.

(b) This subchapter does not apply to:

(1) an identification service that is used in a limited system, including a central office based PBX-type system;

(2) information that is used on a public agency's emergency telephone line or on a line that receives the primary emergency telephone number (911);

(3) information exchanged between telecommunications utilities, enhanced service providers, or other entities that is necessary for the setting up, processing, transmission, or billing of telecommunications or related services;

(4) information provided in compliance with applicable law or legal process; or

(5) an identification service provided in connection with a 700, 800, or 900 access code telecommunications service.

Sec. 55.103. Provision of Service. [Expires September 1, 2023]

(a) A telecommunications utility may offer caller identification services under this subchapter only if the utility obtains written authorization from the commission.

(b) A commercial mobile service provider may offer caller identification services in accordance with Sections 55.104, 55.105, 55.106, 55.1065, and 55.107.

Sec. 55.104. Use of Information. [Expires September 1, 2023]

(a) A person may not use a caller identification service to compile and sell specific local call information without the affirmative approval of the originating telephone customer.

(b) This section does not prohibit a provider of caller identification service from:

(1) verifying network performance or testing the caller identification service;

(2) compiling, using, and disclosing aggregate caller identification information; or

(3) complying with applicable law or legal process.

Sec. 55.105. Per-Call Blocking. [Expires September 1, 2023]

Except as provided by Section 55.1065, the commission shall require that a provider of caller identification service offer free per-call blocking to each telephone subscriber in the specific area in which the service is offered.

Sec. 55.106. Per-Line Blocking. [Expires September 1, 2023]

(a) Except as provided by Section 55.1065, the commission shall require that a provider of caller identification service offer free per-line blocking to a particular customer if the commission receives from the customer written certification that the customer has a compelling need for per-line blocking.

(b) A provider who is ordered to offer per-line blocking under this section shall notify the customer by mail of the date the blocking will begin.

(c) If a customer removes and later reinstates the per-line block, the provider may assess a service order charge in an amount approved by the commission for the provider's administrative expenses relating to the reinstatement.

(d) The commission may impose a fee or assessment on a provider in an amount sufficient to cover the additional expenses the commission incurs in implementing the customer certification provisions of this section.

(e) Information received under this section by the commission or by a provider is confidential and may be used only to administer this section.

Sec. 55.1065. Use of Blocking by Telephone Solicitor [Repealed].

Repealed by Acts 2001, 77th Leg., ch. 1429 (H.B. 472), § 3, effective June 17, 2001.

Sec. 55.107. Limitation on Commission Authority. [Expires September 1, 2023]

The commission may prescribe in relation to blocking only a requirement authorized by Sections 55.105, 55.106, and 55.1065.

Sec. 55.108. Caller ID Consumer Education Panel [Expired].

Expired pursuant to Acts 1997, 75th Leg., ch. 166 (S.B. 1751), § 1, effective September 1, 1997.

Sec. 55.109. Implementation of Panel Recommendations. [Expires September 1, 2023]

The commission may implement the recommendations of the Caller ID Consumer Education Panel and interested parties to the extent consistent with the public interest.

Sec. 55.110. Report of Blocking Failure. [Expires September 1, 2023]

(a) A provider of caller ID services who becomes aware of the failure of per-call or per-line blocking to block identification of a customer shall report that failure to the commission, the Caller ID Consumer Education Panel, and the customer whose identification was not blocked.

(b) The provider shall make a reasonable effort to notify the customer within 24 hours after the provider becomes aware of the failure. The provider is not required to notify the customer if the customer reported the failure.

(c) In this section, "caller ID service" means a service that permits the called party to determine the identity, telephone number, or address of the calling party. The term does not include 911 services.

TITLE 4 DELIVERY OF UTILITY SERVICES

SUBTITLE B PROVISIONS REGULATING DELIVERY OF SERVICES

CHAPTER 186 PROVISIONS TO ENSURE THE RELIABILITY AND INTEGRITY OF UTILITY SERVICE

SUBCHAPTER B MANIPULATION OF SERVICE FOR CERTAIN LAW ENFORCEMENT PURPOSES

Utilities Code

Sec. 186.021. Emergency Involving Hostage or Armed Suspect.

(a) In an emergency in which the supervising law enforcement official having jurisdiction in the geographical area has probable cause to believe that an armed and barricaded suspect or a person holding a hostage is committing a crime, the supervising law enforcement official may order a designated telephone company security official to cut or otherwise control telephone lines to prevent telephone communication by the armed suspect or the hostage holder with a person other than a peace officer or person authorized by a peace officer.

(b) The serving telephone company in the geographical area of a law enforcement unit shall designate a telephone company security official and an alternate to provide all required assistance to law enforcement officials to carry out this section.

(c) Good faith reliance on an order given by a supervising law enforcement official under this section is a complete defense to a civil or criminal action brought against a telephone company or the company's director, officer, agent, or employee as a result of compliance with the order.

SUBCHAPTER C FRAUDULENT OBTAINING OF SERVICE

Sec. 186.031. Definitions.

In this subchapter:

(1) "Publish" means to communicate information to another by any means.

(2) "Telecommunications service" means the transmission of a message or other information by a public utility, including a telephone or telegraph company.

Sec. 186.032. Fraudulently Obtaining Telecommunications Services.

(a) A person commits an offense if:

(1) knowing that another will use the published information to avoid payment of a charge for telecommunications service, the person publishes:

(A) an existing, cancelled, revoked, or nonexistent telephone number;

(B) a credit number or other credit device; or

(C) a method of numbering or coding that is used in issuing telephone numbers or credit devices, including credit numbers; or

(2) the person makes or possesses equipment specifically designed to be used fraudulently to avoid charges for telecommunications service.

(b) An offense under this section is a misdemeanor punishable by a fine of not more than $500, by confinement in jail for not more than 60 days, or by both, unless the person has been previously convicted of an offense under this section. A second or subsequent offense is a felony punishable by a fine of not more than $5,000, by imprisonment in the Texas Department of Criminal Justice for not less than two years and not more than five years, or by both.

(c) This section does not apply to an employee of a public utility who provides telecommunications service while acting in the course of employment.

Sec. 186.033. Disposition of Certain Equipment.

(a) A peace officer may seize equipment described by Section 186.032(a)(2) under a warrant or incident to a lawful arrest.

(b) If the person who possessed equipment seized under Subsection (a) is convicted under Section 186.032, the court entering the judgment of conviction shall order the sheriff to destroy the equipment.

SUBCHAPTER D AVAILABILITY OF EMERGENCY TELEPHONE SERVICE

Sec. 186.041. Definitions.

In this subchapter:

(1) "Emergency" means a situation in which property or human life is in jeopardy and the prompt summoning of aid is essential.

(2) "Party line" means a subscriber's telephone circuit, consisting of two or more main telephone stations connected with the circuit, each station with a distinctive ring or telephone number.

Sec. 186.042. Obstruction of Emergency Telephone Call; Penalty.

(a) A person commits an offense if:

(1) the person wilfully refuses to relinquish a party line immediately on being informed that the line is needed for an emergency call described by Subdivision (2); and

(2) the party line is needed for an emergency call:

(A) to a fire or police department; or

(B) for medical aid or an ambulance service.

(b) An offense under this section is a misdemeanor punishable by:

(1) a fine of not less than $25 and not more than $500;

(2) confinement in the county jail for not more than one month; or

(3) both fine and confinement.

Sec. 186.043. Falsification of Emergency Telephone Call; Penalty.

(a) A person commits an offense if the person secures the use of a party line by falsely stating that the line is needed for an emergency call:

(1) to a fire or police department; or

(2) for medical aid or an ambulance service.

(b) An offense under this section is a misdemeanor punishable by:

(1) a fine of not less than $25 and not more than $500;

(2) confinement in the county jail for not more than one month; or

(3) both fine and confinement.

Sec. 186.044. Notice of Certain Offenses Required.

(a) A telephone directory distributed to the public in this state that lists the telephone numbers of an exchange located in this state must contain a notice explaining the offenses under Sections 186.042 and 186.043. The notice must be:

(1) printed in type not smaller than the smallest type on the same page; and

(2) preceded by the word "warning" printed in type at least as large as the largest type on the same page.

(b) At least once each year, a person providing telephone service shall enclose in the telephone bill mailed to each person who uses a party line telephone a notice of Sections 186.042 and 186.043.

(c) This section does not apply to a directory, commonly known as a classified directory, that is distributed solely for business advertising purposes.

Sec. 186.045. Failure to Provide Notice; Penalty.

(a) A person providing telephone service commits an offense if the person:

(1) distributes copies of a telephone directory subject to Section 186.044(a) from which the notice required by that section is wilfully omitted; or

(2) wilfully fails to enclose in telephone bills the notice required by Section 186.044(b).

(b) An offense under this section is a misdemeanor punishable by a fine of not less than $25 and not more than $500.

WATER CODE

TITLE 2
WATER ADMINISTRATION

SUBTITLE D
WATER QUALITY CONTROL

CHAPTER 26
WATER QUALITY CONTROL

SUBCHAPTER I
UNDERGROUND AND ABOVEGROUND STORAGE TANKS

Sec. 26.3574. Fee on Delivery of Certain Petroleum Products.

(a) In this section:

(1) "Bulk facility" means a facility in this state, including pipeline terminals, refinery terminals, rail and barge terminals, and associated underground and aboveground tanks, connected or separate, from which petroleum products are withdrawn from bulk and delivered into a cargo tank or a barge used to transport those products. This term does not include petroleum products consumed at an electric generating facility.

(2) "Cargo tank" means an assembly that is used for transporting, hauling, or delivering liquids and that consists of a tank having one or more compartments mounted on a wagon, truck, trailer, railcar, or wheels.

(2-a) "Supplier" has the meaning assigned by Section 162.001, Tax Code.

(3) "Withdrawal from bulk" means the removal of a petroleum product from a bulk facility storage tank for delivery directly into a cargo tank or a barge to be transported to another location other than another bulk facility for distribution or sale in this state.

(b) A fee is imposed on the delivery of a petroleum product on withdrawal from bulk of that product as provided by this subsection. Each supplier on withdrawal from bulk of a petroleum product shall collect from the person who orders the withdrawal a fee in an amount determined as follows:

(1) not more than $3.75 for each delivery into a cargo tank having a capacity of less than 2,500 gallons;

(2) not more than $7.50 for each delivery into a cargo tank having a capacity of 2,500 gallons or more but less than 5,000 gallons;

(3) not more than $11.75 for each delivery into a cargo tank having a capacity of 5,000 gallons or more but less than 8,000 gallons;

(4) not more than $15.00 for each delivery into a cargo tank having a capacity of 8,000 gallons or more but less than 10,000 gallons; and

(5) not more than $7.50 for each increment of 5,000 gallons or any part thereof delivered into a cargo tank having a capacity of 10,000 gallons or more.

(b-1) The commission by rule shall set the amount of the fee in Subsection (b) in an amount not to exceed the amount necessary to cover the agency's costs of administering this subchapter, as indicated by the amount appropriated by the legislature from the petroleum storage tank remediation account for that purpose, not including any amount appropriated by the legislature from the petroleum storage tank remediation account for the purpose of the monitoring or remediation of releases occurring on or before December 22, 1998.

(c) The fee collected under Subsection (b) of this section shall be computed on the net amount of a petroleum product delivered into a cargo tank.

(d) A person who imports a petroleum product in a cargo tank or a barge destined for delivery into an underground or aboveground storage tank, regardless of whether or not the tank is exempt from regulation under Section 26.344 , other than a storage tank connected to or part of a bulk facility in this state, shall pay to the comptroller a fee on the number of gallons imported, computed as provided by Subsections (b) and (c). If a supplier imports a petroleum product in a cargo tank or a barge, the supplier is not required to pay the fee on that imported petroleum product if the petroleum product is delivered to a bulk facility from which the petroleum product will be withdrawn from bulk.

(e) A supplier who receives petroleum products on which the fee has been paid may take credit for the fee paid on monthly reports.

(f) Subsection (b) does not apply to a delivery of a petroleum product destined for export from this

Water Code

state if the petroleum product is in continuous movement to a destination outside this state. For purposes of this subsection, a petroleum product ceases to be in continuous movement to a destination outside this state if the product is delivered to a destination in this state. The person that directs the delivery of the product to a destination in this state shall pay the fee imposed by this section on that product.

(g) Each supplier and each person covered by Subsection (d) shall file an application with the comptroller for a permit to deliver a petroleum product into a cargo tank destined for delivery to an underground or aboveground storage tank, regardless of whether or not the tank is exempt from regulation under Section 26.344 . A permit issued by the comptroller under this subsection is valid on and after the date of its issuance and until the permit is surrendered by the holder or canceled by the comptroller. An applicant for a permit issued under this subsection must use a form adopted or approved by the comptroller that contains:

(1) the name under which the applicant transacts or intends to transact business;

(2) the principal office, residence, or place of business in this state of the applicant;

(3) if the applicant is not an individual, the names of the principal officers of an applicant corporation, or the name of the member of an applicant partnership, and the office, street, or post office address of each; and

(4) any other information required by the comptroller.

(h) A permit must be posted in a conspicuous place or kept available for inspection at the principal place of business of the owner. A copy of the permit must be kept at each place of business or other place of storage from which petroleum products are delivered into cargo tanks and in each motor vehicle used by the permit holder to transport petroleum products by him for delivery into petroleum storage tanks in this state.

(i) Each supplier and each person covered by Subsection (d) shall:

(1) list, as a separate line item on an invoice or cargo manifest required under this section, the amount of the delivery fee due under this section; and

(2) on or before the 25th day of the month following the end of each calendar month, file a report with the comptroller and remit the amount of fees required to be collected or paid during the preceding month.

(j) Each supplier or the supplier's representative and each person covered by Subsection (d) shall prepare the report required under Subsection (i) on a form provided or approved by the comptroller.

(k) The cargo manifests or invoices or copies of the cargo manifests or invoices and any other records required under this section or rules of the comptroller must be maintained for a period of four years after the date on which the document or other record is prepared and be open for inspection by the comptroller at all reasonable times.

(*l*) As provided by the rules of the comptroller, the owner or lessee of a cargo tank or a common or contract carrier transporting a petroleum product shall possess a cargo manifest or an invoice showing the delivery point of the product, the amount of the required fee, and other information as required by rules of the comptroller.

(m) The comptroller shall adopt rules necessary for the administration, collection, reporting, and payment of the fees payable or collected under this section.

(n) A person who fails to file a report as provided by Subsection (i) of this section or who possesses a fee collected or payable under this section and who fails to remit the fee to the comptroller at the time and in the manner required by this section and rules of the comptroller shall pay a penalty of five percent of the amount of the fee due and payable. If the person fails to file the report or pay the fee before the 30th day after the date on which the fee or report is due, the person shall pay a penalty of an additional five percent of the amount of the fee due and payable.

(o) Chapters 101 and 111—113, and Sections 162.005, 162.007, and 162.111(b)—(k), Tax Code, apply to the administration, payment, collection, and enforcement of fees under this section in the same manner that those chapters apply to the administration, payment, collection, and enforcement of taxes under Title 2, Tax Code.

(p) The comptroller may add a penalty of 75 percent of the amount of the fee, penalty, and interest due if failure to file the report or pay the fee when it comes due is attributable to fraud or an intent to evade the application of this section or a rule made under this section or Chapter 111, Tax Code.

(q) The comptroller may require a bond or other security from a permittee and may establish the amount of the bond or other security.

(r) A person forfeits to the state a civil penalty of not less than $25 nor more than $200 if the person:

(1) refuses to stop and permit the inspection and examination of a motor vehicle transporting petroleum products on demand of a peace officer or the comptroller;

(2) fails or refuses to comply with or violates a provision of this section; or

(3) fails or refuses to comply with or violates a comptroller's rule for administering or enforcing this section.

(s) A person commits an offense if the person:

(1) refuses to stop and permit the inspection and examination of a motor vehicle transporting petroleum products on the demand of a peace officer or the comptroller;

(2) makes a delivery of petroleum products into cargo tanks on which he knows the fee is required to be collected, if at the time the delivery is made he does not hold a valid permit issued under this section;

(3) makes a delivery of petroleum products imported into this state on which he knows a fee is required to be collected, if at the time the delivery is made he does not hold a valid permit issued under this section;

(4) refuses to permit the comptroller or the attorney general to inspect, examine, or audit a book or record required to be kept by any person required to hold a permit under this section;

(5) refuses to permit the comptroller or the attorney general to inspect or examine any plant, equipment, or premises where petroleum products are stored or delivered into cargo tanks;

(6) refuses to permit the comptroller or the attorney general to measure or gauge the contents of or take samples from a storage tank or container on premises where petroleum products are stored or delivered into cargo tanks;

(7) is required to hold a permit under this section and fails or refuses to make or deliver to the comptroller a report required by this section to be made and delivered to the comptroller;

(8) refuses, while transporting petroleum products, to stop the motor vehicle he is operating when called on to do so by a person authorized to stop the motor vehicle;

(9) transports petroleum products for which a cargo manifest is required to be carried without possessing or exhibiting on demand by an officer authorized to make the demand a cargo manifest containing the information required to be shown on the manifest;

(10) mutilates, destroys, or secretes a book or record required by this section to be kept by any person required to hold a permit under this section;

(11) is required to hold a permit under this section or is the agent or employee of that person and makes a false entry or fails to make an entry in the books and records required under this section to be made by the person;

(12) transports in any manner petroleum products under a false cargo manifest;

(13) engages in a petroleum products transaction that requires that the person have a permit under this section without then and there holding the required permit;

(14) makes and delivers to the comptroller a report required under this section to be made and delivered to the comptroller, if the report contains false information;

(15) forges, falsifies, or alters an invoice or manifest prescribed by law; or

(16) fails to remit any fees collected by any person required to hold a permit under this section.

(t) The following criminal penalties apply to the offenses enumerated in Subsection (s) of this section:

(1) an offense under Subdivision (1) is a Class C misdemeanor;

(2) an offense under Subdivisions (2) through (7) is a Class B misdemeanor;

(3) an offense under Subdivisions (8) and (9) is a Class A misdemeanor;

(4) an offense under Subdivisions (10) through (15) is a felony of the third degree;

(5) an offense under Subdivision (16) is a felony of the second degree; and

(6) violations of three or more separate offenses under Subdivisions (10) through (15) committed pursuant to one scheme or continuous course of conduct may be considered as one offense and are punished as a felony of the second degree.

(u) The court may not fine a corporation or association under Section 12.51(c), Penal Code, unless the amount of the fine under that subsection is greater than the amount that could be fixed by the court under Section 12.51(b), Penal Code.

(v) In addition to a sentence imposed on a corporation, the court shall give notice of the conviction to the attorney general as required by Article 17A.09, Code of Criminal Procedure.

(w) The comptroller shall deduct two percent of the amount collected under this section as the state's charge for its services and shall credit the amount deducted to the general revenue fund. The balance of the fees, penalties, and interest collected by the comptroller shall be deposited in the state treasury to the credit of the petroleum storage tank remediation account.

(x) [Repealed.]

TITLE 4
GENERAL LAW DISTRICTS

CHAPTER 49
PROVISIONS APPLICABLE TO ALL DISTRICTS

SUBCHAPTER H
POWERS AND DUTIES

Sec. 49.217. Operation of Certain Motor Vehicles on or Near Public Facilities.

(a) In this section, "motor vehicle" means a self-propelled device in, upon, or by which a person or property is or may be transported or drawn on a road or highway.

(b) Except as provided in Subsections (c) and (d), a person may not operate a motor vehicle on a levee, in a drainage ditch, or on land adjacent to a levee, canal, ditch, exposed conduit, pipeline, pumping plant, storm water facility, or other facility for the transmission, storage, treatment, or distribution of water, sewage, or storm water owned or controlled by a district.

(c) A district may authorize the use of motor vehicles on land that it owns or controls by posting signs on the property.

(d) This section does not prohibit a person from:

(1) driving on a public road or highway; or

(2) operating a motor vehicle used for repair or maintenance of public water, sewer, or storm water facilities.

(e) A person who operates a motor vehicle in violation of Subsection (b) commits an offense. An offense under this section is a Class C misdemeanor, except that if a person has been convicted of an offense under this section, a subsequent offense is a Class B misdemeanor.

TEXAS RULES OF EVIDENCE

IN THE SUPREME COURT OF TEXAS

Misc. Docket No. 15-9048

FINAL APPROVAL OF REVISIONS TO THE TEXAS RULES OF EVIDENCE

ORDERED that:

1. By order dated November 19, 2014, in Misc. Docket No. 14-9232, the Supreme Court of Texas approved amendments to the Texas Rules of Evidence and invited public comment. After receiving public comments, the Supreme Court made revisions to the rules. This order incorporates those revisions and contains the final version of the rules. The amendments are effective April 1, 2015.

2. Except for the amendments to Rules 511 and 613, which include substantive amendments, these amendments comprise a general restyling of the Texas Rules of Evidence. They seek to make the rules more easily understood and to make style and terminology consistent throughout. The restyling changes are intended to be stylistic only.

The Restyling Project

Following a lengthy restyling process, the Federal Rules of Evidence were amended effective December 1, 2011. The Texas Rules of Evidence restyling project was initiated with the aim of keeping the Texas Rules as consistent as possible with Federal Rules, but without effecting any substantive change in Texas evidence law.

General Guidelines

Following the lead of the drafters of the restyled Federal Rules, the drafters of the restyled Texas Rules were guided in their drafting, usage, and style by Bryan Garner, Guidelines for Drafting and Editing Court Rules, Administrative Office of the United States Courts (1996) and Bryan Garner, Dictionary of Modern Legal Usage (2d ed. 1995).

Formatting Changes

Many of the changes in the restyled rules result from using format to achieve clearer presentations. The rules are broken down into constituent parts, using progressively indented subparagraphs with headings and substituting vertical for horizontal lists.

"Hanging indents" are used throughout. These formatting changes make the structure of the rules graphic and make the restyled rules easier to read and understand even when the words are not changed. Rules 103, 404(b), 606(b), and 612 illustrate the benefits of formatting changes.

Changes to Reduce Inconsistent, Ambiguous, Redundant, Repetitive, or Archaic Words

The restyled rules reduce the use of inconsistent terms that say the same thing in different ways. Because different words are presumed to have different meanings, inconsistent usage can result in confusion. The restyled rules reduce inconsistencies by using the same words to express the same meaning. For example, consistent expression is achieved by not switching between "accused" and "defendant" or between "party opponent" and "opposing party" or between the various formulations of civil and criminal action/case/proceeding.

The restyled rules minimize the use of inherently ambiguous words. For example, the word "shall" can mean "must," "may," or something else, depending on context. The restyled rules replace "shall" with "must," "may," or "should," depending on which one the context and established interpretation make correct in each rule.

The restyled rules minimize the use of redundant "intensifiers." These are expressions that attempt to add emphasis, but instead state the obvious and create negative implications for other rules. The absence of intensifiers in the restyled rules does not change their substantive meaning. See, e.g., Rule 602 (omitting "but need not").

The restyled rules also remove words and concepts that are outdated or redundant.

Rule Numbers

The restyled rules keep the same numbers to minimize the effect on research. Subdivisions have been rearranged within some rules to achieve greater clarity and simplicity.

3. The amendments to Rule 511 align Texas law on waiver of privilege by voluntary disclosure with Federal Rule of Evidence 502.

4. In response to public comments, the Court made the following changes to the version of the restyled rules proposed by Misc. Docket No. 14-9232.

a. The comment to Rule 509 has been revised to add the following sentence to the end of the comment: "Finally, reconciling the provisions of Rule 509 with the parts of Tex. Occ. Code ch. 159 that address a physician-patient privilege applicable to court proceedings is beyond the scope of the restyling project."

b. The comment to Rule 510 has been revised to add the following paragraph: "Tex. Health & Safety Code ch. 611 addresses confidentiality rules for communications between a patient and a mental-health professional and for the professional's treatment records. Many of these provisions apply in contexts other than court proceedings. Reconciling the provisions of Rule 510 with the parts of chapter 611 that address a mental-health-information privilege applicable to court proceedings is beyond the scope of the restyling project."

c. The comment to Rule 613 has been revised. The comment now reads: "The amended rule retains the requirement that a witness be given an opportunity to explain or deny (a) a prior inconsistent statement or (b) the circumstances or a statement showing the witness's bias or interest, but this requirement is not imposed on the examining attorney. A witness may have to wait until redirect examination to explain a prior inconsistent statement or the circumstances or a statement that shows bias. But the impeaching attorney still is not permitted to introduce extrinsic evidence of the witness's prior inconsistent statement or bias unless the witness has first been examined about the statement or bias and has failed to unequivocally admit it. All other changes to the rule are intended to be stylistic only."

d. The Court revised Rule 804(b)(1)(A)(i) to remove redundant language. The change is stylistic only.

e. The Court revised Rule 902(10)(B) to add the following sentence to the text of the rule: "The proponent may use an unsworn declaration made under penalty of perjury in place of an affidavit."

5. The Clerk is directed to:

a. file a copy of this order with the Secretary of State;

b. cause a copy of this order to be mailed to each registered member of the State Bar of Texas by publication in the *Texas Bar Journal*.

c. send a copy of this order to each elected member of the Legislature; and

d. submit a copy of the order for publication in the *Texas Register*.

Dated: March 10, 2015.

Nathan L. Hecht, Chief Justice
Paul W. Green, Justice
Phil Johnson, Justice
Don R. Willett, Justice
Eva M. Guzman, Justice
Debra H. Lehrmann, Justice
Jeffrey S. Boyd, Justice
John P. Devine, Justice
Jeffrey V. Brown, Justice

IN THE COURT OF CRIMINAL APPEALS OF TEXAS

Misc. Docket No. 15-001

IN THE COURT OF CRIMINAL APPEALS OF TEXAS

ORDERED that:

1. By order dated November 19, 2014, in Misc. Docket No. 14-9232, the Supreme Court of Texas approved amendments to the Texas Rules of Evidence and invited public comment. After receiving public comments, the Supreme Court made revisions to the rules. This order incorporates those revisions and contains the final version of the rules. The amendments are effective April 1, 2015.

2. Except for the amendments to Rules 511 and 613, which include substantive amendments, these amendments comprise a general restyling of the Texas Rules of Evidence. They seek to make the rules more easily understood and to make style and terminology consistent throughout. The restyling changes are intended to be stylistic only.

The Restyling Project

Following a lengthy restyling process, the Federal Rules of Evidence were amended effective December 1, 2011. The Texas Rules of Evidence restyling project was initiated with the aim of keeping the Texas Rules as consistent as possible with Federal Rules, but without effecting any substantive change in Texas evidence law.

General Guidelines

Following the lead of the drafters of the restyled Federal Rules, the drafters of the restyled Texas Rules were guided in their drafting, usage, and style by Bryan Garner, Guidelines for Drafting and Editing Court Rules, Administrative Office of the United States Courts (1996) and Bryan Garner, Dictionary of Modern Legal Usage (2d ed. 1995).

Formatting Changes

Many of the changes in the restyled rules result from using format to achieve clearer presentations. The rules are broken down into constituent parts, using progressively indented subparagraphs with headings and substituting vertical for horizontal lists.

"Hanging indents" are used throughout. These formatting changes make the structure of the rules graphic and make the restyled rules easier to read and understand even when the words are not changed. Rules 103, 404(b), 606(b), and 612 illustrate the benefits of formatting changes.

Changes to Reduce Inconsistent, Ambiguous, Redundant, Repetitive, or Archaic Words

The restyled rules reduce the use of inconsistent terms that say the same thing in different ways. Because different words are presumed to have different meanings, inconsistent usage can result in confusion. The restyled rules reduce inconsistencies by using the same words to express the same meaning. For example, consistent expression is achieved by not switching between "accused" and "defendant" or between "party opponent" and "opposing party" or between the various formulations of civil and criminal action/ case/ proceeding.

The restyled rules minimize the use of inherently ambiguous words. For example, the word "shall" can mean "must," "may," or something else, depending on context. The restyled rules replace "shall" with "must," "may," or "should," depending on which one the context and established interpretation make correct in each rule.

The restyled rules minimize the use of redundant "intensifiers." These are expressions that attempt to add emphasis, but instead state the obvious and create negative implications for other rules. The absence of intensifiers in the restyled rules does not change their substantive meaning. See, e.g., Rule 602 (omitting "but need not").

The restyled rules also remove words and concepts that are outdated or redundant.

Rule Numbers

The restyled rules keep the same numbers to minimize the effect on research. Subdivisions have been rearranged within some rules to achieve greater clarity and simplicity.

3. The amendments to Rule 511 align Texas law on waiver of privilege by voluntary disclosure with Federal Rule of Evidence 502.

4. In response to public comments, the Court made the following changes to the version of the restyled rules proposed by Misc. Docket No. 14-9232.

a. The comment to Rule 509 has been revised to add the following sentence to the end of the comment: "Finally, reconciling the provisions of Rule 509 with the parts of Tex. Occ. Code ch. 159 that address a physician-patient privilege applicable to court proceedings is beyond the scope of the restyling project."

b. The comment to Rule 510 has been revised to add the following paragraph: "Tex. Health & Safety Code ch. 611 addresses confidentiality rules for communications between a patient and a mental-health professional and for the professional's treatment records. Many of these provisions apply in contexts other than court proceedings. Reconciling the provisions of Rule 510 with the parts of chapter 611 that address a mental-health-information privilege applicable to court proceedings is beyond the scope of the restyling project."

c. The comment to Rule 613 has been revised. The comment now reads: "The amended rule retains the requirement that a witness be given an opportunity to explain or deny (a) a prior inconsistent statement or (b) the circumstances or a statement showing the witness's bias or interest, but this requirement is not imposed on the examining attorney. A witness may have to wait until redirect examination to explain a prior inconsistent statement or the circumstances or a statement that shows bias. But the impeaching attorney still is not permitted to introduce extrinsic evidence of the witness's prior inconsistent statement or bias unless the witness has first been examined about the statement or bias and has failed to unequivocally admit it. All other changes to the rule are intended to be stylistic only."

d. The Court revised Rule 804(b)(1)(A)(i) to remove redundant language. The change is stylistic only.

e. The Court revised Rule 902(10)(B) to add the following sentence to the text of the rule: "The proponent may use an unsworn declaration made under penalty of perjury in place of an affidavit."

5. The Clerk is directed to:

a. file a copy of this order with the Secretary of State;

b. cause a copy of this order to be mailed to each registered member of the State Bar of Texas by publication in the *Texas Bar Journal*.

c. send a copy of this order to each elected member of the Legislature; and

d. submit a copy of the order for publication in the *Texas Register*.

Dated: March 10, 2015.

Nathan L. Hecht, Chief Justice
Paul W. Green, Justice
Phil Johnson, Justice
Don R. Willett, Justice
Eva M. Guzman, Justice
Debra H. Lehrmann, Justice
Jeffrey S. Boyd, Justice
John P. Devine, Justice
Jeffrey V. Brown, Justice

ARTICLE I. GENERAL PROVISIONS

Rule 101. Title, Scope, and Applicability of the Rules; Definitions

(a) ***Title.*** --These rules may be cited as the Texas Rules of Evidence.

(b) ***Scope.*** --These rules apply to proceedings in Texas courts except as otherwise provided in subdivisions (d)-(f).

(c) ***Rules on Privilege.*** --The rules on privilege apply to all stages of a case or proceeding.

(d) ***Exception for Constitutional or Statutory Provisions or Other Rules.*** --Despite these rules, a court must admit or exclude evidence if required to do so by the United States or Texas Constitution, a federal or Texas statute, or a rule prescribed by the United States or Texas Supreme Court or the Texas Court of Criminal Appeals. If possible, a court should resolve by reasonable construction any inconsistency between these rules and applicable constitutional or statutory provisions or other rules.

(e) ***Exceptions.*** --These rules - except for those on privilege - do not apply to:

(1) the court's determination, under Rule 104(a), on a preliminary question of fact governing admissibility;

(2) grand jury proceedings; and

(3) the following miscellaneous proceedings:

(A) an application for habeas corpus in extradition, rendition, or interstate detainer proceedings;

(B) an inquiry by the court under Code of Criminal Procedure article 46B.004 to determine whether evidence exists that would support a finding that the defendant may be incompetent to stand trial;

(C) bail proceedings other than hearings to deny, revoke, or increase bail;

(D) hearings on justification for pretrial detention not involving bail;

(E) proceedings to issue a search or arrest warrant; and

(F) direct contempt determination proceedings.

(f) ***Exception for Justice Court Cases.*** --These rules do not apply to justice court cases except as authorized by Texas Rule of Civil Procedure 500.3.

(g) ***Exception for Military Justice Hearings.*** --The Texas Code of Military Justice, Tex. Gov't Code §§ 432.001-432.195, governs the admissibility of evidence in hearings held under that Code.

(h) ***Definitions.*** --In these rules:

(1) "civil case" means a civil action or proceeding;

(2) "criminal case" means a criminal action or proceeding, including an examining trial;

(3) "public office" includes a public agency;

(4) "record" includes a memorandum, report, or data compilation;

(5) a "rule prescribed by the United States or Texas Supreme Court or the Texas Court of Criminal Appeals" means a rule adopted by any of those courts under statutory authority;

(6) "unsworn declaration" means an unsworn declaration made in accordance with Tex. Civ. Prac. & Rem. Code § 132.001; and

(7) a reference to any kind of written material or any other medium includes electronically stored information.

Rule 102. Purpose

These rules should be construed so as to administer every proceeding fairly, eliminate unjustifiable expense and delay, and promote the development of evidence law, to the end of ascertaining the truth and securing a just determination.

Rule 103. Rulings on Evidence

(a) ***Preserving a Claim of Error.*** --A party may claim error in a ruling to admit or exclude evidence only if the error affects a substantial right of the party and:

(1) if the ruling admits evidence, a party, on the record:

(A) timely objects or moves to strike; and

(B) states the specific ground, unless it was apparent from the context; or

(2) if the ruling excludes evidence, a party informs the court of its substance by an offer of proof, unless the substance was apparent from the context.

(b) ***Not Needing to Renew an Objection.*** --When the court hears a party's objections outside the presence of the jury and rules that evidence is admissible, a party need not renew an objection to preserve a claim of error for appeal.

(c) ***Court's Statement About the Ruling; Directing an Offer of Proof.*** --The court may make any statement about the character or form of the evidence, the objection made, and the ruling. The court must allow a party to make an offer of proof as soon as practicable. In a jury trial, the court must allow a party to make the offer outside the jury's presence and before the court reads its charge to the jury. At a party's request, the court must direct that an offer of proof be made in question-and-answer form. Or the court may do so on its own.

(d) ***Preventing the Jury from Hearing Inadmissible Evidence.*** --To the extent practicable, the court must conduct a jury trial so that inadmissible evidence is not suggested to the jury by any means.

(e) ***Taking Notice of Fundamental Error in Criminal Cases.*** --In criminal cases, a court may take notice of a fundamental error affecting a substantial right, even if the claim of error was not properly preserved.

Rule 104. Preliminary Questions

(a) ***In General.*** --The court must decide any preliminary question about whether a witness is qualified, a privilege exists, or evidence is admissible. In so deciding, the court is not bound by evidence rules, except those on privilege.

(b) ***Relevance That Depends on a Fact.*** --When the relevance of evidence depends on whether a fact exists, proof must be introduced sufficient to support a finding that the fact does exist. The court may admit the proposed evidence on the condition that the proof be introduced later.

(c) ***Conducting a Hearing So That the Jury Cannot Hear It.*** --The court must conduct any hearing on a preliminary question so that the jury cannot hear it if:

(1) the hearing involves the admissibility of a confession in a criminal case;

(2) a defendant in a criminal case is a witness and so requests; or

(3) justice so requires.

(d) ***Cross-Examining a Defendant in a Criminal Case.*** --By testifying outside the jury's hearing on a preliminary question, a defendant in a criminal case does not become subject to cross-examination on other issues in the case.

(e) ***Evidence Relevant to Weight and Credibility.*** --This rule does not limit a party's right to introduce before the jury evidence that is relevant to the weight or credibility of other evidence.

Rule 105. Evidence That is Not Admissible Against Other Parties or for Other Purposes

(a) ***Limiting Admitted Evidence.*** --If the court admits evidence that is admissible against a party or for a purpose - but not against another party or for another purpose - the court, on request, must restrict the evidence to its proper scope and instruct the jury accordingly.

(b) ***Preserving a Claim of Error.***

(1) ***Court Admits the Evidence Without Restriction.*** --A party may claim error in a ruling to admit evidence that is admissible against a party or for a purpose - but not against another party or for another purpose - only if the party requests the court to restrict the evidence to its proper scope and instruct the jury accordingly.

(2) ***Court Excludes the Evidence.*** --A party may claim error in a ruling to exclude evidence that is admissible against a party or for a purpose - but not against another party or for another purpose - only if the party limits its offer to the party against whom or the purpose for which the evidence is admissible.

Rule 106. Remainder of or Related Writings or Recorded Statements

If a party introduces all or part of a writing or recorded statement, an adverse party may introduce, at that time, any other part - or any other writing or recorded statement - that in fairness ought to be considered at the same time. "Writing or recorded statement" includes depositions.

Rule 107. Rule of Optional Completeness

If a party introduces part of an act, declaration, conversation, writing, or recorded statement, an adverse party may inquire into any other part on the same subject. An adverse party may also introduce any other act, declaration, conversation, writing, or recorded statement that is necessary to explain or allow the trier of fact to fully understand the part offered by the opponent. "Writing or recorded statement" includes a deposition.

ARTICLE II. JUDICIAL NOTICE

Rule 201. Judicial Notice of Adjudicative Facts

(a) ***Scope.*** --This rule governs judicial notice of an adjudicative fact only, not a legislative fact.

(b) ***Kinds of Facts That May Be Judicially Noticed.*** --The court may judicially notice a fact that is not subject to reasonable dispute because it:

(1) is generally known within the trial court's territorial jurisdiction; or

(2) can be accurately and readily determined from sources whose accuracy cannot reasonably be questioned.

(c) ***Taking Notice.*** --The court:

(1) may take judicial notice on its own; or

(2) must take judicial notice if a party requests it and the court is supplied with the necessary information.

(d) ***Timing.*** --The court may take judicial notice at any stage of the proceeding.

(e) ***Opportunity to Be Heard.*** --On timely request, a party is entitled to be heard on the propriety of taking judicial notice and the nature of the fact to be noticed. If the court takes judicial notice before notifying a party, the party, on request, is still entitled to be heard.

(f) ***Instructing the Jury.*** --In a civil case, the court must instruct the jury to accept the noticed fact as conclusive. In a criminal case, the court must instruct the jury that it may or may not accept the noticed fact as conclusive.

Rule 202. Judicial Notice of Other States' Law

(a) ***Scope.*** --This rule governs judicial notice of another state's, territory's, or federal jurisdiction's:
-- Constitution;
-- public statutes;
-- rules;
-- regulations;
-- ordinances;
-- court decisions; and
-- common law.

(b) ***Taking Notice.*** --The court:
(1) may take judicial notice on its own; or
(2) must take judicial notice if a party requests it and the court is supplied with the necessary information.

(c) ***Notice and Opportunity to Be Heard.***
(1) ***Notice.*** --The court may require a party requesting judicial notice to notify all other parties of the request so they may respond to it.
(2) ***Opportunity to Be Heard.*** --On timely request, a party is entitled to be heard on the propriety of taking judicial notice and the nature of the matter to be noticed. If the court takes judicial notice before a party has been notified, the party, on request, is still entitled to be heard.

(d) ***Timing.*** --The court may take judicial notice at any stage of the proceeding.

(e) ***Determination and Review.*** --The court - not the jury - must determine the law of another state, territory, or federal jurisdiction. The court's determination must be treated as a ruling on a question of law.

Rule 203. Determining Foreign Law

(a) ***Raising a Foreign Law Issue.*** --A party who intends to raise an issue about a foreign country's law must:
(1) give reasonable notice by a pleading or other writing; and
(2) at least 30 days before trial, supply all parties a copy of any written materials or sources the party intends to use to prove the foreign law.

(b) ***Translations.*** --If the materials or sources were originally written in a language other than English, the party intending to rely on them must, at least 30 days before trial, supply all parties both a copy of the foreign language text and an English translation.

(c) ***Materials the Court May Consider; Notice.*** --In determining foreign law, the court may consider any material or source, whether or not admissible. If the court considers any material or source not submitted by a party, it must give all parties notice and a reasonable opportunity to comment and submit additional materials.

(d) ***Determination and Review.*** --The court - not the jury - must determine foreign law. The court's determination must be treated as a ruling on a question of law.

(e) ***Suits Brought Under the Family Code Involving a Marriage Relationship or Parent-Child Relationship.*** --Subsections (a) and (b) of this rule do not apply to an action to which Rule 308b, Texas Rules of Civil Procedure, applies.

Rule 204. Judicial Notice of Texas Municipal and County Ordinances, Texas Register Contents, and Published Agency Rules

(a) ***Scope.*** --This rule governs judicial notice of Texas municipal and county ordinances, the contents of the Texas Register, and agency rules published in the Texas Administrative Code.

(b) ***Taking Notice.*** --The court:
(1) may take judicial notice on its own; or
(2) must take judicial notice if a party requests it and the court is supplied with the necessary information.

(c) ***Notice and Opportunity to Be Heard.***
(1) ***Notice.*** --The court may require a party requesting judicial notice to notify all other parties of the request so they may respond to it.
(2) ***Opportunity to Be Heard.*** --On timely request, a party is entitled to be heard on the propriety of taking judicial notice and the nature of the matter to be noticed. If the court takes judicial notice before a party has been notified, the party, on request, is still entitled to be heard.

(d) ***Determination and Review.*** --The court - not the jury - must determine municipal and county ordinances, the contents of the Texas Register, and published agency rules. The court's determination must be treated as a ruling on a question of law.

ARTICLE IV. RELEVANCY AND ITS LIMITS

Rule 401. Test for Relevant Evidence

Evidence is relevant if:

(a) it has any tendency to make a fact more or less probable than it would be without the evidence; and

(b) the fact is of consequence in determining the action.

Rule 402. General Admissibility of Relevant Evidence

Relevant evidence is admissible unless any of the following provides otherwise:

-- the United States or Texas Constitution;

-- a statute;

-- these rules; or

-- other rules prescribed under statutory authority.

Irrelevant evidence is not admissible.

Rule 403. Excluding Relevant Evidence for Prejudice, Confusion, or Other Reasons

The court may exclude relevant evidence if its probative value is substantially outweighed by a danger of one or more of the following: unfair prejudice, confusing the issues, misleading the jury, undue delay, or needlessly presenting cumulative evidence.

Rule 404. Character Evidence; Crimes or Other Acts

(a) ***Character Evidence.***

(1) ***Prohibited Uses.*** --Evidence of a person's character or character trait is not admissible to prove that on a particular occasion the person acted in accordance with the character or trait.

(2) ***Exceptions for an Accused.***

(A) In a criminal case, a defendant may offer evidence of the defendant's pertinent trait, and if the evidence is admitted, the prosecutor may offer evidence to rebut it.

(B) In a civil case, a party accused of conduct involving moral turpitude may offer evidence of the party's pertinent trait, and if the evidence is admitted, the accusing party may offer evidence to rebut it.

(3) ***Exceptions for a Victim.***

(A) In a criminal case, subject to the limitations in Rule 412, a defendant may offer evidence of a victim's pertinent trait, and if the evidence is admitted, the prosecutor may offer evidence to rebut it.

(B) In a homicide case, the prosecutor may offer evidence of the victim's trait of peacefulness to rebut evidence that the victim was the first aggressor.

(C) In a civil case, a party accused of assaultive conduct may offer evidence of the victim's trait of violence to prove self-defense, and if the evidence is admitted, the accusing party may offer evidence of the victim's trait of peacefulness.

(4) ***Exceptions for a Witness.*** --Evidence of a witness's character may be admitted under Rules 607, 608, and 609.

(5) *Definition of "Victim."* --In this rule, "victim" includes an alleged victim.

(b) ***Crimes, Wrongs, or Other Acts.***

(1) ***Prohibited Uses.*** --Evidence of a crime, wrong, or other act is not admissible to prove a person's character in order to show that on a particular occasion the person acted in accordance with the character.

(2) ***Permitted Uses; Notice in Criminal Case.*** --This evidence may be admissible for another purpose, such as proving motive, opportunity, intent, preparation, plan, knowledge, identity, absence of mistake, or lack of accident. On timely request by a defendant in a criminal case, the prosecutor must provide reasonable notice before trial that the prosecution intends to introduce such evidence - other than that arising in the same transaction - in its case-in-chief.

Rule 405. Methods of Proving Character

(a) ***By Reputation or Opinion.***

(1) ***In General.*** --When evidence of a person's character or character trait is admissible, it may be proved by testimony about the person's reputation or by testimony in the form of an opinion. On cross-examination of the character witness, inquiry may be made into relevant specific instances of the person's conduct.

(2) ***Accused's Character in a Criminal Case.*** --In the guilt stage of a criminal case, a witness may testify to the defendant's character or character trait only if, before the day of the offense, the witness was familiar with the defendant's reputation or the facts or information that form the basis of the witness's opinion.

(b) ***By Specific Instances of Conduct.*** --When a person's character or character trait is an essential element of a charge, claim, or defense, the character or trait may also be proved by relevant specific instances of the person's conduct.

Rule 406. Habit; Routine Practice

Evidence of a person's habit or an organization's routine practice may be admitted to prove that on a particular occasion the person or organization acted in accordance with the habit or routine practice. The court may admit this evidence regardless of whether it is corroborated or whether there was an eyewitness.

Rule 407. Subsequent Remedial Measures; Notification of Defect

(a) ***Subsequent Remedial Measures.*** --When measures are taken that would have made an earlier injury or harm less likely to occur, evidence of the subsequent measures is not admissible to prove:
-- negligence;
-- culpable conduct;
-- a defect in a product or its design; or
-- a need for a warning or instruction.

But the court may admit this evidence for another purpose, such as impeachment or - if disputed - proving ownership, control, or the feasibility of precautionary measures.

(b) ***Notification of Defect.*** --A manufacturer's written notification to a purchaser of a defect in one of its products is admissible against the manufacturer to prove the defect.

Rule 408. Compromise Offers and Negotiations

(a) ***Prohibited Uses.*** --Evidence of the following is not admissible either to prove or disprove the validity or amount of a disputed claim:

(1) furnishing, promising, or offering - or accepting, promising to accept, or offering to accept - a valuable consideration in compromising or attempting to compromise the claim; and

(2) conduct or statements made during compromise negotiations about the claim.

(b) ***Permissible Uses.*** --The court may admit this evidence for another purpose, such as proving a party's or witness's bias, prejudice, or interest, negating a contention of undue delay, or proving an effort to obstruct a criminal investigation or prosecution.

Rule 409. Offers to Pay Medical and Similar Expenses

Evidence of furnishing, promising to pay, or offering to pay medical, hospital, or similar expenses resulting from an injury is not admissible to prove liability for the injury.

Rule 410. Pleas, Plea Discussions, and Related Statements

(a) ***Prohibited Uses in Civil Cases.*** --In a civil case, evidence of the following is not admissible against the defendant who made the plea or was a participant in the plea discussions:

(1) a guilty plea that was later withdrawn;

(2) a nolo contendere plea;

(3) a statement made during a proceeding on either of those pleas under Federal Rule of Criminal Procedure 11 or a comparable state procedure; or

(4) a statement made during plea discussions with an attorney for the prosecuting authority if the discussions did not result in a guilty plea or they resulted in a later-withdrawn guilty plea.

(b) ***Prohibited Uses in Criminal Cases.*** --In a criminal case, evidence of the following is not admissible against the defendant who made the plea or was a participant in the plea discussions:

(1) a guilty plea that was later withdrawn;

(2) a nolo contendere plea that was later withdrawn;

(3) a statement made during a proceeding on either of those pleas under Federal Rule of Criminal Procedure 11 or a comparable state procedure; or

(4) a statement made during plea discussions with an attorney for the prosecuting authority if the discussions did not result in a guilty or nolo contendere plea or they resulted in a later-withdrawn guilty or nolo contendere plea.

(c) ***Exception.*** --In a civil case, the court may admit a statement described in paragraph (a)(3) or (4) and in a criminal case, the court may admit a statement described in paragraph (b)(3) or (4), when another statement made during the same plea or plea discussions has been introduced and in fairness the statements ought to be considered together.

Rule 411. Liability Insurance

Evidence that a person was or was not insured against liability is not admissible to prove whether the person acted negligently or otherwise wrongfully. But the court may admit this evidence for another purpose, such as proving a witness's bias or prejudice or, if disputed, proving agency, ownership, or control.

Rule 412. Evidence of Previous Sexual Conduct in Criminal Cases

(a) ***In General.*** --The following evidence is not admissible in a prosecution for sexual assault, aggravated sexual assault, or attempt to commit sexual assault or aggravated sexual assault:

(1) reputation or opinion evidence of a victim's past sexual behavior; or

(2) specific instances of a victim's past sexual behavior.

(b) ***Exceptions for Specific Instances.*** --Evidence of specific instances of a victim's past sexual behavior is admissible if:

(1) the court admits the evidence in accordance with subdivisions (c) and (d);

(2) the evidence:

(A) is necessary to rebut or explain scientific or medical evidence offered by the prosecutor;

(B) concerns past sexual behavior with the defendant and is offered by the defendant to prove consent;

(C) relates to the victim's motive or bias;

(D) is admissible under Rule 609; or

(E) is constitutionally required to be admitted; and

(3) the probative value of the evidence outweighs the danger of unfair prejudice.

(c) ***Procedure for Offering Evidence.*** --Before offering any evidence of the victim's past sexual behavior, the defendant must inform the court outside the jury's presence. The court must then conduct an in camera hearing, recorded by a court reporter, and determine whether the proposed evidence is admissible. The defendant may not refer to any evidence ruled inadmissible without first requesting and gaining the court's approval outside the jury's presence.

(d) ***Record Sealed.*** --The court must preserve the record of the in camera hearing, under seal, as part of the record.

(e) *Definition of "Victim."* --In this rule, "victim" includes an alleged victim.

ARTICLE V. PRIVILEGES

Rule 501. Privileges in General

Unless a Constitution, a statute, or these or other rules prescribed under statutory authority provide otherwise, no person has a privilege to:

(a) refuse to be a witness;

(b) refuse to disclose any matter;

(c) refuse to produce any object or writing; or

(d) prevent another from being a witness, disclosing any matter, or producing any object or writing.

Rule 502. Required Reports Privileged By Statute

(a) ***In General.*** --If a law requiring a return or report to be made so provides:

(1) a person, corporation, association, or other organization or entity - whether public or private - that makes the required return or report has a privilege to refuse to disclose it and to prevent any other person from disclosing it; and

(2) a public officer or agency to whom the return or report must be made has a privilege to refuse to disclose it.

(b) ***Exceptions.*** --This privilege does not apply in an action involving perjury, false statements, fraud in the return or report, or other failure to comply with the law in question.

Rule 503. Lawyer-Client Privilege

(a) ***Definitions.*** --In this rule:

(1) A "client" is a person, public officer, or corporation, association, or other organization or entity - whether public or private - that:

(A) is rendered professional legal services by a lawyer; or

(B) consults a lawyer with a view to obtaining professional legal services from the lawyer.

(2) A "client's representative" is:

(A) a person who has authority to obtain professional legal services for the client or to act for the client on the legal advice rendered; or

(B) any other person who, to facilitate the rendition of professional legal services to the client, makes or receives a confidential communication while acting in the scope of employment for the client.

(3) A "lawyer" is a person authorized, or who the client reasonably believes is authorized, to practice law in any state or nation.

(4) A "lawyer's representative" is:

(A) one employed by the lawyer to assist in the rendition of professional legal services; or

(B) an accountant who is reasonably necessary for the lawyer's rendition of professional legal services.

(5) A communication is "confidential" if not intended to be disclosed to third persons other than those:

(A) to whom disclosure is made to further the rendition of professional legal services to the client; or

(B) reasonably necessary to transmit the communication.

(b) ***Rules of Privilege.***

(1) ***General Rule.*** --A client has a privilege to refuse to disclose and to prevent any other person from disclosing confidential communications made to facilitate the rendition of professional legal services to the client:

(A) between the client or the client's representative and the client's lawyer or the lawyer's representative;

Texas Rules of Evidence

(B) between the client's lawyer and the lawyer's representative;

(C) by the client, the client's representative, the client's lawyer, or the lawyer's representative to a lawyer representing another party in a pending action or that lawyer's representative, if the communications concern a matter of common interest in the pending action;

(D) between the client's representatives or between the client and the client's representative; or

(E) among lawyers and their representatives representing the same client.

(2) ***Special Rule in a Criminal Case.*** --In a criminal case, a client has a privilege to prevent a lawyer or lawyer's representative from disclosing any other fact that came to the knowledge of the lawyer or the lawyer's representative by reason of the attorney-client relationship.

(c) ***Who May Claim.*** --The privilege may be claimed by:

(1) the client;

(2) the client's guardian or conservator;

(3) a deceased client's personal representative; or

(4) the successor, trustee, or similar representative of a corporation, association, or other organization or entity - whether or not in existence.

The person who was the client's lawyer or the lawyer's representative when the communication was made may claim the privilege on the client's behalf - and is presumed to have authority to do so.

(d) ***Exceptions.*** --This privilege does not apply:

(1) ***Furtherance of Crime or Fraud.*** --If the lawyer's services were sought or obtained to enable or aid anyone to commit or plan to commit what the client knew or reasonably should have known to be a crime or fraud.

(2) ***Claimants Through Same Deceased Client.*** --If the communication is relevant to an issue between parties claiming through the same deceased client.

(3) ***Breach of Duty By a Lawyer or Client.*** --If the communication is relevant to an issue of breach of duty by a lawyer to the client or by a client to the lawyer.

(4) ***Document Attested By a Lawyer.*** --If the communication is relevant to an issue concerning an attested document to which the lawyer is an attesting witness.

(5) ***Joint Clients.*** --If the communication:

(A) is offered in an action between clients who retained or consulted a lawyer in common;

(B) was made by any of the clients to the lawyer; and

(C) is relevant to a matter of common interest between the clients.

Rule 504. Spousal Privileges

(a) ***Confidential Communication Privilege.***

(1) ***Definition.*** --A communication is "confidential" if a person makes it privately to the person's spouse and does not intend its disclosure to any other person.

(2) ***General Rule.*** --A person has a privilege to refuse to disclose and to prevent any other person from disclosing a confidential communication made to the person's spouse while they were married. This privilege survives termination of the marriage.

(3) ***Who May Claim.*** --The privilege may be claimed by:

(A) the communicating spouse;

(B) the guardian of a communicating spouse who is incompetent; or

(C) the personal representative of a communicating spouse who is deceased.

The other spouse may claim the privilege on the communicating spouse's behalf - and is presumed to have authority to do so.

(4) ***Exceptions.*** --This privilege does not apply:

(A) ***Furtherance of Crime or Fraud.*** --If the communication is made - wholly or partially - to enable or aid anyone to commit or plan to commit a crime or fraud.

(B) ***Proceeding Between Spouse and Other Spouse or Claimant Through Deceased Spouse.*** --In a civil proceeding:

(i) brought by or on behalf of one spouse against the other; or

(ii) between a surviving spouse and a person claiming through the deceased spouse.

(C) ***Crime Against Family, Spouse, Household Member, or Minor Child.*** --In a:

(i) proceeding in which a party is accused of conduct that, if proved, is a crime against the person of the other spouse, any member of the household of either spouse, or any minor child; or

(ii) criminal proceeding involving a charge of bigamy under Section 25.01 of the Penal Code.

(D) ***Commitment or Similar Proceeding.*** --In a proceeding to commit either spouse or otherwise to place the spouse or the spouse's property under another's control because of a mental or physical condition.

(E) ***Proceeding to Establish Competence.*** --In a proceeding brought by or on behalf of either spouse to establish competence.

(b) ***Privilege Not to Testify in Criminal Case.***

(1) ***General Rule.*** --In a criminal case, an accused's spouse has a privilege not to be called to testify for the state. But this rule neither prohibits a spouse from testifying voluntarily for the state

nor gives a spouse a privilege to refuse to be called to testify for the accused.

(2) ***Failure to Call Spouse.*** --If other evidence indicates that the accused's spouse could testify to relevant matters, an accused's failure to call the spouse to testify is a proper subject of comment by counsel.

(3) ***Who May Claim.*** --The privilege not to testify may be claimed by the accused's spouse or the spouse's guardian or representative, but not by the accused.

(4) ***Exceptions.*** --This privilege does not apply:

(A) ***Certain Criminal Proceedings.*** --In a criminal proceeding in which a spouse is charged with:

(i) a crime against the other spouse, any member of the household of either spouse, or any minor child; or

(ii) bigamy under Section 25.01 of the Penal Code.

(B) ***Matters That Occurred Before the Marriage.*** --If the spouse is called to testify about matters that occurred before the marriage.

Rule 505. Privilege For Communications to a Clergy Member

(a) ***Definitions.*** --In this rule:

(1) A "clergy member" is a minister, priest, rabbi, accredited Christian Science Practitioner, or other similar functionary of a religious organization or someone whom a communicant reasonably believes is a clergy member.

(2) A "communicant" is a person who consults a clergy member in the clergy member's professional capacity as a spiritual adviser.

(3) A communication is "confidential" if made privately and not intended for further disclosure except to other persons present to further the purpose of the communication.

(b) ***General Rule.*** --A communicant has a privilege to refuse to disclose and to prevent any other person from disclosing a confidential communication by the communicant to a clergy member in the clergy member's professional capacity as spiritual adviser.

(c) ***Who May Claim.*** --The privilege may be claimed by:

(1) the communicant;

(2) the communicant's guardian or conservator; or

(3) a deceased communicant's personal representative.

The clergy member to whom the communication was made may claim the privilege on the communicant's behalf - and is presumed to have authority to do so.

Rule 506. Political Vote Privilege

A person has a privilege to refuse to disclose the person's vote at a political election conducted by secret ballot unless the vote was cast illegally.

Rule 507. Trade Secrets Privilege

(a) ***General Rule.*** --A person has a privilege to refuse to disclose and to prevent other persons from disclosing a trade secret owned by the person, unless the court finds that nondisclosure will tend to conceal fraud or otherwise work injustice.

(b) ***Who May Claim.*** --The privilege may be claimed by the person who owns the trade secret or the person's agent or employee.

(c) ***Protective Measure.*** --If a court orders a person to disclose a trade secret, it must take any protective measure required by the interests of the privilege holder and the parties and to further justice.

Rule 508. Informer's Identity Privilege

(a) ***General Rule.*** --The United States, a state, or a subdivision of either has a privilege to refuse to disclose a person's identity if:

(1) the person has furnished information to a law enforcement officer or a member of a legislative committee or its staff conducting an investigation of a possible violation of law; and

(2) the information relates to or assists in the investigation.

(b) ***Who May Claim.*** --The privilege may be claimed by an appropriate representative of the public entity to which the informer furnished the information. The court in a criminal case must reject the privilege claim if the state objects.

(c) ***Exceptions.***

(1) ***Voluntary Disclosure; Informer a Witness.*** --This privilege does not apply if:

(A) the informer's identity or the informer's interest in the communication's subject matter has been disclosed - by a privilege holder or the informer's own action - to a person who would have cause to resent the communication; or

(B) the informer appears as a witness for the public entity.

(2) ***Testimony About the Merits.***

(A) ***Criminal Case.*** --In a criminal case, this privilege does not apply if the court finds a reasonable probability exists that the informer can give testimony necessary to a fair determination of guilt or innocence. If the court so finds and the public entity elects not to disclose the informer's identity:

(i) on the defendant's motion, the court must dismiss the charges to which the testimony would relate; or

(ii) on its own motion, the court may dismiss the charges to which the testimony would relate.

(B) ***Certain Civil Cases.*** --In a civil case in which the public entity is a party, this privilege does not apply if the court finds a reasonable probability exists that the informer can give testimony necessary to a fair determination of a material issue on the merits. If the court so finds and the public entity elects not to disclose the informer's identity, the court may make any order that justice requires.

(C) ***Procedures.***

(i) If it appears that an informer may be able to give the testimony required to invoke this exception and the public entity claims the privilege, the court must give the public entity an opportunity to show in camera facts relevant to determining whether this exception is met. The showing should ordinarily be made by affidavits, but the court may take testimony if it finds the matter cannot be satisfactorily resolved by affidavits.

(ii) No counsel or party may attend the in camera showing.

(iii) The court must seal and preserve for appeal evidence submitted under this subparagraph (2)(C). The evidence must not otherwise be revealed without the public entity's consent.

(3) ***Legality of Obtaining Evidence.***

(A) ***Court May Order Disclosure.*** --The court may order the public entity to disclose an informer's identity if:

(i) information from an informer is relied on to establish the legality of the means by which evidence was obtained; and

(ii) the court is not satisfied that the information was received from an informer reasonably believed to be reliable or credible.

(B) ***Procedures.***

(i) On the public entity's request, the court must order the disclosure be made in camera.

(ii) No counsel or party may attend the in camera disclosure.

(iii) If the informer's identity is disclosed in camera, the court must seal and preserve for appeal the record of the in camera proceeding. The record of the in camera proceeding must not otherwise be revealed without the public entity's consent.

Rule 509. Physician-Patient Privilege

(a) ***Definitions.*** --In this rule:

(1) A "patient" is a person who consults or is seen by a physician for medical care.

(2) A "physician" is a person licensed, or who the patient reasonably believes is licensed, to practice medicine in any state or nation.

(3) A communication is "confidential" if not intended to be disclosed to third persons other than those:

(A) present to further the patient's interest in the consultation, examination, or interview;

(B) reasonably necessary to transmit the communication; or

(C) participating in the diagnosis and treatment under the physician's direction, including members of the patient's family.

(b) ***Limited Privilege in a Criminal Case.*** --There is no physician-patient privilege in a criminal case. But a confidential communication is not admissible in a criminal case if made:

(1) to a person involved in the treatment of or examination for alcohol or drug abuse; and

(2) by a person being treated voluntarily or being examined for admission to treatment for alcohol or drug abuse.

(c) ***General Rule in a Civil Case.*** --In a civil case, a patient has a privilege to refuse to disclose and to prevent any other person from disclosing:

(1) a confidential communication between a physician and the patient that relates to or was made in connection with any professional services the physician rendered the patient; and

(2) a record of the patient's identity, diagnosis, evaluation, or treatment created or maintained by a physician.

(d) ***Who May Claim in a Civil Case.*** --The privilege may be claimed by:

(1) the patient; or

(2) the patient's representative on the patient's behalf.

The physician may claim the privilege on the patient's behalf - and is presumed to have authority to do so.

(e) ***Exceptions in a Civil Case.*** --This privilege does not apply:

(1) ***Proceeding Against Physician.*** --If the communication or record is relevant to a claim or defense in:

(A) a proceeding the patient brings against a physician; or

(B) a license revocation proceeding in which the patient is a complaining witness.

(2) ***Consent.*** --If the patient or a person authorized to act on the patient's behalf consents in writing to the release of any privileged information, as provided in subdivision (f).

(3) ***Action to Collect.*** --In an action to collect a claim for medical services rendered to the patient.

(4) ***Party Relies on Patient's Condition.*** --If any party relies on the patient's physical, mental, or emotional condition as a part of the party's claim or defense and the communication or record is relevant to that condition.

(5) ***Disciplinary Investigation or Proceeding.*** --In a disciplinary investigation of or proceeding against a physician under the Medical Practice Act, Tex.Occ. Code § 164.001 et seq., or a registered nurse under Tex.Occ. Code § 301.451 et seq. But the board conducting the investigation or proceeding must protect the identity of any patient whose medical records are examined unless:

(A) the patient's records would be subject to disclosure under paragraph (e)(1); or

(B) the patient has consented in writing to the release of medical records, as provided in subdivision (f).

(6) ***Involuntary Civil Commitment or Similar Proceeding.*** --In a proceeding for involuntary civil commitment or court-ordered treatment, or a probable cause hearing under Tex. Health & Safety Code:

(A) chapter 462 (Treatment of Persons With Chemical Dependencies);

(B) title 7, subtitle C (Texas Mental Health Code); or

(C) title 7, subtitle D (Persons With an Intellectual Disability Act).

(7) ***Abuse or Neglect of "Institution" Resident.*** --In a proceeding regarding the abuse or neglect, or the cause of any abuse or neglect, of a resident of an "institution" as defined in Tex.Health & Safety Code § 242.002.

(f) ***Consent For Release of Privileged Information.***

(1) Consent for the release of privileged information must be in writing and signed by:

(A) the patient;

(B) a parent or legal guardian if the patient is a minor;

(C) a legal guardian if the patient has been adjudicated incompetent to manage personal affairs;

(D) an attorney appointed for the patient under Tex. Health & Safety Code title 7, subtitles C and D;

(E) an attorney ad litem appointed for the patient under Tex. Estates Code title 3, subtitle C;

(F) an attorney ad litem or guardian ad litem appointed for a minor under Tex. Fam. Code chapter 107, subchapter B; or

(G) a personal representative if the patient is deceased.

(2) The consent must specify:

(A) the information or medical records covered by the release;

(B) the reasons or purposes for the release; and

(C) the person to whom the information is to be released.

(3) The patient, or other person authorized to consent, may withdraw consent to the release of any information. But a withdrawal of consent does not affect any information disclosed before the patient or authorized person gave written notice of the withdrawal.

(4) Any person who receives information privileged under this rule may disclose the information only to the extent consistent with the purposes specified in the consent.

Rule 510. Mental Health Information Privilege in Civil Cases

(a) ***Definitions.*** --In this rule:

(1) A "professional" is a person:

(A) authorized to practice medicine in any state or nation;

(B) licensed or certified by the State of Texas in the diagnosis, evaluation, or treatment of any mental or emotional disorder;

(C) involved in the treatment or examination of drug abusers; or

(D) who the patient reasonably believes to be a professional under this rule.

(2) A "patient" is a person who:

(A) consults, or is interviewed by, a professional for purposes of diagnosis, evaluation, or treatment of any mental or emotional condition or disorder, including alcoholism and drug addiction; or

(B) is being treated voluntarily or being examined for admission to voluntary treatment for drug abuse.

(3) A "patient's representative" is:

(A) any person who has the patient's written consent;

(B) the parent of a minor patient;

(C) the guardian of a patient who has been adjudicated incompetent to manage personal affairs; or

(D) the personal representative of a deceased patient.

(4) A communication is "confidential" if not intended to be disclosed to third persons other than those:

(A) present to further the patient's interest in the diagnosis, examination, evaluation, or treatment;

(B) reasonably necessary to transmit the communication; or

(C) participating in the diagnosis, examination, evaluation, or treatment under the professional's direction, including members of the patient's family.

(b) ***General Rule; Disclosure.***

(1) In a civil case, a patient has a privilege to refuse to disclose and to prevent any other person from disclosing:

(A) a confidential communication between the patient and a professional; and

(B) a record of the patient's identity, diagnosis, evaluation, or treatment that is created or maintained by a professional.

(2) In a civil case, any person-other than a patient's representative acting on the patient's behalf-who receives information privileged under this rule may disclose the information only to the extent consistent with the purposes for which it was obtained.

(c) ***Who May Claim.*** --The privilege may be claimed by:

(1) the patient; or

(2) the patient's representative on the patient's behalf.

The professional may claim the privilege on the patient's behalf-and is presumed to have authority to do so.

(d) ***Exceptions.*** --This privilege does not apply:

(1) ***Proceeding Against Professional.*** --If the communication or record is relevant to a claim or defense in:

(A) a proceeding the patient brings against a professional; or

(B) a license revocation proceeding in which the patient is a complaining witness.

(2) ***Written Waiver.*** --If the patient or a person authorized to act on the patient's behalf waives the privilege in writing.

(3) ***Action to Collect.*** --In an action to collect a claim for mental or emotional health services rendered to the patient.

(4) ***Communication Made in Court-Ordered Examination.*** --To a communication the patient made to a professional during a court-ordered examination relating to the patient's mental or emotional condition or disorder if:

(A) the patient made the communication after being informed that it would not be privileged;

(B) the communication is offered to prove an issue involving the patient's mental or emotional health; and

(C) the court imposes appropriate safeguards against unauthorized disclosure.

(5) ***Party Relies on Patient's Condition.*** --If any party relies on the patient's physical, mental, or emotional condition as a part of the party's claim or defense and the communication or record is relevant to that condition.

(6) ***Abuse or Neglect of "Institution" Resident.*** --In a proceeding regarding the abuse or neglect, or the cause of any abuse or neglect, of a resident of an "institution" as defined in Tex.Health & Safety Code § 242.002.

Rule 511. Waiver by Voluntary Disclosure

(a) ***General Rule.*** A person upon whom these rules confer a privilege against disclosure waives the privilege if:

(1) the person or a predecessor of the person while holder of the privilege voluntarily discloses or consents to disclosure of any significant part of the privileged matter unless such disclosure itself is privileged; or

(2) the person or a representative of the person calls a person to whom privileged communications have been made to testify as to the person's character or character trait insofar as such communications are relevant to such character or character trait.

(b) ***Lawyer-Client Privilege and Work Product; Limitations on Waiver.*** Notwithstanding paragraph (a), the following provisions apply, in the circumstances set out, to disclosure of a communication or information covered by the lawyer-client privilege or work-product protection.

(1) ***Disclosure Made in a Federal or State Proceeding or to a Federal or State Office or Agency; Scope of a Waiver.*** --When the disclosure is made in a federal proceeding or state proceeding of any state or to a federal office or agency or state office or agency of any state and waives the lawyer-client privilege or work-product protection, the waiver extends to an undisclosed communication or information only if:

(A) the waiver is intentional;

(B) the disclosed and undisclosed communications or information concern the same subject matter; and

(C) they ought in fairness to be considered together.

(2) ***Inadvertent Disclosure in State Civil Proceedings.*** --When made in a Texas state proceeding, an inadvertent disclosure does not operate as a waiver if the holder followed the procedures of Rule of Civil Procedure 193.3 (d).

(3) ***Controlling Effect of a Court Order.*** --A disclosure made in litigation pending before a federal court or a state court of any state that has entered an order that the privilege or protection is not waived by disclosure connected with the litigation pending before that court is also not a waiver in a Texas state proceeding.

(4) ***Controlling Effect of a Party Agreement.*** --An agreement on the effect of disclosure in a state proceeding of any state is binding only on the parties to the agreement, unless it is incorporated into a court order.

Rule 512. Privileged Matter Disclosed Under Compulsion or Without Opportunity to Claim Privilege

A privilege claim is not defeated by a disclosure that was:

(a) compelled erroneously; or

(b) made without opportunity to claim the privilege.

Rule 513. Comment On or Inference From a Privilege Claim; Instruction

(a) ***Comment or Inference Not Permitted.*** --Except as permitted in Rule 504(b)(2), neither the court nor counsel may comment on a privilege claim-whether made in the present proceeding or previously-and the factfinder may not draw an inference from the claim.

(b) ***Claiming Privilege Without the Jury's Knowledge.*** --To the extent practicable, the court must conduct a jury trial so that the making of a privilege claim is not suggested to the jury by any means.

(c) ***Claim of Privilege Against Self-Incrimination in a Civil Case.*** --Subdivisions (a) and (b) do not apply to a party's claim, in the present civil case, of the privilege against self-incrimination.

(d) ***Jury Instruction.*** --When this rule forbids a jury from drawing an inference from a privilege claim, the court must, on request of a party against whom the jury might draw the inference, instruct the jury accordingly.

ARTICLE VI. WITNESSES

Rule 601. Competency to Testify in General; "Dead Man's Rule"

(a) ***In General.*** --Every person is competent to be a witness unless these rules provide otherwise. The following witnesses are incompetent:

(1) ***Insane Persons.*** --A person who is now insane or was insane at the time of the events about which the person is called to testify.

(2) ***Persons Lacking Sufficient Intellect.*** --A child - or any other person - whom the court examines and finds lacks sufficient intellect to testify concerning the matters in issue.

(b) *The "Dead Man's Rule."*

(1) ***Applicability.*** --The "Dead Man's Rule" applies only in a civil case:

(A) by or against a party in the party's capacity as an executor, administrator, or guardian; or

(B) by or against a decedent's heirs or legal representatives and based in whole or in part on the decedent's oral statement.

(2) ***General Rule.*** --In cases described in subparagraph (b)(1)(A), a party may not testify against another party about an oral statement by the testator, intestate, or ward. In cases described in subparagraph (b)(1)(B), a party may not testify against another party about an oral statement by the decedent.

(3) ***Exceptions.*** --A party may testify against another party about an oral statement by the testator, intestate, ward, or decedent if:

(A) the party's testimony about the statement is corroborated; or

(B) the opposing party calls the party to testify at the trial about the statement.

(4) ***Instructions.*** --If a court excludes evidence under paragraph (b)(2), the court must instruct the jury that the law prohibits a party from testifying about an oral statement by the testator, intestate, ward, or decedent unless the oral statement is corroborated or the opposing party calls the party to testify at the trial about the statement.

Rule 602. Need for Personal Knowledge

A witness may testify to a matter only if evidence is introduced sufficient to support a finding that the witness has personal knowledge of the matter. Evidence to prove personal knowledge may consist of the witness's own testimony. This rule does not apply to a witness's expert testimony under Rule 703.

Rule 603. Oath or Affirmation to Testify Truthfully

Before testifying, a witness must give an oath or affirmation to testify truthfully. It must be in a form designed to impress that duty on the witness's conscience.

Rule 604. Interpreter

An interpreter must be qualified and must give an oath or affirmation to make a true translation.

Rule 605. Judge's Competency as a Witness

The presiding judge may not testify as a witness at the trial. A party need not object to preserve the issue.

Rule 606. Juror's Competency as a Witness

(a) ***At the Trial.*** --A juror may not testify as a witness before the other jurors at the trial. If a juror is called to testify, the court must give a party an opportunity to object outside the jury's presence.

(b) ***During an Inquiry into the Validity of a Verdict or Indictment.***

(1) ***Prohibited Testimony or Other Evidence.*** --During an inquiry into the validity of a verdict or indictment, a juror may not testify about any statement made or incident that occurred during the jury's deliberations; the effect of anything on that juror's or another juror's vote; or any juror's mental processes concerning the verdict or indictment. The court may not receive a juror's affidavit or evidence of a juror's statement on these matters.

(2) ***Exceptions.*** --A juror may testify:

(A) about whether an outside influence was improperly brought to bear on any juror; or

(B) to rebut a claim that the juror was not qualified to serve.

Rule 607. Who May Impeach a Witness

Any party, including the party that called the witness, may attack the witness's credibility.

Rule 608. A Witness's Character for Truthfulness or Untruthfulness

(a) ***Reputation or Opinion Evidence.*** --A witness's credibility may be attacked or supported by testimony about the witness's reputation for having a character for truthfulness or untruthfulness, or by testimony in the form of an opinion about that character. But evidence of truthful character is admissible only after the witness's character for truthfulness has been attacked.

(b) ***Specific Instances of Conduct.*** --Except for a criminal conviction under Rule 609, a party may not inquire into or offer extrinsic evidence to prove specific instances of the witness's conduct in order to attack or support the witness's character for truthfulness.

Rule 609. Impeachment by Evidence of a Criminal Conviction

(a) ***In General.*** --Evidence of a criminal conviction offered to attack a witness's character for truthfulness must be admitted if:

(1) the crime was a felony or involved moral turpitude, regardless of punishment;

(2) the probative value of the evidence outweighs its prejudicial effect to a party; and

(3) it is elicited from the witness or established by public record.

(b) ***Limit on Using the Evidence After 10 Years.*** --This subdivision (b) applies if more than 10 years have passed since the witness's conviction or release from confinement for it, whichever is later. Evidence of the conviction is admissible only if its probative value, supported by specific facts and circumstances, substantially outweighs its prejudicial effect.

(c) ***Effect of a Pardon, Annulment, or Certificate of Rehabilitation.*** --Evidence of a conviction is not admissible if:

(1) the conviction has been the subject of a pardon, annulment, certificate of rehabilitation, or other equivalent procedure based on a finding that the person has been rehabilitated, and the person has not been convicted of a later crime that was classified as a felony or involved moral turpitude, regardless of punishment;

(2) probation has been satisfactorily completed for the conviction, and the person has not been convicted of a later crime that was classified as a felony or involved moral turpitude, regardless of punishment; or

(3) the conviction has been the subject of a pardon, annulment, or other equivalent procedure based on a finding of innocence.

(d) ***Juvenile Adjudications.*** --Evidence of a juvenile adjudication is admissible under this rule only if:

(1) the witness is a party in a proceeding conducted under title 3 of the Texas Family Code; or

(2) the United States or Texas Constitution requires that it be admitted.

(e) ***Pendency of an Appeal.*** --A conviction for which an appeal is pending is not admissible under this rule.

(f) ***Notice.*** --Evidence of a witness's conviction is not admissible under this rule if, after receiving from the adverse party a timely written request specifying the witness, the proponent of the conviction fails to provide sufficient written notice of intent to use the conviction. Notice is sufficient if it provides a fair opportunity to contest the use of such evidence.

Rule 610. Religious Beliefs or Opinions

Evidence of a witness's religious beliefs or opinions is not admissible to attack or support the witness's credibility.

Rule 611. Mode and Order of Examining Witnesses and Presenting Evidence

(a) ***Control by the Court; Purposes.*** --The court should exercise reasonable control over the mode and order of examining witnesses and presenting evidence so as to:

(1) make those procedures effective for determining the truth;

(2) avoid wasting time; and

(3) protect witnesses from harassment or undue embarrassment.

(b) ***Scope of Cross-Examination.*** --A witness may be cross-examined on any relevant matter, including credibility.

(c) ***Leading Questions.*** --Leading questions should not be used on direct examination except as necessary to develop the witness's testimony. Ordinarily, the court should allow leading questions:

(1) on cross-examination; and

(2) when a party calls a hostile witness, an adverse party, or a witness identified with an adverse party.

Rule 612. Writing Used to Refresh a Witness's Memory

(a) ***Scope.*** --This rule gives an adverse party certain options when a witness uses a writing to refresh memory:

(1) while testifying;

(2) before testifying, in civil cases, if the court decides that justice requires the party to have those options; or

(3) before testifying, in criminal cases.

(b) ***Adverse Party's Options; Deleting Unrelated Matter.*** --An adverse party is entitled to have the writing produced at the hearing, to inspect it, to cross-examine the witness about it, and to introduce in evidence any portion that relates to the witness's testimony. If the producing party claims that the writing includes unrelated matter, the court must examine the writing in camera, delete any unrelated portion, and order that the rest be delivered to the adverse party. Any portion deleted over objection must be preserved for the record.

(c) ***Failure to Produce or Deliver the Writing.*** --If a writing is not produced or is not delivered as ordered, the court may issue any appropriate order. But if the prosecution does not comply in a criminal case, the court must strike the witness's testimony or - if justice so requires - declare a mistrial.

Rule 613. Witness's Prior Statement and Bias or Interest

(a) ***Witness's Prior Inconsistent Statement.***

(1) ***Foundation Requirement.*** --When examining a witness about the witness's prior inconsistent statement - whether oral or written - a party must first tell the witness:

(A) the contents of the statement;

(B) the time and place of the statement; and

(C) the person to whom the witness made the statement.

(2) ***Need Not Show Written Statement.*** --If the witness's prior inconsistent statement is written, a party need not show it to the witness before inquiring about it, but must, upon request, show it to opposing counsel.

(3) ***Opportunity to Explain or Deny.*** --A witness must be given the opportunity to explain or deny the prior inconsistent statement.

(4) ***Extrinsic Evidence.*** --Extrinsic evidence of a witness's prior inconsistent statement is not admissible unless the witness is first examined about the statement and fails to unequivocally admit making the statement.

(5) ***Opposing Party's Statement.*** --This subdivision (a) does not apply to an opposing party's statement under Rule 801(e)(2).

(b) ***Witness's Bias or Interest.***

(1) ***Witness's Bias or Interest.*** --When examining a witness about the witness's bias or interest, a party must first tell the witness the circumstances or statements that tend to show the witness's bias or interest. If examining a witness about a statement - whether oral or written - to prove the witness's bias or interest, a party must tell the witness:

(A) the contents of the statement;

(B) the time and place of the statement; and

(C) the person to whom the statement was made.

(2) ***Need Not Show Written Statement.*** --If a party uses a written statement to prove the witness's bias or interest, a party need not show the statement to the witness before inquiring about it, but must, upon request, show it to opposing counsel.

(3) ***Opportunity to Explain or Deny.*** --A witness must be given the opportunity to explain or deny the circumstances or statements that tend to show the witness's bias or interest. And the witness's proponent may present evidence to rebut the charge of bias or interest.

(4) ***Extrinsic Evidence.*** --Extrinsic evidence of a witness's bias or interest is not admissible unless the witness is first examined about the bias or interest and fails to unequivocally admit it.

(c) ***Witness's Prior Consistent Statement.*** --Unless Rule 801(e)(1)(B) provides otherwise, a witness's prior consistent statement is not admissible if offered solely to enhance the witness's credibility.

Rule 614. Excluding Witnesses

At a party's request, the court must order witnesses excluded so that they cannot hear other witnesses' testimony. Or the court may do so on its own. But this rule does not authorize excluding:

(a) a party who is a natural person and, in civil cases, that person's spouse;

(b) after being designated as the party's representative by its attorney:

(1) in a civil case, an officer or employee of a party that is not a natural person; or

(2) in a criminal case, a defendant that is not a natural person;

(c) a person whose presence a party shows to be essential to presenting the party's claim or defense; or

(d) the victim in a criminal case, unless the court determines that the victim's testimony would be materially affected by hearing other testimony at the trial.

Rule 615. Producing a Witness's Statement in Criminal Cases

(a) ***Motion to Produce.*** --After a witness other than the defendant testifies on direct examination, the court, on motion of a party who did not call the witness, must order an attorney for the state Page 2 or the defendant and the defendant's attorney to produce, for the examination and use of the moving party, any statement of the witness that:

(1) is in their possession;

(2) relates to the subject matter of the witness's testimony; and

(3) has not previously been produced.

(b) ***Producing the Entire Statement.*** --If the entire statement relates to the subject matter of the witness's testimony, the court must order that the statement be delivered to the moving party.

(c) ***Producing a Redacted Statement.*** --If the party who called the witness claims that the statement contains information that does not relate to the subject matter of the witness's testimony, the court must inspect the statement in camera. After excising any unrelated portions, the court must order delivery of the redacted statement to the moving party. If a party objects to an excision, the court must preserve the entire statement with the excised portion indicated, under seal, as part of the record.

(d) ***Recess to Examine a Statement.*** --If the court orders production of a witness's statement, the court, on request, must recess the proceedings to allow the moving party time to examine the statement and prepare for its use.

(e) ***Sanction for Failure to Produce or Deliver a Statement.*** --If the party who called the witness disobeys an order to produce or deliver a statement, the court must strike the witness's testimony from the record. If an attorney for the state disobeys the order, the court must declare a mistrial if justice so requires.

(f) ***"Statement" Defined.*** --As used in this rule, a witness's "statement" means:

(1) a written statement that the witness makes and signs, or otherwise adopts or approves;

(2) a substantially verbatim, contemporaneously recorded recital of the witness's oral statement that is contained in any recording or any transcription of a recording; or

(3) the witness's statement to a grand jury, however taken or recorded, or a transcription of such a statement.

ARTICLE VII. OPINIONS AND EXPERT TESTIMONY

Rule 701. Opinion Testimony by Lay Witnesses

If a witness is not testifying as an expert, testimony in the form of an opinion is limited to one that is:

(a) rationally based on the witness's perception; and

(b) helpful to clearly understanding the witness's testimony or to determining a fact in issue.

Rule 702. Testimony by Expert Witnesses

A witness who is qualified as an expert by knowledge, skill, experience, training, or education may testify in the form of an opinion or otherwise if the expert's scientific, technical, or other specialized knowledge will help the trier of fact to understand the evidence or to determine a fact in issue.

Rule 703. Bases of an Expert's Opinion Testimony

An expert may base an opinion on facts or data in the case that the expert has been made aware of, reviewed, or personally observed. If experts in the particular field would reasonably rely on those kinds of facts or data in forming an opinion on the subject, they need not be admissible for the opinion to be admitted.

Rule 704. Opinion on an Ultimate Issue

An opinion is not objectionable just because it embraces an ultimate issue.

Rule 705. Disclosing the Underlying Facts or Data and Examining an Expert About Them

(a) ***Stating an Opinion Without Disclosing the Underlying Facts or Data.*** --Unless the court orders otherwise, an expert may state an opinion - and give the reasons for it - without first testifying to the underlying facts or data. But the expert may be required to disclose those facts or data on cross-examination.

(b) ***Voir Dire Examination of an Expert About the Underlying Facts or Data.*** --Before an expert states an opinion or discloses the underlying facts or data, an adverse party in a civil case may-or in a criminal case must-be permitted to examine the expert about the underlying facts or data. This examination must take place outside the jury's hearing.

(c) ***Admissibility of Opinion.*** --An expert's opinion is inadmissible if the underlying facts or data do not provide a sufficient basis for the opinion.

(d) ***When Otherwise Inadmissible Underlying Facts or Data May Be Disclosed; Instructing the Jury.*** --If the underlying facts or data would otherwise be inadmissible, the proponent of the opinion may not disclose them to the jury if their probative value in helping the jury evaluate the opinion is outweighed by their prejudicial effect. If the court allows the proponent to disclose those facts or data the court must, upon timely request, restrict the evidence to its proper scope and instruct the jury accordingly.

Rule 706. Audit in Civil Cases

Notwithstanding any other evidence rule, the court must admit an auditor's verified report prepared under Rule of Civil Procedure 172 and offered by a party. If a party files exceptions to the report, a party may offer evidence supporting the exceptions to contradict the report.

ARTICLE VIII. HEARSAY

Rule 801. Definitions That Apply to This Article; Exclusions from Hearsay

(a) ***Statement.*** --"Statement" means a person's oral or written verbal expression, or nonverbal conduct that a person intended as a substitute for verbal expression.

(b) ***Declarant.*** --"Declarant" means the person who made the statement.

(c) ***Matter Asserted.*** --"Matter asserted" means:

(1) any matter a declarant explicitly asserts; and

(2) any matter implied by a statement, if the probative value of the statement as offered flows from the declarant's belief about the matter.

(d) ***Hearsay.*** --"Hearsay" means a statement that:

(1) the declarant does not make while testifying at the current trial or hearing; and

(2) a party offers in evidence to prove the truth of the matter asserted in the statement.

(e) ***Statements That are Not Hearsay.*** --A statement that meets the following conditions is not hearsay:

(1) ***A Declarant-Witness's Prior Statement.*** --The declarant testifies and is subject to cross-examination about a prior statement, and the statement:

(A) is inconsistent with the declarant's testimony and:

(i) when offered in a civil case, was given under penalty of perjury at a trial, hearing, or other proceeding or in a deposition; or

(ii) when offered in a criminal case, was given under penalty of perjury at a trial, hearing, or other proceeding - except a grand jury proceeding - or in a deposition;

(B) is consistent with the declarant's testimony and is offered to rebut an express or implied charge that the declarant recently fabricated it or acted from a recent improper influence or motive in so testifying; or

(C) identifies a person as someone the declarant perceived earlier.

(2) ***An Opposing Party's Statement.*** --The statement is offered against an opposing party and:

(A) was made by the party in an individual or representative capacity;

(B) is one the party manifested that it adopted or believed to be true;

(C) was made by a person whom the party authorized to make a statement on the subject;

(D) was made by the party's agent or employee on a matter within the scope of that relationship and while it existed; or

(E) was made by the party's coconspirator during and in furtherance of the conspiracy.

(3) ***A Deponent's Statement.*** --In a civil case, the statement was made in a deposition taken in the same proceeding. "Same proceeding" is defined in Rule of Civil Procedure 203.6 (b). The deponent's

unavailability as a witness is not a requirement for admissibility.

Rule 802. The Rule Against Hearsay

Hearsay is not admissible unless any of the following provides otherwise:
-- a statute;
-- these rules; or
-- other rules prescribed under statutory authority.

Inadmissible hearsay admitted without objection may not be denied probative value merely because it is hearsay.

Rule 803. Exceptions to the Rule Against Hearsay -- Regardless of Whether the Declarant is Available as a Witness

The following are not excluded by the rule against hearsay, regardless of whether the declarant is available as a witness:

(1) ***Present Sense Impression.*** --A statement describing or explaining an event or condition, made while or immediately after the declarant perceived it.

(2) ***Excited Utterance.*** --A statement relating to a startling event or condition, made while the declarant was under the stress of excitement that it caused.

(3) ***Then-Existing Mental, Emotional, or Physical Condition.*** --A statement of the declarant's then-existing state of mind (such as motive, intent, or plan) or emotional, sensory, or physical condition (such as mental feeling, pain, or bodily health), but not including a statement of memory or belief to prove the fact remembered or believed unless it relates to the validity or terms of the declarant's will.

(4) ***Statement Made for Medical Diagnosis or Treatment.*** --A statement that:

(A) is made for - and is reasonably pertinent to-medical diagnosis or treatment; and

(B) describes medical history; past or present symptoms or sensations; their inception; or their general cause.

(5) ***Recorded Recollection.*** --A record that:

(A) is on a matter the witness once knew about but now cannot recall well enough to testify fully and accurately;

(B) was made or adopted by the witness when the matter was fresh in the witness's memory; and

(C) accurately reflects the witness's knowledge, unless the circumstances of the record's preparation cast doubt on its trustworthiness.

If admitted, the record may be read into evidence but may be received as an exhibit only if offered by an adverse party.

(6) ***Records of a Regularly Conducted Activity.*** --A record of an act, event, condition, opinion, or diagnosis if:

(A) the record was made at or near the time by - or from information transmitted by - someone with knowledge;

(B) the record was kept in the course of a regularly conducted business activity;

(C) making the record was a regular practice of that activity;

(D) all these conditions are shown by the testimony of the custodian or another qualified witness, or by an affidavit or unsworn declaration that complies with Rule 902(10); and

(E) the opponent fails to demonstrate that the source of information or the method or circumstances of preparation indicate a lack of trustworthiness.

"Business" as used in this paragraph includes every kind of regular organized activity whether conducted for profit or not.

(7) ***Absence of a Record of a Regularly Conducted Activity.*** --Evidence that a matter is not included in a record described in paragraph (6) if:

(A) the evidence is admitted to prove that the matter did not occur or exist;

(B) a record was regularly kept for a matter of that kind; and

(C) the opponent fails to show that the possible source of the information or other circumstances indicate a lack of trustworthiness.

(8) ***Public Records.*** --A record or statement of a public office if:

(A) it sets out:

(i) the office's activities;

(ii) a matter observed while under a legal duty to report, but not including, in a criminal case, a matter observed by lawenforcement personnel; or

(iii) in a civil case or against the government in a criminal case, factual findings from a legally authorized investigation; and

(B) the opponent fails to demonstrate that the source of information or other circumstances indicate a lack of trustworthiness.

(9) ***Public Records of Vital Statistics.*** --A record of a birth, death, or marriage, if reported to a public office in accordance with a legal duty.

(10) ***Absence of a Public Record.*** --Testimony - or a certification under Rule 902 - that a diligent search failed to disclose a public record or statement if the testimony or certification is admitted to prove that:

(A) the record or statement does not exist; or

(B) a matter did not occur or exist, if a public office regularly kept a record or statement for a matter of that kind.

(11) ***Records of Religious Organizations Concerning Personal or Family History.*** --A statement of birth, legitimacy, ancestry, marriage, divorce, death, relationship by blood or marriage, or similar facts of personal or family history, contained in a regularly kept record of a religious organization.

(12) ***Certificates of Marriage, Baptism, and Similar Ceremonies.*** --A statement of fact contained in a certificate:

(A) made by a person who is authorized by a religious organization or by law to perform the act certified;

(B) attesting that the person performed a marriage or similar ceremony or administered a sacrament; and

(C) purporting to have been issued at the time of the act or within a reasonable time after it.

(13) ***Family Records.*** --A statement of fact about personal or family history contained in a family record, such as a Bible, genealogy, chart, engraving on a ring, inscription on a portrait, or engraving on an urn or burial marker.

(14) ***Records of Documents That Affect an Interest in Property.*** --The record of a document that purports to establish or affect an interest in property if:

(A) the record is admitted to prove the content of the original recorded document, along with its signing and its delivery by each person who purports to have signed it;

(B) the record is kept in a public office; and

(C) a statute authorizes recording documents of that kind in that office.

(15) ***Statements in Documents That Affect an Interest in Property.*** --A statement contained in a document that purports to establish or affect an interest in property if the matter stated was relevant to the document's purpose-unless later dealings with the property are inconsistent with the truth of the statement or the purport of the document.

(16) ***Statements in Ancient Documents.*** --A statement in a document that is at least 20 years old and whose authenticity is established.

(17) ***Market Reports and Similar Commercial Publications.*** --Market quotations, lists, directories, or other compilations that are generally relied on by the public or by persons in particular occupations.

(18) ***Statements in Learned Treatises, Periodicals, or Pamphlets.*** --A statement contained in a treatise, periodical, or pamphlet if:

(A) the statement is called to the attention of an expert witness on crossexamination or relied on by the expert on direct examination; and

(B) the publication is established as a reliable authority by the expert's admission or testimony, by another expert's testimony, or by judicial notice.

If admitted, the statement may be read into evidence but not received as an exhibit.

(19) ***Reputation Concerning Personal or Family History.*** --A reputation among a person's family by blood, adoption, or marriage - or among a person's associates or in the community - concerning the person's birth, adoption, legitimacy, ancestry, marriage, divorce, death, relationship by blood, adoption, or marriage, or similar facts of personal or family history.

(20) ***Reputation Concerning Boundaries or General History.*** --A reputation in a community - arising before the controversy - concerning boundaries of land in the community or customs that affect the land, or concerning general historical events important to that community, state, or nation.

(21) ***Reputation Concerning Character.*** --A reputation among a person's associates or in the community concerning the person's character.

(22) ***Judgment of a Previous Conviction.*** --Evidence of a final judgment of conviction if:

(A) it is offered in a civil case and:

(i) the judgment was entered after a trial or guilty plea, but not a nolo contendere plea;

(ii) the conviction was for a felony;

(iii) the evidence is admitted to prove any fact essential to the judgment; and

(iv) an appeal of the conviction is not pending; or

(B) it is offered in a criminal case and:

(i) the judgment was entered after a trial or a guilty or nolo contendere plea;

(ii) the conviction was for a criminal offense;

(iii) the evidence is admitted to prove any fact essential to the judgment;

(iv) when offered by the prosecutor for a purpose other than impeachment, the judgment was against the defendant; and

(v) an appeal of the conviction is not pending.

(23) ***Judgments Involving Personal, Family, or General History or a Boundary.*** --A judgment that is admitted to prove a matter of personal, family, or general history, or boundaries, if the matter:

(A) was essential to the judgment; and

(B) could be proved by evidence of reputation.

(24) ***Statement Against Interest.*** --A statement that:

(A) a reasonable person in the declarant's position would have made only if the person believed it to be true because, when made, it was so contrary to the declarant's proprietary or pecuniary interest or had so great a tendency to invalidate the declarant's claim against someone else or to expose the declarant to civil or criminal liability or to make the declarant an object of hatred, ridicule, or disgrace; and

(B) is supported by corroborating circumstances that clearly indicate its trustworthiness, if it is offered in a criminal case as one that tends to expose the declarant to criminal liability.

Rule 804. Exceptions to the Rule Against Hearsay -- When the Declarant is Unavailable as a Witness

(a) ***Criteria for Being Unavailable.*** --A declarant is considered to be unavailable as a witness if the declarant:

(1) is exempted from testifying about the subject matter of the declarant's statement because the court rules that a privilege applies;

(2) refuses to testify about the subject matter despite a court order to do so;

(3) testifies to not remembering the subject matter;

(4) cannot be present or testify at the trial or hearing because of death or a thenexisting infirmity, physical illness, or mental illness; or

(5) is absent from the trial or hearing and the statement's proponent has not been able, by process or other reasonable means, to procure the declarant's attendance or testimony.

But this subdivision (a) does not apply if the statement's proponent procured or wrongfully caused the declarant's unavailability as a witness in order to prevent the declarant from attending or testifying.

(b) ***The Exceptions.*** --The following are not excluded by the rule against hearsay if the declarant is unavailable as a witness:

(1) ***Former Testimony.*** --Testimony that:

(A) when offered in a civil case:

(i) was given as a witness at a trial or hearing of the current or a different proceeding or in a deposition in a different proceeding; and

(ii) is now offered against a party and the party - or a person with similar interest - had an opportunity and similar motive to develop the testimony by direct, cross-, or redirect examination.

(B) when offered in a criminal case:

(i) was given as a witness at a trial or hearing of the current or a different proceeding; and

(ii) is now offered against a party who had an opportunity and similar motive to develop it by direct, cross-, or redirect examination; or

(iii) was taken in a deposition under - and is now offered in accordance with - chapter 39 of the Code of Criminal Procedure.

(2) ***Statement Under the Belief of Imminent Death.*** --A statement that the declarant, while believing the declarant's death to be imminent, made about its cause or circumstances.

(3) ***Statement of Personal or Family History.*** --A statement about:

(A) the declarant's own birth, adoption, legitimacy, ancestry, marriage, divorce, relationship by blood, adoption or marriage, or similar facts of personal or family history, even though the declarant had no way of acquiring personal knowledge about that fact; or

(B) another person concerning any of these facts, as well as death, if the declarant was related to the person by blood, adoption, or marriage or was so intimately associated with the person's family that the declarant's information is likely to be accurate.

Rule 805. Hearsay Within Hearsay

Hearsay within hearsay is not excluded by the rule against hearsay if each part of the combined statements conforms with an exception to the rule.

Rule 806. Attacking and Supporting the Declarant's Credibility

When a hearsay statement - or a statement described in Rule 801(e)(2)(C), (D), or (E), or, in a civil case, a statement described in Rule 801(e)(3) - has been admitted in evidence, the declarant's credibility may be attacked, and then supported, by any evidence that would be admissible for those purposes if the declarant had testified as a witness. The court may admit evidence of the declarant's statement or conduct, offered to impeach the declarant, regardless of when it occurred or whether the declarant had an opportunity to explain or deny it. If the party against whom the statement was admitted calls the declarant as a witness, the party may examine the declarant on the statement as if on cross-examination.

ARTICLE IX. AUTHENTICATION AND IDENTIFICATION

Rule 901. Authenticating or Identifying Evidence

(a) ***In General.*** --To satisfy the requirement of authenticating or identifying an item of evidence, the proponent must produce evidence sufficient to support a finding that the item is what the proponent claims it is.

(b) ***Examples.*** --The following are examples only-not a complete list-of evidence that satisfies the requirement:

(1) ***Testimony of a Witness with Knowledge.*** --Testimony that an item is what it is claimed to be.

(2) ***Nonexpert Opinion About Handwriting.*** --A nonexpert's opinion that handwriting is genuine, based on a familiarity with it that was not acquired for the current litigation.

(3) ***Comparison by an Expert Witness or the Trier of Fact.*** --A comparison by an expert witness or the trier of fact with a specimen that the court has found is genuine.

(4) ***Distinctive Characteristics and the Like.*** --The appearance, contents, substance, internal patterns, or other distinctive characteristics of the item, taken together with all the circumstances.

(5) ***Opinion About a Voice.*** --An opinion identifying a person's voice - whether heard firsthand or through mechanical or electronic transmission or recording - based on hearing the voice at any time under circumstances that connect it with the alleged speaker.

(6) ***Evidence About a Telephone Conversation.*** --For a telephone conversation, evidence that a call was made to the number assigned at the time to:

(A) a particular person, if circumstances, including self-identification, show that the person answering was the one called; or

(B) a particular business, if the call was made to a business and the call related to business reasonably transacted over the telephone.

(7) ***Evidence About Public Records.*** --Evidence that:

(A) a document was recorded or filed in a public office as authorized by law; or

(B) a purported public record or statement is from the office where items of this kind are kept.

(8) ***Evidence About Ancient Documents or Data Compilations.*** --For a document or data compilation, evidence that it:

(A) is in a condition that creates no suspicion about its authenticity;

(B) was in a place where, if authentic, it would likely be; and

(C) is at least 20 years old when offered.

(9) ***Evidence About a Process or System.*** --Evidence describing a process or system and showing that it produces an accurate result.

(10) ***Methods Provided by a Statute or Rule.*** --Any method of authentication or identification allowed by a statute or other rule prescribed under statutory authority.

Rule 902. Evidence That is Self-Authenticating

The following items of evidence are self-authenticating; they require no extrinsic evidence of authenticity in order to be admitted:

(1) ***Domestic Public Documents That are Sealed and Signed.*** --A document that bears:

(A) a seal purporting to be that of the United States; any state, district, commonwealth, territory, or insular possession of the United States; the former Panama Canal Zone; the Trust Territory of the Pacific Islands; a political subdivision of any of these entities; or a department, agency, or officer of any entity named above; and

(B) a signature purporting to be an execution or attestation.

(2) ***Domestic Public Documents That are Not Sealed But Are Signed and Certified.*** --A document that bears no seal if:

(A) it bears the signature of an officer or employee of an entity named in Rule 902(1)(A); and

(B) another public officer who has a seal and official duties within that same entity certifies under seal - or its equivalent - that the signer has the official capacity and that the signature is genuine.

(3) ***Foreign Public Documents.*** --A document that purports to be signed or attested by a person who is authorized by a foreign country's law to do so.

(A) ***In General.*** --The document must be accompanied by a final certification that certifies the genuineness of the signature and official position of the signer or attester - or of any foreign official whose certificate of genuineness relates to the signature or attestation or is in a chain of certificates of genuineness relating to the signature or attestation. The certification may be made by a secretary of a United States embassy or legation; by a consul general, vice consul, or consular agent of the United States; or by a diplomatic or consular official of the foreign country assigned or accredited to the United States.

(B) ***If Parties Have Reasonable Opportunity to Investigate.*** --If all parties have been given a reasonable opportunity to investigate the document's authenticity and accuracy, the court may, for good cause, either:

(i) order that it be treated as presumptively authentic without final certification; or

(ii) allow it to be evidenced by an attested summary with or without final certification.

(C) ***If a Treaty Abolishes or Displaces the Final Certification Requirement.*** --If the United States and the foreign country in which the official record is located are parties to a treaty or convention that abolishes or displaces the final certification requirement, the record and attestation must be certified under the terms of the treaty or convention.

(4) ***Certified Copies of Public Records.*** --A copy of an official record - or a copy of a document that was recorded or filed in a public office as authorized by law - if the copy is certified as correct by:

(A) the custodian or another person authorized to make the certification; or

(B) a certificate that complies with Rule 902(1), (2), or (3), a statute, or a rule prescribed under statutory authority.

(5) ***Official Publications.*** --A book, pamphlet, or other publication purporting to be issued by a public authority.

(6) ***Newspapers and Periodicals.*** --Printed material purporting to be a newspaper or periodical.

(7) ***Trade Inscriptions and the Like.*** --An inscription, sign, tag, or label purporting to have been affixed in the course of business and indicating origin, ownership, or control.

(8) ***Acknowledged Documents.*** --A document accompanied by a certificate of acknowledgment that is lawfully executed by a notary public or another officer who is authorized to take acknowledgments.

(9) ***Commercial Paper and Related Documents.*** --Commercial paper, a signature on it, and related documents, to the extent allowed by general commercial law.

(10) ***Business Records Accompanied by Affidavit.*** --The original or a copy of a record that meets the requirements of Rule 803(6) or (7), if the record is accompanied by an affidavit that complies with subparagraph (B) of this rule and any other requirements of law, and the record and affidavit are served in accordance with subparagraph (A). For good cause shown, the court may order that a business record be treated as presumptively authentic even if the proponent fails to comply with subparagraph (A).

(A) ***Service Requirement.*** --The proponent of a record must serve the record and the accompanying affidavit on each other party to the case at least 14 days before trial. The record and affidavit may be served by any method permitted by Rule of Civil Procedure 21a.

(B) ***Form of Affidavit.*** --An affidavit is sufficient if it includes the following language, but this form is not exclusive. The proponent may use an unsworn declaration made under penalty of perjury in place of an affidavit.

1. I am the custodian of records [*or* I am an employee or owner] of and am familiar with the manner in which its records are created and maintained by virtue of my duties and responsibilities.

2. Attached are pages of records. These are the original records or exact duplicates of original records.

3. The records were made at or near the time of each act, event, condition, opinion, or diagnosis set forth. [*or* It is the regular practice of to make this type of record at or near the time of each act, event, condition, opinion, or diagnosis set forth in the record.]

4. The records were made by, or from information transmitted by, persons with knowledge of the matters set forth. [*or* It is the regular practice of for this type of record to be made by, or from information transmitted by, persons with knowledge of the matters set forth in them.]

5. The records were kept in the course of regularly conducted business activity. [*or* It is the regular practice of to keep this type of record in the course of regularly conducted business activity.]

6. It is the regular practice of the business activity to make the records.

(11) ***Presumptions Under a Statute or Rule.*** --A signature, document, or anything else that a statute or rule prescribed under statutory authority declares to be presumptively or prima facie genuine or authentic.

Rule 903. Subscribing Witness's Testimony

A subscribing witness's testimony is necessary to authenticate a writing only if required by the law of the jurisdiction that governs its validity.

ARTICLE X. CONTENTS OF WRITINGS, RECORDINGS, AND PHOTOGRAPHS

Rule 1001. Definitions That Apply to This Article

In this article:

(a) A "writing" consists of letters, words, numbers, or their equivalent set down in any form.

(b) A "recording" consists of letters, words, numbers, or their equivalent recorded in any manner.

(c) A "photograph" means a photographic image or its equivalent stored in any form.

(d) An "original" of a writing or recording means the writing or recording itself or any counterpart intended to have the same effect by the person who executed or issued it. For electronically stored information, "original" means any printout - or other output readable by sight - if it accurately reflects the information. An "original" of a photograph includes the negative or a print from it.

(e) A "duplicate" means a counterpart produced by a mechanical, photographic, chemical, electronic, or other equivalent process or technique that accurately reproduces the original.

Rule 1002. Requirement of the Original

An original writing, recording, or photograph is required in order to prove its content unless these rules or other law provides otherwise.

Rule 1003. Admissibility of Duplicates

A duplicate is admissible to the same extent as the original unless a question is raised about the original's authenticity or the circumstances make it unfair to admit the duplicate.

Rule 1004. Admissibility of Other Evidence of Content

An original is not required and other evidence of the content of a writing, recording, or photograph is admissible if:

(a) all the originals are lost or destroyed, unless the proponent lost or destroyed them in bad faith;

(b) an original cannot be obtained by any available judicial process;

(c) an original is not located in Texas;

(d) the party against whom the original would be offered had control of the original; was at that time put on notice, by pleadings or otherwise, that the original would be a subject of proof at the trial or hearing; and fails to produce it at the trial or hearing; or

(e) the writing, recording, or photograph is not closely related to a controlling issue.

Rule 1005. Copies of Public Records to Prove Content

The proponent may use a copy to prove the content of an official record - or of a document that was recorded or filed in a public office as authorized by law - if these conditions are met: the record or document is otherwise admissible; and the copy is certified as correct in accordance with Rule 902(4) or is testified to be correct by a witness who has compared it with the original. If no such copy can be obtained by reasonable diligence, then the proponent may use other evidence to prove the content.

Rule 1006. Summaries to Prove Content

The proponent may use a summary, chart, or calculation to prove the content of voluminous writings, recordings, or photographs that cannot be conveniently examined in court. The proponent must make the originals or duplicates available for examination or copying, or both, by other parties at a reasonable time and place. And the court may order the proponent to produce them in court.

Rule 1007. Testimony or Statement of a Party to Prove Content

The proponent may prove the content of a writing, recording, or photograph by the testimony, deposition, or written statement of the party against whom the evidence is offered. The proponent need not account for the original.

Rule 1008. Functions of the Court and Jury

Ordinarily, the court determines whether the proponent has fulfilled the factual conditions for admitting other evidence of the content of a writing, recording, or photograph under Rule 1004 or 1005. But in a jury trial, the jury determines - in accordance with Rule 104(b) - any issue about whether:

(a) an asserted writing, recording, or photograph ever existed;

(b) another one produced at the trial or hearing is the original; or

(c) other evidence of content accurately reflects the content.

Rule 1009. Translating a Foreign Language Document

(a) ***Submitting a Translation.*** --A translation of a foreign language document is admissible if, at least 45 days before trial, the proponent serves on all parties:

(1) the translation and the underlying foreign language document; and

(2) a qualified translator's affidavit or unsworn declaration that sets forth the translator's qualifications and certifies that the translation is accurate.

(b) ***Objection.*** --When objecting to a translation's accuracy, a party should specifically indicate its inaccuracies and offer an accurate translation. A party must serve the objection on all parties at least 15 days before trial.

(c) ***Effect of Failing to Object or Submit a Conflicting Translation.*** --If the underlying foreign language document is otherwise admissible, the court must admit - and may not allow a party to attack the accuracy of - a translation submitted under subdivision (a) unless the party has:

(1) submitted a conflicting translation under subdivision (a); or

(2) objected to the translation under subdivision (b).

(d) ***Effect of Objecting or Submitting a Conflicting Translation.*** --If conflicting translations are submitted under subdivision (a) or an objection is made under subdivision (b), the court must determine whether there is a genuine issue about the accuracy of a material part of the translation. If so, the trier of fact must resolve the issue.

(e) ***Qualified Translator May Testify.*** --Except for subdivision (c), this rule does not preclude a party from offering the testimony of a qualified translator to translate a foreign language document.

(f) ***Time Limits.*** --On a party's motion and for good cause, the court may alter this rule's time limits.

(g) ***Court-Appointed Translator.*** --If necessary, the court may appoint a qualified translator. The reasonable value of the translator's services must be taxed as court costs.

TEXAS TRANSPORTATION CODE, CIVIL STATUTES, AND RELATED STATUTES FOR LAW/CODE ENFORCEMENT OFFICERS

How to use this CHART

This publication has been designed to help you find offenses, section numbers and penalties of the **Texas Transportation Code.** Also included are references to the vehicle laws (V) of the Civil Statutes, the Penal Code (P.C.), the Alcoholic Beverage Code (ABC), the Family Code (FAM), and the Health and Safety Code (HSC). Refer to the Key on the following page regarding the penalties abbreviations.

KEY

M = Misdemeanor
Class A
(fine not to exceed $4,000, jail term not to exceed 1 year, or both)
Class B
(fine not to exceed $2,000, jail term not to exceed 180 days, or both)
Class C
(fine not to exceed $500)

F = Felony
Capital
(death or life imprisonment)
1st degree
(prison term of life or not less than 5 years nor more than 99 years, fine not to exceed $10,000.)
2nd degree
(prison term of not less than 2 years nor more than 20 years, fine not to exceed $10,000.)
3rd degree
(prison term of not less than 2 years nor more than 10 years, fine not to exceed $10,000.)
State jail (SJ)
(confinement in state jail for not less than 180 days nor more than 2 years, fine not to exceed $10,000.)

— = Reference Only

S = Suspension of License
(See § 521.292 and § 521.294. See § 521.341 for automatic suspension.)

R = Revocation of License

CP = Civil Penalty
Penalties are generally the maximum penalties for first offenses.

Offense Titles

OFFENSE	ARTICLE OR SECTION	PENALTY
ABANDONED VEHICLES		
Definitions	683.001	—
Demolition	683.051 to 683.057	—
Records, failure to keep	683.057	M(B)
Officers authorized		
To auction	683.014, 683.015	—
To take into custody	683.011 to 683.013	—
To use	683.016	—
Storage fees, unauthorized	683.033	M(B)
ACCIDENTS, TRAFFIC		
Aid, duty to render	550.023	—
Investigation by peace officer	550.041	—
Leaving scene of		
Accident involving serious injury or death	550.021	F(3)/S
Accidents involving injury	550.021	_/S
Accident involving damage to vehicle	550.022	M(C), (B)/S
Liability, determination of	601.154	—
Report, by officer	550.062	—
Provide false information	601.004	M(A)
Striking fixtures or highway landscaping	550.025	M(C), (B)/S
Striking unattended vehicle	550.024	M(C), (B)/S
ADVERTISING, OUTDOOR		
Defined	391.001(10)	—
Public nuisance	391.034	CP
Unlicensed	391.061	M(B)/R/S
Without permit	391.067	M(B)/R/S
AIRCRAFT		
Flying while intoxicated	P.C. 49.05	M(B), (A), F(3)
Fuel tank, illegal, operation with	24.013	F(3)
Highway, road or street, operation on	24.021	M(C)
Identification numbers,		
Operation without	24.012	F(3)
Tampering with	P.C. 31.11	M(A)
Illumination by intense light	P.C. 42.14	M(C)
Impair ability to control	P.C. 42.14	M(A)
Manslaughter	P.C. 49.08 F(2)	
Possession, duty to determine right of	501.156	M(C)
Unauthorized use of	P.C. 31.07	F(SJ)
Unregistered, operation	24.011	F(3)
ALCOHOL AND DRUGS		
Alcohol		
Alcoholic; operation of vehicle by	521.319	R
Amusement ride, operating or assembling while intoxicated	49.065	M(B)
Breath test; refusal to submit to	522.081	R/S
	724.035	S
Consuming while driving	P.C. 49.03	M(C)/S
By minor	729.001, ABC 106.041, P.C. 8.07, FAM 54.042	M(C)/S

With open container in possession	P.C. 49.04	M(B)
Intoxicated, Boating	P.C. 49.06	M(B)/S
Consent to taking of specimen	724.011	—
Driving	P.C. 49.04	M(B)/S
During commission of offense	545.421(d), (e)	M(A)/S
Flying	P.C. 49.05	M(B)/S
Intoxication, Assault	P.C. 49.07	F(3)/S
Manslaughter	P.C. 49.08	F(2)/S
Cause death of peace officer, firefighter or EMS personnel	P.C. 49.09	F(1)/S
Public	P.C. 49.02	M(C)
Penalties, enhanced		
Serious injury to peace officer, firefighter or EMS personnel	P.C. 49.09	F(2)/S
Second offense	P.C. 49.09	M(A)/S
Third or greater	P.C. 49.09	F(3)/S
Drugs		
Addict; operation of vehicle by	521.319	R
Controlled substance violation, conviction of	521.372	S
Minors	729.001, ABC 106.041, P.C. 8.07, FAM 54.042	M(C)/S
Operating a commercial vehicle with drugs in system	522.081	R/S
ANTIQUE VEHICLES		
Failure to register	504.502	M(C)
APPLICABILITY OF TRAFFIC REGULATIONS		
Animals and animal-drawn vehicles	542.003	—
Bicycles	551.103	—
Emergency vehicles	546.001	—
Highway workers	542.004	—
Implements of husbandry	504.504	—
Pedestrians	552.001 to 552.009	—
Road machinery	504.504	—
Streetcars	545.201 to 545.206	—
Tractors, farm	547.371	—
BICYCLES		
Brakes, absent or insufficient	551.104(a)	M(C)
Clinging to vehicle while riding	551.102(d)	M(C)
Lamps and reflectors, absent or insufficient	551.104(b)	M(C)
Riding unsafely	551.103	M(C)
Carrying articles which prevent driver from keeping at least one hand on handlebars	551.102(c)	M(C)
Failure to keep right	551.103(a)	M(C)
Riding more than two abreast	551.103(c)	M(C)
Too many riders	551.102(b)	M(C)
Traffic laws, application	551.103	—
BRIBERY		
Of county officer or agent	502.411, P.C. 36.02	F(2)/S
Offers or accepts	P.C. 36.02	F(2)/S

Offense Titles

BRIDGES		
Operating vehicle that does not clear	621.504	M(C)
BURGLARY		
Vehicle	P.C. 30.04	M(A)
Vehicle of wholesale drug distributor	P.C. 30.04	F(3)
CHILDREN		
Failure to use safety seat	545.412	M(C)
Leaving unattended in vehicle	P.C. 22.10	M(C)
Permitting to ride in open bed of truck or trailer	545.414	M(C)
(See also Minors)		
CITATIONS, TRAFFIC, failure to comply	702.004	R
Quotas prohibited	720.002	—
COMMERCIAL VEHICLES		
Commercial driver's license		
Application, false information	522.021	M(C)
Change of name or address	522.032	M(C)
Endorsements, violation of	522.042	M(C)
More than one	522.026	M(C)
Operation without	522.011	M
Restrictions, violation of	522.043	M(C)
Disqualifications	522.081, 522.105	R/S
Disqualified, driving while	522.071	M(B)
Foreign		
Annual permits	502.353	M(C)
Border commercial zone, registration exemption	648.101	—
Operation without permit	502.352	M(C)
Identifying markings,		
absence of	642.002	M(C)
Inspection, generally	548.202	—
Operation without		
License plate or registration insignia	502.404	M(C)
Permit	522.011	M(C)
COURT		
Failure to appear		
Denial of license renewal	706.004	R
For felony	P.C. 38.10(f)	F(3)/S
For misdemeanor punishable by jail term	P.C. 38.10(d)	M(A)
For offense punishable by fine only	P.C. 38.10(e)	M(C)
Notice to appear	543.003, 543.004	—
DEALERS, MOTOR VEHICLE		
Auctions, unlicensed purchase of vehicles at	503.037	M(A)/CP
Distinguishing number		
Application for drive-a-way operator	503.023	—
	503.029	—
Cancellation	503.038	M(A)/CP
Engaging in business without	503.021, 503.027	M(A)/CP
Duty of on sale	501.0234	M(C)
License plates, tags		
Failure to display	503.069	M(A)/CP
Out-of-state, removal	503.070	M(A)/CP

Offense Titles

Notice of		
Change of address	503.006	M(A)/CP
Driving or towing from out-of-state	503.071	M(A)/CP
Sale or transfer	503.005	M(A)/CP
Temporary cardboard tags		
Buyer's	503.063	M(A)/CP
Dealer's	503.062	M(A)/CP
Unauthorized	503.067	M(A)/CP
DIMENSIONS AND WEIGHTS OF VEHICLES		
Exceptions	622.901 to 622.953	—
Height, exceeding maximum	621.207	M(C), (B)
Length		
Exceeding maximum	621.203	M(C), (B)
Extended load	621.206	M(C), (B)
Semitrailer or trailer	621.204	M(C), (B)
Vehicle combination	621.205	M(C), (B)
Operation, restricted on certain holidays	621.006	M(C)
Oversize or overweight vehicles transporting		
Cotton or cotton processing equipment	622.101	—
Lumber	622.081	—
Milk	622.031 to 622.033	M(C)
Poles or pipe	622.061 to 622.063	M(C), (B)
Ready-mixed concrete	622.011 to 622.017	M(C), (B)
Timber or timber products	622.041 to 622.044	M(C), (B)
Recreational vehicles	622.903	—
Registration, additional gross weight	621.406	—
Registration receipt		
Failure to carry or present	621.002	M(C), (B)
Prima facie evidence	621.002	—
Size and weight		
Construction and equipment	621.502	M(C), (B)
Containers, exceeding limit	621.505	M
Special mobile equipment		GRADED
	622.071 to 622.074	M(C), (B)
Vehicle clearance	621.504	M(C)
Certificate	621.004	—
Weight, exceeding maximum	621.101	M(C), (B)
Width, exceeding maximum	621.201	M(C), (B)
DISABLED AND HANDICAPPED PERSONS		
Architectural improvement for disabled, blocking	681.011	M(C)
International symbol of access	681.007	—
Mentally incompetent, operation of vehicle while	521.319	R
Parking placard		
Failure to display	681.002	M(C)
Manufacture, sale, possession, or use of counterfeit	681.0111	M(C), (A)
Parking privileges	681.006	—
Unauthorized parking		
Enforcement by certain appointed persons	681.0101	—
In space for disabled	681.011	M(C)
Where prohibited	681.006	M(C)
DISPOSAL OF MOTOR VEHICLES		
Certificate of title, surrender	683.056	—
Failure to keep records	683.057	M(B)

DOCUMENTS		
Application, false information	521.451, 521.454	M(A)/S
Auction license and number, conducting motor vehicle auctions without	503.022	M(C)/CP
Certificate of title		
Agreement, rights of survivorship	501.031	—
Alteration	501.154	M(C)
Applying for on stolen or concealed vehicle	501.153	M(C)
Failure to deliver at time of sale	520.022	M(C)
False information; forgery on application	501.155	F(3)
False name on application	501.155	F(3)
Issuance of receipt; procedural violation:		
without importer's certificate	501.026	M(C)
Without manufacturer's certificate	501.025	M(C)
Lost or destroyed, copy obtained	501.134	—
Motor vehicle title service		
Failure to hold license	520.053	M(A)
Failure to maintain records	520.057	M(A)
Motor vehicles brought into state	501.030	M(C)
Receipt, alteration	501.154	M(C)
Sale without	501.152	M(C)
Refusal to issue	501.051	—
Grounds for	501.051	—
Required	501.022	M(C)
Revocation or suspension	501.051	—
Rights of survivorship	501.031	—
Sale or offer without	501.152	M(C)
Transporters, failure to determine right of possession	501.156	M(C)
Used vehicles, delivery of		
receipt and title	520.022	M(C)
Transfer documents	520.035	M(C)
Disabled person parking card	681.004	—
Driver's license		
Altered, possession of	521.451	M(A)/S
Classifications	521.081 to 521.085	—
Commercial license		
Application, false information	522.021	M(C)/S
Change of name or address	522.032	M/C
Disqualifications	522.081	R/S
Driving while disqualified	522.071	M(B)/S
Driving with alcohol in system	522.081	R/S
Driving without	522.011	M(C)
Endorsements, violation of	522.042	M(C)
Limitation on number of	522.026	M(C)
Notification of conviction		
To department or employer	522.061	—
To licensing authority in other state	522.062	—
Permitting unauthorized driving	522.072	—
Restrictions, violation of	522.043	M(C)
Driving with improper	521.457	M(B), (A)/S
Employment of unlicensed driver	521.459	M(C)
Failure to carry when driving	521.025	M(C)
False swearing to application information	521.454	M(A)/S
Fictitious; possession or use of	521.451, 521.453	M(A)/S
Fraudulent use; permitting	521.455	M(A)/S
General violation	521.451	M(A)/S

Illegally obtained; use of	521.455	M(A)/S
Lending to another	521.451	M(A)/S
Minor, driving without	729.002	M(C)
Procedure	729.003	—
More than one	521.451	M(A)/S
Notice of change of address or name	521.054	—
Occupational license		
Certified copy, failure to carry	521.253	M(B)
Order requirements	521.248	—
On material relating to suspension of driving privilege	521.291 to 521.320, 521.341 to 521.350	—
Permitting use by unauthorized person	521.458	M(C)
Restrictions; violations of	521.221	M(C)
Sex offenders, revocation	521.348	—
Surrender, failure to	521.451	M(A)/S
Suspended, revoked or expired; driving while	521.451, 521.457	M(A)/S
Unauthorized use of driver's license information	521.126	M(A)
Forgery		
Counterfeit documents, use of	521.451	M(A)/S
Counterfeit instrument, defined	521.456(d)	—
Manufacture	521.456	F(3)
Possession of	521.456	M(C)
Generally	P.C. 32.21	M(A)/F(SJ), (3)
Identification required for vehicle near Mexican border	600.002	—
Importer's certificate, alteration	501.154	M(C)
Inspection certificate		
Failure to display	548.602	M(C)
Fictitious	548.603	M(B)
Forgery	548.603(b)	F(3), (2)
Issued for another vehicle	548.603	M(B)
Operating without	548.605	M(C)
Prerequisite to issuance	548.104	—
Motor vehicle records, prohibition on use of personal information	730.004	—
Motorcycle license, restricted	521.084	—
Permit violations		
Advertising signs; outdoor	391.067, 391.068	M(B)
Commercial vehicle; operating	522.011	M(C)
Bordering Mexico	502.353	M(C)
Nonresident owned	502.355	M(C)
Single or 30-day trip	502.354	M(C)
Transporting		
Farm products	501.004(b)(1), 502.351, 502.355, 623.017	M(C)
Equipment	623.071	M(C)
Manufactured house	623.095	M(C)/CP
Oversize load	621.201, 621.206, 621.207	M(C)
Portable buildings	623.121	—

Proof of financial responsibility		
Failure to maintain evidence of, while driving	601.195	M(B)/S
Insufficient	601.057	S
Requirement	601.051	—
Registration		
Application for	502.151	—
Driving without	502.402(a)	M(C)
Improper, driving under	502.403	M(C)
Operation of vehicles without license plate	502.404	M(C)
Release of information	502.008	M(C)
Serial number		
Placement with intent to change identity	501.151	F(3)
Seizure of vehicle with altered	501.158	—
Tamper with	P.C. 31.11	M(A)
DRIVER RESPONSIBILITY PROGRAM		
License points surcharges	708.052 to 708.054 708.102 to 708.104	—
DRIVER'S LICENSE		
(See Documents)		
DRIVING WHILE INTOXICATED		
(See Alcohol and Drugs)		
DUMPING, ILLEGAL		
In cave	H.S.C. 365.016	M(C)
Second offense	H.S.C. 365.016	M(A)
Third or greater offense	H.S.C. 365.016	F(3)
On highway, 15 lbs/13 gals. or less	H.S.C. 365.012(d)	M(C)
15-500 lbs/13 gals.-100 cu. ft.	H.S.C. 365.012(e)	M(B)
500+ lbs/100+ cu. ft.	H.S.C. 365.012(f)(1)	M(A)
5+ lbs./13+ gals., disposed for commercial purposes	H.S.C. 365.012(f)(2)	M(A)
Repeat offense	H.S.C. 365.012(g)	1 cat. higher
ELECTRIC PERSONAL ASSISTIVE MOBILITY DEVICES	551.201 to 551.203	—
EMERGENCY VEHICLES		
Additional equipment requirements	547.702	—
On being approached by	545.156	M(C)
Passing	545.157	M(C), (B)
Permissible conduct	546.001	—
Speed limit	545.365	—
EMPLOYER RESPONSIBILITIES		
Employee information, required	522.063, 522.064	—
Permitting unauthorized driving	522.072	—
Transfer of ownership of emergency vehicles	728.021	M(C)
Unlicensed driver, employment of	521.459	M(C)
ENGINE NUMBER		
(See Serial Number)		
EQUIPMENT VIOLATIONS		
(See Motor Vehicle Equipment Violations)		

EXAMINATION		
Exemption from certain requirements for non-residents	521.164	—
Failure to take or pass when required	521.161	—
FALSE OR INCORRECT INFORMATION		
Title for a nonrepairable motor vehicle or salvage motor vehicle	501.109	F(3)
FALSE SWEARING		
On application for original, renewal or duplicate driver's license	521.454	M(A)/S
FARM PRODUCTS		
Transporting a greater distance or different route than permitted by permit	502.355	M(C)
FARM VEHICLES		
Fee, permitted uses	502.163	M(C)
Lights, combination vehicles	547.372	M(C)
Equipment requirements	547.371	M(C)
Registration requirements	502.276	—
FELONY		
Commercial vehicle, using in commission of	522.081	R/S
FINE, defaulting payment	CCP 43.03, 43.08	—
FIRE HOSE, crossing	545.408	M(C)
FIRE VEHICLES		
Signal lamps, failure to equip with	547.702	M(C)
HABITUAL VIOLATION of Traffic Law	521.292	S
IDENTIFICATION NUMBERS,		
Altering to change identity of vehicle	P.C. 31.11	M(A)
Tampering with	P.C. 31.11	M(A)
IGNITION KEYS, sale of master key	728.011	M(C)
IMPLIED CONSENT	724.011	—
INSPECTION, MECHANICAL		
Commercial vehicles	548.201 to 548.203	—
Failure to display certificate	548.602	M(C)
Failure to furnish evidence of financial responsibility	548.105	M(C)
Failure to have vehicle inspected as required	548.051	M(C)
Fees for certificate; overcharging	548.501, 548.601	M(C)
Fictitious inspection certificate	548.603	M(B)
Inspection station, operation without certification	548.401	M(C)
Violations by	548.405	R/S
Offense generally	548.601	M(C)
Periods of inspection	548.101 to 548.103	—
Reinspection, following repairs	548.053	—
INSURANCE		
Failure to maintain	601.191	M(C)/R/S
	601.195(a)(2)	M(C), (B)

Minimum coverage amounts	601.072	—
Proof of financial responsibility		
Furnishing evidence of	601.053	—
Submitted with registration application	601.083	—
Requirements	601.071	—
INTERFERENCE WITH PEACE OFFICER.		
investigation of highway racing or reckless driving exhibition	545.4205	M(B)
INTOXICATION ASSAULT,		
serious bodily injury while operating vehicle	P.C. 49.07	F(3)/S
INTOXICATION MANSLAUGHTER	P.C. 49.08	F(2)/S
JUNKED VEHICLES		
Defined	683.071	—
Disposal of	683.078	—
Public nuisance,		
abatement and removal	683.072 to 683.078	—
Creating	683.072	—
Hearing	683.076	—
Maintaining	683.073	M(C)
Notice	683.075	—
LAW ENFORCEMENT VEHICLE		
Unauthorized sale or transfer	728.022	CP
LICENSE PLATES		
Off-highway vehicles; number sticker or decal	502.406	M(C)
Altering, intentionally	502.409(b)	M(B)
Antique vehicles	504.502	M(C)
Blurring or reflective material	502.409	M(B)
Dealer's; fraudulent use of	503.068	M(A)/CP
Use on service vehicles carrying load	503.068	M(A)/CP
Dealer's temporary cardboard tags, misuse of	503.038(a)(12), 503.068	M(A)/CP
Display of, operation without	503.069	M(A)/CP
Drive-a-way in-transit;		
operation without	503.069	M(A)/CP
Exempt, seizure of certain vehicles	502.2015	—
Expired, driving when	502.407	M(C)
Failure to surrender		
dealer's plates	503.038(c)	M(A)/CP
False information, using on application	503.038(a)(6)	M(A)/CP
Fictitious; use of	502.409	M(B)
Obscured; use of	502.409	M(C)
Operation of vehicle without plates	502.404	M(C)
Out-of-state; failure of dealer to remove	503.070	M(A)/CP
Temporary, transporting property	503.065(c)	M(A)/CP
Temporary cardboard tags, dealer's,		
failure to display	503.069	M(A)/CP
Unauthorized reproduction	503.067	M(A)/CP
MANUFACTURED AND INDUSTRIALIZED HOUSING		
Transportation, caution lights,		
failure to provide	623.098	M(C)/CP
Equipment violations	623.102	M(C)

Offense Titles

Excessive speed	623.101	M(C)
Insurance coverage, insufficient	623.103	M(C)/CP
No escort flag vehicle	623.099	M(C)/CP
Oversized	623.093	M(C)
Permit, failure to obtain	623.092	M(C)/CP
Registration/certificate number, failure to display	623.094	M(C)
Unauthorized time	623.100	M(C)
MIGRANT AGRICULTURAL WORKERS, MOTOR TRANSPORTATION OF		
Equipment required	647.012	M(C)*
Limitation on operation of vehicle	647.009	M(C)*
Operator physical requirements	647.007	M(C)*
Passenger seating	647.014, 647.015	M(C)*
Protection from weather	647.016	M(C)*
Type of vehicle allowed	647.003	M(C)*
Vehicle other than bus, passenger safety provisions	647.013	M(C)*
*Fine: $5 to $50		
MINORS		
Common carrier, operation by person under 18	521.024	M(B)
Driving under the influence of alcohol	ABC 106.041, P.C. 8.07 (a)(2), FAM 54.042	M(C)/S
Driving without valid license	729.002	M(C)
Operating in violation of traffic laws	729.001	M(C)
Permitting to drive when unauthorized	521.458	M(C)
Restrictions on driving license	521.204	—
Supervision of operator holding instruction permit	521.222	M(C)
MOTOR CARRIERS		
Cab-card, failure to carry	643.059	M(C)
Operation without	643.059	M(C)
Inspection of documents	642.254	—
MOTOR VEHICLE EQUIPMENT VIOLATIONS		
Air-conditioning equipment, unsafe	547.610	M(C)
Allowing vehicle to be driven with equipment violations	547.004	M(C)
Brakes		
Absence	547.401	M(C)
Bicycles; absent or insufficient	551.104	M(C)
Emergency application of brakes; air and vacuum	547.405	M(C)
Insufficient	547.401	M(C)
Maintenance; insufficient	547.402	M(C)
Motorcycles; absent or insufficient	547.408, 547.802	M(C)
Parking brakes; absent or insufficient	547.404	M(C)
Reservoir for air or vacuum brakes; absent or insufficient	547.406	M(C)
Service brakes; absent or insufficient	547.403	M(C)
Single control to operate all brakes; absent	547.403	M(C)
Warning devices; absent or insufficient	547.407	M(C)
Child safety seats, failure to use when required	545.412	M(C)
Driving vehicle with equipment violations	547.004	M(C)
Exhaust system, defective	547.605	M(C)

Horns, absent or insufficient	547.501(a)	M(C)
Lamps and reflectors		
Absent or insufficient	547.302	M(C)
On buses and trucks 80' or more in width	547.352(1)	M(C)
On buses and trucks 30' or more in length	547.352(2)	M(C)
On pole trailers	547.352(4)	M(C)
On trailers and semitrailers 30' or more in length	547.352(3)	M(C)
On truck tractors	547.352(5)	M(C)
On vehicles 80"or more in width	547.352(6)	M(C)
Auxiliary passing lamps; more than two	547.329	M(C)
Bicycles; absent or insufficient	551.104(b)	M(C)
Clearance lamps; insufficient	547.352	M(C)
Mounted incorrectly	547.354(c)	M(C)
Distract or blind other driver; lamps mounted so as to	547.333(b)(2)(B)	M(C)
Distribution of lights; misuse or lack of control	547.333	M(C)
Failure to display at night or during low visibility	547.302, 547.355	M(C)
Farm vehicles; insufficient lights	547.334	M(C)
Flashing lights on unauthorized vehicle	547.305	M(C)
Fog lamps; more than two	547.328	M(C)
Hazard warning lights	547.331	—
Failure to display when required	547.503	M(C)
Headlamps; absent or insufficient	547.321	M(C)
Multiple-beam road lighting equipment	547.333	M(C)
Absent or insufficient on motorcycle	547.801	M(C)
Obstructed lights on combination vehicle	547.372	M(C)
Parked vehicle; failure to display lights	547.383	M(C)
Projecting load lights; absent or insufficient	547.382	M(C)
Red light on front of vehicle when not authorized	547.305(b)	M(C)
Reflectors; absent or insufficient	547.325	M(C)
Running board lamps; more than one on each side	547.332(2)	M(C)
Selling when not in compliance with safety standards	547.201	—
Side cowl or fender lamps; more than two	547.332(1)	M(C)
Side marker lamps; insufficient	547.352	M(C)
Signal lamps; school bus, absent or insufficient	547.701	M(C)
Single-beam road lighting equipment	547.334	M(C)
Snow removal equipment; absent or insufficient lighting	547.305(e)	M(C)
Spot lamps; more than two	547.327	M(C)
Stop lamps; absent or insufficient	547.323	M(C)
Tail lamps; absent or insufficient	547.322	M(C)
Turn signal lamps; absent	547.324	M(C)
Testing	547.203	—
License plates *(See main entry)*		
Mirrors, absent or insufficient	547.602	M(C)
Mudflaps, insufficient	547.606	M(C)
Mufflers		
Absence	547.604	M(C)
Maintenance; insufficient	547.604	M(C)
Permitting crankcase emissions	547.605(b)	M(C)
Permitting escape of excessive fumes or smoke	547.605(a)	M(C)
Sunscreening device, affixed improperly	547.609	M(C)

Tires		
Metal tire	547.612(b)	M(C)
Protuberances; prohibited	547.612(c)	M(C)
Regrooved tires; selling	547.612(e)	M(B)
Solid rubber; not entirely covered	547.612(a)	M(C)
Trademarks and brand names, selling equipment without	547.201(b)	M(C)
Windshield and windows, obstructed	547.613	M(C)
Windshield wipers, absent or insufficient	547.603	M(C)
MOTORCYCLES		
Brakes, absent or insufficient	502.005(b), 547.802	M(C)
Headgear, failure to wear	661.003	M(C)
Inspection by peace officer	521.227	—
License plate, absent	502.404(c)	M(C)
Lighting equipment, insufficient	547.801	M(C)
Passenger without helmet	661.003	M(C)
Registration seal, absent	502.405	M(C)
Too many riders	545.416	M(C)
MOVING VIOLATIONS		
Backing, unsafe	545.415	M(C)
Coasting	545.406	M(C)
Committed in a construction or maintenance zone	542.404	FINE DOUBLED
Crossing firehose	545.205, 545.408	M(C)
Crossing property	545.423	M(C)
Crossing sidewalk	545.422	M(C)
Following too closely	545.062	M(C)
Lane change, unsafe	545.104	M(C)
Median or divider; crossing	545.063	M(C)
One-way roads; disregarding direction indicated	545.059	M(C)
Passing		
No-passing zones; disregarding	545.055	M(C)
On left	545.053	M(C)
On right	545.057	M(C)
Passing school bus	545.066	M(B)
Causing bodily injury	545.066	M(A)/F(SJ)
Second and subsequent offenses	545.066	S
Passing streetcar to left	545.201	M(C)
Passing vehicle moving in opposite direction	545.052	M(C)
Streetcars; unsafely or without authorization	545.202	M(C)
Racing		
On highway	545.420	M(B), (A)/F(SJ)
Causing bodily injury or death	545.420(g), (h)	F(3), (2)
While intoxicated or with an open container	545.420(e)	M(A)
Reckless driving	545.401	M(B)
Restricted access	545.064	M(C)
Riding in trailer or semitrailer	545.4191	M(B)
Right-of-way, failure to yield		
According to traffic control device	544.004	M(C)
At green signal	544.007	M(C)
At intersection	545.151	M(C)
By pedestrian to vehicle when not in crosswalk	552.005	M(C)
Collision or interference as a result of	545.151(f), 545.153(d)	M(C)
Entering highway from private road or driveway	545.155	M(C)

Entering or leaving limited-access or controlled-access highway	545.154	M(C)
Entering roadway from alley, building, private road or driveway	545.256	M(C)
Left turn	545.152	M(C)
On multiple-laned roadway	545.061	M(C)
To emergency vehicle	545.156	M(C)
To pedestrian if control signal present	552.002	M(C)
To pedestrian in crosswalk	552.003	M(C)
To pedestrian on sidewalk	552.006	M(C)
Right side of roadway		
Failure to remain on	545.051	M(C)
While passing around rotary traffic island	545.059	M(C)
Shoulder, improved; operating vehicle on unsafely	545.058	M(C)
Sidewalk; driving upon	545.422	M(C)
Speed violations		
Driving too fast for conditions or safety	545.351	M(C)
On bridge	545.361(c)	M(C)
With inadequate headlamps	545.361(a)	M(C)
With solid rubber or cushion tires	545.361(b)	M(C)
Driving too slowly	545.363	M(C)
Motor-driven cycle	545.361(a)	M(C)
Prima facie speed limits	545.352	M(C)
Speed limit, exceeding	545.351	M(C)
With machine designed for applying plant food or chemicals	545.361(d)	M(C)
Within county park in county bordering Gulf of Mexico	750.002	M(C)
Stopping		
Failure: before reaching a standing school bus operating a visual sign	545.066	M(B)/S
Causing bodily injury	545.066	M(A)/F(SJ)
For approaching train	545.252	M(C)
For pursuing police vehicle	545.421	M(B), (A)
When approached by authorized emergency vehicle	545.156, 545.204	M(C)
When emerging from alley, driveway or building	545.256	M(C)
In an intersection	545.151, 545.302(a)(3)	M(C)
In or near safety zone	545.302(a)(5)	M(C)
Near street excavation	545.302(a)(6)	M(C)
Next to parked or stopped vehicle at curb	545.302(a)(1)	M(C)
On bridge or in tunnel	545.302(a)(7)	M(C)
On crosswalk	545.302(a)(4)	M(C)
On highway, unnecessarily	545.301	M(C)
On railroad tracks	545.302(a)(8)	M(C)
On sidewalk	545.302(a)(2)	M(C)
Stop signs, disregarding	544.010, 545.302(b)(4)	M(C)
Where prohibited by signs	545.302(a)(9)	M(C)
Without signal	545.105	M(C)
Turning		
At intersection	545.101	M(C)
On curve or crest of grade	545.102	M(C)
Signal, failure to	545.104	M(C)
Hand and arm	545.106(a)	—
Improper	545.104(c)	M(C)
Lamp	545.106	—
Unsafe	545.103	M(C)

ODOMETER		
Failure to disclose reading at time of transfer	501.072	M(C)
Failure to record reading at time of transfer	501.072	M(C)
Tampering with	727.002	M(B)
OFF-HIGHWAY VEHICLES		
Crossing street or highway unsafely	663.037	M(C)
Equipment violations	663.033	M(C)
Helmet, operation without	663.034	M(C)
Minors, operation by	663.032	M(C)
Operation on beach	663.0371	M(C)
on public highway or street without authorization	502.006	M(C)
On public property without registration decal	502.406	M(C)
Without safety certificate	663.031	M(C)
Passenger, operation with	663.036	M(C)
Reckless operation	663.035	M(C)
OFFENSES		
Accident, failure to report	550.026	M(C)
Leaving scene of		
Involving damage to vehicle	550.022	M(C), (B)/S
Involving personal injury or death	550.021	F(3)/S
On striking unattended vehicle	550.024	M(C), (B)
Alcohol		
Alcoholic, operation of vehicle by	521.319	R/S
Consumption or possession of, while driving	P.C. 49.03	M(C)
By minor	P.C. 8.07, FAM 54.042	S
Driving while intoxicated	P.C. 49.04	M(B)/S
By minor	ABC 106.041	M(C)/S
Driving while under the influence, commercial motor vehicle	522.081	M(B)/S
Intoxication assault	P.C. 49.07	F(3)/S
Intoxication manslaughter	P.C. 49.08	F(2)/S
Penalties, enhanced	P.C. 49.09	—
Second offense	P.C. 49.09	M(A)/S
Third or greater	P.C. 49.09	F(3)/S
Taking of specimen, refusal	522.104, 724.035	S
Children, leaving unattended in vehicle	P.C. 22.10	M(C)
Safety seat system, failure to secure	545.412	M(C)
Commercial vehicle		
Disqualified, driving while	522.071	M(B)/R/S
Driver's license, operation without	522.011	M(C)
Identifying markings, absent	642.002	M(C)
Committed in construction or maintenance zone	542.404	FINE DOUBLED
Driving license		
Cancelled, revoked, suspended, altered; driving while	521.451	M(A)/S
Failure to carry	521.025	M(C)
By driver of commercial vehicle	522.011	M(C)
By minor	729.002	M(C)
Fictitious	521.453	M(C)/S
More than one	521.451	M(A)/S

Drugs		
Addict, operation of vehicle by	521.319	R/S
Driving under the influence, commercial motor vehicle	522.081	R/S
Minors	P.C. 8.07, FAM 54.042	S
Emergency vehicle, on being approached by	545.156	M(C)
Excessive motor vehicle emissions	548.306	M(C)
Inspection certificate, failure to display	548.602	M(C)
Minor		
Operating a motor vehicle		
In violation of traffic laws	729.001	M(C)
Without license	729.002	M(C)
Motor vehicle		
Operation, in violation of suspension	601.371	M(B)
Second offense	601.371	M(A)
Permitting dangerous driver to borrow	705.001	M(C)
Serial numbers, placement with intent to change identity	501.151	F(3)
Unregistered, operation of	502.402	M(C)
Motorcycle, operator or passenger not wearing helmut	661.003	M(C)
Police officer, fleeing or attempting to elude	545.421	M(B), (A)
Racing		
On highway	545.420	M(B), (A)/F(SJ)
Causing bodily injury or death	545.420(g), (h)	F(3), (2)
While intoxicated or with an open container	545.420(e)	M(A)
Reckless driving	545.401	M(B)
Rest area, unauthorized use of	545.411	M(C)
Safety belts, failure to use	545.413	M(C)
School bus, passing	545.066	M(B)
Causing bodily injury	545.066	M(A)/F(SJ)
Second and subsequent offenses	545.066	M(B)/S
Unauthorized parking, in space for disabled	681.011	M(C)
Unauthorized signs, markings signals or display of	544.006	M(C)
OVERSIZE LOAD		
Extending too far to front, rear or sides	621.206	M(C)
Holidays, designated; transportation on	621.006	M(C)
Maximum load, exceeding	621.101, 621.506	GRADED
Permits, operating without	623.011	—
PARKING		
At angle where prohibited	545.303(c)	M(C)
Blocking curb or access designed to aid disabled	681.011(c)	M(C)
Double parking	545.302(a)(1)	M(C)
In a restricted traffic zone, by commissioner's court of a county	251.156	M(C)
In an intersection	545.302(a)(3)	M(C)
In front of driveway	545.302(b)(1)	M(C)
In or near safety zone	545.302(a)(5)	M(C)
In parking facility, unauthorized	684.011	M(C)

In parking space reserved		
for disabled, unauthorized	681.011	M(C)
Where prohibited	681.006	M(C)
In wrong direction	545.303(b)	M(C)
Interfering with emergency vehicle	545.407(2)	M(C)
Near crosswalk	545.302(a)(4)	M(C)
Near fire hydrant	545.302(b)(2)	M(C)
Near fire station entrance	545.302(b)(5)	M(C)
Near railroad crossing	545.302(c)(1)	M(C)
Near roadside traffic-control device	545.302(b)(4)	M(C)
Near street excavation	545.302(a)(6)	M(C)
Not parallel with curb	545.303(a)	M(C)
On bridge or in tunnel	545.302(a)(7)	M(C)
On crosswalk	545.302(a)(4)	M(C)
On highway, unnecessarily	545.301	M(C)
On railroad tracks	545.302(a)(8)	M(C)
On sidewalk	545.302(a)(2)	M(C)
Too far from curb	545.303(a)	M(C)
Where prohibited by signs	545.302(a)(9), (b)(6), (c)(2)	M(C)
Without setting brakes	547.404	M(C)
Without stopping engine	545.404	M(C)
PEDESTRIAN(S)		
Accident involving pedestrian within crosswalk	545.428	M(A)/F
Crossing against pedestrian control signal	552.002	M(C)
Crossing against red signal	552.001	M(C)
Crosswalks; failure to use		
right half	552.004	M(C)
Right-of-way in	552.003	M(C)
Jaywalking	552.005	M(C)
Soliciting, prohibited	552.007	M(C)
Walking on roadway where sidewalks provided	552.006	M(C)
POLICE OFFICER		
Disobeying	542.501	M(C)
Fleeing or attempting to elude	545.421(a)	M(B)
Placing another in danger of serious bodily injury	545.421(d)	M(A)
While intoxicated, during commission of offense	545.421(e)	M(A)
Giving false report to	P.C. 37.08	M(B)
PUBLIC TRANSPORTATION		
Driving on certain authority right of way	451.113	M(C)
Use without appropriate fare	451.0611, 452.0611	M(C)
RACING		
On highway	545.420	M(B),(A)/F(SJ)
Causing bodily injury or death	545.420(g), (h)	F(3), (2)
While intoxicated or with an open container	545.420(e)	M(A)
RAILROADS		
Duty to stop and render aid		
at accident	V 6419b	M(C)
Grade crossing		
Buses; failure to stop when required	545.253	M(C)
Crossing unsafely	545.251	M(C)
By heavy equipment, without required precautions	545.255	M(C)

Failure to reduce speed and stop by vehicles carrying hazardous substances	545.254	M(C)
Failure to stop	545.252	M(C)
Interference with signal	544.005	M(C)
Operation without permit	V 6419a, Secs. 1, 2, 3	M(C)
REGISTRATION SEAL		
Issued for other vehicle, use of	502.408	M(C)
Motorcycle, driving without	502.405	M(C)
Obscured, use of	502.409	M(C)
Sale or use of imitation	502.409	M(B)
Use of unauthorized	502.404	M(C)
RENTING VEHICLE, to unlicensed driver	521.460	M(C)
REST AREA		
Erection of a structure without authorization	545.411	M(C)
Remaining at for excessive time	545.411	M(C)
RESTRICTED ACCESS ROADWAYS		
Entering or leaving by unauthorized entrance or exit	545.064	M(C)/S
SAFETY EQUIPMENT		
Barricades; tampering with or disregarding	472.021	M(A)
Equipment violations *(See Motor Vehicle Equipment Violations)*		
Fire extinguishers; absent or insufficient	547.607	M(C)
In school bus	547.607	M(C)
In vehicle for hire	547.607	M(C)
Flares or lanterns; carrying flares in vehicle transporting explosives	547.502(b)(2)	M(C)
Disabled or stopped vehicle; failure to display when required	547.504 to 547.507	M(C)
Failure to carry when required	547.502	M(C)
Removing, damaging or destroying without authorization	547.508	M(C)
Helmet; operating motorcycle without	661.003	M(C)
Horn, unnecessary use	547.501	M(C)
Mudflaps; absent or insufficient	547.606	M(C)
Red flags; failure to carry when required	547.505	M(C)
Safety equipment, off-highway vehicle	663.033	M(C)
Safety glazing		
Camper without safety glazing; attaching to vehicle	547.608(d)	M(C)
Replacement of glass with improper glazing material	547.608(c)	M(C)
Selling imperfect safety glass without notification	547.608(e)	M(C)
Selling vehicle without	547.608(a)	M(C)
Seat belts; allowing child to ride without	545.412	M(C)
Failure to carry when required	547.601	M(C)
Failure to use when required	545.413	M(C)
Slow-moving vehicle emblems; failure to display when required	547.703	M(C)
Mounted incorrectly	547.703(a)(2)	M(C)
Use on unauthorized vehicle	547.005(a)	M(C)

Warning signs, damaging, removing or tampering with	472.021	M(C), (B), (A)
Disobeying	472.022	M(C), (B)
SAFETY STANDARDS		
Bicycles *(See main entry)*		
Crossing guards, failure to obey	542.501	M(C)
Dangerous driver, lending vehicle to	705.001	M(C)
Doors, opening unsafely	545.418	M(C)
Due care for pedestrians, failure of driver to exercise	552.008	M(C)
Equipment standards, selling in violation of	547.201	M(C)
Headlights, failure to dim	547.333	M(C)
Using incorrect beam	547.333	M(C)
Incapability to drive	521.292	R/S
Loose materials		
Spillage or residue; failure to remove	725.022	M(C)
Transporting in violation of requirements	725.003	M(C)
With tailgate open	725.021	M(C)
With unenclosed, unsecured or uncovered bed	725.021	M(C)
Motor carrier safety standards; failure to comply	644.151	M(C)/CP
Motorcycles *(See main entry)*		
Mountain highways; driving unsafely	545.405	M(C)
Off-highway vehicles *(See main entry)*		
Reckless driving	545.401	M(B)
Safety zone; driving through	545.403	M(C)
Television receiver, screen located within driver's view	547.611	M(C)
Towing safety chains	545.410	M(C)
Unattended motor vehicle	545.404	M(C)
Unauthorized person, permitting to drive	521.458	M(C)
Vehicle in unsafe condition; driving or permitting to be driven	547.004	M(C)
View		
Driving while obstructed	545.417(a)	M(C)
Obstructing driver's	545.417(b)	M(C)
Windshields, driving while obstructed	547.613	M(C)
SALE OF MOTOR VEHICLE without certificate	501.152	M(C)
SALVAGED VEHICLES	501.0911 to 501.0931	—
Theft, in conjunction with	P.C. 31.03(c)(6)	GRADED
SCHOOL BUSES		
Dismissal of expired license charge	521.026	—
Employment of unlicensed driver	521.021	M(C)
Fire extinguisher, absence of	547.607	M(C)/S
Junior college buses	521.023	—
Mirrors, absence of	547.701	M(C)/S
Operation by person under 18	521.022	M(C)
By person who has not been examined	521.022	M(C)
Without training school certificate	521.022	M(C)
Passing when prohibited	545.066	M(B)
Causing bodily injury	545.066	M(A)/F(SJ)
Railroad grade crossings, failure to stop	545.252	M(C)
Sign	547.7011	M(C)

Stop arms,		
when vehicle moving	547.701	M(C)
Warning lamps, unauthorized use of	547.701	M(C)
Warning signal light, absent or insufficient	547.701	M(C)
Failure to activate when required	547.701	M(C)
Unlawful use of	547.701	M(C)
SEAT BELTS *(See Safety Equipment)*		
SECONDHAND VEHICLE		
Selling, trading or transferring with incomplete documents	520.022, 520.035	M(C)
Without delivering license receipt to transferee	520.022	M(C)
Without registration	520.021	M(C)
SERIAL NUMBER		
Motorcycles; sale when numbers improperly affixed or filed	680.002	M(C)
Placement, with intent to change	501.151 F(3)	
Removed, altered or obliterated, seizure by peace officer	501.158	—
Tampering with	P.C. 31.11	M(A)
SIRENS, WHISTLES AND BELLS		
Unauthorized use	547.702(a)	M(C)
Unnecessary use by emergency vehicle	547.702(b)	M(C)
SPECIAL MOBILE EQUIPMENT		
Documents, failure to display upon peace officer's demand	622.073	M(B)
Serial number, absence	622.072	M(C)
SPEEDING *(See Moving Violations)*		
STANDARDS, FAILURE TO CONFORM TO		
Camping establishment, Must conform to standards	391.093(e)	—
Equipment, motor vehicle *(See Motor Vehicle Equipment Violations)*		
Farm vehicles *(See main entry)*		
Gas station, must provide certain services	391.093(b)	—
Junkyard, failure to screen		
after notice	391.125	CP
too near a right-of-way	391.121	M(B)
Motorcycles *(See main entry)*		
School buses *(See main entry)*		
Trailers *(See main entry)*		
STANDING (VEHICLE)		
In an intersection	545.302(a)(3)	M(C)
In front of driveway	545.302(b)(1)	M(C)
In or near safety zone	545.302(a)(5)	M(C)
Near crosswalk	545.302(b)(3)	M(C)
Near fire hydrant	545.302(b)(2)	M(C)
Near fire station entrance	545.302(b)(5)	M(C)
Near roadside traffic-control device	545.302(b)(4)	M(C)
Near street excavation	545.302(a)(6)	M(C)
Next to parked or stopped vehicle at curb	545.302(a)(1)	M(C)

On bridge or in tunnel	545.302(a)(7)	M(C)
On crosswalk	545.302(a)(4)	M(C)
On highway, unnecessarily	545.301	M(C)
On railroad tracks	545.302(a)(8)	M(C)
On sidewalk	545.302(a)(2)	M(C)
Unattended	545.305(a)(5)	M(C)
On parking facility of apartment complex	684.0125	—
Where prohibited by signs	545.302(a)(9)	M(C)
STICKER indicating vehicle has been driven or towed from place of manufacture; failure to place on windshield	503.071	M(A)/CP
STORAGE OF VEHICLES		
Fees, overcharging	683.033	M(C), (B)
Notification of vehicle owner, failure to provide	684.012	M(C)
Vehicle storage facility, unlicensed operation Duty to report	684.015	M(C)
STREETCARS		
Crossing fire hose	545.205	M(C)
Passing unsafely, to left	545.201	M(C)
To right	545.202	M(C)
Tracks, driving on unsafely	545.203	M(C)
When approached by authorized emergency vehicle	545.204	M(C)
SUSPENDED DRIVER, operating motor vehicle	601.371	M(B)
Driver's license, refuse to surrender	521.451	M(A)/S
TEXTING, While driving	545.4251	M(C),(A)
THEFT OF MOTOR VEHICLE	P.C. 31.03	GRADED
Salvage dealers; violations in conjunction with theft	P.C. 31.03(c)(6)	GRADED
TOWING		
Financial interest by parking facility owner or towing company	684.081	M(C)
Tow truck, unregistered operation	684.001(5)	M(C)
Without authorization	684.014, 684.054	M(C)
TRAFFIC CONTROL DEVICES		
Altering, damaging or destroying, without authorization	544.005	M(C)
Construction warning signs, damaging, removing	472.021	M(A)
Disregarding	544.007	M(C)
Green signal	544.007(b), 552.001(b)	M(C)
Lane direction control signal, disregarding	544.009	M(C)
Pedestrian crossing against	552.001(a)	M(C)
Red signal, flashing, failure to stop at	544.008	M(C)
Red signal, steady, failure to stop at	544.007(d), 552.001(c)	M(C)
Stop sign, disregarding	544.010	M(C)
Turning in disregard of	544.007(d), 545.101	M(C)
Unauthorized devices		
Placement or display of	544.006	M(C)

Yellow signal	544.007(e)	M(C)
Yield signs, failure to yield right-of-way	544.010	M(C)
TRAILERS		
Drawbar or other connection of insufficient strength or length	545.409(a)	M(C)
House trailer, occupying while being moved	545.419	M(C)
License plates, absent	502.404(c)	M(C)
Lighting equipment, absent or insufficient	547.352	M(C)
More than three drawn by triple saddle mount method	545.409(c)	M(C)
White flag, failure to display	545.409(b)	M(C)
TRANSFER OF VEHICLE, failure by dealer to notify Texas Department of Transportation	503.005	M(C)
TRANSPORTATION OF VEHICLE, without inquiring as to ownership	501.156	M(C)
UNAUTHORIZED USE OF VEHICLE	P.C. 31.07	F(SJ)
VANDALISM, highway fixtures	472.021	M(B), (A)
VEHICLE IDENTIFICATION NUMBER		
Altering, erasing or falsifying	501.151	F(3)
Tampering with	P.C. 31.11	M(A)
VEHICLE STORAGE FACILITY		
Failure to report to police	684.015	M(C)
VENDOR, ROADSIDE		
Violation of regulations	285.001, 285.002	M(C)

Offense Titles

TEXAS PENAL CODE PENALTY CHART

OFFENSE	PENAL CODE SECTION	PENALTY
911 abuse	42.061	MB
Abandoning or endangering child	22.041	F2/F3/F
Aggravated assault	22.02	F1/F2
Aggravated sexual assault	22.021	F1
Arson	28.02	F1/F2/F3/F
Assault	22.01	F2/F3/MA
Attack on assistance dog	42.091	F3/MA
Attempt	15.01	F2/F3/F/MA
Bad check	32.41	MB/MC
Bail jumping/Failure to appear	38.10	F3/MA/MC
Bestiality	21.09	F2/F
Body armor—Possession by felon	46.041	F3
Brass knuckles	46.05	MA
Breach of computer security	33.02	F1/F2/F3/F/MA/MB/MC
Burglary	30.02	F1/F2/F3
Burglary of coin-operated machine	30.03	MA
Burglary of vehicle	30.04	F3/MA
BWI	49.06	F3/MA/MB
Capital murder	19.03	CF
Cargo theft	31.18	F1/F2/F3/F
Child erotica	43.262	F2/F3/F
Child porn	43.26	F1/F2/F3
Cockfighting	42.105	F/MA/MC
Conspiracy	15.02	F2/F3//MA
Contraband in correctional facility	38.114	MB/MC
Credit card or debit card abuse	32.31	F3/F
Criminal mischief	28.03	F1/F2/F3/F/MA/MB/MC
Criminal nonsupport	25.05	F
Criminal street gang—coerce, induce or solicit member	71.022	F2/F3
Criminal street gang—Directing activity	71.023	F1
Cruelty to animals	42.092	F3/F/MA
Deadly conduct	22.05	F3/MA
Decryption—Unlawful	33.024	F1/F2/F3/F/MA/MB/MC
Disarming officer	38.14	F/F3
Disclosure of shelter location	42.075	MA
Disorderly conduct	42.01	MB/MC
Disrupting meeting or procession	42.05	MB
Dog fighting	42.10	F/MA
DWI	49.04	F3/MA/MB
DWI—Child passenger	49.045	F
Educator/student/—Improper relationship	21.12	F2
Electronic access interference	33.022	F3
Electronic data tampering	33.023	F1/F2/F3/F/MA/MB/MC
Enticing child	25.04	F3/MB
Escape	38.06	F1/F2/F3/MA
Evading arrest or detention	38.04	F2/F3/F/MA
Evidence tampering or fabrication	37.09	MA
Explosives components	46.09	F3
Failure to identify	38.02	MA/MB

Failure to report felony	38.171	MA
False alarm or report	42.06	F/MA
False caller identification information display	33A.051	MA
False identification as peace officer	37.12	MB
False report to induce emergency response	42.0601	MA/F/F3
False statement regarding missing child or person	37.081	MC
False statement to law enforcement	37.08	MB
Financial abuse of elderly individual	32.55	F1/F2/F3/F/MA/MB
Firearm smuggling	46.14	F2/F3
Firearm—Accessible to child	46.13	MA/MC
Firearm—Unlawful possession	46.04	MA
Fireworks—Unlawful use	50.02	F1/F2/F
Forgery	32.21	F3/F/MA
Gambling	47.02	MC
Gambling device	47.06	MA
Gambling place	47.04	MA
Gambling promotion	47.03	MA
Gambling—Communicating information	47.05	MA
Graffiti	28.08	F1/F2/F3/F/MA/MB/MC
Handgun—Unlawful carrying by license holder	46.035	F3/MA
Harassment	42.07	MA/MB
Harboring runaway	25.06	MA
Harmful materials to minors	43.24	F3/MA
Hindering apprehension or prosecution	38.05	F3/MA
Hindering prosecution by disorderly conduct	38.13	MA
Hoax bomb	46.08	MA
Homicide—Criminally negligent	19.05	F
Identity theft	32.51	F1/F2/F3/F
Impersonating public servant	37.11	F3
Improper contact with victim	38.111	F3/MA
Indecency with child	21.11	F2/F3
Indecent assault	22.012	MA
Indecent exposure	21.08	MB
Injury to child, elderly individual or disabled individual	22.04	F1/F2/F3/F
Interference with custody	25.03	F
Interference with emergency call	42.062	F/MA
Interference with police animal	38.151	F2/F/MA/MB
Interference with public duties	38.15	MB
Interference with radio frequency	38.152	F/MA
Interference with rights of guardian or parent	25.10	F
Intimate visual image—Disclosure or promotion	21.16	MC/MB/MA
Intoxication assault	49.07	F1/F2/F3
Intoxication manslaughter	49.08	F1/F2
Invasive video recording	21.15	F
Joyriding	31.07	F
Kidnapping	20.03	F3
Kidnapping—Aggravated	20.04	F1/F2
Laser pointers	32.13	MC
Leaving child in vehicle	22.10	MC
Mail theft	31.20	F1/F2/F3/MA

Offense Titles

Manslaughter	19.04	F2
Misrepresenting a child as family member	37.082	MB
Murder	19.02	F1/F2
Obscene display or distribution	43.22	MC
Obscenity	43.23	F2/F3/MA
Obstructing emergency vehicle	42.03	F
Obstructing highway	42.03	MB
Obstruction or retaliation	36.06	F3/F2
Online impersonation	33.07	F1/F3/MA
Online solicitation of minor	33.021	F2/F3
Open container	49.031	MC
Organized retail theft	31.16	F1/F2/F3/F/MA/MB
Petroleum products—Appropriation	31.19	F1/F2/F3/F
Preventing execution of civil process	38.16	MC
Prohibited camping	48.05	MC
Prostitution	43.02	F/MA/MB
Prostitution—Aggravated promotion	43.04	F1/F3
Prostitution—Compelling	43.05	F1/F2
Prostitution—Promotion	43.03	F2/F3/F
Prostitution—Solicitation	43.021	F2/F3/F
Public intoxication	49.02	MC
Public lewdness	21.07	MA
Reckless damage or destruction	28.04	MC
Reckless discharge of firearm	42.12	MA
Resisting arrest	38.03	F3/MA
Retail theft devices	31.15	MA
Robbery	29.02	F2
Robbery—Aggravated	29.03	F1
Sexting	43.261	MA/MB/MC
Sexual abuse of child—Continuing	21.02	F1
Sexual assault	22.011	F1/F2
Sexual performance by child	43.25	F1/F2/F3
Skimming	31.17	MA/MB
Smoking in prohibited place	48.01	MC
Smuggling of persons	20.05	F1/F2/F3
Smuggling of persons—Continuous	20.06	F1/F2
Solicitation	15.03	F1/F2
Solicitation of minor	15.031	F2/F3
Stalking	42.072	F2/F3
Tampering with consumer product	22.09	F1/F2/F3/MC
Tampering with identification number	31.11	MA
Terroristic threat	22.07	F3/F/MA/MB
Theft	31.03	F1/F2/F3/F/MA/MB/MC
Theft of services	31.04	F1/F2/F3/F/MA/MB/MC
Trafficking of persons	20A.02	F1/F2
Trafficking of persons—Continuous	20A.03	F1
Trespass	30.05	MA/MB/MC
Trespass with concealed handgun	30.06	MA/MC
Trespass with openly carried handgun	30.07	MA/MC
Unlawful electronic transmission of sexually explicit visual material	21.19	MC
Unlawful restraint	20.02	F2/F3/F/MA
Violation of protective or magistrate's order	25.07	F3/MA
Violence against family—Continuous	25.11	F3
Voyeurism	21.16	MC/MB/F

Weapon—Prohibited place	46.03	F3
Weapons—Prohibited	46.05	F3
Weapons—Unlawful transfer	46.06	F/MA
Weapon—Unlawful carry	46.02	F3/MA
Witness tampering	36.05	F3

Index

INDEX

INDEX

INDEX

INDEX

INDEX

INDEX

INDEX

INDEX

INDEX

INDEX

INDEX

INDEX

H

INDEX

I

J

K

O

P

INDEX

T

U

W

Y

Z